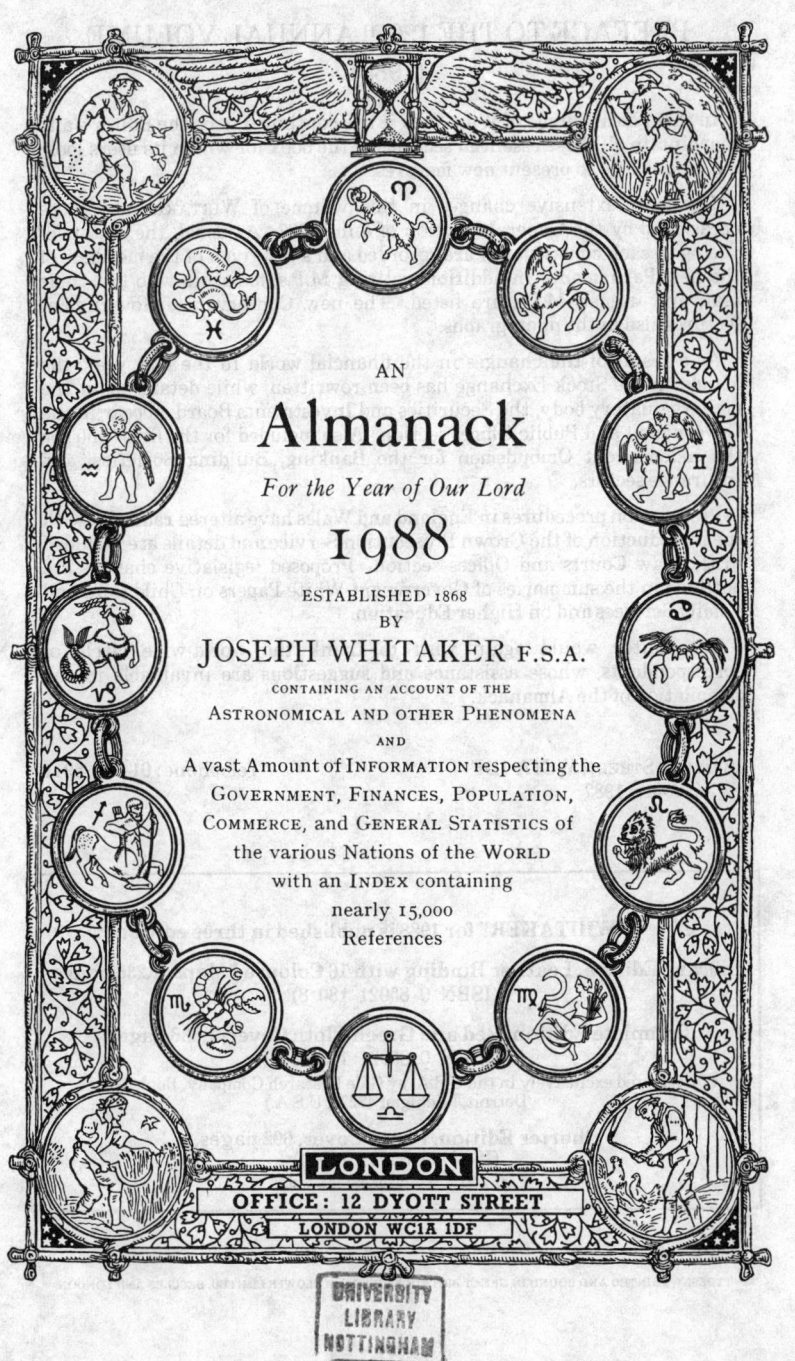

AN

Almanack

For the Year of Our Lord

1988

ESTABLISHED 1868

BY

JOSEPH WHITAKER F.S.A.

CONTAINING AN ACCOUNT OF THE

ASTRONOMICAL AND OTHER PHENOMENA

AND

A vast Amount of INFORMATION respecting the
GOVERNMENT, FINANCES, POPULATION,
COMMERCE, and GENERAL STATISTICS of
the various Nations of the WORLD
with an INDEX containing
nearly 15,000
References

LONDON

OFFICE: 12 DYOTT STREET

LONDON WC1A 1DF

PREFACE TO THE 120TH ANNUAL VOLUME
(1988)

In this 120th volume of WHITAKER it has continued to be the Editor's aim to maintain all those essential sections of the book for which its users look, but to seek also to present new features.

The most extensive changes in this volume of WHITAKER are those occasioned by the General Election of June 1987. As usual, the results of voting in each constituency are recorded and a list given of the members of the new Parliament. In addition, retiring M.P.s, members who lost their seat, and women M.P.s are listed. The new Conservative Government features also in the photographs.

As a result of the changes in the financial world in the past year, the article on the Stock Exchange has been rewritten, while details about the main regulatory body, the Securities and Investments Board, appear in the Government and Public Offices section. Also included for the first time are the independent Ombudsmen for the Banking, Building Societies, and Insurance sectors.

Prosecution procedures in England and Wales have altered radically with the introduction of the Crown Prosecution Service and details are included in the Law Courts and Offices section. Proposed legislative changes are outlined in the summaries of Government White Papers on Child Care and Family Services and on Higher Education.

The Editor would again wish to thank the world-wide circle of correspondents, whose assistance and suggestions are invaluable in the compilation of the Almanack.

12 DYOTT STREET, WC1A 1DF   Telephone: 01-836 8911
October, 1987

Note—"WHITAKER" for 1988 is published in three editions:

Library Edition, Leather Binding with 16 Coloured Maps, 1,236 pages.
(ISBN 0 85021 180 8)

Complete Edition, Red and Green Cloth Cover, 1,236 pages.
(ISBN 0 85021 178 6)

(Distributed exclusively in the U.S.A. by Gale Research Company, Book Tower, Detroit, Michigan 48226, U.S.A.)

Shorter Edition, Paper Cover, 692 pages.
(ISBN 0 85021 179 4)

© 1987 J. Whitaker & Sons, Ltd.

TYPESET, PRINTED AND BOUND IN GREAT BRITAIN BY WILLIAM CLOWES LIMITED, BECCLES AND LONDON

TABLE OF CONTENTS

And in "Complete Edition" and "Library Edition"

INDEX

AA

AL

Pages 693–1236 are omitted from the Shorter Edition

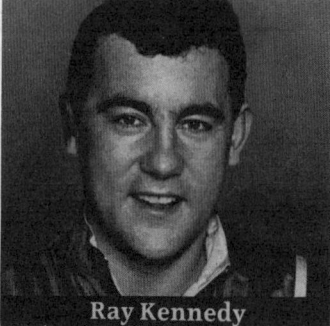

Pages 693–1236 are omitted from the Shorter Edition

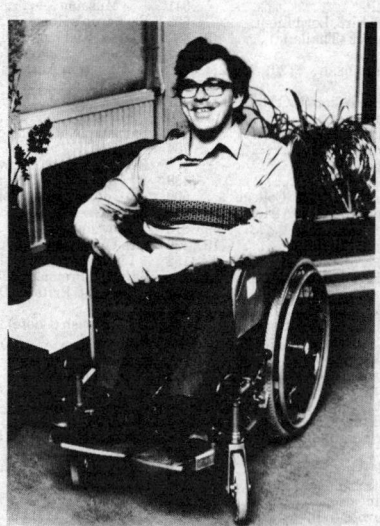

Pages 693–1236 are omitted from the Shorter Edition

Pages 693–1236 are omitted from the Shorter *Edition*

10

Unwanted —
and left to starve

Now loved and cared for in a new home!

Rosie was given as a present. But – like so many other pets every year
– she was unwanted, and was turned out into the streets.

She was one of the lucky ones; rescued and looked after by the Animal
Welfare Trust until a new home was found for her. But there are so
many others like Rosie. We look after hundreds of unwanted pets –
for however long it may take to find them a new home. We never 'put
down' a healthy animal.

But all this costs money! Please help us with a donation or a legacy.
And if you would like to know more about our work and how you can
help us, please write

Animal Welfare Trust

Tyler's Way, Watford by-pass, Watford, Herts. WD2 8HO
Tel. 01-950 8215/0177. Charity Reg. 262999.

Pages 693–1236 *are omitted from the* Shorter *Edition*

Pages 693–1236 are omitted from the Shorter Edition

Pages 693–1236 are omitted from the Shorter Edition

Pages 693–1236 are omitted from the Shorter Edition

Pages 693–1236 are omitted from the Shorter Edition

Pages 693–1236 *are omitted from the* Shorter Edition

Pages 693–1236 *are omitted from the* Shorter Edition

Pages 693–1236 are omitted from the Shorter Edition

Pages 693–1236 *are omitted from the* Shorter Edition

Pages 693–1236 *are omitted from the* Shorter Edition

Pages 693–1236 *are omitted from the* Shorter Edition

Pages 693–1236 are omitted from the Shorter Edition

Pages 693–1236 *are omitted from the* Shorter Edition

Pages 693–1236 are omitted from the Shorter Edition

Pages 693–1236 are omitted from the Shorter Edition

Pages 693–1236 *are omitted from the* Shorter Edition

Pages 693–1236 are omitted from the Shorter Edition

Pages 693–1236 are omitted from the Shorter Edition

Pages 693–1236 are omitted from the Shorter Edition

Pages 693–1236 are omitted from the Shorter Edition

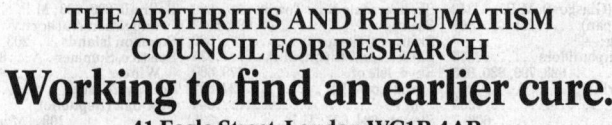

Pages 693–1236 are omitted from the Shorter Edition

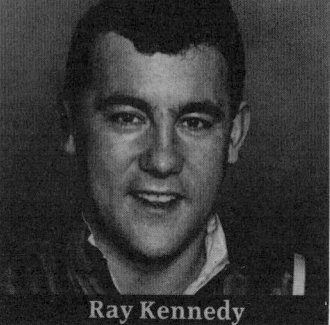

Pages 693–1236 *are omitted from the* Shorter *Edition*

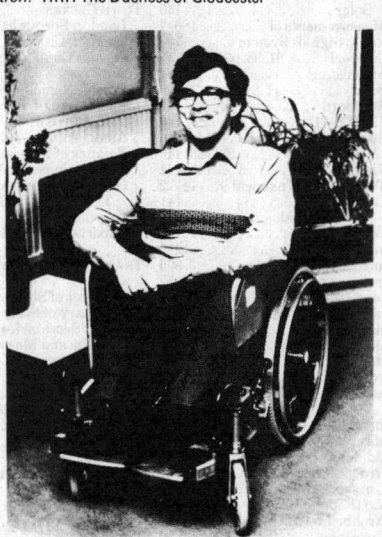

Pages 693–1236 are omitted from the Shorter Edition

Pages 693–1236 are omitted from the Shorter Edition

60

Pages 693–1236 *are omitted from the* Shorter Edition

Pages 693–1236 *are omitted from the* Shorter Edition

64

Pages 693–1236 *are omitted from the* Shorter Edition

OCCURRENCES DURING PRINTING

EVENTS

Sept. 3. President Bagaza of Burundi ousted in a military coup and replaced by a Military Committee for National Redemption led by Maj. Pierre Buyoya, who became President on Sept. 9. **7.** President Honecker of East Germany started an official visit to West Germany. The T.U.C. Congress opened in Blackpool. **8.** General Election in Denmark: an inconclusive result led to Mr. Schluter forming a centre-right minority coalition Government. **9.** 25 Liverpool soccer fans charged with manslaughter in Belgium. **10.** Ethiopia declared a Republic with Col. Mengistu Haile Mariam the first President. **11.** The U.N. Secretary General arrived in Iran to begin attempts to negotiate a ceasefire beween Iran and Iraq. Death reported of Brazilian Minister for Agrarian Reform, Marcos Freire. **12.** Referendum in New Caledonia on future of links with France. **13.** Terry Marsh announced his retirement from boxing. **14.** U.S. Transportation Secretary Elizabeth Dole resigned. The Liberal Party Conference opened in Harrogate. **16.** Cabinet reshuffle in Argentina. **17.** New Philippine Cabinet announced. **18.** U.S.A. and U.S.S.R. announced an accord to eliminate intermediate-range nuclear missiles. **20.** New civilian Cabinet in Ethiopia announced. **21.** N.U.M. began overtime ban. The Open College began broadcasting. **22.** U.S. helicopter fired on an Iranian ship allegedly laying mines in the Gulf. **22.** Cabinet reshuffle in Greece. **25.** Col. Rabuka led a second coup in Fiji: on Oct. 6 he declared Fiji a republic and on Oct. 7 announced a new Cabinet. **26.** It was announced that dealings in B.P. shares would begin on Oct. 30. David Alton, M.P. resigned as Liberal Chief Whip and was replaced by Jim Wallace, M.P. on Oct. 6. **27.** A Colombian landslip killed at least 350. King Mswati III dissolved the Swaziland Parliament and announced elections for Nov. 5. **28.** The Labour Party Conference opened in Brighton. **29.** Alderman Col. Greville Spratt, T.D. elected Lord Mayor of London 1987–88.

Oct. 1. An earthquake centered on Los Angeles, California, killed seven people. Tibetan demonstrations in Lhasa against Chinese rule resulted in several deaths. **2.** President Bourguiba of Tunisia named Mr. Zine al-Abidine Ben Ali as Prime Minister. **3.** An S.A.S. assault team rescued a prison officer from Peterhead prison after a week-long siege by prisoners. **4.** The England golf team won the Dunhill Cup. **5.** The Conservative Party Conference opened in Blackpool. **6.** Three killed in a shooting incident in Wolverhampton. **8.** Tamil guerrillas killed over 200 in two days of violence in northern and eastern Sri Lanka.

APPOINTMENTS

Government and Public Offices

D. Rayner and J. Welsby to be members of British Railways Board from Nov. 1, 1987.

Miss S. Beesley to be a member of the Advisory Council on Public Records.

Miss J. Fookes, M.P. and Sir Derek Day to be members of the Commonwealth War Graves Commission.

Legal

The Hon. Lord Justice MacDermott to become a Privy Counsellor and to be knighted on his appointment as Lord Justice of the Northern Ireland Court of Appeal.

Church

Rev. Canon A. J. Russell to be Bishop of Dorchester from November 1, 1987.

Commonwealth

His Excellency John Manduca accredited as Malta's High Commissioner in London.

OBITUARIES

September

1. Prof. Arnaldo Momigliano, *aged* 78.
4. Bill Bowes, *aged* 79.
5. Bill Fraser, *aged* 79.
6. Sir William Haley, *aged* 86.
—. Maj.-Gen. Sir James d'Avigdor-Goldsmid, Bt., *aged* 76.
8. The Rt. Hon. Sir David Cairns, *aged* 85.
—. Al Read, *aged* 78.
11. Lord Rhodes, *aged* 92.
12. Marshal of the R.A.F. Sir William Dickson, *aged* 88.
—. Gen. J. Lawton Collins, *aged* 91.
13. Lorne Greene, *aged* 72.
14. 2nd Baron Mancroft, *aged* 73.
16. Lord Soames, *aged* 66.
—. Sir William Cook, *aged* 82.
22. 6th Earl of Carnarvon, *aged* 88.
—. Louis Kentner, *aged* 82.
23. Bob Fosse, *aged* 60.
25. Emlyn Williams, *aged* 81.
—. Mary Astor, *aged* 81.
29. Henry Ford II, *aged* 70.

October

1. Sir Geoffrey Jackson, *aged* 72.
2. Sir Peter Medawar, *aged* 72.
3. Jean Anouilh, *aged* 77.
4. Catherine Bramwell-Booth, *aged* 104.
—. Dr. Kenneth Slack, *aged* 70.
8. Sir Rolf Dudley-Williams, *aged* 79.
9. Clare Boothe Luce, *aged* 84.

VOTES CAST FOR MAIN PARTIES, BY STANDARD REGION

	Con.	Lab.	Alli-ance	SNP/PC	Other	Total
England	12,546,134*	8,006,468	6,466,874	—	113,518	27,132,994
North	578,970	830,785	376,675	—	4,635	1,791,065
Yorkshire & Humberside	1,040,749	1,128,875	602,709	—	7,811	2,780,144
East Midlands	1,127,237	696,780	486,768	—	9,128	2,319,913
East Anglia	601,421	249,894	297,041	—	5,217	1,153,573
Greater London	1,680,093*	1,136,892	770,009	—	26,679	3,613,673
Rest of South East ...	3,382,849	1,023,521	1,653,544	—	27,603	6,087,517
South West	1,386,857	436,356	906,288	—	13,048	2,742,549
West Midlands	1,346,505	984,667	615,699	—	10,401	2,957,272
North West	1,401,453	1,518,698	758,141	—	8,996	3,687,288
Wales	501,302	765,344	304,225	123,589	3,742	1,698,202
Scotland	713,089	1,258,132	570,053	416,873	10,069	2,968,216
Northern Ireland	—	—	—	—	730,152	730,152

*Includes the Speaker who was opposed by Labour and SDP candidates.

PERCENTAGE DISTRIBUTION OF VOTES CAST IN EACH REGION BY MAIN PARTY

	Con.	Lab.	Alli-ance	SNP/PC	Other	Total
England	46·2*	29·5	23·8	—	0·4	100·0
North	32·3	46·4	21·0	—	0·3	100·0
Yorks & Humberside	37·4	40·6	21·7	—	0·3	100·0
East Midlands	48·6	30·0	21·0	—	0·4	100·0
East Anglia	52·1	21·7	25·7	—	0·5	100·0
Greater London	46·5*	31·5	21·3	—	0·7	100·0
Rest of South East	55·6	16·8	27·2	—	0·5	100·0
South West	50·6	15·9	33·0	—	0·5	100·0
West Midlands	45·5	33·3	20·8	—	0·4	100·0
North West	38·0	41·2	20·6	—	0·2	100·0
Wales	29·5	45·1	17·9	7·3	0·2	100·0
Scotland	24·0	42·4	19·2	14·0	0·3	100·0
Northern Ireland	—	—	—	—	100·0	100·0

*Includes the Speaker who was opposed by Labour and SDP candidates.

CHANGES SINCE JUNE 1983 IN MAJOR PARTIES' SHARE OF VOTE BY REGION (PERCENT)

	Con.	Lab.	Alli-ance	Other
England	+0·3 (a)	+2·6	−2·5	−0·3
North	−2·3	+6·2	−4·0	+0·1
York & Humberside	−1·2	+5·3	−3·9	−0·2
East Midlands	+1·4	+2·1	−3·1	−0·4
East Anglia	+1·1	+1·2	−2·5	+0·2
Greater London	+2·6 (a)	+1·6	−3·4	−0·9
Rest of South East	+1·1	+0·9	−1·8	−0·2
South West	−0·8	+1·2	−0·1	−0·3
West Midlands	+0·5	+2·1	−2·6	−0·1
North West	−2·0	+5·2	−2·8	−0·4
Wales	−1·5	+7·5	−5·3	−0·7 (b)
Scotland	−4·4	+7·3	−5·3	+2·4 (c)
Northern Ireland	—	—	—	—
United Kingdom	−0·1	+3·3	−2·8	−0·3

(a) 1987 vote includes the Speaker who was opposed by Labour and SDP candidates.
(b) The Plaid Cymru share fell by 0·5 per cent.
(c) The SNP share rose by 2·3 per cent.

SEATS WON BY PARTY AND STANDARD REGION OF GREAT BRITAIN

	Speaker	Con.	Lab.	Alli-ance (a)	SNP/PC	Total
England	1	357	155	10	—	523
North	—	8	27	1	—	36
Yorks & Humberside	—	21	33	—	—	54
East Midlands	—	31	11	—	—	42
East Anglia	—	19	1	—	—	20
Greater London	1	57	23	3	—	84
Rest of South East	—	107	1	—	—	108
South West	—	44	1	3	—	48
West Midlands	—	36	22	—	—	58
North West	—	34	36	3	—	73
Wales	—	8	24	3	3	38
Scotland	—	10	50	9	3	72
Great Britain	1	375	229	22	6	633

(a) The SDP seats are distributed as follows:—

Greater London	2
South West	1
Scotland	2

The other 17 seats are held by Liberals.

DEFENCE MANPOWER STRENGTHS

At 1 April   Thousands

	1980	1981	1982	1983	1984	1985	1986
U.K. SERVICE PERSONNEL							
All services: total	320·6	333·8	327·6	320·6	325·9	326·2	322·5
Female	16·2	16·9	15·7	15·4	16·2	16·4	16·0
Royal Navy: total	64·4	66·4	65·1	64·0	63·7	62·8	60·3
Female	3·8	4·1	4·0	3·9	3·9	3·7	3·4
Royal Marines: total	7·6	7·9	7·9	7·8	7·6	7·6	7·6
Army: total	159·0	166·0	163·2	159·1	161·5	162·4	161·4
Female	6·3	6·6	6·0	6·1	6·6	6·8	6·6
Royal Air Force: total	89·6	93·5	91·5	89·8	93·1	93·4	93·2
Female	6·1	6·3	5·8	5·4	5·7	6·0	6·0
Personnel locally entered overseas:							
total	8·2	9·7	10·1	10·1	9·6	10·2	9·8
Regular Reserves*: total	192·6	196·5	196·4	193;4	198·0	205·5	–
Royal Navy	27·0	26·8	24·7	23·9	23·5	23·3	–
Royal Marines	2·2	2·2	2·2	2·2	2·2	2·2	–
Army	133·1	137·5	140·2	138·3	143·2	150·1	–
Royal Air Force	30·3	30·1	29·3	28·9	29·0	29·8	–
Volunteer Reserves and Auxilliary							
Forces*: total	77·0	83·9	86·3	87·3	85·7	88·5	–
Royal Navy	5·0	5·4	5·4	5·4	5·2	5·2	–
Royal Marines	0·8	0·9	1·1	1·1	1·0	1·1	–
Territorial Army	63·3	69·5	72·1	72·8	71·4	73·7	–
Ulster Defence Regiment	7·4	7·5	7·1	7·1	6·8	6·4	–
Home Service Force	–	–	–	0·3	0·3	0·9	–
Royal Air Force	0·5	0·6	0·6	0·6	1·0	1·1	–
Cadet Forces*: total	141·5	144·1	144·6	142·0	141·2	144·9	–
Royal Navy	22·7	24·5	24·6	22·4	23·1	28·7	–
Army	74·6	75·1	74·1	74·5	73·8	72·1	–
Royal Air Force	44·1	44·4	45·9	45·1	44·3	44·1	–
Ministry of Defence civilians:							
total	276·2	264·9	251·7	242·7	232·5	206·5	201·7
U.K. based	239·8	229·6	216·9	208·9	199·1	174·1	169·4
Non-industrial	118·5	113·5	108·1	105·6	103·2	94·9	93·8
Industrial	121·2	116·1	108·8	103·3	95·9	79·1	75·6
Locally engaged overseas	36·4	35·3	34·8	33·8	33·4	32·4	32·2
Non-industrial	11·0	10·9	10·7	10·5	10·4	10·2	10·3
Industrial	25·5	24·4	24·1	23·3	23·0	22·2	22·0

* Figures unavailable for 1986.

Recruitment of U.K. Service personnel to each Service

Number

	1979/80	1980/81	1981/82	1982/83	1983/84	1984/85	1985/86
All Services: total	50,652	50,488	22,607	21,647	36,991	34,721	32,651
Female	4,446	3,795	1,419	2,305	3,231	2,645	2,244
Royal Navy: total	8,526	9,088	3,805	3,584	4,785	4,582	4,276
Female	825	958	452	506	562	351	289
Royal Marines: total	1,676	1,674	699	447	447	954	1,093
Army: total	29,189	28,871	14,204	13,071	22,348	22,278	20,268
Female	2,025	1,630	601	1,392	1,537	1,364	1,095
Royal Air Force: total	11,261	10,855	3,899	4,545	9,411	6,907	7,014
Female	1,596	1,207	366	407	1,132	930	860

CRIMINAL STATISTICS
ENGLAND AND WALES
Notifiable offences recorded by the police (thousands)

	1981	1982	1983	1984	1985
Total	2,963·8	3,262·4	3,247·0	3,499·1	3,611·9
Violence against the person	100·2	108·7	111·3	114·2	121·7
Sexual offences	19·4	19·7	20·4	20·2	21·5
Burglary	723·2	810·6	813·4	897·5	871·3
Robbery	20·3	22·8	22·1	24·9	27·5
Theft and handling stolen goods	1,603·2	1,755·9	1,705·9	1,808·0	1,884·1
Fraud and forgery	106·7	123·1	121·8	126·1	134·8
Criminal damage	386·7	417·8	443·3	497·8	539·0
Other offences	4·1	3·8	8·7	10·4	12·2

SCOTLAND
Crimes and offences recorded by the police (thousands)

	1981	1982	1983	1984	1985
Total crimes and offences	744·7	762·5	799·6	809·4	800·4
Total crimes	408·2	435·1	448·3	474·9	462·0
Non-sexual crimes of violence against the person	12·2	12·1	13·0	13·7	15·1
Crimes involving indecency	4·8	5·0	5·5	5·7	5·7
Crimes involving dishonesty	320·0	340·1	342·5	359·2	342·3
Fire-raising, malicious and reckless conduct	61·7	66·0	73·1	79·1	79·5
Other crimes	9·5	11·9	14·3	17·3	19·2
Total offences	336·8	327·4	351·3	334·5	338·4
Miscellaneous offences	118·2	115·4	114·8	114·9	118·1
Motor vehicle offences	218·3	212·0	236·5	219·6	220·3

PRISONS
Receptions into prison: by number of previous convictions (England and Wales)

Number of previous convictions	1977	1978	1979	1980	1981	1982	1983*	1984*	1985*
Males: total	33,906	34,832	36,412	38,016	43,388	46,779	42,716	39,930	43,626
None	2,135	1,936	1,634	1,731	1,518	1,773	1,848	1,765	1,686
1–2 sentences	2,516	2,500	2,484	2,685	3,002	3,164	2,969	2,924	3,394
3–5 sentences	5,401	5,399	5,652	6,092	7,161	7,312	6,104	5,694	6,273
6–10 sentences	9,177	9,470	9,412	9,665	11,152	11,845	10,048	9,009	9,861
11 or more sentences	10,893	11,011	11,340	11,905	13,343	14,057	13,632	13,169	13,835
Previous conviction information not recorded	3,784	4,516	5,890	5,938	7,212	8,628	8,115	7,369	8,577
Females: total	1,839	2,000	2,109	2,265	2,533	2,692	2,349	2,388	2,475
None	231	240	156	155	177	176	271	289	208
1–2 sentences	152	149	148	172	234	261	273	252	241
3–5 sentences	285	279	293	322	423	445	419	374	347
6–10 sentences	279	253	287	331	434	443	401	397	360
11 or more sentences	207	189	196	195	267	322	294	265	261
Previous conviction information not recorded	685	890	1,029	1,090	998	1,045	691	811	1,058

*From 1983 data are not comparable with previous years because of the Criminal Justice Act 1982.

HALLMARKS ON GOLD, SILVER AND PLATINUM WARES
London (Goldsmiths' Hall) Date Letters
From 1498

𝕬	Black letter, small	1498–9 to 1517–8	𝖉	Roman letter, small	1739–40 to 1755–6
𝕬	Lombardic	1518–9 „ 1537–8	𝕬	Old English, capitals ..	1756–7 to 1775–6
𝕬	Roman and other capitals	1538–9 „ 1557–8	𝖆	Roman letter, small	1776–7 „ 1795–6
𝕬	Black letter, small	1558–9 „ 1577–8	A	Roman letter, capitals .	1796–7 „ 1815–6
A	Roman letter, capitals .	1578–9 „ 1597–8	𝖆	Roman letter, small ...	1816–7 „ 1835–6
𝖠	Lombardic, external cusps	1598–9 „ 1617–8	𝕬	Old English, capitals ..	1836–7 „ 1855–6
𝑒	Italic letter, small	1618–9 „ 1637–8	𝖆	Old English, small	1856–7 „ 1875–6
𝕭	Court hand	1638–9 „ 1657–8	A	Roman letter, capitals [A to M square shield N to Z as shown]	1876–7 „ 1895–6
𝕬	Black letter, capitals ..	1658–9 „ 1677–8	𝖆	Roman letter, small ...	1896–7 „ 1915–6
𝖆	Black letter, small	1678–9 „ 1696–7	𝖆	Black letter, small	1916–7 „ 1935–6
𝕭	Court hand	1697 „ 1715–6	A	Roman letter, capitals .	1936–7 „ 1955–6
A	Roman letter, capitals	1716–7 „ 1735–6	𝑎	Italic letter, small	1956–7 „ 1974
𝑎	Roman letter, small ...	1736–7 „ 1738–9	𝒜	Italic letter, capitals ..	1975 „ ...

Hallmarks are the symbols stamped on gold, silver, or platinum articles to indicate that they have been chemically tested and that they conform to one of the legal standards. With certain exceptions, all gold, silver, or platinum articles are required by law to be hallmarked before they are offered for sale. Hallmarking was instituted in 1300 under a statute of Edward I.

Normally a complete modern hallmark consists of four symbols—the maker's mark or sponsor's mark, assay office mark, standard mark and date letter.

Additional marks have been authorized from time to time.

Maker's Mark.—Instituted in 1363, the maker's mark was originally a device such as a bird or *fleur-de-lys* and now consists invariably of the initial letters of the name or names of the maker or sponsor, or of the firm.

Assay Office Mark.—The existing assay offices and their distinguishing marks are:—

LONDON (Goldsmiths' Hall).

A leopard's head (uncrowned from 1300 to 1478–9, when it became crowned until 1821, since when it has been uncrowned). From 1697 to 1974 a lion's head erased was used on silver of the higher (Britannia) standard.

BIRMINGHAM (Newhall Street, B3 1SB) . An anchor
SHEFFIELD (137 Portobello Street, S1 4DS) . . A rose
EDINBURGH (9 Granton Road, EH5 3QJ) . . A castle

Offices formerly existed in other towns, e.g. Chester, Glasgow, Newcastle, Exeter, York and Norwich, each having its own distinguishing mark.

Standard Mark.—Instituted in 1544. The current legal standards and their marks are as follows:—

PLATINUM

SILVER.—Sterling silver (92·5 per cent. silver) is marked by English assay offices with a *lion passant* and by the Edinburgh Assay Office with a *lion rampant*. A full-length figure of *Britannia* was impressed on silver of a higher standard (95·84 per cent. silver) between 1697 and 1720 and this mark is still used occasionally by all British assay offices.

GOLD.—Since 1975 gold articles are marked with a crown followed by the millesimal figure for the standard, i.e. 916 for 22 carat, 750 for 18 carat, 585 for 14 carat and 375 for 9 carat.

Date Letter.—Instituted in 1478. The date letter denotes the year in which an article was assayed and hallmarked. Each alphabetical cycle has a distinctive style of lettering or shape of shield. The date letters were different at the various assay offices and the particular office must be established from the assay office mark before reference is made to tables of date letters. Specimen shields and letters used by the London Office on silver articles in each period from 1498 to date are shown on the previous page. The same letters are found on gold articles but the surrounding shield may differ.

OTHER MARKS

Duty Mark.—In 1784 an additional mark of the reigning sovereign's head was introduced to signify that the excise duty had been paid. The mark became obsolete on the abolition of the duty in 1890.

Commemorative Marks.—There are three other marks to commemorate special events, the Silver Jubilee of King George V and Queen Mary in 1935, the Coronation of Queen Elizabeth II in 1953 and her Silver Jubilee in 1977.

Foreign Wares.—Since 1842 foreign wares imported into Great Britain have been required to be hallmarked before sale. The marks consist of the importer's mark, a special assay office mark (*see below*), the figures denoting fineness and the annual date letter. The current assay office marks for foreign wares are as follows:—

LONDON.—The sign of the Constellation Leo.
BIRMINGHAM.—Equilateral triangle.
SHEFFIELD.—The sign of the Constellation Libra.
EDINBURGH.—St. Andrew's Cross.

Common Control Mark.—Special marks at authorised Assay Offices of the signatory countries of the International Convention—United Kingdom, Austria, Denmark (from Jan. 1, 1988), Finland, Ireland, Portugal, Norway, Sweden and Switzerland—are legally recognised in the United Kingdom as approved hallmarks. These marks consist of a Sponsor's Mark, a Common Control Mark, a Fineness Mark (arabic numerals showing the standard in parts per thousand) and an Assay Office Mark. There is no date letter.

POETS LAUREATE

Samuel Daniel	1599	Rev. Laurence Eusden	1718	Lord Tennyson	1850
Ben Jonson	1619	Colley Cibber	1730	Alfred Austin	1890
Sir William D'Avenant	1637	William Whitehead	1757	Robert Bridges	1913
John Dryden	1670	Rev. Thomas Warton	1785	John Masefield	1930
Thomas Shadwell	1688	Henry James Pye	1790	Cecil Day Lewis	1967
Nahum Tate	1692	Robert Southey	1813	Sir John Betjeman	1972
Nicholas Rowe	1715	William Wordsworth	1843	Edward (Ted) Hughes	1984

MASTERS OF THE QUEEN'S/KING'S MUSIC

	Apptd.		Apptd.
Nicholas Lanier	1626	Francois (Franz) Cramer	1834
Louis Grabu	1666	George Frederick Anderson	1848
Nicholas Staggins	1674	Sir William George Cusins	1870
John Eccles	1700	Sir Walter Parratt	1893
Maurice Greene	1735	Sir Edward Elgar	1924
William Boyce	1755 (1757)	Sir Henry Walford Davies	1934
John Stanley	1779	Sir Arnold Edward Trevor Bax	1941
Sir William Parsons	1786	Sir Arthur Bliss	1953
William Shield	1817	Malcolm Williamson	1975
Christian Kramer	1829		

SYMBOLS FOR CORRECTING PROOFS

Supplied by WILLIAM CLOWES LTD, Beccles, Suffolk, Printers of "WHITAKER'S ALMANACK"

Letter(s) or word(s) requiring alteration should be struck through IN INK in the text and the substitution should be written in the nearest margin followed by / (the symbol used to denote that the marginal mark is concluded). Insertions should be indicated by / or ∧ at the conclusion of the marginal mark *and* at the desired place in the text.

Alteration required	Mark in margin	Mark in text	Alteration required	Mark in margin	Mark in text
Delete (take out)	∂ or ∂|	/	Take letter(s) or word(s) from beginning of one line to end of preceding line	*back* or *take back*	
		or —— Vertical stroke to delete one or two letters; horizontal line to delete more	Begin a new paragraph	*n.p.*	before first word of new paragraph
Delete and close up	∂ or ∂|	Strike out letter(s) not required and add "close up" mark above and below	No new para. here or run on with previous matter with later matter	*run on*	between paras. or other matter
Close up: delete space between letters	⌒	linking letters or words	Spell out in full the abbreviation, contraction, or figure	*spell out*	Encircle words, etc., or figures concerned
Use ligature (fi, fl, ffl, etc.) or diphthong (æ, œ)	⌒ *enclosing ligature or diphthong required*	⌒ enclosing letters to be altered	Insert omitted portion of copy	*out – see copy*	Attach the relevant copy to the proof, indicating omitted portion
Insert space between letters or words	#∧	∧	Inserted or substituted letter(s), figure(s), or sign(s) under which this is placed to be superscript (i.e. high alignment)[1]	⅂ *(see footnote)*	for insertions For substitutions encircle letter(s). figure(s). or sign(s) to be altered
Leave as printed (i.e. a cancellation of previous marking)	.... *stet*	under letter(s) or word(s) crossed out but to be retained			
Invert type (of letter(s) upside down)	℃	Encircle letter(s) to be altered	Inserted or substituted letter(s), figure(s), or sign(s) over which this is placed to be subscript (low alignment)[2]	⅂ *(see footnote)*	for insertions For substitutions encircle letter(s), figure(s), etc., to be altered
"Battered" letter(s) to be replaced by similar but undamaged characters	✕	Encircle letter(s) or word(s) to be replaced and write the correct letter(s) in the margin			
Push down space or "high" letter(s) or word(s)	⊥	Encircle space, letter(s), or word(s) affected	Change to lower case	*l.c.*	Encircle letter(s) to be altered
Transpose	*tr.* or *trs.*	between letters or words, numbered when necessary	Replace "wrong fount" by letter(s) of correct fount	*w.f.*	Encircle letter(s) or word(s) to be altered
			Change to capital letters	*caps.*	≡ under letter(s) or word(s) to be altered
Take letter(s) or word(s) from end of one line to beginning of next line	*take over* or *over*		Change to small capitals	*s.c.*	═ under letter(s) or word(s) to be altered

⅂ indicates a superior (superscript) figure one   ⅂ indicates an inferior (subscript) figure two

Alteration required	Mark in margin	Mark in text	Alteration required	Mark in margin	Mark in text
Use capital letters for initial letter(s) (as desired) and small capitals for rest of word(s)	*caps* & *s.c.*	☰ under initial letter(s) and ☰ under the remainder of the word(s)	Move lines to the left	⌐⌐	at right side of group of lines to be moved (indicating approx. position)
Change to bold type	*bold*	∿ Draw wavy line under letter(s) or word(s) to be altered	Move portion of matter so that it is positioned as indicated	[ ]	at limits of required position
Change to roman type	*rom.*	Encircle letter(s) or word(s) to be altered	Raise lines	*raise*	⤉ over lines to be raised
Change to italic type	*italic*	─ Draw this straight line under letter(s) or word(s) to be altered	Lower lines	*lower*	⤈ under lines to be lowered
Letter(s) or word(s) to be underlined	*underline*	under letter(s), word(s), etc. to be underlined	Correct the vertical alignment	‖	‖
			Straighten lines	═	through lines to be straightened
Equalize space between words	*eq. #*	⌐ between words	Insert parentheses (round-shaped brackets)	(/) or (/)/	⋏ or ⋏⋏
Reduce space	*less #*	⌐ between words	Insert [square] brackets	[/] or [/]/	⋏ ⋏
Space to be inserted between lines or paragraphs	# >	*Amount of space should be indicated*	Insert hyphen	⊦-/	⋏
To be placed in centre of line, etc.	*centre*	Position to be indicated by	Insert en (=half-em) rule (*see above*)	*en* ─ /	⋏
Indent one en (approx. space occupied by n of type in use)	*en* □⋏	[indicating approximate position	Insert one-em rule (*see above*)	*em* ─ /	⋏
Indent one em (approx. space occupied by M of type in use)	*em* □⋏	[Ditto	Insert two-em rule (*see above*)	*2 em* ─ /	⋏
Indent two ems (approx. space occupied by MM of type in use)	□□⋏	[Ditto	Insert apostrophe	᾿	⋏
Move to the left	⌐	⊢ Ditto	Insert single quotation marks	⸜ ⸝	⋏ ⋏
Move to the right	⌐	⌐ Ditto	Insert double quotation marks	⸜⸜ ⸝⸝	⋏ ⋏
Move lines to the right	[	at left side of group of lines to be moved (indicating approx. position)	Insert ellipsis	... /	⋏
			Insert leader (*visual guide to alignment in contents pages, etc.*)	⊙⊙⊙ ⊙⊙ ⊙	⋏ (*three, two, or one dot*)
			Insert oblique stroke	Ⓞ	⋏

Punctuation	⸲⋏	⸲/	⸵⋏	⸵/	⊙	⊙	?⋏	?/	!⋏	!/

WEIGHTS AND MEASURES

The Weights and Measures Act, 1985, enacts the legal measures for the United Kingdom. The United Kingdom primary standards are the yard or the metre as the unit of measurement of length, and the pound or the kilogram as the unit of measurement of mass. Other units of measurement are defined by reference to the primary standards. Responsibility for the maintenance of the primary standards and for the determination or redetermination of their value rests with the Secretary of State for Trade and Industry.

The definition of the U.K. primary standards is as follows:

YARD = 0·9144 metre.

METRE is the length of the path travelled by light in vacuum during a time interval of 1/299 792 458 of a second.

POUND = 0·453 592 37 kilogram.

KILOGRAM is equal to the mass of the international prototype of the kilogram.

The following table shows the definitions of measures set out in Schedule 1 of the Weights and Measures Act, 1985.

Measurement of Length

Imperial Units
Mile = 1,760 yards.
YARD (*yd.*) = 0·9144 metre.
Foot (*ft.*) = 1/3 yard.
Inch (*in.*) = 1/36 yard.

Metric Units
Kilometre (*km.*) = 1,000 metres.
METRE (*m.*) is the length of the path travelled by light in vacuum during a time interval of 1/299 792 458 of a second.
Decimetre (*dm.*) = 1/10 metre.
Centimetre (*cm.*) = 1/100 metre.
Millimetre (*mm.*) = 1/1000 metre.

Measurement of Area

Imperial Units
Acre = 4,840 square yards.
SQUARE YARD = a superficial area equal to that of a square each side of which measures one yard.
Square foot = 1/9 square yard.

Metric Units
Hectare (*ha.*) = 100 ares.
Decare = 10 ares.
Are (*a.*) = 100 square metres.
SQUARE METRE = a superficial area equal to that of a square each side of which measures one metre.
Square decimetre = 1/100 square metre.
Square centimetre = 1/100 square decimetre.
Square millimetre = 1/100 square centimetre.

Measurement of Volume

Metric Units
CUBIC METRE (*m*³) = a volume equal to that of a cube each edge of which measures one metre.
Cubic decimetre = 1/1000 cubic metre.
Cubic centimetre = 1/1000 cubic decimetre.
Hectolitre = 100 litres.
LITRE = a cubic decimetre.
Decilitre = 1/10 litre.
Centilitre = 1/100 litre.
Millilitre = 1/1000 litre.

Measurement of Capacity

Imperial Units
GALLON = 4·546 09 cubic decimetres.
Quart = 1/4 gallon.

Pint (*pt.*) = 1/2 quart.
Gill = 1/4 pint.
Fluid ounce (*fl. oz.*) = 1/20 pint.

Metric Units
Hectolitre (*hl.*) = 100 litres.
LITRE (*l.*) = a cubic decimetre.
Decilitre = 1/10 litre.
Centilitre (*cl.*) = 1/100 litre.
Millilitre (*ml.*) = 1/1000 litre.

Measurement of Mass or Weight

Imperial Units
POUND (*lb.*) = 0·453 592 37 kilogram.
Ounce (*oz.*) = 1/16 pound.
*Ounce troy = 12/175 pound.

Metric Units
Tonne, metric tonne (*t.*) = 1000 kilograms.
KILOGRAM (*kg.*) is the unit of mass; it is equal to the mass of the international prototype of the kilogram.
Hectogram (*hg.*) = 1/10 kilogram.
Gram (*g.*) = 1/1000 kilogram.
**Carat (metric) = 1/5 gram.
Milligram (*mg.*) = 1/1000 gram.
  *used only for transactions in gold, silver or other precious metals, and articles made therefrom.
  **used only for transactions in precious stones or pearls.

Certain units of measurement may no longer be used for trade although the measure may still be used, *e.g.* it is legal to sell a 112 lb quantity of a commodity but it must be referred to in invoices, etc., as 112 lb, not as a cwt. These units are defined as follows:

Measurement of Length

Furlong = 220 yards.
Chain = 22 yards.

Measurement of Area

Square mile = 640 acres.
Rood = 1210 square yards.
Square inch = 1/144 square foot.

Measurement of Volume

Cubic yard = a volume equal to that of a cube each edge of which measures one yard.
Cubic foot = 1/27 cubic yard.
Cubic inch = 1/1728 cubic foot.

Measurement of Capacity

Bushel = 8 gallons.
Peck = 2 gallons.
Fluid drachm = 1/8 fluid ounce.
Minim (*min.*) = 1/60 fluid drachm.

Measurement of Mass or Weight

Ton = 2,240 pounds.
Hundredweight (*cwt.*) = 112 pounds.
Cental = 100 pounds.
Quarter = 28 pounds.
Stone = 14 pounds.
Dram (*dr.*) = 1/16 ounce.
Grain (*gr.*) = 1/7000 pound.
Pennyweight (*dwt.*) = 24 grains.
Ounce apothecaries = 480 grains.
Drachm (ʒ1) = 1/8 ounce apothecaries.
Scruple(℈1) = 1/3 drachm.

Metric ton = 1,000 kilograms.
Quintal (*q.*) = 100 kilograms.

Measurement of Electricity

Units of measurement of electricity are defined by the Weights and Measures Act, 1985, as follows:
An AMPERE (*A.*) is that constant current which, if maintained in two straight parallel conductors of infinite length, of negligible circular cross-section and placed 1 metre apart in vacuum, would produce between these conductors a force equal to 2×10^{-7} newton per metre of length.
An OHM (Ω) is the electric resistance between two points of a conductor when a constant potential difference of 1 volt, applied between the two points, produces in the conductor a current of 1 ampere, the conductor not being the seat of any electromotive force.
A VOLT (*V.*) is the difference of electric potential between two points of a conducting wire carrying a constant current of 1 ampere when the power dissipated between these points is equal to 1 watt.
A WATT (*W.*) is the power which in one second gives rise to energy of 1 joule.
Kilowatt (*kW.*) = 1,000 watts.
Megawatt (*MW.*) = one million watts.

Water Measures

1 cubic foot = 62·321 lb.
1 gallon = 160 fluid ounces.
      = 10 lb. (distilled).
1 cubic cm. = 1 gram.
1,000 cubic cm. = 1 litre; 1 kilogram.
1 cubic metre = 1,000 litres; 1,000 kg.; 1 tonne.
    An inch of rain on the surface of an acre (43,560 sq. ft.) = 3,630 cubic ft. = 100·992 tons.
    Cisterns: A cistern 4 × 2½ feet and 3 feet deep will hold brimful 186·963 gallons, weighing 1,869·63 lbs. in addition to its own weight.

Water for Ships
Kilderkin = 18 gallons.
Barrel = 36 gallons.
Puncheon = 72 gallons.
Butt = 110 gallons.
Tun = 210 gallons.

Bottles of Wine
Equivalent in standard champagne bottles (litres in brackets)
Magnum = 2 (1·6).
Jeroboam = 4 (3·2).
Rehoboam = 6 (4·8).
Methuselah = 8 (6·4).
Salmanazar = 12 (9·6).
Balthazar = 16 (12·8).
Nebuchadnezzar = 20 (16).
A quarter of a bottle is known as a *nip*.

NAUTICAL MEASURES

Distance at sea is measured in nautical miles. The British standard nautical mile was 6,080 feet (the length of a minute of an arc of a great circle of the earth, rounded off to a mean value to allow for the length varying at different latitudes). This measure has been obsolete since 1970 when the international nautical mile of 1,852 metres was adopted by the Hydrographic Department of the Ministry of Defence as a result of a recommendation by the International Hydrographic Bureau.
The cable (600 feet or 100 fathoms) was a measure approximately one tenth of a nautical mile. Such distances are now expressed in decimal parts of a sea mile or in metres.
Soundings at sea were recorded in fathoms (6 feet). Depths are now expressed in metres on new Admiralty charts.
Speed is measured in nautical miles per hour, called knots. A ship moving at the rate of 30 nautical miles per hour is said to be doing 30 knots.

Knots	m.p.h.	Knots	m.p.h.
1	1·1515	9	10·3636
2	2·3030	10	11·5151
3	3·4545	15	17·2727
4	4·6060	20	23·0303
5	5·7575	25	28·7878
6	6·9090	30	34·5454
7	8·0606	35	40·3030
8	9·2121	40	46·0606

The tonnage of a vessel is measured in tons of 100 cubic feet.
Gross tonnage = the total volume of all the enclosed spaces of a vessel.
Net tonnage = gross tonnage less deductions for crew space, engine room, water ballast and other spaces not used for passengers or cargo.

Million, Billion, etc.

Value in the United Kingdom
Million . . . . thousand × thousand (10^6)
Billion . . . . million × million (10^{12})
Trillion . . . . million × billion (10^{18})
Quadrillion . . . . million × trillion (10^{24})

Value in U.S.A.
Million . . . . thousand × thousand (10^6)
Billion . . . . thousand × million (10^9)
Trillion . . . . million × million (10^{12})
Quadrillion . . . . million × billion U.S. (10^{15})

Angular or Circular Measures

60 seconds (″) = 1 minute (′).
60 minutes = 1 degree (°).
90 degrees = 1 right angle or quadrant.
Diameter of circle × 3·141 6 = circumference.
Diameter squared × 0·7854 = area of circle.
Diameter squared × 3·141 6 = surface of sphere.
Diameter cubed × 0·523 = solidity of sphere.
One degree of circumference × 57·3 = radius.*
Diameter of cylinder × 3·141 6; product by length or height, gives the surface.
Diameter squared × 0·7854; product by length or height, gives solid content.

* Or, one radian (the angle subtended at the centre of a circle by an arc of the circumference equal in length to the radius) = 57·3 degrees, nearly.

THERMOMETER COMPARISONS

Comparison between Scales of Fahrenheit, Réaumur and Centigrade

CENT.	FAH'T.	RMR.	CENT.	FAH'T.	RMR.
°	°	°	°	°	°
100B.	212B.	80B.	25	77	20
99	210·2	79·2	24	75·2	19·2
98	208·4	78·4	23	73·4	18·4
97	206·6	77·6	22	71·6	17·6
96	204·8	76·8	21	69·8	16·8
95	203	76	20	68	16
94	201·2	75·2	19	66·2	15·2
93	199·4	74·4	18	64·4	14·4
92	197·6	73·6	17	62·6	13·6
91	195·8	72·8	16	60·8	12·8
90	194	72	15	59	12
89	192·2	71·2	14	57·2	11·2
88	190·4	70·4	13	55·4	10·4
87	188·6	69·6	12	53·6	9·6
86	186·8	68·8	11	51·8	8·8
85	185	68	10	50	8
84	183·2	67·2	9	48·2	7·2
83	181·4	66·4	8	46·4	6·4
82	179·6	65·6	7	44·6	5·6
81	177·8	64·8	6	42·8	4·8
80	176	64	5	41	4
79	174·2	63	4	39·2	3·2
78	172·4	62·4	3	37·4	2·4
77	170·6	61·6	2	35·6	1·6
76	168·8	60·8	1	33·8	0·8
75	167	60	*zero*	32	*zero*
74	165·2	59·2	1	30·2	0·8
73	163·4	58·4	2	28·4	1·6
72	161·6	57·6	3	26·6	2·4
71	159·8	56·8	4	24·8	3·2
70	158	56	5	23	4
69	156·2	55·2	6	21·2	4·8
68	154·4	54·4	7	19·4	5·6
67	152·6	53·6	8	17·6	6·4
66	150·8	52·8	9	15·8	7·2
65	149	52	10	14	8
64	147·2	51·2	11	12·2	8·8
63	145·4	50·4	12	10·4	9·6
62	143·6	49·6	13	8·6	10·4
61	141·8	48·8	14	6·8	11·2
60	140	48	15	5	12
59	138·2	47·2	16	3·2	12·8
58	136·4	46·4	17	1·4	13·6
57	134·6	45·6	18	0·4	14·4
56	132·8	44·8	19	2·2	15·2
55	131	44	20	4	16
54	129·2	43·2	21	5·8	16·8
53	127·4	42·4	22	7·6	17·6
52	125·6	41·6	23	9·3	18·4
51	123·8	40·8	24	11·2	19·2
50	122	40	25	13	20
49	120·2	39·2	26	14·8	20·8
48	118·4	38·4	27	16·6	21·6
47	116·6	37·6	28	18·4	22·4
46	114·8	36·8	29	20·2	23·2
45	113	36	30	22	24
44	111·2	35·2	31	23·8	24·8
43	109·4	34·4	32	25·6	25·6
42	107·6	33·6	33	27·4	26·4
41	105·8	32·8	34	29·2	27·2
40	104	32	35	31	28
39	102·2	31·2	36	32·8	28·8
38	100·4	30·4	37	34·6	29·6
37	98·6	29·6	38	36·4	30·4
36	96·8	28·8	39	38·2	31·2
35	95	28	40	40	32
34	93·2	27·2	41	41·8	32·8
33	91·4	26·4	42	43·6	33·6
32	89·6	25·6	43	45·4	34·4
31	87·8	24·8	44	47·2	35·2
30	86	24	45	49	36
29	84·2	23·2	46	50·8	36·8
28	82·4	22·4	47	52·6	37·6
27	80·6	21·6	48	54·4	38·4
26	78·8	20·8	49	56·2	39·2

CONVERSION: Let F = Fahr., " C = Cent., " R = Réaum.

$F = C + R + 32$

$^*F = \frac{9C}{5} + 32$ $\quad F = \frac{9R}{4} + 32$

$C = 5\frac{(F-32)}{9}$ $\quad R = \frac{4(F-32)}{9}$

NOTE.—The *normal* temperature of the *human body* is 98·4°F., or 37° (36·9°) C., or 29·5° R. *Freezing* point = 32°F. = 0°C. = 0°R.; *Boiling* point = 212° F. = 100° C. = 80° R.

"*Absolute*" Temperature is Temperature reckoned from "*Absolute Zero*," which is at 273° C. below 0° C., 459·4° below 0° F., and 218·4° below 0° R. and is denoted by the letter "K."

* Below 32° F. *subtract* 32.

PAPER MEASURES

Writing Paper	*Printing Paper*
480 sheets = 1 ream	516 sheets = 1 ream
24 sheets = 1 quire	2 reams = 1 bundle
20 quires = 1 ream	5 bundles = 1 bale

Sizes of Writing and Drawing Papers

Emperor	= 72 × 48	inches
Antiquarian	= 53 × 31	"
Double Elephant	= 40 × 27	"
Grand Eagle	= 42 × 28¾	"
Atlas	= 34 × 26	"
Colombier	= 34½ × 23½	"
Imperial	= 30 × 22	"
Elephant	= 28 × 23	"
Cartridge	= 26 × 21	"
Super Royal	= 27 × 19	"
Royal	= 24 × 19	"
Medium	= 22 × 17½	"
Large Post	= 21 × 16½	"
Copy or Draft	= 20 × 16	"
Demy	= 20 × 15½	"
Post	= 19 × 15¼	"
Pinched Post	= 18½ × 14¾	"
Foolscap	= 17 × 13½	"
Double Foolscap	= 26½ × 16½	"
Double Post	= 30½ × 19	"
Double Large Post	= 33 × 21	"
Double Demy	= 31 × 20	"
Brief	= 16½ × 13¼	"
Pott	= 15 × 12½	"

Sizes of Printing Papers

Foolscap	= 17 × 13½	inches
Double Foolscap	= 27 × 17	"
Quad Foolscap	= 34 × 27	"
Crown	= 20 × 15	"
Double Crown	= 30 × 20	"
Quad Crown	= 40 × 30	"
Double Quad Crown	= 60 × 40	"
Post	= 19¼ × 15½	"
Double Post	= 31½ × 19½	"
Double Large Post	= 33 × 21	"
Demy	= 22½ × 17½	"
Double Demy	= 35 × 22½	"
Quad Demy	= 45 × 35	"
Music Demy	= 20 × 15½	"
Medium	= 23 × 18	"
Royal	= 25 × 20	"
Super Royal	= 27½ × 20½	"
Elephant	= 28 × 23	"
Imperial	= 30 × 22	"

Sizes of Brown Papers

Casing	= 46 × 36	inches
Double Imperial	= 45 × 29	"
Elephant	= 34 × 24	"
Double Four Pound	= 31 × 21	"
Imperial Cap	= 29 × 22	"
Haven Cap	= 26 × 21	"
Bag Cap	= 24 × 19½	"
Kent Cap	= 21 × 18	"

INTERNATIONAL PAPER SIZES

The basis of the international series of paper sizes is a rectangle having an area of one square metre, the sides of which are in the proportion of $1:\sqrt{2}$. The proportions $1:\sqrt{2}$ have a geometrical relationship, the side and diagonal of any square being in this proportion. The effect of this arrangement is that if the area of the sheet of paper is doubled or halved, the shorter side and the longer side of the new sheet are still in the same proportion $1:\sqrt{2}$. This feature is useful where photographic enlargement or reduction is used, as the proportions remain the same.

Description of the A series is by capital A followed by a figure. The basic size has the description A0 and the higher the figure following the letter, the greater is the number of sub-divisions and therefore the smaller the sheet. Half A0 is A1 and half A1 is A2. Where larger dimensions are required the A is *preceded* by a figure. Thus 2A means twice the size A0; 4A is four times the size of A0.

Subsidiary Series.—A series of B sizes has been devised for use in exceptional circumstances when sizes intermediate between any two adjacent sizes of the A series are needed.

In addition there is a series of C sizes which is used much less. A is for magazines and books, B for posters, wall charts and other large items, C for envelopes particularly where it is necessary for an envelope (in C series) to fit into another envelope. The size recommended for business correspondence is A4.

Long Sizes.—Long sizes are obtainable by dividing any appropriate sizes from the two series above into three, four or eight equal parts parallel with the shorter side in such a manner that the proportions mentioned in paragraph 2 (above) are not maintained, the ratio between the longer and the shorter sides being greater than $\sqrt{2}$:1. In practice long sizes should be produced from the A series only.

It is an essential feature of these series that the dimensions are of the trimmed or finished size.

'A' Series

	mm	*inches*
A0	841 × 1189	33·11 × 46·81
A1	594 × 841	23·39 × 33·11
A2	420 × 594	16·54 × 23·39
A3	297 × 420	11·69 × 16·54
A4	210 × 297	8·27 × 11·69
A5	148 × 210	5·83 × 8·27
A6	105 × 148	4·13 × 5·83
A7	74 × 105	2·91 × 4·13
A8	52 × 74	2·05 × 2·91
A9	37 × 52	1·46 × 2·05
A10	26 × 37	1·02 × 1·46

'B' Series

	mm	*inches*
B0	1000 × 1414	39·37 × 55·67
B1	707 × 1000	27·83 × 39·37
B2	500 × 707	19·68 × 27·83
B3	353 × 500	13·90 × 19·68
B4	250 × 353	9·84 × 13·90
B5	176 × 250	6·93 × 9·84
B6	125 × 176	4·92 × 6·93
B7	88 × 125	3·46 × 4·92
B8	62 × 88	2·44 × 3·46
B9	44 × 62	1·73 × 2·44
B10	31 × 44	1·22 × 1·73

SIZES OF BOUND BOOKS

The book sizes most commonly used are listed below. Approximate centimetre equivalents are in brackets. International sizes are converted to their nearest Imperial Size (*e.g.* A4 = D4; A5 = D8).

		inches	*cms*
Crown 32mo	C32	2½ × 3¾	6 × 6
Crown 16mo	C16	3¾ × 5	9 × 13
Foolscap 8vo	F8	4¼ × 6¾	11 × 17
Demy 16mo	D16	4⅜ × 5⅝	11 × 14
Crown 8vo	C8	5 × 7½	13 × 19
Demy 8vo	D8	5⅝ × 8¾	14 × 22
Medium 8vo	M8	5¾ × 9	15 × 23
Royal 8vo	R8	6¼ × 10	16 × 25
Super Royal 8vo	suR8	6¾ × 10	17 × 25
Foolscap 4to	F4	6¾ × 8½	17 × 22
Crown 4to	C4	7½ × 10	19 × 25
Imperial 8vo	Imp8	7½ × 11	19 × 28
Demy 4to	D4	8¾ × 11¼	22 × 29
Royal 4to	R4	10 × 12½	25 × 31
Super Royal 4to	suR4	10 × 13½	25 × 34
Crown Folio	Cfol	10 × 15	25 × 38
Imperial Folio	Impfol	11 × 15	28 × 38

Folio means a sheet folded in half, *quarto* (4to) folded into four, *octavo* (8vo) folded into eight. Books are usually bound up in sheets of 16 or 32 pages. Octavo books are generally printed 64 pages at a time—32 pages on each side of a sheet of quad.

A TABLE OF THE NUMBER OF DAYS FROM ANY DAY IN ONE MONTH TO THE SAME IN ANY OTHER MONTH IN ORDINARY YEARS

	Jan.	Feb.	Mar.	April	May	June	July	Aug.	Sept.	Oct.	Nov.	Dec.
January	365	31	59	90	120	151	181	212	243	273	304	334
February	334	365	28	59	89	120	150	181	212	242	273	303
March	306	337	365	31	61	92	122	153	184	214	245	275
April	275	306	334	365	30	61	91	122	153	183	214	244
May	245	276	304	335	365	31	61	92	123	153	184	214
June	214	245	273	304	334	365	30	61	92	122	153	183
July	184	215	243	274	304	335	365	31	62	92	123	153
August	153	184	212	243	273	304	334	365	31	61	92	122
September	122	153	181	212	242	273	303	334	365	30	61	91
October	92	123	151	182	212	243	273	304	335	365	31	61
November	61	92	120	151	181	212	242	273	304	334	365	30
December	31	62	90	121	151	182	212	243	274	304	335	365

CONVERSION TABLES FOR WEIGHTS AND MEASURES

NOTE.—The central figures in heavy type represent either of the two columns beside them, as the case may be.
Examples:—1 centimetre=0·394 inch and 1 inch=2·540 centimetres. 1 metre=1·094 yards and 1 yard=
0·914 metre. 1 kilometre=0·621 mile and 1 mile=1·609 kilometres.

Length			Area			Volume			Weight (Mass)		
Centi-metres		Inches	Square Centi-metres		Square Inches	Cubic Centi-metres		Cubic Inches	Kilo-grams		Pounds
2·540	1	0·394	6·452	1	0·155	16·387	1	0·061	0·454	1	2·205
5·080	2	0·787	12·903	2	0·310	32·774	2	0·122	0·907	2	4·409
7·620	3	1·181	19·355	3	0·465	49·161	3	0·183	1·361	3	6·614
10·160	4	1·575	25·806	4	0·620	65·548	4	0·244	1·814	4	8·819
12·700	5	1·969	32·258	5	0·775	81·936	5	0·305	2·268	5	11·023
15·240	6	2·362	38·710	6	0·930	98·323	6	0·366	2·722	6	13·228
17·780	7	2·756	45·161	7	1·085	114·710	7	0·427	3·175	7	15·432
20·320	8	3·150	51·613	8	1·240	131·097	8	0·488	3·629	8	17·637
22·860	9	3·543	58·064	9	1·395	147·484	9	0·549	4·082	9	19·842
25·400	10	3·937	64·516	10	1·550	163·871	10	0·610	4·536	10	22·046
50·800	20	7·874	129·032	20	3·100	327·742	20	1·220	9·072	20	44·092
76·200	30	11·811	193·548	30	4·650	491·613	30	1·831	13·608	30	66·139
101·600	40	15·748	258·064	40	6·200	655·484	40	2·441	18·144	40	88·185
127·000	50	19·685	322·580	50	7·750	819·355	50	3·051	22·680	50	110·231
152·400	60	23·622	387·096	60	9·300	983·226	60	3·661	27·216	60	132·277
177·800	70	27·559	451·612	70	10·850	1147·097	70	4·272	31·752	70	154·324
203·200	80	31·496	516·128	80	12·400	1310·968	80	4·882	36·287	80	176·370
228·600	90	35·433	580·644	90	13·950	1474·839	90	5·492	40·823	90	198·416
254·000	100	39·370	645·160	100	15·500	1638·710	100	6·102	45·359	100	220·464

Metres		Yards	Square Metres		Square Yards	Cubic Metres		Cubic Yards	Metric Tonnes		Tons (U.K.)
0·914	1	1·094	0·836	1	1·196	0·765	1	1·308	1·016	1	0·984
1·829	2	2·187	1·672	2	2·392	1·529	2	2·616	2·032	2	1·968
2·743	3	3·281	2·508	3	3·588	2·294	3	3·924	3·048	3	2·953
3·658	4	4·374	3·345	4	4·784	3·058	4	5·232	4·064	4	3·937
4·572	5	5·468	4·181	5	5·980	3·823	5	6·540	5·080	5	4·921
5·486	6	6·562	5·017	6	7·176	4·587	6	7·848	6·096	6	5·905
6·401	7	7·655	5·853	7	8·372	5·352	7	9·156	7·112	7	6·889
7·315	8	8·749	6·689	8	9·568	6·116	8	10·464	8·128	8	7·874
8·230	9	9·843	7·525	9	10·764	6·881	9	11·772	9·144	9	8·858
9·144	10	10·936	8·361	10	11·960	7·646	10	13·080	10·161	10	9·842
18·288	20	21·872	16·723	20	23·920	15·291	20	26·159	20·321	20	19·684
27·432	30	32·808	25·084	30	35·880	22·937	30	39·239	30·481	30	29·526
36·576	40	43·745	33·445	40	47·840	30·582	40	52·318	40·642	40	39·368
45·720	50	54·681	41·806	50	59·799	38·228	50	65·398	50·802	50	49·210
54·864	60	65·617	50·168	60	71·759	45·873	60	78·477	60·963	60	59·052
64·008	70	76·553	58·529	70	83·719	53·519	70	91·557	71·123	70	68·894
73·152	80	87·489	66·890	80	95·679	61·164	80	104·636	81·284	80	78·737
82·296	90	98·425	75·251	90	107·639	68·810	90	117·716	91·444	90	88·579
91·440	100	109·361	83·613	100	119·599	76·455	100	130·795	101·605	100	98·421

Kilo-metres		Miles	Hectares		Acres	Litres		Gallons	Metric Tonnes		Tons (U.S.)
1·609	1	0·621	0·405	1	2·471	4·546	1	0·220	0·907	1	1·102
3·219	2	1·243	0·809	2	4·942	9·092	2	0·440	1·814	2	2·205
4·828	3	1·864	1·214	3	7·413	13·638	3	0·660	2·722	3	3·305
6·437	4	2·485	1·619	4	9·844	18·184	4	0·880	3·629	4	4·409
8·047	5	3·107	2·023	5	12·355	22·730	5	1·100	4·536	5	5·521
9·656	6	3·728	2·428	6	14·826	27·276	6	1·320	5·443	6	6·614
11·265	7	4·350	2·833	7	17·297	31·822	7	1·540	6·350	7	7·716
12·875	8	4·971	3·327	8	19·769	36·368	8	1·760	7·257	8	8·818
14·484	9	5·592	3·642	9	22·240	40·914	9	1·980	8·165	9	9·921
16·093	10	6·214	4·047	10	24·711	45·460	10	2·200	9·072	10	11·023
32·187	20	12·427	8·094	20	49·421	90·919	20	4·400	18·144	20	22·046
48·280	30	18·641	12·140	30	74·132	136·379	30	6·599	27·216	30	33·069
64·374	40	24·855	16·187	40	98·842	181·839	40	8·799	36·287	40	44·092
80·467	50	31·069	20·234	50	123·555	227·298	50	10·999	45·359	50	55·116
96·561	60	37·282	24·281	60	148·263	272·758	60	13·199	54·431	60	66·139
112·654	70	43·496	28·328	70	172·974	318·217	70	15·398	63·503	70	77·162
128·748	80	49·710	32·375	80	197·684	363·677	80	17·598	72·575	80	88·185
144·841	90	55·923	36·422	90	222·395	409·137	90	19·798	81·647	90	99·208
160·934	100	62·137	40·469	100	247·105	454·596	100	21·998	90·719	100	110·231

FOREIGN EXCHANGE RATES

Country	Denomination	1939 Average Rate to £ (approx.)	15 September, 1987 Middle Rate
A. London Market Rates			
Austria	Schilling	—	20·9650
Belgium	Franc	26·49 Belgas	61·85
Canada	Canadian Dollar	4·545	2·1540
Denmark	Krone	22·26	11·4750
Finland	Markka	217½	7·2150
France	Franc	176·10	9·9410
Germany (West)	Deutsche Mark	—	2·9775
Greece	Drachma	545	227·50
Italy	Lira	85	2,149·50
Japan	Yen	½d	236·50
Netherlands	Guilder	8·34	3·3515
Netherlands (Antilles)	Antillian Guilder	8·34	2·9466
Norway	Krone	19·45	10·9150
Portugal	Escudo	110·07	234·50
Spain	Peseta	42·45	199·60
Sweden	Krona	18·59	10·4850
Switzerland	Franc	19·87	2·4705
U.S.A.	Dollar	4·485	1·6355
B. Former Scheduled Territories			
Australia	Australian Dollar	A£1·2525	2·2445
Bahamas	Bahamas Dollar	—	1·6370
Barbados	Barbados Dollar	—	3·2925
Belize	Belize Dollar	—	3·2740
Bermuda	Bermuda Dollar	—	1·6370
Cyprus	Cyprus £	—	0·7790
Ghana	New Cedi	—	275·8560
Hong Kong	Hong Kong Dollar	—	12·7590
Iceland	Króna	—	63·83
India	Rupee	13·38	21·30
Jamaica	Jamaica Dollar	—	8·8425
Jordan	Dinar	Par	0·5620
Kenya	Shilling	—	27·00
Kuwait	Dinar	—	0·4599
Libya	Dinar	—	0·4837
Malawi	Kwacha	—	3·6700
Malaysia	Malaysian Dollar	—	4·1295
Malta	Maltese Lira	—	0·5665
New Zealand..............	New Zealand Dollar	£1·2425	2·5956
Nigeria	Naira	—	6·9975
Pakistan	Rupee	—	28·20
South Africa..............	Rand	S.A.£1	3·3560
Tanzania	Shilling	—	112·00
Trinidad	Trinidad and Tobago $	—	5·8932
Uganda	Shilling	—	98·00
Yemen, North	Riyal	—	16·85
Zambia	Kwacha	—	12·60
C. Other Rates			
Algeria	Dinar	—	7·6518
Argentina	Austral	19	3·9615
Bolivia	Peso	141·50	3·4528
Brazil	Cruzado	—	80·2095
Bulgaria	Lev	375	1·3860
Burma	Kyat	13·38	10·8865
Chile	Peso	116½	368·18
China	Renminbi (Yuan)	4½	6·1524
Colombia	Peso	7·59	413·80
Costa Rica	Colon	25·16	104·42
Cuba	Peso	4·386	1·2857
Czechoslovakia	Koruna	—	8·90
Ecuador	Sucre	66	259·60
Egypt	Egyptian £	97½ (per £100 London)	3·618
Ethiopia	Birr	—	3·3925
Germany (East)	Ostmark	—	2·9750

Country	Denomination	1939 Average Rate to £ (approx.)	15 September, 1987 Middle Rate
Guatemala	*Quetzal*	4·386	1·6370
Guinea	*Franc Guineen*	—	557·09
Haiti	*Gourde*	22·4	8·1890
Honduras	*Lempira*	8½	3·2691
Hungary	*Forint*	20½	78·2174
Indonesia	*Rupiah*	—	2,710·98
Iran	*Rial*	80·50 (Persian)	117·50
Iraq	*Dinar*	Par	0·5109
Israel	*Shekel*	—	2·815
Lebanon	*Lebanese £*	9·65	440·73
Madagascar	*Franc M. G.*	17 (F. Fr.)	1880·25
Mexico	*Peso*	—	2489·00
Morocco	*Dirham*	176·10 (F. Fr.)	13·60
Nicaragua	*Córdoba*	24	3,589·65
Paraguay	*Guarani*	—	523·04
Peru	*Inti*	24½	47·55
Philippines	*Peso*	—	32·80
Poland	*Zloty*	23¼	476·79
Romania	*Leu*	655	16·26
Salvador, El	*Colon*	11·20	8·1753
Saudi Arabia	*Riyal*	—	6·1325
Sudan	*Sudan £*	97½ (per 100)	4·0925
Syria	*Syrian £*	—	6·4252
Thailand	*Baht*	10·91	41·70
Tunisia	*Tunisian Dinar*	—	1·3858
Turkey	*Turkish Lira*	—	1,489·09
Uruguay	*New Peso*	9	393·62
U.S.S.R.	*Rouble*	23·75	1·0410
Venezuela	*Bolivar*	14·15	12·28
Vietnam	*Dông*	—	131·08
Yugoslavia	*Yugoslav Dinar*	197¼ (YD)	1,345·00
Zaire	*Zaïre*	—	196·630

BUCHAN'S WEATHER PERIODS OR RECURRENCES OF WEATHER

Dr. Alexander Buchan, F.R.S., Secretary of the Scottish Meteorological Society, published in 1867 a paper in the Journal of that Society entitled "Interruptions in the regular rise and fall of temperature in the course of the year". Buchan gave six cold periods and three warm periods, based on his examination of the mean daily temperature as recorded at stations in Scotland covering long periods. The cold periods were February 7–14, April 11–14, May 9–14, June 29–July 4, August 6–11, November 6–13, and the warm periods July 12–15, August 12–15, and December 3–14. This early work aroused considerable interest later. It should be noted, however, that Buchan claimed no more than the existence of tendencies for short spells of relatively cold and warm weather to occur at certain times of the year.

In recent years these smaller fluctuations of weather super-imposed on the normal seasonal changes have been examined from the aspect of tendencies to stormy or anticyclonic spells over the British Isles and have been referred to as "singularities". Stormy periods are relatively warm in winter and cool in summer. The following tendencies have been given:—Jan. 5–17 stormy; Jan. 18–24 anticyclonic; Jan. 24–Feb. 1 stormy; Feb. 8–16 anticyclonic; Feb. 21–25 cold; Feb. 26–Mar. 9 stormy; Mar. 12–19 anticyclonic; Mar. 24–31 stormy; April 10–15 stormy; April 23–26 unsettled; June 1–21 summer monsoon; July 10–24 warm; Aug. 20–30 stormy; Sept. 1–17 anticyclonic; Sept. 17–24 stormy; Sept. 24–Oct. 4 anticyclonic; Oct. 5–12 stormy; Oct. 16–20 anticyclonic; Oct. 24–Nov. 13 stormy; Nov. 15–21 anticyclonic; Nov. 24–Dec. 14 stormy; Dec. 18–24 anticyclonic; Dec. 25–Jan. 1 stormy.

ABBREVIATIONS

Ψ = Seaport.

A

A.—Associate of.
A.A.—Automobile Association; Anti-Aircraft.
A.A.A.—Amateur Athletic Association.
A. and M.—(Hymns) Ancient and Modern.
A.B.—Able-bodied seaman.
A.B.A.—Amateur Boxing Association.
abbrev.—abbreviation.
A.B.M.—Anti-ballistic missile defence system.
Abr.—abridged.
a.c.—alternating current.
a/c.—accounts.
A.C.—Companion, Order of Australia; Aircraftman.
A.C.A.S.—Advisory, Conciliation and Arbitration Service.
A.C.T.—Australian Capital Territory.
A.C.T.T.—Association of Cinematograph, Television and Allied Technicians.
ad(vert)—advertisement.
A.D.—(*Anno Domini*) In the year of our Lord.
A.D.C.—Aide-de-Camp.
A.D.C.(P).—Personal A.D.C. to The Queen.
adj.—adjective.
Adjt.—Adjutant.
Ad lib.—(*ad libitum*) at pleasure.
Adm.—Admiral; Admission.
adv.—adverb.
A.E.—Air Efficiency Award.
A.E.A.—Atomic Energy Authority.
A.E.M.—Air Efficiency Medal.
A.E.R.E.—Atomic Energy Research Establishment.
A.F.C.—Air Force Cross; Association Football Club.
A.F.M.—Air Force Medal.
A.F.V.—Armoured fighting vehicle.
A.G.—Adjutant-General.
A.H.—(*Anno Hegirae*) In the year of the Hegira.
A.I.D.S.—Acquired Immune Deficiency Syndrome.
alt.—altitude.
a.m.—(*ante meridiem*) before noon.
A.M.—(*Anno mundi*) In the year of the world.
A.M.D.G.—(*Ad majorem Dei gloriam*) To the greater glory of God.
amp.—ampere.
A.N.C.—African National Congress.
anon.—anonymous.
A.N.Z.A.C.—Australian and New Zealand Army Corps.
A.O.—Officer, Order of Australia.
A.O.C.—Air Officer Commanding.
A.R.C.—Agricultural Research Council.
A.S.—Anglo-Saxon.
A.S.A.—Amateur Swimming Association.
A.S.B.—Alternative Service Book.

A.S.E.A.N.—Association of South East Asian Nations.
A.S.H.—Action on Smoking and Health.
A.S.L.E.F.—Associated Society of Locomotive Engineers and Firemen.
A.S.L.I.B.—Association for Information Management (*formerly* Association of Special Libraries and Information Bureaux).
A.S.T.M.S.—Association of Scientific, Technical and Managerial Staffs.
A.T.C.—Air Training Corps.
A.U.C.—(*ab urbe condita*) In the year from the foundation of Rome; (*anno urbis conditae*) In the year of the founding of the city.
A.U.E.W.—Amalgamated Union of Engineering Workers.
A.U.T.—Association of University Teachers.
A.V.—Authorized Version.
A.V.R.—Army Volunteer Reserve.
A.W.O.L.—Absent without leave.

B

b.—born; bowled.
B.A.—Bachelor of Arts.
B.A.A.—British Astronomical Association; British Airports Authority.
B. Acc.—Bachelor of Accountancy.
B.A.F.—British Athletic Federation.
B.A.F.T.A.—British Academy of Film and Television Arts.
B.A.O.R.—British Army of the Rhine.
B. Arch.—Bachelor of Architecture.
B.A.S.—British Antarctic Survey.
B.B.—Boys' Brigade.
B.B.C.—British Broadcasting Corporation.
B.C.—Before Christ; British Columbia.
B. Ch. (or Ch.B.)—Bachelor of Surgery.
B.C.L.—*do*, of Civil Law.
B. Com.—*do*, of Commerce.
B.D.—*do*, of Divinity.
B.D.A.—British Dental Association.
B.D.S. (or B.Ch.D.)—Bachelor of Dental Surgery.
B. Ed.—*do*, of Education.
B.E.M.—British Empire Medal.
B. Eng.—Bachelor of Engineering.
B.F.I.—British Film Institute.
B.F.P.O.—British Forces Post Office.
B.I.M.—British Institute of Management.
B.L.A.I.S.E.—British Library Automated Information Service.
B. Litt.—Bachelor of Literature *or* of Letters.
B.M.—*do*, of Medicine; British Museum.

B.M.A.—British Medical Association.
B. Mus.—Bachelor of Music.
B.O.T.B.—British Overseas Trade Board.
Bp.—Bishop.
B. Pharm.—Bachelor of Pharmacy.
B. Phil.—*do*, of Philosophy.
Br. (*or* Brit.)—British.
B.R.—British Rail.
B.R.C.S.—British Red Cross Society.
Brig.—Brigadier.
B.Sc.—Bachelor of Science.
B.S.C.—British Steel Corporation.
B.S.I.—British Standards Institution.
B.S.T.—British Summer Time.
Bt. (*or* Bart.)—Baronet.
B.T.G.—British Technology Group.
B. Th.—Bachelor of Theology.
B.t.u.—British thermal unit.
B.U.P.A.—British United Provident Association.
B.V.M.—Blessed Virgin Mary.
B.V.M.S.—Bachelor of Veterinary Medicine and Surgery.
B.W.B.—British Waterways Board.

C

c.—(*circa*) about.
C.—Celsius; Centigrade.
C. (*or* Con.)—Conservative.
C.A.—Chartered Accountant (*Scottish Institute*).
C.A.A.—Civil Aviation Authority.
C.A.B.—Citizens' Advice Bureau.
Cantab.—(of) Cambridge.
Cantuar.—of Canterbury (*Archbishop*).
C.A.P.—Common Agricultural Policy.
Capt.—Captain.
Caricom—Caribbean Community and Common Market.
Carliol.—of Carlisle (*Bishop*).
C.A.S.—Chief of Air Staff.
C.B.—Companion, Order of the Bath.
C.B.E.—Commander, Order of the British Empire.
C.B.I.—Confederation of British Industry.
cc.—cubic centimetres.
C.C.—County Council; County Councillor; Chamber of Commerce.
C.C.C.—County Cricket Club.
C. Chem.—Chartered Chemist.
C.D.—Civil Defence.
Cdr.—Commander.
Cdre.—Commodore.
C.E.—Civil Engineer.
C.E.G.B.—Central Electricity Generating Board.
C. Eng.—Chartered Engineer.
C.E.N.T.O.—Central Treaty Organization.
C.E.T.—Common External Tariff; Central European Time.
Cestr.—of Chester (*Bishop*).
cf.—confer; compare.

C.F.—Chaplain to the Forces.
C.G.M.—Conspicuous Gallantry Medal.
C.G.S.—Chief of General Staff; Centimetre-gramme-second (system).
C.H.—Companion of Honour.
Ch.B./M.—Bachelor/Master of Surgery.
C.I.—The Imperial Order of the Crown of India; Channel Islands.
C.I.A.—Central Intelligence Agency.
C.I.D.—Criminal Investigation Department.
C.I.E.—Companion, Order of the Indian Empire.
c.i.f.—cost, insurance and freight.
C.-in-C.—Commander-in-Chief.
C.I.P.F.A.—Chartered Institute of Public Finance and Accountancy.
Cicestr.—of Chichester (*Bishop*).
C.L. (*or* C. Litt.)—Companion of Literature.
C.L.J.—Commander, Order of St. Lazarus of Jerusalem.
C.M.—(*Chirurgiae Magister*) Master of Surgery.
C.M.G.—Companion, Order of St. Michael and St. George.
C.M.S.—Church Missionary Society.
C.N.A.A.—Council for National Academic Awards.
C.N.D.—Campaign for Nuclear Disarmament.
c/o—care of.
C.O.—Commanding Officer; Conscientious Objector.
C.O.D.—Cash on delivery.
C. of E.—Church of England.
C.O.H.S.E.—Confederation of Health Service Employees.
C.O.I.—Central Office of Information.
Col.—Colonel.
Comecon.—Council for Mutual Economic Assistance (East European).
C.P.—Communist Party.
Cpl.—Corporal.
C.P.M.—Colonial Police Medal.
C.P.R.E.—Council for the Protection of Rural England.
C.R.E.—Council for Racial Equality.
C.S.E.—Certificate of Secondary Education.
C.S.I.—Companion, Order of the Star of India.
C.T.—Civic Trust.
C.T.C.—Cyclists' Touring Club.
C.V.O.—Commander, Royal Victorian Order.
cwt.—hundredweight.

D

d.—(*denarius*) penny.
D.B.E.—Dame Commander, Order of the British Empire.
d.c.—direct current.
D.C.—District of Columbia.
D.C.B.—Dame Commander, Order of the Bath.
D. Ch.—(*Doctor Chirurgiae*) Doctor of Surgery.

D.C.L.—Doctor of Civil Law.
D.C.M.—Distinguished Conduct Medal.
D.C.M.G.—Dame Commander, Order of St. Michael and St. George.
D.C.V.O.—Dame Commander, Royal Victorian Order.
D.D.—Doctor of Divinity.
D.D.S.—*do*, of Dental Surgery.
D.D.T.—dichlorodiphenyl-trichloroethane (insecticide).
del.—(*delineavit*) he/she drew it.
D.E.S.—Department of Education and Science.
D.F.C.—Distinguished Flying Cross.
D.F.M.—Distinguished Flying Medal.
D.G.—(*Dei gratia*) By the grace of God; Director-General.
D.H.Q.—District Headquarters.
D.H.S.S.—Department of Health and Social Security.
Dip. Ed.—Diploma in Education.
Dip. H. E.—Diploma in Higher Education.
Dip. Tech.—Diploma in Technology.
D.J.—Disc jockey.
D.L.—Deputy-Lieutenant.
D. Litt.—Doctor of Letters *or* of Literature.
D. Mus.—*do*, of Music.
D.N.A.—deoxyribonucleic acid.
D.N.B.—Dictionary of National Biography.
Do.—(*ditto*) the same.
D.o.E.—Department of the Environment.
D.O.M.—(*Dominus Omnium Magister*) God the Master of All.
D. Phil.—Doctor of Philosophy.
D.P.P.—Director of Public Prosecutions.
Dr.—Doctor.
D.Sc.—Doctor of Science.
D.S.C.—Distinguished Service Cross.
D.S.M.—Distinguished Service Medal.
D.S.O.—Companion, Distinguished Service Order.
D.Th.—Doctor of Theology.
Dunelm.—of Durham (*Bishop*).
D.V.—(*Deo volente*) God willing.

E

E. (*or* O.E.)—Errors and omissions excepted.
Ebor.—of York (*Archbishop*).
E.C.—European Community; Electricity Council.
E.C.G.—Electrocardiograph.
E.C.S.C.—European Coal and Steel Community.
E.C.T.U.—European Confederation of Trade Unions.
E.D.—Efficiency Decoration.
E.E.C.—European Economic Community.
E.E.G.—Electroencephalograph.
E.F.T.A.—European Free Trade Association.
e.g.—(*exempli gratia*) for the sake of example.
Elien.—of Ely (*Bishop*).
E.M.S.—European Monetary System.

E.N.E.A.—European Nuclear Energy Agency.
E.R.—Elizabeth Regina.
E.R.D.—Emergency Reserve Decoration.
E.R.N.I.E.—Electronic random number indicator equipment.
E.S.A.—European Space Agency.
E.S.P.—Extra-sensory perception.
E.S.R.C.—Economic and Social Research Council.
et al.—(*et alibi*) and elsewhere; (*et alii*) and others.
etc.—(*et cetera*) and the other things.
et seq.—(*et sequentia*) and the following.
Euratom—European Atomic Energy Commission.
ex lib.—(*ex libris*) from the books of.
Exon.—of Exeter (*Bishop*).

F

f (ff)—and the following page(s).
F.—Fahrenheit; Fellow of.
F.A.—Football Association.
F.A.N.Y.—First Aid Nursing Yeomanry.
F.A.O.—Food and Agriculture Organization.
F.B.A.—Fellow of British Academy.
F.B.A.A.—*do*, of the British Association of Accountants.
F.B.I.—Federal Bureau of Investigation.
F.B.I.M.—Fellow of the British Institute of Management.
F.B.S.—*do*, of Botanical Society.
F.C.A.—*do*, of Institute of Chartered Accountants (of England and Wales).
F.C.C.A.—*do*, of Association of Certified Accountants.
F.C.G.I.—*do*, of City and Guilds Institute.
F.C.I.A.—*do*, of Corporation of Insurance Agents.
F.C.I.B.—*do*, of Chartered Institute of Bankers; of Corporation of Insurance Brokers.
F.C.I.B.S.—*do*, of Chartered Institution of Building-Services Engineers.
F.C.I.I.—*do*, of Chartered Insurance Institute.
F.C.I.S.—*do*, of Chartered Institute of Secretaries and Administrators.
F.C.I.T.—*do*, of Chartered Institute of Transport.
F.C.M.A.—*do*, of Institute of Cost and Management Accountants.
F.C.O.—Foreign and Commonwealth Office.
fcp.—foolscap.
F.C.P.—Fellow of the College of Preceptors.
F.D.—(*Fidei Defensor*) Defender of the Faith.
fec.—(*fecit*) he did it/made it.
F.Eng.—Fellow of the Fellowship of Engineering.
F.F.A.S.—*do*, of the Faculty of Architects and Surveyors.

F.F.R.—*do*, of Faculty of Radiologists.

F.G.S.—*do*, of Geological Society.

F.H.—Fire hydrant.

F.H.S.—Fellow of the Heraldry Society.

F.I.A.—*do*, of Institute of Actuaries.

F.I.Arb.—*do*, of Institute of Arbitrators.

F.I.Biol.—*do*, of Institute of Biology.

F.I.C.E.—*do*, of Institution of Civil Engineers.

F.I.C.S.—*do*, of Institution of Chartered Shipbrokers.

F.I.E.E.—*do*, of Institution of Electrical Engineers.

F.I.M.—*do*, of Institute of Metals.

F.I.M.M.—*do*, of Institution of Mining and Metallurgy.

F.Inst.F.—*do*, of the Institute of Fuel.

F.Inst.P.—*do*, of Institute of Physics.

F.I.Q.S.—*do*, of Institute of Quantity Surveyors.

F.I.E.R.E.—*do*, of the Institution of Electronic and Radio Engineers.

F.I.S.—*do*, of Institute of Statisticians; Family Income Supplement.

F.J.I.—*do*, of Institute of Journalists.

fl.—*(floruit)* he/she flourished.

F.L.A.—Fellow of Library Association.

F.L.S.—*do*, of Linnean Society.

F.M.—Field Marshal.

fo.—folio.

F.O.—Flying Officer.

f.o.b.—free on board.

F.P.A.—Family Planning Association.

F.Ph.S.—Fellow of the Philosophical Society.

F.P.S.—*do*, of Pharmaceutical Society.

F.R.A.D.—*do*, of Royal Academy of Dancing.

F.R.A.I.—*do*, of Royal Anthropological Institute.

F.R.A.M.—*do*, of Royal Academy of Music.

F.R.A.S.—*do*, of Royal Astronomical Society.

F.R.Ae.S.—*do*, of Royal Aeronautical Society.

F.R.B.S.—*do*, of Royal Society of British Sculptors.

F.R.C.M.—*do*, of Royal College of Music.

F.R.C.O.—*do*, of Royal College of Organists.

F.R.C.O.G.—*do*, of Royal College of Obstetricians and Gynaecologists.

F.R.C.P., (Ed.), (I.)—*do*, of Royal College of Physicians (in Edinburgh), (of Ireland).

F.R.C.P.S.G.—*do*, of Royal College of Physicians and Surgeons of Glasgow.

F.R.C.S., (Ed.), (I.)—*do*, of Royal College of Surgeons (in Edinburgh), (of Ireland).

F.R.C.V.S.—*do*, of Royal College of Veterinary Surgeons.

F.R.Econ.S.—*do*, of Royal Economic Society.

F.R.G.S.—*do*, of Royal Geographical Society.

F.R.H.S.—*do*, of Royal Horticultural Society.

F.R.Hist.S.—*do*, of the Royal Historical Society.

F.R.I.B.A.—*do*, of Royal Institute of British Architects.

F.R.I.C.S.—*do*, of Royal Institution of Chartered Surveyors.

F.R.M.S.—*do*, of Royal Microscopical Society.

F.R.Met.S.—*do*, of Royal Meteorological Society.

F.R.N.S.—*do*, of Royal Numismatic Society.

F.R.P.S.—*do*, of Royal Photographic Society.

F.R.S.—*do*, of Royal Society.

F.R.S.A.—*do*, of Royal Society of Arts.

F.R.S.C.—*do*, of Royal Society of Chemistry.

F.R.S.E.—*do*, of Royal Society of Edinburgh.

F.R.S.L.—*do*, of Royal Society of Literature.

F.R.T.P.I.—*do*, of Royal Town Planning Institute.

F.S.A.—*do*, of Society of Antiquaries.

F.S.S.—*do*, of Statistical Society.

F.S.V.A.—*do*, of Society of Valuers and Auctioneers.

F.T.—*Financial Times*.

F.T.I.—Fellow of the Textile Institute.

F.T.I.I.—*do*, of the Taxation Institute Inc.

F.Z.S.—*do*, of Zoological Society.

G

G.A.T.T.—General Agreement on Tariffs and Trade.

G.B.E.—Knight/Dame Grand Cross, Order of the British Empire.

G.C.—George Cross.

G.C.B.—Knight/Dame Grand Cross, Order of the Bath.

G.C.E.—General Certificate of Education.

G.C.H.Q.—Government Communications Headquarters.

G.C.I.E.—Knight Grand Commander, Order of the Indian Empire.

G.C.L.J.—Knight Grand Cross, Order of St. Lazarus of Jerusalem.

G.C.M.G.—Knight/Dame Grand Cross, Order of St. Michael and St. George.

G.C.S.E.—General Certificate of Secondary Education.

G.C.S.I.—Knight Grand Commander, Order of the Star of India.

G.C.V.O.—Knight/Dame Grand Cross, Royal Victorian Order.

G.D.I.—Gross domestic income.

G.D.P.—Gross domestic product.

G.D.R.—German Democratic Republic (E. Germany).

Gen.—General.

G.H.Q.—General Headquarters.

Gib.—Gibraltar.

G.M.—George Medal.

G.M.T.—Greenwich Mean Time.

G.N.P.—Gross national product.

G.O.C.—General Officer Commanding.

G.P.—General Practitioner.

Gp. Capt.—Group Captain.

G.S.O.—General Staff Officer.

H

H.A.C.—Honourable Artillery Company.

H.B.M.—Her Britannic Majesty('s).

H.C.F.—Highest common factor.

H.E.—His/Her Excellency; His Eminence; high explosive.

H.H.—His/Her Highness.

H.I.M.—His/Her Imperial Majesty.

H.J.S.—*(hic jacet sepultus)* here lies buried.

H.M.—His/Her Majesty.

H.M.A.S.—Her Majesty's Australian Ship.

H.M.C.—Headmasters'Conference.

H.M.I.—Her Majesty's Inspector.

H.M.L.—Her Majesty's Lieutenant.

H.M.S.—Her Majesty's Ship.

H.M.S.O.—Her Majesty's Stationery Office.

H.N.C.—Higher National Certificate.

H.N.D.—Higher National Diploma.

H.O.L.M.E.S.—Home Office Large Major Enquiry System.

Hon.—Honourable; Honorary.

h.p.—horse power.

H.P.—Hire purchase.

H.Q.—Headquarters.

H.R.H.—His/Her Royal Highness.

H.S.E.—*(hic sepultus est)* here lies buried. *cf.* H.J.S.

H.T.R.—High temperature reactor.

H.W.M.—High water mark.

I

I.A.A.S.—Incorporated Association of Architects and Surveyors.

I.A.E.A.—International Atomic Energy Agency.

I.A.T.A.—International Air Transport Association.

I.B.A.—Independent Broadcasting Authority.

Ibid.—*(ibidem)* in the same place.

I.B.R.D.—International Bank for Reconstruction and Development.

I.C.A.O.—International Civil Aviation Organization.

I.C.B.M.—Inter-continental ballistic missile.

I.C.I.—Imperial Chemical Industries.

I.C.J.—International Court of Justice.

I.C.R.C.—International Committee of the Red Cross.

I.C.T.—International Computers and Tabulators.

Id.—*(idem)* the same.

i.e.—*(id est)* that is.

I.E.A.—International Energy Agency.

I.F.C.—International Finance Corporation.

I.H.S.—(*Iesus Hominum Salvator*) Jesus the Saviour of Mankind; originally, these were the Greek capital letters, I H Σ.

I.L.E.A.—Inner London Education Authority.

I.L.O.—International Labour Organization.

I.M.C.O.—Inter-Governmental Maritime Consultative Organization.

I.M.F.—International Monetary Fund.

Inc.—Incorporated.

Incog.—(*incognito*) unknown, unrecognized.

I.N.L.A.—Irish National Liberation Army.

In loc.—(*in loco*) in its place.

I.N.R.I.—(*Iesus Nazarenus Rex Iudaeorum*) Jesus of Nazareth, King of the Jews.

Inst.—(*instant*) current month.

Intelsat—International Telecommunications Satellite Consortium.

Interpol—International Criminal Police Commission.

I.O.M.—Isle of Man.

I.O.U.—I owe you.

I.O.W.—Isle of Wight.

I.Q.—Intelligence quotient.

I.R.A.—Irish Republican Army.

I.R.C.—International Red Cross.

I.S.B.N.—International Standard Book Number.

I.S.O.—Imperial Service Order.

I.T.U.—International Telecommunication Union.

I.T.V.—Independent Television.

J

J.—Judge.

J.P.—Justice of the Peace.

K

K.—Köchel numeration (of Mozart's works).

K.A.N.U.—Kenyan African National Union.

K.B.E.—Knight Commander, Order of the British Empire.

K.C.B.—*do*, Order of the Bath.

K.C.I.E.—*do*, Order of the Indian Empire.

K.C.L.J.—Knight Commander, Order of St. Lazarus of Jerusalem.

K.C.M.G.—*do*, Order of St. Michael and St. George.

K.C.S.I.—*do*, Order of the Star of India.

K.C.V.O.—*do*, Royal Victorian Order.

K.G.—Knight of the Garter.

K.G.B.—Soviet State Security Service.

K.K.K.—Ku Klux Klan.

K.L.J.—Knight, Order of St. Lazarus of Jerusalem.

k.o.—knock out (boxing).

K.P.—Knight, Order of St. Patrick.

K.St.J.—Knight, Order of St. John of Jerusalem.

Kt.—Knight.

K.T.—Knight, Order of the Thistle.

K.V.—Kilovolt.

K.W.—Kilowatt.

K.W.h.—Kilowatt hour.

L

L. (*or* Lib.)—Liberal.

Lab.—Labour.

Lat.—Latitude.

L.A.M.D.A.—London Academy of Music and Dramatic Art.

lb.—(*libra*) pound weight.

l.b.w.—leg before wicket.

l.c.—lower case (*printing*).

L.C.J.—Lord Chief Justice.

L.C.M.—Least common multiple.

L.D.S.—Licentiate in Dental Surgery.

L.E.A.—Local Education Authority.

L.H.D.—(*Litterarum Humaniorum Doctor*) Doctor of Humane Letters.

Lic. Med.—Licentiate in Medicine.

Lic. S.—*do*, in Surgery.

Lit.—Literary.

Lit. Hum.—(*Litterae Humaniores*) study of the classics.

Litt. D.—Doctor of Letters.

L.J.—Lord Justice.

LL.B.—Bachelor of Laws; LL.D.—Doctor of Laws; LL.M.—Master of Laws.

L.M.—Licentiate in Midwifery.

L.M.S.S.A.—*do*, in Medicine and Surgery, Society of Apothecaries.

loc. cit.—(*loco citato*) in the place cited.

log.—logarithm.

Londin.—of London (*Bishop*).

L.S.—(*loco sigilli*) place of the seal.

L.S.A.—Licentiate of Society of Apothecaries.

L.s.d.—(*Librae, solidi, denarii*) £, shillings and pence.

L.S.E.—London School of Economics.

L.S.O.—London Symphony Orchestra.

Lt.—Lieutenant.

L.T.A.—Lawn Tennis Association.

Ltd.—Limited liability.

L.Th.—Licentiate in Theology.

L.T.M.—*do*, of Tropical Medicine.

L.V.O.—Lieutenant, Royal Victorian Order.

L.W.M.—Low water mark.

M

M.—Member of; Monsieur.

M.A.—Master of Arts.

M.A.F.F.—Ministry of Agriculture, Fisheries and Food.

Maj.—Major.

max.—maximum.

M.B./D.—Bachelor/Doctor of Medicine.

M.B.E.—Member, Order of the British Empire.

M.C.—Master of Ceremonies; Military Cross.

M.C.C.—Marylebone Cricket Club.

M.Ch.(D.)—Master of (Dental) Surgery.

M.D.S.—*do*, of Dental Surgery.

M.E.—Middle English.

M.E.C.—Member of Executive Council.

M.Ed.—Master of Education.

mega—one million times.

M.E.P.—Member of the European Parliament.

M.F.H.—Master of Foxhounds.

Mgr.—Monsignor.

M.I.—Military Intelligence.

micro—one-millionth part.

milli—one-thousandth part.

min.—minimum.

M.L.A.—Member of Legislative Assembly.

M.L.C.—Member of Legislative Council.

Mlle.—Mademoiselle.

M.L.R.—Minimum lending rate.

M.M.—Military Medal.

Mme.—Madame.

M.N.—Merchant Navy.

M.O.—Medical Officer/Orderly.

M.O.D.—Ministry of Defence.

M.O.T.—Ministry of Transport.

M.P.—Member of Parliament; Military Police.

m.p.h.—miles per hour.

M.R.—Master of the Rolls.

M.R.C.—Medical Research Council.

M.S.—Master of Surgery; Manuscript (pl. MSS).

M.Sc.—*do*, of Science.

M.T.B.—Motor Torpedo Boat.

M.Th.—Master of Theology.

Mus. B./D.—Bachelor/Doctor of Music.

M.V.—million volts (*or* megavolts); Merchant Vessel; Motor Vessel.

M.V.O.—Member, Royal Victorian Order.

M.W.—million watts (*or* megawatts).

N

N.A.A.F.I.—Navy Army and Air Force Institutes.

N.A.B.M.—National Association of British Manufacturers.

N.A.L.G.O.—National and Local Government Officers Association.

N.A.S.A.—National Aeronautics and Space Administration.

N.A.T.O.—North Atlantic Treaty Organization.

N.B.—(*Nota bene*) note well; New Brunswick.

N.C.B.—National Coal Board.

N.C.O.—Non-commissioned Officer.

n.d.—no date (*of books*).

N.E.B.—New English Bible.

N.E.D.C.—National Economic Development Council.

Nem. con.—(*Nemine contradicente*) no one contradicting.

N.E.R.C.—Natural Environment Research Council.

N.F.T.—National Film Theatre.

N.G.A.—National Graphical Association.

N.H.S.—National Health Service.

N.I.—Northern Ireland.

No.—(*numero*) number.

Non seq.—(*Non sequitur*) it does not follow.

Norvic.—of Norwich (*Bishop*).

N.P.—Notary Public.

N.R.A.—National Rifle Assoc.

N.S.—New Style (calendar); Nova Scotia.

N.S.P.C.C.—National Society for the Prevention of Cruelty to Children.

N.S.W.—New South Wales.

N.T.—National Theatre; New Testament.

N.U.J.—National Union of Journalists.

N.U.M.—*do*, of Mineworkers.

N.U.P.E.—*do*, of Public Employees.

N.U.R.—*do*, of Railwaymen.

N.U.S.—*do*, of Seamen; *do*, of Students.

N.U.T.—*do*, of Teachers.

N.W.T.—Northwest Territory.

N.Y.—New York.

N.Z.—New Zealand.

O

O. and M.—Organization and method.

O.A.P.E.C.—Organization of Arab Petroleum Exporting Countries.

O.A.S.—Organization of American States.

O.A.U.—Organization of African Unity.

Ob. (*or* obit.)—died.

O.B.E.—Officer, Order of the British Empire.

O.C.—Officer Commanding.

O.E.—Old English.

O.E.C.D.—Organization for Economic Co-operation and Development.

O.E.D.—Oxford English Dictionary.

O.F.M.—Order of Friars Minor (Franciscans).

O.H.M.S.—On Her Majesty's Service.

O.M.—Order of Merit.

O.P.—Order of Preachers (Dominicans); opposite prompt side (of theatre); out of print (of books).

op.—(*opus*) work.

op. cit.—(*opere citato*) in the work cited.

O.P.C.S.—Office of Population Censuses and Surveys.

O.P.E.C.—Organization of Petroleum Exporting Countries.

O.S.—Old Style (calendar).

O.S.A.—Order of St. Augustine.

O.S.B.—Order of St. Benedict.

O. St. J.—Officer, Order of St. John of Jerusalem.

O.T.—Old Testament.

O.T.C.—Officer Training Corps.

Oxon.—(of) Oxford; Oxfordshire.

Oz.—ounce.

P

P.A.—Press Association.

p.c.—per cent.

P.C.—Privy Counsellor; Police Constable.

P.D.S.A.—People's Dispensary for Sick Animals.

P.E.—Physical Education.

Petriburg—of Peterborough (*Bishop*).

Ph.D.—Doctor of Philosophy.

pinx(it)—he/she painted it.

P.L.A.—Port of London Authority.

P.L.C.—Public Limited Company.

P.L.O.—Palestine Liberation Organization.

p.m.—(*post meridiem*) afternoon.

P.M.—Prime Minister.

P.M.R.A.F.N.S.—Princess Mary's Royal Air Force Nursing Service.

P.O.—Post Office; Postal Order; Petty Officer; Pilot Officer.

P. & O.—Peninsular and Oriental Steamship Co.

P.O.U.N.C.—Post Office Users' National Council.

P.O.W.—Prisoner of War.

p.p. (or per pro)—(*per procurationem*) by proxy.

P.P.S.—Parliamentary Private Secretary.

P.R.—Proportional Representation; Public Relations.

P.R.A.—President of the Royal Academy.

Pro tem.—(*pro tempore*) for the time being.

P.R.S.—President of the Royal Society.

P.R.S.E.—*do*, of Edinburgh.

Prox.—(*proximo*) next month.

Ps.—Psalm.

P.S.—(*Post scriptum*) postscript.

P.S.B.R.—Public sector borrowing requirement.

p.s.c.—passed Staff College.

Pte.—Private.

P.T.O.—Please turn over.

Q

Q.A.R.(A.)N.C.—Queen Alexandra's Royal (Army) Nursing Corps.

Q.A.R.N.N.S.—Queen Alexandra's Royal Naval Nursing Service.

Q.B.—Queen's Bench.

Q.C.—Queen's Counsel.

Q.e.d.—(*quod erat demonstrandum*) which was to be proved.

Q.G.M.—Queen's Gallantry Medal.

Q.H.C.—Honorary Chaplain to the Queen.

Q.H.D.S.—Honorary Dental Surgeon to the Queen.

Q.H.N.S.—Honorary Nursing Sister to the Queen.

Q.H.P.—Honorary Physician to the Queen.

Q.H.S.—Honorary Surgeon to the Queen.

Q.M.G.—Quartermaster General.

Q.P.M.—Queen's Police Medal.

Q.S.—Quarter Sessions.

Q.S.O.—Quasi-stellar object (quasar).

Q.S.S.s—Quasi-stellar radio sources (quasar).

q.v.—(*quod vide*) which see.

R

R.—(*Rex*) King; (*Regina*) Queen.

R.A.—Royal Artillery; Royal Academy/Academician.

R.A.C.—Royal Armoured Corps; Royal Automobile Club.

R.A.D.A.—Royal Academy of Dramatic Art.

R.A.D.C.—Royal Army Dental Corps.

R.A.E.—Royal Aircraft Establishment.

R.A.E.C.—Royal Army Education Corps.

R.Ae.S.—Royal Aeronautical Society.

R.A.F.—Royal Air Force.

R.A.M.—Royal Academy of Music.

R.A.M.C.—Royal Army Medical Corps.

R.A.N.—Royal Australian Navy.

R. and D.—Research and Development.

R.A.O.C.—Royal Army Ordnance Corps.

R.A.P.C.—Royal Army Pay Corps.

R.A.V.C.—Royal Army Veterinary Corps.

R.B.A.—Royal Society of British Artists.

R.B.S.—Royal Society of British Sculptors.

R.C.—Roman Catholic; Red Cross.

R.C.M.—Royal College of Music.

R.C.N.—Royal Canadian Navy.

R.C.N.C.—Royal Corps of Naval Constructors.

R.C.T.—Royal Corps of Transport.

R.D.—Naval Reserve Decoration; Rural Dean; refer to drawer (*banking*).

R.D.I.—Designer for Industry of the Royal Society of Arts.

R.E.—Royal Engineers.

R.E.M.E.—Royal Electrical and Mechanical Engineers.

Rep.—Republican; Representative.

Rev.—Reverend.

R.G.N.—Registered General Nurse.

R.G.S.—Royal Geographical Society.

R.H.S.—Royal Horticultural Society; Royal Humane Society.

R.I.—Royal Institution; Royal Institute of Painters in Watercolours; Rhode Island.

R.I.A.—Royal Irish Academy.

R.I.B.A.—Royal Institute of British Architects.

R.I.P.—(*Requiescat in pace*) May he/she rest in peace.

R.L.—Rugby League.

R.M.—Royal Marines.

R.M.A.—Royal Military Academy.

R.M.S.—Royal Mail Steamer.

R.N.—Royal Navy.

R.N.I.B.—Royal National Institute for the Blind.

R.N.L.I.—Royal National Lifeboat Institution.

R.N.R.—Royal Naval Reserve.

R.N.V.R.—Royal Naval Volunteer Reserve.

R.N.Z.N.—Royal New Zealand Navy.

Ro.—(*Recto*) on the right-hand page.

R.O.C.—Royal Observer Corps.

Roffen.—of Rochester (*Bishop*).

R.O.I.—Royal Institute of Oil Painters.

Ro. S.P.A.—Royal Society for the Prevention of Accidents.

R.P.—Royal Society of Portrait Painters.

r.p.m.—revolutions per minute.
R.R.C.—Lady of Royal Red Cross.
R.R.E.—Royal Radar Establishment.
R.S.A.—Royal Society of Arts; Royal Scottish Academician; Republic of South Africa.
R.S.C.—Royal Shakespeare Company.
R.S.E.—Royal Society of Edinburgh.
R.S.M.—Regimental Sergeant Major.
R.S.P.B.—Royal Society for the Protection of Birds.
R.S.P.C.A.—Royal Society for the Prevention of Cruelty to Animals.
R.S.V.P.—(*Respondez s'il vous plait*) Answer, if you please.
R.S.W.—Royal Scottish Society of Painters in Watercolours.
R.T.P.I.—Royal Town Planning Institute.
R.U.—Rugby Union.
R.U.C.—Royal Ulster Constabulary.
R.V.—Revised Version (of Bible).
R.W.S.—Royal Water Colour Society.
R.Y.S.—Royal Yacht Squadron.

S

s.—(*solidus*) shilling.
S.A.—Salvation Army; Sex Appeal; South Africa; South America; South Australia.
Salop.—Shropshire.
S.A.L.T.—Strategic Arms Limitation Treaty.
Sarum.—of Salisbury (*Bishop*).
S.A.S.—Special Air Service Regiment.
S.B.S.—Special Boat Squadron.
Sc.D.—Doctor of Science.
S.C.M.—State Certified Midwife.
S.D.I.—Strategic Defence Initiative ("Star Wars").
S.D.P.—Social Democratic Party.
S.D.L.P.—Social Democratic and Labour Party (N. Ireland).
S.E.A.T.O.—South East Asia Treaty Organization.
S.E.N.—State Enrolled Nurse.
S.E.R.C.—Science and Engineering Research Council.
S.H.A.P.E.—Supreme Headquarters, Allied Powers, Europe.
S.I.—(*Système International d'Unités*) International System of Units; Statutory Instruments.
Sic.—So written.
Sig.—Signalman.
S.J.—Society of Jesus (Jesuits).
S.N.P.—Scottish National Party.
S.O.G.A.T.—Society of Graphical and Allied Trades.
S.O.S.—Save Our Souls (distress signal).
s.p.—(*sine prole*) without issue.
S.P.C.K.—Society for the Promotion of Christian Knowledge.
sp.gr.—specific gravity.
S.P.Q.R.—(*Senatus Populusque Romanus*) The Senate and People of Rome.

Sqn. Ldr.—Squadron Leader.
S.R.N.—State Registered Nurse.
SS.—Saints.
S.S.—Steamship.
S.S.A.F.A.—Soldiers', Sailors', and Airmen's Families Association.
S.S.C.—Solicitor before Supreme Court (Scotland).
S.S.F.—Society of St. Francis.
St.—Saint; Street.
S.T.A.R.—Satellites for Telecommunications, Applications and Research.
Stet.—Let it stand.
S.T.D.—Subscriber Trunk Dialling.
s.t.p.—Standard temperature and pressure.
S.T.P.—(*Sacrae Theologiae Professor*) Doctor of Divinity.
Sub Lt.—Sub-Lieutenant.
S.W.A.P.O.—South West Africa People's Organization.

T

T.A.—Territorial Army.
T.B.—Tuberculosis.
T.C.C.B.—Test and County Cricket Board.
T.D.—Territorial Decoration.
temp.—temperature; temporary employee.
T.E.S.—*Times Education Supplement.*
T.G.W.U.—Transport and General Workers Union.
T.L.S.—*Times Literary Supplement.*
T.N.T.—trinitrotoluene (explosive).
Toc. H.—Talbot House.
tr.—transpose (*printing*).
Truron—of Truro (*Bishop*).
T.T.—Teetotal; Tubercular tested.
T.U.C.—Trades Union Congress.
T.V.—Television.

U

U.—Unionist.
U.A.E.—United Arab Emirates.
u.c.—upper case (*printing*).
U.C.C.A.—University Central Council on Admissions.
U.C.L.—University College, London.
U.D.I.—Unilateral Declaration of Independence.
U.D.R.—Ulster Defence Regiment.
U.F.O.—Unidentified flying object.
U.G.C.—University Grants Committee.
u.h.f.—ultra-high frequency.
U.K.—United Kingdom.
U.K.A.E.A.—United Kingdom Atomic Energy Authority.
Ult.—(*ultimo*) in the preceding month.
U.N.E.S.C.O.—United Nations Educational, Scientific and Cultural Organization.
U.N.I.C.E.F.—United Nations International Children's Emergency Fund.
Unita.—National Union for the Total Independence of Angola.
U.N.O.—United Nations Organization.

U.P.U.—Universal Postal Union.
U.S. (*or* U.S.A.)—United States (of America).
U.S.P.G.—United Society for the Propagation of the Gospel.
U.S.S.R.—Union of Soviet Socialist Republics.
U.U.—Ulster Unionist.

V

v.—(*versus*) against.
V.—Volt.
V.A.—Vicar Apostolic; Victoria and Albert Order.
V. and A.—Victoria and Albert Museum.
V.A.D.—Voluntary Aid Detachment.
V.A.T.—Value added tax.
V.C.—Victoria Cross.
V.D.—Volunteer Officers' Decoration; venereal disease.
V.D.U.—Visual display unit.
Ven.—Venerable.
Verb. sap.—(*Verbum sapienti satis est*) A word to the wise is enough.
v.h.f.—very high frequency.
V.I.P.—Very important person.
Viz.—(*videlicet*) namely.
Vo.—(*Verso*) on the left-hand page.
V.R.D.—Volunteer Reserve Decoration.
V.S.O.—Voluntary Service Overseas.
V.T.O.L.—Vertical take-off and landing (*aircraft*).

W

W.C.C.—World Council of Churches.
W.E.U.—Western European Union.
W.H.O.—World Health Organization.
W.I.—West Indies; Women's Institutes.
Winton.—of Winchester (*Bishop*).
W.M.O.—World Meteorological Organization.
W.O.—Warrant Officer.
W.R.A.C.—Women's Royal Army Corps.
W.R.A.F.—Women's Royal Air Force.
W.R.N.S.—Women's Royal Naval Service.
W.R.V.S.—Women's Royal Voluntary Service.
W.S.—Writer to the Signet.

Y

Y.H.A.—Youth Hostels Assoc.
Y.M.C.A.—Young Men's Christian Association.
Y.W.C.A.—Young Women's Christian Association.

Z

Z.A.N.U.—Zimbabwe African National Union.
Z.A.P.U.—Zimbabwe African People's Union.

BEING BISSEXTILE OR LEAP YEAR

Golden Number	.. .. ..	XIII
Epact	.. .. ..	11
Dominical Letter	.. .. ..	CB
Solar Cycle	.. .. ..	9
Roman Indiction	.. .. ..	11
Julian Period	.. .. ..	6701
Julian Day, Jan. 1 (begins at noon)	..	2,447,162
New Year's Day	.. ..	Jan. 1
Accession of Queen Elizabeth II (1952)	..	Feb. 6
Ash Wedesday	.. ..	,, 17
Ancient Chinese New Year (Dragon)	..	,, 17
Duke of York's Birthday (1960)	..	,, 19
Prince Edward's Birthday (1964)	..	March 10
Commonwealth Day	.. ..	,, 14
Good Friday	.. ..	April 1
Passover, first day	.. ..	,, 2
Easter Day	.. ..	,, 3
Ramadan, first day	.. ..	,, 18
Birthday of Queen Elizabeth II (1926)	..	,, 21

Ascension Day ..	.. ..	May 12
Whit Sunday ..	.. ..	,, 22
Trinity Sunday	.. ..	,, 29
Corpus Christi ..	.. ..	June 2
Duke of Edinburgh's Birthday (1921)	..	,, 10
Queen's Official Birthday	..	,, 11
Prince William of Wales's Birthday		
(1982)	.. ..	,, 21
Princess of Wales's Birthday (1961)	..	July 1
The Queen Mother's Birthday (1900)	..	Aug. 4
Islamic New Year (1409)	..	,, 14
Princess Royal's Birthday (1950)	..	,, 15
Jewish New Year (5749)	..	Sept. 12
Prince Henry of Wales's Birthday (1984)	..	,, 15
Day of Atonement (Yom Kippur)	..	,, 21
Remembrance Sunday ..	..	Nov. 13
Prince of Wales's Birthday (1948)	..	,, 14
First Sunday in Advent	..	,, 27
Christmas Day ..	.. ..	Dec. 25

Spring Equinox	Sun enters Sign Aries .... March 20d 10h	⎫
Summer Solstice	,, ,, ,, Cancer ...... June 21d 04h	⎬ G.M.T.
Autumn Equinox	,, ,, ,, Libra .... Sept. 22d 19h	
Winter Solstice	,, ,, ,, Capricornus .. Dec. 21d 15h	⎭

CALENDAR FOR THE YEAR 1988

January		*April*		*July*		*October*	
Su.	.. — 3 10 17 24 31	Su.	.. — 3 10 17 24	Su.	.. — 3 10 17 24 31	Su.	.. — 2 9 16 23 30
M.	.. — 4 11 18 25 —	M.	.. — 4 11 18 25	M.	.. — 4 11 18 25 —	M.	.. — 3 10 17 24 31
Tu.	.. — 5 12 19 26 —	Tu.	.. — 5 12 19 26	Tu.	.. — 5 12 19 26 —	Tu.	.. — 4 11 18 25 —
W.	.. — 6 13 20 27 —	W.	.. — 6 13 20 27	W.	.. — 6 13 20 27 —	W.	.. — 5 12 19 26 —
Th.	.. — 7 14 21 28 —	Th.	.. — 7 14 21 28	Th.	.. — 7 14 21 28 —	Th.	.. — 6 13 20 27 —
F.	1 8 15 22 29 —	F.	1 8 15 22 29	F.	1 8 15 22 29 —	F.	— 7 14 21 28 —
S.	2 9 16 23 30 —	S.	2 9 16 23 30	S.	2 9 16 23 30 —	S.	1 8 15 22 29 —

February		*May*		*August*		*November*	
Su.	.. — 7 14 21 28	Su.	1 8 15 22 29	Su.	.. — 7 14 21 28	Su.	.. — 6 13 20 27
M.	.. 1 8 15 22 29	M.	2 9 16 23 30	M.	.. 1 8 15 22 29	M.	.. — 7 14 21 28
Tu.	.. 2 9 16 23 —	Tu.	3 10 17 24 31	Tu.	.. 2 9 16 23 30	Tu.	.. 1 8 15 22 29
W.	.. 3 10 17 24 —	W.	4 11 18 25 —	W.	.. 3 10 17 24 31	W.	.. 2 9 16 23 30
Th.	.. 4 11 18 25 —	Th.	5 12 19 26 —	Th.	.. 4 11 18 25 —	Th.	.. 3 10 17 24 —
F.	.. 5 12 19 26 —	F.	6 13 20 27 —	F.	.. 5 12 19 26 —	F.	.. 4 11 18 25 —
S.	.. 6 13 20 27 —	S.	7 14 21 28 —	S.	.. 6 13 20 27 —	S.	.. 5 12 19 26 —

March		*June*		*September*		*December*	
Su.	.. — 6 13 20 27	Su.	.. — 5 12 19 26	Su.	.. — 4 11 18 25	Su.	.. — 4 11 18 25
M.	.. — 7 14 21 28	M.	.. — 6 13 20 27	M.	.. — 5 12 19 26	M.	.. — 5 12 19 26
Tu.	.. 1 8 15 22 29	Tu.	.. — 7 14 21 28	Tu.	.. — 6 13 20 27	Tu.	.. — 6 13 20 27
W.	.. 2 9 16 23 30	W.	1 8 15 22 29	W.	.. — 7 14 21 28	W.	.. — 7 14 21 28
Th.	.. 3 10 17 24 31	Th.	2 9 16 23 30	Th.	.. 1 8 15 22 29	Th.	.. 1 8 15 22 29
F.	.. 4 11 18 25 —	F.	3 10 17 24 —	F.	.. 2 9 16 23 30	F.	.. 2 9 16 23 30
S.	.. 5 12 19 26 —	S.	4 11 18 25 —	S.	.. 3 10 17 24 —	S.	.. 3 10 17 24 31

PUBLIC HOLIDAYS 1988

	ENGLAND & WALES	N. IRELAND	SCOTLAND
New Year ..	Jan. 1	Jan. 1	Jan. 1, 4
St. Patrick ..	—	March 17	—
Good Friday	April 1*	April 1*	April 1
Easter Monday	April 4	April 4	—
May Day	May 2	May 2	May 30
Spring ..	May 30	May 30	May 2
Battle of Boyne	.. ..	July 12	—
Summer	Aug. 29	Aug. 29	Aug. 1
Christmas ..	Dec. 26, 27	Dec. 26, 27	Dec. 26, 27

*In England and Wales, and Northern Ireland, Good Friday and Christmas Day are common law holidays. In the CHANNEL ISLANDS Liberation Day (May 9) is a bank and public holiday.

QUARTER DAYS (England, Wales, N. Ireland)		**TERM DAYS** (Scotland)	
Lady Day..............................	March 25	Candlemas...............................	Feb. 2
Midsummer.............................	June 24	Whitsunday	May 15
Michaelmas.............................	Sept. 29	Lammas	Aug. 1
Christmas	Dec. 25	Martinmas	Nov. 11
		(*Removal Terms* are May 28 and Nov. 28).	

Janus, god of the portal, facing two ways, past and future.

Sun's Longitude 300° ♒ 20ᵈ 20ʰ

Day of Month	Day of Week	
1	F.	**Naming of Jesus.** James Stuart d. 1766.
2	S.	Sir Michael Tippett b. 1905.
3	**S.**	**2nd S. after Christmas.** Herbert Morrison b.
4	M.	Sir Isaac Pitman b. 1813. T. S. Eliot d. 1965. [1888.*
5	Tu.	Edward the Confessor d. 1066. Catherine de Medici d. 1589.
6	W.	**The Epiphany.** Twelfth Day. Richard II b. 1367.
7	Th.	Calais regained by the French 1558.
8	F.	Galileo d. 1642. Wilkie Collins b. 1824.
9	S.	Gracie Fields b. 1898. Simone de Beauvoir b. 1908.
10	**S.**	**1st S. after Epiphany.** Archbp. Laud exec. 1645.
11	M.	HILARY LAW SITTINGS BEGIN. Thomas Hardy d. 1928.
12	Tu.	Edmund Burke b. 1729. Agatha Christie d. 1976.
13	W.	Stephen Foster d. 1864. James Joyce d. 1941.
14	Th.	Albert Schweitzer b. 1875. Anthony Eden d. 1977.
15	F.	British Museum opened 1759. Ivor Novello b. 1893.
16	S.	Arturo Toscanini d. 1957.
17	**S.**	**2nd S. after Epiphany.** Lloyd George b. 1863.
18	M.	Capt. Scott reaches S. Pole 1912. Gaitskill d. 1963.
19	Tu.	James Watt b. 1736. Paul Cezanne b. 1839.
20	W.	John Ruskin d. 1900. George V d. 1936.
21	Th.	Lenin d. 1924. George Orwell d. 1950.
22	F.	Lord Byron b. 1788.* Victoria I d. 1901.
23	S.	William Pitt d. 1806. Vietnam War Treaty 1973.
24	**S.**	**3rd S. after Epiphany.** Winston Churchill d. 1965.
25	M.	**Conversion of St. Paul.** Robert Boyle b. 1627.
26	Tu.	Proclamation of Republic of India 1950.
27	W.	Mozart b. 1756. Jerome Kern b. 1885.
28	Th.	Henry VII b. 1457. Henry VIII d. 1547.
29	F.	Emmanuel Swedenborg b. 1688.* Robert Frost d.
30	S.	Edward Lear d. 1888.* Gandhi assas. 1948. [1963.
31	**S.**	**9th S. before Easter.** Charles Edward Stuart d. 1788.*

*Centenary

PHENOMENA

January 4ᵈ 00ʰ Earth at Perihelion (147,000,000 kilometres).

15ᵈ 16ʰ Mars in conjunction with the Moon. Mars 5°N.

17ᵈ 04ʰ Saturn in conjunction with the Moon. Saturn 6°N.

20ᵈ 09ʰ Mercury in conjunction with the Moon. Mercury 2°N.

21ᵈ 19ʰ Venus in conjunction with the Moon. Venus 0°·07 N.

25ᵈ 02ʰ Jupiter in conjunction with the Moon. Jupiter 4°S.

26ᵈ 17ʰ Mercury at greatest eastern elongation (19°).

CONSTELLATIONS

The following constellations are near the meridian at

	d	h		d	h
Dec.	1	24	Dec.	16	23
Jan.	1	22	Jan.	16	21
Feb.	1	20	Feb.	15	19

Draco (below the Pole), Ursa Minor (below the Pole), Camelopardus, Perseus, Auriga, Taurus, Orion, Eridanus and Lepus.

MINIMA OF ALGOL

d	h	d	h
3	14	17	22
6	11	20	19
9	7	23	15
12	4	26	12
15	1	29	9

PHASES OF THE MOON

	d	h	m
○ Full Moon	4	01	40
☾ Last Quarter	12	07	04
● New Moon	19	05	26
☽ First Quarter	25	21	53
	d	h	
Apogee (405,980 kilometres)	7	06	
Perigee (357,510 „)	19	21	

Mean Longitude of Ascending Node on Jan. 1, 357°.

MONTHLY NOTES

Jan. 1. Bank Holiday in England, Scotland, Wales and Northern Ireland.

4. Bank Holiday, Scotland.

26. Australia Day. Republic Day, India.

Day	Right Ascension	Dec. −	Equation of Time	Rise 52°	Rise 56°	Transit	Set 52°	Set 56°	Sidereal Time	Transit of First Point of Aries
	h m s	° ′	m s	h m	h m	h m	h m	h m	h m s	h m s
1	18 42 32	23 05	− 3 02	8 08	8 31	12 03	15 58	15 35	6 39 30	17 17 39
2	18 46 57	23 00	− 3 31	8 08	8 31	12 04	15 59	15 36	6 43 27	17 13 43
3	18 51 22	22 55	− 3 59	8 08	8 31	12 04	16 01	15 38	6 47 23	17 09 48
4	18 55 46	22 49	− 4 26	8 08	8 31	12 05	16 02	15 39	6 51 20	17 05 52
5	19 00 10	22 43	− 4 54	8 08	8 30	12 05	16 03	15 40	6 55 16	17 01 56
6	19 04 34	22 37	− 5 21	8 07	8 30	12 06	16 04	15 42	6 59 13	16 58 00
7	19 08 57	22 30	− 5 47	8 07	8 29	12 06	16 05	15 43	7 03 10	16 54 04
8	19 13 19	22 22	− 6 13	8 06	8 28	12 06	16 07	15 45	7 07 06	16 50 08
9	19 17 41	22 15	− 6 39	8 06	8 28	12 07	16 08	15 46	7 11 03	16 46 12
10	19 22 03	22 06	− 7 04	8 05	8 27	12 07	16 10	15 48	7 14 59	16 42 16
11	19 26 24	21 57	− 7 28	8 05	8 26	12 08	16 11	15 50	7 18 56	16 38 20
12	19 30 45	21 48	− 7 52	8 04	8 25	12 08	16 12	15 51	7 22 52	16 34 24
13	19 35 05	21 39	− 8 16	8 03	8 24	12 08	16 14	15 53	7 26 49	16 30 28
14	19 39 24	21 29	− 8 39	8 03	8 23	12 09	16 15	15 55	7 30 45	16 26 33
15	19 43 43	21 18	− 9 01	8 02	8 22	12 09	16 17	15 57	7 34 42	16 22 37
16	19 48 01	21 07	− 9 23	8 01	8 21	12 10	16 19	15 59	7 38 39	16 18 41
17	19 52 19	20 56	− 9 43	8 00	8 20	12 10	16 20	16 00	7 42 35	16 14 45
18	19 56 35	20 45	−10 04	7 59	8 19	12 10	16 22	16 02	7 46 32	16 10 49
19	20 00 52	20 33	−10 23	7 58	8 17	12 11	16 23	16 04	7 50 28	16 06 53
20	20 05 07	20 20	−10 42	7 57	8 16	12 11	16 25	16 06	7 54 25	16 02 57
21	20 09 22	20 07	−11 00	7 56	8 15	12 11	16 27	16 08	7 58 21	15 59 01
22	20 13 36	19 54	−11 18	7 55	8 13	12 11	16 29	16 10	8 02 18	15 55 05
23	20 17 49	19 41	−11 34	7 54	8 12	12 12	16 30	16 12	8 06 14	15 51 09
24	20 22 01	19 27	−11 50	7 52	8 10	12 12	16 32	16 14	8 10 11	15 47 13
25	20 26 12	19 12	−12 05	7 51	8 09	12 12	16 34	16 16	8 14 08	15 43 17
26	20 30 23	18 58	−12 19	7 50	8 07	12 12	16 36	16 19	8 18 04	15 39 22
27	20 34 33	18 43	−12 32	7 49	8 05	12 13	16 37	16 21	8 22 01	15 35 26
28	20 38 42	18 27	−12 45	7 47	8 04	12 13	16 39	16 23	8 25 57	15 31 30
29	20 42 50	18 12	−12 57	7 46	8 02	12 13	16 41	16 25	8 29 54	15 27 34
30	20 46 58	17 56	−13 08	7 44	8 00	12 13	16 43	16 27	8 33 50	15 23 38
31	20 51 04	17 39	−13 18	7 43	7 58	12 13	16 45	16 29	8 37 47	15 19 42

THE SUN   s.d. 16′·3

Duration of Civil (C), Nautical (N), and Astronomical (A), Twilight (in minutes)

Lat. °	Jan. 1 C	N	A	Jan. 11 C	N	A	Jan. 21 C	N	A	Jan. 31 C	N	A
52	41	84	125	40	82	123	38	80	120	37	78	117
56	47	96	141	45	93	138	43	90	134	41	87	130

ASTRONOMICAL NOTES

MERCURY reaches its greatest eastern elongation (19°) on the 26th. Thus for the last two weeks of the month it may be seen at the end of evening civil twilight low in the south-western sky. During this period its magnitude falls from −0·9 to +0·3.

VENUS, magnitude −4·0, is a brilliant object in the evening sky, visible above the west-south-west horizon after sunset, the period available for observation increasing from two to three hours during the month. On the evening of the 21st the crescent Moon, only 2½ days old, passes just S. of the planet.

MARS, magnitude +1·4, is a morning object and visible low in the south-eastern sky after about 05ʰ. During the month the planet moves from Libra, through the northern part of Scorpius and thence into Sagittarius. It passes 5°N. of Antares on the 21st.

JUPITER, magnitude −2·4, is visible in the southern and western sky in the evenings, crossing the meridian shortly after sunset. Jupiter is in the constellation of Pisces.

SATURN is too close to the Sun for observation at the beginning of the year. After the middle of January it gradually becomes visible as a morning object, magnitude +0·6. It may be glimpsed low in the south-eastern sky for a short while before the morning twilight inhibits observation.

THE MOON

Day	R.A.	Dec.	Hor. Par.	Semi-diam.	Sun's Co-long.	P.A. of Bright Limb	Phase	Age	Rise 52°	Rise 56°	Transit	Set 52°	Set 56°
	h m	°	'	'	°	°		d	h m	h m	h m	h m	h m
1	4 09	+25·7	55·6	15·2	50	266	91	11·2	13 15	12 41	22 16	6 19	6 52
2	5 04	+27·8	55·2	15·0	62	276	96	12·2	13 57	13 18	23 10	7 28	8 07
3	5 59	+28·4	54·8	14·9	74	292	99	13·2	14 52	14 14	—	8 24	9 02
4	6 54	+27·7	54·5	14·9	86	356	100	14·2	15 59	15 25	0 03	9 04	9 38
5	7 47	+25·6	54·3	14·8	98	77	99	15·2	17 11	16 45	0 54	9 33	10 00
6	8 38	+22·5	54·1	14·7	111	95	97	16·2	18 26	18 06	1 42	9 53	10 14
7	9 25	+18·4	54·0	14·7	123	103	92	17·2	19 39	19 26	2 27	10 08	10 23
8	10 10	+13·6	54·0	14·7	135	108	87	18·2	20 51	20 43	3 09	10 20	10 29
9	10 54	+ 8·4	54·2	14·8	147	112	80	19·2	22 02	21 59	3 49	10 29	10 34
10	11 36	+ 2·8	54·5	14·9	159	113	72	20·2	23 13	23 15	4 28	10 39	10 39
11	12 18	− 3·0	55·0	15·0	171	114	63	21·2	..	..	5 08	10 48	10 43
12	13 02	− 8·7	55·6	15·1	183	113	53	22·2	0 26	0 34	5 49	10 58	10 48
13	13 48	−14·3	56·3	15·4	196	110	43	23·2	1 43	1 57	6 33	11 11	10 55
14	14 38	−19·4	57·2	15·6	208	107	33	24·2	3 05	3 26	7 22	11 28	11 06
15	15 33	−23·7	58·2	15·9	220	101	23	25·2	4 31	5 01	8 17	11 53	11 23
16	16 32	−26·9	59·2	16·1	232	94	15	26·2	5 57	6 34	9 17	12 33	11 55
17	17 37	−28·4	60·0	16·4	244	84	7	27·2	7 11	7 52	10 22	13 33	12 52
18	18 44	−28·0	60·8	16·6	256	70	2	28·2	8 07	8 43	11 28	14 55	14 20
19	19 51	−25·5	61·2	16·7	269	26	0	29·2	8 44	9 11	12 32	16 31	16 05
20	20 54	−21·1	61·3	16·7	281	272	1	0·8	9 08	9 27	13 32	18 09	17 53
21	21 54	−15·4	61·1	16·7	293	255	5	1·8	9 26	9 37	14 27	19 44	19 35
22	22 49	− 8·9	60·6	16·5	305	249	11	2·8	9 39	9 44	15 18	21 14	21 12
23	23 41	− 2·0	59·9	16·3	317	247	20	3·8	9 51	9 50	16 06	22 41	22 44
24	0 31	+ 4·8	59·1	16·1	330	246	30	4·8	10 02	9 56	16 53	..	..
25	1 21	+11·2	58·2	15·8	342	248	40	5·8	10 15	10 03	17 41	0 05	0 15
26	2 11	+16·9	57·3	15·6	354	250	51	6·8	10 30	10 11	18 30	1 28	1 45
27	3 03	+21·6	56·5	15·4	6	255	61	7·8	10 49	10 24	19 20	2 51	3 15
28	3 56	+25·2	55·8	15·2	18	260	71	8·8	11 16	10 44	20 12	4 10	4 42
29	4 50	+27·6	55·3	15·1	30	267	80	9·8	11 53	11 15	21 06	5 22	6 00
30	5 46	+28·5	54·8	14·9	43	274	87	10·8	12 44	12 05	21 59	6 21	7 01
31	6 41	+28·1	54·5	14·8	55	282	93	11·8	13 48	13 12	22 50	7 06	7 42

MERCURY ☿

Day	R.A.	Dec. −	Diam.	Phase	Transit		Day	R.A.	Dec. −	Diam.	Phase	Transit	5° high 52°	5° high 56°
	h m	°	″		h m			h m	°	″		h m	h m	h m
1	19 05	24·6	—	—	12 28		16	20 50	19·6	5	87	13 12	16 46	16 21
4	19 27	24·1	—	—	12 37	Mercury is too	19	21 08	17·9	6	80	13 19	17 05	16 43
7	19 48	23·3	—	—	12 47	close to the	22	21 26	16·2	6	71	13 24	17 22	17 03
10	20 09	22·3	5	94	12 56	Sun for	25	21 40	14·3	7	62	13 26	17 36	17 19
13	20 30	21·0	5	91	13 04	observation	28	21 51	12·6	7	48	13 25	17 44	17 29
16	20 50	19·6	5	87	13 12		31	21 58	11·2	8	35	13 18	17 45	17 32

VENUS ♀

Day	R.A.	Dec. −	Diam.	Phase	Transit	5° high 52°	5° high 56°
	h m	°	″		h m	h m	h m
1	21 00	18·9	12	85	14 21	17 59	17 34
6	21 25	17·1	13	83	14 26	18 17	17 56
11	21 49	15·0	13	82	14 30	18 35	18 17
16	22 12	12·8	13	81	14 34	18 53	18 37
21	22 35	10·5	14	80	14 37	19 10	18 57
26	22 58	8·0	14	78	14 40	19 27	19 17
31	23 20	5·5	14	77	14 42	19 43	19 35

MARS ♂

Day	R.A.	Dec. −	Diam.	Phase	Transit	5° high 52°	5° high 56°
	h m	°	″		h m	h m	h m
1	15 31	18·5	4	95	8 51	5 13	5 37
6	15 44	19·4	5	95	8 45	5 13	5 38
11	15 58	20·1	5	94	8 39	5 12	5 40
16	16 12	20·8	5	94	8 33	5 12	5 41
21	16 26	21·4	5	94	8 27	5 11	5 42
26	16 40	22·0	5	93	8 22	5 10	5 42
31	16 55	22·4	5	93	8 16	5 09	5 42

SUNRISE AND SUNSET

Day	London a.m. h m	London p.m. h m	Bristol a.m. h m	Bristol p.m. h m	Birmingham a.m. h m	Birmingham p.m. h m	Manchester a.m. h m	Manchester p.m. h m	Newcastle a.m. h m	Newcastle p.m. h m	Glasgow a.m. h m	Glasgow p.m. h m	Belfast a.m. h m	Belfast p.m. h m
1	8 06	4 01	8 16	4 11	8 18	4 02	8 26	3 59	8 32	3 47	8 48	3 53	8 48	4 07
2	8 06	4 02	8 16	4 12	8 18	4 03	8 25	4 00	8 31	3 48	8 48	3 54	8 47	4 08
3	8 06	4 03	8 16	4 13	8 18	4 04	8 25	4 01	8 31	3 49	8 47	3 55	8 47	4 09
4	8 06	4 04	8 16	4 14	8 18	4 06	8 25	4 03	8 31	3 51	8 47	3 57	8 47	4 11
5	8 06	4 05	8 15	4 16	8 18	4 07	8 25	4 04	8 31	3 52	8 47	3 58	8 47	4 12
6	8 06	4 06	8 15	4 17	8 17	4 08	8 24	4 05	8 30	3 53	8 46	3 59	8 46	4 13
7	8 05	4 07	8 15	4 18	8 17	4 10	8 24	4 07	8 30	3 55	8 46	4 01	8 46	4 15
8	8 05	4 09	8 15	4 19	8 16	4 11	8 23	4 08	8 29	3 56	8 45	4 02	8 45	4 16
9	8 04	4 10	8 14	4 21	8 16	4 12	8 23	4 09	8 28	3 58	8 44	4 04	8 44	4 18
10	8 04	4 11	8 14	4 22	8 15	4 14	8 22	4 11	8 28	3 59	8 44	4 05	8 44	4 19
11	8 03	4 12	8 13	4 23	8 14	4 15	8 21	4 12	8 27	4 01	8 43	4 07	8 43	4 21
12	8 03	4 14	8 13	4 25	8 14	4 17	8 21	4 14	8 26	4 03	8 42	4 09	8 42	4 23
13	8 02	4 15	8 12	4 26	8 13	4 18	8 20	4 15	8 25	4 04	8 41	4 10	8 41	4 24
14	8 01	4 17	8 11	4 28	8 13	4 20	8 19	4 17	8 24	4 06	8 40	4 12	8 40	4 26
15	8 01	4 18	8 11	4 29	8 12	4 21	8 19	4 18	8 23	4 08	8 39	4 14	8 39	4 28
16	8 00	4 20	8 10	4 30	8 11	4 23	8 18	4 20	8 22	4 09	8 38	4 16	8 38	4 29
17	7 59	4 21	8 09	4 32	8 10	4 24	8 17	4 21	8 21	4 11	8 37	4 18	8 37	4 31
18	7 58	4 23	8 08	4 33	8 09	4 26	8 16	4 23	8 20	4 13	8 36	4 20	8 36	4 33
19	7 57	4 25	8 07	4 35	8 08	4 28	8 15	4 25	8 19	4 15	8 34	4 21	8 35	4 35
20	7 56	4 26	8 06	4 37	8 07	4 29	8 14	4 27	8 18	4 17	8 33	4 23	8 34	4 37
21	7 55	4 28	8 05	4 38	8 06	4 31	8 13	4 28	8 16	4 18	8 31	4 25	8 33	4 38
22	7 54	4 30	8 04	4 40	8 05	4 33	8 11	4 30	8 15	4 20	8 30	4 27	8 31	4 40
23	7 53	4 31	8 03	4 41	8 04	4 34	8 10	4 32	8 14	4 22	8 29	4 29	8 30	4 42
24	7 51	4 33	8 01	4 43	8 02	4 36	8 09	4 34	8 12	4 25	8 27	4 32	8 29	4 44
25	7 50	4 35	8 00	4 45	8 01	4 38	8 07	4 36	8 11	4 27	8 26	4 34	8 27	4 46
26	7 49	4 37	7 59	4 47	8 00	4 40	8 06	4 38	8 09	4 29	8 24	4 36	8 26	4 48
27	7 47	4 39	7 57	4 49	7 58	4 42	8 04	4 40	8 07	4 31	8 22	4 38	8 24	4 50
28	7 46	4 40	7 56	4 50	7 57	4 43	8 03	4 42	8 06	4 33	8 21	4 40	8 23	4 52
29	7 45	4 42	7 55	4 52	7 56	4 45	8 01	4 44	8 04	4 35	8 19	4 42	8 21	4 54
30	7 43	4 44	7 53	4 54	7 54	4 47	8 00	4 46	8 03	4 37	8 17	4 44	8 19	4 56
31	7 42	4 46	7 52	4 56	7 53	4 49	7 58	4 48	8 01	4 39	8 15	4 46	8 17	4 58

JUPITER ♃   SATURN ♄

Day	R.A. h m	Dec. + °	Transit h m	5° high 52° h m	5° high 56° h m	R.A. h m	Dec. − °	Transit h m	5° high 52° h m	5° high 56° h m
1	1 17	6·7	18 34	0 39	0 41	17 40	22·2	10 59	7 50	8 23
11	1 19	7·0	17 58	0 04	0 06	17 45	22·3	10 25	7 16	7 49
21	1 23	7·5	17 22	23 27	23 30	17 50	22·3	9 50	6 42	7 15
31	1 28	8·0	16 48	22 55	22 59	17 54	22·3	9 15	6 07	6 40

Equatorial diameter of Jupiter 40″; of Saturn 15″.   Diameters of Saturn's rings 34″ and 15″.

URANUS ♅   NEPTUNE ♆

Day	R.A. h m	Dec. ° ′	Transit h m		R.A. h m	Dec. ° ′	Transit h m	
1	17 49·8	23 35	11 09		18 33·7	22 16	11 52	
11	17 52·4	23 36	10 32	Uranus is too close to the Sun for observation	18 35·3	22 14	11 15	Neptune is too close to the Sun for observation
21	17 54·8	23 37	9 55		18 36·9	22 13	10 37	
31	17 57·0	23 37	9 18		18 38·4	22 11	9 59	

Diameter 4″   Diameter 2″

Februa, Roman festival
of Purification
Sun's Longitude 330° ♓ 19ᵈ 11ʰ

Month	Week		
1	M.	Clark Gable b. 1901. Sir Stanley Matthews b. 1915.	
2	Tu.	**Presentation of Christ.** Bertrand Russell d. 1970.	
3	W.	Beau Nash d. 1762. Felix Mendelssohn b. 1809.	
4	Th.	Carlyle d. 1881. End of sweet rationing 1953.	
5	F.	Robert Peel b. 1788.* Adm. Lord Fraser b. 1888.*	
6	S.	QUEEN'S ACCESSION 1952. Ronald Reagan b. 1911.	
7	☉.	**8th S. before Easter.** Charles Dickens b. 1812.	
8	M.	Mary, Queen of Scots exec. 1587.	
9	Tu.	Edward Carson b. 1854. Alban Berg b. 1885.	
10	W.	Treaty of Paris 1763. Harold Macmillan b. 1894.	
11	Th.	Thomas Edison b. 1847. Sir Vivian Fuchs b. 1908.	
12	F.	Lady Jane Grey exec. 1554. Charles Darwin b. 1809.	
13	S.	Accession of William III and Mary II 1689.	
14	☉.	**7th S. before Easter.** VALENTINE'S DAY.	
15	M.	Galileo b. 1564. Sir Ernest Shackleton b. 1874.	
16	Tu	SHROVE TUESDAY. Lord Hore-Belisha d. 1957.	
17	W.	**Ash Wednesday.** Sir Edward German b. 1862.	
18	Th.	Mary I b. 1516. Count Alessandro Volta b. 1745.	
19	F.	DUKE OF YORK b. 1960. Cdr. Robert Peary d. 1920.	
20	S.	Benedict Spinoza d. 1677. Percy Grainger d. 1961.	
21	☉.	**1st S. in Lent.** Léo Delibes b. 1836.	
22	M.	Arthur Schopenhauer b. 1788.* Hugo Wolf d. 1903.	
23	Tu.	G. F. Handel b. 1865. Sir Edward Elgar d. 1934.	
24	W.	Wilhelm Grimm b. 1786. Henry Cavendish d. 1810.	
25	Th.	Enrico Caruso b. 1873. John Foster Dulles b. 1888.*	
26	F.	Victor Hugo b. 1802. Frank Bridge b. 1879.	
27	S.	Labour Party founded 1900. Ivan Pavlov d. 1936.	
28	☉.	**2nd S. in Lent.** Relief of Ladysmith 1900.	
29	M.	Giacchino Rossini b. 1792.	

*Centenary

PHENOMENA

February 11ᵈ 04ʰ Mercury in inferior conjunction.

13ᵈ 09ʰ Mars in conjunction with the Moon. Mars 5° N.

13ᵈ 19ʰ Saturn in conjunction with the Moon. Saturn 6° N.

20ᵈ 17ʰ Venus in conjunction with the Moon. Venus 1°·9 S.

21ᵈ 18ʰ Jupiter in conjunction with the Moon. Jupiter 4° S.

23ᵈ 13ʰ Mars in conjunction with Saturn. Mars 1°·3 S.

CONSTELLATIONS

The following constellations are near the meridian at

	d h		d h
Jan.	1 24	Jan.	16 23
Feb.	1 22	Feb.	15 21
Mar.	1 20	Mar.	16 19

Draco (below the Pole), Camelopardus, Auriga, Taurus, Gemini, Orion, Canis Minor, Monoceros, Lepus, Canis Major and Puppis.

MINIMA OF ALGOL

d	h	d	h
1	6	18	11
4	3	21	8
7	0	24	4
9	20	27	1
12	17	29	22
15	14		

PHASES OF THE MOON

	d h m
○ Full Moon	2 20 51
☽ Last Quarter.......	10 23 01
● New Moon.........	17 15 54
☽ First Quarter	24 12 15

	d h
Apogee (406,390 kilometres)	3 10
Perigee (356,910 „)	17 10

Mean Longitude of Ascending Node on Feb. 1, 356°

MONTHLY NOTES

Feb.   1. Pheasant and partridge shooting ends.
      6. National Day, New Zealand.
    17. First Day of Lent.
       Ancient Chinese New Year (Year of the Dragon).

Day	Right Ascension	Dec. −	Equation of Time	Rise 52°	Rise 56°	Transit	Set 52°	Set 56°	Sidereal Time	Transit of First Point of Aries
	h m s	° ′	m s	h m	h m	h m	h m	h m	h m s	h m s
1	20 55 10	17 23	−13 27	7 41	7 56	12 14	16 46	16 31	8 41 43	15 15 46
2	20 59 15	17 06	−13 35	7 40	7 55	12 14	16 48	16 33	8 45 40	15 11 50
3	21 03 19	16 49	−13 43	7 38	7 53	12 14	16 50	16 36	8 49 37	15 07 54
4	21 07 23	16 31	−13 50	7 36	7 51	12 14	16 52	16 38	8 53 33	15 03 58
5	21 11 25	16 13	−13 55	7 35	7 49	12 14	16 54	16 40	8 57 30	15 00 02
6	21 15 27	15 55	−14 01	7 33	7 47	12 14	16 56	16 42	9 01 26	14 56 07
7	21 19 28	15 37	−14 05	7 31	7 45	12 14	16 58	16 44	9 05 23	14 52 11
8	21 23 28	15 18	−14 09	7 30	7 43	12 14	16 59	16 47	9 09 19	14 48 15
9	21 27 27	14 59	−14 11	7 28	7 40	12 14	17 01	16 49	9 13 16	14 44 19
10	21 31 26	14 40	−14 13	7 26	7 38	12 14	17 03	16 51	9 17 12	14 40 23
11	21 35 24	14 21	−14 15	7 24	7 36	12 14	17 05	16 53	9 21 09	14 36 27
12	21 39 21	14 01	−14 15	7 22	7 34	12 14	17 07	16 55	9 25 06	14 32 31
13	21 43 17	13 41	−14 15	7 20	7 32	12 14	17 09	16 58	9 29 02	14 28 35
14	21 47 12	13 21	−14 14	7 19	7 29	12 14	17 11	17 00	9 32 59	14 24 39
15	21 51 07	13 01	−14 12	7 17	7 27	12 14	17 12	17 02	9 36 55	14 20 43
16	21 55 01	12 41	−14 10	7 15	7 25	12 14	17 14	17 04	9 40 52	14 16 47
17	21 58 55	12 20	−14 06	7 13	7 23	12 14	17 16	17 06	9 44 48	14 12 52
18	22 02 47	11 59	−14 03	7 11	7 20	12 14	17 18	17 09	9 48 45	14 08 56
19	22 06 39	11 38	−13 58	7 09	7 18	12 14	17 20	17 11	9 52 41	14 05 00
20	22 10 31	11 17	−13 53	7 07	7 16	12 14	17 22	17 13	9 56 38	14 01 04
21	22 14 21	10 55	−13 47	7 05	7 13	12 14	17 24	17 15	10 00 35	13 57 08
22	22 18 11	10 33	−13 40	7 03	7 11	12 14	17 25	17 17	10 04 31	13 53 12
23	22 22 00	10 12	−13 33	7 01	7 08	12 13	17 27	17 20	10 08 28	13 49 16
24	22 25 49	9 50	−13 25	6 58	7 06	12 13	17 29	17 22	10 12 24	13 45 20
25	22 29 37	9 28	−13 16	6 56	7 04	12 13	17 31	17 24	10 16 21	13 41 24
26	22 33 24	9 05	−13 07	6 54	7 01	12 13	17 33	17 26	10 20 17	13 37 28
27	22 37 11	8 43	−12 57	6 52	6 59	12 13	17 35	17 28	10 24 14	13 33 32
28	22 40 57	8 20	−12 47	6 50	6 56	12 13	17 36	17 30	10 28 10	13 29 37
29	22 44 43	7 58	−12 36	6 48	6 54	12 13	17 38	17 32	10 32 07	13 25 41

THE SUN　　s.d. 16′·2

Duration of Civil (C), Nautical (N), and Astronomical (A), Twilight (in minutes)

Lat. °	Feb. 1 C	N	A	Feb. 11 C	N	A	Feb. 21 C	N	A	Feb. 28 C	N	A
52	37	77	117	35	75	114	34	74	113	34	73	112
56	41	86	130	39	83	126	38	81	125	38	81	124

ASTRONOMICAL NOTES

MERCURY, magnitude about +1, will only be visible as an evening object for the first few days of the month. Even then it will only be seen low above the south-western horizon for a very short while around the time of end of evening civil twilight.

VENUS continues to be a bright evening object, magnitude −4·1, visible in the western sky for several hours after sunset. On the evening of the 20th the three-day old crescent Moon passes 2° N. of the planet.

MARS, magnitude +1·2, continues to be visible low in the south-eastern sky for a while before the morning twilight inhibits observation. The reddish tint of the planet is a useful aid to its identification.

JUPITER, magnitude −2·2, continues to be visible in the south-western sky in the evenings. On the evening of the 21st the crescent Moon, 4 days old, passes 4° N. of the planet.

SATURN, magnitude +0·6, is a morning object and visible low in the south-eastern sky until it is obliterated by the morning twilight. Observers will note that Mars is approaching Saturn in February and actually passes 1°·3 S. of the giant planet on the 23rd. Note that Saturn is about half a magnitude brighter than Mars.

ZODIACAL LIGHT. The evening cone may be observed in the western sky after the end of twilight from the 5th to the 18th. This faint phenomenon is only visible under good conditions, in the absence of both moonlight and artificial lighting.

THE MOON

Day	R.A.	Dec.	Hor. Par.	Semi-diam.	Sun's Co-long.	P.A. of Bright Limb	Phase	Age	Rise 52°	Rise 56°	Transit	Set 52°	Set 56°
	h m	°	'	'	°	°		d	h m	h m	h m	h m	h m
1	7 34	+26·3	54·2	14·8	67	291	97	12·8	14 59	14 30	23 38	7 37	8 07
2	8 25	+23·4	54·0	14·7	79	306	99	13·8	16 13	15 51	..	7 59	8 22
3	9 13	+19·5	54·0	14·7	91	41	100	14·8	17 27	17 12	0 24	8 15	8 32
4	9 59	+14·9	54·0	14·7	103	99	99	15·8	18 40	18 30	1 07	8 28	8 39
5	10 42	+ 9·7	54·1	14·7	115	109	96	16·8	19 51	19 47	1 48	8 38	8 44
6	11 25	+ 4·1	54·3	14·8	127	113	92	17·8	21 02	21 03	2 27	8 47	8 49
7	12 07	− 1·6	54·6	14·9	140	114	86	18·8	22 14	22 20	3 06	8 56	8 53
8	12 50	− 7·3	55·0	15·0	152	114	78	19·8	23 28	23 40	3 47	9 05	8 57
9	13 34	−12·9	55·5	15·1	164	113	70	20·8	..	..	4 29	9 17	9 03
10	14 22	−18·1	56·2	15·3	176	110	60	21·8	0 46	1 05	5 15	9 31	9 11
11	15 13	−22·6	57·0	15·5	188	105	50	22·8	2 09	2 35	6 05	9 52	9 25
12	16 09	−26·1	57·9	15·8	200	100	39	23·8	3 32	4 06	7 00	10 23	9 48
13	17 10	−28·2	58·8	16·0	213	92	29	24·8	4 50	5 30	8 01	11 11	10 30
14	18 15	−28·5	59·7	16·3	225	84	19	25·8	5 53	6 33	9 05	12 21	11 41
15	19 20	−27·0	60·5	16·5	237	76	11	26·8	6 38	7 10	10 09	13 49	13 18
16	20 25	−23·4	61·1	16·6	249	67	4	27·8	7 08	7 31	11 11	15 27	15 05
17	21 26	−18·3	61·4	16·7	261	54	1	28·8	7 28	7 43	12 09	17 05	16 52
18	22 24	−11·9	61·4	16·7	274	269	0	0·3	7 43	7 52	13 03	18 40	18 34
19	23 18	− 5·0	61·0	16·6	286	248	3	1·3	7 56	7 58	13 54	20 11	20 11
20	0 11	+ 2·2	60·4	16·4	298	245	8	2·3	8 08	8 04	14 43	21 39	21 47
21	1 02	+ 9·0	59·5	16·2	310	245	15	3·3	8 20	8 11	15 32	23 07	23 21
22	1 54	+15·2	58·5	16·0	322	248	25	4·3	8 34	8 18	16 22	..	..
23	2 47	+20·4	57·6	15·7	334	251	35	5·3	8 52	8 30	17 14	0 33	0 54
24	3 41	+24·5	56·7	15·4	347	256	45	6·3	9 17	8 46	18 07	1 56	2 25
25	4 36	+27·2	55·9	15·2	359	262	55	7·3	9 51	9 14	19 01	3 13	3 49
26	5 32	+28·6	55·2	15·0	11	269	65	8·3	10 38	9 58	19 54	4 17	4 57
27	6 27	+28·4	54·7	14·9	23	275	74	9·3	11 38	11 00	20 46	5 06	5 44
28	7 21	+27·0	54·3	14·8	35	282	82	10·3	12 47	12 16	21 35	5 41	6 14
29	8 12	+24·3	54·1	14·7	47	288	88	11·3	14 01	13 37	22 22	6 06	6 31

MERCURY ☿

Day	R.A.	Dec. −	Diam.	Phase	Transit		Day	R.A.	Dec. −	Diam.	Phase	Transit	
	h m	°	"		h m			h m	°	"		h m	
1	21 58	10·8	—	—	13 15	Mercury is too close to the Sun for observation	16	21 11	12·6	—	—	11 26	Mercury is too close to the Sun for observation
4	21 57	10·1	—	—	13 00		19	21 02	13·7	10	14	11 07	
7	21 49	10·0	—	—	12 40		22	20 58	14·6	9	23	10 52	
10	21 37	10·5	—	—	12 15		25	20 59	15·2	9	31	10 41	
13	21 23	11·4	—	—	11 50		28	21 03	15·6	8	38	10 34	
16	21 11	12·6	—	—	11 26		31	21 10	15·7	8	45	10 30	

VENUS ♀

Day	R.A.	Dec.	Diam.	Phase	Transit	5° high. 52°	5° high. 56°
	h m	°	"		h m	h m	h m
1	23 24	− 5·0	14	76	14 43	19 46	19 39
6	23 46	− 2·4	15	75	14 45	20 02	19 47
11	0 07	+ 0·2	15	73	14 46	20 17	20 14
16	0 28	+ 2·9	16	72	14 48	20 32	20 31
21	0 49	+ 5·5	16	70	14 49	20 47	20 48
26	1 10	+ 8·0	17	68	14 50	21 01	21 05
31	1 31	+10·5	18	66	14 51	21 15	21 21

MARS ♂

Day	R.A.	Dec. −	Diam.	Phase	Transit	5° high. 52°	5° high. 56°
	h m	°	"		h m	h m	h m
1	16 58	22·5	5	93	8 15	5 08	5 42
6	17 12	22·9	5	92	8 10	5 06	5 41
11	17 27	23·2	5	92	8 05	5 04	5 40
16	17 41	23·4	5	91	8 00	5 01	5 38
21	17 56	23·6	5	91	7 55	4 57	5 34
26	18 11	23·6	6	91	7 50	4 53	5 30
31	18 25	23·6	6	90	7 45	4 47	5 25

SUNRISE AND SUNSET

Day	London a.m.	London p.m.	Bristol a.m.	Bristol p.m.	Birmingham a.m.	Birmingham p.m.	Manchester a.m.	Manchester p.m.	Newcastle a.m.	Newcastle p.m.	Glasgow a.m.	Glasgow p.m.	Belfast a.m.	Belfast p.m.
	h m	h m	h m	h m	h m	h m	h m	h m	h m	h m	h m	h m	h m	h m
1	7 41	4 48	7 50	4 58	7 52	4 51	7 57	4 50	8 00	4 41	8 14	4 48	8 16	5 00
2	7 39	4 50	7 49	5 00	7 50	4 53	7 55	4 52	7 58	4 43	8 12	4 51	8 14	5 03
3	7 38	4 51	7 47	5 01	7 48	4 55	7 53	4 54	7 56	4 45	8 10	4 53	8 12	5 05
4	7 37	4 53	7 46	5 03	7 46	4 57	7 51	4 56	7 54	4 47	8 08	4 55	8 10	5 07
5	7 35	4 55	7 44	5 05	7 44	4 59	7 49	4 58	7 52	4 49	8 06	4 57	8 08	5 09
6	7 33	4 57	7 42	5 07	7 43	5 01	7 48	5 00	7 50	4 51	8 04	4 59	8 07	5 11
7	7 32	4 58	7 41	5 08	7 41	5 03	7 46	5 02	7 48	4 54	8 02	5 02	8 05	5 13
8	7 30	5 00	7 39	5 10	7 39	5 05	7 44	5 04	7 46	4 56	8 00	5 04	8 03	5 15
9	7 28	5 02	7 38	5 12	7 37	5 07	7 42	5 06	7 44	4 58	7 58	5 06	8 01	5 17
10	7 26	5 04	7 36	5 14	7 35	5 08	7 40	5 07	7 42	5 00	7 56	5 08	7 59	5 19
11	7 24	5 05	7 34	5 15	7 33	5 10	7 38	5 09	7 40	5 02	7 54	5 10	7 57	5 21
12	7 23	5 07	7 32	5 17	7 32	5 12	7 37	5 11	7 38	5 04	7 52	5 12	7 55	5 23
13	7 21	5 09	7 31	5 19	7 30	5 14	7 35	5 13	7 36	5 06	7 50	5 14	7 53	5 25
14	7 19	5 11	7 29	5 21	7 28	5 16	7 33	5 15	7 34	5 08	7 48	5 16	7 51	5 27
15	7 17	5 13	7 27	5 23	7 26	5 18	7 31	5 17	7 32	5 10	7 46	5 18	7 49	5 29
16	7 15	5 15	7 25	5 25	7 24	5 20	7 29	5 19	7 29	5 12	7 43	5 20	7 47	5 31
17	7 13	5 16	7 23	5 26	7 22	5 21	7 27	5 21	7 27	5 14	7 41	5 22	7 45	5 33
18	7 11	5 18	7 21	5 28	7 20	5 23	7 25	5 23	7 25	5 17	7 39	5 25	7 43	5 35
19	7 09	5 20	7 19	5 30	7 18	5 25	7 22	5 25	7 22	5 19	7 36	5 27	7 40	5 37
20	7 07	5 22	7 17	5 32	7 16	5 27	7 20	5 27	7 20	5 21	7 34	5 29	7 38	5 39
21	7 05	5 24	7 15	5 34	7 14	5 29	7 18	5 29	7 18	5 23	7 32	5 31	7 36	5 41
22	7 03	5 26	7 13	5 36	7 12	5 31	7 16	5 31	7 16	5 25	7 29	5 33	7 33	5 43
23	7 01	5 28	7 11	5 38	7 10	5 33	7 14	5 33	7 14	5 27	7 27	5 36	7 31	5 46
24	6 59	5 29	7 09	5 39	7 08	5 34	7 11	5 35	7 11	5 29	7 24	5 38	7 28	5 48
25	6 57	5 31	7 07	5 41	7 06	5 36	7 09	5 37	7 09	5 31	7 22	5 40	7 26	5 50
26	6 54	5 33	7 04	5 43	7 03	5 38	7 07	5 39	7 07	5 33	7 20	5 42	7 24	5 52
27	6 52	5 35	7 02	5 45	7 01	5 40	7 04	5 41	7 04	5 35	7 17	5 44	7 21	5 54
28	6 50	5 37	7 00	5 47	6 59	5 42	7 02	5 43	7 02	5 37	7 15	5 46	7 19	5 56
29	6 48	5 39	6 58	5 49	6 57	5 44	7 00	5 45	6 59	5 39	7 12	5 48	7 17	5 58

		JUPITER ♃						SATURN ♄			
Day	R.A.	Dec. +	Transit	5° high.		R.A.	Dec.	Transit	5° high.		
				52°	56°				52°	56°	
	h m	°	h m	h m	h m	h m	°	h m	h m	h m	
1	1 28	8·0	16 44	22 52	22 56	17 55	22·3	9 12	6 03	6 36	
11	1 34	8·6	16 11	22 22	22 26	17 59	22·3	8 36	5 28	6 01	
21	1 41	9·3	15 38	21 53	21 57	18 02	22·3	8 01	4 52	5 25	
31	1 48	10·0	15 06	21 24	21 29	18 05	22·3	7 24	4 16	4 49	

Equatorial diameter of Jupiter 37″; of Saturn 16″. Diameters of Saturn's rings 36″ and 16″.

		URANUS ♅					NEPTUNE ♆		
Day	R.A.	Dec. −	Transit		R.A.	Dec. −	Transit		
	h m	° ′	h m		h m	° ′	h m		
1	17 57·3	23 37	9 14	Uranus is too close to the Sun for observation	18 38·5	22 11	9 55	Neptune is too close to the Sun for observation	
11	17 59·3	23 37	8 37		18 39·9	22 10	9 17		
21	18 01·0	23 37	7 59		18 41·4	22 09	8 39		
31	18 02·4	23 37	7 21		18 42·1	22 07	8 01		

Diameter 4″   Diameter 2″

Mars, Roman god of battle

Sun's Longitude 0° ♈ 20^d 10^h

Day of Month	Day of Week	
1	Tu.	ST. DAVID'S DAY. Paul Scott d. 1978.
2	W.	Cardinal Archbishop of Westminster b. 1923.
3	Th.	William Macready b. 1793. Sir Henry Wood b. 1869.
4	F.	Opening of Forth Railway Bridge 1890.
5	S.	Geraldus Mercator b. 1512. Sergei Prokofiev d. 1953.
6	𝔖.	**3rd S. in Lent.** Louisa M. Alcott d. 1888.*
7	M.	Sir John Herschel b. 1792. Ravel b. 1875.
8	Tu.	Hector Berlioz d. 1869. Sir William Walton d. 1983.
9	W.	William Cobbett b. 1763. Ernest Bevin b. 1881.
10	Th.	PRINCE EDWARD b. 1964. Dame Eva Turner b. 1892.
11	F.	Alexander Fleming d. 1955. Haydn Wood d. 1959.
12	S.	Bp. George Berkeley b. 1685. Thomas Arne b. 1710.
13	𝔖.	**4th S. in Lent.** MOTHERING SUNDAY.
14	M.	C. P. E. Bach b. 1714. Albert Einstein b. 1879.
15	Tu.	Julius Caesar assas. 44 B.C. Bessemer d. 1898.
16	W.	Georg Ohm b. 1787. Aubrey Beardsley d. 1898.
17	Th.	ST. PATRICK'S DAY. Christian Doppler d. 1853.
18	F.	Rimsky-Korsakov b. 1844. Rudolf Diesel b. 1858.
19	S.	**St. Joseph of Nazareth.** Dr. Livingstone b. 1813.
20	𝔖.	**5th S. in Lent.** Sir Isaac Newton d. 1727.
21	M.	J. S. Bach b. 1685. Modest Mussorgsky b. 1839.
22	Tu.	Sir Anthony van Dyke b. 1599. Stendal d. 1842.
23	W.	Donald Campbell b. 1921. Roger Bannister b. 1929.
24	Th.	Elizabeth I d. 1603. William Morris b. 1834.
25	F.	**The Annunciation.** Claude Debussey d. 1918.
26	S.	Beethoven d. 1827. Cecil Rhodes d. 1902.
27	𝔖.	**Palm Sunday.** John Bright d. 1889.
28	M.	Serge Rachmaninoff d. 1943. Neil Kinnock b. 1942.
29	Tu.	Charles Wesley d. 1788.* Sir Edwin Lutyens b. 1869.
30	W.	HILARY LAW SITTINGS END. Stainer d. 1901.
31	Th.	**Maundy Thursday.** Eiffel Tower completed 1889.

*Centenary

PHENOMENA

March 6^d 20^h Venus in conjunction with Jupiter. Venus 2° N.

8^d 06^h Mercury at greatest western elongation (27°).

12^d 06^h Saturn in conjunction with the Moon. Saturn 6° N.

13^d 00^h Mars in conjunction with the Moon. Mars 5° N.

16^d 05^h Mercury in conjunction with the Moon. Mercury 0°·5 N.

20^d 10^h Equinox.

20^d 14^h Jupiter in conjunction with the Moon. Jupiter 5° S.

21^d 12^h Venus in conjunction with the Moon. Venus 2° S.

CONSTELLATIONS

The following are near the meridian at

	d	h		d	h
Feb.	1	24	Feb.	15	23
Mar.	1	22	Mar.	16	21
Apr.	1	20	Apr.	15	19

Cepheus (below the Pole), Camelopardus, Lynx, Gemini, Cancer, Leo, Canis Minor, Hydra, Monoceros, Canis Major and Puppis.

MINIMA OF ALGOL

d	h	d	h
3	19	18	3
6	16	21	0
9	13	23	21
12	9	26	18
15	6	29	14

PHASES OF THE MOON

	d	h	m
○ Full Moon	3	16	01
☾ Last Quarter	11	10	56
● New Moon	18	02	02
☽ First Quarter	25	04	41

	d	h
Apogee (406,250 kilometres)	1	12
Perigee (359,520 „)	16	21
Apogee (405,470 „)	29	00

Mean Longitude of Ascending Node on March 1, 354°.

Summer Time in 1988 (*see* p. 142).—Begins: March 27^d 01^h G.M.T. Ends: October 23^d 01^h G.M.T.

MONTHLY NOTES

March 14. Commonwealth Day.

17. Bank Holiday in Northern Ireland.

25. Lady Day. Quarter Day.

31. Financial Year 1987–88 ends.

Day	Right Ascension	Dec.	Equation of Time	Rise 52°	Rise 56°	Transit	Set 52°	Set 56°	Sidereal Time	Transit of First Point of Aries
	THE SUN						s.d. 16'·1			

Day	h m s	° '	m s	h m	h m	h m	h m	h m	h m s	h m s
1	22 48 28	− 7 35	−12 25	6 46	6 51	12 12	17 40	17 35	10 36 04	13 21 45
2	22 52 13	− 7 12	−12 13	6 43	6 49	12 12	17 42	17 37	10 40 00	13 17 49
3	22 55 57	− 6 49	−12 00	6 41	6 46	12 12	17 44	17 39	10 43 57	13 13 53
4	22 59 40	− 6 26	−11 47	6 39	6 44	12 12	17 45	17 41	10 47 53	13 09 57
5	23 03 24	− 6 03	−11 34	6 37	6 41	12 11	17 47	17 43	10 51 50	13 06 01
6	23 07 06	− 5 40	−11 20	6 34	6 38	12 11	17 49	17 45	10 55 46	13 02 05
7	23 10 49	− 5 17	−11 06	6 32	6 36	12 11	17 51	17 47	10 59 43	12 58 09
8	23 14 31	− 4 53	−10 51	6 30	6 33	12 11	17 53	17 49	11 03 39	12 54 13
9	23 18 12	− 4 30	−10 36	6 28	6 31	12 10	17 54	17 51	11 07 36	12 50 17
10	23 21 54	− 4 06	−10 21	6 25	6 28	12 10	17 56	17 53	11 11 33	12 46 22
11	23 25 35	− 3 43	−10 05	6 23	6 25	12 10	17 58	17 56	11 15 29	12 42 26
12	23 29 15	− 3 19	− 9 50	6 21	6 23	12 10	18 00	17 58	11 19 26	12 38 30
13	23 32 56	− 2 56	− 9 33	6 19	6 20	12 09	18 01	18 00	11 23 22	12 34 34
14	23 36 36	− 2 32	− 9 17	6 16	6 18	12 09	18 03	18 02	11 27 19	12 30 38
15	23 40 16	− 2 08	− 9 00	6 14	6 15	12 09	18 05	18 04	11 31 15	12 26 42
16	23 43 55	− 1 44	− 8 43	6 12	6 12	12 09	18 07	18 06	11 35 12	12 22 46
17	23 47 35	− 1 21	− 8 26	6 09	6 10	12 08	18 08	18 08	11 39 08	12 18 50
18	23 51 14	− 0 57	− 8 09	6 07	6 07	12 08	18 10	18 10	11 43 05	12 14 54
19	23 54 53	− 0 33	− 7 51	6 05	6 05	12 08	18 12	18 12	11 47 02	12 10 58
20	23 58 32	− 0 10	− 7 34	6 02	6 02	12 07	18 13	18 14	11 50 58	12 07 02
21	0 02 11	+ 0 14	− 7 16	6 00	5 59	12 07	18 15	18 16	11 54 55	12 03 07
22	0 05 49	+ 0 38	− 6 58	5 58	5 57	12 07	18 17	18 18	11 58 51	11 59 11
23	0 09 28	+ 1 02	− 6 40	5 55	5 54	12 07	18 19	18 20	12 02 48	11 55 15
24	0 13 06	+ 1 25	− 6 22	5 53	5 51	12 06	18 20	18 22	12 06 44	11 51 19
25	0 16 45	+ 1 49	− 6 04	5 51	5 49	12 06	18 22	18 24	12 10 41	11 47 23
26	0 20 23	+ 2 12	− 5 46	5 48	5 46	12 06	18 24	18 26	12 14 37	11 43 27
27	0 24 02	+ 2 36	− 5 28	5 46	5 43	12 05	18 26	18 28	12 18 34	11 39 31
28	0 27 40	+ 2 59	− 5 09	5 44	5 41	12 05	18 27	18 30	12 22 31	11 35 35
29	0 31 18	+ 3 23	− 4 51	5 42	5 38	12 05	18 29	18 32	12 26 27	11 31 39
30	0 34 57	+ 3 46	− 4 33	5 39	5 36	12 04	18 31	18 35	12 30 24	11 27 43
31	0 38 35	+ 4 09	− 4 15	5 37	5 33	12 04	18 32	18 37	12 34 20	11 23 47

Duration of Civil (C), Nautical (N), and Astronomical (A), Twilight (in minutes)

Lat. °	Mar. 1 C	N	A	Mar. 11 C	N	A	Mar. 21 C	N	A	Mar. 31 C	N	A
52	34	73	112	34	73	113	34	74	116	34	76	120
56	38	81	124	37	80	125	37	82	129	38	84	136

ASTRONOMICAL NOTES

MERCURY, despite the fact that it reaches greatest western elongation (27°) on the 8th, is not suitably placed for observation.

VENUS is a magnificent object, completely dominating the western sky in the evenings and by the end of the month is visible for four hours after sunset. Its magnitude is −4·2. Venus passes 2° N. of Jupiter on the evening of the 6th. On the evenings of the 20th and 21st the crescent Moon is in the vicinity of the planet.

MARS, magnitude +0·9, is a morning object in the constellation of Sagittarius.

JUPITER is an evening object, magnitude −2·1, still visible in the western sky for several hours after sunset. The four Galilean satellites are readily observable with any small telescope, or even a good pair of binoculars provided that they are held rigidly. Times of eclipses and shadow transits of these satellites are given on page 147.

SATURN, magnitude +0·5, continues to be visible as a morning object, low in the south-eastern sky before dawn.

ECLIPSE. A total eclipse of the Sun occurs on the 17th–18th. See page 148 for details.

ZODIACAL LIGHT. The evening cone may be observed in the western sky after the end of twilight from the 5th to the 18th.

THE MOON

Day	R.A.	Dec.	Hor. Par.	Semi-diam.	Sun's Co-long.	P.A. of Bright Limb	Phase	Age	Rise 52°	Rise 56°	Tran-sit	Set 52°	Set 56°
	h m	°	′	′	°	°		d	h m	h m	h m	h m	h m
1	9 01	+20·6	54·0	14·7	60	˙293	94	12·3	15 15	14 58	23 05	6 23	6 42
2	9 47	+16·1	54·0	14·7	72	297	97	13·3	16 28	16 17	23 47	6 37	6 50
3	10 31	+11·0	54·1	14·7	84	304	100	14·3	17 40	17 34	..	6 47	6 55
4	11 14	+ 5·5	54·3	14·8	96	105	100	15·3	18 52	18 51	0 27	6 56	7 00
5	11 56	− 0·2	54·5	14·9	108	116	98	16·3	20 03	20 08	1 06	7 05	7 04
6	12 39	− 6·0	54·8	14·9	120	117	95	17·3	21 17	21 27	1 46	7 14	7 08
7	13 23	−11·7	55·2	15·1	132	115	90	18·3	22 34	22 50	2 28	7 25	7 13
8	14 10	−16·9	55·7	15·2	145	113	83	19·3	23 54	..	3 12	7 38	7 20
9	15 00	−21·6	56·3	15·3	157	109	75	20·3	..	0 18	4 00	7 56	7 31
10	15 54	−25·3	57·0	15·5	169	104	66	21·3	1 16	1 48	4 53	8 22	7 50
11	16 52	−27·8	57·7	15·7	181	97	55	22·3	2 35	3 14	5 50	9 02	8 22
12	17 53	−28·7	58·4	15·9	193	90	44	23·3	3 42	4 24	6 51	10 01	9 19
13	18 57	−27·8	59·2	16·1	206	83	33	24·3	4 33	5 09	7 53	11 19	10 44
14	19 59	−25·1	59·9	16·3	218	76	23	25·3	5 07	5 35	8 53	12 50	12 24
15	21 00	−20·7	60·5	16·5	230	70	14	26·3	5 31	5 50	9 51	14 26	14 09
16	21 58	−14·9	60·9	16·6	242	66	6	27·3	5 48	6 00	10 46	16 01	15 51
17	22 53	− 8·3	61·0	16·6	254	64	2	28·3	6 01	6 07	11 38	17 33	17 31
18	23 46	− 1·1	60·8	16·6	267	81	0	29·3	6 13	6 13	12 29	19 04	19 08
19	0 39	+ 6·0	60·3	16·4	279	240	1	0·9	6 25	6 19	13 19	20 34	20 44
20	1 31	+12·6	59·6	16·2	291	243	5	1·9	6 39	6 26	14 09	22 03	22 21
21	2 25	+18·5	58·7	16·0	303	247	11	2·9	6 55	6 36	15 02	23 31	23 57
22	3 20	+23·1	57·8	15·7	315	252	19	3·9	7 17	6 50	15 56	..	..
23	4 17	+26·5	56·9	15·5	328	258	29	4·9	7 47	7 13	16 51	0 54	1 28
24	5 14	+28·3	56·0	15·3	340	264	38	5·9	8 30	7 51	17 46	2 06	2 45
25	6 11	+28·6	55·3	15·1	352	271	48	6·9	9 27	8 47	18 40	3 02	3 42
26	7 06	+27·5	54·8	14·9	4	277	58	7·9	10 34	10 00	19 31	3 43	4 17
27	7 58	+25·2	54·4	14·8	16	283	67	8·9	11 47	11 20	20 18	4 11	4 38
28	8 48	+21·7	54·2	14·8	29	288	76	9·9	13 01	12 42	21 03	4 30	4 51
29	9 34	+17·5	54·1	14·7	41	291	83	10·9	14 15	14 01	21 45	4 45	5 00
30	10 19	+12·5	54·1	14·8	53	294	90	11·9	15 27	15 19	22 25	4 56	5 06
31	11 02	+ 7·1	54·3	14·8	65	294	95	12·9	16 39	16 36	23 05	5 06	5 11

MERCURY ☿

Day	R.A.	Dec. −	Diam.	Phase	Tran-sit		Day	R.A.	Dec. −	Diam.	Phase	Tran-sit	
	h m	°	″		h m			h m	°	″		h m	
1	21 08	15·7	8	43	10 31		16	22 09	13·2	6	67	10 34	
4	21 16	15·7	8	49	10 28	Mercury is too	19	22 24	12·0	6	70	10 38	Mercury is too
7	21 27	15·4	7	54	10 28	close to the	22	22 40	10·7	6	73	10 42	close to the
10	21 40	14·9	7	59	10 29	Sun for	25	22 57	9·1	6	77	10 48	Sun for
13	21 54	14·1	7	63	10 31	observation	28	23 15	7·4	6	80	10 53	observation
16	22 09	13·2	6	67	10 34		31	23 33	5·5	5	83	10 59	

VENUS ♀

Day	R.A.	Dec. +	Diam.	Phase	Tran-sit	5° high. 52°	5° high. 56°
	h m	°	″		h m	h m	h m
1	1 27	10·0	18	67	14 51	21 12	21 18
6	1 48	12·4	18	64	14 52	21 26	21 33
11	2 09	14·7	19	62	14 54	21 40	21 49
16	2 30	16·8	20	60	14 55	21 53	22 04
21	2 51	18·8	21	58	14 56	22 05	22 19
26	3 12	20·7	22	55	14 58	22 17	22 32
31	3 33	22·3	23	53	14 59	22 28	22 45

MARS ♂

Day	R.A.	Dec. −	Diam.	Phase	Tran-sit	5° high. 52°	5° high. 56°
	h m	°	″		h m	h m	h m
1	18 22	23·6	6	90	7 46	4 48	5 26
6	18 37	23·5	6	90	7 41	4 43	5 20
11	18 52	23·4	6	90	7 36	4 36	5 12
16	19 06	23·1	6	89	7 31	4 29	5 04
21	19 21	22·8	6	89	7 26	4 21	4 55
26	19 35	22·4	7	88	7 21	4 12	4 45
31	19 50	21·9	7	88	7 15	4 03	4 35

SUNRISE AND SUNSET

Day	London a.m.	London p.m.	Bristol a.m.	Bristol p.m.	Birmingham a.m.	Birmingham p.m.	Manchester a.m.	Manchester p.m.	Newcastle a.m.	Newcastle p.m.	Glasgow a.m.	Glasgow p.m.	Belfast a.m.	Belfast p.m.
	h m	h m	h m	h m	h m	h m	h m	h m	h m	h m	h m	h m	h m	h m
1	6 46	5 40	6 56	5 50	6 55	5 46	6 58	5 47	6 57	5 42	7 10	5 51	7 15	6 00
2	6 44	5 42	6 54	5 52	6 52	5 47	6 55	5 48	6 54	5 43	7 07	5 53	7 12	6 01
3	6 42	5 44	6 51	5 54	6 50	5 49	6 53	5 50	6 52	5 45	7 05	5 55	7 10	6 03
4	6 40	5 46	6 49	5 56	6 47	5 51	6 50	5 52	6 49	5 47	7 02	5 57	7 07	6 05
5	6 38	5 47	6 47	5 57	6 45	5 53	6 48	5 54	6 47	5 49	6 59	5 59	7 05	6 07
6	6 36	5 49	6 45	5 59	6 43	5 55	6 46	5 56	6 45	5 51	6 57	6 01	7 03	6 09
7	6 33	5 50	6 43	6 00	6 40	5 57	6 43	5 58	6 42	5 53	6 54	6 03	7 00	6 11
8	6 31	5 52	6 41	6 02	6 38	5 59	6 41	6 00	6 40	5 55	6 52	6 05	6 58	6 13
9	6 29	5 54	6 39	6 04	6 36	6 00	6 39	6 01	6 37	5 57	6 49	6 07	6 55	6 15
10	6 27	5 55	6 36	6 05	6 34	6 02	6 37	6 03	6 35	5 59	6 47	6 09	6 53	6 17
11	6 24	5 57	6 34	6 07	6 31	6 04	6 34	6 05	6 32	6 02	6 44	6 12	6 50	6 20
12	6 22	5 59	6 32	6 09	6 29	6 06	6 32	6 07	6 29	6 04	6 41	6 14	6 47	6 22
13	6 20	6 00	6 30	6 10	6 27	6 07	6 30	6 09	6 27	6 06	6 39	6 16	6 45	6 24
14	6 17	6 02	6 27	6 12	6 24	6 09	6 27	6 11	6 24	6 08	6 36	6 18	6 42	6 26
15	6 15	6 04	6 25	6 14	6 22	6 11	6 25	6 12	6 22	6 09	6 33	6 20	6 40	6 27
16	6 13	6 06	6 23	6 16	6 20	6 13	6 22	6 14	6 19	6 11	6 31	6 22	6 37	6 29
17	6 11	6 07	6 21	6 17	6 18	6 14	6 20	6 16	6 17	6 13	6 28	6 24	6 35	6 31
18	6 08	6 09	6 18	6 19	6 15	6 16	6 17	6 18	6 14	6 15	6 26	6 26	6 32	6 33
19	6 06	6 11	6 16	6 21	6 13	6 18	6 15	6 20	6 12	6 17	6 23	6 28	6 30	6 35
20	6 04	6 13	6 14	6 23	6 11	6 20	6 12	6 22	6 09	6 19	6 20	6 30	6 27	6 37
21	6 01	6 14	6 11	6 24	6 08	6 21	6 10	6 24	6 07	6 21	6 18	6 32	6 25	6 39
22	5 59	6 16	6 09	6 26	6 06	6 23	6 07	6 26	6 04	6 23	6 15	6 34	6 22	6 41
23	5 57	6 18	6 07	6 28	6 04	6 25	6 05	6 27	6 02	6 24	6 12	6 36	6 20	6 42
24	5 54	6 20	6 04	6 30	6 01	6 27	6 03	6 29	6 00	6 26	6 10	6 38	6 18	6 44
25	5 52	6 21	6 02	6 31	5 59	6 28	6 00	6 31	5 57	6 28	6 07	6 40	6 15	6 46
26	5 50	6 23	6 00	6 33	5 57	6 30	5 58	6 33	5 55	6 30	6 05	6 42	6 13	6 48
27	5 47	6 25	5 57	6 34	5 54	6 32	5 55	6 35	5 52	6 32	6 02	6 44	6 10	6 50
28	5 45	6 26	5 55	6 36	5 52	6 33	5 53	6 36	5 49	6 34	5 59	6 46	6 07	6 52
29	5 43	6 28	5 53	6 38	5 50	6 35	5 51	6 38	5 46	6 36	5 56	6 48	6 04	6 54
30	5 41	6 30	5 51	6 39	5 48	6 37	5 49	6 40	5 44	6 38	5 54	6 51	6 02	6 57
31	5 39	6 31	5 49	6 41	5 45	6 38	5 46	6 41	5 41	6 40	5 51	6 53	5 59	6 58

	JUPITER ♃					SATURN ♄				
Day	R.A.	Dec. +	Transit	5° high. 52°	5° high. 56°	R.A.	Dec. −	Transit	5° high. 52°	5° high. 56°
	h m	°	h m	h m	h m	h m	°	h m	h m	h m
1	1 47	10·0	15 09	21 27	21 32	18 05	22·3	7 28	4 19	4 52
11	1 55	10·7	14 38	21 00	21 05	18 08	22·3	6 51	3 42	4 15
21	2 03	11·5	14 06	20 32	20 39	18 09	22·3	6 14	3 05	3 38
31	2 12	12·3	13 36	20 06	20 13	18 11	22·3	5 35	2 26	2 59

Equatorial diameter of Jupiter 34″; of Saturn 16″. Diameters of Saturn's rings 37″ and 16″.

	URANUS ♅					NEPTUNE ♆				
Day	R.A.	Dec. −	Transit	10° high. 52°	10° high. 56°	R.A.	Dec. −	Transit	10° high. 52°	10° high. 56°
	h m	° ′	h m	h m	h m	h m	° ′	h m	h m	h m
1	18 02·3	23 37	7 25	5 26	6 49	18 42·0	22 08	8 05	5 47	6 44
11	18 03·4	23 38	6 47	4 48	6 11	18 42·9	22 06	7 26	5 09	6 05
21	18 04·2	23 38	6 08	4 09	5 32	18 43·5	22 06	6 47	4 30	5 26
31	18 04·5	23 38	5 29	3 30	4 53	18 43·9	22 05	6 09	3 51	4 47

Diameter 4″   Diameter 2″

DAY OF		
Month	Week	

Aperire, to open. Earth opens to receive seed.

Sun's Longitude 30° ♉ 19ᵈ 21ʰ

1	F	**Good Friday.** End of Spanish Civil War 1939.
2	S.	**Easter Eve.** Neville Cardus b. 1889.
3	♄.	**Easter Day.** Henry IV b. 1367.
4	M.	Atlantic Treaty signed 1949.
5	Tu.	Thomas Hobbes b. 1588.* Joseph Lister b. 1827.
6	W.	Richard II d. 1199. Igor Stravinsky d. 1971.
7	Th.	William Wordsworth b. 1770. Henry Ford d. 1947.
8	F.	Sir Adrian Boult b. 1889. Pablo Picasso d. 1973.
9	S.	Francis Bacon d. 1626. Isambard K. Brunel b. 1806.
10	♄.	**1st S. after Easter.** Ben Nicholson b. 1894.
11	M.	Treaty of Utrecht 1713. Charles Hallé b. 1819.
12	Tu.	EASTER LAW SITTINGS BEGIN. Chaliapin d. 1938.
13	W.	Thomas Jefferson b. 1743. Samuel Beckett b. 1906.
14	Th.	G. F. Handel d. 1759. Arnold Toynbee b. 1889.
15	F.	Matthew Arnold d. 1888.* *Titanic* sunk 1912.
16	S.	Culloden 1746. Sir Charles Chaplin b. 1889.
17	♄.	**2nd S. after Easter.** Diet of Worms 1521.
18	M.	Judge Jeffreys d. 1689. Albert Einstein d. 1955.
19	Tu.	Primrose Day. Charles Darwin d. 1882.
20	W.	Napolean III b. 1808. Adolf Hitler b. 1889.
21	Th.	QUEEN ELIZABETH II b. 1926. Henry VII d. 1509.
22	F.	Kathleen Ferrier b. 1912. Yehudi Menuhin b. 1916.
23	S.	ST. GEORGE'S DAY. Shakespeare b. 1564; d. 1616.
24	♄.	**3rd S. after Easter.** Sir Stafford Cripps b. 1889.
25	M.	**St. Mark.** Guglielmo Marconi b. 1874.
26	Tu.	David Hume b. 1711. Alfred Krupp b. 1812.
27	W.	Magellan killed 1521. Samuel Morse b. 1791.
28	Th.	Edward IV b. 1442. Mutiny on the *Bounty* 1789.
29	F.	Thomas Beecham b. 1879. Malcolm Sargent b. 1895.
30	S.	Mary II b. 1662. Franz Lehar b. 1870.

*Centenary

PHENOMENA

April 3ᵈ 08ʰ Venus at greatest eastern elongation (46°).

8ᵈ 13ʰ Saturn in conjunction with the Moon. Saturn 6° N.

10ᵈ 15ʰ Mars in conjunction with the Moon. Mars 3° N.

20ᵈ 00ʰ Venus in conjunction with the Moon. Venus 1° S.

20ᵈ 15ʰ Mercury in superior conjunction.

CONSTELLATIONS

The following constellations are near the meridian at

	d h		d h
Mar.	1 24	Mar.	16 23
Apr.	1 22	Apr.	15 21
May	1 20	May	16 19

Cepheus (below the Pole), Cassiopeia (below the Pole), Ursa Major, Leo Minor, Leo, Sextans, Hydra and Crater.

MINIMA OF ALGOL

d	h	d	h
1	11	18	16
4	8	21	13
7	5	24	10
10	2	27	7
12	22	30	3
15	19		

PHASES OF THE MOON

		d	h	m
○	Full Moon	2	09	21
☾	Last Quarter.......	9	19	21
●	New Moon.........	16	12	00
☽	First Quarter	23	22	32

	d	h
Perigee (364,310 kilometres)	13	23
Apogee (404,510 „)	25	19

Mean Longitude of Ascending Node on April 1, 352°.

See note on *Summer Time*, p. 98.

MONTHLY NOTES

April 1. Bank Holiday, Scotland.
  2. Lent ends at Midnight. First day of Passover.
  4. Bank Holiday, England, Wales and Northern Ireland.
  5. Income Tax Year (1987–88) ends.
  10. Greek Orthodox Easter.
  18. First day of Ramadân.

				THE SUN		s.d. 16′·0					
Day	Right Ascension	Dec. +	Equation of Time	Rise		Transit	Set		Sidereal Time	Transit of First Point of Aries
				52°	56°		52°	56°		
	h m s	° ′	m s	h m	h m	h m	h m	h m	h m s	h m s
1	0 42 14	4 33	− 3 57	5 35	5 30	12 04	18 34	18 39	12 38 17	11 19 52
2	0 45 52	4 56	− 3 39	5 32	5 28	12 04	18 36	18 41	12 42 13	11 15 56
3	0 49 31	5 19	− 3 21	5 30	5 25	12 03	18 37	18 43	12 46 10	11 12 00
4	0 53 10	5 42	− 3 04	5 28	5 22	12 03	18 39	18 45	12 50 06	11 08 04
5	0 56 49	6 04	− 2 46	5 25	5 20	12 03	18 41	18 47	12 54 03	11 04 08
6	1 00 28	6 27	− 2 29	5 23	5 17	12 02	18 43	18 49	12 58 00	11 00 12
7	1 04 08	6 50	− 2 12	5 21	5 15	12 02	18 44	18 51	13 01 56	10 56 16
8	1 07 48	7 12	− 1 55	5 19	5 12	12 02	18 46	18 53	13 05 53	10 52 20
9	1 11 28	7 35	− 1 38	5 16	5 09	12 02	18 48	18 55	13 09 49	10 48 24
10	1 15 08	7 57	− 1 22	5 14	5 07	12 01	18 49	18 57	13 13 46	10 44 28
11	1 18 48	8 19	− 1 06	5 12	5 04	12 01	18 51	18 59	13 17 42	10 40 33
12	1 22 29	8 41	− 0 50	5 10	5 02	12 01	18 53	19 01	13 21 39	10 36 37
13	1 26 10	9 03	− 0 35	5 07	4 59	12 00	18 55	19 03	13 25 35	10 32 41
14	1 29 52	9 25	− 0 20	5 05	4 57	12 00	18 56	19 05	13 29 32	10 28 45
15	1 33 34	9 46	− 0 05	5 03	4 54	12 00	18 58	19 07	13 33 28	10 24 49
16	1 37 16	10 07	+ 0 09	5 01	4 52	12 00	19 00	19 09	13 37 25	10 20 53
17	1 40 58	10 29	+ 0 23	4 59	4 49	12 00	19 01	19 11	13 41 22	10 16 57
18	1 44 41	10 50	+ 0 37	4 57	4 47	11 59	19 03	19 13	13 45 18	10 13 01
19	1 48 25	11 11	+ 0 50	4 54	4 44	11 59	19 05	19 15	13 49 15	10 09 05
20	1 52 09	11 31	+ 1 03	4 52	4 42	11 59	19 07	19 17	13 53 11	10 05 09
21	1 55 53	11 52	+ 1 15	4 50	4 39	11 59	19 08	19 19	13 57 08	10 01 13
22	1 59 37	12 12	+ 1 27	4 48	4 37	11 58	19 10	19 21	14 01 04	9 57 18
23	2 03 22	12 32	+ 1 39	4 46	4 34	11 58	19 12	19 23	14 05 01	9 53 22
24	2 07 08	12 52	+ 1 50	4 44	4 32	11 58	19 13	19 26	14 08 57	9 49 26
25	2 10 54	13 12	+ 2 00	4 42	4 30	11 58	19 15	19 28	14 12 54	9 45 30
26	2 14 40	13 31	+ 2 10	4 40	4 27	11 58	19 17	19 30	14 16 51	9 41 34
27	2 18 27	13 50	+ 2 20	4 38	4 25	11 58	19 18	19 32	14 20 47	9 37 38
28	2 22 14	14 09	+ 2 29	4 36	4 23	11 57	19 20	19 34	14 24 44	9 33 42
29	2 26 02	14 28	+ 2 38	4 34	4 20	11 57	19 22	19 36	14 28 40	9 29 46
30	2 29 51	14 46	+ 2 46	4 32	4 18	11 57	19 23	19 38	14 32 37	9 25 50

Duration of Civil (C), Nautical (N), and Astronomical (A), Twilight (in minutes)

Lat. °	Apr. 1			Apr. 11			Apr. 21			Apr. 30		
	C	N	A	C	N	A	C	N	A	C	N	A
52	34	76	121	35	79	128	37	84	138	39	89	152
56	38	85	137	40	90	148	42	96	167	44	105	200

ASTRONOMICAL NOTES

MERCURY passes through superior conjunction on the 20th and therefore is unsuitably placed for observation.

VENUS reaches its maximum eastern elongation (46°) from the Sun on the 3rd and thus continues to be visible as a magnificent object, magnitude − 4·4, in the western sky for several hours after sunset. Venus is well north of the ecliptic which means even later setting times in these latitudes: indeed towards the end of April observers in Scotland will note Venus setting in the north-west *after* midnight. On the evening of the 19th the crescent Moon will be seen passing extremely close to the planet, an actual occultation being visible from places nearer the north pole.

MARS continues to be visible low in the south-eastern sky in the mornings and by the end of the month should be visible by 03ʰ. Its magnitude is +0·5.

JUPITER, magnitude − 2·0, is still visible for a short while in the western sky in the evenings for the first half of April until it is lost in the lengthening evening twilight.

SATURN, magnitude +0·4, continues to be visible as a morning object low in the south-eastern sky. By the end of the month it should be possible to observe the planet very low in the south-east, shortly after midnight. Saturn is in the western part of the constellation of Sagittarius.

THE MOON

Day	R.A.	Dec.	Hor. Par.	Semi-diam.	Sun's Co-long.	P.A. of Bright Limb	Phase	Age	Rise 52°	Rise 56°	Tran-sit	Set 52°	Set 56°
	h m	°	′	′	°	°		d	h m	h m	h m	h m	h m
1	11 45	+ 1·4	54·6	14·9	77	292	98	13·9	17 51	17 54	23 45	5 15	5 15
2	12 27	− 4·4	54·9	15·0	89	276	100	14·9	19 05	19 13	..	5 24	5 19
3	13 12	−10·2	55·3	15·1	102	131	100	15·9	20 21	20 36	0 26	5 34	5 24
4	13 58	−15·6	55·8	15·2	114	120	97	16·9	21 42	22 03	1 10	5 46	5 31
5	14 48	−20·5	56·3	15·3	126	114	93	17·9	23 04	23 33	1 57	6 03	5 40
6	15 41	−24·5	56·8	15·5	138	108	87	18·9	..	..	2 49	6 26	5 56
7	16 38	−27·3	57·3	15·6	150	102	79	19·9	0 24	1 01	3 45	7 01	6 24
8	17 39	−28·6	57·8	15·8	162	94	70	20·9	1 35	2 16	4 44	7 53	7 12
9	18 40	−28·2	58·4	15·9	175	87	59	21·9	2 30	3 08	5 45	9 04	8 26
10	19 42	−26·0	58·9	16·1	187	80	48	22·9	3 08	3 39	6 44	10 29	9 59
11	20 42	−22·2	59·4	16·2	199	74	37	23·9	3 34	3 56	7 41	12 00	11 40
12	21 38	−17·0	59·8	16·3	211	70	26	24·9	3 53	4 07	8 35	13 32	13 19
13	22 33	−10·8	60·1	16·4	223	67	16	25·9	4 07	4 15	9 26	15 02	14 56
14	23 25	− 4·0	60·2	16·4	236	67	9	26·9	4 19	4 22	10 16	16 31	16 32
15	0 17	+ 3·0	60·1	16·4	248	70	3	27·9	4 31	4 28	11 05	18 00	18 07
16	1 08	+ 9·8	59·7	16·3	260	87	0	28·9	4 44	4 34	11 55	19 29	19 44
17	2 02	+16·0	59·2	16·1	272	223	0	0·5	4 58	4 43	12 47	20 59	21 21
18	2 57	+21·3	58·5	15·9	284	242	3	1·5	5 18	4 55	13 41	22 26	22 56
19	3 54	+25·2	57·7	15·7	297	250	8	2·5	5 44	5 14	14 37	23 46	..
20	4 52	+27·7	56·9	15·5	309	258	15	3·5	6 22	5 45	15 34	..	0 23
21	5 50	+28·6	56·1	15·3	321	266	23	4·5	7 14	6 34	16 30	0 51	1 31
22	6 47	+27·9	55·4	15·1	333	273	32	5·5	8 18	7 42	17 23	1 39	2 15
23	7 41	+25·9	54·9	14·9	346	279	41	6·5	9 31	9 01	18 12	2 12	2 42
24	8 32	+22·8	54·5	14·8	358	284	51	7·5	10 46	10 23	18 58	2 35	2 58
25	9 20	+18·8	54·3	14·8	10	288	60	8·5	12 00	11 44	19 41	2 51	3 08
26	10 05	+14·0	54·2	14·8	22	291	69	9·5	13 12	13 02	20 22	3 04	3 15
27	10 49	+ 8·7	54·3	14·8	34	293	78	10·5	14 24	14 19	21 02	3 14	3 20
28	11 31	+ 3·1	54·6	14·9	47	293	85	11·5	15 35	15 36	21 41	3 23	3 25
29	12 14	− 2·7	55·0	15·0	59	292	91	12·5	16 48	16 54	22 22	3 32	3 29
30	12 58	− 8·5	55·4	15·1	71	288	96	13·5	18 04	18 16	23 06	3 42	3 34

MERCURY ☿

Day	R.A.	Dec.	Diam.	Phase	Tran-sit		Day	R.A.	Dec. +	Diam.	Phase	Tran-sit	
	h m	°	″		h m			h m	°	″		h m	
1	23 39	−4·9	5	84	11 02		16	1 20	7·1	—	—	11 44	
4	23 58	−2·7	5	87	11 09	Mercury is too	19	1 43	9·8	—	—	11 55	Mercury is too
7	0 17	−0·5	5	90	11 16	close to the	22	2 06	12·5	—	—	12 07	close to the
10	0 37	+1·9	5	93	11 25	Sun for	25	2 30	15·1	—	—	12 20	Sun for
13	0 58	+4·5	—	—	11 34	observation	28	2 55	17·5	—	—	12 32	observation
16	1 20	+7·1	—	—	11 44		31	3 19	19·7	—	—	12 45	

VENUS ♀

Day	R.A.	Dec. +	Diam.	Phase	Tran-sit	5° high. 52°	5° high. 56°
	h m	°	″		h m	h m	h m
1	3 37	22·6	23	67	14 59	22 30	22 48
6	3 58	24·0	24	65	15 00	22 39	22 59
11	4 18	25·1	26	63	15 00	22 47	23 08
16	4 37	26·1	27	60	14 59	22 52	23 15
21	4 55	26·8	29	57	14 58	22 56	23 19
26	5 12	27·3	31	55	14 55	22 56	23 20
31	5 28	27·6	34	53	14 50	22 53	23 18

MARS ♂

Day	R.A.	Dec. −	Diam.	Phase	Tran-sit	5° high. 52°	5° high. 56°
	h m	°	″		h m	h m	h m
1	19 53	21·8	7	88	7 14	4 01	4 32
6	20 07	21·2	7	88	7 09	3 51	4 21
11	20 21	20·6	7	87	7 03	3 40	4 09
16	20 35	19·9	7	87	6 57	3 29	3 56
21	20 49	19·2	8	87	6 52	3 18	3 43
26	21 03	18·4	8	86	6 46	3 06	3 30
31	21 16	17·5	8	86	6 39	2 54	3 16

SUNRISE AND SUNSET

Day	London a.m. h m	London p.m. h m	Bristol a.m. h m	Bristol p.m. h m	Birmingham a.m. h m	Birmingham p.m. h m	Manchester a.m. h m	Manchester p.m. h m	Newcastle a.m. h m	Newcastle p.m. h m	Glasgow a.m. h m	Glasgow p.m. h m	Belfast a.m. h m	Belfast p.m. h m
1	5 37	6 33	5 47	6 42	5 43	6 40	5 44	6 43	5 39	6 42	5 49	6 55	5 57	7 00
2	5 35	6 35	5 45	6 44	5 40	6 42	5 41	6 45	5 36	6 44	5 46	6 57	5 54	7 02
3	5 32	6 36	5 42	6 46	5 38	6 44	5 39	6 47	5 34	6 46	5 43	6 59	5 52	7 04
4	5 30	6 38	5 40	6 47	5 35	6 46	5 36	6 49	5 31	6 48	5 41	7 01	5 49	7 06
5	5 28	6 39	5 38	6 49	5 33	6 48	5 34	6 51	5 29	6 50	5 38	7 03	5 47	7 08
6	5 25	6 41	5 35	6 51	5 31	6 50	5 32	6 53	5 27	6 52	5 36	7 05	5 45	7 10
7	5 23	6 43	5 33	6 52	5 28	6 51	5 29	6 54	5 24	6 54	5 33	7 07	5 42	7 11
8	5 21	6 44	5 31	6 54	5 26	6 53	5 27	6 56	5 21	6 56	5 30	7 09	5 40	7 13
9	5 19	6 46	5 29	6 56	5 24	6 55	5 24	6 58	5 19	6 58	5 28	7 11	5 37	7 15
10	5 16	6 48	5 26	6 58	5 21	6 57	5 22	7 00	5 16	7 00	5 25	7 13	5 35	7 17
11	5 14	6 49	5 24	6 59	5 19	6 58	5 20	7 02	5 14	7 02	5 23	7 15	5 33	7 19
12	5 12	6 51	5 22	7 01	5 17	7 00	5 17	7 04	5 11	7 04	5 20	7 17	5 30	7 21
13	5 10	6 53	5 20	7 03	5 15	7 02	5 15	7 05	5 09	7 05	5 17	7 19	5 27	7 23
14	5 07	6 54	5 17	7 04	5 12	7 03	5 12	7 07	5 06	7 07	5 15	7 21	5 24	7 25
15	5 05	6 56	5 15	7 06	5 10	7 05	5 10	7 09	5 04	7 09	5 12	7 23	5 22	7 27
16	5 03	6 58	5 13	7 08	5 08	7 07	5 08	7 11	5 02	7 11	5 10	7 25	5 20	7 29
17	5 01	6 59	5 11	7 09	5 06	7 08	5 05	7 13	4 59	7 13	5 07	7 27	5 17	7 31
18	4 59	7 01	5 09	7 11	5 04	7 10	5 03	7 15	4 57	7 15	5 05	7 29	5 15	7 33
19	4 57	7 03	5 07	7 13	5 02	7 12	5 01	7 17	4 54	7 17	5 02	7 31	5 13	7 35
20	4 54	7 05	5 04	7 15	4 59	7 14	4 58	7 18	4 51	7 19	5 00	7 33	5 10	7 36
21	4 52	7 06	5 02	7 16	4 57	7 15	4 56	7 20	4 49	7 21	4 57	7 35	5 08	7 38
22	4 50	7 08	5 00	7 18	4 55	7 17	4 54	7 22	4 47	7 23	4 55	7 37	5 06	7 40
23	4 48	7 10	4 58	7 20	4 53	7 19	4 52	7 24	4 45	7 25	4 53	7 39	5 04	7 42
24	4 46	7 11	4 56	7 21	4 51	7 20	4 50	7 25	4 42	7 27	4 50	7 41	5 01	7 44
25	4 44	7 13	4 54	7 23	4 49	7 22	4 48	7 27	4 40	7 29	4 48	7 43	4 59	7 46
26	4 42	7 15	4 52	7 24	4 47	7 24	4 46	7 29	4 38	7 31	4 46	7 45	4 57	7 48
27	4 40	7 16	4 50	7 26	4 45	7 26	4 44	7 31	4 36	7 33	4 44	7 47	4 55	7 50
28	4 38	7 18	4 48	7 27	4 43	7 28	4 42	7 32	4 34	7 34	4 42	7 48	4 53	7 51
29	4 37	7 20	4 47	7 29	4 40	7 29	4 39	7 34	4 31	7 36	4 39	7 50	4 50	7 53
30	4 35	7 21	4 45	7 30	4 35	7 31	4 37	7 36	4 29	7 38	4 37	7 52	4 48	7 55

	JUPITER ♃					SATURN ♄				
Day	R.A.	Dec. +	Transit	5° high. 52°	5° high. 56°	R.A.	Dec. −	Transit	5° high. 52°	5° high. 56°
	h m	°	h m	h m	h m	h m	°	h m	h m	h m
1	2 13	12·3	13 33	20 03	20 10	18 11	22·3	5 32	2 23	2 55
11	2 22	13·1	13 02	19 37	19 45	18 11	22·3	4 53	1 44	2 16
21	2 31	13·9	12 32	19 11	19 19	18 11	22·3	4 13	1 04	1 37
31	2 40	14·6	12 02	18 45	18 54	18 10	22·3	3 32	0 23	0 56

Equatorial diameter of Jupiter 33″; of Saturn 17″. Diameters of Saturn's rings 39″ and 17″.

	URANUS ♅					NEPTUNE ♆				
Day	R.A.	Dec. −	Transit	10° high. 52°	10° high. 56°	R.A.	Dec. −	Transit	10° high. 52°	10° high. 56°
	h m	° ′	h m	h m	h m	h m	° ′	h m	h m	h m
1	18 04·5	23 38	5 25	3 27	4 49	18 43·9	22 05	6 05	3 47	4 43
11	18 04·5	23 38	4 46	2 47	4 10	18 44·0	22 04	5 25	3 08	4 03
21	18 04·1	23 38	4 06	2 08	3 31	18 43·9	22 04	4 46	2 28	3 24
31	18 03·3	23 38	3 26	1 28	2 51	18 43·6	22 04	4 06	1 48	2 44

Diameter 4″   Diameter 2″

DAY OF		

Maia, goddess of growth and increase.

Sun's Longitude 60° II 20ᵈ 20ʰ

PHENOMENA

May 2ᵈ 21ʰ Jupiter in conjunction with the Sun.

5ᵈ 17ʰ Saturn in conjunction with the Moon. Saturn 6° N.

6ᵈ 20ʰ Venus at greatest brilliancy.

9ᵈ 06ʰ Mars in conjunction with the Moon. Mars 0°.8 N.

17ᵈ 17ʰ Mercury in conjunction with the Moon. Mercury 3° S.

18ᵈ 13ʰ Venus in conjunction with the Moon. Venus 1°.2 S.

19ᵈ 02ʰ Mercury at greatest eastern elongation (22°).

Month	Week	
1	☽.	**4th S. after Easter.** Khachaturyan d. 1978.
2	M.	**SS. Philip and James.** Leonardo da Vinci d. 1519.
3	Tu.	Machiavelli b. 1469. Start of Festival of Britain 1951.
4	W.	Start of General Strike 1926.
5	Th.	Karl Marx b. 1818. Napoleon Bonaparte d. 1821.
6	F.	Bannister runs first 4-minute mile 1954.
7	S.	Antonio Salieri d. 1825. Johannes Brahms b. 1833.
8	☽.	**5th S. after Easter.** V.E. Day 1945.
9	M.	Treaty of Windsor 1386. Gay-Lussac d. 1850.
10	Tu.	Indian Mutiny begins 1857.
11	W.	Irving Berlin b. 1888.* Paul Nash b. 1889.
12	Th.	**Ascension Day.** Gabriel Fauré b. 1845.
13	F.	Arthur Sullivan b. 1842. Fridtjof Nansen d. 1930.
14	S.	**St. Matthias.** Gabriel Farenheit b. 1686.
15	☽.	**S. after Ascension (6th after Easter).**
16	M.	Academy Awards first presented 1929.
17	Tu.	Niccolo Paganini d. 1840. Paul Dukas d. 1935.
18	W.	Pope John Paul II b. 1920. Gustav Mahler d. 1911.
19	Th.	Anne Boleyn exec. 1536. Clara Schumann d. 1896.
20	F.	First Chelsea Flower Show 1913.
21	S.	Henry VI killed 1471. Alexander Pope b. 1688.*
22	☽.	**Pentecost. Whit Sunday.** Wagner b. 1813.
23	M.	Carl Linnaeus b. 1707. Herbert Austin d. 1941.
24	Tu.	Copernicus d. 1543. Duke Ellington d. 1974.
25	W.	Lord Lytton b. 1803. Gustav Holst d. 1934.
26	Th.	Last public hanging in England 1868.
27	F.	EASTER LAW SITTINGS END. Nehru d. 1964.
28	S.	George I b. 1660. Ian Fleming b. 1908.
29	☽.	**Trinity Sunday.** Mt. Everest conquered 1953.
30	M.	Joan of Arc exec. 1431. Wilbur Wright d. 1912.
31	Tu.	F. J. Haydn d. 1809. Joseph Grimaldi d. 1837.

CONSTELLATIONS

The following constellations are near the meridian at

	d h		d h
Apr.	1 24	Apr.	15 23
May	1 22	May	16 21
June	1 20	June	15 19

Cepheus (below the Pole), Cassiopeia (below the Pole), Ursa Minor, Ursa Major, Canes Venatici, Coma Berenices, Bootes, Leo, Virgo, Crater, Corvus, and Hydra.

ALGOL

ALGOL is inconveniently situated for observation during May.

* Centenary.

PHASES OF THE MOON

		d	h	m
○ Full Moon	....	1	23	41
☾ Last Quarter	....	9	01	23
● New Moon	....	15	22	11
☽ First Quarter	......	23	16	49
○ Full Moon	....	31	10	53

	d	h
Perigee (369,070 kilometres)	10	22
Apogee (404,100 ,,)	23	14

Mean Longitude of Ascending Node on May 1, 351°.

See note on *Summer Time,* p. 98.

MONTHLY NOTES

May 2. Bank Holiday, England, Wales, N. Ireland and Scotland.

9. Liberation Day, Channel Islands.

15. Whitsunday (Scotland). Scottish Term Day.

22. Jewish Festival of Weeks begins.

28. Removal Day, Scotland.

30. Bank Holiday, England, Wales, N. Ireland and Scotland.

Day	Right Ascension	Dec. +	Equation of Time	Rise 52°	Rise 56°	Transit	Set 52°	Set 56°	Sidereal Time	Transit of First Point of Aries
	h m s	° ′	m s	h m	h m	h m	h m	h m	h m s	h m s
1	2 33 39	15 05	+ 2 54	4 30	4 16	11 57	19 25	19 40	14 36 33	9 21 54
2	2 37 29	15 23	+ 3 01	4 28	4 13	11 57	19 27	19 42	14 40 30	9 17 58
3	2 41 19	15 41	+ 3 08	4 26	4 11	11 57	19 28	19 44	14 44 26	9 14 03
4	2 45 09	15 58	+ 3 14	4 24	4 09	11 57	19 30	19 46	14 48 23	9 10 07
5	2 49 00	16 15	+ 3 19	4 23	4 07	11 57	19 32	19 48	14 52 20	9 06 11
6	2 52 52	16 32	+ 3 24	4 21	4 05	11 57	19 33	19 50	14 56 16	9 02 15
7	2 56 44	16 49	+ 3 28	4 19	4 03	11 57	19 35	19 52	15 00 13	8 58 19
8	3 00 37	17 05	+ 3 32	4 17	4 01	11 56	19 37	19 54	15 04 09	8 54 23
9	3 04 31	17 22	+ 3 35	4 16	3 59	11 56	19 38	19 56	15 08 06	8 50 27
10	3 08 25	17 37	+ 3 38	4 14	3 56	11 56	19 40	19 58	15 12 02	8 46 31
11	3 12 19	17 53	+ 3 40	4 12	3 55	11 56	19 42	19 59	15 15 59	8 42 35
12	3 16 14	18 08	+ 3 41	4 11	3 53	11 56	19 43	20 01	15 19 55	8 38 39
13	3 20 10	18 23	+ 3 42	4 09	3 51	11 56	19 45	20 03	15 23 52	8 34 43
14	3 24 06	18 38	+ 3 42	4 07	3 49	11 56	19 46	20 05	15 27 49	8 30 47
15	3 28 03	18 52	+ 3 42	4 06	3 47	11 56	19 48	20 07	15 31 45	8 26 52
16	3 32 01	19 06	+ 3 41	4 04	3 45	11 56	19 49	20 09	15 35 42	8 22 56
17	3 35 59	19 20	+ 3 39	4 03	3 43	11 56	19 51	20 11	15 39 38	8 19 00
18	3 39 58	19 33	+ 3 37	4 01	3 41	11 56	19 52	20 12	15 43 35	8 15 04
19	3 43 57	19 46	+ 3 35	4 00	3 40	11 56	19 54	20 14	15 47 31	8 11 08
20	3 47 57	19 59	+ 3 31	3 59	3 38	11 57	19 55	20 16	15 51 28	8 07 12
21	3 51 57	20 11	+ 3 28	3 57	3 37	11 57	19 57	20 18	15 55 25	8 03 16
22	3 55 58	20 23	+ 3 24	3 56	3 35	11 57	19 58	20 19	15 59 21	7 59 20
23	3 59 59	20 35	+ 3 19	3 55	3 33	11 57	19 59	20 21	16 03 18	7 55 24
24	4 04 01	20 46	+ 3 14	3 54	3 32	11 57	20 01	20 23	16 07 14	7 51 28
25	4 08 03	20 57	+ 3 08	3 53	3 30	11 57	20 02	20 24	16 11 11	7 47 32
26	4 12 06	21 08	+ 3 02	3 51	3 29	11 57	20 03	20 26	16 15 07	7 43 37
27	4 16 09	21 18	+ 2 55	3 50	3 28	11 57	20 05	20 28	16 19 04	7 39 41
28	4 20 12	21 28	+ 2 48	3 49	3 26	11 57	20 06	20 29	16 23 00	7 35 45
29	4 24 16	21 37	+ 2 41	3 48	3 25	11 57	20 07	20 31	16 26 57	7 31 49
30	4 28 21	21 46	+ 2 33	3 47	3 24	11 58	20 08	20 32	16 30 54	7 27 53
31	4 32 26	21 55	+ 2 24	3 47	3 23	11 58	20 09	20 33	16 34 50	7 23 57

Duration of Civil (C), Nautical (N), and Astronomical (A), Twilight (in minutes)

Lat. °	May 1 C	N	A	May 11 C	N	A	May 21 C	N	A	May 31 C	N	A
52	39	90	154	41	97	179	44	106	T.A.N.	46	116	T.A.N.
56	45	106	209	49	121	T.A.N.	53	143	T.A.N.	57	T.A.N.	T.A.N.

ASTRONOMICAL NOTES

MERCURY, magnitude −1·3 to +2·0, is visible through the month almost to the very end: in fact this evening apparition is the most favourable one of the year for observers in the northern hemisphere. It may be seen low above the W.N.W. horizon at the end of civil twilight and the best chance of locating the planet will be during the third week of the month.

VENUS reaches its greatest brilliancy, magnitude −4·5, on the 6th and continues to dominate the western evening sky for several hours after sunset at the beginning of the month though the period available for observation is shortening rapidly. There is another close conjunction with the crescent Moon on the 18th.

MARS, magnitude 0·0, continues to be visible as a morning object in the south-eastern sky. On the morning of the 9th the Moon, at Last Quarter, rises with the planet and passes only about 1°S. of it.

JUPITER is not visible at first since it passes through conjunction on the 2nd. Towards the end of the month Jupiter may be glimpsed, low down in the eastern sky, for a very short while before dawn.

SATURN, magnitude +0·2, continues to be visible as a morning object low in the southern skies, in the constellation of Sagittarius.

THE MOON

Day	R.A.	Dec.	Hor. Par.	Semi-diam.	Sun's Co-long.	P.A. of Bright Limb	Phase	Age	Rise		Tran-sit	Set	
									52°	56°		52°	56°
	h m	°	′	′	°	°		d	h m	h m	h m	h m	h m
1	13 44	−14·0	55·9	15·2	83	276	99	14·5	19 24	19 42	23 52	3 54	3 40
2	14 33	−19·2	56·5	15·4	95	196	100	15·5	20 47	21 13	..	4 09	3 49
3	15 26	−23·5	57·0	15·5	107	124	99	16·5	22 10	22 44	0 43	4 30	4 03
4	16 23	−26·6	57·5	15·7	120	110	95	17·5	23 26	..	1 39	5 02	4 27
5	17 24	−28·3	58·0	15·8	132	100	90	18·5	..	0 06	2 38	5 49	5 09
6	18 26	−28·3	58·4	15·9	144	92	82	19·5	0 26	1 05	3 39	6 55	6 16
7	19 28	−26·4	58·7	16·0	156	84	73	20·5	1 09	1 42	4 39	8 16	7 45
8	20 28	−23·0	59·0	16·1	168	77	62	21·5	1 38	2 03	5 36	9 46	9 23
9	21 25	−18·2	59·2	16·1	181	72	51	22·5	1 59	2 15	6 30	11 16	11 01
10	22 18	−12·4	59·4	16·2	193	69	39	23·5	2 14	2 24	7 21	12 44	12 36
11	23 10	− 5·9	59·4	16·2	205	67	28	24·5	2 26	2 31	8 10	14 10	14 09
12	0 00	+ 0·9	59·3	16·2	217	67	19	25·5	2 38	2 37	8 57	15 36	15 41
13	0 50	+ 7·6	59·2	16·1	229	70	11	26·5	2 50	2 43	9 46	17 03	17 14
14	1 42	+13·9	58·8	16·0	242	76	5	27·5	3 03	2 50	10 36	18 31	18 49
15	2 35	+19·4	58·4	15·9	254	90	1	28·5	3 20	3 01	11 28	19 58	20 24
16	3 31	+23·8	57·8	15·8	266	178	0	0·1	3 43	3 16	12 23	21 22	21 55
17	4 29	+26·8	57·2	15·6	278	241	2	1·1	4 16	3 42	13 20	22 34	23 13
18	5 28	+28·3	56·5	15·4	291	256	5	2·1	5 02	4 23	14 17	23 30	..
19	6 26	+28·2	55·9	15·2	303	266	11	3·1	6 02	5 25	15 12	..	0 08
20	7 22	+26·6	55·3	15·1	315	274	17	4·1	7 13	6 41	16 04	0 09	0 42
21	8 15	+23·8	54·8	14·9	327	281	25	5·1	8 28	8 03	16 51	0 37	1 02
22	9 04	+20·0	54·5	14·8	340	286	34	6·1	9 43	9 25	17 36	0 55	1 15
23	9 50	+15·4	54·3	14·8	352	289	44	7·1	10 56	10 44	18 17	1 10	1 23
24	10 34	+10·3	54·3	14·8	4	292	53	8·1	12 08	12 01	18 57	1 21	1 29
25	11 17	+ 4·9	54·4	14·8	16	293	62	9·1	13 18	13 17	19 37	1 30	1 34
26	11 59	− 0·8	54·8	14·9	29	293	71	10·1	14 30	14 34	20 17	1 39	1 38
27	12 42	− 6·6	55·2	15·0	41	292	80	11·1	15 44	15 54	20 59	1 49	1 43
28	13 27	−12·2	55·8	15·2	53	289	87	12·1	17 02	17 18	21 44	2 00	1 49
29	14 15	−17·5	56·5	15·4	65	283	93	13·1	18 24	18 47	22 33	2 14	1 57
30	15 07	−22·1	57·2	15·6	77	273	97	14·1	19 49	20 19	23 28	2 32	2 08
31	16 04	−25·7	57·8	15·8	89	241	100	15·1	21 09	21 47	..	3 00	2 28

MERCURY ☿

Day	R.A.	Dec. +	Diam.	Phase	Tran-sit	5° high.		Day	R.A.	Dec. +	Diam.	Phase	Tran-sit	5° high.	
						52°	56°							52°	56°
	h m	°	″		h m	h m	h m		h m	°	″		h m	h m	h m
1	3 19	19·7	6	—	12 45	20 01	20 16	16	5 03	25·2	8	45	13 28	21 15	21 36
4	3 43	21·5	6	79	12 57	20 23	20 40	19	5 17	25·3	8	37	13 30	21 17	21 38
7	4 06	23·0	6	70	13 08	20 42	21 01	22	5 29	25·2	9	30	13 29	21 14	21 35
10	4 27	24·1	7	61	13 16	20 57	21 17	25	5 38	24·9	9	24	13 25	21 08	21 28
13	4 46	24·8	7	53	13 23	21 08	21 29	28	5 43	24·3	10	18	13 19	20 57	21 16
16	5 03	25·2	8	45	13 28	21 15	21 36	31	5 46	23·6	11	12	13 09	20 42	21 00

VENUS ♀

Day	R.A.	Dec. +	Diam.	Phase	Tran-sit	5° high.		Day	R.A.	Dec. −	Diam.	Phase	Tran-sit	5° high.	
						52°	56°							52°	56°
	h m	°	″		h m	h m	h m		h m	°	″		h m	h m	h m
1	5 28	27·6	33	33	14 50	22 53	23 18	1	21 16	17·5	8	86	6 39	2 54	3 16
6	5 41	27·7	36	28	14 43	22 46	23 11	6	21 30	16·7	8	86	6 33	2 41	3 02
11	5 51	27·7	39	24	14 34	22 36	23 00	11	21 43	15·7	9	86	6 26	2 28	2 48
16	5 58	27·4	43	19	14 21	22 20	22 45	16	21 56	14·8	9	85	6 20	2 15	2 34
21	6 02	26·9	46	15	14 04	22 00	22 23	21	22 08	13·8	9	85	6 12	2 02	2 19
26	6 01	26·3	50	10	13 43	21 34	21 56	26	22 21	12·8	10	85	6 05	1 49	2 05
31	5 56	25·5	53	6	13 18	21 03	21 24	31	22 33	11·8	10	85	5 58	1 35	1 50

MARS ♂

SUNRISE AND SUNSET

Day	London a.m.	London p.m.	Bristol a.m.	Bristol p.m.	Birmingham a.m.	Birmingham p.m.	Manchester a.m.	Manchester p.m.	Newcastle a.m.	Newcastle p.m.	Glasgow a.m.	Glasgow p.m.	Belfast a.m.	Belfast p.m.
	h m	h m	h m	h m	h m	h m	h m	h m	h m	h m	h m	h m	h m	h m
1	4 33	7 23	4 43	7 32	4 36	7 33	4 35	7 38	4 27	7 40	4 35	7 54	4 46	7 57
2	4 31	7 24	4 41	7 34	4 34	7 35	4 33	7 40	4 24	7 42	4 32	7 56	4 44	7 59
3	4 29	7 26	4 39	7 35	4 32	7 36	4 31	7 42	4 22	7 44	4 30	7 58	4 42	8 01
4	4 27	7 27	4 37	7 37	4 30	7 38	4 29	7 43	4 20	7 46	4 28	8 00	4 40	8 02
5	4 26	7 29	4 36	7 39	4 29	7 40	4 27	7 45	4 18	7 48	4 26	8 02	4 38	8 04
6	4 24	7 30	4 34	7 40	4 27	7 41	4 25	7 47	4 16	7 50	4 24	8 04	4 36	8 06
7	4 22	7 32	4 32	7 42	4 25	7 43	4 23	7 49	4 14	7 52	4 22	8 06	4 34	8 08
8	4 20	7 34	4 30	7 44	4 23	7 45	4 21	7 50	4 12	7 53	4 19	8 08	4 31	8 10
9	4 18	7 35	4 28	7 45	4 21	7 46	4 19	7 52	4 10	7 55	4 17	8 10	4 29	8 12
10	4 17	7 37	4 27	7 47	4 20	7 48	4 17	7 54	4 08	7 57	4 15	8 12	4 27	8 14
11	4 15	7 38	4 25	7 48	4 18	7 49	4 16	7 56	4 06	7 59	4 13	8 14	4 26	8 16
12	4 13	7 40	4 23	7 50	4 16	7 51	4 14	7 58	4 04	8 01	4 11	8 16	4 24	8 18
13	4 12	7 42	4 22	7 52	4 15	7 53	4 12	7 59	4 02	8 03	4 09	8 18	4 22	8 19
14	4 10	7 43	4 20	7 53	4 13	7 54	4 10	8 01	4 01	8 05	4 08	8 20	4 20	8 21
15	4 08	7 45	4 18	7 55	4 11	7 56	4 09	8 03	3 59	8 07	4 06	8 22	4 19	8 23
16	4 07	7 46	4 17	7 56	4 10	7 57	4 07	8 04	3 57	8 08	4 04	8 24	4 17	8 24
17	4 05	7 48	4 16	7 58	4 08	7 59	4 05	8 06	3 55	8 10	4 02	8 25	4 15	8 26
18	4 04	7 49	4 14	7 59	4 07	8 00	4 04	8 07	3 54	8 12	4 00	8 27	4 14	8 28
19	4 03	7 51	4 13	8 01	4 06	8 02	4 03	8 09	3 52	8 13	3 58	8 29	4 12	8 29
20	4 01	7 52	4 12	8 02	4 04	8 03	4 01	8 10	3 51	8 15	3 57	8 31	4 11	8 31
21	4 00	7 54	4 11	8 04	4 03	8 05	4 00	8 12	3 49	8 17	3 55	8 33	4 09	8 33
22	3 59	7 55	4 10	8 05	4 02	8 06	3 59	8 13	3 48	8 18	3 54	8 34	4 08	8 34
23	3 57	7 56	4 08	8 06	4 00	8 07	3 57	8 14	3 46	8 20	3 52	8 36	4 06	8 36
24	3 56	7 58	4 07	8 08	3 59	8 09	3 56	8 16	3 44	8 22	3 50	8 38	4 04	8 38
25	3 55	7 59	4 06	8 09	3 58	8 10	3 55	8 17	3 43	8 23	3 49	8 39	4 03	8 39
26	3 54	8 00	4 05	8 10	3 57	8 11	3 54	8 19	3 42	8 25	3 48	8 41	4 02	8 41
27	3 53	8 02	4 04	8 11	3 55	8 13	3 52	8 20	3 40	8 26	3 46	8 43	4 00	8 42
28	3 52	8 03	4 03	8 12	3 54	8 15	3 51	8 22	3 39	8 28	3 45	8 44	3 59	8 44
29	3 51	8 04	4 02	8 14	3 53	8 16	3 50	8 23	3 38	8 29	3 44	8 46	3 58	8 45
30	3 51	8 05	4 01	8 15	3 52	8 17	3 49	8 24	3 37	8 30	3 42	8 47	3 57	8 46
31	3 50	8 07	4 00	8 16	3 51	8 18	3 48	8 26	3 36	8 32	3 41	8 48	3 56	8 48

	JUPITER ♃				SATURN ♄				
Day	R.A.	Dec. +	Transit		R.A.	Dec. −	Transit	5° high. 52°	5° high. 56°
	h m	°	h m		h m	°	h m	h m	h m
1	2 40	14·6	12 02	Jupiter is too close to the Sun for observation	18 10	22·3	3 32	0 23	0 56
11	2 50	15·3	11 32		18 08	22·3	2 52	23 38	0 15
21	2 59	16·0	11 02		18 06	22·3	2 10	22 57	23 30
31	3 08	16·7	10 32		18 03	22·3	1 28	22 15	22 48

Equatorial diameter of Jupiter 33″; of Saturn 18″.   Diameters of Saturn's rings 41″ and 18″.

	URANUS ♅					NEPTUNE ♆				
Day	R.A.	Dec. −	Transit	10° high. 52°	10° high. 56°	R.A.	Dec. −	Transit	10° high. 52°	10° high. 56°
	h m	° ′	h m	h m	h m	h m	° ′	h m	h m	h m
1	18 03·3	23 38	3 26	1 28	2 51	18 43·6	22 04	4 06	1 48	2 44
11	18 02·3	23 39	2 46	0 47	2 11	18 43·0	22 05	3 26	1 09	2 05
21	18 00·9	23 39	2 05	0 07	1 30	18 42·3	22 05	2 46	0 29	1 25
31	17 59·4	23 39	1 24	23 22	0 49	18 41·4	22 06	2 06	23 45	0 45

Diameter 4″   Diameter 2″

Junius, Roman *gens* (family).

Sun's Longitude 90° ♋ $21^{d}\ 04^{h}$

Day of Month	Day of Week	
1	W.	Michael Glinka b. 1804. Sir Frank Whittle b. 1907.
2	Th.	CORONATION DAY 1953. CORPUS CHRISTI.
3	F.	William Harvey d. 1657. Georges Bizet d. 1875.
4	S.	George III b. 1738. Kaiser Wilhelm II d. 1941.
5	𝕾.	**1st S. after Trinity.** Orlando Gibbons d. 1625.
6	M.	Capt. Robert Scott b. 1868. D-Day 1944.
7	Tu.	TRINITY LAW SITTINGS BEGIN.
8	W.	Robert Schumann b. 1810. Norman Hartnell d.1979.
9	Th.	Charles Dickens d. 1870. Lord Beaverbrook d. 1964.
10	F.	DUKE OF EDINBURGH b. 1921. James Stuart b. 1688.*
11	S.	**St. Barnabas.** Richard Strauss b. 1864.
12	𝕾.	**2nd S. after Trinity.** John Wayne d. 1979.
13	M.	Alexander the Great d. 323 B.C. Eugene Goossens d. 1962.
14	Tu.	G. K. Chesterton d. 1936. James Logie Baird d. [1946.
15	W.	Magna Carta sealed 1215. Greig b. 1843.
16	Th.	First woman in space 1963.
17	F.	Edward I b. 1239. Charles Gounod b. 1818.
18	S.	Waterloo 1815. Roald Amundsen d. 1928.
19	𝕾.	**3rd S. after Trinity.** Blaise Pascal b. 1623.
20	M.	Black Hole of Calcutta 1756. Offenbach b. 1819.
21	Tu.	PRINCE WILLIAM OF WALES b. 1982.
22	W.	Sir Peter Pears b. 1910. Darius Milhaud d. 1974.
23	Th.	Jean Anouilh b. 1910. Sir Len Hutton b. 1916.
24	F.	**St. John the Baptist.** Bannockburn 1314.
25	S.	Earl Mountbatten of Burma b. 1900.
26	𝕾.	**4th S. after Trinity.** Ford Madox Ford d. 1939.
27	M.	Charles Parnell b. 1846. Helen Keller b. 1880.
28	Tu.	Henry VIII b. 1491. Treaty of Versailles 1919.
29	W.	**St. Peter.** Ignace Jan Paderewski d. 1941.
30	Th.	William Barents d. 1597. Tower Bridge opened 1894.

PHENOMENA

June $1^{d}\ 22^{h}$ Saturn in conjunction with the Moon. Saturn 6° N.

$6^{d}\ 20^{h}$ Mars in conjunction with the Moon. Mars 2° S.

$12^{d}\ 03^{h}$ Jupiter in conjunction with the Moon. Jupiter 6° S.

$13^{d}\ 00^{h}$ Venus in inferior conjunction.

$13^{d}\ 04^{h}$ Mercury in inferior conjunction.

$20^{d}\ 04^{h}$ Uranus at opposition.

$20^{d}\ 09^{h}$ Saturn at opposition.

$21^{d}\ 04^{h}$ Solstice.

$29^{d}\ 04^{h}$ Saturn in conjunction with the Moon. Saturn 6° N.

$30^{d}\ 10^{h}$ Neptune at opposition.

CONSTELLATIONS

The following constellations are near the meridian at

	d	h		d	h
May	1	24	May	16	23
June	1	22	June	15	21
July	1	20	July	16	19

Cassiopeia (below the Pole), Ursa Minor, Draco, Ursa Major, Canes Venatici, Bootes, Corona, Serpens, Virgo and Libra.

ALGOL

ALGOL is inconveniently situated for observation during June.

*Centenary.

PHASES OF THE MOON

	d	h	m
☾ Last Quarter	7	06	21
● New Moon	14	09	14
☽ First Quarter	22	10	23
○ Full Moon	29	19	46

	d	h
Perigee (368,480 kilometres)	05	00
Apogee (404,540 „)	20	08

Mean Longitude of Ascending Node on June 1, 349°.

See note on *Summer Time*, p. 98.

MONTHLY NOTES

June 11. Queen's Official Birthday.

21. Longest day.

24. Midsummer Day. Quarter Day.

	THE SUN						s.d. 15'·8			Transit

Day	Right Ascension	Dec. +	Equa- tion of Time	Rise 52°	Rise 56°	Tran- sit	Set 52°	Set 56°	Sidereal Time	Transit of First Point of Aries
	h m s	° '	m s	h m	h m	h m	h m	h m	h m s	h m s
1	4 36 31	22 03	+ 2 15	3 46	3 22	11 58	20 11	20 35	16 38 47	7 20 01
2	4 40 37	22 11	+ 2 06	3 45	3 21	11 58	20 12	20 36	16 42 43	7 16 05
3	4 44 43	22 19	+ 1 57	3 44	3 20	11 58	20 13	20 37	16 46 40	7 12 09
4	4 48 50	22 26	+ 1 47	3 44	3 19	11 58	20 14	20 39	16 50 36	7 08 13
5	4 52 57	22 33	+ 1 36	3 43	3 18	11 58	20 15	20 40	16 54 33	7 04 17
6	4 57 04	22 39	+ 1 26	3 42	3 17	11 59	20 16	20 41	16 58 29	7 00 22
7	5 01 11	22 45	+ 1 15	3 42	3 17	11 59	20 16	20 42	17 02 26	6 56 26
8	5 05 19	22 51	+ 1 03	3 41	3 16	11 59	20 17	20 43	17 06 23	6 52 30
9	5 09 27	22 56	+ 0 52	3 41	3 15	11 59	20 18	20 44	17 10 19	6 48 34
10	5 13 36	23 01	+ 0 40	3 40	3 15	11 59	20 19	20 45	17 14 16	6 44 38
11	5 17 44	23 05	+ 0 28	3 40	3 14	12 00	20 19	20 46	17 18 12	6 40 42
12	5 21 53	23 09	+ 0 15	3 40	3 14	12 00	20 20	20 46	17 22 09	6 36 46
13	5 26 02	23 13	+ 0 03	3 40	3 13	12 00	20 21	20 47	17 26 05	6 32 50
14	5 30 12	23 16	− 0 10	3 39	3 13	12 00	20 21	20 48	17 30 02	6 28 54
15	5 34 21	23 19	− 0 23	3 39	3 13	12 00	20 22	20 48	17 33 58	6 24 58
16	5 38 31	23 21	− 0 36	3 39	3 13	12 01	20 22	20 49	17 37 55	6 21 02
17	5 42 40	23 23	− 0 49	3 39	3 13	12 01	20 23	20 49	17 41 52	6 17 06
18	5 46 50	23 25	− 1 02	3 39	3 13	12 01	20 23	20 50	17 45 48	6 13 11
19	5 51 00	23 26	− 1 15	3 39	3 13	12 01	20 23	20 50	17 49 45	6 09 15
20	5 55 09	23 26	− 1 28	3 40	3 13	12 02	20 24	20 50	17 53 41	6 05 19
21	5 59 19	23 27	− 1 41	3 40	3 13	12 02	20 24	20 50	17 57 38	6 01 23
22	6 03 28	23 26	− 1 54	3 40	3 13	12 02	20 24	20 51	18 01 34	5 57 27
23	6 07 38	23 26	− 2 07	3 40	3 14	12 02	20 24	20 51	18 05 31	5 53 31
24	6 11 47	23 25	− 2 20	3 41	3 14	12 02	20 24	20 51	18 09 27	5 49 35
25	6 15 57	23 24	− 2 33	3 41	3 14	12 03	20 24	20 51	18 13 24	5 45 39
26	6 20 06	23 22	− 2 45	3 41	3 15	12 03	20 24	20 51	18 17 21	5 41 43
27	6 24 15	23 20	− 2 58	3 42	3 16	12 03	20 24	20 50	18 21 17	5 37 47
28	6 28 24	23 17	− 3 10	3 42	3 16	12 03	20 24	20 50	18 25 14	5 33 51
29	6 32 32	23 14	− 3 22	3 43	3 17	12 03	20 24	20 50	18 29 10	5 29 56
30	6 36 41	23 11	− 3 34	3 44	3 18	12 04	20 23	20 49	18 33 07	5 26 00

Duration of Civil (C), Nautical (N), and Astronomical (A), Twilight (in minutes)

Lat. °	June 1 C	June 1 N	June 1 A	June 11 C	June 11 N	June 11 A	June 21 C	June 21 N	June 21 A	June 30 C	June 30 N	June 30 A
52	47	117	T.A.N.	48	125	T.A.N.	49	128	T.A.N.	49	125	T.A.N.
56	58	T.A.N.	T.A.N.	61	T.A.N.	T.A.N.	63	T.A.N.	T.A.N.	62	T.A.N.	T.A.N.

ASTRONOMICAL NOTES

MERCURY is unsuitably placed for observation throughout the month.

VENUS, magnitude −4, is visible for the first week of the month, low above the west-north-west horizon for a short while after sunset. After passing rapidly through inferior conjunction on the 13th the planet becomes visible as a morning object, magnitude −4·2, during the last week of the month, when it may be seen for a short while before sunrise, low on the east-north-east horizon.

MARS is a morning object in the south-eastern sky and by the end of the month rises shortly before midnight. During the month its magnitude increases from −0·3 to −0·8. The Moon, at Last Quarter, is in the vicinity of Mars on the morning of the 7th.

JUPITER, magnitude −2·1, is visible low in the eastern sky in the mornings. During the month Jupiter moves from Aries into Taurus.

SATURN, magnitude 0·0, is at opposition on the 20th and thus visible throughout the hours of darkness, though never at any great altitude above the horizon, since its declination is −22°. The near Full Moon passes 6° S. of Saturn late on the evening of the 1st and again in the early morning of the 29th.

URANUS is at opposition on the 20th, in the western part of Sagittarius. Uranus is barely visible to the naked-eye since its magnitude is +5·5 but it is readily located with only small optical aid.

NEPTUNE is at opposition on the 30th, in Sagittarius. It is not visible to the naked-eye since its magnitude is +7·9.

THE MOON

Day	R.A.	Dec.	Hor. Par.	Semi-diam.	Sun's Co-long.	P.A. of Bright Limb	Phase	Age	Rise 52°	Rise 56°	Transit	Set 52°	Set 56°
	h m	°	′	′	°	°		d	h m	h m	h m	h m	h m
1	17 05	−27·9	58·4	15·9	102	131	99	16·1	22 17	22 57	0 27	3 42	3 03
2	18 08	−28·3	58·9	16·0	114	102	97	17·1	23 07	23 42	1 29	4 42	4 03
3	19 12	−26·9	59·2	16·1	126	90	92	18·1	23 41	..	2 31	6 01	5 28
4	20 13	−23·8	59·4	16·2	138	81	84	19·1	..	0 08	3 31	7 31	7 06
5	21 12	−19·2	59·5	16·2	150	74	75	20·1	0 04	0 23	4 27	9 02	8 45
6	22 06	−13·5	59·4	16·2	163	70	64	21·1	0 21	0 33	5 19	10 31	10 22
7	22 58	− 7·2	59·3	16·2	175	67	53	22·1	0 34	0 40	6 07	11 58	11 54
8	23 48	− 0·5	59·0	16·1	187	67	42	23·1	0 45	0 46	6 55	13 22	13 25
9	0 37	+ 6·1	58·7	16·0	199	68	31	24·1	0 57	0 52	7 42	14 47	14 56
10	1 28	+12·4	58·4	15·9	212	70	21	25·1	1 10	0 59	8 30	16 12	16 28
11	2 19	+18·0	58·0	15·8	224	75	13	26·1	1 25	1 08	9 20	17 38	18 01
12	3 14	+22·6	57·5	15·7	236	83	7	27·1	1 45	1 21	10 14	19 02	19 33
13	4 10	+26·0	57·0	15·5	248	95	2	28·1	2 14	1 42	11 09	20 18	20 55
14	5 08	+27·9	56·5	15·4	261	132	0	29·1	2 54	2 16	12 06	21 20	21 59
15	6 06	+28·3	56·0	15·2	273	237	1	0·6	3 49	3 10	13 01	22 06	22 40
16	7 03	+27·2	55·4	15·1	285	263	3	1·6	4 56	4 22	13 55	22 37	23 06
17	7 57	+24·7	55·0	15·0	297	275	7	2·6	6 10	5 43	14 44	22 59	23 21
18	8 48	+21·2	54·6	14·9	310	282	13	3·6	7 26	7 06	15 30	23 15	23 30
19	9 35	+16·8	54·3	14·8	322	287	20	4·6	8 40	8 26	16 13	23 27	23 37
20	10 20	+11·8	54·2	14·8	334	290	28	5·6	9 52	9 44	16 53	23 37	23 43
21	11 02	+ 6·5	54·2	14·8	346	293	37	6·6	11 03	10 59	17 32	23 46	23 47
22	11 44	+ 0·9	54·4	14·8	358	293	46	7·6	12 13	12 15	18 12	23 55	23 51
23	12 27	− 4·8	54·8	14·9	11	293	56	8·6	13 25	13 32	18 52	..	23 57
24	13 10	−10·4	55·3	15·1	23	291	65	9·6	14 40	14 53	19 35	0 06	..
25	13 57	−15·8	56·0	15·3	35	288	74	10·6	15 59	16 19	20 22	0 18	0 03
26	14 47	−20·6	56·7	15·5	47	284	83	11·6	17 22	17 50	21 14	0 34	0 13
27	15 41	−24·5	57·6	15·7	59	277	90	12·6	18 45	19 21	22 11	0 57	0 29
28	16 41	−27·3	58·4	15·9	72	267	95	13·6	20 00	20 40	23 13	1 32	0 56
29	17 44	−28·4	59·1	16·1	84	248	99	14·6	20 59	21 37	..	2 24	1 44
30	18 49	−27·6	59·7	16·3	96	148	100	15·6	21 40	22 10	0 16	3 38	3 01

MERCURY ☿

Day	R.A.	Dec. +	Diam.	Phase	Transit		Day	R.A.	Dec. +	Diam.	Phase	Transit	
	h m	°	″		h m			h m	°	″		h m	
1	5 46	23·4	—	—	13 05		16	5 21	19·2	—	—	11 40	
4	5 45	22·6	—	—	12 51	Mercury is too	19	5 15	18·7	—	—	11 23	Mercury is too
7	5 41	21·7	—	—	12 35	close to the	22	5 12	18·5	11	7	11 08	close to the
10	5 35	20·8	—	—	12 17	Sun for	25	5 10	18·4	11	12	10 55	Sun for
13	5 28	19·9	—	—	11 59	observation	28	5 12	18·7	10	17	10 45	observation
16	5 21	19·2	—	—	11 40		31	5 16	19·1	9	23	10 38	

VENUS ♀

Day	R.A.	Dec. +	Diam.	Phase	Transit	
	h m	°	″		h m	
1	5 54	25·3	53	5	13 12	
6	5 44	24·2	55	2	12 42	
11	5 32	22·9	57	1	12 10	Venus is too
16	5 18	21·6	57	1	11 37	close to the
21	5 07	20·3	56	3	11 06	Sun for
26	4 58	19·2	53	6	10 39	observation
31	4 53	18·4	50	10	10 14	

MARS ♂

Day	R.A.	Dec. −	Diam.	Phase	Transit	5° high. 52°	5° high. 56°
	h m	°	″		h m	h m	h m
1	22 35	11·6	10	85	5 56	1 33	1 47
6	22 46	10·6	11	85	5 48	1 19	1 32
11	22 59	9·6	11	85	5 40	1 05	1 17
16	23 10	8·6	12	85	5 32	0 51	1 02
21	23 21	7·6	12	85	5 23	0 37	0 47
26	23 32	6·7	12	85	5 14	0 23	0 32
31	23 42	5·8	13	86	5 05	0 08	0 17

SUNRISE AND SUNSET

Day	London		Bristol		Birmingham		Manchester		Newcastle		Glasgow		Belfast	
	a.m.	p.m.	a.m.	p.m.	a.m.	p.m.	a.m.	p.m.	a.m.	p.m.	a.m.	p.m.	a.m.	p.m.
	h m	h m	h m	h m	h m	h m	h m	h m	h m	h m	h m	h m	h m	h m
1	3 49	8 08	3 59	8 17	3 50	8 20	3 47	8 27	3 35	8 33	3 40	8 50	3 55	8 49
2	3 48	8 09	3 58	8 18	3 49	8 21	3 46	8 28	3 34	8 34	3 39	8 51	3 54	8 50
3	3 47	8 10	3 57	8 19	3 48	8 22	3 45	8 29	3 33	8 35	3 38	8 52	3 53	8 51
4	3 47	8 11	3 57	8 20	3 48	8 23	3 44	8 30	3 32	8 37	3 37	8 54	3 52	8 52
5	3 46	8 12	3 56	8 21	3 47	8 24	3 44	8 31	3 31	8 38	3 36	8 55	3 52	8 53
6	3 45	8 12	3 55	8 22	3 46	8 25	3 43	8 32	3 30	8 39	3 35	8 56	3 51	8 54
7	3 45	8 13	3 55	8 23	3 46	8 26	3 42	8 33	3 30	8 40	3 35	8 57	3 50	8 55
8	3 44	8 14	3 54	8 24	3 45	8 27	3 42	8 34	3 29	8 41	3 34	8 58	3 50	8 56
9	3 44	8 15	3 54	8 24	3 45	8 27	3 41	8 35	3 28	8 42	3 33	8 59	3 49	8 57
10	3 43	8 16	3 53	8 25	3 44	8 28	3 41	8 36	3 28	8 43	3 33	9 00	3 49	8 58
11	3 43	8 16	3 53	8 26	3 44	8 29	3 40	8 37	3 27	8 44	3 32	9 01	3 48	8 59
12	3 43	8 17	3 53	8 27	3 44	8 30	3 40	8 38	3 27	8 45	3 32	9 02	3 48	9 00
13	3 43	8 17	3 53	8 27	3 44	8 30	3 39	8 38	3 26	8 45	3 31	9 02	3 47	9 00
14	3 42	8 18	3 52	8 28	3 43	8 31	3 39	8 39	3 26	8 46	3 31	9 03	3 47	9 01
15	3 42	8 19	3 52	8 28	3 43	8 31	3 39	8 40	3 26	8 47	3 31	9 04	3 47	9 02
16	3 42	8 19	3 52	8 29	3 43	8 32	3 39	8 40	3 26	8 47	3 31	9 04	3 47	9 02
17	3 42	8 19	3 52	8 29	3 43	8 32	3 39	8 41	3 26	8 48	3 30	9 05	3 47	9 03
18	3 42	8 20	3 52	8 30	3 43	8 33	3 39	8 41	3 26	8 48	3 30	9 05	3 47	9 03
19	3 42	8 20	3 52	8 30	3 43	8 33	3 39	8 41	3 26	8 48	3 30	9 06	3 47	9 03
20	3 42	8 20	3 52	8 30	3 43	8 33	3 39	8 42	3 26	8 49	3 31	9 06	3 47	9 04
21	3 42	8 21	3 52	8 31	3 43	8 34	3 39	8 42	3 26	8 49	3 31	9 06	3 47	9 04
22	3 43	8 21	3 53	8 31	3 44	8 34	3 39	8 42	3 26	8 49	3 31	9 07	3 47	9 04
23	3 43	8 21	3 53	8 31	3 44	8 34	3 39	8 42	3 26	8 49	3 31	9 07	3 47	9 04
24	3 43	8 21	3 53	8 31	3 44	8 34	3 40	8 42	3 27	8 49	3 32	9 07	3 48	9 04
25	3 44	8 21	3 54	8 31	3 45	8 34	3 40	8 42	3 27	8 49	3 32	9 07	3 48	9 04
26	3 44	8 21	3 54	8 31	3 45	8 34	3 41	8 42	3 28	8 49	3 32	9 07	3 49	9 04
27	3 44	8 21	3 54	8 31	3 45	8 34	3 41	8 42	3 28	8 49	3 33	9 06	3 49	9 04
28	3 45	8 21	3 55	8 31	3 46	8 34	3 42	8 42	3 29	8 49	3 34	9 06	3 50	9 04
29	3 46	8 21	3 56	8 31	3 47	8 34	3 42	8 42	3 29	8 49	3 34	9 06	3 50	9 04
30	3 46	8 21	3 56	8 30	3 47	8 33	3 43	8 41	3 30	8 48	3 35	9 05	3 51	9 03

JUPITER ♃ — SATURN ♄

Day	R.A.	Dec. +	Transit	5° high.		R.A.	Dec. −	Transit	5° high.	
				52°	56°				52°	56°
	h m	°	h m	h m	h m	h m	°	h m	h m	h m
1	3 09	16·7	10 29	3 35	3 24	18 03	22·3	1 24	22 11	22 44
11	3 18	17·3	9 59	3 02	2 50	18 00	22·3	0 41	21 28	22 01
21	3 27	17·9	9 28	2 28	2 16	17 57	22·3	23 55	20 46	21 19
31	3 36	18·4	8 58	1 54	1 42	17 53	22·3	23 12	20 04	20 37

Equatorial diameter of Jupiter 34″; of Saturn 18″. Diameters of Saturn's rings 42″ and 18″.

URANUS ♅ — NEPTUNE ♆

Day	R.A.	Dec. −	Transit	10° high.		R.A.	Dec. −	Transit	10° high.	
				52°	56°				52°	56°
	h m	° ′	h m	h m	h m	h m	° ′	h m	h m	h m
1	17 59·2	23 39	1 20	23 18	0 45	18 41·3	22 06	2 02	23 41	0 41
11	17 57·5	23 39	0 39	22 37	0 04	18 40·3	22 07	1 22	23 00	0 01
21	17 55·7	23 39	23 54	21 55	23 19	18 39·2	22 08	0 41	22 20	23 17
31	17 54·0	23 39	23 13	21 14	22 38	18 38·0	22 10	0 01	21 40	22 37

Diameter 4″ — Diameter 2″

Day of Month	Day of Week	♋  *Julius* Caesar, formerly *Quintilis*, 5th month (from March).  ♌ *Sun's Longitude* 120° ♌ 22ᵈ 15ʰ
1	F.	Princess of Wales b. 1961. Amy Johnson b. 1903.
2	S.	Archbishop Cranmer b. 1489. Gluck b. 1714.
3	𝕾.	**5th S. after Trinity. St. Thomas.**
4	M.	Independence Day, U.S.A., 1776. William Byrd d. [1623.
5	Tu.	N.H.S. started 1948. Jean Cocteau b. 1889.
6	W.	Henry II d. 1189. Sedgemoor 1685.
7	Th.	Mahler b. 1860. Gian Carlo Menotti b. 1911
8	F.	Joseph Chamberlain b. 1836. von Zeppelin b. 1838.
9	S.	Ottorino Respighi b. 1879. Edward Heath b. 1916.
10	𝕾.	**6th S. after Trinity.** Joe Davis d. 1978.
11	M.	Robert the Bruce b. 1274. George Gershwin d. 1937.
12	Tu.	Julius Caesar b. 102 B.C. Kirsten Flagstad b. 1895.
13	W.	Sidney Webb b. 1859. Arnold Schönberg d. 1951.
14	Th.	Fête Nationale, France. Storming of Bastille [1789.
15	F.	St. Swithin's Day. Indigo Jones b. 1573.
16	S.	Jean Corot b. 1796. Hilaire Belloc d. 1953.
17	𝕾.	**7th S. after Trinity.** Isaac Watts b. 1674.
18	M.	Gilbert White b. 1720. Dr. W. G. Grace b. 1848.
19	Tu.	*Mary Rose* sank 1545. Edgar Degas b. 1834.
20	W.	Petrarch b. 1304. Calouste Gulbenkian d. 1955.
21	Th.	Tate Gallery opened 1897. Henry Longhurst d. 1978.
22	F.	**St. Mary Magdalen.** Rev. Wm. Spooner b. 1844.
23	S.	Raymond Chandler b. 1888.* Olivia Manning d. 1980.
24	𝕾.	**8th S. after Trinity.** Capt. M. Webb d. 1883.
25	M.	**St. James.** First cross-Channel flight 1909.
26	Tu.	Carl Jung b. 1875. Aldous Huxley b. 1894.
27	W.	John Dalton d. 1844. Korean War ended 1953.
28	Th.	Thomas Cromwell exec. 1540. J. S. Bach d. 1750.
29	F.	Defeat of Spanish Armada 1588.*
30	S.	William Penn d. 1718. Denis Diderot d. 1784.
31	𝕾.	**9th S. after Trinity.** Trinity Law Sittings End.

PHENOMENA

July 5ᵈ 07ʰ Mars in conjunction with the Moon. Mars 5° S.

6ᵈ 00ʰ Earth at aphelion (152,000,000 kilometres).

6ᵈ 16ʰ Mercury at greatest western elongation (21°).

9ᵈ 19ʰ Jupiter in conjunction with the Moon. Jupiter 6° S.

11ᵈ 01ʰ Venus in conjunction with the Moon. Venus 10° S.

12ᵈ 04ʰ Mercury in conjunction with the Moon. Mercury 7° S.

19ᵈ 18ʰ Venus at greatest brilliancy.

26ᵈ 11ʰ Saturn in conjunction with the Moon. Saturn 6° N.

CONSTELLATIONS

The following constellations are near the meridian at

	d	h		d	h
June	1	24	June	15	23
July	1	22	July	16	21
Aug.	1	20	Aug.	16	19

Ursa Minor, Draco, Corona, Hercules, Lyra, Serpens, Ophiuchus, Libra, Scorpius and Sagittarius.

MINIMA OF ALGOL

d	h	d	h
2	5	19	10
5	2	22	7
7	23	25	4
10	20	28	1
13	17	30	21
16	13		

* Centenary.

PHASES OF THE MOON

	d	h	m
☾ Last Quarter	6	11	36
● New Moon	13	21	53
☽ First Quarter	22	02	14
○ Full Moon	29	03	25

	d	h
Perigee (363,670 kilometres)	2	06
Apogee (405,510 ,,)	18	01
Perigee (359,330 ,,)	30	08

Mean Longitude of Ascending Node on July 1, 348°

See note on *Summer Time*, p. 98.

MONTHLY NOTES

July 1. National Day, Canada.

3. Dog Days begin (end Aug. 15).

5. Tynwald Day, Isle of Man.

12. Bank Holiday, Northern Ireland.

| | THE SUN | | | | | s.d. 15′·8 | | | Sidereal Time | Transit of First Point of Aries |
| Day | Right Ascension | Dec. + | Equation of Time | Rise | | Transit | Set | | | |
				52°	56°		52°	56°		
	h m s	° ′	m s	h m	h m	h m	h m	h m	h m s	h m s
1	6 40 49	23 07	−3 46	3 44	3 18	12 04	20 23	20 49	18 37 03	5 22 04
2	6 44 57	23 02	−3 57	3 45	3 19	12 04	20 23	20 48	18 41 00	5 18 08
3	6 49 05	22 58	−4 08	3 46	3 20	12 04	20 22	20 48	18 44 57	5 14 12
4	6 53 12	22 53	−4 19	3 47	3 21	12 04	20 22	20 47	18 48 53	5 10 16
5	6 57 19	22 47	−4 30	3 47	3 22	12 05	20 21	20 46	18 52 50	5 06 20
6	7 01 26	22 42	−4 40	3 48	3 23	12 05	20 21	20 46	18 56 46	5 02 24
7	7 05 32	22 35	−4 50	3 49	3 24	12 05	20 20	20 45	19 00 43	4 58 28
8	7 09 38	22 29	−4 59	3 50	3 26	12 05	20 19	20 44	19 04 39	4 54 32
9	7 13 44	22 22	−5 08	3 51	3 27	12 05	20 19	20 43	19 08 36	4 50 36
10	7 17 50	22 14	−5 17	3 52	3 28	12 05	20 18	20 42	19 12 32	4 46 40
11	7 21 54	22 07	−5 25	3 53	3 29	12 05	20 17	20 41	19 16 29	4 42 45
12	7 25 59	21 58	−5 33	3 54	3 31	12 06	20 16	20 40	19 20 26	4 38 49
13	7 30 03	21 50	−5 41	3 56	3 32	12 06	20 15	20 38	19 24 22	4 34 53
14	7 34 06	21 41	−5 48	3 57	3 33	12 06	20 14	20 37	19 28 19	4 30 57
15	7 38 10	21 32	−5 54	3 58	3 35	12 06	20 13	20 36	19 32 15	4 27 01
16	7 42 12	21 22	−6 00	3 59	3 36	12 06	20 12	20 35	19 36 12	4 23 05
17	7 46 14	21 12	−6 06	4 00	3 38	12 06	20 11	20 33	19 40 08	4 19 09
18	7 50 16	21 02	−6 11	4 02	3 40	12 06	20 10	20 32	19 44 05	4 15 13
19	7 54 16	20 51	−6 15	4 03	3 41	12 06	20 09	20 30	19 48 01	4 11 17
20	7 58 17	20 40	−6 19	4 04	3 43	12 06	20 07	20 29	19 51 58	4 07 21
21	8 02 17	20 28	−6 22	4 06	3 44	12 06	20 06	20 27	19 55 55	4 03 25
22	8 06 16	20 17	−6 25	4 07	3 46	12 06	20 05	20 26	19 59 51	3 59 30
23	8 10 14	20 05	−6 27	4 09	3 48	12 06	20 03	20 24	20 03 48	3 55 34
24	8 14 12	19 52	−6 28	4 10	3 50	12 06	20 02	20 22	20 07 44	3 51 38
25	8 18 10	19 39	−6 29	4 11	3 51	12 06	20 01	20 20	20 11 41	3 47 42
26	8 22 07	19 26	−6 29	4 13	3 53	12 06	19 59	20 19	20 15 37	3 43 46
27	8 26 03	19 13	−6 29	4 14	3 55	12 06	19 58	20 17	20 19 34	3 39 50
28	8 29 58	18 59	−6 28	4 16	3 57	12 06	19 56	20 15	20 23 30	3 35 54
29	8 33 53	18 45	−6 26	4 17	3 59	12 06	19 55	20 13	20 27 27	3 31 58
30	8 37 48	18 31	−6 24	4 19	4 00	12 06	19 53	20 11	20 31 24	3 28 02
31	8 41 42	18 16	−6 21	4 20	4 02	12 06	19 51	20 09	20 35 20	3 24 06

Duration of Civil (C), Nautical (N), and Astronomical (A), Twilight (in minutes)

| Lat. ° | July 1 | | | July 11 | | | July 21 | | | July 31 | | |
	C	N	A	C	N	A	C	N	A	C	N	A
52	48	124	T.A.N.	46	116	T.A.N.	44	107	T.A.N.	41	98	180
56	61	T.A.N.	T.A.N.	58	T.A.N.	T.A.N.	53	144	T.A.N.	49	122	T.A.N.

ASTRONOMICAL NOTES

MERCURY is not suitably placed for observation this month.

VENUS is a brilliant morning object, reaching its greatest brilliancy, magnitude −4·5, on the 19th. Through a telescope the planet's appearance changes markedly during the month as its diameter decreases from 50″ to 31″ while the fraction illuminated increases from 10 per cent to 36 per cent.

MARS, its magnitude brightening from −0·8 to −1·5 during July, continues to be visible as a prominent object in the mornings. During the month it moves from Aquarius, through the southern part of Pisces and into Cetus. The Moon passes 5° N. of Mars on the morning of the 5th.

JUPITER, magnitude −2·2, is now a brilliant morning object. By the end of the month it will be seen rising above the east-north-east horizon around midnight.

SATURN, magnitude +0·2, is visible for most of the night in the southern skies though by the end of the month it will not be visible for long after midnight as it moves slowly towards the south-western horizon.

TWILIGHT. Reference to the section just above these notes shows that astronomical twilight lasts all night for some time around the summer solstice (i.e. in June and July), even in southern England. Under these conditions the sky never gets completely dark since the Sun is always less than 18° below the horizon.

THE MOON

Day	R.A.	Dec.	Hor. Par.	Semi-diam.	Sun's Co-long.	P.A. of Bright Limb	Phase	Age	Rise 52°	Rise 56°	Tran-sit	Set 52°	Set 56°
	h m	°	′	′	°	°		d	h m	h m	h m	h m	h m
1	19 53	−24·9	60·1	16·4	108	93	98	16·6	22 07	22 29	1 19	5 07	4 38
2	20 54	−20·6	60·3	16·4	120	79	93	17·6	22 26	22 40	2 18	6 41	6 21
3	21 51	−15·0	60·2	16·4	133	72	86	18·6	22 41	22 48	3 13	8 14	8 02
4	22 45	− 8·6	60·0	16·3	145	68	77	19·6	22 53	22 55	4 04	9 44	9 38
5	23 36	− 1·9	59·6	16·2	157	66	67	20·6	23 05	23 01	4 52	11 10	11 11
6	0 26	+ 4·8	59·1	16·1	169	66	56	21·6	23 17	23 07	5 40	12 35	12 42
7	1 16	+11·2	58·5	15·9	182	68	44	22·6	23 31	23 16	6 28	14 00	14 14
8	2 07	+17·0	57·9	15·8	194	72	34	23·6	23 49	23 27	7 17	15 25	15 46
9	3 00	+21·8	57·3	15·6	206	76	24	24·6	. .	23 45	8 09	16 49	17 17
10	3 55	+24·4	56·8	15·5	218	83	15	25·6	0 15	. .	9 03	18 07	18 42
11	4 52	+27·7	56·3	15·3	230	91	9	26·6	0 50	0 14	9 58	19 13	19 52
12	5 50	+28·4	55·8	15·2	243	101	4	27·6	1 39	1 00	10 54	20 03	20 40
13	6 47	+27·6	55·3	15·1	255	118	1	28·6	2 43	2 06	11 48	20 39	21 09
14	7 41	+25·5	54·9	15·0	267	204	0	0·1	3 55	3 25	12 38	21 03	21 27
15	8 33	+22·2	54·6	14·9	279	269	1	1·1	5 11	4 48	13 26	21 21	21 38
16	9 21	+18·1	54·3	14·8	292	282	4	2·1	6 26	6 09	14 09	21 34	21 46
17	10 06	+13·2	54·1	14·8	304	288	9	3·1	7 38	7 28	14 50	21 45	21 52
18	10 49	+ 7·9	54·1	14·7	316	292	15	4·1	8 49	8 44	15 30	21 54	21 56
19	11 31	+ 2·4	54·1	14·8	328	294	22	5·1	9 59	9 59	16 09	22 03	22 00
20	12 13	− 3·3	54·4	14·8	341	294	30	6·1	11 10	11 15	16 48	22 12	22 05
21	12 56	− 8·8	54·7	14·9	353	293	40	7·1	12 22	12 33	17 29	22 23	22 11
22	13 40	−14·2	55·3	15·1	5	291	49	8·1	13 38	13 55	18 13	22 37	22 19
23	14 28	−19·1	55·9	15·2	17	288	59	9·1	14 58	15 22	19 02	22 56	22 31
24	15 20	−23·3	56·8	15·5	30	283	69	10·1	16 20	16 52	19 55	23 24	22 51
25	16 16	−26·5	57·7	15·7	42	277	78	11·1	17 38	18 17	20 54	. .	23 28
26	17 17	−28·2	58·6	16·0	54	269	87	12·1	18 45	19 25	21 56	0 07	. .
27	18 21	−28·2	59·5	16·2	66	259	93	13·1	19 34	20 08	23 00	1 10	0 30
28	19 26	−26·3	60·2	16·4	78	247	98	14·1	20 07	20 32	. .	2 33	2 00
29	20 29	−22·5	60·8	16·6	91	197	100	15·1	20 30	20 47	0 02	4 08	3 44
30	21 29	−17·2	61·0	16·6	103	82	99	16·1	20 46	20 57	1 00	5 44	5 29
31	22 25	−10·9	61·0	16·6	115	71	95	17·1	21 00	21 04	1 54	7 19	7 11

MERCURY ☿

Day	R.A.	Dec. +	Diam.	Phase	Tran-sit		Day	R.A.	Dec. +	Diam.	Phase	Tran-sit	
	h m	°	″		h m			h m	°	″		h m	
1	5 16	19·1	9	23	10 38		16	6 24	22·4	6	65	10 49	
4	5 24	19·7	8	30	10 34	Mercury is too	19	6 46	22·7	6	74	10 59	Mercury is too
7	5 34	20·4	8	38	10 34	close to the	22	7 10	22·8	6	82	11 12	close to the
10	5 48	21·1	7	46	10 36	Sun for	25	7 35	22·4	—	—	11 26	Sun for
13	6 04	21·8	7	55	10 41	observation	28	8 02	21·7	—	—	11 41	observation
16	6 24	22·4	6	65	10 49		31	8 29	20·6	—	—	11 56	

VENUS ♀ / MARS ♂

Day	R.A.	Dec. +	Diam.	Phase	Tran-sit	5° high. 52°	5° high. 56°	Day	R.A.	Dec. −	Diam.	Phase	Tran-sit	5° high. 52°	5° high. 56°
	h m	°	″		h m	h m	h m		h m	°	″		h m	h m	h m
1	4 53	18·4	50	10	10 14	3 12	2 59	1	23 42	5·8	13	86	5 05	0 08	0 17
6	4 53	17·9	46	15	9 54	2 54	2 42	6	23 52	4·9	14	86	4 55	23 51	0 01
11	4 56	17·8	43	19	9 38	2 38	2 27	11	0 01	4·1	14	86	4 44	23 36	23 43
16	5 02	17·8	39	24	9 25	2 25	2 13	16	0 10	3·3	15	87	4 33	23 21	23 27
21	5 12	18·1	36	28	9 15	2 13	2 01	21	0 18	2·7	15	87	4 22	23 06	23 11
26	5 24	18·4	34	32	9 08	2 04	1 51	26	0 26	2·0	16	88	4 10	22 50	22 55
31	5 38	18·8	32	36	9 02	1 56	1 43	31	0 32	1·5	17	89	3 57	22 34	22 39

SUNRISE AND SUNSET

Day	London a.m. h m	London p.m. h m	Bristol a.m. h m	Bristol p.m. h m	Birmingham a.m. h m	Birmingham p.m. h m	Manchester a.m. h m	Manchester p.m. h m	Newcastle a.m. h m	Newcastle p.m. h m	Glasgow a.m. h m	Glasgow p.m. h m	Belfast a.m. h m	Belfast p.m. h m
1	3 47	8 21	3 57	8 30	3 48	8 33	3 44	8 41	3 31	8 48	3 36	9 05	3 52	9 03
2	3 47	8 20	3 57	8 30	3 48	8 33	3 44	8 41	3 32	8 48	3 37	9 05	3 52	9 03
3	3 48	8 20	3 58	8 29	3 49	8 32	3 45	8 40	3 33	8 47	3 38	9 04	3 53	9 02
4	3 49	8 19	3 59	8 29	3 50	8 32	3 46	8 40	3 33	8 46	3 38	9 03	3 54	9 02
5	3 50	8 19	4 00	8 28	3 51	8 31	3 47	8 39	3 34	8 46	3 39	9 03	3 55	9 01
6	3 51	8 18	4 01	8 28	3 52	8 31	3 48	8 39	3 35	8 45	3 40	9 02	3 56	9 01
7	3 52	8 18	4 02	8 27	3 53	8 30	3 49	8 38	3 37	8 44	3 42	9 01	3 57	9 00
8	3 53	8 17	4 03	8 27	3 54	8 30	3 50	8 37	3 38	8 43	3 43	9 00	3 58	8 59
9	3 54	8 17	4 04	8 26	3 55	8 29	3 51	8 36	3 39	8 43	3 44	9 00	3 59	8 58
10	3 55	8 16	4 05	8 25	3 56	8 28	3 52	8 35	3 40	8 41	3 45	8 58	4 00	8 57
11	3 56	8 15	4 06	8 24	3 57	8 27	3 53	8 35	3 41	8 41	3 46	8 57	4 01	8 57
12	3 57	8 14	4 07	8 24	3 58	8 26	3 55	8 34	3 43	8 40	3 48	8 56	4 03	8 56
13	3 58	8 14	4 08	8 23	3 59	8 26	3 56	8 33	3 44	8 39	3 49	8 55	4 04	8 55
14	3 59	8 13	4 09	8 22	4 00	8 25	3 57	8 32	3 45	8 38	3 51	8 54	4 05	8 54
15	4 00	8 12	4 10	8 21	4 01	8 24	3 58	8 31	3 46	8 37	3 52	8 53	4 06	8 53
16	4 01	8 11	4 11	8 20	4 03	8 22	4 00	8 29	3 48	8 35	3 54	8 51	4 08	8 51
17	4 02	8 10	4 13	8 19	4 04	8 21	4 01	8 28	3 49	8 34	3 55	8 50	4 09	8 50
18	4 03	8 08	4 14	8 18	4 05	8 20	4 02	8 27	3 51	8 33	3 57	8 49	4 11	8 49
19	4 04	8 07	4 15	8 17	4 07	8 19	4 04	8 26	3 52	8 31	3 58	8 47	4 12	8 47
20	4 06	8 06	4 16	8 16	4 08	8 17	4 05	8 24	3 54	8 30	4 00	8 46	4 14	8 46
21	4 07	8 05	4 18	8 15	4 10	8 16	4 07	8 23	3 55	8 28	4 01	8 44	4 15	8 44
22	4 08	8 04	4 19	8 14	4 11	8 15	4 08	8 22	3 57	8 27	4 03	8 43	4 17	8 43
23	4 10	8 02	4 20	8 12	4 13	8 13	4 10	8 20	3 59	8 25	4 05	8 41	4 19	8 41
24	4 11	8 01	4 22	8 11	4 14	8 12	4 11	8 19	4 00	8 23	4 06	8 39	4 20	8 39
25	4 12	7 59	4 23	8 09	4 15	8 10	4 12	8 17	4 02	8 22	4 08	8 38	4 22	8 38
26	4 14	7 58	4 24	8 08	4 17	8 09	4 14	8 16	4 04	8 20	4 10	8 36	4 24	8 36
27	4 15	7 56	4 26	8 06	4 18	8 07	4 15	8 14	4 05	8 19	4 12	8 34	4 25	8 35
28	4 17	7 55	4 27	8 05	4 20	8 06	4 17	8 13	4 07	8 17	4 13	8 32	4 27	8 33
29	4 19	7 53	4 29	8 03	4 22	8 04	4 19	8 11	4 09	8 15	4 15	8 30	4 29	8 31
30	4 20	7 52	4 30	8 02	4 23	8 03	4 20	8 10	4 10	8 13	4 17	8 28	4 30	8 30
31	4 21	7 50	4 31	8 00	4 24	8 01	4 22	8 08	4 12	8 12	4 19	8 27	4 32	8 28

JUPITER ♃ / SATURN ♄

Day	JUPITER R.A. h m	JUPITER Dec. + °	JUPITER Transit h m	JUPITER 5° high. 52° h m	JUPITER 5° high. 56° h m	SATURN R.A. h m	SATURN Dec. − °	SATURN Transit h m	SATURN 5° high. 52° h m	SATURN 5° high. 56° h m
1	3 36	18·4	8 58	1 54	1 42	17 53	22·3	23 12	2 25	1 52
11	3 44	18·8	8 26	1 21	1 08	17 50	22·3	22 30	1 43	1 10
21	3 51	19·2	7 54	0 46	0 33	17 48	22·3	21 48	1 01	0 28
31	3 58	19·5	7 22	0 12	23 55	17 46	22·3	21 07	0 19	23 42

Equatorial diameter of Jupiter 36″; of Saturn 18″.　　Diameters of Saturn's rings 41″ and 18″.

URANUS ♅ / NEPTUNE ♆

Day	URANUS R.A. h m	URANUS Dec. − ° ′	URANUS Transit h m	URANUS 10° high. 52° h m	URANUS 10° high. 56° h m	NEPTUNE R.A. h m	NEPTUNE Dec. − ° ′	NEPTUNE Transit h m	NEPTUNE 10° high. 52° h m	NEPTUNE 10° high. 56° h m
1	17 54·0	23 39	23 13	1 16	23 48	18 38·0	22 10	0 01	2 18	1 21
11	17 52·3	23 39	22 32	0 35	23 07	18 36·9	22 11	23 16	1 37	0 20
21	17 50·7	23 38	21 51	23 50	22 27	18 35·7	22 12	22 36	0 57	23 55
31	17 49·4	23 38	21 11	23 09	21 46	18 34·7	22 13	21 56	0 16	23 15

Diameter 4″　　　　　　Diameter 2″

DAY OF		
Month	Week	Julius Caesar *Augustus*, formerly *Sextilis*, 6th month (from March). Sun's Longitude 150° ♍ 22ᵈ 22ʰ

1	M.	Anne I d. 1714. Louis Bleriot d. 1936.
2	Tu.	Gainsborough d. 1788.* Sir Arthur Bliss b. 1891.
3	W.	Discovery of Lake Victoria 1858.
4	Th.	QUEEN ELIZABETH THE QUEEN MOTHER b. 1900.
5	F.	Friedrich Engels d. 1895. Neil Armstrong b. 1930.
6	S.	**The Transfiguration.** First atomic bomb 1945.
7	♑.	**10th S. after Trinity.** Joseph Jacquard d. 1834.
8	M.	Great Train Robbery 1963.
9	Tu.	Thomas Telford b. 1757. Dmitry Shostakovich b. 1906.
10	W.	Sir Charles Napier b. 1782. Charles Keene b. 1823.
11	Th.	Charlotte Yonge b. 1823. Andrew Carnegie d. 1919.
12	F.	Glorious Twelfth. Ian Fleming d. 1964.
13	S.	John Ireland b. 1879. John Logie Baird b. 1888.*
14	♑.	**11th S. after Trinity.** Japan surrenders 1945.
15	M.	PRINCESS ROYAL b. 1950. T. E. Lawrence b. 1888.*
16	Tu.	Andrew Marvell d. 1678. Robert van Bunsen d. 1899.
17	W.	Davy Crockett b. 1786. Scawen Blunt b. 1840.
18	Th.	Lord Russell b. 1792. Godfrey Evans b. 1920.
19	F.	John Flamsteed b. 1646. James Watt d. 1819.
20	S.	Invasion of Czechoslovakia 1968.
21	♑.	**12th S. after Trinity.** PRINCESS MARGARET b. 1930.
22	M.	Viscount Nuffield d. 1963. Dr. Bronowski d. 1974.
23	Tu.	Constant Lambert b. 1905. Michel Fokine d. 1942.
24	W.	**St. Bartholomew.** Vesuvius erupted A.D. 79.
25	Th.	Sir Wm. Herschel d. 1822. Leonard Bernstein b. 1918.
26	F.	Lavoisier b. 1743. Charles Lindberg d. 1974.
27	S.	Eric Coates b. 1886. Earl Mountbatten assass. 1979.
28	♑.	**13th S. after Trinity.** Count Leo Tolstoy b. 1828.
29	M.	First motorcycle patented 1885.
30	Tu.	Mary Shelley b. 1797. Lord Rutherford b. 1871.
31	W.	John Bunyan d. 1688.* Rocky Marciano d. 1969.

*Centenary.

PHENOMENA

August 2ᵈ 11ʰ Mars in conjunction with the Moon. Mars 8° S.

3ᵈ 04ʰ Mercury in superior conjunction.

6ᵈ 08ʰ Jupiter in conjunction with the Moon. Jupiter 6° S.

8ᵈ 12ʰ Venus in conjunction with the Moon. Venus 9° S.

22ᵈ 12ʰ Venus at greatest western elongation (46°).

22ᵈ 19ʰ Saturn in conjunction with the Moon. Saturn 6° N.

30ᵈ 03ʰ Mars in conjunction with the Moon. Mars 9° S.

CONSTELLATIONS

The following constellations are near the meridian at

	d	h		d	h
July	1	24	July 16	23	
Aug.	1	22	Aug. 16	21	
Sept.	1	20	Sept. 15	19	

Draco, Hercules, Lyra, Cygnus, Sagitta, Ophiuchus, Serpens, Aquila and Sagittarius.

MINIMA OF ALGOL

d	h	d	h
2	18	19	23
5	15	22	20
8	12	25	17
11	9	28	13
14	5	31	10
17	2		

PHASES OF THE MOON

	d	h	m
☾ Last Quarter	4	18	22
● New Moon	12	12	31
☽ First Quarter	20	15	51
○ Full Moon	27	10	56

	d	h
Apogee (406,320 kilometres)	14	12
Perigee (357,100 „)	27	17

Mean Longitude of Ascending Node on Aug. 1, 346°.

See note on *Summer Time*, p. 98.

MONTHLY NOTES

Aug.   1. Lammas. Scottish Term Day. Bank Holiday, Scotland.

12. Grouse shooting begins.

14. Islamic New Year (A.H. 1409).

29. Bank and General Holiday, England, Wales and N. Ireland.

Day	Right Ascension	Dec. +	Equation of Time	Rise 52°	Rise 56°	Transit	Set 52°	Set 56°	Sidereal Time	Transit of First Point of Aries
	h m s	° ′	m s	h m	h m	h m	h m	h m	h m s	h m s
1	8 45 35	18 01	− 6 18	4 22	4 04	12 06	19 50	20 07	20 39 17	3 20 10
2	8 49 27	17 46	− 6 14	4 23	4 06	12 06	19 48	20 05	20 43 13	3 16 14
3	8 53 19	17 30	− 6 09	4 25	4 08	12 06	19 46	20 03	20 47 10	3 12 19
4	8 57 11	17 15	− 6 04	4 27	4 10	12 06	19 44	20 01	20 51 06	3 08 23
5	9 01 01	16 58	− 5 59	4 28	4 12	12 06	19 43	19 59	20 55 03	3 04 27
6	9 04 52	16 42	− 5 52	4 30	4 14	12 06	19 41	19 57	20 58 59	3 00 31
7	9 08 41	16 25	− 5 45	4 31	4 15	12 06	19 39	19 55	21 02 56	2 56 35
8	9 12 30	16 09	− 5 38	4 33	4 17	12 06	19 37	19 52	21 06 53	2 52 39
9	9 16 19	15 51	− 5 30	4 34	4 19	12 05	19 35	19 50	21 10 49	2 48 43
10	9 20 07	15 34	− 5 21	4 36	4 21	12 05	19 33	19 48	21 14 46	2 44 47
11	9 23 54	15 16	− 5 12	4 38	4 23	12 05	19 31	19 46	21 18 42	2 40 51
12	9 27 41	14 58	− 5 02	4 39	4 25	12 05	19 30	19 43	21 22 39	2 36 55
13	9 31 27	14 40	− 4 52	4 41	4 27	12 05	19 28	19 41	21 26 35	2 32 59
14	9 35 13	14 22	− 4 41	4 43	4 29	12 05	19 26	19 39	21 30 32	2 29 04
15	9 38 58	14 03	− 4 30	4 44	4 31	12 04	19 24	19 36	21 34 28	2 25 08
16	9 42 43	13 44	− 4 18	4 46	4 33	12 04	19 21	19 34	21 38 25	2 21 12
17	9 46 27	13 25	− 4 05	4 47	4 35	12 04	19 19	19 32	21 42 22	2 17 16
18	9 50 10	13 06	− 3 52	4 49	4 37	12 04	19 17	19 29	21 46 18	2 13 20
19	9 53 54	12 47	− 3 39	4 51	4 39	12 04	19 15	19 27	21 50 15	2 09 24
20	9 57 36	12 27	− 3 25	4 52	4 41	12 03	19 13	19 24	21 54 11	2 05 28
21	10 01 18	12 07	− 3 10	4 54	4 43	12 03	19 11	19 22	21 58 08	2 01 32
22	10 05 00	11 47	− 2 55	4 56	4 45	12 03	19 09	19 19	22 02 04	1 57 36
23	10 08 41	11 27	− 2 40	4 57	4 47	12 03	19 07	19 17	22 06 01	1 53 40
24	10 12 21	11 06	− 2 24	4 59	4 49	12 02	19 05	19 14	22 09 57	1 49 44
25	10 16 02	10 46	− 2 08	5 00	4 51	12 02	19 02	19 12	22 13 54	1 45 49
26	10 19 41	10 25	− 1 51	5 02	4 53	12 02	19 00	19 09	22 17 51	1 41 53
27	10 23 21	10 04	− 1 34	5 04	4 55	12 01	18 58	19 07	22 21 47	1 37 57
28	10 27 00	9 43	− 1 16	5 05	4 57	12 01	18 56	19 04	22 25 44	1 34 01
29	10 30 39	9 22	− 0 58	5 07	4 59	12 01	18 54	19 02	22 29 40	1 30 05
30	10 34 17	9 00	− 0 40	5 09	5 00	12 01	18 51	18 59	22 33 37	1 26 09
31	10 37 55	8 39	− 0 21	5 10	5 02	12 00	18 49	18 57	22 37 33	1 22 13

THE SUN   s.d. 15′·8

Duration of Civil (C), Nautical (N), and Astronomical (A), Twilight (in minutes)

Lat. °	Aug. 1 C	N	A	Aug. 11 C	N	A	Aug. 21 C	N	A	Aug. 31 C	N	A
52	41	97	177	39	89	153	37	83	138	35	79	127
56	48	120	T.A.N.	45	106	205	42	96	166	40	89	147

ASTRONOMICAL NOTES

MERCURY is unsuitably placed for observation during August.

VENUS continues to be visible as a brilliant morning object, magnitude − 4·4, reaching its greatest western elongation from the Sun on the 22nd.

MARS is becoming a bright object in the second part of the night as its magnitude brightens from − 1·5 to − 2·3 during the month. Mars is in the constellation of Cetus.

JUPITER continues to be visible as a brilliant object in the morning skies, magnitude − 2·3. By the end of the month it is visible low in the E.N.E., shortly after 22ʰ. Jupiter is moving eastwards in the constellation of Taurus, passing between the Hyades and the Pleiades.

SATURN, magnitude + 0·3, continues to be visible in the evenings in the southern and south-western sky. The rings of Saturn present a beautiful spectacle to the observer with only a small telescope. The rings are now open to their widest extent for many years.

ECLIPSE. A partial eclipse of the Moon occurs on the 27th. See page 148 for details.

METEORS. The maximum of the famous Perseid meteor shower occurs on August 12th so the night of the 11th–12th will be the best time for observation. There will be no interference from moonlight.

THE MOON

Day	R.A.	Dec.	Hor. Par.	Semi-diam.	Sun's Co-long.	P.A. of Bright Limb	Phase	Age	Rise 52°	Rise 56°	Transit	Set 52°	Set 56°
	h m	°	′	′	°	°		d	h m	h m	h m	h m	h m
1	23 19	− 4·0	60·6	16·5	127	66	88	18·1	21 12	21 10	2 45	8 49	8 48
2	0 11	+ 3·0	60·1	16·4	139	65	80	19·1	21 24	21 16	3 35	10 18	10 23
3	1 02	+ 9·8	59·4	16·2	152	66	69	20·1	21 37	21 24	4 24	11 45	11 57
4	1 54	+15·8	58·6	16·0	164	69	59	21·1	21 54	21 34	5 14	13 12	13 31
5	2 47	+20·9	57·8	15·8	176	73	48	22·1	22 17	21 50	6 05	14 37	15 04
6	3 43	+24·9	57·1	15·5	188	78	37	23·1	22 49	22 15	6 59	15 58	16 32
7	4 39	+27·4	56·4	15·4	200	85	27	24·1	23 34	22 55	7 54	17 08	17 47
8	5 37	+28·5	55·8	15·2	213	92	19	25·1	..	23 55	8 49	18 03	18 41
9	6 33	+28·0	55·3	15·1	225	99	11	26·1	0 33	..	9 43	18 42	19 15
10	7 28	+26·2	54·9	14·9	237	107	6	27·1	1 43	1 10	10 34	19 09	19 35
11	8 20	+23·2	54·5	14·9	249	115	2	28·1	2 57	2 32	11 22	19 28	19 48
12	9 08	+19·2	54·2	14·8	262	132	0	29·1	4 13	3 54	12 07	19 42	19 56
13	9 54	+14·5	54·1	14·7	274	272	0	0·5	5 26	5 14	12 49	19 53	20 02
14	10 38	+ 9·3	54·0	14·7	286	290	2	1·5	6 38	6 31	13 29	20 03	20 07
15	11 20	+ 3·8	54·0	14·7	298	294	5	2·5	7 48	7 46	14 07	20 12	20 11
16	12 01	− 1·8	54·1	14·7	311	295	11	3·5	8 58	9 01	14 46	20 21	20 15
17	12 43	− 7·4	54·3	14·8	323	295	17	4·5	10 09	10 18	15 26	20 30	20 20
18	13 27	−12·8	54·7	14·9	335	294	25	5·5	11 23	11 37	16 09	20 43	20 27
19	14 13	−17·8	55·2	15·0	347	291	34	6·5	12 40	13 01	16 54	20 59	20 36
20	15 02	−22·2	55·8	15·2	359	287	43	7·5	13 59	14 28	17 44	21 22	20 52
21	15 56	−25·7	56·6	15·4	12	282	54	8·5	15 18	15 54	18 39	21 56	21 19
22	16 54	−27·9	57·5	15·7	24	275	64	9·5	16 29	17 09	19 39	22 48	22 08
23	17 55	−28·5	58·5	15·9	36	268	74	10·5	17 24	18 02	20 40	..	23 24
24	18 59	−27·4	59·4	16·2	48	260	83	11·5	18 04	18 34	21 42	0 01	..
25	20 02	−24·4	60·3	16·4	60	253	91	12·5	18 31	18 52	22 42	1 30	1 01
26	21 03	−19·8	60·9	16·6	73	246	97	13·5	18 50	19 04	23 38	3 06	2 46
27	22 01	−13·8	61·3	16·7	85	237	100	14·5	19 05	19 12	..	4 42	4 30
28	22 56	− 6·9	61·4	16·7	97	68	100	15·5	19 17	19 19	0 32	6 16	6 12
29	23 50	+ 0·3	61·1	16·7	109	63	96	16·5	19 30	19 25	1 23	7 49	7 51
30	0 43	+ 7·4	60·6	16·5	121	63	90	17·5	19 43	19 32	2 14	9 19	9 28
31	1 36	+13·9	59·8	16·3	134	66	82	18·5	19 59	19 41	3 05	10 50	11 06

MERCURY ☿

Day	R.A.	Dec. +	Diam.	Phase	Transit		Day	R.A.	Dec.	Diam.	Phase	Transit	
	h m	°	″		h m			h m	°	″		h m	
1	8 37	20·2	—	—	12 01		16	10 33	+10·6	—	—	12 56	
4	9 03	18·6	—	—	12 14	Mercury is too	19	10 52	+ 8·3	—	—	13 03	Mercury is too
7	9 28	16·8	—	—	12 27	close to the	22	11 11	+ 6·1	5	86	13 10	close to the
10	9 51	14·9	—	—	12 38	Sun for	25	11 28	+ 3·9	5	83	13 15	Sun for
13	10 13	12·7	—	—	12 48	observation	28	11 44	+ 1·7	6	80	13 20	observation
16	10 33	10·6	—	—	12 56		31	12 00	− 0·5	6	77	13 23	

VENUS ♀

Day	R.A.	Dec. +	Diam.	Phase	Transit	5° high. 52°	5° high. 56°
	h m	°	″		h m	h m	h m
1	5 41	18·8	31	37	9 01	1 55	1 42
6	5 57	19·2	29	40	8 58	1 49	1 36
11	6 14	19·5	27	43	8 55	1 45	1 31
16	6 33	19·6	25	47	8 55	1 43	1 29
21	6 53	19·7	24	49	8 55	1 43	1 29
26	7 13	19·5	23	52	8 55	1 45	1 31
31	7 34	19·2	22	55	8 57	1 48	1 34

MARS ♂

Day	R.A.	Dec. −	Diam.	Phase	Transit	5° high. 52°	5° high. 56°
	h m	°	″		h m	h m	h m
1	0 34	1·4	17	89	3 54	22 31	22 36
6	0 39	1·0	18	90	3 40	22 15	22 19
11	0 44	0·7	19	91	3 25	21 58	22 02
16	0 47	0·4	19	92	3 08	21 40	21 44
21	0 49	0·3	20	93	2 51	21 22	21 26
26	0 50	0·3	21	94	2 32	21 03	21 07
31	0 50	0·4	22	96	2 12	20 44	20 47

SUNRISE AND SUNSET

Day	London a.m.	London p.m.	Bristol a.m.	Bristol p.m.	Birmingham a.m.	Birmingham p.m.	Manchester a.m.	Manchester p.m.	Newcastle a.m.	Newcastle p.m.	Glasgow a.m.	Glasgow p.m.	Belfast a.m.	Belfast p.m.
	h m	h m	h m	h m	h m	h m	h m	h m	h m	h m	h m	h m	h m	h m
1	4 23	7 49	4 33	7 59	4 26	8 00	4 23	8 06	4 14	8 10	4 21	8 25	4 33	8 26
2	4 24	7 47	4 34	7 57	4 27	7 58	4 25	8 04	4 16	8 08	4 23	8 23	4 35	8 24
3	4 26	7 45	4 36	7 55	4 29	7 56	4 27	8 02	4 18	8 05	4 25	8 20	4 37	8 22
4	4 27	7 43	4 37	7 53	4 30	7 54	4 28	8 00	4 19	8 03	4 26	8 18	4 38	8 20
5	4 29	7 42	4 39	7 52	4 32	7 53	4 30	7 59	4 21	8 02	4 28	8 16	4 40	8 18
6	4 31	7 40	4 41	7 50	4 34	7 51	4 32	7 57	4 23	8 00	4 30	8 14	4 42	8 16
7	4 32	7 38	4 42	7 48	4 35	7 49	4 34	7 55	4 25	7 58	4 32	8 12	4 44	8 14
8	4 34	7 37	4 44	7 46	4 37	7 47	4 35	7 53	4 26	7 56	4 34	8 10	4 46	8 12
9	4 35	7 35	4 45	7 44	4 38	7 45	4 37	7 51	4 28	7 54	4 36	8 08	4 48	8 10
10	4 37	7 33	4 47	7 42	4 40	7 43	4 39	7 48	4 30	7 51	4 38	8 05	4 50	8 07
11	4 39	7 31	4 49	7 40	4 42	7 41	4 41	7 46	4 32	7 49	4 40	8 03	4 52	8 05
12	4 40	7 29	4 50	7 39	4 44	7 39	4 43	7 44	4 34	7 47	4 42	8 01	4 54	8 03
13	4 42	7 28	4 52	7 37	4 46	7 37	4 45	7 42	4 36	7 44	4 44	7 58	4 55	8 01
14	4 43	7 26	4 53	7 35	4 47	7 35	4 46	7 40	4 38	7 42	4 46	7 56	4 57	7 59
15	4 45	7 24	4 55	7 33	4 49	7 33	4 48	7 38	4 40	7 40	4 48	7 54	4 59	7 57
16	4 46	7 22	4 56	7 31	4 51	7 31	4 50	7 36	4 42	7 38	4 50	7 52	5 01	7 55
17	4 48	7 20	4 58	7 29	4 52	7 29	4 51	7 34	4 43	7 36	4 51	7 50	5 02	7 53
18	4 49	7 17	4 59	7 27	4 54	7 26	4 53	7 31	4 45	7 33	4 53	7 48	5 04	7 50
19	4 51	7 15	5 01	7 25	4 56	7 24	4 55	7 29	4 47	7 31	4 55	7 45	5 06	7 48
20	4 52	7 13	5 02	7 23	4 57	7 22	4 56	7 27	4 49	7 29	4 57	7 43	5 08	7 46
21	4 54	7 11	5 04	7 21	4 59	7 20	4 58	7 25	4 51	7 26	4 59	7 40	5 10	7 43
22	4 56	7 09	5 06	7 19	5 01	7 18	5 00	7 23	4 53	7 24	5 01	7 38	5 11	7 41
23	4 57	7 07	5 07	7 17	5 02	7 16	5 01	7 21	4 55	7 21	5 03	7 35	5 13	7 39
24	4 59	7 05	5 09	7 15	5 04	7 14	5 03	7 19	4 56	7 19	5 04	7 33	5 15	7 37
25	5 00	7 03	5 10	7 13	5 05	7 12	5 05	7 16	4 58	7 16	5 06	7 30	5 17	7 34
26	5 02	7 00	5 12	7 10	5 07	7 09	5 07	7 14	5 00	7 14	5 08	7 28	5 19	7 32
27	5 04	6 58	5 14	7 08	5 09	7 07	5 08	7 12	5 02	7 12	5 10	7 25	5 20	7 29
28	5 05	6 56	5 15	7 06	5 10	7 05	5 10	7 09	5 04	7 09	5 12	7 23	5 22	7 27
29	5 07	6 54	5 17	7 04	5 12	7 03	5 12	7 07	5 06	7 07	5 14	7 20	5 24	7 24
30	5 09	6 52	5 19	7 02	5 14	7 01	5 14	7 04	5 08	7 04	5 16	7 18	5 26	7 22
31	5 10	6 49	5 20	6 59	5 15	6 58	5 15	7 02	5 09	7 02	5 18	7 15	5 28	7 19

JUPITER ♃ / SATURN ♄

Day	Jupiter R.A.	Jupiter Dec. +	Jupiter Transit	Jupiter 5° high. 52°	Jupiter 5° high. 56°	Saturn R.A.	Saturn Dec. −	Saturn Transit	Saturn 5° high. 52°	Saturn 5° high. 56°
	h m	°	h m	h m	h m	h m	°	h m	h m	h m
1	3 59	19·6	7 19	0 09	23 51	17 45	22·3	21 02	0 15	23 38
11	4 05	19·8	6 45	23 30	23 16	17 44	22·4	20 22	23 30	22 57
21	4 10	20·0	6 11	22 54	22 40	17 43	22·4	19 41	22 49	22 16
31	4 14	20·2	5 35	22 18	22 04	17 42	22·4	19 02	22 10	21 36

Equatorial diameter of Jupiter 39″; of Saturn 18″. Diameters of Saturn's rings 40″ and 18″.

URANUS ♅ / NEPTUNE ♆

Day	Uranus R.A.	Uranus Dec. −	Uranus Transit	Uranus 10° high. 52°	Uranus 10° high. 56°	Neptune R.A.	Neptune Dec. −	Neptune Transit	Neptune 10° high. 52°	Neptune 10° high. 56°
	h m	° ′	h m	h m	h m	h m	° ′	h m	h m	h m
1	17 49·3	23 38	21 06	23 05	21 42	18 34·6	22 13	21 52	0 12	23 11
11	17 48·2	23 38	20 26	22 25	21 02	18 33·7	22 14	21 12	23 28	22 30
21	17 47·5	23 38	19 46	21 45	20 22	18 33·0	22 15	20 31	22 47	21 50
31	17 47·1	23 38	19 06	21 05	19 43	18 32·5	22 16	19 52	22 07	21 10

Diameter 4″ Diameter 2″

Septem (seven), 7th month of Roman (pre-Julian) Calendar.

Sun's Longitude 180° ♎ $22^d\ 19^h$

Day of Month	Day of Week	
1	Th.	Ponchielli b. 1834. Englebert Humperdinck b. 1854.
2	F.	Fire of London 1666. Frederick Soddy b. 1877.
3	S.	Start of World War II 1939.
4	S.	**14th S. after Trinity.** Anton Bruckner b. 1824.
5	M.	Jesse James b. 1847. John Gilpin d. 1983.
6	Tu.	James II d. 1701. Walford Davies b. 1869.
7	W.	Elizabeth I b. 1533. Holman Hunt d. 1910.
8	Th.	**Blessed Virgin Mary.** Antonin Dvořák b. 1841.
9	F.	William I d. 1087. Soap rationing ended 1950.
10	S.	Treaty of St. Germain 1919.
11	S.	**15th S. after Trinity.** David Ricardo d. 1823.
12	M.	H. H. Asquith b. 1852. Maurice Chevalier b. 1888.*
13	Tu.	Quebec captured. Gen. Wolfe d. 1759.
14	W.	Dante Aligheri d. 1321. Isadora Duncan d. 1927.
15	Th.	PRINCE HENRY OF WALES b. 1984. BATTLE OF BRITAIN DAY.
16	F.	Henry V b. 1387. Maria Callas d. 1977.
17	S.	Smollett d. 1771. W. H. Fox Talbot d. 1877.
18	S.	**16th S. after Trinity.** William Hazlitt d. 1830.
19	M.	George Cadbury b. 1839. Sir James Dewar b. 1842.
20	Tu.	Mungo Park b. 1771. Jean Sibelius d. 1957.
21	W.	**St. Matthew.** Girolamo Savonarola b. 1452.
22	Th.	Zutphen 1586. Michael Faraday b. 1791.
23	F.	Wilkie Collins d. 1889. Sigmund Freud d. 1939.
24	S.	Horace Walpole b. 1717. Scott Fitzgerald b. 1896.
25	S.	**17th S. after Trinity.** Johann Strauss b. 1849.
26	M.	T. S. Eliot b. 1888.* Béla Bartok d. 1945.
27	Tu.	Edward II d. 1327. Sylvia Pankhurst d. 1960.
28	W.	Cyril McNeile (Sapper) b. 1888.* Pasteur d. 1895.
29	Th.	**St. Michael and All Angels.** Lord Clive b. 1725.
30	F.	Pierre Corneille d. 1684. Lord Raglan b. 1788.*

PHENOMENA

September $2^d\ 20^h$ Jupiter in conjunction with the Moon. Jupiter 6° S.

$6^d\ 23^h$ Venus in conjunction with the Moon. Venus 6° S.

$13^d\ 16^h$ Mercury in conjunction with the Moon. Mercury 0°·6 N.

$15^d\ 22^h$ Mercury at greatest eastern elongation (27°).

$19^d\ 03^h$ Saturn in conjunction with the Moon. Saturn 6° N.

$22^d\ 19^h$ Equinox.

$26^d\ 04^h$ Mars in conjunction with the Moon. Mars 7° S.

$28^d\ 04^h$ Mars at opposition.

$30^d\ 05^h$ Jupiter in conjunction with the Moon. Jupiter 6° S.

CONSTELLATIONS

The following constellations are near the meridian at

	d	h		d	h
Aug.	1	24	Aug.	16	23
Sept.	1	22	Sept.	15	21
Oct.	1	20	Oct.	16	19

Draco, Cepheus, Lyra, Cygnus, Vulpecula, Sagitta, Delphinus, Equuleus, Aquila, Aquarius and Capricornus.

MINIMA OF ALGOL

d	h	d	h
3	7	17	15
6	4	20	12
8	1	23	9
11	22	26	6
14	18	29	2

* Centenary.

PHASES OF THE MOON

	d	h	m
☾ Last Quarter	3	03	50
● New Moon	11	04	49
☽ First Quarter	19	03	18
○ Full Moon	25	19	07

	d	h
Apogee (406,480 kilometres)	10	15
Perigee (357,680 „)	25	04

Mean Longitude of Ascending Node on Sept. 1, 344°

See note on *Summer Time*, p. 98.

MONTHLY NOTES

Sept. 1. Partridge shooting begins.
12. Jewish New Year (A.M. 5749).
21. Jewish Day of Atonement (Yom Kippur).
26. First Day of Tabernacles.
29. Michaelmas. Quarter day.

Day	Right Ascension	Dec.	Equation of Time	Rise 52°	Rise 56°	Transit	Set 52°	Set 56°	Sidereal Time	Transit of First Point of Aries
	h m s	° ′	m s	h m	h m	h m	h m	h m	h m s	h m s
1	10 41 32	+8 17	− 0 03	5 12	5 04	12 00	18 47	18 54	22 41 30	1 18 17
2	10 45 10	+7 55	+ 0 17	5 13	5 06	12 00	18 45	18 51	22 45 26	1 14 21
3	10 48 47	+7 33	+ 0 36	5 15	5 08	11 59	18 42	18 49	22 49 23	1 10 25
4	10 52 24	+7 11	+ 0 56	5 17	5 10	11 59	18 40	18 46	22 53 20	1 06 29
5	10 56 01	+6 49	+ 1 15	5 18	5 12	11 59	18 38	18 44	22 57 16	1 02 34
6	10 59 37	+6 27	+ 1 36	5 20	5 14	11 58	18 35	18 41	23 01 13	0 58 38
7	11 03 13	+6 04	+ 1 56	5 22	5 16	11 58	18 33	18 38	23 05 09	0 54 42
8	11 06 49	+5 42	+ 2 16	5 23	5 18	11 58	18 31	18 36	23 09 06	0 50 46
9	11 10 25	+5 19	+ 2 37	5 25	5 20	11 57	18 28	18 33	23 13 02	0 46 50
10	11 14 01	+4 56	+ 2 58	5 27	5 22	11 57	18 26	18 30	23 16 59	0 42 54
11	11 17 37	+4 34	+ 3 19	5 28	5 24	11 57	18 24	18 28	23 20 55	0 38 58
12	11 21 12	+4 11	+ 3 40	5 30	5 26	11 56	18 21	18 25	23 24 52	0 35 02
13	11 24 48	+3 48	+ 4 01	5 31	5 28	11 56	18 19	18 23	23 28 49	0 31 06
14	11 28 23	+3 25	+ 4 22	5 33	5 30	11 55	18 17	18 20	23 32 45	0 27 10
15	11 31 58	+3 02	+ 4 43	5 35	5 32	11 55	18 15	18 17	23 36 42	0 23 14
16	11 35 34	+2 39	+ 5 05	5 36	5 34	11 55	18 12	18 15	23 40 38	0 19 19
17	11 39 09	+2 15	+ 5 26	5 38	5 36	11 54	18 10	18 12	23 44 35	0 15 23
18	11 42 44	+1 52	+ 5 47	5 40	5 38	11 54	18 07	18 09	23 48 31	0 11 27
19	11 46 19	+1 29	+ 6 09	5 41	5 40	11 54	18 05	18 07	23 52 28	0 07 31
20	11 49 54	+1 06	+ 6 30	5 43	5 41	11 53	18 03	18 04	23 56 24	0 03 35
21	11 53 30	+0 42	+ 6 51	5 44	5 43	11 53	18 00	18 01	0 00 21	{ 23 59 39 / 23 55 43 }
22	11 57 05	+0 19	+ 7 13	5 46	5 45	11 53	17 58	17 59	0 04 18	23 51 47
23	12 00 40	−0 04	+ 7 34	5 48	5 47	11 52	17 56	17 56	0 08 14	23 47 51
24	12 04 16	−0 28	+ 7 55	5 49	5 49	11 52	17 53	17 53	0 12 11	23 43 55
25	12 07 52	−0 51	+ 8 16	5 51	5 51	11 52	17 51	17 51	0 16 07	23 40 00
26	12 11 27	−1 14	+ 8 36	5 53	5 53	11 51	17 49	17 48	0 20 04	23 36 04
27	12 15 03	−1 38	+ 8 57	5 54	5 55	11 51	17 46	17 45	0 24 00	23 32 08
28	12 18 40	−2 01	+ 9 17	5 56	5 57	11 51	17 44	17 43	0 27 57	23 28 12
29	12 22 16	−2 25	+ 9 37	5 58	5 59	11 50	17 42	17 40	0 31 53	23 24 16
30	12 25 53	−2 48	+ 9 57	5 59	6 01	11 50	17 39	17 37	0 35 50	23 20 20

Duration of Civil (C), Nautical (N), and Astronomical (A), Twilight (in minutes)

Lat. °	Sept. 1 C	N	A	Sept. 11 C	N	A	Sept. 21 C	N	A	Sept. 30 C	N	A
52	35	79	127	34	76	120	34	74	115	34	73	113
56	39	89	146	38	84	135	37	82	129	37	80	126

ASTRONOMICAL NOTES

MERCURY is unfavourably placed for observation from these latitudes even though it attains greatest eastern elongation on the 15th.

VENUS is still a brilliant object in the morning skies, magnitude −4·2, and visible in the eastern sky for several hours before dawn.

MARS is at opposition on the 28th, although because of the eccentricity of its orbit, it is actually closest to the Earth six days earlier. It will then be 59 million kilometres from the Earth—closer than at any time for the rest of this century. Mars reaches a magnitude of −2·8 at opposition and is thus a brilliant object visible throughout the hours of darkness. The Full Moon passes 7° N. of Mars on the morning of the 26th.

JUPITER, magnitude −2·5, continues to be visible as a prominent object in the night sky. Jupiter is in Taurus.

SATURN continues to be visible as an evening object, magnitude +0·5, low in the south-western sky.

ECLIPSE. An annular eclipse of the Sun occurs on the 11th. See page 148 for details.

ZODIACAL LIGHT. The morning cone may be seen stretching up from the eastern horizon before the beginning of morning twilight from the 9th to the 24th. This faint phenomenon is only visible under good conditions, in the absence of both moonlight and artifical lighting.

THE MOON

Day	R.A.	Dec.	Hor. Par.	Semi-diam.	Sun's Co-long.	P.A. of Bright Limb	Phase	Age	Rise 52°	Rise 56°	Transit	Set 52°	Set 56°
	h m	°	′	′	°	°		d	h m	h m	h m	h m	h m
1	2 31	+19·6	58·9	16·0	146	69	73	19·5	20 20	19 55	3 58	12 19	12 43
2	3 27	+24·0	58·0	15·8	158	74	62	20·5	20 49	20 16	4 52	13 44	14 16
3	4 24	+27·0	57·1	15·6	170	81	52	21·5	21 30	20 52	5 48	15 00	15 38
4	5 23	+28·4	56·3	15·3	182	87	41	22·5	22 25	21 46	6 44	16 00	16 40
5	6 20	+28·3	55·6	15·1	195	94	32	23·5	23 32	22 58	7 39	16 44	17 19
6	7 15	+26·8	55·0	15·0	207	100	23	24·5	..	..	8 31	17 14	17 43
7	8 07	+24·1	54·6	14·9	219	106	15	25·5	0 46	0 18	9 20	17 35	17 57
8	8 57	+20·3	54·3	14·8	231	110	9	26·5	2 01	1 41	10 06	17 51	18 06
9	9 43	+15·8	54·1	14·7	243	114	4	27·5	3 15	3 01	10 48	18 02	18 13
10	10 27	+10·7	54·0	14·7	256	115	1	28·5	4 27	4 19	11 28	18 12	18 18
11	11 09	+ 5·2	53·9	14·7	268	108	0	29·5	5 38	5 34	12 07	18 21	18 22
12	11 51	− 0·4	54·0	14·7	280	302	1	0·8	6 48	6 50	12 46	18 30	18 26
13	12 33	− 6·1	54·2	14·8	292	300	3	1·8	7 59	8 06	13 26	18 40	18 31
14	13 16	−11·5	54·4	14·8	305	298	7	2·8	9 11	9 24	14 07	18 51	18 37
15	14 01	−16·7	54·8	14·9	317	295	13	3·8	10 27	10 46	14 51	19 05	18 45
16	14 49	−21·2	55·3	15·1	329	291	20	4·8	11 45	12 11	15 39	19 25	18 55
17	15 41	−24·8	55·8	15·2	341	286	29	5·8	13 03	13 37	16 32	19 55	19 20
18	16 37	−27·4	56·5	15·4	353	279	38	6·8	14 15	14 55	17 28	20 38	19 58
19	17 35	−28·5	57·3	15·6	6	273	49	7·8	15 16	15 55	18 27	21 40	21 01
20	18 36	−28·0	58·2	15·8	18	265	59	8·8	16 00	16 34	19 26	23 00	22 27
21	19 38	−25·8	59·0	16·1	30	259	70	9·8	16 31	16 56	20 25	..	..
22	20 38	−21·9	59·9	16·3	42	253	80	10·8	16 53	17 10	21 21	0 30	0 06
23	21 35	−16·5	60·6	16·5	54	249	89	11·8	17 09	17 20	22 15	2 04	1 49
24	22 31	−10·1	61·1	16·6	67	247	95	12·8	17 23	17 27	23 07	3 38	3 30
25	23 25	− 3·1	61·3	16·7	79	250	99	13·8	17 35	17 33	23 59	5 11	5 10
26	0 19	+ 4·2	61·2	16·7	91	32	100	14·8	17 48	17 40	..	6 44	6 49
27	1 13	+11·1	60·8	16·6	103	57	98	15·8	18 03	17 49	0 51	8 16	8 29
28	2 08	+17·4	60·1	16·4	115	63	93	16·8	18 22	18 00	1 44	9 49	10 09
29	3 06	+22·4	59·2	16·1	127	69	86	17·8	18 48	18 19	2 40	11 20	11 48
30	4 05	+26·1	58·2	15·9	140	76	77	18·8	19 25	18 49	3 37	12 43	13 19

MERCURY ☿

Day	R.A.	Dec. −	Diam.	Phase	Transit		Day	R.A.	Dec. −	Diam.	Phase	Transit	
	h m	°	″		h m			h m	°	″		h m	
1	12 05	1·2	6	76	13 24		16	13 09	10·2	7	57	13 28	
4	12 20	3·2	6	73	13 27	Mercury is too	19	13 19	11·6	7	52	13 26	Mercury is too
7	12 34	5·2	6	70	13 29	close to the	22	13 27	12·7	8	46	13 21	close to the
10	12 46	7·0	6	66	13 30	Sun for	25	13 32	13·5	8	39	13 15	Sun for
13	12 58	8·7	7	62	13 30	observation	28	13 35	13·9	9	31	13 05	observation
16	13 09	10·2	7	57	13 28		31	13 34	13·8	9	22	12 52	

VENUS ♀ — MARS ♂

Day	R.A.	Dec. +	Diam.	Phase	Transit	5° high. 52°	5° high. 56°	Day	R.A.	Dec. −	Diam.	Phase	Transit	5° high. 52°	5° high. 56°
	h m	°	″		h m	h m	h m		h m	°	″		h m	h m	h m
1	7 39	19·2	21	55	8 57	1 49	1 35	1	0 50	0·4	22	96	2 08	20 40	20 43
6	8 01	18·6	20	58	9 00	1 54	1 41	6	0 48	0·6	23	97	1 46	20 19	20 23
11	8 23	17·9	19	60	9 02	2 01	1 49	11	0 44	0·9	23	98	1 23	19 57	20 01
16	8 45	16·9	19	62	9 05	2 09	1 58	16	0 40	1·3	23	99	0 59	19 35	19 39
21	9 08	15·8	18	64	9 08	2 18	2 08	21	0 35	1·6	24	99	0 34	19 12	19 16
26	9 30	14·4	17	66	9 10	2 28	2 19	26	0 29	2·0	24	100	0 09	18 48	18 53
31	9 53	12·9	17	68	9 13	2 39	2 32	31	0 23	2·3	23	100	23 38	18 24	18 29

Day														SUNRISE AND SUNSET			

SUNRISE AND SUNSET

Day	London a.m.	London p.m.	Bristol a.m.	Bristol p.m.	Birmingham a.m.	Birmingham p.m.	Manchester a.m.	Manchester p.m.	Newcastle a.m.	Newcastle p.m.	Glasgow a.m.	Glasgow p.m.	Belfast a.m.	Belfast p.m.
	h m	h m	h m	h m	h m	h m	h m	h m	h m	h m	h m	h m	h m	h m
1	5 12	6 47	5 22	6 57	5 17	6 56	5 17	7 00	5 11	7 00	5 20	7 13	5 30	7 17
2	5 13	6 45	5 23	6 55	5 18	6 54	5 19	6 57	5 13	6 57	5 22	7 10	5 32	7 14
3	5 15	6 43	5 25	6 53	5 20	6 52	5 21	6 55	5 15	6 54	5 24	7 07	5 34	7 12
4	5 17	6 40	5 27	6 50	5 22	6 49	5 23	6 52	5 17	6 52	5 26	7 05	5 36	7 09
5	5 18	6 38	5 28	6 48	5 23	6 47	5 24	6 50	5 19	6 49	5 28	7 02	5 37	7 07
6	5 20	6 36	5 30	6 46	5 25	6 44	5 26	6 47	5 21	6 47	5 30	7 00	5 39	7 04
7	5 22	6 34	5 32	6 43	5 27	6 42	5 28	6 45	5 23	6 44	5 32	6 57	5 41	7 02
8	5 23	6 32	5 33	6 41	5 29	6 40	5 30	6 43	5 25	6 41	5 34	6 54	5 43	7 00
9	5 25	6 30	5 35	6 39	5 31	6 37	5 32	6 40	5 27	6 39	5 36	6 52	5 45	6 57
10	5 27	6 27	5 37	6 36	5 32	6 35	5 33	6 38	5 28	6 37	5 38	6 49	5 46	6 55
11	5 28	6 25	5 38	6 34	5 34	6 32	5 35	6 35	5 30	6 34	5 40	6 46	5 48	6 52
12	5 30	6 23	5 40	6 32	5 36	6 30	5 37	6 33	5 32	6 32	5 42	6 44	5 50	6 50
13	5 31	6 20	5 41	6 30	5 37	6 27	5 38	6 30	5 34	6 29	5 44	6 41	5 52	6 47
14	5 32	6 18	5 42	6 28	5 39	6 25	5 40	6 28	5 36	6 26	5 46	6 38	5 54	6 44
15	5 34	6 16	5 44	6 26	5 41	6 23	5 42	6 26	5 38	6 24	5 48	6 36	5 56	6 42
16	5 36	6 13	5 46	6 23	5 42	6 20	5 43	6 23	5 40	6 21	5 50	6 33	5 58	6 39
17	5 37	6 11	5 47	6 21	5 44	6 18	5 45	6 21	5 42	6 18	5 52	6 30	6 00	6 36
18	5 39	6 09	5 49	6 19	5 46	6 16	5 47	6 19	5 43	6 16	5 53	6 28	6 02	6 34
19	5 40	6 06	5 50	6 16	5 47	6 13	5 48	6 16	5 45	6 14	5 55	6 25	6 03	6 31
20	5 42	6 04	5 52	6 14	5 49	6 11	5 50	6 14	5 47	6 11	5 57	6 22	6 05	6 29
21	5 44	6 02	5 54	6 12	5 51	6 09	5 52	6 11	5 49	6 08	5 59	6 20	6 07	6 26
22	5 45	5 59	5 55	6 09	5 52	6 06	5 54	6 09	5 51	6 06	6 01	6 17	6 09	6 24
23	5 47	5 57	5 57	6 07	5 54	6 04	5 56	6 06	5 53	6 03	6 03	6 14	6 11	6 21
24	5 48	5 55	5 58	6 05	5 55	6 02	5 57	6 04	5 54	6 01	6 05	6 12	6 12	6 19
25	5 50	5 52	6 00	6 02	5 57	5 59	5 59	6 01	5 56	5 58	6 07	6 09	6 14	6 16
26	5 52	5 50	6 02	6 00	5 59	5 57	6 01	5 59	5 58	5 56	6 09	6 06	6 16	6 14
27	5 54	5 48	6 04	5 58	6 01	5 55	6 03	5 56	6 00	5 53	6 11	6 04	6 18	6 11
28	5 55	5 46	6 05	5 56	6 02	5 53	6 05	5 54	6 02	5 51	6 13	6 01	6 20	6 09
29	5 57	5 44	6 07	5 54	6 04	5 51	6 06	5 52	6 03	5 48	6 15	5 59	6 21	6 06
30	5 58	5 41	6 08	5 51	6 05	5 48	6 08	5 49	6 05	5 46	6 17	5 56	6 23	6 04

JUPITER ♃ — SATURN ♄

Day	JUPITER R.A.	JUPITER Dec. +	JUPITER Transit	JUPITER 5° high. 52°	JUPITER 5° high. 56°	SATURN R.A.	SATURN Dec. −	SATURN Transit	SATURN 5° high. 52°	SATURN 5° high. 56°
	h m	°	h m	h m	h m	h m	°	h m	h m	h m
1	4 14	20·2	5 32	22 14	22 00	17 42	22·4	18 58	22 06	21 32
11	4 16	20·3	4 55	21 37	21 22	17 43	22·4	18 19	21 27	20 53
21	4 18	20·3	4 17	20 59	20 44	17 44	22·5	17 41	20 48	20 15
31	4 17	20·3	3 37	20 19	20 04	17 46	22·5	17 03	20 10	19 37

Equatorial diameter of Jupiter 43″; of Saturn 17″. Diameters of Saturn's rings 38″ and 17″.

URANUS ♅ — NEPTUNE ♆

Day	URANUS R.A.	URANUS Dec. −	URANUS Transit	URANUS 10° high. 52°	URANUS 10° high. 56°	NEPTUNE R.A.	NEPTUNE Dec. −	NEPTUNE Transit	NEPTUNE 10° high. 52°	NEPTUNE 10° high. 56°
	h m	° ′	h m	h m	h m	h m	° ′	h m	h m	h m
1	17 47·1	23 38	19 03	21 01	19 39	18 32·5	22 16	19 48	22 03	21 06
11	17 47·2	23 38	18 23	20 22	19 00	18 32·2	22 17	19 08	21 24	20 26
21	17 47·5	23 38	17 44	19 43	18 21	18 32·1	22 17	18 29	20 44	19 46
31	17 48·3	23 38	17 06	19 05	17 42	18 32·3	22 17	17 50	20 05	19 07

Diameter 4″ — Diameter 2″

DAY OF		
Month	Week	*Octo* (eight), 8th month of Roman (pre-Julian) Calendar. ♎ ♏ *Sun's Longitude* 210° ♏ 23ᵈ 05ʰ

1	S.	First issue of *News of the World* 1843.
2	℟.	**18th S. after Trinity.** Archbp. of Canterbury
3	M.	MICHAELMAS LAW SITTINGS BEGIN. [b. 1921.
4	Tu.	Max Planck d. 1947. *Sputnik I* launched 1957.
5	W.	R101 disaster 1930. Tea rationing ended 1952.
6	Th.	Jenny Lind b. 1820. Thor Heyerdahl b. 1914.
7	F.	Sir Hubert Parry d. 1918. Marie Lloyd d. 1922.
8	S.	Great Fire of Chicago 1871.
9	℟.	**19th S. after Trinity.** John Lennon b. 1940.
10	M.	Henry Cavendish b. 1731. Giusseppe Verdi b. 1813.
11	Tu.	James Joule d. 1889. Jean Cocteau d. 1963.
12	W.	Vaughan Williams d. 1872. Robert Stephenson d.
13	Th.	Margaret Thatcher b. 1925. [1859.
14	F.	de Valera b. 1882. Katherine Mansfield b. 1888.*
15	S.	Dr. Marie Stopes b. 1880. Cole Porter d. 1964.
16	℟.	**20th S. after Trinity.** Eugene O'Neill b. 1888.*
17	M.	Saratoga 1777. Frederic Chopin d. 1849.
18	Tu.	**St. Luke.** Charles Babbage d. 1871.
19	W.	John I d. 1216. Charles I b. 1600.
20	Th.	Sir Christopher Wren b. 1632. Grace Darling d.
21	F.	Trafalgar 1805. Sir Georg Solti b. 1912. [1842.
22	S.	Franz Liszt b. 1811. Pablo Casals d. 1973.
23	℟.	**21st S. after Trinity.** Edgehill 1642.
24	M.	Alessandro Scarlatti d. 1725. Tito Gobbi b. 1915.
25	Tu.	Geoffrey Chaucer d. 1400. Richard Byrd b. 1888.*
26	W.	Royal Marines founded 1664.
27	Th.	Dylan Thomas b. 1914.
28	F.	**SS. Simon and Jude.** Capt. Cook b. 1728.
29	S.	Edmund Halley b. 1656. Wall Street Crash 1929.
30	℟.	**22nd S. after Trinity.** Sir Barnes Wallis d. 1979.
31	M.	HALLOWMASS EVE. Indira Gandhi assass. 1984.

*Centenary.

PHENOMENA

October 7ᵈ 03ʰ Venus in conjunction with the Moon. Venus 0°·6 S.

11ᵈ 07ʰ Mercury in inferior conjunction.

16ᵈ 12ʰ Saturn in conjunction with the Moon. Saturn 6° N.

23ᵈ 04ʰ Mars in conjunction with the Moon. Mars 5° S.

26ᵈ 21ʰ Mercury at greatest western elongation (18°).

27ᵈ 12ʰ Jupiter in conjunction with the Moon. Jupiter 6° S.

CONSTELLATIONS

The following constellations are near the meridian at

	d	h		d	h
Sept.	1	24	Sept.	15	23
Oct.	1	22	Oct.	16	21
Nov.	1	20	Nov.	15	19

Ursa Major (below the Pole), Cepheus, Cassiopeia, Cygnus, Lacerta, Andromeda, Pegasus, Capricornus, Aquarius and Piscis Austrinus.

MINIMA OF ALGOL

d	h	d	h
1	23	19	4
4	20	22	1
7	17	24	22
10	14	27	19
13	10	30	15
16	7		

PHASES OF THE MOON

		d	h	m
☾	Last Quarter.......	2	16	58
●	New Moon.........	10	21	49
☽	First Quarter	18	13	01
○	Full Moon	25	04	35

	d	h
Apogee (405,980 kilometres)	7	20
Perigee (361,110 „)	23	12

Mean Longitude of Ascending Node on Oct. 1, 343°

MONTHLY NOTES

Oct. 1. Pheasant shooting begins.

     23. *Summer Time* ends at 01ʰ G.M.T.

Day	Right Ascension	Dec. −	Equation of Time	Rise 52°	Rise 56°	Transit	Set 52°	Set 56°	Sidereal Time	Transit of First Point of Aries
	h m s	° ′	m s	h m	h m	h m	h m	h m	h m s	h m s
1	12 29 30	3 11	+10 17	6 01	6 03	11 50	17 37	17 35	0 39 47	23 16 24
2	12 33 07	3 34	+10 36	6 03	6 05	11 49	17 35	17 32	0 43 43	23 12 28
3	12 36 45	3 58	+10 55	6 04	6 07	11 49	17 32	17 30	0 47 40	23 08 32
4	12 40 23	4 21	+11 13	6 06	6 09	11 49	17 30	17 27	0 51 36	23 04 36
5	12 44 01	4 44	+11 32	6 08	6 11	11 48	17 28	17 24	0 55 33	23 00 40
6	12 47 40	5 07	+11 49	6 09	6 13	11 48	17 26	17 22	0 59 29	22 56 45
7	12 51 19	5 30	+12 07	6 11	6 15	11 48	17 23	17 19	1 03 26	22 52 49
8	12 54 59	5 53	+12 24	6 13	6 17	11 47	17 21	17 17	1 07 22	22 48 53
9	12 58 39	6 16	+12 40	6 15	6 19	11 47	17 19	17 14	1 11 19	22 44 57
10	13 02 19	6 39	+12 57	6 16	6 21	11 47	17 17	17 12	1 15 16	22 41 01
11	13 06 00	7 01	+13 12	6 18	6 23	11 47	17 14	17 09	1 19 12	22 37 05
12	13 09 41	7 24	+13 27	6 20	6 25	11 46	17 12	17 06	1 23 09	22 33 09
13	13 13 23	7 46	+13 42	6 21	6 27	11 46	17 10	17 04	1 27 05	22 29 13
14	13 17 06	8 09	+13 56	6 23	6 29	11 46	17 08	17 01	1 31 02	22 25 17
15	13 20 49	8 31	+14 10	6 25	6 32	11 46	17 06	16 59	1 34 58	22 21 21
16	13 24 32	8 53	+14 23	6 27	6 34	11 45	17 03	16 56	1 38 55	22 17 25
17	13 28 16	9 15	+14 35	6 28	6 36	11 45	17 01	16 54	1 42 51	22 13 30
18	13 32 01	9 37	+14 47	6 30	6 38	11 45	16 59	16 51	1 46 48	22 09 34
19	13 35 46	9 59	+14 58	6 32	6 40	11 45	16 57	16 49	1 50 45	22 05 38
20	13 39 32	10 20	+15 09	6 34	6 42	11 45	16 55	16 47	1 54 41	22 01 42
21	13 43 18	10 42	+15 19	6 36	6 44	11 45	16 53	16 44	1 58 38	21 57 46
22	13 47 05	11 03	+15 29	6 37	6 46	11 44	16 51	16 42	2 02 34	21 53 50
23	13 50 53	11 24	+15 38	6 39	6 48	11 44	16 49	16 39	2 06 31	21 49 54
24	13 54 42	11 45	+15 46	6 41	6 50	11 44	16 47	16 37	2 10 27	21 45 58
25	13 58 31	12 06	+15 53	6 43	6 52	11 44	16 45	16 35	2 14 24	21 42 02
26	14 02 21	12 27	+16 00	6 44	6 55	11 44	16 43	16 32	2 18 20	21 38 06
27	14 06 11	12 47	+16 06	6 46	6 57	11 44	16 41	16 30	2 22 17	21 34 10
28	14 10 03	13 07	+16 11	6 48	6 59	11 44	16 39	16 28	2 26 14	21 30 15
29	14 13 55	13 27	+16 15	6 50	7 01	11 44	16 37	16 26	2 30 10	21 26 19
30	14 17 48	13 47	+16 19	6 52	7 03	11 44	16 35	16 23	2 34 07	21 22 23
31	14 21 41	14 06	+16 22	6 53	7 05	11 44	16 33	16 21	2 38 03	21 18 27

Duration of Civil (C), Nautical (N), and Astronomical (A), Twilight (in minutes)

Lat. °	Oct. 1 C	N	A	Oct. 11 C	N	A	Oct. 21 C	N	A	Oct. 31 C	N	A
52	34	73	113	34	73	112	34	74	113	36	75	114
56	37	80	125	37	80	124	38	81	124	40	83	126

ASTRONOMICAL NOTES

MERCURY is at inferior conjunction on the 11th but then moves rapidly westwards from the Sun and for the last two weeks of the month it is visible as a morning object. It may be located low above the east-south-east horizon at the time of beginning of morning civil twilight. This morning apparition is the most favourable one of the year for observers in these latitudes. Its magnitude increases from +2 to −1 during its period of visibility.

VENUS, magnitude −4·1, is a brilliant morning object, visible in the eastern sky for several hours before dawn. On the morning of the 4th Venus will be seen approaching Regulus, passing only 0°·2 S. of it shortly after sunrise. On the morning of the 7th Venus and the old crescent Moon rise together, between 02^h and 03^h; in fact countries to the east of the British Isles will see an actual occultation.

MARS, magnitude −2, is a brilliant object, visible as soon as it is dark and remaining so for most of the night. Mars is in Pisces.

JUPITER, magnitude −2·7, is a brilliant object in Taurus. It is visible for the greater part of the night.

SATURN, magnitude +0·6, is still visible low in the south-western sky in the early part of the evening.

THE MOON

Day	R.A.	Dec.	Hor. Par.	Semi-diam.	Sun's Co-long.	P.A. of Bright Limb	Phase	Age	Rise 52°	Rise 56°	Transit	Set 52°	Set 56°
	h m	°	′	′	°	°		d	h m	h m	h m	h m	h m
1	5 04	+28·1	57·3	15·6	152	83	67	19·8	20 16	19 37	4 35	13 51	14 31
2	6 03	+28·5	56·4	15·4	164	90	57	20·8	21 21	20 44	5 32	14 42	15 19
3	7 00	+27·3	55·6	15·2	176	96	47	21·8	22 33	22 04	6 26	15 17	15 48
4	7 54	+24·9	55·0	15·0	188	102	37	22·8	23 49	23 26	7 17	15 41	16 05
5	8 44	+21·3	54·5	14·9	201	107	28	23·8	..	..	8 03	15 58	16 16
6	9 31	+17·0	54·2	14·8	213	110	20	24·8	1 03	0 47	8 47	16 11	16 23
7	10 16	+12·0	54·1	14·7	225	112	13	25·8	2 16	2 06	9 28	16 22	16 29
8	10 58	+ 6·7	54·0	14·7	237	113	7	26·8	3 27	3 22	10 07	16 31	16 33
9	11 40	+ 1·1	54·1	14·7	249	111	3	27·8	4 37	4 37	10 46	16 40	16 37
10	12 22	− 4·6	54·2	14·8	262	102	1	28·8	5 48	5 53	11 25	16 49	16 42
11	13 05	−10·2	54·5	14·8	274	4	0	0·1	7 00	7 11	12 06	17 00	16 48
12	13 50	−15·4	54·8	14·9	286	308	1	1·1	8 15	8 32	12 50	17 14	16 55
13	14 38	−20·1	55·2	15·0	298	298	4	2·1	9 33	9 56	13 37	17 32	17 07
14	15 29	−24·0	55·6	15·2	310	291	9	3·1	10 51	11 22	14 28	17 58	17 26
15	16 23	−26·8	56·1	15·3	323	284	16	4·1	12 05	12 43	15 23	18 37	17 58
16	17 21	−28·3	56·7	15·4	335	277	24	5·1	13 09	13 49	16 20	19 32	18 52
17	18 21	−28·2	57·3	15·6	347	270	34	6·1	13 58	14 33	17 18	20 44	20 09
18	19 20	−26·5	58·0	15·8	359	263	44	7·1	14 32	15 00	18 15	22 08	21 41
19	20 19	−23·1	58·7	16·0	11	257	55	8·1	14 56	15 16	19 10	23 37	23 19
20	21 16	−18·4	59·4	16·2	24	252	66	9·1	15 13	15 27	20 03	..	..
21	22 10	−12·6	60·0	16·3	36	249	77	10·1	15 28	15 35	20 54	1 08	0 56
22	23 03	− 6·0	60·4	16·5	48	247	86	11·1	15 40	15 41	21 44	2 38	2 33
23	23 55	+ 1·1	60·7	16·5	60	249	93	12·1	15 53	15 48	22 35	4 08	4 10
24	0 48	+ 8·1	60·7	16·5	72	256	98	13·1	16 07	15 56	23 27	5 39	5 48
25	1 43	+14·6	60·4	16·5	84	303	100	14·1	16 24	16 06	..	7 12	7 28
26	2 40	+20·3	59·9	16·3	97	50	99	15·1	16 46	16 21	0 22	8 45	9 09
27	3 39	+24·6	59·2	16·1	109	66	95	16·1	17 19	16 46	1 20	10 14	10 47
28	4 40	+27·3	58·3	15·9	121	76	90	17·1	18 05	17 26	2 20	11 32	12 10
29	5 41	+28·4	57·4	15·6	133	84	82	18·1	19 05	18 20	3 19	12 33	13 11
30	6 41	+27·7	56·5	15·4	145	92	73	19·1	20 17	19 45	4 16	13 15	13 48
31	7 37	+25·6	55·7	15·2	157	98	64	20·1	21 33	21 08	5 09	13 44	14 10

MERCURY ☿

Day	R.A.	Dec. −	Diam.	Phase	Transit		Day	R.A.	Dec. −	Diam.	Phase	Transit	5° high 52°	5° high 56°
	h m	°	″		h m			h m	°	″		h m	h m	h m
1	13 34	13·8	—	—	12 52		16	12 49	5·4	9	7	11 07	6 09	6 16
4	13 29	13·1	—	—	12 34	Mercury is too	19	12 44	4·0	9	19	10 52	5 46	5 53
7	13 21	11·7	—	—	12 13	close to the	22	12 46	3·4	8	33	10 43	5 33	5 40
10	13 09	9·7	—	—	11 50	Sun for	25	12 53	3·6	7	48	10 38	5 30	5 37
13	12 58	7·5	—	—	11 27	observation	28	13 04	4·6	7	61	10 38	5 35	5 42
16	12 49	5·4	—	—	11 07		31	13 18	5·9	6	72	10 40	5 45	5 53

VENUS ♀

Day	R.A.	Dec. +	Diam.	Phase	Transit	5° high 52°	5° high 56°
	h m	°	″		h m	h m	h m
1	9 53	12·9	17	68	9 13	2 39	2 32
6	10 15	11·2	16	70	9 16	2 51	2 45
11	10 38	9·4	16	72	9 19	3 03	2 59
16	11 00	7·4	15	74	9 21	3 16	3 13
21	11 22	5·3	15	75	9 24	3 29	3 28
26	11 45	3·2	14	77	9 27	3 43	3 44
31	12 07	0·9	14	78	9 29	3 57	4 00

MARS ♂

Day	R.A.	Dec. −	Diam.	Phase	Transit	5° high 52°	5° high 56°
	h m	°	″		h m	h m	h m
1	0 23	2·3	23	100	23 38	4 58	4 53
6	0 17	2·5	23	100	23 13	4 31	4 26
11	0 12	2·6	22	99	22 49	4 06	4 01
16	0 08	2·7	21	98	22 25	3 42	3 37
21	0 05	2·6	20	97	22 03	3 20	3 15
26	0 04	2·3	19	96	21 42	3 00	2 55
31	0 03	2·0	18	95	21 22	2 42	2 37

SUNRISE AND SUNSET

Day	London a.m. h m	London p.m. h m	Bristol a.m. h m	Bristol p.m. h m	Birmingham a.m. h m	Birmingham p.m. h m	Manchester a.m. h m	Manchester p.m. h m	Newcastle a.m. h m	Newcastle p.m. h m	Glasgow a.m. h m	Glasgow p.m. h m	Belfast a.m. h m	Belfast p.m. h m
1	6 00	5 38	6 10	5 48	6 07	5 45	6 10	5 46	6 07	5 43	6 19	5 53	6 25	6 01
2	6 02	5 36	6 12	5 46	6 09	5 43	6 12	5 44	6 09	5 41	6 21	5 51	6 27	5 59
3	6 03	5 34	6 13	5 44	6 10	5 41	6 13	5 42	6 11	5 38	6 23	5 48	6 29	5 56
4	6 05	5 32	6 15	5 42	6 12	5 38	6 15	5 39	6 13	5 35	6 25	5 45	6 31	5 53
5	6 07	5 30	6 17	5 40	6 14	5 36	6 17	5 37	6 15	5 33	6 27	5 43	6 33	5 51
6	6 08	5 27	6 18	5 37	6 15	5 34	6 18	5 35	6 17	5 30	6 29	5 40	6 35	5 48
7	6 10	5 25	6 20	5 35	6 17	5 32	6 20	5 33	6 19	5 28	6 31	5 38	6 37	5 46
8	6 12	5 23	6 21	5 33	6 19	5 29	6 22	5 30	6 21	5 25	6 33	5 35	6 39	5 43
9	6 14	5 21	6 23	5 31	6 21	5 27	6 24	5 28	6 23	5 23	6 35	5 33	6 41	5 41
10	6 15	5 19	6 24	5 29	6 23	5 24	6 26	5 25	6 25	5 20	6 37	5 30	6 43	5 38
11	6 17	5 17	6 26	5 27	6 25	5 22	6 28	5 23	6 27	5 18	6 39	5 27	6 45	5 36
12	6 19	5 14	6 28	5 24	6 26	5 20	6 29	5 21	6 28	5 16	6 41	5 25	6 46	5 34
13	6 20	5 12	6 30	5 22	6 28	5 17	6 31	5 18	6 30	5 13	6 43	5 22	6 48	5 31
14	6 22	5 10	6 31	5 20	6 30	5 15	6 33	5 16	6 32	5 11	6 45	5 20	6 50	5 29
15	6 23	5 08	6 33	5 18	6 32	5 13	6 35	5 14	6 34	5 08	6 47	5 17	6 52	5 27
16	6 25	5 06	6 35	5 16	6 34	5 11	6 37	5 11	6 36	5 06	6 49	5 15	6 54	5 24
17	6 27	5 03	6 37	5 13	6 36	5 08	6 39	5 09	6 39	5 03	6 52	5 12	6 56	5 22
18	6 28	5 01	6 38	5 11	6 37	5 06	6 41	5 07	6 41	5 01	6 54	5 10	6 58	5 20
19	6 30	4 59	6 40	5 09	6 39	5 04	6 43	5 04	6 43	4 58	6 56	5 07	7 00	5 17
20	6 32	4 57	6 42	5 07	6 41	5 02	6 45	5 02	6 45	4 56	6 58	5 05	7 02	5 15
21	6 34	4 55	6 44	5 05	6 43	5 00	6 47	5 00	6 47	4 54	7 00	5 03	7 04	5 13
22	6 35	4 53	6 45	5 03	6 44	4 58	6 48	4 58	6 48	4 52	7 02	5 00	7 06	5 10
23	6 37	4 51	6 47	5 01	6 46	4 56	6 50	4 55	6 50	4 49	7 04	4 58	7 08	5 08
24	6 39	4 49	6 49	4 59	6 48	4 54	6 52	4 53	6 52	4 47	7 06	4 55	7 10	5 05
25	6 41	4 47	6 51	4 57	6 50	4 52	6 54	4 51	6 54	4 45	7 08	4 53	7 12	5 03
26	6 42	4 45	6 52	4 55	6 51	4 50	6 56	4 49	6 56	4 43	7 10	4 51	7 14	5 01
27	6 44	4 43	6 54	4 53	6 53	4 48	6 58	4 47	6 59	4 40	7 13	4 48	7 16	4 59
28	6 46	4 41	6 56	4 51	6 55	4 46	7 00	4 45	7 01	4 38	7 15	4 46	7 18	4 57
29	6 48	4 39	6 58	4 49	6 57	4 44	7 02	4 43	7 03	4 36	7 17	4 44	7 20	4 55
30	6 49	4 37	6 59	4 47	6 58	4 42	7 03	4 41	7 05	4 34	7 19	4 42	7 22	4 53
31	6 51	4 35	7 01	4 45	7 00	4 40	7 05	4 39	7 07	4 32	7 21	4 40	7 24	4 51

JUPITER ♃   SATURN ♄

Day	R.A. h m	Dec. + °	Transit h m	5° high. 52° h m	5° high. 56° h m	R.A. h m	Dec. − °	Transit h m	5° high. 52° h m	5° high. 56° h m
1	4 17	20·3	3 37	20 19	20 04	17 46	22·5	17 03	20 10	19 37
11	4 16	20·2	2 56	19 38	19 24	17 48	22·6	16 27	19 33	19 00
21	4 13	20·1	2 14	18 57	18 43	17 51	22·6	15 50	18 57	18 23
31	4 09	19·9	1 31	18 15	18 00	17 55	22·6	15 15	18 21	17 47

Equatorial diameter of Jupiter 46″; of Saturn 16″. Diameters of Saturn's rings 36″ and 16″.

URANUS ♅   NEPTUNE ♆

Day	R.A. h m	Dec. − ° ′	Transit h m	10° high. 52° h m	10° high. 56° h m	R.A. h m	Dec. − ° ′	Transit h m	10° high. 52° h m	10° high. 56° h m
1	17 48·3	23 38	17 06	19 05	17 42	18 32·3	22 17	17 50	20 05	19 07
11	17 49·4	23 38	16 28	18 26	17 03	18 32·7	22 17	17 11	19 26	18 28
21	17 50·9	23 38	15 50	17 48	16 25	18 33·3	22 17	16 32	18 48	17 49
31	17 52·6	23 39	15 12	17 11	15 48	18 34·2	22 17	15 54	18 09	17 11

Diameter 4″   Diameter 2″

Novem (nine), 9th month of Roman (pre-Julian) Calendar.

Sun's Longitude 240° ♐ 22^d 02^h

Day of Month	Day of Week	
1	Tu.	**All Saints.** First hydrogen bomb exploded 1952.
2	W.	ALL SOULS. Marie Antoinette b. 1755.
3	Th.	First dog in space in *Sputnik II* 1957.
4	F.	William III b. 1650. Gabriel Fauré d. 1924.
5	S.	Guy Fawkes Night (1605). Lester Piggott b. 1935.
6	S.	**23rd S. after Trinity.** Tchaikovsky d. 1893.
7	M.	Marie Curie b. 1867. Gene Tunney d. 1978.
8	Tu.	César Franck d. 1890. Edward Ardizzone d. 1979.
9	W.	Edward VII b. 1841. Neville Chamberlain d. 1940.
10	Th.	Kamâl Atatürk d. 1938. Leonid Brezhnev d. 1982.
11	F.	ARMISTICE DAY 1918. Denis Wheatley d. 1977.
12	S.	Canute d. 1035. *Tirpitz* sunk 1944.
13	S.	**24th S. after Trinity.** Edward III b. 1312.
14	M.	PRINCE OF WALES b. 1948. Jawaharlal Nehru b. 1889.
15	Tu.	Brazil declared a Republic 1889.
16	W.	Opening of Suez Canal 1869.
17	Th.	Mary I d. 1558. Heitor Villa-Lobos d. 1959.
18	F.	Carl von Weber b. 1786. Louis Daguerre b. 1789.
19	S.	Franz Schubert d. 1828. Indira Gandhi b. 1917.
20	S.	**25th S. after Trinity.** QUEEN'S WEDDING DAY 1947.
21	M.	Sir Arthur Quiller Couch b. 1863.
22	Tu.	Pres. John F. Kennedy assass. 1963.
23	W.	Thomas Tallis d. 1585. Manuel de Falla b. 1876.
24	Th.	John Knox d. 1572. Baruch Spinoza b. 1632.
25	F.	Lilian Baylis d. 1937. Sir Anton Dolin d. 1983.
26	S.	William Cowper b. 1731. John McAdam d. 1836.
27	S.	**Advent Sunday.** Anders Celsius b. 1701.*
28	M.	Founding of Royal Society 1660.
29	Tu.	Claudio Monteverdi d. 1643. Gaetano Donizetti b.
30	W.	**St. Andrew.** Joyce Grenfell d. 1979. [1798.

* Centenary.

PHENOMENA

November 6^d 15^h Venus in conjunction with the Moon. Venus 5° N.

12^d 21^h Saturn in conjunction with the Moon. Saturn 6° N.

19^d 16^h Mars in conjunction with the Moon. Mars 3° S.

23^d 03^h Jupiter at opposition.

23^d 17^h Jupiter in conjunction with the Moon. Jupiter 6° S.

CONSTELLATIONS

The following constellations are near the meridian at

	d	h		d	h
Oct.	1	24	Oct.	16	23
Nov.	1	22	Nov.	15	21
Dec.	1	20	Dec.	16	19

Ursa Major (below the Pole), Cepheus Cassiopeia, Andromeda, Pegasus, Pisces, Aquarius and Cetus.

MINIMA OF ALGOL

d	h	d	h
2	12	16	20
5	9	19	17
8	6	22	14
11	3	25	11
13	23	28	7

PHASES OF THE MOON

	d	h	m
☾ Last Quarter.......	1	10	11
● New Moon.........	9	14	20
☽ First Quarter......	16	21	35
○ Full Moon.........	23	15	53

	d	h
Apogee (405,070 kilometres)	4	11
Perigee (366,480 „)	20	10

Mean Longitude of Ascending Node on Nov. 1, 341°.

MONTHLY NOTES

Nov. 1. Fox-hunting begins.
11. Martinmas. Scottish Term Day.
12. Lord Mayor's Show.
13. Remembrance Sunday.
28. Removal Day, Scotland.

Day	THE SUN s.d. 16′·2 Right Ascension	Dec. −	Equation of Time	Rise 52°	Rise 56°	Transit	Set 52°	Set 56°	Sidereal Time	Transit of First Point of Aries
	h m s	° ′	m s	h m	h m	h m	h m	h m	h m s	h m s
1	14 25 36	14 26	+16 24	6 55	7 07	11 44	16 31	16 19	2 42 00	21 14 31
2	14 29 31	14 45	+16 25	6 57	7 09	11 44	16 29	16 17	2 45 56	21 10 35
3	14 33 27	15 04	+16 26	6 59	7 12	11 44	16 28	16 15	2 49 53	21 06 39
4	14 37 24	15 22	+16 25	7 01	7 14	11 44	16 26	16 13	2 53 49	21 02 43
5	14 41 22	15 41	+16 24	7 02	7 16	11 44	16 24	16 11	2 57 46	20 58 47
6	14 45 21	15 59	+16 22	7 04	7 18	11 44	16 22	16 09	3 01 43	20 54 51
7	14 49 20	16 17	+16 19	7 06	7 20	11 44	16 21	16 07	3 05 39	20 50 55
8	14 53 20	16 34	+16 15	7 08	7 22	11 44	16 19	16 05	3 09 36	20 47 00
9	14 57 22	16 52	+16 11	7 10	7 24	11 44	16 18	16 03	3 13 32	20 43 04
10	15 01 24	17 09	+16 05	7 11	7 26	11 44	16 16	16 01	3 17 29	20 39 08
11	15 05 27	17 25	+15 59	7 13	7 29	11 44	16 14	15 59	3 21 25	20 35 12
12	15 09 30	17 42	+15 52	7 15	7 31	11 44	16 13	15 57	3 25 22	20 31 16
13	15 13 35	17 58	+15 44	7 17	7 33	11 44	16 11	15 55	3 29 18	20 27 20
14	15 17 40	18 14	+15 35	7 18	7 35	11 44	16 10	15 53	3 33 15	20 23 24
15	15 21 47	18 29	+15 25	7 20	7 37	11 45	16 09	15 52	3 37 12	20 19 28
16	15 25 54	18 44	+15 14	7 22	7 39	11 45	16 07	15 50	3 41 08	20 15 32
17	15 30 02	18 59	+15 03	7 24	7 41	11 45	16 06	15 48	3 45 05	20 11 36
18	15 34 10	19 14	+14 51	7 25	7 43	11 45	16 05	15 47	3 49 01	20 07 40
19	15 38 20	19 28	+14 38	7 27	7 45	11 45	16 03	15 45	3 52 58	20 03 44
20	15 42 30	19 42	+14 24	7 29	7 47	11 46	16 02	15 44	3 56 54	19 59 49
21	15 46 41	19 55	+14 10	7 30	7 49	11 46	16 01	15 42	4 00 51	19 55 53
22	15 50 53	20 08	+13 54	7 32	7 51	11 46	16 00	15 41	4 04 47	19 51 57
23	15 55 06	20 21	+13 38	7 34	7 53	11 47	15 59	15 40	4 08 44	19 48 01
24	15 59 19	20 33	+13 21	7 35	7 55	11 47	15 58	15 38	4 12 41	19 44 05
25	16 03 33	20 45	+13 04	7 37	7 57	11 47	15 57	15 37	4 16 37	19 40 09
26	16 07 48	20 57	+12 45	7 38	7 58	11 47	15 56	15 36	4 20 34	19 36 13
27	16 12 04	21 08	+12 26	7 40	8 00	11 48	15 55	15 35	4 24 30	19 32 17
28	16 16 21	21 18	+12 06	7 42	8 02	11 48	15 54	15 34	4 28 27	19 28 21
29	16 20 38	21 29	+11 45	7 43	8 04	11 48	15 53	15 33	4 32 23	19 24 25
30	16 24 56	21 39	+11 24	7 45	8 06	11 49	15 53	15 32	4 36 20	19 20 29

Duration of Civil (C), Nautical (N), and Astronomical (A), Twilight (in minutes)

Lat.	Nov. 1			Nov. 11			Nov. 21			Nov. 30		
°	C	N	A	C	N	A	C	N	A	C	N	A
52	36	75	115	37	78	117	38	80	120	39	82	123
56	40	84	127	41	87	130	43	90	134	45	93	137

ASTRONOMICAL NOTES

MERCURY, magnitude −0·8, continues to be visible as a morning object for the first ten days of the month, low above the east–south–east horizon at the beginning of morning civil twilight. On the morning of the 1st it passes 4° N. of Spica, though the star is two magnitudes fainter than the planet.

VENUS continues to be visible as a brilliant morning object, magnitude −4·0, visible in the eastern sky before sunrise. Venus passes 4° N. of Spica on the morning of the 17th.

MARS, magnitude about −1·3, is a bright object in the evening sky, though it actually fades by a whole magnitude during the month. By the end of November it sets at 02^h. On the early evening of the 16th the gibbous Moon passes 3° N. of the planet.

JUPITER, magnitude −2·9, is at opposition on the 23rd and is therefore visible throughout the night. It is moving slowly westwards in the constellation of Taurus, between the Pleiades and the Hyades. Also, on the evening of the 23rd the Full Moon passes 6° N. of the planet shortly after sunset.

SATURN, magnitude +0·5, is still visible low in the south-western sky in the early part of the evening, but is coming towards the end of its period of visibility and by the end of the month is not visible after 17^h.

THE MOON

Day	R.A.	Dec.	Hor. Par.	Semi-diam.	Sun's Co-long.	P.A. of Bright Limb	Phase	Age	Rise 52°	Rise 56°	Transit	Set 52°	Set 56°
	h m	°	′	′	°	°		d	h m	h m	h m	h m	h m
1	8 29	+22·3	55·1	15·0	169	104	54	21·1	22 49	22 31	5 58	14 03	14 23
2	9 17	+18·2	54·6	14·9	182	108	45	22·1	..	23 50	6 43	14 18	14 32
3	10 03	+13·4	54·3	14·8	194	111	35	23·1	0 03	..	7 25	14 29	14 38
4	10 46	+ 8·1	54·1	14·8	206	112	27	24·1	1 14	1 07	8 05	14 39	14 43
5	11 28	+ 2·6	54·2	14·8	218	113	19	25·1	2 24	2 22	8 44	14 48	14 47
6	12 10	− 3·0	54·3	14·8	230	111	12	26·1	3 34	3 38	9 23	14 58	14 52
7	12 52	− 8·6	54·6	14·9	243	108	7	27·1	4 46	4 55	10 04	15 08	14 58
8	13 37	−14·0	54·9	15·0	255	101	3	28·1	6 00	6 15	10 46	15 21	15 05
9	14 24	−18·8	55·3	15·1	267	−77	1	29·1	7 18	7 39	11 33	15 38	15 15
10	15 15	−23·0	55·8	15·2	279	331	0	0·4	8 37	9 06	12 23	16 02	15 32
11	16 10	−26·1	56·3	15·3	291	297	2	1·4	9 54	10 30	13 18	16 37	16 01
12	17 07	−27·9	56·8	15·5	304	284	6	2·4	11 02	11 42	14 15	17 27	16 48
13	18 07	−28·2	57·2	15·6	316	275	12	3·4	11 56	12 32	15 13	18 35	17 59
14	19 07	−26·8	57·7	15·7	328	267	20	4·4	12 34	13 04	16 11	19 56	19 27
15	20 06	−23·8	58·2	15·9	340	260	30	5·4	13 00	13 22	17 06	21 23	21 02
16	21 02	−19·5	58·6	16·0	352	254	40	6·4	13 19	13 34	17 58	22 51	22 37
17	21 55	−14·0	59·0	16·1	5	250	51	7·4	13 34	13 43	18 48	..	..
18	22 47	− 7·8	59·4	16·2	17	248	63	8·4	13 46	13 50	19 36	0 18	0 11
19	23 38	− 1·1	59·7	16·3	29	247	73	9·4	13 58	13 56	20 25	1 44	1 43
20	0 29	+ 5·7	59·8	16·3	41	249	83	10·4	14 11	14 03	21 15	3 11	3 17
21	1 21	+12·2	59·8	16·3	53	253	91	11·4	14 26	14 12	22 07	4 40	4 53
22	2 16	+18·1	59·6	16·2	65	261	96	12·4	14 46	14 25	23 03	6 11	6 31
23	3 14	+22·9	59·2	16·1	77	283	99	13·4	15 13	14 44	..	7 42	8 10
24	4 14	+26·3	58·7	16·0	90	31	100	14·4	15 53	15 17	0 01	9 06	9 41
25	5 16	+28·0	58·0	15·8	102	70	98	15·4	16 48	16 09	1 02	10 16	10 54
26	6 17	+28·0	57·2	15·6	114	84	93	16·4	17 56	17 22	2 01	11 07	11 42
27	7 15	+26·4	56·5	15·4	126	93	87	17·4	19 13	18 45	2 57	11 42	12 11
28	8 10	+23·4	55·8	15·2	138	100	80	18·4	20 30	20 10	3 49	12 06	12 28
29	9 00	+19·5	55·1	15·0	150	105	71	19·4	21 46	21 32	4 36	12 23	12 38
30	9 47	+14·8	54·7	14·9	162	109	62	20·4	22 59	22 50	5 20	12 35	12 46

MERCURY ☿

Day	R.A.	Dec. −	Diam.	Phase	Transit	5° high. 52°	5° high. 56°	Day	R.A.	Dec. −	Diam.	Phase	Transit	
	h m	°	″		h m	h m	h m		h m	°	″		h m	
1	13 23	6·4	6	74	10 42	5 49	5 58	16	14 51	15·5	—	—	11 11	
4	13 39	8·2	6	82	10 46	6 03	6 14	19	15 10	17·2	—	—	11 18	Mercury is too
7	13 56	10·0	5	88	10 52	6 19	6 32	22	15 29	18·7	—	—	11 25	close to the
10	14 14	11·9	5	92	10 58	6 36	6 51	25	15 48	20·1	—	—	11 33	Sun for
13	14 33	13·7	5	95	11 04	6 54	7 11	28	16 08	21·4	—	—	11 41	observation
16	14 51	15·5	5	97	11 11	7 12	7 32	31	16 28	22·5	—	—	11 49	

VENUS ♀ / MARS ♂

Day	R.A.	Dec.	Diam.	Phase	Transit	5° high. 52°	5° high. 56°	Day	R.A.	Dec.	Diam.	Phase	Transit	5° high. 52°	5° high. 56°
	h m	°	″		h m	h m	h m		h m	°	″		h m	h m	h m
1	12 11	+ 0·5	14	79	9 30	4 00	4 03	1	0 03	−1·9	18	95	21 18	2 38	2 33
6	12 34	− 1·8	13	80	9 32	4 15	4 20	6	0 04	−1·4	17	94	20 59	2 22	2 18
11	12 56	− 4·1	13	81	9 35	4 30	4 37	11	0 06	−0·9	16	93	20 42	2 08	2 04
16	13 19	− 6·4	13	83	9 38	4 45	4 54	16	0 09	−0·2	16	92	20 26	1 54	1 51
21	13 42	− 8·6	13	84	9 42	5 01	5 12	21	0 14	+0·5	15	91	20 10	1 43	1 40
26	14 06	−10·8	12	85	9 45	5 17	5 31	26	0 19	+1·3	14	90	19 56	1 32	1 30
31	14 29	−12·9	12	87	9 50	5 34	5 50	31	0 24	+2·2	13	90	19 42	1 23	1 21

SUNRISE AND SUNSET

Day	London a.m. h m	London p.m. h m	Bristol a.m. h m	Bristol p.m. h m	Birmingham a.m. h m	Birmingham p.m. h m	Manchester a.m. h m	Manchester p.m. h m	Newcastle a.m. h m	Newcastle p.m. h m	Glasgow a.m. h m	Glasgow p.m. h m	Belfast a.m. h m	Belfast p.m. h m
1	6 53	4 34	7 03	4 44	7 02	4 38	7 07	4 37	7 09	4 30	7 23	4 38	7 26	4 49
2	6 55	4 32	7 05	4 42	7 04	4 36	7 09	4 35	7 11	4 28	7 25	4 36	7 28	4 47
3	6 57	4 30	7 06	4 40	7 06	4 35	7 11	4 34	7 13	4 26	7 27	4 34	7 30	4 45
4	6 59	4 29	7 08	4 39	7 08	4 33	7 13	4 32	7 15	4 24	7 29	4 32	7 32	4 43
5	7 00	4 27	7 10	4 37	7 10	4 31	7 15	4 30	7 17	4 22	7 31	4 30	7 34	4 41
6	7 02	4 25	7 11	4 35	7 12	4 29	7 17	4 28	7 19	4 20	7 33	4 28	7 36	4 39
7	7 04	4 24	7 13	4 34	7 14	4 27	7 19	4 26	7 21	4 18	7 35	4 26	7 38	4 37
8	7 06	4 22	7 15	4 32	7 16	4 25	7 21	4 24	7 23	4 16	7 37	4 24	7 40	4 35
9	7 07	4 20	7 17	4 30	7 17	4 24	7 22	4 23	7 25	4 14	7 39	4 22	7 41	4 34
10	7 09	4 19	7 18	4 29	7 19	4 22	7 24	4 21	7 27	4 12	7 41	4 20	7 43	4 32
11	7 11	4 17	7 20	4 27	7 21	4 20	7 26	4 19	7 29	4 10	7 43	4 18	7 45	4 30
12	7 12	4 16	7 22	4 26	7 23	4 19	7 28	4 17	7 31	4 08	7 46	4 16	7 48	4 28
13	7 14	4 14	7 24	4 24	7 25	4 17	7 30	4 16	7 33	4 07	7 48	4 14	7 50	4 26
14	7 16	4 13	7 26	4 23	7 27	4 16	7 32	4 14	7 35	4 05	7 50	4 13	7 52	4 25
15	7 17	4 11	7 27	4 21	7 28	4 14	7 34	4 13	7 37	4 04	7 52	4 11	7 54	4 23
16	7 19	4 10	7 29	4 20	7 30	4 13	7 36	4 11	7 39	4 02	7 54	4 09	7 56	4 21
17	7 21	4 09	7 31	4 19	7 32	4 12	7 38	4 09	7 41	4 00	7 56	4 07	7 58	4 19
18	7 23	4 07	7 33	4 17	7 34	4 10	7 40	4 08	7 43	3 59	7 58	4 06	8 00	4 18
19	7 24	4 06	7 34	4 16	7 35	4 09	7 42	4 07	7 45	3 57	8 00	4 04	8 02	4 17
20	7 26	4 05	7 36	4 15	7 37	4 08	7 43	4 05	7 47	3 56	8 02	4 03	8 03	4 15
21	7 28	4 04	7 38	4 14	7 39	4 07	7 45	4 04	7 49	3 54	8 04	4 01	8 05	4 14
22	7 29	4 02	7 39	4 13	7 40	4 05	7 47	4 03	7 51	3 53	8 06	4 00	8 07	4 13
23	7 31	4 01	7 41	4 12	7 42	4 04	7 49	4 01	7 53	3 51	8 08	3 58	8 09	4 11
24	7 33	4 00	7 43	4 11	7 44	4 03	7 51	4 00	7 55	3 50	8 10	3 57	8 11	4 10
25	7 34	3 59	7 44	4 10	7 45	4 02	7 52	3 59	7 56	3 49	8 12	3 56	8 12	4 09
26	7 36	3 58	7 46	4 09	7 47	4 01	7 54	3 58	7 58	3 48	8 13	3 55	8 14	4 08
27	7 37	3 58	7 47	4 08	7 48	4 01	7 55	3 58	8 00	3 47	8 15	3 53	8 16	4 07
28	7 39	3 57	7 49	4 07	7 50	4 00	7 57	3 57	8 01	3 46	8 17	3 52	8 17	4 06
29	7 40	3 56	7 50	4 07	7 51	3 59	7 58	3 56	8 03	3 45	8 19	3 51	8 19	4 05
30	7 42	3 55	7 52	4 06	7 53	3 58	8 00	3 55	8 05	3 44	8 21	3 50	8 21	4 04

JUPITER ♃ / SATURN ♄

Day	Jupiter R.A. h m	Jupiter Dec. + °	Jupiter Transit h m	Jupiter 5° high 52° h m	Jupiter 5° high 56° h m	Saturn R.A. h m	Saturn Dec. − °	Saturn Transit h m	Saturn 5° high 52° h m	Saturn 5° high 56° h m
1	4 08	19·9	1 26	18 10	17 56	17 55	22·6	15 11	18 17	17 43
11	4 03	19·7	0 42	17 27	17 13	17 59	22·6	14 36	17 42	17 08
21	3 58	19·4	23 52	16 44	16 30	18 04	22·7	14 01	17 07	16 33
31	3 52	19·2	23 08	16 00	15 47	18 09	22·7	13 26	16 32	15 58

Equatorial diameter of Jupiter 49″; of Saturn 15″. Diameters of Saturn's rings 35″ and 16″.

URANUS ♅ / NEPTUNE ♆

Day	Uranus R.A. h m	Uranus Dec. − ° ′	Uranus Transit h m		Neptune R.A. h m	Neptune Dec. − ° ′	Neptune Transit h m	
1	17 52·8	23 39	15 08	Uranus is too close to the Sun for observation	18 34·3	22 17	15 50	Neptune is too close to the Sun for observation
11	17 54·9	23 39	14 31		18 35·4	22 16	15 12	
21	17 57·1	23 39	13 54		18 36·6	22 16	14 33	
31	18 00·0	23 39	13 17		18 38·0	22 15	13 56	

Diameter 4″   Diameter 2″

Month	Week		

Decem (ten), 10th month
of Roman (pre-Julian)
Calendar.
Sun's Longitude 270° ♑ 21ᵈ 15ʰ

1	Th.	Henry I d. 1135. David Ben-Gurion d. 1973.
2	F.	Opening of St. Paul's Cathedral 1697.
3	S.	Crompton b. 1753. Mary Baker Eddy d. 1910.
4	☉.	**2nd S. in Advent.** Benjamin Britton d. 1976.
5	M.	Christina Rossetti b. 1830. Walt Disney b. 1901.
6	Tu.	Warren Hastings b. 1732. Will Hay b. 1888.*
7	W.	Joyce Cary b. 1888.* Robert Graves d. 1985.
8	Th.	Jean Sibelius b. 1865. Golda Meir d. 1978.
9	F.	Milton b. 1608. Elisabeth Schwarzkopf b. 1915.
10	S.	Alfred Nobel d. 1896. Oliver Messiaen b. 1908.
11	☉.	**3rd S. in Advent.** Hector Berlioz b. 1803.
12	M.	Browning d. 1889. Douglas Fairbanks d. 1939.
13	Tu.	New Zealand discovered 1642. River Plate 1939.
14	W.	Amundsen reaches S. Pole 1911. C. P. E. Bach d. 1788.*
15	Th.	Izaak Walton d. 1683. Harold Abrahams b. 1899.
16	F.	Beethoven b. 1770. Camille Saint-Saens d. 1921.
17	S.	First flight by Wright brothers 1903.
18	☉.	**4th S. in Advent.** Sir John Alcock d. 1919.
19	M.	Emily Brontë d. 1848. J. M. W. Turner d. 1851.
20	Tu.	John Steinbeck d. 1968. Artur Rubinstein d. 1982.
21	W.	MICHAELMAS LAW SITTINGS END.
22	Th.	Giacomo Puccini b. 1858. J. Arthur Rank b. 1888.*
23	F.	Richard Arkwright b. 1732. Malthus d. 1834.
24	S.	CHRISTMAS EVE. Vasco da Gama d. 1524.
25	☉.	**Christmas Day.** Humphrey Bogart b. 1889.
26	M.	**St. Stephen.** Discovery of radium 1898.
27	Tu.	**St. John.** Johann Kepler b. 1571.
28	W.	**The Holy Innocents.** Paul Hindemith d. 1963.
29	Th.	Thomas à Becket d. 1170. Harvey Smith b. 1938.
30	F.	Amelia Bloomer d. 1894. Richard Rodgers d. 1979.
31	S.	Wycliffe d. 1384. Sir Malcolm Campbell d. 1948.

PHENOMENA

December 1ᵈ 09ʰ Mercury
in superior conjunction.

7ᵈ 00ʰ Venus in conjunc-
tion with the Moon. Venus
7° N.

17ᵈ 16ʰ Mars in conjunc-
tion with the Moon. Mars
3° S.

20ᵈ 20ʰ Jupiter in conjunction with the Moon. Jupiter
6° S.

21ᵈ 15ʰ Solstice.

26ᵈ 12ʰ Saturn in conjunction with the Sun.

CONSTELLATIONS

The following constella-
tions are near the meridian
at

	d	h		d	h
Nov.	1	24	Nov.	15	23
Dec.	1	22	Dec.	16	21
Jan.	1	20	Jan.	16	19

Ursa Major (below the
Pole), Ursa Minor (below the
Pole), Cassiopeia, Androm-
eda, Perseus, Triangulum,
Aries, Taurus, Cetus and
Eridanus.

MINIMA OF ALGOL

d	h	d	h
1	4	18	9
4	1	21	6
6	22	24	3
9	19	27	0
12	16	29	20
15	12		

* Centenary.

PHASES OF THE MOON

		d	h	m
☾	Last Quarter......	1	06	49
●	New Moon........	9	05	36
☽	First Quarter	16	05	40
○	Full Moon	23	05	29
☾	Last Quarter......	31	04	57

Apogee (404,360 kilometres)   2 06
Perigee (370,350   „   ) 16 04
Apogee (404,380   „   ) 30 04
Mean Longitude of Ascending
  Node on Dec. 1, 339°.

MONTHLY NOTES

Dec. 10. Grouse shooting ends.

21. Shortest day.

25. Quarter day.

26, 27. Bank Holiday, England, Wales, N. Ireland and Scotland.

31. Various licences expire.

Day	Right Ascension	Dec. −	Equation of Time	Rise 52°	Rise 56°	Transit	Set 52°	Set 56°	Sidereal Time	Transit of First Point of Aries
	h m s	° ′	m s	h m	h m	h m	h m	h m	h m s	h m s
1	16 29 14	21 48	+11 02	7 46	8 07	11 49	15 52	15 31	4 40 16	19 16 34
2	16 33 34	21 57	+10 39	7 47	8 09	11 50	15 51	15 30	4 44 13	19 12 38
3	16 37 53	22 06	+10 16	7 49	8 10	11 50	15 51	15 29	4 48 10	19 08 42
4	16 42 14	22 14	+ 9 52	7 50	8 12	11 50	15 50	15 28	4 52 06	19 04 46
5	16 46 35	22 22	+ 9 28	7 51	8 13	11 51	15 50	15 28	4 56 03	19 00 50
6	16 50 57	22 30	+ 9 03	7 53	8 15	11 51	15 50	15 27	4 59 59	18 56 54
7	16 55 19	22 37	+ 8 37	7 54	8 16	11 52	15 49	15 27	5 03 56	18 52 58
8	16 59 42	22 43	+ 8 11	7 55	8 18	11 52	15 49	15 26	5 07 52	18 49 02
9	17 04 05	22 49	+ 7 44	7 56	8 19	11 52	15 49	15 26	5 11 49	18 45 06
10	17 08 29	22 55	+ 7 17	7 57	8 20	11 53	15 49	15 25	5 15 45	18 41 10
11	17 12 53	23 00	+ 6 49	7 58	8 21	11 53	15 48	15 25	5 19 42	18 37 14
12	17 17 17	23 05	+ 6 22	7 59	8 23	11 54	15 48	15 25	5 23 39	18 33 19
13	17 21 42	23 09	+ 5 53	8 00	8 24	11 54	15 48	15 25	5 27 35	18 29 23
14	17 26 07	23 13	+ 5 25	8 01	8 25	11 55	15 48	15 25	5 31 32	18 25 27
15	17 30 32	23 16	+ 4 56	8 02	8 26	11 55	15 49	15 25	5 35 28	18 21 31
16	17 34 58	23 19	+ 4 27	8 03	8 26	11 56	15 49	15 25	5 39 25	18 17 35
17	17 39 24	23 21	+ 3 58	8 03	8 27	11 56	15 49	15 25	5 43 21	18 13 39
18	17 43 50	23 23	+ 3 28	8 04	8 28	11 57	15 49	15 26	5 47 18	18 09 43
19	17 48 16	23 25	+ 2 59	8 05	8 29	11 57	15 50	15 26	5 51 15	18 05 47
20	17 52 42	23 26	+ 2 29	8 05	8 29	11 58	15 50	15 26	5 55 11	18 01 51
21	17 57 08	23 26	+ 1 59	8 06	8 30	11 58	15 50	15 27	5 59 08	17 57 55
22	18 01 35	23 27	+ 1 30	8 06	8 30	11 59	15 51	15 27	6 03 04	17 53 59
23	18 06 01	23 26	+ 1 00	8 07	8 31	11 59	15 52	15 28	6 07 01	17 50 03
24	18 10 27	23 25	+ 0 30	8 07	8 31	12 00	15 52	15 28	6 10 57	17 46 08
25	18 14 54	23 24	0 00	8 08	8 31	12 00	15 53	15 29	6 14 54	17 42 12
26	18 19 20	23 22	− 0 29	8 08	8 32	12 01	15 54	15 30	6 18 50	17 38 16
27	18 23 46	23 20	− 0 59	8 08	8 32	12 01	15 54	15 31	6 22 47	17 34 20
28	18 28 12	23 17	− 1 28	8 08	8 32	12 02	15 55	15 32	6 26 44	17 30 24
29	18 32 38	23 14	− 1 58	8 08	8 32	12 02	15 56	15 33	6 30 40	17 26 28
30	18 37 03	23 10	− 2 27	8 08	8 32	12 03	15 57	15 34	6 34 37	17 22 32
31	18 41 29	23 06	− 2 55	8 08	8 31	12 03	15 58	15 35	6 38 33	17 18 36

THE SUN   s.d. 16′·3

Duration of Civil (C), Nautical (N), and Astronomical (A), Twilight (in minutes)

Lat. °	Dec. 1 C	N	A	Dec. 11 C	N	A	Dec. 21 C	N	A	Dec. 31 C	N	A
52	40	82	123	41	84	125	41	85	126	41	84	125
56	45	93	138	47	96	141	47	97	142	47	96	141

ASTRONOMICAL NOTES

MERCURY is unsuitably placed for observation throughout the month.

VENUS, magnitude −4·0, is still visible as a brilliant object in the eastern sky before dawn. It is drawing closer to the Sun, thus moving southwards in declination, so that the interval of time from the rising of Venus to sunrise shortens markedly during the month.

MARS, magnitude −0·5, continues to be visible as an evening object in the western sky. Mars ends the year in the constellation of Pisces. On the early evening of the 17th the Moon, just after First Quarter, passes 3° N. of the planet.

JUPITER is only just past opposition and is therefore visible for the greater part of the night. It is a brilliant object, magnitude −2·8, in Taurus.

SATURN is already very low in the south west as soon as it is dark enough to observe and it is unlikely to be seen at all after the first week of the month.

METEORS. The maximum of the well-known Geminid meteor shower occurs on December 13. The Moon, only a few days old, will not interfere with observation.

THE MOON

Day	R.A.	Dec.	Hor. Par.	Semi-diam.	Sun's Co-long.	P.A. of Bright Limb	Phase	Age	Rise 52°	Rise 56°	Tran-sit	Set 52°	Set 56°
	h m	°	′	′	°	°		d	h m	h m	h m	h m	h m
1	10 31	+ 9·6	54·4	14·8	175	112	53	21·4	..	..	6 01	12 46	12 51
2	11 14	+ 4·2	54·2	14·8	187	113	43	22·4	0 09	0 05	6 40	12 55	12 56
3	11 56	− 1·4	54·3	14·8	199	113	34	23·4	1 19	1 20	7 19	13 05	13 01
4	12 38	− 7·0	54·5	14·8	211	112	26	24·4	2 29	2 36	7 59	13 15	13 06
5	13 22	−12·4	54·8	14·9	223	109	18	25·4	3 42	3 54	8 40	13 26	13 13
6	14 08	−17·4	55·3	15·1	235	105	11	26·4	4 58	5 17	9 25	13 42	13 22
7	14 58	−21·8	55·9	15·2	248	97	6	27·4	6 17	6 43	10 14	14 03	13 36
8	15 51	−25·2	56·5	15·4	260	84	2	28·4	7 37	8 10	11 08	14 34	14 00
9	16 49	−27·5	57·1	15·5	272	37	0	29·4	8 50	9 28	12 05	15 20	14 41
10	17 49	−28·2	57·6	15·7	284	297	1	0·8	9 50	10 28	13 05	16 23	15 45
11	18 51	−27·2	58·1	15·8	296	275	4	1·8	10 33	11 05	14 04	17 42	17 11
12	19 51	−24·5	58·5	59·9	309	264	9	2·8	11 03	11 28	15 01	19 10	18 46
13	20 49	−20·4	58·8	16·0	321	257	17	3·8	11 25	11 42	15 55	20 38	20 23
14	21 43	−15·1	59·0	16·1	333	252	26	4·8	11 41	11 51	16 46	22 06	21 57
15	22 35	− 9·0	59·2	16·1	345	248	36	5·8	11 54	11 59	17 34	23 31	23 29
16	23 26	− 2·4	59·2	16·1	357	247	47	6·8	12 06	12 05	18 21	..	..
17	0 16	+ 4·2	59·2	16·1	9	247	59	7·8	12 18	12 11	19 09	0 56	1 00
18	1 06	+10·7	59·1	16·1	22	249	70	8·8	12 31	12 19	19 59	2 22	2 32
19	1 59	+16·6	58·9	16·0	34	253	79	9·8	12 49	12 30	20 52	3 49	4 06
20	2 54	+21·6	58·6	16·0	46	259	88	10·8	13 12	12 46	21 48	5 18	5 43
21	3 52	+25·3	58·3	15·9	58	267	94	11·8	13 45	13 12	22 47	6 43	7 16
22	4 53	+27·6	57·8	15·8	70	281	98	12·8	14 33	13 55	23 46	7 58	8 36
23	5 53	+28·1	57·3	15·6	82	328	100	13·8	15 36	14 59	—	8 57	9 34
24	6 53	+27·1	56·7	15·4	94	72	99	14·8	16 50	16 20	0 44	9 38	10 10
25	7 49	+24·5	56·1	15·3	106	92	97	15·8	18 09	17 45	1 38	10 07	10 31
26	8 42	+20·8	55·5	15·1	119	101	92	16·8	19 26	19 10	2 28	10 26	10 44
27	9 30	+16·3	55·0	15·0	131	107	86	17·8	20 41	20 30	3 13	10 41	10 53
28	10 16	+11·3	54·6	14·9	143	111	79	18·8	21 53	21 47	3 56	10 52	10 59
29	10 59	+ 5·8	54·3	14·8	155	113	70	19·8	23 03	23 02	4 36	11 02	11 05
30	11 41	+ 0·3	54·2	14·8	167	114	61	20·8	..	..	5 14	11 11	11 09
31	12 23	− 5·3	54·3	14·8	179	113	52	21·8	0 13	0 17	5 53	11 21	11 14

MERCURY ☿

Day	R.A.	Dec. −	Diam.	Phase	Tran-sit		Day	R.A.	Dec. −	Diam.	Phase	Tran-sit	
	h m	°	″		h m			h m	°	″		h m	
1	16 28	22·5	—	—	11 49		16	18 10	25·4	—	—	12 33	
4	16 48	23·5	—	—	11 57	Mercury is too	19	18 31	25·4	—	—	12 42	Mercury is too
7	17 08	24·3	—	—	12 06	close to the	22	18 52	25·1	5	94	12 51	close to the
10	17 29	24·8	—	—	12 15	Sun for	25	19 13	24·6	5	92	13 00	Sun for
13	17 50	25·2	—	—	12 24	observation	28	19 33	23·9	5	89	13 08	observation
16	18 10	25·4	—	—	12 33		31	19 53	22·9	6	85	13 16	

VENUS ♀ / MARS ♂

Day	R.A.	Dec. −	Diam.	Phase	Tran-sit	5° high. 52°	5° high. 56°	Day	R.A.	Dec. +	Diam.	Phase	Tran-sit	5° high. 52°	5° high. 56°
	h m	°	″		h m	h m	h m		h m	°	″		h m	h m	h m
1	14 29	12·9	12	87	9 50	5 34	5 50	1	0 24	2·2	13	90	19 42	1 23	1 21
6	14 54	14·9	12	88	9 54	5 51	6 09	6	0 31	3·1	12	90	19 29	1 14	1 14
11	15 18	16·7	12	89	9 59	6 08	6 29	11	0 38	4·1	12	89	19 17	1 07	1 07
16	15 44	18·3	11	90	10 05	6 25	6 49	16	0 46	5·1	11	89	19 05	1 00	1 01
21	16 09	19·7	11	91	10 11	6 41	7 08	21	0 54	6·1	11	88	18 53	0 54	0 55
26	16 35	21·0	11	92	10 17	6 57	7 27	26	1 03	7·1	10	88	18 42	0 48	0 51
31	17 02	21·9	11	93	10 24	7 12	7 44	31	1 12	8·2	10	88	18 32	0 43	0 46

Day	London a.m. h m	London p.m. h m	Bristol a.m. h m	Bristol p.m. h m	Birmingham a.m. h m	Birmingham p.m. h m	Manchester a.m. h m	Manchester p.m. h m	Newcastle a.m. h m	Newcastle p.m. h m	Glasgow a.m. h m	Glasgow p.m. h m	Belfast a.m. h m	Belfast p.m. h m
						SUNRISE AND SUNSET								
1	7 43	3 54	7 53	4 05	7 54	3 57	8 01	3 54	8 06	3 43	8 22	3 49	8 22	4 03
2	7 45	3 54	7 55	4 05	7 56	3 57	8 03	3 54	8 08	3 42	8 24	3 48	8 24	4 02
3	7 46	3 53	7 56	4 04	7 57	3 56	8 04	3 53	8 10	3 42	8 26	3 48	8 26	4 02
4	7 47	3 53	7 57	4 04	7 59	3 55	8 06	3 52	8 11	3 41	8 27	3 47	8 28	4 01
5	7 49	3 52	7 58	4 03	8 00	3 55	8 07	3 52	8 13	3 40	8 29	3 46	8 29	4 00
6	7 50	3 52	8 00	4 03	8 01	3 54	8 08	3 51	8 14	3 40	8 30	3 46	8 30	4 00
7	7 51	3 52	8 01	4 02	8 03	3 54	8 10	3 51	8 16	3 39	8 32	3 45	8 32	3 59
8	7 52	3 52	8 02	4 02	8 04	3 53	8 11	3 50	8 17	3 38	8 33	3 44	8 33	3 58
9	7 54	3 51	8 03	4 02	8 05	3 53	8 12	3 50	8 18	3 38	8 34	3 44	8 34	3 58
10	7 55	3 51	8 04	4 02	8 06	3 53	8 13	3 50	8 19	3 38	8 36	3 44	8 35	3 58
11	7 56	3 51	8 05	4 02	8 08	3 53	8 15	3 50	8 21	3 38	8 37	3 43	8 37	3 58
12	7 57	3 51	8 06	4 02	8 09	3 53	8 16	3 50	8 22	3 38	8 38	3 43	8 38	3 58
13	7 58	3 51	8 07	4 02	8 10	3 53	8 17	3 50	8 23	3 38	8 39	3 43	8 39	3 58
14	7 59	3 51	8 08	4 02	8 11	3 53	8 18	3 50	8 24	3 38	8 40	3 43	8 40	3 58
15	8 00	3 52	8 09	4 02	8 12	3 53	8 19	3 50	8 25	3 38	8 41	3 43	8 41	3 58
16	8 01	3 52	8 10	4 02	8 12	3 53	8 19	3 50	8 25	3 38	8 42	3 43	8 41	3 58
17	8 01	3 52	8 10	4 02	8 13	3 53	8 20	3 50	8 26	3 38	8 43	3 43	8 42	3 58
18	8 02	3 52	8 11	4 02	8 14	3 53	8 21	3 50	8 27	3 38	8 44	3 43	8 43	3 58
19	8 03	3 53	8 12	4 03	8 15	3 54	8 22	3 50	8 28	3 38	8 45	3 44	8 44	3 58
20	8 03	3 53	8 12	4 03	8 15	3 54	8 22	3 51	8 28	3 39	8 45	3 44	8 44	3 59
21	8 04	3 53	8 13	4 03	8 16	3 54	8 23	3 51	8 29	3 39	8 46	3 45	8 45	3 59
22	8 04	3 54	8 13	4 04	8 16	3 55	8 24	3 52	8 30	3 40	8 46	3 45	8 46	4 00
23	8 05	3 54	8 14	4 04	8 17	3 55	8 24	3 52	8 30	3 40	8 47	3 46	8 46	4 00
24	8 05	3 55	8 14	4 05	8 17	3 56	8 24	3 53	8 30	3 41	8 47	3 46	8 46	4 01
25	8 06	3 56	8 15	4 06	8 18	3 57	8 25	3 54	8 31	3 42	8 47	3 47	8 47	4 02
26	8 06	3 56	8 15	4 06	8 18	3 57	8 25	3 54	8 31	3 42	8 48	3 48	8 47	4 02
27	8 06	3 57	8 15	4 07	8 18	3 58	8 25	3 54	8 31	3 43	8 48	3 48	8 47	4 03
28	8 06	3 58	8 15	4 08	8 18	3 59	8 25	3 56	8 31	3 44	8 48	3 49	8 47	4 04
29	8 06	3 59	8 16	4 09	8 18	4 00	8 25	3 57	8 31	3 45	8 48	3 50	8 47	4 05
30	8 06	4 00	8 16	4 10	8 18	4 01	8 26	3 58	8 32	3 46	8 48	3 51	8 48	4 06
31	8 06	4 01	8 16	4 11	8 18	4 02	8 25	3 59	8 31	3 47	8 48	3 52	8 47	4 07

JUPITER ♃

Day	R.A. h m	Dec. + °	Transit h m	5° high. 52° h m	5° high. 56° h m
1	3 52	19·2	23 08	6 19	6 33
11	3 47	18·9	22 23	5 33	5 46
21	3 42	18·7	21 39	4 48	5 01
31	3 39	18·6	20 57	4 05	4 18

SATURN ♄

Day	R.A. h m	Dec. − °	Transit h m	5° high. 52° h m	5° high. 56° h m
1	18 09	22·7	13 26	16 32	15 58
11	18 14	22·7	12 52	15 58	15 24
21	18 19	22·6	12 18	15 24	14 50
31	18 24	22·6	11 44	14 50	14 16

Equatorial diameter of Jupiter 48″; of Saturn 15″. Diameters of Saturn's rings 34″ and 15″.

URANUS ♅

Day	R.A. h m	Dec. − ° ′	Transit h m	
1	18 00·0	23 39	13 17	Uranus is too close to the Sun for observation
11	18 02·1	23 39	12 41	
21	18 04·8	23 39	12 04	
31	18 07·4	23 39	11 27	

Diameter 4″

NEPTUNE ♆

Day	R.A. h m	Dec. − ° ′	Transit h m	
1	18 38·0	22 15	13 56	Neptune is too close to the Sun for observation
11	18 39·5	22 13	13 18	
21	18 41·1	22 12	12 40	
31	18 42·7	22 10	12 02	

Diameter 2″

INTRODUCTION TO ASTRONOMICAL SECTION
GENERAL

The astronomical data are given in a form suitable for those who practise naked-eye astronomy or use small telescopes. No attempt has been made to replace the *Astronomical Almanac* for professional astronomers. Positions of the heavenly bodies are given only to the degree of accuracy required by amateur astronomers for setting telescopes, or for plotting on celestial globes or star atlases. Where intermediate positions are required, linear interpolation may be employed.

All data are, unless otherwise stated, for 0^h Greenwich Mean Time (G.M.T.), *i.e.* at the midnight at the beginning of the day named.

(*See notes on British Summer Time, p. 142.*)

Definitions of the terms used cannot be given in an ephemeris of this nature. They must be sought in astronomical literature and text-books. Probably the best source for the amateur is Norton's *Star Atlas and Reference Book* (Longman, 17th edition, 1986; £12·96), which contains an excellent introduction to observational astronomy, and the finest series of star maps yet produced for showing stars visible to the naked eye. Certain more extended ephemerides are available in the British Astronomical Association Handbook, an annual very popular among amateur astronomers. (Secretary: Burlington House, Piccadilly, London, W1V 9AG)

A special feature has been made of the times when the various heavenly bodies are visible in the British Isles. Since two columns, calculated for latitudes 52° and 56°, are devoted to risings and settings, the range 50° to 58° can be covered by interpolation and extrapolation. The times given in these columns are G.M.T.'s for the meridian of Greenwich. An observer west of this meridian must add his longitude (in time) and vice versa.

In accordance with the usual convention in astronomy, + and − indicate respectively north and south latitudes or declinations.

PAGE ONE OF EACH MONTH

The Zodiacal signs through which the Sun is passing during each month are illustrated. The date of transition from one sign to the next, to the nearest hour, is also given.

The **festivals and holy days** in black-letter type are those observed by the Church of England.

Under the heading PHENOMENA will be found particulars of the more important conjunctions of the Sun, Moon and planets with each other, and also the dates of eclipses and other astronomical phenomena of special interest.

The CONSTELLATIONS listed each month are those that are near the meridian at the beginning of the month at 22^h local mean time. Allowance must be made for Summer Time if necessary. The fact that any star crosses the meridian 4^m earlier each night or 2^h earlier each month may be used, in conjunction with the lists given each month, to find what constellations are favourably placed at any moment.

The table preceding the list of constellations may be extended indefinitely at the rate just quoted.

Times of MINIMA OF ALGOL are approximate times of the middle of the period of diminished light.

The Principal PHASES OF THE MOON are the G.M.T.'s when the difference between the longitude of the Moon and that of the Sun is 0°, 90°, 180° or 270°. The times of perigee and apogee are those when the Moon is nearest to, and farthest from, the Earth, respectively. The nodes or points of intersection of the Moon's orbit and the ecliptic make a complete retrograde circuit of the ecliptic in about 19 years. From a knowledge of the longitude of the ascending node and the inclination, whose value does not vary much from 5°, the path of the Moon among the stars may be plotted on a celestial globe or star atlas.

The MONTHLY NOTES are self-explanatory.

PAGE TWO OF EACH MONTH

The Sun's semi-diameter, in arc, is given once a month.

The right ascension given is that of the true Sun. The right ascension of the mean Sun is obtained by applying the equation of time, with the sign given, to the right ascension of the true Sun, or, more easily, by applying 12^h to the column Sidereal Time. The direction in which the equation of time has to be applied in different problems is a frequent source of confusion and error. Apparent Solar Time is equal to the Mean Solar Time plus the Equation of Time. For example at noon on Aug. 8 the Equation of Time is $-5^m 34^s$ and thus at 12^h Mean Time on that day the Apparent Time is $12^h - 5^m 34^s = 11^h 54^m 26^s$.

The Greenwich Sidereal Time at 0^h and the Transit of the First Point of Aries (which is really the mean time when the sidereal time is 0^h) are used for converting mean time to sidereal time and vice versa.

The G.M.T. of transit of the Sun at Greenwich may also be taken as the local mean time (L.M.T.) of transit in any longitude. It is independent of latitude. The G.M.T. of transit in any longitude is obtained by adding the longitude to the time given if west, and vice versa.

The legal importance of SUNRISE and SUNSET is that the Road Vehicles Lighting Regulations 1984 (S.I. 1984 No. 812) requires lights on vehicles to be used during the hours of darkness; that means the time between half an hour after sunset and half an hour before sunrise, throughout the year. In all laws and regulations "sunset" refers to the local sunset, i.e. the time at which the Sun sets at the place in question. This common-sense interpretation has been upheld by legal tribunals. Thus the necessity for providing for different latitudes and longitudes, as already described, is evident.

The times of SUNRISE and SUNSET are those when the Sun's upper limb, as affected by refraction, is on the true horizon of an observer at sea-level. Assuming the mean refraction to be 34′, and the Sun's semi-diameter to be 16′, the time given is that when the true zenith distance of the Sun's centre is $90° + 34′ + 16′$ or $90° 50′$, or, in other words, when the depression of the Sun's centre below the true horizon is 50′. The upper limb is then 34′ below the true horizon, but is brought there by refraction. It is true, of course, that an observer on a ship might see the Sun for a minute or so longer, because of the dip of the horizon, while another viewing the sunset over hills or mountains would record an earlier time. Nevertheless, the moment when the true zenith distance of the Sun's centre is 90° 50′ is a precise time dependent only on the latitude and longitude of the place, and independent of its altitude above sea-level, the contour of its horizon, the vagaries of refraction or the small seasonal change in the Sun's semi-diameter; this moment is suitable in every way as a definition of sunset (or sunrise) for all statutory purposes. On page 144 is given a method for calculating sunrise and sunset times for any other place.

It is well known that light reaches us before sunrise and also continues to reach us for some time after sunset. The interval between darkness and sunrise or sunset and darkness is called twilight. Astronomically speaking, twilight is considered to begin or end when the Sun's centre is 18° below the horizon, as no light from the Sun can then reach the observer. As thus defined twilight may last several hours; in high latitudes at the summer solstice the depression of 18° is not reached, and twilight lasts from sunset to sunrise.

The need for some sub-division of twilight was met some years ago by dividing the gathering darkness into four steps.

(1) *Sunrise or Sunset*, defined as above.

(2) *Civil twilight*, which begins or ends when the Sun's centre is 6° below the horizon. This marks the time when operations requiring daylight may commence or must cease. In England it varies from about 30 to 60 minutes after sunset and the same interval before sunrise.

Lighting-up time is a crude attempt to approximate to civil twilight over the British Isles.

(3) *Nautical twilight*, which begins or ends when the Sun's centre is 12° below the horizon. This marks the time when it is, to all intent and purposes, completely dark.

(4) *Astronomical twilight*, which begins or ends when the Sun's centre is 18° below the horizon. This marks theoretical perfect darkness. It is of little practical importance, especially if nautical twilight is tabulated.

To assist observers the durations of civil, nautical and astronomical twilights are given at intervals of ten days. The beginning of a particular twilight is found by subtracting the duration from the time of sunrise, while the end is found by adding the duration to the time of sunset. Thus the beginning of astronomical twilight in latitude 52°, on the Greenwich meridian, on March 11 is found as $06^h 23^m - 113^m = 04^h 30^m$ and similarly the end of civil twilight as $17^h 58^m + 34^m = 18^h 32^m$.

The letters T.A.N. (twilight all night) are printed when twilight lasts all night.

Under the heading ASTRONOMICAL NOTES will be found notes describing the position and visibility of all the planets and also of other phenomena; these are intended to guide naked-eye observers, or those using small telescopes.

PAGE THREE OF EACH MONTH

The Moon moves so rapidly among the stars that its position is given only to the degree of accuracy that permits linear interpolation. The right ascension and declination are geocentric, i.e. for an imaginary observer at the centre of the Earth. To an observer on the surface of the Earth the position is always different, as the altitude is always less on account of parallax which may reach 1°.

The lunar terminator is the line separating the bright from the dark part of the Moon's disk. Apart from irregularities of the lunar surface, the terminator is elliptical, because it is a circle seen in projection. It becomes the full circle forming the limb, or edge, of the Moon at New and Full Moon. The selenographic longitude of the terminator is measured from the mean centre of the visible disk, which may differ from the visible centre by as much as 8°, because of libration.

Instead of the longitude of the terminator the Sun's selenographic colongitude is tabulated. It is numerically equal to the selenographic longitude of the morning terminator, measured eastward from the mean centre of the disk. Thus its value is approximately 270° at New Moon, 360° at First Quarter, 90° at Full Moon and 180° at Last Quarter.

The Position Angle of the Bright Limb is the position angle of the midpoint of the illuminated limb, measured eastward from the north point on the disk. The column PHASE shows the percentage of the area of the Moon's disk illuminated; this is also the illuminated percentage of the diameter at right angles to the line of cusps. The terminator is a semi-ellipse whose major axis is the line of cusps, and whose semi-minor axis is determined by the tabulated percentage; from New Moon to Full Moon the east limb is dark, and vice versa.

The times given as moonrise and moonset are those when the upper limb of the Moon is on the horizon of an observer at sea-level. The Sun's horizontal parallax is about 9″, and is negligible when considering sunrise and sunset, but that of the Moon averages about 57′. Hence the computed time represents the moment when the true zenith distance of the Moon is 90° 50′ (as for the Sun) minus the horizontal parallax. The time required for the Sun or Moon to rise or set is about four minutes (except in high latitudes). On page 145 is given a method for calculating moonrise and moonset times for any other place.

The tables have been constructed for the meridian of Greenwich, and for latitudes 52° and 56°. They give Greenwich Mean Time (G.M.T.) throughout the year. To obtain the G.M.T. of the phenomenon as seen from any other latitude and longitude, first interpolate or extrapolate for latitude by the usual rules of proportion. To the time thus found the longitude (expressed in time) is to be *added* if west (as it usually is in Great Britain) or *subtracted* if east. If the longitude is expressed in degrees and minutes of arc, it must be converted to time at the rate of $1° = 4^m$ and $15′ = 1^m$.

The G.M.T. of transit of the Moon over the meridian of Greenwich is given: these times are independent of latitude, but must be corrected for longitude. For places in the British Isles it suffices to add the longitude if west, and vice versa. For more remote places a further correction is necessary because of the rapid movement of the Moon relative to the stars. The entire correction is conveniently determined by first finding the west longitude λ of the place. If the place is in west longitude, λ is the ordinary west longitude; if the place is in east longitude λ is the complement to 24^h (or $360°$) of the longitude and will be greater than 12^h (or $180°$). The correction then consists of two positive portions, namely λ and the fraction $\lambda/24$ (or $\lambda°/360$) multiplied by the difference between consecutive transits. Thus for Sydney, N.S.W., the longitude is $10^h\ 05^m$ east, so $\lambda = 13^h\ 55^m$ and the fraction $\lambda/24$ is 0·58. The transit on the local date 1988 January 27 is found as follows:

	d	h	m
G.M.T. of transit at Greenwich .....Jan.	26	18	30
λ		13	55
$0.58 \times (19^h\ 20^m - 18^h\ 30^m)$			29
G.M.T. of transit at Sydney	27	08	54
Corr. to N.S.W. Standard Time		10	00
Local standard time of transit	27	18	54

It is evident of course, that for any given place the quantities λ and the correction to local standard time may be combined permanently, being here $23^h\ 55^m$.

Positions of Mercury are given for every third day, and those of Venus and Mars for every fifth day; they may be interpolated linearly. The column PHASE shows the illuminated percentage of the disk. In the case of the inner planets this approaches 100 at superior conjunction and 0 at inferior conjunction. When the phase is less than 50 the planet is crescent-shaped or horned; for greater phases it is gibbous. In the case of the exterior planet Mars, the phase approaches 100 at conjunction and opposition, and is a minimum at the quadratures.

Since the planets cannot be seen when on the horizon, the actual times of rising and setting are not given; instead, the time when the planet has an apparent altitude of 5° has been tabulated. If the time of transit is between 00^h and 12^h the time refers to an altitude of 5° above the eastern horizon: if between 12^h and 24^h, to the western horizon. The phenomenon tabulated is the one that occurs between sunset and sunrise; unimportant exceptions to these rules may occur because changes are not made during a month, except in the case of Mercury. The times given may be interpolated for latitude and corrected for longitude as in the case of the Sun and Moon.

The G.M.T. at which the planet transits the Greenwich meridian is also given. The times of transit are to be corrected to local meridians in the usual way, as already described.

PAGE FOUR OF EACH MONTH

The G.M.T.'s of Sunrise and Sunset may be used not only for these phenomena, but also for lighting-up times, which, under the Road Vehicles Lighting Regulations, 1984, are from half an hour after sunset to half an hour before sunrise throughout the year.

The particulars for the four outer planets resemble those for the planets on Page Three of each month,

except that, under Uranus and Neptune, times when the planet is 10° high instead of 5° high are given; this is because of the inferior brightness of these planets. The polar diameter of Jupiter is about 3″ less than the equatorial diameter, while that of Saturn is about 2″ less. The diameters given for the rings of Saturn are those of the major axis (in the plane of the planet's equator) and the minor axis respectively. The former has a small seasonal change due to the slightly varying distance of the Earth from Saturn, but the latter varies from zero when the Earth passes through the ring plane every 15 years to its maximum opening half-way between these periods. The rings are open at their widest extent in 1988.

TIME

From the earliest ages, the natural division of time into recurring periods of day and night has provided the practical time scale for the everyday activities of mankind. Indeed, if any alternative means of time measurement is adopted, it must be capable of adjustment so as to remain in general agreement with the natural time scale defined by the diurnal rotation of the Earth on its axis. Ideally the rotation should be measured against a fixed frame of reference; in practice it must be measured against the background provided by the celestial bodies. If the Sun is chosen as the reference point, we obtain Apparent Solar Time, which is the time indicated by a sundial. It is not a uniform time, but is subject to variations which amount to as much as a quarter of an hour in each direction. Such wide variations cannot be tolerated in a practical time scale, and this has led to the concept of Mean Solar Time in which all the days are exactly the same length and equal to the average length of the Apparent Solar Day.

The positions of the stars in the sky are specified in relation to a fictitious reference point in the sky known as the First Point of Aries (or the Vernal Equinox). It is therefore convenient to adopt this same reference point when considering the rotation of the Earth against the background of the stars. The time scale so obtained is known as Apparent Sidereal Time.

Greenwich Mean Time

The daily rotation of the Earth on its axis causes the Sun and the other heavenly bodies to appear to cross the sky from East to West. It is convenient to represent this relative motion as if the Sun really performed a daily circuit around a fixed Earth. Noon in Apparent Solar Time may then be defined as the time at which the Sun transits across the observer's meridian. In Mean Solar Time, noon is similarly defined by the meridian transit of a fictitious Mean Sun moving uniformly in the sky with the same average speed as the true Sun. Mean Solar Time observed on the meridian of the transit circle telescope of the Old Royal Observatory at Greenwich is called Greenwich Mean Time (G.M.T.). The mean solar day is divided into 24 hours and, for astronomical and other scientific purposes, these are numbered 0 to 23, commencing at midnight. Civil time is usually reckoned in two periods of 12 hours, designated a.m. (*ante meridiem*, i.e. before noon) and p.m. (*post meridiem*, i.e. after noon).

Universal Time

Before 1925 January 1 G.M.T. was reckoned in 24 hours commencing at noon: since that date it has been reckoned from midnight. In view of the risk of confusion in the use of the designation G.M.T. before and after 1925, the International Astronomical Union recommended in 1928 that astronomers should employ the term Universal Time, U.T. (or Weltzeit, W.Z.) to denote G.M.T. measured from Greenwich Mean Midnight.

In precision work it is necessary to take account of small variations in Universal Time. These arise from small irregularities in the rotation of the Earth. Observed astronomical time is designated U.T.0. Observed time corrected for the effects of the motion of the poles (giving rise to a "wandering" in longitude) is designated U.T.1. There is also a seasonal fluctuation in the rate of rotation of the Earth arising from meteorological causes, often called the annual fluctuation. U.T.1 corrected for this effect is designated U.T.2 and provides a time scale free from short-period fluctuations. It is still subject to small secular and irregular changes.

Apparent Solar Time

As has been mentioned on page 140, the time shown by a sundial is called Apparent Solar Time. It differs from Mean Solar Time by an amount known as the Equation of Time, which is the total effect of two causes which make the length of the apparent solar day non-uniform. One cause of variation is that the orbit of the Earth is not a circle, but an ellipse, having the Sun at one focus. As a consequence, the angular speed of the Earth in its orbit is not constant; it is greatest at the beginning of January when the Earth is nearest the Sun. The other cause is due to the obliquity of the ecliptic; the plane of the equator (which is at right-angles to the axis of rotation of the Earth) does not coincide with the ecliptic (the plane defined by the apparent annual motion of the Sun around the celestial sphere) but is inclined to it at an angle of $23°\,26'$. As a result, the apparent solar day is shorter than average at the equinoxes and longer at the solstices. From the combined effects of the components due to obliquity and eccentricity, the equation of time reaches its maximum values in February (-14 mins.) and early November ($+16$ mins.). It has a zero value on four dates during the year, and it is only on these dates (approx. April 15, June 14, Sept. 1, and Dec. 25) that a sundial shows Mean Solar Time.

Sidereal Time

A sidereal day is the duration of a complete rotation of the Earth with reference to the First Point of Aries. The term sidereal (or "star") time is perhaps a little misleading since the time scale so defined is not exactly the same as that which would be defined by successive transits of a selected star, as there is a small progressive motion between the stars and the First Point of Aries due to the precession of the Earth's axis. This makes the length of the sidereal day shorter than the true period of rotation by 0.008 seconds. Superimposed on this steady precessional motion are small oscillations called nutation, giving rise to fluctuations in apparent sidereal time amount-

ing to as much as 1.2 seconds. It is therefore customary to employ Mean Sidereal Time, from which these fluctuations have been removed. The conversion of G.M.T. to Greenwich sidereal time (G.S.T.) may be performed by adding the value of the G.S.T. at 0^h on the day in question (Page Two of each month) to the G.M.T. converted to sidereal time using the table on p. 146.

Example. To find the G.S.T. at August $8^d\,02^h\,41^m\,11^s$ G.M.T.

					h	m	s
G.S.T. at 0^h	..	..	..	..	21	06	53
G.M.T.	..	..	..	..	2	41	11
Acceleration for 2^h	..	..	..			20
,, ,, $41^m\,11^s$	..	..	..				7
Sum = G.S.T. =	..	..	..		23	48	31

If the observer is not on the Greenwich meridian then his longitude, measured positively westwards from Greenwich, must be subtracted from the G.S.T. to obtain Local Sidereal Time (L.S.T.). Thus, in the above example, an observer 5^h east of Greenwich, or 19^h west, would find his L.S.T. as $4^h\,48^m\,31^s$.

Ephemeris Time

In the study of the motions of the Sun, Moon and planets, observations taken over an extended period are used in the preparation of tables giving the apparent position of the body each day. A table of this sort is known as an ephemeris, and may be used in the comparison of current observations with tabulated positions. A detailed examination of the observations made over the past 300 years shows that the Sun, Moon and planets appear to depart from their predicted positions by amounts proportional to their mean motions. The only satisfactory explanation is that the time scale to which the observations were referred was not uniform as had been supposed. Since the time scale was based on the rotation of the Earth, it follows that this rotation is subject to irregularities. The fact that the discrepancies between the observed and ephemeris positions were proportional to the mean motions of the bodies made it possible to secure agreement by substituting a revised time scale and recomputing the ephemeris positions. The time scale which brings the ephemeris into agreement with the observations is known as Ephemeris Time (E.T.).

The new unit of time has been defined in terms of the apparent annual motion of the Sun. Thus the second is now defined in terms of the annual motion of the Earth in its orbit around the Sun ($1/31556925.9747$ of the Tropical Year for 1900 January $0^d\,12^h$ E.T.) instead of in terms of the diurnal rotation of the Earth on its axis ($1/86\,400$ of the Mean Solar Day). In many branches of scientific work other than astronomy there has been a demand for a unit of time that is invariable, and the second of Ephemeris time was adopted by the Comité International des Poids et Mésures in 1956. The length of the unit has been chosen to provide general agreement with U.T. throughout the 19th and 20th centuries. During 1988 the estimated difference E.T. $-$ U.T. is 57 seconds. The precise determination of E.T. from astronomical observations is a lengthy process, as the accuracy with which a single observation of the Sun can be made is far less than that obtainable in, for instance, a comparison between clocks. It is therefore necessary to average the observations over an extended period. Largely on account of its faster motion, the position of the Moon may be observed with greater accuracy, and a close approximation to Ephemeris Time may be obtained by comparing observations of the moon with its ephemeris position. Even in this case, however, the requisite standard of accuracy can only be achieved by averaging over a number of years.

Atomic Time

The fundamental standards of time and frequency must be defined in terms of a periodic motion adequately uniform, enduring and susceptible of measurement. This has led in the past to the adoption of standards based on the observed motions in the Solar System. Recent progress has made it possible to consider the use of other natural standards, such as atomic or molecular oscillations. The oscillations so far employed are not in fact continuous periodic motions such as the revolution of the electrons in their orbits around the nuclei. The continuous oscillations are generated in an electrical circuit, the frequency of which is then compared or brought into coincidence with the frequency characteristic of the absorption or emission by the atoms or molecules when they change between two selected energy levels. At the National Physical Laboratory regular comparisons have been made since the middle of 1955 between quartz clocks of high stability and a frequency defined by atoms of caesium. The standard has proved of great value in the precise calibration of frequencies and time intervals: it has also been possible to build up a scale of "atomic time" by using continuously-running quartz clocks calibrated in terms of the caesium frequency standard.

Terrestrial Dynamical Time

A new time scale, known as Terrestrial Dynamical Time (T.D.T.) has recently been defined in terms of international atomic time in such a way that, for most purposes, it can be regarded as a continuation of atomic time.

Radio Time Signals

The establishment of a uniform time system by the assessment of the performance of standard clocks in terms of astronomical observations is the work of a national observatory, and standard time is then made generally available by means of radio time signals. In the United Kingdom, the Royal Greenwich Observatory controls the "6-pips" radio signals emitted by the British Broadcasting Corporation. The British Telecom Speaking Clock "Timeline" is corrected by the National Physical Laboratory caesium beam atomic frequency standard at the British Telecom International Radio Station at Rugby.

For survey and scientific purposes, in which the highest accuracy is required, special signals are transmitted on behalf of the National Physical Laboratory from Rugby Radio Station. The signals

consist of a standard frequency carrier of 60 kHz (MSF) which switches off for half a second to denote the passing of one minute and for a tenth of a second to denote the passing of one second. Also transmitted are two binary coded decimal (BCD) time codes giving time of day and calendar information. The service is continuous except for a maintenance period from 1000–1400 UTC on the first Sunday of each month.

In addition, a standard frequency and time service is transmitted for 5 minutes in every 10 minutes on 2·5, 5 and 10 MHz (MSF). This facility, however, is scheduled to be withdrawn on February 29, 1988.

The Coordinated Universal Time (UTC) system standard frequency emissions and radio time signals are broadcast on MSF, GBR, and by other national transmitters, eg. by WWV and WWVH in the U.S.A. in conformity with the International Atomic Time Scale. The time intervals between pips correspond exactly to the seconds defined as follows: "The second is the duration of 9 192 631 770 periods of the radiation corresponding to the transition between the 2 hyperfine levels of the ground state of the caesium 133 atom."

As the rate of rotation of the Earth is variable the time signals are adjusted by the introduction of a leap second when necessary in order that UTC shall not depart from UT by more than $0^s·9$. For convenience leap seconds are introduced when necessary, on the last second of a month preferably on Dec. 31 and/or June 30. In the case of a positive leap second $23^h 59^m 60^s$ is followed one second later by $0^h 00^m 00^s$ of the first day of the month. In the case of a negative leap second (required if the Earth were to have a sudden change of rate and begin to gain relative to UTC) $23^h 59^m 58^s$ is followed one second later by $0^h 00^m 00^s$ of the first day of the month.

From 1972 Jan. 1 the six pips on the BBC have consisted of 5 short pips from second 55 to second 59 followed by one lengthened pip, the start of which indicates the exact minute.

SUMMER TIME

In the United Kingdom, in 1988, Summer Time, one hour in advance of G.M.T. will be in force from March $27^d 01^h$ to October $23^d 01^h$.

Variations from the standard time of some countries occurs during part of the year: they are decided annually and are usually referred to as Summer Time or Daylight Saving Time. These variations occur in:

The Commonwealth.—Parts of Australia; Bahamas; Canada; Channel Islands; Gibraltar; New Zealand; Bermuda; Malta.

Foreign Countries.—Albania; Austria; Azores; Belgium; Brazil; Bulgaria; Canary Is.; Chile; parts of China; Corsica; Cuba; Cyprus Ercan; Cyprus Larnaca; Czechoslovakia; Denmark; Faroe; Finland; France; Germany; Greece; Greenland; Guatemala; Haiti; Hungary; Iraq; Israel; Italy; Jordan; Lebanon; Libya; Luxembourg; Madeira; Monaco; Mongolia; Netherlands; New Caledonia; Norway; Paraguay; Peru; Poland; Portugal; Romania; Sicily; Sweden; Switzerland; Syria; Taiwan; Turkey; Uruguay; parts of U.S.A.; U.S.S.R.; Yugoslavia.

In the Irish Republic, and Paraguay, the variation occurs in winter and is called Winter Time.

In the year 1880 it was enacted by statute that the word "time", when it occurred in any legal document relating to Great Britain, was to be interpreted, unless otherwise specifically stated, as the Mean Time of the Greenwich meridian.* Since the year 1883 the system of Standard Time by Zones has been gradually accepted, and now almost throughout the world a Standard Time which differs from that of Greenwich by an integral number of hours, either fast or slow, is used.

The large territories of the United States and Canada are divided into zones approximately 7½° on either side of central meridians. The important ones are given below; there are in addition zones from 3 to 12 hours fast in the U.S.S.R.

Fast on Greenwich Time

12 hours fast
Caroline Is. (E. of 160° E.); Fiji; Kiribati; Marshall Is.; Nauru; New Zealand.

11½ hours fast
Norfolk I.

11 hours fast
Caroline Is. (150°E. to 160° E.); New Caledonia; Sakhalin; Solomon Is.; Vanuatu.

10 hours fast
Admiralty Is.; Australian Capital Territory; Caroline Is. (135° E. to 150° E.); Mariana Is.; New South Wales (except Broken Hill Area); Queensland; Tasmania; Victoria.

9½ hours fast
New South Wales (Broken Hill Area); Northern Territory (Aus); South Australia.

9 hours fast
Caroline Is. (W. of 135° E.); Irian Jaya; Japan; Korea; Kuril Is.; Molucca Is.

8 hours fast
China; Hong Kong; Kalimantan†; Macao; Malaysia; Philippines; Sulawesi; Taiwan; Timor; Western Australia.

7 hours fast
Cambodia; Christmas I. (Indian Ocean); Java; Laos; Sumatra; Thailand; Vietnam.

6½ hours fast
Burma; Cocos-Keeling Is.

6 hours fast
Bangladesh.

5½ hours fast
India; Sri Lanka.

5 hours fast
Pakistan.

4½ hours fast
Afghanistan.

4 hours fast
Mauritius; Réunion; Seychelles; United Arab Emirates.

3½ hours fast
Iran.

3 hours fast
Bahrain; Comoro Is.; Ethiopia; Iraq; Kenya; Madagascar; Somalia; Tanzania; Uganda; Yemen.

2 hours fast
Botswana; Bulgaria; Burundi; Crete; Cyprus; Egypt; Finland; Greece; Israel; Jordan; Lebanon; Lesotho; Malawi; Mozambique; Romania; Rwanda; South Africa; Sudan; Syria; Turkey; Zambia; Zimbabwe.

1 hour fast
Albania; Algeria; Angola; Austria; Belgium; Benin; Cameroon; Central African Republic; Czechoslovakia; Denmark; France; Germany; Gibraltar; Hungary; Ireland (Republic); Italy; Libya; Luxembourg; Malta; Monaco; Netherlands; Niger; Nigeria; Norway; Poland; Spain; Svalbard; Sweden; Switzerland; Tunisia; Yugoslavia; Zaire;

Greenwich Time

Ascension I.; Canary Is.; Channel Is.; Côte d'Ivoire; Faroe Is.; Gambia; Ghana; Guinea; Guinea Bissau; Iceland; Liberia; Madeira; Mali; Mauritania; Morocco; Portugal; St. Helena; São Tomé & Principe I.; Senegal; Sierra Leone; Togo; U.K.

Slow on Greenwich time

1 hour slow
Azores; Cape Verde Is.

2 hours slow
Fernando Noronha I.; South Georgia.

3 hours slow
Argentina; Brazil (eastern); French Guiana; Greenland (except Thule); Guyana; Uruguay.

3½ hours slow
Newfoundland; Suriname.

4 hours slow (Atlantic time)
Bermuda; Bolivia; Brazil (central); Canada (E. of 68° W); Chile; Dominican Republic; Falkland Is.; Greenland (west); Labrador; Paraguay; Puerto Rico; Venezuela; Windward Is.

5 hours slow
Bahama Is.; Brazil (western); Canada (68° W. to 85° W.); Cayman Is.; Colombia; Cuba; Ecuador; Haiti; Jamaica; Panama; Peru; U.S.A. (eastern time).

6 hours slow
Canada (85° W. to 102° W.); Costa Rica, Guatemala; Honduras; Mexico (eastern); Nicaragua; El Salvador; U.S.A. (central time).

7 hours slow
Canada (102° W. to 120° W.); Mexico (central); U.S.A. (mountain time).

8 hours slow
Alaska (S.E. coast); Canada (W. of 120° W.); Mexico (western); U.S.A. (Pacific time); Yukon.

9 hours slow
Alaska (E. of 169°30′W.).

10 hours slow
Aleutian Is. (W. of 169°30′ W.); Christmas Is. (Pacific Ocean); Hawaii; Society Is.; Tuamotu archipelago; Tubuai Is.

11 hours slow
Midway Is.; Samoa.

11½ hours slow
Banaba (Kiribati).

12 hours slow
Tabuaeran Atoll (Kiribati).

In the Tonga Islands the time 13*h* fast and in Chatham Is. 12*h* 45*m* fast on Greenwich is used, as the Date line is to the East of them.

The Date or Calendar Line

The line where the change of date occurs is a modification of the 180th meridian, and is drawn so as to include islands of any one group on the same side of the line, or for political reasons. It is indicated by joining up the following nine points:

Lat.	Long.	Lat.	Long.	Lat.	Long.
60° S.	180°	15° S.	172½° W.	53° N.	170° E.
51° S.	180°	5° S.	180°	65½° N.	169° W.
45° S.	172½° W.	48° N.	180°	75° N.	180°

* Summer Time is the "legal" time during the period in which its use is ordained. † The Indonesian territory on Borneo I.

RISING AND SETTING TIMES

Table 1. Hour Angle

Dec.	Latitude and Declination of Opposite Signs						0°	Latitude and Declination of Same Signs					
	50°	45°	40°	30°	20°	10°		10°	20°	30°	40°	45°	50°
°	h m	h m	h m	h m	h m	h m	h m	h m	h m	h m	h m	h m	h m
0	6 00	6 00	6 00	6 00	6 00	6 00	6 00	6 00	6 00	6 00	6 00	6 00	6 00
1	5 55	5 56	5 57	5 58	5 59	5 59	6 00	6 01	6 01	6 02	6 03	6 04	6 05
2	5 50	5 52	5 53	5 55	5 57	5 58	6 00	6 02	6 03	6 05	6 07	6 08	6 10
3	5 45	5 48	5 50	5 53	5 56	5 58	6 00	6 02	6 04	6 07	6 10	6 12	6 15
4	5 40	5 44	5 46	5 51	5 54	5 57	6 00	6 03	6 06	6 09	6 14	6 16	6 20
5	5 36	5 40	5 43	5 48	5 52	5 56	6 00	6 04	6 08	6 12	6 17	6 20	6 24
6	5 31	5 36	5 39	5 46	5 51	5 56	6 00	6 04	6 09	6 14	6 21	6 24	6 29
7	5 26	5 32	5 36	5 44	5 50	5 55	6 00	6 05	6 10	6 16	6 24	6 28	6 34
8	5 21	5 27	5 33	5 41	5 48	5 54	6 00	6 06	6 12	6 19	6 27	6 33	6 39
9	5 16	5 23	5 29	5 39	5 47	5 53	6 00	6 07	6 13	6 21	6 31	6 37	6 44
10	5 11	5 19	5 26	5 37	5 45	5 53	6 00	6 07	6 15	6 23	6 34	6 41	6 49
11	5 06	5 15	5 22	5 34	5 44	5 52	6 00	6 08	6 16	6 26	6 38	6 45	6 54
12	5 01	5 11	5 19	5 32	5 42	5 51	6 00	6 09	6 18	6 28	6 41	6 49	6 59
13	4 56	5 06	5 15	5 29	5 40	5 51	6 00	6 09	6 20	6 31	6 45	6 54	7 04
14	4 51	5 02	5 12	5 27	5 39	5 50	6 00	6 10	6 21	6 33	6 48	6 58	7 09
15	4 46	4 58	5 08	5 24	5 38	5 49	6 00	6 11	6 22	6 36	6 52	7 02	7 14
16	4 40	4 53	5 04	5 22	5 36	5 48	6 00	6 12	6 24	6 38	6 56	7 07	7 20
17	4 35	4 49	5 00	5 19	5 35	5 48	6 00	6 12	6 25	6 41	7 00	7 11	7 25
18	4 29	4 44	4 57	5 17	5 33	5 47	6 00	6 13	6 27	6 43	7 03	7 16	7 31
19	4 23	4 39	4 53	5 14	5 31	5 46	6 00	6 14	6 29	6 46	7 07	7 21	7 37
20	4 17	4 35	4 49	5 11	5 30	5 45	6 00	6 15	6 30	6 49	7 11	7 25	7 43
21	4 11	4 30	4 44	5 09	5 28	5 44	6 00	6 16	6 32	6 51	7 16	7 30	7 49
22	4 04	4 25	4 40	5 06	5 26	5 44	6 00	6 16	6 34	6 54	7 20	7 35	7 56
23	3 58	4 19	4 36	5 03	5 24	5 43	6 00	6 17	6 36	6 57	7 24	7 41	8 02
24	3 52	4 14	4 32	5 00	5 23	5 42	6 00	6 18	6 37	7 00	7 28	7 46	8 08
25	3 45	4 09	4 28	4 58	5 21	5 41	6 00	6 19	6 39	7 02	7 32	7 51	8 15
26	3 38	4 03	4 24	4 55	5 19	5 40	6 00	6 20	6 41	7 05	7 36	7 57	8 22
27	3 30	3 57	4 19	4 52	5 17	5 39	6 00	6 21	6 43	7 08	7 41	8 03	8 30
28	3 23	3 51	4 14	4 48	5 15	5 38	6 00	6 22	6 45	7 12	7 46	8 09	8 37
29	3 15	3 45	4 09	4 45	5 14	5 38	6 00	6 22	6 46	7 15	7 51	8 15	8 45

SUNRISE AND SUNSET

The local mean time of sunrise or sunset (as defined on page 138) may be found by determining the appropriate hour angle from the table above and applying it to the time of transit given in the ephemeris for each month. The hour angle is negative for sunrise and positive for sunset. A small correction to the hour angle, which always has the effect of increasing it numerically, is necessary to allow for the Sun's semi-diameter (16′) and for refraction (34′). This correction may be obtained from Table 2. The resulting local mean time may be converted into the standard time of the country by taking the difference between the longitude of the standard meridian of the country and that of the place, and adding it to the local mean time if the place is west of the standard meridian, and subtracting it if the place is east of the standard meridian.

Example.—Required the N.Z. Mean Time (12h fast on G.M.T.) of sunset on May 24 at Auckland. The latitude is 36° 50′ south (or minus) and the longitude 11h 39m east. Taking the declination as +20°·7, we find

		h m
Tabular entry for 30° Lat. and Dec. 20°, opposite signs	+	5 11
Proportional part for 6° 50′ of Lat.	−	15
Proportional part for 0°·7 of Dec.	−	3
Correction (Table 2)	+	6
Hour angle		4 59
Sun transits		11 57
Longitudinal correction	+	21
N.Z. Mean Time		17 17

Table 2. Correction for Refraction and Semi-Diameter

Latitude	Declination			
	0°	10°	20°	29°
°	m	m	m	m
0	3	3	4	4
20	4	4	4	4
30	4	4	4	5
40	4	4	5	6
50	5	5	6	8

MOONRISE AND MOONSET

It is possible to calculate the times of moonrise and moonset using Table 1 though the method is more complicated because the apparent motion of the Moon is much more rapid and also more variable than that of the Sun.

The parallax of the Moon, about 57′, is near to the sum of the semi-diameter and refraction but has the opposite effect on these times. It is thus convenient to neglect all three quantities in the method outlined below.

Table 3. Longitude Correction

A \ X	40^m	45^m	50^m	55^m	60^m	65^m	70^m
h	m	m	m	m	m	m	m
1	2	2	2	2	3	3	3
2	3	4	4	5	5	5	6
3	5	6	6	7	8	8	9
4	7	8	8	9	10	11	12
5	8	9	10	11	13	14	15
6	10	11	13	14	15	16	18
7	12	13	15	16	18	19	20
8	13	15	17	18	20	22	23
9	15	17	19	21	23	24	26
10	17	19	21	23	25	27	29
11	18	21	23	25	28	30	32
12	20	23	25	28	30	33	35
13	22	24	27	30	33	35	38
14	23	26	29	32	35	38	41
15	25	28	31	34	38	41	44
16	27	30	33	37	40	43	47
17	28	32	35	39	43	46	50
18	30	34	38	41	45	49	53
19	32	36	40	44	48	51	55
20	33	38	42	46	50	54	58
21	35	39	44	48	53	57	61
22	37	41	46	50	55	60	64
23	38	43	48	53	58	62	67
24	40	45	50	55	60	65	70

Notation

φ = latitude of observer
λ = longitude of observer (measured positively towards the west)
T_{-1} = time of transit of Moon on previous day
T_0 = time of transit of Moon on day in question
T_1 = time of transit of Moon on following day
δ_0 = approximate declination of Moon
δ_R = declination of Moon at moonrise
δ_S = declination of Moon at moonset
h_0 = approximate hour angle of Moon
h_R = hour angle of Moon at moonrise
h_S = hour angle of Moon at moonset
t_R = time of moonrise
t_S = time of moonset

Method

1. With arguments φ, δ_0 enter Table 1 on p. 144 to determine h_0 where h_0 is negative for moonrise and positive for moonset.

2. Form approximate times from
$$t_R = T_0 + \lambda + h_0$$
$$t_S = T_0 + \lambda + h_0$$

3. Determine δ_R, δ_S for times t_R, t_S respectively.

4. Re-enter Table 1 on p. 144 with—
   (a) arguments φ, δ_R to determine h_R
   (b) arguments φ, δ_S to determine h_S

5. Form $t_R = T_0 + \lambda + h_R + AX$
$$t_S = T_0 + \lambda + h_S + AX$$

where $A = (\lambda + h)$

$X = (T_0 - T_{-1})$ if $(\lambda + h)$ is negative
and $X = (T_1 - T_0)$ if $(\lambda + h)$ is positive

AX is the respondent in Table 3.

Example.—To find the times of moonrise and moonset at Vancouver ($\varphi = +49°$, $\lambda = +8^h\ 12^m$) on 1988 March 14. The starting data (from p. 100) are

$$\begin{aligned} & \quad\quad\quad h\ \ m \\ T_{-1} &= 7\ \ 53 \\ T_0 &= 8\ \ 53 \\ T_1 &= 9\ \ 51 \\ \delta &= -25° \end{aligned}$$

1. $h_0 = 3^h\ 50^m$

2. Approximate values
$$\begin{aligned} t_R &= 14^d\ 08^h\ 53^m + 8^h\ 12^m + (-3^h\ 50^m) \\ &= 14^d\ 13^h\ 15^m \\ t_S &= 14^d\ 08^h\ 53^m + 8^h\ 12^m + (+3^h\ 50^m) \\ &= 14^d\ 20^h\ 55^m \end{aligned}$$

3. $\delta_R = -22°\cdot 7$
   $\delta_S = -21°\cdot 3$

4. $h_R = -4^h\ 04^m$
   $h_S = +4^h\ 13^m$

5. $t_R = 14^d\ 08^h\ 53^m + 8^h\ 12^m + (-4^h\ 04^m) + 10^m$
   $= 14^d\ 13^h\ 11^m$
   $t_S = 14^d\ 08^h\ 53^m + 8^h\ 12^m + (+4^h\ 13^m) + 30^m$
   $= 14^d\ 21^h\ 48^m$

To get the L.M.T. of the phenomenon the longitude is subtracted from the G.M.T. thus
Moonrise $= 14^d\ 13^h\ 11^m - 8^h\ 12^m = 14^d\ 04^h\ 59^m$
Moonset $= 14^d\ 21^h\ 48^m - 8^h\ 12^m = 14^d\ 13^h\ 36^m$

ASTRONOMICAL CONSTANTS

Solar Parallax .... 8″·794
Precession for the year 1988 .... 50″·288
    ,,   in R.A. .... 3ˢ·075
    ,,   in Declination .... 20″·044
Constant of Nutation .... 9″·202
Constant of Aberration .... 20″·496
Mean Obliquity of Ecliptic (1988) .... 23° 26′ 27″
Moon's Equatorial Hor. Parallax .... 57′ 02″·70
Velocity of Light in vacuo *per sec* ..... 299792·5 km.
Solar motion *per sec* .... 20·0 km.
Equatorial radius of the Earth .... 6378·140 km.
Polar radius of the Earth .... 6356·755 km.

North Galactic Pole ⎱ R.A. 12ʰ 49ᵐ (1950·0).
(I.A.U. *Standard*). ⎰ Dec. 27°·4 N.
Solar Apex .... R.A. 18ʰ 06ᵐ Dec. +30°
Length of Year ... Tropical .... 365·24220
(*In Mean*   Sidereal .... 365·25636
 Solar Days)   Anomalistic ... 365·25964
        (*Perihelion to Perihelion*)
        Eclipse .... 346·6200

		d h m s
Length of Month	New Moon to New	29 12 44 02·9
(*Mean Values*)	Sidereal	27 07 43 11·5
	Anomalistic	27 13 18 33·2
	(*Perigee to Perigee*)	

MEAN AND SIDEREAL TIME

Acceleration						Retardation						MEAN REFRACTION	
h	m s	h	m s	m s s	s	h	m s	h	m s	m s s	s	Alt. Ref.	Alt. Ref.
1	0 10	13	2 08	0 00	0	1	0 10	13	2 08	0 00	0	° ′	° ′
2	0 20	14	2 18	3 02	1	2	0 20	14	2 18	3 03	1	1 20 / 21	4 30 / 10
3	0 30	15	2 28	9 07	2	3	0 29	15	2 27	9 09	2	1 30 / 20	5 06 / 9
				15 13	3					15 15	3	1 41 / 19	5 50 / 8
4	0 39	16	2 38	21 18	4	4	0 39	16	2 37	21 21	4	1 52 / 18	6 44 / 7
5	0 49	17	2 48	27 23	5	5	0 49	17	2 47	27 28	5	2 05 / 17	7 54 / 6
6	0 59	18	2 57	33 28	6	6	0 59	18	2 57	33 34	6	2 19 / 16	9 27 / 5
7	1 09	19	3 07	39 34	7	7	1 09	19	3 07	39 40	7	2 35 / 15	11 39 / 4
8	1 19	20	3 17	45 39	8	8	1 19	20	3 17	45 46	8	2 52 / 14	15 00 / 3
9	1 29	21	3 27	51 44	9	9	1 28	21	3 26	51 53	9	3 12 / 13	20 42 / 2
10	1 39	22	3 37	57 49	10	10	1 38	22	3 36	57 59	10	3 34 / 12	32 20 / 1
11	1 48	23	3 47	60 00		11	1 48	23	3 46	60 00		4 00 / 11	62 17 / 0
12	1 58	24	3 57			12	1 58	24	3 56			4 30 /	90 00 /

The length of a sidereal day in mean time is 23h 56m 04s.09. Hence 1h M.T. = 1h + 9s.86 S.T. and 1h S.T. = 1h − 9s.83 M.T.

To convert an interval of mean time to the corresponding interval of sidereal time, enter the acceleration table with the given mean time (taking the hours and the minutes and seconds separately) and add the acceleration obtained to the given mean time. To convert an interval of sidereal time to the corresponding interval of mean time, take out the retardation for the given sidereal time and subtract.

The columns for the minutes and seconds of the argument are in the form known as Critical Tables. To use these tables, find in the appropriate left-hand column the two entries between which the given number of minutes and seconds lies; the quantity in the right-hand column between these two entries is the required acceleration or retardation. Thus the acceleration for 11m26s (which lies between the entries 9m07s and 15m13s) is 2s. If the given number of minutes and seconds is a tabular entry, the required acceleration or retardation is the entry in the right-hand column *above* the given tabular entry; e.g. the retardation for 45m46s is 7s.

Example.—Convert 14h27m35s from S.T. to M.T.

	h m s
Given S.T.	14 27 35
Retardation for 14h	2 18
Retardation for 27m35s	5
Corresponding M.T.	14 25 12

For further explanation, see p. 141.
The refraction table is also in the form of a critical table.

THE SUMMER TIME ACTS

In 1916 an Act ordained that during a defined period of that year the legal time for general purposes in Great Britain should be one hour in advance of Greenwich Mean Time. The *Summer Time Acts*, 1922 to 1925, defined the period during which Summer Time was to be in force, stabilizing practice until the war.

During the Second World War the duration of Summer Time was extended and in the years 1941–45 and in 1947, Double Summer Time (2 hrs. in advance of Greenwich Mean Time) was in force. After the war, Summer Time was extended in each year from 1948–1952 and 1961–1964 by Order in Council.

British Standard Time, during which clocks were kept one hour ahead of Greenwich Mean Time throughout the year, was in force between Oct. 27, 1968 and Oct. 31, 1971.

The most recent legislation is the Summer Time Act, 1972, which enacted that "the period of summer time for the purposes of this Act is the period beginning at two o'clock, Greenwich mean time, in the morning of the day after the third Saturday in March or, if that day is Easter Day, the day after the second Saturday in March, and ending at two o'clock, Greenwich mean time, in the morning of the day after the fourth Saturday in October."

The duration of Summer Time can be varied by Order in Council and in recent years alterations have been made to bring the operation of Summer Time in Britain closer to similar provisions in other countries of the European Community. The latest Order in Council is the Summer Time Order, 1986, stipulating the duration of Summer Time in 1986–1988. In 1988 Summer Time will be in force from May 27 to October 23 and, as in recent years, the hour of changeover will be 1 a.m. Greenwich Mean Time.

The duration of Summer Time during the last few years is given in the following table.

1978 Mar. 19—Oct. 29	1983 Mar. 27—Oct. 23
1979 Mar. 18—Oct. 28	1984 Mar. 25—Oct. 28
1980 Mar. 16—Oct. 26	1985 Mar. 31—Oct. 27
1981 Mar. 29—Oct. 25	1986 Mar. 30—Oct. 26
1982 Mar. 28—Oct. 24	1987 Mar. 29—Oct. 25

ASTRONOMERS ROYAL

John Flamsteed, first Astronomer Royal	1675–1719	Sir William Henry Mahoney Christie	1881–1910
Edmund Halley	1720–1742	Sir Frank Watson Dyson	1910–1933
James Bradley	1742–1762	Sir Harold Spencer Jones	1933–1955
Nathaniel Bliss	1762–1764	Sir Richard van der Riet Woolley	1955–1971
Nevil Maskelyne	1765–1811	Sir Martin Ryle	1972–1982
John Pond	1811–1835	Prof. Sir Francis Graham Smith	1982–
Sir George Biddell Airy	1835–1881		

PHENOMENA OF JUPITER'S SATELLITES, 1988

G.M.T. Sat. Phen.

January

d	h	m	Sat	Phen.
5	01	10	I	Sh.I.
5	17	39	III	Sh.I.
5	19	55	III	Sh.E.
5	20	51	II	Sh.I.
5	23	09	II	Sh.E.
6	00	37	I	Ec.R.
6	19	39	I	Sh.I.
6	21	49	I	Sh.E.
7	17	43	II	Ec.R.
7	19	05	I	Ec.R.
8	16	18	I	Sh.E.
12	21	43	III	Sh.I.
12	23	27	II	Sh.I.
12	23	58	III	Sh.E.
13	21	35	I	Sh.I.
13	23	45	I	Sh.E.
14	18	02	II	Ec.D.
14	20	22	II	Ec.R.
14	21	01	I	Ec.R.
15	18	14	I	Sh.E.
20	23	31	I	Sh.I
21	20	41	II	Ec.D.
21	22	56	I	Ec.R.
21	23	01	II	Ec.R.
22	18	00	I	Sh.I.
22	20	10	I	Sh.E.
23	17	25	I	Sh.E.
23	17	39	II	Sh.E.
28	23	21	II	Ec.D.
29	19	56	I	Sh.I.
29	22	06	I	Sh.E.
30	17	58	II	Sh.I.
30	19	20	I	Ec.R.
30	19	43	III	Ec.D.
30	20	15	II	Sh.E.
30	21	59	III	Ec.R.

February

d	h	m	Sat	Phen.
5	21	53	I	Sh.I.
6	20	34	II	Sh.I.
6	21	16	I	Ec.R.
6	22	51	II	Sh.E.
7	18	31	I	Sh.E.
8	17	38	II	Ec.R.
14	18	18	I	Sh.I.
14	20	27	I	Sh.E.
15	17	40	I	Ec.R.
15	17	58	II	Ec.D.
15	20	17	II	Ec.R.
17	17	56	III	Sh.I.
17	20	08	III	Sh.E.

G.M.T. Sat. Phen.

February

d	h	m	Sat	Phen.
21	20	13	I	Sh.I.
21	22	23	I	Sh.E.
22	19	35	I	Ec.R.
22	22	56	II	Ec.R.
24	21	58	III	Sh.I.
29	21	30	I	Ec.R.

March

d	h	m	Sat	Phen.
1	18	48	I	Sh.E.
2	19	57	II	Sh.E.
6	18	06	III	Ec.R.
8	18	34	I	Sh.I.
8	20	44	I	Sh.E.
9	20	17	II	Sh.I.
13	19	56	III	Ec.D.
15	20	30	I	Sh.I.
16	19	49	I	Ec.R.
18	20	11	II	Ec.R.
24	19	04	I	Sh.E.
31	18	50	I	Sh.I.
31	20	18	III	Sh.E.

October

d	h	m	Sat	Phen.
1	22	27	I	Sh.E.
2	00	03	II	Sh.I.
2	02	19	II	Sh.E.
4	02	24	III	Sh.I.
4	04	31	III	Sh.E.
7	03	43	I	Sh.I.
8	01	00	I	Ec.D.
8	22	12	I	Sh.I.
9	00	20	I	Sh.E.
9	02	40	II	Sh.I.
9	04	56	II	Sh.E.
10	20	59	II	Ec.D.
14	20	23	III	Ec.D.
14	22	32	III	Ec.R.
15	02	54	I	Ec.D.
16	00	05	I	Sh.I.
16	02	14	I	Sh.E.
16	05	16	II	Sh.I.
16	21	23	I	Ec.D.
17	20	43	I	Sh.E.
17	23	33	II	Ec.D.
19	20	52	II	Sh.E.
22	00	24	III	Sh.I.
22	02	33	III	Ec.R.
22	04	49	I	Ec.D.
23	01	59	I	Sh.I.
23	04	08	I	Sh.E.
23	23	17	I	Ec.D.

G.M.T. Sat. Phen.

October

d	h	m	Sat	Phen.
24	20	27	I	Sh.I.
24	22	37	I	Sh.E.
25	02	08	II	Ec.D.
26	21	11	II	Sh.I.
26	23	29	II	Sh.E.
29	04	24	III	Ec.D.
30	03	53	I	Sh.I.
30	06	02	I	Sh.E.
31	01	12	I	Ec.D.
31	22	21	I	Sh.I.

November

d	h	m	Sat	Phen.
1	00	31	I	Sh.E.
1	04	33	II	Ec.D.
1	19	41	I	Ec.D.
1	20	32	III	Sh.E.
2	23	48	II	Sh.I.
3	02	06	II	Sh.E.
6	05	47	I	Sh.I.
7	03	07	I	Ec.D.
8	00	15	I	Sh.I.
8	02	25	I	Sh.E.
8	21	35	I	Ec.D.
8	22	24	III	Sh.I.
9	00	34	III	Sh.E.
9	18	44	I	Sh.I.
9	20	54	I	Sh.E.
10	02	24	II	Sh.I.
10	04	43	II	Sh.E.
11	20	36	II	Ec.D.
14	05	01	I	Ec.D.
15	02	10	I	Sh.I.
15	04	20	I	Sh.E.
15	23	30	I	Ec.D.
16	02	24	III	Sh.I.
16	04	34	III	Sh.E.
16	20	38	I	Sh.I.
16	22	48	I	Sh.E.
17	05	01	II	Sh.I.
17	17	59	I	Ec.D.
18	23	11	II	Ec.D.
20	20	38	II	Sh.E.
22	04	04	I	Sh.I.
22	06	14	I	Sh.E.
23	01	25	I	Ec.D.
23	03	35	I	Ec.R.
23	06	24	III	Sh.I.
23	22	33	I	Sh.I.
24	00	43	I	Sh.E.
24	22	04	I	Ec.R.
25	19	11	I	Sh.E.

G.M.T. Sat. Phen.

November

d	h	m	Sat	Phen.
26	04	06	II	Ec.R.
26	22	38	III	Ec.R.
27	20	57	II	Sh.I.
27	23	15	II	Sh.E.
29	05	59	I	Sh.I.
29	17	24	II	Ec.R.

December

d	h	m	Sat	Phen.
1	23	59	I	Ec.R.
2	18	56	I	Sh.I.
2	21	06	I	Sh.E.
3	18	27	I	Ec.R.
4	02	40	III	Ec.R.
4	23	33	II	Sh.I.
5	01	52	II	Sh.E.
6	20	01	II	Ec.R.
7	16	36	III	Sh.I.
9	01	54	I	Ec.R.
9	20	51	I	Sh.I.
9	23	01	I	Sh.E.
10	20	22	I	Ec.R.
11	17	30	I	Sh.E.
12	02	10	II	Sh.I.
12	04	29	II	Sh.E.
13	22	37	II	Ec.R.
14	18	26	III	Sh.I.
14	20	38	III	Sh.E.
15	04	17	I	Sh.I.
15	17	47	II	Sh.E.
16	22	46	I	Sh.I.
17	00	56	I	Sh.E.
17	22	17	I	Ec.R.
18	17	15	I	Sh.I.
18	19	25	I	Sh.E.
21	01	14	II	Ec.R.
21	22	27	III	Sh.I.
22	00	40	III	Sh.E.
22	18	05	II	Sh.I.
22	20	24	II	Sh.E.
24	00	41	I	Sh.I.
24	02	51	I	Sh.E.
25	00	13	I	Ec.R.
25	19	10	I	Sh.I.
25	21	20	I	Sh.E.
26	18	41	I	Ec.R.
28	03	52	II	Ec.R.
29	02	29	III	Sh.I.
29	04	42	III	Sh.E.
29	20	41	II	Sh.I.
29	23	00	II	Sh.E.
31	17	11	II	Ec.R.

Jupiter's satellites transit across the disk from east to west, and pass behind the disk from west to east. The shadows that they cast also transit across the disk. With the exception at times of Satellite IV, the satellites also pass through the shadow of the planet, i.e. they are eclipsed. Just before opposition the satellite disappears in the shadow to the west of the planet, and reappears from occultation on the east limb. Immediately after opposition the satellite is occulted at the west limb, and reappears from eclipse to the east of the planet. At times approximately two to four months before and after opposition, both phases of eclipses of Satellite III may be seen. When Satellite IV is eclipsed, both phases may be seen.

The list of phenomena gives most of the eclipses and shadow transits visible in the British Isles under favourable conditions.

Ec.	= Eclipse	R	= Reappearance
Sh.	= Shadow transit	I	= Ingress
D	= Disappearance	E	= Egress

CELESTIAL PHENOMENA FOR OBSERVATION IN 1988

ECLIPSES

There will be three eclipses during 1988, two of the Sun and one of the Moon. *Penumbral eclipses are not mentioned in this section as they are difficult to observe.*

1. A total eclipse of the Sun on March 17–18. The path of totality begins in the Indian Ocean to the west of Sumatra, crosses Sumatra, Borneo and the southern part of the Philippine Islands, passes close to the Mariana Islands and south of the Aleutian Islands and ends in the Gulf of Alaska. The partial phase is visible from eastern Asia, Indonesia, north-western Australia, New Guinea, Micronesia, the extreme north-west of North America and the western Hawaiian Islands. The eclipse begins on March 17 at 23^h 24^m and ends on March 18 at 04^h 32^m; the total phase begins on March 18 at 00^h 23^m and ends at 03^h 32^m. The maximum duration of totality is 3^m 46^s.

2. A partial eclipse of the Moon on August 27 is visible from North America except the eastern part, Central America, the western part of South America, part of Antarctica, the Pacific Ocean, Australasia and the eastern part of Asia. The eclipse begins at 10^h 08^m and ends at 12^h 00^m. The time of maximum eclipse is 11^h 04^m, when 0.29 of the Moon's diameter is obscured.

3. An annular eclipse of the Sun on September 11 is visible as a partial eclipse from the eastern part of Africa except for most of Egypt and western Sudan, the southern part of Asia, the Indian and Southern Oceans, Indonesia, Australia except for the extreme north-east, New Zealand and part of Antarctica. The eclipse begins at 01^h 46^m and ends at 07^h 41^m. The annular phase begins at the coast of Somalia at 02^h 59^m, crosses the Indian and Southern Oceans and ends at 06^h 28^m between New Zealand and Antarctica. The maximum duration of the annular phase is 6^m 52^s.

LUNAR OCCULTATIONS

The only bright star occulted during the year is z.c. 1487 (α Leonis = Regulus). No planets are occulted by the Moon in 1988.

Observations of the times of these occultations are made by both amateur and professional astronomers. Such observations are later analysed to yield accurate positions of the Moon: this is one method of determining the difference between ephemeris time and universal time.

Many of the observations made by amateurs are obtained with the use of a stop-watch which is compared with a time signal immediately after the observation. Thus an accuracy of about one-fifth of a second is obtainable, though the observer's personal equation may amount to one-third or one-half of a second.

The list on the opposite page includes most of the occultations visible under favourable conditions in the British Isles. No occultation is included unless the star is at least 10° above the horizon and the Sun sufficiently far below the horizon to permit the star to be seen with the naked eye or in a small telescope. The altitude limit is reduced from 10° to 2° for stars and planets brighter than magnitude 2·0 and such occultations are also predicted in daylight.

The column Phase shows whether a disappearance (1) or reappearance (2) is to be observed. The column headed "El. of Moon" gives the elongation of the Moon from the Sun, in degrees. The elongation increases from 0° at New Moon to 180° at Full Moon and on to 360° (or 0°) at New Moon again. Times and position angles (P), reckoned from the north point in the direction north, east, south, west, are given for Greenwich (Lat. 51° 30′, Long. 0°) and Edinburgh (Lat. 56° 00′, Long. 3° 12′ west).

The coefficients a and b are the variations in the G.M.T. for each degree of longitude (positive to the west) and latitude (positive to the north) respectively: they enable approximate times (to within about 1^m generally) to be found for any point in the British Isles. If the point of observation is $\Delta\lambda$ degrees west and $\Delta\phi$ degrees north, the approximate time is found by adding $a.\Delta\lambda + b.\Delta\phi$ to the given G.M.T.

As an illustration the disappearance of z.c. 435 on January 26 at Liverpool will be found from both Greenwich and Edinburgh.

	Greenwich	Edinburgh
	°	°
Longitude	0·0	+3·2
Long. of Liverpool	+3·0	+3·0
$\Delta\lambda$	+3·0	−0·2
Latitude	+51·5	+56·0
Lat. of Liverpool	+53·4	+53·4
$\Delta\phi$	+1·9	−2·6
	h m	h m
G.M.T.	22 00·3	21 48·8
$a.\Delta\lambda$	−2·7	+0·2
$b.\Delta\phi$	−4·4	+3·9
	21 53·2	21 52·9

If the occultation is given for one station but not the other, the reason for the suppression is given by the following code.

N = star not occulted.

A = star's altitude less than 10° (2° for bright stars and planets).

S = Sun not sufficiently below the horizon.

G = occultation is of very short duration.

It will be noticed that in some cases the coefficients a and b are not given: this is because the occultation is so short that prediction for other places by means of these coefficients would not be reliable.

LUNAR OCCULTATIONS, 1988

Date	Z.C. No.	Mag.	Phase	El. of Moon	Greenwich U.T.	a	b	P	Edinburgh U.T.	a	b	P
				°	h m	m	m	°	h m	m	m	°
Jan. 26	435	5·9	D.D.	102	22 0·3	−0·9	−2·3	109	21 48·8	−1·0	−1·5	92
27	537	3·8	D.D.	112	17 56·0	−1·3	1·3	71	17 59·4	−0·9	1·7	57
27	536	5·4	D.D.	112	18 10·8	−0·8	2·6	32	18 23·2	−0·1	3·9	10
27	541	4·0	D.D.	112	18 46·3	−1·0	2·3	37	18 56·5	−0·5	3·5	16
27	545	4·3	D.D.	112	..				18 54·6	..	..	130
27	552	3·0	D.D.	113	19 47·0	..	..	139	19 29·7	−1·7	−1·0	111
27	561	5·2	D.D.	113	..				20 54·9	..	..	160
30	885	5·7	D.D.	138	2 33·7	−0·2	−1·6	91	2 25·8	−0·3	−1·6	86
30	890	4·5	D.D.	139	..				3 57·0	..	..	177
30	1008	5·1	D.D.	147	20 29·8	−1·3	3·2	45	..			
Feb. 25	797	6·3	D.D.	104	18 24·9	−1·7	−0·3	104	18 20·7	−1·4	0·6	88
27	1088	5·6	D.D.	127	18 16·3	−1·5	−0·2	123	18 13·6	−1·1	0·7	107
Mar. 22	552	3·0	D.D.	57	9 46·7	0·1	1·6	75	9 54·5	0·2	1·7	69
22	552	3·0	R.B.	58	10 42·7	−0·0	1·8	242	10 50·7	−0·1	1·8	249
27	1308	4·7	D.D.	120	21 28·6	−1·0	−2·0	135	21 17·1	−1·1	−1·6	128
29	1418	5·9	D.D.	132	1 39·0	−0·5	−1·8	97	1 29·2	−0·6	−1·8	97
Apr. 18	537	3·8	D.D.	31	20 40·3	0·1	−1·1	79	20 35·4	−0·0	−1·1	72
18	536	5·4	D.D.	31	20 49·6	−0·3	−0·1	35	20 48·5	−0·5	0·2	24
18	545	4·3	D.D.	31	21 19·6	0·8	−2·1	130	21 12·5	0·5	−2·0	121
18	541	4·0	D.D.	31	21 20·5	..	..	18	21 27·0	..	..	353
18	541	4·0	R.D.	31	A				21 28·4	..	..	350
18	552	3·0	D.D.	32	A				21 35·5	0·4	−1·4	93
27	1663	5·2	D.D.	133	21 30·0	−1·3	−1·1	121	21 21·8	−1·2	−0·7	118
May 24	1547	3·9	D.D.	93	0 9·7	0·3	−2·3	172	0 0·5	0·2	−2·2	171
30	2287	3·0	R.B.	171	21 26·0	−0·7	0·2	315	A			
Jun. 27	2383	2·9	D.D.	154	21 21·1	−1·0	−0·2	143	A			
27	2383	2·9	R.B.	155	22 28·5	−1·6	0·0	251	22 14·7	−1·5	0·2	244
Aug. 6	537	3·8	R.D.	285	0 04·4	0·3	1·5	254	0 12·0	0·3	1·5	260
6	545	4·3	R.D.	285	0 12·3	..	..	178	0 25·9	0·8	2·1	192
6	552	3·0	D.B.	285	0 16·5	−0·1	1·1	117	0 22·0	0·0	1·3	109
6	541	4·0	R.D.	285	0 26·1	−0·2	1·2	296	0 30·8	−0·2	1·2	305
6	552	3·0	R.D.	286	0 53·7	0·6	2·2	203	1 4·5	0·4	2·0	212
21	2406	6·0	D.D.	104	20 5·1	−1·4	−0·6	79	A			
30	105	4·6	R.D.	218	3 5·7	−1·5	−0·1	261	2 58·9	−1·6	−0·6	279
Sep. 9	1487	1·3	D.B.	342	14 4·8	−0·4	−2·2	147	13 53·8	−0·4	−2·1	146
9	1487	1·3	R.D.	343	15 6·9	−0·6	−1·8	280	14 56·7	−0·6	−1·8	280
20	2848	5·6	D.D.	112	20 35·9	−1·1	−0·2	59	20 31·8	−1·0	−0·1	52
24	3307	4·9	D.D.	155	0 0·4	0·3	1·9	357	..			
Oct. 17	2784	3·4	D.D.	80	18 24·9	−0·6	0·4	22	18 25·5	..	..	10
20	3237	4·4	D.D.	121	22 10·3	−1·3	−0·9	87	22 3·5	−1·0	−0·5	72
21	3379	6·4	D.D.	135	23 4·9	−1·7	−1·6	102	22 55·3	−1·2	−0·7	84
23	105	4·6	D.D.	163	23 51·8	−1·0	0·7	47	23 52·5	−0·7	1·1	31
27	541	4·0	R.D.	207	3 2·2	−1·2	2·0	209	3 4·3	−1·1	0·8	228
Nov. 3	1487	1·3	D.B.	288	..				1 44·9	..	..	185
3	1487	1·3	R.D.	288	..				2 4·9	..	..	222
15	3031	5·9	D.D.	75	16 48·7	−0·4	1·3	6	16 55·1	..	..	351
Dec. 19	399	5·7	D.D.	135	17 36·7	−0·4	2·1	42	17 45·6	−0·2	2·2	31
20	440	4·6	D.D.	140	2 31·6	−0·1	−1·8	101	2 23·4	−0·3	−1·6	89
20	536	5·4	D.D.	149	19 41·6	−1·4	0·8	95	19 42·7	−1·0	1·3	81
20	537	3·8	D.D.	149	..				19 51·3	−1·8	−0·4	126
20	539	4·4	D.D.	149	19 57·6	−1·0	1·5	66	20 2·5	−0·7	1·9	52
20	541	4·0	D.D.	150	20 14·8	−1·5	0·5	98	20 14·2	−1·1	1·1	83
20	542	5·9	D.D.	150	20 21·8	−1·1	1·6	61	20 26·9	−0·7	2·0	46
24	1170	3·7	R.D.	200	21 1·4	−0·7	0·9	290	21 2·7	−0·7	0·6	306

NAME	Mag.	R.A.	Dec.	Spectrum	
		h m	° ′		The positions of heavenly bodies
α Andromedæ *Alpheratz*	2·1	0 07·8	+29 02	A0p	on the celestial sphere are defined by
β Cassiopeiæ *Caph*	2·3	0 08·6	+59 05	F5	two co-ordinates, right ascension
γ Pegasi *Algenib*	2·8	0 12·6	+15 07	B2	and declination, which are anal-
α Phœnicis	2·4	0 25·7	−42 22	K0	ogous to longitude and latitude on
α Cassiopeiæ *Schedar*	2·2	0 39·8	+56 28	K0	the surface of the Earth. If we
					imagine the plane of the terrestrial
β Ceti *Diphda*	2·0	0 43·0	−18 03	K0	equator extended indefinitely, it will
γ Cassiopeiæ*	Var.	0 56·0	+60 39	B0p	cut the celestial sphere in a great
β Andromedæ *Mirach*	2·1	1 09·1	+35 34	M0	circle known as the celestial equator.
δ Cassiopeiæ	2·7	1 25·1	+60 11	A5	Similarly the plane of the Earth's
α Eridani *Achernar*	0·5	1 37·3	−57 18	B5	orbit, when extended, cuts in the
					great circle called the ecliptic. The
β Arietis *Sheratan*	2·6	1 54·0	+20 45	A5	two intersections of these circles are
γ Andromedæ *Almak*	2·3	2 03·2	+42 16	K0	known as the First Point of Aries
α Arietis *Hamal*	2·0	2 06·5	+23 25	K2	and the First Point of Libra. If from
α Ursæ Minoris *Polaris*	2·0	2 19·8	+89 13	F8	any star a perpendicular be drawn
β Persei *Algol**	Var.	3 07·4	+40 55	B8	to the celestial equator, the length
					of this perpendicular is the star's
α Persei *Mirfak*	1·8	3 23·5	+49 49	F5	declination. The arc, measured east-
η Tauri *Alcyone*	2·9	3 46·8	+24 04	B5p	wards along the equator from the
α Tauri *Aldebaran*	0·9	4 35·3	+16 29	K5	First Point of Aries to the foot of
β Orionis *Rigel*	0·1	5 14·0	− 8 13	B8p	this perpendicular, is the right as-
α Aurigæ *Capella*	0·1	5 15·8	+45 59	G0	cension. An alternative definition
					of right ascension is that it is the
γ Orionis *Bellatrix*	1·6	5 24·5	+ 6 20	B2	angle at the celestial pole (where the
β Tauri *Elnath*	1·7	5 25·6	+28 36	B8	Earth's axis, if prolonged, would
δ Orionis	2·2	5 31·4	− 0 18	B0	meet the sphere) between the great
α Leporis	2·6	5 32·2	−17 50	F0	circles to the First Point of Aries
ε Orionis	1·7	5 35·6	− 1 13	B0	and to the star.
					The plane of the Earth's equator
ζ Orionis	1·8	5 40·2	− 1 57	B0	has a slow movement, so that our
κ Orionis	2·1	5 47·2	− 9 40	B0	reference system for right ascension
α Orionis *Betelgeuse**	Var.	5 54·5	+ 7 24	M0	and declination is not fixed. The
β Aurigæ *Menkalinan*	1·9	5 58·7	+44 57	A0p	consequent alteration in these quan-
β Canis Majoris *Mirzam*	2·0	6 22·2	−17 57	B1	tities from year to year is called
					precession. In right ascension it is
α Carinæ *Canopus*	−0·7	6 23·7	−52 41	F0	an increase of about 3ˢ a year for
γ Geminorum *Alhena*	1·9	6 37·0	+16 25	A0	equatorial stars, and larger or
α Canis Majoris *Sirius*	−1·5	6 44·6	−16 42	A0	smaller changes in either direction
ε Canis Majoris	1·5	6 58·2	−28 57	B1	for stars near the poles, depending
δ Canis Majoris	1·9	7 07·9	−26 22	F8p	on the right ascension of the star. In
					declination it varies between +20″
α Geminorum *Castor*	1·6	7 33·9	+31 55	A0	and −20″ according to the right
α Canis Minoris *Procyon*	0·4	7 38·7	+ 5 15	F5	ascension of the star.
β Geminorum *Pollux*	1·1	7 44·6	+28 03	K0	A star or other body crosses the
ζ Puppis	2·3	8 03·2	−39 58	Od	meridian when the sidereal time is
γ Velorum	1·8	8 09·2	−47 18	Oap	equal to its right ascension. The
					altitude is then a maximum, and may
ε Carinæ	1·9	8 22·3	−59 28	K0	be deduced by remembering that the
δ Velorum	2·0	8 44·4	−54 40	A0	altitude of the elevated pole is nu-
λ Velorum *Suhail*	2·2	9 07·6	−43 23	K5	merically equal to the latitude, while
β Carinæ	1·7	9 13·1	−69 40	A0	that of the equator at its intersection
ι Carinæ	2·2	9 16·8	−59 14	F0	with the meridian is equal to the co-
					latitude, or complement of the lati-
α Hydræ *Alphard*	2·0	9 27·0	− 8 37	K2	tude.
α Leonis *Regulus*	1·3	10 07·8	+12 01	B8	
γ Leonis *Algeiba*	1·9	10 19·3	+19 54	K0	
β Ursæ Majoris *Merak*	2·4	11 01·2	+56 27	A0	
α Ursæ Majoris *Dubhe*	1·8	11 03·0	+61 49	K0	

* γ Cassiopeiæ, 1987 mag. 2·5.   β Persei, mag. 2·2 to 3·2.
α Orionis, mag. 0·1 to 1·2.

MEAN PLACES OF STARS, 1988-5

Name	Mag.	R.A.	Dec.	Spectrum	
		h m	° ′		
δ Leonis	2·6	11 13·5	+ 20 35	A3	Thus in London (Lat. 51° 30′) the
β Leonis *Denebola*	2·1	11 48·5	+ 14 38	A2	meridian altitude of *Sirius* is found
γ Ursæ Majoris *Phecda*	2·4	11 53·2	+ 53 46	A0	as follows:
γ Corvi	2·6	12 15·2	− 17 29	B8	
α Crucis	1·0	12 26·0	− 63 02	B1	
					Altitude of equator 38 30
γ Crucis	1·6	12 30·5	− 57 03	M3	Declination south 16 42
γ Centauri	2·2	12 40·9	− 48 54	A0	
γ Virginis	2·7	12 41·1	− 1 23	F0	Difference 21 48
β Crucis	1·3	12 47·0	− 59 38	B1	
ε Ursæ Majoris *Alioth*	1·8	12 53·5	+ 56 01	A0*p*	The altitude of *Capella* (Dec.
					+45° 59′) at lower transit is:
α Canum Venaticorum	2·9	12 55·5	+ 38 23	A0*p*	
ζ Ursæ Majoris *Mizar*	2·1	13 23·5	+ 54 59	A2*p*	Altitude of pole 51 30
α Virginis *Spica*	1·0	13 24·6	− 11 06	B2	Polar distance of star 44 01
η Ursæ Majoris *Alkaid*	1·9	13 47·1	+ 49 22	B3	
β Centauri *Hadar*............	0·6	14 03·0	− 60 19	B1	Difference 7 29
					The brightness of a heavenly body
θ Centauri	2·1	14 06·0	− 36 19	K0	is denoted by its magnitude. Omit-
α Boötis *Arcturus*	0·0	14 15·1	+ 19 15	K0	ting the exceptionally bright stars
α Centauri *Rigil Kent*.	0·1	14 38·8	− 60 47	G0	*Sirius* and *Canopus*, the twenty
ε Boötis.....................	2·4	14 44·5	+ 27 07	K0	brightest stars are of the first mag-
β Ursæ Minoris *Kochab*	2·1	14 50·7	+ 74 12	K5	nitude, while the faintest stars vis-
					ible to the naked eye are of the sixth
α Coronæ Borealis *Alphecca* ..	2·2	15 34·2	+ 26 45	A0	magnitude. The magnitude scale is
δ Scorpii	2·3	15 59·7	− 22 35	B0	a precise one, as a difference of five
β Scorpii	2·6	16 04·8	− 19 46	B1	magnitudes represents a ratio of 100
α Scorpii *Antares*	1·0	16 28·7	− 26 24	M0	to 1 in brightness. Typical second
α Trianguli Australis.........	1·9	16 47·4	− 69 00	K2	magnitude stars are *Polaris* and the
					stars in the Belt of Orion. The scale
ε Scorpii	2·3	16 49·4	− 34 16	K0	is most easily fixed in memory by
α Herculis*..................	Var.	17 14·1	+ 14 24	M3	comparing the stars with Norton's
λ Scorpii	1·6	17 32·8	− 37 06	B2	*Star Atlas* (see page 138). The stars
α Ophiuchi *Rasalhague*	2·1	17 34·4	+ 12 34	A5	*Sirius* and *Canopus* and the planets
θ Scorpii	1·9	17 36·5	− 42 59	F0	Venus and Jupiter are so bright that
					their magnitudes are expressed by
κ Scorpii	2·4	17 41·7	− 39 01	B2	negative numbers. A small telescope
γ Draconis	2·2	17 56·3	+ 51 29	K5	will show stars down to the ninth or
ε Sagittarii *Kaus Australis* ...	1·9	18 23·4	− 34 23	A0	tenth magnitude, while stars fainter
α Lyræ *Vega*	0·0	18 36·5	+ 38 46	A0	than the twentieth magnitude may
σ Sagittarii..................	2·0	18 54·6	− 26 19	B3	be photographed by long exposures
					with the largest telescopes.
β Cygni *Albireo*.............	3·1	19 30·3	+ 27 56	K0	
α Aquilæ *Altair*	0·8	19 50·2	+ 8 50	A5	Some of the astronomical infor-
α Capricorni	3·8	20 17·4	− 12 35	G5	mation in this ALMANACK has been
γ Cygni	2·2	20 21·8	+ 40 13	F8*p*	taken from *Astronomical Phenom-*
α Pavonis	1·9	20 24·7	− 56 46	B3	*ena*, and is published here by ar-
					rangement with, and with the
α Cygni *Deneb*..............	1·3	20 41·0	+ 45 14	A2*p*	permission of, the Controller of H.M.
α Cephei *Alderamin*	2·4	21 18·3	+ 62 32	A5	Stationery Office.
ε Pegasi.....................	2·4	21 43·6	+ 9 49	K0	
δ Capricorni	2·9	21 46·4	− 16 11	A5	
α Gruis	1·7	22 07·5	− 47 01	B5	
δ Cephei*....................	3·7	22 28·7	+ 58 21	*	
β Gruis	2·1	22 42·0	− 46 57	M3	
α Piscis Austrini *Fomalhaut* ..	1·2	22 57·0	− 29 41	A3	
β Pegasi *Scheat*	2·4	23 03·2	+ 28 01	M0	
α Pegasi *Markab*	2·5	23 04·2	+ 15 09	A0	

* α Herculis, mag. 3·1 to 3·9.

δ Cephei, mag. 3·7 to 4·4, Spectrum F5 to G0.

ELEMENTS OF THE SOLAR SYSTEM

Orb	Mean Distance from Sun (Earth=1)	km. 10⁶	Sidereal Period	Synodic Period	Incl. of Orbit to Ecliptic	Diameter	Mass (Earth=1)	Period of Rotation on Axis
			y d	Days	° ′	km.		d h m
Sun	...	...	...	...	...	1,392,000	332,948	25 09
Mercury	0·39	58	88	116	7 00	4,880	0·055	59
Venus...........	0·72	108	225	584	3 24	12,100	0·815	243
Earth	1·00	150	1 0	...	...	12,756eq.	1·00	23 56
Mars............	1·52	228	1 322	780	1 51	6,790	0·107	24 37
Jupiter..........	5·20	778	11 315	399	1 18	{142,800eq. 134,200p.	318	{ 9 50 9 56
Saturn	9·54	1427	29 167	378	2 29	{120,000eq. 108,000p.	95	{ 10 14 10 38
Uranus..........	19·19	2870	84 6	370	0 46	52,000	14·6	16—28
Neptune.........	30·07	4497	164 288	367	1 46	48,400	17·2	18—20
Pluto	39·46	5950	247 255	367	17 09	3,000?	0·01	6 09

THE SATELLITES

Name	Star Mag.	Mean distance from Primary	Sidereal Period of Revolution	Name	Star mag.	Mean distance from Primary	Sidereal Period of Revolution
Earth		km.	d	*Saturn*		km.	d
Moon	—	384,400	27·322	Janus	14	151,000	0·695
				Epimetheus.......	15	151,000	0·694
Mars				Mimas	13	186,000	0·942
Phobos	12	9,400	0·319	Enceladus	12	238,000	1·370
Deimos	13	23,500	1·262	Tethys	10	295,000	1·888
				Telesto	19	295,000	1·888
Jupiter				Calypso	18	295,000	1·888
XVI. Metis	17	128,000	0·295	Dione	10	377,000	2·737
XV. Adrastea	19	129,000	0·298	—...............	18	377,000	2·737
V. Amalthea	14	181,000	0·498	Rhea.............	10	527,000	4·518
XIV. Thebe	15	222,000	0·675	Titan	8	1,222,000	15·945
I. Io	5	422,000	1·769	Hyperion	14	1,481,000	21·277
II. Europa	5	671,000	3·551	Iapetus..........	11	3,561,000	79·331
III. Ganymede ...	5	1,070,000	7·155	Phoebe	16	12,954,000	550·4
IV. Callisto	6	1,880,000	16·689				
XIII. Leda	20	11,090,000	239	*Uranus*			
VI. Himalia.......	15	11,480,000	251	Miranda	17	129,000	1·414
X. Lysithea	18	11,720,000	259	Ariel.............	14	191,000	2·520
VII. Elara	17	11,740,000	260	Umbriel	15	266,000	4·144
XII. Ananke	19	21,200,000	631	Titania	14	436,000	8·706
XI. Carme	18	22,600,000	692	Oberon	14	583,000	13·463
VIII. Pasiphae	18	23,500,000	735				
IX. Sinope	18	23,700,000	758	*Neptune*			
				Triton	14	355,000	5·877
Saturn				Nereid	19	5,510,000	360·21
Atlas.............	18	138,000	0·602				
—................	16	139,000	0·613	*Pluto*			
—................	16	142,000	0·629	Charon...........	17	19,700	6·387

THE EARTH

The shape of the Earth is that of an oblate spheroid or solid of revolution whose meridian sections are ellipses not differing much from circles, whilst the sections at right angles are circles. The length of the equatorial axis is about 12,756 kilometres, and that of the polar axis is 12,714 kilometres. The mean density of the Earth is 5·5 times that of water, although that of the surface layer is less. The Earth and Moon revolve about their common centre of gravity in a lunar month; this centre in turn revolves round the Sun in a plane known as the ecliptic, that passes through the Sun's centre. The Earth's equator is inclined to this plane at an angle of 23½°. This tilt is the cause of the seasons. In mid-latitudes, when the Sun is high above the Equator, not only does the high noon altitude make the days longer, but the Sun's rays fall more directly on the Earth's surface; these effects combine to produce summer. In equatorial regions the noon altitude is large throughout the year, and there is little variation in the length of the day. In higher latitudes the noon altitude is lower, and the days in summer are appreciably longer than those in winter.

The average velocity of the Earth in its orbit is 30 kilometres a second. It makes a complete rotation on its axis in about 23ʰ 56ᵐ of mean time, which is the sidereal day. Because of its annual revolution round the Sun, the rotation with respect to the Sun, or the solar day, is more than this by about four minutes (*see* p. 140). The extremity of the axis of rotation, or the North Pole of the Earth, is not rigidly fixed, but wanders over an area roughly 20 metres in diameter.

TERRESTRIAL MAGNETISM

A magnetic compass points along the horizontal component of a magnetic line of force. These directions converge on the "magnetic dip-poles". At these poles a freely suspended magnetized needle would become vertical. Not only do the positions of these poles change with time, but their exact location is ill-defined, particularly so in the case of the north dip-pole where the lines of force, on the north side of it, instead of converging radially, tend to bunch into a channel. Although it is therefore unrealistic to attempt to specify the locations of the dip-poles exactly, the present adopted positions are 77°·0 N., 102°·4 W. and 65°·3 S., 140°·0 E. The two magnetic dip-poles are thus not antipodal, the line joining them passing the centre of the Earth at a distance of about 1,200 kilometres. The distances of the magnetic dip-poles from the north and south geographical poles are about 1,400 and 2,700 kilometres respectively.

There is also a "magnetic equator", at all points of which the vertical force is zero and a magnetized needle remains horizontal. This line runs between 2° and 10° north of the geographical equator in the eastern hemisphere, turns sharply south off the West African coast, and crosses South America through Brazil, Bolivia and Peru; it recrosses the geographical equator in mid-Pacific.

Reference has already been made to secular changes in the Earth's field. The following table indicates the changes in magnetic declination (or variation of the compass). Similar, though much smaller, changes have occurred in "dip" or magnetic inclination. Secular changes differ throughout the world. Although the London observations strongly suggest a cycle of several hundred years, an exact repetition is unlikely.

London			Greenwich		
1580	11°	15′ E.	1850	22°	24′ W.
1622	5	56 E.	1900	16	29 W.
1665	1	22 W.	1925	13	10 W.
1730	13	00 W.	1950	9	07 W.
1773	21	09 W.	1975	6	39 W.

In order that up-to-date information on the variation of the compass may be available, many governments publish magnetic charts on which there are lines (called isogonic) passing through all places at which specified values of declination will be found at the date of the chart.

In the British Isles, isogonic lines now run approximately north-east to south-west. Though there are considerable local deviations due to geographical causes, a rough value of magnetic declination may be obtained by assuming that at 50° N. on the meridian of Greenwich, the value in 1988 is 4° 28′ west and allowing an increase of 13′ for each degree of latitude northwards and one of 27′ for each degree of longitude westwards. For example, at 53° N., 5° W., declination will be about 4° 28′ + 39′ + 135′, i.e. 7° 22′ west. The average annual change at the present time is about 9′ decrease.

The number of magnetic observatories now approaches 200—widely scattered over the globe. There are three in Great Britain maintained by the Government: at Hartland, North Devon, at Eskdalemuir in Dumfriesshire, Scotland, and at Lerwick, Shetland Islands. Some recent annual mean values of the magnetic elements for Hartland are given below.

The normal worldwide terrestrial magnetic field corresponds approximately to that of a very strong small bar magnet near the centre of the Earth but with appreciable smooth spatial departures. The origin and slow secular change of the normal field is not yet fully understood but is generally ascribed to electric currents associated with fluid motions within the Earth's core. Superposed on the normal field are local and regional anomalies whose magnitudes may in places exceed that of the normal field; these are due to the influence of mineral deposits in the Earth's crust. A small proportion of the field is of external origin, mostly associated with electric currents in the ionosphere. The configuration of the external field and the ionization of the atmosphere depend on the incident particle and radiation flux. There are, therefore, short-term and non-periodic as well as diurnal, 27-day, seasonal and 11-year periodic changes in the magnetic field, dependent upon the position of the Sun and the degree of solar activity.

Year	Declination West	Dip or Inclination	Horizontal Force	Vertical Force
	° ′	° ′	oersted	oersted
1950	11 06	66 54	0·1848	0·4334
1955	10 30	66 49	0·1859	0·4340
1960	9 59	66 44	0·1871	0·4350
1965	9 30	66 34	0·1887	0·4354
1970	9 06	66 26	0·1903	0·4364
1975	8 32	66 17	0·1921	0·4373
1980	7 44	66 10	0·1933	0·4377
1985	6 56	66 08	0·1938	0·4380
1986	6 47	66 08	0·1938	0·4381

Magnetic Storms. Occasionally—sometimes with great suddenness—the Earth's magnetic field is subject for several hours to marked disturbance. In extreme cases, departures in field intensity as much as one tenth the normal value are experienced. In many instances, such disturbances are accompanied by widespread displays of aurorae, marked changes in the incidence of cosmic rays, an increase in the reception of "noise" from the Sun at radio frequencies together with rapid changes in the ionosphere and induced electric currents within the earth which adversely affect radio and telegraphic communications. The disturbances are generally ascribed to flux changes in the stream of neutral and ionized particles which emanates from the Sun and through which the Earth is continuously passing. Some of these changes are associated with visible eruptions on the Sun, usually in the region of sun-spots. There is a marked tendency for disturbances to recur after intervals of about 27 days, the apparent period of rotation of the Sun on its axis, which is consistent with the sources being located on particular areas of the Sun.

Artificial Satellites Launched in 1985–6

Desig-nation	Satellite	Launch date	i	P	e	Perigee height (km)
1985–		1985	°	m		
86	Cosmos 1686, rocket	September 27	51·6	90·5	0·002	291
87	Intelsat 5A F-12, rocket	September 28	0·2	1435·9	0·000	35,767
88	Cosmos 1687, launcher rocket, launcher, rocket	September 30	63·0	717·7	0·736	635
89	Cosmos 1688, rocket	October 2	50·7	93·4	0·014	344
90	Cosmos 1689, rocket	October 3	98·0	97·1	0·006	574
91	Molniya 3-26, launcher rocket, launcher, rocket	October 3	62·9	717·6	0·737	609
92	STS-51J, USA 11, USA12	October 3	28·5	94·3	0·003	476
93	Navstar 11, rocket	October 9	63·4	717·9	0·014	19,822
94	Cosmos 1690-1695, rocket	October 9	82·6	113·8	0·002	1,382
95	Cosmos 1696, rocket, engine	October 16	70·4	89·6	0·004	230
96	China 17, rocket	October 21	63·0	90·1	0·016	171
97	Cosmos 1697, rocket	October 22	71·0	102·0	0·000	849
98	Cosmos 1698, launcher rocket, launcher, rocket	October 22	62·9	717·2	0·737	603
99	Molniya 1-65, launcher rocket, launcher, rocket	October 23	63·0	717·9	0·736	631
100	Meteor 3-01, rocket	October 24	82·5	110·3	0·002	1,227
101	Cosmos 1699, rocket	October 25	67·1	89·5	0·013	166
102	Cosmos 1700, launcher rocket, launcher, rocket	October 25	1·4	1,435·8	0·001	35,758
103	Molniya 1-66, launcher rocket, launcher, rocket	October 28	62·8	718·0	0·741	508
104	STS-61A, GLOMR	October 30	57·0	91·0	0·001	322
105	Cosmos 1701, launcher rocket, launcher, rocket	November 9	63·1	717·5	0·736	632
106	Cosmos 1702, rocket, engine	November 13	72·9	92·3	0·004	356
107	Raduga 17, launcher rocket, launcher, rocket	November 15	1·3	1,436·3	0·000	35,792
108	Cosmos 1703, rocket	November 22	82·5	97·8	0·002	635
109	STS-61B, Morelos 2, Aussat 2, RCA Satcom K2	November 27	28·5	91·4	0·004	323
110	Cosmos 1704, rocket	November 28	82·9	104·9	0·003	965
111	Cosmos 1705, rocket, engine	December 3	72·9	92·3	0·003	356
112	Cosmos 1706, rocket	December 11	67·2	89·5	0·013	167
113	Cosmos 1707, rocket	December 12	82·5	97·8	0·002	635
114	ITV-1, ITV-2, rocket	December 13	37·0	95·4	0·032	319
115	Cosmos 1708, rocket, engine	December 13	82·3	90·0	0·001	256
116	Cosmos 1709, rocket	December 19	82·9	104·9	0·003	965
117	Molniya 3-27, launcher rocket, launcher, rocket	December 24	62·9	735·7	0·746	477
118	Cosmos 1710-2, launcher rocket, launcher, rocket	December 24	64·8	675·4	0·001	19,096
119	Meteor 2-13, rocket	December 26	82·5	104·1	0·002	939
120	Cosmos 1713, rocket	December 27	62·8	90·7	0·014	216
121	Cosmos 1714	December 28	71·0	94·7	0·049	164
1986–		1986				
01	Cosmos 1715, rocket	January 8	72·8	89·6	0·004	227
02	Cosmos 1716-1723, rocket	January 9	74·0	115·5	0·002	1,465
03	STS-61C, RCA Satcom K1	January 12	28·5	91·0	0·002	324
04	Cosmos 1724, rocket	January 15	67·1	89·5	0·012	168
05	Cosmos 1725, rocket	January 16	82·9	104·9	0·002	972
06	Cosmos 1726, rocket	January 17	82·5	97·7	0·002	632

Artificial Satellites Launched in 1986—(*cont.*)

Desig-nation	Satellite	Launch date	i	P	e	Perigee height (km)
1986–		1986	°	m		
07	Raduga 18, launcher rocket, launcher, rocket	January 17	1·3	1,476·7	0·002	36,501
08	Cosmos 1727, rocket	January 23	82·9	104·9	0·004	962
09	Cosmos 1728, rocket, engine	January 28	70·0	89·5	0·004	225
10	China 18, rocket	February 1	0·1	1,435·9	0·000	35,778
11	Cosmos 1729, launcher, launcher rocket, rocket	February 1	62·9	718·0	0·736	633
12	Cosmos 1730, rocket, engine	February 4	72·8	89·9	0·006	228
13	Cosmos 1731, rocket	February 7	64·8	88·9	0·006	179
14	NOSS 7, rocket, USA 16, USA 17	February 9	63·4	107·4	0·006	1,065
15	Cosmos 1732, rocket	February 11	73·6	116·1	0·003	1,480
16	Yuri 2B	February 12	0·9	1,434·3	0·003	35,640
17	Mir, rocket	February 19	51·6	91·1	0·001	324
18	Cosmos 1733, rocket	February 19	82·5	97·7	0·002	633
19	Spot 1, Viking	February 22	98·7	101·5	0·000	824
20	Cosmos 1734, rocket	February 26	67·1	89·6	0·014	162
21	Cosmos 1735, rocket	February 27	65·0	92·8	0·001	406
22	Soyuz T15, rocket	March 13	51·6	89·7	0·004	239
23	Progress 25, rocket	March 19	51·6	89·7	0·005	227
24	Cosmos 1736, rocket, platform	March 21	65·0	89·7	0·001	250
25	Cosmos 1737, rocket	March 25	73·4	93·1	0·001	416
26	G Star 2, Brasilsat 2	March 28	0·6	1,417·4	0·015	34,816
27	Cosmos 1738, launcher rocket, launcher, rocket	April 4	1·4	1,435·9	0·000	35,747
28	Cosmos 1739, rocket	April 9	64·9	89·5	0·012	173
29	Cosmos 1740, rocket, engine	April 15	72·9	92·3	0·004	355
30	Cosmos 1741, rocket	April 17	74·0	100·8	0·002	782
31	Molniya 3-28, launcher rocket, launcher, rocket	April 18	62·8	717·1	0·737	613
32	Progress 26, rocket	April 23	51·6	91·3	0·001	338
33	Cosmos 1742, rocket, engine	May 14	72·9	92·3	0·005	353
34	Cosmos 1743, rocket	May 15	82·5	97·8	0·002	633
35	Soyuz TM1, rocket	May 21	51·6	91·2	0·001	332
36	Cosmos 1744, rocket, engine	May 21	62·8	90·4	0·012	219
37	Cosmos 1745, rocket	May 23	83·0	104·9	0·003	966
38	Ekran 15, launcher rocket, launcher, rocket	May 24	0·4	1,436·3	0·000	35,771
39	Meteor 2-14, rocket	May 27	82·5	104·1	0·001	941
40	Cosmos 1746, rocket, engine	May 28	82·3	89·9	0·001	259
41	Cosmos 1747, rocket, engine	May 29	70·3	89·7	0·006	223
42	Cosmos 1748-1755, rocket	June 6	74·0	115·2	0·001	1,454
43	Cosmos 1756, rocket	June 6	64·9	89·7	0·013	173
44	Gorizont 12, launcher rocket, launcher, rocket	June 10	1·4	1,477·4	0·001	36,568
45	Cosmos 1757, rocket, engine	June 11	82·3	90·1	0·017	159
46	Cosmos 1758, rocket	June 12	82·5	97·8	0·003	631
47	Cosmos 1759, rocket	June 18	82·9	104·9	0·002	969
48	Cosmos 1760, rocket, engine	June 19	70·0	92·2	0·005	349
49	Molniya 3-29, launcher rocket, launcher, rocket	June 19	62·9	736·8	0·741	614
50	Cosmos 1761, launcher rocket, launcher, rocket	July 5	62·9	717·6	0·737	599
51	Cosmos 1762, rocket, engine	July 10	82·5	89·9	0·001	259
52	Cosmos 1763, rocket	July 16	74·0	100·5	0·003	757
53	Cosmos 1764, rocket	July 17	64·9	89·7	0·013	175
54	Cosmos 1765, rocket, engine	July 24	72·9	92·3	0·004	356
55	Cosmos 1766, rocket	July 28	82·5	97·8	0·002	635
56	Cosmos 1767, rocket	July 30	64·9	88·5	0·001	197

Artificial Satellites Launched in 1986—(cont.)

Desig-nation	Satellite	Launch date	i	P	e	Perigee height (km)
1986–		1986	°	m		
57	Molniya 1-67, launcher, launcher rocket, rocket	July 30	62·8	735·9	0·741	623
58	Cosmos 1768, rocket, engine	August 2	82·6	89·9	0·001	259
59	Cosmos 1769, rocket	August 4	65·0	93·3	0·001	429
60	Cosmos 1770, rocket	August 6	64·8	89·6	0·007	209
61	Ajisai, Fuji, rocket	August 12	50·0	115·7	0·001	1,479
62	Cosmos 1771, rocket, platform	August 20	65·0	89·6	0·001	251
63	Cosmos 1772, rocket, engine	August 21	72·9	92·3	0·004	356
64	Cosmos 1773, rocket	August 27	64·9	89·5	0·012	172
65	Cosmos 1774, launcher rocket, launcher, rocket	August 28	63·0	717·5	0·737	616
66	Cosmos 1775, rocket, engine	September 3	70·4	92·2	0·005	348
67	Cosmos 1776, rocket	September 3	74·0	94·6	0·003	474
68	Molniya 1-68, launcher, launcher rocket, rocket	September 5	62·9	717·7	0·736	630
69	USA 19, rocket	September 5	28·6	88·6	0·002	206
70	Cosmos 1777, rocket	September 10	74·0	100·8	0·003	777
71	Cosmos 1778–1780	September 16	64·8	675·0	0·001	19,082
72	Cosmos 1781 rocket, engine	September 17	70·4	92·2	0·005	346
73	NOAA 10	September 17	98·7	101·3	0·001	808
74	Cosmos 1782, rocket	September 30	82·5	97·8	0·002	636
75	Cosmos 1783, launcher rocket, launcher, rocket	October 3	62·8	358·1	0·582	598
76	China 19, rocket	October 6	57·0	90·1	0·016	172
77	Cosmos 1784, rocket	October 6	64·8	89·4	0·005	211
78	Cosmos 1785, launcher, launcher rocket, rocket	October 15	63·0	717·4	0·737	595
79	Molniya 3-30, launcher rocket, launcher, rocket	October 20	62·8	717·0	0·736	627
80	Cosmos 1786, rocket	October 22	64·9	113·3	0·153	190
81	Cosmos 1787, rocket, engine	October 22	70·0	89·6	0·004	230
82	Raduga 19, launcher rocket, launcher, rocket	October 25	1·2	1,436·1	0·001	35,763
83	Cosmos 1788, rocket	October 27	65·8	94·4	0·004	461
84	Cosmos 1789, rocket, engine	October 31	82·6	91·2	0·001	322
85	Cosmos 1790, rocket, engine	November 4	72·9	89·6	0·004	228
86	Cosmos 1791, rocket	November 13	82·9	104·8	0·004	953
87	Cosmos 1792, rocket	November 13	64·9	89·6	0·012	173
88	Polar BEAR, rocket	November 14	89·5	105·0	0·004	963
89	Molniya 1-69, launcher rocket, launcher, rocket	November 15	62·8	717·9	0·742	462
90	Gorizont 13, launcher rocket, launcher, rocket	November 18	1·4	1,435·8	0·000	35,769
91	Cosmos 1793, launcher rocket, launcher, rocket	November 20	63·0	709·0	0·736	584
92	Cosmos 1794-1801, rocket	November 21	74·0	115·7	0·002	1,467
93	Cosmos 1802, rocket	November 24	82·9	105·0	0·004	963
94	Cosmos 1803, rocket	December 2	82·6	116·0	0·000	1,498
95	Cosmos 1804, rocket, engine	December 4	70·0	92·2	0·005	347
96	Fleetsatcom 7, rocket	December 5	5·2	1,436·0	0·006	35,551
97	Cosmos 1805, rocket	December 10	82·5	97·7	0·002	635
98	Cosmos 1806, launcher rocket, launcher, rocket	December 12	62·8	717·6	0·737	617
99	Cosmos 1807, rocket	December 16	67·1	89·6	0·013	166
100	Cosmos 1808, rocket	December 17	82·9	105·1	0·003	973
101	Cosmos 1809, rocket	December 18	82·5	104·2	0·001	944
102	Cosmos 1810, rocket	December 26	64·7	89·6	0·001	249
103	Molniya 1-70, launcher rocket, launcher, rocket	December 26	62·8	701·0	0·739	447

SATELLITE ORBITS

To consider the orbit of an artificial satellite it is best to imagine that one is looking at the Earth from a distant point in space. The Earth would then be seen to be rotating about its axis inside the orbit described by the rapidly revolving satellite. The inclination of a satellite orbit to the Earth's equator (which generally remains almost constant throughout the satellite's lifetime) gives at once the maximum range of latitudes over which the satellite passes. Thus a satellite whose orbit has an inclination of 53° will pass overhead all latitudes between S. 53° and N. 53°, but would never be seen in the zenith of any place nearer the poles than these latitudes. If we consider a particular place on the earth, whose latitude is less than the inclination of the satellite's orbit then the Earth's rotation carries this place first under the northbound part of the orbit and then under the southbound position of the orbit, these two occurrences being always less than 12 hours apart for satellites moving in direct orbits (*i.e.* to the east). (For satellites in retrograde orbits the words "northbound" and "southbound" should be interchanged in the preceding statement.) As the value of the latitude of the observer increases and approaches the value of the inclination of the orbit, so this interval gets shorter until (when the latitude is equal to the inclination) only one overhead passage occurs each day.

SATELLITE LAUNCHINGS

Apart from their names, *e.g.* Cosmos 6 Rocket, the satellites are also classified according to their date of launch. Thus 1961 α refers to the first satellite launching of 1961. A number following the Greek letter indicated the relative brightness of the satellites put in orbit. From the beginning of 1963 the Greek letters were replaced by numbers and the numbers by roman letters *e.g.* 1963–01A. In this table are given the designation and names of the main objects in orbit (in the order A, B, C ... etc.), the launch date and some initial orbital data. These are the inclination to the equator (*i*), the nodal period of revolution (*P*), the eccentricity, *e*, and the perigee height.

OBSERVATION OF SATELLITES

The regression of the orbit around the Earth causes alternate periods of visibility and invisibility, though this is of little concern to the radio or radar observer. To the visual observer the following cycle of events normally occurs (though the cycle may start in any position): invisibility, morning observations before dawn, invisibility, evening observations after dusk, invisibility, morning observations before dawn, and so on. With reasonably high satellites and for observers in high latitudes around the summer solstice the evening observations follow the morning observations without interruption as sunlight passing over the polar regions can still illuminate satellites which are passing over temperate latitudes at local midnight. At the moment all satellites rely on sunlight to make them visible though a satellite with a flashing light has been suggested for a future launching. The observer must be in darkness or twilight in order to make any useful observations and the durations of twilight and the sunrise, sunset times given on page 2 of each month will be a useful guide.

Some of the satellites are visible to the naked eye and much interest has been aroused by the spectacle of a bright satellite disappearing into the Earth's shadow. The event is even more fascinating telescopically as the disappearance occurs gradually as the satellite traverses the Earth's penumbral shadow, and during the last few seconds before the eclipse is complete the satellite may change colour (under suitable atmospheric conditions) from yellow to red. This is because the last rays of sunlight are refracted through the denser layers of our atmosphere before striking the satellite.

Some satellites rotate about one or more axes so that a periodic variation in brightness is observed. This was particularly noticeable in several of the U.S.S.R. satellites.

Satellite research has provided some interesting results. Among them may be mentioned a revised value of the Earth's oblateness, 1/298·2, and the discovery of the Van Allen radiation belts.

ROYAL OBSERVATORIES

Royal Greenwich Observatory
Herstmonceux, East Sussex, BN27 1RP
[0323 833171]

The Royal Observatory was founded at Greenwich by Charles II in 1675. Because of smog and light pollution, the Observatory was moved to Herstmonceux in East Sussex after the Second World War. The traditional work in positional astronomy and the determination of time remain as activities of the Observatory. The well-known "Greenwich 6 pips" are sent from Herstmonceux to the B.B.C. by land line. The rate of rotation of the Earth and other geophysical parameters are monitored by the satellite laser ranging telescope. Various almanacs and other astronomical data are prepared by H.M. Nautical Almanac Office, which is part of the Royal Greenwich Observatory. However, as an establishment of the Science and Engineering Research Council, the main task of the Observatory now is the provision of facilities for research in optical astronomy for astronomers in the universities. In particular, this involves the running of the Isaac Newton group of telescopes with its associated instrumentation at the Roque de los Muchachos Observatory on the island of La Palma in the Canary Islands. This group comprises the 4·2 m. William Herschel telescope, the 2·5 m. Isaac Newton telescope and the 1·0 m Jacobus Kapteyn telescope. The running of these is shared

with the Netherlands, and, in the case of the Jacobus Kapteyn telescope, with the Republic of Ireland also. At Herstmonceux, there are facilities for the processing of astronomical data obtained from the telescopes on La Palma and elsewhere; these include a node of the STARLINK computing network. The Royal Greenwich Observatory is to move from Herstmonceux to Cambridge. Relocation will take until at least 1991. *Dir.*, Prof. A. Boksenberg, F.R.S.

Royal Observatory
Blackford Hill, Edinburgh

The Observatory was founded by the Astronomical Institution in 1818 and its Royal Charter dates from 1822. It is now responsible for some major national astronomical facilities funded by the Science and Engineering Research Council, including a 1·2 m. Schmidt telescope in Australia, a 15·0 m. millimetrewave telescope and a 3·8 m. infra-red telescope in Hawaii and COSMOS, a fast automatic plate measuring machine, in Edinburgh. The Observatory is also part of the U.K. Starlink network for astronomical image and data processing. The Observatory specializes in the development of advanced technologies and the application of these to studies of the properties of matter in extreme environments in space. *Dir., and Astronomer Royal for Scotland*, Prof. M. S. Longair.

WEATHER IN THE UNITED KINGDOM, 1986–1987

(1986) **July**—Rainfall totals were below normal everywhere except in East Anglia and most of Wales where they were above normal. On the 2nd overnight fog formed in some eastern areas and on the 3rd hail was reported in southeast England. The 4th and 5th were wet over England and Wales resulting in a number of accidents on motorways in southern England on the 5th. At Wimbledon rain stopped play for the first time in the fortnight and the Henley Regatta was affected by a downpour for some hours. The 8th brought thunderstorms to central, southern and eastern areas of England when very heavy rain caused flooding in Kent. There was hail in southwest England. Overnight fog formed in some central and southwestern areas between the 13th and 16th. On the 16th gales occurred in the Western Isles of Scotland and on the 17th a gust of 80 knots (92 mph.) was recorded at Cairngorm (Highland). Rain or drizzle on the 20th became heavy on the 21st and 22nd followed by heavy showers with hail and thunder over much of England and Wales on the 23rd. Hailstones of between 10 and 20 mm. (0·4 and 0·8 ins.) in diameter were reported at Watnall (Notts.), Cawood (N. Yorks.) and Bradford (W. Yorks.) Hail was reported from places as far apart as Northumberland, Powys and Kent. Hail was reported in Lancashire on the 24th. From the 29th to 31st there was heavy rain in Scotland and 55 mm. (2·2 ins.) fell at Drummond Castle (Tayside) on the 30th. In Hampshire there was a whirlwind on the 31st which lifted glass cold frames at Titchfield and damaged roof tiles at Fareham. Monthly mean temperatures were near normal in most areas. The month started hot in many regions and in parts of Scotland the highest temperatures were on the 1st when 28·1°C. (82·6°F.) was recorded at Kelso (Borders). It became cooler on the 4th but after the 13th became hot again in most areas. The temperature reached 33°C. (91·4°F.) at Morley St. Botolph (Norfolk) on the 15th and 30°C. (86°F.) at Hull (Humberside) on the 16th. The temperature fell to −2·5°C. (27·5°F.) at St. Harmon (Powys) on the 9th. Sunshine totals were normal in England but below normal in Wales, Northern Ireland and most of Scotland. The 1st was the sunniest day generally with most places recording from 9 to 13 hours of sunshine. The highest daily total was 16·5 hours at Kirkwall (Orkney) on the 12th and the highest monthly total was 233 hours at Eastbourne (E. Sussex).

August—Rainfall totals were above normal everywhere except in northern Scotland where they were generally below normal. On the 1st a gust of 60 knots (69 mph.) was recorded at Pendennis Point (Cornwall) and on the 2nd, 61 knots (70 mph.) was recorded at Fair Isle (Shetland). On the 2nd caravans and camping equipment were damaged by gales as far apart as north Wales and southeast England. On the 3rd and 4th rain, followed by showers, made driving hazardous on motorways and multiple collisions occurred on the M4 and M25. Many sporting events were cancelled. On the 10th there were some heavy thundery showers in central England and East Anglia with lightning damage. A massive electrical storm caused havoc in Berkshire with trees being struck by lightning, power lines brought down and houses set on fire. On the 12th the Lowestoft trawler *Pescado* sank in a gale off Aldeburgh (Suffolk). Funnel clouds were seen in the mouth of the Bristol Channel on the 19th and there was a tornado at Winkfield (Berkshire) on the 22nd. Torrential rain on the 22nd brought chaos to main roads and motorways in the Midlands and the south. On the 25th force 10 winds disrupted shipping in the Irish Sea. At Abersoch (Cardigan Bay) 60 boats were driven ashore onto the rocks

causing an estimated £500,000 damage. Widespread rain on the 25th and 26th brought more disruption to traffic and sporting events. In England and Wales the Bank Holiday Monday (25th) was the wettest on record. Southwest Wales had the worst of the storm as houses and roads were flooded. Much of Whitland (Dyfed) was flooded to a depth of nearly 2 metres (6·6 feet) causing widespread damage and necessitating the evacuation of the inhabitants. 135 mm. (5·3 ins.) of rain fell at Aber (Gwynedd) on the 25th. Hail was very widespread in parts of the west Midlands and central southern England on the 27th and 28th. Monthly mean temperatures were below normal everywhere with means ranging from 3·1°C. (5·6°F.) below normal at Huddersfield (W. Yorks.) to 0·6°C. (1·1°F.) below normal at Lerwick (Shetland). On the 17th temperatures were 7 or 8°C. (13 or 14°F.) below normal in places, especially in the north. In Northern Ireland it was the coldest August since 1912. In central England and London it was the coldest since 1963 and the night of the 29th was the coldest in London since 1940. The temperature fell to −3·3°C. (26·1°F.) at Kinbrace (Highland) on the 25th and to 0°C. (32°F.) at Alwen (Clwyd) on the 1st. Sunshine totals were below normal in all areas except northern Scotland. The highest daily amount was 14·6 hours at Scalpay (Western Isles) on the 9th and the highest monthly total was 213 hours at Tiree (Strathclyde).

September—Rainfall totals were below normal everywhere except in the far north of Scotland and the Channel Islands. Most of the United Kingdom had less than half the normal amount and in north Wales, northwest England and Northern Ireland there was less than 10 per cent of the average amount. It was the driest September in Wales since 1959, in England and Wales since 1971 and in Northern Ireland this century. Monthly totals were as little as 3 mm. (0·1 ins.) at Ronaldsway (Isle of Man) and Valley (Gwynedd) and 6 mm. (0·2 ins.) at Aldergrove (Co. Antrim). On the 2nd and 3rd there was rain in most places, heavy in southern Scotland and northern England. Thunder was reported at Aspatria (Cumbria) on the 3rd and hail fell at Knockanrock (Highland) on the 6th, Fair Isle (Shetland) on the 9th and at Lagganlia (Highland) on the 11th. There were showers in the Northern Isles around the 10th and on the 12th there were snow showers in northern Scotland. Also on the 12th there was some rain on the south coast of England and in the Channel Islands. On the 13th rain affected all southern areas from south Wales to the Wash. After further rain on the 14th, heavy in southern England and in the Channel Islands, it became generally sunny and dry with occasional rain in the Channel Islands and northwest Scotland. On the 20th a gust of 60 knots (69 mph.) was recorded at Butt of Lewis (Western Isles) and on the 22nd fog was dense in central southern and southeast England at dawn. Apart from some rain in northern England on the 21st and heavy rain in northern Scotland on the 26th the rest of the month was mainly dry. On the 23rd fog was slow to clear from southern areas and there were thick fog patches at first on the 29th and 30th. Monthly mean temperatures were below normal over the whole of the United Kingdom. On the 15th many places in southern coastal areas had their coldest September day since 1952 with daily mean temperatures more than 8°C.(14°F.) below normal. North Wyke (Devon) had its coldest September since records began there and Worthing (W. Sussex) had its coldest since 1880. Bournemouth (Dorset) had its coldest September since 1928. The temperature rose to 25°C. (77°F.) at Newcastle upon Tyne on the 30th but fell to −5·5°C. (22·1°F.) at St. Harmon (Powys) on the 19th.

Sunshine totals were above average everywhere except for northern Scotland and the Channel Islands where they were just below. At Morecambe (Lancs.) 12·6 hours of sunshine were recorded on the 9th and the 11th. Aldergrove Airport (Co. Antrim) had its sunniest September since records began there in 1927. The highest daily total was 12·7 hours at Slapton (Devon) on the 4th and the highest monthly total was 217 hours at Tynemouth (Tyne and Wear).

October—Rainfall totals were generally above average in Great Britain but parts of eastern Scotland and northeast England were dry and parts of Wales and southwest England had totals below normal. The weather was mainly dry and mild in the first half of the month. Fog formed frequently overnight between the 4th and 18th mainly in Wales and southern England. The 14th brought some heavy rain to the southeast where it was the first measurable rain for 30 days in some places. The 19th was the wettest day in England and Wales and there were widespread thunderstorms between the 19th and 24th in many areas. The first snow of the season in England fell in West Yorkshire and Derbyshire on the 19th. On the 19th and 20th there were gales in south Wales and western and southwestern England causing structural damage. A gust of 69 knots (80 mph.) was recorded at Aberporth (Dyfed) on the 20th. In south Wales the gales were accompanied by torrential rain and roads and houses were flooded. Fresh falls of snow from the 19th onwards left snow lying on the Scottish hills above 300 m. (984 ft.) which was cleared by overnight rain on the 23rd. There was a slight snow cover on the Yorkshire moors on the 23rd. Rain spread to all areas on the 24th. On the 23rd and 24th there were gales in the west reaching storm force at times. On the 29th hailstones 2 cm. (0·8 ins.) in diameter fell at Kneep (Highland). In northern and northwestern Scotland the windiest day was the 30th when gusts of over 70 knots (81 mph.) were recorded, the highest being 78 knots (90 mph.) at Butt of Lewis (Western Isles), 76 knots (88 mph.) at Fair Isle (Shetland) and 75 knots (86 mph.) at Stornoway (Western Isles). Monthly mean temperatures were near or above normal in England and Wales and about normal in Scotland and Northern Ireland. The warmest day was the 4th. On the 16th and 17th there was a sharp fall in temperature overnight when several places recorded minima below −4°C. (24·8°F.). The temperature reached 23·4°C. (74·1°F.) at St. Helier (Jersey), 22·6°C. (72·7°F.) at Nantmor (Gwynedd) on the 4th and 22·6°C. (72·7°F.) at Hoddesdon (Herts.) and Liphook (Hants.) on the 7th. Sunshine totals were above average except in southern coastal areas of England and in south Wales. Tynemouth with 150 hours had its highest total since 1936 while Leuchars (Fife) and Dyce (Grampian) had their highest totals since 1922 and 1941 respectively. The highest daily total was 10·4 hours at Bramham (W. Yorks.) on the 3rd and the highest monthly total was 159 hours at Craibstone (Grampian).

November—Rainfall totals were above average everywhere except for eastern areas of England and eastern Scotland. In Scotland the 4th was wet and 92 mm. (3·6 ins.) of rain fell at Onich (Highland). On the 5th Butt of Lewis (Western Isles) had a gust of 68 knots (78 mph.) and on the 9th 74 knots (85 mph.) was recorded at Edinburgh. A gust of 60 knots (69 mph.) was recorded at Whithorn (Dumfries and Galloway) on the 10th. The 14th was a wet day everywhere and parts of Devon, Cornwall and south Wales were flooded, blocking roads and leaving thousands of acres of farmland under water. Hailstones between 10 and 20 mm. (0·4 and 0·8 ins.) in diameter fell at Lerwick (Shetland) and Towy Castle (Dyfed) on the 14th. Further heavy rain fell in Scotland on the 15th

and 16th when 70 mm. (2·8 ins.) fell at Inverailort (Highland) on the 15th and 74 mm. (2·9 ins.) fell at Aros (Strathclyde) on the 16th. Winds reached gale force in many areas on the 18th especially in southwest England and Wales. A gust of 78 kts. (90 mph.) was recorded at Gwennap Head (Cornwall). Heavy rain on the 18th over Wales and southwest England gave falls of 79 mm. (3·1 ins.) at Princetown (Devon) and 73 mm. (2·9 ins.) at Moel Cynnedd (Powys). On the 19th houses at Cwmaman (Mid Glamorgan) were cut off by flood water and at Ystalyfera (W. Glamorgan) heavy rain caused a landslide damaging two houses. The heavy rain and gales of the 19th caused disruption in many southern areas with homes flooded, cross-Channel ferries suspended and overhead cables brought down. Power to more than 700 homes was lost when a transformer at Fittleton (Wilts.) was damaged. On the 21st severe storms caused widespread damage and flooding in southern England and Wales. Hundreds of acres of farmland were flooded in East Sussex and Hampshire. A crude-oil storage tank at Pembroke (Dyfed) was set on fire by lightning and tons of shingle and seaweed were hurled onto the seafront at Southsea (Hants.) while at Cowes (Isle of Wight) waves breached the sea-wall. Also on the 21st a tornado swept through Selsey (W. Sussex) causing damage to 250 houses, flattening walls and uprooting trees. More than 30 houses were damaged, some badly, by a whirlwind near Swindon (Wilts.). On the 29th fog brought chaos to airports especially in the southeast and caused severe disruption on roads in Kent, Surrey, Essex and Derbyshire. Monthly mean temperatures were above normal everywhere. Bournemouth (Dorset) had its first November since 1974 without an air frost. The temperature rose to 16·7°C. (62·1°F.) at Hoddesdon (Herts.) on the 10th but fell to −8·6°C. (16·5°F.) at Carnwath (Strathclyde) on the 2nd. Sunshine totals were above normal generally in England and Wales and eastern areas of Scotland but below normal over much of western and southern Scotland. The highest daily total was 9 hours at Eastbourne (E. Sussex) on the 2nd and the highest monthly total was 100 hours at Newcastle upon Tyne.

December—Rainfall totals were above normal nearly everywhere in the United Kingdom ranging from about normal in northern Kent to twice the norm in northwest England and central and southern areas of Scotland. It was the wettest December in England and Wales since 1979, in Northern Ireland since 1966 and in Scotland since 1876. The 1st was a windy day in the north when a gust of 82 knots (94 mph.) was recorded at Kirkwall (Orkney). Gales occurred somewhere in Scotland on more than half the days of the month. On the 3rd 45 mm. (1·8 ins.) of rain fell at Trawsfynydd (Gwynedd). On the 8th precipitation turned to snow over the Central Highlands and a depth of 15 cms. (5·9 ins.) of level snow was measured in the Cairngorm car park. On the 15th sleet and snow fell at low levels and at Pitlochry (Tayside) the 5 cm. (2 ins.) that fell on that day did not disappear until Christmas Day. At Gwennap Head (Cornwall) a gust of 77 knots (89 mph.) was recorded on the 15th. On the 18th there were isolated thunderstorms in southeast England and on the 19th hailstones of between 10 and 20 mm. (0·4 and 0·8 ins.) in diameter fell at Lough Navar Forest (Co. Fermanagh). On the 20th Holme Moss (W. Yorks.) had a depth of 9 cms. (3·5 ins.) of level snow. Wintry showers over England and Wales were widespread from the 18th to 23rd. On the 21st a thunderstorm over northern Wales caused considerable damage especially to television sets and domestic wiring in the village of Rhes-y-Cae (Clwyd). On the 24th 43 mm. (1·7 ins.) of rain fell at Nantmor (Gwynedd). The 24th brought mild weather to give a wet Christmas which melted the snow below levels of around 600 m. (1,969 ft.). A gust of 68 knots (78 mph.) was recorded at Sumburgh (Shetland) on the 28th. On the 29th heavy rain fell in northern Wales and the Midlands when 105 mm. (4·1 ins.) fell at Nantmor (Gwynedd) and 88 mm. (3·5 ins.) fell at Trawsfynydd (Gwynedd). This rain caused floods which cut off villages, blocked roads and left a trail of damage in northern and western areas of Wales. Machynlleth (Powys) was cut off by road and the railway from Machynlleth to Tywyn was closed. Monthly mean temperatures were above normal everywhere except in northern Scotland where they were just below normal. The first few days of the month were mild especially on the 4th when southern areas had temperatures up to 15°C. (59°F.). The highest temperature in the United Kingdom during the month was 15·6°C. (60°F.) at Mansfield (Notts.) on the 4th. The lowest temperature was −7·8°C. (18°F.) at Drumelog (Strathclyde) on the 22nd. Sunshine totals were above normal in England and Wales but generally below normal in Scotland and Northern Ireland. The highest daily total was 7·5 hours at Bognor Regis (W. Sussex) and Herne Bay (Kent) on the 6th. The highest monthly total was 87 hours at Folkestone (Kent).

Year (1986)—Rainfall totals were generally above average and the total for Scotland was the 5th largest for a year since 1869 and for Wales it was the 7th largest since 1910. Annual mean temperatures ranged from 0·5°C. (0·9°F.) to 1·0°C (1·8°F.) below normal everywhere. Sunshine totals for the year were near normal everywhere. January was mostly unsettled with rain, snow or sleet at times. Snow on the 7th/8th produced depths of 20 cms. (7·9 ins.) in the Midlands. Hail was reported extensively on the 11th from the Orkneys to Cornwall. On the 12th rain brought extensive flooding around Tewkesbury and on the 29th flooding disrupted rail traffic in south Wales and the west of England. Snow fell somewhere in the United Kingdom on every day of the month. Temperatures were slightly above normal in southern England but below normal elsewhere. Sunshine ranged from about 50 per cent of normal in eastern Scotland to over 150 per cent in the Midlands. February was a dry month with rainfall well below normal. In the Midlands and Wales it was the driest February for 20 years and in parts of Northern Ireland it was the driest for 100 years. It snowed somewhere in the United Kingdom on every day of the month. At Braemar 49 cms. (18·9 ins.) of snow lay on the 6th and 15 cms. (5·9 ins.) lay on the Isle of Wight on the 7th. On the 22nd and 23rd drifts of up to 1·5 m. (4·9 ft.) lay on the moors of southwest England. On the 25th there were 50 cms. (19·7 ins.) of snow at Cairngorm. It was the coldest February in England and Wales since 1947 and the second coldest this century. Lerwick had its sunniest February since 1923 but sunshine was below normal in many areas. March was a windy, unsettled month. In northwest England and parts of western Scotland it was very wet. On the 20th a gust of 150 knots (173 mph.) was recorded on the top of Cairngorm and on the 24th the Severn Bridge was closed for the first time to all traffic. 18 cms. (7·1 ins.) of snow fell in northern England on the 24th. Fog was frequent throughout the month and dense at times. Temperatures were below normal except in northern Scotland and sunshine was mostly above normal except for parts of northwest Scotland, Shetland, northern Wales and southern England. April was a cold, wet month with frequent showers. Sleet and snow occurred on every day with England and Wales more affected than Scotland. On the 21st a tornado damaged houses in Camelford (Cornwall). Hailstones more than 20 mm. (0·8 ins.) in diameter fell in

Northern Ireland on the 29th. It was the coldest April in central England since 1922 and in Northern Ireland this century. Sunshine was below or near normal everywhere. May was wet and rather windy. At Tiree it was the wettest May since 1926 and in Scotland it was the wettest since 1869. On the 20th there were widespread thunderstorms and power supplies were disrupted in the Midlands. Hailstones more than 20 mm. (0·8 ins.) in diameter fell at Kielder Castle on the 22nd. Temperatures were around normal but sunshine was only above normal in eastern areas of England and Scotland. June was another unsettled month but rainfall varied from only 17 per cent of normal in Northamptonshire to nearly 300 per cent at Guernsey. On the 10th 15 cms. (5·9 ins.) of snow brought snowploughs out in Scotland. On the 23rd Steart Church (Somerset) was severely damaged by lightning and on the 29th the Opera House and several houses were struck by lightning in Jersey. Hailstones 30 mm. (1·2 ins.) in diameter fell at Whitechurch (Dyfed) and some of almost 40 mm. (1·6 ins.) fell in Jersey. Temperatures were near normal and sunshine was above normal in the east but below in the west. July was a mainly dry month with rainfall below normal except in East Anglia and Wales. On the 31st a whirlwind caused damage in Hampshire. Temperatures were near normal in most areas and sunshine was normal in England but below elsewhere. August was a cool, unsettled month with gales at times. The worst weather was on the 25th and 26th. On the 2nd caravans in Wales and southeast England were damaged by gales and on the 10th a severe storm caused havoc in Berkshire with trees and power lines brought down and houses set on fire. On the 12th a trawler sank off Aldeburgh and on the 22nd torrential rain brought chaos to roads and motorways in the Midlands and southern England. On the 25th 60 boats were driven onto the rocks in Cardigan Bay. The Bank Holiday Monday was the wettest this century in England and Wales. It was the coolest August in Northern Ireland since 1912 and the 29th was the coldest August night in London since 1940. Sunshine was below normal except in northern Scotland. September was generally cool, dry and sunny. On the 19th gales caused damage in south Wales, western and southwestern England. It was the coldest September in England and Wales since 1952 and Worthing had its coldest September since 1880. Aldergrove had its sunniest September since 1927. October started dry and mild but became cool and wet. On the 20th roads and houses in southwest Wales were flooded after gales and heavy rain. There were widespread thunderstorms between the 19th and 24th. Hailstones 20 mm. (0·8 ins.) in diameter fell at Kneep (Highland) on the 29th. Temperatures were generally near or above normal. Leuchars had its sunniest October since 1922 and Tynemouth its sunniest since 1936. November was another unsettled month, very wet with gales on 19 days. The wettest days were the 18th and 20th when there was much damage and at least three people were killed. On the 14th there were floods in Devon, Cornwall and south Wales. There were further floods in south Wales on the 19th. On the 21st an oil storage tank at Pembroke was set on fire by lightning and damage was caused by a tornado at Selsey and a whirlwind at Swindon. Temperatures were above normal and sunshine was above normal except in western and southern Scotland. December was a mild, wet and windy month. On the 21st a thunderstorm caused considerable damage in north Wales. Widespread damage was caused by torrential rain in northern and central Wales and northern England on the 29th and 30th. Temperatures were above normal except in northern Scotland and sunshine was above normal except in Scotland and Northern Ireland.

(1987) January—Rainfall totals were below normal except in Edinburgh (Lothian) where rainfall was slightly above normal. It was the driest January in Hampstead (Greater London) since 1914. However, the weather was very severe at times. Thunder occurred at Tregastick (Cornwall) and St. Helier (Jersey) on the 2nd when winds reached gale force in the southwest. On the 4th torrential rain brought flooding to mid Wales when the river Dovey burst its banks and blocked roads between Aberystwyth (Dyfed) and Machynlleth (Powys). On the 5th gales were severe on exposed coasts and hills especially in western areas and thunder occurred in Northern Ireland and western Scotland. On the 8th freezing fog in southeast England disrupted road traffic and closed Heathrow and Gatwick airports. On the 9th and 10th there were frequent sleet and snow showers and snow fell on each day from the 11th to the 14th. On the 12th there were heavy snow showers along the east coast and in Cornwall. A depth of 39 cms. (15·35 ins.) was measured at Penzance and 30 cms. (11·8 ins.) was measured at Falmouth. Heavy snow falling in the area of Sittingbourne and the Isle of Sheppey (Kent) combined with strong winds to give drifts of over 6 m. (20 ft.). Level depths of 38 cms. (15 ins.) at Shoeburyness (Essex) and 37 cms. (14·6 ins.) at Ulcombe (Kent) were measured. Further heavy snow on the 13th gave the worst conditions in Kent for over 20 years. At East Malling (Kent) a depth of 52 cms. (20·5 ins.) was measured, probably the greatest depth of level snow in the area for 40 years. On the 14th snow fell almost everywhere with very heavy falls in the Midlands and Wales where traffic was almost at a standstill with some areas cut off altogether. There was further snow during the next few days but on the 18th and 19th rain brought a thaw to all areas. Monthly mean temperatures were below normal everywhere and on the 12th the highest temperature in the United Kingdom was 0·1°C. (32·2°F.) at Butt of Lewis (Western Isles). The night of the 11th/12th was the coldest night in London since 1940 with a minimum temperature of −11°C. (12·2°F.). In Hampstead (Greater London) the 12th was the coldest day since 1909 and the 13th was the second coldest January day since 1947. At Okehampton (Devon) the maximum temperature on the 13th was −8·5°C. (16·7°F.). The lowest temperature of the month was −17·6°C. (0·3°F.) at Fyvie Castle (Grampian) on the 12th and the highest of the month was 14·5°C. (58·1°F.) at Oldpark Filters (Belfast) on the 17th. Sunshine totals were generally above normal except in some eastern coastal districts. The dull weather of the 13th to 28th broke records in many places for the longest January spell without sunshine. Among places with 15 sunless days were Elmdon (West Midlands), Arborfield (Berks.) and Faversham (Kent). The highest daily total was 10·5 hours at Bastreet (Cornwall) on the 26th and the highest monthly total was 73 hours at Southsea (Hants.).

February—Rainfall totals were above normal in northern and southwestern Scotland, Cumbria, Humberside, Dorset and Somerset but below normal in all other areas. Some heavy falls of rain occurred in northern areas on the 5th and 6th. Thunder was reported at Gogerddan (Dyfed) on the 6th and gusts of 72 knots (83 mph.) were recorded at Leeds (W. Yorks.) and Blyth (Northumberland). Rain fell in all areas on the 9th and there were gales in the far southwest of England where a gust of 63 knots (73 mph.) was recorded at Gwennap Head (Cornwall). On the 10th a belt of rain crossed Scotland turning to sleet or snow on higher ground. Overnight fog formed frequently between the 3rd and 13th mainly in southern and central areas. On the 3rd and 4th fog was thick and slow to clear and caused three

collisions at sea, one off Harwich (Essex) and two in the English Channel off the coasts of Kent and East Sussex. From the 14th to 17th there were frequent, but mostly light snow showers in eastern and central areas. The period from 21st to 24th was dry in most areas. Rain preceded by snow over higher ground moved into southwest England on the 25th and into Wales on the 26th. At Grizedale (Cumbria) 65 mm. (2·6 ins.) of rain fell on the 27th and 70 mm. (2·8 ins.) fell on the 28th to give 164 mm. (6·5 ins.) in all during the last three days of the month. The total for the month at Grizedale was 266 mm. (10·5 ins.). From the 26th to the end of the month it was very misty with hill and coastal fog especially in the west. Monthly mean temperatures were generally about normal over the whole of the United Kingdom. The month began cold and frosty and −11°C. (12·2°F.) was recorded at Eskdalemuir (Dumfries and Galloway) on the night of the 1st. The temperature rose to 14·5°C. (58·1°F.) at Torbay (Devon) on the 8th. It was cold everywhere with frequent widespread frosts about the 14th to 26th. On the 28th the 16°C. (60·8°F.) recorded at London Weather Centre made it the warmest February day in London since 1961. 16·3°C. (61·3°F.) was recorded at Liphook (Hants.) on the 28th. The lowest temperature of the month was −12·7°C. (9·1°F.) at Santon Downham (Norfolk) on the 1st. Sunshine totals were generally above normal in eastern and central areas of England and Scotland, in Shetland, parts of Strathclyde and Northern Ireland but near or below normal elsewhere. The highest daily totals were nearly 10 hours at Penzance and Culdrose (Cornwall) on the 18th and 20th and at Brawdy (Dyfed) on the 21st. The highest monthly total was 97 hours at Ventnor Park (Isle of Wight).

March—Rainfall totals were above normal almost everywhere except for parts of East Anglia and southwest England. Western Scotland had nearly 2½ times the normal amount. Weather was unsettled for most of the month. Rain turned to snow on the 3rd and there was a snow cover everywhere except the far west on the 4th. There were gales in the north and west on the 6th and 7th. Sleet affected all areas on the 7th with heavy and prolonged falls in north Wales, the Midlands and northern England. Roads across the Pennines were blocked; the A6 into Cumbria was closed; northbound traffic on the M6 and M62 was halted and the Snake Pass in Derbyshire was blocked. Early morning snow in the west closed many minor roads and disrupted traffic on main roads including the M4 in Wiltshire. Depths of 15 cms. (5·9 ins.) were reported. Hail and thunder were widespread on the 18th. On the 19th a band of snow crossed Avon, Wiltshire, Dorset, Hampshire and the Isle of Wight disrupting traffic. Rain and drizzle were heavy in southwest England on the 23rd. On the 26th 73 mm. (2·9 ins.) of rain fell at Bronydd Mawr (Powys), 67 mm. (2·64 ins.) at Cilfynydd (Mid Glamorgan) and 66 mm. (2·6 ins.) fell at Grizedale (Cumbria) and Princetown (Devon). On the 27th many roads in north Wales were closed by floods. There were gale force winds in all areas on the 27th, especially in southern and southwest England. 85 knots (98 mph.) was recorded at Rhoose (S. Glamorgan), the highest gust ever recorded there. A gust of 87 knots (100 mph.) at Burrington (Devon) was the highest since records began there in 1977. A gust of 93 knots (107 mph.) was recorded at Gwennap Head (Cornwall) the highest March gust since 1972. At least 11 other anemograph stations recorded gusts of 70 knots (81 mph.) or more and at Oxford a gust of 72 knots (83 mph.) was recorded about the time a mature beech tree was completely uprooted in the garden of Keble College. Also on the 27th the 30 m. (98 ft.) spire of St. James's Church, Waresley (Cambs.) was demolished. The Severn Bridge was closed to all traffic (only the second time in 20 years). On the 28th lightning struck a B.B.C. outside broadcast tower as rain, hail and strong winds accompanied the University Boat Race. Monthly mean temperatures were below normal everywhere. The temperature at Glenlivet (Grampian) fell to −11°C. (12·2°F.) and to −13·5°C. (7·7°F.) at Dalwhinnie (Highland) on the 21st. Coventry (West Midlands) had its coldest March since 1976. Sunshine totals were below normal in England and Wales and Northern Ireland but above normal in Scotland. The highest daily total was 11·4 hours at Sutton Bonington (Notts.) on the 29th and the highest monthly total was 139·8 hours at Penzance (Cornwall).

April—Rainfall totals were generally just above average in England and Wales but below average in Scotland. Most of the month's rainfall fell in the first 10 days with some record breaking totals especially in northeast England and the Exeter area of Devon. Snow fell in northeast England on the 1st and 2nd. On the 2nd sleet followed by rain moved into southwest England and south Wales when 50 mm. (2 ins.) fell at Princetown (Devon). By the 6th some places in the southwest had received almost twice their normal April rainfall. There was considerable flooding around Exeter and other areas of Devon and Cornwall. Thunder occurred on the 9th over central and eastern England when hail was widespread. There was isolated thunder on the 10th and there was local flooding at Whitchester (Borders) after heavy rain. Also on the 10th snow fell on high ground and a depth of 24 cms. (9·5 ins.) lay in the Cairngorm car park on the 11th. Wintry precipitation fell in eastern coastal areas as far south as the Humber on the 11th and gusts of over 70 knots (81 mph.) were recorded at St. Abb's Head (Borders). The rainfall, which had been almost daily, ended on the 12th to give a dry spell with some places in central and southern England having no measurable rain for 16 days. On the 20th, hailstones of 10–20 mm. (0·4—0·8 ins.) in diameter were reported at Widdybank Fell (Co. Durham). A dust devil was seen at Towy Castle (Dyfed) on the 24th and on the 25th fog affected eastern parts of Great Britain and was unusually dense. Overnight fog was widespread on the 27th. The fine spell in the south was broken by thundery activity on the 28th and 29th. Funnel clouds were seen near Watford (Herts.) on the 29th. Monthly mean temperatures were above normal in all parts of the United Kingdom. The lowest temperature of the month was −5·4°C. (22·3°F.) at Carnwath (Strathclyde) on the 12th. On the 17th London with 22·6°C. (72·7°F.) and Bristol with 21·5°C. (70·7°F.) enjoyed one of the warmest Good Fridays since the 1940s. Bidston (Merseyside) had its warmest April since 1867, Hampstead (Greater London) had its warmest since 1949 and Oxford had its warmest since 1944. The 27th was a very warm day and several long-term records were broken in northeastern areas. At Aberdeen Airport 23·7°C. (74·7°F.) was the highest April temperature since 1942 and at Newcastle upon Tyne 22·7°C. (72·9°F.) was the highest since 1952. The highest temperature of the month was 24·9°C. (76·8°F.) at Kelso and Floors Castle (Borders). Sunshine totals were above average in central and southern England and south Wales, northeast England and eastern Scotland but below average elsewhere. The highest daily total was 13·7 hours at Cawood (N. Yorks.) on the 27th and the highest monthly total was 220·3 hours at Guernsey (Channel Islands).

May—Rainfall totals were generally below normal. On the 1st, two cross-Channel ferries collided in thick fog outside Dover harbour and on the 2nd there were gales in exposed places on western coasts. A gust of 62 knots (71 mph.) was recorded at West Freugh

(Dumfries and Galloway). Snow fell on higher ground in Scotland on the 3rd. In Scotland some light rain moved southwards towards the end of the first week then rain and showers spread to most areas on the 11th and 12th with hail and thunder in some places. There were further showers on the 13th especially in northern and eastern areas accompanied by hail and thunder in places. On the 12th and 13th sleet was reported as far south as Wingfield (Suffolk) and snow fell on the mountains. It remained unsettled with showers or periods of rain on the 14th and 15th and thunder was reported on both days. More general rain affected areas of central and eastern England on the 17th and 18th. Further rain affected most parts of England and Wales on the 21st and 22nd and southwestern areas on the 23rd. There was thunder in Devon and Cornwall on the 24th and more general thundery outbreaks on the 26th affected parts of the south and southwest of England. Fog spread inland from the North Sea on the 25th. Rain spread across all areas on the 28th, and there was extensive fog on coasts and hills in the southwest on the 29th. Further rain spread from the west on the 29th and became heavy in places early on the 30th. On the 31st there was heavy rain in southern areas. Monthly mean temperatures were below normal everywhere ranging from 0·5°C. (0·9°F.) below normal on the coast of Dorset and the Isle of Wight to 1·5°C. (2·7°F.) below normal in Kent and East Anglia. The month as a whole was cool but on the 26th the temperature rose to 24°C. (75·2°F.) at Southampton and all areas remained warm for the rest of the month. The highest temperature of the month was 24·7°C. (76·5°F.) at Cookstown (Co. Tyrone) on the 8th and the lowest was −3·8°C. (25·2°F.) at Eskdalemuir (Dumfries and Galloway) on the 4th. Sunshine totals were about normal everywhere but totals reached 14 or 15 hours on 15 days of the month. The highest daily total was 15·9 hours at Hillsborough (Co. Down) on the 20th and the highest monthly total was 269 hours at Gorey Castle (Jersey).

June—Rainfall totals were above normal except in northern Scotland and the Western Isles. Ringway (Greater Manchester) had 289 per cent of normal. Worthing (W. Sussex) had its fourth wettest June since 1887 and Silsoe (Beds.) had its wettest since 1958. Sheffield had its greatest number of consecutive days of rainfall since 1935. The month began with rain and drizzle and on the 2nd rain spread to all areas. On the 3rd and 4th heavy showers with hail and thunder caused flooding in places. On the 5th and 6th gales swept across much of Britain and a gust of 85 knots (98 mph.) was recorded at Berry Head (Devon). On the 6th and 7th the worst weather was in the south where many roads were flooded. There were thunderstorms over the Midlands and southeast on the 8th. Funnel clouds were seen northeast of Valley (Gwynedd) and near Wittering (Cambs.) on the 11th. From the 11th to 13th thunderstorms were widespread over Wales, the Midlands and southeast England. Intense thundery activity occurred on the 14th. London and the southeast were badly hit as the storms caused flooding. On the 15th 71 mm. (2·8 ins.) of rain fell at Sudbury (Suffolk) and there was extensive flooding in Essex and Suffolk. Thunderstorms were again widespread on the 16th. There was rain in southwest England on the 18th which spread to Wales and most of England on the 19th. There were isolated thundery showers on the 20th and 21st. There was further rain on the 22nd, 23rd and 25th. Rain again spread across the country on the 26th and 27th and northern areas had heavy rain on the 28th. On the 26th a whirlwind at Aston (Nr. Sheffield) tore apple trees out of the ground and destroyed greenhouses. On the 27th and 28th fog affected southwest England and the Channel Islands where Jersey airport was closed. Monthly mean temperatures were below normal everywhere. On the 9th a maximum temperature of 12°C. (53·6°F.) gave London its coldest June day since 1964. The highest temperature of the month was 30°C. (86°F.)

at Jersey on the 29th and the lowest was −0·8°C. (30·6°F.) at St. Harmon (Powys) on the 13th. Sunshine was below normal except in parts of northern Scotland and the Western Isles. The highest daily total was 16·9 hours at Cape Wrath (Highland) on the 16th.

AVERAGE AND GENERAL VALUES, 1985–1987 (June)

Month	Rainfall (mm.)				Temperature (°C.)				Bright Sunshine (hrs. per day)			
	Aver. 1941–1970	1985	1986	1987	Aver. 1951–1980	1985	1986	1987	Aver. 1951–1980	1985	1986	1987
England and Wales												
January	86	72	120	30	4·0	1·3	4·1	1·4	1·6	1·7	1·9	1·7
February	65	29	17	59	4·1	2·8	−0·4	4·1	2·3	2·9	2·7	2·3
March	59	66	80	90	5·9	5·0	5·4	4·6	3·6	3·7	4·0	3·3
April	58	70	84	64	8·2	8·7	6·2	10·3	5·1	4·5	4·5	5·3
May	67	65	85	45	11·3	11·0	11·3	10·3	6·3	5·5	6·4	6·3
June	61	94	43	105	14·3	12·9	14·8	13·1	6·7	5·7	6·8	4·1
July	73	73	54	—	16·0	16·4	16·1	—	5·9	6·3	5·4	—
August	90	117	117	—	15·9	15·0	14·1	—	5·5	5·2	4·6	—
September	83	46	26	—	14·0	14·9	11·9	—	4·6	4·5	5·7	—
October	83	48	95	—	11·0	11·4	11·4	—	3·3	3·4	3·7	—
November	97	77	124	—	7·1	4·7	8·3	—	2·1	2·7	2·5	—
December	90	128	143	—	5·1	6·7	6·3	—	1·5	1·2	1·7	—
YEAR	912	885	988	—	9·8	9·2	9·1	—	4·1	3·9	4·2	—
Scotland												
January	137	85	192	73	3·5	1·6	2·9	2·0	1·3	1·5	1·1	1·2
February	104	47	21	88	3·4	3·4	0·5	3·5	2·4	2·8	2·9	2·2
March	92	95	169	153	5·1	4·2	5·0	3·8	3·3	3·3	3·7	3·5
April	90	111	80	68	7·1	7·2	5·2	8·5	5·0	3·8	4·3	4·1
May	91	73	176	75	9·9	9·7	10·0	9·3	5·7	5·4	5·1	5·7
June	92	84	63	98	12·7	11·4	13·0	11·0	5·9	5·6	6·5	4·6
July	112	167	87	—	13·9	14·1	13·8	—	4·9	3·8	4·2	—
August	129	224	120	—	13·9	13·2	12·1	—	4·6	4·0	4·5	—
September	137	200	63	—	12·2	11·9	10·7	—	3·7	3·0	4·3	—
October	149	85	161	—	9·8	10·3	9·8	—	2·6	3·1	3·2	—
November	142	141	232	—	6·0	3·4	7·1	—	1·7	1·6	1·6	—
December	156	193	277	—	4·5	4·9	4·7	—	1·1	0·9	0·9	—
YEAR	1431	1505	1641	—	8·5	7·9	7·9	—	3·5	3·3	3·5	—

TEMPERATURE AND RAINFALL RECORDS

WORLD: The maximum air temperature recorded is 57·8°C. (136°F.) at San Louis, Mexico on August 11, 1933; the minimum air temperature recorded is −89·2°C. (−128·56°F.) at Vostok, Antarctica on July 21, 1983. The greatest rainfall recorded in one day is 1870 mm. (73·62 ins.) at Cilaos, Isle de Réunion on March 16, 1952; the greatest rainfall in one calendar month is 9,300 mm. (366·14 ins.) at Cherrapunji, Assam in July 1861, the greatest annual total being 22,990 mm. (905·12 ins.) also at Cherrapunji in 1861.

UNITED KINGDOM: The maximum air temperature recorded is 38·1°C. (100·5°F.) at Tonbridge, Kent on July 22 1868; the minimum air temperature recorded is −27·2°C. (−17°F.) at Braemar (Grampian) on February 11, 1895 and 10th January 1982. The greatest rainfall recorded in one day is 280 mm. (11 ins.) at Martinstown, Dorset on July 18, 1955. The greatest annual total is 6,528 mm. (257 ins.) at Sprinkling Tarn, Cumbria in 1954.

WIND FORCE MEASURES

The *Beaufort Scale* of wind force has been accepted internationally and is used in communicating weather conditions. Devised originally by Admiral Sir Francis Beaufort in 1805, it now consists of the numbers 0–17, each representing a certain strength or velocity of wind at 10 m. (33 ft.) above ground in the open.

Scale No.	Wind Force	M.p.h.	Knots	Scale No.	Wind Force	M.p.h.	Knots
0	Calm	1	1	9	Strong gale	47–54	41–47
1	Light air	1–3	1–3	10	Whole gale	55–63	48–55
2	Slight breeze	4–7	4–6	11	Storm	64–72	56–63
3	Gentle breeze	8–12	7–10	12	Hurricane	73–82	64–71
4	Moderate breeze	13–18	11–16	13	—	83–92	72–80
5	Fresh breeze	19–24	17–21	14	—	93–103	81–89
6	Strong breeze	25–31	22–27	15	—	104–114	90–99
7	High wind	32–38	28–33	16	—	115–125	100–108
8	Gale	39–46	34–40	17	—	126–136	109–118

TEMPERATURE, RAINFALL AND SUNSHINE
IN THE UNITED KINGDOM

The following table gives mean air temperature (°C.), total monthly rainfall (mm.) and mean daily bright sunshine (hrs.) at a representative selection of climatological reporting stations in the United Kingdom during the year July 1986 to June 1987 and the calendar year 1986. The heights (in metres) of the reporting stations above mean sea level are also given.

		1986											
		July			August			September			October		
Station	Ht. in mtrs.	Temp. °C.	Rain mm.	Sun hrs.	Temp. °C.	Rain mm.	Sun hrs.	Temp. °C.	Rain mm.	Sun hrs.	Temp. °C.	Rain mm.	Sun hrs.
Aberdeen (Dyce) .	65	14·2	50	5·9	11·7	99	4·9	11·1	22	5·6	9·3	40	5·0
Aberporth	134	14·1	41	4·2	12·7	105	4·6	11·2	9	5·4	11·2	82	3·5
Aldergrove	68	14·4	59	2·8	12·1	111	4·4	11·1	6	5·9	10·1	74	3·6
Aspatria	61	14·3	51	4·5	12·5	80	4·6	10·3	23	6·0	10·3	140	4·0
Bala	163	13·9	57	3·7	11·7	135	3·1	9·5	10	4·7	9·9	129	2·8
Birmingham (Elmdon)	98	16·2	35	5·9	13·5	113	4·2	10·8	12	5·9	10·5	69	3·4
Boulmer..........	23	14·7	45	5·8	12·3	131	4·4	11·4	35	6·8	10·1	27	5·0
Bournemouth (Hurn)	10	16·5	43	6·1	14·3	108	5·5	11·1	29	5·4	11·3	77	3·6
Bradford	134	15·0	39	4·7	12·6	129	3·8	11·1	7	5·6	10·1	84	3·0
Braemar	339	12·3	32	4·6	10·1	114	3·5	9·3	14	4·4	7·9	60	—
Buxton..........	307	13·9	71	4·8	11·7	132	3·9	9·7	15	4·4	8·9	164	3·3
Cambridge......	24	16·9	43	5·6	14·7	71	4·5	11·8	29	5·6	11·0	70	3·7
Cheltenham	65	16·7	50	5·1	14·3	126	3·9	11·7	20	4·6	11·3	55	3·4
Clacton-on-Sea...	16	17·4	37	6·4	15·7	70	5·9	12·7	29	5·8	12·1	81	4·2
Douglas	85	13·6	69	3·6	12·4	94	5·2	11·5	6	6·2	10·7	125	4·4
Dumfries	49	13·9	77	3·1	12·3	106	4·3	10·5	13	4·7	9·7	111	3·5
Dundee	45	14·8	47	6·3	12·7	53	4·9	11·7	9	5·5	9·9	39	4·4
Durham	102	15·0	24	4·3	12·3	169	3·6	11·3	28	6·4	10·0	31	4·5
East Malling	33	17·6	70	6·5	15·0	76	6·1	11·9	38	5·2	11·9	77	3·8
Edinburgh.......	134	14·6	58	5·0	12·3	61	4·3	11·2	44	5·4	10·3	56	4·1
Glasgow	107	13·8	72	3·3	12·6	105	3·8	10·7	40	5·0	9·3	132	2·7
Gogerddan	31	14·7	111	3·8	13·1	121	4·2	10·7	11	5·1	11·1	107	3·1
Hastings	45	16·7	29	—	15·5	53	6·2	13·1	41	5·3	12·7	102	4·0
Hull	2	16·7	46	—	13·9	103	4·2	12·3	21	—	11·2	50	—
Inverness	4	14·5	32	4·1	12·5	57	3·6	11·2	23	3·3	9·9	52	3·4
Leeming..........	32	15·6	30	5·0	13·1	89	3·3	11·3	13	6·6	10·3	46	3·6
Lerwick..........	82	11·4	75	3·5	11·1	77	4·2	8·9	133	3·8	8·1	156	2·2
London (Heathrow)	25	17·9	55	5·8	15·7	67	5·1	12·7	23	5·3	12·5	72	3·7
Long Ashton.....	51	15·9	66	6·5	14·0	91	5·3	11·5	31	5·3	11·5	98	3·0
Lowestoft	25	16·7	55	5·7	14·9	61	5·5	12·6	25	5·3	11·7	62	3·3
Manchester (Ringway)	75	15·3	46	4·1	13·3	84	3·7	11·3	11	5·1	10·7	95	3·4
Manston	44	17·3	40	6·8	15·3	45	6·0	12·9	59	5·3	12·3	68	4·0
Melbury	143	14·7	63	4·6	12·8	130	3·8	10·5	31	5·6	10·9	165	2·9
Morecambe	7	14·9	76	3·9	13·6	87	4·8	11·6	17	6·1	10·8	148	3·3
Nottingham (Watnall)......	117	15·6	62	5·9	13·4	102	4·3	11·3	9	5·5	10·3	59	3·4
Oxford	63	17·1	37	6·5	14·7	114	4·7	12·1	39	5·7	11·5	75	3·9
Penzance........	19	15·8	58	5·1	13·9	120	5·5	12·3	28	5·5	12·5	103	3·1
Plymouth	27	15·6	43	5·7	13·9	140	5·2	12·1	31	5·6	12·3	89	3·3
Prestwick	16	14·0	74	3·9	12·2	70	5·2	10·6	35	5·7	10·3	129	3·2
Rhoose	65	15·7	72	6·2	13·9	105	5·3	11·3	26	5·1	11·3	126	2·9
St. Mawgan......	103	15·0	64	5·4	13·5	133	4·7	12·0	28	5·6	12·1	93	3·3
Scarborough.....	52	15·5	32	6·1	13·1	87	—	12·1	23	7·1	10·8	41	4·4
Shawbury	72	15·6	41	5·1	13·1	93	3·9	10·6	2	5·6	9·9	52	3·5
Sheffield	131	15·9	25	5·7	13·4	110	4·3	11·9	9	6·1	10·8	86	3·6
Skegness	5	15·1	49	6·1	14·1	71	4·8	11·9	16	6·5	11·1	45	4·3
Southampton	3	17·1	53	6·0	15·4	104	5·4	12·8	31	4·9	12·5	74	3·4
Stornoway.......	15	12·5	58	3·6	11·3	89	5·1	10·5	55	3·1	9·3	133	2·6
Tenby	5	14·8	66	4·9	13·1	167	4·9	11·4	12	5·1	11·3	127	3·5
Tiree............	9	12·7	66	4·1	12·0	71	6·9	10·9	47	4·5	10·3	138	3·0
Torbay..........	8	16·7	33	6·1	14·3	105	5·1	12·5	55	5·5	12·4	67	3·1
Trawscoed.......	63	14·4	106	3·2	12·5	119	3·8	10·3	14	4·4	10·9	131	2·8
Ventnor.........	135	15·8	36	6·5	15·1	97	5·8	12·9	40	5·7	12·7	106	3·3
Waddington.....	68	16·1	43	4·8	13·6	86	4·6	11·6	17	6·4	10·5	40	4·0
Weymouth	21	15·6	42	6·9	14·7	98	5·5	11·9	31	5·5	12·4	74	3·4
Worthing	2	16·4	23	6·8	14·9	62	6·1	12·1	28	5·7	12·2	94	3·9
Writtle..........	35	16·9	57	6·3	14·9	82	5·0	11·3	25	5·2	11·7	67	3·9

TEMPERATURE, RAINFALL AND SUNSHINE IN THE UNITED KINGDOM—*contd.*

Mean Temperature of the air (°C.), Rainfall (mm.) and Bright Sunshine (as mean hours per day) at a representative selection of reporting stations during the year July 1986 to June 1987. Fuller details of the weather are given in the *Monthly Weather Report* published by the Meteorological Office.

| | 1986 | | | | | | | | | 1987 | | | | | |
| | November | | | December | | | Year | | | January | | | February | | |
Station	Temp. °C.	Rain mm.	Sun hrs.	Temp. °C.	Rain mm.	Sun hrs.	Temp. °C.	Rain mm.	Sun hrs.	Temp. °C.	Rain mm.	Sun hrs.	Temp. °C.	Rain mm.	Sun hrs.
Aberdeen (Dyce)	6·2	44	2·4	3·8	144	1·5	7·5	759	4·3	1·5	55	1·3	2·9	55	2·1
Aberporth	8·1	134	2·3	6·9	188	1·3	8·6	885	4·0	2·1	18	2·0	4·1	48	2·7
Aldergrove	6·7	87	2·8	5·1	94	1·2	8·2	884	3·8	2·9	32	1·9	3·8	48	2·7
Aspatria	7·5	157	1·8	5·5	183	1·1	8·1	1063	4·2	0·5	39	1·6	3·3	67	2·4
Bala	7·1	230	1·7	5·7	275	0·8	—	1406	3·3	0·9	51	1·3	2·3	83	1·5
Birmingham (Elmdon)	7·2	83	2·7	5·8	98	1·9	8·5	726	4·1	0·2	16	2·1	3·4	36	2·2
Boulmer	7·3	34	3·3	5·0	91	1·9	8·0	667	4·5	2·0	51	1·7	3·6	45	3·2
Bournemouth (Hurn)	8·0	138	2·7	6·2	125	2·1	9·0	888	4·4	1·1	10	2·1	3·9	65	2·9
Bradford	7·5	88	2·3	5·5	141	1·2	8·1	989	3·4	0·7	37	1·0	3·3	46	1·7
Braemar	4·5	99	1·4	2·0	150	0·8	5·6	958	—	−1·5	36	1·1	0·7	29	2·1
Buxton	6·3	174	2·2	4·3	261	1·3	6·9	1473	3·6	−0·5	64	1·6	2·1	64	1·9
Cambridge	7·7	55	2·5	5·8	54	2·0	—	577	—	0·3	9	1·4	—	28	2·1
Cheltenham	8·5	93	2·7	7·0	79	1·7	9·3	828	3·7	0·9	13	1·7	4·3	39	1·9
Clacton-on-Sea	8·3	54	2·6	5·9	53	2·4	9·4	608	4·8	1·1	26	1·4	3·6	19	2·7
Douglas	8·1	153	2·8	6·3	152	1·7	8·4	1093	4·3	2·9	54	1·8	4·1	88	2·7
Dumfries	7·3	181	2·1	5·1	207	0·9	7·9	1190	3·4	0·9	52	1·4	3·3	73	2·2
Dundee	7·0	41	2·6	4·4	113	1·4	—	598	—	1·6	58	1·8	3·5	46	3·0
Durham	7·4	36	3·0	5·1	74	1·7	8·0	709	4·0	0·7	39	1·7	3·3	35	2·5
East Malling	8·4	91	2·3	6·4	61	2·1	—	713	4·5	0·4	53	1·3	3·8	29	2·1
Edinburgh	7·3	44	2·7	4·5	110	1·3	8·0	793	3·9	1·6	44	1·5	3·6	45	2·4
Glasgow	6·7	144	1·3	4·1	204	0·9	7·7	1187	2·9	0·9	69	1·1	3·1	76	2·1
Gogerddan	8·5	170	2·3	6·9	231	1·1	8·9	1153	3·7	2·1	27	1·7	4·3	77	2·3
Hastings	9·5	133	3·0	6·9	93	2·6	9·7	810	—	1·1	38	1·8	4·1	49	2·8
Hull	7·9	59	—	5·8	94	—	9·1	716	—	1·7	40	—	3·9	61	—
Inverness	6·9	56	2·0	4·1	111	0·9	8·2	614	3·4	2·3	21	1·1	3·9	43	2·6
Leeming	7·7	43	3·1	5·5	84	1·5	8·4	638	4·0	0·7	16	1·5	3·2	30	2·0
Lerwick	6·0	182	0·7	4·0	194	0·5	6·7	1282	3·0	2·4	124	0·8	2·6	51	2·6
London (Heathrow)	8·7	66	2·4	6·5	61	1·8	9·9	638	4·1	1·3	11	1·7	4·5	32	2·1
Long Ashton	8·3	151	2·5	7·1	124	1·8	9·1	959	4·2	1·3	17	1·7	4·3	62	1·9
Lowestoft	7·9	45	1·7	5·5	72	1·6	—	—	—	0·9	22	1·0	4·2	26	2·5
Manchester (Ringway)	7·5	89	2·7	6·1	157	1·4	8·7	836	3·9	1·3	23	2·2	3·9	34	2·3
Manston	8·1	68	2·7	5·9	52	2·7	9·4	576	4·8	0·5	11	1·3	3·7	24	2·7
Melbury	8·1	226	2·1	7·2	246	1·2	8·6	1444	3·7	1·6	31	1·7	4·3	108	2·5
Morecambe	8·1	116	2·7	6·1	207	1·1	8·9	1067	4·0	1·3	30	1·8	3·6	79	2·7
Nottingham (Watnall)	7·1	77	2·5	5·4	104	1·7	8·3	781	4·1	0·5	25	1·9	3·4	48	2·3
Oxford	8·4	78	2·6	6·5	64	2·1	9·4	702	4·4	0·8	10	2·2	4·1	34	2·4
Penzance	9·5	175	—	8·7	182	2·2	10·1	1279	—	4·5	44	2·0	6·5	97	2·9
Plymouth	9·1	143	2·7	8·1	160	1·9	9·7	1157	4·3	3·1	13	1·8	5·4	85	2·7
Prestwick	7·5	150	1·7	5·2	196	1·0	8·0	1075	3·9	1·5	34	1·8	3·6	56	2·6
Rhoose	8·4	149	2·6	6·9	128	2·0	9·0	1052	4·2	1·4	15	1·9	4·1	95	2·4
St. Mawgan	9·1	171	3·0	8·1	177	1·7	9·5	1160	4·3	2·8	14	2·0	5·3	68	2·7
Scarborough	7·6	43	—	5·3	107	—	8·5	675	—	1·7	28	—	6·5	52	—
Shawbury	7·3	92	2·9	5·5	89	1·7	8·3	640	4·0	0·3	14	1·8	3·2	38	2·1
Sheffield	7·7	93	1·9	5·9	142	1·0	8·7	997	3·7	1·1	53	1·3	3·9	35	1·9
Skegness			—	5·7	88	2·2	—	—	—	1·7	15	1·7	3·8	41	2·8
Southampton	9·1	117	2·8	7·0	112	2·0	10·0	816	4·3	1·9	10	2·0	4·9	55	2·8
Stornoway	6·7	216	1·3	4·7	186	0·7	7·6	1302	3·5	3·7	55	1·0	4·0	66	1·7
Tenby	8·8	165	2·5	7·3	210	1·6	—	1228	4·4	3·5	26	1·9	4·5	117	2·7
Tiree	7·8	196	1·5	5·7	229	0·7	7·8	1314	4·0	3·9	62	1·7	4·7	81	2·9
Torbay	9·3	157	2·8	8·0	128	2·3	10·0	1015	4·4	3·3	11	1·3	5·7	73	2·1
Trawscoed	7·9	192	1·9	6·5	220	0·8	—	—	—	1·9	37	1·4	4·1	64	2·1
Ventnor	9·5	123	2·8	7·5	104	2·2	—	—	—	2·1	13	2·1	4·7	67	3·5
Waddington	7·3	57	2·9	5·5	74	2·0	8·5	625	4·7	0·5	33	1·8	3·1	44	2·5
Weymouth	7·5	120	2·8	7·6	139	1·9	9·4	870	4·5	2·1	12	2·2	4·7	69	3·0
Worthing	9·1	118	2·9	6·7	94	2·4	9·4	746	4·8	1·3	14	2·2	4·1	39	3·2
Writtle	8·1	63	2·4	6·1	57	1·8	9·1	631	4·3	0·3	18	1·5	3·5	24	2·5

TEMPERATURE, RAINFALL AND SUNSHINE IN THE UNITED KINGDOM—*contd.*

Mean Temperature of the air (°C.), Rainfall (mm.) and Bright Sunshine (as mean hours per day) at a representative selection of reporting stations during the year July 1986 to June 1987. Fuller details of the weather are given in the *Monthly Weather Report* published by the Meteorological Office.

	1987											
	March			April			May			June		
Station	Temp. °C.	Rain mm.	Sun hrs.	Temp. °C.	Rain mm.	Sun hrs.	Temp. °C.	Rain mm.	Sun hrs.	Temp. °C.	Rain mm.	Sun hrs.
Aberdeen (Dyce)	3·3	102	3·8	8·6	89	5·2	8·5	40	5·5	10·1	84	4·2
Aberporth	4·7	80	3·5	10·0	51	5·4	7·9	20	6·3	11·7	67	5·4
Aldergrove	4·5	84	2·6	9·3	40	3·7	10·0	30	6·7	11·5	81	3·9
Aspatria	3·9	129	4·3	8·9	54	4·9	9·3	40	7·3	11·9	88	4·8
Bala	3·7	122	2·1	8·8	50	4·7	8·7	40	5·8	11·2	87	2·3
Birmingham (Elmdon)	3·8	50	3·5	10·0	72	4·7	9·9	32	5·4	12·7	107	4·0
Boulmer	3·9	99	3·7	8·0	90	5·4	8·4	43	6·1	10·6	59	4·5
Bournemouth (Hurn)	4·9	88	4·0	9·4	65	6·6	11·0	18	7·8	13·6	60	5·7
Bradford	3·9	94	2·9	9·7	60	4·2	9·7	29	5·5	12·1	104	2·6
Braemar	0·7	67	3·5	6·7	57	4·6	7·6	70	6·0	—	84	—
Buxton.............	2·3	158	2·8	8·6	71	5·2	8·4	89	5·4	10·9	217	3·5
Cambridge..........	—	45	3·1	10·4	43	4·9	10·1	47	5·4	13·4	93	3·3
Cheltenham	4·8	54	2·5	11·3	59	5·1	10·6	46	4·5	13·8	107	3·6
Clacton-on-Sea......	3·9	35	3·1	9·8	43	5·2	10·2	41	6·2	13·7	85	4·7
Douglas	4·5	139	3·0	8·9	42	4·7	9·8	26	7·9	11·4	108	6·0
Dumfries	3·9	129	3·3	8·9	63	3·5	—	37	6·2	11·6	107	3·9
Dundee	4·2	74	3·7	8·7	59	4·8	9·9	52	5·8	11·3	102	3·5
Durham	3·9	81	3·2	9·3	59	5·3	9·1	43	5·3	11·4	92	3·0
East Malling	4·4	47	3·3	10·7	41	5·6	10·8	43	6·1	14·1	66	4·9
Edinburgh..........	4·1	70	3·5	8·7	56	4·4	9·2	38	4·9	11·3	107	3·5
Glasgow............	3·5	125	2·8	8·6	58	—	9·8	51	—	11·7	106	3·0
Gogerddan	5·1	129	3·2	10·2	61	5·2	9·8	41	7·3	12·2	95	4·6
Hastings	4·5	72	3·6	10·5	34	6·2	11·1	43	6·9	14·0	63	5·7
Hull	4·3	75	—	10·1	60	—	9·8	27	—	12·9	73	—
Inverness	4·1	64	3·8	8·9	28	4·0	9·5	52	4·1	12·0	76	4·2
Leeming	3·9	69	3·0	9·7	51	4·3	9·6	30	5·8	12·1	83	3·2
Lerwick	2·7	188	2·6	6·9	37	2·7	7·1	40	5·7	8·8	56	3·9
London (Heathrow).......	4·9	43	3·4	11·2	40	5·1	11·6	54	6·4	14·6	70	4·4
Long Ashton........	5·0	79	3·4	10·7	65	6·3	10·7	31	7·0	13·6	94	5·3
Lowestoft	3·7	36	3·0	9·5	35	4·9	9·9	56	5·5	13·7	55	3·8
Manchester (Ringway)........	4·4	73	3·3	10·6	54	5·1	10·3	51	6·2	12·6	68	4·7
Manston	3·7	37	3·3	—	—	—	—	—	—	—	—	—
Melbury............	4·7	136	3·3	9·2	66	5·9	9·5	55	7·0	12·3	99	4·8
Morecambe	4·3	113	3·5	—	—	—	—	—	—	—	—	—
Nottingham (Watnall)..........	3·7	80	3·0	10·1	58	4·7	9·8	27	6·0	12·5	110	3·4
Oxford	4·9	54	3·6	10·9	51	5·1	10·8	49	5·4	14·1	86	4·3
Penzance	7·2	110	4·5	10·5	68	6·3	11·3	36	8·1	13·2	118	4·6
Plymouth	6·1	97	4·2	10·2	88	6·2	11·1	37	8·1	12·8	81	5·4
Prestwick	4·2	132	3·6	8·8	41	4·1	9·5	53	7·2	11·2	80	5·2
Rhoose	4·7	88	3·5	10·0	63	5·8	10·4	45	2·7	13·1	90	6·3
St. Mawgan.........	6·1	80	4·1	10·4	67	6·6	10·3	46	7·9	12·7	77	4·7
Scarborough........	4·0	72	—	9·8	67	5·1	9·7	31	6·2	14·5	85	4·0
Shawbury	3·9	63	3·0	9·9	53	5·0	9·4	44	5·8	12·5	87	3·5
Sheffield	4·3	89	3·6	10·3	65	5·2	10·2	33	6·4	12·7	140	4·1
Skegness	4·1	57	3·3	9·3	36	5·8	9·1	53	—	12·9	81	—
Southampton	5·4	97	3·6	10·5	73	6·3	12·1	30	7·0	14·4	66	5·2
Stornoway	3·7	147	3·8	7·6	44	4·1	8·3	65	5·9	9·9	57	5·9
Tenby.............	5·3	120	3·9	9·3	58	5·7	10·3	27	6·9	—	—	—
Tiree	4·5	181	3·3	8·2	36	3·9	9·3	67	7·1	10·9	48	7·8
Torbay	6·3	67	3·7	10·3	72	6·2	11·5	25	7·1	14·1	55	5·7
Trawscoed..........	4·9	130	2·4	9·9	85	4·3	9·0	56	5·6	—	—	—
Ventnor............	4·9	88	4·1	—	—	—	—	—	—	—	—	—
Waddington	3·9	66	3·5	9·9	50	5·2	9·8	51	6·1	12·8	104	4·5
Weymouth	5·5	74	4·0	9·5	57	6·3	11·4	20	7·9	13·3	54	5·9
Worthing	4·7	90	3·8	9·7	65	6·2	11·1	31	7·3	13·6	99	5·8
Writtle.............	3·9	40	3·0	—	—	—	—	—	—	—	—	—

METEOROLOGICAL OBSERVATIONS, LONDON (HEATHROW)

Weather Record, July, 1986

Day	Max. °C.	Min. °C.	Wind Speed knots	Rain-fall mm.	Sun-shine hrs.
1	26·5	12·7	3·5	0·0	11·3
2	27·1	12·9	3·1	0·0	11·9
3	25·0	15·6	4·7	0·0	13·4
4	25·6	13·4	7·0	21·2	3·7
5	19·0	15·4	5·3	1·6	0·2
6	21·3	13·4	4·6	0·0	6·8
7	20·5	11·4	4·5	0·0	5·1
8	22·3	13·0	3·7	1·1	4·4
9	20·7	8·2	4·2	0·0	7·7
10	23·3	13·5	5·0	4·8	5·6
11	21·5	12·9	2·8	0·3	3·6
12	20·0	13·7	2·7	1·6	0·2
13	21·9	13·2	2·6	0·0	3·6
14	25·3	16·0	2·7	0·0	1·4
15	29·1	17·3	3·3	0·0	9·9
16	28·0	18·3	5·7	0·0	13·0
17	21·9	15·2	4·9	0·0	12·7
18	19·6	10·6	3·8	0·0	5·2
19	20·4	11·1	3·3	0·1	3·5
20	23·8	13·1	4·6	0·0	3·5
21	22·1	12·7	2·8	13·6	5·6
22	20·6	14·2	2·7	0·2	6·1
23	17·4	10·0	4·0	4·5	3·2
24	22·5	7·4	6·3	0·2	11·9
25	21·9	15·2	7·4	0·2	3·2
26	23·3	15·8	6·3	0·0	2·7
27	23·0	12·5	7·1	0·0	5·6
28	21·2	17·2	6·8	4·7	0·1
29	22·0	15·2	7·7	0·0	7·1
30	20·6	10·3	5·4	0·2	2·9
31	21·6	14·0	8·1	0·3	5·4
Total	—	—	—	54·6	180·5
Mean	22·5	13·4	4·7	—	—
Temp. °F.	72·5	56·1	—	—	—
Average	22·0	12·9	8·2	51·0	189·7

Weather Record, August, 1986

Max. °C.	Min. °C.	Wind Speed knots	Rain-fall mm.	Sun-shine hrs.	Day
21·5	9·7	7·0	0·0	9·2	1
22·6	15·0	10·8	0·0	10·4	2
15·2	11·9	3·6	20·0	0·1	3
19·3	10·9	3·3	1·4	3·5	4
21·2	9·6	5·7	0·0	10·2	5
24·5	11·0	9·3	0·3	9·8	6
20·6	13·5	9·2	0·0	1·5	7
22·4	11·5	4·6	0·0	8·6	8
22·3	11·5	2·5	0·0	6·6	9
25·0	13·6	5·5	1·5	3·2	10
20·9	15·6	5·2	0·2	1·8	11
20·0	14·5	3·2	0·0	0·2	12
22·9	13·6	4·8	0·0	3·2	13
22·6	15·5	6·7	0·0	0·9	14
22·3	12·2	7·8	0·0	10·9	15
21·7	9·5	5·9	0·0	12·0	16
21·2	12·0	2·4	0·9	1·9	17
17·0	14·0	2·4	5·8	0·0	18
18·8	12·1	2·8	0·0	2·4	19
20·5	8·6	2·3	0·0	11·9	20
19·4	9·2	3·6	2·8	0·2	21
19·7	12·7	3·0	2·9	5·1	22
17·9	11·3	3·7	2·3	5·9	23
19·1	11·3	3·7	0·0	7·9	24
16·6	11·5	8·1	25·4	0·0	25
16·6	12·8	11·5	1·3	0·3	26
17·9	8·8	6·5	1·0	7·6	27
17·4	7·8	3·4	0·7	4·0	28
17·6	5·9	5·0	0·0	8·1	29
15·8	11·0	3·4	0·2	0·1	30
18·4	8·8	2·8	0·0	10·8	31
—	—	—	66·7	158·3	Total
20·0	11·5	5·1	—	—	Mean
68·0	52·7	—	—	—	Temp. °F.
21·6	12·7	8·0	58·0	176·4	Average

Weather Record, September, 1986

Day	Max. °C.	Min. °C.	Wind Speed knots	Rain-fall mm.	Sun-shine hrs.
1	15·9	10·0	6·7	0·1	0·0
2	21·5	11·0	7·5	2·0	10·2
3	16·5	11·6	8·0	0·0	3·9
4	19·6	6·0	2·8	0·0	10·6
5	19·3	6·8	2·7	0·0	8·6
6	17·3	9·0	3·6	0·0	1·6
7	19·8	8·1	3·4	0·0	10·8
8	16·5	8·1	2·6	0·0	1·7
9	17·2	5·1	2·3	0·0	9·3
10	17·0	4·5	2·3	0·0	6·4
11	18·0	6·6	3·5	0·0	6·0
12	16·4	7·9	5·5	0·0	5·9
13	14·9	7·9	6·0	16·8	1·5
14	16·0	10·8	3·9	0·1	1·1
15	11·2	9·2	5·0	3·8	0·0
16	15·0	7·5	6·7	0·0	4·5
17	14·0	6·9	4·6	0·0	0·0
18	16·0	5·7	5·0	0·0	9·4
19	16·9	5·2	2·6	0·0	10·0
20	20·2	3·9	2·2	0·0	10·4
21	20·5	5·5	2·6	0·0	9·8
22	20·3	5·7	2·1	0·0	7·7
23	20·1	9·2	2·1	0·0	4·5
24	14·9	11·4	7·3	0·0	0·1
25	16·9	9·8	4·2	0·0	7·1
26	17·0	5·8	2·0	0·0	6·8
27	19·2	8·5	2·4	0·0	6·9
28	19·6	11·7	3·7	0·0	2·6
29	16·7	12·4	2·2	0·0	0·0
30	15·8	12·4	3·3	0·0	0·0
31					
Total	—	—	—	22·8	157·4
Mean	17·3	8·1	4·0	—	—
Temp. °F.	63·1	46·6	—	—	—
Average	19·2	10·6	7·9	56·0	144·7

Weather Record, October, 1986

Max. °C.	Min. °C.	Wind Speed knots	Rain-fall mm.	Sun-shine hrs.	Day
15·7	12·3	2·6	0·0	0·0	1
19·0	11·8	2·5	0·0	4·7	2
19·9	10·9	4·6	0·0	8·8	3
19·4	10·1	6·7	0·0	9·2	4
17·2	10·7	3·3	0·0	0·0	5
20·7	10·4	4·1	0·0	5·5	6
22·0	11·3	4·1	0·0	7·1	7
20·9	13·1	3·0	0·0	4·6	8
21·7	12·8	5·7	0·0	6·6	9
19·6	10·5	3·9	0·4	1·9	10
17·6	9·0	2·6	0·0	7·3	11
16·8	6·5	4·2	0·0	1·2	12
17·0	9·7	2·6	0·0	2·2	13
17·6	11·6	2·1	21·4	0·0	14
15·4	12·1	4·5	0·0	4·0	15
15·0	4·6	3·0	0·0	7·2	16
16·4	4·1	3·6	1·6	7·5	17
14·8	10·6	5·5	4·9	0·8	18
15·1	5·9	8·5	7·0	6·3	19
15·9	7·7	11·5	0·4	5·5	20
14·9	6·6	8·0	18·7	0·0	21
14·5	10·6	6·3	2·1	2·5	22
11·6	4·1	7·8	0·0	8·0	23
12·1	2·5	7·7	4·3	0·1	24
11·9	8·2	11·1	0·0	0·7	25
13·5	4·4	5·5	0·2	7·4	26
15·3	7·8	7·0	5·2	0·0	27
16·0	14·3	8·5	2·7	0·0	28
12·8	4·5	7·0	0·0	6·7	29
14·0	9·0	11·0	0·7	0·2	30
13·2	5·7	5·5	2·8	0·3	31
—	—	—	72·4	116·3	Total
16·4	8·8	5·6	—	—	Mean
59·4	47·8	—	—	—	Temp. °F.
15·2	7·6	7·8	56·0	104·4	Average

Entries of Maximum Temperature cover the day period 9–21 h.; Minimum Temperature the night period 21–9 h. entered to the day of reading; Rainfall is for the 24 hours commencing at 9 h. on the day of entry; Sunshine is for the 24 hours 0–24 h.; Mean Wind Speed is 10 metres above the ground. 100 knots = 115·1 m.p.h.; 100 mm. = 3·94 ins.; °F. = 9/5°C. + 32.
Averages are for the period 1951–1980 except for mean wind speed which is for 1961–1980.

Weather Record, November, 1986

Day	Temperature Max. °C.	Temperature Min. °C.	Wind Speed knots	Rain-fall mm.	Sun-shine hrs.	Day
1	13·6	11·1	9·7	3·4	0·1	1
2	9·6	2·5	3·3	0·0	4·1	2
3	11·4	3·4	3·2	3·6	0·1	3
4	11·7	1·9	2·2	0·0	7·5	4
5	11·9	5·4	6·7	0·2	0·0	5
6	11·9	4·6	2·3	0·0	8·0	6
7	14·8	3·2	6·3	4·2	0·0	7
8	10·2	6·1	8·3	0·0	6·6	8
9	11·1	4·6	11·5	0·3	0·3	9
10	16·2	10·0	11·0	6·2	2·3	10
11	14·1	12·5	8·5	0·3	0·1	11
12	13·4	2·8	4·8	0·0	7·1	12
13	13·6	10·1	7·9	3·5	0·0	13
14	14·1	8·4	8·0	13·3	0·0	14
15	12·7	6·8	3·3	0·0	5·5	15
16	12·5	5·5	7·3	1·2	0·0	16
17	10·9	3·6	5·1	4·7	4·1	17
18	12·3	5·4	12·0	7·1	1·0	18
19	13·1	10·8	7·8	5·3	0·0	19
20	9·4	2·8	5·0	7·6	6·5	20
21	7·9	3·6	6·3	0·3	2·8	21
22	10·8	5·2	10·3	2·2	3·3	22
23	9·1	2·8	9·9	0·6	0·0	23
24	13·7	6·1	8·9	0·6	0·0	24
25	13·6	11·9	13·3	1·5	0·0	25
26	10·2	6·5	8·1	0·0	5·5	26
27	12·0	3·5	3·5	0·0	4·7	27
28	10·8	1·7	2·1	0·0	5·3	28
29	4·2	2·6	2·1	0·0	0·0	29
30	7·5	2·1	2·8	0·0	0·0	30
31						31
Total	—	—	—	66·1	74·9	Total
Mean	11·6	5·6	6·7	—	—	Mean
Temp. °F.	52·9	42·1	—	—	—	Temp. °F.
Average	10·2	3·9	8·9	62·0	64·0	Average

Weather Record, December, 1986

Day	Temperature Max. °C.	Temperature Min. °C.	Wind Speed knots	Rain-fall mm.	Sun-shine hrs.	Day
1	12·7	6·7	7·3	0·2	0·3	1
2	13·2	9·2	5·2	0·0	0·0	2
3	13·2	9·0	11·4	0·0	0·0	3
4	14·8	12·4	12·9	0·0	0·0	4
5	13·8	12·2	10·7	7·1	0·0	5
6	8·5	1·8	2·1	0·0	6·2	6
7	12·4	0·5	5·8	0·7	0·0	7
8	13·2	11·4	10·0	2·6	0·1	8
9	9·3	5·4	7·3	1·0	6·4	9
10	7·9	-0·7	2·9	0·0	6·5	10
11	9·1	3·0	6·4	4·1	0·0	11
12	9·3	0·0	4·5	4·7	1·3	12
13	10·2	6·7	6·4	0·0	4·3	13
14	7·0	1·2	2·0	0·1	4·2	14
15	9·7	-1·0	9·7	8·4	0·0	15
16	7·1	1·8	7·0	0·0	5·7	16
17	9·3	1·2	6·9	3·8	0·0	17
18	10·9	5·1	10·0	1·2	0·0	18
19	6·6	2·4	9·4	0·0	6·5	19
20	7·4	0·8	5·8	0·0	6·8	20
21	4·2	-1·1	5·2	1·4	0·7	21
22	3·7	1·0	6·3	0·0	0·8	22
23	4·8	0·8	4·0	0·0	0·0	23
24	5·4	0·0	2·5	5·4	2·8	24
25	10·2	4·2	5·3	3·6	0·0	25
26	6·7	0·8	3·7	0·4	2·3	26
27	6·4	0·6	5·7	0·0	0·1	27
28	10·9	4·4	6·6	0·0	0·0	28
29	11·0	7·2	8·5	2·1	0·1	29
30	11·5	10·5	11·4	3·5	0·0	30
31	10·6	7·2	9·5	10·3	0·0	31
Total	—	—	—	60·6	55·1	Total
Mean	9·4	4·0	6·9	—	—	Mean
Temp. °F.	48·9	39·2	—	—	—	Temp. °F.
Average	7·9	2·2	7·0	55·0	43·9	Average

Weather Record, January, 1987

Day	Temperature Max. °C.	Temperature Min. °C.	Wind Speed knots	Rain-fall mm.	Sun-shine hrs.	Day
1	11·1	6·9	8·1	0·6	0·0	1
2	7·7	4·2	8·4	0·0	0·1	2
3	5·0	1·0	3·2	0·1	6·0	3
4	10·6	-1·2	9·8	5·0	0·0	4
5	8·7	5·1	9·1	0·0	2·8	5
6	6·1	3·1	9·8	0·0	5·7	6
7	4·4	-1·4	3·9	0·0	3·1	7
8	-0·1	-3·5	2·0	0·0	0·0	8
9	3·2	-2·8	5·0	0·0	0·0	9
10	1·5	0·1	8·6	0·1	0·4	10
11	-3·0	-5·7	6·3	0·6	3·7	11
12	-6·2	-8·9	5·1	0·1	7·1	12
13	-3·3	-9·1	8·8	3·0	0·4	13
14	-2·7	-6·5	14·0	3·6	0·0	14
15	0·7	-3·6	16·6	0·0	0·0	15
16	1·5	-0·6	9·4	0·0	0·0	16
17	-1·3	-1·5	3·5	0·0	0·0	17
18	-0·8	-2·5	3·8	0·0	0·0	18
19	-0·5	-3·7	3·2	0·0	0·0	19
20	2·2	-1·0	2·3	0·0	0·0	20
21	7·2	1·2	2·1	0·3	0·0	21
22	7·6	4·2	2·7	0·8	0·0	22
23	7·6	4·8	2·9	0·1	0·0	23
24	5·7	4·7	6·1	0·0	0·0	24
25	4·8	3·8	2·6	0·0	0·0	25
26	7·0	2·4	3·3	0·0	0·0	26
27	4·2	2·6	2·9	0·0	0·0	27
28	6·2	0·0	3·1	0·0	3·8	28
29	5·5	-2·5	6·8	0·0	4·9	29
30	2·2	-3·7	6·7	0·0	8·4	30
31	5·5	-6·2	2·5	0·0	8·0	31
Total	—	—	—	14·3	54·4	Total
Mean	3·5	-0·7	5·9	—	—	Mean
Temp. °F.	38·3	30·7	—	—	—	Temp. °F.
Average	6·7	1·1	8·6	51·0	48·8	Average

Weather Record, February, 1987

Day	Temperature Max. °C.	Temperature Min. °C.	Wind Speed knots	Rain-fall mm.	Sun-shine hrs.	Day
1	5·4	-5·1	4·2	0·0	5·3	1
2	6·7	2·5	4·5	0·0	0·1	2
3	9·1	3·4	2·2	0·0	0·3	3
4	9·5	6·2	3·5	0·0	0·0	4
5	9·3	6·3	9·0	0·0	0·0	5
6	12·5	8·5	10·4	0·2	0·0	6
7	9·7	1·5	4·1	0·1	4·6	7
8	12·9	5·6	6·6	1·7	0·0	8
9	10·3	8·5	8·8	0·2	0·0	9
10	10·2	4·9	10·3	0·3	6·5	10
11	8·6	1·8	2·9	1·8	1·0	11
12	5·7	2·9	2·6	0·0	0·3	12
13	7·2	-0·4	4·9	11·5	0·1	13
14	5·1	1·5	7·0	0·4	0·2	14
15	5·7	-0·1	4·5	0·0	7·4	15
16	3·7	-1·3	4·3	0·1	0·1	16
17	3·8	-0·5	6·8	0·0	1·0	17
18	4·2	-0·1	7·3	0·0	4·5	18
19	3·7	-2·7	4·5	0·0	2·6	19
20	3·5	-1·9	9·0	0·0	7·4	20
21	5·6	-1·1	8·7	0·1	3·6	21
22	7·3	3·2	5·3	0·5	0·0	22
23	5·8	0·4	3·5	0·0	3·2	23
24	5·2	0·0	6·7	0·0	1·8	24
25	6·1	-2·2	5·2	0·0	5·4	25
26	10·0	-0·8	5·8	4·9	0·0	26
27	12·0	9·4	6·8	7·7	0·0	27
28	14·9	8·8	4·5	2·9	2·6	28
29						29
30						30
31						31
Total	—	—	—	32·4	58·0	Total
Mean	7·6	2·1	5·9	—	—	Mean
Temp. °F.	45·7	35·8	—	—	—	Temp. °F.
Average	7·3	1·3	9·3	38·0	62·6	Average

Weather Record, March, 1987

Day	Max. °C.	Min. °C.	Wind Speed knots	Rainfall mm.	Sunshine hrs.
1	11·9	7·7	6·4	3·5	0·0
2	9·4	7·6	12·8	0·0	4·0
3	3·0	0·2	9·2	0·6	8·4
4	3·9	−3·5	3·1	0·3	0·1
5	8·6	−0·2	3·4	1·5	1·6
6	3·8	2·2	8·3	2·4	0·0
7	4·6	2·0	11·4	4·2	0·0
8	4·8	0·1	6·2	0·1	0·0
9	5·0	−0·1	8·0	0·0	7·3
10	7·6	−0·7	7·1	0·0	9·2
11	7·4	−0·9	5·9	0·0	8·4
12	8·1	−3·0	3·5	0·0	8·1
13	5·9	−4·0	4·0	0·0	1·0
14	7·2	−2·8	2·3	0·0	7·0
15	8·6	0·1	5·8	0·0	0·1
16	8·6	1·5	5·3	0·0	4·8
17	13·0	−5·2	9·3	1·4	1·0
18	8·4	2·6	7·6	0·7	6·0
19	7·9	−0·5	5·2	0·1	7·2
20	8·4	−1·0	5·7	0·0	7·6
21	8·7	−0·6	2·5	0·0	3·4
22	10·0	−1·3	6·2	4·8	2·3
23	11·2	6·7	5·6	5·8	0·0
24	12·2	8·0	3·5	4·8	0·0
25	10·8	9·5	6·0	0·2	0·4
26	12·3	1·8	13·1	7·1	0·1
27	12·0	6·7	21·6	1·7	3·0
28	9·0	4·0	11·3	0·5	1·6
29	8·9	1·2	7·3	0·3	9·6
30	11·8	−0·3	4·5	0·0	2·9
31	11·3	4·2	5·2	2·7	0·1
Total	—	—	—	42·7	105·2
Mean	8·5	1·7	7·0	—	—
Temp. °F.	47·3	35·1	—	—	—
Average	10·2	2·6	9·5	43·0	110·8

Weather Record, April, 1987

Max. °C.	Min. °C.	Wind Speed knots	Rainfall mm.	Sunshine hrs.	Day
9·4	7·3	8·0	7·0	0·0	1
11·1	3·2	6·2	0·0	7·1	2
9·8	4·2	11·9	3·6	0·4	3
9·5	8·0	5·4	7·5	0·0	4
15·1	3·0	4·0	0·2	7·0	5
13·8	7·9	5·8	13·1	2·4	6
13·1	6·0	7·4	0·6	0·5	7
13·0	7·4	9·6	0·4	0·0	8
13·9	8·0	6·5	0·5	3·3	9
12·6	2·1	9·1	2·6	8·4	10
12·2	3·7	10·8	0·0	9·8	11
11·2	3·0	5·8	0·0	6·2	12
11·9	4·7	4·1	0·0	0·0	13
13·9	4·0	2·3	0·0	1·5	14
13·5	5·9	3·0	0·0	2·3	15
14·5	4·6	2·9	0·0	7·2	16
22·1	7·2	4·0	0·0	11·9	17
17·7	6·5	5·5	0·0	4·7	18
16·7	11·4	10·3	0·3	6·6	19
13·4	8·2	8·9	0·0	4·6	20
15·8	3·6	3·4	0·0	1·6	21
16·8	10·0	4·5	0·0	4·3	22
21·0	6·6	4·5	0·0	12·3	23
22·2	7·3	6·3	0·0	10·1	24
20·0	10·1	3·7	0·0	5·4	25
22·2	8·0	3·2	0·0	11·3	26
21·0	10·3	5·4	0·0	5·6	27
23·4	7·5	6·8	0·0	12·0	28
21·6	11·3	4·7	4·1	6·4	29
14·2	11·7	6·7	0·0	0·1	30
—	—	—	39·9	153·0	Total
15·8	6·8	6·0	—	—	Mean
60·4	44·2	—	—	—	Temp. °F.
13·2	4·6	8·3	41·0	146·9	Average

Weather Record, May, 1987

Day	Max. °C.	Min. °C.	Wind Speed knots	Rainfall mm.	Sunshine hrs.
1	17·2	12·0	5·8	1·6	0·2
2	14·5	3·0	8·4	1·9	11·7
3	10·1	4·3	9·8	2·2	6·2
4	12·3	2·2	9·2	0·0	12·1
5	14·2	6·0	5·8	0·0	3·1
6	17·7	6·0	3·8	0·0	5·3
7	17·6	6·7	4·4	0·0	13·7
8	20·4	3·8	3·4	0·0	14·1
9	23·7	6·6	4·4	0·0	13·9
10	14·9	7·2	5·2	0·0	8·2
11	15·2	5·9	7·9	2·5	0·1
12	14·8	11·0	8·5	2·8	6·3
13	13·8	4·0	5·2	9·9	8·6
14	14·5	5·4	7·0	5·2	5·7
15	12·3	6·6	6·9	0·3	7·5
16	14·6	4·0	4·4	0·0	4·9
17	13·8	7·9	5·8	4·7	0·1
18	13·2	8·1	7·5	2·2	1·2
19	17·2	6·6	6·0	0·0	7·4
20	13·6	5·3	6·0	0·1	10·0
21	14·6	6·1	8·4	0·1	3·6
22	13·1	6·3	8·1	5·9	2·6
23	11·7	7·9	5·4	2·5	0·0
24	18·9	7·2	8·6	0·0	5·9
25	17·5	7·6	3·2	0·0	0·9
26	22·6	9·1	7·4	0·3	5·1
27	19·9	9·9	4·8	0·0	12·3
28	18·8	8·1	3·5	0·0	3·4
29	19·9	8·5	5·6	0·0	10·4
30	20·6	12·9	8·3	11·9	5·8
31	20·9	11·4	5·1	0·0	7·9
Total	—	—	—	54·1	198·2
Mean	16·3	7·0	6·2	—	—
Temp. °F.	61·3	44·6	—	—	—
Average	17·1	7·8	8·5	48·0	196·1

Weather Record, June, 1987

Max. °C.	Min. °C.	Wind Speed knots	Rainfall mm.	Sunshine hrs.	Day
20·5	10·3	5·9	0·0	7·7	1
15·5	11·9	5·5	3·7	0·0	2
19·0	11·9	7·3	0·3	2·7	3
19·1	11·9	4·9	13·2	6·7	4
15·6	7·8	6·9	6·5	0·0	5
18·3	12·1	15·3	0·0	7·8	6
14·7	11·2	9·2	2·2	4·9	7
14·2	9·9	4·0	4·2	0·3	8
13·0	9·1	3·2	1·9	0·2	9
17·3	5·3	4·4	2·8	8·7	10
17·2	10·5	3·2	3·6	3·3	11
18·2	6·7	3·4	0·0	8·7	12
17·1	8·8	4·2	0·0	6·0	13
17·9	9·8	3·6	0·3	5·5	14
18·0	6·3	4·6	0·0	4·2	15
16·5	6·9	5·2	5·5	10·3	16
16·2	9·0	4·7	3·6	2·8	17
18·2	8·7	5·2	7·3	2·6	18
16·1	11·4	8·0	1·7	0·1	19
20·0	8·8	5·1	2·8	8·7	20
19·7	10·1	4·4	0·0	4·4	21
15·9	10·5	5·1	3·8	2·9	22
19·6	12·0	3·8	0·2	0·1	23
19·1	11·9	6·1	1·5	8·0	24
17·6	11·2	6·0	4·5	0·2	25
21·3	12·1	6·0	0·3	3·4	26
22·1	13·7	7·6	0·0	0·1	27
25·1	16·9	9·1	0·0	2·5	28
28·5	17·8	6·0	0·0	9·4	29
24·4	17·4	6·0	0·0	10·3	30
—	—	—	69·9	132·9	Total
18·6	10·7	5·8	—	—	Mean
65·5	51·3	—	—	—	Temp. °F.
20·5	10·9	8·4	51·0	206·0	Average

TIDAL CONSTANTS

THE TIME OF HIGH WATER *at the undermentioned Ports and Places may be* approximately *found by taking the appropriate Time of High Water at the Standard Port (as shown on pp. 172, 173, etc.) and* adding thereto *the quantities annexed. The columns headed "Springs" and "Neaps" show the height of the tide above datum for Mean High Water Springs and Mean High Water Neaps respectively.*

EXAMPLE.—Required times of high water at Stranraer on *January* 2, 1988:—

(a) *Morning Tide.*
    Appropriate time of high
        water at *Greenock* .... 1055 hrs. (*Jan.* 2)
    Tidal difference .... −0020 hrs.

    H.W at *Stranraer* ... 1035 hrs.

(b) *Afternoon Tide.*
    Appropriate time of high
        water at *Greenock* .... 2339 hrs. (*Jan* 2).
    Tidal difference .... −0020 hrs.

    H.W. at *Stranraer* .. 2319 hrs.

Port	Diff.	Springs	Neaps	Port	Diff.	Springs	Neaps
	h.m.	metres	metres		h.m.	metres	metres
Aberdeen.........*Leith*	−1 19	4·3	3·4	Coulport ...... *Greenock*	−0 05	3·4	2·9
Aberdovey..... *Liverpool*	−3 00	5·0	3·5	Coverack.... *Avonmouth*	−2 02	5·3	4·2
Aberystwyth .. *Liverpool*	−3 30	5·0	3·5	Cowes.......... *London*	−2 23	4·2	3·5
Aldeburgh...... *London*	−3 05	2·8	2·7	Cromarty........*Leith*	−2 56	4·3	3·4
Alloa.............*Leith*	+0 47	5·6	4·2	Cromer........... *Hull*	+0 19	5·2	4·1
Amlwch.....*Liverpool*	−0 33	7·3	5·8	Dartmouth ..... *London*	+4 37	4·7	3·8
Anstruther Easter . *Leith*	−0 22	5·5	4·4	Deal .... *London*	−2 37	6·1	5·0
Antwerp .... *London*	+0 50	5·8	4·2	Dieppe .... *London*	−3 03	9·3	7·2
Appledore ... *Avonmouth*	−1 15	7·5	5·2	Dingle Hbr... *Liverpool*	+5 38	3·9	2·9
Arbroath.........*Leith*	−0 33	5·0	4·1	Donegal Hbr. . *Liverpool*	−5 24	3·9	3·0
Ardrossan .... *Greenock*	−0 15	3·2	2·7	Douglas .... *Liverpool*	−0 04	6·9	5·4
†Arundel....... *London*	−2 03	3·1	2·2	Dover........ *London*	−2 52	6·7	5·3
Avonmouth ....*A'mouth*	0 00	13·2	10·0	Duclair........ *London*	−1 13	7·7	6·5
Ayr .... *Greenock*	−0 25	3·0	2·6	Duddon Bar ... *Liverpool*	+0 03	8·5	6·6
Baie de Lampaul . *London*	+2 30	7·5	5·8	Dunbar..........*Leith*	−0 07	5·2	4·2
Ballycotton.. *Avonmouth*	−1 43	4·2	3·3	Dundalk (Sldr's Pt) *L'pool*	+0 22	5·1	4·2
Banff............*Leith*	−2 44	3·5	2·8	Dundee ....*Leith*	+0 11	5·3	4·3
Bantry ....*Liverpool*	+5 59	3·5	2·6	Dungeness....... *London*	−3 04	7·7	5·9
Bardsey Island . *Liverpool*	−3 18	4·5	3·3	Dunkirk .... *London*	−1 54	5·8	4·8
Barmouth .... *Liverpool*	−2 57	5·0	3·5	Eastbourne...... *London*	−2 50	7·3	5·6
Barnstaple .. *Avonmouth*	−1 00	4·1	1·4	East Loch Tarbert *G'nock*	+0 05	3·4	2·9
Barrow ..... *Liverpool*	+0 15	9·1	7·1	Exmouth Dock .. *London*	+4 55	4·0	2·8
Barry .... *Avonmouth*	−0 22	11·4	8·7	Eyemouth.........*Leith*	−0 20	4·7	3·7
Belfast .... *London*	−2 45	3·5	3·0	Falmouth ...... *London*	+3 35	5·3	4·2
Berwick..........*Leith*	−0 02	4·7	3·8	Ferryside.... *Avonmouth*	−0 58	6·7	4·5
Bideford.... *Avonmouth*	−1 15	5·9	3·6	Filey Bay ....*Leith*	+1 50	5·8	4·9
Blackpool .... *Liverpool*	−0 10	8·9	7·0	Fishguard ..... *Liverpool*	−4 00	4·8	3·4
Blacktoft......... *Hull*	+0 32	5·7	3·9	Flushing ...... *London*	−0 40	4·9	4·0
Blakeney......... *Hull*	+0 44	3·4	2·0	Folkestone ..... *London*	−3 04	7·1	5·7
Blyth ....*Leith*	+0 50	5·0	3·9	Formby .... *Liverpool*	−0 12	9·0	7·3
Boscastle ... *Avonmouth*	−1 20	7·3	5·6	Fowey .... *London*	+3 53	5·4	4·3
Boulogne ...... *London*	−2 44	8·9	7·2	Fraserburgh ......*Leith*	−2 19	3·9	3·1
Bovisand Pier... *London*	+3 55	5·3	4·3	*Freshwater Bay London*	−4 33	2·6	2·3
Bowling....... *Greenock*	+0 15	4·0	3·4	Galway ...... *Liverpool*	−0 08	5·1	3·9
Braye .... *London*	+5 33	6·3	4·7	Glasgow....... *Greenock*	+0 28	4·7	4·1
Brest .... *London*	+2 28	7·5	5·9	Goole .... *Hull*	+0 59	5·7	3·7
Bridgwater .. *Avonmouth*	−0 22	4·6	1·9	Gorleston ...... *London*	−5 00	2·4	2·0
Bridlington........*Leith*	+2 03	6·1	4·7	Granton...........*Leith*	0 00	5·6	4·5
Bridport .... *London*	+4 37	4·1	3·0	Granville...... *London*	+4 32	12·8	9·6
Brighton .. *London*	−2 50	6·5	5·1	Grimsby........... *Hull*	−0 28	7·0	5·6
Buckie ....*Leith*	−2 56	4·1	3·2	Hartlepool........*Leith*	+0 58	5·1	4·0
Bude Haven . *Avonmouth*	−1 33	7·7	5·8	Harwich ...... *London*	−2 02	4·0	3·4
Bull Sand Fort ..... *Hull*	−0 46	6·9	5·5	Hastings ...... *London*	−2 57	7·5	5·8
Burntisland ......*Leith*	0 00	5·6	4·5	Haverfordwest . *Liverpool*	−4 50	2·2	0·3
Calais .... *London*	−2 04	7·2	6·0	Hestan Islet ... *Liverpool*	+0 25	8·3	6·3
Campbeltown .. *Greenock*	+0 07	2·9	2·6	Hilbre Island.. *Liverpool*	−0 13	9·0	7·2
Cape Cornwall .. *A'mouth*	−2 30	6·0	4·3	Holyhead...... *Liverpool*	−0 48	5·7	4·5
Cardiff ...... *Avonmouth*	−0 15	12·2	9·4	Hook of Holland . *London*	−0 01	2·3	1·8
Cardigan, Port . *Liverpool*	−3 37	4·7	3·4	*Hurst Point ... London*	−3 38	2·7	2·3
Carmarthen . *Avonmouth*	−0 48	2·6	0·4	Ijmuiden .... *London*	+1 09	2·0	1·7
Cayeux........ *London*	−2 55	10·2	7·9	Ilfracombe... *Avonmouth*	−1 10	9·2	6·9
Chatham(N.Lock)*London*	−1 10	6·0	4·9	Inveraray ..... *Greenock*	+0 11	3·3	3·0
Chepstow... *Avonmouth*	+0 20	No Data		Invergordon ....*Leith*	−2 49	4·4	3·5
Cherbourg...... *London*	−6 00	6·3	5·0	Ipswich .... *London*	−1 42	4·2	3·4
Chester ..... *Liverpool*	+1 05	4·0	2·0	Itchenor .... *London*	−2 23	4·8	3·8
Chichester Hbr. . *London*	−2 25	4·9	4·0	Kinsale .... *Liverpool*	−6 03	4·1	3·2
Christchurch Hbr. *L'don*	−4 53	1·8	1·4	Kirkcudbright . *Liverpool*	+0 15	7·5	5·9
Cobh .... *Liverpool*	−5 56	4·1	3·3	Kirkwall ....*Leith*	−4 15	2·9	2·2

Port	Diff.	Springs	Neaps	Port	Diff.	Springs	Neaps
	h.m.	metres	metres		h.m.	metres	metres
Knights Town . *Liverpool*	+5 36	3·9	3·0	Ramsey (I.O.M.) *Liverpool*	+0 04	7·2	5·7
Lamlash .... *Greenock*	−0 26	3·2	2·7	Ramsgate....... *London*	−2 32	4·9	3·8
Le Havre .... *London*	−3 55	7·8	6·5	†Rosslare...... *Liverpool*	−5 23	1·9	1·4
Lerwick .... *Leith*	−3 49	2·2	1·6	Rosyth .... *Leith*	+0 07	5·8	4·7
Limerick Dock . *Liverpool*	−4 24	5·9	4·5	Ryde........... *London*	−2 23	4·5	3·7
Littlehampton .. *London*	−2 33	5·5	4·3	St. Helier ..... *London*	+4 48	11·1	8·1
Lizard Point . *Avonmouth*	−2 17	5·3	4·2	St. Ives ...... *Avonmouth*	−1 55	6·6	4·9
Llanddwyn Island *L'pool*	−1 53	5·0	4·0	St. Malo ...... *London*	+4 27	12·1	9·1
Llanelli ..... *Avonmouth*	−0 56	7·8	5·8	St. Peter Port ... *London*	+4 54	9·0	6·7
Loch Moidart .. *Greenock*	+6 00	4·8	3·5	Salcombe .... *London*	+4 10	5·3	4·1
Londonderry ... *London*	−5 37	2·7	2·0	Saltash .... *London*	+4 10	5·6	4·5
Looe .... *London*	+3 55	5·4	4·2	Scarborough...... *Leith*	+1 33	5·7	4·6
Lossiemouth ...... *Leith*	−3 01	4·1	3·2	Scheveningen... *London*	+0 29	2·1	1·8
Lowestoft ...... *London*	−4 25	2·4	2·1	Scrabster ...... *Leith*	+6 04	5·0	3·7
Lulworth Cove.. *London*	+5 00	2·3	1·5	Seaham .... *Leith*	+0 53	5·2	4·1
Lundy Island *Avonmouth*	−1 23	8·0	5·9	Selsey Bill ...... *London*	−2 28	5·3	4·4
Lyme Regis ..... *London*	+4 55	4·3	3·1	Sennen Cove . *Avonmouth*	−2 30	6·1	4·8
*Lymington ... *London*	−3 33	3·0	2·6	Sharpness Dock . *A'mouth*	+0 42	9·3	5·8
Margate........ *London*	−1 52	4·8	3·9	Sheerness ...... *London*	−1 16	5·7	4·8
Maryport...... *London*	+0 24	8·6	6·6	Shoreham ...... *London*	−2 43	6·2	5·0
Menai Bridge .. *Liverpool*	−0 28	7·4	5·9	Silloth .... *Liverpool*	+0 35	9·2	7·1
Mevagissey ..... *London*	+3 53	5·4	4·3	Southampton ... *London*	−2 52	4·5	3·7
Middlesbrough..... *Leith*	+1 09	5·6	4·5	Southend ...... *London*	−1 22	5·7	4·8
Milford Haven . *Liverpool*	−5 07	7·0	5·2	Southwold..... *London*	−3 50	2·5	2·2
Minehead .... *Avonmouth*	−0 40	10·6	8·1	Stirling .... *Leith*	+1 13	2·9	1·6
Montrose......... *Leith*	−0 19	4·8	3·9	Stonehaven........ *Leith*	−1 09	4·5	3·6
Morecambe .. *Liverpool*	+0 01	9·5	7·6	Stornoway ... *Liverpool*	−4 15	4·8	3·7
Mostyn Quay .. *Liverpool*	−0 17	8·5	6·7	Stranraer ...... *Greenock*	−0 20	3·0	2·5
Newburgh........ *Leith*	+0 48	4·1	3·0	Stromness ..... *Leith*	−5 34	3·6	2·7
Newcastle on Tyne . *Leith*	+0 54	5·3	4·1	Sunderland........ *Leith*	+0 51	5·2	4·2
Newhaven ...... *London*	−2 48	6·6	5·2	*Swanage ..... *London*	−5 13	2·0	1·6
Newlyn .... *Avonmouth*	−2 24	5·6	4·4	Swansea..... *Avonmouth*	−0 49	9·6	7·3
Newport(Gwent) *A'mouth*	−0 15	12·1	9·0	Tarn Point ... *Liverpool*	+0 05	8·3	6·4
Newquay ...... *Avonmouth*	−1 58	7·0	5·3	Tay River (Bar) .....*Leith*	−0 21	5·2	4·2
New Quay (Card.) . *L'pool*	−3 30	4·9	3·4	Tees R. (Ent.) ......*Leith*	+1 08	5·5	4·3
North Shields ...... *Leith*	+0 51	5·0	3·9	Teignmouth .... *London*	+4 37	4·8	3·6
North Sunderland .. *Leith*	+0 05	4·8	3·7	Tenby .... *Avonmouth*	−1 05	8·4	6·3
N. Woolwich .... *London*	−0 20	7·0	5·7	Tilbury.......... *London*	−0 49	6·4	5·3
Oban .... *Greenock*	+5 45	4·0	2·9	Tobermory ... *Liverpool*	−5 12	4·4	3·3
Old Lynn Road..... *Hull*	+0 05	7·3	5·8	Torquay........ *London*	+4 40	4·9	3·7
Orfordness ..... *London*	−2 50	2·8	2·7	*Totland Bay ... *London*	−3 53	2·7	2·3
Ostend .... *London*	−1 32	5·1	4·2	Troon .... *Greenock*	−0 25	3·2	2·7
Padstow ...... *Avonmouth*	−1 45	7·3	5·6	Truro .... *London*	+3 43	5·3	4·2
Peel........... *Liverpool*	−0 02	5·3	4·2	Tyne River (Ent.)... *Leith*	+0 56	5·1	3·9
Peterhead .... *Leith*	−1 59	3·8	3·1	Walton-on-Naze. *London*	−2 10	4·2	3·4
Plymouth ...... *London*	+4 05	5·5	4·4	Waterford Hbr . *Liverpool*	−4 54	4·6	3·6
Poole (Entrance) *London*	−5 03	2·0	1·6	Weston S. Mare . *A'mouth*	−0 25	12·0	9·0
Porlock Bay . *Avonmouth*	−0 50	10·2	7·8	†Wexford Hbr.. *Liverpool*	−5 03	1·7	1·4
Porthcawl .. *Avonmouth*	−0 53	9·9	7·5	Whitby......... *Leith*	+1 22	5·4	4·3
Portmadoc..... *Liverpool*	−2 45	5·1	3·4	Whitehaven ... *Liverpool*	+0 10	8·0	6·3
Portland .... *London*	+5 10	2·1	1·4	Wick........... *Leith*	−3 26	3·4	2·7
Portpatrick.... *Liverpool*	+0 22	3·8	3·0	Wisbech Cut .... *Hull*	+0 01	7·0	5·1
Portsmouth....... *London*	−2 23	4·7	3·8	Workington ... *Liverpool*	+0 20	8·2	6·4
Port Talbot . *Avonmouth*	−0 53	9·6	7·3	Worthing ..... *London*	−2 38	6·1	4·8
Preston ...... *Liverpool*	+0 10	5·3	3·3	*Yarmth.(I.O.W.) *London*	−2 53	3·1	2·5
Pwllheli .... *Liverpool*	−3 07	5·0	3·4	Youghal .... *Liverpool*	−5 50	4·2	3·3

† Very Approximate.   * 1st H.W. (Springs).

Tidal data is no longer available for a number of places which formerly appeared in the list above. These places (with the name of the substitute now recorded) are: *Air Point* (Mostyn Quay); *Alderney* (Braye); *Ardrishaig* (East Loch Tarbert); *Arisaig* (Loch Moidart); *Ayr Pt.*, I.o.M. (Peel); *Beachy Head* (Eastbourne); *Beaumaris* (Menai Bridge); *Brieile* (Scheveningen); *Broughty Ferry* (Newburgh); *Burryport* (Whiteford Lighthouse); *Caen* (Cayeux); *Caernarvon* (Llanddwyn Is.); *Devonport* (Plymouth); *Dumbarton* (Bowling); *Fareham* (Itchenor); *Fifeness* (Anstruther Easter); *Glasson Dock* (Tarn Pt.); *Gravesend* (Tilbury); *Greenwich* (R. Albert Dock); *Honfleur Harbour* (Duclair); *Hythe* (Totland Bay); *Lancaster* (Duddon Bar); *Loch Long* (Coulport); *Lynmouth* (Porlock Bay); *Nash Pt.* (Chepstow); *Neath* (Porthcawl); *Needles Pt.* (Freshwater Bay); *Nore Lt.* (Chatham); *Pembroke Dock* (Milford Haven); *Penzance* (Newlyn); *Plymouth Breakwater* (Bovisand Pier); *Port Harrington* (Hestan Islet); *Portishead* (Avonmouth); *St. Agnes* (Coverack); *St. Annes* (Blackpool); *St. Mary's* (Sennen Cove); *Spurn Head* (Bull Sand Fort); *Start Pt.* (Lulworth Cove); *Stockton* (Seaham); *Sutton Bridge* (Blacktoft); *Torbay* (Torquay); *Ushant* (Baie de Lampaul); *Valentia Harbour* (Knights Town); *Woolwich* (N. Woolwich); *Worms Head* (Ferryside); *Yarmouth Roads* (Gorleston).

Tidal predictions (pp. 172–183) for London Bridge, Liverpool, Avonmouth, Hull, Dún Laoghaire and Leith are computed by the Proudfoot Oceanographic Laboratory, copyright reserved. Those for Greenock have been supplied by the Hydrographer of the Navy and are crown copyright.

JANUARY, 1988

High Water at the undermentioned Places (G.M.T.*)—

Day of Month	Day of Week	LONDON BRIDGE †Datum of Predictions 3·20 m. below				LIVERPOOL †Datum of Predictions 4·93 m. below				AVONMOUTH †Datum of Predictions 6·50 m. below				HULL (Albert Dock) †Datum of Predictions 3·90 m. below				GREENOCK †Datum of Predictions 1·62 m. below				LEITH †Datum of Predictions 2·90 m. below				DUN LAOGHAIRE ‡Datum of Predictions 0·20 m. above			
		Mn. h.m.	Ht.	Aft. h.m.	Ht.	Mn. h.m.	Ht.	Aft. h.m.	Ht.	Mn. h.m.	Ht.	Aft. h.m.	Ht.	Mn. h.m.	Ht.	Aft. h.m.	Ht.	Mn. h.m.	Ht.	Aft. h.m.	Ht.	Mn. h.m.	Ht.	Aft. h.m.	Ht.	Mn. h.m.	Ht.	Aft. h.m.	Ht.
1	F	1150	6·3			912	8·1	2134	8·3	454	11·4	1725	11·6	356	6·5	1638	6·5	1010	3·2	2248	3·2	010	5·0	1245	5·0	942	3·8	22 5	3·8
2	Sa	022	6·5	1245	6·4	1000	8·4	2223	8·4	547	11·8	1815	11·8	455	6·6	1725	6·7	1055	3·3	2339	3·2	1 5	5·1	1334	5·1	1025	3·9	2249	3·8
3	Su	110	6·5	1331	6·5	1044	8·6	2305	8·5	635	12·1	1900	12·1	546	6·6	18 7	6·8	1138	3·4			155	5·1	1419	5·1	11 3	3·9	2327	3·7
4	M	151	6·5	1412	6·6	1123	8·8	2343	8·6	717	12·3	1942	12·2	631	6·6	1843	6·8	026	3·2	1218	3·5	240	5·1	1458	5·2	1140	3·9		
5	Tu	227	6·6	1450	6·7	1158	8·9			755	12·4	2019	12·4	710	6·6	1916	6·8	111	3·1	1255	3·6	320	5·2	1534	5·2	0 4	3·6	1216	4·0
6	W	3 3	6·7	1527	6·7	019	8·6	1234	8·9	829	12·3	2053	12·3	744	6·6	1945	7·0	152	3·1	1332	3·6	355	5·2	16 7	5·2	037	3·6	1251	3·9
7	Th	335	6·7	1602	6·7	053	8·6	1306	8·8	9 0	12·1	2122	12·2	815	6·6	2015	7·1	231	3·1	1407	3·6	428	5·1	1640	5·0	113	3·5	1326	3·9
8	F	4 9	6·6	1637	6·7	127	8·5	1340	8·7	929	12·0	2152	12·1	847	6·6	2047	7·1	3 5	3·0	1442	3·5	5 1	4·9	1715	4·9	147	3·5	14 1	3·8
9	Sa	441	6·5	1711	6·6	2 1	8·3	1413	8·5	1000	11·8	2221	11·6	921	6·5	2122	6·7	338	3·0	1518	3·5	537	4·8	1752	4·8	224	3·4	1439	3·7
10	Su	513	6·6	1746	6·4	236	8·1	1449	8·3	1033	11·3	2254	11·3	957	6·2	2203	6·5	4 9	3·0	1555	3·4	615	4·7	1831	4·7	3 3	3·4	1518	3·7
11	M	546	6·4	1822	6·2	314	7·8	1527	8·0	1108	11·2	2327	10·6	1038	6·0	2244	6·4	441	3·0	1637	3·4	658	4·5	1914	4·7	347	3·3	1603	3·6
12	Tu	622	6·0	19 4	6·0	357	7·6	1614	7·8	1147	10·8			1123	6·0			518	3·0	1725	3·3	744	4·5	20 1	4·6	440	3·3	1656	3·5
13	W	7 0	5·8	1958	5·8	452	7·4	1713	7·6	010	9·9	1239	10·4	038	6·0	1219	6·0	6 4	3·0	1820	3·3	837	4·5	2057	4·6	543	3·3	18 3	3·5
14	Th	8 9	5·8	21 8	5·8	6 0	7·4	1827	7·5	114	10·0	1358	10·5	155	6·2	1328	6·2	7 3	3·0	1924	3·3	939	4·5	2318	4·6	651	3·3	1915	3·5
15	F	932	5·9	2220	5·9	714	7·5	1942	7·7	250	10·7	1522	11·5	310	6·4	1442	6·6	820	3·1	2036	3·3	1047	4·5			754	3·4	2021	3·7
16	Sa	1047	6·2	2327	6·1	822	7·9	2050	8·1	4 4	11·5	1633	12·3	420	6·8	1549	7·0	932	3·3	2146	3·3	1155	4·7			848	3·6	2119	3·8
17	Su	1157	6·2			921	8·5	2149	8·6	511	12·3	1740	13·4	520	7·4	1649	7·7	1030	3·4	2250	3·3	028	4·8	1255	5·0	938	3·8	2211	3·9
18	M	032	6·4	13 0	7·5	1016	9·4	2244	9·0	612	13·4	1842	13·6	614	7·6	1740	8·0	1122	3·3	2349	3·3	129	5·1	1348	5·2	1025	4·0	2259	4·0
19	Tu	127	6·7	1355	7·5	11 6	9·4	2334	9·1	7 9	13·7	1935	13·5	7 2	7·6	1825	8·0			1212	3·7	221	5·4	1523	5·7	1110	4·2	2347	4·0
20	W	218	6·9	1444	7·6	1154	9·8			758	13·9	2023	13·6	747	7·7	19 9	8·0	046	3·4	13 4	3·8	3 9	5·6	16 8	5·7	1157	4·3		
21	Th	3 4	7·2	1532	7·6	1232	9·5	1242	9·9	843	13·8	21 8	13·6	830	7·6	1949	8·0	141	3·4	1352	3·9	439	5·7	1655	5·7	035	3·9	1244	4·4
22	F	348	7·3	1619	7·4	1 9	9·5	1327	9·8	928	13·7	2150	13·7	912	7·4	2032	7·7	232	3·4	1440	3·9	526	5·6	1744	5·5	123	3·9	1333	4·4
23	Sa	431	7·3	1705	7·3	154	9·4	1412	9·5	1010	13·4	2233	13·5	957	7·1	2115	7·3	318	3·4	1525	3·8	616	5·5	1835	5·3	213	3·8	1424	4·2
24	Su	515	7·2	1751	7·1	239	9·0	1457	9·2	1054	12·7	2315	12·7	1044	7·1	2159	6·8	4 0	3·4	16 9	3·8	7 9	5·1	1927	5·1	3 0	3·7	1517	4·0
25	M	558	7·0	1838	6·9	324	8·6	1545	8·9	1137	12·4	2356	12·4	1137	6·8	2248	6·4	440	3·2	1655	3·4	8 4	5·0	2022	5·0	4 0	3·5	1616	4·0
26	Tu	645	6·7	1928	6·6	413	8·1	1638	8·5	1222	12·2			1044	6·3	2248	6·1	520	3·1	1746	3·8	9 4	4·7	2127	4·7	5 4	3·5	1721	3·8
27	W	738	6·4	2026	6·4	512	7·6	1743	8·1	042	11·0	1317	10·8	057	6·3	1355	6·0	6 6	3·1	1849	3·1	1015	4·6	2243	4·7	616	3·4	1838	3·6
28	Th	844	6·1	2134	6·2	627	7·3	19 3	7·7	142	10·4	1427	10·3	219	6·1	1512	6·0	828	2·9	2010	3·0	1129	4·6	2357	4·7	727	3·4	1956	3·5
29	F	10 4	5·9	2252	6·0	748	7·3	2022	7·7	3 1	10·1	1552	10·5	342	6·1	1620	6·4	944	2·9	2133	2·9			1233	4·7	832	3·5	21 2	3·5
30	Sa	1129	6·0			858	7·7	2127	7·7	426	10·5	17 5	10·7	449	6·1	1712	6·4	1041	3·2	2240	2·9	1 0	4·8	1233	4·7	927	3·5	2159	3·5
31	Su	0 0	6·1	1231	6·2	952	8·1	2216	8·1	530	11·1	18 1	11·3							2337	3·1			1325	4·9	1014	3·7	2243	3·6

*All times shown are Greenwich Mean Time.   †Difference of height in metres from Ordnance Datum (Newlyn).
‡Difference of height in metres from Ordnance Datum (Dublin).

FEBRUARY, 1988

High Water at the undermentioned Places (G.M.T.*)—

Day of Month	Day of Week	LONDON BRIDGE †Datum 3·20 m. below Mn.	Ht.	Aft.	Ht.	LIVERPOOL †Datum 4·93 m. below Mn.	Ht.	Aft.	Ht.	AVONMOUTH †Datum 6·50 m. below Mn.	Ht.	Aft.	Ht.	HULL (Albert Dock) †Datum 3·90 m. below Mn.	Ht.	Aft.	Ht.	GREENOCK †Datum 1·62 m. below Mn.	Ht.	Aft.	Ht.	LEITH †Datum 2·90 m. below Mn.	Ht.	Aft.	Ht.	DUN LAOGHAIRE ‡Datum 0·20 m. above Mn.	Ht.	Aft.	Ht.
1	M	053	6·3	1319	6·4	1034	8·5	2257	8·4	621	11·7	1848	11·8	540	6·3	1753	6·7	1126	3·3	12 7	3·4	150	4·9	1411	5·0	1053	3·8	2319	3·6
2	Tu	135	6·4	1359	6·6	1112	8·7	2332	8·6	7 3	12·1	1927	12·1	621	6·5	1828	6·9	025	3·1	1244	3·5	232	5·0	1447	5·1	1127	3·9	2350	3·6
3	W	212	6·6	1436	6·8	1146	8·9	—	—	740	12·4	20 2	12·2	655	6·6	1857	7·1	1 7	3·1	1320	3·5	3 8	5·1	1519	5·2	1159	3·9	—	—
4	Th	246	6·8	1510	6·9	0 3	9·0	1217	9·0	812	12·6	2032	12·3	724	6·9	1926	7·3	144	3·1	1351	3·5	336	5·1	1547	5·3	018	3·6	1230	4·0
5	F	318	6·9	1541	6·9	034	8·8	1248	9·0	840	12·7	2128	12·4	752	7·0	1954	7·4	217	3·0	1422	3·5	4 4	5·2	1615	5·3	046	3·6	1332	4·0
6	Sa	349	6·9	1612	6·9	1 3	8·7	1316	9·0	910	12·6	2156	12·4	820	7·0	2026	7·4	244	3·0	1452	3·5	433	5·1	1645	5·2	115	3·6	1414	3·9
7	Su	419	6·8	1642	6·8	133	8·5	1345	8·9	938	12·3	2223	12·2	853	6·8	2058	7·3	310	3·0	1526	3·5	5 4	5·0	1719	5·1	149	3·6	1440	3·8
8	M	448	6·6	1713	6·7	2 2	8·3	1415	8·7	10 7	11·8	2249	11·7	925	6·6	2132	7·0	335	3·1	1604	3·5	538	4·9	1754	5·0	222	3·5	1521	3·7
9	Tu	516	6·5	1746	6·5	234	8·0	1447	8·4	1037	11·2	2322	11·2	10 0	6·3	2249	6·7	4 3	3·1	1648	3·4	616	4·8	1832	4·9	3 3	3·5	1611	3·5
10	W	549	6·3	1822	6·3	311	7·7	1527	8·1	11 8	10·6	—	—	1037	6·0	2346	6·4	436	3·2	1741	3·3	656	4·6	1914	4·7	350	3·3	1717	3·4
11	Th	627	6·0	19 7	6·2	359	7·4	1620	7·7	1149	9·6	1253	10·0	1123	5·9	—	—	516	3·1	1842	3·2	746	4·5	2012	4·5	449	3·3	1841	3·3
12	F	720	5·7	2011	5·9	5 4	7·2	1739	7·3	0 8	9·7	1440	9·9	1 7	5·9	1228	6·0	607	3·0	2132	3·1	850	4·3	2129	4·4	602	3·2	20 2	3·5
13	Sa	844	5·6	2136	5·7	634	7·6	1916	7·3	149	11·1	1729	10·5	250	6·2	14 2	6·4	718	3·0	2247	3·1	1012	4·5	23 1	4·4	718	3·5	21 9	3·7
14	Su	1017	5·7	23 1	5·9	759	8·3	2037	7·8	332	12·1	1923	11·5	413	6·8	1528	7·0	9 1	3·2	12 5	3·2	1134	4·5	1243	4·8	825	3·5	22 5	3·9
15	M	1143	6·2	—	—	10 4	9·0	2142	8·5	452	13·1	20 8	12·5	515	7·2	1634	7·5	1017	3·4	1255	3·8	120	5·1	1337	5·2	924	4·0	2252	4·0
16	Tu	015	6·3	1250	6·5	1142	9·6	2235	9·1	6 1	13·4	2049	13·3	604	7·6	1725	8·0	1114	3·6	1343	3·9	211	5·1	1423	5·6	1012	4·2	2336	—
17	W	114	6·7	1345	7·2	0 32	10·0	2323	9·5	656	13·8	2128	13·8	648	7·8	18 8	8·3	041	3·3	1427	3·9	255	5·7	15 6	6·0	1058	4·4	—	—
18	Th	2 4	7·1	1433	7·5	050	9·8	1225	10·2	742	14·4	2242	14·1	728	7·8	1849	8·4	131	3·4	1547	4·0	336	5·8	1547	6·0	1143	4·1	1228	4·5
19	F	247	7·4	1517	7·7	130	9·8	1348	10·2	826	14·4	2316	14·0	8 8	7·6	1928	8·2	216	3·4	1628	4·0	418	5·8	1718	5·8	019	4·1	1314	4·4
20	Sa	329	7·5	16 0	7·7	249	9·6	1429	9·9	946	13·5	2353	13·6	847	7·6	20 9	7·8	256	3·5	1713	3·6	5 1	5·6	18 6	5·5	1 1	4·0	1452	4·2
21	Su	410	7·5	1642	7·4	331	8·7	1510	9·5	1026	12·6	1225	12·8	927	6·8	2051	6·9	332	3·5	18 8	3·5	548	5·5	1855	5·2	146	3·9	1546	3·9
22	M	449	7·1	1723	7·1	424	8·1	1557	8·8	11 2	11·4	1334	10·8	10 9	5·9	2135	6·5	4 6	3·5	1926	3·6	636	5·2	1948	4·8	233	3·7	1649	3·7
23	Tu	529	6·7	18 3	6·7	540	7·5	1834	8·1	1140	10·0	1518	10·4	1054	5·9	2221	6·3	441	3·3	1926	3·0	727	4·7	2053	4·5	324	3·5	18 9	3·6
24	W	611	6·7	1846	6·3	721	7·0	20 9	7·3	042	9·4	1645	9·5	1149	5·5	2315	5·6	521	3·3	2123	3·0	824	4·5	2219	4·4	533	3·3	1937	3·3
25	Th	7 0	6·3	1935	6·0	842	7·4	2114	6·9	211	9·7	1742	9·4	024	5·8	13 2	5·6	612	3·0	2241	2·7	936	4·3	2346	4·5	652	3·3	2051	3·4
26	F	8 2	5·9	2039	5·7	935	7·9	22 0	7·5	4 2	10·6	1742	10·1	152	5·5	1434	5·9	724	2·8	2333	3·0	1106	4·3	1218	4·7	8 7	3·3	2146	3·4
27	Sa	924	5·6	22 6	5·6	935	7·9	22 0	8·0	512	10·6	1742	10·9	332	5·8	1557	6·3	917	2·9	—	—	048	4·6	1311	—	9 9	3·4	2226	3·5
28	Su	11 6	5·8	2336	6·1	—	—	—	—	—	—	—	—	437	6·3	1651	—	1028	3·0	2333	—	—	—	—	—	956	3·6	—	—
29	M	—	—	1212	—	—	—	—	—	—	—	—	—	—	—	—	—	—	—	—	—	—	—	—	—	—	—	—	—

*All times shown are Greenwich Mean Time.   †Difference of height in metres from Ordnance Datum (Newlyn).
‡Difference of height in metres from Ordnance Datum (Dublin).

MARCH, 1988

High Water at the undermentioned Places (G.M.T.*)—

Day of Month	Day of Week	London Bridge Mn.	Ht.	Aft.	Ht.	Liverpool Mn.	Ht.	Aft.	Ht.	Avonmouth Mn.	Ht.	Aft.	Ht.	Hull (Albert Dock) Mn.	Ht.	Aft.	Ht.	Greenock Mn.	Ht.	Aft.	Ht.	Leith Mn.	Ht.	Aft.	Ht.	Dun Laoghaire Mn.	Ht.	Aft.	Ht.
		*Datum of Predictions 3·20 m. below				†Datum of Predictions 4·93 m. below				†Datum of Predictions 6·50 m. below				†Datum of Predictions 3·90 m. below				†Datum of Predictions 1·62 m. below				†Datum of Predictions 2·90 m. below				‡Datum of Predictions 0·20 m. above			
		h.m.	m.	h.m.	m.	h.m.	m.	h.m.	m.	h.m.	m.	h.m.	m.	h.m.	m.	h.m.	m.	h.m.	m.	h.m.	m.	h.m.	m.	h.m.	m.	h.m.	m.	h.m.	m.
1	Tu	031	6·2	13·0	6·5	1016	8·4	2237	8·4	6 1	11·4	1827	11·6	522	6·2	1730	6·6	1114	3·2	1152	3·3	134	4·8	1353	4·9	1033	3·8	2258	3·6
2	W	114	6·4	1338	6·7	1051	8·7	23 9	8·7	642	12·1	1937	12·3	558	6·5	1832	7·0	013	3·0	1227	3·4	212	4·9	1426	5·1	11 6	3·9	2324	3·6
3	Th	149	6·5	1412	6·7	1122	8·9	2339	8·9	716	12·3	20 5	12·6	629	6·8	19 0	7·3	048	3·1	1258	3·4	243	5·1	1455	5·3	1134	3·9	2350	3·7
4	F	222	6·8	1443	6·9	1153	9·1			747	12·6	2033	12·8	657	7·0	1930	7·5	119	3·0	1329	3·5	311	5·2	1521	5·4	016	3·7	1230	4·0
5	Sa	253	6·9	1512	7·0	0 7	9·0	1221	9·2	815	12·8	21 1	12·8	724	7·2	1958	7·5	148	3·0	1357	3·5	335	5·2	1547	5·4	044	3·7	13 0	4·0
6	Su	321	7·0	1542	7·0	035	9·0	1249	9·2	843	13·0	2111	12·8	752	7·3	2001	7·5	212	3·1	1427	3·5	4 2	5·2	1616	5·4	114	3·7	1333	3·9
7	M	350	6·9	1612	7·0	1 3	9·0	1316	9·0	912	12·9	2129	12·5	823	7·3	2032	7·3	235	3·1	1459	3·5	432	5·1	1648	5·3	149	3·7	1408	3·8
8	Tu	419	6·8	1642	6·9	133	8·9	1345	9·0	941	12·6	2155	12·0	853	7·0	21 4	7·1	3 0	3·3	1538	3·5	5 5	5·0	1722	5·3	227	3·6	1452	3·7
9	W	449	6·7	1713	6·8	2 4	8·6	1418	8·6	1009	12·2	2220	11·3	925	6·7	2138	6·8	328	3·3	1623	3·3	540	4·9	18 0	5·0	314	3·5	1543	3·5
10	Th	523	6·5	1750	6·5	239	8·3	1457	8·3	1040	11·3	2251	10·7	959	6·4	2221	6·4	4 2	3·3	1715	3·1	619	4·7	1846	4·7	411	3·2	1652	3·3
11	F	6 3	6·2	1832	6·0	325	7·9	1552	7·6	1119	10·5	2336	9·8	1044	6·1	2319	6·0	443	3·1	1816	3·1	7 9	4·5	1949	4·5	525	3·2	1823	3·2
12	Sa	659	5·8	1934	5·6	433	7·4	1716	7·2	120	9·4	1415	9·6	1150	5·7			532	3·1	1939	2·9	817	4·3	2117	4·4	649	3·3	1953	3·3
13	Su	825	5·6	21 5	5·5	6 8	7·2	19 3	7·8	3 8	9·9	1553	10·3	048	5·7	1333	5·6	639	3·0	2136	2·9	949	4·2	2252	4·4	8 6	3·5	2153	3·7
14	M	10 2	5·6	2240	5·6	742	7·6	2029	8·5	437	11·0	1716	11·5	246	5·9	15 8	5·8	841	2·9	2244	3·1	1119	4·3			9 7	3·7	2237	3·9
15	Tu	1130	6·3	2358	6·4	853	8·3	2131	9·1	544	12·3	1810	12·7	4 6	6·4	1613	6·5	10 7	3·4	2335	3·1	0 8	4·7	1226	4·9	1043	4·0	2317	4·0
16	W	056	6·9	1328	7·2	949	9·1	2220	9·6	636	13·3	18 5	13·5	547	6·9	17 2	7·2	1151	3·4			1 4	5·1	1319	5·1	1126	4·2	2357	4·1
17	Th	144	7·2	1413	7·4	1037	9·7	2304	9·8	721	14·0	1945	14·0	627	7·3	1744	7·7	022	3·3	1238	3·7	151	5·4	1343	5·4			1251	4·3
18	F	226	7·4	1456	7·6	1120	10·1	2346	10·2	2 3	14·3	2025	14·2	740	7·6	1824	8·1	1 7	3·4	1324	3·8	233	5·7	14 3	5·7	036	4·1	1337	4·3
19	Sa	3 5	7·5	1536	7·6	025	9·8	1242	10·1	843	14·4	2101	14·1	819	7·8	19 4	8·1	148	3·5	14 7	3·9	311	5·8	1443	5·9	117	4·1	1425	4·1
20	Su	345	7·5	1614	7·5	1 3	9·6	1321	9·8	921	14·0	2138	13·6	857	7·6	1945	8·1	224	3·5	1446	3·8	351	5·8	1523	6·0	2 1	3·9	1618	3·9
21	M	424	7·4	1652	7·2	140	9·2	1359	9·3	957	13·5	2212	12·6	936	7·3	2029	7·8	257	3·6	16 1	3·7	434	5·8	16 5	6·0	250	3·7	1739	3·7
22	Tu	5 2	7·1	1729	6·9	216	8·9	1440	8·6	1031	12·7	2242	11·6	1017	6·8	2112	7·6	329	3·5	1645	3·6	518	5·7	1651	5·8	345	3·5	18 6	3·4
23	W	543	6·8	18 5	6·3	256	8·1	1525	7·8	11 5	11·6	2313	10·6	936	6·3	2159	6·8	4 4	3·5	1737	3·4	6 4	5·6	1738	5·4	452	3·3	2023	3·2
24	Th	629	6·3	1850	5·8	345	7·5	1627	7·1	1144	10·9	2357	9·6	1017	6·1	2251	6·5	444	3·3	1849	3·3	652	5·3	1826	4·7	345	3·3	1618	3·4
25	F	730	5·8	1952	5·5	458	6·9	18 1	7·0	1250	9·0			124	5·9	2357	5·9	532	3·1	2112	3·0	746	4·9	1919	4·5	452	3·3	1739	3·2
26	Sa	847	5·8	2114	5·5	645	6·9	1942	7·4	127	8·9	1442	9·6	310	5·2	1215	5·5	636	3·0	2226	2·7	857	4·6	2023	4·2	614	3·4	1913	3·1
27	Su	1031	5·6	2259	5·6	8 9	7·2	2046	7·9	325	9·2	1613	9·5	412	5·3	1342	5·5	830	2·8	23 9	2·9	1029	4·1	2151	4·3	736	3·4	2028	3·2
28	M	1142	6·1			9 3	7·8	2129	8·4	440	10·1	17 9	10·5	412	5·7	1522	5·6	959	2·7	2226	2·6	1146	4·3	2317	4·3	838	3·4	2119	3·3
29	Tu	0 0	6·0	1229	6·5	943	8·3	22 6	8·4	529	11·1	1751	11·3	454	6·1	1619	6·6	1044	2·9	2343	2·9	016	4·5	1240	4·5	925	3·5	2156	3·4
30	W	043	6·4	13 9	6·7	1019	8·6	2237	8·7	6 8	11·7	1831	11·9	529	6·5	1658	7·0	1122	3·2	2343	3·0	1 1	4·7	1320	4·7	10 2	3·7	2250	3·7
31	Th	137	6·4	1329	6·7	1019	8·6	2237	8·7	529	11·7	1831	11·9	529	6·5	1732	7·0	1122	3·2	2343	3·0	137	4·9	1353	4·9	1033	3·8	2250	3·7

*All times shown are Greenwich Mean Time.   †Difference of height in metres from Ordnance Datum (Newlyn).   ‡Difference of height in metres from Ordnance Datum (Dublin).

APRIL, 1988

High Water at the undermentioned Places (G.M.T.*)—

Day of Month	Day of Week	LONDON BRIDGE †Datum of Predictions 3·20 m. below				LIVERPOOL †Datum of Predictions 4·93 m. below				AVONMOUTH †Datum of Predictions 6·50 m. below				HULL (Albert Dock) †Datum of Predictions 3·90 m. below				GREENOCK †Datum of Predictions 1·62 m. below				LEITH †Datum of Predictions 2·90 m. below				DUN LAOGHAIRE ‡Datum of Predictions 0·20 m. above			
		Mn. h.m.	Ht. m.	Aft. h.m.	Ht. m.	Mn. h.m.	Ht. m.	Aft. h.m.	Ht. m.	Mn. h.m.	Ht. m.	Aft. h.m.	Ht. m.	Mn. h.m.	Ht. m.	Aft. h.m.	Ht. m.	Mn. h.m.	Ht. m.	Aft. h.m.	Ht. m.	Mn. h.m.	Ht. m.	Aft. h.m.	Ht. m.	Mn. h.m.	Ht. m.	Aft. h.m.	Ht. m.
1	F	120	6·6	1341	6·8	1051	8·9	2306	8·9	642	12·2	1903	12·3	558	6·9	18 3	7·3	014	3·0	1155	3·3	2 8	5·1	1420	5·2	11 2	3·9	2316	3·8
2	Sa	151	6·8	1412	6·9	1120	9·1	2336	9·1	714	12·6	1934	12·6	625	7·1	1832	7·4	043	3·0	1227	3·3	236	5·2	1447	5·3	1130	3·9	2343	3·8
3	Su	220	6·9	1440	7·0	1150	9·2	—	—	745	12·8	20 4	12·8	653	7·3	19 3	7·4	110	3·0	1259	3·3	3 2	5·3	1516	5·4	1159	4·0	—	—
4	M	250	7·0	1511	7·1	0 5	9·2	1219	9·2	816	12·9	2034	12·8	723	7·3	1935	7·2	135	3·1	1329	3·4	330	5·3	1548	5·4	012	3·9	1232	3·9
5	Tu	321	7·0	1542	7·1	035	9·1	1250	9·2	847	12·9	21 4	12·6	754	7·2	20 8	6·9	159	3·1	14 0	3·4	4 3	5·1	1621	5·4	044	3·9	13 7	3·9
6	W	353	7·0	1614	6·9	106	9·0	1323	8·9	918	12·5	2134	12·0	825	7·0	2042	6·7	227	3·3	1437	3·4	436	4·9	1659	5·1	122	3·8	1347	3·8
7	Th	428	6·8	1648	6·7	141	8·8	1359	8·6	950	11·8	2204	11·4	857	6·7	2121	6·4	259	3·3	1518	3·4	514	4·5	1743	5·0	2 3	3·7	1435	3·8
8	F	5 8	6·6	1727	6·4	220	8·4	1444	8·1	1027	11·1	2242	10·6	935	6·4	22 9	6·3	336	3·4	16 7	3·3	557	4·4	1837	4·7	252	3·6	1532	3·6
9	Sa	556	6·2	1814	6·0	311	7·8	1545	7·6	1116	10·3	2344	9·9	1026	5·8	2313	6·0	421	3·3	17 0	3·2	653	4·4	1947	4·5	350	3·4	1643	3·4
10	Su	657	5·9	1920	5·7	424	7·5	1715	7·2	120	9·7	1234	9·7	1134	5·8	—	—	512	3·2	18 2	3·0	8 6	4·4	2111	4·5	5 4	3·3	1813	3·3
11	M	820	5·8	2049	5·6	557	7·2	1853	7·4	251	10·2	1535	10·2	048	5·8	1312	5·7	618	3·0	1936	2·8	933	4·6	2236	4·4	628	3·4	1939	3·2
12	Tu	950	6·0	2219	6·5	723	7·5	2011	8·0	416	12·4	1654	12·7	234	6·1	1442	6·1	826	2·9	2131	2·9	1066	4·6	12 1	5·6	746	3·5	2132	3·3
13	W	1112	6·6	2334	7·1	830	7·8	2156	8·0	520	13·7	1750	13·7	346	6·5	1546	6·5	948	3·1	2228	3·1	039	5·4	1252	5·4	848	4·0	2215	3·5
14	Th	1221	6·9	—	—	924	9·1	2240	9·4	612	13·9	1838	13·8	440	7·0	1635	7·0	1040	3·3	2311	3·4	125	5·6	1337	5·6	937	4·2	2253	3·7
15	F	032	6·9	1307	7·4	1012	9·6	2319	9·6	657	13·8	1958	13·7	523	7·5	1719	7·6	1127	3·5	2353	3·6	2 5	5·7	1418	5·8	1022	4·3	2331	4·1
16	Sa	120	7·1	1351	7·4	1137	9·9	—	—	738	13·4	2034	13·4	6 1	7·9	18 0	7·9	035	3·5	1214	3·6	245	5·6	1458	5·8	1105	4·3	—	—
17	Su	2 2	7·3	1432	7·4	035	9·7	1217	9·4	818	13·2	2111	13·2	638	8·1	1842	8·1	114	3·5	1259	3·6	4 7	5·6	1528	5·8	1147	4·3	1230	4·2
18	M	242	7·4	1511	7·3	114	9·4	1256	8·9	856	13·4	2145	13·3	714	7·6	1926	7·6	149	3·6	1341	3·5	450	5·2	1626	5·3	0 9	4·1	1315	4·1
19	Tu	321	7·4	1548	7·1	149	8·8	1335	8·6	932	13·3	2216	11·3	752	7·4	2011	7·5	223	3·6	1420	3·5	535	4·6	1714	4·9	050	3·9	14 3	3·8
20	W	4 0	7·2	1623	6·9	229	8·1	1415	8·3	10 7	10·6	2247	10·7	832	7·1	2056	7·0	256	3·5	1457	3·4	621	4·6	18 2	4·6	135	3·8	1454	3·6
21	Th	440	6·9	1658	6·5	318	7·6	1501	7·6	1041	9·6	2329	9·6	910	6·7	2142	6·4	332	3·4	1537	3·3	712	4·2	1854	4·3	221	3·6	1553	3·1
22	F	520	6·6	1733	6·2	424	7·1	16 0	6·7	1119	9·0	—	—	949	6·3	2233	6·2	413	3·3	1621	3·1	816	4·2	1955	4·2	314	3·4	1643	3·0
23	Sa	6 7	6·2	1815	5·9	550	6·8	1719	6·7	046	9·0	1218	9·0	1033	5·9	2330	5·9	501	3·1	1712	3·0	932	4·3	21 7	4·4	414	3·3	1831	3·1
24	Su	703	5·9	1912	5·6	711	6·9	1849	6·8	229	10·7	1352	10·7	043	5·7	1250	5·4	601	3·0	1820	2·8	1048	4·3	2222	4·4	527	3·3	1944	3·2
25	M	812	5·6	2029	5·4	813	7·4	1957	7·2	342	11·4	1515	11·4	215	5·5	1415	5·5	725	2·8	2029	2·9	1145	4·5	2324	4·4	647	3·3	2034	3·4
26	Tu	932	5·6	2159	5·5	858	7·6	2044	7·6	437	12·0	1617	12·0	328	5·5	1528	6·0	904	2·9	2144	3·0	1145	4·5	—	—	750	3·4	2111	3·4
27	W	1052	5·9	2312	5·8	936	8·4	2124	8·2	522	12·5	17 5	12·5	413	5·7	1614	6·4	957	3·0	2227	2·9	011	4·6	1229	4·7	840	3·6	2142	3·6
28	Th	1147	6·2	—	—	1012	8·7	2157	8·5	6 1	12·0	1747	12·0	448	6·4	1652	6·8	1037	3·1	23 0	3·0	050	4·8	13 7	4·9	918	3·7	2211	3·7
29	F	0 1	6·2	1228	6·5	—	—	—	—	—	—	1824	12·1	519	6·8	1727	7·1	1114	3·2	2330	3·0	125	5·0	1340	5·1	952	3·7	2240	3·8
30	Sa	041	6·4	13 3	6·7	—	8·8	2230	8·8	—	—	—	—	—	—	—	—	—	—	2359	—	—	—	—	—	1025	3·8	—	—

*All times shown are Greenwich Mean Time.   †Difference of height in metres from Ordnance Datum (Newlyn).   ‡Difference of height in metres from Ordnance Datum (Dublin).

MAY, 1988

High Water at the undermentioned Places (G.M.T.*)—

Day of Month	Day of Week	London Bridge (†Datum 3·20 m. below) Mn.	Ht.	Aft.	Ht.	Liverpool (†Datum 4·93 m. below) Mn.	Ht.	Aft.	Ht.	Avonmouth (†Datum 6·50 m. below) Mn.	Ht.	Aft.	Ht.	Hull (Albert Dock) (†Datum 3·90 m. below) Mn.	Ht.	Aft.	Ht.	Greenock (†Datum 1·62 m. below) Mn.	Ht.	Aft.	Ht.	Leith (†Datum 2·90 m. below) Mn.	Ht.	Aft.	Ht.	Dun Laoghaire (‡Datum 0·20 m. above) Mn.	Ht.	Aft.	Ht.
1	Su	114	6·4	1335	6·8	1045	8·9	23 2	9·0	638	12·4	1900	12·4	550	7·0	1801	7·2	1149	3·2	—	—	157	5·2	1412	5·3	1056	3·9	2310	3·9
2	M	147	6·7	14 8	6·9	1119	9·0	2336	9·1	714	12·6	1935	12·6	622	7·1	1838	7·2	028	3·0	1225	3·3	228	5·3	1447	5·4	1131	3·9	2344	3·9
3	Tu	220	6·8	1442	7·0	1153	9·1	—	—	751	12·6	2011	12·6	656	7·1	1913	7·1	057	3·1	1301	3·3	3 1	5·3	1523	5·4	—	—	1208	3·9
4	W	256	6·9	1517	7·0	011	9·2	1229	9·0	827	12·6	2046	12·4	730	7·1	1951	7·0	127	3·1	1338	3·3	338	5·3	16 3	5·4	019	3·9	1249	3·8
5	Th	335	7·0	1555	7·0	049	9·1	13 9	8·8	9 5	12·7	2124	11·7	8 5	6·9	2032	6·8	2 0	3·3	1421	3·3	416	5·3	1650	5·2	1 0	3·9	1335	3·7
6	F	416	6·9	1634	6·7	128	9·0	1354	8·5	946	11·7	2206	11·4	843	6·7	2117	6·4	238	3·4	1508	3·3	511	5·0	1739	5·0	147	3·8	1427	3·6
7	Sa	5 4	6·7	1719	6·4	215	8·5	1446	8·1	1033	11·1	2258	10·8	927	6·5	2210	6·3	320	3·4	1559	3·2	551	4·8	1839	4·8	239	3·7	1525	3·4
8	Su	557	6·4	1811	6·1	312	8·2	1550	7·7	1130	10·6	—	—	1020	6·3	2313	6·1	4 8	3·4	1654	3·1	650	4·7	1943	4·6	339	3·6	1638	3·3
9	M	700	6·2	1917	5·9	423	8·0	1711	7·5	0 1	10·5	1236	10·3	1126	6·0	—	—	5 2	3·2	1756	2·9	758	4·6	2056	4·6	449	3·5	1759	3·3
10	Tu	815	6·1	2033	5·9	540	7·9	1831	7·5	114	10·5	1351	10·5	043	6·0	1248	6·1	610	3·0	1928	2·8	913	4·6	2209	4·7	6 6	3·5	1916	3·4
11	W	932	6·3	2152	6·2	655	8·0	1941	8·1	232	10·8	1510	11·0	211	6·5	14 9	6·4	758	3·0	2103	2·8	1024	4·8	2312	4·7	720	3·7	2017	3·6
12	Th	1047	7·0	2305	6·5	759	8·6	2039	8·8	348	11·6	1623	11·7	317	6·9	1512	6·8	917	3·1	2156	2·9	0 7	5·1	1221	5·3	823	3·9	21 8	3·7
13	F	1150	7·0	—	—	856	8·9	2128	8·8	451	12·3	1720	12·4	410	7·1	16 6	7·1	1010	3·2	2238	3·1	055	5·3	1310	5·5	915	3·9	2152	3·9
14	Sa	0 5	6·8	1242	6·8	945	9·1	2213	9·1	546	13·0	1810	13·0	457	7·2	1655	7·4	1059	3·3	2320	3·2	139	5·4	1355	5·6	10 3	4·1	2232	4·0
15	Su	055	6·9	1328	7·0	1031	9·3	2255	9·2	632	13·0	1853	13·0	536	7·2	1742	7·5	1146	3·4	—	—	221	5·5	1439	5·6	1046	4·1	23 9	4·0
16	M	140	6·9	14 9	7·1	1115	9·3	2334	9·2	714	13·0	1933	13·1	615	7·2	1827	7·3	0 1	3·3	1232	3·4	3 2	5·5	1525	5·5	1128	4·0	2348	3·9
17	Tu	220	7·0	1447	7·0	1156	9·2	—	—	755	12·9	2012	13·0	653	7·1	1913	7·3	041	3·4	1317	3·3	345	5·4	1610	5·4	—	—	1257	3·9
18	W	3 1	7·0	1524	6·9	014	9·1	1236	8·9	834	12·6	2049	12·6	733	6·9	1959	6·9	117	3·5	1357	3·3	426	5·1	1656	5·1	029	4·0	1344	3·8
19	Th	342	6·8	1600	6·5	052	8·9	1317	8·6	914	12·0	2125	11·9	812	6·6	2044	6·6	154	3·6	1438	3·2	510	4·9	1742	4·8	113	3·8	1433	3·6
20	F	423	6·8	1635	6·5	130	8·6	1357	8·2	949	11·5	2157	11·2	849	6·4	2127	6·2	228	3·5	1520	3·1	555	4·7	1830	4·6	2 0	3·6	1525	3·5
21	Sa	5 5	6·5	1711	6·0	213	8·2	1442	7·8	1024	10·9	2231	10·5	927	6·2	2212	5·9	3 7	3·5	16 4	2·9	643	4·5	1920	4·4	249	3·5	1624	3·4
22	Su	547	6·3	1750	5·7	256	7·8	1532	7·4	11 2	9·9	2312	10·0	10 7	5·9	2258	5·7	348	3·4	1652	2·7	735	4·3	2015	4·3	340	3·5	1728	3·3
23	M	636	6·0	1839	5·7	350	7·5	1633	7·1	1149	9·4	—	—	1058	5·7	2354	5·7	435	3·2	1749	2·6	833	4·3	2115	4·3	438	3·3	1837	3·3
24	Tu	733	5·8	1942	5·8	454	7·3	1740	7·0	0 7	9·6	1255	9·2	—	—	1201	5·4	528	3·0	1906	2·5	935	4·3	2214	4·4	542	3·3	1933	3·4
25	W	836	5·7	2056	5·9	6 3	7·2	1848	7·2	123	9·5	14 9	9·4	059	5·4	1312	5·5	631	2·8	2033	2·6	1034	4·5	23 9	4·5	645	3·4	2017	3·5
26	Th	942	5·8	22 3	6·1	8 2	7·4	1945	7·5	236	9·9	1514	9·9	3 8	5·9	1419	5·9	748	2·8	2127	2·7	1127	4·8	2356	4·6	740	3·5	2055	3·6
27	F	1042	6·0	23 1	6·4	849	8·1	2032	7·9	336	10·4	16 9	10·5	355	6·2	1518	6·2	854	2·9	2207	2·8	—	—	1215	4·8	827	3·6	2132	3·7
28	Sa	1133	6·2	—	—	931	8·4	2114	8·3	428	11·1	1658	11·2	437	6·5	1651	6·5	944	3·0	2240	2·9	039	4·9	1259	5·0	949	3·7	2207	3·8
29	Su	034	6·2	1217	6·4	1012	8·6	2153	8·6	516	11·6	1744	11·6	516	6·6	1734	6·7	1028	3·1	2313	3·0	120	5·1	1342	5·2	1028	3·8	2243	3·9
30	M	116	6·5	1259	6·6	1052	8·8	2233	8·6	6 3	12·0	1828	12·2	556	6·8	1817	6·9	1110	3·2	2348	3·1	158	5·2	1425	5·3	11 7	3·9	2320	3·9
31	Tu	—	—	1340	6·7	—	—	2313	9·1	648	12·3	1912	12·4					1153	3·2	—	—								

* All times shown are Greenwich Mean Time. † Difference of height in metres from Ordnance Datum (Newlyn).
‡ Difference of height in metres from Ordnance Datum (Dublin).

JUNE, 1988

High Water at the undermentioned Places (G.M.T.*)—

Day of Month	Day of Week	London Bridge †Datum 3·20 m. below — Mn. h.m.	Ht. m.	Aft. h.m.	Ht. m.	Liverpool †Datum 4·93 m. below — Mn. h.m.	Ht. m.	Aft. h.m.	Ht. m.	Avonmouth †Datum 6·50 m. below — Mn. h.m.	Ht. m.	Aft. h.m.	Ht. m.	Hull (Albert Dock) †Datum 3·90 m. below — Mn. h.m.	Ht. m.	Aft. h.m.	Ht. m.	Greenock †Datum 1·62 m. below — Mn. h.m.	Ht. m.	Aft. h.m.	Ht. m.	Leith †Datum 2·90 m. below — Mn. h.m.	Ht. m.	Aft. h.m.	Ht. m.	Dun Laoghaire ‡Datum 0·20 m. above — Mn. h.m.	Ht. m.	Aft. h.m.	Ht. m.
1	W	158	6·7	1420	6·8	1134	9·0	2354	9·2	733	12·4	1955	12·5	635	7·0	19 0	7·0	024	3·2	1238	3·2	239	5·3	15 9	5·4	1151	3·8	1237	3·8
2	Th	242	6·9	15 3	6·9	—	—	1218	9·0	816	12·4	2039	12·5	716	7·0	1944	7·0	1 2	3·3	1324	3·2	321	5·3	1556	5·4	0 2	4·0	1328	3·6
3	F	327	7·0	1545	6·8	038	9·2	13 4	8·9	9 3	12·3	2124	12·3	755	6·9	2030	7·0	142	3·3	1414	3·2	4 5	5·3	1644	5·3	047	4·0	1421	3·6
4	Sa	413	7·0	1630	6·8	124	9·1	1354	8·7	949	12·1	2212	11·8	839	6·9	2118	6·9	226	3·5	15 4	3·4	454	5·1	1736	5·2	137	3·9	1518	3·5
5	Su	5 4	7·0	1718	6·4	215	8·9	1447	8·4	1038	11·8	23 2	11·2	924	6·7	22 9	6·8	313	3·5	1650	3·5	546	5·1	1831	5·0	229	3·9	1624	3·5
6	M	557	6·8	18 8	6·4	310	8·7	1546	8·1	1130	11·5	—	—	1014	6·7	23 8	6·4	4 2	3·5	1747	3·3	643	5·0	1929	4·9	328	3·9	1733	3·4
7	Tu	655	6·6	19 6	6·3	410	8·5	1651	8·0	057	11·4	1218	11·4	1111	6·5	—	—	454	3·4	1855	3·1	743	4·9	2031	4·8	431	3·8	1844	3·5
8	W	758	6·4	20 9	6·3	515	8·3	1758	7·9	2 5	11·5	1328	11·5	021	6·3	1219	6·5	557	3·2	—	—	846	4·9	2136	4·9	541	3·7	1948	3·5
9	Th	9 7	6·5	2121	6·3	621	8·3	19 6	8·0	314	11·5	1439	11·8	135	6·3	1333	6·6	719	3·0	2014	2·9	951	4·9	2239	4·9	652	3·8	2042	3·7
10	F	1016	6·6	2233	6·5	727	8·4	20 8	8·2	420	12·0	1548	12·0	242	6·4	1440	6·6	838	3·0	2116	2·8	1055	5·1	2337	5·0	758	3·8	2130	3·5
11	Sa	1120	6·7	2337	6·7	827	8·5	21 1	8·4	518	12·0	1649	12·3	338	6·6	1541	6·7	938	3·1	2250	3·0	1155	5·2	1250	5·3	946	3·8	2212	3·8
12	Su	—	—	1217	6·7	922	8·6	2152	8·6	610	12·1	1743	12·3	430	6·8	1638	6·8	1033	3·1	2333	3·1	029	5·1	1341	5·3	1033	3·8	2253	3·9
13	M	034	6·5	13 6	6·6	1013	8·7	2237	8·8	656	12·1	1831	12·3	516	6·8	1732	6·9	1124	3·2	13 0	3·1	117	5·1	1430	5·3	1119	3·8	2333	3·9
14	Tu	123	6·5	1349	6·6	1059	8·8	2319	8·9	740	12·2	1914	12·3	6 0	6·9	1822	6·9	015	3·3	1345	3·1	2 3	5·2	1516	5·3	015	3·9	12 2	3·7
15	W	2 8	6·6	1429	6·6	1143	8·7	—	—	822	12·0	1955	12·3	641	6·9	19 9	6·9	054	3·5	1429	3·3	248	5·2	16 1	5·2	056	3·9	1244	3·5
16	Th	250	6·7	15 7	6·6	0 0	8·9	1224	8·6	9 0	11·7	2034	11·9	720	6·8	1951	6·8	133	3·5	15 9	3·5	329	5·2	1641	5·1	139	3·8	1328	3·4
17	F	331	6·7	1543	6·6	038	8·8	1340	8·5	935	11·3	2111	11·4	757	6·8	2030	6·8	210	3·6	1550	3·4	410	5·0	1721	5·0	222	3·7	1410	3·3
18	Sa	410	6·8	1619	6·5	116	8·6	1419	8·5	10 9	11·0	2143	11·1	830	6·6	21 7	6·7	247	3·6	1630	3·4	450	4·8	1843	4·7	3 4	3·6	1453	3·3
19	Su	448	6·8	1654	6·4	154	8·5	15 0	8·4	1041	10·6	2216	10·6	9 4	6·6	2143	6·6	327	3·5	1711	3·2	530	4·7	1926	4·6	350	3·5	1538	3·2
20	M	526	6·4	1730	6·2	233	8·2	1545	8·0	1118	10·3	2251	10·0	942	6·6	2223	6·2	4 8	3·4	1756	2·8	611	4·5	2014	4·5	438	3·4	1626	3·1
21	Tu	6 7	6·4	1810	6·0	315	8·0	1635	7·7	021	10·3	2332	10·0	1024	6·5	23 6	6·1	453	3·3	1848	2·8	654	4·5	21 7	4·4	533	3·4	1720	3·2
22	W	650	6·0	1853	5·8	4 2	7·7	1734	7·5	123	10·1	12 0	9·8	1115	6·1	2358	5·9	543	3·3	1953	2·8	741	4·5	22 4	4·4	634	3·4	1820	3·3
23	Th	740	5·9	1948	5·7	455	7·5	1836	7·3	233	10·2	1255	9·1	059	5·7	1214	5·7	640	3·3	2056	2·9	831	4·5	2311	4·5	734	3·6	1918	3·4
24	F	837	5·8	2053	5·6	554	7·4	1937	7·5	336	10·6	14 5	10·1	2 2	5·8	1320	5·8	744	3·2	2148	3·0	925	4·5	2357	4·7	828	3·6	20 9	3·6
25	Sa	936	5·8	2157	5·7	657	7·5	2033	7·7	435	10·6	1512	10·7	3 1	6·0	1425	6·0	847	3·1	2233	3·0	1025	4·5	1226	5·0	919	3·7	2055	3·7
26	Su	1035	6·0	2257	5·8	759	7·7	2122	8·0	533	11·3	1612	11·3	357	6·3	1525	6·3	944	3·0	2317	3·1	1127	4·6	1322	5·0	10 5	3·7	2138	3·9
27	M	1132	6·2	2356	6·1	854	8·0	2210	8·4	628	11·6	17 9	11·9	4 4	6·5	1621	6·5	1038	3·1	—	—	—	—	1414	5·3	1053	3·8	2221	4·1
28	Tu	—	—	1227	6·2	946	8·4	2257	8·7	721	12·0	18 4	11·9	536	6·7	1715	6·7	1131	3·0	1224	3·1	049	4·9	15 2	5·3	1138	3·8	23 3	3·9
29	W	052	6·4	1320	6·6	1034	8·7	2344	8·9	8 9	12·3	1856	12·6	621	6·9	18 5	6·6	0 2	3·2	1320	3·1	137	4·9	1414	5·3	1223	3·8	2348	4·1
30	Th	144	6·7	14 8	6·7	1122	8·9	—	—	855	12·3	1945	12·6	—	—	1853	7·0	1 1	3·1	1224	3·1	224	5·3	15 2	5·3	053	3·8	1224	4·1

* All times shown are Greenwich Mean Time. †Difference of height in metres from Ordnance Datum (Newlyn). ‡Difference of height in metres from Ordnance Datum (Dublin).

JULY, 1988

High Water at the undermentioned Places (G.M.T.*)—

Day of Month	Day of Week	LONDON BRIDGE †Datum of Predictions 3·20 m. below				LIVERPOOL †Datum of Predictions 4·93 m. below				AVONMOUTH †Datum of Predictions 6·50 m. below				HULL (Albert Dock) †Datum of Predictions 3·90 m. below				GREENOCK †Datum of Predictions 1·62 m. below				LEITH †Datum of Predictions 2·90 m. below				DUN LAOGHAIRE ‡Datum of Predictions 0·20 m. above			
		Mn. h.m.	Ht. m.	Aft. h.m.	Ht. m.	Mn. h.m.	Ht. m.	Aft. h.m.	Ht. m.	Mn. h.m.	Ht. m.	Aft. h.m.	Ht. m.	Mn. h.m.	Ht. m.	Aft. h.m.	Ht. m.	Mn. h.m.	Ht. m.	Aft. h.m.	Ht. m.	Mn. h.m.	Ht. m.	Aft. h.m.	Ht. m.	Mn. h.m.	Ht. m.	Aft. h.m.	Ht. m.
1	F	233	6·9	1454	6·9			1211	9·1	811	12·6	2033	12·9	7 3	7·1	1938	7·2	047	3·4	1318	3·1	310	5·4	1549	5·5	035	4·1	1228	3·8
2	Sa	321	7·2	1539	7·0	031	9·5	1259	9·2	858	12·8	2118	13·0	747	7·3	2025	7·2	134	3·5	1411	3·1	355	5·5	1635	5·5	125	4·2	1317	3·8
3	Su	4 9	7·3	1624	7·0	119	9·5	1347	9·1	943	12·9	22 4	13·0	829	7·4	2110	7·2	221	3·6	15 2	3·1	443	5·5	1723	5·4	215	4·2	14 7	3·8
4	M	457	7·2	17 8	7·0	2 6	9·4	1436	8·9	1028	12·7	2251	12·8	912	7·4	2157	7·2	3 8	3·6	1551	3·1	534	5·4	1815	5·3	310	4·1	15 1	3·7
5	Tu	544	7·0	1754	6·7	256	9·2	1527	8·6	1115	12·4	2339	12·4	959	7·3	2248	6·7	355	3·6	1637	3·0	626	5·2	19 8	5·1	4 7	4·0	1559	3·6
6	W	635	6·5	1843	6·7	348	8·9	1620	8·3			12 3	11·9	1049	7·0	2347	6·7	444	3·5	1723	2·9	721	5·2	20 3	5·0	511	3·9	17 2	3·6
7	Th	731	6·5	1938	6·4	442	8·6	1720	7·9	031	11·9	1256	11·4	1149	6·9			536	3·3	1814	2·9	817	5·0	21 2	4·9	623	3·8	18 9	3·5
8	F	832	6·4	2043	6·4	544	8·2	1828	7·8	128	11·4	1358	10·9	055	6·5	1257	6·6	641	3·1	1916	2·9	918	4·9	22 6	4·8	734	3·7	1916	3·5
9	Sa	938	6·3	2156	6·2	655	8·0	1938	7·8	237	11·0	15 8	10·8	2 2	6·3	1411	6·5	757	2·9	2029	2·8	1027	4·9	2311	4·8	841	3·7	2017	3·6
10	Su	1048	6·3	2312	6·2	8 5	7·9	2043	8·0	349	10·9	1620	10·9	3 7	6·3	1524	6·5	911	2·9	2134	2·8	1136	4·9			938	3·6	2112	3·6
11	M	1153	6·3			9 8	8·1	2139	8·3	455	11·1	1722	11·3	410	6·4	1633	6·5	1015	2·9	2228	3·0			1240	5·0	1029	3·6	22 0	3·7
12	Tu	018	6·3	1249	6·3	10 4	8·3	2227	8·5	554	11·4	1815	11·6	5 4	6·5	1730	6·6	1113	2·9	2316	3·1	013	5·0	1336	5·1	1113	3·6	2244	3·8
13	W	113	6·3	1335	6·4	1052	8·4	2311	8·7	645	11·6	19 2	12·0	550	6·7	1819	6·7			12 6	2·9	156	5·1	1428	5·1	1154	3·6	2324	3·9
14	Th	158	6·6	1416	6·5	1133	8·6	2349	8·9	728	11·8	1944	12·1	631	6·8	19 2	6·8	0 1	3·3	1255	2·9	241	5·2	1511	5·1				
15	F	239	6·6	1453	6·6			1211	8·6	8 9	11·9	2020	12·1	7 6	6·9	1938	6·9	042	3·4	1341	3·3	320	5·2	1549	5·2	0 2	3·9	1230	3·6
16	Sa	317	6·8	1528	6·7	025	8·9	1245	8·6	844	12·0	2054	12·1	738	7·0	2011	6·9	121	3·4	1420	3·4	355	5·1	1623	5·2	040	3·9	13 4	3·5
17	Su	353	6·8	16 0	6·7	059	8·8	1319	8·5	917	12·1	2124	11·9	8 9	7·0	2042	7·0	157	3·5	1456	3·4	428	5·1	1656	5·1	115	3·9	1340	3·5
18	M	427	6·6	1633	6·6	131	8·6	1351	8·4	946	11·9	2153	11·7	840	7·1	2112	7·1	232	3·4	1529	3·4	5 2	5·1	1730	5·0	152	3·8	1414	3·4
19	Tu	459	6·5	17 5	6·5	2 5	8·4	1425	8·1	1016	11·7	2224	11·4	915	7·0	2148	7·0	3 5	3·3	1559	3·3	538	4·9	18 5	4·9	227	3·7	1452	3·4
20	W	533	6·3	1737	6·3	237	8·1	15 0	8·0	1045	11·5	2257	11·0	952	6·8	2224	6·8	340	3·2	1630	3·2	615	4·8	1843	4·7	3 4	3·6	1532	3·3
21	Th	6 8	6·3	1811	6·1	314	7·8	1541	7·7	1116	10·7	2332	10·5	1033	6·6	23 6	6·3	418	3·1	17 4	3·1	655	4·7	1924	4·6	346	3·5	1618	3·3
22	F	646	6·0	1850	5·9	355	7·7	1628	7·5	1151	10·2			1119	6·1	2356	5·9	5 2	3·0	1742	2·9	738	4·5	2011	4·5	435	3·4	1714	3·3
23	Sa	733	5·8	1942	5·7	447	7·3	1730	7·3	014	10·0	1241	9·8			1217	5·7	551	3·0	1831	2·8	830	4·4	2107	4·4	535	3·3	1820	3·3
24	Su	832	5·7	2056	5·6	557	7·3	1845	7·3	117	10·0	14 6	9·7	1 2	5·7	1334	5·7	649	2·9	1936	2·8	934	4·4	2214	4·4	645	3·4	1926	3·4
25	M	942	5·7	2213	5·9	717	7·7	1958	7·7	244	10·3	1529	10·3	216	6·0	1453	6·1	755	2·9	2056	2·8	1051	4·4	2325	4·5	757	3·5	2024	3·5
26	Tu	1052	5·9	2326	5·9	829	8·2	21 0	8·2	4 0	10·5	1640	10·9	327	6·3	16 4	6·5	9 9	3·0	22 3	3·0			12 6	4·9	858	3·6	2116	3·6
27	W			12 3	6·1	929	8·7	2155	8·7	511	11·1	1746	11·7	427	6·7	17 5	6·7	1018	3·1	2258	3·0	029	4·7	1311	5·2	952	3·6	22 3	4·1
28	Th	035	6·4	13 4	6·5	1024	9·1	2245	9·1	617	11·9	1843	12·5	519	7·1	1756	7·1	1120	3·3	2349	3·0	124	5·0	14 5	5·4	1042	3·8	2249	4·2
29	F	133	6·8	1355	6·8	1113	9·6	2333	9·6	712	12·6	1934	13·1	6 5	7·5	1843	7·5			1218	—	213	5·3	1452	5·5	1127	3·9	2333	4·2
30	Sa	223	7·2	1442	7·1			12 0	9·4	759	13·1	2019	13·6	648	7·8	1927	7·8	039	3·5	1313	3·1	257	5·6	1536	5·5			1213	4·0
31	Su	310	7·4	1525	7·3	018	9·9	1246	9·5	844	13·5	21 4	13·9	728	7·8	20 9	7·6	128	3·6	14 4	3·1	341	5·7	1619	5·7	019	4·3	1258	4·0

* All times shown are Greenwich Mean Time.   †Difference of height in metres from Ordnance Datum (Newlyn).   ‡Difference of height in metres from Ordnance Datum (Dublin).

AUGUST, 1988

High Water at the undermentioned Places (G.M.T.*)—

Heights in metres. †Datum of Predictions: London Bridge 3·20 m. below; Liverpool 4·93 m. below; Avonmouth 6·50 m. below; Hull (Albert Dock) 3·90 m. below; Greenock 1·62 m. below; Leith 2·90 m. below. ‡Dun Laoghaire 0·20 m. above.

Day of Month	Day of Week	London Bridge Mn.	Ht.	Aft.	Ht.	Liverpool Mn.	Ht.	Aft.	Ht.	Avonmouth Mn.	Ht.	Aft.	Ht.	Hull Mn.	Ht.	Aft.	Ht.	Greenock Mn.	Ht.	Aft.	Ht.	Leith Mn.	Ht.	Aft.	Ht.	Dun Laoghaire Mn.	Ht.	Aft.	Ht.
1	M	355	7·5	16 7	7·4	1 3	10·0	1330	9·5	927	13·6	2146	13·9	8 9	8·0	2050	7·5	215	3·7	1452	3·2	426	5·8	17 4	5·6	1 7	4·4	1346	4·0
2	Tu	440	7·4	1649	7·3	148	9·9	1413	9·2	10 9	13·4	2228	13·5	851	8·0	2134	7·3	3 0	3·8	1534	3·3	514	5·5	1751	5·5	156	4·4	1435	3·9
3	W	523	7·1	1732	7·1	232	9·6	1457	8·8	1049	12·9	2312	12·8	936	7·7	2219	6·9	342	3·7	1614	3·3	6 3	5·6	1842	5·2	247	4·3	1528	3·8
4	Th	6 8	6·8	1815	6·8	317	9·1	1545	8·4	1132	12·1	2357	12·0	1023	7·3	2309	6·5	426	3·6	1652	3·3	656	5·4	1934	5·0	342	4·1	1626	3·7
5	F	657	6·5	1904	6·6	4 7	8·5	1640	7·9	—	—	1215	11·2	1119	6·8	—	—	512	3·3	1735	3·0	750	5·1	2031	4·8	445	3·9	1733	3·5
6	Sa	751	6·2	20 6	6·3	5 9	7·9	1750	7·5	048	10·9	1310	10·5	010	6·8	1228	6·4	6 7	3·0	1824	2·9	850	4·8	2137	4·6	557	3·7	1845	3·5
7	Su	854	6·0	2122	6·0	628	7·5	1914	7·4	155	10·2	1427	10·0	121	6·0	1351	6·0	719	2·8	1934	2·8	10 6	4·7	2252	4·6	718	3·5	1957	3·5
8	M	1012	5·9	2252	5·9	754	7·4	2032	7·5	319	10·2	1556	10·0	240	6·2	1519	6·0	853	2·7	21 5	2·8	1128	4·7	—	—	832	3·5	2058	3·6
9	Tu	1130	6·0	—	—	9 5	7·7	2132	8·1	440	10·3	17 8	10·8	355	6·2	1633	6·1	1013	2·7	2217	2·8	0 3	4·7	1239	4·8	935	3·6	2158	3·8
10	W	0 5	6·1	1232	6·2	989	8·1	2219	8·5	542	11·0	18 4	11·5	452	6·4	1726	6·3	1115	2·8	23 9	3·1	1 3	4·8	1334	4·9	1025	3·6	2235	3·9
11	Th	1 0	6·3	1320	6·4	1041	8·4	2258	8·8	632	11·6	1849	12·3	537	6·7	18 8	6·5	12 6	2·9	2352	3·2	150	5·0	1421	5·0	11 5	3·6	2312	3·9
12	F	145	6·5	1359	6·6	1118	8·7	2332	9·0	713	12·0	1927	12·4	614	6·9	1843	6·6	—	—	1249	2·9	231	5·1	1458	5·1	1138	3·7	2345	4·0
13	Sa	223	6·6	1434	6·7	1151	8·8	—	—	749	12·2	20 1	12·4	646	7·1	1916	6·8	031	3·3	1328	2·9	3 3	5·2	1530	5·2	—	—	12 8	3·7
14	Su	257	6·7	15 5	6·8	0 4	9·1	1222	8·9	822	12·3	2030	12·5	714	7·2	1944	6·9	1 8	3·3	14 3	2·8	333	5·3	1558	5·2	016	4·0	13 4	3·7
15	M	330	6·7	1536	6·8	035	9·1	1252	8·8	851	12·3	2058	12·5	744	7·3	2011	7·0	141	3·4	1432	2·8	4 1	5·3	1625	5·1	047	4·0	1335	3·7
16	Tu	357	6·6	16 4	6·7	1 4	9·0	1320	8·7	918	12·3	2127	12·5	813	7·3	2040	7·0	211	3·4	1459	2·9	431	5·2	1655	5·0	117	4·0	14 8	3·6
17	W	428	6·6	1634	6·5	133	8·9	1349	8·6	945	12·1	2155	12·3	846	7·2	2112	6·8	241	3·3	1523	2·9	5 0	5·1	1728	4·8	150	3·9	1446	3·6
18	Th	458	6·6	17 4	6·5	2 1	8·7	1419	8·3	1010	11·7	2221	11·7	918	6·9	2145	6·6	310	3·3	1549	2·9	537	5·0	18 3	4·8	224	3·8	1531	3·5
19	F	529	6·4	1736	6·3	230	8·4	1453	8·0	1035	11·1	2249	11·0	953	6·5	2220	6·3	345	3·3	1620	3·0	613	4·9	1840	4·6	3 3	3·7	1625	3·4
20	Sa	6 4	6·2	1812	6·0	3 7	8·0	1536	7·7	11 1	10·5	2323	10·4	1033	6·2	23 1	6·0	426	3·2	1657	3·0	656	4·7	1925	4·5	350	3·5	1731	3·3
21	Su	643	5·9	1859	5·7	355	7·6	1635	7·3	1140	9·9	—	—	1125	5·8	—	—	514	3·1	1744	2·9	749	4·5	2023	4·3	452	3·3	1848	3·3
22	M	738	5·6	20 9	5·5	5 4	7·2	18 3	7·2	017	9·8	1256	9·4	0 0	5·7	1245	5·6	611	3·0	1843	2·9	852	4·3	2138	4·3	611	3·4	2057	3·4
23	Tu	856	5·5	2139	5·5	646	7·1	1933	7·5	154	9·5	1451	9·4	134	5·6	1433	5·7	719	2·9	2011	2·9	1033	4·6	23 3	4·4	736	3·5	2146	3·5
24	W	1021	5·6	23 8	5·5	813	7·6	2044	8·1	332	9·5	1619	10·6	3 3	5·8	1553	6·1	850	2·9	2145	3·0	1155	4·7	—	—	847	3·7	2232	3·8
25	Th	1144	6·1	—	—	918	8·2	2141	8·8	457	11·0	1730	11·8	4 9	6·1	1654	6·6	1014	3·0	2246	3·2	014	4·7	1259	4·9	941	4·1	2316	4·0
26	F	022	6·5	1248	6·6	1012	8·9	2230	9·5	6 3	12·1	1827	12·9	5 1	6·8	1743	7·1	—	—	2338	3·4	110	5·1	1352	5·3	1028	4·2	2359	4·2
27	Sa	119	7·1	1337	7·1	1058	9·7	2315	9·9	656	13·0	1916	13·7	544	7·3	1825	7·5	028	3·6	1208	3·1	156	5·5	1435	5·6	1110	4·4	1235	4·4
28	Su	2 6	7·5	1422	7·4	1142	9·9	2358	10·0	741	13·7	20 1	14·2	625	7·8	19 4	7·8	116	3·7	1259	3·1	239	5·8	1515	5·8	1152	4·5	1317	4·5
29	M	251	7·6	1504	7·5	—	—	1224	9·8	823	14·0	2042	14·4	704	8·2	1944	8·2	2 2	3·8	1346	3·2	319	6·0	1556	5·8	—	—	14 4	4·1
30	Tu	334	7·6	1543	7·6	041	10·3	13 4	9·7	904	14·1	2122	14·3	745	8·4	2023	8·4	245	3·8	15 7	3·4	4 0	6·0	1640	5·7	044	4·6	1317	4·2
31	W	416	7·4	1624	7·5	123	10·1	1345	9·4	943	13·7	22 3	13·7	827	8·2	21 4	7·7	—	—	15 7	3·4	448	5·9	1726	5·5	132	4·5	14 4	4·1

*All times shown are Greenwich Mean Time. †Difference of height in metres from Ordnance Datum (Newlyn). ‡Difference of height in metres from Ordnance Datum (Dublin).

SEPTEMBER, 1988

High Water at the undermentioned Places (G.M.T.*)—

Day of Month	Day of Week	London Bridge †Datum 3.20 m. below Mn.	Ht.	Aft.	Ht.	Liverpool †Datum 4.93 m. below Mn.	Ht.	Aft.	Ht.	Avonmouth †Datum 6.50 m. below Mn.	Ht.	Aft.	Ht.	Hull (Albert Dock) †Datum 3.90 m. below Mn.	Ht.	Aft.	Ht.	Greenock †Datum 1.62 m. below Mn.	Ht.	Aft.	Ht.	Leith †Datum 2.90 m. below Mn.	Ht.	Aft.	Ht.	Dun Laoghaire ‡Datum 0.20 m. above Mn.	Ht.	Aft.	Ht.
1	Th	457	7.1	17 5	7.2	2 4	9.7	1425	8.9	1021	13.0	2242	12.7	911	7.8	2146	7.0	324	3.7	1543	3.4	537	5.7	1814	5.2	221	4.4	1454	4.0
2	F	539	6.7	1747	6.8	247	9.1	15 8	8.4	1058	12.0	2322	11.5	959	7.2	2233	6.5	4 4	3.6	1619	3.3	629	5.3	19 6	4.9	315	4.1	1550	3.8
3	Sa	621	6.3	1835	6.5	335	8.3	16 0	7.8	1136	10.9	—	—	1054	6.6	2329	6.1	448	3.3	1658	3.2	723	5.0	20 1	4.6	417	3.8	1657	3.6
4	Su	710	6.0	1935	6.1	437	7.5	1713	7.2	0 7	10.3	1224	9.9	042	5.7	12 5	5.9	539	3.0	1746	3.0	828	4.6	2110	4.4	535	3.5	1817	3.5
5	M	811	5.7	2051	5.8	6 5	7.0	1855	7.1	114	9.4	1349	9.3	215	5.7	1338	5.5	649	2.6	1849	2.8	952	4.5	2236	4.5	7 3	3.4	1936	3.5
6	Tu	931	5.5	2231	5.8	745	7.1	2019	7.5	254	9.2	1536	9.6	338	5.9	1517	5.9	849	2.6	2034	2.7	1122	4.5	2353	4.6	825	3.4	2042	3.6
7	W	1108	5.8	2347	6.2	854	7.6	2115	8.1	424	9.9	1652	10.5	433	6.3	1623	6.2	1019	2.7	22 6	2.9	—	—	1228	4.7	926	3.5	2134	3.8
8	Th	—	—	1211	6.6	942	8.1	2159	8.6	525	10.8	1744	11.5	549	6.7	1746	6.6	1111	2.7	2256	3.2	050	4.8	1319	4.9	10 9	3.6	2215	3.9
9	F	041	6.6	1257	6.8	1020	8.5	2234	8.9	610	11.6	1827	12.1	619	6.9	1818	6.9	1152	2.9	2336	3.2	134	5.0	14 0	5.0	1044	3.7	2250	4.0
10	Sa	123	6.5	1335	6.7	1054	8.8	23 6	9.1	649	12.1	19 2	12.4	648	7.3	1913	7.2	—	—	1228	3.2	210	5.1	1433	5.1	1112	3.8	2319	4.1
11	Su	158	6.7	14 9	6.9	1123	9.0	2336	9.2	723	12.4	1934	12.6	716	7.5	1940	7.2	012	3.3	13 1	3.2	239	5.2	15 1	5.2	1137	3.8	2347	4.1
12	M	230	6.9	1439	6.9	1153	9.0	—	—	754	12.6	20 2	12.8	745	7.4	20 8	7.2	046	3.3	1332	3.1	3 5	5.3	1526	5.3	—	—	12 1	3.9
13	Tu	258	6.9	15 5	6.9	0 5	9.0	1219	9.0	820	12.6	2029	12.9	816	7.4	2037	7.0	117	3.3	1358	3.1	330	5.4	1552	5.3	015	4.1	1228	3.9
14	W	325	6.9	1534	6.9	032	9.0	1248	9.0	847	12.6	2057	12.8	847	7.4	21 7	6.9	145	3.3	1422	3.1	359	5.3	1619	5.3	043	4.0	1257	3.9
15	Th	353	6.9	16 2	6.9	1 0	9.0	1316	8.8	914	12.4	2125	12.4	919	7.3	2138	6.7	213	3.3	1445	3.1	429	5.1	1652	5.1	114	4.0	1330	3.8
16	F	423	6.8	1633	6.8	127	8.8	1345	8.6	939	11.8	2150	11.7	959	6.9	2219	6.2	243	3.3	1512	3.1	5 3	5.1	1727	4.9	150	3.9	14 8	3.7
17	Sa	455	6.6	17 8	6.7	158	8.5	1418	8.3	10 2	11.2	2219	11.0	1052	6.5	2318	6.0	317	3.2	1545	3.1	541	4.9	18 4	4.7	232	3.7	1453	3.6
18	Su	529	6.0	1746	6.1	234	8.1	15 1	7.9	1027	10.5	2252	10.3	—	—	1215	5.5	4 0	3.2	1625	3.1	626	4.6	1850	4.5	321	3.6	1549	3.5
19	M	610	5.4	1836	5.4	324	7.6	1734	7.5	128	9.9	2347	9.5	056	5.5	1419	5.8	450	3.0	1712	3.0	727	4.4	1954	4.3	426	3.4	1657	3.4
20	Tu	7 3	5.6	1948	5.6	441	7.1	1912	7.1	311	9.9	1426	10.7	239	5.8	1539	6.0	547	2.9	1811	2.9	850	4.4	2117	4.3	552	3.3	1818	3.4
21	W	823	5.6	2122	5.6	629	7.1	2023	7.6	440	12.1	1711	12.1	345	6.0	1637	7.0	658	2.8	1942	3.0	1021	4.4	2244	4.5	722	3.4	1936	3.6
22	Th	959	6.2	2255	6.2	759	7.6	2117	8.4	543	13.4	18 5	13.2	435	7.0	1722	7.2	849	2.8	2132	3.0	1140	4.7	2354	4.8	832	3.6	2037	3.9
23	F	1125	6.8	—	—	952	8.4	2251	9.6	634	13.9	1853	13.9	519	7.5	18 3	7.6	10 8	3.0	2232	3.3	—	—	1239	5.0	925	3.8	2127	4.1
24	Sa	0 4	6.8	1225	6.8	1035	9.6	22 7	10.1	719	14.2	1937	14.3	558	7.8	1839	7.8	11 1	3.3	2322	3.5	049	5.2	1329	5.4	10 9	4.0	2212	4.4
25	Su	059	7.3	1314	7.3	1118	9.8	2251	10.3	759	14.2	2018	14.4	639	8.0	1916	7.9	1148	3.6	—	—	134	5.6	1410	5.6	1049	4.3	2255	4.5
26	M	145	7.6	1358	7.6	1158	9.9	2333	10.3	839	14.1	2057	14.1	721	8.3	1955	7.7	011	3.8	1234	3.3	214	5.9	1450	5.8	1127	4.3	2337	4.6
27	Tu	229	7.6	1439	7.6	—	—	1238	9.7	915	14.1	2136	13.3	8 5	8.4	2034	7.4	058	3.8	1318	3.4	254	6.1	1530	5.9	—	—	12 6	4.3
28	W	310	7.5	1518	7.5	015	10.3	1316	9.7	953	13.7	2214	12.3	851	8.1	2117	—	142	3.7	1358	3.5	337	6.1	1613	5.7	021	4.6	1249	4.3
29	Th	349	7.3	1559	7.3	056	10.0	1355	9.4	—	—	—	—	—	—	—	—	224	3.7	1435	3.6	424	5.9	1658	5.5	1 7	4.5	1335	4.2
30	F	428	7.0	1641	7.0	137	9.7	1435	9.0	—	—	—	—	—	—	—	—	3 2	3.7	1510	3.6	512	5.6	1747	5.2	157	4.3	1422	4.1

* All times shown are Greenwich Mean Time.   † Difference of height in metres from Ordnance Datum (Newlyn).   ‡ Difference of height in metres from Ordnance Datum (Dublin).

OCTOBER, 1988

High Water at the undermentioned Places (G.M.T.*)—

Day of Month	Day of Week	LONDON BRIDGE †Datum of Predictions 3.20 m below Mn. h.m.	Ht. m.	Aft. h.m.	Ht. m.	LIVERPOOL †Datum of Predictions 4.93 m below Mn. h.m.	Ht. m.	Aft. h.m.	Ht. m.	AVONMOUTH †Datum of Predictions 6.50 m below Mn. h.m.	Ht. m.	Aft. h.m.	Ht. m.	HULL (Albert Dock) †Datum of Predictions 3.90 m below Mn. h.m.	Ht. m.	Aft. h.m.	Ht. m.	GREENOCK †Datum of Predictions 1.62 m below Mn. h.m.	Ht. m.	Aft. h.m.	Ht. m.	LEITH †Datum of Predictions 2.90 m below Mn. h.m.	Ht. m.	Aft. h.m.	Ht. m.	DUN LAOGHAIRE ‡Datum of Predictions 0.20 m above Mn. h.m.	Ht. m.	Aft. h.m.	Ht. m.
1	Sa	5 8	6.6	1723	6.8	219	8.8	1437	8.4	1028	11.7	2252	11.0	941	6.9	22 2	6.5	342	3.5	1547	3.5	6 5	5.2	1837	4.9	252	4.0	1518	3.8
2	Su	549	6.2	1811	6.3	3 7	8.0	1529	7.7	11 4	10.6	2336	10.4	1035	6.2	2254	6.0	425	3.2	1627	3.3	7 2	4.8	1934	4.6	354	3.7	1625	3.6
3	M	634	5.8	1910	5.9	410	7.3	1642	7.2	1149	9.6	—	—	1146	5.6	—	—	516	2.9	1715	3.1	8 8	4.5	2042	4.3	511	3.4	1746	3.5
4	Tu	733	5.5	2023	5.6	542	6.8	1824	7.1	043	8.9	1317	9.0	0 1	5.5	1319	5.2	627	2.6	1816	2.7	1056	4.4	2323	4.5	647	3.4	19 8	3.6
5	W	851	5.4	2157	5.7	720	7.0	1948	7.5	223	8.8	15 5	9.3	133	5.5	1457	5.3	844	2.6	1954	2.6	1159	4.4	—	—	8 6	3.4	2014	3.6
6	Th	1031	5.6	2318	6.1	826	7.5	2044	8.0	352	9.6	1621	10.3	3 7	5.8	1557	5.7	10 3	2.7	2137	2.5	020	4.6	1247	4.8	9 1	3.7	21 5	3.8
7	F	1140	6.1	—	—	912	8.1	2127	8.5	452	10.6	1713	11.3	4 3	6.2	1641	6.1	1048	2.9	2229	2.8	1 2	4.9	1325	5.0	941	3.7	2145	3.9
8	Sa	011	6.5	1227	6.5	949	8.5	22 2	8.8	537	11.5	1754	12.1	444	6.6	1715	6.5	1122	2.9	23 7	3.0	135	5.0	1358	5.1	1011	3.8	2218	4.0
9	Su	052	6.8	13 4	6.8	1021	8.8	2234	9.0	617	12.1	1829	12.4	518	7.0	1746	6.9	1153	3.0	2342	3.0	2 4	5.1	1426	5.2	1037	3.9	2247	4.1
10	M	127	6.9	1338	6.9	1051	9.0	23 4	9.2	650	12.4	19 2	12.7	549	7.3	1812	7.1	015	3.3	1225	3.2	230	5.2	1452	5.3	11 2	3.9	2314	4.1
11	Tu	158	6.9	14 6	6.9	1119	9.1	2333	9.2	721	12.6	1931	12.8	618	7.4	1839	7.3	046	3.3	1252	3.0	258	5.3	1519	5.4	1127	4.0	2343	4.1
12	W	225	6.9	1433	6.9	1149	9.1	—	—	749	12.7	20 1	12.8	648	7.4	19 7	7.3	115	3.3	1319	3.0	328	5.4	1550	5.4	1155	4.0	—	—
13	Th	253	6.9	15 3	6.9	031	9.1	1217	9.1	819	12.7	2030	12.7	720	7.3	1937	7.1	145	3.3	1343	3.0	4 2	5.3	1623	5.3	013	4.0	1226	4.0
14	F	322	6.9	1535	6.9	1 2	8.8	1248	8.8	847	12.6	2129	11.7	751	7.1	20 6	6.9	219	3.3	1410	3.1	439	5.2	1659	5.2	047	4.0	1342	4.0
15	Sa	353	6.8	1610	6.8	137	8.8	1320	8.5	914	11.9	21 0	11.0	823	6.9	2037	6.5	258	3.3	1441	3.2	523	4.7	1741	5.0	126	3.9	1428	3.9
16	Su	428	6.7	1648	6.6	218	8.5	1357	8.1	942	11.2	2129	10.6	9 0	6.5	2111	6.4	344	3.2	1518	3.3	615	4.4	1833	4.8	211	3.7	1525	3.8
17	M	5 5	6.4	1733	6.3	314	8.1	1444	7.6	1016	10.6	2245	9.7	943	6.2	2155	5.8	435	3.2	1602	3.3	722	4.4	1940	4.5	3 6	3.6	1633	3.6
18	Tu	549	6.0	1828	6.0	434	7.6	1549	7.3	11 8	9.9	2353	9.6	1041	5.9	2258	5.8	534	2.9	1652	3.2	840	4.5	2059	4.4	413	3.4	1752	3.6
19	W	646	5.7	1941	5.7	601	7.3	1718	7.3	120	9.6	1236	9.6	027	5.7	1358	5.7	649	2.9	1753	3.1	10 2	4.4	2219	4.5	538	3.4	19 9	3.7
20	Th	8 6	5.5	2111	5.6	735	7.3	1845	7.8	253	10.3	14 9	10.3	2 5	6.0	1514	6.0	843	2.9	1926	2.9	1113	4.8	2325	4.7	7 3	3.7	2013	4.0
21	F	938	5.8	2235	6.3	836	7.8	1955	8.5	414	11.4	1536	11.4	312	6.5	1610	6.5	950	3.2	2111	3.1	811	5.1	1210	5.0	811	3.9	21 5	4.2
22	Sa	1058	6.4	2342	6.9	925	8.5	2051	9.0	6 8	12.5	1645	12.3	4 6	7.1	1655	7.1	1036	3.2	2218	3.2	9 2	5.3	1259	5.3	9 2	4.1	2252	4.4
23	Su	1158	6.9	—	—	10 9	9.0	2141	9.5	653	13.7	1740	13.0	451	7.5	1736	7.5	1120	3.3	2346	3.5	946	5.7	1423	5.7	946	4.3	2235	4.5
24	M	035	7.2	1249	7.2	1051	9.5	2226	9.7	734	13.8	1913	13.7	534	7.7	1814	7.7	034	3.7	12 2	3.6	1025	5.9	15 4	5.8	1025	4.3	2316	4.5
25	Tu	123	7.4	1333	7.4	1132	9.7	2351	9.7	813	13.8	1954	13.9	618	7.9	1852	7.7	2 0	3.7	1245	3.6	1141	6.0	1547	5.5	1141	4.5	—	—
26	W	2 5	7.4	1415	7.4	034	9.6	1212	9.6	851	13.6	2034	13.8	749	8.0	1931	7.5	241	3.5	1325	3.7	315	5.7	1634	5.5	0 1	4.5	1223	4.3
27	Th	244	7.3	1456	7.3	114	9.5	1252	9.2	929	13.5	2115	13.6	837	7.9	2012	7.7	323	3.6	1439	3.6	451	5.7	1720	5.2	047	4.3	13 8	4.2
28	F	324	7.2	1538	7.2	158	9.1	1331	8.9	10 6	12.5	2155	13.2	927	7.2	2053	7.5	4 7	3.4	1518	3.5	544	5.1	1811	5.1	137	4.1	1357	4.1
29	Sa	4 3	6.9	1621	6.9	246	8.5	1415	7.9	1042	10.5	2233	11.8	1019	6.6	2135	6.9	323	3.4	1518	3.4	640	4.8	19 6	4.6	229	3.8	1453	3.9
30	Su	442	6.6	17 6	6.7			15 4				2315	9.7			2221	6.1			16 11						332	3.6	1554	3.7
31	M	522	6.2	1754	6.2													4 7											

* All times shown are Greenwich Mean Time. †Difference of height in metres from Ordnance Datum (Newlyn). ‡Difference of height in metres from Ordnance Datum (Dublin).

NOVEMBER, 1988

High Water at the undermentioned Places (G.M.T.*)—

Day of Month	Day of Week	London Bridge †Datum 3.20 m. below Mn h.m	Ht	Aft h.m	Ht	Liverpool †Datum 4.93 m. below Mn h.m	Ht	Aft h.m	Ht	Avonmouth †Datum 6.50 m. below Mn h.m	Ht	Aft h.m	Ht	Hull (Albert Dock) †Datum 3.90 m. below Mn h.m	Ht	Aft h.m	Ht	Greenock †Datum 1.62 m. below Mn h.m	Ht	Aft h.m	Ht	Leith †Datum 2.90 m. below Mn h.m	Ht	Aft h.m	Ht	Dun Laoghaire ‡Datum 0.20 m. above Mn h.m	Ht	Aft h.m	Ht
1	Tu	6 4	5.8	1848	5.9	345	7.3	1610	7.4	1127	9.6	1241	9.2	1118	5.5	2319	5.8	459	2.9	1649	3.3	742	4.5	20 8	4.4	443	3.3	17 6	3.6
2	W	659	5.5	1951	5.6	5 11	6.9	1732	7.2	014	9.0	14 9	9.3	031	5.6	1229	5.5	6 6	2.7	1748	3.0	852	4.3	2118	4.3	610	3.3	1824	3.5
3	Th	8 9	5.4	21 7	5.5	628	7.0	1852	7.3	134	8.9	1524	10.0	159	5.7	1514	6.0	8 2	2.6	19 7	2.9	10 4	4.4	2230	4.3	726	3.3	1932	3.6
4	F	934	5.5	2228	5.9	737	7.3	1955	7.7	253	9.4	1623	10.8	314	6.0	1524	6.0	921	2.7	2044	2.9	11 7	4.5	2328	4.6	820	3.4	2024	3.7
5	Sa	1052	5.9	2329	6.3	827	7.8	2042	8.1	359	10.2	1723	10.8	4 2	6.4	1637	6.7	10 6	2.9	2143	3.0	1157	4.7			9 0	3.6	21 5	3.8
6	Su	1146	6.3			911	8.2	2121	8.5	451	11.0	17 9	11.4	440	6.8	1737	7.0	1042	3.0	2225	3.1	014	4.8	1238	4.9	931	3.7	2139	3.9
7	M	012	6.5	1227	6.6	943	8.5	2156	8.7	534	11.7	1749	12.1	515	7.0	1839	7.1	1113	3.1	23 2	3.2	051	5.0	1315	5.1	10 0	3.8	2211	4.0
8	Tu	049	6.7	13 0	6.7	1016	8.8	2230	8.9	612	12.2	1825	12.4	549	7.2	1913	7.2	1142	3.1	2337	3.1	124	5.1	1347	5.2	1028	4.0	2243	4.0
9	W	120	6.8	1333	6.8	1047	9.0	23 2	9.0	646	12.4	19 0	12.6	622	7.2	1945	7.1			1212	3.1	157	5.2	1418	5.3	1056	4.0	2314	4.0
10	Th	151	6.8	14 5	6.8	1119	9.1	2334	9.0	720	12.5	1934	12.6	657	7.1	2022	6.8	012	3.3	1241	3.2	231	5.3	1451	5.4	1128	4.1	2350	4.0
11	F	223	6.9	1439	6.9	1153	9.1			754	12.5	2009	12.5	734	7.1	2149	6.6	046	3.3	1310	3.2	3 6	5.4	1525	5.4			12 2	4.1
12	Sa	258	6.9	1517	6.9	010	8.9	1228	9.1	827	12.3	2046	11.8	812	6.8	2247	6.2	122	3.3	1343	3.3	346	5.4	16 3	5.3	028	3.9	1242	4.1
13	Su	334	6.9	1556	6.9	046	8.8	13 6	8.9	9 3	12.0	2124	11.3	854	6.6	1324	6.1	2 2	3.3	1419	3.4	428	5.2	1644	5.2	111	3.8	1325	4.0
14	M	412	6.7	1641	6.8	128	8.5	1349	8.6	942	11.5	22 6	11.3	942	6.4	1437	6.3	247	3.3	15 1	3.5	516	5.1	1731	5.0	2 1	3.7	1414	4.0
15	Tu	454	6.5	1730	6.5	215	8.3	1442	8.3	1028	11.0	2258	10.5	1038	6.0	1536	6.7	336	3.5	1547	3.5	612	4.9	1826	4.8	257	3.6	1510	3.9
16	W	542	6.2	1827	6.2	314	7.8	1543	8.0	1126	10.7	2358	10.5	1151	6.0	1627	7.1	428	3.2	1640	3.4	712	4.7	1929	4.8	4 1	3.5	1613	3.9
17	Th	639	6.0	1934	6.1	426	7.6	1658	8.0	1 9	10.4	1234	10.8	0 0	6.1	1712	7.2	526	3.1	1741	3.4	821	4.6	2036	4.8	517	3.4	1725	3.8
18	F	749	5.9	2051	6.0	546	7.6	1812	8.1	227	10.8	1348	11.1	123	6.3	1753	7.3	637	3.0	19 4	3.2	930	4.7	2146	4.9	635	3.5	1840	3.8
19	Sa	910	6.1	22 7	6.2	7 0	7.9	1921	8.5	343	11.5	15 7	12.1	234	6.7	1834	7.3	812	3.0	2038	3.2	1038	4.9	2250	5.1	743	3.7	1947	4.0
20	Su	1026	6.4	2315	6.5	8 2	8.4	2020	8.9	448	12.8	1616	12.7	334	7.1	1914	7.4	918	3.1	2140	3.4	1136	5.1	2348	5.3	837	3.8	2044	4.1
21	M	1130	7.0			857	9.1	2114	9.5	542	13.1	1715	13.1	427	7.4	1955	6.9	10 5	3.3	2232	3.5			1229	5.3	924	4.0	2132	4.2
22	Tu	011	7.0	1225	6.9	945	9.3	22 3	9.5	628	13.1	1852	13.2	516	7.6	2034	6.4	1049	3.3	2322	3.5	038	5.5	1315	5.5	10 5	4.1	2218	4.3
23	W	0 1	7.0	1313	7.0	1030	9.3	2249	9.5	712	13.2	1935	13.2	6 5	7.6	2112	6.1	1132	3.4			127	5.7	14 0	5.6	1044	4.2	2312	4.3
24	Th	144	7.0	1357	7.0	1112	9.3	2334	9.4	754	13.2	2018	12.9	653	7.4	2153	6.5	011	3.5	1216	3.5	211	5.7	1444	5.6	1124	4.2	2347	4.2
25	F	225	6.9	1440	7.1	1154	9.3			834	12.3	21 0	11.7	741	7.4	2238	5.8	058	3.5	1257	3.6	3 1	5.5	1529	5.5			12 5	4.2
26	Sa	3 5	6.9	1525	7.1	1 0	9.2	1235	9.2	914	12.3	2139	10.9	827	6.8			142	3.5	1337	3.7	349	5.5	1614	5.4	033	4.0	1250	4.2
27	Su	345	6.8	16 9	7.0	142	8.8	1316	8.9	950	11.6	2217	10.2	912	6.4			226	3.4	1416	3.7	438	5.3	17 0	5.2	122	3.9	1339	4.1
28	M	424	6.6	1652	6.8	142	8.4	1358	8.5	1027	10.9	2257	9.8	955	6.1			310	3.3	1456	3.7	526	5.1	1746	5.1	211	3.8	1428	3.9
29	Tu	5 2	6.3	1736	6.4	227	8.0	1443	8.2	11 6	10.3	2340	9.8	1040	5.8			355	3.1	1538	3.6	615	4.8	1834	4.7	3 4	3.5	1523	3.8
30	W	542	6.0	1822	6.1	315	7.6	1534	7.8									442	3.0	1626	3.4	7 6	4.5	1925	4.6	4 3	3.3	1620	3.6

* All times shown are Greenwich Mean Time.   †Difference of height in metres from Ordnance Datum (Newlyn).

‡Difference of height in metres from Ordnance Datum (Dublin).

DECEMBER, 1988

High Water at the undermentioned Places (G.M.T.*)—

Day of Month	Day of Week	London Bridge †Datum 3.20 m. below Mn.	Ht.	Aft.	Ht.	Liverpool †Datum 4.93 m. below Mn.	Ht.	Aft.	Ht.	Avonmouth †Datum 6.50 m. below Mn.	Ht.	Aft.	Ht.	Hull (Albert Dock) †Datum 3.90 m. below Mn.	Ht.	Aft.	Ht.	Greenock †Datum 1.62 m. below Mn.	Ht.	Aft.	Ht.	Leith †Datum 2.90 m. below Mn.	Ht.	Aft.	Ht.	Dun Laoghaire ‡Datum 0.20 m. above Mn.	Ht.	Aft.	Ht.
1	Th	627	5.8	1914	5.8	412	7.3	1633	7.5	1157	10.0	13 4	9.8	1130	5.5	2333	6.0	537	2.8	1718	2.9	8 0	4.4	2020	4.5	5 9	3.2	1723	3.5
2	F	724	5.6	2015	5.7	515	7.1	1737	7.4	038	9.5	1415	10.0	042	5.8	1231	5.5	646	2.7	1819	3.0	857	4.4	2118	4.4	618	3.2	1828	3.5
3	Sa	833	5.5	2119	5.7	624	7.1	1845	7.4	147	9.5	1518	10.4	155	6.1	1342	5.8	8 9	2.8	1932	3.0	958	4.4	2216	4.5	719	3.3	1927	3.5
4	Su	943	5.6	2223	5.9	726	7.7	1944	7.7	253	10.4	1613	10.9	3 1	6.4	1451	6.1	951	2.9	2041	3.1	1144	4.7	2312	4.6	8 6	3.4	2017	3.6
5	M	1045	5.9	2316	6.1	818	7.7	2033	8.0	352	10.9	17 4	11.5	355	6.6	1542	6.4	1028	3.0	2133	3.1	0 1	4.7	1228	4.9	847	3.6	2138	3.7
6	Tu	1136	6.1			9 1	8.1	2117	8.3	445	11.5	1749	11.9	440	6.8	1624	6.6	11 1	3.1	2218	3.2	046	4.8	1310	5.0	924	3.7	2216	3.8
7	W	0 1	6.3	1219	6.3	941	8.5	2157	8.5	532	11.9	1834	12.3	520	6.9	17 2	6.7	1134	3.2	23 0	3.3	128	5.1	1350	5.2	958	3.9	2255	3.8
8	Th	042	6.6	13 0	6.5	1019	8.8	2237	8.7	615	12.3	1916	12.5	6 3	6.9	1740	6.8	024	3.3	2342	3.3	212	5.2	1430	5.3	1032	3.9	2334	3.9
9	F	123	6.7	1342	6.7	1057	9.0	2316	8.9	657	12.5	1958	12.5	643	7.0	1818	6.9	1 8	3.3	12 9	3.3	253	5.3	15 9	5.4	11 7	4.0	1228	3.9
10	Sa	2 4	6.8	1425	6.8	1136	9.2	2357	8.9	738	12.5	2040	12.4	724	7.0	1856	7.0	154	3.3	1246	3.4	338	5.4	1551	5.4	1147	4.0	1313	4.1
11	Su	244	6.9	15 8	7.0			1217	9.2	819	12.5	2124	12.3	8 8	7.0	1935	7.0	242	3.3	1325	3.5	421	5.4	1636	5.3	018	3.9	14 3	4.1
12	M	325	6.9	1553	7.0	041	8.9	13 0	9.0	9 1	12.4	22 9	12.4	851	6.9	2015	7.1	333	3.3	14 7	3.6	5 9	5.3	1723	5.2	1 3	3.8	1454	4.1
13	Tu	4 7	6.9	1638	7.0	126	8.7	1347	8.9	945	12.1	2257	12.1	938	6.8	2057	7.1	422	3.2	1452	3.7	559	5.1	1814	5.1	153	3.7	1553	4.1
14	W	451	6.7	1726	6.8	215	8.6	1437	8.8	1031	11.8	2349	12.2	1028	6.6	2142	6.8	513	3.1	1540	3.7	655	5.0	1910	5.0	246	3.7	1657	4.1
15	Th	536	6.6	1818	6.6	3 7	8.3	1531	8.5	1122	11.4	1218	11.2	1127	6.4	2233	6.4	610	3.0	1631	3.6	753	4.9	20 9	5.0	343	3.6	18 7	3.9
16	F	627	6.4	1917	6.3	4 6	8.1	1631	8.3	046	11.2	1321	11.1	042	6.6	1241	6.7	721	3.0	1727	3.3	855	4.8	2111	5.1	449	3.5	1919	3.9
17	Sa	726	6.3	2023	6.3	511	7.9	1736	8.1	154	11.1	1433	11.3	155	6.9	1354	6.9	835	3.1	1836	3.3	959	4.8	2216	5.1	559	3.5	2023	3.9
18	Su	836	6.3	2135	6.4	621	7.9	1845	8.3	3 8	11.5	1543	11.5	3 4	7.1	15 0	7.1	933	3.1	1958	3.0	11 3	5.0	2321	5.2	7 8	3.7	2119	3.9
19	M	950	6.4	2244	6.5	728	7.8	1951	8.5	417	11.8	1648	11.8	4 9	7.1	16 0	7.1	1023	3.1	21 9	3.1	020	5.3	12 2	5.1	8 9	3.7	22 9	3.9
20	Tu	11 1	6.5	2346	6.5	830	8.3	2053	8.6	516	12.3	1746	12.3	5 9	7.1	1654	7.1	1110	3.4	22 9	3.1	116	5.4	1256	5.3	9 1	3.8	2256	3.9
21	W			12 4	6.6	925	8.6	2148	8.8	610	12.5	1838	12.4	6 3	7.0	1740	6.9	1155	3.5	23 4	3.3	2 7	5.4	1346	5.4	949	4.0	2341	4.0
22	Th	041	6.6	1348	6.6	1016	8.9	2238	9.0	657	12.6	1924	12.5	650	6.8	1824	7.0	047	3.6	2356	3.4	256	5.3	1434	5.4	1033	4.1	1239	3.9
23	F	128	6.6	1433	6.6	11 2	9.1	2326	9.0	741	12.6	20 8	12.6	735	6.6	19 4	7.1	134	3.7	1238	3.6	342	5.3	1518	5.3	1114	3.8	1323	4.1
24	Sa	212	6.7	1515	7.0	1144	9.0	13 3	8.9	822	12.6	2047	11.9	815	6.4	1941	7.0	219	3.7	1320	3.7	424	5.3	16 0	5.3	1157	3.7	14 6	4.1
25	Su	253	6.8	1556	7.0	0 8	8.9	1225	8.8	9 0	11.9	2125	11.9	851	6.3	2016	6.8	3 1	3.6	14 0	3.8	5 5	4.9	1641	5.1	025	3.6	1449	4.1
26	M	331	6.8	1635	6.9	049	8.8	1341	8.6	935	11.5	2159	11.5	927	6.3	2050	6.5	340	3.5	1440	3.7	544	4.8	1720	4.9	1 7	3.5	1532	4.0
27	Tu	4 7	6.8	1713	6.6	127	8.6	1418	8.2	10 7	11.7	2231	11.2	10 2	6.4	2125	6.2	419	3.3	1519	3.6	625	4.7	18 0	4.8	150	3.3	1618	4.1
28	W	444	6.5	1751	6.4	2 4	8.1	1457	8.2	1041	11.4	23 5	11.4	1040	6.3	22 3	6.5	458	3.0	1559	3.5	713	4.5	1842	4.7	233	3.2	1711	3.8
29	Th	518	6.3	1834	6.3	242	8.1	1539	7.9	1118	11.0	2343	11.0	1126	5.9	2245	6.5	540	2.9	1644	3.3	753	4.4	1925	4.6	317		1618	3.6
30	F	556	6.1	1920	5.9	322	7.7	1627	7.6			12 1	10.6			2339	5.9			1732	3.2	625		2011	4.5	4 3		1711	3.4
31	Sa	638	5.9			4 9	7.4															713				456			

*All times shown are Greenwich Mean Time. †Difference of height in metres from Ordnance Datum (Newlyn). ‡Difference of height in metres from Ordnance Datum (Dublin).

CHRONOLOGICAL NOTES

GEOLOGICAL TIME

The earth is thought to have come into existence approximately 4,600 million years ago, but for nearly half this time, the ARCHEAN era, it was uninhabited; life is generally believed to have emerged in the succeeding PROTEROZOIC era. The Archean and the Proterozoic eras are often together referred to as the PRECAMBRIAN. Although primitive forms of life e.g. algae and bacteria, existed during the Proterozoic era, it is not until the strata of Palaeozoic rocks is reached that abundant fossilized remains appear, initially of small shellfish, followed by plants, primitive fishes and, in the Devonian period (c.400 million B.C.), land-living plants and amphibia.

Since the Precambrian, there have been three great geological eras:

PALAEOZOIC ("ancient life") c.570–c.250 million B.C.
   (i) *Cambrian.* Mainly sandstones, slate and shales; limestones in Scotland. Shelled fossils and invertebrates e.g. trilobites and brachiopods appear.
   (ii) *Ordovician.* Mainly shales and mudstones (exemplified in N. Wales); limestones in Scotland.
   (iii) *Silurian.* Shales, mudstones and some limestones, found mostly in Wales and southern Scotland.
   (iv) *Devonian.* Old red sandstone, shale, limestone and slate, e.g. in S. Wales and the West Country. "The age of fishes"—proliferation of fish fossils. First traces of land-living life.
   (v) *Carboniferous.* Coal-bearing rocks, millstone grit, limestone and shale.
   (vi) *Permian.* Marls, sandstones and clays, named after the area of Russia where these strata are widespread. First large-scale appearance of reptile fossils.

There were two great phases of mountain building in the Palaeozoic area: the *Caledonian*, characterized in Britain by N.E.–S.W. lines of hills and valleys; and the later *Hercyian*, widespread in W. Germany and adjacent areas, and in Britain exemplified in E.–W. lines of hills and valleys.

The end of the Palaeozoic was marked by the extensive glaciations of the Permian period in the southern continents and the decline of amphibians; it was succeeded by an era of warm conditions.

MESOZOIC ("middle forms of life") c.250-c.65 million B.C.
   (i) *Triassic.* Mostly sandstone, e.g. in the W. Midlands.
   (ii) *Jurassic.* Mainly limestones and clays, typically displayed in the Jura Mts. and in England in a N.E.–S.W. belt from Lincolnshire and the Wash to the Severn and the Dorset coast.
   (iii) *Cretaceous.* Mainly chalk, clay and sands, e.g. in Kent and Sussex.

Giant reptiles were dominant during the Mesozoic, but it was at this time that marsupial mammals first appeared, as well as *Archaeopteryx lithographica*, the earliest known species of bird. Coniferous trees and flowering plants also developed during the era and, with the birds and the mammals, were the main species to survive into the Caenozoic (or Cenozoic) era. The giant reptiles became extinct.

CAENOZOIC ("recent life") from c.65 million B.C.
   (i) *Eocene.* The emergence of new forms of life, i.e. existing species.
   (ii) *Oligocene.* Fossils of a few still existing species.
   (iii) *Miocene.* Fossil remains show a balance of existing and extinct species.

   (iv) *Pliocene.* Fossil remains show a majority of still existing species.
   (v) *Pleistocene.* The majority of remains are those of still existing species.
   (vi) *Holocene.* The present, post-glacial period. Existing species only, except for a few exterminated by man.

In the last 25 million years, from the Miocene through the Pliocene, the Alpine-Himalayan and the circum-Pacific phases of mountain building reached their climax. During the Pleistocene period ice sheets repeatedly locked up masses of water as land ice; its weight depressed the land, but the locking-up of the water lowered the sea-level by 100–200 metres. The glaciations and interglacials of the Ice Age are extremely difficult to date and classify, but recent scientific opinion considers the Pleistocene to have begun approximately 1·7 million years ago. The last glacial retreat, merging into the Holocene period, was 10,000 years ago.

EARLY MAN

Any consideration of the history of man must start with the fact that all members of the human race belong to one species of animal, i.e. *homo sapiens*, the definition of a species being in biological terms that all its members can interbreed. As a species of mammal it is possible to group man with other similar types, known as the primates. Amongst these is found a sub-group, the apes, which includes, in addition to man, the chimpanzees, gorillas, orang-utans and gibbons. All lack a tail, have shoulder blades at the back, and a Y-shaped chewing pattern on the surface of their molars, as well as showing the more general primate characteristics of four incisors, a thumb which is able to touch the fingers of the same hand, and finger and toe nails instead of claws. All the factors available to scientific study suggest that human beings have chimpanzees and gorillas as their nearest relatives in the animal world. However, there remains the possibility that there once lived creatures, now extinct, which were closer to modern man than the chimpanzees and gorillas. To decide whether or not this is the case it is necessary to consider the fossil evidence to see if any extinct ape-like forms shared with modern man the characteristics of having flat faces (*i.e.* the absence of a pronounced muzzle), being bipedal, and possessing large brains.

There are two broad groups of extinct apes recognised by specialists. First the ramapithecines, the remains of which, mainly jaw fragments, have been found in East Africa, Asia, and Turkey. They lived about 14 to 8 million years ago, and from the evidence of their teeth it seems they chewed more in the manner of modern man than the other presently living apes. The second group, the australopithecines, have left much more numerous remains amongst which sub-groups may be detected, although the geographic spread is limited to South and East Africa. Living between 5 and 1·5 million years ago, they were closer relatives of modern man to the extent that they walked upright, did not have an extensive muzzle, and had similar types of pre-molars. The first australopithecine remains were recognised at Taung in South Africa in 1924, and subsequent discoveries include those at the famous site of Olduvai Gorge in Tanzania. Perhaps the most impressive discovery was made at Hadar in Ethiopia in 1974 when about half a skeleton, known as "Lucy", was found.

Also in East Africa, between 2 million and 1·5 million years ago, lived a hominid group which not only walked upright, had a flat face, and a large brain case, but also made simple pebble and flake stone tools. On present evidence these habilines seem to have been the first people to make tools, however crude. This facility is related to the larger brain size and human beings are the only animals to make implements to be used in other processes. These early pebble tool users, because of their distinctive characteristics, have been grouped as a separate sub-species, now extinct, of the genus *homo*, and are known as *homo habilis*.

The use of fire, again a human characteristic, is associated with another group of extinct hominids whose remains, about a million years old, are found in South and East Africa, China, Indonesia, North Africa and Europe. No doubt the mastery of the techniques of making fire helped the colonisation of the colder northern areas and in this respect the site of Vertesszollos in Hungary is of particular importance. *Homo erectus* is the name given to this group of fossils and it now includes a number of famous individual discoveries from earlier decades, for example, Solo Man, Heidelberg Man, and especially Peking Man who lived at the cave site at Choukou-tien, which has yielded evidence of fire and burnt bone.

The well known group, Neanderthal Man, or *homo sapiens neandertalensis*, is an extinct form of modern man who lived between about 100,000 and 40,000 years ago, thus spanning the last Ice Age. Indeed, its ability to adapt to the cold climate on the edge of the ice sheets is one of its characteristic features, the remains being only found in Europe, Asia and the Middle East. Complete neanderthal skeletons were found during excavations at Tabun in Israel together with evidence of tool-making and the use of fire. Distinguished by very large brains, it seems that neanderthal man was the first to develop recognisable social customs, especially deliberate burial rites. Why the neanderthalers became extinct is not clear, but it may be connected with the climatic changes at the end of the Ice Ages which would have seriously affected their food supplies; possibly they became too specialised for their own good.

The Swanscombe skull is the only known human fossil remains found in England. Some specialists see Swanscombe Man (or, more probably, woman) as a neanderthaler. Others group these remains together with the Steinheim skull from Germany seeing both as a separate sub-species, *homo-sapiens steinheimenses*. Unfortunately there is just too little evidence as yet on which to form a final judgment.

Modern Man, *homo sapiens sapiens*, the surviving sub-species of *homo sapiens* had evolved to our present physical condition and had colonised much of the world by about 30,000 years ago. There are many previously distinguished individual specimens, for example Cromagnon Man, which may now be grouped together as *homo sapiens sapiens*. It was modern man who spread to the New World by crossing the landbridge between Siberia and Alaska and thence moved south through North and into South America. Equally it is modern man who over the last 30,000 years has been responsible for the major developments in technology, art and civilisation generally.

One of the problems for those studying fossil man is the lack in many cases of sufficient quantities of fossil bone for analysis. It is important that theories should be tested against evidence, and not the evidence made to fit the theory. The celebrated Piltdown hoax is perhaps the best known example of "fossils" being forged to fit what was seen in some quarters as the correct theory of man's evolution.

HUMAN CULTURAL DEVELOPMENT

The Eurocentric bias of early archaeologists meant that the search for a starting point for the development and transmission of cultural ideas, especially by migration, trade and warfare, concentrated unduly on Europe and the Near East. The Three Age System, whereby pre-history was divided into a Stone Age, Bronze Age, and Iron Age, was devised by Christian Thomsen, Curator of the National Museum of Denmark in the early nineteenth century, to facilitate the classification of the Museum's collections. The descriptive adjectives referred to the materials from which the implements and weapons were made, and came to be regarded as the dominant features of the societies to which they related. The refinement of the Three Age System once dominated archaeological thought and still remains a generally accepted concept in the popular mind. However, it is now seen by archaeologists as an inadequate model for human development.

Common sense alone suggests that there were no complete breaks between one so-called "Age" and another, any more than contemporaries would have regarded 1485 as a complete break between medieval and modern English history. Nor can the Three Age System be applied universally. In some areas it is necessary to insert a Copper Age, while in Africa south of the Sahara there would seem to be no Bronze Age at all; in Australia, Old Stone Age societies survived, while in South America, New Stone Age communities existed into modern times. The civilisations in other parts of the world clearly invalidate a Eurocentric theory of human development.

The concept of the "Neolithic Revolution", associated with the domestication of plants and animals, was a development of particular importance in the human cultural pattern. It reflected change from the primitive hunter/gatherer economies to a more settled agricultural way of life and therefore, so the argument goes, made possible the development of urban civilisation. However, it can no longer be argued that this "Revolution" took place only in one area from which all development stemmed. Though it appears that the cultivation of wheat and barley was first undertaken, together with the domestication of cattle and goats/sheep in the Fertile Crescent, there is evidence that rice was first deliberately planted and pigs domesticated in South East Asia; maize first cultivated in Central America and llamas first domesticated in South America. It has been recognized increasingly in recent years that cultural changes can take place independently of each other in different parts of the world at different rates and different times. There is no need for a general diffusionist theory.

Although scholars will continue to study the particular societies which interest them, it may be possible to obtain a reliable chronological framework, in absolute terms of years, against which the cultural development of any particular area may be set. The development and refinement of radio-carbon dating and other scientific methods of producing absolute chronologies is enabling the cross-referencing of societies to be undertaken. As the techniques of dating become more rigorous in application and the number of scientifically obtained dates increases, the attainment of an absolute chronology for prehistoric societies throughout the world comes closer to being achieved.

TIME MEASUREMENT AND CALENDARS

MEASUREMENTS OF TIME

Measurements of Time are based on the time taken by the earth to rotate on its axis (*Day*); by the moon to revolve round the earth (*Month*); and by the earth to revolve round the sun (*Year*). From these, which are not commensurable, certain average or mean intervals have been adopted for ordinary use.

The Day begins at midnight and is divided into 24 hours of 60 minutes, each of 60 seconds. The hours are counted from midnight up to 12 noon (when the sun crosses the meridian), and these hours are designated A.M. (*ante meridiem*); and again from noon up to 12 at midnight, which hours are designated P.M. (*post meridiem*), except when the *Twenty-four Hour* reckoning is employed. The 24-hour reckoning ignores A.M. and P.M., and the hours are numbered 0 to 23 from midnight to midnight.

Colloquially the 24 hours are divided into *day* and *night*, day being the time while the sun is above the horizon (including the four stages of twilight defined on p. 139). Day is subdivided further into *morning*, the early part of daytime, ending at noon; *afternoon* from noon to 6 p.m. and *evening*, which may be said to extend from 6 p.m. until midnight. *Night*, the dark period between day and day, begins at the close of Astronomical Twilight (*see* p. 139) and extends beyond midnight to sunrise the next day.

The names of the Days—Sunday, Monday, Tuesday (Tiw = God of War), Wednesday (Woden or Odin), Thursday (Thor), Friday (Frig = wife of Odin), and Saturday—are derived from Old English translations or adaptions of the Roman titles (Sol, Luna, Mars, Mercurius, Jupiter, Venus and Saturnius).

The Week is a period of 7 days.

The Month in the ordinary calendar is approximately the twelfth part of a year, but the lengths of the different months vary from 28 (or 29) days to 31.

The Year.—The *Equinoctial or Tropical Year* is the time that the earth takes to revolve round the sun from equinox to equinox, or 365·2422 mean solar days. The *Calendar Year* consists of 365 days, but a year the date of which is divisible by 4, without remainder, is called *bissextile* (see Roman Calendar) or *Leap Year* and consists of 366 days, one day being added to the month February, so that a date "leaps over" a day of the week. The last year of a century is not a leap year unless its number is divisable by 400 (e.g. the years 1800 and 1900 had only 365 days).

The Solstice.—A Solstice is the point in the Tropical Year at which the Sun attains its greatest distance, north or south, from the Equator. In the northern hemisphere the greatest distance north of the Equator is the Summer Solstice and the greatest distance south is the Winter Solstice.

The Summer Solstice is also the *Longest Day*, measured from sunrise to sunset. At the Solstice the Sun, reaching its greatest northern declination, appears to stand still, the times of sunrise and sunset and the consequent length of the day showing no variation for several days together, before and after the longest day (June 21 or 22). For the remainder of this century the longest day will fall each year on June 21.

The date of the Solstice varies according to locality. If the Solstice falls on June 21 late in the day by Greenwich time, that day will be the longest of the year at Greenwich even though it may be by only a second of time or a fraction thereof, but it will be on June 22, local date, in Japan, and so June 22 will be the longest day there and at places in Eastern longitudes.

Leaving aside the question of locality, the date of the Solstice is also affected by the length of the Tropical Year, which is 365¼ days less about 11 minutes. If a Solstice happens late on June 21 in one year, it will be nearly six hours later in the next, *i.e.* early on June 22, and that will be the longest day. This delay of the Solstice is not permitted to continue because the extra day in Leap Year brings it back a day in the Calendar.

However, because of the 11 minutes above mentioned the additional day in Leap Year brings the Solstice back too far by 44 minutes, and the time of the Solstice in the Calendar is earlier as the century progresses. (In the year 2000 the Summer Solstice reaches its earliest date for 100 years, *i.e.*, June 21^d 02^h.) To remedy this the last year of a century is in most cases not a Leap Year, and the omission of the extra day puts the date of the Solstice later by about six hours too much, compensation for which is made by making the fourth centennial year a Leap Year.

Similar considerations apply to the day of the Winter Solstice, or the *Shortest Day* of the year. For the remainder of this century the shortest day will fall on Dec. 21 in two years of four and on Dec. 22 in the remaining two years. In the year 2000 the Winter Solstice reaches its earliest date, *i.e.*, Dec. 21^d 13^h. The difference due to locality also prevails in the same sense as for the longest day.

At Greenwich the Sun sets at its earliest by the clock about ten days before the shortest day, which is a circumstance that may require explanation. The daily change in the time of sunset is due in the first place to the Sun's movement southwards at this time of the year, which diminishes the interval between the Sun's transit, and its setting, and, secondly, because of the daily decrease of the Equation of Time which causes the time of Apparent noon to be continuously later, day by day, and so in a measure counteracts the first effect. The rates of change of these two quantities are not equal, nor are they uniform, but are such that their combination causes the date of earliest sunset to be Dec. 12 or 13 at Greenwich. In more southerly latitudes the effect of the movement of the Sun is less, and the change in the time of sunset depends on that of the Equation of Time to a greater degree, and the date of earliest sunset is earlier than it is at Greenwich.

The Equinox is the point at which the Sun crosses the Equator and day and night are of equal length all over the world. This occurs in March (Vernal Equinox—about March 21) and September (Autumnal Equinox—about September 21).

The Historical Year.—Before the year 1752, two Calendar systems were in use in England. The Civil or Legal Year began on March 25, while the Historical Year began on January 1. Thus the Civil or Legal date 1658 March 24, was the same day as 1659 March 24 Historical; and a date in that portion of the year is written as: March 24 165⅞, the lower figure showing the Historical year.

The New Year.—In England in the seventh century, and as late as the thirteenth, the year was reckoned from Christmas Day, but in the twelfth century the Anglican Church began the year with the Feast of The Annunciation of the Blessed Virgin (Lady Day) on March 25 and this practice was adopted generally in the fourteenth century. The Civil or Legal year in the British Dominions (exclusive of Scotland) began with "Lady Day" until 1751. But in and since 1752 the civil year has begun with Jan. 1. Certain dividends are still paid by the Bank of England on dates based on Old Style. New Year's Day in *Scotland* was changed from March 25 to Jan. 1 in 1600.

On the Continent of Europe Jan. 1 was adopted as the first day of the year by Venice in 1522, Germany in 1544, Spain, Portugal, and the Roman Catholic Netherlands in 1556, Prussia, Denmark and Sweden in 1559, France 1564, Lorraine 1579, Protestant Netherlands 1583, Russia 1725, and Tuscany 1751.

The Masonic Year.—Two dates are quoted in warrants, dispensations etc., issued by the United Grand Lodge of England, those for the current year being expressed as *Anno Domini* 1988—*Anno Lucis* 5988. This *Year of Light* is based on the Book of Genesis I: 3, the 4000 year difference being derived, in modified form, from *Ussher's Notation*, published in 1654, which place the Creation of the World in 4,004 B.C.

Regnal Years.—These are the years of a sovereign's reign, and each begins on the anniversary of his or her accession: *e.g.* Regnal year 37 of the present Queen begins on Feb. 6, 1988. The system was used for dating Acts of Parliament until 1962. Since 1962 Acts of Parliament have been dated by the calendar year. The *Summer Time Act* of 1925, for example, is quoted as 15 and 16 Geo. V. c. 64, because it became law in the session which extended over part of both of these regnal years. The regnal years of Edward VII began on January 22, which was the day of Queen Victoria's death in 1901, so that Acts passed in that reign are, in general, quoted with only one year number, but year 10 of the series ended on May 6, 1910, being the day on which King Edward died, and Acts of the Parliamentary Session 1910 are headed 10 Edw. VII. and 1 Geo. V.; Acts passed in 1936 were dated 1 Edw. VIII. and 1 Geo. VI.; Acts passed in 1952 were dated 16 Geo. VI. and 1 Elizabeth II.

Lord Mayor's Day.—The Lord Mayor of London was previously elected on the Feast of St. Simon and St. Jude (Oct. 28), and from the time of Edward I, at least, was presented to the King or to the Barons of the Exchequer on the following day, except that day be a Sunday. The day of election was altered to Oct. 16 in 1346, and after some further changes was fixed for Michaelmas Day in 1546, but the ceremonies of admittance and swearing-in of the Lord Mayor continued to take place on Oct. 28 and 29 respectively until 1751. In 1752, at the reform of the Calendar (*see* page 188), the Lord Mayor was continued in office until Nov. 8, the "New Style" equivalent of Oct. 28. The Lord Mayor is now presented to the Lord Chief Justice at the Royal Courts of Justice on the second Saturday in November to make the final declaration of office, having been sworn in at Guildhall on the preceding day.

Dog Days.—The days about the heliacal rising of the Dog Star, noted from ancient times as the hottest and most unwholesome period of the year in the Northern Hemisphere. Their incidence has been variously calculated as depending on the Greater or Lesser Dog Star (Sirius or Procyon) and their duration has been reckoned as from 30 to 54 days. A generally accepted period is from July 3 to Aug. 15.

Metonic (Lunar, or Minor) **Cycle.**—In the year 432 B.C. Meton, an Athenian astronomer, found that 235 Lunations are very nearly, though not exactly

equal in duration to 19 Solar Years, and, hence, after 19 years the Phases of the Moon recur on the same days of the month (nearly). The dates of Full Moon in a cycle of nineteen years were inscribed in *figures of gold* on public monuments in Athens, and the number showing the position of a year in the Cycle is called the **Golden Number** of that year.

Roman Indication.—A period of fifteen years, instituted for fiscal purposes about A.D. 300.

Solar (or Major) **Cycle.**—A period of twenty-eight years, in any corresponding year of which the days of the week recur on the same day of the month.

Julian Period.—Proposed by Joseph Scaliger in 1582. The period is 7980 Julian years, and its first year coincides with the year 4713 B.C. 7980 is the product of the number of years in the Solar Cycle, the Metonic Cycle and the cycle of the Roman Indication (28 × 19 × 15).

Epact.—The age of the calendar Moon, diminished by one day, on January 1, in the ecclesiastical lunar calendar.

THE FOUR SEASONS

Spring, the first season of the year, is defined astronomically to begin in the *Northern Hemisphere* at the Vernal Equinox when the Sun enters the sign Aries and to terminate at the Summer Solstice. In Great Britain, Spring in popular parlance comprises the months of February, March and April. In the *Southern Hemisphere* Spring corresponds with Autumn in the Northern Hemisphere.

Summer, the second and warmest season, begins astronomically at the Summer Solstice when the Sun enters the sign of Cancer. Summer terminates at the Autumnal Equinox. In popular parlance Summer in Great Britain includes the months of May, June, July and August, Midsummer Day being June 24.

Autumn, the third season, begins astronomically at the Autumnal Equinox when the Sun enters the sign Libra and ends at the Winter Solstice. In Great Britain it is popularly held to include the months of September and October. A warm period sometimes occurs round about St. Luke's Day (Oct. 18) and is known as "St. Luke's Summer." In the *Southern Hemisphere* it corresponds with Spring of the Northern.

Winter, the fourth and coldest season, begins astronomically at the Winter Solstice when the Sun enters the sign of Capricornus, and ends at the Vernal Equinox. In Great Britain the season is popularly held to comprise the months of November, December and January, mid-winter being marked by the Shortest Day. A warm period sometimes occurs round about Martinmas (Nov. 11) and is known as "St. Martin's Summer." In the *Southern Hemisphere* it corresponds with Summer of the Northern.

THE CHRISTIAN CALENDAR

In the Christian chronological system the years are distinguished by cardinal numbers before or after the Incarnation, the period being denoted by the letters B.C. (Before Christ) or, more rarely, A.C. (*Ante Christum*), and A.D. (*Anno Domini*—In the Year of Our Lord). The correlative dates of the epoch are the 4th year of the 194th Olympiad, the 753rd year from the Foundation of Rome, A.M. 3761 (Jewish Chronology), and the 4714th year of the Julian Period.

The system was introduced into Italy in the sixth century, and though first used in France in the seventh it was not universally established there until about the eighth century. It has been said that the system was introduced into England by St. Augustine (A.D. 596), but was probably not generally used until some centuries later. It was ordered to be used by the Bishops at the Council of Chelsea, A.D. 816. The actual date of the birth of Christ is somewhat uncertain.

The Julian Calendar.—In the Julian Calendar all the centennial years were Leap Years, and for this reason towards the close of the sixteenth century there was a difference of 10 days between the tropical and calendar years; the equinox fell on March 11 of the Calendar, whereas at the time of the Council of Nicaea, A.D. 325, it had fallen on March 21. In 1582 Pope Gregory ordained that Oct. 5th should be called Oct. 15th and that of the end-century years only the fourth should be a Leap Year (*see* p. 186).

The Gregorian Calendar was adopted by Italy, France, Spain, and Portugal in 1582; by Prussia, the German Roman Catholic States, Switzerland, Holland, and Flanders on Jan. 1, 1583, Poland 1586, Hungary 1587, the German and Netherland Protestant States and Denmark 1700, Sweden (gradually) by the omission of eleven leap days, 1700–1740; Great Britain and her Dominions (including the North American Colonies) in 1752, by the omission of eleven days (Sept. 3 being reckoned as Sept. 14). Japan adopted the calendar in 1872, China in 1912, Bulgaria in 1915, Turkey and Soviet Russia in 1918, Yugoslavia and Romania in 1919, and Greece in February, 1923.

In the same year that the change was made in England from the Julian to the Gregorian Calendar, the beginning of the new year was also changed from March 25 to January 1 (*see* p. 186).

The Orthodox Churches.—Some Orthodox Churches still use the Julian reckoning, but the majority of Greek Churches and the Romanian Orthodox Church have adopted a modified "New Calendar", observing the Gregorian Calendar for fixed feasts and the Julian for movable feasts.

The Orthodox Church year begins on September 1. There are four fast periods, and in addition to Pascha (Easter), twelve great feasts, as well as numerous commemorations of the Saints of the Old and New Testaments throughout the year.

The Dominical Letter is one of the letters A–G which are used to denote the Sundays in successive years. If the first day of the year is a Sunday the letter is A; if the second, B; the third, C; and so on. Leap year requires two letters, the first for Jan. 1—Feb. 29, the second for March 1—Dec. 31.

Epiphany.—The Feast of the Epiphany, commemorating the manifestation of Christ, later became associated with the offering of gifts by the Magi. The day was of exceptional importance from the time of the Council of Nicaea (A.D. 325) as the primate of Alexandria was charged at every Epiphany Feast with the announcement in a letter to the Churches of the date of the forthcoming Easter. The day was of considerable importance in Britain as it influenced dates, ecclesiastical and lay, *e.g.* **Plow Monday**, when work was resumed in the fields, falls upon the Monday in the first full week after the Epiphany.

Lent.—The Teutonic word *Lent*, which denotes the Fast preceding Easter, originally meant no more than the Spring season; but from Anglo-Saxon times, at least, it has been used as the equivalent of the more significant Latin term **Quadragesima**, meaning the "Forty Days" or, more literally, the fortieth day. As early as the fifth century some of the Fathers of the Church put forward the view that the forty days Fast is of Apostolic origin, but this is not supported or believed by modern scholars; and it appears to some that it dates from the early years of the fourth century. There is some suggestion that the Fast was kept originally for only forty hours. **Ash Wednesday** is the first day of Lent, which ends at midnight before Easter Day.

Sexagesima and Septuagesima.—It has been suggested that the unmeaning application of the names *Sexagesima* and *Septuagesima* to the second and third Sundays before Lent was made by analogy with the names *Quadragesima* and *Quinquagesima*. Another less likely conjecture is that *Septuagesima* means the seventh day before the Octave of Easter. It is not certain whether the name *Quinquagesima* is due to the fact that the Sunday in question is the fiftieth day before Easter (reckoned inclusive) or was simply formed on the analogy of *Quadragesima* (*New English Dictionary*).

Palm Sunday, the Sunday before Easter and the beginning of Holy Week, commemorates the triumphal entry of Christ into Jerusalem and is celebrated in Britain (when palm is not available) by branches of willow gathered for use in the decoration of churches on that day.

Maundy Thursday, the day before Good Friday, the name itself being a corruption of *dies mandati* (day of the mandate) when Christ washed the feet of the disciples and gave them the mandate to love one another.

Easter Day is the first Sunday after the full moon which happens upon, or next after, the 21st day of March; and if the full moon happens upon a Sunday, Easter-Day is the Sunday after. This definition is contained in an Act of Parliament (24 Geo. II., cap. 23), and explanation is given in the preamble to the Act that the day of Full Moon depends on certain tables that have been prepared. These are the tables whose essential points are given in the early pages of the Book of Common Prayer. The Moon referred to is not the real Moon of the heavens, but a hypothetical Moon on whose "Full" the date of Easter depends, and the lunations of this "Calendar" Moon consist of twenty-nine and thirty days alternately with certain necessary modifications to make the date of its Full agree as nearly as possible with that of the real Moon, which is known as the **Paschal Full Moon**. As at present ordained, Easter falls on one of 35 days— (March 22–April 25).

A Fixed Easter.—On June 15, 1928, the House of Commons agreed to a motion for the third reading of the Bill that Easter Day shall, in the Calendar year next but one after the commencement of the Act and in all subsequent years, be *the first Sunday after the second Saturday in April.* Easter would thus fall between April 9 and 15, both inclusive—that is, on the second or third Sunday in April. A clause in the Bill provided that before it shall come into operation regard shall be had to any opinion expressed officially by the various Christian Churches. Efforts by the

World Council of Churches to secure a unanimous choice of date for Easter by its member Churches have so far been unsuccessful.

Holy Days and Saints Days were the normal factors in early times for settling the dates of future and recurrent appointments, *e.g.* the **Quarter Days** in England and Wales are the Feast of the Nativity, the Feast of the Annunciation, the Feast of St. John the Baptist and the Feast of St. Michael and All the Holy Angels, while **Term Days** in Scotland are Candlemas (Feast of the Purification), Whitsunday (a fixed date), Lammas (Loaf Mass) and Martinmas (St. Martin's Day). **Law Sittings** in England and Wales commence on the Feast of St. Hilary and the term which begins on Old Michaelmas Day ends on the former feast of St. Thomas the Apostle.

Red Letter Days (*see also* p. 225) were Holy Days and Saints Days indicated in early ecclesiastical calendars by letters printed in red ink. The days to be distinguished in this way were finally approved at the Council of Nicaea, A.D. 325.

Rogation Days.—These are the Monday, Tuesday and Wednesday preceding Ascension Day (Holy Thursday) and in the fifth century were ordered by the Church to be observed as Public Fasts with solemn processions and supplications. The processions were discontinued as religious observances at the Reformation, but survive in the ceremony known as "Beating the Parish Bounds". **Rogation Sunday** is the Sunday before Ascension Day.

Ascension Day is forty days after Easter Day.

Ember Days.—The Ember Days at the Four Seasons are the Wednesday, Friday and Saturday before (*a*) the third Sunday in Advent, (*b*) the second Sunday in Lent, and (*c*) the Sundays nearest to the Festivals of St. Peter, and St. Michael and All Angels.

Whit Sunday or **Pentecost** is seven weeks after Easter Day. It is generally said that this name is a variant of White Sunday, and was so called from the albs or white robes of the newly baptized, but other derivations have been suggested.

Trinity Sunday is eight weeks after Easter Day, on the Sunday following Whit Sunday, and subsequent Sundays are sometimes reckoned in the Church of England as "after Trinity".

Thomas Becket (1118–1170) was consecrated Archbishop of Canterbury on the Sunday after Whit Sunday and his first act was to ordain that the day of his consecration should be held as a new festival in honour of the Holy Trinity. The observance thus originated spread from Canterbury throughout the whole of Christendom.

Advent Sunday is the Sunday nearest to St. Andrew's Day, Nov. 30, which allows three Sundays between Advent and Christmas Day in all cases. The Sunday preceding Advent is the 27th after Trinity if Easter falls on one of the days, March 22–26 inclusive. It is the 22nd after Trinity when Easter Day is on April 24 or 25. If the date of Easter were determined as proposed (*see Fixed Easter*) there would generally be 24 Sundays after Trinity, the number being 25 only in the years when Easter fell on April 9. With a Fixed Easter there would never be a sixth Sunday after Epiphany. There would be a fifth Sunday when Easter Day fell on April 15 or April 14, the year being a leap year.

A TABLE OF THE MOVABLE FEASTS TO THE YEAR 2000

Year	Ash Wednesday	Easter	Ascension	Whit Sunday	Sundays after Trinity	Advent
1983........	Feb. 16	April 3	May 12	May 22	xxv	Nov. 27
1984........	March 7	April 22	May 31	June 10	xxiii	Dec. 2
1985........	Feb. 20	April 7	May 16	May 26	xxv	Dec. 1
1986........	Feb. 12	March 30	May 8	May 18	xxvi	Nov. 30
1987........	March 4	April 19	May 28	June 7	xxiii	Nov. 29
1988........	Feb. 17	April 3	May 12	May 22	xxv	Nov. 27
1989........	Feb. 8	March 26	May 4	May 14	xxvii	Dec. 3
1990........	Feb. 28	April 15	May 24	June 3	xxiv	Dec. 2
1991........	Feb. 13	March 31	May 9	May 19	xxvi	Dec. 1
1992........	March 4	April 19	May 28	June 7	xxiii	Nov. 29
1993........	Feb. 24	April 11	May 20	May 30	xxiv	Nov. 28
1994........	Feb. 16	April 3	May 12	May 22	xxv	Nov. 27
1995........	March 1	April 16	May 25	June 4	xxiv	Dec. 3
1996........	Feb. 21	April 7	May 16	May 26	xxv	Dec. 1
1997........	Feb. 12	March 30	May 8	May 18	xxvi	Nov. 30
1998........	Feb. 25	April 12	May 21	May 31	xxiv	Nov. 29
1999........	Feb. 17	April 4	May 13	May 23	xxv	Nov. 28
2000........	March 8	April 23	June 1	June 11	xxiii	Dec. 3

NOTES CONCERNING TABLE OF MOVABLE FEASTS

Ash Wednesday (first day in Lent) can fall at earliest on February 4 and at latest on March 10.
Easter Day can fall at earliest on March 22 and at latest on April 25.
Ascension Day can fall at earliest on April 30 and at latest on June 3.
Whit Sunday can fall at earliest on May 10 and at latest on June 13.
Trinity Sunday is the Sunday next after *Whit Sunday*.
Corpus Christi falls on the Thursday next after *Trinity Sunday*.
There are not less than 22 and not more than 27 *Sundays after Trinity*.
Advent Sunday is the Sunday nearest to November 30.

A TABLE OF EASTER DAYS AND SUNDAY LETTERS, 1500 TO 2025

		1500—1599	1600—1699	1700—1799	1800—1899	1900—1999	2000—2025
d	Mar. 22	1573	1668	1761	1818		
e	„ 23	1505-16	1600	1788	1845-56	1913	2008
f	„ 24		1611-95	1706-99		1940	
g	„ 25	1543-54	1627-38-49	1722-33-44	1883-94	1951	
A	„ 26	1559-70-81-92	1654-65-76	1749-58-69-80	1815-26-37	1967-78-89	
b	Mar. 27	1502-13-24-97	1608-87-92	1785-96	1842-53-64	1910-21-32	2005-16
c	„ 28	1529-35-40	1619-24-30	1703-14-25	1869-75-80	1937-48	
d	„ 29	1551-62	1635-46-57	1719-30-41-52	1807-12-91	1959-64-70	
e	„ 30	1567-78-89	1651-62-73-84	1746-55-66-77	1823-34	1902-75-86-97	
f	„ 31	1510-21-32-83-94	1605-16-78-89	1700-71-82-93	1839-50-61-72	1907-18-29-91	2002-13-24
g	April 1	1526-37-48	1621-32	1711-16	1804-66-77-88	1923-34-45-56	2018
A	„ 2	1553-64	1643-48	1727-38-52(NS)	1809-20-93-99	1961-72	
b	„ 3	1575-80-86	1659-70-81	1743-63-68-74	1825-31-36	1904-83-88-94	
c	„ 4	1507-18-91	1602-13-75-86-97	1708-79-90	1847-58	1915-20-26-99	2010-21
d	„ 5	1523-34-45-56	1607-18-29-40	1702-13-24-95	1801-63-74-85-96	1931-42-53	2015
e	April 6	1539-50-61-72	1634-45-56	1729-35-40-60	1806-17-28-90	1947-58-69-80	
f	„ 7	1504-77-88	1667-72	1751-65-76	1822-33-44	1901-12-85-96	
g	„ 8	1509-15-20-99	1604-10-83-94	1705-87-92-98	1849-55-60	1917-28	2007-12
A	„ 9	1531-42	1615-26-37-99	1710-21-32	1871-82	1939-44-50	2023
b	„ 10	1547-58-69	1631-42-53-64	1726-37-48-57	1803-14-87-98	1955-66-77	
c	April 11	1501-12-63-74-85-96	1658-69-80	1762-73-84	1819-30-41-52	1909-71-82-93	2004
d	„ 12	1506-17-28	1601-12-91-96	1789	1846-57-68	1903-14-25-36-98	2009-20
e	„ 13	1533-44	1623-28	1707-18	1800-73-79-84	1941-52	
f	„ 14	1555-60-66	1639-50-61	1723-34-45-54	1805-11-16-95	1963-68-74	
g	„ 15	1571-82-93	1655-66-77-88	1750-59-70-81	1827-38	1900-06-79-90	2001
A	April 16	1503-14-25-36-87-98	1609-20-82-93	1704-75-86-97	1843-54-65-76	1911-22-33-95	2006-17
b	„ 17	1530-41-52	1625-36	1715-20	1808-70-81-92	1927-38-49-60	2022
c	„ 18	1557-68	1647-52	1731-42-56	1802-13-24-97	1954-65-76	
d	„ 19	1500-79-84-90	1663-74-85	1747-67-72-78	1829-35-40	1908-81-87-92	
e	„ 20	1511-22-95	1606-17-79-90	1701-12-83-94	1851-62	1919-24-30	2003-14-25
f	April 21	1527-38-49	1622-33-44	1717-28	1867-78-89	1935-46-57	2019
g	„ 22	1565-76	1660	1739-53-64	1810-21-32	1962-73-84	
A	„ 23	1508	1671		1848	1905-16	2000
b	„ 24	1519	1603-14-98	1709-91	1859		2011
c	„ 25	1546	1641	1736	1886	1943	

THE JEWISH CALENDAR

Origin.—The story in the Book of Genesis that the Flood began on the seventeenth day of the second month; that after the end of 150 days the waters were abated; and that on the seventeenth day of the seventh month the Ark rested on Mount Ararat, indicates a calendar of some kind and that the writers recognized 30 days as the length of a lunation. There is other mention of months by their original numbers in the Book of Genesis and in establishing the rite of the Passover Moses spoke of *Abib* as the month when the Israelites came out from Egypt and Abib was to be the first month of the year. In the first Book of Kings three months are mentioned by name, Zif the second month, Ethanim the seventh and Bul the eighth, but these are not names now in use. After the Dispersion, Jewish communities were left in considerable doubt as to the times of Fasts and Festivals, and this led to the formation of the Jewish Calendar as used to-day, which, it is said, was done in A.D. 358 by Rabbi Hillel II, a descendant of Gamaliel—though some assert that it did not happen until much later. This calendar is luni-solar, and is based on the lengths of the lunation and of the tropical year as found by Hipparchus (*Circ.* 120 B.C.) which differ little from those adopted at the present day. The year 5748 A.D. (1987–88) is the 10th year of the 304th *Metonic* (Minor or Lunar) *Cycle* of 19 years and the 8th year of the 207th *Solar* (or Major) *Cycle* of 28 years since the Era of the Creation, which the Jews hold to have occurred at the time of the Autumnal Equinox in the year known in the Christian Calendar as 3760 B.C. (954 of the Julian Period) and the epoch or starting point of Jewish Chronology corresponds to Oct. 7, 3761 B.C. At the beginning of each Solar Cycle the *Teku ah* of Nisan (the vernal equinox) returns to the same day and to the same hour.

The hour is divided into 1080 *minims* and the month between one new moon and the next is reckoned as 29 days, 12 hours, 793 minims. The normal calendar year, called a Common Regular year, consists of 12 months of 30 days and 29 days alternately. Since 12 months such as these comprise only 354 days, in order that each of them shall not diverge greatly from an average place in the solar year, a thirteenth month is occasionally added after the fifth month of the Civil year (which commences on the first day of the month Tishri), or as the penultimate month of the Ecclesiastical (which commences on the first day of month Nisan), the years when this happens being called Embolismic or Leap years. Of the 19 years that form a Metonic cycle, 7 are leap years; they occur at places in the cycle indicated by the numbers 3, 6, 8, 11, 14, 17, 19, these places being chosen so that the accumulated excesses of the solar years should be as small as possible. The first of each month is called the day of New Moon, though it is not necessarily the day of astronomical New Moon, that being the day on which conjunction of Sun and Moon occurs, but there is generally a difference of a day or two. In practice, in a month which follows one of 30 days, the day preceding its first day is also observed as a day of New Moon. The dates on which the first days of the months fall depend on that of the first of Tishri, which therefore controls the dates of fasts and festivals in the Jewish year. For certain ceremonial reasons connected with these, the first of Tishri must not fall on a Sunday, Wednesday or Friday, and if this should happen as the result of the computation it is postponed to the following day. Also, if the New Moon of Tishri falls on any day of the week at noon or later than noon, then the following day is to be taken for the celebration of that New Moon and is Tishri 1, provided that it is not one of the forbidden days, in which case there is a further postponement of a day. These rules and others have been considered in detail, and finally a calendar scheme has been drawn up in which a Jewish year is of one of the following six types: Minimal Common (353 days), Regular Common (354 days), Full Common (355 days), Minimal Leap (383 days), Regular Leap (384 days), or Full Leap (385 days).

The Regular year has an alternation of 30 and 29 days. In a full year, whether Common or Leap, Marcheshvan, the second month of the Civil year, has 30 days instead of 29; in Minimal years Kislev, the third month, has 29 instead of 30. The additional month in Leap years which is called Adar I., and precedes the month called Adar in Common years and Adar II., or Ve-Adar, in Leap, always has 30 days, but neither this, nor the other variations mentioned, is allowed to change the number of days in the other months which still follow the alternation of the normal twelve. In Leap years the month intercalated precedes Adar and usurps its name, but the usual Adar festivals are kept in Ve-Adar.

These are the main features of the Jewish Calendar which must be considered permanent, because as a Jewish law it cannot be altered except by a great Synhedrion.

The Jewish day begins between sunset and night-fall. The time used is that of the meridian of Jerusalem, which is $2h. 21m.$ in advance of Greenwich Mean Time. Rules for the beginning of Sabbaths and Festivals were laid down for the latitude of London in the eighteenth century and hours for nightfall are now fixed annually by the Chief Rabbi.

Jewish Calendar 5748–49

Jewish Month					A.M. 5748				A.M. 5749	
Tishri	1	..	..	..	1987	September 24	..	..	1988	September 12
Marcheshvan	1	..	..	..		October 24	..	..		October 12
Kislev	1	..	..	..		November 22	..	..		November 10
Tebet	1	..	..	..		December 22	..	..		December 9
Shebat	1	..	..	..	1988	January 20	..	..	1989	January 7
Adar	1	..	..	..		February 19	..	..		February 6
Ve-Adar	1	..	..	..			..	..		March 8
Nisan	1	..	..	..		March 19	..	..		April 6
Iyar	1	..	..	..		April 18	..	..		May 6
Sivan	1	..	..	..		May 17	..	..		June 4
Tammuz	1	..	..	..		June 16	..	..		July 4
Ab	1	..	..	..		July 15	..	..		August 2
Elul	1	..	..	..		August 14	..	..		September 1

A.M. 5748 (748) is a Regular Common Year of 12 months, 51 Sabbaths and 354 days. A.M. 5749 (749) is a Minimal Leap Year of 13 months, 53 Sabbaths and 383 days.

Jewish Fasts and Festivals

Tishri	1	Rosh Hoshanah (New Year).	Tebet	10	Fast of Tebet.
,,	3	*Fast of Gedaliah.	Ve-Adar	13	§Fast of Esther.
,,	10	Yom Kippur (Day of Atonement).	,, ,,	14	Purim.
,,	15–22	Succoth (Feast of Tabernacles).	,, ,,	15	Shushan Purim.
,,	21	Hoshana Rabba.	Nisan	15–22	Passover.
,,	22	Solemn Assembly.	Sivan	6 and 7	Shavuot (Pentecost or Feast of Weeks).
,,	23	Rejoicing of the Law.	Tammuz	17	*Fast of Tammuz.
Kislev	25	Dedication of the Temple	Ab	9	*Fast of Ab.

NOTES.—* If these dates fall on the Sabbath the Fast is kept on the following day.
§ This fast is observed on Adar 11 (or Ve-Adar 11 in Leap years) if Adar 13 falls on a Sabbath.

THE ROMAN CALENDAR

Roman historians adopted as an epoch the Foundation of Rome, which is believed to have happened in the year 753 B.C., and the ordinal number of the years in Roman reckoning is followed by the letters A.U.C. (*Ab Urbe Condita*), so that the year 1988 is 2741 A.U.C. (MMDCCXLI). The Calendar that we know has developed from one established by Romulus, who is said to have used a year of 304 days divided into ten months, beginning with March, to which Numa added January and February, making the year consist of 12 months of 30 and 29 days alternately, with an additional day so that the total was 355. It is also said that Numa ordered an intercalary month of 22 or 23 days in alternate years, making 90 days in eight years, to be inserted after Feb. 23, but there is some doubt as to the origination and the details of the intercalation in the Roman Calendar, though it is certain that some scheme of this kind was inaugurated and not fully carried out, for in the year 46 B.C. Julius Cæsar, who was then Pontifex Maximus,

found that the Calendar had been allowed to fall into some confusion. He therefore sought the help of the Egyptian astronomer Sosigenes, which led to the construction and adoption (45 B.C.) of the Julian Calendar, and, by a slight alteration, to the Gregorian now in use. The year 46 B.C. was made to consist of 445 days, and is called the *Year of Confusion.* In the Roman (Julian) Calendar the days of the month were counted backwards from three fixed points, or days, and an intervening day was said to be so many days *before* the next coming point, the first *and* last being counted. These three points were (*a*) the Kalends; (*b*) the Nones; and (*c*) the Ides. Their positions in the months and the method of counting from them will be seen in the table below. The year containing 366 days was called *bissextillis annus,* as it had a doubled sixth day (*bissextus dies*) before the March Kalends on Feb. 24—*ante diem sextum Kalendas Martias,* or VI Kal. Mart.

Present Days of the Month	March, May, July, October have thirty-one days	January, August, December have thirty-one days	April, June, September, November have thirty days	February has twenty-eight days, and in Leap Year twenty-nine
1	Kalendis.	Kalendis.	Kalendis.	Kalendis.
2	VI.⎱ Ante	IV.⎱ Ante	IV.⎱ Ante	IV.⎱ Ante
3	V.⎰ Nonas.	III.⎰ Nonas.	III.⎰ Nonas.	III.⎰ Nonas.
4	IV. Nonas.	Pridie Nonas.	Pridie Nonas.	Pridie Nonas.
5	III.	Nonis.	Nonis.	Nonis.
6	Pridie Nonas.	VIII.	VIII.	VIII.
7	Nonis.	VII.	VII.	VII.
8	VIII.	VI. Ante	VI. Ante	VI. Ante
9	VII.	V. Idus.	V. Idus.	V. Idus.
10	VI. Ante	IV.	IV.	IV.
11	V. Idus.	III.	III.	III.
12	IV.	Pridie Idus.	Pridie Idus.	Pridie Idus.
13	III.	Idibus.	Idibus.	Idibus.
14	Pridie Idus.	XIX.	XVIII.	XVI.
15	Idibus.	XVIII.	XVII.	XV.
16	XVII.	XVII.	XVI.	XIV.
17	XVI.	XVI.	XV.	XIII.
18	XV.	XV.	XIV.	XII.
19	XIV.	XIV.	XIII.	XI.
20	XIII. (of the month following).	XIII. (of the month following).	XII. (of the month following).	X. Ante Kalendas Martias.
21	XII.	XII.	XI.	IX.
22	XI.	XI.	X.	VIII.
23	X.	X.	IX.	VII.
24	IX. Ante Kalendas	IX. Ante Kalendas	VIII. Ante Kalendas	VI.
25	VIII.	VIII.	VII.	V.
26	VII.	VII.	VI.	IV.
27	VI.	VI.	V.	III.
28	V.	V.	IV.	Pridie Kalendas Martias.
29	IV.	IV.	III.	
30	III.	III.	Pridie Kalendas (of the month following).	
31	Pridie Kalendas (of the month following).	Pridie Kalendas (of the month following).		

ROMAN NUMERALS

1	I	9	IX	17	XVII	70	LXX	600	DC
2	II	10	X	18	XVIII	80	LXXX	700	DCC
3	III	11	XI	19	XIX	90	XC	800	DCCC
4	IV	12	XII	20	XX	100	C	900	CM
5	V	13	XIII	30	XXX	200	CC	1000	M
6	VI	14	XIV	40	XL	300	CCC	1500	MD
7	VII	15	XV	50	L	400	CD	1900	MCM
8	VIII	16	XVI	60	LX	500	D	2000	MM

Other Examples: 43 = XLIII; 66 = LXVI; 98 = XCVIII.
339 = CCCXXXIX; 619 = DCXIX; 988 = CMLXXXVIII; 996 = CMXCVI.
1674 = MDCLXXIV; 1962 = MCMLXII; 1988 = MCMLXXXVIII.
A bar placed over a numeral has the effect of multiplying the number by 1,000, *e.g.*:

6,000 = V̄I; 16,000 = X̄V̄I; 160,000 = C̄LX; 666,000 = D̄C̄LXVI.

THE MOSLEM CALENDAR

The basic date of the Moslem Calendar is the *Hejira*, or Flight of Muhammad from Mecca to Medina, the corresponding date of which is A.D. 622, July 16, in the Julian Calendar. Hejira years are used principally in Iran, Turkey, Egypt, in various Arabian states, in certain parts of India and in Malaysia. The system was adopted about A.D. 632, commencing from the first day of the month preceding the Hejira. The years are purely lunar and consist of 12 months containing in alternate sequence 30 or 29 days, with the intercalation of one day at the end of the 12th month at stated intervals in each cycle of 30 years, the object of the intercalation being to reconcile the date of the first of the month with the date of the actual New Moon. Some adherents still take the date of the evening of the first visibility of the crescent as that of the first of the month. In each cycle of 30 years 19 are common and contain 354 days and 11 are intercalary (355 days), the latter being called *kabishah*.

The mean length of the Hejira year is 354 days, 8 hours, 48 minutes and the period of mean lunation is 29 days, 12 hours, 44 minutes.

To ascertain if a Hejira year is common or *kabishah* divide it by 30; the quotient gives the number of completed cycles and the remainder shows the place of the year in the current cycle. If the remainder is 2, 5, 7, 10, 13, 16, 18, 21, 24, 26 or 29 the year is *kabishah* and consists of 355 days.

Hejira year A.H. 1408 (remainder 28) is a common year and A.H. 1409 (remainder 29) is a *kabishah* year.

Hejira Years 1408 and 1409

Name and Length of Month	A.H. 1408		A.H. 1409	
Muharram (30)......1987	Aug.	26	1988 Aug.	14
Safar (29)...........	Sept.	25	Sept.	13
Rabia I (30)	Oct.	24	Oct.	12
Rabia II (29)	Nov.	23	Nov.	11
Jumâda I (30)	Dec.	22	Dec.	10
Jumâda II (29)	Jan.	21	1989 Jan.	9
Rajab (30)	Feb.	19	Feb.	7
Shaabân (29)........	Mar.	20	Mar.	9
Ramadân (30)	April	18	April	7
Shawwâl (29)	May	18	May	7
Dhû'l-Qa'da (30).....	June	16	June	5
Dhû'l-Hijja (29 or 30)	July	16	July	5

OTHER EPOCHS AND CALENDARS

China.—Until the year A.D. 1911 a lunar calendar was in force in China, but with the establishment of the Republic the Government adopted the Gregorian Calendar, and the new and old systems were used simultaneously by the people for several years. Since 1930 the publication and use of the old Calendar have been banned by the Government, and an official Chinese Calendar, corresponding with the European or Western system, is compiled, but the old lunar calendar is still in use to some extent in China. The old Chinese Calendar, with a cycle of 60 years, is still in use in Tibet, Hong Kong, Singapore, Malaysia and elsewhere in South-East Asia.

Ethiopia.—In the Coptic Calendar, which is used by part of the population of Egypt and Ethiopia, the year is made up of 12 months of 30 days each, followed, in general, by 5 complementary days. Every fourth year is an Intercalary or Leap year and in these years there are 6 complementary days. The Intercalary year of the Coptic Calendar immediately precedes the Leap year of the Julian Calendar. The Era is that of Diocletian or the Martyrs, the origin of which is fixed at A.D. 284, Aug. 29 (Julian date).

Greece.—Ancient Greek chronology was reckoned in *Olympiads*, cycles of 4 years corresponding with the periodic Olympic Games held on the plain of Olympia in Elis once in 4 years, the intervening years being the first, second, etc., of the Olympiad which received the name of the victor at the Games. The first recorded Olympiad is that of Choroebus, 776 B.C.

India.—In addition to the Moslem reckoning there are six eras used in India. The principal astronomical system was the *Kaliyuga Era*, which appears to have been adopted in the fourth century A.D. It began on Feb. 18, 3102 B.C. The chronological system of Northern India, known as the *Vikrama Samvat Era*, prevalent in Western India, began on Feb. 23, 57 B.C. The year A.D. 1988 is, therefore, the year 2045 of the Vikrama Era.

The *Saka Era* of Southern India dating from March 3, A.D. 78, was declared the uniform national calendar of the Republic of India with effect from March 22, 1957, to be used concurrently with the Gregorian Calendar. As revised, the year of the new *Saka Era*

begins at the spring equinox, with five successive months of 31 days and seven of 30 days in ordinary years; six months of each length in leap years. The year A.D. 1988 is 1910 of the revised *Saka Era*.

In the Hills, the *Saptarshi Era* dates from the moment when the Saptarshi, or saints, were translated and became the stars of the Great Bear in 3076 B.C.

The *Buddhists* reckoned from the death of Buddha in 543 B.C. (the actual date being 487 B.C.); and the epoch of the *Jains* was the death of Vardhamana, the founder of their faith, in 527 B.C.

Iran.—The chronology of Iran is the Era of Hejira, which began on A.D. 622, July 16. The *Zoroastrian Calendar* was used in pre-Moslem days and is still employed by Zoroastrians in Iran and India (Parsees) with era beginning A.D. 632, June 16.

Japan.—The Japanese Calendar is the Gregorian, and is essentially the same as that in use by Western nations, the years, months and weeks being of the same length and beginning on the same days as those of the Western Calendar. The numeration of the years is different, for Japanese chronology is based on a system of epochs or periods, each of which begins at the accession of an Emperor or other important occurrence, the method being not unlike the former British system of Regnal years, but differing from it in the particular that each year of a period closes on Dec. 31. The Japanese scheme begins about A.D. 650 and the three latest epochs are defined by the reigns of Emperors, whose actual names are not necessarily used:

Epoch Meiji	from 1868 Oct. 13 to 1912 July 31	
„ Taishō	„ 1912 Aug. 1 to 1926 Dec. 25	
„ Shōwa	„ 1926 Dec. 26	

Hence the year Shōwa 63 begins 1988 Jan. 1. The months are not named. They are known as First Month, Second Month, etc., first month being the equivalent to January. The days of the week are Nichiyōbi (Sun-day), Getsuyōbi (Moon-day), Kayōbi (Fire-day), Suiyōbi (Water-day), Mokuyōbi (Wood-day), Kinyōbi (Metal-day), Doyōbi (Earth-day).

for any year between 1770 and 2025 together with the dates of Easter in each of those years.
To select the correct calendar for any year consult the Index below

INDEX TO CALENDARS

Year		Year		Year		Year		Year		Year	
1770	C	1813	K	1856	F*	1899	A	1942	I	1985	E
1771	E	1814	M	1857	I	1900	C	1943	K	1986	G
1772	H*	1815	A	1858	K	1901	E	1944	N*	1987	I
1773	K	1816	D*	1859	M	1902	G	1945	C	1988	L*
1774	M	1817	G	1860	B*	1903	I	1946	E	1989	A
1775	A	1818	I	1861	E	1904	L*	1947	G	1990	C
1776	D*	1819	K	1862	G	1905	A	1948	J*	1991	E
1777	G	1820	N*	1863	I	1906	C	1949	M	1992	H*
1778	I	1821	C	1864	L*	1907	E	1950	A	1993	K
1779	K	1822	E	1865	A	1908	H*	1951	C	1994	M
1780	N*	1823	G	1866	C	1909	K	1952	F*	1995	A
1781	C	1824	J*	1867	E	1910	M	1953	I	1996	D*
1782	E	1825	M	1868	H*	1911	A	1954	K	1997	G
1783	G	1826	A	1869	K	1912	D*	1955	M	1998	I
1784	J*	1827	C	1870	M	1913	G	1956	B*	1999	K
1785	M	1828	F*	1871	A	1914	I	1957	E	2000	N*
1786	A	1829	I	1872	D*	1915	K	1958	G	2001	C
1787	C	1830	K	1873	G	1916	N*	1959	I	2002	E
1788	F*	1831	M	1874	I	1917	C	1960	L*	2003	G
1789	I	1832	B*	1875	K	1918	E	1961	A	2004	J*
1790	K	1833	E	1876	N*	1919	G	1962	C	2005	M
1791	M	1834	G	1877	C	1920	J*	1963	E	2006	A
1792	B*	1835	I	1878	E	1921	M	1964	H*	2007	C
1793	E	1836	L*	1879	G	1922	A	1965	K	2008	F*
1794	G	1837	A	1880	J*	1923	C	1966	M	2009	I
1795	I	1838	C	1881	M	1924	F*	1967	A	2010	K
1796	L*	1839	E	1882	A	1925	I	1968	D*	2011	M
1797	A	1840	H*	1883	C	1926	K	1969	G	2012	B*
1798	C	1841	K	1884	F*	1927	M	1970	I	2013	E
1799	E	1842	M	1885	I	1928	B*	1971	K	2014	G
1800	G	1843	A	1886	K	1929	E	1972	N*	2015	I
1801	I	1844	D*	1887	M	1930	G	1973	C	2016	L*
1802	K	1845	G	1888	B*	1931	I	1974	E	2017	A
1803	M	1846	I	1889	E	1932	L*	1975	G	2018	C
1804	B*	1847	K	1890	G	1933	A	1976	J*	2019	E
1805	E	1848	N*	1891	I	1934	C	1977	M	2020	H*
1806	G	1849	C	1892	L*	1935	E	1978	A	2021	K
1807	I	1850	E	1893	A	1936	H*	1979	C	2022	M
1808	L*	1851	G	1894	C	1937	K	1980	F*	2023	A
1809	A	1852	J*	1895	E	1938	M	1981	I	2024	D*
1810	C	1853	M	1896	H*	1939	A	1982	K	2025	G
1811	E	1854	A	1897	K	1940	D*	1983	M		
1812	H*	1855	C	1898	M	1941	G	1984	B*		

* Leap Year

A

	January	May	September
Su.	1 8 15 22 29	7 14 21 28	3 10 17 24
M.	2 9 16 23 30	1 8 15 22 29	4 11 18 25
Tu.	3 10 17 24 31	2 9 16 23 30	5 12 19 26
W.	4 11 18 25	3 10 17 24 31	6 13 20 27
Th.	5 12 19 26	4 11 18 25	7 14 21 28
F.	6 13 20 27	5 12 19 26	1 8 15 22 29
S.	7 14 21 28	6 13 20 27	2 9 16 23 30

	February	June	October
Su.	5 12 19 26	4 11 18 25	1 8 15 22 29
M.	6 13 20 27	5 12 19 26	2 9 16 23 30
Tu.	7 14 21 28	6 13 20 27	3 10 17 24 31
W.	1 8 15 22	7 14 21 28	4 11 18 25
Th.	2 9 16 23	1 8 15 22 29	5 12 19 26
F.	3 10 17 24	2 9 16 23 30	6 13 20 27
S.	4 11 18 25	3 10 17 24	7 14 21 28

	March	July	November
Su.	5 12 19 26	2 9 16 23 30	5 12 19 26
M.	6 13 20 27	3 10 17 24 31	6 13 20 27
Tu.	7 14 21 28	4 11 18 25	7 14 21 28
W.	1 8 15 22 29	5 12 19 26	1 8 15 22 29
Th.	2 9 16 23 30	6 13 20 27	2 9 16 23 30
F.	3 10 17 24 31	7 14 21 28	3 10 17 24
S.	4 11 18 25	1 8 15 22 29	4 11 18 25

	April	August	December
Su.	2 9 16 23 30	6 13 20 27	3 10 17 24 31
M.	3 10 17 24	7 14 21 28	4 11 18 25
Tu.	4 11 18 25	1 8 15 22 29	5 12 19 26
W.	5 12 19 26	2 9 16 23 30	6 13 20 27
Th.	6 13 20 27	3 10 17 24 31	7 14 21 28
F.	7 14 21 28	4 11 18 25	1 8 15 22 29
S.	1 8 15 22 29	5 12 19 26	2 9 16 23 30

Easter Days

March 26.	1815 1826 1837 1967 1978 1989.
April 2.	1809 1893 1899 1961.
April 9.	1871 1882 1939 1950 2023.
April 16.	1775 1786 1797 1843 1854 1865 1911
April 23.	1905. [1922 1933 1995 2006 2017.

B (Leap year)

	January	May	September
Su.	1 8 15 22 29	6 13 20 27	2 9 16 23 30
M.	2 9 16 23 30	7 14 21 28	3 10 17 24
Tu.	3 10 17 24 31	1 8 15 22 29	4 11 18 25
W.	4 11 18 25	2 9 16 23 30	5 12 19 26
Th.	5 12 19 26	3 10 17 24 31	6 13 20 27
F.	6 13 20 27	4 11 18 25	7 14 21 28
S.	7 14 21 28	5 12 19 26	1 8 15 22 29

	February	June	October
Su.	5 12 19 26	3 10 17 24	7 14 21 28
M.	6 13 20 27	4 11 18 25	1 8 15 22 29
Tu.	7 14 21 28	5 12 19 26	2 9 16 23 30
W.	1 8 15 22 29	6 13 20 27	3 10 17 24 31
Th.	2 9 16 23	7 14 21 28	4 11 18 25
F.	3 10 17 24	1 8 15 22 29	5 12 19 26
S.	4 11 18 25	2 9 16 23 30	6 13 20 27

	March	July	November
Su.	4 11 18 25	1 8 15 22 29	4 11 18 25
M.	5 12 19 26	2 9 16 23 30	5 12 19 26
Tu.	6 13 20 27	3 10 17 24 31	6 13 20 27
W.	7 14 21 28	4 11 18 25	7 14 21 28
Th.	1 8 15 22 29	5 12 19 26	1 8 15 22 29
F.	2 9 16 23 30	6 13 20 27	2 9 16 23 30
S.	3 10 17 24 31	7 14 21 28	3 10 17 24

	April	August	December
Su.	1 8 15 22 29	5 12 19 26	2 9 16 23 30
M.	2 9 16 23 30	6 13 20 27	3 10 17 24 31
Tu.	3 10 17 24	7 14 21 28	4 11 18 25
W.	4 11 18 25	1 8 15 22 29	5 12 19 26
Th.	5 12 19 26	2 9 16 23 30	6 13 20 27
F.	6 13 20 27	3 10 17 24 31	7 14 21 28
S.	7 14 21 28	4 11 18 25	1 8 15 22 29

Easter Days

April 1.	1804 1888 1956.
April 8.	1792 1860 1928 2012.
April 22.	1832 1984.

C

	January	May	September
Su.	7 14 21 28	6 13 20 27	2 9 16 23 30
M.	1 8 15 22 29	7 14 21 28	3 10 17 24
Tu.	2 9 16 23 30	1 8 15 22 29	4 11 18 25
W.	3 10 17 24 31	2 9 16 23 30	5 12 19 26
Th.	4 11 18 25	3 10 17 24 31	6 13 20 27
F.	5 12 19 26	4 11 18 25	7 14 21 28
S.	6 13 20 27	5 12 19 26	1 8 15 22 29

	February	June	October
Su.	4 11 18 25	3 10 17 24	7 14 21 28
M.	5 12 19 26	4 11 18 25	1 8 15 22 29
Tu.	6 13 20 27	5 12 19 26	2 9 16 23 30
W.	7 14 21 28	6 13 20 27	3 10 17 24 31
Th.	1 8 15 22	7 14 21 28	4 11 18 25
F.	2 9 16 23	1 8 15 22 29	5 12 19 26
S.	3 10 17 24	2 9 16 23 30	6 13 20 27

	March	July	November
Su.	4 11 18 25	1 8 15 22 29	4 11 18 25
M.	5 12 19 26	2 9 16 23 30	5 12 19 26
Tu.	6 13 20 27	3 10 17 24 31	6 13 20 27
W.	7 14 21 28	4 11 18 25	7 14 21 28
Th.	1 8 15 22 29	5 12 19 26	1 8 15 22 29
F.	2 9 16 23 30	6 13 20 27	2 9 16 23 30
S.	3 10 17 24 31	7 14 21 28	3 10 17 24

	April	August	December
Su.	1 8 15 22 29	5 12 19 26	2 9 16 23 30
M.	2 9 16 23 30	6 13 20 27	3 10 17 24 31
Tu.	3 10 17 24	7 14 21 28	4 11 18 25
W.	4 11 18 25	1 8 15 22 29	5 12 19 26
Th.	5 12 19 26	2 9 16 23 30	6 13 20 27
F.	6 13 20 27	3 10 17 24 31	7 14 21 28
S.	7 14 21 28	1 8 15 22 29	1 8 15 22 29

Easter Days

March 25.	1883	1894	1951.			
April 1.	1866	1877	1923	1934	1945	2018.
April 8.	1787	1798	1849	1855	1917	2007.
April 15.	1770	1781	1827	1838	1900	1906 1979
April 22.	1810	1821	1962	1973.	[1990	2001.

D (Leap year)

	January	May	September
Su.	7 14 21 28	5 12 19 26	1 8 15 22 29
M.	1 8 15 22 29	6 13 20 27	2 9 16 23 30
Tu.	2 9 16 23 30	7 14 21 28	3 10 17 24
W.	3 10 17 24 31	1 8 15 22 29	4 11 18 25
Th.	4 11 18 25	2 9 16 23 30	5 12 19 26
F.	5 12 19 26	3 10 17 24 31	6 13 20 27
S.	6 13 20 27	4 11 18 25	7 14 21 28

	February	June	October
Su.	4 11 18 25	2 9 16 23 30	6 13 20 27
M.	5 12 19 26	3 10 17 24	7 14 21 28
Tu.	6 13 20 27	4 11 18 25	1 8 15 22 29
W.	7 14 21 28	5 12 19 26	2 9 16 23 30
Th.	1 8 15 22 29	6 13 20 27	3 10 17 24 31
F.	2 9 16 23	7 14 21 28	4 11 18 25
S.	3 10 17 24	1 8 15 22 29	5 12 19 26

	March	July	November
Su.	3 10 17 24 31	7 14 21 28	3 10 17 24
M.	4 11 18 25	1 8 15 22 29	4 11 18 25
Tu.	5 12 19 26	2 9 16 23 30	5 12 19 26
W.	6 13 20 27	3 10 17 24 31	6 13 20 27
Th.	7 14 21 28	4 11 18 25	7 14 21 28
F.	1 8 15 22 29	5 12 19 26	1 8 15 22 29
S.	2 9 16 23 30	6 13 20 27	2 9 16 23 30

	April	August	December
Su.	7 14 21 28	4 11 18 25	1 8 15 22 29
M.	1 8 15 22 29	5 12 19 26	2 9 16 23 30
Tu.	2 9 16 23 30	6 13 20 27	3 10 17 24 31
W.	3 10 17 24	7 14 21 28	4 11 18 25
Th.	4 11 18 25	1 8 15 22 29	5 12 19 26
F.	5 12 19 26	2 9 16 23 30	6 13 20 27
S.	6 13 20 27	3 10 17 24 31	7 14 21 28

Easter Days

March 24	1940.			
March 31.	1872	2024.		
April 7.	1776	1844	1912	1996.
April 14.	1816	1968.		

E

	January	May	September
Su.	6 13 20 27	5 12 19 26	1 8 15 22 29
M.	7 14 21 28	6 13 20 27	2 9 16 23 30
Tu.	1 8 15 22 29	7 14 21 28	3 10 17 24
W.	2 9 16 23 30	1 8 15 22 29	4 11 18 25
Th.	3 10 17 24 31	2 9 16 23 30	5 12 19 26
F.	4 11 18 25	3 10 17 24 31	6 13 20 27
S.	5 12 19 26	4 11 18 25	7 14 21 28

	February	June	October
Su.	3 10 17 24	2 9 16 23 30	6 13 20 27
M.	4 11 18 25	3 10 17 24	7 14 21 28
Tu.	5 12 19 26	4 11 18 25	1 8 15 22 29
W.	6 13 20 27	5 12 19 26	2 9 16 23 30
Th.	7 14 21 28	6 13 20 27	3 10 17 24 31
F.	1 8 15 22	7 14 21 28	4 11 18 25
S.	2 9 16 23	1 8 15 22 29	5 12 19 26

	March	July	November
Su.	3 10 17 24 31	7 14 21 28	3 10 17 24
M.	4 11 18 25	1 8 15 22 29	4 11 18 25
Tu.	5 12 19 26	2 9 16 23 30	5 12 19 26
W.	6 13 20 27	3 10 17 24 31	6 13 20 27
Th.	7 14 21 28	4 11 18 25	7 14 21 28
F.	1 8 15 22 29	5 12 19 26	1 8 15 22 29
S.	2 9 16 23 30	6 13 20 27	2 9 16 23 30

	April	August	December
Su.	7 14 21 28	4 11 18 25	1 8 15 22 29
M.	1 8 15 22 29	5 12 19 26	2 9 16 23 30
Tu.	2 9 16 23 30	6 13 20 27	3 10 17 24 31
W.	3 10 17 24	7 14 21 28	4 11 18 25
Th.	4 11 18 25	1 8 15 22 29	5 12 19 26
F.	5 12 19 26	2 9 16 23 30	6 13 20 27
S.	6 13 20 27	3 10 17 24 31	7 14 21 28

Easter Days

March 24.	1799.		[1918	1929	1991	2002	2013.
March 31.	1771	1782	1793	1839	1850	1861	1907
April 7.	1822	1833	1901	1985.			
April 14.	1805	1811	1895	1963	1974.		
April 21.	1867	1878	1889	1935	1946	1957	2019.

F (Leap year)

	January	May	September
Su.	6 13 20 27	4 11 18 25	7 14 21 28
M.	7 14 21 28	5 12 19 26	1 8 15 22 29
Tu.	1 8 15 22 29	6 13 20 27	2 9 16 23 30
W.	2 9 16 23 30	7 14 21 28	3 10 17 24
Th.	3 10 17 24 31	1 8 15 22 29	4 11 18 25
F.	4 11 18 25	2 9 16 23 30	5 12 19 26
S.	5 12 19 26	3 10 17 24 31	6 13 20 27

	February	June	October
Su.	3 10 17 24	1 8 15 22 29	5 12 19 26
M.	4 11 18 25	2 9 16 23 30	6 13 20 27
Tu.	5 12 19 26	3 10 17 24	7 14 21 28
W.	6 13 20 27	4 11 18 25	1 8 15 22 29
Th.	7 14 21 28	5 12 19 26	2 9 16 23 30
F.	1 8 15 22 29	6 13 20 27	3 10 17 24 31
S.	2 9 16 23	7 14 21 28	4 11 18 25

	March	July	November
Su.	2 9 16 23 30	6 13 20 27	2 9 16 23 30
M.	3 10 17 24 31	7 14 21 28	3 10 17 24
Tu.	4 11 18 25	1 8 15 22 29	4 11 18 25
W.	5 12 19 26	2 9 16 23 30	5 12 19 26
Th.	6 13 20 27	3 10 17 24 31	6 13 20 27
F.	7 14 21 28	4 11 18 25	7 14 21 28
S.	1 8 15 22 29	5 12 19 26	1 8 15 22 29

	April	August	December
Su.	6 13 20 27	3 10 17 24 31	7 14 21 28
M.	7 14 21 28	4 11 18 25	1 8 15 22 29
Tu.	1 8 15 22 29	5 12 19 26	2 9 16 23 30
W.	2 9 16 23 30	6 13 20 27	3 10 17 24 31
Th.	3 10 17 24	7 14 21 28	4 11 18 25
F.	4 11 18 25	1 8 15 22 29	5 12 19 26
S.	5 12 19 26	2 9 16 23 30	6 13 20 27

Easter Days

March 23.	1788	1856	2008.
April 6.	1828	1980.	
April 13.	1884	1952.	
April 20.	1924.		

G

	January	May	September
Su.	.. 5 12 19 26	4 11 18 25	7 14 21 28
M.	.. 6 13 20 27	5 12 19 26	1 8 15 22 29
Tu.	.. 7 14 21 28	6 13 20 27	2 9 16 23 30
W.	.1 8 15 22 29	7 14 21 28	3 10 17 24
Th.	.2 9 16 23 30	1 8 15 22 29	4 11 18 25
F.	.3 10 17 24 31	2 9 16 23 30	5 12 19 26
S.	.4 11 18 25	3 10 17 24 31	6 13 20 27

	February	June	October
Su.	.2 9 16 23	1 8 15 22 29	5 12 19 26
M.	.3 10 17 24	2 9 16 23 30	6 13 20 27
Tu.	.4 11 18 25	3 10 17 24	7 14 21 28
W.	.5 12 19 26	4 11 18 25	1 8 15 22 29
Th.	.6 13 20 27	5 12 19 26	2 9 16 23 30
F.	.7 14 21 28	6 13 20 27	3 10 17 24 31
S.	1 8 15 22	7 14 21 28	4 11 18 25

	March	July	November
Su.	.2 9 16 23 30	6 13 20 27	2 9 16 23 30
M.	.3 10 17 24 31	7 14 21 28	3 10 17 24
Tu.	.4 11 18 25	1 8 15 22 29	4 11 18 25
W.	.5 12 19 26	2 9 16 23 30	5 12 19 26
Th.	.6 13 20 27	3 10 17 24 31	6 13 20 27
F.	.7 14 21 28	4 11 18 25	7 14 21 28
S.	1 8 15 22 29	5 12 19 26	1 8 15 22 29

	April	August	December
Su.	.6 13 20 27	3 10 17 24 31	7 14 21 28
M.	.7 14 21 28	4 11 18 25	1 8 15 22 29
Tu.	1 8 15 22 29	5 12 19 26	2 9 16 23 30
W.	.2 9 16 23 30	6 13 20 27	3 10 17 24 31
Th.	.3 10 17 24	7 14 21 28	4 11 18 25
F.	.4 11 18 25	1 8 15 22 29	5 12 19 26
S.	.5 12 19 26	2 9 16 23 30	6 13 20 27

Easter Days

March 23. 1845 1913.
March 30. 1777 1823 1834 1902 1975 1986 1997.
April 6 1806 1817 1890 1947 1958 1969.
April 13. 1800 1873 1879 1941. [2014 2025.
April 20. 1783 1794 1851 1862 1919 1930 2003

H (Leap year)

	January	May	September
Su.	.. 5 12 19 26	3 10 17 24 31	6 13 20 27
M.	.. 6 13 20 27	4 11 18 25	7 14 21 28
Tu.	.. 7 14 21 28	5 12 19 26	1 8 15 22 29
W.	.1 8 15 22 29	6 13 20 27	2 9 16 23 30
Th.	.2 9 16 23 30	7 14 21 28	3 10 17 24
F.	.3 10 17 24 31	1 8 15 22 29	4 11 18 25
S.	.4 11 18 25	2 9 16 23 30	5 12 19 26

	February	June	October
Su.	.2 9 16 23	7 14 21 28	4 11 18 25
M.	.3 10 17 24	1 8 15 22 29	5 12 19 26
Tu.	.4 11 18 25	2 9 16 23 30	6 13 20 27
W.	.5 12 19 26	3 10 17 24	7 14 21 28
Th.	.6 13 20 27	4 11 18 25	1 8 15 22 29
F.	.7 14 21 28	5 12 19 26	2 9 16 23 30
S.	1 8 15 22 29	6 13 20 27	3 10 17 24 31

	March	July	November
Su.	1 8 15 22 29	5 12 19 26	1 8 15 22 29
M.	.2 9 16 23 30	6 13 20 27	2 9 16 23 30
Tu.	.3 10 17 24 31	7 14 21 28	3 10 17 24
W.	.4 11 18 25	1 8 15 22 29	4 11 18 25
Th.	.5 12 19 26	2 9 16 23 30	5 12 19 26
F.	.6 13 20 27	3 10 17 24 31	6 13 20 27
S.	.7 14 21 28	4 11 18 25	7 14 21 28

	April	August	December
Su.	.5 12 19 26	2 9 16 23 30	6 13 20 27
M.	.6 13 20 27	3 10 17 24 31	7 14 21 28
Tu.	.7 14 21 28	4 11 18 25	1 8 15 22 29
W.	1 8 15 22 29	5 12 19 26	2 9 16 23 30
Th.	.2 9 16 23 30	6 13 20 27	3 10 17 24 31
F.	.3 10 17 24	7 14 21 28	4 11 18 25
S.	.4 11 18 25	1 8 15 22 29	5 12 19 26

Easter Days

March 29. 1812 1964.
April 5. 1896.
April 12. 1868 1936 2020.
April 19. 1772 1840 1908 1992.

I

	January	May	September
Su.	.. 4 11 18 25	3 10 17 24 31	6 13 20 27
M.	.. 5 12 19 26	4 11 18 25	7 14 21 28
Tu.	.. 6 13 20 27	5 12 19 26	1 8 15 22 29
W.	.. 7 14 21 28	6 13 20 27	2 9 16 23 30
Th.	1 8 15 22 29	7 14 21 28	3 10 17 24
F.	.2 9 16 23 30	1 8 15 22 29	4 11 18 25
S.	.3 10 17 24 31	2 9 16 23 30	5 12 19 26

	February	June	October
Su.	1 8 15 22	7 14 21 28	4 11 18 25
M.	.2 9 16 23	1 8 15 22 29	5 12 19 26
Tu.	.3 10 17 24	2 9 16 23 30	6 13 20 27
W.	.4 11 18 25	3 10 17 24	7 14 21 28
Th.	.5 12 19 26	4 11 18 25	1 8 15 22 29
F.	.6 13 20 27	5 12 19 26	2 9 16 23 30
S.	.7 14 21 28	6 13 20 27	3 10 17 24 31

	March	July	November
Su.	1 8 15 22 29	5 12 19 26	1 8 15 22 29
M.	.2 9 16 23 30	6 13 20 27	2 9 16 23 30
Tu.	.3 10 17 24 31	7 14 21 28	3 10 17 24
W.	.4 11 18 25	1 8 15 22 29	4 11 18 25
Th.	.5 12 19 26	2 9 16 23 30	5 12 19 26
F.	.6 13 20 27	3 10 17 24 31	6 13 20 27
S.	.7 14 21 28	4 11 18 25	7 14 21 28

	April	August	December
Su.	.5 12 19 26	2 9 16 23 30	6 13 20 27
M.	.6 13 20 27	3 10 17 24 31	7 14 21 28
Tu.	.7 14 21 28	4 11 18 25	1 8 15 22 29
W.	1 8 15 22 29	5 12 19 26	2 9 16 23 30
Th.	.2 9 16 23 30	6 13 20 27	3 10 17 24 31
F.	.3 10 17 24	7 14 21 28	4 11 18 25
S.	.4 11 18 25	1 8 15 22 29	5 12 19 26

Easter Days

March 22. 1818.
March 29. 1807 1891 1959 1970.
April 5. 1795 1801 1863 1874 1885 1931 1942 [1953 2015.
April 12. 1789 1846 1857 1903 1914 1925 1998
April 19. 1778 1829 1835 1981 1987. [2009.

J (Leap year)

	January	May	September
Su.	.. 4 11 18 25	2 9 16 23 30	5 12 19 26
M.	.. 5 12 19 26	3 10 17 24 31	6 13 20 27
Tu.	.. 6 13 20 27	4 11 18 25	7 14 21 28
W.	.. 7 14 21 28	5 12 19 26	1 8 15 22 29
Th.	1 8 15 22 29	6 13 20 27	2 9 16 23 30
F.	.2 9 16 23 30	7 14 21 28	3 10 17 24
S.	.3 10 17 24 31	1 8 15 22 29	4 11 18 25

	February	June	October
Su.	1 8 15 22 29	6 13 20 27	3 10 17 24 31
M.	.2 9 16 23	7 14 21 28	4 11 18 25
Tu.	.3 10 17 24	1 8 15 22 29	5 12 19 26
W.	.4 11 18 25	2 9 16 23 30	6 13 20 27
Th.	.5 12 19 26	3 10 17 24	7 14 21 28
F.	.6 13 20 27	4 11 18 25	1 8 15 22 29
S.	.7 14 21 28	5 12 19 26	2 9 16 23 30

	March	July	November
Su.	.7 14 21 28	4 11 18 25	7 14 21 28
M.	1 8 15 22 29	5 12 19 26	1 8 15 22 29
Tu.	.2 9 16 23 30	6 13 20 27	2 9 16 23 30
W.	.3 10 17 24 31	7 14 21 28	3 10 17 24
Th.	.4 11 18 25	1 8 15 22 29	4 11 18 25
F.	.5 12 19 26	2 9 16 23 30	5 12 19 26
S.	.6 13 20 27	3 10 17 24 31	6 13 20 27

	April	August	December
Su.	.4 11 18 25	1 8 15 22 29	5 12 19 26
M.	.5 12 19 26	2 9 16 23 30	6 13 20 27
Tu.	.6 13 20 27	3 10 17 24 31	7 14 21 28
W.	.7 14 21 28	4 11 18 25	1 8 15 22 29
Th.	1 8 15 22 29	5 12 19 26	2 9 16 23 30
F.	.2 9 16 23 30	6 13 20 27	3 10 17 24 31
S.	.3 10 17 24	7 14 21 28	4 11 18 25

Easter Days

March 28. 1880 1948.
April 4. 1920.
April 11. 1784 1852 2004.
April 18. 1824 1976.

K

January / May / September

Day	January	May	September
Su.	3 10 17 24 31	2 9 16 23 30	5 12 19 26
M.	4 11 18 25	3 10 17 24 31	6 13 20 27
Tu.	5 12 19 26	4 11 18 25	7 14 21 28
W.	6 13 20 27	5 12 19 26	1 8 15 22 29
Th.	7 14 21 28	6 13 20 27	2 9 16 23 30
F.	1 8 15 22 29	7 14 21 28	3 10 17 24
S.	2 9 16 23 30	1 8 15 22 29	4 11 18 25

February / June / October

Day	February	June	October
Su.	7 14 21 28	6 13 20 27	3 10 17 24 31
M.	1 8 15 22	7 14 21 28	4 11 18 25
Tu.	2 9 16 23	1 8 15 22 29	5 12 19 26
W.	3 10 17 24	2 9 16 23 30	6 13 20 27
Th.	4 11 18 25	3 10 17 24	7 14 21 28
F.	5 12 19 26	4 11 18 25	1 8 15 22 29
S.	6 13 20 27	5 12 19 26	2 9 16 23 30

March / July / November

Day	March	July	November
Su.	7 14 21 28	4 11 18 25	7 14 21 28
M.	1 8 15 22 29	5 12 19 26	1 8 15 22 29
Tu.	2 9 16 23 30	6 13 20 27	2 9 16 23 30
W.	3 10 17 24 31	7 14 21 28	3 10 17 24
Th.	4 11 18 25	1 8 15 22 29	4 11 18 25
F.	5 12 19 26	2 9 16 23 30	5 12 19 26
S.	6 13 20 27	3 10 17 24 31	6 13 20 27

April / August / December

Day	April	August	December
Su.	4 11 18 25	1 8 15 22 29	5 12 19 26
M.	5 12 19 26	2 9 16 23 30	6 13 20 27
Tu.	6 13 20 27	3 10 17 24 31	7 14 21 28
W.	7 14 21 28	4 11 18 25	1 8 15 22 29
Th.	1 8 15 22 29	5 12 19 26	2 9 16 23 30
F.	2 9 16 23 30	6 13 20 27	3 10 17 24 31
S.	3 10 17 24	7 14 21 28	4 11 18 25

Easter Days

March 28.	1869 1875 1937.	[2010 2021.
April 4.	1779 1790 1847 1858 1915 1926 1999	
April 11.	1773 1819 1830 1841 1909 1971 1982	
April 18	1802 1813 1897 1954 1965.	[1993.
April 25.	1886 1943.	

L (Leap year)

January / May / September

Day	January	May	September
Su.	3 10 17 24 31	1 8 15 22 29	4 11 18 25
M.	4 11 18 25	2 9 16 23 30	5 12 19 26
Tu.	5 12 19 26	3 10 17 24 31	6 13 20 27
W.	6 13 20 27	4 11 18 25	7 14 21 28
Th.	7 14 21 28	5 12 19 26	1 8 15 22 29
F.	1 8 15 22 29	6 13 20 27	2 9 16 23 30
S.	2 9 16 23 30	7 14 21 28	3 10 17 24

February / June / October

Day	February	June	October
Su.	7 14 21 28	5 12 19 26	2 9 16 23 30
M.	1 8 15 22 29	6 13 20 27	3 10 17 24 31
Tu.	2 9 16 23	7 14 21 28	4 11 18 25
W.	3 10 17 24	1 8 15 22 29	5 12 19 26
Th.	4 11 18 25	2 9 16 23 30	6 13 20 27
F.	5 12 19 26	3 10 17 24	7 14 21 28
S.	6 13 20 27	4 11 18 25	1 8 15 22 29

March / July / November

Day	March	July	November
Su.	6 13 20 27	3 10 17 24 31	6 13 20 27
M.	7 14 21 28	4 11 18 25	7 14 21 28
Tu.	1 8 15 22 29	5 12 19 26	1 8 15 22 29
W.	2 9 16 23 30	6 13 20 27	2 9 16 23 30
Th.	3 10 17 24 31	7 14 21 28	3 10 17 24
F.	4 11 18 25	1 8 15 22 29	4 11 18 25
S.	5 12 19 26	2 9 16 23 30	5 12 19 26

April / August / December

Day	April	August	December
Su.	3 10 17 24	7 14 21 28	4 11 18 25
M.	4 11 18 25	1 8 15 22 29	5 12 19 26
Tu.	5 12 19 26	2 9 16 23 30	6 13 20 27
W.	6 13 20 27	3 10 17 24 31	7 14 21 28
Th.	7 14 21 28	4 11 18 25	1 8 15 22 29
F.	1 8 15 22 29	5 12 19 26	2 9 16 23 30
S.	2 9 16 23 30	6 13 20 27	3 10 17 24 31

Easter Days

March 27.	1796 1864 1932 2016.
April 3.	1836 1904 1988.
April 17.	1808 1892 1960.

M

January / May / September

Day	January	May	September
Su.	2 9 16 23 30	1 8 15 22 29	4 11 18 25
M.	3 10 17 24 31	2 9 16 23 30	5 12 19 26
Tu.	4 11 18 25	3 10 17 24 31	6 13 20 27
W.	5 12 19 26	4 11 18 25	7 14 21 28
Th.	6 13 20 27	5 12 19 26	1 8 15 22 29
F.	7 14 21 28	6 13 20 27	2 9 16 23 30
S.	1 8 15 22 29	7 14 21 28	3 10 17 24

February / June / October

Day	February	June	October
Su.	6 13 20 27	5 12 19 26	2 9 16 23 30
M.	7 14 21 28	6 13 20 27	3 10 17 24 31
Tu.	1 8 15 22	7 14 21 28	4 11 18 25
W.	2 9 16 23	1 8 15 22 29	5 12 19 26
Th.	3 10 17 24	2 9 16 23 30	6 13 20 27
F.	4 11 18 25	3 10 17 24	7 14 21 28
S.	5 12 19 26	4 11 18 25	1 8 15 22 29

March / July / November

Day	March	July	November
Su.	6 13 20 27	3 10 17 24 31	6 13 20 27
M.	7 14 21 28	4 11 18 25	7 14 21 28
Tu.	1 8 15 22 29	5 12 19 26	1 8 15 22 29
W.	2 9 16 23 30	6 13 20 27	2 9 16 23 30
Th.	3 10 17 24 31	7 14 21 28	3 10 17 24
F.	4 11 18 25	1 8 15 22 29	4 11 18 25
S.	5 12 19 26	2 9 16 23 30	5 12 19 26

April / August / December

Day	April	August	December
Su.	3 10 17 24	7 14 21 28	4 11 18 25
M.	4 11 18 25	1 8 15 22 29	5 12 19 26
Tu.	5 12 19 26	2 9 16 23 30	6 13 20 27
W.	6 13 20 27	3 10 17 24 31	7 14 21 28
Th.	7 14 21 28	4 11 18 25	1 8 15 22 29
F.	1 8 15 22 29	5 12 19 26	2 9 16 23 30
S.	2 9 16 23 30	6 13 20 27	3 10 17 24 31

Easter Days

March 27.	1785 1842 1853 1910 1921 2005.
April 3.	1774 1825 1831 1983 1994.
April 10.	1803 1814 1887 1898 1955 1966 1977.
April 17.	1870 1881 1927 1938 1949 2022.
April 24.	1791 1859 2011.

N (Leap year)

January / May / September

Day	January	May	September
Su.	2 9 16 23 30	7 14 21 28	3 10 17 24
M.	3 10 17 24 31	1 8 15 22 29	4 11 18 25
Tu.	4 11 18 25	2 9 16 23 30	5 12 19 26
W.	5 12 19 26	3 10 17 24 31	6 13 20 27
Th.	6 13 20 27	4 11 18 25	7 14 21 28
F.	7 14 21 28	5 12 19 26	1 8 15 22 29
S.	1 8 15 22 29	6 13 20 27	2 9 16 23 30

February / June / October

Day	February	June	October
Su.	6 13 20 27	4 11 18 25	1 8 15 22 29
M.	7 14 21 28	5 12 19 26	2 9 16 23 30
Tu.	1 8 15 22 29	6 13 20 27	3 10 17 24 31
W.	2 9 16 23	7 14 21 28	4 11 18 25
Th.	3 10 17 24	1 8 15 22 29	5 12 19 26
F.	4 11 18 25	2 9 16 23 30	6 13 20 27
S.	5 12 19 26	3 10 17 24	7 14 21 28

March / July / November

Day	March	July	November
Su.	5 12 19 26	2 9 16 23 30	5 12 19 26
M.	6 13 20 27	3 10 17 24 31	6 13 20 27
Tu.	7 14 21 28	4 11 18 25	7 14 21 28
W.	1 8 15 22 29	5 12 19 26	1 8 15 22 29
Th.	2 9 16 23 30	6 13 20 27	2 9 16 23 30
F.	3 10 17 24 31	7 14 21 28	3 10 17 24
S.	4 11 18 25	1 8 15 22 29	4 11 18 25

April / August / December

Day	April	August	December
Su.	2 9 16 23 30	6 13 20 27	3 10 17 24 31
M.	3 10 17 24	7 14 21 28	4 11 18 25
Tu.	4 11 18 25	1 8 15 22 29	5 12 19 26
W.	5 12 19 26	2 9 16 23 30	6 13 20 27
Th.	6 13 20 27	3 10 17 24 31	7 14 21 28
F.	7 14 21 28	4 11 18 25	1 8 15 22 29
S.	1 8 15 22 29	5 12 19 26	2 9 16 23 30

Easter Days

March 26.	1780.
April 2.	1820 1972.
April 9.	1944.
April 16.	1876.
April 23.	1848 1916 2000.

The World

The **Superficial Area** of the Earth is estimated to be 196,836,000 square miles, of which 55,786,000 square miles are Land and 141,050,000 square miles Water. The **Diameter** of the Earth at the Equator is 7,926$\frac{1}{2}$ English miles, and at the Poles 7,900 English miles. The Equatorial **Circumference** is 24,901·8 English miles, divided into 360 Degrees of Longitude, each of 69·17 English (or 60 Geographical) miles; these Degrees are measured from the Meridian of Greenwich, and numbered East and West of that point to meet in the Antipodes at the 180th Degree. Distance North and South of the Equator is marked by Parallels of Latitude, which proceed from zero (at the Equator) to 90° at the Poles.

The velocity of a given point of the Earth's surface at the Equator exceeds 1,000 miles an hour (24,901·8 miles in 24 hours); the Earth's velocity in its orbit round the Sun is about 66,600 miles an hour (584,000,000 miles in 365$\frac{1}{4}$ days). The Earth is distant from the Sun 93,000,000 miles, on the average.

AREA AND POPULATION

The total population of the world in mid-1985, was estimated at 4,837,500,000 compared with 3,003,000,000 in 1960 and 2,070,000,000 in 1930.

Continent, etc.	Area		Estimated Population, mid-1985
	Sq. km. '000	Sq. miles '000	
Europe[1]	4,961	1,915	497,000,000
Asia[2]	27,549	10,637	2,813,000,000
U.S.S.R.	22,402	8,649	279,000,000
Africa	30,313	11,704	555,000,000
North America[3]	21,525	8,311	264,000,000
Latin America[4]	20,547	7,933	405,000,000
Oceania	8,510	3,286	24,500,000
TOTAL	135,807	52,435	4,837,500,000

[1] Includes European Turkey, excludes U.S.S.R.
[2] Includes Asiatic Turkey, excludes U.S.S.R.
[3] Includes Greenland and Hawaii.
[4] Mexico and the remainder of the Americas south of the U.S.A.
Source: *U.N. Demographic Yearbook 1985 (pub. 1987).*

A United Nations report (*The Future Growth of World Population*) in 1958, pointed out that the population of the world had increased since the beginning of the 20th Century at an unprecedented rate: in 1850 it was estimated at 1,094,000,000 and in 1900 at 1,550,000,000, an increase of 42 per cent in 50 years. By 1925 it had risen to 1,907,000,000—23 per cent in 25 years—and by 1950 it had reached 2,500,000,000, an increase of 31 per cent in 25 years. Levels of population and the trend in distribution of the population by continents as forecast for the year 2000 were:—

Continent, etc.	[millions] 2000	
	Estimated Population	Per cent
Europe (including U.S.S.R.)	947	15·1
Asia (excluding U.S.S.R.). . .	3,870	61·8
Africa	517	8·2
N. America	312	5·0
Latin America†	592	9·4
Oceania	29	0·5
World	6,267	100

† Mexico and the remainder of America south of U.S.A.

THE CONTINENTS

Europe (including European Russia) forms about one-fourteenth of the land surface of the globe. Its length from the North Cape, 71° 12′ N., to Cape Matapan, in the south of Greece, 36° 23′ N., is about 2,400 miles, and its breadth from Cape St. Vincent to the Urals is about 3,300 miles. The boundary between Europe and Asia is the Urals in the north, while in the south-east it follows the valley of the Manych, north of the Caucasus.

Asia (including Asiatic Russia) extends over nearly one-third of the land surface of the globe. The distance between its extreme longitudes, the west coast of Asia Minor (26° E.) and the East Cape (170° W.), is 6,000 miles. The extreme latitudes, Cape Chelyuskin (78° 30′ N.) and Cape Bulus (76 miles north of the Equator), are 5,350 miles apart. Asia is bounded by the ocean on all sides except the west, where the isthmus of Suez connects it with Africa. The land boundary between Europe and Asia is formed on the west mainly by the Ural Mountains, the Ural River and in the south-west the valley of the Manych, which stretches from the Caspian Sea to the mouth of the Don. The islands of the archipelago which lie in the south-east between the continents of Asia and Australia may be divided into two groups by a line passing east of Timor, Timor Laut, the Kei Islands and the Moluccas.

Africa is about three times the area of Europe. Its extreme longitudes are 17° W. at Cape Verde and 51° 27′ 52″ E. at Ras Hafun. The extreme latitudes are Cape Blanco in 37° N. and Cape Agulhas in 35° S., at a distance of about 5,000 miles. It is surrounded by seas on all sides, except in the narrow isthmus of Suez, through which is cut the Suez Canal.

North America, including Mexico, is a little less than twice the size of Europe. Its extreme longitudes extend from a little west of 170° W. to 52$\frac{1}{2}$° W. in the east of Newfoundland, and its extreme latitudes from about 80° N. lat. to 15° N. lat. in the south of Mexico. It is surrounded by seas on all sides except in the south, where it joins the isthmian States of *Central America*, which have an area of about 200,000 square miles. The area of the *West Indies* is about 65,000 square miles, a little more than half that of the United Kingdom. They extend from about 27° N. latitude to 10° N. latitude.

South America is a little more than 1$\frac{3}{4}$ times the size of Europe. The extreme longitudes are Cape Branco 35° W. and Punta Parina 81° W., and the extreme latitudes, Punta Gallinas, 12$\frac{1}{2}$° N. and Cape Horn 56° S. South America is surrounded by the ocean, except where it is joined to Central America by the narrow isthmus through which is cut the Panama Canal.

Oceania extends over an area 1$\frac{1}{2}$ times the size of Europe, from Australia (in the West) to the most easterly islands of Polynesia, and from New Zealand (in the south) to the Sandwich Islands (Hawaii) in the north.

Countries and Their Capitals

No complete survey of many countries has yet been achieved and consequently accurate area figures are not always available. Similarly, many countries have not recently, or have never, taken a census. The areas and populations of countries given below are derived from estimated figures published by the United Nations.

Accurate and up-to-date data for the populations of capital cities are scarce, and definitions of cities' extent differ. The figures given below are the latest estimates available, and where it is known that the figure applies to an urban agglomeration this is indicated.

Where later information becomes available during printing, the new figures are given in the overseas sections of the ALMANACK.

e. estimate   *latest census result   *u.a.* urban-agglomeration   Ψ seaport

AFRICA

COUNTRY	AREA		POPULATION ('000) (mid-1985e)	CAPITAL	POPULATION OF CAPITAL
	Sq. Miles	Sq. Km.			
Algeria...............	919,595	2,381,741	21,718	Algiers	3,250,000
Angola	481,354	1,246,700	8,754	Ψ Luanda	1,000,000
Benin	43,484	112,622	3,932	Ψ Porto Novo.......	208,258
Botswana	224,607	581,730	1,085	Gaborone	94,700
Burkina	105,869	274,200	6,639	Ouagadougou ...	375,001
Burundi..............	10,747	27,834	4,718	Bujumbura	150,000
Cameroon	183,569	475,442	10,106	Yaoundé	522,000
Cape Verde Islands	1,557	4,033	326	Ψ Praia	57,748
Central African Rep. ..	240,535	622,984	2,608	Bangui	473,817
Chad	495,755	1,284,000	5,018	Ndjaména.........	303,000
Comoros..............	838	2,171	444	Moroni	20,112
Congo	132,047	342,000	1,740	Brazzaville	500,000
Côte d'Ivoire..........	124,503	322,463	9,810	Ψ Abidjan	2,000,000
Djibouti	8,494	22,000	430	Ψ Djibouti.........	200,000
Egypt	386,662	1,001,449	48,503	Cairo	14,000,000
Equatorial Guinea	10,830	28,051	392	Ψ Malabo	34,980
Ethiopia	471,778	1,221,900	43,350	Addis Ababa......	1,464,901
Gabon................	103,347	267,667	1,151	Ψ Libreville	251,000
Gambia	4,361	11,295	643	Ψ Banjul (u.a.)	147,394
Ghana	92,100	238,537	13,588	Ψ Accra (u.a.)	1,420,066*
Guinea	94,926	245,857	6,075	Ψ Conakry	763,000
Guinea-Bissau	13,948	36,125	890	Ψ Bissau	109,486*
Kenya	224,961	582,646	20,333	Nairobi	1,103,554
Lesotho	11,720	30,355	1,528	Maseru	277,307
Liberia	43,000	111,369	2,189	Ψ Monrovia	425,000
Libya	679,362	1,759,540	3,605	Ψ Tripoli..........	1,000,000
Madagascar	226,669	587,041	9,985	Antananarivo	1,000,000
Malawi...............	45,747	118,484	7,059	Lilongwe.........	102,924*
Mali	478,791	1,240,000	8,206	Bamako..........	600,000
Mauritania	397,955	1,030,700	1,888	Nouakchott	500,000
Mauritius	790	2,045	1,020	Ψ Port Louis	138,272
Mayotte	144	372	50†	Dzaoudzi	4,147
Morocco..............	172,414	446,550	21,941	Ψ Rabat	893,402*
Western Sahara	102,703	266,000	155	Laayoune	24,000
Mozambique	309,495	801,590	13,961	Ψ Maputo	850,000
Namibia..............	318,261	824,292	1,550	Windhoek........	61,260
Niger	489,191	1,267,080	6,115	Niamey	399,100
Nigeria	356,669	923,768	95,198	Ψ Lagos	3,000,000
Réunion..............	969	2,510	531	St. Denis	109,072
Rwanda	10,169	26,338	6,070	Kigali	156,000
St. Helena	47	122	6	Ψ Jamestown.......	1,516
Ascension I.	34	88	1	Ψ Georgetown	..
Tristan da Cunha ...	40	104	310 (total)	Ψ Edinburgh	..
Sao Tomé & Príncipe ..	372	964	108	Ψ São Tomé	25,000
Senegal	75,750	196,192	6,444	Ψ Dakar	1,000,000
Seychelles	108	280	65	Ψ Victoria	24,733
Sierra Leone..........	27,699	71,740	3,602	Ψ Freetown	469,776
Somalia	246,201	637,657	4,653	Ψ Mogadishu	1,000,000
South Africa..........	471,445	1,221,031	32,392	{ Pretoria (u.a.) .... Ψ Cape Town (u.a.)..	563,384 1,107,764
Sudan	967,500	2,505,813	21,550	Khartoum (u.a.) ..	2,000,000
Swaziland	6,704	17,363	647	Mbabane	30,000
Tanzania	364,900	945,087	21,733	Ψ Dar-es-Salaam	1,096,000
Togo	21,925	56,785	2,960	Lomé	366,476
Tunisia	63,170	163,610	7,081	Ψ Tunis............	1,394,749
Uganda	91,259	236,036	15,477	Kampala (u.a.) ...	460,000
Zaire.................	905,567	2,345,409	30,363	Kinshasa.........	2,778,281
Zambia	290,586	752,614	6,666	Lusaka (u.a.)	641,000
Zimbabwe	150,804	390,580	8,300	Harare...........	656,000

† 1980 e.

AMERICA

(For symbols, etc., *see* introductory note on page 199.)

COUNTRY	AREA		POPULATION ('000) (mid-1985e)	CAPITAL	POPULATION OF CAPITAL
	Sq. Miles	Sq. Km.			
North America					
Canada	3,851,809	9,976,139	25,379	Ottawa (*u.a.*)	769,900
Greenland	840,004	2,175,600	53	ψ Godthab	8,425
Mexico	761,605	1,972,547	78,524	Mexico City (*u.a.*)	18,748,000
St. Pierre and Miquelon	93	242	6	ψ St. Pierre	..
United States	3,618,787	9,372,614	239,283	Washington, D.C. (*u.a.*)	3,490,000
Central America and the West Indies					
Anguilla	35	91	7	The Valley	500
Antigua and Barbuda	170	440	80	ψ St. John's	30,000
Bahamas	5,380	13,935	231	ψ Nassau	135,437*
Barbados	166	431	253	ψ Bridgetown	7,466
Belize	8,867	22,965	166	Belmopan	2,935
Bermuda	20	53	56	ψ Hamilton	1,669
Cayman Islands	100	259	20	ψ George Town	8,200
Costa Rica	19,575	50,700	2,600	San José (*u.a.*)	890,434*
Cuba	42,804	110,861	10,090	ψ Havana	1,992,620
Dominica	290	751	76	ψ Roseau	8,346*
Dominican Republic	18,816	48,734	6,243	ψ Santo Domingo (*u.a.*)	1,313,172*
Grenada	133	344	112	ψ St. George's	7,500
Guadeloupe	687	1,779	334	ψ Basse-Terre	15,778
Guatemala	42,042	108,889	7,963	Guatemala	1,300,000
Haiti	10,714	27,750	6,585	ψ Port au Prince	1,000,000
Honduras	43,277	112,088	4,372	Tegucigalpa	539,600
Jamaica	4,244	10,991	2,337	ψ Kingston (*u.a.*)	696,300
Martinique	425	1,102	328	ψ Fort de France	100,576
Montserrat	38	98	12	ψ Plymouth	1,623
Netherlands Antilles	371	961	260	ψ Willemstad	154,928
Nicaragua	50,193	130,000	3,272	Managua	615,000
Panama	29,762	77,082	2,180	ψ Panama City	608,890
Puerto Rico	3,435	8,897	3,451	ψ San Juan (*u.a.*)	1,816,300
St. Kitts and Nevis	101	261	46	ψ Basseterre	15,000
St. Lucia	238	616	130	ψ Castries	50,798
St. Vincent	150	388	104	ψ Kingstown	33,694
El Salvador	8,124	21,041	4,819	San Salvador	425,119
Trinidad and Tobago	1,981	5,130	1,185	ψ Port of Spain	59,649
Turks and Caicos Is.	166	430	8	ψ Grand Turk	3,146
Virgin Islands:—					
British	59	153	13	ψ Road Town	2,479
U.S.	132	342	105	ψ Charlotte Amalie	11,842
South America					
Argentina	1,068,302	2,766,889	30,564	ψ Buenos Aires (*u.a.*)	9,967,826
Bolivia	424,165	1,098,581	6,429	La Paz	1,000,000
Brazil	3,286,488	8,511,965	135,564	Brasilia	1,576,657
Chile	292,258	756,945	12,074	Santiago	4,132,293
Colombia	439,737	1,138,914	28,624	Bogotá	4,169,000
Ecuador	109,484	283,561	9,378	Quito	1,003,875
Falkland Islands	4,700	12,173	2	ψ Stanley	1,050
South Georgia	1,580	4,092	500 (total)	Stanley	..
Guyana, *French*	34,749	90,000	82	ψ Cayenne	38,135
Guyana	83,000	214,969	790	ψ Georgetown	185,000
Paraguay	157,048	406,752	3,681	ψ Asunción (*u.a.*)	729,307*
Peru	496,225	1,285,216	19,698	Lima (*u.a.*)	5,258,600
Suriname	63,037	163,265	375	ψ Paramaribo	110,000
Uruguay	68,037	176,215	3,012	ψ Montevideo	1,355,312
Venezuela	352,144	912,050	17,317	Caracas	1,816,901

ASIA

(For symbols, etc., *see* introductory note on page 199.)

COUNTRY	AREA Sq. Miles	AREA Sq. Km.	POPULATION ('000) (mid-1985e)	CAPITAL	POPULATION OF CAPITAL
Afghanistan	250,000	647,497	18,136	Kabul............	2,000,000
Bahrain	240	622	417	Ψ Manama	400,000
Bangladesh	55,598	143,998	98,657	Dhaka	4,023,000
Bhutan	18,147	47,000	1,417	Thimphu	8,922
Brunei	2,226	5,765	224	Ψ Bandar Seri Begawan	58,000
Burma	261,218	676,552	37,153	Ψ Rangoon	2,458,712*
Cambodia	69,898	181,035	7,284	Ψ Phnom Penh	500,000
China[1]	3,705,408	9,596,961	1,059,521	Peking (*u.a.*)	9,179,660
Taiwan	13,800	35,742	19,135	Taipei	2,450,000
Macao	6	16	392	Ψ Macao	..
Hong Kong	403	1,045	5,548	Ψ Victoria	767,000
India	1,269,346	3,287,590	750,900	Delhi	6,220,000*
Indonesia	735,358	1,904,569	163,393	Ψ Jakarta	6,503,449
Iran	636,296	1,648,000	44,212	Tehran	5,734,199
Iraq................	167,925	434,924	15,898	Baghdad	3,205,645
Israel	8,019	20,770	4,233	Jerusalem........	472,900
Japan	145,834	377,708	120,754	Tokyo (*u.a.*)	11,806,729
Jordan	37,738	97,740	3,515	Amman	812,500
Korea, North	46,540	120,538	20,385	Pyongyang	1,500,000
Korea, South	38,025	98,484	41,209	Seoul	9,200,000
Kuwait	6,880	17,818	1,710	Ψ Kuwait (city)	400,000
Laos	91,429	231,800	4,117	Vientiane	120,000
Lebanon.............	4,015	10,400	2,668	Ψ Beirut	702,000
Malaysia	127,317	329,749	15,557	Kuala Lumpur....	1,103,200*
Maldives	115	298	177	Ψ Malé............	46,334
Mongolia	604,250	1,565,000	1,891	Ulan Bator	480,000
Nepal	54,342	140,747	16,625	Kathmandu	235,000
Oman	82,030	212,457	1,242	Ψ Muscat	200,000
Pakistan	307,374	746,045	96,180	Islamabad (*u.a.*)...	350,000
Philippine Islands	115,831	300,000	54,378	Ψ Manila (*u.a.*)	6,720,050
Qatar	4,247	11,000	315	Doha	220,000
Saudi Arabia	830,000	2,149,640	11,542	Riyadh	1,000,000
Singapore	224	581	2,558	..	..
Sri Lanka	25,332	65,610	15,837	Ψ Colombo	643,000
Syria................	71,498	185,180	10,267	Damascus	2,250,000
Thailand	198,457	514,000	51,301	Ψ Bangkok	5,400,000
Turkey (in Asia)	292,261	756,953	44,272	Ankara	3,196,460
United Arab Emirates .	32,278	83,600	1,327	..	..
U.S.S.R. (in Asia)......	6,498,486	16,831,000	69,500	..	..
Vietnam	127,242	329,556	59,713	Hanoi............	925,000
Yemen A.R. (North) ...	75,290	195,000	6,849	Sana'a	427,185
Yemen P.D.R. (South) .	128,560	332,968	2,294	Ψ Aden	270,000

[1] Including Tibet.

THE OLYMPIC GAMES

The XXIV Olympic Games take place in Seoul, S. Korea from Sept. 17–Oct. 2, 1988, and the Winter Olympics in Calgary, Canada, from Feb. 13–28, 1988.

Previous Games have been held as follows: I, Athens, 1896; II, Paris, 1900; III, St. Louis, 1904; IV, London, 1908; V, Stockholm, 1912; VII, Antwerp, 1920; VIII, Paris, 1924; IX, Amsterdam, 1928; X, Los Angeles, 1932; XI, Berlin, 1936; XIV, London, 1948;

XV, Helsinki, 1952; XVI, Melbourne, 1956; XVII, Rome, 1960; XVIII, Tokyo, 1964; XIX, Mexico, 1968; XX, Munich, 1972; XXI, Montreal, 1976; XXII, Moscow, 1980; XXIII, Los Angeles, 1984.

The VIth Games scheduled for Berlin in 1916, the XIIth for Tokyo and then Helsinki in 1940, and the XIIIth for London in 1944 did not take place owing to World Wars.

EUROPE AND THE MEDITERRANEAN

(For symbols, etc., *see* introductory notes on page 199.)

COUNTRY	AREA		POPULATION ('000) (mid-1985e)	CAPITAL	POPULATION OF CAPITAL
	Sq. Miles	Sq. Km.			
Albania	11,099	28,748	2,962	Tirana	210,757
Andorra..............	175	453	35	Andorra La Vella .	16,000
Austria	32,374	83,849	7,555	Vienna	1,531,346
Belgium	11,781	30,513	9,903	Brussels (*u.a.*)	1,000,221
Bulgaria	42,823	110,912	8,957	Sofia.............	1,097,791
Cyprus	3,572	9,251	665	Nicosia	233,500
Czechoslovakia	49,370	127,869	15,500	Prague...........	1,190,576
Denmark	16,629	43,069	5,114	Ψ Copenhagen (*u.a.*).	478,615
Faroe Is.	540	1,399	46	Ψ Thorshavn	10,726
Finland	137,851	337,032	4,908	Ψ Helsinki (*u.a.*)	937,603
France	211,208	547,026	54,621	Paris (*u.a.*)	8,707,000
German Democratic Republic	41,768	108,178	16,644	East Berlin	1,202,895
Germany, Federal Republic of[1]	95,976	248,577	61,015	Bonn	291,700
Gibraltar..............	2	6	31	Ψ Gibraltar	..
Greece	50,944	131,944	9,935	Athens (*u.a.*)	3,027,331*
Hungary	35,919	93,030	10,649	Budapest.........	2,072,000
Iceland	39,768	103,000	241	Ψ Reykjavik (*u.a.*) ..	130,175
Irish Republic..........	27,136	70,283	3,552	Ψ Dublin (*u.a.*)	915,115
Italy	116,304	301,225	57,128	Rome (*u.a.*)	2,821,420
Liechtenstein.........	61	157	28	Vaduz	4,927
Luxembourg	998	2,586	366	Luxembourg	78,900
Malta and Gozo	122	316	383	Ψ Valletta	14,013
Monaco	0·4	1	27	Monaco-ville	..
Netherlands	15,770	40,844	14,484	Amsterdam (*u.a.*) ..	996,096
Norway[2]	125,181	324,219	4,152	Ψ Oslo	447,351
Poland	120,725	312,677	37,203	Warsaw..........	1,644,626
Portugal[3]..............	35,553	92,082	10,229	Ψ Lisbon	807,937
Romania	91,699	237,500	23,017	Bucharest........	1,961,189
San Marino...........	23	61	22	San Marino	..
Spain[4]	194,897	504,782	38,602	Madrid (*u.a.*)	3,188,297
Sweden	173,732	449,964	8,350	Ψ Stockholm (*u.a.*) ..	1,420,198
Switzerland	15,943	41,293	6,374	Berne (*u.a.*)	301,100
Turkey (in Europe)	9,121	23,623	5,000	..	..
UNITED KINGDOM[5]	94,227	244,046	56,125	Ψ London (*u.a.*)	6,696,008*
England.............	50,363	130,439	47,112		
Wales	8,018	20,768	2,812	Ψ Cardiff	278,900
Scotland	30,414	78,772	5,137	Ψ Edinburgh	439,679
Northern Ireland	5,452	14,121	1,558	Ψ Belfast	303,600
U.S.S.R. (Europe)......	2,150,975	5,571,000	208,500	Moscow	8,642,000
Vatican City State	0·2	0·44	1	Vatican City	..
Yugoslavia	98,766	255,804	23,123	Belgrade	1,455,000

[1] Data include West Berlin. [2] Excludes Svalbard and Jan Mayen Is. (approx. 24,101 sq. miles (62,422 sq. km.) and 3,000 population). [3] Includes Madeira (314 sq. miles) and the Azores (922 sq. miles). [4] Includes Balearic Is., Canary Is., Ceuta and Melilla. [5] Includes Isle of Man (227 sq. miles (588 sq. km.), 65,000 population), and Channel Is. (75 sq. miles (195 sq. km.), 130,000 population).

THE SEVEN WONDERS OF THE WORLD

I. THE PYRAMIDS OF EGYPT.—From Gizeh (near Cairo) to a southern limit 60 miles distant. The oldest is that of Zoser, at Saqqara, built about 2,700 B.C. The Great Pyramid of Cheops covers more than 12 acres and was originally 481 ft. in height and 756 × 756 ft. at the base.

II. THE HANGING GARDENS OF BABYLON.—Adjoining Nebuchadnezzar's palace, 60 miles south of Baghdad. Terraced gardens, ranging from 75 to 300 ft. above ground level, watered from storage tanks on the highest terrace.

III. THE TOMB OF MAUSOLUS.—At Halicarnassus, in Asia Minor. Built by the widowed Queen Artemisia about 350 B.C. The memorial originated the term mausoleum.

IV. THE TEMPLE OF ARTEMIS AT EPHESUS.—Ionic temple erected about 350 B.C. in honour of the goddess and burned by the Goths in A.D. 262.

V. THE COLOSSUS OF RHODES.—A bronze statue of Apollo, set up about 280 B.C. According to legend it stood at the harbour entrance of the seaport of Rhodes.

VI. THE STATUE OF ZEUS.—At Olympia in the plain of Elis, constructed of marble inlaid with ivory and gold by the sculptor Phidias, about 430 B.C.

VII. THE PHAROS OF ALEXANDRIA.—A marble watch tower and lighthouse on the island of Pharos in the harbour of Alexandria.

OCEANIA

(For symbols, etc., *see* introductory notes on page 199.)

COUNTRY	AREA		POPULATION ('000) (mid-1985e)	CAPITAL	POPULATION OF CAPITAL
	Sq. Miles	Sq. Km.			
Australia............	2,967,909	7,686,848	15,752	Canberra.........	273,600
Norfolk Island	14	36	2	Ψ Kingston........	..
Fiji	7,055	18,274	696	Ψ Suva.............	75,000
French Polynesia	1,544	4,000	163	Ψ Papeete	22,967
Guam	212	549	114	Agaña	896
Kiribati	281	728	64	Tarawa	24,400
Mariana, Caroline and Marshall Islands† ...	687	1,779	154	Saipan	..
Nauru	8	21	8	Ψ Nauru	..
New Caledonia........	7,358	19,058	153	Ψ Noumea	60,112*
New Zealand.........	103,736	268,676	3,254	Ψ Wellington	352,000
Cook Islands	91	236	18	Avarua	..
Niue	100	259	3	Alofi.............	956
Ross Dependency....	175,000	453,247	..	..	..
Papua New Guinea	178,260	461,691	3,329	Ψ Port Moresby	139,300
Pitcairn Islands	1·9	5	57 (total)	..	..
Samoa:—					
Eastern (U.S.).......	76	197	35	Ψ Pago Pago	3,055
Western	1,097	2,842	163	Ψ Apia	33,100*
Solomon Islands.......	10,983	28,446	270	Ψ Honiara	24,975
Tonga, etc.	270	699	97	Ψ Nuku'alofa	27,815
Tuvalu	61	158	8	Ψ Funafuti	2,120
Vanuatu	5,700	14,763	142	Ψ Vila	18,796
Wallis and Futuna Is...	106	274	12	Ψ Mata-Utu	..

† Former Trust Territory of the Pacific Islands.

THE LARGEST CITIES OF THE WORLD

Ψ = Seaport	Population	Ψ = Seaport	Population
MEXICO CITY, Mexico	18,748,000	São Paulo, Brazil	8,490,763
CAIRO, Egypt	14,000,000	SEOUL, Korea	9,200,000
TOKYO, Japan	11,806,729	Ψ Bombay, India	8,202,000
Ψ Shanghai, China	11,630,000	Tianjin, China	7,630,000
PARIS, France.....................	10,073,059	Ψ New York, U.S.A.	7,164,742
TEHRAN, Iran	10,000,000	Ψ Surabaya, Indonesia	7,027,913
Ψ BUENOS AIRES, Argentina	9,677,200	Ψ LONDON, U.K.	6,776,000
Ψ Calcutta, India	9,166,000	Ψ JAKARTA, Indonesia	6,503,449
PEKING, China	9,020,000	DELHI, India	6,220,000
Moscow, U.S.S.R.	8,642,000	Chongqing, China	6,200,000

WORLD GEOGRAPHICAL STATISTICS

North America
River.......	Mississippi–Missouri– Red Rock	3,741 miles
Lake	Superior	31,000 sq miles
Mountain ..	McKinley	20,320 ft
Waterfall ...	Yosemite, California	2,425 ft

South America
River.......	Amazon	4,007 miles
Lake	Titicaca	3,205 sq miles
Mountain ..	Aconcagua	22,834 ft
Waterfall ...	Angel, Venezuela	3,212 ft

Africa
River......	Nile	4,145 miles
Lake	Victoria	26,800 sq miles
Mountain ..	Kilimanjaro	19,340 ft
Waterfall ...	Tugela, Natal	3,110 ft

Europe
River.......	Volga, USSR	2,293 miles
Lake	Ladoga, USSR	6,826 sq miles
Mountain ..	Elbruz, Caucasus	18,481 ft
Waterfall ...	Utigardd, Norway	2,625 ft

Asia
River.......	Yenisei, Mongolia– USSR	3,442 miles
Lake	Aral Sea, USSR	25,500 sq miles
Mountain ..	Everest	29,028 ft
Waterfall ...	Gersoppa, India	830 ft

Oceania
River.......	Murray-Darling, Australia	2,350 miles
Lake	Eyre, Australia	3,700 sq miles
Mountain ..	Cook, New Zealand	12,349 ft
Waterfall ...	Sutherland, New Zealand	1,904 ft

OCEAN AREAS AND DEPTHS

Oceans

Name	Area of Basin (sq. miles)	Greatest Depth (feet)
Pacific	63,800,000	Mariana Trench, 36,198
Atlantic	31,830,000	Milwaukee Deep 30,238
Indian	28,360,000	Java Trench 25,344
Arctic	5,500,000	 18,050

Seas

Name	Area of Basin (sq. miles)	Greatest Depth (feet)
South China	1,148,500	 16,452
Caribbean[1]	1,020,000	Cayman Trench, 25,216

Seas

Name	Area of Basin (sq. miles)	Greatest Depth (feet)
Mediterranean.[2]	966,750	Ionian Basin, 16,801
Bering	875,750	 13,442
Gulf of Mexico	590,000	Sigsbee Deep, 17,070
Okhotsk	589,800	Kuril Trough, 11,069
East China	482,300	Okinawa Trench, 8,914
Hudson Bay	475,800	.... c. 1,500
Japan	389,000	 12,276
Andaman	308,000	 14,500
North Sea	222,125	Skaggerak, 2,400
Banda Sea	180,000	Weber Basin, 24,400
Black Sea (and Sea of Azov)	178,500	 7,257
Red Sea	169,000	 8,984

[1] Excluding the Gulf of Mexico.
[2] Excluding the Black Sea.

PRINCIPAL LAND AREAS OF THE WORLD BELOW SEA LEVEL
(With approx. greatest depth in feet below Mean Sea Level.)

Europe: Netherlands coastal areas (15).
Asia: Jordan Valley, Dead Sea (1290)*.
  China: Sinkiang, Turfan Basin (980).
  U.S.S.R.–Iran: Caspian Sea (85)*.
  Arabia: Trucial Oman-U.A.E. (70).
Africa: Libyan Desert Depressions:—
  Qattara (440), Faiyum (150).
  Wadi Ryan (140), Sittra (110).

Africa: Libyan Desert Depressions (*continued*)—
  Areg (80), Wadi Natrun (75).
  Melfa (60), Siwa (55), Bahrain (50).
  Eritrea: Salt Plains depression (385).
  Algeria-Tunisia: Shott Melghir and El Gharsa (90)*.
America: Death Valley (275), Salton Sea (245)*.
Australia: Lake Eyre (40).

* Water surface

PRINCIPAL HEIGHTS ABOVE SEA LEVEL

	Feet
Europe: Alps—Mont Blanc	15,771
England: Scafell Pike	3,210
Wales: Snowdon	3,560
Scotland: Ben Nevis	4,406
Ireland: Carrantuohill	3,414
Asia: Everest	29,028
Africa: Kilimanjaro	19,340
North America: McKinley	20,320

	Feet
South America: Aconcagua	22,834
Australia: Kosciusko	7,316
New Zealand: Cook	12,349
Oceania: Jayakusumu[1]	16,500
Antarctica: Vinson Massif	16,864

[1] Variously known as Ngga Pulu, Carstensz Pyramid, Puntjak Sukarno.

THE LARGEST ISLANDS

Name of Island	Ocean	Area in Sq. Miles
Greenland	Arctic	840,004
New Guinea	Pacific	300,000
Borneo	Pacific	280,100
Madagascar	Indian	226,658
Baffin Island	Arctic	183,810
Sumatra	Indian	182,860
Honshu	Pacific	88,031
Great Britain[1]	Atlantic	84,186
Victoria Island	Arctic	81,930
Ellesmere Island	Arctic	75,767

Name of Island	Ocean	Area in Sq. Miles
Celebes (Sulawesi)	Indian	72,987
South Island, N.Z.	Pacific	58,093
Java (Indian)	Indian	48,763
North Island, N.Z.	Pacific	44,281
Newfoundland	Atlantic	43,359
Cuba	Atlantic	42,804
Luzon	Pacific	40,420
Iceland	Atlantic	39,769
Mindanao	Pacific	36,381
Ireland	Atlantic	32,595

[1] Mainland only.

THE WORLD'S LARGEST LAKES

The areas of some of these lakes are subject to seasonal variation.

Name	Locality	Length (Miles)	Area (Sq. Miles)	Name	Locality	Length (Miles)	Area (Sq. Miles)
Caspian Sea	Asia	760	143,000	Balkhash	U.S.S.R.	376	6,700
Superior	North America	383	31,800	Nettilling	Baffin Island	120	5,000
Victoria	Africa	210	26,800	Amadjuak	Baffin Island	75	4,000
Aral	U.S.S.R.	280	25,500	Bangweulu[1]	Africa	150	3,800
Huron	North America	206	23,100				(max)
Michigan	North America	321	22,300	Onega	U.S.S.R.	145	3,753
Tanganyika	Africa	430	12,700	Eyre[1]	Australia	130	3,700
Great Bear	Canada	200	12,275	Titicaca	South America	110	3,205
Baikal	U.S.S.R.	395	12,200	Nicaragua	Nicaragua	110	3,190
Malawi	Africa	363	11,430	Athabasca	Canada	208	3,120
Great Slave	Canada	300	11,030	Gairdner	Australia	100	3,000
Erie	North America	241	9,910	Turkana			
Winnipeg	Canada	264	9,465	(Rudolf)	Africa	154	2,473
Chad[1]	Africa	175	9,000	Reindeer	Canada	152	2,467
			(max)	Issyk-Kul	U.S.S.R.	115	2,445
Ontario	North America	193	7,550	Koko-Nor[1]	China	68	2,300
Ladoga	U.S.S.R.	136	6,826				(max)

[1] Area varies considerably according to season.

THE WORLD'S HIGHEST VOLCANOES

ACTIVE

Volcano	Locality	Height in Feet	Volcano	Locality	Height in Feet
Antofalla	Argentina	21,162	Nyamuragira	Zaire	10,150
Guallatiri	Chile	19,882	Mt. St. Helens	Cascade Range, U.S.A.	9,677
Cotopaxi	Ecuador	19,347	Tambora	Indonesia	9,351
Kluchevskaya	U.S.S.R.	15,913	Villarrica	Chile	9,325
Mt Wrangell	Alaska	14,000	Ruapehu	New Zealand	9,175
Mauna Loa	Hawaii	13,680	Paricutin	Mexico	9,100
Cameroon	Cameroon	13,350	Asama	Japan	8,340
Erebus	Antarctica	12,450	Ngauruhoe	New Zealand	7,515
Nyiragongo	Zaire	11,385	Hecla	Iceland	4,747
Iliamna	Aleutian Range, U.S.A.	11,000	Vesuvius	Italy	4,198
Etna	Sicily	10,853	Kilauea	Hawaii	4,077
Chillan	Chile	10,500	Stromboli	Lipari Is. Italy	3,038

DORMANT

Volcano	Locality	Height in Feet	Volcano	Locality	Height in Feet
Llullaillaco	Chile	22,057	Haleakala	Hawaii	10,022
Cayembe	Ecuador	18,982	The Peak	Tristan da Cunha	6,760
Demavend	Iran	18,384	Tongariro	New Zealand	6,458
Popocatepetl	Mexico	17,887	Pelée	Martinique	4,800
Pico de Teide	Tenerife	12,198	Soufrière	St Vincent Is., W.I.	4,200
Semerou	Java	12,060			

BELIEVED EXTINCT

Volcano	Locality	Height in Feet	Volcano	Locality	Height in Feet
Aconcagua	Andes	22,834	Antisana	Ecuador	18,713
Chimborazo	Ecuador	20,561	Citlaltepetl	Mexico	18,700
Kilimanjaro	Tanzania	19,340	Elbruz	Caucasus	18,481

THE WORLD'S HIGHEST MOUNTAINS

The following list contains some of the principal peaks of such ranges as the Himalayas and the Andes, and the highest mountains in other ranges.

Name	Range or Country	Height in Feet	Name	Range or Country	Height in Feet
Everest	Himalayas	29,028	Llullaillaco	Andes	22,057
K 2	Karakoram	28,250	Sajama	Andes	21,463
Kanchenjunga	Himalayas	28,208	Illimani	Andes	21,200
Makalu I	Himalayas	27,824	Chimborazo	Andes	20,561
Dhaulagiri	Himalayas	26,810	McKinley	Alaska	20,320
Nanga Parbat	Himalayas	26,660	Logan	Yukon	19,850
Annapurna	Himalayas	26,504	Cotopaxi	Andes	19,347
Nanda Devi	Himalayas	25,646	Kilimanjaro	Tanzania	19,340
Kamet	Himalayas	25,446	Citlaltepetl	Sierra Madre	18,700
Namcha Barwa	China	25,445	Elbruz	Caucasus	18,481
Minya Konka	China	24,890	St. Elias	Alaska	18,008
Communism Peak	Pamirs	24,590	Popocatepetl	Mexico	17,887
Pobedy Peak	Tian Shan	24,406	Foraker	Alaska	17,395
Lenin Peak	Pamirs	23,406	Lucania	Yukon	17,150
Aconcagua	Andes	22,834	Kenya	Kenya	17,058
Ojos del Salado	Andes	22,588	Ararat	Armenia	16,945
Bonete	Andes	22,545	Vinson Massif	Antarctica	16,864
Huascaran	Andes	22,204	Mont Blanc	Alps	15,771

THE WORLD'S LARGEST WATERFALLS

Greatest in height		Total height ft.	Greatest single drop ft.
Angel	Venezuela	3,212	2,648
Tugela	S. Africa	3,110	1,350
Utigard	Norway	2,625	1,970
Mongefossen	Norway	2,540	
Yosemite	California, U.S.A.	2,425	1,430
Mardalsfoss	Norway	2,154	974
Tyssestrengane	Norway	2,120	948
Kukenaam	Venezuela	2,000	
Sutherland	New Zealand	1,904	815
Takkakaw	Canada	1,650	1,200
Ribbon	California, U.S.A.	1,612	1,612
King George VI	Guyana	1,600	
Wollomombi	Australia	1,580	1,100
Roraima	Guyana	1,500	
Gavarnie	France	1,385	

Greatest in height	Total height ft.	Greatest single drop ft.
BRITISH ISLES		
Eas Coul Aulin	Scotland	658	
Caldron Snout*	England	450	
Powerscourt	Ireland	350	
Pistyll Rhaeadr	Wales	300	
* Cataracts—no sheer drop.		

Greatest in volume		Width yd.
Khone Cataracts	Laos	11,667
Guayra	Brazil	5,300
Victoria	Zimbabwe-Zambia	1,534
Niagara	Canada–U.S.A.	1,200

THE LONGEST RIVERS

River	Outflow	Length in Miles
Nile	Mediterranean	4,145
Amazon	Atlantic	4,007
Mississippi-Missouri– Red Rock	Gulf of Mexico	3,741
Yenisei	Arctic	3,442
Yangtze	North Pacific	3,436
Ob-Irtysh	Arctic	3,362
Hwang-ho (Yellow River)	North Pacific	3,000
Zaire (Congo)	Atlantic	2,920
Lena	Arctic	2,734
Amur	North Pacific	2,700
Mackenzie-Peace	Beaufort Sea	2,635
Mekong	China Sea	2,600
Niger	Gulf of Guinea	2,600
Rio de la Plata-Parana	Atlantic	2,485
Murray-Darling	Southern Ocean	2,350
Volga	Caspian Sea	2,293
Zambezi	Indian Ocean	2,200
Madeira	(1)	2,100
Purus (Coxiuara)	(1)	2,000
Yukon	Bering Sea	1,979
St. Lawrence	Gulf of St. Lawrence	1,945
Rio Grande del Norte	Gulf of Mexico	1,885
Ganges-Brahmaputra	Bay of Bengal	1,800
São Francisco	Atlantic	1,800
Indus	Arabian Sea	1,790
Danube	Black Sea	1,770
Salween (No Chiang)	Gulf of Martaban	1,750
Tigris-Euphrates	Persian Gulf	1,700
Tocantins	Pará River	1,700
Orinoco	Atlantic	1,700

Great Britain

Severn	Bristol Channel	220
Thames	North Sea	215

(1) Tributaries of the Amazon.

SOME FAMOUS BRIDGES

Among the outstanding *suspension bridges* of the World are the Verrazano Narrows Bridge, New York (main span, 4,260 ft.); the Golden Gate Bridge, San Francisco (4,200 ft.); Mackinac Bridge, Michigan (3,800 ft.); Bosporus, Turkey (3,523 ft.); George Washington Bridge, New York (3,500 ft.); the Ponte 25 April (Tagus Bridge), Portugal (3,323 ft.); Forth Road Bridge, Scotland (3,300 ft.); Severn Bridge, England (3,240 ft.); Tacoma Bridge, Washington, U.S.A. (2,800 ft.); Orinoco Bridge, Venezuela (2,336 ft.) and the Kanmon Bridge, Japan (2,336 ft.). Lengths shown above are all those of the main or longest span. The Humber Bridge was opened in 1981 and has the longest single central span, 4,626 ft., of any suspension bridge in the world.

The Transbay Bridge (*suspension and cantilever*), crossing San Francisco Bay from Oakland to San Francisco is 7½ miles long, with spans of 2,310 ft. each.

Among important *steel arch* bridges are the New River Gorge Bridge, Virginia, U.S.A. (1,700 ft); the Bayonne Bridge, from New Jersey to Staten Island, U.S.A. (1,652 ft.); Sydney Harbour Bridge, Australia (1,650 ft.); the Runcorn-Widnes Bridge, England (1,082 ft.); and the Glen Canyon Bridge over the Colorado River, U.S.A. (1,028 ft.). Major *concrete trestle* bridges include the Lake Pontchartrain Causeway, U.S.A. of 2,170 spans extending 23·87 miles and the Oosterscheldebrug, Netherlands, 3·12 miles long. Gladesville Bridge, Sydney, Australia, is a *concrete arch* bridge of 1,000 ft. span. The Tay Bridge in Scotland is a *steel box girder* bridge supported on twin piers (42 spans), 7,365 ft long.

The Chesapeake Bay Bridge-Tunnel (17·6 miles long) joining Cape Charles, Virginia, to Chesapeake Beach has 12·5 miles of *concrete trestle* bridge.

GREAT SHIP CANALS OF THE WORLD

Canal	Opened	Length, miles	Depth (ft.)†	Width (ft.)†
North Sea (Netherlands)	1876	14½	43	148
Corinth (Greece)	1893	4	26	72
Kiel (Germany)	1895	61	31	132
Manchester (England)	1894	35½	30	120
Panama	1914	50½	39·5	500
Suez (Egypt)	1869	100	42	197
Terneuzen-Ghent (Netherlands–Belgium)	1895	18½	38	102
St. Lawrence Seaway (Canada)	1959	378*	27	200

† Of largest vessels permitted.   * Includes Lake Ontario and Welland Canal.

INLAND WATERWAYS.—The British Waterways Board are the navigational authority for nearly 2,000 miles of canals and river navigations in England, Scotland and Wales. Some 340 miles are maintained and are being developed as Commercial Waterways for use by freight-carrying vessels, and another 1,200 miles, the Cruising Waterways, are being developed for boating, fishing and other amenities. The remaining 500 miles, the Remainder Waterways, are maintained with due regard to safety, public health and the preservation of amenities. Over a third of this mileage is navigable or has been restored to navigation. The Manchester Ship Canal, Bridgewater Canal, Rochdale Canal, River Thames and Fenland Waterways are among those which are the responsibility of other authorities.

LONGEST RAILWAY TUNNELS

E.R. = Eastern Region; L.M.R. = London Midland Region;
S.R. = Southern Region; W.R. = Western Region

United Kingdom

		Miles	Yards			Miles	Yards
Severn	W.R.	4	484	Bradway	E.R.	1	267
Totley	E.R.	3	950	Sough	L.M.R.	1	255
Standedge	E.R.	3	66	Watford, New	L.M.R.	1	230
Sodbury	W.R.	2	924	Llangyfelach	W.R.	1	193
Disley	L.M.R.	2	346	Caerphilly	W.R.	1	173
Ffestiniog	L.M.R.	2	338	Abbot's Cliff	S.R.	1	182
Bramhope	E.R.	2	241	Halton	L.M.R.	1	176
Cowburn	L.M.R.	2	182	Corby	L.M.R.	1	160
Sevenoaks	S.R.	1	1693	Wenvoe	W.R.	1	107
Morley	E.R.	1	1609	Sapperton	W.R.	1	100
Box	W.R.	1	1452	Wymington	L.M.R.	1	100
Dove Holes	L.M.R.	1	1224				
Littleborough (Summit)	L.M.R.	1	1125				
Anderston	S.R.	1	1010				
Ponsbourne	E.R.	1	924				
Bleamoor	L.M.R.	1	869				
Polhill	S.R.	1	851				
Queensbury	E.R.	1	741				
Kilsby	L.M.R.	1	666				
Lydden	S.R.	1	609				
Strood	S.R.	1	569				
Oxted	S.R.	1	501				
Clayton	S.R.	1	499				
Penge	S.R.	1	381				
Merstham New (Quarry)	S.R.	1	353				
Greenock	Scottish Region	1	351				

The London Underground *Northern Line* between Morden and East Finchley by the City Branch serves 25 stations and uses tunnels totalling 17¼ miles in length).

The World
(Submarine tunnels are not included)

		Miles	Yards
Simplon	Switzerland–Italy	12	560
Apennine	Italy	11	880
St. Gotthard	Switzerland	9	550
Lötschberg	Switzerland	9	130
Mont Cenis	Italy	8	870
Cascade	United States	7	1410
Arlberg	Austria	6	650
Moffat	United States	6	200
Shimizu	Japan	6	70

THE ARCTIC OCEAN

The Arctic Ocean consists of a deep sea over 2,000 fathoms, on the southern margin of which there is a broad continental shelf with numerous islands. Into this deeper sea there is only one broad channel, about 700 miles, between Greenland and Scandinavia. Bering Strait is only 49 miles wide and 27 fathoms deep. The southern boundary of the Arctic Ocean is the Wyville-Thomson and Faeroe-Icelandic submarine ridge, which separates the North Atlantic from the Norwegian and Greenland Seas. The Norwegian Deep lies between Norway and Jan Mayen and Iceland; it exceeds 1,500 fathoms. The Greenland Deep, of similar depth, lies between Spitsbergen and Greenland. These two depressions are separated by a somewhat deeply submerged ridge from the east of Jan Mayen to Bear Island, south of Spitsbergen. A shallow ridge from the north-west of Spitsbergen to Greenland separates the Greenland Sea from the deep North Polar Basin. This extends from the north of Spitsbergen and Franz Josef Land to the north of the New Siberia Islands and of the North American Arctic Archipelago. Another more shallow depression is Baffin Bay, less than 1,000 fathoms. This is separated from the North Atlantic by a submarine ridge. Barent's Sea, between Spitsbergen, Norway and Novaya Zemlya, and the Kara Sea, between Novaya Zemlya and the Siberian coast, are respectively below 200 and 100 fathoms. The total area of the Arctic Sea is about 5·5 million square miles, of which 2·3 million square miles are probably covered with floating ice.

DISTANCE OF THE HORIZON

The limit of distance to which one can see varies with the height of the spectator. The greatest distance at which an object on the surface of the sea, or of a level plain, can be seen by a person whose eyes are at a height of five feet from the same level is nearly three miles. At a height of 20 feet the range is increased to nearly six miles, and an approximate rule for finding the range of vision for small heights is to increase the square root of the number of feet that the eye is above the level surface by a third of itself, the result being the distance of the horizon in miles, but is slightly in excess of that in the table below, which is computed by a more precise formula. The table may be used conversely to show the distance of an object of given height that is just visible from a point in the surface of the earth or sea. Refraction is taken into account both in the approximate rule and in the Table.

At a height of	the range is	At a height of	the range is	At a height of	the range is
5 ft.	2·9 miles	500 ft.	29·5 miles	4,000 ft.	83·3 miles
20 ft.	5·9 „	1,000 ft.	41·6 „	5,000 „	93·1 „
50 „	9·3 „	2,000 „	58·9 „	20,000 „	186·2 „
100 „	13·2 „	3,000 „	72·1 „		

MIGRATION
Acceptances for settlement by nationality

Geographical region and nationality	Number of persons			Geographical region and nationality	Number of persons		
	1983	1984	1985		1983	1984	1985
Belgium	70	120	100	Morocco	150	130	160
Denmark	140	140	150	Nigeria	360	320	500
France	520	590	580	Sierra Leone	60	80	70
Germany (Federal				Somalia	20	20	20
Republic)	680	640	750	South Africa	840	690	790
Greece	200	220	250	Sudan	50	50	110
Italy	600	520	540	Tanzania	320	300	330
Luxembourg	—	—	—	Tunisia	50	60	40
Netherlands	460	540	460	Uganda	100	40	50
				Zambia	90	110	100
European Community	**2,680**	**2,770**	**2,820**	Zimbabwe	280	280	320
Austria	110	140	120	**Africa: total**	**4,670**	**4,380**	**4,710**
Cyprus	560	470	420				
Finland	130	100	110	Bangladesh	4,870	4,180	5,330
Malta	200	210	180	India	5,380	5,140	5,500
Norway	230	210	230	Pakistan	6,440	5,510	6,680
Portugal	390	230	230				
Spain	480	530	440	**Indian sub-continent**	**16,690**	**14,840**	**17,510**
Sweden	330	400	390				
Switzerland	170	180	170	Iran	1,980	1,670	2,210
Turkey	580	530	480	Iraq	430	400	550
Yugoslavia	140	130	130	Israel	310	290	340
				Jordan	150	120	90
Other Western Europe	**3,310**	**3,130**	**2,900**	Kuwait	—	10	10
				Lebanon	260	260	250
Bulgaria	10	10	20	Saudi Arabia	30	50	30
Czechoslovakia	30	30	20	Syria	100	70	90
German Democratic							
Republic	10	10	10	**Middle East**	**3,280**	**2,870**	**3,580**
Hungary	20	40	50				
Poland	390	310	370	China	160	140	140
Romania	20	20	20	Indonesia	60	60	60
U.S.S.R.	40	50	50	Japan	1,010	1,100	1,010
				Malaysia	780	680	630
Eastern Europe	**520**	**470**	**540**	Philippines	680	630	780
				Singapore	140	160	160
Europe: total	**6,520**	**6,370**	**6,270**	Sri Lanka	920	760	930
				Thailand	260	300	340
Argentina	80	40	50	BDTC Hong Kong*	1,050	1,040	950
Barbados	40	50	60				
Brazil	140	190	170	**Remainder of Asia**	**5,070**	**4,860**	**5,000**
Canada	1,140	1,400	1,500				
Chile	120	60	70	**Asia: total**	**25,040**	**22,570**	**26,090**
Colombia	180	140	170				
Cuba	—	—	—	Australia	2,680	3,590	3,780
Guyana	190	190	200	New Zealand	1,980	2,460	2,880
Jamaica	310	290	350				
Mexico	70	70	70	**Australasia: total**	**4,660**	**6,040**	**6,660**
Peru	50	60	80				
Trinidad and Tobago	170	150	160	British Overseas citizens	3,280	2,690	2,180
U.S.A.	3,940	3,750	4,170	Other countries not else-			
Uruguay	—	—	10	where specified†	820	860	900
Venezuela	70	50	50	Stateless†	1,930	1,600	1,420
West Indies Associated							
States	40	—	—	**All nationalities**	**53,460**	**50,950**	**55,360**
Americas: total	**6,530**	**6,440**	**7,130**	Foreign	26,560	24,230	26,840
				Commonwealth	26,910	26,720	28,520
Algeria	100	60	70				
Egypt	380	350	350	Old Commonwealth	5,800	7,440	8,160
Ethiopia	50	40	30	New Commonwealth and			
Ghana	560	690	660	Pakistan	27,550	24,800	27,050
Kenya	640	610	520	Foreign excluding			
Libya	100	70	170	Pakistan	20,120	18,720	20,150
Mauritius	520	470	410				

*British Dependant Territories Citizens.   †Includes refugees from South-East Asia.

Migration into and out from the United Kingdom (Thousands)

In-flow	Total			Professional & managerial			Manual & clerical			Not gainfully employed†		
	Persons	Males	Females	Persons	Males	Females	Persons	Males	Females	Persons	Males	Females
1980	174	92	82	44	32	12	32	19	14	97	41	56
1981	153	83	71	45	32	13	24	14	10	85	37	48
1982	202	100	101	44	35	9	38	18	20	120	48	73
1983	202	107	95	55	40	15	36	21	15	111	46	64
1984	201	102	99	59	41	18	32	15	17	111	46	64
1985	270	118	153	77	46	31	38	19	19	155	52	103
Out-flow												
1980	229	134	95	65	49	16	62	42	20	102	43	59
1981	233	133	100	67	50	17	60	38	22	105	44	61
1982	259	135	124	67	48	19	66	37	29	126	50	76
1983	185	90	95	51	32	18	36	19	16	99	38	60
1984	164	80	84	51	32	19	34	16	19	79	32	47
1985	174	91	83	51	36	15	36	18	17	87	36	51

† Includes housewives, students, children and retired persons.

DISTANCES FROM LONDON (Heathrow) BY AIR

A list of the distances in statute miles from London to various places abroad. They have been supplied by the publishers of *The International Aeradio Air Distances Manual*, Southall, Middx.

To	Miles	To	Miles	To	Miles
Abu Dhabi	3,425	Doha	3,253	Nairobi	4,248
Addis Ababa	3,675	Dubai	3,414	Naples	1,011
Algiers	1,035	Dublin	279	Nassau	4,333
Amman	2,287	Durban	5,937	New York (J. F. Kennedy)	3,440
Amsterdam	230	Düsseldorf	310	Nice	645
Ankara	1,770	Entebbe	4,033	Oporto	806
Athens	1,500	Frankfurt	406	Oslo (Fornebu)	723
Auckland	11,404	Freetown	3,046	Palma/Majorca	836
Baghdad	2,551	Geneva	468	Paris	215; (Orly 227)
Bahrain	3,163	Gibraltar	1,084	Perth/Australia	9,008
Bangkok	5,928	Gothenburg (Landvetter)	664	Port of Spain/Trinidad	4,405
Barbados	4,193	Hamburg	463	Prague	649
Barcelona	712	Harare	5,156	Rangoon	5,582
Basle	447	Havana	4,647	Reykjavik	1,167
Beirut	2,161	Helsinki (Vantaa)	1,147	Rhodes	1,743
Belfast	325	Hong Kong	5,990	Rome (Fiumicino)	895
Belgrade	1,056	Honolulu	7,220	Salzburg	651
Berlin (Tegel)	588	Istanbul	1,560	Shannon	369
Bermuda	3,428	Jeddah	2,947	Singapore	6,756
Bombay	4,478	Johannesburg	5,634	Sofia	1,266
Brisbane	10,273	Karachi	3,935	Stockholm (Arlanda)	908
Brussels	217	Khartoum	3,071	Sydney, Australia	10,568
Bucharest	1,307	Kingston/Jamaica	4,668	Tangier	1,120
Budapest	923	Kuala Lumpur	6,557	Teheran	2,741
Cairo	2,194	Kuwait	2,903	Tel Aviv	2,227
Calcutta	4,958	Lagos	3,107	Tokyo (Narita)	5,956
Canberra	10,563	Larnaca/Cyprus	2,036	Toronto	3,545
Caracas	4,639	Leningrad	1,314	Tripoli	1,468
Casablanca	1,300	Lima	6,303	Turin (Caselle)	570
Chicago (O'Hare)	3,941	Lisbon	972	Valencia	826
Cologne	331	Lomé	3,129	Vancouver	4,707
Colombo	5,411	Madrid	773	Venice (Tessera)	715
Copenhagen	608	Malta	1,305	Vienna (Schwechat)	790
Dakar	2,706	Marseilles	614	Warsaw	912
Damascus	2,223	Mauritius	6,075	Washington	3,665
Dar-es-Salaam	4,662	Milan	609	Wellington	11,692
Darwin	8,613	Montego Bay	4,687	Zagreb	848
Delhi	4,180	Montreal (Mirabel)	3,241	Zürich	490
Detroit	3,754	Moscow (Sheremetievo)	1,557		
Dhaka	4,976	Munich	588		

ENGLISH KINGS AND QUEENS A.D. 827 TO 1603

Name	DYNASTY	MARRIED	Access.	Died	Age	Rgnd. Yrs.
	Saxons and Danes					
EGBERT	King of Wessex and all England		827	839	—	12
ETHELWULF	Son of Egbert		839	858	—	19
{ ETHELBALD	Son of Ethelwulf		858	860	—	2
{ ETHELBERT	Son of Ethelwulf		858	866	—	8
ETHELRED	Son of Ethelwulf		866	871	—	5
ALFRED THE GREAT	Son of Ethelwulf	Ealhswith of Gaini	871	899	52	28
EDWARD THE ELDER	Son of Alfred the Great	1, Egwyn; 2, Elfled; 3, Eadgifu	899	925	55	26
ATHELSTAN	Eldest son of Edward the Elder (by 1)		925	940	45	15
EDMUND	Third son of Edward the Elder (by 3)	1, Elgiva; 2, Ethefled	940	946	25	6
EDRED	Fourth son of Edward the Elder (by 3)		946	955	32	9
EDWY	Son of Edmund (by 1)		955	959	18	3
EDGAR	Second son of Edmund (by 1)	1, Ethelfled; 2, Elfthryth	959	975	32	17
EDWARD THE MARTYR	Son of Edgar (by 1)		975	978	17	4
ETHELRED II	Younger son of Edgar (by 2)	1, Elfgifu; 2, Emma, dau. of Richard, Duke of Normandy	978	1016	48	37
EDMUND IRONSIDE	Eldest son of Ethelred II (by 1)		1016	1016	27	0
CANUTE THE DANE	By conquest and election	1, Elfgifu of Deira; 2, Emma, widow of Ethelred II	1017	1035	40	18
HAROLD I	Son of Canute (by 1)		1035	1040	—	5
HARDICANUTE	Son of Canute (by 2)		1040	1042	24	2
EDWARD THE CONFESSOR	Son of Ethelred II (by 2)	Edith, dau. of Earl Godwin	1042	1066	62	24
HAROLD II	Son of Earl Godwin		1066	1066	44	0
	The House of Normandy					
WILLIAM I	Obtained the Crown by Conquest	Matilda, dau. of Baldwin, Count of Flanders	1066	1087	60	21
WILLIAM II	Third son of William I	(Died unmarried)	1087	1100	43	13
HENRY I	Youngest son of William I	1st Matilda, dau. of Malcolm Canmore, K. of Scotland; 2nd Adelicia, dau. of Godfrey, D. of Louvaine	1100	1135	67	35
STEPHEN	Third son of Stephen, Count of Blois, by Adela, fourth dau. of William I.	Matilda, dau. of Eustace, Count of Boulogne	1135	1154	50	19
	The House of Plantagenet					
HENRY II	Son of Geoffrey Plantagenet by Matilda, only dau. of Henry I; his grandmother, Matilda of Scotland, was a lineal descendant of Alfred and Egbert.	Eleanor, dau. of Guienne and divorced Queen of Louis VII of France	1154	1189	56	35
RICHARD I	Eldest surviving son of Henry II	Berengaria, dau. of Sancho VI, K. of Navarre	1189	1199	42	10
JOHN	Sixth and youngest son of Henry II	1st Avisa, dau. of E. of Gloucester, divorced upon grounds of consanguinity; 2nd Isabella dau. of Aymer, Count of Angoulême	1199	1216	50	17
HENRY III	Elder son of John	Eleanor, dau. of Raymond, Count of Provence	1216	1272	65	56
EDWARD I	Eldest surviving son of Henry III	1st Eleanor, dau. of Ferdinand III, K. of Castile; 2nd Margaret, dau. of Philip III, the Hardy, K. of France	1272	1307	68	35
EDWARD II	Eldest surviving son of Edward I	Isabella, dau. of Philip IV, the Fair, K. of France	1307	1327	43	20

Name	DYNASTY	MARRIED	Access.	Died	Age	Rgnd.
EDWARD III	Eldest son of Edward II	Philippa, dau. of William, Count of Holland and Hainault.	1327	1377	65	Yrs. 50
RICHARD II	Son of the Black Prince, eldest son of Edward III	1st Anne, dau. of Emp. Charles IV; 2nd Isabel, dau. of Charles VI of France.	1377	dep. 1399 (d. 1400)	34	22
	The House of Lancaster					
HENRY IV	Son of John of Gaunt, 4th son of Edward III	1st Mary de Bohun, dau. of the E. of Hereford; 2nd Joanna of Navarre, widow of John de Montfort, D. of Brittany.	1399	1413	47	13
HENRY V	Eldest surviving son of Henry IV	Katherine, dau. of Charles VI, K. of France	1413	1422	34	9
HENRY VI	Only son of Henry V (died 1471)	Margaret of Anjou, dau. of René, D. of Anjou	1422	dep. 1461	49	39
	The House of York					
EDWARD IV	Son of Richard, grandson of Edmund, fifth son of Edward III; and of Anne, great-grand-daughter of Lionel, third son of Edward III	Elizabeth Widvile (or Woodville), dau. of Sir Richard Widvile and widow of Sir John Grey of Groby.	1461	1483	41	22
EDWARD V	Eldest son of Edward IV	(Died unmarried)	1483	1483	13	75 days
RICHARD III	Younger brother of Edward IV	Anne, dau. of the E. of Warwick, and widow of Edward, Prince of Wales, s. of Henry VI	1483	1485	32	2
	The House of Tudor					
HENRY VII	Son of Edmund, eldest son of Owen Tudor, by Katherine, widow of Henry V; his mother, Margaret Beaufort, was great-grand-daughter of John of Gaunt.	Elizabeth, dau. of Edward IV.	1485	1509	53	24
HENRY VIII	Only surviving son of Henry VII	1st Katherine of Aragon, widow of his elder brother Arthur, (divorced); 2nd Anne, dau. of Sir Thomas Boleyn, (beheaded); 3rd Jane, dau. of Sir John Seymour, (died in childbirth of a son, aft. Edward VI); 4th Anne, sister of William, D. of Cleves, (divorced); 5th Catherine Howard, niece of the Duke of Norfolk, (beheaded); 6th Catherine, dau. of Sir Thomas Parr and widow of Edward Nevill, Lord Latimer.	1509	1547	56	38
EDWARD VI	Son of Henry VIII by Jane Seymour	(Died unmarried)	1547	1553	16	6
JANE	Grand-daughter of Mary, younger sister of Henry VIII, (beheaded Feb. 12, 1554).	Lord Guildford Dudley.	1553	1554	17	14 days
MARY I	Daughter of Henry VIII by Katherine of Aragon	Philip II of Spain	1553	1558	43	5
ELIZABETH I	Daughter of Henry VIII by Anne Boleyn	(Died unmarried)	1558	1603	69	44

BRITISH KINGS AND QUEENS FROM 1603

Name	DYNASTY	MARRIED	Access.	Died	Age	Rgnd.
	The House of Stuart					Yrs.
JAMES I (VI or Scot.)	Son of Mary, Queen of Scots, grand-daughter of James IV and Margaret, daughter of Henry VII.	Anne, dau. of Frederick II of Denmark	1603	1625	59	22
CHARLES I	Only surviving son of James I	Henrietta-Maria, dau. of Henry IV of France	1625	Beh. 1649	48	24
	Commonwealth declared May 19, 1649					
	Oliver Cromwell, Lord Protector, 1653—8; Richard Cromwell, Lord Protector, 1658—9					
CHARLES II	Eldest son of Charles I (restored 1660)	The Infanta Catharine of Portugal, dau. of John IV and sister of Alphonso VI.	1649	1685	55	36
JAMES II (VII or Scot.)	Second son of Charles I (Interregnum, Dec. 11, 1688—Feb. 13, 1689)	1st Lady Anne Hyde, dau. of Edward, E. of Clarendon, who died before James ascended the throne; 2nd Mary Beatrice Eleanor d'Este, dau. of Alphonso, D. of Modena.	1685	dep. 1688 d. 1701	68	3
WILLIAM III and	Son of William Prince of Orange and grandson of Charles I		1689	1702	51	13
MARY II	Eldest daughter of James II			1694	33	6
ANNE	Second daughter of James II	Prince George of Denmark	1702	1714	49	12
	The House of Hanover					
GEORGE I	Son of Elector of Hanover, by Sophia, daughter of Elizabeth, daughter of James I	Sophia, dau. of George William, D. of Celle.	1714	1727	67	13
GEORGE II	Only son of George I	Wilhelmina Caroline, dau. of John Frederick, Margrave of Brandenburg-Anspach.	1727	1760	77	33
GEORGE III	Grandson of George II	Charlotte Sophia, dau. of Charles Lewis Frederick, D. of Mecklenburg-Strelitz	1760	1820	81	59
GEORGE IV	Eldest son of George III (Regent from February 5, 1811)	Caroline, dau. of Charles William Ferdinand, D. of Brunswick-Wolfenbuttel.	1820	1830	67	10
WILLIAM IV	Third son of George III	Adelaide, dau. of George Frederick Charles, D. of Saxe-Meiningen.	1830	1837	71	7
VICTORIA	Daughter of Edward, 4th son of George III	Francis Albert Augustus Charles Emmanuel, D. of Saxe, Pr. of Saxe-Cobourg and Gotha.	1837	1901	81	63
	The House of Saxe-Coburg					
EDWARD VII	Eldest son of Victoria	Princess Alexandra of Denmark	1901	1910	68	9
	The House of Windsor					
GEORGE V	Surviving son of Edward VII	H.S.H. Princess Victoria Mary of Teck	1910	1936	70	25
EDWARD VIII	Eldest son of George V (abdicated 1936)	(Mrs. Wallis Warfield, June 3, 1937.)	1936	1972	77	325 days
GEORGE VI	Second son of George V	The Lady Elizabeth Angela Marguerite, dau. of the 14th Earl of Strathmore and Kinghorne (HER MAJESTY QUEEN ELIZABETH THE QUEEN MOTHER).	1936	1952	56	15
ELIZABETH II	Elder daughter of George VI	Philip, son of Prince Andrew of Greece (H.R.H. THE DUKE OF EDINBURGH).	1952	WHOM GOD PRESERVE.		

SCOTTISH KINGS AND QUEENS A.D. 1057 to 1603

Name	SOVEREIGN	MARRIED	Access.	Died
MALCOLM III (CANMORE)	Son of Duncan I	1st Ingibiorg, widow of Thorfinn, Earl of Orkney; 2nd Margaret, sister of Edgar the Atheling.	1057	1093
DONALD BÁN	Brother of Malcolm Canmore	....	1093	1094
DUNCAN II	Son of Malcolm Canmore, by first marriage	....	1094	1094
DONALD BÁN	(Restored)	....	1094	1097
EDGAR	Son of Malcolm Canmore, by second marriage	Died unmarried	1097	1107
ALEXANDER I	Son of Malcolm Canmore	Sybilla, natural daughter of Henry I of England	1107	1124
DAVID I	Son of Malcolm Canmore	Matilda, daughter of Waltheof, Earl of Northumbria widow of Simon, Earl of Northampton	1124	1153
MALCOLM IV (THE MAIDEN)	Son of Henry, eldest son of David I	Died unmarried	1153	1165
WILLIAM I (THE LION)	Brother of Malcolm the Maiden	Ermengarde, daughter of Richard, Viscount of Beaumont	1165	1214
ALEXANDER II	Son of William the Lion	1st Joanna, daughter of King John; 2nd Mary, daughter of Ingelram de Coucy (Picard)	1214	1249
ALEXANDER III	Son of Alexander II, by second marriage	1st Margaret, daughter of Henry III of England; 2nd Joleta, daughter of the Count de Dreux	1249	1286
MARGARET, MAID OF NORWAY	Daughter of Eric II of Norway, grand-daughter of Alexander III.	Died unmarried	1286	1290
JOHN BALIOL	Grandson of eldest daughter of David, Earl of Huntingdon, brother of William the Lion	....	1292	1296
ROBERT I (BRUCE)	Great-grandson of 2nd daughter of David, Earl of Huntingdon, brother of William the Lion	1st Isabella, daughter of Donald, Earl of Mar; 2nd Elizabeth de Burgh, sister of Earl of Ulster.	1306	1329
DAVID II	Son of Robert I, by second marriage	1st Joanna, daughter of Edward II of England; 2nd Margaret, widow of Sir John Logie (divorced, 1369).	1329	1371
ROBERT II (STEWART)	Son of Marjorie, daughter of Robert I by first marriage, and Walter the Steward.	1st Elizabeth, dau. of Sir Robert Mure (or More) of Rowallan; 2nd Euphemia, dau., of Hugh, Earl of Ross, widow of John, Earl of Moray.	1371	1390
ROBERT III	(John, Earl of Carrick) son of Robert II	Annabella, daughter of Sir John Drummond of Stobhall, niece of Margaret Logie.	1390	1406
JAMES I	Son of Robert III	Jane Beaufort, daughter of John, Earl of Somerset, 4th son of John of Gaunt and grandson of Edward III of England.	1406	1437
JAMES II	Son of James I	Mary, daughter of Arnold, Duke of Gueldres	1437	1460
JAMES III	Eldest son of James II	Margaret, daughter of Christian I of Denmark, Norway and Sweden.	1460	1488
JAMES IV	Eldest son of James III	Margaret Tudor, daughter of Henry VII	1488	1513
JAMES V	Son of James IV	1st Madeleine, daughter of Francis I of France; 2nd Mary of Lorraine, daughter of Duc de Guise, widow of Duc de Longueville.	1513	1542
MARY	Daughter of James V, by second marriage	1st Francis, Dauphin of France; 2nd Henry, Lord Darnley; 3rd James, Earl of Bothwell	1542	1587
JAMES VI (Ascended the Throne of England 1603)	Son of Mary, by second marriage	Anne, daughter of Frederick II of Denmark	1567	1625

WELSH SOVEREIGNS AND PRINCES

WALES was ruled by Sovereign Princes from the "earliest times" until the death of Llywelyn in 1282. The first English Prince of Wales was the son of Edward I, and was born in Caernarvon town on April 25, 1284. According to a discredited legend, he was presented to the Welsh chieftains as their Prince, in fulfilment of a promise that they should have a Prince who "could not speak a word of English" and should be native born. This son, who afterwards became Edward II, was created "Prince of Wales and Earl of Chester" at the famous Lincoln Parliament on February 7, 1301. The title Prince of Wales is borne after individual conferment and is not inherited at birth, though some Princes have been declared and styled Prince of Wales but never formally so created (*s.*). The title was conferred on Prince Charles by Her Majesty the Queen on July 26, 1958. He was invested at Caernarvon on July 1, 1969.

Independent Princes, A.D. 844 to 1282

Rhodri the Great	844–878
Anarawd, son of Rhodri	878–916
Hywel Dda, the Good	916–950
Iago ab Idwal (or Ieuaf)	950–979
Hywel ab Ieuaf, the Bad	979–985
Cadwallon, his brother	985–986
Maredudd ab Owain ap Hywel Dda	986–999
Cynan ap Hywel ab Ieuaf	999–1008
Llywelyn ap Seisyll	1018–1023
Iago ab Idwal ap Meurig	1023–1039
Gruffydd ap Llywelyn ap Seisyll	1039–1063
Bleddyn ap Cynfyn	1063–1075
Trahaern ap Caradog	1075–1081
Gruffydd ap Cynan ab Iago	1081–1137
Owain Gwynedd	1137–1170
Dafydd ab Owain Gwynedd	1170–1194
Llywelyn Fawr, the Great	1194–1240
Dafydd ap Llywelyn	1240–1246
Llywelyn ap Gruffydd ap Llywelyn	1246–1282

English Princes, since A.D. 1301

Edward, b. 1284 (Edwd. II), cr. Pr. of Wales	1301
Edward the Black Prince, s. of Edward III	1343
Richard (Richard II), s. of the Black Prince	1376
Henry of Monmouth (Henry V)	1399
Edward of Westminster, son of Henry VI	1454
Edward of Westminster (Edward V)	1471
Edward, son of Richard III (d. 1484)	1483
Arthur Tudor, son of Henry VII	1489
Henry Tudor (Hen. VIII), s. of Henry VII	1504
Henry Stuart, son of James I (d. 1612)	1610
Charles Stuart (Charles I), s. of James I	1616
Charles (Charles II), son of Charles I ... (*s.*) *c.* 1638
James Francis Edward, "The Old Tender" (d. 1766) .... (*s.*) 1688
George Augustus (Geo. II), s. of George I	1714
Frederick Lewis, s. of George II (d. 1751)	1729
George William Frederick (George III)	1751
George Augustus Frederick (George IV)	1762
Albert Edward (Edward VII)	1841
George (George V)	1901
Edward (Edward VIII)	1910
Charles Philip Arthur George	1958

THE FAMILY OF QUEEN VICTORIA

QUEEN VICTORIA *was born* May 24, 1819; *succeeded* to the Throne June 20, 1837; *married* Feb. 10, 1840 Albert, PRINCE CONSORT (*born* Aug. 26, 1819, *died* Dec. 14, 1861); *died* Jan. 22, 1901. Her Majesty had *issue*:—

1. H.R.H. Princess Victoria (*Princess Royal*) (1840–1901), *m.*, 1858, Frederick, *German Emperor* 1888. *Issue*:—

(1) H.I.M. William II (1859–1941), *German Emperor* 1888–1918, *m.*, 1st, 1881, Princess Augusta Victoria of Schleswig-Holstein-Sonderburg-Augustenburg (1858–1921), and 2nd, 1922, Princess Hermine of Reuss (1887–1947); *issue*:—

  (a) Prince William (1882–1951), (*Crown Prince* 1888–1918), *m.* Duchess Cecilia of Mecklenburg-Schwerin (d. 1954); *issue*:—Prince Wilhelm (1906–1940); Prince Louis Ferdinand, b. 1907, *m.*, 1938, Grand Duchess Kira (see p. 215); Prince Hubertus (1909–1950); Prince Frederick George (1911–1966); Princess Alexandrine Irene (b. 1915); Princess Cecilia (1917–1975).

  (b) Prince Eitel Frederick (1883–1942), *m.* Duchess Sophie of Oldenburg (marriage dissolved 1926).

  (c) Prince Adalbert (1884–1948), *m.* Duchess Adelaide of Saxe-Meiningen; *issue*:—Princess Victoria Marina (b. 1917); Prince William Victor (b. 1919).

  (d) Prince Augustus William (1887–1949), *m.* Princess Alexandra of Schleswig-Glucksburg (marriage dissolved 1920); *issue*:—Prince Alexander (b. 1912).

  (e) Prince Oscar (1888–1958), *m.* Countess von Ruppin; *issue*:—Prince Oscar (1915–1939); Prince Burchard (b. 1917); Princess Herzeleide (b. 1918); Prince William (b. 1922).

  (f) Prince Joachim (1890–1920), *m.* Princess Marie of Anhalt; *issue*:—Prince Karl Franz Joseph (1916–75).

  (g) Princess Victoria (1892–1980), *m.*, 1913, Ernst, Duke of Brunswick; *issue*:—Prince Ernest (b. 1914); Prince George (b. 1915); Princess Frederica (1917–1981), *m.* Paul I, King of the Hellenes (*see* below); Prince Christian Oskar (1919–1981); Prince Welf Heinrich (b. 1923).

(2) Princess Charlotte (1860–1919), *m.*, 1878, Bernhard, Duke of Saxe-Meiningen (1851–1914). *Issue*:—Princess Feodora (1879–1945), *m.*, 1898, the Prince Henry XXX. of Reuss.

(3) Prince Henry (1862–1929), *m.*, 1888, Princess Irene of Hesse. *Issue*:—

  (a) Prince Waldemar (1889–1945), *m.* Princess Calixsta of Lippe.

  (b) Prince Sigismund (1896–1978), *m.* Princess Charlotte of Saxe-Altenberg; *issue*:—Princess Barbe (b. 1920); Prince Alfred (b. 1924).

(4) Princess Victoria (1866–1929), *m.*, 1st, 1890, Prince Adolphus of Schaumburg-Lippe, and 2nd, 1927, Alexander Zubkov.

(5) Prince Waldemar (1868–1879).

(6) Princess Sophia (1870–1932), *m.*, 1889, Constantine I, *King of the Hellenes*, 1913–17, 1920–22. *Issue*:—

  (a) George II (1890–1947), *King of the Hellenes* 1922–24 and 1935–47, *m.* Princess Elisabeth of Roumania (marriage dissolved 1935).

  (b) Alexander (1893–1920), *King of the Hellenes* 1917–1920, *m.*, 1919, Aspasia Manos; *issue*:—Princess Alexandra (b. 1921), *m.*, 1944, King Petar II. of Yugoslavia.

  (c) Princess Helena (1896–1982), *m.*, 1921, King Carol of Roumania, (marriage dissolved 1928); *issue*:—Michael (b. 1921), *King of Roumania* 1927–30, 1940–47; *m.*, 1948, Princess Anne of Bourbon Parma, and has *issue*:—five daughters.

  (d) Paul I (1901–1964), *King of the Hellenes* 1947–1964, *m.*, 1938, Princess Frederica of Brunswick (*see* above); *issue*:—King Constantine (*Constantine XIII.*), b. 1940, *m.*, 1964, Princess Anne-Marie of Denmark, and has *issue*:—Princess Sophia, *b.* 1938, *m.*, 1962, Juan Carlos I, KING OF SPAIN, and has *issue*:—Princess Irene, *b.* 1942.

(e) Princess Eirene (1904–1974), *m.*, 1939, 4th Duke of Aosta; *issue*:—Prince Amedeo (*b.* 1943).

(f) Princess Katherine (*Lady Katherine Brandram*), *b.* 1913, *m.*, 1947, Major R. C. A. Brandram; *issue*:—R. Paul G. A. Brandram (*b.* 1948).

(7) Princess Margarete (1872–1954), *m.*, 1893, Prince Frederick Charles of Hesse (1863–1940). *Issue*:—

(a) Prince Frederick William (1893–1916).

(b) Prince Maximilian (1894–1914).

(c) Prince Philipp (1896–1980), *m.*, 1925, Princess Mafalda of Italy; *issue*, three sons and one daughter.

(d) Prince Wolfgang, *b.* 1896, *m.*, 1st, 1924, Princess Marie of Baden; 2nd, 1948, Ottilie Möller.

(e) Prince Richard (1901–).

(f) Prince Christoph (1901–1943), *m.*, 1930, Princess Sophie of Greece (*see* p. 216).

2. H.M. KING EDWARD VII (*see* p. 216).

3. H.R.H. Princess Alice (1843–1878), *m.*, 1862, Prince Louis, *Grand Duke of Hesse*, 1877–1892. *Issue*:—

(1) Victoria Alberta (1863–1950), *m.*, 1884, Admiral of the Fleet the Marquess of Milford Haven. *Issue*:—

(a) Alice (1885–1969), *m.*, 1903, Prince Andrew of Greece; having issue (*see* p. 216).

(b) Louise (1889–1965), *m.*, 1923, Gustav VI Adolf, *King of Sweden* 1950–73.

(c) George, 2nd Marquess of Milford Haven, G.C.V.O., (1892–1938), Capt. R.N., *m.*, 1916, Countess Nadejda, daughter of Grand Duke Michael of Russia; *issue*:—Lady Elizabeth (*b.* 1917); David Michael, 3rd Marquess (1919–1970).

(d) Louis, 1st Earl Mountbatten of Burma (1900–1979), *m.*, 1922, Edwina Ashley, daughter of Lord Mount Temple; *issue*:—Patricia (*b.* 1924), Pamela (*b.* 1929).

(2) Elizabeth (1864–1918), *m.*, 1884, Grand Duke Sergius of Russia.

(3) Irene (1866–1953), *m.* Prince Henry of Prussia (*see* p. 214).

(4) Ernest Ludwig (1868–1937) Grand Duke of Hesse 1892–1918, *m.*, 1st, 1894, Princess Victoria of Saxe Coberg; 2nd, 1905, Princess Eleonore of Solms-Hohensolmslich. *Issue*:—

(a) George, Grand Duke of Hesse (1906–1937), *m.* Princess Cecilie of Greece and Denmark (*see* p. 216).

(b) Ludwig, Grand Duke of Hesse (1908–1968), *m.*, 1937, Margaret, daughter of 1st Lord Geddes.

(5) Frederick William (1870–1873).

(6) Alix (*Tsaritsa of Russia*) (1872–1918), *m.*, 1894, Nicholas II. (*Tsar of All the Russias*), assassinated July 16, 1918. *Issue*:—

(a) Grand Duchess Olga (*b.* 1895).

(b) Grand Duchess Tatiana (*b.* 1897).

(c) Grand Duchess Marie (*b.* 1899).

(d) Grand Duchess Anastasia (*b.* 1901).

(e) Alexis, Tsarevitch of Russia (*b.* 1904).

(7) Mary (1874–1878).

4. Admiral of the Fleet H.R.H. Prince Alfred, *Duke of Edinburgh* (1844–1900), *m.*, 1874, Grand Duchess Marie Alexandrovna of Russia; succeeded as *Duke of Saxe-Coburg and Gotha* Aug. 22, 1893. *Issue*:—

(1) Alfred (*Prince of Saxe-Coburg*) (1874–1899).

(2) Marie (1875–1938), *m.*, 1893, King Ferdinand of Roumania; *issue*:—

(a) Carol II (1893–1953), *King of Roumania* 1930–40, *m.*, 1st, 1918, Joana Lambrino; 2nd, 1921, Princess Helena of Greece (*see* p. 214); 3rd, 1947, Mrs. Elena Tampeanu.

(b) Elizabeth (1894–1956), *m.*, 1921, King George II of the Hellenes (*see* p. 214).

(c) Marie (1900–1961), *m.*, 1922, King Alexander of Yugoslavia; *issue*:—Petar, King of Yugoslavia (1923–1970); Prince Tomislav (*b.* 1928), *m.*, 1957, Princess Margarita of Baden (*see* p. 216); Prince Andrej (*b.* 1929).

(d) Prince Nicolas, *b.* 1903.

(e) Princess Ileana, *b.* 1909, *m.*, 1st, 1931, Archduke Anton of Austria; and 2nd, 1954, Dr. Stefan Issarescu; *issue*, two sons and three daughters.

(f) Prince Mircea (1913–1916).

(3) Victoria (1876–1936), *m.*, 1st, 1894, Grand Duke of Hesse and 2nd, 1905, the Grand Duke Cyril of Russia. *Issue*:—

(a) Marie (1907–1951), *m.*, 1925, Prince Friedrich Carl of Leiningen; *issue*, three sons and three daughters.

(b) Kira Cyrillovna (1909–1967), *m.*, 1938, Prince Ludwig of Germany; *issue*, four sons and two daughters.

(c) Vladimir Cyrillovitch, *b.* 1917, *m.*, 1948, Princess Leonida Bagration-Moukhransky; *issue*, a daughter.

(4) Alexandra (1878–1942), *m.*, 1896, Prince of Hohenlohe Langenburg; *issue*:—

(a) Gottfried (1897–1960), *m.*, Princess Margarita of Greece (*see* p. 216); *issue*, three sons and one daughter.

(b) Maria (1899–1967), *m.* Prince Frederick of Holstein-Glucksburg; *issue*, one son and one daughter.

(c) Princess Alexandra (1901–1963).

(d) Princess Irma, *b.* 1902.

(5) Princess Beatrice (1884–1966), *m.*, 1909, Prince Alfonso, Infante of Spain; *issue*:—

(a) Prince Alvaro (*b.* 1910), *m.* Carla Parodi-Delfino; *issue*, two sons and two daughters.

(b) Prince Alonso (*b.* 1912).

(c) Prince Ataulfo (*b.* 1913).

5. H.R.H. Princess Helena Augusta Victoria (1846–1923), *m.*, 1866, Prince Christian of Schleswig-Holstein. *Issue*:—

(1) Prince Christian Victor (1867–1900).

(2) Prince Albert (1869–1931).

(3) Princess Helena Victoria (1870–1948).

(4) Princess Marie Louise (1872–1956).

(5) Prince Harold (May 12–20, 1876).

6. H.R.H. Princess Louise (1848–1939), *m.*, 1871, the Marquess of Lorne, afterwards *9th Duke of Argyll* (1845–1914); without *issue*.

7. Field Marshal H.R.H. Prince Arthur, *Duke of Connaught* (1850–1942), *m.*, 1879, Princess Louisa of Prussia (1860–1917). *Issue*:—

(1) Princess Margaret (1882–1920), *m.*, 1905, Gustav VI Adolf, *King of Sweden* 1950–73; *issue*:—

(a) Duke of Westerbotten (1906–1947), *m.*, 1932, Princess Sybil of Saxe-Coburg-Gotha; *issue*:—Carl XVI Gustaf, KING OF SWEDEN, and four daughters.

(b) Duke of Upland (*Count Sigvard Bernadotte*), *b.* 1907.

(c) Princess Ingrid (*Queen Mother of Denmark*), *b.* 1910, *m.*, 1935, Frederick IX, *King of Denmark* (1899–72); *issue*:—Margrethe II, QUEEN OF DENMARK (*b.* 1940); Princess Benedikte (*b.* 1944); Princess Anne-Marie (*Queen of the Hellenes*) (*b.* 1946).

(d) Duke of Halland, *b.* 1912.

(e) Duke of Dalecarlia (*Count Carl Bernadotte*), *b.* 1916.

(2) Prince Arthur (1883–1938), *m.*, 1913, H.H. the Duchess of Fife (*see* below).

(3) Princess Patricia (1886–1974), *m.*, 1919, Adm. Hon. Sir Alexander Ramsay; *issue*:—Hon. Alexander Ramsay of Mar (*b.* 1919), *m.*, 1956, Hon. Flora Fraser (*Lady Saltoun*).

8. H.R.H. Prince Leopold, *Duke of Albany* (1853–1884), *m.*, 1882, Princess Helena of Waldeck (died 1922). *Issue*:—

(1) Princess Alice (1883–1981), *m.*, 1904, Prince Alexander of Teck, afterwards *1st Earl of Athlone; issue:*—

(a) Lady May, *b.* 1906, *m.*, 1931, Sir Henry Abel-Smith, K.C.M.G., K.C.V.O., D.S.O., and has *issue* a son and 2 daughters.

(b) *Viscount Trematon* (1907–1928).

(2) Charles Edward (1884–1954), *Duke of Saxe-Coburg-Gotha* 1900–1918, *m.*, 1905, Princess Victoria of Schleswig-Holstein; *issue:*—Prince Johann (1906–1972); Princess Sibylle (1908–); Prince Dietmar (1909–); Princess Caroline (1912–1983); Prince Frederick (*b.* 1918).

9. H.R.H. Princess Beatrice (1857–1944), *m.*, 1885,

Prince Henry of Battenberg (1858–1896); having *issue:*—

(1) Alexander, *1st Marquess of Carisbrooke* (1886–1960), *m.*, 1917, Lady Irene Denison; *issue:*—Lady Iris Mountbatten (1920–1982).

(2) Victoria Eugénie (1887–1969), *m.*, 1906, Alfonso XIII (1886–1941) *King of Spain* 1886–1931; *issue:*—Alfonso (1907–); Prince Jaime (1908–75); Princess Beatrice (*b.* 1909); Princess Maria (*b.* 1911); Prince Juan (*b.* 1913); Prince Gonzale (1914–).

(3) Major Lord Leopold Mountbatten (1889–1922).

(4) Maurice (1891–1914), died of wounds received in action.

THE FAMILY OF KING EDWARD VII

KING EDWARD VII, eldest son of Queen Victoria, *born* Nov. 9, 1841; *married* March 10, 1863, Her Royal Highness Princess Alexandra of Denmark (*Queen Alexandra*, *born* Dec. 1, 1844; *died* Nov. 20, 1925); *succeeded* to the Throne Jan. 22, 1901; *died* May 6, 1910. *Issue:*—

1. H.R.H. Prince Albert Victor, *Duke of Clarence and Avondale and Earl of Athlone* (1864–1892).

2. H.M. KING GEORGE V (*see* below). Assumed by Royal Proclamation (June 17, 1917) for his House and Family as well as for all descendants in the male line of Queen Victoria who are subjects of these Realms, the name of WINDSOR; (*see* p. 217).

3. H.R.H. Louise, *Princess Royal* (1867–1931), *m.*, 1889, *1st Duke of Fife* (1849–1912). *Issue:*—

(1) H.H. Princess Alexandra, Duchess of Fife (1891–1959), *m.*, 1913, H.R.H. Prince Arthur of Connaught (*see,* above). *Issue:*—

(a) Alastair Arthur, Duke of Connaught (1914–1943).

(2) H.H. Princess Maud (1893–1945), *m.*, 1923, 11th

Earl of Southesk. *Issue:*—

(a) THE DUKE OF FIFE (*b.* 1929).

4. H.R.H. Princess Victoria (1868–1935).

5. H.R.H. Princess Maud (1869–1938), *m.*, 1896, Haakon VII., *King of Norway* (1905–1957). *Issue:*—

(1) H.M. Olav V., K.G., K.T., G.C.B., G.C.V.O., KING OF NORWAY, *b.* 1903, *m.*, 1929, H.R.H. Princess Marthe of Sweden (died 1954). *Issue:*—

(a) H.R.H. Princess Ragnhild, *b.* 1930.

(b) H.R.H. Princess Astrid, *b.* 1932.

(c) H.R.H. Harald, Crown Prince of Norway, G.C.V.O., *b.* 1937.

6. H.R.H. Prince Alexander John Charles Albert (April 6–7, 1871).

THE FAMILY OF PRINCE ANDREW OF GREECE

Prince Andrew of Greece (1882–1944), *m.*, 1903, Princess Alice of Battenberg (*H.R.H. Princess Andrew of Greece*), (1885–1969); *issue:*—

(1) Princess Margarita (1905–1981), *m.*, 1931, Prince Gottfried of Hohenlohe-Langenburg (*see* p. 215); *issue:*—Prince Kraft, *b.* 1935, Princess Beatrix, *b.* 1936, Prince George, *b.* 1938, Prince Ruprecht and Prince Albrecht, *b.* 1944.

(2) Princess Theodora (1906–1969), *m.*, 1931, Prince Berthold of Baden (*d.* 1963); *issue:*—Princess Margarita, *b.* 1932 (*m.*, 1957, Prince Tomislav of Yugoslavia (*see* p. 215)), Prince Max, *b.* 1933, Prince Louis, *b.* 1937.

(3) Princess Cecilie (1911–1937), *m.*, George, Grand

Duke of Hesse (*see* p. 215), accidentally killed with husband and two sons, 1937.

(4) Princess Sophie, *b.* 1914, *m.*, 1st, 1930, Prince Christopher of Hesse (1901–43); *issue:*—Princess Christina, *b.* 1933, Princess Dorothea, *b.* 1934, Prince Charles, *b.* 1937, Prince Rainer, *b.* 1939, Princess Clarissa, *b.* 1944; *m.*, 2nd, 1946, Prince George of Hanover; *issue:*—Prince George (*b.* 1949); Princess Friederike (*b.* 1954).

(5) Prince Philip (*H.R.H. the Prince Philip, Duke of Edinburgh*), *b.* 1921 (*see* p. 218).

THE FAMILY OF KING GEORGE V

KING GEORGE V., second son of King Edward VII., *born* June 3, 1865; *married* July 6, 1893, Her Serene Highness Princess Victoria Mary Augusta Louise Olga Pauline Claudine Agnes (*Queen Mary*, *born* May 26, 1867; *died* March 24, 1953); *succeeded* to the Throne May 6, 1910; *died* Jan. 20, 1936. *Issue:*—

H.R.H. The Duke of Windsor (Edward Albert Christian George Andrew Patrick David), *born* June 23, 1894, *succeeded* to the Throne as KING EDWARD VIII., Jan. 20, 1936; *abdicated* Dec. 11, 1936; *married* June 3, 1937, Mrs. Wallis Warfield (Her Grace The Duchess of Windsor, *born* June 19, 1896; *died* April 24, 1986), *died* May 28, 1972.

H.M. KING GEORGE VI. (Albert Frederick Arthur George) *born* at York Cottage, Sandringham, Dec. 14, 1895; *married* April 26, 1923, Lady Elizabeth Angela Marguerite (HER MAJESTY QUEEN ELIZABETH THE QUEEN MOTHER), daughter of the 14th Earl of Strathmore and Kinghorne, *succeeded* to the throne Dec. 11, 1936; *died* Feb. 6, 1952, having had issue (*see* pp. 218 and 219).

H.R.H. The Princess Royal (Victoria Alexandra Alice MARY), *born* April 25, 1897, *married* Feb. 28, 1922, the 6th Earl of Harewood (*born* Sept. 9, 1882; *died* May 24, 1947), *died* Mar. 28, 1965, leaving issue:—

(1) George Henry Hubert Lascelles, 7TH EARL OF HAREWOOD, K.B.E., *born* Feb. 7, 1923; *married* 1st, Sept. 29, 1949, Maria (Marion) Stein (marriage dissolved 1967); *issue*, (i) David Henry George, Viscount Lascelles, *born* Oct. 21, 1950; (ii) James Edward, *born* Oct. 5, 1953; (iii) Robert Jeremy Hugh, *born* Feb. 14, 1955; 2nd, July 31, 1967, Mrs. Patricia Tuckwell; *issue*, Mark Hubert, *born* July 5, 1964.

(2) Gerald David Lascelles, *born* Aug. 21, 1924, *married* 1st, July 15, 1952, Miss Angela Dowding (marriage dissolved, 1978); *issue*, Henry Ulick, *born* May 19, 1953; 2nd, Nov. 17, 1978, Mrs. Elizabeth Colvin; *issue*, Martin David, born Feb. 9, 1962.

H.R.H. The Duke of Gloucester (Henry William Frederick Albert), Duke of Gloucester, Earl of Ulster and Baron Culloden, *born* March 31, 1900, *married* Nov. 6, 1935, Lady Alice Montagu-Douglas-Scott, daughter of the 7th Duke of Buccleuch (H.R.H. PRINCESS ALICE, DUCHESS OF GLOUCESTER, C.I., G.C.B., G.C.V.O., G.B.E., Grand Cordon of Al Kamal, Colonel-in-Chief of The Royal Hussars (Prince of Wales's Own), The King's Own Scottish Borderers, Royal Corps of Transport, Deputy Colonel-in-Chief, The Royal Anglian Regt., Air Chief Commandant W.R.A.F., *born* Dec. 25, 1901); *died* June 10, 1974. Issue:

(1) H.R.H. Prince WILLIAM Henry Andrew Frederick, *born* Dec. 18, 1941; *accidentally killed* Aug. 28, 1972.

(2) H.R.H. Prince Richard Alexander Walter George (H.R.H. THE DUKE OF GLOUCESTER), G.C.V.O., Colonel-in-Chief, The Gloucestershire Regiment, Royal Pioneer Corps, Honorary Colonel Royal Monmouthshire Royal Engineers (Militia), Grand Prior of the Order of St. John of Jerusalem. *Born* Aug. 26, 1944, *married* July 8, 1972, Birgitte van Deurs, Colonel-in-Chief, Royal Army Educational Corps, and has issue, (i) Alexander Patrick Gregers Richard, Earl of Ulster, *born* Oct. 24, 1974, (ii) Davina Elizabeth Alice Benedikte (Lady Davina Windsor), *born* Nov. 19, 1977 and (iii) Rose Victoria Birgitte Louise (Lady Rose Windsor), *born* March 1, 1980. *Residences*—Kensington Palace, W.8.; Barnwell Manor, Peterborough.

H.R.H. The Duke of Kent (George Edward Alexander Edmund), Duke of Kent, Earl of St. Andrews and Baron Downpatrick, *born* Dec. 20, 1902, *married* Nov. 29, 1934, H.R.H. Princess Marina of Greece and Denmark (*born* Nov. 30, O.S., 1906; *died* Aug. 27, 1968). *Killed on Active Service*, Aug. 25, 1942. Issue:—

(1) H.R.H. Prince Edward George Nicholas Paul Patrick (H.R.H. THE DUKE OF KENT), K.G., G.C.M.G., G.C.V.O., Lt.-Col. Personal A.D.C. to the Queen, Major General, Air Vice-Marshal, Colonel-in-Chief The Royal Regiment of Fusiliers, The Devonshire and Dorset Regiment, The Lorne Scots Regiment (Peel, Dufferin and Hamilton Regiment), Colonel Scots Guards. *Born* Oct. 9, 1935, *married* June 8, 1961, Katharine Lucy Mary, G.C.V.O., Hon. Major General, Colonel-in-Chief 4th/7th Royal Dragoon Guards, The Prince of Wales's Own Regiment of Yorkshire, Army Catering Corps, Controller Commandant Women's Royal Army Corps, Hon. Colonel The Yorkshire Volunteers, daughter of Sir William Worsley, Bt., and has issue, (i) George Philip Nicholas, Earl of St. Andrews, *born* June 26, 1962; (ii) Helen Marina Lucy (Lady Helen Windsor), *born* April 28, 1964; (iii) Nicholas Charles Edward Jonathan (Lord Nicholas Windsor), *born* July 25, 1970. *Residences*—York House, St. James's Palace, S.W.1.; Anmer Hall, Norfolk.

(2) H.R.H. Princess ALEXANDRA Helen Elizabeth Olga Christabel, G.C.V.O., Colonel-in-Chief, 17th/21st Lancers, The King's Own Royal Border Regiment, The Queen's Own Rifles of Canada, The Canadian Scottish Regiment (Princess Mary's), Deputy Colonel-in-Chief The Light Infantry, Deputy Hon. Colonel The Royal Yeomanry, Air Chief Commandant Princess Mary's Royal Air Force Nursing Service. *Born* Dec. 25, 1936, *married* April 24, 1963, Hon. Angus Ogilvy, son of the 12th Earl of Airlie, *born* Sept. 14, 1928, and has issue, (i) James Robert Bruce, *born* Feb. 29, 1964 and (ii) Marina Victoria Alexandra, *born* July 31, 1966. *Residence*—Thatched House Lodge, Richmond, Surrey. *Office*—22 Friary Court, St. James's Palace, S.W.1.

(3) H.R.H. Prince MICHAEL George Charles Franklin, *born* July 4, 1942, Major, Royal Hussars, *married* June 30, 1978, Baroness Marie-Christine von Reibnitz, and has issue, (i) Frederick Michael George David Louis (Lord Frederick Windsor), *born* April 6, 1979 and (ii) Gabriella Marina Alexandra Ophelia (Lady Gabriella Windsor), *born* April 23, 1981. *Residences*—Kensington Palace, W.8.; Nether Lypiatt Manor, Stroud, Glos.

H.R.H. Prince John Charles Francis, *born* July 12, 1905; *died* Jan. 18, 1919.

THE HOUSE OF WINDSOR

Her Most Excellent Majesty **ELIZABETH THE SECOND** (Elizabeth Alexandra Mary of Windsor) by the Grace of God, of the United Kingdom of Great Britain and Northern Ireland and of Her other Realms and Territories Queen, Head of the Commonwealth, Defender of the Faith, Sovereign of the British Orders of Knighthood and Sovereign Head of the Order of St. John, Lord High Admiral of the United Kingdom, Colonel-in-Chief of The Life Guards, The Blues and Royals (Royal Horse Guards and 1st Dragoons), The Royal Scots Dragoon Guards (Carabiniers and Greys), 16th/5th The Queen's Royal Lancers, Royal Tank Regiment, Corps of Royal Engineers, Grenadier Guards, Coldstream Guards, Scots Guards, Irish Guards, Welsh Guards, The Royal Welch Fusiliers, The Queen's Lancashire Regiment, The Argyll and Sutherland Highlanders (Princess Louise's), The Royal Green Jackets, Royal Army Ordnance Corps, Corps of Royal Military Police, The Queen's Own Mercian Yeomanry, The Duke of Lancaster's Own Yeomanry, Canadian Forces Military Engineers Branch, The King's Own Calgary Regiment, Royal 22e Regiment, Governor-General's Foot Guards, The Canadian Grenadier Guards, Le Régiment de la Chaudière, 2nd Bn. Royal New Brunswick Regt. (North Shore), The 48th Highlanders of Canada, The Argyll and Sutherland Highlanders of Canada (Princess Louise's), The Calgary Highlanders, Royal Australian Engineers, Royal Australian Infantry Corps, Royal Australian Army Ordnance Corps, Royal Australian Army Nursing Corps, The Corps of Royal New Zealand Engineers, Royal New Zealand Infantry Regiment, Royal New Zealand Army Ordnance Corps, Royal Malta Artillery, The Malawi Rifles, Captain-General of Royal Regiment of Artillery, The Honourable Artillery Company, Combined Cadet Force, Royal Regiment of Canadian Artillery, Royal Regiment of Australian Artillery, Royal Regiment of New Zealand Artillery, Royal New Zealand Armoured Corps, Air-Commodore-in-Chief, R. Aux.A.F., R.A.F. Regiment, Royal Observer Corps, Air Reserve (of Canada), Australian Citizen Air Force, Commandant-in-Chief, Royal Air Force College, Cranwell, Hon. Air Commodore, R.A.F. Marham, Hon. Commissioner, Royal Canadian Mounted Police, Master of the Merchant Navy and Fishing Fleets, Head of the Civil Defence Corps.

Elder daughter of His late Majesty King George VI and of Her Majesty Queen Elizabeth the Queen Mother; *born* at 17 Bruton Street, London, W.1, April 21, 1926, *succeeded* to the throne February 6, 1952, *crowned* June 2, 1953; having *married*, November 20, 1947, in Westminster Abbey, Philip, Duke of Edinburgh, Earl of

Merioneth and Baron Greenwich (H.R.H. THE PRINCE PHILIP, DUKE OF EDINBURGH, *born* June 10, 1921), K.G., P.C., K.T., O.M., G.B.E., Q.S.O., Admiral of the Fleet, Field Marshal, Marshal of the Royal Air Force, Admiral of the Fleet, Royal Australian Navy, Field Marshal, Australian Military Forces, Marshal of the Royal Australian Air Force, Admiral of the Fleet, Royal New Zealand Navy, Field Marshal New Zealand Army, Marshal of the Royal New Zealand Air Force, Captain General, Royal Marines, Colonel-in-Chief, The Queen's Royal Irish Hussars, The Duke of Edinburgh's Royal Regiment (Berkshire and Wiltshire), The Queen's Own Highlanders (Seaforth and Camerons), Corps of Royal Electrical and Mechanical Engineers, Intelligence Corps, Army Cadet Force, The Royal Canadian Regiment, The Royal Hamilton Light Infantry (Wentworth Regt.), The Cameron Highlanders of Ottawa, The Queen's Own Cameron Highlanders of Canada, The Seaforth Highlanders of Canada, The Royal Canadian Army Cadets, The Royal Australian Electrical and Mechanical Engineers, The Australian Cadet Corps, Corps of Royal New Zealand Electrical and Mechanical Engineers, Colonel of Grenadier Guards, Hon. Colonel, Edinburgh and Heriot-Watt Universities Officers' Training Corps, The Trinidad and Tobago Regiment, Admiral, Royal Canadian Sea Cadets, Air Commodore-in-Chief, Royal New Zealand Air Force, Air Training Corps, Royal Canadian Air Cadets, Hon. Air Commodore, R.A.F. Kinloss, Master of the Corporation of Trinity House, Ranger of Windsor Park, Admiral Sea Cadet Corps, Hon. Colonel Leicester and Derbyshire Yeomanry PAQ Sqn. *See* p. 216.

Residences—Buckingham Palace, S.W.1.; Windsor Castle, Berks.; Balmoral Castle, Aberdeenshire; Sandringham, Norfolk.

CHILDREN OF HER MAJESTY

H.R.H. THE PRINCE OF WALES (CHARLES Philip Arthur George), K.G., K.T., G.C.B, A.K., Q.S.O., A.D.C., Prince of Wales and Earl of Chester, Duke of Cornwall and Duke of Rothesay, Earl of Carrick and Baron Renfrew, Lord of the Isles and Great Steward of Scotland, Personal A.D.C. to the Queen, Great Master of the Order of the Bath, Commander Royal Navy, Wing Commander Royal Air Force, Colonel-in-Chief 5th Royal Inniskilling Dragoon Guards, The Cheshire Regiment, The Royal Regiment of Wales (24th/41st Foot), The Gordon Highlanders, The Parachute Regiment, 2nd King Edward VII's Own Gurkha Rifles (The Sirmoor Rifles), The Royal Canadian Dragoons, Lord Strathcona's Horse (Royal Canadians), Royal Regiment of Canada, Royal Winnipeg Rifles, Royal Australian Armoured Corps, The Royal Pacific Islands Regiment, Colonel, Welsh Guards, Air Reserve Group of Air Command (Canada), Air Commodore-in-Chief Royal New Zealand Air Force, Hon. Air Commodore, R.A.F. Brawdy.

Born November 14, 1948, *married* July 29, 1981, Lady Diana Frances Spencer (H.R.H. THE PRINCESS OF WALES, *born* July 1, 1961), Colonel-in-Chief The Royal Hampshire Regiment, The Princess of Wales's Own Regiment (of Canada), Hon. Air Commodore, R.A.F. Wittering, youngest daughter of the 8th Earl Spencer and the Hon. Mrs. Shand Kydd; and has issue, (i) William Arthur Philip Louis (H.R.H. PRINCE WILLIAM OF WALES), *born* June 21, 1982, and (ii) Henry Charles Albert David (H.R.H. PRINCE HENRY OF WALES), *born* Sept. 15, 1984.

Residences—Highgrove, Doughton, Tetbury, Glos.; Kensington Palace, W.8. *Office*—Buckingham Palace, S.W.1.

H.R.H. THE PRINCESS ROYAL (ANNE Elizabeth Alice Louise), G.C.V.O. Chief Commandant Women's Royal Naval Service, Colonel-in-Chief 14th/20th King's Hussars, Royal Corps of Signals, The Royal Scots (The Royal Regiment), The Worcestershire and Sherwood Foresters Regiment (29th/45th Foot), 8th Canadian Hussars (Princess Louise's), Canadian Forces Communications and Electronics Branch, Grey and Simcoe Foresters Militia, The Royal Regina Rifle Regiment, Royal Australian Corps of Signals, Royal New Zealand Corps of Signals, Royal New Zealand Nursing Corps, Hon. Air Commodore, R.A.F. Lyneham, Commandant-in-Chief, (Ambulance and Nursing Cadets) St. John Ambulance, Commandant-in-Chief, Women's Transport Service (FANY), Dame of Justice, Order of St. John.

Born August 15, 1950, *married* Nov. 14, 1973, Capt. Mark Anthony Peter Phillips, C.V.O. (*born* Sept. 22, 1948), Personal A.D.C. to the Queen, and has issue, (i) Peter Mark Andrew, *born* Nov. 15, 1977, and (ii) Zara Anne Elizabeth, *born* May 15, 1981.

Residence—Gatcombe Park, Minchinhampton, Stroud, Glos. *Office*—Buckingham Palace, S.W.1.

H.R.H. THE DUKE OF YORK (ANDREW Albert Christian Edward), Duke of York, Earl of Inverness and Baron Killyleagh, C.V.O., Personal A.D.C. to the Queen, Lieutenant, Royal Navy. *Born* Feb. 19, 1960, *married* July 23, 1986, Miss Sarah Margaret Ferguson (H.R.H. THE DUCHESS OF YORK, *born* October 15, 1959), younger daughter of Major Ronald Ferguson and Mrs. Hector Barrantes.

H.R.H. PRINCE EDWARD ANTONY RICHARD LOUIS, *born* March 10, 1964.

MOTHER OF HER MAJESTY

H.M. QUEEN ELIZABETH THE QUEEN MOTHER (Elizabeth Angela Marguerite) (daughter of the 14th Earl of Strathmore and Kinghorne), Lady of the Garter, Lady of the Thistle, Order of the Crown of India, Grand Master of the Royal Victorian Order, Dame Grand Cross of the Order of the British Empire, Dame, Grand Cross of the Order of St. John, Royal Victorian Chain, Doctor of Civil Law, Doctor of Literature, Colonel-in-Chief 1st The Queen's Dragoon Guards, The Queen's Own Hussars, 9th/12th Royal Lancers (Prince of Wales's) The King's Regiment, The Royal Anglian Regiment, The Light Infantry, The Black Watch (Royal Highland Regiment), Royal Army Medical Corps, The Black Watch (Royal Highland Regiment) of Canada, The Toronto Scottish Regiment, Canadian Forces Medical Services, Royal Australian Army Medical Corps, Royal New Zealand Army Medical Corps, Hon. Colonel The Royal Yeomanry, The London Scottish, University of London Officers' Training Corps, Commandant-in-Chief R.A.F. Central Flying School, W.R.N.S., W.R.A.C., W.R.A.F., Air Chief Commandant, Women's Royal Australian Air Force, Patron St. Andrew's Ambulance Association, Commandant-in-Chief Nursing Corps and Divisions, Commandant-in-Chief (Nursing) St. John's Ambulance, Lord Warden and Admiral of the Cinque Ports and Constable of Dover Castle. *Born* August 4, 1900, *married* April 26, 1923, Prince Albert Frederick Arthur George of Windsor, Duke of York (*see* King GEORGE VI).

Residences.—Clarence House, St. James's Palace, S.W.1.; Royal Lodge, Windsor Great Park, Berks.; Castle of Mey, Caithness, Scotland.

SISTER OF HER MAJESTY

H.R.H. THE PRINCESS MARGARET, COUNTESS OF SNOWDON (Margaret Rose), C.I., G.C.V.O., Colonel-in-Chief, 15th/19th The King's Royal Hussars, The Royal Highland Fusiliers (Princess Margaret's Own Glasgow and Ayrshire Regiment), Queen Alexandra's Royal Army Nursing Corps, The Highland Fusiliers of Canada, The Princess Louise Fusiliers, The Bermuda Regiment, Deputy Colonel-in-Chief, The Royal Anglian Regiment, Hon. Air Commodore, R.A.F. Coningsby, Commandant-in-Chief, St. John Ambulance Brigade Cadets, Grand President, St. John Ambulance, Dame Grand Cross of the Order of St. John of Jerusalem, President of the Girl Guides Association.

Born Aug. 21, 1930; *married* May 6, 1960 Anthony Charles Robert Armstrong-Jones, G.C.V.O. (*born* March 7, 1930, son of the late Ronald Armstrong-Jones, Q.C. and the Countess of Rosse, *created* Earl of Snowdon, 1961, Constable of Caernarvon Castle, *marriage dissolved*, 1978); and has issue, (i) David Albert Charles, Viscount Linley, *born* Nov. 3, 1961, and (ii) Sarah Frances Elizabeth (Lady Sarah Armstrong-Jones), *born* May 1, 1964.

Residence.—Kensington Palace, W.8.

Order of Succession to the Throne

1. H.R.H. Prince of Wales; 2. H.R.H. Prince William of Wales; 3. H.R.H. Prince Henry of Wales; 4. H.R.H. Duke of York; 5. H.R.H. Prince Edward; 6. H.R.H. Princess Royal; 7. Master Peter Phillips; 8. Miss Zara Phillips; 9. H.R.H. Princess Margaret, Countess of Snowdon; 10. Viscount Linley; 11. Lady Sarah Armstrong-Jones; 12. H.R.H. Duke of Gloucester; 13. Earl of Ulster; 14. Lady Davina Windsor; 15. Lady Rose Windsor; 16. H.R.H. Duke of Kent; 17. Earl of St. Andrews; 18. Lord Nicholas Windsor; 19. Lady Helen Windsor; 20. Lord Frederick Windsor; 21. Lady Gabriella Windsor; 22. H.R.H. Princess Alexandra, Hon. Mrs Angus Ogilvy; 23. Mr James Ogilvy; 24. Miss Marina Ogilvy.

Precedence in England

The Sovereign
The Prince Philip, Duke of Edinburgh.
The Prince of Wales; The Prince Andrew, Duke of York; The Prince Edward.
Princes of the Blood Royal.
Archbishop of Canterbury.
Lord High Chancellor.
Archbishop of York.
The Prime Minister.
Lord President of the Council.
Speaker of the House of Commons.
Lord Privy Seal.
High Commissioners of Commonwealth Countries and Ambassadors of Foreign States.
Dukes, according to their Patents of Creation:
(1) Of England; (2) of Scotland; (3) of Great Britain; (4) of Ireland; (5) those created since the Union.
Ministers and Envoys.
Eldest sons of Dukes of Blood Royal.
Marquesses, in same order as Dukes.
Dukes' eldest Sons.
Earls, in same order as Dukes.
Younger sons of Dukes of Blood Royal.
Marquesses' eldest Sons.
Dukes' younger Sons.
Viscounts, in same order as Dukes.
Earls' eldest Sons.
Marquesses' younger Sons.
Bishops of London, Durham and Winchester.
All other English Bishops, according to their seniority of Consecration.
Secretaries of State, if of the degree of a Baron.
Barons, in same order as Dukes.
Treasurer of H.M.'s Household.
Comptroller of H.M.'s Household.
Vice-Chamberlain of H.M.'s Household.

Secretaries of State under the degree of Baron.
Viscounts' eldest Sons.
Earls' younger Sons.
Barons' eldest Sons.
Knights of the Garter if Commoners.
Privy Councillors if of no higher rank.
Chancellor of the Exchequer.
Chancellor of the Duchy of Lancaster.
Lord Chief Justice of England.
Master of the Rolls.
President of the Family Division.
Vice-Chancellor.
The Lords Justices of Appeal.
Judges of the High Court.
Vice-Chancellor of County Palatine of Lancaster.
Viscounts' younger Sons.
Barons' younger Sons.
Sons of Life Peers.
Baronets of either Kingdom, according to date of Patents.
Knights of the Thistle if Commoners.
Knights Grand Cross of the Bath.
Members of the Order of Merit.
Knights Grand Commanders of the Star of India.
Knights Grand Cross of St. Michael and St. George.
Knights Grand Commanders of the Indian Empire.
Knights Grand Cross of the Royal Victorian Order.
Knights Grand Cross of Order of the British Empire.
Companions of Honour.
Knights Commanders of the above Orders.
Knights Bachelor.
Official Referees of The Supreme Court.
Circuit judges and judges of the Mayor's and City of London Court.

Companions and Commanders *e.g.* C.B.; C.S.I.; C.M.G.; C.I.E.; C.V.O.; C.B.E.; D.S.O.; L.V.O.; O.B.E.; I.S.O.
Eldest Sons of younger Sons of Peers.
Baronets' eldest Sons.
Eldest Sons of Knights in the same order as their Fathers.
M.V.O.; M.B.E.
Younger Sons of the younger Sons of Peers.
Baronets' younger Sons.
Younger Sons of Knights in the same order as their Fathers.
Naval, Military, Air, and other Esquires by Office.

WOMEN

Women take the same rank as their husbands or as their brothers; but the daughter of a Peer marrying a Commoner retains her title as Lady or Honourable. Daughters of Peers rank next immediately after the wives of their elder brothers, and before their younger brothers' wives. Daughters of Peers marrying Peers of lower degree take the same order of precedency as that of their husbands; thus the daughter of a Duke marrying a Baron becomes of the rank of Baroness only while her sisters married to commoners retain their rank and take precedence of the Baroness. Merely official rank on the husband's part does not give any similar precedence to the wife.

Peeresses in their own right take the same Precedence as Peers of the same rank, i.e. from their date of creation.

THE QUEEN'S HOUSEHOLD

Lord Chamberlain, The Earl of Airlie, K.T., P.C., G.C.V.O.
Lord Steward, The Duke of Northumberland, K.G., P.C., G.C.V.O., T.D., F.R.S.
Master of the Horse, The Earl of Westmorland, K.C.V.O.
Treasurer of the Household, D. Hunt, M.B.E.
Comptroller of the Household, Hon. Robert Boscawen, M.C., M.P.
Vice Chamberlain, T. Garel-Jones, M.P.

Gold Stick, Maj.-Gen. Lord Michael Fitzalan Howard, G.C.V.O., C.B., C.B.E., M.C.; General Sir Desmond Fitzpatrick, G.C.B., D.S.O., M.B.E., M.C.
Vice-Adm. of the United Kingdom, Adm. Sir Derek Empson, G.B.E., K.C.B.
Rear-Adm. of the United Kingdom, Adm. Sir Anthony Griffin, G.C.B.
First and Principal Naval Aide-de-Camp, Adm. Sir William Staveley, G.C.B.
Flag Aide de Camp, Adm. Sir John Woodward, K.C.B.
Aides-de-Camp General, Gen. Sir Nigel Bagnall, G.C.B., C.V.O., M.C.; Gen. Sir Edward Burgess, K.C.B., O.B.E.; Gen. Sir David Mostyn, K.C.B., C.B.E.
Air Aides-de-Camp, Air Chief Marshal Sir David Grieg, G.C.B., O.B.E.; Air Chief Marshal Sir Michael Knight, K.C.B., A.F.C.

Mistress of the Robes, The Duchess of Grafton, G.C.V.O.
Ladies of the Bedchamber, The Countess of Airlie, C.V.O.; The Lady Farnham, (*temp.*).
Extra Ladies of the Bedchamber, The Marchioness of Abergavenny, D.C.V.O.; The Countess of Cromer, C.V.O.
Women of the Bedchamber, Hon. Mary Morrison, D.C.V.O.; Lady Susan Hussey, D.C.V.O.; The Lady Elton, (*temp.*); Mrs. John Dugdale, D.C.V.O.
Extra Women of the Bedchamber, Mrs. John Woodroffe, C.V.O.; Lady Rose Baring, D.C.V.O., Mrs. Michael Wall, D.C.V.O.; Lady Abel Smith, D.C.V.O.; Mrs Philippa de Pass, (*temp.*).
Extra Equerries, Vice-Adm. Sir Peter Ashmore, K.C.B., K.C.V.O., D.S.C.; Rear-Adm. the Earl Cairns, G.C.V.O., C.B.; Lt.-Col. The Lord Charteris of Amisfield, P.C., G.C.B., G.C.V.O., O.B.E., Q.S.O.; Vice-Adm. Sir Peter Dawnay, K.C.V.O., C.B., D.S.C.; Sir Edward Ford, K.C.B., K.C.V.O., E.R.D.; Rear-Adm. Sir Paul Greening, K.C.V.O.; Brig. Sir Geoffrey Hardy-Roberts, K.C.V.O., C.B., C.B.E.; The Rt. Hon. Sir William Heseltine, K.C.B., K.C.V.O.; Rear-Adm. Sir Hugh Janion, K.C.V.O.; Lt.-Col. Sir John Johnston, G.C.V.O., M.C.; Maj. Sir Rennie Maudslay, G.C.V.O., K.C.B., M.B.E.; Air Cdre. Sir Dennis Mitchell, K.B.E., C.V.O., D.F.C., A.F.C.; The Lord Moore of Wolvercote G.C.B., G.C.V.O., C.M.G., Q.S.O.; Rear-Adm. Sir Patrick Morgan, K.C.V.O., C.B., D.S.C.; Lt.-Col. Ririd Myddleton, L.V.O.; Lt.-Col. Sir Eric Penn, G.C.V.O., O.B.E., M.C.; Cdr. Sir Philip Row, K.C.V.O., O.B.E., R.N.; Air Vice-Marshal John Severne, L.V.O., O.B.E., A.F.C.; Group Capt. Peter Townsend, C.V.O., D.S.O., D.F.C.; Rear Adm. Sir Richard John Trowbridge, K.C.V.O.; Lt.-Col. G. West; Air Cdre. Sir Archie Little Winskill, K.C.V.O., C.B.E., D.F.C., A.E.

THE PRIVATE SECRETARY'S OFFICE
Buckingham Palace, S.W.1.

Private Secretary to The Queen, The Rt. Hon. Sir William Heseltine, K.C.B., K.C.V.O.
Deputy Private Secretary, R. Fellowes, C.B., L.V.O.
Assistant Private Secretary, K. Scott, C.M.G.
Defence Services Secretary, Air Vice-Marshal Richard Peirse, C.B.
Press Secretary, R. Janvrin, L.V.O.
Assistant Press Secretaries, J. Haslam, L.V.O.; P. Mackie.
Chief Clerk, Miss J. M. Damrel, M.V.O.
Secretary to the Private Secretary, Miss E. Pearce, M.V.O.
Head of Information and Correspondence Section, Mrs. J. Bean, M.V.O.
Clerks, Mrs. W. I. Eldridge, M.V.O.; Mrs. C. N. Good; Miss A. Kennedy; Miss K. E. May-Smith; J. Mordant, M.V.O.; Miss C. Pole.
Press Office, Miss K. McGrigor; Mrs. R. Murdo-Smith, L.V.O.; Mrs. A. Neal, L.V.O.
Lady in Waiting's Office, (vacant).

The Queen's Archives
Round Tower, Windsor Castle.

Keeper of The Queen's Archives, The Rt. Hon. Sir William Heseltine, K.C.B., K.C.V.O.
Assistant Keeper, O. Everett, L.V.O.
Registrar, Miss E. Cuthbert, M.V.O.
Assistant Registrars, Lady de Bellaigue; Miss P. Clark.
Curator of the Photographic Collection, Miss F. Dimond, M.V.O.

THE PRIVY PURSE AND TREASURER'S OFFICE
Buckingham Palace, S.W.1.

Keeper of the Privy Purse and Treasurer to The Queen, Sir Peter Miles, K.C.V.O.
Deputy Keeper of the Privy Purse, Maj. S. G. B. Blewitt, L.V.O.
Asst. Treasurer to the Queen, J. Parsons.
Chief Accountant and Paymaster, F. Mintram, L.V.O.
Establishment Officer, P. Wright, C.V.O.
Personnel Officer (designate), G. Franklin, L.V.O.
Administrative Officer, D. Waters, L.V.O.
Asst. Chief Accountant and Paymaster, D. Walker, M.V.O.
Superintendent of Public Enterprises, E. Hewlett.
Accountants, J. Atwell; Mrs. J. Maitland, M.V.O.; Mrs. D. Mowbray.
Clerks, Mrs. C. Auton, M.V.O.; Miss C. Critchley; Miss L. Greenacre; Miss C. McCarthy; Miss C. Mackenzie; Miss N. Mooney; Miss G. Wickham.
Reprographic Unit, Miss I. Hoaen, M.V.O.; D. Groves.
Land Agent, Sandringham, J. Loyd, C.V.O.
Resident Factor, Balmoral, M. Leslie, L.V.O.

Royal Almonry

Lord High Almoner, The Rt. Rev. the Lord Bishop of Rochester.
Hereditary Grand Almoner, The Marquess of Exeter.
Sub-Almoner, Rev. Canon A. D. Caesar, F.R.C.O.
Secretary, P. Wright, C.V.O.
Assistant Secretary, D. Waters, L.V.O.

THE LORD CHAMBERLAIN'S OFFICE
St. James's Palace, S.W.1.

Comptroller, Lt.-Col. G. West.
Assistant Comptroller, Lt.-Col. M. Ross.
Secretary, J. E. P. Titman, c.v.o.
Assistant Secretary, P. D. Hartley, m.v.o.
Registrar, Capt. D. Rankin-Hunt.
State Invitations Assistant, Maj. J. C. Leech.
Clerks, Miss S. Hay, m.v.o.; Miss S. Bowring; Miss J. Churchill; Miss F. Juniper; Miss C. Hunter-Craig; Mrs. J. Marsham; Miss D. Davis.
Permanent Lords in Waiting, The Lord Cobbold, k.g., g.c.v.o.; Lt. Col. The Lord Charteris of Amisfield, p.c., g.c.b., g.c.v.o., o.b.e., q.s.o.; The Lord Maclean, p.c., k.t., g.c.v.o., k.b.e.
Lords in Waiting, The Lord Somerleyton; The Viscount Boyne; The Viscount Long; The Lord Hesketh; The Lord Beaverbrook; The Earl of Dundee; The Earl of Arran.
Gentlemen Ushers, C. Greig, c.v.o., c.b.e.; Lt.-Col. Sir Julian Paget, Bt., c.v.o.; Air Chief Marshal Sir Neville Stack, k.c.b., c.v.o., c.b.e., a.f.c.; Group Capt. J. Slessor; Maj. N. Chamberlayne-Macdonald, l.v.o., o.b.e.; Air Chief Marshal Sir Roy Austen-Smith, k.b.e., c.b., d.f.c.; Vice-Adm. Sir David Loram, k.c.b., l.v.o.; Capt. M. Barrow, d.s.o., r.n.; Capt. M. Fulford-Dobson, r.n.; Lt. Gen. Sir Richard Vickers, k.c.b., l.v.o., o.b.e.
Extra Gentlemen Ushers, Capt. A. Yates, l.v.o., r.n.; Maj. T. Harvey, c.v.o., d.s.o.; Air Vice-Marshal Sir Ranald Reid, k.c.b., d.s.o., m.c.; E. Butler, c.v.o.; Maj.-Gen. Sir Cyril Colquhoun, k.c.v.o., c.b., o.b.e.; Lt.-Col. Sir John Hugo, k.c.v.o., o.b.e.; Vice-Adm. Sir Ronald Brockman, k.c.b., c.s.i., c.i.e., c.v.o., c.b.e.; Air Marshal Sir Maurice Heath, k.b.e., c.b., c.v.o.; Maj.-Gen. Sir Peter Gillett, k.c.v.o., c.b., o.b.e.; Sir James Scholtens, k.c.v.o.; Sir Patrick O'Dea, k.c.v.o.; Brig.-Gen. S. Cooper, c.v.o., o.b.e., c.d.; Adm. Sir David Williams, g.c.b.; Capt. M. Tufnell, c.v.o., d.s.c., r.n.; H. Davis, c.v.o., c.m.; Maj.-Gen. R. Reid, c.v.o., m.c., c.d.; Lt.-Cdr. J. Holdsworth, c.v.o., o.b.e., r.n.; Capt. P. Blackman, r.a.n.; Col. G. Leigh, c.v.o., c.b.e.; Lt.-Cdr. Sir Russell Wood, k.c.v.o., v.r.d.
Gentleman Usher to the Sword of State, Air Chief Marshal Sir John Barraclough, k.c.b., c.b.e., d.f.c., a.f.c.
Gentleman Usher of the Black Rod, Air Chief Marshal Sir John Gingell, g.b.e., k.c.b.
Serjeants at Arms, P. A. Wright, c.v.o.; J. E. P. Titman, c.v.o.; M. Tims, c.v.o.

Marshal of the Diplomatic Corps, Lt.-Gen. Sir John Richards, k.c.b.
Vice-Marshal, R. Hervey, c.m.g.

Constable & Governor of Windsor Castle, Marshal of the Royal Air Force Sir John Grandy, g.c.b., k.b.e., d.s.o.
Keeper of the Jewel House, Tower of London, Maj. Gen. Patrick MacLellan, c.b., m.b.e.
Master of The Queen's Music, Malcolm Williamson, c.b.e.
Poet Laureate, Ted Hughes, o.b.e.
Bargemaster, E. Hunt.
Keeper of the Swans, F. J. Turk, m.v.o.
Superintendent of the State Apartments, St. James's Palace, T. Taylor, m.v.o., m.b.e.

ROYAL COLLECTION DEPARTMENT
St. James's Palace, S.W.1.

Director of Royal Collection and Surveyor of The Queen's Pictures, Sir Oliver Millar, k.c.v.o., f.b.a., f.s.a.
Asst. and Surveyor of Pictures, C. Noble.

Surveyor of The Queen's Works of Art, Sir Geoffrey de Bellaigue, k.c.v.o., f.s.a.
Assist. Surveyors, Mrs J. Harland; Miss S. de Falbe.
Advisor for The Queen's Works of Art, Sir Francis Watson, k.c.v.o., f.s.a.
Librarian, O. Everett, l.v.o.
Librarian Emeritus, Sir Robin Mackworth-Young, g.c.v.o., f.s.a.
Curator of the Print Room, The Hon. Mrs. Roberts, m.v.o.
Registrar, M. Bishop, m.v.o.
Personal Sec. to Dir., Miss C. Crichton-Stuart.
Personal Sec. to Surveyor of Works of Art, Miss S. Williams.
Lady Clerks, Miss A. Dickson, Miss C. Hunter-Craig.

ASCOT OFFICE
St. James's Palace, S.W.1.

Her Majesty's Representative at Ascot, Col. Sir Piers Bengough, k.c.v.o., o.b.e.
Secretary, Miss L. Thompson-Royd.

ECCLESIASTICAL HOUSEHOLD
The College of Chaplains.

Clerk of the Closet, Rt. Rev. John Bickersteth.
Deputy Clerk of the Closet, Rev. Canon A. D. Caesar, f.r.c.o.
Chaplains to The Queen, Ven. E. J. G. Ward, l.v.o.; Rev. J. R. W. Stott; Rev. A. H. H. Harbottle, l.v.o.; Prof. Canon G. R. Dunstan, d.d., f.s.a.; Ven. D. N. Griffiths, r.d.; Canon A. Glendining, l.v.o.; Canon J. G. Grimwade; Canon D. Landreth, t.d.; Canon J. V. Bean; Canon P. A. Welsby, ph.d.; Canon P. W. Miller; Canon G. Carnell; Rev. K. Huxley; Ven. R. Simpson, l.v.o.; Ven. P. Ashford; Canon G. A. Elcoat; Canon D. C. Gray, t.d.; Canon S. Wilkinson; Canon J. Treadgold; Ven. D. Scott; Canon A. Russell, d.phil.; Canon E. James; Canon J. Hester; Rev. S. Pedley; Rev. D. Tonge; Rev. Canon C. Craston; Rev. Canon N. M. Ramm; Rev. Canon D. N. Hole; Rev. M. A. Moxon; Canon R. J. W. Bevan; Canon R. T. W. McDermid; Canon R. H. C. Lewis; Rev. D. J. Burgess; Rev. E. R. Ayerst; Rev. C. G. R. Hall; Rev. R. S. Clarke; Rev. Canon C. J. Hill.
Extra Chaplains, Canon J. S. D. Mansel, k.c.v.o., f.s.a.; Preb. S. A. Williams, c.v.o.

Chapels Royal

Dean of the Chapels Royal, The Bishop of London.
Sub-Dean of Chapels Royal, Rev. Canon A. D. Caesar, f.r.c.o.
Priests in Ordinary, Rev. W. Booth; Rev. A. Ford; Rev. G. Watkins.
Organist, Choirmaster and Composer, R. J. Popplewell, f.r.c.o., f.r.c.m.
Domestic Chaplain—Buckingham Palace, Rev. Canon A. D. Caesar, f.r.c.o.
Domestic Chaplain—Windsor Castle, The Dean of Windsor.
Domestic Chaplain—Sandringham, Canon G. R. Hall.
Chaplain—Royal Chapel, Windsor Great Park, Rev. Canon J. Treadgold.
Chaplain—Hampton Court Palace, Rev. Canon M. Moore.
Chaplain—Tower of London, Rev. J. F. M. Llewellyn, l.v.o.
Organist and Choirmaster—Hampton Court Palace, Gordon Reynolds, l.v.o., a.r.c.m.

MEDICAL HOUSEHOLD

Head of the Medical Household and Physician, Sir John Batten, k.c.v.o., m.d., f.r.c.p.
Physicians, A. M. Dawson, m.d., f.r.c.p.; R. W. Davey, m.b., b.s.

Serjeant Surgeon, W. Slack, M.CH., F.R.C.S.
Surgeon Oculist, P. Holmes Sellors, B.M., B.CH., F.R.C.S.
Surgeon Gynaecologist, G. D. Pinker, C.V.O., F.R.C.S.(Edin.), F.R.C.O.G.
Surgeon Dentist, N. A. Sturridge, C.V.O., L.D.S., B.D.S., D.D.S.
Physician to the Household, R. Thompson, D.M., F.R.C.P.
Surgeon to the Household, B. Jackson, M.S., F.R.C.S.
Surgeon Oculist to the Household, T. J. ffytche, F.R.C.S., L.R.C.P.
Apothecary to The Queen and to the Household, N. R. Southward, L.V.O., M.B., B.CHir., M.R.C.P.
Apothecary to the Household at Windsor, J. H. D. Briscoe, M.A., M.B., B.chir., M.R.C.G.P., D.obst., R.C.O.G.
Apothecary to the Household at Sandringham, H. K. Ford, L.V.O., M.B., F.R.C.G.P.
Coroner of The Queen's Household, J. Burton, M.B., B.S., M.R.C.S., L.R.C.P..

CENTRAL CHANCERY
OF THE ORDERS OF KNIGHTHOOD
St. James's Palace, S.W.1.

Secretary, Maj. Gen. D. H. G. Rice, C.V.O., C.B.E.
Assistant Secretary, Sqn. Ldr. B. Sowerby, M.V.O.
Insignia Clerk, M. G. P. Kelly, L.V.O.
Clerks, J. McGurk, M.V.O.; Miss S. Koller; Miss R. A. Wells; Miss T. Perfect; Miss H. Weir.

The Honorable Corps of Gentlemen at Arms
St. James's Palace, S.W.1.

Captain, The Lord Denham, P.C.; *Lieutenant*, Maj. D. Jamieson, V.C.; *Standard Bearer*, Lt.-Col. J. Eagles; *Clerk of the Cheque & Adjutant*, Maj. T. St. Aubyn; *Harbinger*, Col. P. Pardoe.

Gentlemen of the Corps

Brigadier, A. N. Breitmeyer.
Colonels, A. G. Way, M.C.; T. Hall, O.B.E.; Sir Piers Gengough, K.C.V.O., O.B.E.; Hon. N. Crossley, T.D.; T. Wilson; D. Fanshawe.
Lieutenant-Colonels, D. A. St. G. Laurie, O.B.E., M.C.; P. Hodgson; R. Steele, M.B.E.; W. S. P. Lithgow; Sir James Scott, Bt.; R. Mayfield, D.S.O.; B. Lockhart.
Majors, Sir Richard Carne Rasch, Bt.; J. D. Dillon, D.S.C., R.M.; The Lord Suffield, M.C.; Sir Torquhil Matheson of Matheson, Bt.; F. J. H. Matheson; J. A. J. Nunn; Sir Philip Duncombe, Bt.; I. B. Ramsden, M.B.E.; M. J. Drummond-Brady; A. Arkwright; G. M. B. Colenso-Jones; T. Gosch.
Captain, The Lord Monteagle of Brandon.

The Queen's Bodyguard of the Yeoman of the Guard
St. James's Palace, S.W.1.

Captain, The Viscount Davidson; *Lieutenant*, Col. A. B. Pemberton, M.B.E.; *Clerk of the Cheque and Adjutant*, Col. G. W. Tufnell; *Ensign*, Lt.-Col. R. S. Longsdon; *Exons.*, Maj. C. Marriott; Maj. C. Enderby.

MASTER OF THE HOUSEHOLD'S
DEPARTMENT
Board of Green Cloth
Buckingham Palace, S.W.1.

Master of the Household, Rear-Adm. Sir Paul Greening, K.C.V.O.
Deputy Master of the Household, Lt.-Col. B. A. Stewart-Wilson, L.V.O.
Assistants to the Master of the Household, M. D. Tims, C.V.O.; M. Parker.
Chief Clerk, A. Hancock, M.V.O.
Deputy to Assistant, M. Jephson, M.V.O.
Senior Clerks, M. Dibben; S. Stacey.

Clerks, Miss S. Derry, M.V.O.; Miss S. Fergus; Mrs. H. Toler; Miss J. Colville; Miss S. Crossley.
Superintendent, Windsor Castle, Maj. B. Eastwood, M.B.E.
Assistant to Superintendent, Capt. R. McClosky.
Palace Steward, C. S. Dickman, R.V.M..
Chief Housekeeper, Miss H. Colebrook.

ROYAL MEWS DEPARTMENT
Buckingham Palace, S.W.1.

Crown Equerry, Lt.-Col. S. Gilbert-Denham.
Equerries, Lt.-Col. B. A. Stewart-Wilson, L.V.O.; Maj. Hugh Lindsay, M.V.O.; Capt. S. Holborow (*temp.*).
Veterinary Surgeon, P. S. Dunn, L.V.O., M.R.C.V.S.
Supt. Royal Mews, Buckingham Palace, Maj. A. Smith, M.B.E.
Comptroller of Stores, Maj. L. Marsham.
Chief Clerk, P. Almond.
Deputy Chief Clerk, J. Spencer.
Office Keeper, P. M. Goodman, M.V.O.

HER MAJESTY'S HOUSEHOLD
IN SCOTLAND

Hereditary Lord High Constable, The Earl of Erroll.
Hereditary Master of the Household, The Duke of Argyll.
Lord Lyon King of Arms, Malcolm R. Innes of Edinight, C.V.O., W.S.
Hereditary Bearer of the Royal Banner of Scotland, The Earl of Dundee.
Hereditary Bearer of the Scottish National Flag, The Earl of Lauderdale.
Hereditary Keepers:—
  Holyrood, The Duke of Hamilton and Brandon.
  Falkland, N. J. Crichton-Stuart.
  Stirling, The Earl of Mar and Kellie.
  Dunstaffnage, The Duke of Argyll.
Hereditary Carver, Sir Ralph Anstruther, K.C.V.O., M.C.
Keeper of Dumbarton Castle, Brig. A. S. Pearson, C.B., D.S.O., O.B.E., M.C., T.D.
Governor of Edinburgh Castle, Lt.-Gen. Sir Norman Arthur, K.C.B.
Dean of the Order of the Thistle, The Very Rev. Prof. J. McIntyre, C.V.O., D.D., D.Litt, F.R.S.E.
Dean of the Chapel Royal, Very Rev. Prof. R. A. S. Barbour, M.C., D.D.
Chaplains in Ordinary, Very Rev. R. A. S. Barbour, M.C., D.D.; Rev. W. J. Morris, D.D., LL.D., Ph.D.; Rev. H. W. M. Cant; Rev. K. MacVicar, M.B.E., D.F.C., T.D.; Rev. A. J. C. Macfarlane; Rev. J. McLeod; Rev. G. I. Macmillan; Very Rev. W. B. Johnston, D.D.; Rev. C. Forrester-Paton; Rev. M. D. Craig.
Extra Chaplains, Very Rev. the Lord MacLeod of Fuinary, M.C., D.D.; Very Rev. Prof. J. S. Stewart, D.D.; Rev. Prof. E. P. Dickie, M.C., D.D.; Very Rev. R. L. Small, C.B.E., D.D.; Very Rev. W. R. Sanderson, D.D.; Very Rev. R. W. V. Selby Wright, C.V.O., T.D., D.D., F.R.S.E., F.S.A.(scot.); Rev. T. J. T. Nicol, M.V.O., M.B.E., M.C., T.D.; Very Rev. G. T. H. Reid, M.C., D.D.; Very Rev. Prof. J. McIntyre, C.V.O., D.D., F.R.S.E.
Domestic Chaplain, Balmoral, Rev. J. A. K. Angus, T.D.
Historiographer, Prof. G. Donaldson, Ph.D., F.B.A., F.R.S.E.
Botanist, Prof. D. Henderson, C.B.E., F.R.S.E.
Painter and Limner, D. A. Donaldson, R.S.A., R.P.
Sculptor in Ordinary, Prof. E. Paolozzi.
Astronomer, Prof. M. S. Longair, Ph.D.
Physicians in Scotland, P. Brunt, M.D., F.R.C.P.; A. L. Muir, M.D., F.R.C.P.
Surgeons in Scotland, T. J. McNair, M.D., F.R.C.S.; J. Engeset, Ch.M., F.R.C.S.

Extra Surgeons in Scotland, Prof. Sir Charles Illingworth, C.B.E., M.D., F.R.C.S.ed.; Prof. Sir Donald Douglas, M.B.E., ch.M., M.S., D.SC., F.R.C.S.
Apothecary to the Household at Balmoral, P. Crawford, M.B., ch.B., D.obst., R.C.O.G.
Apothecary to the Household at the Palace of Holyroodhouse, Dr. H. Gebbie, M.B., M.R.C.G.P.

THE QUEEN'S BODY GUARD FOR SCOTLAND

Royal Company of Archers.
Archers' Hall, Edinburgh.

Captain General and Gold Stick for Scotland, Col. The Earl of Stair, K.C.V.O., M.B.E.
Captains, Maj. The Lord Home of the Hirsel, K.T.; The Duke of Buccleuch and Queensberry, K.T., V.R.D.; Lt.-Col. Sir John Gilmour, Bt., D.S.O., T.D.; Col. The Lord Clydesmuir, K.T., C.B., M.B.E., T.D.
Lieutenants, Maj. The Lord Maclean, P.C., K.T., G.C.V.O., K.B.E.; Maj. Sir Hew Hamilton-Dalrymple, Bt., K.C.V.O.; Maj. The Earl of Wemyss and March, K.T.; The Earl of Airlie, K.T., G.C.V.O.
Ensigns, The Earl of Dalhousie, K.T., G.C.V.O., G.B.E., M.C.; Capt. Sir Iain Tennant, K.T.; Maj.-Gen. The Earl Cathcart, C.B., D.S.O., M.C.; Capt. N. E. F. Dalrymple-Hamilton, C.V.O., M.B.E., D.S.C., R.N.
Brigadiers, The Marquess of Lothian, K.C.V.O.; Cdre. Sir John Clerk of Penicuik, Bt., C.B.E., V.R.D., R.N.R.; The Earl of Elgin and Kincardine, K.T.; Col. G. R. Simpson, D.S.O., L.V.O., T.D.; Maj. D. H. Butter, M.C.; The Earl of Minto, O.B.E.; Maj.-Gen. Sir John Swinton, K.C.V.O., O.B.E.; Gen. Sir Michael Gow, G.C.B.; The Hon. Lord Elliott, M.C.; Maj. The Hon. L. H. C. Maclean; The Rt. Hon. George Younger, T.D., M.P.; Capt. G. Burnet, L.V.O.; The Marquess of Graham.
Adjutant, Maj. The Hon. L. H. C. Maclean.
Surgeon, Dr. M. D. Finlay.
Chaplain, Very Rev. R. W. V. Selby Wright, C.V.O., D.D., T.D., F.R.S.E.
President of the Council and Silver Stick for Scotland, Col. the Lord Clydesmuir, K.T., C.B., M.B.E., T.D.
Vice-President, Major Sir Hew Hamilton-Dalrymple, Bt., K.C.V.O.
Secretary, Col. H. F. O. Bewsher, O.B.E..
Treasurer, R. A. G. Douglas-Miller.

HOUSEHOLD OF THE PRINCE PHILIP, DUKE OF EDINBURGH

Private Secretary and Treasurer, B. H. McGrath.
Assistant Private Secretary, Brig. C. Robertson.
Equerry, Maj. R. A. F. P. Jackson, R.M.
Extra Equerries, J. B. V. Orr, C.V.O.; Sir Richard H. Davies, K.C.V.O., C.B.E.; Lord Buxton of Alsa.
Temporary Equerries, Capt. A. J. Fraser, Grenadier Guards; Capt. M. O. M. Chitty.
Chief Clerk and Accountant, V. G. Jewell, M.V.O.

HOUSEHOLD OF QUEEN ELIZABETH THE QUEEN MOTHER

Lord Chamberlain, Maj. the Earl of Dalhousie, K.T., G.C.V.O., G.B.E., M.C.
Comptroller and Extra Equerry, Capt. Sir Alastair S. Aird, K.C.V.O.
Private Secretary and Equerry, Lt.-Col. Sir Martin Gilliat, G.C.V.O., M.B.E.
Treasurer and Equerry, Maj. Sir Ralph Anstruther, Bt., K.C.V.O., M.C.
Equerry, Maj. R. Seymour, L.V.O.
Press Secretary and Extra Equerry, Maj. A. J. S. Griffin, C.V.O.
Extra Equerry, The Lord Sinclair, L.V.O.
Equerry (Temp.), Capt. N. Hall.

Apothecary to the Household, Dr. N. Southward, L.V.O., M.B., B.chir., M.R.C.P.
Surgeon-Apothecary to the Household (Royal Lodge, Windsor), Dr. J. Briscoe, M.R.C.G.P., D.obst., R.C.O.G.
Mistress of the Robes, The Dowager Duchess of Abercorn, G.C.V.O.
Ladies of the Bedchamber, The Dowager Viscountess Hambleden, D.C.V.O.; The Lady Grimthorpe, C.V.O.
Women of the Bedchamber, Ruth, Lady Fermoy, D.C.V.O., O.B.E.; Mrs Patrick Campbell-Preston, C.V.O.; Lady Elizabeth Basset, C.V.O; Lady Angela Oswald.
Extra Women of the Bedchamber, Lady Victoria Wemyss, C.V.O.; The Hon. Mrs. Geoffrey Bowlby, C.V.O.; Lady Jean Rankin, D.C.V.O.; Miss Jane Walker-Okeover
Clerk Comptroller, M. Blanch, L.V.O.
Chief Accountant, J. P. Kyle, M.V.O.
Clerks, Mrs. R. Murphy, L.V.O.; Miss F. Fletcher, M.V.O.

HOUSEHOLD OF THE PRINCE AND PRINCESS OF WALES

Private Secretary and Treasurer to The Prince and Princess of Wales Sir John Riddell, Bt.
Deputy Private Secretary, H. Mews.
Assistant Private Secretary, The Hon. Rupert Fairfax.
Secretary to the Duchy of Cornwall and Keeper of the Records, D. Landale.
Equerry to The Prince of Wales, Lt.-Col. B. R. Anderson.
Extra Equerries to The Prince of Wales, The Hon. Edward Adeane, C.V.O.; Sqn. Ldr. Sir David Checketts, K.C.V.O.
Lady in Waiting and Assistant Private Secretary to the Princess of Wales, Miss Anne Beckwith-Smith.
Equerry to The Princess of Wales, Lt. Cdr. R. Aylard, R.N.
Extra Ladies in Waiting, Mrs. George West; Viscountess Campden; Mrs. Max Pike; Miss Alexandra Loyd.

HOUSEHOLD OF THE DUKE AND DUCHESS OF YORK

Private Secretary and Equerry to the Duke and Duchess of York, Lt.-Col. S. O'Dwyer.
Ladies in Waiting, Miss Helen Hughes; Mrs. John Floyd.

HOUSEHOLD OF THE PRINCE EDWARD

Private Secretary and Equerry to the Prince Edward, Lt.-Col. S. O'Dwyer.

HOUSEHOLD OF THE PRINCESS ROYAL

Private Secretary, Lt.-Col. P. Gibbs.
Ladies in Waiting, Mrs. Richard Carew Pole, L.V.O.; The Hon. Mrs. Legge-Bourke; The Countess of Lichfield; Mrs. Malcolm Wallace; Mrs. Timothy Holderness-Roddam; Mrs. Charles Ritchie (*temp.*).
Extra Ladies in Waiting, Mrs. Andrew Feilden, L.V.O.; Miss Victoria Legge-Bourke, L.V.O.; Mrs. Malcolm Innes.
Personal Secretary, Mrs. David Hodgson, M.V.O.

HOUSEHOLD OF THE PRINCESS MARGARET, COUNTESS OF SNOWDON

Private Secretary and Comptroller, The Lord Napier and Ettrick, C.V.O.
Personal Secretary, Miss M. Murray Brown, C.V.O.

Extra Ladies in Waiting, The Lady Elizabeth Cavendish, L.V.O.; Mrs. Alastair Aird, L.V.O.; Mrs. Robin Benson, L.V.O.; The Lady Juliet Townsend, L.V.O.; Mrs. Jane Stevens; The Hon. Mrs. Wills, L.V.O.; The Lady Glenconner; The Hon. Mrs. Whitehead, L.V.O.; The Countess Alexander of Tunis; Mrs. Elizabeth Blair.

HOUSEHOLD OF THE DUKE AND DUCHESS OF GLOUCESTER

Comptroller, Private Secretary and Equerry, Lt.-Col. Sir Simon Bland, K.C.V.O.
Personal Secretary to The Duchess of Gloucester, Miss Suzanne Marland.
Ladies in Waiting, Mrs. Michael Wigley, L.V.O.; Mrs. Euan McCorquodale; Mrs. Howard Page.
Extra Lady in Waiting, Miss Jennifer Thomson.

HOUSEHOLD OF PRINCESS ALICE, DUCHESS OF GLOUCESTER

Comptroller, Private Secretary and Equerry, Lt.-Col. Sir Simon Bland, K.C.V.O.
Ladies in Waiting, Dame Jean Maxwell-Scott, D.C.V.O.; Mrs. Michael Harvey.
Extra Ladies in Waiting, Miss Dorothy Meynell, C.V.O.; Mrs. Cedric Holland, C.V.O.; Miss Diana Harrison; The Hon. Jane Walsh, L.V.O.; Miss Jane Egerton Warburton, L.V.O.

HOUSEHOLD OF THE DUKE AND DUCHESS OF KENT

Private Secretary, Lt.-Cdr. Sir Richard Buckley, K.C.V.O., R.N.
Ladies in Waiting, Mrs. Alan Henderson, C.V.O.; Mrs. David Napier, L.V.O.; Miss Sarah Partridge.
Extra Lady in Waiting, Mrs. Peter Wilmot-Sitwell.

HOUSEHOLD OF PRINCESS ALEXANDRA

Lady in Waiting, The Lady Mary Mumford, C.V.O.
Private Secretary and Extra Lady in Waiting, Miss Mona Mitchell, C.V.O.
Extra Equerry, Maj. P. C. Clarke, C.V.O.

HOUSEHOLD OF PRINCE AND PRINCESS MICHAEL OF KENT

Private Secretary, Col. Michael Farmer.
Ladies in Waiting, The Hon. Mrs. Leatham; Miss Anne Frost.

THE QUEEN'S BIRTHDAY, 1988

The date for the observance of the Queen's Birthday in 1988 both at home and abroad will be Saturday, June 11.

ROYAL SALUTES

On the Anniversaries of the Birth, Accession and Coronation of the Sovereign and on the Anniversaries of the birth of H.M. the Queen Mother and H.R.H. the Duke of Edinburgh a salute of 62 guns is fired on the wharf at the Tower of London.

On extraordinary and triumphal occasions, such as on the occasion of the Sovereign opening, proroguing or dissolving Parliament in Person, or when passing through London in procession, except when otherwise ordered, 41 guns only are fired.

On the occasion of the birth of a Royal infant a salute of 41 guns is fired from the two Saluting Stations in London, *i.e.* Hyde Park and the Tower of London.

Constable of the Royal Palace and Fortress of London, Field Marshal Sir Roland Gibb, G.C.B., C.B.E., D.S.O., M.C.
Lieutenant of the Tower of London, Gen. Sir Peter Hudson, K.C.B., C.B.E.
Resident Governor and Keeper of the Jewel House, Maj.-Gen. A. P. W. MacLellan, C.B., M.B.E.
Master Gunner of St. James's Park, Lt.-Gen. Sir Thomas Morony, K.C.B., O.B.E.
Master Gunner within the Tower, Col. G. E. Codbold, T.D.

THE ROYAL ARMS

QUARTERLY.—1st and 4th *gules*, three lions passant guardant in pale *or* (*England*); 2nd *or*, a lion rampant within a double tressure flory counterflory *gules* (*Scotland*); 3rd *azure*, a harp *or*, stringed *argent* (*Ireland*); the whole encircled with the Garter.

SUPPORTERS.—*Dexter*: a lion rampant guardant *or*, imperially crowned. *Sinister*: a unicorn *argent*, armed crined and unguled *or*, gorged with a coronet composed of crosses patées and fleurs de lis, a chain affixed passing between the forelegs and reflexed over the back.

BADGES.—The red and white rose united (*England*), a thistle (*Scotland*); a harp *or*, the strings *argent*, with a shamrock leaf *vert* (*Ireland*); upon a mount *vert*, a dragon passant wings elevated *gules* (*Wales*).

THE UNION JACK

The national flag of the United Kingdom is the Union Flag, generally known as the Union Jack, the name deriving from the use of the Union Flag on the jack-staff of naval vessels. It is a combination of the cross of the patron saint of England, St. George (*cross gules in a field argent*), the cross of the patron saint of Scotland, St. Andrew (*saltire argent in a field azure*) and a cross similar to that of St. Patrick, patron saint of Ireland (*saltire gules in a field argent*). The Union Flag was first introduced in 1606 after the union of England and Scotland, the cross of St. Patrick being added in 1801.

ANNUITIES TO THE ROYAL FAMILY

The annuity payable to Her Majesty is known as the Civil List, and is payable out of the Consolidated Fund under the authority of a Civil List Act following the recommendation of a Parliamentary Select Committee.

The allocation for the calendar year 1987 was as follows:—

The Queen	£4,326,100
Queen Elizabeth The Queen Mother	375,300
The Duke of Edinburgh	209,300
Prince Andrew	50,000
Prince Edward	20,000
The Princess Royal	130,400
The Princess Margaret	127,000
Princess Alice, Duchess of Gloucester	51,400
*Duke of Gloucester	102,200
*Duke of Kent	138,000
*Princess Alexandra	131,500
	5,661,200
*Refunded by The Queen	371,700
Total	5,289,500

These figures combine the sums payable directly from the Consolidated Fund with the supplements provided by the Royal Trustees from the grant made to them in the vote for economic and financial administration in the Estimates.

THE FLYING OF FLAGS

Days for hoisting the Union Flag on Government Buildings (from 8 a.m. to sunset).

February 6 (1952).—Her Majesty's Accession.
February 19 (1960).—Birthday of The Duke of York.
March 1.—St. David's Day (in Wales only).
March 10 (1964).—Birthday of The Prince Edward.
March 14.—Commonwealth Day 1988.
April 21 (1926).—Birthday of Her Majesty the Queen.
April 23.—St. George's Day (in England only). Where a building has two or more flagstaffs the Cross of St. George may be flown in addition to the Union Jack but not in a superior position.
June 2 (1953).—Coronation Day.
June 10 (1921).—Birthday of The Duke of Edinburgh.
June 11.—Queen's Official Birthday, 1988.
July 1 (1961).—Birthday of The Princess of Wales.
Aug. 4 (1900).—Birthday of Her Majesty Queen Elizabeth the Queen Mother.
Aug. 15 (1950).—Birthday of The Princess Royal.
Aug. 21 (1930).—Birthday of The Princess Margaret.
Nov. 13.—Remembrance Sunday, 1988.
Nov. 14 (1948).—Birthday of The Prince of Wales.
Nov. 20 (1947).—Her Majesty's Wedding Day.
Nov. 30.—St. Andrew's Day (in Scotland only).
And on the occasion of the opening and closing of Parliament by the Queen, flags should be flown on Government buildings in the Greater London area, whether or not Her Majesty performs the ceremony in person.

The only additions to the above list will be those notified to the Department of the Environment by Her Majesty's command and communicated by the Ministry to the other Departments. The list applies to all Government Buildings in London and elsewhere in the United Kingdom. In cases where it has been the practice to fly the Union Flag daily, *e.g.* on some Custom Houses, that practice may continue.

Flags will be flown at half-mast on the following occasions:...

(*a*) From the announcement of the death up to the funeral of the Sovereign, except on Proclamation Day, when they are hoisted right up from 11 A.M. to sunset.

(*b*) The funerals of members of the Royal Family, subject to special commands from Her Majesty in each case.

(*c*) The funerals of Foreign Rulers, subject to special commands from Her Majesty in each case.

(*d*) The funerals of Prime Ministers and ex-Prime Ministers of the United Kingdom.

(*e*) Other occasions by special command of Her Majesty.

On occasions when days for flying flags coincide with days for flying flags at half mast the following rules will be observed. Flags will be flown: (*a*) although a member of the Royal Family, or a near relative of the Royal Family, may be lying dead, unless special commands be received from Her Majesty to the contrary, and (*b*) although it may be the day of the funeral of a Foreign Ruler. If the body of a very distinguished subject is lying at a Government Office the flag may fly at half mast on that office until the body has left (provided it is a day on which the flag would fly) and then the flag is to be hoisted right up. On all other Government Buildings the flag will fly as usual.

The *Royal Standard* is only to be hoisted when the Queen is actually present in the building, and never when Her Majesty is passing in procession.

RED-LETTER DAYS

Scarlet Robes are worn by the Judges of the Queen's Bench Division on *Red-Letter Days*.

RED-LETTER DAYS AND STATE OCCASIONS, 1988.

Jan. 25. Conversion of St. Paul.	„ 14. St. Matthias.	*July* 25. St. James.
Feb. 2. Purification.	*June* 2. Coronation Day.	*Aug.* 4. Birthday of Queen Elizabeth the Queen Mother.
„ 6. Queen's Accession.	„ 10. Birthday of The Duke of Edinburgh.	*Oct.* 18. St. Luke.
„ 17. Ash Wednesday.	„ 11. St. Barnabas.	„ 28. St. Simon and St. Jude.
Mar. 1. St. David.	„ 11. Queen's Official Birthday (1988).	*Nov.* 1. All Saints.
„ 25. Annunciation.	„ 24. St. John the Baptist.	„ 12. Lord Mayor's Day.
Apr. 21. Queen's Birthday.	„ 29. St. Peter.	„ 14. Birthday of The Prince of Wales.
„ 25. St. Mark.	*July* 3. St. Thomas.	„ 30. St. Andrew.
May 2. St. Philip and St. James.		
„ 12. Ascension Day.		

THE MILITARY KNIGHTS OF WINDSOR

Founded in 1348 after the Wars in France to assist English Knights, who, having been prisoners in the hands of the French, had become impoverished by the payments of heavy ransoms. They received a pension and quarters in Windsor Castle. Edward III founded the Order of the Garter later in the same year, incorporating the Knights of Windsor and the College of St. George into its foundation and raising the number of Knights to 26 to correspond with the number of the Knights of the Garter. Known later as the Alms Knights or Poor Knights of Windsor, their establishment was reduced under the will of King Henry VIII to 13 and Statutes were drawn up by Queen Elizabeth I.

In 1833 King William IV changed their designation to The Military Knights and granted them their present uniform which consists of a scarlet tail-coat with white cross sword-belt, crimson sash and cocked hat with plume. The badges are the Shield of St. George and the Star of the Order of the Garter. The Knights receive a small stipend in addition to their Army pensions and quarters in Windsor Castle. They take part in all ceremonies of the Noble Order of the Garter and attend Sunday morning service in St. George's Chapel as representatives of the Knights of the Garter.

Applications for appointment should be made to The Military Secretary, Ministry of Defence, Army Dept.

Governor, Maj.-Gen. Sir Peter Gillett, K.C.V.O., C.B., O.B.E.
Military Knights, Lt.-Col. R. W. Dobbin, O.B.E.; Maj. H. Smith, M.B.E., R.V.M.; Lt.-Col. A. R. Clark, M.C.; Maj. A. E. Wollaston, M.V.O.; Brig. A. L. Atkinson, O.B.E.; Brig. J. F. Linders, O.B.E., M.C; Brig. A. C. Tyler, C.B.E., M.C., D.L.; Maj. W. L. Thompson, M.V.O., M.B.E., D.C.M.; Maj. L. W. Dickerson; Maj. J. C. Cowley, D.C.M.; Lt.-Col. N. L. West.
Supernumerary, Lt.-Col. A. R. Clark, M.C.

THE PEERAGE

The rules which govern the creation and succession of Peerages are extremely complicated. There are, technically, five separate Peerages, the Peerage of England, of Scotland, of Ireland, of Great Britain, and of the United Kingdom. The Peerage of Great Britain dates from 1707 when an Act of Union combined the two Kingdoms of England and Scotland and separate Peerages were discontinued; and the Peerage of the United Kingdom from 1801 when Great Britain and Ireland were combined under an Act of Union. Some Scottish Peers have received additional Peerages of Great Britain or of the United Kingdom since 1707, and some Irish Peers additional Peerages of the United Kingdom since 1801. The Peerage of Ireland was not entirely discontinued from 1801 but holders of Irish Peerages, whether pre-dating or created subsequent to the Union of 1801, are not entitled to sit in the House of Lords if they have no additional English, Scottish, Great Britain or United Kingdom Peerage. (However, they are eligible for election to the House of Commons and to vote in Parliamentary elections, which other Peers are not.) An Irish Peer holding a Peerage of a lower grade which enables him to sit in the House of Lords is introduced there by the title which enables him to sit, though for all other purposes he is known by his higher title. In the Peerage of Scotland there is no rank of Baron; the equivalent rank is Lord of Parliament, abbreviated to "Lord" (the female equivalent is "Lady"). All Peers of England, Scotland, Great Britain or the United Kingdom who are of full age (21 years) and of British nationality are entitled to sit in the House of Lords. Certain ancient Peerages pass on death to the nearest heir, male or female, and several are held by women (see also p. 247). Since the Peerage Act, 1963, Peeresses in their own Right have been entitled to sit in the House of Lords, subject to the qualifications applying to Peers.

Non-hereditary or Life Peerages, in the degree of Baron or Baroness, have been conferred by the Crown since 1876 on eminent judges, the Lords of Appeal or Law Lords, to enable them to carry out the judicial functions of the House of Lords, and since 1958 on

men and women of distinction in public life, giving them seats in the House of Lords. Life Peers and Peeresses are addressed identically as an hereditary Peer or Peeress, and their children have the same courtesy style as the children of an hereditary Peer or Peeress.

No fees for Dignities have been payable since 1937. The House of Lords surrendered the ancient right of peers to be tried for treason or felony by their peers in 1948.

Peerages Extinct Since the Last Issue

BARONIES.—Fraser of Allander (cr. 1964).

Disclaimer of Peerages

The Peerage Act, 1963, enables Peers or Peeresses to disclaim their Peerages for life. Peers alive in 1963 could disclaim within 12 months after the passing of the Act (July 31, 1963); a person subsequently succeeding to a Peerage may disclaim within 12 months (one month if an M.P.) after the date of succession, or of attaining his or her majority, if later. The disclaimer is irrevocable but does not affect the descent of the Peerage after the disclaimant's death, and children of a disclaimed Peer may, if they wish, retain their precedence and any courtesy titles and styles borne as children of a Peer.

EARLS: Durham (1970); Home (1963); Sandwich (1964).
VISCOUNTS: Hailsham (1963); Stansgate (1963).
BARONS: Altrincham (1963); Archibald (1975); Merthyr (1977); Reith (1972); Sanderson of Ayot (1971); Silkin (1972); Southampton (1964).

Peers Who Are Minors

EARLS (1): Hardwicke (b. 1971).
VISCOUNTS (1): Dillon (b. 1973).
BARONS (1): Wrottesley (b. 1968).

COMPOSITION OF THE HOUSE OF LORDS (At Aug. 31, 1987)

Archbishops and Bishops	26	
Peers by Succession	763	(20 women)
Hereditary Peers of first creation (including the Prince of Wales)	29	
Life Peers under the Appellate Jurisdiction Act 1876	21	
Life Peers under the Life Peerages Act 1958	346	(47 women)
TOTAL	1185	
Of whom:		
Peers without Writs of Summons	90	
Peers on Leave of Absence from the House	—	

Contractions and Symbols.—S. or I. appended to the date of creation denotes a *Scottish* or *Irish* title, the further addition of a * implies that the Peer in question holds also an *Imperial* title, which is specified (after the name) by its more definite description as *Engl., Brit.,* or *U.K.* When both titles are alike, as in the case of Argyll, this star is appended to the conjoined date below, and it then denotes that such date is that of the imperial creation. The mark ° signifies that there is no "of" in the Marquessate or Earldom so designated; *b.* signifies born; *s.,* succeeded; *m.,* married; *w.,* widower or widow; *M.,* minor; † Information on *Eldest Son or Heir* not ascertained at time of going to press.

ROYAL DUKES

Style, His Royal Highness The Duke of ——.
Addressed as, Sir, or more formally, May it please your Royal Highness.

1947   *Edinburgh,* The Prince Philip, Duke of Edinburgh, K.G., P.C., K.T., O.M., G.B.E., *b.* 1921, *m.* (see p. 217).
1337   *Cornwall,* Charles, Prince of Wales, Duke of Cornwall (*Scottish Duke, Rothesay,* 1398). K.G., P.C., K.T., G.C.B., *b.* 1948, *m.* (see p. 218).
1986   *York,* The Prince Andrew, Duke of York, C.V.O., *b.* 1960, *m.* (see p. 218).
1928   *Gloucester* (2nd), Richard, Duke of Gloucester, G.C.V.O., *b.* 1944, *s.* 1974, *m.* (see p. 217.)
1934   *Kent* (2nd), Edward, Duke of Kent, K.G., G.C.M.G., G.C.V.O., *b.* 1935, *s.* 1942, *m.* (see p. 217).

ARCHBISHOPS

Style, The Most Rev. His Grace The Lord Archbishop of——.
Addressed as, My Lord Archbishop; or, Your Grace.

Introd. to House
of Lords

1973   *Canterbury* (102nd), Robert Alexander Kennedy Runcie. P.C., M.C.,
       b. 1921, *m.* Consecrated Bishop of St. Albans, 1970, *trans.* 1980.

1973   *York* (95th), John Stapylton Habgood, P.C., PH.D., *b.* 1927, *m.*
       Consecrated Bishop of Durham, 1973, trans. 1983.

DUKES

Style, His Grace The Duke of——. *Addressed as,* My Lord Duke; or, Your Grace. The
eldest sons of Dukes and Marquesses take, by courtesy, their father's second title. The
other sons and the daughters are styled Lord Edward, Lady Caroline. etc.

Created.	Title, Order of Succession, Name, etc.	Eldest Son or Heir.
1868 I.*	*Abercorn* (5th), James Hamilton (6th *Brit. Marq.,* 1790, and 14th *Scott. Earl,* 1606 both *Abercorn*), *b.* 1934, *s.* 1979, *m.*	Marquess of Hamilton, *b.* 1969.
1701 S. ⎱ 1892* ⎰	*Argyll,* Ian Campbell (12th *Scottish* and 5th *U.K. Duke, Argyll*), *b.* 1937, *s.* 1973, *m.*	Marquess of Lorne, *b.* 1968.
1703 S.	*Atholl* (10th), George Iain Murray, *b.* 1931, *s.* 1957.	Godfrey P. *M.,* D.S.O., *b.* 1901.
1682	*Beaufort* (11th), David Robert Somerset, *b.* 1928, *s.* 1984, *m.*	Marquess of Worcester, *b.* 1952.
1694	*Bedford* (13th), John Robert Russell, *b.* 1917, *s.* 1953, *m.*	Marquess of Tavistock, *b.* 1940.
1663 S.*	*Buccleuch* (9th) & (11th) *Queensberry* (1684), Walter Francis John Montagu Douglas Scott, K.T., V.R.D. (8th *Engl. Earl, Doncaster,* 1662), *b.* 1923, *s.* 1973, *m.*	Earl of Dalkeith, *b.* 1954.
1694	*Devonshire* (11th), Andrew Robert Buxton Cavendish, P.C., M.C., *b.* 1920, *s.* 1950, *m.*	Marquess of Hartington, *b.* 1944.
1900	*Fife* (3rd), James George Alexander Bannerman Carnegie, *b.* 1929, *s.* 1959. (see *p.* 216).	Earl of Macduff, *b.* 1961.
1675	*Grafton* (11th), Hugh Denis Charles FitzRoy, K.G., *b.* 1919, *s.* 1970, *m.*	Earl of Euston, *b.* 1947.
1643 S.*	*Hamilton* (15th), Angus Alan Douglas Douglas-Hamilton (*Premier Peer of Scotland;* 12th *Brit. Duke, Brandon,* 1711), *b.* 1938, *s.* 1973, *m.*	Marquess of Douglas and Clydesdale, *b.* 1978.
1766 I.*	*Leinster* (8th), Gerald FitzGerald (*Premier Duke, Marquess and Earl of Ireland;* 8th *Brit. Visct., Leinster,* 1747) *b.* 1914, *s.* 1976, *m.*	Marquess of Kildare, *b.* 1948.
1719	*Manchester* (12th), Angus Charles Drogo Montagu, *b.* 1938, *s.* 1985, *m.*	Viscount Mandeville, *b.* 1962.
1702	*Marlborough* (11th), John George Vanderbilt Henry Spencer-Churchill, *b.* 1926, *s.* 1972, *m.*	Marquess of Blandford, *b.* 1955.
1707 S.*	*Montrose* (7th), James Angus Graham (5th *Brit. Earl, Graham,* 1722), *b.* 1907, *s.* 1954, *m.*	Marquess of Graham, *b.* 1935.
1756	*Newcastle (under Lyme)* (9th), Henry Edward Hugh Pelham-Clinton-Hope, O.B.E., *b.* 1907, *s.* 1941, *m.*	Edward C. *Pelham-Clinton, b.* 1920
1483	*Norfolk* (17th), Miles Francis Stapleton Fitzalan-Howard, K.G., G.C.V.O., C.B., C.B.E., M.C. (*Premier Duke and Earl;* 12th *Eng. Baron Beaumont,* 1309; 4th *U.K. Baron Howard of Glossop,* 1869), *b.* 1915, *s.* 1975, *m.* (*Earl Marshal*).	Earl of Arundel and Surrey, *b.* 1956.
1766	*Northumberland* (10th), Hugh Algernon Percy, K.G., P.C., G.C.V.O., T.D., F.R.S., *b.* 1914, *s.* 1940, *m.* (*Lord Steward*).	Earl Percy, *b.* 1953.
1716	*Portland* (9th), Victor Frederick William Cavendish-Bentinck, C.M.G. *b.* 1897, *s.* 1980, *m.*	(None to Dukedom), to Earldom of Portland, Henry N. *B., b.* 1919.
1675	*Richmond* (9th) & *Gordon* (4th, 1876), Frederick Charles Gordon-Lennox (9th *Scott. Duke, Lennox.* 1675), *b.* 1904, *s.* 1935, *m.*	Earl of March and Kinrara, *b.* 1929.
1707 S.*	*Roxburghe* (10th), Guy David Innes-Ker (5th *U.K. Earl, Innes,* 1837), *b.* 1954, *s.* 1974, *m.* (*Premier Baronet of Scotland*).	Marquess of Bowmont, *b.* 1981.
1703	*Rutland* (10th), Charles John Robert Manners, C.B.E., *b.* 1919, *s.* 1940, *m.*	Marquess of Granby, *b.* 1959.
1684	*St. Albans* (13th), Charles Frederick Aubrey de Vere Beauclerk, O.B.E., *b.* 1915, *s.* 1964, *m.*	Earl of Burford, *b.* 1939.
1547	*Somerset* (19th), John Michael Edward Seymour, *b.* 1952, *s.* 1984, *m.*	Lord Seymour, *b.* 1982.
1833	*Sutherland* (6th), John Sutherland Egerton, T.D. (5th *U.K. Earl Ellesmere,* 1846), *b.* 1915, *s.* 1963, *m.*	Cyril R. *E., b.* 1905.
1814	*Wellington* (8th), Arthur Valerian Wellesley, M.V.O., O.B.E., M.C. (9th *Irish Earl, Mornington,* 1760), *b.* 1915, *s.* 1972, *m.*	Marquess of Douro, *b.* 1945.
1874	*Westminster* (6th), Gerald Cavendish Grosvenor, *b.* 1951, *s.* 1979, *m.*	(None to Dukedom), to Marquessate, Earl of Wilton, *b.* 1921 (see, p. 233).

MARQUESSES

Style, The Most Hon. The Marquess of——. *Addressed as,* My Lord Marquess.
In titles marked ° the "of" is *not* used. For the style of Marquesses' sons and daughters,
see under "DUKES,"above.

Created.	Title, Order of Succession, Name, etc.	Eldest Son or Heir.
1916	*Aberdeen and Temair* (6th), Alastair Ninian John Gordon (12th *Scott. Earl, Aberdeen,* 1682), *b.* 1920, *s.* 1984, *m.*	Earl of Haddo, *b.* 1955.
1876	*Abergavenny* (5th), John Henry Guy Nevill, K.G., O.B.E., *b.* 1914, *s.* 1954, *m.*	Guy R. G. N., *b.* 1945.
1821	*Ailesbury* (8th), Michael Sidney Cedric Brudenell-Bruce, *b.* 1926, *s.* 1974, *m.*	Earl of Cardigan, *b.* 1952.
1831	*Ailsa* (7th), Archibald David Kennedy, O.B.E., (19th *Scott. Earl, Cassillis,* 1509), *b.* 1925, *s.* 1957, *m.*	Earl of Cassillis, *b.* 1956.
1815	*Anglesey* (7th), George Charles Henry Victor Paget, *b.* 1922, *s.* 1947, *m.*	Earl of Uxbridge, *b.* 1950.
1789	*Bath* (6th), Henry Frederick Thynne, *b.* 1905, *s.* 1946, *m.*	Viscount Weymouth, *b.* 1932.
1826	*Bristol* (7th), Frederick William John Augustus Hervey, *b.* 1954, *s.* 1985, *m.*	Lord Frederick W. C. N. W. H., *b.* 1961.
1796	*Bute* (6th), John Crichton-Stuart (11th *Scott. Earl, Dumfries,* 1633), *b.* 1933, *s.* 1956, *m.*	Earl of Dumfries, *b.* 1958.
1812	°*Camden* (6th), David George Edward Henry Pratt, *b.* 1930, *s.* 1983.	Earl of Brecknock, *b.* 1965.
1815	*Cholmondeley* (6th), George Hugh Cholmondeley, G.C.V.O., M.C. (10th *Irish Viscount, Cholmondeley,* 1661), *b.* 1919, *s.* 1968, *m.* (*Lord Great Chamberlain*).	Earl of Rocksavage, *b.* 1960.
1816 I.*	°*Conyngham* (7th), Frederick William Henry Francis Conyngham (7th *U.K. Baron, Minster, U.K.* 1821), *b.* 1924, *s.* 1974, *w.*	Earl of Mount Charles, *b.* 1951.
1791 I.*	*Donegall* (7th), Dermot Richard Claud Chichester, L.V.O. (7th *Brit. Baron, Fisherwick,* 1790, 6th *Brit. Baron, Templemore,* 1831), *b.* 1916, *s.* to Marquessate, 1975: to Templemore Barony, 1953, *m.*	Earl of Belfast, *b.* 1952.
1789 I.*	*Downshire* (7th), Arthur Wills Percy Wellington Blundell Trumbull Sandys Hill (7th *Brit. Earl, Hillsborough,* 1772), *b.* 1894, *s.* 1918, *w.*	A. Robin I. H., *b.* 1929.
1888	*Dufferin & Ava* (5th), Sheridan Frederick Terence Hamilton-Temple-Blackwood (11th *Irish Baron, Dufferin & Clandeboye,* 1800), *b.* 1938, *s.* 1945, *m.*	(None to Marquessate), to Irish Barony, Sir Francis G. *Blackwood,* Bt., *b.* 1916.
1801 I.*	*Ely* (8th) Charles John Tottenham (8th *U.K. Baron, Loftus,* 1801), *b.* 1913, *s.* 1969, *m.*	Viscount Loftus, *b.* 1943.
1801	*Exeter* (7th), William Martin Alleyne Cecil, *b.* 1909, *s.* 1981, *m.*	Lord Burghley, *b.* 1935.
1800 I.*	*Headfort* (6th), Thomas Geoffrey Charles Michael Taylour (4th *U.K. Baron, Kenlis,* 1831), *b.* 1932, *s.* 1960, *m.*	Earl of Bective, *b.* 1959.
1793	*Hertford* (8th), Hugh Edward Conway Seymour (9th *Irish Baron, Conway,* 1712), *b.* 1930, *s.* 1940, *m.*	Earl of Yarmouth, *b.* 1958.
1599 S.*	*Huntly* (13th), Granville Charles Gomer Gordon (*Premier Marquess of Scotland*) (5th *U.K. Baron, Meldrum,* 1815), *b.* 1944, *s.* 1987, *m.*	Earl of Aboyne, *b.* 1973.
1784	*Lansdowne* (8th), George John Charles Mercer Nairne Petty-Fitzmaurice, P.C. (8th *Irish Earl. Kerry,* 1723), *b.* 1912, *s.* 1944, *w.*	Earl of Shelburne, *b.* 1941.
1902	*Linlithgow* (4th), Adrian John Charles Hope (10th *Scott. Earl, Hopetoun* 1703), *b.* 1946, *s.* 1987, *m.*	Earl of Hopetoun, *b.* 1969.
1816 I.*	*Londonderry* (9th), Alexander Charles Robert Vane-Tempest-Stewart (4th *U.K. Earl, Vane,* 1823), *b.* 1937, *s.* 1955, *m.*	Viscount Castlereagh, *b.* 1972.
1701 S.*	*Lothian* (12th), Peter Francis Walter Kerr, K.C.V.O. (6th *U.K. Baron, Kerr,* 1821), *b.* 1922, *s.* 1940, *m.*	Earl of Ancram, *b.* 1945.
1917	*Milford Haven* (4th), George Ivar Louis Mountbatten, *b.* 1961, *s.* 1970.	Lord Ivar A. M. M., *b.* 1963.
1838	*Normanby* (4th), Oswald Constantine John Phipps, K.G., C.B.E. (8th *Irish Baron, Mulgrave,* 1767), *b.* 1912, *s.* 1932, *m.*	Earl of Mulgrave, *b.* 1954.
1812	*Northampton* (7th), Spencer Douglas David Compton, *b.* 1946, *s.* 1978, *m.*	Earl Compton, *b.* 1973.
1825 I.*	*Ormonde* (7th), James Hubert Theobald Charles Butler, M.B.E. (7th *U.K. Baron, Ormonde,* 1821), *b.* 1899, *s.* 1971, *w.*	(None to Marquessate), to Earldoms of Ormonde and Ossory, Viscount Mountgarret, *b.* 1936.
1682 S.	*Queensberry* (12th), David Harrington Angus Douglas, *b.* 1929, *s.* 1954.	Viscount Drumlanrig, *b.* 1967.
1926	*Reading* (4th), Simon Charles Henry Rufus Isaacs, *b.* 1942, *s.* 1980, *m.*	Viscount Erleigh, *b.* 1986.
1789	*Salisbury* (6th), Robert Edward Peter Gascoyne-Cecil, *b.* 1916, *s.* 1972, *m.*	Viscount Cranborne, *b.* 1946.
1800 I.*	*Sligo* (10th), Denis Edward Browne (10th *U.K. Baron, Monteagle,* 1806), *b.* 1908, *s.* 1952, *m.*	Earl of Altamont, *b.* 1939.
1787	°*Townshend* (7th), George John Patrick Dominic Townshend, *b.* 1916, *s.* 1921, *m.*	Viscount Raynham, *b.* 1945.
1694 S.*	*Tweeddale* (13th), Edward Douglas John Hay (4th *U.K. Baron, Tweeddale,* 1881), *b.* 1947, *s.* 1979.	Lord Charles D. M. H., *b.* 1947.
1789 I.*	*Waterford* (8th), John Hubert de la Poer Beresford (8th *Brit. Baron, Tyrone,* 1786), *b.* 1933, *s.* 1934, *m.*	Earl of Tyrone, *b.* 1958.
1551	*Winchester* (18th), Nigel George Paulet (*Premier Marquess of England*), *b.* 1941, *s.* 1968, *m.*	Earl of Wiltshire, *b.* 1969.
1892	*Zetland* (3rd), Lawrence Aldred Mervyn Dundas (5th *U.K. Earl of Zetland,* 1838, 6th *Brit. Baron Dundas,* 1794), *b.* 1908, *s.* 1961, *m.*	Earl of Ronaldshay, *b.* 1937.

EARLS

Style (*see also* note, p. 247). The Right Hon. The Earl of ——. *Addressed as*, My Lord. The eldest sons of Earls take, by courtesy, their father's second title, the younger sons being styled the Hon., *e.g.* the Hon. John ——, but the daughters Lady Elizabeth ——, etc. Where marked ° the "of" is not used.

Created.	*Title, Order of Succession, Name, etc.*	*Eldest Son or Heir.*
1639 s.	*Airlie* (13th), David George Coke Patrick Ogilvy, K.T., G.C.V.O., P.C., b. 1926, s. 1968, m.	Lord Ogilvy, b. 1958.
1696	*Albemarle* (10th), Rufus Arnold Alexis Keppel, b. 1965, s. 1979.	Crispian W. J. K., b. 1948.
1952	°*Alexander of Tunis* (2nd), Shane William Desmond Alexander, b. 1935, s. 1969, m.	Hon. Brian J. A., b. 1939.
1826	°*Amherst* (5th), Jeffery John Archer Amherst, M.C., b. 1896, s. 1927.	(None.)
1662 s.	*Annandale and Hartfell* (11th), Patrick Andrew Wentworth Hope Johnstone, b. 1941, *claim established* 1985, m.	Lord Johnstone, b. 1971.
1789 i.	°*Annesley* (10th), Patrick Annesley, b. 1924, s. 1979, m.	Hon. Philip H.A., b. 1927.
1785 i.	*Antrim* (9th), Alexander Randal Mark McDonnell, b. 1935, s. 1977, m. (*Viscount Dunluce*.)	Hon. Randal A. St. J. M., b. 1967.
1762 i.*	*Arran* (9th), Arthur Desmond Colquhoun Gore (5th *U.K. Baron Sudley*, 1884), b. 1938, s. 1983, m.	Paul A. G., C.M.G., C.V.O., b. 1921.
1955	°*Attlee* (2nd), Martin Richard Attlee, b. 1927, s. 1967, m.	Viscount Prestwood, b. 1956.
1714	*Aylesford* (11th), Charles Ian Finch-Knightley, b. 1918, s. 1958, m.	Lord Guernsey, b. 1947.
1937	°*Baldwin of Bewdley* (4th), Edward Alfred Alexander Baldwin, b. 1938, s. 1976, m.	Viscount Corvedale, b. 1973.
1922	*Balfour* (4th), Gerald Arthur James Balfour, b. 1925, s. 1968, m.	Eustace A. G. B., b. 1921.
1772	°*Bathurst* (8th), Henry Allen John Bathurst, b. 1927, s. 1943, m.	Lord Apsley, b. 1961.
1919	°*Beatty* (3rd), David Beatty, b. 1946, s. 1972.	Viscount Borodale, b. 1973.
1797 i.	*Belmore* (8th), John Armar Lowry-Corry, b. 1951, s. 1960, m.	Viscount Corry, b. 1985.
1739 i.* 1937	} *Bessborough*, Frederick Edward Neuflize Ponsonby (10th *Irish* and 2nd *U.K. Earl Bessborough*), b. 1913, s. 1956, m.	Arthur M. L. P., b. 1912 (to Irish Earldom only).
1815	*Bradford* (7th), Richard Thomas Orlando Bridgeman, b. 1947, s. 1981, m.	Viscount Newport, b.1980.
1677 s.	*Breadalbane and Holland* (10th), John Romer Boreland Campbell, b. 1919, s. 1959.	(None.)
1469 s.*	*Buchan* (17th), Malcolm Harry Erskine, (8th *U.K. Baron Erskine* 1806), b. 1930, s. 1984, m.	Lord Cardross, b. 1960.
1746	*Buckinghamshire* (10th), (George) Miles Hobart-Hampden, b. 1944, s. 1983, m.	Sir Robert Hobart, Bt., b. 1915.
1800	°*Cadogan* (7th), William Gerald Charles Cadogan, M.C., b. 1914, s. 1933, m.	Viscount Chelsea, b. 1937.
1878	°*Cairns* (5th), David Charles Cairns, G.C.V.O., C.B., b. 1909, s. 1946, m.	Viscount Garmoyle, b. 1939.
1455 s.	*Caithness* (20th), Malcolm Ian Sinclair, b. 1948, s. 1965, m.	Lord Berriedale, b. 1981.
1800 i.	*Caledon* (7th), Nicholas James Alexander, b. 1955, s. 1980.	Earl Alexander of Tunis (*see above*).
1661	*Carlisle* (12th), Charles James Ruthven Howard, M.C. (12th *Scott. Baron, Ruthven of Freeland*, 1651), b. 1923, s. 1963, m.	Viscount Morpeth, b. 1949.
1793	*Carnarvon* (6th), Henry George Alfred Marius Victor Francis Herbert, b. 1898, s. 1923.	Lord Porchester, K.C.V.O., K.B.E., b. 1924.
1748 i.*	*Carrick* (9th), Brian Stuart Theobald Somerset Caher Butler (3rd *U.K. Baron, Butler*, 1912), b. 1931, s. 1957.	Viscount Ikerrin, b. 1953.
1800 i.	°*Castle Stewart* (8th), Arthur Patrick Avondale Stuart, b. 1928, s. 1961, m.	Viscount Stuart, b. 1953.
1814	°*Cathcart* (6th), Alan Cathcart, C.B., D.S.O., M.C. (15th *Scott. Baron, Cathcart*, 1447), b. 1919, s. 1927, m.	Lord Greenock, b. 1952.
1647 i.	*Cavan* (12th), Michael Edward Oliver Lambart, T.D., b. 1911, s. 1950, m.	Roger C. L., b. 1944.
1827	°*Cawdor* (6th), Hugh John Vaughan Campbell, b. 1932, s. 1970, m.	Viscount Emlyn, b. 1962.
1801	*Chichester* (9th), John Nicholas Pelham, b. 1944, s. 1944, m.	Richard A. H. P., b. 1952.
1803 i.*	*Clancarty* (8th), William Francis Brinsley Le Poer Trench (7th *U.K. Visct. Clancarty*, 1823), b. 1911, s. 1975, m.	Nicholas P. R. *Le P. T.*, b. 1952.
1776 i.*	*Clanwilliam* (6th), John Charles Edmund Carson Meade (4th *U.K. Baron Clanwilliam*, 1828), b. 1914, s. 1953, m.	John H. M., b. 1919.
1776	*Clarendon* (7th), George Frederick Laurence Hyde Villiers, b. 1933, s. 1955, m.	Lord Hyde, b. 1976.
1620 i.*	*Cork & Orrery* (1660), Patrick Reginald Boyle (13th *Irish Earl* and 9th *Brit. Baron, Boyle of Marston*, 1711), b. 1910, s. 1967, m.	Hon. John W. B., D.S.C., b. 1916.
1850	*Cottenham* (8th), Kenelm Charles Everard Digby Pepys, b. 1948, s. 1968, m.	Viscount Crowhurst, b. 1983.
1762 i.*	*Courtown* (9th), James Patrick Montagu Burgoyne Winthrop Stopford (8th *Brit. Baron, Saltersford*, 1796), b. 1954, s. 1975, m.	Hon. Jeremy N. S., M.V.O., b. 1958.
1697	*Coventry* (11th), George William Coventry, b. 1934, s. 1940, m.	Viscount Deerhurst, b. 1957.
1857	°*Cowley* (7th), Garret Graham Wellesley, b. 1934, s. 1975, m.	Viscount Dangan, b. 1965.
1892	*Cranbrook* (5th), Gathorne Gathorne-Hardy, b. 1933, s. 1978, m.	Lord Medway, b. 1968.
1801	*Craven* (8th), Simon George Craven, b. 1961, s. 1983.	Rupert J. E. C., b. 1926.
1398 s.*	*Crawford* (29th) *and Balcarres* (12th), Robert Alexander Lindsay, P.C., (*Premier Earl on Union Roll and* 5th *U.K. Baron, Wigan*, 1826), b. 1927, s. 1975, m.	Lord Balniel, b. 1958.

Created.	Title, Order of Succession, Name, etc.	Eldest Son or Heir.
1861	*Cromartie* (4th), Roderick Grant Francis Mackenzie, M.C., T.D., *b.* 1904, *s.* 1962, *m.*	Viscount Tarbat, *b.* 1948.
1901	*Cromer* (3rd), George Rowland Stanley Baring, K.G., G.C.M.G., M.B.E., P.C., *b.* 1918, *s.* 1953, *m.*	Viscount Errington, *b.* 1946.
1633 s.*	*Dalhousie* (16th), Simon Ramsay, K.T., G.C.V.O., G.B.E., M.C. (4th *U.K. Baron, Ramsay*, 1875), *b.* 1914, *s.* 1950, *m.*	Lord Ramsay, *b.* 1948.
1725 I.*	*Darnley* (11th), Adam Ivo Stuart Bligh (20th *English Baron, Clifton of Leighton Bromswold*, 1608), *b.* 1941, *s.* 1980, *m.*	Lord Clifton, *b.* 1968.
1711	*Dartmouth* (9th), Gerald Humphry Legge, *b.* 1924, *s.* 1962, *m.*	Viscount Lewisham, *b.* 1949.
1761	°*De La Warr* (10th), William Herbrand Sackville, *b.* 1921, *s.* 1976, *m.*	Lord Buckhurst, *b.* 1948.
1622	*Denbigh* (11th) *and Desmond* (10th), William Rudolph Michael Feilding (10th *Irish Earl, Desmond*, 1622), *b.* 1943, *s.* 1966, *m.*	Viscount Feilding, *b.* 1970.
1485	*Derby* (18th), Edward John Stanley, M.C., *b.* 1918, *s.* 1948, *m.*	Edward R. W. S., *b.* 1962.
1553	*Devon* (17th), Charles Christopher Courtenay, *b.* 1916, *s.* 1935, *m.*	Lord Courtenay, *b.* 1942.
1800 I.*	*Donoughmore* (8th), Richard Michael John Hely-Hutchinson (8th *U.K. Visct., Hutchinson*, 1821), *b.* 1927, *s.* 1981, *m.*	Viscount Suirdale, *b.* 1952.
1661 I.*	*Drogheda* (11th), Charles Garrett Ponsonby Moore, K.G., K.B.E. (2nd *U.K. Baron. Moore*, 1954), *b.* 1910, *s.* 1957, *m.*	Viscount Moore, *b.* 1937.
1837	*Ducie* (6th), Basil Howard Moreton, *b.* 1917, *s.* 1952, *m.*	Lord Moreton, *b.* 1951.
1860	*Dudley* (4th), William Humble David Ward, *b.* 1920, *s.* 1969, *m.*	Viscount Ednam, *b.* 1947.
1660 s.*	*Dundee* (12th), Alexander Henry Scrymgeour, (2nd *U.K. Baron, Glassary*, 1954), *b.* 1949, *s.* 1983, *m.*	Lord Scrymgeour, *b.* 1982.
1669 s.	*Dundonald* (15th), Iain Alexander Douglas Blair Cochrane, *b.* 1961, *s.* 1986, *m.*	†
1686 s.	*Dunmore* (11th), Kenneth Randolph Murray, *b.* 1913, *s.* 1981, *w.*	Viscount Fincastle, *b.* 1946.
1822 I.	*Dunraven and Mount-Earl* (7th), Thady Windham Thomas Wyndham-Quin, *b.* 1939, *s.* 1965, *m.*	(None).
1837	*Effingham* (6th), Mowbray Henry Gordon Howard (16th *E. Baron, Howard of Effingham*, 1554), *b.* 1905, *s.* 1946, *m.*	Lt.-Cmdr. David P. M. A. H., *b.* 1939.
1507 s. ⎫ 1859* ⎭	*Eglinton* (18th) & (9th) *Winton* (1600), Archibald George Montgomerie (6th *U.K. Earl Winton*, 1859), *s.* 1939, *s.* 1966, *m.*	Lord Montgomerie, *b.* 1966.
1733 I.*	*Egmont* (11th), Frederick George Moore Perceval (9th *Brit. Baron, Lovel & Holland*, 1762), *b.* 1914, *s.* 1932, *m.*	Viscount Perceval, *b.* 1934.
1821	*Eldon* (5th), John Joseph Nicholas Scott, *b.* 1937, *s.* 1976, *m.*	Viscount Encombe, *b.* 1962.
1633 s.*	*Elgin* (11th), & *Kincardine* (15th) (1647), Andrew Douglas Alexander Thomas Bruce, (4th *U.K. Baron, Elgin*, 1849), K.T., *b.* 1924, *s.* 1968, *m.*	Lord Bruce, *b.* 1961.
1789 I.*	*Enniskillen* (6th), David Lowry Cole, M.B.E., (4th *U.K. Baron, Grinstead*, 1815) *b.* 1918, *s.* 1963, *m.*	Viscount Cole, *b.* 1942.
1789 I.*	*Erne* (6th), Henry George Victor John Crichton (3rd *U.K. Baron, Fermanagh*, 1876), *b.* 1937, *s.* 1940, *m.*	Viscount Crichton, *b.* 1971.
1452 s.	*Erroll* (24th), Merlin Sereld Victor Gilbert Hay (*Hereditary Lord High Constable and Knight Marischal of Scotland*), *b.* 1948, *s.* 1978, *m.*	Lord Hay, *b.* 1984.
1661	*Essex* (10th), Robert Edward de Vere Capell, *b.* 1920, *s.* 1981, *m.*	Viscount Malden, *b.* 1944.
1711	°*Ferrers* (13th), Robert Washington Shirley, P.C., *b.* 1929, *s.* 1954, *m.*	Viscount Tamworth, *b.* 1952.
1789	°*Fortescue* (7th), Richard Archibald Fortescue, *b.* 1922, *s.* 1977, *m.*	Viscount Ebrington, *b.* 1951.
1841	*Gainsborough* (5th), Anthony Gerard Edward Noel, *b.* 1923, *s.* 1927, *m.*	Viscount Campden, *b.* 1950.
1623 s.*	*Galloway* (13th), Randolph Keith Reginald Stewart (6th *Brit. Baron, Stewart of Garlies*, 1796), *b.* 1928, *s.* 1978, *m.*	Andrew C. S., *b.* 1949.
1703 s.*	*Glasgow* (10th), Patrick Robin Archibald Boyle (4th *U.K. Baron, Fairlie*, 1897), *b.* 1939, *s.* 1984, *m.*	Viscount of Kelburn, *b.* 1978.
1806 I.*	*Gosford* (7th), Charles David Nicholas Alexander John Sparrow Acheson (5th *U.K. Baron, Worlingham*, 1835), *b.* 1942, *s.* 1966, *m.*	Hon. Patrick B. V. M. *A.*, *b.* 1915.
1945	*Gowrie* (2nd), Alexander Patric Greysteil Hore-Ruthven, P.C. (3rd *U.K. Baron, Ruthven of Gowrie*, 1919), *b.* 1939, *s.* 1955, *m.*	Viscount Ruthven of Canberra, *b.* 1964.
1684 I.*	*Granard* (9th), Arthur Patrick Hastings Forbes, A.F.C. (4th *U.K. Baron, Granard*, 1806), *b.* 1915, *s.* 1948, *m.*	Peter A. E. H. *F.*, *b.* 1957.
1833	°*Granville* (5th), Granville James Leveson-Gower, M.C., *b.* 1918, *s.* 1953, *m.*	Lord Leveson, *b.* 1959.
1806	°*Grey* (6th), Richard Fleming George Charles Grey, *b.* 1939, *s.* 1963, *m.*	Philip K. *G.*, *b.* 1940.
1752	*Guilford* (9th), Edward Francis North, *b.* 1933, *s.* 1949, *m.*	Lord North, *b.* 1971.
1619 s.	*Haddington* (13th), John George Baillie-Hamilton, *b.* 1941, *s.* 1986, *m.*	Lord Binning, *b.* 1985.
1919	°*Haig* (2nd), George Alexander Eugene Douglas Haig, O.B.E., *b.* 1918, *s.* 1928, *m.*	Viscount Dawick, *b.* 1961.
1944	*Halifax* (3rd), Charles Edward Peter Neil Wood (5th *U.K. Viscount, Halifax*, 1866), *b.* 1944, *s.* 1980, *m.*	Lord Irwin, *b.* 1977.
1898	*Halsbury* (3rd), John Anthony Hardinge Giffard, F.R.S., *b.* 1908, *s.* 1943, *w.*	Adam E. *G.*, *b.* 1934.
1754	*Hardwicke* (10th), Joseph Philip Sebastian Yorke, *b.* 1971, *s.* 1974, *M.*	Richard C. J. *Y.*, *b.* 1916.
1812	*Harewood* (7th), George Henry Hubert Lascelles, K.B.E., *b.* 1923, *s.* 1947, *m.* (*See also* p. 216).	Viscount Lascelles, *b.* 1950.

Created.	Title, Order of Succession, Name, etc.	Eldest Son or Heir.
1742	*Harrington* (11th), William Henry Leicester Stanhope (8th *Brit. Viscount, Stanhope of Mahon*, 1717), *b.* 1922, *s.* 1929, *m.*	Viscount Petersham, *b.* 1945.
1809	*Harrowby* (7th), Dudley Danvers Granville Coutts Ryder, T.D., *b.* 1922, *s.* 1987, *m.*	Viscount Sandon, *b.* 1951.
1821	°*Howe* (7th), Frederick Richard Penn Curzon, *b.* 1951, *s.* 1984, *m.*	Charles M. P. C., *b.* 1967.
1529	*Huntingdon* (15th), Francis John Clarence Westenra Plantagenet Hastings, *b.* 1901, *s.* 1939, *m.*	Lt. Col. R. H. W. S. *H.*, D.S.O., O.B.E., M.C., *b.* 1917.
1885	*Iddesleigh* (4th), Stafford Henry Northcote, *b.* 1932, *s.* 1970, *m.*	Viscount St. Cyres, *b.* 1957.
1756	*Ilchester* (9th), Maurice Vivian de Touffreville Fox-Strangways, *b.* 1920, *s.* 1970, *m.*	Hon. Raymond G. *F.-S.*, *b.* 1921.
1929	*Inchcape* (3rd), Kenneth James William Mackay, *b.* 1917, *s.* 1939, *m.*	Viscount Glenapp, *b.* 1943.
1919	*Iveagh* (3rd), Arthur Francis Benjamin Guinness, *b.* 1937, *s.* 1967.	Viscount Elveden, *b.* 1969.
1925	°*Jellicoe* (2nd), George Patrick John Rushworth Jellicoe, K.B.E., P.C., D.S.O., M.C., *b.* 1918, *s.* 1935, *m.*	Viscount Brocas, *b.* 1950.
1697	*Jersey* (9th), George Francis Child-Villiers (12th *Irish Visct., Grandison*, 1620), *b.* 1910, *s.* 1923, *m.*	Viscount Villiers, *b.* 1948.
1822 I.	*Kilmorey* (6th), Richard Francis Needham, M.P., *b.* 1942, *s.* 1977, *m.*	Viscount Newry and Morne, *b.* 1966.
1866	*Kimberley* (4th), John Wodehouse, *b.* 1924, *s.* 1941, *m.*	Lord Wodehouse, *b.* 1951.
1768 I.	*Kingston* (11th), Barclay Robert Edwin King-Tenison, *b.* 1943, *s.* 1948.	Viscount Kingsborough, *b.* 1969.
1633 S.*	*Kinnoull* (15th), Arthur William George Patrick Hay (9th *Brit. Baron, Hay of Pedwardine*, 1711), *b.* 1935, *s.* 1938, *m.*	Viscount Dupplin, *b.* 1962.
1677 S.*	*Kintore* (12th), (James) Ian Keith (2nd *U.K. Visct., Stonehaven*, 1938), *b.* 1908, *s.* to Viscountcy, 1941, to Earldom, 1974, *m.*	Lord Inverurie, *b.* 1939.
1914	°*Kitchener of Khartoum* (3rd), Henry Herbert Kitchener, T.D., *b.* 1919, *s.* 1937.	(None.)
1756 I.	*Lanesborough* (9th), Denis Anthony Brian Butler, T.D., *b.* 1918, *s.* 1950.	Cdr. T. B. J. D. *B.*, *b.* 1913.
1624 S.	*Lauderdale* (17th), Patrick Francis Maitland, *b.* 1911, *s.* 1968, *m.*	Viscount Maitland, *b.* 1937.
1837	*Leicester* (6th), Anthony Louis Lovel Coke, *b.* 1909, *s.* 1976, *m.*	Viscount Coke, *b.* 1936.
1641 S.	*Leven* (14th) & (13th) *Melville* (1690), Alexander Robert Leslie Melville, *b.* 1924, *s.* 1947, *m.*	Lord Balgonie, *b.* 1954.
1831	*Lichfield* (5th), Thomas Patrick John Anson, *b.* 1939, *s.* 1960.	Viscount Anson, *b.* 1978.
1803 I.*	*Limerick* (6th), Patrick Edmund Pery, K.B.E. (6th *U.K. Baron, Foxford*, 1815), *b.* 1930, *s.* 1967, *m.*	Viscount Glentworth, *b.* 1963.
1633 S.	*Lindsay* (15th), David Lindesay-Bethune, *b.* 1926, *s.* 1985, *m.*	Viscount Garnock, *b.* 1955.
1626	*Lindsey* (14th) *and Abingdon* (9th) (1682), Richard Henry Rupert Bertie, *b.* 1931, *s.* 1963, *m.*	Lord Norreys, *b.* 1958.
1776 I.	*Lisburne* (8th), John David Malet Vaughan, *b.* 1918, *s.* 1965, *m.*	Viscount Vaughan, *b.* 1945.
1822 I.*	*Listowel* (5th), William Francis Hare, P.C., G.C.M.G. (3rd *U.K. Baron, Hare*, 1869), *b.* 1906, *s.* 1931, *m.*	Viscount Ennismore, *b.* 1964.
1905	*Liverpool* (5th), Edward Peter Bertram Savile Foljambe, *b.* 1944, *s.* 1969, *m.*	Viscount Hawkesbury, *b.* 1972.
1945	°*Lloyd George of Dwyfor* (3rd), Owen Lloyd George, *b.* 1924, *s.* 1968, *m.*	Viscount Gwynedd, *b.* 1951.
1785 I.*	*Longford* (7th), Francis Aungier Pakenham, K.G., P.C. (6th *U.K. Baron, Silchester*, 1821; 1st *U.K. Baron, Pakenham*, 1945), *b.* 1905, *s.* 1961, *m.*	Thomas F. D. *P.*, *b.* 1933.
1807	*Lonsdale* (7th), James Hugh William Lowther, *b.* 1922, *s.* 1953, *m.*	Viscount Lowther, *b.* 1949.
1838	*Lovelace* (5th), Peter Axel William Locke King (12th *British Baron, King*, 1725), *b.* 1951, *s.* 1964, *m.*	(None.)
1795 I.*	*Lucan* (7th), Richard John Bingham (3rd *U.K. Baron, Bingham*, 1934), *b.* 1934, *s.* 1964, *m.*	Lord Bingham, *b.* 1967.
1880	*Lytton* (5th), John Peter Michael Scawen Lytton (18th *English Baron, Wentworth*, 1529), *b.* 1950, *s.* 1985, *m.*	Hon. T. Roland C. L. *L.* *b.* 1954.
1721	*Macclesfield* (8th), George Roger Alexander Thomas Parker, *b.* 1914, *s.* 1975, *m.*	Viscount Parker, *b.* 1943.
1800	*Malmesbury* (6th), William James Harris, T.D., *b.* 1907, *s.* 1950, *m.*	Viscount FitzHarris, *b.* 1946.
1776 & 1792	*Mansfield and Mansfield* (8th), William David Mungo James Murray (14th *Scott. Visct., Stormont*, 1621), *b.* 1930, *s.* 1971, *m.*	Viscount Stormont, *b.* 1956.
1565 S.	*Mar* (13th) & (15th) *Kellie* (1616), John Francis Hervey Erskine, *b.* 1921, *s.* 1955, *m.*	Lord Erskine, *b.* 1949.
1785 I.	*Mayo* (10th), Terence Patrick Bourke, *b.* 1929, *s.* 1962, *m.*	Lord Naas, *b.* 1953.
1627 I.*	*Meath* (14th), Anthony Windham Normand Brabazon (5th *U.K. Baron, Chaworth*, 1831), *b.* 1910, *s.* 1949, *m.*	Lord Ardee, *b.* 1941.
1766 I.	*Mexborough* (8th), John Christopher George Savile, *b.* 1931, *s.* 1980, *m.*	Viscount Pollington, *b.* 1959.
1813	*Minto* (6th), Gilbert Edward George Lariston Garnet Elliot-Murray-Kynynmound, O.B.E., *b.* 1928, *s.* 1975, *w.*	Viscount Melgund, *b.* 1953.
1562 S.*	*Moray* (20th) Douglas John Moray Stuart (12th *Brit. Baron, Stuart of Castle Stuart*, 1796), *b.* 1928, *s.* 1974, *m.*	Lord Doune, *b.* 1966.
1815	*Morley* (6th), John St. Aubyn Parker, *b.* 1923, *s.* 1962, *m.*	Visct. Boringdon, *b.* 1956.
1458 S.	*Morton* (22nd), John Charles Sholto Douglas, *b.* 1927, *s.* 1976, *m.*	Lord Aberdour, *b.* 1952.
1789	*Mount Edgcumbe* (8th), Robert Charles Edgcumbe, *b.* 1939, *s.* 1982, *m.*	Piers V. *E.*, *b.* 1946.

Created.	Title, Order of Succession, Name, etc.	Eldest Son or Heir.
1831	*Munster* (7th), Anthony Charles FitzClarence, *b.* 1926, *s.* 1983, *m.*	(None).
1805	°*Nelson* (9th), Peter John Horatio Nelson, *b.* 1941, *s.* 1981, *m.*	Viscount Merton, *b.* 1971.
1660 s.	*Newburgh* (12th), Prince Filippo Giambattista Camillo Francesco Aldo Maria Rospigliosi, *b.* 1942, *s.* 1986, *m.*	Princess Benedetta F. M. *R.*, *b.* 1974.
1827 I.	*Norbury* (6th), Noel Terence Graham-Toler, *b.* 1939, *s.* 1955, *m.*	Viscount Glandine, *b.* 1967.
1806 I.*	*Normanton* (6th), Shaun James Christian Welbore Ellis Agar (9th *Brit. Baron, Mendip,* 1791) (4th *U.K. Baron, Somerton,* 1873), *b.* 1945, *s.* 1967, *m.*	Viscount Somerton, *b.* 1982.
1647 s.	*Northesk* (13th), Robert Andrew Carnegie, *b.* 1926, *s.* 1975, *m.*	Lord Rosehill, *b.* 1954.
1801	*Onslow* (7th), Michael William Coplestone Dillon Onslow, *b.* 1938, *s.* 1971, *m.*	Viscount Cranley, *b.* 1967.
1696 s.	*Orkney* (8th), Cecil O'Bryen Fitz-Maurice, *b.* 1919, *s.* 1951, *m.*	Oliver P. St. J. *F-M.,* *b.* 1938
1925	*Oxford & Asquith* (2nd), Julian Edward George Asquith, K.C.M.G., *b.* 1916, *s.* 1928, *m.*	Viscount Asquith, *b.* 1952.
1929	°*Peel* (3rd), William James Robert Peel (4th *U.K. Viscount Peel,* 1895), *b.* 1947, *s.* 1969, *m.*	Viscount Clanfield, *b.* 1976.
1551	*Pembroke* (17th) & (14th) *Montgomery* (1605), Henry George Charles Alexander Herbert, *b.* 1939, *s.* 1969.	Lord Herbert, *b.* 1978.
1605 s.	*Perth* (17th), John David Drummond, P.C., *b.* 1907, *s.* 1951, *m.*	Viscount Strathallan, *b.* 1935.
1905	*Plymouth* (3rd), Other Robert Ivor Windsor-Clive (15th *English Baron, Windsor,* 1529), *b.* 1923, *s.* 1943, *m.*	Viscount Windsor, *b.* 1951.
1785 I.	*Portarlington* (7th), George Lionel Yuill Seymour Dawson-Damer, *b.* 1938, *s.* 1959, *m.*	Viscount Carlow, *b.* 1965.
1743	*Portsmouth* (10th), Quentin Gerard Carew Wallop, *b.* 1954, *s.* 1984, *m.*	Viscount Lymington, *b.* 1981.
1804	*Powis* (6th), Christian Victor Charles Herbert (7th *Irish Baron, Clive,* 1762), *b.* 1904, *s.* 1974.	George W. *H.,* *b.* 1925.
1765	*Radnor* (8th), Jacob Pleydell-Bouverie, *b.* 1927, *s.* 1968, *m.*	Viscount Folkestone, *b.* 1955.
1831 I.*	*Ranfurly* (6th), Thomas Daniel Knox, K.C.M.G. (7th *U.K. Baron, Ranfurly,* 1826), *b.* 1913, *s.* 1933, *m.*	Gerald F. N. *K.,* *b.* 1929.
1771 I.	*Roden* (9th), Robert William Jocelyn, *b.* 1909, *s.* 1956, *m.*	Viscount Jocelyn, *b.* 1938.
1801	*Romney* (7th), Michael Henry Marsham, *b.* 1910, *s.* 1975, *m.*	Julian C. *M.,* *b.* 1948.
1703 s.*	*Rosebery* (7th), Neil Archibald Primrose (3rd *U.K. Earl, Midlothian,* 1911), *b.* 1929, *s.* 1974, *m.*	Lord Dalmeny, *b.* 1967.
1806 I.	*Rosse* (7th), William Brendan Parsons, *b.* 1936, *s.* 1979, *m.*	Lord Oxmantown, *b.* 1969.
1801	*Rosslyn* (7th), Peter St. Clair-Erskine, *b.* 1958, *s.* 1977, *m.*	Jonathan H. *St. C.-E.,* *b.* 1949.
1457 s.	*Rothes* (21st), Ian Lionel Malcolm Leslie, *b.* 1932, *s.* 1975, *m.*	Lord Leslie, *b.* 1958.
1861	°*Russell* (4th), John Conrad Russell, *b.* 1921, *s.* 1970.	Hon. Conrad S. R. *R.,* *b.* 1937.
1915	°*St. Aldwyn* (2nd), Michael John Hicks Beach, P.C., G.B.E., T.D., *b.* 1912, *s.* 1916, *m.*	Viscount Quenington, *b.* 1950.
1815	*St. Germans* (9th), Nicholas Richard Michael Eliot, *b.* 1914, *s.* 1960, *m.*	Lord Eliot, *b.* 1941.
1690	*Scarbrough* (12th), Richard Aldred Lumley (13th *Irish Visct., Lumley,* 1628), *b.* 1932, *s.* 1969, *m.*	Viscount Lumley, *b.* 1973.
1701 s.	*Seafield* (13th), Ian Derek Francis Ogilvie-Grant, *b.* 1939, *s.* 1969, *m.*	Visct. Reidhaven, *b.* 1963.
1882	*Selborne* (4th), John Roundell Palmer, K.B.E., *b.* 1940, *s.* 1971, *m.*	Viscount Wolmer, *b.* 1971.
1646 s.	*Selkirk* (10th), (George) Nigel Douglas-Hamilton, P.C., K.T., G.C.M.G., G.B.E., A.F.C., Q.C., *b.* 1906, *s.* 1940, *m.*	The Master of Selkirk, *b.* 1939.
1672	*Shaftesbury* (10th), Anthony Ashley-Cooper, *b.* 1938, *s.* 1961, *m.*	Lord Ashley, *b.* 1977.
1756 I.*	*Shannon* (9th), Richard Bentinck Boyle (8th *Brit. Bn., Carleton* 1786), *b.* 1924, *s.* 1963.	Viscount Boyle, *b.* 1960.
1442	*Shrewsbury* (22nd) & *Waterford* (I. 1446), Charles Henry John Benedict Crofton Chetwynd Chetwynd-Talbot (*Premier Earl of England and Ireland; Earl Talbot,* 1784), *b.* 1952, *s.* 1980, *m.*	Viscount Ingestre, *b.* 1978.
1961	*Snowdon* (1st), Antony Charles Robert Armstrong-Jones, G.C.V.O., *b.* 1930, *m.* (See also p. 219).	Viscount Linley, *b.* 1961 (*see also* p. 219).
1880	°*Sondes* (5th), Henry George Herbert Milles-Lade, *b.* 1940, *s.* 1970.	(None.)
1633 s.*	*Southesk* (11th), Charles Alexander Carnegie, K.C.V.O. (3rd *U.K. Baron, Balinhard,* 1869), *b.* 1893, *s.* 1941, *m.*	The Duke of Fife, *b.* 1929 (*see* pp. 216 and 227).
1765	°*Spencer* (8th), Edward John Spencer, L.V.O., *b.* 1924, *s.* 1975, *m.*	Viscount Althorp, *b.* 1964.
1703 s.*	*Stair* (13th), John Aymer Dalrymple, K.C.V.O., M.B.E (6th *U.K. Baron, Oxenfoord,* 1841), *b.* 1906, *s.* 1961, *m.*	Viscount Dalrymple, *b.* 1961.
1984	*Stockton* (2nd), Alexander Daniel Alan Macmillan, *b.* 1943, *s.* 1986, *m.*	Viscount Macmillan of Ovenden, *b.* 1974.
1821	*Stradbroke* (6th), Robert Keith Rous, *b.* 1937, *s.* 1983, *m.*	Viscount Dunwich, *b.* 1961.
1847	*Strafford* (8th), Thomas Edmund Byng, *b.* 1936, *s.* 1984, *m.*	Viscount Enfield, *b.* 1964.
1606 s.*	*Strathmore and Kinghorne* (18th), Michael Fergus Bowes-Lyon (16th *Scottish Earl, Strathmore,* 1677, & 18th *Kinghorne,* 1606; 5th *U.K. Earl, Strathmore & Kinghorne,* 1937), *b.* 1957, *s.* 1987, *m.*	Lord Glamis, *b.* 1986.
1603	*Suffolk* (21st) & (14th) *Berkshire* (1626), Michael John James George Robert Howard, *b.* 1935, *s.* 1941, *m.*	Viscount Andover, *b.* 1974.
1955	*Swinton* (2nd), David Yarburgh Cunliffe-Lister, *b.* 1937, *s.* 1972, *m.*	Hon. Nicholas J. *C.-L.,* *b.* 1939.

Created.	Title, Order of Succession, Name, etc.	Eldest Son or Heir.
1714	*Tankerville* (10th), Peter Grey Bennet, *b.* 1956, *s.* 1980.	Rev. the Hon. George A. G. B., *b.* 1925.
1822	°*Temple of Stowe* (7th), Ronald Stephen Brydges Temple-Gore-Langton, *b.* 1910, *s.* 1966.	W. Grenville A. *T.-G.-L.*, *b.* 1924.
1815	*Verulam* (7th), John Duncan Grimston (11th *Irish Visct.*, *Grimston*, 1719; 16th *Scott. Baron, Forrester of Corstorphine*, 1633), *b.* 1951, *s.* 1973, *m.*	Viscount Grimston, *b.* 1978.
1729	°*Waldegrave* (12th), Geoffrey Noel Waldegrave, K.G., G.C.V.O., T.D., *b.* 1905, *s.* 1936, *m.*	Viscount Chewton, *b.* 1940.
1759	*Warwick &* °*Brooke* (1746), David Robin Francis Guy Greville (8th *Earl Brooke* and 8th *Earl of Warwick*), *b.* 1934, *s.* 1984.	Lord Brooke, *b.* 1957.
1633 s.*	*Wemyss* (12th) *&* (8th) *March* (1697), Francis David Charteris, K.T. (5th *U.K. Baron, Wemyss*, 1821), *b.* 1912, *s.* 1937, *m.*	Lord Neidpath, *b.* 1948.
1621 i.	*Westmeath* (13th), William Anthony Nugent, *b.* 1928, *s.* 1971, *m.*	Hon. Sean C. W. *N.*, *b.* 1965.
1624	*Westmorland* (15th), David Anthony Thomas Fane, K.C.V.O., *b.* 1924, *s.* 1948, *m.* (*Master of the Horse*).	Lord Burghersh, *b.* 1951.
1876	*Wharncliffe* (5th), Alan Ralph Montagu-Scott-Wortley, *b.* 1927, *s.* 1987, *m.*	Viscount Carlton, *b.* 1953.
1801	*Wilton* (7th), Seymour William Arthur John Egerton, *b.* 1921, *s.* 1927, *m.*	Baron Ebury, *b.* 1934 (*see* p. 240).
1628	*Winchilsea* (16th) *&* (11th) *Nottingham* (1681), Christopher Denys Stormont Finch-Hatton, *b.* 1936, *s.* 1950, *m.*	Viscount Maidstone, *b.* 1967.
1766 i.	°*Winterton* (7th), Robert Chad Turnour, *b.* 1915, *s.* 1962, *m.*	N. Cecil *T.*, D.F.M., C.D., *b.* 1919.
1956	*Woolton* (3rd), Simon Frederick Marquis, *b.* 1958, *s.* 1969, *m.*	(None.)
1837	*Yarborough* (7th), John Edward Pelham, *b.* 1920, *s.* 1966, *m.*	Lord Worsley, *b.* 1963.
1922	*Ypres* (3rd), John Richard Charles Lambart French, *b.* 1921, *s.* 1948, *m.*	(None.)

VISCOUNTS

Style (*see also* note, p. 247), The Right Hon. The Viscount ——. *Addressed as*, My Lord.
The eldest sons of Viscounts and Barons have no distinctive title; they, as well as
their brothers and sisters, are styled the Hon. Robert, Hon. Mary, &c.

Created.	Title, Order of Succession, Name, etc.	Eldest Son or Heir.
1945	*Addison* (3rd), Michael Addison, *b.* 1914, *s.* 1976, *m.*	Hon. William M. W. *A.*, *b.* 1945.
1946	*Alanbrooke* (3rd), Alan Victor Harold Brooke, *b.* 1932, *s.* 1972.	(None.)
1919	*Allenby* (3rd), Lt.-Col. Michael Jaffray Hynman Allenby, *b.* 1931, *s.* 1984, *m.*	Hon. Henry J. H. *A.*, *b.* 1968.
1911	*Allendale* (3rd), Wentworth Hubert Charles Beaumont, *b.* 1922, *s.* 1956, *m.*	Hon. Wentworth P. I. *B.*, *b.* 1948.
1642 s.	*Arbuthnott* (16th), John Campbell Arbuthnott, C.B.E., D.S.C., *b.* 1924, *s.* 1966, *m.*	Master of Arbuthnott, *b.* 1950.
1751 i.	*Ashbrook* (10th), Desmond Llowarch Edward Flower, K.C.V.O., M.B.E., *b.* 1905, *s.* 1936, *m.*	Hon. Michael L. W. *F.*, *b.* 1935.
1917	*Astor* (4th), William Waldorf Astor, *b.* 1951, *s.* 1966, *m.*	Hon. William W. *A.*, *b.* 1979.
1781 i.	*Bangor* (7th), Edward Henry Harold Ward, *b.* 1905, *s.* 1950, *m.*	Hon. William M. D. *W.*, *b.* 1948.
1720 i.*	*Barrington* (11th), Patrick William Daines Barrington (5th *U.K. Baron Shute*, 1880), *b.* 1908, *s.* 1960.	(None.)
1925	*Bearsted* (4th), Peter Montefiore Samuel, M.C., T.D., *b.* 1911, *s.* 1986, *m.*	Hon. Nicholas A. *S.*, *b.* 1950.
1963	*Blakenham* (2nd), Michael John Hare, *b.* 1938, *s.* 1982, *m.*	Hon. Caspar J. *H.*, *b.* 1972.
1935	*Bledisloe* (3rd), Christopher Hiley Ludlow Bathurst, Q.C., *b.* 1934, *s.* 1979.	Hon. Rupert E. L. *B.*, *b.* 1964.
1712	*Bolingbroke & St. John* (7th), Kenneth Oliver Musgrave St. John, *b.* 1927, *s.* 1974, *m.*	Hon. Henry F. *St. J.*, *b.* 1957.
1960	*Boyd of Merton* (2nd), Simon Donald Rupert Neville Lennox-Boyd, *b.* 1939, *s.* 1983, *m.*	Hon. Benjamin A. *L.-B.*, *b.* 1964.
1717 i.*	*Boyne* (10th), Gustavus Michael George Hamilton-Russell (4th *U.K. Baron, Brancepeth*, 1866), *b.* 1931, *s.* 1942, *m.*	Hon. Gustavus M. S. *H.-R.*, *b.* 1965.
1929	*Brentford* (4th), Crispin William Joynson-Hicks, *b.* 1933, *s.* 1983, *m.*	Hon. Paul W. *J.-H.*, *b.* 1971.
1929	*Bridgeman* (3rd), Robin John Orlando Bridgeman, *b.* 1930, *s.* 1982, *m.*	Hon. William O. C. *B.*, *b.* 1968.
1868	*Bridport* (4th), Alexander Nelson Hood (7th *Duke of Brontë in Sicily*, 1799, *and* 6th *Irish Baron, Bridport* 1794), *b.* 1948, *s.* 1969, *m.*	Hon. Peregrine A. N. *H.*, *b.* 1974.
1952	*Brookeborough* (3rd), Alan Henry Brooke, *b.* 1952, *s.* 1987, *m.*	Hon. Christopher A. *B.*, *b.* 1954.
1933	*Buckmaster* (3rd), Martin Stanley Buckmaster, O.B.E., *b.* 1921, *s.* 1974.	Hon. Colin J. *B.*, *b.* 1923.
1939	*Caldecote* (2nd), Robert Andrew Inskip, K.B.E., D.S.C., *b.* 1917, *s.* 1947, *m.*	Hon. Piers J. H. *I.*, *b.* 1947.

Created.	Title, Order of Succession, Name, etc.	Eldest Son or Heir.
1941	*Camrose* (2nd), (John) Seymour Berry, T.D., *b.* 1909, *s.* 1954, *m.*	Baron Hartwell, M.B.E., T.D., *b.* 1911 (*see* p. 249).
1952	*Chandos* (3rd), Thomas Orlando Lyttelton, *b.* 1953, *s.* 1980, *m.*	Hon. Matthew P. A. *L.*, *b.* 1956.
1665 I.	*Charlemont* (14th), John Day Caulfeild (18th *Irish Baron*, *Caulfeild of Charlemont*, 1620), *b.* 1934, *s.* 1985, *m.*	Hon. John D. *C.*, *b.* 1966.
1921	*Chelmsford* (3rd), Frederic Jan Thesiger, *b.* 1931, *s.* 1970, *m.*	Hon. Frederic C. P. *T.*, *b.* 1962.
1717 I.	*Chetwynd* (10th), Adam Richard John Casson Chetwynd, *b.* 1935, *s.* 1965, *m.*	Hon. Adam D. *C.*, *b.* 1969.
1911	*Chilston* (4th), Alastair George Akers-Douglas, *b.* 1946, *s.* 1982, *m.*	Hon. Oliver I. *A.-D.*, *b.* 1973.
1902	*Churchill* (3rd), Victor George Spencer (5th *U.K. Baron Churchill*, 1815), *b.* 1934, *s.* 1973.	None to Viscountcy; to Barony, R. Harry R. *S.*, *b.* 1926.
1718	*Cobham* (11th), John William Leonard Lyttelton (8th *Irish Baron*, *Westcote*, 1776), *b.* 1943, *s.* 1977, *m.*	Hon. Christopher C. *L.*, *b.* 1947.
1902	*Colville of Culross* (4th), John Mark Alexander Colville, Q.C. (13th *Scott. Baron*, *Colville of Culross*, 1604), *b.* 1933, *s.* 1945, *m.*	Master of Colville, *b.* 1959.
1826	*Combermere* (5th), Michael Wellington Stapleton-Cotton, *b.* 1929, *s.* 1969, *m.*	Hon. Thomas R. W. *S.-C.*, *b.* 1969.
1917	*Cowdray* (3rd), Weetman John Churchill Pearson, T.D. (3rd *U.K. Baron, Cowdray*, 1910), *b.* 1910, *s.* 1933, *m.*	Hon. Michael O. W. *P.*, *b.* 1944.
1927	*Craigavon* (3rd), Janric Fraser Craig, *b.* 1944, *s.* 1974.	(None).
1886	*Cross* (3rd), Assheton Henry Cross, *b.* 1920, *s.* 1932, *m.*	(None).
1943	*Daventry* (3rd), Francis Humphrey Maurice FitzRoy Newdegate, *b.* 1921, *s.* 1986, *m.*	Hon. James E. *F-N.*, *b.* 1960.
1937	*Davidson* (2nd), John Andrew Davidson, *b.* 1928, *s.* 1970, *m.*	Hon. Malcolm W. M. *D.*, *b.* 1934.
1956	*De L'Isle* (1st), William Philip Sidney, V.C., K.G., P.C., G.C.M.G., G.C.V.O., (6th *Baron De L'Isle and Dudley*, 1835), *b.* 1909, *m.*	Maj. Hon. Philip J. A. *S.*, M.B.E., *b.* 1945.
1776 I.	*De Vesci* (7th), Thomas Eustace Vesey (8th *Irish Baron, Knapton*, 1750), *b.* 1955, *s.* 1983.	Nicholas I. *V.*, *b.* 1954.
1917	*Devonport* (3rd), Terence Kearley, *b.* 1944, *s.* 1973.	Chester D. H. *K.*, *b.* 1932.
1964	*Dilhorne* (2nd), John Mervyn Manningham-Buller, *b.* 1932, *s.* 1980, *m.*	Hon. James E. *M.-B.*, *b.* 1956.
1622 I.	*Dillon* (22nd), Henry Benedict Charles Dillon, *b.* 1973, *s.* 1982, *M.*	Hon. Richard A. L. *D.*, *b.* 1948.
1785 I.	*Doneraile* (10th), Richard Allen St. Leger, *b.* 1946, *s.* 1983, *m.*	Hon. Nathaniel W. R. St. J. *St. L.*, *b.* 1971.
1680 I.*	*Downe* (11th), John Christian George Dawnay (4th *U.K. Baron, Dawnay*, 1897), *b.* 1935, *s.* 1965, *m.*	Hon. Richard H. *D.*, *b.* 1967.
1959	*Dunrossil* (2nd), John William Morrison, C.M.G., *b.* 1926, *s.* 1961, *m.*	Hon. Andrew W. R. *M.*, *b.* 1953.
1964	*Eccles* (1st), David McAdam Eccles, K.C.V.O., C.H., P.C., *b.* 1904, *m.*	Hon. John D. *E.*, C.B.E., *b.* 1931.
1897	*Esher* (4th), Lionel Gordon Baliol Brett, C.B.E., *b.* 1913. *s.* 1963, *m.*	Hon. Christopher L. B. *B.*, *b.* 1936.
1816	*Exmouth* (10th), Paul Edward Pellew, *b.* 1940, *s.* 1970, *m.*	Hon. Edward F. *P.*, *b.* 1978.
1620 s.	*Falkland* (15th), Lucius Edward William Plantagenet Cary (*Premier Scottish Viscount on the Roll*), *b.* 1935, *s.* 1984, *m.*	Master of Falkland, *b.* 1963.
1720	*Falmouth* (9th), George Hugh Boscawen (26th *Eng. Baron, Le Despencer*, 1264), *b.* 1919, *s.* 1962, *m.*	Hon. Evelyn A. H. *B.*, *b.* 1955.
1918	*Furness* (2nd), William Anthony Furness, *b.* 1929, *s.* 1940.	(None.)
1720 I.*	*Gage* (7th), George John St. Clere Gage, (6th *Brit. Baron, Gage*, 1790), *b.* 1932, *s.* 1982, *m.*	Hon. Henry N *G.*, *b.* 1934.
1727 I.	*Galway* (12th), George Rupert Monckton-Arundell, *b.* 1922, *s.* 1980, *m.*	Hon. John P. *M.-A.*, *b.* 1952.
1478 I.*	*Gormanston* (17th), Jenico Nicholas Dudley Preston (*Premier Viscount of Ireland*; 5th *U.K. Baron, Gormanston*, 1868), *b.* 1939, *s.* 1940, *w.*	Hon. Jenico F. T. *P.*, *b.* 1974.
1816 I.	*Gort* (8th), Colin Leopold Prendergast Vereker, *b.* 1916, *s.* 1975, *m.*	Hon. Foley R.S.P. *V.*, *b.* 1951.
1900	*Goschen* (4th), Giles John Harry Goschen, *b.* 1965, *s.* 1977.	(None.)
1849	*Gough* (5th), Shane Hugh Maryon Gough, *b.* 1941, *s.* 1951.	(None.)
1937	*Greenwood* (2nd), David Henry Hamar Greenwood, *b.* 1914, *s.* 1948.	Hon. Michael G. H. *G.*, *b.* 1923.
1891	*Hambleden* (4th), William Herbert Smith, *b.* 1930, *s.* 1948, *m.*	Hon. William H. B. *S.*, *b.* 1955.
1884	*Hampden* (6th), Anthony David Brand, *b.* 1937, *s.* 1975, *m.*	Hon. Francis A. *B.*, *b.* 1970.
1936	*Hanworth* (2nd), David Bertram Pollock, *b.* 1916, *s.* 1936, *m.*	Hon. David S. G. *P.*, *b.* 1946.
1791 I.	*Harberton* (10th), Thomas de Vautort Pomeroy, *b.* 1910, *s.* 1980, *m.*	Hon. Robert W. *P.*, *b.* 1916.
1846	*Hardinge* (6th), Charles Henry Nicholas Hardinge, *b.* 1956, *s.* 1984.	Hon. Andrew H. *H.*, *b.* 1960.
1791 I.	*Hawarden* (8th), Robert Leslie Eustace Maude, *b.* 1926, *s.* 1958, *m.*	Hon. Robert C. W. L. *M.*, *b.* 1961.
1960	*Head* (2nd), Richard Antony Head, *b.* 1937, *s.* 1983, *m.*	Hon. Henry J. *H.*, *b.* 1980.

Created.	Title, Order of Succession, Name, etc.	Eldest Son or Heir.
1550	*Hereford* (18th), Robert Milo Leicester Devereux (*Premier Viscount of England*), b. 1932, s. 1952.	Hon. Charles R. de B. D., b. 1975.
1842	*Hill* (8th), Antony Rowland Clegg-Hill, b. 1931, s. 1974, m.	Peter D. R. C. C.-H., b. 1945.
1796	*Hood* (7th), Alexander Lambert Hood (7th *Irish Baron, Hood*, 1782), b. 1914, s. 1981, m.	Hon. Henry L. A. H., b. 1958.
1956	*Ingleby* (2nd), Martin Raymond Peake, b. 1926, s. 1966, m.	(None.)
1945	*Kemsley* (2nd), (Geoffrey) Lionel Berry, b. 1909, s. 1968, m.	Richard G. B., b. 1951.
1911	*Knollys* (3rd), David Francis Dudley Knollys, b. 1931, s. 1966, m.	Hon. Patrick N. M. K., b. 1962.
1895	*Knutsford* (6th), Michael Holland-Hibbert, b. 1926, s. 1986, m.	Hon. Henry T. H.-H., b. 1959.
1945	*Lambert* (2nd), George Lambert, T.D., b. 1909, s. 1958, m.	Hon. Michael J. L., b. 1912.
1954	*Leathers* (2nd), Frederick Alan Leathers, b. 1908, s. 1965, m.	Hon. Christopher G. L., b. 1941.
1922	*Leverhulme* (3rd), Philip William Bryce Lever, T.D., b. 1915, s. 1949, w.	(None.)
1781 I.	*Lifford* (9th), (Edward) James Wingfield Hewitt, b. 1949, s. 1987, m.	Hon. James T. W. H., b. 1979.
1921	*Long* (4th), Richard Gerard Long, b. 1929, s. 1967, m.	Hon. James R. L., b. 1960.
1957	*Mackintosh of Halifax* (3rd), (John) Clive Mackintosh, b. 1958, s. 1980, m.	Hon. Thomas H. G. M., b. 1985.
1955	*Malvern* (3rd), Ashley Kevin Godfrey Huggins, b. 1949, s. 1978.	Hon. M. James H., b. 1928.
1945	*Marchwood* (3rd), David George Staveley Penny, b. 1936, s. 1979, m.	Hon. Peter G. W. P., b. 1965.
1942	*Margesson* (2nd), Francis Vere Hampden Margesson, b. 1922, s. 1965, m.	Lt. Hon. Richard F. D. M., b. 1960.
1660 I.*	*Massereene* (13th) & (6th) *Ferrard* (1797), John Clotworthy Talbot Foster Whyte-Melville Skeffington (6th *U.K. Baron, Oriel*, 1821), b. 1914, s. 1956, m.	Hon. John D. C. W.-M. F. S., b. 1940.
1802	*Melville* (9th), Robert David Ross Dundas, b. 1937, s. 1971, m.	Hon. Robert H. K. D., b. 1984.
1916	*Mersey* (4th), Richard Maurice Clive Bigham, b. 1934, s. 1979, m.	Hon. Edward J. H. B., b. 1966.
1717 I.*	*Midleton* (11th), Trevor Lowther Brodrick (8th *Brit. Baron, Brodrick of Peper Harow*, 1796), b. 1903, s. 1979, m.	Alan H. B., b. 1949.
1962	*Mills* (2nd), Roger Clinton Mills, b. 1919, s. 1968, m.	Hon. Christopher P. R. M., b. 1956.
1716 I.	*Molesworth* (11th), Richard Gosset Molesworth, b. 1907, s. 1961, w.	Hon. Robert B. K. M., b. 1959.
1801 I.*	*Monck* (7th), Charles Stanley Monck (4th *U.K. Baron, Monck*, 1866), b. 1953, s. 1982.	Hon. George S. M., b. 1957.
1957	*Monckton of Brenchley* (2nd), Gilbert Walter Riversdale Monckton, C.B., O.B.E., M.C., b. 1915, s. 1965, m.	Hon Christopher W. M., b. 1952.
1935	*Monsell* (2nd), Henry Bolton Graham Eyres Monsell, b. 1905, s. 1969.	(None.)
1946	*Montgomery of Alamein* (2nd), David Bernard Montgomery, C.B.E., b. 1928, s. 1976, m.	Hon. Henry D. M., b. 1954.
1550 I.*	*Mountgarret* (17th), Richard Henry Piers Butler (4th *U.K. Baron, Mountgarret*, 1911), b. 1936, s. 1966, m.	Hon. Piers J. R. B., b. 1961.
1964	*Muirshiel* (1st), John Scott Maclay, P.C., K.T., C.H., C.M.G., b. 1905, w.	(None.)
1952	*Norwich* (2nd), John Julius Cooper, b. 1929, s. 1954.	Hon. Jason C. D. B. C., b. 1959.
1651 S.	*Oxfuird* (13th), George Hubbard Makgill, b. 1934, s. 1986, m.	Ian A. A. M., b. 1969.
1873	*Portman*, (9th), Edward Henry Berkeley Portman, b. 1934, s. 1967, m.	Hon. Christopher E. B. P., b. 1958.
1743 I.*	*Powerscourt* (10th), Mervyn Niall Wingfield (4th *U.K. Baron, Powerscourt*, 1885), b. 1935, s. 1973, m.	Hon. Mervyn A. W., b. 1963.
1900	*Ridley* (4th), Matthew White Ridley, T.D., b. 1925, s. 1964, m.	Hon. Matthew W. R., b. 1958.
1960	*Rochdale* (1st), John Durival Kemp, O.B.E., T.D. (2nd *U.K. Baron, Rochdale*, 1913), b. 1906, m.	Hon. St. John D. K., b. 1938.
1919	*Rothermere* (3rd), Vere Harold Esmond Harmsworth, b. 1925, s. 1978, m.	Hon. Harold J. E. V. H., b. 1967.
1937	*Runciman of Doxford* (2nd), Walter Leslie Runciman, O.B.E., A.F.C. (3rd *U.K. Baron, Runciman*, 1933), b. 1900, s. 1949, m.	Hon. Walter G. R., C.B.E., F.B.A., b. 1934.
1918	*St. Davids* (2nd), Jestyn Reginald Austen Plantagenet Philipps (19th *English Baron, Strange of Knokin* 1299, 7th *English Baron, Hungerford*, 1426 *and De Moleyns*, 1445), b. 1917, s. 1938, m.	Hon. Colwyn J. J. P., b. 1939.
1801	*St. Vincent* (7th), Ronald George James Jervis, b. 1905, s. 1940, m.	Hon. Edward R. J. J., b. 1951.
1937	*Samuel* (3rd), David Herbert Samuel, PH.D., b. 1922, s. 1978, m.	Hon. Dan J. S., b. 1925.
1911	*Scarsdale* (3rd), Francis John Nathaniel Curzon (7th *Brit. Baron, Scarsdale*, 1761), b. 1924, s. 1977, m.	Hon. Peter G. N. C., b. 1949.
1905	*Selby* (4th), Michael Guy John Gully, b. 1942, s. 1959, m.	Hon. Edward T. W. G., b. 1967.
1805	*Sidmouth* (7th), John Tonge Anthony Pellew Addington, b. 1914, s. 1976, m.	Hon. Jeremy F. A., b. 1947.
1940	*Simon* (2nd), John Gilbert Simon, C.M.G., b. 1902, s. 1954, m.	Hon. Jan D. S., b. 1940.
1960	*Slim* (2nd), John Douglas Slim, O.B.E., b. 1927, s. 1970, m.	Hon. Mark W. R. S., b. 1960.

Created.	Title, Order of Succession, Name, etc.	Eldest Son or Heir.
1954	*Soulbury* (2nd), James Herwald Ramsbotham, *b.* 1915, *s.* 1971, *w.*	Hon. Sir Peter E. *R.*, G.C.M.G., G.C.V.O., *b.* 1919.
1776 I.	*Southwell* (7th), Pyers Anthony Joseph Southwell, *b.* 1930, *s.* 1960, *m.*	Hon. Richard A. P. *S.*, *b.* 1956.
1959	*Stuart of Findhorn* (2nd), David Randolph Moray Stuart, *b.* 1924, *s.* 1971, *m.*	Hon. James D. *S.*, *b.* 1948.
1957	*Tenby* (3rd), William Lloyd George, *b.* 1927, *s.* 1983, *m.*	Hon. Timothy H. G. *L. G.*, *b.* 1962.
1952	*Thurso* (2nd), Robin Macdonald Sinclair, *b.* 1922, *s.* 1970, *m.*	Hon. John A. *S.*, *b.* 1953.
1983	*Tonypandy* (1st), (Thomas) George Thomas, P.C., *b.* 1909.	(None).
1721	*Torrington* (11th), Timothy Howard St. George Byng, *b.* 1943, *s.* 1961, *m.*	John L. *B.*, M.C., *b.* 1919.
1936	*Trenchard* (3rd), Hugh Trenchard, *b.* 1951, *s.* 1987, *m.*	Hon. Alexander T. *T.*, *b.* 1978.
1921	*Ullswater* (2nd), Nicholas James Christopher Lowther, *b.* 1942, *s.* 1949, *m.*	Hon. Benjamin J. *L.*, *b.* 1975.
1621 I.	*Valentia* (15th), Richard John Dighton Annesley, *b.* 1929, *s.* 1983, *m.*	Hon. Francis W. D. *A.*, *b.* 1959.
1960	*Ward of Witley* (1st), George Reginald Ward, P.C., *b.* 1907, *w.*	(None).
1964	*Watkinson* (1st), Harold Arthur Watkinson, P.C., C.H., *b.* 1910, *m.*	(None.)
1952	*Waverley* (2nd), David Alastair Pearson Anderson, *b.* 1911, *s.* 1958, *m.*	Hon. John D. F. *A.*, *b.* 1949.
1938	*Weir* (3rd), William Kenneth James Weir, *b.* 1933, *s.* 1975, *m.*	Hon. James W. H. *W.*, *b.* 1965.
1983	*Whitelaw* (1st), William Stephen Ian Whitelaw, P.C., C.H., M.C., *b.* 1918, *m.*	(None).
1918	*Wimborne* (3rd), Ivor Fox-Strangways Guest (4th *U.K. Baron, Wimborne,* 1880), *b.* 1939, *s.* 1967, *m.*	Hon. Ivor M.V.*G.*, *b.* 1968.
1923	*Younger of Leckie* (3rd), Edward George Younger, O.B.E., T.D., *b.* 1906, *s.* 1946, *w.*	Rt. Hon. George K. H. *Y.*, T.D., M.P., *b.* 1931.

BISHOPS

Style, The Right Rev. The Lord Bishop of ——. *Addressed as,* My Lord.

The Bishops of London, Durham and Winchester always have seats in the House of Lords: the other 21 seats are filled by the remaining diocesan Bishops in order of seniority. The Bishop of Sodor and Man and the Bishop of Gibraltar are not eligible to sit in the House of Lords.

Introd. to House of Lords		Election as Diocesan Bp. confirmed	Trans. to present See
1977	*London* (130th), Graham Douglas Leonard, P.C., *b.* 1921, *cons.* 1964, *m.*	1973	1981
1984	*Durham* (92nd), David Edward Jenkins, *b.* 1925, *cons.* 1984, *m.*	1984	—
1982	*Winchester* (95th), Colin Clement Walter James, *b.* 1926, *cons.* 1973, *m.*	1977	1985
1969	*Rochester* (104th), Richard David Say, D.D., *b.* 1914, *cons.* 1961, *m.*	1961	
1973	*Derby* (4th), Cyril William Johnston Bowles, *b.* 1916, *cons.* 1969, *m.*	1969	
1976	*Carlisle* (64th), Henry David Halsey, *b.* 1919, *cons.* 1968, *m.*	1972	
1976	*Southwark* (7th), Ronald Oliver Bowlby, *b.* 1926, *cons.* 1973, *m.*	1973	1980
1979	*Hereford* (102nd), John Richard Gordon Eastaugh, *b.* 1920, *cons.* 1974, *m.*	1974	
1979	*Chichester* (102nd), Eric Waldram Kemp, D.D., *b.* 1915, *cons.* 1974, *m.*	1974	
1980	*Liverpool* (6th), David Stuart Sheppard, *b.* 1929, *cons.* 1969, *m.*	1975	
1981	*Gloucester* (37th), John Yates, *b.* 1925, *cons.* 1972, *m.*	1975	
1981	*Bath and Wells (74th), John Monier Bickersteth, *b.* 1921, *cons.* 1970, *m.*	1975	
1984	*Ripon* (11th), David Nigel de Lorentz Young, *b.* 1931, *cons.* 1977, *m.*	1977	
1984	*Ely* (66th), Peter Knight Walker, *b.* 1919, *cons.* 1972, *m.*	1977	
1985	*Chelmsford* (7th), John Waine, *b.* 1930, *cons.* 1975, *m.*	1978	1986
1985	*Manchester* (9th), Stanley Eric Francis Booth-Clibborn, *b.* 1924, *cons.* 1979, *m.*	1979	
1985	*Leicester* (4th), Cecil Richard Rutt, C.B.E., *b.* 1925, *cons.* 1966, *m.*	1979	
1985	*Sheffield* (5th), David Ramsay Lunn, *b.* 1930, *cons.* 1980.	1980	
1985	*St. Albans* (8th), John Bernard Taylor, *b.* 1929, *cons.* 1980, *m.*	1980	
1985	*Newcastle* (10th), Andrew Alexander Kenny Graham, *b.* 1929, *cons.* 1977.	1981	
1985	*Truro* (12th), Peter Mumford, *b.* 1922, *cons.* 1974, *m.*	1981	
1986	*Salisbury* (76th), John Austin Baker, *b.* 1928, *cons.* 1982, *m.*	1982	
1986	*Blackburn* (6th), David Stewart Cross, *b.* 1928, *cons.* 1976, *m.*	1982	
1987	*Worcester* (111th), Philip Harold Ernest Goodrich, *b.* 1929, *cons.* 1973, *m.*	1982	

Bishops awaiting seats, in order of seniority

Chester (39th), Michael Alfred Baughen, *b.* 1930, *cons.* 1982, *m.*		1982
Guildford (7th), Michael Edgar Adie, *b.* 1929, *cons.* 1983, *m.*		1983
Bradford (7th), Robert Kerr Williamson, *b.* 1932, *cons.* 1984, *m.*		1984
Lichfield (97th), Keith Norman Sutton, *b.* 1934, *cons.* 1978, *m.*		1984

	Election as Diocesan Bp. confirmed	Trans. to present See
Peterborough (36th), William John Westwood, *b.* 1925, *cons.* 1975, *m.*	1984	
Portsmouth (7th), Timothy John Bavin, *b.* 1935, *cons.* 1974.	1985	
Southwell (8th), Michael Humphrey Dickens Whinney, *b.* 1930, *cons.* 1982.	1985	
Exeter (69th), (Geoffrey) Hewlett Thompson, *b.* 1929, *cons.* 1974, *m.*	1985	
Bristol (54th), Barry Rogerson, *b.* 1936, *cons.* 1979, *m.*	1985	
Wakefield (10th), David Michael Hope, D.Phil., *b.* 1940, *cons.* 1985.	1985	
Coventry (7th), Simon Barrington-Ward, *b.* 1930, *cons.* 1985, *m.*	1985	
Norwich (70th), Peter John Nott, *b.* 1933, *cons.* 1977, *m.*	1985	
St. Edmundsbury and Ipswich (8th), John Dennis, *b.* 1931, *cons.* 1979, *m.*	1986	
Lincoln (70th), Robert Maynard Hardy, *b.* 1936, *cons.* 1980, *m.*	1987	
Oxford (41st), Richard Douglas Harries, *b.* 1936, *cons.* 1987, *m.*	1987	
Birmingham (7th), Mark Santer, *b.* 1936, *cons.* 1981, *m.*	1987	

* The Bishop of Bath and Wells retires in Oct. 1987.

BARONS

Style (see *also* note, p. 247), The Right Hon. The Lord ——.
Addressed as, My Lord.

Created.	Title, Order of Succession, Name, etc.	Eldest Son or Heir.
1911	*Aberconway* (3rd), Charles Melville McLaren, *b.* 1913, *s.* 1953, *m.*	Hon. Henry C. *McL.*, *b.* 1948.
1873	*Aberdare* (4th), Morys George Lyndhurst Bruce, P.C., K.B.E., *b.* 1919, *s.* 1957, *m.*	Hon. Alastair J. L. *B.*, *b.* 1947.
1835	*Abinger* (8th), James Richard Scarlett, *b.* 1914, *s.* 1943, *m.*	Hon. James H. *S.*, *b.* 1959.
1869	*Acton* (3rd), John Emerich Henry Lyon-Dalberg-Acton, C.M.G., M.B.E., T.D., *b.* 1907, *s.* 1924, *m.*	Hon. Richard G. *L.-D.-A.*, *b.* 1941.
1887	*Addington* (6th), Dominic Bryce Hubbard, *b.* 1963, *s.* 1982.	Hon. Michael W. L. *H.*, *b.* 1965.
1955	*Adrian* (2nd), Richard Hume Adrian, F.R.S., *b.* 1927, *s.* 1977, *m.*	(None.)
1921	*Ailwyn* (4th), Carol Arthur Fellowes, T.D., *b.* 1896, *s.* 1976, *w.*	(None.)
1907	*Airedale* (4th), Oliver James Vandeleur Kitson, *b.* 1915, *s.* 1958.	(None.)
1896	*Aldenham* (6th), and (4th) *Hunsdon of Hunsdon* (1923), Vicary Tyser Gibbs, *b.* 1948, *s.* 1986, *m.*	Hon. George H. P. *G.*, *b.* 1950.
1962	*Aldington* (1st), Toby Austin Richard William Low, P.C., K.C.M.G., C.B.E., D.S.O., T.D., *b.* 1914, *m.*	Hon Charles H. S. *L.*, *b.* 1948.
1902	*Allerton* (3rd), George William Lawies Jackson, *b.* 1903, *s.* 1925, *m.*	(None).
1929	*Alvingham* (2nd), Maj.-Gen. Robert Guy Eardley Yerburgh, C.B.E., *b.* 1926, *s.* 1955, *m.*	Capt. Hon. Robert R. G. *Y.*, *b.* 1956.
1892	*Amherst of Hackney* (4th), William Hugh Amherst Cecil, *b.* 1940, *s.* 1980, *m.*	Hon. Hugh W. A. *C.*, *b.* 1968.
1881	*Ampthill* (4th), Geoffrey Denis Erskine Russell, C.B.E., *b.* 1921, *s.* 1973, *m.*	Hon. David W. E. *R.*, *b.* 1947.
1947	*Amwell* (2nd), Frederick Norman Montague, *b.* 1912, *s.* 1966, *m.*	Hon. Keith N. *M.*, *b.* 1943.
1863	*Annaly* (5th), Luke Robert White, *b.* 1927, *s.* 1970, *m.*	Hon. Luke R. *W.*, *b.* 1954.
1903	*Armstrong* (3rd), William Henry Cecil John Robin Watson-Armstrong, *b.* 1919, *s.* 1972, *m.*	(None.)
1885	*Ashbourne* (4th), Edward Barry Greynville Gibson, *b.* 1933, *s.* 1983, *m.*	Hon. Edward C. D'O. *G.*, *b.* 1967.
1835	*Ashburton* (6th), Alexander Francis St. Vincent Baring, K.G., K.C.V.O., *b.* 1898, *s.* 1938, *w.*	Hon. Sir John F. H. *B.*, C.V.O., *b.* 1928.
1892	*Ashcombe* (4th), Henry Edward Cubitt, *b.* 1924, *s.* 1962, *m.*	M. Robin *C.*, *b.* 1936.
1911	*Ashton of Hyde* (3rd), Thomas John Ashton, T.D., *b.* 1926, *s.* 1983, *m.*	Hon. Thomas H. *A.*, *b.* 1958.
1800 I.	*Ashtown* (6th), Christopher Oliver Trench, *b.* 1931, *s.* 1979.	Sir Nigel C. C. *T.*, K.C.M.G., *b.* 1916.
1956	*Astor of Hever* (3rd), John Jacob Astor, *b.* 1946, *s.* 1984, *m.*	Hon. Philip D. P. *A.*, *b.* 1959.
1789 I. / 1793*	*Auckland* (9th), Ian George Eden (9th *Brit. Baron, Auckland*), *b.* 1926, *s.* 1957, *m.*	Hon. Robert I. B. *E.*, *b.* 1962.
1313	*Audley* (25th), Richard Michael Thomas Souter, *b.* 1914, *s.* 1973, *m.*	Three co-heiresses.
1900	*Avebury* (4th), Eric Reginald Lubbock, *b.* 1928, *s.* 1971.	Hon. Lyulph A. J. *L.*, *b.* 1954.
1718 I.	*Aylmer* (13th), Michael Anthony Aylmer, *b.* 1923, *s.* 1982, *m.*	Hon. A. Julian *A.*, *b.* 1951.
1929	*Baden-Powell* (3rd), Robert Crause Baden-Powell, *b.* 1936, *s.* 1962, *m.*	Hon. David M. *B.-P.*, *b.* 1940.
1780	*Bagot* (9th), Heneage Charles Bagot, *b.* 1914, *s.* 1979, *m.*	Hon. Charles H. S. *B.*, *b.* 1944.
1953	*Baillieu* (3rd), James William Latham Baillieu, *b.* 1950, *s.* 1973, *m.*	Hon. Robert L. *B.*, *b.* 1979.
1607 S.	*Balfour of Burleigh* (8th), Robert Bruce, *b.* 1927, *s.* 1967, *m.*	Hon. Victoria *B.*, *b.* 1973.
1945	*Balfour of Inchrye* (1st), Harold Harington Balfour, P.C., M.C., *b.* 1897, *m.*	Hon. Ian *B.*, *b.* 1924.
1924	*Banbury of Southam* (3rd), Charles William Banbury, *b.* 1953, *s.* 1981, *m.*	(None.)
1698	*Barnard* (11th), Harry John Neville Vane, T.D., *b.* 1923, *s.* 1964, *m.*	Hon. Henry F. C. *V.*, *b.* 1959.
1887	*Basing* (5th), Neil Lutley Sclater-Booth, *b.* 1939, *s.* 1983, *m.*	Hon. Stuart W. *S.-B.*, *b.* 1969.

Created.	Title, Order of Succession, Name, etc.	Eldest Son or Heir.

1917   *Beaverbrook* (3rd), Maxwell William Humphrey Aitken, *b.* 1951, *s.* 1985, *m.* — Hon. Maxwell F. *A*, *b.* 1977.

1647 s.   *Belhaven & Stenton* (13th), Robert Anthony Carmichael Hamilton, *b.* 1927, *s.* 1961, *m.* — Master of Belhaven, *b.* 1953.

1848 I.   *Bellew* (7th), James Bryan Bellew, *b.* 1920, *s.* 1981, *m.* — Hon. Bryan E. *B.*, *b.* 1943.

1856   *Belper* (4th), (Alexander) Ronald George Strutt, *b.* 1912, *s.* 1956. — Hon. Richard H. *S.*, *b.* 1941.

1938   *Belstead* (2nd), John Julian Ganzoni, P.C., *b.* 1932, *s.* 1958. — (None.)

1922   *Bethell* (4th), Nicholas William Bethell, *b.* 1938, *s.* 1967. — Hon. James N. *B.*, *b.* 1967.

1938   *Bicester* (3rd), Angus Edward Vivian Smith, *b.* 1932, *s.* 1968. — Hugh C. V. *S.*, *b.* 1934.

1903   *Biddulph* (4th), Robert Michael Christian Biddulph, *b.* 1931, *s.* 1972, *m.* — Hon. Anthony N. C. M.*B.*, *b.* 1959.

1938   *Birdwood* (3rd), Mark William Ogilvie Birdwood, *b.* 1938, *s.* 1962, *m.* — (None.)

1958   *Birkett* (2nd), Michael Birkett, *b.* 1929, *s.* 1962, *m.* — Hon. Thomas *B.*, *b.* 1982.

1935   *Blackford* (4th), William Keith Mason, *b.* 1962, *s.* 1977. — (None.)

1907   *Blyth* (4th), Anthony Audley Rupert Blyth, *b.* 1931, *s.* 1977, *m.* — Hon. Riley A. J. *B.*, *b.* 1955.

1797   *Bolton* (7th), Richard William Algar Orde-Powlett, *b.* 1929, *s.* 1963, *m.* — Hon. Harry A. N. *O.-P.*, *b.* 1954.

1452 s.   *Borthwick* (23rd), John Henry Stuart Borthwick, T.D., *b.* 1905, *claim succeeded* 1986. *w.* — Master of Borthwick, *b.* 1940.

1922   *Borwick* (4th), James Hugh Myles Borwick, M.C., *b.* 1917, *s.* 1961, *m.* — Hon. George S. *B.*, *b.* 1922.

1761   *Boston* (10th), Timothy George Frank Boteler Irby, *b.* 1939, *s.* 1978, *m.* — Hon. George W. E. B. *I.*, *b.* 1971.

1942   *Brabazon of Tara* (3rd), Ivon Anthony Moore-Brabazon, *b.* 1946, *m.* — Hon. Benjamin R. *M.-B.*, *b.* 1983.

1880   *Brabourne* (7th), John Ulick Knatchbull, *b.* 1924, *s.* 1943, *m.* — Lord Romsey, *b.* 1947, *see* p. 247.

1925   *Bradbury* (2nd), John Bradbury, *b.* 1914, *s.* 1950, *m.* — Hon. John *B.*, *b.* 1940.

1962   *Brain* (2nd), Christopher Langdon Brain, *b.* 1926, *s.* 1966, *m.* — Hon. Michael C. *B.*, D.M., *b.* 1928.

1938   *Brassey of Apethorpe* (3rd), David Henry Brassey, *b.* 1932, *s.* 1967, *m.* — Hon. Edward *B.*, *b.* 1964.

1788   *Braybrooke* (9th), Henry Seymour Neville, *b.* 1897, *s.* 1943, *w.* — Hon. Robin H. C. *N.*, *b.* 1932.

1957   *Bridges* (2nd), Thomas Edward Bridges, K.C.M.G., *b.* 1927, *s.* 1969, *m.* — Hon. Mark T. *B.*, *b.* 1954.

1945   *Broadbridge* (3rd), Peter Hewett Broadbridge, *b.* 1938, *s.* 1972, *m.* — Martin H. *B.*, *b.* 1929.

1933   *Brocket* (3rd), Charles Ronald George Nall-Cain, *b.* 1952, *s.* 1967, *m.* — Hon. Alexander C. C. *N.-C.*, *b.* 1984.

1860   *Brougham and Vaux* (5th), Michael John Brougham, *b.* 1938, *s.* 1967. — Hon. Charles W. *B.*, *b.* 1971.

1945   *Broughshane* (2nd), Patrick Owen Alexander Davison, *b.* 1903, *s.* 1953, *m.* — Hon. Alexander *D.*, *b.* 1936.

1776   *Brownlow* (7th), Edward John Peregrine Cust, *b.* 1936, *s.* 1978, *m.* — Hon. Peregrine E. Q. *C.*, *b.* 1974.

1942   *Bruntisfield* (1st), Victor Alexander George Anthony Warrender, M.C., *b.* 1899, *m.* — Col. Hon. John R. *W.*, O.B.E., M.C., T.D., *b.* 1921.

1950   *Burden* (2nd), Philip William Burden, *b.* 1916, *s.* 1970, *m.* — Hon. Andrew P. *B.*, *b.* 1959.

1529   *Burgh* (7th), Alexander Peter Willoughby Leith, *b.* 1935, *s.* 1959, *m.* — Hon. Alexander G. D. *L.*, *b.* 1958.

1903   *Burnham* (5th), William Edward Harry Lawson, *b.* 1920, *s.* 1963, *m.* — Hon. Hugh J. F. *L.*, *b.* 1931.

1897   *Burton* (3rd), Michael Evan Victor Baillie, *b.* 1924, *s.* 1962, *m.* — Hon. Evan M. R. *B.*, *b.* 1949.

1643   *Byron* (12th), Richard Geoffrey Gordon Byron, D.S.O., *b.* 1899, *s.* 1983, *w.* — Hon. Robert J. *B.*, *b.* 1950.

1937   *Cadman* (3rd), John Anthony Cadman, *b.* 1938, *s.* 1966, *m.* — Hon. Nicholas A. J. *C.*, *b.* 1977.

1796   *Calthorpe* (10th), Peter Waldo Somerset Gough-Calthorpe, *b.* 1927, *s.* 1945, *m.* — (None.)

1945   *Calverley* (3rd), Charles Rodney Muff, *b.* 1946, *s.* 1971, *m.* — Hon. Jonathan E. *M.*, *b.* 1975.

1383   *Camoys* (7th), (Ralph) Thomas (Campion George Sherman) Stonor, *b.* 1940, *s.* 1976, *m.* — Hon. William *S.*, *b.* 1974.

1715 I.   *Carbery* (11th), Peter Ralfe Harrington Evans-Freke, *b.* 1920, *s.* 1970, *m.* — Hon. Michael P. *E.-F.*, *b.* 1942.

1834 I. ⎱   *Carew* (6th), William Francis Conolly-Carew, C.B.E. (6th *U.K. Baron*, 1838* ⎰   Carew, 1838), *b.* 1905, *s.* 1927, *m.* — Hon. Patrick T. *C.-C.*, *b.* 1938.

1916   *Carnock* (4th), David Henry Arthur Nicolson, *b.* 1920, *s.* 1982. — Nigel *N.*, M.B.E., *b.* 1917.

1796 I. ⎱   *Carrington* (6th), Peter Alexander Rupert Carington, K.G., P.C., C.H., 1797* ⎰   K.C.M.G., M.C. (6th *Brit. Baron*, Carrington, 1797), *b.* 1919, *s.* 1938, *m.* — Hon. Rupert F. J. *C.*, *b.* 1948.

1812 I.   *Castlemaine* (8th), Roland Thomas John Handcock, *b.* 1943, *s.* 1973, *m.* — Terence R. *H.*, *b.* 1902.

1936   *Catto* (2nd), Stephen Gordon Catto, *b.* 1923, *s.* 1959, *m.* — Hon. Innes G. *C.*, *b.* 1950.

1918   *Cawley* (3rd), Frederick Lee Cawley, *b.* 1913, *s.* 1954, *m.* — Hon. John F. *C.*, *b.* 1946.

1937   *Chatfield* (2nd), Ernle David Lewis Chatfield, *b.* 1917, *s.* 1967, *m.* — (None.)

1858   *Chesham* (5th), John Charles Compton Cavendish, P.C., *b.* 1916, *s.* 1952, *m.* — Hon. Nicholas C. *C.*, *b.* 1941.

1945   *Chetwode* (2nd), Philip Chetwode, *b.* 1937, *s.* 1950. — Hon. Roger *C.*, *b.* 1968.

1945   *Chorley* (2nd), Roger Richard Edward Chorley, *b.* 1930, *s.* 1978, *m.* — Hon. Nicholas R. D. *C.*, *b.* 1966.

1858   *Churston* (4th), Richard Francis Roger Yarde-Buller, V.R.D., *b.* 1910, *s.* 1930, *m.* — Hon. John F. *Y.-B.*, *b.* 1934.

1946   *Citrine* (2nd), Norman Arthur Citrine, *b.* 1914, *s.* 1983, *m.* — Hon. Ronald E. *C.*, *b.* 1919.

Created.	*Title, Order of Succession, Name, etc.*	*Eldest Son or Heir.*

1800 I.   *Clanmorris* (7th), John Michael Ward Bingham, *b.* 1908, *s.* 1960, *m.*   Hon. Simon J. W. *B.*, *b.* 1937.

1672   *Clifford of Chudleigh* (13th), (Lewis) Hugh Clifford, O.B.E., *b.* 1916, *s.* 1964, *m.*   Hon. Thomas H. *C.*, *b.* 1948.

1299   *Clinton* (22nd), Gerard Nevile Mark Fane Trefusis, *b.* 1934, *title called out of abeyance* 1965, *m.*   Hon. Charles P. R. F. *T.*, *b.* 1962.

1955   *Clitheroe* (2nd), Ralph John Assheton, *b.* 1929, *s.* 1984, *m.*   Hon. Ralph C. *A.*, *b.* 1962.

1919   *Clwyd* (3rd), (John) Anthony Roberts, *b.* 1935, *s.* 1987, *m.*   Hon. John M. *R.*, *b.* 1971.

1948   *Clydesmuir* (2nd), Ronald John Bilsland Colville, K.T., C.B., M.B.E., T.D., *b.* 1917, *s.* 1954, *m.*   Hon. David R. *C.*, *b.* 1949.

1960   *Cobbold* (1st), Cameron Fromanteel Cobbold, K.G., P.C., G.C.V.O., *b.* 1904, *m.*   Hon. David A. F. *Lytton-Cobbold*, *b.* 1937.

1919   *Cochrane of Cults* (3rd), Thomas Charles Anthony Cochrane, *b.* 1922, *s.* 1968.   Hon. R. H. Vere *C.*, *b.* 1926.

1954   *Coleraine* (2nd), (James) Martin (Bonar) Law, *b.* 1931, *s.* 1980, *m.*   Hon. James P. B. *L.*, *b.* 1975.

1873   *Coleridge* (5th), William Duke Coleridge, *b.* 1937, *s.* 1984, *m.*   Hon. James D. *C.*, *b.* 1967.

1946   *Colgrain* (3rd), David Colin Campbell, *b.* 1920, *s.* 1973, *m.*   Hon. Alastair C. L. *C.*, *b.* 1951.

1917   *Colwyn* (3rd), (Ian) Anthony Hamilton-Smith, *b.* 1942, *s.* 1966, *m.*   Hon. Craig P. *H.-S.*, *b.* 1968.

1956   *Colyton* (1st), Henry Lennox D'Aubigné Hopkinson, P.C., C.M.G., *b.* 1902, *m.*   Hon. Nicholas H. E. *H.*, *b.* 1932.

1841   *Congleton* (8th), Christopher Patrick Parnell, *b.* 1930, *s.* 1967, *m.*   Hon. John P. C. *P.*, *b.* 1959.

1927   *Cornwallis* (3rd), Fiennes Neil Wykeham Cornwallis, O.B.E., *b.* 1921, *s.* 1982, *m.*   Hon. F. W. Jeremy *C.*, *b.* 1946.

1874   *Cottesloe* (4th), John Walgrave Halford Fremantle, G.B.E., T.D., *b.* 1900, *s.* 1956, *m.*   Hon. John T. *F.*, *b.* 1927.

1929   *Craigmyle* (3rd), Thomas Donald Mackay Shaw, *b.* 1923, *s.* 1944, *m.*   Hon. Thomas C. *S.*, *b.* 1960.

1899   *Cranworth* (3rd), Philip Bertram Gurdon, *b.* 1940, *s.* 1964, *m.*   Hon. Sacha W. R. *G.*, *b.* 1970.

1959   *Crathorne* (2nd), Charles James Dugdale, *b.* 1939, *s.* 1977, *m.*   Hon. Thomas A. J. *D.*, *b.* 1977.

1892   *Crawshaw* (4th), William Michael Clifton Brooks, *b.* 1933, *s.* 1946.   Hon. David G. *B.*, *b.* 1934.

1940   *Croft* (2nd), Michael Henry Glendower Page Croft, *b.* 1916, *s.* 1947, *w.*   Hon. Bernard W. H. P. *C.*, *b.* 1949.

1797 I.   *Crofton* (6th), Charles Edward Piers Crofton, *b.* 1949, *s.* 1974, *m.*   Hon. Guy P. G. *C.*, *b.* 1951.

1375   *Cromwell* (7th), Godfrey John Bewicke-Copley, *b.* 1960, *s.* 1982.   Hon. Thomas D. *B.-C.*, *b.* 1964.

1947   *Crook* (1st), Reginald Douglas Crook, *b.* 1901, *w.*   Hon. Douglas E. *C.*, *b.* 1926.

1920   *Cullen of Ashbourne* (2nd), Charles Borlase Marsham Cokayne, M.B.E., *b.* 1912, *s.* 1932, *m.*   Hon. Edmund W. M. *C.*, *b.* 1916.

1914   *Cunliffe* (3rd), Roger Cunliffe, *b.* 1932, *s.* 1963, *m.*   Hon. Henry *C.*, *b.* 1962.

1927   *Daresbury* (2nd), Edward Greenall, *b.* 1902, *s.* 1938, *w.*   Hon. Edward G. *G.*, *b.* 1928.

1924   *Darling* (2nd), Robert Charles Henry Darling, *b.* 1919, *s.* 1936, *m.*   Hon. Robert J. H. *D.*, *b.* 1944.

1946   *Darwen* (2nd), Cedric Percival Davies, *b.* 1915, *s.* 1950, *m.*   Hon. Roger M. *D.*, *b.* 1938.

1923   *Daryngton* (2nd), Jocelyn Arthur Pike Pease, *b.* 1908, *s.* 1949.   (None.)

1932   *Davies* (3rd), David Davies, *b.* 1940, *s.* 1944, *m.*   Hon. David D. *D.*, *b.* 1975.

1812 I.   *Decies* (6th), Arthur George Marcus Douglas de la Poer Beresford, *b.* 1915, *s.* 1944, *m.*   Hon. Marcus H. T. *de la P.B.*, *b.* 1948.

1299   *de Clifford* (27th), John Edward Southwell Russell, *b.* 1928, *s.* 1982, *m.*   Hon. William S. *R.*, *b.* 1930.

1851   *De Freyne* (7th), Francis Arthur John French, *b.* 1927, *s.* 1935, *m.*   Hon. Fulke C. A. J. *F.*, *b.* 1957.

1821   *Delamere* (5th), Hugh George Cholmondeley, *b.* 1934, *s.* 1979, *m.*   Hon. Thomas P. G. *C.*, *b.* 1968.

1838   *de Mauley* (6th), Gerald John Ponsonby, *b.* 1921, *s.* 1962, *m.*   Col. Hon. Thomas M. *P.*, T.D., *b.* 1930.

1937   *Denham* (2nd), Bertram Stanley Mitford Bowyer, P.C., *b.* 1927, *s.* 1948, *m.*   Hon. Richard G. *B.*, *b.* 1959.

1834   *Denman* (5th), Charles Spencer Denman, C.B.E., M.C., T.D., *b.* 1916, *s.* 1971, *m.*   Hon. Richard T. S. *D.*, *b.* 1946.

1885   *Deramore* (6th), Richard Arthur de Yarburgh-Bateson, *b.* 1911, *s.* 1964, *m.*   (None.)

1887   *De Ramsey* (3rd), Ailwyn Edward Fellowes, K.B.E., T.D., *b.* 1910, *s.* 1925, *m.*   Hon. John A. *F.*, *b.* 1942.

1264   *de Ros* (28th), Peter Trevor Maxwell, *b.* 1958, *s.* 1983 (*Premier Baron of England*).   Hon. Diana E. *M.*, *b.* 1957.

1881   *Derwent* (5th), Robin Evelyn Leo Vanden-Bempde-Johnstone, L.V.O., *b.* 1930, *s.* 1986, *m.*   Hon. Francis P. H. *V.-B.-J.*, *b.* 1965.

1831   *De Saumarez* (6th), James Victor Broke Saumarez, *b.* 1924, *s.* 1969, *m.*   Hon. Eric D. *S.*, *b.* 1956.

1910   *de Villiers* (3rd), Arthur Percy de Villiers, *b.* 1911, *s.* 1934.   Hon. Alexander C. *de V.*, *b.* 1940.

1930   *Dickinson* (2nd), Richard Clavering Hyett Dickinson, *b.* 1926, *s.* 1943, *m.*   Hon. Martin H. *D.*, *b.* 1961.

1620 I.   ⎱ *Digby* (12th), Edward Henry Kenelm Digby, (6th *Brit. Baron, Digby*), *b.* 1924, *s.* 1964, *m.*   Hon. Henry N. K. *D.*, *b.* 1954.
1765*   ⎰

1615   *Dormer* (16th), Joseph Spencer Philip Dormer, *b.* 1914, *s.* 1975.   Geoffrey H. *D.*, *b.* 1920.

1943   *Dowding* (2nd), Derek Hugh Tremenheere Dowding, *b.* 1919, *s.* 1970, *m.*   Hon. Piers H. T. *D.*, *b.* 1948.

Created.	*Title, Order of Succession, Name, etc.*	*Eldest Son or Heir.*
1963	*Drumalbyn* (1st), Niall Malcolm Stewart Macpherson, P.C., K.B.E., *b.* 1908, *m.*	(None.)
1929	*Dulverton* (2nd), (Frederick) Anthony Hamilton Wills, C.B.E., T.D., *b.* 1915, *s.* 1956, *m.*	Hon. G. Michael H. *W.*, *b.* 1944.
1800 I.	*Dunalley* (6th), Henry Desmond Graham Prittie, *b.* 1912, *s.* 1948, *m.*	Hon. Henry F. C. *P.*, *b.* 1948.
1324 I.	*Dunboyne* (28th), Patrick Theobald Tower Butler, *b.* 1917, *s.* 1945, *m.*	Hon. John F. *B.*, *b.* 1951.
1802	*Dunleath* (4th), Charles Edward Henry John Mulholland, T.D., *b.* 1933, *s.* 1956, *m.*	Sir Michael H. *M.*, Bt., *b.* 1915.
1439 I.	*Dunsany* (19th), Randal Arthur Henry Plunkett (20th *Irish, Baron, Killeen,* 1449), *b.* 1906, *s.* 1957, *m.*	Hon. Edward J. C. *P.*, *b.* 1939.
1780	*Dynevor* (9th), Richard Charles Uryan Rhys, *b.* 1935, *s.* 1962.	Hon. Hugo G. U. *R.*, *b.* 1966.
1928	*Ebbisham* (2nd), Rowland Roberts Blades, T.D., *b.* 1912, *s.* 1953, *m.*	(None.)
1857	*Ebury* (6th), Francis Egerton Grosvenor, *b.* 1934, *s.* 1957, *m.*	Hon. Julian F. M. *G.*, *b.* 1959.
1643	*Elibank* (14th), Alan d'Ardis Erskine-Murray, *b.* 1923, *s.* 1973, *m.*	Master of Elibank, *b.* 1964.
1802	*Ellenborough* (8th), Richard Edward Cecil Law, *b.* 1926, *s.* 1945, *m.*	Capt. Hon. Rupert E. H. *L.*, *b.* 1955.
1509 s.*	*Elphinstone* (18th), James Alexander Elphinstone (4th *U.K. Baron Elphinstone,* 1885), *b.* 1953, *s.* 1975, *m.*	Master of Elphinstone, *b.* 1980.
1934	*Elton* (2nd), Rodney Elton, T.D., *b.* 1930, *s.* 1973, *m.*	Hon. Edward P. *E.*, *b.* 1966.
1964	*Erroll of Hale* (1st), Frederick James Erroll, P.C., T.D., *b.* 1914, *m.*	(None.)
1964	*Erskine of Rerrick* (2nd), Iain Maxwell Erskine, *b.* 1926, *s.* 1980, *m.*	(None.)
1627 s.	*Fairfax of Cameron* (14th), Nicholas John Albert Fairfax, *b.* 1956, *s.* 1964, *m.*	Hon. Edward N. T. *F.*, *b.* 1984.
1961	*Fairhaven* (3rd), Ailwyn Henry George Broughton, *b.* 1936, *s.* 1973, *m.*	Hon. James H. A. *B.*, *b.* 1963.
1916	*Faringdon* (3rd), Charles Michael Henderson, *b.* 1937, *s.* 1977, *m.*	Hon. James H. *H.*, *b.* 1961.
1756 I.	*Farnham* (12th), Barry Owen Somerset Maxwell, *b.* 1931, *s.* 1957, *m.*	Hon. Simon K. *M.*, *b.* 1933.
1856 I.	*Fermoy* (6th), Patrick Maurice Burke Roche, *b.* 1967, *s.* 1984.	Hon. E. Hugh B. *R.*, *b.* 1972.
1826	*Feversham* (6th), Charles Antony Peter Duncombe, *b.* 1945, *s.* 1963, *m.*	Hon. Jasper O. S. *D.*, *b.* 1968.
1798 I.	*ffrench* (8th), Robuck John Peter Charles Mario ffrench, *b.* 1956, *s.* 1986.	Hon. John C. M. J. F. *ff.*, *b.* 1928.
1909	*Fisher* (3rd), John Vavasseur Fisher, D.S.C., *b.* 1921, *s.* 1955, *m.*	Hon. Patrick V. *F.*, *b.* 1953.
1295	*Fitzwalter* (21st), Fitzwalter Brook Plumptre, *b.* 1914, *called out of abeyance,* 1953, *m.*	Hon. Julian B. *P.*, *b.* 1952.
1776	*Foley* (8th), Adrian Gerald Foley, *b.* 1923, *s.* 1927, *m.*	Hon. Thomas H. *F.*, *b.* 1961.
1445 s.	*Forbes* (22nd), Nigel Ivan Forbes, K.B.E. (*Premier Baron of Scotland*), *b.* 1918, *s.* 1953, *m.*	Master of Forbes, *b.* 1946.
1821	*Forester* (8th), (George Cecil) Brooke Weld-Forester, *b.* 1938, *s.* 1977, *m.*	Hon. Charles R. G. *W.-F.*, *b.* 1975.
1922	*Forres* (4th), Alastair Stephen Grant Williamson, *b.* 1946, *s.* 1978, *m.*	Hon. George A. M. *W.*, *b.* 1972.
1917	*Forteviot* (3rd), Henry Evelyn Alexander Dewar, M.B.E., *b.* 1906, *s.* 1947, *w.*	Hon. John J. E. *D.*, *b.* 1938.
1951	*Freyberg* (2nd), Paul Richard Freyberg, O.B.E., M.C., *b.* 1923, *s.* 1963, *m.*	Hon. Valerian B. *F.*, *b.* 1970.
1917	*Gainford* (3rd), Joseph Edward Pease, *b.* 1921, *s.* 1971, *m.*	Hon. George *P.*, *b.* 1926.
1818 I.	*Garvagh* (5th), (Alexander Leopold Ivor) George Canning, *b.* 1920, *s.* 1956, *m.*	Hon. Spencer G. S. de R. *C.*, *b.* 1953.
1942	*Geddes* (3rd), Euan Michael Ross Geddes, *b.* 1937, *s.* 1975, *m.*	Hon. James G. N. *G.*, *b.* 1969.
1876	*Gerard* (4th), Robert William Frederick Alwyn Gerard, *b.* 1918, *s.* 1953.	Anthony R. H. *G.*, *b.* 1949.
1824	*Gifford* (6th), Anthony Maurice Gifford, Q.C., *b.* 1940, *s.* 1961, *m.*	Hon. Thomas A. *G.*, *b.* 1967.
1917	*Gisborough* (3rd), Thomas Richard John Long Chaloner, *b.* 1927, *s.* 1951, *m.*	Hon. Thomas P. L. *C.*, *b.* 1961.
1960	*Gladwyn* (1st), (Hubert Miles) Gladwyn Jebb, G.C.M.G., G.C.V.O., C.B., *b.* 1900, *m.*	Hon. Miles A. G. *J.*, *b.* 1930.
1899	*Glanusk* (4th), David Russell Bailey, *b.* 1917, *s.* 1948, *m.*	Hon. Christopher R. *B.*, *b.* 1942.
1918	*Glenarthur* (4th), Simon Mark Arthur, *b.* 1944, *s.* 1976, *m.*	Hon. Edward A. *A.*, *b.* 1973.
1911	*Glenconner* (3rd), Colin Christopher Paget Tennant, *b.* 1926, *s.* 1983, *m.*	Hon. Charles E. P. *T.*, *b.* 1957.
1964	*Glendevon* (1st), John Adrian Hope, P.C., *b.* 1912, *m.*	Hon. Julian J. S. *H.*, *b.* 1950.
1922	*Glendyne* (3rd), Robert Nivison, *b.* 1926, *s.* 1967, *m.*	Hon. John *N.*, *b.* 1960.
1939	*Glentoran* (2nd), Daniel Stewart Thomas Bingham Dixon, P.C. (N.I.), K.B.E., *b.* 1912, *s.* 1950, *w.*	Hon. Thomas R. V. *D.*, M.B.E., *b.* 1935.
1909	*Gorell* (4th), Timothy John Radcliffe Barnes, *b.* 1927, *s.* 1963, *m.*	Hon. Ronald A. H. *B.*, *b.* 1931.
1953	*Grantchester* (2nd), Kenneth Bent Suenson-Taylor, C.B.E., Q.C., *b.* 1921, *s.* 1976, *m.*	Hon. Christopher J. *S.-T.*, *b.* 1951.
1782	*Grantley* (7th), John Richard Brinsley Norton, M.C., *b.* 1923, *s.* 1954, *m.*	Hon. Richard W. B. *N.*, *b.* 1956.
1794 I.	*Graves* (8th), Peter George Wellesley Graves, *b.* 1911, *s.* 1963, *m.*	Evelyn P. *G.*, *b.* 1926.
1445 s.	*Gray* (22nd), Angus Diarmid Ian Campbell-Gray, *b.* 1931, *s.* 1946, *m.*	Master of Gray, *b.* 1964.
1950	*Greenhill* (2nd), Stanley Ernest Greenhill, M.D., *b.* 1917, *s.* 1967, *m.*	Hon. Malcolm *G.*, *b.* 1924.
1927	*Greenway* (4th), Ambrose Charles Drexel Greenway, *b.* 1941, *s.* 1975, *m.*	Hon. Mervyn S. K. *G.*, *b.* 1942.
1902	*Grenfell* (3rd), Julian Pascoe Francis St. Leger Grenfell, *b.* 1935, *s.* 1976, *m.*	Francis P. J. *G.*, *b.* 1938.

Created.	Title, Order of Succession, Name, etc.	Eldest Son or Heir.
1944	*Gretton* (3rd), John Henrik Gretton, *b.* 1941, *s.* 1982, *m.*	Hon. John L. *G.*, *b.* 1975.
1869	*Greville* (4th), Ronald Charles Fulke Greville, *b.* 1912, *s.* 1952.	(None.)
1955	*Gridley* (2nd), Arnold Hudson Gridley, *b.* 1906, *s.* 1965, *m.*	Hon. Richard D. A. *G.*, *b.* 1956.
1964	*Grimston of Westbury* (2nd), Robert Walter Sigismund Grimston, *b.* 1925, *s.* 1979, *m.*	Hon. Robert J. S. *G.*, *b.* 1951.
1886	*Grimthorpe* (4th), Christopher John Beckett, O.B.E., *b.* 1915, *s.* 1963, *m.*	Hon. Edward J. *B.*, *b.* 1954.
1945	*Hacking* (3rd), Douglas David Hacking, *b.* 1938, *s.* 1971, *m.*	Hon. Douglas F. *H.*, *b.* 1968.
1950	*Haden-Guest* (4th), Peter Haden Haden-Guest, *b.* 1913, *s.* 1987, *m.*	Hon. Christopher *H.-G.*, *b.* 1948.
1886	*Hamilton of Dalzell* (3rd), John d'Henin Hamilton, G.C.V.O., M.C., *b.* 1911, *s.* 1952, *m.*	Hon. James L. *H.*, *b.* 1938.
1874	*Hampton* (6th), Richard Humphrey Russell Pakington, *b.* 1925, *s.* 1974, *m.*	Hon. John H. A. *P.*, *b.* 1964.
1939	*Hankey* (2nd), Robert Maurice Alers Hankey, K.C.M.G., K.C.V.O., *b.* 1905, *s.* 1963, *m.*	Hon. Donald R. A. *H.*, *b.* 1938.
1958	*Harding of Petherton* (1st), John Harding, G.C.B., C.B.E., D.S.O., M.C., Field-Marshal, *b.* 1896, *w.*	Hon. John C. *H.*, *b.* 1928.
1910	*Hardinge of Penshurst* (3rd), George Edward Charles Hardinge, *b.* 1921, *s.* 1960, *m.*	Hon. Julian A. *H.*, *b.* 1945.
1876	*Harlech* (6th), Francis David Ormsby-Gore, *b.* 1954, *s.* 1985.	Hon. John J. S. *O.-G.*, *b.* 1925.
1939	*Harmsworth* (2nd), Cecil Desmond Bernard Harmsworth, *b.* 1903, *s.* 1948, *m.*	Hon. Eric B. N. *H.*, *b.* 1905.
1815	*Harris* (6th), George Robert John Harris, *b.* 1920, *s.* 1984.	Derek M. *H.*, *b.* 1916.
1954	*Harvey of Tasburgh* (2nd), Peter Charles Oliver Harvey, *b.* 1921, *s.* 1968, *m.*	Hon. John W. *H.*, *b.* 1923.
1295	*Hastings* (22nd), Edward Delaval Henry Astley, *b.* 1912, *s.* 1956, *m.*	Hon. Delaval T. H. *A.*, *b.* 1960.
1835	*Hatherton* (8th), Edward Charles Littleton, *b.* 1950, *s.* 1985, *m.*	Hon. Thomas E. *L.*, *b.* 1977.
1776	*Hawke* (10th), (Julian Stanhope) Theodore Hawke, *b.* 1904, *s.* 1985, *m.*	Hon. Edward G. *H.*, *b.* 1950.
1927	*Hayter* (3rd), George Charles Hayter Chubb, K.C.V.O., C.B.E., *b.* 1911, *s.* 1967, *m.*	Hon. George W. M. *C.*, *b.* 1943.
1945	*Hazlerigg* (2nd), Arthur Grey Hazlerigg, M.C., *b.* 1910, *s.* 1949, *w.*	Hon. Arthur G. *H.*, *b.* 1951.
1797 I.	*Headley* (7th), Charles Rowland Allanson-Winn, *b.* 1902, *s.* 1969, *m.*	Hon. John R. *A.-W.*, *b.* 1934.
1943	*Hemingford* (3rd), Dennis Nicholas Herbert, *b.* 1934, *s.* 1982, *m.*	Hon. Christopher D. C. *H.*, *b.* 1973.
1906	*Hemphill* (5th), Peter Patrick Fitzroy Martyn Martyn-Hemphill, *b.* 1928, *s.* 1957, *m.*	Hon. Charles A. M. *M.-H.*, *b.* 1954.
1799 I.*	*Henley* (8th), Oliver Michael Robert Eden (6th *U.K. Baron, Northington*, 1885), *b.* 1953, *s.* 1977, *m.*	Hon. Andrew F. *E.*, *b.* 1955.
1800 I.*	*Henniker* (8th), John Patrick Edward Chandos Henniker-Major, K.C.M.G., C.V.O., M.C. (4th *U.K. Baron, Hartismere*, 1866), *b.* 1916, *s.* 1980, *m.*	Hon. Mark I. P. C. *H.-M.*, *b.* 1947.
1886	*Herschell* (3rd), Rognvald Richard Farrer Herschell, *b.* 1923, *s.* 1929, *m.*	(None.)
1935	*Hesketh* (3rd), Thomas Alexander Fermor-Hesketh, *b.* 1950, *s.* 1955, *m.*	Hon. Robert *F.-H.*, *b.* 1951.
1828	*Heytesbury* (6th), Francis William Holmes à Court, *b.* 1931, *s.* 1971, *m.*	Hon. James W. *H. à C.*, *b.* 1967.
1886	*Hindlip* (5th), Henry Richard Allsopp, *b.* 1912, *s.* 1966, *m.*	Hon. Charles H. *A.*, *b.* 1940.
1950	*Hives* (2nd), John Warwick Hives, *b.* 1913, *s.* 1965, *m.*	Matthew P. *H.*, *b.* 1971.
1912	*Hollenden* (3rd), Gordon Hope Hope-Morley, *b.* 1914, *s.* 1977, *m.*	Hon. Ian H. *H.-M.*, *b.* 1946.
1897	*Holm Patrick* (3rd), James Hans Hamilton, *b.* 1928, *s.* 1942, *m.*	Hon. Hans. J. D. *H.*, *b.* 1955.
1933	*Horder* (2nd), Thomas Mervyn Horder, *b.* 1910, *s.* 1955.	(None.)
1797 I.	*Hotham* (8th), Henry Durand Hotham, *b.* 1940, *s.* 1967, *m.*	Hon. William B. *H.*, *b.* 1972.
1881	*Hothfield* (5th), George William Anthony Tufton, T.D., *b.* 1904, *s.* 1986, *m.*	Hon. Anthony C. S. *T.*, *b.* 1939.
1597	*Howard de Walden* (9th), John Osmael Scott-Ellis (5th *U.K. Baron, Seaford*, 1826), *b.* 1912, *s.* 1946, *m.*	Co-heiresses. To U.K. Barony, Colin H. F. *Ellis*, *b.* 1946.
1930	*Howard of Penrith* (2nd), Francis Philip Howard, *b.* 1905, *s.* 1939, *m.*	Hon. Philip E. *H.*, *b.* 1945.
1960	*Howick of Glendale* (2nd), Charles Evelyn Baring, *b.* 1937, *s.* 1973, *m.*	Hon. David E. C. *B.*, *b.* 1975.
1796 I.	*Huntingfield* (6th), Gerard Charles Arcedeckne Vanneck, *b.* 1915, *s.* 1969, *m.*	Hon. Joshua C. *V.*, *b.* 1954.
1866	*Hylton* (5th), Raymond Hervey Jolliffe, *b.* 1932, *s.* 1967, *m.*	Hon. William H. M. *J.*, *b.* 1967.
1933	*Iliffe* (2nd), Edward Langton Iliffe, *b.* 1908, *s.* 1960, *m.*	Robert P. R. *I.*, *b.* 1944.
1543 I.	*Inchiquin* (18th), Conor Myles John O'Brien, *b.* 1943, *s.* 1982.	Murrough R. *O'B.*, *b.* 1910.
1962	*Inchyra* (1st), Frederick Robert Hoyer Millar, G.C.M.G., C.V.O., *b.* 1900, *m.*	Hon. Robert C. R. H. *M.*, *b.* 1935.
1964	*Inglewood* (1st), William Morgan Fletcher-Vane, T.D., *b.* 1909, *w.*	Hon. W. Richard *F.-V.*, *b.* 1951.
1919	*Inverforth* (4th), Andrew Peter Weir, *b.* 1966, *s.* 1982.	Hon. John V. *W.*, *b.* 1935.
1941	*Ironside* (2nd), Edmund Oslac Ironside, *b.* 1924, *s.* 1959, *m.*	Hon. Charles E. G. *I.*, *b.* 1956.
1952	*Jeffreys* (3rd), Christopher Henry Mark Jeffreys, *b.* 1957, *s.* 1986.	Hon. Alexander C. D. *J.*, *b.* 1959.

Created.	Title, Order of Succession, Name, etc.	Eldest Son or Heir.
1924	*Jessel* (2nd), Edward Herbert Jessel, C.B.E., *b.* 1904, *s.* 1950, *m.*	(None).
1906	*Joicey* (4th), Michael Edward Joicey, *b.* 1925, *s.* 1966, *m.*	Hon. James M. *J.*, *b.* 1953.
1937	*Kenilworth* (4th), John Randle Siddeley, *b.* 1954, *s.* 1981, *m.*	(None).
1935	*Kennet* (2nd), Wayland Hilton Young, *b.* 1923, *s.* 1960, *m.*	Hon. William A. T. *Y.*, *b.* 1957.
1776 I. 1886* }	*Kensington* (8th), Hugh Ivor Edwardes (5th *U.K. Baron, Kensington*), *b.* 1933, *s.* 1981, *m.*	Hon. William O. A. *E.*, *b.* 1964.
1951	*Kenswood* (2nd), John Michael Howard Whitfield, *b.* 1930, *s.* 1963, *m.*	Hon. Michael C. *W.*, *b.* 1955.
1788	*Kenyon* (5th), Lloyd Tyrell-Kenyon, C.B.E., *b.* 1917, *s.* 1927, *m.*	Hon. Lloyd *T.-K.*, *b.* 1947.
1947	*Kershaw* (4th), Edward John Kershaw, *b.* 1936, *s.* 1962, *m.*	Hon. John C. E. *K.*, *b.* 1971.
1943	*Keyes* (2nd), Roger George Bowlby Keyes, *b.* 1919, *s.* 1945, *m.*	Hon. Charles W. P. *K.*, *b.* 1951.
1909	*Kilbracken* (3rd), John Raymond Godley, D.S.C., *b.* 1920, *s.* 1950, *m.*	Hon. Christopher J. *G.*, *b.* 1945.
1900	*Killanin* (3rd), Michael Morris, M.B.E., T.D., *b.* 1914, *s.* 1927, *m.*	Hon. G. Redmond F. *M.*, *b.* 1947.
1943	*Killearn* (2nd), Graham Curtis Lampson, *b.* 1919, *s.* 1964, *m.*	Hon. Victor M. G. A. *L.*, *b.* 1941.
1789 I.	*Kilmaine* (7th), John David Henry Browne, *b.* 1948, *s.* 1978, *m.*	Hon. John F. S. *B.*, *b.* 1983.
1831	*Kilmarnock* (7th), Alastair Ivor Gilbert Boyd, *b.* 1927, *s.* 1975, *m.*	Hon. Robin J. *B.*, *b.* 1941.
1941	*Kindersley* (3rd), Robert Hugh Molesworth Kindersley, *b.* 1929, *s.* 1976, *m.*	Hon. Rupert J. M. *K.*, *b.* 1955.
1223 I.	*Kingsale* (35th), John de Courcy (*Premier Baron of Ireland*), *b.* 1941, *s.* 1969.	Nevinson R. *de C.*, *b.* 1920.
1682 s. 1860* }	*Kinnaird* (13th), Graham Charles Kinnaird (5th *U.K. Baron, Kinnaird*), *b.* 1912, *s.* 1972, *m.*	(None).
1902	*Kinross* (5th), Christopher Patrick Balfour, *b.* 1949, *s.* 1985, *m.*	Hon. Alan I. *B.*, *b.* 1978.
1951	*Kirkwood* (3rd), David Harvie Kirkwood, PH.D., *b.* 1931, *s.* 1970, *m.*	Hon. James S. *K.*, *b.* 1937.
1800 I.	*Langford* (9th), Geoffrey Alexander Rowley-Conwy, O.B.E., *b.* 1912, *s.* 1953, *m.*	Hon. Owen G. *R.-C.*, *b.* 1958.
1942	*Latham* (2nd), Dominic Charles Latham, *b.* 1954, *s.* 1970.	Anthony M. *L.*, *b.* 1954.
1431	*Latymer* (8th), Hugo Neville Money-Coutts, *b.* 1926, *s.* 1987, *m.*	Hon. Crispian J. A. N. *M.-C.*, *b.* 1955.
1869	*Lawrence* (5th), David John Downer Lawrence, *b.* 1937, *s.* 1968.	(None).
1947	*Layton* (2nd), Michael John Layton, *b.* 1912, *s.* 1966, *m.*	Hon. Geoffrey M. *L.*, *b.* 1947.
1859	*Leconfield* (7th), John Max Henry Scawen Wyndham (2nd *U.K. Baron, Egremont*, 1963), *b.* 1948, *s.* 1972, *m.*	Hon. George R. V. *W.*, *b.* 1983.
1839	*Leigh* (5th), John Piers Leigh, *b.* 1935, *s.* 1979, *m.*	Hon. Christopher D. P. *L.*, *b.* 1960.
1962	*Leighton of St. Mellons* (2nd), (John) Leighton Seager, *b.* 1922, *s.* 1963, *m.*	Hon. Robert W. H. L. *S.*, *b.* 1955.
1797	*Lilford* (7th), George Vernon Powys, *b.* 1931, *s.* 1949, *m.*	Hon. Mark V. *P.*, *b.* 1975.
1945	*Lindsay of Birker* (2nd), Michael Francis Morris Lindsay, *b.* 1909, *s.* 1952, *m.*	Hon. James F. *L.*, *b.* 1945.
1758 I.	*Lisle* (7th), John Nicholas Horace Lysaght, *b.* 1903, *s.* 1919, *m.*	Patrick J. *L.*, *b.* 1931.
1895	*Loch* (4th), Spencer Douglas Loch, M.C., *b.* 1920, *s.* 1982, *m.*	(None).
1850	*Londesborough* (9th), Richard John Denison, *b.* 1959, *s.* 1968.	(None).
1541 I.	*Louth* (16th), Otway Michael James Oliver Plunkett, *b.* 1929, *s.* 1950, *m.*	Hon. Jonathan O. *P.*, *b.* 1952.
1458 s. 1837* }	*Lovat* (15th), Simon Christopher Joseph Fraser, D.S.O., M.C., T.D. (4th *U.K. Baron, Lovat*), *b.* 1911, *s.* 1933, *m.*	Master of Lovat, *b.* 1939.
1946	*Lucas of Chilworth* (2nd), Michael William George Lucas, *b.* 1926, *s.* 1967, *m.*	Hon. Simon W. *L.*, *b.* 1957.
1929	*Luke* (2nd), Ian St. John Lawson-Johnston, K.C.V.O., T.D., *b.* 1905, *s.* 1943, *m.*	Hon. Arthur C. St. J. *L.-J.*, *b.* 1933.
1839	*Lurgan* (5th), John Desmond Cavendish Brownlow, O.B.E., *b.* 1911, *s.* 1984.	(None).
1914	*Lyell* (3rd), Charles Lyell, *b.* 1939, *s.* 1943.	(None).
1859	*Lyveden* (6th), Ronald Cecil Vernon, *b.* 1915, *s.* 1973, *m.*	Hon. Jack L. *V.*, *b.* 1938.
1959	*MacAndrew* (2nd), Colin Nevil Glen MacAndrew, *b.* 1919, *s.* 1979, *m.*	Hon. Christopher A. C. *MacA.*, *b.* 1945.
1776 I.	*Macdonald* (8th), Godfrey James Macdonald, *b.* 1947, *s.* 1970, *m.*	Hon. Godfrey E. H. T. *M.*, *b.* 1982.
1949	*Macdonald of Gwaenysgor* (2nd), Gordon Ramsay Macdonald, *b.* 1915, *s.* 1966, *m.*	Hon. Kenneth L. *M.*, *b.* 1921.
1937	*McGowan* (3rd), Harry Duncan Cory McGowan, *b.* 1938, *s.* 1966, *m.*	Hon. Harry J. C. *McG.*, *b.* 1971.
1922	*Maclay* (3rd), Joseph Paton Maclay, *b.* 1942, *s.* 1969, *m.*	Hon. Joseph P. *M.*, *b.* 1977.
1955	*McNair* (2nd), (Clement) John McNair, *b.* 1915, *s.* 1975, *m.*	Hon. Duncan J. *McN.*, *b.* 1947.
1951	*Macpherson of Drumochter* (2nd), (James) Gordon Macpherson, *b.* 1924, *s.* 1965, *m.*	Hon. James A. *M.*, *b.* 1979.
1937	*Mancroft* (2nd), Stormont Mancroft Samuel Mancroft, K.B.E., T.D., *b.* 1914, *s.* 1942, *m.*	Hon. Benjamin L. S. *M.*, *b.* 1957.
1807	*Manners* (5th), John Robert Cecil Manners, *b.* 1923, *s.* 1972, *m.*	Hon. John H. R. *M.*, *b.* 1956.

Created.	Title, Order of Succession, Name, etc.	Eldest Son or Heir.
1922	*Manton* (3rd), Joseph Rupert Eric Robert Watson, *b.* 1924, *s.* 1968, *m.*	Capt. Hon. Miles R. M. *W.*, *b.* 1958.
1908	*Marchamley* (3rd), John William Tattersall Whiteley, *b.* 1922, *s.* 1949, *m.*	Hon. William F. *W.*, *b.* 1968.
1964	*Margadale* (1st), John Granville Morrison, T.D., *b.* 1906, *w.*	Hon. James I. *M.*, T.D., *b.* 1930.
1961	*Marks of Broughton* (2nd), Michael Marks, *b.* 1920, *s.* 1964, *m.*	Hon. Simon R. *M.*, *b.* 1950.
1930	*Marley* (2nd), Godfrey Pelham Leigh Aman, *b.* 1913, *s.* 1952, *m.*	(None.)
1964	*Martonmere* (1st), (John) Roland Robinson, P.C., G.B.E., K.C.M.G., *b.* 1907, *w.*	John S. *R.*, *b.* 1963.
1776 I.	*Massy* (9th), Hugh Hamon John Somerset Massy, *b.* 1921, *s.* 1958, *m.*	Hon. David H. S. *M.*, *b.* 1947.
1935	*May* (3rd), Michael St. John May, *b.* 1931, *s.* 1950, *m.*	Hon. Jasper B. St. J. *M.*, *b.* 1965.
1928	*Melchett* (4th), Peter Robert Henry Mond, *b.* 1948, *s.* 1973.	(None.)
1925	*Merrivale* (3rd), Jack Henry Edmond Duke, *b.* 1917, *s.* 1951, *m.*	Hon. Derek J. P. *D.*, *b.* 1948.
1919	*Meston* (3rd), James Meston, *b.* 1950, *s.* 1984, *m.*	Hon. Thomas J. D. *M.*, *b.* 1977.
1838	*Methuen* (6th), Anthony John Methuen, *b.* 1925, *s.* 1975.	Hon. Robert A. H. *M.*, *b.* 1931.
1711	*Middleton* (12th), (Digby) Michael Godfrey John Willoughby, M.C., *b.* 1921, *s.* 1970, *m.*	Hon. Michael C. J. *W.*, *b.* 1948.
1939	*Milford* (2nd), Wogan Philipps, *b.* 1902, *s.* 1962, *m.*	Hon. Hugo J. L. *P.*, *b.* 1929.
1933	*Milne* (2nd), George Douglass Milne, T.D., *b.* 1909, *s.* 1948, *m.*	Hon. George A. *M.*, *b.* 1941.
1951	*Milner of Leeds* (2nd), Arthur James Michael Milner, *b.* 1923, *s.* 1967, *m.*	Hon. Richard J. *M.*, *b.* 1959.
1947	*Milverton* (2nd), Rev. Fraser Arthur Richard Richards, *b.* 1930, *s.* 1978, *m.*	Hon. Michael H. *R.*, *b.* 1936.
1873	*Moncreiff* (5th), Harry Robert Wellwood Moncreiff, *b.* 1915, *s.* 1942, *w.*	Hon. Rhoderick H. W. *M.*, *b.* 1954.
1884	*Monk Bretton* (3rd), John Charles Dodson, *b.* 1924, *s.* 1933, *m.*	Hon. Christopher M. *D.*, *b.* 1958.
1885	*Monkswell* (5th), Gerard Collier, *b.* 1947, *s.* 1984, *m.*	Hon. James A. *C.*, *b.* 1977.
1728	*Monson* (11th), John Monson, *b.* 1932, *s.* 1958, *m.*	Hon. Nicholas J. *M.*, *b.* 1955.
1885	*Montagu of Beaulieu* (3rd), Edward John Barrington Douglas-Scott-Montagu, *b.* 1926, *s.* 1929, *m.*	Hon. Ralph *D.-S.-M.*, *b.* 1961.
1839	*Monteagle of Brandon* (6th), Gerald Spring Rice, *b.* 1926, *s.* 1946, *m.*	Hon. Charles J. S. *R.*, *b.* 1953.
1943	*Moran* (2nd), (Richard) John (McMoran) Wilson, K.C.M.G., *b.* 1924, *s.* 1977, *m.*	Hon. James McM. *W.*, *b.* 1952.
1918	*Morris* (3rd), Michael David Morris, *b.* 1937, *s.* 1975, *m.*	Hon. Thomas A. S. *M.*, *b.* 1982.
1950	*Morris of Kenwood* (2nd), Philip Geoffrey Morris, *b.* 1928, *s.* 1954, *m.*	Hon. Jonathan D. *M.*, *b.* 1968.
1945	*Morrison* (2nd), Dennis Morrison, *b.* 1914, *s.* 1953.	(None.)
1831	*Mostyn* (5th), Roger Edward Lloyd Lloyd-Mostyn, M.C., *b.* 1920, *s.* 1965, *m.*	Hon. Llewellyn R. L. *L.-M.*, *b.* 1948.
1933	*Mottistone* (4th), David Peter Seely, C.B.E., *b.* 1920, *s.* 1966, *m.*	Hon. Peter J. P. *S.*, *b.* 1949.
1945	*Mountevans* (3rd), Edward Patrick Broke Evans, *b.* 1943, *s.* 1974, *m.*	Hon. Jeffrey de C. R. *E.*, *b.* 1948.
1283	*Mowbray* (26th), *Segrave* (27th) (1283), & *Stourton* (23rd) (1448), Charles Edward Stourton, C.B.E., *b.* 1923, *s.* 1965, *m.*	Hon. Edward W. S. *S.*, *b.* 1953.
1932	*Moyne* (2nd), Bryan Walter Guinness, *b.* 1905, *s.* 1944, *m.*	Hon. Jonathan B. *G.*, *b.* 1930.
1929	*Moynihan* (3rd), Antony Patrick Andrew Cairnes Berkeley Moynihan, *b.* 1936, *s.* 1965.	Hon. Colin B. *M.*, M.P., *b.* 1955.
1781 I.	*Muskerry* (8th), Hastings Fitzmaurice Tilson Deane, *b.* 1907, *s.* 1966, *m.*	Hon. Robert F. *D.*, *b.* 1948.
1627 s.*	*Napier and Ettrick* (14th), Francis Nigel Napier, C.V.O. (5th *U.K. Baron, Ettrick*, 1872), *b.* 1930, *s.* 1954, *m.*	Master of Napier, *b.* 1962.
1868	*Napier of Magdala* (5th), (Robert) John Napier, O.B.E., *b.* 1904, *s.* 1948, *m.*	Hon. Robert A. *N.*, *b.* 1940.
1940	*Nathan* (2nd), Roger Carol Michael Nathan, *b.* 1922, *s.* 1963, *m.*	Hon. Rupert H. B. *N.*, *b.* 1957.
1960	*Nelson of Stafford* (2nd), Henry George Nelson, *b.* 1917, *s.* 1962, *m.*	Hon. Henry R. G. *N.*, *b.* 1943.
1959	*Netherthorpe* (3rd), James Frederick Turner, *b.* 1964, *s.* 1982.	Hon. Patrick A. *T.*, *b.* 1971.
1946	*Newall* (2nd), Francis Storer Eaton Newall, *b.* 1930, *s.* 1963, *m.*	Hon. Richard H. E. *N.*, *b.* 1961.
1776 I.	*Newborough* (7th), Robert Charles Michael Vaughan Wynn, D.S.C., *b.* 1917, *s.* 1965, *m.*	Hon. Robert V. *W.*, *b.* 1949.
1892	*Newton* (4th), Peter Richard Legh, *b.* 1915, *s.* 1960, *m.*	Hon. Richard T. *L.*, *b.* 1950.
1930	*Noel-Buxton* (3rd), Martin Connal Noel-Buxton, *b.* 1940, *s.* 1980.	Hon. Charles C. *N.-B.*, *b.* 1975.
1957	*Norrie* (2nd), (George) Willoughby Moke Norrie, *b.* 1936, *s.* 1977, *m.*	Hon. Mark W. J. *N.*, *b.* 1972.
1884	*Northbourne* (5th), Christopher George Walter James, *b.* 1926, *s.* 1982, *m.*	Hon. Charles W. H. *J.*, *b.* 1960.
1866	*Northbrook* (5th), Francis John Baring, *b.* 1915, *s.* 1947, *m.*	Hon. Francis T. *B.*, *b.* 1954.
1878	*Norton* (7th), John Arden Adderley, O.B.E., *b.* 1915, *s.* 1961, *m.*	Hon. James N. A. *A.*, *b.* 1947.
1906	*Nunburnholme* (4th), Ben Charles Wilson, *b.* 1928, *s.* 1974, *m.*	Hon. Charles T. *W.*, *b.* 1935.
1950	*Ogmore* (2nd), Gwilym Rees Rees-Williams, *b.* 1931, *s.* 1976, *m.*	Hon. Morgan *R.-W.*, *b.* 1937.
1870	*O'Hagan* (4th), Charles Towneley Strachey, *b.* 1945, *s.* 1961.	Hon. Richard T. *S.*, *b.* 1950.

Created.	Title, Order of Succession, Name, etc.	Eldest Son or Heir.
1868	*O'Neill* (4th), Raymond Arthur Clanaboy O'Neill, T.D., b. 1933, s. 1944, m.	Hon. Shane S. C. *O'N.*, b. 1965.
1836 I.*	*Oranmore and Browne* (4th), Dominick Geoffrey Edward Browne (2nd U.K. Baron Mereworth, 1926), b. 1901, s. 1927, m.	Hon. Dominick G. T. *B.*, b. 1929.
1933	*Palmer* (3rd), Raymond Cecil Palmer, O.B.E., b. 1916, s. 1950, m.	Hon. Gordon W. N. *P.*, O.B.E., T.D., b. 1918.
1914	*Parmoor* (4th), (Frederick Alfred) Milo Cripps, b. 1929, s. 1977.	M. Anthony L. *C.*, C.B.E., D.S.O., T.D., Q.C., b. 1913.
1937	*Pender* (3rd), John Willoughby Denison-Pender, b. 1933, s. 1965, m.	Hon. Henry J. R. *D.-P.*, b. 1968.
1866	*Penrhyn* (6th), Malcolm Frank Douglas-Pennant, D.S.O., M.B.E., b. 1908, s. 1967, m.	Hon. Nigel *D.-P.*, b. 1909.
1603	*Petre* (17th), Joseph William Lionel Petre, b. 1914, s. 1915, m.	Hon. John P. L. *P.*, b. 1942.
1918	*Phillimore* (3rd), Robert Godfrey Phillimore, b. 1939, s. 1947.	Hon. Claud S. *P.*, b. 1911.
1945	*Piercy* (3rd), James William Piercy, b. 1946, s. 1981.	Hon. Mark E. P. *P.*, b. 1953.
1827	*Plunket* (8th), Robin Rathmore Plunket, b. 1925, s. 1975, m.	Hon. Shaun A. F. S. *P.*, b. 1931.
1831	*Poltimore* (7th), Mark Coplestone Bampfylde, b. 1957, s. 1978, m.	Hon. Henry A. W. *B.*, b. 1985.
1690 S.	*Polwarth* (10th), Henry Alexander Hepburne-Scott, T.D., b. 1916, s. 1944, m.	Master of Polwarth, b. 1947.
1930	*Ponsonby of Shulbrede* (3rd), Thomas Arthur Ponsonby, b. 1930, s. 1976, m.	Hon. Frederick M. T. *P.*, b. 1958.
1958	*Poole* (1st), Oliver Brian Sanderson Poole, P.C., C.B.E., T.D., b. 1911, m.	Hon. David C. *P.*, b. 1945.
1852	*Raglan* (5th), FitzRoy John Somerset, b. 1927, s. 1964.	Hon. Geoffrey *S.*, b. 1932.
1932	*Rankeillour* (4th), Peter St. Thomas More Henry Hope, b. 1935, s. 1967.	Michael R. *H.*, b. 1940.
1953	*Rathcavan* (2nd), Phelim Robert Hugh O'Neill, P.C. (N.I.), b. 1909, s. 1982, m.	Hon. Hugh D. T. *O'N.*, b. 1939.
1916	*Rathcreedan* (2nd), Charles Patrick Norton, T.D., b. 1905, s. 1930, m.	Hon. Christopher J. *N.*, b. 1949.
1868 I.	*Rathdonnell* (5th), Thomas Benjamin McClintock Bunbury, b. 1938, s. 1959, m.	Hon. William L. McC. *B.*, b. 1966.
1911	*Ravensdale* (3rd), Nicholas Mosley, M.C., b. 1923, s. 1966, m.	Hon. Shaun N. *M.*, b. 1949.
1821	*Ravensworth* (8th), Arthur Waller Liddell, b. 1924, s. 1950, m.	Hon. Thomas A. H. *L.*, b. 1954.
1821	*Rayleigh* (5th), John Arthur Strutt, b. 1908, s. 1947, w.	John G. *S.*, b. 1960.
1937	*Rea* (3rd), John Nicolas Rea, M.D., b. 1928, s. 1981, m.	Hon. Matthew J. *R.*, b. 1956.
1628 S.	*Reay* (14th), Hugh William Mackay, b. 1937, s. 1963, m.	Master of Reay, b. 1965.
1902	*Redesdale* (5th), Clement Napier Bertram Mitford, b. 1932, s. 1963, m.	Hon. Rupert B. *M.*, b. 1967.
1928	*Remnant* (3rd), James Wogan Remnant, C.V.O., b. 1930, s. 1967, m.	Hon. Philip J. *R.*, b. 1954.
1806 I.	*Rendlesham* (8th), Charles Anthony Hugh Thellusson, b. 1915, s. 1943, w.	Hon. Charles W. B. *T.*, b. 1954.
1933	*Rennell* (3rd), (John Adrian) Tremayne Rodd, b. 1935, s. 1978, m.	Hon. James R. D. T. *R.*, b. 1978.
1964	*Renwick* (2nd), Harry Andrew Renwick, b. 1935, s. 1973, m.	Hon. Robert J. *R.*, b. 1966.
1885	*Revelstoke* (4th), Rupert Baring, b. 1911, s. 1934.	Hon. John *B.*, b. 1934.
1905	*Ritchie of Dundee* (5th), (Harold) Malcolm Ritchie, b. 1919, s. 1978, m.	Hon. Charles R. R. *R.*, b. 1958.
1935	*Riverdale* (2nd), Robert Arthur Balfour, b. 1901, s. 1957, m.	Hon. Mark R. *B.*, b. 1927.
1961	*Robertson of Oakridge* (2nd), William Ronald Robertson, b. 1930, s. 1974, m.	Hon. William B. E. *R.*, b. 1975.
1938	*Roborough* (2nd), Massey Henry Edgcumbe Lopes, b. 1903, s. 1938, m.	Hon. Henry M. *L.*, b. 1940.
1931	*Rochester* (2nd), Foster Charles Lowry Lamb, b. 1916, s. 1955, m.	Hon. David C. *L.*, b. 1944.
1934	*Rockley* (3rd), James Hugh Cecil, b. 1934, s. 1976, m.	Hon. Anthony R. *C.*, b. 1961.
1782	*Rodney* (9th), John Francis Rodney, b. 1920, s. 1973, m.	Hon. George B. *R.*, b. 1953.
1651 S.*	*Rollo* (13th), Eric John Stapylton Rollo (4th U.K. Baron, Dunning, 1869), b. 1915, s. 1947, m.	Master of Rollo, b. 1943.
1959	*Rootes* (2nd), William Geoffrey Rootes, b. 1917, s. 1964, m.	Hon. Nicholas G. *R.*, b. 1951.
1796 I. ⎫ 1838* ⎭	*Rossmore* (7th), William Warner Westenra (6th U.K. Baron, Rossmore), b. 1931, s. 1958, m.	Hon. Benedict W. *W.*, b. 1983.
1939	*Rotherwick* (2nd), (Herbert) Robin Cayzer, b. 1912, s. 1958, w.	Hon. H. Robin *C.*, b. 1954.
1885	*Rothschild* (3rd), Nathaniel Mayer Victor Rothschild, G.B.E., G.M., F.R.S., b. 1910, s. 1937, m.	Hon. N. C. Jacob *R.*, b. 1936.
1911	*Rowallan* (3rd), Arthur Cameron Corbett, b. 1919, s. 1977.	Hon. John P. C. *C.*, b. 1947.
1947	*Rugby* (2nd), Alan Loader Maffey, b. 1913, s. 1969, m.	Hon. Robert C. *M.*, b. 1951.
1919	*Russell of Liverpool* (3rd), Simon Gordon Jared Russell, b. 1952, s. 1981, m.	Hon. Edward C. S. *R.*, b. 1985.
1876	*Sackville* (6th), Lionel Bertrand Sackville-West, b. 1913, s. 1965, m.	Hugh R. I. *S.-W.*, M.C., b. 1919.
1964	*St. Helens* (2nd), Richard Francis Hughes-Young, b. 1945, s. 1980, m.	Hon. Henry T. *H.-Y.*, b. 1986.
1559	*St. John of Bletso* (21st), Anthony Tudor St. John, b. 1957, s. 1978.	Edmund O. *St. J.*, b. 1927.
1852	*St. Leonards* (4th), John Gerard Sugden, b. 1950, s. 1972.	Edward C. S., b. 1902.
1887	*St. Levan* (4th), John Francis Arthur St. Aubyn, D.S.C., b. 1919, s. 1978, m.	Hon. O. Piers *St. A.*, M.C., b. 1920.
1885	*St. Oswald* (5th), Derek Edward Anthony Winn, b. 1919, s. 1984, m.	Hon. Charles R. A. *W.*, b. 1959.
1945	*Sandford* (2nd), Rev. John Cyril Edmondson, D.S.C., b. 1920, s. 1959, m.	Hon. James J. M. *E.*, b. 1949.

Created.	Title, Order of Succession, Name, etc.	Eldest Son or Heir.
1871	*Sandhurst* (5th), (John Edward) Terence Mansfield, D.F.C., *b.* 1920, *s.* 1964, *m.*	Hon. Guy R. J. *M.*, *b.* 1949.
1802	*Sandys* (7th), Richard Michael Oliver Hill, *b.* 1931, *s.* 1961, *m.*	Marcus T. *H.*, *b.* 1931.
1888	*Savile* (3rd), George Halifax Lumley-Savile, *b.* 1919, *s.* 1931.	Hon. Henry L. T. *L.-S.*, *b.* 1923.
1447	*Saye and Sele* (21st), Nathaniel Thomas Allen Fiennes, *b.* 1920, *s.* 1968, *m.*	Hon. Richard I. *F.*, *b.* 1959.
1932	*Selsdon* (3rd), Malcolm McEacharn Mitchell-Thomson, *b.* 1937, *s.* 1963, *m.*	Hon. Callum M. M. *M.-T.*, *b.* 1969.
1916	*Shaughnessy* (3rd), William Graham Shaughnessy, *b.* 1922, *s.* 1938, *m.*	Hon. Michael J. *S.*, *b.* 1946.
1783 I.	*Sheffield* (8th), Thomas Henry Oliver Stanley (8th *U.K. Baron, Stanley*	Hon. Richard O. *S.*, *b.* 1956.
1839*	*of Alderley and 7th U.K. Baron Eddisbury*, 1848), *b.* 1927, *s.* 1971, *m.*	
1946	*Shepherd* (2nd), Malcolm Newton Shepherd, P.C., *b.* 1918, *s.* 1954, *m.*	Hon. Graeme G. *S.*, *b.* 1949.
1964	*Sherfield* (1st), Roger Mellor Makins, G.C.B., G.C.M.G., *b.* 1904, *w.*	Hon. Christopher J. *M.*, *b.* 1942.
1902	*Shuttleworth* (5th), Charles Geoffrey Nicholas Kay-Shuttleworth, *b.* 1948, *s.* 1975, *m.*	Hon. Thomas E. *K.-S.*, *b.* 1976.
1963	*Silsoe* (2nd), David Malcolm Trustram Eve, Q.C., *b.* 1930, *s.* 1976, *m.*	Hon. Simon R. T. *E.*, *b.* 1966.
1947	*Simon of Wythenshawe* (2nd), Roger Simon, *b.* 1913, *s.* 1960, *m.*	Hon. Matthew *S.*, *b.* 1955.
1449 s.	*Sinclair* (17th), Charles Murray Kennedy St. Clair, L.V.O., *b.* 1914, *s.* 1957, *m.*	Master of Sinclair, *b.* 1968.
1957	*Sinclair of Cleeve* (3rd), John Lawrence Robert Sinclair, *b.* 1953, *s.* 1985.	(None.)
1919	*Sinha* (3rd), Sudhindro Prosanno Sinha, *b.* 1920, *s.* 1967, *m.*	Hon. Sushanto *S.*, *b.* 1953.
1828	*Skelmersdale* (7th), Roger Bootle-Wilbraham, *b.* 1945, *s.* 1973, *m.*	Hon. Andrew *B.-W.*, *b.* 1977.
1916	*Somerleyton* (3rd), Savile William Francis Crossley, *b.* 1928, *s.* 1959, *m.*	Hon. Hugh F. S. *C.*, *b.* 1971.
1784	*Somers* (8th), John Patrick Somers Cocks, *b.* 1907, *s.* 1953, *m.*	Philip S. S. *C.*, *b.* 1948.
1917	*Southborough* (4th), Francis Michael Hopwood, *b.* 1922, *s.* 1982, *w.*	(None.)
1959	*Spens* (3rd), Patrick Michael Rex Spens, *b.* 1942, *s.* 1984, *m.*	Hon. Patrick N. G. *S.*, *b.* 1968.
1640	*Stafford* (15th), Francis Melfort William Fitzherbert, *b.* 1954, *s.* 1986, *m.*	Hon. Benjamin *F.*, *b.* 1983.
1938	*Stamp* (3rd), Trevor Charles Stamp, M.D., *b.* 1907, *s.* 1941, *m.*	Hon. Trevor C. B. *S.*, M.D., *b.* 1935.
1318	*Strabolgi* (11th), David Montague de Burgh Kenworthy, *b.* 1914, *s.* 1953, *m.*	Rev. the Hon. Jonathan M. A. *K.*, *b.* 1916.
1954	*Strang* (2nd), Colin Strang, *b.* 1922, *s.* 1978, *m.*	(None.)
1955	*Strathalmond* (3rd), William Roberton Fraser, *b.* 1947, *s.* 1976, *m.*	Hon. William G. *F.*, *b.* 1976.
1936	*Strathcarron* (2nd), David William Anthony Blyth Macpherson, *b.* 1924, *s.* 1937, *m.*	Hon. Ian D. P. *M.*, *b.* 1949.
1955	*Strathclyde* (2nd), Thomas Galloway Dunlop du Roy de Blicquy Galbraith, *b.* 1960, *s.* 1985.	Charles W. du R. de B. *G.*, *b.* 1962.
1900	*Strathcona and Mount Royal* (4th), Donald Euan Palmer Howard, *b.* 1923, *s.* 1959, *m.*	Hon. Donald A. S. *H.*, *b.* 1961.
1836	*Stratheden & Campbell* (1841) (5th), Gavin Campbell, *b.* 1901, *s.* 1981, *m.*	Hon. Donald *C.*, *b.* 1934.
1884	*Strathspey* (5th), Donald Patrick Trevor Grant, *b.* 1912, *s.* 1948, *m.*	Hon. James P. *G.*, *b.* 1943.
1838	*Sudeley* (7th), Merlin Charles Sainthill Hanbury-Tracy, *b.* 1939, *s.* 1941, *m.*	Claud E. F. *Hanbury-Tracy-Domvile*, T.D., *b.* 1904.
1786	*Suffield* (11th), Anthony Philip Harbord-Hamond, M.C., *b.* 1922, *s.* 1951, *m.*	Hon. Charles A. A. *H.-H.*, *b.* 1953.
1893	*Swansea* (4th), John Hussey Hamilton Vivian, *b.* 1925, *s.* 1934, *m.*	Hon. Richard A. H. *V.*, *b.* 1957.
1907	*Swaythling* (3rd), Stuart Albert Samuel Montagu, O.B.E., *b.* 1898, *s.* 1927, *m.*	Hon. David C. S. *M.*, *b.* 1928.
1919	*Swinfen* (3rd), Roger Mynors Swinfen Eady, *b.* 1938, *s.* 1977, *m.*	Hon. Charles R. P. S. *E.*, *b.* 1971.
1935	*Sysonby* (3rd), John Frederick Ponsonby, *b.* 1945, *s.* 1956.	(None.)
1831 I	*Talbot of Malahide* (10th), Reginald John Richard Arundell, *b.* 1931, *s.* 1987, *m.*	Hon. Richard J. T. *A.*, *b.* 1957.
1946	*Tedder* (2nd), John Michael Tedder, SC.D., PH.D., D.SC., *b.* 1926, *s.* 1967, *m.*	Hon. Robin J. *T.*, *b.* 1955.
1884	*Tennyson* (4th), Harold Christopher Tennyson, *b.* 1919, *s.* 1951.	Hon. Mark A. *T.*, D.S.C., *b.* 1920.
1918	*Terrington* (4th), (James Allen) David Woodhouse, *b.* 1915, *s.* 1961, *m.*	Hon. C. Montague *W.*, D.S.O., O.B.E., *b.* 1917.
1940	*Teviot* (2nd), Charles John Kerr, *b.* 1934, *s.* 1968, *m.*	Hon. Charles R. *K.*, *b.* 1971.
1616	*Teynham* (20th), John Christopher Ingham Roper-Curzon, *b.* 1928, *s.* 1972, *m.*	Hon. David J. H. I. *R.-C.*, *b.* 1965.
1964	*Thomson of Fleet* (2nd), Kenneth Roy Thomson, *b.* 1923, *s.* 1976, *m.*	Hon. David K. R. *T.*, *b.* 1957.
1792	*Thurlow* (8th), Francis Edward Hovell-Thurlow-Cumming-Bruce, K.C.M.G., *b.* 1912, *s.* 1971, *m.*	Hon. Roualeyn R. *H.-T.-C.-B.*, *b.* 1952.
1876	*Tollemache* (5th), Timothy John Edward Tollemache, *b.* 1939, *s.* 1975, *m.*	Hon. Edward J. H. *T.*, *b.* 1976.
1564 s.	*Torphichen* (15th), James Andrew Douglas Sandilands, *b.* 1946, *s.* 1975, *m.*	Douglas R. A. *S.*, *b.* 1926.

Created.	Title, Order of Succession, Name, etc.	Eldest Son or Heir.
1947	*Trefgarne* (2nd), David Garro Trefgarne, *b.* 1941, *s.* 1960, *m.*	Hon. George G. *T.*, *b.* 1970.
1921	*Trevethin* (4th), *and Oaksey* (2nd), John Geoffrey Tristram Lawrence (2nd *U.K. Baron, Oaksey,* 1947), *b.* 1929, *s.* 1971, *m.*	Hon. Patrick J. T. *L.*, *b.* 1960.
1880	*Trevor* (4th), Charles Edwin Hill-Trevor, *b.* 1928, *s.* 1950, *m.*	Hon. Marke C. *H.-T.*, *b.* 1970.
1461 I.	*Trimlestown* (19th), Charles Aloysius Barnewall, *b.* 1899, *s.* 1937, *m.*	Hon. Anthony E. *B.*, *b.* 1928.
1940	*Tryon* (3rd), Anthony George Merrik Tryon, *b.* 1940, *s.* 1976, *m.*	Hon. Charles G. B. *T.*, *b.* 1976.
1935	*Tweedsmuir* (2nd), John Norman Stuart Buchan, C.B.E., C.D., *b.* 1911, *s.* 1940, *m.*	Hon. William *B.*, *b.* 1916.
1523	*Vaux of Harrowden* (10th), John Hugh Philip Gilbey, *b.* 1915, *s.* 1977, *m.*	Hon. Anthony W. *G.*, *b.* 1940.
1800 I.	*Ventry* (8th), Andrew Wesley Daubeny de Moleyns, *b.* 1943, *s.* 1987, *m.*	Hon. Francis W. *D. de M.*, *b.* 1965.
1762	*Vernon* (10th), John Lawrance Vernon, *b.* 1923, *s.* 1963, *m.*	Robert V. *Harcourt*, *b.* 1918.
1922	*Vestey* (3rd), Samuel George Armstrong Vestey, *b.* 1941, *s.* 1954, *m.*	Hon. William G. *V.*, *b.* 1983.
1841	*Vivian* (5th), Anthony Crespigny Claude Vivian, *b.* 1906, *s.* 1940, *w.*	Hon. Nicholas *V.*, *b.* 1935.
1934	*Wakehurst* (3rd), (John) Christopher Loder, *b.* 1925, *s.* 1970, *m.*	Hon. Timothy W. *L.*, *b.* 1958.
1723	*Walpole* (9th), Robert Henry Montgomerie Walpole, T.D., *b.* 1913, *s.* 1931, *m.*	Hon. Robert H. *W.*, *b.* 1938.
1780	*Walsingham* (9th), John de Grey, M.C., *b.* 1925, *s.* 1965, *m.*	Hon. Robert *de G.*, *b.* 1969.
1936	*Wardington* (2nd), Christopher Henry Beaumont Pease, *b.* 1924, *s.* 1950, *m.*	Hon. William S. *P.*, *b.* 1925.
1792 I.	*Waterpark* (7th), Frederick Caryll Philip Cavendish, *b.* 1926, *s.* 1948, *m.*	Hon. Roderick A. *C.*, *b.* 1959.
1942	*Wedgwood* (4th), Piers Anthony Weymouth Wedgwood, *b.* 1954, *s.* 1970.	John *W.*, M.D., *b.* 1919.
1861	*Westbury* (5th), David Alan Bethell, M.C., *b.* 1922, *s.* 1961, *m.*	Hon. Richard N. *B.*, M.B.E., *b.* 1950.
1944	*Westwood* (2nd), William Westwood, *b.* 1907, *s.* 1953, *m.*	Hon. William G. *W.*, *b.* 1944.
1935	*Wigram* (2nd), (George) Neville (Clive) Wigram, M.C., *b.* 1915, *s.* 1960, *w.*	Maj. Hon. Andrew F. C. *W.*, *b.* 1949.
1491	*Willoughby de Broke* (21st), Leopold David Verney, *b.* 1938, *s.* 1986, *m.*	Hon. Rupert G. *V.*, *b.* 1966.
1946	*Wilson* (2nd), Patrick Maitland Wilson, *b.* 1915, *s.* 1964, *m.*	(None.)
1937	*Windlesham* (3rd), David James George Hennessy, P.C., C.V.O., *b.* 1932, *s.* 1962, *w.*	Hon. James *H.*, *b.* 1968.
1951	*Wise* (2nd), John Clayton Wise, *b.* 1923, *s.* 1968, *m.*	Hon. Christopher J. C. *W.*, PH.D., *b.* 1949.
1869	*Wolverton* (6th), John Patrick Riversdale Glyn, C.B.E., *b.* 1913, *s.* 1986, *m.*	Hon. Christopher R. *G.*, *b.* 1938.
1928	*Wraxall* (2nd), George Richard Lawley Gibbs, *b.* 1928, *s.* 1931.	Hon. Eustace H. B. *G.*, C.M.G., *b.* 1929.
1915	*Wrenbury* (3rd), John Burton Buckley, *b.* 1927, *s.* 1940, *m.*	Hon. William E. *B.*, *b.* 1966.
1838	*Wrottesley* (6th), Clifton Hugh Lancelot de Verdon Wrottesley, *b.* 1968, *s.* 1977, *M.*	Hon. Mark *W.*, *b.* 1951.
1919	*Wyfold* (3rd), Hermon Robert Fleming Hermon-Hodge, *b.* 1915, *s.* 1942.	(None.)
1829	*Wynford* (8th), Robert Samuel Best, M.B.E., *b.* 1917, *s.* 1943, *m.*	Hon. John P. *B.*, *b.* 1950.
1308	*Zouche* (18th), James Assheton Frankland, *b.* 1943, *s.* 1965, *m.*	Hon. William T. A. *F.*, *b.* 1984.

PEERESSES IN THEIR OWN RIGHT

Peerages falling under this heading are the result of regular inheritance in lines which are open to females in default of males. A Peeress in her Own Right retains her title after marriage, and if her husband's rank is the superior she is designated by the two titles jointly, the inferior one last: her hereditary claim still holds good in spite of any marriage whether higher or lower. No rank held by a woman can confer any title or even precedence upon her husband but the rank of a Peeress in her Own Right is inherited by her eldest son (or perhaps daughter), to whomsoever she may have been married.

COUNTESSES IN THEIR OWN RIGHT

Style, The Countess of —— *Addressed as,* My Lady.

Created.	Title, Name, etc.	Eldest Son or Heir.
1643 s.	*Dysart* (11th in line), Rosamund Agnes Greaves, *b.* 1914, *s.* 1975.	Lady Katherine *Grant*, *b.* 1918.
1633 s.	*Loudoun* (13th in line), Barbara Huddleston Abney-Hastings, *b.* 1919, *s.* 1960, *m.*	Lord Mauchline, *b.* 1942.
c. 1115 s.	*Mar* (31st in line), Margaret of Mar (*Premier Earldom of Scotland*), *b.* 1940, *s.* 1975, *m.*	The Mistress of Mar, *b.* 1963.
1947	*Mountbatten of Burma* (2nd in line), Patricia Edwina Victoria Knatchbull, *b.* 1924, *s.* 1979, *m.*	Lord Romsey, *b.* 1947.
c. 1235 s.	*Sutherland* (24th in line), Elizabeth Millicent Sutherland, *b.* 1921, *s.* 1963, *m.*	Lord Strathnaver, *b.* 1947.

BARONESSES IN THEIR OWN RIGHT

Style, The Baroness —— *Addressed as*, My Lady.

Created.	*Title, Name, etc.*	*Eldest Son or Heir.*
1421	*Berkeley* (17th in line), Mary Lalle Foley-Berkeley, *b.* 1905, *title called out of abeyance*, 1967.	Hon. Cynthia E. *Gueterbock*, *b.* 1909.
1455	*Berners* (15th in line), Vera Ruby Williams, *b.* 1901, *s.* 1950, *m.*	Two co-heiresses.
1529	*Braye* (8th in line), Mary Penelope Aubrey Fletcher, *b.* 1941, *s.* 1985, *m.*	Hon. Ambrose J. *Verney-Cave, b.* 1906.
1321	*Dacre* (27th in line), Rachel Leila Douglas-Home, *b.* 1929, *title called out of abeyance*, 1970, *m.*	Hon. James T. A. *D.-H., b.* 1952.
1332	*Darcy de Knayth* (18th in line), Davina Marcia Ingrams, *b.* 1938, *s.* 1943, *w.*	Hon. Caspar D. *I., b.* 1962.
1439	*Dudley* (14th in line), Barbara Amy Felicity Hamilton, *b.* 1907, *s.* 1972, *m.*	Hon. Jim. A. H. *Wallace, b.* 1930.
1490 s.	*Herries of Terregles* (14th in line), Anne Elizabeth Fitzalan-Howard, *b.* 1938, *s.* 1975.	Lady Mary K. *F.-H.*, C.V.O., *b.* 1940.
1602 s.	*Kinloss* (12th in line), Beatrice Mary Grenville Freeman-Grenville, *b.* 1922, *s.* 1944, *m.*	Master of Kinloss, *b.* 1953.
1663	*Lucas of Crudwell* (& *Scottish Lordship, Dingwall* 1609), Anne Rosemary Palmer, *b.* 1919, *s.* 1958, *m.*	Hon. Ralph M. *P., b.* 1951.
1681 s.	*Nairne* (12th in line), Katherine Evelyn Constance Bigham (*Katherine, Viscountess Mersey*), *b.* 1912, *s.* 1944, *m.*	Viscount Mersey, *b.* 1934 (*see* p. 235).
1945	*Portal of Hungerford* (2nd in line), Rosemary Ann Portal, *b.* 1923, *s.* 1971.	(None).
1445 s.	*Saltoun* (20th in line), Flora Marjory Fraser, *b.* 1930, *s.* 1979, *m.*	Hon. Katharine I. M. I. *F., b.* 1957.
1489 s.	*Sempill* (20th in line), Ann Moira Sempill, *b.* 1920, *s.* 1965, *m.*	Master of Sempill, *b.* 1949.
1628	*Strange* (16th in line), Jean Cherry Drummond of Megginch, *b.* 1928, *title called out of abeyance*, 1986, *m.*	Hon. Adam H. *D., b.* 1953.
1313	*Willoughby de Eresby* (27th in line), Nancy Jane Marie Heathcote-Drummond-Willoughby, *b.* 1934, *s.* 1983.	Two co-heiresses.

LIFE PEERS

Created under the Appellate Jurisdiction Act, 1876 (as amended)

BARONS

Created		
1986	*Ackner*, Desmond James Conrad Ackner, P.C., *b.* 1920, *m.*	Lord of Appeal in Ordinary.
1981	*Brandon of Oakbrook*, Henry Vivian Brandon, P.C., M.C., *b.* 1920, *m.*	Lord of Appeal in Ordinary.
1980	*Bridge of Harwich*, Nigel Cyprian Bridge, P.C., *b.* 1917, *m.*	Lord of Appeal in Ordinary.
1982	*Brightman*, John Anson Brightman, P.C., *b.* 1911, *m.*	Lord of Appeal in Ordinary.
1971	*Cross of Chelsea*, (Arthur) Geoffrey (Neale) Cross, P.C., *b.* 1904, *m.*	Lord of Appeal (retired).
1957	*Denning*, Alfred Thompson Denning, P.C., *b.* 1899, *m.*	Lord of Appeal (retired).
1961	*Devlin*, Patrick Arthur Devlin, P.C., F.B.A., *b.* 1905, *m.*	Lord of Appeal (retired).
1974	*Edmund-Davies*, (Herbert) Edmund Edmund-Davies, P.C., *b.* 1906, *m.*	Lord of Appeal (retired).
1975	*Fraser of Tullybelton*, Walter Ian Reid Fraser, P.C., *b.* 1911, *m.*	Lord of Appeal (retired).
1986	*Goff of Chieveley*, Robert Lionel Archibald Goff, P.C., *b.* 1926, *m.*	Lord of Appeal in Ordinary.
1985	*Griffiths*, (William) Hugh Griffiths, P.C., M.C., *b.* 1923, *m.*	Lord of Appeal in Ordinary.
1977	*Keith of Kinkel*, Henry Shanks Keith, P.C., *b.* 1922, *m.*	Lord of Appeal in Ordinary.
1971	*Kilbrandon*, Charles James Dalrymple Shaw, P.C., *b.* 1906, *m.*	Lord of Appeal (retired).
1979	*Lane*, Geoffrey Dawson Lane, P.C., A.F.C., *b.* 1918, *m.*	Lord of Appeal (Lord Chief Justice).
1986	*Oliver of Aylmerton*, Peter Raymond Oliver, P.C., *b.* 1921, *m.*	Lord of Appeal in Ordinary.
1962	*Pearce*, Edward Holroyd Pearce, P.C., *b.* 1901, *w.*	Lord of Appeal (retired).
1980	*Roskill*, Eustace Wentworth Roskill, P.C., *b.* 1911, *m.*	Lord of Appeal (retired).
1972	*Salmon*, Cyril Barnet Salmon, P.C., *b.* 1903, *m.*	Lord of Appeal (retired).
1977	*Scarman*, Leslie George Scarman, P.C., O.B.E., *b.* 1911, *m.*	Lord of Appeal (retired).
1982	*Templeman*, Sydney William Templeman, P.C., M.B.E., *b.* 1920, *m.*	Lord of Appeal in Ordinary.
1964	*Wilberforce*, Richard Orme Wilberforce, P.C., C.M.G., O.B.E., *b.* 1907, *m.*	Lord of Appeal (retired).

Created under Life Peerages Act, 1958

BARONS

† A number of Life Peerages were announced in the Dissolution Honours in July 1987 but titles had not been gazetted at the time of going to press.

1974 *Alexander of Potterhill*, William Picken Alexander, ph.d., b. 1905, m.
1976 *Allen of Abbeydale*, Philip Allen, g.c.b., b. 1912, m.
1961 *Alport*, Cuthbert James McCall Alport, p.c., t.d., b. 1912, w.
1965 *Annan*, Noel Gilroy Annan, o.b.e., b. 1916, m.
1970 *Ardwick*, John Cowburn Beavan, b. 1910, m.
1973 *Ashby*, Eric Ashby, d.sc., f.r.s., b. 1904, m.
†1987 *Atkins*, Humphrey Edward Gregory Atkins, p.c., k.c.m.g., b. 1922, m.
1967 *Aylestone*, Herbert William Bowden, p.c., c.h., c.b.e., b. 1905, m.
1982 *Bancroft*, Ian Powell Bancroft, g.c.b., b. 1922, m.
1974 *Banks*, Desmond Anderson Harvie Banks, c.b.e., b. 1918, m.
1974 *Barber*, Anthony Perrinott Lysberg Barber, p.c., t.d., b. 1920, w.
1983 *Barnett*, Joel Barnett, p.c., b. 1923, m.
1987 *Basnett*, David Basnett, b. 1924, m.
1982 *Bauer*, Prof. Peter Thomas Bauer, b. 1915.
1967 *Beaumont of Whitley*, Timothy Wentworth Beaumont, b. 1928, m.
1979 *Bellwin*, Irwin Norman Bellow, b. 1923, m.
1981 *Beloff*, Max Beloff, b. 1913, m.
1981 *Benson*, Henry Alexander Benson, g.b.e., b. 1909, m.
1969 *Bernstein*, Sidney Lewis Bernstein, b. 1899, m.
1971 *Blake*, Robert Norman William Blake, f.b.a., b. 1916, m.
1983 *Blanch*, Rt. Rev. Stuart Yarworth Blanch, p.c., b. 1918, m.
1978 *Blease*, William John Blease, b. 1914, m.
1964 *Blyton*, William Reid Blyton, b. 1899, m.
1980 *Boardman*, Thomas Gray Boardman, m.c., t.d., b. 1919, m.
1986 *Bonham-Carter*, Hon. Mark Raymond Bonham Carter, b. 1922, m.
1976 *Boston of Faversham*, Terence George Boston, q.c.,b. 1930, m.
1983 *Bottomley*, Arthur George Bottomley, p.c., o.b.e., b. 1907, m.
1963 *Bowden*, Bertram Vivian Bowden, ph.d., b. 1910.
1972 *Boyd-Carpenter*, John Archibald Boyd-Carpenter, p.c., b. 1908, m.
1987 *Bramall*, Edwin Noel Westby Bramall, g.c.b., o.b.e., m.c., *Field Marshal*, b. 1923, m.
1976 *Briggs*, Asa Briggs, b. 1921, m.
1974 *Briginshaw*, Richard William Briginshaw, m.
1976 *Brimelow*, Thomas Brimelow, g.c.m.g., o.b.e., b. 1915, m.
1964 *Brockway*, (Archibald) Fenner Brockway, b. 1888, m.
1975 *Brookes*, Raymond Percival Brookes, b. 1909, m.
1979 *Brooks of Tremorfa*, John Edward Brooks, b. 1927, m.
1983 *Broxbourne*, Derek Colclough Walker-Smith, p.c., t.d., q.c., b. 1910, m.
1974 *Bruce of Donington*, Donald William Trevor Bruce, b. 1912, m.
1983 *Bruce-Gardyne*, John, (Jock), Bruce-Gardyne, b. 1930, m.
1976 *Bullock*, Alan Louis Charles Bullock, f.b.a., b. 1914, m.
1985 *Butterworth*, John Blackstock Butterworth, c.b.e., b. 1918, m.
1978 *Buxton of Alsa*, Aubrey Leland Oakes Buxton, m.c., b. 1918, w.
1965 *Caccia*, Harold Anthony Caccia, g.c.m.g., g.c.v.o., b. 1905, m.
†1987 *Callaghan*, (Leonard) James Callaghan, k.g., p.c., b. 1912, m.
1984 *Cameron of Lochbroom*, Kenneth John Cameron, p.c., q.c., b. 1931, m.
1981 *Campbell of Alloway*, Alan Robertson Campbell, q.c., b. 1917, m.
1974 *Campbell of Croy*, Gordon Thomas Calthrop Campbell, p.c., m.c., b. 1921, m.
1966 *Campbell of Eskan*, John Middleton Campbell, b. 1912, w.
1964 *Caradon*, Hugh Mackintosh Foot, p.c., g.c.m.g., k.c.v.o., o.b.e., b. 1907, w.
†1987 *Carlisle*, Mark Carlisle, p.c., q.c., b. 1929, m.
1983 *Carmichael of Kelvingrove*, Neil George Carmichael, b. 1921, m.
1975 *Carr of Hadley*, (Leonard) Robert Carr, p.c., b. 1916, m.
1987 *Carter*, Denis Victor Carter.
1977 *Carver*, (Richard) Michael (Power) Carver, g.c.b., c.b.e., d.s.o., m.c., *Field Marshal*, b. 1915, m.
1982 *Cayzer*, (William) Nicholas Cayzer, b. 1910, m.
1964 *Chalfont*, (Alun) Arthur Gwynne Jones, p.c., o.b.e., m.c., b. 1919, m.
1985 *Chapple*, Frank Joseph Chapple, b. 1921, m.
1978 *Charteris of Amisfield*, Martin Michael Charles Charteris, p.c., g.c.b., g.c.v.o., o.b.e., b. 1913, m.
1963 *Chelmer*, Eric Cyril Boyd Edwards, m.c., t.d., b. 1914, m.
1974 *Chelwood*, Tufton Victor Hamilton Beamish, m.c., b. 1917, m.
1987 *Chilver*, (Amos) Henry Chilver, f.r.s., b. 1926, m.
1977 *Chitnis*, Pratap Chidamber Chitnis, b. 1936, m.
1979 *Cledwyn of Penrhos*, Cledwyn Hughes, p.c., c.h., b. 1916, m.
1978 *Cockfield*, (Francis) Arthur Cockfield, p.c., b. 1916, m.
†1987 *Cocks*, Michael Francis Lovell Cocks, p.c., b. 1929, m.
1980 *Coggan*, Rt. Rev. (Frederick) Donald Coggan, p.c., d.d., Royal Victorian Chain, b. 1909, m.
1964 *Collison*, Harold Francis Collison, c.b.e., b. 1909, m.
1981 *Constantine of Stanmore*, Theodore Constantine, c.b.e., b. 1910, m.
1966 *Cooper of Stockton Heath*, John Cooper, b. 1908, m.
1959 *Craigton*, Jack Nixon Browne, p.c., c.b.e., b. 1904, m.
1978 *Croham*, Douglas Albert Vivian Allen, g.c.b., b. 1917, m.
1974 *Cudlipp*, Hugh Cudlipp, o.b.e., b. 1913, m.

1979 *Dacre of Glanton*, Hugh Redwald Trevor-Roper, b. 1914, m.
1986 *Dainton*, Frederick Sydney Dainton, PH.D., SC.D., F.R.S., b. 1914, m.
1974 *Davies of Penrhys*, Gwilym Elfed Davies, b. 1913, m.
1983 *Dean of Beswick*, Joseph Jabez Dean, b. 1923.
1986 *Deedes*, William Francis Deedes, P.C., M.C., b. 1913, m.
1976 *Delfont*, Bernard Delfont, b. 1909, m.
1970 *Diamond*, John Diamond, P.C., b. 1907, m.
1967 *Donaldson of Kingsbridge*, John George Stuart Donaldson, O.B.E., b. 1907, m.
1985 *Donoughue*, Bernard Donoughue, b. 1934, m.
†1987 *Dormand*, John Donkin Dormand, b. 1919, m.
1974 *Duncan-Sandys*, Duncan Edwin Duncan-Sandys, P.C., C.H., b. 1908, m.
1983 *Eden of Winton*, John Benedict Eden, P.C., b. 1925, m.
†1987 *Edwards*, (Roger) Nicholas, P.C., b. 1934, m.
1985 *Elliott of Morpeth*, Robert William Elliott, b. 1920, m.
1972 *Elworthy*, (Samuel) Charles Elworthy, K.G., G.C.B., C.B.E., D.S.O., L.V.O., D.F.C., A.F.C., *Marshal of the Royal Air Force*, b. 1911, w.
1974 *Elwyn-Jones*, Frederick Elwyn-Jones, P.C., C.H., b. 1909, m.
1981 *Elystan-Morgan*, Dafydd Elystan Elystan-Morgan, b. 1932, m.
1980 *Emslie*, George Carlyle Emslie, P.C., M.B.E., b. 1919, m. (*Lord Justice-General of Scotland*).
1983 *Ennals*, David Hedley Ennals, P.C., b. 1922, m.
1978 *Evans of Claughton*, (David Thomas) Gruffydd Evans, b. 1928, m.
1983 *Ezra*, Derek Ezra, M.B.E., b. 1919, m.
1983 *Fanshawe of Richmond*, Anthony Henry Fanshawe Royle, K.C.M.G., b., 1927, m.
1958 *Ferrier*, Victor Ferrier Noel-Paton, E.D., b. 1900, m.
1983 *Fitt*, Gerard Fitt, b. 1926, m.
1970 *Fletcher*, Eric George Molyneux Fletcher, P.C., Ll.D., b. 1903, m.
1979 *Flowers*, Brian Hilton Flowers, F.R.S., b. 1924, m.
1967 *Foot*, John Mackintosh Foot, b. 1909, m.
1982 *Forte*, Charles Forte, b. 1908, m.
1962 *Franks*, Oliver Shewell Franks, O.M., G.C.M.G., K.C.B., K.C.V.O., C.B.E., P.C., F.B.A., b. 1905, m.
1974 *Fraser of Kilmorack*, (Richard) Michael Fraser, C.B.E., b. 1915, m.
1982 *Gallacher*, John Gallacher, b. 1920, m.
1979 *Galpern*, Myer Galpern, b. 1903.
1963 *Gardiner*, Gerald Austin Gardiner, P.C., C.H., b. 1900, m.
1975 *Gibson*, (Richard) Patrick (Tallentyre) Gibson, b. 1916, m.
1979 *Gibson-Watt*, (James) David Gibson-Watt, P.C., M.C., b. 1918, m.
1977 *Glenamara*, Edward Watson Short, P.C., C.H., b. 1912, m.
1965 *Goodman*, Arnold Abraham Goodman, C.H., b. 1913.
1987 *Goold*, James Duncan Goold, b. 1934, m.
1982 *Gormley*, Joseph Gormley, O.B.E., b. 1917, m.
1976 *Grade*, Lew Grade, b. 1906, m.
1983 *Graham of Edmonton*, (Thomas) Edward Graham, b.1925, m.
1967 *Granville of Eye*, Edgar Louis Granville, b. 1899, m.
1983 *Gray of Contin*, James (Hamish) Hector Northey Gray, P.C., b. 1927, m.
1974 *Greene of Harrow Weald*, Sidney Francis Greene, C.B.E., b. 1910, m.
1974 *Greenhill of Harrow*, Denis Arthur Greenhill, G.C.M.G., O.B.E., b. 1913, m.
1975 *Gregson*, John Gregson, b. 1924.
1968 *Grey of Naunton*, Ralph Francis Alnwick Grey, G.C.M.G., G.C.V.O., O.B.E., b. 1910, m.
1983 *Grimond*, Joseph Grimond, P.C., T.D., b. 1913, m.
1970 *Hailsham of St. Marylebone*, Quintin McGarel Hogg, P.C., C.H., b. 1907, m.
1983 *Hanson*, James Edward Hanson, b. 1922, m.
1974 *Harmar-Nicholls*, Harmar Harmar-Nicholls, b. 1912, m.
1974 *Harris of Greenwich*, John Henry Harris, b. 1930, m.
1979 *Harris of High Cross*, Ralph Harris, b. 1924, m.
1968 *Hartwell*, (William) Michael Berry, M.B.E., T.D., b. 1911, w.
1971 *Harvey of Prestbury*, Arthur Vere Harvey, C.B.E., b. 1906, m.
1974 *Harvington*, Robert Grant Grant-Ferris, P.C., b. 1907, m.
1978 *Hatch of Lusby*, John Charles Hatch, b. 1917.
1987 *Havers*, (Robert) Michael (Oldfield) Havers, P.C., b. 1923, m. (*Lord High Chancellor*).
1983 *Henderson of Brompton*, Peter Gordon Henderson, K.C.B., b. 1922, m.
1967 *Heycock*, Llewellyn Heycock, C.B.E., b. 1905, m.
1963 *Hill of Luton*, Charles Hill, P.C., M.D., b. 1904, m.
1979 *Hill-Norton*, Peter John Hill-Norton, G.C.B., *Admiral of the Fleet*, b. 1915, m.
1967 *Hirshfield*, Desmond Barel Hirshfield, b. 1913, m.
1979 *Holderness*, Richard Frederick Wood, P.C., b. 1920, m.
1974 *Home of the Hirsel*, Alexander Frederick Douglas-Home, P.C., K.T., b. 1903, m.
1979 *Hooson*, (Hugh) Emlyn Hooson, Q.C., b. 1925, m.
1974 *Houghton of Sowerby*, (Arthur Leslie Noel) Douglas Houghton, P.C., C.H., b. 1898, m.
1978 *Howie of Troon*, William Howie, b. 1924, m.
1961 *Hughes*, William Hughes, P.C., C.B.E., b. 1911, m.
1966 *Hunt*, (Henry Cecil) John Hunt, K.G., C.B.E., D.S.O., b. 1910, m.
1973 *Hunt of Fawley*, John Henderson Hunt, b.B.E., D.M., b. 1905, m.
1980 *Hunt of Tanworth*, John Joseph Benedict Hunt, G.C.B., b. 1919, m.
1978 *Hunter of Newington*, Robert Brockie Hunter, M.B.E., F.R.C.P., b. 1915, m.
1978 *Hutchinson of Lullington*, Jeremy Nicolas Hutchinson, Q.C., b. 1915, m.
1982 *Ingrow*, John Aked Taylor, O.B.E., T.D., b. 1917, m.
1987 *Irvine of Lairg*, Alexander Andrew Mackay Irvine, Q.C., b. 1940, m.

1979 *Irving of Dartford*, Sydney Irving, P.C., *b.* 1918, *m.*
1975 *Jacobson*, Sydney Jacobson, M.C., *b.* 1908, *m.*
1968 *Jacques*, John Henry Jacques, *b.* 1905, *m.*
1959 *James of Rusholme*, Eric John Francis James, *b.* 1909, *m.*
†1987 *Jay*, Douglas Patrick Thomas Jay, P.C., *b.* 1907, *m.*
†1987 *Jenkin*, (Charles) Patrick (Fleeming) Jenkin, P.C., *b.* 1926, *m.*
†1987 *Jenkins*, Roy Harris Jenkins, P.C., *b.* 1920, *m.*
1981 *Jenkins of Putney*, Hugh Gater Jenkins, *b.* 1908, *m.*
1981 *John-Mackie*, John John-Mackie, *b.* 1909, *m.*
1987 *Johnston of Rockport*, Charles Collier Johnston, T.D., *b.* 1915, *m.*
†1987 *Joseph*, Keith Sinjohn Joseph, P.C., C.H., *b.* 1918.
1983 *Kaberry of Adel*, Donald Kaberry, T.D., *b.* 1907, *m.*
1981 *Kadoorie*, Lawrence Kadoorie, C.B.E., *b.* 1899, *m.*
1976 *Kagan*, Joseph Kagan, *b.* 1915, *m.*
1965 *Kahn*, Richard Ferdinand Kahn, C.B.E., F.B.A., *b.* 1905.
1970 *Kearton*, (Christopher) Frank Kearton, O.B.E., F.R.S., *b.* 1911, *m.*
1980 *Keith of Castleacre*, Kenneth Alexander Keith, *b.* 1916, *m.*
1985 *Kimball*, Marcus Richard Kimball, *b.* 1928, *m.*
1983 *King of Wartnaby*, John Leonard King, *m.*
1965 *Kings Norton*, Harold Roxbee Cox, PH.D., *b.* 1902, *m.*
1975 *Kirkhill*, John Farquharson Smith, *b.* 1930, *m.*
1974 *Kissin*, Harry Kissin, *b.* 1912, *m.*
1987 *Knights*, Philip Douglas Knights, C.B.E., Q.P.M., *b.* 1920, *m.*
1964 *Leatherland*, Charles Edward Leatherland, O.B.E., *b.* 1898, *m.*
1979 *Lever of Manchester*, Harold Lever, P.C., *b.* 1914, *m.*
1982 *Lewin*, Terence Thornton Lewin, K.G., G.C.B., L.V.O., D.S.C., *Admiral of the Fleet*, *b.* 1920, *m.*
1965 *Lloyd of Hampstead*, Dennis Lloyd, Q.C., LL.D., *b.* 1915, *m.*
1973 *Lloyd of Kilgerran*, Rhys Gerran Lloyd, C.B.E., Q.C., *b.* 1907, *m.*
1974 *Lovell-Davis*, Peter Lovell Lovell-Davis, *b.* 1924, *m.*
1979 *Lowry*, Robert Lynd Erskine Lowry, P.C., *b.* 1919, *w.* (*Lord Chief Justice of Northern Ireland*).
1980 *McAlpine of Moffat*, (Robert) Edwin McAlpine, *b.* 1907, *w.*
1983 *McAlpine of West Green*, (Robert) Alistair McAlpine, *b.* 1942, *m.*
1975 *McCarthy*, William Edward John McCarthy, *b.* 1925, *m.*
1976 *McCluskey*, John Herbert McCluskey, Q.C., *b.* 1929, *m.*
1966 *McFadzean*, William Hunter McFadzean, K.T., *b.* 1903, *m.*
1980 *McFadzean of Kelvinside*, Francis Scott McFadzean, *b.* 1915, *m.*
1978 *McGregor of Durris*, Oliver Ross McGregor, *b.* 1921, *m.*
1982 *McIntosh of Haringey*, Andrew Robert McIntosh, *b.* 1933, *m.*
1979 *Mackay of Clashfern*, James Peter Hymers Mackay, P.C., Q.C., *b.* 1927, *m.* (*Lord of Appeal*).
1974 *Mackie of Benshie*, George Yull Mackie, C.B.E., D.S.O., D.F.C., *b.* 1919, *w.*
1971 *Maclean*, Charles Hector Fitzroy Maclean, P.C., K.T., G.C.V.O., K.B.E., Royal Victorian Chain, *b.* 1916, *m.*
1982 *MacLehose of Beoch*, (Crawford) Murray MacLehose, K.T., G.B.E., K.C.M.G., K.C.V.O., *b.* 1917, *m.*
1967 *MacLeod of Fuinary*, Very Rev. George Fielden MacLeod, M.C., D.D., *b.* 1895, *m.*
1967 *Mais*, Alan Raymond Mais, G.B.E., T.D., E.R.D., *b.* 1911, *m.*
1981 *Marsh*, Richard William Marsh, P.C., *b.* 1928, *m.*
1985 *Marshall of Goring*, Walter Charles Marshall, C.B.E., F.R.S., *b.* 1932, *m.*
1980 *Marshall of Leeds*, Frank Shaw Marshall, *b.* 1915, *m.*
†1987 *Mason*, Roy Mason, P.C., *b.* 1924, *m.*
1980 *Matthews*, Victor Collin Matthews, *b.* 1919, *m.*
1983 *Maude of Stratford-upon-Avon*, Angus Edmund Upton Maude, P.C., T.D., *b.* 1912, *m.*
1981 *Mayhew*, Christopher Paget Mayhew, *b.* 1915, *m.*
1985 *Mellish*, Robert Joseph Mellish, P.C., *b.* 1913, *m.*
1979 *Miles*, Bernard James Miles, C.B.E., *b.* 1907, *m.*
1978 *Mishcon*, Victor Mishcon, *b.* 1915, *m.*
1981 *Molloy*, William John Molloy, *b.* 1918, *m.*
1961 *Molson*, (Arthur) Hugh (Elsdale) Molson, P.C., *b.* 1903, *m.*
1986 *Moore of Wolvercote*, Philip Brian Cecil Moore, G.C.B., G.C.V.O., C.M.G., P.C., *b.* 1921, *m.*
1967 *Morris of Grasmere*, Charles Richard Morris, K.C.M.G., *b.* 1898, *m.*
1985 *Morton of Shuna*, Hugh Drennan Baird Morton, Q.C., *b.* 1930, *m.*
1971 *Moyola*, James Dawson Chichester-Clark, P.C. (N.I.), *b.* 1923, *m.*
1983 *Mulley*, Frederick William Mulley, P.C., *b.* 1918, *m.*
1985 *Murray of Epping Forest*, Lionel Murray, P.C., O.B.E., *b.* 1922, *m.*
1964 *Murray of Newhaven*, Keith Anderson Hope Murray, K.C.B., PH.D., *b.* 1903.
1979 *Murton of Lindisfarne*, (Henry) Oscar Murton, P.C., O.B.E., T.D., *b.* 1914, *m.*
1975 *Northfield*, (William) Donald Chapman, *b.* 1923.
1966 *Nugent of Guildford*, (George) Richard (Hodges) Nugent, P.C., *b.* 1907, *m.*
1973 *O'Brien of Lothbury*, Leslie Kenneth O'Brien, P.C., G.B.E., *b.* 1908, *m.*
1970 *Olivier*, Laurence Kerr Olivier, O.M., *b.* 1907, *m.*
1970 *O'Neill of the Maine*, Terence Marne O'Neill, P.C (N.I.), *b.* 1914, *m.*
1976 *Oram*, Albert Edward Oram, *b.* 1913, *m.*
1971 *Orr-Ewing*, (Charles) Ian Orr-Ewing, O.B.E., *b.* 1912, *m.*
1974 *Paget of Northampton*, Reginald Thomas Paget, Q.C., *b.* 1908, *m.*
1975 *Parry*, Gordon Samuel David Parry, *b.* 1925, *m.*
1976 *Peart*, (Thomas) Frederick Peart, P.C., *b.* 1914, *m.*
1967 *Penney*, William George Penney, O.M., K.B.E., PH.D., D.SC., F.R.S., *b.* 1909, *m.*
1982 *Pennock*, Raymond (William) Pennock, *b.* 1920, *m.*
1979 *Perry of Walton*, Walter Laing Macdonald Perry, O.B.E., M.D., D.SC., F.R.S.E., F.R.C.P., *b.* 1921, *m.*

1987 *Peston*, Maurice Harry Peston.
1983 *Peyton of Yeovil*, John Wynne William Peyton, P.C., b. 1919, m.
1975 *Pitt of Hampstead*, David Thomas Pitt, b. 1913, m.
1959 *Plowden*, Edwin Noel Plowden, K.C.B., G.B.E., b. 1907, m.
1987 *Plumb*, Charles Henry Plumb, b. 1925, m.
1981 *Plummer of St. Marylebone*, (Arthur) Desmond (Herne) Plummer, T.D., b. 1914, m.
1973 *Porritt*, Arthur Espie Porritt, G.C.M.G., G.C.V.O., C.B.E., b. 1900, m.
†1987 *Prior*, James Michael Leathes Prior, P.C., b. 1927, m.
1975 *Pritchard*, Derek Wilbraham Pritchard, b. 1910, m.
1982 *Prys-Davies*, Gwilym Prys Prys-Davies, b. 1923, m.
†1987 *Pym*, Francis Leslie Pym, P.C., M.C., b. 1922, m.
1982 *Quinton*, Anthony Meredith Quinton, b. 1925, m.
1974 *Ramsey of Canterbury*, Rt. Rev. Arthur Michael Ramsey, P.C., D.D., Royal Victorian Chain, b. 1904, m.
1978 *Rawlinson of Ewell*, Peter Anthony Grayson Rawlinson, P.C., Q.C., b. 1919, m.
1976 *Rayne*, Max Rayne, b. 1918, m.
1983 *Rayner*, Derek George Rayner, b. 1926.
†1987 *Rees*, Peter Wynford Innes Rees, P.C., Q.C., b. 1926, m.
1970 *Reigate*, John Kenyon Vaughan-Morgan, P.C., b. 1905, m.
1978 *Reilly*, Paul Reilly, b. 1912, m.
1979 *Renton*, David Lockhart-Mure Renton, P.C., K.B.E., T.D., Q.C., b. 1908, w.
1964 *Rhodes*, Hervey Rhodes, K.G., P.C., D.F.C., b. 1895, w.
1979 *Richardson*, John Samuel Richardson, L.V.O., M.D., F.R.C.P., b. 1910, m.
1983 *Richardson of Duntisbourne*, Gordon William Humphreys Richardson, K.G., P.C., M.B.E., T.D, b. 1915, m.
†1987 *Rippon*, (Aubrey) Geoffrey (Frederick) Rippon, P.C., Q.C., b. 1924, m.
1961 *Robens of Woldingham*, Alfred Robens, P.C., b. 1910, m.
1969 *Roberthall*, Robert Lowe Roberthall, K.C.M.G., C.B., b. 1901, m.
1977 *Roll of Ipsden*, Eric Roll, K.C.M.G., C.B., b. 1907, m.
†1987 *Ross*, Stephen Sherlock Ross, b. 1926, m.
1979 *Ross of Marnock*, William Ross, P.C., M.B.E., b. 1911, m.
1975 *Ryder of Eaton Hastings*, Sydney Thomas Franklin (Don) Ryder, b. 1916, m.
1962 *Sainsbury*, Alan John Sainsbury, b. 1902, m.
1977 *Saint Brides*, John Morrice Cairns James, P.C., G.C.M.G., C.V.O., M.B.E., b. 1916, m.
†1987 *St. John-Stevas*, Norman Antony Francis St. John-Stevas, P.C., b. 1929.
1985 *Sanderson of Bowden*, Charles Russell Sanderson, b. 1933, m.
1979 *Scanlon*, Hugh Parr Scanlon, b. 1913, m.
1976 *Schon*, Frank Schon, b. 1912, m.
1972 *Seebohm*, Frederic Seebohm, T.D., b. 1909, m.
1978 *Sefton of Garston*, William Henry Sefton, b. 1915, m.
1958 *Shackleton*, Edward Arthur Alexander Shackleton, K.G., P.C., O.B.E., b. 1911, m.
1959 *Shawcross*, Hartley William Shawcross, P.C., G.B.E., Q.C., b. 1902, w.
1980 *Sieff of Brimpton*, Marcus Joseph Sieff, O.B.E., b. 1918, m.
1985 *Silkin of Dulwich*, Samuel Charles Silkin, P.C., Q.C, b. 1918, m.
1971 *Simon of Glaisdale*, Jocelyn Edward Salis Simon, P.C., b. 1911, m. (*Lord of Appeal, retired*).
1978 *Smith*, Rodney Smith, K.B.E., F.R.C.S., b. 1914, m.
1978 *Soames*, (Arthur) Christopher (John) Soames, P.C., C.H., G.C.M.G., G.C.V.O., C.B.E., b. 1920, m.
1965 *Soper*, Rev. Donald Oliver Soper, PH.D., b. 1903, m.
1983 *Stallard*, Albert William Stallard, b. 1921, m.
1987 *Stevens of Ludgate*, David Robert Stevens, b. 1936, m.
1979 *Stewart of Fulham*, Robert Michael Maitland Stewart, P.C., C.H., b. 1906, w.
1981 *Stodart of Leaston*, James Anthony Stodart, P.C., b. 1916, m.
1983 *Stoddart of Swindon*, David Leonard Stoddart, b. 1926, m.
1969 *Stokes*, Donald Gresham Stokes, T.D., b. 1914, m.
1979 *Strauss*, George Russell Strauss, P.C., b. 1901, m.
1981 *Swann*, Michael Meredith Swann, PH.D., F.R.S., b. 1920, m.
1971 *Tanlaw*, Simon Brooke Mackay, b. 1934, m.
1958 *Taylor*, Stephen James Lake Taylor, M.D., b. 1910, m.
1978 *Taylor of Blackburn*, Thomas Taylor, C.B.E., b. 1929, m.
1968 *Taylor of Gryfe*, Thomas Johnston Taylor, b. 1912, m.
1982 *Taylor of Hadfield*, Francis Taylor, b. 1905, m.
1966 *Taylor of Mansfield*, Harry Bernard Taylor, C.B.E., b. 1895, w.
†1987 *Thomas*, Peter John Mitchell Thomas, P.C., Q.C., b. 1920, w.
1981 *Thomas of Swynnerton*, Hugh Swynnerton Thomas, b. 1931, m.
1977 *Thomson of Monifieth*, George Morgan Thomson, P.C., K.T., b. 1921, m.
1967 *Thorneycroft*, (George Edward) Peter Thorneycroft, P.C., C.H., b. 1909, m.
1962 *Todd*, Alexander Robertus Todd, O.M., D.SC., D.Phil., F.R.S., b. 1907, w.
1981 *Tordoff*, Geoffrey Johnson Tordoff, b. 1928, m.
1987 *Trafford*, Joseph Anthony Porteous Trafford, b. 1932, m.
1974 *Tranmire*, Robert Hugh Turton, P.C., K.B.E., M.C., b. 1903, m.
1979 *Underhill*, (Henry) Reginall Underhill, C.B.E., b. 1914, m.
1985 *Vinson*, Nigel Vinson, L.V.O., b. 1931, m.
1964 *Wade*, Donald William Wade, b. 1904, m.
1974 *Wallace of Campsie*, George Wallace, b. 1915, m.
1974 *Wallace of Coslany*, George Douglas Wallace, b. 1906, m.
1961 *Walston*, Henry David Leonard George Walston, C.V.O., b. 1912, m.
1972 *Watkins*, Tudor Elwyn Watkins, b. 1903, m.
1977 *Wedderburn of Charlton*, Kenneth William Wedderburn, b. 1927, m.
1976 *Weidenfeld*, (Arthur) George Weidenfeld, b. 1919.

1980   *Weinstock*, Arnold Weinstock, *b.* 1924, *m.*
1965   *Wells-Pestell*, Reginald Alfred Wells-Pestell, *b.* 1910, *m.*
1978   *Whaddon*, John Derek Page, *b.* 1927, *m.*
1970   *Wheatley*, John Wheatley, P.C., *b.* 1908, *m.*
1974   *Wigoder*, Basil Thomas Wigoder, Q.C., *b.* 1921, *m.*
1985   *Williams of Elvel*, Charles Cuthbert Powell Williams, C.B.E., *b.* 1933, *m.*
1963   *Willis*, Edward Henry Willis, *b.* 1918, *m.*
1969   *Wilson of Langside*, Henry Stephen Wilson, P.C., Q.C., *b.* 1916, *m.*
1983   *Wilson of Rievaulx*, (James) Harold Wilson, K.G., P.C., O.B.E., F.R.S., *b.* 1916, *m.*
1975   *Winstanley*, Michael Platt Winstanley, *b.* 1918, *m.*
1965   *Winterbottom*, Ian Winterbottom, *b.* 1913, *m.*
1985   *Wolfson*, Leonard Gordon Wolfson, *b.* 1927, *m.*
1987   *Wyatt of Weeford*, Woodrow Lyle Wyatt, *b.* 1918, *m.*
1978   *Young of Dartington*, Michael Young, PH.D., *b.* 1915, *m.*
1984   *Young of Graffham*, David Ivor Young, P.C., *b.* 1932, *m.*
1971   *Zuckerman*, Solly Zuckerman, O.M., K.C.B., F.R.S., M.D., D.SC., *b.* 1904, *m.*

BARONESSES

1979   *Airey of Abingdon*, Diana Josceline Barbara Neave Airey, *b.* 1919, *w.*
1970   *Bacon*, Alice Martha Bacon, P.C., C.B.E., *b.* 1911.
1967   *Birk*, Alma Birk, *b.* 1921, *m.*
1987   *Blackstone*, Tessa Ann Vosper Blackstone, PH.D., *b.* 1942.
1987   *Blatch*, Emily May Blatch, C.B.E.
1964   *Brooke of Ystradfellte*, Barbara Muriel Brooke, D.B.E., *b.* 1908, *w.*
1962   *Burton of Coventry*, Elaine Frances Burton, *b.* 1904.
1982   *Carnegy of Lour*, Elizabeth Patricia Carnegy of Lour, *b.* 1925.
1982   *Cox*, Caroline Anne Cox, *b.* 1937, *m.*
1978   *David*, Nora Ratcliff David, *b.* 1913, *m.*
1974   *Delacourt-Smith of Alteryn*, Margaret Rosalind Delacourt-Smith, *b.* 1916, *m.*
1978   *Denington*, Evelyn Joyce Denington, D.B.E., *b.* 1907, *m.*
1972   *Elles*, Diana Louie Elles, *b.* 1921, *m.*
1958   *Elliot of Harwood*, Katharine Elliot, D.B.E., *b.* 1903, *w.*
1981   *Ewart-Biggs*, (Felicity) Jane Ewart-Biggs, *b.* 1929, *w.*
1975   *Faithfull*, Lucy Faithfull, O.B.E., *b.* 1910.
1974   *Falkender*, Marcia Matilda Falkender, C.B.E., *b.* 1932.
1974   *Fisher of Rednal*, Doris Mary Gertrude Fisher, *b.* 1919, *w.*
1963   *Gaitskell*, Anna Dora Gaitskell, *w.*
1981   *Gardner of Parkes*, (Rachel) Trixie (Anne) Gardner, *b.* 1927, *m.*
1985   *Hooper*, Gloria Hooper, *b.* 1939.
†1987   *Hart*, Judith Constance Mary Hart, P.C., D.B.E., *b.* 1924, *m.*
1965   *Hylton-Foster*, Audrey Pellew Hylton-Foster, *b.* 1908, *w.*
1979   *Jeger*, Lena May Jeger, *b.* 1915, *w.*
1981   *Lane-Fox*, Felicity Lane-Fox, O.B.E., *b.* 1918.
1970   *Lee of Asheridge*, Janet Bevan, P.C., *b.* 1904, *w.*
1967   *Llewelyn-Davies of Hastoe*, Annie Patricia Llewelyn-Davies, P.C., *b.* 1915, *w.*
1978   *Lockwood*, Betty Lockwood, *b.* 1924, *m.*
1979   *McFarlane of Llandaff*, Jean Kennedy McFarlane, *b.* 1926.
1971   *Macleod of Borve*, Evelyn Hester Macleod, *b.* 1915, *w.*
1970   *Masham of Ilton*, Susan Lilian Primrose Cunliffe-Lister, *b.* 1935, *m.* (*Countess of Swinton*).
1982   *Nicol*, Olive Mary Wendy Nicol, *b.* 1923, *m.*
1964   *Phillips*, Norah Phillips, *b.* 1910, *w.*
1974   *Pike*, (Irene) Mervyn (Parnicott) Pike, D.B.E., *b.* 1918.
1981   *Platt of Writtle*, Beryl Catherine Platt, C.B.E., *b.* 1923, *m.*
1974   *Robson of Kiddington*, Inga-Stina Robson, *b.* 1919, *w.*
1979   *Ryder of Warsaw*, (Sue Ryder), C.M.G., O.B.E., *b.* 1924, *m.*
1971   *Seear*, (Beatrice) Nancy Seear, P.C., *b.* 1913.
1967   *Serota*, Beatrice Serota, *b.* 1919, *m.*
1973   *Sharples*, Pamela Sharples, *b.* 1923, *m.*
1974   *Stedman*, Phyllis Stedman, O.B.E., *b.* 1916, *m.*
1980   *Trumpington*, Jean Alys Barker, *b.* 1922, *m.*
1985   *Turner of Camden*, Muriel Winifred Turner.
1974   *Vickers*, Joan Helen Vickers, D.B.E., *b.* 1907.
1985   *Warnock*, Helen Mary Warnock, D.B.E., *b.* 1924, *m.*
1970   *White*, Eirene Lloyd White, *b.* 1909, *w.*
1958   *Wootton of Abinger*, Barbara Frances Wright, C.H., *b.* 1897, *w.*
1971   *Young*, Janet Mary Young, P.C., *b.* 1926, *m.*

COURTESY TITLES

Holders of Courtesy Titles are addressed in the same manner as holders of substantive titles.

From this list it will be seen that, for example, the "Marquess of Blandford" *is heir to the Dukedom of Marlborough*, and "Viscount Althorp" *to the Earldom of Spencer. Titles of second heirs are also given, and the Courtesy Title of the father of a second heir is indicated by* *; *e.g.,* Earl of Burlington, *eldest son of* *Marquess of Hartington.

Marquesses

Blandford—*Marlborough*
Bowmont—*Roxburghe*
Douglas and Clydesdale—*Hamilton*
*Douro—*Wellington*
*Graham—*Montrose*
Granby—*Rutland*
Hamilton—*Abercorn*
*Hartington—*Devonshire*
*Kildare—*Leinster*
Lorne—*Argyll*
*Tavistock—*Bedford*
Worcester—*Beaufort*

Earls

*Aboyne—*Huntly*
Altamont—*Sligo*
Ancram—*Lothian*
Arundel and Surrey—*Norfolk*
Bective—*Headfort*
Belfast—*Donegall*
*Brecknock—*Camden*
*Burford—*St. Albans*
Burlington—*Hartington
Cardigan—*Ailesbury*
Cassillis—*Ailsa*
Compton—*Northampton*
Dalkeith—*Buccleuch*
Dumfries—*Bute*
*Euston—*Grafton*
Haddo—*Aberdeen and Temair*
*Hopetoun—*Linlithgow*
Jermyn—*Bristol*
Macduff—*Fife*
*March and Kinrara—*Richmond*
*Mount Charles—*Conyngham*
Mornington—*Douro
Mulgrave—*Normanby*
Offaly—*Kildare
Percy—*Northumberland*
Rocksavage—*Cholmondeley*
*Ronaldshay—*Zetland*
St. Andrews—*Kent*
*Shelburne—*Lansdowne*
Tyrone—*Waterford*
Ulster—*Gloucester*
Uxbridge—*Anglesey*
Wiltshire—*Winchester*
Yarmouth—*Hertford*

Viscounts

Aithrie—*Hopetoun
Althorp—*Spencer*
Andover—*Suffolk and Berkshire*
Anson—*Lichfield*
Asquith—*Oxford & Asquith*
Bayham—*Brecknock
Boringdon—*Morley*
Borodale—*Beatty*
Boyle—*Shannon*
Brocas—*Jellicoe*
Calne and Calstone—*Shelburne
Campden—*Gainsborough*
Carlow—*Portarlington*
Castlereagh—*Londonderry*
Chelsea—*Cadogan*
Chewton—*Waldegrave*
Clanfield—*Peel*
Coke—*Leicester*
Cole—*Enniskillen*
Corry—*Belmore*
Corvedale—*Baldwin of Bewdley*
Cranborne—*Salisbury*
Cranley—*Onslow*
Crichton—*Erne*
Crowhurst—*Cottenham*
Dalrymple—*Stair*
Dawick—*Haig*
Deerhurst—*Coventry*
Drumlanrig—*Queensberry*
Dunwich—*Stradbroke*
Dupplin—*Kinnoull*
Ebrington—*Fortescue*
Ednam—*Dudley*
Elveden—*Iveagh*
Emlyn—*Cawdor*
Encombe—*Eldon*
Ennismore—*Listowel*
Enfield—*Strafford*
Erleigh—*Reading*
Errington—*Cromer*
Feilding—*Denbigh*
Fincastle—*Dunmore*
FitzClarence—*Munster*
FitzHarris—*Malmesbury*
Folkestone—*Radnor*
Garmoyle—*Cairns*
Garnock—*Lindsay*
Glandine—*Norbury*
Glenapp—*Inchcape*
Glentworth—*Limerick*
Grimston—*Verulam*
Gwynedd—*Lloyd George of Dwyfor*
Hawkesbury—*Liverpool*
Ikerrin—*Carrick*
Ingestre—*Shrewsbury*

Ipswich—*Euston
Jocelyn—*Roden*
Kelburn—*Glasgow*
Kingsborough—*Kingston*
Knebworth—*Lytton*
Kynnaird—*Newburgh*
Lascelles—*Harewood*
Lewisham—*Dartmouth*
Linley—*Snowdon*
Loftus—*Ely*
Lowther—*Lonsdale*
Lumley—*Scarbrough*
Lymington—*Portsmouth*
Macmillan of Ovenden—*Stockton*
Maidstone — *Winchilsea and Nottingham*
Maitland—*Lauderdale*
Malden—*Essex*
Mandeville—*Manchester*
Melgund—*Minto*
Merton—*Nelson*
Moore—*Drogheda*
Morpeth—*Carlisle*
Newport—*Bradford*
Newry and Mourne—*Kilmorey*
Parker—*Macclesfield*
Perceval—*Egmont*
Petersham—*Harrington*
Pollington—*Mexborough*
Prestwood—*Attlee*
Quenington—*St. Aldwyn*
Raynham—*Townshend*
Reidhaven—*Seafield*
Ruthven of Canberra and Dirleton—*Gowrie*
St. Cyres—*Iddesleigh*
Sandon—*Harrowby*
Slane—*Mount Charles
Stormont—*Mansfield*
Strathallan—*Perth*
Stuart—*Castle Stewart*
Sudley—*Arran*
Suirdale—*Donoughmore*
Tamworth—*Ferrers*
Tarbat—*Cromartie*
Tiverton—*Halsbury*
Vaughan—*Lisburne*
Villiers—*Jersey*
Weymouth—*Bath*
Windsor—*Plymouth*
Wolmer—*Selborne*

Barons (Lord—)

Aberdour—*Morton*
Apsley—*Bathurst*
Ardee—*Meath*
Ashley—*Shaftesbury*

Balgonie—*Leven & Melville*
Berriedale—*Caithness*
Bingham—*Lucan*
Binning—*Haddington*
Brooke—*Warwick*
Bruce—*Elgin*
Buckhurst—*De La Warr*
Burghersh—*Westmorland*
Burghley—*Exeter*
Cardross—*Buchan*
Clifton—*Darnley*
Cochrane—*Dundonald*
Courtenay—*Devon*
Dalmeny—*Rosebery*
Delvin—*Westmeath*
Doune—*Moray*
Dundas—*Ronaldshay
Eliot—*St. Germans*
Erskine—*Mar & Kellie*
Fintrie—*Graham
Glamis—*Strathmore*
Greenock—*Cathcart*
Guernsey—*Aylesford*
Hay—*Erroll*
Herbert—*Pembroke*
Howland—*Tavistock
Hyde—*Clarendon*
Inverurie—*Kintore*
Irwin—*Halifax*
Leslie—*Rothes*
Leveson—*Granville*
Mauchline—*Loudoun*
Medway—*Cranbrook*
Montgomerie—*Eglinton and Winton*
Moreton—*Ducie*
Naas—*Mayo*
Neidpath—*Wemyss & March*
Norreys—*Lindsey & Abingdon*
North—*Guilford*
Ogilvy—*Airlie*
Oxmantown—*Rosse*
Porchester—*Carnarvon*
Ramsay—*Dalhousie*
Romsey—*Mountbatten of Burma*
Rosehill—*Northesk*
Scrymgeour—*Dundee*
Settrington—**March and Kinrara*
Seymour—*Somerset*
Silchester—*Longford*
Strathavon and Glenlivet—*Aboyne
Strathnaver—*Sutherland*
Vere of Hanworth—*Burford
Wodehouse—*Kimberley*
Worsley—*Yarborough*

Surnames of Peers and Peeresses differing from their Titles

Abney Hastings—Loudoun
Acheson—Gosford
Adderley—Norton
Addington—Sidmouth
Agar—Normanton
Akers Douglas—Chilston
Alexander—Alexander of Potterhill*
Alexander—Alexander of Tunis
Alexander—Caledon
Allen—Allen of Abbeydale*
Allen—Croham*
Allanson Winn—Headley
Allsopp—Hindlip
Aman—Marley
Anderson—Waverley
Annesley—Valentia
Anson—Lichfield
Armstrong Jones—Snowdon
Arthur—Glenarthur
Ashley Cooper—Shaftesbury
Ashton—Ashton of Hyde
Asquith—Oxford & A.
Assheton—Clitheroe
Astley—Hastings
Astor—Astor of Hever
Aubrey Fletcher—Braye
Bailey—Glanusk
Baillie—Burton
Baille Hamilton—Haddington
Baldwin—Baldwin of Bewdley
Balfour—Kinross
Balfour—Riverdale
Balfour—Balfour of Inchrye
Bampfylde—Poltimore
Banbury—Banbury of Southam
Baring—Ashburton
Baring—Cromer
Baring—Howick of Glendale
Baring—Northbrook
Baring—Revelstoke
Barker—Trumpington*
Barnes—Gorell
Barnewall—Trimlestown
Bathurst—Bledisloe
Beamish—Chelwood*
Beauclerk—St. Albans
Beaumont—Allendale
Beaumont—Beaumont of Whitley*
Beavan—Ardwick*
Beckett—Grimthorpe
Bellow—Bellwin*
Bennet—Tankerville
Beresford—Decies
Beresford—Waterford
Berry—Camrose
Berry—Hartwell*
Berry—Kemsley
Bertie—Lindsey
Best—Wynford
Bethell—Westbury
Bevan—Lee of Asheridge*

Bewicke Copley—Cromwell
Bigham—Mersey
Bigham—Nairne
Bingham—Clanmorris
Bingham—Lucan
Blades—Ebbisham
Bligh—Darnley
Bootle Wilbraham—Skelmersdale
Boscawen—Falmouth
Boston—Boston of Faversham*
Bourke—Mayo
Bowden—Aylestone*
Bowes Lyon—Strathmore
Bowyer—Denham
Boyd—Kilmarnock
Boyle—Cork and Orrery
Boyle—Glasgow
Boyle—Shannon
Brabazon—Meath
Brand—Hampden
Brassey—Brassey of Apethorpe
Brett—Esher
Bridgeman—Bradford
Brodrick—Midleton
Brooke—Alanbrooke
Brooke—Brooke of Ystradfellte*
Brooke—Brookeborough
Brooks—Brooks of Tremorfa*
Brooks—Crawshaw
Brougham—Brougham and Vaux
Broughton—Fairhaven
Browne—Craigton*
Browne—Kilmaine
Browne—Oranmore and Browne
Browne—Sligo
Brownlow—Lurgan
Bruce—Aberdare
Bruce—Balfour of Burleigh
Bruce—Bruce of Donington*
Bruce—Elgin and Kincardine
Brudenell Bruce—Ailesbury
Buchan—Tweedsmuir
Buckley—Wrenbury
Burton—Burton of Coventry*
Butler—Carrick
Butler—Dunboyne
Butler—Lanseborough
Butler—Mountgarret
Butler—Ormonde
Buxton—Buxton of Alsa*
Buxton—Noel-Buxton
Byng—Strafford
Byng—Torrington
Cameron—Cameron of Lochbroom*
Campbell—Argyll
Campbell—Breadalbane and Holland
Campbell—Campbell of Alloway*

Campbell—Campbell of Croy*
Campbell—Campbell of Eskan*
Campbell—Cawdor
Campbell—Colgrain
Campbell—Stratheden and Campbell
Campbell Gray—Gray
Canning—Garvagh
Capell—Essex
Carington—Carrington
Carmichael—Carmichael of Kelvingrove*
Carnegie—Fife
Carnegie—Northesk
Carnegie—Southesk
Carr—Carr of Hadley*
Cary—Falkland
Caulfeild—Charlemont
Cavendish—Chesham
Cavendish—Devonshire
Cavendish—Waterpark
Cavendish Bentinck—Portland
Cayzer—Rotherwick
Cecil—Amherst of Hackney
Cecil—Exeter
Cecil—Rockley
Chaloner—Gisborough
Chapman—Northfield*
Charteris—Charteris of Amisfield*
Charteris—Wemyss and March
Cheshire—Ryder of Warsaw*
Chetwynd Talbot—Shrewsbury
Chichester—Donegall
Chichester Clark—Moyola*
Child Villiers—Jersey
Cholmondeley—Delamere
Chubb—Hayter
Clegg Hill—Hill
Clifford—Clifford of Chudleigh
Clifton of Mar—Mar
Cochrane—Cochrane of Cults
Cochrane—Dundonald
Cocks—Somers
Cokayne—Cullen of Ashbourne
Coke—Leicester
Cole—Enniskillen
Colville—Clydesmuir
Colville—Colville of Culross
Compton—Northampton
Conolly Carew—Carew
Constantine—Constantine of Stanmore*
Cooper—Norwich
Cooper—Cooper of Stockton Heath*
Corbett—Rowallan
Courtenay—Devon
Cox—Kings Norton*
Craig—Craigavon

Crawshaw—Crawshaw of Aintree*
Crichton—Erne
Crichton Stuart—Bute
Cripps—Parmoor
Cross—Cross of Chelsea
Crossley—Somerleyton
Cubitt—Ashcombe
Cunliffe Lister—Masham of Ilton*
Cunliffe Lister—Swinton
Curzon—Howe
Curzon—Scarsdale
Cust—Brownlow
Dalrymple—Stair
Darling—Darling of Hillsborough*
Davidson—Northchurch*
Davies—Darwen
Davies—Davies of Penrhys*
Davison—Broughshane
Dawnay—Downe
Dawson Damer—Portarlington
De Courcy—Kingsale
De Grey—Walsingham
Delacourt Smith—Delacourt Smith of Alteryn*
De Yarburgh Bateson—Deramore
Dean—Dean of Beswick*
Deane—Muskerry
Denison—Londesborough
Denison Pender—Pender
Devereux—Hereford
Dewar—Forteviot
Dixon—Glentoran
Dodson—Monk Bretton
Donaldson—Donaldson of Kingsbridge*
Douglas—Morton
Douglas—Queensberry
Douglas Hamilton—Hamilton
Douglas Hamilton—Selkirk
Douglas Home—Dacre
Douglas-Home—Home of the Hirsel*
Douglas Pennant—Penrhyn
Douglas Scott Montagu—Montagu of Beaulieu
Drummond—Perth
Dugdale—Crathorne
Duke—Merrivale
Duncombe—Feversham
Dundas—Melville
Dundas—Zetland
Dutton—Sherborne
Eady—Swinfen
Eden—Auckland
Eden—Avon
Eden—Henley
Eden—Eden of Winton*
Edgcumbe—Mount Edgcumbe
Edmondson—Sandford
Edwardes—Kensington
Edwards—Chelmer*
Egerton—Sutherland

Egerton—*Wilton*
Eliot—*St. Germans*
Elliot—*Elliot of Harwood**
Elliot-Murray-Kynymound—*Minto*
Elliott—*Elliott of Morpeth**
Erroll—*Errol of Hale*
Erskine—*Buchan*
Erskine—*Erskine of Rerrick*
Erskine—*Mar & Kellie*
Erskine Murray—*Elibank*
Evans—*Evans of Claughton**
Evans—*Mountevans*
Evans Freke—*Carbery*
Eve—*Silsoe*
Eveleigh de Moleyns—*Ventry*
Eyres Monsell—*Monsell*
Fairfax—*Fairfax of Cameron*
Fane—*Westmorland*
Feilding—*Denbigh*
Fellowes—*Ailwyn*
Fellowes—*De Ramsey*
Fermor Hesketh—*Hesketh*
Fiennes—*Saye & Sele*
Finch Hatton—*Winchilsea*
Finch Knightley—*Aylesford*
Fisher—*Fisher of Rednal**
Fitzalan Howard—*Herries*
Fitzalan Howard—*Norfolk*
FitzClarence—*Munster*
FitzGerald—*Leinster*
Fitzherbert—*Stafford*
FitzRoy—*Daventry*
FitzRoy—*Grafton*
Fletcher Vane—*Inglewood*
Flower—*Ashbrooke*
Foley Berkeley—*Berkeley*
Foljambe—*Liverpool*
Foot—*Caradon**
Forbes—*Granard*
Fox Strangways—*Ilchester*
Frankland—*Zouche*
Fraser—*Fraser of Kilmorack**
Fraser—*Fraser of Tullybelton*
Fraser—*Lovat*
Fraser—*Saltoun*
Fraser—*Strathalmond*
Freeman Grenville—*Kinloss*
Freeman Mitford—*Redesdale*
Fremantle—*Cottesloe*
French—*De Freyne*
French—*Ypres*
Galbraith—*Strathclyde*
Ganzoni—*Belstead*
Gardner—*Gardner of Parkes**

Gascoyne Cecil—*Salisbury*
Gathorne Hardy—*Cranbrook*
Gibbs—*Alderham*
Gibbs—*Wraxall*
Gibson—*Ashbourne*
Giffard—*Halsbury*
Gilbey—*Vaux of Harrowden*
Glyn—*Wolverton*
Godley—*Kilbracken*
Gordon—*Aberdeen*
Gordon—*Huntly*
Gordon Lennox—*Richmond*
Gore—*Arran*
Gough Calthorpe—*Calthorpe*
Graham—*Graham of Edmonton**
Graham—*Montrose*
Graham Toler—*Norbury*
Grant—*Strathspey*
Grant Ferris—*Harvington**
Granville—*Granville of Eye**
Gray—*Gray of Contin**
Greaves—*Dysart*
Greenall—*Daresbury*
Greene—*Greene of Harrow Weald**
Greenhill—*Greenhill of Harrow**
Grenfell—*St. Just*
Greville—*Warwick*
Grey—*Grey of Naunton**
Grimston—*Grimston of Westbury*
Grimston—*Verulam*
Grosvenor—*Ebury*
Grosvenor—*Westminster*
Guest—*Wimborne*
Guinness—*Iveagh*
Guinness—*Moyne*
Gully—*Selby*
Gurdon—*Cranworth*
Gwynne Jones—*Chalfont**
Hamilton—*Abercorn*
Hamilton—*Belhaven and Stenton*
Hamilton—*Hamilton of Dalzell*
Hamilton—*Holm Patrick*
Hamilton Russel—*Boyne*
Hamilton Temple Blackwood—*Dufferin*
Hanbury Tracy—*Sudeley*
Handcock—*Castlemaine*
Harbord Hamond—*Suffield*
Harding—*Harding of Petherton*
Hardinge—*Hardinge of Penshurst*
Hare—*Blakenham*
Hare—*Listowel*
Harmsworth—*Rothermere*
Harris—*Harris of Greenwich**

Harris—*Harris of High Cross**
Harris—*Malmesbury*
Harvey—*Harvey of Prestbury**
Harvey—*Harvey of Tasburgh*
Hastings—*Huntingdon*
Hatch—*Hatch of Lusby**
Hay—*Erroll*
Hay—*Kinnoull*
Hay—*Tweeddale*
Heathcote-Drummond-Willoughby—*Willoughby de Eresby*
Hely Hutchinson—*Donoughmore*
Henderson—*Henderson of Brompton**
Henderson—*Faringdon*
Hennessy—*Windlesham*
Henniker Major—*Henniker*
Hepburne Scott—*Polwarth*
Herbert—*Carnarvon*
Herbert—*Hemingford*
Herbert—*Pembroke*
Herbert—*Powis*
Hermon Hodge—*Wyfold*
Hicks Beach—*St. Aldwyn*
Hervey—*Bristol*
Hewitt—*Lifford*
Hill—*Downshire*
Hill—*Hill of Luton**
Hill—*Sandys*
Hill Trevor—*Trevor*
Hobart Hampden—*Buckinghamshire*
Hogg—*Hailsham of St. Marylebone**
Holland Hibbert—*Knutsford*
Holms à Court—*Heytesbury*
Hood—*Bridport*
Hope—*Glendevon*
Hope—*Linlithgow*
Hope—*Rankeillour*
Hope Morley—*Hollenden*
Hopkinson—*Colyton*
Hopwood—*Southborough*
Hore Ruthven—*Gowrie*
Houghton—*Houghton of Sowerby**
Hovell Thurlow Cumming Bruce—*Thurlow*
Howard—*Carlisle*
Howard—*Effingham*
Howard—*Howard of Penrith*
Howard—*Strathcona*
Howard—*Suffolk and Berkshire*
Howie—*Howie of Troon**
Hoyer Millar—*Inchyra*
Hubbard—*Addington*
Huggins—*Malvern*
Hughes—*Cledwyn of Penrhos**
Hughes Young—*St. Helens*
Hunt—*Hunt of Fawley*

Hunt—*Hunt of Tanworth**
Hunter—*Hunter of Newington**
Hutchinson—*Hutchinson of Lullington**
Ingrams—*Darcy de Knayth*
Innes Ker—*Roxburghe*
Inskip—*Caldecote*
Irby—*Boston*
Irving—*Irving of Dartford**
Isaacs—*Reading*
Jackson—*Allerton*
James—*James of Rusholme**
James—*Saint Brides**
James—*Northbourne*
Jebb—*Gladwyn*
Jervis—*St. Vincent*
Jocelyn—*Roden*
Jolliffe—*Hylton*
Joynson Hicks—*Brentford*
Kaberry—*Kaberry of Adel**
Kay Shuttleworth—*Shuttleworth*
Kearley—*Devonport*
Keith—*Keith of Castleacre**
Keith—*Keith of Kinkel*
Keith—*Kintore*
Kemp—*Rochdale*
Kennedy—*Ailsa*
Kenworthy—*Strabolgi*
Keppel—*Albemarle*
Kerr—*Lothian*
Kerr—*Teviot*
King—*Lovelace*
King—*King of Wartnaby**
King Tenison—*Kingston*
Kitchener—*Kitchener of Khartoum*
Kitson—*Airedale*
Knatchbull—*Brabourne*
Knatchbull-Mountbatten of Burma
Knox—*Ranfurly*
Lamb—*Rochester*
Lambart—*Cavan*
Lampson—*Killearn*
Larnach Nevill—*Abergavenny*
Lascelles—*Harewood*
Law—*Coleraine*
Law—*Ellenborough*
Lawrence—*Trevethin and Oaksey*
Lawson—*Burnham*
Lawson Johnston—*Luke*
Lee—*Lee of Asheridge**
Le Poer Trench—*Clancarty*
Legge—*Dartmouth*
Legh—*Newton*
Leith—*Burgh*
Lennox Boyd—*Boyd of Merton*
Leslie—*Rothes*
Leslie Melville—*Leven*
Lever—*Lever of Manchester**

Lever—*Leverhulme*
Leveson Gower—*Granville*
Liddell—*Ravensworth*
Lindesay Bethune—*Lindsay*
Lindsay—*Crawford*
Lindsay—*Lindsay of Birker*
Littleton—*Hatherton*
Llewelyn-Davies—*Llewelyn-Davies of Hastoe**
Lloyd—*Lloyd of Hampstead**
Lloyd—*Lloyd of Kilgerran**
Lloyd George—*Lloyd George of Dwyfor*
Lloyd George—*Tenby*
Lloyd Mostyn—*Mostyn*
Loder—*Wakehurst*
Lopes—*Roborough*
Low—*Aldington*
Lowry Corry—*Belmore*
Lowther—*Lonsdale*
Lowther—*Ullswater*
Lubbock—*Avebury*
Lucas—*Lucas of Chilworth*
Lumley—*Scarbrough*
Lumley Savile—*Savile*
Lyon Dalberg Acton—*Acton*
Lysaght—*Lisle*
Lyttelton—*Chandos*
Lyttelton—*Cobham (Viscountcy)*
McAlpine—*McAlpine of Moffat**
McAlpine—*McAlpine of West Green**
McClintock Bunbury—*Rathdonnell*
Macdonald—*Macdonald of Gwaenysgor*
McDonnell—*Antrim*
McFadzean—*McFadzean of Kelvinside**
McFarlane—*McFarlane of Llandaff**
McGregor—*McGregor of Durris*
McIntosh—*McIntosh of Haringey**
Mackay—*Inchcape*
Mackay—*Mackay of Clashfern**
Mackay—*Reay*
Mackay—*Tanlaw**
Mackie—*John-Mackie**
Mackie—*Mackie of Benshie**
Mackintosh—*Mackintosh of Halifax*
McLaren—*Aberconway*
MacLehose—*MacLehose of Beoch**
Macleod—*Macleod of Borve**
MacLeod—*Macleod of Fuinary**
Maclay—*Muirshiel*
Macmillan—*Stockton*
Macpherson—*Drumalbyn*

Macpherson—*Macpherson of Drumochter*
Macpherson—*Strathcarron*
Maffey—*Rugby*
Maitland—*Lauderdale*
Makgill—*Oxfuird*
Makins—*Sherfield*
Manners—*Rutland*
Manningham Buller—*Dilhorne*
Mansfield—*Sandhurst*
Marks—*Marks of Broughton*
Marquis—*Woolton*
Marshall—*Marshall of Goring**
Marshall—*Marshall of Leeds**
Marsham—*Romney*
Martyn Hemphill—*Hemphill*
Mason—*Blackford*
Maude—*Hawarden*
Maude—*Maude of Stratford-upon-Avon**
Maxwell—*De Ros*
Maxwell—*Farnham*
Meade—*Clanwilliam*
Milles Lade—*Sondes*
Milner—*Milner of Leeds*
Mitchell Thomson—*Selsdon*
Monckton—*Galway*
Monckton—*Monckton of Brenchley*
Monckton—*Ruthven of Freeland*
Mond—*Melchett*
Money-Coutts—*Latymer*
Montagu—*Manchester*
Montagu—*Swaythling*
Montagu Douglas Scott—*Buccleuch*
Montagu Stuart Wortley Mackenzie—*Wharncliffe*
Montague—*Amwell*
Montgomerie—*Eglinton*
Montgomery—*Montgomery of Alamein*
Moore—*Drogheda*
Moore—*Moore of Wolvercote**
Moore Brabazon—*Brabazon of Tara*
Moreton—*Ducie*
Morris—*Killanin*
Morris—*Morris of Grasmere**
Morris—*Morris of Kenwood*
Morrison—*Dunrossil*
Morrison—*Margadale*
Morton—*Morton of Shuna**
Mosley—*Ravensdale*
Mountbatten—*Edinburgh*
Mountbatten—*Milford Haven*
Muff—*Calverley*
Mulholland—*Dunleath*
Murray—*Atholl*

Murray—*Dunmore*
Murray—*Mansfield and Mansfield*
Murray—*Murray of Epping Forest**
Murray—*Murray of Newhaven**
Murton—*Murton of Lindisfarne**
Nall Cain—*Brocket*
Napier—*Napier and Ettrick*
Napier—*Napier of Magdala*
Neave—*Airey of Abingdon**
Needham—*Kilmorey*
Nelson—*Nelson of Stafford*
Neville—*Braybrooke*
Nicolson—*Carnock*
Nivison—*Glendyne*
Noel—*Gainsborough*
Noel Paton—*Ferrier**
North—*Guilford*
Northcote—*Iddesleigh*
Norton—*Grantley*
Norton—*Rathcreedan*
Nugent—*Nugent of Guildford**
Nugent—*Westmeath*
O'Brien—*Inchiquin*
O'Brien—*O'Brien of Lothbury**
Ogilvie Grant—*Seafield*
Ogilvy—*Airlie*
O'Neill—*O'Neill of the Maine**
O'Neill—*Rathcavan*
Orde Powlett—*Bolton*
Ormsby Gore—*Harlech*
Page—*Whaddon**
Paget—*Anglesey*
Paget—*Paget of Northampton**
Pakenham—*Lonford*
Pakington—*Hampton*
Palmer—*Lucas of Crudwell*
Palmer—*Selborne*
Parker—*Macclesfield*
Parker—*Morley*
Parnell—*Congleton*
Parsons—*Rosse*
Paulet—*Winchester*
Peake—*Ingleby*
Pearson—*Cowdray*
Pease—*Daryngton*
Pease—*Gainford*
Pease—*Wardington*
Pelham—*Chichester*
Pelham—*Yarborough*
Pelham Clinton Hope—*Newcastle*
Pellew—*Exmouth*
Penny—*Marchwood*
Pepys—*Cottenham*
Perceval—*Egmont*
Percy—*Northumberland*
Perry—*Perry of Walton**
Pery—*Limerick*
Petty Fitzmaurice—*Lansdowne*
Peyton—*Peyton of Yeovil**

Philipps—*Milford*
Philipps—*St. Davids*
Phipps—*Normanby*
Pitt—*Pitt of Hampstead**
Platt—*Platt of Writtle**
Pleydell Bouverie—*Radnor*
Plummer—*Plummer of St. Marylebone**
Plumptre—*Fitzwalter*
Pluckett—*Dunsany*
Plunkett—*Fingall*
Plunkett—*Louth*
Pollock—*Hanworth*
Pomeroy—*Harberton*
Ponsonby—*Bessborough*
Ponsonby—*De Mauley*
Ponsonby—*P. of Shulbrede*
Ponsonby—*Sysonby*
Portal—*Portal of Hungerford*
Powys—*Lilford*
Pratt—*Camden*
Preston—*Gormanston*
Primrose—*Rosebery*
Prittie—*Dunalley*
Ramsay—*Dalhousie*
Ramsey—*Ramsey of Canterbury**
Ramsbotham—*Soulbury*
Rawlinson—*Rawlinson of Ewell**
Rees Williams—*Ogmore*
Rhys—*Dynevor*
Richards—*Milverton*
Richardson—*Richardson of Duntisbourne**
Ritchie—*Ritchie of Dundee*
Robens—*Robens of Woldingham*
Roberts—*Clwyd*
Robertson—*Robertson of Oakridge*
Robinson—*Martonmere*
Robson—*Robson of Kiddington**
Roche—*Fermoy*
Rodd—*Rennell*
Roll—*Roll of Ipsden**
Roper Curzon—*Teynham*
Rospigliosi—*Newburgh*
Ross—*Ross of Marnock**
Rous—*Stradbroke*
Rowley Conwy—*Langford*
Royle—*Fanshawe of Richmond**
Runciman—*Runciman of Doxford*
Russell—*Ampthill*
Russell—*Bedford*
Russell—*De Clifford*
Russell—*Russell of Killowen*
Russell—*R. of Liverpool*
Ryder—*Harrowby*
Ryder—*Ryder of Eaton Hastings**
Sackville—*De La Warr*
Sackville West—*Sackville*
St. Aubyn—*St. Levan*
St. Clair—*Sinclair*

St. Clair Erskine—
  Rosslyn
St. John—*St. J. of Blesto*
St. John—*Bolingbroke*
  and St. John
St. Leger—*Doneraile*
Samuel—*Bearsted*
Sanderson—*Sanderson of*
  Bowden*
Sandilands—*Torphichen*
Saumarez—*De Saumarez*
Savile—*Mexborough*
Scarlett—*Abinger*
Sclater Booth—*Basing*
Scott—*Eldon*
Scott Ellis—*Howard de*
  Walden
Scrymgeour
  Wedderburn—*Dundee*
Seager—*Leighton of St.*
  Mellons
Seely—*Mottistone*
Sefton—*Sefton of*
  Garston*
Seymour—*Hertford*
Seymour—*Somerset*
Shaw—*Craigmyle*
Shaw—*Kilbrandon*
Shirley—*Ferrers*
Short—*Glenamara**
Siddeley—*Kenilworth*
Sidney—*De L'Isle*
Sieff—*Sieff of Brimpton**
Silkin—*Silkin of*
  Dulwich*
Simon—*Simon of*
  Glaisdale*
Simon—*Simon of*
  Wythenshawe
Sinclair—*Caithness*
Sinclair—*Sinclair of*
  Cleeve
Sinclair—*Thurso*
Skeffington—*Massereene*
Smith—*Bicester*
Smith—*Birkenhead*
Smith—*Colwyn*
Smith—*Hambleden*
Smith—*Kirkhill**
Somerset—*Beaufort*
Somerset—*Raglan*
Souter—*Audley*

Spencer—*Churchill*
Spencer Churchill—
  Marlborough
Spring Rice—*Monteagle*
  of Brandon
Stanhope—*Harrington*
Stanley—*Derby*
Stanley—*Sheffield*
Stapleton Cotton—
  Combermere
Stern—*Michelham*
Stewart—*Galloway*
Stewart—*Stewart of*
  Fulham*
Stodart—*Stodart of*
  Leaston*
Stoddart—*Stoddart of*
  Swindon*
Stonor—*Camoys*
Stopford—*Courtown*
Stourton—*Mowbray*
Strachey—*O'Hagan*
Strutt—*Belper*
Strutt—*Rayleigh*
Stuart—*Castle Stewart*
Stuart—*Moray*
Stuart—*Stuart of*
  Findhorn
Suenson Taylor—
  Grantchester
Sugden—*St. Leonards*
Talbot—*T. of Malahide*
Taylor—*Taylor of*
  Blackburn*
Taylor—*Taylor of Gryfe**
Taylor—*Taylor of*
  Hadfield*
Taylor—*Taylor of*
  Mansfield*
Taylour—*Headfort*
Temple Gore Langton—
  Temple of Stowe
Tennant—*Glenconner*
Thellusson—*Rendlesham*
Thesiger—*Chelmsford*
Thomas—*Thomas of*
  Swynnerton*
Thomas—*Tonypandy*
Thomson—*Thomson of*
  Fleet
Thomson—*Thomson of*
  Monifieth*

Thynne—*Bath*
Tottenham—*Ely*
Trefusis—*Clinton*
Trench—*Ashtown*
Trevor Roper—*Dacre of*
  Glanton*
Tufton—*Hothfield*
Turner—*Netherthorpe*
Turner—*Turner of*
  Camden*
Turnour—*Winterton*
Turton—*Tranmire**
Tyrell Kenyon—*Kenyon*
Vanden Bempde
  Johnstone—*Derwent*
Vane—*Barnard*
Vane Tempest Stewart—
  Londonderry
Vanneck—*Huntingfield*
Vaughan—*Lisburne*
Vaughan Morgan—
  Reigate*
Vavasseur Fisher—
  Fisher
Vereker—*Gort*
Verney—*Willoughby de*
  Broke
Vernon—*Lyveden*
Vesey—*De Vesci*
Villiers—*Clarendon*
Vintcent—*Wharton*
Vivian—*Swansea*
Walker-Smith—
  Broxbourne*
Wallace—*Dudley*
  (Barony)
Wallace—*Wallace of*
  Campsie*
Wallace—*Wallace of*
  Coslany*
Wallop—*Portsmouth*
Ward—*Bangor*
Ward—*Dudley (Earldom)*
Ward—*Ward of Witley*
Warrender—*Bruntisfield*
Watson—*Manton*
Watson Armstrong—
  Armstrong
Wedderburn—
  Wedderburn of
  Charlton*

Weir—*Inverforth*
Weld Forester—*Forester*
Wellesley—*Cowley*
Wellesley—*Wellington*
West—*Granville-West**
Westenra—*Rossmore*
White—*Annaly*
Whiteley—*Marchamley*
Whitfield—*Kenswood*
Willey—*Barnby*
Williams—*Berners*
Williams—*Williams of*
  Elvel*
Williamson—*Forres*
Willoughby—*Middleton*
Wills—*Dulverton*
Wilson—*Moran*
Wilson—*Nunburnholme*
Wilson—*Wilson of*
  Langside*
Wilson—*Wilson of*
  Rievaulx*
Windsor—*Cornwall*
Windsor—*Gloucester*
Windsor—*Kent*
Windsor Clive—
  Plymouth
Wingfield—*Powerscourt*
Winn—*St. Oswald*
Winn—*Headley*
Wodehouse—*Kimberley*
Wood—*Halifax*
Wood—*Holderness**
Woodhouse—*Terrington*
Wright—*Wootton of*
  Abinger*
Wyndham—*Leconfield*
Wyndham Quin—
  Dunraven
Wynn—*Newborough*
Yarde Buller—*Churston*
Yerburgh—*Alvingham*
Yorke—*Hardwicke*
Young—*Kennet*
Young—*Young of*
  Dartington*
Young—*Young of*
  Graffham*
Younger—*Y. of Leckie*

* Life Peer created under Life Peerages Act, 1958

THE PREFIX RIGHT HONOURABLE

"Right Honourable."—By long established custom, or courtesy, members of her Majesty's Most Honourable Privy Council are entitled to be designated "The Right Honourable," but, in practice, this prefix is sometimes absorbed in other designations; for example, a Prince of the Blood admitted a Privy Counsellor remains "His Royal Highness"; a Duke remains "His Grace"; a Marquess is still styled "Most Honourable". The style of all other Peers whether Privy Counsellors or not, is "Right Honourable", although it is more usual to describe them with the prefix "The", omitting the more elaborate styles. A Privy Counsellor who is not a Peer should be addressed as The Right (or Rt.) Hon.——. A Peer below the rank of Marquess who is a Privy Counsellor should be addressed as The Right (or Rt). Hon. the Lord (or Earl or Viscount)——, P.C., or, less elaborately, The Lord (or Earl or Viscount)——P.C.

THE PRIVY COUNCIL

Apart from Cabinet Ministers, who must be Privy Counsellors and are sworn in on first assuming office, membership of the Council (retained for life) is accorded by the Sovereign on the recommendation of the Prime Minister to eminent people in independent monarchical countries of the Commonwealth. Cabinet Ministers principally form the active Privy Council.

H.R.H. The Duke of Edinburgh	1951	Carr of Hadley, Lord	1963	Foot, Michael	1974
		Carrington, Lord	1959	Fowler, Norman	1979
H.R.H. The Prince of Wales	1977	Casey, M. Eugene	1986	Fox, Sir Michael	1981
		Castle, Barbara	1964	Franks, Lord	1949
Aberdare, Lord	1974	Cato, Robert	1981	Fraser of Tullybelton, Lord	1975
Ackner, Lord	1980	Chalfont, Lord	1964	Fraser, Malcolm	1976
Adams-Schneider, Sir Lancelot	1980	Chalker, Lynda	1987	Fraser, Thomas	1964
		Chan, Sir Julius	1981	Freeman, John	1966
Ademola, Sir Adetokunbo	1963	Channon, Paul	1980	Freeson, Reginald	1976
Airlie, Earl of	1984	Charteris of Amisfield, Lord	1972	Gairy, Sir Eric	1977
Aldington, Lord	1954	Chataway, Christopher	1970	Gardiner, Lord	1964
Alison, Michael	1981	Chesham, Lord	1964	Georges, Telford	1986
Alport, Lord	1960	Clarke, Kenneth	1983	Gibbs, Sir Harry	1972
Amery, Julian	1960	Cledwyn of Penrhos, Lord	1966	Gibbs, Sir Humphrey	1969
Anthony, John Douglas	1971	Cobbold, Lord	1959	Gibson, Sir Ralph	1985
Archer, Peter	1977	Cockfield, Lord	1982	Gibson-Watt, Lord	1974
Armstrong, Ernest	1979	Cocks, Lord	1976	Gilbert, John William	1978
Arnold, Sir John	1979	Coggan, Rt. Rev. Lord	1961	Gilmour, Sir Ian, Bt	1973
Ashley, Jack	1979	Colman, Fraser	1986	Glenamara, Lord	1964
Atkins, Lord	1973	Colyton, Lord	1952	Glendevon, Lord	1959
Avonside, Lord	1962	Compton, John	1983	Glidewell, Sir Iain	1985
Aylestone, Lord	1962	Concannon, John	1978	Goff of Chieveley, Lord	1982
Azikiwe, Nnamdi	1960	Cooke, Sir Robin	1977	Gordon, John Bowie	1978
Bacon, Baroness	1966	Cooper, Sir Frank	1983	Gorton, Sir John Grey	1968
Baker, Kenneth	1984	Corfield, Sir Frederick	1970	Gowrie, Earl of	1984
Balcombe, Sir John	1985	Cowen, Sir Zelman	1981	Gray of Contin, Lord	1982
Balfour of Inchrye, Lord	1941	Craigton, Lord	1961	Griffiths, Lord	1980
Barber, Lord	1963	Crawford and Balcarres, Earl of	1972	Grimond, Lord	1961
Barnett, Lord	1975			Gummer, John	1986
Barwick, Sir Garfield	1964	Cromer, Earl of	1966	Hailsham of St. Marylebone, Lord	1956
Belstead, Lord	1983	Croom-Johnson, Sir David	1984	Harrison, Walter	1977
Benn, Anthony	1964	Cross of Chelsea, Lord	1969	Hart, Lady	1967
Bennett, Sir Frederic	1985	Cumming-Bruce, Sir Roualeyn	1977	Harvington, Lord	1971
Bevins, John Reginald	1959			Hasluck, Sir Paul	1966
Biffen, John	1979	Davies, Denzil	1978	Hattersley, Roy	1975
Bingham, Sir Thomas	1986	Davison, Sir Ronald	1978	Havers, Lord	1977
Bird, Vere	1982	Deedes, Lord	1962	Hayhoe, Barney	1985
Blaize, Herbert	1986	De L'Isle, Viscount	1951	Healey, Denis Winston	1964
Blaker, Sir Peter	1983	Dell, Edmund	1970	Heath, Edward	1955
Blanch, Rt. Rev. Lord	1975	Denham, Lord	1981	Herbison, Margaret	1964
Booth, Albert	1976	Denning, Lord	1948	Heseltine, Michael	1979
Bottomley, Lord	1952	Devlin, Lord	1960	Heseltine, Sir William	1986
Boyd-Carpenter, Lord	1954	Devonshire, Duke of	1964	Higgins, Terence	1979
Boyson, Sir Rhodes	1987	Diamond, Lord	1965	Hill of Luton, Lord	1955
Braine, Sir Bernard	1985	Dillon, Sir Brian	1982	Holderness, Lord	1959
Brandon of Oakbrook, Lord	1978	Donaldson, Sir John	1979	Home of the Hirsel, Lord	1951
Bridge of Harwich, Lord	1975	Douglas, Sir William	1977	Houghton of Sowerby, Lord	1964
Brightman, Lord	1979	Drumalbyn, Lord	1962		
Brittan, Leon	1981	du Cann, Sir Edward	1964	Howe, Sir Geoffrey	1972
Brown, Sir Stephen	1983	Duff, Sir Antony	1980	Howell, David	1979
Browne, Sir Patrick	1974	Duncan-Sandys, Lord	1944	Howell, Denis	1976
Browne-Wilkinson, Sir Nicolas	1983	Dunn, Sir Robin	1980	Hughes, Lord	1970
		Eccles, Viscount	1951	Hurd, Douglas	1982
Broxbourne, Lord	1957	Eden of Winton, Lord	1972	Irvine, Sir Bryant Godman	1982
Buchanan-Smith, Alick	1981	Edmund-Davies, Lord	1966	Irving of Dartford, Lord	1969
Buckley, Sir Denys	1970	Edwards, Lord	1979	Jay, Lord	1952
Butler, Sir Adam	1984	Ellison, Rt. Rev. Gerald	1973	Jellicoe, Earl	1963
Cairns, Sir David	1970	Elwyn-Jones, Lord	1964	Jenkin, Lord	1973
Callaghan, Lord	1964	Emslie, Lord	1972	Jenkins, Lord	1964
Cameron of Lochbroom, Lord	1984	Ennals, Lord	1970	Jones, Aubrey	1955
		Erroll of Hale, Lord	1960	Jones, Sir Edward	1979
Campbell of Croy, Lord	1970	Esquivel, Manuel	1986	Jopling, Michael	1979
Canterbury, The Archbishop of	1980	Eveleigh, Sir Edward	1977	Joseph, Lord	1962
		Fernyhough, Ernest	1970	Jugnauth, Aneerood	1987
Caradon, Lord	1968	Ferrers, Earl	1982	Kaufman, Gerald	1978
Carlisle, Lord	1979	Fletcher, Lord	1967	Keith of Kinkel, Lord	1976

Clerk of the Council, G. I. de Deney, c.v.o.   *Deputy Clerk of the Council,* C. E. S. Horsford, c.v.o.

ORDERS OF CHIVALRY

The Most Noble Order of the Garter (1348)—K.G.

Ribbon, Garter Blue. *Motto*, Honi soit qui mal y pense (*Shame on him who thinks evil of it*).
The number of Knights Companions is limited to 24.

SOVEREIGN OF THE ORDER—THE QUEEN

Lady of the Garter—H.M. QUEEN ELIZABETH THE QUEEN MOTHER, 1936.
Extra Ladies of the Garter—H.M. JULIANA, QUEEN OF THE NETHERLANDS, 1958
H.M. THE QUEEN OF DENMARK, 1979

Royal Knights

H.R.H. The Duke of Edinburgh, 1947.
H.R.H. The Prince of Wales, 1958.
H.R.H. The Duke of Kent, 1985.

Extra Knights

H.M. The King of Norway, 1959.
H.M. The King of The Belgians, 1963.
H.I.M. The Emperor of Japan, 1971.
H.R.H. The Grand Duke of Luxemburg, 1972.
H.M. The King of Sweden, 1983

Knights Companions

The Duke of Northumberland, 1959.
The Viscount De L'Isle, 1968.

The Lord Ashburton, 1969.
The Lord Cobbold, 1970.
Sir Cennydd Traherne, 1970.
The Earl Waldegrave, 1971.
The Earl of Longford, 1971.
The Lord Rhodes, 1972.
The Earl of Drogheda, 1972.
The Lord Shackleton, 1974.
The Marquess of Abergavenny, 1974.
The Lord Wilson of Rievaulx, 1976.
The Duke of Grafton, 1976.
The Earl of Cromer, 1977.
The Lord Elworthy, 1977.
The Lord Hunt, 1979.
Sir Paul Hasluck, 1979.
Sir Richard Hull, 1980
The Duke of Norfolk, 1983

The Lord Lewin, 1983
The Lord Richardson of Duntisbourne, 1983
The Marquess of Normanby, 1985
The Lord Carrington, 1985
The Lord Callaghan, 1987.
Prelate, The Bishop of Winchester.
Chancellor, The Marquess of Abergavenny, K.G., O.B.E.
Register, The Dean of Windsor.
Garter King of Arms, Lt.-Col. Sir Colin Cole, K.C.V.O., T.D.
Gentleman Usher of the Black Rod, Air Chief Marshal Sir John Gingell, G.B.E., K.C.B.
Secretary, Sir Walter Verco, K.C.V.O.

The Most Ancient and Most Noble Order of the Thistle—K.T.

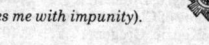

Ribbon, Green. *Motto*, Nemo me impune lacessit (*No one provokes me with impunity*).
The number of Knights is limited to 16.

SOVEREIGN OF THE ORDER—THE QUEEN

Lady of the Thistle—H.M. QUEEN ELIZABETH THE QUEEN MOTHER, 1937

Royal Knights

H.R.H. The Duke of Edinburgh, 1952.
H.R.H. The Prince of Wales (*Duke of Rothesay*), 1977.

Extra Knight

H.M. The King of Norway, 1962.

Knights

The Lord Home of the Hirsel, 1962.
The Earl of Wemyss and March, 1966.

The Lord Maclean, 1969.
The Earl of Dalhousie, 1971.
The Lord Clydesmuir, 1972.
The Viscount Muirshiel, 1973.
Sir Donald Cameron of Lochiel, 1973.
The Earl of Selkirk, 1976.
The Lord McFadzean, 1976.
The Hon. Lord Cameron, 1978.
The Duke of Buccleuch and Queensberry, 1978.
The Earl of Elgin and Kincardine, 1981.
The Lord Thomson of Monifieth, 1981.

The Lord MacLehose of Beoch, 1983.
The Earl of Airlie, 1985.
Capt. Sir Iain Tennant, 1986.
Chancellor, The Lord Home of the Hirsel.
Dean, The Very Rev. Prof. J. McIntyre, C.V.O., D.Litt.
Secretary and Lord Lyon King of Arms, Malcolm R. Innes of Edingight, C.V.O., W.S.
Usher of the Green Rod, Rear-Admiral D.A. Dunbar-Nasmith, C.B., D.S.C.

The Most Honourable Order of the Bath (1725)

Ribbon, Crimson. *Motto*, Tria juncta in uno (*Three joined in one*). (Remodelled 1815, and enlarged many times since. The Order is divided into civil and military divisions.)

G.C.B. Mil.   G.C.B. Civ.   K.C.B. Mil.   K.C.B. Civ.   C.B. Mil.

THE SOVEREIGN; *Great Master and First or Principal Knight Grand Cross*, H.R.H. The Prince of Wales, K.G., K.T., G.C.B., A.K.; *Dean of the Order*, The Dean of Westminster; *Bath King of Arms*, Air Chief Marshal Sir David Evans, G.C.B., C.B.E.; *Registrar and Secretary*, Air Marshal Sir Denis Crowley-Milling, K.C.B., C.B.E., D.S.O., D.F.C.; *Genealogist*, Dr. C. Swan, C.V.O., PH.D.; *Gentleman Usher of the Scarlet Rod*, Rear-Admiral D. E. Macey, C.B.; *Deputy Secretary*, Maj.-Gen. D. H. G. Rice, C.V.O., C.B.E.; *Chancery*, Central Chancery of the Orders of Knighthood, St. James's Palace, SW1A 1BH.—G.C.B., Knight (or Dame) Grand Cross; K.C.B., Knight Commander; D.C.B., Dame Commander; C.B., Companion. Women became eligible for the Order from Jan. 1, 1971.

The Order of Merit (1902)—O.M.
Ribbon, Blue and Crimson.

O.M.Mil.   This Order is designed as a special distinction for eminent men and women—without conferring a knighthood upon them. The Order is limited in numbers to 24, with the addition of foreign honorary members. Membership is of two kinds, Military and Civil, the badge of the former having crossed swords, and the latter oak leaves. Membership is denoted by the suffix O.M., which follows the first class of the Order of the Bath and precedes the letters designating membership of the inferior classes of the Bath and all classes of the lesser Orders of Knighthood.   O.M.Civ.

THE SOVEREIGN
H.R.H. THE DUKE OF EDINBURGH (1968)

Dorothy Hodgkin, 1965.	The Lord Todd, 1977.	Sir Michael Tippett, 1983.
The Lord Zuckerman, 1968.	The Lord Franks, 1977.	Rev. Prof. Owen Chadwick, K.B.E.,
The Lord Penney, 1969.	Sir Frederick Ashton, 1977.	1983.
Dame Veronica Wedgwood, 1969.	The Lord Olivier, 1981.	Graham Greene, 1986.
Sir Isaiah Berlin, 1971.	Sir Peter Medawar, 1981.	Frederick Sanger, 1986.
Sir George Edwards, 1971.	Gp. Capt. L. Cheshire, v.c., 1981.	Air Commodore Sir Frank Whittle,
Sir Alan Hodgkin, 1973.	Sir Andrew Huxley, 1983.	1986.
Sir Ronald Syme, 1976.	Sir Sidney Nolan, 1983.	Sir Yehudi Menuhin, 1987.

Secretary and Registrar, Sir Edward Ford, K.C.B., K.C.V.O.
Chancery, Central Chancery of the Orders of Knighthood, St. James's Palace, SW1A 1BH.

The Most Exalted Order of the Star of India (1861)

Ribbon, Light Blue, with White Edges. *Motto*, Heaven's Light our Guide.
THE SOVEREIGN; *Registrar*, Maj.-Gen. D. H. G. Rice, C.V.O., C.B.E.; G.C.S.I. Knight Grand
G.C.S.I.   Commander; K.C.S.I., Knight Commander; C.S.I., Companion. No conferments since 1947.

The Most Distinguished Order of St. Michael and St. George (1818)

Ribbon, Saxon Blue, with Scarlet centre. *Motto*, Auspicium melioris ævi (Token of a better age)
THE SOVEREIGN; *Grand Master*, H.R.H. The Duke of Kent, K.G., G.C.M.G., G.C.V.O., A.D.C.; *Prelate*,
The Rt. Rev. R. Woods, K.C.V.O.; *Chancellor*, The Lord Carrington, P.C., C.H., K.C.M.G., M.C.; *Secretary*,
Sir Patrick Wright, K.C.M.G.; *Registrar*, Sir John Graham, Bt., G.C.M.G.; *King of Arms*, Sir Oliver
Wright, G.C.M.G., G.C.V.O., D.S.C.; *Gentleman Usher of the Blue Rod*, Sir John Moreton, K.C.M.G.,
K.C.V.O., M.C.; *Dean*, The Dean of St. Paul's; *Deputy Secretary*, Maj.-Gen. D. H. G. Rice, C.V.O., C.B.E.
Chancery, Central Chancery of the Orders of Knighthood, St. James's Palace, SW1A 1BH.—G.C.M.G.,
Knight (or Dame) Grand Cross; K.C.M.G., Knight Commander; D.C.M.G., Dame Commander;
C.M.G., Companion.

The Most Eminent Order of the Indian Empire (1868)

Ribbon, Imperial Purple. *Motto*, Imperatricis auspiciis (*Under the auspices of the Empress*).
THE SOVEREIGN; *Registrar*, Maj.-Gen. D. H. G. Rice, C.V.O., C.B.E.; G.C.I.E., Knight Grand
G.C.I.E.   Commander; K.C.I.E., Knight Commander; C.I.E., Companion. No conferments since 1947.

The Royal Victorian Order (1896)

Ribbon, Blue, with Red and White Edges. *Motto*, Victoria.
THE SOVEREIGN; *Grand Master*, H.M. Queen Elizabeth The Queen Mother; *Chancellor*,
The Lord Chamberlain; *Secretary*, The Keeper of the Privy Purse; *Registrar*, The Secretary
of the Central Chancery of the Orders of Knighthood; *Chaplain*, The Rev. J. H. Williams.
Hon. Genealogist, Sir Walter Verco, K.C.V.O.; G.C.V.O., Knight or Dame Grand Cross;
K.C.V.O., Knight Commander; D.C.V.O., Dame Commander; C.V.O., Commander; L.V.O.,
Lieutenant; M.V.O., Member.

The Royal Victorian Chain (1902)

Founded by King Edward VII, in 1902. It confers no precedence on its holders.
H.M. THE QUEEN
H.M. QUEEN ELIZABETH THE QUEEN MOTHER (1937).

H.M. Juliana, Queen of the Netherlands (1950).	Rt. Hon. Roland Michener (1973).	Ratu Sir George Cakobau (1982).
	H.M. The Queen of Denmark (1974).	H.M. The Queen of the Netherlands (1982).
H.M. The King of Norway (1955).	The Right Rev. The Lord Ramsey of Canterbury (1974).	
H.M. The King of Thailand (1960).		The Lord Maclean (1984).
H.I.H. The Crown Prince of Ethiopia (1965).	H.M. The King of Nepal (1975).	General Antonio Eanes (1985).
	H.M. The King of Sweden (1975).	H.M. The King of Spain (1986).
H.M. The King of Jordan (1966).	The Right Rev. The Lord Coggan (1980).	H.M. The King of Saudi Arabia (1987).
H.M. King Zahir Shah of Afghanistan (1971).		

The Most Excellent Order of the British Empire (1917)

Ribbon, Rose pink edged with pearl grey with vertical pearl stripe in centre (Military Division); without vertical pearl stripe (Civil Division). *Motto,* For God and the Empire.

G.B.E.   K.B.E.

THE SOVEREIGN: *Grand Master,* H.R.H. The Prince Philip, Duke of Edinburgh, K.G., P.C., K.T., O.M., G.B.E.; *Prelate,* The Bishop of London; *King of Arms,* Admiral Sir Anthony Morton, G.B.E., K.C.B.; *Registrar,* Maj.-Gen. D. H. G. Rice, C.V.O., C.B.E.; *Secretary,* Sir Robert Armstrong, G.C.B., C.V.O.; *Dean,* The Dean of St. Paul's; *Gentleman Usher of the Purple Rod,* Sir Robin Gillett, G.B.E.; *Chancery,* Central Chancery of the Orders of Knighthood, St. James's Palace, SW1A 1BH. G.B.E., Knight or Dame Grand Cross; K.B.E. Knight Commander; D.B.E., Dame Commander; C.B.E., Commander; O.B.E., Officer; M.B.E., Member. The Order was divided into *Military* and *Civil* divisions in Dec. 1918.

Order of the Companions of Honour (June 4, 1917)—C.H.

Ribbon, Carmine, with Gold Edges.

This Order consists of one Class only and carries with it no title. It ranks after the 1st Class of the Order of the British Empire, *i.e.,* Knights and Dames Grand Cross (Mil. and Civ. Div.). The number of awards is limited to 65 (excluding honorary members) and the Order is open to both sexes. *Secretary and Registrar,* The Secretary of the Central Chancery of the Orders of Knighthood.

Anthony, Rt. Hon. John Douglas, 1982.
Ashley, Rt. Hon. Jack, 1975.
Ashton, Sir Frederick, 1970.
Aylestone, The Lord, 1975.
Brenner, Sydney, 1987.
Carrington, The Lord, 1983.
Casson, Sir Hugh, 1985.
Cledwyn of Penrhos, The Lord, 1977.
de Valois, Dame Ninette, 1982.
Duncan-Sandys, The Lord, 1973.
Eccles, The Viscount, 1984.
Elwyn-Jones, The Lord, 1976.
Fraser, Rt. Hon. Malcolm, 1977.
Freud, Lucian, 1983.
Gardiner, The Lord, 1975.
Gielgud, Sir John, 1977.
Glenamara, The Lord, 1976.
Goodman, The Lord, 1972.
Gorton, Rt. Hon. Sir John Grey, 1971.
Greene, Graham, 1966.
Hailsham of St. Marylebone, The Lord, 1974.

von Hayek, *Prof.* Friedrich, 1984.
Healey, Rt. Hon. Denis, 1979.
Houghton of Sowerby, The Lord, 1967.
Jones, James Larkin, 1978.
Joseph, The Lord, 1986.
McMahon, Rt. Hon. Sir William, 1972.
Marshall, Rt. Hon. Sir John Ross, 1973.
Medawar, Sir Peter, 1972.
Muirshiel, The Viscount, 1962.
Muldoon, Rt. Hon. Sir Robert, 1977.
Pasmore, Victor, 1981.
Perutz, *Prof.* Max Ferdinand, 1975.
Piper, John Egerton Christmas, 1972.
Popper, *Prof.* Sir Karl, 1982.
Powell, Sir Philip, 1984.
Rahman, Tunku Abdul, 1960.
Runciman, *Hon.* Sir Steven, 1984.
Rylands, George, 1987.
Sanger, Frederick, 1981.

Scott, Sir Peter, 1987.
Sitwell, Sir Sacheverell, 1984.
Smith, Arnold Cantwell, 1975.
Soames, The Lord, 1980.
Somare, Rt. Hon. Michael Thomas, 1978.
Stewart of Fulham, The Lord, 1969.
Summerson, Sir John, 1987.
Talboys, Rt. Hon. Brian Edward, 1981.
Tebbit, Rt. Hon. Norman, 1987.
Thorneycroft, The Lord, 1980
Tippett, Sir Michael, 1979.
Trudeau, Rt. Hon. Pierre Elliot, 1984.
Watkinson, The Viscount, 1962.
Whitelaw, The Viscount, 1974.
Wootton of Abinger, The Baroness, 1977.
Honorary Members, M. René Massigli, 1954; Lee Kuan Yew, 1970; Dr. Joseph Luns, 1971; Jean Monnet, 1972.

The Royal Victoria and Albert (for Ladies)—V.A.

Instituted in 1862, and enlarged in 1864, 1865, and 1880. Badge, a medallion of Queen Victoria and the Prince Consort, surmounted by a crown, which was attached to a bow of white moiré ribbon. The honour did not confer any rank or title upon the recipient. The last holder of the honour, H.R.H. The Princess Alice, Countess of Athlone, died in 1981.

The Imperial Order of the Crown of India (for Ladies)—C.I.

Instituted Dec. 31, 1877. Badge, the royal cipher in jewels within an oval, surmounted by an Heraldic Crown and attached to a bow of light blue watered ribbon, edged white. The honour does not confer any rank or title upon the recipient. No conferments have been made since 1947.

H.M. THE QUEEN, 1947.
H.M. Queen Elizabeth the Queen Mother, 1931.

H.R.H. The Princess Margaret, Countess of Snowdon, 1947.
H.R.H. The Princess Alice, Duchess of Gloucester, 1937.

H.H. Maharani of Travancore, 1929.
Eugenie Marie, Countess Wavell, 1943.

The Imperial Service Order (1902)—I.S.O.

Ribbon, Crimson, with Blue Centre.

Appointment of Companion of this Order shall be open to those members of the Civil Services whose eligibility shall be determined by the grade held by such persons. The Order consists of THE SOVEREIGN and Companions (not exclusively male) to a number not exceeding 1,700 of whom 1,100 may belong to the Home Civil Services and 600 to Overseas Civil Services. *Secretary,* Sir Robert Armstrong, G.C.B., C.V.O. *Registrar,* Maj.-Gen. D. H. G. Rice, C.V.O., C.B.E., St. James's Palace, SW1A 1BH.

BARONETS, KNIGHTS GRAND CROSS, KNIGHTS GRAND COMMANDERS, KNIGHTS COMMANDERS AND KNIGHTS BACHELOR

    Badge of Baronets
of England, Great Britain, U.K.,
(and Ireland marked I.).

Badge of Baronets
of Scotland or Nova Scotia
(marked S. or N.S.).

NOTES CONCERNING BARONETS

Clause II. of the Royal Warrant of February 8, 1910, ordains as follows:—"That no person whose name is not entered upon the Official Roll shall be received as a Baronet, or shall be addressed or mentioned by that title in any Civil or Military Commission, Letters Patent or other official document." When an obelisk (†) precedes a name it indicates that, *at the time of going to press*, the Baronet concerned has not been registered on the Official Roll of the Baronetage. The date of creation of the Baronetcy is given in parenthesis ( ).

Baronets are addressed as "Sir" (with Christian name) and in writing as "Sir Robert *A*—, Bt." Baronet's wives are addressed (formally) as "Your Ladyship" or "Lady *A*—," without any Christian name unless a daughter of a Duke, Marquess or Earl, in which case "The Lady Mary *A*—"; if daughter of a Viscount or Baron "The Hon. Lady *A*—."

NOTES CONCERNING KNIGHTS GRAND CROSS, ETC.

Knights Grand Cross, Knights Grand Commanders and Knights Commanders are addressed in the same manner as Baronets (*q.v.*), but in writing the appropriate initials (G.C.B., K.C.B., &c.) are appended to surname after "Bt." if they are also baronets or in place of "Bt." if they are not. Knights Bachelor are addressed as "Sir —— (first or Christian name)" and in writing as "Sir —— B ——." The wife of a Knight Grand Cross, Knight Grand Commander, Knight Commander or Knight Bachelor is addressed as stated for the wife of a Baronet.

NOTES CONCERNING KNIGHTS BACHELOR

The Knights Bachelor do not constitute a Royal Order, but comprise the surviving representation of the ancient State Orders of Knighthood. The Register of Knights Bachelor, instituted by James I in the 17th century, lapsed, and in 1908 a voluntary Association under the title of "The Society of Knights" (now "The Imperial Society of Knights Bachelor" by Royal command) was formed with the primary objects of continuing the various registers dating from 1257 and obtaining the uniform registration of every created Knight Bachelor. In 1926 a design for a badge to be worn by Knights Bachelor was approved and adopted, a miniature reproduction being shown above; in 1974 a neck badge and miniature were added. The Officers of the Society are:—*Knight Principal*, Sir Colin Cole, K.C.V.O., T.D.; *Chairman of the Council*, Sir Alexander Durie, C.B.E.; *Prelate*, Rt. Rev. and Rt. Hon. Graham D. Leonard, D.D.; *Hon. Registrar*, Sir Roger Falk, O.B.E.; *Hon. Treasurer*, Sir Peter Lane; *Clerk to the Council*, R. M. Esden; *Office*, 21 Old Buildings, Lincoln's Inn, WC2A 3UJ.

BARONETAGE AND KNIGHTAGE
(Revised to Aug. 31, 1987)
Peers are not included in this list

A full entry in italic type indicates that the recipient of a Knighthood died/was ennobled during the year in which the honour was conferred. The name is included for purposes of record.

Aarvold, *Hon.* Sir Carl Douglas, Kt., O.B.E., T.D.

Abal, Sir Tei, Kt., C.B.E.

Abbott, Sir Albert Francis, Kt., C.B.E.

Abdy, Sir Valentine Robert Duff, Bt. (1850).

Abel, Sir Seselo (Cecil) Charles Geoffrey, Kt., O.B.E.

Abeles, Sir (Emil Herbert) Peter, Kt.

Abell, Sir Anthony Foster, K.C.M.G.

Abell, Sir George Edmond Brackenbury, K.C.I.E., O.B.E.

Abercromby, Sir Ian George, Bt. (s. 1636).

Abraham, Sir Edward Penley, Kt., C.B.E., F.R.S.

Acheson, *Prof.* Sir (Ernest) Donald, K.B.E.

Ackers, Sir James George, Kt.

Ackroyd, Sir John Robert Whyte, Bt. (1956).

Acland, Sir Antony Arthur, G.C.M.G., K.C.V.O.

Acland, *Maj.* Sir Christopher Guy Dyke, Bt. (1890).

Acland, *Maj.-Gen.* Sir John Hugh Bevil, K.C.B., C.B.E.

Acland, Sir Richard Thomas Dyke, Bt. (1644).

Acton, Sir Harold Mario Mitchell, Kt., C.B.E.

Adair, *Maj.-Gen.* Sir Allan Henry Shafto, Bt., G.C.V.O., C.B., D.S.O., M.C. (1838).

Adam, Sir Christopher Eric Forbes, Bt. (1917).

Adams, Sir Philip George Doyne, K.C.M.G.

Adams-Schneider, *Rt. Hon.* Sir Lancelot Raymond, K.C.M.G.

Adamson, Sir (William Owen) Campbell, Kt.

Adcock, Sir Robert Henry, Kt., C.B.E.

Addison, Sir William Wilkinson, Kt.

Ademola, *Rt. Hon.* Sir Adetokunbo Adegboyega, K.B.E.

Adrien, *Hon.* Sir Maurice Latour-, Kt.

Agnew, Sir Crispin Hamlyn, Bt. (s. 1629).

Agnew, Sir (John) Anthony Stuart, Bt. (1895).

Agnew, *Cdr.* Sir Peter Garnett, Bt. (1957).

Agnew, Sir (William) Godfrey, K.C.V.O., C.B.

Ah-Chuen, Sir Moi Lin Jean Etienne, Kt.

Aiken, *Air Chief Marshal* Sir John Alexander Carlisle, K.C.B.

Ainley, Sir (Alfred) John, Kt., M.C.

Ainsworth, Sir (Thomas) David, Bt. (1916).

Aird, *Capt.* Sir Alastair Sturgis, K.C.V.O.

Aird, Sir (George) John, Bt. (1901).

Airey, Sir Lawrence, K.C.B.

Aisher, Sir Owen Arthur, Kt.

Aitchison, Sir Charles Walter de Lancey, Bt. (1938).

Aitken, Sir Robert Stevenson, Kt., M.D., D.Phil.

Akehurst, *Gen.* Sir John Bryan, K.C.B., C.B.E.

Akers-Jones, Sir David, K.B.E., C.M.G.

Albert, Sir Alexis François, Kt., C.M.G., V.R.D.

Albery, Sir Donald Arthur Rolleston, Kt.

Albu, Sir George, Bt. (1912).

Aldington, Sir Geoffrey William, K.B.E., C.M.G.

Alexander, Sir Alexander Sandor, Kt.

Alexander, Sir Charles Gundry, Bt. (1945).

Alexander, Sir Claud Hagart-, Bt. (1886).

Alexander, *Hon.* Sir Darnley Arthur Raymond, Kt., C.B.E.

Alexander, Sir Desmond William Lionel Cable, Bt. (1809).

Alexander, Sir Douglas, Bt. (1921).

Alexander, Sir (John) Lindsay, Kt.

Alexander, *Prof.* Sir Kenneth John Wilson, Kt.

Alexander, Sir Norman Stanley, Kt., C.B.E.

Allan, Sir Anthony James Allan Havelock-, Bt. (1858).

Allan, Sir Colin Hamilton, K.C.M.G., O.B.E.

Allard, Sir Gordon Laidlaw, Kt.

Allcroft, Sir Philip Magnus-, Bt., C.B.E. (1917).

Allen, *Prof.* Sir Geoffrey, Kt., Ph.D., F.R.S.

Allen, Sir George Oswald Browning, Kt., C.B.E., T.D.

Allen, Sir Peter Austin Philip Jermyn, Kt.

Allen, Sir Peter Christopher, Kt.

Allen, Sir Richard Hugh Sedley, K.C.M.G.

Allen, Sir William Guilford, Kt.

Allen, Sir (William) Kenneth (Gwynne), Kt.

Alleyne, *Rev.* John Olpherts Campbell, Bt., (1769).

Allinson, Sir (Walter) Leonard, K.C.V.O., C.M.G.

Alliott, *Hon.* Sir John Downes, Kt.

Alment, Sir (Edward) Anthony John, Kt.

Alun-Jones, Sir (John) Derek, Kt.

Anderson, *Prof.* Sir (James) Norman (Dalrymple), Kt., O.B.E., Q.C., F.B.A.

Anderson, *General* Sir John D'Arcy, G.B.E., K.C.B., D.S.O.

Anderson, *Maj.-Gen.* Sir John Evelyn, K.B.E.

Anderson, Sir John Muir, K.B.E., C.M.G.

Anderson, Sir Kenneth, K.B.E., O.B.E.

Anderson, *Hon.* Sir Kevin Victor, Kt.

Anderson, *Vice-Adm.* Sir Neil Dudley, K.B.E., C.B.

Anderson, *Prof.* Sir (William) Ferguson, Kt., O.B.E.

Andrew, Sir Robert John, K.C.B.

Andrewes, Sir Christopher Howard, Kt., M.D., F.R.S.

Andrews, *Hon.* Sir Dormer George, Kt.

Ansell, *Col.* Sir Michael Picton Kt., C.B.E., D.S.O.

Anson, *Vice-Adm.* Sir Edward Rosebery, K.C.B.

Anson, *Rear-Admiral* Sir Peter, Bt., C.B. (1831).

Anstey, *Brig.* Sir John, Kt., C.B.E., T.D.

Anstruther, Sir Ralph Hugo, Bt. K.C.V.O., M.C. (s. 1694).

Anthony, Sir (Michael) Mobolaji Bank-, K.B.E.

Antico, Sir Tristan Venus, Kt.

Antrobus, Sir Philip Coutts, Bt. (1815).

Appleyard, Sir Raymond Kenelm, K.B.E.

Arbuthnot, Sir John Sinclair-Wemyss, Bt., M.B.E., T.D. (1964).

Arbuthnot, Sir Keith Robert Charles, Bt. (1823).

Archdale, *Comdr.* Sir Edward Folmer, Bt., D.S.C., R.N. (1928).

Archer, *General* Sir (Arthur) John, K.C.B., O.B.E.

Archer, Sir Clyde Vernon Harcourt, Kt.

Arculus, Sir Ronald, K.C.M.G., K.C.V.O.

Armitage, *Air Chief Marshal* Sir Michael John, K.C.B., C.B.E.

Armitage, Sir Robert Perceval, K.C.M.G., M.B.E.

†Armstrong, Sir Andrew Clarence Francis, Bt., C.M.G. (1841).

Armstrong, Sir Robert Temple, G.C.B., C.V.O.

Armstrong, Sir Thomas Henry Wait, Kt., D.MUS.

Armytage, Sir John Martin, Bt. (1738).

Arnold, *Rt. Hon.* Sir John Lewis, Kt.

Arnott, Sir Alexander John Maxwell, Bt. (1896).

Arnott, *Prof.* Sir (William) Melville, Kt., T.D., M.D.

Arrindell, Sir Clement Athelston, G.C.M.G., G.C.V.O.

Arrowsmith, Sir Edwin Porter, K.C.M.G.

Arthur, Sir Stephen John, Bt. (1841).

Arthur, *Lt.-Gen.* Sir (John) Norman Stewart, K.C.B.

Arundell, *Brig.* Sir Robert Duncan Harris, K.C.M.G., O.B.E.

Arup, Sir Ove Nyquist, Kt., C.B.E.

Ashburnham, Sir Denny Reginald, Bt. (1661).

Ashe, Sir Derick Rosslyn, K.C.M.G.

Ashley, Sir Bernard Albert, Kt.

Ashmore, *Admiral of the Fleet* Sir Edward Beckwith, G.C.B., D.S.C.

Ashmore, *Vice-Adm.* Sir Peter William Beckwith, K.C.B., K.C.V.O., D.S.C.

Ashton, Sir Frederick William Mallandaine, Kt., O.M., C.H., C.B.E.

Ashworth, Sir Herbert, Kt.

Aske, *Rev.* Sir Conan, Bt. (1922).

Astley, Sir Francis Jacob Dugdale, Bt. (1821).

Aston, Sir Harold George, Kt., C.B.E.

Aston, *Hon.* Sir William John, K.C.M.G.

Astor, *Hon.* Sir John Jacob, Kt., M.B.E.

Astwood, *Hon.* Sir James Rufus, Kt.

Astwood, *Lt.-Col.* Sir Jeffrey Carlton, Kt., C.B.E., E.D.

Atcherley, Sir Harold Winter, Kt.

Atiyah, Sir Michael Francis, Kt., Ph.D., F.R.S.

Atkins, Sir William Sydney Albert, Kt., C.B.E.

Atkinson, *Air Marshal* Sir David William, K.B.E., Q.H.P.

Atkinson, Sir Frederick John, K.C.B.

Atkinson, Sir John Alexander, K.C.B., D.F.C.

Atkinson, Sir (John) Kenneth, Kt.

Atkinson, *Maj.-Gen.* Sir Leonard Henry, K.B.E.

Atkinson, Sir Robert, Kt., D.S.C.

Attenborough, Sir David Frederick, Kt., C.B.E., F.R.S.

Attenborough, Sir Richard Samuel, Kt., C.B.E.

Atwell, Sir John William, Kt., C.B.E., F.R.S.E.

Atwill, Sir (Milton) John (Napier), Kt.

Audland, Sir Christopher John, K.C.M.G.

Audley, Sir George Bernard, Kt.

Austin, Sir William Ronald, Bt. (1894).

Austin, *Vice-Admiral* Sir Peter Murray, K.C.B.

Ayer, *Prof.* Sir Alfred Jules, Kt., F.B.A.

Aykroyd, Sir Cecil William, Bt. (1929).

Aykroyd, Sir William Miles, Bt., M.C. (1920).

Aylmer, Sir Fenton Gerald, Bt. (I 1622).

Backhouse, Sir Jonathan Roger, Bt. (1901).

Bacon, Sir Nicholas Hickman Ponsonby, Bt. *Premier Baronet of England* (1611 and 1627).

Bacon, Sir Ranulph Robert Maunsell, Kt.

Bacon, Sir Sidney Charles, Kt., C.B.

Baddeley, Sir John Wolsey Beresford, Bt. (1922).

Baddiley, *Prof.* Sir James, Kt., Ph.D., D.S.C., F.R.S., F.R.S.E.

Badenoch, Sir John, Kt., D.M., F.R.C.P.

Badger, Sir Geoffrey Malcolm, Kt.

Bagge, Sir John Alfred Picton, Bt. (1867).

Bagnall, *Gen.* Sir Nigel Thomas, G.C.B., C.V.O., M.C.

Bailey, Sir Alan Marshall, K.C.B.

Bailey, Sir Brian Harry, Kt., O.B.E.

Bailey, Sir Derrick Thomas Louis, Bt., D.F.C. (1919).

Bailey, *Prof.* Sir Harold Walter, Kt., D.Phil., F.B.A.

Bailey, Sir John Bilsland, Kt.

Bailey, Sir Richard John, Kt., C.B.E.

Bailey, Sir Stanley Ernest, Kt., C.B.E., Q.P.M.

Baillie, Sir Gawaine George Hope, Bt. (1823).

Baines, *Prof.* Sir George Grenfell-, Kt., O.B.E.

Baird, Sir David Charles, Bt. (1809).

Baird, *Lt.-Gen.* Sir James Parlane, K.B.E., M.D.

Baird, Sir James Richard Gardiner, Bt., M.C. (s. 1695).

Baird, *Vice-Adm.* Sir Thomas Henry Eustace, K.C.B.

Bairsto, *Air Marshal* Sir Peter Edward, K.B.E., C.B.

Baker, Sir (Allan) Ivor, Kt., C.B.E.

Baker, Sir Humphrey Dodington Benedict Sherston-, Bt. (1796).

Baker, Sir (Stanislaus) Joseph, Kt., C.B.

Balcombe, *Rt. Hon.* Sir (Alfred) John, Kt.

Balderstone, Sir James Schofield, Kt.

Baldwin, Sir Peter Robert, K.C.B.

Balfour, *General* Sir (Robert George) Victor FitzGeorge-, K.C.B., C.B.E., D.S.O., M.C.

Ball, *Air Marshal* Sir Alfred Henry Wynne, K.C.B., D.S.O., D.F.C.

Ball, Sir Charles Irwin, Bt. (1911).

Ball, *Prof.* Sir Robert James, Kt., Ph.D.

Balmer, Sir Joseph Reginald, Kt.

Banks, Sir Maurice Alfred Lister, Kt.

Banner, Sir George Knowles Harmood-, Bt. (1924).

Bannerman, *Lt.-Col.* Sir Donald Arthur Gordon, Bt. (s. 1682).

Bannister, Sir Roger Gilbert, Kt., C.B.E., D.M., F.R.C.P.

Barber, Sir Derek Coates, Kt.

Barber, *Hon.* Sir (Edward Hamilton) Esler, Kt.

Barber, Sir William Francis, Bt., T.D. (1960).

Barclay, Sir Colville Herbert Sanford, Bt. (s. 1668).

Barclay, Sir Roderick Edward, G.C.V.O., K.C.M.G.

Barford, Sir Leonard, Kt.

Baring, Sir Charles Christian, Bt. (1911).

Baring, *Hon.* Sir John Francis Harcourt, Kt., C.V.O.

Baring, Sir Mark, K.C.V.O.

Barker, Sir Alwyn Bowman, Kt., C.M.G.

Barker, Sir Harry Heaton, Kt., K.B.E.

Barker, Sir William, K.C.M.G., O.B.E.

Barlow, Sir Christopher Hilaro, Bt. (1803).

Barlow, Sir (George) William, Kt.

Barlow, Sir John Kemp, Bt. (1907).

Barlow, Sir Thomas Erasmus, Bt., D.S.C. (1902).

Barnard, Sir (Arthur) Thomas, Kt., C.B., O.B.E.

Barnard, *Capt.* Sir George Edward, Kt.

Barnard, Sir Joseph Brian, Kt.

Barnes, Sir Denis Charles, K.C.B.

Barnes, Sir (Ernest) John (Ward), K.C.M.G., M.B.E.

Barnes, Sir James George, Kt., M.B.E.

Barnes, Sir Kenneth, K.C.B.

Barnett, *Air Chief Marshal* Sir Denis Hensley Fulton, G.C.B., C.B.E., D.F.C.

Barnett, Sir Oliver Charles, Kt., C.B.E., Q.C.

Barnewall, Sir Reginald Robert, Bt. (I 1623).

Barraclough, *Air Chief Marshal* Sir John, K.C.B., C.B.E., D.F.C., A.F.C.

Barraclough, Sir Kenneth James Priestley, Kt., C.B.E., T.D.

Barran, Sir David Haven, Kt.

Barran, Sir John Napoleon Ruthven, Bt. (1895).

Barratt, Sir Lawrence Arthur, Kt.

Barrett, *Lt.-Gen.* Sir David William Scott-, K.B.E., M.C.

Barrett, *Lt.-Col.* Sir Dennis Charles Titchener, Kt., T.D.

Barrie, Sir Walter, Kt.

Barrington, Sir Alexander (Fitzwilliam Croker), Bt. (1831).

Barrington, Sir Kenneth Charles Peto, Kt.

Barritt, Sir David Thurlow, Kt.

Barron, Sir Donald James, Kt.

Barrow, *Capt.* Sir Richard John Uniacke, Bt. (1835).

Barry, Sir (Lawrence) Edward (Anthony Tress), Bt. (1899).

Barry, Sir (Philip) Stuart Milner-, K.C.V.O., C.B., O.B.E.

Bartlett, Sir Henry David Hardington, Bt., M.B.E (1913).

Barton, Sir Charles Newton, Kt., O.B.E., E.D.

Barton, *Prof.* Sir Derek Harold Richard, Kt., F.R.S., F.R.S.E.

Barttelot, *Lt.-Col.* Sir Brian Walter de Stopham, Bt., O.B.E. (1875).

Barwick, *Rt. Hon.* Sir Garfield Edward John, G.C.M.G.

Basten, Sir Henry Bolton, Kt., C.M.G.

Batchelor, Sir Ivor Ralph Campbell, Kt., C.B.E.

Bate, Sir David Lindsay, K.B.E.

Bate, Sir (Walter) Edwin, Kt., O.B.E.

Bateman, Sir Cecil Joseph, K.B.E.

Bateman, Sir Charles Harold, K.C.M.G., M.C.

Bateman, Sir Geoffrey Hirst, Kt., F.R.C.S.

Bateman, Sir Ralph Melton, K.B.E.

Bates, *Prof.* Sir David Robert, Kt., D.S.C., F.R.S.

Bates, *Maj.-Gen.* Sir (Edward) John (Hunter), K.B.E., C.B., M.C.

Bates, Sir Geoffrey Voltelin, Bt., M.C. (1880).

Bates, Sir John David, Kt., C.B.E., V.R.D.

Bates, Sir (John) Dawson, Bt., M.C. (1937).

Bates, Sir (Julian) Darrell, Kt., C.M.G., C.V.O.

Batho, Sir Maurice Benjamin, Bt. (1928).

Bathurst, *Vice-Adm.* Sir (David) Benjamin, K.C.B.

Bathurst, Sir Frederick Peter Methuen Hervey-, Bt. (1818).

Bathurst, Sir Maurice Edward, Kt., C.M.G., C.B.E., Q.C.

Batsford, Sir Brian Caldwell Cook, Kt.

Batten, Sir John Charles, K.C.V.O.

Batty, Sir William Bradshaw, Kt., T.D.

Baxendell, Sir Peter Brian, Kt., C.B.E.

Baxter, *Prof.* Sir (John) Philip, K.B.E., C.M.G.

Bayliss, *Prof.* Sir Noel Stanley, Kt., C.B.E.

Bayliss, Sir Richard Ian Samuel, K.C.V.O., M.D., F.R.C.P.

Bayly, *Vice-Adm.* Sir Patrick Uniacke, K.B.E., C.B., D.S.C.

Baynes, Sir John Christopher Malcolm, Bt. (1801).

Bazley, Sir Thomas Stafford, Bt. (1869).

Beach, *General* Sir (William Gerald) Hugh, G.B.E., K.C.B., M.C.

Beale, Sir William Francis, Kt., O.B.E.

Beament, Sir James William Longman, Kt., SC.D., F.R.S.

Beattie, *Hon.* Sir Alexander Craig, Kt.

Beattie, *Hon.* Sir David Stuart, G.C.M.G., G.C.V.O.

Beauchamp, Sir Christopher Radstock Proctor-, Bt. (1745).

Beaumont, Sir George (Howland Francis), Bt. (1661).

Beaumont, Sir Richard Ashton, K.C.M.G., O.B.E.

Beavis, *Air Chief Marshal* Sir Michael Gordon, K.C.B., C.B.E., A.F.C.

Becher, Sir William Fane Wrixon, Bt., M.C. (1831).

Beck, Sir Edgar Charles, Kt., C.B.E.

Beckett, *Capt.* Sir (Martyn) Gervase, Bt., M.C. (1921).

Beckett, Sir Terence Norman, Kt., K.B.E.

Bedbrook, Sir George Montario, Kt., O.B.E.

Bedingfeld, *Capt.* Sir Edmund George Felix Paston-, Bt. (1661).

Beecham, John Stratford Roland, Bt. (1914).

Beeley, Sir Harold, K.C.M.G., C.B.E.

Beetham, *Marshal of the Royal Air Force* Sir Michael James, G.C.B., C.B.E., D.F.C., A.F.C.

Beevor, Sir Thomas Agnew, Bt. (1784).

Begg, Sir Neil Colquhoun, K.B.E.

Begg, *Admiral of the Fleet* Sir Varyl Cargill, G.C.B., D.S.O., D.S.C.

Beit, Sir Alfred Lane, Bt. (1924).

Beith, Sir John Greville Stanley, K.C.M.G.

Beldam, *Hon.* Sir (Alexander) Roy (Asplan), Kt.

Bell, Sir Charles William, Kt., C.B.E.

Bell, Sir Gawain Westray, K.C.M.G., C.B.E.

Bell, Sir (George) Raymond, K.C.M.G., C.B.

Bell, Sir John Lowthian, Bt. (1885).

Bell, Sir (William) Ewart, K.C.B.

Bell, Sir William Hollin Dayrell Morrison-, Bt. (1905).

Bellew, *Hon.* Sir George Rothe, K.C.B., K.C.V.O., F.S.A.

Bellew, Sir Henry Charles Gratton-, Bt. (1838).

Bellinger, Sir Robert Ian, G.B.E.

Bellingham, Sir Noel Peter Roger, Bt. (1796).

Bengough, *Col.* Sir Piers, K.C.V.O., O.B.E.

Benn, *Capt.* Sir (Patrick Ion) Hamilton, Bt. (1920).

Benn, Sir James Jonathan, Bt. (1914).

Bennett, *Rt. Hon.* Sir Charles Moihi Te Arawaka, Kt., D.S.O.

Bennett, *Rt. Hon.* Sir Frederic Mackarness, Kt.

Bennett, Sir Hubert, Kt.

Bennett, *Lt.-Gen.* Sir Phillip Harvey, K.B.E.

Bennett, Sir Reginald Frederick Brittain, Kt., V.R.D.

Bennett, Sir Ronald Wilfrid Murdoch, Bt. (1929).

Benson, Sir Arthur Edward Trevor, G.C.M.G.

Benson, Sir (William) Jeffrey, Kt.

Benthall, Sir (Arthur) Paul, K.B.E.

Bentley, Sir William, K.C.M.G.

Berger, *Vice-Adm.* Sir Peter Egerton Capel, K.C.B., M.V.O., D.S.C.

Berkeley, Sir Lennox Randal Francis, Kt., C.B.E.

Berlin, Sir Isaiah, Kt., O.M., C.B.E.

Bernard, Sir Dallas Edmund, Bt. (1954).

Berney, Sir Julian Reedham Stuart, Bt. (1620).

Berrill, Sir Kenneth Ernest, K.C.B.

Berthon, *Vice-Adm.* Sir Stephen Ferrier, K.C.B.

Berthoud, Sir Eric Alfred, K.C.M.G.

Berthoud, Sir Martin Seymour, K.C.V.O., C.M.G.

Bethune, Sir Alexander Maitland Sharp, Bt. (s. 1683).

Bethune, *Hon.* Sir (Walter) Angus, Kt.

Bevan, Sir Martyn Evan Evans, Bt. (1958).

Bevan, Sir Timothy Hugh, Kt.

Beynon, *Prof.* Sir (William John) Granville, Kt., C.B.E., Ph.D., D.SC., F.R.S.

Bibby, Sir Derek James, Bt., M.C. (1959).

Biddulph, Sir Ian D'Olier, Bt. (1664).

Bide, Sir Austin Ernest, Kt.

Biggs, Sir Norman Paris, Kt.

Biggs-Davison, Sir John Alec, Kt., M.P.

Bing, Sir Rudolf Franz Josef, K.B.E.

Bingham, *Rt. Hon.* Sir Thomas Henry, Kt.

Bird, Sir Richard Geoffrey Chapman, Bt. (1922).

Bird, *Col.* Sir Richard Dawnay Martin-, Kt., C.B.E., T.D.

Birkin, Sir John Christian William, Bt. (1905).

Birkmyre, Sir Henry, Bt. (1921).

Bishop, Sir Frederick Arthur, Kt., C.B., C.V.O.

Bishop, Sir George Sidney, Kt., C.B., O.B.E.

Bishop, *Instructor Rear-Adm.* Sir William, K.B.E., C.B.

Bjelke-Petersen, *Hon.* Sir Johannes, K.C.M.G.

Black, Sir Cyril Wilson, Kt.

Black, *Prof.* Sir Douglas Andrew Kilgour, Kt., M.D., F.R.C.P.

Black, Sir Hermann David, Kt.

Black, Sir James Whyte, Kt., F.R.C.P., F.R.S..

Black, *Vice-Adm.* Sir John Jeremy, K.C.B., D.S.O., M.B.E.

Black, Sir Robert Brown, G.C.M.G., O.B.E.

Black, Sir Robert David, Bt. (1922).

Blackburn, *Hon.* Sir Richard Arthur, Kt., O.B.E.

Blacker, *General* Sir Cecil Hugh, G.C.B., O.B.E., M.C.

Blackett, Sir George William, Bt. (1673).

Blackman, Sir Frank Milton, K.C.V.O., O.B.E.

Blackwell, Sir Basil Davenport, Kt.

Blackwood, Sir Francis (George), Bt. (1814).

Blair, Sir Alastair Campbell, K.C.V.O., T.D., W.S.

Blair, *Lt.-Gen.* Sir Chandos, K.C.V.O., O.B.E., M.C.

Blair, Sir Edward Thomas Hunter, Bt. (1786).

Blake, Sir Alfred Lapthorn, K.C.V.O., M.C.

Blake, Sir Francis Michael, Bt. (1907).

Blake, Sir (Thomas) Richard (Valentine), Bt. (1 1622).

Blaker, Sir John, Bt. (1919).

Blaker, *Rt. Hon.* Sir Peter Allan Renshaw, K.C.M.G., M.P.

Blakiston, Sir Ferguson Arthur James, Bt. (1763).

Bland, Sir Henry Armand, Kt., C.B.E.

Bland, *Lt.-Col.* Sir Simon Claud Michael, K.C.V.O.

Blaxter, Sir Kenneth Lyon, Kt., F.R.S., F.R.S.E.

Blelloch, Sir John Nial Henderson, K.C.B.

Blennerhassett, Sir (Marmaduke) Adrian Francis William, Bt. (1809).

Blois, Sir Charles Nicholas Gervase, Bt. (1686).

Blomefield, Sir Thomas Charles Peregrine, Bt. (1807).

Bloomfield, *Hon.* Sir John Stoughton, Kt., Q.C.

Bloomfield, Sir Kenneth Percy, K.C.B.

Blosse, *Capt.* Sir Richard Hely Lynch-, Bt. (1622).

Blount, Sir Walter Edward Alpin, Bt., D.S.C. (1642).

Blundell, Sir Michael, K.B.E.

Blunden, Sir George, Kt.

Blunden, Sir Philip Overington, Bt. (1 1766).

Blunt, Sir David Richard Reginald Harvey, Bt. (1720).

Blyth, Sir James, Kt.

Boardman, Sir Kenneth Ormrod, Kt.

Bodily, *Hon.* Sir Jocelyn, Kt., V.R.D.

Bodmer, Sir Walter Fred, Kt., Ph.D., F.R.S.

Body, Sir Richard Bernard Frank Stewart, Kt., M.P.

Boevey, Sir Thomas Michael Blake Crawley-, Bt. (1784).

Boileau, Sir Guy (Francis), Bt. (1838).

Boles, Sir Jeremy John Fortescue, Bt. (1922).

Boles, Sir John Dennis, Kt., M.B.E.

Bolland, Sir Edwin, K.C.M.G.

Bollers, *Hon.* Sir Harold Brodie Smith, Kt.

Bolte, *Hon.* Sir Henry Edward, G.C.M.G.

Bolton, Sir Frederic Bernard, Kt., M.C.

Bonallack, Sir Richard Frank, Kt., C.B.E.

Bonar, Sir Herbert Vernon, Kt., C.B.E.

Bond, Sir Kenneth Raymond Boyden, Kt.

Bondi, *Prof.* Sir Hermann, K.C.B., F.R.S.

Bonham, *Maj.* Sir Antony Lionel Thomas, Bt. (1852).

Bonsall, Sir Arthur Wilfred, K.C.M.G., C.B.E.

Bonsor, Sir Nicholas Cosmo, Bt., M.P. (1925).

Boolell, Sir Satcam, Kt.

Boon, Sir Peter Coleman, Kt.

Boord, Sir Nicolas John Charles, Bt. (1896).

Boorman, *Lt.-Gen.* Sir Derek, K.C.B.

†Booth, Sir Angus Josslyn Gore-, Bt. (1 1760).

Booth, Sir Christopher Charles, Kt., M.D., F.R.C.P.

Booth, Sir Douglas Allen, Bt. (1916).

Booth, Sir Gordon, K.C.M.G., C.V.O.

Booth, Sir Robert Camm, Kt., C.B.E., T.D.

Boothby, Sir Brooke Charles, Bt. (1660).

Boreel, Sir Francis David, Bt. (1645).

Boreham, Sir (Arthur) John, K.C.B.

Boreham, *Hon.* Sir Leslie Kenneth Edward, Kt.

Bornu, The Waziri of, K.C.M.G., C.B.E.

Borrie, Sir Gordon Johnson, Kt., Q.C.

Borthwick, Sir John Thomas, Bt. M.B.E. (1908).

Bossom, *Hon.* Sir Clive, Bt. (1953).

Boswall, Sir (Thomas) Alford Houstoun-, Bt. (1836).

Boswell, *Lt.-Gen.* Sir Alexander Crawford Simpson, K.C.B., C.B.E.

Bosworth, Sir Neville Bruce Alfred, Kt., C.B.E.

Bottomley, Sir James Reginald Alfred, K.C.M.G.

Boughey, Sir John George Fletcher, Bt. (1798).

Boulton, Sir (Harold Hugh) Christian, Bt. (1905).

Boulton, Sir William Whytehead, Bt., C.B.E., T.D. (1944).

Bourne, Sir (John) Wilfrid, K.C.B.

Bovell, *Hon.* Sir (William) Stewart, Kt.

Bowater, Sir (John) Vansittart, Bt. (1914).

Bowater, Sir Euan David Vansittart, Bt. (1939).

Bowden, Sir Frank, Bt. (1915).

Bowen, Sir Geoffrey Fraser, Kt.

Bowen, *Hon.* Sir Nigel Hubert, K.B.E.

Bowen, Sir Thomas Frederic Charles, Bt. (1921).

Bower, *Air Marshal* Sir Leslie William Clement, K.C.B., D.S.O., D.F.C.

Bower, *Lt.-Gen.* Sir Roger Herbert, K.C.B., K.B.E.

Bowes, Sir (Harold) Leslie, K.C.M.G., C.B.E.

Bowlby, Sir Anthony Hugh Mostyn, Bt. (1923).

Bowman, Sir George, Bt. (1961).

Bowman, Sir John Paget, Bt. (1884).

Bowman-Shaw, Sir (George) Neville, Kt.

Bowmar, Sir Charles Erskine, Kt.

Bowness, Sir Peter Spencer, Kt., C.B.E.

Boxer, *Air Vice-Marshal* Sir Alan Hunter Cachemaille, K.C.V.O., C.B., D.S.O., D.F.C.

Boyce, Sir Robert Charles Leslie, Bt. (1952).

Boyd, Sir Alexander Walter, Bt. (1916).

Boyd, Sir John McFarlane, Kt., C.B.E.

Boyd, *Prof.* Sir Robert Lewis Fullarton, Kt., C.B.E., D.SC., F.R.S.

Boyes, Sir Brian Gerald Barratt-, K.B.E.

Boyle, *Marshal of the Royal Air Force* Sir Dermot Alexander, G.C.B., K.C.V.O., K.B.E., A.F.C.

Boyle, Sir Lawrence, Kt., Ph.D.

Boyle, Sir Stephen Gurney, Bt. (1904).

Boyne, Sir Henry Brian, Kt., C.B.E.

Boynton, Sir John Keyworth, Kt., M.C.

Boyson, Sir Rhodes, Kt., M.P.

Brabham, Sir John Arthur, Kt., O.B.E.

Bradbury, *Surgeon Vice-Adm.* Sir Eric Blackburn, K.B.E., C.B.

Bradford, Sir Edward Alexander Slade, Bt. (1902).

Bradlaw, *Prof.* Sir Robert Vivian, Kt., C.B.E.

Bradman, Sir Donald George, Kt.

Bradshaw, Sir Kenneth Anthony, K.C.B.

Bradshaw, *Lt.-Gen.* Sir Richard Phillip, K.B.E.

Brain, Sir (Henry) Norman, K.B.E., C.M.G.

Braine, *Rt. Hon.* Sir Bernard Richard, Kt., M.P.

Braithwaite, Sir (Joseph) Franklin Madders, Kt.

Bramall, Sir (Ernest) Ashley, Kt.

Bramley, *Prof.* Sir Paul Anthony, Kt.

Branch, Sir William Allan Patrick, Kt.

Brancker, Sir (John Eustace) Theodore, Kt., Q.C.

Branigan, Sir Patrick Francis, Kt., Q.C.

Brassey, *Col.* Sir Hugh Trefusis, K.C.V.O., O.B.E., M.C.

Bray, Sir Theodor Charles, Kt., C.B.E.

Braynen, Sir Alvin Rudolph, Kt.

Brearley, Sir Norman, Kt., C.B.E., D.S.O., M.C., A.F.C.

Bremridge, Sir John Henry, K.B.E.

Brennan, *Hon.* Sir (Francis) Gerard, K.B.E.

Brett, Sir Lionel, Kt.

Brickwood, Sir Basil Greame, Bt. (1927).

Bridges, *Hon.* Sir Phillip Rodney, Kt., C.M.G.

Brierley, Sir Zachry, Kt., C.B.E.

Briggs, *Hon.* Sir Geoffrey Gould, Kt.

Bright, Sir Keith, Kt.

Brinckman, Sir Theodore George Roderick, Bt. (1831).

Brisco, Sir Donald Gilfrid, Bt. (1782).

Briscoe, Sir John Leigh Charlton, Bt., D.F.C. (1910).

Brise, Sir John Archibald Ruggles-, Bt., C.B., O.B.E., T.D. (1935).

Bristow, *Hon.* Sir Peter Henry Rowley, Kt.

Britton, Sir Edward Louis, Kt., C.B.E.

Broackes, Sir Nigel, Kt.

Broadbent, Sir Ewen, K.C.B., C.M.G.

Broadbent, Sir George Walter, Bt. (1893).

Broadhurst, *Air Chief Marshal* Sir Harry, G.C.B., K.B.E., D.S.O., D.F.C., A.F.C.

Brockhoff, Sir Jack Stuart, Kt.

Brocklebank, Sir Aubrey Thomas, Bt. (1885).

Brockman, *Vice-Adm.* Sir Ronald Vernon, K.C.B., C.V.O., C.S.I., C.I.E., C.B.E.

Brockman, *Hon.* Sir Thomas Charles Drake-, Kt., D.F.C.

Brodie, Sir Benjamin David Ross, Bt. (1834).

Brogan, *Lt.-Gen.* Sir Mervyn Francis, K.B.E., C.B.

Bromhead, Sir John Desmond Gonville, Bt. (1806).

Bromley, Sir Rupert Charles, Bt. (1757).

Brook, Sir Robin, Kt., C.M.G., O.B.E.

†Brooke, Sir Alistair Weston, Bt. (1919).

Brooke, Sir Francis George Windham, Bt. (1903).

Brooke, Sir (Norman) Richard (Rowley), Kt., C.B.E.

Brooke, Sir Richard Neville, Bt. (1662).

Brookes, Sir Wilfred Deakin, Kt., C.B.E., D.S.O.

Brooksbank, Sir (Edward) Nicholas, Bt. (1919).

Broom, *Air Marshal* Sir Ivor Gordon, K.C.B., C.B.E., D.S.O., D.F.C., A.F.C.

Broughton, *Air Marshal* Sir Charles, K.B.E., C.B.

Broughton, Sir Evelyn Delves, Bt. (1661).

Broun, Sir Lionel John Law, Bt. (s. 1686).

Brown, Sir Allen Stanley, Kt., C.B.E.

Brown, Sir (Arthur James) Stephen, K.B.E.

Brown, *Lt.-Col.* Sir Charles Frederick Richmond, Bt. (1863).

Brown, Sir (Cyril) Maxwell Palmer, K.C.B., C.M.G.

Brown, Sir David, Kt.

Brown, *Vice-Adm.* Sir David Worthington, K.C.B.

Brown, Sir Derrick Holden-, Kt.

Brown, Sir Douglas Denison, Kt.

Brown, Sir Edward Joseph, Kt., M.B.E.

Brown, *Prof.* Sir (Ernest) Henry Phelps, Kt., M.B.E., F.B.A.

Brown, Sir (Frederick Herbert) Stanley, Kt., C.B.E.

Brown, *Prof.* Sir (George) Malcolm, Kt., F.R.S

Brown, Sir John Douglas Keith, Kt.

Brown, Sir John Gilbert Newton, Kt., C.B.E.

Brown, Sir Mervyn, K.C.M.G., O.B.E..

Brown, *Hon.* Sir Ralph Kilner, Kt., O.B.E., T.D.

Brown, Sir Raymond Frederick, Kt., O.B.E.

Brown, Sir Robert Crichton-, K.C.M.G., C.B.E., T.D.

Brown, *Hon.* Sir Simon Denis, Kt.

Brown, *Rt. Hon.* Sir Stephen, Kt.

Brown, Sir Thomas, Kt.

Brown, Sir William Brian Piggott-, Bt. (1903).

Browne, *Rt. Hon.* Sir Patrick Reginald Evelyn, Kt., O.B.E., T.D.

Browne, Sir Thomas Anthony Gore, Kt.

Brownrigg, Sir Nicholas (Gawen), Bt. (1816).

Bruce, Sir Arthur Atkinson, K.B.E., M.C.

Bruce, Sir (Francis) Michael Ian, Bt. (s. 1628).

Bruce, Sir Hervey James Hugh, Bt. (1804).

Bruce, *Rt. Hon.* Sir (James) Roualeyn Hovell-Thurlow-Cumming-, Kt.

Brunner, Sir John Henry Kilian, Bt. (1895).

Brunton, Sir (Edward Francis) Lauder, Bt. (1908).

Brunton, Sir Gordon Charles, Kt.

Bryan, Sir Andrew Meikle, Kt.

Bryan, Sir Arthur, Kt.

Bryan, Sir Paul Elmore Oliver, Kt., D.S.O., M.C.

Bryce, *Hon.* Sir (William) Gordon, Kt., C.B.E.

Bryson, *Vice-Adm.* Sir Lindsay Sutherland, K.C.B.

Buchan, Sir John, Kt., C.M.G.

Buchanan, Sir Charles Alexander James Leith-, Bt. (1775).

Buchanan, Sir Andrew George, Bt. (1878).

Buchanan, *Prof.* Sir Colin Douglas, Kt., C.B.E.

Buchanan, *Vice-Adm.* Sir Peter William, K.B.E.

Buck, Sir (Philip) Antony (Fyson), Kt., Q.C., M.P.

Buckley, *Rt. Hon.* Sir Denys Burton, Kt., M.B.E.

Buckley, Sir John William, Kt.

Buckley, *Rear-Adm.* Sir Kenneth Robertson, K.B.E.

Buckley, *Lt.-Comdr.* Sir (Peter) Richard, K.C.V.O.

Bulkeley, Sir Richard Harry David Williams-, Bt., T.D. (1661).

Bull, Sir Graham MacGregor, Kt., M.D., F.R.C.P.

†Bull, Sir Simeon George, Bt. (1922).

Bull, Sir Walter Edward Avenon, K.C.V.O.

Bullard, Sir Giles Lionel, K.C.V.O., G.M.G.

Bullard, Sir Julian Leonard, G.C.M.G.

Bullus, Sir Eric Edward, Kt.

Bulmer, Sir William Peter, Kt.

Bultin, Sir Bato, Kt., M.B.E.

Bunbury, Sir Michael William, Bt. (1681).

Bunbury, Sir (Richard David) Michael Richardson-, Bt. (I 1787).

Bunch, Sir Austin Wyeth, Kt., C.B.E.

Bunting, Sir (Edward) John, K.B.E.

Burbidge, Sir Herbert Dudley, Bt. (1916).

Burbury, *Hon.* Sir Stanley Charles, K.C.M.G., K.C.V.O., K.B.E.

Burder, Sir John Henry, Kt.

Burdett, Sir Savile Aylmer, Bt. (1665).

Burgen, Sir Arnold Stanley Vincent, Kt., F.R.S.

Burgess, *General* Sir Edward Arthur, K.C.B., O.B.E.

Burgh, Sir John Charles, K.C.M.G., C.B.

Burke, Sir Aubrey Francis, Kt., O.B.E.

Burke, *Prof.* Sir Joseph Terence, K.B.E.

Burke, Sir Thomas Stanley, Bt. (I 1797).

Burley, Sir Victor George, Kt., C.B.E.

Burman, Sir (John) Charles, Kt.

Burman, Sir Stephen France, Kt., C.B.E.

Burnet, Sir James William Alexander (Sir Alastair Burnet), Kt.

Burnett, *Air Chief Marshal* Sir Brian Kenyon, G.C.B., D.F.C., A.F.C.

Burnett, Sir David Humphery, Bt., M.B.E., T.D. (1913).

Burnett, Sir John Harrison, Kt.

Burney, Sir Anthony George Bernard, Kt., O.B.E.

Burney, Sir Cecil Denniston, Bt. (1921).

Burns, Sir Charles Ritchie, K.B.E., M.D.

Burns, Sir John Crawford, Kt.

Burns, Sir Malcolm McRae, K.B.E.

Burns, Sir Terence, Kt.

Burns, *Maj.-Gen.* Sir (Walter Arthur) George, K.C.V.O., C.B., D.S.O., O.B.E., M.C.

Burrell, *Vice-Adm.* Sir Henry Mackay, K.B.E., C.B.

Burrell, Sir John Raymond, Bt. (1774).

Burrenchobay, Sir Dayendranath, K.B.E., C.M.G., C.V.O.

Burrows, Sir Bernard Alexander Brocas, G.C.M.G.

Burrows, Sir (Robert) John (Formby), Kt.

Burston, Sir Samuel Gerald Wood, Kt., O.B.E.

Burt, *Hon.* Sir Francis Theodore Page, K.C.M.G.

Burton, Sir Carlisle Archibald, Kt., O.B.E.

Burton, Sir George Vernon Kennedy, Kt., C.B.E.

Burton, *Air Marshal* Sir Harry, K.C.B., C.B.E., D.S.O.

Burton-Chadwick, Sir Joshua Kenneth, Bt. (1935).

Busby, Sir Matthew, Kt., C.B.E.

Bush, *Hon.* Sir Brian Drex, Kt.

Bush, *Admiral* Sir John Fitzroy Duyland, G.C.B., D.S.C.

Busk, Sir Douglas Laird, K.C.M.G.

Butler, *Rt. Hon.* Sir Adam Courtauld, Kt.

Butler, Sir Clifford Charles, Kt., PH.D., F.R.S.

Butler, Sir Michael Dacres, G.C.M.G.

Butler, Sir (Reginald) Michael (Thomas), Bt. (1922).

Butler, *Hon.* Sir Richard Clive, Kt.

Butler, *Col.* Sir Thomas Pierce, Bt., C.V.O., D.S.O., O.B.E. (1628).

Butt, Sir (Alfred) Kenneth Dudley, Bt. (1929).

Butterfield, *Prof.* Sir (William) John (Hughes), Kt., O.B.E., D.M., F.R.C.P.

Butterworth, Sir (George) Neville, Kt.

Buxton, Sir Thomas Fowell Victor, Bt. (1840).

Buzzard, Sir Anthony Farquhar, Bt. (1929).

Byatt, Sir Hugh Campbell, K.C.V.O., C.M.G.

Byers, Sir Maurice Hearne, Kt., C.B.E., Q.C.

Byford, Sir Lawrence, Kt., C.B.E., Q.P.M.

Byrne, Sir Clarence Askew, Kt., O.B.E., D.S.C.

Cable, Sir James Eric, K.C.V.O., C.M.G.

Cadbury, Sir (George) Adrian (Hayhurst), Kt.

Cadell, *Vice-Adm.* Sir John Frederick, K.B.E.

Cadwallader, Sir John, Kt.

Caffyn, *Brig.* Sir Edward Roy, K.B.E., C.B., T.D.

Cahn, Sir Albert Jonas, Bt. (1934).

Cain, Sir Edward Thomas, Kt., C.B.E.

Cain, Sir Henry Edney Conrad, Kt.

Caine, Sir Sydney, K.C.M.G.

Cairncross, Sir Alexander Kirkland, K.C.M.G.

Cairns, *Rt. Hon.* Sir David Arnold Scott, Kt.

Cakobau, *Ratu* Sir George, G.C.M.G., G.C.V.O., O.B.E., Royal Victorian Chain.

Caldicott, *Hon.* Sir John Moore, K.B.E., C.M.G.

Caldwell, *Surgeon Vice-Adm.* Sir (Eric) Dick, K.B.E., C.B.

Callaghan, Sir Allan Robert, Kt., C.M.G.

Callaghan, Sir Bede Bertrand, Kt., C.B.E.

Callaghan, *Rt. Hon.* Sir (Leonard) James, K.G.

Callard, Sir Eric John, Kt.

Callaway, *Prof.* Sir Frank Adams, Kt., C.M.G., O.B.E.

Calley, Sir Henry Algernon, Kt., D.S.O., D.F.C.

Callinan, Sir Bernard James, Kt., C.B.E., D.S.O., M.C.

Calne, *Prof.* Sir Roy Yorke, Kt., F.R.S.

Calthorpe, Sir Euan Hamilton Anstruther-Gough-, Bt. (1929).

Cameron of Lochiel, Sir Donald Hamish, K.T., C.V.O., T.D.

Cameron, Sir (Eustace) John, Kt., C.B.E.

Cameron, Sir James Clark, Kt., C.B.E., T.D.

Cameron, *Hon.* Sir John, Kt., D.S.C., Q.C. (Lord Cameron).

Cameron, Sir John Watson, Kt., O.B.E.

Camilleri, *His Hon.* Sir Luigi Antonio, Kt, LL.D.

Campbell, Sir Alan Hugh, G.C.M.G.

Campbell, Sir Clifford Clarence, G.C.M.G., G.C.V.O.

Campbell, Sir Colin Moffat, Bt., M.C. (s. 1668).

Campbell, *Col.* Sir Guy Theophilus Halswell, Bt., O.B.E., M.C. (1815).

Campbell, *Maj.-Gen.* Sir Hamish Manus, K.B.E., C.B.

Campbell, Sir Ilay Mark, Bt. (1808).

Campbell, Sir Matthew, K.B.E., C.B., F.R.S.E.

Campbell, Sir Niall Alexander Hamilton, Bt. (1831).

Campbell, Sir Ralph Abercromby, Kt.

Campbell, Sir Robin Auchinbreck, Bt. (s 1628).

Campbell, Sir Thomas Cockburn-, Bt. (1821).

Campbell, *Hon.* Sir Walter Benjamin, Kt.

Campion, Sir Harry, Kt., C.B., C.B.E.

Cantley, *Hon.* Sir Joseph Donaldson, Kt., O.B.E.

Carberry, Sir John Edward Doston, Kt.

Carden, *Lt.-Col.* Sir Henry Christopher, Bt., O.B.E. (1887).

Carden, Sir John Craven, Bt. (I 1787).

Carew, Sir Rivers Verain, Bt. (1661).

Carey, Sir Peter Willoughby, G.C.B.

Carlill, *Vice-Adm.* Sir Stephen Hope, K.B.E., C.B., D.S.O.

Carlisle, Sir John Michael, Kt.

Carmichael, Sir David Peter William Gibson-Craig-, Bt. (s. 1702 and 1831).

Carmichael, Sir John, K.B.E.

Carnac, *Rev. Canon* Sir (Thomas) Nicholas Rivett-, Bt. (1836).

Carnegie, *Lt.-Gen.* Sir Robin Macdonald, K.C.B., O.B.E.

Carnegie, Sir Roderick Howard, Kt.

Carnwath, Sir Andrew Hunter, K.C.V.O.

Caro, Sir Anthony Alfred, Kt., C.B.E.

Carŏe, Sir (Einar) Athelstan (Gordon), Kt., C.B.E.

Carpenter, *Very Rev.* Edward Frederick, K.C.V.O.

Carr, Sir (Albert) Raymond (Maillard), Kt.

Carr, *Air Marshal* Sir John Darcy Baker-, K.B.E., C.B., A.F.C.

Carreras, *Lt.-Col.* Sir James, K.C.V.O., M.B.E.

Carrick, *Hon.* Sir John Leslie, K.C.M.G.

Carter, Sir Charles Frederick, Kt., F.B.A.

Carter, Sir Derrick Hunton, Kt., T.D.

Carter, *Hon.* Sir Douglas Julian, K.C.M.G.

Carter, Sir John, Kt., Q.C.

Carter, Sir William Oscar, Kt.

Cartland, Sir George Barrington, Kt., C.M.G.

Cartledge, Sir Bryan George, K.C.M.G.

Cary, Sir Roger Hugh, Bt. (1955).

Cash, Sir Gerald Christopher, G.C.M.G., G.C.V.O., O.B.E.

Cass, Sir John Patrick, Kt., O.B.E.

Cassel, Sir Harold Felix, Bt., T.D., Q.C. (1920).

Cassels, *Field Marshal* Sir (Archibald) James Halkett, G.C.B., K.B.E., D.S.O.

Cassels, *Admiral* Sir Simon Alastair Cassillis, K.C.B., C.B.E.

Cassidi, *Admiral* Sir (Arthur) Desmond, G.C.B.

Casson, Sir Hugh Maxwell, C.H., K.C.V.O., P.P.R.A., F.R.I.B.A.

Cater, Sir Jack, K.B.E.

Cater, Sir John Robert, Kt.

Catherwood, Sir (Henry) Frederick (Ross), Kt.

Catling, Sir Richard Charles, Kt., C.M.G., O.B.E.

Cato, *Hon.* Sir Arnott Samuel, K.C.M.G.

Caughey, Sir Thomas Harcourt Clarke, K.B.E.

Caulfield, *Hon.* Sir Bernard, Kt.

Cave, Sir Charles Edward Coleridge, Bt. (1896).

Cave, Sir (Charles) Philip Haddon-, K.B.E., C.M.G.

Cave, Sir Richard Phillip, K.C.V.O., C.B.

Cave, Sir Robert Cave-Browne-, Bt. (1641).

Cawley, Sir Charles Mills, Kt., C.B.E., Ph.D.

Cayley, Sir Digby William David, Bt. (1661).

Cayzer, Sir James Arthur, Bt. (1904).

Cecil, *Rear-Adm.* Sir (Oswald) Nigel Amherst, K.B.E., C.B.

Chacksfield, *Air Vice-Marshal* Sir Bernard Albert, K.B.E., C.B.

Chadwick, *Rev. Prof.* (William) Owen, O.M., K.B.E., F.B.A.

Chalk, *Hon.* Sir Gordon William Wesley, K.B.E.

Chamberlain, *Hon.* Sir Reginald Roderic St. Clair, Kt.

Chan, *Rt. Hon.* Sir Julius, K.B.E.

†Chance, Sir (George) Jeremy ffolliott, Bt. (1900).

Chancellor, Sir Christopher John, Kt., C.M.G.

Chandler, Sir Geoffrey, Kt., C.B.E.

Chaney, *Hon.* Sir Frederick Charles, K.B.E., A.F.C.

†Chapman, Sir David Robert Macgowan, Bt. (1958).

Chapman, Sir George Alan, Kt.

Chapman, *Hon.* Sir Stephen, Kt.

Chapple, *Gen.* Sir John Lyon, K.C.B., C.B.E.

Charles, Sir Joseph Quentin, Kt.

Charnley, Sir (William) John, Kt., C.B.

Chau, *Hon.* Sir Sik-Nin, Kt., C.B.E.

Chaytor, Sir George Reginald, Bt. (1831).

Cheadle, Sir Eric Wallers, Kt., C.B.E.

Cheeketts, *Sqn. Ldr.* Sir David John, K.C.V.O.

Cheetham, Sir Nicolas John Alexander, K.C.M.G.

Chesterman, Sir (Dudley) Ross, Kt., Ph.D.

Chesterton, Sir Oliver Sidney, Kt., M.C.

Chetwood, Sir Clifford Jack, Kt.

Chetwynd, Sir Arthur Ralph Talbot, Bt. (1795).

Cheung, Sir Oswald Victor, Kt., C.B.E.

Cheyne, Sir Joseph Lister Watson, Bt., O.B.E. (1908).

Chichester, Sir (Edward) John, Bt. (1641).

Child, Sir (Coles John) Jeremy, Bt. (1919).

Chilton, *Air Marshal* Sir (Charles) Edward, K.B.E., C.B.

Chilton, *Brig.* Sir Frederick Oliver, Kt., C.B.E., D.S.O.

Chitty, Sir Thomas Willes, Bt. (1924).

Cholmeley, Sir Montague John, Bt. (1806).

Christie, Sir George William Langham, Kt.

Christie, *Hon.* Sir Vernon Howard Colville, Kt.

Christie, Sir William, Kt., M.B.E.

Christison, *Gen.* Sir (Alexander Frank) Philip, Bt., G.B.E., C.B., D.S.O., M.C. (1871).

Christofas, Sir Kenneth Cavendish, K.C.M.G., M.B.E.

Christopherson, Sir Derman Guy, Kt., O.B.E., D.Phil., F.R.S.

Chung, Sir Sze-yuen, Kt., C.B.E.

Clapham, Sir Michael John Sinclair, K.B.E.

Claringbull, Sir (Gordon) Frank, Kt., Ph.D.

Clark, Sir George Anthony, Bt. (1917).

Clark, Sir John Allen, Kt.

Clark, Sir John Douglas, Bt. (1886).

Clark, Sir John Stewart-, Bt. (1918).

Clark, Sir Robert Anthony, Kt., D.S.C.

Clark, Sir Robin Chichester-, Kt.

Clark, Sir Thomas Edwin, Kt.

Clark, Sir William Gibson, Kt., M.P.

Clarke, Sir (Charles Mansfield) Tobias, Bt. (1831).

Clarke, *Prof.* Sir Cyril Astley, K.B.E., M.D., SC.D., F.R.S., F.R.C.P.

Clarke, Sir Ellis Emmanuel Innocent, G.C.M.G.

Clarke, Sir (Henry) Ashley, G.C.M.G., G.C.V.O.

Clarke, Sir Jonathan Dennis, Kt.

Clarke, Sir Rupert William John, Bt., M.B.E. (1882).

Clay, Sir Richard Henry, Bt. (1841).

Clayson, Sir Eric Maurice, Kt.

Clayton, Sir David Robert, Bt., (1732).

Clayton, *Air Marshal* Sir Gareth Thomas Butler, K.C.B., D.F.C.

Clayton, Sir Robert James, Kt., C.B.E.

Cleary, Sir Joseph Jackson, Kt.

Clegg, Sir Walter, Kt.

Clements, Sir John Selby, Kt., C.B.E.

Cleminson, Sir James Arnold Stacey, Kt., M.C.

Clerk, Sir John Dutton, Bt., C.B.E., V.R.D. (s. 1679).

Clerke, Sir John Edward Longueville, Bt. (1660).

Clifford, Sir Roger Joseph, Bt. (1887).

Clothier, Sir Cecil Montacute, K.C.B., Q.C.

Clowes, *Col.* Sir Henry Nelson, K.C.V.O., D.S.O., O.B.E.

Clucas, Sir Kenneth Henry, K.C.B.

Clutterbuck, *Vice-Adm.* Sir David Granville, K.B.E., C.B.

Coates, Sir Ernest William, Kt., C.M.G.

Coates, Sir Frederick Gregory Lindsay, Bt. (1921).

Coats, Sir Alastair Francis Stuart, Bt. (1905).

Coats, Sir William David, Kt.

Cobban, Sir James Macdonald, Kt., C.B.E., T.D.

Cochrane, Sir (Henry) Marc (Sursock), Bt. (1903).

Cockburn, Sir John Elliot, Bt. (s. 1671).

Cockburn, Sir Robert, K.B.E., C.B., Ph.D.

Cockcroft, Sir Wilfred Halliday, Kt., D.Phil.

Cockerell, Sir Christopher Sydney, Kt., C.B.E., F.R.S.

Cockram, Sir John, Kt.

Cocks, Sir (Thomas George) Barnett, K.C.B., O.B.E.

Codrington, Sir Simon Francis Bethell, Bt. (1876).

Codrington, Sir William Alexander, Bt. (1721).

Coghill, Sir Egerton James Nevill Tobias, Bt. (1778).

Cohen, Sir Bernard Nathaniel Waley-, Bt. (1961).

Cohen, Sir Edward, Kt.

Cohen, Sir Rex Arthur Louis, K.B.E.

Coldstream, Sir George Phillips, K.C.B., K.C.V.O., Q.C.

Cole, Sir (Alexander) Colin, K.C.V.O., T.D.

Cole, Sir David Lee, K.C.M.G., M.C.

Cole, Sir (Robert) William, Kt.

Coles, Sir Norman Cameron, Kt.

Colfox, Sir (William) John, Bt. (1939).

Collett, Sir Ian Seymour, Bt. (1934).

Collins, Sir Arthur James Robert, K.C.V.O.

Collins, *Vice-Adm.* Sir John Augustine, K.B.E., C.B.

Collyear, Sir John Gowen, Kt.

Colman, Sir Michael Jeremiah, Bt. (1907).

Colquhoun, *Maj.-Gen.* Sir Cyril Harry, K.C.V.O., C.B., O.B.E.

Colquhoun of Luss, Sir Ivar Iain, Bt. (1786).

Colt, Sir Edward William Dutton Bt. (1694).

Colthurst, Sir Richard La Touche, Bt. (1744).

Colville, Sir John Rupert, Kt., C.B., C.V.O.

Combs, Sir Willis Ide, K.C.V.O., C.M.G.

Compston, *Vice-Adm.* Sir Peter Maxwell, K.C.B.

Compton, Sir Edmund Gerald, G.C.B., K.B.E.

Compton Miller, Sir John (Francis), Kt., M.B.E., T.D.

Comyn, *Hon.* Sir James, Kt.

Conant, Sir John Ernest Michael, Bt. (1954).

Conran, Sir Terence Orby, Kt.

Constable, Sir Robert Frederick Strickland-, Bt. (1641).

Constantine, *Air Chief Marshal* Sir Hugh Alex, K.B.E., C.B., D.S.O.

Cook, Sir Christopher Wymondham Rayner Herbert, Bt. (1886).

Cook, Sir (Philip) Halford, Kt., O.B.E.

Cook, Sir William Richard Joseph, K.C.B., F.R.S.

Cooke, Sir Charles Fletcher-, Kt., Q.C.

Cooke, *Lt.-Col.* Sir David William Perceval, Bt. (1661).

Cooke, Sir John Fletcher-, Kt., C.M.G.

Cooke, *Rt. Hon.* Sir Robin Brunskill, K.B.E.

Cooley, Sir Alan Sydenham, Kt., C.B.E.

Coop, Sir Maurice Fletcher, Kt.

Cooper, *Rt. Hon.* Sir Frank, G.C.B., C.M.G.

Cooper, *General* Sir George Leslie Conroy, G.C.B., M.C.

Cooper, Sir Gilbert Alexander, Kt., C.B.E., E.D.

Cooper, Sir Patrick Graham Astley, Bt. (1821).

†Cooper, Sir Richard Powell, Bt. (1905).

Cooper, Sir William Daniel Charles, Bt. (1863).

Cooper, Sir William Henry, Kt., C.B.E.

Cooper, *Prof.* Sir (William) Mansfield, Kt.

Coote, Sir Christopher John, Bt., *Premier Baronet of Ireland* (1621).

Copas, *Most Rev.* Virgil, K.B.E., D.D.

Corbet, Sir John Vincent, Bt., M.B.E. (1808).

Corfield, *Rt. Hon.* Sir Frederick Vernon, Kt., Q.C.

Corfield, Sir Kenneth George, Kt.

Cork, Sir Kenneth Russell, G.B.E.

Corley, Sir Kenneth Sholl Ferrand, Kt.

Cormack, Sir Magnus Cameron, K.B.E.

Corness, Sir Colin Ross, Kt.

Cornford, Sir (Edward) Clifford, K.C.B.

Cornforth, Sir John Warcup, Kt., C.B.E., D.Phil., F.R.S.

†Corry, Sir William James, Bt. (1885).

Cortazzi, Sir (Henry Arthur) Hugh, G.C.M.G.

Cory, Sir Clinton James Donald, Bt. (1919).

Coslett, *Air Marshal* Sir (Thomas) Norman, K.C.B., O.B.E.

Costar, Sir Norman Edgar, K.C.M.G.

Cotter, *Lt.-Col.* Sir Delaval James Alfred, Bt., D.S.O. (1763).

Cotterell, Sir John Henry Geers, Bt. (1805).

Cotton, Sir John Richard, K.C.M.G., O.B.E.

Cotton, *Hon.* Sir Robert Carrington, K.C.M.G.

Cottrell, Sir Alan Howard, Kt., Ph.D., F.R.S.

Cotts, Sir (Robert) Crichton Mitchell, Bt. (1921).

Coulson, Sir John Eltringham, K.C.M.G.

Couper, Sir (Robert) Nicholas (Oliver), Bt. (1841).

Court, *Hon.* Sir Charles Walter Michael, K.C.M.G., O.B.E.

Coutts, Sir Walter Fleming, G.C.M.G., M.B.E.

Couzens, Sir Kenneth Edward, K.C.B.

Covacevich, Sir (Anthony) Thomas, Kt., D.F.C.

Cowen, *Rt. Hon. Prof.* Sir Zelman, G.C.M.G., G.C.V.O., Q.C.

Cowley, *Lt.-Gen.* Sir John Guise, K.B.E., C.B.

Cowper, Sir Norman Lethbridge, Kt., C.B.E.

Cowperthwaite, Sir John James, K.B.E., C.M.G.

Cox, Sir Anthony Wakefield, Kt., C.B.E., F.R.I.B.A.

Cox, *Prof.* Sir David Roxbee, Kt., F.R.S.

Cox, Sir (Ernest) Gordon, K.B.E., T.D., D.S.C., F.R.S.

Cox, Sir Geoffrey Sandford, Kt., C.B.E.

Cox, Sir (George) Trenchard, Kt., C.B.E., F.S.A.

Cox, *Vice-Adm.* Sir John Michael Holland, K.C.B.

Cox, Sir John William, Kt., C.B.E.

Cox, Sir Mencea Ethereal, Kt.

Cradock, Sir Percy, G.C.M.G.

Craig, Sir (Albert) James (Macqueen), G.C.M.G.

Craig, *Air Chief Marshal* Sir David Brownrigg, G.C.B., O.B.E.

Cramer, *Hon.* Sir John Oscar, Kt.

Crane, Sir James William Donald, Kt., C.B.E.

Craufurd, Sir Robert James, Bt. (1781).

Craven, *Air Marshal* Sir Robert Edward, K.B.E., C.B., D.F.C.

Crawford, *Prof.* Sir Frederick William, Kt.

Crawford, *Hon.* Sir George Hunter, Kt.

Crawford, Sir (Robert) Stewart, G.C.M.G., C.V.O

Crawford, *Prof.* Sir Theodore, Kt.

Crawford, *Vice-Adm.* Sir William Godfrey, K.B.E., C.B., D.S.C.

Crawshaw, *Hon.* Sir (Edward) Daniel (Weston), Kt.

Crawshay, *Col.* Sir William Robert, Kt., D.S.O., E.R.D., T.D.

Creagh, *Maj.-Gen.* Sir (Kilner) Rupert Brazier-, K.B.E., C.B., D.S.O.

Crichton, Sir Andrew James Maitland-Makgill-, Kt.

Crill, Sir Peter Leslie, Kt., C.B.E.

Cripps, Sir John Stafford, Kt., C.B.E.

Crisp, Sir (John) Peter, Bt. (1913).

Critchett, Sir Ian (George Lorraine), Bt. (1908).

Croft, Sir John Archibald Radcliffe, Bt. (1818).

Croft, Sir Owen Glendower, Bt. (1671).

†Crofton, Sir Hugh Denis, Bt. (1801).

Crofton, *Prof.* Sir John Wenman, Kt.

Crofton, Sir Malby Sturges, Bt. (1838).

Croker, Sir Walter Russell, K.B.E.

Crookenden, *Lt.-Gen.* Sir Napier, K.C.B., D.S.O., O.B.E.

Cross, Sir Cecil Lancelot Stewart, Kt., C.B.E.

Cross, *Air Chief Marshal* Sir Kenneth Brian Boyd, K.C.B., C.B.E., D.S.O., D.F.C.

Crossland, Sir Leonard, Kt.

Crossley, Sir Christopher John, Bt. (1909).

Crossman, Sir Douglas Peter, Kt., T.D.

Crosthwaite, Sir (Ponsonby) Moore, K.C.M.G.

Crouch, Sir David Lance, Kt.

Crowe, Sir Colin Tradescant, G.C.M.G.

Cruthers, Sir James Winter, Kt.

Cubbon, Sir Brian Crossland, G.C.B.

Cubitt, Sir Hugh Guy, Kt., C.B.E.

Cuckney, Sir John Graham, Kt.

Cumber, Sir John Alfred, Kt., C.M.G., M.B.E., T.D.

Cumming, Sir William Gordon Gordon-, Bt. (1804).

Cunard, Sir Guy Alick, Bt. (1859).

Cuninghame, Sir John Christopher Foggo Montgomery-, Bt. (N.S. 1672).

†Cuninghame, Sir William Henry Fairlie-, Bt., (s. 1630).

Cunliffe, Sir David Ellis, Bt. (1759)

Cunningham, Sir Charles Craik, G.C.B., K.B.E., C.V.O.

Cunningham, *Lt.-Gen.* Sir Hugh Patrick, K.B.E.

Cunynghame, Sir Andrew David Francis, Bt. (s. 1702).

Cunynghame, Sir James Ogilvy Blair-, Kt., O.B.E.

Curle, Sir John Noel Ormiston, K.C.V.O., C.M.G.

Curran, Sir Samuel Crowe, Kt., D.SC., Ph.D., F.R.S., F.R.S.E.

Currie, *Prof.* Sir Alastair Robert, Kt., F.R.C.P., F.R.C.P.E., F.R.S.E.

Currie, Sir Neil Smith, Kt., C.B.E.

Currie, Sir William George Cubitt, Bt. (1847).

Curtis, Sir (Edward) Leo, Kt.

Curtis, Sir William Peter, Bt. (1802).

Curtiss, *Air Marshal* Sir John Bagot, K.C.B., K.B.E.

Curwen, Sir Christopher Keith, K.C.M.G.

Cuthbert, *Vice-Adm.* Sir John Wilson, K.B.E., C.B.

Cuthbertson, Sir David Paton, Kt., C.B.E., M.D., D.SC.

Cuthbertson, Sir Harold Alexander, Kt.

Cutler, Sir (Arthur) Roden, V.C., K.C.M.G., K.C.V.O., C.B.E.

Cutler, Sir Charles Benjamin, K.B.E., E.D.

Cutler, Sir Horace Walter, Kt., O.B.E.

Dacie, *Prof.* Sir John Vivian, Kt., M.D., F.R.S.

Daldry, Sir Leonard Charles, K.B.E.

Dale, Sir William Leonard, K.C.M.G.

Dalrymple, *Maj.* Sir Hew Fleetwood Hamilton-, Bt., K.C.V.O. (s. 1697).

Dalton, Sir Alan Nugent Goring, Kt., C.B.E.

Dalton, *Maj.-Gen.* Sir Charles James George, Kt., C.B., C.B.E.

Dalton, *Vice-Adm.* Sir Geoffrey Thomas James Oliver, K.C.B.

Dalton, *Vice-Adm.* Sir Norman Eric, K.C.B., O.B.E.

Daly, *Lt.-Gen.* Sir Thomas Joseph, K.B.E., C.B., D.S.O.

Dalyell, Sir Tam, Bt., M.P. (N.S. 1685).

Daniel, Sir Goronwy Hopkin, K.C.V.O., C.B., D.Phil.

Daniell, Sir Peter Averell, Kt., T.D.

Danks, Sir Alan John, K.B.E.

Darby, Sir Peter Howard, Kt., C.B.E., Q.F.S.M.

Darell, Sir Jeffrey Lionel, Bt., M.C. (1795).

Dargie, Sir William Alexander, Kt., C.B.E.

Darling, Sir Clifford, Kt.

Darling, Sir James Ralph, Kt., C.M.G., O.B.E.

Darling, *General* Sir Kenneth Thomas, G.B.E., K.C.B., D.S.O.

Darlington, *Rear-Adm.* Sir Charles Roy, K.B.E.

Darvall, Sir (Charles) Roger, Kt., C.B.E.

Dashwood, Sir Francis John Vernon Hereward, Bt., *Premier Baronet of Great Britain* (1707).

Dashwood, Sir Richard James, Bt. (1684).

Davenport, *Lt.-Col.* Sir Walter Henry Bromley-, Kt., T.D.

David, Sir Jean Marc, Kt., C.B.E., Q.C.

Davie, *Rev.* Sir Arthur Patrick Ferguson-, Bt. (1847).

Davie, Sir Paul Christopher, Kt.

Davies, *Air Marshal* Sir Alan Cyril, K.C.B., C.B.E.

Davies, *Hon.* Sir (Alfred William) Michael, Kt.

Davies, Sir Alun Talfan, Kt., Q.C.

Davies, Sir (David) Arthur, K.B.E.

Davies, Sir David Henry, Kt.

Davies, *Hon.* Sir (David Herbert) Mervyn, Kt., M.C., T.D.

Davies, Sir David Joseph, Kt.

Davies, *Vice-Adm.* Sir Lancelot Richard Bell, K.B.E.

Davies, Sir Oswald, Kt., C.B.E.

Davies, Sir Peter Maxwell, Kt., C.B.E.

Davies, Sir Richard Harries, K.C.V.O., C.B.E.

Davies, Sir Victor Caddy, Kt., O.B.E.

Davis, Sir Charles Sigmund, Kt., C.B.

Davis, Sir Colin Rex, Kt., C.B.E.

Davis, *Hon.* Sir (Dermot) Renn, Kt., O.B.E.

Davis, Sir (Ernest) Howard, Kt., C.M.G., O.B.E.

Davis, Sir John Gilbert, Bt. (1946).

Davis, *Air Chief Marshal* Sir John Gilbert, G.C.B., O.B.E.

Davis, Sir John Henry Harris, Kt.

Davis, Sir Maurice Herbert, Kt., O.B.E.

Davis, Sir Rupert Charles Hart-, Kt.

Davis, *Hon.* Sir Thomas Robert Alexander Harries, K.B.E.

Davis, Sir (William) Allan, G.B.E.

Davis, *Admiral* Sir William Wellclose, G.C.B., D.S.O.

Davison, *Rt. Hon.* Sir Ronald Keith, G.B.E., C.M.G.

Dawbarn, Sir Simon Yelverton, K.C.V.O., C.M.G.

Dawnay, *Vice-Adm.* Sir Peter, K.C.V.O., C.B., D.S.C.

Dawson, *Hon.* Sir Daryl Michael, K.B.E., C.B.

Dawson, Sir Hugh Michael Trevor, Bt. (1920).

Dawson, *Air Chief Marshal* Sir Walter Lloyd, K.C.B., C.B.E., D.S.O.

Dawtry, Sir Alan (Graham), Kt., C.B.E., T.D.

Day, Sir Derek Malcolm, K.C.M.G.

Day, Sir Robin, Kt.

Deakin, Sir (Frederick) William (Dampier), Kt., D.S.O.

Dean, Sir (Arthur) Paul, Kt., M.P.

Dean, Sir John Norman, Kt.

Dean, Sir Patrick Henry, G.C.M.G.

Deane, *Hon.* Sir William Patrick, K.B.E.

Dearing, Sir Ronald Ernest, Kt., C.B.

de Bellaigue, Sir Geoffrey, K.C.V.O.

Debenham, Sir Gilbert Ridley, Bt. (1931).

De Bunsen, Sir Bernard, Kt., C.M.G.

Deer, Sir (Arthur) Frederick, Kt., C.M.G.

de Hoghton, Sir (Richard) Bernard (Cuthbert), Bt. (1611).

De la Bère, Sir Cameron, Bt. (1953).

Delacombe, *Maj.-Gen.* Sir Rohan, K.C.M.G., K.C.V.O., K.B.E., C.B., D.S.O.

de la Mare, Sir Arthur James, K.C.M.G., K.C.V.O.

de la Rue, Sir Eric Vincent, Bt. (1898).

de Lotbinière, *Lt.-Col.* Sir Edmond Joly, Kt.

Delve, Sir Frederick William, Kt., C.B.E.

de Montmorency, Sir Arnold Geoffroy, Bt. (I 1631).

Denman, Sir (George) Roy, K.C.B., C.M.G.

Denning, *Lt.-Gen.* Sir Reginald Francis Stewart, K.C.V.O., K.B.E., C.B.

Denny, Sir Alistair Maurice Archibald, Bt. (1913).

Denny, Sir Anthony Coningham de Waltham, Bt. (I 1782).

Dent, Sir John, Kt., C.B.E.

Denton, *Prof.* Sir Eric James, Kt., C.B.E., F.R.S.

Derbyshire, Sir Andrew George, Kt.

Derham, Sir Peter John, Kt.

de Trafford, Sir Dermot Humphrey, Bt. (1841).

Deverell, Sir Colville Montgomery, G.B.E., K.C.M.G., C.V.O.

Devesi, Sir Baddeley, G.C.M.G., G.C.V.O.

Devitt, Sir Thomas Gordon, Bt. (1916).

Dewes, Sir Herbert John Salisbury, Kt., C.B.E.

Dewey, Sir Anthony Hugh, Bt. (1917).

Dewhurst, *Prof.* Sir (Christopher) John, Kt.

D'Eyncourt, Sir (John) Jeremy (Eustace) Tennyson-, Bt. (1930).

de Zulueta, Sir Philip Francis, Kt.

Dhenin, *Air Marshal* Sir Geoffrey Howard, K.B.E., A.F.C., G.M., M.D.

Dhrangadhra, H.H. the Maharaja Raj Saheb of, K.C.I.E.

Dibela, *Hon.* Sir Kingsford, G.C.M.G.

Dick, Sir John Alexander, M.C.

Dickens, Sir Louis Walter, Kt., D.F.C., A.F.C.

Dickinson, Sir Harold Herbert, Kt.

Dickinson, Sir Samuel Benson, Kt.

Dickson, *Marshal of the Royal Air Force* Sir William Forster, G.C.B., K.B.E., D.S.O., A.F.C.

Dilbertson, Sir Geoffrey, C.B.E.

Dilke, Sir John Fisher Wentworth, Bt. (1862).

Dill, Sir Nicholas Bayard, Kt., C.B.E.

Dillon, *Rt. Hon.* Sir (George) Brian (Hugh), Kt.

Dillon, Sir John Vincent, Kt., C.M.G.

Dillon, Sir Max, Kt.

Diver, *Hon.* Sir Leslie Charles, Kt.

Dixon, *Air Vice-Marshal* Sir (Francis Wilfred) Peter, K.B.E.

Dixon, Sir John George, Bt. (1919).

Dobson, Sir Denis William, K.C.B., O.B.E., Q.C.

Dobson, *General* Sir Patrick John Howard-, G.C.B.

Dobson, Sir Richard Portway, Kt.

Dodds, Sir Ralph Jordan, Bt. (1964).

Dodson, Sir Derek Sherborne Lindsell, K.C.M.G., M.C.

Dodsworth, Sir John Christopher Smith-, Bt. (1784).

Doll, *Prof.* Sir (William) Richard (Shaboe), Kt., O.B.E., F.R.S., D.M., M.D., D.SC.

Dollery, Sir Colin Terence, Kt.

Donald, *Air Marshal* Sir John George, K.B.E.

Donaldson, Sir Dawson, K.C.M.G.

Donaldson, *Rt. Hon.* Sir John Francis, Kt.

Donne, *Hon.* Sir Gaven John, K.B.E.

Donne, Sir John Christopher, Kt.

Donner, Sir Patrick William, Kt.

Dookun, Sir Dewoonarain, Kt.

Dorman, *Lt.-Col.* Sir Charles Geoffrey, Bt., M.C. (1923).

Dorman, Sir Maurice Henry, G.C.M.G., G.C.V.O.

Dos Santos, Sir Errol Lionel, Kt., C.B.E.

Dougherty, *Maj.-Gen.* Sir Ivan Noel, Kt., C.B.E., D.S.O., E.D.

Douglas, *Prof.* Sir Donald Macleod, Kt., M.B.E.

Douglas, Sir (Edward) Sholto, Kt.

Douglas, Sir Robert McCallum, Kt., O.B.E.

Douglas, *Rt. Hon.* Sir William Randolph, K.C.M.G.

Dove, Sir Clifford Alfred, Kt., C.B.E., E.R.D.

Dover, *Prof.* Sir Kenneth James, Kt., D.Litt., F.B.A., F.R.S.E.

Down, Sir Alastair Frederick, Kt., O.B.E., M.C., T.D.

Downey, Sir Gordon Stanley, K.C.B.

Downs, Sir Diarmuid, Kt., C.B.E.

Downward, Sir William Atkinson, Kt.

Dowson, Sir Philip Manning, Kt., C.B.E., A.R.A.

†D'Oyly, Sir Nigel Hadley Miller, Bt. (1663).

Drake, Sir (Arthur) Eric (Courtney), Kt., C.B.E.

Drake, *Hon.* Sir (Frederick) Maurice, Kt., D.F.C.

Drake, Sir James, Kt., C.B.E.

Drew, Sir Arthur Charles Walter, K.C.B.

Drew, Sir Ferdinand Caire, Kt., C.M.G.

Drew, *Lt.-Gen.* Sir (William) Robert (Macfarlane), K.C.B., C.B.E., F.R.C.P.

Dreyer, *Admiral* Sir Desmond Parry, G.C.B., C.B.E., D.S.C.

Dring, *Lt.-Col.* Sir Arthur John, K.B.E., C.I.E.

Driver, Sir Antony Victor, Kt.

Driver, Sir Arthur John, Kt.

Driver, Sir Eric William, Kt.

Drummond, *Lieut.-Gen.* Sir (William) Alexander (Duncan), K.B.E., C.B.

Dryden, Sir John Stephen Gyles, Bt. (1733 and 1795).

du Cann, *Rt. Hon.* Sir Edward Dillon Lott, K.B.E.

Duckmanton, Sir Talbot Sydney, Kt., C.B.E.

Duckworth, *Maj.* Sir Richard Dyce, Bt. (1909).

du Cros, Sir Claude Philip Arthur Mallet, Bt. (1916).

Duff, *Rt. Hon.* Sir (Arthur) Antony, G.C.M.G., C.V.O., D.S.O., D.S.C.

Duffus, *Hon.* Sir William Algernon Holwell, Kt.

Dugdale, Sir William Stratford, Bt., M.C. (1936).

du Heaume, Sir Francis Herbert, Kt., C.I.E., O.B.E.

Duke, *Maj.-Gen.* Sir Gerald William, K.B.E., C.B., D.S.O.

Dunbar, Sir Archibald Ranulph, Bt. (s 1700).

Dunbar, Sir David Hope-, Bt. (s 1664).

Dunbar, Sir Drummond Cospatrick Ninian, Bt., M.C. (s 1698).

Dunbar, Sir Jean Ivor, Bt. (s 1694).

Dunbar of Hempriggs, Dame Maureen Daisy Helen, Bt. (s 1706).

Duncan, Sir James Blair, Kt.

Duncombe, Sir Philip Digby Pauncefort-, Bt. (1859).

Dundas, Sir Hugh Spencer Lisle, Kt., C.B.E., D.S.O., D.F.C.

Dunham, Sir Kingsley Charles, Kt., Ph.D., F.R.S., F.R.S.E.

Dunlop, Sir (Ernest) Edward, Kt., C.M.G., O.B.E.

Dunlop, Sir Thomas, Bt. (1916).

Dunlop, Sir William Norman Gough, Kt.

Dunn, *Air Marshal* Sir Eric Clive, K.B.E., C.B., B.E.M.

Dunn, *Lt.-Col.* Sir (Francis) Vivian, K.C.V.O., O.B.E.

Dunn, *Air Marshal* Sir Patrick Hunter, K.B.E., C.B., D.F.C.

Dunn, *Rt. Hon.* Sir Robin Horace Walford, Kt., M.C.

Dunnett, Sir (Ludovic) James, G.C.B., C.M.G.

Dunning, Sir Simon William Patrick, Bt. (1930).

Dunphie, *Maj.-Gen.* Sir Charles Anderson Lane, Kt., C.B., C.B.E., D.S.O.

Dunstan, *Lt.-Gen.* Sir Donald Beaumont, K.B.E., C.B.

Duntze, Sir John Alexander, Bt. (1774).

Dupree, Sir Peter, Bt. (1921).

Dupuch, Sir (Alfred) Etienne (Jerome), Kt., O.B.E.

Durand, *Rev.* Sir (Henry Mortimer) Dickon, Bt. (1892).

Durham, Sir Kenneth, Kt.

Durie, Sir Alexander Charles, Kt., C.B.E.

Durkin, *Air Marshal* Sir Herbert, K.B.E., C.B.

Durrant, Sir William Henry Estridge, Bt. (1784).

Duthie, *Prof.* Sir Herbert Livingstone, Kt.

Duthie, Sir Robert Grieve (Robin), Kt., C.B.E.

Duval, Sir (Charles) Gaetan, Kt.

Duxbury, *Air Marshal* Sir (John) Barry, K.C.B., C.B.E.

Dyer, *Prof.* Sir (Henry) Peter (Francis) Swinnerton-, Bt., K.B.E., F.R.S. (1678).

Dyke, Sir Derek William Hart, Bt. (1677).

Earle, *Air Chief Marshal* Sir Alfred, G.B.E., C.B.

Earle, Sir (Hardman) George (Algernon), Bt. (1869).

East, Sir (Lewis) Ronald, Kt., C.B.E.

Eastham, *Hon.* Sir (Thomas) Michael, Kt.

Eastick, *Brig.* Sir Thomas Charles, Kt., C.M.G., D.S.O., E.D.

Easton, *Admiral* Sir Ian, K.C.B., D.S.C.

Easton, *Air Commodore* Sir James Alfred, K.C.M.G., C.B., C.B.E.

Eastwood, Sir John Bealby, Kt.

Eberle, *Admiral* Sir James Henry Fuller, G.C.B.

Ebrahim, Sir (Mahomed) Currimbhoy, Bt. (1910).

Eburne, Sir Sidney Alfred William, Kt., M.C.

Eccles, Sir John Carew, Kt., D.Phil., F.R.S.

Echlin, Sir Norman David Fenton, Bt. (1721).

Eckersley, Sir Donald Payze, Kt., O.B.E.

Edden, *Vice-Adm.* Sir (William) Kaye, K.B.E., C.B.

†Edge, Sir William, Bt. (1937).

Edmenson, Sir Walter Alexander, Kt., C.B.E.

Edmonstone, Sir Archibald Bruce Charles, Bt. (1774).

Edwardes, Sir Michael Owen, Kt.

Edwards, Sir Christopher John Churchill, Bt. (1866).

Edwards, Sir George Robert, Kt., O.M., C.B.E., F.R.S.

Edwards, Sir (John) Clive (Leighton), Bt. (1921).

Edwards, Sir Llewellyn Roy, Kt.

Edwards, *Prof.* Sir Samuel Frederick, Kt., F.R.S.

Egan, Sir John Leopold, Kt.

Egerton, Sir John Alfred Roy, Kt.

Egerton, Sir (Philip) John (Caledon) Grey-, Bt. (1617).

Egerton, Sir Seymour John Louis, G.C.V.O.

Eggleston, *Hon.* Sir Richard Moulton, Kt.

Eley, Sir Geoffrey Cecil Ryves, Kt., C.B.E.

Elliot, Sir Gerald Henry, Kt.

Elliot, Sir John Blumenfeld, Kt.

Eliott of Stobs, Sir Arthur Francis Augustus Boswell, Bt. (s 1666).

Elliott, Sir Hugh Francis Ivo, Bt., O.B.E. (1917).

Elliott, Sir Norman Randall, Kt., C.B.E.

Elliott, Sir Randal Forbes, K.B.E.

Elliott, *Prof.* Sir Roger James, Kt., F.R.S.

Elliott, Sir Ronald Stuart, Kt.

Ellis, Sir John Rogers, Kt., M.B.E., M.D., F.R.C.P.

Ellis, Sir Ronald, Kt.

Ellison, *Rt. Rev.* and *Rt. Hon.* Gerald Alexander, K.C.V.O.

Ellison, *Col.* Sir Ralph Harry Carr-, Kt., T.D.

Ellwood, *Air Marshal* Sir Aubrey Beauclerk, K.C.B., D.S.C.

Elphinstone, Sir John, Bt. (s 1701).

Elphinstone, Sir (Maurice) Douglas (Warburton), Bt., T.D. (1816).

Elstub, Sir St. John de Holt, Kt., C.B.E.

Elton, Sir Arnold, Kt., C.B.E.

Elton, Sir Charles Abraham Grierson, Bt. (1717).

Elton, *Prof.* Sir Geoffrey Rudolph, Kt., F.B.A.

Elyan, Sir (Isadore) Victor, Kt.

Emery, Sir Peter Frank Hannibal, Kt., M.P.

Empson, *Admiral* Sir (Leslie) Derek, G.B.E., K.C.B.

Emson, *Air Marshal* Sir Reginald Herbert, K.B.E., C.B., A.F.C.

Engholm, Sir Basil Charles, K.C.B.

Engineer, Sir Noshirwan Phiroz-shah, Kt.

Engle, Sir George Lawrence Jose, K.C.B., Q.C.

English, Sir Cyril Rupert, Kt.

English, Sir David, Kt.

Entwistle, Sir (John Nuttall) Max-well, Kt.

Ereaut, Sir (Herbert) Frank Cob-bold, Kt.

Errington, *Col.* Sir Geoffrey Fred-erick, Bt. (1963).

Errington, Sir Lancelot, K.C.B.

Erskine, Sir (Thomas) David, Bt. (1821).

†Esmonde, Sir Thomas Francis Grattan, Bt. (I 1629).

Espie, Sir Frank Fletcher, Kt., O.B.E.

Esplen, Sir William Graham, Bt. (1921).

Eustace, Sir Joseph Lambert, G.C.M.G., G.C.V.O.

Evans, Sir Anthony Adney, Bt. (1920).

Evans, Sir Athol Donald, K.B.E.

Evans, *Hon.* Sir Anthony Howell Meurig, Kt., R.D.

Evans, *Air Chief Marshal* Sir David George, G.C.B., C.B.E.

Evans, Sir Geraint Llewellyn, Kt., C.B.E.

Evans, *Hon.* Sir Haydn Tudor, Kt.

Evans, Sir Hywel Wynn, K.C.B.

Evans, Sir Richard Mark, K.C.M.G., K.C.V.O.

Evans, Sir (Robert) Charles, Kt.

Evans, Sir (William) Vincent (John), G.C.M.G., M.B.E., Q.C.

Eveleigh, *Rt. Hon.* Sir Edward Wal-ter, Kt., E.R.D.

Everard, *Maj.-Gen.* Sir Christopher Earle Welby-, K.B.E., C.B.

Everard, Sir Robin Charles, Bt. (1911).

Everson, Sir Frederick Charles, K.C.M.G.

Every, Sir John Simon, Bt. (1641).

Evetts, *Lt.-Gen.* Sir John Fullerton, Kt., C.B., C.B.E., M.C.

Ewans, Sir Martin Kenneth, K.C.M.G.

Ewart, Sir (William) Ivan (Cecil), Bt., D.S.C. (1887).

Ewbank, *Hon.* Sir Anthony Bruce, Kt.

Ewin, Sir (David) Ernest Thomas Floyd, Kt., O.B.E., M.V.O.

Ewing, *Vice-Adm.* Sir (Robert) Alastair, K.B.E., C.B., D.S.C.

Ewing, Sir Ronald Archibald Orr-, Bt. (1886).

Eyre, *Maj.-Gen.* Sir James Ains-worth Campden Gabriel, K.C.V.O., C.B.E.

Eyre, Sir Reginald Edwin, Kt.

Faber, Sir Richard Stanley, K.C.V.O., C.M.G.

Fadahunsi, Sir Joseph Odeleye, K.C.M.G.

Fagge, Sir John William Frederick, Bt. (1660).

Fairbairn, *Hon.* Sir David Eric, K.B.E., D.F.C.

Fairbairn, Sir (James) Brooke, Bt. (1869).

Fairbairn, Sir Robert Duncan, Kt.

Fairfax, Sir Vincent Charles, Kt., C.M.G.

Fairgrieve, Sir (Thomas) Russell, Kt., C.B.E., T.D.

Fairhall, *Hon.* Sir Allen, K.B.E.

Falconer, *Hon.* Sir Douglas Wil-liam, Kt., M.B.E.

Falk, Sir Roger Salis, Kt., O.B.E.

†Falkiner, Sir Edmond Charles, Bt. (I 1778).

Falkner, Sir (Donald) Keith, Kt.

Falle, Sir Samuel, K.C.M.G., K.C.V.O., D.S.C.

Falvey, *Hon.* Sir John Neil, K.B.E., Q.C.

Faridkot, *Col.* H.H. the Raja of, K.C.S.I.

Farmer, Sir (Lovedin) George Thomas, Kt.

Farndale, *General* Sir Martin Baker, K.C.B.

Farquhar, Sir Michael Fitzroy Henry, Bt. (1796).

Farquharson, *Hon.* Sir Donald Henry, Kt.

Farquharson, Sir James Robbie, K.B.E.

Farr, Sir John Arnold, Kt., M.P.

Farrar-Hockley, *General* Sir An-thony Heritage, G.B.E., K.C.B., D.S.O., M.C.

Farrer, Sir Charles Matthew, K.C.V.O.

Farrington, Sir Henry Francis Col-den, Bt. (1818).

Faulkner, Sir Eric Odin, Kt., M.B.E.

Faulkner, Sir Percy, K.B.E., C.B.

Fawcus, Sir (Robert) Peter, K.B.E., C.M.G.

Fawkes, Sir Randol Francis, Kt.

Fawcett, Sir James Edmund Sand-ford, Kt., D.S.C., Q.C.

Fayrer, Sir John Lang Macpherson, Bt., (1896).

Feilden, Sir Bernard Melchior, Kt., C.B.E.

Feilden, Sir Henry Wemyss, Bt., (1846).

Feldman, Sir Basil Samuel, Kt.

Fell, Sir Anthony, Kt.

Fennessy, Sir Edward, Kt., C.B.E.

Ferens, Sir Thomas Robinson, Kt., C.B.E.

Ferguson, *Lt.-Col.* Sir Neil Edward Johnson-, Bt., T.D. (1906).

Fergusson of Kilkerran, Sir Charles, Bt. (s. 1703).

Fergusson, Sir Ewan Alastair John, K.C.M.G.

Fergusson, Sir James Herbert Hamilton Colyer-, Bt. (1866).

Feroze, Sir Rustam Moolan, Kt., F.R.C.S.

ffolkes, Sir Robert Francis Alex-ander, Bt. (1774)

Fieldhouse, Sir Harold, K.B.E., C.B.

Fieldhouse, *Admiral of the Fleet* Sir John David Elliott, G.C.B., G.B.E.

Fielding, Sir Colin Cunningham, Kt., C.B.

Fiennes, Sir John Saye Wingfield Twisleton-Wykeham-, K.C.B., Q.C.

Fiennes, Sir Maurice Alberic Twis-leton-Wykeham-, Kt.

Fiennes, Sir Ranulph Twisleton-Wykeham-, Bt. (1916).

Figg, Sir Leonard Clifford William, K.C.M.G.

Figgess, Sir John George, K.B.E., C.M.G.

Figgures, Sir Frank Edward, K.C.B., C.M.G.

Figures, Sir Colin Frederick, K.C.M.G., O.B.E.

Fingland, Sir Stanley James Gunn, K.C.M.G.

Finlay, Sir David Ronald James Bell (1964).

Finley, Sir Peter Hamilton, Kt., O.B.E., D.F.C.

Finniston, Sir (Harold) Montague, Kt., PH.D., F.R.S.

Finsberg, Sir Geoffrey, Kt., M.B.E., M.P.

Firth, *Prof.* Sir Raymond William, Kt., PH.D., F.B.A.

Fisher, Sir George Read, Kt., C.M.G.

Fisher, *Hon.* Sir Henry Arthur Pears, Kt.

Fisher, Sir Nigel Thomas Lover-idge, Kt., M.C.

Fison, Sir (Richard) Guy, Bt., D.S.C. (1905).

Fitch, *Admiral* Sir Richard George Alison, K.C.B.

Fitzgerald, *Rev.* (Sir) Edward Thomas, Bt. (1903).

FitzGerald, Sir George Peter Maur-ice, Bt., M.C., *The Knight of Kerry* (1880).

FitzGerald, Sir William James, Kt., M.C., Q.C.

FitzHerbert, Sir John Richard Frederick, Bt. (1784).

Fitzmaurice, *Lt.-Col.* Sir Desmond FitzJohn, Kt., C.I.E.

Fitzpatrick, *General* Sir (Geoffrey Richard) Desmond, G.C.B., D.S.O., M.B.E., M.C.

Fitzpatrick, *Air Marshal* Sir John Bernard, K.B.E., C.B.

Flanagan, Sir James Bernard, Kt., C.B.E.

Flavelle, Sir (Joseph) David Ell-sworth, Bt. (1917).

Fleming, Sir Charles Alexander, K.B.E., F.R.S.

Fleming, *Instr. Rear-Adm.* Sir John, K.B.E., D.S.C.

Fleming, *Rt. Rev.* (William) Laun-celot Scott, K.C.V.O., D.D.

Fletcher, *Hon.* Sir Alan Roy, Kt.

Fletcher, Sir Alexander Mac-Pherson, Kt.

Fletcher, Sir James Muir Cameron, Kt.

Fletcher, Sir John Henry Lancelot Aubrey-, Bt. (1782).

Fletcher, Sir Leslie, Kt., D.S.C.

Fletcher, Sir Norman Seymour, Kt.

Fletcher, *Air Chief Marshal* Sir Peter Carteret, K.C.B., O.B.E., D.F.C., A.F.C.

Floyd, Sir Giles Henry Charles, Bt. (1816).

Foley, Sir (Thomas John) Noel, Kt., C.B.E.

Foot, Sir Geoffrey James, Kt.

Foots, Sir James William, Kt.

Forbes, *Hon.* Sir Alastair Granville, Kt.

Forbes, Sir Archibald Finlayson, G.B.E.

Forbes of Pitsligo, Sir Charles Edward Stuart-, Bt. (s 1626).

Forbes of Brux, *Hon.* Sir Ewan, Bt. (s 1630).

Forbes, *Vice-Adm.* Sir John Morrison, O.B.E.

Forbes, *Maj.* Sir Hamish Stewart, Bt., M.B.E., M.C. (1823).

Ford, *Capt.* Sir Aubrey St. Clair-, Bt., D.S.O., R.N. (1793).

Ford, *Maj.* Sir Edward William Spencer, K.C.B., K.C.V.O.

Ford, *Air Marshal* Sir Geoffrey Harold, K.B.E., C.B.

Ford, Sir Henry Russell, Bt. (1929).

Ford, *Prof.* Sir Hugh, Kt., F.R.S.

Ford, Sir John Archibald, K.C.M.G., M.C.

Ford, *Maj.-Gen.* Sir Peter St. Clair-, K.B.E., C.B., D.S.O.

Ford, Sir Richard Brinsley, Kt., C.B.E.

Ford, *General* Sir Robert Cyril, G.C.B., C.B.E.

Foreman, Sir Philip Frank, Kt., C.B.E.

Forman, Sir John Denis, Kt., O.B.E.

Forrest, *Prof.* Sir (Andrew) Patrick (McEwen), Kt.

Forrest, Sir James Alexander, Kt.

Forrest, *Rear Adm.* Sir Ronald Stephen, K.C.V.O.

Forster, Sir Archibald William, Kt.

Forster, Sir Oliver Grantham, K.C.M.G., M.V.O.

Forwood, Sir Dudley Richard, Bt. (1895).

Foster, *Prof.* Sir Christopher David, Kt.

Foster, Sir John Gregory, Bt. (1930).

Foster, Sir Robert Sidney, G.C.M.G., K.C.V.O.

Foulis, Sir Ian Primrose Liston-, Bt. (s 1634).

Foulkes, Sir Nigel Gordon, Kt.

Fowden, Sir Leslie, Kt., F.R.S.

Fowke, Sir Frederick (Woollaston Rawdon), Bt. (1814).

Fowler, Sir (Edward) Michael Coulson, Kt.

Fox, Sir (Henry) Murray, G.B.E.

Fox, Sir (John) Marcus, Kt., M.B.E., M.P.

Fox, *Rt. Hon.* Sir Michael John, Kt.

Fox, Sir Theodore Fortescue, Kt., M.D., Ll.D.

Frame, Sir Alistair Gilchrist, Kt.

France, Sir Arnold William, G.C.B.

Francis, Sir Frank Chalton, K.C.B., F.S.A.

Frank, Sir Douglas George Horace, Kt., Q.C.

Frank, Sir (Frederick) Charles, Kt., O.B.E., F.R.S.

†Frank, Sir Robert Andrew, Bt. (1920).

Frankel, Sir Otto Herzberg, Kt., D.SC., F.R.S.

Franklin, Sir Eric Alexander, Kt., C.B.E.

Franklin, Sir Michael David Milroy, K.C.B., C.M.G.

Franks, Sir Arthur Temple, K.C.M.G.

Fraser, Sir Angus McKay, K.C.B., T.D.

Fraser, Sir Basil Malcolm, Bt. (1921).

Fraser, Sir Bruce Donald, K.C.B.

Fraser, *General* Sir David William, G.C.B., O.B.E.

Fraser, Sir Douglas Were, Kt., I.S.O.

Fraser, *Air Marshal Rev.* Sir (Henry) Paterson, K.B.E., C.B., A.F.C.

Fraser, Sir Ian, Kt., D.S.O., O.B.E.

Fraser, Sir Ian James, Kt., C.B.E., M.C.

Fraser, Sir (James) Campbell, Kt.

Fraser, *Prof.* Sir James David, Bt. (1943).

Fraser, Sir William Kerr, G.C.B.

Frederick, Sir Charles Boscawen, Bt. (1723).

Freeland, Sir John Redvers, K.C.M.G.

Freeman, *His Eminence Cardinal* James Darcy, K.B.E.

Freeman, Sir James Robin, Bt. (1945).

Freeman, Sir Ralph, Kt., C.V.O., C.B.E.

Freer, *Air Chief Marshal* Sir Robert William George, G.B.E., K.C.B.

Freeth, *Hon.* Sir Gordon, K.B.E.

French, *Hon.* Sir Christopher James Saunders, Kt.

Fretwell, Sir George Herbert, K.B.E., C.B.

Fretwell, Sir (Major) John (Emsley), G.C.M.G.

Freud, Sir Clement Raphael, Kt.

Froggatt, Sir Leslie Trevor, Kt.

Froggatt, Sir Peter, Kt.

Frossard, Sir Charles Keith, Kt.

Frost, *Hon.* Sir (Thomas) Sydney, Kt.

Fry, *Hon.* Sir William Gordon, Kt.

Fryberg, Sir Abraham, Kt., M.B.E.

Fuchs, Sir Vivian Ernest, Kt., Ph.D.

Fuller, *Hon.* Sir John Bryan Munro, Kt.

Fuller, Sir John William Fleetwood, Bt. (1910).

Fung, *Hon.* Sir Kenneth Ping-Fan, Kt., C.B.E.

Furness, Sir Stephen Roberts, Bt. (1913).

Gadsden, Sir Peter Drury Haggerston, G.B.E.

Gage, Sir Berkeley Everard Foley, K.C.M.G.

Gairy, *Rt. Hon.* Sir Eric Matthew, Kt.

Gallwey, Sir Philip Frankland Payne-, Bt. (1812).

Galsworthy, Sir John Edgar, K.C.V.O., C.M.G.

Gamble, Sir David Hugh Norman, Bt. (1897).

Gandell, Sir Alan Thomas, Kt., C.B.E.

Ganilau, *Ratu* Sir Penaia Kanatabatu, G.C.M.G., K.C.V.O., K.B.E., D.S.O.

Gardner, Sir Douglas Bruce Bruce-, Bt. (1945).

Gardner, Sir Edward Lucas, Kt., Q.C.

Gardner-Thorpe, *Col.* Sir Ronald, G.B.E., T.D.

Garland, *Hon.* Sir Patrick Neville, Kt.

Garland, *Hon.* Sir Ransley Victor, K.B.E.

Garlick, Sir John, K.C.B.

Garner, Sir Anthony Stuart, Kt.

Garran, Sir (Isham) Peter, K.C.M.G.

Garrett, *Hon.* Sir Raymond William, Kt., A.F.C.

Garrioch, Sir (William) Henry, Kt.

Garthwaite, Sir William Francis Cuthbert, Bt., D.S.C. (1919).

Garvey, Sir Ronald Herbert, K.C.M.G., K.C.V.O., M.B.E.

Gascoigne, *Maj.-Gen.* Sir Julian Alvery, K.C.M.G., K.C.V.O., C.B., D.S.O.

Gatehouse, *Hon.* Sir Robert Alexander, Kt.

Geddes, Sir (Anthony) Reay (Mackay), K.B.E.

Gentry, *Maj.-Gen.* Sir William George, K.B.E., C.B., D.S.O.

George, Sir Arthur Thomas, Kt.

Gerken, *Vice-Adm.* Sir Robert William Frank, K.C.B., C.B.E.

Gethin, *Lt.-Col.* Sir Richard Patrick St. Lawrence, Bt. (I 1665).

Ghurburrun, Sir Rabindrah, Kt.

Gibb, Sir Francis Ross (Frank), Kt., C.B.E.

Gibbon, *General* Sir John Houghton, G.C.B., O.B.E.

Gibbons, Sir (John) David, K.B.E.

Gibbons, Sir William Edward Doran, Bt. (1752).

Gibbs, *Hon.* Sir Eustace Hubert Beilby, K.C.V.O., C.M.G.

Gibbs, *Air Marshal* Sir Gerald Ernest, K.B.E., C.I.E., M.C.

Gibbs, *Rt. Hon.* Sir Harry Talbot, G.C.M.G., K.B.E.

Gibbs, *Rt. Hon.* Sir Humphrey Vicary, G.C.V.O., K.C.M.G., O.B.E.

Gibbs, *Field-Marshal* Sir Roland Christopher, G.C.B., C.B.E., D.S.O., M.C.

Gibson, Sir Alexander Drummond, Kt., C.B.E.

Gibson, Sir Christopher Herbert, Bt. (1931).

Gibson, *Rev.* Sir David, Bt. (1926).

Gibson, *Vice-Adm.* Sir Donald Cameron Ernest Forbes, K.C.B., D.S.C.

Gibson, Sir Donald Evelyn Edward, Kt., C.B.E.

Gibson, *Hon.* Sir Marcus George, Kt.

Gibson, Sir Peter Leslie, Kt.

Gibson, *Rt. Hon.* Sir Ralph Brian, Kt.

Gibson, Sir Ronald George, Kt., C.B.E., F.R.C.S.

Giddings, *Air Marshal* Sir (Kenneth Charles) Michael, K.C.B., O.B.E., D.F.C., A.F.C.

Gielgud, Sir (Arthur) John, Kt., C.H.

Giffard, Sir (Charles) Sydney (Rycroft), K.C.M.G.

Gilbert, *Brig.* Sir Herbert Ellery, K.B.E., D.S.O.

Gilbert, *Air Chief Marshal* Sir Joseph Alfred, K.C.B., C.B.E.

Gilbertson, Sir Geoffrey, Kt., C.B.E.

Gilbey, Sir (Walter) Derek, Bt. (1893).

Gilchrist, Sir Andrew Graham, K.C.M.G.

Giles, Sir Alexander Falconer, K.B.E., C.M.G.

Gilkison, Sir Alan Fleming, Kt., C.B.E.

Gillett, *Maj.-Gen.* Sir Peter Bernard, K.C.V.O., C.B., O.B.E.

Gillett, Sir Robin Danvers Penrose, Bt., G.B.E., R.D. (1959).

Gilliat, *Lt.-Col.* Sir Martin John, G.C.V.O., M.B.E.

Gilmour, *Rt. Hon.* Sir Ian Hedworth John Little, Bt., M.P. (1926).

Gilmour, Sir John Edward, Bt., D.S.O., T.D. (1897).

Gingell, *Air Chief Marshal* Sir John, G.B.E., K.C.B.

Gladstone, Sir (Erskine) William, Bt. (1846).

Glass, Sir Leslie Charles, K.C.M.G.

Glasspole, Sir Florizel Augustus, G.C.M.G., G.C.V.O.

Glen, Sir Alexander Richard, K.B.E., D.S.C.

Glenn, Sir (Joseph Robert) Archibald, Kt., O.B.E.

Glidewell, *Rt. Hon.* Sir Iain Derek Laing, Kt.

Glock, Sir William Frederick, Kt., C.B.E.

Glover, *General* Sir James Malcolm, K.C.B., M.B.E.

Glyn, Sir Anthony Geoffrey Leo Simon, Bt. (1927).

Glyn, Sir Richard Lindsay, Bt., (1759 and 1800).

Goad, Sir (Edward) Colin (Viner), K.C.M.G.

Godber, Sir George Edward, G.C.B., D.M.

Goff, Sir Robert (William) Davis-, Bt. (1905).

Gold, Sir Arthur Abraham, Kt., C.B.E.

Gold, Sir Joseph, Kt.

Goldberg, *Prof.* Sir Abraham, Kt., M.D., D.SC., F.R.C.P.

Golding, Sir John Simon Rawson, Kt., O.B.E.

Goldman, Sir Samuel, K.C.B.

Goldsmid, *Maj.-Gen.* Sir James Arthur d'Avigdor-, Bt., C.B., O.B.E., M.C. (1934).

Goldsmith, Sir James Michael, Kt.

Gombrich, *Prof.* Sir Ernst Hans Josef, Kt., C.B.E., PH.D., F.B.A., F.S.A.

Gooch, Sir (Richard) John Sherlock, Bt. (1746).

Gooch, Sir Robert Douglas, Bt. (1866).

Goodall, Sir (Arthur) David Saunders, K.C.M.G.

Goodall, Sir Reginald, Kt., C.B.E.

Goodenough, Sir Richard Edmund, Bt. (1943).

Goodhart, Sir Philip Carter, Kt., M.P.

Goodhart, Sir Robert Anthony Gordon, Bt. (1911).

Goodhew, Sir Victor Henry, Kt.

Goodison, Sir Alan Clowes, K.C.M.G.

Goodison, Sir Nicholas Proctor, Kt.

Goodson, Sir Mark Weston Lassam, Bt. (1922).

Goody, *Most Rev.* Launcelot John, K.B.E.

Goold, Sir George Leonard, Bt. (1801).

Goold, Sir James Duncan, Kt.

Gordon, Sir Andrew Cosmo Lewis Duff-, Bt. (1813).

Gordon, Sir Charles Addison Somerville Snowden, K.C.B.

Gordon, Sir Keith Lyndell, Kt., C.M.G.

Gordon, Sir (Lionel) Eldred (Peter) Smith-, Bt. (1838).

Gordon, Sir Robert James, Bt. (s 1706).

Gordon, Sir Sidney Samuel, Kt., C.B.E.

Gore, Sir Richard Ralph St. George, Bt. (I 1622).

Goring, Sir William Burton Nigel, Bt. (1627).

Gorton, *Rt. Hon.* Sir John Grey, G.C.M.G., C.H.

Goschen, Sir Edward Christian, Bt., D.S.O. (1916).

Gosling, Sir (Frederick) Donald, Kt.

Goulding, Sir (Ernest) Irvine, Kt.

Goulding, Sir (William) Lingard Walter, Bt. (1904).

Gourlay, *General* Sir (Basil) Ian (Spencer), K.C.B., O.B.E., M.C., R.M.

Govan, Sir Lawrence Herbert, Kt.

Gow, *Gen.* Sir (James) Michael, G.C.B.

Gowans, *Hon.* Sir (Urban) Gregory, Kt.

Gowans, Sir James Learmonth, Kt., C.B.E., F.R.C.P., F.R.S.

Gower, Sir (Herbert) Raymond, Kt., M.P.

Gowing, *Prof.* Sir Lawrence Burnett, Kt., C.B.E.

Graaff, Sir de Villiers, Bt., M.B.E. (1911).

Grace, Sir John Te Herekiekie, K.B.E., M.V.O.

Graesser, *Col.* Sir Alastair Stewart Durward, Kt., D.S.O., O.B.E., M.C., T.D.

Graham, Sir Charles Spencer Richard, Bt. (1783).

Graham, Sir James Bellingham, Bt. (1662).

Graham, Sir John Alexander Noble, Bt., K.G.M.G. (1906).

Graham, Sir John Moodie, Bt. (1964).

Graham, Sir (John) Patrick, Kt.

Graham, Sir Norman William, Kt., C.B.

Graham, Sir Peter Alfred, Kt., O.B.E.

Graham, Sir Ralph Wolfe, Bt. (1629).

Grandy, *Marshal of the Royal Air Force* Sir John, G.C.B., K.B.E., D.S.O.

Grant, Sir Archibald, Bt. (s 1705).

Grant, Sir Clifford, Kt.

Grant, Sir (John) Anthony, Kt., M.P.

Grant, Sir Kenneth Lindsay, Kt., O.B.E.

Grant, Sir Patrick Alexander Benedict, Bt. (s 1688).

Grantham, *Admiral* Sir Guy, G.C.B., C.B.E., D.S.O.

Granville, Sir Keith, Kt., C.B.E.

Gray, Sir John Archibald Browne, Kt., SC.D., F.R.S.

Gray, *Vice-Adm.* Sir John Michael Dudgeon, K.B.E., C.B.

Gray, *Lt.-Gen.* Sir Michael Stuart, K.C.B., O.B.E.

Gray, Sir William Hume, Bt. (1917).

Gray, Sir William Stevenson, Kt.

†Grayson, Sir Rupert Stanley Harrington, Bt. (1922).

Greatbatch, Sir Bruce, Kt., K.C.V.O., C.M.G., M.B.E.

Green, Sir (Edward) Stephen (Lycett), Bt., C.B.E. (1886).

Green, Sir George Ernest, Kt.

Green, *Hon.* Sir Guy Stephen Montague, K.B.E.

Green, Sir Owen Whitley, Kt.

Green, Sir Peter James Frederick, Kt.

Greenaway, Sir Derek Burdick, Bt., C.B.E. (1933).

Greenborough, Sir John, K.B.E.

Greene, Sir (John) Brian Massy-, Kt.

Greengross, Sir Alan David, Kt.

Greening, *Rear-Adm.* Sir Paul Woollven, K.C.V.O.

Greenwell, Sir Edward Bernard, Bt. (1906).

Greeves, *Maj.-Gen.* Sir Stuart, K.B.E., C.B., D.S.O., M.C.

Grenside, Sir John Peter, Kt., C.B.E.

Gretton, *Vice-Adm.* Sir Peter William, K.C.B., D.S.O., O.B.E., D.S.C.

Grey, Sir Anthony Dysart, Bt. (1814).

Grey, Sir Paul Francis, K.C.M.G.

†Grierson, Sir Michael John Bewes, Bt. (s 1685).

Grieve, *Prof.* Sir Robert, Kt.

Griffin, *Admiral* Sir Anthony Templer Frederick Griffith, G.C.B.

Griffin, Sir (Charles) David, Kt., C.B.E.

Griffin, Sir John Bowes, Kt., Q.C.

Griffiths, Sir Eldon Wylie, Kt., M.P.

Griffiths, Sir (Ernest) Roy, Kt.

Griffiths, Sir Percival Joseph, K.B.E., C.I.E.

Griffiths, Sir John Norton-, Bt. (1922).

Griffiths, Sir Reginald Ernest, Kt., C.B.E.

Grimwade, Sir Andrew Sheppard, Kt., C.B.E.

Grindrod, *Most Rev.* John Basil Rowland, K.B.E.

Grinstead, Sir Stanley Gordon, Kt.

Groom, Sir (Thomas) Reginald, Kt.

Groom, *Air Marshal* Sir Victor Emmanuel, K.C.V.O., K.B.E., C.B., D.F.C.

Grotrian, Sir Philip Christian Brent, Bt. (1934).

Grove, Sir Charles Gerald, Bt. (1874).

Grove, Sir Edmund Frank, K.C.V.O.

Groves, Sir Charles Barnard, Kt., C.B.E.

Grugeon, Sir John Drury, Kt.

Guinness, Sir Alec, Kt., C.B.E.

Guinness, Sir Howard Christian Sheldon, Kt., V.R.D.

Guinness, Sir Kenelm Ernest Lee, Bt. (1867).

Guise, Sir John, G.C.M.G., K.B.E.

Guise, Sir John Grant, Bt. (1783).

Gujadhur, Sir Radhamohun, Kt., C.M.G.

Gull, Sir Michael Swinnerton Cameron, Bt. (1872).

Gunn, *Prof.* Sir John Currie, Kt., C.B.E.

Gunn, Sir William Archer, K.B.E., C.M.G.

Gunning, Sir Robert Charles, Bt. (1778).

Gunston, Sir Richard Wellesley, Bt. (1938).

Gurden, Sir Harold Edward, Kt.

Gutch, Sir John, K.C.M.G., O.B.E.

Guthrie, Sir Malcolm Connop, Bt., (1936)

Guthrie, *Hon.* Sir Rutherford Campbell, Kt., C.M.G.

Guy, *General* Sir Roland Kelvin, G.C.B., C.B.E., D.S.O.

Gwynne-Evans, Sir Francis Loring, Bt. (1913).

Habakkuk, Sir John Hrothgar, Kt., F.B.A.

Hackett, *General* Sir John Winthrop, G.C.B., C.B.E., D.S.O., M.C.

Hadley, Sir Leonard Albert, Kt.

Hadow, Sir Gordon, Kt., C.M.G., O.B.E.

Hadow, Sir (Reginald) Michael, K.C.M.G.

Hague, *Prof.* Sir Douglas Chalmers, Kt., C.B.E.

Haines, Sir Cyril Henry, K.B.E.

Hale, *Prof.* Sir John Rigby, Kt.

Haley, Sir William John, K.C.M.G.

Hall, Sir Arnold Alexander, Kt., F.R.S.

Hall, Sir Basil Brodribb, K.C.B., M.C., T.D.

Hall, *Air Marshal* Sir Donald Percy, K.C.B., C.B.E., A.F.C.

Hall, Sir Douglas Basil, Bt., K.C.M.G. (s 1687)

Hall, Sir (Frederick) John (Frank), Bt. (1923).

Hall, Sir John Bernard, Bt. (1919).

Hall, Sir Peter Reginald Frederick, Kt., C.B.E.

Hall, Sir Robert de Zouche, K.C.M.G.

Hall, *Brig.* Sir William Henry, K.B.E., D.S.O., E.D.

Halliday, Sir George Clifton, Kt.

Halliday, *Vice-Adm.* Sir Roy William, K.B.E., D.S.C.

Hallifax, *Admiral* Sir David John, K.C.B., K.B.E.

Hallinan, Sir (Adrian) Lincoln, Kt.

Halpern, Sir Ralph Mark, Kt.

Halsey, *Rev.* Sir John Walter Brooke, Bt. (1920).

Halstead, Sir Ronald, Kt., C.B.E.

Hambling, Sir (Herbert) Hugh, Bt. (1924).

Hamburger, Sir Sidney Cyril, Kt., C.B.E.

Hamer, *Hon.* Sir Rupert James, K.C.M.G., E.D.

Hamill, Sir Patrick, Kt., Q.P.M.

Hamilton, Sir (Charles) Denis, Kt., D.S.O.

Hamilton, Sir Edward Sydney, Bt. (1776 and 1819).

Hamilton, Sir James Arnot, K.C.B., M.B.E.

Hamilton, *Admiral* Sir John Graham, G.B.E., C.B.

Hamilton, Sir Michael Aubrey, Kt.

Hamilton, Sir Patrick George, Bt. (1937).

Hamilton, Sir (Robert Charles) Richard Caradoc, Bt. (s 1646).

Hamilton, Sir Bruce Stirling-, Bt. (s 1673).

Hammett, *Hon.* Sir Clifford James, Kt.

Hammick, Sir Stephen George, Bt. (1834).

Hampshire, Sir Stuart Newton, Kt., F.B.A.

Hanbury, Sir John Capel, Kt., C.B.E.

Hancock, *Lt.-Col.* Sir Cyril Percy, K.C.I.E., O.B.E., M.C.

Hancock, Sir David John Stowell, K.C.B.

Hancock, *Air Marshal* Sir Valston Eldridge, K.B.E., C.B., D.F.C.

Hancock, *Prof.* Sir (William) Keith, K.B.E., F.B.A.

Hand, *Most Rev.* Geoffrey David, K.B.E.

Handley, Sir David John Davenport-, Kt., O.B.E.

Hanham, Sir Michael William, Bt., D.F.C. (1667).

Hanley, Sir Michael Bowen, K.C.B.

Hanmer, Sir John Wyndham Edward, Bt. (1774).

Hannay, Sir David Hugh Alexander, K.C.M.G.

Hanson, Sir Anthony Leslie Oswald, Bt. (1887).

Hanson, Sir (Charles) John, Bt. (1918).

Harcourt-Smith, *Air Chief Marshal* Sir David, K.C.B., D.F.C.

Harders, Sir Clarence Waldemar, Kt., O.B.E.

Hardie, Sir Charles Edgar Mathewes, Kt., C.B.E.

Harding, Sir George William, K.C.M.G., C.V.O.

Harding, *Air Chief Marshal* Sir Peter Robin, K.C.B.

Harding, Sir Roy Pollard, Kt., C.B.E.

Hardinge, Sir Robert Arnold, Bt. (1801).

Hardingham, Sir Robert Ernest, Kt., C.M.G., O.B.E.

Hardman, Sir Fred, Kt., M.B.E.

Hardman, Sir Henry, K.C.B.

Hardy, Sir James Gilbert, Kt., O.B.E.

Hardy, Sir Rupert John, Bt., (1876).

Hare, Sir Thomas, Bt. (1818).

Harford, Sir James Dundas, K.B.E., C.M.G.

Harford, Sir (John) Timothy, Bt. (1934).

Hargroves, *Brig.* Sir Robert Louis, Kt., C.B.E.

Harington, *General* Sir Charles Henry Pepys, G.C.B., C.B.E., D.S.O., M.C.

Harington, Sir Nicholas John, Bt. (1611).

Harland, *Air Marshal* Sir Reginald Edward Wynyard, K.B.E., C.B.

Harley, Sir Thomas Winlack, Kt., M.B.E., M.C.

Harman, *General* Sir Jack Wentworth, G.C.B., O.B.E., M.C.

Harman, *Hon.* Sir Jeremiah LeRoy, Kt.

Harmer, Sir Frederic Evelyn, Kt., C.M.G.

Harmer, Sir (John) Dudley, Kt., O.B.E.

Harmsworth, Sir Hildebrand Harold, Bt. (1922).

Harper Gow, Sir Leonard Maxwell, Kt., M.B.E.

Harpham, Sir William, K.B.E., C.M.G.

Harris, *Prof.* Sir Alan James, Kt., C.B.E.

Harris, Sir Anthony Kyrle Travers, Bt. (1953).

Harris, *Prof.* Sir Charles Herbert Stuart-, Kt., C.B.E., M.D.

Harris, *Lt.-Gen.* Sir Ian Cecil, K.B.E., C.B., D.S.O.

Harris, Sir Jack Wolfred Ashford, Bt. (1932).

Harris, Sir Philip Charles, Kt.

Harris, Sir Ronald Montague Joseph, K.C.V.O., C.B.

Harris, Sir William Gordon, K.B.E., C.B.

Harris, Sir William Woolf, Kt., O.B.E.

Harrison, Sir Ernest Thomas, Kt., O.B.E..

Harrison, Sir Francis Alexander Lyle, Kt., M.B.E., Q.C.

Harrison, Sir Geoffrey Wedgwood, G.C.M.G., K.C.V.O.

Harrison, *Surgeon Vice-Adm.* Sir John Albert Bews, K.B.E.

Harrison, *Hon.* Sir (John) Richard, Kt., E.D.

Harrison, Sir Michael James Harwood, Bt. (1961).

Harrison, *Prof.* Sir Richard John, Kt., F.R.S.

Harrison, Sir (Robert) Colin, Bt. (1922).

Harrop, Sir Peter John, K.C.B.

Hart, Sir Byrne, Kt., C.B.E., M.C.

Hart, Sir Francis Edmund Turton-, K.B.E.

Hartley, *Air Marshal* Sir Christopher Harold, K.C.B., C.B.E., D.F.C., A.F.C.

Hartley, Sir Frank, Kt., C.B.E., Ph.D.

Hartopp, Sir John Edmund Cradock-, Bt. (1796).

Hartwell, Sir Brodrick William Charles Elwin, Bt. (1805).

Harvey, Sir Charles Richard Musgrave, Bt. (1933).

Harvey-Jones, Sir John Henry, Kt., M.B.E.

Haskard, Sir Cosmo Dugal Patrick Thomas, K.C.M.G., M.B.E.

Haslam, *Hon.* Sir Alec Leslie, Kt.

Haslam, *Rear-Adm.* Sir David William, K.B.E., C.B.

Haslam, Sir Robert, Kt.

Hasluck, *Rt. Hon.* Sir Paul Meernaa Caedwalla, K.G., G.C.M.G., G.C.V.O.

Hassan, Sir Joshua Abraham, K.C.M.G., C.B.E., L.V.O., Q.C.

Hassett, *General* Sir Francis George, K.B.E., C.B., D.S.O., M.V.O.

Hastings, Sir Stephen Lewis Edmonstone, Kt., M.C.

Hatty, *Hon.* Sir Cyril James, Kt.

Haughton, Sir James, Kt., C.B.E., Q.P.M.

Havelock, Sir Wilfrid Bowen, Kt.

Hawker, Sir (Frank) Cyril, Kt.

Hawkings, Sir (Francis) Geoffrey, Kt.

Hawkins, Sir Arthur Ernest, Kt.

Hawkins, Sir Humphry Villiers Caesar, Bt. (1778).

Hawkins, Sir Paul Lancelot, Kt., T.D.

Hawkins, *Vice-Adm.* Sir Raymond Shayle, K.C.B.

Hawley, *Maj.* Sir David Henry, Bt. (1795).

Hawley, Sir Donald Frederick, K.C.M.G., M.B.E.

†Haworth, Sir Philip, Bt. (1911).

Hawthorne, *Prof.* Sir William Rede, Kt., C.B.E., SC.D., F.R.S.

Hay, Sir Arthur Thomas Erroll, Bt., I.S.O. (s 1663).

Hay, Sir David Osborne, Kt., C.B.E., D.S.O.

Hay, Sir James Brian Dalrymple-, Bt. (1798).

†Hay, Sir Ronald Nelson, Bt. (s 1703).

Hayday, Sir Frederick, Kt., C.B.E.

Haydon, Sir Walter Robert, K.C.M.G.

Hayes, Sir Brian David, K.C.B.

Hayes, Sir Claude James, K.C.M.G.

Hayes, *Vice-Adm.* Sir John Osier Chattock, K.C.B., O.B.E.

Hayhoe, *Rt. Hon.* Sir Bernard John (Barney), Kt., M.P.

Hayman, Sir Peter Telford, K.C.M.G., C.V.O., M.B.E.

Hayter, Sir William Goodenough, K.C.M.G.

Hayward, Sir Alfred, K.B.E.

Hayward, Sir Anthony William Byrd, Kt.

Hayward, Sir Jack Arnold, Kt., O.B.E.

Hayward, Sir Richard Arthur, Kt., C.B.E.

Head, Sir Francis David Somerville, Bt. (1838).

Healey, Sir Charles Edward Chadwyck-, Bt. (1919).

Heap, Sir Desmond, Kt.

Heath, Sir Barrie, Kt., D.F.C.

Heath, Sir Mark Evelyn, K.C.V.O., C.M.G.

Heath, *Air Marshal* Sir Maurice Lionel, K.B.E., C.B., C.V.O.

Heathcoat Amory, Sir Ian, Bt. (1874).

Heathcote, *Brig.* Sir Gilbert Simon, Bt., C.B.E. (1733).

Heathcote, Sir Michael Perryman, Bt. (1733).

Heaton, Sir Yvo Robert Henniker-, Bt. (1912).

Heiser, Sir Terence Michael, K.C.B.

Hele, Sir Ivor Thomas Henry, Kt., C.B.E.

Hellaby, Sir (Frederick Reed) Alan, Kt.

Hellings, *General* Sir Peter William Cradock, K.C.B., D.S.C., M.C., R.M.

Henare, Sir James Clendon Tau, K.B.E., D.S.O.

Henderson, Sir Guy Wilmot McLintock, Kt., Q.C.

Henderson, Sir James Thyne, K.B.E., C.M.G.

Henderson, Sir (John) Nicholas, G.C.M.G.

Henderson, *Admiral* Sir Nigel Stuart, G.B.E., K.C.B.

Henderson, Sir William MacGregor, Kt., D.SC., F.R.S.

Henley, Sir Douglas Owen, K.C.B.

Henley, *Rear-Adm.* Sir Joseph Charles Cameron, K.C.V.O., C.B.

Hennessy, Sir James Patrick Ivan, K.B.E., C.M.G.

Hennessy, Sir John Wyndham Pope-, Kt., C.B.E., F.B.A., F.S.A.

Henniker, *Brig.* Sir Mark Chandos Auberon, Bt., C.B.E., D.S.O., M.C. (1813).

Henry, Sir Denis Aynsley, Kt., O.B.E., Q.C.

Henry, *Hon.* Denis Robert Maurice, Kt.

Henry, Sir James Holmes, Bt., C.M.G., M.C., T.D., Q.C. (1923).

Henry, *Hon.* Sir Trevor Ernest, Kt.

Hepburn, Sir Ninian Buchan Archibald John Buchan-, Bt. (1815).

Herbecq, Sir John Edward, K.C.B.

Herbert, *Admiral* Sir Peter Geoffrey Marshall, K.C.B., O.B.E.

Hermon, Sir John Charles, Kt., K.C.B.

Heron, Sir Conrad Frederick, K.C.B., O.B.E.

Herries, Sir Michael Alexander Robert Young-, Kt., O.B.E., M.C.

Heseltine, *Rt. Hon.* Sir William Frederick Payne, K.C.B., K.C.V.O.

Hetherington, Sir Arthur Ford, Kt., D.S.C.

Hetherington, Sir Thomas Chalmers, K.C.B., C.B.E., T.D., Q.C.

Heward, *Air Chief Marshal* Sir Anthony Wilkinson, K.C.B., O.B.E., D.F.C., A.F.C.

Hewetson, Sir Christopher Raynor, Kt., T.D.

Hewetson, *General* Sir Reginald Hackett, G.C.B., C.B.E., D.S.O.

Hewett, Sir John George, Bt., M.C. (1813).

Hewitt, Sir (Cyrus) Lenox (Simson), Kt., O.B.E.

Hewitt, Sir Nicholas Charles Joseph, Bt. (1921).

Heygate, Sir George Lloyd, Bt. (1831).

Heyman, Sir Horace William, Kt.

Heywood, Sir Oliver Kerr, Bt. (1838).

Hezlet, *Vice-Adm.* Sir Arthur Richard, K.B.E., C.B., D.S.O., D.S.C.

Hibbert, Sir Reginald Alfred, G.C.M.G.

Hickey, Sir Justin, Kt.

Hickman, Sir (Richard) Glenn, Bt. (1903).

Hicks, Sir John Richard, Kt., F.B.A.

Hielscher, Sir Leo Arthur, Kt.

Higgins, Sir Christopher Thomas, Kt.

Higgs, Sir (John) Michael (Clifford), Kt.

Hildreth, *Maj.-Gen.* Sir (Harold) John (Crossley), K.B.E.

Hildyard, Sir David Henry Thoroton, K.C.M.G., D.F.C.

Hiley, *Hon.* Sir Thomas Alfred, K.B.E.

Hilgendorf, Sir Charles, Kt., C.M.G.

Hill, *Prof.* Sir Austin Bradford, Kt., C.B.E., Ph.D., D.SC., F.R.S.

Hill, Sir James Frederick, Bt. (1917).

Hill, Sir John McGregor, Kt., Ph.D.

Hill, Sir John Maxwell, Kt., C.B.E., D.F.C.

Hill, Sir Richard George Rowley, Bt., M.B.E. (1779).

Hill, Sir Robert Erskine-, Bt. (1945).

Hillary, Sir Edmund, K.B.E.

Himsworth, Sir Harold Percival, K.C.B., M.D., F.R.S.

Hine, *Air Chief Marshal* Sir Patrick Bardon, K.C.B.

Hines, Sir Colin Joseph, Kt., O.B.E.

Hinsley, *Prof.* Sir Francis Harry, Kt., O.B.E., F.B.A.

Hirsch, *Prof.* Sir Peter Bernhard, Kt., Ph.D., F.R.S.

Hirst, *Hon.* Sir David Cozens-Hardy, Kt.

Hoare, Sir Peter Richard David, Bt. (1786).

Hoare, Sir Timothy Edward Charles, Bt. (1 1784).

Hobart, *Lt.-Cdr.* Sir Robert Hampden, Bt., R.N. (1914).

Hobday, Sir Gordon Ivan, Kt.

Hobhouse, Sir Charles Chisholm, Bt., T.D. (1812).

Hobson, Sir Harold, Kt., C.B.E.

Hockaday, Sir Arthur Patrick, K.C.B., C.M.G.

Hodge, Sir John Rowland, Bt., M.B.E. (1921).

Hodge, Sir Julian Stephen Alfred, Kt.

Hodges, *Air Chief Marshal* Sir Lewis MacDonald, K.C.B., C.B.E., D.S.O., D.F.C.

Hodgkin, *Prof.* Sir Alan Lloyd, O.M., K.B.E., F.R.S., SC.D.

Hodgkinson, *Air Chief Marshal* Sir (William) Derek, K.C.B., C.B.E., D.F.C., A.F.C.

Hodgson, Sir Maurice Arthur Eric, Kt.

Hodgson, *Hon.* Sir (Walter) Derek (Thornley), Kt.

Hodson, Sir Michael Robin Adderley, Bt. (1 1789).

Hoffenberg, *Prof.* Sir Raymond, K.B.E.

Hoffman, *Hon.* Sir Leonard Hubert, Kt.

Hogg, *Maj.* Sir Arthur Ramsay, Bt., M.B.E. (1846).

Hogg, Sir Christopher Anthony, Kt.

Hogg, *Vice-Adm.* Sir Ian Leslie Trower, K.C.B., D.S.C.

Hogg, Sir John Nicholson, Kt., T.D.

Hogg, Sir William Lindsay Lindsay-, Bt. (1905).

Holcroft, Sir Peter George Culcheth, Bt. (1921).

Holden, Sir David Charles Beresford, K.B.E., C.B., E.R.D.

Holden, Sir Edward, Bt. (1893).

Holden, Sir John David, Bt. (1919).

Holder, Sir John Henry, Bt. (1898).

Holder, *Air Marshal* Sir Paul Davie, K.B.E., C.B., D.S.O., D.F.C., ph.D.

Holderness, Sir Richard William, Bt. (1920).

Holdsworth, Sir (George) Trevor, Kt.

Holland, Sir Clifton Vaughan, Kt.

Holland, Sir Guy (Hope), Bt. (1917).

Holland, Sir Kenneth Lawrence, Kt., C.B.E., Q.F.S.M.

Holland, Sir Philip Welsby, Kt.

Hollings, *Hon.* Sir (Alfred) Kenneth, Kt., M.C.

Hollis, *Hon.* Sir Anthony Barnard, Kt.

Hollom, Sir Jasper Quintus, K.B.E.

Holloway, *Hon.* Sir Barry Blyth, K.B.E.

Holm, Sir Carl Henry, Kt., O.B.E.

Holmes, *Prof.* Sir Frank Wakefield, Kt.

Holmes, Sir Maurice Andrew, Kt.

Holt, Sir James Richard, K.B.E.

Holt, Sir John Anthony Langford-, Kt.

Home, Sir David George, Bt. (s 1671).

Hone, *Maj.-Gen.* Sir (Herbert) Ralph, K.C.M.G., K.B.E., M.C., T.D., Q.C.

Honywood, Sir Filmer Courtenay William, Bt. (1660).

Hood, Sir Alexander William Fuller-Acland-, Bt. (1806).

Hood, Sir Harold Joseph, Bt., T.D. (1922).

Hookway, Sir Harry Thurston, Kt.

Hoole, Sir Arthur Hugh, Kt.

Hooper, Sir Leonard James, K.C.M.G., C.B.E.

Hooper, Sir Robin William John, K.C.M.G., D.S.O., D.F.C.

Hope, Sir (Charles) Peter, K.C.M.G., T.D.

†Hope, Sir John Carl Alexander, Bt. (s 1628).

Hope, Sir Robert Holms-Kerr, Bt. (1932)

Hopkin, Sir David Armand, Kt.

Hopkin, Sir (William Aylsham) Bryan, Kt., C.B.E.

Hopkins, *Admiral* Sir Frank Henry Edward, K.C.B., D.S.O., D.S.C.

Hopkins, Sir James Sidney Rawdon Scott-, Kt.

Hopkinson, Sir (Henry) Thomas, Kt., C.B.E.

Hordern, Sir Michael Murray, Kt., C.B.E.

Hordern, Sir Peter Maudslay, Kt., M.P.

Horlick, *Vice-Adm.* Sir Edwin John, K.B.E.

Horlick, Sir John James Macdonald, Bt. (1914).

Hornby, Sir (Roger) Antony, Kt.

Horne, Sir Alan Gray Antony, Bt. (1929).

Horsfall, Sir John Musgrave, Bt., M.C., T.D. (1909).

Horsley, *Air Marshal* Sir (Beresford) Peter (Torrington), K.C.B., C.B.E., M.V.O., A.F.C.

Hort, Sir James Fenton, Bt. (1767).

Hoskyns, Sir Benedict Leigh, Bt. (1676).

Hoskyns, Sir John Austin Hungerford Leigh, Kt.

Houldsworth, Sir (Harold) Basil, Bt. (1956).

Houldsworth, Sir Reginald Douglas Henry, Bt., O.B.E., T.D. (1887).

Hounsfield, Sir Godfrey Newbold, Kt., C.B.E.

House, *Lt.-Gen.* Sir David George, G.C.B., K.C.V.O., C.B.E., M.C.

Houssemayne du Boulay, Sir Roger William, K.C.V.O., C.M.G.

How, Sir Friston Charles, Kt., C.B.

Howard, Sir Douglas Frederick, K.C.M.G., M.C.

Howard, Sir (Hamilton) Edward de Coucey, Bt., G.B.E. (1955).

Howard, *Prof.* Sir Michael Eliot, Kt., C.B.E., M.C.

Howard, *Maj.-Gen.* Lord Michael Fitzalan-, G.C.V.O., C.B., C.B.E., M.C.

Howard, Sir Walter Stewart, Kt., M.B.E.

Howe, *Rt. Hon.* Sir (Richard Edward) Geoffrey, Kt., Q.C., M.P.

Howie, Sir James William, Kt., M.D.

Howlett, *Gen.* Sir Geoffrey Hugh Whitby, K.B.E., M.C.

Hoyle, *Prof.* Sir Fred, Kt., F.R.S.

Hoyos, *Hon.* Sir Fabriciano Alexander, Kt.

Huckle, Sir (Henry) George, Kt., O.B.E.

Huddie, Sir David Patrick, Kt.

Hudleston, *Air Chief Marshal* Sir Edmund Cuthbert, G.C.B., C.B.E.

Hudson, Sir Havelock Henry Trevor, Kt.

Hudson, *Lt.-Gen.* Sir Peter, K.C.B., C.B.E.

Huggins, *Hon.* Sir Alan Armstrong, Kt.

Hugh-Jones, Sir Wynn Normington, Kt., M.V.O.

Hughes, Sir David Collingwood, Bt. (1773).

Hughes, *Prof.* Sir Edward Stuart Reginald, Kt., C.B.E.

Hughes, Sir Jack William, Kt.

Hughes, *Air Marshal* Sir (Sidney Weetman) Rochford, K.C.B., C.B.E., A.F.C.

Hughes, Sir Trevor Poulton, K.C.B.

Hughes, Sir Trevor Denby Lloyd-, Kt.

Hugo, *Lt.-Col.* Sir John Mandeville, K.C.V.O., O.B.E.

Hull, *Field Marshal* Sir Richard Amyatt, K.G., G.C.B., D.S.O.

Hulme, *Hon.* Sir Alan Shallcross, K.B.E.

Hulse, Sir (Hamilton) Westrow, Bt. (1739).

Hulton, Sir Edward George Warris, Kt.

Hulton, Sir Geoffrey Alan, Bt. (1905).

Hume, Sir Alan Blyth, Kt., C.B.

Humphreys, Sir Olliver William, Kt., C.B.E.

Humphreys, Sir (Raymond Evelyn) Myles, Kt.

Hunn, Sir Jack Kent, Kt., C.M.G.

Hunt, Sir David Wathen Stather, K.C.M.G., O.B.E.

Hunt, *Admiral* Sir Nicholas John Streynsham, G.C.B., L.V.O.

Hunt, *General* Sir Peter Mervyn, G.C.B., D.S.O., O.B.E.

Hunt, Sir Rex Masterman, Kt., C.M.G.

Hunt, Sir Robert Frederick, Kt., C.B.E.

Hunter, *Hon.* Sir Alexander Albert, K.B.E.

Hunter, Sir Ian Bruce Hope, Kt., M.B.E.

Hurley, Sir John Garling, Kt., C.B.E.

Hurrell, Sir Anthony Gerald, K.C.V.O., C.M.G.

Hutchinson, Sir Joseph Burtt, Kt., C.M.G., SC.D., F.R.S.

Hutchinson, *Hon.* Sir Ross, Kt., D.F.C.

Hutchison, *Lt.-Cdr.* Sir (George) Ian Clark, Kt., R.N.

Hutchison, *Hon.* Sir Michael, Kt.

Hutchison, Sir Peter, Bt. (1939).

Hutchison, Sir Peter Craft, Bt. (1956).

Hutchison, Sir (William) Kenneth, Kt., C.B.E., F.R.S.

Hutson, Sir Francis Challenor, Kt., C.B.E.

Hutton, Sir Leonard, Kt.

Huxley, *Prof.* Sir Andrew Fielding, Kt., O.M., F.R.S.

Huxley, Sir Leonard George Holden, K.B.E., D.Phil., ph.D.

Huxtable, *Gen.* Sir Charles Richard, K.C.B., C.B.E.

Hyatali, *Hon.* Sir Isaac Emanuel, Kt.

Ibbs, Sir (John) Robin, Kt.

Illingworth, *Prof.* Sir Charles Frederick William, Kt., C.B.E.

Inch, Sir John Ritchie, Kt., C.V.O., C.B.E.

Ingilby, Sir Thomas Colvin William, Bt. (1866).

Inglefield, Sir Gilbert Samuel, G.B.E., T.D.

Inglefield, *Col.* Sir John Frederick Crompton-, Kt., T.D.

Inglis, Sir Brian Scott, Kt.

Inglis of Glencorse, Sir Roderick John, Bt. (s 1703).

Ingram, Sir James Herbert Charles, Bt. (1893).

Innes, Sir Charles Kenneth Gordon, Bt. (N.S. 1686).

Innes, Sir (Ronald Gordon) Berowald, Bt., O.B.E. (s 1628).

Inniss, *Hon.* Sir Clifford de Lisle, Kt.

Irish, Sir Ronald Arthur, Kt., O.B.E.

Irvine, *Rt. Hon.* Sir Bryant Godman, Kt.

Irving, *Rear-Adm.* Sir Edmund George, K.B.E., C.B.

Irwin, Sir James Campbell, Kt., O.B.E., E.D.

Isaac, Sir Neil, Kt.

Isham, Sir Ian Vere Gyles, Bt. (1627).

Issigonis, Sir Alec Arnold Constantine, Kt., C.B.E., F.R.S.

Jack, *Hon.* Sir Alieu Sulayman, Kt.

Jackman, *Air Marshal* Sir (Harold) Douglas, K.B.E., C.B.

Jackson, *Air Marshal* Sir Brendan James, K.C.B.

Jackson, Sir Geoffrey Holt Seymour, K.C.M.G.

Jackson, Sir (John) Edward, K.C.M.G.

Jackson, *Hon.* Sir Lawrence Walter, K.C.M.G.

Jackson, Sir Michael Roland, Bt. (1902).

Jackson, Sir Nicholas Fane St. George, Bt. (1913).

Jackson, *Air Vice-Marshal* Sir Ralph Coburn, K.B.E., C.B.

Jackson, Sir Robert, Bt. (1815).

Jackson, *Comdr.* Sir Robert Gillman Allen, K.C.V.O., C.M.G., O.B.E.

Jackson, *General* Sir William Godfrey Fothergill, G.B.E., K.C.B., M.C.

Jackson, Sir William Thomas, Bt. (1869).

Jacob, *Lt.-Gen.* Sir (Edward) Ian (Claud), G.B.E., C.B.

Jacob, Sir Isaac Hai, Kt., Q.C.

Jacobs, *Hon.* Sir Kenneth Sydney, K.B.E.

Jacobs, Sir Wilfred Ebenezer, G.C.M.G., G.C.V.O., O.B.E., Q.C.

Jacomb, Sir Martin Wakefield, Kt.

Jaffray, Sir William Otho, Bt. (1892).

Jagatsingh, *Hon.* Sir Kher, Kt.

Jakeway, Sir (Francis) Derek, K.C.M.G., O.B.E.

Jakobovits, Rabbi Immanuel, Kt.

James, Sir Cynlais Morgan, K.C.M.G.

James, Sir Gerard Bowes Kingston, Bt. (1823).

Jamieson, *Air Marshal* Sir David Ewan, K.B.E., C.B.

Janion, *Rear-Adm.* Sir Hugh Penderel, K.C.V.O.

Janvrin, *Vice-Adm.* Sir (Hugh) Richard Benest, K.C.B., D.S.C.

Jardine, *Maj.* Sir (Andrew) Rupert (John) Buchanan-, Bt., M.C. (1885).

Jardine, Sir Andrew Colin Douglas, Bt. (1916).

Jardine of Applegirth, Sir Alexander Maule, Bt. (s 1672).

Jarratt, Sir Alexander Anthony, Kt., C.B.

Jarrett, Sir Clifford George, K.B.E., C.B.

Jawara, *Hon.* Sir Dawda Kairaba, Kt.

Jeewoolall, Sir Ramesh, Kt.

Jeffcoate, Sir (Thomas) Norman (Arthur), Kt., M.D., F.R.C.S.

Jefferson, Sir George Rowland, Kt., C.B.E.

Jefferson, Sir Mervyn Stewart Dunnington-, Bt. (1958).

Jeffreys, Sir Harold, Kt., D.SC., F.R.S.

Jehangir, Sir Hirji, Bt. (1908).

Jejeebhoy, Sir Rustom, Bt. (1857).

Jellicoe, Sir Geoffrey Alan, Kt., C.B.E., F.R.I.B.A.

Jenkins, Sir Owain Trevor, Kt.

Jenkinson, Sir Anthony Banks, Bt. (1661).

Jenks, Sir Richard Atherley, Bt. (1932).

Jennings, Sir Albert Victor, Kt.

Jennings, Sir Raymond Winter, Kt., Q.C.

Jennings, *Prof.* Sir Robert Yewdall, Kt., Q.C.

Jenour, Sir (Arthur) Maynard (Chesterfield), Kt., T.D.

Jephcott, *Hon.* Sir Bruce Reginald, Kt., C.B.E.

Jephcott, Sir (John) Anthony, Bt. (1962).

Jessel, Sir Charles John, Bt. (1883).

Joel, *Hon.* Sir Asher Alexander, K.B.E.

John, Sir Rupert Godfrey, Kt.

Johnson, *Rt. Hon.* Sir David Powell Croom-, Kt., D.S.C., V.R.D.

Johnson, Sir Henry Cecil, K.B.E.

Johnson, Sir Peter Colpoys Paley, Bt. (1755).

†Johnson, Sir Robin Eliot, Bt. (1818).

Johnson, Sir Ronald Ernest Charles, Kt., C.B.

Johnson Smith, Sir Geoffrey, Kt., M.P.

Johnston, Sir Alexander, G.C.B., K.B.E.

Johnston, Sir Charles Collier, Kt., T.D.

Johnston, Sir (David) Russell, Kt., M.P.

Johnston, Sir John Baines, G.C.M.G., K.C.V.O.

Johnston, *Lt.-Col.* Sir John Frederick Dame, G.C.V.O., M.C.

Johnston, *Lt.-Gen.* Sir Maurice Robert, K.C.B., O.B.E.

Johnston, Sir Thomas Alexander, Bt. (s 1626).

Johnstone, Sir Frederic Allan George, Bt. (s 1700).

Jolliffe, Sir Anthony Stuart, G.B.E.

Jones, Sir Brynmor, Kt., Ph.D., SC.D.

Jones, *General* Sir Charles Phibbs, G.C.B., C.B.E., M.C.

Jones, Sir Christopher Lawrence-, Bt. (1831).

Jones, *Air Marshal* Sir Edward Gordon, K.C.B., C.B.E., D.S.O., D.F.C.

Jones, *Rt. Hon.* Sir Edward Warburton, Kt.

Jones, Sir (Edward) Martin Furnival, Kt., C.B.E.

Jones, Sir Ewart Ray Herbert, Kt., D.SC., Ph.D., F.R.S.

Jones, Sir Francis Avery, Kt., C.B.E., F.R.C.P.

Jones, *Air Marshal* Sir George, K.B.E., C.B., D.F.C.

Jones, Sir Glyn Smallwood, G.C.M.G., M.B.E.

Jones, Sir Harry Ernest, Kt., C.B.E.

Jones, Sir Henry Frank Harding, G.B.E.

Jones, Sir James Duncan, K.C.B.

Jones, Sir (John) Kenneth (Trevor), Kt., C.B.E., Q.C.

Jones, Sir John Lewis, K.C.B.

Jones, Sir John Prichard-, Bt. (1910).

Jones, Sir Keith Stephen, Kt.

Jones, *Hon.* Sir Kenneth George Illtyd, Kt.

Jones, *Air Marshal* Sir Laurence Alfred, K.C.B., C.B., A.F.C.

Jones, Sir (Owen) Trevor, Kt.

Jones, Sir Samuel Owen, Kt.

Jones, Sir Simon Warley Frederick Benton, Bt. (1919).

Jones, Sir (Thomas) Philip, Kt., C.B.

Jones, Sir (William) Elwyn (Edwards), Kt.

Jones, Sir (William) Emrys, Kt.

Jones, *Hon.* Sir William Lloyd Mars-, Kt., M.B.E.

Jordan, *Air Marshal* Sir Richard Bowen, K.C.B., D.F.C.

Joseph, *Maj.* Sir (Herbert) Leslie, Kt.

Jungius, *Vice-Adm.,* Sir James George, K.B.E.

Junor, Sir John Donald Brown, Kt.

Jupp, *Hon.* Sir Kenneth Graham, Kt., M.C.

Kalo, Sir Kwamala, Kt., M.B.E.

Kan Yuet-Keung, Sir, G.B.E.

Karimjee, Sir Tayabali Hassanali Alibhoy, Kt.

Katsina, The Emir of, K.B.E., C.M.G.

Katz, Sir Bernard, Kt., F.R.S.

Kavali, Sir Thomas, Kt., O.B.E.

Kay, *Prof.* Sir Andrew Watt, Kt.

Kaye, Sir Emmanuel, Kt., C.B.E.

Kaye, Sir John Phillip Lister Lister-, Bt. (1812).

Kaye, Sir David Alexander Gordon, Bt. (1923).

Keane, Sir Richard Michael, Bt. (1801).

Keatinge, Sir Edgar Mayne, Kt., C.B.E.

Keeble, Sir (Herbert Ben) Curtis, G.C.M.G.

Kellett, Sir Brian Smith, Kt.

Kellett, Sir Stanley Charles, Bt. (1801).

Kelliher, Sir Henry Joseph, Kt.

Kelly, *Rt. Hon.* Sir (John William) Basil, Kt.

Kelly, Sir William Theodore, Kt., O.B.E.

Kemp, Sir Leslie Charles, K.B.E.

Kemsley, *Col.* Sir Alfred Newcombe, K.B.E., C.M.G., E.D.

Kendrew, *Maj.-Gen.* Sir Douglas Anthony, K.C.M.G., C.B., C.B.E., D.S.O.

Kendrew, Sir John Cowdery, Kt., C.B.E., SC.D., F.R.S.

Kenilorea, *Rt. Hon.* Sir Peter, K.B.E.

Kennard, *Lt.-Col.* Sir George Arnold Ford, Bt. (1891).

Kennaway, Sir John Lawrence, Bt. (1791).

Kennedy, Sir Albert Henry, Kt.

Kennedy, Sir Clyde David Allen, Kt.

Kennedy, Sir Francis, K.C.M.G., C.B.E.

Kennedy, Sir George Ronald Derrick, Bt., O.B.E. (1836).

Kennedy, *Hon.* Sir Ian Alexander, Kt.

Kennedy, *Hon.* Sir Paul Joseph Morrow, Kt.

Kennedy, *Air Chief Marshal* Sir Thomas Lawrie, G.C.B., A.F.C.

Kennedy-Good, Sir John, K.B.E.

Kennon, *Vice-Adm.* Sir James Edward Campbell, K.C.B., C.B.E.

Kenny, *Gen.* Sir Brian Leslie Graham, K.C.B., C.B.E.

Kenny, Sir Patrick John, Kt.

Kent, Sir Harold Simcox, G.C.B., Q.C.

Kenyon, Sir George Henry, Kt.

Kermode, Sir Ronald Graham Quale, K.B.E.

Kerr, *Rt. Hon.* Sir John Robert, G.C.M.G., G.C.V.O.

Kerr, *Rt. Hon.* Sir Michael Robert Emanuel, Kt.

Kerr, *Hon.* Sir Alastair Blair-, Kt.

Kerruish, Sir (Henry) Charles, Kt., O.B.E.

Kerry, Sir Michael James, K.C.B., Q.C.

Kershaw, Sir (John) Anthony, Kt., M.C.

Keswick, Sir William Johnston, Kt.

Keville, Sir (William) Errington, Kt., C.B.E.

Kidd, Sir Robert Hill, K.B.E., C.B.

Kidu, *Hon.* Sir Buri (William), Kt.

Kikau, *Ratu* Sir Jone Latianara, K.B.E.

Kiki, *Hon.* Sir (Albert) Maori, K.B.E.

Killen, *Hon.* Denis James, K.C.M.G.

Killick, Sir John Edward, G.C.M.G.

Kilpatrick, *Prof.* Sir Robert, Kt., C.B.E.

Kilpatrick, Sir William John, K.B.E. (1904).

Kimber, Sir Charles Dixon, Bt. (1904).

Kinahan, Sir Robert George Caldwell, Kt., E.R.D.

King, Sir Albert, Kt., O.B.E.

King, *General* Sir Frank Douglas, G.C.B., M.B.E.

King, Sir James Granville Le Neve, Bt., T.D. (1888).

King, Sir Richard Brian Meredith, K.C.B., M.C.

King, Sir Sydney Percy, Kt., O.B.E.

King, Sir Wayne Alexander, Bt. (1815).

Kingman, *Prof.* Sir John Frank Charles, Kt., F.R.S.

Kingsland, Sir Richard, Kt., C.B.E., D.F.C.

Kingsley, Sir Patrick Graham Toler, K.C.V.O.

Kininmonth, Sir William Hardie, Kt., P.P.R.S.A., F.R.I.B.A.

Kinloch, Sir David, Bt. (s 1686).

Kinloch, Sir John, Bt. (1873).

Kirby, *Hon.* Sir Richard Clarence, Kt.

Kirkley, Sir (Howard) Leslie, Kt., C.B.E.

Kirkpatrick, Sir Ivone Elliott, Bt. (s 1685).

Kirwan, Sir (Archibald) Laurence Patrick, K.C.M.G., T.D.

Kitson, *General* Sir Frank Edward, G.B.E., K.C.B., M.C.

Kitson, Sir Timothy Peter Geoffrey, Kt.

Kitto, *Rt. Hon.* Sir Frank Walters, K.B.E.

Kleinwort, Sir Kenneth Drake, Bt. (1909).

Knight, Sir Allan Walton, Kt., C.M.G.

Knight, Sir Arthur William, Kt.

Knight, Sir Harold Murray, K.B.E., D.S.C.

Knight, *Air Marshal* Sir Michael William Patrick, K.C.B., A.F.C.

Knill, Sir John Kenelm Stuart, Bt. (1893).

Knipe, Sir Leslie Francis, Kt., M.B.E.

Knott, Sir John Laurence, Kt., C.B.E.

Knowles, Sir Charles Francis, Bt. (1765).

Knowles, Sir Leonard Joseph, Kt., C.B.E.

Knox, *Hon.* Sir John Leonard, Kt.

Knox, *Hon.* Sir William Edward, Kt.

Kornberg, *Prof.* Sir Hans Leo, Kt., D.SC., SC.D., Ph.D., F.R.S.

Krusin, Sir Stanley Marks, Kt., C.B.

Kurongku, *Most. Rev.* Peter, K.B.E.

Kyle, *Air Chief Marshal* Sir Wallace Hart, G.C.B., K.C.V.O., C.B.E., D.S.O., D.F.C.

Labouchere, Sir George Peter, G.B.E., K.C.M.G.

Lacon, Sir Edmund Vere, Bt. (1818).

Lacy, Sir Hugh Maurice Pierce, Bt. (1921).

Lagesen, *Air Marshal* Sir Philip Jacobus, K.C.B., D.F.C., A.F.C.

Laidlaw, Sir Christophor Charles Fraser, Kt.

Laing, Sir Hector, Kt.

Laing, Sir (John) Maurice, Kt.

Laing, Sir (William) Kirby, Kt.

Lake, Sir (Atwell) Graham, Bt. (1711).

Laker, Sir Frederick Alfred, Kt.

Lakin, Sir Michael, Bt. (1909).

Laking, Sir George Robert, K.C.M.G.

Lamb, Sir Albert (Larry), Kt.

Lamb, Sir Albert Thomas, K.B.E., C.M.G., D.F.C.

Lamb, Sir Lionel Henry, K.C.M.G., O.B.E.

Lambert, Sir Anthony Edward, K.C.M.G.

Lambert, Sir Edward Thomas, K.B.E., C.V.O.

Lambert, Sir Greville Foley, Bt. (1711).

Lambert, Sir John Henry, K.C.V.O., C.M.G.

Lancaster, *Vice-Adm.* Sir John Strike, K.B.E., C.B.

Landau, Sir Dennis Marcus, Kt.

Lane, Sir David William Stennis Stuart, Kt.

Lane, Sir Peter Stewart, Kt.

Lang, *Lt.-Gen.* Sir Derek Boileau, K.C.B., D.S.O., M.C.

Langham, Sir James Michael, Bt. (1660).

Langley, *Maj.-Gen.* Sir Henry Desmond Allen, K.C.V.O., M.B.E.

Langrishe, Sir Hercules Ralph Hume, Bt. (1 1777).

Lapsley, *Air Marshal* Sir John Hugh, K.B.E., C.B., D.F.C., A.F.C.

Lapun, *Hon.* Sir Paul, Kt.

Larcom, Sir (Charles) Christopher Royde, Bt. (1868).

Larmour, Sir Edward Noel, K.C.M.G.

Lartigue, Sir Louis Cools-, Kt., O.B.E.

Lasdun, Sir Denys Louis, Kt., C.B.E., F.R.I.B.A.

Laskey, Sir Denis Seward, K.C.M.G., C.V.O.

Latey, *Rt. Hon.* Sir John Brinsmead, Kt., M.B.E.

Latham, Sir Joseph, Kt., C.B.E.

Latham, Sir Richard Thomas Paul, Bt. (1919).

Latimer, Sir (Courtenay) Robert, Kt., C.B.E.

Latimer, Sir Graham Stanley, K.B.E.

Laucke, *Hon.* Sir Condor Louis, K.C.M.G.

Lauder, Sir Piers Robert Dick-, Bt. (s 1690).

Laughton, Sir Anthony Seymour, Kt.

Laurantus, Sir Nicholas, Kt., M.B.E.

Laurence, Sir Peter Harold, K.C.M.G., M.C.

Laurie, Sir Robert Bayley Emilius, Bt. (1834).

Lavan, *Hon.* Sir John Martin, Kt.

Law, *Hon.* Sir Eric John Ewan, Kt.

Law, *Admiral* Sir Horace Rochfort, G.C.B., O.B.E., D.S.C.

Lawes, Sir (John) Michael Bennet, Bt. (1882).

Lawler, Sir Peter James, Kt., O.B.E.

Lawrence, Sir David Roland Walter, Bt. (1906).

Lawrence, Sir Guy Kempton, Kt., D.S.O., O.B.E., D.F.C.

Lawrence, Sir John Waldemar, Bt., O.B.E. (1858).

Lawrence, Sir William Fettiplace, Bt. (1867).

Lawson, Sir Christopher Donald, Kt.

Lawson, *Col.* Sir John Charles Arthur Digby, Bt., D.S.O., M.C. (1900).

Lawson, *Hon.* Sir Neil, Kt.

Lawson, *Gen.* Sir Richard George, K.C.B., D.S.O., O.B.E.

Lawson, Sir William Howard, Bt. (1841).

Lawton, *Prof.* Sir Frank Ewart, Kt.

Lawton, *Rt. Hon.* Sir Frederick Horace, Kt.

Layfield, Sir Frank Henry Burland Willoughby, Kt., Q.C.

Lazarus, Sir Peter Esmond, K.C.B.

Lea, *Lt.-Gen.* Sir George Harris, K.C.B., D.S.O., M.B.E.

Lea, *Vice-Adm.*, Sir John Stuart Crosbie, K.B.E.

†Lea, Sir (Thomas) Julian, Bt. (1892).

Leach, *Prof.* Sir Edmund Ronald, Kt., Ph.D., F.B.A.

Leach, *Admiral of the Fleet* Sir Henry Conyers, G.C.B.

Leach, Sir Ronald George, G.B.E.

Leahy, Sir John Henry Gladstone, K.C.M.G.

Lean, Sir David, Kt., C.B.E.

Leask, *Lt.-Gen.* Sir Henry Lowther Ewart Clark, K.C.B., D.S.O., O.B.E.

Leather, Sir Edwin Hartley Cameron, K.C.M.G., K.C.V.O.

Leaver, Sir Christopher, G.B.E.

Le Bailly, *Vice-Adm.* Sir Louis Edward Stewart Holland, K.B.E., C.B.

Le Cheminant, *Air Chief Marshal* Sir Peter de Lacey, G.B.E., K.C.B., D.F.C.

Lechmere, Sir Berwick Hungerford, Bt. (1818).

Ledger, Sir Frank, (Joseph Francis), Kt.

Ledwidge, Sir (William) Bernard (John), K.C.M.G.

Lee, Sir Arthur James, K.B.E., M.C.

Lee, *Air Chief Marshal* Sir David John Pryer, G.B.E., C.B.

Lee , *Col.* Tun Sir Henry Hau Shik, K.B.E.

Lee, Sir (Henry) Desmond (Pritchard), Kt.

Lee, *Brig.* Sir Leonard Henry, Kt., C.B.E.

Lee, *Col.* Sir William Allison, Kt., O.B.E., T.D.

Leeds, Sir Christopher Anthony, Bt. (1812).

Lees, *Air Marshal* Sir Ronald Beresford, K.C.B., C.B.E., D.F.C.

Lees, Sir Thomas Edward, Bt. (1897).

Lees, Sir Thomas Harcourt Ivor, Bt. (1804).

Lees, Sir (William) Antony Clare, Bt. (1937).

Leese, Sir John Henry Vernon, Bt. (1908).

Le Fanu, *Maj.* Sir (George) Victor (Sheridan), K.C.V.O.

le Fleming, Sir William Kelland, Bt. (1705).

Legard, Sir Charles Thomas, Bt. (1660).

Leggatt, *Hon.* Sir Andrew Peter, Kt.

Leggett, Sir Clarence Arthur Campbell, Kt., M.B.E.

Leigh, Sir John, Bt. (1918).

Leigh, Sir Neville Egerton, K.C.V.O.

Leighton, Sir Michael John Bryan, Bt. (1693).

Leitch, Sir George, K.C.B., O.B.E.

Leith, Sir Andrew George Forbes-, Bt. (1923).

†Le Marchant, Sir Francis Arthur, Bt. (1841).

Le Masurier, Sir Robert Hugh, Kt., D.S.C.

Lemon, Sir (Richard) Dawnay, Kt., C.B.E.

Leng, *General* Sir Peter John Hall, K.C.B., M.B.E., M.C.

Lennard, *Rev.* Sir Hugh Dacre Barrett-, Bt. (1801).

Lennox, *Lt.-Gen.* Sir George Charles Gordon, K.B.E., C.B., C.V.O., D.S.O.

Leon, Sir John Ronald, Bt. (1911).

Leonard, *Hon.* Sir (Hamilton) John, Kt.

Le Quesne, Sir (Charles) Martin, K.C.M.G.

Le Quesne, Sir (John) Godfray, Kt., Q.C.

Leslie, Sir Colin Alan Bettridge, Kt.

Leslie, Sir John Norman Ide, Bt. (1876).

†Leslie, Sir (Percy) Theodore, Bt. (s 1625).

Lethbridge, Sir Thomas Periam Hector Noel, Bt. (1804).

Leuchars, Sir William Douglas, K.B.E.

Leupena, Sir Tupua, G.C.M.G., M.B.E.

Lever, Sir (Tresham) Christopher Arthur Lindsay, Bt. (1911).

Levey, Sir Michael Vincent, Kt., M.V.O.

Levine, Sir Montague Bernard, Kt.

Levinge, Sir Richard George Robin, Bt. (1 1704).

Levy, Sir (Enoch) Bruce, Kt., O.B.E.

Levy, Sir Ewart Maurice, Bt. (1913).

Lewando, Sir Jan Alfred, Kt., C.B.E.

Lewis, Sir Allen Montgomery, G.C.M.G., G.C.V.O., Q.C.

Lewis, *Admiral* Sir Andrew Mackenzie, K.C.B.

Lewis, Sir Ian Malcolm, Kt.

Lewis, *Prof.* Sir Jack, Kt., F.R.S.

Lewis, Sir Kenneth, Kt.

Lewis, Sir Terence Murray, Kt., O.B.E., Q.P.M.

Lewis, Sir William Arthur, Kt.

Lewthwaite, Sir William Anthony, Bt. (1927).

Ley, Sir Francis Douglas, Bt., M.B.E., T.D. (1905).

Leyland, Sir Vivyan Edward Naylor-, Bt. (1895).

Lickley, Sir Robert Lang, Kt., C.B.E.

Lidbury, Sir John Towersey, Kt.

Lidderdale, Sir David William Shuckburgh, K.C.B.

Liddle, Sir Donald Ross, Kt.

Liggins, Sir Edmund Naylor, Kt., T.D.

Lighthill, Sir (Michael) James, Kt., F.R.S.

Lighton, Sir Christopher Robert, Bt., M.B.E. (1 1791).

Lim, Sir Han-Hoe, Kt., C.B.E.

Linacre, Sir (John) Gordon (Seymour), Kt., C.B.E., A.F.C., D.F.M.

Lincoln, Sir Anthony Handley, K.C.M.G., C.V.O.

Lincoln, *Hon.* Sir Anthony Leslie Julian, Kt.

Lindley, Sir Arnold Lewis George, Kt.

Lindop, Sir Norman, Kt.

Lindsay, Sir James Harvey Kincaid Stewart, Kt.

Lindsay, Sir Ronald Alexander, Bt., (1962).

Lindsay-Fynn, Sir Basil Mortimer, Kt.

Lintott, Sir Henry John Bevis, K.C.M.G.

Lithgow, Sir William James, Bt. (1925).

Little, *Hon.* Sir Douglas Macfarlan, Kt.

Little, *Most Rev.* Thomas Francis, K.B.E.

Littler, Sir (James) Geoffrey, K.C.B.

Livermore, Sir Harry, Kt.

Llewellyn, Sir David Treharne, Kt.

Llewellyn, Sir (Frederick) John, K.C.M.G.

Llewellyn, Sir Henry Morton, Bt., C.B.E. (1922).

Llewellyn, Sir John Michael Dillwyn-Venables-, Bt. (1890).

Llewellyn, *Lt.-Col.* Sir Michael Rowland Godfrey, Bt. (1959).

Lloyd, *Rt. Hon.* Sir Anthony John Leslie, Kt.

Lloyd, *Maj.* Sir (Ernest) Guy (Richard), Bt., D.S.O. (1960).

Lloyd, Sir Ian Stewart, Kt., M.P.

Lloyd, Sir (John) Peter (Daniel), Kt.

Loader, Sir Leslie Thomas, Kt., C.B.E.

Loane, *Most Rev.* Marcus Lawrence, K.B.E.

Lobo, Sir Rogerio Hyndman, Kt., C.B.E.

Lock, *Comdr.* Sir (John) Duncan, Kt.

†Lockhart, Sir Simon John Edward Francis Sinclair-, Bt. (s 1636).

Lockhart-Mummery, Sir Hugh Evelyn, K.C.V.O., M.D., F.R.C.S.

Lockspeiser, Sir Ben, K.C.B., F.R.S.

Lockwood, Sir Joseph Flawith, Kt.

Loder, Sir Giles Rolls, Bt. (1887).

Lodge, Sir Thomas, Kt.

Loehnis, Sir Clive, K.C.M.G.

Logan, Sir Donald Arthur, K.C.M.G.

Logan, Sir Douglas William, Kt., D.Phil.

Logan, Sir Raymond Douglas, Kt.

Lokoloko, Sir Tore, G.C.M.G., G.C.V.O., O.B.E.

Lomax, Sir John Garnett, K.B.E., C.M.G., M.C.

Long, Sir Ronald, Kt.

Longden, Sir Gilbert James Morley, M.B.E.

Longland, Sir David Walter, Kt., C.M.G.

Longland, Sir John Laurence, Kt.

Longley, Sir Norman, Kt., C.B.E.

Looker, Sir Cecil Thomas, Kt.

Loram, *Vice-Adm.* Sir David Anning, K.C.B., M.V.O.

Lorimer, Sir (Thomas) Desmond, Kt.

Lousada, Sir Anthony Baruh, Kt.

Love, Sir Makere Rangiatea Ralph, Kt.

Lovell, Sir (Alfred Charles) Bernard, Kt., O.B.E., F.R.S.

Lovelock, Sir Douglas Arthur, K.C.B.

Loveridge, Sir John Henry, Kt., C.B.E.

Lovill, Sir John Roger, Kt., C.B.E.

Low, Sir Alan Roberts, Kt.

Low, Sir James Richard Morrison-, Bt. (1908).

Lowe, *Air Chief Marshal* Sir Douglas Charles, G.C.B., D.F.C., A.F.C.

Lowe, *Air Vice-Marshal* Sir Edgar Noel, K.B.E., C.B.

Lowe, Sir Thomas William Gordon, Bt. (1918).

Lowry, Sir John Patrick, Kt., C.B.E.

Lowson, Sir Ian Patrick, Bt. (1951).

Lowther, *Maj.* Sir Charles Douglas, Bt. (1824).

Loyd, Sir Francis Alfred, K.C.M.G., O.B.E.

Lubbock, Sir Alan, Kt., F.S.A.

Lucas, Sir Cyril Edward, Kt., C.M.G., F.R.S.

Lucas, Sir Thomas Edward, Bt. (1887).

Luckhoo, *Hon.* Sir Joseph Alexander, Kt.

Luckhoo, Sir Lionel Alfred, K.C.M.G., C.B.E., Q.C.

Lucy, Sir Edmund John William Hugh Cameron-Ramsay-Fairfax-, Bt. (1836).

Luddington, Sir Donald Collin Cumyn, K.B.E., C.M.G., C.V.O.

Luke, *Hon.* Sir Emile Fashole, K.B.E.

Luke, Sir Stephen Elliot Vyvyan, K.C.M.G.

Lumby, Sir Henry, Kt., C.B.E.

Lumsden, Sir David James, Kt.

Lus, *Hon.* Sir Pita, Kt., O.B.E.

Lush, *Hon.* Sir George Hermann, Kt.

Lushington, Sir Henry Edmund Castleman, Bt. (1791).

Lusty, Sir Robert Frith, Kt.

Luyt, Sir Richard Edmonds, G.C.M.G., K.C.V.O., D.C.M.

Lyell, Sir Nicholas Walter, Kt., M.P.

Lygo, *Admiral* Sir Raymond Derek, K.C.B.

Lyle, Sir Gavin Archibald, Bt. (1929).

Lyons, Sir Edward Houghton, Kt.

Lyons, Sir (Isidore) Jack, Kt., C.B.E.

Lyons, Sir James Reginald, Kt.

Lyons, Sir John, Kt.

Lyons, *His Hon.* Sir Rudolph, Kt., Q.C.

McAdam, Sir Ian William James, Kt., O.B.E.

Macadam, Sir Peter, Kt.

McAlpine, Sir Robin, Kt., C.B.E.

Macara, Sir (Charles) Douglas, Bt. (1911).

Macartney, Sir John Barrington, Bt. (1 1799).

McAvoy, Sir (Francis) Joseph, Kt., C.B.E.

McCaffrey, Sir Thomas Daniel, Kt.

McCall, Sir (Charles) Patrick Home, Kt., M.B.E., T.D.

McCamley, Sir Graham Edward, Kt., M.B.E.

McCarthy, *Rt. Hon.* Sir Thaddeus Pearcey, K.B.E.

McCauley, *Air Marshal* Sir John Patrick Joseph, K.B.E., C.B.

McCaw, *Hon.* Sir Kenneth Malcolm, Kt., Q.C.

McClellan, *Col.* Sir Herbert Gerard Thomas, Kt., C.B.E., T.D.

McClintock, Sir Eric Paul, Kt.

McConnell, *Cdr.* Sir Robert Melville Terence, Bt., V.R.D. (1900).

McCowan, *Hon.* Sir Anthony James Denys, Kt.

McCowan, Sir Hew Cargill, Bt. (1934).

McCrea, *Prof.* Sir William Hunter, Kt., F.R.S.

McCullough, *Hon.* Sir (Iain) Charles (Robert), Kt.

McCusker, Sir James Alexander, Kt.

MacDermot, Sir Dermot Francis, K.C.M.G., C.B.E.

McDermott, Sir (Lawrence) Emmet, K.B.E.

MacDonald, *General* Sir Arthur Leslie, K.B.E., C.B.

McDonald, *Air Chief Marshal* Sir Arthur William Baynes, K.C.B., A.F.C.

McDonald, Sir Duncan, Kt., C.B.E.

Macdonald, Sir Herbert George deLorme, K.B.E.

Macdonald of Sleat, Sir Ian Godfrey Bosville, Bt. (s 1625).

McDonald, Sir James, K.B.E.

Macdonald, *Vice-Adm.* Sir Roderick Douglas, K.B.E.

McDonald, *Hon.* Sir William John Farquhar, Kt.

MacDougall, Sir (George) Donald (Alastair), Kt., C.B.E., F.B.A.

McDowell, Sir Henry McLorinan, K.B.E.

McEvoy, *Air Chief Marshal* Sir Theodore Newman, K.C.B., C.B.E.

McEwen, Sir John Roderick Hugh, Bt. (1953).

McEwin, *Hon.* Sir (Alexander) Lyell, K.B.E.

McFarland, Sir John Talbot, Bt. (1914).

McFarlane, Sir Ian, Kt.

Macfarlane, Sir George Gray, Kt., C.B.

Macfarlane, Sir James Wright, Kt.

Macfarlane, Sir Norman Somerville, Kt.

McGeoch, *Vice-Adm.* Sir Ian Lachlan Mackay, K.C.B., D.S.O., D.S.C.

Macgregor, Sir Edwin Robert, Bt. (1828).

MacGregor of MacGregor, Sir Gregor, Bt. (1795).

McGregor, Sir Ian Alexander, Kt., C.B.E., F.R.S.

MacGregor, Sir Ian Kinloch, Kt.

McGrigor, *Capt.* Sir Charles Edward, Bt. (1831).

McInerney, *Hon.* Sir Murray Vincent, Kt.

McIntosh, *Vice-Adm.* Sir Ian Stewart, K.B.E., C.B., D.S.O., D.S.C.

Macintosh, Sir Robert Reynolds, Kt., M.D.

McIntosh, Sir Ronald Robert Duncan, K.C.B.

McKaig, *Admiral* Sir (John) Rae, K.C.B., C.B.E.

McKay, *Hon.* Sir Donald Norman, K.C.M.G.

Mackay, Sir (George Patrick) Gordon, Kt., C.B.E.

McKay, Sir James Wilson, Kt.

McKay, Sir John Andrew, Kt., C.B.E.

Mackay, Sir William Calder, Kt., O.B.E., M.C.

McKee, *Air Marshal* Sir Andrew, K.C.B., C.B.E., D.S.O., D.F.C., A.F.C.

McKee, *Maj.* Sir (William) Cecil, Kt., E.R.D.

MacKenna, Sir Bernard Joseph Maxwell, Kt.

McKenzie, Sir Alexander, K.B.E.

Mackenzie, Sir Alexander Alwyne Henry Charles Brinton Muir-, Bt. (1805).

Mackenzie, Sir (Alexander George Anthony) Allan, Bt. (1890).

Mackenzie, *Vice-Adm.* Sir Hugh Stirling, K.C.B., D.S.O., D.S.C.

Mackenzie, Sir Robert Evelyn, Bt. (s 1673).

†Mackenzie, Sir Roderick McQuhae, Bt. (s 1703).

Mackeson, Sir Rupert Henry, Bt. (1954).

Mackie, Sir Maitland, Kt., C.B.E.

MacKinlay, Sir Bruce, Kt., C.B.E.

McKissock, Sir Wylie, Kt., O.B.E., F.R.C.S.

Macklin, Sir Bruce Roy, Kt., O.B.E.

Mackworth, *Cdr.* Sir David Arthur Geoffrey, Bt. (1776).

Maclaren, Sir Hamish Duncan, K.B.E., C.B., D.F.C.

Maclean, Sir Donald Og Grant, Kt.

Maclean, Sir Fitzroy Hew, Bt., C.B.E. (1957).

McLean, Sir Francis Charles, Kt., C.B.E.

MacLean, *Vice-Adm.* Sir Hector Charles Donald, K.B.E., C.B., D.S.C.

Maclean, Sir Robert Alexander, K.B.E.

MacLellan, Sir (George) Robin (Perronet), Kt., C.B.E.

McLennan, Sir Ian Munro, K.C.M.G., K.B.E.

McLeod, Sir Charles Henry, Bt. (1925).

McLeod, Sir Ian George, Kt.

†McLintock, Sir Michael William, Bt. (1934).

Maclure, Sir John Robert Spencer, Bt. (1898).

McMahon, Sir Brian Patrick, Bt. (1817).

McMahon, Sir Christopher William, Kt.

McMahon, *Rt. Hon.* Sir William, G.C.M.G., C.H.

McMichael, Sir John, Kt., M.D., F.R.S., F.R.C.P.

MacMillan, Sir Kenneth, Kt.

Macmillan, Sir Alexander McGregor Graham, Kt.

Macmillan, Sir (James) Wilson, K.B.E.

McMullin, *Rt. Hon.* Sir Duncan Wallace, Kt.

Macnab, *Brig.* Sir Geoffrey Alex Colin, K.C.M.G., C.B.

Macnaghten, Sir Patrick Alexander, Bt. (1836).

McNamara, *Air Chief Marshal* Sir Neville Patrick, K.B.E.

Macnaughton, *Prof.* Sir Malcolm Campbell, Kt.

McNee, Sir David Blackstock, Kt., Q.P.M.

McNeice, Sir (Thomas) Percy (Fergus), Kt., C.M.G., O.B.E.

McNeill, *Hon.* Sir David Bruce, Kt.

McNicoll, *Vice-Adm.* Sir Alan Wedel Ramsay, K.B.E., C.B., G.M.

McPetrie, Sir James Carnegie, K.C.M.G., O.B.E.

MacPherson, Sir Keith Duncan, Kt.

Macpherson, *Hon.* Sir William Alan, Kt., T.D.

McQuarrie, Sir Albert, Kt.

Macready, Sir Nevil John Wilfrid, Bt. (1923).

Macrory, Sir Patrick Arthur, Kt.

McShine, *Hon.* Sir Arthur Hugh, Kt.

Mactaggart, Sir John Auld, Bt. (1938).

McTiernan, *Rt. Hon.* Sir Edward Aloysius, K.B.E.

Madden, *Admiral* Sir Charles Edward, Bt., G.C.B. (1919).

Maddock, Sir Ieuan, Kt., C.B., O.B.E., F.R.S.

Maddocks, Sir Kenneth Phipson, K.C.M.G., K.C.V.O.

Maddox, Sir (John) Kempson, Kt., V.R.D., M.D.

Madigan, Sir Russel Tullie, Kt., O.B.E.

Magarey, Sir James Rupert, Kt.

Maguire, *Air Marshal* Sir Harold John, K.C.B., D.S.O., O.B.E.

Mahon, Sir George Edward John, Bt. (1819).

Mahon, Sir (John) Denis, Kt., C.B.E.

Main, Sir Peter Tester, Kt., E.R.D.

Maini, Sir Amar Nath, Kt., C.B.E.

Mais, *Hon.* Sir (Robert) Hugh, Kt.

Maitland, Sir Donald James Dundas, G.C.M.G., O.B.E.

Maitland, Sir Richard John, Bt. (1818).

Makins, Sir Paul Vivian, Bt. (1903).

Malcolm, Sir David Peter Michael, Bt. (s. 1665).

Malet, *Col.* Sir Edward William St. Lo, Bt., O.B.E. (1791).

Mallabar, Sir John Frederick, Kt.

Mallet, Sir (William) Ivo, G.B.E., K.C.M.G.

Mallinson, Sir (William) Paul, Bt. (1935).

Malone, *Hon.* Sir Denis Eustace Gilbert, Kt.

Mamo, Sir Anthony Joseph, Kt., O.B.E.

Manchester, Sir William Maxwell, K.B.E.

Mander, Sir Charles Marcus, Bt. (1911).

Mann, *Hon.* Sir Michael, Kt.

Mann, Sir Rupert Edward, Bt. (1905).

Mansel, *Rev. Canon* James Seymour Denis, K.C.V.O.

Mansel, Sir Philip, Bt. (1622).

Mansergh, *Vice-Adm.* Sir (Cecil) Aubrey (Lawson), K.B.E., C.B., D.S.C.

Mansfield, *Vice-Adm.* Sir (Edward) Gerard (Napier), K.B.E., C.V.O.

Mansfield, Sir Philip (Robert Aked), K.C.M.G.

Mant, Sir Cecil George, Kt., C.B.E.

Manzie, Sir (Andrew) Gordon, K.C.B.

Mara, *Rt. Hon. Ratu* Sir Kamisese Kapaiwai Tuimacilai, G.C.M.G., K.B.E.

Marchant, Sir Herbert Stanley, K.C.M.G., O.B.E.

Margetson, Sir John William Denys, K.C.M.G.

Marjoribanks, Sir James Alexander Milne, K.C.M.G.

Mark, Sir Robert, G.B.E.

Markham, Sir Charles John, Bt. (1911).

Marking, Sir Henry Ernest, K.C.V.O., C.B.E., M.C.

Marling, Sir Charles William Somerset, Bt., (1882).

Marr, Sir Leslie Lynn, Bt. (1919).

Marre, Sir Alan Samuel, K.C.B.

Marriner, Sir Neville, Kt., C.B.E.

Marriott, Sir Ralph George Cavendish Smith-, Bt. (1774).

Marsack, Sir Charles Croft, K.B.E.

Marsden, Sir Nigel John Denton, Bt., (1924).

Marshall, Sir Arthur Gregory George, Kt., O.B.E.

Marshall, Sir Colin Marsh, Kt.

Marshall, Sir Denis Alfred, Kt.

Marshall, *Rt. Hon.* Sir John Ross, G.B.E., C.H.

Marshall, *Prof.* Sir (Oshley) Roy, Kt., C.B.E.

Marshall, Sir Peter Harold Reginald, K.C.M.G.

Marshall, Sir Robert Braithwaite, K.C.B., M.B.E.

Martell, *Vice-Adm.* Sir Hugh Colenso, K.B.E., C.B.

Martin, *Air Marshal* Sir Harold Brownlow, K.C.B., D.S.O., D.F.C., A.F.C.

Martin, *Vice-Adm.* Sir John Edward Ludgate, K.C.B., D.S.C.

Martin, *Prof.* Sir (John) Leslie, Kt., PH.D.

Martin, Sir John Miller, K.C.M.G., C.B., C.V.O.

Martin, Sir Sidney Launcelot, Kt.

Marwick, Sir Brian Allan, K.B.E., C.M.G.

Marychurch, Sir Peter Harvey, K.C.M.G.

Masefield, Sir Peter Gordon, Kt.

Mason, *Hon.* Sir Anthony Frank, K.B.E.

Mason, Sir (Basil) John, Kt., C.B., D.S.C., F.R.S.

Mason, *Vice-Adm.* Sir Frank Trowbridge, K.C.B.

Mason, Sir Frederick Cecil, K.C.V.O., C.M.G.

Mason, Sir John Charles Moir, K.C.M.G.

Mason, *Prof.* Sir Ronald, K.C.B., F.R.S.

Matane, Sir Paulias Nguna, Kt., C.M.G., O.B.E.

Mather, Sir (David) Carol (Macdonell), Kt., M.C.

Mather, *Prof.* Sir Kenneth, C.B.E., D.SC., F.R.S.

Mather, Sir William Loris, Kt., C.V.O., O.B.E., M.C., T.D.

Mathers, Sir Robert William, Kt.

Matheson, Sir (James Adam) Louis, K.B.E., C.M.G.

Matheson of Matheson, Sir Torquhil Alexander, Bt. (1882).

Mathias, Sir Richard Hughes, Bt. (1917).

Matthews, Sir Peter Alec, Kt.

Matthews, Sir Peter Jack, Kt., C.V.O., O.B.E., Q.P.M.

Matthews, Sir Russell, Kt., O.B.E.

Matthews, Sir Stanley, Kt., C.B.E.

Maudslay, *Major* Sir (James) Rennie, G.C.V.O., K.C.B., M.B.E.

Mavor, *Air Marshal* Sir Leslie Deane, K.C.B., A.F.C.

†Maxwell, Sir Michael Eustace George, Bt. (s 1681).

Maxwell, Sir Nigel Mellor Heron-, Bt. (s 1683).

Maxwell, Sir Robert Hugh, K.B.E.

May, *Rt. Hon.* Sir John Douglas, Kt.

May, Sir Kenneth Spencer, Kt., C.B.E.

Mayall, Sir (Alexander) Lees, K.C.V.O., C.M.G.

Mayhew, *Rt. Hon.* Sir Patrick Barnabas Burke, Kt., Q.C., M.P.

Mayhew-Sanders, Sir John Reynolds, Kt.

Maynard, *Air Chief Marshal* Sir Nigel Martin, K.C.B., C.B.E., D.F.C., A.F.C.

Meade, Sir (Richard) Geoffrey (Austin), K.B.E., C.M.G., C.V.O.

Meaney, Sir Patrick Michael, Kt.

Medawar, Sir Peter Brian, Kt., O.M., C.H., C.B.E., D.SC., F.R.S.

Medlycott, Sir Mervyn Tregonwell, Bt. (1808).

Megarry, *Rt. Hon.* Sir Robert Edgar, Kt., F.B.A.

Megaw, *Rt. Hon.* Sir John, Kt., C.B.E., T.D.

Meinertzhagen, Sir Peter, Kt., C.M.G.

Mellor, Sir John Francis, Bt. (1924).

Melville, Sir Harry Work, K.C.B., PH.D., D.SC., F.R.S.

Melville, Sir Leslie Galfreid, K.B.E.

Melville, Sir Ronald Henry, K.C.B.

Mensforth, Sir Eric, Kt., C.B.E., F.Eng.

Menter, Sir James Woodham, Kt., PH.D., SC.D., F.R.S.

Menteth, Sir James Wallace Stuart-, Bt. (1838).

Menuhin, Sir Yehudi, K.B.E., O.M.

Menzies, Sir Peter Thomson, Kt.

Merrison, Sir Alexander Walter, Kt., F.R.S.

Messervy, Sir (Roney) Godfrey (Collumbell), Kt.

Meyer, Sir Anthony John Charles, Bt., M.P. (1910).

Meyjes, Sir Richard Anthony, Kt.

Meyrick, *Lt.-Col.* Sir George David Elliott Tapps-Gervis-, Bt., M.C. (1791).

Meyrick, Sir David John Charlton, Bt. (1880).

Michelmore, Sir Walter Harold Strachan, Kt., M.B.E.

Micklethwait, Sir Robert Gore, Kt., Q.C.

Middleton, Sir George Humphrey, K.C.M.G.

Middleton, Sir George Proctor, K.C.V.O.

Middleton, Sir Peter Edward, K.C.B.

Middleton, Sir Stephen Hugh, Bt. (1662).

Miers, Sir (Henry) David Alastair Capel, K.B.E., C.M.G.

Milbank, Sir Anthony Frederick, Bt. (1882).

Milburn, Sir Anthony Rupert, Bt. (1905).

Miles, Sir (Arnold) Ashley, Kt., C.B.E., M.D., F.R.S.

Miles, Sir Peter Tremayne, K.C.V.O.

Miles, Sir William Napier Maurice, Bt. (1859).

Millais, Sir Ralph Regnault, Bt. (1885).

Millar, Sir Oliver Nicholas, K.C.V.O., F.B.A.

Millar, Sir Ronald Graeme, Kt.

Millard, Sir Guy Elwin, K.C.M.G., C.V.O.

Miller, Sir Douglas Sinclair, K.C.V.O., C.B.E.

Miller, Sir (Ian) Douglas, Kt.

Miller, Sir John Holmes, Bt. (1705).

Miller, Lt.-Col. Sir John Mansel, G.C.V.O., D.S.O., M.C.

Miller, Sir (Joseph) Holmes, Kt., O.B.E.

Miller, Sir (Oswald) Bernard, Kt.

Miller, Sir Richard Hope, Kt.

Miller, Sir Stephen James Hamilton, K.C.V.O., M.D., F.R.C.S.

Miller of Glenlee, Sir (Frederick William) Macdonald, Bt. (1788).

Millett, Hon. Sir Peter Julian, Kt.

Milling, Air Marshal Sir Denis Crowley-, K.C.B., C.B.E., D.S.O., D.F.C.

Mills, Vice-Adm. Sir Charles Piercy, K.C.B., C.B.E., D.S.C.

Mills, Sir Frank, K.C.V.O., C.M.G.

Mills, Sir John Lewis Ernest Watts, Kt., C.B.E.

Mills, Sir Peter Frederick Leighton, Bt. (1921).

Mills, Sir Peter McLay, Kt.

Milman, Sir Dermot Lionel Kennedy, Bt. (1800).

Milmo, Hon. Sir Helenus Patrick Joseph, Kt.

Milne, Sir John Drummond, Kt.

Milner, Sir (George Edward) Mordaunt, Bt. (1717).

Milnes Coates, Sir Anthony Robert, Bt. (1911).

Minhinnick, Sir Gordon Edward George, K.B.E.

Minogue, Hon. Sir John Patrick, Kt., Q.C.

Miskin, Hon. Sir James William, Kt., Q.C.

Mitchell, Air Cdre. Sir (Arthur) Dennis, K.B.E., C.V.O., D.F.C., A.F.C.

Mitchell, Sir Derek Jack, K.C.B., C.V.O.

Mitchell, Sir Hamilton, K.B.E.

Mitchell, Sir (Seton) Steuart Crichton, K.B.E., C.B.

Mobbs, Sir (Gerald) Nigel, Kt.

Moberly, Sir John Campbell, K.B.E., C.M.G.

Moberly, Sir Patrick Hamilton, K.C.M.G.

Mocatta, Sir Alan Abraham, Kt., O.B.E.

Moffat, Lt.-Gen. Sir (William) Cameron, K.B.E.

Mogg, General Sir (Herbert) John, G.C.B., C.B.E., D.S.O.

Moir, Sir Ernest Ian Royds, Bt. (1916).

Moller, Hon. Sir Lester Francis, Kt.

†Molony, Sir Thomas Desmond, Bt. (1925).

Monro, Sir Hector Seymour Peter, Kt., M.P.

Monson, Sir (William Bonnar) Leslie, K.C.M.G., C.B.

Montgomery, Sir (Basil Henry) David, Bt. (1801).

Montgomery, Sir (William) Fergus, Kt., M.P.

Mookerjee, Sir Birendra Nath, Kt.

Moollan, Sir Abdool Hamid Adam, Kt.

Moollan, Hon. Sir Cassam (Ismael), Kt.

Moon, Sir Edward, Bt., M.C. (1887).

Moon, Sir Peter James Scott, K.C.V.O., C.M.G.

Moon, Sir Peter Wilfred Giles Graham-, Bt. (1855).

Moore, Sir Edward Stanton, Bt., O.B.E. (1923).

Moore, Sir Francis Thomas, Kt.

Moore, Sir Henry Roderick, Kt., C.B.E.

Moore, Hon. Sir John Cochrane, Kt.

Moore, Maj.-Gen. Sir (John) Jeremy, K.C.B., O.B.E., M.C.

Moore, Sir John Michael, K.C.V.O., C.B., D.S.C.

Moore, Prof. Sir Norman Winfrid, Bt. (1919).

Moore, Sir William Roger Clotworthy, Bt., T.D. (1932).

Moores, Sir John, Kt., C.B.E.

Mootham, Sir Orby Howell, Kt.

Mordaunt, Sir Richard Nigel Charles, Bt. (1611).

Mordecai, Sir John Stanley, Kt., C.M.G.

More, Sir Jasper, Kt.

Moreton, Sir John Oscar, K.C.M.G., K.C.V.O., M.C.

Morgan, Maj.-Gen. Sir David John Hughes-, Bt., C.B., C.B.E. (1925).

Morgan, Sir Ernest Dunstan, K.B.E.

Morgan, Rear-Adm. Sir Patrick John, K.C.V.O., C.B., D.S.C.

Morgan-Giles, Rear-Adm. Sir Morgan Charles, Kt., D.S.O., O.B.E., G.M.

Morley, Sir Godfrey William Rowland, Kt., O.B.E., T.D.

Morony, Gen. Sir Thomas Lovett, K.C.B., O.B.E.

Morpeth, Sir Douglas Spottiswoode, Kt., T.D.

Morris, Air Marshal Sir Arnold Alec, K.B.E., C.B.

Morris, Air Marshal Sir Douglas Griffith, K.C.B., C.B.E., D.S.O., D.F.C.

Morris, Sir Robert Byng, Bt. (1806).

Morrow, Sir Ian Thomas, Kt.

Morse, Sir Christopher Jeremy, K.C.M.G.

Morton, Admiral Sir Anthony Storrs, G.B.E., K.C.B.

Morton, Sir Brian, Kt.

Morton, Sir Ralph John, Kt., C.M.G., O.B.E., M.C.

Moseley, Sir George Walker, K.C.B.

Moser, Prof. Sir Claus Adolf, K.C.B., C.B.E., F.B.A.

Moses, Sir Charles Joseph Alfred, Kt., C.B.E.

Moss, Sir John Herbert Theodore Edwards-, Bt. (1868).

Mostyn, Sir Jeremy John Anthony, Bt. (1670).

Mostyn, Gen. Sir (Joseph) David Frederick, K.C.B., C.B.E.

Mott, Sir John Harmer, Bt. (1930).

Mott, Sir Nevill Francis, Kt., F.R.S.

Mount, Sir James William Spencer, Kt., C.B.E., B.E.M.

Mount, Sir William Malcolm, Bt. (1921).

Mountain, Sir Denis Mortimer, Bt. (1922).

Mowbray, Sir John, Kt.

Mowbray, Sir John Robert, Bt. (1880).

Moynihan, Sir Noel Henry, Kt.

Muir, Sir John Harling, Bt. (1892).

Muir, Sir Laurence Macdonald, Kt.

Muir Wood, Sir Alan Marshall, Kt., F.R.S.

Muirhead, Sir David Francis, K.C.M.G., C.V.O.

Muldoon, Rt. Hon. Sir Robert David, G.C.M.G., C.H.

Mulholland, Sir Michael Henry, Bt. (1945).

Mumford, Sir Albert Henry, K.B.E.

Munn, Sir James, Kt., O.B.E.

Munro, Sir Alasdair Thomas Ian, Bt. (1825).

Munro, Sir Ian Talbot, Bt. (s 1634).

Munro, Hon. Sir Robert Lindsay, Kt., C.B.E.

Munro, Sir Sydney Douglas Gun-, G.C.M.G., M.B.E.

Murley, Sir Reginald Sydney, K.B.E., T.D., F.R.C.S.

Murphy, Sir Leslie Frederick, Kt.

Murray, Rear-Adm. Sir Brian Stewart, K.C.M.G.

Murray, Sir Donald Frederick, K.C.V.O., C.M.G.

Murray, General Sir Horatius, G.C.B., K.B.E., D.S.O.

Murray, Sir James, K.C.M.G.

Murray, Sir John Antony Jerningham, Kt., C.B.E.

Murray, Sir Nigel Andrew Digby, Bt. (s 1628).

Murray, Sir Patrick Ian Keith, Bt. (s 1673).

Murray, Sir Rowland William Patrick, Bt. (s 1630).

Murrie, Sir William Stuart, G.C.B., K.B.E.

Mursell, Sir Peter, Kt., M.B.E.

Musgrave, Sir Christopher Patrick Charles, Bt. (1611).

Musgrave, Sir Richard James, Bt. (1 1782).

Musker, Sir John, Kt.

Musson, General Sir Geoffrey Randolph Dixon, G.C.B., C.B.E., D.S.O.

Mustill, Rt. Hon. Sir Michael John, Kt.

Myers, Sir Kenneth Ben, Kt., M.B.E.

Myers, Sir Philip Alan, Kt., O.B.E., Q.P.M.

Myers, *Prof.* Sir Rupert Horace, K.B.E.

Mynors, Sir Humphrey Charles Baskerville, Bt. (1964).

Mynors, *Prof.* Sir Roger Aubrey Baskerville, Kt., F.B.A.

Nabarro, Sir John David Nunes, Kt., M.D., F.R.C.P.

Nairn, Sir Michael, Bt. (1904).

Nairn, Sir Robert Arnold Spencer-, Bt. (1933).

Nairne, *Rt. Hon.* Sir Patrick Dalmahoy, G.C.B., M.C.

Nalder, *Hon.* Sir Crawford David, Kt.

Nall, Sir Michael Joseph, Bt., R.N. (1954).

Napier, Sir Oliver John, Kt.

Napier, Sir Robin Surtees, Bt. (1867).

Napier, Sir William Archibald, Bt. (s 1627).

Napley, Sir David, Kt.

Narain, Sir Sathi, K.B.E.

Neal, Sir Eric James, Kt.

Neal, Sir Leonard Francis, Kt., C.B.E.

Neale, Sir Alan Derrett, K.C.B., M.B.E.

Neave, Sir Arundell Thomas Clifton, Bt. (1795).

Nedd, *Hon.* Sir Robert Archibald, Kt.

Neill, *Rt. Hon.* Sir Brian Thomas, Kt.

Neill, Sir Francis Patrick, Kt., Q.C.

Neill, *Rt. Hon.* Sir Ivan, Kt.

Nelson, *Maj.-Gen.* Sir (Eustace) John (Blois), K.C.V.O., C.B., D.S.O., O.B.E., M.C.

Nelson, *Air Marshal* Sir (Sidney) Richard (Carlyle), K.C.B., O.B.E., M.D.

Nelson, *Maj.* Sir William Vernon Hope, Bt., O.B.E. (1912).

Nepean, *Lt.-Col.* Sir Evan Yorke, Bt. (1802).

Ness, *Air Marshal* Sir Charles Ernest, K.C.B., C.B.E.

Neville, Sir Richard Lionel John Baines, Bt. (1927).

Newbold, Sir Charles Demorée, K.B.E., C.M.G., Q.C.

Newman, Sir Geoffrey Robert, Bt. (1836).

Newman, Sir Gerard Robert Henry Sigismund, Bt. (1912).

Newman, Sir Jack, Kt., C.B.E.

Newman, Sir Kenneth Leslie, Kt., G.B.E.

Newns, Sir (Alfred) Foley (Francis Polden), K.C.M.G., C.V.O.

Newsam, Sir Peter Anthony, Kt.

Newton, Sir (Harry) Michael (Rex), Bt. (1900).

Newton, Sir Hubert, Kt.

Newton, Sir Kenneth Garnar, Bt., O.B.E., T.D. (1924).

Newton, Sir (Leslie) Gordon, Kt.

Ngata, Sir Henare Kohere, K.B.E.

Niall, Sir Horace Lionel Richard, Kt., C.B.E.

Nicholas, Sir Herbert Richard, O.B.E.

Nicholas, Sir John William, K.C.V.O., C.M.G.

Nicholls, *Rt. Hon.* Sir Donald James, Kt.

Nicholls, Sir Douglas Ralph, K.C.V.O., O.B.E.

Nicholls, *Air Marshal* Sir John Moreton, K.C.B., C.B.E., D.F.C., A.F.C.

Nichols, Sir Edward Henry, Kt., T.D.

Nicholson, Sir Bryan Hubert, Kt.

Nicholson, *Hon.* Sir David Eric, Kt.

Nicholson, Sir Godfrey, Bt. (1958).

Nicholson, Sir John Norris, Bt., K.B.E., C.I.E. (1912).

Nicholson, Sir Robin Buchanan, Kt., Ph.D., F.R.S.

Nickerson, Sir Joseph, Kt.

Nickson, Sir David Wigley, K.B.E.

Nicolson, Sir David Lancaster, Kt.

Nield, Sir Basil Edward, Kt., C.B.E., Q.C.

Nield, Sir William Alan, G.C.M.G., K.C.B.

Nightingale, Sir Charles Manners Gamaliel, Bt. (1628).

Nightingale, Sir John Cyprian, Kt., C.B.E., B.E.M., Q.P.M.

Nimmo, *Hon.* Sir John Angus, Kt., C.B.E.

Niven, Sir (Cecil) Rex, Kt., C.M.G., M.C.

Nixon, Sir Edwin Ronald, Kt., C.B.E.

Nixon, *Rev.* Sir Kenneth Michael John Basil, Bt. (1906).

Noad, Sir Kenneth Beeson, Kt., M.D.

Noble, Sir Iain Andrew, Bt. (1923).

Noble, Sir Marc Brunel, Bt. (1902).

Noble, Sir (Thomas Alexander) Fraser, Kt., M.B.E.

Nock, Sir Norman Lindfield, Kt.

Noel, Sir Claude, Kt., C.M.G.

Nolan, *Hon.* Sir Michael Patrick, Kt.

Nolan, Sir Sidney Robert, O.M., Kt., C.B.E.

Nordmeyer, *Hon.* Sir Arnold Henry, K.C.M.G.

Norman, Sir Arthur Gordon, K.B.E., D.F.C.

Norman, *Vice-Adm.* Sir (Horace) Geoffrey, K.C.V.O., C.B., J.P.

Norman, Sir Mark Annesley, Bt. (1915).

Norman, *Prof.* Sir Richard Oswald Chandler, K.B.E., F.R.S.

Norman, Sir Robert Wentworth, Kt.

Normanton, Sir Tom, Kt., T.D.

Norris, Sir Alfred Henry, K.B.E.

Norris, *Vice-Adm.* Sir Charles Fred Wivell, K.B.E., C.B., D.S.O.

Norris, *Air Chief Marshal* Sir Christopher Neil Foxley-, G.C.B., D.S.O., O.B.E.

Norris, Sir Eric George, K.C.M.G.

Norris, *Hon.* Sir John Gerald, Kt., E.D.

North, Sir Thomas Lindsay, Kt.

North, Sir (William) Jonathan (Frederick), Bt. (1920).

Northam, Sir William Herbert, Kt., C.B.E.

Norton, Sir Clifford John, K.C.M.G., C.V.O.

Norwood, Sir Walter Neville, Kt.

Nossal, Sir Gustav Joseph Victor, Kt., C.B.E.

Nott, *Rt. Hon.* Sir John William Frederic, K.C.B.

Nourse, *Rt. Hon.* Sir Martin Charles, Kt.

Nugent, Sir John Edwin Lavallin, Bt. (t 1795).

Nugent, *Maj.* Sir Peter Walter James, Bt. (1831).

Nugent, Sir Robin George Colborne, Bt. (1806).

Nuttall, Sir Nicholas Keith Lillington, Bt. (1922).

Nutting, *Rt. Hon.* Sir (Harold) Anthony, Bt. (1903).

†Oakeley, Sir John Digby Atholl, Bt. (1790).

Oakes, Sir Christopher, Bt. (1939).

Oakeshott, Sir Walter Fraser, Kt., F.B.A., F.S.A.

Oakshott, *Hon.* Sir Anthony Hendrie, Bt. (1959).

Oates, Sir Thomas, Kt., C.M.G., O.B.E.

Oatley, Sir Charles William, Kt., O.B.E., F.R.S.

Obolensky, *Prof.* Sir Dimitri, Kt.

O'Brien, Sir Frederick William Fitzgerald, Kt.

O'Brien, Sir Timothy John, Bt. (1849).

O'Brien, Sir Richard, Kt., D.S.O., M.C.

O'Brien, *Admiral* Sir William Donough, K.C.B., D.S.C.

O'Connell, Sir Morgan Donal Conail, Bt. (1869).

O'Connor, *Lt.-Gen.* Sir Denis Stuart Scott, K.B.E., C.B.

O'Connor, *Rt. Hon.* Sir Patrick McCarthy, Kt.

O'Dea, Sir Patrick Jerad, K.C.V.O.

Odell, Sir Stanley John, Kt.

Ogilvie, Sir Alec Drummond, Kt.

Ogilvy, Sir David John Wilfrid, Bt. (s 1626).

Ognall, *Hon.* Sir Harry Henry, Kt.

O'Halloran, Sir Charles Ernest, Kt.

Ohlson, Sir Brian Eric Christopher, Bt. (1920).

Okeover, *Capt.* Sir Peter Ralph Leopold Walker-, Bt. (1886).

Oldman, *Col.* Sir Hugh Richard Deare, K.B.E., M.C.

Olewale, *Hon.* Sir Niwia Ebia, Kt.

Oliphant, Sir Mark (Marcus Laurence Elwin), K.B.E., F.R.S.

Oliver, Sir (Frederick) Ernest, Kt., C.B.E., T.D.

O'Loghlen, Sir Colman Michael, Bt. (1838).

Olver, Sir Stephen John Linley, K.B.E., C.M.G.

O'Neil, *Hon.* Sir Desmond Henry, Kt.

O'Neill, *Hon.* Sir Con Douglas Walter, G.C.M.G.

Ongley, Sir Joseph Augustine, Kt.

Onslow, Sir John Roger Wilmot, Bt. (1797).

Oppenheim, Sir Alexander, Kt., O.B.E., D.SC., F.R.S.E.

Oppenheim, Sir Duncan Morris, Kt.

Oppenheimer, Sir Michael Bernard Grenville, Bt. (1921).

Oppenheimer, Sir Philip Jack, Kt.

Opperman, *Hon.* Sir Hubert Ferdinand, Kt., O.B.E.

Orde, Sir John Alexander Campbell-, Bt. (1790).

O'Regan, *Hon.* Sir John Barry, Kt.

Organe, *Prof.* Sir Geoffrey Stephen William, Kt., M.D.

Ormond, Sir John Davies Wilder, Kt., B.E.M.

Ormrod, *Rt. Hon.* Sir Roger Fray Greenwood, Kt.

Orr, *Rt. Hon.* Sir Alan Stewart, Kt., O.B.E.

Orr, Sir David Alexander, Kt., M.C.

Orr, Sir John Henry, Kt., O.B.E., Q.P.M.

Osborn, Sir Richard Henry Danvers, Bt. (1662).

Osborn, Sir John Holbrook, Kt.

Osborne, Sir Basil, Kt., C.B.E.

Osborne, Sir Peter George, Bt. (I 1629).

Osifelo, Sir Frederick Aubarua, Kt., M.B.E.

Osman, Sir (Abdool) Raman Mahomed, G.C.M.G., C.B.E.

Osmond, Sir Douglas, Kt., C.B.E.

Osmond, Sir (Stanley) Paul, Kt., C.B.

Oswald, *Admiral* Sir John Julian Robertson, K.C.B.

Otton, Sir Geoffrey John, K.C.B.

Otton, *Hon.* Sir Philip Howard, Kt.

Oulton, Sir Antony Derek Maxwell, K.C.B., Q.C.

Outerbridge, *Col. Hon.* Sir Leonard Cecil, Kt., C.B.E., D.S.O.

Outram, Sir Alan James, Bt. (1858).

Overall, Sir John Wallace, Kt., C.B.E., M.C.

Overton, Sir Hugh Thomas Arnold, K.C.M.G.

Owen, Sir Hugh Bernard Pilkington, Bt. (1813).

†Owen, Sir Hugo Dudley Cunliffe-, Bt. (1920).

Owen, *Hon.* Sir John Arthur Dalziel, Kt.

Owen, Sir Ronald Hugh, Kt.

Owo, The Olowo of, Kt.

Packard, *Lieut.-Gen.* Sir (Charles) Douglas, K.B.E., C.B., D.S.O.

Padmore, Sir Thomas, G.C.B.

Page, Sir Alexander Warren, Kt., M.B.E.

Page, Sir (Arthur) John, Kt.

Page, Sir Frederick William, Kt., C.B.E.

Page, Sir John Joseph Joffre, Kt., O.B.E.

Paget, Sir John Starr, Bt. (1886).

Paget, Sir Julian Tolver, Bt., C.V.O. (1871).

Pain, *Lt.-Gen.* Sir (Horace) Rollo (Squarey), K.C.B., M.C.

Pain, *Hon.* Sir Peter Richard, Kt.

Palliser, *Rt. Hon.* Sir (Arthur) Michael, G.C.M.G.

Palmar, Sir Derek James, Kt.

Palmer, Sir (Charles) Mark, Bt. (1886).

Palmer, *Lt.-Gen.* Sir (Charles) Patrick (Ralph), K.B.E.

Palmer, Sir Geoffrey Christopher John, Bt. (1660).

Palmer, Sir John Chance, Kt.

Palmer, Sir John Edward Somerset, Bt. (1791).

Palmer, *Maj.-Gen.* Sir (Joseph) Michael, K.C.V.O.

Panckridge, *Surgeon Vice-Adm.* Sir (William) Robert (Silvester), K.B.E., C.B.

Pao, Sir Yue-Kong, Kt., C.B.E.

Pape, *Hon.* Sir George Augustus, Kt.

Pararajasingam, Sir Sangarapillai, Kt.

Parbo, Sir Arvi Hillar, Kt.

Parham, *Admiral* Sir Frederick Robertson, G.B.E., K.C.B., D.S.O.

Parish, Sir David Elmer Woodbine, Kt., C.B.E.

Park, *Hon.* Sir Hugh Eames, Kt.

Parker, Sir (Arthur) Douglas Dodds-, Kt.

Parker, Sir Douglas William Leigh, Kt., O.B.E.

Parker, Sir Karl Theodore, Kt., C.B.E., Ph.D., F.B.A.

Parker, Sir Peter, Kt., M.V.O.

Parker, Sir Richard (William) Hyde, Bt. (1681).

Parker, *Rt. Hon.* Sir Roger Jocelyn, Kt.

Parker, *Vice-Adm.* Sir (Wilfred) John, K.B.E., C.B., D.S.C.

Parker, Sir (William) Alan, Bt. (1844).

Parkes, Sir Alan Sterling, Kt., C.B.E., Ph.D., D.Sc., Sc.D., F.R.S.

Parkes, Sir Basil Arthur, Kt., O.B.E.

Parkes, Sir Edward Walter, Kt.

Parkinson, Sir Nicholas Fancourt, Kt.

Parry, Sir Ernest Jones-, Kt.

Parry, Sir (Frank) Hugh (Nigel), Kt., C.B.E.

Parry-Evans, *Air Marshal* Sir David, K.C.B., C.B.E.

Parsons, Sir Anthony Derrick, G.C.M.G., M.V.O., M.C.

Parsons, Sir (John) Michael, Kt.

Parsons, Sir Richard Edmund (Clement Fownes), K.C.M.G.

Part, Sir Antony Alexander, Kt., G.C.B.

Pascoe, *Lt. Gen.* Sir Robert Alan, K.C.B., M.B.E.

Pasley, Sir John Malcolm Sabine, Bt. (1794).

Patch, *Air Chief Marshal* Sir Hubert Leonard, K.C.B., C.B.E.

Paterson, Sir Dennis Craig, Kt.

Paterson, Sir George Mutlow, Kt., O.B.E., Q.C.

Paterson, Sir John Valentine Jardine, Kt.

Paton, Sir (Thomas) Angus (Lyall), Kt., C.M.G., F.R.S.

Paton, *Prof.* Sir William Drummond Macdonald, Kt., C.B.E., D.M., F.R.S., F.R.C.P.

Pattie, *Rt. Hon.* Sir Geoffrey Edwin, Kt., M.P.

Pattinson, *Hon.* Sir Baden, K.B.E.

Paul, Sir John Warburton, G.C.M.G., O.B.E., M.C.

Payne, Sir Norman John, Kt., C.B.E.

Peacock, Sir Alan Turner, Kt., D.S.C.

Peacock, Sir Geoffrey Arden, Kt., C.V.O.

Pearce, Sir Austin William, Kt., C.B.E., Ph.D.

Pearce, Sir Eric Herbert, Kt., O.B.E.

Peard, *Rear-Adm.* Sir Kenyon Harry Terrell, K.B.E.

Pearman, *Hon.* Sir James Eugene, Kt., C.B.E.

Pearson, Sir Francis Fenwick, Bt., M.B.E. (1964).

Pearson, Sir (James) Denning, Kt.

Pearson, *General* Sir Thomas Cecil Hook, K.C.B., C.B.E., D.S.O.

Peart, *Prof.* Sir William Stanley, Kt., M.D., F.R.S.

Pease, Sir (Alfred) Vincent, Bt. (1882).

Pease, Sir Richard Thorn, Bt. (1920).

Peat, Sir Henry, K.C.V.O., D.F.C.

Peck, Sir Edward Heywood, G.C.M.G.

Peck, Sir John Howard, K.C.M.G.

Pedder, *Vice-Adm.* Sir Arthur Reid, K.B.E., C.B.

Pedder, *Air Marshal* Sir Ian Maurice, K.C.B., O.B.E., D.F.C.

Pedler, Sir Frederick Johnson, Kt.

Peek, Sir Francis Henry Grenville, Bt. (1874).

Peek, *Vice-Adm.* Sir Richard Innes, K.B.E., C.B., D.S.C.

Peel, Sir John Harold, K.C.V.O.

Peel, Sir (William) John, Kt.

Peierls, Sir Rudolf Ernst, Kt., C.B.E., D.SC., D.Phil., F.R.S.

Peile, *Vice-Adm.* Sir Lancelot Arthur Babington, K.B.E., C.B., D.S.O., M.V.O.

Peirse, Sir Henry Grant de la Poer Beresford-, Bt. (1814).

Pelly, Sir John Alwyne, Bt. (1840).

Pemberton, Sir Francis Wingate William, Kt., C.B.E.

Penn, *Lt.-Col.* Sir Eric Charles William Mackenzie, G.C.V.O., O.B.E., M.C.

Penruddock, Sir Clement Frederick, Kt., C.B.E.

Percival, Sir Anthony Edward, Kt., C.B.

Percival, *Rt. Hon.* Sir (Walter) Ian, Kt., Q.C.

Pereira, Sir (Herbert) Charles, Kt., D.S.C., F.R.S.

Perkins, *Surgeon Vice-Adm.* Sir Derek Duncombe Steele-, K.C.B., K.C.V.O.

Perkins, Sir (Walter) Robert Dempster, Kt.

Perrin, Sir Michael Willcox, Kt., C.B.E.

Perring, Sir Ralph Edgar, Bt. (1963).

Perris, Sir David (Arthur), Kt., M.B.E.

Perry, Sir David Howard, K.C.B.

Perry, Sir (David) Norman, Kt., M.B.E.

Pestell, Sir John Richard, K.C.V.O.

Peterkin, Sir Neville, Kt.

Petersen, Sir Jeffrey Charles, K.C.M.G.

Petit, Sir Dinshaw Manockjee, Bt. (1890).

Peto, Sir Henry George Morton, Bt. (1855).

Peto, Sir Michael Henry Basil, Bt. (1927).

Petrie, Sir (Charles) Richard (Borthwick), Bt., T.D. (1918).

Pettigrew, Sir Russell Hilton, Kt.

Pettingel, Sir William Walter, Kt., C.B.E.

Pettit, Sir Daniel Eric Arthur, Kt.

Philips, *Prof.* Sir Cyril Henry, Kt.

Philipson, Sir Robert James, (Sir Robin Philipson), Kt., R.A.

Phillips, *Prof.* Sir David Chilton, Kt., PH.D., F.R.S.

Phillips, Sir Fred Albert, Kt., C.V.O.

Phillips, Sir Henry Ellis Isidore, Kt., C.M.G., M.B.E.

Phillips, Sir Horace, K.C.M.G.

Phillips, *Hon.* Sir Nicholas Addison, Kt.

Phillips, Sir Robin Francis, Bt. (1912).

Phipps, *Vice-Adm.* Sir Peter, K.B.E., D.S.C., V.R.D.

Pickard, Sir Cyril Stanley, K.C.M.G.

Pickering, Sir Edward Davies, Kt.

Pickthorn, Sir Charles William Richards, Bt. (1959).

Piers, Sir Charles Robert Fitzmaurice, Bt. (I 1661).

†Pigot, Sir George Hugh, Bt. (1764).

Pigott, Sir Berkeley Henry Sebastian, Bt. (1808).

Pike, Sir Philip Ernest Housden, Kt., Q.C.

Pike, Sir Theodore Ouseley, K.C.M.G.

Pike, *Lt.-Gen.* Sir William Gregory Huddleston, K.C.B., C.B.E., D.S.O.

Pilcher, Sir (Charlie) Dennis, Kt., C.B.E.

Pilcher, Sir John Arthur, G.C.M.G.

Pilditch, Sir Richard Edward, Bt. (1929).

Pile, Sir Frederick Devereux, Bt. M.C. (1900).

Pile, Sir William Dennis, G.C.B., M.B.E.

Pilkington, Sir Lionel Alexander Bethune, (Sir Alastair), Kt., F.R.S.

Pilkington, Sir Thomas Henry Milborne-Swinnerton-, Bt. (s 1635).

Pillar, *Admiral* Sir William Thomas, G.B.E., K.C.B.

Pindling, *Rt. Hon.* Sir Lynden Oscar, K.C.M.G.

Pinsent, Sir Christopher Roy, Bt. (1938).

Piper, Sir David Towry, Kt., C.B.E.

Pippard, *Prof.* Sir (Alfred) Brian, Kt., F.R.S.

Pirbhai, Sir Eboo, Kt., O.B.E.

Pirie, *Gp. Capt.* Sir Gordon Hamish, Kt., C.V.O., C.B.E.

Pitblado, Sir David Bruce, K.C.B., C.V.O.

Pitoi, Sir Sere, Kt., C.B.E.

Pitt, Sir Harry Raymond, Kt., PH.D., F.R.S.

Pitts, Sir Cyril Alfred, Kt.

Pixley, Sir Neville Drake, Kt., M.B.E., V.R.D.

Pizey, *Admiral* Sir (Charles Thomas) Mark, G.B.E., C.B., D.S.O.

Plaister, Sir Sydney, Kt., C.B.E.

Plastow, Sir David Arnold Stuart, Kt.

†Platt, Sir (Frank) Lindsey, Bt. (1958).

Platt, *Prof.* Hon. Sir Peter, Bt. (1959).

Playfair, Sir Edward Wilder, K.C.B.

Pleass, Sir Clement John, K.C.M.G., K.C.V.O., K.B.E.

Pliatzky, Sir Leo, K.C.B.

Plimmer, Sir Clifford Ulric, K.B.E.

Plowman, Sir (John) Anthony, Kt.

Plowman, *Hon.* Sir John Robin, Kt., C.B.E.

Plumb, Sir (Charles) Henry, Kt.

Plumb, *Prof.* Sir John Harold, Kt.

Pochin, Sir Edward Eric, Kt., C.B.E., M.D., F.R.C.P.

Poett, *General* Sir (Joseph Howard) Nigel, K.C.B., D.S.O.

Pole, *Col.* Sir John Gawen Carew, Bt., D.S.O., T.D. (1628).

Pole, Sir Peter Van Notten, Bt. (1791).

Pollard, Sir (Charles) Herbert, Kt., C.B.E.

Pollen, Sir John Michael Hungerford, Bt. (1795).

Pollock, Sir George, Kt., Q.C.

Pollock, Sir George Frederick, Bt. (1866).

Pollock, Sir Giles Hampden Montagu-, Bt. (1872).

Pollock, *Admiral of the Fleet* Sir Michael Patrick, G.C.B., M.V.O., D.S.C.

Pollock, Sir William Horace Montagu-, K.C.M.G.

Ponsonby, Sir Ashley Charles Gibbs, Bt., M.C. (1956).

Pontin, Sir Frederick William, Kt.

Poore, Sir Herbert Edward, Bt. (1795).

Pope, *Vice-Adm.* Sir (John) Ernle, K.C.B.

Pope, Sir Joseph Albert, Kt., D.SC., PH.D.

Popper, *Prof.* Sir Karl Raimund, Kt., C.H., PH.D., F.R.S.

Popplewell, *Hon.* Sir Oliver Bury, Kt.

Portal, Sir Jonathan Francis, Bt. (1901).

Porter, Sir John Simon Horsbrugh-, Bt. (1902).

Porter, *Prof.* Sir George, Kt., F.R.S., PH.D., SC.D.

Porter, Sir Leslie, Kt.

Porter, *Air Marshal* Sir (Melvin) Kenneth (Drowley), K.C.B., C.B.E.

Porter, *Hon.* Sir Murray Victor, Kt.

Porter, *Rt. Hon.* Sir Robert Wilson, Kt., Q.C.

Posnett, Sir Richard Neil, K.B.E., C.M.G.

Potter, Sir (Joseph) Raymond (Lynden), Kt.

Potter, *Maj.-Gen.* Sir (Wilfrid) John, K.B.E., C.B.

Potter, Sir (William) Ian, Kt.

Potts, *Hon.* Sir Francis Humphrey, Kt.

Pound, Sir John David, Bt. (1905).

Fountain, Sir Eric John, Kt.

Powell, Sir (Arnold Joseph) Philip, Kt., C.H., O.B.E., R.A., F.R.I.B.A.

Powell, Sir Nicholas Folliott Douglas, Bt. (1897).

Powell, Sir Richard Royle, G.C.B., K.B.E., C.M.G.

Power, Sir Alastair John Cecil, Bt. (1924).

Powles, Sir Guy Richardson, K.B.E., C.M.G., E.D.

Poynton, Sir (Arthur) Hilton, G.C.M.G.

Prain, Sir Ronald Lindsay, Kt., O.B.E.

Prendergast, Sir John Vincent, K.B.E., C.M.G., G.M.

Prentice, *Rt. Hon.* Sir Reginald Ernest, Kt.

Prentice, *Hon.* Sir William Thomas, Kt., M.B.E.

Prescott, Sir Mark, Bt. (1938).

Preston, Sir Kenneth Huson, Kt.

Preston, Sir Peter Sansome, K.C.B.

Preston, Sir Ronald Douglas Hildebrand, Bt. (1815).

Pretyman, Sir Walter Frederick, K.B.E.

Prevost, Sir Christopher Gerald, Bt. (1805).

Price, Sir Charles Keith Napier Rugge-, Bt. (1804).

Price, Sir David Ernest Campbell, Kt., M.P.

Price, Sir Francis Caradoc Rose, Bt. (1815).

Price, Sir Frank Leslie, Kt.

Price, Sir (James) Robert, K.B.E.

Price, Sir Leslie Victor, Kt., O.B.E.

Price, Sir Norman Charles, K.C.B.

Price, Sir Robert John Green-, Bt. (1874).

Prichard, Sir Montague Illtyd, Kt., C.B.E., M.C.

Prickett, *Air Chief Marshal* Sir Thomas Other, K.C.B., D.S.O., D.F.C.

Prideaux, Sir Humphrey Povah Treverbian, Kt., O.B.E.

Prideaux, Sir John Francis, Kt., O.B.E.

Primrose, Sir Alasdair Neil, Bt. (1903).

Pringle, *Air Marshal* Sir Charles Norman Seton, K.B.E.

Pringle, *Lt.-Gen.* Sir Steuart (Robert), Bt., K.C.B., R.M. (s 1683).

Pritchard, Sir Asa Hubert, Kt.

Pritchard, Sir John Michael, Kt., C.B.E.

Pritchard, Sir Neil, K.C.M.G.

Pritchett, Sir Victor Sawdon, Kt., C.B.E.

Proby, Sir Peter, Bt. (1952).

Proctor, Sir Roderick Consett, Kt., M.B.E.

Proud, Sir John Seymour, Kt.

Pryke, Sir David Dudley, Bt. (1926).

Pugh, Sir Idwal Vaughan, K.C.B.

Pugsley, *Prof.* Sir Alfred Grenvile, Kt., O.B.E., D.SC., F.R.S.

Pullen, Sir William Reginald James, K.C.V.O.

Pullinger, Sir (Francis) Alan, Kt., C.B.E.

Pumphrey, Sir (John) Laurence, K.C.M.G.

Purchas, *Rt. Hon.* Sir Francis Brooks, Kt.

Pyke, Sir Louis Frederick, Kt., E.D.

Quayle, Sir (John) Anthony, Kt., C.B.E.

Quilter, Sir Anthony Raymond Leopold Cuthbert, Bt. (1897).

Quinlan, Sir Michael Edward, K.C.B.

Quirk, *Prof.* Sir (Charles) Randolph, C.B.E., F.B.A.

Rabukawaqa, Sir Josua Rasilau, K.B.E., M.V.O.

Raby, Sir Victor Harry, K.B.E., C.B., M.C.

Radcliffe, Sir Sebastian Everard, Bt. (1813).

Radclyffe, Sir Charles Edward Mott-, Kt.

Radford, Sir Ronald Walter, K.C.B., M.B.E.

Radzinowicz, *Prof.* Sir Leon, Kt., LL.D.

Rae, *Hon.* Sir Wallace Alexander Ramsay, Kt.

Raeburn, Sir Michael Edward Norman, Bt. (1923).

Raeburn, *Maj.-Gen.* Sir (William) Digby (Manifold), K.C.V.O., C.B., D.S.O., M.B.E.

Raffray, Sir Piat Joseph Raymond Andre, Kt.

Raikes, *Vice-Adm.* Sir Iwan Geoffrey, K.C.B., C.B.E., D.S.C.

Ralli, Sir Godfrey Victor, Bt., T.D. (1912).

Ramphal, Sir Shridath Surendranath, Kt., C.M.G.

Rampton, Sir Jack Leslie, K.C.B.

Ramsay, Sir Alexander William Burnett, Bt. (1806).

Ramsay, Sir Thomas Meek, Kt., C.M.G.

Ramsbotham, *Lt.-Gen.* Sir David John, K.C.B., C.B.E.

Ramsbotham, *Hon.* Sir Peter Edward, G.C.M.G., G.C.V.O.

Ramsden, Sir Geoffrey Charles Frescheville, Kt., C.I.E.

Ramsden, Sir John Charles Josslyn, Bt. (1689).

Ramsey, Sir Alfred Ernest, Kt.

Randle, *Prof.* Sir Philip John, Kt.

Ranger, Sir Douglas, Kt., F.R.C.S.

Rank, Sir Benjamin Keith, Kt., C.M.G.

Rankin, Sir Hugh (Charles Rhys), Bt. (1898).

Raper, *Vice-Adm.* Sir (Robert) George, K.C.B.

Rasch, *Maj.* Sir Richard Guy Carne, Bt. (1903).

Rashleigh, Sir Richard Harry, Bt. (1831).

Rault, Sir Louis Joseph Maurice, Kt.

Rawlins, *Surgeon Vice-Adm.* Sir John Stuart Pepys, K.B.E.

Rawlinson, Sir Anthony Henry John, Bt. (1891).

Raymond, Sir Stanley Edward, Kt.

Read, *Air Marshal* Sir Charles Frederick, K.B.E., C.B., D.F.C., A.F.C.

Read, *General* Sir (John) Antony (Jervis), G.C.B., C.B.E., D.S.O., M.C.

Read, Sir John Emms, Kt.

Reade, Sir Clyde Nixon, Bt. (1661).

Readhead, Sir James Templeman, Bt. (1922).

Reay, *Lt.-Gen.* Sir (Hubert) Alan John, K.B.E.

Redfearn, Sir Herbert, Kt.

Redgrave, *Maj.-Gen.* Sir Roy Michael Frederick, K.B.E., M.C.

Redmayne, Sir Nicholas, Bt. (1964).

Redmond, Sir James, Kt.

Redshaw, Sir Leonard, Kt.

Redwood, Sir Peter Boverton, Bt. (1911).

Reece, Sir James Gordon, Kt.

Reed, *Hon.* Sir Nigel Vernon, Kt., C.B.E.

Rees, Sir (Charles William) Stanley, Kt., T.D.

Rees-Mogg, Sir William, Kt.

Reeve, *Hon.* Sir (Charles) Trevor, Kt.

Reeves, *Most Rev.* Paul Alfred, G.C.M.G., G.C.V.O.

Reffell, *Vice-Adm.* Sir Derek Roy, K.C.B.

Refshauge, *Maj-Gen.* Sir William Dudley, Kt., C.B.E.

Reid, Sir Alexander James, Bt. (1897).

Reid, *Hon.* Sir George Oswald, Kt., Q.C.

Reid, *Air Vice-Marshal* Sir (George) Ranald Macfarlane, K.C.B., D.S.O., M.C.

Reid, Sir (Harold) Martin (Smith), K.B.E., C.M.G.

Reid, Sir Hugh, Bt. (1922).

Reid, Sir John James Andrew, K.C.M.G., C.B., T.D.

Reid, Sir Norman Robert, Kt.

Reid, Sir Robert Basil, Kt., C.B.E.

Reilly, Sir (D'Arcy) Patrick, G.C.M.G., O.B.E.

Reilly, *Lt.-Gen.* Sir Jeremy Calcott, K.C.B., D.S.O.

Reiss, Sir John Anthony Ewart, Kt., B.E.M.

Renals, Sir Stanley, Bt. (1895).

Rendell, Sir William, Kt.

Rennie, Sir Alfred Baillie, Kt.

Rennie, Sir John Shaw, G.C.M.G., O.B.E.

Renouf, Sir Francis Henry, Kt.

Renshaw, Sir (Charles) Maurice Bine, Bt. (1903).

Renwick, Sir Richard Eustace, Bt. (1921).

Reporter, Sir Shapoor Ardeshirji, K.B.E.

Revans, Sir John, Kt., C.B.E.

Rex, *Hon.* Sir Robert Richmond, K.B.E., C.M.G.

Reynolds, Sir David James, Bt. (1923).

Reynolds, Sir Peter William John, Kt., C.B.E.

Rhodes, Sir Basil Edward, Kt., C.B.E., T.D.

Rhodes, Sir John Christopher Douglas, Bt. (1919).

Rhodes, Sir Peregrine Alexander, K.C.M.G.

Richards, *Hon.* Sir Edward Trenton, Kt., C.B.E.

Richards, Sir (Francis) Brooks, K.C.M.G., D.S.C.

Richards, Sir James Maude, Kt., C.B.E.

Richards, *Lt.-Gen.* Sir John Charles Chisholm, K.C.B., R.M.

Richards, Sir Rex Edward, Kt., D.SC., F.R.S.

Richardson, Sir Anthony Lewis, Bt. (1924).

Richardson, *General* Sir Charles Leslie, G.C.B., C.B.E., D.S.O.

Richardson, *Air Marshal* Sir (David) William, K.B.E.

Richardson, Sir Egerton Rudolf, Kt., C.M.G.

Richardson, Sir (Horace) Frank, Kt.

Richardson, *Rt. Hon.* Sir Ivor Lloyd Morgan, Kt.

Richardson, Sir (John) Eric, Kt., C.B.E.

Richardson, Sir (Lionel) Earl George, Kt.

Richardson, *Lt.-Gen.* Sir Robert Francis, K.C.B., C.V.O., C.B.E.

Richardson, Sir Simon Alaisdair Stewart-, Bt. (s 1630).

Riches, Sir Derek Martin Hurry, K.C.M.G.

Riches, Sir Eric William, Kt., M.C.

Riches, *General* Sir Ian Hurry, K.C.B., D.S.O.

Richmond, Sir Alan James, Kt.

Richmond, *Rt. Hon.* Sir Clifford Parris, K.B.E.

Richmond, Sir John Christopher Blake, K.C.M.G.

Richmond, Sir John Frederick, Bt. (1929).

Richmond, *Prof.* Sir Mark Henry, Kt., F.R.S.

Rickett, Sir Denis Hubert Fletcher, K.C.M.G., C.B.

Ricketts, Sir Robert Cornwallis Gerald St. Leger, Bt. (1828).

Ricks, Sir John Plowman, Kt.

Riddell, Sir John Charles Buchanan, Bt. (s 1628).

Ridley, Sir Adam (Nicholas), Kt.

Ridley, Sir Sidney, Kt.

Ridsdale, Sir Julian Errington, Kt., C.B.E., M.P.

Rigby, *Lt.-Col.* Sir (Hugh) John (Macbeth), Bt. (1929).

Riley, Sir Ralph, Kt., F.R.S.

Ring, Sir Lindsay Roberts, G.B.E.

Ringadoo, *Hon.* Sir Veerasamy, G.C.M.G.

Ripley, Sir Hugh, Bt. (1880).

Risk, Sir Thomas Neilson, Kt.

Risson, *Maj.-Gen.* Sir Robert Joseph Henry, Kt., C.B., C.B.E., D.S.O., E.D.

Ritchie, Sir James Edward Thomson, Bt., T.D. (1918).

Rix, Sir Brian Norman Roger, Kt., C.B.E.

Rix, Sir John, Kt., M.B.E.

Roberts, Sir Bryan Clieve, K.C.M.G., Q.C.

Roberts, *Hon.* Sir Denys Tudor Emil, K.B.E., Q.C.

Roberts, Sir (Edward Fergus) Sidney, Kt., C.B.E.

Roberts, Sir Frank Kenyon, G.C.M.G., G.C.V.O.

Roberts, Sir Geoffrey Newland, Kt., C.B.E., A.F.C.

Roberts, *Brig.* Sir Geoffrey Paul Hardy-, K.C.V.O., C.B., C.B.E.

Roberts, Sir Gilbert Howland Rookehurst, Bt. (1809).

Roberts, Sir Gordon James, Kt., C.B.E.

Roberts, Sir Samuel, Bt. (1919).

Roberts, Sir Stephen James Leake, Kt.

Roberts, Sir William James Denby, Bt. (1909).

Robertson, *Prof.* Sir Alexander, Kt., C.B.E.

Robertson, Sir James Anderson, Kt., C.B.E.

Robertson, *Prof.* Sir Rutherford Ness, Kt., C.M.G.

Robinson, Sir Albert Edward Phineas, Kt.

Robinson, Sir Dove-Myer, Kt.

Robinson, *Prof.* Sir (Edward) Austin (Gossage), Kt., C.M.G., O.B.E., F.B.A.

Robinson, Sir John Beverley, Bt. (1854).

Robinson, Sir John James Michael Laud, Bt. (1660).

Robinson, *Rt. Hon.* Sir Kenneth, Kt.

Robinson, Sir Niall Bryan Lynch-, Bt., D.S.C. (1920).

Robinson, Sir Wilfred Henry Frederick, Bt. (1908).

Robotham, *Hon.* Sir Lascelles Lister, Kt.

Robson, *Prof.* Sir James Gordon, Kt., C.B.E.

Robson, Sir Thomas Buston, Kt., M.B.E.

Robson, *Vice-Adm.* Sir (William) Geoffrey (Arthur), K.B.E., C.B., D.S.O., D.S.C.

Roch, *Hon.* Sir John Ormond, Kt.

Roche, Sir David O'Grady, Bt. (1838).

Rodger, Sir William Glendinning, Kt., O.B.E.

Rodgers, Sir John Charles, Bt. (1964).

Rodrigues, Sir Alberto Maria, Kt., C.B.E., E.D.

Roe, *Air Chief Marshal* Sir Rex David, G.C.B., A.F.C.

Rogers, *Air Chief Marshal* Sir John Robson, K.C.B., C.B.E.

Rogers, Sir Philip, G.C.B., C.M.G.

Rogers, Sir Philip James, Kt., C.B.E.

Roll, *Rev.* Sir James William Cecil, Bt. (1921).

Rooke, Sir Denis Eric, Kt., C.B.E.

Roper, *Hon.* Sir Clinton Marcus, Kt.

Ropner, Sir John Bruce Woollacott, Bt. (1952).

Ropner, Sir Robert Douglas, Bt. (1904).

Roscoe, Sir Robert Bell, K.B.E.

Rose, Sir Alec Richard, Kt.

Rose, *Hon.* Sir Christopher Dudley Roger, Kt.

Rose, Sir Clive Martin, G.C.M.G.

Rose, Sir David Lancaster, Bt. (1874).

Rose, Sir Julian Day, Bt. (1872 and 1909).

Rosier, *Air Chief Marshal* Sir Frederick Ernest, G.C.B., C.B.E., D.S.O.

Roskill, Sir Ashton Wentworth, Kt., Q.C.

Ross, Sir Alexander, Kt.

Ross, Sir Archibald David Manisty, K.C.M.G.

Ross, Sir (James) Keith, Bt., R.D., F.R.C.S. (1960).

Ross, Sir Lewis Nathan, Kt., C.M.G.

Rosser, Sir Melvyn Wynne, Kt.

Rossi, Sir Hugh Alexis Louis, Kt., M.P.

Rossiter, *Hon.* Sir John Frederick, K.B.E.

Rostron, Sir Frank, Kt., M.B.E.

Roth, *Prof.* Sir Martin, Kt., M.D., F.R.C.P.

Rothenstein, Sir John Knewstub Maurice, Kt., C.B.E., Ph.D.

Rothnie, Sir Alan Keir, K.C.V.O., C.M.G.

Rougier, *Hon.* Sir Richard George, Kt.

Rous, Sir Anthony Gerald Roderick, K.C.M.G., O.B.E.

Row, *Hon.* Sir John Alfred, Kt.

Row, *Cdr.*, Sir Philip John, K.C.V.O., O.B.E., R.N.

Rowe, Sir Henry Peter, K.C.B., Q.C.

Rowe-Ham, Sir David Kenneth, G.B.E.

Rowell, Sir John Joseph, Kt., C.B.E.

Rowland, *Air Marshal* Sir James Anthony, K.B.E., D.F.C., A.F.C.

Rowlands, *Air Marshal* Sir John Samuel, K.B.E., G.C.

Rowley, Sir Charles Robert, Bt. (1836).

Rowley, Sir Joshua Francis, Bt. (1786).

Rowling, *Rt. Hon.* Sir Wallace Edward, K.C.M.G.

Rowntree, Sir Norman Andrew Forster, Kt.

Roxburgh, *Vice-Adm.* Sir John Charles Young, K.C.B., C.B.E., D.S.O., D.S.C.

Royden, Sir Christopher John, Bt. (1905).

Rucker, Sir Arthur Nevil, K.C.M.G., C.B., C.B.E.

Rumbold, Sir (Horace) Algernon (Fraser), K.C.M.G., C.I.E.

Rumbold, Sir Henry John Sebastian, Bt. (1779).

Rumbold, Sir Jack Seddon, Kt.

Runciman, *Hon.* Sir Steven (James Cochran Stevenson), Kt., C.H.

Rusby, *Vice-Adm.* Sir Cameron, K.C.B., M.V.O.

Russell, Sir Archibald Edward, Kt., C.B.E., F.R.S.

Russell, Sir Charles Ian, Bt. (1916).

Russell, Sir Evelyn Charles Sackville, Kt.

Russell, Sir George Michael, Bt. (1812).

Russell, Sir (Robert) Mark, K.C.M.G.

Russell, *Rt. Hon.* Sir (Thomas) Patrick, Kt.

Russo, Sir Peter George, Kt., C.B.E.

Rutter, Sir Frank William Eden, K.B.E.

Ryan, Sir Derek Gerald, Bt. (1919).

Rycroft, Sir Richard Newton, Bt. (1784).

Ryland, Sir (Albert) William (Cecil), Kt., C.B.

Rymill, Sir Arthur Campbell, Kt.

Ryrie, Sir William Sinclair, K.C.B.

Sainsbury, *Hon.* Sir John Davan, Kt.

Sainsbury, Sir Robert James, Kt.

St. Aubyn, Sir (John) Arscott Molesworth-, Bt. (1689).

St. George, Sir Denis Howard, Bt. (1766).

Sainty, Sir John Christopher, K.C.B.

Sakzewski, Sir Albert, Kt.

Salt, Sir Anthony Houlton, Bt. (1869).

Salt, Sir (Thomas) Michael John, Bt. (1899).

Samuel, Sir Jon Michael Glen, Bt. (1898).

Samuelson, Sir (Bernard) Michael (Francis), Bt. (1884).

Sandberg, Sir Michael Graham Ruddock, Kt., C.B.E.

Sanders, Sir Robert Tait, K.B.E., C.M.G.

Sanderson, Sir (Frank Philip) Bryan, Bt. (1920).

Sandilands, Sir Francis Edwin Prescott, Kt., C.B.E.

Sarei, Sir Alexis Holyweek, Kt., C.B.E.

Sarell, Sir Roderick Francis Gisbert, K.C.M.G., K.C.V.O.

Sargant, Sir (Henry) Edmund, Kt.

Saunders, *Hon.* Sir John Anthony Holt, Kt., C.B.E., D.S.O., M.C.

Saunders, Sir Owen Alfred, Kt., D.S.C., F.R.S.

Saunders, Sir Peter, Kt.

Sauzier, Sir (André) Guy, Kt., C.B.E., E.D.

Savage, Sir Ernest Walter, Kt.

Saville, *Hon.* Sir Mark Oliver, Kt.

Savory, Sir Reginald Charles Frank, Kt., C.B.E.

Scarlett, Sir Peter William Shelley Yorke, K.C.M.G., K.C.V.O.

Schiemann, *Hon.* Sir Konrad Hermann Theodor, Kt.

Scholey, Sir David Gerald, Kt., C.B.E.

Scholey, Sir Robert, Kt., C.B.E.

Scholtens, Sir James Henry, K.C.V.O.

Schubert, Sir Sydney, Kt.

Schultz, Sir (Joseph) Leopold, Kt., O.B.E.

Schuster, Sir (Felix) James Moncrieff, Bt., O.B.E. (1906).

Scipio, Sir Hudson Rupert, Kt.

Scoon, Sir Paul, G.C.M.G., G.C.V.O., O.B.E.

Scoones, *Maj.-Gen.* Sir Reginald Laurence, K.B.E., C.B., D.S.O.

Scopes, Sir Leonard Arthur, K.C.V.O., C.M.G., O.B.E.

Scott, Sir Anthony Percy, Bt. (1913).

Scott, Sir Bernard Francis William, Kt., C.B.E., T.D.

Scott, Sir (Charles) Hilary, Kt.

Scott, Sir (Charles) Peter, K.B.E., C.M.G.

Scott, Sir David Aubrey, G.C.M.G.

Scott, Sir George Edward, Kt., C.B.E.

Scott, Sir Ian Dixon, K.C.M.G., K.C.V.O., C.I.E.

Scott, Sir James Walter, Bt. (1962).

Scott, Sir Michael, K.C.V.O., C.M.G.

Scott, Sir Michael Fergus Maxwell, Bt. (1642).

Scott, Sir Oliver Christopher Anderson, Bt. (1909).

Scott, Sir Peter Markham, Kt., C.B.E., C.H., D.S.C.

Scott, *Hon.* Sir Richard Rashleigh Folliott, Kt.

Scott, Sir Terence Charles Stuart Morrison-, Kt., D.S.C., D.SC.

Scott, Sir Walter, Bt. (1907).

Scott, *Rear-Adm.* Sir (William) David (Stewart), K.B.E., C.B.

Scowen, Sir Eric Frank, Kt., M.D., D.SC., LL.D., F.R.C.P., F.R.C.S.

Scragg, *Air Vice-Marshal* Sir Colin, K.B.E., C.B., A.F.C.

Scrivenor, Sir Thomas Vaisey, Kt., C.M.G.

Seale, Sir John Henry, Bt. (1838).

Seaman, Sir Keith Douglas, K.C.V.O., O.B.E.

Sebright, Sir Peter Giles Vivian, Bt. (1626).

Secombe, Sir Harry Donald, Kt., C.B.E.

Seconde, Sir Reginald Louis, K.C.M.G., C.V.O.

Seely, Sir Nigel Edward, Bt. (1896).

Seeyave, Sir Rene Sow Choung, Kt., C.B.E

Selby, Sir Kenneth, Kt.

Seligman, Sir Peter Wendel, Kt., C.B.E.

Sellors, Sir Thomas Holmes, D.M.

Sells, Sir David Perronet, Kt.

Senior, Sir Edward Walters, Kt., C.M.G.

Sergeant, Sir Patrick, Kt.

Series, Sir (Joseph Michel) Emile, Kt., C.B.E.

Serpell, Sir David Radford, K.C.B., C.M.G., O.B.E.

Seton, Sir (Christopher) Bruce, Bt. (s 1663).

Seton, Sir Robert James, Bt. (s 1683).

Sewell, Sir (John) Allan, Kt., I.S.O.

Seymour, *Cdr.* Sir Michael Culme-, Bt., R.N. (1809).

Shakerley, Sir Geoffrey Adam, Bt. (1838).

Shakespeare, Sir William Geoffrey, Bt. (1942).

Shann, Sir Keith Charles Owen, Kt., C.B.E.

Shapland, Sir William Arthur, Kt.

Sharp, Sir Adrian, Bt. (1922).

Sharp, Sir Eric, Kt., C.B.E.

Sharp, Sir George, Kt., O.B.E.

Sharp, Sir Kenneth Johnston, Kt., T.D.

Sharp, Sir Milton Reginald, Bt. (1920).

Sharp, Sir Richard Lyall, K.C.V.O., C.B.

Sharp, Sir (William Harold) Angus, K.B.E., Q.P.M.

Sharpe, Sir Frank Victor, Kt., C.M.G., O.B.E., E.D.

Sharpe, *Hon.* Sir John Henry, Kt., C.B.E.

Sharpe, Sir Reginald Taaffe, Kt., Q.C.

Shattock, Sir Gordon, Kt.

Shaw, Sir Brian Piers, Kt.

Shaw, Sir (Charles) Barry, Kt., C.B., Q.C.

Shaw, Sir (John) Giles (Dunkerley), Kt., M.P.

Shaw, Sir John Michael Robert Best-, Bt. (1665).

Shaw, Sir Michael Norman, Kt., M.P.

Shaw, Sir Robert, Bt. (1821).

Shaw, Sir Roy, Kt.

Shaw, Sir Run Run, Kt., C.B.E.

Sheen, *Hon.* Sir Barry Cross, Kt.

Sheffield, Sir Reginald Adrian Berkeley, Bt. (1755).

Shehadie, Sir Nicholas Michael, Kt., O.B.E.

Shelbourne, Sir Philip, Kt.

Sheldon, *Hon.* Sir (John) Gervase (Kensington), Kt.

Shelley, Sir John Richard, Bt. (1611).

Shepheard, Sir Peter Faulkner, Kt., C.B.E.

Shepheard, Sir Victor George, K.C.B.

Shepherd, Sir Peter Malcolm, Kt., C.B.E.

Sherlock, Sir Philip Manderson, K.B.E.

Sherman, Sir Alfred, Kt.

Sherman, Sir Louis, Kt., O.B.E.

Shields, Sir Neil Stanley, Kt., M.C.

Shiffner, Sir Henry David, Bt. (1818).

Shillington, Sir (Robert Edward) Graham, Kt., C.B.E.

Sholl, *Hon.* Sir Reginald Richard, Kt.

Shone, Sir Robert Minshull, Kt., C.B.E.

Short, *Brig.* Sir Noel Edward Vivian, Kt., M.B.E., M.C.

Shuckburgh, Sir (Charles Arthur) Evelyn, G.C.M.G., C.B.

Shuckburgh, Sir Charles Gerald Stewkley, Bt. (1660).

Sich, Sir Rupert Leigh, Kt., C.B.

Siddall, Sir Norman, Kt., C.B.E.

Sidey, *Air Marshal* Sir Ernest Shaw, K.B.E., C.B., M.D.

Sie, Sir Banja Tejan-, G.C.M.G.

Simeon, Sir John Edmund Barrington, Bt. (1815).

Simogun, Sir Petar, Kt., M.B.E., B.E.M.

Simonet, Sir Louis Marcel Pierre, Kt., C.B.E.

Simpson, *Hon.* Sir Alfred Henry, Kt.

Simpson, Sir William James, Kt.

Sinclair, Sir Clive Marles, Kt.

Sinclair, Sir George Evelyn, Kt., C.M.G., O.B.E.

Sinclair, Sir Ian McTaggart, K.C.M.G., Q.C.

Sinclair, Sir John Rollo Norman Blair, Bt. (s 1704).

Sinclair, *Prof.* Sir Keith, Kt., C.B.E.

Sinclair, *Air Vice-Marshal* Sir Laurence Frank, K.C.B., G.C., C.B.E., D.S.O.

Sinclair, Sir Ronald Ormiston, K.B.E.

Singh, *Hon.* Sir Vijay Raghubir, Kt.

Singhania, Sir Padampat, Kt.

Singhateh, *Alhaji* Sir Farimang, G.C.M.G.

Singleton, Sir Edward Henry Sibbald, Kt.

Sinnamon, Sir Hercules, Kt., O.B.E.

Sisson, Sir Roy, Kt.

Sitwell, Sir Sacheverell, Bt., C.H. (1808).

Skeet, Sir Trevor Herbert Harry, Kt., M.P.

Skeggs, Sir Clifford George, Kt.

Skelhorn, Sir Norman John, K.B.E., Q.C.

Skellerup, Sir Valdemar Reid, Kt., C.B.E.

Skingsley, *Air Marshal* Sir Anthony Gerald, K.C.B.

Skinner, Sir Thomas Edward, K.B.E.

Skinner, Sir (Thomas) Keith (Hewitt), Bt. (1912).

Skipwith, Sir Patrick Alexander d'Estoteville, Bt. (1622).

Skyrme, Sir (William) Thomas (Charles), K.C.V.O., C.B., C.B.E.,T.D.

Slade, Sir Benjamin Julian Alfred, Bt. (1831).

Slade, *Rt. Hon.* Sir Christopher John, Kt.

Slaney, *Prof.* Sir Geoffrey, K.B.E.

Slattery, *Rear-Adm.* Sir Matthew Sausse, K.B.E., C.B.

Sleight, Sir John Frederick, Bt. (1920).

Slimmings, Sir William Kenneth MacLeod, Kt., C.B.E.

Sloman, Sir Albert Edward, Kt., C.B.E.

Slynn, *Hon.* Sir Gordon, Kt.

Smallpeice, Sir Basil, K.C.V.O.

Smallwood, *Air Chief Marshal* Sir Denis Graham, G.B.E., K.C.B., D.S.O., D.F.C.

Smart, *Prof.* Sir George Algernon, Kt., M.D., F.R.C.P.

Smart, Sir Jack, Kt., C.B.E.

Smedley, Sir Harold, K.C.M.G., M.B.E.

Smeeton, *Vice-Adm.* Sir Richard Michael, K.C.B., M.B.E.

Smiley, Sir Hugh Houston, Bt. (1903).

Smirk, Sir (Frederick) Horace, K.B.E., M.D.

Smith, Sir Alan, Kt., C.B.E., D.F.C.

Smith, Sir Alexander Mair, Kt., Ph.D.

Smith, Sir (Alexander) Rowland, Kt.

Smith, Sir Arthur Henry, Kt.

Smith, *Maj.-Gen.* Sir Cecil Miller, K.B.E., C.B., M.C.

Smith, Sir Charles Bracewell-, Bt. (1947).

Smith, Sir Christopher Sydney Winwood, Bt. (1809).

Smith, *Prof.* Sir David Cecil, Kt., F.R.S.

Smith, Sir Dudley (Gordon), Kt., M.P.

Smith, *Maj.-Gen.* Sir (Francis) Brian Wyldbore-, Kt., C.B., D.S.O., O.B.E.

Smith, *Prof.* Sir (Francis) Graham, Kt., F.R.S.

Smith, Sir (Frank) Ewart, Kt.

Smith, *Col.* Sir Henry Abel, K.C.M.G., K.C.V.O., D.S.O.

Smith, Sir Howard Frank Trayton, G.C.M.G.

Smith, *Hon.* Sir James Alfred, Kt., C.B.E., T.D.

Smith, Sir (James) Eric., Kt., C.B.E., SC.D., F.R.S.

Smith, Sir John Hamilton-Spencer-, Bt. (1804).

Smith, Sir John Kenneth Newson-, Bt. (1944).

Smith, Sir Laurence Barton Grafftey-, K.C.M.G., K.B.E.

Smith, Sir Leonard Herbert, Kt., C.B.E.

Smith, Sir Leslie Edward George, Kt.

Smith, *Hon.* Sir Murray Stuart-, Kt.

Smith, Sir Raymond Horace, K.B.E.

Smith, Sir Reginald Beaumont, Kt.

Smith, Sir Richard Rathbone Vassar-, Bt., T.D. (1917).

Smith, Sir (Richard) Robert Law-, Kt., C.B.E., A.F.C.

Smith, Sir Robert Courtney, Kt., C.B.E.

Smith, Sir Robert Hill, Bt., (1945).

Smith, *Air Marshal* Sir Roy David Austen-, K.B.E., C.B., D.F.C.

Smith, *Prof.* Sir Thomas Broun, Kt., Q.C.

Smith, Sir (Thomas) Gilbert. Bt. (1897).

Smith, *Admiral* Sir Victor Alfred Trumper, K.B.E., C.B., D.S.C.

Smith, Sir William Reardon Reardon-, Bt. (1920).

Smith, Sir (William) Reginald Verdon, Kt.

Smith, Sir (William) Richard Prince-, Bt. (1911).

Smithers, *Prof.* Sir David Waldron, Kt., M.D.

Smithers, Sir Peter Henry Berry Otway, Kt., V.R.D., D.Phil.

Smithers, *Hon.* Sir Reginald Allfree, Kt.

Smyth, Sir Thomas Weyland Bowyer-, Bt., (1661).

Smyth, Sir Timothy John, Bt. (1955).

Snelling, Sir Arthur Wendell, K.C.M.G., K.C.V.O.

Snelson, Sir Edward Alec Abbott, K.B.E.

Soame, Sir Charles John Buckworth-Herne-, Bt. (1697).

Sobell, Sir Michael, Kt.

Sobers, Sir Garfield St. Auburn, Kt.

Solomon, Sir David Arnold, Kt., M.B.E.

Solomons, *Hon.* Sir (Louis) Adrian, Kt.

Solti, Sir Georg, K.B.E.

Somerset, Sir Henry Beaufort, Kt., C.B.E.

Somerville, *Brig.* Sir John Nicholas, Kt., C.B.E.

Somerville, Sir Robert, K.C.V.O.

Sopwith, Sir Charles Ronald, Kt.

Sopwith, Sir Thomas Octave Murdoch, Kt., C.B.E.

Sorsbie, Sir Malin, Kt., C.B.E.

Soutar, *Air Marshal* Sir Charles John Williamson, K.B.E.

South, Sir Arthur, Kt.

Southby, Sir (Archibald) Richard (Charles), Bt., O.B.E., (1937).

Southern, Sir Richard William, Kt., F.B.A.

Southern, Sir Robert, Kt., C.B.E.

Southey, Sir Robert John, Kt., C.M.G.

Southwood, Sir Leonard Bingley, Kt., O.B.E.

Southward, Sir Ralph, K.C.V.O., F.R.C.P.

Southwood, *Prof.* Sir (Thomas) Richard (Edmund), Kt., F.R.S.

Southworth, Sir Frederick, Kt., Q.C.

Souyave, *Hon.* Sir (Louis) Georges, Kt.

Sowrey, *Air Marshal* Sir Frederick Beresford, K.C.B., C.B.E., A.F.C.

Soysa, Sir Warusahennedige Abraham Bastian, Kt., C.B.E.

Sparkes, Sir Robert Lyndley, Kt.

Sparrow, Sir John, Kt.

Spearman, Sir Alexander Young Richard Mainwaring, Bt. (1840).

Speed, Sir Robert William Arney, Kt., C.B., Q.C.

Speelman, *Jonkheer* Sir Cornelis Jacob, Bt. (1686).

Speight, *Hon.* Sir Graham Davies, Kt.

Speir, Sir Rupert Malise, Kt.

Spencer, Sir Kelvin Tallent, Kt., C.B.E., M.C.

Spender, *Prof.* Sir Stephen Harold, Kt., C.B.E.

Spicer, Sir Peter James, Bt. (1906).

Spooner, Sir James Douglas, Kt.

Spotswood, *Marshal of the Royal Air Force* Sir Denis Frank, G.C.B., C.B.E., D.S.O., D.F.C.

Springer, Sir Hugh Worrell, G.C.M.G., G.C.V.O., C.B.E.

Spry, *Brig.* Sir Charles Chambers Fowell, Kt., C.B.E., D.S.O.

Spry, *Hon.* Sir John Farley, Kt.

Stabb, *Hon.* Sir William Walter, Kt., Q.C.

Stack, *Air Chief Marshal* Sir (Thomas) Neville, K.C.B., C.V.O., C.B.E., A.F.C.

Staine, *Hon.* Sir Albert Llewellyn, Kt., C.B.E.

Stainton, Sir Anthony Nathaniel, K.C.B., Q.C.

Stainton, Sir (John) Ross, Kt., C.B.E.

Stallard, Sir Peter Hyla Gawne, K.C.M.G., C.V.O., M.B.E.

Stallworthy, Sir John Arthur, Kt., F.R.C.S.

Stamer, Sir (Lovelace) Anthony, Bt. (1809).

Stanbridge, *Air Vice-Marshal* Sir Brian Gerald Tivy, K.C.V.O., C.B.E., A.F.C.

Stanford, *Admiral* Sir Peter Maxwell, G.C.B., L.V.O.

Stanier, *Brig.* Sir Alexander Beville Gibbons, Bt., D.S.O., M.C. (1917).

Stanier, *Field-Marshal* Sir John Wilfred, G.C.B., M.B.E.

Staples, Sir John Richard, Bt. (I. 1628).

Stapleton, Sir (Henry) Alfred, Bt. (1679).

Stark, Sir Andrew Alexander Steel, K.C.M.G., C.V.O.

Starke, *Hon.* Sir John Erskine, Kt.

Starkey, Sir John Philip, Bt. (1935).

Starrit, Sir James, K.C.V.O.

Statham, Sir Norman, K.C.M.G., C.V.O.

Staughton, *Hon.* Sir Christopher Stephen Thomas Jonathan Thayer, Kt.

Staveley, Sir John Malfroy, K.B.E., M.C.

Staveley, *Admiral* Sir William Doveton Minet, G.C.B.

Stebbings, Sir John Chalmer, Kt.

Steedman, *Air Chief Marshal* Sir Alasdair (Alexander McKay Sinclair), G.C.B., C.B.E., D.F.C.

Steel, Sir David Edward Charles, Kt., D.S.O., M.C., T.D.

Steel, *Maj.* Sir (Fiennes) William Strang, Bt. (1938).

Steel, Sir James, Kt., C.B.E.

Steele, Sir (Philip John) Rupert, Kt.

Steere, Sir Ernest Henry Lee-, K.B.E.

Stenhouse, Sir Nicol, Kt.

Stening, *Col.* Sir George Grafton Lees, Kt., E.D.

Stephen, *Rt. Hon.* Sir Ninian Martin, G.C.M.G., G.C.V.O., K.B.E.

Stephens, Sir David, K.C.B., C.V.O.

Stephenson, Sir Henry Upton, Bt. (1936).

Stephenson, *Rt. Hon.* Sir John Frederick Eustace, Kt.

Stephenson, Sir William Samuel, Kt., M.C., D.F.C.

Sterling, Sir Jeffrey Maurice, Kt., C.B.E.

Sternberg, Sir Sigmund, Kt.

Stevens, *Vice-Adm.* Sir John Felgate, K.B.E., C.B.

Stevens, Sir Laurence Houghton, Kt., C.B.E.

Stevenson, *Rt. Hon.* Sir (Aubrey) Melford (Steed), Kt.

Stevenson, *Vice-Adm.* Sir (Hugh) David, K.B.E.

Stevenson, Sir Simpson, Kt.

Stewart, Sir Alan, K.B.E.

Stewart, Sir Alan d'Arcy, Bt. (I. 1623).

Stewart, Sir David Brodribb, Bt., T.D. (1960).

Stewart, Sir David James Henderson-, Bt. (1957).

Stewart, Sir Edward Jackson, Kt.

Stewart, *Prof.* Sir Frederick Henry, Kt., Ph.D., F.R.S., F.R.S.E.

Stewart, Sir Herbert Ray, Kt., C.I.E.

Stewart, Sir Houston Mark Shaw-, Bt., M.C., T.D. (s. 1667)

Stewart, Sir Hugh Charlie Godfray, Bt. (1803).

Stewart, Sir James Douglas, Kt.

Stewart, Sir James Watson, Bt. (1920).

Stewart, Sir Michael Norman Francis, K.C.M.G., O.B.E.

Stewart, Sir Robertson Huntly, Kt., C.B.E.

Stewart, Sir Ronald Compton, Bt. (1937).

Steyn, *Hon.* Sir Johan Van Zyl, Kt.

Stinson, Sir Charles Alexander, K.B.E.

Stirling, Sir Alexander John Dickson, K.B.E., C.M.G.

Stoby, Sir Kenneth Sievewright, Kt.

Stockdale, Sir Arthur Noel, Kt.

Stockdale, Sir Edmund Villiers Minshull, Bt. (1960).

Stocker, *Rt. Hon.* Sir John Dexter, Kt., M.C., T.D.

Stoker, *Prof.* Sir Michael George Parke, Kt., C.B.E., F.R.C.P., F.R.S., F.R.S.E.

Stone, *Prof.* Sir (John) Richard (Nicholas), Kt., C.B.E.

Stonhouse, Sir Philip Allan, Bt. (1628).

Storey, *Hon.* Sir Richard, Bt. (1960).

Stormonth Darling, Sir James Carlisle, Kt., C.B.E., M.C., T.D.

Stott, Sir Adrian George Ellingham, Bt. (1920).

Stow, Sir Christopher Philipson-, Bt., D.F.C. (1907).

Stow, Sir John Montague, G.C.M.G., K.C.V.O.

Stowe, Sir Kenneth Ronald, G.C.B., C.V.O.

Stracey, Sir John Simon, Bt. (1818).

Strachey, Sir Charles, Bt. (1801).

Stradling Thomas, Sir John, Kt., M.P.

Straker, Sir Michael Ian Bowstead, Kt., C.B.E.

Strasser, Sir Paul, Kt.

Stratton, Sir Richard James, K.C.M.G.

Stratton, *Lt.-Gen.* Sir William Henry, K.C.B., C.V.O., C.B.E., D.S.O.

Strawson, *Prof.* Sir Peter Frederick, Kt., F.B.A.

Street, *Hon.* Sir Laurence Whistler, K.C.M.G.

Strong, Sir Charles Love, K.C.V.O.

Strong, Sir Roy Colin, Kt., Ph.D., F.S.A.

Stronge, Sir James Anselan Maxwell, Bt. (1803).

Strutt, Sir Nigel Edward, Kt., T.D.

Stuart, Sir James Keith, Kt.

Stuart, Sir Kenneth Lamonte, Kt.

†Stuart, Sir Phillip Luttrell, Bt. (1660).

Stuart-Smith, *Hon.* Sir Murray, Kt.

Stubblefield, Sir (Cyril) James, Kt., D.SC., F.R.S.

Stubbs, Sir James Wilfrid, K.C.V.O., T.D.

Stucley, *Lt.* Sir Hugh George Coplestone Bampfylde, Bt. (1859).

Studd, Sir Edward Fairfax, Bt. (1929).

Studd, Sir Peter Malden, G.B.E., K.C.V.O.

Studholme, Sir Henry Gray, Bt., C.V.O. (1956).

Style, *Lt. Cdr.* Sir Godfrey William, Kt., C.B.E., D.S.C., R.N.

†Style, Sir William Frederick, Bt. (1627).

Suffield, Sir (Henry John) Lester, Kt.

Sugden, Sir Arthur, Kt.

Sullivan, Sir Desmond John, Kt.

Sullivan, Sir Richard Arthur, Bt. (1804).

Summerfield, *Hon.* Sir John Crampton, Kt., C.B.E.

Summerhayes, Sir Christopher Henry, K.B.E., C.M.G.

Summers, Sir Felix Roland Brattan, Bt. (1952).

Summerson, Sir John Newenham, Kt., C.H., C.B.E., F.B.A., F.S.A.

Sunderland, *Prof.* Sir Sydney, Kt., C.M.G.

Surridge, Sir (Ernest) Rex (Edward), Kt., C.M.G.

Sutherland, Sir John Brewer, Bt. (1921).

Sutherland, Sir Maurice, Kt.

Suttie, Sir (George) Philip Grant-, Bt. (s 1702).

Sutton, Sir Frederick Walter, Kt., O.B.E.

Sutton, *Air Marshal* Sir John Matthias Dobson, K.C.B.

Sutton, Sir Richard Lexington, Bt. (1772).

Sutton, Sir Stafford William Powell Foster-, K.B.E., C.M.G., Q.C.

Swaffield, Sir James Chesebrough, Kt., C.B.E., R.D.

Swallow, Sir William, Kt.

Swann, Sir Anthony Charles Christopher, Bt., C.M.G., O.B.E., (1906).

Swanwick, Sir Graham Russell, Kt., M.B.E.

Swartz, *Hon.* Sir Reginald William Colin, K.B.E., E.D.

Swayne, Sir Ronald Oliver Carless, Kt., M.C.

Swinson, Sir John Henry Alan, Kt., O.B.E.

Swinton, *Maj.-Gen.* Sir John, K.C.V.O., O.B.E.

Swire, Sir Adrian Christopher, Kt.

Swiss, Sir Rodney Geoffrey, Kt., O.B.E.

Swynnerton, Sir Roger John Massy, Kt., C.M.G., O.B.E., M.C.

Sykes, Sir Francis Godfrey, Bt. (1781).

Sykes, Sir John Charles Anthony le Gallais, Bt. (1921).

Sykes, Sir Tatton Christopher Mark, Bt. (1783).

Syme, Sir Ronald, Kt., O.M., F.B.A.

Symington, *Prof.* Sir Thomas, Kt., M.D., F.R.S.E.

Symons, *Vice-Adm.* Sir Patrick Jeremy, K.B.E.

Synge, Sir Robert Carson, Bt. (1801).

Tait, *Admiral* Sir (Allan) Gordon, K.C.B., D.S.C.

Tait, Sir James Sharp, Kt., D.SC., LlD., Ph.D.

Tait, Sir Peter, K.B.E.

Tait, *Air Vice-Marshal* Sir Victor Hubert, K.B.E., C.B.

Talbot, *Vice-Adm.* Sir (Arthur Allison) FitzRoy, K.B.E., C.B., D.S.O.

Talbot, *Hon.* Sir Hilary Gwynne, Kt.

Tallack, Sir Hugh Mackay, Kt.

Tancred, Sir Henry Lawson-, Bt. (1662).

Tang, Sir Shiu-kin, Kt., C.B.E.

Tangaroa, *Hon.* Sir Tangaroa, M.B.E.

Tange, Sir Arthur Harold, Kt., C.B.E.

Tansley, Sir Eric Crawford, Kt., C.M.G.

Tapp, *Maj.-Gen.* Sir Nigel Prior Hanson, K.B.E., C.B., D.S.O.

Tapsell, Sir Peter Hannay Bailey, Kt., M.P.

Tate, *Lt.-Col.* Sir Henry, Bt. (1898).

Taukala, Sir David Dawea, Kt., M.B.E.

Tavaiqia, *Ratu* Sir Josaia, K.B.E.

Taylor, *Lt.-Gen.* Sir Allan Macnab, K.B.E., M.C.

Taylor, Sir Alvin Burton, Kt.

Taylor, Sir (Arthur) Godfrey, Kt.

Taylor, Sir Charles Stuart, Kt., T.D.

Taylor, Sir George, Kt., D.SC., F.R.S., F.R.S.E.

Taylor, Sir Henry Milton, Kt.

Taylor, Sir James, Kt., M.B.E., D.SC.

Taylor, Sir John Lang, K.C.M.G.

Taylor, Sir Nicholas Richard Stuart, Bt. (1917).

Taylor, *Hon.* Sir Peter Murray, Kt.

Tebbit, Sir Donald Claude, G.C.M.G.

Te Heuheu, Sir Hepi Hoani, K.B.E.

Telford, Sir Robert, Kt., C.B.E.

Temple, Sir John Meredith, Kt.

Temple, Sir Rawden John Afamado, Kt. C.B.E., Q.C.

Temple, *Maj.* Sir Richard Anthony Purbeck, Bt., M.C. (1876).

Templeton, Sir John Marks, Kt.

Tennant, *Capt.* Sir Iain Mark, Kt.

Tennant, Sir Mark Dalcour, K.C.M.G., C.B.

Tennant, Sir Peter Frank Dalrymple, Kt., C.M.G., O.B.E.

Teo, Sir Fiatau Penitala, G.C.M.G., G.C.V.O., I.S.O., M.B.E.

Terry, Sir George Walter Roberts, Kt., C.B.E., Q.P.M.

Terry, Sir John Elliott, Kt.

Terry, Sir Michael Edward Stanley Imbert-, Bt. (1917).

Terry, *Air Chief Marshal* Sir Peter David George, G.C.B., A.F.C.

Tetley, Sir Herbert, K.B.E., C.B.

Tett, Sir Hugh Charles, Kt.

Thiess, Sir Leslie Charles, Kt., C.B.E.

Thomas, Sir Derek Morison David, K.C.M.G.

Thomas, Sir Frederick William, Kt.

Thomas, Sir (Godfrey) Michael (David) Bt. (1694).

Thomas, Sir Jeremy Cashel, K.C.M.G.

Thomas, Sir John Maldwyn, Kt.

Thomas, Sir Patrick Muirhead, Kt., D.S.O., T.D.

Thomas, Sir Robert Evan, Kt.

Thomas, *Hon.* Sir Swinton Barclay, Kt.

Thomas, Sir William James Cooper, Bt., T.D. (1919).

Thomas, Sir (William) Michael (Marsh), Bt. (1918).

Thomas, *Vice-Adm.* Sir William Richard Scott, K.C.B., O.B.E.

Thompson, Sir Christopher Peile, Bt. (1890).

Thompson, Sir Edward Hugh Dudley, Kt., M.B.E., T.D.

Thompson, Sir Edward Walter, Kt.

Thompson, *Vice-Adm.* Sir Hugh Leslie Owen, K.B.E.

Thompson, Sir (Humphrey) Simon Meysey-, Bt. (1874).

Thompson, *Hon.* Sir John, Kt.

Thompson, Sir Paul Anthony, Bt. (1963).

Thompson, Sir Peter Anthony, Kt.

Thompson, Sir Ralph Patrick, Kt.

Thompson, Sir Richard Hilton Marler, Bt. (1963).

Thompson, Sir Robert Grainger Ker, K.B.E., C.M.G., D.S.O., M.C.

Thompson, Sir (Thomas) Lionel Tennyson, Bt. (1806).

Thomson, Sir Adam, Kt., C.B.E.

Thomson, Sir Evan Rees Whitaker, Kt.

Thomson, Sir (Frederick Douglas) David, Bt. (1929).

Thomson, Sir Ivo Wilfrid Home, Bt. (1925).

Thomson, Sir John, K.B.E., T.D.

Thomson, Sir John Adam, G.C.M.G.

Thomson, Sir John (Ian) Sutherland, K.B.E., C.M.G.

Thorley, Sir Gerald Bowers, Kt., T.D.

Thorn, Sir John Samuel, Kt., O.B.E.

Thorne, *Maj.-Gen.* Sir David Calthrop, K.B.E.

Thorne, Sir Peter Francis, K.C.V.O., C.B.E.

Thornton, *Lt.-Gen.* Sir Leonard Whitmore, K.C.B., C.B.E.

Thornton, Sir Peter Eustace, K.C.B.

Thorold, Sir Anthony Henry, Bt., O.B.E., D.S.C. (1642).

Thouron, Sir John Rupert Hunt, K.B.E.

Throckmorton, Sir Robert George Maxwell, Bt. (1642).

Thwaites, Sir Bryan, Kt., Ph.D.

Thwin, Sir U, Kt.

Tibbits, *Capt.* Sir David Stanley, Kt., D.S.C., R.N.(*ret*).

Tickell, Sir Crispin Charles Cervantes, K.C.V.O.

Tikaram, Sir Moti, K.B.E.

Tilney, Sir John Dudley Robert Tarleton, Kt., T.D.

Tippet, *Vice-Adm.* Sir Anthony Sanders, K.C.B.

Tippett, Sir Michael Kemp, Kt., O.M., C.H., C.B.E.

Tirvengadum, Sir Harry Krishnan, Kt.

Titterton, *Prof.* Sir Ernest William, Kt., C.M.G.

Tizard, Sir John Peter Mills, Kt.

Tod, *Air Marshal* Sir John Hunter Hunter-, K.B.E., C.B.

Todd, Sir Bryan James, Kt.

Todd, *Hon.* Sir (Reginald Stephen) Garfield, Kt.

Tollemache, *Maj.-Gen.* Sir Humphry Thomas, Bt., C.B., C.B.E., R.M. (1793).

Tololo, Sir Alkan, K.B.E.

Tombs, Sir Francis Leonard, Kt.

Tomkins, Sir Alfred George, Kt., C.B.E.

Tomkins, Sir Edward Emile, G.C.M.G., C.V.O.

Tomlinson, Sir (Frank) Stanley, K.C.M.G.

Tooley, Sir John, Kt.

†Tooth, Sir Hugh John Lucas-, Bt. (1920).

Tooth, *Hon.* Sir (Seymour) Douglas, Kt.

ToRobert, Sir Henry Thomas, K.B.E.

Tory, Sir Geofroy William, K.C.M.G.

Touche, Sir Anthony George, Bt. (1920).

Touche, Sir Rodney Gordon, Bt. (1962).

Tovey, Sir Brian John Maynard, K.C.M.G.

ToVue, Sir Ronald, Kt., O.B.E.

Townley, Sir John Barton, Kt.

Townsend, *Rear-Adm.* Sir Leslie William, K.C.V.O., C.B.E.

Townsing, Sir Kenneth Joseph, Kt., C.M.G.

Trafford, Sir (Joseph) Anthony Porteous, Kt.

Traherne, Sir Cennydd George, K.G., T.D.

Traill, Sir Alan Towers, G.B.E.

Trant, *General* Sir Richard Brooking, K.C.B.

Travancore, *Maj.-Gen.* H.H. the Maharajah of, G.C.S.I., G.C.I.E.

Travers, Sir Thomas à'Beckett, Kt.

Treacher, *Admiral* Sir John Devereux, K.C.B.

Trehane, Sir (Walter) Richard, Kt.

Trelawny, Sir John Barry Salusbury-, Bt. (1628).

Trench, Sir David Clive Crosbie, G.C.M.G., M.C.

Trench, Sir Nigel Clive Cosby, K.C.M.G.

Trench, Sir Peter Edward, Kt., C.B.E., T.D.

Trescowthick, Sir Donald Henry, K.B.E.

Trethowan, Sir (James) Ian (Raley), Kt.

Trethowan, *Prof.* Sir William Henry, Kt. C.B.E., F.R.C.P.

Trevaskis, Sir (Gerald) Kennedy (Nicholas), K.C.M.G., O.B.E.

Trevelyan, Sir George Lowthian, Bt. (1874).

Trevelyan, Sir Norman Irving, Bt. (1662).

Trewby, *Vice-Adm.* Sir (George Francis) Allan, K.C.B.

Trinder, Sir (Arnold) Charles, G.B.E.

Tritton, Sir Anthony John Ernest, Bt. (1905).

Trollope, Sir Anthony Owen Clavering, Bt. (1642).

Trotter, Sir Ronald Ramsay, Kt.

Troubridge, Sir Peter, Bt. (1799).

Troughton, Sir Charles Hugh Willis, Kt., C.B.E., M.C., T.D.

Troup, *Vice-Adm.* Sir (John) Anthony (Rose), K.C.B., D.S.C.

Trowbridge, *Rear-Adm.* Sir Richard John, K.C.V.O.

Truscott, Sir Denis Henry, G.B.E., T.D.

Truscott, Sir George James Irving, Bt. (1909).

Tuck, Sir Bruce Adolph Reginald, Bt. (1910).

Tucker, *Hon.* Sir Richard Howard, Kt.

Tuckwell, Sir Edward George, K.C.V.O., F.R.C.S.

Tudor, *Hon.* Sir James Cameron, K.C.M.G.

Tuite, Sir Christopher Hugh, Bt., Ph.D. (1622).

Tuivaga, Sir Timoci Uluiburotu, Kt.

Tuke, Sir Anthony Favill, Kt.

Tupper, Sir Charles Hibbert, Bt. (1888).

Turbott, Sir Ian Graham, Kt., C.M.G., C.V.O.

Turing, Sir John Leslie, Bt., M.C. (s 1638).

Turnbull, Sir Francis Fearon, K.B.E., C.B., C.I.E.

Turnbull, Sir Richard Gordon, G.C.M.G.

Turner, *Rt. Hon.* Sir Alexander Kingcome, K.B.E.

Turner, *Admiral* Sir (Arthur) Francis, K.C.B., D.S.C.

Turner, *Hon.* Sir Michael John, Kt.

Turner, *Lt.-Gen.* Sir William Francis Robert, K.B.E., C.B., D.S.O.

Tuttle, *Air Marshal* Sir Geoffrey William, K.B.E., C.B., D.F.C.

Tuzo, *General* Sir Harry Craufurd, G.C.B., O.B.E., M.C.

Twiss, *Admiral* Sir Frank Roddam, K.C.B., K.C.V.O., D.S.C.

Tyler, *Maj.-Gen.* Sir Leslie Norman, K.B.E., C.B.

Tymms, Sir Frederick, K.C.I.E., M.C.

Tyree, Sir (Alfred) William, Kt., O.B.E.

Tyrrell, Sir Murray Louis, K.C.V.O., C.B.E.

Tyrwhitt, Sir Reginald Thomas Newman, Bt. (1919).

Udoma, *Hon.* Sir (Egbert) Udo, Kt.

Unsworth, Hon. Sir Edgar Ignatius Godfrey, Kt., C.M.G.

Unwin, Sir Keith, K.B.E., C.M.G.

Ure, Sir John Burns, K.C.M.G., L.V.O.

Urquhart, Sir Andrew, K.C.M.G., M.B.E.

Urquhart, Sir Brian Edward, K.C.M.G., M.B.E.

Urwick, Sir Alan Bedford, K.C.V.O., C.M.G.

Usher, Sir Leonard Gray, K.B.E.

Usher, Sir Peter Lionel, Bt. (1899).

Vallat, Sir Francis Aimé, G.B.E., K.C.M.G., Q.C.

Vallings, *Vice-Adm.* Sir George Montague Francis, K.C.B.

Vanderfelt, Sir Robin Victor, K.B.E.

van der Post, Sir Laurens Jan, Kt., C.B.E.

Vane, Sir John Robert, Kt., D.Phil., D.SC., F.R.S.

Vangeke, *Most Rev.* Louis, K.B.E.

Vanneck, *Air Commodore* Hon. Sir Peter Beckford Rutgers, G.B.E., C.B., A.F.C.

van Straubenzee, Sir William Radcliffe, Kt., M.B.E.

Vaughan, Sir (George) Edgar, K.B.E.

Vaughan, Sir Gerard Folliott, Kt., M.P., F.R.C.P.

Vavasour, *Cdr.* Sir Geoffrey William, Bt., D.S.C., R.N. (1828).

Veale, Sir Alan John Ralph, Kt.

Verco, Sir Walter John George, K.C.V.O.

Verney, Sir John, Bt., M.C., T.D. (1946).

Verney, Sir Ralph Bruce, Bt., K.B.E. (1818).

Vernon, Sir James, Kt., C.B.E.

Vernon, Sir Nigel John Douglas, Bt. (1914).

Vesey, Sir (Nathaniel) Henry (Peniston), Kt., C.B.E.

Vestey, Sir (John) Derek, Bt. (1921).

Vial, Sir Kenneth Harold, Kt., C.B.E.

Vick, Sir (Francis) Arthur, Kt., O.B.E., Ph.D.

Vickers, *Lt.-Gen.* Sir Richard Maurice Hilton, K.C.B., M.V.O., O.B.E.

Victoria, Sir (Joseph Aloysius) Donatus, Kt., C.B.E.

Villiers, Sir Charles Hyde, Kt., M.C.

Villiers, *Vice-Adm.* Sir (John) Michael, K.C.B., O.B.E.

Vincent, *Gen.* Sir Richard Frederick, K.C.B., D.S.O.

Vincent, Sir William Percy Maxwell, Bt. (1936).

Vinelott, *Hon.* Sir John Evelyn, Kt.

Vines, Sir William Joshua, Kt., C.M.G.

Virtue, *Hon.* Sir John Evenden, K.B.E.

Vyse, *Lt.-Gen.* Sir Edward Dacre Howard-, K.B.E., C.B., M.C.

Vyvyan, Sir John Stanley, Bt. (1645).

Waddell, Sir Alexander Nicol Anton, K.C.M.G., C.B.E.

Waddell, Sir James Henderson, Kt., C.B.

Wade, *Prof.* Sir Henry William Rawson, Kt., Q.C., F.B.A.

Wade, *Air Chief Marshal* Sir Ruthven Lowry, K.C.B., D.F.C.

Wade, Sir (William) Oulton, Kt.

Wade-Gery, Sir Robert Lucian, K.C.M.G., K.C.V.O.

Waechter, Sir (Harry Leonard) d'Arcy, Bt. (1911).

Wagner, Sir Anthony Richard, K.C.B., K.C.V.O.

Waite, *Hon.* Sir John Douglas, Kt.

Wake, Sir Hereward, Bt., M.C., (1621).

Wakefield, Sir (Edward) Humphry (Tyrell), Bt. (1962).

Wakefield, Sir Peter George Arthur, K.B.E., C.M.G.

Wakeford, *Air Marshal* Sir Richard Gordon, K.C.B., M.V.O., O.B.E., A.F.C.

Wakeley, Sir John Cecil Nicholson, Bt., F.R.C.S. (1952).

Wakeman, Sir (Offley) David, Bt. (1828).

Walker, *Rev.* Alan Edgar, Kt., O.B.E.

Walker, Sir Allan Grierson, Kt., Q.C.

Walker, *Lt.-Gen.* Sir Antony Kenneth Frederick, K.C.B.

Walker, Sir Baldwin Patrick, Bt. (1856).

Walker, Sir (Charles) Michael, G.C.M.G.

Walker, *Vice-Adm.* Sir (Charles) Peter (Graham), K.B.E., C.B., D.S.C.

Walker, Sir Edward Ronald, Kt., C.B.E.

Walker, Sir Gervas George, Kt.

Walker, *Maj.* Sir Hugh Ronald, Bt. (1906).

Walker, Sir James Graham, Kt., M.B.E.

Walker, Sir James Heron, Bt. (1868).

Walker, Sir Michael Leolin Forestier-, Bt. (1835).

Walker, *General* Sir Walter Colyear, K.C.B., C.B.E., D.S.O.

Walker, Sir William Giles Newsom, Kt., T.D.

Wall, Sir David William, Kt., O.B.E.

Wall, *Dr.* Sir Gerard Aloysius, Kt.

Wall, Sir Patrick Henry Bligh, Kt., M.C., V.R.D.

Wallace, Sir Gordon, Kt.

Wallace, Sir Ian James, Kt., C.B.E.

Waller, *Rt. Hon.* Sir George Stanley, Kt., O.B.E.

Waller, Sir (John) Keith, Kt., C.B.E.

Waller, Sir John Stainer, Bt. (1815).

Waller, Sir Robert William, Bt. (1780).

Walley, Sir John, K.B.E., C.B.

Walsh, Sir Alan, Kt., D.SC., F.R.S.

Walsh, Sir David Philip, K.B.E., C.B.

Walsh, Prof. Sir John Patrick, K.B.E.

Walsham, *Rear-Adm.* Sir John Scarlett Warren, Bt., C.B., O.B.E. (1831).

Walter, Sir Harold Edward, Kt.

Walters, *Prof.* Sir Alan Arthur, Kt.

Walters, Sir Frederick Donald, Kt.

Walters, Sir Peter Ingram, Kt.

Walters, Sir Roger Talbot, K.B.E., F.R.I.B.A.

Walton, *Prof.* Sir John Nicholas, Kt., T.D., F.R.C.P.

Walton, Sir John Robert, Kt.

Walton, *Hon.* Sir Raymond Henry, Kt.

Wan, Sir Wamp, Kt., M.B.E.

Wanstall, *Hon.* Sir Charles Gray, Kt.

Ward, Sir Arthur Hugh, K.B.E.

Ward, *General* Sir Dudley, G.C.B., K.B.E., D.S.O.

Ward, Sir John Guthrie, G.C.M.G.

Ward, Sir Joseph James Laffey, Bt. (1911).

Ward, *Maj.-Gen.* Sir Philip John Newling, K.C.V.O., C.B.E.

Ward, *General* Sir Richard Erskine, G.B.E., K.C.B., D.S.O., M.C.

Ward, Sir Terence George, Kt., C.B.E.

Wardale, Sir Geoffrey Charles, K.C.B.

Wardlaw, Sir Henry (John), Bt. (s 1631).

Wardle, Sir Thomas Edward Jewell, Kt.

Ware, Sir Henry Gabriel, K.C.B.

Waring, Sir (Alfred) Holburt, Kt. (1935).

Warmington, *Lt.-Cdr.* Sir Marshall George Clitheroe, Bt., R.N. (1908).

Warner, Sir (Edward Courtenay) Henry, Bt. (1910).

Warner, Sir Edward Redston, K.C.M.G., O.B.E.

Warner, Sir Frederick Archibald, G.C.V.O., K.C.M.G.

Warner, Sir Frederick Edward, Kt., F.R.S.

Warner, *Hon.* Sir Jean-Pierre Frank Eugene, Kt.

Warnock, Sir Geoffrey James, Kt.

Warren, Sir Alfred Henry, Kt., C.B.E.

Warren, Sir Brian Charles Pennefather, Bt. (1784).

Warren, Sir Frederick Miles, K.B.E.

Warren, Sir (Harold) Brian (Seymour), Kt.

Wass, Sir Douglas William Gretton, G.C.B.

Waterhouse, *Hon.* Sir Ronald Gough, Kt.

Waterlow, Sir Christopher Rupert, Bt. (1873).

Waterlow, Sir (James) Gerard, Bt. (1930).

Watkins, *Rt. Hon.* Sir Tasker, Kt., V.C.

Watson, Sir Bruce Dunstan, Kt.

Watson, Sir Francis John Bagott, K.C.V.O., F.B.A., F.S.A.

Watson, Sir (James) Andrew, Bt. (1866).

Watson, Sir John Forbes, Bt. (1895).

Watson, Sir Michael Milne-, Bt., C.B.E. (1937).

Watson, Sir (Noel) Duncan, K.C.M.G.

Watson, *Vice-Admiral* Sir Philip Alexander, K.B.E., M.V.O.

Watson, *Vice-Adm.* Sir (Robert) Dymock, K.C.B., C.B.

Watt, Sir Alan Stewart, Kt., C.B.E.

Watt, Sir George Steven Harvie-, Bt., T.D., Q.C. (1945).

Watt, *Surgeon Vice-Adm.* Sir James, K.B.E., F.R.C.S.

Wauchope, Sir Patrick George Don-, Bt. (s 1667).

Way, Sir Richard George Kitchener, K.C.B., C.B.E.

Wayne, *Prof.* Sir Edward Johnson, Kt., M.D., Ph.D.

Weatherall, *Prof.* Sir David John, Kt., F.R.S.

Weaver, Sir Tobias Rushton, Kt., C.B.

Webb, *Lt.-Gen.* Sir Richard James Holden, K.B.E., C.B.

Webb, Sir Thomas Langley, Kt.

Webster, *Vice-Adm.* Sir John Morrison, K.C.B.

Webster, *Hon.* Sir Peter Edlin, Kt.

Wedderburn, Sir Andrew John Alexander Ogilvy-, Bt. (1803).

Wedderspoon, Sir Thomas Adam, Kt.

Wedgwood, Sir John Hamilton, Bt., T.D. (1942).

Weeks, Sir Hugh Thomas, Kt., C.M.G.

Weinberg, Sir Mark Aubrey, Kt.

Weipers, *Prof.* Sir William Lee, Kt.

Weir, Sir Michael Scott, K.C.M.G.

Weir, Sir Roderick Bignell, Kt.

Weiss, Sir Eric, Kt.

Welby, Sir (Richard) Bruno Gregory, Bt. (1801).

Welch, Sir John Reader, Bt. (1957).

Weld, *Col.* Sir Joseph William, Kt., O.B.E., T.D.

Weldon, Sir Anthony William, Bt. (I. 1723).

Welensky, *Rt. Hon.* Sir Roy, (Roland), K.C.M.G.

Wellings, Sir Jack Alfred, Kt., C.B.E.

Wells, Sir Charles Maltby, Bt., T.D. (1944).

Wells, Sir John Julius, Kt.

West-Russell, *Hon.* Sir David Sturrock, Kt.

Westerman, Sir (Wilfred) Alan, Kt., C.B.E.

Wheatley, Sir (George) Andrew, Kt., C.B.E.

Wheeler, Sir Ernest Richard, K.C.V.O., M.B.E.

Wheeler, Sir Frederick Henry, Kt., C.B.E.

Wheeler, *Air Chief Marshal* Sir (Henry) Neil (George), G.C.B., C.B.E., D.S.O., D.F.C., A.F.C.

Wheeler, Sir John Hieron, Bt. (1920).

Wheeler, *Hon.* Sir Kenneth Henry, Kt.

Wheler, Sir Edward Woodford, Bt. (1660).

Whishaw, Sir Charles Percival Law, Kt.

Whitaker, *Maj.* Sir James Herbert Ingham, Bt. (1936).

White, *Hon.* Sir Alfred John, Kt.

White, Sir Christopher Robert Meadows, Bt. (1937).

White, Sir Dick Goldsmith, K.C.M.G., K.B.E.

White, Sir Frederick William George, K.B.E., Ph.D., F.R.S.

White, Sir George Stanley James, Bt. (1904).

White, Sir Harold Leslie, Kt., C.B.E.

White, *Wing-Cdr.* Sir Henry Arthur Dalrymple-, Bt., D.F.C. (1926).

White, *Hon.* Sir John Charles, Kt., M.B.E.

White, Sir John Woolmer, Bt. (1922).

White, Sir Lynton Stuart, Kt., M.B.E.. T.D.

White, *Admiral* Sir Peter, G.B.E.

White, Sir Thomas Astley Woollaston, Bt. (1802).

White, Sir (Vincent) Gordon (Lindsay), K.B.E.

Whitehead, Sir John Stainton, K.C.M.G., C.V.O.

Whitehead, Sir Rowland John Rathbone, Bt. (1889).

Whiteley, Sir Hugo Baldwin Huntington-, Bt. (1918).

Whiteley, *General* Sir Peter John Frederick, G.C.B., O.B.E., R.M.

Whitford, *Hon.* Sir John Norman Keates, Kt.

Whitley, *Air Marshal* Sir John René, K.B.E., C.B., D.S.O., A.F.C.

Whitmore, Sir Clive Anthony, K.C.B., C.V.O.

Whitmore, Sir John Henry Douglas, Bt. (1954).

Whitteridge, Sir Gordon Coligny, K.C.M.G., O.B.E.

Whittle, *Air Commodore* Sir Frank, O.M., K.B.E., C.B., F.R.S.

Whyte, Sir William Erskine Hamilton, K.C.M.G.

Wickerson, Sir John Michael, Kt.

Wicks, *Hon.* Sir James, Kt.

Wicks, Sir James Albert, Kt.

Wigan, Sir Alan Lewis, Bt. (1898).

Wiggin, Sir John Henry, Bt., M.C. (1892).

Wigglesworth, Sir Vincent Brian, Kt., C.B.E., M.D., F.R.S.

Wigram, *Rev. Canon* Sir Clifford Woolmore, Bt. (1805).

Wilbraham, Sir Richard Baker, Bt. (1776).

Wilford, Sir (Kenneth) Michael, G.C.M.G.

Wilkins, Sir Graham John, Kt.

Wilkins, *Lt.-Gen.* Sir Michael Compton Lockwood, K.C.B., O.B.E.

Wilkinson, Sir (David) Graham (Brook) Bt. (1941).

Wilkinson, *Prof.* Sir Denys Haigh, Kt., F.R.S.

Wilkinson, *Prof.* Sir Geoffrey, Kt., F.R.S.

Wilkinson, *Rt. Hon.* Sir Nicolas Christopher Henry Browne-, Kt.

Wilkinson, Sir Peter Allix, K.C.M.G., D.S.O., O.B.E.

Wilkinson, Sir (Robert Francis) Martin, Kt.

Willatt, Sir (Robert) Hugh, Kt.

Willcocks, Sir David Valentine, Kt., C.B.E., M.C.

Williams, Sir Alwyn, Kt., Ph.D., F.R.S.

Williams, Sir Anthony James, K.C.M.G.

Williams, Sir Brandon Meredith Rhys-, Bt., M.P. (1918).

Williams, *Prof.* Sir Bruce Rodda, K.B.E.

Williams, *Admiral* Sir David, G.C.B.

Williams, Sir David Innes, Kt.

Williams, *Hon.* Sir Denys Ambrose, Kt.

Williams, Sir Donald Mark, Bt. (1866).

Williams, Sir Edgar Trevor, Kt., C.B., C.B.E., D.S.O.

Williams, *Hon.* Sir Edward Stratten, K.C.M.G., K.B.E.

Williams, Sir Francis John Watkin, Bt., Q.C. (1798).

Williams, Sir Gwilym Tecwyn, Kt., C.B.E.

Williams, Sir Henry Morton Leech, Kt., M.B.E.

Williams, Sir Henry Sydney, Kt., O.B.E.

Williams, Sir (John) Leslie, Kt., C.B.E.

Williams, *Capt.* Sir John Protheroe, Kt., C.M.G., O.B.E.

Williams, Sir John Robert, K.C.M.G.

Williams, Sir Leonard, K.B.E., C.B.

Williams, Sir Osmond, Bt., M.C. (1909).

Williams, Sir Peter Watkin, Kt.

Williams, *Prof.* Sir Robert Evan Owen, Kt., M.D., F.R.C.P.

Williams, Sir (Robert) Philip Nathaniel, Bt. (1915).

Williams, Sir Robin Philip, Bt. (1953).

Williams, Sir Rolf Dudley-, Bt. (1964).

Williams, Sir (William) Maxwell (Harries), Kt.

Williamson, *Marshal of the Royal Air Force* Sir Keith Alec, G.C.B., A.F.C.

Williamson, Sir (Nicholas Frederick) Hedworth, Bt. (1642).

Willink, Sir Charles William, Bt. (1957).

Willis, *Hon.* Sir Eric Archibald, K.B.E., C.M.G.

Willis, *Vice-Adm.* Sir (Guido) James, K.B.E.

Willis, Sir John Ramsay, Kt.

Willison, *Lt.-Gen.* Sir David John, K.C.B., O.B.E., M.C.

Willison, Sir John Alexander, Kt., O.B.E.

Willoughby, *Maj.-Gen.* Sir John Edward Francis, K.B.E., C.B.

Wills, Sir David Seton, Bt. (1904).

Wills, Sir (Hugh) David Hamilton, Kt., C.B.E., T.D.

Wills, Sir John Spencer, Kt.

Wills, Sir John Vernon, Bt., T.D. (1923).

Wilmot, Sir Henry Robert, Bt. (1759).

Wilmot, *Cdr.* Sir John Assheton Eardley-, Bt., M.V.O., D.S.C., R.N. (1821).

Wilson, Sir Alan Herries, Kt., F.R.S.

Wilson, *Lt.-Gen.* Sir (Alexander) James, K.B.E., M.C.

Wilson, Sir Angus Frank Johnstone, Kt., C.B.E.

Wilson, Sir Austin George, Kt., O.B.E.

Wilson, Sir Charles Haynes, Kt.

Wilson, Sir David, Bt. (1920).

Wilson, Sir David Clive, K.C.M.G.

Wilson, Sir David Mackenzie, Kt.

Wilson, Sir Geoffrey Masterman, K.C.B., C.M.G.

Wilson, Sir James William Douglas, Bt. (1906).

Wilson, Sir John Foster, Kt., C.B.E.

Wilson, Sir John Gardiner, Kt., C.B.E.

Wilson, Sir John Martindale, K.C.B.

Wilson, Sir Keith Cameron, Kt.

Wilson, Sir (Mathew) Martin, Bt. (1874).

Wilson, Sir Reginald Holmes, Kt.

Wilson, Sir Robert Donald, Kt.

Wilson, *Rt. Rev.* Roger Plumpton, K.C.V.O., D.D.

Wilson, Sir Roland, K.B.E.

Wilson, *Hon.* Sir Ronald Darling, K.B.E., C.M.G.

Wilton, Sir (Arthur) John, K.C.M.G., K.C.V.O., M.C.

Wiltshire, Sir Frederick Munro, Kt., C.B.E.

Windeyer, Sir Brian Wellingham, Kt.

Windeyer, *Rt. Hon.* Sir (William John) Victor, K.B.E., C.B., D.S.O., E.D.

Wingate, *Capt.* Sir Miles Buckley, K.C.V.O.

Winnifrith, Sir (Alfred) John (Digby), K.C.B.

Winnington, Sir Francis Salwey William, Bt. (1755).

Winskill, *Air Commodore* Sir Archibald Little, K.C.V.O., C.B.E., D.F.C.

Winterbottom, Sir Walter, Kt., C.B.E.

Winterton, *Maj.-Gen.* Sir (Thomas) John (Willoughby), K.C.B., K.C.M.G., C.B.E.

Wiseman, Sir John William, Bt. (1628).

Wolfson, Sir David, Kt.

Wolfson, Sir Isaac, Bt., F.R.S. (1962).

Wolseley, Sir Charles Garnet Richard Mark, Bt. (1628).

Wolseley, Sir Garnet, Bt. (1745).

Wolstenholme, Sir Gordon Ethelbert Ward, Kt., O.B.E.

Wombwell, Sir George Philip Frederick, Bt. (1778).

Womersley, Sir Peter John Walter, Bt. (1945).

Wontner, Sir Hugh Walter Kingwell, G.B.E., C.V.O.

Wood, Sir Anthony John Page, Bt. (1837).

Wood, Sir David Basil Hill-, Bt. (1921).

Wood, Sir Frederick Ambrose Stuart, Kt.

Wood, Sir Henry Peart, Kt., C.B.E.

Wood, *Prof.* Sir John Crossley, Kt., C.B.E.

Wood, *Hon.* Sir John Kember, Kt., M.C.

Wood, Sir Martin Francis, Kt., O.B.E.

Wood, Sir Russell Dillon, K.C.V.O., V.R.D.

Wood, Sir William Alan, K.C.V.O., C.B.

Woodfield, Sir Philip John, K.C.B., C.B.E.

Woodhouse, *Rt. Hon.* Sir (Arthur) Owen, K.B.E., D.S.C.

Woodroffe, *Most Rev.* George Cuthbert Manning, K.B.E.

Woodroofe, Sir Ernest George, Kt., Ph.D.

Woodruff, *Prof.* Sir Michael Francis Addison, Kt., D.SC., F.R.S., F.R.C.S.

Woods, Sir Colin Philip Joseph, K.C.V.O., C.B.E.

Woods, *Most Rev.* Frank, K.B.E., D.D.

Woods, *Rt. Rev.* Robert Wilmer, K.C.V.O.

Woodward, *Hon.* Sir (Albert) Edward, Kt., O.B.E.

Woodward, *Admiral.* Sir John Forster, K.C.B.

Woolf, *Rt. Hon.* Sir Harry Kenneth, Kt.

Woolf, Sir John, Kt.

Woollaston, Sir (Mountford) Tosswill, Kt.

Wordie, Sir John Stewart, Kt., C.B.E., V.R.D.

Worsley, *General* Sir Richard Edward, G.C.B., O.B.E.

Worsley, Sir (William) Marcus (John), Bt. (1838).

Worthington, *Air Vice Marshal* Sir Geoffrey Luis, K.B.E., C.B.

Wraight, Sir John Richard, K.B.E., C.M.G.

Wraxall, Sir Charles Frederick Lascelles, Bt. (1813).

Wrey, Sir (Castel Richard) Bourchier, Bt. (1628).

Wright, Sir Allan Frederick, K.B.E.

Wright, Sir Denis Arthur Hepworth, G.C.M.G.

Wright, Sir Edward Maitland, Kt., D.Phil.,Ll.D., D.SC., F.R.S.E.

Wright, Sir (John) Oliver, G.C.M.G., G.C.V.O., D.S.C.

Wright, Sir Patrick Richard Henry, K.C.M.G.

Wright, Sir Paul Hervé Giraud, K.C.M.G., O.B.E.

Wright, *Hon.* Sir Reginald Charles, Kt.

Wright, Sir Richard Michael Cory-, Bt. (1903).

Wright, Sir Rowland Sydney, Kt., C.B.E.

Wrightson, Sir Charles Mark Garmondsway, Bt. (1900).

Wykeham, *Air Marshal* Sir Peter Guy, K.C.B., D.S.O., O.B.E., D.F.C., A.F.C.

Wylie, Sir Campbell, Kt., E.D., Q.C.

Wyndham, Sir Harold Stanley, Kt., C.B.E.

Wynn, *Col.* Sir (Owen) Watkin Williams-, Bt., C.B.E. (1688).

Wynter, Sir Luther Reginald, Kt., C.B.E.

Yapp, Sir Stanley Graham, Kt.

Yarrow, Sir Eric Grant, Bt., M.B.E. (1916).

Yeend, Sir Geoffrey John, Kt., C.B.E.

Yellowlees, Sir Henry, K.C.B.

Yocklunn, Sir John (Soong Chung), K.C.V.O.

Youde, *Sir Edward*, G.C.M.G., G.C.V.O., M.B.E.

Youens, Sir Peter William, Kt., C.M.G., O.B.E.

Young, Sir Brian Walter Mark, Kt.

Young, *Lt.-Gen.* Sir David Tod, K.B.E., C.B., D.F.C.

Young, *Prof.* Sir Frank George, Kt., D.SC., Ph.D., F.R.S.

Young, Sir George Samuel Knatchbull, Bt., M.P. (1813).

Young, *Most Rev.* Guilford, K.B.E.

Young, *Hon.* Sir Harold William, K.C.M.G.

Young, Sir John Kenyon Roe, Bt. (1821).

Young, *Hon.* Sir John McIntosh, K.C.M.G.

Young, Sir Leslie Clarence, Kt., C.B.E.

Young, Sir Norman Smith, Kt.

Young, Sir Richard Dilworth, Kt.

Young, Sir Robert Christopher Mackworth-, G.C.V.O.

Young, Sir Roger William, Kt.

Young, Sir Stephen Stewart Templeton, Bt. (1945).

Young, Sir William Neil, Bt. (1769).

Younger, *Maj.-Gen.* Sir John William, Bt., C.B.E. (1911).

Younger, Sir William McEwan, Bt., D.S.O. (1964).

Zeidler, Sir David Ronald, Kt. C.B.E.

Zoleveke, Sir Gideon Pitabose, K.B.E.

Zurenuo, *Rt. Rev.* Zurewe Kamong, Kt., O.B.E.

Baronetcies Extinct (Since last issue).—Lambart (U.K., 1911); Hoare (U.K., 1962); Stafford-King-Harman (U.K., 1914); Fraser (U.K., 1961); Doyle (U.K., 1828); Fry (U.K., 1894); Hooper (U.K., 1962); Middlemore (U.K., 1919); Stephen (U.K., 1891).

Dames Grand Cross and Dames Commanders of the Order of the Bath, the Order of St. Michael and St. George, the Royal Victorian Order and the Order of the British Empire

NOTE.—Dames Grand Cross (G.C.B., G.C.M.G., G.C.V.O. or G.B.E.) and Dames Commanders (D.C.B., D.C.M.G., D.C.V.O. or D.B.E.) are addressed in a manner similar to that of Knights Grand Cross or Knights Commanders, *e.g.* "Miss Florence Smith" after receiving the honour would be addressed as "Dame Florence", and in writing as "Dame Florence Smith, G. (or D.) C.B., G. (or D.) C.M.G., G. (or D.) C.V.O., OR G. (or D.) B.E." Where such award is made to a lady already in enjoyment of a higher title the appropriate letters are appended to her name, *e.g.* "The Countess of —— G.C.V.O." Peeresses in their own right, and Life Peeresses, are not included in this list. Dames Grand Cross rank after wives of Baronets and before wives of Knights Grand Cross. Dames Commanders rank after the wives of Knights Grand Cross and before the wives of Knights Commanders.

DAMES GRAND CROSS AND DAMES COMMANDERS

H.M. Queen Elizabeth The Queen Mother, K.G., K.T., C.I., G.M.V.O.

H.R.H. The Princess Margaret, Countess of Snowdon, C.I., G.C.V.O.

H.R.H. The Princess Alice, Duchess of Gloucester, G.C.B., C.I., G.C.V.O., G.B.E.

H.R.H. The Princess Alexandra of Kent, G.C.V.O.

H.R.H. The Princess Royal, G.C.V.O.

H.R.H. The Duchess of Kent, G.C.V.O.

Abercorn, Mary, Duchess of, G.C.V.O.

Albemarle, The Countess of, D.B.E.

Anderson, Dame Judith, D.B.E.

Anderson, *Brig.* Hon. Dame Mary Mackenzie (Mrs. Pihl), D.B.E.

Anglesey, (Elizabeth) Shirley Vaughan, Marchioness of, D.B.E.

Ashcroft, Dame Peggy (Mrs. Hutchinson), D.B.E.

Austin, Dame (Mary) Valerie Hall, D.B.E.

Baker, Dame Janet Abbott (Mrs. Shelley), D.B.E.

Baring, Lady Rose Gwendolen Louisa, D.C.V.O.

Barnes, Dame (Alice) Josephine (Mary Taylor), (Dame Josephine Warren), D.B.E., F.R.C.P., F.R.C.S.

Bate, Dame Zara Kate, D.B.E.

Beaurepaire, Dame Beryl Edith, D.B.E.

Berry, Dame Alice Miriam, D.B.E.

Bishop, Dame (Margaret) Joyce, D.B.E.

Blaxland, Dame Helen Frances, D.B.E.

Booth, *Hon.* Dame Margaret Myfanwy Wood, D.B.E.

Bottomley, Dame Bessie Ellen, D.B.E.

Boyd, Dame Vivienne Myra, D.B.E.

Brazill, Dame Josephine (Sister Mary Philippa), D.B.E.

Brecknock, Marjorie, Countess of, D.B.E.

Breen, Dame Marie Freda, D.B.E.

Bridges, Dame Mary Patricia, D.B.E.

Brown, Dame Beryl Paston, D.B.E.

Browne, Lady Moyra Blanche Madeleine, D.B.E.

Bryans, Dame Anne Margaret, D.B.E.

Bryce, Dame Isabel Graham, D.B.E.

Burnside, Dame Edith, D.B.E.

Butler-Sloss, *Hon.* Dame (Ann) Elizabeth (Oldfield), D.B.E.

Buttfield, Dame Nancy Eileen, D.B.E.

Bynoe, Dame Hilda Louisa, D.B.E.

Cartwright, Dame Mary Lucy, D.B.E., SC.D., D.Phil., F.R.S.

Cayford, Dame Florence Evelyn, D.B.E.

Chesterton, Dame Elizabeth Ursula, D.B.E.

Clay, Dame Marie Mildred, D.B.E.

Cleland, Dame Rachel, D.B.E.

Clode, Dame (Emma) Frances (Heather), D.B.E.

Cockayne, Dame Elizabeth, D.B.E.

Coker, Dame Elizabeth, D.B.E.

Coles, Dame Mabel Irene, D.B.E.

Colvin, *Brig.* Dame Mary Katherine Rosamond, D.B.E., T.D.

Cooper, Dame Whina, D.B.E.

Coulshed, Dame (Mary) Frances, D.B.E., T.D.

Cozens, *Brig.* Dame (Florence) Barbara, D.B.E., R.R.C.

Crowe, Dame Sylvia, D.B.E.

Daws, Dame Joyce Margaretta, D.B.E.

De La Warr, Sylvia, Countess, D.B.E.

Dell, Dame Miriam Patricia, D.B.E.

de Valois, Dame Ninette, C.H., D.B.E.

Devonshire, Mary Alice, Duchess of, G.C.V.O., C.B.E.

Dickson, Dame Violet Penelope, D.B.E.

Donaldson, Dame (Dorothy) Mary, G.B.E.

Doyle, *Air Commandant* Dame Jean Lena Annette Conan (Lady Bromet), D.B.E.

Drake, *Brig.* Dame Jean Elizabeth Rivett Rivett-, D.B.E.

Dugdale, Dame Kathryn Edith Helen, D.C.V.O.

du Maurier, Dame Daphne (Lady Browning), D.B.E.

Durack, Dame Mary (Mrs. H. C. Miller), D.B.E.

Elgin & Kincardine, Katherine, Countess of, D.B.E.

Evans, Lady Olwen Elizabeth Carey, D.B.E.

Fenner, Dame Peggy Edith, D.B.E., M.P.

Fermoy, Ruth Sylvia, Lady, D.C.V.O., O.B.E.

Fitton, Dame Doris Alice (Mrs. Mason), D.B.E.

Fonteyn, Dame Margot, D.B.E.

Fraser, Dame Dorothy Rita, D.B.E.

Friend, Dame Phyllis Muriel, D.B.E.

Frink, Dame Elisabeth, D.B.E., R.A.

Frost, Dame Phyllis Irene, D.B.E.

Gallagher, Dame Monica Josephine, D.B.E.

Gardiner, Dame Helen Louisa, D.B.E., M.V.O.

Gardner, Dame Frances, D.B.E.

Gibbs, Dame Molly Peel, D.B.E.

Giles, *Air Commandant* Dame Pauline (Mrs. Parsons), D.B.E., R.R.C.

Godwin, Dame (Beatrice) Anne, D.B.E.

Golding, Dame (Cecilie) Monica, D.B.E.

Gordon, Dame Minita Elmira, G.C.M.G., G.C.V.O.

Grafton, The Duchess of, G.C.V.O.

Green, Dame Mary Georgina, D.B.E.

Guilfoyle, Dame Margaret Georgina Constance. D.B.E.

Hall, Dame Catherine Mary, D.B.E.

Hambleden, Patricia, Viscountess, D.C.V.O.

Hammond, Dame Joan Hood, D.B.E.

Harris, Dame (Muriel) Diana Reader-, D.B.E.

Heilbron, *Hon.* Dame Rose, D.B.E.

Henrison, Dame Anne Elizabeth Rosina, D.B.E.

Herbison, Dame Jean Marjory, D.B.E., C.M.G.

Hill, Dame Elizabeth Mary, D.B.E.

Hill, *Air Commodore* Dame Felicity Barbara, D.B.E.

Hiller, Dame Wendy (Mrs. Gow), D.B.E.

Holland-Martin, Rosamund Mary, Lady, D.B.E.

Horsman, Dame Dorothea Jean, D.B.E.

Howard, Dame Rosemary Christian, D.B.E.

Hunter, Dame Pamela, D.B.E.

Hussey, Lady Susan Katharine, D.C.V.O.

Isaacs, Dame Albertha Madeline, D.B.E.

James, Dame Naomi Christine, D.B.E.

Jenkins, Dame (Mary) Jennifer, D.B.E.

Jessel, Dame Penelope, D.B.E.

Jones, Dame Gwyneth (Mrs. Haberfeld-Jones), D.B.E.

Kekedo, Dame Mary, D.B.E., B.E.M.

Kelleher, Dame Joan, D.B.E.

Kettlewell, *Commandant* Dame Marion Mildred, D.B.E.

Kidd, Dame Margaret Henderson (Mrs. Macdonald), D.B.E., Q.C.

Kilroy, Dame Alix Hester Marie (Lady Meynell), D.B.E.

Kirk, Dame (Lucy) Ruth, D.B.E.

Knight, Dame (Joan Christabel) Jill, D.B.E., M.P.

Kramer, *Prof.* Dame Leonie Judith, D.B.E.

Lancaster, Dame Jean, D.B.E.

Lane, Dame Elizabeth Kathleen, D.B.E.

Lister, Dame Unity Viola, D.B.E.

Litchfield, Dame Ruby Beatrice, D.B.E.

Lloyd, Dame Hilda Nora, D.B.E.

Lowrey, *Air Commandant* Dame Alice, D.B.E., R.R.C.

Lynn, Dame Vera (Mrs. Lewis), D.B.E.

Mackinnon, Dame (Una) Patricia, D.B.E.

Macknight, Dame Ella Annie Noble, D.B.E., M.D.

Macmillan of Ovenden, Katharine, Viscountess, D.B.E.

Maconchy, Dame Elizabeth Violet (Mrs. Le Fanu), D.B.E.

Mann, Dame Ida Caroline, D.B.E., D.SC., F.R.C.S.

Markova, Dame Alicia, D.B.E.

Maxwell-Scott, Dame Jean Mary Monica, D.C.V.O.

Menzies, Dame Pattie Maie, G.B.E.

Metge, Dr. Dame (Alice) Joan, D.B.E.

Miles, Dame Margaret, D.B.E.

Miller, Dame Mabel Flora Hobart, D.B.E.

Mitchell, *Hon.* Dame Roma Flinders, D.B.E.

Morrison, *Hon.* Dame Mary Anne, D.C.V.O.

Munro, Dame Alison, D.B.E.

Murdoch, Dame Elisabeth Joy, D.B.E.

Murdoch, Dame (Jean) Iris (Mrs. Bayley), D.B.E.

Murray, Dame (Alice) Rosemary, D.B.E., D.Phil.

Niccol, Dame Kathleen Agnes, D.B.E.

Norris, Dame Ada May, D.B.E., C.M.G.

Ollerenshaw, Dame Kathleen Mary, D.B.E., D.Phil.

Origo, *Marchesa* Iris, D.B.E.

Park, Dame Merle Florence (Mrs. Bloch), D.B.E.

Parker, Dame Marjorie Alice Collett, D.B.E.

Paterson, Dame Betty Fraser Ross, D.B.E.

Pepys, Lady (Mary) Rachel, D.C.V.O.

Pickerill, Dame Cecily Mary Wise, D.B.E.

Plowden, The Lady, D.B.E.

Prendergast, Dame Simone Ruth, D.B.E.

Prentice, Dame Winifred Eva, D.B.E.

Purves, Dame Daphne Helen, D.B.E.

Pyke, The Lady, D.B.E.

Quinn, Dame Sheila Margaret Imelda, D.B.E.

Railton, *Brig.* Dame Mary, D.B.E.

Railton, Dame Ruth (Mrs. King), D.B.E.

Rankin, Lady Jean Margaret Florence, D.C.V.O.

Raven, Dame Kathleen Annie (Mrs. Ingram), D.B.E.

Reader, Dame Audrey Tattie Hinchcliff, D.B.E.

Rees, Dame Dorothy Mary, D.B.E.

Riddelsdell, Dame Mildred, D.C.B., C.B.E.

Ridley, Dame (Mildred) Betty, D.B.E.

Roberts, Dame Jean, D.B.E.

Roberts, Dame Joan Howard, D.B.E.

Roberts, Dame Shelagh Marjorie, D.B.E.

Robertson, *Commandant* Dame Nancy Margaret, D.B.E.

Roe, Dame Raigh Edith, D.B.E.

Saunders, Dame Cicely Mary Strode, D.B.E., F.R.C.P.

Scott, Dame Catherine Campbell, D.B.E.

Scott, Dame Margaret, (Dame Catherine Margaret Mary Denton), D.B.E.

Seccombe, Dame Joan Anna Dalziel, D.B.E.

Shenfield, Dame Barbara Estelle, D.B.E.

Shepherd, Dame Margaret Alice, D.B.E.

Sherlock, *Prof.* Dame Sheila Patricia Violet, D.B.E., M.D., F.R.C.P.

Smieton, Dame Mary Guillan, D.B.E.

Smith, Lady Abel, D.C.V.O.

Smith, Dame Enid Mary Russell Russell-, D.B.E.

Smith, Dame Margot, D.B.E.

Snagge, Dame Nancy Marion, D.B.E.

Soames, The Lady, D.B.E.

Stark, Dame Freya (Mrs. Perowne), D.B.E.

Stephens, *Air Commandant* Dame Anne, D.B.E.

Stevenson, Dame Hilda Mabel, D.B.E.

Stewart, Dame Muriel Acadia, D.B.E.

Sutherland, Dame Joan (Mrs. Bonynge), D.B.E.

Taylor, Dame Jean Elizabeth, D.C.V.O.

Te Atairangikaahu, Arikinui, D.B.E.

Te Kanawa, Dame Kiri Janette (Mrs. Park), D.B.E.

Tilney, Guinevere, Lady, D.B.E.

Tizard, Dame Catherine Anne, D.B.E.

Tokiel, Dame Rosa, D.B.E.

Turner, Dame Eva, D.B.E.

Turner, *Brig.* Dame Margot, D.B.E., R.R.C.

Tyrwhitt, *Brig.* Dame Mary Joan Caroline, D.B.E., T.D.

Uatioa, Dame Mere, D.B.E.

Uvarov, Dame Olga, D.B.E.

Van Praagh, Dame Peggy, D.B.E.

Varley, Dame Joan Fleetwood, D.B.E.

Vaughan, Dame Janet Maria, (Mrs. Gourlay), D.B.E., F.R.S.

Wakehurst, Margaret, Lady, D.B.E.

Walker, Dame Susan Armour, D.B.E.

Wall, (Alice) Anne, (Mrs. Michael Wall), D.C.V.O.

Warburton, Dame Anne Marion, D.C.V.O., C.M.G.

Wedega, Dame Alice, D.B.E.

Wedgwood, Dame (Cicely) Veronica, O.M., D.B.E.

Weston, Dame Margaret Kate, D.B.E.

Williamson, Dame (Elsie) Marjorie, D.B.E., Ph.D.

Winner, Dame Albertine Louise, D.B.E., M.D.

Wormald, Dame Ethel May, D.B.E.

Yarwood, Dame Elizabeth Ann, D.B.E.

Yonge, Dame (Ida) Felicity (Ann), D.B.E.

THE VICTORIA CROSS, V.C.

For Conspicuous Bravery

The ribbon *is Crimson* for all Services (until 1918 it was *Blue* for Royal Navy).

Instituted on January 29, 1856, the Victoria Cross was awarded retrospectively to 1854, the first being held by Lieut. C. D. Lucas, R.N. for bravery in the Baltic Sea on June 21, 1854 (gazetted Feb. 24, 1857). The first 62 Crosses were presented by Queen Victoria in Hyde Park, London, on June 26, 1857.

The V.C. is worn before all other decorations, on the left breast, and consists of a cross-pattée of bronze, 1¼ inches in diameter, with the Royal Crown surmounted by a lion in the centre, and beneath there is the inscription "For Valour." Holders of the V.C. receive a tax-free annuity of £100, irrespective of need or other conditions. In 1911, the right to receive the Cross was extended to Indian soldiers, and in 1920 a Royal Warrant extended the right to Matrons, Sisters and Nurses, and the Staff of the Nursing Services and other services pertaining to Hospitals and Nursing, and to Civilians of either sex regularly or temporarily under the orders, direction or supervision of the Naval, Military, or Air Forces of the Crown.

Surviving Recipients of the Victoria Cross

Agansing Rai, *Havildar* (Gurkha Rifles), *World War*....................................1944

Ali Haidar, *Jemadar* (Frontier Force Rifles), *World War*.............................1945

Anderson, *Lt.-Col.* C. G. W., M.C. (Australian M.F.), *World War*.........................1942

Annand, *Capt.* R. W. (Durham L.I.), *World War*....................................1940

Bhanbhagta Gurung, *Capt.* (2nd Gurkha Rifles), *World War*.........................1945

Bhandari Ram, *Capt.* (Baluch R.), *World War* ..1944

Burton, *Corpl.* R. H. (Duke of Wellington's R.), *World War* 1944

Campbell, *Brigadier* L. M., D.S.O., O.B.E., T.D. (A. & S. Highrs.), *World War*.............1943

Chapman, *Sergt.* E. T., B.E.M. (Monmouthshire R.), *World War*.........................1945

Cheshire, *Group Capt.* G. L., D.S.O., D.F.C. (R.A.F.), *World War* 1944

Cruickshank, *Fl. Lt.* J. A. (R.A.F.V.R.), *World War*....................................1944

Cutler, Sir A. R., K.C.M.G., K.C.V.O., C.B.E. (Australia), *World War* 1941

De L'Isle, *Maj.* The Viscount, K.G., P.C., G.C.M.G., G.C.V.O. (*Hon.* W. P. Sidney) (Gren. Gds.), *World War* 1944

Eardley, *Sergt.* G. H., M.M. (K.S.L.I.), *World War* 1944

Elliott, *Lt.* the Rev. K. (N.Z.M.F.), *World War* ..1942

Ervine-Andrews, *Lt.-Col.* H. M. (E. Lancs. R.), *World War* 1940

Foote, *Maj.-Gen.* H. R. B., C.B., D.S.O. (R. Tank R.), *World War*..........................1942

Foote, Rev. J. W. (Canada), *World War* 1942

Fraser, *Cdr.* I. E., D.S.C. (R.N.R.), *World War* 1945

Ganju Lama, *Jemadar*, M.M. (Gurkha Rifles), *World War* 1944

Gardner, *Capt.* P. J., M.C. (R.T.R.), *World War* ..1941

Ghale, *Subedar* Gaje (Gurkha Rifles), *World War*............................1943
Gian Singh, *Jemadar* (Punjab R.), *World War* ..1945
Gould, *Lt.* T. W. (R.N.), *World War* 1942
Hinton, *Sergt.* J. D. (N.Z.M.F.), *World War* 1941
Jackson, *W.O.* N. C. (R.A.F.V.R.), *World War* ...1944
Jamieson, *Maj.* D. A. (R. Norfolk R.), *World War*............................1944
Kenna, *Pte.* E. (Australian M.F.), *World War* ..1945
Kenneally, *C.-Q.-M.-S.* J. P. (Irish Gds.), *World War*............................1943
Lachiman Gurung, *Rifleman* (Gurkha Rifles), *World War*............................1945
Laurent, *Lt.* H. J. (N.Z. Rif. Bgde.), *Gt. War*.....1918
Learoyd, *Wing-Cmdr.* R. A. B. (R.A.F.), *World War*............................1940
Mahony, *Lt.-Col.* J. K., C.D. (Westminster R., Canada), *World War* 1944
Merritt, *Lt.-Col.* C. C. I., C.D. (S. Saskatchewan R.), *World War* 1942
Norton, *Capt.* G. R., M.M. (S.A.M.F.), *World War*............................1944
Parkash Singh, *Maj.* (Punjab R.), *World War* ...1943
Payne, *W.O.* K. (Australian Army), *Vietnam* ...1969
Place, *Rear-Adm.* B. C. G., C.B., D.S.C. (R.N.), *World War* 1943
Porteous, *Brig.* P. A. (R.A.), *World War* 1942

Rambahadur Limbu, *Lt.* (Gurkha Rifles), *Sarawak* 1965
Reid, *Fl.-Lt.* W. (R.A.F.V.R.), *World War*.......1943
Rutherford, *Capt.* C. S., M.C., M.M. (Quebec R.), *Gt. War* 1918
Smith, *Sergt.* E. A., C.D. (Seaforth Highrs. of Canada), *World War* 1944
Smythe, *Capt.* Q. G. M. (S.A.M.F.), *World War* ..1942
Speakman, *Sergt.* W. (Black Watch), *Korea* 1951
Starcevich, *Pte.* L. T. (Australia), *World War* 1945
Tilston, *Col.* F. A. (Essex Scottish, Canada), *World War* 1945
Tulbahadur Pun, *W.O. I.* (Gurkha Rifles), *World War* 1944
Umrao Singh, *Sub-Major* (I.A.), *World War* 1944
Upham, *Capt.* C. H. (and Bar, 1942), (N.Z.M.F.), *World War* 1941
Watkins, *Maj. Rt. Hon.* Sir Tasker (Welch R.), *World War* 1944
West, *Air Commodore* Ferdinand M. F., C.B.E., M.C. (R.A.F.), *Gt. War* 1918
Wilson, *Lt.-Col.* E. C. T. (E. Surrey R.), *World War* 1940
Wright, *C.S.M.* P. H. (Coldstream Gds.), *World War* 1943

THE GEORGE CROSS, G.C. (1940)

For Gallantry

The ribbon is *dark blue* threaded through a bar adorned with laurel leaves.
Instituted *September, 24th,* 1940 (with amendments, *November 3rd,* 1942).

The George Cross is worn before all other decorations (except the V.C.) on the left breast § and consists of a plain silver cross with four equal limbs, the cross having in the centre a circular medallion bearing a design showing St. George and the Dragon. The inscription "For Gallantry" appears round the medallion and in the angle of each limb of the cross is the Royal cypher "G VI" forming a circle concentric with the medallion. The reverse is plain and bears the name of the recipient and the date of the award. The cross is suspended by a ring from a bar adorned with laurel leaves on dark blue ribbon 1½ inches wide.

The cross is intended primarily for civilians and awards to the fighting services are confined to actions for which purely military honours are not normally granted. It is awarded only for acts of the greatest heroism or of the most conspicuous courage in circumstances of extreme danger. From April 1, 1965, holders of the Cross have received a tax-free annuity of £100.

§ When worn by a woman it may be worn on the left shoulder from a ribbon of the same width and colour fashioned into a bow.

Empire Gallantry Medal.—The Royal Warrant which ordained that the grant of the Empire Gallantry Medal should cease authorized holders of that medal to return it to the Central Chancery of the Orders of Knighthood and to receive in exchange the George Cross. A similar provision applied to posthumous awards of the Empire Gallantry Medal made after the outbreak of war in 1939.

In October 1971 all surviving holders of the Albert Medal and the Edward Medal exchanged those decorations for the George Cross.

THE DISTINGUISHED SERVICE ORDER (1886)—D.S.O.

Ribbon, Red, with Blue Edges.

Bestowed in recognition of especial services in action of commissioned officers in the Navy, Army and Royal Air Force and (1942) Mercantile Marine. The members are Companions only and rank immediately before the 4th Class of the Royal Victorian Order. A Bar may be awarded for any additional act of service.

THE ORDER OF ST. JOHN

The Most Venerable Order of the Hospital of St. John of Jerusalem

St. John's Gate, Clerkenwell, EC1M 4DA

Grand Prior, H.R.H. The Duke of Gloucester, G.C.V.O.

Lord Prior, The Earl Cathcart, C.B., D.S.O., M.C.   *Chancellor,* The Lord Grey of Naunton, G.C.M.G., G.C.V.O., O.B.E.

300 [1988

PRINCIPAL DECORATIONS AND MEDALS (in order of Precedence)

Victoria Cross. (V.C.)—1856.

George Cross. (G.C.)—1940.

British Orders of Knighthood, Etc. (For D.S.O. *see* p. 252).

Baronet's Badge

Knight Bachelor's Badge

Decorations

Royal Red Cross. (Class I—R.R.C.)—1883.—For ladies.

Distinguished Service Cross. (D.S.C.)—1914.—For officers of R.N. below the rank of Captain, and Warrant Officers.

Military Cross. (M.C.)—Dec. 1914.—Awarded to Captains, Lieutenants, and Warrant Officers (Cl I. and II.) in the Army and Indian and Colonial Forces.

Distinguished Flying Cross. (D.F.C.)—1918.—For officers and Warrant Officers in the R.A.F. (and Fleet Air Arm from April 9, 1941) for acts of gallantry when flying in active operations against the enemy.

Air Force Cross. (A.F.C.)—1918.—Instituted as preceding but for acts of courage or devotion to duty when flying, although not in active operations against the enemy (extended to Fleet Air Arm since April 9, 1941).

Royal Red Cross (Class II—A.R.R.C.).

Order of British India.

Kaisar-i-Hind Medal.

Order of St. John.

Medals for Gallantry and Distinguished Conduct

Union of South Africa Queen's Medal for Bravery, in Gold.

Distinguished Conduct Medal. (D.C.M.)—1854.—Awarded to warrant officers, non-commissioned officers and men of the Army and R.A.F.

Conspicuous Gallantry Medal. (C.G.M.)—1874.—Is bestowed upon warrant officers and men of the R.N. and since 1942 of Mercantile Marine and R.A.F.

The George Medal. (G.M.)—1940.

Queen's Police Medal for Gallantry.

Queen's Fire Service Medal for Gallantry.

Royal West African Frontier Force Distinguished Conduct Medal.

King's African Rifles Distinguished Conduct Medal.

Indian Distinguished Service Medal.

Union of South Africa Queen's Medal for Bravery, in Silver.

Distinguished Service Medal. (D.S.M.)—1914.—For chief petty officers, petty officers and men, of all branches of the Royal Navy, and since 1942 of Mercantile Marine; non-commissioned officers and men of the Royal Marines; all other persons holding corresponding positions in Her Majesty's Service afloat.

Military Medal. (M.M.)—1916.—For warrant and non-commissioned officers and men and serving women.

Distinguished Flying Medal. (D.F.M.)—1918.—and the Air Force Medal. (A.F.M.)—For warrant and non-commissioned officers and men for equivalent services as for D.F.C. and A.F.C. (extended to Fleet Air Arm, 1941).

Constabulary Medal (Ireland).

Medal for Saving Life at Sea.

Indian Order of Merit (Civil).

Indian Police Medal for Gallantry.

Ceylon Police Medal for Gallantry.

Sierra Leone Police Medal for Gallantry.

Sierra Leone Fire Brigades Medal for Gallantry.

Colonial Police Medal for Gallantry. (C.P.M.)

Queen's Gallantry Medal.—1974.

Royal Victorian Medal.—(Gold, Silver and Bronze).

British Empire Medal. (B.E.M.)—(formerly the Medal of the Order of the British Empire, for Meritorious Service; also includes the Medal of the Order awarded before Dec. 29, 1922).

Queen's Police (Q.P.M.) and Fire Services Medals for Distinguished Service, (Q.F.S.M.).

Queen's Medal for Chiefs.

War Medals and Stars (in order of date).

Polar Medals (in order of date).

Imperial Service Medal.

Police Medals for Valuable Service.

Badge of Honour.

Jubilee, Coronation and Durbar Medals.

King George V, King George VI and Queen Elizabeth II Long and Faithful Service Medals.

Efficiency and Long Service Decorations and Medals.

Medal for Meritorious Service.

Long Service and Good Conduct Medal—(Military).

Naval Long Service and Good Conduct Medal.

Royal Marine Meritorious Service Medal.

Royal Air Force Meritorious Service Medal.

Royal Air Force Long Service and Good Conduct Medal.

Medal for Long Service and Good Conduct (Ulster Defence Regiment).

Police and Fire Brigade Long Service and Good Conduct Medal.

Colonial Police and Fire Brigades Long Service Medal.

Colonial Prison Service Medal.

Army Emergency Reserve Decoration.—(E.R.D.)

Volunteer Officer's Decoration.—(V.D.)

Volunteer Long Service Medal.

Volunteer Officer's Decoration (for India and the Colonies).

Volunteer Long Service Medal (for India and the Colonies).

Colonial Auxiliary Forces Officer's Decoration.

Colonial Auxiliary Forces Long Service Medal.

Medal for Good Shooting (Naval).

Militia Long Service Medal.

Imperial Yeomanry Long Service Medal.

Territorial Decoration.—(T.D.)—1908.

Efficiency Decoration.—(E.D.)

Territorial Efficiency Medal.

Efficiency Medal.

Special Reserve Long Service and Good Conduct Medal.

Decoration for Officers, Royal Navy Reserve. (R.D.)—1910.

Decoration for Officers, R.N.V.R.—(V.R.D.)

Royal Naval Reserve Long Service and Good Conduct Medal.

R.N.V.R. Long Service and Good Conduct Medal.

Royal Naval Auxiliary Sick Berth Reserve Long Service and Good Conduct Medal.

Royal Fleet Reserve Long Service and Good Conduct Medal.

Royal Naval Wireless Auxiliary Reserve Long Service and Good Conduct Medal.

Air Efficiency Award. (A.E.)—1942.

Ulster Defence Regiment Medal.

The Queen's Medal.—(For champion shots in the R.N., R.M., R.N.Z.N., Army, R.A.F.)

Cadet Forces Medals.—1950.

Coast Life Saving Corps Long Service Medal.—1911.

Special Constabulary Long Service Medal.

Royal Observer Corps Medal.

Civil Defence Long Service Medal.

Royal Ulster Constabulary Service Medal.

Service Medal of the Order of St. John.

Badge of the Order of the League of Mercy.

Voluntary Medical Service Medal.—1932.

Women's Royal Voluntary Service Medal.

Colonial Special Constabulary Medal.

Foreign Orders, Decorations and Medals (in order of date).

THE UNITED KINGDOM CONSTITUTION

The United Kingdom constitution is not contained in any single document but has evolved in the course of time, formed partly by statute, partly by common law and partly by convention. A constitutional monarchy, the United Kingdom is governed by Ministers of the Crown in the name of the Sovereign, who is head both of the state and the government.

The organs of government are the *legislature* (Parliament), the *executive* and the *judiciary*. The executive consists of Her Majesty's Government (Cabinet and other Ministers), government departments (*see* pp. 367–447), local authorities (*see* Index), and public corporations operating nationalised industries or social or cultural services (*see* pp. 367–447). The judiciary, *i.e.* judges, pronounce on the law, both written and unwritten, interpret statutes and are responsible for the enforcement of the law; the judiciary is independent of both the legislature and the executive (*see* Law Courts and Offices).

THE MONARCHY

The Sovereign personifies the state and is, in law, an integral part of the legislature, head of the executive, head of the judiciary, the Commander-in-Chief of all armed forces of the Crown and the 'Supreme Governor' of the Church of England. The seat of the monarchy is in the United Kingdom. In the Channel Islands and the Isle of Man, which are Crown dependencies, the Sovereign is represented by a Lieutenant-Governor; in the member states of the Commonwealth of which the Sovereign is head of state, her representative is a Governor-General (*see also* p. 693); in United Kingdom dependencies the Sovereign is usually represented by a Governor, who is responsible to the British Government.

Although the powers of the monarchy are now very limited, restricted mainly to the advisory and ceremonial, there are important acts of government which require the participation of the Sovereign. These include summoning, proroguing and dissolving Parliament, giving Royal Assent to Bills passed by Parliament, appointing important office-holders, e.g. government ministers, judges, bishops, and governors, conferring peerages, knighthoods and other honours, and granting pardon to a person wrongly convicted of a crime. An important function is appointing a Prime Minister, by convention the leader of the political party which enjoys, or can secure, a majority of votes in the House of Commons. In international affairs the Sovereign as head of State has the power to declare war and make peace, to recognise foreign states and governments, to conclude treaties and to annex or cede territory. However, as the Sovereign entrusts executive power to Ministers of the Crown and acts on the advice of her Ministers, which she cannot ignore, in practice royal prerogative powers are exercised by Ministers, who are responsible to Parliament.

Ministerial responsibility does not diminish the Sovereign's importance to the smooth working of government. She holds meetings of the Privy Council, gives audiences to her Ministers and other officials at home and overseas, receives accounts of Cabinet decisions, reads dispatches and signs state papers; she must be informed and consulted on every aspect of national life; and she must show complete impartiality.

In the event of the Sovereign's absence abroad, it is necessary to appoint *Counsellors of State* under Letters Patent to carry out the chief functions of the Monarch, including the holding of Privy Councils and giving Royal Assent to Acts passed by Parliament. The normal procedure is to appoint as Counsellors three or four members of the Royal Family among those remaining in the United Kingdom. In the event of the Sovereign on accession being under the age of eighteen years, or at any time unavailable or incapacitated by infirmity of mind or body for the performance of the royal functions, provision is made for a Regency.

THE PRIVY COUNCIL

The Sovereign in Council, or Privy Council, was the chief source of executive power until the system of Cabinet government developed. Now its main function is to advise the Sovereign to approve Orders in Council and to advise on the issue of royal proclamations. The Council's own statutory responsibilities (independent of the powers of the Sovereign in Council) include powers of supervision over the registering bodies for the medical and allied professions. A full Council is summoned only on the death of the Sovereign or when the Sovereign announces his or her intention to marry (for full list of Counsellors, see pp. 258–259).

There are a number of advisory Privy Council committees, whose meetings the Sovereign does not attend. Some are prerogative committees, such as those dealing with legislative matters submitted by the legislatures of the Channel Islands and the Isle of Man or with applications for charters of incorporation; and some are provided for by statute, *e.g.* those for the universities of Oxford and Cambridge and the Scottish universities.

The Judicial Committee of the Privy Council is the final court of appeal from courts of the United Kingdom dependencies, courts of independent Commonwealth countries which have retained the right of appeal, courts of the Channel Islands and the Isle of Man, some professional and disciplinary committees, and church sources. The Committee is composed of all Privy Counsellors who hold, or have held, high judicial office, although usually only three or five hear each case.

Administrative work is carried out by the Privy Council Office under the direction of the Lord President of the Council, a Cabinet Minister.

PARLIAMENT

Parliament is the supreme law-making authority and can legislate for the United Kingdom as a whole or for any parts of it separately (the Channel Islands and the Isle of Man are Crown dependencies and not part of the United Kingdom). The main functions of Parliament are to pass laws, to provide (by voting taxation) the means of carrying on the work of government and to scrutinise government policy and administration, particularly proposals for expenditure. By custom, Parliament is also consulted before the ratification of international treaties and agreements.

Parliament emerged during the late thirteenth and early fourteenth centuries. The nucleus of early Parliaments were the officers of the King's household and the King's judges, joined by such ecclesiastical and lay magnates as the King might summon, and occasionally by the knights of the shires, burgesses and proctors of the lower clergy. By the end of Edward III's reign a "House of Commons" was beginning to appear: the first known Speaker was elected in 1377.

Parliamentary procedure is based on custom and precedent, partly formulated in the Standing Orders of both Houses (*see* p. 307), and each House has the right to control its own internal proceedings and to commit for contempt. The system of debate in the two Houses is similar; when a motion has been moved, the Speaker proposes the question as the subject of a debate. Members speak from wherever they have been sitting. Questions are decided by a vote on a simple majority. Draft legislation is introduced, in either House, as a public Bill. Public Bills can be introduced by a Government Minister or a private Member, but in practice the majority of Bills which become law are introduced by the Government. To become law, a Bill must be passed by each House (for parliamentary stages, *see* Bill, p. 305) and then sent to the Sovereign for the Royal Assent, after receipt of which it becomes an Act of Parliament.

Proceedings of both Houses are public, except on extremely rare occasions. The minutes (called Votes and Proceedings in the Commons, and Minutes of Proceedings in the Lords) and the speeches (The Official Report of Parliamentary Debates, *Hansard*) are published daily. Proceedings are also recorded for sound transmission on radio and television; a Parliamentary Sound Archive has been established. Since January 1985, the House of Lords has allowed television cameras into its debates and Select Committees.

By the Parliament Act of 1911, the maximum duration of a Parliament is five years, if not previously dissolved, the term being reckoned from the date given on the writs for the new Parliament. The maximum life has been prolonged by legislation in such rare circumstances as the two world wars (Jan. 31, 1911–Nov. 25, 1918; Nov. 26, 1935–June 15, 1945). Dissolution and writs for a general election are ordered by the Queen on the advice of the Prime Minister. The life of a Parliament is divided into *sessions*, usually of one year in length, beginning and ending most often in October or November.

THE HOUSE OF LORDS

The House of Lords consists of the Lords Spiritual and Temporal. The Lords Spiritual are the Archbishops of Canterbury and York, the Bishops of London, Durham and Winchester, and the 21 senior diocesan Bishops of the Church of England. The Lords Temporal consist of all hereditary Peers and Peeresses of England, Scotland, Great Britain and the United Kingdom who have not disclaimed their Peerages, Life Peers and Peeresses created under the Life Peerages Act 1958, and those Lords of Appeal in Ordinary created Life Peers under the Appellate Jurisdiction Act 1876, as amended (Law Lords).

Disclaimants of an hereditary Peerage lose their right to sit in the House of Lords but gain the right to vote at Parliamentary elections and to offer themselves for election to the House of Commons. (*See also* p. 226). Peers who do not wish to attend sittings of the House of Lords may apply for leave of absence for the duration of a Parliament.

Until the beginning of this century the House of Lords had considerable power, being able to veto any Bill submitted to it by the House of Commons, but those powers were greatly reduced by the Parliament Act of 1911 and subsequently by the Parliament Act of 1949 (*see* **Parliament Acts 1911 and 1949**, p. 306).

Combined with its legislative role, the House of Lords has judicial powers as the ultimate Court of Appeal for Courts in Great Britain and Northern Ireland, except for criminal cases in Scotland. These powers are exercised by the Lord Chancellor and the Law Lords.

Members of the House of Lords are unpaid. However, they are entitled to reimbursement of travelling expenses on parliamentary business within the U.K. and certain other expenses incurred for the purpose of attendance at sittings of the House, within a maximum for each day of £52·00 for overnight subsistence, £20·00 for day subsistence and incidental travel, and £22·00 for secretarial costs, postage and certain additional expenses.

The House is presided over by the Lord Chancellor, who is *ex officio* Speaker of the House. A panel of deputy Speakers is appointed by Royal Commission. The first deputy Speaker is the Lord Chairman of Committees, appointed at the beginning of each session, a salaried officer of the House who takes the chair in Committee of the whole House and in some Select Committees. He is assisted by a panel of Deputy Chairmen, headed by the salaried Principal Deputy Chairman of Committees, who is also Chairman of the European Communities Committee of the House. The permanent officers include the Clerk of the Parliaments and other Clerks who, with other officers of the House, are collectively known as the Parliament Office; the Gentleman-Usher of the Black Rod, who is also Serjeant-at-Arms in attendence upon the Lord Chancellor and is responsible for security and for accommodation and services in the House of Lords; and the Yeoman Usher who is Deputy Serjeant-at-Arms and assists Black Rod in his duties.

OFFICERS OF THE HOUSE OF LORDS

Speaker, The Rt. Hon. The Lord Havers.
    Private Secretary, R. C. Stoate.
Chairman of Committees, The Rt. Hon. Lord Aberdare, K.B.E. £30,640
Principal Deputy Chairman of Committees, The Baroness Serota £27,530

Clerk of the Parliaments, Sir John Sainty,
    K.C.B. £65,000
*Clerk Assistant and Principal Clerk, Public
    Bills,* J. E. Grey, C.B. .... £43,500–£45,500
Reading Clerk and Clerk of the Journals,
    M. A. J. Wheeler-Booth .... £34,000–£37,000
Counsel to Chairman of Committees, D.
    Rippengal, C.B., Q.C. .... £43,500–£45,500
Second Counsel, K. Newman, C.B. .. £34,000–£37,000
Assistant Counsel, G. A. Preston ... £26,230–£29,680
Principal Clerks, J. A. Vallance White
    (*Judicial Office and Fourth Clerk at the
    Table*); J. M. Davies (*Private Bills and
    Overseas Offices*); P. D. G. Hayter (*Com-
    mittees*) .... £34,000–£37,000
Chief Clerks, C. A. J. Mitchell; M. G.
    Pownall; B. P. Keith; R. H. Walters,
    D.PHIL.; (*Seconded as Secretary to the
    Leader of the House and Chief Whip*)
                      £26,230–£29,680

Senior Clerks, D. R. Beamish; D. F. Slater;
    Miss F. P. Tudor .... £16,495–£21,757
Clerk of the Records, H. S. Cobb, F.S.A.
                      £26,230–£29,680
Deputy Clerk of the Records, D. J. Johnson,
    F.S.A. .... £20,251–£26,800
Assistant Clerks of the Records, J. C.
    Morgan (*Sound Archives*); S. K. Ellison
                      £16,495–£21,757
Accountant, E. W. Field, O.B.E. ..... £26,230–£29,680
Assistant Accountant, C. Preece ... £13,615–£16,965
Judicial Taxing Clerk, C. G. Osborne
                      £13,615–£16,965
Librarian, R. H. V. C. Morgan ..... £26,230–£29,680
Deputy Librarian, D. L. Jones. ..... £20,251–£26,800
Library Clerks, P. G. Davis, PH.D.; Miss I. L.
    Victory, PH.D. .... £12,828–£16,665/£16,495–£21,757
Examiners of Petitions for Private Bills, H.
    M. Barclay; J. M. Davies.

Gentleman-Usher of the Black Rod and
Serjeant-at-Arms, Air Chief Marshal Sir
John Gingell, G.B.E., K.C.B. . . . . £34,000–£37,000
Yeoman Usher of the Black Rod and Deputy
Serjeant-at-Arms, Brigadier D. M. Stile-
man, O.B.E. . . . . £16,495–£21,757
Staff Superintendent, Maj. F. P. Horsfall, M.B.E.
Shorthand Writer, Mrs. E. M. C. Holland . . . . . . fees
Editor, Official Report (Hansard), Mrs.
M. E. E. C. Villiers. . . . . £24,744–£27,987
Deputy do. G. R. Goodbarne . . . . £18,372–£24,267

THE HOUSE OF COMMONS

The Members of the House of Commons are elected
by universal adult suffrage. For electoral purposes,
the United Kingdom is divided into constituencies,
each of which returns one Member to the House of
Commons, the Member being the candidate who
obtains the largest number of votes cast in the
constituency. To ensure equitable representation
the four Boundary Commissions keep constituency
boundaries under review and recommend any redistribution of seats which may seem necessary due to
population movements, etc. The number of seats was
raised to 640 in 1945, then reduced to 625 in 1948, and
subsequently rose to 630 in 1955, 635 in 1970 and 650
in 1983. Of the present 650 seats there are 523 for
England, 38 for Wales, 72 for Scotland and 17 for
Northern Ireland. Elections are by secret ballot, each
elector casting one vote: voting is not compulsory.
When a seat becomes vacant between General
Elections, a by-election is held.

British subjects and citizens of the Irish Republic
can stand for election as Members of Parliament
(M.P.s) provided they are 21 or over and not subject
to disqualification. Those disqualified from sitting in
the House include undischarged bankrupts, people
sentenced to more than one year's imprisonment,
clergy of the Church of England, Church of Scotland,
Church of Ireland and Roman Catholic Church,
peers, and holders of certain offices listed in the House
of Commons Disqualification Act 1975 (e.g. members
of the judiciary, Civil Service, regular armed forces,
police forces, some local government officers and some
members of public corporations and government
commissions). A candidate does not require any
party backing but his or her nomination for election
must be supported by the signatures of ten people
registered in the constituency. A candidate must
also deposit with the returning officer £500, which is
forfeit if the candidate does not receive more than
5 per cent of the votes cast. All election expenses,
except the candidate's personal expenses, are subject
to a statutory limit of £3,370, plus 2·9 pence for each
elector in a borough constituency or 3·8 pence for
each elector in a county constituency. (See pp. 311–
318 for an alphabetical list of M.P.s, pp. 319–345 for
the results of the last General Election and subsequent by-elections).

The week's business of the House is outlined each
Thursday by the Leader of the House, after consultation between the Chief Government Whip and the
Chief Opposition Whip. A quarter to third of the
time will be taken up by the Government's legislative
programme, and the rest by other business, e.g.
question time. As a rule Bills likely to raise political
controversy are introduced in the Commons before
going on to the Lords, and the Commons claims
exclusive control in respect of national taxation and
expenditure. Bills such as the Finance Bill, which
imposes taxation, and the Consolidated Fund Bills,
which authorise expenditure, must begin in the
Commons. A Bill of which the financial provisions
are subsidiary may begin in the Lords; and the
Commons may waive their rights in regard to Lords'
amendments affecting finance.

The Commons has a public register of M.P.s'
financial, and certain other, interests. Members must
also disclose any relevant financial interest or benefit
in a matter before the House when taking part in a
debate, in certain other proceedings of the House or
in consultations with other Members, with Ministers
or civil servants.

Since 1911 Members of the House of Commons have
received payments and travelling facilities; they are
entitled to claim income tax relief on expenses
incurred in the course of their Parliamentary duties.
Salary rates since 1911 as follows:

	p.a.		p.a.
1911.	£400	1978 June	£9,450
1937.	600	1980 June	11,750
1946.	1,000	1981 June	13,950
1957.	1,750	1982 June	14,510
1964.	3,250	1983 June	15,308
1972 Jan	4,500	1984 Jan	16,106
1975 June	5,750	1985 Jan	16,904
1976 June	6,062	1986 Jan	17,702
1977 July	6,270	1987 Jan	18,500
1978 June	6,897		

In October 1969 Members were granted an allowance for secretarial and research expenses.

	p.a.		p.a.
1969 Oct	£500	1980 Feb	£6,750
1972 Jan	1,000	1980 Aug	8,000
1974 Aug	1,750	1981 June	8,480
1975 June	3,200	1982 June	8,820
1976 June	3,512	1983 June	12,000
1977 June	3,687	1984 June	12,546
1978 June	4,200	1985 April	13,211
1979 June	4,600	1986 April	20,140

Also, since January 1972, Members can claim
reimbursement for the additional cost of staying
overnight away from their main residence while on
Parliamentary business. Since 1984 this has been
non-taxable.

	p.a.		p.a.
1972.	£750	1980 Aug	£4,903
1974 Aug	1,050	1981 Aug	5,206
1975 July	1,814	1982 Aug	5,674
1976 July	2,038	1983 Aug	6,163
1977 July	2,534	1984 Aug	6,696
1978 July	3,046	1985 Aug	7,351
1979 July	3,866	1986 Aug	7,855

From March 1980 provision was made enabling
each Member in receipt of Secretarial and Research
Allowance to contribute sums to an approved pension
scheme for the provision of a pension, or other
benefits, for or in respect of persons whose salary is
met by him, from the office secretarial research
allowance.

To 31 Mar.	1981	£786 p.a.	1985	£1,200 p.a.
	1982	838	1986	1,321
	1983	875	1987	2,014
	1984	1,136		

The cost of travel allowances for 1986–87 was stated
in June 1987 to be £4,725,802 (car mileage claims
£3,088,718, rail travel £564,430 and air travel
£471,506, spouse/children travel £360,877, extended
travel within U.K. £83,279, and secretarial travel
£156,992).

The Ministerial Salaries and Members' Pensions
Act 1965 established a contributory pension fund
providing pensions for former Members of Parliament
and for dependents of deceased former Members. The
Fund was reconstituted and the scheme restructured
to bring it into line with pension schemes in the
public sector by the Parliamentary and Other Pen-

sions Acts 1972: further Acts modifying the arrangements for Members, Ministers and certain office-holders are the Parliamentary and Other Pensions and Salaries Act 1976; the Parliamentary Pensions Act 1978; the House of Commons Members' Fund and Parliamentary Pensions Act 1981 and the Parliamentary Pensions, etc., Act 1984. The arrangements now provide a pension of one-fiftieth of salary for each year of pensionable service with a maximum of two-thirds of salary at age 65. Pension is normally payable at age 65, for men and women, or on later retirement. Pensions may be paid earlier e.g. on ill-health retirement. The widow/widower of a former Member receives a pension of one-half of the late Member's pension. Pensions are index-linked. Members contribute 9 per cent of salary to the pension fund: there is an Exchequer contribution, currently twice the amount contributed by Members.

The House of Commons Members' Fund provides for annual or lump sum grants to ex-Members, their widows or widowers, and children whose incomes are below certain limits. Alternatively, payments of £1,428 per annum to ex-Members with at least ten years service and who left the House of Commons before October 1964 and £714 per annum to their widows or widowers are made as of right. Members contribute £24 per annum and the Exchequer £115,000 per annum to the Fund. The income of the Fund in 1985–86 was £213,703 and estimated expenditure on grants and payments was £145,275. The net assets of the Fund as at September 30, 1986 amounted to £1,254,123.

The House of Commons is presided over by the Speaker, who has considerable powers to maintain order in the House. His deputy, the Chairman of Ways and Means, and two Deputy Chairmen, all of whom may preside over sittings of the House of Commons, are elected by the House; they, like the Speaker, neither speak nor vote other than in their official capacity. The staff of the House are employed by a Commission chaired by the Speaker. The Clerk of the House of Commons, the Serjeant-at-Arms and the other Heads of Departments (*see* below) are permanent officers of the House, not M.P.s. The Clerk of the House is the principal adviser to the Speaker on the privileges and procedures of the House and his department's responsibilities relate to the conduct of the business of the House and its Committees. The Serjeant-at-Arms, who attends upon the Speaker on ceremonial occasions, is responsible for security and for accommodation and services in the Commons part of the building.

OFFICERS AND OFFICIALS OF THE HOUSE OF COMMONS

Speaker, The Rt. Hon. Bernard Weatherill, M.P. for Croydon North East £48,750
Chairman of Ways and Means, The Rt. Hon. Harold Walker, M.P. for Doncaster Central £37,773
First Deputy Chairman of Ways and Means, Sir Paul Dean, M.P. for Woodspring £34,763
Second Deputy Chairman of Ways and Means, Miss Betty Boothroyd, M.P. for West Bromwich West .. £34,763

Offices of the Speaker and Chairman of Ways and Means

Speaker's Secretary, P. J. Kitcatt, C.B.
                      £26,230–£29,680
Speaker's Counsel, H. Knorpel, C.B.; G. E. Gammie, C.B. .... £33,725–£36,852
Chaplain to the Speaker, The Rev. Canon D. Gray.

Department of the Clerk of the House

Clerk of the House of Commons, C. J. Boulton, C.B. £64,739
Clerk Asst., J. F. Sweetman, T.D. .... £43,264–£45,349
Clerk of Committees, (vacant) ...... £43,264–£45,349
Principal Clerks—
  Public Bills, J. H. Willcox
  Table Office, D. W. Limon
  Private Bills, H. M. Barclay
  Journals, M. T. Ryle
  Financial Committees, W. R. McKay
                     £33,725–£36,852
  Select Committees, C. B. Winnifrith
  Overseas Office, (vacant)
  Second Clerk, Select Committees, A. J. Hastings .... £31,809–£33,309
Deputy Principal Clerks, R. J. Willoughby; S. A. L. Panton; R. B. Sands; G. Cubie; M. R. Jack, PH.D.; D. G. Millar; Mrs. J. Sharpe; Ms. A. Milner-Barry; R. W. G. Wilson; W. A. Proctor; F. A. Cranmer; R. J. Rogers; C. R. M. Ward, PH.D.; Ms. H. E. Irwin; D. W. N. Doig; A. Sandall; E. P. Silk
                   £26,230–£29,680
Senior Clerks, M. H. Cooper, PH.D.; D. L. Natzler; Mrs. S. A. de Ste. Croix; A. R. Kennon; D. W. Robson; L. C. Laurence Smyth; A. R. Gren; S. J. Patrick; D. J. Gerhold; C. J. Poyser; D. F. Harrison; S. J. Priestley; C. P. R. Bennett; A. H. Doherty; P. A. Evans; R. I. S. Phillips; R. G. James; J. Hallowell

(*acting*); J. B. Ingram (*acting*); P. D. Austwick (*acting*); W. Deakins (*acting*)
                   £16,495–£21,757
Examiners of Private Bills, H. M. Barclay; J. M. Davies.
Taxing Officer, H. M. Barclay.

Department of the Serjeant-at-Arms

Serjeant-at-Arms, Sir Victor Le Fanu, K.C.V.O.
                   £33,725–£36,852
Deputy Serjeant-at-Arms, Major P. N. W. Jennings .... £26,230–£29,680
Assistant Serjeant-at-Arms, M. J. A. Cummins .... £19,312–£25,533
Deputy Assistant Serjeants-at-Arms, P. A. J. Wright; J. F. Collins .... £16,495–£21,757

Department of the Library

Librarian, D. Menhennet, D.Phil ... £33,725–£36,852
Deputy Librarian, D. J. T. Englefield
                   £26,230–£29,680

Library and Information Service

Assistant Librarians, G. F. Lock; Miss J. B. Tanfield .... £26,230–£29,680
Deputy Assistant Librarians, J. B. Poole, PH.D.; S. Z. Young; Mrs. H. R. Coates; Miss P. J. Baines; K. G. Cuningham; Mrs. J. M. Wainwright; C. C. Pond, PH.D.; Mrs. C. B. Andrews; R. C. Clements ..... £20,251–£29,800
Senior Library Clerks, Miss E. K. Andrews, D.Phil.; Mrs. B. L. Miller; Mrs. J. M. Lourie; Ms. F. Poole; Mrs. J. M. Fiddick; C. R. Barclay; Mrs. C. M. Gillie; Miss C. E. Nield; R. J. Ware, D.Phil; Ms. D. Gore, PH.D; R. J. Twigger; B. K. Winetrobe; T. N. Edmonds; R. J. Cracknell; Miss O. M. Gay; Miss E. M. McInnes; Mrs. G. L. Allen (*temp.*)
                   £16,495–£21,757

Vote Office

Deliverer of the Vote, G. R. Russell . £20,251–£26,800
Deputy Deliverer of the Vote, H. C. Foster
£14,992–£19,728

Administration Department

Head of Administration Department, A. C. J.
Poole .... £33,725–£36,852
Accountant, J. L. G. Dobson .... £31,809–£33,309
Deputy Accountant, A. J. Lewis.... £26,230–£29,680
Senior Assistant Accountant, G. P. Brown
(temp.) .... £20,251–£26,800
Assistant Accountants, F. W. Brewer; A. R.
Marskell; M. J. Barram; Miss M. M. McColl
(temp.) .... £16,495–£21,757
Head of Establishments Office, G. A. Roberts
£26,230–£29,680
Deputy Head of Establishments Office, J. A.
Robb .... £20,251–£26,800

Computer Officer, R. S. Morgan .... £25,735–£29,116
Internal Auditor, Miss C. Stone .... £16,495–£21,757
Staff Inspector, R. C. Collins .... £16,495–£21,757

Department of the Official Report

Editor, K. S. Morgan .... £31,809–£33,309
Deputy Editor, L. R. Johns .... £20,251–£26,800
Principal Assistant Editors, R. V. Hadlow; J.
Gourley; F. G. Brotherston, o.b.e.; C. R. G.
Watson, o.b.e. .... £18,936–£25,027
Assistant Editors, P. Walker; E. Holland; I.
Church; J. Withers .... £17,057–£22,493

Refreshment Department

General Manager, W. J. J. Smillie .. £20,251–£26,800
Deputy General Manager, E. J. Nash
£16,495–£21,757
Catering Accountant, D. R. W. Wood
£16,495–£21,757

PARLIAMENTARY INFORMATION
The following is a short glossary of aspects of work of Parliament:
(*Unless otherwise stated, references are to* House of Commons *procedures.*)

Adjournment Debate.—Usually a half-hour debate introduced by a backbencher at the end of business for the day. The subjects raised are often local or personal issues.

Bill.—Proposed legislation is termed a *Bill*. The stages of a Public Bill in the House of Commons are as follows:
First Reading: There is no debate at this stage, which nowadays merely constitutes an order to have the Bill printed.
Second Reading: The debate on the principles of the Bill.
Committee Stage: The detailed examination of a Bill, clause by clause. In most cases this takes place in a *Standing Committee*, or the whole House may act as a Committee. A *Special Standing Committee* may take evidence before embarking on detailed scrutiny of the Bill. Rarely, a Bill may be examined by a *Select Committee* (*see* below).
Report Stage: Detailed review of a Bill as amended in Committee.
Third Reading: Final debate on a Bill.
Public Bills go through the same stages in the House of Lords, except that in almost all cases the Committee Stage is taken in the Committee of the Whole House.
Some Public Bills may start in the House of Lords, in which case the Lords stages are taken first.
Both Houses have to agree the same text of a Bill, so that the *Amendments* made by the second House are then considered in the originating House and if not agreed, sent back or themselves amended, until agreement is reached.

Chiltern Hundreds.—A legal fiction, a nominal office of profit under the Crown, the acceptance of which requires a Member to vacate his seat. The Manor of Northstead is similar. These are the only means by which an M.P. may resign.

Closure & Guillotine.—To prevent deliberate waste of time of either House, a motion may be made that the question be now put. In the House of Commons, if the Speaker decides that the rights of a minority are not being prejudiced and 100 members support the closure motion in a division, if carried, the original motion is put to the House, without further debate. The *Guillotine* represents a more

rigorous and systematic application of the Closure. Under this system, a Bill proceeds in accordance with a rigid timetable and discussion is limited to the time allotted to each group of clauses. The Closure is possible in the House of Lords, but is hardly ever used. There is, however, no procedure for a guillotine. The completion of business in the Lords is traditionally ensured by mutual agreement from all sides of the House.

Consolidated Fund Bill.—A Bill to authorize issue of sums to maintain Government service. The Bill is dealt with without debate, but afterwards members may raise topics of public or local importance.

Delegated Legislation.—This consists, principally, of Statutory Instruments within the meaning of the Statutory Instruments Act 1946. These fall into three broad categories:—(i) Affirmative Instruments, which are subject to approval by resolutions of both Houses before they can come into or remain in force; (ii) Negative Instruments, which are subject to annulment by resolution of either House; and (iii) General Instruments, which include those not required to be laid before Parliament and those which are required to be so laid but are not subject to approval or annulment. There are in addition Special Procedure Orders, which are another form of delegated legislation, subject to procedures which allow time for petitions to be lodged against them.

Dissolution.—Parliament comes to an end either by Dissolution by the Sovereign, on the advice of the Prime Minister, or the expiration of the term of five years for which the House of Commons was elected. Dissolution is normally effected by a Royal Proclamation.

Early Day Motion.—A motion put on the Notice Paper by an M.P. without in general the real prospect of its being debated. Such motions are expressions of backbench opinion.

Emergency Debate.—In the Commons a method of obtaining prompt discussion of a matter of urgency is by moving the adjournment under Standing Order No. 10 for the purpose of discussing a specific and important matter that should have urgent consideration. A member may ask leave to make this motion by giving written notice to the Speaker, usually before 12 noon, and if the Speaker considers the matter of sufficient importance and it obtains the support of 40 members, it is discussed usually at 7 p.m. on the following day.

Father of the House.—The Member whose continuous service in the House of Commons, is the longest. The present Father of the House is the Rt. Hon. Sir Bernard Braine, elected first in 1950.

General Synod Measure.—A measure passed by the national assembly of the Church of England under the Church of England Assembly (Powers) Act 1919. These measures are considered by the Ecclesiastical Committee, who make a report. They are then considered by both Houses, and if approved, sent for the Royal Assent.

Hansard.—The official report of debates in both Houses (and in Standing Committees) published by H.M.S.O., normally on the day after the sitting concerned.

Hours of Meeting.—The House of Commons meets on Monday, Tuesday, Wednesday and Thursday at 2.30 p.m., and on Friday at 9.30 a.m. The House of Lords normally meets during the Session at 2.30 p.m. on Monday, Tuesday and Wednesday and at 3 p.m. on Thursday. In the latter part of the Session, the House sometimes sits on Fridays at 11 a.m.

Hybridity.—A Public Bill which is considered to affect specific private or local interests, as distinct from *all* such interests of a single category, is called a Hybrid Bill and is subject to a special form of scrutiny.

Leader of the Opposition.—In 1937 the office of Leader of the Opposition was recognized and a salary of £2,000 per annum was assigned to the post, thus following a practice which had prevailed in the Dominion of Canada since 1906. In June 1987 the salary was £44,100. The present Leader of the Opposition is the Rt. Hon. Neil Kinnock.

The Lord Chancellor.—The Lord High Chancellor of Great Britain is (*ex officio*) the Speaker of the House of Lords. Unlike the Speaker of the House of Commons, he is a member of the Government, takes part in debates and votes in divisions. He has none of the powers to maintain order that the Speaker in the Commons has, these powers being exercised in the Lords by the House as a whole. The Lord Chancellor sits in the Lords on one of the *Woolsacks*, couches covered with red cloth and stuffed with wool. If he wishes to address the House in any way except formally as Speaker, he leaves the Woolsack and steps towards his place as a peer.

Naming.—When a member has been named, i.e. contrary to the practice of the House called by surname and not addressed as the "Hon. Member for ... (his/her constituency)", the Leader of the House moves that the offender "be suspended from the service of the House" for (in the case of a first offence) a period of a week. Should the member offend again, the period of suspension is increased.

Opposition Day.—A day on which the topic for debate is chosen by the Opposition. There are 20 such days in a normal session. On 17 days, subjects are chosen by the Leader of the Opposition; on the remaining three days by the leader of the next largest opposition party.

Parliament Acts 1911 and 1949.—Under these Acts certain Bills may become law without the consent of the Lords.

Since at least the 18th century the Commons have had the privilege of having bills concerned with supply (i.e. taxation and money matters) passed without amendment by the Lords; though until 1911 the Lords retained the right to reject such bills outright.

By the Parliament Act 1911 a Bill which has been endorsed by the Speaker of the House of Commons as a Money Bill and has been passed by the Commons and sent up to the Lords at least one month before the end of a session can become law without the consent of the Lords if it is not passed by them without amendment within a month.

Under the Parliament Act 1911 and 1949, if the Lords reject any other Public Bill (except those dealing with certain subjects such as the prolongation of Parliament) which has been passed by the Commons in two successive sessions then that Bill shall (unless the Commons direct to the contrary) become law without the consent of the Lords.

The effect of the Parliament Acts is therefore that the Lords have power to delay a Public Bill for thirteen months from its first Second Reading in the House of Commons.

Prime Minister's Questions.—The Prime Minister answers questions from 3.15 to 3.30 pm on Tuesdays and Thursdays. Nowadays the "open question" predominates. Members ask the Prime Minister what are his or her official engagements for the day or whether an official visit will be made to such and such a place. A supplementary question on virtually any topic can then be put.

Private Bill.—A Bill promoted by a body or an individual to give powers additional to, or in conflict with, the general law, and to which a separate procedure applies.

Private Members' Bill.—A Public Bill promoted by a Member who is not a member of H.M. Government.

Private Notice Question.—A question adjudged of urgent importance on submission to Mr. Speaker, answered at the end of oral questions—usually at 3.30 p.m.

Privilege.—The following are covered by the privilege of Parliament: (i) freedom from interference in going to, attending at, and going from, Parliament; (ii) freedom of speech; (iii) the printing and publishing of anything relating to the proceedings of the two Houses is subject to privilege; (iv) each House is the guardian of its dignity and may punish any insult to the House as a whole.

Prorogation.—The bringing to an end, by the Sovereign on the advice of the Government, of a Session of Parliament. All Public Bills which have not completed their stages lapse on Prorogation.

Queen's Speech.—The Speech delivered by H.M. The Queen at the State Opening of Parliament, in which the Government's programme for the year is set forth. The Speech is, of course, drafted for and approved by the Cabinet.

Question Time.—Oral questions are answered in the Commons from 2.30 to 3.30 pm every day except Friday. They are also taken at the start of the Lords sittings, with a daily limit of four oral questions.

Royal Assent.—The Royal Assent is signified by Letters Patent to such Bills and Measures as have passed both Houses of Parliament (or Bills which have been passed under the Parliament Acts 1911 and 1949). The Sovereign has not given Royal Assent in person since 1854. On occasion, for instance in the Prorogation of Parliament, Royal Assent may be pronounced to the two Houses by Lords Commissioners; but more usually Royal Assent is notified to each House sitting separately in accordance with the Royal Assent Act 1967. The Norman formulae for Royal Assent are then endorsed on the Acts by the Clerk of the Parliaments.

The power to withhold assent (colloquially known as the Royal Veto) resides with the Sovereign, but has not been exercised in the United Kingdom since 1707, in the reign of Queen Anne.

Select Committees consisting usually of 10–15 members of all parties are a means used by both Houses in order to investigate certain matters.

Most Select Committees in the House of Commons are now tied to Departments—each Committee investigates subjects within a Government Department's remit. These are: Agriculture, Defence, Education Science and Arts, Employment, Energy, Environment, Foreign Affairs, Home Affairs, Scottish Affairs, Social Services, Trade and Industry, Transport, Treasury and Civil Service, Welsh Affairs.

There are other House of Commons Select Committees dealing with Public Accounts (i.e. the spending by H.M. Government of money voted by Parliament), European Legislation and Statutory Instruments, and also domestic committees dealing, for example, with Privilege and Services. Major Select Committees usually take evidence in public: their evidence and reports are published by H.M.S.O.

The principal Select Committee in the House of Lords is that on the European Communities, which has, at present, six sub-committees dealing with all areas of community policy. The House of Lords also has a Select Committee on Science and Technology, which appoints sub-committees to deal with specific subjects. In addition, *ad hoc* Select Committees have been set up from time to time to investigate specific subjects, e.g. unemployment, overseas trade. There are also some Joint Committees of the two Houses, e.g. the Joint Committee on Statutory Instruments.

The Speaker.—The Speaker of the House of Commons is the spokesman and president of the Chamber. He is elected by the House at the beginning of each Parliament or when the previous Speaker retires or dies. He neither speaks in debates nor votes in divisions except when the voting is equal.

Standing Orders.—Rules which have from time to time been agreed by each House of Parliament to regulate the conduct of its business. These orders are not irrevocable, may be revised, amended or repealed, and are from time to time suspended or dispensed with.

State Opening.—This marks the start of each new Parliament or new session of Parliament. Parliament is normally opened, in the presence of both Houses, by the Queen in person, who makes the Speech from the Throne which outlines the Government's policies for the coming session (*see* **Queen's Speech**). In the

absence of the Queen, Parliament is opened by Royal Commission, and the Queen's Speech is read by one of the Lords Commissioners specially appointed by Letters Patent for the occasion.

Strangers.—Anyone who is not a Member or Officer of the House is a *stranger*. Visitors are generally admitted to debates of both Houses but may be excluded if the House so decides. In practice this happens only in time of war.

Ten Minute Rule.—A colloquial term for Standing Order No. 19, under which backbenchers have an opportunity on Tuesdays and Wednesdays to introduce a Bill and speak in its favour for about ten minutes. Time is also available for a short opposing speech.

Vacant Seats.—When a vacancy occurs in the House of Commons during a session of Parliament the Writ for the by-election is moved, by a Whip of the party to which the member whose seat has been vacated belonged. If the House is in recess, the Speaker can issue a warrant for a writ, should two members certify to him that a seat is vacant.

Whips.—In order to secure the attendance of Members of a particular party in Parliament on all occasions, and particularly on the occasion of an important division, Whips (originally known as "Whippers-in") are appointed. The written appeal or circular letter issued by them is also known as a "whip", its urgency being denoted by the number of times it is underlined. Failure to respond to a three-line whip, headed "Most important", is tantamount in the Commons to secession (at any rate temporarily) from the party. Whips are officially recognized by Parliament and are provided with office accommodation in both Houses. In both Houses, Government and some Opposition Whips receive salaries from public funds.

PUBLIC INFORMATION SERVICE.—Enquiries from the general public and organizations of all kinds about the work, composition and history of the House of Commons are answered by the Public Information Office, House of Commons, SW1A 0AA (01-219 4272). This office also edits the House of Commons Weekly Information Bulletin (published by H.M.S.O.). A series of free leaflets on the work and processes of the House is available. The Information Office, House of Lords, SW1A 0PW (01-219 3107) answers queries relating to the procedure and practice of the Lords.

HER MAJESTY'S GOVERNMENT

Her Majesty's Government is the body of Ministers responsible for the administration of national affairs, determining policy and introducing into Parliament any legislation necessary to give effect to government policy. The majority of Ministers are members of the House of Commons but members of the House of Lords may also hold Ministerial responsibility, and certain offices, e.g. Lord Chancellor, are always held by members of the House of Lords. The Prime Minister is, by recent convention, always a member of the House of Commons.

THE PRIME MINISTER

The office of Prime Minister, which had been in existence for nearly 200 years, was officially recognised in 1905 and its holder was granted a place in the Table of Precedence. The Prime Minister, by tradition also First Lord of the Treasury and Minister for the Civil Service, is appointed by the Sovereign

and is usually the leader of the party which enjoys, or can secure, a majority in the House of Commons. Other Ministers are appointed by the Sovereign on the recommendation of the Prime Minister, who also allocates functions amongst Ministers and has the power to obtain their resignation or dismissal individually.

The Prime Minister informs the Sovereign of state and political matters, advises on the dissolution of Parliament, and makes recommendations for important Crown appointments, the award of honours, etc.

As the chairman of Cabinet meetings and leader of a political party, the Prime Minister is responsible for translating party policy into government activity: and as leader of the Government the Prime Minister is responsible to Parliament and to the electorate for the policies and their implementation.

The Prime Minister also represents the nation in international affairs, e.g. summit conferences.

THE CABINET

The Cabinet developed during the 18th century as an inner committee of the Privy Council, which was the chief source of executive power until that time. It is composed of about 20 Ministers chosen by the Prime Minister, usually the heads of government departments (generally known as Secretaries of State unless they have a special title, e.g. Chancellor of the Exchequer) and the holders of various traditional offices.

The Cabinet's functions are the final determination of policy, control of government and co-ordination of government departments. The exercise of its functions is dependent upon enjoying majority support in the House of Commons. Cabinet meetings are held in private, taking place once or twice a week during parliamentary sittings and less often during a recess. Proceedings are confidential, the members being bound by their oath as Privy Counsellors not to disclose information about the proceedings.

The convention of collective responsibility means that the Cabinet acts unanimously even when Cabinet Ministers do not all agree on a subject. The policies of departmental Ministers must be consistent with the policies of the Government as a whole, and once the Government's policy has been decided, each Minister is expected to support it or resign.

The convention of Ministerial responsibility holds a Minister, as the political head of his or her department, accountable to Parliament for the department's work. Departmental Ministers usually decide all matters within their responsibility, although on matters of political importance they normally consult their colleagues collectively. A decision by a departmental Minister is binding on the Government as a whole.

HER MAJESTY'S GOVERNMENT

THE CABINET

Prime Minister, First Lord of the Treasury and Minister for the Civil Service, THE RT. HON. MRS MARGARET HILDA THATCHER, M.P., F.R.S, *born* Oct. 13, 1925.

Lord President of the Council and Leader of the House of Lords, The Rt. Hon. the Viscount Whitelaw, C.H., M.C., *born* June 28, 1918.

Lord High Chancellor, The Rt. Hon. the Lord Havers, *born* March 10, 1923.

Secretary of State for Foreign and Commonwealth Affairs, The Rt. Hon. Sir (Richard Edward) Geoffrey Howe, Q.C., M.P., *born* Dec. 20, 1926.

Chancellor of the Exchequer, The Rt. Hon. Nigel Lawson, M.P., *born* March 11, 1932.

Secretary of State for the Home Department, The Rt. Hon. Douglas Richard Hurd, C.B.E., M.P., *born* March 8, 1930.

Secretary of State for Energy, The Rt. Hon. Cecil Edward Parkinson, M.P., *born* Sept. 1, 1931.

Secretary of State for Defence, The Rt. Hon. George Kenneth Hotson Younger, T.D., M.P., *born* Sept. 22, 1931.

Secretary of State for Wales, The Rt. Hon. Peter Edward Walker, M.B.E., M.P., *born* March 25, 1932.

Lord Privy Seal and Leader of the House of Commons, The Rt. Hon. John Wakeham, M.P., *born* June 22, 1932.

Secretary of State for Social Services, The Rt. Hon. John Edward Michael Moore, M.P., *born* Nov. 26, 1937.

Chancellor of the Duchy of Lancaster, The Rt. Hon. Kenneth Harry Clarke, Q.C., M.P., *born* July 2, 1940 (*and Minister of Trade and Industry.*

Secretary of State for Northern Ireland, The Rt. Hon. Thomas Jeremy King, M.P., *born* June 13, 1933.

Minister of Agriculture, Fisheries and Food, The Rt. Hon. John Roddick Russell MacGregor, O.B.E., M.P., *born* Feb. 14, 1937.

Secretary of State for the Environment, The Rt. Hon. Nicholas Ridley, M.P., *born* Feb. 17, 1929.

Secretary of State for Employment, The Rt. Hon. (Peter) Norman Fowler, M.P., *born* Feb. 2, 1938.

Secretary of State for Education and Science, The Rt. Hon. Kenneth Wilfred Baker, M.P., *born* Nov. 3, 1934.

Chief Secretary to the Treasury, The Rt. Hon. John Major, M.P., *born* March 29, 1943.

Secretary of State for Scotland, The Rt. Hon. Malcolm Leslie Rifkind, Q.C., M.P., *born* June 21, 1946.

Secretary of State for Trade and Industry, The Rt. Hon. the Lord Young of Graffham, *born* Feb. 27, 1932.

Secretary of State for Transport, The Rt. Hon. (Henry) Paul Guinness Channon, M.P., *born* Oct. 9, 1935.

LAW OFFICERS

Attorney-General, The Rt. Hon. Sir Patrick Barnabas Burke Mayhew, Q.C., M.P.

Lord Advocate, The Rt. Hon. the Lord Cameron of Lochbroom, Q.C.

Solicitor-General, Sir Nicholas Walter Lyell, Q.C., M.P.

Solicitor-General for Scotland, Peter Lovat Fraser, Q.C.*

(* not a member of the House of Commons)

OTHER MINISTERS

Parliamentary Secretary to the Treasury, The Rt. Hon. David Waddington, Q.C., M.P.

Financial Secretary to the Treasury, The Rt. Hon. Norman Lamont, M.P.

Paymaster General, The Hon. Peter Brooke, M.P.

MINISTERS OF STATE

Agriculture, Fisheries and Food, The Rt. Hon. John Gummer, M.P.

Defence, Ian Stewart, R.D., M.P., (*Armed Forces*); The Lord Trefgarne (*Defence Procurement*).

Education and Science, Mrs. Angela Rumbold, C.B.E., M.P.

Employment, John Cope, M.P.

Energy, The Hon. Peter Morrison, M.P.

Environment, Michael Howard, Q.C., M.P. (*Local Government*); Hon. William Waldegrave, M.P. (*Housing and Planning*); The Rt. Hon. the Lord Belstead (*Water, Environment Protection, Countryside and Heritage*).

Foreign and Commonwealth Affairs, The Rt Hon. Mrs Lynda Chalker, M.P.; The Lord Glenarthur; David Mellor, M.P.; Christopher Patten, M.P. (*Minister for Overseas Development*).

Health and Social Security, Antony Newton, O.B.E., M.P. (*Health*); Nicholas Scott, M.B.E., M.P. (*Social Security and the Disabled*).

Home Office, The Earl of Caithness; John Patten, M.P.; Timothy Renton, M.P.

Northern Ireland, The Rt. Hon. John Stanley, M.P.

Privy Council Office, The Rt. Hon. Richard Luce, M.P. (*Minister for the Arts*).

Scottish Office, Ian Lang, M.P.; The Lord Sanderson of Bowden.

Trade and Industry, The Hon. Alan Clark, M.P. (*Trade*).

Transport, David Mitchell, M.P.

Treasury, Peter Lilley, M.P. (*Economic Secretary*).

Welsh Office, Wyn Roberts, M.P.

UNDER-SECRETARIES OF STATE

Agriculture, Fisheries and Food, Donald Thompson, M.P.; The Baroness Trumpington.

Defence, Roger Freeman, M.P. (*Armed Forces*); The Hon. Timothy Sainsbury, M.P. (*Defence Procurement*).

Education and Science, Robert Dunn, M.P.; The Baroness Hooper; Robert Jackson, M.P.

Employment, John Lee, M.P.; Patrick Nicholls, M.P.

Energy, Michael Spicer, M.P.

Environment, Christopher Chope, O.B.E., M.P.; The Hon. Colin Moynihan, M.P. (*Minister for Sport*); Mrs. Marion Roe, M.P.; David Trippier, R.D., M.P.

Foreign and Commonwealth Affairs, Timothy Eggar, M.P.

Health and Social Security, Mrs. Edwina Currie, M.P.; Michael Portillo, M.P.; The Lord Skelmersdale.

Home Office, The Hon. Douglas Hogg, M.P.

Northern Ireland Office, The Lord Lyell; Dr. Brian Mawhinney, M.P.; Richard Needham, M.P.; Peter Viggers, M.P.

Scottish Office, Michael Forsyth, M.P.; Lord James Douglas-Hamilton, M.P.

Trade and Indusry, Robert Atkins, M.P.; John Butcher, M.P.; The Hon. Francis Maude, M.P.

Transport, Peter Bottomley, M.P. The Lord Brabazon of Tara.

Treasury, The Lords Commissioners (*see* Government Whips).

Welsh Office, Ian Grist, M.P.

GOVERNMENT WHIPS

HOUSE OF LORDS

Captain of the Gentlemen-at-Arms (Chief Whip), The Rt. Hon. the Lord Denham.

Captain of the Queen's Bodyguard of the Yeoman of the Guard (Deputy Chief Whip), The Viscount Davidson.

Lords in Waiting, The Viscount Long; The Lord Hesketh; The Lord Beaverbrook; The Earl of Dundee; The Earl of Arran.

HOUSE OF COMMONS

Parliamentary Secretary to the Treasury (Chief Whip), The Rt. Hon. David Waddington, Q.C., M.P.

Treasurer of the H.M. Household (Deputy Chief Whip), David Hunt, M.B.E., M.P.

Comptroller of H.M. Household, The Hon. Robert Boscawen, M.C., M.P.

Vice-Chamberlain of H.M. Household, Tristan Garel-Jones, M.P.

Lords Commissioners, Anthony Durant, M.P.; The Hon. Mark Lennox-Boyd, M.P.; David Lightbown, M.P.; Peter Lloyd, M.P.; Michael Neubert, M.P.

Assistant Whips, Kenneth Carlisle, M.P.; Stephen Dorrell, M.P.; Alan Howarth, C.B.E., M.P.; David Maclean, M.P.; Richard Ryder, O.B.E., M.P.

GOVERNMENT BY PARTY

Before the reign of William and Mary the principal Officers of State were chosen by and were responsible to the Sovereign alone and not to Parliament or the nation at large. Such officers acted sometimes in concert with one another, but more often independently, and the fall of one did not, of necessity, involve that of others, although all were liable to be dismissed at any moment.

In 1693 the Earl of Sunderland recommended to William III the advisability of selecting a Ministry from the political party which enjoyed a majority in the House of Commons and the first united Ministry was drawn in 1696 from the Whigs, to which party the King owed his throne, the principal members being Russell (the Admiral), Somers (the Advocate), Lord Wharton and Charles Montague (afterwards Chancellor of the Exchequer). This group became known as the *Junto* and was regarded with suspicion as a novelty in the political life of the nation, being a small section meeting in secret apart from the main body of Ministers. It may be regarded as the forerunner of the *Cabinet* and in course of time it led to the establishment of the principle of joint responsibility of Ministers, so that internal disagreement caused a change of personnel or resignation of the whole body of Ministers.

The accession of George I, who was unfamiliar with the English language, led to a disinclination on the part of the Sovereign to preside at meetings of his Ministers and caused the appearance of a *Prime Minister*, a position first acquired by Robert Walpole in 1721 and retained without interruption for 20 years and 326 days.

In 1828 the old party of the Whigs became known as *Liberals*, a name originally given to it by its

opponents to imply laxity of principles, but gradually accepted by the party to indicate its claim to be pioneers and champions of political reform and progressive legislation. In 1861 a Liberal Registration Association was founded and Liberal Associations became widespread. As the outcome of a conference at Birmingham in 1877 a National Liberal Federation was formed, with headquarters in London. The Liberal Party was in power for long periods during the second half of the nineteenth century in spite of the set-back during the Home Rule crisis of 1886, which resulted in the secession of the Liberal Unionists, and for several years during the first quarter of the twentieth century, but after a further split into National and Independent Liberals it numbered only 59 in all after the General Election of 1929, with a further fall to 12 (excluding National Liberals) after the 1945 Election.

Soon after the change from Whig to Liberal the Tory Party became known as *Conservative*, a name traditionally believed to have been invented by John Wilson Croker in 1830 and to have been generally adopted about the time of the passing of the Reform Act of 1832 to indicate that the preservation of national institutions was the leading principle of the party. After the Home Rule crisis of 1886 the dissentient Liberals entered into a compact with the Conservatives, under which the latter undertook not to contest their seats, but a separate *Liberal Unionist* organization was maintained until 1912, when it was united with the Conservatives.

The Labour Party.—Labour candidates for Parliament made their first appearance at the General Election of 1892, when there were 27 standing as "Labour" or "Liberal-Labour."

In 1900 the *Labour Representation Committee* was set up in order to establish a distinct Labour Group in Parliament, with its own whips, its own policy, and a readiness to co-operate with any party which might be engaged in promoting legislation in the direct interest of labour. In 1906 the L.R.C. became known as *The Labour Party*.

Social Democratic Party.—The Council for Social Democracy was announced by four former Labour Cabinet Ministers—Roy Jenkins, David Owen, William Rodgers and Mrs. Shirley Williams—on Jan. 25, 1981. Subsequently a number of sitting Labour Members of Parliament, together with one Conservative, joined the new group, and on March 26, 1981 the Social Democratic Party was launched in London, followed by eight regional launches. Later in the year the S.D.P. and the Liberal Party formed an electoral *Alliance*, though each party decides its own policy and maintains its own party organisation. At the time of going to press, proposals for a closer union were under discussion.

The government of the day is formed by the party which wins the largest number of seats in the House of Commons at a General Election, or which has the support of a majority of members in the House of Commons. By tradition, the leader of the majority party is asked by the Sovereign to form a government, while the largest minority party becomes the official Opposition with its own leader and own "Shadow Cabinet". Leaders of the Government and Opposition sit on the front benches of the Commons with their supporters (the back-benchers) sitting behind them.

When a party is in Opposition and its leadership becomes vacant, it makes its free choice among the various personalities available; but if the party is in office, the Sovereign's choice may anticipate, and in a certain sense forestall, the decision of the party.

POLITICAL PARTIES

CONSERVATIVE AND UNIONIST PARTY, Central Office, 32 Smith Square, SW1P 3HH.—*Party Chairman,* Rt. Hon. N. Tebbit, C.H., M.P.; *Deputy Chairman,* Hon. P. Morrison, M.P.; *Vice Chairmen,* T. Arnold, M.P.; Dame Joan Seccombe, O.B.E.; J. Spicer, M.P.; *Hon. Treasurers,* Lord McAlpine of West Green; Sir Oulton Wade; Lord Johnston, T.D.

SCOTTISH CONSERVATIVE PARTY, Central Office, 3 Chester Street, Edinburgh EH3 7RF.—*Chairman,* The Lord Goold; *Deputy Chairman,* Sir Donald Maclean; *Hon. Treasurer,* M. D. Goodwin, C.B.E.; *Dir.,* W. R. Henderson, T.D.

LABOUR PARTY, 150 Walworth Road, SE17 1JT.—*Chairman,* S. Tierney; *Vice Chairman,* Rt. Hon. N. Kinnock; *Treasurer,* S. McCluskie; *Gen. Sec.,* L. Whitty; *Parliamentary Party Leader,* Rt. Hon. N. Kinnock, M.P.; *Deputy Leader,* Rt. Hon. R. Hattersley, M.P.; *Leader of the Labour Peers,* Lord Cledwyn of Penrhos, C.H.

SHADOW CABINET, 1987–88.—Rt. Hon. N. Kinnock, M.P. (*Leader of the Opposition*); Rt. Hon. J. Smith, M.P. (*Treasury and Economic Affairs*); Rt. Hon. G. Kaufman, M.P. (*Foreign and Commonwealth Affairs*); Rt. Hon. R. Hattersley, M.P. (*Home Affairs*); F. Dobson, M.P. (*Leader of the House and Campaigns Co-ordinator*); B. Gould, M.P. (*Trade and Industry*); Dr. J. Cunningham, M.P. (*Environment*); M. Meacher, M.P. (*Employment*); R. Hughes, M.P. (*Transport*); Rt. Hon. D. Davies, M.P. (*Defence, Disarmament and Arms Control*); Rt. Hon. P. Archer, M.P. (*Northern Ireland*); B. Jones, M.P. (*Wales*); D. Dewar, M.P. (*Scotland*); R. Cook, M.P. (*Health and Social Security*); J. Straw, M.P. (*Education*); J. Prescott, M.P. (*Energy*); Dr. D. Clark, M.P. (*Agriculture and Rural Affairs*); Ms. J. Richardson, M.P. (*Women*); G. Brown, M.P. (*Chief Secretary to the Treasury*).

Labour Whips in the House of Lords are: *Chief Whip,* Lord Ponsonby of Shulbrede; *Deputy Chief Whip,* Baroness David. Labour Whips in the House of Commons are: *Chief Whip,* D. Foster, M.P.; *Deputy Chief Whip,* D. Dixon, M.P.

LIBERAL PARTY, Headquarters, 1 Whitehall Place, SW1A 2HE.—*Chairman,* T. Clement-Jones; *Vice Chairmen,* P. Harris, D. Hughes; *President,* A. Slade; *Hon. Treasurers,* Sir Hugh Jones, L.V.O., A. Jacobs; *Sec. Gen.,* A. Ellis, O.B.E.; *Parliamentary Party Leader,* Rt. Hon. D. Steel, M.P.; *Deputy Leader,* A. Beith, M.P.; *Leader of the Liberal Peers,* Rt. Hon. the Lady Seear.

The Liberal Whip in the House of Lords is Lord Tordoff. Liberal Whips in the House of Commons are: *Chief Whip,* D. Alton; *Deputy Whip,* J. Wallace.

SCOTTISH LIBERAL PARTY, 4 Clifton Terrace, Edinburgh EH12 5DR.—*Chairman,* Dr. C. Mason; *Vice Chairmen,* I. Macfarlane, A. Robinson, Ms. A. Singh; *Hon. Treasurer,* E. Bennett; *Political Director,* R. Waddell.

WELSH LIBERAL PARTY, Dumfries Chambers, 91 St. Mary's Street, Cardiff CF1 1DW.—*Chairman,* N. Phillips; *Vice Chairman,* G. Griffiths; *Hon. Treasurers,* P. Davies, Dr. G. Morrison; *Sec.,* Ms. K. Lloyd.

PLAID CYMRU, 51 Cathedral Road, Cardiff CF1 9HD.—*Chairman,* D. Huws; *Deputy Chairman,* Ms. J. Davies; *Hon. Treasurer,* D. Watkins; *Sec.,* D. Williams; *Party President,* D. E. Thomas, M.P.; *Vice-President,* D. Iwan.

SCOTTISH NATIONAL PARTY, 6 North Charlotte Street, Edinburgh EH2 4JH.—*Chairman,* G. Wilson; *Deputy Chairman,* Mrs. M. Ewing; *Hon. Treasurer,* A. Morgan; *National Sec.,* J. Swinney; *Parliamentary Party Leader,* Mrs. M. Ewing, M.P.; *Chief Whip,* A. Welsh, M.P.

SOCIAL DEMOCRATIC PARTY, 4 Cowley Street, SW1P 3NB.—*President,* Rt. Hon. Mrs. S. Williams; *Vice-Presidents,* Rt. Hon. W. Rodgers, J. Cartwright, M.P.; *National Sec.,* R. Newby; *Parliamentary Party Leader,* R. Maclennan, M.P.; *Leader of the S.D.P. Peers,* Lord Diamond.

The S.D.P. Whip in the House of Lords is Baroness Stedman. The S.D.P. Whip in the House of Commons is J. Cartwright, M.P.

NORTHERN IRELAND

SOCIAL DEMOCRATIC AND LABOUR PARTY, 38 University Street, Belfast BT7 1FZ.—*Chairman,* A. Maginness; *Deputy Chairmen,* M. Durkan, A. Colton; *Hon. Treasurer,* P. Brannigan; *Gen. Sec.,* Ms. P. McGlone; *Parliamentary Party Leader,* J. Hume, M.P.; *Deputy Leader,* S. Mallon, M.P.

ULSTER DEMOCRATIC UNIONIST PARTY, 296 Albertbridge Road, Belfast BT5 4GW.—*Chairman,* J. McClure; *Deputy Chairman,* S. Gibson; *Hon. Treasurer,* D. Herron; *Sec.,* A. Kane; *Parliamentary Party Leader,* Dr. I. Paisley, M.P.; *Deputy Leader,* P. Robinson, M.P.

ULSTER UNIONIST COUNCIL, 3 Glengall Street, Belfast BT12 5AE.—*Chairman,* J. Allen; *Deputy Chairman,* Dr. W. Brownlees; *Hon. Treasurer,* J. Cunningham; *Gen. Sec.,* F. Millar; *Party Leader,* Rt. Hon. J. H. Molyneaux, M.P.

ALPHABETICAL LIST OF MEMBERS OF THE HOUSE OF COMMONS

(as at end July 1987)
For abbreviations, *see* page 320

	Maj.
Abbott, Ms. Diane J. (*b.* 1953), *Lab.*, *Hackney, N. and Stoke Newington*	7,678
*Adams, Allen S. (*b.* 1946), *Lab.*, *Paisley, N.*	14,442
*Adams, Gerard (*b.* 1948), *S.F.*, *Belfast, W.* .	2,221
*Adley, Robert J. (*b.* 1935), *C.*, *Christchurch*	22,374
*Aitken, Jonathan W. P. (*b.* 1942), *C.*, *Thanet, S.*	13,683
*Alexander, Richard T. (*b.* 1934), *C.*, *Newark*	13,543
*Alison, Rt. Hon. Michael J. H. (*b.* 1926), *C.*, *Selby*	13,779
Allason, Rupert W. S. (*b.* 1951), *C.*, *Torbay*	8,820
Allen, Graham W. (*b.* 1953), *Lab.*, *Nottingham, N.*	1,665
*Alton, David P. P.(*b.* 1951), *L/All.*, *Liverpool, Mossley Hill*	2,226
*Amery, Rt. Hon. H. Julian (*b.* 1919), *C.*, *Brighton, Pavilion*	9,142
*Amess, David A. A. (*b.* 1952), *C.*, *Basildon*	2,649
Amos, Alan T. (*b.* 1952), *C.*, *Hexham*	8,066
*Anderson, Donald (*b.* 1939), *Lab.*, *Swansea, E.*	19,338
Arbuthnot, James N. (*b.* 1952), *C.*, *Wanstead and Woodford*	16,412
*Archer, Rt. Hon. Peter K., Q.C. (*b.* 1926), *Lab.*, *Warley, W.*	5,393
Armstrong, Ms. Hilary J. (*b.* 1945), *Lab.*, *Durham, N.W.*	10,162
Arnold, Jacques A. (*b.* 1947), *C.*, *Gravesham*	8,792
*Arnold, Thomas R. (*b.* 1947), *C.*, *Hazel Grove*	1,840
*Ashby, David G. (*b.* 1940), *C.*, *Leicestershire, N. W.*	7,828
*Ashdown, J. J. D. (Paddy) (*b.* 1941), *L/All.*, *Yeovil*	5,700
*Ashley, Rt. Hon. Jack, C. H. (*b.* 1922), *Lab.*, *Stoke-on-Trent, S.*	5,053
*Ashton, Joseph W. (*b.* 1933), *Lab.*, *Bassetlaw*	5,613
*Aspinwall, Jack H. (*b.* 1933), *C.*, *Wansdyke*	16,144
*Atkins, Robert J. (*b.* 1946), *C.*, *S. Ribble* .	8,430
*Atkinson, David A. (*b.* 1940), *C.*, *Bournemouth, E.*	14,683
*Baker, Rt. Hon. Kenneth W. (*b.* 1934), *C.*, *Mole Valley*	16,076
*Baker, Nicholas B. (*b.* 1938), *C.*, *Dorset, N.*	11,907
*Baldry, Antony B. (*b.* 1950), *C.*, *Banbury* .	17,330
*Banks, Robert G. (*b.* 1937), *C.*, *Harrogate*	11,902
*Banks, Tony L. (*b.* 1943), *Lab.*, *Newham, N. W.*	8,496
Barnes, Harold (*b.* 1936), *Lab.*, *Derbyshire, N.E.*	3,720
*Barnes, Mrs. Rosemary S. (*b.* 1946), *S.D.P./All.*, *Greenwich*	2,141
*Barron, Kevin J. (*b.* 1946), *Lab.*, *Rother Valley*	15,790
*Batiste, Spencer L. (*b.* 1945), *C.*, *Elmet*	5,356
Battle, John D. (*b.* 1951), *Lab.*, *Leeds, W.* .	4,692
*Beaumont-Dark, Anthony M. (*b.* 1932), *C.*, *Birmingham, Selly Oak*	2,584
*Beckett, Mrs. Margaret M. (*b.* 1943), *Lab.*, *Derby, S.*	1,516
*Beggs, J. Roy (*b.* 1936), *O.U.P.*, *Antrim, E.*	15,360
*Beith, Alan J. (*b.* 1943), *L./All.*, *Berwickupon-Tweed*	9,503
*Bell, Stuart (*b.* 1938), *Lab.*, *Middlesbrough*	14,958
*Bellingham, Henry C. (*b.* 1955), *C.*, *Norfolk, N.W.*	10,825
*Bendall, Vivian W. H. (*b.* 1938), *C.*, *Ilford, N.*	12,090
*Benn, Rt. Hon. Anthony N. W. (*b.* 1925), *Lab.*, *Chesterfield*	8,577

	Maj.
*Bennett, Andrew F. (*b.* 1939), *Lab.*, *Denton and Reddish*	8,250
Bennett, Nicholas J. (*b.* 1949), *C.*, *Pembroke*	5,700
*Benyon, William R. (*b.* 1930), *C.*, *Milton Keynes*	13,701
*Bermingham, Gerald E. (*b.* 1940), *Lab.*, *St. Helens, S.*	13,801
*Bevan, A. David G. (*b.* 1928), *C.*, *Birmingham, Yardley*	2,522
*Bidwell, Sydney J. (*b.* 1917), *Lab.*, *Ealing, Southall*	7,977
*Biffin, Rt. Hon. W. John (*b.* 1930), *C.*, *Shropshire, N.*	14,415
*Biggs-Davison, Sir John A. (*b.* 1918), *C.*, *Epping Forest*	21,513
*Blackburn, John G. (*b.* 1933), *C.*, *Dudley, W.*	10,244
*Blair, Anthony C. L. (*b.* 1953), *Lab.*, *Sedgefield*	13,058
*Blaker, Rt. Hon. Sir Peter A. R., K.C.M.G. (*b.* 1922), *C.*, *Blackpool, S.*	6,744
Blunkett, David (*b.* 1947), *Lab.*, *Sheffield, Brightside*	24,191
Boateng, Paul Y. (*b.* 1951), *Lab.*, *Brent, S.*	7,931
*Body, Sir Richard B. F. S. (*b.* 1927), *C.*, *Holland with Boston*	17,595
*Bonsor, Sir Nicholas C., Bt. (*b.* 1942), *C.*, *Upminster*	16,857
*Boothroyd, Miss Betty (*b.* 1929), *Lab.*, *West Bromwich, W.*	5,253
*Boscawen, Hon. Robert T., M.C. (*b.* 1923), *C.*, *Somerton and Frome*	9,538
Boswell, Timothy E. (*b.* 1942), *C.*, *Daventry*	19,690
*Bottomley, Peter J. (*b.* 1944), *C.*, *Eltham* .	6,460
*Bottomley, Mrs. Virginia H. B. M. (*b.* 1948), *C.*, *Surrey, S. W.*	14,343
*Bowden, Andrew, M.B.E. (*b.* 1930), *C.*, *Brighton, Kemptown*	9,260
*Bowden, Gerald F., T.D. (*b.* 1935), *C.*, *Dulwich*	180
Bowis, John C. (*b.* 1945), *C.*, *Battersea*	857
*Boyes, Roland (*b.* 1937), *Lab.*, *Houghton and Washington*	20,193
*Boyson, Rt. Hon. Sir Rhodes (*b.* 1925), *C.*, *Brent, N.*	15,720
Bradley, Keith J. C. (*b.* 1950), *Lab.*, *Manchester, Withington*	3,391
*Braine, Rt. Hon. Sir Bernard R. (*b.* 1914), *C.*, *Castle Point*	19,248
*Brandon-Bravo, Martin M. (*b.* 1932), *C.*, *Nottingham, S.*	2,234
*Bray, Dr. Jeremy W. (*b.* 1930), *Lab.*, *Motherwell, S.*	16,930
Brazier, Julian W. H. (*b.* 1953), *C.*, *Canterbury*	14,891
*Bright, Graham F. J. (*b.* 1942), *C.*, *Luton, S.*	5,115
*Brittan, Rt. Hon. Leon, Q.C. (*b.* 1939), *C.*, *Richmond, Yorks.*	19,576
*Brooke, Hon. Peter L. (*b.* 1934), *C.*, *City of London and Westminster, S.*	12,042
*Brown, Dr. James G. (*b.* 1951), *Lab.*, *Dunfermline, E.*	19,589
*Brown, Michael R. (*b.* 1951), *C.*, *Brigg and Cleethorpes*	12,248
*Brown, Nicholas H. (*b.* 1950), *Lab.*, *Newcastle upon Tyne, E.*	12,500
*Brown, Ronald D. M. (*b.* 1940), *Lab.*, *Edinburgh, Leith*	11,327

Maj.

*Browne, John E. D. D. (b. 1938), C., Winchester 7,479
Bruce, Ian C. (b. 1947), C., Dorset, S. 15,067
*Bruce, Malcolm G. (b. 1944), L./All., Gordon 9,519
*Buchan, Norman F. (b. 1922), Lab., Paisley, S. 15,785
*Buchanan-Smith, Rt. Hon. Alick L. (b. 1932), C., Kincardine and Deeside 2,063
*Buck, Sir P. Antony F., Q.C. (b. 1928), C., Colchester, N. 13,623
Buckley, George J. (b. 1935), Lab., Hemsworth 20,700
*Budgen, Nicholas W. (b. 1937), C., Wolverhampton, S.W. 10,318
Burns, Simon H. M. (b. 1952), C., Chelmsford 7,761
*Burt, Alistair J. H. (b. 1955), C., Bury, N. . 6,911
*Butcher, John P. (b. 1946), C., Coventry, S.W. 3,210
Butler, Christopher J. (b. 1950), C., Warrington, S. 3,609
*Butterfill, John V. (b. 1941), C., Bournemouth, W. 12,651
*Caborn, Richard G. (b. 1943), Lab., Sheffield, Central 19,342
*Callaghan, James (b. 1927), Lab., Heywood and Middleton 6,848
Campbell, Ronald (b. 1943), Lab., Blyth Valley 853
Campbell, W. Menzies, C.B.E., Q.C. (b. 1941), L./All., Fife, N.E. 1,447
*Campbell-Savours, Dale N. (b. 1943), Lab., Workington 7,019
*Canavan, Dennis A. (b. 1942), Lab., Falkirk, W. 13,552
*Carlile, Alexander C., Q.C. (b. 1948), L./All., Montgomery 2,558
*Carlisle, John R. (b. 1942), C., Luton, N. .. 15,573
*Carlisle, Kenneth M. (b. 1941), C., Lincoln 7,483
Carrington, Matthew H. M. (b. 1947), C., Fulham 6,322
*Carttiss, Michael R. H. (b. 1938), C., Great Yarmouth 10,083
*Cartwright, John C. (b. 1933), S.D.P./All., Woolwich 1,937
*Cash, William N. P. (b. 1940), C., Stafford . 13,707
*Chalker, Rt. Hon. Mrs. Lynda (b. 1942), C., Wallasey 279
*Channon, Rt. Hon. H. Paul G. (b. 1935), C., Southend, W. 8,400
*Chapman, Sydney B. (b. 1935), C., Chipping Barnet 14,871
*Chope, Christopher R., O.B.E. (b. 1947), C., Southampton, Itchen 6,716
*Churchill, Winston S. (b. 1940), C., Davyhulme 8,199
*Clark, Hon. Alan K. M. (b. 1928), C., Plymouth, Sutton 4,013
*Clark, Dr. David G. (b. 1939), Lab., South Shields 13,851
*Clark, Dr. Michael (b. 1935), C., Rochford . 19,694
*Clark, Sir William G. (b. 1917), C., Croydon, S. 19,063
*Clarke, Rt. Hon. Kenneth H., Q.C. (b. 1940), C., Rushcliffe 20,839
*Clarke, Thomas, C.B.E. (b. 1941), Lab., Monklands, W. 18,333
*Clay, Robert A. (b. 1946), Lab., Sunderland, N. 14,672
*Clelland, David G. (b 1943), Lab., Tyne Bridge 15,573
*Clwyd, Mrs. Ann (b. 1937), Lab., Cynon Valley 21,571
*Cohen, Harry M. (b. 1949), Lab., Leyton .. 4,641
*Coleman, Donald R., C.B.E. (b. 1925), Lab., Neath 20,578

Maj.

*Colvin, Michael K. B. (b. 1932), C., Romsey and Waterside 15,272
*Conway, Derek L. (b. 1953), C., Shrewsbury and Atcham 9,064
*Cook, Francis (b. 1935), Lab., Stockton, N. 8,801
*Cook, R. F. (Robin) (b. 1946), Lab., Livingston 11,105
Coombs, Anthony M. V. (b. 1952), C., Wyre Forest 7,224
*Coombs, Simon C. (b. 1947), C., Swindon .. 4,857
*Cope, John A. (b. 1937), C., Northavon 14,270
*Corbett, Robin (b. 1933), Lab., Birmingham, Erdington 2,467
*Corbyn, Jeremy B. (b. 1949), Lab., Islington, N. 9,657
*Cormack, Patrick T. (b. 1939), C., Staffordshire, S. 25,268
*Couchman, James R. (b. 1942), C., Gillingham 12,549
Cousins, James M. (b. 1944), Lab., Newcastle upon Tyne, Central 2,483
*Cox, Thomas M. (b. 1930), Lab., Tooting .. 1,441
Cran, James D. (b. 1944), C., Beverley 12,595
*Critchley, Julian M. G. (b. 1930), C., Aldershot 17,784
*Crowther, J. Stanley (b. 1925), Lab., Rotherham 16,012
Cryer, G. Robert (b. 1934), Lab., Bradford, S. 309
Cummings, John S. (b. 1943), Lab., Easington 24,639
*Cunliffe, Lawrence F. (b. 1929), Lab., Leigh 16,606
*Cunningham, Dr. John A. (b. 1939), Lab., Copeland 1,894
*Currie, Mrs. Edwina (b. 1946), C., Derbyshire, S. 10,311
Curry, David M. (b. 1944), C., Skipton and Ripon 17,174
*Dalyell, Tam (Sir Thomas Dalyell of the Binns, Bt.) (b. 1932), Lab., Linlithgow ... 10,373
*Darling, Alistair M. (b. 1953), Lab., Edinburgh, Central 2,262
*Davies, Rt. Hon. D. J. Denzil (b. 1938), Lab., Llanelli 20,935
Davies, J. Quentin (b. 1944), C., Stamford and Spalding 13,991
*Davies, Ronald (b. 1946), Lab., Caerphilly . 19,167
Davis, David M. (b. 1948), C., Boothferry .. 18,970
*Davis, Terence A. G. (b. 1938), Lab., Birmingham, Hodge Hill 4,789
Day, Stephen R. (b. 1948), C., Cheadle 10,631
*Dean, Sir A. Paul (b. 1924), C., Woodspring 17,852
Devlin, Timothy R. (b. 1959), C., Stockton, S. 774
*Dewar, Donald C. (b. 1937), Lab., Glasgow, Garscadden 18,977
*Dickens, Geoffrey K. (b. 1931), C., Littleborough and Saddleworth 6,202
*Dicks, Terence P. (b. 1937), C., Hayes and Harlington 5,965
*Dixon, Donald (b. 1929), Lab., Jarrow 18,795
*Dobson, Frank G. (b. 1940), Lab., Holborn and St. Pancras 8,853
Doran, Frank (b. 1949), Lab., Aberdeen, S. 1,198
*Dorrell, Stephen J. (b. 1952), C., Loughborough 17,648
*Douglas, Richard G. (b. 1932), Lab., Dunfermline, W. 9,402
*Douglas-Hamilton, Lord James (b. 1942), C., Edinburgh, W. 1,234
*Dover, Densmore R. (b. 1938), C., Chorley . 8,057
*Duffy, A. E. Patrick (b. 1920), Lab., Sheffield, Attercliffe 17,191
*Dunn, Robert J. (b. 1946), C., Dartford 14,929
Dunnachie, James F. (b. 1930), Lab., Glasgow, Pollok 17,983

Maj.

Dunwoody, Hon. Mrs. Gwyneth P. (b. 1930), Lab., Crewe and Nantwich 1,092
Durant, R. Anthony B. (b. 1928), C., Reading, W. 16,753
Dykes, Hugh J. M. (b. 1939), C., Harrow, E. 18,273
Eadie, Alexander, B.E.M. (b. 1920), Lab., Midlothian 12,253
Eastham, Kenneth (b. 1927), Lab., Manchester, Blackley 10,122
Eggar, Timothy J. C. (b. 1951), C., Enfield, N. 14,015
Emery, Sir Peter F. H. (b. 1926), C., Honiton 16,562
Evans, David J. (b. 1935), C., Welwyn Hatfield* 10,903
Evans, John (b. 1930), Lab., St. Helens, N. 14,260
Evennett, David A. (b. 1949), C., Erith and Crayford 6,994
*Ewing, Harry (b. 1931), Lab., Falkirk, E. .. 14,023
Ewing, Mrs. Margaret A. (b. 1945), S.N.P., Moray* 3,685
Fairbairn, Nicholas H., Q.C. (b. 1933), C., Perth and Kinross 5,676
Fallon, Michael C. (b. 1952), C., Darlington 2,661
Farr, Sir John A. (b. 1922), C., Harborough 18,810
Fatchett, Derek J. (b. 1945), Lab., Leeds, Central 11,505
Faulds, Andrew M. W. (b. 1923), Lab., Warley, E. 5,585
Favell, Anthony R. (b. 1939), C., Stockport 2,853
Fearn, Ronald C. (b. 1931), L./All., Southport* 1,849
Fenner, Dame Peggy E., D.B.E. (b. 1940), C., Medway 9,929
Field, Barry J. A. (b. 1946), C., Isle of Wight* 6,442
*Field, Frank (b. 1942), Lab., Birkenhead .. 15,372
Fields, Terence (b. 1937), Lab., Liverpool, Broadgreen 6,047
Finsberg, Sir Geoffrey, M.B.E. (b. 1926), C., Hampstead and Highgate 2,221
Fisher, Mark (b. 1944), Lab., Stoke-on-Trent, Central 9,770
Flannery, Martin H. (b. 1918), Lab., Sheffield, Hillsborough 3,286
Flynn, Paul P. (b. 1935), Lab., Newport, W.* 2,708
Fookes, Miss Janet E. (b. 1936), C., Plymouth, Drake 3,125
Foot, Rt. Hon. Michael M. (b. 1913), Lab., Blaenau Gwent 27,861
Forman, F. Nigel (b. 1943), C., Carshalton and Wallington 14,409
*Forsyth, Michael B. (b. 1954), C., Stirling . 948
Forsythe, Clifford (b. 1929), O.U.P., Antrim, S. 19,587
Forth, M. Eric (b. 1944), C., Worcestershire, Mid 14,911
Foster, Derek (b. 1937), Lab., Bishop Auckland 7,035
Foulkes, George (b. 1942), Lab., Carrick, Cumnock and Doon Valley 16,802
Fowler, Rt. Hon. P. Norman (b. 1938), C., Sutton Coldfield 21,183
Fox, Sir J. Marcus, M.B.E. (b. 1927), C., Shipley 12,630
Franks, Cecil S. (b. 1935), C., Barrow and Furness 3,927
*Fraser, John D. (b. 1934), Lab., Norwood .. 4,723
Freeman, Roger N. (b. 1942), C., Kettering 11,327
French, Douglas C. (b. 1944), C., Gloucester* 12,035
Fry, Peter D. (b 1931), C., Wellingborough 14,070
Fyfe, Mrs. Maria (b. 1938), Lab., Glasgow, Maryhill* 19,364
Galbraith, Samuel L. (b. 1945), Lab., Strathkelvin and Bearsden* 2,452
*Gale, Roger J. (b. 1943), C., Thanet, N. 17,480
Galloway, George (b. 1954), Lab., Glasgow, Hillhead* 3,251

Maj.

*Gardiner, George A. (b. 1935), C., Reigate . 18,173
Garel-Jones, W. A. T, Tristan (b. 1941), C., Watford 11,736
Garrett, John L. (b. 1931), Lab., Norwich, S.* 336
Garrett, William E. (b. 1920), Lab., Wallsend 19,384
George, Bruce T. (b. 1942), Lab., Walsall, S. 1,116
Gilbert, Dr. The Rt. Hon. John W. (b. 1927), Lab., Dudley, E. 3,473
Gill, Christopher J. F., R.D. (b. 1936), C., Ludlow* 11,699
Gilmour, Rt. Hon. Sir Ian H. J. L., BT. (b. 1926), C., Chesham and Amersham 19,440
Glyn, Dr. Alan, E.R.D. (b. 1918), C., Windsor and Maidenhead 17,836
Godman, Norman A. (b. 1937), Lab., Greenock and Port Glasgow 20,055
Golding, Mrs. Llinos (b. 1933), Lab., Newcastle-under-Lyme 5,132
Goodhart, Sir Philip C. (b. 1925), C., Beckenham 13,464
Goodlad, Alastair R. (b. 1943), C., Eddisbury 15,835
Goodson-Wickes, Dr. Charles (b. 1945), C., Wimbledon* 11,301
Gordon, Mrs. Mildred (b. 1923), Lab., Bow and Poplar* 4,631
Gorman, Mrs. Theresa E. (b. 1941), C., Billericay* 17,986
*Gorst, John M. (b. 1928), C., Hendon, N. .. 20,155
Gould, Bryan C. (b. 1939), Lab., Dagenham 2,469
Gow, Ian R. E., T.D. (b. 1937), C., Eastbourne 16,923
Gower, Sir H. Raymond (b. 1916), C., Vale of Glamorgan 6,251
Graham, Thomas (b. 1944), Lab., Renfrew, W. and Inverclyde* 4,053
Grant, Bernard A. M. (b. 1944), Lab., Tottenham* 4,141
Grant, Sir J. Anthony (b. 1925), C., Cambridgeshire, S.W. 18,251
Greenway, Harry (b. 1934), C., Ealing, N. 15,153
Greenway, John R. (b. 1946), C., Ryedale . 9,740
*Gregory, Conal R. (b. 1947), C., York 147
Griffiths, Sir Eldon W. (b. 1925), C., Bury St. Edmunds 21,458
Griffiths, Nigel (b. 1955), Lab., Edinburgh, S.* 1,859
Griffiths, Peter H. S. (b. 1928), C., Portsmouth, N. 18,401
Griffiths, Winston J. (b. 1943), Lab., Bridgend* 4,380
*Grist, Ian (b. 1938), C., Cardiff, Central ... 1,986
Grocott, Bruce J. (b. 1940), Lab., The Wrekin* 1,456
Ground, R. Patrick, Q.C. (b. 1932), C., Feltham and Heston 5,430
Grylls, W. Michael J. (b. 1934), C., Surrey, N.W. 23,575
Gummer, Rt. Hon. John S. (b. 1939), C., Suffolk, Coastal 15,280
Hamilton, Hon. Archibald G. (b. 1941), C., Epsom and Ewell 20,761
*Hamilton, M. Neil (b. 1949), C., Tatton 17,094
Hampson, Dr. Keith (b. 1943), C., Leeds, N.W. 5,201
Hanley, Jeremy J. (b. 1945), C., Richmond and Barnes 1,766
*Hannam, John G. (b. 1929), C., Exeter 7,656
*Hardy, Peter (b. 1931), Lab., Wentworth .. 20,092
Hargreaves, Andrew R. (b. 1955), C., Birmingham, Hall Green* 7,621
Hargreaves, Joseph K. (b. 1939), C., Hyndburn 2,220
Harman Ms. Harriet R. (b. 1950), Lab., Peckham 9,489
*Harris, David A. (b. 1937), C., St. Ives 7,555

Maj.

*Moore, Rt. Hon. John E. M. (*b.* 1937), *C.*, Croydon, Central* 12,617

Morgan, H. Rhodri (*b.* 1939), *Lab.*, *Cardiff, W.* 4,045

Morley, Elliot A. (*b.* 1952), *Lab.*, *Glanford and Scunthorpe* 512

*Morris, Rt. Hon. Alfred (*b.* 1928), *Lab.*, Manchester, Wythenshawe* 11,855

*Morris, Rt. Hon. John, Q.C. (*b.* 1931), *Lab.*, Aberavon* 20,609

*Morris, Michael W. L. (*b.* 1936), *C.*, *Northampton, S.* 17,803

*Morrison, Hon. Charles A. (*b.* 1932), *C.*, Devizes* 17,830

*Morrison, Hon. Peter H. (*b.* 1944), *C.*, *City of Chester* 4,855

Moss, Malcolm D. (*b.* 1943), *C.*, *Cambridgeshire, N.E.* 1,428

Mowlam, Dr. Marjorie (*b.* 1949), *Lab.*, Redcar* 7,735

*Moynihan, Hon. Colin B. (*b.* 1955), *C.*, Lewisham, E.* 4,814

*Mudd, W. David (*b.* 1933), *C.*, *Falmouth and Camborne* 5,039

Mullin, Christopher J. (*b.* 1947), *Lab.*, Sunderland, S.* 12,613

Murphy, Paul P. (*b.* 1948), *Lab.*, *Torfaen* .. 17,550

*Neale, Gerrard A. (*b.* 1941), *C.*, *Cornwall, N.* 5,682

*Needham, Richard F. (*b.* 1942), *C.*, *Wiltshire, N.* 10,939

*Nellist, David J. (*b.* 1952), *Lab.*, *Coventry S. E.* 6,653

*Nelson, R. Anthony (*b.* 1948), *C.*, *Chichester* 20,177

*Neubert, Michael J. (*b.* 1933), *C.*, *Romford* 13,471

*Newton, Antony H., O.B.E. (*b.* 1937), *C.*, Braintree* 16,857

*Nicholls, Patrick C. M. (*b.* 1948), *C.*, *Teignbridge* 10,425

Nicholson, David J. (*b.* 1944), *C.*, *Taunton* 10,380

Nicholson, Miss Emma H. (*b.* 1941), *C.*, Devon, W. and Torridge* 6,468

*Oakes, Rt. Hon. Gordon J. (*b.* 1931), *Lab.*, Halton* 14,578

*O'Brien, William (*b.* 1929), *Lab.*, *Normanton* 7,287

*O'Neill, Martin J. (*b.* 1945), *Lab.*, *Clackmannan* 12,401

*Onslow, Cranley G. D. (*b.* 1926), *C.*, *Woking* 16,544

*Oppenheim, Phillip A. C. L. (*b.* 1955), *C.*, Amber Valley* 9,500

*Orme, Rt. Hon. Stanley (*b.* 1923), *Lab.*, Salford, E.* 12,056

*Owen, Dr. The Rt. Hon. David A. L. (*b.* 1938), *S.D.P./All.*, *Plymouth, Devonport* 6,470

*Page, Richard L. (*b.* 1941), *C.*, *Hertfordshire, S.W.* 15,784

Paice, James E. T. (*b.* 1949), *C.*, *Cambridge, S. E.* 17,502

*Paisley, Rev. Ian R. K. (*b.* 1926), *D.U.P.*, Antrim, N.* 23,234

*Parkinson, Rt. Hon. Cecil E. (*b.* 1931), *C.*, Hertsmere* 18,106

*Parry, Robert (*b.* 1933), *Lab.*, *Liverpool, Riverside* 20,689

*Patchett, Terry (*b.* 1940), *Lab.*, *Barnsley, E.* 23,511

Patnick, Cyril I. (*b.* 1929), *C.*, *Sheffield, Hallam* 7,637

*Patten, Christopher F. (*b.* 1944), *C.*, *Bath* . 1,412

*Patten, John H. C. (*b.* 1945), *C.*, *Oxford, W. and Abingdon* 4,878

*Pattie, Rt. Hon. Sir Geoffrey E. (*b.* 1936), *C.*, *Chertsey and Walton* 17,469

*Pawsey, James F. (*b.* 1933), *C.*, *Rugby and Kenilworth* 16,264

Maj.

*Peacock, Mrs. Elizabeth J. (*b.* 1937), *C.*, Batley and Spen* 1,363

*Pendry, Thomas (*b.* 1934), *Lab.*, *Stalybridge and Hyde* 5,663

*Pike, Peter L. (*b.* 1937), *Lab.*, *Burnley* 7,557

Porter, David J. (*b.* 1948), *C.*, *Waveney* 11,783

*Porter, George B. (*b.* 1948), *C.*, *Wirral, S.* . 10,963

*Portillo, Michael D. X. (*b.* 1953), *C.*, *Enfield, Southgate* 18,345

*Powell, Raymond (*b.* 1928), *Lab.*, *Ogmore* . 22,292

*Powell, William R. (*b.* 1948), *C.*, *Corby* 1,805

*Prescott, John L. (*b.* 1938), *Lab.*, *Kingston upon Hull, E.* 14,689

*Price, Sir David E. C. (*b.* 1924), *C.*, *Eastleigh* 13,355

Primarolo, Ms. Dawn (*b.* 1954), *Lab.*, *Bristol, S.* 1,404

Quin, Miss Joyce G. (*b.* 1944), *Lab.*, *Gateshead, E.* 17,228

*Radice, Giles H. (*b.* 1936), *Lab.*, *Durham, N.* 18,433

*Raffan, Keith, W. T. (*b.* 1949), *C.*, *Delyn* ... 1,224

*Raison, Rt. Hon. Timothy H. F. (*b.* 1929), *C.*, *Aylesbury* 16,558

*Randall, Stuart J. (*b.* 1938), *Lab.*, *Kingston upon Hull, W.* 8,130

*Rathbone, J. R. (Tim) (*b.* 1933), *C.*, *Lewes* . 13,620

*Redmond, Martin (*b.* 1937), *Lab.*, *Don Valley* 11,467

Redwood, John A. (*b.* 1951), *C.*, *Wokingham* 20,387

*Rees, Rt. Hon. Merlyn (*b.* 1920), *Lab.*, *Leeds, S. and Morley* 6,711

Reid, John (*b.* 1947), *Lab.*, *Motherwell, N.* . 23,595

*Renton, R. Timothy (*b.* 1932), *C.*, *Sussex, Mid* 18,292

*Rhodes James, Robert V. (*b.* 1933), *C.*, Cambridge* 5,060

*Rhys Williams, Sir Brandon M., BT. (*b.* 1927), *C.*, *Kensington* 4,447

*Richardson, Ms. Josephine (*b.* 1923), *Lab.*, Barking* 3,409

Riddick, Graham E. G. (*b.* 1955), *C.*, *Colne Valley* 1,677

*Ridley, Rt. Hon. Nicholas (*b.* 1929), *C.*, Cirencester and Tewkesbury* 12,662

*Ridsdale, Sir Julian E., C.B.E. (*b.* 1915), *C.*, Harwich* 12,082

*Rifkind, Rt. Hon. Malcolm L., Q.C. (*b.* 1946), *C.*, *Edinburgh, Pentlands* 3,745

*Roberts, Allan (*b.* 1943), *Lab.*, *Bootle* 24,477

*Roberts, I. Wyn P. (*b.* 1930), *C.*, *Conwy* 3,024

*Robertson, George I. M. (*b.* 1946), *Lab.*, Hamilton* 21,662

*Robinson, Geoffrey (*b.* 1938), *Lab.*, *Coventry, N.W.* 5,663

*Robinson, Peter D. (*b.* 1948), *D.U.P.*, *Belfast, E.* 9,798

*Roe, Mrs. Marion A. (*b.* 1936), *C.*, *Broxbourne* 22,995

*Rogers, Allan R. (*b.* 1932), *Lab.*, *Rhondda* . 30,754

*Rooker, Jeffrey W. (*b.* 1941), *Lab.*, *Birmingham, Perry Barr* 6,933

*Ross, Ernest (*b.* 1942), *Lab.*, *Dundee, W.* .. 16,526

*Ross, William (*b.* 1936), *O.U.P.*, *Londonderry, E.* 20,157

*Rossi, Sir Hugh A. L. (*b.* 1927), *C.*, *Hornsey and Wood Green* 1,779

*Rost, Peter L. (*b.* 1930), *C.*, *Erewash* 9,754

*Rowe, Andrew J. B. (*b.* 1935), *C.*, *Kent, Mid.* 14,768

*Rowlands, Edward (*b.* 1940), *Lab.*, *Merthyr Tydfil and Rhymney* 28,130

Ruddock, Ms. Joan M. (*b.* 1943), *Lab.*, Lewisham, Deptford* 6,771

*Rumbold, Mrs. Angela C. R., C.B.E. (*b.* 1932), *C.*, *Mitcham and Morden* 6,183

*Ryder, Richard A., O.B.E. (*b.* 1949), *C.*, Norfolk, Mid* 18,008

	Maj.		Maj.
*Wallace, James R. (b. 1954), L./All., Orkney and Shetland	3,922	*Wilkinson, John A. D. (b. 1940), C., Ruislip-Northwood	16,971
*Waller, Gary P. A. (b. 1945), C., Keighley ..	5,606	*Williams, Rt. Hon. Alan J. (b. 1930), Lab., Swansea, W.	7,062
Walley, Ms. Joan L. (b. 1949), Lab., Stoke-on-Trent, N.	8,513	Williams, Alan W. (b. 1945), Lab., Carmarthen	4,317
*Walters, Dennis M., M.B.E. (b. 1928), C., Westbury	10,097	Wilshire, David (b. 1943), C., Spelthorne ..	20,050
*Ward, John D., C.B.E. (b. 1925), C., Poole ..	14,808	Wilson, Brian D. H. (b. 1948), Lab., Cunninghame, N.	4,467
*Wardell, Gareth L. (b. 1944), Lab., Gower .	5,764	*Winnick, David J. (b. 1933), Lab., Walsall, N.	1,790
*Wardle, Charles F. (b. 1939), C., Bexhill and Battle	20,519	*Winterton, Mrs. J. Ann (b. 1941), C., Congleton	7,969
*Wareing, Robert N. (b. 1930), Lab., Liverpool, West Derby	20,496	*Winterton, Nicholas R. (b. 1938), C., Macclesfield	19,092
*Warren, Kenneth R. (b. 1926), C., Hastings and Rye	7,347	Wise, Mrs. Audrey (b. 1935), Lab., Preston	10,645
*Watts, John A. (b. 1947), C., Slough	4,090	*Wolfson, G. Mark (b. 1934), C., Sevenoaks .	17,345
*Weatherill, Rt. Hon. B. Bernard (b. 1920), The Speaker, Croydon, N.E.	12,519	*Wood, Timothy J. R. (b. 1940), C., Stevenage	5,340
*Wells, Bowen (b. 1935), C., Hertford and Stortford	17,140	*Woodcock, Michael (b. 1943), C., Ellesmere Port and Neston	1,853
Welsh, Andrew (b. 1944), S.N.P., Angus, E.	1,544	Worthington, Anthony (b. 1941), Lab., Clydebank and Milngavie	16,304
*Welsh, Michael C. (b. 1926), Lab., Doncaster, N.	19,935	Wray, James (b. 1938), Lab., Glasgow, Provan	18,372
*Wheeler, John D. (b. 1940), C., Westminster, N.	3,310	*Yeo, Timothy S. K. (b. 1945), C., Suffolk, S.	16,243
*Whitney, Raymond W., O.B.E. (b. 1930), C., Wycombe	13,819	*Young, David W. (b. 1930), Lab., Bolton, S.E.	11,381
Widdecombe, Miss Ann N. (b. 1947), C., Maidstone	10,364	*Young, Sir George S. K., Bt. (b. 1941), C., Ealing, Acton	12,243
*Wiggin, A. W. (Jerry), T.D. (b. 1937), C., Weston-super-Mare	7,998	*Younger, Rt. Hon. George K. H., T.D. (b. 1931), C., Ayr	182
*Wigley, Dafydd W. (b. 1943), P.C., Caernarfon	12,802		

SMALL MAJORITIES

The following Members were returned in June 1987 with majorities of fewer than 1,000 votes.

*Richard Livsey (L/All., Brecon and Radnor) .	56	Timothy Janman (C., Thurrock)	690
Alan Meale (Lab., Mansfield)	56	Edward McGrady (S.D.L.P., Down, S.)	731
*Conal Gregory (C., York)	147	Timothy Devlin (C., Stockton, S.)	774
*Gerald Bowden (C., Dulwich)	180	*Christopher Smith (Lab., Islington, S. and Finsbury)	805
*Rt. Hon. George Younger (C., Ayr)	182	*Peter Thurnham (C., Bolton, N.E.)	813
Mrs. Maureen Hicks (C., Wolverhampton N.E.)	204	Ronald Campbell (Lab., Blyth Valley)	853
David Martin (C., Portsmouth, S.)	205	John Bowis (C., Battersea)	857
*Mrs. Lynda Chalker (C., Wallasey)	279	Michael Irvine (C., Ipswich)	874
Robert Cryer (Lab., Bradford S.)	309	Eric Martlew (Lab., Carlisle)	916
John Garrett (Lab., Norwich, S.)	336	*Michael Forsyth (C., Stirling)	948
Mrs. Ann Taylor (Lab., Dewsbury)	445	*Peter Snape (Lab., West Bromwich, E)	983
*Michael Knowles (C., Nottingham, E.)	456		
Elliott Morley (Lab., Glanford and Scunthorpe)	512		

WOMEN MEMBERS

The number of women M.P.s returned in June 1987 (41) is the highest ever.

Ms. Diane Abbott (Lab., Hackney N. and Stoke Newington); Ms. Hilary Armstrong (Lab., Durham N.W.); *Mrs. Rosemary Barnes (SDP/All., Greenwich); *Mrs. Margaret Beckett (Lab., Derby S.); *Miss Betty Boothroyd (Lab., West Bromwich W.); *Mrs. Virginia Bottomley (C., Surrey S.W.); *Mrs. Lynda Chalker (C., Wallasey); *Mrs. Ann Clwyd (Lab., Cynon Valley); *Mrs. Edwina Currie (C., Derbyshire S.); *Hon. Mrs. Gwyneth Dunwoody (Lab., Crewe and Nantwich); Mrs. Margaret Ewing (S.N.P., Moray); *Dame Peggy Fenner (C., Medway); *Miss Janet Fookes (C., Plymouth Drake); Mrs. Maria Fyfe (Lab., Glasgow Maryhill); *Mrs. Llinos Golding (Lab., Newcastle-under-Lyme); Mrs. Mildred Gordon (Lab., Bow and Poplar); Mrs. Theresa Gorman (C., Billericay); *Ms. Harriet Harman (Lab., Peckham); Mrs. Maureen Hicks (C., Wolverhampton N.E.); *Mrs. Elaine Kellett-Bowman (C., Lancaster); *Dame Jill Knight (C., Birmingham Edgbaston).

Miss Joan Lestor (Lab., Eccles); Mrs. Alice Mahon (Lab., Halifax); Mrs. Ray Michie (L./All., Argyll and Bute); Dr. Marjorie Mowlam (Lab., Redcar); Miss Emma Nicholson (C., Devon W. and Torridge); *Mrs. Elizabeth Peacock (C., Batley and Spen); Ms. Dawn Primarolo (Lab., Bristol S.); Miss Joyce Quin (Lab., Gateshead E.); *Ms. Jo Richardson (Lab., Barking); *Mrs. Marion Roe (C., Broxbourne); Ms. Joan Ruddock (Lab., Lewisham Deptford); *Mrs. Angela Rumbold (C., Mitcham and Morden); Mrs. Gillian Shephard (C., Norfolk S.W.); *Ms. Clare Short (Lab., Birmingham Ladywood); Mrs. Ann Taylor (Lab., Dewsbury); *Rt. Hon. Mrs. Margaret Thatcher (C., Finchley); Ms. Joan Walley (Lab., Stoke-on-Trent); Miss Ann Widdecombe (C., Maidstone); *Mrs. Ann Winterton (C., Congleton); Mrs. Audrey Wise (Lab., Preston).

THE HOUSE OF COMMONS BY CONSTITUENCIES, JUNE 1987

The figures following the name of the Constituency denote the total number of *Electors* in the Parliamentary Division at the General Election of June 11, 1987.

ABBREVIATIONS — *C.* = Conservative; *D.U.P.* = Democratic Unionist Party; *Ind.* = Independent; *L./All., S.D.P./All.* = Liberal and Social Democratic Alliance; *Lab.* = Labour; *O.U.P.* = Official Unionist Party; *P.C.* = Plaid Cymru; *S.D.L.P.* = Social Democratic and Labour Party; *S.F.* = Sinn Fein; *S.N.P.* = Scottish National Party; *U.P.U.P* = Ulster Popular Unionist Party.

All. = Alliance Party (N.I.); *B.N.* = British Nationalist; *Bread* = Creek Road Fresh Bread Party; *B.T.* = Blancmange Thrower; *C.D.* = Christian Democrat; *C.M.N.H.Y.* = Common Market No, Hanging Yes; *Comm.* = Communist Party; *C.P.R.P.* = Capital Punishment Referendum Party; *C.P.W.S.M.L.* = Capital Punishment Will Save More Lives; *C.S.* = Christian Socialist Opposing Secret Masonic Government; *D.C.* = Democratic Commonwealth Party; *Dem.* = Independent Democrat; *Ecol.* = Ecology (N.I.); *Ex. Lab. Mod.* = Ex Labour Moderate; *Falk.* = Right of Falkland Islands to elect Westminster M.P.; *F.D.P.* = Fancy Dress Party; *Fell.* = Fellowship Party; *F.P.* = Feudal Party; *Gait. Lab.* = Gaitskell Labour; *Gold* = Gold Party; *Grem.* = Gremloid; *Grn.* = Green Party; *H.P.* = Human Party; *I.C.C.* = Independent Community Campaigner, East Oxford People; *I.C.N.* = Independent Christian Nationalist; *L.A.O.* = Law and Order; *L.A.P.P.* = Let's Have Another Party Party; *L.M.* = Loony Official Monster Raving Party; *M.L.* = Moderate Labour Party; *N.F.F.G.* = National Front Flag Group; *N.P.R.* = National People's Rally; *O.F.P.* = Official Fidgeyitous Party; *O.O.B.P.C.* = Only Official Best Party Candidate; *O.S.M.* = Orkney and Shetland Movement; *P.I.P.* = Public Independent Plaintiff; *Prot. U.* = Protestant Unionist; *P.R.P.* = Protestant Reformation Party; *R.A.B.I.E.S.* = Rainbow Alliance Brixton Insane Extremist Section; *R.C.P.* = Return Capital Punishment; *Real U.* = Real Unionist; *R.F.* = Red Front; *Ret.* = Retired; *R.R.P.R.C.* = Revolutionary Reform Party Representative of Christ; *S.E.* = Spare the Earth; *S.P.G.B.* = Socialist Party of Great Britain; *W.P.* = Workers' Party (N.I.); *W.R.P.* = Workers' Revolutionary Party.

An asterisk * denotes membership of the last House. The majority in the 1983 General Election (and in any subsequent by-election) is shown below the 1987 result.

ENGLAND

Aldershot (Hants)
E. 80,797

*J. M. G. Critchley, *C.*		35,272
R. A. Hargreaves, *L./All.*		17,488
I. H. Pearson, *Lab.*		7,061
C. maj.		17,784
(June '83, C. maj. 12,218)		

Aldridge-Brownhills
(W. Midlands)
E. 62,129

*R. C. S. Shepherd, *C.*		26,434
C. Duncan, *Lab.*		14,038
G. Betteridge, *S.D.P./All.*		9,084
C. maj.		12,396
(June '83, C. maj. 12,284)		

Altrincham and Sale
(Gtr. Manchester)
E. 67,611

*Sir F. Montgomery, *C.*		27,746
J. Mulholland, *L./All.*		13,518
D. Hinder, *Lab.*		10,617
C. Maj.		14,228
(June '83, C. maj. 10,911)		

Amber Valley (Derbys)
E. 58,674

*P. A. C. L. Oppenheim, *C.*		28,603
D. M. Bookbinder, *Lab.*		19,103
S. Reynolds, *L./All.*		7,904
C. maj.		9,500
(June '83, C. maj. 3,318)		

Arundel (W. Sussex)
E. 78,683

*R. M. Marshall, *C.*		34,356
Dr. J. M. M. Walsh, *L./All.*		15,476
P. Slowe, *Lab.*		6,177
C. maj.		18,880
(June '83, C. maj. 15,705)		

Ashfield (Notts)
E. 70,937

*D. F. Haynes, *Lab.*		22,812
B. G. Coleman, *C.*		18,412
Mrs. F. B. Stein, *L./All.*		13,542
Lab. maj.		4,400
(June '83, Lab. maj. 6,087)		

Ashford (Kent)
E. 70,052

*H. K. Speed, *C.*		29,978
N. N. Macmillan, *S.D.P./ All.*		14,490
M. J. Wiggins, *Lab.*		7,775
Dr. C. A. Porter, *Grn.*		778
C. maj.		15,488
(June '83, C. maj. 13,911)		

Ashton-under-Lyne
(Gtr. Manchester)
E. 58,440

*Rt. Hon. R. E. Sheldon, *Lab.*		22,389
H. L. Cadman, *C.*		13,103
M. J. Hunter, *L./All.*		7,760
Lab. maj.		9,286
(June '83, Lab. maj. 7,697)		

Aylesbury (Bucks)
E. 76,919

*Rt. Hon. T. H. F. Raison, *C.*		32,970
M. A. Soole, *S.D.P./All.*		16,412
Ms. J. Larner, *Lab.*		7,936
C. maj.		16,558
(June '83, C. maj. 14,920)		

Banbury (Oxon)
E. 69,455

*A. B. Baldry, *C.*		29,716
D. C. Rowland, *S.D.P./All.*		12,386
J. A. Honeybone, *Lab.*		10,789
C. maj.		17,330
(June '83, C. maj. 13,025)		

Barking (Gtr. London)
E. 51,639

*Ms. J. Richardson, *Lab.*		15,307
W. K. Sharp, *C.*		11,898
J. K. Gibb, *L./All.*		7,336
Lab. maj.		3,409
(June '83, Lab. maj. 4,026)		

Barnsley (S. Yorks)

CENTRAL E. 55,902

E. E. Illsley, *Lab.*		26,139
Mrs. V. Prais, *C.*		7,088
Mrs. S. A. M. Holland, *L./ All.*		5,928
Lab. maj.		19,051
(June '83, Lab. maj. 14,173)		

EAST E. 53,505

*T. Patchett, *Lab.*		28,948
W. J. Clappison, *C.*		5,437
G. J. Griffiths, *L./All.*		4,482
Lab. maj.		23,511
(June '83, Lab. maj. 17,492)		

WEST AND PENISTONE E. 61,091

*A. McKay, *Lab.*		26,498
A. J. C. Duncan, *C.*		12,307
R. Hall, *S.D.P./All.*		7,409
Lab. maj.		14,191
(June '83, Lab. maj. 10,342)		

Barrow and Furness (Cumbria)
E. 69,288

*C. S. Franks, *C.*		25,431
P. Phizacklea, *Lab.*		21,504
R. W. Phelps, *S.D.P./All.*		7,799
C. maj.		3,927
(June '83, C. maj. 4,577)		

Basildon (Essex)
E. 68,500

*D. A. A. Amess, *C.*		21,858
J. G. H. Fulbrook, *Lab.*		19,209
R. M. Auvray, *L./All.*		9,139
C. maj.		2,649
(June '83, C. maj. 1,379)		

Basingstoke (Hants)
E. 78,003

*A. R. F. Hunter, C.	....	33,657
D. Bennett, S.D.P./All.	...	15,764
P. Daden, Lab.	....	10,632
C. maj.	....	17,893

(June '83, C. maj. 12,450)

Bassetlaw (Notts)
E. 68,043

*J. W. Ashton, Lab.	....	25,385
D. R. J. Selves, C.		19,772
W. G. Smith, S.D.P./All.	.	7,616
Lab. maj.	....	5,613

(June '83, Lab. maj. 3,831)

Bath (Avon)
E. 65,246

*C. F. Patten, C.	....	23,515
J. M. Dean, S.D.P./All.	...	22,103
Mrs. J. Smith, Lab.	......	5,507
D. N. Wall, Grn.	....	687
C. maj.	....	1,412

(June '83, C. maj. 5,304)

Batley and Spen (W. Yorks)
E. 74,347

*Mrs. E. J. Peacock, C.	....	25,512
K. J. Woolmer, Lab.	......	24,150
K. Burke, S.D.P./All.	....	8,372
A. Harrison, M.L.	....	689
C. maj.	....	1,363

(June '83, C. maj. 870)

Battersea (Gtr. London)
E. 66,979

J. C. Bowis, C.	....	20,945
*A. Dubs, Lab.	....	20,088
D. I. Harries, S.D.P./All.	.	5,634
Ms. S. G. Willington, Grn.		559
A. B. Bell, W.R.P.	....	116
C. maj.	....	857

(June '83, Lab. maj. 3,276)

Beaconsfield (Bucks)
E. 67,713

*T. J. Smith, C.	....	33,324
D. H. Ive, L./All.	....	11,985
K. J. Harper, Lab.	....	5,203
C. maj.	....	21,339

(June '83, C. maj. 18,300)

Beckenham (Gtr. London)
E. 60,110

*Sir P. C. Goodhart, C.	....	24,903
C. G. Darracott, L./All.	...	11,439
K. G. Ritchie, Lab.	....	7,888
C. maj.	....	13,464

(June '83, C. maj. 12,670)

Bedfordshire
MID E. 80,673

*N. W. Lyell, q.c., C.	......	37,411
N. C. Hills, S.D.P./All.	...	14,560
J. Heywood, Lab.	....	11,463
C. maj.	....	22,851

(June '83, C. maj. 17,381)

NORTH E. 73,491

*Sir T. H. H. Skeet, C.	.....	29,845
Mrs. J. V. Lennon, L./All.		13,340
C. B. Henderson, Lab.	.....	13,140
C. D. Slee, O.O.B.P.C.	....	435
C. maj.	....	16,505

(June '83, C. maj. 13,849)

SOUTH WEST E. 78,956

*W. D. Madel, C.	....	36,140
J. R. Burrow, S.D.P./All.	.	13,835
P. H. Dimoldenberg, Lab.	.	11,352
P. J. Rollings, Grn.	....	822
C. maj.	....	22,305

(June '83, C. maj. 15,731)

Berkshire East
E. 87,820

*A. J. MacKay, C.	....	39,094
Mrs. L. A. Murray, S.D.P./ All.		16,468
R. J. E. Evans, Lab.	......	9,287
C. maj.	....	22,626

(June '83, C. maj. 16,099)

Berwick-upon-Tweed (Nthmb)
E. 54,378

*A. J. Beith, L./All.	....	21,903
T. Middleton, C.	....	12,400
S. Lambert, Lab.	....	7,360
N. Pamphilion, Grn.	.....	379
L./All. maj.	....	9,503

(June '83, L./All. maj. 8,215)

Bethnal Green and Stepney
(Gtr. London)
E. 55,769

*Rt. Hon. P. D. Shore, Lab.		15,490
J. A. Shaw, L./All.	....	10,206
Lady O. H. Maitland, C.	..	6,176
Ms. S. Gasquoine, Comm.	.	232
Lab. maj.	....	5,284

(June '83, Lab. maj. 6,358)

Beverley (Humberside)
E. 78,923

J. D. Cran, C.	....	31,459
J. Bryant, L./All.	....	18,864
M. Shaw, Lab.	....	9,901
C. maj.	....	12,595

(June '83, C. maj. 13,869)

Bexhill and Battle
(E. Sussex)
E. 65,288

*C. F. Wardle, C.	....	33,570
R. Kiernan, S.D.P./All.	..	13,051
D. K. Watts, Lab.	....	3,903
C. maj.	....	20,519

(June '83, C. maj. 19,746)

Bexleyheath
(Gtr. London)
E. 59,448

*C. D. Townsend, C.	......	24,866
B. C. Standen, L./All.	....	13,179
J. F. Little, Lab.	....	8,218
C. maj.	....	11,687

(June '83, C. maj. 10,258)

Billericay (Essex)
E. 79,535

Mrs. T. E. Gorman, C.	....	33,741
M. Birch, S.D.P./All.	.....	15,755
R. Howitt, Lab.	....	11,942
C. maj.	....	17,986

(June '83, C. maj. 14,615)

Birkenhead (Merseyside)
E. 65,662

*F. Field, Lab.	....	27,883
K. J. Costa, C.	....	12,511
R. Kemp, L./All.	....	7,095
Lab. maj.	....	15,372

(June '83, Lab. maj. 9,714)

Birmingham (W. Midlands)
EDGBASTON E. 54,416

*Dame J. C. J. Knight, D.B.E., C.	....	18,595
J. Wilton, Lab.	....	10,014
J. C. Binns, S.D.P./All.	...	7,843
P. Simpson, Grn.	....	559
S. T. Hardwick, Ind. C.	...	307
C. maj.	....	8,581

(June '83, C. maj. 11,418)

ERDINGTON E. 54,179

*R. Corbett, Lab.	....	17,037
P. J. Johnston, C.	....	14,570
N. Biddlestone, S.D.P./All.		5,530
Lab. maj.	....	2,467

(June '83, Lab. maj. 231)

HALL GREEN E. 61,148

A. R. Hargreaves, C.	.....	20,478
Mrs. E. Brook, Lab.	......	12,857
M. Wilkes, S.D.P./All.	...	12,323
C. maj.	....	7,621

(June '83, C. maj. 9,373)

HODGE HILL E. 59,296

*T. A. G. Davis, Lab.	......	19,872
S. Eyre, C.	....	15,083
K. G. Hardeman, L./All.	..	5,868
Lab. maj.	....	4,789

(June '83, Lab. maj. 5,092)

LADYWOOD E. 58,761

*Ms. C. Short, Lab.	....	21,971
S. T. Lee, C.	....	11,943
G. S. Sangha, S.D.P./All.	.	3,532
Ms. J. Millington, Grn.	...	650
Lab. maj.	....	10,028

(June '83, Lab. maj. 9,030)

NORTHFIELD E. 73,319

*R. D. King, C.	....	24,024
J. F. Spellar, Lab.	....	20,889
J. Gordon, S.D.P./All.	....	8,319
C. maj.	....	3,135

(June '83, C. maj. 2,760)

PERRY BARR E. 73,767

*J. W. Rooker, Lab.	....	25,894
J. D. B. Taylor, C.	....	18,961
D. D. Webb, L./All.	......	6,514
Lab. maj.	....	6,933

(June '83, Lab. maj. 7,402)

SELLY OAK E. 72,213
*A. M. Beaumont-Dark, C. 23,305
A. Bore, Lab. 20,721
Mrs. C. Cane, L./All. 8,128
Ms. M. Hackett, Grn 611
    C. maj. 2,584
    (June '83, C. maj. 5,396)

SMALL HEATH E. 56,722
*Rt. Hon. D. H. Howell,
    Lab. 22,787
P. Nischal, C. 7,266
J. A. M. Hemming, L./All. 3,600
A. Clawley, Grn. 559
P. R. Sheppard, Comm. ... 154
    Lab. maj. 15,521
    (June '83, Lab. maj. 15,252)

SPARKBROOK E. 53,093
*Rt. Hon. R. S. G. Hattersley,
    Lab. 20,513
N. A. Khan, C. 8,654
R. Dimmick, S.D.P./All. 3,803
R. Ambler, Grn. 526
P. Khan, R.F. 229
    Lab. maj. 11,859
    (June '83, Lab. maj. 10,548)

YARDLEY E. 56,957
*A. D. G. Bevan, C. 17,931
G. Edge, Lab. 15,409
L. Smith, L./All. 8,734
    C. maj. 2,522
    (June '83, C. maj. 2,865)

Bishop Auckland (Durham)
E. 72,147
*D. Foster, Lab. 25,648
R. Wight, C. 18,613
G. Irwin, L./All. 9,195
    Lab. maj. 7,035
    (June '83, Lab. maj. 4,306)

Blaby (Leics)
E. 77,094
*Rt. Hon. N. Lawson, C. ... 37,732
R. E. Lustig, L./All. 15,556
J. M. Roberts, Lab. 9,046
    C. maj. 22,176
    (June '83, C. maj. 17,116)

Blackburn (Lancs)
E. 74,801
*J. W. Straw, Lab. 27,965
Mrs. A. C. Cheetham, C. .. 22,468
M. A. Ali, S.D.P./All. 5,602
    Lab. maj. 5,497
    (June '83, Lab. maj. 3,055)

Blackpool (Lancs)
NORTH E. 58,893
*N. A. Miscampbell, Q.C., C. 20,680
E. Kirton, Lab. 13,359
C. J. Heyworth, L./All. .. 9,032
    C. maj. 7,321
    (June '83, C. maj. 10,152)

SOUTH E. 57,567
*Rt. Hon. Sir P. A. R. Blaker,
    K.C.M.G., C. 20,312
Mrs. S. Baugh, Lab. 13,568
J. Allitt, S.D.P./All. 8,405
    C. maj. 6,744
    (June '83, C. maj. 10,138)

Blaydon (Tyne & Wear)
E. 66,301
*J. D. McWilliam, Lab. ... 25,277
V. P. Nunn, S.D.P./All. .. 12,789
P. R. Pescod, C. 12,147
    Lab. maj. 12,488
    (June '83, Lab. maj. 7,222)

Blyth Valley (Nthmb)
E. 59,104
R. Campbell, Lab. 19,604
Miss R. M. Brownlow,
    S.D.P./All. 18,751
Dr. R. Kinghorn, C. 7,823
    Lab. maj. 853
    (June '83, Lab. maj. 3,243)

Bolsover (Derbys)
E. 65,452
*D. E. Skinner, Lab. 28,453
M. R. Lingens, C. 14,333
M. H. Fowler, S.D.P./All. . 7,836
    Lab. maj. 14,120
    (June '83, Lab. maj. 13,848)

Bolton (Gtr. Manchester)
NORTH EAST E. 59,382
*P. G. Thurnham, C. 20,742
F. R. White, Lab. 19,929
J. H. Alcock, S.D.P./All. .. 6,060
    C. maj. 813
    (June '83, C. maj. 2,443)

SOUTH EAST E. 65,932
*D. W. Young, Lab. 26,791
S. Windle, C. 15,410
F. Harasiwka, L./All. 7,161
    Lab. maj. 11,381
    (June '83, Lab. maj. 8,753)

WEST E. 69,843
*T. G. Sackville, C. 24,779
G. J. Harkin, Lab. 20,186
D. T. Eccles, S.D.P./All. .. 10,936
    C. maj. 4,593
    (June '83, C. maj. 7,152)

Boothferry (Humberside)
E. 75,176
D. M. Davis, C. 31,716
Mrs. J. D. Davies, L./All. .. 12,746
R. Donson, Lab. 12,498
    C. maj. 18,970
    (June '83, C. maj. 17,420)

Bootle (Merseyside)
E. 71,765
*A. Roberts, Lab. 34,975
P. R. Papworth, C. 10,498
P. Denham, S.D.P./All. ... 6,820
    Lab. maj. 24,477
    (June '83, Lab. maj. 15,139)

Bosworth (Leics)
E. 77,186
D. A. S. Tredinnick, C. ... 34,145
D. C. Bill, L./All. 17,129
R. S. Hall, Lab. 10,787
Mrs. D. Freer, Grn 660
    C. maj. 17,016
    (June '83, C. maj. 17,294)

Bournemouth (Dorset)
EAST E. 75,232
*D. A. Atkinson, C. 30,925
Dr. J. Millward, L./All. ... 16,242
I. A. Taylor, Lab. 5,885
    C. maj. 14,683
    (June '83, C. maj. 11,416)

WEST E. 74,444
*J. V. Butterfill, C. 30,117
P. G. M. Craven, S.D.P./
    All. 17,466
R. W. Jones, Lab. 7,018
    C. maj. 12,651
    (June '83, C. maj. 13,331)

Bow and Poplar (Gtr. London)
E. 59,178
Ms. M. Gordon, Lab. 15,746
E. Flounders, L./All. 11,115
D. C. Hughes, C. 6,810
P. S. Chappell, W.R.P. ... 274
    Lab. maj. 4,631
    (June '83, Lab. maj. 5,861)

Bradford (W. Yorks)
NORTH E. 67,430
C. P. Wall, Lab. 21,009
*G. J. Lawler, C. 19,376
A. M. Berkeley, S.D.P./All. 8,656
    Lab. maj. 1,633
    (June '83, C. maj. 1,602)

SOUTH E. 69,588
G. R. Cryer, Lab. 21,230
G. T. Hall, C. 20,921
T. Lindley, S.D.P./All. ... 9,109
    Lab. maj. 309
    (June '83, Lab. maj. 110)

WEST E. 70,763
*M. F. Madden, Lab. 25,775
I. Duncan-Smith, C. 18,224
M. Moghal, S.D.P./All. ... 5,657
    Lab. maj. 7,551
    (June '83, Lab. maj. 3,337)

Braintree (Essex)
E. 76,994
*A. H. Newton, O.B.E., C. ... 32,978
I. G. Bing, S.D.P./All. 16,121
B. Stapleton, Lab. 11,764
    C. maj. 16,857
    (June '83, C. maj. 13,441)

Brent (Gtr. London)
EAST E. 61,020
K. R. Livingstone, Lab. ... 16,772
Miss H. S. Crawley, C. 15,119
D. W. Finkelstein, S.D.P./
    All. 5,710
R. Q. Dooley, Ind. Lab. ... 1,035
M. Litvinoff, Grn. 716
    Lab. maj. 1,653
    (June '83, Lab. maj. 4,834)

NORTH E. 63,081
*Dr. R. Boyson, C. 26,823
P. Patel, Lab. 11,103
C. Mularczyk, S.D.P./All. 6,868
    C. maj. 15,720
    (June '83, C. maj. 14,651)

SOUTH *E.* 62,772

P. Y. Boateng, *Lab.*	......	21,140
A. J. Paterson, *C.*	....	13,209
M. T. Harskin, *L./All.*	....	6,375
Lab. maj.	....	7,931
(June '83, Lab. maj. 10,519)		

Brentford and Isleworth
(Gtr. London)
E. 71,715

Rt. Hon. Sir B. J. Hayhoe,		
C.	....	26,230
Ms. A. Keen, *Lab.*	....	18,277
Dr. D. M. W. Wilks, *S.D.P./*		
All.	....	9,626
T. Cooper, *Grn.*	....	849
C. maj.	....	7,953
(June '83, C. maj. 9,387)		

Brentwood and Ongar (Essex)
E. 67,521

R. A. McCrindle, C.	......	32,258
N. R. Amor, *L./All.*	......	13,337
J. W. Orpe, *Lab.*	....	7,042
Mrs. M. E. Willis, *Grn.*	...	686
C. maj.	....	18,921
(June '83, C. maj. 14,202)		

Bridgwater (Somerset)
E. 67,480

Rt. Hon. T. J. King, C.	....	27,177
C. Clarke, *S.D.P./All.*	....	15,982
J. Turner, *Lab.*	....	9,594
C. maj.	....	11,195
(June '83, C. maj. 10,697)		

Bridlington (Humberside)
E. 80,126

J. E. Townend, C.	....	32,351
E. I. Marshall, *S.D.P./All.*	15,030
L. M. Bird, *Lab.*	....	10,653
R. D. Myerscough, *Grn.*	...	983
C. maj.	....	17,321
(June '83, C. maj. 16,609)		

Brigg and Cleethorpes
(Humberside)
E. 80,096

M. R. Brown, C.	....	29,723
I. Powney, *L./All.*	....	17,475
T. Geraghty, *Lab.*	....	13,876
C. maj.	....	12,248
(June '83, C. maj. 12,189)		

Brighton (E. Sussex)

KEMPTOWN *E.* 60,271

A. Bowden, M.B.E., *C.*	.....	24,031
J. S. Bassam, *Lab.*	....	14,771
C. Berry, *L./All.*	....	6,080
C. maj.	....	9,260
(June '83, C. maj. 9,378)		

PAVILION *E.* 58,910

Rt. Hon. H. J. Amery, C.	...	22,056
D. S. Hill, *Lab.*	....	12,914
K. F. Carey, *S.D.P./All.*	...	8,459
C. maj.	....	9,142
(June '83, C. maj. 11,132)		

Bristol (Avon)

EAST *E.* 63,840

J. Sayeed, C.	....	21,906
R. R. Thomas, *Lab.*	......	17,783
D. M. E. Foster, *L./All.*	....	10,247
P. M. Kingston, *N.F.F.G.*		286
C. maj.	....	4,123
(June '83, C. maj. 1,789)		

NORTH WEST *E.* 72,876

M. C. Stern, C.	....	26,953
T. W. Walker, *Lab.*	......	20,001
J. M. G. Kirkaldy, *S.D.P./*		
All.	....	10,885
C. maj.	....	6,952
(June '83, C. maj. 6,327)		

SOUTH *E.* 68,733

Ms. D. Primalo, *Lab.*	.....	20,798
P. S. Cutcher, *C.*	....	19,394
Mrs. H. S. Long, *S.D.P./All.*	9,952
G. R. Vowles, *Grn.*	....	600
Ms. C. M. Meghji, *R.F.*	...	149
Lab. maj.	....	1,404
(June '83, Lab. maj. 4,419)		

WEST *E.* 72,357

Hon. W. A. Waldegrave, C.	24,695
G. R. P. Ferguson, *L./All.*	.	16,992
Mrs. M. C. Georghiou, *Lab.*	11,337
Mrs. G. A. Dorey, *Grn.*	...	1,096
Ms. V. Ralph, *Comm.*	.....	134
C. maj.	....	7,703
(June '83, C. maj. 10,178)		

Bromsgrove (H & W)
E. 69,494

H. D. Miller, C.	....	29,051
J. D. Ward, *Lab.*	....	12,366
D. L. Cropp, *S.D.P./All.*	..	11,663
C. maj.	....	16,685
(June '83, C. maj. 17,175)		

Broxbourne (Herts)
E. 70,631

Mrs. M. A. Roe, C.	....	33,567
Mrs. E. Yates, *L./All.*	....	10,572
P. Parry, *Lab.*	....	8,984
C. maj.	....	22,995
(June '83, C. maj. 17,466)		

Broxtowe (Notts)
E. 71,780

J. T. Lester, C.	....	30,462
K. Fleet, *Lab.*	....	13,811
K. M. Melton, *L./All.*	.....	12,562
C. maj.	....	16,651
(June '83, C. maj. 15,078)		

Buckingham
E. 70,036

G. G. H. Walden, C.M.G.,		
C.	....	32,162
C. M. Burke, *L./All.*	......	13,636
M. Groucutt, *Lab.*	....	9,053
C. maj.	....	18,526
(June '83, C. maj. 13,968)		

Burnley (Lancs)
E. 65,956

P. L. Pike, Lab.	....	25,140
H. Elletson, *C.*	....	17,583
R. H. Baker, *S.D.P./All.*	..	9,241
Lab. maj.	....	7,557
(June '83, Lab. maj. 770)		

Burton (Staffs)
E. 73,252

I. J. Lawrence, Q.C., *C.*	.....	29,160
D. Heptonstall, *Lab.*	.....	19,330
K. A. Hemsley, *L./All.*	....	9,046
C. maj.	....	9,830
(June '83, C. maj. 11,647)		

Bury (Gtr. Manchester)

NORTH *E.* 67,961

A. J. H. Burt, C.	....	28,097
D. Crausby, *Lab.*	....	21,186
D. Vasmer, *L./All.*	....	6,804
C. maj.	....	6,911
(June '83, C. maj. 2,792)		

SOUTH *E.* 65,039

D. A. G. Sumberg, C.	.....	23,878
D. Boden, *Lab.*	....	21,199
D. A. Eyre, *S.D.P./All.*	...	6,772
C. maj.	....	2,679
(June '83, C. maj. 3,720)		

Bury St. Edmunds (Suffolk)
E. 76,619

Sir E. W. Griffiths, C.	.....	33,672
Sir R. Harland, *S.D.P./All.*	12,214
C. L. Greene, *Lab.*	....	9,841
Ms. I. M. J. Wakelam, *Grn.*	1,057
C. maj.	....	21,458
(June '83, C. maj. 16,122)		

Calder Valley (W. Yorks)
E. 73,398

D. Thompson, C.	....	25,892
D. M. Chaytor, *Lab.*	.....	19,847
D. T. Shutt, *L./All.*	....	13,761
C. maj.	....	6,045
(June '83, C. maj. 7,999)		

Cambridge
E. 69,336

R. V. Rhodes James, C.	...	21,624
Mrs. S. V. T. B. Williams,		
S.D.P./All.	....	16,564
C. J. Howard, *Lab.*	......	15,319
Ms. M. E. Wright, *Grn.*	...	597
C. maj.	....	5,060
(June '83, C. maj. 5,968)		

Cambridgeshire

NORTH EAST *E.* 74,231

M. D. Moss, *C.*	....	26,983
C. R. Freud, L./All.	.....	25,555
R. J. Harris, *Lab.*	....	4,891
C. maj.	....	1,428
(June '83, L./All. maj. 5,195)		

SOUTH EAST *E.* 73,216

J. E. T. Paice, *C.*	....	32,901
P. C. Lee, *S.D.P./All.*	.....	15,399
T. G. Ling, *Lab.*	....	7,694
C. maj.	....	17,502
(June '83, C. maj. 13,764)		

SOUTH WEST *E.* 81,658
*Sir J. A. Grant, C. 36,622
D. C. Nicholls, *L./All.* 18,371
Ms. J. Billing, *Lab.* 8,434
   C. maj. 18,251
   (June '83, C. maj. 13,867)

Cannock and Burntwood (Staffs)
E. 68,137

*J. G. D. Howarth, C. 24,186
G. E. Roberts, *Lab.* 21,497
N. Stanley, *L./All.* 8,698
   C. maj. 2,689
   (June '83, C. maj. 2,045)

Canterbury (Kent)
E. 76,062

J. W. H. Brazier, C. 30,273
J. Purchese, *L./All.* 15,382
Ms. L. A. Keen, *Lab.* 9,494
S. Dawe, *Grn.* 957
Miss J. M. White, *I.C.N.* .. 147
   C. maj. 14,891
   (June '83, C. maj. 15,742)

Carlisle (Cumbria)
E. 55,053

E. A. Martlew, *Lab.* 18,311
W. G. Hodgson, C. 17,395
R. S. Hunt, *S.D.P./All* 7,655
   Lab. maj. 916
   (June '83, Lab. maj. 71)

Carshalton and Wallington
(Gtr. London)
E. 69,120

*F. N. Forman, C. 27,984
J. D. Grant, *S.D.P./All.* .. 13,575
Mrs. J. G. Baker, *Lab.* 9,440
R. W. Steel, *Grn.* 843
   C. maj. 14,409
   (June '83, C. maj. 10,755)

Castle Point (Essex)
E. 65,992

*Rt. Hon. Sir B. R. Braine,
  C. 29,681
Miss A. P. Bastow, *S.D.P./*
  All. 10,433
W. A. Deal, *Lab.* 9,422
   C. maj. 19,248
   (June '83, C. maj. 15,417)

Cheadle
(Gtr. Manchester)
E. 68,332

S. R. Day, C. 30,484
A. B. Leah, *L./All.* 19,853
Ms. A. Coffey, *Lab.* 5,037
   C. maj. 10,631
   (June '83, C. maj. 9,380)

Chelmsford (Essex)
E. 82,564

S. H. M. Burns, C. 35,231
S. G. Mole, *L./All.* 27,470
C. E. Playford, *Lab.* 4,642
A. C. Slade, *Grn.* 486
   C. maj. 7,761
   (June '83, C. maj. 378)

Chelsea (Gtr. London)
E. 49,534

*N. P. Scott, M.B.E., C. 18,443
Mrs. J. M. Ware, *L./All.* .. 5,124
D. J. Ward, *Lab.* 4,406
Ms. N. Kortvelyessy, *Grn.* 587
   C. maj. 13,319
   (June '83, C. maj. 12,021)

Cheltenham (Glos)
E. 79,234

*C. G. Irving, C. 31,371
R. G. Holme, *L./All.* 26,475
M. Luker, *Lab.* 4,701
   C. maj. 4,896
   (June '83, C. maj. 5,518)

Chertsey and Walton (Surrey)
E. 71,448

*G. E. Pattie, C. 32,119
Mrs. S. K. Stapely, *S.D.P./*
  All. 14,650
H. G. Trace, *Lab.* 7,185
   C. maj. 17,469
   (June '83, C. maj. 15,699)

Chesham and Amersham
(Bucks)
E. 71,751

*Rt. Hon. Sir I. H. J. L.
  Gilmour, BT., C. 34,504
A. T. Ketteringham, *L./All.* 15,064
P. A. Goulding, *Lab.* 5,170
Mrs. A. G. Darnbrough,
  Grn. 760
   C. maj. 19,440
   (June '83, C. maj. 15,879)

Chester, City of
E. 65,845

*Hon. P. H. Morrison, C. .. 23,582
D. Robinson, *Lab.* 18,727
R. A. Stunell, *L./All.* 10,262
   C. maj. 4,855
   (June '83, C. maj. 9,099)

Chesterfield (Derbys)
E. 70,357

*Rt. Hon. A. N. W. Benn,
  Lab. 24,532
A. H. Rogers, *L./All.* 15,955
R. P Grant, C. 13,472
   Lab. maj. 8,577
   (June '83, Lab. maj. 7,763)
   (March '84, Lab. maj. 6,264)

Chichester (W. Sussex)
E. 81,019

*R. A. Nelson, C. 37,274
P. F. Weston, *L./All.* 17,097
D. Morrison, *Lab.* 4,751
I. F. N. Bagnall, *Grn.* 1,196
   C. maj. 20,177
   (June '83, C. maj. 20,117)

Chingford (Gtr. London)
E. 56,797

*Rt. Hon. N. B. Tebbit, C. .. 27,110
J. G. Williams, *L./All.* 9,155
Ms. M. I. Cosin, *Lab.* 6,650
Ms. E. Newton, *Grn.* 634
   C. maj. 17,955
   (June '83, C. maj. 12,414)

Chipping Barnet (Gtr. London)
E. 60,876

*S. B. Chapman, C. 24,686
J. Skinner, *L./All.* 9,815
D. Perkin, *Lab.* 8,115
   C. maj. 14,871
   (June '83, C. maj. 12,393)

Chislehurst (Gtr. London)
E. 55,535

*R. E. Sims, C. 24,165
R. A. Younger-Ross, *L./All.* 9,658
S. H. Ward, *Lab.* 8,115
   C. maj. 14,507
   (June '83, C. maj. 12,061)

Chorley (Lancs)
E. 78,541

*D. R. Dover, C. 29,015
A. J. Watmough, *Lab.* 20,958
I. A. Simpson, *L./All.* 9,706
A. S. Holgate, *Grn.* 714
   C. maj. 8,057
   (June '83, C. maj. 10,275)

Christchurch (Dorset)
E. 70,964

*R. J. Adley, C. 35,656
Miss H. J. McKenzie,
  S.D.P./All. 13,282
Ms. C. E. Longhurst, *Lab.* 5,174
   C. maj. 22,374
   (June '83, C. maj. 19,738)

Cirencester and Tewkesbury
(Glos)
E. 84,071

*Rt. Hon. N. Ridley, C. 36,272
P. T. Beckerlegge, *L./All.* . 23,610
J. D. Naysmith, *Lab.* 5,342
M. A. Curtis, *Male O.A.P.* 283
   C. maj. 12,662
   (June '83, C. maj. 13,827)

**The City of London and
Westminster South**
E. 57,428

*Hon. P. L. Brooke, C. 19,333
Ms. J. C. G. Smithard,
  S.D.P./All 7,291
Ms. R. E. Bush, *Lab.* 6,821
   C. maj. 12,042
   (June '83, C. maj. 13,387)

Colchester (Essex)

NORTH *E.* 82,420
*Sir P. A. F. Buck, Q.C., C. . 32,747
A. Hayman, *S.D.P./All.* ... 19,124
R. A. Green, *Lab.* 10,768
   C. maj. 13,623
   (June '83, C. maj. 15,048)

SOUTH, AND MALDON *E.* 84,392
*Rt. Hon. J. Wakeham, C. 34,894
J. W. Stevens, *S.D.P./All.* 19,411
Ms. S. Bigwood, *Lab.* 9,229
   C. maj. 15,483
   (June '83, C. maj. 12,165)

Colne Valley (W. Yorks)
E. 70,199

G. E. G. Riddick, C.	......	20,457
N. J. Priestley, L./All.	....	18,780
J. A. Harman, Lab.	......	16,353
M. R. Mullany, Grn.	.....	614
C. maj.	....	1,677

(June '83, L./All. maj. 3,146)

Congleton (Cheshire)
E. 68,172

*Mrs. J. A. Winterton, C.	..	26,513
I. M. Brodie-Browne, L./		
All.	....	18,544
M. Knowles, Lab.	....	9,810
C. maj.	....	7,969

(June '83, C. maj. 8,459)

Copeland (Cumbria)
E. 54,695

*Dr. J. A. Cunningham,		
Lab.	....	20,999
A. R. M. Toft, C.	......	19,105
E. T. Colgan, S.D.P./All.	..	4,052
R. A. Gibson, Grn.	....	319
Lab. maj.	....	1,894

(June '83, Lab. maj. 1,837)

Corby (Northants)
E. 66,119

*W. R. Powell, C.	....	23,323
H. A. Feather, Lab.	......	21,518
T. G. Whittington, L./		
All.	....	7,805
C. maj.	....	1,805

(June '83, C. maj. 3,168)

Cornwall

NORTH E. 72,375

*G. A. Neale, C.	....	29,862
M. N. Mitchell, L./All.	...	24,180
Ms. C. Herries, Lab.	.....	3,719
C. maj.	....	5,682

(June '83, C. maj. 5,059)

SOUTH EAST E. 70,248

*R. A. Hicks, C.	....	28,818
I. P. Tunbridge, L./All.	...	22,211
P. A. Clark, Lab.	....	4,847
C. maj.	....	6,607

(June '83, C. maj. 8,354)

Coventry (W. Midlands)

NORTH EAST E. 67,479

J. Hughes, Lab.	....	25,832
C. Prior, C.	....	13,965
S. Wood, L./All.	....	7,502
A. McNally, Comm.	......	310
Lab. maj.	....	11,867

(June '83, Lab. maj. 8,775)

NORTH WEST E. 53,090

*G. Robinson, Lab.	....	19,450
J. Powell, C.	....	13,787
T. Jones, S.D.P./All.	.....	6,455
Lab. maj.	....	5,663

(June '83, Lab. maj. 3,038)

SOUTH EAST E. 51,880

*D. J. Nellist, Lab.	....	17,969
A. Grant, C.	....	11,316
F. Devine, S.D.P./All.	....	8,095
N. Hutchinson, Grn.	.....	479
Lab. maj.	....	6,653

(June '83, Lab. maj. 2,682)

SOUTH WEST E. 65,567

*J. P. Butcher, C.	....	22,318
R. E. G. Slater, Lab.	......	19,108
R. Wheway, L./All.	......	10,166
C. maj.	....	3,210

(June '83, C. maj. 6,447)

Crawley (W. Sussex)
E. 72,076

*Hon. A. N. W. Soames, C.	.	29,259
P. J. Leo, Lab.	....	17,121
D. N. Simmons, S.D.P./All.		12,674
C. maj.	....	12,138

(June '83, C. maj. 11,814)

Crewe and Nantwich (Cheshire)
E. 72,961

*Hon. Mrs. G. P. Dunwoody,		
Lab.	....	25,457
Mrs. A. F. Browning, C.	..	24,365
Dr. K. N. Roberts, S.D.P./		
All.	....	8,022
Lab. maj.	....	1,092

(June '83, Lab. maj. 290)

Crosby (Merseyside)
E. 83,914

*G. M. Thornton, C.	....	30,836
A. F. S. Donovan, S.D.P./		
All.	....	23,989
C. W. Cheetham, Lab.	....	11,992
C. maj.	....	6,847

(June '83, C. maj. 3,401)

Croydon (Gtr. London)

CENTRAL E. 55,410

*Rt. Hon. J. E. M. Moore, C.		22,133
Ms. B. T. Prentice, Lab.	..	9,516
T. Burgess, S.D.P./All.	...	7,435
C. maj.	....	12,617

(June '83, C. maj. 11,821)

NORTH EAST E. 63,129

*Rt. Hon. B. B. Weatherill,		
(The Speaker)	....	24,188
Miss C. Patrick, Lab.	.....	11,669
J. D. Goldie, S.D.P./All.	..	8,128
The Speaker maj.	.....	12,519

(June '83, C. maj. 11,627)

NORTH WEST E. 57,369

*H. J. Malins, C.	....	18,665
M. H. Wicks, Lab.	....	14,677
L. A. Rowe, L./All.	......	6,363
C. maj.	....	3,988

(June '83, C. maj. 4,092)

SOUTH E. 65,085

*Sir W. G. Clark, C.	....	30,732
I. Morrison, L./All.	......	11,669
G. R. Davies, Lab.	......	4,679
P. C. Baldwin, Grn.	......	900
C. maj.	....	19,063

(June '83, C. maj. 17,440)

Dagenham (Gtr. London)
E. 61,714

*B. C. Gould, Lab.	....	18,454
R. J. M. Neill, C.	....	15,985
J. Carter, S.D.P./All	......	7,088
Lab. maj.	....	2,469

(June '83, Lab. maj. 2,997)

Darlington (Durham)
E. 65,940

*M. C. Fallon, C.	....	24,831
O. O'Brien, Lab.	....	22,170
A. Collinge, L./All.	......	6,289
C. maj.	....	2,661

(June '83, C. maj. 3,438)

Dartford (Kent)
E. 72,632

*R. J. Dunn, C.	....	30,685
B. J. Clarke, Lab.	......	15,756
M. G. Bruce, S.D.P./All.	..	10,439
K. J. Davenport, F.D.P.	..	491
C. maj.	....	14,929

(June '83, C. maj. 13,563)

Daventry (Northants)
E. 69,241

T. E. Boswell, C.	....	31,353
I. R. Miller, L./All.	......	11,663
Mrs. L. M. A. W. Koumi,		
Lab.	....	11,097
C. maj.	....	19,690

(June '83, C. maj. 13,136)

Davyhulme (Gtr. Manchester)
E. 65,558

*W. S. Churchill, C.	....	23,633
J. Nicholson, Lab.	......	15,434
D. I. Wrigley, L./All.	.....	11,637
C. maj.	....	8,199

(June '83, C. maj. 9,014)

Denton and Reddish
(Gtr. Manchester)
E. 69,533

*A. F. Bennett, Lab.	......	26,023
P. Slater, C.	....	17,773
T. I. Huffer, S.D.P./All.	..	8,697
Lab. maj.	....	8,250

(June '83, Lab. maj. 5,125)

Derby

NORTH E. 71,738

*G. Knight, C.	....	26,561
P. Whitehead, Lab.	......	20,236
S. F. Connolly, L./All.	....	7,268
E. Wall, Grn.	....	291
C. maj.	....	6,325

(June '83, C. maj. 3,506)

SOUTH E. 68,825

*Mrs. M. M. Beckett, Lab.	.	21,003
P. F. Leighton, C.	....	19,487
Ms. P. N. Mellor, S.D.P./		
All.	....	7,608
Lab. maj.	....	1,516

(June '83, Lab. maj. 421)

Derbyshire

NORTH EAST E. 70,314

H. Barnes, Lab.	....	24,747
J. H. Hayes, C.	....	21,027
S. P. Hardy, S.D.P./All.	..	9,985
Lab. maj.	....	3,720

(June '83, Lab. maj. 2,006)

SOUTH E. 80,045

*Mrs. E. Currie, C.	....	31,927
J. D. Whitby, Lab.	....	21,616
J. Edgar, S.D.P./All.	.....	11,509
C. maj.	....	10,311

(June '83, C. maj. 8,613)

WEST *E.* 70,782

*P. A. McLoughlin, C.	...	31,224
C. R. Walmsley, *L./All.*	...	20,697
W. Moore, *Lab.*	...	6,875
C. maj.	...	10,527

(June '83, C. maj. 15,325)
(May '86, C. maj. 100)

Devizes (Wilts)
E. 86,047

*Hon. C. A. Morrison, C.	..	36,372
Mrs. L. E. Siegle, *L./All.*	..	18,542
R. W. Buxton, *Lab.*	...	11,487
C. maj.	...	17,830

(June '83, C. maj. 15,624)

Devon

NORTH *E.* 67,474

*A. Speller, C	...	28,071
M. A. Pinney, *L./All.*	...	23,602
Ms. A. Marjoram, *Lab.*	...	3,467
C. maj.	...	4,469

(June '83, C. maj. 8,727)

WEST AND TORRIDGE *E.* 74,550

Miss E. H. Nicholson, C.	..	29,484
J. P. A. Burnett, *L./All.*	...	23,016
D. G. Brenton, *Lab.*	...	4,990
F. Williamson, *Grn.*		1,168
C. maj.	...	6,468

(June '83, C. maj. 12,351)

Dewsbury (W. Yorks)
E. 70,836

Mrs. W. A. Taylor, *Lab.*	..	23,668
*J. Whitfield, C.	...	23,223
A. Mills, *S.D.P./All.*	...	8,907
Lab. maj.	...	445

(June '83, C. maj. 2,086)

Doncaster (S. Yorks)

CENTRAL *E.* 69,699

*Rt. Hon. H. Walker, *Lab.*	...	26,266
Miss P. E. Rawlings, C.	...	18,070
J. A. Gore-Browne, *S.D.P./*		
All.	...	7,004
Lab. maj.	...	8,196

(June '83, Lab. maj. 2,508)

NORTH *E.* 72,986

*M. C. Welsh, *Lab.*	...	32,950
R. J. Shepherd, C.	...	13,015
P. Norwood, *S.D.P./All.*	..	7,394
Lab. maj.	...	19,935

(June '83, Lab. maj. 12,711)

Don Valley (S. Yorks)
E. 74,500

*M. Redmond, *Lab.*	...	29,200
C. H. Gallagher, C.	...	17,733
W. K. Whitaker, *L./All.*	..	8,027
Lab. maj.	...	11,467

(June '83, Lab. maj. 6,466)

Dorset

NORTH *E.* 72,844

*N. B. Baker, C.	...	32,854
Dr. G. W. Tapper, *L./All.*	..	20,947
J. Hanley, *Lab.*	...	3,819
C. maj.	...	11,907

(June '83, C. maj. 11,380)

SOUTH *E.* 72,855

I. C. Bruce, C.	...	30,184
B. Ellis, *L./All.*	...	15,117
Ms. B. Dench, *Lab.*	...	9,494
A. Hayler, *Ind.*	...	244
C. maj.	...	15,067

(June '83, C. maj. 15,098)

WEST *E.* 64,360

*J. W. Spicer, C.	...	28,305
T. Jones, *L./All.*	...	15,941
D. Watson, *Lab.*	...	6,123
C. maj.	...	12,364

(June '83, C. maj. 13,952)

Dover (Kent)
E. 68,997

D. L. Shaw, C.	...	25,343
S. S. E. W. Love, *Lab.*	...	18,802
G. Nice, *S.D.P./All.*	...	10,942
C. maj.	...	6,541

(June '83, C. maj. 9,220)

Dudley (W. Midlands)

EAST *E.* 75,206

*Rt. Hon. Dr. J. W. Gilbert,		
Lab.	...	24,942
Mrs. E. Jones, C.	...	21,469
K. Monks, *S.D.P./All.*	...	7,965
Lab. maj.	...	3,473

(June '83, Lab. maj. 5,816)

WEST *E.* 81,789

*J. G. Blackburn, C.	...	32,224
G. Titley, *Lab.*	...	21,980
G. P. T. Lewis, *L./All.*	...	10,477
C. maj.	...	10,244

(June '83, C. maj. 8,723)

Dulwich (Gtr. London)
E. 56,355

*G. F. Bowden, C.	...	16,563
Miss C. L. Hoey, *Lab.*	...	16,383
Dr. A. N. G. Harris, *S.D.P./*		
All.	...	5,664
A. Goldie, *Grn.*	...	432
C. maj.	...	180

(June '83, C. maj. 1,859)

Durham

CITY OF *E.* 66,567

G. N. Steinberg, *Lab.*	...	23,382
D. Stoker, *S.D.P./All.*	...	17,257
C. M. Colquhoun, C.	...	11,408
Lab. maj.	...	6,125

(June '83, Lab. maj. 1,973)

NORTH *E.* 72,115

*G. H. Radice, *Lab.*	...	30,798
Dr. D. Jeary, *S.D.P./All.*	.	12,365
N. C. Gibbon, C.	...	11,602
Lab. maj.	...	18,433

(June '83, Lab. maj. 13,437)

NORTH WEST *E.* 61,302

Ms. H. J. Armstrong, *Lab.*		22,947
D. Iceton, C.	...	12,785
C. Foote Wood, *L./All.*	...	9,349
Lab. maj.	...	10,162

(June '83, Lab. maj. 6,356)

Ealing (Gtr. London)
E. 67,176

ACTON *E.* 67,176

*Sir G. S. K. Young, BT., C.	.	25,499
P. J. Portwood, *Lab.*	...	13,256
S. R. D. Brooks, *S.D.P./All.*		8,973
C. maj.	...	12,243

(June '83, C. maj. 10,092)

NORTH *E.* 71,634

*H. Greenway, C.	...	30,100
H. J. Benn, *Lab.*	...	14,947
A. H. J. Miller, *L./All.*	...	8,149
Mrs. K. Fitzherbert, *Grn.*		577
C. maj.	...	15,153

(June '83, C. maj. 6,291)

SOUTHALL *E.* 74,843

*S. J. Bidwell, *Lab.*	...	26,480
M. A. Truman, C.	...	18,503
Mrs. M. Howes, *L./All.*	...	6,947
R. F. Lugg, *W.R.P.*	...	256
Lab. maj.	...	7,977

(June '83, Lab. maj. 11,116)

Easington (Durham)
E. 64,863

J. S. Cummings, *Lab.*	...	32,396
W. J. Perry, C.	...	7,757
G. Morpeth, *L./All.*	...	7,447
Lab. maj.	...	24,639

(June '83, Lab. maj. 14,792)

Eastbourne (E. Sussex)
E. 74,144

*I. R. E. Gow, T.D., C.	...	33,587
P. G. Driver, *L./All.*	...	16,664
A. Patel, *Lab.*	...	4,928
Ms. R. Addison, *Grn.*	...	867
C. maj.	...	16,923

(June '83, C. maj. 13,486)

Eastleigh (Hants)
E. 87,552

*Sir D. E. C. Price, C.	...	35,584
M. J. Kyrle, *L./All.*	...	22,229
D. J. C. Bull, *Lab.*	...	11,599
C. maj.	...	13,355

(June '83, C. maj. 13,008)

Eccles (Gtr. Manchester)
E. 66,961

Miss J. Lestor, *Lab.*	...	25,346
Mrs. M. E. J. Packalow, C.		15,647
P. C. W. Beatty, *S.D.P./All.*		8,924
Lab. maj.	...	9,699

(June '83, Lab. maj. 6,005)

Eddisbury (Cheshire)
E. 73,894

*A. R. Goodlad, C.	...	29,474
R. I. Fletcher, *L./All.*	...	13,639
Mrs. C. Grigg, *Lab.*	...	13,574
A. Basden, *Grn.*	...	976
C. maj.	...	15,835

(June '83, C. maj. 14,846)

Edmonton (Gtr. London)
E. 66,080

*Dr. I. D. Twinn, C.	...	24,556
B. G. Grayston, *Lab.*	...	17,270
M. Lawson, *S.D.P./All.*	...	6,115
C. maj.	...	7,286

(June '83, C. maj. 1,193)

Ellesmere Port and Neston
(Cheshire)
E. 71,344

*M. Woodcock, C.		25,664
Miss H. M. Jones, Lab.		23,811
S. A. Holbrook, S.D.P./All.		8,143
D. J. E. Carson, P.R.P.		185
C. maj.		1,853

(June '83, C. maj. 7,087)

Elmet (W. Yorks)
E. 69,024

*S. L. Batiste, C.		25,658
C. Burgon, Lab.		20,302
J. D. Macarthur, S.D.P./All.		8,755
C. maj.		5,356

(June '83, C. maj. 7,856)

Eltham (Gtr. London)
E. 54,063

*P. J. Bottomley, C.		19,752
D. Vaughan, Lab.		13,292
E. J. Randall, L./All.		8,542
C. maj.		6,460

(June '83, C. maj. 7,592)

Enfield (Gtr. London)
NORTH E. 69,488

*T. J. C. Eggar, C.		28,758
M. Upham, Lab.		14,743
Ms. H. Leighter, S.D.P./All.		7,633
M. Chantler, Grn.		644
C. maj.		14,015

(June '83, C. maj. 11,716)

SOUTHGATE E. 66,600

*M. D. X. Portillo, C.		28,445
N. Harvey, L./All.		10,100
R. Course, Lab.		9,114
S. Rooney, Grn.		696
C. maj.		18,345

(June '83, C. maj. 15,819)
(Dec. '84, C. maj. 4,711)

Epping Forest (Essex)
E. 67,804

*Sir J. A. Biggs-Davison, C.		31,536
A. Humphris, S.D.P./All.		10,023
S. Murray, Lab.		9,499
R. Denhard, Grn.		695
C. maj.		21,513

(June '83, C. maj. 15,378)

Epsom and Ewell (Surrey)
E. 70,683

*Hon. A. G. Hamilton, C.		33,145
Mrs. M. J. Joachim, L./All.		12,384
Mrs. D. B. Follett, Lab.		7,751
C. maj.		20,761

(June '83, C. maj. 17,195)

Erewash (Derbys)
E. 76,545

*P. L. Rost, C.		28,775
R. W. Jones, Lab.		19,021
Ms. C. P. Moss, S.D.P./All.		11,442
C. maj.		9,754

(June '83, C. maj. 11,319)

Erith and Crayford
(Gtr. London)
E. 59,292

*D. A. Evennett, C.		20,203
C. F. Hargrave, Lab.		13,209
*A. J. Wellbeloved, S.D.P./All.		11,300
C. maj.		6,994

(June '83, C. maj. 920)

Esher (Surrey)
E. 62,117

I. C. Taylor, M.B.E., C.		31,334
A. J. Barnett, L./All.		12,266
N. J. V. Lucas, Lab.		4,197
C. maj.		19,068

(June '83, C. maj. 15,912)

Exeter (Devon)
E. 75,208

*J. G. Hannam, C.		26,922
M. S. Thomas, S.D.P./All.		19,266
J. A. Vincent, Lab.		13,643
R. J. Vail, Grn.		597
N. D. Byles, L.A.P.P.		209
C. maj.		7,656

(June '83, C. maj. 9,880)

Falmouth and Camborne
(Cornwall)
E. 68,612

*W. D. Mudd, C.		23,725
J. C. Marks, S.D.P./All.		18,686
J. Cosgrove, Lab.		11,271
F. Zapp, L.M.		373
C. maj.		5,039

(June '83, C. maj. 11,025)

Fareham (Hants)
E. 76,974

*P. R. C. Lloyd, C.		36,781
T. Slack, L./All.		17,986
M. Merritt, Lab.		5,451
C. maj.		18,795

(June '83, C. maj. 16,316)

Faversham (Kent)
E. 79,039

*R. D. Moate, C.		31,074
E. M. Goyder, S.D.P./All.		17,096
P. Dangerfield, Lab.		12,616
C. maj.		13,978

(June '83, C. maj. 14,597)

Feltham and Heston
(Gtr. London)
E. 81,062

*R. P. Ground, Q.C., C.		27,755
C. Hinds, Lab.		22,325
J. Daly, S.D.P./All.		9,623
C. maj.		5,430

(June '83, C. maj. 2,148)

Finchley (Gtr. London)
E. 57,727

*Rt. Hon. Mrs. M. H. Thatcher, C.		21,603
J. Davies, Lab.		12,690
D. Howarth, L./All.		5,580
Lord Buckethead, Grem.		131
Miss M. St. Vincent, Gold		59
C. maj.		8,913

(June '83, C. maj. 9,314)

Folkestone and Hythe (Kent)
E. 64,406

*M. Howard, Q.C., C.		27,915
J. R. MacDonald, L./All.		18,789
V. S. Anand, Lab.		3,720
C. maj.		9,126

(June '83, C. maj. 11,670)

Fulham (Gtr. London)
E. 54,498

M. H. M. Carrington, C.		21,752
*W. R. N. Raynsford, Lab.		15,430
P. A. C. Marshall, S.D.P./All.		4,365
Ms. J. Grimes, Grn.		465
C. maj.		6,322

(June '83, C. maj. 4,789)
(April '86, Lab. maj. 3,503)

Fylde (Lancs)
E. 63,246

J. M. Jack, C.		29,559
Mrs. E. A. Smith, L./All.		11,787
G. Smith, Lab.		6,955
H. Fowler, R.C.P.		405
C. maj.		17,772

(June '83, C. maj. 17,102)

Gainsborough and Horncastle
(Lincs)
E. 69,760

*E. J. E. Leigh, C.		28,621
D. A. Grace, L./All.		18,898
R. Naylor, Lab.		6,156
C. maj.		9,723

(June '83, C. maj. 5,067)

Gateshead East (Tyne & Wear)
E. 67,953

Miss J. G. Quin, Lab.		28,895
F. W. Rogers, C.		11,667
N. G. Rippeth, S.D.P./All.		8,231
Lab. maj.		17,228

(June '83, Lab. maj. 10,322)

Gedling (Notts)
E. 68,398

A. J. B. Mitchell, C.		29,492
V. R. Coaker, Lab.		12,953
D. Morton, S.D.P./All.		11,684
C. maj.		16,539

(June '83, C. maj. 14,664)

Gillingham (Kent)
E. 71,847

*J. R. Couchman, C.		28,711
L. R. Andrews, L./All.		16,162
D. J. Bishop, Lab.		9,230
C. maj.		12,549

(June '83, C. maj. 10,843)

Glanford and Scunthorpe
(Humberside)
E. 72,816

E. A. Morley, Lab.		24,733
*R. S. Hickmet, C.		24,221
C. Nottingham, S.D.P./All.		7,762
K. S. Trivedi, Ind.		104
Lab. maj.		512

(June '83, C. maj. 637)

Gloucester
E. 76,910

D. C. French, C.	29,826
D. Hulme, *Lab.*	17,791
J. Hilton, *L./All.*	12,417
C. maj.	12,035
(June '83, C. maj. 12,537)	

Gloucestershire West
E. 77,994

P. Marland, C.	29,257
P. E. S. Nielson, *Lab.*	17,578
J. T. Watkinson, *S.D.P./ All.*	16,440
C. maj.	11,679
(June '83, C. maj. 9,652)	

Gosport (Hants)
E. 68,113

P. J. Viggers, C.	29,804
P. J. Chegwyn, *L./All.*	16,081
A. Lloyd, *Lab.*	5,053
C. maj.	13,723
(June '83, C. maj. 14,451)	

Grantham (Lincs)
E. 79,434

Hon. D. M. Hogg, C.	33,988
J. P. Heppell, *L./All.*	12,685
M. B. Gent, *Lab.*	12,197
Mrs. P. A. Hewis, *Grn.*	700
C. maj.	21,303
(June '83, C. maj. 18,911)	

Gravesham (Kent)
E. 72,759

J. A. Arnold, *C.*	28,891
M. A. Coleman, *Lab.*	20,099
R. I. Crawford, *L./All.*	8,724
C. maj.	8,792
(June '83, C. maj. 8,463)	

Great Grimsby (Humberside)
E. 68,501

A. V. Mitchell, Lab.	23,463
C. F. Robinson, *C.*	14,679
P. W. Genney, *S.D.P./All.*	13,457
Lab. maj.	8,784
(June '83, Lab. maj. 731)	

Great Yarmouth
(Norfolk)
E. 65,770

M. R. H. Carttiss, C.	25,336
J. Cannell, *Lab.*	15,253
S. D. Maxwell, *S.D.P./All.*	8,387
C. maj.	10,083
(June '83, C. maj. 11,200)	

Greenwich (Gtr. London)
E. 50,830

Mrs. R. S. Barnes, S.D.P./ All.	15,149
Mrs. D. F. M. Wood, *Lab.*	13,008
J. G. C. Antcliffe, *C.*	8,695
Ms. J. Thomas, *Grn.*	346
R. Mallone, *Fell.*	59
Ms. P. Clinton, *Comm.*	58
S.D.P./All. maj.	2,141
(June '83, Lab. maj. 1,211)	
(Feb. '87, S.D.P./All. maj. 6,611)	

Guildford (Surrey)
E. 77,872

Rt. Hon. D. A. R. Howell, C.	32,504
Mrs. M. L. Sharp, *S.D.P./ All.*	19,897
R. J. Wolverson, *Lab.*	6,216
C. maj.	12,607
(June '83, C. maj. 11,824)	

Hackney (Gtr. London)

NORTH AND STOKE NEWINGTON
E. 66,771

Ms. D. J. Abbott, *Lab.*	18,912
O. Letwin, *C.*	11,234
S. H. Taylor, *S.D.P./All.*	7,446
D. J. Fitzpatrick, *Grn.*	997
Ms. Y. T. Anwar, *R.F.*	228
Lab. maj.	7,678
(June '83, Lab. maj. 8,545)	

SOUTH AND SHOREDITCH *E.* 70,873

B. C. J. Sedgemore, Lab.	18,799
M. C. Northcroft-Brown, *C.*	11,277
J. D. Roberts, *L./All.*	8,812
D. Green, *Comm.*	403
Lab. maj.	7,522
(June '83, Lab. maj. 7,691)	

Halesowen and Stourbridge
(W. Midlands)
E. 78,017

J. H. R. Stokes, C.	31,037
T. J. Sunter, *Lab.*	17,229
D. C. A. Simon, *S.D.P./All.*	13,658
C. maj.	13,808
(June '83, C. maj. 13,316)	

Halifax (W. Yorks)
E. 73,392

Mrs. A. Mahon, *Lab.*	24,741
R. Galley, C.	23,529
F. L. Cockcroft, *S.D.P./All.*	8,758
Lab. maj.	1,212
(June '83, Lab. maj. 1,869)	

Halton (Cheshire)
E. 73,848

Rt. Hon. G. J. Oakes, Lab.	32,065
J. Hardman, *C.*	17,487
Ms. H. Clucas, *S.D.P./All.*	8,272
Lab. maj.	14,578
(June '83, Lab. maj. 6,829)	

Hammersmith (Gtr. London)
E. 48,285

C. S. Soley, Lab.	15,811
N. J. A. Deva, *C.*	13,396
S. H. J. A. Knott, *L./All.*	5,241
D. P. Kirk, *Grn.*	453
P. J. F. Fitzpatrick, *R.F.*	125
Miss M. M. A. Carrick, *Humanist*	98
Lab. maj.	2,415
(June '83, Lab. maj. 1,954)	

Hampshire

EAST *E.* 86,363

M. J. Mates, C.	43,093
R. Booker, *L./All.*	19,307
C. Lloyd, *Lab.*	4,443
C. maj.	23,786
(June '83, C. maj. 18,327)	

NORTH WEST *E.* 69,965

D. B. Mitchell, C.	31,470
I. H. Wills, *L./All.*	18,033
Ms. A. Burnage, *Lab.*	4,980
C. maj.	13,437
(June '83, C. maj. 12,122)	

Hampstead and Highgate
(Gtr. London)
E. 63,301

Sir G. Finsberg, M.B.E., C.	19,236
P. J. Turner, *Lab.*	17,015
Mrs. A. Sofer, *S.D.P./All.*	8,744
G. Weiss, *Rainbow*	137
Ms. S. Ellis, *Humanist*	134
C. maj.	2,221
(June '83, C. maj. 3,370)	

Harborough (Leics)
E. 74,700

Sir J. A. Farr, C.	35,216
T. J. Swift, *L./All.*	16,406
P. Harley, *Lab.*	7,646
C. maj.	18,810
(June '83, C. maj. 18,485)	

Harlow (Essex)
E. 70,286

J. J. J. Hayes, C.	26,017
A. S. Newens, *Lab.*	20,140
Mrs. M. C. Eden-Green, *S.D.P./All.*	8,915
C. maj.	5,877
(June '83, C. maj. 3,674)	

Harrogate (N. Yorks)
E. 75,761

R. G. Banks, C.	31,167
J. R. Leach, *S.D.P./All.*	19,265
A. J. Wright, *Lab.*	5,671
C. maj.	11,902
(June '83, C. maj. 15,888)	

Harrow (Gtr. London)

EAST *E.* 81,124

H. J. M. Dykes, C.	32,302
D. J. Brough, *Lab.*	14,029
Mrs. Z. Gifford, *L./All.*	13,251
C. maj.	18,273
(June '83, C. maj. 12,668)	

WEST *E.* 74,041

R. G. Hughes, *C.*	30,456
S. P. Bayliss, *S.D.P./All.*	15,012
C. Bastin, *Lab.*	9,665
C. maj.	15,444
(June '83, C. maj. 11,021)	

Hartlepool (Cleveland)
E. 68,686

E. Leadbitter, Lab.	24,296
P. C. Catchpole, *C.*	17,007
A. Preece, *L./All.*	7,047
I. J. Cameron, *Ind.*	1,786
Lab. maj.	7,289
(June '83, Lab. maj. 3,090)	

Harwich (Essex)
E. 77,149

Sir J. E. Ridsdale, C.B.E., C.	29,344
Miss E. Lynne, *L./All.*	17,262
R. Knight, *Lab.*	9,920
C. A. Humphrey, *O.F.P.*	161
C. maj.	12,082
(June '83, C. maj. 12,502)	

Hastings and Rye (E. Sussex)
E. 72,758

*K. R. Warren, C.	26,163
D. J. Amies, *L./All.*	18,816
Ms. J. Hurcombe, *Lab.*	6,825
D. Howell, *L.M.*	242
S. P. Davies, *N.P.R.*	194
C. maj.	7,347
(June '83, C. maj. 10,980)	

Havant (Hants)
E. 76,344

*Sir I. S. Lloyd, C.	32,527
Mrs. E. E. Cleaver, *S.D.P./ All.*	16,017
J. A. Phillips, *Lab.*	8,030
G. W. Fuller, *Bread*	373
C. maj.	16,510
(June '83, C. maj. 11,956)	

Hayes and Harlington
(Gtr. London)
E. 58,240

*T. P. Dicks, C.	21,355
P. F. Fagan, *Lab.*	15,390
Ms. S. Slipman, *S.D.P./All.*	6,641
C. maj.	5,965
(June '83, C. maj. 4,234)	

Hazel Grove (Gtr. Manchester)
E. 65,717

*T. R. Arnold, C.	24,396
A. M. Vos, *L./All.*	22,556
J. G. Ford, *Lab.*	6,354
Ms. F. K. Chapman, *Grn.*	346
C. maj.	1,840
(June '83, C. maj. 2,022)	

Hemsworth (W. Yorks)
E. 54,951

G. J. Buckley, *Lab.*	27,859
E. H. Garnier, *C.*	7,159
J. D. Wooffindin, *L./All.*	6,568
Lab. maj.	20,700
(June '83, Lab. maj. 14,190)	

Hendon (Gtr. London)

NORTH *E.* 55,095

*J. M. Gorst, C.	20,155
Ms. J. Manson, *Lab.*	9,223
Ms. E. Davies, *S.D.P./All.*	6,859
C. maj.	10,932
(June '83, C. maj. 9,025)	

SOUTH *E.* 54,560

J. L. Marshall, *C.*	19,341
M. O. Palmer, *L./All.*	8,217
Miss L. Christian, *Lab.*	7,261
C. maj.	11,124
(June '83, C. maj. 6,433)	

Henley (Oxon)
E. 65,443

*Rt. Hon. M. R. D. Heseltine, C.	29,978
J. Madeley, *L./All.*	12,896
M. B. Barber, *Lab.*	6,173
C. maj.	17,082
(June '83, C. maj. 13,781)	

Hereford
E. 67,075

*C. R. Shepherd, C.	24,865
C. F. Green, *L./All.*	23,452
V. S. Woodell, *Lab.*	4,031
C. maj.	1,413
(June '83, C. maj. 2,277)	

Hertford and Stortford
E. 75,508

*B. Wells, C.	33,763
R. E. Wotherspoon, *S.D.P./ All.*	16,623
Mrs. P. R. E. Sumner, *Lab.*	7,494
G. C. Cole, *Grn.*	814
C. maj.	17,140
(June '83, C. maj. 12,929)	

Hertfordshire

NORTH *E.* 78,694

*B. H. I. H. Stewart, R.D., C.	31,750
G. W. Binney, *L./All.*	20,308
A. Gorst, *Lab.*	11,782
C. maj.	11,442
(June '83, C. maj. 9,943)	

SOUTH WEST *E.* 75,643

*R. L. Page, C.	32,791
I. M. Blair, *L./All.*	17,007
I. Willmore, *Lab.*	8,966
C. maj.	15,784
(June '83, C. maj. 12,194)	

WEST *E.* 78,966

*R. B. Jones, C.	31,760
N. A. Hollinghurst, *S.D.P./ All.*	16,836
A. McBrearty, *Lab.*	15,317
C. maj.	14,924
(June '83, C. maj. 9,576)	

Hertsmere (Herts)
E. 73,367

*Rt. Hon. C. E. Parkinson, C.	31,278
L. S. Brass, *L./All.*	13,172
F. Ward, *Lab.*	10,835
C. maj.	18,106
(June '83, C. maj. 14,870)	

Hexham (Nthmb)
E. 56,360

A. T. Amos, *C.*	22,370
E. M. Robson, *L./All.*	14,304
M. R. Wood, *Lab.*	8,103
Mrs. S. M. Wood, *Grn.*	336
C. maj.	8,066
(June '83, C. maj. 8,308)	

Heywood and Middleton
(Gtr. Manchester)
E. 59,487

*J. Callaghan, Lab.	21,900
R. E. Walker, *C.*	15,052
I. Greenhalgh, *S.D.P./All.*	6,953
Lab. maj.	6,848
(June '83, Lab. maj. 3,974)	

High Peak (Derbys)
E. 69,926

*C. J. Hawkins, C.	25,715
Mrs. J. McCrindle, *Lab.*	16,199
Dr. J. Oldham, *S.D.P./All.*	14,389
C. maj.	9,516
(June '83, C. maj. 9,940)	

Holborn and St. Pancras
(Gtr. London)
E. 70,589

*F. G. Dobson, Lab.	22,966
P. J. Luff, *C.*	14,113
S. McGrath, *L./All.*	7,994
M. J. Gavan, *R.F.*	300
Lab. maj.	8,853
(June '83, Lab. maj. 7,259)	

Holland with Boston (Lincs)
E. 65,539

*Sir R. B. F. S. Body, C.	27,412
Mrs. C. Le Brun, *L./All.*	9,817
J. D. Hough, *Lab.*	9,734
D. James, *Local Voice*	405
C. maj.	17,595
(June '83, C. maj. 11,736)	

Honiton (Devon)
E. 77,259

*Sir P. F. H. Emery, C.	34,931
G. Tatton-Brown, *S.D.P./ All.*	18,369
S. Pollentine, *Lab.*	4,988
S. Hughes, *L.M.*	747
C. maj.	16,562
(June '83, C. maj. 14,769)	

Hornchurch (Gtr. London)
E. 62,397

*R. C. Squire, C.	24,039
A. R. Williams, *Lab.*	13,345
M. L. C. Long, *L./All.*	9,609
C. maj.	10,694
(June '83, C. maj. 9,184)	

Hornsey and Wood Green
(Gtr. London)
E. 80,594

*Sir H. A. L. Rossi, C.	25,397
Mrs. B. M. R. Roche, *Lab.*	23,618
D. Eden, *S.D.P./All.*	8,928
Ms. E. Crosbie, *Grn.*	1,154
C. maj.	1,779
(June '83, C. maj. 3,899)	

Horsham (W. Sussex)
E. 86,135

*Sir P. M. Hordern, C.	39,775
Mrs. J. Pearce, *S.D.P./All.*	15,868
M. Shrimpton, *Lab.*	5,435
T. Metheringham, *Grn.*	1,383
C. maj.	23,907
(June '83, C. maj. 21,785)	

Houghton and Washington
(Tyne & Wear)
E. 77,906

*R. Boyes, Lab.	32,805
J. M. Callanan, *C.*	12,612
R. F. Kenyon, *S.D.P./All.*	10,090
Lab. maj.	20,193
(June '83, Lab. maj. 13,821)	

Hove (E. Sussex)
E. 72,626

*Hon. T. A. D. Sainsbury, C.	28,952	
Mrs. M. E. Collins, S.D.P./		
All.	....	10,734
D. K. Turner, Lab.	....	9,010
T. A. Layton, S.E.	....	522
C. maj.	....	18,218
(June '83, C. maj. 17,219)		

Huddersfield (W. Yorks)
E. 66,413

*B. J. Sheerman, Lab.	.....	23,019
N. J. Hawkins, C.	....	15,741
J. Smithson, L./All.	......	10,773
N. A. L. Harvey, Grn.	....	638
Lab. maj.	....	7,278
(June '83, Lab. maj. 3,955)		

Huntingdon (Cambs)
E. 86,186

*Rt. Hon. J. Major, C.	.....	40,530
A. J. Nicholson, S.D.P./All.	13,486	
D. M. Brown, Lab.	....	8,883
B. Lavin, Grn.	....	874
C. maj.	....	27,044
(June '83, C. maj. 20,348)		

Hyndburn (Lancs)
E. 60,529

*J. K. Hargreaves, C.	......	21,606
K. Coombes, Lab.	....	19,386
J. Strak, S.D.P./All.	.....	7,423
F. Smith, Grn.	....	297
C. maj.	....	2,220
(June '83, C. maj. 21)		

Ilford (Gtr. London)

NORTH   E. 60,433

*V. W. H. Bendall, C.	.....	24,110
P. Jeater, Lab.	....	12,020
G. Tobbell, S.D.P./All.	...	7,757
C. maj.	....	12,090
(June '83, C. maj. 11,201)		

SOUTH   E. 58,572

*N. G. Thorne, O.B.E., T.D., C.	20,351	
K. Jones, Lab.	....	15,779
R. J. Scott, L./All.	......	5,928
C. maj.	....	4,572
(June '83, C. maj. 4,566)		

Ipswich (Suffolk)
E. 68,165

M. F. Irvine, C.	....	23,328
*K. T. Weetch, Lab.	......	22,454
H. P. Nicholson, S.D.P./All.	6,596	
D. T. Lettice, W.R.P.	.....	174
C. maj.	....	874
(June '83, Lab. maj. 1,077)		

Isle of Wight
E. 98,694

B. J. A. Field, C.	....	40,175
M. Young, L./All.	....	33,733
K. Pearson, Lab.	....	4,626
C. maj.	....	6,442
(June '83, L./All. maj. 3,503)		

Islington (Gtr. London)

NORTH   E. 58,917

*J. B. Corbyn, Lab.	....	19,577
E. G. Noad, C.	....	9,920
A. Whelan, S.D.P./All.	...	8,560
C. Ashby, Grn.	....	1,131
Lab. maj.	....	9,657
(June '83, Lab. maj. 5,607)		

SOUTH AND FINSBURY   E. 57,910

*C. R. Smith, Lab.	....	16,511
G. Cunningham, S.D.P./		
All.	....	15,706
A. Mitchell, C.	....	8,482
P. Powell, Grn.	....	382
S. Dowsett, S.P.G.B.	.....	81
Ms. J. Early, H.P.	....	56
Lab. maj.	....	805
(June '83, Lab. maj. 363)		

Jarrow (Tyne & Wear)
E. 62,845

*D. Dixon, Lab.	....	29,651
P. Yeoman, C.	....	10,856
P. Freitag, L./All.	....	6,230
Lab. maj.	....	18,795
(June '83, Lab. maj. 13,877)		

Keighley (W. Yorks)
E. 65,831

*G. P. A. Waller, C.	....	23,903
A. Rye, Lab.	....	18,297
J. H. Wells, L./All.	....	10,041
C. maj.	....	5,606
(June '83, C. maj. 2,774)		

Kensington (Gtr. London)
E. 48,212

*Sir B. M. Rhys Williams,		
BT., C.	....	14,818
B. T. Bousquet, Lab.	.....	10,371
W. H. Goodhart, S.D.P./		
All.	....	5,379
R. E. Shorter, Grn.	......	528
Miss L. Carrick, Humanist	65	
Mrs. M. Hughes, P.I.P.	...	30
C. maj.	....	4,447
(June '83, C. maj. 5,101)		

Kent Mid
E. 72,456

*A. J. B. Rowe, C.	....	28,719
G. D. Colley, L./All.	......	13,951
J. A. Hazelgrove, Lab.	...	9,420
C. maj.	....	14,768
(June '83, C. maj. 12,543)		

Kettering (Northants)
E. 65,965

*R. N. Freeman, C.	....	26,532
Mrs. C. M. Goodhart,		
S.D.P./All.	....	15,205
A. M. Minto, Lab.	....	10,229
C. maj.	....	11,327
(June '83, C. maj. 8,586)		

Kingston-upon-Hull

EAST   E. 68,657

*J. L. Prescott, Lab.	....	27,287
P. Jackson, C.	....	12,598
T. Wright, L./All.	....	8,572
Lab. maj.	....	14,689
(June '83, Lab. maj. 10,074)		

NORTH   E. 73,288

*J. K. McNamara, Lab.	...	26,123
Miss A. O'Brien, C.	......	13,954
S. W. Unwin, S.D.P./All.	.	10,962
Lab. maj.	....	12,169
(June '83, Lab. maj. 6,028)		

WEST   E. 55,636

*S. J. Randall, Lab.	....	19,527
M. R. C. Humphrys, C.	...	11,397
M. Bond, S.D.P./All.	.....	6,669
Lab. maj.	....	8,130
(June '83, Lab. maj. 3,654)		

Kingston upon Thames
(Gtr. London)
E. 54,839

*Rt. Hon. N. S. H. Lamont,		
C.	....	24,198
R. M. Hayes, L./All.	......	13,012
R. Markless, Lab.	....	5,676
J. Baker, C.P.W.S.M.L.	..	175
C. maj.	....	11,186
(June '83, C. maj. 8,872)		

Kingswood (Avon)
E. 73,089

*R. A. Hayward, C.	....	26,300
R. L. Berry, Lab.	....	21,907
Mrs. P. Whittle, S.D.P./All.	10,382	
C. maj.	....	4,393
(June '83, C. maj. 1,797)		

Knowsley (Merseyside)

NORTH   E. 52,960

*G. E. Howarth, Lab.	.....	27,454
Ms. R. Cooper, L./All.	...	6,356
R. C. A. Brown, C.	......	4,922
D. Hallsworth, R.F.	......	538
Lab. maj.	....	21,098
(June '83, Lab. maj. 17,191)		
(Nov. '86, Lab. maj. 6,724)		

SOUTH   E. 65,643

*S. F. Hughes, Lab.	....	31,378
A. J. Hall, C.	....	10,532
Mrs. R. Watmough, S.D.P./		
All.	....	6,760
Lab. maj.	....	20,846
(June '83, Lab. maj. 11,769)		

Lancashire West
E. 76,094

*K. H. Hind, C.	....	26,500
C. Pickthall, Lab.	....	25,147
R. Jermyn, S.D.P./All.	...	8,972
C. maj.	....	1,353
(June '83, C. maj. 6,858)		

Lancaster (Lancs)
E. 57,229

*Mrs. M. E. Kellett-Bow-		
man, C.	....	21,142
J. Gallacher, Lab.	....	14,689
Mrs. K. C. Brooks, L./All.	.	9,003
P. F. F. Jones, Grn.	......	473
C. maj.	....	6,453
(June '83, C. maj. 10,636)		

Langbaurgh (Cleveland)
E. 79,193

*J. R. Holt, C.		26,047
P. Harford, Lab.		23,959
R. A. J. Ashby, L./All.		12,405
C. maj.		2,088
(June '83, C. maj. 6,024)		

Leeds (W. Yorks)

CENTRAL E. 59,019

*D. J. Fatchett, Lab.		21,270
D. Schofield, C.		9,765
Dr. Karen Lee, S.D.P./All.		6,853
W. Innis, Comm.		355
Lab. maj.		11,505
(June '83, Lab. maj. 8,222)		

EAST E. 61,178

*Rt. Hon. D. W. Healey, C.H., M.B.E., Lab.		20,932
J. S. W. Sheard, C.		11,406
Miss M. G. Clay, L./All.		10,630
Lab. maj.		9,526
(June '83, Lab. maj. 6,095)		

NORTH EAST E. 64,631

T. J. R. Kirkhope, C.		22,196
P. M. Crystal, S.D.P./All.		13,777
O. B. Glover, Lab.		12,292
Ms. C. D. Nash, Grn.		416
C. maj.		8,419
(June '83, C. maj. 8,995)		

NORTH WEST E. 68,227

*Dr. K. Hampson, C.		22,480
B. Peters, L./All.		17,279
Ms. J. Thomas, Lab.		11,210
A. Stevens, Grn.		663
C. maj.		5,201
(June '83, C. maj. 8,537)		

SOUTH AND MORLEY E. 60,726

*Rt. Hon. M. Rees, Lab.		21,551
Mrs. T. C. Holdroyd, C.		14,840
E. J. V. Dawson, S.D.P./All.		7,099
Lab. maj.		6,711
(June '83, Lab. maj. 5,854)		

WEST E. 66,344

J. D. Battle, Lab.		21,032
*M. J. Meadowcroft, L./All.		16,340
P. D. Allott, C.		11,276
Lab. maj.		4,692
(June '83, L./All. maj. 2,048)		

Leicester

EAST E. 66,372

N. K. A. S. Vaz, Lab.		24,074
*P. N. E. Bruinvels, C.		22,150
Mrs. A. M. Ayres, S.D.P./All.		5,935
Lab. maj.		1,924
(June '83, C. maj. 933)		

SOUTH E. 73,236

J. Marshall, Lab.		24,901
*D. H. Spencer, Q.C., C.		23,024
R. Pritchard, L./All.		7,773
B. Fewster, Grn.		390
M. M. Mayat, Ind. Lab.		192
Ms. R. F. Manners, W.R.P.		96
Lab. maj.		1,887
(June '83, C. maj. 7)		

WEST E. 67,829

*G. E. Janner, Q.C., Lab.		22,156
J. S. W. Cooper, C.		20,955
W. Edgar, S.D.P./All.		6,708
Lab. maj.		1,201
(June '83, Lab. maj. 1,712)		

Leicestershire North West
E. 70,633

*D. G. Ashby, C.		27,872
Mrs. S. A. Waddington, Lab.		20,044
D. S. Emmerson, L./All.		10,034
Miss H. T. Michetschlager, Grn.		570
C. maj.		7,828
(June '83, C. maj. 6,662)		

Leigh (Gtr. Manchester)
E. 69,155

*L. F. Cunliffe, Lab.		30,064
L. B. A. Browne, C.		13,458
S. D. Jones, S.D.P./All.		7,743
Lab. maj.		16,606
(June '83, Lab. maj. 12,314)		

Leominster (H & W)
E. 69,977

*P. Temple-Morris, C.		31,396
S. C. Morris, L./All.		17,321
A. C. R. Chappell, Lab.		4,444
Mrs. F. M. Norman, Grn.		1,102
C. maj.		14,075
(June '83, C. maj. 9,786)		

Lewes (E. Sussex)
E. 73,181

*J. R. Rathbone, C.		32,016
D. F. Bellotti, L./All.		18,396
R. P. Taylor, Lab.		4,973
A. G. P. Sherwood, Grn.		970
C. maj.		13,620
(June '83, C. maj. 13,904)		

Lewisham (Gtr. London)

DEPTFORD E. 58,151

Ms. J. M. Ruddock, Lab.		18,724
M. C. Punyer, C.		11,953
Ms. A. M. E. Braun, S.D.P./All.		6,513
P. K. Makepeace, Grn.		568
Lab. maj.		6,771
(June '83, Lab. maj. 6,032)		

EAST E. 59,627

*Hon. C. B. Moynihan, C.		19,873
M. R. Profitt, Lab.		15,059
Mrs. V. W. Stone, S.D.P./All.		9,118
C. maj.		4,814
(June '83, C. maj. 1,909)		

WEST E. 62,923

*J. C. Maples, C.		20,995
J. P. Dowd, Lab.		17,223
Ms. S. C. Titley, L./All.		7,247
C. maj.		3,772
(June '83, C. maj. 2,506)		

Leyton (Gtr. London)
E. 57,662

*H. M. Cohen, Lab.		16,536
S. Banks, L./All.		11,895
D. N. Gilmartin, C.		11,692
Lab. maj.		4,641
(June '83, Lab. maj. 4,516)		

Lincoln
E. 77,049

*K. M. Carlisle, C.		27,097
N. J. Butler, Lab.		19,614
P. Zentner, S.D.P./All.		11,319
T. B. Kyle, R.R.P.R.C.		232
C. maj.		7,483
(June '83, C. maj. 10,286)		

Lindsey East (Lincs)
E. 74,027

*Sir P. H. B. Tapsell, C.		29,048
J. C. L. Sellick, L./All.		20,432
K. Stevenson, Lab.		6,206
C. maj.		8,616
(June '83, C. maj. 7,517)		

Littleborough and Saddleworth
(Gtr. Manchester)
E. 66,074

*G. K. Dickens, C.		22,027
C. Davies, L./All.		15,825
P. Stonier, Lab.		13,299
C. maj.		6,202
(June '83, C. maj. 5,650)		

Liverpool

BROADGREEN E. 63,091

*T. Fields, Lab.		23,262
R. Pine, L./All.		17,215
M. R. G. Seddon, C.		7,413
Lab. maj.		6,047
(June '83, Lab. maj. 3,800)		

GARSTON E. 61,280

*E. Loyden, Lab.		24,848
P. B. Feather, C.		11,071
R. Isaacson, S.D.P./All.		10,370
K. Timlin, W.R.P.		98
Lab. maj.		13,777
(June '83, Lab. maj. 4,002)		

MOSSLEY HILL E. 60,954

*D. P. P. Alton, L./All.		20,012
J. A. Devaney, Lab.		17,786
W. M. Lightfoot, C.		8,005
L./All. maj.		2,226
(June '83, L./All. maj. 4,195)		

RIVERSIDE E. 53,328

*R. Parry, Lab.		25,505
S. Fitzsimmons, C.		4,816
B. S. Chahal, S.D.P./All.		3,912
Ms. C. A. Gardner, Comm.		601
Lab. maj.		20,689
(June '83, Lab. maj. 17,378)		

WALTON E. 73,118

*E. S. Heffer, Lab.		34,661
P. R. Clark, L./All.		11,408
I. A. Mays, C.		7,738
Lab. maj.		23,253
(June '83, Lab. maj. 14,115)		

WEST DERBY E. 60,522
*R. N. Wareing, Lab. 29,021
J. E. Backhouse, C. 8,525
M. Ferguson, S.D.P./All. .. 6,897
   Lab. maj. 20,496
   (June '83, Lab. maj. 11,843)

Loughborough (Leics)
E. 73,660

*S. J. Dorrell, C. 31,931
C. J. Wrigley, Lab. 14,283
R. G. Fox, S.D.P./All. 11,499
R. Gupta, Grn. 656
   C. maj. 17,648
   (June '83, C. maj. 16,180)

Ludlow (Salop)
E. 66,187

C. J. F. Gill, R.D., C. 27,499
D. Phillips, L./All. 15,800
K. Harrison, Lab. 7,724
   C. maj. 11,699
   (June '83, C. maj. 11,303)

Luton (Beds)
NORTH E. 74,235

*J. R. Carlisle, C. 30,997
M. Wright, Lab. 15,424
J. D. Stephen, S.D.P./All. .. 11,166
   C. maj. 15,573
   (June '83, C. maj. 11,981)

SOUTH E. 71,231
*G. F. J. Bright, C. 24,762
W. D. McKenzie, Lab. 19,647
P. Chapman, L./All. 9,146
   C. maj. 5,115
   (June '83, C. maj. 4,621)

Macclesfield (Cheshire)
E. 76,093

*N. R. Winterton, C. 33,208
A. B. Haldane, L./All. 14,116
Ms. C. Pinder, Lab. 11,563
   C. maj. 19,092
   (June '83, C. maj. 20,679)

Maidstone (Kent)
E. 72,987

Miss A. N. Widdecombe, C. 29,100
C. J. Sutton-Mattocks, L./
   All. 18,736
K. P. Brooks, Lab. 6,935
Mrs. P. A. Kemp, Grn. 717
   C. maj. 10,364
   (June '83, C. maj. 7,226)

Makerfield (Gtr. Manchester)
E. 70,819

I. McCartney, Lab. 30,190
L. A. Robertson, C. 14,632
B. Hewer, L./All. 8,838
   Lab. maj. 15,558
   (June '83, Lab. maj. 10,876)

Manchester
BLACKLEY E. 58,814
*K. Eastham, Lab. 22,476
K. Nath, C. 12,354
H. Showman, S.D.P./All. .. 8,041
   Lab. maj. 10,122
   (June '83, Lab. maj. 6,456)

CENTRAL E. 62,928
*R. K. Litherland, Lab. ... 27,428
M. R. W. Banks, C. 7,561
B. W. McColgan, S.D.P./
   All. 5,250
   Lab. maj. 19,867
   (June '83, Lab. maj. 18,485)

GORTON E. 64,243
*Rt. Hon. G. B. Kaufman,
   Lab. 24,615
J. Kershaw, C. 10,550
K. A. Whitmore, L./All. .. 9,830
Ms. P. Lawrence, R.F. 253
   Lab. maj. 14,065
   (June '83, Lab. maj. 9,965)

WITHINGTON E. 65,343
K. J. C. Bradley, Lab. 21,650
*F. J. Silvester, C. 18,259
Mrs. A. Jones, L./All. 9,978
M. T. Abberton, Grn. 524
   Lab. maj. 3,391
   (June '83, C. maj. 2,373)

WYTHENSHAWE E. 58,287
*Rt. Hon. A. Morris, Lab. .. 23,881
D. G. Sparrow, C. 12,026
Ms. J. Butterworth,
   S.D.P./All. 5,921
Ms. S. Connelly, R.F. 216
   Lab. maj. 11,855
   (June '83, Lab. maj. 10,684)

Mansfield (Notts)
E. 66,764

J. A. Meale, Lab. 19,610
C. Hendry, C. 19,554
B. Answer, S.D.P./All. 11,604
B. Marshall, M.L. 1,580
   Lab. maj. 56
   (June '83, Lab. maj. 2,216)

Medway (Kent)
E. 64,103

*Dame P. Fenner, D.B.E., C. 23,889
V. Hull, Lab. 13,960
Mrs. J. Horne-Roberts,
   S.D.P./All. 8,450
Ms. J. V. Rosser, Grn. 504
   C. maj. 9,929
   (June '83, C. maj. 8,656)

Meriden (W. Midlands)
E. 78,444

*I. C. Mills, C. 31,935
R. H. Burden, Lab. 15,115
Ms. C. E. Parkinson,
   S.D.P./All. 10,896
   C. maj. 16,820
   (June '83, C. maj. 15,018)

Middlesbrough (Cleveland)
E. 60,789

*S. Bell, Lab. 25,747
R. J. Orr-Ewing, C. 10,789
P. A. Hawley, L./All. 6,594
   Lab. maj. 14,958
   (June '83, Lab. maj. 9,669)

Milton Keynes (Bucks)
E. 97,041

*W. R. Benyon, C. 35,396
W. T. Rodgers, S.D.P./All. 21,695
Ms. Y. V. A. Brownfield-
   Pope, Lab. 16,111
A. H. Francis, Grn. 810
   C. maj. 13,701
   (June '83, C. maj. 11,522)

Mitcham and Morden
(Gtr. London)
E. 63,089

*Mrs. A. C. R. Rumbold,
   C.B.E., C. 23,002
Ms. S. McDonagh, Lab. ... 16,819
B. L. H. Douglas-Mann,
   S.D.P./All. 7,930
   C. maj. 6,183
   (June '83, C. maj. 6,451)

Mole Valley (Surrey)
E. 67,715

*Rt. Hon. K. W. Baker, C. .. 31,689
Mrs. S. P. Thomas, L./All. 15,613
C. M. B. King, Lab. 4,846
   C. maj. 16,076
   (June '83, C. maj. 14,718)

Morecambe and Lunesdale
(Lancs)
E. 55,718

*Hon. M. A. Lennox-Boyd,
   C. 22,327
Mrs. J. Greenwell, S.D.P./
   All. 10,542
D. Smith, Lab. 9,535
   C. maj. 11,785
   (June '83, C. maj. 12,194)

Newark (Notts)
E. 67,555

*R. T. Alexander, C. 28,070
D. Barton, Lab. 14,527
G. A. Emerson, S.D.P./All. 9,833
   C. maj. 13,543
   (June '83, C. maj. 14,283)

Newbury (Berks)
E. 75,187

*R. M. C. McNair-Wilson, C. 35,266
D. D. Rendel, L./All. 18,608
R. C. Stapley, Lab. 4,765
   C. maj. 16,658
   (June '83, C. maj. 13,038)

Newcastle-under-Lyme (Staffs)
E. 66,053

*Mrs. L. Golding, Lab. 21,618
A. L. Thomas, L./All. 16,486
P. C. J. Ridgway, C. 14,863
M. J. Nicklin, Ex Lab.
   Mod. 397
   Lab. maj. 5,132
   (June '83, Lab. maj. 2,804)
   (July '86, Lab. maj. 799)

Newcastle upon Tyne
CENTRAL E. 63,682
J. M. Cousins, Lab. 20,416
*P. R. G. Merchant, C. 17,933
Dr. N. Martin, S.D.P./All. 7,304
R. J. Bird, Grn. 418
K. Williams, R.F. 111
   Lab. maj. 2,483
   (June '83, C. maj. 2,228)

EAST *E.* 59,369
*N. H. Brown, Lab. 23,677
Miss J. G. A. Riley, *C.* 11,177
P. J. Arnold, *L./All.* 6,728
J. Keith, *Comm.* 362
Lab. maj. 12,500
(June '83, Lab. maj. 7,492)

NORTH *E.* 69,178
D. J. Henderson, *Lab.* 22,424
J. W. Shipley, *L./All.* 17,181
J. W. Tweddle, *C.* 12,915
Lab. maj. 5,243
(June '83, Lab. maj. 2,556)

New Forest (Hants)
E. 75,083
**P. M. E. D. McNair-Wilson,
C.* 37,188
R. Karn, *L./All.* 15,456
J. I. Hampton, *Lab.* 4,856
C. maj. 21,732
(June '83, C. maj. 20,925)

Newham (Gtr. London)
NORTH EAST *E.* 60,787
*R. Leighton, Lab. 20,220
P. Davis, *C.* 11,984
Ms. H. Steele, *L./All.* 6,772
Lab. maj. 8,236
(June '83, Lab. maj. 8,509)

NORTH WEST *E.* 47,568
*T. L. Banks, Lab. 15,677
J. C. Wylie, *C.* 7,181
R. H. Redden, *S.D.P./All.* . 4,920
Ms. A. V. Degrandis-
Harrison, *Grn.* 497
Lab. maj. 8,496
(June '83, Lab. maj. 6,918)

SOUTH *E.* 50,244
*N. J. Spearing, Lab. 12,935
J. Fairrie, *C.* 10,169
A. J. Kellaway, *S.D.P./All.* 6,607
Lab. maj. 2,766
(June '83, Lab. maj. 7,311)

Norfolk
MID *E.* 73,893
*R. A. Ryder, O.B.E., C. ... 32,758
G. J. E. Graham, *S.D.P./
All.* 14,750
K. Luckey, *Lab.* 10,272
C. maj. 18,008
(June '83, C. maj. 15,515)

NORTH *E.* 69,790
*R. F. Howell, C. 28,822
N. R. Anthony, *S.D.P./All.* 13,512
A. Earle, *Lab.* 10,765
M. G. Filgate, *Grn.* 960
C. maj. 15,310
(June '83, C. maj. 13,223)

NORTH WEST *E.* 73,739
*H. C. Bellingham, C. 29,393
C. Brocklebank-Fowler,
S.D.P./All. 18,568
F. Dignan, *Lab.* 10,184
C. maj. 10,825
(June '83, C. maj. 3,147)

SOUTH *E.* 78,372
**Rt. Hon. J. R. R. Mac-
Gregor,* O.B.E., *C.* 33,912
R. A. P. Carden, *L./All.* ... 21,494
L. Addison, *Lab.* 8,047
C. maj. 12,418
(June '83, C. maj. 12,135)

SOUTH WEST *E.* 74,240
Mrs. G. P. Shephard, C. .. 32,519
M. Scott, *L./All.* 12,083
Ms. M. Page, *Lab.* 11,844
C. maj. 20,436
(June '83, C. maj. 14,910)

Normanton (W. Yorks)
E. 62,899
*W. O'Brien, Lab. 23,303
M. D. M. Smith, *C.* 16,016
R. J. Macey, *S.D.P./All.* .. 7,717
Lab. maj. 7,287
(June '83, Lab. maj. 4,183)

Northampton
NORTH *E.* 69,294
*A. R. Marlow, C. 24,816
O. J. Granfield, *Lab.* 15,560
A. S. Rounthwaite, *L./All.* 10,690
M. Green, *Grn.* 471
S. Colling, *W.R.P.* 156
C. maj. 9,256
(June '83, C. maj. 9,860)

SOUTH *E.* 76,071
*M. W. L. Morris, C. 31,864
J. Dickie, *Lab.* 14,061
G. Hopkins, *S.D.P./All.* .. 10,639
Mrs. M. Hamilton, *Grn.* .. 647
C. maj. 17,803
(June '83, C. maj. 15,126)

Northavon (Avon)
E. 78,483
*J. A. Cope, C. 34,224
Mrs. C. Willmore, *L./All.* . 19,954
D. Norris, *Lab.* 8,762
C. maj. 14,270
(June '83, C. maj. 12,983)

Norwich (Norfolk)
NORTH *E.* 62,725
*H. P. Thompson, C. 22,772
Miss M. H. R. Honeyball,
Lab. 14,996
T. P. Nicholls, *L./All.* 11,922
C. maj. 7,776
(June '83, C. maj. 5,879)

SOUTH *E.* 64,421
J. L. Garrett, *Lab.* 19,666
*J. A. Powley, C. 19,330
C. J. M. Hardie, *S.D.P./All.* 12,896
Lab. maj. 336
(June '83, C. maj. 1,712)

Norwood (Gtr. London)
E. 56,602
*J. D. Fraser, Lab. 18,359
D. C. R. Grieve, *C.* 13,636
M. M. Noble, *S.D.P./All.* .. 12,579
F. M. Jackson, *R.A.B.I.E.S.* 171
R. J. Hammond, *C.D.* 151
Lab. maj. 4,723
(June '83, Lab. maj. 2,883)

Nottingham
EAST *E.* 68,266
*M. Knowles, C. 20,162
M. Aslam, *Lab.* 19,706
S. Parkhouse, *L./All.* 6,887
K. Malik, *R.F.* 212
C. maj. 456
(June '83, C. maj. 1,464)

NORTH *E.* 69,620
G. W. Allen, *Lab.* 22,713
*R. G. J. Ottaway, C. 21,048
S. C. Fernando, *S.D.P./All.* 5,912
J. H. Peck, *Comm.* 879
Lab. maj. 1,665
(June '83, C. maj. 362)

SOUTH *E.* 72,807
*M. M. Brandon-Bravo, C. . 23,921
A. Simpson, *Lab.* 21,687
L. V. Williams, *S.D.P./All.* . 7,517
C. maj. 2,234
(June '83, C. maj. 5,715)

Nuneaton (Warwicks)
E. 68,287
*L. D. Stevens, M.B.E., C. ... 24,630
Mrs. V. A. Veness, *Lab.* .. 18,975
A. Trembath, *S.D.P./All.* .. 10,550
Dr. J. Morrissey, *Grn.* 719
C. maj. 5,655
(June '83, C. maj. 5,061)

Old Bexley and Sidcup
(Gtr. London)
E. 50,831
*Rt. Hon. E. R. G. Heath,
M.B.E., *C.* 24,350
T. H. Pearce, *L./All.* 8,076
H. J. A. Stoate, *Lab.* 6,762
C. maj. 16,274
(June '83, C. maj. 12,718)

Oldham (Gtr. Manchester)
CENTRAL AND ROYTON
E. 65,277
*J. A. Lamond, Lab. 21,759
J. A. Farquhar, *C.* 15,480
Mrs. A. Dunn, *S.D.P./All.* . 7,956
Lab. maj. 6,279
(June '83, Lab. maj. 3,312)

WEST *E.* 57,178
*M. H. Meacher, Lab. 20,291
Mrs. J. M. Jacobs, *C.* 14,324
Miss M. R. Mason, *L./All.* . 6,478
Lab. maj. 5,967
(June '83, Lab. maj. 3,180)

Orpington (Gtr. London)
E. 59,608
*I. R. Stanbrook, C. 27,261
J. H. Fryer, *L./All.* 14,529
S. J. Cowan, *Lab.* 5,020
C. maj. 12,732
(June '83, C. maj. 10,151)

Oxford
EAST *E.* 62,145
A. D. Smith, Lab. 21,103
*S. J. Norris, C. 19,815
Mrs. M. Godden, *L./All.* ... 7,648
D. Dalton, *Grn.* 441
P. S. Mylvaganam, *I.C.C.* .. 60
Lab. maj. 1,288
(June '83, C. maj. 1,267)

West and Abingdon *E.* 69,193
**J. H. C. Patten, C. 25,171
C. M. P. Huhne, *S.D.P./All.* 20,293
J. G. Power, *Lab.* 8,108
D. Smith, *Grn.* 695
C. maj. 4,878
(June '83, C. maj. 7,151)

Peckham (Gtr. London)
E. 59,261
*Ms. H. Harman, Lab. 17,965
Mrs. L. K. F. Ingram, *C.* .. 8,476
R. H. Shearman, *L./All.* .. 5,878
Miss D. Robinson, *Grn.* ... 628
Lab. maj. 9,489
(June '83, Lab. maj. 8,824)

Pendle (Lancs)
E. 63,588
*J. R. L. Lee, C. 21,009
Mrs. S. Renilson, *Lab.* 18,370
A. G. Lishman, *L./All.* ... 12,662
C. maj. 2,639
(June '83, C. maj. 6,135)

Penrith and The Border
(Cumbria)
E. 70,994
*D. J. Maclean, C. 33,148
D. J. Ivison, *L./All.* 15,782
J. M. P. Hutton, *Lab.* 6,075
C. maj. 17,366
(June '83, C. maj. 15,421)
(July '83, C. maj. 552)

Peterborough (Cambs)
E. 84,284
*Dr. B. S. Mawhinney, C. . 30,624
A. MacKinlay, *Lab.* 20,840
D. W. Green, *L./All.* 9,984
N. A. Callaghan, *Grn.* 506
C. maj. 9,784
(June '83, C. maj. 10,439)

Plymouth (Devon)
DEVONPORT *E.* 64,741
*Rt. Hon. Dr. D. A. L. Owen,
S.D.P./All. 21,039
T. Jones, *C.* 14,569
I. Flintoff, *Lab.* 14,166
S.D.P./All. maj. 6,470
(June '83, S.D.P./All. maj. 4,936)

DRAKE *E.* 51,186
*Miss J. E. Fookes, C. 16,195
D. Astor, *S.D.P./All.* 13,070
D. Jamieson, *Lab.* 9,451
Ms. P. Barber, *Grn.* 493
C. maj. 3,125
(June '83, C. maj. 8,585)

SUTTON *E.* 64,120
*Hon. A. K. M. Clark, C. .. 23,187
B. Tidy, *L./All.* 19,174
R. D. Maddern, *Lab.* 8,310
C. maj. 4,013
(June '83, C. maj. 11,687)

Pontefract and Castleford
(W. Yorks)
E. 64,414
*G. Lofthouse, Lab. 31,656
J. H. Mallins, *C.* 10,030
M. F. Taylor, *L./All.* 5,334
D. M. Lees, *R.F.* 295
Lab. maj. 21,626
(June '83, Lab. maj. 13,691)

Poole (Dorset)
E. 76,673
*J. D. Ward, C.B.E., C. 34,159
R. J. Whitley, *S.D.P./All.* . 19,351
M. Shutler, *Lab.* 5,901
C. maj. 14,808
(June '83, C. maj. 14,429)

Portsmouth (Hants)
NORTH *E.* 80,501
*P. H. S. Griffiths, C. 33,297
Mrs. E. Mitchell, *S.D.P./*
All. 14,896
D. Miles, *Lab.* 12,016
C. maj. 18,401
(June '83, C. maj. 17,999)

SOUTH *E.* 76,292
D. Martin, *C.* 23,534
*M. T. Hancock, S.D.P./All. 23,329
K. Gardiner, *Lab.* 7,047
R. Hughes, *657 Party* 455
C. maj. 205
(June '83, C. maj. 12,335)
(June '84, S.D.P./All. maj. 1,341)

Preston (Lancs)
E. 64,459
Mrs. A. Wise, Lab. 23,341
Dr. R. T. Chandran, *C.* ... 12,696
J. P. Wright, *L./All.* 8,452
Lab. maj. 10,645
(June '83, Lab. maj. 6,978)

Pudsey (W. Yorks)
E. 71,681
*J. G. D. Shaw, C. 25,457
J. P. F. Cummins, *L./All.* . 19,021
N. Taggart, *Lab.* 11,461
C. maj. 6,436
(June '83, C. maj. 5,314)

Putney (Gtr. London)
E. 63,108
*D. J. Mellor, C. 24,197
P. G. Hain, *Lab.* 17,290
Ms. S. Harlow, *L./All.* 5,934
S. Desorgher, *Grn.* 508
C. maj. 6,907
(June '83, C. maj. 5,019)

Ravensbourne (Gtr. London)
E. 59,365
*J. L. Hunt, C. 28,295
G. Campbell, *S.D.P./All.* .. 11,376
M. D'Arcy, *Lab.* 5,087
A. Waide, *B.N.* 184
C. maj. 16,919
(June '83, C. maj. 15,512)

Reading (Berks)
EAST *E.* 72,311
*Sir G. Vaughan, C. 28,515
Mrs. S. M. Baring, *S.D.P./*
All. 12,298
M. J. Salter, *Lab.* 11,371
P. J. Unsworth, *Grn.* 667
A. B. Shone, *C.S.* 125
C. maj. 16,217
(June '83, C. maj. 11,508)

WEST *E.* 70,391
*R. A. B. Durant, C. 28,122
K. H. Lock, *L./All.* 11,369
M. E. Orton, *Lab.* 10,819
E. P. Wilson, *Grn.* 542
C. maj. 16,753
(June '83, C. maj. 11,399)

Redcar (Cleveland)
E. 63,393
Dr. Marjorie Mowlam, Lab. 22,824
P. J. Bassett, *C.* 15,089
G. Nightingale, *S.D.P./All.* 10,298
Lab. maj. 7,735
(June '83, Lab. maj. 3,104)

Reigate (Surrey)
E. 71,940
*G. A. Gardiner, C. 30,925
Mrs. E. A. Pamplin, *S.D.P./*
All. 12,752
R. P. Spencer, *Lab.* 7,460
G. Brand, *Grn.* 1,026
C. maj. 18,173
(June '83, C. maj. 16,307)

Ribble Valley (Lancs)
E. 62,644
*Rt. Hon. D. C. Waddington,
Q.C., *C.* 30,136
M. Carr, *S.D.P./All.* 10,608
G. Pope, *Lab.* 8,781
C. maj. 19,528
(June '83, C. maj. 18,591)

Richmond and Barnes
(Gtr. London)
E. 54,700
*J. J. Hanley, C. 21,729
A. J. Watson, *L./All.* 19,963
M. D. Gold, *Lab.* 3,227
Miss C. M. Matthews, *Grn.* 610
C. maj. 1,766
(June '83, C. maj. 74)

Richmond (N. Yorks)
E. 79,277
*Rt. Hon. L. Brittan, Q.C.,
C. 34,995
D. Lloyd-Williams, *L./All.* 15,419
F. Robson, *Lab.* 6,737
C. maj. 19,576
(June '83, C. maj. 18,066)

Rochdale (Gtr. Manchester)
E. 68,703
*C. Smith, M.B.E., L./All. .. 22,245
D. Williams, *Lab.* 19,466
C. Condie, *C.* 9,561
L./All. maj. 2,779
(June '83, L./All. maj. 7,587)

Rochford (Essex)
E. 76,048

*Dr. M. Clark, C.	....	35,872
P. Young, L./All.	......	16,178
D. Weir, Lab.	....	7,308
C. maj.	....	19,694
(June '83, C. maj. 13,102)		

Romford (Gtr. London)
E. 55,668

*M. J. Neubert, C.	....	22,745
N. J. M. Smith, Lab.	.....	9,274
J. H. Bates, L./All.	......	8,195
F. J. Gibson, Grn.	....	385
C. maj.	....	13,471
(June '83, C. maj. 10,574)		

Romsey and Waterside (Hants)
E. 79,136

*M. K. B. Colvin, C.	....	35,303
A. T. Bloss, S.D.P./All.	...	20,031
S. J. Roberts, Lab.	....	7,213
C. maj.	....	15,272
(June '83, C. maj. 13,690)		

Rossendale and Darwen (Lancs)
E. 75,038

*D. A. Trippier, C.	....	28,056
Mrs. J. Anderson, Lab.	...	23,074
P. J. Hulse, L./All.	....	9,097
C. maj.	....	4,982
(June '83, C. maj. 8,821)		

Rotherham (S. Yorks)
E. 61,521

*J. S. Crowther, Lab.	......	25,422
J. C. C. Stevens, C.	......	9,410
P. J. Bowler, L./All.	......	7,766
Lab. maj.	....	16,012
(June '83, Lab. maj. 11,709)		

Rother Valley (S. Yorks)
E. 66,416

*K. J. Barron, Lab.	....	28,292
P. R. Rayner, C.	....	12,502
J. R. Boddy, S.D.P./All.	..	9,240
M. R. Driver, W.R.P.	.....	145
Lab. maj.	....	15,790
(June '83, Lab. maj. 8,625)		

Rugby and Kenilworth
(Warwicks)
E. 76,654

*J. F. Pawsey, C.	....	31,485
J. Airey, Lab.	....	15,221
D. R. Owen-Jones, L./All.	...	14,343
C. maj.	....	16,264
(June '83, C. maj. 14,241)		

Ruislip-Northwood
(Gtr. London)
E. 56,365

*J. A. D. Wilkinson, C.	....	27,418
Mrs. D. Darby, L./All.	....	10,447
Ms. H. A. Smith, Lab.	....	5,913
C. maj.	....	16,971
(June '83, C. maj. 12,982)		

Rushcliffe (Notts)
E. 72,797

*Rt. Hon. K. H. Clarke, Q.C.,		
C.	....	34,214
L. George, S.D.P./All.	....	13,375
P. Tipping, Lab.	....	9,631
Ms. H. Wright, Grn.	.....	991
C. maj.	....	20,839
(June '83, C. maj. 20,220)		

Rutland and Melton (Leics)
E. 77,846

*M. A. Latham, C.	....	37,073
R. C. Renold, L./All.	.....	14,051
L. C. Burke, Lab.	....	8,680
C. maj.	....	23,022
(June '83, C. maj. 18,353)		

Ryedale (N. Yorks)
E. 83,205

J. R. Greenway, C.	....	35,149
*Mrs. E. L. Shields, L./All.	.	25,409
J. Beighton, Lab.	....	5,340
C. maj.	....	9,740
(June '83, C. maj. 16,142)		
(May '86, L./All. maj. 4,940)		

Saffron Walden (Essex)
E. 73,185

*A. G. B. Haselhurst, C.	...	33,354
M. P. Hayes, L./All.	......	16,752
R. Gifford, Lab.	....	6,674
G. B. Hannah, Grn.	......	816
W. O. Smedley, C.M.N.H.Y.		217
C. maj.	....	16,602
(June '83, C. maj. 15,363)		

St. Albans (Herts)
E. 75,281

*P. B. Lilley, C.	....	31,726
A. S. B. Walkington, L./All.		20,845
A. McWalter, Lab.	....	6,922
Ms. E. V. Field, Grn.	.....	788
W. H. Pass, C.P.R.P.	.....	110
C. maj.	....	10,881
(June '83, C. maj. 8,561)		

St. Helens (Merseyside)

NORTH E. 70,836

*J. Evans, Lab.	....	28,989
Miss M. J. Libby, C.	......	14,729
N. P. Derbyshire, L./All.	..	10,300
Lab. maj.	....	14,260
(June '83, Lab. maj. 9,259)		

SOUTH E. 69,449

*G. E. Bermingham, Lab.	..	27,027
A. J. Brown, C.	....	13,226
P. J. Briers, S.D.P./All.	.	9,252
Lab. maj.	....	13,801
(June '83, Lab. maj. 9,662)		

St. Ives (Cornwall)
E. 67,448

*D. A. Harris, C.	....	25,174
H. H. J. Carter, S.D.P./All.		17,619
I. Hope, Lab.	....	9,275
C. maj.	....	7,555
(June '83, C. maj. 7,859)		

Salford East
(Gtr. Manchester)
E. 58,087

*Rt. Hon. S. Orme, Lab.	...	22,555
C. W. H. McFall, C.	......	10,499
P. Keaveney, S.D.P./All.	.	5,105
S. G. Murray, W.R.P.	....	201
Lab. maj.	....	12,056
(June '83, Lab. maj. 9,541)		

Salisbury (Wilts)
E. 76,221

*S. R. Key, C.	....	31,612
P. A. Mitchell, S.D.P./All.		20,169
Ms. T. E. Seabourne, Lab.		5,455
S. W. Fletcher, Ind.	......	372
C. maj.	....	11,443
(June '83, C. maj. 7,174)		

Scarborough (N. Yorks)
E. 74,612

*Sir M. N. Shaw, C.	....	27,672
Mrs. H. Callan, S.D.P./All.		14,046
M. Wolstenholme, Lab.	..	12,913
C. maj.	....	13,626
(June '83, C. maj. 13,929)		

Sedgefield (Durham)
E. 60,866

*A. C. L. Blair, Lab.	......	25,965
N. B. S. Hawkins, C.	.....	12,907
R. I. Andrew, S.D.P./All.	.	7,477
Lab. maj.	....	13,058
(June '83, Lab. maj. 8,281)		

Selby (N. Yorks)
E. 71,378

*Rt. Hon. M. J. H. Alison,		
C.	....	28,611
J. T. Grogan, Lab.	....	14,832
J. E. F. Longman, L./All.	.	12,010
C. maj.	....	13,779
(June '83, C. maj. 15,965)		

Sevenoaks (Kent)
E. 73,179

*G. M. Wolfson, C.	....	32,945
S. R. Jakobi, L./All.	......	15,600
G. A. Green, Lab.	....	7,379
C. maj.	....	17,345
(June '83, C. maj. 15,706)		

Sheffield (S. Yorks)

ATTERCLIFFE E. 67,051

*A. E. P. Duffy, Lab.	......	28,266
G. J. Perry, C.	....	11,075
Ms. H. E. Woolley, S.D.P./		
All.	....	9,549
Lab. maj.	....	17,191
(June '83, Lab. maj. 11,612)		

BRIGHTSIDE E. 64,982

D. Blunkett, Lab.	....	31,208
Miss M. C. Glyn, C.	......	7,017
J. A. Leeman, L./All.	.....	6,434
Lab. maj.	....	24,191
(June '83, Lab. maj. 15,209)		

CENTRAL *E.* 61,156
*R. G. Caborn, Lab. 25,872
B. Oxley, *C.* 6,530
Ms. F. C. Hornby, *S.D.P./
All.* 5,314
C. T. Dingle, *R.F.* 278
K. E. Petts, *Comm.* 203
Lab. maj. 19,342
(June '83, Lab. maj. 16,790)

HALLAM *E.* 74,158
C. I. Patnick, *C.* 25,649
P. J. Gold, *L./All.* 18,012
M. C. Savani, *Lab.* 11,290
Ms. L. M. Spencer, *Grn.* .. 459
C. maj. 7,637
(June '83, C. maj. 11,774)

HEELEY *E.* 73,931
*W. Michie, Lab. 28,425
N. P. Mearing-Smith, *C.* .. 13,985
P. Moore, *S.D.P./All.* 10,811
Lab. maj. 14,440
(June '83, Lab. maj. 8,368)

HILLSBOROUGH *E.* 76,312
*M. H. Flannery, Lab. 26,208
D. Chadwick, *L./All.* 22,922
J. D. Sykes, *C.* 10,396
Lab. maj. 3,286
(June '83, Lab. maj. 1,546)

Sherwood (Notts)
E. 71,378
*A. S. Stewart, C. 26,816
W. S. G. Bach, *Lab.* 22,321
S. R. Thompstone, *S.D.P./
All.* 9,343
C. maj. 4,495
(June '83, C. maj. 658)

Shipley (W. Yorks)
E. 68,705
*Sir J. M. Fox, M.B.E., C. ... 26,941
W. J. L. Wallace, *L./All.* .. 14,311
C. R. B. Butler, *Lab.* 12,669
C. M. Harris, *Grn.* 507
C. maj. 12,630
(June '83, C. maj. 11,445)

Shoreham (W. Sussex)
E. 71,318
*Rt. Hon. R. N. Luce, C. ... 33,660
J. A. Ingram, *L./All.* 16,590
P. Godwin, *Lab.* 5,053
C. maj. 17,070
(June '83, C. maj. 15,766)

Shrewsbury and Atcham (Salop)
E. 70,689
*D. L. Conway, C. 26,027
R. Hutchison, *L./All.* 16,963
Mrs. E. Owen, *Lab.* 10,797
G. Hardy, *Grn.* 660
C. maj. 9,064
(June '83, C. maj. 8,624)

Shropshire North
E. 77,122
*Rt. Hon. W. J. Biffen, C. .. 30,385
G. Smith, *L./All.* 15,970
R. Hawkins, *Lab.* 11,866
C. maj. 14,415
(June '83, C. maj. 11,667)

Skipton and Ripon
(N. Yorks)
E. 72,199

D. M. Curry, *C.* 33,128
S. J. Cooksey, *L./All.* 15,954
T. L. Whitfield, *Lab.* 6,264
Ms. L. S. Williams, *Grn.* .. 825
C. maj. 17,174
(June '83, C. maj. 15,046)

Slough (Berks)
E. 73,424
*J. A. Watts, C. 26,166
E. Lopez, *Lab.* 22,076
M. Goldstone, *S.D.P./All* .. 7,490
C. maj. 4,090
(June '83, C. maj. 3,106)

Solihull (W. Midlands)
E. 78,123
*J. M. Taylor, C. 35,844
G. E. Gadie, *L./All.* 14,058
Mrs. S. E. Knowles, *Lab.* . 8,791
C. maj. 21,786
(June '83, C. maj. 17,394)

Somerton and Frome
(Somerset)
E. 68,773
**Hon. R. T. Boscawen, M.C.,
C.* 29,351
R. G. Morgan, *L./All.* 19,813
I. S. Kelly, *Lab.* 5,461
C. maj. 9,538
(June '83, C. maj. 9,227)

ITCHEN *E.* 72,687
*C. R. Chope, O.B.E., C. 24,419
J. Y. Denham, *Lab.* 17,703
R. C. Mitchell, *S.D.P./All.* 13,006
C. maj. 6,716
(June '83, C. maj. 5,290)

TEST *E.* 73,918
*S. J. A. Hill, C. 25,722
A. P. V. Whitehead, *Lab.* . 18,768
Mrs. V. Rayner, *L./All.* .. 11,950
C. maj. 6,954
(June '83, C. maj. 9,346)

Southend (Essex)

EAST *E.* 59,073
*E. M. Taylor, C. 23,753
H. J. Berkeley, *S.D.P./All.* 9,906
D. R. Scully, *Lab.* 7,296
C. maj. 13,847
(June '83, C. maj. 10,691)

WEST *E.* 68,415
**Rt. Hon. H. P. G. Channon,
C.* 28,003
G. Grant, *L./All.* 19,603
Mrs. A. Smith, *Lab.* 3,899
C. maj. 8,400
(June '83, C. maj. 8,033)

South Hams (Devon)
E. 78,583
*A. D. Steen, C. 34,218
R. F. Chave, *L./All.* 21,072
*W. W. Hamilton, Lab. 5,060
C. G. Titmuss, *Grn.* 1,178
T. C. Langsford, *L.M.* 277
C. maj. 13,146
(June '83, C. maj. 12,401)

Southport (Merseyside)
E. 71,443

R. C. Fearn, *L./All.* 26,110
N. M. Thomas, *C.* 24,261
Mrs. A. Moore, *Lab.* 3,483
J. R. G. Walker, *Grn.* 653
L./All. maj. 1,849
(June '83, C. maj. 5,039)

South Ribble (Lancs)
E. 72,177
*R. J. Atkins, C. 28,133
D. F. Roebuck, *Lab.* 19,703
J. A. Holleran, *L./All.* 11,746
C. maj. 8,430
(June '83, C. maj. 12,659)

South Shields (Tyne & Wear)
E. 60,754
*Dr. D. G. Clark, Lab. 24,882
M. L. D. Fabricant, *C.* 11,031
Ms. M. Meling, *S.D.P./All.* 6,654
E. G. Dunn, *Dem.* 408
Lab. maj. 13,851
(June '83, Lab. maj. 6,402)

Southwark and Bermondsey
(Gtr. London)
E. 55,438
*S. H. W. Hughes, L./All. .. 17,072
J. Bryan, *Lab.* 14,293
O. Heald, *C.* 4,522
P. N. Power, *Comm.* 108
L./All. maj. 2,779
(June '83, L./All. maj. 5,164)

Spelthorne (Surrey)
E. 72,967
D. Wilshire, *C.* 32,440
Mrs. M. Cunningham,
S.D.P./All. 12,390
D. F. J. Welfare, *Lab.* 9,227
C. maj. 20,050
(June '83, C. maj. 13,506)

Stafford
E. 72,431
*W. N. P. Cash, C. 29,541
C. B. Phipps, *S.D.P./All.* .. 15,834
Ms. N. Hafeez, *Lab.* 12,177
C. maj. 13,707
(June '83, C. maj. 14,227)
(May '84, C. maj. 3,980)

Staffordshire

MID *E.* 71,252
*B. J. Heddle, C. 28,644
C. R. St. Hill, *Lab.* 13,990
T. A. Jones, *L./All.* 13,114
J. G. Bazeley, *Ind. C.* 836
C. maj. 14,654
(June '83, C. maj. 13,880)

MOORLANDS *E.* 74,302
*D. L. Knox, C. 31,613
Mrs. V. Ivers, *Lab.* 17,186
J. P. Corbett, *S.D.P./All.* . 10,950
C. maj. 14,427
(June '83, C. maj. 16,566)

SOUTH *E.* 79,261
*P. T. Cormack, C. 37,708
Mrs. F. Oborski, *L./All.* .. 12,440
P. Bateman, *Lab.* 11,805
C. maj. 25,268
(June '83, C. maj. 19,760)

SOUTH EAST *E.* 66,176

*D. L. Lightbown, C.		25,115
Miss E. Gluck, *S.D.P./All.*		14,230
D. Spilsbury, *Lab.*		13,874
C. maj.		10,885

(June '83, C. maj. 10,898)

Stalybridge and Hyde
(Gtr. Manchester)
E. 67,983

T. Pendry, Lab.		24,401
R. N. Greenwood, *C.*		18,738
P. J. Ashenden, *S.D.P./All.*		7,311
Lab. maj.		5,663

(June '83, Lab. maj. 4,362)

Stamford and Spalding (Lincs)
E. 70,560

J. Q. Davies, *C.*		31,000
Miss R. Bryan, *L./All.*		17,009
P. E. Lowe, *Lab.*		6,882
C. maj.		13,991

(June '83, C. maj. 11,756)

Stevenage (Herts)
E. 69,525

T. J. R. Wood, C.		23,541
B. R. M. Stoneham, *S.D.P./ All.*		18,201
M. R. C. Withers, *Lab.*		14,229
C. maj.		5,340

(June '83, C. maj. 1,755)

Stockport (Gtr. Manchester)
E. 60,059

A. R. Favell, C.		19,410
Mrs. S. Haines, *Lab.*		16,557
J. L. Begg, *S.D.P./All.*		10,365
M. Shipley, *Grn.*		573
C. maj.		2,853

(June '83, C. maj. 5,786)

Stockton (Cleveland)

NORTH *E.* 70,329

F. Cook, Lab.		26,043
D. J. C. Faber, *C.*		17,242
N. F. G. Bosanquet, *S.D.P./ All.*		9,712
Lab. maj.		8,801

(June '83, Lab. maj. 1,870)

SOUTH *E.* 75,279

T. R. Devlin, *C.*		20,833
I. W. Wrigglesworth, S.D.P./All.		20,059
J. M. Scott, *Lab.*		18,600
C. maj.		774

(June '83, S.D.P./All. maj. 102)

Stoke-on-Trent (Staffs)

CENTRAL *E.* 65,987

M. Fisher, Lab.		23,842
D. Stone, *C.*		14,072
I. Cundy, *S.D.P./All.*		7,462
Lab. maj.		9,770

(June '83, Lab. maj. 8,250)

NORTH *E.* 74,184

Ms. J. L. Walley, Lab.		25,459
R. Davies, *C.*		16,946
S. J. Simmonds, *S.D.P./All.*		11,665
Lab. maj.		8,513

(June '83, Lab. maj. 8,203)

SOUTH *E.* 70,806

Rt. Hon. J. Ashley, C.H., Lab.		24,794
D. Hartshorne, *C.*		19,741
P. Wild, *L./All.*		7,669
Lab. maj.		5,053

(June '83, Lab. maj. 7,105)

Stratford-upon-Avon (Warwicks)
E. 81,263

A. T. Howarth, C.B.E., C.		38,483
D. G. Cowcher, *L./All.*		17,318
R. H. Rhodes, *Lab.*		6,335
C. maj.		21,165

(June '83, C. maj. 17,917)

Streatham (Gtr. London)
E. 60,519

W. J. M. Shelton, C.		18,916
Ms. A. Tapsall, *Lab.*		16,509
M. Tuffrey, *L./All.*		6,663
C. maj.		2,407

(June '83, C. maj. 5,902)

Stretford (Gtr. Manchester)
E. 57,568

A. J. Lloyd, Lab.		22,831
D. Dougherty, *C.*		13,429
D. Lee, *S.D.P./All.*		5,125
Lab. maj.		9,402

(June '83, Lab. maj. 4,342)

Stroud (Glos)
E. 81,275

R. M. Knapman, *C.*		32,883
A. A. Walker-Smith, *L./ All.*		20,508
T. Levitt, *Lab.*		12,145
C. maj.		12,375

(June '83, C. maj. 11,714)

Suffolk

CENTRAL *E.* 79,199

M. N. Lord, C.		32,422
T. Dale, *L./All.*		16,132
M. Walker, *Lab.*		11,817
C. maj.		16,290

(June '83, C. maj. 14,731)

COASTAL *E.* 75,684

Rt. Hon. J. S. Gummer, C.		32,834
Mrs. J. M. Miller, *S.D.P./ All.*		17,554
Mrs. S. A. Reeves, *Lab.*		7,534
J. W. Holloway, *Grn.*		1,049
C. maj.		15,280

(June '83, C. maj. 15,622)

SOUTH *E.* 81,954

T. S. K. Yeo, C.		33,972
C. M. N. Bradford, *L./All.*		17,729
A. C. Bavington, *Lab.*		11,876
C. maj.		16,243

(June '83, C. maj. 11,269)

Sunderland
(Tyne & Wear)

NORTH *E.* 75,674

R. A. Clay, Lab.		29,767
I. S. Picton, *C.*		15,095
T. Jenkinson, *L./All.*		8,518
Lab. maj.		14,672

(June '83, Lab. maj. 7,196)

SOUTH *E.* 74,947

C. J. Mullin, *Lab.*		28,823
G. E. Howe, *C.*		16,210
K. Hudson, *S.D.P./All.*		7,768
D. N. Jacques, *Grn.*		516
Lab. maj.		12,613

(June '83, Lab. maj. 5,548)

Surbiton (Gtr. London)
E. 45,428

R. P. Tracey, C.		19,861
D. T. Burke, *S.D.P./All.*		10,120
A. McGowan, *Lab.*		5,111
Ms. J. Vidler, *Grn.*		465
C. maj.		9,741

(June '83, C. maj. 8,749)

Surrey

EAST *E.* 59,528

Rt. Hon. Sir R. E. G. Howe, Q.C., C.		29,126
M. A. J. Anderson, *L./All.*		11,000
M. Davis, *Lab.*		4,779
D. Newell, *Grn.*		1,044
C. maj.		18,126

(June '83, C. maj. 15,436)

NORTH WEST *E.* 83,083

W. M. J. Grylls, C.		38,535
C. Brodie, *L./All.*		14,960
J. Cooper, *Lab.*		6,751
C. maj.		23,575

(June '83, C. maj. 21,018)

SOUTH WEST *E.* 73,018

Mrs. V. H. B. M. Bottomley, C.		34,024
G. D. Scott, *L./All.*		19,681
J. K. P. Evers, *Lab.*		3,224
M. J. Green, *Ind. C.*		299
C. maj.		14,343

(June '83, C. maj. 14,351)
(May '84, C. maj. 2,599)

Sussex Mid
E. 80,147

R. T. Renton, C.		37,781
N. S. E. Westbrook, *L./All.*		19,489
R. Hughes, *Lab.*		4,573
C. maj.		18,292

(June '83, C. maj. 16,744)

Sutton and Cheam
(Gtr. London)
E. 63,850

D. N. Macfarlane, C.		29,710
R. D. Grieg, *L./All.*		13,992
Ms. L. Monk, *Lab.*		5,202
C. maj.		15,718

(June '83, C. maj. 10,264)

Sutton Coldfield (W. Midlands)
E. 72,329

Rt. Hon. P. N. Fowler, C.		34,475
T. Bick, *L./All.*		13,292
P. McLoughlin, *Lab.*		6,104
C. maj.		21,183

(June '83, C. maj. 18,984)

Swindon (Wilts)
E. 86,150

*S. C. Coombs, C.	....	29,385
Ms. G. Johnston, *Lab.*	....	24,528
D. J. Scott, *S.D.P./All.*	...	13,114
C. maj.	....	4,857

(June '83, C. maj. 1,395)

Tatton (Cheshire)
E. 71,904

*M. N. Hamilton, C.	......	30,128
Ms. B. Gaskin, *S.D.P./All.*		13,034
Ms. H. A. Blears, *Lab.*	....	11,760
M. G. Gibson, *F.P.*		263
C. maj.	....	17,094

(June '83, C. maj. 13,960)

Taunton (Somerset)
E. 74,145

D. J. Nicholson, C.	....	30,248
M. A. K. Cocks, *S.D.P./All.*		19,868
Dr. G. Reynolds, *Lab.*	....	8,754
C. maj.	....	10,380

(June '83, C. maj. 12,567)

Teignbridge (Devon)
E. 71,872

*P. C. M. Nicholls, C.	.....	30,693
R. D. Ryder, *L./All.*	......	20,268
J. Greenwood, *Lab.*	....	6,413
A. Hope, *L.M.*	....	312
C. maj.	....	10,425

(June '83, C. maj. 8,218)

Thanet (Kent)

NORTH E. 69,723

*R. J. Gale, C.	....	29,225
N. R. M. Cranston, *S.D.P./ All.*		11,745
A. M. Bretman, *Lab.*	.....	8,395
D. R. Condor, *Grn.*	....	996
C. maj.	....	17,480

(June '83, C. maj. 14,545)

SOUTH E. 62,761

*J. W. P. Aitken, C.	......	25,135
W. H. Pitt, *L./All.*	....	11,452
C. Wright, *Lab.*	....	9,673
C. maj.	....	13,683

(June '83, C. maj. 14,051)

Thurrock (Essex)
E. 67,594

T. S. Janman, C.	....	20,527
Dr. O. A. McDonald, *Lab.*		19,837
D. S. Benson, *S.D.P./All.*		7,970
C. maj.	....	690

(June '83, Lab. maj. 1,722)

Tiverton (Devon)
E. 68,210

*R. J. Maxwell-Hyslop, C.	.	29,875
D. J. Morrish, *L./All.*	....	20,663
Mrs. J. A. Northam, *Lab.*	.	3,400
W. J. Jones, *L.A.O.*	......	434
C. maj.	....	9,212

(June '83, C. maj. 7,886)

Tonbridge and Malling (Kent)
E. 76,797

*Rt. Hon. J. P. Stanley, C.	..	33,990
M. J. Ward, *S.D.P./All.*	..	17,561
D. G. Still, *Lab.*	....	7,803
M. D. S. Easter, *B.N.*	.....	369
C. maj.	....	16,429

(June '83, C. maj. 13,520)

Tooting (Gtr. London)
E. 78,116

*T. M. Cox, *Lab.*	....	21,457
M. A. Winter, C.	....	20,016
J. N. Ambache, *S.D.P./All.*		6,423
Ms. M. Vickery, *Grn.*	.....	621
Lab. maj.	....	1,441

(June '83, Lab. maj. 2,659)

Torbay (Devon)
E. 70,435

R. W. S. Allason, C.	......	29,029
N. D. Bye, *L./All.*	....	20,209
G. R. Taylor, *Lab.*	....	4,538
C. maj.	....	8,820

(June '83, C. maj. 6,555)

Tottenham (Gtr. London)
E. 76,092

B. A. L. Grant, *Lab.*	......	21,921
P. L. Murphy, C.	....	17,780
S. Etherington, *L./All.*	...	8,983
D. Nicholls, *Grn.*	....	744
P. Nealon, *Gait. Lab.*	.....	638
Ms. C. L. Dixon, *W.R.P.*	.	205
Lab. maj.	....	4,141

(June '83, Lab. maj. 9,396)

Truro (Cornwall)
E. 72,432

*M. O. J. Taylor, *L./All.*	..	28,368
N. F. St. Aubyn, C.	....	23,615
J. R. King, *Lab.*	....	5,882
L./All. maj.	....	4,753

(June '83, L./All. maj. 10,480)
(March '87, L./All. maj. 14,617)

Tunbridge Wells (Kent)
E. 76,291

*Sir P. B. B. Mayhew, Q.C., C.	....	33,111
Mrs. D. A. Buckrell, *L./All.*		16,989
P. L. Sloman, *Lab.*	....	6,555
C. maj.	....	16,122

(June '83, C. maj. 15,126)

Twickenham (Gtr. London)
E. 64,661

*T. F. H. Jessel, C.	....	27,331
J. Waller, *L./All.*	....	20,204
Ms. V. C. M. Vaz, *Lab.*	...	4,415
D. S. Batchelor, *Grn.*	.....	746
C. maj.	....	7,127

(June '83, C. maj. 4,792)

Tyne Bridge
(Tyne & Wear)
E. 58,152

*D. G. Clelland, *Lab.*	......	23,131
M. W. Bates, C.	....	7,558
J. C. Mansfield, *S.D.P./All.*		6,005
Lab. maj.	....	15,573

(June '83, Lab. maj. 11,693)
(Dec '85, Lab. maj. 6,575)

Tynemouth
(Tyne & Wear)
E. 74,407

*N. G. Trotter, C.	....	25,113
P. Cosgrove, *Lab.*	....	22,530
D. F. Mayhew, *L./All.*	....	10,446
C. maj.	....	2,583

(June '83, C. maj. 9,609)

Upminster (Gtr. London)
E. 66,613

*Sir N. C. Bonsor, BT., C.	..	27,946
J. Martin, *S.D.P./All.*	....	11,089
D. R. O'Flynn, *Lab.*	......	11,069
C. maj.	....	16,857

(June '83, C. maj. 12,814)

Uxbridge (Gtr. London)
E. 63,157

*J. M. Shersby, C.	....	27,292
D. Keys, *Lab.*	....	11,322
A. Goodman, *S.D.P./All.*	.	9,164
I. Flindall, *Grn.*	....	549
C. maj.	....	15,970

(June '83, C. maj. 12,837)

Vauxhall (Gtr. London)
E. 66,538

*S. K. Holland, *Lab.*	......	21,364
D. R. Lidington, C.	......	12,345
S. H. V. Acland, *S.D.P./All.*		7,764
Ms. J. Owens, *Grn.*	......	770
D. J. S. Cook, *Comm.*	....	223
K. Oluremi, *R.F.*	....	117
Lab. maj.	....	9,019

(June '83, Lab. maj. 7,780)

Wakefield (W. Yorks)
E. 69,580

D. M. Hinchliffe, *Lab.*	....	24,509
N. J. Hazell, C.	....	21,720
Dr. L. Kamal, *S.D.P./All*	.	6,350
Lab. maj.	....	2,789

(June '83, Lab. maj. 360)

Wallasey (Merseyside)
E. 67,216

*Mrs. L. Chalker, C.	......	22,791
L. Duffy, *Lab.*	....	22,512
J. K. Richardson, *S.D.P./ All.*		8,363
C. maj.	....	279

(June '83, C. maj. 6,708)

Wallsend (Tyne & Wear)
E. 76,688

*W. E. Garrett, *Lab.*	....	32,709
D. Milburn, C.	....	13,325
Mrs. J. Phylactou, *S.D.P./ All.*		11,508
Lab. maj.	....	19,384

(June '83, Lab. maj. 12,514)

Walsall (W. Midlands)

NORTH E. 68,331

*D. J. Winnick, *Lab.*	....	21,458
Mrs. L. Hertz, C.	....	19,668
I. Shires, *L./All.*	....	9,285
Lab. maj.	....	1,790

(June '83, Lab. maj. 2,824)

SOUTH E. 67,257

*B. T. George, *Lab.*	....	22,629
G. E. Postles, C.	....	21,513
L. A. King, *L./All.*	....	6,241
Lab. maj.	....	1,116

(June '83, Lab. maj. 702)

Walthamstow (Gtr. London)
E. 48,691

H. H. F. Summerson, C.	..	13,748
*E. P. Deakins, *Lab.*	......	12,236
P. L. Leighton, *S.D.P./All.*		8,852
Dr. Z. I. Malik, *D.C.*	......	396
C. maj.	....	1,512
(June '83, Lab. maj. 1,305)		

Wansbeck (Nthmb)
E. 62,639

*J. Thompson, *Lab.*	....	28,080
Mrs. S. Mitchell, *L./All.*	..	11,291
D. Walton, C.		9,490
Lab. maj.	....	16,789
(June '83, Lab. maj. 7,831)		

Wansdyke (Avon)
E. 75,239

*J. H. Aspinwall, C.	......	31,537
R. B. Blackmore, *L./All.*	..	15,393
I. White, *Lab.*	....	14,231
C. maj.	....	16,144
(June '83, C. maj. 13,066)		

Wanstead and Woodford
(Gtr. London)
E. 57,921

J. N. Arbuthnot, C.	....	25,701
J. R. Bastick *L./All.*	......	9,289
Mrs. L. Hilton, *Lab.*	.....	6,958
C. maj.	....	16,412
(June '83, C. maj. 14,354)		

Wantage (Oxon)
E. 66,499

*R. V. Jackson, C.	....	27,951
Mrs. W. Tumin, *S.D.P./All.*	15,795
S. Ladyman, *Lab.*	....	8,055
C. maj.	....	12,156
(June '83, C. maj. 10,125)		

Warley (W. Midlands)

EAST   E. 55,706

*A. M. W. Faulds, *Lab.*	...	19,428
A. Antoniou, C.	....	13,843
J. J. Jordan, *S.D.P./All.*	..	5,396
Lab. maj.	....	5,585
(June '83, Lab. maj. 3,391)		

WEST   E. 57,526

*Rt. Hon. P. K. Archer, Q.C., *Lab.*		19,825
W. Williams, C.	......	14,432
Miss E. Todd, *L./All.*	.....	6,027
Lab. maj.	....	5,393
(June '83, Lab. maj. 5,268)		

Warrington (Cheshire)

NORTH   E. 75,627

*E. D. H. Hoyle, *Lab.*	......	27,422
L. Jones, C.		19,409
C. Bithel, *S.D.P./All.*	.....	10,046
Lab. maj.	....	8,013
(June '83, Lab. maj. 5,277)		

SOUTH   E. 76,219

C. J. Butler, C.	....	24,809
A. Booth, *Lab.*	....	21,200
I. Marks, *L./All.*	....	13,112
C. maj.	....	3,609
(June '83, C. maj. 6,465)		

Warwick and Leamington
E. 72,763

*Sir D. G. Smith, C.	....	27,530
K. P. O'Sullivan, *S.D.P./ All.*	....	13,548
Ms. A. Christina, *Lab.*	...	13,019
Ms. J. A. Alty, *Grn.*	......	1,214
C. maj.	....	13,982
(June '83, C. maj. 13,032)		

Warwickshire

NORTH   E. 70,687

*Hon. F. A. A. Maude, C.	..	25,453
M. O'Brien, *Lab.*	....	22,624
Mrs. S. J. Neale, *S.D.P./All.*	8,382
C. maj.	....	2,829
(June '83, C. maj. 2,585)		

Watford (Herts)
E. 73,540

*W. A. T. T. Garel-Jones, C.	....	27,912
M. J. Jackson, *Lab.*	......	16,176
Mrs. F. M. Beckett, *S.D.P./ All.*	....	13,202
C. maj.	....	11,736
(June '83, C. maj. 12,006)		

Waveney (Suffolk)
E. 81,889

D. J. Porter, C.	....	31,067
J. A. Lark, *Lab.*	....	19,284
D. Beaven, *S.D.P./All.*	...	13,845
C. maj.	....	11,783
(June '83, C. maj. 14,298)		

Wealden (E. Sussex)
E. 73,057

*Sir G. J. Johnson Smith, C.	....	35,154
D. Sinclair, *S.D.P./All.*	...	15,044
C. Ward, *Lab.*	....	4,563
C. maj.	....	20,110
(June '83, C. maj. 17,185)		

Wellingborough (Northants)
E. 70,450

*P. D. Fry, C.	....	29,038
J. Currie, *Lab.*	....	14,968
L. E. Stringer, *L./All.*	.....	11,047
C. maj.	....	14,070
(June '83, C. maj. 12,056)		

Wells (Somerset)
E. 67,195

*D. P. Heathcoat-Amory, C.		28,624
A. A. S. Butt Philip, *L./All.*	20,083
P. James, *Lab.*	....	4,637
J. S. Fish, *Falk.*	....	134
C. maj.	....	8,541
(June '83, C. maj. 6,575)		

Welwyn Hatfield (Herts)
E. 73,607

D. J. Evans, C.	....	27,164
Miss L. P. Granshaw, *S.D.P./All.*	....	16,261
C. R. Pond, *Lab.*	....	15,699
B. I. Dyson, *Ind. C.*	....	401
C. maj.	....	10,903
(June '83, C. maj. 12,246)		

Wentworth (S. Yorks)
E. 63,886

*P. Hardy, *Lab.*	....	30,205
W. J. Hague, C.	....	10,113
D. M. Eglin, *S.D.P./All.*	..	6,031
Lab. maj.	....	20,092
(June '83, Lab. maj. 15,935)		

West Bromwich (W. Midlands)

EAST   E. 58,239

*P. C. Snape, *Lab.*	....	18,162
R. F. Woodhouse, C.	......	17,179
M. G. Smith, *L./All.*	......	7,268
Lab. maj.	....	983
(June '83, Lab. maj. 298)		

WEST   E. 58,944

*Miss B. Boothroyd, *Lab.*	..	19,925
F. A. Betteridge, C.	......	14,672
A. Collingbourne, *S.D.P./ All.*	....	4,877
Lab. maj.	....	5,253
(June '83, Lab. maj. 6,639)		

Westbury (Wilts)
E. 84,860

*D. M. Walters, M.B.E., C.	..	34,256
D. J. Hughes, *L./All.*	......	24,159
H. W. Thomas, *Lab.*	......	7,982
C. maj.	....	10,097
(June '83, C. maj. 8,506)		

Westminster North
(Gtr. London)
E. 59,263

*J. D. Wheeler, C.	....	19,941
Ms. J. F. Edwards, *Lab.*	..	16,631
R. J. De Ste Croix, *S.D.P./ All.*	....	5,116
D. Stutchfield, *Grn.*	......	450
C. maj.	....	3,310
(June '83, C. maj. 1,710)		

Westmorland and Lonsdale
(Cumbria)
E. 70,237

*Rt. Hon. T. M. Jopling, C.	..	30,259
S. Collins, *L./All.*	....	15,339
C. Halfpenny, *Lab.*	......	6,968
C. maj.	....	14,920
(June '83, C. maj. 16,587)		

Weston-super-Mare (Avon)
E. 76,341

*A. W. Wiggin, T.D., C.	....	28,547
J. R. Crockford-Hawley, *S.D.P./All.*	....	20,549
P. J. Loach, *Lab.*	....	6,584
Dr. R. H. Lawson, *Grn.*	...	2,067
C. maj.	....	7,998
(June '83, C. maj. 9,491)		

Wigan (Gtr. Manchester)
E. 72,064

*R. Stott, C.B.E., *Lab.*	......	33,955
K. R. Wade, C.	....	13,493
K. J. White, *L./All.*	......	7,732
Lab. maj.	....	20,462
(June '83, Lab. maj. 17,305)		

Wiltshire

NORTH *E.* 80,712

*R. F. Needham, C.	......	35,309
C. S. M. Graham, *L./All.*	.	24,370
Mrs. C. Reid, *Lab.*	....	4,343
C. maj.	....	10,939

(June '83, C. maj. 7,232)

Wimbledon (Gtr. London)

E. 63,353

Dr. C. Goodson-Wickes, C.	24,538
A. C. Slade, *L./All.*	....	13,237
Ms. C. M. Bickerstaff, *Lab.*	10,428
C. maj.	....	11,301

(June '83, C. maj. 11,546)

Winchester (Hants)

E. 76,507

J. E. D. D. Browne, C.	....	32,195
J. L. MacDonald, *S.D.P./*
All.	....	24,716
F. C. Inglis, *Lab.*	.....	4,028
Ms. J. P. Walker, *Grn.*	....	565
C. maj.	....	7,479

(June '83, C. maj. 13,047)

Windsor and Maidenhead
(Berks)

E. 79,319

Dr. A. Glyn, E.R.D., *C.*	....	33,980
S. J. Jackson, *L./All.*	.....	16,144
Ms. H. B. De Lyon, *Lab.*	..	6,678
W. O. Board, *Ind. C.*	.....	1,938
P. Gordon, *Grn.*	....	711
Ms. P. H. Stephenson, *B.T.*	328
C. maj.	....	17,836

(June '83, C. maj. 18,203)

Wirral (Merseyside)

SOUTH *E.* 62,251

G. B. Porter, C.	......	24,821
J. S. Swarbrooke, *Lab.*	...	13,858
P. N. Gilchrist, *L./All.*	...	10,779
C. maj.	....	10,963

(June '83, C. maj. 13,838)

WEST *E.* 63,597

D. J. F. Hunt, M.B.E., *C.*	...	25,736
A. H. Dunn, *Lab.*	....	13,013
A. J. Brame, *L./All.*	.....	10,015
D. Burton, *Grn.*	....	806
C. maj.	....	12,723

(June '83, C. maj. 15,151)

Witney (Oxon)

E. 75,284

Rt. Hon. D. R. Hurd, C.B.E.,
C.	....	33,458
Miss M. E. Burton, *L./All.*	14,994
Ms. C. Collette, *Lab.*	.....	9,733
C. maj.	....	18,464

(June '83, C. maj. 12,712)

Woking (Surrey)

E. 82,476

C. G. D. Onslow, C.	......	35,990
P. Goldenberg, *L./All.*	.....	19,446
Miss A. J. Pollack, *Lab.*	..	6,537
C. maj.	....	16,544

(June '83, C. maj. 16,237)

Wokingham (Berks)

E. 85,474

J. A. Redwood, C.	......	39,808
J. C. Leston, *L./All.*	......	19,421
P. J. Morgan, *Lab.*	....	5,622
C. maj.	....	20,387

(June '83, C. maj. 15,698)

Wolverhampton (W. Midlands)

NORTH EAST *E.* 63,464

Mrs. M. P. Hicks, C.	...	19,857
K. Purchase, *Lab.*	....	19,653
M. Pearson, *L./All.*	......	7,623
C. maj.	....	204

(June '83, Lab. maj. 214)

SOUTH EAST *E.* 55,710

D. Turner, Lab.	....	19,760
J. P. Mellor, *C.*	....	13,362
R. F. Whitehouse, *L./All.*	.	7,258
Lab. maj.	....	6,398

(June '83, Lab. maj. 5,012)

SOUTH WEST *E.* 68,586

N. W. Budgen, C.	....	26,235
R. Lawrence, *Lab.*	....	15,917
B. Lamb, *S.D.P./All.*	.....	9,616
C. maj.	....	10,318

(June '83, C. maj. 11,520)

Woodspring (Avon)

E. 76,289

Sir P. Dean, C.	....	34,134
Mrs. C. R. Coleman, *L./All.*	16,282
D. L. T. Chapple, *Lab.*	....	8,717
Dr. B. R. Keeble, *Grn.*	....	1,208
C. maj.	....	17,852

(June '83, C. maj. 15,132)

Woolwich (Gtr. London)

E. 58,071

J. C. Cartwright, S.D.P./
All.	....	17,137
J. Austin Walker, *Lab.*	...	15,200
A. Salter, *C.*	....	8,723
S.D.P./All. maj.	....	1,937

(June '83, S.D.P./All. maj. 2,725)

Worcester

E. 68,980

Rt. Hon. P. E. Walker,
M.B.E., *C.*	....	25,504
M. J, Webb, *Lab.*	....	15,051
J. J. Caiger, *S.D.P./All.*	..	12,386
C. maj.	....	10,453

(June '83, C. maj. 10,871)

Worcestershire

MID *E.* 80,591

M. E. Forth, C.	....	31,854
P. Pinfield, *Lab.*	....	16,943
E. Harwood, *S.D.P./All.*	..	12,954
C. maj.	....	14,911

(June '83, C. maj. 14,205)

SOUTH *E.* 77,237

W. M. Spicer, C.	....	32,277
P. J. Chandler, *L./All.*	....	18,632
R. J. Garnett, *Lab.*	....	6,374
G. M. H. Woodford, *Grn.*	.	1,089
C. maj.	....	13,645

(June '83, C. maj. 11,389)

Workington (Cumbria)

E. 56,911

D. N. Campbell-Savours,
Lab.	....	24,019
Miss A. C. B. McIntosh, *C.*	17,000
G. W. Badger, *L./All.*	.....	4,853
Lab. maj.	....	7,019

(June '83, Lab. maj. 7,128)

Worsley (Gtr. Manchester)

E. 73,208

T. Lewis, Lab.	....	27,157
Mrs. V. Horman, *C.*	......	19,820
D. Cowpe, *L./All.*	....	9,507
Lab. maj.	....	7,337

(June '83, Lab. maj. 4,139)

Worthing (W. Sussex)

E. 77,000

Rt. Hon. T. L. Higgins, C.	.	34,573
B. A. Clare, *L./All.*	....	16,072
J. Deen, *Lab.*	....	5,387
C. maj.	....	18,501

(June '83, C. maj. 15,253)

The Wrekin (Salop)

E. 82,520

B. J. Grocott, Lab.	......	27,681
P. W. Hawksley, C.	....	26,225
G. Cook, *S.D.P./All.*	.....	10,737
Lab. maj.	....	1,456

(June '83, C. maj. 1,331)

Wycombe (Bucks)

E. 71,918

R. W. Whitney, O.B.E., *C.*	..	28,209
T. E. G. Hayhoe, *S.D.P./*
All.	....	14,390
J. R. W. Huddart, *Lab.*	...	9,773
C. maj.	....	13,819

(June '83, C. maj. 13,197)

Wyre (Lancs)

E. 67,066

K. D. R. Mans, C.	......	26,800
I. C. Murdoch, *S.D.P./All.*	12,139
P. Ainscough, *Lab.*	......	10,725
R. Brown, *Grn.*	....	874
C. maj.	....	14,661

(June '83, C. maj. 14,811)

Wyre Forest (H & W)

E. 70,784

A. M. V. Coombs, C.	....	25,877
A. J. Batchelor, *L./All.*	...	18,653
N. Knowles, *Lab.*	....	10,365
C. maj.	....	7,224

(June '83, C. maj. 8,177)

Yeovil (Somerset)

E. 70,390

J. J. D. Ashdown, L./All.	.	28,841
G. D. S. Sandeman, *C.*	....	23,141
J. Fitzmaurice, *Lab.*	.....	4,099
L./All. maj.	....	5,700

(June '83, L./All. maj. 3,406)

York (N. Yorks)

E. 79,297

C. R. Gregory, C.	....	25,880
H. Bayley, *Lab.*	....	25,733
J. V. Cable, *S.D.P./All.*	..	9,898
A. D. Dunnett, *Grn.*	.....	637
C. maj.	....	147

(June '83, C. maj. 3,647)

WALES

Aberavon (W. Glam)
E. 52,280

Rt. Hon. J. Morris, Q.C.,		
Lab.		27,126
Mrs. M. Harris, *L./All.*		6,517
P. Warrick, *C.*		5,861
Miss A. Howells, *P.C.*		1,124
Lab. maj.		20,609
(June '83, Lab. maj. 15,539)		

Alyn and Deeside (Clwyd)
E. 58,674

S. B. Jones, Lab.		22,916
N. J. Twilley, *C.*		16,500
E. C. H. Owen, *S.D.P./All.*		7,273
J. D. Rogers, *P.C.*		478
Lab. maj.		6,416
(June '83, Lab. maj. 1,368)		

Blaenau Gwent
E. 56,011

Rt. Hon. M. M. Foot, Lab.		32,820
A. R. Taylor, *C.*		4,959
D. I. McBride, *L./All.*		3,847
S. Morgan, *P.C.*		1,621
Lab. maj.		27,861
(June '83, Lab. maj. 23,705)		

Brecon and Radnor (Powys)
E. 49,394

R. A. L. Livsey, L./All.		14,509
J. P. Evans, *C.*		14,453
F. R. Willey, *Lab.*		12,180
J. H. Davies, *P.C.*		535
L./All. maj.		56
(June '83, C. maj. 8,784)		
(July '84, L./All. maj. 559)		

Bridgend (Mid Glam)
E. 57,389

W. J. Griffiths, Lab.		21,893
P. C. Hubbard-Miles, C.		17,513
R. Smart, *S.D.P./All.*		5,590
Miss L. McAllister, *P.C.*		1,065
Lab. maj.		4,380
(June '83, C. maj. 1,327)		

Caernarfon (Gwynedd)
E. 45,661

D. W. Wigley, P.C.		20,338
F. F. E. Aubel, *C.*		7,536
D. Rhys Williams, *Lab.*		5,632
J. H. Parsons, *L./All.*		2,103
P.C. maj.		12,802
(June '83, P.C. maj. 10,989)		

Caerphilly (Mid Glam)
E. 64,154

R. Davies, Lab.		28,698
M. E. Powell, *C.*		9,531
M. G. Butlin, *L./All.*		6,923
L. G. Whittle, *P.C.*		3,955
Lab. maj.		19,167
(June '83, Lab. maj. 11,553)		

Cardiff (S. Glam)
CENTRAL *E.* 52,980

I. Grist, C.		15,241
J. O. Jones, *Lab.*		13,255
M. J. German, *L./All.*		12,062
Ms. S. M. Caiach, *P.C.*		535
C. maj.		1,986
(June '83, C. maj. 3,452)		

NORTH *E.* 54,704

G. H. Jones, C.		20,061
S. H. Tarbet, *Lab.*		11,827
A. W. Jeremy, *S.D.P./All.*		11,725
Ms. E. M. Bush, *P.C.*		692
C. maj.		8,234
(June '83, C. maj. 6,848)		

SOUTH AND PENARTH *E.* 58,714

A. E. Michael, Lab.		20,956
G. J. J. Neale, *C.*		16,382
Mrs. J. E. Randerson, *L./All.*		6,900
Ms. S. A. Edwards, *P.C.*		599
Lab. maj.		4,574
(June '83, Lab. maj. 2,276)		

WEST *E.* 57,363

H. R. Morgan, Lab.		20,329
S. Terlezki, C.		16,284
R. G. Drake, *S.D.P./All.*		7,300
P. J. Keelan, *P.C.*		736
Lab. maj.		4,045
(June '83, C. maj. 1,774)		

Carmarthen (Dyfed)
E. 65,252

A. W. Williams, Lab.		19,128
R. Richards, *C.*		14,811
H. T. Edwards, *P.C.*		12,457
G. G. Jones, *S.D.P./All.*		7,203
G. E. Oubridge, *Grn.*		481
Lab. maj.		4,317
(June '83, Lab. maj. 1,154)		

Ceredigion and Pembroke North (Dyfed)
E. 63,141

G. W. Howells, L./All.		17,683
O. J. Williams, *C.*		12,983
J. R. Davies, *Lab.*		8,965
C. G. Davis, *P.C.*		7,848
Mrs. M. A. Wakefield, *Grn.*		821
L./All. maj.		4,700
(June '83, L./All. maj. 5,639)		

Clwyd
NORTH WEST *E.* 66,118

Sir A. J. C. Meyer, BT., C.		24,116
K. L. Thomas, *Lab.*		12,335
O. G. Griffiths, *L./All.*		11,279
R. K. Davies, *P.C.*		1,966
C. maj.		11,781
(June '83, C. maj. 9,989)		

SOUTH WEST *E.* 58,158

M. D. Jones, Lab.		16,701
R. L. Harvey, C.		15,673
R. T. Ellis, *S.D.P./All.*		10,778
E. L. Jones, *P.C.*		3,987
Lab. maj.		1,028
(June '83, C. maj. 1,551)		

Conwy (Gwynedd)
E. 52,862

I. W. P. Roberts, C.		15,730
J. R. Roberts, *L./All.*		12,706
Ms. E. Williams, *Lab.*		9,049
R. Davies, *P.C.*		3,177
C. maj.		3,024
(June '83, C. maj. 4,268)		

Cynon Valley (Mid Glam)
E. 49,621

Mrs. A. Clwyd, Lab.		26,222
K. D. Butler, *S.D.P./All.*		4,651
M. A. Bishop, *C.*		4,638
Mrs. D. L. Richards, *P.C.*		2,549
Lab. maj.		21,571
(June '83, Lab. maj. 13,074)		
(May '84, Lab. maj. 12,835)		

Delyn (Clwyd)
E. 63,541

K. W. T. Raffan, C.		21,728
D. G. Hanson, *Lab.*		20,504
D. J. Evans, *L./All.*		8,913
D. J. Owen, *P.C.*		1,329
C. maj.		1,224
(June '83, C. maj. 5,944)		

Gower (W. Glam)
E. 58,871

G. L. Wardell, Lab.		22,138
G. A. L. Price, *C.*		16,374
D. H. O. Elliott, *S.D.P./All.*		7,645
J. G. M. Edwards, *P.C.*		1,341
Lab. maj.		5,764
(June '83, Lab. maj. 1,205)		

Islwyn (Gwent)
E. 50,414

Rt. Hon. N. G. Kinnock, Lab.		28,901
J. Twitchen, *C.*		5,954
Ms. J. Gasson, *S.D.P./All.*		3,746
A. Richards, *P.C.*		1,932
Lab. maj.		22,947
(June '83, Lab. maj. 14,380)		

Llanelli (Dyfed)
E. 63,845

Rt. Hon. D. J. D. Davies, Lab.		29,506
P. J. Circus, *C.*		8,571
M. J. Shrewsbury, *L./All.*		6,714
A. Price, *P.C.*		5,088
Lab. maj.		20,935
(June '83, Lab. maj. 13,606)		

Meirionnydd Nant Conwy (Gwynedd)
E. 31,632

D. E. Thomas, P.C.		10,392
D. T. Jones, *C.*		7,366
H. G. Roberts, *Lab.*		4,397
D. L. Roberts, *S.D.P./All.*		3,847
P.C. maj.		3,026
(June '83, P.C. maj. 2,643)		

Merthyr Tydfil and Rhymney (Mid Glam)
E. 58,285

E. Rowlands, Lab.		33,400
N. M. Walters, *C.*		5,270
P. Verma, *L./All.*		3,573
Mrs. J. Davies, *P.C.*		2,085
Lab. maj.		28,130
(June '83, Lab. maj. 22,730)		

Monmouth (Gwent)
E. 58,468

*Sir J. Stradling Thomas, C.		22,387
Ms. K. Gass, Lab.		13,037
C. Lindley, S.D.P./All.		11,313
Mrs. S. Meredudd, P.C.		363
C. maj.		9,350
(June '83, C. maj. 9,343)		

Montgomery (Powys)
E. 39,808

*A. C. Carlile, Q.C. L./All.		14,729
D.M. Evans, C.		12,171
E. D. W. Llewellyn Jones, Lab.		3,304
C. Clowes, P.C.		1,412
L./All. maj.		2,558
(June '83, L./All. maj. 668)		

Neath (W. Glam)
E. 55,261

*D. R. Coleman, Lab.		27,612
M. R. T. Howe, C.		7,034
J. Warman, S.D.P./All.		6,132
H. John, P.C.		2,792
Lab. maj.		20,578
(June '83, Lab. maj. 13,604)		

Newport (Gwent)
EAST E. 52,199

*R. J. Hughes, Lab.		20,518
G. R. Webster-Gardiner, C.		13,454
Mrs. F. A. David, S.D.P./All.		7,383
G. Butler, P.C.		458
Lab. maj.		7,064
(June '83, Lab. maj. 2,630)		

WEST E. 55,455

P. P. Flynn, Lab.		20,887
*M. N. F. Robinson, C.		18,179
G. W. Roddick, L./All.		5,903
D. J. Bevan, P.C.		377
Lab. maj.		2,708
(June '83, Lab. maj. 581)		

Ogmore (Mid Glam)
E. 51,255

*R. Powell, Lab.		28,462
M. F. Barratt, C.		6,170
Ms. M. James, S.D.P./All.		3,954
J. G. Jones, P.C.		1,791
T. H. Spence, Ind. Lab.		652
Lab. maj.		22,292
(June '83, Lab. maj. 17,364)		

Pembroke (Dyfed)
E. 70,360

N. J. Bennett, C.		23,314
B. J. Rayner, Lab.		17,614
P. E. C. Jones, L./All.		14,832
O. Osmond, P.C.		1,119
C. maj.		5,700
(June '83, C. maj. 9,356)		

Pontypridd (Mid Glam)
E. 61,255

*B. T. John, Lab.		26,422
D. Swayne, C.		9,145
P. G. Sain-Ley-Berry, S.D.P./All.		8,865
D. L. Bowen, P.C.		2,498
Lab. maj.		17,277
(June '83, Lab. maj. 8,744)		

Rhondda (Mid Glam)
E. 60,931

*A. R. Rogers, Lab.		35,015
G. R. Davies, P.C.		4,261
J. R. YorkWilliams, S.D.P./All.		3,930
S. H. Reid, C.		3,611
A. True, Comm.		869
Lab. maj.		30,754
(June '83, Lab. maj. 21,370)		

Swansea (W. Glam)
EAST E. 57,200

*D. Anderson, Lab.		27,478
R. D. Lewis, C.		8,140
Rev. D. W. Thomas, L./All.		6,380
C. Reid, P.C.		1,145
Lab. maj.		19,338
(June '83, Lab. maj. 13,535)		

WEST E. 59,836

*Rt. Hon. A. J. Williams, Lab.		22,089
N. M. Evans, C.		15,027
M. Ford, L./All.		7,019
N. Williams, P.C.		902
Mrs. J. V. Harman, Grn.		469
Lab. maj.		7,062
(June '83, Lab. maj. 2,350)		

Torfaen (Gwent)
E. 59,896

P. P. Murphy, Lab.		26,577
G. R. Blackburn, L./All.		9,027
R. Gordon, C.		8,632
J. Evans, P.C.		577
M. Witherden, Grn.		450
Lab. maj.		17,550
(June '83, Lab. maj. 8,285)		

Vale of Glamorgan (S. Glam)
E. 65,310

*Sir H. R. Gower, C.		24,229
J. W. P. Smith, Lab.		17,978
D. K. Davies, S.D.P./All.		8,633
P. G. Williams, P.C.		946
C. maj.		6,251
(June '83, C. maj. 10,393)		

Wrexham (Clwyd)
E. 62,401

*Dr. J. C. Marek, Lab.		22,144
R. H. W. Graham-Palmer, C.		17,992
M. Thomas, L./All.		9,808
D. Watkins, P.C.		539
Lab. maj.		4,152
(June '83, Lab. maj. 424)		

Ynys Môn/Anglesey (Gwynedd)
E. 52,633

I. W. Jones, P.C.		18,580
R. Evans, C.		14,282
C. Parry, Lab.		7,252
I. L. Evans, S.D.P./All.		2,863
P.C. maj.		4,298
(June '83, C. maj. 1,684)		

SCOTLAND

Aberdeen (Grampian)
NORTH E. 63,214

*R. Hughes, Lab.		24,145
R. Smith, S.D.P./All.		7,867
Mrs. G. E. C. Scanlan, C.		6,330
P. Greenhorn, S.N.P.		5,827
Lab. maj.		16,278
(June '83, Lab. maj. 9,144)		

SOUTH E. 62,943

F. Doran, Lab.		15,917
*G. P. Malone, C.		14,719
I. G. Philip, S.D.P./All.		8,844
M. F. Weir		2,776
Lab. maj.		1,198
(June '83, C. maj. 3,581)		

Angus East (Tayside)
E. 61,060

A. Welsh, S.N.P.		19,536
*P. L. Fraser, C.		17,992
R. Mennie, Lab.		4,971
I. Mortimer, S.D.P./All.		3,592
S.N.P. maj.		1,544
(June '83, C. maj. 3,527)		

Argyll and Bute (S'clyde)
E. 48,700

Mrs. J. R. Michie, L./All.		13,726
*J. J. MacKay, C.		12,332
R. Shaw, S.N.P.		6,297
D. Tierney, Lab.		4,437
L./All. maj.		1,394
(June '83, C. maj. 3,844)		

Ayr (S'clyde)
E. 66,450

*Rt. Hon. G. K. H. Younger, T.D., C.		20,942
K. MacDonald, Lab.		20,760
K. M. Moody, L./All.		7,859
C. Weir, S.N.P.		3,548
C. maj.		182
(June '83, C. maj. 7,987)		

Banff and Buchan (Grampian)
E. 62,149

A. E. A. Salmond, S.N.P.		19,462
*A. McQuarrie, C.		17,021
G. M. Burness, S.D.P./All.		4,211
J. Livie, Lab.		3,281
S.N.P. maj.		2,441
(June '83, C. maj. 937)		

Caithness and Sutherland (H'land)
E. 31,279

*R. A. R. Maclennan, S.D.P./All.		12,338
R. L. Hamilton, C.		3,844
A. Byron, Lab.		3,437
K. MacGregor, S.N.P.		2,371
W. A. Mowat, Ind. L.		686
B. Planterose, Grn.		333
S.D.P./All. maj.		8,494
(June '83, S.D.P./All. maj. 6,843)		

Carrick, Cumnock and Doon Valley (S'clyde)
E. 56,360

*G. Foulkes, Lab.	25,669
S. Stevenson, C.	8,867
Mrs. M. Ali, S.D.P./All.	4,106
C. D. Calman, S.N.P.	4,094
Lab. maj.	16,802

(June '83, Lab. maj. 11,370)

Clackmannan (Central)
E. 49,083

*M. J. O'Neill, Lab.	20,317
Dr. A. Macartney, S.N.P.	7,916
J. Parker, C.	5,620
Mrs. A. Watters, S.D.P./All.	3,961
Lab. maj.	12,401

(June '83, Lab. maj. 9,639)

Clydebank and Milngavie (S'clyde)
E. 50,152

A. Worthington, Lab.	22,528
K. Hirstwood, C.	6,224
R. Ackland, S.D.P./All.	5,891
S. Fisher, S.N.P.	4,935
Lab. maj.	16,304

(June '83, Lab. maj. 7,715)

Clydesdale (S'clyde)
E. 61,620

J. Hood, Lab.	21,826
R. Robertson, C.	11,324
J. Boyle, S.D.P./All.	7,909
M. Russell, S.N.P.	7,125
Lab. maj.	10,502

(June '83, Lab. maj. 4,866)

Cumbernauld and Kilsyth (S'clyde)
E. 45,427

*N. Hogg, Lab.	21,385
T. Johnston, S.N.P.	6,982
C. S. Deans, S.D.P./All.	4,059
Mrs. A. E. Thomson, C.	3,227
Lab. maj.	14,403

(June '83, Lab. maj. 9,928)

Cunninghame (S'clyde)

NORTH E. 54,817

B. D. H. Wilson, Lab.	19,061
*J. A. Corrie, C.	14,594
D. J. Herbison, S.D.P./All.	5,185
M. Brown, S.N.P.	4,076
Lab. maj.	4,467

(June '83, C. maj. 1,637)

SOUTH E. 49,842

*D. Lambie, Lab.	22,728
E. R. Gibson, C.	6,095
J. A. Boss, L./All.	4,426
Mrs. K. Ullrich, S.N.P.	4,115
Lab. maj.	16,633

(June '83, Lab. maj. 11,768)

Dumbarton (S'clyde)
E. 58,968

J. McFall, Lab.	19,778
R. F. Graham, C.	14,556
R. Mowbray, S.D.P./All.	6,060
Ms. J. Herriot, S.N.P.	5,564
Lab. maj.	5,222

(June '83, Lab. maj. 2,115)

Dumfries (D & G)
E. 59,347

*Sir H. S. P. Monro, C.	18,785
Ms. C. W. Phillips, Lab.	11,292
J. R. McCall, S.D.P./All.	8,064
T. McAlpine, S.N.P.	6,391
P. M. Thomas, Grn.	349
C. maj.	7,493

(June '83, C. maj. 8,694)

Dundee (Tayside)

EAST E. 60,805

J. McAllion, Lab.	19,539
*R. G. Wilson, S.N.P.	18,524
P. Cook, C.	5,938
Mrs. M. von Romberg, L./All.	2,143
Lab. maj.	1,015

(June '83, S.N.P. maj. 5,016)

WEST E. 61,926

*E. Ross, Lab.	24,916
J. A. Donnelly, C.	8,390
A. N. Morgan, S.N.P.	7,164
Ms. R. Lonie, S.D.P./All.	5,922
S. R. Mathewson, Comm.	308
Lab. maj.	16,526

(June '83, Lab. maj. 10,150)

Dunfermline (Fife)

EAST E. 51,175

*Dr. J. G. Brown, Lab.	25,381
C. Shenton, C.	5,792
Ms. E. Harris, L./All.	4,122
Mrs. A. McGarny, S.N.P.	3,901
Lab. maj.	19,589

(June '83, Lab. maj. 11,301)

WEST E. 51,063

*R. G. Douglas, Lab.	18,493
P. R. Gallie, C.	9,091
F. A. Moyes, S.D.P./All.	8,288
G. Hughes, S.N.P.	3,435
Lab. maj.	9,402

(June '83, Lab. maj. 2,474)

East Kilbride (S'clyde)
E. 63,097

A. P. Ingram, Lab.	24,491
D. R. E. Sullivan, S.D.P./All.	11,867
P. M. Walker, C.	7,344
J. H. Taggart, S.N.P.	6,275
Lab. maj.	12,624

(June '83, Lab. maj. 4,336)

East Lothian
E. 65,046

*J. D. Home Robertson, Lab.	24,583
S. M. Langdon, C.	14,478
A. Robinson, L./All.	7,929
A. Burgon-Lyon, S.N.P.	3,727
A. Marland, Grn.	451
Lab. maj.	10,105

(June '83, Lab. maj. 6,241)

Eastwood (S'clyde)
E. 61,872

*J. A. Stewart, C.	19,388
R. Leishman, S.D.P./All.	13,374
P. A. Grant-Hutchison, Lab.	12,305
J. Findlay, S.N.P.	4,033
C. maj.	6,014

(June '83, C. maj. 8,595)

Edinburgh (Lothian)

CENTRAL E. 59,529

A. M. Darling, Lab.	16,502
*Sir A. Fletcher, C.	14,240
A. Myles, L./All.	7,333
B. Shaw, S.N.P.	2,559
Mrs. L. M. Hendry, Grn.	438
Lab. maj.	2,262

(June '83, C. maj. 2,566)

EAST E. 48,895

*G. S. Strang, Lab.	18,257
J. F. Renz, C.	8,962
Mrs. J. Aitken, L./All.	5,592
M. Bovey, S.N.P.	3,434
Lab. maj.	9,295

(June '83, Lab. maj. 5,866)

LEITH E. 60,359

*R. D. M. Brown, Lab.	21,104
D. A. Y. Menzies, C.	9,777
Mrs. S. Wells, S.D.P./All.	7,843
W. Morrison, S.N.P.	4,045
Lab. maj.	11,327

(June '83, Lab. maj. 4,973)

PENTLANDS E. 58,125

*Rt. Hon. M. L. Rifkind, Q.C., C.	17,278
M. Lazarowicz, Lab.	13,533
K. A. Smith, S.D.P./All.	11,072
D. N. MacCormick, S.N.P.	3,264
C. maj.	3,745

(June '83, C. maj. 4,309)

SOUTH E. 63,842

N. Griffiths, Lab.	18,211
*M. A. F. J. K. Ancram (Earl of Ancram), C.	16,352
D. A. Graham, S.D.P./All.	10,900
Mrs. R. Moore, S.N.P.	2,455
Mrs. R. Clark, Grn.	440
Lab. maj.	1,859

(June '83, C. maj. 3,655)

WEST E. 62,214

*Lord James Douglas-Hamilton, C.	18,450
D. G. King, L./All.	17,216
M. McGregor, Lab.	10,957
N. Irons, S.N.P.	2,774
C. maj.	1,234

(June '83, C. maj. 498)

Falkirk (Central)

EAST E. 52,564

*H. Ewing, Lab.	21,379
K. H. Brookes, C.	7,356
R. N. F. Halliday, S.N.P.	6,056
Mrs. E. G. Dick, S.D.P./All.	4,624
Lab. maj.	14,023

(June '83, Lab. maj. 10,061)

WEST E. 50,222

*D. A. Canavan, Lab.	20,256
D. R. D. Thomas, C.	6,704
I. R. Goldie, S.N.P.	6,696
M. J. Harris, L./All.	4,841
Lab. maj.	13,552

(June '83, Lab. maj. 8,978)

Fife

CENTRAL *E.* 56,090

H. B. McLeish, *Lab.*	.....	22,827
R. E. Aird, *C.*	....	7,118
Mrs. T. M. Little, *L./All.*	..	6,487
D. Hood, *S.N.P.*	....	6,296
Lab. maj.	....	15,709

(June '83, Lab. maj. 7,794)

NORTH EAST *E.* 52,266

W. H. Campbell, C.B.E., Q.C.,

L./All.	....	17,868
*J. S. B. Henderson, *C.*	....	16,421
A. M. E. Gannon, *Lab.*	...	2,947
F. D. Roche, *S.N.P.*	......	2,616
L./All. maj.	....	1,447

(June '83, C. maj. 2,185)

Galloway and Upper Nithsdale
(D & G)
E. 53,429

*I. B. Lang, *C.*	....	16,592
S. F. Norris, *S.N.P.*	......	12,919
J. McKercher, *L./All.*	....	6,001
J. Gray, *Lab.*	....	5,298
D. Kenny, *Ret.*	....	230
C. maj.	....	3,673

(June '83, C. maj. 5,461)

Glasgow (S'clyde)

CATHCART *E.* 49,307

*J. A. Maxton, *Lab.*	....	19,623
W. A. Harvey, *C.*	....	8,420
Miss M. Craig, *S.D.P./All.*		5,722
W. A. Steven, *S.N.P.*	......	3,883
Lab. maj.	....	11,203

(June '83, Lab. maj. 4,230)

CENTRAL *E.* 51,137

*R. McTaggart, *Lab.*	......	21,619
B. Jenkin, *C.*	....	4,366
Dr. J. Bryden, *L./All.*	....	3,528
A. Wilson, *S.N.P.*	....	3,339
A. Brooks, *Grn.*	....	290
J. P. McGoldrick, *Comm.*	.	265
D. Owen, *R.F.*	....	126
Lab. maj.	....	17,253

(June '83, Lab. maj. 10,962)

GARSCADDEN *E.* 47,958

*D. C. Dewar, *Lab.*	....	23,118
A. Brophy, *S.N.P.*	......	4,201
T. N. A. Begg, *C.*	....	3,660
S. Callison, *S.D.P./All.*	...	3,211
Lab. maj.	....	18,977

(June '83, Lab. maj. 13,474)

GOVAN *E.* 50,616

*Rt. Hon. B. Millan, *Lab.*	..	24,071
A. Ferguson, *S.D.P./All.*	..	4,562
Mrs. J. R. Girsman, *C.*	....	4,411
F. McCabe, *S.N.P.*	......	3,851
D. Chalmers, *Comm.*	.....	237
Lab. maj.	....	19,509

(June '83, Lab. maj. 13,057)

HILLHEAD *E.* 57,836

G. Galloway, *Lab.*	....	17,958
*Rt Hon. R. H. Jenkins,		
S.D.P./All.	....	14,707
B. D. Cooklin, *C.*	......	6,048
W. Kidd, *S.N.P.*	....	2,713
A. Whitelaw, *Grn.*	....	443
Lab. maj.	....	3,251

(June '83, S.D.P./All. maj. 1,164)

MARYHILL *E.* 52,371

Mrs. M. Fyfe, *Lab.*	.....	23,482
Miss E. M. A. Attwooll, *L./		
All.*	....	4,118
G. Roberts, *S.N.P.*	....	3,895
S. R. R. Kirk, *C.*	....	3,307
D. Spaven, *Grn.*	....	539
Lab. maj.	....	19,364

(June '83, Lab. maj. 11,203)

POLLOK *E.* 51,396

J. Dunnachie, *Lab.*	......	23,239
Mrs. G. French, *C.*	....	5,256
J. Shearer, *L./All.*	....	4,445
A. Doig, *S.N.P.*	....	3,528
D. Fogg, *Grn.*	....	362
Lab. maj.	....	17,983

(June '83, Lab. maj. 11,532)

PROVAN *E.* 43,744

J. Wray, *Lab.*	....	22,032
W. Ramsay, *S.N.P.*	......	3,660
Miss A. Strutt, *C.*	....	2,336
J. Morrison, *S.D.P./All.*	...	2,189
Lab. maj.	....	18,372

(June '83, Lab. maj. 15,385)

RUTHERGLEN *E.* 57,313

T. McAvoy, *Lab.*	....	24,790
R. E. Brown, *L./All.*	......	10,795
G. Hamilton, *C.*	....	5,088
J. Higgins, *S.N.P.*	....	3,584
Lab. maj.	....	13,995

(June '83, Lab. maj. 9,126)

SHETTLESTON *E.* 53,604

*D. Marshall, *Lab.*	....	23,991
J. M. S. Fisher, *C.*	....	5,010
J. MacVicar, *S.N.P.*	......	4,807
Miss P. Clarke, *L./All.*	...	3,942
Lab. maj.	....	18,981

(June '83, Lab. maj. 12,416)

SPRINGBURN *E.* 51,563

*M. J. Martin, *Lab.*	....	25,617
B. O'Hara, *S.N.P.*	....	3,554
M. Call, *C.*	....	2,870
D. Rennie, *L./All.*	....	2,746
Lab. maj.	....	22,063

(June '83, Lab. maj. 17,599)

Gordon (Grampian)
E. 73,479

*M. G. Bruce, *L./All.*	......	26,770
P. R. Leckie, *C.*	....	17,251
Mrs. M. C. Morrell, *Lab.*	..	6,228
G. E. Wright, *S.N.P.*	......	3,876
L./All. maj.	....	9,519

(June '83, L./All. maj. 850)

Greenock and Port Glasgow
(S'clyde)
E. 57,756

*N. A. Godman, *Lab.*	......	27,848
J. H. Moody, *L./All.*	......	7,793
T. J. D. Pearson, *C.*	.....	4,199
T. Lenehan, *S.N.P.*	......	3,721
Lab. maj.	....	20,055

(June '83, Lab. maj. 4,625)

Hamilton (S'clyde)
E. 62,205

*G. I. M. Robertson, *Lab.*	..	28,563
G. S. Mond, *C.*	....	6,901
T. Mackay, *L./All.*	....	6,302
C. Crossley, *S.N.P.*	....	6,093
Lab. maj.	....	21,662

(June '83, Lab. maj. 15,019)

Inverness, Nairn and Lochaber
(H'land)
E. 66,743

*Sir D. R. Johnston, *L./All.*		17,422
D. Stewart, *Lab.*	....	11,991
Mrs. A. T. Keswick, *C.*	...	10,901
N. P. Johnson, *S.N.P.*	....	7,001
L./All. maj.	....	5,431

(June '83, L./All. maj. 7,298)

Kilmarnock and Loudoun
(Grampian)
E. 62,648

*W. McKelvey, *Lab.*	....	23,713
Mrs. A. K. Bates, *C.*	......	9,586
G. Leslie, *S.N.P.*	....	8,881
P. Kerr, *S.D.P./All.*	......	6,698
Lab. maj.	....	14,127

(June '83, Lab. maj. 8,800)

Kincardine and Deeside
(Grampian)
E. 63,587

*Rt. Hon. A. L. Buchanan-

Smith, *C.*	....	19,438
N. R. Stephen, *L./All.*	...	17,375
J. K. Thomaneck, *Lab.*	...	7,624
Mrs. F. E. Duncan, *S.N.P.*	.	3,082
Mrs. L. M. Perica, *Grn.*	...	299
C. maj.	....	2,063

(June '83, C. maj. 7,796)

Kirkcaldy (Fife)
E. 53,439

Dr. L. G. Moonie, *Lab.*	...	20,281
I. G. Mitchell, *C.*	....	8,711
D. Stewart, *S.D.P./All.*	...	7,118
W. A. R. Mullin, *S.N.P.*	...	4,794
Lab. maj.	....	11,570

(June '83, Lab. maj. 5,331)

Linlithgow (Lothian)
E. 59,542

*T. Dalyell, *Lab.*	....	21,869
J. Sillars, *S.N.P.*	....	11,496
T. R. Armstrong Wilson, *C.*		6,828
Mrs. H. McDade, *S.D.P./		
All.*	....	5,840
J. Glassford, *Comm.*	......	154
Lab. maj.	....	10,373

(June '83, Lab. maj. 11,361)

Livingston (Lothian)
E. 56,583

*R. F. Cook, *Lab.*	....	19,110
R. McCreadle, *L./All.*	...	8,005
Dr. M. N. A. Mayall, *C.*	...	7,860
K. MacAskill, *S.N.P.*	......	6,969
Lab. maj.	....	11,105

(June '83, Lab. maj. 4,951)

Midlothian
E. 60,549

*A. Eadie, B.E.M., *Lab.*	....	22,553
A. R. Dewar, *S.D.P./All.*	..	10,300
Dr. F. Riddell, *C.*	....	8,527
I. Chisholm, *S.N.P.*	......	4,947
I. Smith, *Grn.*	....	412
Lab. maj.	....	12,253

(June '83, Lab. maj. 6,156)

Monklands (S'clyde)

EAST *E.* 49,644

Rt. Hon. J. Smith, Q.C., *Lab.*	22,649
J. Love, *C.*	6,260
K. Gibson, *S.N.P.*	4,790
Mrs. S. Grieve, *L./All.*	3,442
Lab. maj.	16,389

(June '83, Lab. maj. 9,799)

WEST *E.* 50,874

T. Clarke, C.B.E., *Lab.*	24,499
G. Lind, *C.*	6,166
Ms. A. McQueen, *S.D.P./*	
All.	4,408
K. Bovey, *S.N.P.*	4,260
Lab. maj.	18,333

(June '83, Lab. maj. 12,264)

Moray (Grampian)
E. 62,201

Mrs. M. Ewing, S.N.P.	19,510
A. Pollock, C.	15,825
C. R. C. Smith, *Lab.*	5,118
D. G. M. Skene, *L./All.*	4,724
S.N.P. maj.	3,685

(June '83, C. maj. 1,713)

Motherwell (S'clyde)

NORTH *E.* 57,632

J. Reid, *Lab.*	29,825
A. Currie, *S.N.P.*	6,230
R. Hargrave, *C.*	4,939
G. Swift, *L./All.*	3,558
Lab. maj.	23,595

(June '83, Lab. maj. 17,894)

SOUTH *E.* 52,127

Dr. J. W. Bray, Lab.	22,957
J. Wright, *S.N.P.*	6,027
J. S. Bercow, *C.*	5,702
W. R. MacGregor, *S.D.P./*	
All.	4,463
R. Somerville, *Comm.*	223
Lab. maj.	16,930

(June '83, Lab. maj. 12,349)

Orkney and Shetland (Islands)
E. 31,047

J. R. Wallace, L./All.	8,881
R. W. A. Jenkins, *C.*	4,959
J. H. Aberdein, *Lab.*	3,995
J. Goodlad, *O.S.M.*	3,095
G. K. Collister, *Grn.*	389
L./All. maj.	3,922

(June '83, L./All. maj. 4,150)

Paisley (S'clyde)

NORTH *E.* 49,487

A. S. Adams, Lab.	20,193
Mrs. E. F. Laing, *C.*	5,751
Miss E. P. McCartin,	
S.D.P./All.	5,741
I. Taylor, *S.N.P.*	4,696
Lab. maj.	14,442

(June '83, Lab. maj. 7,587)

SOUTH *E.* 51,127

N. F. Buchan, Lab.	21,611
A. M. Carmichael, *L./All*	5,826
Miss D. A. Williamson, *C.*	5,644
J. R. Mitchell, *S.N.P.*	5,398
Lab. maj.	15,785

(June '83, Lab. maj. 6,529)

Perth and Kinross (Tayside)
E. 63,443

N. H. Fairbairn, Q.C., *C.*	18,716
J. M. Fairlie, *S.N.P.*	13,040
S. Donaldson, *L./All.*	7,969
J. W. McConnell, *Lab.*	7,490
C. maj.	5,676

(June '83, C. maj. 6,733)

Renfrew West and Inverclyde
(S'clyde)
E. 56,189

T. Graham, Lab.	17,525
Mrs. A. A. McCurley, C.	13,472
Dr. J. D. Mabon, *S.D.P./*	
All.	9,669
C. Campbell, *S.N.P.*	4,578
Lab. maj.	4,053

(June '83, C. maj. 1,322)

Ross, Cromarty and Skye
(H'land)
E. 52,369

C. P. Kennedy, S.D.P./All.	18,809
F. Spencer Nairn, *C.*	7,490
M. M. MacMillan, *Lab.*	7,287
R. M. Gibson, *S.N.P.*	4,492
S.D.P./All. maj.	11,319

(June '83, S.D.P./All. maj. 1,704)

Roxburgh and Berwickshire
(Borders)
E. 43,140

A. J. Kirkwood, L./All.	16,388
Dr. L. Fox, *C.*	12,380
T. Luckhurst, *Lab.*	2,944
M. Douglas, *S.N.P.*	1,586
L./All. maj.	4,008

(June '83, L./All. maj. 3,396)

Stirling (Central)
E. 57,836

M. B. Forsyth, C.	17,591
M. Connarty, *Lab.*	16,644
I. McFarlane, *L./All.*	6,804
I. M. Lawson, *S.N.P.*	4,897
C. maj.	948

(June '83, C. maj. 5,133)

Strathkelvin and Bearsden
(S'clyde)
E. 62,676

S. L. Galbraith, *Lab.*	19,639
M. W. Hirst, C.	17,187
J. Bannerman, *L./All.*	11,034
G. Paterson, *S.N.P.*	3,654
Lab. maj.	2,452

(June '83, C. maj. 3,700)

Tayside North
E. 53,985

W. C. Walker, C.	18,307
K. J. N. Guild, *S.N.P.*	13,291
P. F. Regent, *L./All.*	5,201
J. Whytock, *Lab.*	3,550
C. maj.	5,016

(June '83, C. maj. 10,099)

Tweeddale, Ettrick and Lauderdale (Borders)
E. 37,875

Rt. Hon. D. M. S. Steel, L./	
All.	14,599
Mrs. S. Finlay-Maxwell, *C.*	8,657
N. Glen, *Lab.*	3,320
A. Lumsden, *S.N.P.*	2,660
L./All. maj.	5,942

(June '83, L./All. maj. 8,539)

Western Isles (Islands)
E. 23,507

C. A. MacDonald, *Lab.*	7,041
I. Smith, *S.N.P.*	4,701
K. MacIver, *S.D.P./All.*	3,419
M. Morrison, *C.*	1,336
Lab. maj.	2,340

(June '83, S.N.P. maj. 3,712)

NORTHERN IRELAND

Antrim

EAST *E.* 60,587

J. R. Beggs, O.U.P.	23,942
S. Neeson, *All.*	8,582
A. Kelly, *W.P.*	936
O.U.P. maj.	15,360

(June '83, OUP. maj. 367)
(Jan. '86, O.U.P. maj. 24,981)

NORTH *E.* 65,733

Rev. I. R. K. Paisley,	
D.U.P.	28,383
S. Farren, *S.D.L.P.*	5,149
G. Williams, *All.*	5,140
S. Reagan, *S.F.*	2,633
D.U.P. maj.	23,234

(June '83, D.U.P. maj. 13,173)
(Jan. '86, D.U.P. maj. 33,024)

SOUTH *E.* 61,649

C. Forsythe, O.U.P.	25,395
G. Mawhinney, *All.*	5,808
D. McClelland, *S.D.L.P.*	3,611
H. Cushinan, *S.F.*	1,592
O.U.P. maj.	19,587

(June '83, O.U.P. maj. 6,792)
(Jan. '86, O.U.P. maj. 28,217)

Belfast

EAST *E.* 54,628

P. D. Robinson, D.U.P.	20,372
Dr. J. Alderdice, *All.*	10,574
F. Cullen, *W.P.*	1,314
J. O'Donnell, *S.F.*	649
D.U.P. maj.	9,798

(June '83, D.U.P. maj. 7,989)
(Jan. '86, D.U.P. maj. 21,690)

NORTH *E.* 59,124

A. C. Walker, O.U.P.	14,355
A. Maginness, *S.D.L.P.*	5,795
G. Seawright, *Prot. U.*	5,671
P. McManus, *S.F.*	5,062
S. Lynch, *W.P.*	3,062
T. Campbell, *All.*	2,871
O.U.P. maj.	8,560

(June '83, O.U.P. maj. 7,079)
(Jan. '86, O.U.P. maj. 16,577)

SOUTH *E.* 54,208
Rev. W. M. Smyth, O.U.P.	18,917
D. Cook, *All.*	6,963
Dr. A. McDonnell, *S.D.L.P.*	4,268
G. Carr, *W.P.*	1,528
S. McKnight, *S.F.*	1,030
O.U.P. maj.	11,954

(June '83, O.U.P. maj. 9,724)
(Jan. '86, O.U.P. maj. 14,136)

WEST *E.* 59,324
G. Adams, S.F.	16,862
Dr. J. G. Hendron, *S.D.L.P.*	14,641
F. Miller, *O.U.P.*	7,646
Mrs. M. McMahon, *W.P.*	1,819
S.F. maj.	2,221

(June '83, S.F. maj. 5,445)

Down

NORTH *E.* 65,018
J. A. Kilfedder, U.P.U.P.	18,420
R. McCartney, *Real U.*	14,467
J. Cushnahan, *All.*	7,932
U.P.U.P. maj.	3,953

(June '83, U.P.U.P. maj. 13,846)
(Jan. '86, U.P.U.P. maj. 22,727)

SOUTH *E.* 71,235
E. K. McGrady, *S.D.L.P.*	26,579
Rt. Hon. J. E. Powell, M.B.E., O.U.P.	25,848
Ms. G. Ritchie, *S.F.*	2,363
Miss S. E. Laird, *All.*	1,069
D. O'Hagan, *W.P.*	675
S.D.L.P. maj.	731

(June '83, O.U.P. maj. 548)
(Jan. '86, O.U.P. maj. 1,842)

Fermanagh and South Tyrone
E. 68,979
K. Maginnis, O.U.P.	27,446
P. Corrigan, *S.F.*	14,623
Mrs. R. Flanagan, *S.D.L.P.*	10,581
D. Kettyles, *W.P.*	1,784
J. Haslett, *All.*	941
O.U.P. maj.	12,823

(June '83, O.U.P. maj. 7,676)
(Jan. '86, O.U.P. maj. 12,579)

Foyle
E. 70,519
J. Hume, S.D.L.P.	23,743
G. Campbell, *D.U.P.*	13,883
M. McGuiness, *S.F.*	8,707
Mrs. E. Zammitt, *All.*	1,276
E. Melaugh, *W.P.*	1,022
S.D.L.P. maj.	9,860

(June '83, S.D.L.P. maj. 8,148)

Lagan Valley
E. 64,873
Rt. Hon. J. H. Molyneaux, O.U.P.	29,101
S. A. Close, *All.*	5,728
B. McDonnell, *S.D.L.P.*	2,888
P. J. Rice, *S.F.*	2,656
J. T. Lowry, *W.P.*	1,215
O.U.P. maj.	23,373

(June '83, O.U.P. maj. 17,216)
(Jan. '86, O.U.P. maj. 29,186)

Londonderry East
E. 71,031
W. Ross, O.U.P.	29,532
A. Doherty, *S.D.L.P.*	9,375
J. Davey, *S.F.*	5,464
P. McGowan, *All.*	3,237
F. Donnelly, *W.P.*	935
M. H. Samuel, *Ecol.*	281
O.U.P. maj.	20,157

(June '83, O.U.P. maj. 7,262)
(Jan. '86, O.U.P. maj. 28,921)

Newry and Armagh
E. 66,027
S. Mallon, S.D.L.P.	25,137
J. F. Nicholson, O.U.P.	19,812
J. McAllister, *S.F.*	6,173
W. H. Jeffrey, *All.*	664
J. O'Hanion, *W.P.*	482
S.D.L.P. maj.	5,325

(June '83, O.U.P. maj. 1,554)
(Jan. '86, S.D.L.P. maj. 2,583)

Strangford
E. 64,429
Rt. Hon. J. D. Taylor, O.U.P.	28,199
A. J. Morrow, *All.*	7,553
Miss I. E. Hynds, *W.P.*	1,385
O.U.P. maj.	20,646

(June '83, O.U.P. maj. 7,370)
(Jan. '86, O.U.P. maj. 30,634)

Ulster, Mid-
E. 67,256
Rev. R. T. W. McCrea, D.U.P.	23,004
P. D. Haughey, *S.D.L.P.*	13,644
S. Begley, *S.F.*	12,449
P. Bogan, *All.*	1,846
P. J. McClean, *W.P.*	1,133
D.U.P. maj.	9,360

(June '83, D.U.P. maj. 78)
(Jan. '86, D.U.P. maj. 9,697)

Upper Bann
E. 64,540
J. H. McCusker, O.U.P.	26,037
Mrs. B. Rodgers, *S.D.L.P.*	8,676
B. P. Curran, *S.F.*	3,126
Mrs. M. F. A. Cook, *All.*	2,487
T. French, *W.P.*	2,004
O.U.P. maj.	17,361

(June '83, O.U.P. maj. 17,081)
(Jan. '86, O.U.P. maj. 22,333)

BY-ELECTIONS (Since last edition)

Knowsley, North
(November 13, 1986)
G. Howarth, *Lab.*	17,403
Rosemary Cooper, *L./All.*	10,679
R. Brown, *C.*	1,960
D. Hallsworth, *Revolutionary Communist Party*	664
R. Weiss, *Rainbow Alliance*	111
D. Cory, *Ind.*	88
Lab. maj.	6,724

Greenwich
(February 26, 1987)
Rosemary S. Barnes, *S.D.P/ All.*	18,287
Deirdre Wood, *Lab.*	11,676
J. G. Antcliffe, *C.*	3,852
G. J. E. Bell, *Green Party*	264
M. G. Hardee, *Rainbow Alliance*	124
T. B. Dell, *British National Party*	116
J. A. Pearce, *National Front*	103
Ms. K. Marshall, *Revolutionary Communist*	91
S.D.P./All. maj.	6,611

Truro
(March 12, 1987)
M. Taylor, *L./All.*	30,599
N. St. Aubyn, *C.*	15,982
J. King, *Lab.*	3,603
H. Hoptrough, *Green Party*	403
Helen Anscomb, *Death off Roads, Freight on Rail*	75
L./All. maj.	14,617

EUROPEAN PARLIAMENT (U.K. MEMBERS AND ELECTIONS)

UNITED KINGDOM MEMBERS OF THE EUROPEAN PARLIAMENT

An asterisk* denotes membership of the previous parliament.

*Gordon J. Adam (*Lab.*), Northumbria; *Richard A. Balfe (*Lab.*), London, South Inner; *Robert C. Battersby (C.), Humberside; Christopher J. P. Beazley (*C.*), Cornwall and Plymouth; *Peter G. Beazley (*C.*), Bedfordshire, S.; *The Lord Bethell (*C.*), London, N.W.; John Bird (*Lab.*), Midlands, W.; *Miss Beata A. Brookes (*C.*), Wales, N.; *Mrs. Janey Buchan (*Lab.*), Glasgow; Bryan M. D. Cassidy (*C.*), Dorset E. and Hampshire W.; *Rt. Hon. Mrs. Barbara A. Castle (*Lab.*), Greater Manchester, W.; *Sir Frederick Catherwood (*C.*), Cambridge and Bedfordshire N.; *Kenneth D. Collins (*Lab.*), Strathclyde, E.; *Richard J. Cottrell (*C.*), Bristol; Mrs. Christine M. Crawley (*Lab.*), Birmingham, E.; G. Robert Cryer (*Lab.*), Sheffield; *David M. Curry (*C.*), Essex, N.E.; Mrs. Margaret M. Daly (*C.*), Somerset and Dorset W.; *John de Courcy Ling (*C.*), Midlands, Central; *Basil R. V. Z. de Ferranti (*C.*), Hampshire, Central; *The Marquess of Douro (*C.*), Surrey, W.

*The Baroness Elles (*C.*), Thames Valley; James E. M. Elles (*C.*), Oxford and Buckinghamshire; Michael N. Elliott (*Lab.*), London, W.; *Mrs. Winifred M. Ewing (*S.N.P.*), Highlands and Islands; Mrs. I. Sheila Faith (*C.*), Cumbria and Lancashire, N.; Alec Falconer (*Lab.*), Scotland Mid and Fife; J. Glyn Ford (*Lab.*), Greater Manchester, W.; *Winston J. Griffiths (*Lab.*), Wales, S.; Michael J. Hindley (*Lab.*), Lancashire, E.; Geoffrey W. Hoon (*Lab.*), Derbyshire; *Paul F. Howell (*C.*), Norfolk; Leslie J. Huckfield (*Lab.*), Merseyside, E.; Stephen S. Hughes (*Lab.*), Durham; *John Hume (*S.D.L.P.*), N. Ireland; *Alasdair H. Hutton (*C.*), Scotland, S.; Mrs. Caroline F. Jackson (*C.*), Wiltshire; *Christopher M. Jackson (*C.*), Kent, E.; Michael L. Kilby (*C.*), Nottingham.

*Alfred Lomas (*Lab.*), London, N.E.; Michael McGowan (*Lab.*), Leeds; Hugh McMahon (*Lab.*), Strathclyde, W.; Edward H. C. Macmillan Scott (*C.*), York; *John L. Marshall (*C.*), London, N.; David W. Martin (*Lab.*), Lothians; *Thomas Megahy (*Lab.*), Yorkshire, S.W.; C. James O. Moorhouse (*C.*), London S. and Surrey E.; D. Richard Morris (*Lab.*), Wales, Mid and W.; A. Stanley Newens (*Lab.*), London, Central; Edward Newman (*Lab.*), Greater Manchester, Central; *William F. Newton Dunn (*C.*), Lincolnshire; *Sir Tom Normanton (*C.*), Cheshire, E.; *The Lord O'Hagan (*C.*), Devon; *Rev. Ian R. K. Paisley (*D.U.P.*), N. Ireland; *George B. Patterson (*C.*), Kent, W.; *Andrew Pearce (*C.*), Cheshire, W.; Lord Plumb (*C.*), The Cotswolds; *Derek Prag (*C.*), Hertfordshire; *Peter N. Price (*C.*), London, S.E.; *Christopher J. Prout (*C.*), Shropshire and Stafford; *James L. C. Provan (*C.*), Scotland, N.E.; *Miss Joyce G. Quin (*Lab.*), Tyne and Wear; *Dame Shelagh M. Roberts (*C.*), London, S.W.

*Sir James Scott-Hopkins (*C.*), Hereford and Worcester; *Barry H. Seal (*Lab.*), Yorkshire, W.; *R. Madron Seligman (*C.*), Sussex, W.; *Dr. Alexander Sherlock (*C.*), Essex, S.W.; *Richard J. Simmonds (*C.*), Wight and Hampshire, E.; *Anthony. M. H. Simpson (*C.*), Northamptonshire; Llewellyn Smith (*Lab.*), Wales, S.E.; George W. Stevenson (*Lab.*), Staffordshire, E.; Kenneth Stewart (*Lab.*), Merseyside, W.; *Sir John Stewart-Clark, Bt. (*C.*), Sussex, E.; *Rt. Hon. John Taylor (*O.U.P.*), N. Ireland; John E. Tomlinson (*Lab.*), Birmingham, W.; Mrs. Carol Tongue (*Lab.*), London, E.; *Frederick A. Tuckman (*C.*), Leicester; *Amédée E. Turner (*C.*), Suffolk; *Hon. Sir Peter B. R. Vanneck (*C.*), Cleveland and Yorkshire N.; *Michael J. Welsh (*C.*), Lancashire, Central; Norman West (*Lab.*), Yorkshire, South.

UNITED KINGDOM ELECTIONS TO EUROPEAN PARLIAMENT (June 14, 1984)

An asterisk * denotes membership of the previous Parliament. (*Eco.* = Ecology Party; *W. Reg.* = Wessex Regionalists; for other abbreviations, *see* p. 319

Bedfordshire, South
E. 524,974

*P. G. Beazley, C.	72,088
W. Cochrane, *Lab.*	57,106
P. A. Dixon, *L./All.*	36,444
C. maj.	*14,982*

Birmingham, East
E. 548,899

Mrs. C. M. Crawley, *Lab.*	76,377
*Miss N. E. Forster, C.	54,994
D. A. Bennett *S.D.P./All.*	21,927
Miss D. Howell, *Ind.*	1,440
Lab. maj.	*21,383*

Birmingham, West
E. 518,707

J. E. Tomlinson, *Lab.*	61,946
C. Hart, *C.*	55,702
J. C. Binns, *S.D.P./All.*	19,422
Lab. maj.	*6,244*

Bristol
E. 569,765

*R. J. Cottrell, C.	94,652
R. L. Berry, *Lab.*	77,008
P. J. Farley, *S.D.P./All.*	33,698
C. maj.	*17,644*

Cambridge and Bedfordshire North
E. 523,899

*Sir Frederick Catherwood, C.	86,117
H. G. Bottomley, *Lab.*	38,901
A. N. Duff, *L./All.*	36,341
C. maj.	*47,216*

Cheshire, East
E. 498,568

*T. Normanton, C.	71,182
A. Stephenson, *Lab.*	52,806
J. P. Corbett, *S.D.P./All.*	31,374
C. maj.	*18,376*

Cheshire, West
E. 539,761

*A. Pearce, C.	74,579
D. G. Hanson, *Lab.*	64,887
E. C. H. Owen, *S.D.P./All.*	30,470
C. maj.	*9,692*

Cleveland and Yorkshire North
E. 566,083

*Hon. Sir P. Vanneck,, C.	73,217
P. F. Tinnion, *Lab.*	70,592
C. Beever, *S.D.P./All.*	35,916
C. maj.	*2,625*

Cornwall and Plymouth
E. 506,004

C. J. P. Beazley, C.	81,627
J. C. Marks, *S.D.P./All.*	63,876
J. D. Cosgrove, *Lab.*	35,952
A. I. Parkin, *Ind.*	5,645
R. J. Trevallion, *Ind.*	2,981
J. Whetter, *Ind.*	1,892
C. maj.	*17,751*

The Cotswolds
E. 527,081

*Sir H. Plumb, C.	94,740
Miss M. E. Burton, *L./All.*	45,798
Miss J. A. Royall, *Lab.*	36,738
C. maj.	*48,942*

Cumbria and Lancashire North
E. 547,433

Mrs. I. S. Faith, C.	86,127
J. R. Atkinson, *Lab.*	62,332
Mrs. K. C. Brooks, *L./All.*	39,622
C. maj.	*23,795*

Derbyshire
E. 553,020

G. W. Hoon, *Lab.*	79,466
*T. N. B. Spencer, C.	72,613
Miss J. M. Elles, *S.D.P./All.*	30,824
Lab. maj.	*6,853*

Devon
E. 560,807

*Lord O'Hagan, C.	......	110,129
P. G. Driver, L./All.	.....	53,519
D. A. Gorbutt, Lab.	.....	30,017
P. S. Christie, Eco.	......	6,919
Lady Rous, W. Reg.	....	659
C. maj.	....	56,610

Dorset East and Hampshire West
E. 565,709

B. M. D. Cassidy, C.	......	109,072
J. M. Goss, L./All.	......	49,181
D. T. James, Lab.	....	31,223
C. maj.	....	59,891

Durham
E. 530,104

S. S. Hughes, Lab.	....	106,073
Hon. W. R. Fletcher-Vane, C.		44,846
C. Foote Wood, L./All.	....	32,307
Lab. maj.	....	61,227

Essex, N.E.
E. 574,022

*D. M. Curry, C.	......	97,138
B. L. Stapleton, Lab.	....	42,836
A. E. Ross, S.D.P./All.	..	34,769
C. maj.	....	54,302

Essex, S.W.
E. 557,704

*Dr. A. Sherlock, C.	......	72,190
C. O'Brien, Lab.	....	56,169
A. F. C. Morris, L./All.	...	29,385
C. maj.	....	16,021

Glasgow
E. 518,178

*Mrs. J. Buchan, Lab.	....	91,015
Miss S. Chadd, C.	....	25,282
C. Mason, L./All.	......	20,867
N. MacLeod, S.N.P.	......	16,456
Lab. maj.	....	65,733

Greater Manchester, Central
E. 507,941

E. Newman, Lab.	....	76,830
T. R. M. Sewell, C.	......	48,753
G. E. A. O. Weddell, L./All.	...	24,192
K. J. Martin, Ind.	....	1,430
Lab. maj.	....	28,077

Greater Manchester, East
E. 510,586

J. G. Ford, Lab.	......	65,101
T. K. Thornber, C.	....	56,450
Mrs. B. Gaskin, S.D.P./All.	...	27,801
M. J. Shipley, Eco.	....	3,158
Lab. maj.	....	8,651

Greater Manchester, West
E. 528,896

*Rt. Hon. Mrs. B. A. Castle, Lab.	....	93,740
*W. J. Hopper, C.	......	56,042
J. R. Boddy, S.D.P./All.	...	17,894
Lab. maj.	....	37,698

Hampshire, Central
E. 524,649

*B. R. V. Z. de Ferranti, C.	..	84,086

Hereford and Worcester
E. 560,654

*Sir J. Scott-Hopkins, C.	...	84,077
P. E. S. Nielson, Lab.	.....	44,143
I. D. Phillips, L./All.	.....	37,854
Mrs. F. M. Norman, Eco.	..	8,179
C. maj.	....	39,934

Hertfordshire
E. 505,206

*D. Prag, C.	......	87,603
A. McWalter, Lab.	......	41,671
Mrs. F. M. Beckett, S.D.P./All.	.....	40,877
C. maj.	....	45,932

Highlands and Islands
E. 307,265

*Mrs. W. M. Ewing, S.N.P.	..	49,410
D. R. Johnston, L./All.	...	33,133
D. Webster, C.	....	18,847
Rev. J. McArthur, Lab.	....	16,644
S.N.P. maj.	....	16,277

Humberside
E. 503,080

*R. C. Battersby, C.	....	61,952
P. D. Crampton, Lab.	......	53,937
S. W. Unwin, S.D.P./All.	..	27,318
C. maj.	....	8,015

Kent, East
E. 554,808

*C. M. Jackson, C.	....	92,340
D. A. Enright, Lab.	......	43,473
A. Kinch, S.D.P./All.	.....	34,601
S. Dawe, Eco.	....	5,405
C. maj.	....	48,867

Kent, West
E. 565,693

*G. B. Patterson, C.	....	85,414
A. Woodhams, Lab.	......	50,784
P. H. Billenness, L. All.	...	33,306
Mrs. C. A. Bunyan, Eco.	....	4,991
C. maj.	....	34,630

Lancashire, Central
E. 524,132

*M. J. Welsh, C.	....	82,370
Miss H. M. Jones, Lab.	.....	56,175
*M. Gallagher, S.D.P./All.	..	24,936
C. maj.	....	26,195

Lancashire, East
E. 534,542

M. J. Hindley, Lab.	......	75,711
*E. T. Kellett-Bowman, C.	..	67,806
A. G. Lishman, L./All.	....	26,320
Lab. maj.	....	7,905

Leeds
E. 527,653

M. McGowan, Lab.	......	70,535
J. G. Holt, C.	....	60,178
S. J. Cooksey, L./All.	......	36,097
Lab. maj.	....	10,357

Leicester
E. 564,350

*F. A. Tuckman, C.	......	72,508
P. A. Soulsby, Lab.	....	69,616

D. N. Simmonds, S.D.P./All.

	......	29,656
A. G. Barrett, Ind.	....	3,249
C. maj.	....	2,892

Lincolnshire
E. 551,904

*W. F. Newton Dunn, C.	...	92,606
C. W. Sewell, Lab.	......	47,161
G. Purves, L./All.	......	37,244
C. maj.	....	45,445

London, Central
E. 543,825

A. S. Newens, Lab.	......	77,842
*A. D. Fergusson, C.	......	64,545
E. Wistrich, S.D.P./All.	..	30,269
J. E. Porritt, Eco.	......	5,945
R. J. Maynard, Ind.	....	1,569
Lab. maj.	......	13,297

London, East
E. 537,831

Miss C. Tongue, Lab.	......	73,870
*A. R. Tyrrell, C.	......	61,711
Mrs. J. Horne, S.D.P./All.	..	26,379
Lab. maj.	......	12,159

London, North
E. 564,359

*J. L. Marshall, C.	......	74,846
E. Large, Lab.	......	69,993
J. Skinner, L./All.	......	31,344
P. S. J. Lang, Eco.	....	4,682
C. maj.	....	4,853

London, N.E.
E. 513,781

*A. Lomas, Lab.	......	79,907
M. Batchelor, C.	....	27,242
J. P. Heppell, L./All.	......	17,344
Mrs. J. Lambert, Eco.	......	4,797
Lab. maj.	....	52,665

London, N.W.
E. 518,365

*The Lord Bethell, C.	......	69,803
Ms. P. Healy, Lab.	....	62,381
A. Ketteringham, L./All.	..	29,609
C. maj.	....	7,422

London, S.E.
E. 561,984

*P. N. Price, C.	....	81,508
S. J. Cowan, Lab.	....	61,493
J. H. Fryer, L./All.	....	38,614
W. E. Turner, Ind.	....	989
C. maj.	....	20,015

London, S.W.
E. 499,273

*Dame Shelagh M. Roberts, C.	....	70,490
Miss A. J. Pollack, Lab.	.....	63,623
D. J. Twigg, L./All.	....	32,268
Mrs. S. G. Willington, Eco.	.	3,066
C. maj.	....	6,867

London South and Surrey East
E. 505,393

*C. J. O. Moorhouse, C.	....	82,122
A. S. MacKinlay, Lab.	.....	37,465
J. G. Parry, L./All.	....	34,522
C. maj.	....	44,657

London, South Inner
E.530,672

*R. A. Balfe, *Lab.*	77,661
Mrs. D. Miller, *C.*	46,180
J. Daly, *S.D.P./All.*	25,391
Mrs. J. Owens, *Eco.*	3,281
Lab. maj.	*31,481*

London, West
E.516,661

M. N. Elliot, *Lab.*	79,554
*B. H. Hord, *C.*	74,325
C. Layton, *S.D.P./All.*	36,687
Mrs. D. M. Sutherland, *Eco.*	4,361
Lab. maj.	*5,229*

Lothians
E.516,068

D. W. Martin, *Lab.*	74,989
I. J. Henderson, *C.*	49,065
Dr. J. D. Mabon, *S.D.P./All.*	36,636
Dr. D. Stevenson, *S.N.P.*	22,331
Miss L. Hendry, *Eco.*	2,560
Lab. maj.	*25,924*

Merseyside, East
E.537,285

L. J. Huckfield, *Lab.*	87,086
T. G. D. R. B. Galbraith, *C.*	38,047
T. Bishop, *S.D.P./All.*	17,259
Lab. maj.	*49,039*

Merseyside, West
E.551,532

K. Stewart, *Lab.*	65,915
*Miss G. D. Hooper, *C.*	52,718
P. R. Clark, *L./All.*	37,303
Lab. maj.	*13,197*

Midlands, Central
E.533,798

*J. de Courcy Ling, *C.*	67,884
D. J. Blackman, *Lab.*	55,155
P. Langmead, *S.D.P./All.*	27,912
A. Enstone, *Ind.*	1,494
C. maj.	*12,729*

Midlands, West
E.533,796

T. J. Pitt, *Lab.*	74,091
A. T. Burnside, *C.*	54,406
C. Carter, *L./All.*	17,709
Lab. maj.	*19,685*
(see p. 349 for by-election result)	

Norfolk
E.543,214

*P. F. Howell, *C.*	95,459
A. E. B. Heading, *Lab.*	58,602
L. Williams, *S.D.P./All.*	37,703
C. maj.	*36,857*

Northamptonshire
E.547,188

*A. M. H. Simpson, *C.*	88,668
J. Dickie, *Lab.*	48,809
Mrs. C. M. Goodhart, *S.D.P./All.*	37,421
Mrs. A. Bryant, *Ind.*	3,330
C. maj.	*39,859*

Northumbria
E.512,979

*G. J. Adam, *Lab.*	78,417

C. M. M. Crichton, *C.*	62,717
G. Scott, *L./All.*	42,946
Lab. maj.	*15,700*

Nottingham
E.554,473

M. L. Kilby, *C.*	82,500
K. Coates, *Lab.*	66,374
K. M. Melton, *L./All.*	33,169
C. maj.	*16,126*

Oxford and Buckinghamshire
E.542,343

J. E. M. Elles, *C.*	94,136
R. J. Liddle, *S.D.P./All.*	45,055
J. G. Power, *Lab.*	39,164
C. maj.	*49,081*

Scotland, Mid and Fife
E.528,529

A. Falconer, *Lab.*	80,038
*J. R. Purvis, *C.*	52,872
Mrs. J. T. Jones, *S.N.P.*	30,511
A. A. I. Wedderburn, *S.D.P./All.*	24,220
Lab. maj.	*27,166*

Scotland, North-East
E.548,711

*J. L. C. Provan, *C.*	53,809
F. Doran, *Lab.*	44,638
D. Hood, *S.N.P.*	33,448
I. G. Philip, *S.D.P./All.*	25,490
C. maj.	*9,171*

Scotland, South
E.484,760

*A. H. Hutton, *C.*	60,843
R. Stewart, *Lab.*	57,706
Mrs. E. M. Buchanan, *L./All.*	23,598
I. R. Goldie, *S.N.P.*	22,242
C. maj.	*3,137*

Sheffield
E.558,984

G. R. Cryer, *Lab.*	93,530
D. R. Grayson, *C.*	47,247
Miss M. Holmstedt, *L./All.*	23,935
Lab. maj.	*46,283*

Shropshire and Stafford
E.562,823

*C. J. Prout, *C.*	82,291
D. J. A. Hallam, *Lab.*	57,359
R. M. Burman, *L./All.*	37,209
C. maj.	*24,932*

Somerset and Dorset West
E.540,393

Mrs. M. Daly, *C.*	98,928
R. G. Moore, *L./All.*	58,677
Mrs. J. Linden, *Lab.*	36,836
C. maj.	*40,251*

Staffordshire, East
E.563,376

G. W. Stevenson, *Lab.*	76,753
*R. J. Moreland, *C.*	68,886
R. Fox, *S.D.P./All.*	26,093
Lab. maj.	*7,867*

Strathclyde, East
E.498,458

*K. D. Collins, *Lab.*	90,792
G. Leslie, *S.N.P.*	27,330
P. R. Leckie, *C.*	24,857

Ms. P. de Seume, *L./All.*	11,883
Lab. maj.	*63,462*

Strathclyde, West
E.499,162

H. McMahon, *Lab.*	70,234
Miss J. Lait, *C.*	47,196
Mrs. J. Herriot, *S.N.P.*	28,866
D. J. Herbison, *S.D.P./All.*	25,955
Lab. maj.	*23,038*

Suffolk
E.516,050

*A. E. Turner, *C.*	88,243
W. Moszczynski, *Lab.*	41,145
C. Leakey, *L./All.*	34,084
C. maj.	*47,098*

Surrey, West
E.504,923

*The Marquess of Douro, *C.*	96,675
E. Mortimer, *S.D.P./All.*	44,087
N. K. A. S. Vaz, *Lab.*	22,531
C. maj.	*52,588*

Sussex, East
E.537,397

*Sir J. Stewart-Clark, Bt., *C.*	102,287
J. Busby, *S.D.P./All.*	36,666
H. Spillman, *Lab*	32,213
Mrs. E. Evelyn, *Eco.*	5,401
C. maj.	*65,621*

Sussex, West
E.531,934

*R. M. Seligman, *C.*	104,257
Dr. J. M. M. Walsh, *L./All.*	46,755
G. C. Rees, *Lab.*	22,857
D. Aherne, *Eco.*	3,842
C. maj.	*57,502*

Thames Valley
E.519,564

*The Baroness Elles, *C.*	74,928
R. B. Bastin, *Lab.*	36,123
R. W. Bradnock, *L./All.*	32,704
C. maj.	*38,805*

Tyne and Wear
E.543,955

*Miss J. G. Quin, *Lab.*	89,024
R. R. Cook, *C.*	39,610
B. P. Carroll, *S.D.P./All.*	19,081
Lab. maj.	*49,414*

Wales, Mid and West
E.533,644

D. R. Morris, *Lab.*	89,362
D. Lewis, *C.*	52,910
D. Lloyd, *L./All.*	35,168
Dr. P. Williams, *P.C.*	32,880
Miss M. A. Smith, *Eco.*	4,266
Lab. maj.	*36,452*

Wales, North
E.516,153

*Miss B. A. Brooks, *C.*	69,139
R. T. Ellis, *S.D.P./All.*	56,861
C. I. Campbell, *Lab.*	54,768
D. Iwan, *P.C.*	38,117
C. maj.	*12,278*

Wales, South
E.509,434

*W. J. Griffiths, *Lab.*	99,936
Miss J. R. Pattman, *C.*	55,678

Mrs. J. Davis, *L./All.*	26,588
Dr D. Huws, *P.C.*	13,201
Lab. maj.	*44,258*

Wales, S.E.
E. 565,739

L. Smith, *Lab.*	131,916
R. Whyatt, *C.*	36,359
C. D. Lindley, *S.D.P./All.*	28,330
S. Morgan, *P.C.*	18,833
Lab. maj.	*95,557*

Wight and Hampshire, East
E. 544,189

*R. J. Simmonds, *C.*	96,666
Mrs. S. Ludford, *L./All.*	53,738
J. A. Phillips, *Lab.*	36,445
C. maj.	*42,928*

Wiltshire
E. 531,501

Mrs. C. F. Jackson, *C.*	86,873
J. B. Ainslie, *L./All.*	60,404
P. Whiteside, *Lab.*	35,457
C. maj.	*26,469*

York
E. 517,592

E. H. C. McMillan-Scott, *C.*	80,636
Mrs. S. Haines, *Lab.*	44,234
M. G. Howard, *S.D.P./All.*	33,356
C. maj.	*36,402*

Yorkshire, South
E. 516,431

N. West, *Lab.*	98,020
Mrs. R. P. N. Pockley, *C.*	30,271
D. Eden, *S.D.P./All.*	19,306
Lab. maj.	*67,749*

Yorkshire, S.W.
E. 518,423

*T. Megahy, *Lab.*	88,464
A. J. A. Lodge, *C.*	44,291
J. F. Crossley, *L./All.*	26,964
Lab. maj.	*44,173*

Yorkshire, West
E. 560,190

*B. H. Seal, *Lab.*	86,259
I. C. Bruce, *C.*	65,405
E. Lyons, *S.D.P./All.*	28,709
Lab. maj.	*20,854*

Northern Ireland
E. 1,077,605

First
Preference

Rev. I. R. K. Paisley, D.U.P.	230,251
J. Hume, S.D.L.P.	151,399
Rt. Hon. J. D. Taylor, O.U.P.	147,169
D. Morrison, *S.F.*	91,476
D. Cook, *All.*	34,046
J. Kilfedder, *U.P.U.P.*	20,092
S. Lynch, *W.P.*	8,712
C. McGuigan, *Eco.*	2,172

Rev. I. R. K. Paisley, J. Hume, and Rt. Hon. J. D. Taylor were elected by the single transferable voting system.

BY-ELECTIONS

Midlands, West
(March 5, 1987)

John Bird, *Lab.*	59,761
Michael Whitby, *C.*	55,736
Christopher Carter, *L.*	37,106
Lab. maj.	*4,025*

VOTES CAST AT U.K. GENERAL ELECTIONS, 1974–87

General Election, October, 1974*

Labour	11,456,597
Conservative	10,464,675
Liberal	5,346,800
Scottish Nationalist	839,628
Plaid Cymru	166,321
Others	195,065

General Election, 1979*

Conservative	13,697,753
Labour	11,506,741
Liberal	4,305,324
Scottish Nationalist	504,259
National Front	191,706
Plaid Cymru	132,544
Others	188,063

General Election, 1983*

Conservative	13,012,602
Labour	8,457,124
Liberal/S.D.P. Alliance	7,780,587
Scottish Nationalist	331,975
Plaid Cymru	125,309
Others	198,383

General Election, 1987*

Conservative	13,760,525
Labour	10,029,944
Liberal/S.D.P. Alliance	7,341,152
Scottish Nationalist	416,873
Plaid Cymru	123,589
Green†	89,753
Others	37,576

*Excluding Northern Ireland †Excluding Ecology candidate in Northern Ireland

THE PRINCIPAL PARTIES IN PARLIAMENT (1931–1987)

General Election	Conservative	Liberal	Labour
1931	471	72 (a)	65 (b)
1935	387	54 (c)	166 (d)
1945	189	25 (e)	396 (f)
1950	298 (g)	9	315 (h)
1951	320 (i)	6	296 (h)
1955	344 (i)	6	277 (j)
1959	365 (i)	6	258 (k)
1964	303 (i)	9	317
1966	253 (i)	12	363 (l)
1970	330 (m)	6	287 (n)
1974 (February)	296	14	301 (o)
1974 (October)	276	13	319 (p)
1979	339	11	268 (q)
1983	397	23 (r)	209 (s)
1987	376	22 (t)	229 (u)

NOTES.—(a) Liberal National 35 (Simon); Liberal 33 (Samuel); 4 (Lloyd George). (b) National Labour 13 (MacDonald); Labour 52 (Henderson). (c) Liberal National 33; Liberal 21. (d) National Labour 8; Labour 154; I.L.P. 4. (e) Liberal National 13; Liberal 12. (f) Labour 393; I.L.P. 3. (g) Incl. Nat. Liberal. (h) Irish Nationalists (2) and Speaker make total of 625. (i) Including associates. (j) Sinn Fein (2) and Speaker make total of 630. (k) Independent (1) makes total of 630. (l) Republican Labour (1) makes total of 630. (m) Including Ulster Unionists. (n) Scottish Nationalists (1); Independent (5) and Speaker make total of 630. (o) United Ulster Unionist Council (11), Scottish Nationalists (7), Plaid Cymru (2); Social Democratic and Labour Party (1); Social Democrat (1); Independent Labour (1); and Speaker make total of 635. (p) Scottish Nationalists (11); United Ulster Unionist (10); Plaid Cymru (3); Social Democratic and Labour Party (1); Independent (1) and Speaker make a total of 635. (q) Ulster Unionist (5); Democratic Unionist (3); Plaid Cymru (2); Scottish Nationalists (2); Social Democratic and Labour (1); United Ulster Unionist (1); Independent (2) and Speaker make a total of 635. (r) Liberal 17; S.D.P. 6. (s) Official Unionist (11); Democratic Unionist (3); Scottish Nationalists (2); Plaid Cymru (2); Ulster Popular Unionist (1); Social Democratic and Labour Party (1) and Provisional Sinn Fein (1) make a total of 650. (t) Liberal 17; S.D.P. 5. (u) Ulster Unionist (9); Scottish Nationalists (3); Plaid Cymru (3); Democratic Unionist (3); Social Democratic and Labour Party (3); Ulster Popular Unionist (1); Sinn Fein (1) make a total of 650.

PARLIAMENTARY SUMMARY, LORDS AND COMMONS, 1986–87

The House of Lords re-assembled on Oct. 6, and the Commons returned from the summer recess on Oct. 21, to deal with the outstanding legislative programme before the prorogation of Parliament on Nov. 6, marking the end of the session. On Oct. 24 the Commons was unified in condemning the attempt to blow up an Israeli airliner by an Arab terrorist. The Commons also supported the Government's decision to break off diplomatic relations with Syria because of its involvement in the case. The Foreign Secretary told M.P.s that the Government had given the Syrian Ambassador, Dr. Loutof Haydar, 14 days to leave Britain.

FINANCIAL STATEMENT

The Chancellor of the Exchequer (Mr. Lawson) presented his autumn financial statement in the Commons on Nov. 6 and announced that the outturn for public expenditure for this financial year was expected to be £140·4 billion, about one per cent. above the plans set out in the Budget Report.

The main increases in expenditure compared with the plans were in the current spending of local authorities and in demand-led programmes such as social security. He said, however, "Other items on the expenditure side, the largest of which was debt interest, were likely to fall short of what was forecast at the time of the Budget, thus reducing the total overrun on the expenditure side to about £0·5 billion.

"On the receipts side, the North Sea tax take is likely to be even lower, by about £1 billion, than I envisaged at the time of the Budget, largely because for a long period the oil price has been below the 15 dollars a barrel level on which the Budget arithmetic was explicitly based.

"This shortfall, however, is more than offset by the continuing buoyancy of non-oil tax revenues, in particular V.A.T. and Corporation Tax.

"Non-oil revenues now look likely to exceed the Budget forecast by £2 billion. This would imply a net overrun on the receipts side of about £1 billion, rather more than that on the expenditure side.

"But this will be reduced by a change I propose to make to the North Sea fiscal regime.

"The collapse of the oil price has led to a sharp cutback in investment activity in the North Sea, with inevitable consequences for the U.K. offshore supplies industry both in Scotland and the north-east of England.

"I therefore propose, on a carefully targeted basis, to accelerate the arrangements for the repayment to the oil companies of advance petroleum revenue tax due to them. The new arrangements will have a revenue cost this financial year of some £300 million, which will be fully recouped over the next three years.

"Taking this into account, the public sector borrowing requirement for the current year is still forecast to be about £7 billion, the figure I set in the Budget."

The Chancellor said that since 1982-83 public spending, both before and after deducting the proceeds of privatisation, had been declining as a proportion of G.D.P. It was set to be lower still this year.

"The Government is determined to ensure that this trend continues.

"The plans I am about to announce for the next three years secure that objective.

"But within this overall constraint, and in the context of its policy priorities, the Government has felt it right to allow an increase in the previously announced planning totals for 1987-88 and 1988-89.

"Compared with the prospective outturn for the current year, we are now planning for an average growth in the public expenditure planning total of about 1·25 per cent a year in real terms, well within the prospective growth of the economy as a whole.

"The new planning totals have thus been set at £148·5 billion for 1987-88 and £154·25 billion in 1988-89, an increase of £4·75 billion and £5·5 billion respectively over the totals previously published. For 1989-90, the planning total has been set at £161·5 billion.

"As usual, these totals incorporate estimates for the proceeds of privatisation. Last year I increased the estimate of these proceeds very substantially to £4·75 billion in each of the three survey years, a figure which I expect to be duly achieved this year.

"Though the privatisation programme is now moving ahead more strongly than ever before, I have decided to make only a modest further addition to this estimate, bringing it to £5 billion in each of the next three years."

The new planning totals also contained substantial reserves, rising from £3·5 billion in 1987-88 to £7·5 billion in 1989-90.

"The public expenditure increases I have announced allow us to make realistic provision both for local authority current expenditure, over which the Government has no direct control, and for demand-led programmes such as social security, while still leaving scope for increased spending on services to which the Government attaches particular priority.

"There can be no question of allowing the projected increases in public expenditure over the next two years to undermine the prudence of the Government's overall fiscal stance.

"The Government's fiscal stance has been clearly set out in the medium-term financial strategy published at the time of this year's Budget. There will be no relaxation of that stance."

After detailing the increased spending plans, Mr Lawson said both growth and inflation had turned out to be slightly lower this year than he envisaged at the time of the Budget.

"The principal reason for this slower growth has been the disappointing performance of exports, which were hard hit by the cutback in spending by O.P.E.C. and other primary producers affected by the sharp fall in commodity prices in general and the oil price in particular.

"Combined with a halving in the value of our own oil exports, this has meant a significant deterioration in the current account of the balance of payments, from a surplus of some £3·5 billion in 1985—and a cumulative surplus of some £21 billion over the six years from 1980 to 1985 inclusive—to a forecast of broad balance for 1986.

"Looking ahead to 1987 the prospects are generally encouraging.

"While the necessary adjustment of the exchange rate to the oil price collapse has now taken place, it will inevitably take time before the full benefits come through in higher non-oil exports and lower import growth. This means we can expect the current account of the balance of payments to go into deficit next year, for the first time since 1979, to the tune of some £1·5 billion.

"Even so, non-oil exports are forecast to rise next year by 5·5 per cent, compared with an increase of only one per cent this year, with manufacturing output in consequence up by four per cent. And with domestic demand continuing to expand at the same rate as this year, the economy overall is likely to grow by a further three per cent next year—the sixth successive year of steady growth at an average annual rate of almost three per cent.

"Recorded inflation is likely to edge up a little, to 3·75 per cent in the fourth quarter of 1987. This is almost entirely due to the effect on the Retail Prices Index of the timing of mortgage rate changes. The Government's commitment to a monetary policy that will squeeze out inflation remains unabated.

"Meanwhile, the likelihood of faster growth next year, coming at a time when unemployment already appears to have stopped rising, suggests that the prospects for some fall in unemployment are now more promising. But this promise could still be frustrated by excessive pay settlements."

Mr Lawson said the strategy followed since 1979 had brought inflation down to the lowest level for two decades, combined with sustained growth and steadily rising living standards.

Reaction to the Financial Statement

Mr. Hattersley, Shadow Chancellor, rejected the Chancellor's economic forecasts as "absolutely incredible" and said the economic outturn was worse in a number of crucial areas than was predicted at the time of the Budget. Mr. Wrigglesworth, economic spokesman for the S.D.P., accused the Government of abandoning monetary targets and monetary policies to generate a short-term pre-election boom for party political gain. The exchanges on the statement were followed by a debate on a Labour motion that the Government's economic strategy had failed. Mr. Hattersley condemned the Chancellor's Medium Term Financial Strategy for failing to bring about the economic recovery it was claimed would follow its application. Mr. Jenkins (S.D.P.), a former Labour Chancellor, observed it was almost impossible to tell what the Government's economic policy was. The Opposition motion was rejected by a large Conservative majority. Parliament was prorogued on Nov. 7.

THE QUEEN'S SPEECH

The Queen opened the new session of Parliament on Nov. 12 with one of the shortest speeches of her reign. The Speech which outlined the legislative programme of the Government stated :

"I look forward with much pleasure to receiving H.M. King Fahd of Saudi Arabia and H.M. King Hassan of Morocco on State visits during the next 12 months.

I also look forward to visiting Berlin in May during that city's 750th anniversary year and to being present on the occasion of the Commonwealth Heads of Government Meeting in Canada.

My Government will continue to attach the highest importance to national security and to preserving peace with freedom and justice. They will maintain the United Kingdom's own defences and play an active part in the Atlantic Alliance.

My Government will work for new agreements on arms control and disarmament. They will seek greater co-operation and trust between East and West and work for progress at the Vienna Review Conference on Security and Co-operation in Europe.

My Government will hold the Presidency of the Council of Ministers of the European Community until the end of this year. Within the Community they will work to promote enterprise and employment; to remove barriers to internal trade; for improvements in world trade rules; and for continuing reform of the Common Agricultural Policy.

My Government will honour their commitments to the people of the Falkland Islands while continuing to seek more normal relations with Argentina. They will discharge their obligations to the people of Hong Kong and will work closely with the Chinese Government to carry out the Sino-British Joint Declaration. They will stand by their commitment to the people of Gibraltar.

My Government will continue to work for peaceful and fundamental change in South Africa, in consultation with their partners in the European Community and with the Commonwealth. They will support Namibian independence. They will look for solutions to the problems of the Middle East. They will support attempts to achieve settlements in Afghanistan, in Cambodia, in Cyprus and in Central America.

My Government will make vigorous efforts to combat international terrorism and trafficking in drugs.

My Government will play a constructive role in the Commonwealth and at the U.N. They will maintain a substantial aid programme, play their part in the relief of famine and other natural disasters and encourage investment in the developing countries.

My Government's firm monetary and fiscal policies will continue to restrain inflation and foster the conditions necessary for further sustained economic growth. Within that framework, my Government will continue to promote enterprise, the growth of employment and the education and training of young people.

My Government will maintain firm control of public expenditure, so that it may continue to fall as a proportion of the nation's income and permit further reductions in the burden of taxation. Consistently with this, my Government will continue to seek better value for money in public spending, so that vital services may be further improved.

Action will be taken to further privatisation, both to improve economic efficiency and to encourage wider share ownership.

Legislation will be introduced to improve the system for the supervision of banks.

A Bill will be brought forward to improve the working of criminal justice, to implement certain recommendations made by the Committee on Fraud Trials and to make further provision for the confiscation of the proceeds of crime.

Measures will be proposed to promote further competition in order to secure greater efficiency in the provision of local authorities' services, and to improve the basis for the payment of rate support grant in England and Wales.

Legislation will be brought before you to repeal the Remuneration of Teachers Act 1965 and to introduce new arrangements to settle schoolteachers' pay, duties and conditions of service within the resources available.

A Bill will be introduced to extend the rights of people living in privately-owned flats in England and Wales.

A Bill will be introduced to facilitate the conservation and management of the Norfolk and Suffolk Broads.

Legislation will be introduced to provide further financial assistance to support the coal industry's progress to commercial viability and to enable fair representation of the workforce.

Measures will be proposed to bring up to date the arrangements regulating oil and gas installations and operations.

Measures will be brought forward further to reform family law in England and Wales.

A Bill will be introduced to modify the system for the control of fire risks and to make further provision for safety at sports grounds.

For Scotland, Bills will be introduced to abolish domestic rates, to reform the enforcement of debts due under court orders, and to make various improvements to criminal justice.

My Government will continue through the Anglo-Irish Agreement to co-operate with the Government of the Republic of Ireland. They will encourage elected representatives in Northern Ireland to search for an agreed basis for a return to a devolved administration. They will continue to encourage economic and industrial development. A Bill will be introduced to amend Northern Ireland legislation against terrorism.

Measures will be proposed to reform the administration of marine pilotage.

Legislation will again be brought before you to enable construction of a Channel Tunnel. A Bill will be introduced to authorise the construction of a third crossing of the Thames at Dartford.

Measures will be proposed to strengthen the law on consumer protection.

Other measures will be laid before you."

Debate on the Queen's Speech

The Commons debate on the Speech was opened by Mr. Kinnock, the Opposition leader, who spoke of the growth in poverty under the Conservatives brought about by low pay and unemployment, but he promised full support for action to combat international terrorism and drug trafficking. Mrs. Thatcher replied that the Speech reaffirmed the Government's commitment to prudent financial management and declared the prospects for growth, exports, investment and inflation were good, and the outlook for employment more promising. She denounced Labour's plans to give up Britain's nuclear deterrent and the American nuclear "umbrella". The six-day debate embraced discussions of education, foreign affairs including international terrorism, local government and Scotland, industry and employment, and the economy. On Nov. 19, the concluding day of the debate, a Labour amendment calling for policies to produce sustained improvement in the strength and competitive performance of the real economy, and substantial and persistent reductions in unemployment and poverty was defeated by 354 votes to 206.

The Wright Case

On Nov. 25 the Prime Minister defended the Government's decision to seek an injunction banning publication in Australia of a book by a former MI5 officer, Mr. Peter Wright. Mrs. Thatcher said publication of his manuscript would violate the obligation of confidentiality to the Crown of all present and former members of the security services. The Government, she added, was concerned with upholding the principle of confidentiality and the obligations of staff. Later Mr. Kinnock, the Opposition leader, complained to the Speaker that Mrs. Thatcher had implied that the well-established bi-partisan attitude to national security had been breached, and said that his exposure of the Prime Minister's inconsistencies over the publication of books on espionage had no implications for national security. On Nov. 27 Mrs. Thatcher refused to answer detailed questions from Labour M.P.s about the Government's past actions over the publication of books about MI5, on the grounds that Prime Ministers do not answer questions affecting national security.

Concern about the accountability of the security services led to an Alliance motion on Dec. 3 proposing the appointment of a Select Committee to oversee the security services. Dr. Owen, the S.D.P. leader, suggested a joint committee be set up of Privy Counsellors from the Lords and the Commons. The motion was rejected by 232 votes to 24. The Government's amendment declaring full confidence in the present system was carried by 205 votes to 45.

The controversy over Mr. Wright's book was fuelled by allegations of a "dirty tricks" campaign by the security services. On Dec. 15, Labour M.P.s demanded a judicial inquiry into the allegations that MI5 officers tried to undermine the Labour Government led by Mr. Wilson (now Lord Wilson). This was rejected by Mr. Waddington, Home Office Minister, who pointed out that Mr. Callaghan, who succeeded Mr. Wilson as Prime Minister, had also turned down calls for an inquiry in Dec. 1977, and had told the Commons he was satisfied that at no time had the security service or any other British intelligence or security agency undertaken electronic surveillance in 10 Downing Street or in the Prime Minister's room at the Commons. Mr. Waddington added Mr. Wilson had associated himself with Mr. Callaghan's statement.

The City

There was equal concern over events in the City and on Dec. 2 Labour's motion on "the scandal of insider dealing" occupied the main business. Mr. Cook (Lab.) declared that trading in the shares of Guinness, the brewing and spirits group, should be stopped if the Government was not prepared to disclose the nature of the Department of Trade and Industry investigation into the company. Mr. Howard, Trade and Industry Under-Secretary, said it was entirely a matter for the Stock Exchange who had statutory responsibility for these matters. The Labour motion also expressed concern at the low clear-up rate in cases referred to the D.T.I. and deplored the Government's failure to secure proper supervision of the City in time for de-regulation, but it was defeated by 261 votes to 177.

The Government easily secured a second reading in the Commons on Dec. 8 for the Teachers' Pay and Conditions Bill. However, there was anything but a smooth passage for the remaining stages of the Bill, which opened in the Commons on Dec. 9 and continued for 26 hours 8 minutes in the face of line-by-line opposition by Labour M.P.s. The Bill received a third reading by 235 votes to 152, but the all-night sitting wiped out the business for Dec. 11.

Mr. Gummer, Agriculture Minister, told the Commons on Dec. 17 that dairy farmers in Britain would not be forced out of business by the European Community deal secured by the British Government to reduce food mountains. Although Mr. Gummer regarded the agreement as an historic step forward, M.P.s on both sides were concerned about the effects on British agriculture of measures aimed at reducing milk production in the Community by 9·5 per cent over two years.

The Commons gave approval to the Chancellor of the Exchequer's autumn financial statement on Dec. 17, though the Government's majority dropped to 28 when M.P.s were asked to approve the provision to require newly-unemployed home owners to pay half their mortgage interest for the first 16 weeks they were out of work. Two Tories, Mr. Doverly and Mr. Fry, voted against the Government and about 20 others abstained, although the proposal was approved by 221 votes to 193.

The Defence Secretary, Mr. Younger, made a statement in the Commons on Dec. 18 announcing the Cabinet's decision to reject the British Nimrod early warning system developed by G.E.C. in favour of the American A.W.A.C.S. system. Immediately Mr. Davies, Labour's defence spokesman, sought an emergency debate on the awarding of the contract and called on the Government to agree to an independent technical inquiry into the decision. Mr. Prior, a former Tory Cabinet Minister and now chairman of G.E.C., concentrated on the alleged lack of co-operation between the Defence Ministry and G.E.C. He was supported by two former Cabinet colleagues, Mr. Heath and Mr. Parkinson, who both considered that G.E.C. should have been given more time. Labour pressed their opposition by dividing the House on a technical motion for the adjournment which was defeated by 339 votes to 170. Nine Conservatives abstained including Mr. Heath, Mr. Prior and Mr. Parkinson.

No sooner had the Commons reassembled on Jan. 12 after the Christmas recess than the City was again in the firing-line. Amid claims that the Guinness affair would prove to be the biggest City scandal for a generation, Mr. Kinnock, the Opposition leader, demanded that the City should be subject to statutory supervision. However, Mrs. Thatcher said it was too soon to decide to change to a full statutory system instead of the present self-regulating Securities and Investment Board. Next there emerged pressure from Tory and Labour M.P.s for the proposed merger between B.T.R. and Pilkington to be referred to the Monopolies and Mergers Commission. This was resisted by the Trade and Industry Secretary, Mr. Channon, in line with a recommendation by the Director General of Fair Trading that the merger did not raise significant competition issues. Mr. Kinnock said the gobbling-up of Pilkington by B.T.R. would not be in the national interest.

The Opposition launched a censure motion on the Government's economic policies on Jan. 20. Mr. Hattersley, Shadow Chancellor, attacked the City for its greed, its obsession with short-term speculation and its sleazy undercurrent of corruption, which he said was the inevitable extension of Tory economic policy. Mr. Lawson, the Chancellor, replied that the guilty men in the City of London were a tiny minority. The overwhelming majority who worked there were honest, and eager to root out the wrongdoers in their midst. The Labour motion was defeated by 355 votes to 206, and the Government amendment congratulating it on the success of its economic policies was carried without a division.

A Labour motion condemning the Government's policies regarding the City as irresponsible was debated in the Commons on Jan. 28. Mr. John Smith, Opposition spokesman on trade and industry, committed his party to the replacement of self-regulation by a statutory independent commission to supervise financial services, including Lloyd's. Mr. Channon, Trade and Industry Secretary, accepted there were serious grounds for concern and announced the Government's intention to seek measures to strengthen the regulation of take-overs. The Labour motion, however, was defeated by 283–181 votes. A Government amendment congratulating it on its firm action in establishing a regulatory framework for the City and its determination to root out abuses was carried by 267–192.

Project Zircon

Yet another security row enveloped the Government on Jan. 22. Following publication in the *New Statesman* magazine of details of the £500 million spy satellite programme codenamed Project Zircon, the Government succeeded in preventing a banned B.B.C. film about the project being shown to M.P.s at Westminster. The Government's belated attempt to prevent disclosure about the satellite programme produced noisy and irate exchanges in the Commons.

On Jan. 27 Mrs. Thatcher rejected Labour charges that her complacency and tardiness had led to the *New Statesman*'s revelations and said Mr. Kinnock should be directing his criticisms at left-wing organs which sought to release material contrary to national security. Later, M.P.s debated a Government motion to uphold a ban on the film being shown at Westminster. Labour countered that the ban should be lifted because the information in the film had already been published in the *New Statesman* magazine. (The Speaker ended his ban on the film being shown at

Westminster when the High Court injunctions against Mr. Duncan Campbell, the journalist who made the film, were lifted on Feb. 25.)

There was combined Labour and Alliance condemnation in the Commons on Feb. 2 of the Special Branch raid on B.B.C. offices in Glasgow the previous weekend in connection with the banned Zircon film. The Government was accused of being involved in an authoritarian and inept exercise, and Mr. Kaufman, Shadow Home Secretary, said the raid had given rise to misgivings about the future of civil liberties. Mr. Rifkind, Scottish Secretary, declared that the Government had played no part in the Metropolitan Police decision to apply for search warrants in pursuing their criminal investigation. Tempers were soothed when the Speaker granted an Opposition application for an emergency debate on the incident, which took place on Feb. 3. During the debate Mr. Kaufman claimed that the Attorney-General had been involved in giving the orders for the raid but this accusation was strenuously denied by the Home Secretary, Mr. Hurd, who repeated Government denials that ministers had intervened in the investigation. At the end of a sometimes noisy debate, the Government had a majority of 151 on a formal motion to adjourn.

Wapping

On Jan. 26 Mr. Hurd, Home Secretary, made a statement in the Commons on the weekend's demonstrations at Wapping against News International. He said the vicious attack had nothing to do with peaceful protest or the peaceful furtherance of a dispute within the law. Angry exchanges ensued with Labour M.P.s demanding a public inquiry into the disorders and the Home Secretary declaring his full support for the police. In the Lords, Lord Murray of Epping Forest, former General Secretary of the T.U.C., said the unions concerned would be well advised to call an end to mass picketing at Wapping which only provided a Roman holiday for hooligans and Trotskyites.

The Rates Support Grants Bill received a second reading in the lower House on Feb. 4 by 343–196 votes, and M.P.s gave a third reading to the Channel Tunnel Bill by 94–22 votes, after a lengthy report stage debate. The Bill took nine months to pass through the Commons with much of the time occupied by a select committee hearing of nearly 5,000 objections.

A private member's Bill supported on both sides of the House to incorporate the European Convention on Human Rights into British law failed in the Commons on Feb. 6. A motion of closure on the debate to enable a vote on second reading failed to win enough votes to carry the closure, so the debate was automatically adjourned and the Bill dropped to the end of the list of private members' legislation.

On Feb. 9 the Government announced the relaxation of planning controls in the countryside. Mr. Jopling, Agriculture Minister, said there would be a £25 million-a-year package of measures to enhance environmental protection and encourage alternative uses of farmland. On Feb. 10 Mr. Ridley, Environment Secretary, made a statement on the planning implications of the new policy, but Labour and Alliance M.P.s described the proposals as a speculators' charter.

There was a crowded House of Lords on Feb. 11 when the Duke of York swore his oath of allegiance to the Queen on being introduced. His supporters were the Duke of Gloucester and the Duke of Kent.

An unopposed second reading was given in the Commons on Feb. 13 to a private member's Bill to restore the right to sue for deaths or injuries to Servicemen and women resulting from peacetime training accidents. The Bill followed a Government statement on Dec. 8 (the date from which liability would begin) accepting the need to end Crown immunity. Several M.P.s were critical that those injured or killed before that date would not be allowed to sue.

Peers gave a second reading on Feb. 16 to the Channel Tunnel Bill and Lord Pennock, joint chairman of Eurotunnel, described it as the most uplifting project of the century. They also gave a third reading to the Teachers' Pay and Conditions Bill which empowers the Education Secretary to impose a pay settlement on teachers. An eleventh-hour effort by Lord Henderson of Brompton to limit the lifetime of the measure failed by 151–99 votes.

Sizewell

On Feb. 23 M.P.s debated the report of the Sizewell B public inquiry, conducted by Sir Frank Layfield, which recommended the building of a pressurised water nuclear reactor at Sizewell, Suffolk. Labour and Alliance spokesmen pleaded for rejection of the nuclear reactor and Mr. Orme, Labour's energy spokesman, declared that if the Government decided to proceed with the project, Labour would reverse it. Mr. Steel, the Liberal leader, said they were not convinced on economic or safety grounds of the case for the reactor. When the Lords debated the plan to build a reactor at Sizewell, on March 2, several peers urged caution. Viscount Davidson, Government energy spokesman, observed that forecasts on Britain's energy needs had all proved wrong to date; it was impossible to predict what changes there would be in either the size of the population or in industrialisation in the next century. Lord Bruce of Donington doubted if the conclusions of the Layfield inquiry still applied in the wake of the Chernobyl disaster. Lord Ezra, a former Coal Board chairman, also expressed doubts about this particular choice of reactor when the world price of coal could have dropped considerably by the year 2000. In a maiden speech, Lord Wyatt of Weeford favoured the Sizewell plan, which would open the way for the export of similar reactors.

In the Commons on Feb. 25, Mr. Meacher, Labour's social services spokesman, moved a motion calling on the Government to reverse its policy of reducing the resources devoted to the elderly. He said Labour would reverse the Government's preference for tax cuts which benefitted the better-off rather than pensioners. Mr. Cyril Smith said the Alliance was totally committed to re-introducing pension increases linked with earnings. The Labour motion was defeated by 273 votes to 199.

A private member's measure introduced into and already passed by the Lords, was approved by the Commons on Feb. 27. The Licensing (Restaurant Meals) Bill allows restaurants in England and Wales to serve alcohol with afternoon meals.

The Government announced on March 3 a Bill to curb abuse of Britain's asylum procedures. This evoked noisy exchanges in the Commons with the Opposition demanding that the Home Secretary defer the introduction of the Bill, intended to penalise airlines and other carriers who brought in people without valid entry documents. Alliance and Labour M.P.s condemned the Government's handling of the cases of 64 Tamils who, Mr. Hurd announced, were to be allowed to remain while the U.K. Immigration Advisory Service examined their applications for asylum. On March 26 Labour moves to restrict the impact of the Bill failed and the Bill was given a third reading by 147–57 votes.

Mr. Callaghan, the former Labour Prime Minister, criticised his party's unilateral nuclear disarmament policies on March 9 during a debate initiated by the S.D.P. on the prospects opened up by Mr. Gorbachev's zero option initiative on intermediate nuclear weapons. Mr. Callaghan asserted that recent Russian concessions on nuclear disarmament were the result of the determination of Britain and other governments to deploy cruise and Pershing missiles.

THE BUDGET

On March 17 the Chancellor of the Exchequer (Mr. Lawson) presented his fourth Budget Speech and said the setting for it was more favourable than it had been for many years. He said 1986 had been dominated by the sudden collapse of the oil price and continued:

"Our own economy was affected not only directly, as a major oil producer and exporter, but also by the pause in world growth as the world economy adjusted to what has been described as the third oil shock. Despite the dislocation, however, the economy has developed in most respects as I foreshadowed a year ago.

"In 1986 as a whole output grew by a further 2½ per cent or so, which compares well with the experience of other industrialised countries. During the 1980s, our growth rate has been the highest of all the major European economies.

"And this greatly improved growth performance has been accompanied by falling inflation, which at 3½ per cent in 1986 reached the lowest figure for almost 20 years. Over the lifetime of this Parliament, inflation has averaged less than five per cent.

"During the first half of last year exports and hence output were affected by the pause in world growth. But since the middle of the year exports have grown strongly.

"Indeed, over the last three months the volume of exports of manufactures was six per cent higher than a year earlier. This pattern was reflected in the rapid growth of manufacturing output in the second half of last year.

ECONOMIC GROWTH

"This resurgence of economic growth, coupled with the special measures we have taken, has brought about a welcome fall in the number of people out of work. Since July, unemployment has fallen by more than 100,000; the largest six-monthly fall since 1973. Though the numbers out of work are still far too high, both youth unemployment and long-term unemployment are now lower than they were a year ago.

"There will be more places on the Enterprise Allowance Scheme, and the number of Jobclubs is to be quadrupled. The new Job Training Scheme will eventually give a quarter of a million people vocational training leading to recognised qualifications.

"But the best hope of all for the unemployed is in the continuing vigour of the economy.

"Since the early months of last year, there has been a further surge in manufacturing productivity. This continues the remarkable improvement in productivity growth achieved by British industry throughout the 1980s. During the 1980s, our annual rate of growth of output per head in manufacturing has been the highest of all the seven major industrial countries.

"The recorded current account of the balance of payments went into deficit in 1986 by around £1 billion. This followed a cumulative current account surplus of some £20 billion between 1979 and 1985. Some deterioration in our current account was inevitable in the face of a £4 billion loss of earnings on oil trade virtually overnight. But the significance of this should not be exaggerated.

"The exchange rate adjustment that followed the fall in the oil price is already contributing to an improved non-oil trade performance. And earnings from the massive stock of net overseas assets we have acquired since 1979 will provide a continuing support to the current account in the years ahead. At well over £100 billion our net overseas assets are now greater than at any time since the war, and second only to those of Japan.

"I expect 1987 to be another year of balanced growth with low inflation. Total output is forecast to rise by three per cent, with exports and investment up by rather more than that. By then we will have registered the longest period of steady growth, at a rate approaching three per cent a year, that the British economy has known since the war.

"Manufacturing industry, in particular, should do well in 1987. And with the non-oil economy set to grow 3½ per cent, there is every prospect of unemployment continuing to fall throughout the year.

"Despite the strong growth in exports, it will inevitably take time for the full effect of the exchange rate adjustment to work through. The current account is thus likely to remain in deficit this year, by some £2½ billion, around half of one per cent of G.D.P.

"Inflation may continue to edge up for a time, perhaps exceeding 4½ per cent by the summer, before falling back to four per cent by the end of the year. While short-term fluctuations are inescapable, it remains the Government's prime objective to keep inflation on an underlying downward trend.

"Given the continuation of present policies in this country, the biggest risk to the excellent prospect I have outlined is that of a downturn in the world economy as a whole. There are still serious imbalances afflicting the three major economies—the U.S.A., Japan and Germany—which, if not handled properly, could lead to a simultaneous downturn in all three.

MONETARY POLICY

Mr. Lawson said the Government would keep in place a sound and prudent financial framework. That meant, as it has done since 1980, the medium-term financial strategy (M.T.F.S.).

"The essential instrument of monetary policy must remain short term interest rates. These will continue to be set in the light of monetary conditions as indicated principally by the growth of narrow and broad money and the behaviour of the exchange rate.

"For narrow money, M0, the target range for next year would be two to six per cent, as foreshadowed in last year's medium term financial strategy. For broad money it was probably wiser to eschew an explicit target. But broad money would continue to be taken into account in assessing monetary conditions, as would the exchange rate.

PUBLIC SECTOR BORROWING

"The final outturn for the public sector borrowing requirement (P.S.B.R.) last year, 1985–86, was just under £6 billion, equivalent to 1½ per cent of G.D.P., the lowest level since 1970–71.

"This year's P.S.B.R. looks like turning out at only £4 billion, or one per cent of G.D.P.: the second successive year of significant undershoot. This successful outcome is chiefly attributable to the remarkable buoyancy of non-oil tax revenues in general and of the Corporation Tax paid by an increasing profitable business sector in particular.

"Looking ahead, there is still uncertainty surrounding oil prices, and I have therefore stuck to the assumption I made last year that the North Sea oil price would average $15 a barrel. But it is clear that the increased flow of non-oil tax revenues, coupled with the prospective further growth of the economy in excess of the growth of public expenditure, puts the public finances in a very strong position.

"Since its inception in 1980, the M.T.F.S. has indicated a steadily declining path for the P.S.B.R. expressed as a percentage of G.D.P. We have now reached what I judge to be its appropriate destination: a P.S.B.R. of one per cent of G.D.P. My aim will be to keep it there over the years ahead. This would maintain a degree of fiscal prudence that, until this year, had been achieved on only two occasions since 1950.

"Accordingly, I have decided to provide for a P.S.B.R. in 1987-88 of £4 billion.

"Inevitably, this greatly diminishes the scope I have this year for reducing the burden of taxation, which remains a major objective of Government policy.

"The British economy is now embarking on its seventh successive year of steady growth, at an average rate of getting on for three per cent a year. During that time the P.S.B.R. even if privatisation proceeds are added back, has been deliberately and steadily reduced from a shade under six per cent of G.D.P. to a little over two per cent.

EXCHANGE CONTROLS

"In 1979, a few months after the present Government had first taken office, my predecessor announced the abolition of exchange controls, which had been in continuous operation ever since the outbreak of war in 1939.

"That bold action has, over the past 7½ years, proved wholly beneficial to the British economy; and other European countries are now moving in the same direction.

"But the Exchange Control Act remains on the Statute book. The time has come to repeal it. The necessary legislation will be contained in this year's Finance Bill.

BUSINESS TAXATION

Mr. Lawson dealt first with taxes on business and said: "The fundamental reform of the Corporation Tax system which I introduced in 1984 came fully into effect last April. The new system has undoubtedly improved the quality of business investment decisions in Britain, and is also encouraging more overseas companies to set up here.

The main rate of Corporation Tax in 1987–88 will be unchanged at 35 per cent.

"I propose that, from today, companies' capital gains be charged at the appropriate Corporation Tax rate, without adjustment, save for the indexation which applies to all post-1982 gains.

"Hitherto, companies have not been allowed to set payments of Advanced Corporation Tax against their liability to tax on capital gains. This means that, where companies distribute capital gains as dividends, the gains are in effect taxed twice, once in the hands of the company and once in the hands of the shareholder. I propose that, under the new system, companies should be able to set A.C.T. payments against tax on capital gains.

"Taken together, these changes should yield £60 million in 1988–89.

"I propose that all companies and building societies should be treated the same way, with all liable to pay Corporation Tax nine months after the end of the accounting period on which the tax is due.

While business and industry as a whole are doing well, the North Sea oil sector has inevitably been hard hit by last year's oil price collapse. The Secretary of State for Energy and I have followed closely the effects on North Sea producers and their suppliers.

"I propose two Petroleum Revenue Tax reliefs. First, as from today companies may elect to have up to 10 per cent of the costs of developing certain new fields set against their Petroleum Revenue Tax liabilities in existing fields, until such time as the income of those new fields exceeds the cost incurred. Second, there will be a new relief against P.R.T. for spending on research into U.K. oil extraction that is not related to any particular field.

"Last year I put the Business Expansion Scheme onto a permanent footing. However, the present rules still produce too much end-year bunching of B.E.S. investments, and hence may crowd out some projects and lead to bad decisions on others. I propose, therefore, to permit someone who invests in the first half of the year to claim part of the relief against his previous year's income. This will make it easier for companies to raise B.E.S. finance throughout the year.

"I have to set the 1988–89 car and fuel benefit scales for those with company cars. The car scale charges still fall well short of the true value of the benefit, and as last year I propose to increase them by 10 per cent. There will be no change in the fuel scales which, as already announced, will also be used for V.A.T. purposes from April 6.

"The past few years have seen a remarkable and welcome growth in the number of small businesses and the self-employed. The Government has done a great deal to lighten the burdens on this vitally important sector of the economy. But I am aware that problems remain, not least in the field of V.A.T.

"Accordingly, I asked Customs and Excise to issue a consultative document last autumn canvassing a number of changes. In the light of the responses to that document, I have four proposals to make.

"My first proposal is that, as from Oct. 1, businesses whose annual turnover is under £250,000, which means more than half of all traders registered for V.A.T., will be able to choose to account for V.A.T. on the basis of cash paid and received.

"In other words, they will have no liability to pay V.A.T. until they themselves have received the money from their customers. In addition to easing the cash flow problems caused by late payers, this system will provide automatic V.A.T. relief for bad debts.

"Second, I propose to give these businesses the option of accounting for V.A.T. on an annual basis. Instead of making quarterly returns, they would make regular payments on account, and then file a single return at the end of the year. This option will be available next year.

"Third, the period within which businesses must apply to be registered for V.A.T. will be extended from 10 to 30 days.

"Fourth, there will be changes to the rules for the special V.A.T. schemes for retailers, and more small and medium-sized businesses will be able to make use of the simpler schemes.

"I believe that the changes I have outlined, and in particular the option to move to cash accounting, will be widely welcomed by the small business community. The cost will be £115 million in 1987–88 and £60 million in 1988–89.

"In addition, I propose to increase the V.A.T. threshold to £21,300, to keep it at the maximum permitted under existing European Community law.

"I have one further measure to help the small businessman, unrelated to V.A.T. I propose to increase the limit for Capital Gains Tax retirement relief by 25 per cent, from £100,000 to £125,000.

"The House will be aware that a business that provides a service that is exempt from V.A.T. cannot in turn deduct input tax on its purchases.

"But where the activities of a business are in part liable to V.A.T. and in part exempt, the existing rules are excessively generous as to the amount of input tax that can be deducted; and this generosity is being exploited on a growing scale.

"The rules must therefore be changed, and the changes, which I proposed to the House last December, will come into effect on April 1. There will be special arrangements to deal with the problem of brewers' tied houses.

"I am also taking this opportunity to exclude a significant number of small businesses from the scope of this provision. The yield from this change will be some £300 million in 1987–88 and £400 million in 1988–89.

"Second, I propose to change the law so that companies in multinational groups which enjoy dual residence will no longer be able to secure tax relief twice on one and the same interest payment. Genuine trading companies will not be affected. This change will take effect on April 1. It will yield £125 million in 1988–89.

"Third, I propose to end the present excessively generous treatment of tax credit relief for foreign withholding tax paid on interest on bank loans. In future, banks will be able to offset this tax credit only against tax on the profit on the relevant loan, and not more widely.

"This will bring our rules broadly into line with those in most other countries. The change will apply from April 1 this year for new loans and from April 1 next year for existing loans. It will yield some £20 million in 1988–89.

"Fourth, the tax treatment of Lloyd's syndicates as it applies to the Reinsurance to Close system is clearly unsatisfactory. I therefore propose to bring it into line with that of provisions for outstanding liabilities made by ordinary insurance companies and, indeed, of comparable provisions made by other financial traders.

"The new rules will first apply to premiums payable for the Lloyd's account which closes on Dec. 31 this year.

"Fifth, I propose to implement the Keith Committee's recommendation that interest should be charged in the limited number of cases where an employer does not apply P.A.Y.E. properly and a formal assessment has to be made to recover the tax. The change will take effect from April next year, and the yield in 1988–89 is estimated at £45 million."

The Chancellor also proposed to introduce a scheme of tax relief broadly along the lines floated in the Green Paper on profit-related pay presented in July 1986 in conjunction with the Employment Secretary and the Trade and Industry Secretary.

"My proposals depart from those in the Green Paper in one important respect. I am doubling the proportion of an employee's profit-related pay that will be tax free from a quarter to a half, and I am also increasing the upper limits on the relief.

TAXATION ON SAVINGS

Turning to the taxation of savings, the Chancellor said a central theme and purpose of the Government's policies was the creation of a genuine popular capitalism. That meant wider home ownership, wider share ownership, and wider pension ownership.

He went on: "Over the past eight years, the Government has actively promoted the first two, and has now embarked on the third.

"We know that 63 per cent of households now own their own homes, 2½ million more than in 1979.

"There are now some 8½ million individual shareholders in this country—amounting to one fifth of total adult population, and roughly three times the number there were in 1979.

"And then there is wider pension ownership. We have already introduced a number of important new measures to that end, and the tax changes I am announcing today will complete the picture.

The cornerstone of the Government's pensions

strategy is the introduction of an entirely new means of provision for retirement, developed by the Secretary of State for Social Services. This is the personal pension, which will be launched at the beginning of next year, three months earlier than planned.

"Personal pensions are an important new dimension of ownership. They will enable employees—if they wish—to opt out of their employers' schemes and make their own arrangements, tailored to fit their own circumstances. And they will provide a new opportunity for the 10 million employees who at present do not belong to an occupational scheme to make provision of their own and, if they so wish, to contract out of S.E.R.P.S.

"In my Budget last year I undertook to bring forward proposals to give personal pensions the same favourable tax treatment as is currently enjoyed by retirement annuities. The necessary legislation will be contained in this year's Finance Bill.

"In addition, to encourage a wider spread of occupational schemes, employers will be able to set up simplified schemes with the minimum of red tape. This will be particularly welcome to many small employers.

"Finally, I have decided to go beyond the proposals set out in the consultative document in one important respect. Starting in October, I propose to allow members of occupational pension schemes to make additional voluntary contributions, with full tax relief, to a separate plan of their own choice instead of, as now, being restricted to plans within their employers' schemes. They will be able to top their pensions up to the present tax approval limits.

"But the generous tax treatment of pensions can be justified only if it is not abused. I propose, therefore, to introduce some limited changes to the present rules to restrict the excessive relief which can be obtained in some circumstances, particularly by a few very highly paid people.

"These will include a stricter definition of final salary and, for all arrangements entered into from today, an upper limit of £150,000 on the maximum permissible tax-free lump sum, coupled with more rigorous rules on how pension and lump-sum benefits can be calculated.

"The cost of the overall pensions package will inevitably depend on take-up, but with that proviso is estimated at £65 million in 1988-99.

"For Friendly Societies, I have decided to replace the existing tax-exempt life insurance limit based on the sum assured with a new limit based on annual premiums. I propose to set this at £100 a year, which will greatly increase the scope for the traditional societies to offer life policies to their members.

"The tax-exempt limits governing sickness and accident benefits which trade unions provide for their members have not been changed since 1982. With effect from today, I propose to increase them to £3,000 for lump sums and £625 for annuities."

On inheritance tax, Mr. Lawson recalled that in his Budget last year he abolished the "pernicious" Capital Transfer Tax on lifetime gifts between individuals.

"This year I propose to extend the same exemption from tax, on similar terms, to gifts involving settled property where there is an interest in possession. This will not, however, apply to discretionary trusts. These changes will be of particular benefit to family businesses and to heritage properties, both of which are often held in trust.

"The abolition of the tax on lifetime giving was of the first importance to family businesses. But I remain conscious that it did little to help the smallest taxable estate, where the family home is often the principal asset.

"I therefore propose to make a substantial increase in the threshold for Inheritance Tax, from £71,000 to £90,000, coupled with a simplification of the rate structure from seven rates to four. As a result of this change, the number of estates liable to Inheritance Tax will be cut by roughly a third. The cost will be £75 million in 1987-88 and £170 million in 1988-89.

Dealing with the taxation of spending, Mr Lawson said he had already announced some important changes in V.A.T. to prevent avoidance and to help the small businessman. "I have no other proposals for major changes in V.A.T. this year.

"However, in the light of representations I have received, I have decided to extend slightly the V.A.T. reliefs I introduced last year for certain aspects of charitable work.

"I propose to relieve charities from V.A.T. on certain welfare vehicles used by hospices to transport the terminally ill; on installing or adapting lavatory or bathroom facilities in charity homes for the disabled; on drugs and chemicals used by a charity in medical research; and on specialised location and identification equipment employed by mountain rescue and first aid services.

"This year's Finance Bill will increase the limit on donations to charity under the new payroll giving scheme, which starts next month, from £100 to £120 a year.

"Next, the excise duties. I propose to maintain the revenue from the taxation of gambling, but to make some readjustment within the total. I therefore propose to increase the gaming machine licence duty by about a quarter, which will restore it in real terms to its 1982 level, when it was last increased; and to offset this by abolishing, from March 29, the tax on on-course betting.

"In my Budget Statement last year, I undertook to introduce a tax differential in favour of unleaded petrol, to offset its higher production costs. I can announce that the differential will be 5p a gallon. This means that the pump price of unleaded petrol should be no higher than that of 4-star leaded petrol.

"In my 1985 Budget I announced the first stage in the process of increasing the rates of Vehicle Excise Duty on farmers' heavy lorries to bring them into line with the use they make of the public roads. I introduced the second stage in last year's Budget and propose to complete the process this year. I also propose to increase the rates of duty on trade licences and to rationalise the taxation of recovery vehicles.

"I have no further changes to propose this year in the rates of excise duty."

On income tax, the Chancellor said: "For 1987-88 I propose to raise all the main thresholds and allowances by the statutory indexation factor of 3·7 per cent, rounded up. Thus the single person's allowance will rise by £90 to £2,425 and the married man's allowance by £140 to £3,795. The single age allowance will rise by £110 to £2,960 and the married age allowance by £170 to £4,675. The age allowance income limit becomes £9,800. I propose to raise the first 40 per cent higher rate threshold by £700 to £17,900, in line with statutory indexation; but the threshold for the 45 per cent rate will go up by only £200 to £20,400. The other higher rate thresholds will remain unchanged.

"I propose to give an additional increase in the age allowance for those aged 80 or over. For them, the increase will be double the amount due under statutory indexation, so that, for the very elderly, the single age allowance will rise by £220 to £3,070 and the married age allowance by £340 to £4,845.

"Around 400,000 taxpayers will benefit from this new measure, and up to 25,000 of them will be taken out of income tax altogether.

"The blind person's allowance has remained unchanged since 1981, when it was increased by £180 to its present level of £360. For 1987–88 I propose to increase it by a further £180, to £540.

"In my Budget speech last year I reaffirmed the aim set out by my predecessor in 1979, to reduce the basic rate of income tax to no more than 25 per cent. That remains my firm objective.

However, given my decision to use the greater part of the fiscal scope I now have to reduce the P.S.B.R., that goal cannot be achieved in this Budget.

"I can, however, take a further step towards it, as I did last year. I am therefore reducing the basic rate of income tax by twopence, to 27 per cent. This reduction, which will benefit every taxpayer in the land, will be worth more than £3 a week to a man on average earnings.

"There will, of course, be a consequential reduction in the rate of Advance Corporation Tax, and—as last year—I also propose a corresponding cut in the small companies' rate of Corporation Tax from 29 per cent to 27 per cent. Taken together with the income tax change, this will mean a significant reduction in the tax burden on small businesses, which are so important for future growth and jobs.

"The income tax changes I have just announced will take effect under P.A.Y.E. on the first pay day after 17 May. They will cost a little more than £2 billion in 1987–88 over and above the cost of statutory indexation.

"The total cost of all the measures in this year's Budget, again on an indexed basis, is a little over £2¼ billion.

Mr. Lawson concluded: "This is a Budget built on success, and a Budget for success."

The Debate on the Budget

Mr. Kinnock, the Opposition leader, described it as a "bribes Budget" which had "little to do with the general good and everything to do with the General Election". He said that instead of across-the-board tax cuts, the Chancellor should have been using these funds to combat unemployment, mitigate poverty, stimulate investment, build houses, develop industry, invest in education and encourage and improve training and research. Mr. Bruce, the Alliance employment spokesman, said the Budget was defending the inequality aggravated by eight years of Tory rule. There was nothing in it for the unemployed, the poor, the low-paid, for manufacturing industry or the regions. On March 23 at the end of a four days' debate, the Budget proposals were approved by 351–202 votes.

Protests were made in the Commons on March 25 at Japanese goods being able to flood into the U.K. while British goods were kept out of Japan, and M.P.s urged the Government to take retaliatory moves. Mr. Clark, Trade and Industry Minister, explained that Britain was constrained in taking action by a whole range of international treaties but he held out some hope of early retaliatory action in the field of financial services.

Supporters of licensing law reform obtained a second reading in the Commons on March 27 for the Licensing (Amendment) Bill, a private member's measure which sought to let public houses open for up to 12 hours between 10.30 a.m. and 11.30 p.m. Mondays to Saturdays. Other private members' legislation to make progress that day was the Aids (Control) Bill, which was given an unopposed third reading. A Bill extending the hours of Saturday night sessions of gambling casinos also completed its passage and another private member's measure, the

Agricultural Training Board Bill, passed through all its remaining stages.

An unopposed second reading was given in the Commons on March 30 to the Landlord and Tenant (No. 2) Bill which provides greater rights for some 500,000 people living in privately-owned flats. It was based on the recommendations of the Nugee Committee and followed complaints about the management of privately-owned blocks of flats and particularly mansion blocks.

Death Penalty Debate

On April 1 Sir Ian Percival, a former Solicitor-General, proposed that capital punishment be restored for particularly evil murders, but only when the jury was unanimous in its verdict. As always with death penalty debates there were high emotions, and powerful speeches against restoration were made by the Home Secretary (Mr. Hurd), Mr. Heath, and Mr. Jenkins. The Commons rejected the move for restoration by 342 votes to 230, on a free vote during consideration of the Criminal Justice Bill, which later received an unopposed third reading.

A private member's Bill introduced by Mr. Howarth to increase the scope of the 1959 Obscene Publications Act and extend it to broadcasting, was given a second reading on April 3 by 160 votes to 23, after receiving support from Mr. Mellor, Minister of State, Home Office.

A private member's measure, the Animals (Penalties) Bill, which doubled penalties for the organisation of dog fights, was given an unopposed third reading in the Commons on April 24. The Bill also dealt with cock fights.

Mr. King, Northern Ireland Secretary, made clear in the Commons on April 27 that stronger anti-terrorist measures were being considered following the increase in I.R.A. violence and the murder of Lord Justice Gibson and his wife. There were demands from both sides of the House for more powers for the security forces because of the worsening position, and the Ulster Unionists even broke their voluntary exile from the House to be present for the Secretary of State's statement, intervening to urge a debate on the situation. The debate took place on May 6 when Mr. King announced that the full-time reserve of the R.U.C. was to be increased and that additional helicopter resources and other support were to be provided by the Defence Secretary. Mr. Molyneaux, leader of the Ulster Unionist party, attacked the announcement, claiming that it showed no sign of a determination to win the battle against the terrorists.

The Lords had a constructive debate on April 29 on the Government's Green Paper *Trade Unions and their Powers* during which Lord Murray of Epping Forest, a former T.U.C. General Secretary, made his first speech as an Opposition Front Bench spokesman. Lord Murray claimed the chance to receive fair treatment at work would be reduced if the Green Paper became law, but Lord Boyd-Carpenter, who initiated the debate, commended the proposal to shift the balance of union power from the leadership to the members. In the Commons that day, the clause in the Finance Bill giving legislative effect to the 2p reduction in the standard rate of income tax announced in the Budget was approved by 257 votes to 156.

Wright Again

Mrs. Thatcher turned down renewed calls on April 28 for an official inquiry into allegations of a "dirty tricks" plot by MI5 to destabilise the Labour Government in 1974. She turned aside efforts to involve her in the controversy over allegations of treasonable activities by the security services, stressing that she had no ministerial responsibility for events which occurred before she became Prime Minister in 1979. The Prime Minister repeated her earlier statement that Mr. Callaghan, the former Prime Minister, had investigated the allegations and issued a statement effectively clearing the security services.

On May 6 Labour M.P.s again challenged Mrs Thatcher's refusal to institute a new inquiry into these allegations, but the Prime Minister said the Director General of the Security Service had conducted a thorough investigation and had given her his personal assurance that the stories were false. Detailed inquiries had confirmed the conclusion there were no grounds for lack of confidence in the competence or impartiality of the security service. Sir James Callaghan, who had called the day before for an inquiry into recent allegations involving the security service and the Wilson Government, said Mrs. Thatcher was missing an opportunity to close an unhappy chapter and to open a fresh one. In the Lords, Lord Glenavon, an ex-deputy Labour Prime Minister, also called for a full inquiry into the alleged activities of the security service against the Wilson Government.

Parliament Dissolved

Pre-election fever at Westminster had been rising for some time and by the beginning of May a hustings atmosphere pervaded proceedings. Mr. Banks was even given leave on May 5 to introduce a private member's Bill making voting compulsory in general elections, with fines for those who failed to do so without good reason. On May 11 it was announced from Downing Street that Parliament would be dissolved and a General Election held on June 11.

The announcement of the General Election date necessitated the rearrangement of business. On May 12 a slimmed down Finance Bill was dealt with in under two hours after negotiations between the parties. On May 13 the passage of the Abolition of Domestic Rates (Scotland) Bill was completed after the Government imposed a guillotine to deal with the Lords' amendments. M.P.s also approved an order to allow the Channel Tunnel Bill to be carried over to the new Parliament. On May 14 M.P.s dealt with the Criminal Justice Bill, but the impending General Election again meant a severe truncation of its contents. As the Government had waived the formal prorogation ceremony, the Speaker remained in the Chamber after the last debate on May 15 to shake hands with retiring M.P.s. On May 18 Parliament was officially dissolved.

THE NEW PARLIAMENT

The newly-elected Members of Parliament met at Westminster on June 17 when Mr. Bernard Weatherill was re-elected Speaker of the House of Commons. The swearing-in of M.P.s took place on June 18 and 19 after which the House adjourned until June 24 when the swearing-in of Members continued. On June 25 the Queen opened the first session of the new Parliament and in her speech, outlining the Government's legislative programme, said: "I look forward with great pleasure to receiving H.M. King Hassan II of Morocco and President Cossiga of Italy on State visits this year. I also look forward to being present on the occasion of the Commonwealth Heads of Government meeting in Canada in October and to visiting Australia in connection with the Bicentenary next year.

My Government will stand fully by their obligations to the Nato Alliance. They will sustain Britain's contribution to Western defence by modernising the independent nuclear deterrent through the introduction of the Trident submarine programme and by increasing the effectiveness of the nation's conventional forces.

My Government will strive for balanced and verifiable measures of arms control. They strongly support the United States' proposals for the elimination of intermediate range nuclear missiles, and 50 per cent reductions in American and Soviet strategic nuclear weapons.

They will strive for a world-wide ban on chemical weapons. They will seek balanced reductions leading to lower levels of conventional forces throughout Europe and the elimination of disparities which threaten Western security.

My Government will work for greater trust and confidence between East and West and for progress, especially on human rights, at the Vienna Review Conference on Security and Co-operation in Europe.

My Government will play a leading role in the development of the European Community while safeguarding Britain's essential national interests. They will work for reform of the Common Agricultural Policy.

They will press for strict controls on Community spending and the opening of the market in financial and other services. They will work with our European partners to defend our trading interests and to press for free trade among all nations.

My Government will sustain the fight against international terrorism and trafficking in drugs.

They will stand by their pledges to the people of the Falkland Islands, while seeking more normal relations with Argentina. They will fulfil their responsibilities to the people of Hong Kong and will continue to co-operate with the Chinese Government to carry out the Sino-British Joint Declaration.

They will play their full part in the United Nations and the Commonwealth. They will seek peaceful and lasting solutions to the most difficult international problems, including those of the Middle East and Southern Africa. They will work for the restoration of an independent and non-aligned Afghanistan.

My Government will maintain their substantial aid programme. They will pursue proposals for international action on debt to help some of the poorest countries of sub-Saharan Africa.

My Government will continue to pursue policies of sound financial management designed further to reduce inflation and to promote enterprise and increased employment.

They will maintain firm control of public expenditure so that it continues to fall as a proportion of national income and permits further reductions in the burden of taxation. Legislation will be brought forward shortly to implement the tax changes proposed in the last Budget but not yet enacted.

My Government will consult the Manpower Services Commission with a view to providing a comprehensive employment service for unemployed people. There will be guaranteed places on the Youth Training Scheme for school leavers under 18 who do not go into employment. Legislation will be introduced to enable benefit to be withheld from those who refuse a place.

My Government will take action to raise standards throughout education and to extend parental choice. Legislation will be introduced to provide for a national curriculum for schools, delegation of school budgets and greater autonomy for schools. It will also reform the structure of education in Inner London, give greater independence to polytechnics and certain other colleges and support the establishment of city technology colleges.

Measures will be brought before you to effect a major reform of housing legislation in England and Wales.

In all these policies, my Government will have special regard to the needs of the inner cities. Action will be taken to encourage investment and to increase enterprise and employment in these areas.

A Bill will be introduced to abolish domestic rates in England and Wales and to make new arrangements for the finance of local government.

Measures will be introduced to promote further competition in the provision of local authorities' services.

Legislation will be introduced to enable the water and sewerage functions of the water authorities in England and Wales to be privatised.

My Government remain determined to tackle the problem of crime. They will carry out their plans to increase the resources available to the police and will establish a national organisation to promote crime prevention. A Bill will be introduced to improve the working of criminal justice.

A Bill will be introduced to reinforce the system of firm but fair immigration control.

Legislation will be introduced to give greater flexibility in licensing hours.

Legislation will be introduced to improve the rights of individual members with respect to their trade unions and to provide further protection against trade unions enforcement of closed shops.

A Bill will be introduced to reform the law of copyright and intellectual property.

My Government will maintain and improve the health and social services and will complete the introduction of the reformed social security system.

My Government will continue to support farming. They will help farmers to diversify and will introduce legislation to encourage the planting of farm woodlands.

Legislation will be introduced to improve the provision of rented housing in Scotland. Measures will be introduced to strengthen schools councils in Scotland and to improve the management of Scottish education.

In Northern Ireland, my Government will seek an agreed basis on which greater responsibility can be devolved to representatives of the people. They will work unremittingly for the defeat of terrorism. They will build upon the constructive relations established with the Republic of Ireland in security and other matters.

Measures will be introduced to assist the merchant shipping industry.

My Government will bring forward legislation to improve the arrangements for legal aid.

Other measures will be laid before you."

Debate on the Queen's Speech

When the debate opened in the Commons on the Queen's Speech, the Opposition leader (Mr. Kinnock) said all the signs were that the Government planned to use its powers malevolently. He claimed that it proposed to introduce fees for State education and referred to the community charge as a "poll tax", a tax on the right to vote. The Prime Minister described the claims of fee-paying as mischievous: no fees would be payable at those schools which decided to opt out of local authority control. Mrs. Thatcher said her third Government would be dedicated to extending freedom and choice, particularly in housing and education. The legislative programme of 17 major Bills was one of the most substantial and radical in recent years. The Liberal leader, Mr. Steel, said the programme would do nothing to heal the country's growing social, economic and political divisions.

The six-day debate on the Queen's Speech covered foreign affairs, devolution for Scotland, law and order, immigration, Britain's cities, local services and education, the use of natural resources and the economy. On the last day, July 2, the Government's programme was approved by 347 to 247 votes. A Labour amendment regretting that the proposals would widen divisions in society and neglect key services and industries was defeated by 353 to 255 votes. An Alliance amendment critical of the so-called "poll tax" and the lack of proposals for Scottish and Welsh assemblies was rejected by 351 to 26 votes. The Lords debated the proposals for four days, their discussions including nuclear disarmament, education, economic affairs and employment.

In the Commons on July 6, the Opposition attempted to censure the Government over the decision to allow Mr. Rupert Murdoch to take over the *Today* newspaper without the bid being referred to the Monopolies and Mergers Commission: the amendment was defeated by 291 to 220 votes. On July 8 the Government secured the second reading of the Finance (No. 2) Bill which contained a number of measures dropped from the earlier Bill because of the General Election.

On July 14 the Lords gave an unopposed second reading to the Criminal Justice Bill, a revised version of the original Bill which restored those sections dropped because of the General Election. Lord Elwyn-Jones, a former Labour Lord Chancellor, was afraid the Bill would do little to deal with the rising rate of crime or with dangerously overcrowded prisons. Lord Hailsham, former Lord Chancellor, endorsed a proposal to permit the Court of Appeal to review criminal sentences. Lord Ackner, a Lord of Appeal, supported a right of appeal for the prosecution.

On July 19 the Home Secretary (Mr. Hurd) told M.P.s of plans to reduce prison overcrowding by earlier release of some criminals. A number of Tories were strongly critical of the proposal to increase remission on sentences of up to 12 months, but Mr. Hurd explained that the greatest reduction in a sentence which could result from the proposal would be two months. He also announced the opening of Rollestone camp in Wiltshire, an expansion of the prison building programme, and the involvement of the private sector in the programme. Mr. Hattersley, Shadow Home Secretary, supported the increase in remission.

There was a late-night debate on July 20, continuing into the early hours of July 21, on Members' salaries and allowances at the end of which M.P.s approved by 407 votes to 34 a pay rise for themselves of 22 per cent. A Liberal move to cut the award to M.P.s with jobs outside the Commons was defeated by 275–65. A proposal to increase secretarial and research allowances was approved by 241 to 198 votes. In future M.P.s' salaries will be linked to a senior civil service grade and will be adjusted automatically.

The Environment Secretary (Mr. Ridley) announced in the Commons on July 23 the rate support grant settlement for England. He said that current expenditure provision for 1988–89 would be set at £27·538 billion with the Exchequer grant towards local authority spending rising to £13·775 billion, a £750 million (5·75 per cent.) increase over the 1987–88 amount. On July 24 the Transport Secretary (Mr. Channon) made a statement to M.P.s on the report of the inquiry into the loss of the *Herald of Free Enterprise*. He promised urgent action on the major recommendations of Mr. Justice Sheen's inquiry and announced immediate consultations to make mandatory the fitting of indicator lights and closed circuit television to enable the position of doors to be monitored from the bridge. Members on all sides demanded action for negligence against Townsend Thoresen, the owners of the ferry.

The Lords rose for the summer recess on July 23 and the Commons on July 24.

PUBLIC ACTS OF PARLIAMENT 1986–87

This list of Public Acts commences with five Public Acts which received the Royal Assent before September 1986 and which were mentioned briefly in the last summary. Those Public Acts which follow received the Royal Assent after August 1986. Figures in bold after the name of the Act refer to the chapter number of the Act in the annual *Public and General Acts*. The date stated after each Act is the date on which it came into operation.

Appropriation Act 1986, c. 42 (July 25, 1986) applies a sum out of the Consolidated Fund to the service of the year ending March 31, 1987; appropriates the supplies granted in this session of Parliament; and repeals certain Consolidated Fund and Appropriation Acts.

Insolvency Act 1986, c. 45 (Dec. 15, 1986) consolidates the enactments relating to company insolvency, and winding up for both solvent and insolvent companies and unregistered companies; enactments relating to the insolvency and bankruptcy of individuals; and other enactments bearing on those matters. The Act also deals with the functions and qualifications of insolvency practitioners and the avoidance of certain transactions at an undervalue including those which are undertaken with the objective of defrauding creditors.

Company Directors Disqualification Act 1986, c. 46 (Dec. 15, 1986) consolidates certain enactments relating to the disqualification of persons being directors of companies and from being otherwise concerned with a company's affairs.

Legal Aid (Scotland) Act 1986, c. 47 (various dates). This Act gives effect to most of the proposals in a consultation paper "Legal Aid in Scotland", transferring responsibility for the provision of legal aid in Scotland from the Law Society of Scotland to the Scottish Legal Aid Board set up by this Act. It also establishes the Scottish Legal Aid Fund and makes new provision in connection with the availability of criminal legal aid in Scotland; and for connected purposes.

Social Security Act 1986, c. 50 (various dates) makes provisions in relation to personal pension schemes and amends the law relating to social security, occupational pension schemes and the provision of refreshments for school pupils. For example, additional state pensions are to be based on lifetime average earnings rather than the best twenty years and it will be possible to contract out personal pension schemes in the same way as occupational pension schemes. The Act also abolishes maternity pay under the Employment Protection (Consolidation) Act 1978 and provides for the winding up of the Maternity Pay Fund. It also provides for connected purposes.

Rate Support Grants Act 1986, c. 54 (Oct. 21, 1986) validates certain block grant determinations already approved by the House of Commons; and clarifies and amends the law relating to Rate Support Grants.

Family Law Act 1986, c. 55 (various dates) gives effect to the recommendations of the Law Commission and the Scottish Law Commission in their joint report "Custody of Children—Jurisdiction and Enforcement within the United Kingdom" by, *inter alia*, amending the law relating to the jurisdiction of the Courts in the U.K. to make orders with regard to custody of the children by providing for the recognition and enforcement of such orders throughout the U.K. The Act also amends the law relating to the recognition of divorces, annulments and legal separations. Further, it abolishes the right to petition for jactitation of marriage and provides for various other matters relating to the family.

Parliamentary Constituencies Act 1986, c. 56 (Feb. 7, 1987) consolidates the House of Commons (Redistribution of Seats) Acts 1949 to 1979 and certain related enactments.

Public Trustee and Administration of Funds Act 1986, c. 57 (Jan. 2, 1987) makes provision with respect to certain functions of the Public Trustee, the Accountant General of the Supreme Court and the Court of Protection as regards the management, protection and administration of the funds and other property and, if under disability, the affairs of private persons; and as to the investment expenses of the National Debt Commissioners.

European Communities (Amendment) Act 1986, c. 58 (Jan. 1, 1987) makes the necessary legislative changes to enable the U.K. to comply with the obligations imposed by the Single European Act signed at Luxembourg and the Hague on Feb. 17 and Feb. 28, 1986. *Inter alia*, the Act provides that the definition of "the Treaties" and "the Common Treaties" shall be extended and that the Single European Act be drawn up in a single original in the Danish, Dutch, English, French, German, Greek, Irish, Italian, Portuguese and Spanish languages, the text in each of these languages being equally authentic.

Sex Discrimination Act 1986, c. 59 (Feb. 7, 1987) amends the 1975 Act and the Employment Protection (Consolidation) Act 1978 in order to bring them into line with European Community law. For example, the Act makes it unlawful to discriminate against a woman solely on the grounds of her age, such as by dismissing her or refusing promotion because she is nearing sixty. The Act also repeals protective legislation restricting the hours of work for one sex, such as in the baking industry.

Financial Services Act 1986, c. 60 (various dates) regulates the carrying on of investment business; makes related provision with respect to insurance friendly society business; makes new provision with respect to the official listing of securities, offers of unlisted securities, take-over offers and insider dealing; and makes various other provisions with relation to financial services generally. The Act completely overhauls the regulation of investment business.

Education (No. 2) Act 1986, c. 61 (various dates) amends the law relating to eduction; for example, it provides for a number of schools to be grouped under the same all-governing body and for local educational authorities to state their school curriculum policy.

Housing and Planning Act 1986, c. 63 (various dates) makes further provision with respect to housing, planning and local enquiries; provides for financial assistance for the regeneration of urban areas; and for connected purposes. For example, it amends the "right to buy" provision of the Housing Act 1985; introduces simplified planning zones to allow general planning permission to be granted for part of a planning authority area; and introduces a new system of control over hazardous substances.

Public Order Act 1986, c. 64 (various dates) abolishes the common law against offences of riot, rout, unlawful assembly and affray and certain statutory offences relating to public order; creates new offences relating to public order; controls public possessions and assemblies on the stirring up of racial hatred; provides for the exclusion of certain offenders from sporting events and for other provisions relating to public order.

Housing (Scotland) Act 1986, c. 65 (Jan. 7, 1987) amends the Tenants' Rights Etc. (Scotland) Act 1980, the Housing Associations Act 1985 and the Building (Scotland) Act 1959; makes further provision as regards housing in Scotland; and for connected purposes. *Inter alia*, tenants of most housing associations and regional councils are given a right to buy their property.

National Health Service (Amendment) Act 1986, c. 66 (various dates) applies to certain enactments, orders and regulations relating to food and health and safety to certain health service bodies and premises; makes further provision as to pharmaceutical services under the 1977 Act and the 1978 Scottish Act and for the remuneration of persons providing those services and other services relating to health under those Acts; and makes further provision in Scotland relating to securing and advancing the health of disabled persons, the elderly and others; and for connected purposes.

Consolidated Fund (No. 2) Act 1986, c. 67 (Dec. 18, 1986) applies certain sums out of the Consolidated Fund to the service of the years ending on March 31, 1987 and 1988;

Advance Petroleum Revenue Tax Act 1986, c. 68 (Dec. 18, 1986) provides for the repayment of certain amounts of advance petroleum revenue tax.

Teachers' Pay and Conditions Act 1987, c. 1 (March 2, 1987) repeals the Remuneration of Teachers Act 1965 and makes temporary provision with respect to the remuneration and other conditions of employment of school teachers and certain arrangements for settling the remuneration and other conditions of employment of teachers in further education.

Licensing (Restaurant Meals) Act 1987, c. 2 (May 2, 1987) relaxes the daytime restrictions concerning the hours during which intoxicating liquor may be served with meals in restaurants.

Coal Industry Act 1987, c. 3 (ss. 6–8 on May 5, 1987, the remainder on March 5, 1987) changes the name of the N.C.B. to the British Coal Corporation; makes new provision with respect to grants by the Secretary of State to the Corporation and makes provision with respect to coal industry employee organizations, etc. in the management of trusts and superannuation schemes.

Ministry of Defence Police Act 1987, c. 4 (May 5, 1987) makes fresh provision for the Ministry of Defence Police.

Rate Support Grants Act 1987, c. 5 (March 12, 1987) provides further for the calculation of entitlement to block grant under Part VI of the Local Government Planning and Land Act 1980.

Local Government Finance Act 1987, c. 6 (March 12, 1987) validates things done by the Secretary of State in connection with, and to make further provision as to, rate support grants and the limitation

or reduction of rates and precepts of local authorities in both Scotland, and England and Wales.

Social Fund (Maternity and Funeral Expenses) Act 1987, c. 7 (March 17, 1987) empowers the Secretary of State to prescribe, under Social Security Act 1986, s. 32(2)(a), amounts, whether in respect of prescribed items or otherwise, to meet maternity and funeral expenses.

Consolidated Fund Act 1987, c. 8 (March 25, 1987) applies certain sums out of the Consolidated Fund to the service of the years ending March 31, 1986 and 1987.

Animals (Scotland) Act 1987, c. 9 (June 9, 1987) makes provision for Scotland with respect to civil liability for injury or damage caused by animals, the detention of straying animals, and the protection of persons or livestock from animals.

Broadcasting Act 1987, c. 10 (April 9, 1987) alters the maximum period for which programmes may be provided under contracts with the I.B.A.

Gaming (Amendment) Act 1987, c. 11 (day to be appointed) amends the 1968 Act, s. 18, with respect to the hours of gaming (which are extended).

Petroleum Act 1987, c. 12 (various dates) makes provision with respect to the abandonment of offshore installations and submarine pipelines and of safety zones around offshore installations. It makes provision with respect to licences under the Petroleum (Production) Act 1934; amends the law relating to pipelines and repeals Petroleum and Submarine Pipelines Act 1975, ss. 34–39.

Minors' Contracts Act 1987, c. 13 (June 9, 1987) amends the law relating to minors' contracts. For example, a guarantee of a minor's contract (which contract is unenforceable against the minor, or repudiated by him) will not for that reason alone be unenforceable against the guarantor.

Recognition of Trusts Act 1987, c. 14 (day to be appointed) enables the U.K. to ratify the Convention on the Law Applicable to Trusts and on Their Recognition signed on behalf of the U.K. on January 10, 1986.

Reverter of Sites Act 1987, c. 15 (day to be appointed) amends the law with respect to the reverter of sites that have ceased to be used for particular purposes.

Finance Act 1987, c. 16 (May 15, 1987) grants certain duties, alters others and amends the law relating to the National Debt and the public revenue and makes further provision in connection with finance. For example, the Act reduces the basic rate of tax to 27 per cent, increases retirement relief for capital gains tax purposes to £125,000 and abolishes the Exchange Control Act 1947.

Appropriation Act 1987, c. 17 (May 15, 1987) applies a sum out of the Consolidated Fund to the service of the year ending on March 31, 1988; appropriates the supplies granted in this session of Parliament; and repeals certain Consolidated Fund and Appropriation Acts.

Debtors (Scotland) Act 1987, c. 18 (day or days to be appointed) makes new provision with regard to Scotland for an extension of time for payment of debts and amends the law relating to certain diligences; and makes provision with respect to messengers-at-arms and sheriff officers.

Billiards (Abolition of Restrictions) Act 1987, c. 19 (May 15, 1987) abolishes the restrictions by way of licensing or otherwise on the public playing of billiards, bagatelle and similar games and also the related power of entry.

The Chevening Estate Act 1987, c. 20 (day to be appointed) establishes an incorporated board of trustees of the trust contained in the Schedule to the 1959 Act; confers functions on, and transfers property rights and liabilities to, the board; amends the trust instrument; and for connected purposes.

Pilotage Act 1987, c. 21 (day or days to be appointed) makes new provision in respect of pilotage.

Banking Act 1987, c. 22 (various dates) makes new provision for regulating the acceptance of deposits in the course of a business, for protecting depositors and for regulating the use of banking names and descriptions; amends the Consumer Credit Act 1974, s. 187 in relation to arrangements for the electronic transfer of funds; clarifies the powers conferred by the Financial Services Act 1986, s. 183; and for connected purposes.

Register of Sasines (Scotland) Act 1987, c. 23 (July 15, 1987) makes provision as to the methods of keeping the Register of Sasines.

Immigration (Carrier's Liability) Act 1987, c. 24 (retrospective to March 4, 1987) requires carriers to make payments to the Secretary of State in respect of passengers brought by them to the U.K. without proper documents. The Act extends to Northern Ireland and contains a power to extend any of its provisions to the Channel Islands and the Isle of Man.

Crown Proceedings (Armed Forces) Act 1987, c. 25 (May 15, 1987) repeals the Crown Proceedings Act 1947, s. 10 and provides for the revival of that section in certain circumstances.

Housing (Scotland) Act 1987, c. 26 (Aug. 15, 1987) consolidates, with amendments to give effect to recommendations of the Scottish Law Commission, certain enactments relating to housing in Scotland.

Fire Safety and Safety of Places of Sport Act 1987, c. 27 (day or days to be appointed) amends the Fire Precautions Act 1971 and other enactments relating to fire precautions; amends the Safety of Sports Grounds Act 1975 and makes like provision as respects stands at sports grounds; extends, as respects indoor sports premises, and amends, the statutory provisions regulating entertainment licences; and for connected purposes.

Deer Act 1987, c. 28 (July 15, 1987) makes it lawful for deer kept on deer farms in England and Wales to be killed during a close season.

Agricultural Training Board Act 1987, c. 29 (July 15, 1987) makes further provision with respect to the functions of the Agricultural Training Board.

Northern Ireland (Emergency Provisions) Act 1987, c. 30 (various dates) amends the 1978 Act, confers certain rights on persons detained in police custody under or by virtue of the Prevention of Terrorism (Temporary Provisions) Act 1984 and regulates the provisions of security services in Northern Ireland.

Landlord and Tenant Act 1987, c. 31 (day to be appointed) confers on tenants of flats rights with respect to the acquisition by them of their landlord's reversion. *Inter alia*, the Act also makes provision for the tenants to demand the appointment of a manager, for the variation of their long leases and with respect to service charges.

Crossbows Act 1987, c. 32 (various dates) creates offences relating to the sale and letting on hire of crossbows to, and the purchase, hiring and possession of crossbows by, persons under the age of 17.

AIDS (Control) Act 1987, c. 33 (May 15, 1987) makes provision with respect to Acquired Immune Deficiency Syndrome and human immuno-deficiency virus.

Motor Cycle Noise Act 1987, c. 34 (day or days to be appointed) prohibits the supply of motor cycle exhaust systems and silencers likely to result in the emission of excessive noise.

Protection of Animals (Penalties) Act 1987, c. 35 (July 15, 1987) amends the Protection of Animals Act 1911 by increasing penalties for offences against animals imposed under section 1(1) of that Act.

Prescription (Scotland) Act 1987, c. 36 (May 15, 1987) amends Part I of the Prescription and Limitation (Scotland) Act 1973 by extending the definition of "relevant claim" in section 9 to include, *inter alia*, submission of a claim in a liquidation of a company where the winding up commenced on or after Dec. 29, 1986.

Access to Personal Files Act 1987, c. 37 (May 15, 1987) provides access for individuals to information relating to themselves maintained by certain authorities (such as a Housing Act local authority and Scottish Special Housing Commission), and allows individuals to obtain copies of, and require amendments to, such information.

Criminal Justice Act 1987, c. 38 (various dates, some to be appointed) makes further provision for the investigation and trial of fraud.

Parliamentary and Health Service Commissioners Act 1987, c. 39 (July 15, 1987) makes further provision with respect to the Parliamentary Commissioner for Administration and the Health Service Commissioners for England, Wales and Scotland; and provides for the appointment of persons for limited periods to act as the Ombudsman or as a Health Service Commissioner; extends the period within which complaints may be referred to the Health Service Commissioner for England and Wales by a body subject to investigation and makes fresh provision in relation to references of complaints to the Health Service Commissioner for Scotland.

Registered Establishments (Scotland) Act 1987, c. 40 (day or days to be appointed) makes further provision as to the registration of establishments under the Social Work (Scotland) Act 1968 and the Nursing Homes Registration (Scotland) Act 1938; and for connected purposes.

Criminal Justice (Scotland) Act 1987, c. 41 (day or days to be appointed) makes provision for Scotland as respects the recovery of the proceeds of drug trafficking and makes further provision as regards criminal justice in Scotland. Some sections extend to England and Wales.

Family Law Reform Act 1987, c. 42 (day or days to be appointed) reforms the law relating to the consequences of birth outside marriage; makes further provision with respect to the rights and duties of parents (for example, the right to appoint a guardian) and the determination of parentage, for example, where birth results from artificial insemination by a donor, not the husband. Parts of the Act extend to Scotland and Northern Ireland.

Consumer Protection Act 1987, c. 43 (day or days to be appointed) makes provision with respect to the liability of persons for damage caused by defective products and with respect to the giving of price indications. *Inter alia*, the Consumer Safety Act 1978 and the Consumer Safety (Amendment) Act 1986 are consolidated with amendments and the Trade Descriptions Act 1972 and the Fabrics (Misdescription) Act 1913 are repealed.

Local Government Act 1987, c. 44 (May 15, 1987) amends Part VIII (capital expenditure of local authorities) of the Local Government, Planning and Land Act 1980 and makes further provision about the adjustment of block grant in connection with education.

Parliamentary and Other Pensions Act 1987, c. 45 (day or days to be appointed) provides for the continuance in existence of the Parliamentary Contribution Pension Fund; confers power on the Leader of the House of Commons to make regulations with respect to that Fund and with respect to the application of the assets in that Fund in or towards the provision of pensions; amends Mr. Speaker King's Retirement Act 1971 to provide for the annuity which would have been paid to Una, the late Lady Maybray-King, had she survived Lord Maybray-King, to be paid to his widow, Sheila; and for connected purposes.

Diplomatic and Consular Premises Act 1987, c. 46 (various dates) makes provision as to what land is diplomatic or consular premises; gives the Secretary of State power to vest certain land in himself and imposes on him a duty to sell land vested in him in the exercise of that power; gives the force of law to certain provisions of the Vienna Conventions on Diplomatic Relations and on Consular Relations; and amends the Criminal Law Act 1977.

Abolition of Domestic Rates Etc. (Scotland) Act 1987, c. 47 (day or days to be appointed) abolishes domestic rates in Scotland and provides as to the finance of local government in Scotland (by imposing community charges instead).

Irish Sailors and Soldiers Land Trust Act 1987, c. 48 (day to be appointed) provides for the distribution of the surplus funds of the Irish Sailors and Soldiers Land Trust and makes provision for the winding up and dissolution of the Fund.

Territorial Sea Act 1987, c. 49 (day or days to be appointed) extends the territorial sea adjacent to the British Isles to 12 nautical miles; and for connected purposes.

Appropriation (No. 2) Act 1987, c. 50 (July 23, 1987) applies a sum out of the Consolidated Fund to the service of the year ending March 31, 1988 and appropriates the supplies granted in this session of Parliament.

Finance (No. 2) Act 1987, c. 51 (July 23, 1987) grants certain duties, alters others and amends the law relating to the National Debt and the Public Revenue, and makes further provision in connection with finance. *Inter alia*, the Act brings in provisions dealing with profit-related pay, and personal pension schemes and other provisions which were removed from the Finance Act 1987 in order for it to reach Royal Assent before the General Election.

British Shipbuilders (Borrowing Powers) Act 1987, c. 52 (July 23, 1987) raises the limits imposed by the Aircraft and Shipbuilding Industries Act 1977, s. 11(7) in relation to the finance of British Shipbuilders and its wholly owned subsidiaries.

Channel Tunnel Act 1987, c. 53.

PARLIAMENTARY ASSOCIATIONS

COMMONWEALTH PARLIAMENTARY ASSOCIATION (1911)

The Commonwealth Parliamentary Association consists of 116 branches in the national, state, provincial or territorial parliaments in the countries of the Commonwealth. Commonwealth Parliamentary conferences and general assemblies are held every year in different countries of the Commonwealth.

President (1986–87), Hon. Dato' Shahrir bin Abdul Samad, M.P. (*Malaysia*).

Vice President (1986–87), Senator the Hon. K. W. Sibraa, President of the Senate (*Australia*).

Secretary-General, Dr. the Hon. David Tonkin, 7 Old Palace Yard, S.W.1.

Secretary, United Kingdom Branch, P. Cobb, Westminster Hall, Houses of Parliament, S.W.1.

THE INTER-PARLIAMENTARY UNION (1889)

To facilitate personal contact between Members of all Parliaments in the promotion of representative institutions, peace and international co-operation.

Secretary General, P. Cornillon, Place du Petit-Saconnex, B.P. 99, 1211 Geneva 19, Switzerland.

BRITISH GROUP

Palace of Westminster, SW1

Hon. Presidents, The Lord Chancellor; Mr. Speaker.
President, The Rt. Hon. Margaret Thatcher, M.P.
Chairman, M. Marshall, M.P.
Secretary, Capt. P. J. Shaw, R.N.

RETIRING M.P.s

Of the Members of the last Parliament who did not seek re-election in June 1987, 43 were Conservative M.P.s, 41 Labour M.P.s (including six de-selected by the constituency Labour Party), 2 Liberal M.P.s and 1 Scottish Nationalist.

Leo Abse, *Lab.*, *Torfaen*; Rt. Hon. Ernest Armstrong, *Lab.*, *Durham, N.W.*; Rt. Hon. Sir Humphrey Atkins, *C.*, *Spelthorne*; *Norman Atkinson, *Lab.*, *Tottenham*; Gordon Bagier, *Lab.*, *Sunderland, S*; Rt. Hon. Sir Frederic Bennett, *C.*, *Torbay*; Keith Best, *C.*, *Ynys Môn*; Timothy Brinton, *C.*, *Gravesham*; Hugh Brown, *Lab.*, *Glasgow, Provan*; Robert Brown, *Lab.*, *Newcastle upon Tyne, N.*; Sir Paul Bryan, *C.*, *Boothferry*; Esmond Bulmer, *C.*, *Wyre Forest*; Rt. Hon. Sir Adam Butler, *C.*, *Bosworth*; Rt. Hon. Sir James Callaghan, *Lab.*, *Cardiff, South and Penarth*; Ian Campbell, *Lab.*, *Dumbarton*; Rt. Hon. Mark Carlisle, *C.*, *Warrington, S*; Lewis Carter-Jones, *Lab.*, *Eccles*; Sir Walter Clegg, *C.*, *Wyre*; Eric Cockeram, *C.*, *Ludlow*; *Rt. Hon. Michael Cocks, *Lab.*, *Bristol, S*; Rt. Hon. Don Concannon, *Lab.*, *Mansfield*; Bernard Conlan, *Lab.*, *Gateshead, E.*; James Craigen, *Lab.*, *Glasgow, Maryhill*; Viscount Cranborne, *C.*, *Dorset, S.*; David Crouch, *C.*, *Canterbury*; John Dormand, *Lab.*, *Easington*; Rt. Hon. Sir Edward du Cann, *C.*, *Taunton*; Robert Edwards, *Lab.*, *Wolverhampton, S.E.*; Rt. Hon. Nicholas Edwards, *C.*, *Pembroke*; Raymond Ellis, *Lab.*, *Derbyshire, N.E.*; Sir Reginald Eyre, *C.*, *Birmingham, Hall Green*; *John Forrester, *Lab.*, *Stoke-on-Trent, N.*; Rt. Hon. Reginald Freeson, *Lab.*, *Brent, E.*; Sir Edward Gardner, *C.*, *Fylde*; James Hamilton, *Lab.*, *Motherwell*; Rt. Hon. Walter Harrison, *Lab.*, *Wakefield*; Rt. Hon. Dame Judith Hart, *Lab.*, *Clydesdale*; Rt. Hon. Sir Michael Havers, *C.*, *Wimbledon*; Sir Paul Hawkins, *C.*, *Norfolk, S.W.*; Sir Philip Holland, *C.*, *Gedling*; Mark Hughes, *Lab.*, *Durham, City of*; Rt. Hon. Patrick Jenkin, *C.*, *Wanstead and Woodford*; Rt. Hon. Sir Keith Joseph, *C.*, *Leeds, N.E.*; Sir Anthony Kershaw,

C., *Stroud*; Sir Kenneth Lewis, *C.*, *Stamford and Spalding*; Ronald Lewis, *Lab.*, *Carlisle*; Hugh McCartney, *Lab.*, *Clydebank and Milngavie*; *Michael McGuire, *Lab.*, *Makerfield*; Rt. Hon. Gregor Mackenzie, *Lab.*, *Glasgow, Rutherglen*; Rt. Hon. Roy Mason, *Lab.*, *Barnsley, Central*; Carol Mather, *C.*, *Esher*; Miss Joan Maynard, *Lab.*, *Sheffield, Brightside*; Ian Mikardo, *Lab.*, *Bow and Poplar*; Dr. Maurice Miller, *Lab.*, *East Kilbride*; Sir Peter Mills, *C.*, *Torridge and West Devon*; Christopher Murphy, *C.*, *Welwyn Hatfield*; Tom Normanton, *C.*, *Cheadle*; Rt. Hon. Mrs. Sally Oppenheim, *C.*, *Gloucester*; Sir John Osborn, *C.*, *Sheffield, Hallam*; Sir John Page, *C.*, *Harrow, W.*; George Park, *Lab.*, *Coventry, N.E.*; Laurence Pavitt, *Lab.*, *Brent, S.*; Rt. Hon. Sir Ian Percival, *C.*, *Southport*; Rt. Hon. Reginald Prentice, *C.*, *Daventry*; Rt. Hon. James Prior, *C.*, *Waveney*; Harvey Proctor, *C.*, *Billericay*; Rt. Hon. Francis Pym, *C.*, *Cambridgeshire, S.E.*; Rt. Hon. Peter Rees, *C.*, *Dover*; Rt. Hon. Geoffrey Rippon, *C.*, *Hexham*; *Ernest Roberts, *Lab.*, *Hackney, N. and Stoke Newington*; Stephen Ross, *L/All.*, *Isle of Wight*; John Ryman, *Lab.*, *Blyth Valley*; Rt. Hon. Norman St. John-Stevas, *C.*, *Chelmsford*; Mrs. Renee Short, *Lab.*, *Wolverhampton, N.E.*; Rt. Hon. Donald Stewart, *S.N.P.*, *Western Isles*; Rt. Hon. Peter Thomas, *C.*, *Hendon, S.*; Roger Thomas, *Lab.*, *Carmarthen*; Stanley Thorne, *Lab.*, *Preston*; James Tinn, *Lab.*, *Redcar*; Thomas Torney, *Lab.*, *Bradford, S.*; Sir William van Straubenzee, *C.*, *Wokingham*; Richard Wainwright, *L/All.*, *Colne Valley*; Sir Patrick Wall, *C.*, *Beverley*; John Watson, *C.*, *Skipton and Ripon*; Sir John Wells, *C.*, *Maidstone*; James White, *Lab.*, *Glasgow, Pollok*; *Alec Woodall, *Lab.*, *Hemsworth*.

(* Members de-selected by constituency Labour Party)

Two seats, Kirkcaldy and Lewisham, Deptford, were vacant at the time of the election due to the deaths of Harry Gourlay and Rt. Hon. John Silkin.

DEFEATED MEMBERS

Members of the last House who lost their seats at the General Election were:

Michael Ancram (Earl of Ancram) (*C.*, *Edinburgh S.*); Peter Bruinvels (*C.*, *Leicester E.*); John Corrie (*C.*, *Cunninghame N.*); Eric Deakins (*Lab.*, *Walthamstow*); Alfred Dubs (*Lab.*, *Battersea*); Sir Alexander Fletcher (*C.*, *Edinburgh Central*); Peter Fraser (*C.*, *Angus E.*); Clement Freud (*L/All.*, *Cambridgeshire N.E.*); Roy Galley (*C.*, *Halifax*); Michael Hancock (*SDP/All.*, *Portsmouth S.*); Robert Harvey (*C.*, *Clwyd S.W.*); Warren Hawksley (*C.*, *The Wrekin*); Barry Henderson (*C.*, *Fife N.E.*); Richard Hickmet (*C.*, *Glanford and Scunthorpe*); Michael Hirst (*C.*, *Strathkelvin and Bearsden*); Peter Hubbard-Miles (*C.*, *Bridgend*); Rt. Hon. Roy Jenkins (*SDP/All.*, *Glasgow Hillhead*); Geoffrey Lawler (*C.*, *Bradford N.*); Mrs. Anna McCurley (*C.*, *Renfrew W. and Inverclyde*); Dr. Oonagh McDonald (*Lab.*, *Thurrock*); John MacKay

(*C.*, *Argyll and Bute*); Albert McQuarrie (*C.*, *Banff and Buchan*); Gerald Malone (*C.*, *Aberdeen S.*); Michael Meadowcroft (*L/All.*, *Leeds W.*); Piers Merchant (*C.*, *Newcastle upon Tyne, Central*); Steven Norris (*C.*, *Oxford E.*); Richard Ottaway (*C.*, *Nottingham N.*); Alexander Pollock (*C.*, *Moray*); Rt. Hon. Enoch Powell (*O.U.P.*, *Down S.*); John Powley (*C.*, *Norwich S.*); Nick Raynsford (*Lab.*, *Fulham*); Mark Robinson (*C.*, *Newport W.*); Mrs. Elizabeth Shields (*L/All.*, *Ryedale*); Frederick Silvester (*C.*, *Manchester Withington*); Derek Spencer (*C.*, *Leicester S.*); Stefan Terlezki (*C.*, *Cardiff W.*); Kenneth Weetch (*Lab.*, *Ipswich*); John Whitfield (*C.*, *Dewsbury*); Gordon Wilson (*S.N.P.*, *Dundee E.*); Ian Wrigglesworth (*SDP/All.*, *Stockton S.*).

William Hamilton did not seek re-election in the Fife Central constituency he had previously represented: he did seek election, unsuccessfully, in the South Hams, Devon, constituency.

MAJORITIES IN THE HOUSE OF COMMONS SINCE 1945

Year	Party	Majority	Year	Party	Majority
1945	Labour	146	1970	Conservative	31
1950	Labour	8	1974 (Feb.)	No Majority	
1951	Conservative	16	1974 (Oct.)	Labour	5
1955	Conservative	59	1979	Conservative	43
1959	Conservative	100	1983	Conservative	144
1964	Labour	5	1987	Conservative	102
1966	Labour	99			

CIVIL SERVICE STAFF

Analysis by ministerial responsibility at April 1 in each year

† Full-time equivalents (thousands)

	1980	1981	1982	1983	1984	1985	1986
Total civil and defence departments	704·9	689·6	666·4	648·9	624·0	599·0	594·4
of which Non-industrials	*547·5*	*539·9*	*528·0*	*518·5*	*504·3*	*498·0*	*498·2*
Industrials	*157·4*	*149·7*	*138·4*	*130·4*	*119·7*	*101·0*	*96·2*
Total civil departments	465·1	460·0	449·4	440·0	424·8	425·0	424·9
Agriculture, Fisheries and Food	14·3	13·6	13·1	12·7	12·1	12·1	11·7
Chancellor of the Exchequer's	119·0	114·9	121·0	117·4	112·4	111·9	110·0
Departments:							
Customs and Excise	27·2	26·8	26·2	25·4	25·1	25·4	25·1
Inland Revenue	78·3	75·6	74·0	73·1	69·8	69·8	69·3
Department for National Savings	10·4	10·0	9·1	8·3	8·0	7·8	7·8
Treasury and others	3·1	2·5	11·7	10·6	9·5	8·9	8·8
Education and Science	3·7	3·6	3·5	3·5	2·4	2·4	2·4
Employment	50·7	53·8	58·7	57·9	56·4	54·7	55·7
Energy	1·3	1·2	1·1	1·1	1·1	1·1	1·0
Environment	51·7	47·0	42·1	39·4	36·6	35·8	34·9
Foreign and Commonwealth	11·6	11·4	11·1	11·1	10·0	9·8	9·6
Home	34·1	35·4	34·6	35·1	36·4	36·6	37·5
Industry	9·1	8·8	8·3	7·7	–	–	–
Scotland	13·6	13·6	13·4	13·1	12·8	13·0	12·9
Social Services	98·9	100·1	98·0	96·4	92·6	94·9	94·9
Trade	9·4	9·3	8·9	8·9	–	–	–
Trade and Industry	–	–	–	–	14·7	14·8	14·8
Transport	13·5	13·7	13·0	13·0	14·2	14·4	14·7
Wales	2·5	2·3	2·3	2·2	2·2	2·3	2·3
Other civil departments	31·7	31·3	20·2	20·5	20·9	21·2	21·5
Total Ministry of Defence	239·8	229·6	216·9	208·9	199·2	174·0	169·5

† Part-time employees are counted as half units.

POLICE FORCES

Number

	1979	1980	1981	1982	1983	1984	1985
England and Wales							
Regular police							
Authorised establishment	118,322	118,930	120,008	120,125	120,447	120,679	120,903
Strength:							
Men	102,360	105,563	107,379	108,517	108,519	108,102	107,960
Women...................	9,394	10,355	10,702	10,935	10,995	11,001	11,213
Seconded:							
Men	1,477	1,430	1,424	1,419	1,407	1,388	1,439
Women...................	78	75	70	80	82	82	90
Additional constables:							
Men	114	96	90	89	84	83	79
Women...................	2	1	1	1	2	–	1
Scotland							
Regular police							
Authorised establishment:	13,148	13,187	13,195	13,205	13,261	13,283	13,377
Strength:							
Men	12,280	12,419	12,379	12,433	12,435	12,415	12,455
Women...................	786	771	749	719	713	722	761
Central service:							
Men	56	60	54	55	65	61	69
Women...................	4	5	2	2	2	2	1
Seconded:							
Men	72	69	78	73	68	67	67
Women...................	3	2	5	4	3	3	3
Additional regular police:							
Authorised establishment ..	126	72	67	62	60	88	88
Strength	148	71	66	62	60	88	88
Northern Ireland							
Royal Ulster Constabulary							
Strength:							
Men	5,938	6,224	6,622	7,017	7,328	7,487	7,610
Women...................	676	711	712	701	675	640	649

GOVERNMENT AND PUBLIC OFFICES

All salaries throughout the section were supplied by individual Offices. At the time of going to press, increases in Civil Service salaries had been announced and there is some variation in the figures supplied. Increases in ministerial and M.P.s pay were agreed in July 1987 and come into effect from Jan. 1, 1988. The new salaries are:

Secretaries of State	£34,157
Minister of State (Lords)	£34,688
Minister of State (Commons)	£23,887
Parliamentary Under Secretary (Lords)	£28,688
Parliamentary Under Secretary (Commons)	£17,897

In addition to the ministerial salary, Ministers who are Members of the House of Commons receive a (reduced) parliamentary salary of £16,911 (from Jan. 1, 1988).

The Home Civil Service has adopted a unified pay and grading structure for senior personnel.

Unified Grade	Title
*1	Permanent Secretary.
*1A	Second Permanent Secretary.
*2	Deputy Secretary.
*3	Under Secretary.
4	Chief Scientific Officer B, Professional and Technology Directing A.
5	Assistant Secretary, Deputy Chief Scientific Officer, Professional and Technology Directing B.
6	Senior Principal, Senior Principal Scientific Officer, Professional and Technology Superintending Grade.
7	Principal.

*These grades do not attract London Weighting. London Weighting is currently: Inner zone, £1,465 p.a.; Intermediate zone, £840 p.a.; Outer zone, £615 p.a.

ADVISORY, CONCILIATION AND ARBITRATION SERVICE
11–12 St. James's Square, SW1Y 4LA
[01–210 3600]

The Advisory, Conciliation and Arbitration Service (ACAS) is an independent organisation set up under the Employment Protection Act, 1975, under the management of a Council appointed by the Secretary of State for Employment. The functions of the Service are to provide facilities for conciliation, mediation and arbitration as a means of avoiding and resolving industrial disputes; and to provide advisory services to industry on industrial relations and quality of working life matters.
Chairman, D. B. Smith, C.B.
Chief Conciliation Officer, D. G. Boyd.
Director of Resources and General Policy Branch, E. Norcross.

MINISTRY OF AGRICULTURE, FISHERIES AND FOOD
Whitehall Place, SW1A 2HH†
[01–270 3000]

The Ministry of Agriculture, Fisheries and Food is responsible for administering government policy for agriculture, horticulture and fishing in England and for many food matters in the United Kingdom. Some of the Ministry's responsibilities for animal health and welfare extend to Great Britain. In association with the other Agricultural Departments in the U.K. and the Intervention Board for Agricultural Produce it is responsible for the administration of the E.C.

†Unless otherwise stated, this is the main address of Divisions of the Ministry.

common agricultural and fisheries policies and for various national support schemes. It deals with countryside matters within the responsibilities of the Ministry including agricultural land use and farm woodlands; diversification; pollution; environmental and conservation policy. It administers schemes for the control and eradication of animal and plant diseases and for assistance to capital investment in farm and horticultural businesses and flood defence; it exercises responsibilities relating to applied research and development. The Ministry sponsors the food and drink manufacturing industries and distribution trades. It is concerned with the supply and quality of food, food compositional standards, hygiene, labelling and advertising of food and has certain responsibilities for ensuring public health standards in the manufacture, preparation and distribution of basic foods. The Agricultural Development and Advisory Service (ADAS) is part of the Ministry.

Salary List

Minister	£33,145
Minister of State (Commons)	£22,875
Parliamentary Secretary (Commons)	£16,855
Grade 1	£65,000
Grade 2	£43,500–£45,500
*Grade 3**	£41,000
Grade 3	£34,000–£37,000
Grade 4	£30,344–£31,844
Grade 5	£24,765–£28,215
Grade 6	£18,786–£25,335
Grade 7	£15,030–£20,292

Minister, THE RT. HON. JOHN MACGREGOR, O.B.E., M.P.
  Private Secretary (*G7*), Mrs. S. Stagg.
  Parliamentary Private Secretary, A. Stewart, M.P.
Minister of State, THE RT. HON. JOHN GUMMER, M.P.
  Private Secretary, A. J. Bastian.
Parliamentary Secretary (*Lords*), The Baroness Trumpington.
  Private Secretary, Miss K. J. Williams.
Parliamentary Secretary
  (*Commons*), D. Thompson, M.P.
  Private Secretary, Miss C. J. Bowles.
Parliamentary Clerk Miss B. J. Richards.
Permanent Secretary (*G1*), D. H. Andrews, C.B., C.B.E.
  Private Secretary, W. F. G. Strang.

ESTABLISHMENT DEPARTMENT

Director of Establishments (*G3*), J. W. Hepburn.

Manpower Division
Victory House, 30–34 Kingsway, WC2B 6TU
[01–405 4310]
Head of Division (*G5*), Mrs. A. M. Blackburn.

Establishments (General) Division
Victory House, 30–34 Kingsway, WC2B 6TU
[01–405 4310]
Head of Division (*G5*), Mrs. A. M. Pickering.

Staff Training Branch*
Principal (*G7*), G. F. Buxton.

Welfare Branch
Victory House, 30–34 Kingsway, WC2B 6TU
[01–405 4310]
Chief Welfare Officer (*S.E.O.*), D. J. Jones.

*Units at Great Westminster House, Horseferry Road, SW1P 2AE [01–216 6311] are to be relocated in mid-1988.

Personnel Division
Victory House, 30–34 Kingsway, WC2B 6TU
[01-405 4310]
Head of Division (G5), C. J. A. Barnes.

FINANCE DEPARTMENT

Principal Finance Officer (G3), B. H. B. Dickinson.

Finance Division I*
Head of Division (G5), G. A. Hollis.

Finance Division II*
Head of Division (G5), R. C. McIvor.

Financial Management Team
Head of Division (G5), D. J. Coates.

Audit Division*
Director of Audit (G5), S. T. K. Hester.
Assistant Director of Audit (G6), F. W. Martin.

Purchasing and Supply Unit*
Director (G5), J. J. Frost.

LEGAL DEPARTMENT
55 Whitehall, SW1A 2EY
[01-270 3000]

Legal Adviser and Solicitor (G2), G. J. Jenkins.
Principal Assistant Solicitors (G3), A. E. Munir; J. McElheran.

Legal Division A1
Assistant Solicitor (G5), B. T. Atwood.

Legal Division A2
Assistant Solicitor (G5), A. Yavash.

Legal Division A3
Assistant Solicitor (G5), J. H. Jordan.

Legal Division A4
Assistant Solicitor (G5), J. F. McCleary.

Legal Division B1
Assistant Solicitor (G5), J. E. G. Vaux.

Legal Division B2
Assistant Solicitor (G5), D. J. Pearson.

Legal Division B3
Assistant Solicitor (G5), Miss E. A. Stephens.

Legal Division B4
Assistant Solicitor (G5), Mrs. H. Cornwell-Kelly.

MANAGEMENT SERVICES

Under Secretary (G3), M. Madden.

Computer Services Division
Government Buildings, Epsom Road,
Guildford, Surrey GU1 2LD
[0483 68121]
Head of Division (G5), D. V. Orchard.

Office Services Division
Head of Division (G6), J. E. Nunn, D.F.C.

Management Services Division**
Eagle House, 90–96 Cannon Street, EC4N 6HT
[01-623 4266]
Head of Division (G5), G. B. Hopley.

Information Division
Chief Information Officer (G5), J. Coe.
Chief Press Officer, Mrs. S. Cunningham.
Principal Librarian (G7), T. C. J. Norton.

**Information Technology and Procedures
Division**
Victory House, 30–34 Kingsway, WC2B 6TU
[01-405 4310]
Head of Division (G5), R. J. Wheeler.

CHIEF SCIENTIST'S GROUP

Chief Scientist (Fisheries and Food) (G3), R. N. Crossett, D.phil.*
Chief Scientist (Agriculture and Horticulture) (G3), D. W. F. Shannon, ph.D.*

RESEARCH AND DEVELOPMENT REQUIREMENTS DIVISION*

Head of Division (G5), (vacant).

FOOD SCIENCE DIVISION*

Deputy Chief Scientific Officer (G5), M. E. Knowles, ph.D.

AGRICULTURAL COMMODITIES

Deputy Secretary (G2), D. A. Hadley.

EUROPEAN AND EXTERNAL RELATIONS

Under Secretary (G3), (vacant).

European Community Division I
Head of Division (G5), R. S. Thomas.

European Community Division II
Head of Division (G5), R. E. Melville.

External Relations Division
Head of Division (G5), P. A. Cocking.

External Trade Policy Division
Head of Division (G5), D. P. Hunter.

ARABLE CROPS, PIGS AND POULTRY

Under Secretary (G3), G. E. Myers, C.M.G.

Cereals Division
Head of Division (G5), C. J. Llewelyn.

Sugar, Oils and Fats Division
Head of Division (G5), P. P. Nash.

Pigs, Eggs and Poultry Division
Head of Division (G5), M. Ring.

MEAT

Under Secretary (G3), S. Wentworth.

Beef Division
Head of Division (G5), J. R. Cowan.

Sheep Division
Head of Division (G5), A. R. Burne.

Livestock Subsidies Division
Head of Division (G6), G. Belchamber.

MILK

Under Secretary (G3), P. W. Murphy.

Milk and Milk Products Division I
Head of Division (G5), R. C. Lowson.

Milk and Milk Products Division II
Head of Division (G5), I. C. Redfern.

*Units at Great Westminster House, Horseferry Road, SW1P 2AE [01-216 6311] and **Eagle House are to be relocated in mid-1988.

FISHERIES AND FOOD
Deputy Secretary (G2), W. E. Mason, C.B.

FISHERIES DEPARTMENT*
Fisheries Secretary (G3), C. R. Cann.

Marine Environmental Protection Division
Head of Division (G5), (vacant).

Fisheries Division I
Head of Division (G5), G. W. Noble.

Fisheries Division II
Head of Division (G5), J. C. Edwards.

Fisheries Division III
Head of Division (G5), M. T. Haddon.

Sea Fisheries Inspectorate
Chief Inspector (G6), M. G. Jennings.

Fisheries Research
Director of Fisheries Research and Development for Great Britain (G4), A. Preston.
Deputy Directors of Fisheries Research (G5), H. W. Hill; D. J. Garrod, ph.D.

Fisheries Laboratory
Pakefield Road, Lowestoft, Suffolk NR33 0HT
[0502 62244]

Fisheries Laboratory
Remembrance Avenue, Burnham-on-Crouch,
Essex CM0 8HA
[0621 782658]

Fisheries Experiment Station
Benarth Road, Conwy, Gwynedd LL32 8UB
[049 263 3883]

Fish Diseases Laboratory
The Nothe, Weymouth, Dorset DT4 8UB
[03057 72137]
Officer-in-charge (Principal Scientific Officer) (G7), B. J. Hill, ph.D.

Torry Research Station
P.O. Box 31, 135 Abbey Road,
Aberdeen AB9 8DG
[0224 877071]
Director (G5), G. Hobbs, ph.D.

FOOD, DRINK AND MARKETING POLICY
Under Secretary (G3), D. H. Griffiths.

Food Policy and Exports Promotion Division
Head of Division (G5), B. E. Camp.

Alcoholic Drinks Division
Head of Division (G5), C. R. Bodrell.

Tropical Foods*
Head of Division (G5), F. J. H. Scolles.

Marketing Policy and Potatoes Division*
Head of Division (G5), G. P. McLachlan.

EMERGENCIES, FOOD QUALITY AND PEST CONTROLS*
Under Secretary (G3), Mrs. E. A. J. Attridge.

Standards Division*
Head of Division (G5), C. A. Cockbill.

Emergencies Division
Head of Division (G5), A. Jeffrey Smith.

Pesticides and Infestation Control*
Head of Division (G5), G. M. Trevelyan.

LAND AND RESOURCES
Deputy Secretary (G2), E. J. G. Smith, C.B.

LANDS AND ENVIRONMENTAL AFFAIRS
Under Secretary (G3), J. A. Anderson.*

Rural Structures and Grants Division*
Head of Division (G5), Miss S. E. Brown.

Environmentally Sensitive Areas Task Force
Head of Task Force (G6), B. M. T. White.

Land Use and Tenure Division*
Head of Division (G5), Miss L. J. Neville-Rolfe.

Environmental and Conservation Policy Division*
Head of Division (G5), J. W. Reed, O.B.E.

ANIMAL HEALTH
Under Secretary (G3), A. R. Cruickshank.

Animal Health Division
Government Buildings, Hook Rise South,
Tolworth, Surbiton, Surrey KT6 7NF
[01–337 6611]
Head of Division (G5), J. C. Suich.

Animal Welfare Division
Government Buildings, Hook Rise South,
Tolworth, Surbiton, Surrey KT6 7NF
[01–337 6611]
Head of Division (G5), H. B. Brown.

Animal Medicines Division
Tolworth Tower, Surbiton, Surrey KT6 7DX
[01–399 5191]
Head of Division (G5), K. W. Wilkes.

Meat Hygiene Division
Tolworth Tower, Surbiton, Surrey KT6 7DX
[01–399 5191]
Head of Division (G5), P. M. Boyling.

HORTICULTURE, SEEDS, PLANT HEALTH
AND FLOOD PROTECTION
Under Secretary (G3), G. P. Jupe.

Horticulture Division*
Head of Division (G5), R. E. Mordue.

Plant Variety, Rights Office and Seeds
White House Lane, Huntingdon Road,
Cambridge CB3 0LF
[0223 277151]
Head of Division (G5), J. Harvey.

Plant Health Divison*
Head of Division (G5), Miss E. M. Price.

Flood Defence and Land Sales Division*
Head of Division (G5), R. C. McKinley.

ECONOMICS AND STATISTICS
Under Secretary (G3), C. W. Capstick, C.M.G.

Economics (Farm Business) Division
Senior Economic Adviser (G5), Mrs. S. M. Dickinson.

Economics (International) Division
Senior Economic Adviser (G5), R. W. Irving.

*Units at Great Westminster House, Horseferry
Road, SW1P 2AE [01–216 6311] are to be relocated in
mid-1988.

Economics (Resource Use) Division
55 Whitehall, SW1A 2EY
[01–233 3000]
Senior Economic Adviser (G5), A. P. Power, ph.d.

Statistics (Agricultural Commodities) Division*
Chief Statistician (G5), P. Roberts.

Statistics (Census and Prices) Division
Chief Statistician (G5), D. E. Bradbury.

Economics and Statistics (Food)
Senior Economic Adviser (G5), J. M. Slater, ph.d.

Agricultural Resources Policy Division**
Eagle House, 90/96 Cannon Street, EC4N 6HT
[01–623 4266]
Head of Division (G5), H. R. Neilson.

REGIONAL ADMINISTRATION

Deputy Secretary (G2), E. J. G. Smith, c.b.
Director of Regional Management (G3), R. J. Packer.

Eastern, Block C, Government Buildings, Brooklands Avenue, Cambridge CB2 2DR (0223 358911).— *Chief Regional Officer (G4)*, G. K. Bruce.

Northern, Block 2, Government Buildings, Lawnswood, Leeds LSI6 5PY (0532–611223).—*Chief Regional Officer (G4)*, A. F. Baines.

South Eastern, Block A, Government Offices, Coley Park, Reading RG1 6DT (0734 581222).—*Chief Regional Officer (G4)*, J. A. Bamford.

South Western, Block 3, Government Bldgs., Burghill Road, Westbury-on-Trym, Bristol BS10 6NJ (0272 500000).—*Chief Regional Officer (G4)*, B. F. Shorney.

Midlands and Western, Woodthorne, Wolverhampton WV6 8TQ (0902 754190).—*Chief Regional Officer (G4)*, A. D. Bailey.

AGRICULTURAL DEVELOPMENT AND ADVISORY SERVICE (A.D.A.S.)

Director General of A.D.A.S. and Regional Organisation (G2), Prof. R. L. Bell, ph.d.

Adas Administration

Director of Regional Administration (G3), R. J. Packer.
Chief A.D.A.S. Officer (Wales) (G5), T. M. K. Evans.

Agricultural Development and Advice Division
Head of Division (G5), A. H. Abbott.*

A.D.A.S. Marketing Unit
Head of Unit (G5), D. E. Bawcutt.*

A.D.A.S. Information and Technology Unit
Head of Unit (G5), R. W. Swain.

FARM AND COUNTRYSIDE SERVICE*

Director of F.C.S. (G3), P. Ingram.
Head of Cropping Services (G4), D. J. Fuller.
Head of Livestock Services (G4), J. B. Finney.
Head of Environmental and Land Management Services (G4), B. D. M. Trafford.
Head of Environmental Unit (G5), J. R. Park, ph.d.
Staff Officer (G5), I. M. Tring.

*Units at Great Westminster House, Horseferry Road, SW1P 2AE [01-216 6311] and **Eagle House are to be relocated in mid-1988.

RESEARCH AND DEVELOPMENT SERVICE

Director of R.D.S. (G3), P. J. Bunyan, d.sc., ph.d.*
Deputy Directors of R.D.S. (G4), D. C. Drummond* *(Commercial Funding)*; P. Needham* *(Public Funding)*.
Staff Officer (G5), G. H. Francis.*

Slough Laboratory
London Road, Slough, Berks. SL3 7HJ
[0753–34626]
Director of Slough, Tolworth and Worplesdon Laboratories (G5), P. I. Stanley, ph.d.

Harpenden Laboratory
Hatching Green, Harpenden, Herts. AL5 2BD
[0582–75241]
Director of Harpenden Laboratory (G5), H. J. Gould.

STATE VETERINARY SERVICE
Government Buildings, Hook Rise South,
Tolworth, Surbiton, Surrey KT15 3NB
[01–337 6611]

Chief Veterinary Officer (G3), W. H. G. Rees.
Director of Veterinary Field Services (G3), K. C. Meldrum.

Central Veterinary Laboratory, New Haw,
Weybridge, Surrey KT15 3NB
[09323–41111]
Director of Veterinary Laboratories (G3), W. A. Watson, ph.d.
Staff Officer (G5), J. E. Morris.

Lasswade Veterinary Laboratory,
East of Scotland College of Agriculture,
The Bush Estate, Penicuick,
Midlothian EH26 09N
[031–445 4811]

Cattle Breeding Centre, Shinfield, Reading,
Berks. RG2 9BZ
[0734–883157]

AGRICULTURAL AND FOOD RESEARCH COUNCIL
160 Great Portland Street, W1N 6DT
[01-580 6655]

The Council is an autonomous body established in 1931 as the Agricultural Research Council, adopting its present title in 1983. It is responsible for the organisation and development of agricultural and food research in Great Britain. To this end it directly funds its own institutes and allocates grants to universities and colleges.

The Council is principally financed from the Parliamentary vote of the Department of Education and Science and the Ministry of Agriculture, Fisheries and Food, but is receiving increasing funds from industry and other outside bodies.

The Agricultural and Food Research Service comprises the institutes and units in England, Wales and Scotland which are responsible to the Council. It also encompasses the Scottish Agricultural Research Institutes funded by the Department of Agriculture and Fisheries for Scotland.

Chairman, The Earl of Selborne, k.b.e.
Members, Prof. R. L. Bell; Prof. T. L. Blundell, f.r.s.; Prof. D. Boulter; J. E. Cross; R. N. Crossett; Prof. B. Crossland, c.b.e., f.r.s.; Prof. J. M. M. Cunningham, c.b.e., f.r.s.e.; J. I. Davies; Prof. B. K. Follett, f.r.s.; A. C. Green; L. P. Hamilton; Prof. J. L. Harper, f.r.s.; M. Mackie; J. A. Parry, c.b.e.; G. T. Pryce; B. C. Read, c.b.e.; Dr. D. W. F. Shannon;

Prof. Sir David Smith, F.R.S.; E. J. G. Smith, C.B.;
Prof. E. J. L. Soulsby; Prof. R. Whittenbury.
Assessors, Dr. R. F. Coleman; R. Hall-Williams;
W. H. G. Rees; Prof. W. D. P. Stewart, F.R.S.; Prof.
C. E. Wright.
Acting Secretary (G2), Prof. J. Hearn.
Director of Central Office (G3), B. G. Jamieson, PH.D.
Heads of Divisions (G5), R. Prideaux *(Finance)*; J.
Dickens *(Personnel)*; R. J. Harris *(Science)*.
Policy Group (G5), Dr. J. V. Lake.
Commercial Policy Section (G7), S. M. Lawrie.
Principal Information Officer (G7), M. F. Goodwin.
For institutes and units of the Agricultural and
Food Research Service, *see* Index.

COLLEGE OF ARMS OR HERALDS COLLEGE
Queen Victoria Street, EC4V 4BT
[01–248 2762]

The College of Arms is open Mon.–Fri. 10–4, when
an Officer of Arms is in attendance to deal with
enquiries by the public, though such enquiries may
also be directed to any of the Officers of Arms, either
personally or by letter.

The College is the official repository of the Arms
and pedigrees of English, Northern Irish, and Commonwealth families and their descendants, and its
records include official copies of the records of Ulster
King of Arms, the originals of which remain in
Dublin. The 13 officers of the College specialize in
genealogical and heraldic work for their respective
clients.

Arms have been and still are granted by Letters
Patent from the Kings of Arms under Authority
delegated to them by the Sovereign, such authority
having been expressly conferred on them since at
least the fifteenth century. A right to Arms can only
be established by the registration in the official
records of the College of Arms of a pedigree showing
direct male line descent from an ancestor already
appearing therein as being entitled to Arms, or by
making application through the College of Arms for
a Grant of Arms.
Earl Marshal, His Grace the Duke of Norfolk, K.G.,
G.C.V.O., C.B., C.B.E., M.C.

Kings of Arms

Garter, Sir Colin Cole, K.C.V.O., T.D., F.S.A.
Clarenceux, Sir Anthony Wagner, K.C.B., K.C.V.O.,
F.S.A.
Norroy and Ulster, J. P. B. Brooke-Little, C.V.O., F.S.A.

Heralds

York (and Registrar), C. M. J. F. Swan, C.V.O., PH.D.,
F.S.A.
Chester, D. H. B. Chesshyre, F.S.A.
Windsor, T. D. Mathew.
Richmond, M. Maclagan, F.S.A.
Lancaster, P. L. Gwynn-Jones.
Somerset, T. Woodcock.

Earl Marshal's Secretary, Sir Walter Verco, K.C.V.O.,
Surrey Herald Extraordinary.

Pursuivants

Rouge Dragon, P. L. Dickinson.
Portcullis, P. B. Spurrier.
Bluemantle, T. D. McCarthy.
Rouge Croix, H. E. Paston-Bedingfeld.

COURT OF THE LORD LYON
H.M. New Register House, Edinburgh EH1 3YT
[031–556 7255]

The Scottish Court of Chivalry, including the
genealogical jurisdiction of the *Ri-Sennachie* of
Scotland's Celtic Kings, adjudicates rights to arms
and administration of The Scottish Public Register
of All Arms and Bearings and Public Register of All
Genealogies. The Lord Lyon presides and judicially
establishes rights to existing arms or succession to
Chiefship, or for cadets with scientific "differences"
showing position in clan or family. Pedigrees are also
established by decrees of Lyon Court, and by Letters
Patent. As Royal Commissioner in Armory, he grants
Patents of Arms (which constitute the grantee and
heirs noble in the Noblesse of Scotland) to "virtuous
and well-deserving" Scotsmen, and petitioners (personal or corporate) in Her Majesty's overseas realms
of Scottish connection, and issues birthbrieves.
Lord Lyon King of Arms, Malcolm Rognvald Innes of
Edinight, C.V.O., W.S., F.S.A. *scot.*

Heralds

Marchmont, Maj. D. M. Maitland-Titterton, T.D.,
F.S.A. *scot.*
Albany, J. A. Spens, R.D., W.S.
Rothesay, Sir Crispin Agnew of Lochnaw, Bt.

Pursuivants

Dingwall, C. J. Burnett, F.S.A. *scot.*
Kintyre, J. C. G. George, F.S.A. *scot.*
Unicorn, Alastair Campbell of Ards.

Lyon Clerk and Keeper of Records, Mrs. C. G. W.
Roads, F.S.A. *scot.*
Procurator-Fiscal, I. R. Guild, C.B.E., W.S.
Herald Painter, Mrs. J. Phillips.
Macer, T. C. Gray.

ART GALLERIES, ETC.

OFFICE OF ARTS AND LIBRARIES
Great George Street, SW1P 3AL
[01–270 5866]

The Office of Arts and Libraries, formerly part of
the Department of Education and Science, became a
separate department in 1983. It has general responsibilities for arts policy and its broad objectives are
to assist the provision and development of the
performing and visual arts, to maintain and enhance
the collections of national museums and art galleries,
to help preserve the national heritage and to sustain
and develop national collections of literary and
archive material. It directly funds some 20 bodies
including the Arts Council, the nine national museums and galleries and the British Library. The
Office of Arts and Libraries also has policy responsibilities towards the public library and local museum
services. The Government Art Collection, which is
responsible for the acquisition, maintenance and
display of works of art in major government buildings
in this country and abroad, forms part of the Office of
Arts and Libraries.
Minister for the Arts, The Rt. Hon. Richard Luce, M.P.
  Private Secretary, M. Stark.
  Parliamentary Private Secretary, J. Hanley, M.P.
*Head of the Office of Arts and Libraries (Deputy
Secretary)*, R. W. L. Wilding, C.B.

Arts and Heritage

Assistant Secretary, R. H. Stone.
Principals, P. J. Fallon; Miss M. J. Lamont; D. H. A.
Lodge; Miss C. R. Morrison.

Finance, Establishments and Museums

Assistant Secretary, Mrs. S. D. Brown.
Principals, N. A. Luck; D. M. Mainwood; E. A. Yeo.

Libraries and Information Services

Assistant Secretary, C. C. Leamy.
Principal, A. Poulter.
Library Advisers, P. J. Beauchamp; Miss C. R. Lutyens.

Government Art Collection

Curator, Dr. W. Baron.

ARTS COUNCIL OF GREAT BRITAIN
105 Piccadilly, W1V 0AU
[01-629 9495]

The Arts Council, an independent body established by Royal Charter in 1946, is Great Britain's principal channel for public financial support of the arts. It funds the major arts organizations in England, the Regional Arts Associations and the Scottish and Welsh Arts Councils. It also provides a service of advice, information and help to artists, arts organizations and the general public.

Its aims are to develop and improve the understanding and practice of the arts and to increase their accessibility to the public.

The Council receives a grant-in-aid from the Government, and for the year 1987–88 the amount is £136·4 million.
Chairman, Sir William Rees-Mogg.
Secretary-General, L. Rittner.

ROYAL FINE ART COMMISSION
7 St. James's Square, SW1Y 4JU
[01-839 6537]

Appointed in May, 1924, the Commission is required to advise Departments of State on, and call their attention to, any project or development which might affect national or public amenities.
Chairman, The Lord St. John-Stevas.
Commissioners, The Countess of Airlie, C.V.O.; R. D. Carter, C.B.E.; Miss Elizabeth Chesterton, O.B.E.; Sir Philip Dowson, C.B.E.; Mark Girouard, PH.D.; A. J. Gordon, C.B.E.; The Duke of Grafton, K.G., F.S.A.; M. J. Hopkins; R. MacCormac; P. Nuttgens, C.B.E., PH.D.; Mrs. D. Nutting; Sir David Piper, C.B.E.; Sir Philip Powell, C.H., O.B.E., R.A.; J. Sutherland; Miss W. Taylor; W. Whitfield, C.B.E.; J. Winter, M.B.E.
Secretary (G6), S. Cantacuzino.

ROYAL FINE ART COMMISSION FOR SCOTLAND
9 Atholl Crescent,
Edinburgh EH3 8HA
[031-229 1109]

Chairman, Prof. A. J. Youngson, C.B.E.
Commissioners, Miss K. Borland; J. Boys, F.R.I.B.A.; B. Gasson, O.B.E.; Dr. Deborah Howard, PH.D., F.S.A.; W. K. Mackay; Prof. I. Metzstein; A. Morrocco, R.S.A.; G. Ogilvie-Laing; J. D. Richards, C.B.E.; R. R. Steedman, R.S.A.; Mrs. F. M. E. Walker.
Secretary, C. Prosser.

NATIONAL GALLERY
Trafalgar Square, WC2N 5DN
[01-839 3321]

Hours of opening.—Weekdays 10–6, Sun. 2–6. Closed on Good Friday, Christmas Eve, Christmas Day, Boxing Day, New Year's Day and May Day Bank Holiday.

The National Gallery was founded in 1824, following a Parliamentary grant of £60,000 for the purchase and exhibition of the Angerstein collection of pictures. The present site was first occupied in 1838 and enlarged and improved at various times throughout the years. A substantial extension to the north of the building with a public entrance in Orange Street was opened in 1975. Expenses for 1987–88 are estimated at £7,017,000.

Board of Trustees

Chairman, Hon. J. Rothschild.
Trustees, H.R.H. The Prince of Wales, K.G., P.C., K.T., G.C.B.; Miss B. Riley, C.B.E.; Hon. Sir John Baring, C.V.O.; The Marquess of Dufferin and Ava; Sir Rex Richards, F.R.S., D.Phil.; Mrs. C. Hubbard; M. Cowdy; Sir Nicholas Henderson, G.C.M.G.; R. S. Alexander, Q.C.; F. St. J. Gore.

Officers
Salaries

Grade 3	£41,000
Grade 5	£24,765–£28,215
Grade 6	£18,786–£25,335
Grade 7	£15,030–£20,292

Director (G3), R. N. MacGregor.
Keeper and Deputy Director (G5), A. J. W. Braham, PH.D.
Keeper, Education and Exhibitions (G5), A. J. W. Smith.
Deputy Keepers (G6), Dr. C. P. H. Brown; M. J. Wilson.
Chief Restorer (G5), M. H. Wyld.
Scientific Adviser (G6), Dr. J. S. Mills.
Finance and Establishment (G7), D. C. E. Gunn.

NATIONAL PORTRAIT GALLERY
St. Martin's Place, WC2H 0HE
[01-930 1552]

Open Mon.–Fri. 10–5. Sat. 10–6. Sun. 2–6.

A grant was made in 1856 to form a gallery of the portraits of the most eminent persons in British history. The present building was opened in 1896, £80,000 being contributed to its cost by Mr. W. H. Alexander; an extension erected at the expense of Lord Duveen was opened in 1933.
Chairman, The Lord Kenyon, C.B.E., F.S.A.
Trustees, The Lord President of the Council (*ex officio*); The President of the Royal Academy of Arts (*ex officio*); Prof. Sir Lawrence Gowing, C.B.E.; The Duke of Grafton, K.G., F.S.A.; Sir Oliver Millar, K.C.V.O., F.B.A., F.S.A.; J. Roberts, D.Phil.; Prof. B. R. Morris, D.Phil.; The Rev. Prof. W. O. Chadwick, O.M., K.B.E., F.B.A.; Mrs. S. Crosland; Prof. M. Gowing, C.B.E., F.B.A.; The Marquess of Anglesey, F.S.A; The Lord Rockley; H. Keswick; Prof. N. Lynton; The Lord Sieff of Brimpton, O.B.E.

Director, J. T. Hayes, C.B.E., PH.D., F.S.A £29,680
Keeper and Deputy Director, M. Rogers, D.Phil.
£27,876

TATE GALLERY
Millbank, SW1P 4RG
[01-821 1313]

Hours of opening.—Weekdays 10–5.50. Sun. 2–5.50. Closed on New Year's Day, Good Friday, May Day Holiday, Christmas Eve, Christmas Day and Boxing Day.

The Tate Gallery comprises the National Collections of British painting and 20th century painting and sculpture. Works are displayed at the Gallery as two collections: The British Collection and the

Modern Collection. The Gallery was opened in 1897, the cost of erection (£80,000) being defrayed by Sir Henry Tate, who also contributed the nucleus of the present collection. The Turner Wing, built at the expense of Sir Joseph Duveen was opened in 1920. Lord Duveen defrayed the cost of galleries to contain the collection of modern foreign painting, completed in 1926, and a new sculpture hall, completed in 1937. The latest extension to the Tate Gallery, the Clore Gallery for the Turner Collection, was opened by H.M. The Queen on April 1, 1987. The Tate Gallery Liverpool, sited in the Albert Dock, is due to open in late May 1988. Expenses for 1987–88 are estimated at £6,500,000.

Board of Trustees

Chairman, R. Rogers.
Trustees, The Countess of Airlie, c.v.o.; A. Caro, c.b.e.; G. de Botton; J. Golding; D. Puttnam, c.b.e.; Sir Rex Richards, d.sc., f.r.s.; M. Weinberg; Mrs. C. Hubbard.

Officers
Salaries

Grade 3	£34,000–£37,000
Grade 5	£24,739–£28,215
Grade 6	£18,786–£25,335

Director (*G3*), A. Bowness, c.b.e.
Keeper of the British Collection (*G5*), M. R. F. Butlin
Keeper of the Modern Collection (*G5*), R. Morphet
Keeper of Museum Services (*G5*), M. G. Compton
Keeper of Conservation (*G5*), The Viscount Dunluce
Curator of the Turner Collection (*G6*), A. Wilton
Deputy Keepers (*G6*), L. A. Parris; Miss R. Rattenbury; R. Perry.
Head of Administration (*G6*), R. Aylward.

WALLACE COLLECTION
Hertford House, Manchester Square, W1M 6BN
[01–935 0687]

Admission free. Open on weekdays 10–5: Sun. 2–5. Closed on Good Friday, December 24–26, January 1 and May Day.

The Wallace Collection was bequeathed to the nation by the widow of Sir Richard Wallace, Bt., on her death in 1897, and Hertford House was subsequently acquired by the Government. The collection includes pictures, drawings and miniatures, French furniture, sculpture, bronzes, porcelain, armour and miscellaneous *objets d'art*. The total net expenses were estimated at £939,000 in 1987–88.
Director, J. A. S. Ingamells.
Assistants to Director, P. Hughes; Miss R. J. Savill.
Establishment and Finance Officer, A. W. Houldershaw.

NATIONAL GALLERIES OF SCOTLAND
The Mound, Edinburgh EH2 2EL
[031–556 8921]

Chairman of the Trustees, R. W. Begg, c.b.e.
Trustees, Prof. H. A. D. Miles; The Countess of Rosebery; J. Packer, o.b.e.; A. M. Grossart; A. R. Cole-Hamilton; Mrs. L. W. Gibbs; Sir Norman Macfarlane; J. D. Richards, c.b.e.

Salaries

Director	£27,065
Keeper	£18,786–£25,335
Assistant Keeper/Curator	£14,927–£20,292

Director, T. Clifford.
Keeper of Conservation, J. P. Dick.

Keeper of Information (*Asst. Keeper*), R. Dalrymple.
Secretary (*Asst. Keeper*), W. J. Sinclair.
Comprising:

National Gallery of Scotland
The Mound, Edinburgh
[031–556 8921]

Open: Mon.–Sat. 10–5; Sun. 2–5; Closed December 25, 26, 27, 31; January 1, 2, 3.
Keeper, M. Clarke.
Assistant Keepers, Miss L. M. Errington, ph.d.; (vacant).
Keeper of Prints and Drawings, H. Macandrew.

Scottish National Portrait Gallery
1 Queen Street, Edinburgh
[031–556 8921]

Hours—as for National Gallery of Scotland.
Keeper, D. Thomson, ph.d.
Assistant Keepers, Miss R. K. Marshall, ph.d.; J. E. Holloway.
Curator of Photography, Miss S. F. Stevenson.

Scottish National Gallery of Modern Art
Belford Road, Edinburgh EH4 3DR
[031 556 8921]

Hours—as for National Gallery of Scotland.
Keeper, R. Calvocoressi.
Assistant Keeper, K. S. Hartley.

(For other British Art Galleries, *see* Index.)

UNITED KINGDOM ATOMIC ENERGY AUTHORITY
11 Charles II Street, SW1Y 4QP
[01–930 5454]

Established by the Atomic Energy Authority Act, 1954, the Authority is responsible for providing research and development support for the U.K. nuclear power programme. It also undertakes work on other civil applications of nuclear energy and on various projects outside the nuclear field on repayment. Since April 1986 UKAEA has been required by the Government on a quasi-commercial footing. The UKAEA has eight laboratories and a London headquarters employing some 14,000 people.
Chairman, J. G. Collier £65,000
Members (*Full-time*), Dr. T. N. Marsham, c.b.e., f.r.s.; Dr. G. G. E. Low; R. N. Simeone, c.b.e.
(*Part-time*) *Prof. Sir Peter Hirsch, f.r.s.; J. Bullock; *R. E. J. Roberts, c.b.e.; *Sir Alan Cottrell, f.r.s.; M. J. B. Parker; R. Sanderson, o.b.e. (*each* £5,400).
Secretary, M. A. W. Baker.
* Appointment ends late 1987.

THE BANK OF ENGLAND
Threadneedle Street, EC2R 8AH

The Bank of England was incorporated in 1694 under Royal Charter. It is the banker of the Government on whose behalf it manages the Note Issue and the National Debt. As central reserve bank of the country, the Bank keeps the accounts of British banks, who maintain with it a proportion of their cash resources, and of most overseas central banks.
Governor, Rt. Hon. Robin Leigh-Pemberton.
Deputy Governor, Sir George Blunden.
Directors, Dr. D. V. Atterton, c.b.e.; Hon. Sir John Baring, c.v.o.; Sir Adrian Cadbury; F. B. Corby; Sir Colin Corness; R. D. Galpin; E. A. J. George; Sir Robert Haslam; Sir Martin Jacomb; Sir Hector

Laing; G. H. Laird; A. D. Loehnis; Sir David Scholey, C.B.E.; D. A. Walker; D. V. Weyer, C.B.E.; Sir Leslie Young, C.B.E.

Associate Director, Banking Supervision, W. P. Cooke.
Adviser to the Governor, Economics, J. S. Flemming.
Assistant Directors, A. L. Coleby; B. Quinn; I. Plenderleith; R. A. Barnes.
Chief Adviser, Industrial Finance, J. P. Charkham.
Chief of Banking Department (Chief Cashier), D. H. F. Somerset.
Chief Registrar, J. G. Drake.
General Manager, Printing Works, A. W. Jarvis.
Secretary, G. A. Croughton.
Head of Information Division, P. J. Warland.
The Auditor, L. G. Lloyd.

BOUNDARY COMMISSIONS

The Commissions are constituted under the Parliamentary Constituencies Act, 1986. The Speaker of the House of Commons is ex-officio chairman of all four Commissions in the United Kingdom. Each of the four Commissions is required by law to keep the parliamentary constituencies in their part of the United Kingdom under review. Each of the three Commissions in Great Britain is required by law to keep the European Assembly constituencies in their part of Great Britain under review.

England
St. Catherines House, 10 Kingsway, WC2B 6JP
[01–242 0262]

Deputy Chairman, The Hon. Mr. Justice Knox.
Joint Secretaries, R. McLeod; Mrs. M. E. Moxon.

Wales
St. Catherines House, 10 Kingsway, WC2B 6JP
[01–242 0262]

Deputy Chairman, The Hon. Mr. Justice Kenneth Jones.
Joint Secretaries, R. McLeod; Mrs. M. E. Moxon.

Scotland
St. Andrew's House, Edinburgh EH1 3DE
[031–556 8400]

Deputy Chairman, The Hon. Lord Davidson.
Secretary, A. Simmen.

Northern Ireland
c/o Northern Ireland Office,
Whitehall, SW1A 2AZ
[01–210 6569]

Deputy Chairman, The Hon. Mr. Justice Hutton.
Secretary, G. D. Fergusson.

BRITISH BROADCASTING CORPORATION
Broadcasting House, W1A 1AA
[01–580 4468]

The B.B.C. was incorporated under Royal Charter as successor to the British Broadcasting Company, Ltd., whose licence expired Dec. 31, 1926. Its present Charter came into force Aug. 1, 1981, for 15 years. The Chairman, Vice-Chairman and other Governors are appointed by the Queen in Council. The B.B.C. is financed by revenue from receiving licences for the Home services and by grant-in-aid from Parliament for the External services. The total number of receiving licences in the U.K. at March 31, 1987 was 18,953,161, of which 2,414,496 were for monochrome receivers and 16,538,665 for colour receivers. Annual television fees are: monochrome £18; colour £58.

Television licence fees are to be index-linked from April 1, 1988.

Board of Governors
(as at Aug. 1, 1987)

Chairman, M. Hussey. £33,820
Vice-Chairman, The Lord Barnett, P.C. £8,670
Governors, W. Peat, C.B.E. *(Scotland)*; J. Kincade, PH.D. *(N. Ireland)*; J. Parry *(Wales)* .. *(each)*£8,670
Miss J. Barrow, O.B.E.; M. McAlpine; The Lady Parkes; Sir Curtis Keeble .... *(each)* £4,340

Board of Management
(as at Aug. 1, 1987)

Director-General, M. Checkland.
Deputy Director-General, J. Birt.
Managing Directors, W. F. Cotton, O.B.E. *(Television)*; B. Wenham *(Radio)*; J. Tusa *(External Broadcasting)*; G. Stanley Jones *(Regional Broadcasting)*.
Assistant Director-General, A. Protheroe, M.B.E., T.D.
Directors, F. Fitzpatrick *(Finance)*; M. Grade *(Programmes, Television)*; D. Hatch *(Programmes, Network Radio)*; C. Martin *(Personnel)*; W. Denny *(Engineering)*.

Other Senior Staff

Deputy Managing Director, External Broadcasting, C. Bell.
Deputy Director of Engineering, C. Sandbank.
Deputy Director of Personnel, R. Chase.
Deputy Director, Resources Radio, D. Thomas.
Deputy Director, Planning and Resource Management, Television, C. Taylor.
Secretary, Patricia Hodgson.
Chief Assistant to Director-General, Margaret Douglas.
Legal Adviser, A. Jennings.
Controller BBC-2, G. McDonald.
Controller Radio 1, J. Beerling.
Controller Radio 2, B. Marriott.
Controller Radio 3, J. Drummond.
Controller Radio 4, M. Green.
Controller, Scotland, P. Chalmers.
Controller, Wales, G. Price.
Controller, N. Ireland, J. Hawthorne, C.B.E.
Controller, Editorial Policy, J. Wilson.
Controller Information Services, M. Bunce.
Chief Executive, B.B.C. Enterprises, J. Arnold-Baker.

BRITISH COAL CORPORATION
Hobart House, Grosvenor Place, SW1X 7AE
[01–235 2020]

The National Coal Board was constituted in 1946. It took over the mines on January 1, 1947. In 1986, the name was changed to the British Coal Corporation.
Chairman, Sir Robert Haslam.
Deputy Chairman, Sir Kenneth Couzens, K.C.B.
Members, M. H. Butler; M. J. Edwards, C.B.E.; K. Moses; J. H. Northard, O.B.E.
Members (part-time), Sir Melvyn Rosser; D. K. Newbigging, O.B.E.; C. Barker; Dr. D. V. Atterton, C.B.E.; T. J. Parker.
Secretary, D. G. Brandrick, C.B.E.

THE BRITISH COUNCIL
10 Spring Gardens, SW1A 2BN
[01–930 8466]

The British Council was established in 1934 and incorporated by Royal Charter in 1940. Its principal aims and functions are: to promote a wider knowledge

of Britain and the English language abroad, to develop closer cultural relations between Britain and other countries and to administer educational aid programmes. The Council receives grants from the Foreign and Commonwealth Office and the Overseas Development Administration (estimated for 1987–88 at £97,700,000); acts as the agent of the Overseas Development Administration in specific aid programmes (totalling £96,000,000); as the agent of the Foreign and Commonwealth Office in specific student support programmes (£8,600,000); and gains, from sources other than the British taxpayer, earnings from English language teaching, paid educational services, and acting for international organizations, including U.N. agencies (£57,600,000).
Chairman, Sir David Orr, M.C.
Director-General, R. Francis £59,500

BRITISH RAILWAYS BOARD
Euston Square, P.O. Box 100, NW1 2DZ
[01–262 3232]

The British Railways Board came into being on Jan. 1, 1963 under the terms of the Transport Act, 1962. The Board became responsible for the provision of railway services in Great Britain and for catering and other services formerly carried on by the British Transport Commission.
Chairman, Sir Robert Reid, C.B.E. £78,600
Vice-Chairmen, D. Fowler, C.B.E.; G. Myers, C.B.E.
Members, H. G. DeVille, C.B.E.*; S. D. Jenkins*; D. P. Hornby*; A. J. G. Sheppard*; R. W. Tookey, C.B.E.*; Ms. A. Bliss*; Miss K. T. Kantor*; D. L. Davies; D. D. Kirby, J. J. O'Brien (*Joint Managing Directors, Railways*).
    * Part-time members, paid *pro rata*.

BRITISH SHIPBUILDERS
Headquarters: Benton House, 136 Sandyford Road, Newcastle upon Tyne, NE2 1QE
[091 2326772]

Established under the Aircraft and Shipbuilding Industries Act of 1977, British Shipbuilders is a national corporation responsible for all publicly-owned shipyards, etc. in England and Scotland.
Chairman and Chief Executive, J. Lister.
Corporation Secretary, M. Day.

B.S.I. (BRITISH STANDARDS INSTITUTION)
2 Park Street, W1A 2BS
[Enquiry Section: B.S.I., Linford Wood, Milton Keynes, MK14 6LE. Tel. 0908 221166]

B.S.I. (the British Standards Institution) is the recognized authority in the U.K. for the preparation and publication of national standards for industrial and consumer products. In consultation with the interests concerned, B.S.I. prepares standards relating to nearly every sector of the nation's industry and trade.

British Standards are issued for voluntary adoption though in a number of cases compliance with a British Standard is required by legislation. B.S.I. operates certification schemes under which industrial and consumer products are certified as complying with the relevant British Standard and manufacturers satisfying the requirements of such schemes may use the Institution's certification trade marks known as the "Kitemark" and the "Safety Mark".

B.S.I. is financed by voluntary subscriptions, an annual Government grant, the sale of its publications and fees for testing and certification. There are more than 20,000 subscribing members of B.S.I.
Director General, Dr. I. Dunstan.

BRITISH STEEL CORPORATION
9 Albert Embankment, SE1 7SN
[01–735 7654]

The British Steel Corporation was established under the Iron and Steel Act 1967 which vested in the Corporation the shares of the fourteen major steel companies. The Corporation's main duty is to supply such iron and steel products as it thinks fit in sufficient quantities and at such prices as will meet reasonable demand.
Chairman, R. Scholey, C.B.E. £100,000
Deputy Chairman (*part-time*), Sir Ronald Halstead, C.B.E.
Chief Executive, M. E. Llowarch.
Members (*full-time*), Dr. F. Fitzgerald; Dr. D. Grieves; G. H. Sambrook, C.B.E.; J. G. Stewart.
Members (*part-time*), J. D. Birkin; J. F. Eccles, C.B.E.; The Lord Gregson; S. J. Gross, C.M.G.; H. L. I. Runciman; A. E. Wheatley.
Secretary, T. J. MacDonald.

BRITISH TECHNOLOGY GROUP
101 Newington Causeway, SE1 6BU
[01–403 6666]

British Technology Group (B.T.G.) is a self-financing public organization appointed by the Government to license new scientific and engineering products and processes discovered through research at U.K. universities, polytechnics, research councils and Government research establishments. B.T.G. provides finance where further development is needed before inventions can be licensed to industry. B.T.G. can also offer finance to companies that want to develop new products and processes based on their own technology.
Chairman, C. Barker.
Chief Executive, I. A. Harvey.

BRITISH TOURIST AUTHORITY
Thames Tower, Black's Road, W6 9EL
[01–846 9000]

Under the Development of Tourism Act, 1969, four co-equal statutory Tourist Boards were established: the British Tourist Authority, the English Tourist Board, the Scottish Tourist Board and the Wales Tourist Board. Each is financed mainly by direct grant-in-aid from Government and is an independent statutory body. The British Tourist Authority has specific responsibility for promoting tourism to Great Britain from overseas. It also has a general responsibility for tourism within Great Britain as a whole.
Chairman, D. R. Y. Bluck, O.B.E. (*part-time*).
Chief Executive, M. G. Medlicott.

English Tourist Board
Thames Tower, Black's Road, W6 9EL

Scottish Tourist Board
23, Ravelston Terrace, Edinburgh EH4 3EU

Wales Tourist Board
Brunel House, 2 Fitzalan Street, Cardiff CF2 1UY

BRITISH WATERWAYS BOARD
Melbury House, Melbury Terrace, NW1 6JX
[01–262 6711]

Vice-Chairman and acting Chairman, Dr. A. Robertson, C.B.E. (*part-time*).
Members (*all part-time*), R. J. Weston; Rear-Adm. D. A. Dunbar-Nasmith; M. Everard; Sir Trevor Hughes, K.C.B.; B. Bean, C.B.E.; J. Gordon.
Chief Executive, B. C. Dice.
Secretary and Deputy Chief Executive, T. T. Luckcuck.

CABINET OFFICE

The Cabinet Office comprises the Secretariat, who support Ministers collectively in the conduct of Cabinet business; the Central Statistical Office; and the Management and Personnel Office (M.P.O.) which is responsible for the management and organization of the Civil Service and recruitment into it, efficiency, and senior appointments. Other functions are from time to time laid on the Office, some ephemerally and some permanently. Non-departmental Ministers may be attached to the Office.

The functions of the Cabinet Office (M.P.O.) are in support of the Prime Minister in her capacity as Minister for the Civil Service, with responsibility for day-to-day supervision delegated to the Minister of State, Privy Council Office.

Salaries

Prime Minister	£33,145
Head of Home Civil Service	£81,000
Grade 1A	£59,500
Grade 2	£43,500–£45,500
Grade 3	£34,000–£37,000
Grade 5	£24,765–£28,215
Grade 6	£18,786–£25,335

Prime Minister's Office

The Prime Minister.
Principal Private Secretary to the Prime Minister, N. L. Wicks, C.B.E.
Private Secretaries to the Prime Minister, C. Powell (*Overseas Affairs*); D. R. Norgrove (*Economic Affairs*); M. E. Addison (*Parliamentary Affairs*).
Personal Assistant to the Prime Minister, Mrs. C. M. Ryder.
Secretary for Appointments, J. R. Catford.
Political Secretary, S. Sherbourne.
Foreign Affairs Adviser, Sir Percy Cradock, G.C.M.G.
Policy Unit, D. Willets; P. T. Warry; J. B. Wybrew; D. Hobson; H. Booth; N. Blackwell; P. J. Stredder; G. Guise; Prof. B. Griffiths; A. J. O'Sullivan.
Chief Press Secretary, B. Ingham.
Deputy Chief Press Secretary, T. J. Perks.
Assistant Private Secretaries to Prime Minister, Miss J. Drever; Mrs J. Cole.
Parliamentary Private Secretary, Hon. A. Hamilton, M.P.
Adviser on Efficiency, Sir Robin Ibbs.
Secretary to the Cabinet and Head of Home Civil Service, Sir Robert Armstrong, G.C.B., C.V.O. (retires Dec. 1987.)

Ceremonial Branch

Ceremonial Officer (G5), Mrs. M. E. Hedley-Miller, C.B.

SECRETARIAT
70 Whitehall, SW1A 2AS
[01–233 3000]

Second Permanent Secretary (G1A), The Rt. Hon. Sir Antony Duff, G.C.M.G., C.V.O., D.S.O., D.S.C.
Chief Scientific Adviser, J. W. Fairclough.
Deputy Secretaries (G2), Sir Colin Figures, K.C.M.G., O.B.E.; C.L.G. Mallaby, C.M.G.; D. F. Williamson, C.B.; R. Wilson.
Under Secretaries (G3), J. H. Holroyd; A. J. Langdon; P.E. Hall, C.M.G.; G. Monger; N. H. Nicholls; H. V. B. Brown.
Assistant Secretaries (G5), C. R. Budd; Brig. J. A. J. Budd; H. Burke; Mrs. C. M. Cunningham; B. Dinwiddy; R. E. Escritt; Brig. C. L. G. Henshaw, C.B.E.; J. S. Hibberd; F. M. Merrifield; J. Morrison; M. Nicholson; P. B. Preece; A. Quigley; M. W. Townley; S. J. Wright.
Senior Principals (G6), Mrs. M. Bloom; C. K. Davies; Dr. G. W. D. Findlay; P. C. F. Gilbert.

Efficiency Unit
70 Whitehall, SW1A 2AS

Head of Unit (G3), Miss K. Jenkins.
Assistant Secretary (G5), Miss K. Caines.

ESTABLISHMENT OFFICER'S GROUP

Principal Establishment and Finance Officer, (G3), J. W. Stevens.

Information Services

Chief Press Officer (G6), J. B. Wright.

Establishment Division

Deputy Establishment Officer (G5), A. Phillips.

Finance

Senior Finance Officer (G6), C. J. Parry.

Internal Audit

Principal (G7), A. K. Holman.

Historical Section
Hepburn House, Marsham Street, SW1P 4HW
[01–211 6605]

Departmental Records Adviser (G6), Miss. P. Andrews.

CENTRAL STATISTICAL OFFICE
Government Offices, Great George Street, SW1P 3AQ
[01–233 3000]

Director and Head of the Government Statistical Service (G1A), J. Hibbert.
Private Secretary, Mrs. R. Passmore.
Under Secretaries (G3), D. W. Flaxen; M. J. M. Erritt; J. D. Wells.
Assistant Secretaries (G5), P. Altobell; Miss S. P. Carter; A. A. Croxford; T. J. Griffin; P. B. Kenny; K. Mansell; Dr. J. H. Ludley; D. C. K. Stirling.

MANAGEMENT AND PERSONNEL OFFICE
Government Offices, Great George Street, SW1P 3AL
[01–233 3000]

Second Permanent Secretary (G1A), Miss A. E. Mueller, C.B.
Deputy Secretary, Top Management Programme (G2), H. Phillips.
Assistant Secretaries, Top Management Programme (G5), Miss I. Nisbet; Miss A. J. Brimelow.
Security Adviser, Air Vice Marshal B. G. Lock, C.B., C.B.E., A.F.C.

Personnel Management

Under Secretary (G3), R. Wilson.
Assistant Secretaries (G5), E. Ferguson; G. J. Court; P. D. Ewins.

Senior and Public Appointments
Management and Efficiency Group

Director, Public Appointments Unit (G3), G. T. Morgan.
Assistant Secretary (G5), G. H. Wollen.
Senior Principal (G6), E. Brown.

Joint M.P.O./H.M. Treasury
Management Unit

Head of Unit (G3), Mrs. V. Strachan.

Central Unit on Purchasing

Director (G2), M. J. O. Willacy.
Deputy Director (G5), R. B. Brown.
Assistant Secretary (G5), T. D. P. Twyman.

Machinery of Government

Assistant Secretary (G5), Dr. J. P. Spencer.

Security Division

Assistant Secretary (G5), S. R. Davie.

Occupational Health Service
Tilbury House, Petty France, SW1H 9EU

Medical Adviser and Acting Director of Occupational Health Service, Dr. G. S. Sorrie.
Principal Medical Officers, Dr. P. J. Constable (*Deputy Medical Adviser*); Dr. A. N. Hepburn.

Civil Service Commission
Alencon Link, Basingstoke, Hants. RG21 1JB
[0256–29222]

First Commissioner (G2), D. J. Trevelyan, C.B.
Commissioners (G3), N. B. J. Gurney; (*G4*), J. K. Moore (*Director, Civil Service Selection Board*).
Commissioners (part-time), D. P. Hornby; Dr. J. S. MacFarlane; Miss D. Whittingham.
Assistant Secretary (G5), A. A. Carter.
Senior Principals (G6), A. S. Halford; R. B. M. Payne; S. Royston; P. J. Wiggett.

Civil Service Selection Board
Kirkland House, 22 Whitehall, SW1A 2ED

Director (G4), J. K. Moore.
Deputy Director (G5), D. M. Williams.
Chief Psychologist (G6), J. McLeod.

Training and Civil Service College
Sunningdale Park, Ascot, Berks SL5 0QE
[0990–23444]
London : 11 Belgrave Road, SW1V 1RB
[01-834 6644]

Principal (G3), R. Jackling.
Head of Training Division (G5), P. R. Coster.
College Secretary (G6), P. Cook.
Directors (G5), J. Allen; E. J. Henstridge; G. Gammon; Dr. P. Lund.

CABLE AUTHORITY
Gillingham House, 38–44 Gillingham Street, SW1V 1HU
[01-821 6161]

The Cable Authority is the statutory body established by the Cable and Broadcasting Act, 1984 to grant franchises for the operation of new cable systems and to licence and regulate the provision of cable programme services.
Chairman, R. Burton.
Deputy Chairman, Prof. J. Ring, C.B.E.
Members, Mrs. A. Ballard; P. Johnson; Mrs. E. MacDonald-Brown; P. Paine, C.B.E., D.F.C; P. Darwin.
Director-General, J. Davey.

CHARITY COMMISSION
St. Alban's House, 57–60 Haymarket, SW1Y 4QX
[01–210 3000]

Northern Office:
Graeme House, Derby Square, Liverpool L2 7SB
[051–227 3191]

The Charity Commissioners are appointed under the Charities Act, 1960, principally to further the work of charities in England and Wales by giving advice and information, and by investigating and checking abuses. The Commissioners maintain a register of charities; give consent to land transactions; help to modernize the purposes and administrative machinery of charities; and, in the name of the Official Custodian for Charities, hold investments for charities.

Salaries

Grade 5	£24,739–£28,215
Grade 6	£18,736–£25,335
Grade 7	£14,927–£20,292

Chief Commissioner, D. A. Peach ... £40,058–£41,000
Commissioners, C. A. H. Parsons; J. Farquharson £30,207–£37,000
Deputy Commissioners (G5), R. W. Groves; J. A. Dutton; M. A. Rao; J. F. Claricoat; Mrs. J. F. R. Quint; G. S. Goodchild.
Assist. Commissioners (G6), Mrs. F. E. Middleton; H. K. Udvadia; Mrs. H. M. Phillips; Miss D. F. Taylor; S. K. Sen; K. M. Dibble; P. P. White; N. M. Mackenzie; D. C. Raikes; R. W. Tomlinson; Miss V. A. Nuttall; Miss V. D. Mayson; S. Slack; M. Woodward; M. J. Harbottle.
Secretary and Asst. Commissioner (G5), D. Forrest.
Office Manager and Asst. Commissioner (G5), J. H. Vining.
Asst. Commissioners (G7), R. E. Hatton; D. Mc-Naught; Miss S. M. St. C. Smith; M. C. T. Seymour; Miss C. F. Byrne.
Official Custodian for Charities (G6), R. J. Crick.
Deputy Official Custodian (G7), R. E. Edwards.
Establishment Officer (G6), J. M. Samuels.

CHURCH COMMISSIONERS

1 Millbank, SW1P 3JZ
[01–222 7010]

The Church Commissioners were established on April 1, 1948, by the amalgamation of *Queen Anne's Bounty* (established 1704) and the *Ecclesiastical Commissioners* (established 1836).

The Commissioners' main task is to improve the stipends and housing of the Church of England clergy and to provide them and their widows with adequate pensions and assistance with housing in retirement. They also carry out administrative duties in connection with pastoral reorganization and redundant churches, and have been designated by the General Synod as the Central Stipends Authority of the Church of England.

The Commissioners' income for the year ended Dec. 31, 1986, was derived from the following sources:—

	£'s million
Stock exchange investments	45·5
Land and property	44·8
Mortgages, loans, etc.	9·7
Trust income, and diocesan/parish contributions for stipends	50·8
	£150·8

This income was applied as follows:—	
Clergy stipends	85·8
Clergy and widows' pensions	35·0
Clergy houses	12·4
Episcopal administration and payments to Chapters	5·4
Church buildings	2·5
Administrative expenses of the Commissioners and related bodies	8·3
Carried forward	1·4
	£150·8

Constitution

The 2 Archbishops, the 41 diocesan Bishops, 5 deans or provosts, 10 other clergy and 10 laymen appointed by the General Synod; 4 laymen nominated by the Queen; 4 persons nominated by the Archbishop of Canterbury; The Lord Chancellor; The Lord President of the Council; the First Lord of the Treasury; The Chancellor of the Exchequer; The Secretary of State for the Home Dept; The Speaker of the House of Commons; The Lord Chief Justice; The Master of the Rolls; The Attorney-General; The Solicitor-General; The Lord Mayor and two Aldermen of the City of London; The Lord Mayor of York and one representative from each of the Universities of Oxford and Cambridge.

Church Estates Commissioners

First, Sir Douglas Lovelock, K.C.B.
Second, Rt. Hon. Michael Alison, M.P.
Third, Mrs. B. E. Haworth.

Officers

Secretary, J. E. Shelley.
Private Secretary, J. N. Neil-Smith.
Deputy Secretary, P. Locke.
Assistant Secretaries, D. I. Archer (*Chief Accountant*); P. H. P. Shaw, L.V.O. (*Estates*); R. M. Hutchings (*Commercial Property*); W. R. Herbert (*Establishment Officer*); J. M. Davies (*Redundant Churches*); D. J. Day (*Pastoral*); M. D. Elengorn (*Stipends and Allocations*); J. W. Ferguson (*Computer*); D. N. Goodwin (*Houses*); C. P. Canton (*Bishoprics*); P. G. Brealey (*Investments*).
Deputy Accountant and Trust Officer, G. C. Baines.
Deputy Establishment Officer, Mrs. B. A. Bartlett.
Press & Information Officer, R. S. Hopgood.
Principals, A. W. Atkins; P. D. Chadwick; M. G. S. Farrell; Miss A. M. Mackie; E. G. Peacock.

Legal Department

Official Solicitor, E. W. Wills.
Deputy Solicitor, J. P. Guy.
Senior Legal Assistants, Miss J. M. Bland; J. D. Carter; Rev. B. G. Hall; Miss S. M. S. Jones; R. D. C. Murray; Mrs. S. E. Prosser; Miss I. E. Slaughter.

Main Agents

Messrs. Cluttons, 5 Great College Street, S.W.1; Messrs. Smiths Gore, The King's Lodgings, Minster Precincts, Peterborough; Messrs. Chesterton, Lalonde, 54 Brooke Street, W.1.

CIVIL AVIATION AUTHORITY
C.A.A. House, 45–59 Kingsway, WC2B 6TE
[01–379 7311]

The C.A.A. is responsible for the economic regulation of U.K. airlines by licensing air routes, air travel organisers and approving fares; for the safety regulation of U.K. civil aviation by the certification of airlines and aircraft, and by licensing aerodromes, flight crew and aircraft engineers; and, through the National Air Traffic Services, for the provision of air traffic control and telecommunications services.

Chairman, C. Tugendhat (*part-time*) £41,800
Managing Director, T. Murphy.
Secretary, Miss G. M. E. White.

COMMONWEALTH DEVELOPMENT CORPORATION
33 Hill Street, W1A 3AR
[01–629 8484]

The Corporation's area of operations covers British dependent territories and, with Ministerial approval, any Commonwealth or other developing country. At present, the Corporation is authorised to operate in 38 Commonwealth and 15 non-Commonwealth countries in addition to the remaining British dependent

territories. The Corporation is authorized to borrow up to £750,000,000.
Chairman (part-time), The Lord Kindersley.
Deputy Chairman (part-time), Sir Colin Campbell, Bt., M.C.
Members (part-time), H.R.H. The Prince of Wales; J. M. Clay; C. F. Sedcole; Mrs. A. Wright; V. Robertson, O.B.E.; D. Warburton; M. H. Caine; M. D. Nightingale, O.B.E.
General Manager, J. D. Eccles, C.B.E.

COMMONWEALTH SECRETARIAT
(*see* p. 694)

COUNTRYSIDE COMMISSION
John Dower House, Crescent Place,
Cheltenham, Glos. GL50 3RA
[0242 521381]

The Countryside Commission is an independent agency set up in 1968 to promote the conservation and enhancement of landscape beauty in England and Wales, to encourage the provision and improvement of facilities in the countryside for enjoyment, including the need to secure access for open air recreation. Since April 1982 the Commission has been funded by annual grant from the Department of the Environment. Members of the Commission are appointed by the Secretary of State for the Environment and the Secretary of State for Wales acting jointly.

Chairman, Sir Derek Barber £18,809
Director, A. A. C. Phillips £36,852
Assistant Directors, R. Clarke (*Policy*); M. J. Kirby (*Regions*) .... £24,739–£28,215
National Heritage Adviser, Mrs. M. D. Laverack
.... £18,020 to £24,302
Secretary, M. J. Burchell.
Head of Conservation Branch, M. E. Taylor.
Head of Recreation & Access Branch, J. W. B. Worth.
Head of Communications Branch, C. Pugsley.
Regional Officers, (vacant) (*Newcastle*); B. Walbank (*Cambridge*); Dr. S. A. Bucknall (*Leeds*); R. J. Lloyd (*Bristol*); R. T. Thomas (*Manchester*); D. E. Coleman (*London*); F. S. Walmsley (*Birmingham*).

Office for Wales
Ladywell House, Newtown, Powys, SY16 1RD
[0686 26799]

Chairman, R. E. M. Rees £10,530
Principal Officer, A. M. H. Fitton.
(*Salary: £14,927–£20,292*)

COUNTRYSIDE COMMISSION FOR SCOTLAND
Battleby, Redgorton, Perth, PH1 3EW
[0738 27921]

Established under the Countryside (Scotland) Act, 1967, with functions for the provision, development and improvement of facilities for the enjoyment of the Scottish countryside, and for the conservation and enhancement of the natural beauty and amenity thereof.

Chairman, J. R. Carr (*part-time*).
Commissioners, J. M. S. Arnott (*Vice-Chairman*); Mrs. F. Ballantyne; Dr. D. J. Bennet; I. R. Thomson; Prof. C. H. Gimingham; D. Ross; R. R. Steedman; G. G. Stewart; Prof. J. I. Cunningham; Q. Brown; D. Grainger.
Secretary, W. B. Prior.
Asst. Directors, J. M. Fladmark (*Research and Development*); J. R. Turner (*Planning*); M. A. Payne (*Communications and Training*).

COVENT GARDEN MARKET AUTHORITY
Covent House, New Covent Garden Market,
SW8 5NX
[01–720 2211]

The Covent Garden Market Authority is constituted under the Covent Garden Market Acts, 1961 to 1966, the members being appointed by the Minister of Agriculture, Fisheries and Food. The Authority owns and operates the 60-acre New Covent Garden Markets (fruit, vegetable, flowers) which have been trading since 1974.

Chairman, P. Firmston-Williams, C.B.E. (*part-time*) £19,902
Members (*part-time*), Sir Adrian Cadbury; P. J. Hunt; E. I. Kingston; R. Pierson; J. A. Harvey ... £5,000
General Manager, C. M. G. Allen, C.B.E.
Secretary, Dr. P. M. Liggins.

CRIMINAL INJURIES COMPENSATION BOARD
Whittington House, 19 Alfred Place, WC1E 7LG
[01–636 9501 and 01–631 4467]

The Board was constituted in 1964 to administer the Government scheme for *ex gratia* payments of compensation to victims of crimes of violence.
Chairman, M. Ogden, Q.C.
Members, J. F. A. Archer, Q.C.; M. S. R. Bruce, Q.C.; D. Calcutt, Q.C.; H. Carlisle, Q.C.; B. W. Chedlow, Q.C.; Miss B. Cooper, Q.C.; J. D. Crowley, Q.C.; C. Fawcett, Q.C.; G. M. Hamilton, Q.C.; Sir Arthur Hoole; J. Law, Q.C.; M. E. Lewer, Q.C.; J. Leighton Williams, Q.C.; Sir Denis Marshall; M. Morland, Q.C.; The Lord Morton of Shuna, Q.C.; Sir John Palmer; I. M. S. Park, C.B.E.; Miss S. Ritchie, Q.C.; D. B. Robertson, Q.C.; C. Seagroatt, Q.C.; L. Stuart Shields, Q.C.; D. M. Thomas, O.B.E., Q.C.; D. O. Thomas, Q.C.; P. Weitzman, Q.C.; C. H. Whitby, Q.C.
Secretary and Solicitor, D. M. North.
Deputy Secretary, D. J. White.
Chief Executive, T. F. Corbett.

CROWN AGENTS FOR OVERSEA GOVERNMENTS AND ADMINISTRATIONS
St. Nicholas House, St. Nicholas Road, Sutton,
Surrey, SM1 1EL
[01–643 3311]

The Crown Agents are financial, commercial and professional agents to governments and public authorities in the developing world and to international aid agencies. They do not act for individuals or for commercial concerns in the private sector.

The Crown Agents also act on behalf of the International Bank for Reconstruction and Development (The World Bank), the International Development Association and regional development banks.
Chairman, Sir Peter Graham, O.B.E.

CROWN ESTATE COMMISSIONERS
13/15 Carlton House Terrace, SW1Y 5AH
[01–210 3000]
78 Pall Mall, SW1Y 5ES

The Land Revenues of the Crown in England and Wales have been collected on the public account since 1760, when George III surrendered them and received a fixed annual payment or *Civil List*. At the time of the surrender the gross revenues amounted to about £89,000 and the net return to about £11,000.

In the year ended March 31, 1987, the gross income from the Crown Estate totalled £55,932,000. The expenditure was £26,527,000. The sum of £30,000,000 was paid to the Exchequer in 1986–87 as Surplus Revenue.

The Land Revenues in Ireland have been carried to the Consolidated Fund since 1820; from April 1, 1923, as regards Southern Ireland, they have been collected and administered by the Irish Government.

The Land Revenues in Scotland were transferred to the Commissioners in 1833.
First Commissioner and Chairman (*part-time*), The Earl of Mansfield and Mansfield.
Second Commissioner and (and Secretary), Dr. K. Dexter, C.B. £45,349
Commissioners (*part-time*), R. B. Caws, C.B.E.; P. Sober; O. H. Colburn; G. D. Lillingston, C.B.E.; Capt. Sir Iain Tennant, K.T.; J. N. C. James.
Deputy Commissioners, D. J. Chapman; R. G. L. Osborne .... £24,739–£28,215
Crown Estate Surveyor, C. F. Hynes £18,786–£25,335
Principals (G7), J. Stumbke; F. G. Parrish; J. S. Ellingford .... £14,927–£20,292
Organization and Establishments Officer and Clerk to the Board (G7), R. Blake .... £14,927–£20,292
Accountant and Receiver-General, R. G. Bell £24,739–£28,215
Legal Adviser and Assistant Solicitor, M. L. Davies £24,739–£28,215
Senior Principal (G6), I. R. Colquhoun; H. Turnsek; J. B. Postgate.
Principal (G7), R. T. Haywood.
Senior Legal Assistants, M. A. J. Cordingley; A. M. Spratt .... £16,629–£22,575
Crown Estate Receiver for Scotland (G7), M. J. Gravestock (10 Charlotte Square, Edinburgh) £14,927–£20,292
Solicitor, Scotland, D. F. Stewart.

Windsor Estate
Surveyor and Deputy Ranger, A. R. Wiseman, M.V.O. £30,475
Crown Estate Forestry Officer and Chief Forester, Windsor, J. J. Taylor .... £15,989–£18,914

BOARD OF CUSTOMS AND EXCISE
King's Beam House, Mark Lane, EC3R 7HE
[01–626 1515]

Commissioners of Customs were first appointed in 1671 and housed by the King in London. The present "Long Room" in the Custom House, Lower Thames Street, E.C.3, replaced that built by Charles II and was rebuilt after destruction by fire in 1718 and 1814. The Excise Department was formerly under the Inland Revenue Department and was amalgamated with the Customs Department on April 1, 1909.

H.M. Customs and Excise is responsible for collecting and administering customs and excise duties and value added tax and advises the Chancellor of the Exchequer on any matters connected with them. The Department is also responsible for preventing and detecting the evasion of revenue laws and for enforcing a range of prohibitions and restrictions on the importation of certain classes of goods. In addition, the Department undertakes certain agency work on behalf of other departments, including the compilation of U.K. overseas trade statistics from customs import and export documents.

Salaries
Grade 1 .... £64,739
Grade 2 .... £43,264–£45,349
Grade 3 .... £33,725–£36,852
Grade 5 .... £24,739–£28,215
Grade 6 .... £18,786–£25,335
Grade 7 .... £14,927–£20,292

The Board

Chairman (G1), J. B. Unwin, c.b.
  Private Secretaries, J. L. Railton; Ms. C. W. Appleton.
Deputy Chairmen (G2), B. H. Knox, c.b.; Mrs. V. P. M. Strachan.
Commissioners (G3), D. J. Howard; P. Jefferson Smith; P. Nash; A. W. Russell; R. Weston; C. C. Finlinson.

Headquarters Office

Assistant Secretaries (G5), I. D. Savins; P. R. H. Allen; J. Vaughan; R. I. Bolt; P. Kent; P. St. Quinton; D. A. Walton; P. Hammond; R. A. Mechem; P. J. Webb; D. F. O. Battle; D. J. Fellingham; R. H. C. Stiff; P. Wilmott; V. Matthews; B. J. Cockerell; E. N. Taylor; J. W. Tracey; W. D. Whitmore; W. F. McGuigan; G. F. Taylor; D. F. W. Fryett; R. D. Goddard; P. Hogg; D. E. Barratt; L. G. Bentley; J. C. Stevenson; F. D. Tweddle; W. Crawford; K. Berry; P. Trevett; A. G. H. Paynter.
Head of Press and Information Division (G7), G. G. Hammond.

V.A.T. Central Unit

Controller, Projects (G5), R. A. Huband.
Controller, Operations (G5), M. J. Wardle.
Deputy Controller (G6), J. P. Hall.

Solicitor's Office

Solicitor (G2), P. V. H. Smith.
Principal Assistant Solicitors (G3), G. F. Butt; D. E. J. Nissen.
Assistant Solicitors (G5), P. Breuer; P. J. C. Ellis; M. Michael; Miss E. S. Thomas; R. D. S. Wylie; M. A. Cooper; G. W. M. McFarlane; D. E. T. S. Keefe; M. C. K. Gasper; R. L. Barlow; Miss A. E. Bolt; G. Fotherby.

Accountant and Comptroller-General's Office

Accountant and Comptroller-General (G5), C. A. Bray.
Deputy Accountant-Generals (G6), M. H. Smith; J. E. Ebery.

Statistical Office

Controller (G5), (vacant).

Investigation Division

Chief Investigation Officer (G5), R. L. H. Lawrence.

Collectors of Customs and Excise (G5)
England and Wales

Birmingham: M. W. Summers.
Dover: R. Crossley.
East Anglia: R. N. Lewis.
East Midlands: C. J. Packman.
Leeds: N. T. Hodson.
Liverpool: P. J. Little.
London Airports: R. Craggs.
London City and South: A. Collie.
London Port: A. C. Morrow.
London North and West: A. G. Smith.
Manchester: D. Smith.
Northampton: G. D. Town.
Northern England: D. R. Inglis.
Reading: J. H. Tee.
Southampton: S. J. C. Jones.
South Wales and the Borders: A. Ferguson.
South West England: M. G. W. Lloyd.

Scotland

Aberdeen: G. W. Sharpe.
Edinburgh: A. C. Sawyer.
Glasgow & Clyde: I. McLeod.

Northern Ireland

Belfast: B. E. Barclay.

OFFICE OF THE DATA PROTECTION REGISTRAR
Springfield House, Water Lane, Wilmslow, Cheshire SK9 5AX
[Admin.: 0625–535711; Enquiries: 0625–535777]

The Office of the Data Protection Registrar was created by the Data Protection Act, 1984. It is the Registrar's duty to compile and maintain the Register of Data Users and Computer Bureaux and provide facilities for members of the public to examine the Register; promote observance of the data protection principles; consider complaints made by data subjects; disseminate information about the Act; encourage the production of codes of practice by trade associations and other bodies, to guide data users in complying with the data protection principles; co-operate with other parties to the Council of Europe Convention and act as U.K. authority for the purposes of Article 13 of the Convention; report annually to Parliament on the performance of his functions under the Act.
Registrar, E. J. Howe.

MINISTRY OF DEFENCE
See **Armed Forces Section**

DESIGN COUNCIL
28 Haymarket, SW1Y 4SU
[01-839-8000]

The Design Council's aim is to improve the design of British products by: advising companies on up-to-date practice in engineering and industrial design; selecting well-designed British goods for The Design Centre and for the annual British Design Awards; publishing information to help manufacturers, designers, and others professionally involved in design; and promoting improvements in design education at all levels. There are Design Centres in London, Glasgow and Cardiff, and offices in Belfast, Wolverhampton and Manchester. The Design Council is funded partly by a Government grant-in-aid and partly by earned revenues.
Chairman, S. Hornby.
Director, K. Grant.

DEVELOPMENT COMMISSION FOR RURAL ENGLAND
11 Cowley Street, SW1P 3NA
[01-222 9134]

The Development Commission for Rural England is a statutory body funded by Government grant-in-aid which undertakes to alleviate economic and social problems in rural areas and advises the Government on related rural matters in England. It concentrates its resources in priority areas—Rural Development Areas—but some assistance, particularly through its main agency, the Council for Small Industries in Rural Areas, is available both within and outside the RDAs.
Chairman, The Lord Vinson, l.v.o.
Other Commissioners, Mrs. P. Batty Shaw, c.b.e.; Prof. M. D. I. Chisholm; D. J. C. Davenport; The Lord Gisborough; M. Schreiber; R. Thompson; A. Leavett.
Chief Executive, J. V. Williams.

THE DUCHY OF CORNWALL
10 Buckingham Gate, SW1E 6LA
[01-834 7346]

The Duchy of Cornwall was instituted by Edward III in 1337 for the support of his eldest son, Edward, the Black Prince, and since 1503 the eldest surviving son of the Sovereign has, as heir apparent, succeeded to the Dukedom by inheritance. As the oldest of the English Duchies, it has enjoyed a long association with the Crown. Before elevation to a dukedom, it was an earldom from 1227, when Richard, King of the Romans and younger brother of Henry III, was created Earl of Cornwall.

The Prince's Council

H.R.H. The Prince of Wales, K.G., K.T., G.C.B; Sir Nicholas Henderson, G.C.M.G. (*Lord Warden of the Stannaries*); Hon. Sir John Baring, C.V.O. (*Receiver General*); Sir Peter Miles, K.C.V.O.; R. A. Morritt, Q.C. (*Attorney-General to the Prince of Wales*); D. W. N. Landale (*Secretary and Keeper of the Records*); Sir John Riddell, Bt.; J. E. Pugsley; J. N. C. James; A. M. J. Galsworthy.

Other Officers of the Duchy of Cornwall

Auditors, J. H. Bowman; P. L. Ainger; H. Hughes.
Solicitor, M. H. Boyd-Carpenter.
Assistant Secretary, K. J. S. Knott.
Sheriff (1987–88), Rt. Hon. The Viscountess Boyd of Merton.

THE DUCHY OF LANCASTER
Lancaster Place, Strand, WC2E 7ED
[01–836 8277]

The estates and jurisdiction known as the Duchy and County Palatine of Lancaster have been attached to the Crown since 1399, when John of Gaunt's son came to the throne as Henry IV. As the Lancaster inheritance it goes back to 1265. Edward III erected Lancashire into a County Palatine in 1351.

Chancellor of the Duchy of Lancaster, THE RT. HON. KENNETH CLARKE, Q.C., M.P.
Private Secretary, A. Lansley.
Attorney-General and Attorney and Serjeant within the County Palatine of Lancaster, D. K. Rattee, Q.C.
Receiver-General, Sir Peter Miles, K.C.V.O.
Vice-Chancellor, His Hon. Mr. Justice Scott.
Clerk of the Council and Keeper of Records, M. K. Ridley.
Solicitor, W. O. Farrer.
Asst. Solicitor, I. J. Dicker.
Chief Clerk, P. C. Clarke, C.V.O.

ECONOMIC AND SOCIAL RESEARCH COUNCIL
160 Great Portland Street, W1N 6BA
[01–637 1499]

The E.S.R.C. was set up by Royal Charter in 1965 for the promotion of social science research. The Council carries out its role by awarding research grants, by initiating research and research contracts, by funding designated research centres, and by awarding postgraduate studentships and bursaries. In addition, the Council provides advice and disseminates knowledge on the social sciences.
Chairman, (vacant).
Secretary, Mrs. S. Reeve.

DEPARTMENT OF EDUCATION AND SCIENCE
Elizabeth House, York Road, SE1 7PH
[01–934 9000]

The Government Department of Education was, until the establishment of a separate office, a Committee of the Privy Council appointed in 1839 to supervise the distribution of certain grants which had been made by Parliament since 1834. The Act of 1899 established the Board of Education, with a President and Parliamentary Secretary, and created a Consultative Committee. The Education Act of 1944 estab-

lished the Ministry of Education. In April 1964 the office of the Minister of Science was combined with the Ministry to form the Department of Education and Science. The cost of administration for the financial year 1987–88 was estimated at £58,309,000.

Salary List

Secretary of State	£33,145
Minister of State (Commons)	£22,875
Parliamentary Under Secretaries	£16,885
Grade 1	£64,739
Grade 2	£43,264–£45,349
Grade 3	£33,725–£36,852
Grade 4	£30,207–£31,770
Grade 5	£24,739–£28,215
Grade 6	£18,786–£25,335
Grade 7	£14,927–£20,292

Secretary of State for Education and Science, THE RT. HON. KENNETH BAKER, M.P.
Private Sec., R. L. Smith.
Parliamentary Private Secretary, A. Burt, M.P.
Minister of State, MRS ANGELA RUMBOLD, C.B.E., M.P.
Private Secretary, J. Johnstone.
Parliamentary Private Secretary, E. Forth, M.P.
Parliamentary Under Secretaries of State, R. Dunn, M.P.; R. Jackson, M.P.; Baroness Hooper.
Permanent Secretary (*G1*), Sir David Hancock, K.C.B.
Deputy Secretaries (*G2*), R. H. Bird, C.B.; P. H. Halsey, M.V.O.; N. W. Stuart.
Under Secretaries (*G3*), J. H. Thompson (*Director of Establishments*); Miss J. H. Bacon; A. E. D. Chamier; C. A. Clark (*Accountant General*); J. I. Langtry; D. G. Libby; B. M. Norbury; N. Summers; D. W. Tanner; N. B. W. Thompson; W. B. Wakefield (*Director of Statistics*); A. J. Wiggins.

Schools Branch 1

Assistant Secretaries (*G5*), Mrs. H. K. Douglas; Miss J. A. Gilbey; R. J. Green.
Principals (*G7*), Miss A. M. J. Benham; Miss J. F. Cramphorn; G. H. N. Evans; D. H. Griffiths; J. S. Harris; M. H. Sharpe; J. S. Street; D. K. Timms; Mrs. S. J. Trundle; A. Wilshaw.

Schools Branch 2

Assistant Secretaries (*G5*), Mrs. C. M. Chattaway; Miss P. I. Laidlaw.
Principals (*G7*), D. Barwick; Miss C. A. Bienkowska; W. M. Caldow; Mrs. G. W. Dishart; Mrs. K. H. Jameson; P. S. Lewis; I. A. Loveless; Mrs. P. A. Masters; J. K. Sawtell; J. N. Walmsley.

Schools Branch 3

Assistant Secretaries (*G5*), M. M. Capey; Mrs. H. M. Williams; M. D. Phipps; Miss C. E. Hodkinson.
Staff Inspector (*G5*), A. Clegg.
H.M. Inspectors (*G6*), Mrs. J. McLean; P. J. Silvester.
Principals (*G7*), Miss M. d'Armenia; S. N. Jardine; J. F. Bird; Miss A. M. J. Benham; Mrs. C. K. Saville; S. T. Crowne; Miss G. G. Beauchamp.

Architects and Building Branch

Chief Architect (*G5*), P. Benwell.
Deputy Chief Architect, R. L. Thompson.
Superintending Architects, R. Clynes; D. H. Griffin; M. S. Hacker; J. J. Wilson.
Superintending Engineer (*Mechanical and Electrical*), (vacant).
Chief Quantity Surveyor, B. G. Whitehouse.
Principals (*G7*), K. L. R. English; A. G. Myatt.
Principal Architects, R. W. U. Alcock; A. J. Branton; Miss C. G. Edwards; Miss E. J. Lloyd-Jones; P. Lenssen; D. S. Nightingale; G. J. Parker; T. W. Prosser; Miss B. M. T. Sanders; A. C. Thompson; D. F. Wicks.

Principal Quantity Surveyors, T. W. A. Carden; A. A. Jones; J. L. S. Sinclair.
Principal Engineer, M. J. Patel.
S.P.T.O. Architects, S. Aswat; A. J. Benson-Wilson; E. C. Bissell; J. R. C. Brooke; Mrs. D. Holt; G. E. Hughes; Miss L. Watson; T. J. Williamson.
S.P.T.O. Quantity Surveyors, E. W. Lawless; M. Sturt.
S.P.T.O. Engineers, R. Heard; R. L. Daniels.
S.P.T.O. Furniture Designer, N. J. Carter.

Further and Higher Education Branch 1

Assistant Secretaries (G5), A. N. Brown; E. R. Morgan; G. J. Mungeam.
Senior Principal (G6), E. J. Herbert.
Principals (G7), K. Baxter; A. Clarke; Miss L. M. Clarke; Mrs. S. G. Evans; P. J. Hodgman; W. A. Irvine; M. Kerin; M. F. Neale; P. W. Syme.

Further and Higher Education Branch 2

Assistant Secretaries (G5), A. G. B. Woollard; R. D. Hull; K. Clarke.
Principals (G7), J. K. Bushnell; A. J. Coles; M. McBride; S. A. Marston; D. R. Pollard; A. J. Shaw; R. E. Troedson; J. P. Vann; D. T. Wood.

Further and Higher Education Branch 3

Assistant Secretaries (G5), M. B. Baker; G. Etheridge; D. V. Stafford.
Principals (G7), Miss N. Bartman; Miss L. Butler; C. J. Dowse; P. W. Fulford-Jones; D. I. B. Hardy; Mrs. M. E. Jackson; A. J. Sargent.

Science Branch

Assistant Secretaries (G5), R. P. Ritzema; P. J. Thorpe.
Principals (G7), A. Callaghan; Miss S. P. Gane; K. C. Humphrey; L. J. R. Dando; K. D. J. Root.

Teachers Pay and General Branch

Assistant Secretaries (G5), R. W. Chattaway; P. A. Shaw.
Principals (G7), A. D. Adamson; R. S. Daruwalla; M. J. F. Rabarts; A. J. Wye.

Pensions Branch
Mowden Hall, Staindrop Road,
Darlington, Co. Durham DL3 9BG
[Darlington: 460155]

Assistant Secretary (G5), J. Wilde.
Principals (G7), D. G. Halladay; K. M. Miles.

Teachers Supply and Training Branch

Assistant Secretaries (G5), M. J. Richardson; J. W. Whitaker.
Senior Economic Adviser (G5), B. D. Cullen.
Senior Principal Scientific Officer (G6), R. B. Ladley.
Principals (G7), B. D. Glickman; H. C. H. Hodge; T. B. Jeffery; J. S. Street; M. Williams.
Economic Advisers (G7), K. J. Sear; J. Tarsh.

Information Technology Branch

Assistant Secretary (G5), F. M. Scott.
Senior Principals (G6), B. Bekhradnia; A. Cowan.
Principals (G7), A. Allison; K. Coombs; A. M. Cooper; B. Lillburn; Mrs. N. A. T. Malt; Mrs. J. D. Nisbet.

Statistics Branch

Assistant Secretary (G5), W. B. Wakefield.
Chief Statisticians (G5), P. L. Turnbull; J. W. Gardner.
Statisticians (G7), W. H. Barron; R. E. Dew; R. K. Jain; Mrs. S. Keith; T. C. Knight; Mrs. I. M. MacDonald-Davies; Mrs. I. R. Magill; Mrs. A. E. Mellor.
Principal Research Officer (G7), D. J. Hodges.
Principal (G7), P. D. Gott.

Legal Branch
Assistant Legal Adviser (G5), A. G. Jones.
Assistant Solicitors (G6), F. L. Croft; R. S. Cumming.
Senior Legal Assistant (G6), Miss M. E. Trefgarne; A. D. Preston; M. A. Widdrington.

Library
Librarian, D. N. Allum.

Finance Branch
Assistant Secretaries (G5), R. D. Horne; N. J. Sanders (*Deputy Accountant General*).
Senior Principals (G6), W. Gamble; P. Smith.
Principals (G7), E. A. Alcock; P. J. Edwards; B. M. Ellington; J. P. Partington; G. R. E. Stewart; C. E. Treen.

H.M. Inspectorate (England)
Senior Chief Inspector (G2), E. J. Bolton, c.b.
Chief Inspectors (G4), B. C. Arthur; J. A. Everson; A. R. Marshall; T. P. Melia; Miss A. C. Millett; A. J. Rose; B. D. Short.
Divisional Inspectors (G5), B. A. Chaplin; E. C. Cordell; Miss V. J. Evans; B. W. Howes; L. Jackson; E. Scott; D. E. Walker.
Staff Inspectors (G5), T. H. Bennetts; R. G. Booth; P. L. Bradbury; R. J. Brake; P. Brown; P. R. Clarke; A. G. Clegg; D. A. Cormican; A. T. Cox; L. S. Crickmore; D. A. Denegri; B. Denton; Mrs. G. M. Dolden; Mrs. G. Everson; J. H. Fairhurst; D. Flanagan; G. R. Frater; A. Gibson; G. Goldstein; J. G. Goulding; V. Green; R. A. S. Hennessey; G. A. Hicks; P. Highfield; M. W. Himsworth; D. Hollingsworth; Miss B. J. Lewis; D. J. Marjoram; P. F. Marlow; C. P. Marshall; J. H. Mayhew; R. W. Mycock; P. J. Pearson; G. T. Peaker; C. M. Richards; M. V. Salter; C. H. Selby; P. Singh; Mrs. M. M. Smart; D. E. Soulsby; Mrs. B. Staniland; D. W. Taylor; K. W. Thomas; M. J. Tomlinson; D. R. Trainor; A. F. Turberfield; A. D. J. Turner; Mrs. S. P. Twite; J. R. Ungoed-Thomas; D. G. Vallis; D. L. West; J. B. Willcock; R. C. Williams; T. Wylie; R. E. Young.
H.M. Inspectors (G6), Mrs. C. A. Agambar; W. Agnew; D. W. Airey; Miss J. A. Aldwinckle; Mrs. G. M. V. Alexander; D. J. Allen; K. J. Anglesey; P. T. Armitstead; Miss J. L. Atkin; D. Baillie; W. G. Bakehouse; Mrs. C. A. Baker; C. Banks; Miss D. M. L. Barlow; A. M. Barnes; Mrs. J. M. Barnes; J. N. Barnes; G. Barratt; R. E. Barrett; Ms. E. P. Baxell; Mrs. J. M. Bell; P. E. B. Belshaw; D. A. Bennett; J. F. Bennett; S. G. L. Bignell; D. B. F. Billimore; Miss. V. Blackburn; A. J. Boddington; Mrs. C. M. Bond; Miss J. M. Bonner; P. R. Booth; A. C. Boucher; Mrs. E. J. Boucher; Miss E. Bourne; C. Bowring-Carr; Mrs. M. T. Boyd-Clarke; G. R. H. Boys; D. J. Bradbury; M. H. Bradley; T. E. Brand; Mrs. H. S. Bridge; E. F. H. Brittain; J. Broadbent; F. Brook; Mrs. J. M. Brookes; Miss C. M. Brooks; A. W. Brown; Mrs. M. A. Buckingham; D. G. Buckland; M. J. Buckley; Miss K. Bull; T. A. Burdett; J. M. Burgess; Mrs. G. M. Burke; J. E. Butler; Ms. M. E. Caistor; R. A. Callender; M. J. Campbell; P. Candlish; N. Carr; Mrs. J. Carswell; M. J. Caton; Mrs. E. Cave; B. Chandler; Miss J. A. Cheong; B. J. Chopping; Miss D. H. Chorley; D. Clare; P. R. Clarke; G. Clay; R. S. W. Clements; D. G. Close; D. A. Coe; J. E. M. Cohn; B. Colbeck; M. J. Collier; Mrs. P. M. Collins; M. J. Convey; Mrs. M. A. Cooke; P. Cradock; G. Cranmer; Mrs. G. K. Crawford; J. Creedy; Mrs. M. E. Crisp; Miss K. Cross; R. S. Crowcroft; D. K. Danna; Mrs. J. Darroch; C. M. Davies; T. Dickinson; T. Dillon; A. Dobson; Lady Donoughue; J. A. S. Dossett; R. G. Dyke; Mrs. M. E. Eade; P. D. Edwards; Mrs. C. Elliott; D. L. Elliott; J. A. Elliott; M. A. Emery;

Mrs. V. E. Emmett; Mrs. J. E. Ensing; K. J. Evans; Mrs. G Everson; J. H. Fairhurst; Mrs. C. Farrell; V. A. Farthing; Mrs. B. E. Fawcett; B. P. Fitzgerald; J. Fitzpatrick; I. G. Forrest; D. H. M. Foster; Ms. C. M. Fraser; D. Fraser; P. S. Friend; B. Frost; C. C. Frost; D. J. Frost; R. C. Frost; B. S. Furness; P. Gannon; D. A. Gardiner; P. H. W. Garwood; I. Gera; Mrs. P. M. Gibbon; Mrs. J. E. A. Gifford; G. A. Gill; C. R. Gillings; Ms. S. Girling; C. Goodhead; Mrs E. M. Goodwin; Mrs. K. N. Gosling; C. D. Gould; C. Goulding; Miss S. Gracey; D. I. Grant; J. D. Green; B. Gregson-Allcott; N. Grenyer; P. Griffiths; R. H. Griffiths; Mrs. P. E. Guest-Jones; Mrs. F. Hadley; Miss C. E. Hague; E. E. J. Haidon; D. S. Hale; D. J. Halligan; N. J. Hallmark; J. A. Hamer; J. N. Hardwick; J. S. Hardwick; R. A. Hargreaves; B. R. Harris; C. R. Hart; D. J. Hart; R. Hartley; A. Harvey; B. P. Hayes; Mrs. G. M. Hayes; G. M. Hearnshaw; Miss L. M. Hencher; M. L. Hening; J. F. Herbert; Mrs. J. S. Herbert; J. A. Hertrich; P. M. Hesketh; D. Hibbert; T. Higginbottom; J. F. H. Hilbourne; W. J. Hill; Mrs. G. A. Hindhaugh; D. G. Holford; J. R. Holmes; C. Hooper; F. X. Horan; J. E. Hosegood; D. J. House; M. J. Howarth; B. A. F. Hubbard; B. R. Hudson; V. C. Hughes; J. E. Hunt; P. J. Hunt; J. B. Huskins; J. N. Hutchinson; J. S. Ingleson; P. F. J. Irvine; A. R. Ivatts; M. J. Ive; H. A. James; T. M. Jardine; B. D. Jelly; D. W. John; Miss S. H. Johns; P. W. R. Johnson; H. B. Joicey; D. A. Jones; Mrs. M. E. Jones; M. G. Jones; R. Kapadia; W. D. Kaye; Mrs. A. C. Keelan-Towner; M. Kerrigan; M. A. Khan; B. L. King; D. P. King; K. King; A. V. Kirwan; D. Knighton; J. B. Knox; D. G. Labon; A. J. Lacey; G. N. E. Lageard; B. M. Lane; J. W. Langley; J. W. F. Learmonth; E. H. Leaton; J. P. Leigh; D. Lewis; D. F. Lewis; D. J. Lewis; Mrs. J. M. Lingard; E. R. B. Little; A. W. Littlewood; W. G. K. Lloyd; Miss B. M. Lockwood; A. B. Lomax; R. Long; Mrs. E. M. Lowe; T. L. Lusty; J. A. Mabey; Mrs. H. M. Macdonald; Mrs. P. R. Maclay; M. E. Madden; R. H. Manser; G. D. Marrow; J. G. Marshall; E. S. Martin; Mrs. M. M. Martin; T. W. Martin; W. P. Massam; Miss E. M. Matthews; J. E. Mattick; M. R. E. Mealing; B. R. Meech; Miss B. E. Megson; Mrs. R. Melling; G. Merlane; B. E. Merton; K. Miller; H. Millington; J. K. Millington; D. Mills; Miss H. A. Moffat; A. R. H. Monk; P. Muschamp; H. Myers; C. McCall; Mrs. J. C. McGinty; D. C. McIntosh; M. McLaughlin; Mrs. J. McLean; I. A. McNally; C. Needham; Miss D. A. Nelson; R. Nicholls; Ms. S. M. Nicholls; A. J. Nisbett; P. M. Nixon; M. Norman; Mrs. G. I. Oldham; P. I. Orr; A. Owen; W. E. Owen; Ms. J. H. Paraskeva; Miss P. Park; K. Parker; D. J. Parks; J. M. Parsons; I. M. Paterson; Mrs. D. M. Penn; Miss J. M. Phillips; P. Piddock; K. Pinder; M. W. A. Pitts; E. A. Pollard; M. R. Potter; C. Potts; C. P. Power; A. A. Price; Mrs. M. P. Pryce; M. E. Pullee; W. J. Rea; C. J. Redman; J. Reynolds; J. C. Richardson; A. S. Robertson; G. Robson; I. A. Rodger; S. J. A. Rogers; A. C. Rowe; C. Rowe; D. H. Rutt; M. J. Ryder; M. V. Salter; Mrs. J. Sartain; Mrs. K. J. Saunders; B. Sayer; Ms. M. Sayer; J. C. Schenk; D. J. Scott; P. L. Seaborne; G. W. Searle; D. T. V. Sharman; D. I. Shelton; A. R. Shirley; J. R. Shirtcliff; Mrs. V. M. Sida; P. J. Silvester; Mrs. D. E. Simmonds; G. Sleightholme; B. J. Smith; P. J. C. Smith; P. R. Smith; J. D. Stannard; O. M. Stannard; J. Stanyer; J. W. Steel; J. M. Steels; J. B. Stevenson; Miss M. T. Stiles; R. W. Stockdale; M. M. Stone; C. F. Stoneman; Mrs. J. E. Storrie; R. Storrs; Ms. M. E. Stride; R. Summersby; D. P. Swain; A. Sykes; D. W. Sylvester; F. Taylor; J. A. Taylor; R. S. Taylor; A. F. Thomas; D. L. Thorburn; R. M. Thorpe; J. Tierney; M. J. Todd; B. D. Tomkins; J. V. Townshend; J. E. Trickey; Mrs. J. W. Turner; E.

A. Vallis; B. C. L. Walker; C. V. Wall; A. Walmsley; Miss P. Walters; M. Wardlow; Mrs. A. P. Warren; R. K. Warren; N. G. Warwick; J. M. Watson; M. R. Webb; Mrs. J. M. Webberley; R. R. Weir; D. J. Wells; P. E. Weston; R. Whitburn; Miss F. White; J. White; F. Whiteman; D. G. Whittaker; Mrs. O. Whittingham; C. C. B. Wightwick; Ms. S. M. Wiles; J. B. Willcock; D. G. Williams; J. R. Williams; K. G. Williams; Mrs. S. A. Williams; G. Wilson-Pratt; D. P. T. Woodgate; J. D. Woodhouse; Mrs. S. A. Woodroffe; J. A. Woodrow; J. I. Wragg; Miss B. M. Wright; Miss A. P. Yeomans; F. P. Young; A. J. Youngs.

Attached to H.M. Inspectorate, S. R. C. Jones (*Staff Inspector attached*); G. A. N. Smith; T. Vincent; Mrs. J. A. Wisker.

H.M. Inspectorate Support Services

Principal (G7), P. J. Thorpe.
Senior Executive Officer, Miss M. Osborne.

H.M. Inspectorate (Wales)
(*See* Welsh Office)

Establishments and Organization Branch

Assistant Secretaries (G5), E. B. Granshaw; H. W. B. Davies.
Senior Principal (G6), R. E. Judd.
Principals (G7), H. H. Barrick; Miss S. A. Clarke; K. R. Fitzgerald; P. L. Jones; R. M. King; P. Ramsden; B. C. Willett.

ELECTRICITY AUTHORITIES

THE ELECTRICITY COUNCIL
30 Millbank, SW1P 4RD
[01–834 2333]

The Electricity Council, a non-trading body, is the central council of the supply industry for the formulation of general policy. It is a federal body with representation from both the generation and distribution boards which provides a forum for common problems to be resolved with independent guidance from Central Members and their supporting staff. The Council's main functions are to advise the Secretary of State for Energy on matters affecting the supply industry and "to promote and assist the maintenance and development by electricity boards in England and Wales of an efficient, co-ordinated and economical system of electricity supply".

Chairman, Sir Philip Jones, C.B. £66,500
Deputy Chairman, D. G. Jefferies . £55,000 to £60,000
Members, R. W. Orson, C.B.E.; R. A. Farrance; D. G. C. Gronow. . . . . £40,000 to £45,000
Members from the Central Electricity Generating Board, The Lord Marshall of Goring, C.B.E., F.R.S.; G. A. W. Blackman, C.B.E.
Secretary, R. Savinson.

CENTRAL ELECTRICITY GENERATING BOARD
Sudbury House, 15 Newgate Street, EC1A 7AU
[01–634 5111]

The Central Electricity Generating Board owns and operates the power stations and grid system of main transmission lines. It is responsible for bulk supply of electricity to the twelve area boards; and also, for traction purposes, to the railways. Its duties also include (i) planning the provision of new generating and transmission capacity, including research, (ii) siting and constructing new power stations (conventional and nuclear) and (iii) siting and constructing extensions to the transmission network. The C.E.G.B. is a highly capitalized process industry—engaged in converting primary fuels into electricity, of which they are the "wholesalers". Among its main problems are the choice of primary fuels for the power stations; the development of new technology (for example, nuclear generation); and problems concerned with amenity, as in siting of power stations and grid-lines, the disposal of effluents, and smoke elimination.

Chairman, The Lord Marshall of Goring, C.B.E., F.R.S. £66,500
Deputy Chairman and Production Managing Director, G. A. W. Blackman, C.B.E. ... £55,000 to £60,000
Members, D. A. Davis; F. Ledger, O.B.E.; J. W. Baker.
Part-time Members, R. M. Dantzic; Sir Eric Sharp, C.B.E.; R. V. Giordano (*each*).
Secretary, G. H. Hadley.

ELECTRICITY BOARDS
The 12 Area Electricity Boards

(The Chairmen of Area Boards receive a salary of £30,000 to £45,000).
London, Templar House, 81–87 High Holborn, WC1V 6NU. *Chairman*, J. J. Wilson. *Sec.*, D. G. Rees.
South Eastern, Grand Avenue, Hove, East Sussex BN3 2LS. *Chairman*, G. A. Squair. *Sec.*, S. M. Wide.
Southern, Southern Electricity House, Littlewick Green, Maidenhead, Berks. *Chairman*, D. A. Ross. *Sec.*, R. C. Collier.
South Western, Electricity House, Colston Avenue, Bristol BS1 4TS. *Chairman*, K. F. Whittle. *Sec. and Solicitor*, S. G. Marshall.
Eastern, P.O. Box 40, Wherstead, Ipswich, Suffolk IP9 2AQ. *Chairman*, J. C. Smith. *Sec.*, W. L. M. French.
East Midlands, P.O. Box 4, North P.D.O., 398 Coppice Road, Arnold, Nottingham NG5 7HX. *Chairman*, J. F. Harris. *Sec.*, T. F. C. Walker.
Midlands, P. O. Box 8 Mucklow Hill, Halesowen, West Midlands B62 8BP. *Chairman*, B. S. Townsend. *Sec.*, R. K. Young.
South Wales, St. Mellons, Cardiff CF3 9XW. *Chairman*, J. Wynford Evans. *Sec.*, A. Worth.
Merseyside and North Wales, Sealand Road, Chester. *Chairman*, B. H. Weston, *Sec.*, C. W. Leonard.
Yorkshire, Wetherby Road, Scarcroft, Leeds LS14 3HS. *Chairman*, J. Porteous. *Sec. and Solicitor*, R. Dickinson.
North Eastern, Carliol House, Newcastle upon Tyne NE99 1SE. *Chairman*, T. Rutherford, C.B.E., *Sec.*, J. W. Dalgleish.
North Western, Cheetwood Road, Manchester M8 8BA. *Chairman*, B. R. Hastings. *Sec.*, B. Benson.

NORTH OF SCOTLAND HYDRO-ELECTRIC BOARD
16 Rothesay Terrace, Edinburgh EH3 7SE
[031–225 1361]

Chairman, M. Joughin, C.B.E. (*part-time*) £23,000
Deputy Chairman and Chief Executive, K. R. Vernon, C.B.E.
Members (*part-time*), A. T. H. Tulloch; Christine A. M. Davis (*Chairman of Consultative Council*).; M. G. N. Walker, C.B.E.; D. J. Miller; C. S. Macphie; D. F. Myles; G. Barrie (£3,750 to £5,750).
Secretary, J. E. M. Watts.

SOUTH OF SCOTLAND ELECTRICITY BOARD
Spean Street, Glasgow G44 4BE
[041–637 7177]

Chairman, D. J. Miller £52,750
Deputy Chairman, I. M. H. Preston £44,250
Non-Executive Members, A. Barr; N. C. Kuenssberg; I. H. Macdonald, O.B.E.; J. Neumann, C.B.E.; Mrs. J.

A. Thomson (£3,750); M. Joughin, C.B.E.; G. B. Whyte (*unpaid*).
Secretary, D. A. S. MacLaren.

DEPARTMENT OF EMPLOYMENT
Caxton House, Tothill Street, SW1H 9NF
[01–213 3000]

The Department of Employment is responsible for Government policies on the working of the labour market and the needs and conditions of people at work. These policies include the encouragement of employment and of effective training for it, the provision of special measures to deal with unemployment, and the promotion of good industrial relations and a healthy and safe working environment. The Department publishes a wide range of statistics and other information bearing on these matters, including the movement of prices and earnings.

Many of the executive functions carried out in the Department's area of policy interest are exercised by separate public agencies reporting to the Secretary of State for Employment.

Salaries

Secretary of State £33,145
Minister of State £22,875
Under Secretary of State £16,885
Grade 1 .... £64,739
Grade 2 .... £43,264–£45,349
Grade 3 .... £33,725–£36,852
Grade 4 .... £28,975–£30,475
Grade 5 .... £24,739–£28,215
Grade 6 .... £18,786–£25,335

Secretary of State for Employment, THE RT. HON. NORMAN FOWLER, M.P.
Private Secretary (G5), J. Turner.
Assistant Private Secretaries, P. Baldwinson; B. Evans.
Parliamentary Private Secretary, P. Thurnam, M.P.
Minister of State, JOHN COPE, M.P.
Under Secretaries of State, J. Lee, M.P.; P. Nicholls, M.P.
Permanent Secretary (G1), Sir Michael Quinlan, K.C.B.
Deputy Secretaries (G2), R. J. Dawe, O.B.E.; I. Manley, C.B.
Legal Adviser (G3), M. Harris.

Industrial Relations

Grade 3, R. S. Allison; E. G. Whybrew.
Grade 5, D. W. Brown; N. H. Reed; A. G. Johnson.
Chief Wages Inspector (G6), J. A. Dyble.
Secretary of Wages Councils, S. Cottingham.

Manpower Policy

Grade 3 (Division 1), C. R. Walker.
Grade 3 (Division 2), M. E. G. Fogden.
Chief Executive of Unemployment Benefit Service (G4), J. W. Cooper.
Grade 5, M. J. Miller; R. A. David; L. Lewis; H. Miller.

Overseas Division

Grade 3, W. R. B. Robinson.
Grade 5, J. B. Sahw; G. Kahan.

Economic and Social Division

Chief Economic Adviser (G3), G. L. Reid.
Grade 5, Dr. V. G. Keddie; Mrs. Z. Hornstein; D. Stanton.

Employment Policy Division

Grade 3, C. F. Tucker.

Personnel and Business Services Division

Director of Personnel (G3), A. W. Brown.
Head of Business Services (G4), M. Davies.
Head of Group Personnel Unit (G5), S. Tolson.
Director of Computing (G5), S. Elliott.
Head of Personnel Services Branch (G5), D. Lifton.

Information Division

Head of Information (G5), B. Sutlieff.
Deputy Head of Information (G6), S. Reardon.

Finance Division

Director of Finance and Resource Management (G3),
D. G. Talintyre.
Grade 5, R. H. Chambers; K. J. Jordan.

Solicitor's Office

Legal Adviser (G3), M. Harris.

Statistics Division

Director of Statistics (G3), P. D. Dworkin.
Chief Statisticians (G5), M. J. Hughes; Mrs. A. V.
Wheatcroft; D. J. Sellwood; D. E. Allnutt.

Small Firms and Tourism Division

Grade 3, R. A. Lingard.
Grade 5, I. M. Jones; Dr. P. J. Graham; Mrs. J. Peretz.

DEPARTMENT OF ENERGY
Thames House South,
Millbank, SW1P 4QJ (unless otherwise stated)
[01–211 3000]

The Department of Energy is responsible within
the Government for the development of policies in
relation to all forms of energy. It also discharges
governmental functions connected with the publicly-
owned coal and electricity industries. It is responsible for the Atomic Energy Authority; is the sponsoring Department for the nuclear power industry and
is responsible for the development of oil and gas
resources on the British sector of the Continental
Shelf. It is the sponsoring Department for the oil
industry and is responsible for international aspects
of energy problems, including relations and co-
operation with oil producing countries. The Department is the co-ordinating body for energy efficiency
policy and for encouraging the development of new
sources of energy.

Salaries

Secretary of State	£33,145
Minister of State (Commons)	£22,875
Parliamentary Under Secretary	£16,885
Grade 1	£64,739
Grade 2	£43,264–£45,349
Grade 3	£33,725–£36,852
Grade 4	£28,975–£30,475
Grade 5	£24,739–£28,215
Grade 6	£18,786–£25,335
Head of P.E.D.	£44,947
Reservoir Evaluation Specialist I	£39,400
Reservoir Evaluation Specialist II	£29,560–£37,100
Petroleum Specialist II	£25,834–£32,400
A.D./Accounts	£18,562–£25,106

Secretary of State for Energy, THE RT. HON. CECIL
PARKINSON, M.P.
  Principal Private Secretary, G. S. Dart.
  Parliamentary Private Secretary, M. Fallon, M.P.
  Assistant Private Secretaries, Miss P. K. Jones; S.
  Sklaroff; R. Major.
Minister of State for Energy, THE RT. HON. PETER
MORRISON, M.P.
  Private Secretary, S. J. Whiting.
  Parliamentary Private Secretary, Dr. I. Twinn, M.P.

Parliamentary Under-Secretary of State, M. Spicer,
M.P.
Permanent Under Secretary of State (G1), P. Gregson,
C.B.
  Private Secretary, E. F. Quilty.
Deputy Secretaries (G2), J. R. S. Guinness; G. H.
Chipperfield.
Chief Scientific Adviser, Sir Sam Edwards.
Parliamentary Clerk, A. D. Proud.

Establishment and Finance Division

Principal Establishment and Finance Officer (G3), C.
E. Henderson.
Director of Resource Management (G4), C. C. Wilcock.
Assistant Secretaries (G5), R. Beasley; Dr. W. S.
Burroughs; J. Morris; Dr. F. R. Heathcote; P. D.
Atkinson.

Electricity Division

Under Secretary (G3), J. H. Pownall.
Assistant Secretaries (G5), G. W. Thynne; Dr. A.
Eggington; W. J. Rickett.
Chief Electrical Engineering Inspector (G5), D. C.
Gore.

Coal Division

Under Secretary (G3), M. S. Buckley.
Assistant Secretaries (G5), M. H. Atkinson; E. Pash.

Atomic Energy Division

Under Secretary (G3), D. I. Morphet.
Assistant Secretaries (G5), P. H. Agrell; B. Hampton;
Dr. E. G. Finer; Dr. J. G. Wright.

Energy Technology Division

Chief Scientist (G3), Dr. J. Rae.
Deputy Chief Scientific Officers (G5), Dr. R. G. S.
Skipper; G. Bevan.
Assistant Secretary (G5), Dr. W. D. Evans.
Senior Principal Scientific Officers (G6), H. F. Fergu-
son; R. A. Meir; Dr. S. E. R. Hiscocks; G. S.
Dearnley; W. Macpherson; Dr. D. Fairmaner.

International Unit

Assistant Secretary (G5), S. W. Freemantle.

Nationalised Industry Policy

Assistant Secretary (G5), J. Whaley, C.B.E.

Energy Efficiency Office

Director General (G3), W. I. MacIntyre.
Directors (G5), P. G. P. D. Fullerton; M. Keay; Mr. J.
E. P. Miles.
Director (G6), Dr. D. Hauser.

Economics and Statistics Division

Under Secretary (G3), E. H. M. Price.
Chief Statistician (G5), T. S. Simmons.
Senior Economic Advisers (G5), A. J. Meyrick; S. A.
Price; Dr. P. A. Rowlatt.

Oil Division

Under Secretary (G3), B. D. Emmett.
Assistant Secretaries (G5), Dr. C. J. Myerscough; P.
T. Harding; W. C. F. Butler; Ms. A. Beaton.

Gas Division

Under Secretary (G3), D. R. Davis.
Assistant Secretary (G5), J. R. Wakely.

Gas and Oil Measurement Branch
Government Buildings, Saffron Road, Wigston,
Leicester
[0533 785354]

Director (G5), J. Plant.
Senior Chief Examiner (G6), G. A. Paul-Clerk.

Petroleum Engineering Division

Director of P.E.D., P. J. Walmsley, M.B.E..
Reservoir Evaluation Specialist I, K. R. J. Trott.
Reservoir Evaluation Specialists II, J. R. V. Brooks;
D. W. Mann.
Reservoir Evaluation Specialist I, J. R. Petrie.
Petroleum Specialists II, R. Giles; D. R. Clementson;
B. B. Moore; N. G. Marguerie.
Senior Principal Scientific Officer (G6), J. N. Mansfield.
Assistant Director Engineer (G6), G. N. Marriott.

Offshore Supplies Office

Alhambra House, 45 Waterloo Street,
Glasgow G2 6AS
[041–221 8777]

Director General (G3), J. E. d'Ancona.
Director Industry (G5), W. E. Allison.
Director Policy and Administration (G5), A. E. Maule.
Director Research and Development (G5), C. P. Carter.
Director China Unit (G6), Dr. K. P. Forrest.
Senior Principal Business Development (G6), H.
Holden.
Senior Principal Scientific Officer (G6), Dr. K. Tregonning.
Assistant Director Engineers (G6), H. M. Whiteside;
P. R. Taylor.

Information Division

Head of Information (G5), M. S. D. Granatt.
Deputy Head of Information (G6), Mrs. A. Wadsworth.
Chief Press Officer (G7), Ms. M. Palau.

DEPARTMENT OF THE ENVIRONMENT
2 Marsham Street, SW1P 3EB
[01–212 3434]

The Department of the Environment is responsible for planning and land use; local government; housing, construction; inner city areas; new towns; environmental protection; conservation areas and countryside affairs; royal parks and palaces; historic buildings and ancient monuments; sport and recreation. The Property Services Agency is responsible for all construction activities, supplies and transport at home and abroad for all Government departments including the Ministry of Defence and some repayment clients including British Telecom.

Salaries

Secretary of State	£33,145
Minister of State (Lords)	£30,640
Minister of State (Commons)	£22,875
Parliamentary Under Secretary	£16,885
Grade 1	£65,000
*Grade 1*A	£59,500
Grade 2	£43,500–£45,500
Grade 3	£34,000–£37,000
Grade 4	£30,344–£31,844
Grade 5	£24,765–£28,215
Grade 6	£18,786–£25,355
Director, B.R.S., U.I.P.P.L.	£41,000
Chief Inspector, Pollution Inspectorate	£29,577–£30,537

Secretary of State for the Environment, THE RT. HON.
NICHOLAS RIDLEY, M.P.
Private Secretary, R. U. Young.
Special Adviser, Mrs. K. Ramsay.
Parliamentary Private Secretary, Hon. N. Soames,
M.P.

Minister for Housing and Planning, THE HON.
WILLIAM WALDEGRAVE, M.P.
Private Secretary, Mrs. H. Gosh.
Special Adviser, (vacant).

Minister for Local Government, MICHAEL HOWARD,
M.P.
Private Secretary, N. A. J. Kinghan.

Minister for Environment, Countryside and Water,
THE RT. HON. LORD BELSTEAD.
Private Secretary, S. Watts.
Parliamentary Under Secretaries of State:—
The Hon. Colin Moynihan, M.P.; *(also Minister for
Sport)*; D. Trippier, R.D., M.P.; C. Chope, O.B.E., M.P.;
Mrs. M. Roe, M.P.
Private Secretaries, P. J. Heron *(to Hon. C. Moyni-
han)*; Mrs. T. E. Vokes *(to D. Trippier)*; N.
Ledgerwood *(to C. Chope)*; J. R. Tillson *(to Mrs.
Roe)*.
Parliamentary Clerk, A. Mitcheson.
Permanent Secretary (G1), Sir Terence Heiser, K.C.B.
Private Secretary, Ms. A. J. Rutherford.
*Second Permanent Secretary, (G1*A*),* Sir Gordon
Manzie, K.C.B.
Private Secretary, P. Handley.

Information

Director (G4), D. A. McDonald.
*Head of Publicity, Promotions and Administration
(G5),* G. N. Bendon.
Head of News (G6), J. Gee.

MERSEYSIDE TASK FORCE

Under Secretary (G3), D. C. Renshaw.
Controller (G5), D. J. Morrison.

PLANNING, INNER CITIES, NEW TOWNS, REGIONAL DEVELOPMENT

Deputy Secretary (G2), J. Delafons, C.B.

Inner Cities

Under Secretary (G3), K. E. C. Sorensen.
Head of Divisions (G5), J. S. Parker; W. B. Solesbury;
Ms. D. S. Kahn; Mrs. D. S. Phillips; A. D. Whetnall.

Land and Property

Director (G4), C. K. Howes.
Grade 6, J. C. White.

Planning Land Use Policy

Under Secretary (G3), N. W. Summerton.
Grade 5, D. N. Donaldson; A. H. Corner; J. J. Rendall;
A. D. Fagin.

Planning Services

Director (G4), S. P. Byrne, C.B.E.
Grade 5, R. A. Bird; R. C. Mabey; J. A. Zetter.
Grade 6, P. Morgan; D. C. Stroud.

HOUSING, CONSTRUCTION AND THE BUILT HERITAGE

Deputy Secretary (G2), P. F. Owen.

Housing Associations and Private Sector

Director (G3), F. A. Osborn.
Heads of Divisions (G5), P. J. J. Britton; R. J. Gibson;
J. Vaughan; G. L. Laufer.
Grade 7, D. T. Jones; A. A. Brown.

Housing Monitoring and Analysis

Under Secretary (G3), D. C. L. Wroe.
Grade 5, J. E. Turner; A. E. Holmans; W. H. Stott; R.
F. Sellwood; D. T. I. G. Davies; N. Dorling.
Grade 6, Mrs. J. Littlewood.

Public Sector Housing

Under Secretary (G3), A. G. Watson.
Heads of Divisions (G5) D. R. Lewis; J. K. Stoker; R. Williams; P. F. Everall.

Housing Policy Studies

Under Secretary (G3), J. Hobson.
Grade 5, R. M. F. Bright.

Construction Industry

Director (G3), A. A. Pelling.
Heads of Divisions (G5), J. M. Hope; Mrs. J. M. Williams; S. T. McQuillin; I. C. Macpherson; F. D. Sando.

Sport and Recreation Division

Director (G3), A. A. Pelling.
Head of Division (G5), R. Jones.

Building Research Establishment

Director (G3), Dr. R. G. H. Watson, C.B.
Deputy Director (G4), R. G. Courtney.
Heads of Departments and Stations (G5), Dr. J. B. Menzies; N. O. Milbank; K. N. Palmer; J. M. Baker.
Heads of Services/Research (G6), A. J. M. Harrison; B. O. Hall; I. L. Freeman; Mrs. J. Lemessany; Dr. H. W. Pratt; Dr. R. F. Stevens; J. B. Bowden; Dr. J. K. Eaton; Dr. J. F. A. Moore; Dr. A. B. Birtles; R. E. Baldwin; Dr. V. A. C. Crisp; C. J. D. Webster; Dr. W. H. Gutt; Dr. L. H. Everett; B. B. Pigott; P. F. Thorne; Dr. W. D. Woolley; J. F. S. Carruthers; Dr. J. M. W. Morgan; Dr. A. J. Majumdar, M.B.E.

Ancient Monuments and Historic Buildings

Director (G3), Ms. E. C. Turton.
Head of Royal Parks, Palaces, Presentation and Central Services Division (G5), (vacant).
Grade 6, A. Cornwell.
Grade 7, J. A. Goodburn.
Bailiff of the Royal Parks Office (G6), R. A. Stephenson, M.V.O.
Grade 7, Miss M. E. Gree; Miss A. S. Mitchell.

Heritage Sponsorship Division

Head of Division (G5), T. E. Radice.
Grade 7, N. F. Digance; M. A. L. Ross; P. H. Denton.

CHIEF ARCHITECTURAL ADVISER ON THE BUILT ENVIRONMENT

Grade 2, J. B. Jefferson.
Grade 5, J. E. Turner.

FINANCE AND LOCAL GOVERNMENT

Deputy Secretary, Principal Finance Officer (G2), K. F. J. Ennals, C.B.

Local Government Finance Policy

Under Secretary (G3), C. J. S. Brearley.
Grade 4 (temp), Mrs. M. McDonald.
Grade 5, D. L. H. Roberts; A. C. B. Ramsey; P. D. Ward; J. E. Roberts; I. C. McBrayne; J. Adams.

Housing, Water and Central Finance

Under Secretary (G3), P. J. Fletcher.
Grade 5, I. G. Urquhart; D. A. C. Heigham; R. S. Dudding.
Director Accountant (G5), B. Redfern.
Grade 6, G. Knowles.

Local Government

Under Secretary (G3), R. J. A. Sharp.
Grade 5, R. Compton; C. J. Griffin; Mrs. L. A. Heath; A. H. Davis; A. J. C. Simcock.
Grade 6, P. G. Iredale.

CHIEF ENVIRONMENTAL SCIENTISTS

Deputy Secretary (G2), Dr. M. W. Holdgate, C.B.
Deputy Chief Scientist (G3), Dr. D. J. Fisk.
Grade 5, C. L. Robson.

ENVIRONMENT PROTECTION

Deputy Secretary (G2), Dr. M. W. Holdgate, C.B.

H.M. Inspectorate of Pollution

Director (G3), B. D. Ponsford.
Chief Inspector (Air, Wastes, Water), R. J. Perriman.
Chief Inspector (Radioactive Substances) (G5), F. S. Feates; J. P. Henry; D. A. Mills.
Deputy Chief Inspectors, J. M. Thayer; M. F. Tunnicliffe; L. N. Stuffins.
Grade 6, Dr. P. D. Johnston; A. Windsor; Dr. A. G. Duncan; J. Bentley.
District Inspectors, S. D. Phillips; G. G. Jones; M. R. Walters; J. Downs; Dr. L. A. Hales; J. E. Hooper; B. T. Head; Dr. K. Speakman; E. F. Tomlinson; A. H. Brown; Dr. E. Hutton; J. Barrett.

Central Directorate of Environmental Protection

Under Secretary (G3), J. P. G. Rowcliff.
Grade 5, Miss F. McConnell; Dr. N. J. King; P. S. MacCormack; J. A. Colley.
Grade 6, Dr. D. L. Simms; Dr. A. J. Apling.

Air, Noise and Wastes Directorate

Under Secretary (G3), Dr. D. J. Fisk.
Grade 5, N. Sanders; R. C. Argent.

Directorate of Rural Affairs

Under Secretary (G3), T. R. Hornsby.
Grade 5, A. Flexman; R. Bunce.
Grade 6, J. C. Peters.

Water Directorates

Director (G3), J. A. L. Gunn.
Grade 5, M. G. Healey; R. J. Smith; M. J. C. Faulkner; D. R. Ritchie; R. J. Dorrington.

LEGAL

Solicitor and Legal Adviser (G2), M. J. Ware.
Principal Assistant Solicitors (G3), J. G. Medcalf; J. G. Roscoe.
Assistant Solicitors (G5), R. S. Cumming; Ms. S. D. Underman; J. L. Comber; Mrs. J. L. Weinberg; J. A. Catlin; Mrs. I. M. Watson; P. J. Szell; D. K. Sergeant; I. D. Day; Miss A. Brett-Holt.

PROPERTY SERVICES AGENCY

Chief Executive (G1A), Sir Gordon Manzie, K.C.B..
Private Secretary, P. Handley.

DEPUTY CHIEF EXECUTIVE 1

Deputy Chief Executive (G2), A. R. Atherton.

Home Regional Services

Director (G3), A. J. Aveling.
Grade 5, J. W. Deane; R. Kent; E. R. Turtle.
Head of Works Division (G6), J. P. Hammond.

Scottish Services

Director (G3), A. G. Gosling.
Grade 5, D. R. Smith; P. M. Livesey; J. S. Wilson.

Central Office for Wales

Director (G4), J. H. Clemits.
Works Officer (G5), A. N. Towers.
Admin. Officer (G6), A. L. S. Richard.

Regions

Director (G3):
  London, G. Hopkinson.
Directors (G4):
  Eastern, A. J. B. Staveley
  Midland, K. H. A. Allen.
  North East, G. Flanagan.
  North West, M. M. Harrison.
  South East, P. J. M. Butter.
  South West, M. Baggott.
  Southern, M. R. Newey.

DEPUTY CHIEF EXECUTIVE 2

Deputy Chief Executive (G2), H. P. Johnston, C.B.

Civil Accommodation

Director (G3), R. G. S. Johnston.
Chief Estate Surveyor (G4), R. P. Hore.
Grade 5, F. Boonham; Mrs. L. A. C. Simcock; D. J. Phillips; W. H. M. Clarke; G. H. Sowden.
Grade 6, R. M. Hosangady; G. Southey; J. D. Turfitt; L. G. Collett; M. H. Bowles.

Defence Services I

Director (G3), R. A. Gomme.
Grade 5, H. L. Froome-Lewis; M. Clayton; D. C. P. Izsatt; R. Gray; D. Ashwoth.
Grade 6, R. K. Houghton.
Germany:
Director (G4), R. B. Perry.
Regional Works Officer (G5), P. W. Berrington.
Regional Admin. Officer (G6), D. C. Falvey.

Defence Services II

Director (G3), A. S. Kennedy.
Grade 5, P. Kitchen; G. D. Miles; S. G. D. Duguid; M. R. Sutton; D. K. Warren; A. K. W. Morgan.
Grade 6, K. A. Holme.

Defence Estates Services Division

Grade 5, M. D. Clarke.

DIRECTOR GENERAL OF DESIGN SERVICES

Director General (G2), J. B. Jefferson, C.B.E.

Directorate of Architectural Services

Director (G4), J. E. Jeavons.
Director (G5), C. A. P. Crooke.

Building and Quantity Surveying Services

Director (G4), K. A. Miles.
Grade 5, M. Barney; M. G. Stuart.

Civil Engineering Services

Director (G4), R. F. Hughes.
Grade 5, D. A. Woodward.

Mechanical and Electrical Engineering Services

Director (G4), R. C. Cracknell.
Grade 5, J. Fisher.

PSA ESTABLISHMENTS AND INFORMATION TECHNOLOGY MANAGEMENT OFFICE SERVICES

Principal Establishment Officer (G3), P. S. Draper.
Grade 5, R. A. Stead; G. J. Skinner; F. M. Rymill.

Information Technology and Office Systems

Grade 4, Mrs. E. M. Causley Cooper.
Computing Division:
Grade 5, D. Evans.
Grade 6, M. Nelson; F. J. H. Brown; A. L. Cole.

PSA FINANCE

Principal Finance Officer (G3), R. A. Munday.
Grade 5, A. E. Coules; M. L. Taylor.
Controller of Accounts (G5), J. A. Pearson.
Director of Contracts (G4), C. Pink.
Deputy Director (G5), M. J. Wanstall.
Head of Internal Audit (G5), J. W. C. Wilton.
Public Expenditure (G5), J. E. Kidgell.
Grade 6, P. Ashton.

THE CROWN SUPPLIERS

Controller (G3), D. T. Routh.
Financial Controller (G5), J. Cousins.
Assistant Controllers (G5), E. L. Pinfold; A. H. Pollington; P. L. Leonard.
Grade 6, R. Thrower.

DEPARTMENTS OF THE ENVIRONMENT AND TRANSPORT REGIONAL OFFICES

West Midlands, Birmingham.—*Regional Director (G3)*, H. F. Ellis-Rees. *Regional Controllers (G5)*, S. Jones; D. L. Saunders; Mrs. P. M. Holland.
Yorkshire and Humberside, Leeds.—*Regional Director (G3)*, J. F. Ballard. *Regional Controllers (G5)*, J. B. Wilson; K. Beaumont.
North West, Manchester.—*Regional Director (G3)*, F. Kendall. *Regional Controllers (G5)*, B. C. Isherwood; D. J. Morrison; J. W. Glester.
Northern, Newcastle upon Tyne.—*Regional Director (G3)*, A. G. Balls. *Regional Controllers (G5)*, J. A. M. Hastings; R. G. Bell.
South West, Bristol.—*Regional Director (G3)*, G. M. Wedd. *Regional Controller (G5)*, G. Ashbridge.
East Midlands, Nottingham.—*Regional Director (G4)*, P. M. Hewitt, O.B.E. *Regional Controller (G6)*, G. Meynell, M.B.E.; Miss R. M. Whittaker.
South East, W.14.—*Regional Director (G3)*, D. Grufydd Jones. *Regional Controllers (G5)*, N. Thompson; M. W. M. Cairns.
Eastern, W.14.—*Regional Director (G3)*, G. D. Crane. *Regional Controllers (G5)*, J. J. Parsons; A. F. Richardson.

GREATER LONDON REGIONAL OFFICES

Under Secretary (G3), P. C. McQuail.
Grade 5, J. G. Grevatt; M. B. Gahagan; D. R. Bradley; B. Strong.

DEPARTMENTS OF THE ENVIRONMENT AND TRANSPORT—COMMON SERVICES
2 Marsham Street, SW1P 3EB
[01–212 3434]

ORGANIZATION AND ESTABLISHMENTS

Director General of Organisation and Establishments (G2), D. J. Burr.

Establishments Organisation Division
Grade 5, P. D. Burgess.

Senior Staff Management
Under Secretary (G3), R. J. Green.
Grade 5, H. D. Hallett.
Chief Librarian (G6), P. Kirwan.
Grade 6, F. R. Gill.

Personnel Management and Training
Director (G3), E. B. C. Osmotherly.
Grade 5, P. Stringfellow; G. D. Edmonds; D. A. R. Peel; A. S. D. Whybrow; L. B. Hicks.
Grade 6, B. L. W. Dexter; G. R. Wells; G. Bray; M. S. Barratt; R. E. Vidler.

Directorate of Administrative Resources
Director (G3), Miss D. A. Nichols.
Grade 4, P. Leonard.
Grade 5, A. Z. Levy; C. P. Evans; Miss L. F. Bell.

PLANNING INSPECTORATE
Chief Planning Inspector (G3), Miss E. B. Haran.
Deputy Chief Planning Inspector (G4), P. J. Roberts.
Director of Operations (G4), A. J. M. Morgan.
Assistant Chief Planning Inspectors (G5), M. M. Cross; H. S. Crow; T. M. Millington; J. Mossop; Miss G. M. Pain; G. Lidbury; J. G. Greenfield.
Head of Administration (G5), B. E. Fensome.

ROYAL COMMISSION ON ENVIRONMENTAL POLLUTION
Church House, Great Smith Street, SW1P 3BL
[01–212 8620]

Set up on Feb. 20, 1970, "to advise on matters, both national and international, concerning the pollution of the environment; on the adequacy of research in this field; and the future possibilities of danger to the environment."
Chairman, Prof. Sir Jack Lewis, F.R.S.
Members, Prof. B. E. Clayton; Prof. G. R. Conway; The Earl of Cranbrook; J. W. Edmonds; The Lord Nathan; Prof. D. E. Newland; J. J. R. Pope, O.B.E.; Dr. C. W. Suckling, F.R.S.; Prof. M. P. Vessey; Prof. H. Charnock, F.R.S.; L. C. G. Gilling, O.B.E.; J. M. Raisman, C.B.E.; Prof. E. M. Rothschild; Prof. Z. A. Silberston; Prof. W. D. P. Stewart, F.R.S.
Secretary, G. I. Fuller.

EQUAL OPPORTUNITIES COMMISSION
Overseas House, Quay Street, Manchester M3 3HN
[061–833 9244]

PRESS OFFICE: 1 Bedford Street. W.C.2 [01–379 6323]
REGIONAL OFFICES: St. Andrew House, 141 West Nile Street, Glasgow G1 2RN [041–332 8018]
Caerwys House, Windsor Place, Cardiff [0222–43552]

The Commission was set up by Parliament in 1975 as a result of the passing of the Sex Discrimination Act. It works towards the elimination of discrimination by virtue of sex or marital status and to promote equality of opportunity between men and women generally.
Chairman, The Baroness Platt of Writtle . . £36,050†
Deputy Chairman, Mrs. J. O'Dell £15,132
Members, K. Boardman; Mrs. R. Brown; J. Dunlop; D. Guereca; Prof. G. Powell; A. Simpkin; Mrs. P. Turner; Mrs. E. Walker; Dame Anne Warburton, D.C.V.O., C.M.G.; Miss M. Monk; Mrs. M. Prosser; Baroness Turner of Camden.
Chief Executive, A. E. Hart.

† Official salary, but only claims £33,479.

EXCHEQUER AND AUDIT DEPARTMENT
See National Audit Office

EXPORT CREDITS GUARANTEE DEPARTMENT
P.O. Box 272, Export House,
50 Ludgate Hill, EC4M 7AJ
[01–382 7000]

The Export Credits Guarantee Department is responsible to the Secretary of State for Trade. The Export Guarantees and Overseas Investment Act 1978 enables E.C.G.D. to encourage U.K. exports by making available export credit insurance to British firms engaged in selling overseas and to guarantee repayment to banks in Britain providing finance for export credit for goods sold on credit terms of two years or more. Guarantees under Section 1 of the Act are given after consultation with an Advisory Council of bankers and businessmen.
The Act also empowers E.C.G.D. to insure British private investment overseas against political risks, such as war, expropriation and restrictions on remittances.

Export Guarantees Advisory Council
Chairman, P. E. Lesley.
Deputy Chairman, T. W. B. Sallitt.
Other Members, E. L. Brooks; P. W. Bulfield; R. H. George, C.B.E.; W. Hogbin; C. E. Blundell (*ex officio*).

Chief Executive, M. G. Stephens.
Directors, F. J. Chapman; R. G. Codd; C. Foxall; R. T. Kemp; D. H. Twyford . . . . £34,000–£37,000
Heads of Divisions, K. G. Lockwood; C. M. Bossom; G. Bromley; G. E. J. Breach; J. G. M. Cochrane; R. Wild; J. W. Coggins; R. A. Ranson; A. K. Sedman; W. J. C. Pinnell; A. J. Bray; B. J. Davison; J. R. Weiss; A. P. Fowell; J. H. Hall; P. Henley; A. J. Holloway; Dr. R. Van Slooten; R. I. Fear; M. J. Long; R. W. MacGregor . . . . £24,765–£28,215
Senior Principals, G. C. Bird; D. C. Cooper; K. Dixey; A. P. G. Hare; R. F. Lethbridge; L. S. W. Montgomery; J. S. Snowdon . . . . £18,786–£25,335
Principals, Miss J. Albutt; P. Armstrong; J. S. Astruc; D. D. Baird; R. Bennett; T. R. Black; G. Blackburn; D. Q. Bryars; P. J. Callaghan; J. D. Cameron; A. P. Carcas; A. L. Childs; D. Collins; D. R. Coombe; Mrs. A. C. Cowie; D. M. Cox; A. B. Coyne; M. J. Crane; R. P. D. Crick; J. C. W. Croall; Mrs. R. Q. Davies; R. A. Dew; R. X. Fear; J. M. Foster; P. C. Gaudoin; N. F. George; R. Gotts; D. A. Green; R. T. Griffiths; P. Hambleton; R. Hardy; G. H. Hill; R. Holloway; P. Jackson; T. M. Jaffray; P. F. Jennings; Miss S. J. Johnson; G. G. Jones; R. Jones; N. A. Lambert; V. P. Lunn-Rockliffe; I. Mackay; J. S. McKibbin; Mrs. M. Maddox; S. Merchack; D. W. Miller; J. P. Moon; D. J. Morris; A. J. E. Muckersie; P. L. Neal; G. A. Newhouse; D. W. Overy; M. D. Pentecost; R. J. Pomeroy; S. C. Pond; Mrs. V. A. Randall; A. B. Redmayne; I. S. Robertson; S. Rosenthal; M. Russell; M. Scales; R. Scott; B. M. Sidwell, T.D.; K. Smith; K. R. Smith; B. C. Southwell; R. M. Sutton; P. K. Terry; C. M. Thorogood; D. A. H. Tickner; D. L. Townley; J. A. Tyler; E. J. Walsby; A. R. Watt; R. A. Watt; Miss J.West; T. J. M. West; J. M. Willis; D. L. Wyatt; G. A. Young . . . . £15,030–£20,292
Principal Information Officer, G. Hicks.

Regional Offices
Belfast: Windsor House, 9–15 Bedford Street, BT2 7EG (0232 231743); *Birmingham:* Colmore Centre, 115 Colmore Row, B3 3SB (021–233 1771); *Bristol:* Robinson Building, 1 Redcliffe Street, BS1 6NP (0272–299971); *Cambridge:* Three Crowns House, 72–80

Hills Road, CB2 1NJ (0223–68801); *City of London:* Export House, 50 Ludgate Hill, EC4M 7AY (01–726 4050); *Croydon:* Sunley House, Bedford Park, Croydon, CR9 4HL (01–680 5030); *Glasgow:* Fleming House, 134 Renfrew Street, G3 6TL (041–332 8707); *Leeds:* West Riding House, 67 Albion Street, LS1 5AA (0532–450631); *Manchester:* Townbury House, Blackfriars Street, Salford M3 5AL (061–834 8181).

OFFICE OF FAIR TRADING
Field House, Bream's Buildings, EC4A 1PR
[01–242 2858]

The Office of Fair Trading is a government department responsible for the administration of the Fair Trading Act, 1973, the Consumer Credit Act, 1974, the Restrictive Trade Practices Act, 1976, the Estate Agents Act, 1979, and the Competition Act, 1980. Under the supervision of the Director General of Fair Trading the office keeps under review commercial activities in the U.K. and aims to protect the consumer against unfair practices and is divided between five main areas: consumer affairs, consumer credit, monopolies and mergers, restrictive trade practices and anti-competitive practices.

Director General, Sir Gordon Borrie, Q.C. ... £62,000
Deputy Director General, A. J. Lane £43,500

Consumer Affairs Division
Director, R. J. Thomas .... £31,000 to £34,000
Assistant Directors, H. J. Charman; S. G. Linstead, M. Z. Wasilewski .... £23,730 to £27,065

Competition Policy Division
Director, Dr. M. Howe .... £31,000 to £34,000
Assistant Directors, Mrs. E. C. Jones; D. W. Lightfoot; J. C. Octon; M. Borland .... £23,730 to £27,065

Legal Division
Director, B. J. O'Toole .... £31,000 to £34,000
Assistant Directors, A. J. Perrett; G. Vaughan Davies .... £23,730–£27,065

Chief Information Officer, J. E. Perry
£18,020 to £24,302
Senior Economic Adviser, A. G. Atkinson
£23,730 to £27,065
Establishment and Finance Officer, B. A. Hennah
£14,318 to £19,465

FOREIGN AND COMMONWEALTH OFFICE
Downing Street, SW1A 2AL
[01-270 3000]

The Foreign and Commonwealth Office provides, mainly through diplomatic missions, the means of communication between the British Government and other governments and international governmental organizations for the discussion and negotiation of all matters falling within the field of international relations. It is responsible for alerting the British Government to the implications of developments overseas; for protecting British interests overseas; for protecting British citizens abroad; for explaining British policies to, and cultivating friendly relations with, Governments overseas and for the discharge of British responsibilities to the dependent territories.

Salaries
Secretary of State £33,145
Minister of State (Lords) £30,640
Minister of State (Commons) £22,875
Parliamentary Under Secretary £16,885

Diplomatic Service
Permanent Under Secretary and Head of the Diplomatic Service £75,750
Senior Grade Salary Point 1 (SP1) £65,000
Deputy to the Permanent Under Secretary ... £59,500
Senior Grade Salary Point 2 (SP2) £54,000
Senior Grade Salary Point 3 (SP3) .. £43,500–£45,500
Senior Grade Salary Point 4 (SP4) £41,000
Senoir Grade Salary Point 5 (SP5) .. £34,000–£37,000
Diplomatic Service Grade 4 (DS4) .. £24,765–£28,215
Diplomatic Service Grade 5 (DS5) .. £15,030–£20,292

Secretary of State, THE RT. HON. SIR GEOFFREY HOWE, Q.C., M.P.
Private Secretary, A. C. Galsworthy, C.M.G.
Assistant Private Secretaries, R. N. Culshaw, M.V.O.; J. Houston; L. Parker.
Social Secretary, Mrs. L. McBride.
Ministers of State for Foreign and Commonwealth Affairs, RT. HON. LYNDA CHALKER, M.P.; THE LORD GLENARTHUR; DAVID MELLOR, M.P.
Minister of State for Foreign and Commonwealth Affairs (Minister for Overseas Development), CHRISTOPHER PATTEN, M.P.
Parliamentary Under Secretary of State, T. Eggar, M.P.
Parliamentary Relations Unit, P. J. Bacon (*Head*); J. G. Rice (*Deputy Head and Parliamentary Clerk*).
Permanent Under Secretary of State and Head of the Diplomatic Service, Sir Patrick Wright, K.C.M.G.
Private Secretary, S. L. Cowper-Coles.
Deputy to the Permanent Under Secretary and Political Director, Sir John Fretwell, G.C.M.G.
Deputy Under Secretaries (SP2), Sir Mark Russell, K.C.M.G.; (*Chief Clerk*); D. H. Gillmore, C.M.G.; A. G. Munro, C.M.G.; R. Q. Braithwaite, C.M.G.; J. D. I. Boyd, C.M.G.
H.M. Vice-Marshal of the Diplomatic Corps, R. Hervey, C.M.G.
Assistant Under Secretaries (SP5), Miss C. E. Pestell, C.M.G.; B. J. P. Fall, C.M.G.; P. R. Fearn, C.M.G.; C. W. Long, C.M.G. (*Deputy Chief Clerk and Chief Inspector*); W. R. Tomkys, C.M.G. (*Principal Finance Officer*); Hon. H. Maud, C.M.G.; Sir David Miers, K.B.E., C.M.G.; D. J. E. Ratford, C.M.G., C.V.O.; A. Reeve, C.M.G.; J. O. Kerr, C.M.G.; D. Slater, C.M.G.; R. J. T. McLaren, C.M.G.; I. S. Winchester C.M.G. (*Director of Communications & Technical Services*).
Legal Adviser, A. D. Watts, C.M.G.
Second Legal Adviser, H. G. Darwin, C.M.G.
Deputy Legal Advisers, D. H. Anderson; P. R. N. Fifoot, C.M.G.
Legal Counsellors, F. D. Berman, C.M.G.; M. C. Wood; A. I. Aust; I. D. Hendry; K. J. Chamberlain; J. Fiddle.
International Labour Adviser, A. E. Smith.
Overseas Police Adviser (DS4), J. W. Kelland, L.V.O., Q.P.M.

Signals Department (Government Communications Headquarters)
Priors Road, Cheltenham, Glos. GL52 5AJ
[0242–521491]

Director (G2), Sir Peter Marychurch, K.C.M.G.
Principal Establishment Officer (G3), J. Adye.

Heads of Departments (DS4) and Assistant Heads of Department (DS5)
*Aid Policy Dept., B. Ireton; *Asst.,* J. Thompson, M.B.E.
Arms Control and Disarmament Dept., P. D. R. Davies; *Asst.,* P. Dunn.
Central African Dept., C. A. K. Cullimore; *Asst.,* N. R. Jarrold.
Claims Dept., J. Thomas.
Commonwealth Co-ordination Dept., T. T. Macan.

Communications Administration Dept., B. B. Bushell; *Assts.*, R. J. Saltwell; D. Hughes.

Communications Engineering Dept., R. Castle-Smith, M.B.E.

Communications Operations Dept., B. P. Austin; *Assts.*, G. Feast; E. G. B. Jarman.

Communications Planning Staff, D. J. Briggs.

Communications Technical Services Dept., P. Mason; *Assts.*, N. L. Allen; R. Read.

Conference on Security and Co-operation in Europe Unit, P. W. Summerscale.

Consular Dept., J. Harrison, L.V.O.; *Assts.*, J. R. Jamieson; T. W. Abbott.

Cultural Relations Dept., J. N. Elam; *Assts.*, J. M. Candlish; Ms. S. G. Falconer.

Defence Dept., P. Lever; *Assts.*, A. D. Sprake; W. G. Ehrman.

Defence Dept. (General), P. Yarnold.

East African Dept., W. Marsden; *Asst.*, T. C. S. Stitt.

Eastern European Dept., A. St. J. H. Figgis; *Asst.*, R. P. Nash.

**Economic Advisers*, S. H. Broadbent; *Deputy Head*, J. M. C. Rollo.

**Economic Relations Dept.*, T. L. Richardson; *Asst.*, J. White.

Energy Science and Space Dept., P. H. D. Wetton; *Assts.*, M. F. Sullivan, M.B.E.; M. J. Robinson.

European Community Dept. (External), Miss R. J. Spencer; *Asst.*, G. G. Wetherell.

European Community Dept. (Internal), J. S. Wall, L.V.O.; *Asst.*, M. I. P. Webb.

Falkland Islands Dept., A. J. Beamish; *Deputy Head*, D. Broad.

Far Eastern Dept., R. F. Cooper, M.V.O.; *Asst.*, K. Sullivan.

Finance Dept., C. D. Crabbie; *Deputy Head of Dept.*, G. F. Griffiths (£22,329 to £26,898); *Assts.*, I. Knight Smith; A. H. Ellis.

Hong Kong Dept., C. O. Hum; *Asst.*, R. D. Lavers.

Information Dept., R. J. S. Muir; *Assts.* Mrs. G. S. Wright; C. K. Woodfield, O.B.E.

Information Technology Dept., K. R. Willis; *Asst.*, T. Gould.

**Internal Audit Unit*, L. E. Fitzpatrick.

Library and Records Dept., Miss P. M. Barnes; *Assts.*, R. L. E. Foreman; Miss M. Clay, O.B.E.

**Management Review Staff*, (vacant); *Associate*, (vacant)

Maritime, Aviation and Environment Dept., R. C. Beetham, L.V.O.; *Asst.*, H. G. Hogger.

Mexico and Central America Dept., A. L. S. Coltman; *Asst.*, Miss M. L. Croll.

Middle East Dept., J. R. Young; *Asst.*, I. L. Blackley.

Migration and Visa Dept., D. M. Harrison, O.B.E.; *Asst.*, B. B. Low.

Nationality and Treaty Dept., P. V. Rollitt; *Asst.*, A. R. Kaye.

Near East and North Africa Dept., A. F. Goulty; *Asst.*, J. S. Laing.

News Dept., C. J. R. Meyer; *Deputy Head*, J. M. Cresswell.

North America Dept., P. Fowler; *Asst.*, M. R. Crompton.

Nuclear Energy Dept., J. K. Gordon; *Asst.*, D. C. B. Beaumont.

Office Services and Transport Unit, I. McCluney; *Asst.*, A. E. Gay (£19,257)

Overseas Estate Dept., M. H. R. Bertram; *Deputy Head*, M. E. Cook.

Overseas Inspectorate, C. W. Long, C.M.G. (*Deputy Chief Clerk and Chief Inspector*); *Inspectors*, R. Thomas; Miss M. I. Rothwell; G. M. Gowlland, L.V.O.; B. Smith, O.B.E.

---

*Joint Foreign and Commonwealth Office/Overseas Development Administration Dept.

Permanent Under Secretary's Dept., P. G. Wallis; *Deputy Head*, C. C. R. Battiscombe.

Personnel Operations Dept., D. B. C. Logan; *Deputy Head*, R. P. Ralph; *Assts.*, H. J. S. Pearce; P. V. Rollitt; P. A. Heald, M.B.E.

Personnel Policy Dept., A. M. Goodenough; *Asst.*, D. W. Fall.

Personnel Services Dept., D. J. Wright; *Assts.*, B. E. Bowley; G. C. Fedrick.

Planning Staff, Hon. D. Gore-Booth; *Asst.*, Dr. V. Caton.

Protocol Dept., D. MacLeod; *Asst.*, J. S. Jasper, O.B.E.; S. W. F. Martin, L.V.O. (*First Assistant Marshal of the Diplomatic Corps*).

Republic of Ireland Dept., T. J. B. George.

Research Dept., *Director*, J. Ling; *Regional Directors*, J. P. Bannerman (*Africa & Middle East*); K. C. Walker (*Asia*); R. M. Bone (*Atlantic*); G. D. G. Murrell (*Soviet Union & E. Europe*).

Security Dept., A. Ford; *Asst.*, V. A. Lister, M.B.E.

Security Co-ordination Dept., I. A. Roberts; *Asst.*, D. R. Upton.

South America Dept., P. McLean; *Asst.*, C. R. L. de Chassiron.

South Asian Dept., R. A. Burns; *Asst.*, W. B. Sinton.

South-East Asian Dept., C. C. W. Adams; *Asst.*, R. T. Fell.

Southern African Dept., W. K. Prendergast; *Asst.*, C. T. W. Humfrey.

Southern European Dept., M. C. S. Weston, C.V.O.; *Asst.*, P. J. Torry.

South Pacific Dept., A. E. Furness; *Asst.*, M. J. Peart, L.V.O.

Soviet Dept., M. J. Llewelyn Smith; *Asst.*, A. J. Longrigg.

Trade Relations and Exports Dept., G. N. Smith; *Assts.*, R. K. Buist; P. Sullivan.

Training Dept., Mrs. J. J. Campbell; *Director of Language Centre*, J. Moore.

United Nations Dept., P. K. Williams; *Assts.*, Mrs. S. F. Morphet; D. A. Lamont.

West African Dept., Miss M. G. Fort; *Asst.*, F. X. Gallagher, O.B.E.

West Indian and Atlantic Dept., A. J. H. Ramsay; *Asst.*, A. F. Smith.

Western European Dept., D. J. M. Dain; *Assts.*, G. H. Fry; P. J. Sullivan.

CORPS OF QUEEN'S MESSENGERS

Superintendent of the Corps of Queen's Messengers, Lt.-Col. E. M. T. Crump.

Queen's Diplomatic Service Messengers, Maj. J. E. A. Andre; R. J. Angel; Col. B. C. F. Arkle, M.B.E., T.D.; Maj. I. G. M. Bamber; Cdr. R. D. D. Bamford; Maj. G. M. Benson; Lt.-Cdr. B. R. Bezance; Capt. D. F. A. Bloom, G.M.; Capt. G. Courtauld; Maj. F. C. W. Courtenay-Thompson; Col. J. M. Deans; Maj. P. T. Dunn; Maj. A. M. Farmer; Lt.-Col. J. W. A. Fleming, O.B.E.; Capt. N. C. E. Gardner; J. W. Hannah, M.B.E.; J. O. Hollis; Wg.-Cdr. J. O. Jewiss; Lt.-Col. P. S. Kerr-Smiley; Lt.-Col. J. M. C. Kimmins; Lt.-Col. R. C. Letchworth; G. F. Miller; Maj. J. K. Nairne; Wg.-Cdr. R. A. Nash; Maj. D. R. Nevile; Maj. L. M. Phillips; Lt.-Col. H. M. L. Smith; Maj. P. M. O. Springfield; Col. W. H. F. Stevens, O.B.E., A.D.C.; Col. D. W. F. Taylor; Sqn.-Ldr. J. A. Watson.

FOREIGN COMPENSATION COMMISSION
Alexandra House, Kingsway, WC2B 6TT
[01–438 7045]

The Commission was set up by the Foreign Compensation Act 1950 primarily to distribute under Orders in Council funds received from other governments in accordance with agreements to pay compensation for expropriated British property and other losses sustained by British nationals.

The Commission has the further duty of registering claims for British-owned property in contemplation of agreements with other countries, and it has done so in seven instances since 1950.

Chairman, A. W. E. Wheeler, c.b.e.
Commissioners, J. A. S. Hall, d.f.c., q.c.; Sir Alan Leslie.
Secretary and Chief Examiner, D. H. Wright.

FORESTRY COMMISSION
231 Corstorphine Road, Edinburgh EH12 7AT
[031–334 0303]

The Forestry Commissioners are charged with the general duty of promoting in Great Britain the interests of forestry, the development of afforestation, the production and supply of timber and, in discharging their functions, endeavouring to achieve a reasonable balance between the needs of forestry and conservation. The Commission manages some 890,000 hectares of productive forest and has a continuing policy of developing its forests for recreation by the general public. It is also the Forestry Authority for Great Britain with responsibility for a range of regulatory functions, including the administration of grant-aid schemes for planting by private owners, the licensing of tree felling and the control of tree pests and diseases.

Chairman, Sir David Montgomery (*part-time*)
 £24,382
Director-General and Deputy Chairman, G. J. Francis £43,264
Commissioner for Private Forestry and Development, R. T. Bradley £35,289
Commissioner for Administration and Finance, D. T. J. Rutherford £36,825
Commissioner for Operations, D. L. Foot £33,725
Secretary to the Commissioners, P. J. Clarke . £28,215

REGISTRY OF FRIENDLY SOCIETIES
15 Great Marlborough Street, W1V 2AX
[01–437 9992]

The Registry of Friendly Societies is a Government department serving two statutory bodies, the Building Societies Commission, and the Central Office of the Registry of Friendly Societies, together with the Assistant Registrar of Friendly Societies for Scotland.

The Building Societies Commission was established by the Building Societies Act, 1986. The Commission is responsible for the supervision of building societies on the Commission, and administers the system of regulations. It also advises the Treasury and other Government departments on matters relating to building societies.

The Central Office of the Registry of Friendly Societies provides a public registry for mutual organizations registered under the Building Societies Act, 1986, Friendly Societies Act, 1974, and the Industrial and Provident Societies Act, 1965. It is responsible for the supervision of friendly societies and credit unions, and advises the Government on issues affecting those societies. The Chief Registrar has certain powers to arbitrate in disputes between members and registered societies. He also acts as the Industrial Assurance Commissioner.

Salaries

Grade 2	£43,264–£45,349
Grade 3	£33,725–£36,852
Grade 4	£30,207–£31,770
Grade 5	£24,739–£28,215
Grade 6	£18,786–£25,335
Grade 7	£14,927–£20,292

Building Societies Commission

Chairman, J. M. Bridgeman.
Deputy Chairman, G. W. Watson.
Commissioners, R. L. Devlin; D. Hobson; S. Proctor, c.b.e.; G. Sammons; H. R. C. Walden, c.b.e.

Central Office

Chief Registrar, J. M. Bridgeman.
Assistant Registrars, A. Wilson; P. D. Davis; R. N. Williams.

The Registry

First Commissioner and Chief Registrar (*G2*), J. M. Bridgeman.

Staff serving the Building Societies Commission:
Grade 3, G. W. Watson.
Grade 5, R. L. Devlin; T. Mathews.
Grade 7, D. B. Severn; F. da Rocha; A. G. Tebbutt.

Staff serving the Central Office:
Assistant Registrar (*G4*), A. Wilson.
Grade 7, R. E. Merrick; T. R. Richards.

Central Services

Assistant Registrar (*G5*), P. D. Davis.
Legal Staff (*G6*), W. H. Godwin; R. C. Perkins.
Establishment and Finance Officer (*G6*), M. L. Battenti.
Computer Project Manager (*G7*), F. Gold.

Registry of Friendly Societies, Scotland
58 Frederick Street, Edinburgh, EH2 1NB
[031–226 3224]

Assistant Registrar (*G5*), J. L. J. Craig, w.s.

GAMING BOARD FOR GREAT BRITAIN
Berkshire House, 168–173 High Holborn,
WC1V 7AA
[01–240 0821]

Established on October 25, 1968, to maintain a broad oversight of developments in gaming in Great Britain, to check prospective gaming licensees management and staff, and to advise the Home Secretary on making regulations which may be needed for the further control of gaming.

Chairman, N. A. Ward Jones, v.r.d. (*part-time*)
 £21,630
Members, P. B. Kavanagh, c.b.e., q.p.m.; Lady Ibbs; W. N. Hunter Smart; M. H. Hogan (*part-time*)
 £8,670
Secretary, J. V. Dance.

OFFICE OF GAS SUPPLY
Southside, 105 Victoria Street, SW1E 6QT
[01–828 0898]

The Office of Gas Supply (OFGAS) is a regulatory body set up under the Gas Act 1986. It is headed by the Director General of Gas Supply who is independent of Ministerial control.

The principal function of OFGAS is to monitor British Gas's activities as a public gas supplier and, where necessary, enforce the conditions of that company's authorisation to act as a public gas supplier. Other functions are to grant authorisations to other suppliers of gas through pipes; to investigate complaints on matters where enforcement powers may be exercisable; to fix and publish maximum charges for reselling gas; to publish information and advice for the benefit of tariff customers; to keep under review developments concerning the gas supply industry; to settle the terms on which other suppliers have access to British Gas' pipelines in the event of disagreement.

Director General, J. McKinnon.
Deputy Director General, Dr. D. H. Metz.
Legal Adviser, D. R. M. Long.
Business Adviser, P. T. Gittins.
Public Affairs Adviser, N. W. Hayes.
Consumer Affairs Adviser, W. Macleod.
Commercial Affairs Adviser, R. A. Field.

BRITISH GAS p.l.c.
152 Grosvenor Road, SW1V 3JL
[01–821 1444]

British Gas was privatised following the Gas Act, 1986. Its primary activities are the purchase, distribution and sale of gas. It also explores for and produces hydrocarbons.
Chairman, Sir Denis Rooke, C.B.E., F.R.S. £175,000
Chief Executive, R. Evans, C.B.E.
Secretary, G. C. Hogg.

GAS REGIONS

Scotland, Granton House, 4 Marine Drive, Edinburgh EH5 1YB. *Chairman,* R. W. Hill.
Northern, P.O. Box 1GB, Killingworth, Newcastle upon Tyne NE99 1GB. *Chairman,* K. Summersgill.
North Western, Welman House, Altrincham, Cheshire WA15 8AE. *Chairman,* R. H. Greenfield.
North Eastern, New York Road, Leeds LS2 7PE. *Chairman,* N. Blacker.
East Midlands, P.O. Box 145, De Montfort Street, Leicester LE1 9DB. *Chairman,* D. R. Atkinson.
West Midlands, Wharf Lane, Solihull, West Midlands B91 2JP. *Chairman,* C. H. Brown.
Wales, Helmont House, Churchill Way, Cardiff CF1 4NB. *Chairman,* G. H. Langshaw.
Eastern, Star House, Potters Bar, Herts. EN6 2PD. *Chairman,* D. H. Griffiths, O.B.E.
North Thames, North Thames House, London Road, Staines, Middx. TW18 4AE. *Chairman,* J. Gadd.
South Eastern, Katherine Street, Croydon CR9 1JU. *Chairman,* A. A. Dove.
Southern, 80 St. Mary's Road, Southampton SO9 5AT. *Chairman,* D. A. Young.
South Western, Riverside, Temple Street, Keynsham, Bristol BS18 1EQ. *Chairman,* A. I. D. Frith.

THE GOVERNMENT ACTUARY
22 Kingsway, WC2B 6LE
[01–242 6828]

The Government Actuary provides a consulting service to Government departments, nationalised industries and Commonwealth Governments. His actuaries advise on social security schemes and superannuation arrangements within the public sector at home and abroad, on population and other statistical studies, and on Government supervision of insurance companies and friendly societies.
Government Actuary, E. A. Johnston, C.B. ... £54,000
Directing Actuaries, C. D. Daykin; D. H. Loades; G. G. Newton £37,000
Chief Actuaries, D. G. Ballantine; C. L. Cannon; J. L. Field; R. T. Foster; M. A. Pickford; A. G. Young
£33,309

Senior Actuaries, P. L. Burt; B. J. Coode; C. A. Harris*; T. W. Hewitson; P. H. Hinton*; F. A. Honeysett; A. I. Johnston; Mrs. I. W. Lane; A. P. Pavelin; D. F. Renn*; Miss P. M. Webster
£20,302–£26,800
*£24,631–£29,680

GOVERNMENT HOSPITALITY FUND
8 Cleveland Row, SW1A 1DH
[01–210 3000]

Instituted in 1908 for the purpose of organizing official hospitality on a regular basis, with a view to the promotion of international goodwill.
Minister in Charge, The Lord Glenarthur.
Secretary, Brig. A. Cowan, M.B.E. .... £22,329–£26,898

HEALTH AND SAFETY COMMISSION
Baynards House, 1 Chepstow Place,
Westbourne Grove, W2 4TF
[01–229 3456]

The Health and Safety Commission is made up of eight representatives of trade unions, employers and local authorities and a full-time chairman appointed by the Secretary of State for Employment. Its primary functions are: to secure the health, safety and welfare of people at work; to protect the public from risks arising from work activities; to control the storage and use of explosives, highly flammable or other dangerous substances.
Chairman, Dr. J. Cullen.
Members, D. Mason; Dr. M. C. Shannon; Dr. C. M. Thomas; R. Eberlie; P. Jacques; Dr. A. H. Raper; Miss A. Maddocks; A. Tuffin.
Secretary, A. J. Lord

Health and Safety Executive
Broad Lane, Sheffield S3 7HQ
[0742–768141]

The Health and Safety Executive is a statutory body consisting of a deputy general and two other people appointed by the Commission. It advises the Commission, and its staff are the primary instrument for carrying out the Commission's policies.
Through a network of 20 area offices, H.S.E. inspectors visit and review work activities, giving expert advice and guidance and, where necessary, issuing enforcement notices and initiating prosecutions. The Employment Medical Advisory Services, the operational arm of the Medical Division, is also based on the area offices. Other inspectorates within H.S.E. monitor or enforce standards and give advice and guidance in specific sectors of industry or employment.
Director General, J. D. Rimington.
Deputy Director General, J. D. G. Hammer.
Director, Resources and Planning Division, A. B. Martin.

Responsible to the Director General:

H.M. Factory Inspectorate
H.M. Chief Inspector of Factories, D. C. T. Eves.

H.M. Agricultural Inspectorate
H.M. Chief Agricultural Inspector, C. Boswell.

H.M. Mines and Quarries Inspectorate
H.M. Chief Inspector of Mines and Quarries, Dr. M. B. Jones.

H.M. Nuclear Installations Inspectorate
H.M. Chief Inspector of Nuclear Installations (G3), E. A. Ryder.

Safety Policy and Information Services Division
Director, D. J. Hodgkins.

Hazardous Substances Division
Director, C. D. Burgess.

Responsible to the Deputy Director General:

Technology Division
(includes H.M. Explosives Inspectorate and Major Hazards Unit).
Director, A. C. Barrell.

Research and Laboratory Services Division
Director (G3), Dr. J. McQuaid.

Medical Division
(includes the Employment Medical Advisory Service).
Director of Medical Services, Dr. J. T. Carter.

Responsible to Director, Resources and Planning Division:

Resources and Planning Division
(including the Accident Prevention Advisory Unit).
Director, A. B. Martin.

Public enquiry points: London (01–221 0870); Sheffield (0742–753259); Bootle (051–951 4381).

DEPARTMENT OF HEALTH AND SOCIAL SECURITY
Alexander Fleming House, Elephant and Castle,
SE1 6BY
[01–407 5522]

The Department of Health and Social Security was created on November 1, 1968, from the Ministry of Health and Ministry of Social Security. The Department performs the functions of the two former Ministries.

The Department is responsible for the administration of the National Health Service in England and for the personal social services run by local authorities in England for children, the elderly, infirm, handicapped and other persons in need. It has functions relating to food hygiene and welfare foods. The Department is also concerned with the medical treatment of war pensioners, and is responsible for the ambulance and first aid services in emergency, under the Civil Defence Act, 1948. The Department represents the U.K. on the World Health Organization. Responsibility for the administration of the Health Services in Wales was transferred to the Welsh Office on April 1, 1969.

The Department is responsible for the social security services in England, Scotland and Wales. These services comprise schemes for war pensions, national insurance, child benefit, industrial injuries, attendance allowances, mobility allowances and supplementary benefits.

Salary List

Secretary of State	£33,145
Minister of State (Commons)	£22,875
Parliamentary Under Secretary of State	£16,885
Grade 1	£64,739
Grade 1A	£59,214
Grade 2	£43,264–£45,349
Grade 3*	£40,058
Grade 3	£34,000–£37,000
Grade 4	£30,344–£31,844
Grade 5	£24,765–£28,215
Grade 6	£18,786–£25,335
Grade 7	£15,030–£20,292

Secretary of State for Social Services, THE RT. HON. JOHN MOORE, M.P.
Private Secretary, G. J. F. Podger.

Assistant Private Secretaries, Ms. J. McKessack; B. Calderwood.
Parliamentary Private Secretary, J. Ward, C.B.E., M.P.
Special Adviser to the Secretary of State, A. Turner.
Minister of State for Health, ANTONY HAROLD NEWTON, O.B.E., M.P.
Minister of State for Social Security, NICHOLAS SCOTT, M.B.E., M.P.
Parliamentary Under Secretaries of State, Mrs. E. Currie, M.P. (*Health*); M. Portillo, M.P. (*Social Security*); The Lord Skelmersdale (*Lords*).
Permanent Secretary (G1), C. W. France, C.B.
Private Secretary (G7), B. Slater.
Second Permanent Secretary (G1A), M. J. A. Partridge.
Private Secretary (G7), J. Nightingale.
Chief Medical Officer (G1A), Prof. Sir Donald Acheson, K.B.E.
Chief Scientist, Prof. F. W. O'Grady, C.B.E., T.D.

NATIONAL HEALTH SERVICE MANAGEMENT BOARD

Chairman, The Minister of State (Health).
Deputy Chairman, Sir Roy Griffiths.
Chief Executive and Director of Personnel, L. H. Peach.
Chief Medical Officer, Sir Donald Acheson, K.B.E.
Director of Operations, G. A. Hart, C.B.
Director of Planning & Information Technology, M. J. Fairy.
Director of Operations (Personnel), P. J. Wormald.
Director of Financial Management, G. I. Mills.
Director of Health Authority Finance, J. James.
Director of Health Authority Liaison, A. J. Merifield.
Director of N.H.S. Procurement, T. Critchley.
Chief Nursing Officer, Mrs A. A. B. Poole.
Property Adviser, D. N. I. Pearce.
Non Executive Director, D. Nichol.
Secretary, A. M. McKeever.
Assistant Secretary, M. Jarvis.

SOCIAL SECURITY OPERATIONS GROUP

Deputy Secretary (G2), N. E. Clarke.

Regional Directorate

Under Secretary (G3), B. W. Taylor.
Assistant Secretaries (G5), Miss A. E. Perkins; J. F. Jones; J. R. Moyes.

Operational Strategy Directorate

Director (G3*), E. Caines.
Assistant Directors (G5), W. A. Healey; J. Y. Marshall; D. E. Thomas.
Assistant Secretary, NUBS (G5), B. Gibb.
Assistant Secretary, LOP (G5), G. H. Bardwell.

North Fylde Central Office

Controller (G5), J. M. Bankier.

Newcastle upon Tyne Central Office

Controller (G3), S. Thorpe-Tracey.
Assistant Secretaries (G5), J. Wailes; J. W. W. Nairn; B. Heaney; A. Laurance.

NHS Information Technology and Planning Division

Director of Planning and Information Technology (G2), M. J. Fairey.
Family Practitioner Services Information Technology (G3), J. F. Shaw.
Assistant Secretaries (G5), R. W. D. Venning; R. T. Rogers; D. J. Clark.
Senior Principals (G6), M. A. O'Flynn; C. M. O'Rourke.

International Relations (Health)

Assistant Secretary (G5), G. C. M. Lupton.

Health Service Division

Under Secretary (G3), J. P. Cashman.
Assistant Secretaries (G5), M. A. Harris; P. M. C. Winterton; G. J. Brechin.
Senior Principal (G6), L. G. T. Weir.

Community/Childrens Services Division

Under Secretary (G3), Mrs. J. M. Firth.
Assistant Secretaries (G5), C. E. Stone; J. H. Garlick; R. P. S. Hughes; Mrs. L. Fosh; D. M. Woolley.

Priority Care Division

Under Secretary (G3), E. B. McGinnis.
Assistant Secretaries (G5), Miss M. R. Edwards; Mrs. P. M. Williamson; Mrs. M. A. J. Pearson.

Children, Maternity and Prevention Division

Under Secretary (G3), C. H. Wilson.
Assistant Secretaries (G5), N. Teller; Mrs. E. Shaw; R. Cunningham; A. Barton.

Procurement Directorate

Director of Procurement and Distribution (G3), T. Critchley.
Director of Scientific and Technical Services Branch (G4), G. R. Higson.
Superintendents (G6), R. W. B. Allen; Miss M. N. Duncan; Dr. D. C. Potter; Dr. N. A. Slark; A. D. C. Shipley.

Regional Liaison Division

Under Secretary (G3), A. Merifield.
Assistant Secretaries (G5), A. J. Davies; N. Glass; J. C. Middleton.

N.H.S. Personnel Divisions

Deputy Secretary (G2), B. R. Rayner.

Division FPS

Under Secretary (G3), J. F. Shaw.
Assistant Secretaries (G5), J. A. Parker; J. Sharpe; Mrs. P. Petrie; B. A. R. Smith.

Division HAP

Under Secretary (G3), P. J. Wormald.
Assistant Secretaries (G5), N. Illingworth; B. A. R. Smith; R. M. Drury; J. H. Rogers.

Division FPS2

Under Secretary (G3), J. I. Langtry.
Assistant Secretaries (G5), P. Allen; K. J. Guinness; B. A. Harrison.

Medicines Division

Under Secretary (G3), C. H. Wilson.
Assistant Secretaries (G5), D. O. Hagger; W. Robertson.

ADMINISTRATION AND FINANCE GROUP

Principal Establishments and Finance Officer (G2), J. F. Mayne, C.B.

Finance Division A

Under Secretary (Health) (G3), J. H. James.
Assistant Secretaries (G5), Ms. P. Stewart; R. K. Alder.

Finance Division B

Under Secretary (Health) (G4), M. G. Lillywhite.
Assistant Secretaries (G5), A. J. Ratcliffe; R. Smith; A. T. Skinner; Ms. M. Stuart.

Financial Management Directorate

Director of Financial Management (G2), I. Mills.
Deputy Directors (G3), A. Black; J. S. Catterell; R. Spurgeon.

Finance Division C

Under Secretary (Social Security) (G3), D. Chislett.
Assistant Secretaries (G5), G. R. L. Osborne; R. A. Wallace; M. Whippman.

Statistics and Research Division

Director of Statistics and Information Management (G3), R. Gibbs.
Chief Statisticians (G5), Miss P. W. Annesley; R. J. Scott; C. P. Hogan; J. N. Lithgow; R. Willmer; T. Orchard.
Senior Statistician (G6), Miss A. J. Cleveland.

Economic Adviser's Office

Chief Economic Adviser (G3), C. H. Smee.
Senior Economic Advisers (G5), G. C. Fiegehen; J. W. Hurst; D. Todd.

Operational Research Service

Under Secretary (G3), C. H. Smee.
Director (G4), Dr. A. A. Holt.
Branch Heads (G6), F. M. Gayton; Dr. G. H. D. Royston; Dr. D. J. Hughes.

Personnel Management (Headquarters)

Director of Personnel Management (Headquarters) (G3), M. C. Malone-Lee.
Assistant Secretaries (G5), I. Magee; B. Gilbert.

Departmental Establishments and Personnel

Director of Establishment and Personnel (Departmental) (G3), B. Bridges.
Assistant Secretaries (G5), R. J. Tilney; J. M. Wray; G. R. West.

Central Management Support

Assistant Secretary (G5), I. D. Alexander.

Superannuation Branch

Deputy Secretary (G2), N. E. Clarke.
Assistant Secretary (G5), J. M. Bankier.
Senior Principal (G6), D. Napier.

SOCIAL SECURITY POLICY GROUP

Deputy Secretary (G2), Mrs. A. E. Bowtell.

Social Security Division A

Under Secretary (G3), D. G. Storer.
Assistant Secretaries (G5), J. E. Knight; P. L. Adeane; Mrs. A. De Peyer; Miss K. E. W. Blunt.

Social Security Division B

Under Secretary (G3), R. Birch.
Assistant Secretaries (G5), J. W. White; S. H. F. Hickey; T. Whiteley; Mrs. S. P. Maunsell.

Social Security Division C

Under Secretary (G3), N. L. J. Montagu.
Assistant Secretaries (G5), Mrs. M. Evans; D. S. Fanning; I. D. Alexander.
Senior Principal (G6), J. M. Hewlett; P. I. Blakey.

Social Security Supplementary Benefits Division

Under Secretary (G3), B. Walmsley.
Assistant Secretaries (G5), J. Tross; D. Brereton; Mrs. E. A. Woods.

Research Management Division

Chief Scientist (*G2*), Prof. F. W. O'Grady, C.B.E., T.D.
Deputy Chief Scientist, Director of Research Management (*G3*), Dr. J. S. Metters.
Assistant Secretary (*G5*), V. J. Harley.
Senior Medical Officers (*G5*), Dr. M. B. Dastgir; Dr. M. Graveney; Dr. D. Rothman, O.B.E.; Dr. M. E. Smith.
Senior Principal (*G6*), J. G. Hall.
Senior Principal Research Officers (*G6*), Ms. H. Houghton; Ms. H. Canter.

Solicitor's Office

Solicitor (*G2*), J. St. L. Brockman.
Principal Assistant Solicitors (*G3*), P. K. J. Thompson; Mrs. M. A. Morgan.
Proceedings Operational Director (*G4*), G. E. Beaven.

MEDICAL DIVISIONS (HEALTH AND PERSONAL SOCIAL SERVICES)

Chief Medical Officer (*G1*A), Sir Donald Acheson, K.B.E.
Deputy Chief Medical Officers (*G2*), Dr. M. E. Abrams; Dr. R. M. Oliver; Dr. E. L. Harris, C.B.

MEDICAL DIVISIONS UNDER DR. ABRAMS
Division CDPNM

Senior Principal Medical Officer (*G3*), Dr. P. R. Greenfield.
Principal Medical Officer (*G4*), Dr. J. M. Graham.
Senior Medical Officers (*G5*), Dr. E. Cloake; Dr. B. S. Ely; Dr. D. Ernaelsteen; Dr. P. Clarke; Dr. L. B. Hunt; Dr. W. J. Modle; Dr. S. Munday; Dr. A. Rawson; Dr. I. A. F. Lister Cheese.
Medical Officers (*G6*), Dr. J. G. Ablett; Dr. R. Young.
Principal Research Officer (*G7*), R. Wenlock.

Division MHI

Senior Principal Medical Officer (*G3*), Dr. J. L. Reed.
Principal Medical Officers (*G4*), Dr. R. J. Wawman; Dr. J. Shanks.
Senior Medical Officers (*G5*), Dr. D. F. M. Black; Dr. P. G. Mason; Dr. J. R. Lissamore; Dr. L. J. F. Warnants.

Division PCR

Senior Principal Medical Officer (*G3*), Dr. G. C. Rivett.
Principal Medical Officer (*G4*), Dr. R. H. Smith.
Senior Medical Officers (*G5*), Dr. W. G. Griffiths; Dr. R. G. Troup; Dr. G. E. Singer; Dr. W. Miller; Dr. M. F. Cuthbert; Dr. J. D. F. Bellamy.

Toxicology and Environmental Protection

Senior Principal Medical Officer (*G3*), Dr. B. Mac-Gibbon.
Principal Medical Officers (*G4*), Dr. G. Matthew; Dr. J. Steadman.

Division E

Principal Medical Officer (*G4*), Dr. J. L. Hunt, O.B.E.
Medical Officer (*G6*), Dr. R. Young.

MEDICAL DIVISIONS UNDER DR. OLIVER
Division HPS

Senior Principal Medical Officer (*G3*), Dr. N. P. Halliday.
Principal Medical Officer (*G4*), Dr. G. Pincherle.
Senior Medical Officers (*G5*), Dr. M. Prophet; Dr. N. Melia; Dr. P. Bourdillon; Dr. P. Simpson.
Medical Officer (*G6*), Dr. J. Mettle.
Principal Scientific Officer (*G7*), M. R. Godfrey.

Division MPO

Principal Medical Officer (*G4*), Dr. E. Winyard.
Senior Medical Officers (*G5*), Dr. J. P. Doyle; Dr. L. J. Martin; Dr. W. Thorne.
Medical Officers (*G6*), Dr. F. S. Goldby; Dr. D. Macpherson; Dr. E. Smales.

Division MME

Senior Principal Medical Officers (*G3*), Dr. A. J. Isaacs.
Senior Medical Officers (*G5*), Dr. T. K. Sweeney; Dr. C. Swinson; Dr. D. McInnes; Dr. R. B. Singh; Dr. D. P. Mason.

MEDICAL DIVISIONS UNDER DR. HARRIS
Division MD

Senior Principal Medical Officer (*G3*), Dr. G. Jones.
Principal Medical Officer (*G4*), Dr. D. Jefferys; Dr. W. J. Jenkins; Dr. R. D. Mann.
Senior Medical Officers (*G5*), Dr. P. N. Adams; Dr. G. H. Burton; Dr. T. H. Corn; Dr. K. Fowler; Dr. J. Hilton; Dr. D. Looi; Dr. A. Nath; Dr. J. A. Nicholson; Dr. J. M. Raine; Dr. L. Robinson; Dr. F. Rotblat; Dr. R. Shah; Dr. D. I. Slovick; Dr. K. A. Winship; Dr. S. Wood.
Medical Officer (*G6*), Dr. M. Glen-Bott.

Division IMCD

Senior Principal Medical Officer (*G3*), Dr. D. Walford.
Principal Medical Officer (*G4*), Dr. H. Pickles.
Senior Medical Officers (*G5*), Dr. J. Barnes; Dr. A. Fenton Lewis; Dr. P. A. Hyzler; Dr. H. Murrell; Dr. R. G. Penn; Dr. P. Exon; Dr. J. Berrie; Dr. G. Greenberg; Dr. D. M. Salisbury; Dr. H. Williams.
Medical Officers (*G6*), Dr. A. Dawson; Dr. H. Raynes; Dr. H. R. Playfair.
Environmental Health Officers, M. Jacob; E. W. Kingcott.

Division SEB

Senior Principal Medical Officer (*G3*), (vacant).
Chief Scientific Officer, Dr. F. P. Woodford.
Principal Medical Officers (*G4*), Dr. J. Heckford; Dr. A. Smithies.
Senior Medical Officers (*G5*), Dr. P. R. Dendy; Dr. P. M. Furnell; Dr. D. H. Holt; Dr. R. Skinner; Dr. S. P. Vahl.
Medical Officer (*G6*), Dr. S. Lader.

Disablement Services Division

General Manager (*G3*), I. M. Burns.
Disablement Services Branch A (*G5*), Miss A. Edwards.
Disablement Services Branch B (*G5*), J. Harley.
Disablement Services, Medical (*G4*), Dr. A. W. G. English.
Disablement Service, Operations (*G5*), J. Kenworthy.

Medical Division (Social Security)

Chief Medical Adviser (*G3**), Dr. W. R. O. Eggington.
Principal Medical Officers, Dr. K. A. Cameron; Dr. P. Castaldi; D. F. Rice; T. J. G. Phillips.

Dental Division

Chief Dental Officer, Dr. M. C. Downer.
Deputy Chief Dental Officer, D. R. Whittington.
Senior Dental Officers, W. G. Everett; Dr. A. S. Atkinson; R. B. Mouatt.

Nursing Division

Chief Nursing Officer, Mrs. A. A. B. Poole ... £37,000
Deputy Chief Nursing Officer, Miss S. P. C. Wright-Warren £31,352
Principal Nursing Officers, M. A. Clark; Mrs. D. A. Patey; Mrs. E. B. Rivett; J. Tait; Mrs. A. Dawar
£27,958

Social Services Inspectorate

Chief Inspector (G2), W. B. Utting.
Deputy Chief Inspectors (G4), J. H. Barnes; M. Phillips.
Assistant Chief Inspectors (HQ), Miss J. Baraclough; J. Cypher; Mrs. P. K. Hall; Ms. W. Jones; J. G. Smith.
Assistant Chief Inspectors (Regions), S. Allard; J. K. Corcoran; D. Gilroy; B. D. Harrison; Miss C. M. Hey; D. G. Lambert; Miss S. Markham; B. E. Stimpson; Miss A. Taylor ..... £20,213 to £25,332

Pharmaceutical Division

Chief Pharmaceutical Officer, Dr. B. A. Wills
£30,293
Deputy Chief Pharmaceutical Officers (G5), B. H. Hartley; Dr. C. A. Johnson; Dr. P. R. Noyce; A. G. Stewart.
Superintending Pharmaceutical Officers (G6), K. J. Ayling; A. C. Cartwright; Miss M. N. Duncan; Dr. B. R. Matthews; J. R. V. Merrills; Dr. J. Purves; Dr. A. R. Rogers; S. L. Turner.
Principal Pharmaceutical Officers (G7), D. T. Britton; Miss R. Coulson; Miss P. O. Creed; B. A. Curran; Mrs. L. Davidson; D. Haythornthwaite; Miss D. Hepburn; W. J. Hewlett; D. J. Hurrell; Dr. C. R. Hutton; Dr. A. Islam; D. E. Jenkins; Dr. M. L. Kavanagh; Miss M. J. E. Millar; Miss S. A. Norton; J. P. O'Brien; K. Preece; Miss M. L. Rabouhans; Dr. N. Richardson; Dr. M. I. Robertson; Miss R. J. Smith; R. L. Smith; R. B. Trigg; G. Wade; J. A. Wandless; D. R. Warburton; M. G. Willows.

Hotel and Dietetic Services Branch

Chief Officer, D. G. Thomson.
Deputy Chief Officer, Hotel and Dietetic Services (G7), R. Brown.
Deputy Chief Officer, Domestic Services (G7), Miss I. D. Oliver.

Information Division

Director of Information (G4), Miss R. Christopherson.
Deputy Directors (G6), C. P. Wilson (*news*); G. Meredith (*publicity*).

HEALTH BUILDING DIRECTORATE

Director of Health Building (G3*), R. H. Goodman.

NHS Building Procurement Branch

Assistant Director (G5) and Chief Surveyor, D. A. Butler.
Superintending Architect (G6), W. R. Hyslop.
Superintending Engineers (G6), R. J. Tuthill; R. S. Body.
T/Superintending Surveyor (G6), R. W. Davis.

Nucleus Hospitals Development Branch

Assistant Director (G5), P. L. Ward.
Superintending Architect (G6), G. F. Mayers.
Superintending Engineer (G6), J. M. Singh.
Superintending Surveyor (G6), D. A. Eastwood.

Building Guidance, Engineering Standards and Cost Allowances Branch

Assistant Director (G5) and Chief Architect, M. A. Meager.
Superintending Architect (G6), A. J. Noakes.
Superintending Engineer (G6), G. D. Fisher.
Superintending Surveyor (G6), K. J. I. McSweeney.

Technology and Safety Branch

Assistant Director (G5) and Chief Engineer, I. E. G. Mahon.
Superintending Engineers (G6), B. C. Oliver; L. W. Arrowsmith; D. W. Luscombe.

Administrative Support, Fire, Building Regulations Branch

Assistant Secretary (G5), P. R. Gant.
Superintending Architect (G6), M. F. Kemp.

ESTATE AND PROPERTY MANAGEMENT DIRECTORATE

Property Adviser to the NHS Management Board (G2), D. N. I. Pearce (PT).

Policy Branch

Assistant Director (G5), C. Davies.
Superintending Engineer (G6), T. Wagstaff.

Performance Branch

Assistant Secretary (G5), A. Bacon.
Superintending Architect (G6), B. Hitchcox.
Superintending Estate Surveyor (G6), J. C. Ellis.

REGIONAL ORGANIZATION

Scotland

Argyle House, 3 Lady Lawson Street, Edinburgh
Controller (G4), R. Walton.

England and Wales

North Eastern, Government Buildings, Lawnswood, Leeds. *Regional Controller (G5)*, P. Nelmes.
London North, Olympic House, Olympic Way, Wembley, Middx. *Regional Controller*, Mrs. M. A. Robinson (*Middx.*).
London South, Sutherland House, 29–37 Brighton Road, Sutton, Surrey and Grosvenor House, Basing View, Basingstoke, Hants. *Regional Controller*, M. F. Archer.
Wales and South Western, Gabalfa, Cardiff. *Regional Controller*, G. Griffiths.
Midlands, Five Ways Tower, Frederick Road, Edgbaston, Birmingham. *Regional Controller*, J. T. Green.
North Western, St. Martin's House, Stanley Precinct, Bootle, Merseyside. *Regional Controller*, J. B. Griffin.

INDUSTRIAL INJURIES ADVISORY COUNCIL
Friars House, 157–168 Blackfriars Road,
SE1 8EU
[01–703 6380]

The Industrial Injuries Advisory Council is a statutory body under the Social Security Act, 1975, which considers and advises the Secretary of State for Social Services on Regulations and other questions relating to industrial injuries benefits or their administration.

Chairman, Prof. J. M. Harrington.
Members, Mrs. S. M. Anderson; G. Applebey; J. R. Boddy, M.B.E.; Miss J. C. Brown; Prof. M. J. Cinnamond; Dr. R. J. Donaldson, O.B.E.; Dr. P. C. Elmes; Dr. G. A. Hard; P. R. A. Jacques; Dr. C. P. Juniper; G. Lloyd, C.B.E.; T. W. Mawer; Dr. M. L. Newhouse; Dr. A. J. Newman Taylor; Dr. A. Sinclair; G. M. Thompson.
Secretary, A. L. Perl.

NATIONAL INSURANCE JOINT AUTHORITY
151 Great Titchfield Street, W1P 8AD
[01–636 1696]

The Authority's function is to co-ordinate the operation of social security legislation in Great

Britain and Northern Ireland, including the necessary financial adjustments between the two National Insurance Funds.

Members, The Secretary of State for Social Services; the Head of the Department of Health and Social Services for Northern Ireland.

Secretary, Miss K. E. W. Blunt.

SOCIAL SECURITY—OFFICE OF THE CHIEF ADJUDICATION OFFICER
Cumberland House,
15/17 Cumberland Place, Southampton SO9 2DD
[0703–330066]

The Chief Adjudication Officer is an independent authority under the Social Security Act, 1975 (as amended) appointed by the Secretary of State for Social Services to give advice to adjudication officers (who make decisions of first instance on all claims for Social Security cash benefits), to keep under review the operation of the system of adjudication and to report annually to the Secretary of State on adjudication standards. The Office also enters written observations on all appeals made to the Social Security Commissioners.

Chief Adjudication Officer, M. E. H. Platt.

SOCIAL SECURITY ADVISORY COMMITTEE
New Court, Carey Street, WC2A 2LS
[01–831 6111]

The Social Security Advisory Committee (SSAC) was established by the Social Security Act 1980 to advise the Secretary of State for Social Services and the Department of Health and Social Services for Northern Ireland on all Social Security matters except those relating to benefits for industrial injuries and diseases and occupational pensions. The Social Security Housing Benefit Act 1982 added housing benefit to the Committee's responsibilities.

Chairman, P. M. Barclay, C.B.E.

Members, Prof. J. Cheetham; Dr. R. J. Donaldson, O.B.E.; Mrs. S. Flather; Rev. G. H. Good, O.B.E.; H. Hodge; J. Hughes; P. Jacques; Hon. Mrs. R. H. P. Price; Dr. A. V. Stokes, O.B.E.; Prof. Olive Stevenson; R. G. Wendt.

Secretary, Mrs. U. Brennan.

NATIONAL HEALTH SERVICE
Regional Health Authorities

The Chairmen, and members of Regional Health Authorities are appointed by the Secretary of State for Social Services.

Northern, Benfield Road, Walker Gate, Newcastle upon Tyne. *Chairman*, Prof. B. E. Tomlinson, C.B.E., M.D. *Regional General Manager*, D. Hague.

Yorkshire, Park Parade, Harrogate. *Chairman*, B. Askew. *Regional General Manager*, A. Stokes.

Trent, Fulwood House, Old Fulwood Road, Sheffield. *Chairman*, Sir Michael Carlisle. *Regional General Manager*, B. Edwards.

East Anglia, Union Lane, Chesterton, Cambridge. *Chairman*, Sir Arthur South. *Regional General Manager*, M. W. King.

North East Thames, 40 Eastbourne Terrace, W2. *Chairman*, D. Berriman. *Regional General Manager*, T. Hunt.

North West Thames, 40 Eastbourne Terrace, W2. *Chairman*, W. Doughty. *Regional General Manager*, D. J. Kenny.

South East Thames, Thrift House, Collington Avenue, Bexhill-on-Sea, E. Sussex. *Chairman*, Sir Peter Baldwin, K.C.B. *Regional General Manager*, P. H. J. Le Fleming.

South West Thames, 40 Eastbourne Terrace, W2. *Chairman*, Sir Antony Driver. *Regional General Manager*, A. J. Kember.

Wessex, Highcroft, Romsey Road, Winchester, Hants. *Chairman*, Prof. Sir Bryan Thwaites, Ph.D. *Regional General Manager*, J. Hoare.

Oxford, Old Road, Headington, Oxford. *Chairman*, Sir Gordon Roberts, C.B.E. *Regional General Manager*, Dr. R. Rue, C.B.E., F.R.C.P., F.F.C.M.

South Western, King Square House, 26–27 King Square, Bristol. *Chairman*, W. V. S. Seccombe. *Regional General Manager*, Miss C. E. Hawkins.

West Midlands, Arthur Thompson House, 146–150 Hagley Road, Birmingham. *Chairman*, Sir James Ackers. *Regional General Manager*, K. F. Bales.

Mersey, Hamilton House, 24 Pall Mall, Liverpool. *Chairman*, Sir Donald Wilson. *Regional General Manager*, D. Nichol.

North Western, Gateway House, Piccadilly South, Manchester. *Chairman*, Sir John Page, O.B.E. *Regional General Manager*, D. Allison.

Special Health Authorities

Health Education Authority, 78 New Oxford Street, WC1A 1AH. *Chairman*, Sir Brian Bailey, O.B.E.; *Chief Executive*, Dr. Spencer Hagard.

Disablement Services Authority, 14 Russell Square, WC1. *Chairman*, Lord Holderness, K.G., P.C.; *Chief Executive*, M. G. Jeremiah.

The Special Hospitals Service is provided by four hospitals: Rampton; Broadmoor; Moss Side; and Park Lane. The Boards of these hospitals are Special Health Authorities. (There is a single Board for Moss Side and Park Lane). Chairmen and members are appointed by the Secretary of State for Social Services.

Rampton Hospital, Retford, Notts. *Chairman*, Dr. D. E. Edmond. *Administrator*, D. Atha.

Broadmoor Hospital, Crowthorne, Berks. *Chairman*, Sir David Brown, K.C.B. *Administrator*, J. R. Roberts.

Moss Side and Park Lane Hospitals, Maghull, Liverpool. *Chairman*, R. F. McConnell. *Administrator*, C. P. Tattersall.

SCOTTISH HOME AND HEALTH DEPARTMENT
and
NATIONAL HEALTH SERVICE, SCOTLAND
See Scottish Office

NATIONAL HERITAGE MEMORIAL FUND
10 St James's Street, SW1A 1EF
[01–930 0963]

The National Heritage Memorial Fund was established in 1980 as an independent body, and is intended as a memorial to those who have died for the U.K. The Fund is empowered, by the National Heritage Act 1980, to give financial assistance towards the cost of acquiring, maintaining or preserving land, buildings, works of art and other objects of outstanding interest which are also of importance to the national heritage. The Fund is administered by up to eleven Trustees, appointed by the Prime Minister.

The Fund's major sources of money are the Department of the Environment and the Office of Arts and Libraries, each of which gives annual grants. In its first seven years, the Fund spent £83 million in carrying out its responsibilities.

Trustees

The Lord Charteris of Amisfield (*Chairman*); The Baroness Airey of Abingdon; Prof. F. G. T. Holliday; Sir Martin Jacomb; C. Jenkins; C. Kinahan; Prof.

B. R. Morris; Sir Norman Macfarlane; M. McCrum; Cdr. L. M. M. Saunders Watson; M. Wright.
Secretary, B. Lang.

HIGHLANDS AND ISLANDS DEVELOPMENT BOARD
Bridge House, 27 Bank Street,
Inverness IV1 1QR
[0463 234171]

The Board, a grant-aided body, responsible to the Secretary of State for Scotland, has two broad objectives. These are (1) to assist the people of the Highlands and Islands to improve their economic and social conditions; (2) to enable the Highlands and Islands to play a more effective part in the economic and social development of the nation. To this end the Board will concert, promote, assist or undertake measures for economic and social development.
Chairman, R. Cowan.
Secretary, J. A. MacAskill.

HISTORIC BUILDINGS AND MONUMENTS COMMISSION FOR ENGLAND
Fortress House,
23 Savile Row, W1X 2HE
[01–734 6010]

Under the National Heritage Act, 1983, the duties of the Commission are: (i) to secure the preservation of ancient monuments and historic buildings; (ii) to promote the preservation and enhancement of conservation areas; (iii) to promote the public's enjoyment of, and advance their knowledge of, ancient monuments and historic buildings and their preservation. The Commission has advisory committees on historic buildings, ancient monuments, historic areas, and London.
Chairman, The Lord Montagu of Beaulieu.
Deputy Chairman, H.R.H. The Duke of Gloucester, G.C.V.O.
Commissioners, J. Beecham; J. Benson; P. M. Burnham; The Lord Camoys; Prof. R. Cramp; Prof. B. Cunliffe; A. H. Emery; D. W. Insall; S. D. Jenkins; Sir George Moseley; J. Newman; The Earl of Shelburne; R. L. Vigars; Prof. W. Whitfield.
Chief Executive, P. W. Rumble, C.B.

HISTORIC BUILDINGS COUNCIL (WALES)
Brunel House, 2 Fitzalan Road,
Cardiff CF2 1UY
[0222–465511]

Chairman, The Marquess of Anglesey, F.S.A.
Members, W. Lindsay Evans; Prof. J. Eynon, F.R.I.B.A., F.S.A.; The Earl Lloyd George of Dwyfor; T. Lloyd; Prof. G. Williams, C.B.E., D.Litt., F.S.A.; R. Haslam.
Secretary, R. J. Bolus.

HISTORIC BUILDINGS COUNCIL (SCOTLAND)
20 Brandon Street, Edinburgh EH3 5RA
[031–556 8400]

Chairman, The Marquess of Bute.
Members, I. Begg; Mrs. K. Dalyell; Prof. J. Dunbar-Nasmith, C.B.E.; M. Ellington; I. Hutchison, O.B.E.; The Hon. Lord Jauncey; Dr. M. Lindsay, C.B.E., T.D.; K. Newis, C.B., C.V.O.; Rev. K. Nugent, S.J.; H. F. Smith, M.B.E.
Secretary, I. G. Dewar.

ROYAL COMMISSION ON THE HISTORICAL MONUMENTS OF ENGLAND
Fortress House, 23 Savile Row, W1X 1AB
[01–734 6010]

The Royal Commission on the Historical Monuments of England was established in 1908. The Royal Commission is the national body charged with the recording and analysing of ancient and historical monuments and buildings. The results of these surveys are published. It also compiles, preserves and makes publicly available the national archive of such material, which is housed in the National Monuments Record.
Chairman, The Earl Ferrers, P.C.
Commissioners, Prof. M. W. Beresford, F.B.A.; R. Bradley, F.S.A.; R. A. Buchanan, Ph.D.; Prof. J. D. Evans, Ph.D., Litt.D, F.B.A., F.S.A.; D. J. Keene, Ph.D.; P. Kidson, Ph.D., F.S.A.; Prof. G. H. Martin, C.B.E., D.Phil., F.S.A.; Prof. G. I. Meirion-Jones, Ph.D., F.S.A.; Sir Harry Hookway, Ph.D., Prof. J. K. Downes, Ph.D., F.S.A.; Prof. A. C. Thomas, D.Litt., F.S.A.; Prof. M. Biddle, F.B.A., F.S.A.; Prof. P. E. Lasko, C.B.E., F.B.A., F.S.A.; Prof. M. Todd, F.S.A.
Secretary, T. G. Hassall, F.S.A.

ROYAL COMMISSION ON ANCIENT AND HISTORICAL MONUMENTS IN WALES
Edleston House, Queens Road,
Aberystwyth SY23 2HP
[Aberystwyth : 4381]

The Commission was appointed in 1908 to make an inventory of the ancient and historical monuments in Wales and Monmouthshire. The Commission also includes the National Monuments Record for Wales.
Chairman, Prof. G. Williams C.B.E., D.Litt., F.S.A.
Commissioners, Prof. L. Alcock, F.S.A.; M. R. Apted, Ph.D., F.S.A.; G. C. Boon, F.S.A.; R. W. Brunskill, Ph.D.; Prof. D. Ellis Evans, D.Phil., F.B.A.; R. M. Haslam, F.S.A.; J. G. Jenkins, D.SC., F.S.A.; J. B. Smith; G. J. Wainwright, Ph.D., F.S.A.; Prof. J. G. Williams.
Secretary, P. Smith, F.S.A.

ROYAL COMMISSION ON ANCIENT AND HISTORICAL MONUMENTS OF SCOTLAND
54 Melville Street, Edinburgh EH3 7HF
[031–225 5994]

The Commission was appointed in 1908 to make an inventory of the ancient and historical monuments of Scotland and to specify those that seem most worthy of preservation. The Commission also includes the National Monuments Record of Scotland.
Chairman, The Earl of Crawford and Balcarres, P.C.
Commissioners, Prof. A. A. M. Duncan; Prof. J. D. Dunbar-Nasmith, C.B.E., F.R.I.B.A.; Prof. Rosemary Cramp, C.B.E., F.S.A.; H. M. Colvin, C.V.O., C.B.E., F.B.A.; Prof. L. Alcock, F.S.A., F.R.S.E.; Prof. G. Jobey, D.S.O., F.S.A.; Prof. J. Butt; Mrs. P. E. Durham; Prof. T. C. Smout.
Secretary, J. G. Dunbar, F.S.A.

ANCIENT MONUMENTS BOARD (WALES)
Brunel House, 2 Fitzalan Road, Cardiff CF2 1UY
[0222–465511]

Chairman, Prof. G. Williams, C.B.E., D.Litt., F.S.A.
Members, G. C. Boon, F.S.A.; R. B. Heaton, F.R.I.B.A.; Prof. R. R. Davies, D.Phil.; R. G. Keen; Mrs. F. Lynch-Llewellyn, F.S.A.; D. Moore, R.D., F.S.A.; P. Smith, F.S.A.
Secretary, I. Gibson.

ANCIENT MONUMENTS BOARD (SCOTLAND)
20 Brandon Street, Edinburgh EH3 5RA
[031 244 3076]

Chairman, M. Magnusson, F.R.S.E., F.S.A.Scot.
Members, J. G. Dunbar, F.S.A., F.S.A.Scot.; Prof. G. Jobey, D.S.O., F.S.A., F.S.A.Scot.; A. Fenton, C.B.E., D.Litt., F.S.A., F.S.A.Scot.; H. F. Smith, M.B.E.; The Lady Grimond; Prof. L. Alcock, F.S.A., F.R.S.E., F.S.A.Scot.; J. Simpson, F.S.A.Scot.; Sir Jamie Stormonth Darling, C.B.E., M.C., T.D., W.S.; Prof. J. J. Wilkes, Ph.D., F.S.A., F.S.A.Scot.; Prof. E. C. Fernie, F.S.A., F.S.A.Scot.; Mrs. E. W. Proudfoot, F.S.A., F.S.A.Scot.; Miss R. Fothergill, F.S.A.Scot.
Secretary, J. C. Judson.

HOME-GROWN CEREALS AUTHORITY
Hamlyn House, Highgate Hill, N19 5PR

Constituted under the Cereals Marketing Act, 1965, the Authority consists of 9 members representing U.K. cereal growers, 9 representing dealers in, or processors of, grain and 3 independent members. The purpose of the Authority is to improve the production and marketing of U.K. grain. The Authority also acts as the agent of the Intervention Board for Agricultural Produce in respect of intervention buying, storage and disposal of cereals and oilseed rape within the U.K. under the Common Agricultural Policy and for certain other aspects of the E.C. arrangements for cereals in the U.K.
Chairman, A. Laing, C.B.E.
General Manager, C. J. Ames.

HOME OFFICE
50 Queen Anne's Gate, SW1H 9AT
[01–213 3000]

The Home Office deals with those internal affairs in England and Wales which have not been assigned to other Government Departments. The Home Secretary is particularly concerned with the administration of justice; criminal law; the treatment of offenders including probation and the prison service; the police; immigration and nationality; passport policy matters; community relations; certain public safety matters; fire and civil defence services and also with broad questions of national broadcasting policy. He personally is the link between The Queen and the public and exercises certain powers on her behalf including that of the Royal Pardon.

Other subjects dealt with include electoral arrangements; addresses and petitions to The Queen; ceremonial and formal business connected with honours; requests for extradition of criminals; scrutiny of local authority byelaws; grant of licences for scientific experiments on animals; cremations, burials and exhumations; firearms; dangerous drugs and poisons, general policy on laws relating to shops, liquor licensing, gaming and lotteries, charitable collections and marriage; theatre and cinema licensing; co-ordination of government action in relation to the voluntary social services; and sex discrimination and race relations policy.

The Home Secretary is also the link between the U.K. Government and the governments of the Channel Islands and the Isle of Man.

Salary List

Secretary of State	£33,145
Ministers of State (Commons)	£22,875
Parliamentary Under Secretary	£16,855
Grade 1	£64,739–£65,000
Grade 2	£43,500–£45,550
Grade 3	£34,000–£37,000
Grade 5	£24,765–£28,215
Grade 6	£18,786–£25,335
Grade 7	£15,030–£20,292
H.M. Chief Inspector of Constabulary	£48,154
H.M. Inspectors of Constabulary	£43,539
H.M. Chief Inspector of Prisons	£38,425
Prison Governor I	£25,159
Prison Governor II	£18,872–£22,575
Prison Governor III	£15,323–£18,636
Prison Governor IV	£12,912–£14,976

Secretary of State for the Home Department, THE RT. HON. DOUGLAS HURD, C.B.E., M.P.
Principal Private Secretary (G5), P. C. J. Mawer.
Private Secretaries, W. R. Fittall; C. R. Miller.
Parliamentary Private Secretary, D. Heathcoat-Amory, M.P.
Parliamentary Clerk, J. Acton.
Ministers of State, THE EARL OF CAITHNESS; TIMOTHY RENTON, M.P.; JOHN PATTEN, M.P.
Parliamentary Under Secretary of State, Hon. Douglas Hogg, M.P.
Permanent Under Secretary of State (G1), Sir Brian Cubbon, G.C.B.
Private Secretary, Miss C. J. Stewart.
Chief Medical Officer (at Department of Health and Social Security), Prof. Sir Donald Acheson, K.B.E.

Legal Adviser's Branch

Legal Adviser (G2), J. Nursaw, C.B.
Principal Assistant Legal Advisers (G3), A. H. Hammond; J. Pakenham-Walsh, C.B.
Assistant Legal Advisers, D. Bentley; R. J. Clayton; Miss P. Edwards; Mrs. S. A. Evans; A. W. D. Wilson.
Senior Legal Assistants, A. M. C. Inglese; J. O'Meara; C. M. L. Osborne; D. Seymour.

CRIMINAL AND STATISTICS DEPARTMENTS

Deputy Under Secretary (G2), D. E. R. Faulkner, C.B.

Criminal Policy Department

Assistant Under Secretary of State (G3), W. J. Bohan.
Assistant Secretaries (G5), Miss J. M. Goose; B. M. Cafferey; W. A. Jeffry; N. A. Nagler; N. R. Varney.
Principals (G7), N. Benger; A. Cogbill; Miss K. Collins; R. G. W. Cook; D. A. L. Cooke; F. H. Eggleston; Mrs. E. J. Grimsey; R. E. Hawkes; Miss R. E. Henn; Mrs. S. Jarvis; B. Johnson; Mrs. C. A. Lane Kellas; Miss B. Latimer; Mrs. R. M. Mitev; Mrs. G. Moody; S. S. Mundy; G. J. O. Phillpotts; J. M. Potts; Miss J. B. Rumble; P. A. Stanton; Miss S. R. Street; G. Sutton; G. L. Thomas; Miss M. S. Wooldridge; P. Wright; R. G. Yates.
Chief Inspector, Drugs Branch (G6), P. G. Spurgeon.

Research and Planning Unit

Head of Unit (G5), Mrs. M. Tuck.
Grade 6, J. F. Macleod; R. Tarling; K. H. Heal.
Principals (G7), T. J. Hope; J. M. Hough; Mrs. K. E. Howard; A. D. Maclean; T. F. Marshall; Mrs. P. Mayhew; Ms. P. M. Morgan; Miss J. W. Mott; Dr. D. E. Smith; F. P. E. Southgate; Ms. J. Vennard; G. R. Walmsley; Ms. C. Willis.

Statistical Department

Assistant Under Secretary of State (G3), Miss R. J. Maurice.
Chief Statisticians (G5), C. G. Lewis; P. W. Ward; T. J. Kavanagh.
Statisticians (G7), G. G. Barclay; T. Benn; Dr. A. V. Bishop; L. Davidoff; H. P. Redway; K. D. Childs; P. F. Collier; B. J. Derry; Mrs. R. Passmore; D. H. Ward; P. H. Atkinson; Z. J. Frosztega; K. M. Jackson; Mrs. P. A. Penneck; P. E. Ramell; C. F. Woolf.

Criminal Justice and Constitutional Department

Assistant Under Secretary of State (G3), M. E. Head.
Assistant Secretaries (G5), S. S. Bampton; G. K. Sandiford; Miss P. C. Drew.
Principals (G7), Miss M. V. A. Allibone; M. K. Brenchley; M. P. Cook; Miss G. M. Griffith; B. Johnson; Miss B. Latimer; A. J. Lewis; P. Mc-Dermott; A. D. MacFarlane; Miss S. R. Muir; Mrs. E. A. Sanders; C. P. Stevens; J. Wake.
Chief Probation Officer (G5), C. T. Swann.
Assistant Chief Probation Inspectors (G6), R. A. Betteridge; D. F. Duchemin; Miss M. D. Samuels.

Animals (Scientific Procedure) Inspectorate

Chief Inspector, M. A. Richards.
Superintending Inspectors, C. B. Hart; Dr. W. D. Tavernor.

POLICE AND SCIENTIFIC RESEARCH AND DEVELOPMENT BRANCH

Deputy Under Secretary (G2), J. A. Chilcot.

Police Department

Assistant Under Secretaries of State (G3), G. L. Angel; G. J. Wasserman; A. P. Wilson.
Assistant Secretaries (G5), M. J. Addison; B. O. Bubbear; Mrs. E. I. France; P. R. A. Fulton; J. A. Ingram; E. Soden; F. J. Warne.
Senior Principals (G6), K. H. Heal; Dr. R. A. Hinder; J. W. Cane.
Principals (G7), R. J. Baxter; C. E. Birt; D. Brooker; J. I. Chisholm; Mrs. F. Clarkson; T. P. R. Crompton; P. R. Curwen; S. W. Davidson; J. C. Dilling; G. E. Dunkley; B. R. Gange; N. F. M. Home; C. C. R. Hudson; L. T. Hughes; M. W. Jarvis; Dr. G. K. Laycock; K. Mackenzie; Miss E. B. Moody; T. C. Morris; A. Norbury; J. Sibson; R. E. Smith; P. R. C. Storr; A. Townsend; R. C. Yeates.

Scientific Research and Development Branch
Horseferry House,
Dean Ryle Street, S.W.1
[01–211 3000]

Director (G5), A. N. Rapsey.
Deputy Directors (G6), T. R. Mann; Dr. D. M. S. Peace; Dr. J. R. Stealey; Dr. G. Turnbull; Dr. P. A. Young.
Principal Scientific Officers (G7), Dr. B. J. Blain; Dr. G. A. Carr-Hill; R. H. Doney; Dr. S. Hadjipavlou; Dr. J. A. Harwood; D. J. Meakin; K. Millard; D. D. O'Brien; Dr. G. E. Scott; J. E. Simes; R. C. Stephen; Dr. I. P. Williamson.
Principal Professional and Technology Officer, R. Oliver.

Headquarters Forensic Science Service
Horseferry House
Dean Ryle Street, S.W.1.
[01–211 3000]

Controller (G4), Miss M. Pereira, C.B.E.
Assistant to Controller (G6), Dr. D. G. Sanger.
Principal (G7), (vacant).
Principal Scientific Officer, Dr. R. M. Wright.

Police National Computer Unit
Horseferry House,
Dean Ryle Street, S.W.1
[01–211 3000]

Assistant Secretary (G5), A. G. Bailey.
Senior Principals (G6), G. M. Cole; D. W. Punshon; D. A. Quarmby.
Principals (G7), E. L. Brannan; G. T. Coulthard; D. H. Faulks; A. F. G. Hitchman; D. C. Moulton; R. J. Reason; B. G. Stocking; R. H. Watt; M. H. Williams; T. W. Wrighton.

Directorate of Telecommunications
Horseferry House,
Dean Ryle Street, S.W.1
[01–211 3000]

Director of Telecommunications (G5), P. L. T. Owen, O.B.E.
Deputy Directors (G6), I. Aitken; G. E. Guy; D. A. Hendon; R. M. Hughes.
Principals (G7), D. Mullarky; W. Hogg; T. R. Peters.
Senior Communications Officer, (vacant).
Chief Telecommunications Engineers, I. Aitken; C. J. Barron; R. C. Eaton; R. Harry; A. Hulme; A. N. Kent; G. J. Mewett; J. L. Mumford; M. A. Parker; M. J. Phillips; K. Staves; D. C. J. Theobald; P. M. Tomlinson.

H.M. Inspectorate of Constabulary

H.M. Chief Inspector of Constabulary, R. S. Barratt, C.B.E., Q.P.M.
H.M. Inspectors, J. H. Brownlow, C.B.E., Q.P.M.; C. McLachlan, C.B.E., Q.P.M.; Sir Philip Myers, O.B.E., Q.P.M.; B. Weigh, C.B.E., Q.P.M.; J. Woodcock, C.B.E., Q.P.M.

Police Staff College
Bramshill House, Basingstoke, Hampshire
RG27 0JW
[Hartley Wintney 2931]

Commandant, B. N. Pain, C.B.E., Q.P.M.
Deputy Commandant and Director of Courses, D. P. Griffiths.
Secretary (G7), K. J. Sheehan.

BROADCASTING, EQUAL OPPORTUNITIES, IMMIGRATION AND NATIONALITY DEPARTMENTS

Deputy Under Secretary (G2), W. N. Hyde.

Broadcasting and Miscellaneous Department

Assistant Under Secretary of State (G3), Q. J. Thomas.
Assistant Secretaries (G5), E. A. Grant; N. M. Johnson; L. P. Wright.
Principals (G7), D. C. Houghton; N. C. Sanderson; R. Haugh; R. B. Snow; A. G. Thompson.

Equal Opportunities and General Department

Assistant Under Secretary of State (G3), R. J. Fries.
Assistant Secretaries (G5), J. L. Goddard; Mrs. P. A. Lee, C.B.E.; G. P. Pratt.
Principals (G7), M. J. Gillespie; M. J. I. Hill; Mrs. M. E. Moxon; A. N. Pickersgill; D. J. Rigby; K. D. Sutton; W. F. Whiting; D. I. H. Wright.

Voluntary Services Unit

Assistant Secretary (G5), C. H. Taylor.
Senior Principal (G6), P. E. Bolton.
Principal (G7), G. H. Marriage.

Immigration and Nationality Department
Lunar House, 40 Wellesley Road, Croydon, Surrey,
CR9 2BY
[01–686 0333]

Assistant Under Secretaries of State (G3), R. M. Morris; T. C. Platt.
Assistant Secretaries (G5), D. J. Belfall; P. R. Burleigh; Mrs. B. H. Fair; T. J. Flesher; J. M. Lyon; A. R. Rawsthorne.
Senior Principals (G6), R. A. McDowell; D. M. McQueen.
Principals (G7), B. D. Bishop; M. Boyle; J. G. Burgess; J. G. Daley; Miss V. M. Dews; P. Durbin; M. Copley; J. P. Emery; Mrs. J. M. Kidd; D. J. M. McDonough; R. C. Masefield; N. Montgomery-Potts; Mrs. S. Morris; Mrs. E. C. L. Pallett; D. A. Peters; S. Spence; Mrs. B. Turrell; R. S. Weekes.

Immigration Service

Chief Inspector (G4), P. Tompkins.
Deputy Chief Inspectors (G6), C. B. Manchip; A. A. Holton; D. G. Stephens.
Assistant Chief Inspectors, D. Barrell; J. M. Durose; V. Hogg; J. D. Smith.

Passport Department
Clive House, Petty France, SW1H 9HD
[01–213 3000]

Head of Division (G5), A. Holmes, C.B.E.
Deputy Head of Division (G6), W. R. Mann.
Principals (G7), Miss M. A. N. Ashton; N. K. Finlayson; R. I. Henderson; T. Lonsdale; J. F. Nicholson; Miss H. E. Wells.

PRISON SERVICE
Cleland House, Page Street, SW1P 4LN
[01–211 3000]

Director-General of the Prison Service (G2), C. J. Train, C.B.
Deputy Director-General of the Prison Service (G3), G. H. Lakes, M.C.

Prisons Department

Assistant Under Secretaries of State (Directors) (G3), J. G. Pilling *(Personnel and Finance)*; S. Norris *(Operational Policy)*; Miss M. A. Clayton *(Regimes and Services)*; Dr. J. L. Kilgour *(Medical Services)*.
Non-Executive Members, Miss D. N. Barrett; C. J. Ganderton.
Assistant Secretaries (G5), S. W. Boys-Smith; B. O. Bubbear; A. J. Butler; B. A. Emes; P. C. Edwards; Miss J. McNaughton; A. J. Pearson; H. H. Taylor; Miss J. Thompson; A. H. Turney.
Deputy Director of Prison Medical Services (G4), Dr. P. J. Hynes.
Principal Medical Officers (G4), Dr. P. Arrowsmith; Dr. D. A. F. Doherty; Dr. R. J. Wool.
Senior Principals (G6), D. R. Birleson; D. F. Scagell; A. C. Stott; L. A. Scudder.
Governors I, G. D. Dadds; J. H. Rumball; D. A. Brown; J. E. Simmons; W. R. Booth.
Principals (G7), Mrs. P. R. Atkins; W. M. Black; D. J. Blackman; G. Boiling, M.B.E.; A. D. Burgess; B. G. Chaplin; P. Cook; Mrs. C. Crawford; H. M. C. Crudge; R. F. Cumings; P. Done; J. Duke-Evans; R. W. G. Dyke; R. Eagle; D. H. Gannon; Miss L. F. Gill; D. J. Hollis; R. Hulley; J. C. Imber; Miss D. Loudon; M. J. Murphy; Mrs. S. Murray; K. R. North; J. S. Nottingham; P. G. V. Pike; J. Plumridge; J. R. K. de Quidt; M. J. A. Prowse; Miss G. Romney; P. M. Scott; J. Simpson; Miss A. Smith; G. N. Stadlen; R. J. Weatherill; W. F. Whiting; T. J. Wilson; R. A. Wright.
Governors II, R. Clarke; Miss J. M. Fowler; D. G. Longley; A. K. Rawson; J. Shulman; D. Twiner; I. Ward.
Prison Service Chaplaincy (G6), Ven. K. S. Pound.
Director of Psychological Services, P. H. Shapland.
Chief Education Officer, I. G. Benson.
Chief Physical Education Officer (G6), M. W. Denton.
Governors III, T. M. O'Sullivan; M. F. W. Watson-Jackson; R. Daley; G. Gregory-Smith; D. V. Hickson; D. I. Lockwood; D. Wilson; F. Masserick; C. J. Williams.

Chief Architect's Branch and Directorate of Works
Abell House, John Islip Street, SW1P 4LH
[01–211 3000]

Chief Architect and Director of Works (G4), H. J. M. McMaster.
Superintending Architects (G6), J. H. Cooper; A. W. Gillman; R. W. T. Haines; D. W. Harris; M. J. Ireson; S. Mahraj.

Principal Professional and Technology Officers, O. P. Astaniotis; P. J. Attwater; D. G. Baines; H. G. S. Banks; M. J. Bridgford; G. F. Burgess; J. K. Chamberlain; B. D. Charlson; G. W. Chrisp; C. R. Cope; H. J. Davies; J. A. Doohan; C. F. Drewitt; M. C. Hayes; G. E. Hickey; J. V. R. Hillyer; F. Home; M. J. Ireson; J. F. Keeler; R. T. Lewis; A. A. Newman; A. W. Orchard; R. J. Perham; C. A. G. Poole; R. S. Putland; K. T. Stannard; B. A. Stickley; M. Sweeny.
Principals (G7), D. Mannings; P. Luscombe.

Prison Service Industries and Farms
Lunar House, Wellesley Road, Croydon,
Surrey CR9 2BY
[01–686 0333]

Director (G5), Miss A. M. Edwards.
Group Managers (G6), M. Codd; T. S. A. Devon; N. Fennemore; G. C. Robertson; J. H. Smith.
Principals (G7), J. A. Byrd; J. D. Cleary; R. Cunningham; A. Gillcrist; D. E. Neville; J. A. Ward; A. S. Wilson.
Principal Professional & Technology Officers, R. Fisher; G. A. Hallam; T. Senior; A. Sweeney.

Supply and Transport Branch
Crown House, 52 Elizabeth Street,
Corby, Northants.
[Corby 202101]

Director (G6), D. J. Hardwick.
Principals (G7), R. C. Brett; M. Fitzgerald; J. Harvey; A. S. Thompson.

Prison Service Regional Offices

Midland, Birmingham:
Regional Director (G5), J. R. Sandy.
Deputy Regional Director, M. D. Jenkins.
Assistant Regional Directors, (vacant) *(Administration)*; J. Blakey *(Young Offenders)*; C. B. Heald *(Operations)*.

South West, Bristol:
Regional Director (G5), I. Dunbar.
Deputy Regional Director, A. H. Rayfield.
Assistant Regional Directors, T. C. Newell *(Adult Offenders)*; (vacant) *(Administration)*; J. W. Plumb *(Young Offenders)*.

North, Manchester:
Regional Director (G5), A. W. Driscoll, Q.G.M..
Deputy Regional Director, C. J. Jones.
Assistant Regional Directors, L. Edgar *(Administration)*; C. B. Scott *(Locals/Reception Centres)*; G. A. Shore *(Trainers/Dispersal/Open)*; P. J. Rudgard *(Female/Young Offenders)*.

South East, Woking:
Regional Director (G5), C. P. Honey.
Deputy Regional Director, J. F. Perriss.
Assistant Regional Directors, (vacant) *(Administration)*; J. Dugdale *(Operations)*; E. R. Campbell *(Young Offenders)*; B. Hayday *(Women)*; R. H. Jacques, J. Walsh *(Operational Assessment)*.

PRISONS
Governors

Acklington, Northumberland, C. Harder.
Albany, I.O.W., P. J. Kitteridge.
Aldington, Kent, H. G. Bagshaw.
Ashwell, Leics., R. Curtis.
Askham Grange, Yorks., R. Smith.
Bedford, J. L. Uzzell.
Birmingham, P. Buxton.
Blundeston, Suffolk, G. H. Cropper.
Bristol, T. M. O'Sullivan.
Brixton, S.W.2., Miss J. Kinsley.
Camp Hill, I.O.W., D. M. Morrison.
Canterbury, J. M. Reid.

Cardiff, J. M. Williams.
Channings Wood, Devon, C. G. Clark.
Chelmsford, D. B. Sinclair.
Coldingley, Surrey, Mrs. M. M. Donnelly.
Cookham Wood, P. J. Meakings.
Dartmoor, R. J. May.
Dorchester, B. Coatsworth.
Drake Hall, Stafford, R. Mitchell.
Durham, A. H. Papps.
Exeter, D. Alderson.
Featherstone, Wolverhampton, J. W. Dring.
Ford, Sussex, G. W. E. Ellington.
Frankland, Durham, R. Mole.
Full Sutton, B. V. Smith.
Gartree, Leics., R. R. Tilt.
Gloucester, N. W. A. Wall.
Grendon and Spring Hill, Bucks., M. F. G. Selby.
Haverigg, Cumbria, B. McLuckie.
Highpoint, Newmarket, J. Hunter.
Holloway, N.7., C. Allen.
Hull, P. M. Wheatley.
Kingston, Portsmouth, Miss M. R. Allen.
Kirkham, Lancs., F. V. Weigh.
Lancaster, B. A. Wilson.
Leeds, W. A. Martin.
Leicester, J. R. Wilkinson.
Lewes, J. R. Marriott.
Leyhill, Glos., W. E. McEvoy.
Lincoln, P. L. Harrap.
Lindholme (Doncaster), C. F. Lambert.
Littlehay, (vacant).
Liverpool, J. Richardson, O.B.E.
Long Lartin, Worcs., J. Whitty.
Maidstone, J. W. Staples.
Manchester, F. B. O'Friel.
Morton Hall, Lincoln, P. J. Leonard.
Northeye, Sussex, D. C. Ozanne.
Norwich, A. J. Barclay.
Nottingham, H. Reid.
Oxford, M. A. Lewis.
Parkhurst, I.O.W., R. E. Withers.
Pentonville, B. A. Marchant.
Preston, A. N. Joseph.
Ranby, T. Davies.
Reading, D. Myers.
Rudgate, W. Yorks., N. Berry.
Send, Surrey, A. C. Smith.
Shepton Mallet, R. D. Dixon.
Shrewsbury, L. M. Wiltshire.
Stafford, I. A. E. Boon.
Standford Hill, B. W. Sutton.
Stocken, E. P. Polkinghorne.
Styal, Cheshire, G. Walker.
Sudbury, Derbys., L. Stones.
Swansea, S. R. Robinson.
Thorp Arch, W. Yorks, D. Whitehead.
The Verne, Dorset, D. L. Long.
Wakefield, T. J. Gadd.
Wakefield Service College, R. S. Duncan.
Wandsworth, S.W.18., D. A. Marsden.
Wayland, C. A. Brown.
Winchester, M. V. Roberts.
Wormwood Scrubs, W.12., D. Brooke.
Wymott, Preston, Maj. R. B. Coombs.

YOUTH CUSTODY CENTRES
Governors

Aylesbury, T. C. H. Newth.
Bullwood Hall, Essex, Miss U. M. B. McCollam.
Campsfield House, Oxford, K. B. Owen.
Castington, M. R. J. Gander.
Deerbolt, P. A. Whitehouse.
Dover, D. Aram.
East Sutton Park, Kent, G. Gibson.
Erlestoke, Wilts., D. J. Waplington.
Everthorpe, Humberside, T. M. Turner.
Feltham, A. M. E. de Frisching.

Gaynes Hall, Cambs, M. J. Jehan.
Glen Parva, Leics., H. Jones.
Guys Marsh, Dorset, G. Brunskill.
Hatfield, Yorks., W. J. Clark.
Hewell Grange, Worcs., Miss M. A. Carden.
Hindley, Lancs, J. H. M. Anderson.
Hollesley Bay Colony, Suffolk, Miss S. F. McCormick.
Huntercombe and Finnamore Wood, Oxon., F. Crowe.
Lowdham Grange, Notts., W. J. Cooper.
Northallerton, M. A. Mogg.
Onley, Warwicks., T. Abbott.
Portland, Dorset, M. Langdon.
Rochester, M. Manning.
Stoke Heath, Salop, A. Cruikshank.
Styal, Cheshire, G. Walker.
Swinfen Hall, Staffs., J. B. Pudney.
Thorn Cross, D. Hall.
Usk, Gwent, J. Capel.
Wellingborough, E. Martin.
Werrington, Staffs., M. K. Pascoe.
Wetherby, Yorks., A. Holman.

REMAND CENTRES
Governors

Ashford, Middx., S. C. A. Pryor.
Brockhill, Worcs., P. T. Hanglin.
Latchmere House, Surrey, G. Barnard.
Low Newton, Co. Durham, W. J. Mansfield.
Pucklechurch, Bristol, D. C. Leach.
Risley, Cheshire, D. J. Thompson.

DETENTION CENTRES
Governors

Blantyre House, Kent, K. D. Wyatt.
Buckley Hall, Lancs., C. R. Griffiths.
Eastwood Park, Glos., T. B. Thomas.
Foston Hall, Derby, P. Lynch.
Gringley, B. Tyreman.
Haslar, Hants., W. J. Keast.
Kirklevington, Cleveland, D. G. McNaughton.
Medomsley, C. Harder.
New Hall, Yorks., J. D. Yates.
North Sea Camp, Lincs., J. W. Hanson, M.B.E.
Whatton, Notts., F. Abbott.

Inspectorate of Prisons

H.M. Chief Inspector of Prisons, Sir James Hennessy, K.B.E., C.M.G.
H.M. Deputy Chief Inspector of Prisons (G5), M. D. Jenkins.
H.M. Inspectors (G5), D. F. Campbell; S. C. Handley; D. Shaw; B. J. Wells.
Principal (G7), Mrs. C. L. Lehman.

ESTABLISHMENT, FINANCE AND MANPOWER,
FIRE AND EMERGENCY PLANNING
DEPARTMENTS

Deputy Under Secretary (G2), M. J. Moriarty.

Establishment Department

Assistant Under Secretary of State (G3), A. R. Rawsthorne *(Personnel, Organisation and Management Services)*.
Assistant Secretaries (G5), F. J. A. Warne; M. H. Davies; J. L. Goddard; F. H. Keens, O.B.E.; J. S. Smedley.
Senior Principals (G6), S. W. Bennett; F. R. Hayhurst; P. G. Spurgeon.
Principals (G7), D. J. Blackwood; R. C. Case; Miss K. J. Collins; Mrs. C. Cowley; C. I. Dickinson; G. J. Edwards; R. G. Ferguson; A. Fishwick; D. H. Gannon; D. J. Grant; D. Hillier; P. J. Honour; D. G. Jones; B. J. Jordan; J. F. Love; Miss S. Marshall; Mrs. J. Morgan; R. Ritchie; K. E. R. Rogers; D. G. Ross; M. P. Scandrett; J. C. Smith; R. E. Stockdale; S. E. Wharton.

Home Office Unit at Civil Service Selection Board
Kirkland House, 22 Whitehall, SW1A 2ED
[01–210 6671]

Assistant Secretary (G5), R. J. Miles.
Principal Psychologists, R. T. Feltham; F. D. Bedford.

Public Relations Branch

Director of Information Services (G4), B. L. Mower.
Deputy Director, Ms. E. Drummond.
Principal Information Officers (G7), R. Windsor; P. G. Rose.

Finance and Manpower Department

Assistant Under Secretary of State (Principal Finance Officer) (G3), J. F. Halliday.
Assistant Secretaries (G5), C. Farrington; A. Harding; Mrs. V. V. R. Harris; J. E. Hayzelden.
Senior Principals (G6), J. W. Cane; R. M. Hoare; J. P. Nicholson.
Principals (G7), I. J. Babbage; C. W. Bolt; J. Bowles; M. J. Brown; J. I. Chisholm; I. M. Clark; D. R. Dewick; G. B. Fox; P. F. Hewett; S. B. Hickson; M. P. B. Kennedy; J. W. Maloney; M. R. Matthews; Mrs. P. W. Nice; A. Norbury; Mrs. M. R. Ryan; K. J. Sheehan; A. V. H. Stainer.

Fire and Emergency Planning Department

Assistant Under Secretary of State (G3), A. H. Turney.
Assistant Secretaries (G5), P. Canovan; R. R. G. Watts; J. A. Howard; Mrs. J. Thompson.
Grade 6, B. S. Luetchford.
Principals (G7), E. Alley; W. F. Bryant; T. K. Cobley; D. H. Evans; Mrs. D. M. Grice; B. Lockett; D. J. Moss; D. J. Mould.

Fire Service Inspectorate

Chief Inspector, R. D. Doyle, C.B.E.
Inspectors (Grade I), H. R. C. Boyce, Q.F.S.M.; C. G. Burgon; N. F. Roundell, Q.F.S.M.
Inspectors (Grade II), S. D. Christian; J. Dukelow; C. Green; T. Greenwood; A. F. Kilford; P. A. Kilshaw; W. C. Perry, M.B.E.; H. V. Reed; C. H. Sanders; G. J. Tinley.
Senior Engineering Inspector, R. M. Simpson

Fire Service College

Moreton-in-Marsh, Gloucestershire GL56 0RH
[Moreton-in-Marsh : 50831]

Commandant, G. Clarke, C.B.E.
Deputy Commandant, F. N. David.
Secretary (G7), J. A. Gunderson.

Civil Defence College

The Hawkhills, Easingwold, Yorks. YO6 3EG
[Easingwold : 21406]

Head of College (G5), J. B. Bettridge, C.B.E.
Vice-Principal, J. D. Shallow, M.C.

Home Office H.Q. U.K. Warning and Monitoring Organization

James Wolfe Road, Cowley, Oxford OX4 2PT
[Oxford 776005]

Director (G6), R. F. Cooke.
Deputy Director I, W. P. Lawrie.
Deputy Director II, D. L. Warden.

Women's Royal Voluntary Service

234/244 Stockwell Road, SW1P 9SP
[01–733 3388]

National Chairman, Dame Barbara Shenfield, D.B.E.

HORSERACE TOTALISATOR BOARD

74 Upper Richmond Road, SW15 2SU
[01–874 6411]

Established by the Betting, Gaming and Lotteries Act, 1963, as successor in title to the Racecourse Betting Control Board established by the Racecourse Betting Act, 1928.

Its function is to operate totalisators on approved racecourses in Great Britain, and it also provides off-course cash and credit offices. Under the Horserace Totalisator and Betting Levy Board Act, 1972, it is further empowered to offer bets at starting price (or other bets at fixed odds) on any sporting event.
Chairman, Lord Wyatt of Weeford £52,000
Members, The Lord Chapple; Mrs. P. Hastings; Hon. D. Montagu; P. S. Winfield; J. F. Sanderson; H.R.H. Prince Michael of Kent.

HOUSING CORPORATION

149 Tottenham Court Road, W1P 0BN
[01–387 9466]

Established by Parliament in 1964, the Housing Corporation has since had its functions broadened by the Housing Acts of 1974 and 1980. It now registers, supervises and funds non-profit making housing associations throughout Great Britain. The Corporation has registered over 2,600 associations since 1974.

The Corporation also supports housing associations in the rehabilitation of older houses and in new building to help people with special needs, including the elderly, the disabled, and single homeless people, and backs initiatives by housing associations to provide homes for sale to people on lower incomes, through schemes for shared equity, leasehold for the elderly and improvement for sale.
Chairman, Sir Hugh Cubitt, C.B.E.

INDEPENDENT BROADCASTING AUTHORITY

70 Brompton Road, S.W.3
[01–584 7011]

The Independent Television Authority was created by Act of Parliament in 1954 to provide an additional television broadcasting service to that provided by the British Broadcasting Corporation. In 1972 it was renamed the Independent Broadcasting Authority and its functions were extended to cover the provision of independent local radio.

The main functions of the Authority are to appoint the ILR and ITV programme companies; to own and operate transmitters; to supervise the programmes provided by contractors and the Channel Four Television Company and their scheduling; and to control advertising. The programme companies pay the Authority a rental to enable it to carry out its duties.

Fifteen ITV programme companies provide programmes in 14 regions (two companies operate in London, one at the weekends, the other during the week). By June, 1987, 47 Independent Local Radio contractors were broadcasting in the U.K. (in London, there are two companies, one providing a news and information service, and the second general entertainment and information). Both ITV and ILR are financed mainly by the sale of advertising time.

The Authority consists of a Chairman and eleven members appointed by the Home Secretary and a permanent staff under the Director General.
Chairman, The Lord Thomson of Monifieth, K.T., P.C.
Deputy Chairman, Sir Donald Maitland, G.C.M.G., O.B.E.
Members, Mrs. P. Ridley; M. H. Caine; R. A. Grantham; Prof. J. F. Fulton *(Northern Ireland);* J. R. Purvis *(Scotland);* G. R. Peregrine *(Wales);* Prof. A. Cullen, O.B.E., F.R.S., Sir Anthony Jolliffe; Lady Popplewell; R. Sondhi.
Director General, J. Whitney.
Deputy Director General, The Lady Littler.
Director of Television, D. Glencross.

Director of Radio, P. A. C. Baldwin.
Director of Engineering, Dr. J. Forrest.
Director of Finance, P. Rogers.
Controller of Advertising, F. Willis.
Controller of Information Service, Miss C. Bowe.
Secretary, B. Rook.
Regional Officers, M. J. Fay *(Yorkshire)*; E. Lewis *(Wales and West of England)*; A. D. Fleck *(Northern Ireland)*; Miss S. Thane *(East of England)*; D. Lee *(North-West England)*; B. Marjoribanks *(Scotland)*; R. J. F. Lorimer *(North-East England and the Borders)*; N. J. Reedy *(East and West Midlands)*; J. B. Scott *(South of England and Channel Islands)*.

CENTRAL OFFICE OF INFORMATION
Hercules Road, SE1 7DU
[01–928 2345]

The Central Office of Information is a common service department which produces information and publicity material, and supplies publicity services, for other Government departments on a repayment basis. In the U.K. it conducts Government display press, television and poster advertising, produces and distributes booklets, leaflets, films, television material, exhibitions, photographs and other visual material; and distributes departmental press notices. For the overseas departments it supplies British Information posts overseas with press, radio and television material, booklets, magazines, reference services, films, exhibitions, photographs, display and reading room material; arranges tours in the U.K. for official visitors from overseas. Administrative responsibility for the Central Office of Information rests with H.M. Treasury Ministers, while the ministers whose departments it serves are responsible for the policy expressed in its work.

Salary List

Grade 3	£41,000
Grade 4	£30,344–£31,844
Grade 5	£24,765–£28,215
Grade 6	£18,786–£25,335
Grade 7	£15,030–£20,292

Director-General (G3), N. Taylor.
  Private Secretary, Mrs. M. M. Habershon.
Head of Information Officer Management Unit (G5), (vacant).
Deputy Director-General (G4), G. M. Devereau.

Personnel and Office Services Division
Principal Establishment Officer (G5), E. Bridger.

Finance and Management Services Division
Principal Finance Officer (G5), A. H. Robinson.
Director (G6), K. E. Williamson.

OVERSEAS PUBLICITY GROUP
Group Director (G5), P. T. Brazier.

Overseas Press Services
Director (G6), G. L. Strickland.

Overseas Publications & Foreign Languages
Director (G6), R. Smith.

Overseas Visitors & Information Studies
Director (G6), D. A. Smith.

VISUAL MEDIA AND RADIO GROUP
Group Director (G5), R. N. Hooper.

Films & Television
Director (G6), R. J. Hall.

Radio and Photographic Services
Director (G6), J. A. Leys.

Exhibitions
Director (G6), D. A. Loxley.

HOME PUBLICITY GROUP
Group Director (G5), J. Bolitho.

Advertising
Director (G6), K. C. Belben.

Home Publications
Director (G6), D. A. Low.

Research
Director (G6), M. C. Warren.

CLIENT SERVICES GROUP
Director (G6), Miss J. Luke.

REGIONAL OFFICES

North Eastern, Wellbar House, Gallowgate, Newcastle upon Tyne.—*Regional Director (G7)*, J. F. Dougray.
Yorkshire and Humberside, City House, New Station Street, Leeds.—*Regional Director (G6)*, A. S. Poole.
Eastern, Three Crowns House, 72–80 Hills Road, Cambridge.—*Regional Director (G7)*, D. Dowle.
London and South Eastern, Hercules Road, SE1 7DU.—*Regional Director (G6)*, G. E. Moggridge.
South Western, The Pithay, Bristol.—*Regional Director (G7)*, P. D. Yorke.
Midlands, Five Ways Tower, Frederick Road, Edgbaston, Birmingham.—*Regional Director (G6)*, P. J. Woodford.
North Western, Sunley Building, Piccadilly Plaza, Manchester.—*Regional Director (G6)*, O. J. B. Prince-White.

BOARD OF INLAND REVENUE
Somerset House, WC2R 1LB
[01–438 6622]

The Board of Inland Revenue was constituted under the Inland Revenue Board Act, 1849, by the consolidation of the Board of Excise and the Board of Stamps and Taxes. In 1909 the administration of excise duties was transferred to the Board of Customs. The Board of Inland Revenue administers and collects direct taxes—mainly income tax, corporation tax, capital gains tax, inheritance tax, stamp duty, development land tax and petroleum revenue tax— and advises the Chancellor of the Exchequer on policy questions involving them. The Head Office is in London and there are Inspectors of Taxes offices and Collection offices throughout the United Kingdom. The Department's Valuation Office is responsible for valuing property for tax purposes, for compensation and for compulsory purchase and (in England and Wales) for local rating purposes. In 1986–87 Inland Revenue collected over £57,000 million tax.

Salary List

Grade 1	£65,000
Grade 2	£43,500–£45,500
Grade 3	£34,000–£37,000
Grade 4	£30,344–£31,844
Grade 5	£24,765–£28,215
Grade 6	£18,786–£25,335
Grade 7	£15,030–£20,292

The Board

Chairman (G1), A. M. W. Battishill.
  Private Secretary, Ms. B. A. St. Quinton.
Deputy Chairmen (G2), A. J. G. Isaac, c.b.; T. J. Painter.
Directors General (G2), D. B. Rogers, c.b.; B. Pollard.
Commissioners: Chief Valuer (G2), A. B. Fallows, c.b.; *(G3),* J. D. Taylor-Thompson c.b.

Policy Divisions

Grade 3, P. Lewis; C. W. Corlett; B. T. Houghton; E. McGivern; J. D. Taylor-Thompson, c.b.; D. Y. Pitts.
Grade 5, B. A. Mace; Miss A. M. Rhodes; M. Prescott; J. D. Farmer; C. Stewart; C. D. Sullivan; N. C. Munro; D. G. Draper; D. L. Shaw; J. P. Battersby; H. B. Thompson; M. F. Cayley; J. H. Reed; P. S. A. Driscoll; M. J. G. Elliott; I. R. Spence; J. P. B. Bryce; P. W. Fawcett; J. B. Shepherd; Mrs. C. B. Hubbard; Miss M. A. Hill; B. O'Connor.
Controller of Development Land Tax Office (G7), V. Robinson.

Central Division

Grade 3, L. J. H. Beighton.
Grade 5, M. A. Johns; R. R. Martin.
Senior Economic Adviser (G5), R. Weeden.

Technical Division

Directors (G3), J. E. Lawrance; J. H. Roberts.
Assistant Directors (G4), J. C. Campbell; K. A. Skinner; R. E. German; M. D. Whitear; J. Moule; M. D. E. Newstead; E. K. Pearson; E. Pattison; G. F. Hamilton; W. Northend; J. M. L. Davenport; J. K. Duxbury; D. W. Hugo; I. N. Hunter; B. Sadler; J. F. Hall.
Assistant Directors (G5), A. J. O'Brien; R. C. Mountain.
Principal Inspectors of Taxes (G5), M. L. Gordon; M. Templeman; J. Potter; T. R. Evans; K. Hamer; R. E. Creed; J. White; P. C. Fielder; I. R. Drummond; R. A. Reed; B. Carter; K. H. Colmer; J. S. Marshall; D. A. Johnson; R. G. Jasper; R. Thomas; A. Beauchamp; R. E. Haigh; Mrs. M. E. Williams.
Controller of Oil Taxation Office (G4), R. M. Elliss.

Management Divisions

Director of Personnel (G3), P. B. G. Jones.
Assistant Directors (G4), G. Findley; G. J. Lyall; *(G5)* R. A. Hutton, F. W. Newcombe; J. T. Tudor; R. Neilson; M. Jordan.
Controller of Office Services (G6), B. R. Spooner.
Director of Manpower and Support Services (G3), J. M. Crawley.
Assistant Directors (G5); D. Ward; J. Marshall; D. K. Matthews.
Head of Operational Research (G5), R. P. R. Tilley.
Director of Information Technology (G3), S. C. T. Matheson.
Assistant Directors (G5), R. A. Hamilton; J. C. Cockcroft; D. Selwood; J. A. Pinder; C. J. Thompson; B. T. Glassberg; A. M. Paterson.
Director of Operations (G3), C. Cherry.
Assistant Directors (G4), R. N. Page; J. M. Phalp; *(G5)* J. E. Yard; R. H. Allen; P. J. Hodgson; J. C. Jones; J. Gant; Miss M. James; G. H. Bush; R. K. Freeman; J. M. Thomas.
Controller, Enforcement Office (G5), R. F. Bruford.
Head of Communications Group (G4), D. W. Muir.
Press Secretary (G7), Miss F. A. McFarlane.

Finance Division

Principal Finance Officer (G3), J. M. Crawley.
Assistant Secretary (G5), A. G. Nield.
Controller, Central Accounting Office (G6), J. Gray.
Chief Internal Auditor (G6), (vacant).

Statistics Division

Director (G3), J. R. Calder.
Chief Statisticians (G5), J. B. Dearman; R. J. Eason; F. A. Fitzpatrick; W. Gonzalez, c.b.e.
Computing (G6), C. R. Bond.

Office of the Controller of Stamps
Bush House, South-West Wing, Strand, WC2B 4QN
and Barrington Road, Worthing, W. Sussex
BN12 4XH

Controller (G6), D. E. Pipe.

Capital Taxes Office
Minford House, Rockley Road, W14 0DF

Controller (G4), G. A. Spencer.
Deputy Controllers (G5), B. D. Kent; R. J. Draper.
Asst. Controllers (G6), R. Shanks; A. S. Johnson; M. Swann; A. L. Barton; I. P. Gunn; D. J. Ferley; C. A. Oldridge; H. V. Capon; R. T. Kablean; J. Blagden; T. J. Plumb.

Solicitor of Inland Revenue
Somerset House, WC2R 1LB

Solicitor (G2), R. K. Miller.
Principal Assistant Solicitors (G3), J. F. Easton; B. E. Cleave; J. D. H. Johnston.
Assistant Solicitors (G5), C. J. C. Baron; J. C. H. Bates; R. T. Brand; K. Brown; K. O. Butterfield; B. R. D. Clarke; M. C. Furey, c.b.e.; A. J. Gunz; J. F. W. Hinson; N. R. Phillips; P. L. Ridd; A. K. S. Shaw; R. W. Thornhill.

Superannuation Funds Office
Lynwood Road, Thames Ditton, Surrey KT7 0DP

Controller (G5), R. G. Lusk.
Assistant Controllers (G6), I. A. Young; R. C. Fullbrook.

Inspector of Foreign Dividends Office
Lynwood Road, Thames Ditton, Surrey KT7 0DP

Inspector of Foreign Dividends (G6), D. J. Critchley.

Office of the Chief Valuer
New Court, Carey Street, WC2A 2JE

Chief Valuer (G2), A. B. Fallows, c.b.
Deputy Chief Valuers (G3), P. G. Heard, c.b.; R. R. B. Shutler.
Assistant Chief Valuers (G4), S. H. Keith; A. J. Langford; R. J. Sellick.
Superintending Valuers (G5), R. Burrows; P. R. Garrett; D. B. Hardy; M. J. Loveridge; O. T. Morgan; W. J. Reed; A. B. Prior.
Assistant Directors (G5), J. H. Ebdon; D. R. Morrough; T. R. Peckham.

INLAND REVENUE (SCOTLAND)
80 Lauriston Place, Edinburgh EH3 9SL

Controller (G4), W. S. Linkie.
Group Controllers (G5), J. Brown; H. S. MacRae; O. J. Clarke; R. I. Ford.

Controller (Stamps)
16 Picardy Place, Edinburgh EH1 3NF

Controller, D. G. Hunter.

Capital Taxes Office
16 Picardy Place, Edinburgh EH1 3NF

Registrar (G5), J. B. M. McKean.
Deputy Registrar (G6), P. G. Bruce, m.b.e.
Chief Examiners (G7), G. Mackie; Mrs. J. A. Templeton; W. Young; J. Telford; T. E. Naysmith; C. G. Hogg; Miss A. Forbes.

Solicitor's Office
80 Lauriston Place, Edinburgh EH3 9SL

Solicitor, T. H. Scott.
Senior Principals (Legal) (G6), I. K. Laing; Miss E. M. M. McLean.
Senior Legal Assistant, D. S. Wishart.

Office of the Chief Valuer, Scotland
15 Drumsheugh Gardens, Edinburgh EH3 7UN

Chief Valuer (G4), J. A. Sutherland.
Assistant Chief Valuer (G5), M. A. Newbury.

INTERVENTION BOARD FOR AGRICULTURAL PRODUCE
Fountain House, 2 Queen's Walk, Reading RG1 7QW
[0734–583626]

The Board was formed as a Government Department on November 22, 1972, and is responsible under the Agricultural Ministers for the implementation within the U.K. of the guarantee functions of the Common Agricultural Policy of the European Community. Policy matters are the responsibility of the Agricultural Ministers of the U.K.

Salary List
Grade 3	£34,000–£37,000
Grade 4	£30,344–£31,844
Grade 5	£24,765–£28,215
Grade 6	£18,786–£25,335
Grade 7	£15,030–£20,292

Chairman, A. J. Ellis, C.B.E.
Chief Executive (G3), G. Stapleton.
Director of Corporate Services (G4), P. G. Horscroft.

Establishments Branch
Grade 6, J. Bird.

Secretariat and Procurement Services
Grade 6, G. R. Holloway.

Finance Division
Grade 5, J. N. Diserens.
Principals (G7), H. MacKinnon; E. R. Asprey; R. Bryant.

Audit Branch
Principal (G7), G. Evans.

Computer Services
Grade 6, E. M. Abbott.
Principals (G7), D. F. Horler; T. T. Simpson.

Crops Division
Grade 5, D. M. L. Macgregor.
Principals (G7), M. E. Statham; R. W. Roughley.
Commodity Specialists, J. R. Edmunds; B. C. Cook.

Livestock Products Division
Grade 5, R. A. Saunderson.
Principals (G7), P. J. Offer; J. F. Springate; J. A. Sutton.

External Market Division
Grade 5, G. N. Dixon.
Principals (G7), C. D. Perrin; N. P. J. Rowe; G. Donkin.

U.K. Seeds Executive
Chairman, Prof. J. C. Murdoch, O.B.E., Ph.D.
Members, T. M. Clucas; B. R. Cummings; J. Harvey; Prof. J. D. Hayes, Ph.D.; P. R. Hayward, O.B.E.; G. G. Lyall; D. J. Palmer; W. P. Watt.

H.M. LAND REGISTRY
Lincoln's Inn Fields, WC2A 3PH
[01–405 3488]

The registration of title to land was first introduced in England and Wales by the Land Registry Act, 1862: H.M. Land Registry operates today under the Land Registration Acts, 1925 to 1971. The object of registering title to land is to create a register of land owners whose title is guaranteed by the State and to simplify the transfer, mortgage and other dealings with real property. Under the Land Registration Act, 1966, the voluntary first registration of land in non-compulsory areas was curtailed to accelerate the extension of the compulsory system to all built-up areas of the country. The intention is that registration of title shall ultimately be universal throughout England and Wales.

H.M. Land Registry is administered under the Lord Chancellor by the Chief Land Registrar and the work is decentralized to a number of regional offices. The Chief Land Registrar is also responsible for the Land Charges Department and the Agricultural Credits Department.

Salary List
Grade 2	£43,500–£45,500
Grade 3	£34,000–£37,000
Grade 5	£24,765–£28,215
Grade 6	£18,786–£25,335
Senior Legal Assistant	£17,336–£23,534
Grade 7	£15,030–£20,292

Headquarters Office
Chief Land Registrar (G2), E. J. Pryer.
Chief Executive (G3), J. J. Manthorpe.
Senior Land Registrar (G5), Mrs. J. G. Totty.
Land Registrar (G5), M. L. Wood.
Asst. Land Registrars (G6), M. Croker; M. G. Garwood; (SLA), R. B. Fearnley.
Asst. Secretaries (G5), G. N. French (Controller Registration); R. J. Fenn (Controller of Management Services).
Senior Principals (G6), P. J. Smith; J. O. Sheldon.
Principals (G7), W. W. Birnie; M. K. Brown; J. E. Deas; A. W. Howarth; P. R. Laker; I. Leach; B. A. E. Marr; R. J. Martin; P. Morris; A. S. Pemberton.

Establishment and Accounts
Principal Establishment Officer (G5), E. G. Beardsall.
Asst. Establishment Officers (G7), J. Hodder; C. A. McKenzie.
Principal Finance Officer (G7), B. R. Elliott.
Head of Office Services (G7), I. T. Goodall.
Head of Departmental Accommodation (G7), G. A. Tocher.

Birkenhead District Land Registry
Old Market House, Hamilton Street, Birkenhead L41 5JW
[051–647 2377]

District Land Registrar (G5), J. L. Inskipp.
Senior Asst. Land Registrar (G6), G. A. Hughes.
Asst. Land Registrars (SLA/G7), I. E. Hardman; S. R. Coveney; J. L. Griffiths.
Area Manager (G6), J. Eccles.

Croydon District Land Registry
Sunley House, Bedford Park, Croydon CR9 3LE
[01–686 8833]

District Land Registrar (G5), D. M. J. Moss.
Senior Asst. Land Registrar (G6), C. H. Johnson.
Asst. Land Registrars (SLA), A. E. Farwell; Miss W. V. Drake.
Area Manager (G6), G. Hix.

Durham District Land Registry
Southfield House, Southfield Way,
Durham DH1 5TR
[091–3866151]

District Land Registrar (G5), P. H. Curnow.
Senior Asst. Land Registrar (G6), C. W. Martin.
Asst. Land Registrars (SLA/G7), Miss C. A. Lever; H. M. Taylor; R. E. P. Underwood; G. J. Wadsworth; Mrs. R. Flovel; Mrs. A. Bulmer.
Area Manager (G6), D. F. Price.

Gloucester District Land Registry
Twyver House, Bruton Way,
Gloucester GL1 1DQ
[0452–28666]

District Land Registrar (G5), Miss A. M. Phillips.
Senior Asst. Land Registrar (G6), S. G. Taverner.
Asst. Land Registrars (SLA/G7), M. E. Burn; H. G. Parham; P. M. Ratcliffe; W. J. Perry.
Area Manager (G6), M. H. Spooner.

Harrow District Land Registry
Lyon House, Lyon Road, Harrow,
Middx. HA1 2EU
[01–427 8811]

District Land Registrar (G5), H. S. Early.
Senior Asst. Registrars (G6), T. H. O. Lewis; C. Tate.
Asst. Land Registrars (SLA/G7), C. J. T. Brierley; J. H. Gill.
Area Manager (G6), D. I. Whyte.

Land Charges and Agricultural Credits Department
Burrington Way, Plymouth PL6 3LP
[0752–779831]
Superintendent of Land Charges (G7), J. C. O'Brien.

Lytham District Land Registry
Birkenhead House, Lytham St. Annes,
Lancs. FY8 5AB
[0253–736999]

District Land Registrar (G5), J. G. Cooper.
Senior Asst. Registrar (G6), J. G. Dickinson.
Asst. Land Registrars (SLA/G7), J. F. Bamber; J. B. Duckworth; M. Taylor; W. Aldworth; N. J. Allen.
Area Manager (G6), E. J. Stringer.

Nottingham District Land Registry
Chalfont Drive, Nottingham NG8 3RN
[0602–291166]

District Land Registrar (G5), P. J. Timothy.
Senior Asst. Land Registrars (G6), P. A. Brown; Mrs. P. M. Reeson.
Asst. Land Registrars (SLA/G7), D. M. Adams; K. G. Harvey; M. C. Jefferies; P. D. Smith; P. R. Arkwright; Mrs. J. A. Goodfellow; Miss A. M. Walker.
Area Manager, (G6), W. Whitaker.

Peterborough District Land Registry
Touthill Close, City Road,
Peterborough PE1 1XN
[0733 555666]

District Land Registrar (G5), M. Avens.
Asst. Land Registrars (SLA/G7), T. J. Reacher; J. T. Scott; S. T. Abdulhusein; J. M. Richardson.
Area Manager (G6), B. J. Andrews.

Plymouth District Land Registry
Plumer House, Tailyour Road,
Crownhill, Plymouth PL6 5HY
[0752–701234]

District Land Registrar (G5), P. A. Meehan.
Senior Asst. Land Registrar (G6), E. G. Thomas.
Asst. Land Registrars (SLA/G7), S. P. Kelway; L. M. Pope; A. J. Pain; P. R. Ings.
Area Manager(G6), K. Robinson.

Stevenage District Land Registry
Brickdale House, Danestrete, Stevenage,
Herts. SG1 1XG
[0438–313003]

District Land Registrar (G5), D. M. T. Mullett.
Senior Asst. Land Registrar (G6), F. G. D. Emler.
Asst. Land Registrars (SLA/G7), I. M. Jeffrey; O. D. Christopherson; Mrs. J. K. Ralph.
Area Manager (G6), A. Gould.

Swansea District Land Registry
Tybryn Glas High Street,
Swansea, Glam. SA1 1PW
[0792–476677]

District Land Registrar (G5), A. P. Roberts.
Senior Asst. Land Registrar (G6), N. M. Jones.
Asst. Land Registrars (SLA/G7), C. D. Hinds; T. M. Lewis; Mrs. J. Barton; Mrs. S. M. James.
Area Manager (G6), B. E. G. Martin.

Tunbridge Wells District Land Registry
Curtis House, Hawkenbury, Tunbridge Wells,
Kent TN2 5AQ
[0892–510015]

District Land Registrar (G5), C. J. West.
Senior Asst. Land Registrar (G6), G. R. Tooke.
Asst. Land Registrars (SLA/G7), F. M. Twambley; P. L. Cook.
Area Manager (G6), B. E. Kitching.

Weymouth District Land Registry
1 Cumberland Drive, Weymouth,
Dorset DT4 9TT
[03057–76161]

District Land Registrar (G5), K. L. Charles.
Senior Asst. Land Registrar (G6), W. W. Budden.
Asst. Land Registrars, (SLA/G7), S. R. Sehrawat; A. M. Lewis.
Area Manager (G6), R. R. C. Green.

Computer Services Division
Burrington Way,
Plymouth PL5 3LP
[0752–779831]

Head of Division (G6), A. A. Restorick.
Principals (G7), N. G. Worcester; R. J. Smith; R. T. Davis; P. A. Maycock.

LAW COMMISSION

England and Wales
Conquest House, 37–38 John Street,
Theobalds Road, WC1N 2BQ
[01–242 0861]

Set up on June 16, 1965, under the Law Commissions Act, 1965, to make proposals to the Government for the examination of the law and for its revision where it is unsuited for modern requirements, obscure, or otherwise unsatisfactory. It recommends to the Lord Chancellor programmes for the examination of different branches of the law and suggests whether the examination should be carried out by the Commission itself or by some other body. The Commission is also responsible for the preparation of Consolidation and Statute Law (Repeals) Bills.
Chairman, The Hon. Mr. Justice Beldam.
Members, T. M. Aldridge; B. J. Davenport, q.c.; Prof. J. T. Farrand; Mrs. B. M. Hoggett.
Secretary, J. G. H. Gasson.

Scottish Law Commission
140 Causewayside, Edinburgh EH9 1PR
[031-668 2131]

Chairman, The Hon. Lord Maxwell.
Commissioners, Dr. E. M. Clive; C. G. B. Nicholson, q.c. (*full-time*); Prof. P. N. Love, c.b.e.; J. Murray, q.c. (*part-time*).

LAW OFFICERS' DEPARTMENT
Attorney-General's Chambers,
Royal Courts of Justice, WC2A 2LL
[01–936 6602]

The Law Officers of the Crown for England and Wales (the Attorney General and the Solicitor General) are the legal advisers of the Government and represent the Crown in court. The Attorney General also superintends the Director of Public Prosecutions and the Crown Prosecution Service and is the Attorney General for Northern Ireland.

Attorney General, THE RT. HON. SIR PATRICK MAY-
HEW, Q.C., M.P. . . . . £35,345†
  Parliamentary Private Secretary, D. A. Sumberg,
  M.P.
Solicitor General, THE RT. HON. SIR NICHOLAS LYELL,
Q.C., M.P. . . . . £28,625†
  Parliamentary Private Secretary, P. Ground, M.P.
Legal Secretary, M. L. Saunders £35,350
Asst. Legal Sec., C. W. P. Newell £26,106
  † Excluding Parliamentary salary.

THE LAY OBSERVER'S OFFICE
Royal Courts of Justice, Strand, WC2A 2LL
[01–936 6695]

The Lay Observer's Office was established in 1975 and is funded by the Lord Chancellor's Department. The function of the Lay Observer is to monitor the Solicitor's Complaints Bureau's handling of complaints made to it about the conduct of solicitors or solicitors' employees. The Lay Observer is independent and is appointed by the Lord Chancellor.

Lay Observer, L. Lightman £22,000
Clerk, G. R. Bower.

LIBRARIES

OFFICE OF ARTS AND LIBRARIES
(*see* entry on pages 371–2)

THE BRITISH LIBRARY
2 Sheraton Street, W1V 4BH
[01–636 1544]

The British Library is the U.K.'s national library and occupies the central position in the library and information network. The Library aims to serve scholarship, research, industry, commerce and all other major users of information. Its services are based on collections which include over 15·5 million volumes (books, manuscripts, maps, newspapers and other serials, stamps and music), 1 million discs, 40,000 hours of tape recordings, in more than 20 buildings in London and one complex in West Yorkshire, amounting to over 360 miles of shelving growing at the rate of 8 miles every year.

The British Library was established on July 1, 1973 under the British Library Act, 1972. It brought together the library departments of the British Museum, the National Central Library, the National Lending Library for Science and Technology, the British National Bibliography Ltd and, in 1974, the functions of the Office for Scientific and Technical Information. Subsequently the Library took responsibility for other organisations: the India Office Library and Records and the H.M.S.O. Binderies in 1982; and the National Sound Archive in 1983. Since 1985 they have all been regrouped into three service areas, a Research and Development Department plus a corporate administrative centre.

Access to the Humanities and Social Sciences reading rooms in Great Russell Street is limited to holders of a British Library Reader's Pass, and information about eligibility (basically, academic researchers and investigative professionals) is available from the Reader Admissions Office. The Aldwych and Holborn reading rooms of the Science Reference and Information Service are open to the general public without charge or formality.

The Library's exhibition galleries are housed in the British Museum building in Great Russell Street. On permanent display are famous items from the national written archive including the Magna Carta, the Lindisfarne Gospels and Shakespeare's First Folio.

Board Members
Chairman, The Lord Quinton.
Chief Executive and Deputy Chairman, K. R. Cooper.
Directors General, J. M. Smethurst; P. R. Lewis; M. B. Line.
Part-time Members, The Lord Adrian, M.D., F.R.S.; The Lord Windlesham, C.V.O., P.C.; Prof. A. S. Forty, PH.D., D.SC.; Prof. B. Morris; D. Owen; Miss D. Park; Sir Robin Mackworth-Young, K.C.V.O., F.S.A.; N. Higham; R. E. Utiger, C.B.E.; T. J. Rix.

HUMANITIES AND SOCIAL SCIENCES
Director General, J. M. Smethurst.

Planning and Administration
Great Russell Street WC1B 3DG
[01-636 1544]

Director, I. P. Gibb.

Preservation Service
Great Russell Street WC1B 3DG
[01-636 1544]

Director, Dr. D. W. Clements.

Collection Development
Director, B. C. Bloomfield.

  Oriental Collections
  Store Street WC1E 7DG
  [01-636 1544]

  India Office Library and Records
  197 Blackfriars Road SE1 8NG
  [01-928 9531]

  English Language, Western, Eastern European Printed Books
  Great Russell Street WC1B 3DG
  [01-636 1544]

Special Collections
Director, Mrs. S. J. Tyacke.

  Western Manuscripts, Maps, Manuscript and Printed Music, Stamps
  Great Russell Street WC1B 3DG
  [01-636 1544]

  The National Sound Archive
  29 Exhibition Road SW7 2AS
  [01-589 6603]

Public Services
Director, A. Phillips.

  Reading rooms for Great Russell Street collections, Official Publications
  Great Russell Street WC1B 3DG
  [01-636 1544]

  Library Association Library
  7 Ridgmount Street WC1E 7AE
  [01-200 5515]

SCIENCE, TECHNOLOGY AND INDUSTRY
Director General, M. B. Line.

Document Supply Centre
Boston Spa, Wetherby, W. Yorks. LS23 7BQ
[0937 843434]

Director, D. Russon.

Science Reference and Information Service

25 Southampton Buildings, Chancery Lane
WC2A 1AW
[01-405 8721]
and 9 Kean Street WC2B 4AT
[01-636 1544]

Director, A. Gomersall.

BIBLIOGRAPHIC SERVICES

2 Sheraton Street W1V 4BH
[01-636 1544]

Director General, P. R. Lewis.
Director of Automated Services, M. D. Martin.

Research and Development Department

2 Sheraton Street W1V 4BH
[01-636 1544]

Director, B. J. Perry.

NATIONAL LIBRARY OF SCOTLAND
George IV Bridge, Edinburgh EH1 1EW
[031–226 4531]

Open free. Reading Room, weekdays, 9.30–8.30;
Sat. 9.30–1. Map Room, weekdays, 9.30–5; Sat. 9.30–
1. Exhibition, weekdays, 9.30–5; Sat. 9.30–1; Sun. 2–
5 (closed on Sun. Oct.–April).

The Library, which had been founded as the
Advocates' Library in 1682, became the National
Library of Scotland by Act of Parliament in 1925. It
continues to share the rights conferred by successive
Copyright Acts since 1710. Its collections of printed
books and MSS., augmented by purchase and gift, are
very large and it has an unrivalled Scottish collection.
The present building was opened by H.M. the Queen
in 1956.

The Reading Room is for reference and research
which cannot conveniently be pursued elsewhere.
Admission is by ticket issued to an approved applicant.

Salaries

Librarian £28,215
Deputy Librarian .... £24,765–£28,215
Keeper .... £18,786–£25,335
Curator Grade C .... £15,030–£20,292
Chairman of the Trustees, M. F. Strachan, C.B.E.
F.R.S.E.
Librarian and Secretary to the Trustees, Prof. E. F. D.
Roberts, PH.D., F.R.S.E.
Secretary of the Library and Deputy Librarian, B. G.
Hutton.
Curators Grade C, M. C. Graham; J. E. McIntyre.
Keepers of Printed Books, R. Donaldson, PH.D.; I. D.
McGowan; A. M. Marchbank, PH.D.; Ms. A. Mathe-
son, PH.D.
Curators Grade C, M. A. Begg; A. M. Cain, PH.D.; T.
A. F. Cherry; R. Duce; Ms. A. E. Harvey Wood; B.
P. Hillyard, D.Phil.; S. Holland; Ms. R. I. Hope; Ms.
A. F. Howe; W. A. Kelly; J. M. Morris; Ms. J. M.
Wilkes.
Keepers of Manuscripts, P. M. Cadell; T. I. Rae, PH.D.
Curators Grade C, I. G. Brown, PH.D., F.S.A.; I. C.
Cunningham; I. F. Maciver; S. M. Simpson; Ms. E.
D. Yeo.

Director of Scottish Library Network (SCOLCAP)
(*Keeper*), B. Gallivan.
Curator Grade C, R. F. Guy.
Director of Scottish Science Library (*Keeper*), Ms. A.
J. Bunch.

THE NATIONAL LIBRARY OF WALES
Llyfrgell Genedlaethol Cymru
Aberystwyth, Dyfed SY23 3BU
[0970–3816/9]

Readers' room open on weekdays, 9.30 a.m. to 6 p.m.
(Saturdays, 5 p.m.); closed on Sundays and Bank
Holidays. Admission by Reader's Ticket.

Founded by Royal Charter, 1907, and maintained
by annual grant from the Treasury. One of the six
libraries entitled to privileges under Copyright Act.
Contains about 3,000,000 printed books, 40,000 manuscripts, 4,000,000 deeds and documents, and numerous maps, prints and drawings, and audio-visual
collection. Specializes in manuscripts and books
relating to Wales and the Celtic peoples. Repository
for pre-1858 Welsh probate records. Approved by the
Master of the Rolls as a repository for manorial
records and tithe documents, and by the Lord
Chancellor for certain legal records. Bureau of the
Regional Libraries Scheme for Wales.
Librarian, B. F. Roberts, PH.D., F.S.A.
Secretary, D. B. Lloyd.
Heads of Departments, D. Huws (Manuscripts and
Records); P. A. L. Jones (Printed Books); D. H.
Owen (Pictures and Maps).

**COMMISSION FOR LOCAL
ADMINISTRATION IN ENGLAND**
21 Queen Anne's Gate, SW1H 9BU
[01–222 5622]

Local Commissioners are responsible for investigating complaints from members of the public in
England who claim to have suffered injustice because
of maladministration by a local authority, a water
authority or a police authority. Certain types of
action are excluded from investigation, particularly
personnel matters and commercial transactions unless they relate to the purchase or sale of land.
Complaints must normally be made through a member
of the authority against which the complaint is made
although a complaint can be put to a Local Commissioner direct if a member fails or refuses to refer it.
A free booklet "Your Local Ombudsman" is available
from the Commission's office.
Chairman of the Commission and Local Commissioner, D. C. M. Yardley, D.Phil. £65,000
Vice Chairman and Local Commissioner, F. G. Laws
£46,500
Local Commissioner, Mrs. P. A. Thomas £45,500
Member, The Parliamentary Commissioner for Administration
Secretary, G. D. Adams £29,300

LONDON REGIONAL TRANSPORT
55 Broadway, SW1H 0BD
[01–222 5600]

Subject to the financial objectives and principles
approved by the Secretary of State for Transport,
London Regional Transport has a general duty to
provide or secure the provision of public transport
services for Greater London.
Chairman, Sir Keith Bright £59,500
Members, Dr. T. M. Ridley; J. Telford Beasley; B. G.
Dale £46,000

LORD ADVOCATE'S DEPARTMENT
Fielden House, 10 Great College Street,
SW1P 3SL
[01–212 7676]

The Law Officers for Scotland are the Lord Advocate and the Solicitor-General for Scotland. The Lord Advocate's Department is responsible for drafting Scottish legislation, for providing legal advice to other departments on Scottish questions and for assistance to the Law Officers for Scotland in certain of their legal duties.

Lord Advocate, The Lord Cameron of Lochbroom,
P.C., Q.C. £36,460
Solicitor-General for Scotland, P. L. Fraser, Q.C.
£24,085
Legal Secretary and First Parliamentary Draftsman,
N. J. Adamson, C.B., Q.C. £45,500
Senior Asst. Legal Secs. and Parlty. Draftsmen, G. M.
Clark; D. J. S. Duncan; G. Kowalski; P. J. Layden,
T.D.; J. C. McCluskie .... £32,596–£37,000
Asst. Legal Secs. and Deputy Parlty. Draftsmen, J. D.
Harkness; D. C. Macrae; C. A. M. Wilson
£24,139–£28,215

LORD CHANCELLOR'S DEPARTMENT
House of Lords, SW1A 0PW
[01–219 3000]

The Lord Chancellor is responsible for promoting general reforms in the civil law, for the procedure of the civil courts and for the administration of the Supreme Court (Court of Appeal, High Court and Crown Court) and county courts in England and Wales, and for legal aid schemes. He is responsible for advising the Crown on the appointment of judges and certain other officers and is himself responsible for the appointment of Masters and Registrars of the High Court and District and County Court Registrars and magistrates. He is responsible for ensuring that letters patent and other formal documents are passed in the proper form under the Great Seal of the Realm, of which he is the custodian. The work in connection with this is carried out under his direction in the Office of the Clerk of the Crown in Chancery.

Salaries
Grade 2 .... £43,500–£45,500
Grade 3 .... £34,000–£37,000
Grade 5 .... £24,765–£29,465
Grade 6 .... £18,768–£25,335
Grade 7 .... £15,030–£20,292

Lord Chancellor, THE RT. HON. THE LORD HAVERS
£83,000
Private Secretary, J. P. Stockton.
Permanent Secretary, Sir Derek Oulton, K.C.B., Q.C.
£65,000
Private Secretary, G. Pulford.

Crown Office
Clerk of the Crown in Chancery, Sir Derek Oulton,
K.C.B., Q.C.
Deputy Clerk of the Crown in Chancery (G2), T. S.
Legg, C.B.
Clerk of the Chamber, Miss J. L. Waine.

Court Service Management Group
Trevelyan House, 30 Great Peter Street, SW1P 2BY
[01–210 8872]

Deputy Secretary (G2), R. Potter.
Grade 5, D. E. Staff; R. A. Vincent; J. F. Brindley.

Appointments Group
House of Lords, SW1A 0PW
[01–219 3000]

26–28 Old Queen Street, S.W.1.
[01–210 3537]

Deputy Secretary (G2), T. S. Legg, C.B.
Grade 5, J. R. A. Hanratty; R. C. Stoate; R. V. Gobler;
G. Norman.

Legislation Group
26–28 Old Queen Street, S.W.1.
[01–210 3508]

Deputy Secretary (G2), T. S. Legg, C.B.
Grade 3, C. R. Seaton.
Grade 5, M. H. Collon; M. C. L. Carpenter.

Policy and Legal Services Group
Trevelyan House, 30 Great Peter Street, SW1P 2BY
[01–210 8769]

Grade 3, J. G. H. Gasson.
Grade 5, C. W. V. Everett; M. W. Sayers; M. Kron;
R. H. H. White.

Establishment and Finance Group
Trevelyan House, 30 Great Peter Street, SW1P 2BY
[01–210 8512]

Principal Establishment and Finance Officer (G3), D.
J. Wiblin.
Grade 5, Miss J. E. Court; D. S. Mortimer; P. J.
Farmer; Mrs. N. A. Oppenheimer.
Principal Information Officer (G7), A. Goodson.

Public Trust Office
Stewart House, 24 Kingsway, WC2B 6JX
[01–405 4300]

Public Trustee and Accountant General (G3), J.
Boland.
*Asst. Public Trustee and Deputy Accountant General
(G5)*, P. D. Lewis, T.D.
Asst. Public Trustee (G5), R. C. Annis.

22 Kingsway, WC2B 6LE
[01–936 6000]

Head of Courts Funds Office (G7), I. J. MacBean.

Ecclesiastical Patronage
10 Downing Street, S.W.1
[01–233 3000]

Secretary for Ecclesiastical Patronage, J. R. Catford.
Assistant Secretary for Ecclesiastical Patronage (G7),
N. Wheeler.
See also **Law Courts and Offices**

LORD GREAT CHAMBERLAIN'S OFFICE
House of Lords, SW1A 0PW
[01–219 3100]

The Lord Great Chamberlain is a Great Officer of State, the office being hereditary since the grant of Henry I to the family of De Vere, Earls of Oxford.
Lord Great Chamberlain, The Marquess of Cholmon-
deley, G.C.V.O., M.C.
Secretary to the Lord Great Chamberlain, Air Chief
Marshal Sir John Gingell, G.B.E., K.C.B.
Clerk to the Lord Great Chamberlain, Miss J. M.
Drewett.

LORD PRIVY SEAL'S OFFICE
Privy Council Office,
Whitehall, SW1A 2AT

As leader of the House of Commons, the Lord Privy Seal is responsible for supervising the Government's legislative programme. He upholds the rights and privileges of the House as a whole and in this capacity

it falls to him to move motions relating to the procedure of the House.
Lord Privy Seal, and Leader of the House of Commons, THE RT. HON. JOHN WAKEHAM, M.P.
Private Secretary, S. N. Wood.
Assistant Private Secretary, Miss A. J. Smith.

OFFICE OF MANPOWER ECONOMICS
22 Kingsway, WC2B 6JY
[01–405 5944]

The Office of Manpower Economics was set up in 1971. It is an independent non-statutory organization which is responsible for servicing independent review bodies which advise on the pay of various public service groups (*see* entries under "Review Bodies"), the Pharmacists Review Panel, the Police Negotiating Board and the Civil Service Arbitration Tribunal. The Office is also responsible for servicing *ad hoc* bodies of inquiry and for undertaking research into pay and associated matters as requested by Government.
Director, N. Covington.
Assistant Secretaries (G5), D. R. Bower; K. R. Perry; P. J. H. Edwards.

MANPOWER SERVICES COMMISSION
Head Office: Moorfoot, Sheffield S1 4PQ
[0742–753275]

The Manpower Services Commission (M.S.C.) was set up on January 1, 1974 by the Employment and Training Act, 1973, to run the public employment and training services. The Commission is separate from Government but accountable to the Secretary of State for Employment (and to the Secretaries for Scotland and Wales in respect of its operations in Scotland and Wales). The Commission has ten members who each serve for three years.
†*Chairman,* Sir Bryan Nicholson £60,000
Members, M. Bett; M. O. Bury, O.B.E.; Prof. K. Durrands; J. Gilchrist; J. D. Pearman; K. Graham, O.B.E.; R. A. Grantham; J. M. Peake, C.B.E.; R. Todd.
Director, G. Holland, C.B. £48,500
†Sir Bryan Nicholson becomes chairman of the Post Office in Oct. 1987.

Salaries

Grade 3	£31,000 to £34,000
Grade 4	£27,584 to £30,293
Grade 5	£23,730 to £27,065
Grade 6	£18,020 to £24,302

Employment and Enterprise Group

Chief Executive (G3), J. Surr.
Director of Field Operations (G4), S. C. G. Loveman
Head of Planning Branch (G5), J. S. Child
Head of Disabled People's Services Branch (G5), J. A. Robertson
Head of SEPACS and Sheltered Employment Branch (G5), D. J. Sullivan
Director of Special Measures (G4), M. Emmott.
Director of Professional and Executive Recruitment (G6), A. W. P. Bateman
Head of Long-Term Unemployed Branch (G6), D. W. Main
Head of Gateway and Employment Services Branch (G5), E. B. Pearce

Vocational, Educational and Training Group

Chief Executive (G3), I. A. Johnston.
Director of Strategy (G3), R. Hillier.
Heads of Branches (G5):
Policy and Analysis, N. H. W. Davis.
Evaluation, G. MacNair.
Labour Market Intelligence, A. G. Davies.

Infrastructure Development, P. J. Gregory.
Training Access, K. C. J. White.

Director of Education Programmes (G3), J. G. Woolhouse.
Heads of Branches (G5):
Technical and Vocational Education Initiative, I. A. W. Fair.
Higher and Further Education, I. Randall.
N.A.F.E. Unit (G6), R. Wormald.

Director of Field Operations (G4), J. Lambert.
Heads of Branches (G5):
Field Systems Review (G6), M. Christie.
Field Planning and Systems, J. M. Franklin.
Job Training Scheme, J. Walker

Director of Training Programmes (G3), K. N. Atkinson.
Heads of Branches (G5):
Y.T.S. Programmes, J. F. Smith.
Y.T.S. Development, P. R. Lavener.
Adult Training Programmes, Miss S. Newton.

Director of Quality, Standards and Methods (G4), G. Kendall.
Heads of Branches (G5):
Programme Quality, J. K. Fuller.
Occupational Standards, A. T. Wisbey.
Industry Bodies, J. Wiltshire.

Director of Open Learning Branch (G5), Mrs. H. Temple.
Director of Training Standards Advisory Service (G5), J. D. Tinsley.

Skills Training Agency

Chief Executive (G4), T. R. R. O'Conor.
Head of Skillcentre Operations Branch (G5), S. Bishell
Head of Financial and Accounting Services Branch (G6), T. W. Kent
Head of Product Development Branch (G6), P. R. Wells
Head of Marketing and Mobile Training Branch (G6), J. L. P. Davies

Personnel and Central Services Division

Director (G4), D. B. Price
Head of Personnel (G5), D. Grover
Deputy Head of Personnel (G6), K. Baker
Head of Computing Branch (G5), I. E. Turl
Head of Information Services (G5), A. J. Brooks
Head of Psychological Services (G5), Dr. M. C. Killcross
Head of Training (G6), Mrs. A. Le Sage

Planning and Resources Division

Director (G3), J. Wild
Financial Controller (G5), N. L. Gregory
Head of Resource Control Branch (G5), C. P. Thomas
Head of Top Management Support Unit (G5), N. Schofield
Head of Internal Audit Unit (G6), C. Williams

MEDICAL RESEARCH COUNCIL
20 Park Crescent, W1N 4AL
[01–636 5422]

The Medical Research Council is the main Government agency for the promotion of medical and related biological research. The Council employs its own research staff and also provides grants for other institutions and for individuals who are not members of its own staff, thus complementing the research resources of the universities and hospitals.
Chairman, The Earl Jellicoe, K.B.E., P.C., D.S.O., M.C.
Deputy Chairman and Secretary, D. A. Rees, PH.D., D.SC., F.R.S.

Members, Sir Donald Acheson, K.B.E., D.M., F.R.C.P.; Belinda Banham, C.B.E.; Sir Austin Bide; S. Brenner, D.Phil., F.R.C.P., F.R.S.; J. T. Carter; D. L. Crouch, M.P.; M. J. Crumpton, Ph.D., F.R.S.; Prof. C. J. Dickinson, D.M., F.R.C.P.; Prof. R. E. Kendell, M.D., F.R.C.P.; Prof. June Lloyd, M.D., F.R.C.P.; I. S. Macdonald, M.D.; Prof. P. J. Morris, Ph.D., F.R.C.S.; Prof. J. M. Newsom-Davis, M.D., F.R.C.P.; Prof. F. W. O'Grady, C.B.E.; Prof. D. K. Peters, F.R.C.P.; Prof. J. K. Wing, M.D., Ph.D.; Prof. L. Wolpert, Ph.D., F.R.S.
Administrative Secretary, D. Noble.

Neurobiology and Mental Health Board
Chairman, Prof. J. K. Wing, M.D., Ph.D.

Cell Biology and Disorders Board
Chairman, Prof. L. Wolpert, Ph.D., F.R.S.

Physiological Systems and Disorders Board
Chairman, Prof. D. K. Peters, F.R.C.P.

Tropical Medicine Research Board
Chairman, Prof. M. A. Epstein.

HEADQUARTERS OFFICE
Medical Division
Principal Medical Officers, Katherine Levy; Barbara Rashbass; J. Alwen, Ph.D.

Administrative Division
Administrative Secretary, D. Noble.
Assistant Secretaries, Norma Morris; N. H. Winterton; J. E. A. Hay.

Secretariat, Grants and Training Awards
Assistant Secretary, B. C. Dodd.

Headquarters Establishments
Head of Section, Gillian Breen.

National Institute for Medical Research
Mill Hill, N.W.7
[01–959 3666]

Director, (vacant).

Clinical Research Centre
Watford Road, Harrow, Middlesex
[01–864 5311]

Director, Sir Christopher Booth, M.D., F.R.C.P.

Research Units
Anatomical Neuropharmacology Unit, Dept. of Pharmacology, University of Oxford, South Park Road, Oxford OX1 3QT. *Director*, Prof. A. D. Smith, D.Phil.
Applied Psychology Unit, 15 Chaucer Road, Cambridge CB2 2EF. *Director*, A. D. Baddeley, Ph.D.
Biochemical Parasitology Unit, Molteno Institute, Downing Street, Cambridge CB2 3EE. *Director*, B. A. Newton, Sc.D.
Biostatistics Unit, 5 Shaftesbury Road, Cambridge CB2 2BW. *Director*, N. E. Day, Ph.D.
Blood Group Unit, University College, London, Wolfson House, 4 Stephenson Way, N.W.1. *Director*, Patricia Tippett, Ph.D.
Blood Pressure Unit, Western Infirmary, Glasgow G11 6NT. *Director*, A. F. Lever, F.R.C.P.
Brain Metabolism Unit, University Dept. of Pharmacology, 1 George Square, Edinburgh EH8 9JZ. *Director*, G. Fink, M.D., D.Phil.
Cell Biophysics Unit, Dept. of Biophysics, King's College, 26–29 Drury Lane, W.C.2. *Director*, Prof. B. B. Boycott, F.R.S.
Cell Mutation Unit, University of Sussex, Falmer, Brighton BN1 9RR. *Director*, Prof. B. A. Bridges, Ph.D.
Cellular Immunology Unit, Sir William Dunn School

of Pathology, Oxford. *Director*, Dr. A. F. Williams, Ph.D.
Child Psychiatry Unit, Institute of Psychiatry, De Crespigny Park, Denmark Hill, SE5 8AF. *Director*, Prof. M. Rutter, C.B.E., M.D., F.R.C.P.
Clinical and Population Cytogenetics Unit, Western General Hospital, Crewe Road, Edinburgh EH4 2XU. *Director*, Prof. H. J. Evans, Ph.D., F.R.S.E.
Clinical Oncology and Radiotherapeutics Unit, M.R.C. Centre, Hills Road, Cambridge CB2 2QH. *Hon. Director*, Prof. N. M. Bleehen, F.R.C.P., F.R.C.R.
Clinical Pharmacology Unit, University Department of Clinical Pharmacology, Radcliffe Infirmary, Woodstock Road, Oxford OX2 6HE. *Hon. Director*, Prof. D. G. Grahame-Smith, Ph.D., F.R.C.P.
Cognitive Development Unit, 17 Gordon Street, W.C.1. *Director*, Prof. J. Morton, Ph.D.
Cyclotron Unit, Hammersmith Hospital, Ducane Road, W.12. *Director*, D. D. Vonberg, C.B.E.
Dental Research Unit, London Hospital Medical College, 30/32 Newark Street, E1 2AA. *Director*, Prof. N. W. Johnson, Ph.D.
Unit on the Development and Integration of Behaviour, Subdept. of Animal Behaviour, Madingley, Cambridge CB3 8AA. *Hon. Director*, Prof. R. A. Hinde, D.Phil., Sc.D., F.R.S
Developmental Neurobiology Unit, Institute of Neurology, 33 St. John's Mews, W.C.1. *Director*, R. Balázs, D.M., D.Phil.
Dunn Nutrition Unit, Downhams Lane, Milton Road, Cambridge. *Director*, R. G. Whitehead, Ph.D.
Environmental Epidemiology Unit, Southampton General Hospital, Southampton SO9 4XY. *Director*, Prof. D. J. P. Barker, M.D., Ph.D., F.R.C.P.
Epidemiology and Medical Care Unit, Northwick Park Hospital, Watford Road, Harrow, Middx. *Director*, T. W. Meade, D.M., F.R.C.P.
Epidemiology Unit (South Wales), 4 Richmond Road, Cardiff. *Director*, P. C. Elwood, M.D., F.R.C.P.
Unit for Epidemiological Studies in Psychiatry, University Dept. of Psychiatry, Royal Edinburgh Hospital, Morningside Park, Edinburgh EH10 5HF. *Director*, N. B. Kreitman, M.D.
Experimental Embryology and Teratology Unit, M.R.C. Laboratories, Woodmansterne Road, Carshalton, Surrey. *Director*, D. G. Whittingham, D.Sc.
Human Biochemical Genetics Unit, Galton Laboratory, University College London, Wolfson House, 4 Stephenson Way, N.W.1. *Hon. Director*, D. A. Hopkinson, M.D.
Immunochemistry Unit, University Department of Biochemistry, South Parks Road, Oxford OX1 3QU. *Director*, K. B. M. Reid, Ph.D.
Institute of Hearing Research, University of Nottingham, Nottingham NG7 2RD. *Director*, M. P. Haggard, Ph.D.
M.R.C. Laboratories, Carshalton, Woodmansterne Road, Carshalton, Surrey, SM5 4EF. *Laboratory Manager*, T. B. Pendry.
M.R.C. Laboratories, The Gambia, Fajara, near Banjul, The Gambia, W. Africa. *Director*, B. M. Greenwood, M.D., F.R.C.P.
M.R.C. Laboratories, Jamaica, University of the West Indies, Mona, Kingston, Jamaica. *Director*, Prof. G. R. Serjeant, C.M.G., M.D., F.R.C.P.
Leukaemia Unit, Royal Postgraduate Medical School, Ducane Road, W.12. *Hon. Director*, Prof. D. A. G. Galton, M.D., F.R.C.P.
Mammalian Development Unit, University College London, Wolfson House, 4 Stephenson Way, N.W.1. *Director*, Anne McLaren, D.Phil., F.R.S.
Mammalian Genome Unit, Dept. of Zoology, West Mains Road, Edinburgh EH9 3JT. *Acting Director*, A. P. Bird, Ph.D.
Mechanisms in Tumour Immunity Unit, University Medical School, Hills Road, Cambridge CB2 2QH. *Director*, Prof. P. J. Lachmann, Sc.D., F.R.C.P., F.R.S

Medical Sociology Unit, 6, Lilybank Gardens, Glasgow, G12 8QQ. *Director*, Sally Macintyre, Ph.D.

Laboratory of Molecular Biology, Hills Road, Cambridge CB2 2QH. *Director*, A. Klug, Ph.D., F.R.S.

Molecular Genetics Unit, M.R.C. Centre, Hills Road, Cambridge CB2 2QH. *Director*, S. Brenner, D.Phil., D.SC., F.R.C.P., F.R.S.

Molecular Haematology Unit, John Radcliffe Hospital, Headington, Oxford OX3 9DU. *Director*, Prof. D. J. Weatherall, M.D., F.R.C.P., F.R.S.

Molecular Neurobiology Unit, University Medical School, Hills Road, Cambridge CB2 2QH. *Director*, Prof. E. A. Barnard.

Unit on Neural Mechanisms of Behaviour, 3 Malet Place, W.C.1. *Director*, I. Steele Russell, Ph.D.

Neuroendocrinology Unit, Newcastle General Hospital, Westgate Road, Newcastle upon Tyne NE4 6BE. *Director*, Prof. J. A. Edwardson, Ph.D.

Neurological Prostheses Unit, Institute of Psychiatry, De Crespigny Park, Denmark Hill, S.E.5. *Hon. Director*, Prof. G. S. Brindley, M.D., F.R.C.P., F.R.S.

Neuro-Otology Unit, Institute of Neurology, National Hospital, Queen Square, W.C.1. *Director*, J. D. Hood, Ph.D., D.SC.

Neuropathogenesis Unit, Ogston Building, West Mains Road, Edinburgh. *Director*, A. G. Dickinson, Ph.D.

Perceptual and Cognitive Performance Unit, Experimental Psychology Laboratory, University of Sussex, Falmer, Brighton. *Director*, Prof. W. P. Colquhoun, Ph.D.

Radiobiology Unit, Chilton, Didcot, Oxon. OX11 0RD *Director*, Prof. G. E. Adams, Ph.D., D.SC.

Reproductive Biology Unit, Centre for Reproductive Biology, 37 Chalmers St., Edinburgh EH3 9EW. *Director*, D. W. Lincoln, D.SC.

Social and Applied Psychology Unit, Dept. of Psychology, University of Sheffield S10 2TN. *Director*, P. B. Warr, Ph.D.

Social Psychiatry Unit, Institute of Psychiatry, De Crespigny Park, Denmark Hill, S.E.5. *Director*, Prof. J. K. Wing, M.D., Ph.D.

Toxicology Unit, M.R.C. Laboratories, Woodmansterne Road, Carshalton, Surrey SM5 4EF. *Director*, T. A. Connors, D.SC., Ph.D.

Trauma Unit, Stopford Building, University of Manchester, Oxford Road, Manchester M13 9PT. *Acting Director*, R. A. Little, Ph.D.

Tuberculosis and Related Infections Unit, Hammersmith Hospital, Du Cane Road, W12 0HS. *Director*, Dr. J. Ivanyi, M.D., Ph.D.

Virology Unit, Institute of Virology, Church Street, Glasgow G11 5JR. *Hon. Director*, Prof. J. H. Subak-Sharpe, Ph.D., F.R.S.E.

THE ROYAL MINT
Llantrisant, nr. Pontyclun,
Mid-Glamorgan CF7 8YT
[0443–222111]

Master Worker and Warden, The Chancellor of the Exchequer (*ex officio*).
Deputy Master and Comptroller, Dr. D. J. Gerhard.

MONOPOLIES AND MERGERS COMMISSION
48 Carey Street, WC2A 2JT
[01–831 6111]

The Commission was established in 1948 as the Monopolies and Restrictive Practices Commission and was reconstituted on subsequent occasions. It became the Monopolies and Mergers Commission in 1973. The Commission has the duty of investigating and reporting on questions referred to it with respect to (*a*) the existence or possible existence of monopolies not registrable under the Restrictive Trade Practices Act, 1976, and relating to the supply of goods or services in the U.K. or part of the U.K. or to the supply of goods for export; (*b*) the transfer of a newspaper or newspaper's assets; (*c*) the creation or possible creation of a merger qualifying for investigation within the meaning of the Fair Trading Act, 1973.

References may be made to the Commission on the general effect on the public interest of specified monopoly or other uncompetitive practices and of restrictive labour practices.

The Competition Act, 1980, provides for the reference to the Commission of particular anti-competitive practices and of questions of efficiency, costs, service provided and possible abuse of monopolies in the public sector. In respect of recently-privatized industries, references to the Commission may be made in certain circumstances, with regard to their respective industries, by the Director General of Telecommunications, the Civil Aviation Authority and the Director General of Gas Supply.

Chairman, Sir Godfray Le Quesne, Q.C. £65,000
Deputy Chairmen, H. H. Hunt (£22,780); D. G. Richards (£26,197); R. G. Smethurst (£22,780).
Members, Sir James Ackers; C. C. Baillieu; L. Britz; M. B. Bunting; K. S. Carmichael, C.B.E.; Sir Robert Clayton, C.B.E.; P. H. Dean; A. Ferry; P. S. G. Flint; D. G. Goyder; G. D. Gwilt; Miss A. M. Head; J. D. Keir; L. Kelly; M. S. Lipworth; Prof. S. C. Littlechild; Miss P. K. R. Mann; S. McDowall, C.B.E.; L. A. Mills; B. C. Owens; Prof. R. Rees; N. L. Salmon; Sir Ronald Swayne, M.C.; D. P. Thomson; C. A. Unwin, M.B.E.; S. Wainwright, C.B.E.; R. Young .... each £9,171
Secretary, S. N. Burbridge.
(Chairman from Jan. 1, 1988 is S. Lipworth.)

MUSEUMS

MUSEUMS AND GALLERIES COMMISSION
7 St. James's Square, SW1Y 4JU
[01–839 9341]

The Commission was established in 1931 as an advisory body. Since 1981 it has, at the Government's instance, taken on several new executive functions. The Chairman and 14 Commissioners are appointed by the Prime Minister and represent all parts of the U.K. The Commission is funded by the Office of Arts and Libraries and has an annual budget of £6 million, of which nearly 90 per cent is distributed as grants.

The Commission advises the Government and others on a wide range of matters relating to museums and galleries. In addition to its advisory role the Commission's executive functions include the services of the National Museums Security Adviser; funding of the seven Area Museum Councils in England and the Museum Documentation Association; administration of capital and conservation grant schemes for non-national museums, and transitional grants occasioned by the abolition of the G.L.C. and metropolitan county councils. The Commission also administers the arrangements for government indemnities and the acceptance of works of art in lieu of Inheritance Tax, and has responsibility for the two Purchase Funds for local museums administered on its behalf by the V. & A. and Science Museums.

Chairman, Prof. B. Morris, D.Phil.
Members, The Marchioness of Anglesey, D.B.E.; F. Atkinson, O.B.E.; L. Brandes, C.B.; T. Clifford; The Lord Dainton, F.R.S.; Hon. J. Davies; Prof. Sir John Hale, F.B.A.; T. W. I. Hodgkinson, C.B.E.; J. Last; H. F. J. Leggatt; The Lord O'Neill, T.D.; Prof. G. D. Sims, O.B.E.
Secretary, P. Longman.

THE BRITISH MUSEUM
Great Russell Street, WC1B 3DG
[01–636 1555]

Antiquities collections, coins and medals, prints and drawings. Open weekdays (including Bank Holidays) 10–5 and Sun. 2.30–6. Closed on Good Friday, Christmas Eve, Christmas Day, Boxing Day, New Year's Day and the first Monday in May. The ethnographical collections are displayed in The Museum of Mankind at 6 Burlington Gardens, W.1. Opening times as above.

The British Museum may be said to date from 1753, when Parliament granted funds to purchase the collections of Sir Hans Sloane and the Harleian manuscripts, and for their proper housing and maintenance. The building (Montagu House) was opened in 1759. The present buildings were erected between 1823 and the present day, and the original collection has increased to its present dimensions by gifts and purchases. The administrative expenses were estimated at £13,938,000 in 1987–88.

Board of Trustees

Appointed by the Sovereign: H.R.H. The Duke of Gloucester, G.C.V.O. *Appointed by the Prime Minister:* The Lord Windlesham, C.V.O., P.C. (*Chairman*); The Lord Charteris of Amisfield, P.C., G.C.B., G.C.V.O., O.B.E.; Graham C. Greene, C.B.E.; Prof. E. T. Hall, D.Phil., F.S.A., F.B.A.; C. E. A. Hambro; Sir Denis Hamilton, D.S.O.; Sir Peter Harrop, K.C.B.; Prof. Sir Harry Hinsley, O.B.E., F.B.A.; Hon. Mrs. Marten, O.B.E.; Mrs. M. Moore; Prof. G. H. Treitel, D.C.L., F.B.A., Q.C.; Sir Ian Trethowan; The Lord Weinstock; Prof. W. Whitfield, C.B.E.; Sir Oliver Wright, G.C.M.G., G.C.V.O., D.S.C.
Nominated by the learned Societies: The Lord Adrian, M.D., F.R.S. (*Royal Society*); Dame Elisabeth Frink, D.B.E., R.A. (*Royal Academy*); The Lord Blake, F.B.A. (*British Academy*); Prof. W. Watson, C.B.E., F.S.A., F.B.A. (*Society of Antiquaries*)
Appointed by the Trustees of the British Museum: Sir David Attenborough, C.B.E., F.R.S.; Sir Martyn Beckett, Bt., M.C.; Prof. Rosemary Cramp, F.S.A.; Prof. Sir John Hale, F.S.A., F.B.A.; Prof. P. Lasko, C.B.E., F.S.A., F.B.A.

Salaries

Grade 2	£42,000
Grade 5	£25,203–£27,065
Grade 6	£18,078–£22,575
Grade 7	£14,318–£19,465
Head of Press and P.R.	£12,093–£15,200
Press and P.R. Officer	£9,798–£12,407

Officers

Director (G2), Sir David Wilson.
Deputy Director (G5), Ms. J. M. Rankine.
Secretary (G6), G. B. Morris.
Assistant to the Director (G7), Ms. M. L. Caygill.
Head of Public Services (G6), G. A. L. House.
Head of Design (G6), Margaret Hall, O.B.E.
Head of Education (G7), J. F. Reeve.
Head of Press and Public Relations, A. E. Hamilton.
Press and Public Relations Officer, Ms. K. Hudson.
Head of Administration (G6), B. A. Wilson.
Museum Superintendent (G7), P. E. Youngs.
Keeper of Prints and Drawings (G5), J. K. Rowlands.
Deputy Keeper (G6), A. V. Griffiths.
Assistant Keepers (G7), Ms. F. A. Carey; N. J. L. Turner; Ms. L. Stainton; M. B. Royalton-Kisch.
Keeper of Coins and Medals (G5), J. P. C. Kent.
Deputy Keeper (G6), M. J. Price.
Assistant Keepers (G7), M. G. Powell-Jones; Ms. M. M. Archibald; A. M. Burnett; B. J. Cook.
Keeper of Egyptian Antiquities (G5), T. G. H. James.

Deputy Keeper (G6), W. V. Davies.
Assistant Keepers (G7), M. L. Bierbrier; A. J. Spencer.
Keeper of Western Asiatic Antiquities (G5), T. C. Mitchell.
Assistant Keepers (G7), J. E. Curtis; C. B. F. Walker; I. L. Finkel.
Keeper of Greek and Roman Antiquities (G5), B. F. Cook.
Deputy Keeper (G6), K. S. Painter.
Assistant Keepers (G7), Ms. S. E. C. Walker; Ms. V. Tatton-Brown; D. J. R. Williams.
Keeper of Medieval and Later Antiquities (G5), N. M. Stratford.
Deputy Keepers (G6), G. H. Tait; J. Cherry; Ms. L. E. Webster.
Assistant Keepers (G7), D. Kidd; D. Buckton; T. H. Wilson.
Keeper of Prehistoric and Romano-British Antiquities (G5), I. H. Longworth.
Deputy Keeper (G6), I. M. Stead.
Assistant Keepers (G7), I. A. Kinnes; T. W. Potter; Ms. J. M. Cook.
Keeper of Japanese Antiquities (G5), L. R. H. Smith.
Keeper of Oriental Antiquities (G5), Ms. J. M. Rawson (acting).
Deputy Keeper (G6), J. M. Rogers.
Assistant Keepers (G7), W. Zwalf; Ms. A. S. L. Farrer; J. R. Knox.
Keeper of Ethnography (G5), M. D. McLeod.
Deputy Keeper (G6), B. Durrans.
Assistant Keepers (G7), Ms. E. M. Carmichael; Ms. S. G. Weir; Ms. D. Starzecka; J. C. H. King; J. B. Mack; N. F. Barley.
Keeper of Scientific Research and Conservation (G5), M. Tite.
Principal Scientific Officers (G7), P. T. Craddock; M. J. Hughes; I. C. Freestone.
Keeper of Conservation (G5), W. A. Oddy.
Principal Scientific Officer (G7), V. D. Daniels.
Principal Conservator (G7), Ms. H. P. Lane.

THE BRITISH MUSEUM (NATURAL HISTORY)
Cromwell Road, SW7 5BD
[01–589 6323]

Open Mon.–Sat. (except New Year's Day, Good Friday, May Day, Christmas Eve, Christmas Day and Boxing Day) 10–6, Sun. 1–6. Admission, £2.

The Natural History Museum originates from the natural history departments of the British Museum. During the 19th century the natural history collections grew extensively and in 1881 they were moved to South Kensington. In 1963, the Natural History Museum became completely independent with its own body of Trustees. The Zoological Museum, Tring, bequeathed by the second Lord Rothschild, has formed part of the Museum since 1938. The Geological Museum merged with the Natural History Museum in 1985 (opening times are as given above). Research workers are admitted to the libraries and study collections by Student's Ticket, applications for which should be made in writing to the Director.

The administrative expenses were estimated at £11,787,000 in 1986–87.

Salaries

Grade 3	£41,000
Grade 5	£24,765–£28,215
Grade 6	£18,786–£25,335
Grade 7	£15,030–£20,292
Grade 7 (PSO)	£15,354–£18,816

Board of Trustees

Chairman, Prof. Sir Richard Harrison, M.D., F.R.S.
Appointed by the Prime Minister: The Lord Adrian,
M.D., F.R.S.; Sir Walter Bodmer, F.R.S.; Prof. D.
Spencer Smith; Sir Owen Green; Prof. J. M.
Thomas, F.R.S.; G. M. Ronson.
Nominated by the Royal Society: Prof. Sir Andrew
Huxley, O.M., F.R.S.
*Appointed by the Trustees of the British Museum
(Natural History):* Prof. H. B. Whittington, F.R.S.;
Sir James Hamilton, K.C.B., M.B.E.; R. J. Carter.
Director (G3), R. H. Hedley, C.B., D.SC.
Deputy Director (G5), A. C. Bishop, PH.D.
Secretary (G5), C. J. E. Legg.
Co-ordinator of Planning and Development (G6), A.
P. Harvey.
Assistant to the Director (G7), R. F. Eastwood, PH.D.

Department of Zoology

Keeper (G5), J. F. Peake.
Deputy Keepers (G6), C. R. Curds, D.SC.; R. J. Lincoln,
PH.D.
Deputy Chief Scientific Officer (G5), P. H. Greenwood,
D.SC., F.R.S.
Senior Principal Scientific Officer (G6), J. D. Taylor,
PH.D.
Principal Scientific Officers (G7), E. N. Arnold, PH.D.;
I. R. Bishop, O.B.E.; G. A. Boxhall, PH.D.; P. F. S.
Cornelius, PH.D.; A. A. Fincham, PH.D.; J. D. George,
PH.D.; D. I. Gibson, PH.D.; J. E. Hill; R. W. Ingle,
PH.D.; Mrs. J. Jewell, PH.D.; P. B. Mordan, PH.D.; H.
M. Platt, PH.D.; D. M. Roberts, PH.D.; D. Rollinson,
PH.D.; V. R. Southgate, PH.D.; A. C. Wheeler; P. J.
P. Whitehead, PH.D.

Bird Section
Park Street, Tring, Herts.
[Tring: 4181]
Principal Scientific Officer (G7), P. J. K. Burton, PH.D.

Department of Entomology

Keeper (G5), L. A. Mound, D.SC.
Deputy Keepers (G6), D. R. Ragge, PH.D.; R. I. Vane-
Wright.
Senior Principal Scientific Officers (G6), R. L. Black-
man; R. W. Crosskey, D.SC.; V. F. Eastop, D.SC.
Principal Scientific Officers (G7), P. C. Barnard, PH.D.;
B. Bolton; I. D. Gauld, PH.D.; P. M. Hammond; D.
Hollis; W. J. Knight, PH.D.; A. C. Pont; G. S.
Robinson, PH.D.; K. S. O. Sattler, PH.D.; A. J.
Shelley, PH.D.; K. G. V. Smith; N. E. Stork, PH.D.;
R. T. Thompson; W. G. Tremewan; Miss C. M. F.
von Hayek; A. Watson; P. E. S. Whalley, D.SC.

Department of Botany

Keeper (G5), J. F. M. Cannon.
Deputy Keeper (G6), P. W. James.
Principal Scientific Officers (G7), S. Blackmore, PH.D.;
A. O. Chater; A. Eddy; C. J. Humphries, PH.D.; L.
M. Irvine; A. C. Jermy; D. M. John, PH.D.; R. J.
Pankhurst; J. H. Price; N. K. B. Robson, PH.D.; I.
Tittley.

Department of Palaeontology

Keeper (G5), L. R. M. Cocks, D.SC.
Deputy Keepers (G6), M. K. Howarth, PH.D.; H. G.
Owen, PH.D.
Grade 6, C. G. Adams, O.B.E., PH.D.
Senior Principal Scientific Officers (G6), C. Patterson,
PH.D.; R.A. Fortey, SC.D.
Principal Scientific Officers (G7), P. J. Andrews, PH.D.;
C. H. C. Brunton, PH.D.; P. L. Forey, PH.D.; A. W.
Gentry, D.PHIL.; R. P. S. Jefferies, PH.D.; Miss T. I.
Molkeson; N. J. Morris, D.PHIL.; C. P. Nuttall; J. B.
Richardson, PH.D.; B. R. Rosen, PH.D.; A. B. Smith,
PH.D.; C. B. Stringer, PH.D.; P. D. Taylor, PH.D.

Department of Mineralogy

Keeper (G5), A. C. Bishop, PH.D.
Deputy Keeper (G6), P. Henderson, D.PHIL.
Senior Principal Scientific Officer (G6), R. Hutchison,
PH.D.
Principal Scientific Officers (G7), A. M. Clark, PH.D.;
A. J. Criddle; A. L. Graham, PH.D.; R. R. Harding,
D.PHIL.; R. F. Symes, PH.D.; A. R. Woolley, PH.D.

Department of Administrative Services

Head and Finance and Establishment Officer (G5), C.
J. E. Legg.
Administration Officer (G7), K. Davey, PH.D.
Finance and Organization (G7), E. G. Hartman.
Estates Manager (G7), R. G. Nash.

Department of Central Services

Head (G6), G. B. Corbet, PH.D.
Publications Officer (G7), C. A. P. Reynard.
Technical Services (G7), B. S. Martin.

Department of Library Services

Head (G6), A. P. Harvey.
Deputy Head (G7), R. E. R. Banks.
Principal Scientific Officer (G7), Miss P. Gilbert.

Department of Public Services

Head (G5), R. S. Miles, D.SC.
Deputy Head (G7), G. C. S. Clarke, PH.D.
Operations Manager (G7), M. J. Grant.

Geological Museum
Exhibition Road, South Kensington, SW7 2DE
[01-589 3444]

The Museum's three public galleries have major
displays of gems and basic earth science.
Curator (G6), F. W. Dunning, O.B.E.

MUSEUM OF LONDON
London Wall, EC2Y 5HN
[01-600 3699]

The Museum of London opened in 1976. It is based
on the amalgamation of the former Guildhall Museum
and London Museum. The Museum is controlled by
a Board of Governors, appointed (9 each) by the
Government and the Corporation of London. The
exhibition illustrates the history of London from
prehistoric times to the present day.
Chairman of Board of Governors, R. M. Robbins,
C.B.E., F.S.A.
Director, M. G. Hebditch, F.S.A.

THE SCIENCE MUSEUM
South Kensington, SW7 2DD
[01-589 3456]

Open on Mon.–Sat. 10–6; Sun. 2.30–6. Closed on
New Year's Day, Good Friday, May Day Bank
Holiday, Christmas Eve, Christmas Day and Boxing
Day.

The Science Museum, which is the National
Museum of Science and Industry, opened in 1857; to
it were added in 1883 the collections of the Patent
Museum. In 1909 the administration of the Science
Collections was separated from that of the Art
Collections, which were transferred to the Victoria
and Albert Museum. The collections in the Science
Museum illustrate the development of science, medi-
cine, engineering and related industries.

The principal store for the Museum's commercial
aircraft, agricultural machinery, and road and rail
transport collections is at Wroughton, near Swindon,
Wilts., and is open for public viewing on selected
weekends during the summer.

The Museum is responsible for the Concorde Exhibition at the Fleet Air Arm Museum, Yeovilton.

The administrative expenses of the Museum, the Science Museum Library, the National Railway Museum and the National Museum of Photography, Film and Television are estimated at £9,214,000 for 1987–88.

Salaries

Director .... £32,350–£35,350
Keeper .... £23,730–£27,065
Curator B/Grade 6 .... £18,020–£24,302
Curator C/Grade 7 .... £14,318–£19,465

Director, Dr. N. Cossons, O.B.E.
Museum Administrator (G6), K. J. Rhodes, M.B.E.
Deputy Administrator (G7), P. W. Melrose.
Finance Officer (G7), Miss J. M. Quickfall.

Department of Physical Sciences

Keeper, Dr. D. A. Robinson.
Curator B, Dr. R. F. Bud.
Curators C, Dr. D. Vaughan; Dr. A. Q. Morton; Dr. A. K. Newmark; Dr. J. Darius; C. N. Brown.

Department of Medical Sciences

Keeper, Dr. B. Bracegirdle.
Curator C, Dr. G. M. Lawrence.

Department of Engineering

Keeper, Dr. E. J. S. Becklake.
Curators C, Dr. B. P. Bowers; A. E. Butcher; P. D. Stephens; Dr. A. McConnell; D. D. Swade.

Department of Transport

Keeper, Dr. T. Wright.
Curators C, J. A. Bagley; A. Hall-Patch; P. R. Mann.

Public Services Division

Assistant Director (G5), T. Suthers.
Curators C, I. M. Ball; Dr. A. W. Wilson.

Library

A national library of science, specializing in the history of science and technology. Bibliographies supplied. Photocopying and microfilm service.—Open on Mon.–Sat. 10–5.30. Closed on Sundays and Bank Holiday weekends.
Keeper, L. R. Day.
Curators C, Dr. L. D. Will.

National Railway Museum
Leeman Road, York YO2 4XJ
[0904–21261]

Opened in 1975 as the first outstation of the Science Museum. Some 50 locomotives and carriages are displayed to illustrate the technical, social and economic story of the development of railways in Britain. Open Mon.–Sat. 10–6, Sun. 11–6.
Keeper, Dr. J. A. Coiley.
Curator C, R. Shorland-Ball.

National Museum of Photography, Film and Television
Prince's View, Bradford BD5 0TR
[0274 727488]

Opened in 1983, it collects, conserves and displays photography, film and television as documentary records, expansion of human vision and as art forms. The Museum has the only IMAX cinema in the U.K. Open Tues.–Sun. 11–6, with special exhibition galleries open to 7.30.
Keeper (Curator B), C. J. Ford.
Curator C, Miss M. Benton.

THE VICTORIA AND ALBERT MUSEUM
South Kensington, SW7 2RL
[01–589 6371]

Open Mon.–Sat. 10–5.30, Sun. 2.30–5.50. Closed Christmas Eve, Christmas Day, Boxing Day, New Year's Day and May Day. The National Art Library is open Tues.–Sat. 10–5 (closed 1–2 Sat.) and the Print Room Tues.–Fri. 10–5, Sat. 10–1, 2–4.30. Donations are invited.

A museum of all branches of fine and applied art, it descends directly from the Museum of Manufactures, which opened in Marlborough House in 1852 after the Great Exhibition of 1851. The Museum was moved in 1857 to become part of the collective South Kensington Museum. It was renamed the Victoria and Albert Museum in 1899. The branch museum at Bethnal Green was opened in 1872 and the building is the most important surviving example of the type of glass and iron construction used by Paxton for the Great Exhibition. The Victoria and Albert Museum also administers the Wellington Museum (Apsley House), Ham House, Osterley Park, and the Theatre Museum.
†*Director and Secretary*, Sir Roy Strong, PH.D., F.S.A.
Deputy Director, Dr. M. D. Darby.

Department of Ceramics

Keeper, J. V. Mallet............... £24,739–£28,215
Deputy Keeper, D. M. Archer.
Assistant Keepers, Miss A. G. Somers-Cocks; Dr. O. Watson.

Department of Conservation

Keeper, Dr. J. Ashley-Smith .... £24,739–£28,215
Deputy Keeper, Mrs. G. F. Miles.

Far Eastern Department

Keeper, Miss R. Kerr (acting) ...... £24,739–£28,215
Assistant Keeper, A. C. Clunas.

Department of Furniture and Interior Design

Keeper, J. H. Morley .... £24,739–£28,215
Deputy Keeper, S. S. Jervis.

Indian Department

Keeper, R. W. Skelton............. £24,739–£28,215
Assistant Keepers, Dr. D. Swallow; J. S. Guy.

National Art Library

†*Keeper*, Mrs. E. A. L. Esteve-Coll .. £24,739–£28,215
Deputy Keeper, Dr. D. Haldane.
Assistant Keeper, Dr. R. Watson.

Metalwork Department

Keeper, R. Lightbown .... £24,739–£28,215
Assistant Keepers, Mrs. P. Glanville; Miss M. Campbell; E. R. Edgecumbe.

Prints, Drawings, Photographs and Paintings Department

Keeper, J. D. W. Murdoch .... £24,739–£28,215
Assistant Keepers, Miss S. B. Lambert; L. S. Lambourne; M. Haworth-Booth; M. Snodin.

Department of Sculpture

Keeper, A. F. Radcliffe .... £24,739–£28,215
Assistant Keepers, M. Baker; P. E. D. Williamson.

---

†Sir Roy Strong completes his term of office at the end of 1987. His successor is Mrs. E. A. L. Esteve-Coll.

Department of Textiles and Dress

Keeper, Miss S. Levey . . . . £24,739–£28,215
Deputy Keeper, Miss N. K. A. Rothstein.
Assistant Keepers, Mrs. M. Ginsburg; Mrs. V. D. Mendes; Miss W. Hefford.

Administration

Chief Administrative Officer, J. Close
£18,020 to £24,302

Department of Public Services

Keeper, J. Earle . . . . £24,739–£28,215

Bethnal Green Museum of Childhood
Cambridge Heath Road, Bethnal Green, E2 9PA
[01–980 3204]

Open Mon.–Thurs. and on Sat. 10–6, Sun. 2.30–6. Closed every Friday, May Day, Christmas Eve, Christmas Day, Boxing Day and New Year's Day.
Keeper, A. P. Burton . . . . £18,020 to £24,302

Theatre Museum
1E Tavistock Street, WC2E 7PA
[01–836 7891]

Open Tues.–Sun. 11–7. Closed Mon. except Bank Holidays. Admission £2.25, concessions £1.25.
Keeper, A. Schouvaloff . . . . £18,020 to £24,302
Assistant Keeper, Dr. J. Fowler.

THE COMMONWEALTH INSTITUTE
Kensington High Street, W.8
[01–603 4535]

The Commonwealth Institute is a centre for information about the Commonwealth. It is funded by the British Government with contributions from other Commonwealth Governments. The Institute is controlled by a Board of Governors which includes the High Commissioners of all Commonwealth countries represented in London. The Institute has permanent exhibitions on all Commonwealth nations, an arts centre, library and education department.

Open Mon.–Sat. 10–5.30, Sun. 2–5. Admission free. Closed Good Friday, May Day, Christmas Eve, Christmas Day, Boxing Day and New Year's Day.
Director, J. F. Porter.
Deputy Director, R. R. Bourne.
* *Chief Education Officer*, P. L. B. Woodroffe.
* *Chief Exhibition Officer*, A. E. Cobbold.
* *Art Director*, R. Atkins.
* *Chief Administration Officer*, M. J. Dunleavy.
** *Librarian*, M. J. Foster.
** *Senior Education Officer*, Miss M. Butcher.
** *Senior Exhibition Officer*, R. Varney.
(Salaries: * £16,392–£21,757; ** £13,599–£16,665).

IMPERIAL WAR MUSEUM
Lambeth Road, SE1 6HZ
[01–735 8922]

Open daily (except Good Friday, Christmas Eve, Christmas Day, Boxing Day, New Year's Day and May Bank Holiday) 10–5.50 (Sun. 2–5.50). Reference Depts. open Mon.–Fri. (except on public holidays), 10–5.

The Museum, founded in 1917, illustrates and records all aspects of the two world wars and other military operations involving Britain and the Commonwealth since 1914. It was opened in its present home, formerly Bethlem Hospital or Bedlam, in 1936. The Museum also administers H.M.S. *Belfast* in the Pool of London, Duxford Airfield near Cambridge and The Cabinet War Rooms in Westminster.

Expenses for 1987–88 are estimated at £4,727,000.

Salaries

Grade 5 . . . . £23,730–£27,065
Grade 6 . . . . £18,020–£24,302
Grade 7 . . . . £14,318–£19,465

Director (G5), A. C. N. Borg, Ph.D., F.S.A.
Deputy Director and Head of the Research and Information Office (G5), R. W. K. Crawford.
Secretary (G6), J. J. Chadwick.
Special Assistant to the Director, Mrs. S. R. Burgess.
Establishment Officer, G. A. Kelly.
Finance Officer, Mrs. P. A. Whitfield.
Museum Superintendent, D. A. Needham.
Senior Keeper and Keeper of Audio-Visual Records (G5), G. T. C. Coultass.
Keeper of Duxford Airfield (G5), E. O. Inman.
Keeper of H.M.S. Belfast (G5), Capt. A. W. Wheeler, R.N.
Keeper of the Department of Museum Services (G6), C. Dowling, D.Phil.
Keeper of the Department of Documents (G6), R. W. A. Suddaby.
Keeper of the Department of Exhibits and Firearms (G6), D. J. Penn.
Keeper of the Department of Printed Books (G6), G. M. Bayliss, Ph.D.
Keeper of the Department of Art (G6), Miss A. H. Weight.
Keeper of the Department of Film (G6), Miss A. E. Fleming.
Keeper of the Department of Information Retrieval (G6), R. B. N. Smither.
Keeper of the Department of Photographs (G7), Miss K. J. Carmichael.
Keeper of the Department of Sound Records (G7), Mrs. M. A. Brooks.
Curator of the Cabinet War Rooms, E. J. Wenzel.

NATIONAL MARITIME MUSEUM
Greenwich, SE10 9NF
[01–858 4422]

Open Mon.–Sat., 10–6 (10–5 in winter); Sun. 2–6 (2–5 in winter). Closed Jan. 1, Good Friday, May Day Bank Holiday and Dec. 24–26. Admission charge.

Reading Room open Mon.–Fri., 10–5; readers' tickets available on written application to Reader Services Section.

Established by Act of Parliament in 1934, the National Maritime Museum illustrates the maritime history of Great Britain in the widest sense, underlining the importance of the sea and its influence on the nation's power, wealth, culture, technology and institutions. The Museum is in two groups of buildings in Greenwich Park—the main buildings centred around the Queen's House (built by Inigo Jones, 1616–35) and the Old Royal Observatory (including Wren's Flamsteed House) to the south. The collections include paintings, actual craft and ship models, ships' lines, prints and drawings, atlases and charts, navigational and astronomical instruments, uniforms and relics, books and MSS.
Director, R. L. Ormond.

NATIONAL ARMY MUSEUM
Royal Hospital Road, SW3 4HT
[01–730 0717]

Established by Royal Charter (1960). History of five centuries of the British Army: includes the story of the Indian Army up to Independence in 1947. Open, Mon.–Sat., 10–5.30; Sun. 2–5.30. The Indian Army room at R.M.A. Sandhurst, Camberley, Surrey may be viewed by appointment only.

Director, W. Reid, C.B.E., F.S.A.
Personal Assistant to the Director, Miss E. Christie.
Deputy Director and Keeper of Records, B. Mollo, T.D.
Assistant Director and Keeper of Uniform, Mrs. D. B.
Willcox.

ROYAL AIR FORCE MUSEUM
Hendon, NW9 5LL
[01–205 2266]

The museum covers all aspects of the history of the
Royal Air Force and its predecessors, and the history
of aviation generally. The museum occupies part of
the former airfield at Hendon. Its aircraft hall
displays aircraft from the museum's collection. Admission is free. The Battle of Britain Museum
contains a collection of British, German and Italian
aircraft. Admission: £1·00; children and O.A.P.s 50p.
The Bomber Command Museum contains a collection
of bomber aircraft. Admission: £1; children and
O.A.P.s 50p.

Open Mon.–Sat., 10–6. (Sun. 2–6). Closed Dec. 24,
25, 26, Jan. 1, Good Fri. and May Day.
Director, J. Tanner, C.B.E., D.Litt., F.S.A.
Keepers, R. F. Barker; D. C. R. Elliott; P. Murton; R.
Simpson; M. C. Tagg.

THE NATIONAL MUSEUMS AND
GALLERIES ON MERSEYSIDE
William Brown Street, Liverpool L3 8EN
[051–207 0001]

On April 1, 1986 a corporate body, The National
Museums and Galleries on Merseyside, was established, funded directly by the Government, to take
over responsibility for the museums and galleries
previously administered by Merseyside County
Council. Various stores ancillary to the collections
are also the responsibility of the body.

All properties, except the Large Objects Collection,
are open all year except Jan. 1, Dec. 24–26 and Good
Friday. Opening times for all properties (except the
Maritime Museum and the Large Objects Collection)
are Mon.–Sat. 10–5, Sun. 2–5. Opening times for the
Merseyside Maritime Museum are daily 10.30–5.30.
Admission charge. Opening times for the Large
Objects Collection are; Easter–Sept., daily 10–5.
Chairman of the Board of Trustees, Sir Leslie Young,
C.B.E.
Director, R. Foster.
Deputy Director, (vacant).

Liverpool Museum
William Brown Street, Liverpool
[051–207 0001]

Merseyside Maritime Museum
Pier Head, Liverpool
[051–709 1551]

Large Object Collection
Princes Dock, Liverpool
[051–207 0001]

Museum of Labour History
County Sessions House, Islington, Liverpool
[051–207 0001]

Walker Art Gallery
William Brown Street, Liverpool
[051–207 0001]

Lady Lever Art Gallery
Port Sunlight Village, Bebington, Wirral
[051–645 3623]

Sudley Art Gallery
Mossley Hill Road, Liverpool
[051–207 0001]

(For other Museums in England—*see*** Index)**

THE NATIONAL MUSEUM OF WALES
(Amgueddfa Genedlaethol Cymru)
Cardiff CF1 3NP
[0222 397951]

Open Tues.–Sat., 10–5. Sun. 2.30–5. Closed on
Mondays, Christmas Eve, Christmas Day, Boxing
Day, New Year's Day, May Day and Good Friday.
Admission free.
President, W. A. Twiston-Davies.
Vice-President, Hon. J. Davies.
Director, D. W. Dykes, PH.D., F.S.A.
Secretary, G. Morgan.
Keepers, M. G. Bassett, PH.D. (*Geology*); B. A. Thomas,
PH.D. (*Botany*); P. M. Morgan (*Zoology*); H. S.
Green, PH.D. (*acting*) (*Archaeology*); T. J. Stevens
(*Art*).

Welsh Folk Museum
(Amgueddfa Werin Cymru)
St. Fagans, Nr. Cardiff

Open April–Oct., daily 10–5; Nov.–March, week-
days 10–5, Sun. 2.30–5. Admission charge. Closed on
Christmas Eve, Christmas Day, Boxing Day, New
Year's Day, Good Friday and May Day.
Curator, J. G. Jenkins, PH.D.
Keepers, V. H. Phillips; E. Scourfield, PH.D.; E.
William, PH.D.

Roman Legionary Museum, Caerleon
Caerleon, Gwent.

Contains material found on the site of the Roman
fortress of Isca and its suburbs.

Turner House Art Gallery
Plymouth Road, Penarth, Nr. Cardiff

Open Tues.–Sat. 11–12.45 and 2–5, Sun. 2–5. Closed
Mondays, except Bank Holidays, and on Christmas
Eve, Christmas Day, Boxing Day, New Year's Day,
Good Friday, and May Day. Admission free.

Oriel Eryri
Llanberis, Gwynedd

An environmental centre interpreting the natural
history of Snowdonia. Open mid-June to mid-Sept.;
weekdays 10–5; Sun. 2.30–5. Admission free.

Welsh Slate Museum
Llanberis, Gwynedd

Open Easter–Sept. daily 9.30–5.30. Admission 80p;
concessions 40p.

Segontium Roman Fort Museum
Beddgelert Road, Caernarfon, Gwynedd

Open weekdays at 9.30, Sundays at 2. Closes at 6
from May to September, at 5.30 in March, April and
October, at 4 from November to February. Closed
Christmas Eve, Christmas Day, Boxing Day, New
Year's Day, Good Friday and May Day. Admission
free. On the site of the fort, in the guardianship of
the Welsh Office. Contains mostly material excavated
there.

Museum of the Welsh Woollen Industry
Dre-fach Felindre, nr. Llandysul, Dyfed

It occupies part of a working mill. Open April–
Sept., Mon.–Sat. 10–5. Closed May Day. Admission
free.

Welsh Industrial and Maritime Museum
Bute Street, Cardiff

Open Tues.–Sat. 10–5; Sun. 2.30–5. Closed Mondays, Christmas Eve, Christmas Day, Boxing Day, New Year's Day, Good Friday and May Day. Admission free.

Curator, S. Owen-Jones, ph.d., (*acting*).

Yr Hen Gapel
Tre'r-ddôl, nr. Aberystwyth, Dyfed

The museum portrays 19th century religious life in Wales. Open 10–5 Monday–Saturday from April–September. Closed May Day. Admission free.

NATIONAL MUSEUMS OF SCOTLAND
Chambers Street, Edinburgh EH1 1JF
[031–225 7534]
and
Queen Street, Edinburgh EH2 1JD
[031–225 7534]

Open, Mon.–Sat., 10–5 and Sun., 2–5.

The National Museums of Scotland have one Director and one Board of Trustees, and include, besides the Royal Museum of Scotland (an amalgamation of the Royal Scottish Museum and the National Museum of Antiquities), the Scottish United Services Museum, the Scottish Agricultural Museum at Ingliston, the Museum of Flight at East Fortune, Shambellie House Museum of Costume near Dumfries, Leith Custom House Gallery and Biggar Gasworks Museum.

Director, R. G. W. Anderson, d.Phil. £30,475
Research Director, A. Fenton, c.b.e., d.Litt. ... £27,530
Keeper, Department of History & Applied Art, Miss D. Idiens.
Keeper, Department of Geology, W. D. I. Rolfe ph.d.
Keeper, Department of Natural History, M. Shaw, d.Phil.
Keeper, Department of Science, Technology and Working Life, J. D. Storer.
Deputy Keepers, Sheila Brock, ph.d.; H. G. MacPherson, ph.d.; S. C. Wood; D. V. Clarke, ph.d.; Ms C. V. Glenn.
(Salaries: Keepers £24,739–£28,215; Deputy Keepers £18,786–£25,335).

NATIONAL AUDIT OFFICE
157–197 Buckingham Palace Road, SW1W 9SP
[01–798 7000]

The National Audit Office came into existence under the National Audit Act 1983, to replace and continue the work of the former Exchequer and Audit Department. The Act reinforced the Office's total financial and operational independence from the Government and brought its head, the Comptroller and Auditor General, into a closer relationship with Parliament as an Officer of the House of Commons.

The National Audit Office provides independent information, advice and assurance to Parliament and the public about all aspects of the financial operations of government departments and many other bodies receiving public funds. This it does by examining and certifying the accounts of these organizations; and by regularly publishing reports to Parliament on the results of its value for money investigations of the economy, efficiency and effectiveness with which public resources have been used. The National Audit Office is also the auditor by agreement of the accounts of certain international and other organizations. In addition, the office authorizes the issue of public funds to Government departments.

Comptroller and Auditor General, Sir Gordon Downey, k.c.b. £62,100
Private Secretary, T. J. Bristow.
Deputy Comptroller and Auditor General, H. D. Myland £50,620
Assistant Auditor Generals, J. A. Collens; D. A. Dewar; M. J. Goodson; R. N. Le Marechal.
£34,880–£44,880
Directors, P. M. Jefford; P. J. C. Keemer; G. W. Garside; M. R. J. Paul; P. J. Beck; J. A. Davies; I. R. W. Hargest; R. W. Locke; T. Dobson; P. O'Keefe; A. G. Brown; E. S. Young; T. J. Lovett; A. C. Pyatt; G. J. S. Frith; D. A. Reeve; A. I. A. Oyarzabal; C. L. Press; W. D. Turner; B. D. Baker; C. K. Beauchamp; J. A. Higgins; A. K. Bell; L. H. Hughes; M. C. Pfleger .... £26,650–£37,420
Deputy Directors, A. W. Bird; E. J. Weeks; C. J. Day; D. C. Page; G. T. Morgan; J. E. Smith; K. E. Turner; B. Hogg; R. J. McCourt; A. R. Murray; W. L. Ewing; G. J. McKeown; J. M. Pearce; R. M. Bennett; M. V. Pettet; R. E. Spurgeon; A. G. Roberts; R. A. Skeen; A. Cunningham; D. S. Dodge; G. G. Jones; K. Maclean; M. L. Daynes; D. R. Corsby; R. W. Tycer; J. Parsons; S. Clayton; J. J. Jones; D. J. Woodward .... £22,925–£30,650

NATIONAL BUS COMPANY
172 Buckingham Palace Road, SW1W 9TN
[01–730 3453]

The National Bus Company is a statutory body under the provisions of the Transport Act, 1968. It controlled 72 operating companies covering almost every part of England and Wales: these were privatized in phases throughout 1987. A residual body will continue into 1988 to finalize administrative and financial matters before final dissolution.
Chairman, R. C. Lund.
Members (full time), I. Dalton, c.b.e. (*Executive Vice Chairman and Chief Executive (Operations)*); C. J. Campbell (*Executive Member*); (*part-time*): C. R. Hollick; R. T. Kanter; Miss K. Mortimer; Sir Peter Harrop, k.c.b.

NATIONAL CONSUMER COUNCIL
20 Grosvenor Gardens, SW1W 0DH
[01–730 3469]

The National Consumer Council was set up by the Government in 1975 and is funded by a grant-in-aid from the Department of Trade and Industry. The Council watches over consumers' interests and speaks up for the consumer to Government, nationalised industry, independent industry and commerce, and the public and private services.
Chairman, Mrs. S. Oppenheim-Barnes.
Director, M. Healy.

NATIONAL DOCK LABOUR BOARD
22–26 Albert Embankment, SE1 7TE
[01–735 7271]

The National Dock Labour Board administers the scheme for giving permanent employment to dock workers under the Dock Workers (Regulation of Employment) (Amendment) Scheme 1967. The Board was reconstituted as a body corporate on August 1, 1977 under the Dock Work Regulation Act 1976 which made further provision for regulating the allocation and performance of the work of cargo-handling in and about the ports of Great Britain.
Chairman, R. H. Thompson.
General Manager, K. T. Percy.

NATIONAL ECONOMIC DEVELOPMENT OFFICE
Millbank Tower, Millbank, SW1P 4QX
[01–211 6998]

The National Economic Development Council (NEDDY) brings together Government, management and unions to tackle issues vital to jobs and growth. Its organisations help to promote constructive dialogue throughout British industry.

Council

Government Members, The Chancellor of the Exchequer (*Chairman*); the Secretaries of State for Employment, Education and Science, Energy, Environment and Trade and Industry. *Management Members,* J. M. M. Banham; Dr. J. S. McFarlane; D. A. G. Monk; Sir David Nickson, C.B.E.; T. J. O'Connor. *Trade Union Members,* R. Bickerstaffe; J. Edmonds; C. Jenkins; W. Jordan, R. Todd; N. Willis. *Independent Members,* Sir Bryan Nicholson; Sir Robert Haslam; Rt. Hon. Robin Leigh-Pemberton; The Lord Marshall of Goring, C.B.E., F.R.S.; Mrs. R. E. Waterhouse, C.B.E.
Director-General, J. Cassels, C.B.
Secretary, P. V. Dixon.
Industrial Director, I. McDonald.
Economic Director, W. Eltis.

NATIONAL GALLERIES
See **Art Galleries**

NATIONAL INVESTMENT AND LOANS OFFICE
Royex House, Aldermanbury Square, EC2V 7LR
[01–606 7321]

The National Investment and Loans Office was set up on April 1, 1980 by merging the staffs of the National Debt Office and the Public Works Loan Board. The Department provides staff and services for the National Debt Commissioners and the Public Works Loan Commissioners.
Director, I. H. Peattie.
Establishment Officer, A. G. Ladd.

National Debt Office
Comptroller General, I. H. Peattie.

Public Works Loan Board
Chairman, J. E. A. R. Guinness, C.B.E.
Deputy Chairman, W. H. P. Davison.
Other Commissioners, Miss F. M. Cook; R. W. E. Law; Miss V. J. Di Palma; G. Ross Russell; P. Brackfield; S. G. Dunster; D. H. Adams; R. A. Chapman; J. Broadfoot; R. J. Dent; R. Emmett.
Secretary, I. H. Peattie.
Assistant Secretary, D. L. Hammond.

NATIONAL RADIOLOGICAL PROTECTION BOARD
Chilton, Didcot, Oxon. OX11 0RQ
[0235–831600]

The National Radiological Protection Board is an independent statutory body created by the Radiological Protection Act 1970. The Government's purpose was to establish a national point of authoritative reference in radiological protection.
Chairman, Sir Richard Southwood, F.R.S.
Director, Dr. R. H. Clarke.

DEPARTMENT FOR NATIONAL SAVINGS
Charles House, 375 Kensington High Street, W14 8SD
[01–605 9300]

The Department for National Savings was established as a Government Department in 1969. The Department is responsible for the administration of a wide range of schemes for personal savers.

(For details of schemes, *see* **Savings**).

Salaries

Grade 2	£43,264–£45,349
Grade 3	£33,725–£36,852
Grade 5	£24,739–£28,215
Grade 6	£14,927–£20,292

Director of Savings (G2), J. A. Patterson.
Deputy Director (G3), G. R. Wilson.
Establishment Officer (G5), R. T. Rowland.
Finance Officer (G5), D. E. L. Whittall.
Controllers (G5), P. N. S. Hickman Robertson (*Marketing & Information*); R. S. Watts; J. Stamp; E. B. Senior; C. Ward.
Senior Principals (G6), D. W. Kellaway; I. T. Standen; R. H. Lee; J. K. Hill; I. Forsyth; D. H. Monaghan.
Principals (G7), A. G. Muir; M. A. Nicholls; Mrs. H. Brown; P. G. Hutchings; Mrs. S. M. Cullum; W. J. Herd; D. K. Paterson; D. S. Speedie; A. J. Cummings; T. J. Bedeman; W. J. Ferrier; H. Johnson; J. W. Davison; D. Newton; A. B. Wood; P. Finnie; K. M. J. Harbridge; C. E. Funk; I. Jordinson; A. Brown; K. R. Tyerman; T. Threlfall; B. Paley; A. T. Stevenson; H. Webster; J. Wheatley; A. S. McGill; I. B. Arkinstall; T. J. F. McMahon; C. McVey; R. A. Nichol; N. Thistlethwaite; J. B. Dunphy; R. J. McLelland; J. C. Foreman; D. Wilson.

NATURAL ENVIRONMENT RESEARCH COUNCIL
Polaris House, North Star Avenue, Swindon, Wilts. SN2 1EU
[0793–40101]

The Natural Environment Research Council was established in 1965, to encourage, plan and conduct research in the physical and biological sciences which relate to man's natural environment and its resources.

The Council carries out research and training through its own institutes and grant-aided institutes, and by grants, fellowships and post-graduate awards to universities and other institutions of higher education.
Chairman, H. Fish, C.B.E.
Secretary, J. C. Bowman, C.B.E., Ph.D.

RESEARCH INSTITUTES

British Geological Survey
Nicker Hill, Keyworth, Nottingham NG12 5GG
[06077–6111]
Director, F. G. Larminie.

Institute of Oceanographic Sciences
Deacon Laboratory, Wormley, nr. Godalming, GU8 5UB
[042879–4141]
Director, Sir Anthony Laughton, Ph.D., F.R.S.
Proudman Laboratory, Bidston Observatory, Birkenhead L43 7RA
[051–653 8633]

Institute for Marine Environmental Research
Prospect Place, The Hoe, Plymouth PL1 3DH
[0752–221371]
Director, B. L. Bayne, Ph.D.

Institute of Marine Biochemistry
St. Fittick's Road, Aberdeen AB1 3RA
[0224–875695]
Acting Director, Dr. C. B. Cowey.

British Antarctic Survey
Madingley Road, Cambridge CB3 0ET
[0223–61188]
Director, Dr. D. J. Drewry.

Sea Mammal Research Unit
c/o British Antarctic Survey,
[0223–311354]
Director, Dr. D. J. Drewry.

Institute of Hydrology
Maclean Building, Crowmarsh Gifford,
Oxon. OX10 8BB
[0491–38800]
Director, J. S. G. McCulloch, ph.d.

Institute of Terrestrial Ecology (North)
Bush Estate, Penicuik, Midlothian EH26 0QB,
[031–445 4343/6]
Director, Dr. O. W. Heal.

Institute of Terrestrial Ecology (South)
Monks Wood Experimental Station, Abbots Ripton,
Huntingdon PE17 2LS
[04873–381/8]
Director, Dr. J. P. Dempster.
Research Stations: Merlewood; Furzebrook; Banchory; Bangor.

Institute of Virology
Mansfield Road, Oxford OX1 3SR
[0865–512361]
Director, Prof. D. H. L. Bishop, ph.d.

Unit of Comparative Plant Ecology
Department of Botany, University of Sheffield,
Western Bank, Sheffield S10 2TN
[0742–768555]
Head of Unit, Prof. I. H. Rorison, d.phil.

GRANT-AIDED INSTITUTES

Marine Biological Association of the U.K.
The Laboratory, Citadel Hill, Plymouth PL1 2PB
[0752–221761]
Director, Dr. E. D. S. Corner.

Scottish Marine Biological Association
Dunstaffnage Marine Research Laboratory
P.O. Box 3, Oban, Argyll PA34 4AD
[0631–62244]
Director, Prof. R. I. Currie, c.b.e.

Freshwater Biological Association
The Ferry House, Far Sawrey,
Ambleside, Cumbria LA22 0LP
[09662–2468/9]
Director, R. T. Clarke, ph.d.

SPECIAL SERVICES

N.E.R.C. Scientific Services
Polaris House, North Star Avenue,
Swindon, Wilts. SN2 1EU
[0793–40101]
Director, B. J. Hinde.

NATURE CONSERVANCY COUNCIL
Northminster House, Peterborough PE1 1UA
[0733 40345]

Establishes, maintains and manages National Nature Reserves, advises generally on nature conservation, gives advice to the Government on nature conservation policies and on how other policies may

affect nature conservation, and supports, commissions and undertakes relevant research.
Chairman, W. H. N. Wilkinson.
Director General, R. C. Steele.
Chief Scientist, Dr. D. A. Ratcliffe.
Country Headquarters:
England: Northminster House, Peterborough
PE1 1UA.—*Director*, Dr. F. B. O'Connor.
Scotland: 12 Hope Terrace, Edinburgh EH9 2AS.—
Director, Dr. J. Francis.
Wales: Plas Penrhos, Penrhos Road, Bangor, Gwynedd LL57 2LQ.—*Director*, Dr. T. Pritchard.

NORTHERN IRELAND OFFICE
Whitehall, SW1A 2AZ
[01–210 3000]
Stormont House, Belfast BT4 3ST
[0232–63255]
Stormont Castle, Belfast BT4 3ST
[0232–63011]
Dundonald House,
Upper Newtownards Road, Belfast BT4 3SU
[0232–63255]

The Northern Ireland Office is the U.K. government department in which the Secretary of State for Northern Ireland has overall responsibility for the government of Northern Ireland. The Secretary of State is directly responsible for constitutional developments, law and order, security and electoral matters. Under the Northern Ireland Act 1974, the Northern Ireland departments are also subject to the direction and control of the Secretary of State during direct rule.
Secretary of State for Northern Ireland, THE RT. HON.
THOMAS KING, M.P. £33,145
Parliamentary Private Secretary, A. Mackay, M.P.
Minister of State, THE RT. HON. JOHN STANLEY, M.P.
£22,875
Parliamentary Private Secretary, T. Wood, M.P.
Parliamentary Under Secretaries of State, The Lord
Lyell (£24,640); R. Needham, M.P.; Dr. B. Mawhinney, M.P.; P. Viggers, M.P. £16,885
Permanent Under Secretary of State, Sir Robert
Andrew, K.C.B. £65,000
Second Permanent Under Secretary of State, Head of
the NICS, Sir Kenneth Bloomfield, K.C.B.

OMBUDSMAN, see PARLIAMENTARY
COMMISSIONER

ORDNANCE SURVEY
Romsey Road, Maybush, Southampton SO9 4DH
[Southampton 775555]

The Ordnance Survey is the national mapping agency for Britain and it produces over 220,000 large scale maps of the country at three basic scales. These are 1:1,250 (50 inches to 1 mile) for urban areas; 1:2,500 (25 inches to 1 mile) for rural areas; and 1:10,000 (6 inches to 1 mile) for mountain and moorland. Additionally, Ordnance Survey produces a range of small scale maps and other products for general use.
Director-General, P. McMaster.
Directors:
  Surveys and Production, A. S. Macdonald.
  Marketing, Planning and Development, J. Leonard.
  Overseas Surveys, B. E. Furmston.
  Establishments and Finance, K. Nolan.
Heads of Functions:
  Production, E. Gilbert.
  Topographic Surveys, P. Wesley.
  Geodesy, Photogrammetry and Computations, A. P. Atkinson.

Marketing, D. Toft.
Research and Development, M. Sowton.
Head of Finance, J. Evenett.
Establishments, I. Lock.
Overseas Surveys, I. T. Logan.

OVERSEAS DEVELOPMENT ADMINISTRATION
Eland House, Stag Place, SW1E 5DH
[01–213 3000]
Abercrombie House, Eaglesham Road, East Kilbride,
Glasgow G75 8EA
[03552 41199]

The Overseas Development Administration deals with British development assistance to overseas countries. This includes both capital aid on concessional terms and technical assistance (mainly in the form of specialist staff abroad and training facilities in the United Kingdom), whether provided directly to developing countries or through the various multilateral aid organizations, including the United Nations and its specialized agencies.

Salaries

Minister of State	£22,875
*Grade 1*A	£59,214
Grade 2	£43,264–£45,349
Grade 3	£33,725–£36,852
Grade 4	£28,975–£30,475
Grade 5	£24,739–£28,215
Grade 6	£18,786–£25,335
Grade 7	£14,927–£20,292

Minister for Overseas Development, THE RT. HON. CHRISTOPHER PATTEN, M.P.
Private Secretary (G7), M. J. Dinham.
*Permanent Secretary (G1*A), J. Caines, C.B.
Private Secretary, Miss A. V. Curran.
Deputy Secretary (G2), R. M. Ainscow.
Under Secretaries (G3), N. B. Hudson; J. L. F. Buist; J. M. M. Vereker; J. V. Kerby; Dr. J. M. Healey; R. C. Samuel, C.M.G., C.V.O.; A. J. Bennett; Dr. D. G. Osborne.

Economic Service

Head of the Economic Service (G3), Dr. J. M. Healey.
Senior Economic Advisers (G5), J. B. Wilmshurst; J. C. H. Morris; J. T. Roberts; G. P. Sandersley.
Economic Advisers (G7), P. J. Ackroyd; N. D. Bailey; P. D. Balacs; B. Carstairs; D. B. Crapper; A. D. Davis; P. J. Dearden; M. G. Foster; K. E. Gubbins; Dr. G. Haley; E. Hawthorn; P. G. Hill; W. Kingsmill; P. J. A. Landymore; P. L. Owen; J. D. Patel; K. Sparkhall; J. N. Stevens; B. P. Thomson; C. J. B. White; Mrs. J. M. White; D. J. Wood.
Chief Statistician (G5), R. M. Allen.
Statisticians (G7), A. B. Williams; Miss M. O'Connor; J. R. B. King; M. W. Kirsop; P. W. K. Rundell; M. C. Walmsley.

Information Department

Head of Information Dept. (G6), J. C. Machin.
Principal Information Officer (G7), Ms L. J. Sinclair.

Heads of Development Divisions (G5)

Caribbean (Bridgetown), M. G. Bawden; *East Africa (Nairobi)*, M. C. McCulloch; *Pacific (Suva)*, J. Hodges; *South-East Asia (Bangkok)*, V. J. McLean; *Southern Africa (Lilongwe)*, G. M. Stegmann.
Assistant Secretaries (G5), Miss A. M. Archbold; G. A. Beattie; M. L. Cahill; R. F. R. Deare; M. J. Dinham; J. A. L. Faint; P. D. M. Freeman; K. G. W. Frost; W. Hobman; B. R. Ireton; Mrs. S. Jay; C. R. O. Jones; Mrs. B. M. Kelly; R. G. M. Manning; R. G. Pettitt; M. A. Power; C. P. Raleigh; D. L.

Stanton; Ms. S. Unsworth; Mrs. P. M. Wilkinson; R. J. Wilson; R. W. Wootton.
Senior Principals (G6), F. Crampsey; L. E. Fitzpatrick; A. F. Watkins; D. S. Fish; G. A. Williams; D. Sands Smith; J. C. Machin.
Principals (G7), J. D. Aitken; S. I. Alexander; J. A. Anning; G. A. Armstrong; D. W. Baker; D. J. Batt; W. T. Birrell; H. Britton; W. A. Brownlie; P. J. Burton; R. O. Carter; P. H. Charters; Miss D. W. Cherry; D. J. Church; T. F. G. Connor; B. Cook; G. Crabtree; D. R. Curran; J. R. Drummond; J. R. Gilbert; K. D. Grimshaw; Miss J. V. Hanna; P. Harris; Ms. P. J. Hilton; M. I. Holland; N. Hoult; W. Jardine; Mrs. J. Laurance; D. Lawless; G. G. Leader; R. A. Ludford; G. H. Malley; C. A. Metcalf; J. C. Millett; G. A. Mustard; S. C. Pennock; P. T. Perris; B. G. Peskett; S. Ray; D. T. Richards; R. S. Ridgwell; G. F. Roberts; M. K. Robson; C. R. Roth; J. M. Scoular; R. J. Smith; M. J. Sexton; I. F. Stickels; I. D. Stuart; A. J. Sutherland; C. M. Taylor; E. C. N. Taylor; N. Thomas; B. A. Thorpe; D. Trotter; D. P. Turner; Miss M. H. Vowles; R. J. Walsgrove; C. W. Warren; S. A. Wheeler; R. S. White; D. M. Whitecross; M. A. Wickstead; P. M. Wilson; J. M. Winter.

Advisory and Specialist Staff

Principal Education Adviser (G5), Dr. R. O. Iredale.
Education Advisers (G6), M. D. Francis; P. G. Scopes; Dr. B. L. Steele.
Principal Engineering Adviser (G5), T. D. Pike.
Engineering Advisers (G6), J. N. Bulman; A. G. Colley; D. Gillett; B. Dolton; P. H. Hilton; H. B. Jackson; B. G. Little; P. H. Scarlett.
Engineering Advisers (G7), C. I. Ellis; R. J. Cadwallader; C. S. Reid; M. F. Sergeant; P. W. D. H. Roberts; A. Coulthart; A. Barker; J. R. Plumb.
Energy Adviser (G6), Dr. J. L. D. Harrison.
Electrical and Mechanical Engineering Adviser (G6), R. P. Jones.
Architectural Adviser (G6), J. B. Shelley.
Architectural & Planning Adviser (G6), H. W. Housego-Woolgar.
Senior Medical Advisers (G6), Dr. P. Key; Dr. M. R. Owen.
Principal Nursing and Health Services Adviser (G5), Miss M. Pollock.
Nursing and Health Services Adviser (G7), Miss A. Rutter.
Chief Natural Resources Adviser (G3), A. J. Bennett.
Deputy Chief National Resources Adviser (G5), J. R. Goldsack.
Deputy Chief Natural Resources Adviser (G5), Dr. J. C. Davies (*Research*).
Agricultural Advisers (G6), J. R. F. Hansell; R. W. Smith (*Research*); P. Tuley; A. R. Stobbs; A. J. Tainsh; R. L. Waddell; J. B. Warren; M. F. Watson; P. R. Weare; M. J. Wilson.
Assistant Agricultural Advisers (G7), Miss L. C. Brown; Dr. B. E. Grimwood; D. J. Salmon; D. A. Trotman.
Animal Health Advisers (G6), G. G. Freeland; Dr. A. D. Irvin.
Fisheries Advisers (G6), J. Stoneman; Dr. J. Tarbit.
Forestry Advisers (G6), R. H. Kemp; W. J. Howard.
Financial Management Advisers (G6), E. A. Gill; D. W. Heffer.
Senior Procurement Adviser (G7), K. S. Breyer.
Senior Social Development Adviser (G6), Dr. S. J. Conlin.
Social Development Adviser (G7), Dr. R. J. Eyben.

Land Resources Development Centre
Tolworth Tower, Surbiton, Surrey KT6 7DY
[01–399 5281]

Director (G5), A. J. Smyth.

Tropical Development Research Institute
56–62 Gray's Inn Road, WC1X 8LU
[01–242 5412]
College House, Wrights Lane, W.8
Director (*G5*), A. Beattie.

OFFICE OF THE PARLIAMENTARY COMMISSIONER AND HEALTH SERVICE COMMISSIONER
Church House, Great Smith Street, SW1P 3BW
[01–212 7676]

The Parliamentary Commissioner for Administration is responsible for investigating complaints referred to him by Members of the House of Commons from members of the public who claim to have sustained injustice in consequence of maladministration in connection with administrative action taken by or on behalf of Government Departments and certain non-departmental public bodies. Certain types of action by Government Departments or bodies are excluded from investigation. Actions taken by other public bodies (such as local authorities, the police, the Post Office and nationalised industries) are outside the Commissioner's scope.

The Health Service Commissioners for England, for Scotland and for Wales are responsible for investigating complaints against National Health Service authorities that are not dealt with by those authorities to the satisfaction of the complainant. Complaints can be referred direct by the member of the public who claims to have sustained injustice or hardship in consequence of the failure in a service provided by a relevant body, failure of that body to provide a service or in consequence of any other action by that body. Certain types of action are excluded, in particular, action taken solely in consequence of the exercise of clinical judgment. The three offices are presently held by the Parliamentary Commissioner.

Parliamentary Commissioner and Health Service Commissioner, A. R. Barrowclough, Q.C. . . £64,739
Secretaries, D. G. Allen, C.M.G.; G. V. Marsh
£33,725–£36,852
Directors, V. J. Dean; K. H. Green; Mrs. J. M. Fowler; M. D. Randall; J. C. Bateman; J. H. Carruthers
£24,739–£28,215
Principals, P. J. Belsham; G. M. Keil; R. A. Smith; A. Watson; R. Church; P. Godden-Kent; Mrs. C. Bentley; M. H. Hodgkiss; N. J. Jordan; R. L. Fenner; Miss D. M. Pace; R. Paxton; T. J. Corkett; D. S. Burn; A. C. Beer (*Establishment Officer*)
£14,927–£20,292

PARLIAMENTARY COUNSEL
36 Whitehall, SW1A 2AY
[01–210 6633]

Parliamentary Counsel draft all Government Bills (i.e. primary legislation) except common form ones and those relating exclusively to Scotland. They also advise on all aspects of parliamentary procedure in connection with such Bills and draft Government amendments to them as well as any motions (including financial resolutions) necessary to secure their introduction into, and passage through, Parliament.
First Counsel, C. H. de Waal, C.B. £65,000
Second Counsel, P. Graham, C.B. £54,000
Counsel, J. D. M. Rennie, C.B.; J. C. Jenkins, C.B.; J. S. Mason; Miss S. P. Burns; D. W. Saunders; E. G. Caldwell; E. G. Bowman; G. B. Sellers. *up to* £45,500

PAROLE BOARD
Abell House, John Islip Street, SW1P 4LH
[01–211 3000]

The Board was constituted under section 59 of the Criminal Justice Act, 1967.

The function of the Board is to advise the Secretary of State for the Home Department with respect to: (1) Release on licence under section 60 (i) or 61 and recall under section 62 of the Criminal Justice Act, 1967 of persons whose cases have been referred to the Board by the Secretary of State; (2) The conditions of such licences, and the variation and cancellation of such conditions; and (3) any other matter so referred which is connected with release on licence or recall of persons to whom section 60 or 61 of the Act applies.
Chairman, The Lord Windlesham, P.C., C.V.O.
Vice-Chairman, The Hon. Mr. Justice Wood.
Secretary, J. Glaze.

PATENT OFFICE
(and Industrial Property and Copyright Department)
Department of Trade and Industry,
State House, 66–71 High Holborn,
WC1R 4TP
[01–831 2525]
Sale Branch: Orpington, Kent

The duties of the Department consist in the administration of the Patent Acts, the Registered Designs Act and the Trade Marks Act and in dealing with questions relating to the Copyright Acts. The Department also provides an information service about patent specifications. In 1986 the Office granted 16,206 patents and registered 7,167 designs and 17,089 trade marks.
Comptroller-General, P. J. Cooper £38,465
Assistant Comptrollers, T. W. Sage; V. Tarnofsky
£32,349
Superintending Examiners, N. G. Tarnofsky; J. P. Britton; M. F. Vivian; A. Sugden; J. Sharrock; G. K. Lindsey; E. F. Blake; K. E. Panchen; W. J. Lyon £29,680
Principal Examiners, C. S. Richenberg; C. I. C. Byrne; M. G. Currell; J. Winter; A. J. Needs; H. R. Bailey; P. L. Eggington; Miss C. M. Edwards; D. R. Barratt; B. C. Faulkner; S. J. Rutland; C. D. Kopkin; D. H. Rowland; E. J. Lawrence; B. J. Phillips; D. B. Johnson; C. G. M. Hoptroff; S. Southworth; B. G. Harden; J. Hillman; M. W. Hills; L. Lewis; P. S. Michaelis; N. M. Miles; K. C. Thomas; R. S. Vidler; Miss Y. J. Pegler; P. Ferdinando; M. F. Pilgrim; P. J. Herbert; J. K. Dugnolle; G. C. Brown; D. L. Wood; C. Corney; D. Davenport . . . . £26,404–£28,564
Assistant Registrar, Trade Marks, J. M. Myall
£25,195–£28,530
Senior Principals, R. V. Egan; A. Holt
£20,251–£26,800
Senior Examiner, Information Retrieval Services, W. Preacher . . . . £17,439–£24,999

Manchester Office
Room 921A, Sunley Buildings,
Piccadilly Plaza, M1 4BA
[01–236 2171]

PAYMASTER GENERAL
H.M. Treasury, Parliament Street, SW1P 3AG
[01–270 4350]
Sutherland House, Russell Way, Crawley, West
Sussex RH10 1UH
[0293–27833]

The Paymaster General's Office was formed by the consolidation in 1835 of various separate pay departments then existing, some of which dated back at least to the Restoration of 1660. Its function is that of paying agent for Government Departments, other than the Revenue Departments. Most of its payments are made through banks, to whose accounts the necessary transfers are made at the Bank of England. The payment of over one million public service pensions is an important feature of its work.

Paymaster General, THE HON. PETER BROOKE, M.P.

Assistant Paymaster General (G5), L. A. Andrews
£24,765–£28,215

Senior Principals (G6), D. R. L. Breed; A. J. McClatchey .... £18,786–£25,335

Principals (G7), D. R. Alexander; E. D. Hatswell; J. A. Payne; K. Sullens; G. Thomas; M. D. West
£15,030–£20,292

POLICE COMPLAINTS AUTHORITY
10 Great George Street, SW1P 3AB
[01–213 5392]

The Police Complaints Authority was established under the Police and Criminal Evidence Act 1984 to introduce a further independent element into the procedure for dealing with complaints by members of the public against police officers in England and Wales. The Authority has powers to supervise the investigation of certain categories of serious complaints and certain statutory functions in relation to the disciplinary aspects of complaints.

Chairman, Sir Cecil Clothier, K.C.B., Q.C.

Deputy Chairman (Discipline), Brig. J. Pownall.

Deputy Chairman (Investigations), Rt. Hon. R. Moyle.

Members, V. Clements; J. Crawford; Mrs E. Crawley; B. A. Gillman; M. C. Hazlewood; B. V. Moore; K. Singh; Capt. N. Taylor; Mrs. R. Vickers; Mrs. R. Wolff.

POLITICAL HONOURS SCRUTINY COMMITTEE
Cabinet Office, Great George Street, SW1P 3AL
[01–233 3000]

The function of the Political Honours Scrutiny Committee is set out in an Order in Council dated May 31, 1979. The Prime Minister submits certain particulars to the Committee about persons proposed to be recommended for honour for their political services. The Committee, after such enquiry as they think fit, report to the Prime Minister whether, so far as they believe, the persons whose names are submitted to them are fit and proper persons to be recommended.

Chairman, The Lord Shackleton, K.G., P.C., O.B.E.

Members, The Lord Carr of Hadley, P.C.; The Lord Franks, P.C., O.M., G.C.M.G., K.C.B., C.B.E., F.B.A.

Secretary, Mrs. M. Hedley-Miller, C.B.

OFFICE OF POPULATION CENSUSES AND SURVEYS
St. Catherine's House, 10 Kingsway,
WC2B 6JP
[01–242 0262]

The Office of Population Censuses and Surveys was created by a merger in May 1970 of the General Register Office and the Government Social Survey Department. The Registrar General controls the local registration service in England and Wales in the exercise of its registration and marriage duties. Copies of the original registrations of births, stillbirths, marriages and deaths are kept in London. A register of adopted children is held at Titchfield. Central indexes are compiled quarterly and certified copies of entries may be obtained on payment of certain fees. Since 1841 the Registrar General has been responsible for taking the census of population. He also prepares and publishes a wide range of statistics and appropriate commentary relating to population, fertility, births, still-births, marriages, deaths and cause of death, infectious diseases, sickness and injuries. The Registrar General also maintains, at Southport, a central register of persons on doctors' lists, for the purposes of the National Health Service.

Hours of public access, Mon.–Fri., 8.30 a.m.–4.30 p.m.

Director and Registrar General, Mrs. G. T. Banks
£45,550

Deputy Director, F. E. Whitehead; B. J. Ellis
£37,000

Senior Principal Medical Officer, M. R. Alderson
£37,000

Grade 5, R. Barnes; J. Craig; J. P. Hisley (*Establishment Officer*); M. L. Pennington; J. V. Ribbins (*Deputy Registrar General*); I. K. G. Arnold; J. A. Rowntree; B. H. Mahon .... £24,765–£28,215

Senior Statisticians (Medical), J. S. A. Ashley; A. G. McCormick; A. J. Swerdlow £28,215

Grade 6, B. S. T. Alcock; Mrs. K. H. Dunnell; Mrs. W. Jenkins; I. B. Knight; D. L. Pearce; R. K. Thomas; P. R. Wilson; R. McLeod .... £18,786–£25,335

Grade 7, R. I. Armitage; F. L. Ashwood; Mrs. P. E. Astbury; Ms J. Atkinson; N. E. Auckland; R. A. P. Bailey; E. Barton; R. J. Beacham; D. E. Birch; Mrs. M. R. Bone; Mrs. B. J. Botting; M. J. Bradley; M. S. Britton; Miss A. C. Brown; T. B. Bryson; L. Bulusu; R. J. Butcher; A. M. Clark; J. Cloyne; M. J. L. Day; C. J. Denham; J. Denton; T. L. F. Devis; J. M. Dixie; Ms E. M. Goddard; I. Golds; Mrs. J. R. Gregory; J. Haskey; P. J. Heady; Mrs. P. E. John; A. F. Jones; B. G. Little; Miss C. S. J. Lloyd; Miss E. M. McCrossan; Mrs. J. Martin; B. W. Meakings; Mrs. J. S. Morris; R. M. Nicholls; A. Parr (*Chief Inspector of Registration*); J. A. Rampton; Mrs. I. Rauta; R. U. Redpath; T. A. Russell; C. Shaw; K. J. Stalker; D. Stewart; Mrs. D. M. Stobbart; A. W. Tester; Miss J. Todd; Mrs. M. J. Waggett; Miss S. Wallace (*Press Officer*); J. B. Werner
£15,030–£20,292

PORT OF LONDON AUTHORITY
Head Office: Europe House, World Trade Centre,
E1 9AA
[01–481 8484]

Under the Port of London Authority (Constitution) Revision Order 1975, the membership of the Board consists of a minimum of nine and a maximum of 17 members. In addition to the Chairman a minimum of seven and a maximum of 10 nonexecutive members are appointed by the Minister of Transport.

A minimum of one executive member and a maximum of six executive members may be appointed by the Chairman and other non-executive members.

Chairman, Sir Brian Kellett.

Chief Executive, River, D. Jeffery.

Chief Executive Tilbury, J. S. McNab.

Chief Executive, Property, J. C. Jenkinson, M.V.O.

Director of Finance, T. R. MacMaster.

Secretary, G. E. Ennals.

THE POST OFFICE
33 Grosvenor Place, SW1X 1PX
[01–235 8000]

Crown services for the carriage of Government despatches were set up about 1516. The conveyance of public correspondence began in 1635 and the mail service was made a Parliamentary responsibility with the setting up of a Post Office in 1657. Telegraphs came under the Post Office control in 1870 and the

Post Office Telephone Service began in 1880. The National Girobank service of the Post Office began in 1968. The Post Office ceased to be a Government Department on October 1, 1969 and responsibility for the running of the postal, telecommunications, and giro and remittance services was transferred to a public authority called the Post Office. The 1981 British Telecommunications Act separated the functions of the Post Office, making it solely responsible for postal services and National Girobank.

The Chairman and members of the Post Office Board are appointed by the Secretary of State but responsibility for the running of the Post Office as a whole rests with the Board in its corporate capacity.

Post Office Board

Chairman, Sir Ronald Dearing, C.B.†
Vice-Chairman and Member for Personnel and Corporate Resources, K. M. Young, C.B.E.
Members, W. Cockburn, T.D. (*Managing Director, Letters*); A. D. Garrett (*Managing Director, Parcels*); A. J. Roberts (*Managing Director, Counters*); P. E. Sellers (*Corporate Finance and Planning*); G. M. Williamson (*Managing Director, Girobank* P.L.C.)
Part-time Members, A. B. Butler; E. Cole; Sir Clifford Cornford, K.C.B.; D. Hodson.
Secretary, M. MacDonald.
† Replaced Oct. 1987 by Sir Bryan Nicholson.

PRIVY COUNCIL OFFICE
Whitehall, SW1A 2AT
[01-270 3000]

The Office is responsible for the arrangements leading to the making of all Royal Proclamations and Orders in Council; for certain formalities connected with Ministerial changes; for considering applications for the grant (or amendment) of Royal Charters; the scrutiny and approval of bye-laws and statutes of Chartered Bodies; for the appointment of High Sheriffs and many Crown and Privy Council appointments to governing bodies.
Lord President of the Council (and Leader of the House of Lords), THE VISCOUNT WHITELAW, C.H., M.C.
Private Secretary, M. Eland.
Clerk of the Council, G. I. de Deney, C.V.O. £35,350
Deputy Clerk of the Council, C. E. S. Horsford, C.V.O.
                                                              £28,530
Senior Clerk, R. P. Bulling £19,047

PUBLIC HEALTH LABORATORY SERVICE
Headquarters Office:
61 Colindale Avenue, NW9 5EQ
[01–200 1295]

The Public Health Laboratory Service comprises 52 regional or area laboratories distributed through England and Wales, and 23 reference and special laboratories or units. The P.H.L.S. gives a routine microbiological service to several hospitals, and provides reference facilities that are available nationally. It collates information on the incidence of infection, and when necessary it institutes special enquiries into outbreaks and the epidemiology of infectious disease, although executive responsibility for their control is the statutory responsibility of local authorities. It also undertakes bacteriological surveillance of the quality of food and water for local authorities and others. The P.H.L.S. is often called upon to advise central and local government and the hospital service on many aspects of infectious disease.

It maintains close contact with veterinary organizations in areas of mutual interest, and collaborates with the World Health Organization and with national laboratory and epidemiological services overseas.

The Board

Chairman, Dr. C. E. Gordon Smith, C.B., M.D., D.SC, F.R.C.P., F.R.C.Path.
Deputy Chairman, C. C. Stevens, C.B.
Members, Prof. A. R. Buchan, M.D.; D. Cormack, Ph.D.; N. E. Day, Ph.D.; A. E. Eames; P. W. Russell Eggitt, O.B.E., Ph.D.; E. L. Harris, C.B., F.R.C.P.; P. Higham; Dr. Deirdre J. Hine; Prof. Rosalinde Hurley, M.D.; Dr. M. J. Painter; Dr. A. J. Rowland; Prof. H. Smith, Ph.D., D.SC., F.R.S.; Prof. A. J. Zuckerman, M.D., D.SC., F.R.C.P.
Staff Assessors, J. F. R. Graves; M. J. Hill, Ph.D.; D. M. Jones, M.D.
Secretary, K. M. Saunders.
Deputy Secretary, J. M. Harker.
Director, J. W. G. Smith, M.D.
Deputy Directors, Joan R. Davies, M.D.; C. Roberts, M.D.

Central Public Health Laboratory
Colindale Avenue, N.W.9

Director, Prof. A. A. Glynn, M.D.
Division of Enteric Pathogens, B. Rowe, T.D.
Division of Hospital Infection, E. M. Cooke, M.D.
Division of Microbiological Reagents and Quality Control, A. G. Taylor, Ph.D.
Food Hygiene Laboratory, R. J. Gilbert, Ph.D.
Hepatitis Epidemiology Unit (Division of Epidemiology), S. Polakoff, M.D.
Mycological Reference Laboratory, Prof. D. W. R. Mackenzie, Ph.D.
National Collection of Type Cultures, L. R. Hill, D.SC.
Virus Reference Laboratory, P. P. Mortimer, M.D.

Centre for Applied Microbiology and Research
Porton Down, Salisbury

Director, P. M. Sutton.
Bacterial Metabolism Research Laboratory, M. J. Hill, Ph.D.
Experimental Pathology Laboratory, A. Baskerville, D.V.SC., Ph.D.
Microbial Technology Laboratory, Prof. A. Atkinson, Ph.D.
Molecular Genetics Laboratory, P. J. Greenaway, Ph.D.
Quality Control and Safety Laboratory, O. Basarab, Ph.D.
Special Pathogens Research Laboratory, E. T. W. Bowen, O.B.E., Ph.D.
Therapeutic Products Laboratory, H. E. Wade, Ph.D.
Vaccine Research and Production Laboratory, Prof. J. Melling, Ph.D.

Other Special Laboratories and Units

Anaerobe Reference Unit, Public Health Laboratory, Luton: A. T. Willis, M.D.
Communicable Disease Surveillance Centre (Division of Epidemiology), 61 Colindale Avenue, N.W.9: N. S. Galbraith.
Gonococcus Reference Unit, Public Health Laboratory, Bristol: A. E. Jephcott, M.D.
Influenza Research Unit, Public Health Laboratory, Guildford: J. R. Davies, M.D.
Leptospira Reference Unit, Public Health Laboratory, Hereford: S. A. Waitkins, Ph.D.

Malaria Reference Laboratory, London School of Hygiene and Tropical Medicine, W.C.1: Prof. D. J. Bradley, D.M.; Prof. W. Peters, M.D., D.SC.

Mycobacterium Reference Unit, Public Health Laboratory, Cardiff: P. A. Jenkins, PH.D.

Regional Laboratories

Birmingham, J. G. P. Hutchison, M.D.; *Bristol*, A. E. Jephcott, M.D.; *Cambridge*, C. E. D. Taylor, M.D.; *Cardiff*, C. H. L. Howells, M.D.; *Leeds*, R. N. Peel; *Liverpool*, G. C. Turner, M.D.; *Manchester*, D. M. Jones, M.D.; *Newcastle*, A. E. Wright, T.D., M.D.; *Oxford*, J. B. Selkon, M.D.; *Portsmouth*, O. A. Okubadejo, M.D.; *Sheffield*, B. W. Barton.

Area Laboratories

Ashford, C. Dulake; *Bath*, D. G. White; *Brighton*, B. T. Thom; *Carlisle*, M. A. Knowles; *Carmarthen*, H. D. S. Morgan; *Chelmsford*, R. E. Tettmar, D.Path.; *Chester*, J. H. Pennington, M.D.; *Coventry*, P. R. Mortimer, M.D.; *Dorchester*, P. Gill; *Epsom*, E. I. Tanner; *Exeter*, R. J. C. Hart; *Gloucester*, K. A. V. Cartwright; *Guildford*, Prof. R. Y. Cartwright; *Hereford*, I. R. Ferguson; *Hull*, S. L. Mawer; *Ipswich*, P. H. Jones; *Leicester*, C. J. Mitchell; *Lincoln*, J. G. Wallace; LONDON: *Central Middlesex Hospital*, D. A. McSwiggan; *Dulwich*, A. H. C. Uttley, PH.D.; *Tooting*, D. G. Fleck, M.D.; *Whipps Cross*, B. Chattopadhyay, M.D.; *Luton*, A. T. Willis, M.D.; *Middlesbrough*, E. McKay-Ferguson, M.D.; *Norwich*, W. Shepherd, M.D.; *Nottingham*, M. J. Lewis, M.D.; *Peterborough*, R. S. Jobanputra, M.D.; *Plymouth*, P. J. Wilkinson; *Poole*, W. L. Hooper; *Preston*, D. N. Hutchinson; *Reading*, J. V. Dadswell; *Rhyl*, D. N. Looker; *Salisbury*, S. Patrick; *Shrewsbury*, C. A. Morris, M.D.; *Southampton*, J. A. Lowes (*acting*); *Stoke-on-Trent*, J. Gray; *Swansea*, D. H. M. Joynson; *Taunton*, N. F. Lightfoot; *Truro*, W. A. Telfer Brunton; *Watford*, M. T. Moulsdale; *Wolverhampton*, R. G. Thompson.

REGISTRAR OF PUBLIC LENDING RIGHT
Bayheath House,
Prince Regent Street,
Stockton-on-Tees,
TS18 1DF
[0642–604699]

Under the Public Lending Right system, in operation since Jan. 1983, payment is made from public funds to authors whose books are lent out from public libraries. Payment is made once a year (in February) and the amount each author receives is proportionate to the number of times (established from a sample) that each registered book was lent out during the previous year.

The Registrar of PLR, who is appointed by the Minister for the Arts, compiles the register of authors and books. Only living authors resident in the U.K. or West Germany are eligible to apply. (The term "author" covers writers, illustrators, translators, and some editors/compilers.)

A payment of 1·20 pence was made in 1986–87 for each estimated loan of a registered book, up to a top limit of £5,000 for the books of any one registered author: the money for loans above this level is used to augment the remaining PLR payments.

In February 1987, the sum of £2,402,000 was made available for distribution to 11,010 registered authors and assignees as the fourth annual payment of PLR. *Registrar*, J. W. Sumsion.

PUBLIC RECORD OFFICE
See **Record Offices**

PUBLIC TRUST OFFICE
Stewart House, 24 Kingsway, WC2B 6JX
[01–405 4300]

The Public Trustee is a trust Corporation created to undertake the business of executorship and trusteeship; he can act as executor or administrator of the estate of a deceased person, or as trustee of a will or settlement. The Public Trustee is also responsible for the performance of all the administrative, but not the judicial, tasks required of the Court of Protection under Part VII of the Mental Health Act, 1983, relating to the management and administation of the property and affairs of persons suffering from mental disorder. The Public Trustee also acts as Receiver when so directed by the Court, usually where there is no other person willing or able so to act.

The Accountant General of the Supreme Court, through the Court Funds Office, is responsible for the investment and accounting of funds in court for persons under a disability, monies in Court subject to litigation and statutory deposits.

The Court Funds Office is at 22 Kingsway, WC2B 6LE (01-936 6016).

Public Trustee and Accountant General, J. A. Boland.
Assistant Public Trustee (Administration) and Deputy Accountant General, P. D. Lewis, T.D.
Assistant Public Trustee (Legal), H. N. Mather.
Heads of Divisions:
Administration, J. R. Ellis.
Court Funds, I. J. MacBean.
Finance, F. J. Eddy.
Investment, H. Stevenson
Property, A. Nightingale.
Protection, E. J. Dober.
Receivership and Trust, R. A. Cunningham, T.D.

COMMISSION FOR RACIAL EQUALITY
Elliot House, 10–12 Allington Street, SW1E 5EH
[01–828 7022]

Established on June 13, 1977, under the Race Relations Act 1976, to work towards elimination of discrimination and promote equality of opportunity and good relations between different racial groups generally.

Chairman, P. Newsam.
Deputy Chairman, Prof. B. Parekh.
Members, G. E. B. Tyler; L. Crawford; Mrs. L. Khan; G. S. Sarang; Ethel M. Houston, O.B.E.; E. Gilmour Jones; K. R. Whitesides; Q. S. Anisuddin; Prof. B. Hepple; Mrs. E. Nam (*full-time*); D. A. C. Lambert; Dr. D. Ray; C. Lloyd (*part-time*).

RECORD OFFICES, ETC.

THE PUBLIC RECORD OFFICE
Chancery Lane, WC2A 1LR
[01–405 0741]
Ruskin Avenue, Kew,
Richmond, Surrey TW9 4DU
[01–876 3444]

The Office, originally established in 1838 under the Master of the Rolls, was placed by the Public Records Act 1958 under the direction of the Lord Chancellor. He appoints a Keeper of Public Records, whose duties are to co-ordinate and supervise the selection of records of government departments and the English Law Courts for permanent preservation, to safeguard the records under his charge, and to make them available to the public.

The Office holds records of central government dating from *Domesday Book* (1086) to 1987. Under the 1967 Public Records Act they are normally open to inspection when 30 years old, and are then available, without charge, in the reading rooms, Monday to Friday, 9.30–5.

Keeper of Public Records, G. H. Martin, C.B.E., D.Phil., F.S.A. . . . . £34,000–£37,000
Deputy Keeper, M. Roper . . . . £25,605–£29,055
Records Administration Officer, C. D. Chalmers
£25,605–£29,055
Officer-in-Charge, Chancery Lane, Dr. R. F. Hunnisett
£26,230–£29,680
Establishment Officer, J. G. Wickham
£15,870–£21,132
Principal Assistant Keepers, Mrs. J. M. Cox; Dr. N. G. Cox; N. E. Evans; Dr. A. A. H. Knightbridge; Mrs. A. N. Nicol; J. B. Post; J. L. Walford
£19,626–£26,800
Assistant Keepers, Mrs. M. K. Banton; Miss G. L. Beech; Dr. A. S. Bevan; Dr. T. M. Chalmers; Miss M. M. Condon; C. R. H. Cooper; Miss A. Crawford; Dr. D. Crook; Dr. H. Forde; Dr. M. R. Foster; Dr. E. M. Hallam Smith; Ms. S. M. F. Healy; Dr. E. J. Higgs; Mrs. H. E. Jones; Dr. M. J. Jubb; A. J. McDonald; Mrs. A. E. Morton; T. R. Padfield; Dr. N. A. M. Rodger; Dr. D. L. Thomas
scale rising to max. of £21,757
Head, Repository and Reprographic Departments, P. F. McCaffrey . . . . £15,870–£21,132
Principal Inspecting Officer, D. Ashton
£15,870–£21,132
Inspecting Officers, D. Barlow; A. W. H. Medlicott; J. S. Harley; K. J. Smith; F. McCall; Mrs. E. J. Baldwin; Mrs. M. A. Bull; C. J. Edwards; Mrs. H. R. Saw. . . . . £12,479–£15,469
Head of Information Technology Unit, Mrs. M. Wilkinson . . . . £12,479–£15,469
Deputy Establishment Officer, J. A. Keene
£12,479–£15,469

ADVISORY COUNCIL ON PUBLIC RECORDS
Public Record Office, Chancery Lane, WC2A 1LR
[01–405 0741]

Council members are appointed by the Lord Chancellor, under the Public Records Act 1958, to advise him "on matters concerning public records in general and, in particular, on those aspects of the work of the Public Record Office which affect members of the public who make use of the facilities provided by the Public Record Office". The Council meets quarterly and produces an annual report which is published alongside the Report of the Keeper of Public Records as a House of Commons sessional paper.
Chairman, The Master of the Rolls.
Members, The Lord Bancroft, G.C.B.; Miss V. Cromwell; A. Gomersall; J. S. W. Gibson; Prof. P. D. A. Harvey; Prof. Sir Michael Howard, C.B.E., M.C., F.B.A.; Sir Paul Osmond, C.B.; Prof. T. Ranger; Dr. H. Roseveare; Prof. W. Saunders; W. R. Serjeant; R. S. Wainwright; M. A. Latham, M.P.; Prof. E. A. Wrigley.
Assessors, D. J. Wiblin; Dr. G. H. Martin.
Secretary, Dr. M. J. Jubb.

HOUSE OF LORDS RECORD OFFICE
House of Lords, SW1A 0PW
[01–219 3074]

Since 1497, the records of Parliament have been kept within the Palace of Westminster. They are in the custody of the Clerk of the Parliaments, who in 1946 established a record department to supervise their preservation and their production to students.

The Search Room of this office is open to the public Mon.–Fri., 9.30–5.

The records preserved number some 3,000,000 documents, and include Acts of Parliament from 1497, Journals of the House of Lords from 1510, Minutes and Committee proceedings from 1610, and Papers laid before Parliament from 1531. Amongst the records are the Petition of Right, the Death Warrant of Charles I, the Declaration of Breda and the Bill of Rights. The House of Lords Record Office also has charge of the Journals of the House of Commons (from 1547), and other surviving records of the Commons (from 1572), which include plans and annexed documents relating to Private Bill legislation from 1818. Among other documents are the records of the Lord Great Chamberlain, the political papers of certain members of the two Houses (including the papers of Lloyd George, Bonar Law and other statesmen previously preserved in the Beaverbrook Library), and documents relating to Parliament acquired on behalf of the nation. All the manuscripts and other records are preserved in the Victoria Tower of the Houses of Parliament. A permanent exhibition was established in the Royal Gallery in 1979.

Clerk of the Records, H. S. Cobb, F.S.A.
£26,230–£29,680
Deputy Clerk of the Records, D. J. Johnson, F.S.A.
£20,251–£26,800
Assistant Clerks of the Records, J. C. Morgan (*Sound Archives*); S. K. Ellison . . . . £16,495–£21,757

ROYAL COMMISSION ON HISTORICAL MANUSCRIPTS
Quality House, Quality Court, Chancery Lane, WC2A 1HP
[01–242 1198]

The Commission was set up by Royal Warrant in 1869 to enquire and report on collections of papers of value for the study of history in private hands. In 1959 a new warrant enlarged these terms of reference to include all historical records, wherever situated, outside the Public Records and gave it added responsibilities, as a central co-ordinating body, to promote, assist and advise on their proper preservation and storage. The Commission has published over 200 volumes of reports. It holds a further 30,000 unpublished reports in the National Register of Archives, available for consultation in its search room. It also administers the Manorial and Tithe Documents Rules on behalf of the Master of the Rolls.
Chairman, The Lord Blake, F.B.A.
Commissioners, Sir Robert Somerville, K.C.V.O., F.S.A.; The Lord Kenyon, C.B.E., F.S.A.; The Lord Fletcher, P.C., F.S.A.; ; The Duke of Northumberland, K.G., P.C., G.C.V.O., F.R.S.; J. P. W. Ehrman, F.B.A., F.S.A.; Prof. S. F. C. Milsom, F.B.A.; Sir John Habakkuk, F.B.A.; G. E. Aylmer, F.B.A.; P. T. Cormack, F.S.A., M.P.; H. M. Colvin, C.B.E., F.B.A., F.S.A.; Prof. G. W. S. Barrow, F.B.A.; Valerie L. Pearl, F.S.A.; The Marquess of Anglesey; Prof. Owen Chadwick, O.M., K.B.E., F.B.A.; D. G. Vaisey, F.S.A.; The Viscount of Arbuthnot, C.B.E., D.S.C.
Secretary, B. S. Smith, F.S.A.

SCOTTISH RECORD OFFICE
H.M. General Register House, Edinburgh EH1 3YY
[031–556 6585]

The history of the national archives of Scotland can be traced back to the 13th century. The present headquarters of the Scottish Record Office, the General Register House, was founded in 1774. Here are preserved the administrative records of pre-

Union Scotland, the registers of central and local courts of law, the public registers of property rights and legal documents, and many collections of local and church records and private archives. Certain groups of records, mainly the modern records of government departments in Scotland, the Scottish railway records, and the plans collection, are preserved in the branch repository at the West Register House in Charlotte Square. The Search Rooms in both buildings open Mon.–Fri., 9–4.45. A permanent exhibition at the West Register House and changing exhibitions at the General Register House are open to the public on weekdays, 10–4. The National Register of Archives (Scotland), which is a branch of the Scottish Record Office, is based in the West Register House.

Keeper of the Records of Scotland, Dr. A. L. Murray.

DEPARTMENT OF THE REGISTERS OF SCOTLAND
Meadowbank House, 153 London Road,
Edinburgh EH8 7AU
[031–661 6111]

The Registers of Scotland consist of:—
(1) General Register of Sasines and Land Register of Scotland; (2) Register of Deeds in the Books of Council and Session; (3) Register of Protests; (4) Register of English and Irish Judgments; (5) Register of Service of Heirs; (6) Register of the Great Seal; (7) Register of the Quarter Seal; (8) Register of the Prince's Seal; (9) Register of Crown Grants; (10) Register of Sheriffs' Commissions; (11) Register of the Cachet Seal; (12) Register of Inhibitions and Adjudications; (13) Register of Entails; (14) Register of Hornings.

The General Register of Sasines and the Land Register of Scotland form the chief security in Scotland of the rights of land and other heritable (or real) property.

Keeper of the Registers of Scotland, W. Russell
                                 £28,350–£29,850
Deputy Keeper, J. Robertson . . . . . £23,730 to £27,065
Senior Assistant Keepers, R. C. Brown; A. A. Snowdon; G. C. Warrender . . . . £18,020 to £24,302
Assistant Keepers, J. Cogle; B. J. Corr; A. M. Falconer; R. C. Fulton; J. Knox; D. Lorimer; Mrs. A. McDonald; L. J. Morrison; A. G. T. New; D. L. Nicoll; A. W. Ramage; A. G. Rennie; I. M. Tainsh
                               £14,318 to £19,465

CORPORATION OF LONDON RECORDS OFFICE
Guildhall, EC2P 2EJ
[01–260 1251]

Contains the municipal archives of the City of London which are regarded as the most complete collection of ancient municipal records in existence. Includes charters of William the Conqueror, Henry II, and later Kings and Queens to 1957; ancient custumals: Liber Horn, Dunthorne, Custumarum, Ordinacionum, Memorandorum and Albus, Liber de Antiquis Legibus, and collections of Statutes; continuous series of judicial rolls and books from 1252 and Council minutes from 1275; records of the Old Bailey and Guildhall Sessions from 1603, and financial records from the 16th century, together with the records of London Bridge from the 12th century and numerous subsidiary series and miscellanea of historical interest. A Guide was published in 1951. Readers' Room open Mon.–Fri., 9.30–4.45.

Keeper of the City Records, The Town Clerk.
Deputy Keeper, J. R. Sewell.
Assistant Keeper, Mrs. J. M. Bankes.

REVIEW BODIES

ARMED FORCES PAY
The Review Body on Armed Forces Pay was appointed in September 1971 to advise the Prime Minister on the pay and allowances of members of Naval, Military and Air Forces of the Crown and of any women's service administered by the Defence Council.

The members of the Review Body are: Sir Peter Matthews (*Chairman*); M. Bett; D. P. M. Hudson; Mrs. J. Hughes; L. A. Mills; Adm. Sir Anthony Morton, G.B.E., K.C.B.; W. C. Thomson; Prof. J. Little, C.B.E.

DOCTORS' AND DENTISTS' REMUNERATION
The Review Body on Doctors' and Dentists' Remuneration was appointed in July 1971 to advise the Prime Minister on the remuneration of doctors and dentists taking any part in the National Health Service.

The members of the Review Body are: Sir Graham Wilkins (*Chairman*); Dr. Anne Hogg; J. L. Kirkpatrick, C.B.E.; Prof. P. G. Moore, T.D.; D. G. Richards; Prof. G. F. Thomason, C.B.E.; J. K. Warburton, C.B.E.

TOP SALARIES
The Review Body on Top Salaries was appointed in May, 1971 to advise the Prime Minister on the remuneration of the higher judiciary and other judicial appointments; senior civil servants; and senior officers of the armed forces. Until August 1980 the remit also included the Chairmen and members of the Boards of nationalized industries. The Review Body has also been asked on a number of occasions to advise on the remuneration of Members of Parliament and of Ministers and on the level of parliamentary allowances.

The members of the Review Body are: The Lord Plowden, K.C.B., K.B.E. (*Chairman*); J. D. Birkin, T.D.; The Lord Chorley; Sir Robin Ibbs; Sir Peter Matthews, A.O.; A. Morritt, Q.C.; J. J. R. Pope, O.B.E.; Sir Thomas Skyrme, K.C.V.O., C.B., C.B.E., T.D.

NURSING STAFF, MIDWIVES, HEALTH VISITORS AND PROFESSIONS ALLIED TO MEDICINE
The Review Body for nursing staff, midwives, health visitors and professions allied to medicine was set up in July 1983 to advise the Prime Minister on the remuneration of nursing staff, midwives and health visitors employed in the National Health Service; and physiotherapists, radiographers, remedial gymnasts, occupational therapists, orthoptists, chiropodists, dietitians and related grades employed in the National Health Service.

The members of the Review Body are: Sir James Cleminson, M.C. (*Chairman*); Sir John Herbecq, K.C.B. (*Deputy Chairman*); Miss B. Cooper, Q.C.; Mrs. S. Harold; Dr. G. Hills; Mrs. J. Hughes; I. H. Phillipps; Prof. G. F. Thomason, C.B.E.

NOTE.—The secretariat for the above bodies is provided by the Office of Manpower Economics (*see separate entry*).

ROYAL BOTANIC GARDENS, KEW
Richmond, Surrey TW9 3AB
[01-940 1171]
Also at: Wakehurst Place, Ardingly, near Haywards
Heath,
West Sussex RH17 6TN
[0444 892701]

The Royal Botanic Gardens (RBG), Kew were
founded in 1759 by H.R.H. Princess Augusta. In 1841,
they became a public institution; in 1847, the
Museums of Economic Botany were opened, and in
1852, the Herbarium and Library were established.
The Jodrell Laboratory opened in 1876. In 1965, the
garden at Wakehurst Place was acquired; it is owned
by the National Trust and managed by RBG Kew.
From 1903 to 1984, RBG Kew was part of the Ministry
of Agriculture, Fisheries and Food. Under the
National Heritage Act 1983, a Board of Trustees was
set up to administer the Gardens which in 1984
became an independent body supported by a grant-
in-aid.

The functions of RBG Kew are to carry out
research into plant sciences, to disseminate knowledge about plants and to provide the public with the
opportunity to gain knowledge and enjoyment from
the Gardens' collections. There are extensive national reference collections of living and preserved
plants and a comprehensive library and archive. The
main emphasis is on tropical and subtropical plants.

Open daily, except Christmas Day and New Year's
Day, from 9.30 a.m. The closing hour varies from 4
p.m. in mid-winter to 7 p.m. on week-days, and 8 p.m.
at week-ends and Bank Holidays, in mid-summer.
Admission, 50p. Museums open 9.30 a.m.; Glass-
houses, 9.30–4.30 (weekdays); to 5.30 p.m. (Sundays).
No dogs except guide-dogs for the blind.

BOARD OF TRUSTEES

Chairman, Hon. J. D. Eccles, C.B.E.
Members, Sir Leslie Fowden, F.R.S.; Sir David Atten-
borough, C.B.E., F.R.S.; Prof. W. G. Chaloner, F.R.S.;
Prof. E. C. D. Cocking, F.R.S.; J. P. Cousins; Sir
Philip M. Dowson, C.B.E.; Prof. G. E. Fogg, C.B.E.; P.
J. D. Marshall; Prof. Elizabeth B. Robson, PH.D.;
Cdr. L. M. Saunders Watson, R.N. (*ret*).
Director, Prof. E. A. Bell.

Royal Botanic Garden, Edinburgh
Inverleith Row, Edinburgh EH3 5LR
[031–552 7171]

Regius Keeper, Prof. J. McNeill.
Assistant Keeper, J. Cullen, PH.D.

ROYAL COMMISSION FOR THE
EXHIBITION OF 1851
Sherfield Building,
Imperial College of Science and Technology,
SW7 2AZ
[01–589 6483]

Incorporated by Supplemental Charter as a per-
manent Commission after winding up the affairs of
the Great Exhibition of 1851. It has for its object the
promotion of scientific and artistic education by
means of funds derived from its Kensington Estate,
purchased with the surplus left over from the Great
Exhibition.
President, H.R.H. The Duke of Edinburgh, K.G., P.C.,
K.T., O.M., G.B.E.
Chairman, Board of Management, Sir Richard Way,
K.C.B., C.B.E.
Secretary to Commissioners, M. C. Neale, C.B.

SCIENCE AND ENGINEERING
RESEARCH COUNCIL
Polaris House, North Star Avenue,
Swindon, Wilts. SN2 1ET
[0793–26222]

The Science and Engineering Research Council
(S.E.R.C.) is one of five research councils funded
through the Department of Education and Science
"to develop the natural and social sciences, including
engineering, to maintain a fundamental capacity of
research and scholarship and to support relevant
postgraduate education". S.E.R.C.'s role is to encour-
age and support research and advanced training in
U.K. universities and polytechnics in all the basic
areas of science and engineering.
Chairman, Prof. E. W. J. Mitchell.
Members, Prof. Sir Michael Atiyah; Prof. B. L.
Clarkson; Dr. R. F. Coleman; Prof. A. H. Cook;
Prof. D. E. N. Davies; Prof. B. E. F. Fender; C. A. P.
Foxell; Prof. C. Hilsum; Prof. M. A. Jeeves; Dr. C.
Jordan; Dr. H. D. Law; Prof. Sir Richard Norman;
Prof. D. H. Perkins; Dr. C. H. Reece; D. T. Shore;
Prof. J. M. Thomas; Prof. R. Wilson.

SCOTTISH OFFICE

The Secretary of State for Scotland is responsible
in Scotland for a wide range of statutory functions
which in England and Wales are the responsibility of
a number of departmental ministers. He also works
closely with ministers in charge of Great Britain
departments on topics of special significance to
Scotland within their fields of responsibility. His
statutory functions are administered by five main
departments: Department of Agriculture and Fisheries for Scotland, Scottish Development Department, Scottish Education Department, Scottish
Home and Health Department, and Industry Department for Scotland. These Departments (plus Central
Services embracing the Solicitor's Office, the Scottish
Information Office, Establishment, Liaison and
Finance Divisions) are collectively known as the
Scottish Office. In addition there are a number of
other Scottish Departments for which the Secretary
of State has some degree of responsibility: these
include the Scottish Courts Administration, the
Department of the Registrar General for Scotland
(the General Register Office), the Scottish Record
Office and the Department of the Registers of
Scotland. The Secretary of State also bears Ministerial responsibility for the activities in Scotland of
several statutory bodies whose functions extend
throughout Great Britain such as the Manpower
Services Commission and the Forestry Commission.

Salary List

Secretary of State	£33,145
Minister of State (Lords)	£30,640
Minister of State (Commons)	£22,875
Parliamentary Under Secretary	£16,885
Grade 1	£65,000
Grade 2	£43,500–£45,500
Grade 3	£34,000–£37,000
Grade 4	£30,344–£31,844
Grade 5	£27,765–£28,215
Grade 6	£18,786–£25,335
Grade 7	£15,030–£20,292

Dover House, Whitehall, SW1A 2AU
[01–270 3000]
Secretary of State for Scotland, THE RT. HON. MALCOLM
RIFKIND, Q.C., M.P.
Private Secretary (G5), D. J. Crawley
Assistant Private Secretaries, A. Rinning; R.
Weatherston.

Ministers of State, IAN LANG, M.P. (*Industry and Local Government*); LORD SANDERSON OF BOWDEN (*Agriculture and Fisheries, Forestry, the Highlands and Islands, and Tourism*).
Private Secretaries, I. W. Jardine (*I. Lang*); A. C. McLaren (*Lord Sanderson of Bowden*).
Parliamentary Under Secretaries of State, Lord James Douglas–Hamilton, M.P.; M. Forsyth, M.P.
Private Secretaries, I. J. C. Howie (*Lord James Douglas–Hamilton*); D. B. Binnie (*M. Forsyth*).
Parliamentary Clerk, Mrs. M. E. Thomson.
Permanent Under Secretary of State (*G1*), Sir William Fraser, G.C.B.
Private Secretary, D. W. Hamilton.
Liaison Staff:
Assistant Secretary (*G5*), I. C. Freeman.
Principals (*G7*), I. A. Sneddon; A. C. King.

New St. Andrew's House,
Edinburgh EH1 3SX
[031–556 8400]

MANAGEMENT GROUP SUPPORT STAFF

Principal (*G7*), J. D. Gallagher.

CENTRAL SERVICES

Deputy Secretary (*Central Services*) (*G2*), I. D. Penman.

Establishment Division
16 Waterloo Place Edinburgh, EH1 3DN
[031–556 8400]

Principal Establishments Officer (*G3*), A. H. Bishop.
Assistant Secretary (*G5*), Miss M. Maclean.
Senior Principals (*G6*), D. J. Chalmers; J. N. Davison, O.B.E.; A. B. Fairweather, T.D.; G. W. Tucker.
Principals (*G7*), W. E. Bennet; D. A. Christie; J. H. F. Finnie; M. Finnigan; J. R. M. Flucker; A. W. Fraser; J. D. Gallagher; H. J. Graham; C. D. Henderson; I. C. Henderson; J. Meldrum; J. B. Roddin; A. Stephenson.

Directorate of Information Technology
Broomhouse Drive, Edinburgh EH11 3XD
[031–556 8400]

Computer Services
Director (*G5*), J. Duffy.
Deputy Director (*G6*), C. B. Knox.
Principals (*G7*), J. A. Brown; W. Ferguson; A. R. McCowan; B. U. Pearson.

Telecommunications
St. Andrew's House, Edinburgh EH1 3DE
[031–556 8400]

Director (*G6*), A. F. Harrison.

Finance Division
New St. Andrew's House, Edinburgh EH1 3SX
[031–556 8400]

Finance Group

Principal Finance Officer (*G3*), K. J. MacKenzie.
Assistant Secretaries (*G5*), J. W. Elvidge; E. W. Frizzell; I. G. F. Gray; T. E. McGreevy; H. Robertson, M.B.E.; W. T. Toit.
Senior Principal (*G6*), A. Walker.
Principals (*G7*), J. S. Aldridge; E. G. J. Bee; S. W. E. Davidson; J. D. Gallagher; D. A. Howe; T. Hunter; N. J. H. Kernohan; W. A. Lamberton; I. A. McLeod; W. E. M. Maxwell; D. R. Mayer; R. E. Merrall; D. F. Middleton; D. Muir; J. Porter; I. M. Smith; R. K. West.

Local Government Finance Group

Assistant Secretaries (*G5*), G. Robson; A. M. Russell.
Principals (*G6*), D. J. Christie; P. S. Collings; A. G. Dickson; G. A. Paul; J. A. Rennie; T. Winwick.

Solicitor's Office
(*For the Scottish Departments and certain U.K. services including H.M. Treasury, in Scotland.*)

Solicitor (*G2*), R. Brodie.
Deputy Solicitor (*G3*), N. W. Boe.
Divisional Solicitors (*G5*), J. B. Allan; K. F. Barclay; G. C. Duke; *R. Eadie; R. M. Henderson; G. Jackson; J. L. Jamieson; *Mrs. L. A. Lilliker; T. G. Walters.
*Seconded to Scottish Law Commission

Scottish Information Office
(*For the Scottish Departments and certain U.K. services*)

Director (*G5*), C. F. Corbett.
Deputy Director (*G6*), D. C. M. Beveridge.

Statistics

Chief Statistician (*G5*), A. M. Burnside.

Inquiry Reporters
16 Waterloo Place, Edinburgh EH1 3DN
[031–556 8400]

Chief Reporter (*G3*), A. G. Bell.
Deputy Chief Reporter (*G5*), W. D. Campbell.

DEPARTMENT OF AGRICULTURE AND FISHERIES FOR SCOTLAND
Chesser House, 500 Gorgie Road, Edinburgh
EH11 3AW
[031–443 4020]
Dover House, Whitehall, London, SW1A 2AU
[01–270 3000]

Secretary (*G2*), L. P. Hamilton, C.B.
Under Secretary (*G3*), D. J. Essery.
Fisheries Secretary (*G3*), W. A. P. Weatherston.
Assistant Secretaries (*G5*), T. A. Cameron; R. J. W. Clark; A. D. F. Findlay; J. W. L. Lonie; G. G. Lyall; L. V. McEwan; G. M. D. Thomson; E. J. Weeple; J. M. Whitelaw.
Principals (*G7*), D. J. Baird; J. Blaikie; D. R. Dickson; J. G. Donnelly; J. H. B. Fleming, T.D.; A. W. Gladwin; R. A. Grant; A. Johnston; F. J. Lawrie; A. Lister; W. Malcolm; I. F. McEwan; C. K. McIntosh; B. Naylor; D. Reid; W. B. Ritchie; D. M. Rowand; N. A. Stewart; T. A. Titterton; R. J. Walker.
Chief Agricultural Officer (*G3*), J. F. Hutcheson.
Deputy Chief Agricultural Officer (*G5*), W. A. Macgregor.
Assistant Chief Agricultural Officers (*G6*), D. R. J. Craven; J. A. Hardie; J. G. Muir; A. Robb; J. I. Woodrow.
Chief Agricultural Economist (*G6*), J. M. Dunn, D.Phil.
Chief Meat and Livestock Inspector (*G7*), A. Bain.
Chief Food and Dairy Officer (*G7*), M. E. M. Anderson.
Chief Surveyor (*G6*) N. Taylor.
Scientific Adviser (*G5*) A. M. Raven, Ph.D.
Senior Principal Scientific Officers (*G6*), R. J. Dowdell; T. W. Hegarty, Ph.D.; D. Thornton.

Agricultural Scientific Services
East Craigs, Edinburgh EH12 8NJ
[031–339 2355]

Director (*G5*) D. C. Graham, Ph.D., F.R.S.E.
Deputy Director (*G6*), J. R. Cutler.
Senior Principal Scientific Officers (*G6*), J. L. Keppie; M. J. Richardson.

Fisheries Research Services
Marine Laboratory, P.O. Box 101,
Victoria Road, Torry, Aberdeen AB9 8DB
[0224 876544]

Director and Co-ordinator of U.K. Fisheries Research and Development, A. D. Hawkins, Ph.D

Deputy Director (G5), D. N. MacLennan.
Senior Principal Scientific Officers (G6), J. M. Davies, ph.d.; R. Jones; A. L. S. Munro, ph.d.; C. S. Wardle, ph.d.

Freshwater Fisheries Laboratory,
Faskally, Pitlochry, Perthshire PH16 5LB
[0796 2060]

Senior Principal Scientific Officers (G6), R. G. J. Shelton, ph.d.; J. E. Thorpe, ph.d.

Sea Fisheries Inspectorate

Chief Inspector of Sea Fisheries (G6), J. F. Fenton.
Inspector of Salmon and Freshwater Fisheries for Scotland (G7), R. B. Williamson.
Marine Superintendent, Captain D. R. Corse
£23,650 to £24,031

Crofters Commission
4/6 Castle Wynd, Inverness IV2 3EQ
[0463 237231]

Chairman (part-time), A. Macleod, o.b.e. £22,667
Members (part-time), A. I. Macarthur; B. T. Hunter; D. A. Morrison; P. Morrison; I. G. Munro; W. Lawson; A. Bremner.
Secretary (G6), I. A. Macpherson.

Red Deer Commission
Knowsley, 82 Fairfield Road, Inverness IV3 5LH
[0463 231751]

Chairman, I. K. Mackenzie £11,900
Secretary, N. H. McCulloch ...... £11,639 to £14,629

SCOTTISH DEVELOPMENT DEPARTMENT
New St. Andrew's House, Edinburgh EH1 3SZ
[031–556 8400]
Dover House, Whitehall, London, SW1A 2AU
[01–270 3000]

Secretary (G2), T. R. H. Godden, c.b. (to Nov. 1987).
Under Secretaries (G3), H. H. Mills; D. G. MacKay.
Director, Historic Buildings and Monuments, D. Connelly.
Assistant Secretaries (G5), N. G. Campbell; Mrs. E. C. G. Craghill; M. J. P. Cunliffe; J. S. Graham; Mrs. M. B. Gunn; Miss E. A. MacKay; J. S. B. Martin; I. Maxwell; K. W. Moore; R. E. S. Robinson; A. B. Scott; Mrs. G. M. Stewart.
Principals (G7), M. T. Affolter; I. R. Anderson; M. T. S. Batho; I. G. Dewar; Mrs. W. Dickson; P. G. Drumm; M. A. Duffy; W. M. Giles; J. C. Halley; J. L. Helm; I. P. Hetherington; J. C. Judson; G. A. McHugh; I. J. MacKenzie; N. MacLeod; W. R. J. McQueen; D. J. Palmer; G. S. Pearson; Miss T. S. Teale; J. O. Wastle.

Professional Staff
Chief Engineer (G3), R. MacGillivray.
Deputy Chief Engineer (G5), A. C. Paton.
Assistant Chief Engineers (G6), W. Ferguson; N. G. Semple; J. O. Thorburn.
Director of Building and Chief Architect (G3), J. E. Gibbons, ph.d.
Deputy Director of Building and Deputy Chief Architect (G5), M. R. Miller.
Deputy Director of Building and Chief Quantity Surveyor (G5), D. C. Russell.
Assistant Director and Deputy Chief Quantity Surveyor (G6), A. Duncan, o.b.e.
Assistant Directors (G6), A. R. H. Bott; G. Gray; H. R. McGallum; R. W. Naismith.
Chief Planner (G3), A. Mackenzie.
Deputy Chief Planner (G5), D. R. Dare.
Assistant Chief Planners (G6), T. Williamson; A. W. Denham; I. R. Duncan; S. G. Fulton.
Chief Research Officer (G5), C. C. MacDonald.

Senior Principal Research Officers (G6), C. P. A. Levein, ph.d.; C. L. Wood.
Chief Road Engineer (G3), J. A. M. MacKenzie.
Deputy Chief Engineer (Roads) (G5), G. S. Marshall.
Deputy Chief Engineer (Bridges) (G5), W. R. Varley.
Assistant Chief Engineers (G6), J. Patience; R. D. Udall; J. Innes.
H.M. Chief Industrial Pollution Inspector (G5), I. W. W. Wright.
Chief Estates Officer (G6), R. I. K. White.
Principal Inspector of Ancient Monuments for Scotland, I. MacIvor .... £18,517–£21,343
Principal Inspector of Historic Buildings, D. M. Walker .... £18,517–£21,343

INDUSTRY DEPARTMENT
FOR SCOTLAND
New St. Andrew's House, Edinburgh EH1 3TA
[031–556 8400]
and
Dover House, Whitehall, SW1A 2AU
[01–270 3000]

Secretary and Chief Economic Adviser to the Secretary of State for Scotland (G2), R. G. L. McCrone, c.b., ph.d.
Under Secretaries (G3), J. F. Laing; W. W. Scott.
Assistant Secretaries (G5), P. A. Brady; G. D. Calder; Ms. L. Clare; R. S. Crofts; M. J. P. Cunliffe; Miss I. M. Low.
Senior Economic Advisers (G5), J. A. Peat; W. M. McNie.
Principals (G7), C. H. Coulthard; J. A. Ewing; S. W. Fox; M. A. Grant; J. C. Henderson; R. N. Irvine; A. McKean; A. K. MacLeod; Mrs. R. N. Menlowe; D. N. G. Reid; Mrs. A. Robson; D. A. Stewart.

Industrial Expansion
Alhambra House, 45 Waterloo Street, Glasgow
G2 6AT
[041–248 2855]

Under Secretary (G3), G. R. Wilson.
Industrial Adviser, D. E. Guy.
Assistant Secretaries (G5), S. F. Hampson; P. McKinlay.
Senior Principals (G6), J. E. Milne, o.b.e.; D. J. Fowles.
Principals (G7), W. C. Alison; D. A. Brew; J. A. Brown; Mrs. S. M. Quinn.

Locate in Scotland
120 Bothwell Street, Glasgow G2 7JP
[041–248 2700]

Director, Prof. N. Hood £36,500
Senior Principal (G6), J. McGhee.
Principal (G7), W. Malone.
H. Moody (*U.S.A.*)

SCOTTISH EDUCATION DEPARTMENT
New St. Andrew's House,
Edinburgh EH1 3SY
[031–556 8400]
and
Dover House, Whitehall, London, SW1A 2AU
[01–270 3000]

Secretary (G2), J. A. Scott, l.v.o.
Under Secretaries (G3), R. R. Hillhouse; P. MacKay.
Assistant Secretaries (G5), D. A. Campbell; J. R. Cuthbert, ph.d. (*Chief Statistician*); E. C. Davison; I. W. Gordon; K. Macrae; W. Moyes; E. C. Reavley; D. Wishart.
Senior Principal (G6), G. E. Brewerton.
Principals (G7), T. Blacklock; Mrs. M. Brannan; J. R. Brown; D. G. Campbell; W. Davidson; M. Ewart; C. C. Forsyth; J. C. Halley; F. H. Hunter; M. J.

Hunter; Mrs. E. Lewis; A. Lindsey; J. B. Lyall; N. MacLeod; R. E. Merrall; B. R. Morgan; B. J. O'Connor; R. I. Perrett; B. V. Surridge; I. M. Watt; G. P. Walker.

H.M. Inspectors of Schools

Senior Chief Inspector (G3), T. N. Gallagher.
Deputy Senior Chief Inspectors (G4), W. R. Ritchie; S. E. McCelland, PH.D.
Chief Inspectors (G5), W. T. Beveridge; W. F. L. Bigwood; L. Clark; A. H. Ferguson; G. P. D. Gordon; J. Howgego; A. S. McGlynn; D. W. Mack; D. A. Osler; A. M. Rankin.
Inspectors (G6), J. N. Alison; M. T. J. Axford; P. Banks; Mrs. W. Binnie; A. D. Blair; J. Boyes; Miss C. L. Boyle; M. J. Brown; Mrs. M. M. Browning; J. W. Burdin; D. C. Burgess; Miss G. C. Campbell; T. N. Carr; D. G. Carter; M. Q. Cramb; F. Crawford; A. H. B. Davidson; G. B. Debling; G. A. Dell; R. F. Dick; J. C. Dignan; G. H. C. Donaldson; J. T. Donaldson; D. W. Duncan; Miss K. M. Fairweather; B. Fryer; A. R. Gallon; K. G. Gavin; W. Geddes; A. B. Giovanazzi; G. D. Gray, PH.D.; T. O. Greig; R. A. Hawke; J. Hay, PH.D.; K. A. Hope; L. A. Hunter; M. Jack; J. Jackson, PH.D.; E. S. Kelly; D. E. Kelso; Ms. A. Kennedy; D. G. Kirkpatrick; I. Lawson; R. E. Lygo; M. McAllan; I. M. MacAskill; L. McCallum; D. McCalman; H. K. McCorkindale; J. J. McDonald; Mrs. M. A. Macfarlane; Ms. I. S. McGregor; H. M. MacLaren; C. R. MacLean; M. Macleod; D. R. McNicoll; A. J. Macpherson; A. Maltby; H. L. Martin; G. Mathison; W. M. Mein; Mrs. J. M. Millar; A. Milne; S. Milne, PH.D.; J. Mitchell; Miss E. R. Mowat; R. H. Nelson; B. Nickerson, PH.D.; A. M. Noble, PH.D.; I. P. Pascoe; W. M. Patterson; J. Picken; Miss A. H. M. Prain; R. B. Prescott; T. A. Rankin; J. C. Rankine; S. A. Ritchie; W. M. Roach, PH.D.; I. D. S. Robertson; J. N. Robertson; A. L. Robson; M. Roebuck; J. Rorrison; D. M. Russell; A. L. Small; E. P. Spencer; H. Stalker; A. M. Steele; W. Stevenson; Mrs. J. A. Stewart; W. P. Stewart; J. W. Thomson; R. M. S. Tuck; R. S. Weir; Miss G. A. White; R. G. Wilson; J. G. L. Wright; D. B. Young; R. W. J. Young, PH.D.

Social Work Services Group
43 Jeffrey Street, Edinburgh EH1 1DN
[031-556 8400]

The Social Work Services Group, which is attached to the Scottish Education Department, administers the provisions of the Social Work (Scotland) Act, 1968.
Under Secretary (G3), D. A. Leitch.
Assistant Secretaries (G5), D. A. Bennet; J. W. Sinclair; R. E. Smith.
Principals (G7), M. J. Hunter; D. G. Kerr; R. C. Lawson; D. R. Semple; D. Stewart; R. Walker.
Chief Social Work Adviser, D. Colvin
£30,884–£32,980
Senior Advisers, Ms. M. L. Hunt; F. A. O'Leary; I. C. Robertson; A. R. Sabine; J. I. Smith
£21,072–£26,409

SCOTTISH HOME AND HEALTH DEPARTMENT
St. Andrew's House,
Edinburgh EH1 3DE
[031-556 8400]
Dover House, Whitehall, London, SW1A 2AU
[01-270 3000]

Secretary (G2), W. K. Reid, C.B.
Under Secretaries (G3), Miss P. A. Cox; J. E. Fraser; J. Hamill; H. Morison.
Assistant Secretaries (G5), G. P. H. Aitken, T.D.; G. A. Anderson; J. W. Barron; C. M. Baxter; W. J. Fearnley; J. W. H. Irvine; R. D. Jackson; K. W.

McKay; D. Macniven, T.D.; Mrs. N. S. Munro; F. H. Orr; B. V. Philp; P. M. Russell; R. H. Scott; N. E. Sharp; D. Stevenson.
Senior Principal (G6), T. Collinson.
Principals (G7), A. G. Aitken; S. S. Anderson; J. Ballantyne; Mrs. E. E. R. Barnwell; H. W. Bradford; D. H. Brown; J. T. Brown; A. J. Cameron; L. C. Cunning; D. I. Dalgetty; D. J. Davidson; D. H. F. Dee; L. P. S. Dunbar; P. J. Fleming; J. Gilmour; I. W. Goodwin; Miss A. E. Hamilton; N. Harvey; D. M. Henderson; A. Howat; N. D. Ingram; D. K. C. Jeffrey; S. M. Liddle; M. J. Lowndes; C. M. A. Lugton; R. S. T. MacEwen; K. B. T. MacKenzie; P. McLaren; D. C. Macnab; Miss M. M. Marshall; A. J. Matheson; I. F. Munro; R. Patton; G. A. Paul; D. A. Robertson; W. F. Robertson; A. J. Rushworth; A. Simmen; M. P. Sivell; T. Spence; P. D. Stephenson; I. C. Stewart; I. R. N. Stewart; R. S. Stewart; R. Tait; A. W. Wallace; B. F. Warren; A. G. Young.

Medical Services

Chief Medical Officer (G2), I. S. Macdonald.
Deputy Chief Medical Officer (G3), G. A. Scott.
Principal Medical Officers, Margaret Hennigan; A. C. McBlane; A. D. McIntyre; R. A. Ratcliff; A. B. Young .... £29,965–£31,338
Senior Medical Officers, R. E. G. Aitken, T.D.; P. W. Brooks; R. G. Covell; D. C. Drummond; J. B. P. Ferguson; C. F. Fleming; G. I. Forbes; W. Forbes; J. M. Forrester; W. M. Gilmour; G. Gilray; Ms. M. R. Halley; R. M. Melville, O.B.E.; J. S. Patterson; Ms. E. M. K. Sowler; O. A. Thores; A. W. Watt; G. C. M. Watt £28,215
Senior Regional Medical Officers, I. G. Conn; H. McBain .... £28,194 to £29,512
Regional Medical Officers, P. I. Brown; Elspeth C. Carrick; J. A. Fergusson; T. E. S. Fergusson; G. W. G. Hunter; K. Inglis; G. McKay; A. S. Mackenzie; Elizabeth M. Melville; H. D. R. Munro; P. I. T. Walker .... £17,593 to £24,926
Chief Scientist, Prof. R. D. Weir, O.B.E.
Chief Dental Officer, N. K. Colquhoun
£28,194 to £29,512
Deputy Chief Dental Officer, J. R. Wild £27,065
Regional Dental Officers, T. G. L. Bell; F. D. Murray; G. A. Reid .... £17,593 to £24,926
Chief Nursing Officer, Miss M. G. Auld £34,395
Chief Pharmacist (G6), G. Calder.

Miscellaneous Appointments

H.M. Chief Inspector of Constabulary, A. Morrison, C.V.O., Q.P.M. £42,647
H.M. Chief Inspector of Prisons, T. B. Buyers, O.B.E. £16,239
Commandant, Scottish Police College, T. J. Whitson, O.B.E.................................£31,860
H.M. Chief Inspector of Fire Services, R. J. Knowlton, C.B.E., Q.F.S.M. .... £27,574 to £30,759
Commandant, Scottish Fire Service Training School, (vacant) .... £16,296 to £17,046
Secretary, Scottish Health Service Planning Council, W. J. Farquhar.

Prisons Group
St. Margaret's House, 151 London Road,
Edinburgh EH8 7TQ
[031-556 8400]

Director of Scottish Prison Service, A. M. Thomson
£30,793
Assistant Secretary, Deputy Director (Administration), J. W. H. Irvine .... £22,222 to £27,065
Assistant Controller, Deputy Director (Operations), W. McVey £28,315
Deputy Director (Personnel and Supplies) (G5), W. J. Fearnley.
Deputy Director (Regime Services) (G6), T. Collinson.
Deputy Director (Co-ordinator), T. J. Kelly.

Prison Governors

Governor I..............................	£25,159
Governor II..........................	£18,872–£22,575
Governor III......................	£15,323–£18,636

Aberdeen (III), A. S. Ogilvie.
Barlinnie (I), A. R. Walker.
Barlinnie Special Unit (III), E. J. Campbell.
Castle Huntly Young Offenders Institution (III), E. J. Brownsmith.
Cornton Vale (II), J. Meiklejohn.
Dumfries Prison (III), G. R. Bond.
Dungavel, Strathaven (III), R. R. H. Glen.
Edinburgh (I), J. M. Brownlee.
Friarton Prison, R. Park.......... £12,912–£14,976
Glenochil Young Offenders Institution and Detention Centre (I), W. G. Walker.
Greenock (III), A. G. Coyle.
Inverness (III), F. Sankey.
Longriggend Remand Institution (III), R. L. Houghin.
Low Moss (III), A. P. Spence.
Noranside (III), J. C. Stuart.
Penninghame, D. F. Houston...... £12,912–£14,976
Perth (II), A. Thomson.
Peterhead (I), A. J. Smith.
Polmont Young Offenders Institution (II), G. B. Duncan.
Shotts (II), P. L. Abernethy.
Scottish Prison Service College (II), M. J. Milne.

Mental Welfare Commission for Scotland
25 Drumsheugh Gardens, Edinburgh EH3 7NS
[031–225 7034]

Chairman, P. C. Millar, O.B.E.
Commissioners, P. H. Brodie; Prof. T. D. Campbell; R. G. Davis; Dr. L. Dunbar; Mrs. J. B. M. Ellis, O.B.E.; A. Findlay, M.B.E.; Ms. A. M. Green; Mrs. A. I. Huggins; D. A. Macdonald, O.B.E.; Mrs. H. S. Mein; M. O'Reilly; Prof. P. Prophit; Dr. H. S. Ross; J. G. Sutherland.
Medical Commissioners, H. C. Fowlie; W. Boyd.
Secretary, J. S. Graham.

Counsel to the Secretary of State for Scotland under the Private Legislation Procedure (Scotland) Act, 1936 (50 Frederick Street, Edinburgh.—(031–226 6499)).
Senior Counsel, G. S. Douglas, Q.C.
Junior Counsel, N. M. P. Morrison.

NATIONAL HEALTH SERVICE, SCOTLAND

Health Boards
Argyll and Clyde, Gilmour House, Paisley. *Chairman*, J. D. Ryan. *General Manager*, I. C. Smith.

Ayrshire and Arran, P.O. Box 13, Hunters Avenue, Ayr. *Chairman*, W. S. Fyfe. *General Manager*, J. M. Eckford.

Borders, Huntlyburn, Melrose, Roxburghshire. *Chairman*, J. Gibb. *General Manager*, D. A. Peters.

Dumfries and Galloway, Nithbank, Dumfries. *Chairman*, J. A. M. McIntyre. *General Manager*, M. D. Cook.

Fife, Glenrothes House, North Street, Glenrothes. *Chairman*, Mrs. P. A. H. Ferguson. *General Manager*, J. Leigh.

Forth Valley, 33 Spittal Street, Stirling. *Chairman*, L. S. M. Hynd. *General Manager*, A. R. Robertson.

Grampian, 1–7 Albyn Place, Aberdeen. *Chairman*, C. W. Ellis. *General Manager*, H. Fullerton.

Greater Glasgow, 225 Bath Street, Glasgow. *Chairman*, Dr. T. J. Thomson. *General Manager*, L. Peterken.

Highland, Reay House, 17 Old Edinburgh Road, Inverness. *Chairman*, J. McWilliam. *General Manager*, R. R. W. Stewart.

Lanarkshire, 14 Beckford Street, Hamilton, Lanarkshire. *Chairman*, Mrs. B. M. Gunn, O.B.E. *General Manager*, F. Clark.

Lothian, 11 Drumsheugh Gardens, Edinburgh. *Chairman*, R. B. Weatherstone. *General Manager*, W. J. Taylor.

Orkney, Balfour Hospital, New Scapa Road, Kirkwall, Orkney. *Chairman*, J. D. M. Robertson. *General Manager*, Dr. J. I. Cromarty.

Shetland, 28 Burgh Road, Lerwick. *Chairman*, Mrs. F. Grains. *General Manager*, D. C. March.

Tayside, P.O. Box 75, Vernonholme, Riverside Drive, Dundee. *Chairman*, D. B. Grant. *General Manager*, Dr. R. C. Graham.

Western Isles, 37 South Beach Street, Stornoway, Isle of Lewis. *Chairman*, Mrs. M. A. Macmillan. *General Manager*, J. J. Glover.

Common Services Agency
Trinity Park House, South Trinity Road,
Edinburgh EH5 3SE

Secretary, J. R. Y. Mutch. *Treasurer*, J. W. Morrison.

GENERAL REGISTER OFFICE (Scotland)
New Register House, Edinburgh EH1 3YT
[031–556 3952]

Registrar General, Dr. C. M. Glennie
£28,975–£30,475
Deputy Registrar General, J. N. Randall
£24,739–£28,215
Statisticians, D. A. Orr; J. Arrundale; F. G. Thomas
£14,927–£20,292
Principals, G. F. Baird; I. G. Bowie; A. M. Titterington........................ £14,927–£20,292

SEA FISH INDUSTRY AUTHORITY
Sea Fisheries House, 10 Young Street,
Edinburgh EH2 4JQ
[031–225 2515]

Chairman, J. P. Rettie, T.D.
Chief Executive, J. C. H. Richman.
Deputy Chief Executive, P. D. Chaplin.
Finance Director, A. Downie.
Technical Director, A. G. Hopper.
Marketing Director, R. M. Kennedy.
Secretary, R. A. Davie.

SECURITIES AND INVESTMENTS BOARD
3 Royal Exchange Buildings, EC3V 3NL
[01–283 2474]

The Securities and Investments Board was formed in 1985 and is the designated agency, under the Financial Services Act, 1986, to regulate the activities of the investment businesses in the U.K. Although not a statutory body, the Board has transferred powers under the 1986 Act to recognize self-regulating organizations, recognized professional bodies, recognized investment exchanges and recognized clearing houses, and directly to authorize firms to do investment business in the U.K. The Board also has the power to act as a prosecution authority in respect of persons carrying out authorizable business whilst unauthorized.

Members of the Board are appointed by agreement between the Secretary of State for Trade and Industry and the Governor of the Bank of England. The Chairman and Chief Executive are full-time Board members; the others are part-time and non-executive.

The Board

Chairman, Sir Kenneth Berrill, K.C.B.
Deputy Chairmen, Sir Mark Weinberg; R. N. Quartano, C.B.E.
Members (part-time), A. V. Alexander, C.B.E.; Prof. A. Budd; D. M. Child, C.B.E.; J. Clement; A. Cox, Jr.; R. G. Hodgson; J. S. Kerridge; P. J. Manser; W. Proudfoot; E. E. Ray; Hon. W. G. Runciman, C.B.E.; Sir Philip Shelbourne; Mrs R. Waterhouse, C.B.E.; R. B. Williamson.
Chief Executive, R. H. F. Croft, C.B.

Management

The Chairman.
The Chief Executive.
Directors of Divisions:
  Finance, S. A. Carter.
  Futures and Options, M. B. Gittins.
  Information Services, B. W. Smith.
  Intermediaries, M. J. Vile.
  International Securities Regulation, R. J. Britton.
  Investment Management and Products, J. Orme.
  Legal Services, M. Blair.
  Regulation, A. J. Thrall.
Deputy Directors:
  Futures and Options, P.E. Thompson.
  Intermediaries, A. Selman.
  International Securities Regulation, A. King.
  Investment Management, J. Hickman.
  Legal, J. B. Evans; A. Whittaker.
  Personnel and Administration, J. L. Clark.
  Press and Information, B. A. Conway.
  Regulation, H. D. Jenkins.
Secretary to the Board, T. E. Allen.

SOLICITORS COMPLAINTS BUREAU
Portland House, Stag Place, SW1E 5BL
[01-834 2288]

Director, J. P. S. Thompson.

SPORTS COUNCIL
16 Upper Woburn Place, WC1H 0QP
[01–388 1277]

The Sports Council exists to promote the development of sport and foster the provision of facilities for sport and recreation in Great Britain.
Chairman, J. W. Smith, C.B.E.
Director-General, J. D. Wheatley.

HER MAJESTY'S STATIONERY OFFICE
St. Crispins, Duke Street, Norwich NR3 1PD
[0603–622211]

Her Majesty's Stationery Office was established in 1786 and is the British Government's central organization for the supply of printing, binding, office supplies and office machinery of all kinds, for the Public Service at home and abroad; H.M.S.O. is also the Government's publisher and has bookshops for the sale of Government publications in London, Edinburgh, Manchester, Bristol, Birmingham and Belfast. H.M.S.O. obtains most of its supplies from commercial sources by competitive tender, except that about 20 per cent of its printing requirements is done in its own printing works.

Since April 1, 1980, H.M.S.O. has been a trading fund established under the Government Trading Funds Act, 1973.

Salary List

Grade 2	£43,500–£45,500
Grade 4	£30,344–£31,844
Grade 5	£27,765–£28,215
Grade 6	£18,786–£25,335
Grade 7	£15,030–£20,292

Controller and Chief Executive (G2), J. A. Dole.
  Executive Assistant, Mrs. M. E. Nisbet.
Director General of Printing and Publishing (G4), K. A. Allen.
Director General of Corporate Services (G4), M. D. Lynn.

Publications Division

Director (G5), C. J. Penn.
General Manager Publications Centre (G6), S. M. Rae.

Supply Division

Director (G5), D. W. Ray.

Finance and Planning Division

Director (G5), A. J. Davies.

Personnel Services Division

Director (G5), D. J. Balls.

Industrial Personnel Division

Director (G6), D. G. Forbes.

Marketing Services

Head (G6), A. M. Cole.

Information Technology Division

Director (G6), C. N. Southgate.

Production Division

Director (G5), D. J. Wintle.
Director of Parliamentary Printing (G6), E. Hendry.
Director of Reprographics (G7), R. S. Moore.

Technical Services

Head, Origination (G7), T. J. Soutar.
Head, Printing (G7), H. S. Todd.

Print Procurement Division

Director (G5), E. B. McKendrick.

Scotland
Bankhead Avenue, Edinburgh EH11 4AB

Bookshop: 71 Lothian Road, Edinburgh EH3 9AZ
Director (G7), G. A. H. Turner.

Northern Ireland
IDB House, Chichester Street, Belfast BT1 4PS

Retail and Trade Bookshop: 80 Chichester Street, Belfast BT1 4JY
Director (G7), Miss V. J. Wilson.

London
Publications Centre: 51 Nine Elms Lane, SW8 5BR.
Bookshops: Retail—49 High Holborn, WC1V 6HB.
Wholesale and Post Orders—P. O. Box 276, SW8 5DT.

Manchester
Broadway, Chadderton, Oldham, Lancs. OL9 9QH
Bookshop: 9–21 Princess Street, Manchester M60 8AS.

Bristol
Ashton Vale Road, Bristol BS3 2HN
Bookshop: Southey House, Wine Street, Bristol BS1 2BQ.

Birmingham
Bookshop: 258 Broad Street, Birmingham B1 2HE.

STATUTE LAW COMMITTEE
House of Lords, SW1A 0PW

The Committee exercises a general supervision over the form of the statute law and of Statutory Instruments. It is also responsible for the publication of amended editions of the Statutes, including the current official revised edition of the Statutes in Force.

Chairman, The Lord Chancellor.
Vice-Chairman, The Hon. Mr. Justice Beldam.
Members, The Hon. Lord Maxwell; The Attorney General; The Lord Advocate; The Lord Scarman, P.C., O.B.E.; The Lord Mackay of Clashfern, P.C., Q.C.; The Lord Lowry, P.C.; Rt. Hon. J. Morris, Q.C., M.P.; Rt. Hon. P. Archer, Q.C., M.P.; Sir Anthony Buck, Q.C., M.P.; Sir Derek Oulton, K.C.B.; D. Rippengal, C.B., Q.C.; H. Knorpel, C.B.; C. H. de Waal, C.B.; N. J. Adamson, C.B., Q.C.; Sir John Sainty, K.C.B.; Sir Kenneth Bradshaw, K.C.B.; Sir John Bailey, K.C.B.; Sir William Fraser, K.C.B.; Sir Brian Cubbon, G.C.B.; Sir Terence Heiser, K.C.B.; Miss A. Mueller, C.B.; K. A. Allen; H. W. Gamon, C.B.E., M.C.

Secretary, B. P. Keith.

Statutory Publications Office
Queen Anne's Chambers,
28 Broadway, SW1H 9JS
[01–273 3000]

Editor, J. M. Gibson.

OFFICE OF TELECOMMUNICATIONS
Atlantic House, Holborn Viaduct, EC1N 2HQ
[01–353 4020]

OFTEL is a non-Ministerial Government Department headed by a Director General, which is responsible for supervising telecommunications activities in the U.K.

Its principal functions are to ensure that holders of telecommunications licences comply with their licence conditions; to maintain and promote effective competition in telecommunications; to promote, in respect of prices, quality and variety the interests of consumers, purchasers and other users of telecommunication services and apparatus.

The Director General has powers to deal with anti-competitive practices and monopoly situations. He also has a duty to consider all reasonable complaints and representations about telecommunication apparatus and services.

Director General, Prof. B. V. Carsberg.
Deputy Director General, W. R. B. Wigglesworth.
Director of P.T.O. Licensing, G. P. Knight.
Director of Apparatus Approval, J. P. Compton.
Head of Consumer Affairs, Mrs. J. T. Percy-Davis.
Head of Information, D. C. Redding.

NATIONAL THEATRE BOARD
South Bank, SE1 9PX
[01–928 2033]

Chairman, The Lord Rayne.
Members, R. Baird; T. Burrill; The Lord Chorley; R. Clutton; J. Hannam, M.P.; Sonia Melchett; R. M. Mills; The Lord Mishcon; Sir Derek Mitchell, K.C.B., C.V.O.; J. Mortimer, Q.C.; The Lady Plowden, D.B.E.; Lois Sieff; J. Whitney; Sir Peter Parker, M.V.O.

Secretary, D. Gosling.

DEPARTMENT OF TRADE AND INDUSTRY
1 Victoria Street, SW1H 0ET
[01–215 7877]

The Department is responsible for:
(a) international trade policy, including the promotion of U.K. trade interests in the European Community, G.A.T.T., O.E.C.D., U.N.C.T.A.D. and other international organizations.
(b) under the direction of the British Overseas Trade Board, the promotion of U.K. exports and assistance to exporters.
(c) policy in relation to industry, including the general promotion of the interests of industry and assistance to industry; specific interest in all manufacturing and service industries apart from those covered by other Departments; regional policy, Inner Cities Initiative, enterprise and deregulation, and regional industrial assistance (some of this applying only to England); and policy in relation to the public bodies British Shipbuilders, the British Steel Corporation, the Post Office and the British Technology Group.
(d) competition policy and consumer protection, including relations with the Office of Fair Trading and the Monopolies and Mergers Commission, and the National Weights and Measures Laboratory.
(e) policy on science and technology and research and development matters, standards and designs, support for innovation, and the administration of the National Physical Laboratory, National Engineering Laboratory, Warren Spring Laboratory and the Laboratory of the Government Chemist.
(f) the administration of company legislation and the Companies Registration Office; the Insolvency Service; the regulation of the insurance industry; the regulation of radio frequencies; and the Patent Office.
(g) the Business Statistics Office.

Salaries
Secretary of State £33,145
Ministers of State £22,875
Parliamentary Under Secretaries of State . . . £16,885

Grade 1	£64,739
Grade 2	£43,264–£45,349
Grade 3	£33,725–£36,852
Grade 4	£28,975–£30,475
Grade 5	£24,789–£28,215
Grade 6	£18,786–£25,335
Grade 7	£14,927–£20,292
Inspector General of the Insolvency Service	£36,852
Deputy Inspectors General	£29,247
Inspector of Companies	£29,247

Research Establishments

Director, National Physical Laboratory	£40,058
Director, National Engineering Laboratory	£36,852
Government Chemist	£37,825
Director, Warren Spring Laboratory	£35,289

Secretary of State for Trade and Industry and President of the Board of Trade, THE RT. HON. THE LORD YOUNG OF GRAFFHAM.
Principal Private Secretary, Dr. T. Walker.
Parliamentary Private Secretary, N. Baker, M.P.
Chancellor of the Duchy of Lancaster and Minister of Trade and Industry, THE RT. HON. KENNETH CLARKE, Q.C., M.P.
Private Secretary, T. P. Abraham.
Parliamentary Private Secretary, J. Taylor, M.P.
Minister for Trade, THE HON. ALAN CLARK, M.P.
Private Secretary, Miss M. E. K. Davies.
Parliamentary Under Secretary of State for Corporate and Consumer Affairs, The Hon. Francis Maude, M.P.
Private Secretary, D. Roe.
Parliamentary Under Secretary of State for Industry, John Butcher, M.P.
Private Secretary, T. J. Soane.
Parliamentary Under Secretary of State for Industry, Robert Atkins, M.P.
Private Secretary, M. McHardy.
Permanent Secretary (G1), Sir Brian Hayes, K.C.B.
Private Secretary, K. Lussey.
Deputy Secretaries (G2), D. M. Dell; A. J. Macdonald; Dr. R. F. Coleman (*Chief Scientist and Engineer*); R. Mountfield; B. W. Oakley, C.B.E. (*Alvey Directorate*); Miss E. M. Llewellyn-Smith; C. W. Roberts, C.B.; R. Williams; H. H. Liesner, C.B. (*Chief Economic Adviser*); G. A. Hosker (*The Solicitor*); W. M. Knighton, C.B. (*Principal Establishment and Finance Officer*).
Parliamentary Clerk, T. A. Hardbattle.
Head of Policy Planning Unit (G5), Dr. T. E. H. Walker.

International Trade Policy Division
1 Victoria Street, SW1H 0ET
[01–215 7877]

Under Secretary (G3), A. C. Hutton.
Heads of Branch (G5), M. D. C. Johnson; P. Gent; Miss A. E. Stoddart.

Overseas Trade Divisions
1 Victoria Street, SW1H 0ET
[01–215 7877]

Division 1 (*Projects and Export Policy*)

Under Secretary (G3), C. B. Benjamin.
Heads of Branch (G5), C. A. Palmer; F. B. Wheeler; C. E. Blundell.

Division 2
(*N. America, N.E. and S.E. Asia, China, Hong Kong and Export Licensing Branch*)

Under Secretary (G3), J. A. Cooke.
Heads of Branch (G5), W. J. Hall; J. V. Hagestadt; E. W. Beston.

Division 3

Under Secretary (G3), A. J. Hunter.

Administration and Finance
Head of Branch (G5), M. G. Roberts.

Exports to Europe Branch
Head of Branch (G5), K. D. Levinson.

Export Data Branch
Director (G6), M. J. Morrison.

Fairs and Promotions Branch
Head of Branch (G5), G. J. Bradshaw.

Soviet Union and Eastern Europe
Head of Branch (G5), K. W. N. George.

Division 4 (*Middle East, Africa, Latin America, the Caribbean and Australasia*)

Under Secretary (G3), A. Titchener.
Heads of Branch (G5), H. R. Owen; M. Petter; M. A. S. Garrod.

European Policy Division
1 Victoria Street, SW1H 0ET
[01–215 7877]

Under Secretary (G3), Miss M. T. Neville-Rolfe.
Heads of Branch (G5), P. Loughead; R. A. Brown.

British Overseas Trade Board
1 Victoria Street, SW1H 0ET
[01–215 7877]

President, The Secretary of State.
Chairman, Sir James Cleminson, M.C.
Vice-Chairman, H.R.H. The Duke of Kent, K.G., G.C.M.G., G.C.V.O.
Members, R. Q. Braithwaite, C.M.G.; Gisla Burg, C.B.E.; D. M. Dell, C.B.; A. K. Edwards, M.B.E.; T. P. Frost; Dr. A. Hayes; M. R. Hoffman; D. A. Holland, C.B.E.; Sir Philip Jones, C.B.; W. B. Jordan; The Earl of Limerick, K.B.E.; Sir Godfrey Messervy; J. W. Parsons; M. S. Perry, O.B.E.; Dr. N. B. Smith, C.B.E.; M. G. Stephens; G. S. Tucker, C.B.E..
Chief Executive, D. M. Dell, C.B.
Secretary (G5), M. G. Roberts.
Head of Publicity Unit (G6), S. Lyle Smith.

Patent Office and Industrial Property and Copyright Department
State House, 66–71 High Holborn, WC1R 4TP
[01–831 2525]

Comptroller General, P. J. Cooper.
Assistant Comptrollers, T. W. Sage; V. Tarnofsky.
Assistant Registrar of Trade Marks, J. M. Myall.

Insurance Division
10–18 Victoria Street, SW1H 0NN
[01–215 7877]

Under Secretary (G3), T. Muir.
Heads of Branch (G5), V. F. Lane; D. W. Hellings; M. D. Oldham.

Financial Services Division
10–18 Victoria Street, SW1H 0NN
[01–215 7877]

Under Secretary (G3), B. J. G. Hilton.
Heads of Branch (G5), A. C. G. Lowry; R. H. S. Wells; Mrs. S. E. Brown.

Companies Division
10–18 Victoria Street, SW1H 0NN
[01–215 7877]

Under Secretary (G3), Mrs. S. E. Brown.
Heads of Branch (G5), D. L. Gatland; Mrs. M. A. Wilks.

Companies Investigation Branch
2–14 Bunhill Row, EC1Y 8LL
[01–606 4071]

Inspector of Companies, G. Clark.

Companies Registration Office
Companies House, Crown Way, Maindy, Cardiff
CF4 3UZ
[0222–388588]

Registrar of Companies for England and Wales (*G5*),
S. R. Curtis.
London Search Room, 55–71 City Road, EC1Y 1BB
[01–253 9393]

102 George Street, Edinburgh EH2 3DJ
[031–225 5774]
Registrar for Scotland, E. T. K. Lougheed.

**Mechanical Engineering and Manufacturing
Technology Division**
Ashdown House, 123 Victoria Street, SW1E 6RB
[01–212 7676]

Under Secretary (*G3*), J. E. Cammell.
Heads of Branch (*G5*), H. M. Lanyon; B. N. Steel; R.
C. McVickers.

Department of Economic Development
64 Chichester Street, Belfast
[0232–233233]
Registrar for Northern Ireland, C. Stutt.

The Insolvency Service
2–14 Bunhill Row, EC1Y 8LL
[01–606 4071]

Inspector General of the Insolvency Service, M. Clark.
Deputy Inspectors General, P. D. Pink; P. R. Joyce;
A. K. Sales.

Consumer Affairs Division
10–18 Victoria Street, SW1H 0NN
[01–215 7877]

Under Secretary (*G3*), C. T. Newton.
Heads of Branch (*G5*), R. P. Hope; F. W. Willis; R. E.
Palmer; D. Jones.
Trading Standards Adviser (*G5*), D. Jones.

Air Division
Kingsgate House, 66–74 Victoria Street,
SW1E 6SW
[01–215 7877]

Under Secretary (*G3*), M. J. Michell.
Heads of Branch (*G5*), M. K. O'Shea; J. M. Bowder.
Grade 6, J. R. Collingbourne; A. W. R. Allcock.

Research and Technology Policy Division
Ashdown House, 123 Victoria Street, SW1E 6RB
[01–212 7676]

Under Secretary (*G3*), B. Murray.
Heads of Branch (*G5*), J. H. Chapman; R. C. Dobbie;
J. D. Howarth; A. W. Keddie.

National Physical Laboratory
Teddington, Middx. TW11 0LW
[01–977 3222]

Director (*G3*), Dr. P. Dean, C.B.

Laboratory of the Government Chemist
Cornwall House, Waterloo Road, SE1 8XY
[01–211 7900]

Government Chemist (*G3*), A. Williams.

National Engineering Laboratory
East Kilbride, Glasgow G75 0QU
[03552–20222]

Director (*G3*), Dr. D. A. Bell.

Warren Spring Laboratory
Gunnels Wood Road, Stevenage, Herts SG1 2BX
[0438–3388]

Director (*G3*), Dr. J. S. S. Reay.

National Weights and Measures Laboratory
Teddington, Middx. TW11 0JZ
[01–977 3222]

Director (*G5*), Dr. P. B. Clapham.

General Policy Division
1 Victoria Street, SW1H 0ET
[01–215 7877]

Under Secretary (*G3*), S. W. Treadgold.
Heads of Branch (*G5*), J. M. Healey; B. E. Armstrong;
D. J. Hall; R. J. Allpress; R. E. Allen.

Enterprise and Deregulation Unit
1 Victoria Street, SW1H 0ET
[01–215 7877]

Under Secretary (*G3*), R. Hewes.

Quality Design and Education Division
Bridge Place, 88/89 Eccleston Square, SW1V 1PT
[01–212 7676]

Under Secretary (*G3*), Mrs. P. A. Denham.
Heads of Branch (*G5*), Dr. E. B. Bates; M. R. Cohen;
C. L. Jackson; D. M. Forrester.

**Shipbuilding and Electrical Engineering
Division**
Ashdown House, 123 Victoria Street, SW1E 6RB
[01–212 7676]

Under Secretary (*G3*), D. R. C. Durie.
Heads of Branch (*G5*), D. R. Coates; D. M. Hoddinott;
P. Goodman.

British National Space Centre
Millbank Tower, Millbank, SW1P 4QU
[01–211 3000]

Director General (*G2*), (vacant).
Director of Policy and Programmes (*G3*), J. C.
Leeming.
Heads of Branch (*G5*), R. D. Hart; Dr. B. R. Martin;
A. C. Nicholas.

Telecommunications and Posts Division
Kingsgate House, 66–74 Victoria Street,
SW1E 6SW
[01–215 7877]

Under Secretary (*G3*), R. J. Priddle.
Heads of Branch (*G5*), J. E. Avery; L. G. Faulkener;
S. R. Temple; M. J. C. Butcher.

Radiocommunications Division
Waterloo Bridge House, Waterloo Road, SE1 8UA
[01–275 3000]

Under Secretary (*G3*), A. J. Nieduszynski.
Director (*G4*), Dr. K. C. Shotton.
Heads of Branch (*G5*), M. Goddard; M. P. Davies; M.
V. Coolican; R. A. Bedford; B. A. Heatley; (*G6*) Dr.
A. C. D. Whitehouse.

Alvey Directorate
Kingsgate House, 66–74 Victoria Street,
SW1E 6SW
[01–215 7877]

Director (*G2*), B. W. Oakley, C.B.E.
Deputy Director (*G3*), S. L. H. Clark.
Director of Administration (*G5*), R. L. Hird.
Directors of Alvey Programme, K. A. Bartlett; R.
Morland; D. N. Shorter; D. G. Morgan.

Minerals and Metals Division
Ashdown House, 123 Victoria Street, SW1E 6RB
[01–212 7676]

Under Secretary (G3), J. F. Mogg.
Heads of Branch (G5), R. I. Roger; V. F. Lane; R. L. Long; J. P. Spencer.

Chemicals, Textiles, Paper, Timber and Miscellaneous Manufacturing and Service Industries Division
Ashdown House, 123 Victoria Street, SW1E 6RB
[01–212 7676]

Under Secretary (G3), P. M. S. Corley.
Heads of Branch (G5), P. Robinson; Miss V. E. Evans; M. S. Bremner; Miss S. E. Harding; Dr. H. N. M. Stewart.

Vehicles Division
Ashdown House, 123 Victoria Street, SW1E 6RB
[01–212 7676]

Under Secretary (G3), M. J. A. Cochlin.
Heads of Branch (G5), S. J. Bowen; Mrs. C. E. D. Bell; *(G6)* P. Neale.

Industrial Financial Appraisal Division
Bridge Place, 88–89 Eccleston Square, SW1V 1PT

Under Secretary (G3), J. A. Knox.
Heads of Branch (G5), A. Berry; G. T. Pearson; A. W. G. Chatto; *(G6)* N. A. T. Hobbs.
Directors, T. J. Bellamy; A. Bray; P. Mason.

Inner Cities Unit
1 Victoria Street, SW1H 0ET
[01–215 7877]

Under Secretary (G3), N. H. Perry.

Investment and Development Division
Bridge Place, 88/89 Eccleston Square, SW1V 1PT
[01–212 7676]

Under Secretary (G3), F. R. Mingay.
Heads of Branch (G5), B. D. Winkett; M. S. Bremner; J. C. S. Priston; D. Harrison-Harvey.

Information Technology Division
Kingsgate House, 66–74 Victoria Street, SW1E 6SW
[01–215 7877]

Under Secretary (G3), W. B. Willott.
Heads of Branch (G5), R. Foster; M. E. Stanley; H. L. Evans; J. P. Hobday.

Electronics Applications Division
29 Bressenden Place, SW1E 5DT
[01–213 3000]

Under Secretary (G3), J. H. Major.
Heads of Branch (G5), J. G. Noyes; M. E. Farry; H. J. Ivey; A. C. Conway.

DEPARTMENT OF TRADE AND INDUSTRY SERVICES ORGANIZATION
Deputy Secretaries (G2), H. H. Liesner, C.B. (*Chief Economic Adviser*); G. A. Hosker (*The Solicitor*); W. M. Knighton (*Principal Establishment and Finance Officer*).

Personnel Management Division
Allington Towers,
17 Allington Street, SW1
[01–215 7877]

Under Secretary (G3), N. F. Ledsome.
Heads of Branch (G5), P. S. Salvidge; D. W. F. Johnson; J. F. Bailes; Dr. R. Wood.

Management Services and Manpower Division
29 Bressenden Place, SW1E 5DT
[01–215 7877]

Under Secretary (G3), R. M. Rumbelow.
Heads of Branch (G5), K. J. Doyle; N. Bernard; R. J. Meadway; E. W. Pearcey.

Finance and Resource Management Division
Ashdown House, 123 Victoria Street, SW1E 6RB
[01–212 7676]

Under Secretary (G3), A. C. Russell.
Heads of Branch (G5), E. H. Whitaker; N. R. Thornton; A. C. Elkington; P. R. S. Hartnack.

Accounts Branch
24–26 Newport Road, Cardiff CF2 1SY
[0222–492611]

Director of Accounts, A. C. Elkington.

Internal Audit
Ebury Bridge House, 2/18 Ebury Bridge Road, SW1W 8QD
[01–730 9678]

Head of Internal Audit, K. Holt

Solicitor's Office
10–18 Victoria Street, SW1H 0NQ
[01–215 7877]

The Solicitor (G2), G. A Hosker.
Under Secretaries (G3), P. H. Bovey; J. R. Mallinson; J. R. Woolman.
Assistant Solicitors (G5), D. M. Bailey; Mrs. N. M. P. Chappell; C. J. Cook; R. D. Fayers; Miss P. A. E. Granados; R. Higgins; C. S. Kerse; R. M. Malbey; I. K. Mathers; Miss K. Morton; Miss E. N. O'Flynn; Miss J. Richardson; J. W. Roberts; Mrs. F. A. Scarborough; J. M. Stanley; Miss J. V. Stokes; A. M. Susman; E. A. Thompson.

Information Division
1 Victoria Street, SW1H 0ET
[01–215 7877]

Head of Information (G4), Miss C. Bowe.
Deputy Heads of Information Division (G6), Miss G. P. Samuel; T. Bryan.

Economics Divisions
1 Victoria Street, SW1H 0ET
[01–215 7877]

Chief Economic Adviser (G2), H. H. Liesner, C.B.

Division 1
Ashdown House, 123 Victoria Street, SW1E 6RB
[01–212 7676]

Under Secretary (G3), J. R. Shepherd.
Heads of Branch (G5), B. M. Nonehebel; J. M. Barber; J. A. S. Robertson.

Division 2
1 Victoria Street, SW1H 0ET
[01–215 7877]

Under Secretary (G3), A. Whiting.
Heads of Branch (G5), P. J. Goate; M. S. Bradbury; D. A. Miner.

Statistics Divisions
1 Victoria Street, SW1H 0ET
[01–215 7877]

Division 1
Millbank Tower, Millbank, SW1P 4QU
[01–211 3000]

Under Secretary (G3), N. Harvey.
Heads of Branch (G5), R. L. Butchart; J. Walker; J. Astin.

Division 2
1 Victoria Street, SW1H 0ET
[01–215 7877]

Under Secretary (G3), P. J. Stibbard.
Heads of Branch (G5), W. E. Boyd; P. H. Richardson; G. Jenkinson.

Business Statistics Office
Cardiff Road, Newport, Gwent, NP9 1XG
[0633–56111]

Director (G3), R. G. Ward.
Heads of Branch (G5), C. C. Maskall; Dr. B. Mitchell; R. M. Norton; D. R. Lewis; C. J. Spiller.
Grade 6, W. D. Knight.

REGIONAL OFFICES

North East, Stanegate House, 2 Groat Market, Newcastle upon Tyne NE1 1YN. [091–232 4722].—*Regional Director (G3),* R. W. Simpson. *Regional Industrial Adviser,* Dr. A. Chitty.

North West, Sunley Tower, Piccadilly Plaza, Manchester M1 4BA. [061–236 2171].—*Regional Director (G3),* M. M. Baker.

Yorkshire and Humberside, Priestley House, Park Row, Leeds LS1 5LF. [0532 443171].—*Regional Director (G3),* E. Wright.

West Midlands, Ladywood House, Stephenson Street, Birmingham B2 4DT. [021–632 4111].—*Regional Director (G3),* A. J. Pryor.

East Midlands, Severns House, 20 Middle Pavement, Nottingham NG1 7DW. [0602 506181].—*Regional Director (G5),* K. J. Green.

South West, The Pithay, Bristol BS1 2PB. [0272–272666].—*Regional Director (G5),* D. B. Lodge. *South West Industrial Development Office,* Phoenix House, Notte Street, Plymouth PL1 2HF. [0752–221891].—*Director (G7),* M. G. Brown.

South East (Industry), Ebury Bridge House, 2/18 Ebury Bridge Road, SW1W 8QD. [01–730 9678].—*Regional Director (G5),* A. J. Mantle.

South East (Exports), Ebury Bridge House, 2/18 Ebury Bridge Road, SW1W 8QD. [01–730 9678].—*Director (G6),* Dr. H. A. P. Fisher.

DEPARTMENT OF TRANSPORT
2 Marsham Street, SW1P 3EB
[01–212 3434]

The Department of Transport has overall responsibility for land, sea and air transport. This entails general sponsorship of the transport industries, with particular responsibility for the rail and bus industries; domestic and international civil aviation policy; shipping policy and the ports industry; navigation lights; pilotage; H.M. Coastguard; oversight of road transport, including vehicle registration and licensing, driver licensing and road safety; responsibility for construction and maintenance of motorways and trunk roads; and general oversight of the transport planning of local authorities, including payments of grant from central Government.

Salaries

Secretary of State	£33,145
Minister of State	£22,875
Parliamentary Secretary	£16,885
Grade 1	£65,000
Grade 2	£43,500–£45,500
Grade 3	£34,000–£37,000
Grade 4	£30,344–£31,844
Chairman of Traffic Commissioners	£28,215
Grade 5	£24,765–£28,215

Secretary of State for Transport, THE RT. HON. PAUL CHANNON, M.P.
Private Secretary, R. J. Griffin.
Parliamentary Private Secretary, R. Hayward, M.P.
Minister of State, DAVID MITCHELL, M.P.
Private Secretary, K. W. Miller.
Parliamentary Private Secretary, N. Hamilton, M.P.
Parliamentary Under Secretaries, P. Bottomley, M.P.; Lord Brabazon of Tara.
Private Secretaries, N. J. Starling; Miss S. J. Smith.
Lord in Waiting, The Viscount Davidson.
Private Secretary. Miss S. J. Smith.
Parliamentary Clerk, M. Carty.
Permanent Under Secretary of State (G1), Sir Alan Bailey, K.C.B.
Private Secretary, C. Smith.

Information

Head of Information (G5), Miss J. Caines.

PUBLIC TRANSPORT AND RESEARCH

Deputy Secretary (G2), J. Palmer, C.B.

Railways

Under Secretary (G3), J. R. Coates.
Heads of Division (G5), A. J. Nichols; P. G. Hewett.
Chief Inspecting Officer (G4), Maj. C. F. Rose (*retd.*).

Public Transport London and Metropolitan

Under Secretary (G3), A. J. Goldman.
Heads of Division (G5), F. Gale; Mrs. C. M. Dixon; E. C. Neve.

Transport and Road Research Laboratory

Director (G3), G. Margason.
Deputy Director (G4), D. F. Cornelius.
Grade 5, N. W. Lister; Dr. A. J. M. Hitchcock; F. W. Webster; R. S. Hinsley; D. I. Robertson; Dr. G. P. Tilly; Dr. M. A. Crisfield.
Grade 6, J. S. Yerrell.

Science and Research Policy and Programmes

Grade 5, P. G. O'Neill.

CHIEF SCIENTIFIC ADVISER (G2):
Dr. M. W. Holdgate, C.B.

SHIPPING, ROAD SAFETY AND LICENSING

Deputy Secretary (G2), R. C. M. Cooper, C.B.

Shipping Policy and Emergency Planning

Under Secretary (G3), G. R. Sunderland.
Heads of Division (G5), R. A. Allen; R. G. Jones; J. D. Henes.

Marine

Under Secretary (G3), J. W. S. Dempster.
Heads of Division (G5), J. A. Battersby; J. R. Fells; M. W. Jackson.
Grade 6, D. H. Forward.

Marine Emergency Operations and Marine Pollution Control Unit

Director (G4), Rear-Adm. M. L. Stacey, C.B.
Chief Coastguard (G5), Capt. P. C. K. Harris.
Surveyor General, Dr. J. Cowley, C.B.E.
Deputy Surveyors General (G5), D. J. Fowler; P. J. Hambling; G. Thompson.

Road and Vehicle Safety

Under Secretary (G3), Mrs. J. M. Bridgeman.
Heads of Division (G5), D. J. Lyness; D. M. Smith; R. J. Oliver.

Grade 6, D. J. Spragg; B. V. Woolford; J. David; K. Walton; D. Harvey.
Chief Mechanical Engineer (G4), D. V. Jones.
Grade 6, R. J. White.

Driver and Vehicle Licensing

Director (G4), G. R. Wattley.
Heads of Division (G5), M. A. Robinson; R. Bird; R. J. Verge; H. C. S. Derwent.
Grade 6, D. A. Gedrych.

Freight and Bus Licensing

Under Secretary (G3), W. P. Jackson.
Grade 5, M. S. Albu; H. C. T. Fawcett.
Grade 6, J. Winder; D. J. Blackman.

Traffic Area Offices
Traffic Commissioners and Licensing Authorities

Eastern (Nottingham and Cambridge), Brig. C. M. Boyd.
Metropolitan (Acton), Air Vice-Marshal R. G. Ashford, C.B.E.
North Eastern (Newcastle upon Tyne and Leeds), F. Whalley.
North Western (Manchester), (vacant).
Scottish (Edinburgh), H. McNamara.
South Eastern (Eastbourne), Brig. M. H. Turner.
West Midlands (Birmingham), J. M. C. Pugh.
Western (Bristol), Maj.-Gen. V. H. J. Carpenter, C.B., M.B.E.
South Wales (Cardiff), J. M. C. Pugh.

HIGHWAYS AND TRAFFIC

Deputy Secretary (G2), J. E. Hannigan, C.B.

Highways Policy and Programme

Under Secretary (G3), H. J. Blanks.
Heads of Division (G5), M. R. Egerton; B. R. A. Blaxall; B. J. Billington; P. E. Pickering.

Highways, Contracts, Administration and Maintenance

Under Secretary (G3), P. Critchley.
Heads of Division (G5), W. Walker; P. R. Smith; J. W. Fellows; B. J. Bennett.

Highways Engineering

Chief Highway Engineer (G3), K. Sriskandan.
Deputy Chief Highway Engineer (G4), D. A. Holland.
Grade 5, R. S. Wilson; S. Chatterjee; J. Denning; S. Rose; P. H. Dawe.
Grade 6, K. Softly.

Traffic and Greater London Roads

Under Secretary (G3), I. Yass.
Heads of Division (G5), R. M. C. Edridge; N. T. Rees; P. E. Butler; J. A. L. Dawson.

AVIATION INTERNATIONAL

Deputy Secretary (G2), D. Holmes, C.B.

Civil Aviation Policy

Under Secretary (G3), R. E. Clarke.
Grade 5, A. T. Baker; J. A. Rhodes; D. S. Evans; R. J. Griffin; C. J. Harris; B. D'Oliveira, O.B.E.

International Aviation

Under Secretary (G3), H. M. G. Stevens.
Heads of Division (G5), C. R. Hook; M. L. Fielder; D. C. Moss.

Accidents Investigation Branch

Chief Inspector of Accidents (G4), D. A. Cooper.
Deputy Chief Inspector of Accidents (G5), K. P. R. Smart.

International Transport

Under Secretary (G3), J. D. Noulton.
Grade 5, C. M. Woodman; Miss S. J. Lambert; Ms. E. A. Hopkins.
Grade 6, R. Pounder.

Finance

Under Secretary (G3), A. P. Brown.
Grade 4, H. B. Wenban-Smith.
Heads of Division (G5), P. R. Smethurst; L. S. Moyle; C. R. Grimsey; J. W. B. Robins; D. J. Rowlands.
Accounting Adviser (G5), G. M. Dennett.

Internal Audit

Head of Branch (G6), J. Kingdom.

ECONOMICS AND STATISTICS (TRANSPORT)

Chief Economic Adviser (G2), Dr. J. H. Rickard.
Grade 5, G. A. C. Searle; M. B. Egerton; C. T. B. Smith; A. J. Nichols.

Statistics (Transport)

Under Secretary (G3), E. J. Thompson.
Grade 5, H. M. Dale; Miss B. J. Wood; H. Collings; G. R. Emes.

DEPARTMENTS OF THE ENVIRONMENT AND TRANSPORT REGIONAL OFFICES AND COMMON SERVICES

See under **Department of the Environment**

THE TREASURY
Parliament Street, SW1P 3AG
[01–233 3000]

The Office of the Lord High Treasurer has been continuously in commission for well over 200 years: the Lord High Commissioners of H.M. Treasury consist of the First Lord of the Treasury (who is also the Prime Minister), the Chancellor of the Exchequer and five Junior Lords. This Board of Commissioners is assisted at present by the Chief Secretary, a Parliamentary Secretary who is the Chief Whip, a Financial Secretary, an Economic Secretary, a Paymaster General and by the Permanent Secretary.

The Prime Minister and First Lord is not primarily concerned in the day to day aspects of Treasury business. The Parliamentary Secretary and the Junior Lords are Government whips in the House of Commons. The management of the Treasury devolves upon the Chancellor of the Exchequer and, under him, the Chief Secretary, the Financial Secretary, The Economic Secretary and the Paymaster General. The Chief Secretary is responsible for the control of public expenditure; public services and industry groups; overseas aid and export credit; efficiency in the public sector; and procurement policy. The Financial Secretary discharges the traditional responsibility of the Treasury for the largely formal procedure for the voting of funds by Parliament. He also has responsibility for other Parliamentary financial business, Inland Revenue duties and taxes and privatisation policy. The Economic Secretary has responsibility for monetary policy; international financial business; North Sea fiscal regime; Department for National Savings, Registry of Friendly Societies and the National Loans Office; and the Treasury research budget. The Paymaster General deals with Customs & Excise matters; European Community business; civil service pay; the Royal Mint, H.M. Stationery Office, Central Office of Information, Government Actuary's Department and the Paymaster General's Office. All Treasury Ministers are concerned in tax matters.

Prime Minister and First Lord of the Treasury, THE RT. HON. MARGARET HILDA THATCHER, M.P., F.R.S. £33,145

Lord Commissioners of the Treasury, M. Neubert, M.P.; A. Durant, M.P.; P. Lloyd, M.P.; The Hon. Mark Lennox-Boyd, M.P.; D. Lightbown, M.P. £13,815

Chancellor of the Exchequer, THE RT. HON. NIGEL LAWSON, M.P. £33,145
  Principal Private Secretary, A. C. S. Allan.
  Private Secretary, A. W. Kuczys.
Chief Secretary to the Treasury, THE RT. HON. JOHN MAJOR, M.P. £33,145
  Private Secretary, Miss J. K. Rutter.
  Assistant Private Secretary, M. C. Felstead.
Parliamentary Secretary to the Treasury and Government Chief Whip, THE RT. HON. DAVID WADDINGTON, Q.C., M.P. £27,255
  Private Secretary, M. Maclean.
Financial Secretary, THE RT. HON. NORMAN LAMONT, M.P. £22,875
  Private Secretary, J. J. Heywood.
Economic Secretary, PETER LILLEY, M.P.
  Private Secretary, P. D. P. Barnes.
Paymaster General, THE HON. PETER BROOKE, M.P. £22,875
  Private Secretary, S. P. Judge.
Treasurer of H.M. Household and Deputy Chief Whip, David Hunt, M.B.E., M.P. £22,875
Assistant Whips, R. Ryder, O.B.E., M.P.; D. Maclean, M.P.; K. Carlisle, M.P.; A. Howarth, M.P.; S. Dorrell, M.P. £13,815

(NOTE.—(i) All salaries shown above do not include Parliamentary salary: (ii) The Prime Minister is entitled to draw a salary of £44,775.)

Civil Service Salaries

Permanent Secretary of the Treasury £75,750
Grade 1A £59,500
Grade 2 .... £43,500–£45,500
Grade 3 .... £34,000–£37,000
Grade 5 .... £24,765–£28,215
Grade 6 .... £18,786–£25,335
Grade 7 .... £15,030–£20,292

Permanent Secretary of the Treasury, Sir Peter Middleton, K.C.B.
  Private Secretary, R. B. Saunders.
Second Permanent Secretaries (*G1A*), Sir Geoffrey Littler, K.C.B. (*Overseas Finance*); F. E. R. Butler (*Public Services*).
Head of Government Economics Service and Chief Economic Adviser to the Treasury, Sir Terence Burns.
Deputy Secretaries (*G2*), F. Cassell (*Public Finance*); R. G. Lavelle (*Overseas Finance*); J. Anson, C.B. (*Public Services, and General Expenditure*); E. P. Kemp (*Pay and Allowances*); N. J. Monck (*Industry*).
Deputy Chief Economic Adviser to the Treasury (*G2*), I. C. R. Byatt.

Public Services Sector

Industry, Agriculture and Employment Group:
Under Secretary (*G3*), T. U. Burgner.
Assistant Secretaries (*G5*), R. J. Bonney; M. A. Waller; P. R. C. Gray.
Public Enterprises:
Under Secretary (*G3*), D. J. L. Moore.
Assistant Secretaries (*G5*), M. L. Williams; Mrs. M. E. Brown; J. G. Colman.

Social Services and Territorial:
Under Secretary (*G3*), Miss M. E. Peirson.
Assistant Secretaries (*G5*), Miss G. M. Noble; Ms. P. M. Boys; A. M. White.
Local Government:
Under Secretary (*G3*), M. V. Hawtin.
Assistant Secretaries (*G5*), B. H. Potter; D. R. Instone.
Home Transport and Education:
Under Secretary (*G3*), B. T. Gilmore.
Assistant Secretaries (*G5*), D. C. W. Revolta; T. J. Burr.
Public Expenditure Economics and Operational Research:
Under Secretary (*G3*), M. J. Spackman.
Assistant Secretaries (*G5*), M. A. Parsonage; G. M. White.
Deputy Chief Scientific Officer (*G5*), J. B. Jones.
Accounts and Purchasing:
Under Secretary (*G3*), C. H. A. Judd.
Assistant Secretary (*G5*), F. K. Jones.
Central Computer and Telecommunications Agency:
Under Secretary (*G3*), P. I. Freeman.
Assistant Secretaries (*G5*), W. A. Beard; W. Houldsworth; R. Paynter; I. S. Thomson; P. Rayner; R. E. Dibble.
Directing Grade Engineer B (*G5*), C. R. D. Tatham.
General Expenditure Policy:
Under Secretary (*G3*), A. Turnbull.
Assistant Secretaries (*G5*), R. C. Pratt; Mrs. R. Butler.
Senior Principal (*G6*), E. I. Cooper.
Defence Policy and Material:
Under Secretary (*G3*), S. A. Robson.
Assistant Secretaries (*G5*), N. M. Hansford; Ms. D. Seammen.
Civil Service Catering Organization:
Executive Director (*G3*), D. S. B. Simpson.

Overseas Finance Sector

Overseas Finance:
International Finance Group:
Under Secretary (*G3*), H. P. Evans.
Assistant Secretaries (*G5*), H. G. Walsh; S. W. Matthews.
Aid and Export Finance:
Under Secretary (*G3*), P. Mountfield.
Assistant Secretaries (*G5*), Mrs. A. F. Case; P. G. F. Davis.
European Community:
Under Secretary (*G3*), A. J. C. Edwards.
Assistant Secretaries (*G5*), J. E. Mortimer; C. D. Crabbie.

Chief Economic Adviser's Sector

Forecast and Analysis:
Under Secretary (*G3*), P. N. Sedgewick.
Senior Economic Advisers (*G5*), S. J. Davies; A. R. H. Bottrill.
Medium Term and Policy Analysis:
Under Secretary (*G3*), J. C. Odling-Smee.
Senior Economic Advisers (*G5*), C. Mellis; C. J. Riley.

Public Enterprises Analytic Unit and Economics of Taxation and Social Security Division

Deputy Secretary (*G2*), I. C. R. Byatt.
Assistant Secretary (*G5*), G. A. C. D. Houston.
Senior Economic Advisers (*G5*), Mrs. M. F. Haworth; G. P. Smith.
Fiscal Policy:
Under Secretary (*G3*), M. C. Scholar.
Assistant Secretary (*G5*), Miss C. E. C. Sinclair.
Monetary Group:
Under Secretary (*G3*), D. L. C. Peretz.
Assistant Secretaries (*G5*), C. W. Kelly; J. W. Grice.

Financial Institutions and Market Group

Under Secretary (G3), Mrs. R. Lomax.
Assistant Secretaries (G5), Miss G. Noble; N. J. Ilett.

Pay and Allowances Command

Pay:
Deputy Secretary (G3), E. P. Kemp.
Assistant Secretaries (G5), J. F. Gilhooly; C. J. A. Chivers.

Running Costs and Superannuation

Under Secretary (G3), T. R. H. Luce.
Assistant Secretaries (G5), N. M. Hansford; D. A. Truman; J. Dixon.
Grade 6, E. I. Cooper; W. G. Bristow; D. G. Pain.

Central Area

Establishment and Organization:
Under Secretary (G3), C. D. Butler.
Assistant Secretary (G5), C. C. Allan.
Senior Economic Adviser (G5), R. B. Stannard.
Senior Principals (G6), E. J. Needle; R. N. Edwards.
Economic Briefing (G5), Miss M. O'Mara.
Information:
Assistant Secretary (G5), R. P. Culpin.
Deputy Head of Division (G6), S. J. Pickford.

Treasury Representatives in U.S.A.

Economic Minister and U.K. Representative IMF/ IBRD, T. P. Lankester.

Rating of Government Property Department
Jameson House, 69 Notting Hill Gate, W11 3JU

Treasury Valuer, J. F. Olney.
Deputy Treasury Valuer, T. J. Cundall.

THE TREASURY SOLICITOR
Department of H.M. Procurator-General and Treasury Solicitor
Queen Anne's Chambers, 28 Broadway, SW1H 9JS
[01–210 3000]

The Treasury Solicitor's Department provides legal services for many Government Departments. Those that do not have their own lawyers are given legal advice, and both they and many other departments are provided with litigation and conveyancing services. The Department also deals with Bona Vacantia. The Treasury Solicitor is also the Queen's Proctor.

Salaries

Grade 1	£65,000
Grade 2	£43,500–£45,500
Grade 3	£34,000–£37,000
Grade 4	£30,344–£31,844
Grade 5	£24,765–£28,215
Grade 6	£18,786–£25,335
Senior Legal Assistants	£17,336–£23,534
Grade 7	£15,030–£20,292

Procurator-General and Treasury Solicitor (G1), Sir John Bailey, K.C.B.
Deputy Treasury Solicitor (G2), (vacant).

Central Advisory Division

Principal Assistant Solicitor (G3), Miss J. L. Wheldon.
Assistant Solicitors (G5), J. E. Collins; A. S. W. Hyett.
Grade 6, P. C. Jenkins; C. P. J. Muttukunaru.
Senior Legal Assistants, M. R. M. Davis; C. J. Gregory.

Litigation Divisions

Principal Assistant Solicitors (G3), T. J. G. Pratt; R. N. Ricks; J. H. Wilkinson.
Assistant Solicitors (G5), M. A. Blythe; D. A. Hogg; I. Hood; A. Leithead; C. G. Leonard; R. Lines; D. F. W. Pickup; H. R. L. Purse; A. J. Sandal; G. F. Sills.

Grade 6, Mrs. D. Babar; Mrs. G. Dagtoglou; J. N. Desai; Mrs. J. B. C. Douglas; Mrs. S. J. Hay; R. A. D. Jackson; A. D. Lawton; Mrs. A. M. Morris; R. J. Phillips; M. B. Sturdy; P. F. O. Whitehurst.
Senior Legal Assistants, A. P. M. Aylett; N. Beach; Miss P. J. Carroll; Miss. S. Cochrane; P. D. F. Grant; N. J. Harington; J. D. Howes; Mrs. C. Pearson; Miss J. E. Pemberton; R. E. Seely; Mrs. V. Selzer; A. Turek.
Principals (G7), M. W. Benney; Miss J. L. C. Brooks; J. M. Hawkins; Miss A. Lancaster; Mrs. I. G. Letwin; F. G. O'Connell; D. Palmer; A. J. J. Woodcock.

Queen's Proctor Division

Queen's Proctor, Sir John Bailey, K.C.B.
Assistant Queen's Proctor, I. Hood.

Conveyancing Division

Principal Assistant Solicitor (G3), I. T. Lewis.
Assistant Solicitors (G5), D. E. T. Bevan; R. W. M. Cooper; P. L. Noble; A. M. Scarfe; J. Wyer.
Grade 6, M. H. M. Anderson; M. Benmayor; R. L. Coward; Miss R. C. Farmer; D. J. C. Garnett; Miss G. Gilder; D. M. Gleed; J. B. Howe; P. F. Nockles; C. L. Oastler; G. E. Papes; R. M. Pierce; M. F. Rawlins; S. W. Rock; R. J. B. Stenhouse; Miss C. E. M. Troddyn.
Senior Legal Assistants, M. V. Cooper; M. Drayton; I. R. S. Falconer; T. Forrester; A. R. Lilleystone; I. P. Parker; M. R. Rosenfeld; Miss P. E. Slatter; T. J. Sylvester-Jones; B. D. Thurley; S. A. Tobin; W. F. Williams.
Grade 7, I. Adams; H. S. Davis; R. D. Harris; C. R. Irving; P. Page; A. W. Prior; J. M. Williamson.

Statutory Publications Office

Assistant Solicitor (G5), J. M. Gibson.
Grade 6, C. E. J. Carey.

Establishment, Finance and General Services Division

Establishment and Legal Personnel Officer (G5), G. Roberts.
Deputy Establishment Officer (G7), D. A. Stalker.
Chief Accountant (G7), B. C. Shephard.
Head of Costs Branch (G7), A. M. Niven.

Bona Vacantia Division

Assistant Solicitor (G5), Miss S. L. Sargant.
Grade 6, (vacant).
Grade 7, Miss H. Donnelly.

Ministry of Defence Branch
Standard House, 28 Northumberland Avenue, WC2N 5JA
[01-218 4691]

Grade 4, R. P. Ellis.
Grade 6, J. R. Braggins; P. D. Coopman; M. J. Hemming.
Senior Legal Assistant, A. L. Norris.

Department of Education and Science Branch
Elizabeth House, York Road, SE1 7PH
[01–934 9958]

Principal Assistant Solicitor (G3), J. E. Coleman.
Assistant Solicitors (G5), A. G. Jones; F. L. Croft.
Grade 6, A. D. Preston; Miss M. Trefgarne; M. A. Widdrington.

Department of Employment Branch
Caxton House, Tothill Street, SW1H 9NF
[01–213 4675]

Principal Assistant Solicitor (G3), M. Harris.
Assistant Solicitors (G5), R. J. Baker; Mrs. A. Leale; S. G. Milligan; Miss V. Rice-Pyle.

Group 6, R. H. Britten; Mrs. C. V. Fox; C. House; Miss R. A. Jeffreys; C. B. D. Lucas; J. K. Winayak.
Senior Legal Assistants, Miss E. A. Barry; G. W. M. Galliford; J. Hall; N. A. D. Lambert.

Department of Energy Branch
Thames House South, Millbank, SW1P 4QJ
[01–211 6046]

Principal Assistant Solicitor (G3), G. B. Claydon.
Assistant Solicitors (G5), D. Brummell; R. M. C. Venables; D. H. M. Ingham; D. J. Ecclestone.
Grade 6, D. J. Aries; M. R. Brocklehurst; Mrs. P. A. Dayer.
Senior Legal Assistant, Miss V. F. Dewhurst.

Department of Transport Branch
2 Marsham Street, SW1P 3EB
[01–212 4527]

Principal Assistant Solicitor (G3), G. H. Beetham.
Assistant Solicitors (G5), R. G. Bellis; C. W. M. Ingram; B. W. James; D. F. Pascho; L. Oates.
Grade 6, F. D. W. Clarke; Miss A. Lind-Smith; H. R. Morrison.
Senior Legal Assistants, J. H. Francis; B. J. Hammersley; A. K. Johnston; B. E. McHenry.

COUNCIL ON TRIBUNALS
7th Floor, 22 Kingsway, WC2B 6LE
[01-936 7050]

The Council on Tribunals are an independent body established in 1958. They now operate under the Tribunals and Inquiries Act, 1971. Under the Act they keep under review the constitution and working of the various tribunals which have been placed under their general supervision, and consider and report on administrative procedures relating to statutory inquiries. They are also frequently consulted on proposals for legislation affecting tribunals and inquiries and on proposals where the need for an appeals procedure may arise.

The tribunals under the Council's supervision include social security and National Health Service Tribunals, the Lands Tribunal, Industrial Tribunals, Mental Health Review Tribunals, Local Valuation Courts and the Civil Aviation Authority. The Council's jurisdiction is from time to time extended to additional tribunals, inquiries and hearings.

The Scottish Committee of the Council generally considers Scottish tribunals and matters relating only to Scotland.

Members of the Council are appointed by the Lord Chancellor and the Lord Advocate. The Scottish Committee is composed partly of members of the Council designated by the Lord Advocate and partly others appointed by him. The Parliamentary Commissioner for Administration is *ex officio* a member of both the Council and the Scottish Committee.

The Council submit an annual report on their work and that of the Scottish Committee to the Lord Chancellor and the Lord Advocate, which must be laid before Parliament.

Chairman, Sir Cyril Philips.
Members, A. R. Barrowclough, Q.C.; Prof. L. N. Brown; D. Bruce; Miss S. M. Cameron, Q.C.; Mrs. M. P. Case; Sir Kenneth Clucas, K.C.B.; A. C. Heywood; Miss J. Horsham, C.B.E.; G. V. Hyde; Mrs. J. U. Kellock; R. N. M. MacLean, Q.C.; A. L. Rennie, C.B.; M. E. J. Rush; Mrs. S. H. Spence; Prof. A. Webb.
Secretary, C. W. Dyment.

Scottish Committee
20 Walker Street, Edinburgh EH3 7HR
[031–220 1236]

Chairman, R. N. M. MacLean, Q.C.
Members, A. R. Barrowclough, Q.C.; Mrs. E. Anderson; D. Bruce; P. M. Gemmill; A. L. Rennie, C.B.; Mrs. E. Walker.
Secretary, Mrs. E. M. Chalmers.

TRIBUNALS
(see pages 459–60)

CORPORATION OF TRINITY HOUSE
Trinity House, Tower Hill, EC3N 4DH
[01–480 6601]

Trinity House, the first General Lighthouse and Pilotage Authority in the Kingdom, was a body of importance when Henry VIII granted the institution its first charter in 1514. The Corporation is the General Lighthouse Authority for England and Wales, the Channel Islands and Gibraltar, with certain statutory jurisdiction over aids to navigation maintained by local harbour authorities. It is also responsible for dealing with wrecks dangerous to navigation, except those occurring within port limits or wrecks of H.M. ships. The Trinity House Lighthouse Service is maintained out of the General Lighthouse Fund which is provided from light dues levied on ships at ports of the U.K. and Republic of Ireland. The Corporation is also the principal pilotage authority in the U.K. and is responsible for London and 39 other districts. (Under the terms of the Pilotage Act 1987 responsibility for pilotage will be transferred to harbour authorities at a date in 1988 yet to be decided.)

The affairs of the Corporation are controlled by a board of eight Elder Brethren, who are master mariners with long experience of command in the Royal and Merchant Navy, and the Secretary. Separate Boards, which are comprised of Elder Brethren, senior staff and outside representatives currently control the Lighthouse and Pilotage Services. The Boards are assisted by administrative and technical staff. The Elder Brethren also act as nautical assessors in marine causes in the Admiralty Division of the High Court of Justice.

Elder Brethren
Master, H.R.H. the Duke of Edinburgh, K.G. *Deputy Master*, Sir Miles Buckley Wingate, K.C.V.O. *Elder Brethren*, Capt. D. J. Cloke; Capt. I. R. C. Saunders; H.R.H. the Prince of Wales, K.G.; Capt. G. P. McCraith; Capt. Sir George Barnard; Capt. R. N. Mayo, C.B.E.; Capt. Sir David Tibbits, D.S.C., R.N.; Capt. D. A. G. Dickens; Capt. J. E. Bury; Capt. J. A. N. Bezant, D.S.C., R.D., R.N.R. *(ret.)*; The Lord Wilson of Rievaulx, K.G., O.B.E., F.R.S.; Rt. Hon. E. R. G. Heath, M.B.E., M.P.; The Visct. Runciman of Doxford, O.B.E., A.F.C.; Capt. P. F. Mason, C.B.E.; Capt. T. Woodfield, O.B.E.; Sir Arthur Drake, C.B.E.; The Lord Simon of Glaisdale, P.C.; Admiral of the Fleet the Lord Lewin, K.G., G.C.B., M.V.O., D.S.C.; Capt. D. T. Smith, R.N.; Commander Sir Robin Gillett, G.B.E., R.D., R.N.R.; Capt. P. M. Edge; The Lord Shackleton, K.G., O.B.E., P.C.; Sir John Cuckney; Capt. D. J. Orr; The Lord Carrington, K.G., C.H., K.C.M.G., M.C., P.C.

Officers
Secretary, J. R. Backhouse.
Deputy Secretary, J. B. Fuller.
Director of Engineering, E. J. Macnamara.
Director of Finance, K. W. Clark.
Operations Manager, Mrs. B. C. Heesom.

Personnel Manager, M. J. Faulkner.
Finance Manager, J. B. Burke.
Engineering Manager, D. A. S. Vennings.
Surveyor of Shipping, J. K. Rankin.
Principal, Pilotage Department, H. E. Oliver.
Principal, Corporate Department, J. A. Liddle.
Information Officer, Mrs. L. A. Dennison.

CLYDE PORT AUTHORITY
16 Robertson Street, Glasgow G2 8DS
[041-221 8733]

The Authority is a self-governing statutory body established by individual Act of Parliament and provides sea port facilities within a 450 sq. mile area of jurisdiction which encompasses the River Clyde, its estuary and sea lochs.
Chairman, R. W. S. Easton, C.B.E.
Managing Director, J. Mather.
Secretary, G. P. Johnston.

COMMISSIONERS OF NORTHERN LIGHTHOUSES
84 George Street, Edinburgh EH2 3DA.
[031-226 7051]

The Commissioners of Northern Lighthouses are the General Lighthouse Authority for Scotland and the Isle of Man. The present Board owes its origin to an Act of Parliament passed in 1786. At present the Commissioners operate under the Merchant Shipping Act, 1894 and are 19 in number.
The Commissioners control 38 major manned lighthouses, 50 major unmanned lighthouses, 109 minor lights and many lighted and unlighted buoys. They have a fleet of 3 motor vessels.

Commissioners

The Lord Advocate, the Solicitor General, the Lords Provost of Edinburgh, Glasgow and Aberdeen; the Provost of Inverness; the Chairman of Argyll & Bute District Council; the Sheriffs-Principal of North Strathclyde; Tayside, Central & Fife; Grampian, Highlands & Islands: South Strathclyde, Dumfries & Galloway; Lothians & Borders; and Glasgow & Strathkelvin; W. D. H. Gregson, C.B.E.; T. Macgill; Capt. J. A. MacLeod; Capt. A. F. Dickson, O.B.E.; Capt. W. B. Kinley; A. J. Struthers.

Officers

General Manager, Cdr. J. M. Mackay, M.B.E.
Secretary, I. A. Dickson.
Engineer-in-Chief, W. Paterson.

UNIVERSITY GRANTS COMMITTEE
14 Park Crescent, W1N 4DH
[01-636 7799]

The Committee was appointed by the Chancellor of the Exchequer in July, 1919, and its present terms of reference are as follows;
"To enquire into the financial needs of university education in the U.K.; to advise the Government as to the application of any grants made by Parliament towards meeting them; to collect, examine, and make available information relating to university education throughout the United Kingdom; and to assist, in consultation with the universities and other bodies concerned, the preparation and execution of such plans for the development of the universities as may from time to time be required in order to ensure that they are fully adequate to national needs."
Chairman, Sir Peter Swinnerton-Dyer, K.B.E., F.R.S.
£59,500
Other Members, Prof. E. W. Abel; Sir Peter Baxendell, C.B.E.; Prof. C. M. Campbell; Prof. J. Cannon, C.B.E.; Sir Robert Clayton, C.B.E.; Dr. S. Cotson; Prof. C.

T. Dollery; Prof. T. A. Douglas; Prof. K. Entwistle; Prof. P. Haggett; R. S. Johnson, C.B.E.; Prof. P. R. G. Layard; Prof. R. M. Needham, F.R.S.; Prof. M. J. O'Hara, F.R.S., F.R.S.E.; W. D. C. Semple; Prof. J. Sizer; Prof. R. Whittenbury.
Secretary, N. T. Hardyman, C.B. £37,000
Assist. Secretaries, E. C. Appleyard; Mrs. I. Wilde
£24,765–£28,215
Principals, C. R. Doherty; J. G. Gooderham; M. C. Hutchison (*Statistician*); A. H. Prosser; J. Smith; W. A. Smyth; L. B. Webb .... £15,030–£20,292

COMMONWEALTH WAR GRAVES COMMISSION
2 Marlow Road, Maidenhead, Berkshire SL6 7DX
[Maidenhead : 34221]

The Commonwealth War Graves Commission (formerly Imperial War Graves Commission) was founded by Royal Charter in 1917. It is responsible for the commemoration of 1,695,000 members of the forces of the Commonwealth who fell in the two world wars. More than one million graves are maintained in 23,175 burial grounds throughout the world. Over three-quarters of a million men and women who have no known grave or who were cremated are commemorated by name on memorials built by the Commission.
The funds of the Commission are derived from the six Governments participating in its work—the U.K., Canada, Australia, New Zealand, South Africa and India.

President, H.R.H. The Duke of Kent, K.G., G.C.M.G., G.C.V.O.
Chairman, The Secretary of State for Defence.
Vice-Chairman, Adm. Sir David Williams, G.C.B.
Members, The Secretary of State for the Environment; The High Commissioners for Canada, the Commonwealth of Australia, New Zealand, and India; the Ambassador for the Republic of South Africa; Sir Edward Gardner, Q.C., M.P.; Gen. Sir Robert Ford, G.C.B., C.B.E.; Air Chief Marshal Sir John Gingell, G.B.E., K.C.B.; Capt. Sir Miles Wingate, K.C.V.O.; Maj.-Gen. D. Smith, C.B.E., D.S.O.; Sir Donald Maitland, G.C.M.G., O.B.E.; The Baroness McFarlane of Llandaff; Rt. Hon. D. Concannon, M.P.
Director-General, Sir Arthur Hockaday, K.C.B., C.M.G.
Deputy Director-Generals, D. Kennedy (*Administration*); J. Saynor (*Organization*).
Directors, R. Wilson (*Finance*); P. J. Noakes (*Horticulture*); H. Mackay (*Management Services*); T. F. Penfold (*Personnel*); R. J. Dalley (*Secretariat*); N. B. Osborn (*Works*).
Legal Adviser and Solicitor, G. C. Reddie.
Hon. Botanical Adviser, Prof. E. A. Bell, PH.D.
Hon. Artistic Adviser, Prof. Sir Peter Shepheard, C.B.E.

Imperial War Graves Endowment Fund

Trustees, Sir John Hogg, T.D.; E. M. P. Welman; Admiral Sir David Williams, G.C.B.
Hon. Secretary to the Trustees, R. Wilson.

WELSH OFFICE
*Gwydyr House, Whitehall, SW1A 2ER
[01–270 3000]

Cathays Park, Cardiff CF1 3NQ
[0222 825111]

°Ty Glas Road, Llanishen,
Cardiff CF4 5PL
[0222 753271]

†Plas Crug, Aberystwyth,
Dyfed SY23 1NG
[0970 3162]

‡Brunel House, Fitzalan Road,
Cardiff CF2 1UY
[0222 465511]

(All staff are based at Cathays Park unless otherwise
indicated by the symbols used above by the relevant
location.)

The Welsh Office has responsibility in Wales for
ministerial functions relating to health and personal
social services; education, except for terms and
conditions of service, student awards and the University; the Welsh language and culture; local
government; housing; water and sewerage; environmental protection; sport; agriculture and fisheries;
forestry; land use, including town and country
planning, countryside and nature conservation; new
towns; ancient monuments and historic buildings;
roads; tourism; a range of matters affecting the
careers service and the activities of the Manpower
Services Commission in Wales; financial assistance
to industry; the urban programme in Wales; the
operation of the European Regional Development
Fund in Wales and other European Community
matters; civil emergencies, and all financial aspects
of these matters, including Welsh rate support grant.
It has oversight responsibilities for economic affairs
and regional planning in Wales.

Salaries

Secretary of State	£33,145
Minister of State	£22,875
Parliamentary Under Secretary of State	£16,885
Grade 1	£62,100
Grade 2	£41,500–£43,500
Grade 3	£33,725–£36,852
Grade 4	£30,207–£31,770
Grade 5	£24,739–£28,215
Grade 6	£18,786–£25,335
Grade 7	£14,927–£20,292
Principal Social Work Service Officer	£20,213–£25,332
Medical Officer	£17,593–£24,926
Dental Officer	£17,593–£24,926
Chief Nursing Officer	£27,420
Deputy Chief Nursing Officer	£24,125
Nursing Officer	£18,429–£21,676

Secretary of State for Wales, THE RT. HON. PETER
WALKER, M.B.E., M.P.*
Private Secretary, J. D. Shortridge.*
Assistant Private Secretaries, D. A. Powell*; E. K.
Davies.*
Parliamentary Private Secretary, P. Hubbard-Miles,
M.P.*
Minister of State, WYN ROBERTS, M.P.*
Parliamentary Under-Secretary, I. Grist, M.P.*
Parliamentary Clerk, Mrs. S. Rees.*
Permanent Secretary (G1), R. A. Lloyd Jones, C.B.
Private Secretary, J. Howells.
Deputy Secretaries (G2), I. H. Lightman, C.B.; J. W.
Preston.
Head of Permanent Secretary's Division (G5), L. L.
Ginn, T.D.*
Principal (G7), D. H. Jones.

Establishment Group

Principal Establishment Officer (G3), G. C. G. Craig.
Heads of Divisions (G5), W. L. Chapman; M. J.
Clancy.
Senior Economic Adviser (G5), O. T. Hooker.
Chief Statistician (G5), Dr. M. P. G. Pepper.
Principals (G7), R. J. Bolus‡; P. Davenport; Miss E.
M. Jones; Miss C. M. Owen; M. J. Shanahan.
Economic Adviser (G7), V. W. F. McPherson.
Principal Research Officers (G7), I. I. Thomas; E.
Darwin; Mrs. M. A. J. Gronow.
Statisticians (G7), G. J. Cockell; Miss W. K. Fader; J.
T. Fletcher; K. Francombe; P. J. Fullerton; E.

Swires Hennessey; J. D. James; R. Jones; J. D.
Kinder; G. E. Pierce.
Director, Cadw: Welsh Historic Monuments, E. A. J.
Carr‡ £31,164
Conservation Architect (G6), J. D. Hogg‡.
*Principal Inspector of Ancient Monuments and His-
toric Buildings*, J. R. Avent‡ ..... £17,762–£20,473
*Inspectors of Ancient Monuments and Historic Build-
ings*, J. K. Knight; Dr. L. MacInnes; A. D. McLees;
Dr. S. E. Rees .... £10,549–£18,513

Finance Group

Principal Finance Officer (G3), J. F. Craig.
Heads of Divisions (G5), C. L. Jones; L. Pritchard; B.
Wilcox.
Principals (G7), Dr. M. Dunn; M. G. Horlock; P. G. C.
Lunn; D. T. Richards; C. Spillane; C. E. Taylor; B.
O. Valentine; Dr. B. J. M. Wilson.
Head of Internal Audit (G7), B. R. Davies.

Health Professional Group

Chief Medical Officer (G3), G. Crompton.
Deputy Chief Medical Officers (G4), A. M. George;
Deirdre J. Hine.
Senior Medical Officers (G5), G. J. Moses; D. Ferguson
Lewis; Mary Cotter; H. G. Penrhyn Jones; Jennifer
Lloyd.
Chief Dental Officer, D. M. Heap.
Medical Officers, J. D. Andrews; R. Buntwal; J. W.
Crossley; D. E. Davies; T. I. Evans; N. E. Thomas.
Dental Officers, A. Cobb; J. D. O. Parkholm; T. A.
Williams.
Scientific Adviser (G6), Dr. J. A. V. Pritchard.
Pharmaceutical Adviser (G6), Dr. G. B. A. Veitch.

Housing, Health and Social Services Policy Group

Head of Group (G3), J. W. Lloyd.
Heads of Divisions (G5), S. H. Martin; J. C. Price; A.
E. Peat.
Chief Social Work Service Officer (G5), D. G. Evans.
Chief Architect (G6), H. O. M. Coleman.
Principal Social Work Service Officer, J. K. Fletcher
(acting).
Principals (G7), Mrs. J. D. Annand; L. Conway; A. C.
Elmer; P. S. Gray; B. Hilbourne; R. Hughes; A. G.
Huwes; Miss C. Maddocks; Ms. J. H. Roberts; Mrs.
C. Peat.
Social Work Service Officers (G7), D, Barker; G. H.
Davies; I. Forster; J. F. Mooney; Miss A. M.
Perrott; C. D. Vyvyan; A. G. Williams; R. C.
Woodward.
Principal Professional and Technology Officers (G7),
R. Broad; T. A. Campden; C. Eyres; G. N. Harding;
H. D. Harry; W. Ross; E. T. Williams.

National Health Service Directorate

Director of the NHS in Wales, J. W. Owen ... £46,787
Heads of Divisions (G5), P. R. Gregory; N. E. Thomas;
R. J. Davies.
Head of Division (G6), G. T. Evans.
Principals (G7), C. J. Burdett; W. M. Cooper; W. G.
Davies; J. Duggan; M. Harper; N. S. Jones, I.S.O.;
D. McGlinn; K. Orchard; D. Quinlan; A. Thornton;
M. F. Webb.
Ambulance Adviser (G7), P. J. Hunt.
Principal Professional and Technology Officer (G7),
M. W. Grist.

Nursing Division

Chief Nursing Officer, Mrs. Y. Moores.
Deputy Chief Nursing Officer, Mrs. G. M. Stephens.
Nursing Officers, Miss G. Harris; Miss M. Hope; Dr.
D. Keyzer; Mrs. B. Melvin; M. F. Tonkin; Mrs. D.
J. Voss.

Legal Division

Legal Adviser (G3), A. J. Beale.
Assistant Solicitors (G5), D. G. Lambert; P. J. Murrin.
Grade 6, A. B. Cole; J. D. H. Evans; A. K. Gillard; C. P. Jones; C. G. Longville; Mrs. T. C. Shellens; J. H. Turnbull; A. J. Watkins.
Senior Legal Assistants (G7), A. J. Park; Mrs. A. T. Parkes; D. H. J. Williams.
Legal Officer, D. R. G. Thickens.

Information Division

Director of Information (G5), H. G. Roberts.
Chief Press Officer (G7), E. M. Bowen, M.V.O.

Economic and Regional Policy Group

Head of Group (G3), O. Rees.
Heads of Divisions (G5), D. I. Westlake; Miss E. N. M. Davies; F. G. Watson; R. A. Wallace.
Principals (G7), R. O. Evans; Ms. J. M. Gordon; J. A. Grimes; A. Lansdown; R. D. Macey; G. S. Podmore; W. P. Roderick; G. A. Thomas.

Industry Department

Director (G3), C. D. Stevens.
Industrial Director (G4), T. E. Morgan, M.B.E.
Heads of Divisions (G5), R. M. Abel; R. C. Williams.
Senior Principal Scientific Officer (G6), Dr. J. N. M. Firth.
Principals (G7), P. Bishop; R. Callen; R. J. Masefield; D. A. Pritchard; D. Pugh (at Colwyn Bay); K. Smith; C. J. Tudor; R. Waller; J. W. Wallington.
Principal Scientific Officers (G7), P. Bragg; G. A. Madden.

Water and Environmental Protection Division

Head of Division (G5), L. E. Taylor.
Senior Principals (G6), D. M. Timlin; P. R. Marsden; L. A. Pavelin.
Principals (G7), M. D. Evans (*acting*); Miss J. E. Paulett; D. Simpson.
Principal Scientific Officer (G7), R. A. Page.
Principal Professional and Technology Officers (G7), J. A. Atkins; H. R. Payne; J. E. Saunders.

H. M. Inspectorate of Pollution

Inspectors for Wales, Dr. L. A. W. Hales (*Air*); H. G. Taylor (*Waste*); A. A. Houlden (*Water*).

Education Department

Head of Department (G3), R. H. Jones, C.V.O.
Heads of Divisions (G5), H. Evans; C. D. Stephens.
Head of Division (G6), R. C. Simpson.
Principals (G7), Mrs. J. Booker; D. A. Bullen; R. J. Callen; J. B. Davies; M. L. Evans; R. Farrington; J. W. Jones.

H. M. Inspectorate

Chief Inspector (G4), I. R. Lloyd.
Staff Inspectors (G5), S. J. Adams; R. L. James; W. R. Jenkins; T. E. Parry; P. Thomas; R. Thomas; M. J. F. Wynn.
H. M. Inspectors (G6), C. Abbott; G. Adams; R. A. Charles; Mrs. G. Briwnant Jones; H. W. Davies; R. G. Davies; D. G. Evans; J. R. N. Evans; N. B. Evans; Mrs. L. Gainsbury; A. G. George; J. Griffiths; M. G. Haines; A. Hamilton Jones; A. Higgins; I. L. James; Mrs. R. James; W. R. Jenkins; M. John; G. D. Jones; G. T. J. Jones; O. E. Jones; Mrs A. Keane; J. M. Laugharne; M. J. Law; I. M. Lewis; J. R. Lewis; Miss S. Lewis; A. Morgan; I. G. Morgan; J. Nicholas; Miss P. A. Nicholas; Miss E. Ogwen; T. G. Prosser; W. H. Raybould; D. G. H. Rees; G. O. Roberts; Miss D. Selleck; Mrs. V. Scott; M. W. Stone; R. Taylor; G. Thomas; Mrs. I. Thomas; Miss L. Thomas; P. B. Walker; G. Warren; B. Wigley; E. L. Williams; D. P. Williams.

Transport, Highways and Planning Group

Head of Group (G3), R. W. Jarman.
Director of Highways (G4), G. Mercer°.
Heads of Divisions (G5), A. H. H. Jones°; J. C. Lewis; J. A. Morgan°.
Chief Planner (G5), C. J. Curry.
Principal Planning Inspector (G5), R. Pierce.
Superintending Engineers (G6), J. G. Evans°; B. H. Hawker°; R. Lober°.
Superintending Estates Officer (G6), G. K. Hoad.
Senior Housing and Planning Inspectors (G6), T. W. B. Barnes; J. H. Chadwick; J. L. S. Whalley; P. Rosser; D. Sheers; G. Sloan.
Principals (G7), G. Davies°; R. W. Jenkins°; A. V. Price; D. M. Rolph; S. H. Spackman; Mrs. E. A. Taylor°.
Principal Planning Officers (G7), D. B. Courtier; G. Fairhurst; J. O. Pryce.
Principal Research Officers (G7), G. R. Jones; A. S. Dredge.
Principal, Professional and Technology Officers, Highways Directorate (G7), T. A. Dockerty°; P. Dunstan°; J. A. L. Harries; A. L. Howcraft°; D. G. Minas°; B. J. W. Martin°; S. D. Padfield°; A. L. Perry°; R. H. Powell°; J. R. Rees°; D. P. Soane°; C. W. W. Smart°; J. Fitch°.

Agriculture Department

Head of Department (G3), J. I. Davies, M.B.E.
Heads of Divisions (G5), M. E. Bevan; H. R. Bollington; D. J. Palmer†.
Principals (G7), P. Finnigan†; W. K. Griffiths; T. W. Hunter; R. F. Patterson†; J. M. Thomas.
Divisional Executive Officers (G7), J. C. Alexander (*Carmarthen*); D. W. Evans (*Ruthin*); D. Davies (*Cardiff*); D. R. Thomas (*Caernarfon*); R. J. E. Wilcox (*Llandrindod Wells*).

LAND AUTHORITY FOR WALES
The Custom House, Custom House Street, Cardiff CF1 5AP
[0222–223444]

The Authority is responsible for acquiring and disposing of land needed for private development in Wales.
Chairman, G. D. Inkin, O.B.E. (*part-time*) £21,743
Chief Executive, B. Ryan.

LAW COURTS AND OFFICES

LAW SITTINGS (1988)—*Hilary*, Jan. 11 to March 30; *Easter*, April 12 to May 27; *Trinity*, June 7 to July 31; *Michaelmas*, Oct. 1 to Dec. 21.

THE JUDICIAL COMMITTEE OF THE PRIVY COUNCIL

The Judicial Committee of the Privy Council is the final court of appeal from courts of the United Kingdom dependencies, courts of independent Commonwealth countries which have retained the right of appeal, courts of the Channel Islands and the Isle of Man, some professional and disciplinary committees and church sources. The Committee is composed of all Privy Counsellors who hold, or have held, high judicial office, although usually only three or five hear each case.

The Judicial Committee includes the Lord Chancellor, the Lords of Appeal in Ordinary (*see* below) and such other members of the Privy Council as shall from time to time hold or have held "high judicial office," and certain judges from the Commonwealth.

Office—Downing Street, S.W.1.
Registrar of the Privy Council, D. H. O. Owen.
Chief Clerk, D. Rushton.

THE JUDICATURE OF ENGLAND AND WALES

The legal system of England and Wales is separate from those of Scotland and Northern Ireland and differs from them in law, judicial procedure and court structure, although there is a common distinction between civil law (disputes between individuals) and criminal law (acts harmful to the community).

The supreme judicial authority for England and Wales is the House of Lords, which is the ultimate Court of Appeal from all courts in Great Britain and Northern Ireland (except criminal courts in Scotland). As a Court of Appeal it consists of the Lord Chancellor and the Lords of Appeal in Ordinary (Law Lords). The Supreme Court of Judicature comprises the Court of Appeal, the Crown Court and the High Court of Justice. The High Court of Justice is the superior civil court and is divided into three Divisions. The Chancery Division is concerned mainly with equity, bankruptcy and contentious probate business; the Queen's Bench Division deals with commercial and maritime law, with civil cases not assigned to other courts, and hears appeals from lower courts; and the Family Division, which deals with matters relating to family law. Sittings are held at the Royal Courts of Justice in London or at 24 Crown Court centres outside the capital. High Court judges sit alone to hear cases at first instance. Appeals from lower courts are heard by two or three judges, or by single judges of the appropriate Division.

The decision to prosecute in cases tried on indictment and in summary cases of a serious nature rests with the Crown Prosecution Service, an independent prosecuting body established in 1986 to serve all of England and Wales (*see* p. 455–6). At the head of the Service is the Director of Public Prosecutions, who discharges his duties under the superintendence of the Attorney General. Certain categories of offence continue to require the consent for prosecution of the Attorney General.

Minor criminal offences (summary offences) are dealt with in magistrates' courts, which usually consist of three unpaid lay magistrates (justices of the peace) sitting without a jury, who are advised on points of law and procedure by a legally-qualified clerk to the justices: in busier courts a full-time, salaried and legally-qualified stipendiary magistrate presides alone. Cases involving people under 17 are heard in juvenile courts, specially constituted magistrates' courts which sit apart from other courts. Preliminary proceedings in a serious case to decide whether there is evidence to justify committal for trial in the Crown Court are also held in the magistrates' courts. Appeals from magistrates' courts against sentence or conviction are made to the Crown Court. Appeals upon a point of law are made to the High Court, and may go on to the House of Lords.

The Crown Court sits in about 90 centres, divided into six circuits, and is presided over by High Court judges, full-time circuit judges, and part-time recorders, sitting with a jury in all trials which are contested. It deals with trials of the more serious criminal offences, the sentencing of offenders committed for sentence by magistrates' courts (when the magistrates' consider their own power of sentence inadequate), and appeals from lower courts. Magistrates usually sit with a circuit judge or recorder to deal with appeals and committals for sentence. Appeals from the Crown Court, either against sentence or conviction, are made to the Court of Appeal (Criminal Division), presided over by the Lord Chief Justice. A further appeal from the Court of Appeal to the House of Lords can be brought if a point of law of general public importance is considered to be involved.

Most minor civil cases are dealt with by the county courts, of which there are about 300. For cases involving small claims there are special arbitration facilities and simplified procedures: cases involving claims which exceed set limits may be tried in the county courts with the consent of the parties, or in certain circumstances on transfer from the High Court. Undefended divorce cases and, outside London, bankruptcy proceedings can be heard in designated county courts. Magistrates' courts can deal with certain classes of civil case, mostly those relating to the family, and committees of magistrates licence public houses, clubs and betting shops. Appeals in matrimonial, adoption and guardianship proceedings heard in the magistrates' courts go to the Family Division of the High Court: affiliation appeals and appeals from decisions of the licensing committees of magistrates to the Crown Court. Appeals from the High Court and county courts are heard in the Court of Appeal (Civil Division), presided over by the Master of the Rolls, and may go on to the House of Lords, the final court of appeal in civil cases.

Coroners' courts investigate violent and unnatural deaths or sudden deaths where the cause is unknown. Cases may be brought before a local coroner (a senior lawyer or doctor) by doctors, the police, various public authorities or members of the public. Where a death is sudden and the cause is unknown the coroner may order a post-mortem examination to determine the cause of death rather than holding an inquest in court.

THE HOUSE OF LORDS
(as final Court of Appeal)

The Lord High Chancellor—
The Rt. Hon. the Lord Havers (*born* 1923, *apptd*. 1987), £83,000.

Lords of Appeal in Ordinary (each £74,750)

	Apptd.
Rt. Hon. Lord Keith of Kinkel, *born* 1922	1977
Rt. Hon. Lord Bridge of Harwich, *born* 1917 ..	1980
Rt. Hon. Lord Brandon of Oakbrook, M.C., *born* 1920..................................	1981

Rt. Hon. Lord Brightman, *born* 1911 1982
Rt. Hon. Lord Templeman, M.B.E., *born* 1920 . . 1982
Rt. Hon. Lord Griffiths, *born* 1923 1985
Rt. Hon. Lord Mackay of Clashfern, *born* 1927 . .1985
Rt. Hon. Lord Ackner, *born* 1920 1986
Rt. Hon. Lord Oliver of Aylmerton, *born* 1921 . .1986
Rt. Hon. Lord Goff of Chieveley, *born* 1926 1986
Registrar: The Clerk of the Parliaments, Sir John Sainty, K.C.B.

SUPREME COURT OF JUDICATURE
COURT OF APPEAL

Ex officio Judges.—The Lord High Chancellor, the Lord Chief Justice of England, the Master of the Rolls, the President of the Family Division, and the Vice-Chancellor.

The Master of the Rolls (£74,750)
The Rt. Hon. Sir John Donaldson (*born* 1920, *apptd.* 1982).
Secretary, Miss V. Seymour; *Clerk,* K. H. L. Smeeton.

Lords Justices of Appeal (each £71,750)
                                                        Apptd.
Rt. Hon. Sir Tasker Watkins, V.C., *born* 1918 . 1980
Rt. Hon. Sir Patrick McCarthy O'Connor, *born* 1914. 1980
Rt. Hon. Sir Michael John Fox, *born* 1921 1981
Rt. Hon. Sir Michael Robert Emanuel Kerr, *born* 1921 1981
Rt. Hon. Sir John Douglas May, *born* 1923 . . . 1982
Rt. Hon. Sir Christopher John Slade, *born* 1927. 1982
Rt. Hon. Sir Francis Brooks Purchas, *born* 1919. 1982
Rt. Hon. Sir George Brian Hugh Dillon, *born* 1923. 1982
Rt. Hon. Sir Stephen Brown, *born* 1929 1983
Rt. Hon. Sir Roger Jocelyn Parker, *born* 1923 . 1983
Rt. Hon. Sir David Powell Croom-Johnson, D.S.C., V.R.D., *born* 1914 1984
Rt. Hon. Sir Anthony John Leslie Lloyd, *born* 1929. 1984
Rt. Hon. Sir Brian Thomas Neill, *born* 1923 . . 1985
Rt. Hon. Sir Michael John Mustill, *born* 1931 . 1985
Rt. Hon. Sir Martin Charles Nourse, *born* 1932. 1985
Rt. Hon. Sir Iain Derek Laing Glidewell, *born* 1924. 1985
Rt. Hon. Sir Alfred John Balcombe, *born* 1925 1985
Rt. Hon. Sir Ralph Brian Gibson, *born* 1922 1985
Rt. Hon. Sir John Dexter Stocker, M.C., T.D., *born* 1918 1986
Rt. Hon. Sir Harry Kenneth Woolf, *born* 1933 1986
Rt. Hon. Sir Donald James Nicholls, *born* 1933 1986
Rt. Hon. Sir Thomas Henry Bingham, *born* 1933 1986
Rt. Hon. Sir Thomas Patrick Russell, *born* 1926 1986

Court of Appeal (Criminal Division)

Judges, The Lord Chief Justice of England, The Master of the Rolls, Lord Justices of Appeal and the Judges of the Queen's Bench Division.

Courts-Martial Appeal Court

Judges, The Lord Chief Justice of England, The Master of the Rolls, Lords Justice of Appeal, and Judges of the Queen's Bench Division.

HIGH COURT OF JUSTICE
CHANCERY DIVISION
President, The Lord High Chancellor

The Vice-Chancellor (£71,500)
The Rt. Hon. Sir Nicolas Christopher Henry Browne-Wilkinson
(*born* 1930, *apptd.* 1985)

Secretary (vacant); *Clerk,* W. Northfield.

Judges (each £65,000)   Apptd.
Hon. Sir John Norman Keates Whitford, *born* 1913. 1970
Hon. Sir Raymond Henry Walton, *born* 1915 . 1973
Hon. Sir John Evelyn Vinelott, *born* 1923 1978
Hon. Sir Douglas William Falconer, M.B.E., *born* 1914 1981
Hon. Sir Jean-Pierre Frank Eugene Warner, *born* 1924 1981
Hon. Sir Peter Leslie Gibson, *born* 1934 1981
Hon. Sir David Herbert Mervyn Davies, M.C., T.D., *born* 1918 1982
Hon. Sir Jeremiah LeRoy Harman, *born* 1930 . 1982
Hon. Sir Richard Rashleigh Folliott Scott, *born* 1934 1983
Hon. Sir Leonard Hubert Hoffman, *born* 1934 . 1985
Hon. Sir John Knox, *born* 1925 1985
Hon. Sir Peter Julian Millett, *born* 1932 1986

High Court of Justice in Bankruptcy

Judges, The Master of the Rolls, The Vice-Chancellor, the Lord Justices, and other members of the Court of Appeal.

Companies Court

Judges, The Hon. Mr. Justice Vinelott; The Hon. Mr. Justice Mervyn Davies; The Hon. Mr. Justice Harman; The Hon. Mr. Justice Hoffman.

Patent Court (Appellate Section)

Judges, The Hon. Mr. Justice Whitford; The Hon. Mr. Justice Falconer.

QUEEN'S BENCH DIVISION
The Lord Chief Justice of England (£81,000)
The Rt. Hon. The Lord Lane, A.F.C.
(*born* 1918, *apptd.* 1980)

Secretary, Mrs. J. Simpson; *Clerk,* G. Curtis.

Judges (each £71,750)   Apptd.
Hon. Sir Bernard Caulfield, *born* 1914 1968
Hon. Sir William Lloyd Mars-Jones, M.B.E., *born* 1915 1969
Hon. Sir Leslie Kenneth Edward Boreham, *born* 1918 1972
Hon. Sir (Alfred William) Michael Davies, *born* 1921. 1973
Hon. Sir Kenneth George Illtyd Jones, *born* 1921. 1974
Hon. Sir Haydn Tudor Evans, *born* 1920 1974
Hon. Sir Peter Richard Pain, *born* 1913 1975
Hon. Sir Kenneth Graham Jupp, M.C., *born* 1917 1975
Hon. Sir (Walter) Derek (Thornley) Hodgson, *born* 1917. 1977
Hon. Sir (Frederick) Maurice Drake, D.F.C., *born* 1923 1978
Hon. Sir Barry Cross Sheen, *born* 1918 1978
Hon. Sir David Bruce McNeill, *born* 1922 1979
Hon. Sir Christopher James Saunders French, *born* 1925. 1979
Hon. Sir Peter Edlin Webster, *born* 1924 1980
Hon. Sir Peter Murray Taylor, *born* 1930 1981
Hon. Sir Murray Stuart-Smith, *born* 1927 1981
Hon. Sir Christopher Stephen Thomas Jonathan Thayer Staughton, *born* 1933 1981
Hon. Sir Donald Henry Farquharson, *born* 1928 1981
Hon. Sir Anthony James Denys McCowan, *born* 1928 1981
Hon. Sir (Iain) Charles (Robert) McCullough, *born* 1931 1981

Hon. Sir Hamilton John Leonard, *born* 1926 .. 1981
Hon. Sir Alexander Roy Asplan Beldam, *born* 1925 1981
Hon. Sir David Cozens-Hardy Hirst, *born* 1925 1982
Hon. Sir John Stewart Hobhouse, *born* 1932 . . 1982
Hon. Sir Michael Mann, *born* 1930 1982
Hon. Sir Andrew Peter Leggatt, *born* 1930 . . . 1982
Hon. Sir Michael Patrick Nolan, *born* 1928 . . . 1982
Hon. Sir Oliver Bury Popplewell, *born* 1927 . . 1983
Hon. Sir William Alan Macpherson, T.D., *born* 1926 1983
Hon. Sir Philip Howard Otton, *born* 1933 1983
Hon. Sir Paul Joseph Morrow Kennedy, *born* 1935 1983
Hon. Sir Michael Hutchison, *born* 1933 1983
Hon. Sir Simon Denis Brown, *born* 1937 1984
Hon. Sir Anthony Howell Meurig Evans, *born* 1934 1984
Hon. Sir Mark Oliver Saville, *born* 1936...... 1985
Hon. Sir Johan Van Zyl Steyn, *born* 1932 1985
Hon. Sir Christopher Dudley Roger Rose, *born* 1937 1985
Hon. Sir Richard Howard Tucker, *born* 1931 . 1985
Hon. Sir Robert Alexander Gatehouse, *born* 1924 1985
Hon. Sir Patrick Neville Garland, *born* 1929 . . 1985
Hon. Sir John Ormond Roch, *born* 1934 1985
Hon. Sir Michael John Turner, *born* 1931 1985
Hon. Sir John Downes Alliott, *born* 1932..... 1986
Hon. Sir Harry Henry Ognall, *born* 1934 1986
Hon. Sir Konrad Hermann Theodor Schie-mann, *born* 1937...................... 1986
Hon. Sir John Arthur Dalziel Owen, *born* 1925.................................... 1986
Hon. Sir Denis Robert Maurice Henry, *born* 1931 1986
Hon. Sir Francis Humphrey Potts, *born* 1931 . 1986
Hon. Sir Richard George Rougier, *born* 1932 . 1986
Hon. Sir Ian Alexander Kennedy, *born* 1930 .. 1986
Hon. Sir Nicholas Addison Phillips, *born* 1938 1987

FAMILY DIVISION
President (£71,750)

Rt. Hon. Sir John Lewis Arnold (*born* 1915, *apptd.* 1979).
Secretary, Mrs. E. Coles; *Clerk*, C. Beardsmore.

Judges (each £65,000)	Apptd.
Rt. Hon. Sir John Brinsmead Latey, M.B.E., *born* 1914	1965
Hon. Sir (Alfred) Kenneth Hollings, M.C., *born* 1918....................................	1971
Hon. Sir (Charles) Trevor Reeve, *born* 1915 . . .	1973
Hon. Dame Rose Heilbron, D.B.E., *born* 1914 . . .	1974
Hon. Sir Brian Drex Bush, *born* 1925	1976
Hon. Sir John Kember Wood, M.C., *born* 1922 .	1977
Hon. Sir Ronald Gough Waterhouse, *born* 1926....................................	1978
Hon. Sir (John) Gervase (Kensington) Shel-don, *born* 1913	1978
Hon. Sir (Thomas) Michael Eastham, *born* 1920....................................	1978
Hon. Dame Margaret Myfanwy Wood Booth, D.B.E., *born* 1933	1979
Hon. Sir Anthony Leslie Julian Lincoln, *born* 1920....................................	1979
Hon. Dame (Ann) Elizabeth (Oldfield) Butler-Sloss, D.B.E. *born* 1933	1979
Hon. Sir Anthony Bruce Ewbank, *born* 1925 .	1980
Hon. Sir John Douglas Waite, *born* 1932	1982
Hon. Sir Anthony Barnard Hollis, *born* 1927 .	1982
Hon. Sir Swinton Barclay Thomas, *born* 1931 .	1985

RESTRICTIVE PRACTICES COURT

Judicial Members, The Hon. Mr. Justice Anthony Lincoln (*Principal*); The Hon. Mr. Justice Mc-Neill; The Hon. Mr. Justice Warner; Lord Ross.
Lay Members, N. L. Salmon; I. G. Stewart; B. M. Currie; L. Robertson; R. Garrick; Z. A. Silberston.

LORD CHANCELLOR'S DEPARTMENT
See Government and Public Offices.

SUPREME COURT DEPARTMENTS AND OFFICES
Royal Courts of Justice, WC2A 2LL

Administrator, S. Orchard .... £24,765–£29,465

Central Office of the Supreme Court
Royal Courts of Justice, WC2A 2LL

Senior Master of the Supreme Court (Q.B.D.), and Queen's Remembrancer, J. R. Bickford-Smith, T.D. £43,500
Masters of the Supreme Court (Q.B.D.), I. S. Warren; C. W. S. Lubbock; S. J. Waldman; P. B. Creight-more; K. W. Topley; D. L. Prebble; A. A. Grant; G. H. Hodgson; R. L. Turner £33,500
Chief Clerk (Central Office), R. P. Knight £15,030–£20,292
Chief Clerk to the Q.B. Judges in Chambers, C. F. Jones .... £15,030–£20,292

Crown Office of the Supreme Court
Royal Courts of Justice, WC2A 2LL

Master of the Crown Office, and Queen's Coroner and Attorney, D. R. Thompson, C.B., Q.C.

Official Referees of the Supreme Court

His Hon. Judge Hawser, Q.C.; His Hon. Judge Newey, Q.C.; His Hon. Judge Lewis, Q.C.; His Hon. Judge Davies, Q.C.; His Hon. Judge Fox-Andrews, Q.C.

Court of Appeal (Civil Division) Office
Royal Courts of Justice, WC2A 2LL

Registrar, J. D. R. Adams.

Criminal Appeal Office
Royal Courts of Justice, WC2A 2LL

Registrar, D. R. Thompson, C.B., Q.C. £43,500
Assistant Registrars, R. A. Venne; M. Mckenzie £24,765–£29,465
Chief Clerk, J. Read............... £15,030–£20,292

Courts-Martial Appeals Office
Royal Courts of Justice, WC2A 2LL

Registrar, D. R. Thompson, C.B., Q.C. £43,500
Chief Clerk, J. Read.

Supreme Court Taxing Office

Chief Master, F. T. Horne £43,500
Masters of the Supreme Court, M. A. Clews; F. G. Berkeley; A. J. Wright; C. R. N. Martyn; M. N. Devonshire, T.D.; P. T. Hurst; C. A. Prince £33,500
Chief Clerk, D. Hutchings .... £15,030–£20,292

Examiners of the Court
(Empowered to take Examination of Witnesses in all Divisions of the High Court)
M. F. Meredith-Hardy; B. Rathbone; N. W. Briggs; R. Jacobs.

Chancery Chambers,
Royal Courts of Justice, WC2A 2LL

Chief Master of the Supreme Court, R. D. Munro £43,500

Masters of the Supreme Court, M. B. Cholmondeley
Clarke; J. M. Dyson; J. S. Gowers; G. A. Barratt
£33,500
Chief Clerk, D. F. Jupe .... £15,030–£20,292
Conveyancing Counsel of the Supreme Court, J.
Monckton; S. G. Maurice; M. J. Roth.

Bankruptcy Department
Thomas More Building, Royal
Courts of Justice, Strand, WC2A 2LL

Chief Registrar, J. Bradburn £43,500
Chief Clerk, T. Palmer.

Official Receivers' Department

Senior Official Receiver, A. K. Sales.
Official Receivers, D. E. Dolman; P. J. Chillery; J. L.
P. Pope; J. V. F. Norris; R. G. L. Howard.

Companies Court
Thomas More Building,
Royal Courts of Justice, WC2A 2LL

Registrar, J. Bradburn.
Chief Clerk, J. R. Baker .... £15,030–£20,292
Senior Official Receiver, Companies Department,
A. K. Sales.

Restrictive Practices Court
Thomas More Building,
Royal Courts of Justice, WC2A 2LL

Clerk of the Court, J. Bradburn.
Chief Clerk, J. R. Baker.

Principal Registry (Family Division)
Somerset House, WC2R 1LP

Senior Registrar, B. P. Tickle £43,500
Registrars, C. F. Turner; T. G. Guest; D. E. Morris;
J. E. Artro-Morris; R. B. Rowe; G. B. N. A. Angel;
B. P. F. Kenworthy-Browne; G. A. Terian; Mrs.
K. T. Moorhouse; D. T. A. Davies; Mrs. N. Pearce;
M. J. Segal £33,500
Secretary, R. Conn .... £15,030–£20,292

District Probate Registrars

Birmingham and Stoke-on-Trent, C. Marsh.
Brighton and Maidstone, G. R. Garrett.
Bristol, Exeter and Bodmin, P. L. Speyer.
Ipswich, Norwich and Peterborough, E. R. Alexander.
Leeds, Lincoln and Sheffield, A. P. Dawson.
Liverpool, Lancaster and Chester, B. J. Thomas.
Llandaff, Bangor, Carmarthen and Gloucester,
D. W. Jones.
Manchester and Nottingham, M. A. Moran.
Newcastle, Carlisle, York and Middlesbrough, A.
Bertram.
Oxford and Leicester, Miss M. L. Farmborough.
Winchester, A. K. Biggs.

Admiralty Registry and Marshal's Office
Royal Courts of Justice, WC2A 2LL

Registrar, J. D. H. Rochford £33,500
Marshal and Chief Clerk, V. E. Ricks
£15,030–£20,292

Court of Protection
25 Store Street, W.C.1.

Master, Mrs. A. B. MacFarlane.
Chief Clerk, P. D. Lewis, T.D.

Protection Division
Head of Protection Division, E. J. Dober.

Management Division
Stewart House, 24 Kingsway, WC2R 6JX
Head of Management Division, J. R. Ellis.

Official Solicitor's Department
Penderel House, 287 High Holborn, W.C.1.

Official Solicitor to the Supreme Court, H. D. S.
Venables £37,000
Dep. do., H. J. Baker .... £24,765–£29,465
Chief Clerk, T. C. P. Molin .... £15,030–£20,292

OFFICE OF THE LORD CHANCELLOR'S VISITORS
Trevelyan House, 330 Great Peter Street, S.W.1.

Legal Visitor, M. H. Fauvelle.
Medical Visitors, W. A. Heaton-Ward; E. Carr; F. E.
Kenyon; R. J. Kerry; P. A. Morris; D. Parr; H.
Whittet.

OFFICE OF THE JUDGE ADVOCATE OF THE FLEET

Judge Advocate of the Fleet, His Hon. Judge Waley,
V.R.D., Q.C.

OFFICE OF THE JUDGE ADVOCATE GENERAL OF THE FORCES
(*Joint Service for the Army and the Royal Air Force*)
22 Kingsway, WC2B 6LE

Judge Advocate General, J. Stuart-Smith, C.B.
£48,250
Vice Judge Advocate General, G. L. Chapman
£43,500
Assistant Judge Advocates General, C. G. Gould; G.
E. Empson; G. R. Canner; E. G. Moelwyn-Hughes;
A. P. Pitts; S. B. Spence .... £24,765–£28,215
Deputy Judge Advocates, D. M. Berkson; M. A.
Hunter; T. R. King .... £17,336–£23,534

HIGH COURT AND CROWN COURT CENTRES

First-tier centres deal with both civil and criminal
cases and are served by High Court and Circuit
Judges. Second-tier centres deal with criminal cases
only but are served by both High Court and Circuit
Judges. Third-tier centres deal with criminal cases
only and are served only by Circuit Judges.

Midland and Oxford Circuit

First-tier—Birmingham, Lincoln, Nottingham, Ox-
ford, Stafford, Warwick. *Second-tier*—Leicester,
Northampton, Shrewsbury, Worcester. *Third-tier*—
Coventry, Derby, Dudley, Grimsby, Peterborough,
Stoke-on-Trent.
Circuit Administrator, R. E. K. Holmes, 2 Newton
Street, Birmingham B4 7LU.
Courts Administrators, *Birmingham Group*, C. A.
Green; *Nottingham Group*, P. H. Martin; *Stafford
Group*, A. F. Parker.

North Eastern Circuit

First-tier—Leeds, Newcastle upon Tyne, Sheffield,
Teesside. *Second-tier*—York. *Third-tier*—Beverley,
Doncaster, Durham, Huddersfield, Kingston-upon-
Hull, Wakefield.
Circuit Administrator, M. D. Huebner, West Riding
House, 17th Floor, Albion Street, Leeds LS1 5AA.
Courts Administrators, *Leeds Group*, C. A. White;
Newcastle upon Tyne Group, F. I. Lance; *Sheffield
Group*, G. Bingham.

Northern Circuit

First-tier—Carlisle, Liverpool, Manchester, Preston. *Third-tier*—Barrow-in-Furness, Bolton, Burnley, Kendal, Lancaster.

Circuit Administrator, P. M. Harris, Aldine House, West Riverside, New Bailey Street, Salford M3 5EU.

Courts Administrators, Manchester Group, A. H. Howard; *Liverpool Group*, B. H. Whittaker; *Preston Group*, G. Davies.

South Eastern Circuit

First-tier—Greater London, Lewes, Norwich (The High Court in Greater London sits at the Royal Courts of Justice. The Crown Court in Greater London sits at the following locations: Acton, Central Criminal Court, Croydon, Inner London Sessions House, Isleworth, Kingston upon Thames, Knightsbridge, Snaresbrook, Southwark and Wood Green). *Second-tier*—Chelmsford, Ipswich, Maidstone, Reading, St. Albans. *Third-tier*—Aylesbury, Bury St. Edmunds, Cambridge, Canterbury, Chichester, Guildford, King's Lynn, Southend.

Circuit Administrator, J. L. Heritage, New Cavendish House, 18 Maltravers Street, W.C.2.

Deputy Circuit Administrator, J. Howe.

Courts Administrators, Chelmsford Group, G. E. Calvett; *Maidstone Group*, G. R. Nicholls; *Kingston Group*, P. M. Thomas; *London (Civil)*, S. M. Orchard; *London (Crime)*, G. F. Addicott.

Wales and Chester Circuit

First-tier—Caernarfon, Cardiff, Chester, Mold, Swansea. *Second-tier*—Carmarthen, Newport, Welshpool. *Third-tier*—Dolgellau, Haverfordwest, Knutsford, Merthyr Tydfil, Warrington.

Circuit Administrator, S. W. L. James, Churchill House, Churchill Way, Cardiff.

Courts Administrators, Cardiff Group, G. Jones; *Chester Group*, E. R. Walter.

Western Circuit

First-tier—Bodmin, Bristol, Exeter, Winchester. *Second-tier*—Dorchester, Gloucester, Plymouth. *Third-tier*—Barnstaple, Bournemouth/Poole, Devizes, Newport (I.O.W.), Portsmouth, Salisbury, Southampton, Swindon, Taunton.

Circuit Administrator, G. Jones, Bridge House, Clifton, Bristol BS8 4BN.

Courts Administrators, Bristol Group, A. C. Burden; *Exeter Group*, (vacant); *Winchester Group*, K. Henderson.

CIRCUIT JUDGES
(each £43,500)

Midland and Oxford Circuit

W. A. L. Allardice; F. A. Allen; M. J. Astill; I. J. Black, Q.C.; F. A. Blennerhassett, Q.C.; J. F. Blythe, T.D.; F. L. Clark, Q.C.; P. Clark; R. Cole; J. M. Coulson; P. F. Crane; I. T. R. Davidson, Q.C.; A. de Piro, Q.C.; T. M. Dillon, Q.C.; J. F. Evans, Q.C.; B. A. Farrer, Q.C.; J. E. Fletcher; H. G. A. Gosling; M. K. Harrison-Hall; T. R. Heald; J. R. Hopkin; R. H. Hutchinson; J. E. M. Irvine; J. R. O. Jones; E. F. Jowitt, Q.C.; T. O. Kellock, Q.C.; J. T. C. Lee; M. H. Mander; K. Matthewman, Q.C.; R. G. May; P. W. Medd, O.B.E., Q.C.; K. S. W. Mellor, Q.C.; N. Micklem; A. J. H. Morrison; M. D. Mott; P. C. Northcote; C. J. Pitchers; F. M. Potter; D. E. Roberts; J. R. S. Smyth; P. J. Stretton; C. S. Stuart-White; H. C. Tayler, Q.C.; K. J. Taylor; R. J. Toyn; M. B. Ward; R. L. Ward, Q.C.; G. A. Whitehead, D.F.C.; D. J. R. Wilcox; D. H. Wild; H. Wilson; J. W. Wilson; B. Woods; G. H. Wootton; C. G. Young.

Northern Circuit

H. H. Andrew, Q.C.; J. R. Arthur, D.F.C.; A. W. Bell; R. M. Bingham, T.D., Q.C.; M. S. Blackburn; A. J. Blackett-Ord (*Vice Chancellor, County Palatine of Lancaster*); A. S. Booth, Q.C.; D. D. Brown, Q.C.; I. B.

Campbell; F. B. Carter, Q.C.; G. P. Crowe, Q.C.; J. M. Davies, Q.C.; Ann E. Downey; B. Duckworth; Ann M. Ebsworth; A. A. Edmondson; D. M. Evans, Q.C.; S. J. D. Fawcus; J. FitzHugh, Q.C.; D. M. Forster; D. G. F. Franks; J. Hall; R. G. Hamilton; J. A. Hammond; R. J. Hardy; Mary Holt; G. W. Humphries; W. H. W. Jalland; A. C. Jolly; H. A. Kershaw; H. L. Lachs; C. N. Lees; J. M. Lever, Q.C.; R. Lockett; J. H. Lord; I. H. Morris-Jones, Q.C.; F. J. Nance; G. K. Naylor, T.D.; M. O' Donoghue; F. D. Paterson; R. E. I. Pickering; D. A. Pirie; A. M. Prestt, Q.C. (*Recorder of Manchester*); M. A. G. Sachs; N. W. M. Sellers, V.R.D.; H. S. Singer; J. A. Stannard; Anne H. Steel; I. R. Taylor, Q.C.; E. S. Temple, M.B.E., Q.C. (*Recorder of Liverpool*); V. B. Webster; W. R. Wickham.

North Eastern Circuit

T. G. F. Atkinson; P. M. Baker, Q.C.; J. M. A. Barker; H. G. Bennett, Q.C.; B. Bush; M. C. Carr; Myrella Cohen, Q.C.; G. J. K. Coles, Q.C.; J. A. Cotton; J. Crabtree; W. H. R. Crawford, Q.C.; C. R. Dean, Q.C.; A. N. Fricker, Q.C.; S. S. Gill; H. G. Hall; P. H. Hallam; G. F. R. Harkins; J. A. Henham; D. Herrod, Q.C.; H. Hewitt; R. Hunt; V. R. Hurwitz; A. E. Hutchinson, Q.C.; J. R. Johnson; G. M. Lightfoot; A. C. Macdonald; A. L. Myerson, Q.C.; D. A. Orde; Miss H. E. Paling; R. A. Percy; J. Pickles; J. H. E. Randolph; D. M. Savill, Q.C.; A. Simpson; L. B. Stephen; J. Stephenson; R. A. R. Stroyan, Q.C.; R. C. Taylor; G. M. Voss; J. D. Walker; M. Walker; P. H. C. Walker; O. Wrightson.

South Eastern Circuit

F. J. Aglionby; A. K. Allen, O.B.E.; M. J. Anwyl-Davies, Q.C.; M. V. Argyle, M.C., Q.C.; A. P. Babington; J. A. Baker; J. B. Baker, Q.C.; P. V. Baker, Q.C.; A. F. Balston; R. M. N. Band, M.C., Q.C.; R. A. Barr; N. G. A. Bathurst; P. T. S. Batterbury, T.D.; N. E. Beddard; F. E. Beezley; G. J. Binns; M. Birks; J. C. C. Blofeld, Q.C.; J. Bolland; P. N. Brandt; L. J. Bromley, Q.C.; A. E. Brooks; G. N. Butler, Q.C.; N. M. Butter, Q.C.; H. J. Byrt, Q.C.; C. V. Callman; B. E. Capstick, Q.C.; Sir Harold Cassel, Bt., T.D., Q.C.; A. W. Clark; D. J. Clarkson, Q.C.; J. L. Clay, T.D.; Patricia Coles, Q.C.; C. C. Colston, Q.C.; C. D. Compston; M. J. Cook; R. K. Cooke, O.B.E.; G. H. Coombe; M. R. Coombe; Margaret D. Cosgrave; A. G. W. Coulthard; P. H. Counsell; A. E. Cox; P. V. Crocker; D. W. L. Davies, Q.C.; I. H. Davies; L. J. Davies, Q.C.; W. N. Denison, Q.C.; K. M. Devlin; G. L. S. Dobry, C.B.E., Q.C.; C. M. Edwards; Q. T. Edwards, Q.C.; J. K. Q. Evans; P. R. Faulks, M.C.; A. L. Figgis; I. Finestein, Q.C.; J. A. R. Finlay, Q.C.; J. J. Finney; J. J. Fordham; G. C. F. Forrester; J. Fox-Andrews, Q.C.; A. Garfitt; L. Gerber; P. W. Goldstone; M. B. Goodman; J. H. Gower, Q.C.; M. Graham, Q.C.; P. B. Greenwood; D. J. Griffiths; R. B. Groves, T.D., R.D.; Jean G. Hall; P. J. Halnan; J. Hamilton; R. E. Hammerton; J. P. Harris, D.S.C., Q.C.; T. F. Hatton; C. L. Hawser, Q.C.; J. D. W. Hayman; J. B. R. Hazan, Q.C.; A. H. Head; M. R. Hickman; D. E. Hill-Smith, V.R.D.; A. N. Hitching; D. Holden; A. C. W. Hordern, Q.C.; Sir David Hughes-Morgan, Bt., C.B., C.B.E.; J. Hunter; H. J. Hyam; C. P. James; W. Kee; M. Kennedy, Q.C.; J. F. Kingham; L. G. Krikler; L. H. C. Lait; R. Laurie; T. Lawrence; C. G. Lea, M.C.; N. Lermon, Q.C.; E. Lewis, Q.C.; A. C. L. Lewisohn; A. Lipfriend; D. T. Lloyd; G. D. Lovegrove, Q.C.; D. B. D. Lowe; R. H. Lownie; Noreen M. Lowry; R. J. Lowry, Q.C.; R. D. Lymbery, Q.C.; K. M. McHale; I. G. McLean; J. L. E. MacManus, T.D., Q.C.; M. B. MacMullan; M. J. P. Macnair; K. A. Machin, Q.C.; J. R. Main, Q.C.; A. Marder, Q.C.; O. S. Martin, Q.C.; J. H. E. Mendl; A. L. Mildon, Q.C.; Sir James Miskin, Q.C. (*Recorder of London*); E. F. Monier-Williams; D. Morton Jack; J. D. F. Moylan; J. I. Murchie; J. H. R. Newey, Q.C.; C. W. F. Newman, Q.C.; Mrs. M. F. Norrie; Suzanne F. Norwood; C. R. Oddie; A. Owen; D. A. Paiba; R. H. S. Palmer; M. C. Parker, Q.C.; R. B.

H. Pearce, Q.C.; Miss V. A. Pearlman; F. H. L. Petre;
A. L. Phelan; T. H. Pigot, Q.C. (*Common Serjeant*); D.
C. Pitman; H. C. Pownall; B. H. Pryor, Q.C.; J. E.
Pullinger; R. D. Ranking; J. W. Rant, Q.C.; E. V. P.
Reece; G. R. Rice; D. A. H. Rodwell, Q.C.; G. H. Rooke,
T.D., Q.C.; P. C. R. Rountree; K. W. Rubin; J. H. A.
Scarlett; J. D. Sheerin; G. J. Shindler, Q.C.; M. Singh,
Q.C.; J. K. E. Slack, T.D.; P. M. J. Slot; R. J. Southam;
R. O. C. Stable, Q.C.; E. Stockdale; J. H. A. Stucley,
D.S.C.; J. B. Taylor, M.B.E., T.D.; D. A. Thomas, M.B.E.;
A. H. Tibber; A. M. Troup; S. Tumim; J. T. Turner;
M. T. Underhill, Q.C.; J. E. Van der Werff; L. J.
Verney, T.D.; A. O. R. Vick, Q.C.; R. W. Vick; B. J.
Wakley, M.B.E.; A. F. Waley, V.R.D., Q.C.; M. E. Ward;
J. R. Warde; D. B. Watling, Q.C.; V. B. Watts; Sir
David West-Russell; F. J. White; J. E. Williams; S.
M. Willis; G. N. Worthington; E. E. Wrintmore.

Wales and Chester Circuit

T. R. Crowther, Q.C.; G. H. M. Daniel; R. D. G.
David, Q.C.; Lord Elystan-Morgan; T. M. Evans, Q.C.;
W.N.Francis; M.Gibbon, Q.C.; D.W.Howells; G.Jones;
T. E. I. Lewis-Bowen; D. T. Lloyd-Jones, V.R.D.; G.
Morgan; P. T. Hopkin Morgan, Q.C.; D. Morgan
Hughes; D. A. Phillips; C. N. Pitchford; D. W. Powell;
H. W. J. ap Robert; H. E. P. Roberts, Q.C.; J. C. Rutter;
S. M. Stephens, Q.C.; D. B. Williams, T.D., Q.C.; H.
Williams, Q.C.; R. G. Woolley.

Western Circuit

G. B. Best; N. R. Blaker, Q.C.; Joyanne W.
Bracewell, Q.C.; B. R. Braithwaite; Sir Jonathan
Clarke; P. H. F. Clarke; Hazel Counsell; J. A. Cox; J.
W. Da Cunha; M. Dyer; P. Fallon, Q.C.; P. D. Fanner;
B. J. F. Galpin; I. Starforth Hill, Q.C.; G. B. Hutton;
J. H. Inskip, Q.C.; A. C. Lauriston, Q.C.; Sir Ian Lewis;
I. P. Llewellyn Jones; D. McCarraher, V.R.D.; H. E. L.
McCreery, Q.C.; Sheila M. D. McKinney; G. G.
Macdonald; C. B. Mantell, Q.C.; E. G. Neville; D. A.
Smith, Q.C.; K. C. L. Smithies; H. M. J. Tucker, Q.C.;
J. R. Whitley; K. M. Willcock, Q.C..

RECORDERS

J. R. S. Adams; M. F. Addison; I. D. G. Alexander;
W. P. Andreae-Jones, Q.C.; B. J. Appleby, Q.C.; J. F.
Appleton; J. F. A. Archer, Q.C.; The Rt. Hon. P. K.
Archer, Q.C., M.P.; A. J. Arlidge; R. Ashton; P.
Ashworth, Q.C.; N. J. Atkinson; R. E. Auld, Q.C.; M.
G. Austin-Smith; W. S. Aylen, Q.C.; P. Back, Q.C.; P.
G. N. Badge; M. J. D. Baker; N. R. J. Baker; T. S. G.
Baker, Q.C.; A. Barker, Q.C.; B. J. Barker; D. Barker,
Q.C.; R. O. Barlow; D. M. W. Barnes, Q.C.; T. P. Barnes,
Q.C.; C. J. A. Barnett, Q.C.; W. E. Barnett, Q.C.; A. R.
Barrowclough, Q.C.; J. E. Barry; J. C. T. Barton; S.
T. Bates, Q.C.; R. J. A. Batt; J. J. Baughan; P. M.
Beard; C. H. Beaumont; P. J. L. Beaumont, Q.C.; C.
O. M. Bedingfield, T.D., Q.C.; R. E. Bell, Q.C.; The Hon.
M. J. Beloff, Q.C.; P. Bennett, Q.C.; K. C. Bentall; D.
R. Bentley, Q.C.; D. M. Berkson; Miss I. Bernstein; R.
H. Bernstein, D.F.C., Q.C.; M. Bethel, Q.C.; J. C.
Beveridge, Q.C.; J. W. Black, Q.C.; D. M. Blair; J. A.
Blair-Gould; C. Bloom, Q.C.; J. G. Boal; G. T. K.
Boney; C. L. Boothman; L. A. F. Borrett; M. R.
Bowley, Q.C.; P. C. Bowsher, Q.C.; I. R. Boyd; R. W. A.
Bray; D. J. Brennan, Q.C.; G. J. B. G. Brice, Q.C.; J. N.
W. Bridges-Adams; A. N. J. Briggs; P. J. Briggs; S. E.
Brodie, Q.C.; M. J. L. Brodrick; H. Brooke, Q.C.; R.
Brown; D. M. A. Bryant; D. W. Brunning; R. J.
Buckley, Q.C.; J. M. Bull, Q.C.; J. W. M. Bullimore; D.
L. Bulmer; J. P. Burgess; J. P. Burke, Q.C.; J. K.
Burke, Q.C.; M. A. B. Burke-Gaffney, Q.C.; R. D. H.
Bursell, Q.C.; A. J. Butcher, Q.C.; A. N. L. Butterfield,
Q.C.; R. J. Buxton, Q.C.; D. C. Calcutt, Q.C.; Mrs. B. A.
Calvert, Q.C.; D. Calvert-Smith; Miss S. M. C.
Cameron, Q.C.; The Lord Campbell of Alloway, Q.C.;
G. M. C. Carey; A. C. Carlile, Q.C., M.P.; H. B. H.

Carlisle, Q.C.; M. Carlisle, Q.C.; R. C. L. Carr; B. I.
Caulfield; E. S. Cazaler, Q.C.; J. A. Chadwin, Q.C.; J.
R. Chalkley; N. M. Chambers, Q.C.; B. L. Charles,
Q.C.; P. J. Charlesworth; B. W. Chedlow, Q.C.; C. H.
Clark; D. Clark; A. P. Clarke, Q.C.; D. C. Clarke, Q.C.;
P. C. Clegg; R. N. B. Clegg, Q.C.; C. D. Cochrane; D. J.
Cocks, Q.C.; J. R. Cole; N. B. C. Coles, Q.C.; A. D.
Collins, Q.C.; J. M. Collins, Q.C.; J. M. Collins; A. D.
Colman, Q.C.; J. S. Colyer, Q.C.; P. R. C. Coni, Q.C.; T.
A. C. Coningsby, Q.C.; M. B. Connell, Q.C.; J. G.
Connor; Miss B. P. Cooper, Q.C.; Rt. Hon. Sir
Frederick Corfield, Q.C.; Miss D. R. Cotton, Q.C.; J. S.
Coward, Q.C.; B. R. E. Cox, Q.C.; P. J. Cox, D.S.C., Q.C.;
R. C. Cox; P. J. Crawford, Q.C.; C. J. Crespi, Q.C.; P. J.
Cresswell, Q.C.; D. I. Crigman; M. L. S. Cripps; D. L.
Croft, Q.C.; F. P. Crowder, Q.C.; J. D. Crowley, Q.C.; E.
J. R. Crowther, O.B.E., Q.C.; W. R. H. Crowther, Q.C.;
Miss E. A. M. Curnow, Q.C.; R. H. Curtis, Q.C.; S. C.
Darwall-Smith; Mrs. S. P. Darwall-Smith; G. W.
Davey; R. E. Davies, Q.C.; J. J. Deave; J. B. Deby,
Q.C.; C. F. Dehn, Q.C.; P. N. De Mille; W. E. Denny,
C.B.E., Q.C.; S. C. Desch, Q.C.; A. E. J. Diamond, Q.C.; J.
B. S. Diehl; A. M. Donne; D. P. Draycott, Q.C.; J. M.
Drinkwater, Q.C.; R. Du Cann, Q.C.; S. B. Duncan; W.
H. Dunn, Q.C.; C. H. Durman; J. A. Dyson, Q.C.

D. Eady, Q.C.; J. S. Eastwood; H. W. P. Eccles; D. E.
H. Edwards; G. O. Edwards, Q.C.; D. F. Elfer, Q.C.; G.
Elias, Q.C.; B. J. Elliot; G. A. Ensor; D. A. Evans, Q.C.;
F. P. L. Evans; Miss M. A. P. Evans; E. C. Evans-
Lombe, Q.C.; G. N. Eyre, Q.C.; W. D. Fairclough; J. D.
Farnworth; D. J. Farrer, Q.C.; E. J. Faulkes; M. H.
Fauvelle; J. D. A. Fennell, O.B.E., Q.C.; R. Fernyhough,
Q.C.; T. G. Field-Fisher, T.D., Q.C.; Miss E. N. Fisher;
W. R. Fitch; G. D. Flather, Q.C.; P. E. J. Focke, Q.C.;
T. J. Forbes, Q.C.; P. J. Fox, Q.C.; N. H. Freeman; R.
H. K. Frisby, Q.C.; W. M. Gage, Q.C.; M. Gale, Q.C.; M.
S. Garner; L. N. H. George; R. J. H. Gibbs, Q.C.; L.
Giovene; A. T. Glass, Q.C.; W. J. Glover, Q.C.; Miss A.
F. Goddard, Q.C.; H. K. Goddard, Q.C.; S. A. Goldstein;
J. B. Goldring, Q.C.; A. A. Gordon; C. G. M. Gordon;
J. P. Gorman, Q.C.; T. J. C. Gouldie, Q.C.; The Lord
Grantchester, Q.C.; G. Gray, Q.C.; R. I. Gray, Q.C.; R.
M. K. Gray, Q.C.; A. D. Green, Q.C.; B. S. Green, Q.C.;
H. Green; S. P. Grenfell; R. D. Grey, Q.C.; W. P.
Grieve, Q.C.; D. L. Griffiths; J. C. Griffiths, Q.C.; L.
Griffiths; G. D. Grigson; M. G. Grills; Mrs. H. M.
Grindrod, Q.C.; A. S. Hacking, Q.C.; M. F. Haigh; J.
H. Hames, Q.C.; A. W. Hamilton, Q.C.; G. M. Hamilton,
T.D., Q.C.; J. Hampton; W. Hannah; Miss R. S. A.
Hare, Q.C.; B. Hargrove, Q.C.; R. D. Harman,
Q.C.; R. M. Harrison, Q.C.; F. D. Hart, Q.C.; C. S.
Harvey, M.B.E., T.D.; M. L. T. Harvey, Q.C.; R. O.
Havery, Q.C.; T. S. A. Hawkesworth, Q.C.; R. G.
Hawkins, Q.C.; R. W. P. Hay; R. Hayward-Smith; M.
Heald, Q.C.; G. E. Heggs; R. A. Henderson, Q.C.; R. H.
Q. Henriques, Q.C.; R. B. Hickman; J. C. Hicks, Q.C.;
A. B. Hidden, Q.C.; B. J. Higgs, Q.C.; A. M. Hill, Q.C.;
E. M. Hill, Q.C.; A. J. H. Hilton; J. D. Hitchen; T. D.
T. Hodson; P. M. L. Hoffman; D. A. Hollis, V.R.D., Q.C.;
C. G. Hookway; A. T. Hoolahan, Q.C.; A. Hooper, Q.C.;
The Lord Hooson, Q.C.; R. Houlker, Q.C.; M. Howard,
Q.C.; M. J. Hubbard, Q.C.; J. Hugill, Q.C.; J. G. Hull,
Q.C.; P. J. Hunt, Q.C.; I. G. A. Hunter; B. A. Hytner,
Q.C.; N. E. J. Inglis-Jones, Q.C.; The Lord Irvine of
Lairg, Q.C.; F. C. Irwin, Q.C.; M. R. Jackson; P. J. E.
Jackson; I. E. Jacob; C. E. F. James; N. F. B. Jarman,
Q.C.; D. A. Jeffreys, Q.C.; J. Jeffs, Q.C.; D. B. Johnson,
Q.C.; M. H. Johnson; R. L. Johnson, Q.C.; E. S. Jones,
Q.C.; G. R. Jones; N. H. Jones, Q.C.; T. G. Jones; W. H.
Joss; P. S. L. Joyce; I. Judge, Q.C.; M. D. L. Kalisher,
Q.C.; J. W. Kay, Q.C.; D. St. J. Keane, Q.C.; M. L.
Keane; D. N. Keating, Q.C.; R. W. M. Keeling; D. A.
M. Kemp, Q.C.; A. M. Kenny; T. D. Kent-Jones; P. M.
Kershaw, Q.C.; R. I. Kidwell, Q.C.; G. E. Kilfoil; A. W.
P. King; R. C. Klevan, Q.C.; C. F. Kolbert.

D. G. Lane; G. J. H. Langley, Q.C.; D. N. R. Latham,
Q.C.; R. B. Latham; G. F. B. Laughland, Q.C.; J. G. M.

Laws; L. D. Lawton, q.c.; M. K. Lee, q.c.; R. T. L. Lee; C. H. de V. Leigh; Sir Godfrey Le Quesne, q.c.; S. Levine; M. E. Lewer, q.c.; A. K. Lewis, q.c.; M. ap G. Lewis, q.c.; R. S. Lewis; C. C. D. Lindsay, q.c.; B. J. E. Livesey; R. J. D. Livesey, q.c.; C. G. Llewellyn-Jones; J. Lloyd-Eley, q.c.; F. R. Lockhart; A. J. C. Lodge; F. D. L. Loy; J. A. T. Loyd, q.c.; Sir Nicholas Lyell, q.c., M.P.; E. Lyons, q.c.; A. G. MacDuff; D. D. McEvoy, q.c.; S. N. McKinnon, q.c.; I. S. Mackintosh; N. R. B. Macleod, q.c.; N. J. C. McLusky; Miss M. B. MacMurray, q.c.; K. C. Macrae; J. G. McNaught; E. A. Machin, q.c.; B. C. Maddocks; C. J. Mahon; Miss V. H. Mairants; Miss A. Mallalieu; F. J. M. Marr-Johnson; R. G. Marshall-Andrews, q.c.; D. N. N. Martineau; D. Matheson; P. B. Mauleverer, q.c.; R. B. Mawrey, q.c.; A. T. K. May, q.c.; H. R. Mayor, q.c.; N. A. Medawar, q.c.; M. Meggerson; D. J. Mellor; J. M. Meredith; J. T. Milford; D. Q. Miller; R. A. Miller; Mrs. B. J. L. Mills, q.c.; J. B. M. Milmo, q.c.; N. A. Miscampbell, q.c., M.P.; S. G. Mitchell; H. J. Montlake; L. J. J. Morgan; W. G. O. Morgan, q.c.; G. E. Moriarty, q.c.; M. Morland, q.c.; D. G. Morris; The Rt. Hon. J. Morris, q.c., M.P.; T. H. Moseley, q.c.; A. G. Moses; P. C. Mott; F. J. Muller, q.c.; N. J. Mylne, q.c.; R. F. Nelson, q.c.; G. M. Newman, q.c.; J. D. Newton; A. J. D. Nicholl; C. V. Nicholls, q.c.; C. A. A. Nicholls, q.c.; M. C. Nicholson; A. S. T. E. Nicol; J. G. Nutting; D. P. O'Brien, q.c.; R. C. C. O'Rorke; E. M. Ogden, q.c.; B. R. Oliver; S. K. O'Malley; S. K. Overend; G. V. Owen, q.c.; S. R. Page; D. C. J. Paget; A. W. Palmer, q.c.; S. A. B. Parish; T. C. Parkin; E. O. Parry; N. S. K. Pascoe; A. Patience; J. G. Paulusz; Mrs. N. Pearce; D. H. Penry-Davey; J. R. Peppitt, q.c.; Sir Ian Percival, q.c.; D. S. Perrett, q.c.; M. T. Pill, q.c.; Miss E. F. Platt, q.c.; J. R. Playford, q.c.; A. G. S. Pollock, q.c.; P. B. Pollock; D. A. Poole, q.c.; M. H. Potter; M. J. Pratt, q.c.; T. W. Preston, q.c.; J. E. Previté; J. A. Price, q.c.; P. J. Price; A. J. Proctor; E. J. Prosser, q.c.; G. V. Pugh, q.c.; C. P. B. Purchas; A. G. Purnell, q.c.; N. R. Purnell, q.c.; P. O. Purnell, q.c.; Mrs. C. M. Puxon, q.c.; J. R. Pyke.

A. Rankin, q.c.; A. D. Rawley, q.c.; L. F. Read, q.c.; A. R. F. Redgrave; P. Rees; J. R. Reid, q.c.; M. S. Rich, q.c.; D. W. Richards; H. A. Richardson; K. A. Richardson; Miss S. A. Ritchie, q.c.; G. Rivlin, q.c.; J. M. G. Roberts, q.c.; P. B. Roberts; V. Robinson, q.c.; D. E. H. Robson, q.c.; D. A. H. Rodwell, q.c.; J. M. T. Rogers, q.c.; J. W. Rogers, q.c.; P. H. Rolf; J. J. Rowe, q.c.; R. J. Royce, q.c.; J. H. Rucker; J. N. P. J. Rudd; R. R. Russell; G. C. Ryan, q.c.; T. R. G. F. Ryland; N. T. Salts, q.c.; J. E. A. Samuels, q.c.; R. B. Sanders; M. P. Sayers; R. J. Scholes; A. F. B. Scrivener, q.c.; R. J. Seabrook, q.c.; C. Seagroatt, q.c.; H. M. Self, q.c.; Brig. D. M. D. Selwood; J. A. O. Shand; R. M. Shawcross; M. D. Sherrard, q.c.; L. Shield; L. S. Shields, q.c.; J. M. Shorrock; D. R. A. Sich; K. T. Simpson; A. T. Smith, q.c.; R. S. Smith, q.c.; R. E. Snape; R. F. Solman; Miss J. M. Southworth, q.c.; G. C. H. Spafford; M. H. Spence, q.c.; D. H. Spencer, q.c.; M. G. Spencer; S. M. Spencer; J. A. C. Spokes, q.c.; S. A. Stamler, q.c.; D. H. Stembridge; J. S. H. Stewart, q.c.; R. M. Stewart, q.c.; D. M. A. Stokes; E. D. R. Stone, q.c.; M. Stuart-Moore; J. Stuart-Smith; F. R. C. Such; A. B. Suckling, q.c.; C. J. Sumner; D. M. Sumner; L. Swift, q.c.; M. R. Swift; A. B. Taylor; E. Taylor; N. Taylor, q.c.; W. E. M. Taylor; K. J. Tetley; D. M. Thomas, O.B.E., q.c.; D. O. Thomas, q.c.; J. Thomas, q.c.; Rt. Hon. P. J. M. Thomas, q.c.; R. U. Thomas, q.c.; W. F. C. Thomas; A. A. R. Thompson, q.c.; M. A. Thorpe, q.c.; C. H. Tilling; R. N. Titheridge, q.c.; J. K. Toulmin, q.c.; R. G. Toulson, q.c.; J. B. S. Townend, q.c.; J. P. Townend; S. L. Tuckey, q.c.; H. W. Turcan; P. A. Twigg, q.c.; C. J. M. Tyrer; A. R. Tyrrell, q.c.; Mrs. A. P. Uziell-Hamilton; N. P. Valios; A. R. Vandermeer, q.c.; Miss M. S. Viner, q.c.; Rt. Hon. D. C.

Waddington, q.c., M.P.; J. P. Wadsworth, q.c.; D. St. J. R. Wagstaff; R. M. Wakerley, q.c.; W. H. Waldron, q.c.; R. J. Walker, q.c.; T. E. Walker, q.c.; J. J. Walker-Smith; G. M. Waller, q.c.; B. Walsh, q.c.; A. H. Ward, q.c.; C. D. G. P. Waud; D. M. Webster, q.c.; P. A. Webster; M. Weisman; P. Weitzman, q.c.; C. P. C. Whelon; C. H. Whitby, q.c.; P. J. M. Whiteman, T.D.; A. Whitfield, q.c.; D. G. Widdicombe, q.c.; G. H. G. Williams, q.c.; G. W. Williams, q.c.; J. G. Williams, q.c.; J. L. Williams, q.c.; The Hon. J. M. Williams, q.c.; S. W. Williamson, q.c.; J. C. Willis; A. M. Wilson, q.c.; C. Wilson-Smith, q.c.; G. W. Wingate-Saul, q.c.; M. E. Wolff; H. Wolton, q.c.; D. A. Wood, q.c.; D. R. Woolley, q.c.; N. G. Wootton; N. J. Worsley; P. F. Worsley; J. M. Wright, q.c.; G. N. Barr Young; K. H. Zucker, q.c.

STIPENDIARY MAGISTRATES

Greater Manchester, William D. Fairclough (1982); Cecil T. Latham, O.B.E. (1976).
Humberside, Neville H. White (1985).
Merseyside, Norman G. Wootton (1976).
Mid Glamorgan, David P. Rowland (1961); Benjamin R. Oliver (1983).
South Glamorgan, Sir Lincoln Hallinan (1976).
South Yorkshire, Ian W. Crompton (1983); James E. Barry (1985).
West Midlands, Frederick H. Hatchard (1981); William M. Probert (1983); Geoffrey H. Kamil (1987).
West Yorkshire, Francis D. L. Loy (1972); Ian R. Boyd (1982).

INNER LONDON MAGISTRATES

Chief Metropolitan Stipendiary Magistrate and Chairman of Committee of Magistrates for Inner London Area, Sir David Hopkin (*Bow Street*) £43,500

Committee of Magistrates for Inner London Area
3rd Floor, North West Wing,
Bush House, Aldwych, WC2B 4PJ

Principal Chief Clerk and Clerk to the Committee, I. Fowler £33,054
Chief Clerk (Training), J. W. Greenhill £28,734

Magistrates
(each £33,500)

Bow Street, The Chief Magistrate; William E. C. Robins; Ronald D. Bartle; Terence M. English.

Camberwell Green, Roger D. Connor; David B. Meier; Peter Fingret; Mrs. Heather Mitchum; Bruce Morgan.

Clerkenwell, Mark L. R. Romer; Christopher J. Bourke; Michael A. Johnstone.

Greenwich and Woolwich, Miss Pamela M. Long; Timothy H. Workman; Miss Dorothy Quick.

Highbury Corner, David Barr; Graham E. Parkinson; Ronald T. Moss; Geoffrey B. Breen.

Horseferry Road, Eric J. R. Crowther, O.B.E.; Sir Bryan Roberts, K.C.M.G., q.c.; Charles P. M. Davidson.

Marlborough Street, Kenneth J. H. Nichols; Jeremy G. Connor.

Marylebone, Geoffrey L. J. Noel; John Q. Campbell; Stanley G. Clixby; Barrington Black.

Old Street, Roger B. Sanders; Terence Maher.

South Western, Miss Dawn A. Freedman; David Q. Miller; Anura Cooray.

Thames, Peter G. N. Badge; B. J. Canham.

Tower Bridge, Christopher D. Voelcker; Mrs. Jacqueline R. Comyns; David K. Brown.

Wells Street, Christopher Besley; Miss Audrey M. Jennings; David M. Fingleton; Nicholas Crichton.

West London, David Fairbairn; Harold J. Cook.

Unattached Magistrates, Mrs. Norma F. Negus; Keith Maitland-Davies; A. Roger Davies.

CROWN PROSECUTION SERVICE
Headquarters: 4/12 Queen Anne's Gate, SW1H 9AZ
[01-213 3000: *Casework sections,* 01-222 7944]

Fraud Divisions
10 Furnival Street, EC4A 1PE
[01-831 3038]

The Crown Prosecution Service (C.P.S.) handles the prosecution of criminal proceedings instituted by police forces (excluding certain minor road traffic offences). The head of the C.P.S. is the Director of Public Prosecutions: day-to-day administration of the C.P.S. is handled by the Deputy Director. There are four Regional Directors responsible for the 31 areas: each area is headed by a Chief Crown Prosecutor.

Salaries

Grade 1	£64,739
Grade 2	£43,264–£45,349
Grade 3	£33,725–£36,852
Grade 4	£28,975–£30,475
Grade 5	£24,739–£28,215
London Weighting = £1,465 p.a.	

Director of Public Prosecutions (G1), A. D. Green, Q.C..

Deputy Director and Chief Executive (G2), D. S. Gandy, O.B.E.

Principal Establishment and Finance Officer (G3), J. Merchant.

Director, Headquarters Casework (G3), Mrs. M. Phillips.

Head, General Casework (G5), T. Taylor.

Head, Special Casework (G5), K. Horn.

Head, Policy Division (G5), K. Ashken.

Heads, Fraud Divisions (G5), T. Waring; G. Adams.

Head, Police Complaints Division (G5), C. Cleugh.

Head, Financial Services (G5), B. Spratt.

Head, Personnel and Office Services (G5), Mrs. P. Hurley.

In addition, the four Regional Directors are based at C.P.S. headquarters: the Director, Northern Region also has an office in Manchester.

C.P.S. AREAS

Northern Region
Suite 101, Sunlight House, Quay Street
Manchester M3 3JU
Regional Director(G3), B. Crebbin

CHESHIRE, Hamilton House, Hamilton Place, Chester CH1 2BH.—*Chief Crown Prosecutor (G5),* Mrs. N. E. Hollingworth.

CLEVELAND/N. YORKSHIRE, Rydale Buildings, 60 Piccadilly, York YO1 1PA.—*Chief Crown Prosecutor (G5),* C. Mc. C. Sharp.

GREATER MANCHESTER, P.O.Box 491, Sunlight House, Quay Street, Manchester M60 3LU.—*Chief Crown Prosecutor (G4),* A. Taylor.

LANCASHIRE/CUMBRIA, Red Rose House, Lancaster Road, Preston, Lancs. PR1 1ER.—*Chief Crown Prosecutor (G5),* J. V. Bates.

MERSEYSIDE, 7th Floor (South), Royal Liver Building, Liverpool L3 1HN.—*Chief Crown Prosecutor (G4),* E. C. Woodcock.

NORTHUMBRIA/DURHAM, Newgate House, Newgate Street, Newcastle upon Tyne NE1 5UQ.—*Chief Crown Prosecutor (G5),* G. Duff.

N. WALES/DYFED/POWYS, 491 Abergele Road, Old Colwyn, Colwyn Bay, Clwyd LL29 9AE.—*Chief Crown Prosecutor (G5),* A. S. R. Clarke.

S. YORKSHIRE, Belgrave House, 47 Bank Street, Sheffield S1 2EH.—*Chief Crown Prosecutor (G4),* M. J. Rose.

W. YORKSHIRE, Grove Hall, College Grove Road, Wakefield WF1 3RA.—*Chief Crown Prosecutor (G4),* R. Otley.

Midland Region
Regional Director (G3), R. Williamson.

CAMBRIDGESHIRE/LINCOLNSHIRE, The River Mill, St Ives, Huntingdon, Cambs. PE17 4HJ.—*Chief Crown Prosecutor (G5),* D. G. Lewis.

DERBYSHIRE, Celtic House, Heritage Gate, Derby DE1 9BR.—*Chief Crown Prosecutor (G5),* D. R. K. Seddon.

HUMBERSIDE, Queens House, Paragon Street, Hull HU3 3DA.—*Chief Crown Prosecutor (G5),* L. M. Bell.

LEICESTERSHIRE/NORTHAMPTONSHIRE, Leicester House, Lee Circle, Leicester LE1 3RE.—*Chief Crown Prosecutor (G5),* G. Etherington.

NORFOLK/SUFFOLK, Saxon House, 1 Franciscan Way, Ipswich, Suffolk IP1 1TR.—*Chief Crown Prosecutor (G5),* M. F. C. Harvey.

NOTTINGHAMSHIRE, Victoria House, 76 Milton Street, Nottingham NG1 3QZ.—*Chief Crown Prosecutor (G5),* D. C. Beal.

STAFFORDSHIRE/WARWICKSHIRE, Government Building, Millbank, Stafford ST16 8QU.—*Chief Crown Prosecutor (G5),* D. V. Dickenson.

WEST MIDLANDS, The McClaren Building, Dale End, Birmingham B4 7LN.—*Chief Crown Prosecutor (G3),* I. S. Manson.

South and West Region
Regional Director (G3), C. Hoad.

AVON/SOMERSET, Froomsgate House, Rupert Street, Bristol BS1 2PS.—*Chief Crown Prosecutor (G5),* R. O. M. Lovibond.

DEVON/CORNWALL, Bradninch Hall, Castle Street, Exeter EX4 3PL.—*Chief Crown Prosecutor (G5),* R. J. Green.

DORSET/HAMPSHIRE, Black Horse House, 8–10 Leigh Road, Eastleigh, Hants. SO5 4FH.—*Chief Crown Prosecutor (G5),* P. Boeuf.

GLOUCESTERSHIRE/WILTSHIRE, Avonbridge House, Bath Road, Chippenham, Wiltshire SN15 2BB.—*Chief Crown Prosecutor (G5),* R. A. Prickett.

S. WALES/GWENT, Pearl Assurance House, Greyfriars Road, Cardiff CF1 3AG.—*Chief Crown Prosecutor (G4),* H. G. Wallace.

SUSSEX, Unit 3, Clifton Mews, Clifton Hill, Brighton, E. Sussex BN1 3HR.—*Chief Crown Prosecutor (G5),* D. Thompson.

THAMES VALLEY, The Courtyard, Lombard Street, Abingdon, Oxon. OX14 5SE.—*Chief Crown Prosecutor (G5),* P. D. F. Higginbottom.

WEST MERCIA, Orchard House, Victoria Square, Droitwich, Worcester WR9 8QT.—*Chief Crown Prosecutor (G5),* B. G. Coase.

London and South East
Regional Director (G3), R. Gwilliam.

ESSEX, Gemini Centre, 88 New London Road, Chelmsford, Essex CM2 0BR.—*Chief Crown Prosecutor (G5),* J. J. Goodwin.

HERTFORDSHIRE/BEDFORDSHIRE, Queens House, 58 Victoria Street, St Albans AL1 3HZ.—*Chief Crown Prosecutor (G5)*, R. J. Chronnell.

KENT, Kent House, Lower Stone Street, Maidstone, Kent ME15 6JT.—*Chief Crown Prosecutor (G5)*, R. A. Crabb.

LONDON (INNER), New Portland House, Stag Place, SW1.—*Chief Crown Prosecutor (G4)*, B. McArdle.

LONDON (NORTH), Solar House, 1 Romford Road, Stratford E15 4LJ.—*Chief Crown Prosecutor (G4)*, S. J. Wooler.

LONDON (SOUTH)/SURREY, Tolworth Tower, Surbiton KT6 7DS.—*Chief Crown Prosecutor (G4)*, D. E. Dracup.

THE SCOTTISH JUDICATURE

Scotland has a legal system separate and differing greatly from the English legal system in enacted law, judicial procedure and the structure of courts.

There is in Scotland a system of public prosecution headed by the Lord Advocate which is independent of the police, who have no say in the decision to prosecute. The Lord Advocate, discharging his functions through the Crown Office in Edinburgh, is responsible for prosecutions in the High Court, sheriff courts and district courts. Prosecutions in the High Court are prepared by the Crown Office and conducted in court by one of the Law Officers or an advocate-depute. In the inferior courts the decision to prosecute is made and prosecution is preferred by procurators fiscal, who are lawyers and full-time civil servants, subject to the directions of the Crown Office. A permanent legally-qualified civil servant known as the Crown Agent is responsible for the running of the Crown Office and the organization of the Procurator Fiscal Service, of which he is the head.

Scotland is divided into six Sheriffdoms, each with a full-time Sheriff Principal. The Sheriffdoms are further divided into sheriff court districts, each of which has a legally-qualified, resident sheriff or sheriffs, who are the judges of the court.

In criminal cases sheriffs principal and sheriffs have the same powers: sitting with a jury of 15 members, they may try more serious cases on indictment, or, sitting alone, may try lesser cases under summary procedure. Minor summary offences are dealt with in district courts which are administered by the district and the islands local government authorities and presided over by lay justices of the peace, and, in Glasgow only, by stipendiary magistrates. Juvenile offenders (children under 16) may be brought before an informal children's hearing comprising three local lay people. The superior criminal court is the High Court of Justiciary which is both a trial and an appeal court. Cases on indictment are tried by a High Court Judge, sitting with a jury of 15, in Edinburgh and on circuit in other towns. Appeals from the lower courts against conviction or sentence are heard also by the High Court, which sits as an appeal court only in Edinburgh. There is no further appeal to the House of Lords in criminal cases.

In civil cases the jurisdiction of the sheriff court extends to most kinds of action. Appeal against decisions of the sheriff may be made to the Sheriff Principal and thence to the Court of Session, or direct to the Court of Session, which sits only in Edinburgh. The Court of Session is divided into the Inner and the Outer House. The Outer House is a court of first instance in which cases are heard by judges sitting singly, sometimes with a jury of 12. The Inner House, itself subdivided into two Divisions of equal status, is mainly an appeal court. Appeals may be made to the Inner House from the Outer House as well as from the sheriff court: an appeal may be made from the Inner House to the House of Lords.

The Judges of the Court of Session are the same as those of the High Court of Justiciary, the Lord President of the Court of Session also holding the office of Lord Justice General in the High Court.

The office of coroner does not exist in Scotland: the local procurator fiscal inquires privately into sudden and suspicious deaths and may report findings to the Crown Agent. In some cases a fatal accident inquiry may be held before the sheriff.

COURT OF SESSION (Established 1532) and HIGH COURT OF JUSTICIARY

The Lord President and Lord Justice General, The Rt. Hon. The Lord Emslie, M.B.E.

INNER HOUSE.—*First Division.*

The Lord President, The Rt. Hon. The Lord Emslie, (George Carlyle Emslie, M.B.E.) £74,750
Hon. Lord Grieve, (William Robertson Grieve, V.R.D.)
Hon. Lord Brand, (David William Robert Brand).
Hon. Lord Kincraig, (Robert Smith Johnston).

Second Division

Lord Justice Clerk, The Rt. Hon. Lord Ross, (Donald MacArthur Ross) £71,750
Hon. Lord Robertson, (Ian Macdonald Robertson, T.D.)
Hon. Lord Dunpark, (Alastair McPherson Johnston, T.D.)
Hon. Lord McDonald, (Robert Howat McDonald, M.C.)
Hon. Lord Maxwell, (Peter Maxwell) (*seconded to Scottish Law Commission*)

OUTER HOUSE

Rt. Hon. Lord Wylie, (Norman Russell Wylie, V.R.D.)
Hon. Lord Allanbridge, (William Ian Stewart)
Hon. Lord Cowie, (William Lorn Kerr Cowie)
Hon. Lord Jauncey, (Charles Eliot Jauncey)
Rt. Hon. Lord Murray, (Ronald King Murray)
Hon. Lord Mayfield, (Ian MacDonald, M.C.)
Hon. Lord Davidson, (Charles Kemp Davidson)
Rt. Hon. Lord McCluskey, (John Herbert McCluskey).
Hon. Lord Morison, (Alastair Malcolm Morison)
Hon. Lord Sutherland, (Ranald Iain Sutherland)
Hon. Lord Weir, (David Bruce Weir)
Hon. Lord Clyde, (James John Clyde)
Hon. Lord Cullen, (William Douglas Cullen)
Hon. Lord Prosser (William David Prosser).
Hon. Lord Kirkwood (Ian Candlish Kirkwood).
(SALARIES: All judges other than the Lord President and Lord Justice Clerk, £65,000)

Court of Session and High Court of Justiciary
Parliament House, Parliament Square, Edinburgh

Principal Clerk of Session and Justiciary, A. M. Campbell . . . . £24,739–£28,215
Deputy Principal Clerk of Session and Principal Extractor, V. A. Woods . . . . £14,927–£20,292
Deputy Principal Clerk of Justiciary, J. Robertson
£14,927–£20,292
Deputy Principal Clerk (Administration) and Keeper of the Rolls, H. S. Foley . . . . £14,927–£20,292
Depute Clerks of Session and Justiciary, W. Gillon; M. Weir; A. Hogg; N. J. Dowie; M. G. Bonar; I. Smith; J. A. R. Cowie; T. Higgins; E. A. Cumming; B. Watson; P. J. McGonigle; W. McCulloch; T. B. Cruickshank; Q. Oliver; F. Shannly; P. Crow; J. L. Anderson; R. D. Sinclair; Mrs. A. Leighton; J. Clark; T. M. Thomson; D. D. Mackay . . . . £12,150–£15,500

Scottish Courts Administration
26–27 Royal Terrace, Edinburgh EH7 5AH

Director, G. Murray.

SHERIFFS PRINCIPAL, SHERIFFS, SHERIFF CLERKS AND PROCURATORS FISCAL IN SCOTLAND

Sheriffdom and Sheriff Principal	Sheriffs	Sheriff Clerks	Procurators Fiscal
Grampian, Highland and Islands.— S. E. Bell, Q.C.	*Aberdeen, Stonehaven,* A. M. G. Russell, Q.C.; A. L. Stewart; D. J. Risk; D. Bogie; D. Kelbie.	J. Rodden .... I. P. Smith	S. W. Lockhart, C.B.E. (*Regional Procurator Fiscal*). J. D. McNaughton.
	Banff and Peterhead, A. J. Murphy.	W. H. Connon ...... A. H. Hempseed	A. J. M. Colley. I. S. McNaughtan.
	Elgin, N. McPartlin.	I. Munro	A. Wither.
	Inverness, Lochmaddy, Portree, Stornoway, Dingwall, Tain, Wick, Dornoch, W. J. Fulton; D. Booker-Milburn; J. O. A. Fraser; E. Stewart.	J. S. Doigt† .... W. Dunn	D. R. Hingston. C. B. McClory. C. S. Mackenzie. W. M. S. Carnegie. H. T. Westwater. B. Heywood.
	Kirkwall, Lerwick, A. A. MacDonald.	J. Rodden	A. W. Wright. Miss A. Thom.
	Fort William, D. Noble (*also Oban and Campbeltown*)	J. S. Doigt†	J. I. M. MacGillivray.
Tayside, Central and Fife.— R. R. Taylor, Q.C., PH.D.	*Arbroath, Forfar,* S. O. Kermack	B. T. McCabe ...... R. G. Davis	C. D. G. Hillary. A. L. Ingram.
	Dundee, E. F. Bowen; G. L. Cox	B. J. Young†	D. R. Smith (*Regional Procurator Fiscal*).
	Perth, J. F. Wheatley; C. Smith*.	Miss J. Telfer	M. MacPhail.
	Falkirk, A. V. Sheehan; A. B. Wilkinson.	E. G. Appelbe	G. E. Scott.
	Stirling, W. C. Henderson; R. E. G. Younger	K. MacKenzie......	K. Valentine. Miss M. W. Robertson.
	Alloa, R. E. G. Younger	R. G. Young	
	Cupar, J. C. McInnes (*also Perth*)	B. Sullivan	R. A. S. Brown.
	Dunfermline, J. S. Forbes; W. M. Reid.	J. M. Hay	R. T. Hamilton.
	Kirkcaldy, W. J. Christie; C. R. Macarthur, Q.C.	T. Fyffe	Mrs. I. Guild.
Lothian and Borders.— Sir Frederick O'Brien, Q.C.	*Edinburgh,* N. E. D. Thomson; R. D. Ireland, Q.C.; J. L. M. Mitchell; P. G. B. McNeill, PH.D.; Miss H. J. Aronson; R. G. Craik, Q.C.; G. I. W. Shiach; J. A. Farrell*; Miss I. A. Poole; R. J. D. Scott; G. W. S. Presslie; I. A. Cameron.	D. B. White†	J. D. Allan (*Regional Procurator Fiscal*).
	Peebles, N. E. D. Thomson (*also Edinburgh*).	D. B. White†	F. J. M. Brown.
	Linlithgow, I. D. MacPhail; M. Stone	R. Sinclair	H. R. Annan.
	Haddington, G. W. S. Presslie (*also Edinburgh*)	B. W. S. Manthorpe.	I. D. Douglas.
	Jedburgh, Duns, J. V. Paterson.	J. R. Jenkins	J. C. Whitelaw.
	Selkirk, J. V. Paterson	J. R. Jenkins	D. J. F. Howdle.
North Strathclyde.— P. I. Caplan, Q.C.	*Oban and Campbeltown,* D. Noble (*also Fort William*).	G. Waddell .... A. A. Brown†	I. Henderson.
	Dumbarton, J. P. Murphy; J. T. Fitzsimons; C. W. Palmer; F. H. Hamilton*.	N. R. Weir	J. Cardle.
	Paisley, A. K. F. Hunter; H. R. MacLean; R. G. Smith.	A. A. Brown†	J. B. R. Mackinnon (*Regional Procurator Fiscal*).
	Greenock, J. Irvine Smith (*also Rothesay*); Sir Stephen Young.	A. P. McPherson ...	A. T. W. Wilson. W. D. Stewart.
	Kilmarnock, T. M. Croan; D. B. Smith; T. F. Russell.	J. Shaw	J. L. McLeod.

*Floating Sheriffs.   †Regional Sheriff Clerk.

Sheriffdom and Sheriff Principal	Sheriffs	Sheriff Clerks	Procurators Fiscal
Glasgow and Strathkelvin.— N. D. MacLeod, Q.C.	*Glasgow,* N. D. MacLeod; A. C. Horsfall; J. J. Maguire; A. A. Bell, Q.C.; J. S. Mowat; B. Kearney; G. H. Gordon, Q.C.; A. C. McKay; A. Lothian; J. C. M. Jardine; Mrs. D. J. B. Robertson; B. A. Lockhart; I. G. Pirie; Miss A. L. A. Smith; W. G. Stevenson, Q.C.; G. J. Evans; E. H. Galt; F. J. Keane; A. C. Henry; A. M. Bell; J. K. Mitchell; A. G. Johnston; C. Smith*.	C. McLay†.........	A. S. Jessop *(Regional Procurator Fiscal).*
South Strathclyde, Dumfries and Galloway.— M. G. Gillies, T.D., Q.C.	*Hamilton,* J. R. Fiddes, Q.C.; L. S. Lovat; A. C. MacPherson; W. F. Lunny; I. A. MacMillan, C.B.E.; V. J. Canavan *(also Airdrie)*; R. H. Dickson*.	J. Cumming	W. G. Carmichael *(Regional Procurator Fiscal).*
	Lanark, R. G. McEwan, Q.C.	A. S. Morwood	S. R. Houston.
	Ayr, D. M. K. Grant; N. Gow, Q.C.	T. D. McIntosh	N. G. O'Brien.
	Stranraer, Kirkcudbright, J. R. Smith.	L. McFarlane	F. Walkingshaw.
	Dumfries, K. G. Barr.	W. Jones	J. T. MacDougall.
	Airdrie, J. H. Stewart; J. S. Boyle; V. J. Canavan *(also Hamilton)*.	H. Findlay†........	A. C. Normand.

*Floating Sheriffs.   †Regional Sheriff Clerk.

Crown Office
5/7 Regent Road, Edinburgh EH7 5BL

Crown Agent, I. Dean, C.B. £45,349
Deputy Crown Agent, J. D. Lowe £31,844

Companies Registration Office
102 George Street, Edinburgh EH2 3DJ

Registrar, E. T. K. Lougheed.

Sheriff Court of Chancery
16 North Bank Street, Edinburgh

Sheriff of Chancery, Sir Frederick O'Brien, Q.C.

H.M. Commissary Office
16 North Bank Street, Edinburgh

Commissary Clerk, D. B. White.

SCOTTISH LAND COURT
1 Grosvenor Crescent, Edinburgh

Chairman, The Hon. Lord Elliott, M.C.
Members, A. B. Campbell, O.B.E.; D. D. McDiarmid; R. MacDonald.

NORTHERN IRELAND JUDICATURE

In Northern Ireland the legal system and the structure of courts closely resemble those of England and Wales; there are, however, often differences in enacted law.

The Supreme Court of Judicature of Northern Ireland comprises the Court of Appeal, the High Court of Justice and the Crown Court. The practice and procedure of these Courts is similar to those in England. The superior civil court is the High Court of Justice, from which an appeal lies to the Court of Appeal; the House of Lords is the final civil appeal court.

The decision to prosecute in cases tried on indictment and in summary cases of a serious nature rests in Northern Ireland with the Director of Public Prosecutions, who is responsible to the Attorney General. Minor summary offences are prosecuted by the police.

Minor criminal offences are dealt with in magistrates' courts by a full-time, legally qualified resident magistrate and, where an offender is under 17, by juvenile courts consisting of the resident magistrate and two lay members specially qualified to deal with juveniles (at least one of whom must be a woman). Appeals from magistrates' courts are heard by the county court. The Crown Court, served by High Court and county court judges, deals with criminal trials on indictment. Cases are heard before a judge and, except those involving offences specified under emergency legislation, a jury. Appeals from the Crown Court against conviction or sentence are heard by the Northern Ireland Court of Appeal; the House of Lords is the final court of appeal.

Magistrates' courts in Northern Ireland can deal with certain classes of civil case but most minor civil cases are dealt with in county courts. Judgments of all civil courts are enforceable through a centralized procedure administered by the Enforcement of Judgments Office.

SUPREME COURT OF JUDICATURE
The Royal Courts of Justice, Belfast.

Lord Chief Justice of Northern Ireland, The Rt. Hon. The Lord Lowry.
Judges, The Rt. Hon. Lord Justice (Turlough) O'Donnell; The Rt. Hon. Lord Justice (Sir John William Basil) Kelly; The Hon. Lord Justice (John Clarke) MacDermott; The Hon. Mr. Justice (Donald Bruce) Murray; The Hon. Mr. Justice (James Brian Edward) Hutton; The Hon. Mr. Justice (John Patrick Basil) Higgins; The Hon. Mr. Justice (Robert Douglas) Carswell; The Hon. Mr. Justice (James Michael Anthony) Nicholson; The Hon. Mr. Justice (William Paschal) McCollum.

Lord Chief Justice's Office

Principal Secretary to the Lord Chief Justice and Clerk of the Crown for Northern Ireland, J. A. L. McLean, Q.C.

Legal Secretary to the Lord Chief Justice, R. T. Millar.

Master, Central Office, V. A. Care, Q.C.
Master, Office of Care and Protection, F. B. Hall.
Master, Chancery Office, V. G. Bridges.
Master, Bankruptcy and Companies Office, J. B. C. Glass.
Master, Probate and Matrimonial Office, D. W. G. Heatly.
Master, High Court, J. W. Wilson.
Master, Taxing Office, A. E. Anderson, C.B.E.
Accountant, Court Funds Office, J. Teer.

Recorders

Belfast, J. K. Pringle, Q.C.
Londonderry, A. R. Hart, Q.C.

County Court Judges

Judge Babington, D.S.C., Q.C.; Judge Chambers, Q.C.; Judge Curran, Q.C.; Judge Donaldson, Q.C.; Judge Gibson, Q.C.; Judge Hart, Q.C.; Judge McKee, Q.C.; Judge Petrie, Q.C.; Rt. Hon. Judge Sir Robert Porter, Q.C.; Judge Rowland, Q.C.; Judge Russell, Q.C.; Judge Watt, Q.C.

Crown Solicitor, H. A. Nelson.
Director of Public Prosecutions, Sir Barry Shaw, C.B., Q.C.

ECCLESIASTICAL COURTS

Original jurisdiction is exercised by the Consistory Court of each Diocese in England, presided over by the Chancellor of that Diocese. Appellate jurisdiction is exercised by the Provincial Courts detailed below, and by the Court for Ecclesiastical Causes Reserved, and by Commissions of Review (the membership of these being newly constituted for each case).

Arches Court of Canterbury
Registry, 16 Beaumont Street, Oxford.

Dean of the Arches, The Rt. Worshipful Sir John Owen.

Chancery Court of York
Registry, 5 New Street, York.

Auditor, The Rt. Worshipful Sir John Owen.

Court of Faculties
Registry, 1 The Sanctuary, S.W.1.

Office for the issue of special and ordinary marriage licences, appointment of notaries public, etc. Office hours, Mon.–Fri., 10–4.

Master of the Faculties, The Rt. Worshipful Sir John Owen.
Vicar-General of the Province of Canterbury, The Rt. Worshipful Miss S. Cameron, Q.C.
Vicar-General of the Province of York, The Rt. Worshipful T. A. C. Coningsby, Q.C.

TRIBUNALS, ETC

Employment Appeal Tribunal
Central Office, 4 St. James's Square, SW1Y 4JU.
Divisional Office, 11 Melville Crescent, Edinburgh, EH3 7LU.
President, The Hon. Mr. Justice Popplewell.
Registrar, Mrs. J. Harbord.

The Industrial Tribunals
Central Office (England and Wales)
93 Ebury Bridge Road, S.W.1

President, His Honour Judge Sir David West-Russell
£48,250

Central Office (Scotland)
St. Andrew House, 141 West Nile Street, Glasgow

President, R. C. Hay, W.S. £44,500

Immigration Appeal Tribunal
Thanet House, 231 Strand, WC2R 1DA

President, D. L. Neve.
Vice-Presidents, G. W. Farmer; Prof. D. C. Jackson.

Lands Tribunal
48/49 Chancery Lane, WC2A 1JR

President, Sir Douglas Frank, Q.C.
Members, V. G. Wellings, Q.C.; W. H. Rees; C. R. Mallett; W. Hall, D.F.C., J. C. Hill.
Registrar, C. A. McMullan.

Lands Tribunal for Scotland
1 Grosvenor Crescent, Edinburgh EH12 5ER

President, The Hon. Lord Elliott, M.C.
Members, W. Hall, D.F.C.; T. Finlayson (*full-time*); W. D. C. Andrews, C.B.E., W.S.; K. O. Osborne, Q.C.; J. Horsburgh, Q.C. (*part-time*).
Clerk, D. McCallum.

N.H.S. Tribunal

Inquires into representations that the continued inclusion of a family practitioner (doctor, dentist, pharmacist or optician) on a Family Practitioner Committee's list would be prejudicial to the efficiency of the services concerned. The Tribunal sits when required, about eight times a year, and usually in London.

Chairman, B. Hargrove, Q.C.
Clerk, I. D. Keith, Martlets House, 25–26 Queens Square, Crawley, W. Sussex RH10 1EU.

Pensions Appeal Tribunals
48/49 Chancery Lane, WC2A 1JR

Responsibility for hearing appeals in connection with War Pensions.

President, M. H. Fauvelle.

Performing Right Tribunal
Room 1509, State House, 66–71 High Holborn, WC1R 4TP

Chairman, W. Aldons, Q.C.
Secretary, E. J. Barnett.

The Office of the President of Social Security Appeal Tribunals and Medical Appeal Tribunals
Almack House, 26–28 King Street, SW1Y 6QW

An independent statutory authority which exercises judicial and administrative control over social security appeal tribunals and medical appeal tribunals.

President, Hon. Judge Byrt, Q.C.
Secretary, J. Connelly.

The Office of the Social Security Commissioners
London: Harp House, 83/86 Farringdon Street, EC4A 4BL
Cardiff: 16 Park Grove, CF1 3BN
Edinburgh: 23 Melville Street, EH3 7PW

The final statutory authority to decide social security and medical claims.

Chief Commissioner, Hon. Judge Bromley, Q.C.
Secretary, Miss H. A. R. Baker (*London*); I. Erskine (*Edinburgh*).

The Solicitors' Disciplinary Tribunal
60 Carey Street, WC2A 2JB

Independent body appointed by the Master of the Rolls.

President, J. H. Walford.
Clerk, Mrs. S. C. Elson.

Special Commissioners of Income Tax
Turnstile House, 98 High Holborn, WC1V 6LQ

Independent body appointed by the Lord Chancellor to hear appeals concerning income taxes, etc.

Presiding Special Commissioner, R. H. Widdows
£43,264
Special Commissioners, A. K. Tavaré; B. M. F. O'Brien; T. H. K. Everett £34,669
Clerk, R. P. Lester £15,074

Transport Tribunal
4th Floor, Golden Cross House,
Duncannon Street, WC2N 4JF

President, Judge Inskip, Q.C.
Secretary, D. T. R. Evans.

V.A.T. Tribunals
15/17 Great Marlborough Street, W1V 2AP

V.A.T. Tribunals are administered by the Lord Chancellor's Department (the Secretary of State in Scotland) and are intended to determine disputes concerning V.A.T.

President, The Lord Grantchester, C.B.E., Q.C.
Vice-President, Scotland, R. A. Bennett, Q.C.
Registrar, J. M. Busby.

Tribunal Centres

London (including Belfast), 15/17 Great Marlborough Street, W1V 2AP.
Edinburgh, 44 Palmerston Place, Edinburgh EH12 5BJ.
Manchester, Warwickgate House, Warwick Road, Old Trafford, Manchester M16 0GP.

Parliamentary and Local Government Election Petitions Office
Room 120, Royal Courts of Justice, WC2A 2LL

Prescribed Officer, J. R. Bickford Smith, T.D.

POLICE FORCES IN UNITED KINGDOM

METROPOLITAN POLICE OFFICE
New Scotland Yard, Broadway, SW1H 0BG
[01–230 1212]

Commissioner, P. M. Imbert, Q.P.M. £62,100
Deputy Commissioner, J. Dellow, C.B.E. £46,389
Receiver, D. H. J. Hilary £45,349
Deputy Receiver, J. E. Owen £31,770

Territorial Operations Department
Assistant Commissioner, G. D. McLean, Q.P.M.
£40,926
Deputy Assistant Commissioner, C. F. Dinsdale
£32,739
Head of Administration, Miss B. Arnold
£18,786–£25,335
Commanders, N. B. Dickens; J. P. Robinson; W. E. E. Boreham £28,734

Area Headquarters
Deputy Assistant Commissioners, D. H. Cree, Q.P.M.; T. J. Siggs; D. N. Meynell; R. Innes, Q.P.M.; P. L. Condon; R. B. Wells, Q.P.M.; G. W. Jones, Q.P.M. £32,739
Commanders, G. M. Ness; J. A. Coo; D. J. Polkinghorne; P. J. Carson, Q.P.M.; G. E. Howlett, Q.P.M.; Miss T. M. Wagstaff; L. T. Roach; B. Sparks; Miss J. H. Wilton; D. N. Stevens; G. R. Lloyd; M. J. Gough; E. Jones; M. J. Sullivan; R. C. Marsh; J. A. Howley; A. E. Marnoch, Q.P.M.; A. G. Fry; C. J. Rideout, Q.P.M. £28,734
Metropolitan Police Special Constabulary, Chief Commandant, A. A. Hammond, O.B.E.

Specialist Operations Department
Assistant Commissioner, H. N. Annesley, Q.P.M.
£40,926
Deputy Assistant Commissioners, J. H. Cracknell, L.V.O.; S. R. A. Crawshaw, Q.P.M.; B. R. C. Worth, O.B.E.; J. M. M. Huins £32,739
Commanders, M. R. Campbell; K. G. Churchill-Coleman; P. H. Corbett; A. W. F. Hemingway, Q.P.M.; R. A. Dowling; A. McNair; P. Phelan, Q.P.M.; J. J. Plowman; J. M. Allain, Q.P.M.; D. C. Veness; D. C. Gunn £28,734

Metropolitan Police Laboratory

Director, R. L. Williams, C.B.E. £31,178
Deputy Directors, G. J. O. Lee; M. R. Loveland; P. D. Martin; E. F. Pearson .... £18,786–£25,335
Senior Principal Scientific Officer, B. B. Wheals
£18,786–25,335

National Drugs Intelligence Unit

Co-ordinator, B. Price £40,926

Personnel and Training Department
Assistant Commissioner, C. B. J. Sutton, Q.P.M.
£40,926
Deputy Assistant Commissioner, M. J. Evans, Q.P.M.; A. W. Young £32,739
Commanders, D. M. Cansdale; D. J. Osland; A. J. Speed £28,734
Welfare Officer, K. F. T. Rivers, M.B.E £14,927–£20,292

Metropolitan Police Cadet Corps

Commander, D. M. Cansdale £28,734

Medical and Dental Branch

Chief Medical Officer, E. C. A. Bott

Management Support Department
Assistant Commissioner, J. A. Smith, Q.P.M. . £40,926
Deputy Assistant Commissioner, P. J. Winship
£32,739
Commander, E. Mitchell, Q.P.M. £28,734

Complaints Investigation Bureau

Commander, K. J. Merton, Q.P.M. £28,734

Directorate of Public Affairs

Director of Public Affairs, B. D. Goodfellow
£24,739–£28,215
Deputy Director of Public Affairs, J. P. Stubbs
£18,786–25,335

Directorate of Management Services

Director, N. E. Hand .... £24,739–£28,215
Deputy Directors, J. E. Tubb; Mrs. S. M. Merchant
£18,786–£25,385

Force Inspectorate
Deputy Assistant Commissioner, R. A. Hunt, O.B.E.
£32,739
Commanders, E. D. Humphrey; K. E. Hunter. £28,734

Solicitor's Department
Solicitor, C. S. Porteous £31,770
Assistant Solicitors, R. E. Marsh; P. A. Shawdon; D.
S. Hamilton .... £24,739–£28,215

The following departments are responsible to the
Receiver through the Deputy Receiver.

"E" Department
Establishments and Secretariat

Establishment Officer, R. B. Jones .. £24,739–£28,215
Deputy Establishment Officers, E. R. Bright; M. W.
Maidment; P. I. May .... £18,786–£25,335

"F" Department
Finance

Director of Finance, J. A. Crutchlow £24,739–£28,215
Deputy Directors of Finance, J. L. Davies; A. M. J.
Williams; D. Wilson .... £18,786–£25,335

Supplies and Services Department
Director, N. N. I. Batten .... £18,786–£25,335

Catering Department
Director of Catering, Col. R. R. Owens, O.B.E.
£18,786–£25,335

Property Services Department
Director of Property Services, M. L. Belchamber
£24,739–£28,215
Deputy Directors, R. M. Boa; J. A. Chipchase; K. R.
Sewell .... £18,786–£25,335

Chief Engineer's Department
Chief Engineer, D. Hale, O.B.E. ..... £24,739–£28,215
Deputy Chief Engineers, N. Boothman; C. W. Cornock; J. M. Wardle; D. A. Woolgar; G. Sudbury
£18,786–£25,335

Department of Computing Services
Director of Computing Services, R. G. Gregory
£24,739–£28,215
Deputy Directors of Computing Services, D. K. Dun-
kin; T. Egan .... £18,786–£25,335

CITY OF LONDON POLICE
26 Old Jewry, EC2R 8DJ

Commissioner, O. Kelly, Q.P.M. £45,018
Assistant Commissioner, W. Taylor £35,091
Commander, H. J. Moore £28,734
Chief Superintendents, J. E. Conray (*Administra-
tion*); R. Fowlie (*Traffic & Communications*); T.
Hillier ("*B" Divn.*); E. G. Aggar ("*C" Divn.*); B. A.
Tarbun (*C.I.D.*); G. Squires, P. Nove (*C.I.D/Fraud*)
£24,846–£26,352

City of London Special Constabulary
Chief Commandant, F. A. D. Ralfe.
Staff Officer, P. Redman.

BRITISH TRANSPORT POLICE
15 Tavistock Place, WC1H 9SJ
[01–388 7541]

The Force provides a policing service to the British
Railways Board and its wholly-owned subsidiary
companies, London Underground Ltd., and Sealink

U.K. Ltd. Police posts are located throughout Eng-
land, Wales and Scotland.
Chief Constable, K. H. Ogram, Q.P.M.
Deputy Chief Constable, G. E. Coles.
Assistant Chief Constables, T. H. S. Buckle (*Admin-
istration*); W. I. McGregor (*Operations*); J. Nixon
(*Personnel & Training*); W. F. Palmer (*London
Underground Division*); A. M. Mackenzie (*Scottish
Division*).

MINISTRY OF DEFENCE POLICE
Ministry of Defence, Empress State Building,
Lillie Road, SW6 1TR
[01–385 1244]

The Ministry of Defence Police are responsible
chiefly for the policing of naval, military, R.A.F.
establishments, etc. in Great Britain.
Chief Constable, J. Aspinall.
Deputy Chief Constable, N. L. Chapple, Q.P.M.
Head of M.D.P. Secretariat, L. Bone.
Assistant Chief Constable (*Operations*), A. A. J. Scale.

Area Headquarters
Central Area, Apsley House, Stockport, Cheshire.—
Assistant Chief Constable, A. F. Grant.
Northern Area, Hilton Road, Rosyth, Fife.—*Assistant
Chief Constable,* C. Bucke.
Southern Area, Aldershot, Hants.—*Assistant Chief
Constable,* R. E. Murray.
Western Area, Spring Quarry, Copenacre, Hawthorn,
Wilts.—*Assistant Chief Constable,* S. G. Edwards.

STAFF ASSOCIATIONS
ASSOCIATION OF CHIEF POLICE OFFICERS OF ENGLAND,
WALES AND NORTHERN IRELAND, Room 1133, New
Scotland Yard, Broadway, SW1H 0BG.—Repre-
sents the Chief Constables, Deputy Chief Con-
stables and Assistant Chief Constables of England,
Wales and N. Ireland, and officers of the rank of
Commander and above in the Metropolitan and
City of London Police. *Gen. Sec.,* G. Maxted
(*acting*).
THE POLICE SUPERINTENDENTS' ASSOCIATION OF ENG-
LAND AND WALES, 67a Reading Road, Pangbourne
RG8 7JD.—Represents officers of the rank of
Superintendent and Chief Superintendent. *Sec.,*
Chief Supt. K. A. Smith.
THE POLICE FEDERATION OF ENGLAND AND WALES,
15–17 Langley Road, Surbiton, Surrey KT6 6LP.—
Represents officers up to and including the rank of
Chief Inspector. *Gen. Sec.,* W. F. Tanner.
ASSOCIATION OF CHIEF POLICE OFFICERS (SCOTLAND),
Police Headquarters, Fettes Avenue, Edinburgh
EH4 1RB.—Represents the Chief Constables, Dep-
uty Chief Constables and Assistant Chief Con-
stables of the Scottish police forces. *Hon. Sec.,*
Chief Constable W. G. M. Sutherland, Q.P.M.
THE ASSOCIATION OF SCOTTISH POLICE SUPERINTEND-
ENTS, Hon. Secretary's Office, Strathclyde Police,
Divisional Headquarters, Campbell Street, Hamil-
ton ML3 6AT.—Represents officers of the rank of
Superintendent and Chief Superintendent. *Hon.
Sec.,* Chief Supt. J. McNicol.
THE SCOTTISH POLICE FEDERATION, 5 Woodside Place,
Glasgow G3 7PD.—Represents officers up to and
including the rank of Chief Inspector. *Gen. Sec.,*
A. W. A. Wallace.
THE SUPERINTENDENTS ASSOCIATION OF NORTHERN
IRELAND, Ormiston House, Hawthornden Road,
Belfast BT4 3NH.—Represents Superintendents
and Chief Superintendents in the R.U.C. *Hon. Sec.,*
W/Chief Supt. A. Donald.
THE POLICE FEDERATION FOR NORTHERN IRELAND,
Royal Ulster Constabulary, Garnerville, Garner-
ville Road, Belfast BT4 2NX.—Represents officers
up to and including the rank of Chief Inspector.
Gen. Sec., J. Elder.

POLICE AUTHORITIES IN THE UNITED KINGDOM

Police Force	Headquarters	Actual Strength	Chief Constable	Chairman of Police Authority/Committee
England				
Avon and Somerset	Bristol	3,030	R. Broome, O.B.E., Q.P.M.	R. G. Bell
Bedfordshire	Bedford	984	A. Dyer, Q.P.M.	*
Cambridgeshire	Huntingdon	1,147	I. H. Kane, Q.P.M.	D. N. Morris
Cheshire	Chester	1,868	D. J. Graham, Q.P.M.	J. H. Collins, O.B.E.
Cleveland	Middlesbrough	1,464	C. F. Payne, Q.P.M.	Mrs. I. Cole
Cumbria	Penrith	1,119	B. D. K. Price, Q.P.M.	Maj. T. R. Riley
Derbyshire	Derby	1,778	A. O. Smith, Q.P.M.	A. Barnes
Devon and Cornwall	Exeter	2,757	D. Elliott, Q.P.M.	J. R. W. R. Carew-Pole
Dorset	Dorchester	1,207	B. H. Weight, Q.P.M.	Maj. Gen. H. M. G. Bond
Durham	Durham	1,320	E. J. Boothby, Q.P.M.	A. Agar
Essex	Chelmsford	2,784	R. S. Bunyard, C.B.E., Q.P.M.	G. C. Waterer, M.B.E.
Gloucestershire	Cheltenham	1,159	A. H. Pacey, Q.P.M.	C. P. Hay
Hampshire	Winchester	3,104	J. Duke, C.B.E., Q.P.M.	Capt. M. P. R. Boyle
Hertfordshire	Welwyn Garden City	1,587	T. A. Morris, Q.P.M.	D. R. Williams
Humberside	Hull	1,957	D. Hall, C.B.E., Q.P.M.	C. Brady
Kent	Maidstone	2,936	F. L. Jordan, Q.P.M.	J. A. Spence
Lancashire	Preston	3,157	R. B. Johnson, Q.P.M.	J. Entwistle
Leicestershire	Leicester	1,714	M. J. Hirst	R. R. Angrave
Lincolnshire	Lincoln	1,170	S. W. Crump, Q.P.M.	M. D. Kennedy
Greater Manchester	Manchester 16	6,847	C. J. Anderton, C.B.E., Q.P.M.	S. Murphy
Merseyside	Liverpool 69	4,736	K. G. Oxford, C.B.E., Q.P.M.	G. Bundred
Norfolk	Norwich	1,322	G. Charlton, Q.P.M.	J. S. Peel, M.C.
Northamptonshire	Northampton	1,050	D. J. O'Dowd	A. A. Morby
Northumbria	Newcastle upon Tyne	3,483	Sir Stanley Bailey, C.B.E., Q.P.M.	G. Gill
Nottinghamshire	Nottingham	2,235	R. Hadfield	F. Higgins
Staffordshire	Stafford	2,117	C. H. Kelly, C.B.E., Q.P.M.	Miss I. H. Moseley
Suffolk	Ipswich	1,177	S. L. Whiteley, C.B.E., Q.P.M.	Capt. R. J. Sheepshanks
Surrey	Guildford	1,655	B. Hayes, Q.P.M.	J. F. Whitfield
Sussex	Lewes	2,870	R. Birch, C.B.E., Q.P.M.	F. W. E. Keen
Thames Valley	Oxford	3,467	C. Smith, C.V.O.	Lt. Col. J. C. Walton
Warwickshire	Warwick	979	P. D. Joslin, Q.P.M.	H. W. De'Ath
West Mercia	Worcester	1,923	A. A. Mullett, Q.P.M.	Mrs. M. J. T. Hadley, O.B.E.
West Midlands	Birmingham 4	6,684	G. J. Dear, Q.P.M.	D. M. Ablett
Wiltshire	Devizes	1,074	D. Smith, O.B.E., Q.P.M.	J. E. H. Church.
Yorkshire, North	Northallerton	1,368	J. Nobes, Q.P.M.	J. H. G. Parfect, M.B.E.
Yorkshire, South	Sheffield	2,885	P. Wright, O.B.E.	J. Layden
Yorkshire, West	Wakefield	5,154	C. Sampson, Q.P.M.	K. Wilson
Wales				
Dyfed-Powys	Carmarthen	915	D. J. Shattock, Q.P.M.	J. H. Lloyd
Gwent	Cwmbran	967	J. E. Over, Q.P.M.	B. J. Hearth
North Wales	Colwyn Bay	1,287	D. Owen, Q.P.M.	W. R. Pierce
South Wales	Bridgend	3,096	D. A. East, Q.P.M.	D. Allinson
Scotland				
Central Scotland	Stirling	555	I. T. Oliver, Q.P.M., PH.D.	S. Conner
Dumfries and Galloway	Dumfries	331	J. M. Boyd, Q.P.M.	K. A. Kelly
Fife	Kirkcaldy	731	W. M. Moodie, Q.P.M.	W. G. Anderson
Grampian	Aberdeen	1,005	A. G. Lynn, Q.P.M.	W. A. Grant
Lothian and Borders	Edinburgh 4	2,393	W. G. M. Sutherland, Q.P.M.	W. G. Rankine
Northern	Inverness	609	H. C. MacMillan, Q.P.M.	J. S. Munro
Strathclyde	Glasgow 2	6,761	A. Sloan, Q.P.M.	W. Harley
Tayside	Dundee	1,009	J. W. Bowman, Q.P.M.	Mrs. P. Doran
Northern Ireland				
Royal Ulster Constabulary	Belfast 5	8,253	Sir John Hermon, O.B.E.	T. Rainey
Islands				
Isle of Man	Douglas	179	R. E. N. Oake	E. G. Lowey
States of Jersey	St. Helier	212	†D. Parkinson	J. W. Ellis
Guernsey	St. Peter Port	129	†M. Le Moignan	M. W. Torode

† Chief Officer   * Elected at every meeting

THE ARMED FORCES

MINISTRY OF DEFENCE
Main Building, Whitehall, SW1A 2HB
[01–218 9000]

Salaries

Secretary of State	£33,145
Minister of State, Commons	£22,875
Minister of State, Lords	£30,640
Parliamentary Under-Secretaries	£16,885
Grade 1	£64,739
Grade 1A	£59,214
Grade 2	£43,264–£45,349
Grade 3	£33,725–£36,852
Grade 4	£30,207–£31,770

(For Services salaries, *see* pp. 473–8.)

Secretary of State for Defence, THE RT. HON. GEORGE YOUNGER, T.D., M.P.
  Private Secretary, J. F. Howe.
  Parliamentary Private Secretary, G. A. Neale, M.P.
Minister of State for the Armed Forces, IAN STEWART, M.P.
  Private Secretary, J. F. M. Tesh.
  Parliamentary Private Secretary, T. Wood, M.P.
Parliamentary Under-Secretary of State for the Armed Forces, R. N. Freeman, M.P.
  Private Secretary, Dr. A. Cowpe.
Minister of State for Defence Procurement, THE LORD TREFGARNE.
  Private Secretary, C. E. V. Hain-Cole.
  Parliamentary Private Secretary, S. Batiste, M.P.
Parliamentary Under-Secretary of State for Defence Procurement, The Hon. T. Sainsbury, M.P.
  Private Secretary, H. D. Kernohan.

Defence Staff

Permanent Under-Secretary of State (G1), Sir Clive Whitmore, K.C.B., C.V.O.
  Private Sec., J. S. Pitt-Brooke.
Chief Scientific Advisor (G1A), Sir Richard Norman, K.B.E.
  Private Sec., Dr. B. H. Collins.
Chief of Defence Staff, Adm. Sir John Fieldhouse, G.C.B., G.B.E., A.D.C.
Vice Chief of the Defence Staff, Gen. Sir Richard Vincent, K.C.B., D.S.O.
Deputy Chief of the Defence Staff (Commitments), Lt.-Gen. Sir Antony Walker, K.C.B.
Asst. C.D.S. (N.A.T.O/U.K.), Air Vice-Marshal M. J. D. Stear, C.B.E.
Asst. C.D.S. (Overseas), Air Vice-Marshal B. Higgs, C.B.E.
Asst. Under-Sec. of State (Commitments) (G3), N. Bevan.
Asst. C.D.S. (Logistics), Maj.-Gen. I. S. Baxter, C.B.E.
Deputy C.D.S. (Systems), Vice-Adm. Sir Jeremy Black, K.C.B., D.S.O., M.B.E.
Asst. C.D.S. (Concepts), Maj.-Gen. J. R. Templar, O.B.E.
Asst. C.D.S., Operational Requirements (Sea), Rear-Adm. A. Grose, A.D.C.
Asst. C.D.S., Operational Requirements (Land), Maj.-Gen. A R. G. Mullens, O.B.E.
Asst. C.D.S., Operational Requirements (Air), Air Vice Marshal G. C. Williams, A.F.C.
Asst. C.D.S. (C.C.C.I.S.), Air Vice-Marshal D. A. Saunders, C.B.E.
Deputy Under-Sec. of State (Policy) (G2), D. A. Nicholls, C.M.G.
Asst. C.D.S. (Policy and Nuclear), Air Vice-Marshal E. H. Macey, O.B.E.
Asst. Under-Sec. of State (Policy) (G3), J. M. Legge.
Deputy C.D.S. (Programmes and Personnel), Air Marshal Sir David Parry-Evans, K.C.B., C.B.E.
Asst. C.D.S. (Programmes), Rear-Adm. B. N. Wilson.

Surgeon Gen. and Dir. Gen. Army Medical Services, Lt.-Gen. Sir Cameron Moffat, K.B.E., Q.H.S.
Deputy Surgeon Gen. (Ops.), Dir. Gen. Medical Services (R.A.F.), Air Vice-Marshal F. C. Hurrell, C.B., O.B.E., Q.H.P.
Deputy Surgeon Gen. (Research and Training), Medical Dir. Gen. (Navy), Rear-Adm. G. J. Milton-Thompson, Q.H.P.
Chief of Defence Intelligence, Lt.-Gen. Sir Derek Boorman, K.C.B.
Asst. C.D.S. (Intelligence), Air Vice-Marshal R. J. Kemball, C.B.E.
Dir., Management and Support Intelligence, Maj.-Gen. I. O. J. Sprackling, O.B.E.
Dir., Scientific and Technical Intelligence (G3), Dr. J. W. Berry.
Dir., Economic and Logistic Intelligence (G4), D. H. Hills.
Defence Services Sec., Air Vice-Marshal R. C. F. Peirse, C.B.

Naval Staff

Chief of Naval Staff and First Sea Lord, Adm. Sir William Staveléy, G.C.B., A.D.C.
Asst. Chief of Naval Staff, Rear-Adm. M. H. Livesay.
Hydrographer of the Navy, Rear-Adm. R. O. Morris.
Cmdt.-Gen. Royal Marines, Lt.-Gen. J. M. C. Garrod, O.B.E.

General Staff

Chief of the General Staff, General Sir Nigel Bagnall, G.C.B., C.V.O., M.C., A.D.C.
Asst. Chief of the General Staff, Maj.-Gen. C. R. L. Guthrie, L.V.O., O.B.E.
Dir., Military Survey, Maj-Gen. P. F. Fagan, M.B.E.
Dir. Gen., T.A. and Organisation, Maj.-Gen. C. A. Ramsey, O.B.E.
Dir. Gen., Training and Doctrine (Army), Maj-Gen. A. J. G. Pollard, C.B.E.
Dir., Royal Armoured Corps, Maj.-Gen. N. G. P. Ansell, O.B.E.
Dir., Royal Artillery, Maj.-Gen. P. R. F. Bonnet, M.B.E.
Dir., Infantry, Maj.-Gen. Sir David Thorne, K.B.E.
Dir., Army Air Corps, Maj.-Gen. L. F. H. Busk.
Engineer in Chief (Army), Maj.-Gen. C. J. Rougier, C.B.
Signal Officer in Chief (Army), Maj.-Gen. P. D. Alexander, M.B.E.

Air Staff

Chief of the Air Staff, Air Chief Marshal Sir David Craig, G.C.B., O.B.E., A.D.C.
Asst. Chief of Air Staff, Air Vice-Marshal M. G. Simmons, A.F.C.
Cmdt. Gen. (R.A.F. Regt.) and Dir. Gen. of Security, Air Vice-Marshal D. B. Leech, C.B.E.
Controller of National Air Traffic Services, K. R. Mack, (C.A.A.).

Scientific Staff

Deputy Chief Scientific Adviser (G3), J. F. Barnes.
Asst. Chief Scientific Advisers (G3), D. E. Humphries (*Projects and Research*); J. D. Culshaw (*Capabilities*); (*G4*) Dr. R. G. Ridley (*Nuclear*).
Dir., Defence Operational Analysis Establishment (G3), R. J. Poole.
Dir. Gen., Strategic Defence Initiative Participation Office (G3), Dr. S. Orman.

Navy Department

Chief of Naval Personnel and Second Sea Lord, Adm. Sir Richard Fitch, K.C.B.
Naval Secretary, Rear-Adm. N. R. D. King.
Dir. Gen., Naval Manpower and Training, Rear-Adm. B. T. Brown, C.B.E.
Dir. Gen., Naval Personal Services, Rear-Adm. A. M. Norman.
Chief of Fleet Support, Vice-Adm. Sir Benjamin Bathurst, K.C.B.
Dir. Gen., Ship Refitting, Rear-Adm. G. A. F. Hitchens.
Dir. Gen., Supplies and Transport (G3), J. T. Baugh.
  Dir., Supplies and Transport (Armaments and Managements Services) (G4), W. N. Cooke.
  Dir., Supplies and Transport (Stores, Moves and Victualling) (G4), G. E. Miller.
Dir., Fleet Support Policy and Services, Rear-Adm. C. L. Wood.
Dir. Gen., Aircraft (Navy), Rear-Adm. R. V. Holley, C.B.
Chaplain of The Fleet, Ven. N. D. Jones, C.B., Q.H.C.

Army Department

Military Secretary, Lt.-Gen. Sir Patrick Palmer, K.B.E.
Adjutant-General, Gen. Sir David Mostyn, K.C.B., C.B.E., A.D.C.
Dir. Gen., Army Manning & Recruiting, Maj.-Gen. A. B. Crowfoot, C.B.E.
Paymaster in Chief, Maj.-Gen. B. M. Bowen.
Dir. Gen., Personal Services (Army), Maj.-Gen. J. D. G. Pank.
Dir., Army Legal Services, Maj.-Gen. M. T. Fugard.
Dir., Army Education, Maj.-Gen. J. S. Lee, M.B.E.
Quartermaster-General, Lt.-Gen. Sir Charles Huxtable, K.C.B., C.B.E.
Dir. Gen., Logistic Policy (Army), Maj.-Gen. P. W. E. Istead, O.B.E., G.M.
Dir. Gen., Transport and Movements, Maj.-Gen. D. B. H. Colley, C.B.E.
Dir. Gen., Ordnance Services, Maj.-Gen. G. B. Berragan.
Dir. Gen., Electrical and Mechanical Engineering, Maj.-Gen. J. Boyne, C.B., M.B.E.
Chaplain-Gen., Ven. W. F. Johnston, C.B., Q.H.C.

Air Force Department

Air Member for Personnel, Air Marshal Sir Laurence Jones, K.C.B., A.F.C.
Air Secretary, Air Vice-Marshal R. A. Mason, C.B.E.
Dir. Gen., R.A.F. Personal Services, Air Vice-Marshal D. W. Hann.
Dir. Gen., Training, Air Vice-Marshal M. J. Pilkington, C.B.E.
Air Member for Supply and Organisation, Air Chief Marshal Sir Patrick Hine, K.C.B.
Dir. Gen., Communications, Information Systems and Organisation, Air Vice-Marshal R. J. M. Alcock.
Chief Engineer, Air Marshal Sir William Richardson, K.B.E.
Dir. Gen., Supply, Air Vice-Marshal R. C. Allerton.
Chaplain-in-Chief, Ven. G. R. Renowden, C.B., Q.H.C.

Office of Management and Budget

Second Permanent Under-Secretary of State (G1A), Sir John Blelloch, K.C.B.
Deputy Under-Secs. of State (G2), J. G. Ashcroft (*Finance*); R. M. Hastie-Smith, C.B. (*Civilian Management*); J. M. Stewart (*Personnel and Logistics*); K. C. Macdonald, C.B. (*Resources and Programmes*).
Asst. Under-Secs. of State (G3), R. C. Mottram (*Programmes*); W. D. Reeves (*Systems*); C. T. McDonnell (*Resources*); B. H. Cousins, C.B.E. (*General Finance*); J. Roberts, C.B. (*Civilian Management (Administrators)*); J. E. Pestell (*Civilian Management (Specialists)*); R. L. Facer (*Personnel and Logistics*); T. J. Brack (*Naval Personnel*); B. M. Day (*Fleet Support*); M. Gainsborough (*Adjutant General*); J. E. Carruthers (*Supply and Organisation*) (*Air*); K. W. B. Gooderhan (*Security and Common Services*); Dr. M. J. Harte (*Personnel*) (*Air*); D. C. R. Heyhoe (*Dir. Gen., Management Audit*); C. E. Johnson (*Dir. Gen., Defence Accounts*); B. F. Rule (*Dir. Gen., Info. Technology Systems*); B. A. E. Taylor (*Quartermaster*).

PROCUREMENT EXECUTIVE

Chief of Defence Procurement (G1), P. K. Levene.
Private Sec., Miss E. G. Cassidy.

Research and Development Controllerate

Controller Establishments, Research and Nuclear Programmes, D. M. Spiers, C.B., T.D.
Asst. Under Sec. of State Research Establishments and Research Admin. (G3), W. F. Mumford.
Deputy Controller (Nuclear) (G4), J. C. Mabberley.
Deputy Controller (Research) (G3), Dr. T. Buckley.
Dir., Admiralty Research Establishment (G3), I. B. Bott.
Dir., Royal Signals and Radar Establishment (G2), N. H. Hughes.
Dir., Atomic Weapons Research Establishment (G2), Dr. T. P. McLean.
Dir., Chemical Defence Establishment (G3), Dr. G. F. Pearson.
Dir., Royal Armament Research and Development Establishment (G3), Dr. A. C. Baynham.
Commandant, Aeroplane and Armament Experimental Establishment, Air Cdre. P. D. L. Gover.
Dir., Royal Aircraft Establishment (G2), Dr. G. G. Pope, C.B.
Chief Engineer, (G4), R. H. Lovell.

Sea Systems Controllerate

Controller of the Navy, Vice-Adm. Sir Derek Reffell, K.C.B.
Asst. Under-Sec. of State (Material-Naval) (G3), J. Peters.
Principal Dir., Navy and Nuclear Contracts (G4), A. J. Figes.
Chief Strategic Systems Executive, Rear-Adm. J. S. Cooper, O.B.E.
Deputy Chief Strategic Systems Executive, Cdre. J. S. Kelly, O.B.E.
Dir. Gen. Strategic Weapon Systems, Cdre. T. W. Craven.
Deputy Controller Warships, Vice-Adm. Sir Hugh Thompson, K.B.E.
Dir. Gen. Surface Ships (G3), A. J. Creighton.
Dir. Gen. Submarines (G3), W. G. Sanders.
Chief Naval Architect (G3), B. O. Wall.
Chief Naval Weapons Systems Engineer (G4), D. McArthur.
Dir. Gen. Future Material Projects (Naval), Rear-Adm. N. Purvis.
Deputy Controller Warship Equipment (G3), P. E. Chamberlain.
Dir. Gen. Surface Weapons (G4), H. Perkins.
Dir. Gen. Underwater Weapons, Cdre. K. J. Eaton.
Dir. Gen. Marine Engineering, Chief Marine Systems Engineer, Rear-Adm. R. A. Issac.

Land Systems Controllerate

Master General of the Ordnance, Lt.-Gen. J. J. Stibbon, O.B.E.
Vice Master General of the Ordnance, Maj.-Gen. C. N. Last, O.B.E.

Asst. Under-Sec. of State (Ordnance) (G3), M. D. Tidy.
Principal Dir., Contracts (Ordnance) (G4), R. G. Woodman.
Dir. Gen., Guided Weapons and Electronics (G3), Dr. P. G. Smith.
Dir. Gen., Fighting Vehicles and Engineer Equipment, Maj.-Gen. S. R. A. Stopford, M.B.E.
Dir. Gen., Weapons (Army), Maj.-Gen. M. T. Skinner, C.B.

Air Systems Controllerate

Controller Aircraft, Air Chief Marshal Sir David Harcourt-Smith, K.C.B., D.F.C.
Dep. Controller Aircraft (G2), M. T. Peters.
Asst. Under-Sec. of State/Air (Procurement Executive) (G3), J. M. Moss.
Principal Dir., Contracts/Air (G4), D. Grassby.
Dir. Gen. Engines (Procurement Executive) (G3), M. C. Neale.
Dir. Gen. Aircraft 1, Air Vice-Marshal, R. M. Austin.
Dir. Gen. Aircraft 2, Air Vice-Marshal J. A. Porter, O.B.E.
Dir. Gen., Air Weapons Electronic Systems (G3), K. G. Hambleton.
Dir. Gen., Strategic Electronic Systems, Air Vice-Marshal M. J. D. Brown.

Procurement Executive Policy and Administration

Deputy Under-Sec. of State (Defence Procurement) (G2), J. B. Bourn, C.B.
Dir. Gen. Defence Quality Assurance (G3), B. Miller.
Dir. Gen. Defence Contracts (G3), B. J. Slade.
Principal Dir. Accountancy Services (P.E.) (G4), J. V. A. Crawford.
Principal Dir. Technical Costs (G4), R. E. Rowe.
Principal Dir. of Patents (G4), E. J. Mansfield.

Defence Export Services Organisation

Head of Defence Export Services (G2), C. Chandler.
Military Deputy to Head of D.E.S., Air Vice-Marshal F. D. G. Clark, C.B.E., A.F.C. (retd).
Dir. Gen. Saudi Airforce Projects, Air Vice-Marshal R. I. Stuart-Paul, M.B.E.
Dir. Gen., Marketing (G3), T. F. W. B. Knapp.
Asst. Under-Sec. of State (D.S.E. Admin.) (G3), C. Henn.

Equipment Collaboration Staff

Chief of Defence Equipment Collaboration (G1), Sir David Perry, K.C.B.
Private Sec., T. A. McKinnon.
Asst. Under-Sec. of State (Equipment Collaboration) (G3), J. L. Roberts.

METEOROLOGICAL OFFICE

London Road, Bracknell, Berks.
[Bracknell: 420242]

The Meteorological Office is the State Meteorological Service. It forms part of the Ministry of Defence, the Director General being ultimately responsible to the Secretary of State for Defence.

Except for the common services provided by other government departments as part of their normal functions, the cost of the Meteorological Office is borne by Defence Votes.

Of the expenditure chargeable to Defence Votes about £35,000,000 represents expenditure associated with staff and £34,000,000 on stores, communications and miscellaneous services. About £25,500,000 is recovered from outside bodies for special services rendered, sales of meteorological equipment, etc.

Dir. Gen., Dr. J. T. Houghton, C.B.E., D.Phil., F.R.S.
£43,500
Dir. of Services, Dr. D. N. Axford £35,350
Dir. of Research, A. Gilchrist £29,725

RELATIVE RANK—SEA, LAND AND AIR

ROYAL NAVY	ARMY	ROYAL AIR FORCE
1. Admiral of the Fleet.	1. Field Marshal.	1. Marshal of the R.A.F.
2. Admiral.	2. General.	2. Air Chief Marshal.
3. Vice-Admiral.	3. Lieutenant-General.	3. Air Marshal.
4. Rear-Admiral.	4. Major-General.	4. Air Vice-Marshal.
5. Commodore (1st & 2nd Class).	5. Brigadier.	5. Air Commodore.
6. Captain.	6. Colonel.	6. Group Captain.
7. Commander.	7. Lieutenant-Colonel.	7. Wing Commander.
8. Lieutenant Commander.	8. Major.	8. Squadron Leader.
9. Lieutenant.	9. Captain.	9. Flight Lieutenant.
10. Sub-Lieutenant.	10. Lieutenant.	10. Flying Officer.
11. Acting Sub-Lieutenant.	11. Second Lieutenant.	11. Pilot Officer.

THE ROYAL NAVY

THE QUEEN

Admirals of the Fleet

H.R.H. The Prince Philip, Duke of Edinburgh, K.G., P.C., K.T., O.M., G.B.E., *born* June 10, 1921 ..... Jan. 15, 1953
Sir Varyl Begg, G.C.B., D.S.O., D.S.C., *born* Oct. 1, 1908 .... Aug. 12, 1968
The Lord Hill-Norton, G.C.B., *born* Feb. 8, 1915 .... March 12, 1971
Sir Michael Pollock, G.C.B., L.V.O., D.S.C., *born* Oct. 19, 1916 .... March 1, 1974
Sir Edward Ashmore, G.C.B., D.S.C., *born* Dec. 11, 1919 .... Feb. 9, 1977
The Lord Lewin, K.G., G.C.B., L.V.O., D.S.C., *born* Nov. 19, 1920 .... July 6, 1979
Sir Henry Leach, G.C.B., *born* Nov. 18, 1923 .... Dec. 1, 1982
Sir John Fieldhouse, G.C.B., G.B.E., (*Chief of Defence Staff*), *born* Feb. 12, 1928 .... Aug. 2, 1985

Admirals

Staveley, Sir William, G.C.B., A.D.C., (*First Sea Lord and Chief of Naval Staff*).
Fitch, Sir Richard, K.C.B., (*Second Sea Lord and Chief of Naval Personnel, and Admiral President Royal Naval College Greenwich*).
Hallifax, Sir David, K.C.B., K.B.E., (*Comdt. of the Royal College of Defence Studies*).
Woodward, Sir John, K.C.B., (*C.-in-C. Naval Home Command*).
Oswald, Sir Julian, K.C.B., (*C.-in-C. Fleet, Allied C.-in-C. Channel and C-in-C. Eastern Atlantic Area*).

Vice-Admirals

Reffell, Sir Derek, K.C.B., (*Controller of the Navy*).
Symons, Sir Patrick, K.B.E., (*Chief of Staff to Commander, Allied Naval Forces, Southern Europe*).
Vallings, Sir George, K.C.B.
Webster, Sir John, K.C.B. (*Flag Officer, Plymouth, Naval Base Commander Devonport, Commander Central Sub. Area, Eastern Atlantic and Plymouth Sub. Area Channel*)
Thompson, Sir Hugh, K.B.E., (*Deputy Controller Warships, Senior Naval Representative Bath and Chief Naval Engineer Officer*)
Black, Sir Jeremy, K.C.B., D.S.O., M.B.E., (*Deputy Chief of the Defence Staff* (*Systems*)).
Thomas, Sir William, K.C.B., O.B.E., (*Deputy Supreme Allied Commander Atlantic*).
Bathurst, Sir Benjamin, K.C.B., (*Chief of Fleet Support*).

Slater, J. C. K., L.V.O., (*Flag Officer Scotland and N. Ireland, Commander Northern Sub. Area Eastern Atlantic, and Commander NORE Sub. Area Channel, and Naval Base Commander Rosyth*).

Rear-Admirals

Marsh, G. G. W., C.B., O.B.E.
Hogg, R. I. T.
Livesay, M. H., (*Asst. Chief of Naval Staff*).
Kerr, J. B., (*Flag Officer First Flotilla*).
Hitchens, G. A. F., (*Dir. Gen. Ship Refitting*).
Richmond, A. J., C.B.
King, N. R. D., (*Naval Secretary*).
Holley, R. V., C.B., (*Dir. Gen. Aircraft* (*Naval*)).
Morris, R. O., (*Hydrographer of the Navy*).
Dimmock, R. C., (*Flag Officer Naval Air Command*).
Dingemans, R. G. V., D.S.O., (*Chief of Staff to C.-in-C. Fleet*).
Marsden, P. N., (*Senior Naval Member of the Directing Staff, Royal College of Defence Studies*).
Garnier, J., C.B.E., L.V.O., (*Flag Officer Royal Yachts*).
Cooper, J. S., O.B.E., (*Chief Strategic Systems Executive*).
Sherval, D. R., (*Chief Staff Officer* (*Engineering*), *to C.-in-C. Fleet*).
Wheatley, A.
Balfour, H. M., L.V.O., (*Commander, Sultan of Oman's Navy*).
Grenier, P. F., (*Flag Officer Submarines and COMSUBEASTLANT*).
Wilson, B. N., (*Asst. C.D.S.* (*Programmes*)).
Brown, B. T., C.B.E. (*Dir. Gen. Naval Manpower and Training and Chief Naval Supply and Secretariat Officer*).

O'Riordan, J. P. B., C.B.E., (*Military Deputy Commandant, N.A.T.O. Defence College, Rome*).
Wood, C. L., (*Dir. Gen. Fleet Support, Policy and Services*).
Isaac, R. A., (*Dir. Gen. Marine Engineering*).
Layman, C. H., D.S.O., L.V.O., (*Commander British Forces, Falkland Islands*).
Grose, A., (*Asst. Chief of the Defence Staff, Operational Requirements* (*Sea Systems*)).
Norman, A. M., (*Dir. Gen. Naval Personal Services*).
Cole, M. C., (*Commander British Naval Staff Washington, Naval Attaché Washington and U.K. National Liaison Representative to SACLANT*).
Liardet, G. F., C.B.E., (*Flag Officer Second Flotilla*).
Weatherall, J. L. (*Deputy Asst. Chief of Staff* (*Operations*) *on the Staff of the Supreme Allied Commander Europe*).
Purvis, N., (*Dir. Gen. Future Material Projects*).
Howard, C. J., (*Chief of Staff to C.-in-C. Naval Home Command, and Chief Naval Instructor Officer*).
White, H. M., O.B.E., (*Flag Officer Third Flotilla and Commander Anti-Submarine Warfare Striking Force*).
Coward, J. F., D.S.O., (*Flag Officer Sea Training*).
Eaton, K. J., (*Flag Officer Portsmouth, Naval Base Commander Portsmouth and Head of Establishment of the Fleet Maintenance and Repair Organisation*).
Milton-Thompson, G. J., Q.H.P., (*Medical Dir. Gen.* (*Naval*)).
Hampton, T. R. W., Q.H.P.
Snow, R. E., L.V.O., O.B.E., Q.H.P.

HER MAJESTY'S FLEET

Type/Class	No.	Operational or engaged in preparing for service or trials or training	No.	Undergoing restorative or major refit or conversion, on standby etc.
Submarines				
Polaris	4	*Renown, Repulse, Resolution, Revenge*		
Fleet	12	*Warspite, Churchill, Conqueror, Courageous, Sovereign, Swiftsure, Superb, Splendid, Trafalgar, Turbulent, Tireless, Torbay†*	3	*Valiant, Sceptre, Spartan*

Oberon Class	9	Orpheus, Olympus, Opportune, Odin, Onslaught, Otter, Otus, Ocelot, Onyx	3 Oracle, Opossum, Osiris
Porpoise Class	1	Sealion	
ASW Carrier	2	Illustrious, Ark Royal	1 Invincible
Assault Ships	1	Intrepid†	1 Fearless
Guided-Missile Destroyers			
County	1	Fife	
Type 82	1	Bristol	
Type 42	11	Cardiff, Glasgow, Exeter, Birmingham, Southampton, Nottingham, Liverpool, Manchester, York, Gloucester, Edinburgh	1 Newcastle

Frigates

Type 22	11	Broadsword, Battleaxe, Brilliant, Brazen, Boxer, Beaver, Brave, London†, Sheffield*, Cornwall*, Coventry*	
Type 21	4	Amazon, Arrow, Ambuscade, Active	2 Alacrity, Avenger
Leander Class	18	Achilles, Charybdis, Diomede, Euryalus, Naiad, Penelope, Arethusa, Aurora, Phoebe, Sirius, Argonaut, Minerva, Danae, Andromeda, Hermione, Scylla, Apollo, Ariadne	2 Cleopatra, Jupiter
Rothesay Class	2	Rothesay, Plymouth	
Navigation Training Ship ...	1	Juno†	
Offshore Patrol			
Castle Class	2	Dumbarton Castle, Leeds Castle	
Island Class	6	Alderney, Guernsey, Lindisfarne, Orkney, Shetland, Anglesey	1 Jersey

MCMVs

Minesweepers	3	Cuxton, Soberton, Upton	2 Stubbington, Walkerton
River Class	12	Waveney, Carron, Dovey, Helford, Humber, Blackwater, Itchen, Helmsdale, Orwell, Ribble, Spey, Arun	
Minehunters Ton Class	11	Brereton, Brinton, Bronington, Hubberston, Iveston, Kedleston, Kellington, Maxton, Nurton, Sheraton, Wilton	2 Kirkliston, Gavinton
Hunt Class	11	Brecon, Brocklesby, Cattistock, Cottesmore, Dulverton, Middleton, Chiddingfold, Hurworth, Bicester, Atherstone†, Berkeley	1 Ledbury

Patrol Craft

Bird Class	5	Cygnet, Kingfisher, Peterel†, Sandpiper†, Redpole	
Coastal Training Craft	15	Attacker†, Fencer†, Hunter†, Chaser†, Striker†, Archer†, Biter†, Smiter†, Pursuer*, Blazer*, Dasher*, Puncher*, Charger*, Ranger*, Trumpeter*	
Peacock Class	5	Peacock, Plover, Starling, Swallow, Swift	
Gibraltar Search and Rescue Craft	2	Cormorant, Hart	
Support Ships			
Submarine Tender	1	Wakeful	1 Sentinel
MCM Support Ship	1	Abdiel	
Seabed Operations Vessel....	1	Challenger	
Royal Yacht/Hospital Ship ..			1 Britannia
Training Ships			
Fleet Tenders	3	Manly†, Messina†, Milbrook†	1 Mentor
Ice Patrol Ship			1 Endurance
Survey Ships	8	Bulldog, Fawn, Fox, Hecate, Herald, Gleaner, Hecla, Roebuck	1 Beagle

Notes:
(i) This table includes ships due for completion or disposal during the course of 1987/88; the numbers of each type are not therefore an accurate indication of the ships available at any one time. Ships solely engaged in harbour training duties are not included.
(ii) Ships marked * were under construction on April 1, 1987 and are planned to enter service during 1987/88.
(iii) Ships marked † are engaged partially on trials or training.

(iv) Ships approved during 1986/87 for disposal: *Oberon, Walrus, Glamorgan, Leander, Galatea, Yarmouth, Alfriston, Bickington, Hodgeston, Bildeston, Bossington, Protector, Guardian, Hydra.*

Royal Naval Auxiliary Service.—The Royal Naval Auxiliary Service (RNXS) is a uniformed civilian volunteer service, administered by the Ministry of Defence and trained by the Royal Navy to operate at ports and anchorages, for duty in emergencies and war. RNXS units are situated on the coasts of the United Kingdom and organised and run by the Area Flag Officers. The role of the RNXS is to assist with the defence of ports and anchorages by manning local headquarters and supporting the Naval Control of Shipping Organisation. The strength is 3,000.
Patron, H.R.H. Prince Michael of Kent.

ROYAL MARINES

The Corps of Royal Marines, about 7,100 strong, first formed in 1664, is part of the Naval Service. The Royal Marines provide Britain's sea soldiers and in particular 3 Commando Brigade Royal Marines, two thirds of which is trained and equippped for arctic warfare. Royal Marines also serve in H.M. Ships, provide landing craft crews, special boat sections and other detachments for naval and amphibious operations. They also provide the Naval Band Service.

The Royal Marines Reserve of about 1,200 volunteers consists of five main centres in London, Bristol, Liverpool, Newcastle and Glasgow.
Commandant-General, Royal Marines, Lt.-Gen. J. M. C. Garrod, O.B.E.
Major-Generals, J. St. J. Grey, C.B. (*Chief of Staff*); H. Y. La R. Beverley, O.B.E. (*Training, Reserve and Special Forces*); N. F. Vaux, D.S.O. (*Commando Forces*).

QUEEN ALEXANDRA'S ROYAL NAVAL NURSING SERVICE (Q.A.R.N.N.S.)

The first nursing sisters were appointed to naval hospitals in 1884 and the service gained its current title under the patronage of Queen Alexandra in 1902. Nursing ratings were introduced in 1960 and from 1982 a number of men have taken the opportunity to join Q.A.R.N.N.S. as both officers and ratings. Still largely based at the Royal Naval Hospitals, Q.A.R.N.N.S. continue their responsibility for the health and fitness of naval personnel. The strength is about 600.
Patron, H.R.H. Princess Alexandra.
Matron-in-Chief, Miss E. M. Northway, R.R.C., Q.H.N.S., Q.A.R.N.N.S.

WOMEN'S ROYAL NAVAL SERVICE (W.R.N.S.)

Originally founded in 1917, the W.R.N.S. were temporarily disbanded between World Wars I and II. The contribution of the Service is now firmly established as a professional and integral part of the Royal Navy with personnel serving in the United Kingdom and abroad in a wide range of specialist roles. Although W.R.N.S. do not serve at sea, they provide an essential nucleus of about 3,000 trained personnel ashore in order to release men to H.M. Ships.
Chief Commandant, H.R.H. Princess Anne.
Director W.R.N.S., Commandant M. H. Fletcher, A.D.C., W.R.N.S.

THE ARMY

THE QUEEN

Field Marshals

H.R.H. The Prince Philip, Duke of Edinburgh, K.G., P.C., K.T., O.M., G.B.E., *born* June 10, 1921	.....	Jan. 15, 1953
The Lord Harding of Petherton, G.C.B., C.B.E., D.S.O., M.C., *born* Feb. 10, 1896	....	July 21, 1953
Sir Richard A. Hull, K.G., G.C.B., D.S.O., *born* May 7, 1907	....	Feb. 8, 1965
Sir A. James H. Cassels, G.C.B., K.B.E., D.S.O., *born* Feb. 28, 1907	....	Feb. 29, 1968
The Lord Carver, G.C.B., C.B.E., D.S.O., M.C., *born* April 24, 1915	....	July 18, 1973
Sir Roland Gibbs, G.C.B., C.B.E., D.S.O., M.C., *born* June 22, 1921	....	July 13, 1979
The Lord Bramall, G.C.B., O.B.E., M.C., *born* Dec. 18, 1923	....	Aug. 1, 1982
Sir John W. Stanier, G.C.B., M.B.E., *born* Oct. 6, 1925	....	July 10, 1985

Generals

Bagnall, Sir Nigel, G.C.B., C.V.O., M.C., A.D.C. (*Gen.*), Col. Comdt. A.P.T.C., Col. Comdt. R.A.C., (*Chief of the General Staff*).

Mostyn, Sir David, K.C.B., C.B.E., A.D.C. (*Gen.*), Col. Comdt. A.L.C. (*Adjutant General*).

Howlett, Sir Geoffrey, K.B.E., M.C., Col. Comdt. P.A.R.A., Col. Comdt. A.C.C. (*C.-in-C. AFNORTH*).

Vincent, Sir Richard, K.C.B., D.S.O., Col. Comdt. R.A., Col. Comdt.

R.E.M.E., (*Vice Chief of the Defence Staff*).

Chapple, Sir John, K.C.B., C.B.E., Col. 2 GR (*C.-in-C. U.K.L.F.*).

Akehurst, Sir John, K.C.B., C.B.E., Col. R. Anglian (*D. SACEUR*).

Huxtable, Sir Charles, K.C.B., C.B.E., Col. Comdt. The King's Division, Col. D.W.R. (*Quartermaster-General*).

Kenny, Sir Brian, K.C.B., C.B.E., Col. Comdt. R.A.V.C., Col. Q.R.I.H., (*C.-in-C. B.A.O.R. and Commander Northern Army Group*).

Lieutenant-Generals

Boorman, Sir Derek, K.C.B., Col. 6 GR, Col. Staffords (*Chief of Defence Intelligence*).

Arthur Sir Norman, K.C.B., Col. Comdt. M.P.S.C., Col. Comdt. Scots D.G., (*G.O.C. Scotland and Governor of Edinburgh Castle*).

Pascoe, Sir Robert, K.C.B., M.B.E., Col. Comdt. 1 R.G.J., (*G.O.C. & D. Mil. Operations Northern Ireland*).

Moffat, Sir Cameron, K.B.E., Q.H.S., (*Surgeon General*).

Reilly, Sir Jeremy, K.C.B., D.S.O., Col. R.R.F., (*Comd. Training and Arms Directors*).

Palmer, Sir Patrick, K.B.E., Col. A. & S.H., (*Military Secretary*).

Walker, Sir Antony, K.C.B., Col. Comdt. R.T.R., (*Deputy Chief of the Defence Staff (Commitments)*).

Ramsbotham, Sir David, K.C.B., C.B.E., Col. Comdt. 2GR, (*Comd. U.K. Fd. Army and Inspec. Gen. T.A.*).

Inge, P. A. Col. Green Howards, Col. Comdt. R.M.P., (*Comd. 1 (B.R.) Corps.*).

Stibbon, J. J., O.B.E., Col. Comdt. R.A.P.C., Col. Comdt. R.P.C., (*Master General of the Ordnance*).

Billiere, P. E. de la C. de la, C.B.E., D.S.O., M.C., Col. Comdt. The Light Division, (*G.O.C., S.E. District*).

MacMillan, J. R. A., C.B.E., Col. Comdt. The Scottish Division, (*G.O.C. Scotland and Governor Edinburgh Castle (designate)*).

Major-Generals

Watts, J. P. B. C., C.B., C.B.E., M.C. (*C.D.S. & Chief of Mil. Operations Sultan of Oman's Armed Forces*).

Thorne, Sir David, K.B.E., Col. Comdt. The Queen's Division. (*Dir. of Infantry*).

Boyne, J., C.B., M.B.E., (*Dir. Gen. of Electrical and Mechanical Engineering*).

Rougier, C. J., C.B., (*Engineer in Chief (Army)*).

Shortis, C. T., C.B.E., Col. Comdt. P.O.W. Divn., Col. D and D, (*G.O.C. N.W. District*).

Waters, C. J., C.B.E., Col. Glosters (*Comdt. Staff College*).

Cornock, C. G., M.B.E., Col. Comdt. R.A., (*Chief of Staff LIVE OAK*).

Pank, J. D. G., Col. L.I. (*Dir. Gen. of Personal Services (Army)*).

Airy, C. J., C.B.E. (*G.O.C. London District and Maj. Gen. Comd. The Household Divn.*).

Skinner, M. T., C.B., (*Dir. Gen. of Weapons (Army)*).

Cooper, S. C., (*Cmdt. Royal Military Academy Sandhurst.*).

Roberts, D. M., Q.H.P. (*Director Army Medicine*).

Guthrie, C. R. L., L.V.O., O.B.E., Col. Comdt. Int. Corps. (*Asst. Chief of the General Staff*).

Jeapes, A. S., O.B.E., M.C., (*G.O.C. S.W. District*).

Johnson, G. D., O.B.E., M.C., Col. 10 G.R. (*C.B.F. Hong Kong and Maj.-Gen. Brigade of Gurkhas*).

Jones, C. E. W., C.B.E., Col. Comdt. R.A.E.C. (*Comd. 3 Armd. Divn.*).

Learmont, J. H., C.B.E., (*Chief of Staff H.Q. U.K.L.F.*).

Mullens, A. R. G., O.B.E., (*Asst. Chief of Defence Staff O.R. (Land)*).

Ramsay, C. A., O.B.E., (*Dir. Gen., T.A. and Organisation*).

Alexander, P. D., M.B.E., (*Signal Officer in Chief (Army)*).

Beckett, E. H. A., M.B.E., (*Chief of Staff H.Q. B.A.O.R.*).

Berragan, G. B., (*Dir. Gen. Ordnance Services*).

Brooking, P. G., M.B.E., (*G.O.C. Berlin*).

Evans, J. A. M., (*Senior Army Member, Royal College of Defence Studies*).

Stopford, S. R. A., M.B.E., (*Dir. Gen. Fighting Vehicles and Engineer Equipment*).

Bowen, B. M., (*Paymaster-in-Chief*).

Willmott, E. G., O.B.E., (*President Ordnance Board*).

Colley, D. B. H., C.B.E., (*Dir. Gen., Transport and Movements*).

Fawcus, G. B., (*Chief, Jt. Service Liaison Organisation Bonn*).

Ward, R. W., M.B.E., (*G.O.C. W. District*).

Bonnet, P. R. F., M.B.E., (*Dir. Royal Artillery*).

Crowfoot, A. B., C.B.E., (*Dir. Gen., Army Manning and Recruiting*).

Quayle, T. D. G., (*Comd. Arty 1 (B.R.) Corps*).

Templer, J. R., O.B.E., (*Asst. Chief of Defence Staff (Concepts)*).

Busk, L. F. H., (*Dir. Army Air Corps*).

Fugard, M. T., (*Dir. Army Legal Services*).

Graham, P. W., C.B.E., Col. Gordons, (*G.O.C. E. District*).

Pollard, A. J. G., C.B.E., Col. Comdt. S.A.S.C., Dep. Col. R. Anglian, (*Dir. Gen. Training and Doctrine*).

Tyler, C., (*Dep. Chief of Staff (Support) H.Q. AFNORTH*).

Blewett, R. S., O.B.E., (*Comd. Med. B.A.O.R.*).

Coakley, P. K., Q.H.S., (*Dir. Army Surgery*).

Ansell, N. G. P., O.B.E., (*Dir. Royal Armoured Corps*).

Baxter, I. S., C.B.E., (*Asst. Chief of Defence Staff (Logistics)*).

Davies, P. R., Col. King's (*Comd. Comms. B.A.O.R.*).

Hodges, R. J., O.B.E., (*C.L.F. and D.D. Ops. N. Ireland*).

Istead, P. W. E., O.B.E., G.M., (*Dir. Gen. Logistic Policy (Army)*).

Last, C. N., O.B.E., (*Vice Master General of the Ordnance*).

Lee, J. S., M.B.E., (*Dir. Army Education*).

Spackling, I. O. J., O.B.E., (*Dir. Management and Support Intelligence*).

Scott, R., (*Comdt. Royal Army Medical College and Post Graduate Dean*).

Blacker, A. S. J., C.B.E., (*Comdt. R.M.C.S.*).

Carlier, A. N., O.B.E., (*Comdt. British Forces Falkland Is.*).

Fagan, P. F., M.B.E., (*D. Mil. Svy.*).

Llewellyn, R. M., O.B.E., (*G.O.C. Wales*).

Naylor, D. M., M.B.E., (*G.O.C. N.E. District Comd. 2 Inf. Divn.*).

Rous, The Hon. W. E., O.B.E., (*Comd. 4 Armd. Divn.*).

Swinburn, R. H., (*Comd. 1 Armd. Divn.*).

Macphie, D. L., Q.H.S., (*Comd. Med. B.A.O.R.*).

Beale, P. J., (*Comd. Med. U.K.L.F.*).

CONSTITUTION OF THE BRITISH ARMY

The Regular Forces include the following Arms, Branches and Corps. Soldiers' Record Offices are shown at the end of each group; records of officers are maintained at the Ministry of Defence.

The Arms

Household Cavalry.—The Life Guards; The Blues and Royals (Royal Horse Guards and 1st Dragoons). *Records*, Horse Guards, London, S.W.1.

Royal Armoured Corps.—Cavalry Regiments: 1st The Queen's Dragoon Guards; The Royal Scots Dragoon Guards (Carabiniers and Greys); 4th/7th Royal Dragoon Guards; 5th Royal Inniskilling Dragoon Guards; The Queen's Own Hussars; The Queen's Royal Irish Hussars; 9th/12th Royal Lancers (Prince of Wales's); The Royal Hussars (Prince of Wales's Own), 13th/18th Royal Hussars (Queen Mary's Own); 14th/20th King's Hussars; 15th/19th The King's Royal Hussars; 16th/5th The Queen's

Royal Lancers; 17th/21st Lancers; Royal Tank Regiment comprising four regular regiments. *Records*, Queen's Park, Chester.

Artillery.—Royal Regiment of Artillery. *Records*, Imphal Barracks, Fulford Road, York.

Engineers.—Corps of Royal Engineers. *Records*, Kentigern House, Brown Street, Glasgow.

Signals.—Royal Corps of Signals. *Records*, Kentigern House, Brown Street, Glasgow.

Infantry.—The Foot Guards and Regiments of Infantry of the Line are grouped in Divisions as follows:—

Guards Division—Grenadier, Coldstream, Scots, Irish and Welsh Guards. Divisional HQ: HQ Household Division, Horse Guards, S.W.1. *Depot:* Pirbright Camp, Brookwood, Surrey. *Records:* Imphal Barracks, Fulford Road, York.

Scottish Division—The Royal Scots (The Royal Regiment); The Royal Highland Fusiliers (Princess Margaret's Own Glasgow and Ayrshire Regiment);

The King's Own Scottish Borderers; The Black Watch (Royal Highland Regiment); Queen's Own Highlanders (Seaforth and Camerons); The Gordon Highlanders (Seaforth and Camerons); The Argyll and Sutherland Highlanders (Princess Louise's). *Divisional HQ*, The Castle, Edinburgh. *Depots*, Scottish Divisional Depots, Glencorse, Milton Bridge, Midlothian and Albemarle Barracks, Ouston, Newcastle. *Records*, Imphal Barracks, Fulford, York.

Queen's Division—The Queen's Regiment, The Royal Regiment of Fusiliers, The Royal Anglian Regiment. *Divisional HQ*, Bassingbourn Barracks, Royston, Herts. *Depot*, Bassingbourn Barracks, Royston, Herts. *Records*, Higher Barracks, Exeter, Devon.

King's Division—The King's Own Royal Border Regiment, The King's Regiment; The Prince of Wales's Own Regiment of Yorkshire; The Green Howards (Alexandra, Princess of Wales's Own Yorkshire Regiment); The Royal Irish Rangers (27th (Inniskilling) 83rd and 87th); The Queen's Lancashire Regiment; The Duke of Wellington's Regiment (West Riding). *Divisional HQ*, Imphal Barracks, York. *Depots*, The King's Division Depot (Yorkshire), Queen Elizabeth Barracks, Strensall, Yorks., and Albemarle Barracks, Ouston, Newcastle. The King's Division Depot (Royal Irish Rangers), St. Patrick's Barracks, Ballymena, Northern Ireland. *Records*, Imphal Barracks, Fulford, York.

Prince of Wales's Division—The Devonshire and Dorset Regiment; The 22nd (Cheshire) Regiment; The Royal Welch Fusiliers, The Royal Regiment of Wales (24th/41st Foot); The Gloucestershire Regiment; The Worcestershire and Sherwood Foresters Regiment (29th/45th Foot); The Royal Hampshire Regiment; The Staffordshire Regiment (The Prince of Wales's); The Duke of Edinburgh's Royal Regiment (Berkshire and Wiltshire). *Divisional HQ*, Whittington Barracks, Lichfield, Staffs. *Depots*, Mercian Depot, The Prince of Wales's Division, Whittington Barracks, Lichfield, Staffs; Welsh Depot, The Prince of Wales's Division, Cwrt-y-Gollen, Crickhowell, Powys. *Records*, Imphal Barracks, Fulford, York.

Light Division—The Light Infantry; The Royal Green Jackets. *Divisional HQ*, Peninsula Barracks, Winchester, Hants. *Depots*, The Light Division Depot (Shrewsbury), Sir John Moore Barracks, Copthorne, Shrewsbury, Salop. The Light Division Depot (Winchester), Peninsula Barracks, Winchester, Hants. *Records*, Higher Barracks, Exeter.

Brigade of Gurkhas—2nd King Edward VII's Own Gurkha Rifles (The Sirmoor Rifles); 6th Queen Elizabeth's Own Gurkha Rifles; 7th Duke of Edinburgh's Own Gurkha Rifles; 10th Princess Mary's Own Gurkha Rifles, The Queen's Gurkha Engineers, Queen's Gurkha Signals, Gurkha Transport Regt. *Brigade HQ*, H.M.S. *Tamar*, Hong Kong, B.F.P.O. 1. *Depot*, Training Depot, Brigade of Gurkhas, Malaya Lines, Sek Kong, B.F.P.O. 1. *Records*, Record Office, Brigade of Gurkhas, Hong Kong, B.F.P.O. 1.

The Parachute Regiment (Three regular battalions)—*Depot*, Browning Barracks, Aldershot, Hants. *Records*, Higher Barracks, Exeter.

Special Air Service Regiment—*Regimental HQ*, Duke of York's Headquarters, Sloane Square, S.W.3. *Depot*, Stirling Lines, Hereford. *Records*, Higher Barracks, Exeter, Devon.

Army Air Corps—Regimental H.Q. and Depot, Middle Wallop, Hants. *Records*, Higher Barracks, Exeter.

The Services

Royal Army Chaplain's Department—Regimental H.Q. and Depot, Bagshot Park, Surrey.

Royal Corps of Transport, *Records*, Kentigern House, Brown Street, Glasgow.

Royal Army Medical Corps, Royal Army Dental Corps, Queen Alexandra's Royal Army Nursing Corps, and Women's Royal Army Corps. *Records*, Queen's Park, Chester.

Royal Army Ordnance Corps, Corps of Royal Electrical and Mechanical Engineers. *Records*, Glen Parva Barracks, Saffron Road, Wigston, Leicester.

Small Arms School Corps. *Records*, Higher Barracks, Exeter.

General Service Corps. *Records*, Imphal Barracks, Fulford Road, York.

Corps of Royal Military Police, Royal Army Pay Corps, Royal Army Veterinary Corps, Royal Pioneer Corps, Intelligence Corps, Army Catering Corps, Military Provost Staff Corps, Royal Army Educational Corps, Army Physical Training Corps, Army Legal Corps, Sandhurst, Officers Training Corps. *Records*, Higher Barracks, Exeter, Devon.

The Territorial Army (T.A.) is designed to provide a highly trained and well equipped force which will complete the Regular Army order of battle in a time of national emergency. Its establishment is approximately 84,000 and it is planned that this will rise to 86,000 by 1990. A new element of the T.A., The Home Service Force, designed to produce a low cost guard force, is being expanded to some 5,000 posts by 1990.

The Ulster Defence Regiment (U.D.R.) was raised under authority of the *U.D.R. Act* 1969 and assists the Regular Army in Northern Ireland. H.Q., Magheralave Road, Lisburn, Co. Antrim. *Records*, Imphal Barracks, Fulford Road, York.

QUEEN ALEXANDRA'S ROYAL ARMY NURSING CORPS (Q.A.R.A.N.C.)

Founded in 1902 as Q.A.I.M.N.S., became Q.A.R.A.N.C. in 1959. Q.A.R.A.N.C. has trained nurses for the register and roll since 1950 and has four other employment categories. There was an introduction of a non-nursing officer element in 1959 for personnel work. The Q.A.R.A.N.C. provides service in military hospitals world-wide—United Kingdom (including N. Ireland), B.A.O.R., Hong Kong, Dharan, Cyprus, Falkland Islands and Belize.

Colonel-in-Chief, H.R.H. Princess Margaret.
Director of Defence Nursing Services, Brig. M. B. T. Hennessy, M.B.E., R.R.C., Q.H.N.S.

WOMEN'S ROYAL ARMY CORPS (W.R.A.C.)

The W.R.A.C. was formed on February 1, 1949 as a Corps of the Regular Army. The Corps predecessors were Q.M.A.A.C. in World War I, and A.T.S. in World War II. The present role of the W.R.A.C. is to be organised and trained, as an integral part of the Army, to carry out those tasks for which its members are best suited and qualified, so that it will contribute to the maximum efficiency of the Army as a whole. The Corps is approximately 8,500 (Regular and T.A.) and is employed by 36 sponsors in 30 employments in 500 units worldwide in the British Army.

Commandant-in-Chief, H.M. Queen Elizabeth The Queen Mother.
Controller Commandant, H.R.H. The Duchess of Kent.
Deputy Controller Commandant, Brig. A. Field, C.B.
Director, Women's Royal Army Corps, Brig. S. P. Nield, A.D.C.

THE ROYAL AIR FORCE

THE QUEEN

Marshals of the Royal Air Force

H.R.H. the Prince Philip, Duke of Edinburgh, K.G., P.C., K.T., O.M., G.B.E., *born* June 10, 1921 ...... Jan. 15, 1953
Sir William F. Dickson, G.C.B., K.B.E., D.S.O., A.F.C., *born* Sept. 24, 1898 .... June 1, 1954
Sir Dermot A. Boyle, G.C.B., K.C.V.O., K.B.E., A.F.C., *born* Oct. 2, 1904 .... Jan 1, 1958
The Lord Elworthy, K.G., G.C.B., C.B.E., D.S.O., M.V.O., D.F.C., A.F.C., *born* March 23, 1911 .... April 1, 1967
Sir John Grandy, G.C.B., K.B.E., D.S.O., *born* Feb. 8, 1913 (*Governor and Constable of Windsor Castle*) .... April 1, 1971
Sir Denis Spotswood, G.C.B., C.B.E., D.S.O., D.F.C., *born* Sept. 26, 1916 .... March 31, 1974
Sir Michael Beetham, G.C.B., C.B.E., D.F.C., A.F.C., A.D.C., *born* May 17, 1923 .... Oct. 15, 1982
Sir Keith Williamson, G.C.B., A.F.C., *born* Feb. 25, 1928 .... Oct. 15, 1985

Air Chief Marshals

Craig, Sir David, G.C.B., O.B.E., A.D.C., (*Chief of the Air Staff*).

Harding, Sir Peter, K.C.B., (*A.O.C. in C. Strike Command*).

Hine, Sir Patrick, K.C.B., (*Vice Chief of the Defence Staff*).

Knight, Sir Michael, K.C.B., A.F.C., A.D.C. (*U.K. Military Representative, H.Q. N.A.T.O.*).

Armitage, Sir Michael, K.C.B., C.B.E., (*Air Member for Supply and Organisation*).

Gilbert, Sir Joseph, K.C.B., C.B.E., (*Deputy C.-in-C., Allied Forces Central Europe*).

Harcourt-Smith, Sir David, K.C.B., D.F.C., (*Controller Aircraft*).

Air Marshals

Parry-Evans, Sir David, K.C.B., C.B.E., (*Deputy Chief of Defence Staff (Programmes and Personnel)*).

Sutton, Sir John, K.C.B., (*A.O.C.-in-C., R.A.F. Support Command*).

Skingsley, Sir Anthony, K.C.B., (*C.-in-C. R.A.F. Germany and Cmdr. 2 A.T.A.F.*).

Duxbury, Sir Barry, K.C.B., C.B.E., (*A.O.C. No. 18 Group*).

Richardson, Sir William, K.B.E., (*Chief Engineer (R.A.F.)*).

Jackson, Sir Brendan, K.C.B., (*Chief of Staff and Deputy C.-in-C. Strike Command*).

Jones, Sir Laurence, K.C.B., A.F.C., (*Air Member for Personnel*).

Bennett, E. P., C.B., (*Commander Sultan of Oman's Air Force*).

Air Vice-Marshals

Hayr, K. W., C.B., C.B.E., A.F.C. (*Cdr. British Forces Cyprus and Administrator Sovereign Base Areas*).

Peirse, R. C. F., C.B. (*Defence Services Secretary*).

Adams, M. K., C.B., A.F.C. (*Senior Directing Staff, Royal College of Defence*).

Holroyd, F. M., C.B. (*Air Officer Engineering Strike Command*).

Spottiswood, J. D., C.V.O., A.F.C. (*Air Officer Training R.A.F. Support Command*).

Stuart-Paul, R. I., M.B.E. (*Dir. Gen. Saudi Air Force Project*).

Porter, J. A., O.B.E. (*Dir. Gen. Aircraft 2*).

Dick, R. (*Head of British Defence Staff and Defence Attaché Washington*).

Newton, B. H., O.B.E. (*Comdt. Joint Services Defence College*).

Simmons, M. G., A.F.C. (*Asst. Chief of the Air Staff*).

Hann, D. W. (*Dir. Gen of Personal Services*).

Bryant, D. T., C.B., O.B.E. (*Cmdt. R.A.F. Staff College, Bracknell*).

Macey, E. H., O.B.E. (*Asst. Chief of Defence Staff (Policy and Nuclear)*).

Stear, M. J. D., C.B.E. (*Asst. Chief of Defence Staff (N.A.T.O./U.K.)*).

Alcock, R. J. M., (*Director General of Communications Inf. Systems and Organisation (R.A.F.)*).

Campbell, K. A., (*Air Officer Maintenance, R.A.F. Support Command*).

Walker, J. R., C.B.E., A.F.C. (*Deputy Chief of Staff (Ops.)*).

Higgs, B., C.B.E. (*Asst. Chief of the Defence Staff (Overseas)*).

Kemball, R. J., C.B.E., (*Asst. Chief of Defence Staff (Intelligence)*).

Palin, R. H., O.B.E. (*Air Officer Commanding No. 11 Group*).

Mason, R. A., C.B.E. (*Air Secretary and Air Officer Commanding R.A.F. Personnel Management Centre*).

Brook, D. C. G., C.B.E. (*Air Officer Scotland and N. Ireland*).

Whittaker, D., M.B.E. (*Air Officer Admin., R.A.F. Support Command*).

Pilkington, M. J., C.B.E. (*Dir. Gen. of Training (R.A.F.)*).

Graydon, M. J., C.B.E. (*Asst. Chief of Staff (Policy) Supreme H.Q. Allied Powers Europe*).

Brown, M. J. D., (*Dir. Gen. of Strategic Electronic Systems*).

Leech, D. B. (*Cmdt. Gen. R.A.F. Regiment and Dir. Gen. of Security (R.A.F.)*).

Stoner, T. H., (*Deputy Controller, National Air Traffic Services*).

Roberts, A. L., C.B.E., A.F.C., (*Chief of Staff, H.Q. No. 18 Group*).

Wilson, R. A. F., A.F.C., (*Senior Air Strike Officer, Strike Command*).

Thomson, C. J., C.B.E., A.F.C., (*Air Officer Commanding No. 1 Group*).

Honey, R. J., C.B.E., (*Deputy Commander R.A.F. Germany*).

Robson, R. M., O.B.E., (*Air Officer Admin., Strike Command*).

Williams, G. C., A.F.C., (*Asst. Chief of Defence Staff Operational Requirements (Air Systems)*).

Saunders, D. A., C.B.E., (*Asst. Chief of Defence Staff (Command, Control, Communications and Information Systems)*).

Allerton, R. C., (*Dir. Gen. of Supply (R.A.F.)*).

Austin, R. M., A.F.C., (*Dir. Gen. Aircraft 1*).

Wood, R. H., O.B.E., (*Air Officer Commanding and Cmdt. R.A.F. College, Cranwell*).

Hurrell, F. C., C.B., O.B.E., Q.H.P. (*Deputy Surgeon Gen. (Operations) and Dir. Gen. R.A.F. Medical Services*).

Livingston, G., Q.H.S. (*Principal Medical Officer, R.A.F. Support Command*).

Howard, P., O.B.E., Q.H.P. (*Dean of Air Force Medicine*).

Simpson, C. E., Q.H.S. (*Principal Medical Officer, Strike Command*).

Forman, G. N. (*Dir. of Legal Services (R.A.F.)*).

PRINCESS MARY'S ROYAL AIR FORCE NURSING SERVICE (P.M.R.A.F.N.S.)

The Princess Mary's Royal Air Force Nursing Service is open to suitable male and female candidates who hold the Enrolled Nurse Certificate (G). Registered General Nurses are eligible to apply for an initial 4 years' short service commission.

Matron-in-Chief, Princess Mary's R.A.F. Nursing Service, Group Captain M. M. Shaw, Q.H.N.S., R.R.C.

WOMEN'S ROYAL AIR FORCE (W.R.A.F.)

Formed on April 1, 1918, the Women's Royal Air Force was disbanded on April 1, 1920 and reformed on February 1, 1949 from the Women's Auxiliary Air Force, the World War II Service, which had been formed on June 28, 1939, and from the R.A.F. Companies of the Auxiliary Territorial Service.

W.R.A.F. officers and airwomen, respectively, serve in most of the R.A.F. ground branches and trades and also as Air Loadmaster aircrew. W.R.A.F. personnel are employed at R.A.F. stations and higher formations at home and abroad, and they compete, on equal terms, with their R.A.F. counterparts for appointments, promotion and places on training courses.

Commandant-in-Chief, H.M. Queen Elizabeth the Queen Mother.
Air Chief Commandant, H.R.H. Princess Alice, Duchess of Gloucester.
Director, Air Commodore S. A. Jones, A.D.C.

CONSTITUTION OF THE ROYAL AIR FORCE

The Royal Air Force consists of three Commands: Strike Command and Support Command in the United Kingdom, and R.A.F. Germany. Strike Command is responsible for providing the air defence of the United Kingdom and reinforcement forces for N.A.T.O.; its roles include strike/attack, air defence, control and reporting, maritime surveillance, air reconnaissance, air-to-air refuelling, offensive support, air transport, aero-medical facilities, and search and rescue. Support Command is responsible for air and ground training, communications, engineering support, logistics, hospitals and for providing a range of administrative support. R.A.F. Germany provides tactical air support in N.A.T.O.'s Central Region; its roles include strike/attack, interdiction, counter air operations, air defence, close air support of land forces, tactical reconnaissance and helicopter support.

To carry out its tasks, the Royal Air Force is equipped with Victor, Tornado, Buccaneer, Phantom, Lightning, Harrier, Jaguar, Canberra, Nimrod, Shackleton, VC10, Tristar, Hercules, Hawk, Jet Provost, Tuccano, Chipmunk and Bulldog aircraft; Puma, Wessex, Sea King and Chinook helicopters; miscellaneous communications aircraft, etc.; and Bloodhound and Rapier missiles.

ROYAL OBSERVER CORPS
Bentley Priory, Stanmore, Middlesex

Established 1925, the Royal Observer Corps is a uniformed voluntary civilian organization originally set up to identify and track the movement of aircraft in war. In 1955 the Corps assumed the modern role of detecting nuclear bursts and monitoring radioactive fall-out in support of the United Kingdom Warning and Monitoring Organization. The Corps is affiliated to the Royal Air Force and is administered by Strike Command.

Air Commodore-in-Chief, H.M. THE QUEEN.
Commandant, Air Commodore I. Horrocks

SERVICE SALARIES AND PENSIONS

The following rates of pay have been introduced as part of the 1987 pay award for Service personnel. The Government accepted the recommendations of the Armed Forces Pay Review Body, which advises on pay levels for all ranks from April 1, 1987. The Government, however, decided to introduce in two stages the recommendations of the Top Salaries Review Body, which advises on ranks above Brigadier. The first stage took effect from April 1, 1987, with the full amount (shown below) being introduced from Oct. 1, 1987.

Salaries for the Women's Services reflect equal pay for equal work and conditions, but because the X-Factor addition for women is lower than for men (7·5 per cent compared to 10 per cent) women's rates approximate to 98 per cent of the rates for men. Since 1970 the determining factor of the Review Bodies' recommendations has been the relation of forces' salaries to civilian earnings by a carefully detailed process of job evaluation.

ROYAL NAVY AND ROYAL MARINES
Normal Rates

Rank	Daily	Annual
	£	£
Midshipman	16·34	5,980
After 1 year	20·31	7,433
Sub-Lieutenant and Acting Lieu-		
tenant RM	23·28	8,520
After 2 years	30·34	11,104
After 3 years	32·74	11,983
Lieutenant	38·28	14,010
After 1 year	39·31	14,387
After 2 years	40·34	14,764
After 3 years	41·37	15,141
After 4 years	42·40	15,518
After 5 years	43·43	15,895
After 6 years	44·46	16,272
Lieutenant Commander/Captain		
RM	48·66	17,810
After 1 year	49·87	18,252
After 2 years	51·08	18,695
After 3 years	52·29	19,138
After 4 years	53·50	19,581
After 5 years	54·71	20,024
After 6 years	55·92	20,467
After 7 years	57·13	20,910
After 8 years	58·34	21,352
Commander/Major RM	67·43	24,679
After 2 years or 19 years		
service	69·20	25,327
After 4 years or 21 years		
service	70·97	25,975
After 6 years or 23 years		
service	72·74	26,623
After 8 years or 25 years		
service	74·51	27,271
Captain/Lieutenant-Colonel RM	77·73	28,449
After 2 years	79·78	29,199
After 4 years	81·83	29,950
With 6 years seniority/Colonel		
RM	93·14	34,089
Rear-Admiral/Major-General		
RM	101·09	37,000
Vice-Admiral/Lieutenant-Gen-		
eral RM	124·32	45,000
Admiral/General RM	177·60	65,000
Admiral of the Fleet	221·31	81,000

ARMY
Normal Rates

Rank	Daily	Annual
	£	£
Second Lieutenant	23·28	8,520
Lieutenant		
On appointment	30·34	11,104
After 1 year	31·14	11,397
After 2 years	31·94	11,690
After 3 years	32·74	11,983
After 4 years	33·54	12,276
Captain		
On appointment	38·28	14,010
After 1 year	39·31	14,387
After 2 years	40·34	14,764
After 3 years	41·37	15,141
After 4 years	42·40	15,518
After 5 years	43·43	15,895
After 6 years	44·46	16,272
Major		
On appointment	48·66	17,810
After 1 year	49·87	18,252
After 2 years	51·08	18,695
After 3 years	52·29	19,138
After 4 years	53·50	19,581
After 5 years	54·71	20,024
After 6 years	55·92	20,467
After 7 years	57·13	20,910
After 8 years	58·34	21,352
Special List Lieutenant Colonel.	66·60	24,376
Lieutenant-Colonel		
On appointment	67·43	24,679
After 2 years or with 19 years		
service	69·20	25,327
After 4 years or with 21 years		
service	70·97	25,975
After 6 years or with 23 years		
service	72·74	26,623
After 8 years or with 25 years		
service	74·51	27,271
Colonel		
On appointment	77·73	28,499
After 2 years	79·78	29,199
After 4 years	81·83	29,950
After 6 years	83·88	30,700
After 8 years	85·93	31,450
Brigadier	93·14	34,089
Major-General	101·09	37,000
Lieutenant-General	124·32	45,000
General	177·60	65,000
Field Marshal	221·31	81,000

ROYAL AIR FORCE
Normal rates

Rank	Daily	Annual	Rank	Daily	Annual
	£	£		£	£
Acting Pilot Officer............	19·85	7,265	After 4 years................	53·50	19,581
After 6 months in the rank			After 5 years................	54·71	20,024
(aircrew officers only)......	20·31	7,433	After 6 years................	55·92	20,467
Pilot Officer	23·28	8,520	After 7 years................	57·13	20,910
Flying Officer	30·34	11,104	After 8 years................	58·34	21,352
After 1 year or 3 years c.s.	31·14	11,397	Wing Commander		
After 2 years or 4 years c.s. ...	31·94	11,690	On appointment.............	67·43	24,679
After 3 years or 5 years c.s. ...	32·74	11,983	After 2 years or 19 years c.s. ..	69·20	25,327
After 4 years or 6 years c.s. ...	33·54	12,276	After 4 years or 21 years c.s. ..	70·97	25,975
Flight Lieutenant	38·28	14,010	After 6 years or 23 years c.s. ..	72·74	26,623
After 1 year or 7 years c.s.	39·31	14,387	After 8 years or 25 years c.s. ..	75·51	27,271
After 2 years or 8 years c.s. ...	40·34	14,764	Group Captain	77·73	28,449
After 3 years or 9 years c.s. ...	41·37	15,141	After 2 years................	79·78	29,199
After 4 years or 10 years c.s. ..	42·40	15,518	After 4 years................	81·83	29,950
After 5 years or 11 years c.s. ..	43·43	15,895	After 6 years................	83·88	30,700
After 6 years or 12 years c.s. ..	44·46	16,272	After 8 years................	85·93	31,450
Squadron Leader	48·66	17,810	Air Commodore	93·14	34,089
After 1 year.................	49·87	18,252	Air Vice-Marshal	101·09	37,000
After 2 years................	51·08	18,695	Air Marshal	124·32	45,000
After 3 years................	52·29	19,138	Air Chief Marshal	177·60	65,000
			Marshal of the Royal Air Force .	221·31	81,000

c.s. = commissioned service.

ROYAL NAVY AND ROYAL MARINES SPECIAL DUTIES LIST OFFICERS
Army Male Officers commissioned from the ranks, and Royal Air Force Branch Officers

Years of Commissioned service	Years of Non-Commissioned service from age 18					
	Under 12 years		12 years but less than 15 years		15 years and over	
	Daily	Annual	Daily	Annual	Daily	Annual
	£	£	£	£	£	£
On appointment..................	41·70	15,262	43·82	16,038	45·94	16,814
After 1 year....................	42·76	15,650	44·88	16,426	46·74	17,107
After 2 years...................	43·82	16,038	45·94	16,814	47·54	17,400
After 3 years...................	44·88	16,426	46·74	17,107	48·34	17,692
After 4 years...................	45·94	16,814	47·54	17,400	49·14	17,985
After 5 years...................	46·74	17,107	48·34	17,692	49·94	18,278
After 6 years...................	47·54	17,400	49·14	17,985	50·74	18,571
After 8 years...................	48·34	17,692	49·94	18,278	51·54	18,864
After 10 years..................	49·14	17,985	50·74	18,571	51·54	18,864
After 12 years..................	49·94	18,278	51·54	18,864	51·54	18,864
After 14 years..................	50·74	18,571	51·54	18,864	51·54	18,864
After 16 years..................	51·54	18,864	51·54	18,864	51·54	18,864

ROYAL NAVY
Artificers, Medical and Communications Technicians—Daily Rates

Rating	Less than 6 years Scale A	6 years but less than 9 years Scale B	9 years or more Scale C
	£	£	£
FCPO Artificer/Technician	43·44	43·74	44·19
CCPO Artificer/Technician	41·71	42·01	42·46
CPO Artificer........ Scale I .... 1st Class Technician .	40·10	40·40	40·85
CPO Artificer........ Scale II.................... 1st Class Technician .	38·56	38·86	39·31
PO Artificer .... 2nd Class Technician	34·06	34·36	34·81
Probationary or Acting PO Artificer .... 3rd Class Technician .	32·49	32·79	33·24
4th Class Technician (Leading)	28·37	28·67	29·12
Leading Artificer .... Acting/4th Class Technician .	26·60	26·90	27·35
Acting Leading Artificer..........................	24·04	24·34	24·79
5th Class Technician (Able)	22·62	22·92	23·37

ROYAL NAVY AND ROYAL MARINES—OTHER BRANCHES

Daily rates of pay for those committed to serve for:

Rank	Scale	Less than 6 years Scale A	6 years but less than 9 years Scale B	9 years or more Scale C
		£	£	£
Fleet Chief Petty Officer/Warrant Officer Class I	I	40·18	40·48	40·93
Chief Petty Officer	I	35·49	35·79	36·24
Chief Petty Officer	II	34·85	35·15	35·60
Petty Officer/Sergeant	I	31·61	31·91	32·36
Petty Officer/Sergeant	II	31·04	31·34	31·79
Leading Rating/Corporal	I	28·37	28·67	29·12
Leading Rating/Corporal	II	26·60	26·90	27·35
Able Rating/Marine 1st Class	I	22·62	22·92	23·37
Able Rating/Marine 1st Class	II	21·24	21·54	21·99
Able Rating/Marine 1st Class	III	18·77	19·07	19·52
Ordinary Rating/Marine 2nd Class	I	16·07	16·37	16·82
Ordinary Rating/Marine 2nd Class	II	14·76	15·06	15·51

ARMY

Daily rates of pay for those committed to serve for:

Rank	Less than 6 years Scale A			6 years but less than 9 years Scale B			9 years or more Scale C		
	Band 1	Band 2	Band 3	Band 1	Band 2	Band 3	Band 1	Band 2	Band 3
	£	£	£	£	£	£	£	£	£
Private Class IV ...	14·76	—	—	15·06	—	—	15·51	—	—
Class III ...	16·21	18·77	—	16·51	19·07	—	16·96	19·52	—
Class II	17·93	20·49	23·23	18·23	20·79	23·53	18·68	21·24	23·98
Class I	19·37	21·93	24·67	19·67	22·23	24·97	20·12	22·68	25·42
Lance Corporal									
Class III ...	19·37	21·93	—	19·67	22·23	—	20·12	22·68	—
Class II	20·83	23·39	—	21·13	23·69	—	21·58	24·14	—
Class I	22·38	24·94	27·68	22·68	25·24	27·98	23·13	25·69	28·43
Corporal Class II ..	24·04	26·60	—	24·34	26·90	—	24·79	27·35	—
Class I	25·81	28·37	31·11	26·11	28·67	31·41	26·56	29·12	31·86

Rank	Band 4	Band 5	Band 6	Band 7	Band 4	Band 5	Band 6	Band 7	Band 4	Band 5	Band 6	Band 7
	£	£	£	£	£	£	£	£	£	£	£	£
Sergeant	28·25	31·04	34·06	—	28·55	31·34	34·36	—	29·00	31·79	34·81	—
Staff Sergeant	30·05	32·84	35·86	39·12	30·35	33·14	36·16	39·42	30·80	33·59	36·61	39·87
Warrant Officer Class II	32·13	34·92	37·94	41·20	32·43	35·22	38·24	41·50	32·88	35·67	38·69	41·95
Warrant Officer Class I	34·37	37·16	40·18	43·44	34·67	37·46	40·48	43·74	35·12	37·91	40·93	44·19

ROYAL AIR FORCE
Airmen (Aircrew)

Rank	Less than 6 years Scale A			6 years but less than 9 years Scale B			9 years or more Scale C		
	Band 5	Band 6	Band 7	Band 5	Band 6	Band 7	Band 5	Band 6	Band 7
	£	£	£	£	£	£	£	£	£
Pilots, Navigators, Air Electronics Operators and Air Engineers (A)									
Sergeant	—	34·06	—	—	34·36	—	—	34·81	—
Flight Sergeant ..	—	—	40·13	—	—	40·43	—	—	40·88
Master Aircrew ..	—	—	43·44	—	—	43·74	—	—	44·19
Air Signallers and Air Loadmasters									
Sergeant	31·04	—	—	31·34	—	—	31·75	—	—
Flight Sergeant ..	—	36·87	—	—	37·17	—	—	37·62	—
Master Aircrew ..	—	40·18	—	—	40·48	—	—	40·93	—

ROYAL AIR FORCE

Airmen (Ground Trades, Apprentices and P.M.R.A.F.N.S.)

Daily rates of pay for those committed to serve for:

Rank/Category	less than 6 years Scale A			6 years but less than 9 years Scale B			9 years or more Scale C		
	Band 1	Band 2	Band 3	Band 1	Band 2	Band 3	Band 1	Band 2	Band 3
	£	£	£	£	£	£	£	£	£
Aircraftmen over 17½ on entry	14·76	14·76	14·76	15·06	15·06	15·06	15·51	15·51	15·51
Leading Aircraftmen	16·21	18·77	21·51	16·51	19·07	21·81	16·96	19·52	22·26
Senior Aircraftmen	19·37	21·93	24·67	19·67	22·23	24·97	20·12	22·68	25·42
Junior Technician	22·38	24·94	27·68	22·68	25·24	27·98	23·13	25·69	28·43
Corporal	25·49	28·05	31·11	25·79	28·35	31·41	26·24	28·80	31·86

	Band 4	Band 5	Band 6	Band 7	Band 4	Band 5	Band 6	Band 7	Band 4	Band 5	Band 6	Band 7
	£	£	£	£	£	£	£	£	£	£	£	£
Sergeant	28·25	31·04	34·06	—	28·55	31·34	34·36	—	29·00	31·79	34·81	—
Chief Technician	29·66	32·45	35·47	38·73	29·96	32·75	35·77	39·03	30·41	33·20	36·22	39·48
Flight Sergeant	31·06	33·85	36·87	40·13	31·36	34·15	37·17	40·43	31·81	34·60	37·62	40·88
Warrant Officer	34·37	37·16	40·18	43·44	34·67	37·46	40·48	43·74	35·12	37·91	40·93	44·19

Officers of W.R.N.S.

Rank	Daily	Annual
	£	£
Probationary 3rd Officer	22·75	8,326
Third Officer on confirmation	25·05	9,168
After 2 years	29·65	10,852
Second Officer	37·41	13,692
After 1 year	38·42	14,062
After 2 years	39·42	14,428
After 3 years	40·43	14,797
After 4 years	41·44	15,167
After 5 years	42·44	15,533
After 6 years	43·45	15,903
First Officer	47·55	17,403
After 1 year	48·74	17,839
After 2 years	49·92	18,271
After 3 years	51·10	18,703
After 4 years	52·28	19,134
After 5 years	53·47	19,570
After 6 years	54·65	20,002
After 7 years	55·83	20,434
After 8 years	57·01	20,866
Chief Officer	65·90	24,119
After 2 years or with 19 years service	67·63	24,753
After 4 years or with 21 years service	69·36	25,386
After 6 years or with 23 years service	71·13	26,034
After 8 years or with 25 years service	72·90	26,681
Superintendent	76·65	28,054
After 2 years	78·70	28,804
After 4 years	80·75	29,554
After 6 years	82·80	30,305
After 8 years	84·85	31,055
Director, W.R.N.S.	92·60	33,892

Female officers of Q.A.R.N.N.S.

Rank	Daily	Annual
	£	£
Nursing Officer On appointment	29·65	10,852
After 1 year	30·43	11,137
After 2 years	31·21	11,423
After 3 years	32·00	11,712
After 4 years	32·75	11,997
Senior Nursing Officer		
On appointment	37·41	13,692
After 1 year	38·42	14,062
After 2 years	39·42	14,428
After 3 years	40·43	14,797
After 4 years	41·44	15,167
After 5 years	42·44	15,533
After 6 years	43·45	15,903
Superintending Nursing Officer		
On appointment	47·55	17,403
After 1 year	48·74	17,839
After 2 years	49·92	18,271
After 3 years	51·10	18,703
After 4 years	52·28	19,134
After 5 years	53·47	19,570
After 6 years	54·65	20,002
After 7 years	55·83	20,434
After 8 years	57·01	20,866
Chief Nursing Officer		
On appointment	65·90	24,119
After 2 years or with 19 years service	67·63	24,753
After 4 years or with 21 years service	69·36	25,386
After 6 years or with 23 years service	71·13	26,034
After 8 years or with 25 years service	72·90	26,681
Principal Nursing Officer		
On appointment	76·65	28,054
After 2 years	78·70	28,804
After 4 years	80·75	29,554
After 6 years	82·80	30,305
After 8 years	84·85	31,055
Matron-in-Chief	92·60	33,892

Officers of W.R.A.C., and Q.A.R.A.N.C.

Rank	Daily	Annual
	£	£
Second-Lieutenant	22·75	8,326
Lieutenant—On appointment	29·65	10,852
After 1 year	30·43	11,137
After 2 years..................	31·21	11,423
After 3 years..................	32·00	11,712
After 4 years..................	32·78	11,997
Captain—On appointment	37·41	13,692
After 1 year...................	38·42	14,062
After 2 years..................	39·42	14,428
After 3 years..................	40·43	14,797
After 4 years..................	41·44	15,167
After 5 years..................	42·44	15,533
After 6 years..................	43·45	15,903
Major—On appointment	47·55	17,403
After 1 year...................	48·74	17,839
After 2 years..................	49·92	18,271
After 3 years..................	51·10	18,703
After 4 years..................	52·28	19,134
After 5 years..................	53·47	19,570
After 6 years..................	54·65	20,002
After 7 years..................	55·83	20,434
After 8 years..................	57·01	20,866
Lieutenant-Colonel—On appointment	65·90	24,119
After 2 years or with 19 years service	67·63	24,753
After 4 years or with 21 years service	69·36	25,386
After 6 years or with 23 years service	71·13	26,034
After 8 years or with 25 years service	72·90	26,681
Colonel—On appointment........	76·65	28,054
After 2 years..................	78·70	28,804
After 4 years..................	80·75	29,554
After 6 years..................	82·80	30,305
After 8 years..................	84·85	31,055
Brigadier......................	92·60	33,892

Officers of W.R.A.F.

Rank	Daily	Annual
	£	£
Acting Pilot Officer..............	19·40	7,100
Pilot Officer	22·75	8,326
Flying Officer	29·65	10,852
After 1 year or 3 years c.s.	30·43	11,137
After 2 years or 4 years c.s.	31·21	11,423
After 3 years or 5 years c.s.	32·00	11,712
After 4 years or 6 years c.s.	32·78	11,997
Flight Lieutenant	37·41	13,692
After 1 year or 7 years c.s.	38·42	14,062
After 2 years or 8 years c.s.	39·42	14,428
After 3 years or 9 years c.s.	40·43	14,797
After 4 years or 10 years c.s.	41·44	15,167
After 5 years or 11 years c.s.	42·44	15,533
After 6 years or 12 years c.s.	43·45	15,903
Squadron Leader	47·55	17,403
After 1 year....................	48·74	17,839
After 2 years...................	49·92	18,271
After 3 years...................	51·10	18,703
After 4 years...................	52·28	19,134
After 5 years...................	53·47	19,570
After 6 years...................	54·65	20,002
After 7 years...................	55·83	20,434
After 8 years...................	57·01	20,866
Wing Commander On appointment................	65·90	24,119
After 2 years or 19 years c.s.	67·63	24,753
After 4 years or 21 years c.s.	69·36	25,386
After 6 years or 23 years c.s.	71·13	26,034
After 8 years or 25 years c.s.	72·90	26,681
Group Captain	76·65	28,054
After 2 years...................	78·70	28,804
After 4 years...................	80·75	29,554
After 6 years...................	82·80	30,305
After 8 years...................	84·85	31,055
Air Commodore	92·60	33,892

c.s. = commissioned service

W.R.N.S. Ratings and Naval Nurses

Rating	Scale	Band 1	Band 2	Band 3
		£	£	£
Ordinary Rating	under 17½	10·91	—	—
	at 17½	14·42	14·42	—
Able Rating	III	15·84	18·34	21·02
	II	18·25	20·75	23·43
	I	19·60	22·10	24·78
Leading Rating	II	23·49	25·99	28·67
	I	25·22	27·72	30·40

		Band 4	Band 5	Band 6	Band 7
		£	£	£	£
Petty Officer	II	27·29	30·02	32·97	36·16
	I	27·90	30·63	33·58	36·77
Chief Petty Officer	II	29·57	32·30	35·25	38·44
	I	30·29	33·02	35·97	39·16
Fleet Chief Petty Officer	I	33·58	36·31	39·26	42·45

Wrens and Naval Nurses who have served (a) for 6 years but less than 9 years will receive an additional £0·30; (b) for 9 years or more will receive an additional £0·75.

W.R.A.C. and Q.A.R.A.N.C.
Daily rates of pay for those who have served for:

Rank	Less than 6 years			6 years but less than 9 years			9 years or more		
	Band 1	Band 2	Band 3	Band 1	Band 2	Band 3	Band 1	Band 2	Band 3
	£	£	£	£	£	£	£	£	£
Private Class IV Age 17–17½	10·91	—	—	—	—	—	—	—	—
Class IV	14·42	—	—	14·72	—	—	15·17	—	—
Class III	15·84	18·34	—	16·14	18·64	—	16·59	19·09	—
Class II	17·52	20·02	—	17·82	20·32	—	18·27	20·77	—
Class I	18·92	21·42	24·10	19·22	21·72	24·40	19·67	22·17	24·85
Lance Corporal Class III	18·92	21·42	—	19·22	21·72	—	19·67	22·17	—
Class II	20·35	22·85	—	20·65	23·15	—	21·10	23·60	—
Class I	21·87	24·37	27·05	22·17	24·67	27·35	22·62	25·12	27·80
Corporal Class II	23·49	25·99	—	23·79	26·29	—	24·24	26·74	—
Class I	25·22	27·72	30·40	25·52	28·02	30·70	25·97	28·47	31·15

Band	4	5	6	7	4	5	6	7	4	5	6	7
	£	£	£	£	£	£	£	£	£	£	£	£
Sergeant	27·60	30·33	33·28	—	27·90	30·63	33·58	—	28·35	31·08	34·03	—
Staff Sergeant	29·36	32·09	35·04	38·23	29·66	32·39	35·34	38·53	30·11	32·84	35·79	38·98
Warrant Officer Class II	31·39	34·12	37·07	40·26	31·69	34·42	37·37	40·56	32·14	34·87	37·82	41·01
Class I	33·58	36·31	39·26	42·45	33·88	36·61	39·56	42·75	34·33	37·06	40·01	43·20

W.R.A.F. AIRWOMEN (Ground Trades) and P.M.R.A.F.N.S.
Daily rates of pay for those who have served for:

Rank/Category	Less than 6 years			6 years but less than 9 years			9 years or more		
	Band 1	Band 2	Band 3	Band 1	Band 2	Band 3	Band 1	Band 2	Band 3
	£	£	£	£	£	£	£	£	£
Aircraftwoman under age 17½	10·91	—	—	—	—	—	—	—	—
Aircraftwoman at age 17½	14·42	14·42	14·42	—	—	—	—	—	—
Leading Aircraftwoman	15·84	18·34	21·02	16·14	18·64	21·32	16·59	19·09	21·77
Senior Aircraftwoman	18·92	21·42	24·10	19·22	21·72	24·40	19·67	22·17	24·85
Junior Technician	21·87	24·37	27·05	22·17	24·67	27·35	22·62	25·12	27·80
Corporal	24·91	27·41	30·40	25·21	27·71	30·70	25·66	28·16	31·15

	Band 4	Band 5	Band 6	Band 7	Band 4	Band 5	Band 6	Band 7	Band 4	Band 5	Band 6	Band 7
	£	£	£	£	£	£	£	£	£	£	£	£
Sergeant	27·60	30·33	33·28	—	27·90	30·63	33·58	—	28·35	31·08	34·03	—
Chief Technician	28·98	31·71	34·68	37·85	29·28	32·01	34·98	38·15	29·73	32·46	35·41	38·60
Flight Sergeant	30·34	33·07	36·02	39·21	30·64	33·37	36·32	39·51	31·09	33·82	36·77	39·96
Warrant Officer	33·58	36·31	39·26	42·45	33·88	36·61	39·58	42·75	34·33	37·06	40·01	43·20

CHARGES FOR MARRIED AND SINGLE QUARTERS

Married Quarters

Type of quarter	Annual* charge			
	Grade 1	Grade 2	Grade 3	Grade 4
	£	£	£	£
Officers				
I	2,983	2,701	2,064	1,362
II	2,679	2,419	1,852	1,219
III	2,375	2,148	1,647	1,083
IV	2,053	1,859	1,438	937
V	1,782	1,614	1,230	824
Other Ranks				
D/WO	1,405	1,270	988	640
C	1,255	1,135	875	575
B	1,124	1,014	778	512
A	750	677	520	344

Single Quarters

Rank	Annual* charge			
	Grade 1	Grade 2	Grade 3	Grade 4
	£	£	£	£
Major and above	1,186	1,072	820	542
Captain and below	981	886	677	458
Warrant Officer and Senior N.C.O.	703	637	487	322
Corporal and below	377	340	260	172
Young serviceman receiving less than the minimum adult (i.e. Private IV) rate	282	253	194	132

*Annual charges are derived from daily rates in whole pence and rounded to the nearest £.

SERVICE RETIREMENT BENEFITS, ETC.

NOTE—Those who leave the Forces having served at least five years, but not long enough to qualify for the appropriate immediate pension, now qualify for a preserved pension and terminal grant both of which are payable at age 60. The tax-free resettlement grants shown below are payable on release to those who qualify for a preserved pension and who have completed 9 years service from age 21 (officers) or 12 years from age 18 (other ranks).

RETIREMENT BENEFITS (MEN) Officers*—All Services

No. of years reckonable service over age 21	Capt. (incl. Q.M.) and below	Major (incl. Q.M.)	Lt.-Col. (Q.M.)	Lt.-Col.	Col. and Deputy Chaplain General	Brigadier	Major-General, etc.	Lieutenant-General, etc.	General, etc.
	£p.a.	£p.a.	£p.a.	£p.a.	£p.a.	£p.a.	£p.a.	£p.a.	£p.a.
16	4,638	5,581	6,330	7,218					
17	4,854	5,846	6,595	7,552					
18	5,069	6,112	6,861	7,886	9,092				
19	5,285	6,377	7,126	8,219	9,477				
20	5,501	6,642	7,391	8,553	9,862				
21	5,716	6,907	7,656	8,887	10,247				
22	5,932	7,173	7,922	9,221	10,632	11,988			
23	6,148	7,438	8,187	9,554	11,017	12,366			
24	6,383	7,703	8,452	9,888	11,402	12,745	13,834		
25	6,579	7,969	8,718	10,222	11,788	13,124	14,245		
26	6,795	8,234	8,983	10,556	12,173	13,503	14,656		
27	7,010	8,499	9,248	10,890	12,558	13,882	15,067	18,529	
28	7,226	8,764	9,513	11,223	12,943	14,260	15,478	19,035	
29	7,442	9,030	9,779	11,557	13,328	14,539	15,890	19,540	
30	7,657	9,295	10,044	11,891	13,713	15,018	16,301	20,046	28,637
31	7,873	9,560	10,309	12,225	14,098	15,397	16,712	20,551	29,359
32	8,089	9,825	10,574	12,558	14,483	15,775	17,123	21,057	30,082
33	8,304	10,091	10,840	12,892	14,868	16,154	17,534	21,562	30,804
34	8,520	10,356	11,105	13,226	15,253	16,530	17,945	22,068	31,526

* Including those male officers holding equivalent ranks in the Q.A.R.N.N.S.

Ratings, Soldiers and Airmen*

Number of years reckonable service	Below Corporal	Corporal	Sergeant	Staff Sergeant	Warrant Officer Class II	Warrant Officer Class I
	£p.a.	£p.a.	£p.a.	£p.a.	£p.a.	£p.a.
22	2,724	3,492	3,849	4,376	4,501	4,938
23	2,819	3,614	3,983	4,529	4,660	5,116
24	2,914	3,736	4,118	4,681	4,820	5,293
25	3,009	3,858	4,252	4,834	4,979	5,471
26	3,104	3,979	4,387	4,987	5,139	5,649
27	3,199	4,101	4,521	5,140	5,298	5,826
28	3,294	4,223	4,655	5,292	5,458	6,004
29	3,389	4,345	4,790	5,445	5,617	6,182
30	3,485	4,467	4,924	5,598	5,777	6,359
31	3,580	4,589	5,059	5,751	5,936	6,537
32	3,675	4,711	5,193	5,903	6,096	6,715
33	3,770	4,833	5,327	6,056	6,255	6,892
34	3,865	4,954	5,462	6,209	6,415	7,070
35	3,960	5,076	5,596	6,362	6,574	7,248
36	4,055	5,198	5,731	6,514	6,734	7,425
37	4,150	5,320	5,865	6,667	6,893	7,603

* Including male nurses serving in the Q.A.R.N.N.S. holding equivalent rank.

RETIREMENT BENEFITS (WOMEN)

Q.A.R.N.N.S., W.R.N.S., Q.A.R.A.N.C., W.R.A.C., P.M.R.A.F.N.S., W.R.A.F. (The annual rates for W.R.A.C. are given: these apply to equivalent ranks in all Services, including the Nursing Services).

OFFICERS (16–34 years' service).—Captain, £4,534–£8,328; Major, £5,455–£10,123; Lt.-Col., £7,056–£12,928; Colonel, £8,978–£15,062; Brigadier, £11,928–£16,450.

SERVICEWOMEN (22–37 years' service).—Below Corporal, £2,663–£4,057; Corporal, £3,413–£5,200; Sergeant, £3,762–£5,733; Staff Sergeant, £4,278–£6,517; Warrant Officer II, £4,400–£6,738; Warrant Officer I, £4,827–£7,432.

NOTES

Terminal grants are in each case three times the rate of retired pay or pension. There are special rates of retired pay for Chaplains, Flight Lieutenants (Specialist Aircrew), and certain other ranks not shown above. Deductions may be made in cases of voluntary retirement.

The normal rates of gratuity for officers with short service commissions are £1,575 (men) and £1,540 (women) for each year completed. Resettlement grants are: officers £5,424 (men) and £5,302 (women); non-commissioned ranks £3,638 (men), £3,556 (women).

THE CHURCH OF ENGLAND

THE GENERAL SYNOD OF THE CHURCH OF ENGLAND

The General Synod was constituted in 1970, under the Synodical Government Measure 1969, in succession to the former Church Assembly. There are in total some 574 members of the General Synod, divided into three distinct houses—the House of Bishops, the House of Clergy and the House of Laity. It is presided over jointly by the Archbishops of Canterbury and York and normally meets three times each year—in February, July and November.

The function of the General Synod is to consider and make provision for all matters concerning the Church of England, and to consider and express opinion on any other matters of religious or public interest. The Synod appoints a number of Committees, Boards and Councils which deal with, or advise the Synod on, a wide range of matters affecting the Church and its Ministry.

Under the Church of England Assembly (Powers) Act 1919 the General Synod has the power—delegated by Parliament—to frame Statute Law on any matter concerning the Church of England, which are known as Measures. A Measure, once approved by General Synod, must be laid before both Houses of Parliament who may accept or reject it but may not amend it. If the Measure is accepted it is then submitted for Royal Assent and when this has been given the Measure has the full force of Law just as an Act of Parliament.

The Synod also has the power to make Canons and other ecclesiastical regulations provided that they do not conflict with statutory law. Canons have to be submitted to the Crown before they can come into effect.

OFFICES.—Church House, Dean's Yard, SW1P 3NZ—*Presidents*, The Archbishop of Canterbury; The Archbishop of York; *Sec.-Gen.*, W. D. Pattinson. THE HOUSE OF BISHOPS.—*Chairman*, The Archbishop of Canterbury; *Vice-Chairman*, The Archbishop of York. THE HOUSE OF CLERGY.—*Chairman*, The Archdeacon of Leicester; *Vice-Chairman*, Canon P. H. Boulton. THE HOUSE OF LAITY, *Chairman*, Prof. J. D. McClean; *Vice-Chairman*, Mrs. J. Dann.

Stipends (from April 1987)

Archbishop of Canterbury	£30,005
Archbishop of York	£26,190
Bishop of London	£24,355
Bishop of Durham	£21,415
Bishop of Winchester	£17,730
Diocesan Bishop	£15,925
Dean or Provost	£12,965
Canons Residentiary	£10,465

Province of Canterbury

CANTERBURY

102*nd Archbishop and Primate of All England*, Most Rev. and Rt. Hon. Robert Alexander Kennedy Runcie, M.C., *cons.* 1970, *trs.* 1980 (Lambeth Palace, SE1 7JU) [Signs Robert Cantuar:] 1980

Bishops Suffragan

Dover, Rt. Rev. Richard Henry McPhail Third, *cons.* 1976 (Upway, St. Martin's Hill, Canterbury, CT1 1PR) 1980
Maidstone, Rt. Rev. David James Smith, *cons.* 1987 (Bishop's House, Pett Lane, Charing, Ashford TN27 0DL).......................1987

Assistant Bishops

Rt. Rev. Harold Isherwood, M.V.O., O.B.E. (*cons.* 1974), 1979; Rt. Rev. The Lord Coggan, P.C. (*cons.* 1956), 1980; Rt. Rev. Ross Sydney Hook, M.C. (*cons.* 1965), 1986; Rt. Rev. William Alfred Franklin, O.B.E. (*cons.* 1972), 1987.

Dean

Very Rev. John Arthur Simpson 1986

Canons Residentiary

J. H. R. De Sausmarez (1981); P. Brett (1983); Ven. M. Till (1986).
Organist, A. Wicks, F.R.C.O. (1961).

Archdeacons

Canterbury, Ven. M. Till 1986
Maidstone, Ven. A. M. P. Smith 1979
Clergy, 241
Vicar-General of Province and Diocese, Miss S. Cameron, Q.C.
Commissary General, J. H. R. Newey, Q.C. (1971).

Joint Registrars of the Province, F. E. Robson, 16 Beaumont Street, Oxford; B. J. T. Hanson, Church House, Dean's Yard, SW1P 3NZ.
Registrar of the Diocese of Canterbury, A. O. E. Davies, 9 The Precincts, Canterbury CT1 2EQ.

LONDON

130*th Bishop*, Rt. Rev. and Rt. Hon. Graham Douglas Leonard, *cons.* 1964, *trs.* 1973 and 1981 (8 Barton Street, SW1P 3NE) [Signs Graham Londin:] 1981

Bishops Suffragan

Kensington, Rt. Rev. John Hughes 1987
Willesden, Rt. Rev. Thomas Butler, PH.D. (173 Willesden Lane, Brondesbury, NW6 7YN) ...1985
Edmonton, Rt. Rev. Brian John Masters, *cons.* 1982 (13 North Audley Street, W1Y 1FW) 1984
Stepney, Rt. Rev. James Lawton Thompson, *cons.* 1978 (23 Tredegar Square, E3 5AG) 1978
Fulham, Rt. Rev. Charles John Klyberg, *cons.* 1985 (4 Cambridge Place, W8 5PB) 1985

Assistant Bishops

Rt. Rev. Maurice Wood, D.S.C. (*cons.* 1971), 1985; Rt. Rev. George Reindorp (*cons.* 1961); Rt. Rev. Michael Marshall, 1984.

Dean of St. Paul's, (vacant).

Canons Residentiary

K. J. Woollcombe (1981); K. G. Routledge (1982); P. Ball (1984); Ven. G. Cassidy (1987).
Organist, C. H. Dearnley, F.R.C.O. (1968).
Receiver of St. Paul's, Commander C. Shears, O.B.E., R.N. (*ret.*)

Archdeacons

London, Ven. G. Cassidy 1987
Hackney, Ven. R. E. D. Sharpley 1981
Hampstead, Ven. R. Coogan 1984
Middlesex, Ven. T. J. Raphael 1983
Northolt, Ven. E. Shirras 1985
    Beneficed Clergy, 403; Curates, &c., 185
Chancellor and Commissary of the Dean and Chapter, G. H. Newsom, Q.C. (1971).
Registrar, D. W. Faull, 35 Great Peter St., SW1P 3LR.

WESTMINSTER

The Collegiate Church of St. Peter—(A Royal Peculiar)
Dean, Michael Clement Otway Mayne 1986

Canons Residentiary

S. Charles (1978); A. E. Harvey (1982); D. Gray (1987); C. Semper (1987).
Archdeacon, (vacant).
Chapter Clerk and Receiver General, Rear-Adm. K. A. Snow, C.B. (1987).
Organist, M. Neary, F.R.C.O. (1988).
Legal Secretary, C. L. Hodgetts (1973).
Registrar, S. J. Holmes, 20 Dean's Yard, SW1P 3PA.

WINCHESTER

95th Bishop, Rt. Rev. Colin Clement Walter James, cons. 1973, trs. 1977 and 1985 (Wolvesey, Winchester SO23 9ND) [Signs Colin Winton:] 1985

Bishops Suffragan

Southampton, Rt. Rev. Edward David Cartwright, cons. 1984 (Jollers, Winchester SO21 2NS) 1984
Basingstoke, Rt. Rev. Michael Richard John Manktelow, cons. 1977 (1 The Close, Winchester SO23 9LS)............................1977

Dean

Very Rev. Trevor Randall Beeson 1987

Dean of Jersey, Very Rev. Basil Arthur O'Ferrall, C.B., R.N. 1985
Dean of Guernsey, Very Rev. John William Foster, R.N. 1978

Canons Residentiary

Ven. T. G. Nash (1977); E. G. Job (1979); P. A. Britton (1980).
Organist, A. K. Walker (1987).

Archdeacons

Winchester, Ven. A. G. Clarkson 1984
Basingstoke, Ven. T. G. Nash 1982
    Beneficed Clergy, 220; Curates, &c., 55
Chancellor, John Spokes, Q.C. (1985).
Registrar and Legal Secretary, P. M. White, 19 St. Peter St., Winchester SO23 8BU.

BATH AND WELLS

75th Bishop, Rt. Rev. George Leonard Carey, Ph.D., cons. 1988 (The Palace, Wells BA5 2PD) [Signs George Bath & Wells]...............1988

Bishop Suffragan

Taunton, Rt. Rev. Nigel Simeon McCulloch, cons. 1986 (Sherford Farm House, Sherford, Taunton TA1 3RF)....................................1986

Assistant Bishop

Rt. Rev. John Stevens Waller (cons. 1979) 1987

Dean

Very Rev. Patrick Reynolds Mitchell, F.S.A. 1973

Canons Residentiary

D. R. Vicary (1975); S. R. Cutt (1979); C. E. Thomas (1983).
Organist, A. Crossland, F.R.C.O. (1970).

Archdeacons

Wells, Ven. C. E. Thomas 1983
Bath, Ven. J. E. Burgess 1975
Taunton, Ven. L. E. Olyott 1977
    Beneficed Clergy, 225; Other Clergy, 45.
Chancellor, G. H. Newsom, Q.C. (1970).
Registrar, Sec. & Chapt. Clerk, N. M. Cavender, Diocesan Registry, Market Place, Wells BA5 2RE.

BIRMINGHAM

7th Bishop, Rt. Rev. Mark Santer, cons. 1981 (Bishop's Croft, Harborne, Birmingham B17 0BG) [Signs Mark Birmingham] 1987

Bishop Suffragan

Aston, Rt. Rev. Colin Ogilvie Buchanan, cons. 1985 (60 Handsworth Wood Road, Birmingham B20 2DT) 1985

Provost

Very Rev. Peter Austin Berry 1986

Canons Residentiary

D. McLean (1972); L. M. Davies (1981); Ven. J. L. Cooper (1982).

Archdeacons

Aston, Ven. J. L. Cooper 1982
Birmingham, Ven. J. Duncan.................1985
    Beneficed Clergy, 165; Curates, &c., 73
Organist, M. R. Huxley, F.R.C.O. (1986).
Chancellor, His Hon. Judge Aglionby (1970).
Registrar and Legal Secretary, M. Shaw, 85 Cornwall Street, Birmingham B3 3BZ.

BRISTOL

54th Bishop, Rt. Rev. Barry Rogerson, cons. 1979 (Bishop's House, Clifton Hill, Bristol BS8 1BW) [Signs Barry Bristol] 1985

Bishop Suffragan

Malmesbury, Rt. Rev. Peter James Firth, cons. 1983 (7 Ivywell Rd., Bristol BS9 1NX) 1983

Dean

Very Rev. Wesley Arthur Carr 1987

Canons Residentiary

J. M. Free (1982); J. Rogan (1983); A. L. J. Redfern (1987).
Organist, M. Archer, F.R.C.O., A.R.C.M. (1983).

Archdeacons

Bristol, Ven. A. J. Balmforth 1979
Swindon, Ven. K. J. Clark....................1982
    Beneficed Clergy, 123; Curates, &c., 30
Chancellor, D. C. Calcutt, Q.C. (1971).
Registrar and Sec., T. R. Urquhart, 30 Queen Charlotte St., Bristol BS13 8HE

CHELMSFORD

7th Bishop, Rt. Rev. John Waine, *cons.* 1975 (Bishopscourt, Margaretting Ingatestone CM4 0HD) [Signs John Chelmsford] 1986

Bishops Suffragan

Barking, Rt. Rev. James William Roxburgh, *cons.* 1983 (28a Connaught Ave, Loughton, IG10 4DS) 1983
Colchester, (vacant).
Bradwell, Rt. Rev. Charles Derek Bond, *cons.* 1976 (188 New London Road, Chelmsford CM2 0AR) 1976

Provost

Very Rev. J. H. Moses, ph.d. 1982
Organist, G. Elliott, ph.D., f.r.c.o. (1981).

Archdeacons

West Ham, Ven. P. S. Dawes 1980
Colchester, Ven. E. C. F. Stroud 1983
Southend, Ven. J. S. Bailey 1982
    Beneficed Clergy, 384; *Curates, &c.*, 99
Chancellor, Miss S. M. Cameron (1970).
Diocesan Registrar, D. W. Faull, 35 Great Peter Street, Westminster SW1P 3LR.

CHICHESTER

102nd Bishop, Rt. Rev. Eric Waldram Kemp, D.D., *cons.* 1974 (The Palace, Chichester PO19 1PY) [Signs Eric Cicestr:] 1974

Bishops Suffragan

Horsham, Rt. Rev. Ivor Colin Docker, *cons.* 1975 (Bishop's Lodge, Worth, nr. Crawley RH10 4RT) 1975
Lewes, Rt. Rev. Peter John Ball, *cons.* 1977 (Litlington Rectory, nr. Polegate BN26 5RB) .1977

Assistant Bishops

Rt. Rev. William Warren Hunt (*cons.* 1955), 1980; Rt. Rev. Mark Green (*cons.* 1972), 1982; Rt. Rev. Simon Wilton Phipps (*cons.* 1968), 1987; Rt. Rev. Edward George Knapp-Fisher (*cons.* 1960), 1987.

Dean

Very Rev. Robert Tinsley Holtby..............1977

Canons Residentiary

R. T. Greenacre (1975); J. F. Hester (1985).
Organist, A. J. Thurlow, f.r.c.o. (1980).

Archdeacons

Chichester, Ven. K. Hobbs 1981
Horsham, Ven. W. C. L. Filby, ...1983
Lewes and Hastings, Ven. M. L. Godden 1975
    Beneficed Clergy, 320; *Curates, &c.*, 69
Chancellor, Q. T. Edwards, q.c. (1978).
Legal Secretary to the Bishop, and Diocesan Registrar, C. L. Hodgetts, 5 East Pallant, Chichester PO19 1TS.

COVENTRY

7th Bishop, Rt. Rev. Simon Barrington-Ward, *cons.* 1985 (The Bishop's House, 23 Davenport Road, Coventry CV5 6PW) [Signs Simon Coventry] 1985

Bishop Suffragan

Warwick, Rt. Rev. Keith Appleby Arnold, *cons.* 1980 (139 Kenilworth Rd., Coventry CV4 7AF) 1980

Assistant Bishops

Rt. Rev. John Daly (*cons.* 1935), 1968; Rt. Rev. Vernon Nicholls (*cons.* 1974), 1984.
Provost, (vacant).
Organist, P. Wright, f.r.c.o. (1984).

Canons Residentiary

P. Oestreicher (1986); M. Sadgrove (1987).

Archdeacons

Coventry, Ven. A. W. Morgan 1983
Warwick, Ven. P. S. G. Bridges...............1983
    Beneficed Clergy, 104; *Curates, &c.*, 49
Chancellor, W. M. Gage (1980).
Registrar, D. J. Dumbleton, 8 The Quadrant, Coventry CV1 2EL.

DERBY

4th Bishop, Rt. Rev. Cyril William Johnston Bowles, *cons.* 1969 (The Bishop's House, 6 King Street, Duffield, Derby DE6 4EU) [Signs Cyril Derby] 1969
    (Rt. Rev. Cyril Bowles is to retire Nov. 1987.)

Bishop Suffragan

Repton, Rt. Rev. Francis Henry Arthur Richmond, *cons.* 1986 (Repton House, Lea, Matlock DE4 5JP) 1986

Assistant Bishop

Rt. Rev. Cecil Allan Warren (*cons* 1965)........1983

Provost

Very Rev. Benjamin Hugh Lewers 1981

Canons Residentiary

Ven. R. S. Dell (1981); I. Gatford (1984); G. R. Orchard (1986).

Archdeacons

Chesterfield, Ven. G. R. Phizackerley 1978
Derby, Ven. R. S. Dell 1973
Organist, P. Gould, f.r.c.o. (1982).
    Beneficed Clergy, 180; *Curates, &c.*, 26
Chancellor, J. W. M. Bullimore (1981).
Registrar, J. S. Battie, Derby Church House, Full St., Derby DE1 3DR.

ELY

66th Bishop, Rt. Rev. Peter Knight Walker, *cons.* 1972, *trs.* 1977 (The Bishop's House, Ely CB7 4DW) [Signs Peter Ely] 1977

Bishop Suffragan

Huntingdon, Rt. Rev. William Gordon Roe, D.phil., *cons.* 1980 (Powchers Hall, The College, Ely).......................................1980

Dean

Very Rev. William James Patterson 1984

Canons Residentiary

D. J. Green (1980); Ven. R. K. Sledge (1980); M. S. MacDonald (1982).
Organist, A. W. Wills, mus.D., f.r.c.o. (1959).

Archdeacons

Ely, Ven. D. Walser 1981
Huntingdon, Ven. R. K. Sledge................1978
Wisbech, Ven. D. Fleming 1984
    Incumbents, 158; *Curates, &c.*, 10
Chancellor, Rev. Canon K. G. Routledge.
Registrar, W. H. Godfrey.
Joint Registrar, P. F. B. Beesley, 1 The Sanctuary, SW1P 3JT.

EXETER

69th Bishop, Rt. Rev. Geoffrey Hewlett Thompson, cons. 1974 (The Palace, Exeter EX1 1HY) [Signs Hewlett Exon:] 1985

Bishops Suffragan

Crediton, Rt. Rev. Peter Coleman, cons. 1984 (10 The Close, Exeter EX1 1EZ) 1984
Plymouth, Rt. Rev. Kenneth Albert Newing, cons. 1982 (38 Huxhams Cross, Dartington, Devon TQ9 6NT) 1982

Assistant Bishops

Rt. Rev. John Armstrong, C.B., O.B.E. (cons. 1963), 1969; Rt. Rev. Charles Robert Claxton (cons. 1946), 1971; Rt. Rev. Ronald Cedric Osbourne Goodchild (cons. 1964), 1983; Rt. Rev. Philip John Pasterfield (cons. 1971), 1984.

Dean

Very Rev. Richard Montague Stephens Eyre . . .1981

Canons Residentiary

J. A. Thurmer (1973); A. C. Mawson (1979); Ven. J. Richards (1981).
Organist, L. Nethsingha, F.R.C.O. (1972).
Chapter Clerk, J. F. Eden (1966).

Archdeacons

Exeter, Ven. J. Richards 1981
Plymouth, Ven. R. G. Ellis 1982
Barnstaple, Ven. R. G. Herniman 1970
Totnes, Ven. R. S. Hawkins 1981
        Beneficed Clergy, 275; Curates, &c., 38
Chancellor, D. C. Calcutt, Q.C. (1971).
Registrar, J. F. G. Michelmore, T.D., 18 Cathedral Yard, Exeter EX1 1HE.
Diocesan Secretary, Rev. R. R. Huddleson, Diocesan House, Palace Gate, Exeter EX1 1HX.

GIBRALTAR IN EUROPE

1st Bishop, Rt. Rev. John Richard Satterthwaite, cons. 1970 (5A Gregory Place, W8 4NG) [Signs John Gibraltar] 1971

Bishop Suffragan

In Europe, Rt. Rev. Edward Holland, A.K.C.

Auxiliary Bishops

Rt. Rev. E. M. H. Capper, O.B.E., (cons. 1967), 1973; Rt. Rev. D. de Pina Cabral, (cons. 1967), 1976; Rt. Rev. H. Isherwood, M.V.O., O.B.E., (cons. 1974), 1980.
Vicar-General, Rev. Canon P. O. Deacon.
Bishop's Commissaries, Canon J. A. Taylor; Canon L. Tyzack; Preb. D. W. C. Mossman, O.B.E.; Canon J. D. Beckwith.
Dean, Cathedral Church of the Holy Trinity, Gibraltar, Very Rev. A. L. Nind.
Chancellor, Pro-Cathedral of St. Paul, Valletta, Malta, Canon K. W. A. Roberts.
Chancellor, Pro-Cathedral of the Holy Trinity, Brussels, Belgium, Ven. J. Lewis.

Archdeacons

Aegean, Ven. G. B. Evans.
N.W. Europe, Ven. J. Lewis.
N. France, Ven. M. B. Lea.
Gibraltar, Rt. Rev. D. de Pina Cabral.
Italy, Ven. G. L. C. Westwell.
Riviera, Ven. J. Livingstone.
Scandinavia, Ven. B. Horlock, O.B.E.
Switzerland, Ven. P. J. Hawker.

GLOUCESTER

37th Bishop, Rt. Rev. John Yates, cons. 1972 (Bishopscourt, Gloucester GL1 2BQ) [Signs John Gloucestr] 1975

Bishop Suffragan

Tewkesbury, Rt. Rev. Geoffrey David Jeremy Walsh, cons. 1986 (Green Acre, Hempsted, Gloucester GL2 6LS) 1986

Dean

Very Rev. K. N. Jennings 1982

Canons Residentiary

Ven. T. E. Evans (1969); D. C. St. V. Welander (1975); A. L. Dunstan (1978); R. D. M. Grey (1982); P. R. Greenwood (1986).
Organist, J. D. Sanders, F.R.C.O., A.R.C.M. (1967).

Archdeacons

Gloucester, Ven. C. J. H. Wagstaff 1982
Cheltenham, Ven. T. E. Evans 1975
        Beneficed Clergy, 184; Curates, &c., 23
Chancellor & Vicar-Gen., Rev. E. Garth Moore .1957
Diocesan Registry, 34 Brunswick Road, Gloucester GL1 1JW.
Joint Registrars, J. R. Stayt; C. G. Peak.
Diocesan Sec., R. Anderton.

GUILDFORD

7th Bishop, Rt. Rev. Michael Edgar Adie, cons. 1983 (Willow Grange, Woking Road, Guildford GU4 7QS) [Signs Michael Guildford] 1983

Bishop Suffragan

Dorking, Rt. Rev. David Peter Wilcox (13 Pilgrims Way, Guildford GU4 8AD) 1986

Assistant Bishop

Rt. Rev. Kenneth Evans, (cons. 1968) 1986

Dean

Very Rev. Alexander Gillan Wedderspoon 1987

Canons Residentiary

F. S. Telfer (1973); P. G. Croft (1983); A. S. Leak (1986).
Organist, A. T. S. Millington, F.R.C.O. (1983).

Archdeacons

Surrey, Ven. P. E. Barber 1980
Dorking, Ven. P. G. Hogben 1982
        Beneficed Clergy, 148; Curates, &c., 59
Chancellor, M. B. Goodman.
Legal Sec., P. F. B. Beesley.
Registrar, P. F. B. Beesley, 1 The Sanctuary, SW1P 3JT.

HEREFORD

102nd Bishop, Rt, Rev. John Richard Gordon Eastaugh, cons. 1974 (The Palace, Hereford HR4 9BN) [Signs John Hereford]............1974

Bishop Suffragan

Ludlow, Rt. Rev. Ian MacDonald Griggs, cons. 1987 (Halford Vicarage, Craven Arms, Shropshire SY7 9BT)............................1987

Dean

Very Rev. Peter Haynes......................1982

Canons Residentiary

Ven. A. H. Woodhouse (1982); P. Iles (1983); J. Tiller (1984).
Organist, R. Massey, F.R.C.O. (1974).

Archdeacons

Hereford, Ven. A. H. Woodhouse 1982
Ludlow, Ven. J. H. R. Lewis 1987
    Beneficed Clergy, 98; *Curates, &c.*, 43
Chancellor, J. M. Henty.
Joint Registrars, V. T. Jordan, 44 Bridge Street,
    Hereford; P. Beesley, 1 The Sanctuary, West-
    minster, SW1P 3JT.

LEICESTER

4th Bishop, Rt. Rev. Cecil Richard Rutt, C.B.E.,
    cons. 1966 (Bishop's Lodge, Leicester LE2 3BD)
    [Signs Richard Leicester] 1979

Assistant Bishop

Rt. Rev. John Ernest Llewelyn Mort, C.B.E. (*cons.*
    1952) 1972

Provost

Very Rev. Alan Christopher Warren 1978

Canons Residentiary

Rt. Rev. J. E. L. Mort (1970).
Organist, P. White, F.R.C.O. (1968).

Archdeacons

Leicester, Ven. R. D. Silk .1980
Loughborough, Ven. T. H. Jones 1986
    Beneficed Clergy, 163; *Curates, &c.*, 43
Chancellor, N. H. Freeman (1979).
Registrar, G. K. J. Moore, 10 Friar Lane, Leicester
    LE1 5QD.

LICHFIELD

97th Bishop, Rt. Rev. Keith Norman Sutton,
    cons. 1978 (Bishop's House, The Close, Lichfield
    WS13 7LG) [Signs Keith Lichfield] 1984

Bishops Suffragan

Shrewsbury, Rt. Rev. John Dudley Davies, *cons.*
    1987 (Athlone House, 68 London Road, Shrews-
    bury SY2 6PG) 1987
Stafford, Rt. Rev. Michael Charles Scott-Joynt,
    cons. 1987 (Ash Garth, Broughton Crescent,
    Barlaston ST12 9DD) 1987
Wolverhampton, Rt. Rev. Christopher John May-
    field, *cons.* 1986 (61 Richmond Road, Wolver-
    hampton WV3 9JH) 1986

Dean

Very Rev. John Harley Lang 1980

Canons Residentiary

Ven. R. B. Ninis (1974); A. N. Barnard (1977);
    G. M. Smallwood (1978); W. J. Turner (1983).
Organist, J. Rees-Williams, F.R.C.O. (1978).

Archdeacons

Lichfield, Ven. R. B. Ninis 1974
Stoke on Trent, Ven. J. D. Delight 1982
Salop, Ven. G. Frost 1987
    Beneficed Clergy, 352; *Curates, &c.*, 76
Chancellor, Rev. Canon K. G. Routledge.
Diocesan Registrar and Bishop's Sec., M. B. S.
    Exham, 20 St. John St., Lichfield WS13 6PD.

LINCOLN

70th Bishop, Rt. Rev. Robert Maynard Hardy,
    cons. 1980 (Bishop's House, Eastgate, Lincoln
    LN2 1QQ) [Signs Robert Lincoln:] 1987

Bishops Suffragan

Grantham, Rt. Rev. William Ind, *cons.* 1987
    (Fairacre, Barrowby High Road, Grantham
    NG31 8NP) 1987
Grimsby, Rt. Rev. David Tustin, *cons.* 1979 (43
    Abbey Park Road, Grimsby DN32 0HS) 1979

Assistant Bishop

Rt. Rev. Gerald Fitzmaurice Colin (*cons.* 1966), 1979

Dean

Very Rev. the Hon. Oliver William Twisleton-
    Wykeham-Fiennes 1969

Canons Residentiary

D. C. Rutter (1965); B. R. Davis (1977); J. S.
    Nurser, PH.D. (1977); Ven. J. H. C. Laurence
    (1985).
Organist, D. A. Flood, F.R.C.O. (1986).

Archdeacons

Lincoln, Ven. R. J. Milner .1983
Stow, Ven. D. Scott 1975
Lindsey, Ven. J. H. C. Laurence 1985
    Beneficed Clergy, 280; *Curates, &c.*, 50
Chancellor, His Honour Judge M. B. Goodman (1971).
Registrar, D. M. Wellman, 5–6 Bank Street,
    Lincoln LN3 5QX.

NORWICH

70th Bishop (and *111th of East Anglia*), Rt. Rev.
    Peter John Nott, *cons.* 1977 (Bishop's House,
    Norwich, NR3 1SB) [Signs Peter Norvic:] 1985

Bishops Suffragan

Thetford, Rt. Rev. Timothy Dudley-Smith, *cons.*
    1981 (Rectory Meadow, Bramerton, Norwich
    NR14 7DW) 1981
Lynn, Rt. Rev. David Edward Bentley, *cons.* 1986
    (The Old Vic., Castle Acre, King's Lynn PE32
    2AA) 1986

Dean

Very Rev. John Paul Burbridge 1983

Canons Residentiary

D. H. Bishop (1980); C. Beswick (1984); M. S.
    McLean (1986).
Organist, M. B. Nicholas, F.R.C.O. (1971).

Archdeacons

Norwich, Ven. A. M. Handley 1981
Lynn, (vacant).
Norfolk, Ven. P. Dawson .1977
    Beneficed Clergy, 210; *Curates, &c.*, 25
Chancellor, His Hon. J. H. Ellison, V.R.D. (1955).
Joint Registrars and Secs., B. O. L. Prior, M.B.E.,
    T.D.; J. A. Linton, 74 The Close, Norwich NR1
    4DE.

OXFORD

41st Bishop, Rt. Rev. Richard Douglas Harries,
    cons. 1987 (Bishop's House, 27 Linton Rd.,
    Oxford) [Signs Richard Oxon:] 1987

Area Bishops

Reading, Rt. Rev. Ronald Gregory Graham
    Foley, *cons.* 1982 (Greenbanks, Old Bath Road,
    Sonning, Reading RG4 0SY 1982
Buckingham, Rt. Rev. Simon Hedley Burrows,
    cons. 1974 (Sheridan, Grimms Hill, Great
    Missenden HP16 9BD) 1974
Dorchester, (vacant).

Assistant Bishops

Rt. Rev. Sydney Cyril Bulley, D.D. (*cons.* 1959), 1979; Rt. Rev. Albert Kenneth Cragg, D.D., (*cons.* 1970), 1982; Rt. Rev. Eric Wild, (*cons.* 1972), 1982; Rt. Rev. Leonard James Ashton, C.B., (*cons.* 1974), 1984.

Dean of Christ Church

Very Rev. Eric William Heaton 1979

Canons Residentiary

W. R. F. Browning (*Canon of the Cathedral Church*) (1965); M. F. Wiles, (1970); J. C. Fenton (1978); Ven. F. V. Weston (1982); O. M. T. O'Donovan, D.phil. (1982); R. D. Williams, D.phil. (1985).
Organist, S. Darlington, F.R.C.O.

Archdeacons

Bucks., Ven. J. F. E. Bone 1978
Oxford, Ven. F. V. Weston...................1982
Berks., Ven. D. Griffiths......................1987

Chancellor, P. T. S. Boydell, Q.C. (1958).
Registrar and Legal Sec., F. E. Robson, 16 Beaumont St., Oxford OX1 2LZ.

WINDSOR

(*The Queen's Free Chapel of St. George within Her Castle of Windsor—A Royal Peculiar*)
Dean, Rt. Rev. Michael Ashley Mann..........1976

Canons Residentiary

J. D. Treadgold (1981); J. A. White (1982); D. M. Stanesby (1985); A. A. Coldwells (1987).
Organist, C. J. Robinson, L.V.O., F.R.C.O. (1975).
Chapter Clerk, Maj.-Gen. R. L. C. Dixon, C.B., M.C. (1981).

PETERBOROUGH

36*th Bishop*, Rt. Rev. William John Westwood, *cons.* 1975 (The Palace, Peterborough PE1 1YA) [Signs William Petriburg:] 1984

Dean

Very Rev. Randolph George Wise 1981

Canons Residentiary

Ven. B. Fernyhough (1977); T. R. Christie (1980); J. Higham (1983).
Master of the Music, C. S. Gower, F.R.C.O. (1977).

Archdeacons

Northampton, Ven. B. R. Marsh 1964
Oakham, Ven. B. Fernyhough 1977
    Beneficed Clergy, 190; *Curates, &c*, 40
Chancellor, Rev. Canon K. C. Routledge.
Registrar, R. Hemingray, 10 Queen St., Peterborough PE1 1PH.

PORTSMOUTH

7*th Bishop*, Rt. Rev. Timothy John Bavin, *cons.* 1974 (Bishopswood, Fareham, Hants., PO14 1NT) [Signs Timothy Portsmouth] 1985

Provost

Very Rev. David Staffurth Stancliffe 1982
Organist, A. Froggatt, A.R.C.O.

Canons Residentiary

S. G. Platten (1983); R. Eckersley (1984); P. J. Cotton (1984); M. J. Gudgeon (1987).

Archdeacons

Portsmouth, Ven. N. H. Crowder 1985
I. of Wight, Ven. A. H. M. Turner..............1986

Beneficed Clergy, 94; *Curates, &c.*, 67
Chancellor, His Honour Judge Aglionby (1978).
Registrar, Miss H. A. G. Tyler, 175 London Road, North End, Portsmouth PO2 9AE.

ROCHESTER

104*th Bishop*, Rt. Rev. Richard David Say, D.D., *cons.* 1961 (Bishopscourt, Rochester ME1 1TS) [Signs David Roffen:] 1961

Bishop Suffragan

Tonbridge, Rt. Rev. David Henry Bartleet, *cons.* 1982 (Bishop's Lodge, St. Botolph's Road, Sevenoaks TN13 3AG) 1982

Dean

Very Rev. John Robert Arnold 1978

Canons Residentiary

P. A. Welsby, PH.D. (1966); H. E. C. Stapleton (1980); E. R. Turner (1981); Ven. A. M. A. Turnbull (1984).
Organist, B. Ferguson, F.R.C.O. (1977).

Archdeacons

Rochester, Ven. A. M. A. Turnbull.............1984
Tonbridge, Ven. R. J. Mason..................1977
Bromley, Ven. E. R. Francis 1979
    Beneficed Clergy, 200; *Curates, &c.*, 50
Chancellor, His Honour Judge M. B. Goodman (1971).
Registrar, O. R. Woodfield, Rochester.
Sec. D. W. Faull, 35 Great Peter St., SW1P 3LR.

ST. ALBANS

8*th Bishop*, Rt. Rev. John Bernard Taylor, *cons.* 1980 (Abbey Gate House, St. Albans AL3 4HD) [Signs John St. Albans] 1980

Bishops Suffragan

Hertford, Rt. Rev. Kenneth Harold Pillar, *cons.* 1982 (Hertford House, Abbey Mill Lane, St. Albans AL3 4HE)..........................1982
Bedford, Rt. Rev. David John Farmbrough, *cons.* 1981 (168 Kimbolton Rd., Bedford MK41 8DN)....................................1981

Dean

Very Rev. Peter Clement Moore, D.phil.........1973
Organist, C. Walsh, F.R.C.O. (1985).

Canons Residentiary

B. C. E. Pettifer; C. B. Slee (1982); C. Garner (1984).

Archdeacons

St. Albans, Ven. E. M. Norfolk 1982
Bedford, Ven. M. G. Bourke 1986
    Beneficed Clergy, 249; *Curates, &c.*, 83
Chancellor, G. H. Newsom, Q.C. (1958).
Registrar and Legal Sec., D. N. Cheetham, Holywell Lodge, 41 Holywell Hill, St. Albans AL1 1HE.

ST. EDMUNDSBURY AND IPSWICH

8*th Bishop*, Rt. Rev. John Dennis, *cons.* 1979 (Bishop's House, Ipswich IP1 3ST) [Signs John St. Edm. & Ipswich]........................1986

Bishop Suffragan

Dunwich, Rt. Rev. Eric Nash Devenport, *cons.* 1980 (94 Henley Rd., Ipswich IP1 4NJ) 1980

Provost

Very Rev. Raymond Furnell.................1981

Canons Residentiary

D. A. Payne (1973); G. J. Tarris (1982); R. Garrard (1987).

Archdeacons

Sudbury, Ven. D. J. Smith 1984
Suffolk, Ven. N. Robinson 1987
Ipswich, Ven. T. A. Gibson 1987
Organist, P. Treptre, F.R.C.O. (1985).
Beneficed Clergy, 139; *Clergy of incumbent status*, 38; *Curates*, 17
Chancellor, His Honour Judge Blofeld, Q.C. (1974).
Registrar, J. D. Mitson, 22–28 Museum Street, Ipswich IP1 1JA.

SALISBURY

76th Bishop, Rt. Rev. John Austin Baker, *cons.* 1982 (South Canonry, The Close, Salisbury SP1 2ER) [Signs John Sarum]...................1982

Bishops Suffragan

Sherborne, Rt. Rev. John Dudley Galtrey Kirkham, *cons.* 1976 (Little Bailie, Sturminster Marshall, Wimborne BH21 4AD) 1976
Ramsbury, Rt. Rev. John Robert Geoffrey Neale, *cons.* 1974 (Bishop's House, Urchfont, Devizes, Wilts., SN10 4QH) 1974

Dean

Very Rev. the Hon. Hugh Geoffrey Dickinson ..1986

Canons Residentiary

I. G. D. Dunlop, F.S.A. (1972); R. G. Askew (1983); D. J. C. Davies (1985).
Organist, R. G. Seal, F.R.C.O. (1968).

Archdeacons

Sarum, Ven. B. J. Hopkinson 1986
Wilts, Ven. B. J. Smith 1980
Dorset, Ven. G. E. Walton 1982
Sherborne, Ven. J. K. Oliver 1985
Beneficed Clergy, 255; *Curates, &c.*, 38
Chancellor of the Diocese, His Hon. J. H. Ellison, V.R.D. (1955).
Registrar and Legal Secretary, F. M. Broadbent, 42 Castle Street, Salisbury SP1 3TX.

SOUTHWARK

7th Bishop, Rt. Rev. Ronald Oliver Bowlby, *cons.* 1973, *trs.* 1980 (Bishop's House, 38 Tooting Bec Gardens, SW16 1QZ) [Signs Ronald Southwark] 1980

Bishops Suffragan

Croydon, Rt. Rev. Wilfred Denniston Wood, D.D., *cons.* 1985 (St. Matthew's House, George St., Croydon CR0 1PE) 1985
Kingston on Thames, Rt. Rev. Peter Stephen Maurice Selby, PH.D., *cons.* 1984 (24 Albert Drive, SW19 6LS) 1984
Woolwich, Rt. Rev. Albert Peter Hall, *cons.* 1984 (8b Hillyfields Crescent, SE4) 1984

Assistant Bishops

Rt. Rev. Edmund Michael Hubert Capper, O.B.E. (*cons.* 1967), 1981; Rt. Rev. Archibald Ronald McDonald Gordon (*cons.* 1975), 1984; Rt. Rev. John Hughes (*cons.* 1956), 1986; Rt. Rev. Hugh William Montefiore (*cons.* 1970), 1987.

Provost

Very Rev. David Lawrence Edwards 1983

Canons Residentiary

P. H. Penwarden (1971); I. G. Smith-Cameron (1972); G. A. Parrott (1977); J. S. Cox (1983).
Organist, H. Bramma (1976).

Archdeacons

Croydon, Ven. F. R. Hazell....................1984
Kingston, Ven. B. V. Jacob 1977
Lewisham, Ven. C. J. Lacey 1985
Southwark, Ven. D. L. Bartles-Smith 1985
Wandsworth, Ven. P. B. Coombs 1975
Lambeth, (vacant).
Chancellor, Rev. E. Garth Moore (1948).
Registrar, D. W. Faull, 35 Great Peter St., SW1P 3LR.

TRURO

12th Bishop, Rt. Rev. Peter Mumford, *cons.* 1974, (Lis Escop, Truro TR3 6QQ) [Signs Peter Truron:] 1981

Bishop Suffragan

St. Germans, Rt. Rev. Richard Llewellin, *cons.* 1986 (32 Falmouth Road, Truro TR1 2HX) ...1985

Assistant Bishop

Rt. Rev. R. F. Cartwright 1982

Dean

Very Rev. David John Shearlock..............1982

Canons Residentiary

P. L. Maddock (1976); Ven. A. Wood (1981); W. J. P. Boyd, PH.D. (1985).
Organist, J. Winter (1971).

Archdeacons

Cornwall, Ven. A. Wood.....................1981
Bodmin, Ven. G. F. Temple 1981
Beneficed Clergy, 164; *Curates, &c.*, 20
Chancellor, P. T. S. Boydell, Q.C. (1957).
Registrar and Secretary, R. W. Money, 2 Princes Street, Truro TR1 2EZ.

WORCESTER

111th Bishop, Rt. Rev. Philip Harold Ernest Goodrich, *cons.* 1973 (The Bishop's House, Hartlebury Castle, Kidderminster DY11 7XX) [Signs Philip Worcester] 1982

Bishop Suffragan

Dudley, Rt. Rev. Anthony Charles Dumper, *cons.* 1977 (The Bishop's House, Brooklands, Halesowen Road, Cradley Heath B64 7JF)........1977

Assistant Bishops

Rt. Rev. David Howard Nicholas Allenby (*cons.* 1962), 1968; Rt. Rev. Oliver Stratford Tomkins (*cons.* 1959), 1975; Rt. Rev. John Arthur Arrowsmith Maund, C.B.E., M.C. (*cons.* 1950), 1984; Rt. Rev. Stanley Chapman Pickard, C.B.E. (*cons.* 1958), 1984.

Dean

Very Rev. Robert Martin Colquhoun Jeffery ...1987

Canons Residentiary

J. R. Fenwick (1978); Ven. F. Bentley (1984).
Organist, D. Hunt, MUS.D., F.R.C.O. (1975).

Archdeacons

Worcester, Ven. F. Bentley 1984
Dudley, Ven. J. Gathercole 1987
Beneficed Clergy, 120; *Curates, &c.*, 50
Chancellor, P. T. S. Boydell, Q.C. (1959).
Registrar, Rev. J. A. Dale, Diocesan Registry, Little Comberton Rectory, Pershore WR10 3EP.

Province of York

YORK

95th *Archbishop and Primate of England* Most
Rev. and Rt. Hon. John Stapylton Habgood,
ph.d., *cons.* 1973, *trs.* 1983 (Bishopthorpe, York
YO2 1QE) [Signs John Ebor:] 1983

Bishops Suffragan

Selby, Rt. Rev. Clifford Conder Barker, t.d., *cons.*
1976 (8 Bankside Close, Upper Poppleton, York
YO2 6LH) 1983
Hull, Rt. Rev. Donald George Snelgrove, t.d.,
cons. 1981 (Hullen House, Woodfield Lane,
Hessle, Hull HU13 0ES) 1981
Whitby, Rt. Rev. Gordon Bates, *cons.* 1983 (60
West Green, Stokesley, Middlesbrough
TS9 5BD) 1983

Assistant Bishops

Rt. Rev. George Eyles Irwin Cockin (*cons.* 1959),
1969; Rt. Rev. Richard Knyvet Wimbush (*cons.*
1963), 1977; Rt. Rev. George Edward Holderness, e.r.d. (*cons.* 1955), 1980; Rt. Rev. Richard
James Wood (*cons.* 1973), 1985.

Dean

Very Rev. John Eliot Southgate 1984

Canons Residentiary

R. A. Hockley (1976); R. Mayland (1982); J. Toy,
ph.d. (1983).
Organist, P. J. Moore, a.r.c.m., f.r.c.o.

Archdeacons

York, Ven. L. C. Stanbridge 1972
East Riding, Ven. M. E. Vickers...............1981
Cleveland, Ven. R. J. Woodley 1984
   Beneficed Clergy, 256; *Curates, &c.*, 41
*Official Principal and Auditor of the Chancery
Court*, J. A. D. Owen, q.c.
Chancellor of the Diocese, T. A. C. Coningsby
(1977).
*Vicar-General of the Province and Official Prin-
cipal of the Consistory Court*, T. A. C. Con-
ingsby.
Registrar and Legal Secretary, L. P. M. Lennox,
22 High Petergate, York YO1 2EH.

DURHAM

92nd *Bishop*, Rt. Rev. David Edward Jenkins,
cons. 1984 (Auckland Castle, Bishop Auckland
DL14 7NR) [Signs David Dunelm] 1984

Bishop Suffragan

Jarrow, Rt. Rev. Michael Thomas Ball, *cons.* 1980
(Melkridge House, Gilesgate, Durham
DH1 1JB)..................................1980

Dean

Very Rev. Peter Richard Baelz................1980

Canons Residentiary

Ven. M. C. Perry (1970); R. L. Coppin (1974);
Ven. J. D. Hodgson (1983); T. Hart (1983);
D. W. Hardy (1986).
Organist, J. B. Lancelot, f.r.c.o. (1985).

Archdeacons

Durham, Ven. M. C. Perry 1970
Auckland, Ven. J. D. Hodgson 1983
   Clergy, 306
Chancellor, Rev. E. Garth Moore (1954).
Registrar and Legal Secretary, W. K. Wills,
Diocesan Registry, 21a Elvet Bridge, Durham
DH1 3HB (1975).

BLACKBURN

6th *Bishop*, Rt. Rev. David Stewart Cross, *cons.*
1976 (Bishop's House, Ribchester Road, Blackburn BB1 9EF) [Signs Stewart Blackburn] ...1982

Bishops Suffragan

Lancaster, Rt. Rev. Ian Harland, *cons.* 1985
(Wheatfield, Dallas Road, Lancaster
LA1 1TN) 1985
Burnley, (vacant).

Provost

Very Rev. Lawrence Jackson 1973

Canons Residentiary

G. A. Williams (1965); J. M. Taylor (1976); B. M.
Beaumont (1977); G. I. Hirst (1987).

Archdeacons

Blackburn, Ven. W. D. Robinson 1986
Lancaster, Ven. K. H. Gibbons 1981
Organist, D. A. Cooper, f.r.c.o. (1983).
   Beneficed Clergy, 230; *Curates, &c.*, 50
Chancellor, Quentin T. Edwards, q.c. (1977).
Registrar, Leslie Ranson, Diocesan Registry,
Cathedral Close, Blackburn BB1 5AB (1954).

BRADFORD

7th *Bishop*, Rt. Rev. Robert Kerr Williamson,
cons. 1984 (Bishopscroft, Ashwell Road, Heaton, Bradford BD9 4AU) [Signs Robert
Bradford]..................................1984

Provost

Very Rev. Brandon Donald Jackson 1977

Canons Residentiary

K. H. Cook (1977); C. J. Hayward (1983).
Organist, A. Horsey (1986).

Archdeacons

Bradford, Ven. D. H. Shreeve 1984
Craven, Ven. B. A. Smith.....................1987
   Beneficed Clergy, 123; *Curates, &c.*, 23
Chancellor, D. M. Savill, q.c. (1976).
Registrar and Secretary, J. G. H. Mackrell, 6–14
Devonshire Street, Keighley BD21 2AY (1977).

CARLISLE

64th *Bishop*, Rt. Rev. Henry David Halsey, *cons.*
1968 (Rose Castle, Dalston, Carlisle CA5 7BZ),
[Signs David Carliol:]......................1972

Bishop Suffragan

Penrith, Rt. Rev. George Lanyon Hacker, *cons.*
1979 (The Rectory, Gt. Salkeld, Penrith
CA11 9NA) 1979
Dean, (vacant).

Canons Residentiary

R. A. Chapman (1978); R. J. W. Bevan (1982); A.
Smithson (1984); Ven. C. P. Stannard (1984).
Organist, R. A. Seivewright, a.r.c.o. (1960).

Archdeacons

Carlisle, Ven. C. P. Stannard 1984
West Cumberland, Ven. T. R. B. Hodgson 1979
Westmorland and Furness, Ven. P. St. G.
Vaughan 1983
   Beneficed Clergy, 190
Chancellor, His Hon. D. J. Stinson (1971).
Registrar and Sec., I. S. Sutcliffe, Castle St.,
Carlisle CA3 8TW (1964).

CHESTER

39th Bishop, Rt. Rev. Michael Alfred Baughen,
cons. 1982 (Bishop's House, Chester CH1 2JD)
[Signs Michael Cestr:] 1982

Bishops Suffragan

Stockport, Rt. Rev. Frank Pilkington Sargeant,
cons. 1984 (32 Park Gate Drive, Cheadle Hulme,
Cheshire SK8 7DS) 1984
Birkenhead, Rt. Rev. Ronald Brown, *cons.* 1974
(Trafford House, Queen's Park, Chester
CH4 7AX) 1974

Dean

Very Rev. Stephen Stewart Smalley 1986

Canons Residentiary

W. H. Vanstone (1978); L. R. Barker (1984); C. D.
Biddell (1986).
Organist, R. A. Fisher, F.R.C.O. (1967).

Archdeacons

Chester, Ven. H. L. Williams 1975
Macclesfield, Ven. J. S. Gaisford 1986
Chancellor, H. H. Lomas (1977).
Registrar and Legal Secretary, A. K. McAllester,
Friars, 20 White Friars, Chester CH1 1XS.

LIVERPOOL

6th Bishop, Rt. Rev. David Stuart Sheppard,
cons. 1969 (Bishop's Lodge, Woolton Park,
Liverpool L25 6DT) [Signs David Liverpool] ..1975

Bishop Suffragan

Warrington, Rt. Rev. Michael Henshall, *cons.*
1976 (Martinsfield, Elm Avenue, Great Crosby,
Liverpool L23 2SX) 1976

Assistant Bishops

Rt. Rev. William Scott Baker (*cons.* 1943) 1968

Dean

Very Rev. R. D. C. Walters 1983

Canons Residentiary

M. M. Wolfe (1982); D. J. Hutton (1983); K. J.
Riley (1983).
Organist, I. Tracey (1980).

Archdeacons

Liverpool, Ven. G. H. G. Spiers 1979
Warrington, Ven. C. D. S. Woodhouse..........1981
Beneficed Clergy, 246; *Curates, &c.*, 89
Chancellor, R. G. Hamilton.
Registrar and Cathedral Chapter Clerk, R. H.
Arden, 1 Hanover Street, Liverpool L1 3DW.

MANCHESTER

9th Bishop, Rt. Rev. Stanley Eric Francis Booth-
Clibborn, *cons.* 1979 (Bishopscourt, Bury New
Road, Manchester M7 0LE) [Signs Stanley
Manchester] 1979

Bishops Suffragan

Bolton, Rt. Rev. David George Galliford, *cons.*
1984 (4 Sandfield Drive, Lostock, Bolton
BL6 4DU) 1984
Middleton, Rt. Rev. Donald Alexander Tytler,
cons. 1982 (The Hollies, Manchester Road,
Rochdale OL11 3QY) 1982
Hulme, Rt. Rev. Colin John Fraser Scott, *cons.*
1984 (1 Raynham Avenue, Didsbury, Manchester M20 0BW) 1984

Assistant Bishops

Rt. Rev. Edward Ralph Wickham (*cons.* 1959),
1982; Rt. Rev. Kenneth Venner Ramsey (*cons.*
1953), 1975.

Dean

Very Rev. Robert Murray Waddington 1984

Canons Residentiary

Ven. R. B. Harris (1980); J. Nicholls (1983); J. R.
Atherton, PH.D. (1984); B. Duncan (1986).
Organist, G. Stewart.

Archdeacons

Manchester, Ven. R. B. Harris 1980
Rochdale, Ven. D. Bonser 1982
Bolton, Ven. W. S. Brison 1985
Beneficed Clergy, 300; *Curates, &c.*, 110
Chancellor, G. C. H. Spafford (1976).
Registrar and Bishop's Secretary, M. Darlington,
90 Deansgate, Manchester M3 2GH (1986).

NEWCASTLE

10th Bishop, Rt. Rev. Andrew Alexander Kenny
Graham, *cons.* 1977 (Bishop's House, 29 Moor
Road South, Gosforth, Newcastle upon Tyne
NE3 1PA) [Signs A. Newcastle] 1981

Assistant Bishop

Rt. Rev. Kenneth Edward Gill (*cons.* 1972) 1980

Provost

Very Rev. Christopher Garnett Howsin Spafford
1976

Canons Residentiary

D. A. Carrette (1978); W. J. Thomas (1983); R.
Langley (1985); P. R. Strange (1986).
Organist, T. Hone (1987).

Archdeacons

Lindisfarne, Ven. M. E. Bowering 1987
Northumberland, Ven. W. J. Thomas 1983
Beneficed Clergy, 117; *other Clergy of incumbent
status*, 27; *Curates, &c.*, 34
Chancellor, His Hon. A. J. Blackett-Ord (1971).
Registrar and Sec., R. R. V. Nicholson, 46
Grainger Street, Newcastle upon Tyne NE1
5LB.

RIPON

11th Bishop, Rt. Rev. David Nigel de Lorentz
Young, *cons.* 1977 (Bishop Mount, Ripon
HG4 5DP) [Signs David Ripon].............1977

Bishop Suffragan

Knaresborough, Rt. Rev. Malcolm James Men-
nin, *cons.* 1986 (16 Shaftesbury Ave., Round-
hay, Leeds LS8 1DT) 1986

Assistant Bishops

Rt. Rev. John Howe (*cons.* 1955) 1983; Rt. Rev.
Ralph Emmerson (*cons.* 1972) 1987.

Dean

Very Rev. Christopher Russell Campling 1984

Canons Residentiary

R. B. McFadden (1979); D. G. Ford (1980); P. J.
Marshall (1985).
Organist, Ronald Perrin, F.R.C.O. (1966).

Archdeacons

Leeds, Ven. A. J. Comber 1982
Richmond, Ven. N. G. L. R. McDermid.........1983
Beneficed Clergy, 132; *Curates, &c.*, 40
Chancellor, D. M. Savill, Q.C. (1987).
Registrar and Legal Secretary, J. R. Balmforth,
York House, York Place, Knaresborough HG5
0AD.

SHEFFIELD

5th Bishop, Rt. Rev. David Ramsay Lunn, *cons.* 1980 (Bishopscroft, Snaithing Lane, Sheffield S10 3LG) [Signs David Sheffield] 1980

Bishop Suffragan

Doncaster, Rt. Rev. William Michael Dermot Persson, *cons.* 1982 (Bishops Lodge, Rotherham S65 4PF).................................1982

Provost

Very Rev. Wilfred Frank Curtis 1974

Archdeacons

Sheffield, Ven. M. J. M. Paton.................1978
Doncaster, Ven. D. Carnelley 1985
Organist, G. Matthews, F.R.C.O. (1967).
   Beneficed Clergy, 163; *Curates, &c.,* 46
Chancellor, G. B. Graham, Q.C. (1971).
Registrar and Legal Sec. P. T. Ward, 30 Bank Street, Sheffield S1 2DS.

SODOR AND MAN

78th Bishop, Rt. Rev. Arthur Henry Attwell, *cons.* 1983 (Bishop's House, Quarterbridge Road, Douglas, Isle of Man) [Signs Arthur Sodor and Man] 1983

Archdeacon

Ven. D. A. Willoughby 1982

Canons Residentiary

B. H. Kelly (1980); D. Baggaley (1980); J. D. Gelling (1980); B. H. Partington (1985).
   Beneficed Clergy, 20; *Curates, &c.,* 21
Vicar-General and Registrar, P. W. S. Farrant, 24 Athol Street, Douglas.
Assistant Secretary, J. Wilson.

SOUTHWELL

8th Bishop, Rt. Rev. Michael Humphrey Dickens Whinney, *cons.* 1982 (Bishop's Manor, Southwell NG25 0JP) [Signs Michael Southwell] ...1985

Bishop Suffragan

Sherwood, Rt. Rev. Harold Richard Darby, *cons.* 1975 (Applegarth, Halam, Newark NG22 8AN)......................................1975

Provost

Very Rev. John Murray Irvine 1978

Canons Residentiary

D. P. Keene (1981); I. G. Collins (1985).
Organist, K. Beard, F.R.C.O. (1959).

Archdeacons

Nottingham, Ven. G. C. Handford 1984
Newark, Ven. D. Leaning 1980
   Beneficed Clergy, 180; *Curates, &c.,* 52
Chancellor, J. Shand (1981).
Registrar, P. H. Mellors, Diocesan Office, Westgate, Southwell NG25 0JL (1970).

WAKEFIELD

10th Bishop, Rt. Rev. David Michael Hope, D.Phil., *cons.* 1985 (Bishop's Lodge, Woodthorpe Lane, Wakefield WF2 6JJ) [Signs David Wakefield]..................................1985

Bishop Suffragan

Pontefract, Rt. Rev. Thomas Richard Hare, *cons.* 1971 (306 Barnsley Road, Wakefield WF2 6AX).......................................1971

Assistant Bishop, (vacant).

Provost

Very Rev. John Edward Allen. 1982

Archdeacons

Halifax, Ven. A. D. Chesters 1985
Pontefract, Ven. K. Unwin 1981
Organist, J. L. Bielby, F.R.C.O. (1971).
   Beneficed Clergy, 176; *Curates, &c.,* 27
Chancellor, G. B. Graham, Q.C. (1959).
Registrar and Sec., E. Chapman, Burton Street, Wakefield WF1 2DA (1979).

THE CHURCH IN WALES

(Stipend of diocesan bishop of the Church of Wales is £15,457 p.a. from Jan. 1, 1988)

BANGOR

79th Bishop, Rt. Rev. John Cledan Mears, *b.* 1922, *cons.* 1982 (Tŷ'r Esgob, Bangor LL57 2SS) 1982

LLANDAFF

101st Bishop, Rt. Rev. Roy Thomas Davies, *b.* 1934, *cons.* 1985 (Llys Esgob, The Cathedral Green, Llandaff, Cardiff CF5 2YE)...........1985

MONMOUTH

7th Bishop, Rt. Rev. Royston Clifford Wright, *b.* 1922, *cons.* 1986 (Bishopstow, Stow Hill, Newport NPT 4EA)..............................1986

ST. ASAPH

74th Bishop, Rt. Rev. Alwyn Rice Jones, *b.,* 1934, *cons.* 1982 (Esgobty, St. Asaph, Clwyd LL17 0TW) 1982

ST. DAVID'S

124th Bishop and 9th Archbishop of Wales, Rt. Rev. George Noakes, *b.* 1924, *cons.* 1982 (Llys Esgob, Abergwili, Dyfed SA31 2JG) 1982, *elected* Archbishop of Wales, 1987.

SWANSEA AND BRECON

6th Bishop, Rt. Rev. Benjamin Noel Young Vaughan, *b.* 1917, *cons.* 1961 (Ely Tower, Brecon, Powys) 1976

THE EPISCOPAL CHURCH IN SCOTLAND

Primus of the Episcopal Church of Scotland, Most Rev. Lawrence Edward Luscombe, b. 1924, *cons.* 1975, *elected* 1985.

Rt. Rev. Bishops:

Aberdeen and Orkney, Frederick Charles Darwent, b. 1927, *cons.* 1978, *apptd.* 1978, *stipend* £10,248: *Clergy* 13.

Argyll and the Isles, George Kennedy Buchanan Henderson, b. 1921, *cons.* 1977, *apptd.* 1977, *stipend* £12,200: *Clergy* 10.

Brechin, Lawrence Edward Luscombe (as above), *stipend* £7,453: *Clergy* 16.

Edinburgh, Richard Frederick Holloway, b. 1933, *cons.* 1986, *apptd.* 1986, *stipend* £9,522: *Clergy* 65.

Glasgow and Galloway, Derek Alec Rawcliffe, O.B.E.,

b. 1919, *cons.* 1974, *apptd.* 1981, *stipend* £9,900: *Clergy* 41.

Moray, Ross and Caithness, George Minshull Sessford, b. 1928, *cons.* 1970, *apptd.* 1970, *stipend* £8,068: *Clergy* 17.

St. Andrews, Dunkeld and Dunblane, Michael Geoffrey Hare-Duke, b. 1925, *cons.* 1969, *apptd.* 1969, *stipend* £8,500: *Clergy* 28.

Registrar of the Episcopal Synod, I.R. Guild, 16 Charlotte Square, Edinburgh EH2 4YS Churches, Mission Stations, &c., 339. Clergy 217; Communicants, 37,731.

THE CHURCH OF IRELAND

Central Office: Church of Ireland House, Church Avenue, Rathmines, Dublin 6.

Province of Armagh

Archbishop of Armagh and Primate of All Ireland, Most Rev. Robert Henry Alexander Eames, PH.D., b. 1937, *cons.* 1975, *trs.* 1986: *Clergy* 49.

Rt. Rev. Bishops:

Clogher, Brian Desmond Anthony Hannon, b. 1936, *apptd.* 1986: *Clergy* 30.

Connor, William John McCappin, b. 1919, *apptd.* 1981: *Clergy* 94.

Derry and Raphoe, James Mehaffey, PH.D., b. 1931, *apptd.* 1980: *Clergy* 48.

Down and Dromore, Gordon McMullan, PH.D., b. 1934, *apptd.* 1980, *trs.* 1986: *Clergy* 98.

Kilmore, Elphin and Ardagh, William Gilbert Wilson, PH.D., b. 1918, *apptd.* 1981: *Clergy* 22.

Tuam, Killala and Achonry, John Robert Winder Neill, b. 1945, *apptd.* 1986: *Clergy* 10.

Province of Dublin

Archbishop of Dublin, Bishop of Glendalough, and Primate of Ireland, Most Rev. Donald Arthur Caird, b. 1925, *cons.* 1970, *apptd.* 1985: *Clergy* 66.

Rt. Rev. Bishops:

Cashel and Ossory, Noel Vincent Willoughby, b. 1926, *apptd.* 1980: *Clergy* 32.

Cork, Cloyne and Ross, Samuel Greenfield Poyntz, PH.D., b. 1926, *apptd.* 1978: *Clergy* 22.

Limerick and Killaloe, Edward Flewett Darling, b. 1933, *apptd.* 1985: *Clergy* 13.

Meath and Kildare, Walton Newcombe Francis Empey, b. 1934, *cons.* 1981, *trs.* 1985: *Clergy* 20.

St. Patrick's National Cathedral, Dublin: *Dean and Ordinary*, Very Rev. V. G. B. Griffin, PH.D.

ANGLICAN COMMUNION OVERSEAS

Sees	Apptd.

ANGLICAN CHURCH OF AUSTRALIA

Primate of Australia
The Most Rev. John Basil Rowland Grindrod, K.B.E., Archbishop of Brisbane.

Province of New South Wales

Archbishop and Metropolitan

Sydney, D. W. B. Robinson, b. 1922 (*cons.* 1973) . . 1982
Asst. Bps., J. R. Reid, b. 1928 (1972); K. H. Short, b. 1927 (1975); E. D. Cameron, b. 1926 (1975); R. H. Goodhew, b. 1931 (1982).

The Rt. Rev. Bishops

Armidale, P. Chiswell, b. 1934 1976
Bathurst, H. A. J. Witt (*cons.* 1965) 1981
Canberra and Goulburn, O. D. Dowling (*cons.* 1981) 1983
Grafton B. A. Schultz (*cons.* 1985)
Newcastle, A. C. Holland b. 1927 (*cons.* 1970) 1978
Riverina, B. R. Hunter, b. 1927 (*cons.* 1971) 1971

Province of Queensland

Archbishop and Metropolitan

Brisbane, The Most Rev. J. B. R. Grindrod, K.B.E., b. 1919 1980
Bp. for Southern Region, R. Wicks, O.B.E., b. 1921 (1973); *Bp. for Western Region*, A. O. Charles, b. 1926 (1983); *Bp. for Northern Region*, G. V. Browning, b. 1942 (1985).

The Rt. Rev. Bishops

Carpentaria, A. F. B. Hall-Matthews, b. 1940 . . . 1984
N. Queensland, H. J. Lewis, b. 1926 1971
Rockhampton, G. A. Hearn, b. 1935 1981

Province of South Australia

Archbishop and Metropolitan

Adelaide, The Most Rev. Keith Rayner, b. 1929 (*cons.* 1969) 1975

Sees	Apptd.

The Rt. Rev. Bishops
The Murray, R. G. Porter, O.B.E. *b.* 1924 (*cons.* 1967) 1970
Willochra, W. D. H. McCall, *b.* 1940 (*cons.* 1987) .1987

Province of Victoria
Archbishop and Metropolitan

Melbourne, The Most Rev. David John Penman, *b.* 1936 (*cons.* 1982)..........1984

Bps. Coadj., J. A. Grant, *b.* 1931 (1970); D. H. W. Shand; *b.* 1921 (1973); J. C. Stewart *b.* 1940 (1984); R. L. Butterss *b.* 1931 (1985); P. J. Hollingworth *b.* 1935 (1985); J. W. Wilson *b.* 1937 (1985).

The Rt. Rev. Bishops
Ballarat, J. Hazlewood, *b.* 1924..........1975
Bendigo, O. S. Heyward, *b.* 1926..........1975
Gippsland, N. J. Chynoweth, *b.* 1922 (*cons.* 1974) 1980
Wangaratta, R. G. Beal, *b.* 1929..........1985

Province of Western Australia
Archbishop and Metropolitan

Perth, The Most Rev. Peter Frederick Carnley, (*cons.* 1981)..........1981
Asst. Bps., M. B. Challen (1978); B. R. Kyme..1982

The Rt. Rev. Bishops
Bunbury, H. J. U. Jamieson..........1984
N. W. Australia, G. B. Muston..........1982

Extra-Provincial Diocese

Tasmania, P. K. Newell, *b.* 1930 (*cons.* 1982)....1982

EPISCOPAL CHURCH OF BRAZIL
Primate

Southwestern Brazil, Rt. Rev. Olavo Ventura Luiz, *b.* 1938 (*cons.* 1976)..........1986

The Rt. Rev. Bishops
Brasilia, A. G. Sória, *b.* 1922 (*cons.* 1977)......1985
Central Brazil, S. A. Ruiz, *b.* 1932 (*cons.* 1985)..1985
Northern Brazil, C. E. Rodrigues, *b.* 1935 (*cons.* 1985)..........1986
South Central Brazil, S. Takatsu, *b.* 1927 (*cons.* 1977)..........1977
Southern Brazil, C. V. S. Gastal, *b.* 1937 (*cons.* 1984)..........1984

CHURCH OF THE PROVINCE OF BURMA
Archbishop

Rangoon, The Most Rev. Gregory Hla Gyaw, (*cons.* 1973)..........1979

The Rt. Rev. Bishops
Sittwe, B. Theaung Hawi, (*cons.* 1978)..........1980
Mandalay, T. Mya Wah, (*cons.* 1984)..........1984
Pa'an, G. Kyaw Mya, (*cons.* 1979)..........1979

CHURCH OF THE PROVINCE OF BURUNDI, RWANDA AND ZAIRE
Archbishop

Butare, The Most Rev. J. Ndandali (*cons.* 1975)..........1982

The Rt. Rev. Bishops
Boga Zaire, P. Njojo..........1980
Bukavu, B. Dirokpa..........1982
Asst. Bps., K. Mbona..........1980
Bujumbura, S. Sindamuka..........1975
Buye, S. Ndayisenga..........1979
Gitega, J. Nduwayo

Sees	Apptd.

Kigali, A. Sebununguri.
Kisangani, S. T. Mugera..........1980
Shyira, A. Nshamihigo.

ANGLICAN CHURCH OF CANADA
Primate

The Most Rev. Michael Geoffrey Peers..........1986

Province of British Columbia
The Most. Rev. Archbishop

New Westminster, Douglas Walter Hambidge, *b.* 1927 (*cons.* 1969), *Archbishop and Metropolitan*..........1981

The Rt. Rev. Bishops
British Columbia R. F. Shepherd..........1984
Caledonia, J. E. Hannen..........1981
Cariboo, J. S. P. Snowden..........1974
Kootenay, R. E. F. Berry..........1971
Yukon, R. C. Ferris..........1981

Province of Canada
The Most Rev. Archbishop

Fredericton, Harold Lee Nutter, *b.* 1923 (*cons.*1971), *Archbishop and Metropolitan*....1980

The Rt. Rev. Bishops
Central Newfoundland, M. Genge..........1975
Eastern Newfoundland and Labrador, M. Mate.1980
Montreal, R. Hollis..........1975
Nova Scotia, A. G. Peters..........1982
Quebec, A. Goodings..........1977
Western Newfoundland, S. S. Payne, *b.* 1932....1978

Province of Ontario
The Most Rev. Archbishop

Niagara, John Charles Bothwell, (*cons.* 1971), *Archbishop and Metropolitan*..........1985

The Rt. Rev. Bishops
Algoma, L. E. Peterson..........1983
Huron, D. D. Jones (*cons.* 1982)..........1984
Moosonee, C. J. Lawrence..........1980
Ontario, A. A. Read (*cons.* 1972)..........1981
Ottawa, E. K. Lackey..........1981
Toronto L. S. Garnsworthy..........1972

Province of Rupert's Land
The Most Rev. Archbishop

Edmonton, Edwin Kent Clarke, (*cons.* 1976), *Archbishop and Metropolitan*..........1986

The Rt. Rev. Bishops
Arctic, J. R. Sperry, *b.* 1924..........1974
Athabasca, G. F. Woolsey..........1983
Brandon, J. F. S. Conlin..........1975
Calgary, J. B. Curtis..........1983
Keewatin, H. J. P. Allan, *b.* 1928..........1974
Qu' Appelle, E. Bays..........1986
Rupert's Land, W. H. Jones (*cons.* 1970)........1983
Saskatchewan, T. O. Morgan..........1985
Saskatoon, R. A. Wood..........1981

CHURCH OF THE PROVINCE OF CENTRAL AFRICA
Archbishop

Botswana, The Most Rev. W. P. K. Makhulu, *b.* 1935 (*cons.* 1979)..........1980

The Rt. Rev. Bishops
Central Zambia, C. W. H. Shaba
Lake Malawi, P. N. Nyanja, *b.* 1940 (*cons.* 1978) .1978

Sees	Apptd.
Lundi, J. Siyachitema, *b.* 1932 (*cons.* 1981)	1981
Lusaka, S. S. Mumba, *b.* 1939 (*cons.* 1981)	1981
Manicaland, E. Masuko (*cons.* 1981)	1981
Harare, R. P. Hatendi, *b.* 1927 (*cons.* 1979)	1981
Matabeleland, T. T. Naledi (*cons.* 1987)	1987
Northern Zambia, J. Mabula, *b.* 1922 (*cons.* 1971)	1971
Southern Malawi, B. N. Aipa (*cons.* 1987)	1987

CHURCH OF THE PROVINCE OF THE INDIAN OCEAN

Archbishop

Seychelles, F. Chang-Him	1984

The Rt. Rev. Bishops

Antananarivo, R. Rabenirina	1984
Antsiranana, K. Benzies	1982
Mauritius, R. Donat	1984
Toamasina, F. Razakariasy	1984

THE HOLY CATHOLIC CHURCH IN JAPAN

(Nippon Sei Ko Kai)

Primate

Osaka, The Rt. Rev. Christopher Ichiro Kikawada, *b.* 1925 (*cons.* 1975)	1986

The Rt. Rev. Bishops

Chubu, S. W. Hoyo, *b.* 1929 (*cons.* 1987)	1987
Hokkaido, A. H. Amagi, *b.* 1926 (*cons.* 1987)	1987
North Kanto, J. T. Yashiro, *b.* 1931 (*cons.* 1985)	1985
Kobe, P. K. Yashiro, *b.* 1924 (*cons.* 1984)	1984
Kyoto, St. George J. Yagi, *b.* 1928 (*cons.* 1979)	1979
Kyushu, J. N. Iida, *b.* 1929 (*cons.* 1982)	1982
Okinawa, P. S. Nakamura, *b.* 1927 (*cons.* 1972)	1972
Tohoku, C. Y. Tazaki, *b.* 1923 (*cons.* 1979)	1979
Tokyo, J. J. Yamada, *b.* 1917 (*cons.* 1982)	1982
Yokohama, R. S. Kajiwara, *b.* 1932 (*cons.* 1984)	1984

THE EPISCOPAL CHURCH IN JERUSALEM AND THE MIDDLE EAST

President-Bishop, Rt. Rev. S. Kafity	1986
Jerusalem, S. Kafity	1984
Iran, H. B. Dehqani-Tafti	1961
Egypt, G. Abdel Malik	1984
Cyprus and the Gulf, J. Brown	1986

CHURCH OF THE PROVINCE OF KENYA

Archbishop

Nairobi, The Most Rev. Manasses Kuria	1979

The Rt. Rev. Bishops

Eldoret, A. K. Muge	1983
Machakos, B. N. P. Nzimbi	1985
Maseno North, J. Mundia	1970
Maseno South, H. Okullu	1974
Maseno West, D. J. Omolo	1985
Mombasa, C. Nzano	1986
Mount Kenya Central, J. Mahiani	1984
Mount Kenya East, D. Gitari	1975
Mount Kenya South, G. M. Njuguna	1985
Nakuru, L. Kamau	1979

CHURCH OF THE PROVINCE OF MELANESIA

Archbishop

Central Melanesia, The Most Rev. Amos Stanley Waiaru	1987

The Rt. Rev. Bishops

Malaita, W. A. Pwaisiho	1981
Temotu, L. S. Munamua (*cons.* 1987)	1987

Sees	Apptd.
Vanuatu, H. Tevi (*cons.* 1979)	1980
Ysabel, E. Pogo	1981

CHURCH OF THE PROVINCE OF NEW ZEALAND

Primate and Archbishop

Wellington, Brian Newton Davis, *b.* 1934	1986

The Rt. Rev. Bishops

Aotearoa, W. Vercoe, *b.* 1928	1981
Auckland, B. C. Gilberd, *b.* 1938	1985
Christchurch, M. J. Goodall, *b.* 1928	1984
Dunedin, P. W. Mann, *b.* 1924	1976
Nelson, P. E. Sutton, *b.* 1923	1965
Polynesia, J. L. Bryce, *b.* 1935	1975
Waiapu, P. G. Atkins, *b.* 1936	1983
Waikato, R. A. Herft, *b.* 1948	1986

CHURCH OF THE PROVINCE OF NIGERIA

Archbishop

Ibadan, The Most Rev. Timothy Omotayo Olufosoye (*cons.* 1965) *elected Archbp. of Nigeria*	1979

The Rt. Rev. Bishops

Lagos, J. A. Adetiloye	1985
The Niger, J. A. Onyemelukwe	1975
Niger Delta, S. O. Elenwa	1981
Ondo, S. O. Aderin	1981
Kaduna, T. E. Ogbonyomi	1975
Owerri, B. C. Nwankiti	1968
Benin, J. K. George	1985
Ekiti, C. A. Akinbola	1986
Enugu, G. N. Otubelu	1969
Aba, A. O. Iwuagwu	1987
Kwara, H. Haruna	1974
Ilesha, G. I. O. Olajide	1981
Egba-Egbado, T. I. Akintayo	1977
Ijebu-Remo, E. O. I. Ogundana	1984
Asaba, R. N. C. Nwosu	1977
Kano, B. B. Ayam	1980
Jos, T. E. I. Adesola	1985
Warri, J. O. Dafiewhare	1980
Akure, E. B. Gbonigi	1983
Owo, A. O. Awosan	1983
Ijebu, I. O. B. Akintemi	1976
Akoko, J. O. K. Olowokure	1986
Okigwe/Orlu, S. C. N. Ebo	1985
Awka, M. S. C. Anikwenwa	1987
Osun, S. O. Fagbemi	1987

ANGLICAN CHURCH OF PAPUA NEW GUINEA

Archbishop

Popondota, The Most Rev. George S. Ambo O.B.E. (*cons.* 1960)	1984

The Rt. Rev. Bishops

Aipo Rongo, P. Richardson	1987
Asst. Bp., B. Kerina	1981
Dogura, R. Sanana	1976
New Guinea Is., B. S. Meredith	1967
Port Moresby, I. R. Gadebo	1983

CHURCH OF THE PROVINCE OF SOUTHERN AFRICA

Archbishop and Metropolitan

Cape Town, The Most Rev. Desmond Mpilo Boy Tutu, *b.* 1931 (*cons.* 1976), *elected*	1986
Bps. *Suff.*, P. M. Matolengwe, *b.* 1937 (1976); C. H. Albertyn *b.* 1928 (1983).	

The Rt. Rev. Bishops

Bloemfontein, T. S. Stanage, *b.* 1932	1982
George, D. G. Damant *b.* 1933	1985

Sees	Apptd.
Grahamstown, D. P. H. Russell, *b.* 1938	1986
Johannesburg, D. Buchanan	1986
Bps. *Suff.*, M. S. Ndwandwe, *b.* 1928 (1978); J. S. Nkoane, *b.* 1929 (1982).	
Kimberley & Kuruman, G. A. Swartz, *b.* 1928	1983
Lebombo, D. S. Sengulane, *b.* 1946	1976
Lesotho, P. S. Mokuku, *b.* 1935	1978
Bp. *Suff.*, D. P. Nestor, *b.* 1938	1980
Namibia, J. H. Kauluma, *b.* 1933	1981
Natal, M. Nuttall, *b.* 1934	1982
Niassa, P. T. Manhique	1986
Port Elizabeth, B. R. Evans, *b.* 1929	1974
Pretoria, R. A. Kraft, *b.* 1936	1982
Bp. *Suff.*, J. H. G. Ruston, *b.* 1929	1983
St. Helena, J. N. Johnson, *b.* 1932	1985
St. John's, J. Z. Dlamini, *b.* 1935	1985
Swaziland, B. L. N. Mkhabela, *b.* 1926	1975
Zululand, L. B. Zulu, *b.* 1937	1975
Order of Ethiopia, S. Dwane, *b.* 1941	1983

ANGLICAN CHURCH OF THE SOUTHERN CONE OF AMERICA

The Rt. Rev. Bishops

Argentina and Uruguay, R. S. Cutts	1975
Chile, C. F. Bazley (*cons.* 1969)	1977
Asst. *Bp.*, I. Morrison	1977
Northern Argentina, D. Leake (*cons.* 1969)	1980
Asst. *Bp.*, M. Mariño	1975
Paraguay, (vacant).	
Peru and Bolivia, D. R. J. Evans	1978

CHURCH OF THE PROVINCE OF THE SUDAN

Archbishop

Bishop of Juba, Most Rev. Elinana J. Ngalamu, *born c.* 1915 *cons.* 1963, *apptd.* 1976, *elected Archbp.* 1976

The Rt. Rev. Bishops

Khartoum, (vacant).
Rumbek, Benjamin W. Yugusuk, *born* 1927, *cons.* 1971, *apptd.* 1976
Yambio, Daniel M. Zindo, *born* 1942, *cons.* 1984, *apptd.* 1984

CHURCH OF THE PROVINCE OF TANZANIA

Archbishop

Zanzibar and Tanga, The Most Rev. John Acland Ramadhani (*cons.* 1980) ... 1984

The Rt. Rev. Bishops

Central Tanganyika, Y. Madinda, *b.* 1926 (*cons.* 1964)	1971
Dar es Salaam, C. Mlangwa	1984
Kagera, Christoper Ruhuza	1985
Mara, Gershom Nyaronga	1985
Masasi, C. R. Norgate	1984
Morogoro, G. Chitemo	1965
Mount Kilimanjaro, A. Mohamed	1982
Ruvuma, M. Ngahyoma	1971
South West Tanganyika, C. Mwaigoga	1983
Victoria Nyanza, J. Rusibamayila	1976
Western Tanganyika, G. E. Mpango	1983

CHURCH OF THE PROVINCE OF UGANDA

Archbishop

Kampala, The Most Rev. Dr. Yona Okoth (*cons.* 1972) ... 1984
Asst. *Bp.*, A. L. Gonahasa ... 1985

The Rt. Rev. Bishops

East Ankole, A. Betungura	1970
Bukedi, N. E. Okille	1984

Sees	Apptd.
Bunyoro-Kitara, Y. Rwakaikara	1981
Busoga, C. Bamwoze	1972
Karamoja, P. Lomongin	1987
Kigezi, F. Kivengere	1972
Asst. *Bp.*, W. Rukirande	1975
Lango, M. Otim	1976
Asst. *Bp.*, W. Okodi	1979
Madi and West Nile, R. Ringtho (*cons.* 1976)	1977
Mbale, A. M. Wesonga	1981
Mityana, Y. Mukasa	1977
Mukono, L. Mpalanyi-Nkoyoyo	1985
Namirembe, M. Kauma	1985
North Kigezi, Y. Ruhindi	1981
Northern Uganda, B. Ogwal	1974
Asst. *Bp.*, G. Oboma	1979
Ruwenzori, E. Kamanyire	1981
South Ruwenzori, Z. Masereka	1985
Soroti, G. Ilukor	1976
West Ankole, Y. Bamunoba	1977
West Buganda, C. Senyonjo	1974

CHURCH OF THE PROVINCE OF WEST AFRICA

Archbishop

Liberia, The Most Rev. George Daniel Browne, D.D.
Bp. *Suff.*, Rt. Rev. Edward W. Neufville.

The Rt. Rev. Bishops

Accra, F. W. B. Thompson; *Bo*, M. Keili; *Cape Coast*, J. Ackon; *Freetown*, P. E. S. Thompson; *Kumasi*, E. K. Yeboah; *Gambia*, M. E. Millard; *Guinea*, W. Y. Macauley; *Liberia*, (see above); *Koforidua*, R. Okine; *Sekondi*, T. Annobil; *Sunyani/Tamale*, J. Dadson.

As the Province of Nigeria came into being on Feb. 24, 1979, the rest of the Province of West Africa continues to function as the (On-going) Province of West Africa:

CHURCH IN THE PROVINCE OF THE WEST INDIES

Archbishop of West Indies

N. E. Caribbean and Aruba, Orland Lindsay, *b.* 1928 (cons. 1970) ... 1986

The Rt. Rev. Bishops

Barbados, D. W. Gomez, *b.* 1937 (*cons.* 1972)	1972
Belize, K. A. McMillan (cons. 1980)	1980
Guyana, R. O. George, *b.* 1924 (*cons.* 1976)	1980
Jamaica, N. W. de Souza (cons. 1973)	1979
Bps. *Suff.* (*Mandeville*), W. A. Murray (1976); (*Montego Bay*), A. C. Reid (1980)	
Nassau and the Bahamas, M. H. Eldon, C.M.G. (*cons.* 1971)	1972
Trinidad and Tobago, C. O. Abdulah (*cons.* 1970)	1970

OTHER CHURCHES AND EXTRA-PROVINCIAL DIOCESES

Under the Archbishop of Canterbury

The Rt. Rev. Bishops

Bermuda, C. C. Luxmoore.	
Pusan, W. Choi	1974
Kuching, John Leong Chee Yun	
Lusitanian Church in Portugal, F. Soares	1971
Sabah, Chhoa Heng Sze	1971
Seoul, S. S. Kim.	
Singapore, M. Tay	1982
Spanish Reformed Episcopal Church, A. Sanchez	1982
Taejon, M. Pae	1974
West Malaysia, J. G. Savarimuthu	1973

THE PRESBYTERIAN CHURCH OF WALES

The PRESBYTERIAN OR CALVINISTIC METHODIST CHURCH OF WALES is the only Church of purely Welsh origin, and embraces a large section of the Welsh-speaking population. Its form of government is Presbyterian, and it is a constituent of the World Alliance of Reformed Churches.

In 1987 the body numbered—chapels and other buildings, 1,078; ministers in pastoral charge, 152; elders, 4,699; communicants, 68,585; Sunday scholars, 21,148.

The *Association in the East* which includes nine of the English Presbyteries was formed in 1947.
Moderator of General Assembly (1987–88), Rev. H. Williams, Rhuddlan.
Moderators of Associations (1987–88) *South Wales*, Rev. J. D. Jones, Rhydyfelin; *North Wales*, Rev. H. D. Jones, Menai Bridge; *East Wales*, R. Lloyd Davies, Neath.
General Secretary, Rev. D. H. Owen, 53 Richmond Road, Cardiff CF2 3UP

THE CHURCH OF SCOTLAND

Church Office, 121 George Street, Edinburgh EH2 4YN

THE CHURCH OF SCOTLAND is Presbyterian in constitution, and is governed by Kirk Sessions, Presbyteries, Synods, and the General Assembly, which consists of both representative ministers and elders, in equal numbers from each of the Presbyteries. It is presided over by a Moderator chosen annually by the Assembly. The Sovereign, if not present in person, is represented by a Lord High Commissioner, who is appointed each year by the Crown. The country, for Church purposes, is divided into 12 Synods and 46 Presbyteries, and there are about 1,400 ministers and licentiates engaged in ministerial and other work. The figures at Dec. 31, 1986, were:—

Congregations, 1,745; total membership 854,311. There are 130 ministers and other personnel working with partner Churches and in expatriate charges in 26 countries.

LORD HIGH COMMISSIONER (1987), The Viscount of Arbuthnott, C.B.E., D.S.C., F.R.S.E., F.R.S.A.
MODERATOR OF THE GENERAL ASSEMBLY (1987), Right Rev. Dr. D. Shaw.

Principal Clerk, Rev. J. L. Weatherhead.
Deputy Clerk, Rev. A. G. McGillivray.
Procurator, G. Penrose, Q.C.
Law Agent and Solicitor of the Church, R. A. Paterson.
Parliamentary Agent, I. McCulloch (London).
General Treasurer, W. G. P. Colledge.

THE PRESBYTERIAN CHURCH IN IRELAND

The largest of the Presbyterian churches in Ireland consists of 22 presbyteries, 432 ministers, 564 congregations, with 131,326 communicants, 123,570 families and 6,200 Sunday-school teachers. During the 12 months ended Dec. 31, 1986, there was contributed by congregational effort £3,570,409 plus IR£251,848 for religious, charitable, and missionary purposes. The total income for the period raised by congregations for all purposes was £17,856,207 plus IR£1,455,344.—
General Sec., Very Rev. Dr. T. J. Simpson, Church House, Belfast BT1 6DW.

UNITED REFORMED CHURCH

The United Reformed Church was formed by the union of the Congregational Church in England and Wales and the Presbyterian Church of England on October 5, 1972. The Re-formed Association of Churches of Christ were joined to the U.R.C. on September 26, 1981. It is divided into 12 Provinces, each with a Provincial Moderator, and 70 Districts. There are 136,000 members and 1,000 serving ministers of whom 145 are auxiliary and give voluntary service. It shares an international mission through the Council for World Mission and is a member of the British and World Council of Churches. Its ministers

are trained at five recognized colleges.
General Sec., Rev. B. G. Thorogood, 86 Tavistock Place, WC1H 9RT

The Congregational Federation

The majority of those members of the Congregational Church who did not join the United Reformed Church comprise the Congregational Federation.
Sec., J. B. Wilcox, The Congregational Centre, 4 Castle Gate, Nottingham.

THE METHODIST CHURCH

The Methodist Church was founded in 1739 by the two brothers Wesley and rapidly spread throughout the British Isles and to America before 1770. The Methodist Church in Great Britain was united in 1932 by the fusion of the Wesleyan Methodist Church (the original section), the Primitive Methodist Church (1810) and the United Methodist Church (a 1907 fusion of the Methodist New Connexion (1797), the Bible Christian Methodist Church (1815) and the United Methodist Free Churches (1828 and 1849)).

The World Methodist Council, founded 1881, reorganized 1951, associates Methodism throughout the world in 90 countries.

The Methodist Church in Great Britain is governed primarily by the Conference, secondarily by the District Synods (held in the autumn and the spring), consisting of all the ministers and of selected laymen in each district, over which a chairman, who is a minister, is appointed by the Conference; and thirdly

by the circuit meeting of the ministers and lay officers of each circuit. The authority of both Synods and Circuit Meetings is subordinate to the Conference, which has the supreme legislative and judicial power in Methodism.

President of the Conference (July 1987–88), Rev. Dr. W. R. Davies.
Vice-President of the Conference (July 1987–88), D. W. Burrell.
Secretary of the Conference, Rev. B. E. Beck, 1 Central Buildings, Westminster, S.W.1.
President Designate (1988–89), Rev. R. G. Jones.
Vice-President Designate (1988–89), Ms. J. M. Carpenter.

Statistics.—In 1984 in association with the Conference in Great Britain there were 3,457 Ministers, 13,984 Local Preachers, 458,592 Members in 7,659 churches. (Statistics are published triennially.)

Methodist Church in Ireland

The Methodist Church in Ireland has 194 Ministers, 265 Lay Preachers, 20,272 Adult and 12,524 Junior Members.

President, (1987–88), Rev. W. I. Hamilton.

Secretary, Rev. C. G. Eyre, 3 Upper Malone Road, Belfast BT9 6TD.

Independent Methodists

Independent Methodists.—This body is Congregational in its organization, with an unpaid Ministry. Its first Conference was held in 1805. In 1986 there were in Great Britain 138 Ministers, 4,108 Members, 111 Churches and 4,015 Sunday scholars. *Gen. Sec.,* Rev. J. M. Day, The Old Police House, Croxton, Stafford ST21 6PE.

Wesleyan Reform Union

This Union is Methodist in doctrine, Congregational in government, with, if any church desires it, a paid ministry. It is the remnant of the original Reformers expelled from Wesleyan Methodism in 1849. The adherents are mainly in the Midland and Northern counties. In 1987 there were in Great Britain 20 Ministers, 153 Lay Preachers, 3,224 Members, 132 Churches and 2,060 Sunday School scholars.—*President,* Rev. J. W. Goulder, 2 The Hill, Syresham, Brackley, Northants.

General Secretary, Rev. D. A. Morris, Wesleyan Reform Church House, 123 Queen Street, Sheffield 1.

The Baptist Union

The Baptists have over 35,000,000 members in all countries. In Britain they are for the most part grouped in Associations of churches, and the majority of these belong to the Baptist Union, which was formed in 1812. Current statistics show that there are 2,065 churches and 170,318 members. There also exist separate Baptist Unions of Scotland (166 churches and 14,600 members); Wales (593 churches and 31,472 members); Ireland (92 churches and 8,269 members). *President of the Baptist Union of Great Britain and Ireland,* (1987–88), Rev. Margaret Jarman. *Secretary,* Rev. B. Green. *Office,* 4 Southampton Row, WC1B 4AB

LUTHERAN CHURCH

The Lutheran Church is one of the largest Protestant churches, with nearly 60 million members worldwide, although there are only about 27,000 adherents in Great Britain. The government and organisation of the Lutheran Church varies from country to country, some having an episcopal and some a more congregational form.

Very few British people are Lutherans and services in Great Britain are held in many languages to serve members of different nationalities. English-language congregations in Great Britain are members either of the Lutheran Church in Great Britain—United Synod or of the Evangelical Lutheran Church of England. The United Synod and most of the "national churches" are members of the Lutheran Council of Great Britain and through the Council are related to the Lutheran World Federation.

LUTHERAN COUNCIL OF GREAT BRITAIN, 8 Collingham Gardens, SW5 0HW.—*Chairman,* Very Rev. R. J. Patkai.

ORTHODOX CHURCH

Greek Orthodox Church (Archdiocese of Thyateira and Great Britain), Most Rev. Archbishop Methodios Fouyas, ph.d., 5 Craven Hill, W2 3EN.

Serbian Orthodox Church (Patriarchate of Serbia) Right Rev. Bishop Lavrentije, 89 Lancaster Road, W11 1QQ.

Russian Orthodox Church (Patriarchate of Moscow), Most Rev. Metropolitan Anthony of Sourozh, Russian Cathedral, Ennismore Gardens, S.W.7.

Russian Orthodox Church Outside Russia. His Grace Bishop Constantine, Dormition Cathedral, Emperor's Gate, S.W.7. *Mission Administrator,* Hegumen Seraphim, 14 St. Dunstan's Road, N.W.6.

The Poles, Ukrainians, Latvians, Byelorussians and Romanians also have congregations in this country.

OTHER RELIGIOUS DENOMINATIONS

The General Assembly of Unitarian and Free Christian Churches has about 95 ministers, 250 chapels and other places of worship in Great Britain and Ireland. *Gen. Sec.,* Dr. R. W. Smith, Essex Hall, 1–6 Essex Street, WC2R 3HY.

The Salvation Army, first known as the Christian Mission, was founded by William Booth in the East End of London in 1865. In 1878 it took its present name and adopted a quasi-military method of government. Since then it has become established in 89 countries of the world. The world leader, known as the General, is elected by a High Council, consisting of all active Commissioners and Territorial Commanders who have held the rank of Colonel for at least two years. In 1986 there were in Great Britain, 950 Corps (Churches), 133 Social Services Centres and 1,800 Officers engaged in evangelistic and social work. The latest world statistics (1986) are 14,540 Corps, 4,861 Social Services Centres (including institutions and schools) and 24,972 Officers.

General, Eva Burrows. *International Headquarters:*— 101 Queen Victoria Street, EC4P 4EP.

The Religious Society of Friends (Quakers), founded in the 17th century, has no separated ministry. There are in Great Britain 447 places of worship and 18,076 members (world membership 210,398). *Central Offices (Great Britain),* Friends House, Euston Road, NW1 2BJ; (*Ireland*), Swanbrook House, Morehampton Road, Dublin 4.

The First Church of Christ, Scientist, in Boston Massachusetts, U.S.A. (District Manager, Committees on Publication for Great Britain and Ireland, 108 Palace Gardens Terrace, W.8), has about 230 branch churches and societies in Great Britain and Ireland.

The Free Church of England (otherwise called The Reformed Episcopal Church) has 33 churches in England. *Gen. Sec.,* Rt. Rev. A. Ward, 28 Sedgebrook, Swindon, Wilts.

The Seventh Day Adventists (*Hdqrs.,* Stanborough Park, Watford, Herts. WD2 6JP), have more than 230 organized churches and companies and more than 16,500 members in the British Isles. *Executive Sec.,* D. W. McFarlane.

THE ROMAN CATHOLIC CHURCH

HIS HOLINESS POPE JOHN PAUL II (Karol Wojtyla), *born* in Wadowice, Poland, May 18, 1920; *ordained priest* November 1, 1946; appointed *Archbishop of Krakow* January 13, 1964, created *Cardinal* at a Consistory on June 26, 1967. Formally assumed Pontificate October 16, 1978.

THE SACRED COLLEGE OF CARDINALS, when complete, consisted of six Cardinal Bishops, fifty Cardinal Priests and fourteen Cardinal Deacons. This number was fixed by Pope Sixtus V in 1586. Pope John XXIII created 52 new Cardinals. Pope Paul VI created 27 new Cardinals on Feb. 22, 1965, 27 on June 26, 1967, 33 on Apr. 28 1969, 30 on March 5, 1973, 20 on May 24, 1976, 4 on June 27, 1977; Pope John Paul II created 15 new Cardinals on June 30, 1979, 18 on Feb. 2, 1983, 28 on May 25, 1985. In Oct. 1986 there were 151 Cardinals. The Cardinals are advisers and assistants of the Sovereign Pontiff and form the supreme council or Senate of the Church. On the death of the Pope they elect his successor. The assembly of the Cardinals at the Vatican for the election of a new Pope is known as the Conclave in which, in complete seclusion, the Cardinals elect by secret ballot; a two-thirds majority is necessary before the vote can be accepted as final. When a Cardinal receives the necessary votes the Dean of the Sacred College formally asks him if he will accept election and the name by which he wishes to be known. On his acceptance of the office the Conclave is dissolved and the First Cardinal Deacon announces the election to the assembled crowd in St. Peter's Square. On the first Sunday or Holyday following the election the new Pope assumes the pontificate at High Mass in St. Peter's Square. A new pontificate is dated from the assumption of the pontificate.

FORMS OF ADDRESS: *Cardinal*, "His Eminence Cardinal . . ." (if an Archbishop, "His Eminence the Cardinal Archbishop of . . ."); *Archbishop*, "The Most Rev. Archbishop of . . ."; *Bishop*, "The Rt. Rev. Bishop of . . ."

THE CURIA

The Curia or governing body of the Roman Catholic Church is made up of various administrative departments headed by the Secretariat of State and the Sacred Council for the Public Affairs of the Church. Below these are congregations, secretariats and tribunals assisted by commissions and offices. All are headed by Cardinals who have as their British equivalent the Ministers or Secretaries of State heading the various government departments.

The Vatican State has as with any nation its own diplomatic service although its representatives are officially acknowledged in different ways throughout the countries of the World. Where the representation is only to the local churches and not to the government of that country then the man appointed is an Apostolic Delegate as was the case in Britain until recently. However where the representative is recognized as having diplomatic status by a particular government then he is known as either a nuncio, pro nuncio or inter nuncio. Nuncios are Papal Ambassadors who are given precedence over all other ambassadors by their appointed country and are the doyens of the diplomatic corps. In countries where precedence is not recognized, as in Britain, the papal representative is known as a pro nuncio.

THE BISHOPS' CONFERENCES

The Roman Catholic church in **England and Wales** is governed by:

1. **The Bishops' Conference** which consists of the local ordinaries (the Diocesan Bishops) of any rite; coadjutor bishops and auxiliaries; and titular bishops with special tasks. They are headed by the President, Cardinal Basil Hume and Vice President, Archbishop Worlock, Archbishop of Liverpool.

2. **The Bishops' Standing Committee** made up of the Metropolitans (Archbishops) and department heads. It has general responsibility for continuity and policy between the Plenary Sessions of the Conference and for the preparation of the agenda and implementation of Conference decisions. This committee is serviced by the General Secretariat.

There are six departments each with an episcopal chairman which look after the life of the church within England and Wales. The departments and their heads are as follows:

(a) Department for Christian Life and Worship: Archbishop Bowen (*Southwark*).

(b) Department for Mission and Unity: Bishop Clark (*East Anglia*).

(c) Department for Christian Doctrine and Formation: Bishop Konstant (*Leeds*).

(d) Department for Social Responsibility: Bishop Harris (*Middlesbrough*).

(e) Department for Christian Citizenship: Bishop McCartie (*Auxiliary in Birmingham*).

(f) Department for International Affairs: Bishop O'Brien (*Hertfordshire*).

As well as the above the Conference has agencies and consultative bodies affiliated to it and all are serviced by the General Secretariat headed by a General Secretary namely:

England & Wales—Monsignor Vincent Nichols, 39 Eccleston Square, SW1V 1PD.

Scotland—Right Rev. Maurice Taylor, Bishop of Galloway, Candida Casa, 8 Corsehill Road, Ayr, Scotland, KA7 26T.

Ireland—(Executive Secretary) Rev. Gerard Clifford, Iona, 67 Newry Road, Dundalk, Co. Louth.

ENGLAND AND WALES

Apostolic Pro-Nuncio to the United Kingdom of Great Britain and Northern Ireland, The Most Rev. Luigi Barbarito.

	Cons.	Clgy.
The Most Revd. Archbishops		
Westminster, H.E. Cardinal Basil Hume (1976)	1976	926
Auxil., John Crowley	1986	
Auxil., Victor Guazzelli	1970	
Auxil., Philip Harvey	1977	
Auxil., Gerald Mahon	1970	
Auxil., James J. O'Brien	1977	
Birmingham, Maurice Couve de Murville (1982)	1982	526
Auxil., Joseph Cleary	1965	
Auxil., Crispian Hollis	1987	
Auxil., Patrick L. McCartie	1977	
Cardiff, John A. Ward (1983)	1981	186
Liverpool, Derek Worlock (1976)	1965	563
Auxil., Anthony Hitchen	1979	
Auxil., Kevin O'Connor	1979	
Auxil., John Rawsthorne	1982	
Southwark, Michael Bowen (1977)	1970	573
Auxil., Charles Henderson	1972	
Auxil., Howard Tripp	1980	
Auxil., John Jukes	1980	
The Rt. Revd. Bishops		
Arundel and Brighton, Cormac Murphy-O'Connor	1977	331
Brentwood, Thomas McMahon (1980)	1980	214
Clifton, Mervyn Alexander (1975)	1972	246
East Anglia, Alan Clark (1976)	1969	125

	Cons.	Clgy.
Hallam, Gerald Moverley (1980)	1968	106
Hexham and Newcastle, Hugh Lindsay		
(1975)	1970	340
Auxil., Owen Swindelhurst	1977	
Lancaster, John Brewer (1971)	1985	265
Leeds, David Konstant (1985)	1977	299
Menevia (*Wales*), Daniel Mullins (1987)	1970	
Middlesbrough, Augustine Harris (1978)	1966	208
Auxil., Thomas O'Brien	1982	
Northampton, Francis Thomas	1982	182
Nottingham, James McGuinness (1975)	1972	250
Plymouth, Christopher Budd	1986	187
Portsmouth, Anthony Emery (1976)	1968	355
Salford, Patrick Kelly	1984	490
Auxil., Geoffrey Burke	1967	
Shrewsbury, Joseph Gray (1980)	1969	255
Wrexham (*Wales*), James Hannigan	1983	

SCOTLAND

The Most Revd. Archbishops

St. Andrews & Edinburgh, Keith Patrick		
O'Brian	1985	250
Auxil., James Monaghan	1970	
Glasgow, Thomas Winning (1974)	1972	374
Auxil., John Mone	1984	
Auxil., Charles Renfrew	1977	

The Rt. Revd. Bishops

Aberdeen, Mario Conti	1977	57
Argyll & Isles, Colin MacPherson	1969	39
Dunkeld, Vincent Logan	1981	75
Galloway, Maurice Taylor	1981	82
Motherwell, Joseph Devine	1977	203
Paisley, Stephen McGill (1969)	1960	94

IRELAND†

Nuncio to Ireland, Most Rev. Gaetano
Alibrandi (Archbishop of Bindi)

The Most Revd. Archbishops

Armagh, H.E. Cardinal Thomas O'Fiaich	1977	290
Auxil., James Lennon	1980	
Cashel, Thomas Morris	1960	
Coadjutor., Dermot Clifford	1986	
Dublin, vacant		1778
Auxil., Joseph Carroll	1968	
Auxil., James Kavanagh	1973	
Auxil., Donal Murray	1982	
Auxil., Dermot O'Mahony	1975	
Auxil., Desmond Williams	1985	
Tuam, vacant		182

The Rt. Revd. Bishops
(N. Ireland)

Clogher, Joseph Duffy	1979	130
Derry, Edward Daly	1974	158
Down & Connor, Cahil Daly (1982)	1967	329
Dromore, Francis Brooks	1976	75
Kilmore, Francis McKiernan	1972	139

† There is one hierarchy for the whole of Ireland.
Several of the Dioceses have territory partly in the
Republic of Ireland and partly in Northern Ireland.

RESIDENTIAL ARCHBISHOPRICS THROUGHOUT THE WORLD

NOTE: This list is set out with the name of the
relevant country first; then the name of the diocese;
and finally the Archbishop's name. It does not
include England and Wales, Scotland or Ireland
which are above.

Albania

Durrës, vacant. (Apostolic Administrator: Monsignor Nicola Troshani).
Shkodrë, vacant. (Apostolic Administrator: Monsignor Ernesto Coba).

Algeria

Alger, H.E. Cardinal Leon-Etienne Duval.

Angola

Huambo, Francisco Viti.
Luanda, H.E. Cardinal Alexandre do Nascimento.
Lubango, Manuel Franklin da Costa.

Argentina

Bahia Blanca, Jorge Mayer.
Buenos Aires, H.E. Cardinal Juan Carlos Aramburu.
Cordoba, H.E. Cardinal Raúl Francisco Primatesta.
Corrientes, Fortunato A. Rossi.
La Plata, Antonio Quarracino.
Mendoza, Candido Genaro Rubiolo.
Paraná, Estanislao Esteban Karlich.
Resistencia, Juan J. Iriarte.
Rosario, Jorge Manuel López.
Salta, Moises J. Blanchoud.
San Juan de Cuyo, Italo Severino Di Stefano.
Santa Fe, Edgardo Gabriel Storni.
Tucumán, Horatio A. Bozzoli.

Australia

Adelaide, Leonard Anthony Faulkner.
Brisbane, Francis Roberts Rush.
Canberra, Francis P. Carroll.
Hobart, Guilford Clyde Young.
Melbourne, Thomas Francis Little.
Perth, William J. Foley.
Sydney, Edward B. Clancy.

Austria

Salzburg, Karl Berg.
Wien, Hermann Groer.

Bangladesh

Dhaka, Michael Rozario.

Belgium

Malines-Bruxelles, H.E. Cardinal Godfried Danneels.

Benin

Cotonou, Christophe Adimou.

Bolivia

Cochabamba, Gennaro Prata Vuolo.
La Paz, Luis Sainz Hinojosa.
Santa Cruz de la Sierra, Luis Rodriguez Pardo.
Sucre, Rene Fernandez Apaza.

Brazil

Aparacida, Geraldo Maria de Morais Penido.
Aracaju, Luciano José Cabral Duarte.
Belem do Pará, Alberto Guadêncio Ramos.
Belo Horizonte, Serafim Fernandes de Araújo.
Botucatú, Vincent Marchetti Zioni.
Brasilia, Jose Freire Falcao.
Campinas, Gilberto Pereira Lopes.
Campo Grande, Vitorio Pavanello.
Cascavel, Armando Cirio.
Cuiaba, Bonifacio Piccinini.
Curitiba, Pedro Antonio Fedalto.
Diamantina, Geraldo Majelo Reis.
Florianópolis, Afonso Niehues.
Fortaleza, H.E. Cardinal Aloisio Lorscheider.
Goiania, Antonio Ribeiro de Oliveira.
Juiz de Fora, Juvenal Roriz.

Londrina, Geraldo Majela Agnelo.
Maceió, Edvaldo G. Amaral.
Manaus, Clovis Frainer.
Mariana, Oscar de Oliveira.
Maringá, Jaime Luis Coelho.
Natal, Nivaldo Monte.
Niteroi, José Gonçalves da Costa.
Olinda & Recife, José Cardoso Sobrinho.
Paraiba, José M. Pires.
Porto Alegre, Claudio Colling.
Porto Velho, José Martins da Silva.
Pouso Alegre, José D'Angelo Neto.
Ribeirão Preto, Romeu Alberti.
São Luis do Maranhão, Paulo Eduardo Andrade Ponte.
São Paulo, H.E. Cardinal Paulo Evaristo Arns.
São Salvador da Bahia, Lucas Moreira Neves.
São Sebastião do Rio de Janeiro, H.E. Cardinal Eugenio de Araújo Sales.
Teresina, Miguel F. Camara Filho.
Uberaba, Benedito de Ulhôa Vieira.
Vitória, Silvestre L. Scandian.

Burma

Mandalay, Alphonse U. Than Aung.
Rangoon, Gabriel Thohey.

Burundi

Gitega, Joachim Ruhuna.

Cameroon

Bamenda, Paul Verdzekov.
Douala, Simon Tonyé.
Garoua, Christian W. Tumi.
Yaoundé, Jean Zoa.

Canada

Edmonton, Joseph N. MacNeil.
Grouard-McLennon, Henri Légaré.
Halifax, James Martin Hayes.
Keewatin-Le Pas, Peter Alfred Sutton.
Kingston, Francis John Spence.
Moncton, Donat Chiasson.
Montréal, Paul Grégoire.
Ottawa, Joseph Aurèle Plourde.
Québec, H.E. Cardinal Louis-Albert Vachon.
Regina, Charles Halpin.
Rimouski, Gilles Ouellet.
St Boniface, Antoine Hacault.
St Johns, Newfoundland, Alphonsus L. Penney.
Sherbrooke, Jean Marie Fortier.
Toronto, H.E. Cardinal Gerald Emmett Carter.
Vancouver, James Francis Carney.
Winnipeg, Latin Rite–Adam Exner; Ukrainian Rite–Maxim Hermaniuk.

Central Africa

Bangui, Joachim N'Dayen.

Chad

N'Djamena, Charles Vandame.

Chile

Antofagasta, Carlos Oviedo Cavada.
Concepción, José Manuel Santos Ascarza.
La Serena, Bernardino Pinera Carvallo.
Puerto Montt, Eladio Vicuña Aránguiz.
Santiago de Chile, H.E. Cardinal Juan F. Fresno Larrain.

China

Anking, Huai-Ning, vacant.
Canton, Dominic Tang Yee-Ming.
Changsha, vacant.
Chunking, vacant.
Foochow, Min-Hou, vacant.
Hangchow, vacant.

Hankow, vacant.
Kaifeng, vacant.
Kunming, vacant.
Kweyang, vacant.
Lanchow, vacant.
Mukden, vacant.
Nanchang, vacant.
Nanking, vacant.
Nanning, vacant.
Peking, vacant.
Sian, vacant.
Suiyüan, Francis Wong Hsueh-Ming.
Taiyuan, vacant; Bishop Emeritus Dominic Luke Capozi (expelled 11 April 1946, now living in Nazareth, Israel).
Tsinan, vacant.

Colombia

Barranquilla, Felix Maria Torres Parra.
Bogota, Mario Revollo Bravo.
Bucaramanga, Hector Rueda Hernández.
Cali, Pedro Rubiano Sáenz.
Cartagena, Carlos Jose Ruiseco Vieira.
Ibagué, José Joaquin Flórez Hernández.
Manizales, José de Jesús Pimiento Rodriguez.
Medellin, H.E. Cardinal Alfonso López Trujillo.
Nueva Pamplona, Rafael Sarmiento Peralta.
Popayán, Samuel Silverio Buitrago Trujillo.
Tunja, Augusto Trujillo Arango.

Congo

Brazzaville, Barthélémy Batantu.

Costa Rica

San José de Costa Rica, Román Arrieta Villalobos.

Cuba

San Cristóbal de la Habana, Jaime Lucas Ortega y Alamino.
Santiago de Cuba, Pedro Meurice Estiu.

Czechoslovakia

Olomouc, vacant.
Praha, H.E. Cardinal František Tomášek.
Trnava, vacant. (Apostolic Administrator: Monsignor Julius Gábriš).

Dominican Republic

Santo Domingo, Nicolás de Jesús López Rodriguez.

Ecuador

Cuenca, Alberto Luna Tobar.
Guayaquil, Bernardino Echeveria Ruiz.
Quito, Antonio J. González Zumárraga.

El Salvador

San Salvador, Arturo Rivera Damas.

Equatorial Guinea

Malabo, Rafael Nze Abuy.

Ethiopia

Addis Ababa, H.E. Cardinal Paul Tzadua.

Federal Republic of Germany

Bamberg, Elmar Maria Kredel.
Freiburg Im Breisgau, Oskar Saier.
Koln, H.E. Cardinal Joseph Höffner.
Munich & Freising, H.E. Cardinal Friedrich Wetter.
Paderborn, Johannes Joachim Degenhardt.

France

Aix, Bernard Panafieu.
Albi, Joseph Rabine.
Auch, Gabriel Vanel.
Avignon, Raymond Bouchex.
Besançon, Lucien Daloz.

Bordeaux, Marius Maziers.
Bourges, Pierre Plateau.
Cambrai, Jacques Delaporte.
Chambéry, Claude Feidt.
Lyon, H.E. Cardinal Albert Decourtray.
Marseilles, Robert Coffey.
Paris, H. E. Cardinal J. M. Lustiger.
Reims, Jacques Ménager.
Rennes, Jacques Jullien.
Rouen, Joseph Duval.
Sens, Eugene Ernoult.
Toulouse, André Collini.
Tours, Jean Honoré.

French Polynesia
Papeete, Michel Coppenrath.

Gabon
Libreville, André Fernand Anguilé.

Ghana
Cape Coast, John Kodwo Amissah.
Tamale, Peter Poreiku Dery.

Greece
Athenai, Nicola Foscolos.
Corfu, Antonio Varthalitis.
Naxos, Jean Perris.
Ródhos, vacant (Apostolic administrator Michel Pierre Franzidis).

Guatemala
Guatemala, Prospero Penandos del Barrio.

Guinea
Conakry, Robert Sarah.

Haiti
Port au Prince, François-Wolff Ligondé.

Haute Volta
Ouagadougou, H.E. Cardinal Paul Zoungrana.

Honduras
Tegucigalpa, Hector Enrique Santos Hernández.

Hungary
Eger, Istvan Seregely.
Esztergom, Laslo Paskai.
Kalocsa, vacant.

India
Agra, Cecil de Sa.
Bangalore, Alphonsus Mathias.
Bhopal, Eugene D'Souza.
Bombay, Simon Ignatius Pimenta.
Calcutta, Henry Sebastian D'Souza.
Changanacherry, Joseph Powathil.
Cuttack-Bhubaneswar, Raphael Cheenath.
Delhi, Angelo Innocent Fernandes.
Ernakulam, Anthony Padiyara.
Goa and Damao, Raul Nicolau Gonsalves.
Hyderabad, Saminini Arulappa.
Madras and Mylapore, Casimir Gnanadickam.
Madurai, Marianus Arokiasamy.
Nagpur, Leobard D'Souza.
Pondicherry and Cuddalore, Venmani S. Selvanather.
Ranchi, Telesphore P. Toppo.
Shillong-Gauhati, Hubert D'Rosario.
Trivandrum, [Syrian Melekite Rite], Benedict Varghese Mar Gregorios Thangalathil.
Verapoly, Cornelius Elanjikal.

Indonesia
Ende, Donatus Djagom.
Jakarta, Leo Soekoto.
Medan, Alfred Gonti Pius Datubara.
Merauke, Jacobus Duivenvoorde.
Pontianak, Hieronymus Herculanus Bumbun.
Semarang, Julius R. Darmaatmadja.
Ujung Pandang, vacant.

Iran
Ahwaz, Hanna Zora.
Teheran, Youhannan Semaan Issayi.
Urmyä, Thomas Meram.

Iraq
Arbil, Stephane Babeka.
Baghdad, Paul Dahdah.
Basra, Yousif Thomas.
Kerkuk, André Sana.
Mossul, Georges Garmo.

Israel
Akka [Greek Melekite Catholic Rite], Maximos Salloum.

Italy
Acerenza, vacant.
Amalfi, Ferdinand Palatucci.
Ancona, Carlo Maccari.
Bari, Mariano Magrassi.
Benevento, Carlo Minchiatti.
Bologna, H.E. Cardinal Giacomo Biffi.
Brindisi, Settimio Todisco.
Cagliari, vacant.
Camerino, Bruno Frattegiani.
Campobasso-Boiano, Pietro Santoro.
Capua, Luigi Diligenza.
Catania, Domenico Picchinenna.
Catanzaro, Antonio Cantisani.
Chieti, Antonio Valentini.
Conza, Antonio Nuzzi.
Cosenza, Dino Trabalzini.
Fermo, Cleto Bellucci.
Ferrara, Luigi Maverna.
Florence, H.E. Cardinal Silvano Piovanelli.
Foggia, Salvatore De Giorgi.
Gaeta, Vincenzo Farano.
Genoa, Giovanni Canestri.
Gorizia and Gradisca, Antonio Vitale Bommarco.
Lanciano, Enzio d'Antonio.
L'Aquila, Mario Peressin.
Lecce, Michele Mincuzzi.
Lucca, Guiliano Agresti.
Manfredonia, Valentino Vailati.
Matera, vacant.
Messina, Ignazio Cannavó.
Milano, H.E. Cardinal Carlo Maria Martini.
Modena, Santo B. Quadri.
Monreale, Salvatore Cassisa.
Napoli, Michele Giordano.
Oristano, Pier Luigi Tiddia.
Otranto, Vincenzo Franco.
Palermo, H.E. Cardinal Salvatore Pappalardo.
Perugia, Cesare Pagani.
Pescara-Penne, Antonio Jannucci.
Pisa, Alessandro Plotti.
Potenza, Guiseppe Vairo.
Ravenna, Ersilio Tonini.
Reggio Calabria, Aurelio Sorrentino.
Rossano, Serafino Sprovieri.
Salerno, Guerino Grimaldi.
Santa Severina, Giuseppi Agostino.
Sassari, Salvatore Isgrò.
Siena, Ismaele Mario Castellano.
Siracusa, Calogero Lauricella.
Sorrento, Antonio Zama.
Spoleto, Ottorino Pietro Alberti.
Taranto, Guglielmo Motolese.
Torino, H.E. Cardinal Anastasio Alberto Ballestrero.
Trani and Barletta, Giuseppe Carata.

Trento, Alessandro Maria Gottardi.
Udine, Alfredo Battisti.
Urbino, Donato U. Bianchi.
Vercelli, Albino Mensa.

Ivory Coast

Abidjan, H.E. Cardinal Bernard Yago.

Jamaica

Kingston in Jamaica, Samuel Emmanuel Carter.

Japan

Nagasaki, H.E. Cardinal Joseph Asajiro Satowaki.
Osaka, Paul Hisao Yasuda.
Tōkyō, Peter Seiichi Shirayanagi.

Jordan

Petra and Filadelfia [Greek Melekite Catholic Rite], Saba Youakim.

Kenya

Nairobi, H.E. Cardinal Maurice Otunga.

Korea

Kwang Ju, Victorinus Kong-Hi Youn.
Seoul, H.E. Cardinal Stephen Sou Hwan Kim.
Tae Gu, Paul Moun-Hi Ri.

Lebanon

Baalbek, Eliopoli [Greek Melekite Catholic Rite], Elias Zoghbi.
Beirut [Greek Melekite Catholic Rite], Habib Bacha; [Maronite Rite] Khalil Abinader.
Cipro, Joseph Mohsen Bechara.
Saidā [Greek Melekite Catholic Rite], Georges Kwaiter.
Tripoli del Libano [Maronite Rite], Antoine Joubeir; [Greek Melekite Catholic Rite], Elias Nijmé.
Tyr [Greek Melekite Catholic Rite], vacant; [Maronite Rite], Joseph Khoury.
Zahleh and Furzol [Greek Melekite Catholic Rite], Andre Haddad.

Lesotho

Maseru, Alfonso Ligouri Morapeli.

Liberia

Monrovia, Michael Kpakala Francis.

Lithuania

Kaunas, vacant.
Vilna, vacant (Apostolic administrator, Monsignor Edward Kisiel).

Madagascar

Diego Suarez, Albert Joseph Tsiahoana.
Fianarantsoa, Gilbert Ramanantoanina.
Tananarive, H.E. Cardinal Victor Razafimahatratra.

Malawi

Bamako, Luc Auguste Sangaré.

Malaysia

Kuching, Peter Chung Hoan Ting.

Malta

Malta, Joseph Mercieca.

Martinique

Fort de France, Maurice Marie-Sainte.

Mexico

Acapulco, Rafael Bello Ruiz.
Antequera, Bartolomé Carrasco Briseno.
Chihuahua, Adalberto Almeida Merino.
Guadalajara, Juan J.P. Ocampo.
Hermosillo, Carlos Quintero Arce.
Jalapa, Sergio Obeso Rivero.
Mexico, H.E. Cardinal Ernesto Corripio Ahumada.

Monterrey, Adolfo Suarez Rivera.
Morelia, Estanislao Alcarez Figueroa.
Puebla de los Angeles, Rosendo Huesca Pacheco.
Yucatán, Manuel Castro Ruiz.

Monaco

Monaco, Joseph-Marie Sardou.

Morocco

Rabat, Hubert Michon.
Tanger, Antonio J. Peteiro Freire.

Mozambique

Maputo, Alexandre José Maria dos Santos.
Nampula, Manuel Vieira Pinto.

Netherlands

Utrecht, H.E. Cardinal Adrianus J. Simonis.

New Guinea

Port Moresby, Peter Kurongku.

New Zealand

Wellington, H.E. Cardinal Thomas Stafford Williams.

Nicaragua

Managua, H.E. Cardinal Miguel Obando Bravo.

Nigeria

Kaduna, Peter Yariyok Jatau.
Lagos, Anthony Okogie.
Onitsha, Stephen Nweke Ezeanya.

Oceania

Agaña, Anthony Sablan Apuron.
Honiara, Adrian Thomas Smith.
Nouméa, Michel-Marie-Bernard Calvet.
Samoa, Apia and Tokelau, H.E. Cardinal Pio Taofino'u.
Suva, Petero Mataca.

Pakistan

Karachi, H.E. Cardinal Joseph Cordeiro.

Panamá

Panamá, Marcos Gregorio McGrath.

Papua New Guinea

Madang, Leo Arkfeld.
Mount Hagen, Michael Meier.
Rabaul, Albert Bundervoet.

Paraguay

Asuncion, Ismael Blas Rolon Silvero.

Peru

Arequipa, Fernando Vargas Ruiz de Somocurcio.
Ayacucho o Huamanga, Federico Richter Fernandez-Prada.
Cuzco, Alcides Mendoza Castro.
Huancayo, Emilio Vallebuona Merea.
Lima, H.E. Cardinal Juan Landózuri Ricketts.
Piura, Oscar Rolando Cantuarias Pastor.
Trujillo, Manuel Prado Pérez-Rosas.

Philippines

Caceres, Leonardo Legazpi.
Cagayan de Oro, Patrick H. Cronin.
Capiz, Onesimo C. Gordoncillo.
Cebu, Nome di Gesù, H.E. Cardinal Ricardo Vidal.
Cotabato, Philip Frances Smith.
Davao, Antonio Mabutas.
Jaro, Alberto J. Piamonte.
Lingayan-Dagupan, Federico G. Limon.
Lipa, Mariano Gaviola.
Manila, H.E. Cardinal Jaime L. Sin.
Nueva Segovia, Orlando Quevedo.

Ozamis, Jesus Dosado.
Palo, Pedro R. Dean.
San Fernando, Oscar Cruz.
Tuguegarao, Diosdado A. Talamayan.
Zamboanga, Francisco Raval Cruces.

Poland

Gniezno, H.E. Cardinal Józef Glemp. (See also Warszawa).
Kraków, H.E. Cardinal Franciszek Macharski.
Lwów, vacant.
Poznan, Jerzy Stroba.
Warszawa, H.E. Cardinal Józef Glemp.
Wroclaw, H.E. Cardinal Henryk Roman Gulbinowicz.

Portugal

Braga, Eurico Dias Nogueira.
Evora, Maurilio Jorge Quintal de Gouveia.

Puerto Rico

San Juan de Puerto Rico, H.E. Cardinal Luis Aporte Martinez.

Romania

Bucarest, vacant.

Rwanda

Kigali, Vincent Nsengiyumva.

Senegal

Dakar, H.E. Cardinal Hyacinthe Thiandoum.

Sierra Leone

Freetown & Bo, Joseph Ganda.

Singapore

Singapore, Gregory Yong Sooi Nghean.

South Africa

Bloemfontein, Peter John Butelezi.
Cape Town, Stephen Naidoo.
Durban, Denis Eugene Hurley.
Pretoria, George Francis Daniel.

Spain

Barcelona, H.E. Cardinal Narciso Jubany Arnau.
Burgos, Theodoro C. Fernandez.
Granada, José Méndez Asensio.
Madrid, H.E. Cardinal Angel Suquia Goicoechea.
Oviedo, Gabino Diaz Merchán.
Pamplona, José Mariá Cirardo Lachiondo.
Santiago de Compostella, Antonio Rouco Varela.
Sevilla, Carlos Amigo Vallejo.
Tarragona, Ramon Torrella Cascante.
Toledo, H.E. Cardinal Marcelo González Martin.
Valencia, Miguel Roca Cabanellas.
Valladolid, José Delicado Baeza.
Zaragoza, Elíaz Yanez Alvarez.

Sri Lanka

Colombo, Nicholas Marcus Fernando.

Sudan

Khartoum, Gabriel Zubeir Wako.

Syria

Alep, Beroea, Halab [Greek Melekite Catholic Rite], Néophytes Edelby.
Baniyas, vacant.
Bosra, Bostra, Boulos Nassif Borkhoche.
Damascus [Greek Melekite Catholic Rite], vacant.
Hassaké-Nisibi, Georges Habib Hafouri.
Homs, Emesa [Syrian Catholic Rite], Jean Dahi.
Laodicea di Siria [Greek Melekite Catholic Rite], Michel Yatim.

Taiwan

Taipeh, Matthew Kia Yen-Wen.

Tanzania

Dar es Salaam, H.E. Cardinal Laurean Rugambwa.
Tabora, Mario E. A. Mgulunde.

Thailand

Bangkok, H.E. Cardinal Michael Michai Kitbunchu.
Tharé and Nonseng, Lawrence Khai Saen-Phon-On.

Togo

Lomé, Robert Casimir Dosseh-Anyron.

Trinidad

Port of Spain, Gordon Anthony Pantin.

Turkey

Diarbekir, Paul Karatas.
Istanbul, Constantinople, Jean Tcholakian.
Izmir, Giuseppe G. Bernardini.

Uganda

Kampala, H.E. Cardinal Emmanuel Nsubuga.

Uruguay

Montevideo, José Gottardi Cristelli.

U.S.A.

Anchorage, Francis Thomas Hurley.
Atlanta, Thomas A. Donnellan.
Baltimore, William D. Borders.
Boston, H.E. Cardinal Bernard F. Law.
Chicago, H.E. Cardinal Joseph L. Bernardin.
Cincinnati, Daniel E. Pilarczyk.
Denver, James Francis Stafford.
Detroit, Edmund C. Szoka.
Dubuque, Daniel W. Kucera.
Hartford, John F. Whealon.
Indianapolis, Edward T. O'Meara.
Kansas City in Kansas, Ignatius J. Strecker.
Los Angeles, Roger M. Mahony.
Louisville, Thomas C. Kelly.
Miami, Edward A. McCarthy.
Milwaukee, Rembert G. Weakland.
Mobile, Oscar H. Lipscomb.
Newark, Theodore E. McCarrick.
New Orleans, Philip M. Hannan.
New York, H.E. Cardinal John J. O'Connor.
Oklahoma City, Charles A. Salatka.
Omaha, Daniel E. Sheehan.
Philadelphia, H.E. Cardinal John Joseph Krol.
Pittsburgh, Stephen J. Kocisko.
Portland in Oregon, William J. Levada.
St Louis (Missouri), John L. May.
St Paul & Minneapolis, John Robert Roach.
San Antonio, Patrick F. Flores.
San Francisco, John R. Quinn.
Santa Fe, Robert F. Sanchez.
Seattle, Raymond G. Hunthausen.
Washington, James A. Hickey.

U.S.S.R.

Mohilev, there is an **unnamed** Apostolic Administrator in the following Russian Dioceses: Mohilev, Moscow, Leningrad, Kharkov, Kazan, Samara and Simbirsk.

Venezuela

Barquisimeto, Julio Manuel Chirivella Varela.
Caracas, H.E. Cardinal José Ali Lebrún Moratinos.
Ciudad Bolivar, Medardo Luzardo Romero.
Maracaibo, Domingo Roa Pérez.
Merida, Miguel Antonio Salas Salas.
Valencia, Luis Eduardo Henriquez Jiménez.

Vietnam

Hanoi, H.E. Cardinal Joseph-Marie Trinh văn Căn.
Huê, Philippe Nguyen-Kim-Diên.
Thanh-Phô Hôchiminh, Paul Nguyên Van Binh.

West Indies

Castries, Kelvin Edward Felix.

Yugoslavia

Bar, Petar Perkolić.
Beograd, Franc Perco.
Ljubljana, Alojzij Šuštar.
Rijeka-Senj, Josip Paulišić.
Split-Makarska, Frane Franić.
Vrhbosna, Marco Jozinović.
Zadar, Marijan Oblak.
Zagreb, H.E. Cardinal Franjo Kuharić.

Zaire

Bukavu, Mulindwa Mutabesha.
Kananga, Bakole wa Ilunga.
Kinshasa, H.E. Cardinal Joseph Malula.
Kisangani, Fataki Alueka.
Lubumbashi, Kabanga Songasonga.
Mbandaka-Bikoro, Etsou-Nzabi-Bamungwabi.

Zambia

Kasama, Elias Mutale.
Lusaka, Adrian Mungandu.

Zimbabwe

Harare, Patrick Chakaipa.

ARCHBISHOPS OF TITULAR SEES

Acrida, Mario Schierano.
Amasya, James Patrick Carroll.
Amida, Flavien Zacharie Melkie.
Aquileia, Michele Cecchini.
Beroe, Victor Sartre.
Cesarea in Palaestina [Greek Melekite Catholic Rite]:
  Hilarion Capucci.
Claudiopolis in Honoriade, Alfredo Bruniera.
Corinthus, Gennaro Verolino.
Dara, Nicholas T. Elko.
Doclea, Pier Luigi Celata.
Edessa in Osrhoëne [Greek Melekite Catholic Rite]:
  Pierre Rai; [Syrian Catholic Rite]: Gregoire
  Ephrem Jarjour.
Egina, Raffaele Forni.
Ephesus, John Henry Boccella.
Gabala, Gérard de Milleville.
Gangra, Antonio Ferreira de Macedo.
Gortina, Victor F. Foley.
Gradum, José López Ortiz.
Hadrianopolis in Haemimonto, Lino Zanini.
Kaškar, Emmanuel-Karim Delly.
Macra, John Dooley.
Marcianopolis, Teofilo Camomot Bastida.
Mesembria, Loris Francesco Capovilla.
Nazareth, Giuseppe Carata.
Nicaea Parva, Paolino Limongi.
Nicosia, Aurelio Signora.
Nubia, Paul Antaki.
Salamis, Joseph Kuo.
Scytopolis, Joseph Raya.
Selymbria, Emile Socquet.
Soteropolis, Ettore Cunial.
Tarsus [Maronite Rite]: Abdallah Bared; [Greek
  Melekite Catholic Rite]: Loutfi Laham.
Tiburnia, Donato Squicciarini.
Velebusdo, Jose M. Estepa Llaurens.
Viminacium, Franco Brambilla.

THE JEWS

CHIEF RABBI—Sir Immanuel Jakobovits, KT., PH.D.
Office, Adler House, Tavistock Square, WC1H 0EP.   *Executive Officer*, S. Cohen.

It is estimated that about 410,000 Jews are resident in the U.K., some 280,000 being domiciled in Greater London.

The *Board of Deputies of British Jews*, established in 1760, is the representative body of British Jewry and is recognized by H.M. Government. The basis of representation is mainly synagogal, but secular organizations are also represented. It is a deliberative body and its objects are to watch over the interests of British Jewry, to protect Jews against any disability which they may suffer by reason of their creed and to take such action as may be conducive to their welfare.

President, Dr. Lionel Kopelowitz, J.P.
Secretary General, H. Pinner, Woburn House,

Upper Woburn Place, WC1H 0EP.

The *Beth Din* (Court of Judgment) is a rabbinic body consisting of *Dayanim* (Assessors) and the Chief Rabbi, who is President of the Court. The Court arbitrates when requested in cases between Jew and Jew, and Jew and non-Jew, and gives decisions on religious questions. The decisions are based on Jewish Law and practice and do not conflict with the law of the land. The *Beth Din* also deals with matters concerning dietary law and marriages and divorces, according to Jewish Law.

Dayanim, Rabbi C. Ehrentreu; Rabbi Dr. I. Lerner; Rabbi C. D. Kaplin; Rabbi I. D. Berger.
Clerk to the Court, Rabbi B. Berkovits, Adler House, Tavistock Square, WC1H 0EP.

LONDON CATHEDRALS, CHURCHES, ETC.

Church of England

ST. PAUL'S CATHEDRAL, City of London, EC4M 8AD (1675–1710), cost £747,660. The cross on the dome is 365 ft. above the ground level, the inner cupola 218 ft. above the floor. "Great Paul," in S.W. tower weighs 17 tons. Organ by Father Smith (enlarged by Willis and rebuilt by Mander) in case carved by Grinling Gibbons (who also carved the choir stalls). The choir and high altar were restored in 1958 after war damage and the North Transept in 1962. The American War Memorial Chapel was consecrated in November, 1958. The Chapel of the Most Excellent Order of the British Empire in the Crypt of the Cathedral was dedicated on May 20, 1960. Nave and transepts free. The following parts open weekdays 10–4.15 (Sat. 11–4.15). Admission Ambulatory, 50p; Crypt, Treasury and historical display, 75p; whispering gallery, stone gallery, 85p (children reduced price). —Services: Sundays, 8, 10.30, 11.30 and 3.15. Weekdays, 7.30, 8, and 5.

WESTMINSTER ABBEY, S.W.1. (built A.D. 1050–1745). Chapel of Henry VII, Chapter House and Cloisters; King Edward the Confessor's shrine, A.D. 1269, tombs of kings and queens (Henry III, Edward I, Edward III, Henry V, Mary Queen of Scots, Elizabeth I), and many other monuments and objects of interest, including the grave of "The Unknown Warrior" and Poets' Corner. The Coronation Chair encloses the "Stone of Scone", which was removed from Scotland by Edward I in 1296. Open on weekdays 9–6 (9–7.45 Wed). Admission to the Royal Chapels, Poets' Corner, Quire and Statesmen's Aisle £1.60, concessions 80p/40p. Last admission Mon.–Fri. 4 p.m., Sat. 5 p.m. Wed. 6–8 p.m. free. Nave open on Sundays between services. —Services: Sundays, 8, 10.30, 11.40, (sung every second and fourth Sundays in month), 3, 6.30 (generally preceded by an organ recital). Monday–Friday, 7.30, 8, 12.30 (Wednesdays, Lunch-hour Service), 5. Saturdays, 8, 9, 3.

SOUTHWARK CATHEDRAL, south side of the Thames, near London Bridge, SE1 9DE.—Mainly 13th century, but the nave is largely rebuilt. The tomb of John Gower (1330–1408) is between the Bunyan and Chaucer memorial windows, in the N. aisle; Shakespeare effigy backed by view of Southwark and Globe Theatre in S. aisle; the altar screen (erected 1520) has been restored; the tomb of Bishop Andrews (died 1626) is near screen. The Early English Lady Chapel (behind the choir), restored 1930, was the scene of the Consistory Courts of the reign of Mary (Gardiner and Bonner); and is still used as a Consistory Court. John Harvard, after whom Harvard University is named, was baptized here in 1607, and the Chapel by the North Choir Aisle is his memorial chapel. Open 7.30–6 free.—Services: Sundays, 11, 3. Weekdays, 12.30, 12.45, 5.30 (sung on Tuesdays and Fridays), Saturdays, 12 noon.

TEMPLE CHURCH, The Temple, E.C.4.—The nave formed one of five remaining round churches in England, the others being at Cambridge, Northampton, Little Maplestead (Essex), and Ludlow Castle. Rebuilding of the church was completed in 1958. —Services: Sundays, 8.30 and 11.15 except in August and September. *Master of the Temple*, Rev. Canon J. Robinson. *Reader*, Rev. Preb. W. D. Kennedy-Bell.

Church of Scotland

CROWN COURT CHURCH, Russell Street, Covent Garden, WC2B 5EZ.—Services: Sundays, 11.15 and 6.30. Thursdays, 1.10.

ST. COLUMBA'S, Pont Street, SW1X 0BD. —Services: Sundays, 11 and 6.30. *Minister*, Rev. W. A. Cairns.

United Reformed

CITY TEMPLE, Holborn Viaduct, EC1A 2DE.—Sundays, 11 and 6.30 and Thursdays, 1.15. *Minister*, Rev. E. Waugh.

Independent Evangelical

WESTMINSTER CHAPEL, Buckingham Gate, SW1E 6BS—Services: Sundays, 11 and 6.30. *Minister*, Rev. Dr. R. T. Kendall.

Methodist

WESLEY'S CHAPEL, City Road, EC1Y 1AU—Services: Sundays, 11 a.m. *Minister*, Rev. Dr. R. C. Gibbins.

CENTRAL HALL, Westminster, SW1H 9NU— Services: Sundays, 11 and 6.30. *Minister*, Rev. Dr. R. J. Tudor.

WEST LONDON MISSION, Hinde Street Methodist Church, W.1.—Services: Sundays, 10, 11 and 6.30. *Superintendent*, Rev. Dr. L. J. Griffiths.

Baptist

BLOOMSBURY CENTRAL BAPTIST CHURCH, Junction of Shaftesbury Avenue and New Oxford Street, W.C.2.—Services: Sundays, 11 and 6.30. *Minister*, Rev. B. Hibbert.

Religious Society of Friends

FRIENDS HOUSE, Euston Road, N.W.1.

Roman Catholic

WESTMINSTER CATHEDRAL, Ashley Place, Westminster, SW1P 1QW, built 1895–1903 from the designs of J. F. Bentley (the campanile is 283 feet high). Cathedral open 6.45 a.m.–8 p.m.—Masses: Sundays, 7, 8, 9, 10.30 (sung), 12, 5.30 and 7; Solemn Vespers and Benediction 3.30. Monday–Friday, 7, 8, 8.30, 9, 10.30, 12.30, 1.05 and 5.30 (sung). Morning Prayer 7.40, Vespers 5 . Saturdays 7, 8, 8.30, 9, 10.30 (sung), 12.30 and 6, Morning Prayer 7.40, Vespers 5.30. Holy days of obligation, Low Masses 7, 8, 8.30, 9, 10.30, 12.30, 1.05, 5.30 (sung) and 7.

THE ORATORY, Brompton, S.W.7.—Masses: Sundays, 7, 8, 9, 10, 11, 12.30, 4.30, 7; Vespers 3.30. Weekdays, 7, 8, 10, 12.30 and 6 (no 12.30 on Sats.). Service Thurs. 6.30 p.m. Holy days, 7, 10, 12.15, 1.15, 4.30, 6 and 8. On the eve, Vespers 5.30 p.m.

EDUCATION DIRECTORY

UNIVERSITIES

The universities have power to award their own degrees. They grant 70 per cent. of all first degrees awarded in Britain and 95 per cent. of all higher degrees. They provide most of the basic and much of the applied research undertaken in Britain, and are responsible for the initial training of virtually all research workers. The universities make the chief contribution to wholly new knowledge through fundamental research.

THE UNIVERSITY OF OXFORD

FULL TERMS, 1988

Hilary, Jan. 17 to March 12; *Trinity*, April 24 to June 18; *Michaelmas*, Oct. 9 to Dec. 3

Number of Undergraduates in Residence 1986–87: Men, 5,884; Women, 3,846

UNIVERSITY OFFICES, etc.	Elect.
Chancellor, The Lord Jenkins, P.C., *Balliol*	1987
High Steward, The Lord Wilberforce, P.C., C.M.G., O.B.E., M.A., *All Souls*	1967
Vice-Chancellor, Sir Patrick Neill, Q.C., Warden of *All Souls*	1985
Proctors, P. M. Neumann, D.Phil., D.SC., *Queens*; Mrs. G. A. Stoy, D.Phil., *Lady Margaret*	1987
Assessor, J. S. Knowland, D.Phil., *Pembroke*	1987
Public Orator, G. W. Bond, *Pembroke*	1980
Bodley's Librarian, D. G. Vaisey, *Exeter*	1986
Keeper of Archives, (vacant)	
Director of the Ashmolean Museum, C. J. White, *Worcester*	1985
Registrar of the University, A. J. Dorey, D.Phil., *Linacre*	1979
Surveyor to the University, D. W. Bending	1985
Secretary of Faculties, A. P. Weale *Worcester*	1984
Secretary of the Chest and Chief Accountant, I. G. Thompson, *Merton*	1986
Deputy Registrar (Admin.), D. W. Roberts, *Pembroke*	

Oxford Colleges and Halls
(With dates of foundation)

All Souls (1438), Sir Patrick Neill, Q.C., *Warden* (1977).
Balliol (1263), A. J. P. Kenny, D.Phil., D.Litt., F.B.A., *Master* (1978).
Brasenose (1509) Prof. J. K. B. M. Nicholas *Principal* (1978).
Christ Church (1546), Very Rev. E. W. Heaton, *Dean*, (1979).
Corpus Christi (1517), Prof. K. V. Thomas, F.B.A., *President* (1986).
Exeter (1314), Sir Richard Norman, K.B.E., D.SC., F.R.S., *Rector* (1987).
Green (1979), Sir John Walton, D.SC., *Warden* (1983).
Hertford (1874), Sir Geoffrey Warnock, *Principal* (1971).
Jesus (1571), Dr. P. M. North, D.C.L. *Principal* (1984).
Keble (1868), C. J. E. Ball, *Warden* (1979).
Lady Margaret Hall (1878), D. M. Stewart, *Principal* (1979).
Linacre (1962). J. B. Bamborough, *Principal* (1962).
Lincoln (1427), M. Shock, *Rector* (1987).
Magdalen (1458), K. B. Griffin, D.Phil., *President* (1979).
Merton (1264), J. M. Roberts, D.Phil., *Warden* (1985).
New College (1379), H. McGregor, Q.C., D.C.L. *Warden* (1985).
Nuffield (1937), M. G. Brock, C.B.E., *Warden* (1978).

Oriel (1326), Rt. Hon. Sir Zelman Cowen, A.K., G.C.M.G., G.C.V.O., Q.C., D.C.L., *Provost* (1982).
Pembroke (1624), Sir Roger Bannister, C.B.E., D.M., F.R.C.P., *Master* (1985).
Queen's (1340), J. Moffatt, D.Phil., *Provost* (1987).
St. Anne's (1952) (Originally Society of Oxford Home-Students (1879)), Dr. C. Palley, PH.D., *Principal* (1984).
St. Antony's (1950), R. Dahrendorf, K.B.E., PH.D., F.B.A., *Warden* (1987).
St. Catherine's (1962), Rt. Hon. Sir Patrick Nairne, G.C.B., M.C., *Master* (1981).
St. Cross (1965), R. C. Repp, D.Phil., *Master* (1987).
St. Edmund Hall (c. 1278), J. C. B. Gosling, *Principal* (1983).
St. Hugh's (1886), Miss M. R. Trickett, *Principal* (1973).
St. John's (1555), W. Hayes, D.Phil., *President* (1987).
St. Peter's (1929), Prof. G. E. Aylmer, D.Phil., F.B.A., *Master* (1978).
Trinity (1554), Sir John Burgh, K.C.M.G., C.B., *President* (1987).
University (1249), Kingman Brewster, *Master* (1986).
Wadham (1612), Sir Claus Moser, K.C.B., C.B.E., F.B.A., *Warden* (1984).
Wolfson (1966), Sir Raymond Hoffenberg, M.D., PH.D., *President* (1985).
Worcester (1714), The Lord Briggs, F.B.A., *Provost* (1976).
Campion Hall (1896), Rev. P. Hackett, *Master* (1984).
St. Benet's Hall (1897), Rev. P. D. Holdsworth, O.S.B., *Master* (1980).
Mansfield (1886), J. L. Womer, D.Phil., *Principal* (1986).
Regent's Park (1810), Rev. B. R. White, D.Phil., *Principal* (1972).
Greyfriars (1910), Very Rev. T. M. Mann, *Warden* (1981).

COLLEGES FOR WOMEN ONLY

St. Hilda's (1893), Mrs. G. M. Moore, *Principal* (1980).
Somerville (1879), Miss D. M. S. D. Park, C.M.G., O.B.E. *Principal* (1980).

THE UNIVERSITY OF CAMBRIDGE

FULL TERMS, 1988

Lent, Jan. 12 to March 11; *Easter*, April 19 to June 10; *Michaelmas*, Oct. 11 to Dec. 9

Number of Undergraduates in Residence 1986–87: Men, 6,182; Women, 3,624

UNIVERSITY OFFICES, ETC.	Elect.
Chancellor, H.R.H. The Duke of Edinburgh, K.G., K.T., O.M., G.B.E.	1977
† *Vice-Chancellor*, M. W. McCrum, *Master of Corpus Christi*	1985
High Steward, The Lord Devlin, P.C., F.B.A., *Christ's*	1966
Deputy High Steward, The Lord Richardson of Duntisbourne, P.C., M.B.E., T.D.	1983
Commissary, The Lord Salmon, P.C., *Pembroke*.	1979
Proctors, S. K. Newman, *New Hall*; R. W. M. Dias, *Magdalene*.	1987
Orator, J. Diggle, Litt.D., *Queen's*.	1982
Registrary, S. G. Fleet, PH.D., *Downing*	1983
Deputy Registrary, R. F. Holmes, *Darwin*	1972

† Correspondence for the *Vice-Chancellor* and other administrative officers should be sent to the *University Offices*, The Old Schools, Cambridge.

Librarian, F. W. Ratcliffe, PH.D., *Corpus Christi* 1980
Treasurer, M. P. Halstead, PH.D.,*Caius* 1985
Secretary General of the Faculties, J. R. G.
Wright, *St. Catharine's* 1987
Director of the Fitzwilliam Museum, Prof.
A. M. Jaffé, LITT.D., *King's* 1973

Cambridge Colleges
(With dates of foundation)

Christ's (1505), Prof. Sir Hans Kornberg, SC.D., F.R.S.,
Master (1983).
Churchill (1960), Prof. Sir Hermann Bondi, K.C.B.,
F.R.S., *Master* (1982).
Clare (1326), Prof. R. C. O. Matthews, C.B.E., F.B.A.,
Master (1975).
Clare Hall (1966), Prof. D. A. Low, D.Phil., PH.D.,
President (1987).
Corpus Christi (1352), M. W. McCrum, *Master* (1980).
Darwin (1964), Sir Arnold Burgen, M.D., F.R.S.,*Master*
(1982).
Downing (1800), P. Mathias, C.B.E., D.Litt., F.B.A.,
Master (1987).
Emmanuel (1584), Prof. D. S. Brewer, LITT.D., *Master*
(1977).
Fitzwilliam (1966), Prof. J. C. Holt, D.Phil., F.B.A.,
Master (1981).
Girton (1869), The Baroness Warnock, D.B.E., *Mistress*
(1984).
Gonville & Caius (1348), Prof. Sir William Wade,
LL.D., D.C.L., F.B.A., Q.C., *Master* (1976).
Jesus (1496), Prof. A. C. Renfrew, SC.D. *Master* (1986).
King's (1441), Prof. P. P. G. Bateson, SC.D., F.R.S.,
Provost (1987).
Pembroke (1347), Prof. The Lord Adrian, M.D., F.R.S.,
Master (1981).
Peterhouse (1284), Prof. H. Chadwick, D.D., F.B.A.,
Master (1987).
Queens' (1448), Prof. E. R. Oxburgh, F.R.S., *President*
(1982).
Robinson (1977), Prof. Sir Jack Lewis, PH.D., D.SC.,
SC.D., F.R.S., *Warden* (1977).
St. Catharine's (1473), *Master*, Prof. B. E. Supple,
PH.D. (1984).
St. Edmund's (1896), R. M. Laws, C.B.E., PH.D, *Master*
(1986).
St. John's (1511), Prof. Sir Francis Hinsley, O.B.E.,
Master (1979).
Selwyn (1882), Prof. A. H. Cook, SC.D., F.R.S., *Master*
(1983).
Sidney Sussex (1596), Prof. D. H. Northcote, PH.D.,
SC.D., F.R.S., *Master* (1976).
Trinity (1546), Sir Andrew Huxley, O.M., F.R.S., *Master*
(1984).
Trinity Hall (1350), J. Lyons, PH.D., *Master* (1984).
Wolfson (1965), Prof. D. G. T. Williams, *President*
(1980).

COLLEGE FOR MEN ONLY

Magdalene (1542), D. Calcutt, Q.C., *Master* (1985).

COLLEGES FOR WOMEN ONLY

New Hall (1954), Mrs. V. L. Pearl, PH.D., *President*
(1981).
Newnham (1871), Miss S. J. Browne, C.B., *Principal*
(1983).

APPROVED SOCIETIES

Homerton (1824) (for B.Ed. Students), A. G. Bamford.
Principal (1985).
Hughes Hall (1885), (for post-graduate students), B.
M. Herbertson, M.D., *President* (1984).
Lucy Cavendish College (1965) (for women research
students and mature undergraduates), Dame Anne
Warburton, D.C.V.O., C.M.G., *President* (1985).

THE UNIVERSITY OF ASTON IN BIRMINGHAM (1966)
Aston Triangle, Birmingham B4 7ET

Full-time Students (1986–87), 3,949.
Chancellor, Sir Adrian Cadbury (1979).
Vice-Chancellor Prof. Sir Frederick Crawford, PH.D.,
D.Eng., D.SC.
Registrar, (vacant).
Secretary, J. R.Tunley (*acting*).

UNIVERSITY OF BATH (1966)
Claverton Down, Bath BA2 7AY

Full-time Students (1986–87), 3,666.
Chancellor, Lord Kearton, O.B.E., F.R.S. (1980).
Vice-Chancellor, Prof. J. R. Quayle, PH.D., F.R.S.
Registrar and Secretary, R. M. Mawditt, F.R.S.A.

THE UNIVERSITY OF BIRMINGHAM (1900)
P.O. Box 363, Birmingham B15 2TT

Full-time Students (1986-87), 9,016.
Chancellor, Sir Alex Jarratt, C.B.
Vice-Chancellor and Principal, Prof. M. W. Thomp-
son.
Secretary, H. Harris.
Registrar, (vacant).

UNIVERSITY OF BRADFORD (1966)
Bradford BD7 1DP

Full-time Students (1986–87), 4,170.
Chancellor, Sir John Harvey-Jones, M.B.E.,
Vice-Chancellor and Principal, Prof. J. C. West, C.B.E.,
PH.D., D.SC. (1986).
Registrar and Secretary, I. M. Sanderson, M.B.E., .

THE UNIVERSITY OF BRISTOL (1909)
Bristol BS8 1TH

Full-time Students (1986–87), 7,188.
Chancellor, Prof. Dorothy Hodgkin, O.M., PH.D, F.R.S.
(1971).
Vice-Chancellor, Sir John Kingman, F.R.S.
Registrar and Secretary, E. C. Wright.

BRUNEL UNIVERSITY (1966)
Uxbridge, Middx. UB8 3PH

Full-time Students (1986–87), 2,897.
Chancellor, The Earl of Halsbury, F.R.S.
Vice-Chancellor, Prof. R. E. D. Bishop, C.B.E., PH.D.,
SC.D., F.R.S.
Registrar, D. Neave.
Academic Secretary, J. B. Alexander.

UNIVERSITY OF BUCKINGHAM (1983)
(Founded 1976 as University College at
Buckingham). Independent of state finance.
Buckingham MK18 1EG

Full-time Students (1986–87), 662.
Chancellor, The Lord Hailsham of St. Marylebone,
P.C., C.H., F.R.S. (1983).
Vice-Chancellor, Dr. A. M. Barrett, PH.D.
Registrar, S. P. J. Ellis.
Bursar and Secretary to Council, P. Quick.

THE CITY UNIVERSITY (1966)
Northampton Square, EC1V 0HB

Full-time Students (1986–87), 3,164.
Chancellor, The Lord Mayor of London.
Vice-Chancellor, Prof. R. N. Franklin, D.Phil., D.SC.
Academic Registrar, A. H. Seville, PH.D.
Secretary, M. M. O'Hara.

THE UNIVERSITY OF DURHAM
(Founded 1832; re-organized 1908, 1937 and 1963)
Old Shire Hall, Durham DH1 3HP

Full-time Students (1986–87), 5,105.
Chancellor, Dame Margot Fonteyn de Arias (1982).
Vice-Chancellor and Warden, Prof. F. G. T. Holliday, C.B.E., F.R.S.E.
Registrar and Secretary, J. C. F. Hayward.

Colleges
Collingwood, G. H. Blake, Ph.D.
Graduate Society, M. Richardson, Ph.D.
Grey, E. Halladay, *Master*.
Hatfield, J. P. Barber, Ph.D., *Master*.
St. Aidan's, Miss I. Hindmarsh, *Principal*.
St. Chad's, Rev. R. C. Trounson, *Principal*.
St. Cuthbert's Society, J. D. Norton, *Principal*.
St. Hild and St. Bede, J. V. Armitage, Ph.D., *Principal*.
St. John's, Miss D. R. Etchells, *Principal*.
St. Mary's, Miss J. M. Kenworthy, *Principal*.
Trevelyan, Miss D. Lavin, *Principal*.
University, E. C. Salthouse, Ph.D., *Master*
Ushaw, Rt. Rev. Mgr. P. F. J. Walton, *President*.
Van Mildert, A. T. von S. Bradshaw, *Master*.

THE UNIVERSITY OF EAST ANGLIA (1963)
Norwich NR4 7TJ

Full-time Students (1986–87), 4,364.
Chancellor, Rev. Prof. W. O. Chadwick, O.M., K.B.E., D.D., F.B.A. (1985).
Vice-Chancellor, Prof. D. C. Burke, Ph.D.
Registrar and Secretary, M. G. E. Paulson-Ellis.

THE UNIVERSITY OF ESSEX (1964)
Wivenhoe Park, Colchester CO4 3SQ

Full-time Students (1986–87), 2,980.
Chancellor, Rt. Hon. Sir Patrick Nairne G.C.B., M.C. (1983).
Vice-Chancellor, Prof. M. Harris, Ph.D.
Registrar and Sec., E. Newcomb.

THE UNIVERSITY OF EXETER (1955)
Exeter EX4 4QJ

Full-time Students (1986–87), 5,035.
Chancellor, Sir Rex Richards, D.SC., F.R.S. (1981).
Vice-Chancellor, D. Harrison, Ph.D., SC.D.
Academic Registrar and Secretary, M. J. Hislop.

THE UNIVERSITY OF HULL (1954)
Cottingham Road, Hull HU6 7RX

Full-time Students (1986–87), 4,750.
Chancellor, The Lord Wilberforce, P.C., C.M.G., O.B.E. (1978).
Vice-Chancellor, Prof. W. Taylor, C.B.E., Ph.D.
Registrar, F. T. Mattison.

THE UNIVERSITY OF KEELE (1962)
Keele, Staffs. ST5 5BG

Full-time Students (1986–87), 2,401.
Chancellor, Sir Claus Moser, K.C.B., C.B.E., F.B.A. (1986).
Vice-Chancellor, Prof. B. E. F. Fender, C.M.G., Ph.D.
Registrar, D. Cohen, Ph.D.

UNIVERSITY OF KENT AT CANTERBURY
(1965)
Canterbury CT2 7NZ

Full-time Students (1986–87), 4,198.
Chancellor, The Lord Grimond, P.C., T.D. (1969).
Vice-Chancellor, D. J. E. Ingram, D.Phil., D.SC.
Registrar and Finance Officer, A. D. Linfoot.

THE UNIVERSITY OF LANCASTER (1964)
Bailrigg, Lancaster LA1 4YW

Full-time Students (1986–87), 4,589.
Chancellor, H.R.H. The Princess Alexandra, G.C.V.O. (1964).
Vice-Chancellor, Prof. H. J. Hanham, Ph.D.
Registrar, M. D. Forster.
Secretary, G. M. Cockburn.

THE UNIVERSITY OF LEEDS (1904)
Leeds LS2 9JT

Full-time Students (1986–87), 10,292.
Chancellor, H.R.H. The Duchess of Kent, G.C.V.O. (1966).
Vice-Chancellor, Sir Edward Parkes, Ph.D., SC.D.
Registrar, J. J. Walsh.
Bursar, R. Head.

THE UNIVERSITY OF LEICESTER (1957)
Leicester LE1 7RH

Full-time Students (1986–87), 4,851.
Chancellor, Sir George Porter, P.R.S., Ph.D., SC.D. (1985).
Vice-Chancellor, K. J. R. Edwards, Ph.D.
Registrar, (vacant).

THE UNIVERSITY OF LIVERPOOL (1903)
P.O. Box 147, Liverpool L69 3BX

Full-time Students (1986–87), 7,595.
Chancellor, The Viscount Leverhulme, T.D. (1980).
Vice-Chancellor, Prof. G. J. Davies, Ph.D., SC.D.
Registrar, R. A. Nind.
Academic Secretary and Deputy Registrar., D. R. Holmes.

THE UNIVERSITY OF LONDON (1836)
Senate House, WC1E 7HU

Internal Students (1985–86), 50,155, External Students, 24,498.
Visitor, H.M. The Queen in Council.
Chancellor, H.R.H. The Princess Royal, G.C.V.O., F.R.S. (1981).
Vice-Chancellor, The Lord Flowers, F.R.S.
Chairman of the Court, The Lord Goff of Chieveley, P.C., D.C.L.
Chairman of Convocation, Prof. J. P. Quilliam, O.B.E., D.SC.
Principal, P. Holwell.

Principal Officers
Clerk of the Court, P. J. Griffiths.
Clerk of the Senate, P. Taylor.
Academic Registrar, Mrs. G. F. Roberts.
Secretary to University Entrance and School Examinations Council, A. R. Stephenson.
Director of Central Library Services, V. T. H. Parry.

Schools of the University
Birkbeck College, Malet Street, WC1E 7HX, The Baroness Blackstone, Ph.D., *Master*.
Imperial College of Science and Technology, South Kensington, SW7 2AZ, Prof. E. A. Ash, C.B.E., Ph.D., F.R.S., *Rector*.
Institute of Education, 20 Bedford Way, WC1H 0AL, Prof. D. Lawton, Ph.D., *Dir.*
King's College London (includes former Chelsea College and Queen Elizabeth College), Strand, WC2R 2LS, Prof. S. R. Sutherland, *Principal*.
London School of Economics and Political Science, Houghton Street, WC2A 2AE, Dr. I. Patel, *Director*.
Queen Mary College, Mile End Road, E1 4NS, Prof. I. Butterworth, C.B.E., Ph.D., F.R.S., *Principal*.

Royal Holloway and Bedford New College, Egham Hill, Egham, Surrey TW20 0EX, Prof. Dorothy E. C. Wedderburn, D. Litt, *Principal.*

Royal Veterinary College, Royal College Street, NW1 0TU, A. O. Betts, Ph.D., *Principal and Dean.*

School of Oriental and African Studies, Malet Street, WC1E 7HP, Prof. C. D. Cowan, Ph.D., *Dir.*

School of Pharmacy, 29–39 Brunswick Square, WC1N 1AX, F. Fish, Ph.D., *Dean.*

University College, Gower Street, WC1E 6BT, Sir James Lighthill, F.R.S., *Provost.*

Westfield College, Kidderpore Avenue, Hampstead, NW3 7ST, Prof. J. E. Varey, Ph.D., D.Litt., F.B.A., *Principal.*

Wye College, Wye, Ashford, Kent TN25 5AH, I. A. M. Lucas, C.B.E., *Principal.*

*Heythrop College, 11–13 Cavendish Square, W1M 0AN, Rev. B. A. Callaghan, S.J., *Principal.*

General Medical Schools

Charing Cross and Westminster Medical School, The Reynolds Building, St. Dunstan's Road, W6 8RP. *Dean*, Prof. T. W. Glenister, C.B.E., T.D., D.SC.; *Secretary*, G. K. Buckley.

King's College School of Medicine and Dentistry, Denmark Hill, SE5 8RX.

The London Hospital Medical College, Turner Street, E1 2AD.—*Dean*, Prof. R. Duckworth, M.D., F.R.C.S., F.R.C. Path. *Secretary*, J. W. Walmsley.

Royal Free Hospital School of Medicine, Rowland Hill Street, NW3 2PF.—*Dean*, B. B. MacGillivray, F.R.C.P.; *Secretary*, B. A. Blatch.

St. Bartholomew's Hospital Medical College, West Smithfield, EC1A 7BE.—*Dean*, Dr. I. Kelsey Fry, D.M., F.R.C.P.; *Secretary*, D. J. Brown, M.B.E.

St. George's Hospital Medical School, Cranmer Terrace, Tooting, SW17 0RE.—*Dean*, (vacant); *Secretary*, R. B. Hill.

St. Mary's Hospital Medical School, Norfolk Place, Paddington, W2 1PG.—*Dean*, Prof. P. Richards, Ph.D., M.D., F.R.C.P.; *Secretary*, K. Lockyer.

United Medical and Dental Schools of Guy's and St. Thomas's Hospitals, Guy's: London Bridge, SE1 9RT; St. Thomas's: Lambeth Palace Road, SE1 7EH.—*Dean*, Prof. T. J. H. Clark, M.D., F.R.C.P.; *Secretary*, C. S. Argles

University College and Middlesex School of Medicine, Gower Street WC1E 6BT.—*Provost*, Sir James Lighthill, F.R.S.; *Secretary*, I. H. Baker, C.B.E.

Postgraduate Medical Schools

London School of Hygiene and Tropical Medicine, Keppel Street WC1E 7HT. Dr. C. E. Gordon Smith, C.B., M.D., F.R.C.P., *Dean.*

Royal Postgraduate Medical School, Du Cane Road W12 0SH. Prof. D. N. S. Kerr, F.R.C.P., *Dean.*

British Postgraduate Medical Federation (University of London), 33 Millman Street, WC1N 3EJ. Prof. M. J. Peckham, M.D., F.R.C.P.(G), F.R.C.R., *Director.*
Comprises:—

Institute of Cancer Research, Royal Cancer Hospital, 17A Onslow Gardens SW7 3AL. Prof. R. A. Weiss, Ph.D. *Director.*

Cardiothoracic Institute, Fulham Road, SW3 6HP. M. Green, D.M., F.R.C.P., *Dean.*

Institute of Child Health, 30 Guilford Street, WC1N 1EH. Prof. P. J. Graham, F.R.C.P., *Dean.*

Institute of Dental Surgery, Eastman Dental Hospital, Gray's Inn Road, WC1X 8LD. Prof. G. B. Winter, D.Ch., F.D.S., *Dean.*

Hunterian Institute, Royal College of Surgeons of England, Lincoln's Inn Fields, WC2A 3PN. Prof. Sir Gordon Robson, C.B.E., *Master*; Prof. G. P. Lewis, *Academic Dean.*

Institute of Neurology, National Hospital, Queen Square, WC1N 3BG. D. N. Landon, *Dean.*

Institute of Ophthalmology, Judd Street, WC1H 9QS. R. K. Blach, M.D., F.R.C.S., *Dean.*

Institute of Psychiatry, De Crespigny Park, Denmark Hill, SE5 8AF. Dr. R. M. Murray, M.D., *Dean.*

Senate Institutes

British Institute in Paris, 9–11 Rue de Constantine, 75007, Paris, Prof. C. L. Campos, L-ès-L., Ph.D., *Dir.* London office: Senate House, WC1E 7HU.

Courtauld Institute of Art, 20 Portman Square, W1H 0BE, Prof. C. M. Kauffman, Ph.D., *Dir.*

Institute of Advanced Legal Studies, Charles Clore House, 17 Russell Square, WC1B 5DR, Prof. T. C. Daintith, *Dir.*

Institute of Classical Studies, 31–34 Gordon Square, WC1H 0PY, Prof. J. P. Barron, F.S.A., *Dir.*

Institute of Commonwealth Studies, 27–28 Russell Square, WC1B 5DS, Prof. Shula E. Marks, Ph.D., *Dir.*

Institute of Germanic Studies, 29 Russell Square, WC1B 5DP, Prof. R. A. Wisbey, Hon. *Dir.*

Institute of Historical Research, Senate House, Malet Street, WC1E 7HU, Prof. F. M. L. Thompson, D.Phil., F.B.A., *Dir.*

Institute of Latin American Studies, 31 Tavistock Square, WC1H 9HA, Prof. L. M. Bethell, Ph.D., *Dir.*

Institute of United States Studies, 31 Tavistock Square, WC1H 9EZ, Prof. P. J. Parish, *Dir.*

School of Slavonic and E. European Studies, Senate House, WC1E 7HU, Prof. M. A. Branch, Ph.D., *Dir.*

Warburg Institute, Woburn Square, WC1H 0AB, Prof. J. B. Trapp, F.B.A., *Dir.*

Institutions having Recognized Teachers

Goldsmiths' College, Lewisham Way, New Cross, SE14 6NW, A. Rutherford, *Warden.*

Jews' College, 44A Albert Road, NW4 2SJ, Rabbi Dr. J. Sacks, *Principal.*

London Business School, Sussex Place, NW1 4SA, Prof. P. G. Moore, Ph.D., *Principal.*

Royal Academy of Music, Marylebone Road, NW1 5HT, Sir David Lumsden, D.Phil., F.R.C.M., *Principal.*

Royal College of Music, Prince Consort Road, SW7 2BS, M. G. Matthews, F.R.S.A., *Director.*

Trinity College of Music, Mandeville Place, W1M 6AQ, M. Davies, C.B.E., *Principal.*

LOUGHBOROUGH UNIVERSITY OF TECHNOLOGY (1966)
Loughborough LE11 3TU

Full-time Students (1986–87), 5,800.
Chancellor, Sir Arnold Hall, F.R.S. (1980).
Vice-Chancellor, (vacant).
Registrar, H. Brooks.

THE UNIVERSITY OF MANCHESTER
Oxford Road, Manchester MI3 9PL

(Founded 1851; re-organized 1880 and 1903).

Full-time Students (1986–87), 11,123.
Chancellor, Prof. J. A. G. Griffith, F.B.A.
Vice-Chancellor, Prof. Sir Mark Richmond, Ph.D., SC.D., F.R.S.
Registrar, K. E. Kitchen.

---

*Not in receipt of U.G.C. grants.

UNIVERSITY OF MANCHESTER INSTITUTE OF SCIENCE AND TECHNOLOGY
(1824)
P.O. Box 88, Manchester M60 1QD

Full-time Students (1986–87), 4,069.
President, Sir John Mason, C.B., D.SC., F.R.S.
Principal, Prof. H. C. A. Hankins, Ph.D.
Secretary and Registrar, P. C. C. Stephenson.

THE UNIVERSITY OF NEWCASTLE UPON TYNE
(Founded 1852; re-organized 1908, 1937 and 1963)
6 Kensington Terrace, Newcastle upon Tyne
NE1 7RU

Full-time Students (1986–87), 7,776.
Chancellor, The Duke of Northumberland, K.G., P.C., G.C.V.O., T.D., F.R.S. (1963).
Vice-Chancellor, Prof. L. W. Martin, Ph.D.
Registrar, D. E. T. Nicholson.

THE UNIVERSITY OF NOTTINGHAM (1948)
University Park, Nottingham NG7 2RD

Full-time Students (1986–87), 7,000.
Chancellor, Sir Gordon Hobday, Ph.D.
Vice-Chancellor, B. C. L. Weedon, C.B.E., Ph.D., D.SC., F.R.S.
Registrar, G. E. Chandler.

THE UNIVERSITY OF READING (1926)
Whiteknights, P.O. Box 217, Reading RG6 2AH

Full-time Students (1986–87), 5,879.
Chancellor, The Lord Sherfield, G.C.B., G.C.M.G., F.R.S. (1970).
Vice-Chancellor, E. S. Page, Ph.D.
Registrar, T. Bottomley.

UNIVERSITY OF SALFORD (1967)
Salford M5 4WT

Full-time Students (1986–87), 3,760.
Chancellor, H.R.H. The Prince Philip, Duke of Edinburgh, K.G., P.C., K.T., O.M., G.B.E., F.R.S. (1967).
Vice-Chancellor, J. M. Ashworth, Ph.D., D.SC.
Registrar, S. R. Bosworth, O.B.E.

THE UNIVERSITY OF SHEFFIELD (1905)
Sheffield S10 2TN

Full-time Students (1986–87), 7,968.
Chancellor, The Lord Dainton, Ph.D., SC.D., F.R.S. (1979).
Vice-Chancellor, Prof. G. D. Sims, O.B.E., Ph.D.
Registrar and Secretary, J. S. Padley, Ph.D.

THE UNIVERSITY OF SOUTHAMPTON (1952)
Highfield, Southampton SO9 5NH

Full-time Students (1986–87), 6,437.
Chancellor, The Earl Jellicoe, P.C., K.B.E., D.S.O., M.C. (1984).
Vice-Chancellor, Dr. G. R. Higginson, Ph.D.
Secretary and Registrar, D. A. Schofield.
Academic Registrar, Miss A. E. Clarke.

UNIVERSITY OF SURREY (1966)
Guildford, Surrey GU2 5XH

Full-time Students (1986–87), 3,375.
Chancellor, H.R.H. The Duke of Kent, K.G., G.C.M.G., G.C.V.O.
Vice-Chancellor, A. Kelly, Ph.D., SC.D., F.R.S.
Academic Registrar, G. Haigh, Ph.D.
Secretary, L. J. Kail.

THE UNIVERSITY OF SUSSEX (1961)
Falmer, Brighton BN1 9RH

Full-time Students (1986–87), 4,558.
Chancellor, The Earl of March and Kinrara.
Vice-Chancellor, L. Fielding.
Registrar and Secretary, G. Lockwood, D.phil.

THE UNIVERSITY OF WARWICK (1965)
Coventry CV4 7AL

Full-time Students (1986–87), 5,880.
Chancellor, The Lord Scarman, P.C., O.B.E. (1977).
Vice-Chancellor, C. L. Brundin, Ph.D.
Registrar, M. L. Shattock

THE UNIVERSITY OF YORK (1963)
Heslington, York YO1 5DD

Full-time Students (1986–87), 3,417.
Chancellor, The Lord Swann, Ph.D., F.R.S., F.R.S.E.
Vice-Chancellor, Prof. S. B. Saul, Ph.D.
Registrar, D. J. Foster.

ROYAL COLLEGE OF ART (1837)
Kensington Gore, SW7 2EU

Under Royal Charter (1967) the Royal College of Art grants the degrees of Doctor, Doctor of Philosophy, Master of Arts and Master of Design (RCA). Students (1986–87), 633 (all postgraduate).
Provost, The Earl of Gowrie, P.C.
Registrar, F. Higgins.

CRANFIELD INSTITUTE OF TECHNOLOGY (1969)
Cranfield, Bedford MK43 0AL

Under Royal Charter (1969) the Cranfield Institute of Technology grants degrees in applied science, engineering, technology and management.
Full-time Students (1986–87), 2,000.
Chancellor, The Lord Kings Norton, Ph.D., D.I.C. (1969).
Vice-Chancellor, The Lord Chilver, Ph.D., F.R.S.
General Secretary, P. A. Digger.

THE OPEN UNIVERSITY (1969)
Walton Hall, Milton Keynes MK7 6AA

Students and clients (1986), 149,500.

Tuition by correspondence linked with special radio and television programmes, summer schools and a locally-based tutorial and counselling service. Under Royal Charter the University awards degrees of B.A., B.Phil., M.A., M.SC., M.Phil., Ph.D., D.SC. and D.Litt. There are seven faculties—arts, education, mathematics, science, social sciences, technology and management and a wide range of continuing education courses.
Chancellor, The Lord Briggs, F.B.A.
Vice-Chancellor, J. H. Horlock, Ph.D., SC.D., F.R.S.
Secretary, D. J. Clinch.

THE UNIVERSITY OF WALES (1893)
Cathays Park, Cardiff CF1 3NS

Chancellor, H.R.H. The Prince of Wales, K.G., P.C., K.T., G.C.B. (1976).
Pro-Chancellor, The Lord Cledwyn of Penrhos, P.C., C.H. (1985).
Vice-Chancellor, Prof. B. L. Clarkson, Ph.D.
Registrar, M. A. R. Kemp, Ph.D.

Colleges
University College of Wales, Aberystwyth.—*Princ.*, G. Owen, D.SC. (1979).

University College of North Wales, Bangor.—*Princ.*,
Prof. E. Sunderland, ph.d. (1984).
University of Wales Institute of Science and Technology, Cardiff.—*Princ.*, A. F. Trotman-Dickenson,
ph.d., d.sc. (1968).
Cardiff (*University College*).—*Princ.*, A. F. Trotman-Dickenson, ph.d., d.sc. (1987).
Lampeter (*St. David's College*).—*Princ.*, Prof. B. R.
Morris, d.phil. (1980).
Swansea (*University College*).—*Princ.*, Prof. B. L.
Clarkson, ph.d., (1982).
University of Wales College of Medicine, Cardiff.—
Provost, Prof. Sir Herbert Duthie, m.d., ch.m.,
f.r.c.s. (1979).

SCOTLAND

UNIVERSITY OF ABERDEEN (1495)
Regent Walk, Aberdeen AB9 1FX

Full-time Students (1986–87), 5,656.
Chancellor, Sir Kenneth Alexander, f.r.s.e.
Principal, Prof. G. P. McNicol, m.d., ph.d., f.r.s.e.,
f.r.c.p. (1981).
Secretary, W. M. Bradley.
Rector, H. Watt (1984–87).

UNIVERSITY OF DUNDEE (1967)
Dundee DD1 4HN

Full-time Students (1986–87), 3,796.
Chancellor, The Earl of Dalhousie, k.t., g.c.v.o., g.b.e.,
m.c. (1977).
Vice-Chancellor, M. J. Hamlin.
Secretary, R. Seaton.
Rector, M. G. Bruce, m.p. (1986–89).

UNIVERSITY OF EDINBURGH (1583)
Old College, South Bridge, Edinburgh EH8 9YL

Full-time Students (1986–87), 10,091.
Chancellor, H.R.H. The Prince Philip, Duke of
Edinburgh, k.g., p.c., k.t., o.m., g.b.e., f.r.s. (1952).
Vice-Chancellor and Principal, Sir David Smith,
d.phil., f.r.s.
Secretary, A. M. Currie, o.b.e.
Rector, A. MacPherson, (1985–88).

UNIVERSITY OF GLASGOW (1451)
Glasgow G12 8QQ

Full-time Students (1986–87), 10,481.
Chancellor, Sir Alexander Cairncross, k.c.m.g., ph.d.,
f.b.a.
Vice-Chancellor, Sir Alwyn Williams, ph.d., f.r.s.,
f.r.s.e. (1976).
Registrar, J. M. Black.
Secretary, R. Ewen, o.b.e., t.d.
Rector, Mrs. W. Mandela, (1987–90).

HERIOT-WATT UNIVERSITY (1966)
Riccarton, Currie, Edinburgh EH14 4AS

Full-time Students (1986–87), 3,863.
Chancellor, The Lord Thomson of Monifieth, p.c.,
k.t., f.r.s.e. (1977).
Principal and Vice-Chancellor, T. L. Johnston, ph.d.,
f.r.s.e. (1981).
Registrar, D. Sturgeon.
Secretary, D. I. Cameron.

UNIVERSITY OF ST. ANDREWS (1411)
College Gate, St. Andrews KY16 9AJ

Full-time Students (1986–87), 3,811.
Chancellor, Sir Kenneth Dover, d.litt., f.r.s.e., f.b.a.
(1981).

Vice-Chancellor, Prof. S. Arnott, ph.d., f.r.s.
Registrar and Secretary, M. J. B. Lowe, ph.d.
Rector, S. Adams (1985–88).

UNIVERSITY OF STIRLING (1967)
Stirling FK9 4LA

Full-time Students (1986–87), 2,900.
Chancellor, Sir Montague Finniston, ph.d., f.r.s.
(1978).
Vice-Chancellor, Prof. A. J. Forty, ph.d., d.sc.
Deputy Secretary and Registrar, Dr. D. J. Farrington,
d.phil.
Secretary, R. G. Bomont.

UNIVERSITY OF STRATHCLYDE (1964)
16 Richmond Street, Glasgow G1 1XQ

Full-time Students (1986–87), 7,546.
Chancellor, The Lord Todd, o.m., d.sc., d.phil., f.r.s.
(1965).
Principal and Vice-Chancellor, G. J. Hills, ph.d., d.sc.,
f.r.s.e.
Registrar and Secretary, D. W. J. Morrell.

NORTHERN IRELAND

THE QUEEN'S UNIVERSITY OF BELFAST
(1908)

Full-time Students (1986–87), 7,169.
Chancellor, Sir Rowland Wright, k.b., c.b.e., d.sc.
President and Vice-Chancellor, G. S. G. Beveridge,
ph.d., f.r.s.e.
Registrar, F. Smyth.

UNIVERSITY OF ULSTER (1984)
Coleraine, Co. Londonderry BT52 1SA
(Amalgamation of New University of Ulster and
Ulster Polytechnic)

Full-time Students (1986–87), 7,613.
Chancellor, The Lord Grey of Naunton, g.c.m.g.,
g.c.v.o., o.b.e. (1985).
Vice-Chancellor, D. S. Birley.
Academic Registrar, P. J. Conway.
Secretary, J. A. Hunter.

REPUBLIC OF IRELAND

UNIVERSITY OF DUBLIN TRINITY
COLLEGE (1592)
Dublin 2

Full-time Students (1986–87), 6,550.
Chancellor, F. J. C. O'Reilly (1985).
Provost, W. A. Watts, sc.d.
Registrar, W. R. Duncan.
Secretary, G. H. H. Giltrap.

NATIONAL UNIVERSITY OF IRELAND,
DUBLIN (1908)
49 Merrion Square, Dublin 2

Full-time Students (1986–87), 18,796.
Chancellor, Dr. T. K. Whitaker.
Vice-Chancellor, Dr. C. ó h Eocha, ph.d.
Registrar, Dr. M. Gilheany.

Constituent Colleges
Presidents
Univ. Coll., Dublin, P. Masterson, ph.d.
Univ. Coll., Cork, T. ó Ciardha, ph.d.
Univ. Coll. Galway, C.ó h Eocha, ph.d.

THE ASSOCIATION OF COMMONWEALTH UNIVERSITIES
36 Gordon Square, WC1H 0PF

The Association holds quinquennial Congresses of the Universities of the Commonwealth and other meetings in the intervening years; publishes the *Commonwealth Universities Yearbook*, handbooks listing scholarships and fellowships, etc.; acts as a general information centre on universities in U.K. and other Commonwealth countries; provides an advisory service for the filling of university teaching staff appointments overseas; administers travelling fellowships for university administrators as well as electives bursaries for medical students; and runs the Third World Academic Exchange Programme. It also supplies the secretariat for the Commonwealth Scholarship Commission in the U.K. and for the Marshall Aid Commemoration Commission.

Secretary General, A. Christodoulou, C.B.E., D.Univ.

COUNCIL FOR NATIONAL ACADEMIC AWARDS
344–354 Gray's Inn Road, WC1X 8BP

Established in 1964 with powers to award degrees and other academic distinctions equivalent in standard to those awarded by universities. Courses are designed and taught in institutions of higher education (including polytechnics) which are not themselves empowered to award degrees. The Council awards degrees and honours degrees of B.A., B.Ed., B.Sc., LL.B., B.Eng. and M.Eng., and higher and research degrees and doctorates. On Sept. 1, 1974, the Council assumed responsibility for the work formerly undertaken by the National Council for Diplomas in Art and Design, and in September, 1976, for the Diploma of Management Studies.

Chairman, R. Dearing, C.B.
Director and Chief Executive, M. Frazer, Ph.D.

POLYTECHNICS

The 30 polytechnics constitute a substantial part of the higher education system in England and Wales. Overall they provide an educational environment for some 320,000 students each year, about half of them following full-time or sandwich courses. Within the public sector their total entry includes over 70 per cent. of all first-year enrolments to degree courses and others recognised as being of the same standard. In addition the polytechnics play a major part in the national provision of other advanced courses including Higher National awards and professional qualifications. The polytechnics also provide opportunities for postgraduate research in most disciplines.

Courses have a vocational emphasis. Together engineering, science and technology currently account for some 42 per cent. of enrolments. A further 30 per cent. is involved in administrative, business and social studies and some 7 per cent. in education. The remaining 21 per cent. are spread over other professional and vocational subjects (e.g. architecture, librarianship and catering); music, drama and visual arts; languages (3 per cent.) and other arts (4 per cent.).

Full-time and sandwich course students for the year 1986–87 are shown in parentheses.

CITY OF BIRMINGHAM POLYTECHNIC, Perry Barr, Birmingham B42 2SU (5,500).—*Dir.*, Dr. P. C. Knight, D.Phil.

BRIGHTON POLYTECHNIC, Moulsecoomb, Brighton, E. Sussex BN2 4AT (4,747).—*Dir.*, Prof. G. R. Hall, C.B.E.

BRISTOL POLYTECHNIC, Coldharbour Lane, Frenchay, Bristol BS16 1QY (5,900).—*Dir.*, A. Morris.

HATFIELD POLYTECHNIC, College Lane, Hatfield, Herts AL10 9AB (4,500).—*Dir.*, Prof. N. K. Buxton, Ph.D.

HUDDERSFIELD POLYTECHNIC, Queensgate, Huddersfield HD1 3DH (4,700).—*Rector*, K. J. Durrands.

KINGSTON POLYTECHNIC, Gipsy Hill Centre, Kenry House, Kingston Hill, Kingston upon Thames KT2 7LB (5,417).—*Dir.*, R. C. Smith, Ph.D.

LANCASHIRE POLYTECHNIC, Preston PR1 2TQ (4,334).—*Dir.*, E. E. Robinson.

LANCHESTER POLYTECHNIC, Priory Street, Coventry CV1 5FB (6,168).—*Dir.*, M. Goldstein, Ph.D., D.SC., F.R.S.C.

LEEDS POLYTECHNIC, Calverley Street, Leeds LS1 3HE (5,865).—*Dir.*, C. Price.

LEICESTER POLYTECHNIC, P.O. Box 143, Leicester LE1 9BH (6,325).—*Dir.*, K. Barker.

LIVERPOOL POLYTECHNIC, Rodney House, 70 Mount Pleasant, Liverpool L3 5UX (7,119).—*Rector*, P. Toyne.

LONDON:

    CITY OF LONDON POLYTECHNIC, 117–119 Houndsditch EC3A 7BU (3,350).—*Provost*, J. M. Edwards, C.B.E., Q.C.

    MIDDLESEX POLYTECHNIC, 114 Chase Side, N14 5PN (7,227).—*Dir.*, R. M. W. Rickett, C.B.E., Ph.D.

    NORTH EAST LONDON POLYTECHNIC, Romford Road, E15 4LZ (5,200).—*Dir.*, Prof. G. T. Fowler.

    POLYTECHNIC OF CENTRAL LONDON, 309 Regent Street, W1R 8AL (4,296).—*Rector.*, Prof. T. E. Burlin, D.SC., Ph.D.

    POLYTECHNIC OF NORTH LONDON, Holloway Road N7 8DB (7,000).—*Dir.*, L. Wagner.

    SOUTH BANK POLYTECHNIC, Borough Road, SE1 0AA (5,400).—*Dir.*, Mrs. P. Perry.

    THAMES POLYTECHNIC, Wellington Street, Woolwich, SE18 6PF (4,722).—*Dir.*, N. Singer, Ph.D.

MANCHESTER POLYTECHNIC, All Saints, Manchester M15 6BH (10,455).—*Dir.*, K. Green.

NEWCASTLE UPON TYNE POLYTECHNIC, Ellison Place, Newcastle upon Tyne NE1 8ST (6,870).—*Dir.*, Prof. L. Barden.

NORTH STAFFORDSHIRE POLYTECHNIC, Beaconside, Stafford ST18 0AD; College Road, Stoke-on-Trent, ST4 2DE (4,770).—*Dir.*, K. B. Thompson.

OXFORD POLYTECHNIC, Headington, Oxford OX3 0BP (4,320).—*Dir.*, B. L. Tonge, Ph.D.

PLYMOUTH POLYTECHNIC, Drake Circus, Plymouth PL4 8AA (5,216).—*Dir.*, R. F. M. Robbins, C.B.E., Ph.D.

PORTSMOUTH POLYTECHNIC, Ravelin House, Museum Road, Portsmouth PO1 2QQ (6,500).—*Pres.*, H. D. Law, Ph.D.

SHEFFIELD CITY POLYTECHNIC, Pond Street, Sheffield S1 1WB (8,000).—*Principal*, J. M. Stoddart.

SUNDERLAND POLYTECHNIC, Langham Tower, Ryhope Road, Sunderland SR2 7EE (4,230).—*Rector*, E. P. Hart, Ph.D.

TEESSIDE POLYTECHNIC, Borough Road, Middlesbrough, Cleveland TS1 3BA (3,514)—*Dir.*, M. D. Longfield, Ph.D.

TRENT POLYTECHNIC, Burton Street, Nottingham NG1 4BU (7,521).—*Dir.*, Prof. J. O'Neill.

WOLVERHAMPTON POLYTECHNIC, Molineux Street, Wolverhampton WV1 1SB (5,052).—*Dir.*, M. J. Harrison.

POLYTECHNIC OF WALES, Pontypridd, Mid Glamorgan CF37 1DL (4,312).—*Dir.*, J. D. Davies, O.B.E., Ph.D., D.SC.

SCOTTISH CENTRAL INSTITUTIONS

There are no Polytechnics (*see above*) in Scotland but there are 15 Central Institutions which provide most of the advanced full-time courses of higher education there outside the universities and the colleges of education. Most Central Institutions are financed direct by the Scottish Education Department but the three agricultural colleges are funded by the Department of Agriculture and Fisheries for Scotland. Central Institutions are managed by independent boards of governors representing industrial, commercial, professional and educational interests. They are vocationally oriented and do not offer liberal arts courses. Most of their courses lead to degrees awarded by the C.N.A.A. (*see above*) or by neighbouring universities, or to diplomas and certificates granted by the Scottish Vocational Education Council (SCOTVEC) and other bodies. They also provide courses leading to other qualifications.

DUNCAN OF JORDANSTONE COLLEGE OF ART (*B.A., B.Sc., B.Arch.*), Perth Road, Dundee DD1 4HT.—*Principal*, M. Lacome.

DUNDEE COLLEGE OF TECHNOLOGY (*B.A., B.Sc., B.Eng.*), Bell Street, Dundee DD1 1HG.—*Principal*, H. G. Cuming, C.B.E., PH.D.

EAST OF SCOTLAND COLLEGE OF AGRICULTURE, West Mains Road, Edinburgh EH9 3JG.—*Principal*, Prof. P. N. Wilson, PH.D.

EDINBURGH COLLEGE OF ART (*B.A., B.Sc., B.Arch.*), Lauriston Place, Edinburgh EH3 9DF.—*Principal*, J. L. Paterson.

GLASGOW COLLEGE OF TECHNOLOGY (*B.A., B.Sc.*), Cowcaddens Road, Glasgow G4 0BA.—*Director*, Dr. N. G. Meadows.

GLASGOW SCHOOL OF ART (*B.A., B.Arch.*), 167 Renfrew Street, Glasgow G3 6RQ.—*Director*, T. H. Pannell.

NAPIER COLLEGE (*B.A., B.Sc., B.Eng.*), Colinton Road, Edinburgh EH10 5DT.—*Principal*, Dr. W. A. Turmeau.

NORTH OF SCOTLAND COLLEGE OF AGRICULTURE, 581 King Street, Aberdeen AB9 1UD.—*Secretary*, Ms. S. Hannabuss.

PAISLEY COLLEGE OF TECHNOLOGY (*B.A., B.Sc., B.Eng.*), High Street, Paisley PA1 2BE.—*Principal*, R. W. Shaw.

QUEEN MARGARET COLLEGE (*B.A., B.Sc.*), Clerwood Terrace, Edinburgh EH12 8TS.—*Principal*, D. F. Leach.

THE QUEEN'S COLLEGE, GLASGOW (*B.A., B.Sc.*), 1 Park Drive, Glasgow G3 6LP.—*Principal*, G. A. Richardson, PH.D.

ROBERT GORDON'S INSTITUTE OF TECHNOLOGY (*B.A., B.Sc., B.L.E., B.Eng.*), Schoolhill, Aberdeen AB9 1FR.—*Principal*, Dr. D. A. Kennedy.

ROYAL SCOTTISH ACADEMY OF MUSIC AND DRAMA (*B.A.*), 100 Renfrew Street, Glasgow G2 3BD.—*Principal*, P. Ledger, C.B.E.

SCOTTISH COLLEGE OF TEXTILES (*B.A., B.Sc.*), Galashiels, Selkirkshire, TD1 3HF.—*Principal*, J. C. Furniss.

THE WEST OF SCOTLAND AGRICULTURAL COLLEGE, Auchincruive, Ayr KA6 5HW.—*Principal*, Prof. P. C. Thomas, PH.D.

COLLEGES

It is not possible to name here all the colleges offering courses of higher or further education. The list that follows is confined to colleges providing at least one full-time course leading to a *first degree* granted by a university or by the Council for National Academic Awards (C.N.A.A.). It does not include colleges forming part of a polytechnic or a university, nor does it include Scottish central institutions.

After the name of each college the abbreviated title of the appropriate degree or degrees is given, but the very many *other* qualifications for which the colleges also provide courses are not listed.

BATH COLLEGE OF HIGHER EDUCATION (*B.A., B.Sc., B.Ed.*), Newton Park, Bath BA2 9BN.—*Director*, B. L. Gomes da Costa.

BEDFORD COLLEGE OF HIGHER EDUCATION (*B.A., B.Ed.*), Cauldwell Street, Bedford MK42 9AH.—*Director*, Dr. P. Mansell.

BISHOP GROSSETESTE COLLEGE (*B.Ed.*), Lincoln, Lincolnshire LN1 3DY.—*Principal*, L. Marsh.

BOLTON INSTITUTE OF HIGHER EDUCATION (*B.A., B.Sc., B.Ed., B.Eng.*), Deane Road, Bolton BL3 5AB.—*Principal*, Dr. R. Oxtoby.

BRADFORD AND ILKLEY COMMUNITY COLLEGE (*B.A., B.Ed.*), Great Horton Road, Bradford BD7 1AY.—*Principal*, Dr. P. J. Gallagher.

BRETTON HALL COLLEGE OF HIGHER EDUCATION (*B.A., B.Ed.*), West Bretton, Wakefield, W. Yorkshire WF4 4LG.—*Principal*, Dr. J. L. Taylor.

BUCKINGHAMSHIRE COLLEGE OF HIGHER EDUCATION (*B.A., B.Sc.*), Queen Alexandra Road, High Wycombe, Bucks. HP11 2JZ.—*Director*, D. J. Everett, LL.D.

BULMERSHE COLLEGE OF HIGHER EDUCATION (*B.A., B.Ed.*), Woodlands Avenue, Earley, Reading, Berks. RG6 1HY.—*Acting Principal*, B. G. Palmer.

CAMBERWELL SCHOOL OF ART AND CRAFTS (*B.A.*), Peckham Road, London SE5 8UF—*Principal*, A. Harris.

CAMBORNE SCHOOL OF MINES (*B.Eng.*), Pool, Redruth, Cornwall TR15 3SE.—*Principal*, Dr. P. Hackett.

CAMBRIDGESHIRE COLLEGE OF ARTS AND TECHNOLOGY (*B.A., B.Sc.*), East Road, Cambridge CB1 1PT—*Principal*, K. Swinhoe, PH.D.

CENTRAL SCHOOL OF ART AND DESIGN (*B.A.*), Southampton Row, London WC1 4AP.—*Principal*, T. H. Pannell.

CENTRAL SCHOOL OF SPEECH AND DRAMA (B.A., B.Sc., B. Ed), Embassy Theatre, Eton Avenue, London NW3 3HY.—*Acting Principal*, R. S. Fowler.

CHARLOTTE MASON COLLEGE OF EDUCATION (*B.Ed.*), Ambleside, Cumbria LA22 9BB.—*Principal*, J. Thorley, PH.D.

CHELSEA SCHOOL OF ART (*B.A.*), Manresa Road, London SW3 6LS—*Head of School*, J. Barnicoat.

CHESTER COLLEGE (*B.A., B.Sc., B.Ed.*), Cheyney Road, Chester CH1 4BJ.—*Principal*, Rev. E. J. Binks.

CHRIST CHURCH COLLEGE OF HIGHER EDUCATION (*B.A., B.Sc., B.Ed.*), North Holmes Road, Canterbury, Kent CT1 1QU—*Principal*, M. H. A. Berry, T.D.

COLCHESTER INSTITUTE (*B.A.*), Sheepen Road, Colchester, Essex CO3 3LL.—*Director*, J. M. Threlfall.

CRAIGIE COLLEGE OF EDUCATION (*B.Ed.*), Ayr KA8 0SR.—*Principal*, P. C. McNaught.

CREWE AND ALSAGER COLLEGE OF HIGHER EDUCATION (*B.A., B.Sc., B.Ed.*), Crewe Road, Crewe CW1 1DU.—*Director*, Miss B. P. R. Ward, C.B.E.

DARTINGTON COLLEGE OF ARTS (*B.A.*), Totnes, Devon TQ9 6EJ.—*Principal*, C. Roosevelt.

DERBYSHIRE COLLEGE OF HIGHER EDUCATION (*B.Comb.Studs., B.A., B.Sc., B.Eng., B.Ed.*), Kedleston Road, Derby DE3 1GB.—*Director*, J. May, T.D., PH.D.

DORSET INSTITUTE OF HIGHER EDUCATION (*B.A., B.Sc.*), Wallisdown Road, Wallisdown, Poole, Dorset BH12 5BB—*Director*, Dr. B. R. MacManus.

DUNFERMLINE COLLEGE OF PHYSICAL EDUCATION (*B.A., B.Ed.*), Cramond Road North, Edinburgh EH4 6JD.—*Principal*, Miss J. A. Carroll.

EALING COLLEGE OF HIGHER EDUCATION (*B.A., LL.B.*), St. Mary's Road, Ealing, London W5 5RF—*Director*, N. Merritt.

EDGE HILL COLLEGE OF HIGHER EDUCATION (*B.A., B.Sc., B.Ed.*), St. Helens Road, Ormskirk, Lancs. L39 4QP.—*Director*, H. Webster.

ESSEX INSTITUTE OF HIGHER EDUCATION (*B.Sc., B.Ed., LL.B.*), Victoria Road South, Chelmsford, Essex CM1 1LL.—*Director*, M. Salmon.

EXETER COLLEGE OF ART AND DESIGN (*B.A.*), Earl Richards Road North, Exeter EX26AS.—*Principal*, D. Jeremiah, PH.D.

FALMOUTH SCHOOL OF ART AND DESIGN (*B.A.*), Woodlane, Falmouth, Cornwall TR11 4RA—*Principal*, Prof. A. G. Livingston.

GLASGOW COLLEGE OF BUILDING AND PRINTING (*B.Sc.*), 60 North Hanover Street, Glasgow G1 2BP.—*Principal*, D. McEwan.

GLOUCESTERSHIRE COLLEGE OF ARTS AND TECHNOLOGY (*B.A., B.Sc.*), Oxstalls Lane, Gloucester GL2 9HW.—*Principal*, D. Williams.

GWENT COLLEGE OF HIGHER EDUCATION (*B.A., B.Ed., LL.B., B.Eng.*), Clarence Place, Newport, Gwent NP9 0UW.—*Principal*, M. I. Harris, O.B.E.

HARROW COLLEGE OF HIGHER EDUCATION (*B.A.*), Watford Road, Northwick Park, Harrow, Middlesex HA1 3TP.—*Principal*, Dr. H. R. Harris.

HERTFORDSHIRE COLLEGE OF ART AND DESIGN (*B.A.*), 7 Hatfield Road, St. Albans, Herts. AL1 3RS. — *Principal*, C. Hunt.

HUMBERSIDE COLLEGE OF HIGHER EDUCATION (*B.A., B.Sc., B.Eng., B.Ed.*), Cottingham Road, Hull HU6 7RT.—*Director*, J. C. Earls, PH.D.

JEWS' COLLEGE (*B.A.*), Albert Road, Hendon, NW4 2SJ.—*Principal*, Rabbi Dr. J. Sacks.

JORDANHILL COLLEGE OF EDUCATION (*B.A., B.Ed., B.Sc.*), Southbrae Drive, Jordanhill, Glasgow G13 1PP.—*Principal*, Dr. T. R. Bone, C.B.E.

KENT INSTITUTE OF ART AND DESIGN (*B.A.*), New Dover Road, Canterbury; Oakwood Road, Maidstone; Fort Pitt, Rochester.—*Director*, P. Williams.

KIDDERMINSTER COLLEGE (*B.A.*), Hoo Road, Kidderminster, Worcs. DY10 1LX.—*Principal*, Dr. T. Seddon.

KING ALFRED'S COLLEGE OF HIGHER EDUCATION (*B.A., B.Ed.*), Sparkford Road, Winchester SO22 4NR.—*Principal*, J. A. Cranmer.

LABAN CENTRE FOR MOVEMENT AND DANCE, GOLDSMITHS' COLLEGE (*B.A.*), New Cross, London SE14 6NW.—*Director*, Marion North, PH.D.

LA SAINTE UNION COLLEGE OF HIGHER EDUCATION (*B.A., B.Th., B.Ed.*), The Avenue, Southampton SO9 5HB.—*Principal*, Sister Maria Bernard.

COLLEGE OF LIBRARIANSHIP WALES (*B.Lib.*), Llanbadarn Fawr, Aberystwyth SY23 3AS.—*Principal*, F. N. Hogg.

LIVERPOOL INSTITUTE OF HIGHER EDUCATION (*B.A., B.Sc., B.Ed.*), P.O. Box 6, Stand Park Road, Liverpool L16 9JD.—*Rector*, Dr. J. Burke.

LONDON BIBLE COLLEGE (*B.A.*), Green Lane, Northwood, Middlesex HA6 2UW.—*Principal*, M. C. Griffiths.

LONDON COLLEGE OF PRINTING (*B.A.*), Elephant and Castle, London SE1 6SB.—*Head of College and Pro. Rector*, R. Hedley Lewis.

LONDON CONTEMPORARY DANCE SCHOOL (*B.A.*), 16 Flaxman Terrace, WC1H 9AT.—*Principal*, Dr. R. Ralph.

LOUGHBOROUGH COLLEGE OF ART AND DESIGN (*B.A.*), Radmoor, Loughborough, Leics.—*Principal*, R. H. Hampson.

LUTON COLLEGE OF HIGHER EDUCATION (*B.Sc.*), Park Square, Luton LU1 3JU.—*Director*, Dr. A. J. Wood.

MORAY HOUSE COLLEGE OF EDUCATION (*B.Ed.*), Holyrood Road, Edinburgh EH8 8AQ.—*Principal*, G. Kirk.

NENE COLLEGE (*B.A., B.Sc., B.Ed.*), Moulton Park, Northampton NN2 7AL.—*Director*, Dr. E. Ogilvie.

NEW COLLEGE (*B.A., B.Ed.*), Framwellgate Moor Centre, Durham DH1 5ES.—*Principal*, D. L. Turner.

NEWMAN COLLEGE (*B.Ed.*), Genners Lane, Bartley Green, Birmingham B32 3NT.—*Principal*, Joan S. Cuming, PH.D., F.R.G.S.

NORMAL COLLEGE OF HIGHER EDUCATION (*B.A., B.Ed.*), Bangor, North Wales LL57 2PX.—*Principal*, R. Williams.

NORTH CHESHIRE COLLEGE (*B.A.*), Fearnhead, Warrington WA2 0DB.—*Director*, T. R. Keen, PH.D.

NORTH EAST SURREY COLLEGE OF TECHNOLOGY (*B.Sc.*), Reigate Road, Ewell, Surrey KT17 3DS. *Principal*, Dr. J. A. Strickson.

NORTH E. WALES INSTITUTE OF HIGHER EDUCATION (*B.A., B.Sc., B.Ed., B.N.*), Cefn Road, Wrexham, Clwyd LL13 9HL.—*Principal*, Prof. G. O. Phillips, PH.D.

NORTHERN COLLEGE OF EDUCATION (*B.Ed.*). Hilton Place, Aberdeen AB9 1FA; Gardyne Road, Dundee DD5 1NY.—*Principal*, D. A. Adman.

NORTH RIDING COLLEGE (*B.Ed.*), Filey Road, Scarborough, N. Yorkshire YO11 3AZ.—*Principal*, F. W. Wright.

NORWICH CITY COLLEGE OF FURTHER AND HIGHER EDUCATION (*B.A.*), Ipswich Road, Norwich, Norfolk NR2 2LJ.—*Principal*, Dr. J. S. Lewis, R.D., PH.D.

NORWICH SCHOOL OF ART (*B.A.*), St. George Street, Norwich, Norfolk NR3 1BB.—*Principal*, W. G. English.

OAK HILL COLLEGE (*B.A.*), Chase Side, Southgate, N14 4PS.—*Principal*, Rev. G. Bridger.

RAVENSBOURNE COLLEGE OF DESIGN AND COMMUNICATION (*B.A.*), Walden Road, Chislehurst, Kent BR7 5SN.—*Principal*, N. J. Frewing.

RIPON AND YORK ST. JOHN COLLEGE OF HIGHER EDUCATION (*B.A., B.Sc., B.Ed.*), Lord Mayor's Walk, York YO3 7EX.—*Principal*, Dr. G. P. McGregor.

ROEHAMPTON INSTITUTE OF HIGHER EDUCATION (*B.A., B.Sc., B.Ed.*), Senate House, Roehampton Lane, London SW15 5PU.—*Rector*, K. W. Keohane, C.B.E., PH.D.

ROLLE COLLEGE (*B.A., B.Ed.*), Exmouth, Devon EX8 2AT.—*Principal*, M. Preston, PH.D.

ROSE BRUFORD COLLEGE OF SPEECH AND DRAMA (*B.A.*), Lamorbey Park, Burnt Oak Lane, Sidcup, Kent DA15 9DF.—*Principal*, J. N. Benedetti.

ROYAL ACADEMY OF MUSIC (*B.Mus.*), Marylebone Road, London NW1 5HT.—*Principal*, Sir David Lumsden, D.Phil.

ROYAL COLLEGE OF MUSIC (*B.Mus.*), Prince Consort Road, London SW7 2BS.—*Director*, M. G. Matthews, F.R.C.M.

ROYAL NAVAL ENGINEERING COLLEGE (*B.Eng.*), Manadon, Plymouth PL5 3AQ.—*Dean*, Capt. G. C. George.

S. MARTIN'S COLLEGE OF HIGHER EDUCATION (*B.A., B.Ed.*), Bowerham, Lancaster LA1 3JD.—*Principal*, R. Clayton.

ST. ANDREW'S COLLEGE OF EDUCATION (*B.Ed.*), Duntocher Road, Bearsden, Glasgow G61 4QA.—*Principal*, B. J. McGettrick.

ST. JOHN'S SEMINARY (*B.Th.*), Wonersh, Guildford GU5 0QX.—*Rector*, Father P. Smith.

COLLEGE OF ST. MARK AND ST. JOHN (*B.A., B.Ed.*), Derriford Road, Plymouth PL6 8BH.—*Principal*, J. E. Anderson.

ST. MARTIN'S SCHOOL OF ART (*B.A.*), 107 Charing Cross Road, London WC2H 0DU.—*Head*, I. Simpson.

ST. MARY'S COLLEGE (*B.Ed.*), 191 Falls Road, Belfast BT12 6FE.—*Principal*, Very Rev. Canon M. Dallat.

ST. MARY'S COLLEGE (*B.A., B.Sc., B.Ed.*), Strawberry Hill, Twickenham, Middlesex TW1 4SX.—*Principal*, Rev. D. A. Beirne.

COLLEGE OF ST. PAUL AND ST. MARY (*B.A., B.Sc., B.Ed.*), The Park, Cheltenham, Glos. GL50 2RH.—*Principal*, Miss J. O. Trotter.

SALISBURY AND WELLS THEOLOGICAL COLLEGE (*B.Th.*), Salisbury SP1 2EE.—*Principal*, Rev. Canon R. J. A. Askew.

SOUTHAMPTON INSTITUTE OF HIGHER EDUCATION (*B.A., B.Sc.*), East Park Terrace, Southampton SO9 4WW.—*Principal*, J. W. Longden.

SOUTH GLAMORGAN INSTITUTE OF HIGHER EDUCATION (*B.A., B.Sc., B.Ed.*), Western Avenue, Llandaff, Cardiff CF5 2YB.—*Principal*, Dr. E. J. Brent.

SPURGEON'S COLLEGE (*B.A.*), South Norwood Hill, London SE25 6DJ.—*Principal*, Rev. P. Beasley-Murray, PH.D.

STOCKPORT COLLEGE OF TECHNOLOGY (*B.Sc., B.Eng.*), Wellington Road South, Stockport SK1 3UQ. *Principal*, D. A. Humphreys, O.B.E.

STOURBRIDGE COLLEGE OF TECHNOLOGY AND ART (*B.A.*), Hagley Road, Stourbridge, W. Midlands DY8 1QU.—*Principal*, T. H. Jenkins.

STRANMILLIS COLLEGE (*B.Ed.*), Stranmillis Road, Belfast BT9 5DY.—*Principal*, R. J. Rodgers, PH.D.

THEOLOGICAL COLLEGE (*B.Th.*), Chichester PO19 1SG.—*Principal*, Rev. Canon J. W. Hind.

TRINITY AND ALL SAINTS' COLLEGE (*B.A., B.Sc., B.Ed.*), Brownberrie Lane, Horsforth, Leeds LS18 5HD.—*Principal*, Dr. H. M. Hallaway.

TRINITY COLLEGE (*B.A.*), Stoke Hill, Bristol BS9 1JP.—*Principal*, (vacant).

TRINITY COLLEGE (*B.A., B.Ed.*), Carmarthen, Dyfed, SA31 3EP.—*Principal*, D. C. Jones-Davies.

TRINITY COLLEGE OF MUSIC (*B.Mus.*), 11–13 Mandeville Place, London W1M 6AQ.—*Principal*, M. Davies, C.B.E.

WATFORD COLLEGE (*B.Sc.*), Hempstead Road, Watford, WD1 3EZ.—*Principal*, T. J. Howard, PH.D.

WELSH COLLEGE OF MUSIC AND DRAMA (*B.A., B.Ed.*), Castle Grounds, Cathays Park, Cardiff CF1 3ER.—*Principal*, P. Fletcher.

WEST GLAMORGAN INSTITUTE OF HIGHER EDUCATION (*B.A., B.Ed.*), Townhill Road, Swansea SA2 0UT.—*Principal*, G. Stockdale, PH.D.

WESTHILL COLLEGE (*B.Ed.*), Hamilton Building, Weoley Park Road, Selly Oak, Birmingham B29 6LL.—*Principal*, Rev. G. Benfield.

WEST LONDON INSTITUTE OF HIGHER EDUCATION (*B.A., B.Sc., B.Ed.*), Lancaster House, Borough Road, Isleworth, Middlesex TW7 5DU.—*Principal*, J. E. Kane, PH.D.

WEST MIDLANDS COLLEGE OF HIGHER EDUCATION (*B.Ed.*), Gorway, Walsall WS1 3BD.—*Principal*, T. J. Cox.

WESTMINSTER COLLEGE (*B.A., B.Ed.*), North Hinksey, Oxford OX2 9AT.—*Principal*, Rev. Dr. K. B. Wilson.

WEST SURREY COLLEGE OF ART AND DESIGN (*B.A.*), Falkner Road, The Hart, Farnham, Surrey GU9 7DS.—*Principal*, N. J. Taylor.

WEST SUSSEX INSTITUTE OF HIGHER EDUCATION (*B.A., B.Ed.*), The Dome, Upper Bognor Road, Bognor Regis, West Sussex PO21 1HR.—*Director*, J. F. Wyatt.

WIMBLEDON SCHOOL OF ART (*B.A.*), Merton Hall Road, Wimbledon, London SW19 3QA.—*Principal*, Dr. L. Massey.

WINCHESTER SCHOOL OF ART (*B.A.*), Park Avenue, Winchester, Hampshire SO23 8DL.—*Principal*, D. C. Sherlock.

WORCESTER COLLEGE OF HIGHER EDUCATION (*B.A., B.Sc., B.Ed.*), Henwick Grove, Worcester WR2 6AJ.—*Principal*, D. R. Shadbolt, D.Phil.

GRANTS FOR STUDENTS

Post-School

Students in England and Wales who plan to take a full-time or sandwich course of further study after leaving school may be eligible for a grant from their local education authority (L.E.A.). Enquiries should be made to the authority in the area in which the student normally lives. There is a list on pages 513–515. Application forms are available from schools and L.E.A.s. Completed forms should be sent to the appropriate L.E.A. as early as possible. For courses beginning in the autumn, applications should, however, not be made earlier than the preceding January.

Types of grant. Grants are of two kinds: mandatory and discretionary. *Mandatory grants* (387,361 in 1984–85) are those which L.E.A.s *must* pay to students who are attending what are called "designated courses" and who can satisfy certain other conditions; such a grant is normally to enable the student to attend only one designated course and there is no general entitlement to an award for any particular number of years. *Discretionary grants* (47,138 full value awards in 1984–85) are those for which each L.E.A. has discretion to decide its own policy.

Designated courses include those which are *full-time or sandwich* and lead to a university or C.N.A.A. (*see* p. 510) degree; the diploma of higher education; the higher national diploma of the Business & Technician Education Council; and initial teacher-training courses including courses for the postgraduate certificate in education and the art teachers' certificate or diploma.

Eligibility. To be eligible for a grant, students admitted to a designated course must, *inter alia*:—

(a) have been ordinarily resident in the United Kingdom for the three years immediately preceding the academic year in which the course begins. (If the student was absent because his or her family was temporarily employed abroad, or if the student was in the UK primarily for full-time education (and would normally be elsewhere), the L.E.A. should be consulted for advice).

(b) have not previously attended a course of advanced further education of more than two years' duration. Attendance for up to one term on such a course is usually disregarded;

(c) apply for the grant before the end of the first term of the course.

Condition (b) above does not apply to students wishing to take a course leading to a postgraduate certificate in education or the art teachers' certificate.

Value. A means-tested maintenance grant, usually paid once a term through the university or college office, covers periods of attendance during term and the Christmas and Easter vacations but not the summer vacation. It is subject to deduction on account of the student's own income and his/her parents' or spouse's income. Tuition fees in full are usually paid direct to the university or college by the L.E.A.

Cost. Local authority expenditure on student maintenance in 1984–85 was £546 million.

In Scotland corresponding awards are made by the Scottish Education Department and in Northern Ireland by Education and Library Boards.

Postgraduate awards

A number of schemes of postgraduate bursaries or studentships for U.K. residents are administered by the Department of Education and Science and the five research councils (agricultural and food, economic and social science, medical, natural environment, science and engineering). 15,417 awards were made in 1984–85.

LOCAL EDUCATION AUTHORITIES

English and Welsh Counties

AVON, P.O. Box 57, Avon House North, St. James Barton, Bristol BS99 7EB.—*Director*, P. Coleman.

BEDFORDSHIRE, County Hall, Bedford MK42 9AP.—*Chief Education Officer*, D. P. J. Browning, C.B.E.

BERKSHIRE, Shire Hall, Shinfield Park, Reading RG2 9XE.—*Director*, P. E. Edwards.

BUCKINGHAMSHIRE, County Hall, Aylesbury HP20 1UZ.—*Chief Education Officer*, C. M. Garrett.

CAMBRIDGESHIRE, Castle Court, Shire Hall, Cambridge CB3 0AP.—*Chief Education Officer*, G. H. Morris.

CHESHIRE, County Hall, Chester CH1 1SQ.—*Director*, N. J. Fitton.

CLEVELAND, Woodlands Road, Middlesbrough TS1 3BN.—*County Education Officer*, A. H. R. Calderwood.

CLWYD, Shire Hall, Mold CH7 6NB.—*Director*, H. K. Evans.

CORNWALL, County Hall, Truro TR1 3BA.—*Secretary for Education*, N. W. Barr.

CUMBRIA, 5 Portland Square, Carlisle CA1 1PU.—*Director*, P. C. Boulter.

DERBYSHIRE, County Offices, Matlock DE4 3AG.—*Director*, J. G. Evans.

DEVON, County Hall, Exeter EX2 4QD.—*Chief Education Officer*, J. G. Owen, C.B.E.

DORSET, County Hall, Dorchester DT1 1XJ.—*County Education Officer*, P. L. Gedling.

DURHAM, County Hall, Durham DH1 5UJ.—*Director*, K. B. Grimshaw.

DYFED, Pibwrlwyd, Carmarthen SA31 2NH.—*Director*, W. J. Phillips.

ESSEX, Threadneedle House, Market Road, Chelmsford CM1 1LD.—*County Education Officer*, J. O. Morris.

GLOUCESTERSHIRE, Shire Hall, Gloucester GL1 2TP.—*Chief Education Officer*, K. D. Anderson.

GWENT, County Hall, Cwmbran NP44 2XG.—*Director*, G. V. Drought.

GWYNEDD, County Offices, Shirehall Street, Caernarfon LL55 1SH.—*Director*, G. E. Humphreys.

HAMPSHIRE, The Castle, Winchester SO23 8UJ.—*County Education Officer*, R. D. Clark.

HEREFORD AND WORCESTER, Castle Street, Worcester WR1 3AG.—*County Education Officer*, J. W. Turnbull.

HERTFORDSHIRE, County Hall, Hertford SG13 8DF.—*County Education Officer*, D. Fisher, C.B.E.

HUMBERSIDE, County Hall, Beverley HU17 9BA.—*Director*, J. Bower, C.B.E.

ISLE OF WIGHT, County Hall, Newport PO30 1UD.—*County Education Officer*, R. O. Burton.

KENT, Springfield, Maidstone ME14 2LJ.—*County Education Officer*, B. Oatley.

LANCASHIRE, County Hall, Preston PR1 8RJ.—*Chief Education Officer*, A. J. Collier.

LEICESTERSHIRE, County Hall, Glenfield, Leicester LE3 8RF.—*Director*, K. H. Wood-Allum.

LINCOLNSHIRE, County Offices, Newland, Lincoln LN1 1YQ.—*Director*, D. G. Esp.

MID GLAMORGAN, County Hall, Cardiff CF1 3NF.—*Director*, E. Roberts.

NORFOLK, County Hall, Norwich NR1 2DH.—*County Education Officer*, M. H. Edwards.

NORTHAMPTONSHIRE, Northampton House, Northampton.—*County Education Officer*, J. R. Atkinson.

NORTHUMBERLAND, County Hall, Morpeth NE61 2EF.—*Director*, C. C. Tipple.

NOTTINGHAMSHIRE, County Hall, West Bridgford, Nottingham NG2 7QP.—*Director*, A. J. Fox.

OXFORDSHIRE, Macclesfield House, New Road, Oxford OX1 1NA.—*Chief Education Officer*, T. R. P. Brighouse.

POWYS, The Lindens, Spa Road, Llandrindod Wells LD1 5HA.—*Director*, R. W. Bevan.

SHROPSHIRE, Shirehall, Abbey Foregate, Shrewsbury SY2 6ND.—*County Education Officer*, J. Boyers.

SOMERSET, County Hall, Taunton TA1 4DY.—*Director*, (vacant).

SOUTH GLAMORGAN, County Offices, Kingsway, Cardiff CF1 4JG.—*Director*, D. Orrell.

STAFFORDSHIRE, County Education Offices, Tipping Street, Stafford ST16 2DH.—*Chief Education Officer*, Dr. P. J. Hunter.

SUFFOLK, St. Andrew House, County Hall, Ipswich IP4 1LJ.—*County Education Officer*, T. R. Cornthwaite.

SURREY, County Hall, Kingston upon Thames KT1 2DJ.—*County Education Officer*, M. C. Pinchin.

SUSSEX (East), County Hall, St. Anne's Crescent, Lewes BN7 1SG.—*County Education Officer*, J. A. Carter.

SUSSEX (West), County Hall, Chichester PO19 1RF.—*Director*, R. D. C. Bunker.

WARWICKSHIRE, P.O. Box 24, 22 Northgate Street, Warwick CV34 4SR.—*County Education Officer*, M. L. Ridger.

WEST GLAMORGAN, County Hall, Swansea SA1 3SN.—*Director*, J. Beale.

WILTSHIRE, County Hall, Trowbridge BA14 8JN.—*Chief Education Officer*, I. M. Slocombe.

YORKSHIRE, NORTH, County Hall, Northallerton DL7 8AD.—*County Education Officer*, F. F. Evans.

London

INNER LONDON EDUCATION AUTHORITY.—*Controller of Education*, W. H. Stubbs.

Education Officers

BARKING, Town Hall, Barking, Essex IG11 7LU.—A. W. Bush.

BARNET, Town Hall, Friern Barnet N11 3DL.—N. M. Gill.

BEXLEY, Town Hall, Crayford, Kent DA1 4EN.—*Director*, (vacant).

BRENT, Chesterfield House, Park Lane, Wembley, Middx. HA9 7RW.—*Director*, M. Stoten.

BROMLEY, Town Hall, Tweedy Road, Bromley, Kent BR1 1RG.—G. Grainge.

CROYDON, Taberner House, Park Lane, CR9 1TP.—*Director*, D. Naismith.

EALING, Hadley House, 79 Uxbridge Road, W5 5SU.—R. J. Hartles, C.B.E.

ENFIELD, P.O. Box 56, Civic Centre, Silver Street, Enfield EN1 3XQ.—*Director*, G. Hutchinson.

HARINGEY, 48 Station Road, Wood Green, N22 4TY.—*Director*, R. L. Jones.

HARROW, Civic Centre, P.O. Box 22, Harrow HA1 2UW.—*Director*, J. F. Mann.

HAVERING, Mercury House, Mercury Gardens, Romford, Essex RM1 3DR.—*Director*, B. H. Laister.

HILLINGDON, Civic Centre, High Street, Uxbridge, Middx. UB8 1UW.—*Director*, C. J. Rundle (*acting*).

HOUNSLOW, Civic Centre, Lampton Road, Hounslow, Middx. TW3 4DN.—*Director*, J. D. Trickett.

KINGSTON UPON THAMES, Guildhall, KT1 1EU.—*Director*, R. J. McCloy.

MERTON, Crown House, London Road, Morden, Surrey SM4 5DX.—*Director*, R. Davies.

NEWHAM, The Broadway, Stratford, E.15.—*Director*, A. Lockhart.

REDBRIDGE, 255–259 High Road, Ilford, Essex IG1 1NN.—K. G. M. Ratcliffe.

RICHMOND UPON THAMES, Regal House, London Road, Twickenham, Middx. TW1 3QB.—*Director*, I. Waters.

SUTTON, The Grove, Carshalton, Surrey SM5 3AL.—*Director*, C. Melville.

WALTHAM FOREST, Municipal Offices, High Road, E10 5QJ.—*Director*, (vacant).

Metropolitan District Councils

BARNSLEY, Berneslai Close, S70 2TA.—*Education Officer*, T. Brooks.

BIRMINGHAM, Margaret Street, B3 3BU.—*Chief Education Officer*, J. M. Crawford.

BOLTON, Paderborn House, Civic Centre, BL1 1JW.—*Director*, B. Hughes.

BRADFORD, Provincial House, Bradford BD1 1NP.—*Director*, W. R. Knight, C.B.E.

BURY, Athenaeum House, Market Street, BL9 0BN.— *Director,* M. Gray.

CALDERDALE.—Northgate House, Northgate, Halifax HX1 1UN.—*Chief Education Officer,* A. Pickvance.

COVENTRY, New Council Offices, Earl Street, CV1 5RR.—*Education Officer,* C. Farmer.

DONCASTER, Princegate, Doncaster.—*Director,* M. J. Pass.

DUDLEY, Westox House, 1 Trinity Road, Dudley DY1 1JB.—*Chief Education Officer,* R. K. Westerby.

GATESHEAD, Civic Centre, Regent Street, NE8 1HH.—*Education Officer,* H. Cubitt.

KIRKLEES, Oldgate House, 2 Oldgate, Huddersfield HD1 6QW.—*Education Officer,* P. G. Davies.

KNOWSLEY, Huyton Hey Road, Huyton, Merseyside L36 5YH.—*Education Officer,* A. Culley.

LEEDS, Merrion House, Merrion Centre, LS2 8JY.— *Director,* R. S. Johnson, C.B.E.

LIVERPOOL, 14 Sir Thomas Street, L1 6BJ.—*Education Officer,* K. A. Antcliffe.

MANCHESTER, Cumberland House, Crown Square, M60 3BB.—*Chief Education Officer,* G. Hainsworth.

NEWCASTLE UPON TYNE, Civic Centre, NE99 2BM.— *Director,* M. Davies.

NORTH TYNESIDE, The Chase, North Shields NE29 0RW.—*Education Officer,* J. F. Partington.

OLDHAM, Old Town Hall, Chadderton, OL9 6NE.— *Education Officer,* Dr. W. R. Kneen.

ROCHDALE, Municipal Offices, Smith Street, Rochdale.—*Chief Education Officer,* A. N. Naylor.

ROTHERHAM, Norfolk House, Walker Place, Rotherham.—*Education Officer,* K. Snowden.

ST. HELENS, Century House, Hardshaw Street, St. Helens.—*Education Officer,* N. D. Nelson.

SALFORD, Chapel Street, M3 5LT.—*Education Officer,* B. Grady.

SANDWELL, P.O. Box 41, Shaftesbury House, 402 High Street, West Bromwich B70 9LT.—*Education Officer,* G. A. Brinsdon.

SEFTON, Town Hall, Bootle, Merseyside L20 7AE.— *Education Officer,* J. A. Marsden.

SHEFFIELD, P.O. Box 67, Leopold Street, S1 1RJ.— *Education Officer,* W. S. Walton.

SOLIHULL, P.O. Box 20, Council House, B91 3QU.— *Education Officer,* M. E. Sweet.

SOUTH TYNESIDE, Town Hall, Jarrow NE32 3LE.— *Director,* K. Stringer.

STOCKPORT, Town Hall, Wellington Road, SK1 3XE.—*Director of Education,* J. E. Hendy.

SUNDERLAND, P.O. Box 101, Town Hall and Civic Centre, SR2 7DN.—*Education Officer,* J. Hall.

TAMESIDE, Council Offices, Wellington Road, Ashton-under-Lyne OL6 6DL.—*Education Officer,* G. Mayall.

TRAFFORD, P.O. Box 19, Town Hall, Sale M33 1YR.— *Education Officer,* D. J. Hatfield.

WAKEFIELD, 8 Bond Street, WF1 2QL.—*Education Officer,* W. H. Wright.

WALSALL, Civic Centre, Darwall Street, WS1 1DQ.— *Director,* Mrs D. Tuck.

WIGAN, Gateway House, Standishgate, WN1 1XL.— *Director of Education,* J. K. Hampson.

WIRRAL, Municipal Offices, Cleveland Street, Birkenhead L41 6NH.—*Director,* M. G. Nichol.

WOLVERHAMPTON, Civic Centre, St. Peter's Square, WV1 1RR.—*Director,* P. N. Harris.

Scottish Regional and Islands Councils

BORDERS, Regional Headquarters, Newtown St. Boswells, Melrose TD6 0SA.—*Director,* J. McLean.

CENTRAL, Viewforth, Stirling FK8 2ET.—*Director,* I. Collie.

DUMFRIES AND GALLOWAY, 30 Edinburgh Road, Dumfries DG1 1JQ.—*Director,* W. C. Fordyce.

FIFE, Fife House, North Street, Glenrothes KY7 5LT.—*Director,* M. More.

GRAMPIAN, Woodhill House, Westburn Road, Aberdeen AB9 2LU.—*Director,* J. A. D. Michie.

HIGHLAND, Regional Buildings, Glenurquhart Road, Inverness IV3 5NX.—*Director,* Dr. C. E. Stewart.

LOTHIAN, 40 Torphichen Street, Edinburgh EH3 8JJ.—*Director,* W. D. C. Semple.

ORKNEY, Council Offices, Kirkwall KW15 1NY.— *Director,* R. L. Henderson.

SHETLAND, Brentham House, Harbour Street, Lerwick.—*Director,* R. A. B. Barnes.

STRATHCLYDE, Strathclyde House, 20 India Street, Glasgow G2 4PF.—*Director,* E. Miller.

TAYSIDE, Tayside House, 28 Crichton Street, Dundee DD1 3RA.—*Director,* D. G. Robertson.

WESTERN ISLES, Council Offices, Sandwick Road, Stornoway, Isle of Lewis PA87 2BW.—*Director,* N. R. Galbraith.

Northern Ireland

Education and Library Boards

BELFAST, Board Headquarters, 40 Academy Street, Belfast BT1 2NG.—*Chief Officer,* T. G. J. Moag.

NORTH-EASTERN, County Hall, 182 Galgorm Road, Ballymena, Co. Antrim BT42 1HN.—*Chief Officer,* R. A. Hamilton.

SOUTH-EASTERN, 18 Windsor Avenue, Belfast BT9 6EF.—*Chief Officer,* T. Nolan.

SOUTHERN, 3 Charlemont Place, The Mall, Armagh BT61 9AX.—*Chief Officer,* J. G. Kelly.

WESTERN, 1 Hospital Road, Omagh, Co. Tyrone BT79 0AW.—*Chief Officer,* M. H. F. Murphy, O.B.E.

Channel Islands, etc.

GUERNSEY, P.O. Box 32, La Couperderie, St. Peter Port.—*Director,* M. D. Hutchings.

JERSEY, P.O. Box 142, Highlands, St. Saviour.— *Director,* J. S. Rodhouse.

ISLE OF MAN, Government Offices, Bucks Road, Douglas.—*Director,* J. A. Davies.

ISLES OF SCILLY, Town Hall, St. Mary's TR21 0LW.— *Secretary for Education,* I. Glover.

ADULT EDUCATION

'Adult Education' covers a broad spectrum of educational activities ranging from non-vocational courses of general interest, through the acquiring of special vocational skills needed in industry or commerce, to study for a degree at the Open University. It has been defined as "the provision of non-formal and informal education for adult people: that is, courses excluding the normal range of provision in colleges and universities for young people immediately following the statutory school leaving age, but including the full range of recurrent educational opportunities designed for people of more mature years, and related to any or all aspects of adult life".

Providers. Courses specifically for adults are provided by many bodies. They include local education authorities (regional authorities in Scotland, education and library boards in Northern Ireland), residential colleges, the Open University, the extra-mural departments of other universities (and Birkbeck College of the University of London), the BBC, ITV and local radio stations, and various voluntary bodies. The local education authorities operate through 'area' adult education centres, institutes or colleges and the adult studies departments of colleges of further education. The Open University, in partnership with the BBC, provides distance teaching leading to ordinary or honours first degrees, and also offers post-experience and higher degree courses. More than 30 other universities have extra-mural or adult education or continuing education departments which serve their local areas or regions. The BBC has a Continuing Education Advisory Council and the Independent Broadcasting Authority an Educational Advisory Council which has an Adult Education Section. Of the voluntary bodies the biggest and best-known is the Workers' Educational Association (*see below*). There are also the training and retraining facilities provided under the aegis of the Manpower Services Commission and of PICKUP (Professional, Industrial and Commercial Updating Programme).

Courses. Although lengths vary, most courses are part-time. Long-term residential colleges (*see below*) provide full-time courses lasting one or two years. Adult education courses are of two main kinds – those involving face-to-face teaching with teacher and student in the same room and the distance teaching provided through TV and radio, and/or correspondence courses.

Numbers. There are no comprehensive statistics covering all aspects of adult education but it is known that enrolments in November 1985 at L.E.A. adult education in England were about 1,418 million. During 1986, the Open University had about 66,200 students studying for first degrees, 1,000 working for higher degrees, 11,500 associate students and 71,000 other students. In 1984–85, 307,631 students attended courses of liberal adult education provided by university extra-mural departments and the W.E.A. in England and Wales.

NATIONAL INSTITUTE OF ADULT CONTINUING EDUCATION (England and Wales), 19B De Montfort Street, Leicester LE1 7GE. The institute provides a means of consultation and co-operation between all the interests in adult continuing education. It provides information and advice to organizations and individuals on all aspects of adult continuing education; it conducts enquiries into problems of adult continuing education; organizes conferences and other meetings and issues publications. The Institute manages a number of agencies and special units which benefit from funding from the D.E.S. and the Welsh Office, including the Adult Literacy and Basic Skills Unit. It also manages a major part of the D.E.S./W.O.E.D. programme for the adult unemployed (REPLAN).—*Dir.*, A. K. Stock.

SCOTTISH INSTITUTE OF ADULT AND CONTINUING EDUCATION, 30 Rutland Square, Edinburgh EH1 2BW. The institute is a national voluntary organization which aims to advance education amongst adults. It makes policy, conducts research, provides information, arranges conferences, and produces publications.—*Dir.*, Dr. Elisabeth Gerver.

UNIVERSITIES COUNCIL FOR ADULT AND CONTINUING EDUCATION, Dept. of Adult Education, University of Leicester, University Road, Leicester LE1 7RH. The council, consisting of one representative from each university, was established in 1947 for the interchange of ideas and the formulation of common policies on extra-mural education.—*Hon. Secretary*, Prof. W. Forster.

WORKERS EDUCATIONAL ASSOCIATION, Temple House, 9 Upper Berkeley Street, London W1H 8BY. Founded in 1903, the W.E.A. consists of about 900 branches and nearly 1,500 affiliated educational and workers' organisations. Non-sectarian and non-party-political, it aims to stimulate and to satisfy the demands of workers for education, and to further the advancement of education generally. The W.E.A. is organised in 20 districts. The D.E.S. and L.E.A.s make grants towards expenses.—*Gen. Sec.*, R. Lochrie.

RESIDENTIAL COLLEGES FOR ADULT EDUCATION

Long term:
The eight long-term colleges listed below offer one- and two-year courses for adults and are grant-aided by the Department of Education and Science, the Welsh Office or the Scottish Office. Students are eligible for grants under an Adult Education State Bursaries Scheme.

COLEG HARLECH, Harlech, Gwynedd LL46 2PU. (For men and women).—*Warden*, J. W. England.

CO-OPERATIVE COLLEGE, Stanford Hall, Loughborough, Leics. LE12 5QR (For men and women).—*Principal*, Dr. R. Houlton.

FIRCROFT COLLEGE, 1018 Bristol Road, Selly Oak, Birmingham B29 6LH. (For men and women).—*Principal*, B. J. Wicker.

HILLCROFT COLLEGE, Surbiton, Surrey KT6 6DF. (For women).—*Principal*, Ms. P. J. Lambert.

NEWBATTLE ABBEY COLLEGE, Dalkeith, Midlothian EH22 3LL. (For men and women).—*Principal*, A. D. Reid.

NORTHERN COLLEGE, Wentworth Castle, Stainborough, Barnsley, South Yorks. S75 3ET. (For men and women).—*Principal*, R. H. Fryer.

PLATER COLLEGE, Pullens Lane, Oxford OX3 0DT. (For men and women).—*Principal*, D. G. Chiles.

RUSKIN COLLEGE, Oxford OX1 2HE. (For men and women).—*Principal*, J. D. Hughes.

Short term:
The short-term colleges and centres listed below offer residential courses, lasting from a day or two to two or three weeks, in a wide range of subjects. L.E.A.s directly sponsor many of the colleges while others are sponsored by universities or voluntary organizations. A booklet listing such *Residential Short Courses* is published by the National Institute of Adult Education (see above).

ALSTON HALL COLLEGE, Longridge, nr. Preston PR3 3BP; AVONCROFT COLLEGE, Stoke Heath, Bromsgrove, Worcs. B60 4JS; BEAMISH HALL RESIDENTIAL COLLEGE FOR ADULT EDUCATION, Stanley, Co. Durham DH9 0RG; BELSTEAD HOUSE, Belstead, Ipswich, Suffolk IP8 3NA; BENSLOW MUSIC TRUST, Little Benslow Hills, Ibberson Way, Hitchin SG4 9RB; BRAZIERS ADULT COLLEGE, Ipsden, Oxford OX9 6AN; BURTON MANOR, Burton, South Wirral, Cheshire L64 5SJ; BURWELL HOUSE RESIDENTIAL CENTRE, North St., Burwell, Cambridge CB5 0BA; DEBDEN HOUSE, Debden Green, Loughton, Essex IG10 2PA; DENMAN COLLEGE, Marcham, Nr. Abingdon, Oxon. OX13 6NW; DEVON CENTRE FOR CONTINUING EDUCATION, Dartington College of Arts, Totnes; DILLINGTON COLLEGE FOR ADULT EDUCATION, Ilminster, Somerset TA19 9DT; DYFFRYN HOUSE, St. Nicholas, nr. Cardiff CF5 6SU; EARNLEY CONCOURSE, nr. Chichester, Sussex PO20 7JL; EAST-HAMPTEAD PARK EDUCATIONAL CENTRE, Wokingham, Berks. RG11 3DF; GRAFHAM WATER RESIDENTIAL CENTRE, West Perry, Huntingdon PE18 0BX; GRANTLEY HALL, Ripon, N. Yorks.; HAWKWOOD ADULT COLLEGE, Stroud, Glos. GL6 7QW; HIGHAM HALL, Bassenthwaite Lake, Cockermouth, Cumbria CA13 9SH; THE HILL, Pen-y-Pound, Abergavenny, Gwent NP7 7RP; HOLLY ROYDE COLLEGE, West Didsbury, Manchester M20 9JP; HORNCASTLE RESIDENTIAL COLLEGE, Horncastle, Lincs. LN9 6BW; KINGSGATE HOUSE, Convent

Road, Broadstairs, Kent CT10 3PX; KNUSTON HALL, Irchester, Wellingborough, Northants. NN9 7EU; LANCASHIRE COLLEGE FOR ADULT EDUCATION, Southport Road, Chorley PR7 1NB; LOSEHILL HALL, Castleton, Derbys. S30 2WB; MADINGLEY HALL, Madingley, Cambridge CB3 8AQ; MARYLAND, Woburn, Milton Keynes MK17 9JD; THE OLD RECTORY, Fittleworth, Pulborough, Sussex RH20 1HU; PENDRELL HALL, Codsall Wood, Wolverhampton WV8 1QP; REWLEY HOUSE, 1 Wellington Square, Oxford OX1 2JA; THEOBALDS COLLEGE, Waltham Cross, Herts. EN7 5HW; URCHFONT MANOR, nr. Devizes, Wilts.; WANSFELL COLLEGE, Theydon Bois, Epping, Essex CM16 7LF; WEDGWOOD MEMORIAL COLLEGE, Barlaston, Stoke-on-Trent, Staffs. ST12 9DG; WENSUM LODGE, King Street, Norwich, Norfolk NR1 1QW; WEST DEAN COLLEGE, West Dean, Chichester, Sussex; WESTHAM HOUSE COLLEGE, Barford, Warwick. CV35 8DP.

PROFESSIONAL EDUCATION
(excluding *postgraduate* study)

NOTE.—References to courses at universities, polytechnics and colleges in the sections following are not claimed to be comprehensive and cover only *full-time* courses leading to *first degrees*. Full lists appear in the new *University Entrance: the Official Guide* and in the *C.N.A.A. Directory of First Degree and Diploma of Higher Education Courses.* Both are produced annually.

POSTGRADUATE STUDY AND RESEARCH are not treated here. All universities provide facilities for postgraduate study and research. They co-operatively issue each year the *British Universities' Guide to Graduate Study* which lists all "taught courses" but does not cover research. In general, universities can provide facilities for research in at least some aspects of all the subjects in which first degrees are offered.

Courses at postgraduate level leading to master's-level degrees of the Council for National Academic Awards (C.N.A.A.) are offered by polytechnics and other colleges. They are listed in the C.N.A.A.'s annual *Directory of Postgraduate and Post-Experience Courses.* Research is also undertaken at polytechnics leading to an M. Phil. or Ph.D. granted by the C.N.A.A.

ACCOUNTANCY

(*See also* Business, Management and Administration).

First Degrees in *Accounting* or *Accountancy* are granted by the Universities of Aberdeen, Belfast, Birmingham, Dundee, East Anglia (also *Computerized Accountancy*), Exeter, Glasgow, Hull, Kent, Liverpool, Stirling, Strathclyde, Ulster and Wales (Aberystwyth and Cardiff University Colleges and Institute of Science and Technology). At several other universities one of these subjects can be combined with, e.g., Financial Administration, Finance or Economics.

Courses leading to first degrees in *Accounting, Accountancy* or *Accounting and Finance* granted by the C.N.A.A. are provided by City of Birmingham Polytechnic, Brighton Polytechnic, Bristol Polytechnic, City of London Polytechnic, Dorset Institute of Higher Education (*Financial Services*), Dundee College of Technology, Ealing College of Higher Education, Glasgow College of Technology, Huddersfield Polytechnic, Humberside College of Higher Education, Kingston Polytechnic, Lancashire Polytechnic, Leeds Polytechnic, Liverpool Polytechnic, Manchester Polytechnic, Middlesex Polytechnic, Napier College, Newcastle upon Tyne Polytechnic, North East London Polytechnic (*Finance with Accounting*), Polytechnic of North London, Plymouth Polytechnic, Portsmouth Polytechnic, Sheffield City Polytechnic (*Accounting and Management Control*), Trent Polytechnic and Polytechnic of Wales.

Professional Bodies.—The main bodies granting membership on examination after a period of practical work are:

INSTITUTE OF CHARTERED ACCOUNTANTS IN ENGLAND AND WALES, P.O. Box 433, Moorgate Place, EC2P 2BJ.—*Dir.*, E. J. D. Warne, C.B.

INSTITUTE OF CHARTERED ACCOUNTANTS OF SCOTLAND, 27 Queen Street, Edinburgh EH2 1LA.—*Sec.*, E. Tait, M.B.E.

CHARTERED ASSOCIATION OF CERTIFIED ACCOUNTANTS, 29 Lincolns Inn Fields, WC2A 3EE.—*Sec.*, Ms. S. J. Small.

CHARTERED INSTITUTE OF MANAGEMENT ACCOUNTANTS, 63 Portland Place, W1N 4AB.—*Sec.*, T. B. Degenhardt, O.B.E.

CHARTERED INSTITUTE OF PUBLIC FINANCE AND ACCOUNTANCY, 3 Robert Street, WC2N 6BH.—*Sec.*, N. P. Hepworth, O.B.E.

ACTUARIAL SCIENCE

First Degrees in *Actuarial Science* are granted by the City University and the Universities of Kent and London (London School of Economics and Political Science); in *Actuarial Mathematics and Statistics* by Heriot-Watt University, and in *Mathematics with Actuarial Studies* by the University of Southampton.

Two professional organizations grant qualifications after examination:

INSTITUTE OF ACTUARIES, Staple Inn Hall, High Holborn, WC1V 7QJ.—*Sec. Gen.*, C. D. A. Mackie.

FACULTY OF ACTUARIES IN SCOTLAND, 23 St. Andrew Square, Edinburgh EH2 1AQ.—*Sec.*, W. W. Mair.

AERONAUTICS
and Aeronautical Engineering

First Degrees in *Aeronautical Engineering* are granted by the Universities of Bath, Belfast, Bristol, Cambridge, the City University, the Universities of Glasgow (also *Avionics*), London (Imperial College of Science and Technology, Queen Mary College, also *Avionics—Aeronautical/Electrical*), Loughborough (*Aeronautical Engineering and Design*), Manchester, Salford and Southampton (*Aeronautics and Astronautics* and *Aerospace Systems Engineering*) and in *Air Transport Engineering* by the City University.

Courses leading to first degrees in *Aeronautical Engineering* granted by the C.N.A.A. are provided by Hatfield Polytechnic and Kingston Polytechnic (*Aerospace Engineering*).

AGRICULTURE

First Degrees in *Agriculture* or *Agricultural Science(s)* are granted by the Universities of Aberdeen, Belfast, Edinburgh, Glasgow, Leeds, London (Wye College), Newcastle upon Tyne, Nottingham, Reading and Wales (University Colleges of Aberystwyth and Bangor); in *Agricultural Technology and Management* by Cranfield Institute of Technology (Silsoe College); and in *Horticulture* by Bath, London (Wye College), Nottingham, Reading and Strathclyde.

Courses leading to first degrees in *Agriculture* granted by the C.N.A.A. are provided by Plymouth Polytechnic/Seale Hayne College and (*Agricultural Technology*) Wolverhampton Polytechnic/Harper Adams Agricultural College.

ARCHÆOLOGY

First Degrees in *Archæology* or *Archæological Sciences/Studies* are granted by the Universities of Belfast, Bradford, Cambridge, Durham, Edinburgh, Exeter, Glasgow, Leicester, Liverpool, London (University College), Newcastle upon Tyne, Nottingham, Reading, Southampton, Wales (University College Cardiff, also *Archaeological Conservation*), and York. At several other universities archæology can be combined with another subject, e.g. ancient history, classics or anthropology.

ARCHITECTURE

(*See also* Building, and Town and Country Planning).

First Degrees in *Architecture/Architectural Studies* are granted by the universities of Bath, Belfast, Cambridge, Dundee, Edinburgh, Glasgow, Heriot-Watt, Liverpool, London (University College), Manchester, Newcastle, Nottingham, Sheffield, Strathclyde, Wales (UWIST, Cardiff).

Courses leading to first degrees in *Architecture/ Architectural Studies* granted by the C.N.A.A. are provided by City of Birmingham Polytechnic, Brighton Polytechnic (*Architectural Design*), Canterbury College of Art, Polytechnic of Central London, Humberside College of Higher Education, Kingston Polytechnic, Leeds Polytechnic, Leicester Polytechnic, Liverpool Polytechnic, Manchester Polytechnic, North East London Polytechnic, Polytechnic of North London, Oxford Polytechnic, Plymouth Polytechnic, Portsmouth Polytechnic, Robert Gordon's Institute of Technology, Polytechnic of the South Bank, Thames Polytechnic.

Other schools of architecture include:

ARCHITECTURAL ASSOCIATION SCHOOL OF ARCHITECTURE, 34–36 Bedford Square, W.C.1.

The Education and Professional Development Committee of the Royal Institute of British Architects sets standards and guides the whole system of architectural education throughout the United Kingdom. Courses at Schools recognized by the R.I.B.A. exempt students from the R.I.B.A.'s own examinations.

THE ROYAL INSTITUTE OF BRITISH ARCHITECTS, 66 Portland Place, W1N 4AD, *Pres.*, Dr. R. Hackney, PH.D.; *Sec.*, P. K. Harrison, C.B.E.

ART AND DESIGN

First Degrees in *Art, Fine Art* or *History of Art* are granted by the Universities of Aberdeen, Cambridge, East Anglia, Edinburgh, Essex, Glasgow, Lancaster (*Visual Arts*),Leeds, Leicester, London (Courtauld Institute of Art, Birkbeck, University and Westfield Colleges, School of Oriental and African Studies, Goldsmiths' College), Loughborough (*Design and Technology*), Manchester, Manchester Institute of Science and Technology (*Textile Design and Design Management*), Newcastle upon Tyne, Nottingham, Oxford, Reading, St. Andrews, Sussex, Ulster, Wales (University College, Aberystwyth—*Visual Art*) and Warwick. At several other universities art or history of art can be combined with another subject. Courses in *Art and Design* leading to first degrees granted by the University of Leeds are provided at Bretton Hall College of Higher Education. The degrees in *Art* granted by the Royal College of Art are higher degrees.

Courses leading to first degrees in *Art and Design* (*Fine Art, Graphic Design, Textiles/Fashion* or *Three-Dimensional Design*) granted by the C.N.A.A. are provided by more than 40 colleges/schools of art and polytechnics some of which also offer C.N.A.A. degree courses in other subjects in the field of Art and Design, including *Furniture Design, Industrial Design* and *Interior Design*.

ASTRONOMY

First Degrees in *Astronomy* are granted by the Universities of Glasgow, London (University College) and in *Astrophysics* by the Universities of Edinburgh, London (Queen Mary College) and Wales (University College, Cardiff). Various combinations of Astronomy, Mathematics, Physics and Astrophysics are also available.

Astronomy may be taken as part of a C.N.A.A. degree course at certain polytechnics.

BANKING

First Degrees with specialization in *Banking and Finance* are granted by the Universities of Birmingham (*Money, Banking and Finance*), Loughborough, Ulster (*Banking, Finance and Retail Distribution*) and Wales (Institute of Science and Technology), Bangor University College (*Banking, Insurance and Finance*), and the City University (*Banking and International Finance*).

Banking may be taken as part of a C.N.A.A. degree course at certain polytechnics/colleges.

Professional organizations granting qualifications after examination:—

CHARTERED INSTITUTE OF BANKERS, 10 Lombard Street, EC3V 9AS.—*Sec. General*, E. Glover.

INSTITUTE OF BANKERS IN SCOTLAND, 20 Rutland Square, Edinburgh EH1 2DE.—*Sec.*, B. McKenna.

BIOLOGY, CHEMISTRY, PHYSICS

First Degrees in these subjects are granted by many universities. Courses leading to first degrees, granted by the C.N.A.A., are provided by many polytechnics. Professional qualifications are awarded by:—

INSTITUTE OF BIOLOGY, 20 Queensberry Place, SW7 2DZ.—*Gen. Sec.*, P. N. O'Donoghue.

INSTITUTE OF PHYSICS, 47 Belgrave Square, SW1X 8QX.—*Sec.*, Dr. L. Cohen.

ROYAL SOCIETY OF CHEMISTRY, Burlington House, Piccadilly W1V 0BN.—*President*, Prof. Sir Jack Lewis, F.R.S., F.R.S.C., *Sec.*, Dr. J. S. Gow, F.R.S.C., F.R.S.E.

BREWING

First Degrees in Brewing are granted by Heriot-Watt University.

BUILDING

(*See also* Architecture, Estate and Land Management and Surveying)

First Degrees in *Building, Building Engineering* or *Building Technology* are granted by the following Universities: Bath, Heriot-Watt (also *Building Services Engineering* and *Building Economics and Quantity Surveying*), Liverpool (*Building Technology, Building Services Engineering*), London (University College), Manchester (Manchester Institute of Science and Technology, also *Building Services Engineering* and *Construction Management*), Reading (*Building Construction & Management, Quantity Surveying* and *Building Surveying*), Salford (*Building Surveying*, also *Quantity Surveying and Construction Economics*) Strathclyde (*Building Engineering Design*), and Ulster (also *Building Services Engineering* and *Quantity Surveying*).

Courses leading to first degrees in *Building* granted by the C.N.A.A. are provided by Brighton Polytechnic, Bristol Polytechnic, Polytechnic of Central

London, Coventry (Lanchester) Polytechnic, Glasgow College of Technology with Glasgow College of Building and Printing, Leeds Polytechnic, Liverpool Polytechnic, Sheffield City Polytechnic (*Construction*), the Polytechnic of the South Bank, Trent Polytechnic, and Polytechnic of Wales; in *Building Surveying* by Leicester Polytechnic, Liverpool Polytechnic, Polytechnic of the South Bank, Thames Polytechnic; and in *Building Services Engineering* by Newcastle upon Tyne Polytechnic and the Polytechnic of the South Bank (*Environmental Engineering*).

Examinations are also conducted by:—

CHARTERED INSTITUTE OF BUILDING, Englemere, King's Ride, Ascot, Berks., SL5 8BJ.—*Chief Exec.*, Dr. J. D. Hooper.

INSTITUTION OF BUILDING CONTROL, The White House, 41 Carshalton Road, Sutton, Surrey SM1 4TA.—*Sec.*, R. Raywood.

INSTITUTE OF CLERKS OF WORKS OF GREAT BRITAIN, 41 The Mall, Ealing, W5 3TJ.—*Sec.*, A. P. Macnamara.

BUSINESS, MANAGEMENT AND ADMINISTRATION

First Degrees in *Business Studies* are granted by the Universities of Bath (*Business Administration*), Bradford, Buckingham, the City University, the Universities of East Anglia (*Business Information Systems*), Edinburgh, Heriot-Watt (*Business Organization*), Liverpool, Salford (*Business and Management Studies, Business Operation and Control*), Sheffield, Stirling, Strathclyde (*Business and Administration*), Ulster (also *European Business Studies and International Business Communication*), Wales (University College, Aberystwyth, *Business Administration*) (University College, Swansea, also *European Business Studies*), Wales (Institute of Science and Technology) (*Business Administration*, also *Business Economics*); in *Administration* by the Universities of Aston (*Managerial and Administrative Studies*), Birmingham (*Public Policy Making and Administration*), Essex (*Policy-making and Administration*) and Strathclyde (*Business and Administration*); in *Management Sciences/Studies* by the Universities of Aston (*Managerial and Administrative Studies*), Bradford, Cambridge, the City University (*Management & Systems*), the Universities of Hull, Kent (also *Public Administration and Management*, and *European Management Science*), Lancaster, Leeds (also *Textile Management*), London (London School of Economics), Loughborough, Manchester (Institute of Science and Technology), St. Andrews, Salford (*Business and Management Studies*), Stirling, Wales (Cardiff University College; Swansea University College, also *American Management Studies and European Management Science*), and Warwick; in *Marketing* by the Universities of Lancaster, Stirling and Strathclyde; and in *Commerce* by the University of Birmingham. A variety of other combinations in these fields are available at some of these universities and these subjects also form part of degree courses in other universities.

Courses in *Public Administration* leading to first degrees granted by the Universtiy of Wales are provided at Bangor Normal College.

Courses leading to first degrees in *Business Studies* or *Business Administration* granted by the C.N.A.A. are provided by City of Birmingham Polytechnic, Brighton Polytechnic, Bristol Polytechnic, Polytechnic of Central London, City of London Polytechnic, Coventry (Lanchester) Polytechnic, Dorset Institute of Higher Education, Dundee College of Technology (also *Commerce*), Ealing College of Higher Education, Glasgow College of Technology (also *Commerce*), Hatfield Polytechnic, Huddersfield Polytechnic, Humberside College of Higher Education, Kingston Polytechnic, Lancashire Polytechnic, Leeds Polytechnic, Leicester Polytechnic, Liverpool Polytechnic, Manchester Polytechnic, Middlesex Polytechnic, Napier College of Commerce and Technology (also *Commerce*), Newcastle upon Tyne Polytechnic, North East London Polytechnic (also *Manufacturing Studies*), Polytechnic of N. London, N. Staffordshire Polytechnic, Oxford Polytechnic, Paisley College of Technology (*Business Economics*), Plymouth Polytechnic, Portsmouth Polytechnic, Robert Gordon's Institute of Technology (also *Commerce*), Sheffield City Polytechnic (also *Industrial Studies*), Polytechnic of the South Bank, Sunderland Polytechnic, Teesside Polytechnic, Thames Polytechnic, Trent Polytechnic (also *Industrial Studies*), Polytechnic of Wales, West Glamorgan Institute of Higher Education and Wolverhampton Polytechnic.

Courses leading to first degrees in *Business Information Systems/Technology* granted by the C.N.A.A. are provided by Humberside College of Higher Education, Kingston Polytechnic, Lancashire Polytechnic and Manchester Polytechnic (*Information Technology in Business*).

Courses leading to first degrees in *European Business Studies/Administration* granted by the C.N.A.A. are provided by Brighton Polytechnic (*European Business with Technology*), Buckinghamshire College of Higher Education, Humberside College of Higher Education, Middlesex Polytechnic and Trent Polytechnic.

The Thames Polytechnic provides courses for C.N.A.A. first degrees in *International Marketing*; and Manchester Polytechnic in *Retail Marketing*. Huddersfield Polytechnic provides courses for C.N.A.A. degrees in *Marketing (Engineering)* and *Textile Marketing*. Humberside College of Higher Education provides courses for C.N.A.A. degrees in *Secretarial Studies and Office Systems Management*, and Newcastle upon Tyne Polytechnic in *Secretarial Studies*.

Leicester, Manchester, Sheffield City, Teesside and Trent Polytechnics, the Polytechnic of Wales, Glasgow College of Technology, Robert Gordon's Institute of Technology provide courses for C.N.A.A. first degrees in *Public Administration*.

Glasgow College of Technology provides courses for C.N.A.A. first degrees in *Risk Management*.

Professional bodies conducting training and/or examinations in Administration and Management include:

ROYAL INSTITUTE OF PUBLIC ADMINISTRATION, 3 Birdcage Walk, SW1H 9JH.—*Dir. Gen.*, W. Plowden.

INSTITUTE OF ADMINISTRATIVE MANAGEMENT, 40 Chatsworth Parade, Petts Wood, Orpington, Kent BR5 1RW.—*Sec.*, M. J. Ainsworth.

INSTITUTE OF HEALTH SERVICE MANAGEMENT, 75 Portland Place, W1N 4AN.—*Dir.*, Maureen Dixon, PH.D.

INSTITUTE OF HOUSING, 9 White Lion Street, Islington, N1 9XJ.—*Dir.*, P. McGurk.

INSTITUTION OF INDUSTRIAL MANAGERS, Rochester House, 66 Little Ealing Lane, W5 4XX.—*Chief Exec.*, P. V. Crooks.

INSTITUTE OF MARKETING, Moor Hall, Cookham, Maidenhead, Berks. SL6 9QH.—*Dir. Gen.*, P. B. Blood.

INSTITUTE OF PERSONNEL MANAGEMENT, IPM House, Camp Road, Wimbledon SW19 4UW.

HENLEY—THE MANAGEMENT COLLEGE, Greenlands, Henley-on-Thames, Oxon., RG9 3AU.—*Princ.*, Prof. T. Kempner.

LONDON BUSINESS SCHOOL, Sussex Place, Regent's Park, NW1 4SA.—*Princ.*, Prof. P. G. Moore, D.SC., Ph.D.

MANCHESTER BUSINESS SCHOOL, Booth Street West, Manchester M15 6PB.—*Dir.*, Dr. R. G. J. Telfer, C.B.E., Ph.D.

SCOTTISH BUSINESS SCHOOL, 79 St. George's Place, Glasgow G2 1EU.—*Dean*, Prof. A. W. J. Thomson.

Institutions awarding Professional Qualifications in Commerce:—

A. GENERAL

ROYAL SOCIETY OF ARTS EXAMINATIONS BOARD, 8 John Adam Street, WC2N 6EZ.—*Sec.*, W. F. E. Gibbs.

LONDON CHAMBER OF COMMERCE AND INDUSTRY, Examinations Board, Marlowe House, Station Road, Sidcup, Kent DA15 7BJ.—*Dir.*, R. W. Cattell.

EAST MIDLAND FURTHER EDUCATIONAL COUNCIL, Robins Wood House, Robins Wood Road, Aspley, Nottingham NG8 3NH.

NORTH WESTERN REGIONAL ADVISORY COUNCIL FOR FURTHER EDUCATION (incorporating the Union of Lancashire and Cheshire Institutes), Town Hall, Walkden Road, Worsley, Manchester M28 4QE.

NORTHERN COUNCIL FOR FURTHER EDUCATION, 5 Grosvenor Villas, Grosvenor Road, Newcastle upon Tyne NE2 2RU.

WELSH JOINT EDUCATION COMMITTEE, 245 Western Avenue, Cardiff CF5 2YX.

WEST MIDLANDS ADVISORY COUNCIL FOR FURTHER EDUCATION (incorporating Union of Educational Institutions), Norfolk House, Smallbrook Queensway, Birmingham B5 4NB.

YORKSHIRE AND HUMBERSIDE ASSOCIATION FOR FURTHER AND HIGHER EDUCATION, Bowling Green Terrace, Leeds LS11 9SX.

B. SPECIALIZED

INSTITUTE OF PRACTITIONERS IN ADVERTIZING, 44 Belgrave Square SW1X 8QS.—*Dir.*, C. Channon.

THE CAM FOUNDATION, Abford House, 15 Wilton Road SW1V 1NJ.—*Registrar*, Mrs. S. J. Hurford.

INSTITUTE OF EXPORT, Export House, 64 Clifton Street, EC2A 4HB.—*Sec.*, J. R. Wilson.

INSTITUTE OF MARKETING, Moor Hall, Cookham, Maidenhead, Berks., SL6 9QH.—*Dir. Gen.*, T. McBurnie.

INSTITUTE OF PERSONNEL MANAGEMENT, IPM House, Camp Road, Wimbledon, SW19 4UW.

INSTITUTE OF PURCHASING AND SUPPLY, Easton House, Easton on the Hill, Stamford, Lincs., PE9 3NZ.—*Dir. Gen.*, I. G. S. Groundwater.

FACULTY OF SECRETARIES AND ADMINISTRATORS LTD., 15 Church Street, Godalming, Surrey GU7 1EL.—*Sec.*, Mrs. B. D. Lloyd.

INSTITUTE OF CHARTERED SECRETARIES AND ADMINISTRATORS, 16 Park Crescent, W1N 4AH.—*Sec.*, B. Barker, M.B.E.

INSTITUTE OF CHARTERED SHIPBROKERS, 24 St. Mary Axe, EC3A 8DE.—*Sec.*, J. H. Parker.

CHARTERED INSTITUTE OF TRANSPORT, 80 Portland Place, W1N 4DP.—*Dir. Gen.*, J. C. F. Cameron.

BUSINESS AND TECHNICIAN EDUCATION COUNCIL Central House, Upper Woburn Place, WC1H 0HH

The Business & Technician Education Council (BTEC) validates courses leading to nationally recognized qualifications in agriculture; business and finance; caring services; computing and information systems; construction; design; distribution; engineering; home economics; hotel and catering; leisure services; public administration and science, at colleges and polytechnics throughout England, Wales and Northern Ireland.

Chairman, P. Rogers.
Chief Executive, J. E. Sellars.

COMPUTER SCIENCE

First Degrees in *Computer/Computing Science(s)/ Computing, Computational Science* are granted by the Universities of Aberdeen, Aston, Bath (*Computer Software Technology*), Belfast (also *Information Technology*), Birmingham (*Software Engineering*), Bradford (also *Computing & Information Systems Science*), Bristol, Brunel (also *Applied Computer Systems* and *Information Technology*), Buckingham, Cambridge, the City University (also *Business Computing Systems*), Cranfield (*Command and Control Communications and Information Systems* and *Information Technology*) the Universities of Dundee, Durham, East Anglia, Edinburgh, Essex (also *Computer & Microprocessor Systems*), Exeter, Glasgow, Heriot-Watt, Hull, Keele, Kent (also *Computer Systems Engineering* and (provisional) *Computer Communications*) Lancaster, Leeds (also *Data Processing*), Liverpool, London (Imperial (also *Software Engineering*), King's (also *Computer Systems with Microelectronics* and *Computer Science & Digital Electronics*), Queen Mary (also *Computer Systems with Microelectronics*), Royal Holloway and Bedford New, and University Colleges, London School of Economics and Political Science), Loughborough (also *Data Processing* and *Information Technology and Human Factors*), Manchester (also *Computing & Information Systems*), Manchester Institute of Science and Technology, Newcastle upon Tyne, Nottingham, Reading, St. Andrews (also *Information Processing*), Salford (also *Electronic Computer Systems*), Sheffield, Southampton, Stirling, Strathclyde, Sussex, Ulster (also *Computing Science* (*Information Systems*) and *Applied Computing*), Wales (University College, Aberystwyth; University College, Cardiff, also *Computer Systems*; University College, Swansea), Warwick and York (also *Computer Systems & Software Engineering*).

The University of Salford also grants a first degree in *Computer Studies* for which courses are provided at the North East Wales Institute of Higher Education.

Courses leading to first degrees in *Computer Science/Studies* or *Computing* granted by the C.N.A.A. are provided by City of Birmingham Polytechnic (*Computing Information Systems*), Brighton Polytechnic (also *Microelectronics & Information Processing*), Bristol Polytechnic (*Systems Analysis* and *Systems Design*), City of London Polytechnic (*Computing and Information Systems*), Coventry (Lanchester) Polytechnic (also *Information Systems Engineering*), Glasgow College of Technology (*Computer Information Systems*), Hatfield Polytechnic, Huddersfield Polytechnic (*Computing in Business*), Humberside College of Higher Education (*Business Information Systems*), Kingston Polytechnic (also *Information Systems Design*), Lancashire Polytechnic (*Business Information Technology*), Leeds Polytechnic (*Computing and Operational Research*), Leicester Polytechnic (also *Information Technology*), Liverpool Polytechnic, Napier College of Commerce and Technology (*Computing and Data Processing*), Newcastle Polytechnic (*Computing for Industry*), North East London Polytechnic, North Staffordshire Polytechnic (also *Information Systems and Information Technology*), Paisley College of Technology, Plymouth Polytechnic (*Computing and Informatics*), Portsmouth Polytechnic, Sheffield City Polytechnic (also *Information Technology*), Polytechnic of the South Bank (also *Computer and Information Engi-*

neering), Sunderland Polytechnic (*Data Processing*), Teesside Polytechnic (also *Information Technology*), Thames Polytechnic (also *Computer and Communication Systems*), Wolverhampton Polytechnic and Polytechnic of Wales (also *Information Technology*).

These subjects also form part of other degree courses, often as *Mathematics/Statistics and Computer Science*, at many universities, polytechnics and colleges.

DANCE

(*See also* Recreation, Sport, etc.)

First degrees in *Dance in Society* are granted by the University of Surrey.

The University of Kent grants a first degree in *Contemporary Dance* for which courses are provided at the London Contemporary Dance School.

Courses leading to first degrees in *Dance Theatre* granted by the C.N.A.A. are provided by the Laban Centre for Movement and Dance in association with Goldsmiths' College. Dance also forms part of C.N.A.A. degree courses, often called *Performing Arts* or *Creative Arts*, at several polytechnics and colleges. For first degree courses in *Human Movement Studies* see under 'Recreation, Sport and Human Movement Studies'.

ROYAL ACADEMY OF DANCING, 48 Vicarage Crescent, SW11 3LT.—*Directors*, Ms. J. Farron, Ms. P. Yates; D. Wall, C.B.E.

ROYAL BALLET SCHOOL, 155 Talgarth Road, W14 9DE, and White Lodge, Richmond Park.—*Dir.*, Dame Merle Park, D.B.E.

IMPERIAL SOCIETY OF TEACHERS OF DANCING, Euston Hall, Birkenhead Street, WC1H 8BE.—*Dir.*, K. Abraham.

DEFENCE

First Degrees in *Peace Studies* are granted by the Universities of Bradford and Ulster.

Royal Naval Colleges

ROYAL NAVAL COLLEGE, Greenwich, SE10 9NN.— *Admiral President*, Admiral Sir Richard Fitch, K.C.B.; *Dean of the College*, Prof. P. Nailor.

BRITANNIA ROYAL NAVAL COLLEGE, Dartmouth, Devon TQ6 0HJ.—Initial officer training. *Captain*, Capt. J. R. Brigstocke. *Dir. of Studies*, C. I. M. Jones.

ROYAL NAVAL ENGINEERING COLLEGE, Manadon, Plymouth PL5 3AQ.—B.Eng., M.Sc. and specialist training in naval engineering. Students are selected uniformed officers of the Royal Navy, Commonwealth and foreign navies, and civilians. *Captain*, Capt. I. H. Pirnie.
Dean, Capt. G. C. George.
Executive Officer, Cdr. C. D. de Burgh.

INSTITUTE OF NAVAL MEDICINE, Alverstoke, Hants PO12 2DL.—Higher professional and postgraduate training for officers of all three services and some civilians. *Medical Officer-in-Charge*, Surgeon Capt. R. W. F. Paul, Q.H.S.

Military Colleges

STAFF COLLEGE, CAMBERLEY, Surrey GU15 4NP.— *Commandant*, Maj. Gen. C. J. Waters.
Deputy Commandant, Brig. P. R. Davies.

ROYAL MILITARY ACADEMY, SANDHURST, Camberley, Surrey GU15 4PQ.—*Commandant*, Maj.-Gen. S. C. Cooper.

ROYAL MILITARY COLLEGE OF SCIENCE, Shrivenham, nr. Swindon, Wilts SN6 8LA.—Students from U.K. and overseas study from degree to post-graduate levels in management, science and technology. There is an increasing range of research and consultancy activity as the College is now a Faculty of the Cranfield Institute of Technology.
Commandant, Maj.-Gen. J. A. M. Evans.
Dean, Prof. F. R. Hartley, D.Phil.
Academic Registrar, (vacant).

ARMOUR SCHOOL, R.A.C. CENTRE, Bovington Camp, nr. Wareham, Dorset BH20 6LZ.—*Commanding Officer and Chief Instructor*, Col. A. T. Lindsay.

INSTITUTE OF ARMY EDUCATION, Court Road, Eltham, SE9 5NR.—*Director*, Maj.-Gen. D. E. Ryan.

Royal Air Force Colleges

ROYAL AIR FORCE STAFF COLLEGE, Bracknell, Berks, RG12 3DD.—Prepares selected senior officers for high-grade command and staff appointments. The majority of students are R.A.F. officers but officers from the other U.K. services and from foreign air forces also attend.
Air Officer Commanding and Commandant, Air Vice-Marshal D. T. Bryant, C.B., O.B.E.

ROYAL AIR FORCE COLLEGE, Cranwell, Lincs NG34 8HB.—Initial officer training for officers of the R.A.F., W.R.A.F. and P.M.R.A.F.N.S., and initial specialist training for officers of the Engineer and Supply Branches. Advanced specialist training is provided for officers of the General Duties, Engineer and Supply Branches and basic flying training for pilots of the General Duties Branch.
Air Officer Commanding and Commandant, Air Vice-Marshal R. H. Wood, O.B.E.

ROYAL AIR FORCE SCHOOL OF EDUCATION AND TRAINING SUPPORT, R.A.F. Newton, Nottingham NG13 8HL.—*Commanding Officer*, Gp. Capt. D. E. Priestley.

DENTISTRY

First Degrees in Dentistry are granted by the Universities of Belfast, Birmingham, Bristol, Dundee, Edinburgh, Glasgow, Leeds, Liverpool, London (United Medical and Dental Schools of Guy's and St. Thomas's Hospitals, King's College School of Medicine and Dentistry, London Hospital Medical College, University College & Middlesex Hospital Medical School), Manchester, Newcastle upon Tyne, Sheffield, Wales (University College, Cardiff, and Welsh National School of Medicine).

To be entitled to be registered in the Dentists Register a person must hold the degree or diploma in dental surgery of a University in the U.K. or Republic of Ireland or the diploma of any of the Licensing Authorities (The Royal College of Surgeons of England, of Edinburgh and in Ireland, and the Royal College of Physicians and Surgeons of Glasgow). The Dentists Register is maintained by THE GENERAL DENTAL COUNCIL, 37 Wimpole Street, W1M 8DQ.

DIETETICS

(*See also* Food and Nutrition Science)

Courses in *Nutrition and Dietetics* leading to first degrees granted by the University of Wales are provided by South Glamorgan Institute of Higher Education. Courses leading to first degrees in *Dietetics* granted by the C.N.A.A. are provided by Leeds Polytechnic, Queen Margaret College, Paisley College of Technology with Queen's College and Robert Gordon's Institute of Technology (*Nutrition and Dietetics*).

The professional association is THE BRITISH DIE-TETIC ASSOCIATION, Daimler House, Paradise Circus, Birmingham B1 2BJ. Full membership is open to dietitians holding a recognized qualification, who may also become State Registered Dietitians through the Council for Professions Supplementary to Medicine (*q.v.*).

DRAMA

First Degrees in *Drama* are granted by the Universities of Birmingham (*Drama and Theatre Arts*), Bristol, East Anglia, Exeter, Glasgow (*Dramatic Studies*—in conjunction with Royal Scottish Academy of Music and Drama), Hull, Kent (*Drama and Theatre Studies*), Lancaster (*Theatre Studies*), London (Royal Holloway and Bedford New College, *Drama and Theatre Studies*), Loughborough, Manchester and Wales (University Colleges of Aberystwyth and Bangor) and Warwick (*Theatre Studies and Dramatic Arts*). Drama also forms part of degree courses in other universities. Courses in Drama leading to first degrees granted by the University of Leeds are provided at Bretton Hall College of Higher Education.

Courses leading to first degrees granted by the C.N.A.A. are provided by Crewe and Alsager College of Higher Education (*Drama Studies*), Dartington College of Arts (*Theatre*), King Alfred's College of Higher Education (*Drama, Theatre and TV Studies*) and Rose Bruford College of Speech and Drama (*Theatre Arts*).

The national validating body for courses providing training in drama is THE NATIONAL COUNCIL FOR DRAMA TRAINING, 5 Tavistock Place, WC1H 9SS. It currently has accredited, non-degree awarding, courses at the following: Academy of Live and Recorded Arts; Arts Educational Schools; Birmingham School of Speech Training & Dramatic Art; Bristol Old Vic Theatre School; Central School of Speech and Drama; Drama Centre, London; Drama Studio; Guildford School of Acting; Guildhall School of Music and Drama; London Academy of Music and Dramatic Art; Manchester Polytechnic School of Theatre; Middlesex Polytechnic; Mountview Theatre School; Royal Academy of Dramatic Art; Webber Douglas Academy of Dramatic Art; Welsh College of Music and Drama.

ECONOMICS

Almost all universities grant first degrees in Economics. Courses leading to first degrees in Economics granted by the Council for National Academic Awards are provided by some 20 Polytechnics and Colleges.

ENGINEERING
(*See separate subjects below*)

The Council of Engineering Institutions ceased operations in Sept. 1983 and its major functions are now carried on by THE ENGINEERING COUNCIL, 10 Maltravers Street, WC2R 3ER.—*Sec.*, J. Carlill, O.B.E. The fifteen principal qualifying bodies are:—

ROYAL AERONAUTICAL SOCIETY, 4 Hamilton Place, W1V 0BQ.—*Pres.*, Prof. J. L. Stollery. *Sec.*, G. C. May.

ROYAL INSTITUTION OF NAVAL ARCHITECTS, 10 Upper Belgrave Street, SW1X 8BQ.—*Sec.*, P. W. Ayling.

INSTITUTION OF CHEMICAL ENGINEERS, 165/171 Railway Terrace, Rugby, Warwickshire CV21 3HQ; London Office, 12 Gayfere Street, SW1P 3HP.—*Gen. Sec.*, Dr. T. J. Evans.

INSTITUTION OF CIVIL ENGINEERS, 1–7 Great George Street SW1P 3AA.—*Sec.*, J. M. Sutherland.

INSTITUTION OF ELECTRICAL ENGINEERS, Savoy Place, WC2R 0BL.—*Sec.*, H. W. Losty.

INSTITUTION OF ELECTRONIC AND RADIO ENGINEERS, 99 Gower Street, WC1E 6AZ.—*Sec.*, D. D. Duffett.

INSTITUTE OF ENERGY, 18 Devonshire Street, W.1.

INSTITUTION OF GAS ENGINEERS, 17 Grosvenor Crescent, SW1X 7ES.—*Sec.*, D. J. Chapman.

INSTITUTE OF MARINE ENGINEERS, 76 Mark Lane, EC3R 7JN.—*Sec.*, J. E. Sloggett.

INSTITUTION OF MECHANICAL ENGINEERS, 1 Birdcage Walk, SW1H 9JJ.

INSTITUTE OF METALS, 1 Carlton House Terrace SW1Y 5DB.—*Registrar-Sec.*, Sir Geoffrey Ford.

INSTITUTION OF MINING ENGINEERS, Danum House, 6A South Parade, Doncaster DN1 2DY.—*Sec.*, W. J. W. Bourne.

INSTITUTION OF MINING AND METALLURGY, 44 Portland Place, W1N 4BR.—*Sec.*, M. J. Jones.

INSTITUTION OF PRODUCTION ENGINEERS, Rochester House, 66 Little Ealing Lane, W5 4XX.—*Sec.*, R. J. Miskin.

INSTITUTION OF STRUCTURAL ENGINEERS, 11 Upper Belgrave Street, SW1X 8BH.—*Sec.*, D. J. Clark.

ENGINEERING, GENERAL AND ENGINEERING SCIENCE

First Degrees in *General Engineering* or *Engineering Science* are granted by the Universities of Aberdeen, Aston, Cambridge, Durham, Edinburgh, Exeter, Lancaster, Leicester, Liverpool, London (Queen Mary College), Loughborough, Oxford, Reading, Surrey, Ulster and Warwick. Courses leading to first degrees in *Engineering* granted by the C.N.A.A. are provided by polytechnics and colleges.

Aeronautical Engineering

See main heading:
AERONAUTICS AND AERONAUTICAL ENGINEERING

Agricultural Engineering

First Degrees in *Agricultural Engineering* and *Agricultural Mechanization Management* are granted by the University of Newcastle upon Tyne. Courses in *Agricultural Engineering* and *Agricultural Technology & Management* leading to degrees granted by Cranfield Institute of Technology are provided at Silsoe College.

Chemical Engineering

First Degrees are granted by the Universities of Aston (*Chemical Process Engineering*), Bath, Belfast, Birmingham, Bradford, Cambridge, Edinburgh, Exeter, Heriot-Watt, Leeds, London (Imperial College of Science and Technology, University College), Loughborough, Manchester (Manchester Institute of Science and Technology), Newcastle upon Tyne, Nottingham, Salford, Sheffield (*Chemical Process Engineering*), Strathclyde, Surrey and Wales (University College, Swansea).

Courses leading to first degrees granted by the C.N.A.A. are provided by North East London Polytechnic, Polytechnic of the South Bank, Teesside Polytechnic and Polytechnic of Wales.

Civil, Electrical & Mechanical Engineering

First Degrees in *Civil,* (or *Civil and Structural*) *Electrical* (or *Electrical and Electronic*) *and Mechanical Engineering* are granted by the Universities of Aberdeen, Aston, Bath, Belfast, Birmingham, Bradford, Bristol, Brunel (*E. & M.*), Cambridge, the City University, Cranfield Institute, the Universities of

Dundee, Durham, Edinburgh, Exeter, Glasgow, Heriot-Watt, Lancaster, Leeds, Leicester, Liverpool, London (Imperial College of Science and Technology, King's College, Queen Mary College, University College), Loughborough, Manchester, *also* Manchester Institute of Science and Technology, Newcastle upon Tyne, Nottingham, Oxford, Reading (*E. & M.*), Salford, Sheffield, Southampton, Strathclyde, Surrey, Sussex, Ulster, Wales (University Colleges at Cardiff and Swansea, Institute of Science and Technology, Cardiff) and Warwick.

Some 35 polytechnics or colleges provide courses (in one or more of civil, electrical/electronic and mechanical engineering) leading to first degrees granted by the C.N.A.A.

Electronic Engineering & Electronics

First Degrees in *Electronic Engineering* or *Electronics* or *Electrical and Electronic Engineering* or *Electrical Engineering (including Electronics)* are granted by the following universities: Aberdeen, Aston, Bath, Belfast, Birmingham, Bradford, Bristol, Brunel, Cambridge, the City University, Cranfield Institute (*Electrical Systems Engineering*), the Universities of Dundee, Durham, East Anglia (*Electronic Systems Engineering*), Edinburgh, Essex, Exeter, Glasgow, Heriot-Watt, Hull, Keele, Kent, Lancaster, Leeds, Leicester, Liverpool, London (Imperial College of Science and Technology, King's, Queen Mary and University Colleges), Loughborough, Manchester (*also* Manchester Institute of Science and Technology), Newcastle upon Tyne, Nottingham, Oxford, Reading, Salford, Sheffield, Southampton, Strathclyde, Surrey, Sussex, Ulster, Wales (University Colleges of Bangor, Cardiff and Swansea, Institute of Science and Technology), Warwick (also *Engineering Electronics*), York.

Courses leading to first degrees in *Electronic Engineering* or in *Electrical and Electronic Engineering*, granted by the C.N.A.A. are provided by some 30 polytechnics or colleges.

Marine Engineering and Naval Architecture

First Degrees in *Marine Engineering* and *Naval Architecture and Shipbuilding* are granted by the University of Newcastle upon Tyne; in *Naval Architecture and Ocean Engineering* by the Universities of Glasgow and London (University College); in *Naval Architecture* by the University of Strathclyde; in *Offshore Engineering* by Heriot-Watt University; in *Ship Science* by the University of Southampton, in *Maritime Studies* by the University of Wales (Institute of Science and Technology) and in *Civil and Maritime Engineering* by the University of Liverpool.

Courses leading to first degrees in *Mechanical Engineering (Marine)* granted by the C.N.A.A. are provided by Liverpool Polytechnic.

Nuclear Engineering

First Degrees are granted by the University of Manchester.

Production Engineering

First Degrees in *Production Engineering, Manufacturing Engineering* or *Industrial Engineering* are granted by the Universities of Aston, Bath, Birmingham (*Engineering Production*), Brunel, Cambridge, Exeter (*Engineering (Operations & Manufacturing)*), Hull (*Engineering Design and Manufacture*), Loughborough, Manchester and Manchester Institute of Science and Technology, Nottingham, Strathclyde, Ulster, Wales (Institute of Science and Technology) and Warwick (*Engineering (Manufacturing Systems)*).

Courses leading to first degrees in *Production Engineering* granted by the C.N.A.A. are provided by Coventry (Lanchester) Polytechnic, Kingston Polytechnic, Leeds Polytechnic, Trent Polytechnic; in *Industrial Engineering* by Hatfield Polytechnic, Paisley College of Technology; in *Manufacturing Engineering* by Liverpool Polytechnic; in *Manufacturing Studies* by North East London Polytechnic; in *Manufacturing Systems Engineering* by Sheffield City Polytechnic; and in *Plant Engineering* by Trent Polytechnic.

Structural Engineering

First Degrees in *Civil and Structural Engineering* are granted by the Universities of Aberdeen, Bath, Bradford, Heriot-Watt (*Structural Engineering*), Liverpool, London (University College, *Civil, Structural and Environmental Engineering*), Sheffield, Sussex (*Structural Engineering*), and Wales (University College, Cardiff).

ESTATE AND LAND MANAGEMENT, AND SURVEYING
(See also Building)

First Degrees are granted by the Universities of Aberdeen (*Land Economy*), Cambridge (*Land Economy*), Heriot-Watt (*Estate Management*), Reading (*Land Management* and *Rural Land Management*) and Ulster (*Estate Management*).

First Degrees in *Surveying Science* are granted by the University of Newcastle upon Tyne; in *Building Economics and Quantity Surveying* by Heriot-Watt University; in *Quantity Surveying* by Ulster University; in *Property Valuation and Management* by the City University; in *Quantity Surveying and Building Surveying* by the University of Reading and in *Quantity Surveying and Construction Economics* and *Building Surveying* by the University of Salford.

Courses leading to first degrees granted by the C.N.A.A. are provided by the following: in *Estate Management* by the City of Birmingham Polytechnic, Kingston Polytechnic, Newcastle upon Tyne Polytechnic, Oxford Polytechnic, Polytechnic of the South Bank and Thames Polytechnic; in *Housing* by Bristol Polytechnic; in *Housing Studies* by Sheffield City Polytechnic; in *Land Administration* by North East London Polytechnic; in *Land Economics* by Paisley College of Technology; in *Land Management* by Leicester Polytechnic; in *Minerals Estate Management* by Sheffield City Polytechnic; in *Quantity Surveying* by City of Birmingham Polytechnic, Bristol Polytechnic, Polytechnic of Central London, Dundee College of Technology, Glasgow College of Technology with Glasgow College of Building and Printing, Kingston Polytechnic, Leeds Polytechnic, Liverpool Polytechnic, Newcastle upon Tyne Polytechnic, Portsmouth Polytechnic, Robert Gordon's Institute of Technology, Polytechnic of the South Bank, Thames Polytechnic, Trent Polytechnic and Polytechnic of Wales; in *Surveying and Mapping Sciences* by North East London Polytechnic; in *Urban Estate Management* by Polytechnic of Central London, Liverpool Polytechnic and the Polytechnic of Wales; in *Urban Estate Surveying* by Trent Polytechnic; in *Urban Land Administration* by Portsmouth Polytechnic; in *Urban Land Economics* by Sheffield City Polytechnic; and in *Valuation and Estate Management* by Bristol Polytechnic.

Qualifying professional bodies include:

ROYAL INSTITUTION OF CHARTERED SURVEYORS (incorporating The Institute of Quantity Surveyors), 12 Great George Street, SW1P 3AD.—*Sec. Gen.*, M. Pattison.

FACULTY OF ARCHITECTS AND SURVEYORS, with which is incorporated the Institute of Registered Architects, 15 St. Mary Street, Chippenham, Wilts.— *Sec.,* A. D. G. Webb.

INCORPORATED ASSOCIATION OF ARCHITECTS AND SURVEYORS, Jubilee House, Billing Brook Road, Weston Favell, Northampton NN3 4NW.—*Hon. Sec.,* W. A. Black.

RATING AND VALUATION ASSOCIATION, 115 Ebury Street, SW1W 9QT.—*Sec.,* B. L. Hill, R.D.

INCORPORATED SOCIETY OF VALUERS AND AUCTIONEERS, 3 Cadogan Gate, SW1X 0AS.—*Sec.,* M. Astbury.

FISHERY SCIENCE

First Degrees in *Wildlife and Fisheries Management* are granted by the University of Edinburgh.

Courses leading to first degrees in *Fishery Science/ Studies* granted by the C.N.A.A. are provided by Humberside College of Higher Education, and Plymouth Polytechnic.

FOOD AND NUTRITION SCIENCE
(See also Dietetics, Home Economics and Hotelkeeping)

First Degrees in *Food Science* are granted by the Universities of Belfast (also *Food Technology*), Leeds, London (King's College), Newcastle (*Agricultural & Food Marketing*), Nottingham, Reading (also *Food Science, Food Economics & Marketing* and *Food Technology*), Strathclyde, Surrey (*Nutrition & Food Science*), Ulster (*Food Technology Management*) and Wales (University College, Aberystwyth, *Agricultural & Food Marketing*); and in *Nutrition* by the Universities of London (King's College), Nottingham, Surrey and (*Human Nutrition*) Ulster.

Courses leading to first degrees in *Food Manufacture* granted by the C.N.A.A. are provided by Manchester Polytechnic and in *Food Science* by the Polytechnic of the South Bank; in *Catering and Applied Nutrition* by Huddersfield Polytechnic; in *Food and Accommodation Management* by Leeds Polytechnic; in *Food Marketing Sciences* by Sheffield City Polytechnic; in *Food, Textiles & Consumer Studies* by the Polytechnic of the South Bank; in *Industrial Food Technology* by Humberside College of Higher Education; in *Nutrition and Dietetics* by Robert Gordon's Institute of Technology.

Scientific and professional bodies include:

NUTRITION SOCIETY, Grosvenor Gardens House, 35–37 Grosvenor Gardens, SW1W 0BS.—*Hon. Sec.,* Dr. M. Ashwell.

INSTITUTE OF FOOD SCIENCE & TECHNOLOGY, 20 Queensberry Place, SW7 2DR.—*Exec. Sec.,* Ms. H. G. Wild.

FORESTRY AND TIMBER STUDIES

First Degrees in Forestry are granted by the Universities of Aberdeen, Edinburgh (also *Agriculture, Forestry & Rural Economy*), and Wales (University College, Bangor), (also *Wood Science* and *Agroforestry*).

Courses leading to first degrees in *Timber Technology* granted by the C.N.A.A. are provided by Buckinghamshire College of Higher Education.

Professional Organizations

ROYAL FORESTRY SOCIETY OF ENGLAND, WALES AND NORTHERN IRELAND, 102 High Street, Tring, Herts., HP23 4MH.—*Dir.,* E. H. M. Harris.

ROYAL SCOTTISH FORESTRY SOCIETY, 11 Atholl Crescent, Edinburgh EH3 8HE.—*Sec.,* W. B. C. Walker.

COMMONWEALTH FORESTRY ASSOCIATION, c/o Oxford Forestry Institute, South Parks Road, Oxford OX1 3RB.—*Sec.,* W. Hockey.

INSTITUTE OF CHARTERED FORESTERS, 22 Walker Street, Edinburgh EH3 7HR.—*Sec.,* Mrs. M. Dick.

FUEL AND ENERGY STUDIES
(See also Nuclear Engineering)

First Degrees in *Fuel and Combustion Science* and in *Fuel and Energy Engineering* are granted by the University of Leeds; in *Petroleum Engineering* by London (Imperial College of Science and Technology); in *Mining and Petroleum Engineering* by the University of Strathclyde; in *Natural Gas Engineering* by the University of Salford; in *Chemical Process Engineering, Fuel Technology* by the University of Sheffield; and in *Fuel and Energy—Management Studies* by the University of Leeds. These subjects may also form part of other degree courses.

Courses leading to first degrees in *Energy Engineering* granted by the C.N.A.A. are provided by Napier College of Commerce and Technology, and in *Power Engineering* by Derbyshire College of Higher Education.

Courses leading to certificates and qualification by professional bodies are available at many Technical Colleges.

The principal professional bodies are:—

INSTITUTE OF ENERGY, 18 Devonshire Street, W.1.

INSTITUTION OF GAS ENGINEERS, 17 Grosvenor Crescent, SW1X 7ES.

INSTITUTE OF PETROLEUM, 61 New Cavendish Street W1M 8AR.—*Gen. Sec.,* D. C. Payne.

GEOLOGY

First Degrees in *Geology* or *Geological Sciences* or *Applied Geology* are granted by the Universities of Aberdeen (also *Petroleum Geology*), Aston, Belfast, Birmingham, Bristol, Cambridge, Dundee, Durham, Edinburgh, Exeter, Glasgow, Hull, Keele, Leeds, Leicester (also *Mining Geology*), Liverpool, London (Birkbeck College, Goldsmiths' College, Imperial College of Science and Technology (also *Mining Geology*), Queen Mary College, Royal Holloway & Bedford New College, University College), Manchester, Newcastle upon Tyne, Nottingham, Oxford, Reading, St. Andrews, Sheffield, Southampton, Strathclyde, Wales (University Colleges at Aberystwyth, Cardiff and Swansea).

Degree courses in *Geophysics* and *Geophysical Sciences* are also provided by universities.

Courses leading to first degrees in *Geology* granted by the C.N.A.A. are provided by City of London Polytechnic, College of St. Paul and St. Mary (*Geography and Geology*), Derbyshire College of Higher Education (*Earth and Life Studies*), Kingston Polytechnic, Plymouth Polytechnic (*Applied Geology*), and Portsmouth Polytechnic; in *Earth Sciences* by Oxford Polytechnic and in *Engineering Geology and Geotechnics* by Portsmouth Polytechnic.

HOME ECONOMICS AND CATERING
(See also Dietetics, Food, Hotelkeeping and Institutional Management).

First Degrees are granted by the Universities of Ulster (*Home Economics and Catering Administration*), Wales (Cardiff University College, *Home Economics*), Strathclyde (*Hotel and Catering Management*) and Surrey (*Hotel and Catering Management*). Courses leading to first degrees in *Home Economics* granted by the University of Bath are provided at Bath College of Higher Education.

Courses leading to first degrees granted by the C.N.A.A. are provided by Bradford and Ilkley Community College (*Home and Community Studies*), Brighton Polytechnic (*Hotel and Catering Management*), Dorset Institute of Higher Education (*Catering Administration*), Huddersfield Polytechnic (*Catering and Applied Nutrition, Hotel and Catering Administration*); Leeds Polytechnic (*Home Economics*); Liverpool Polytechnic (*Home Economics*), Manchester Polytechnic (*Home Economics* and *Hotel and Catering Studies*); Middlesex Polytechnic (*Hotel and Catering Administration*); Napier College of Commerce and Technology (*Catering and Accommodation Studies*); Newcastle upon Tyne Polytechnic (*Applied Consumer Science*); Oxford Polytechnic (*Catering*); Portsmouth Polytechnic/Highbury College of Technology (*Hotel and Catering Management*); Queen Margaret College (*Home Economics*); Queen's College (*Home Economics* and *Catering and Accommodation Management*); Robert Gordon's Institute of Technology (*Hotel, Catering and Institutional Administration*); and Sheffield City Polytechnic (*Catering Systems*).

HOTELKEEPING
(*See also* Institutional Management)

First Degrees are granted by the Universities of Strathclyde (*Hotel and Catering Management*), Surrey (*Hotel Management and Hotel and Catering Management*), Ulster (*Hotel and Tourism Management*) and Wales (Cardiff University College, *Hotel and Institutional Management*).

Courses leading to first degrees in *Hotel and Catering Administration/Studies/Management* granted by the C.N.A.A. are provided by Brighton, Huddersfield, Manchester and Middlesex Polytechnics and by Portsmouth Polytechnic/Highbury College of Technology; in *Hospitality Management* by Norwich City College of Further and Higher Education; and in *Hotel, Catering and Institutional Management* by Robert Gordon's Institute of Technology.

INDUSTRIAL RELATIONS

First Degrees in Industrial Relations are granted by the Universities of Birmingham, Kent, London (London School of Economics and Political Science), Strathclyde and Wales (Cardiff University College). Industrial relations also forms part of degree courses at other universities.

INSTITUTIONAL MANAGEMENT
(*See also* Hotelkeeping)

First Degrees in Hotel and Institutional Management are granted by the University of Wales (Cardiff University College).

Courses leading to first degrees in *Institutional Management* granted by the C.N.A.A. are provided by the Polytechnic of North London; and in *Hotel, Catering and Institutional Management* by Robert Gordon's Institute of Technology.

Qualifying professional body in the three subjects above is:

HOTEL, CATERING AND INSTITUTIONAL MANAGEMENT ASSOCIATION, 191 Trinity Road, SW17 7HN.—*Dir.*, Ms. E. Gadsby.

INSURANCE

First Degrees in *Banking, Insurance and Finance* are granted by the University of Wales (University College, Bangor) and in *Industrial Economics with Insurance* by the University of Nottingham.

Courses leading to first degrees in *Risk Management* granted by the C.N.A.A. are provided by the Glasgow College of Technology.

Organizations conducting examinations and awarding diplomas:—

ASSOCIATION OF AVERAGE ADJUSTERS, Irongate House, Dukes Place, EC3A 7LP.

CHARTERED INSURANCE INSTITUTE, 20 Aldermanbury, EC2V 7HY.—*Sec. Gen.*, P. V. Saxton.

CHARTERED INSTITUTE OF LOSS ADJUSTERS, Manfield House, 376 Strand, W.C.2.

JOURNALISM

Courses for trainee newspaper journalists are available at 11 centres. One-year full-time courses are available for selected students. Particulars of all these courses are available from the Director of THE NATIONAL COUNCIL FOR TRAINING OF JOURNALISTS, Carlton House, Hemnall Street, Epping, Essex CM16 4NL. Short courses for experienced journalists are also arranged by the National Council.

For periodical journalists, there are four centres running courses approved by THE PERIODICALS TRAINING COUNCIL, Imperial House, 15–19 Kingsway, WC2B 6UN.—*Dir.*, A. R. Sumption.

LANGUAGES

First Degrees in English and in a very wide range of Foreign Languages (including Oriental and African languages) are granted by universities. Degrees in *Linguistics* are awarded by the Universities of Cambridge, East Anglia, Essex (also *Language Studies* and *Psycholinguistics*), Lancaster, Leeds (*Linguistics and Phonetics*), London (School of Oriental and African Studies and University College), Newcastle upon Tyne, Reading (also *Linguistics and Language Pathology*), Sussex and Wales (University College, Bangor, *Applied Linguistics* and *Theoretical Linguistics*); in *Applied Languages* by the University of Ulster; in *Language and Linguistic Science* by the University of York; and in *Languages* (*Interpreting and Translating*) by Heriot-Watt University. These subjects also form part of degree courses at many other universities.

Courses leading to first degrees in various *Foreign Languages* granted by the C.N.A.A. are provided by some 15 Polytechnics and Colleges.

LAW

First Degrees in Law are granted by the Universities of Aberdeen, Belfast, Birmingham, Bristol, Brunel, Buckingham, Cambridge, Dundee, Durham, East Anglia, Edinburgh, Essex, Exeter, Glasgow, Hull, Kent (also *Industrial Relations (Law)*), Lancaster, Leeds, Leicester, Liverpool, London (King's College, London School of Economics and Political Science, Queen Mary College, School of Oriental and African Studies; University College), Manchester, Newcastle upon Tyne, Nottingham, Oxford, Reading, Sheffield, Southampton, Stirling (*Business Law*), Strathclyde (also *Business Law*), Sussex, Wales (University Colleges at Aberystwyth and Cardiff, Institute of Science and Technology) and Warwick.

Courses leading to first degrees in Law granted by the C.N.A.A. are provided by City of Birmingham Polytechnic, Bristol Polytechnic, Polytechnic of Central London, City of London Polytechnic (also *Business Law*), Coventry (Lanchester) Polytechnic (*Business Law*), Ealing College of Higher Education, Essex Institute of Higher Education, Huddersfield Polytechnic (*Business Law*), Kingston Polytechnic, Lancashire Polytechnic, Leeds Polytechnic, Leicester Polytechnic, Liverpool Polytechnic, Manchester Polytechnic, Middlesex Polytechnic, Newcastle upon Tyne Polytechnic, North East London Polytechnic, Polytechnic of North London, North Staffordshire

Polytechnic, Polytechnic of the South Bank, Trent Polytechnic and Wolverhampton Polytechnic; and Polytechnic of Wales.

The Bar

Qualifications for Barrister are obtainable only at one of the Inns of Court or Faculty of Advocates.

THE INNS OF COURT

COUNCIL OF THE INNS OF COURT

President, Rt. Hon. Sir John Donaldson, (*Master of the Rolls*).
Secretary, Rear Adm. J. R. Hill.

THE INNER TEMPLE, EC4Y 7HL

Treasurer, His Honour Judge Hawser, Q.C.
Sub-Treasurer, Capt. P. T. Sheehan, C.B.E., R.N.

THE MIDDLE TEMPLE, EC4Y 9AT

Treasurer, The Rt. Hon. Lord Justice Watkins, V.C.
Under-Treasurer, Rear Adm. J. R. Hill.

GRAY'S INN, WC1R 5EU

Treasurer, The Hon. Sir Kenneth Jones.
Under-Treasurer, Rear Adm. C. M. Bevan, C.B.

LINCOLN'S INN, WC2A 3TL

Treasurer, The Rt. Hon. Mr. Justice Caulfield.
Under-Treasurer, Capt. P. M. Carver, R.N.

THE GENERAL COUNCIL OF THE BAR
11 South Square, Gray's Inn, WC1R 5EL

The governing body of the Barristers' branch of the legal profession, established in 1987 in succession to the Senate of the Inns of Court and the Bar.
Chairman, P. Scott, Q.C.
Vice-Chairman, R. Johnson, Q.C.
Treasurer, J. Griffiths, C.M.G., Q.C.
Chief Executive, J. Mottram.

COUNCIL OF LEGAL EDUCATION
Inns of Court School of Law, 4 Gray's Inn Place, WC1R 5DX

Established by the four Inns of Court to superintend the Education and Examination of Students for the Bar of England and Wales.
Chairman, The Hon. Mr. Justice Hobhouse.
Inns of Court School of Law, Dean, Mrs. M. A. Phillips.
Registrar, R. H. Vaughan.

FACULTY OF ADVOCATES
Advocates Library, Edinburgh EH1 1RF

Application for admission as an Advocate of the Scottish Bar is made by Petition to the Court of Session. The candidate is remitted for examination to the Faculty of Advocates. Enquiries should be addressed to The Clerk of Faculty.
Dean of Faculty, J. A. D. Hope, Q.C.
Clerk of Faculty, P. B. Cullen.

NORTHERN IRELAND

Admission to the Bar of Northern Ireland is controlled by the Honorable Society of the Inn of Court of Northern Ireland, Royal Courts of Justice, Belfast BT1 3JF.
Treasurer, M. Lavery, Q.C.
Under-Treasurer, J. A. L. McLean, Q.C.

Solicitors

Qualifications for Solicitor are obtainable only from the Law Society or its equivalent in Scotland or Northern Ireland.

LAW SOCIETY OF ENGLAND AND WALES
113 Chancery Lane, WC2A 1PL

The Society controls the education and examination of articled clerks, and the admission of solicitors in England and Wales. It also regulates professional standards and conduct. Number of members, over 40,000.
President of the Society (1987–88), J. D. R. Bradbeer.
Vice-President (1987–88), R. K. H. Gaskell.
Secretary-General, J. W. Hayes.

THE COLLEGE OF LAW, Braboeuf Manor, St. Catherine's, Guildford, Surrey GU3 1HA (and at 33–35 Lancaster Gate, W2 3LU, 2 Breams Buildings, Chancery Lane, EC4A 1DP, and Christleton Hall, Chester CH3 7AB), provides courses for The Law Society examinations.

LAW SOCIETY OF SCOTLAND
Law Society's Hall, 26 Drumsheugh Gardens, Edinburgh EH3 7YR

The Society comprises all practising and non-practising solicitors in Scotland. It controls the examination of legal trainees and the admission of solicitors in Scotland and acts as Registrar of solicitors under the Solicitors (Scotland) Act, 1980.
President of the Society (1987–88), J. M. Smith.
Secretary, K. W. Pritchard.
Secretary (*Legal Education*), P. S. B. Niven.

LAW SOCIETY OF NORTHERN IRELAND
Law Society House, 90–106 Victoria Street, Belfast BT1 2JZ

Secretary, M. Davey.

LIBRARIANSHIP AND INFORMATION SCIENCE

First Degrees are granted by the University of Belfast (*Information Studies*), Loughborough (*Library Studies*), and the University of Wales (Aberystwyth) (*Librarianship* with another subject) (jointly with the College of Librarianship, Wales), and by the University of Strathclyde (*Information Science*).

Courses leading to first degrees in *Librarianship/ Library Studies* or *Librarianship/Library Studies and Information Studies/Science* granted by the C.N.A.A. are provided by City of Birmingham Polytechnic, Brighton Polytechnic, Ealing College of Higher Education, Leeds Polytechnic, Liverpool Polytechnic, Manchester Polytechnic, Newcastle upon Tyne Polytechnic, Polytechnic of North London and Robert Gordon's Institute of Technology; and in *Information Science* by Leeds Polytechnic.

THE LIBRARY ASSOCIATION, 7 Ridgmount Street, WC1E 7AE, maintains the professional register of Chartered Members (Fellows and Associates).—*Chief Exec.*, G. Cunningham.

MATERIALS STUDIES (including Metallurgy)

First Degrees in *Materials Science, Materials Technology, or Materials Science and Technology* are granted by the Universities of Bath, Birmingham (also *Metallurgy/Materials Engineering*), Brunel, Cambridge (*Metallurgy and Materials Science*), Leeds, Liverpool (also *Metallurgy and Materials Science*), London (Imperial College of Science and Technology,

Queen Mary College), Loughborough (*Materials Engineering*), Manchester and Manchester Institute of Science and Technology, Newcastle upon Tyne, Nottingham (*Metallurgy and Materials Science*), Oxford (*Metallurgy and Science of Materials*), Sheffield, Strathclyde (*Science of Engineering Materials*), Surrey and Wales (University College, Swansea, and (*Materials Science and Metallurgy*) Cardiff). First Degrees in *Polymer Science and Engineering* are granted by London (Queen Mary College) Manchester Institute of Science and Technology (*Polymer Science and Technology*), and Sheffield. First Degrees in *Ceramics Science and Engineering* are granted by the Universities of Leeds and Sheffield; and in *Science and Engineering of Glasses* by the University of Sheffield. First Degrees in *Metallurgy* and/or *Metallurgical Engineering* are granted by the Universities of Birmingham (*Metallurgy/Materials Engineering*), Brunel, Cambridge (*Metallurgy and Materials Science*), Leeds, Liverpool (*Metallurgy and Materials Science*), London (Imperial College of Science and Technology), Manchester and Manchester Institute of Science and Technology, Newcastle upon Tyne, Nottingham (*Metallurgy and Materials Science*), Oxford (*Metallurgy and Science of Materials*), Salford (*Engineering Metallurgy*), Sheffield, Strathclyde, Surrey, Wales (University College at Cardiff (*Materials Science and Metallurgy*).

Courses leading to first degrees in *Materials Science/Technology* or *Metallurgy* or *Metallurgy and Materials* granted by the C.N.A.A. are provided by the City of London Polytechnic, Coventry (Lanchester) Polytechnic, Sheffield City Polytechnic (*Metallurgy and Microstructural Engineering*), Sunderland Polytechnic, Thames Polytechnic and Wolverhampton Polytechnic (*Materials and Manufacture*). Courses leading to first degrees in *Polymer Science and Technology* granted by the C.N.A.A. are provided by Manchester Polytechnic and the Polytechnic of North London; in *Mineral Process Engineering* by Camborne School of Mines; and in *Timber Technology* by Buckinghamshire College of Higher Education.

INSTITUTE OF METALS, 1 Carlton House Terrace SW1Y 5DB, is a qualifying body.

MATHEMATICS

First Degrees in *Mathematics* and/or *Applied Mathematics* are granted by all universities.

Courses leading to first degrees in *Mathematics* granted by the C.N.A.A. are provided by about a dozen Polytechnics and Colleges.

MEDICINE

First Degrees in *Medicine and Surgery* are granted by the Universities of Aberdeen, Belfast, Birmingham, Bristol, Cambridge, Dundee, Edinburgh, Glasgow, Leeds, Leicester, Liverpool, London (medical schools/colleges:— Charing Cross and Westminster M.S., King's College S.M.D., London H.M.C., Royal Free H.M.S., St. Bart's. H.M.C., St. George's H.M.S., St. Mary's H.M.S., United M.D.S. (Guy's and St. Thomas's), University College and Middlesex S.M.), Manchester, Newcastle upon Tyne, Nottingham, Oxford, Sheffield, Southampton, and University of Wales College of Medicine.

Licensing Corporations granting Diplomas

ROYAL COLLEGE OF PHYSICIANS OF LONDON AND THE ROYAL COLLEGE OF SURGEONS OF ENGLAND, Examining Board in England, 35–43 Lincoln's Inn Fields, WC2A 3PN.

SOCIETY OF APOTHECARIES, Black Friars Lane, EC4V 6EJ.—*Registrar*, D. H. C. Barrie.

ROYAL COLLEGE OF OBSTETRICIANS AND GYNÆCOLOGISTS, 27 Sussex Place, Regent's Park, NW1 4RG.—*President*, G. Pinker; *Sec.*, P. Barnett.

ROYAL COLLEGE OF PHYSICIANS OF EDINBURGH, 9 Queen Street, Edinburgh EH2 1JQ.—*President*, Dr. M. F. Oliver, C.B.E.; *Sec.*, Dr. J. L. Anderton.

ROYAL COLLEGE OF SURGEONS OF EDINBURGH, Nicolson Street, Edinburgh EH8 9DW.—*President*, T. J. McNair, Q.H.S.; *Sec.*, P. Edmond, C.B.E., T.D.

ROYAL COLLEGE OF PHYSICIANS AND SURGEONS OF GLASGOW, 234–242 St. Vincent Street, Glasgow G2 5RJ.—*President*, Prof. A. C. Kennedy; *Sec.*, Dr. A. Beattie.

SCOTTISH TRIPLE QUALIFICATION BOARD, Nicolson Street, Edinburgh EH8 9DW and 242 St. Vincent Street, Glasgow.

Professions Supplementary to Medicine

The standard of professional education in chiropody, dietetics, medical laboratory sciences, occupational therapy, orthoptics, physiotherapy and radiography is the responsibility of seven professional boards, which also publish an annual register of qualified practitioners. The work of the Boards is coordinated by THE COUNCIL FOR PROFESSIONS SUPPLEMENTARY TO MEDICINE, Park House, 184 Kennington Park Road, SE11 4BU. *Registrar*, F. Whitehill.

BIOMEDICAL SCIENCES

First Degrees in *Biomedical Sciences* are granted by the Universities of Bradford, London (King's College), and Ulster.

Courses leading to first degrees in *Medical Laboratory Science* granted by the C.N.A.A. are provided by Portsmouth Polytechnic (*Biomedical Sciences*).

Qualifications from higher or further education establishments and training in medical laboratories are required for progress to the professional examinations and qualifications of THE INSTITUTE OF MEDICAL LABORATORY SCIENCES, 12 Queen Anne Street, W1M 0AU.

CHIROPODY

Professional qualifications are granted by THE SOCIETY OF CHIROPODISTS, 53 Welbeck Street, W1M 7HE, to students who have passed the qualifying examination after attending a course of full-time training for three years at one of the ten recognized schools in England and Wales, two in Scotland and one in Northern Ireland. Qualifications granted by the Society are approved by the Chiropodists Board for the purpose of State Registration, which is a condition of employment within the National Health Service. *Sec.*, G. C. Jenkins.

DIETETICS
(*See* main heading, p. 521)

OCCUPATIONAL HYGIENE

Courses leading to first degrees in *Occupational Hygiene* granted by the C.N.A.A. are provided by the Polytechnic of the South Bank.

OCCUPATIONAL THERAPY

First Degrees in *Occupational Therapy* are granted by the University of Ulster and the University of Wales (College of Medicine) (provisional).

Courses leading to first degrees in *Occupation Therapy* granted by the C.N.A.A. are provided by Queen Margaret College.

Professional qualifications are awarded by THE COLLEGE OF OCCUPATIONAL THERAPISTS, 20 Rede Place, W2 4TU, upon completion of one of the 16 training courses approved by the College.

ORTHOPTICS

First Degrees in *Orthoptics* are granted by the University of Wales (College of Medicine) (provisional).

Orthoptists undertake the diagnosis and treatment of all types of squint and other anomalies of binocular vision, working in close collaboration with ophthalmologists. The training and maintenance of professional standards are the responsibility of the Orthoptists Board of the Council for the Professions Supplementary to Medicine. The examining and qualifying body is the BRITISH ORTHOPTIC SOCIETY, Tavistock House North, Tavistock Square, WC1H 9HX. Training consists of a three-year course at one of nine approved Orthoptic Schools in England and Wales and one in Scotland.

(*See also* Ophthalmic Optics.)

PHYSIOTHERAPY

First Degrees are granted by the University of Ulster and the University of Wales (College of Medicine) (provisional).

Courses leading to first degrees in *Physiotherapy* granted by the C.N.A.A. are provided by North East London Polytechnic, Queen Margaret College and the Queen's College.

Full-time three- or four-year degree or diploma courses are available at 32 recognised Schools in the U.K. Information about examinations leading to eligibility for Membership of The Chartered Society of Physiotherapy and to State Registration is available from THE CHARTERED SOCIETY OF PHYSIOTHERAPY, 14 Bedford Row, London WC1R 4ED.—*Sec.*, T. Simon.

RADIOGRAPHY AND RADIOTHERAPY

First Degrees in *Diagnostic Radiography* and *Therapeutic Radiography* are granted by the University of Wales (College of Medicine) (provisional).

Examinations leading to qualification are conducted by THE COLLEGE OF RADIOGRAPHERS, 14 Upper Wimpole Street, W1M 8BN.

There are recognized training centres in radiography and radiotherapy at many cities and towns in England and Wales, Scotland and Northern Ireland.

METEOROLOGY

First Degrees in *Meteorology* are granted by the University of Reading. The subject is also included in degree courses at some other universities.

MINING AND MINING ENGINEERING

First Degrees in *Mining* or *Mining Engineering* are granted by the following universities: Leeds (also *Mineral Engineering*), London (Imperial College of Science and Technology), Newcastle upon Tyne, Nottingham, Strathclyde (*Mining and Petroleum Engineering*), Wales (University College, Cardiff, also *Mineral Processing*).

Courses leading to first degrees granted by the C.N.A.A. are provided by Camborne School of Mines (*Mining Engineering* and *Mineral Processing Engineering*) and North Staffordshire Polytechnic (*Mining Engineering*).

Miscellaneous Authorities

ENGINEERING COUNCIL, 10 Maltravers Street, WC2R 3ER.

INSTITUTION OF MINING ENGINEERS, Danum House, 6A South Parade, Doncaster DN1 2DY.

MUSIC

First Degrees in *Music* are granted by the Universities of Aberdeen (also *History of Music*), Belfast, Birmingham, Bristol, Cambridge, the City University, the Universities of Durham, East Anglia, Edinburgh, Exeter, Glasgow (also *Music Education* and *Music Performance* in conjunction with Royal Scottish Academy of Music and Drama), Hull, Lancaster, Leeds (also at Bretton Hall College), Leicester (*Musicianship*), Liverpool, London (King's College, Royal Holloway and Bedford New College; *also* Goldsmiths' College, Royal Academy of Music, Royal College of Music, and Trinity College of Music), Manchester, Newcastle upon Tyne, Nottingham, Oxford, Reading, Sheffield, Southampton, Surrey (*Academic & Practical Applications of Music*; *Music & Sound Recording (Tonmeister)*), Sussex, Ulster, Wales (University Colleges at Aberystwyth, Bangor and Cardiff; also at Welsh College of Music and Drama), and York.

Courses leading to first degrees in Music granted by the C.N.A.A. are provided by Bath College of Higher Education, Cambridgeshire College of Arts and Technology, City of Birmingham Polytechnic, Colchester Institute, Dartington College of Arts, Huddersfield Polytechnic and Kingston Polytechnic (*Music Education*).

ASSOCIATED BOARD OF THE ROYAL SCHOOLS OF MUSIC, 14 Bedford Square, WC1B 3JG.—Conducts the local examinations in centres throughout the world in music and speech for the Royal Academy of Music and the Royal College of Music in London, the Royal Northern College of Music, Manchester and the Royal Scottish Academy of Music and Drama, Glasgow.
Chief Exec. and Dir. of Examinations, R. Smith.

ROYAL ACADEMY OF MUSIC, Marylebone Road, NW1 5HT.—*Principal*, Sir David Lumsden, D.Phil.

ROYAL COLLEGE OF MUSIC, Prince Consort Road, South Kensington, S.W.7.—*Director*, M. G. Matthews, F.R.C.M., A.R.C.O.

ROYAL NORTHERN COLLEGE OF MUSIC, 124 Oxford Road, Manchester M13 9RD.—*Principal*, J. Manduell, C.B.E., F.R.A.M., F.R.N.C.M., F.R.C.M., F.R.S.A.M.D.

ROYAL SCOTTISH ACADEMY OF MUSIC AND DRAMA, 100 Renfrew Street, Glasgow G2 3BD.—*Principal*, P. Ledger, C.B.E.

ROYAL COLLEGE OF ORGANISTS, Kensington Gore, SW7 2QS.—*Clerk*, K. B. Lyndon.

GUILDHALL SCHOOL OF MUSIC AND DRAMA, Silk Street, Barbican, EC2Y 8DT.—*Principal*, J. Hosier, C.B.E., F.R.C.M.

LONDON COLLEGE OF MUSIC, 47 Great Marlborough Street, W1V 2AS.—*Director*, J. McCabe, C.B.E. *Secretary*,

TRINITY COLLEGE OF MUSIC, 11–13 Mandeville Place, W1M 6AQ.—*Principal*, M. Davies, C.B.E.

NAUTICAL STUDIES

(*See also* Marine Engineering, Fishery Science)

The University of Wales grants first degrees in *Maritime Studies, Maritime Commerce* and *Maritime Geography* (courses at Institute of Science and Technology).

Courses leading to first degrees in *Nautical Studies* granted by the C.N.A.A. are provided by Liverpool Polytechnic (*Maritime Studies*), Plymouth Polytechnic and Sunderland Polytechnic.

Merchant Navy Training Schools
For Officers

MERCHANT NAVY COLLEGE, Greenhithe, Kent DA9 9NY.—*Principal*, G. Emmons, PH.D.

THE COLLEGE OF MARITIME STUDIES, Warsash, Southampton SO3 6ZL. *Director*, Capt. C. N. Phelan.

For Seamen

INDEFATIGABLE AND NATIONAL SEA TRAINING SCHOOL FOR BOYS, Plas Llanfair, Llanfairpwll, Anglesey.—*Captain Headmaster*, Capt. T. R. Beggs; *Sec.*, L. Dodd, Room 22, Oriel Chambers, 14 Water Street, Liverpool L2 8TD.

NATIONAL SEA TRAINING COLLEGE, Denton, Gravesend, Kent DA12 2HR.—*Princ.*, Capt. C. G. W. Hunter.

NURSING

Courses in which academic study leading to a degree at a University may be combined with nursing training/practical nursing in hospitals are provided by the University of Brunel (*Mental Nursing*), the City University, the Universities of Edinburgh, Glasgow, Hull, Liverpool, London (Goldsmiths', King's and Queen Mary Colleges), Manchester, Southampton, Surrey, Ulster and Wales (College of Medicine).

Courses leading to first degrees in *Nursing* granted by the C.N.A.A. are provided by Bristol Polytechnic, Dundee College of Technology, Glasgow College of Technology, Leeds Polytechnic, Queen Margaret College, Sheffield City Polytechnic and Polytechnic of the South Bank.

Three-year courses for State Registration in general, sick children's mental and mental deficiency nursing. Two-year course for State enrolment. Training schools in many parts of Great Britain.

THE ROYAL COLLEGE OF NURSING
OF THE UNITED KINGDOM
20 Cavendish Square, W1M 0AB

The Royal College of Nursing, within its Institute of Advanced Nursing Education, provides education at post-basic level in hospital, occupational health and community health fields. Advanced courses are held in preparation for senior posts in management and teaching; and other short and special courses.
Director of Education and Principal of the Institute of Advanced Nursing Education, Miss M. Green, O.B.E.

NATIONAL BOARD FOR NURSING, MIDWIFERY AND HEALTH VISITING FOR ENGLAND, 170 Tottenham Court Road, W1P 0HA.—*Chief Exec. Officer*, D. Jones, O.B.E.

NATIONAL BOARD FOR NURSING, MIDWIFERY AND HEALTH VISITING FOR SCOTLAND, 22 Queen Street, Edinburgh EH2 1JX.—*Chief Exec. Officer*, Miss L. Coutts.

WELSH NATIONAL BOARD FOR NURSING, MIDWIFERY AND HEALTH VISITING, Floor 13, Pearl Assurance House, Greyfriars Road, Cardiff CF1 3AG.—*Chief Exec.*, D. A. Ravey.

NATIONAL BOARD FOR NURSING, MIDWIFERY AND HEALTH VISITING FOR NORTHERN IRELAND, 79 Chichester Street, Belfast BT1 4JE.—*Chief Exec. Officer*, J. J. Walsh.

OPHTHALMIC OPTICS

First Degrees in *Ophthalmic Optics* or *Optometry* are granted by the Universities of Aston, Bradford, the City University, Manchester (Manchester Institute of Science and Technology), and Wales (Institute of Science and Technology).

Courses leading to first degrees in *Ophthalmic Optics* granted by the C.N.A.A. are provided by the Glasgow College of Technology.

Examining bodies granting qualifications as an optometrist or ophthalmic optician and higher diplomas:—

THE BRITISH COLLEGE OF OPTOMETRISTS, 10 Knaresborough Place, SW5 0TG.

THE ASSOCIATION OF BRITISH DISPENSING OPTICIANS, 22 Nottingham Place, W1M 4AT.

PHARMACY

First Degrees in *Pharmacy* are granted by the Universities of Aston, Bath, Belfast, Bradford, London (King's College and the School of Pharmacy), Manchester, Nottingham, Strathclyde, Wales (Institute of Science and Technology).

Courses leading to first degrees in Pharmacy granted by the C.N.A.A. are provided by Brighton Polytechnic, Leicester Polytechnic, Liverpool Polytechnic, Portsmouth Polytechnic, Robert Gordon's Institute of Technology, and Sunderland Polytechnic.

Information may be obtained from The Registrar, THE PHARMACEUTICAL SOCIETY OF GREAT BRITAIN, 1 Lambeth High Street, SE1 7JN.

PHOTOGRAPHY, FILM AND TV STUDIES

First Degrees are awarded by the Universities of Glasgow (*Drama/Film & TV Studies*), Kent (*Drama/Film Studies*), Stirling (*Film and Media Studies*), and Wales (College of Medicine, *Medical Photography* (provisional)). At some other universities *Film* may be studied as part of a first degree course.

Courses leading to first degrees granted by the C.N.A.A. are provided by Derbyshire College of Higher Education (*Photographic Studies*), Harrow College of Higher Education/Middlesex Polytechnic (*Applied Photography, Film and TV*), London College of Printing (*Photography; Film and Video*), Napier College of Commerce and Technology (*Photographic Studies*), Polytechnic of Central London (*Film, Video and Photographic Arts* and *Photographic Sciences*), Trent Polytechnic (*Photography*), West Surrey College of Art and Design (*Photography, Film and Video, Animation*).

BRITISH INSTITUTE OF PROFESSIONAL PHOTOGRAPHY, Amwell End, Ware, Herts. SG12 9HN.—*Secretary*, P. A. Large.

PRINTING

First Degrees in *Typography and Graphic Communication* are awarded by the University of Reading.

Courses leading to first degrees in *Printing and Packaging Technology* granted by the C.N.A.A. are provided by Watford College of Technology.

Courses in technical and general, design and administrative aspects of printing are available at technical colleges throughout the United Kingdom. Details can be obtained from the Institute of Printing and the British Printing Industries Federation (*see below*).

In addition to the examining and organizing bodies listed below, examinations are held by various independent regional examining boards in further education.

INSTITUTE OF PRINTING, 8 Lonsdale Gardens, Tunbridge Wells, Kent TN1 1NU.—*Sec.*, C. F. Partridge.
BRITISH PRINTING INDUSTRIES FEDERATION, 11 Bedford Row, WC1R 4DX.

RECREATION, SPORT, AND HUMAN MOVEMENT STUDIES

(*See also* Dance)

First Degrees are granted by the University of Birmingham (*Sport and Recreation Studies*), Liverpool (*Physical Education and Movement Science*), Loughborough (*Physical Education and Sports Science*; also *Physical Education, Sports Science and Recreation Management*) and Ulster (*Sport and Leisure Studies*). *Physical Education* may be studied as part of other first degree courses at several universities.

Courses in *Sports Science/Studies* leading to first degrees granted by the C.N.A.A. are provided by Bedford College of Higher Education, Brighton Polytechnic, Crewe and Alsager College of Higher Education, Jordanhill College of Education (*Sport in the Community*), Liverpool Polytechnic, Newcastle upon Tyne Polytechnic with Sunderland Polytechnic, North Staffordshire Polytechnic (*Sport and Recreation Studies*), Sheffield City Polytechnic, Trent Polytechnic (*Sport—Administration and Science*) and West Sussex Institute of Higher Education.

First Degrees in *Recreation and Environment* are granted by the University of Manchester (courses at North Cheshire College), in *Recreation* by the C.N.A.A. with courses at Dunfermline College of Physical Education, Leeds Polytechnic (*Leisure Studies*), North Staffordshire Polytechnic (*Sport and Recreation Studies*), and College of St. Mark and St. John (*Recreation and Community*), and in *Tourism* with courses at Dorset Institute of Higher Education and (*Travel and Tourism*) Newcastle upon Tyne Polytechnic.

First degrees in *Human Movement Studies* are granted by the University of Wales (courses at South Glamorgan Institute of Higher Education) and by the C.N.A.A. (courses at Leeds Polytechnic).

Physical Education and *Sports Science/Studies* also form part of a degree course at many other colleges/polytechnics.

ROBOTICS

(*See also* Computer Science)

First Degrees in *Electronic Control and Robot Engineering* are granted by the University of Hull.

SOCIAL WORK

First Degrees in *Social Studies* or in *Social Sciences* are granted by most universities. Courses leading to first degrees in *Social Science* or *Social Sciences/Applied Social Science or Sociology* granted by the C.N.A.A. are provided by some 30 polytechnics and colleges.

CENTRAL COUNCIL FOR EDUCATION AND TRAINING IN SOCIAL WORK, Derbyshire House, St. Chad's Street, London WC1H 8AD.—*Dir.*, A. Hall. The Council validates and approves courses, schemes and programmes leading to the C.C.E.T.S.W.'s awards, including the Certificate of Qualification in Social Work. This is the professional qualification for social workers and courses that lead to it are available at universities, polytechnics, colleges and institutes.

SPEECH SCIENCE

(*See also* Languages)

First Degrees in *Speech* are awarded by the University of Newcastle upon Tyne; in *Speech Science* by the University of Sheffield; in *Speech Sciences* by the University of London (University College); in *Speech Pathology* by the University of Manchester; in *Speech Pathology and Therapeutics* (with courses at Jordanhill College of Education) by the University of Glasgow; and in *Speech Therapy* by the University of Ulster and (with courses at South Glamorgan Institute of Higher Education) by the University of Wales. First Degrees in *Clinical Communication Studies* are granted by the City University.

Courses leading to first degrees in *Speech Therapy* granted by the C.N.A.A. are provided by Central School of Speech and Drama, City of Birmingham Polytechnic (*Speech and Language Pathology and Therapeutics*), Leeds Polytechnic (*Clinical Language Sciences*), Leicester Polytechnic (*Speech Pathology and Therapy*), Manchester Polytechnic (*Speech Pathology and Therapy*) and Queen Margaret College (*Speech Pathology and Therapy*).

The Directory of qualified Speech Therapists is published biennially by THE COLLEGE OF SPEECH THERAPISTS, Harold Poster House, 6 Lechmere Road, NW2 5BU. Details of courses leading to certification by The College of Speech Therapists are available from the College.

SURVEYING

(*See* Estate Management and Surveying)

TEACHING

There are two main ways to gain the qualification needed to become a teacher:

(a) The first is to follow a three- or four-year course leading to a B.Ed. degree. B.Ed. courses are provided by colleges of education/institutes of higher education/polytechnics. The degrees are awarded either by universities or by the C.N.A.A.

(b) The second, for those who are already graduates with a degree other than a B.Ed., is to follow a one-year course leading to a postgraduate certificate in education at a college, polytechnic or university.

There is, in addition, a third route which is to take a course at one of the few institutions, mainly universities, that offer concurrent courses (normally four years) leading to a degree (other than B.Ed.) *and* a teaching qualification.

Special arrangements exist for those wishing to teach craft design and technology.

TECHNICAL EDUCATION

First Degrees in one or more technologies are awarded by almost all universities; and many polytechnics and colleges of technology provide courses leading to first degrees granted by the C.N.A.A. Details are given under individual subject headings.

CITY AND GUILDS OF LONDON INSTITUTE
76 Portland Place, W1N 4AA

The Institute offers examinations on its published regulations and syllabuses, and awards certificates of pre-vocational and vocational training in a wide range of technical subjects. The Institute provides the administrative services for the National Examinations Board for Supervisory Studies and the National Examinations Board for Agriculture, Horticulture and Allied Industries. With the Business and Technician Education Council (*see* page 520), it has established the Joint Board for Pre-Vocational Education.

President, H.R.H. the Duke of Edinburgh, K.G., K.T.
Chairman, H. M. Neal.
Director-General, J. A. Barnes.
Secretary, S. J. Westacott.

Regional Advisory Councils

The Councils issue handbooks, etc., giving information about the facilities available within a region or district for various types of technical training. They also have certain responsibilities in connection with the procedure for the approval by the Department of Education and Science of advanced courses.

EAST ANGLIAN.—Regional Advisory Council for Further Education, 2 Looms Lane, Bury St. Edmunds, Suffolk IP33 1HE.

EAST MIDLANDS.—East Midlands Further Education Council, Robins Wood House, Robins Wood Road, Aspley, Nottingham NG8 3NH.

LONDON AND SOUTH EASTERN.—Regional Advisory Council for Further Education, Tavistock House South, Tavistock Square, WC1H 9LR.

NORTH WESTERN.—North Western Regional Advisory Council for Further Education, Town Hall, Walkden Road, Worsley, Manchester M28 4QE.

NORTHERN.—Northern Council for Further Education, 5 Grosvenor Villas, Grosvenor Road, Newcastle upon Tyne NE2 2RU.

SOUTHERN.—Regional Council for Further Education, 26 Bath Road, Reading RG1 6NT.

SOUTH WEST.—Regional Council for Further Education, Wessex Lodge, 11–13 Billetfield, Taunton TA1 3NN.

WALES.—Welsh Joint Education Committee, 245 Western Avenue, Cardiff CF5 2YX.

WEST MIDLANDS.—Advisory Council for Further Education, Norfolk House, Smallbrook Queensway, Birmingham B5 4NB.

YORKSHIRE AND HUMBERSIDE.—Association for Further and Higher Education, Bowling Green Terrace, Leeds LS11 9SX.

Industry Training Boards

AGRICULTURAL, Bourne House, 32–34 Beckenham Road, Beckenham, Kent BR3 4PB.—*Dir.,* D. C. Newman.

CLOTHING AND ALLIED PRODUCTS, Tower House, Merrion Way, Leeds LS2 8NY.—*Chief Exec.,* J. W. Dearden.

CONSTRUCTION, Dewhurst House, 24 West Smithfield, EC1A 9JA.—*Sec.,* J. A. Reynolds, O.B.E.

ENGINEERING, P.O. Box 176, 54 Clarendon Road, Watford, Herts. WD1 1LB.—*Sec.,* E. P. Jones.

HOTEL AND CATERING, International House, High Street, Ealing, W5 5DB.—*Sec.,* W. A. Heaney.

LOCAL GOVERNMENT TRAINING BOARD, Arndale House, Arndale Centre, Luton, Beds. LU1 2TS.—*Dir.,* M. G. Clarke.

MAN-MADE FIBRES INDUSTRY TRAINING ADVISORY BOARD, Gable House, 40 High Street, Rickmansworth, Herts. WD3 1ER.—*Gen. Manager,* D. W. Ashby.

OFFSHORE PETROLEUM, Offshore Training Centre, Forties Road, Montrose, Angus DD10 9ET.—*Sec.,* P. J. Bing, O.B.E.

PLASTICS PROCESSING, Coppice House, Halesfield 7, Telford, Shropshire, TF7 4NA.—*Chief Exec.,* J. C. Shearman.

ROAD TRANSPORT, Capitol House, Empire Way, Wembley, Middx. HA9 0NG.—*Dir. Gen.,* D. C. Barnett.

TEXTILES

First Degrees in *Textiles* are awarded by the Universities of Leeds and Manchester (Manchester Institute of Science and Technology, *Textile Technology* and *Clothing Engineering*).

Courses leading to first degrees in *Textile Marketing* granted by the C.N.A.A. are provided by Huddersfield Polytechnic; in *Textile and Knitwear Technology* by Leicester Polytechnic; in *Textiles with Clothing Studies* by Scottish College of Textiles; in *Clothing Studies* by Manchester Polytechnic; in *Food, Textiles and Consumer Studies* by Polytechnic of the South Bank and Robert Gordon's Institute of Technology, and in various aspects of *Textiles/Fashion* by some 20 Polytechnics and Colleges.

THE TEXTILE INSTITUTE, 10 Blackfriars Street, Manchester M3 5DR.—*Gen. Sec.,* R. G. Denyer.

THEOLOGY

First Degrees in *Theology* or *Divinity* are granted by the Universities of Aberdeen, Belfast, Birmingham, Bristol (*Theology and Religious Studies*), Cambridge (*Theological and Religious Studies*), Durham, Edinburgh, Exeter, Glasgow, Hull, Kent, Leeds (*Theology and Religious Studies*), London (Heythrop and King's Colleges), Manchester (*Theology and Religious Studies*), Nottingham, Oxford, St. Andrews, Southampton (at La Sainte Union College of Higher Education), and Wales (Aberystwyth, Bangor, Cardiff, and, also *Theology and Religious Studies,* St. David's University Colleges); in *Biblical Studies* by the Universities of London (Heythrop and King's Colleges), Manchester, Sheffield and Wales (Bangor University College); and in *Religious Studies* by the Universities of Bristol (*Theology and Religious Studies*), Cambridge (*Theological and Religious Studies*), Edinburgh, Lancaster, Leeds (*Theology and Religious Studies*), London (King's College), Manchester (*Theology and Religious Studies* and *Comparative Religion*), Newcastle upon Tyne, Stirling, and Wales (University College, Cardiff and, also *Theology and Religious Studies,* St. David's University College).

Courses leading to first degrees in *Theology* or *Theological Studies* granted by the C.N.A.A. are provided by London Bible College, Spurgeon's College, Thames Polytechnic, Trinity College, Bristol and Westminster College, Oxford; in *Theological and Pastoral Studies* by Oak Hill College; and in *Jewish Studies* by Jews' College.

Theological Colleges
Church of England and Church in Wales

CHICHESTER THEOLOGICAL COLLEGE, Chichester, W. Sussex PO19 1SG. (56).—*Princ.,* Rev. Canon J. Hind.

CRANMER HALL, St. John's College, Durham DH1 3RJ. (77).—*Princ.,* Miss D. R. Etchells.

LINCOLN THEOLOGICAL COLLEGE, Drury Lane, Lincoln LN1 3BP. (76).—*Warden,* Rev. Canon Dr. W. M. Jacob.

OAK HILL COLLEGE, Chase Side, Southgate, N14 4PS. (112 + 28 part-time).—*Princ.,* Rev. Canon G. F. Bridger.

COLLEGE OF THE RESURRECTION, Mirfield, W. Yorks. WF14 0BW. (44).—*Princ.,* Rev. Fr. D. Lloyd.

RIDLEY HALL, Cambridge CB3 9HG. (60).—*Princ.,* Rev. Canon H. F. de Waal.

RIPON COLLEGE, Cuddesdon, Oxon. OX9 9EX. (70).—*Princ.,* Rev. J. H. Garton.

ST. DEINIOL'S LIBRARY, Hawarden, Deeside, Clwyd CH5 3DF.—*Princ.,* Rev. P. J. Jagger.

ST. JOHN'S COLLEGE, Bramcote, Nottingham NG9
3DS. (128).—*Princ.*, Rev. Dr. A. C. Thiselton.
ST. MICHAEL'S THEOLOGICAL COLLEGE, Llandaff, Cardiff CF5 2YJ. (30).—*Princ.*, Rev. Canon Dr. J. G.
Hughes.
ST. STEPHEN'S HOUSE, 16 Marston Street, Oxford OX4
1JX. (60).—*Princ.*, Rev. E. R. Barnes.
SALISBURY AND WELLS THEOLOGICAL COLLEGE, 19 The
Close, Salisbury, Wilts. SP1 2EE. (150).—*Princ.*,
Rev. Canon R. J. A. Askew.
TRINITY COLLEGE, Stoke Hill, Bristol BS9 1JP. (135).—
Princ., (vacant).
WESTCOTT HOUSE, Jesus Lane, Cambridge CB5 8BP.
(50).—*Princ.*, Rev. Canon Dr. R. W. N. Hoare.
WYCLIFFE HALL, 54 Banbury Road, Oxford OX2 6PW.
(90).—*Princ.*, Rev. Canon G. N. Shaw.

Scottish Episcopal Church

THEOLOGICAL COLLEGE, Roebery Avenue, Edinburgh
EH12 5JT. (28).—*Princ.*, Rev. Canon J. M. Armson.

Interdenominational

QUEEN'S COLLEGE, Somerset Road, Edgbaston, Birmingham B15 2QH. (75).—*Princ.*, Rev. Dr. J. B.
Walker.

Church of Scotland

CHRIST'S COLLEGE, Aberdeen AB1 1YD. (80).—*Master*,
Rev. Dr. H. R. Sefton.
NEW COLLEGE, Mound Place, Edinburgh EH1 2LU.
(270).—*Princ.*, Rev. Prof. D. B. Forrester.
TRINITY COLLEGE, 4 The Square, University of
Glasgow, GL12 8QQ. (140).—*Princ.*, Rev. Prof. R.
Davidson, D.D.

Non-Denominational

COLLEGE OF ST. MARY, The University, St. Andrews
KY16 9JU. (162).—*Princ.*, Rev. Prof. D. W. D. Shaw.

Presbyterian

UNION THEOLOGICAL COLLEGE, Belfast BT7 1JT.
(52).—*Princ.*, Prof. R. F. G. Holmes.

Presbyterian Church of Wales

UNITED THEOLOGICAL COLLEGE, Aberystwyth SY23
2LT. (45).—*Princ.*, Rev. Prof. E. ap Nefydd Roberts.

Methodist

EDGHILL THEOLOGICAL COLLEGE, Belfast. (25).—
Princ., Rev. W. D. D. Cooke, PH.D.
WESLEY COLLEGE, Westbury-on-Trym, Bristol BS10
7QD. (72).—*Princ.*, Rev. Dr. H. McKeating.
WESLEY HOUSE, Cambridge. (34).—*Princ.*, Rev. Dr. I.
H. Jones.

Congregational and United Reformed

BALA-BANGOR INDEPENDENT COLLEGE, Bangor LL57
2EH. (15).—*Princ.*, R. T. Jones, D.PHIL., D.D.
MANSFIELD COLLEGE, Oxford. (160).—*Princ.*, Rev. J.
L. Womer.
MEMORIAL COLLEGE, Aberystwyth. (20).—*Princ.*, Rev.
Dr. D. E. Davies.
NORTHERN COLLEGE, Luther King House, Brighton
Grove, Rusholme, Manchester M14 5JP. (45).—
Princ., Rev. Dr. R. J. McKelvey.
SCOTTISH CONGREGATIONAL COLLEGE, Rosebery Crescent, Edinburgh EH12 5JN. (23).—*Princ.*, Rev. H.
Smith.
WESTMINSTER COLLEGE, Cambridge CB3 0AA. (30).—
Princ., Rev. M. H. Cressey.

Roman Catholic

ALLEN HALL COLLEGE, 28 Beaufort Street, SW3 5AA.
(60).—*Rector*, Rt. Rev. Mgr. P. O'Donoghue.
CAMPION HOUSE COLLEGE, 112 Thornbury Road,
Osterley, Middx. TW7 4NN. (55).—*Rector*, Rev. M.
Barrow, S.J.

CHESTERS COLLEGE, 2 Chesters Road, Bearsden,
Glasgow. (50).—*Rector*, Very Rev. P. Tartaglia.
OSCOTT COLLEGE, Chester Road, Sutton Coldfield, W.
Midlands B73 5AA. (80).—*Rector*, Rt. Rev. Mgr. M.
J. Kirkham.
ST. JOHN'S SEMINARY, Wonersh, Guildford, Surrey
GU5 0QX. (65).—*Rector*, Rt. Rev. Mgr. P. Smith.
ST. JOSEPH'S COLLEGE SCHOOL AND UPHOLLAND
NORTHERN INSTITUTE FOR ADULT CHRISTIAN EDUCATION, Upholland, Skelmersdale, Lancs. WN8
0PZ.—*Dir.*, Mgr. J. Butchard.
USHAW COLLEGE, Durham DH7 9RH. (150).—*Pres.*,
Rt. Rev. Mgr. P. Walton.

Baptist

BRISTOL BAPTIST COLLEGE, Woodland Road, Bristol
BS8 1UN. (40).—*Princ.*, Rev. J. E. Morgan-Wynne.
NORTHERN BAPTIST COLLEGE, Brighton Grove, Rusholme, Manchester M14 5JP. (45).—*Princ.*, Rev. Dr.
B. Haymes.
NORTH WALES BAPTIST COLLEGE, Ffordd Ffriddoedd,
Bangor LL57 2EH. (7).—*Princ.*, Rev. J. R. Rowlands.
REGENT'S PARK COLLEGE, Oxford OX1 2LB. (83).—
Princ., Rev. B. R. White, D.Phil.
THE SCOTTISH BAPTIST COLLEGE, 12 Aytoun Road,
Glasgow G41 5RT. (18).—*Princ.*, Rev. G. W. Martin.
SOUTH WALES BAPTIST COLLEGE, 54 Richmond Road,
Cardiff CF2 3UR. (22).—*Princ.*, Rev. N. Clark.
SPURGEON'S COLLEGE, South Norwood Hill, SE25 6DJ.
(68).—*Princ.*, Rev. Dr. P. Beasley-Murray.

Unitarian

UNITARIAN COLLEGE, Luther King House, Brighton
Grove, Rusholme, Manchester M14 5JP. (3).—
Princ., Rev. A. J. Long.

Jewish

JEWS' COLLEGE, Albert Road, Hendon, NW4 2SJ.
(60).—*Princ.*, Rabbi J. Sacks, PH.D.
LEO BAECK COLLEGE, The Manor House, 80 East End
Road, N3 2SY (20).—*Princ.* Rabbi J. Magonet, PH.D.

TOWN AND COUNTRY PLANNING

First Degrees are granted by the Universities of
Belfast (*Environmental Planning*), Dundee (*Town
and Regional Planning*), East Anglia (*Development
Studies—Regional Analysis & Planning*), Glasgow
(*Planning*), Heriot-Watt (*Town Planning*), Kent
(*Urban Studies*), London (University College, *Environmental Studies* and *Planning*), Manchester (*Town
and Country Planning*), Newcastle upon Tyne (*Town
and Country Planning*), Sheffield (*Urban Studies*),
Stirling (*Urban Studies and Social Policy*), Sussex
(*Urban Studies*), and Wales (Institute of Science and
Technology, *Town Planning Studies*).
Courses leading to first degrees in *Town Planning*
granted by the C.N.A.A. are provided by City of
Birmingham Polytechnic, Leeds Polytechnic and
Polytechnic of the South Bank; in *Town and Country
Planning* by Bristol Polytechnic; in *Planning Studies*
by Oxford Polytechnic; in *Environmental Planning*
by Essex Institute of Higher Education; in *Urban
Planning Studies* by the Polytechnic of Central
London; and in *Urban and Regional Planning* by
Coventry (Lanchester) Polytechnic.
The ROYAL TOWN PLANNING INSTITUTE, 26 Portland Place, W1N 4BE, recognizes a number of degree
and diploma courses in town planning.

TRANSPORT

First Degrees are granted by the Universities of
Aston (*Transport Management*), Loughborough
(*Transport Management and Planning*), Wales (*Institute of Science and Technology: International Transport*) and Ulster (*Transport Technology*). The City

University awards a first degree in *Air Transport Engineering.*

Courses leading to first degrees granted by the C.N.A.A. are provided by Coventry (Lanchester) Polytechnic (*Industrial Design—Transportation*), Huddersfield Polytechnic (*Transport and Distribution*) and Napier College of Commerce and Technology (*Transportation Engineering*).

THE CHARTERED INSTITUTE OF TRANSPORT, 80 Portland Place, London W1N 4DP, conducts qualifying examinations in transport management leading to chartered professional status.

VETERINARY STUDIES

First Degrees in *Veterinary Science/Medicine and Surgery* are granted by the Universities of Bristol, Cambridge, Edinburgh, Glasgow, Liverpool and London (Royal Veterinary College).

ARCHBISHOPS OF CANTERBURY SINCE 1414

1414 Henry Chichele	1633 William Laud	1828 William Howley
1443 John Stafford	1660 William Juxon	1848 John Bird Sumner
1452 John Kemp	1663 Gilbert Sheldon	1862 Charles Thomas Longley
1454 Thomas Bourchier	1678 William Sancroft	1868 Archibald Campbell Tait
1486 John Morton	1691 John Tillotson	1883 Edward White Benson
1501 Henry Dean	1695 Thomas Tenison	1896 Frederick Temple
1503 William Warham	1716 William Wake	1903 Randall Thomas Davidson
1533 Thomas Cranmer	1737 John Potter	1928 Cosmo Gordon Lang
1556 Reginald Pole	1747 Thomas Herring	1942 William Temple
1559 Matthew Parker	1757 Matthew Hutton	1945 Geoffrey Francis Fisher
1576 Edmund Grindal	1758 Thomas Secker	1961 Arthur Michael Ramsey
1583 John Whitgift	1768 Hon. Frederick Cornwallis	1974 Frederick Donald Coggan
1604 Richard Bancroft	1783 John Moore	1980 Robert Runcie
1611 George Abbot	1805 Charles Manners Sutton	

ARCHBISHOPS OF YORK SINCE 1606

1606 Tobias Matthew	1724 Launcelot Blackburn	1891 William Connor Magee
1628 George Montague	1743 Thomas Herring	1891 William Dalrymple Maclagan
1629 Samuel Harsnett	1747 Matthew Hutton	1909 Cosmo Gordon Lang
1632 Richard Neile	1757 John Gilbert	1929 William Temple
1641 John Williams	1761 Robert Hay Drummond	1942 Cyril Forster Garbett
1660 Accepted Frewen	1777 William Markham	1956 Arthur Michael Ramsey
1664 Richard Sterne	1808 Edward Venables Vernon	1961 Frederick Donald Coggan
1683 John Dolben	Harcourt	1975 Stuart Yarworth Blanch
1688 Thomas Lamplugh	1848 Thomas Musgrave	1983 John Stapylton Habgood
1691 John Sharp	1860 Charles Thomas Longley	
1714 William Dawes	1862 William Thomson	

POPES FROM 1800

Sovereign Pontiff	Family Name	Elected	Sovereign Pontiff	Family Name	Elected
Pius VII	Chiaramonti	1800	Pius XII	Pacelli	1939
Leo XII	della Genga	1823	John XXIII	Roncalli	1958
Pius VIII	Castiglioni	1829	Paul VI	Montini	1963
Gregory XVI	Cappellari	1831	John Paul I	Luciani	1978
Pius IX	Mastai-Ferretti	1846	John Paul II	Wojtyla	1978
Leo XIII	Pecci	1878			
Pius X	Sarto	1903	Adrian IV (Nicholas Breakspear, the only English-
Benedict XV	della Chiesa	1914	man elected Pope) was born at Langley, near St.
Pius XI	Ratti	1922	Albans; elected Pope, on the death of Anastasius IV, 1154; died 1159.

HEADMASTERS' CONFERENCE SCHOOLS

THE HEADMASTERS' CONFERENCE.—*Chairman* (1987), M. J. W. Rogers (King Edward's, Birmingham); *Gen. Sec.*, T. P. Snape, Chancery House, 107 St. Paul's Road, N1 2NB; *Deputy Sec.*, R. N. P. Griffiths. The annual meetings are, as a rule, held at the end of September.

In considering applications for election to membership the Committee will have regard to the scheme or other instrument under which the school is administered (taking particularly into consideration the degree of independence enjoyed by the Headmaster and the Governing Body); the number of pupils over thirteen years of age in the school and the number of pupils in proportion to the size of the school who are in the sixth form, *i.e.* engaged on studies at the Advanced Level of the General Certificate of Education.

Name of School	F'ded.	No. of Boys	Annual Fees D = Day Boys		Headmaster (With date of Appointment)
England and Wales					
Abbotsholme School, Staffs.	1889	270†	£6,100	D£4,050	D. J. Farrant (1984)
Abingdon, Oxfordshire	1256	700	£5,502	D£2,751	M. St. J. Parker (1975)
Aldenham, Elstree, Herts.	1597	350†	£6,540	D£4,050	M. Higginbottom (1983)
Alleyn's School, S.E.22	1619	900†	....	D£2,895	D. A. Fenner (1976)
Allhallows, Rousdon, Dorset..........	1515	285†	£5,754	D£2,712	P. S. Larkman,L.V.O. (1983)
Ampleforth College (*R.C.*), York	1802	620	£5,500		Rev. D. L. Milroy, O.S.B. (1980)
Ardingly College, Haywards Heath, Sussex*	1858	490†	£6,435	D£5,040	J. W. Flecker (1980)
Arnold School, Blackpool	1896	740†	£4,080	D£2,043	J. A. B. Kelsall (1987)
Ashville College, Harrogate	1877	450†	£4,905	D£2,664	M. H. Crosby (1987)
Bancroft's, Woodford Green, Essex	1727	686†	....	D£2,920	Dr. P. C. D. Southern (1985)
Barnard Castle, Co. Durham..........	1883	513†	£3,813	D£2,022	F. S. McNamara (1980)
Bedales, Petersfield, Hants.	1893	375†	£6,825	D£4,800	E. A. M. MacAlpine (1981)
Bedford School	1552	760	£5,478	D£3,180	S. J. Miller (1986)
Bedford Modern School	1566	950	£4,095	D£2,199	P. J. Squire (1977)
Berkhamsted, Herts..................	1541	658	£5,310	D£3,024	C. J. Driver (1983)
Birkenhead, Merseyside	1860	713	....	D£2,025	J. A. Gwilliam (1963)
Bishop's Stortford College, Herts.	1868	373†	£5,331	D£3,786	S. G. G. Benson (1984)
Bloxham School, Banbury, Oxon.*	1860	360†	£5,985	D£4,020	M. W. Vallance (1982)
Blundell's, Tiverton	1604	482†	£6,150	D£3,750	A. J. D. Rees (1980)
Bolton	1524	850	....	D£2,196	A. W. Wright (1983)
Bootham, York......................	1823	300†	£5,098	D£3,402	J. H. Gray (1972)
Bradfield College, Berks.	1850	500	£6,600	D£4,620	P. B. Smith (1985)
Bradford Grammar, Yorks.............	1662	1000†	....	D£1,998	D. A. G. Smith (1974)
Brentwood School, Essex..............	1557	809†	£4,821	D£2,775	J. A. E. Evans (1981)
Brighton College, Sussex	1845	485	£5,100	D£3,315	J. D. Leach (1987)
Bristol Cathedral School	1542	450†	....	D£2,097	C. S. Martin (1979)
Bristol Grammar School	1532	982†	....	D£2,134	C. E. Martin (1986)
Bromsgrove, Worcs...................	1553	460†	£5,151	D£3,267	T. M. Taylor (1986)
Bryanston School, Blandford	1928	630†	£6,195 ..	D£4,131°	T. D. Wheare (1983)
Bury Grammar, Lancs................	1634	650	....	D£1,680	J. Robson (1969)
Canford, Wimborne, Dorset	1923	530†	£6,240	D£4,365	M. Marriott (1976)
Caterham, Surrey	1811	425†	£4,539	D£2,493	S. R. Smith (1974)
Charterhouse, Godalming.............	1611	703†	£7,116	D£5,871	P. J. Attenborough (1982)
Cheadle Hulme	1855	870†	£4,740	D£2,280	D. C. Firth (1977)
Cheltenham College	1841	566†	£6,600	D£4,440	R. M. Morgan (1978)
Chigwell, Essex	1629	350†	£4,935	D£3,303	B. J. Wilson (1971)
Christ College, Brecon	1541	320†	£4,590	D£3,450	S. W. Hockey (1982)
Christ's Hospital, Horsham	1553	860†	Various		R. C. Poulton (1987)
Churcher's College, Petersfield, Hants. .	1722	460†	£5,310	D£2,751	J. F. Fishley (1985)
City of London, E.C.4	1442	800	....	D£3,192	J. M. Hammond (1984)
City of London Freemen's School, Ash- tead Park, Surrey	1854	542†	£4,737	D£2,985	D. C. Haywood (1987)
Clifton College, Bristol...............	1862	670†	£7,050	D£4,800	S. M. Andrews (1975)
Colfe's School, S.E.12	1652	650†	....	D£2,475	V. S. Anthony (1976)
Colston's, Bristol	1710	325†	£5,100	D£3,135	G. W. Searle (1975)
Coventry School (Bablake and King Henry VIII, *amal.* 1977)	—	1690†	....	D£1,890	R. Cooke (*Director*) (1977)
Cranleigh, Surrey	1863	560†	£7,065	D£4,920	A. Hart (1984)
Culford School, Bury St. Edmunds	1881	450†	£5,285	D£3,349	D. Robson (1971)
Dame Allan's Sch., Newcastle on Tyne .	1705	440	....	D£2,088	F. Wilkinson (1970)
Dauntsey's, Devizes	1543	540†	£5,685	D£2,991	C. R. Evans (1985)
Dean Close, Cheltenham	1884	400†	£6,615	D£4,230	C. J. Bacon (1979)
Denstone College, Uttoxeter, Staffs.* ...	1873	390†	£5,925	D£4,100	R. M. Ridley (1986)
Douai (*R.C.*), Woolhampton	1903	305	£5,391	D£3,591	Rev. G. Scott, O.S.B. (1987)
Dover College, Kent	1871	370†	£6,240	D£4,125	J. K. Ind (1981)
Downside (*R.C.*), Stratton-on-the-Fosse, Somerset	1607	472	£6,200	D£4,500	Rev. P. Jebb, O.S.B. (1980)

† Pupils.   * A Woodard Corporation School.   ° 1986 figures.

Name of School	F'ded.	No. of Boys	Annual Fees D = Day Boys	Headmaster *(With date of Appointment)*
Dulwich College, S.E.21	1619	1440	£6,435 .... D£3,225	A. C. F. Verity (*Master*) (1986)
Durham	1414	375	£6,138 .... D£4,092	M. A. Lang (1982)
Eastbourne College, Sussex	1867	550†	£6,135 .... D£4,647	C. J. Saunders (1981)
Ellesmere College, Shropshire*	1884	412†	£6,030 .... D£4,260	F. E. Maidment (1982)
Eltham College, S.E.9	1842	516†	£5,853 .... D£1,890	C. D. Waller, ph.d. (1983)
Emanuel School, S.W.11.	1594	715	D£2,688	P. F. Thomson (1984)
Epsom College, Surrey	1855	625†	£5,610 .... D£3,900	J. B. Cook, ph.d. (1982)
Eton College, Windsor	1440	1250	£6,450	Dr. W. E. K. Anderson (1980)
Exeter, Devon	1633	650†	£4,170 .... D£2,280	G. T. Goodall (1979)
Felsted, Dunmow, Essex	1564	500†	£6,306 .... D£4,971	E. J. H. Gould (1983)
Forest School, E.17	1834	436†	£4,587 .... D£3,153	J. C. Gough (*Warden*) (1983)
Framlingham College, Suffolk	1864	500†	£5,265 .... D£3,375	L. I. Rimmer (1971)
Frensham Heights, Farnham, Surrey ...	1925	265†	£5,817 .... D£3,495°	A. L. Pattinson (1973)
Giggleswick, Settle, Yorks.	1512	320†	£6,210 .... D£4,140	P. Hobson (1986)
Gresham's, Holt, Norfolk	1555	460†	£6,540 .... D£4,440	H. R. Wright (1985)
Haberdashers' Aske's, Elstree, Herts. ...	1690	1100	D£3,024	A. K. Dawson (1987)
Haileybury, Herts.	1862	676†	£5,832 .... D£3,651	D. J. Jewell (1987)
Hampton, Middlesex	1557	845	D£2,475	H. G. Alexander (1970)
Harrow, Middlesex	1571	770	£6,750 .... D£4,557	I. D. S. Beer (1981)
Hereford Cathedral School	1384	591†	£4,170 .... D£2,385	Dr. H. C. Tomlinson (1987)
Highgate, N.6	1565	620	£6,228 .... D£3,555	R. C. Giles (1974)
Hulme Grammar School, Oldham	1611	715	D£1,782	G. F. Dunkin (1987)
Hurstpierpoint College, Sussex*	1849	420	£6,210 .... D£4,830	S. A. Watson (1986)
Hymers College, Hull	1889	650†	D£1,602	B. G. Bass (1983)
Ipswich, Suffolk	1390	610†	£4,671 .... D£2,700	Dr. J. M. Blatchly (1972)
The John Lyon School, Harrow	1876	490	D£2,490	Rev. T. J. Wright (1987)
Kelly College, Tavistock	1877	340†	£6,300 .... D£3,675	C. H. Hirst (1985)
Kent College, Canterbury	1885	566†	£5,265 .... D£2,949	R. J. Wicks (1980)
Kimbolton, Cambs.	1600	517†	£4,920 .... D£2,565	R. V. Peel (1987)
King Edward VI School, Southampton .	1553	950†	D£2,370	C. Dobson (1971)
King Edward VII School, Lytham	1908	540	D£1,788	D. Heap (1982)
King Edward's, Bath, Avon	1552	630†	D£2,043	J. P. Wroughton (1982)
King Edward's, Birmingham	1552	736	D£2,430	M. J. W. Rogers (*Chief Master*) (1982)
King Edward's, Witley, Surrey	1553	510†	£5,085 .... D£3,480	Dr. R. W. Wilkinson (1985)
King's College, Taunton*	1880	477†	£5,445 .... D£3,990	J. M. Batten (1969)
King's College School, S.W.19	1829	600	D£3,030	R. M. Reeve (1980)
King's School, Bruton	1519	330†	£6,300 .... D£4,500	A. H. Beadles (1985)
King's School, Canterbury	600	705†	£6,750 .... D£4,725	Rev. Canon A. C. J. Phillips (1986)
King's School, Chester	1541	440	D£2,244	A. R. D. Wickson (1981)
King's School, Ely	970	430†	£6,390 .... D£4,074	H. Ward (1970)
King's School, Macclesfield	1502	860†	D£2,475	A. G. Silcock (1987)
King's School, Rochester	604	450†	£5,097 .... D£3,057	Dr. I. R. Walker (1986)
King's School, Worcester	1541	709†	£4,518 .... D£2,667	Dr. J. M. Moore (1983)
Kingston Grammar, Surrey	1561	552†	D£2,640	A. B. Creber (1987)
Kingswood School, Bath	1748	485†	£5,940 .... D£3,765	G. M. Best (1987)
Lancing College, Sussex*	1848	540†	£6,750 .... D£4,590	J. S. Woodhouse (1981)
Latymer Upper, W.6	1624	1000	D£2,775	M. L. R. Isaac (1971)
Leeds Gr. School, Leeds 6.	1552	1027	D£2,004	B. W. Collins (1987)
Leighton Park School, Reading	1890	337†	£5,850 .... D£4,095	J. A. Chapman (1986)
The Leys School, Cambridge	1875	400†	£6,480 .... D£4,815	T. G. Beynon (1986)
Liverpool College, Liverpool 18	1840	392†	£4,143 .... D£2,184	R. V. Haygarth (1979)
Llandovery College	1848	241†	£4,785 .... D£2,860	R. Brinley Jones, ph.d. (1976)
Lord Wandsworth College, Long Sutton, Hants.	1912	400	£5,280 .... D£3,300	G. A. G. Dodd (1982)
Loughborough Grammar	1495	850	£4,377 .... D£2,088°	D. N. Ireland (1984)
Magdalen College School, Oxford	1480	500	£4,749 .... D£2,448	W. B. Cook (*Master*) (1972)
Malvern College, Worcester	1865	600	£6,450 .... D£4,680	R. de C. Chapman (1983)
Manchester Grammar School	1515	1440	D£2,091	J. G. Parker (*High Master*) (1985)
Marlborough College, Wilts.	1843	871†	£6,640 .... D£4,470	D. R. Cope (*Master*) (1986)
Merchant Taylors', Crosby	1620	650	D£2,079	S. J. R. Dawkins (1986)
Merchant Taylors', Northwood	1561	720	£5,700 .... D£3,720	D. J. Skipper (1982)
Mill Hill, N.W.7	1807	540	£5,685 .... D£3,765°	A. C. Graham (1979)
Monkton Combe, Bath	1868	340†	£5,445 .... D£3,936°	R. A. C. Meredith (1978)
Monmouth	1614	540	£4,755 .... D£2,610	R. D. Lane (1982)
Mount St. Mary's College, Spinkhill, Derbyshire (*R.C.*)	1842	308†	£5,076 .... D£3,465	Rev. J. F. Grumitt, s.j. (1976)
Newcastle-under-Lyme School.........	1874	1200†	D£1,914	J. W. Donaldson (*Principal*) (1974)

† Pupils.   * A Woodard Corporation School.   ° 1986 figures.

Name of School	F'ded.	No. of Boys	Annual Fees D = Day Boys	Headmaster (With date of Appointment)
Norwich School	1250	765	£4,875 .... D£2,355	C. D. Brown (1984)
Nottingham High School	1513	825	.... D£2,040	D. T. Witcombe, ph.d. (1970)
Oakham, Rutland, Leics.	1584	967†	£5,757 .... D£3,021	G. Smallbone (1985)
The Oratory (R.C.), Woodcote, Reading	1859	350	£5,289 .... D£3,681	A. J. Snow (1972)
Oundle, Peterborough, Northants	1556	740	£6,900	D. B. McMurray (1984)
Pangbourne College, Berks.	1917	360	£5,385 .... D£3,795	P. D. C. Points (1969)
Perse School, Cambridge	1615	465	£4,944 .... D£2,418	Dr. G. M. Stephen (1987)
Plymouth College	1877	680	£4,440 .... D£2,340	A. M. Joyce (1983)
Pocklington School, York.	1514	735†	£4,571 .... D£2,340	A. D. Pickering (1981)
Portsmouth Grammar School	1732	730†	.... D£2,085	A. C. V. Evans (1983)
Prior Park College (R.C.), Bath	1830	360†	£5,410 .... D£3,069	P. F. J. Tobin (1981)
Queen Elizabeth's Gr., Blackburn	1567	1100†	.... D£2,000	P. F. Johnston (1978)
Queen Elizabeth Gr. Sch., Wakefield	1591	730	£3,354 .... D£2,043	R. P. Mardling (1985)
Queen Elizabeth's Hospital, Bristol	1590	470	£3,930 .... D£2,205	Dr. R. Gliddon (1985)
Queen's College, Taunton	1843	450†	£5,175 .... D£3,405	A. P. Hodgson (1979)
Radley College, Abingdon	1847	590	£6,600	D. R. W. Silk (*Warden*) (1968)
Ratcliffe College (R.C.), Leicester	1844	390†	£5,138 .... D£3,425	Rev. L. G. Hurdidge (1985)
Reed's, Cobham, Surrey	1813	345	£5,400 .... D£3,900	D. E. Prince (1983)
Reigate Grammar	1675	850†	.... D£2,478	J. G. Hamlin (1982)
Rendcomb College, Cirencester	1920	260†	£5,610	J. Tolputt (1987)
Repton School, Derby	1557	575†	£6,540 .... D£4,833	G. E. Jones (1987)
Rossall, Fleetwood, Lancs.	1844	480†	£6,375 .... D£4,395	R. D. W. Rhodes (1987)
Royal Grammar School, Guildford	1552	750	.... D£2,850	J. Daniel (1975)
Royal Grammar School, Newcastle upon Tyne	1545	950	.... D£1,944	A. S. Cox (1972)
Royal Grammar School, Worcester	1291	744	£4,500 .... D£2,475	T. E. Savage, t.d. (1978)
Rugby, Warwickshire	1567	758†	£6,750 .... D£3,900	O. R. S. Bull (1985)
Rydal, Colwyn Bay, Clwyd	1885	340†	£5,160 .... D£3,768	P. F. Watkinson (1968)
Ryde School, Isle of Wight	1921	369†	£4,080 .... D£2,040	P. D. V. Wilkes (1984)
St. Albans, Herts.	1570	660	.... D£2,685	S. C. Wilkinson (1984)
St. Anselm's Coll., Birkenhead.	1933	647	.... D£1,776	Br. C. J. Sreenan (1987)
St. Bees, Cumbria	1583	400†	£6,045 .... D£4,095	M. T. Thyne (1980)
St. Benedict's, W.5 (R.C.).	1902	600†	.... D£2,310	Dr. A. J. Dachs (1987)
St. Dunstan's, S.E.6	1888	845	.... D£2,565	B. D. Dance (1973)
St. Edmund's, Canterbury	1749	300†	£5,997 .... D£4,107	J. V. Tyson (1978)
St. Edmund's College (R.C.), Ware	1568	370†	£4,725 .... D£3,051	D. J. J. McEwen (1984)
St. Edward' College, Liverpool	1853	654†	.... D£1,926	Rev. Br. B. D. Sassi (1984)
St. Edward's, Oxford	1863	571†	£6,105 .... D£4,575	J. C. Phillips (*Warden*) (1978)
St. George's College, Weybridge (R.C.)	1869	615†	£4,533 .... D£3,057°	Rev. P. C. Hunting (1977)
St. John's, Leatherhead	1851	450	£4,860 .... D£3,432	D. E. Brown (1985)
St. Lawrence College, Ramsgate	1879	350†	£5,955 .... D£3,900	J. H. Binfield (1983)
St. Mary's College, Gt. Crosby	1919	600†	.... D£1,836	Br. P. E. Ryan (1987)
St. Paul's, Lonsdale Rd., S.W.13	1509	750	£5,928 .... D£3,728	Rev. Canon P. Pilkington (*High Master*) (1986)
St. Peter's, York	627	470†	£5,580 .... D£3,441	R. N. Pittman (1985)
Sedbergh, Cumbria	1525	480	£6,345 .... D£4,440	Dr. R. G. Baxter (1982)
Sevenoaks School, Kent.	1418	900†	£6,237 .... D£3,753	R. P. Barker (1981)
Sherborne, Dorset	1550	650	£6,740 .... D£4,200	R. D. Macnaghten (1974)
Shrewsbury School	1552	650	£6,525 .... D£4,665	S. J. B. Langdale (1981)
Silcoates, Wakefield	1820	302†	£4,482 .... D£2,682	J. C. Baggaley (1979)
Solihull, Warwicks	1560	840	£3,687 .... D£2,356	A. Lee (1983)
Stamford, Lincs.	1532	805	£3,912 .... D£1,956	G. J. Timm (1978)
Stockport Grammar School	1487	1012†	.... D£2,187	D. R. J. Bird (1985)
Stonyhurst College (R.C.), nr. Whalley, Lancs.	1794	430	£6,240 .... D£3,240	Dr. R. G. G. Mercer (1985)
Stowe, Bucks.	1923	622†	£6,393 .... D£4,476	C. G. Turner (1979)
Sutton Valence, Kent	1576	420†	£6,036 .... D£3,861	M. R. Haywood (1980)
Taunton School, Somerset	1847	620†	£6,525 .... D£4,224	B. B. Sutton (1987)
Tettenhall College, Staffs.	1863	300†	£4,929 .... D£3,039	W. J. Dale (1968)
Tonbridge, Kent	1553	650	£6,600 .... D£4,650	C. H. D. Everett (1975)
Trent College, Long Eaton, Derbys.	1868	610†	£5,850 .... D£3,264	A. J. Maltby (1968)
Trinity School, Croydon	1596	750	.... D£2,700	R. J. Wilson (1972)
Truro, Cornwall	1879	842†	£4,350 .... D£2,400	B. K. Hobbs (1986)
University College School, N.W.3	1830	520	.... D£3,165	G. D. Slaughter (1985)
Uppingham, Leics.	1584	680†	£6,270	N. R. Bomford (1982)
Warwick	914	800	£5,025 .... D£2,325	J. A. Strover (1977)
Wellingborough, Northants	1595	400†	£5,049 .... D£3,093	G. Garrett (1973)
Wellington College, Crowthorne, Berks.	1856	800†	£5,880 .... D£4,260	Dr. D. H. Newsome, Litt.d. (1980)
Wellington School, Somerset	1841	770†	£4,500 .... D£2,400	J. Kendall-Carpenter (1973)
Wells Cathedral School, Somerset	1180	545†	£4,794 .... D£2,802	J. S. Baxter (1986)
West Buckland School, Barnstaple	1858	420†	£4,665 .... D£2,535	M. Downward (1979)
Westminster, S.W.1	1560	600†	£6,666 .... D£4,335	D. M. Summerscale (1986)

† Pupils.   * A Woodard Corporation School.   ° 1986 figures.

Name of School	F'ded.	No. of Boys	Annual Fees D = Day Boys	Headmaster (With date of Appointment)
Whitgift, Croydon	1596	880	.... D£2,844	D. A. Raeburn (1970)
William Hulme's G. S.	1887	785†	.... D£2,391	P. D. Briggs (1987)
Winchester College	1382	650	£6,999.... D£5,250	J. P. Sabben-Clare (1985)
Wolverhampton Grammar School	1512	630†	.... D£2,800	P. H. Hutton (1978)
Woodbridge School, Suffolk	1662	510†	£5,010.... D£2,880	Dr. D. Younger (1985)
Woodhouse Grove School, Bradford	1812	560†	£4,500.... D£2,775	D. A. Miller (1972)
Worcester College for the Blind	1866	94†	£11,352... D£7,569	Rev. B. R. Manthorp (1980)
Worksop College, Notts.*	1895	400†	£5,250.... D£3,585	A. H. Monro (1986)
Worth School, Crawley, Sussex (R.C.)	1959	330	£5,925..........	Rev. R. S. Ortiger (1983)
Wrekin College, Shropshire	1880	375†	£5,550.... D£3,795	J. H. Arkell (1983)
Wycliffe College, Stonehouse, Glos.	1882	337†	£6,222.... D£4,014	A. P. Millard (1987)

Scotland

Daniel Stewart's and Melville College, Edinburgh	1832	789	£4,476.... D£2,316	R. M. Morgan (1977)
Dollar Academy, Perthshire	1818	912†	£4,056.... D£1,800°	L. Harrison (Rector) (1984)
Dundee High School, Tayside	1239	1172†	.... D£2,034	R. Nimmo (Rector) (1977)
The Edinburgh Academy	1824	630†	£5,595.... D£2,835	L. E. Ellis (Rector) (1977)
Fettes College, Edinburgh	1870	425†	£6,000.... D£4,035	A. J. C. Cochrane (1979)
George Heriot's, Edinburgh	1659	1400†	.... D£2,160	K. P. Pearson (1983)
George Watson's College, Edinburgh	1741	1200†	£4,476.... D£2,316	F. E. Gerstenberg (Principal) (1985)
Glasgow Academy	1845	550	.... D£2,115	C. W. Turner (Rector) (1983)
Glenalmond College, Perthshire	1841	400	£5,700..........	S. R. D. Hall (Warden) (1987)
Gordonstoun, Elgin, Morayshire	1934	483†	£6,540.... D£4,200	M. B. Mavor, c.v.o. (1979)
The High School of Glasgow	1124	560†	.... D£2,205	R. G. Easton (1983)
Hutcheson's Grammar School, Glasgow	1641	1049†	.... D£1,650	D. R. Ward (Rector) (1987)
Kelvinside Academy, Glasgow	1878	500	.... D£2,175	J. H. Duff (Rector) (1980)
Loretto, Musselburgh, E. Lothian	1827	300†	£6,300.... D£3,945	Rev. N. W. Drummond (1984)
Merchiston Castle, Edinburgh	1833	360	£5,970.... D£3,810	D. M. Spawforth (1981)
Morrison's Academy, Perthshire	1860	600†	£4,860.... D£1,860	H. A. Ashmall (Rector) (1979)
Robert Gordon's College, Aberdeen	1729	857	£3,840.... D£1,740	G. A. Allan (1978)
Strathallan, Forgandenny, Perthshire	1913	380†	£6,060.... D£3,520	C. D. Pighills (1975)

Northern Ireland

Bangor Grammar School, Co. Down	1856	890	n/a	T. W. Patton (1979)
Belfast Methodist College	1868	1610†	£3,020.... D£1,120	J. Kincade, ph.d. (1974)
Belfast Royal Academy	1785	1300†	.... D£1,306	W. M. Sillery (1980)
Campbell College, Belfast	1894	464	£4,572.... D£2,022°	B. W. J. G. Wilson (1977)
Coleraine Academical Institution	1856	1000	£2,800...... D£930	R. S. Forsythe (1984)
Portora Royal School, Enniskillen	1618	360†	£4,035.... D£1,260	R. L. Bennett (1983)
Royal Belfast Academical Institution	1810	900	.... D£1,500	T. J. Garrett (1978)

Channel Islands, Isle of Man, etc.

Elizabeth College, Guernsey	1563	530	£2,865...... D£960	R. A. Wheadon (1971)
Victoria College, Jersey	1852	550†	£4,923...... D£996	M. H. Devenport (1967)
King William's College, Isle of Man	1668	350†	£5,709.... D£3,795	P. K. Bregazzi, ph.d. (1979)

OVERSEAS

Africa

Diocesan Coll., Rondebosch, S. Africa	1849	616†	R8,840 ... DR5,040	J. S. B. Peake (1983)
Falcon College, Esigodini, Zimbabwe	1954	450	Z$4,755..........	P. N. Todd (1985)
Peterhouse, Marondera, Zimbabwe	1955	580	Z$5,000 .. DZ$3,500	Dr. A. J. Megahey (Rector) (1984)
St George's College, Harare, Zimbabwe	1896	850	Z$1,800 .. DZ$1,200	J. C. Berry (1983)
St. Stithians College, S. Africa	1953	550	R7,125 ... DR4,065	M. Henning (1969)

Australia

A.C.T.:

Canberra Grammar School	1929	873	$7,650 ... D$3,330	T. C. Murray (1986)

N.S.W.:

Armidale Sch., Armidale	1894	500	$8,340.... D$3,570	K. Langford-Smith (1987)
Church of England G.S., N. Sydney	1889	973	$8,610.... D$4,305	R. A. I. Grant (1984)
Cranbrook School, Sydney	1918	800	$9,045.... D$4,530	Dr. B. N. Carter (1985)
The King's School, Parramatta	1831	900	$8,175.... D$4,380	J. A. Wickham (1985)
Knox Grammar School, Wahroonga	1924	1260	$8,400.... D$4,000	Dr. I. Paterson (1969)
Newington College, Stanmore	1863	1110	$9,000.... D$5,100	A. J. Rae (1972)
St. Patrick's College, Goulburn	1874	572	$3,195.... D$615°	Br. F. D. Marzorini (President) (1975)
The Scots College, Sydney	1893	1050	$9,240.... D$4,890	G. A. W. Renney (1980)
Sydney Grammar School	1857	1180	.... D$5,385	A. M. Mackerras (1969)

† Pupils.   * A Woodard Corporation School.   ° 1986 Figures.

Name of School	F'ded.	No. of Boys	Annual Fees D = Day Boys	Headmaster (With date of Appointment)
Queensland:				
Anglican Church G.S., Brisbane	1912	1261	$5,950 .... D$2,550	C. V. Ellis (1987)
Southport School.....................	1901	908	$7,584 .... D$4,292	P. J. McKeown (1987)
South Australia:				
Prince Alfred College, Adelaide	1869	771	$9,810 .... D$4,500	Dr. B. J. Webber (1988)
St. Peter's College, Adelaide	1847	770	$9,020 .... D$4,120	Dr. A. J. Shinkfield (1978)
Scotch College, Adelaide	1919	660†	$9,300 .... D$4,220	W. M. Miles (197)
Tasmania:				
Hutchins School, Hobart	1846	750	$5,730 .... D$2,955	J. M. Bedmall (1987)
Victoria:				
Ballarat and Clarendon Coll., Ballarat ..	1864	650†	$8,070 .... D$3,870	A. B. Croome (1987)
Brighton Grammar School, Brighton ...	1882	700	.... D$4,000	R. L. Rofe (1977)
Camberwell G. S., Balwyn	1886	875	.... D$3,500	C. F. Black (1987)
Carey Baptist Grammar School, Kew ...	1923	1175†	.... D$4,650	G. L. Cramer (1965)
Caulfield Grammar School, St. Kilda ...	1881	2110†	$7,932 .... D$4,062	Rev. A. S. Holmes (1977)
Eltham College			n/a	
Geelong Church of England G.S., Corio .	1855	1687†	$10,424 .... D$4,888	J. E. Lewis (1980)
Geelong College, Geelong, Corio	1861	931†	$9,340 .... D$4,440	A. P. Sheahan (1986)
Haileybury College, Keysborough	1892	1400	.... D$4,500	A. M. H. Aikman (1974)
Melbourne Church of England G.S.	1856	780	$8,640 .... D$4,560	N. A. H. Creese (1970)
Peninsula School, Mt. Eliza	1961	1054	$8,324 .... D$4,564	H. A. Macdonald (1971)
Scotch College, Hawthorn, Melbourne..	1851	1335	$8,796 .... D$4,536	Dr. F. G. Donaldson (1983)
Wesley College, Melbourne	1866	1721†	.... D$4,890	D. H. Prest (1972)
West Australia:				
Christ Church Grammar School, Claremont........................	1910	1150	$7,640 .... D$3,440	A. J. de V. Hill (1982)
Guildford Grammar Sch.	1896	775	$7,600 .... D$3,560	J. M. Moody (1979)
Hale School, Wembley Downs..........	1858	650	$6,400 .... D$3,200	Dr. K. G. Tregonning, M.B.E. (1967)
Scotch College, Swanbourne...........	1897	745	$7,620 .... D$3,600	W. R. Dickinson (1972)
Canada				
Appleby College, Ontario..............	1911	265	$13,750 .... D$8,950	G. S. McLean (acting) (1987)
Brentwood College School, Vancouver .	1961	360†	n/a	W. T. Ross (1975)
Hillfield Strathallan College, Ontario ..	1901	908†	.... D$6,429	M. B. Wansbrough (1969)
Pickering College, Ontario.	1842	155	$12,000 .... D$6,600	S. H. Clark (1978)
St. Andrew's College, Ontario	1899	455	$13,500 .... D$7,600	R. P. Bedard (1981)
Toronto French School, Ontario	1962	1092†	.... D$6,150	M. Gharghoury, PH.D. (acting) (1986)
Trinity College School, Ontario........	1865	376	$13,700 .... D$8,100	R. C. N. Wright (1983)
Upper Canada College, Toronto	1829	610	$13,850 .... D$7,500	R. H. Sadleir (Principal) (1975)
Europe				
Aiglon College, Switzerland	1949	260†	n/a	P. Parsons (1976)
British School of Brussels	1970	1050†	.... D£6,000	J. Jackson, PH.D. (1983)
British School in the Netherlands		475†	.... DH.fl13,230	B. D. Davidson (1979)
Campion School, Athens	1970	440†	Drachmae1,040,000 D Drachmae520,000	A. F. Eggleston, O.B.E. (1983)
The English School, Cyprus	1900	800†	.... DC£1,057	D. H. Humphreys, O.B.E. (1968)
St. Columba's College, Dublin	1843	295†	IR£4,350D IR£2,265	D. S. Gibbs, O.B.E. (Warden) (1974)
St. George's English School, Rome	1958	450†	......DL10,820,000	Dr. C. Niven (1988)
Far East				
Island School, Hong Kong	1967	1170†	.... D$18,000	Dr. C. H. R. Niven (1983)
India				
Lawrence School, Ootacamund	1858	685†	Rs.9,000	B. S. Bhatnagar (1986)
Lawrence School, Sanawar............	1847	550†	Rs.9,000	S. R. Das (1974)
St. Paul's School, Darjeeling	1823	409	Rs.11,000	J. Gardner (Rector) (1984)
The Scindia School, Gwalior	1897	700	Rs.10,500	Dr. S. D. Singh (1978)
Yadavindra Public School, Patiala	1947	552†	Rs.7,500 DRs.3,000°	H. N. Kashyap (1969)
New Zealand				
Christchurch Boys' High School, Canterbury	1881	1080	$3,360 .... D$44	I. D. Leggat (1976)
Christ's Coll., Christchurch, Canterbury	1850	600	$6,915 .... D$3,750	Dr. M. J. Rosser (1985)
The Collegiate School, Wanganui	1854	502	$7,920 .... D$4,275	I. D. McKinnon (1980)
King's College, Auckland	1896	720†	$7,785 .... D$4,860	J. S. Taylor (1988)

† Pupils.   ° 1986 figures.

Name of School	F'ded.	No. of Boys	Annual Fees D = Day Boys	Headmaster (With date of Appointment)
Rathkeale College, Masterton	1963	448	$9,274 .... D$4,213	R. Nethercole (1988)
St. Andrew's College, Christchurch	1916	670	$8,082 .... D$4,455	A. J. Rentoul, PH.D. (1982)
Waitaki Boys' High School	1883	782	$990......... D$33	G. Tait (1985)
South America				
Markham College, Lima, Peru	1946	1600	.... D$I.32,330	R. C. Pinchbeck, O.B.E. (1966)
St. Andrew's Scots School, Argentina ..		n/a	n/a	n/a
St. George's College, Argentina	1898	225†	U.S.$7,500 .... DU.S.$5,600	G. R. Sims (1986)
St. Paul's School, Brazil	1926	240†	.... D£1,500	P. Gysin (1987)
U.S.A.				
The Rivers School, Weston, Mass.......	1915	280	.... D$9,250	R. A. Bradley (1981)
West Indies				
Harrison College, Barbados	1729	805†	n/a	C. W. Thorpe (1983)
Munro College, Jamaica	1856	694	n/a	V. Forbes (1983)

NOTE.—The Headmasters of the following schools are additional members, by invitation, of the H.M.C.: Cavendish School, Devizes School, High Wycombe R.G.S., Highbury Grove School, London Oratory School, Oxford Upper School, Richmond School, Royal H.S. Edinburgh, Sexey's School, Bruton, Stand College, St. Bartholomew's School, Tiffin School, Watford G.S., Westcliffe H.S.

SOCIETY OF HEADMASTERS OF INDEPENDENT SCHOOLS

Secretary, A. E. R. Dodds, Green Garth, Horsell Rise, Woking, Surrey GU21 4AY.

Name of School	F'ded.	No. of Boys	Annual Fees D = Day Boys	Headmaster (With date of Appointment)
Ackworth, Pontefract	1779	420†	£4,995 .... D£2,898	G. R. McKee (1971)
Austin Friars, Carlisle (R.C.)	1951	290†	£3,927 .... D£2,145	Rev. T. Lyons, O.S.A. (1981)
Bearwood College, Wokingham, Berks. .	1827	345	£5,850 .... D£3,450	The Hon. Martin Penney (1980)
Bedstone College, Shropshire..........	1948	215†	£4,875 .... D£2,955	G. S. Wilson (1971)
Belmont Abbey, Hereford (R.C.)	1926	250	£5,085 .... D£2,880	Rev. S. J. McGurk (1983)
Bembridge, Isle of Wight	1919	180†	£4,245 .... D£2,400	J. High (1986)
Bentham School, N. Yorks	1726	300†	£4,440 .... D£2,220	R. S. Repper (1983)
Bethany School, Goudhurst, Kent	1866	280	£5,040 .... D£3,360	C. A. H. Lanzer (1970)
Box Hill School, Mickleham, Dorking . .	1959	265†	£5,805 .... D£3,405	Dr. R. A. S. Atwood (1987)
Carmel College, Wallingford, Oxon.	1948	315†	£7,500 .... D£4,065	P. D. Skelker (1984)
Chetham's School of Music, Manchester	1653	268†	Various	J. Vallins, O.B.E. (1974)
Claysmore, Iwerne Minster, Blandford	1896	329†	£6,480 .... D£4,560	D. J. Beeby (1986)
Cokethorpe School, Nr. Witney, Oxon. .	1957	170†	£6,420 .... D£4,590	D. F. Goldsmith (1979)
Cranbrook, Kent	1518	740†	£2,490° ...... DNil	M. C. Pavey (1981)
Friends' School, Saffron Walden	1702	340†	£5,046 .... D£3,015	J. C. Woods (1968)
Fulneck Boys' School, W. Yorkshire.....	1753	260	£3,879 .... D£2,049	I. D. Cleland (1980)
Grenville College, Bideford, Devon*	1954	360	£5,205 .... D£2,625	D. C. Powell-Price, T.D., PH.D. (1975)
Keil School, Dumbarton	1915	200†	£4,758 .... D£2,760	C. H. Tongue (1984)
Kingham Hill School, Oxon.	1886	250	£4,320 .... D£2,880	D. Shepherd (1981)
King's School, Gloucester	1541	572†	£4,605 .... D£2,844	Rev. A. C. Charters (1983)
Kirkham Grammar, nr. Preston, Lancs..	1549	485†	£3,486 .... D£1,878	M. J. Summerlee (1971)
Lindisfarne College, Ruabon, Wrexham	1891	200†	£5,277 .... D£2,925	T. R. Wilson (1986)
Lord Mayor Treloar College, Alton, Hants.	1908	280†	£14,979 .. D£11,234	A. Macpherson (1974)
Milton Abbey School, Blandford Forum, Dorset	1954	275	£6,240	R. H. Hardy (1987)
Oswestry, Shropshire	1407	320†	£4,344 .... D£2,586	I. G. Templeton (1985)
Pierrepont School, Farnham, Surrey ...	1947	260†	£4,950 .. D£3,024°	J. D. Payne (1983)
Purcell School (Music), Harrow, Middx.	1962	175†	£6,045 .... D£3,075	K. J. Bain (1983)
Rannoch School, Perthshire...........	1959	240†	£5,460 .... D£3,225	M. Barratt (1982)
Reading Blue Coat School, Berks.	1646	500†	£4,683 .... D£2,637	A. C. E. Sanders (1974)
Rishworth School, Ripponden, W. Yorks.	1724	560†	£4,470 .... D£2,385	A. J. Morsley (1986)
Royal Hospital School, Holbrook, Suffolk	1712	700	£3,051	M. A. B. Kirk (1983)
Royal Russell School, Croydon, Surrey .	1853	421†	£4,770 .... D£2,559	R. D. Balaam (1981)
Royal Wolverhampton School, Staffs....	1850	350†	£4,740 .... D£2,800	P. Gorring (1985)

† Pupils.   * A Woodard Corporation School.   ° 1986 figures.

Name of School	F'ded	No. of Boys	Annual Fees D=Day Boys	Headmaster (With date of Appointment)
Ruthin School, Clwyd	1574	160†	£5,340 .... D£3,390	F. R. Ullmann (1986)
St. David's Coll., Llandudno	1965	240	£5,550 .... D£3,600	J. A. Mayor (1965)
Scarborough College, Yorks.	1898	410†	£5,115 .... D£2,685	Dr. D. S. Hempsall (1985)
Seaford College, Petworth, Sussex	1884	430	£4,944	Rev. C. E. Johnson (1944)
Shebbear College, Beaworthy, Devon	1841	315	£4,605 .... D£2,400	R. J. Buley (1983)
Shiplake College, Henley, Oxon.	1959	340	£6,300 .... D£4,050	P. H. Lapping (1979)
Sidcot School, Winscombe, Somerset	1808	280†	£5,280 .... D£2,775	C. J. Greenfield (1986)
Stanbridge Earls School, Romsey	1952	170†	£6,360 .... D£4,242	H. Moxon (1984)
Warminster School, Wilts.	1707	305†	£4,875 .... D£2,925	D. M. Green (1984)

† Pupils.

NOTE.—The Headmasters of Abbotsholme School, Bedales School, Churcher's College, City of London Freemen's School, Colston's School, Frensham Heights School, Lord Wandsworth College, Pangbourne College, Rendcomb College, Ryde School, St. George's College, Weybridge, Silcoates School, Tettenhall College, Wells Cathedral School, West Buckland School and Woodbridge School are also Members of the Society. Details of these schools are included in the list of Headmasters' Conference Schools.

GIRLS' SCHOOLS ASSOCIATION MEMBERS

THE GIRLS' SCHOOLS ASSOCIATION, 29 Gordon Square, W.C.1.—*President* (1987), Sr. J. Sinclair; *Sec.*, Miss S. M. Chapman.

Name of School	F'ded	No. of Girls	Annual Fees D = Day Girls	Headmistress (a) Headmaster (With date of Appointment)
The Abbey School, Reading	1887	950	.... D£2,277	S. M. Hardcastle, M.B.E. (1960)
Abbots Bromley, Rugeley, Staffs	1874	270	£5,430 .... D£3,420	Mrs. B. Harbron (1984)
Abbot's Hill, Hemel Hempstead	1912	153	£4,950 .... D£3,375	Mrs. J. Kingsley (1979)
Adcote School, Shrewsbury	1907	130	£4,725 .... D£2,850	Mrs. S. B. Cecchet (1979)
The Alice Ottley School, Worcester	1883	650	£4,575 .... D£2,325	C. Sibbit (1986)
All Hallows School, Ditchingham, Bungay, Suffolk	1864	130	£4,245 .... D£2,673	A. C. Harris (1984)
Ashford School, Kent	1910	541	£4,149 .... D£2,367	Mrs A. T. D. Macaire (1984)
Assumption School, Richmond, Yorks	1852	170	£4,614 .... D£2,574	Sr. M. Connor (1978)
The Atherley School, Southampton (CSC)	1926	320	.... D£2,100	A. Ward (1973)
Badminton School, Bristol	1858	310	£5,460 .... D£3,060	(a) C. J. T. Gould (1981)
*Bath High School	1875	523	.... D£1,866	M. A. Winfield (1986)
Battle Abbey School, E. Sussex	1912	140	£4,650 .... D£2,850	(a) D. J. A. Teall (1982)
Bedford High School	1882	830	£4,602 .... D£2,337	D. M. Otter (1987)
Bedgebury School, Goudhurst, Kent	1860	380	£5,568 .... D£3,300	Mrs. M. E. A. Kaye (1987)
*Belvedere School, Liverpool	1880	551	.... D£1,866	S. Downs (1972)
Benenden School, Cranbrook, Kent	1923	400	£6,450	Mrs. G. D. du Charme (1985)
Beresford House, Eastbourne	1902	150	£5,625 .... D£3,195	A. M. Barnett (1964)
Berkhamsted School for Girls	1888	450	£3,909 .... D£1,974°	V. E. M. Shepherd (1980)
*Birkenhead High	1901	925	.... D£1,866	Mrs. K. R. Irving (1986)
*Blackheath High	1880	543	.... D£2,052	Mrs. H. E. W. Williams (1978)
Bolton School, Lancs	1877	845	.... D£2,196	Mrs. M. A. Spurr (1979)
Bradford Grammar School for Girls	1875	640	.... D£1,710°	R. M. Gleave (1976)
*Brighton and Hove High, Brighton	1876	731	£2,232 .... D£1,866	Mrs. J. B. E. Wells (1978)
*Bromley High School	1883	696	.... D£2,052	Mrs. J. Schofield (1984)
Bruton School for Girls, Somerset	1900	585	£3,750 .... D£2,100	Mrs. J. M. Wade (1987)
Burgess Hill, Sussex	1906	306	£4,950 .... D£2,796	Mrs. B. H. Webb (1979)
Bury Grammar School	1884	756	.... D£1,680	J. M. Lawley (1987)
Casterton School, Kirkby Lonsdale, Cumbria	1823	360	£4,560 .... D£2,808	(a) G. Vinestock (1984)
*Central Newcastle High School	1895	763	.... D£1,866	Mrs. A. M. Chapman (1985)
Channing School, Highgate, N.6	1885	286	.... D£2,745	Mrs. I. R. Raphael (1984)
Charters Ancaster College, Bexhill-on-Sea	1906	200	£4,125 .... D£2,220	Mrs. S. V. Chapman (1985)
Cheltenham Ladies' College	1853	845	£6,360 .... D£4,260	E. Castle (1987)
City of London, Barbican, E.C.2	1894	550	.... D£2,550	Mrs. V. E. France (1986)
Clarendon School, Bedford	1898	234	£5,390 .... D£3,105	J. L. Howell (1978)
Clifton High School, Bristol	1877	654	£3,990 .... D£1,950	Mrs. J. D. Walters (1985)
Cobham Hall, Gravesend, Kent	1962	315	£5,820 .... D£3,870	S. Cameron (1985)
Colston's Girls' School, Bristol	1891	640	.... D£1,950	A. C. Parkin (1981)
Combe Bank, Sevenoaks, Kent	1868	250	.... D£2,400	Mrs. A. J. K. Austin (1982)
Commonweal Lodge, Purley, Surrey	1916	135	.... D£2,160	J. M. Brown (1982)
Cranborne Chase, Tisbury, Wilts.	1946	150	£5,985 .... D£2,430	Mrs. M. Simmons (1983)

* Girls Public Day School Trust.   † A Woodard Corporation School.   ° 1986 figures.

Name of School	F'ded.	No. of Girls	Annual Fees D = Day Girls	Headmistress (a) Headmaster (With date of Appointment)
Cranford House, Wallingford	1931	122	.... D£2,280	T. A. Spencer (1980)
Croft House, Shillingstone, Dorset	1941	200	£5,175 .... D£3,600	Mrs. S. Rawlinson (1985)
Croham Hurst, S. Croydon, Surrey	1899	350	.... D£2,085	J. M. Shelmerdine (1986)
*Croydon High School	1874	1078	.... D£2,052	A. M. Mark (1980)
Dame Alice Harpur School, Bedford ...	1882	800	.... D£1,923	S. M. Morse (1970)
Dame Allan's Girls', Newcastle upon Tyne...............................	1705	440	.... D£2,088	J. Graham (1970)
Derby High School	1892	400	.... D£2,445	(a) Dr. G. H. Goddard (1983)
Downe House, Cold Ash, Newbury	1907	435	£6,150 .... D£3,990	S. E. Farr (1978)
Dunottar School, Reigate, Surrey	1926	350	.... D£2,058	J. Burnell (1985)
Durham High School	1884	387	.... D£1,860	B. E. Stephenson (1978)
Edgbaston Church of England College .	1886	320	.... D£2,028	(a) I. J. Walkley (1979)
Edgbaston High School	1876	540	.... D£1,982	Mrs. S. Horsman (1987)
Edgehill College, Bideford, Devon	1884	367	£4,830 .... D£2,535	Mrs. E. M. Burton (1987)
Ellerslie, Great Malvern	1922	260	£4,875 .... D£3,165	P. M. Binyon (1974)
Elmslie School, Blackpool	1918	350	.... D£1,935	E. M. Smithies (1978)
Eothen, Caterham, Surrey (CSC)	1892	220	.... D£2,340	D. C. Raine (1973)
Farlington, Horsham, W. Sussex	1896	220	£4,950 .... D£3,000	Mrs. P. Metham (1987)
Farnborough Hill, Hants.	1889	505	.... D£2,394	Sr. S. Cousins (1983)
Farringtons, Chislehurst............	1911	400	£4,959 .... D£2,790	Mrs. B. J. Stock (1987)
Felixstowe College, Suffolk	1929	334	£4,974 .... D£3,030	E. D. Guinness (1979)
Fernhill Manor, New Milton, Hants. ..	1890	154	£4,185 .... D£2,835	(a) Rev. A. J. Folks (1985)
Francis Holland, N.W.1.	1878	352	.... D£2,520	A. E. Holt (1974)
Francis Holland, S.W.1.	1881	176	.... D£2,610	Mrs. J. A. Anderson (1982)
Gateways School, Harewood, Leeds ...	1941	200	.... D£1,860	L. M. Brown (1984)
Godolphin, Salisbury	1726	320	£5,625 .... D£3,345	E. A. S. Hannay (1980)
Godolphin and Latymer Upper Sch., W.6...............................	1905	700	.... D£2,520	M. Rudland (1986)
Greenacre, Banstead, Surrey	1933	365	£4,515 .... D£2,370	M. E. Haggerty (1977)
The Grove, Hindhead, Surrey	1877	170	£4,329 .... D£2,565	(a) C. Brooks (1984)
Guildford High School (CSC)	1888	435	.... D£2,490	J. E. Dutton (1977)
Haberdashers' Aske's, Elstree	1873	834	.... D£1,710°	Mrs. S. Wiltshire (1974)
Haberdashers' Monmouth School for Girls.............................	1891	620	£3,975 .... D£2,115	H. L. Gichard (1986)
Harrogate Ladies' College	1893	400	£4,995 .... D£3,312	Mrs. J. C. Lawrance (1974)
Headington School, Oxford	1915	540	£4,704 .... D£2,145	E. M. Tucker (1982)
Heathfield School, Ascot	1900	195	£6,300	Mrs. S. E. Watkins (1982)
Heathfield School, Pinner	1900	300	.... D£2,160	Mrs. W. E. Ribchester (1974)
Hethersett Old Hall, Norwich	1928	227	£4,215 .... D£2,415	Mrs. V. M. Redington (1983)
Holy Child School, Edgbaston	1933	251	£3,762 .... D£2,046	J. Johnson (1987)
Howell's School, Denbigh	1859	300	£5,952 .... D£3,720	(a) J. H. Delany (1987)
*Howell's School, Llandaff	1860	659	£2,232 .... D£2,025	J. P. Turner (1978)
Hull High School (CSC)	1890	261	£3,045 .... D£2,175	C. M. B. Radcliffe (1976)
Hulme Grammar School, Oldham	1895	450	.... D£1,782	Mrs. A. Groom (1985)
Hunmanby Hall, nr. Filey	1928	250	£3,570 .... D£2,340	J. Rutherford (1986)
Huyton College, Liverpool	1894	234	£5,115 .... D£2,289	W. E. Edwards (1984)
*Ipswich High School	1878	599	.... D£1,866	P. M. Hayworth (1971)
James Allen's Girls', Dulwich, S.E.22 ..	1741	700	.... D£2,565	Mrs. B. Davies (1984)
School of Jesus and Mary, Ipswich ...	1860	200	.... D£2,130	Mrs. E. A. McKay (1982)
Kent College, Tunbridge Wells	1885	350	£4,860 .... D£2,880	(a) Rev. J. C. A. Barrett (1983)
King Edward VI H.S., Birmingham ...	1883	550	.... D£2,160	E. W. Evans (1977)
King's High School, Warwick	1879	542	.... D£2,025	Mrs. J. M. Anderson (1987)
Kingsley School, Leamington	1884	335	£3,591 .... D£1,875	E. C. Fairhurst (1977)
La Retraite, Salisbury	1953	250	.... D£2,115	Mrs. M. Paisey (1985)
La Sagesse Convent High, Newcastle upon Tyne	1906	350	.... D£1,869	Sr. Pauline (1967)
La Sagesse Convent, Romsey	1896	162	£3,374 .... D£1,464	Sr. T. Cox (1977)
Lady Eleanor Holles, Hampton, Middx.	1711	593	.... D£1,779	E. M. Candy (1981)
Lavant House, Chichester	1952	149	£4,665 .... D£2,775	Mrs. B. M. Gay (1987)
Lawnside, Great Malvern	1818	150	£5,505	D. M. M. Stewart (1971)
Leeds Girls' High	1876	590	.... D£2,316	P. A. Randall (1977)
Leicester High School, Leicester	1906	310	.... D£2,100	Mrs. D. Buchan (1982)
Loughborough High School	1850	530	£3,372 .... D£1,938	J. E. L. Harvatt (1978)
Luckley-Oakfield School, Wokingham .	1895	280	£3,855 .... D£2,385°	(a) R. C. Blake (1984)
Malvern Girls' College	1893	520	£5,130 .... D£3,420	Dr. V. B. Payne (1986)
Manchester High School for Girls	1874	730	.... D£2,160	M. M. Moon (1983)
Maynard School, Exeter	1877	454	.... D£2,142	F. Murdin (1980)
Merchant Taylors' School, Crosby	1888	790	.... D£2,265	Mrs. M. E. Davies (1963)
Micklefield School, Seaford, Sussex	1910	180	£6,300 .... D£3,090	(a) E. Reynolds
Moira House, Eastbourne	1875	300	£4,500 .... D£2,970	(a) A. R. Underwood (1975)
More House School, S.W.1............	1953	247	£3,060	Mrs. P. M. Mathias (1974)

Name of School	F'ded.	No. of Girls	Annual Fees D = Day Girls	Headmistress (a) Headmaster (With date of Appointment)
Moreton Hall, Oswestry	1913	330	£5,790 .... D£3,860	(a) E. J. Cussell (1976)
Mount School, York	1831	309	£5,364 .... D£3,657	B. J. Windle (1986)
New Hall, Chelmsford	1642	550	£5,400 .... D£3,300	Sr. M. M. Horton (1986)
Newcastle upon Tyne Church H.S.	1885	400	.... D£2,040	P. E. Davies (1974)
North Foreland Lodge, Sherfield-on-Loddon, Hants.	1909	180	£5,400	D. Matthews (1983)
North London Collegiate School, Edgware	1850	761	.... D£2,475	Mrs. J. L. Clanchy (1986)
Northampton High School	1878	500	.... D£2,001	S. J. Lightburne (1964)
Northwood College, Middx.	1878	470	£4,038 .... D£2,388	Mrs. D. K. Dalton (1986)
*Norwich High School	1875	717	.... D£1,866	Mrs. V. C. Bidwell (1985)
*Nottingham High School	1875	993	.... D£1,866	Mrs. C. Bowering (1984)
*Notting Hill and Ealing High	1873	750	.... D£2,052	Mrs. C. J. Fitz (1983)
Oakdene, Beaconsfield	1911	400	£3,600 .... D£2,220°	A. M. Tippett (1987)
Old Palace School, Croydon	1887	600	.... D£1,980	K. L. Hilton (1974)
*Oxford High School	1875	609	.... D£1,866	Mrs. J. Townsend (1981)
Palmers Green High School, N.21	1905	104	.... D£2,091	Mrs. A. F. E. Woodings (1984)
Park School, Yeovil	1851	160	£4,380 .... D£2,250	Mrs. M. Hannon (1987)
Parsons Mead, Ashstead, Surrey	1897	450	£4,965 .... D£2,730	M. M. Dees (1979)
Penrhos College, Colwyn Bay	1880	280	£5,460 .... D£3,645	(a) N. C. Peacock (1974)
Perse School for Girls, Cambridge	1881	560	.... D£2,361	M. R. Bateman (1980)
Pipers Corner School, High Wycombe	1930	257	£4,725 .... D£2,565	Dr. M. M. Wilson (1986)
Polam Hall, Darlington	1848	320	£4,785 .... D£2,370	Mrs. H. C. Hamilton (1987)
*Portsmouth High School	1882	642	.... D£1,866	Mrs. J. M. Dawtrey (1984)
Princess Helena Coll., Hitchin, Herts.	1820	181	£5,400 .... D£3,780	(a) D. Clarke, ph.d. (1971)
Prior's Field, Godalming	1902	225	£5,091 .... D£3,141	Mrs. J. M. McCallum (1987)
*Putney High School, S.W.15	1893	769	.... D£2,052	Mrs. P. A. Penney (1987)
Queen Anne's, Caversham	1698	375	£4,818 .... D£2,970	A. M. Scott (1977)
†Queen Ethelburga's, Harrogate	1912	162	£5,400 .... D£3,300	Mrs. M. C. James (1984)
†Queen Margaret's, York	1901	275	£5,460 .... D£3,405	(a) C. S. McGarrigle (1983)
Queen Mary, Lytham	1930	600	.... D£1,788	M. C. Ritchie (1981)
Queen's College, W.1	1848	390	.... D£2,640	Mrs. P. J. Fleming (1983)
Queen's Gate School, S.W.7	1891	177	n/a	Mrs. C. M. Newnham (1971)
Queen's School, Chester	1878	420	.... D£1,866	M. Farra (1973)
Queenswood, Hatfield, Herts.	1894	400	£6,045 .... D£2,015	Mrs. A. M. B. Butler (1981)
Redland High, Bristol	1882	440	.... D£1,917	E. Hobbs (1986)
The Red Maids' School, Bristol	1634	480	£3,513 .... D£1,836	S. Hampton (1987)
Rickmansworth Masonic School	1788	510	£4,740 .... D£2,610	(a) D. L. Curtis (1980)
Roedean School, Brighton	1885	475	£5,802	Mrs. A. R. Longley (1984)
Rosemead, Littlehampton	1919	225	£5,220 .... D£2,925	Mrs. J. Bevis (1987)
Royal Naval School, Haslemere, Surrey	1840	300	£4,599 .. D£3,060°	Dr. J. Clough (1987)
Royal School for Daughters of Officers of the Army, Bath	1864	400	£5,250 .... D£3,150	Dr. J. M'Clure (1987)
Runton Hill, W. Runton, Cromer	1911	170	£4,800 .... D£3,225	Dr. A. Cardew (1987)
Rye St. Anthony School, Oxford	1930	330	£4,185 .... D£2,190	P. M. Sumpter (1976)
Sacred Heart, Tunbridge Wells	1915	233	£5,436 .... D£2,970	(a) Dr. J. A. Fallon (1979)
St. Albans High School	1889	490	.... D£2,400	E. M. Diggory (1983)
St. Andrew's, Bedford	1897	180	.... D£1,635	Mrs. S. E. Cooke (1987)
St. Anne's, Windermere	1863	300	£5,550 .... D£3,660	M. P. Hawkins (1986)
St. Antony's-Leweston, Sherborne, Dorset	1891	399	£4,950 .... D£3,360	Mrs. P. Cartwright (1983)
St. Audries, West Quantoxhead, Somerset	1906	150	£5,175 .... D£2,985	(a) A. J. Tough (1975)
St. Brandon's, Clevedon, Avon	1831	270	£5,475 .... D£2,790	(a) J. S. Davey (1978)
St. Catherine's, Bramley, Guildford	1885	435	£4,560 .... D£2,790	(a) J. R. Palmer (1982)
†School of St. Clare, Penzance	1889	125	£4,455 .... D£2,535	(a) I. Halford (1986)
St. David's, Ashford, Middx.	1716	232	£4,518 .... D£2,622	Mrs. J. G. Osborne (1985)
St. Dunstan's Abbey, Plymouth	1850	240	£3,615 .... D£2,115	H. L. Alsey (1970)
St. Elphin's, Matlock	1844	218	£5,175 .... D£2,925	(a) A. P. C. Pollard (1978)
St. Felix, Southwold, Suffolk	1897	360	£5,400 .... D£3,340	M. Claydon (1987)
St. Francis' College, Letchworth, Herts.	1933	260	£4,575 .... D£2,325	Mrs. J. Frith (1987)
S. Gabriel's, Newbury	1929	140	.... D£2,658	Mrs. P. Gott (1980)
St. George's, Ascot	1923	280	£6,000 .... D£3,525	Mrs. J. M. Goodland (1983)
St. Helen and St. Katharine, Abingdon	1903	504	£3,765 .... D£1,875	Y. Paterson (1973)
St. Helen's, Northwood, Middx.	1899	859	£4,521 .... D£2,436	Dr. Y. Burne (1987)
St. Hilary's, Alderley Edge	1880	240	.... D£2,250	Mrs. J. Tracey (1985)
St. Hilary's, Sevenoaks	1942	180	.... D£2,379	Mrs. P. Miles (1977)
St. James's and the Abbey, W. Malvern	1896	160	£5,550 .... D£3,705	E. M. Mullenger (1986)
St. Joseph's, Lincoln	1905	200	£4,035 .... D£1,950	Mrs. A. Scott (1983)
St. Joseph's Convent, Reading	1909	490	.... D£2,100	M. Ball (1985)
St. Leonards-Mayfield School, E. Sussex	—	540	£5,175 .... D£3,450	Sr. J. Sinclair (1980)

* Girls Public Day School Trust.   † A Woodard Corporation School.   ° 1986 figures.

Name of School	F'ded.	No. of Girls	Annual Fees D = Day Girls	Headmistress (a) Headmaster (With date of Appointment)
St. Margaret's, Bushey, Herts	1749	350	£4,725 .... D£2,910	Mrs. S. Law (1985)
†St. Margaret's, Exeter	1904	370	£3,330 .... D£2,025	Mrs. J. M. Giddings (1984)
St. Martin's, Solihull	1941	350	.... D£2,415	(a) D. J. Cobb (1984)
St. Mary's Hall, Brighton	1836	350	£4,875 .... D£3,090	M. F. C. Harvey (1981)
St. Mary's School, Ascot	1885	320	£5,670 .... D£3,402	Sr. M. M. Orchard (1982)
St. Mary's School, Calne, Wilts........	1872	312	£5,325 .... D£3,165	D. H. Burns (1985)
St. Mary's School, Cambridge.........	1898	600	£3,540 .... D£1,980	Sr. M. C. Kenworthy-Browne (1977)
St. Mary's School, Colchester	1908	300	.... D£1,950	Mrs. G. M. G. Mouser (1981)
St. Mary's School, Gerrards Cross	1872	223	.... D£2,300	Mrs. J. P. G. Smith (1984)
St. Mary's School, Shaftesbury	1945	295	£4,935 .... D£2,961	Sr. M. Campion Livesey (1985)
St. Mary's, Wantage, Oxon.	1873	300	£5,775	Mrs. P. H. Johns (1980)
†St. Michael's, Burton Park, Petworth, W. Sussex	1844	225	£5,550 .... D£3,900	Mrs. M. Steeves (1981)
St. Michael's, Limpsfield, Oxted	1850	200	£4,785	(a) Dr. B. Long (1983)
St. Paul's Girls', Brook Green, W.6	1904	618	.... D£3,435	Mrs. H. Brigstocke (*High Mistress*) (1974)
St. Stephen's College, Broadstairs	1867	140	£4,740 ... D£2,928°	B. Seymour (1974)
St. Swithun's, Winchester	1884	420	£5,805 .... D£3,648	J. E. Jefferson (1986)
*Sheffield High School	1878	687	.... D£1,866	D. M. Skilbeck (1983)
Sherborne School for Girls, Dorset	1899	455	£5,475 .... D£3,660	J. M. Taylor (1985)
*Shrewsbury High School	1885	546	.... D£1,866	E. M. Gill (1982)
Sir William Perkins's, Chertsey	1725	460	.... D£1,990	Mrs. A. F. Darlow (1982)
*South Hampstead High School	1876	643	.... D£2,052	Mrs. D. A. Burgess (1975)
Stamford High School, Lincs.	1876	750	£4,344 .... D£2,172	G. K. Bland (1978)
Stonar, Atworth, Melksham, Wilts.	1921	281	£5,154 .... D£2,658	Mrs. S. Hopkinson (1985)
Stover School, Newton Abbot	1932	250	£4,563 .... D£2,496	Mrs. W. E. Lunel (1984)
Stratford House School, Bromley	1912	250	.... D£2,250	Mrs. A. Williamson (1974)
*Streatham Hill and Clapham High	1887	450	.... D£2,052	G. M. Ellis (1979)
Sunderland High School (*CSC*)	1884	240†	.... D£2,097	Mrs. M. Thrush (1980)
Surbiton High School (*CSC*)	1884	402	.... D£2,340	Mrs. R. A. Thynne (1979)
*Sutton High School, Surrey	1884	822	.... D£2,052	A. E. Cavendish (1980)
*Sydenham High School, S.E.26	1887	635	.... D£2,052	Mr. G. Baker (1988)
Talbot Heath, Bournemouth	1886	538	£4,047 .... D£2,121	C. E. Austin-Smith (1976)
Teesside High, Cleveland.............	1970	382	.... D£2,124	Mrs. H. Coles (1982)
Tormead School, Guildford	1905	388	.... D£2,526	Mrs. J. Crouch-Smith (1976)
Truro High School	1880	432	£4,053 .... D£2,241	Mrs. J. F. Marshall (1984)
Tudor Hall School, Banbury	1850	250	£5,175 .... D£3,294	N. Godfrey (1984)
Upper Chine, Shanklin, I.O.W.........	1799	216	£4,500 .... D£2,460	B. A. Philpott (1981)
Ursuline Convent, Westgate-on-Sea ...	1904	350	£5,133 .... D£2,598	Sr. M. Murphy (1977)
Ursuline High School, Ilford	1903	400	.... D£1,851°	P. Dixon (1984)
Wadhurst College, Sussex	1930	230	£5,385 .... D£3,210	D. Swatman (1972)
Wakefield High School	1878	735	.... D£2,127	Mrs. P. A. Langham (1987)
Walthamstow Hall, Sevenoaks, Kent ..	1838	400	£4,380 ... D£2,370°	Mrs. J. S. Lang (1984)
Wentworth Milton, Bournemouth	1962	322	£4,170 .... D£2,475	M. Vokins (1982)
Westfield, Newcastle upon Tyne	1962	220	.... D£2,070	(a) J. S. Taylor (1986)
West Heath, Sevenoaks, Kent	1867	148	£5,775 .... D£4,050	Mrs. D. Cohn-Sherbok (1988)
Westholme, Blackburn	1923	600	.... D£1,770	Dr. J. Bond (1968)
Westonbirt, Tetbury, Glos.	1928	220	£5,850 .... D£3,795	Mrs. G. Hylson-Smith (1986)
*Wimbledon High School	1880	686	.... D£2,052	Mrs. R. A. Smith (1982)
Wispers School, Haslemere	1946	194	£4,875 .... D£3,000	(a) L. H. Beltran (1979)
Withington School, Manchester	1890	550	.... D£1,998	Mrs. M. Kenyon (1986)
Woldingham School, Surrey	1842	425	£5,460 .... D£3,300	Dr. P. Dineen (1985)
Wroxhall Abbey School, Warwick	1872	150	£5,340 .... D£3,219	Mrs. I. D. M. Iles (1980)
Wycombe Abbey School, Bucks.	1896	498	£6,075	P. M. Lancaster (1974)
York College (*CSC*)..................	1908	287	.... D£2,325	Mrs. J. L. Clare (1982)

Scotland

Name of School	F'ded.	No. of Girls	Annual Fees D = Day Girls	Headmistress
Laurel Bank, Glasgow	1903	240	.... D£2,169	L. G. Egginton (1984)
Mary Erskine School, Edinburgh	1694	580	£4,476 .... D£2,316	R. M. Morgan (*Principal*) (1978)
Park School, Glasgow	1880	300	.... D£2,169	Mrs. M. E. Myatt (1986)
St. Denis and Cranley, Edinburgh.....	1858	225	£4,590 .... D£2,310	Mrs. J. M. Munro (1984)
St. George's, Edinburgh	1888	600	£4,665 .... D£2,340	Mrs. J. G. Scott (1986)
St. Leonards, St. Andrews, Fife	1877	365	£6,060 .... D£3,030	M. Hamilton (1971)
St. Margaret's, Aberdeen	1846	335	£4,101 .... D£1,851	Mrs. M. Bosomworth (1970)
St. Margaret's, Edinburgh	1890	650	£4,575 .... D£2,400	Mrs. M. J. Cameron (1984)

Channel Islands

Name of School	F'ded.	No. of Girls	Annual Fees D = Day Girls	Headmistress
The Ladies' College, Guernsey	1872	350	.... D£960	J. Honey (1976)

---

* Girls' Public Day School Trust, 26 Queen Anne's Gate, SW1H 9AN.

† Woodard Corporation School.

CSC Church Schools Company, 1a Doughty Street, WC1N 2PH.

° 1986 figures.

EVENTS OF THE YEAR (*SEPT. 1, 1986–AUG. 31, 1987*)

THE ROYAL HOUSE

(1986). **Sept. 2.** The Prince of Wales left Dyce Airport for the U.S.A. **18.** Princess Anne visited H.M. Prison Winson Green. **19.** The Princess pf Wales visited Barnardo House, Barkingside, Essex. **25.** The Queen opened the 32nd Commonwealth Parliamentary Conference. The Duke of Edinburgh left for Italy to attend the 25th anniversary conference of the World Wildlife Fund, and subsequently joined the Queen for the China tour. The Prince of Wales visited South Pembrokeshire.

Oct. 3. The Duke and Duchess of York left R.A.F. Northolt for the Netherlands. **11.** The Queen left Heathrow Airport to visit China and Hong Kong. **13.** Princess Anne opened the "Science for Industry" fair. **16.** Princess Anne visited Banbury. **21.** The Queen Mother visited Dundee. **28.** The Prince of Wales opened the 50th anniversary conference of the National Housebuilding Council. **29.** The Prince of Wales visited Widnes and Manchester. **30.** The Queen visited R.A.F. Locking.

Nov. 4. Princess Margaret opened the Cavendish Clinic, London. **5.** The Queen opened the Britten Opera Theatre at the Royal College of Music. **6.** The Duke of Edinburgh, accompanied by Prince Edward, attended a service at Westminster Abbey to celebrate the 30th anniversary of The Duke of Edinburgh's Award Scheme. **8.** The Queen and the Duke of Edinburgh, the Queen Mother, the Prince and Princess of Wales, the Duke and Duchess of York, and Princess Anne were present at the Royal British Legion Festival of Remembrance at the Royal Albert Hall. **9.** The Queen and the Duke of Edinburgh, with the Prince of Wales and the Duke of York, laid wreaths at the Cenotaph on Remembrance Day. Other members of the royal family were present during the ceremony. **10.** The Prince and Princess of Wales left R.A.F. Brize Norton to visit Oman, Qatar, Bahrain, and Saudi Arabia. Princess Anne visited Blackburn. **11.** The Queen Mother was admitted to King Edward VII Hospital for Officers after bruising her leg: she left hospital on Nov. 16. Princess Anne visited the National Council for Voluntary Youth Services on the occasion of its 50th anniversary. **12.** The Queen, accompanied by the Duke of Edinburgh, opened the new session of Parliament. Princess Margaret was present at a service at Southwark Cathedral to mark the centenary of the Salvation Army. **13.** The Queen opened the Swan Theatre at Stratford-upon-Avon. **18.** The Queen, accompanied by the Duke of Edinburgh, opened the new Lloyd's building. **20.** The Queen visited the Imperial Cancer Research Fund. Princess

Anne attended a dinner to celebrate London University's 150th anniversary. **24.** The Queen and the Duke of Edinburgh visited Harrow School. **26.** The biographer of Lord Dawson of Penn, the doctor who attended King George V on his deathbed, disclosed that Lord Dawson had prematurely ended the King's life. **27.** The Queen visited Winchester. Princess Anne visited Bridgwater. The Prince of Wales launched the Inner Cities Trust and addressed the Building Communities Conference. The Prince of Wales, accompanied by the Princess of Wales, attended a dinner to inaugurate the Prince's Trust Youth Business Appeal.

Dec. 2. The Queen and the Duke of Edinburgh visited the Royal Smithfield Show. **3.** The Queen Mother visited the Royal Smithfield Show. The Princess of Wales visited the Downland Housing Society project at Worthing. Princess Anne attended a service at St. Paul's Cathedral to celebrate London University's 150th anniversary. **4.** The Prince of Wales opened Brunel University's Science Park. **5.** The Queen and the Duke of Edinburgh gave a lunch for delegates to the European Council meeting in London. Princess Anne visited Leicestershire and Nottinghamshire. **9.** The Prince of Wales visited Ashington and Newcastle upon Tyne. **11.** The Prince and Princess of Wales visited the production stage of the film *Living Daylights*. **12.** The Queen visited South Yorkshire. **18.** The Queen opened the renovated headquarters of the U.K. Central Council for Nursing, Midwifery and Health Visiting. **19.** Prince Edward, chairman, The Duke of Edinburgh's Award 30th anniversary tribute, visited Northern Ireland. **22.** It was announced that the Queen would not ride at the Trooping of the Colour ceremony in future but would drive in an open carriage. **25.** The Queen made her traditional broadcast to the Commonwealth. **31.** The New Year's Honours List was published.

(1987). **Jan. 12.** It was announced that Prince Edward had decided to resign from the Royal Marines. **27.** The Princess of Wales opened a unit for deaf and visually handicapped children in east London. **30.** Princess Anne left Heathrow Airport to visit Western Australia, United Arab Emirates, Qatar, Kuwait, and Jordan.

Feb. 6. The Prince of Wales visited Bradford, Halifax and Calderdale. **9.** The Prince of Wales visited the Home Office. The Queen Mother opened the new headquarters of the Church of England Children's Society. **11.** The Prince and Princess of Wales left R.A.F. Northolt to visit Portugal and France. The Duke of York took his seat in the House of Lords. **14.** The Prince and Princess of Wales launched the first A320 Airbus at a ceremony in Toulouse, southern France. **17.** The Queen Mother visited the Royal National Institute for the Blind. **20.** The Duke of Edinburgh visited Liverpool. **23.** The Duke of Edinburgh visited Newcastle. **26.** The Duke of Edinburgh left for Rome to visit the N.A.T.O. Defence College.

March 6. The Prince of Wales, accompanied by the Princess of Wales, visited Birmingham. The Prince of Wales also visited the Ironbridge Gorge Museum and the Princess visited West Midlands Police drug squad. **9.** The Queen and the Duke of Edinburgh attended the Commonwealth Day observance service in Westminster Abbey. **10.** The President of Nauru visited the Queen. **11.** The Queen and the Duke of Edinburgh attended a service at St. Paul's Cathedral for the dedication of the Korean War Memorial. The Prince of Wales left R.A.F. Northolt to visit Belgium. He viewed the wreck of *The Herald of Free Enterprise* in Zeebrugge and visited survivors in hospital. **16.** President Moi of Kenya visited the Queen. **18.** The Prince and Princess of Wales visited Cleveland. **19.** The Prince of Wales continued his tour of Cleveland. **20.** The Queen and the Duke of Edinburgh visited Canterbury and the University of Kent. **24.** The King of Saudi Arabia arrived in London for a three-day State visit. **26.** Princess Anne visited North Humberside. **30.** The Princess of Wales opened the new full body scanner at Stoke Mandeville Hospital. Princess Anne visited Cumbria.

April 1. The Queen, accompanied by the Duke of Edinburgh, opened the Clore Gallery for the Turner Collection at the Tate Gallery. The Princess of Wales visited Preston. **7.** The Princess of Wales attended a lunch to mark World Health Day. **8.** The Prince of Wales attended a "Better Made in Britain" reception. Princess Anne visited Birmingham. **9.** The Princess of Wales opened a unit for the care of people with H.I.V. infection at the Middlesex Hospital, London. **15.** The Queen was represented by the Duke of Edinburgh at the Zeebrugge Ferry Memorial Service held in Canterbury Cathedral; Princess Anne was also present. **16.** The Queen and the Duke of Edinburgh attended the Maundy Service at Ely Cathedral where the Queen distributed the Royal Maundy. **19.** The Duke of Edinburgh left Heathrow Airport to visit the Bahamas and the U.S.A. **21.** The Prince and Princess of Wales left Heathrow Airport to visit Spain. **23.** Princess Margaret opened the Theatre Museum at Covent Garden. **28.** Princess Anne visited Edinburgh. **29.** The Princess of Wales visited the *Queen Elizabeth 2.*

May 2. The Duke and Duchess of York started the Jersey international air race. **5.**

Princess Anne attended a concert at H.M. Prison Saughton. **6.** The Queen and the Duke of Edinburgh visited the Joint Services Defence College on its 40th anniversary. The Duke of Edinburgh attended the 200th anniversary dinner of the M.C.C. **7.** The President of Mozambique visited the Queen. The Queen, accompanied by the Duke of Edinburgh, took the salute at a march-past of the Honourable Artillery Company to mark the Company's 450th anniversary. The Queen Mother visited Northamptonshire. **8.** The Queen and the Duke of Edinburgh visited Taunton and Bridgwater. **11.** The Duke of Edinburgh left Heathrow Airport to visit Denmark. **13.** The Queen and the Duke of Edinburgh visited Portsmouth and the Isle of Wight to attend ceremonies to mark the 200th anniversary of the departure for Australia of the First Fleet. **14.** Princess Anne visited Rugby. Princess Margaret left Gatwick Airport to visit China and Hong Kong. **15.** The Prince of Wales, accompanied by the Princess of Wales, attended the 40th International Film Festival in Cannes. **18.** The Queen and the Duke of Edinburgh visited the Chelsea Flower Show. **19.** The President of Costa Rica visited the Queen. **26.** The Queen and the Duke of Edinburgh left Heathrow Airport for Berlin to attend the celebrations of the City's 750th anniversary. **29.** Princess Anne visited Wales.

June 1. The Queen, accompanied by the Duke of Edinburgh, reviewed the King's Troop, Royal Horse Artillery, to mark its 40th anniversary. **3.** The Queen, accompanied by other members of the royal family, was present at Epsom Races. The Duke of Edinburgh left Heathrow Airport to visit Canada. **4.** The Queen Mother left Heathrow Airport to visit Canada. **9.** Princess Anne was admitted a Fellow of the Royal Society. **10.** The Duke and Duchess of Kent announced the betrothal of the Earl of St Andrews to Miss Sylvana Tomaselli. **12.** It was announced that the title Princess Royal had been conferred on Princess Anne by the Queen. The Queen's Birthday Honours List was published. **13.** The Queen was present at her Birthday Parade at Horse Guards Parade. **16, 17, 18.** The Queen was present at Ascot races with other members of the royal family. **21.** The Queen and the Duke of Edinburgh visited the celebrations in Hyde Park of the centenary of the St John Ambulance Brigade. **25.** The Queen, accompanied by the Duke of Edinburgh, opened the first session of the new Parliament. The Queen Mother visited Durham to attend celebrations marking the 1,300th anniversary of the death of St. Cuthbert. The Princess of Wales visited Huddersfield. **26.** The Queen, accompanied by the Duke of Edinburgh, inaugurated the new wet dock at Invergordon. **29.** The Queen visited St Columba's Hospice, Edinburgh. The Princess Royal opened the Orthoptic Congress at Harrogate.

30. The Queen and the Duke of Edinburgh visited Livingston New Town in its 25th anniversary year and the Heriot-Watt University, Edinburgh. The Princess Royal visited H.M. Prison Perth.

July 1. The Queen and the The Duke of Edinburgh visited Dundee. The Prince of Wales visited a number of community employment projects in Spitalfields, east London. **3.** The Queen and the The Duke of Edinburgh visited the Scottish National War Memorial at Edinburgh Castle in its 60th anniversary year. They also visited an exhibition to mark the tercentenary of the revival of the Order of the Thistle. **6.** The Prince of Wales opened the Institute of Medical Genetics for Wales at the University of Wales College of Medicine. **7.** The Queen and the Duke of Edinburgh were entertained at dinner on board *M.V. Pacific Princess* at Greenwich to celebrate 150th anniversary of the Peninsular and Oriental Steam Navigation Company. The Prince and Princess of Wales visited the Brixton Recreation Centre, London. **9.** The Princess of Wales visited the flower festival organized in support of Ely Cathedral. **10.** The Princess Royal opened Alton Water. Princess Margaret launched *H.M.S. Norfolk* at the Yarrow shipyard. **12.** The Princess Royal attended the Fun Day Sunday Celebrities at Ascot racecourse. **14.** The King of Morocco arrived in London for a four-day State visit. **15.** The Duke and Duchess of York left Heathrow airport to visit Canada. Princess Margaret inaugurated the Princess Margaret passenger terminal at King George Dock, Hull. **16.** The Queen visited Milton's Cottage, Chalfont St. Giles, to mark the centenary of Milton's Cottage Trust. The Duke of Edinburgh attended the Globe Theatre ground-breaking ceremony at Southwark, London. The Prince of Wales visited Birtley and Gateshead, Tyne and Wear. **17.** The Queen and the Duke of Edinburgh visited North Humberside. The Princess Royal visited Edinburgh. **24.** The Queen and the Duke of Edinburgh visited Cheshire. **28.** The Princess of Wales opened the Princess of Wales conservatory at the Royal Botanic Gardens, Kew. **30.** The Queen, accompanied by the Duke of Edinburgh, visited Poplar and the Isle of Dogs, London, and opened the Docklands Light Railway. The Prince and Princess of Wales attended a pageant at Trewithen to mark the 650th anniverary of the Duchy of Cornwall. **31.** The Queen opened the Leonard Cheshire Foundation's new home for severely handicapped people at Park House, Sandringham.

Aug. 5. The Queen opened the new Jubilee market in Covent Garden, London. **7.** The Queen opened Britoil's Clyde oilfield from the company's headquarters in Glasgow. **9.** The Queen visited Orkney to mark the 85th

anniversary of St. Magnus Cathedral. **15.** The Queen opened the renovated Albert Hall in Ballater. **18.** The Prince of Wales visited the Lochaber mountain rescue team at Ben Nevis, Fort William. **19.** The Queen Mother visited Orkney.

BRITISH POLITICS

(1986). Sept. 1. The Home Office announced that people from India, Pakistan, Bangladesh, Ghana, and Nigeria would have to obtain a visa before visiting Britain. **4.** Lord Elton, Minister of State, Dept. of Environment, resigned for family reasons. **5.** The Welsh Secretary (Mr. Nicholas Edwards) announced that Welsh farmers would receive up to £5 million compensation for sheep affected by fall-out from the Chernobyl nuclear accident. **10.** Mrs. Thatcher announced a Government reshuffle involving 33 changes. **13.** The Social Democratic Party's annual conference opened in Harrogate. **22.** The Liberal Party annual conference opened at Eastbourne. **28.** The Labour Party annual conference opened in Blackpool with delegates voting for the next Labour Government to include a Minister for Women in the Cabinet. Mr. Kinnock reaffirmed Labour's decision to abandon all nuclear weapons. On Sept. 29 delegates confirmed the expulsion of eight Merseyside Militants from the Labour Party. On Sept. 30 Mr. Kinnock told the conference he would not close U.S. bases on British territory and would keep Britain in N.A.T.O. The N.E.C. reaffirmed Labour's promise to repeal Conservative trade union legislation and replace it with a charter of workers' rights. On Oct. 1 the Conference voted to reject nuclear power and to phase out existing plants.

Oct. 1. Mrs. Thatcher named Mr. Marmaduke Hussey as the new chairman of the B.B.C. **2.** The Government banned all Libyan Arab Airline flights into Britain from the end of Oct. because of "the irrefutable evidence" of the airline's links with terrorism. **3.** The Environment Secretary (Mr. Ridley) announced that the Government was to allow local authorities to spend £300 million more on police forces, especially in inner city areas. **7.** The Conservative Party annual conference opened in Bournemouth: the Education Secretary (Mr. Baker) announced that 20,000 places were to be created in new city colleges specializing in technology and business. On Oct. 8 the Home Secretary (Mr. Hurd) announced new powers to confiscate the assets of criminals and to enable child victims of abuse to give evidence by video. On Oct. 9 the Chancellor of the Exchequer (Mr. Lawson) pledged not to cut taxes at the risk of higher inflation and set a target of zero per cent inflation for the next Parliament. Delegates voted for the proposal to replace rates with a community charge on all adults. On Oct. 10 the conference ended with a declaration by Mrs. Thatcher that the Conservative Party was the only one with an effective defence policy. **11.** It was stated that the Home Secretary (Mr. Hurd) had ordered five Arabs and a Swede, believed to be terrorists, to leave the country. **15.** Alliance and Labour peers voted through an amendment to the National Health Service Bill which removes the Crown immunity from prosecution under health and safety regulations of health authorities' premises. **22.** Liberal M.P.s unanimously supported a new policy commitment to maintain and modernize a minimum nuclear deterrent, reversing the vote at the Eastbourne conference favouring a non-nuclear defence policy in Europe. The Labour Party's National Executive blocked the selection of Mr. Leslie Huckfield as the Labour candidate in the Knowsley North by-election and imposed a nominee of its own, Mr. George Howarth. **24.** Diplomatic relations between the U.K. and Syria were broken off because of Syria's "outrageous role" in the attempt by Nezar Hindawi to blow up an El Al airliner. The Foreign Secretary (Sir Geoffrey Howe) said that there was evidence that the Syrian ambassador (Dr. Loutof Haydar) was personally involved in planning the bombing and that the ambassador and his staff had been ordered to leave the U.K. Syria closed its airspace and territorial waters to British craft but guaranteed the safety of Britons in the country. The U.S. withdrew its ambassador from Syria in protest at Syria's involvement in international terrorism, and Canada recalled its ambassador to Syria for consultations. **26.** Mr. Jeffrey Archer, deputy chairman of the Conservative Party, resigned because of allegations in a Sunday newspaper that he had tried to pay a prostitute to go abroad to avoid a scandal. Mr. Archer explained he had foolishly allowed himself to be trapped into offering money to a women he had never met, and stated that he had never had any association with a prostitute. **29.** The Foreign Secretary (Sir Geoffrey Howe) announced that Britain was to impose controls on fishing in the 150-mile protection zone around the Falklands from Feb. 1. Tam Dalyell, Labour M.P. for Linlithgow, was ordered from the Commons for describing Mrs. Thatcher as "a bounder, a liar, a deceiver, a cheat, and a crook" in her handling of the Westland affair. The Security Commission published its report on measures for improving security at Armed Forces' communications units in the light of the Cyprus secrets trials. **30.** Mr. Tebbit, Conservative Party chairman, published an analysis of television news coverage of the U.S. air raid on Tripoli and accused the B.B.C. of anti-Government and anti-American bias in its news coverage. The B.B.C.'s Director-General, Mr. Alisdair Milne, rejected the accusa-

tions and said the Conservative party was attempting to intimidate the B.B.C. On Nov. 5 the B.B.C. rejected all but one of the 40 complaints but Mr. Tebbit dismissed its defence of its news coverage.

Nov. 6. The Chancellor of the Exchequer (Mr. Lawson) presented his autumn statement to the Commons. **7.** The all-party social services committee of the Commons announced an urgent Parliamentary inquiry into the problem of A.I.D.S. On Nov. 11 a special Cabinet committee on A.I.D.S. decided to distribute a leaflet about A.I.D.S. to nearly 23 million homes, backed by a television and press campaign. **13.** Mr. George Howarth held Knowsley North for Labour in the by-election, but with a greatly reduced majority. **20.** The Attorney General (Sir Michael Havers) announced that a police investigation had started into alleged leaks by former senior officials in MI5 to the author Nigel West. The move followed questions in the Commons over the Government's attempts to ban publication in Australia of a book about alleged Soviet penetration of the security service written by Peter Wright. The Home Secretary told M.P.s that the colour television licence fee would remain at £58 until April 1988. The D.H.S.S. said old people on supplementary benefit would be able to claim an extra £5 a week in periods of exceptionally cold weather during the winter. **21.** Mr. Fowler, Social Services Secretary, announced that the Government was setting up a Special Health Authority to direct a public information campaign about A.I.D.S., at a cost of £20 million. **22.** The Liberal Council voted to endorse Mr. Steel's new nuclear defence policy. **25.** Mr. Derek Hatton, expelled from the Labour party because of his membership of Militant, resigned as deputy leader of Liverpool City Council. **26.** There were questions in the Commons about alleged breaches of confidence by Lord Rothschild and Sir Arthur Franks, former head of MI6, in relation to information on matters of State security given to authors: in a written reply the Attorney General said he was considering the allegations with the Director of Public Prosecutions. On Dec. 3 an Alliance motion in the Commons requesting the appointment of a special commission on the security forces was defeated. On Dec. 4 Lord Rothschild, in a letter to *The Daily Telegraph*, publicly called on the Director General of MI5 to clear him of allegations that he was the "fifth man" in Soviet spy scandals, and declared he was not and never had been a Soviet agent. In the Commons that day the Prime Minister declined to give immediately the public assurance requested but on Dec. 5 in a statement issued from Downing Street she said she was advised that there was no evidence that Lord Rothschild had ever been a Soviet agent. **28.** The Commons select committee on the Channel Tunnel scheme issued its final report, with recommendations for 70 amendments.

Dec. 3. Mr. Ridley, Environment Secretary, announced in the Commons measures to avoid large rate increases by county councils. **8.** Mr. Younger, Defence Secretary, told the Commons that Servicemen were to be given the same right to sue the Crown in cases of personal injury as civilians. **10.** The D.H.S.S. announced comprehensive legislation to control test-tube baby fertilization, experiments on human embryos, and non-commercial surrogacy. **18.** The Defence Secretary announced the cancellation of development work on the G.E.C. Nimrod early warning system in favour of buying the American A.W.A.C.S. system. He also promised a full review of the handling of major defence contracts. The Attorney General (Sir Michael Havers) told the Commons that he and the Director of Public Prosecutions (Sir Thomas Hetherington) were satisfied that there was no evidence to substantiate the allegations that Sir Arthur Franks, former head of MI6, had supplied information on matters of state security to authors of books on espionage. Mrs. Irina Ratushinskaya, the dissident Soviet poet, arrived in Britain : she was received by the Prime Minister at No. 10 Downing Street on Dec. 22. **22.** Mr. Patten, Minister for Housing, announced that the new town programme would be wound-up by April 1992. **29.** Britain and Guatemala resumed full diplomatic relations.

(1987). Jan. 20. The Government announced a second severe weather payment to supplementary benefit claimants and alterations to the scheme to make future claims easier. In the Commons, Mr. Hurd (Home Secretary) announced his decision to reopen the case of the six men jailed for the Birmingham pub bombings in 1975. **21.** The Attorney General obtained a High Court injunction to prevent Mr. Duncan Campbell, a journalist, from publishing details about a secret satellite system, Project Zircon. **22.** An article about the spy satellite project, written by Mr. Campbell, was published in *The New Statesman*. Government lawyers tried, unsuccessfully, to obtain a second injunction preventing the showing of a film about Project Zircon at the Palace of Westminster. However, the Speaker of the Commons banned the showing of the film in the precincts of Parliament until the Commons had debated the matter. The debate took place on Jan. 27. **26.** Mr. Hurd, Home Secretary, rejected Opposition demands for an independent inquiry into the clashes on Jan. 24 between demonstrators and police near News International's Wapping newspaper plant.

Feb. 2. In the Commons, Labour and Alliance M.P.s condemned the Special Branch

raid on the B.B.C. offices in Glasgow on Jan. 31 in which film and documents relating to the Secret Society television series (which included an episode about Project Zircon) were seized. Mr. Rifkind, Scottish Secretary, denied in the Commons that Government Ministers had any responsibility for ordering the raid. Opposition M.P.s successfully applied for an emergency debate on the role of the Special Branch which was held on Feb. 3. **6.** The private member's Bill to incorporate the European Convention on Human Rights into British law failed to receive enough votes to obtain a second reading. **9.** The Government announced a major relaxation of planning controls in the countryside. The Ministry of Agriculture announced measures to enhance environmental protection and encourage alternative uses of farm land. **11.** Eleven new life peers—six Conservative, five Labour—were created. **17.** Mr. Fowler, Social Services Secretary, announced details of a £25 million programme to reduce hospital waiting lists by increasing the number of operations carried out. **19.** Mr. Channon, Trade and Industry Secretary, told the Commons that the Rover Group was to merge its trucks and van business with DAF of Holland. **24.** The all-party War Crimes Group of M.P.s disclosed that six alleged Nazi war criminals had been found to be living in Britain by Home Office officials. **26.** Mr. Rifkind, Scottish Secretary, announced that Scotland's domestic rating system would be replaced by the community charge on April 1, 1989, instead of the change being phased over three years. In the Greenwich by-election, the S.D.P. candidate, Rosie Barnes, won the seat from Labour.

March 2. Mr. Baker, Education Secretary, announced a revised package of pay and conditions for teachers. After meeting members of the Simon Wiesenthal Centre, Mr. Hurd, Home Secretary, promised further investigations into the circumstances in which 17 East Europeans accused of Nazi war crimes came to Britain. **3.** Mr. Newton, Health Minister, announced rises from April 1 in N.H.S. prescription charges and charges for private patients in N.H.S. hospitals but said charges for N.H.S. dental treatment were frozen for a further year. Mr. Hurd, Home Secretary, announced that from midnight airlines would face fines of up to £1,000 for every passenger they brought to Britain without a valid passport and visa. **6.** Labour retained the Midland West seat in the European Parliament by-election but with a smaller majority. **10.** The second report from the trade and industry committee of the Commons on the Westland affair was published. **12.** The Government announced its approval of the building of the Sizewell B nuclear power station in Suffolk. Mr. Matthew Taylor, the Liberal candidate, held Truro for the Alliance in the by-election.

The Queen inspecting 2,000 year-old terracotta warriors in Xian during her visit to China in October.

THE ROYAL VISIT TO CANADA

The Duke and Duchess of York arriving by canoe at Thunder Bay during their visit to Canada in July.

THE PRINCESS ROYAL

In June the Queen conferred the title Princess Royal on Princess Anne for her work for the Save the Children Fund and other charities.

THE GOVERNMENT

The Conservative Party, led by Mrs. Thatcher, won a third term of office at the General Election in June.

Tamil guerrillas surrendered their weapons in August to Indian soldiers monitoring the peace accord.

THE GULF CRISIS

The U.N. Secretary General visited Iran and Iraq in September as tension rose in the Gulf.

Over 180 people died when *The Herald of Free Enterprise* capsized in March.

KOREAN RIOTS

Civil unrest and rioting in Korea throughout the summer of 1987 led the government to promise constitutional changes.

BANGLADESHI FLOODS

Three months of flooding in the summer of 1987 left 600 dead and over three million homeless.

FLIGHT RECORD

In December *Voyager* made the first non-stop flight around the world without refuelling.

BALLOONING RECORD

Virgin Atlantic Flyer set a record for the longest hot-air balloon flight by crossing the Atlantic in July.

OBITUARIES

Lord Stockton (*top left*), Vyacheslav Molotov (*top right*), Lord Maybray-King (*bottom left*) and John Silkin.

Fred Astaire (*top left*), Andrés Segovia (*top right*), Cary Grant (*bottom left*) and Rita Hayworth.

GOLFING TRIUMPHS

Laura Davies was the first British winner of the U.S. Women's Open Championship in July. Nick Faldo won the British Open Championship, also in July.

WIMBLEDON RECORD

Martina Navratilova won the Women's Singles title for the sixth successive year, the record number of consecutive wins.

RECORD BREAKERS

Ben Johnson (*left*) set a new 100 metre world record in August. Said Aouita broke his own 5,000 metre world record in July.

17. The Chancellor of the Exchequer (Mr. Lawson) presented his annual Budget in the Commons: the Budget proposals were approved by 351–202 votes on March 23. **26.** In the Commons, the Immigration (Carriers Liability) Bill was given a third reading by 147 votes to 57. **30.** Mr. Walker, Energy Secretary, announced that West Burton, Notts., and Fawley, near Southampton, were the preferred sites for two new coal-fired power stations.

April 1. A proposal to add to the Criminal Justice Bill a clause reintroducing the death penalty for particularly evil murders was defeated in the Commons. **2.** The Government set a three-week deadline for Japan to open up its financial markets to British firms or face the expulsion of Japanese banks and finance houses from London. The Government sold the State-owned Royal Ordnance munitions business to British Aerospace for £190 million. **4.** Mr. Michael Howard, the Corporate Affairs Minister, visited Tokyo to try to obtain specific undertakings for fair access to Japanese markets for British goods and financial services. **8.** Mr. Keith Best, Conservative M.P. for Ynys Môn, who made multiple applications for British Telecom shares, announced that he would stand down at the next General Election. On April 10 Mr. Eric Cockeram, Conservative M.P. for Ludlow, who also made multiple applications for British Telecom shares, announced his intention to stand down at the next General Election. **9.** The Government announced that it was placing orders worth over £300 million with the Westland helicopter firm as the company confirmed it was to make up to 2,000 workers redundant. **23.** The Cabinet approved the payment in full of salary increases averaging 9·5 per cent. for nurses, midwives and health visitors. They also approved increases of 9·1 per cent. for Health Service professionals, 7·7 per cent. for doctors and dentists, and 5·96 per cent for the armed forces. In a written reply in the Commons, Mrs. Thatcher confirmed that Sir Maurice Oldfield, head of MI6 from 1973 to 1978, was an active homosexual but said there was no evidence that this had compromised national security. **27.** The Government set up eight task forces to co-ordinate Government aid in Coventry, Preston, Doncaster, Hartlepool, Nottingham, Rochdale, Wolverhampton and Tower Hamlets, London, and provided extra finance to five "city action teams" in Birmingham, Liverpool, Salford, Newcastle, and London.

May 1. The Government ordered a search for a deep underground site for the disposal of nuclear waste after Mr. Ridley, Environment Secretary, confirmed that the search for a shallow dump in four rural sites had been abandoned. **6.** The Prime Minister rejected a request by Sir James Callaghan, ex-Labour Prime Minister, for a fresh inquiry into the activities of MI5. She disclosed that an internal investigation by the Director General of the Security Service had cleared it of involvement in a plot to destabilize the Wilson Government in the 1970s. The White Paper on Defence Estimates for 1987 was published. **7.** Voting took place for metropolitan district councils in England and non-metropolitan district councils in England and Wales. The Conservatives made a net gain of 78 seats and won overall control of three more councils: Labour had a net loss of 220 seats and lost overall control of six councils: the Alliance parties had a net gain of 438 seats and won overall control of four more councils. **8.** The Home Secretary announced that 498 Vietnamese "boat people" would be admitted to Britain over the next two years. The Government announced that it is to spend £170 million in a 10-year programme to combat acid rain pollution. **11.** The Prime Minister announced that a General Election would be held on June 11. **12.** The remaining stages of the Finance Bill were completed in under two hours. **13.** The Commons approved an order to allow the Bill authorizing the Channel Tunnel project to be carried over to the new Parliament. **14.** Mr. Channon, Trade and Industry Secretary, announced that British Aerospace was to receive a £450 million Government loan to help finance the Airbus A330/A340 projects. **18.** Parliament was dissolved. The Government announced approval for a £230 million extension at the Naval dockyards in Rosyth, Fife.

June 11. The General Election was won by the Conservative Party; the final state of the parties was: Conservatives 375 seats, Labour 229 seats, Liberals 17, S.D.P. 5, an overall Conservative majority of 101. **13.** Mrs. Thatcher announced her reshuffled Cabinet: this included the replacement of Lord Hailsham as Lord Chancellor by Sir Michael Havers, who was subsequently ennobled. **14.** Mr. Steel, Liberal leader, announced he had called a meeting of Liberal Party officers at which he would set out options for democratic fusion of the S.D.P. and Liberal Parties. Dr. David Owen and other leading members of the S.D.P. made it clear that they were not ready to give up their status as an independent party. **15.** Mrs. Thatcher announced the appointments of junior Ministers. **17.** Mr. Bernard Weatherill was re-elected Speaker of the House of Commons. **24.** S.D.P. M.P.s rejected the Liberals' proposal that the two parties should undertake a full merger but recommended that the Alliance should become a closer-knit partnership under a single leader. **25.** The Queen opened the first session of the new Parliament. **27.** Dr. David Owen, S.D.P. leader, declared that he would play no part in a merged Alliance party. **29.** A meeting of the S.D.P.s National Committee opposed a formal merger with the Liberal Party by 18–13 votes.

July 2. At the end of a six-day debate, the Queen's Speech was approved by 347–247 votes. **4.** Liberal and S.D.P. leaders in Wales supported Mr. David Steel's call for a full merger of the two Alliance parties. **8.** Elections for Labour's Shadow Cabinet resulted in six members of the "soft Left" gaining places at the expense of the centre-right of the party. **9.** The Attorney General (Sir Patrick Mayhew) announced that a police investigation had discovered no evidence to justify bringing proceedings against Lord Rothschild for an alleged breach of the Official Secrets Act: he also ruled out the prosecution of Mr. Chapman Pincher, author of several books on the security services. Mr. Tony Newton, Health Minister, announced that a High Court judge was to head a statutory inquiry into the recent child abuse scandal in Cleveland. Mrs. Justice Butler-Sloss was named as head of the inquiry on July 13. The inquiry opened in Middlesbrough on Aug. 11. **16.** Mr. Hurd, Home Secretary, announced that up to 3,500 prisoners serving short sentences would be released early to reduce the pressure on overcrowded prisons. **20.** Mr. Younger, Defence Secretary, announced that the three Royal Navy warships patrolling the Gulf to protect British shipping had been given orders to defend themselves. **21.** Col. Ivan Djambov, the Bulgarian military attaché, was ordered to leave Britain for spying. M.P.s voted to award a pay rise to themselves of 22 per cent. **23.** Mr. Ridley, Environment Secretary, announced a £13,700 million Government grant towards local council spending and said that five more councils (Ealing, Liverpool, Kingston-upon-Hull, Manchester and Waltham Forest) were to be added to the list of rate-capped councils. **24.** Mr. Channon, Transport Secretary, announced new safety measures for ferries following publication of the report on the capsize of the *Herald of Free Enterprise*. **30.** The Dissolution Honours List was published: 19 life peers and four knights were created. **31.** The Foreign Office stated that the Government was keeping under constant review the situation in the Gulf and the threat to shipping, but had no plans to send minesweepers to the area.

Aug. 6. Dr. David Owen resigned the leadership of the S.D.P. after party members voted in favour of merger talks with the Liberal Party. **11.** Mr. Younger, Defence Secretary announced that four Royal Navy minesweepers were to be sent to the Gulf. **14.** Mr. Hurd, Home Secretary, ordered a police investigation into the jailing of four people for the Guildford and Woolwich pub bombings in 1974. **29.** Mr. Robert Maclennan, M.P. for Caithness and Sutherland, became the new

leader of the S.D.P. **30.** The S.D.P.'s annual conference opened in Portsmouth. Dr. David Owen said he would not join a merged S.D.P. and Liberal Alliance Party but would set up a fourth political force. On Aug. 31 delegates voted overwhelmingly in favour of merger negotiations with the Liberal Party, and voted also against a proposal that the party assets should be shared between the new merged party and the remains of the S.D.P.

IRELAND

(1986). Sept. 4. The Irish Republic banned Libyan students from entering the country for training or education because of the Libyan Government's continued support for the I.R.A. **18.** An agreement was signed by the U.K. and Irish Governments setting up an international fund to provide aid for social and economic development on both sides of the border. **23.** The Irish Government had a two-vote majority in a confidence motion in Parliament, thus avoiding an immediate general election.

Nov. 2. At the Sinn Fein annual conference, delegates voted to lift their boycott of the Dail. Those opposed to the decision later announced the formation of an organization to be known as Republican Sinn Fein. **12.** The Ulster Resistance Organization was launched in Belfast to oppose the Anglo-Irish Agreement. **15.** Forty-eight policemen and 28 civilians were injured, and 110 people arrested, in rioting and looting towards the end of a Loyalist rally in Belfast marking the first anniversary of the Anglo-Irish Agreement. **22.** Ulster's S.D.L.P. renewed its support for the Anglo-Irish Agreement and called for fresh reconciliation talks with the Unionists. **27.** Thirty-five people were injured in an I.R.A. mortar bomb attack in Newry, Co. Down, when six missiles missed their target and hit a housing estate near the Irish border. An Ulster Unionist campaign to disrupt the province's civic administration was defeated when Official Unionist councillors refused to respond to calls from their leader, Mr. James Molyneaux, to resign.

Dec. 2. The Irish High Court rejected a move by the Attorney General (Sir Michael Havers) to ban publication in the Irish Republic of a book, *One Girl's War*, by Joan Miller, a former M15 agent. **10.** The Irish Government lost its parliamentary majority when Mrs. Alice Green (Dublin Central) resigned the Fine Gael whip. **16.** More than 600 homes were damaged when explosives packed into a school bus blew up outside a police station in Lisburn Road, Belfast. **23.** Mrs. Thatcher paid an eight-hour visit to Northern Ireland.

(1987). **Jan. 2.** Ulster Unionists launched a petition to the Queen calling for a referendum on the Anglo-Irish Agreement. **12.** The High Court in Dublin ordered the Irish Government to pay £50,000 to three journalists whose telephones were secretly bugged by the administration of Mr. Charles Haughey, now in Opposition. **20.** The four-year-old Irish coalition Government collapsed when four Labour Party ministers refused to accept cuts to health and social welfare spending: Dr. FitzGerald, the Prime Minister, called a general election for Feb. 17. **31.** Mary McGlinchey, wife of the former leader of the Irish National Liberation Army, was shot dead in Dundalk, in one of a series of murders connected with feuding inside the I.N.L.A.

Feb. 17. The general election in the Irish Republic resulted in victory for Mr. Charles Haughey's Fianna Fail party, which won 81 seats, three short of an overall majority. Fine Gael won 51 seats, and the Progressive Democrats, in their first general election, secured 14 seats. **22.** Loyalists suspects were questioned after the theft of arms and ammunition from an Ulster Defence Regiment base in Coleraine, Co. Londonderry. The weapons and ammunition were recovered when a gang was intercepted at Templepatrick, Co. Antrim. **23.** Belfast City Council was fined £25,000 in the Ulster High Court for its contempt of court in continuing to adjourn meetings in protest at the Anglo-Irish Agreement.

March 9. It was announced the Royal Ulster Constabulary was to pay nearly £250,000 compensation to 31 women police reservists in settlement of a sex discrimination action. The Chief Constable (Sir John Hermon) agreed to change police procedure to ensure equal opportunities in the future. **10.** Mr. Charles Haughey was elected Taoiseach, his third term in the office. **11.** Dr. Garret FitzGerald, former Irish Prime Minister, resigned as leader of the Fine Gael party: on Mar. 21 Mr. Alan Dukes, former Justice Minister, was elected his successor. **15.** Gerard Steenson, believed to be behind killings in the I.N.L.A., was shot dead in Belfast. The Irish People's Liberation Organization, a breakaway faction of I.N.L.A., claimed responsibility. On March 22 the I.N.L.A. retaliated with two murders, bringing to 12 the number of victims of the I.N.L.A. feud. **26.** The Bishop of Derry, the Rt. Rev. Edward Daly, announced that he had banned the bodies of terrorists from Roman Catholic churches during Requiem Masses after a funeral in Londonderry on March 24 during which two masked I.R.A. men fired pistol shots over the coffin from inside the church grounds. **31.** The new Irish Government introduced its Budget, which reduced current

and capital expenditure and imposed new medical charges.

April 8. The three-day siege at Magilligan jail, near Londonderry, ended when 20 Loyalist prisoners gave themselves up and released unharmed a prison officer and a Roman Catholic inmate they had held hostage. **17.** The Provisional I.R.A. announced that shots would no longer be fired over the coffins of dead members on church grounds.

May 8. I.R.A. terrorists attempting to bomb the police station at Loughgall, Co. Armagh, were ambushed by police and troops. In the ensuing gun fight eight I.R.A. men and a civilian caught in crossfire were killed. **26.** In a referendum in the Republic of Ireland the majority voted in favour of ratifying the Single European Act.

June 15. Mr. Ken Maginnis, Ulster Unionist M.P. for Fermanagh and South Tyrone, was jailed for seven days for not paying his car tax in protest at the Anglo-Irish Agreement.

ACCIDENTS AND DISASTERS

(1986). **Sept. 2.** It was announced in Moscow that 79 people had died and 319 were missing after the collision on Aug. 31 of the Soviet cruise ship *Admiral Nakjimov* and a freighter in the Black Sea. **5.** Fourteen people were killed in a hotel fire at Kristiansand, Norway. **16.** An underground fire at Kinross gold mine in South Africa killed 177 miners. **19.** Two inter-city express trains crashed at Colwich Junction, Staffs., killing the driver of one train.

Oct. 3. A Russian nuclear-powered submarine exploded and caught fire in the Atlantic Ocean near Bermuda: three crew members were reported to have died. On Oct. 6 the submarine sank in 18,000 feet of water. **10.** An earthquake in El Salvador caused 890 deaths. **11.** Mother Teresa of Calcutta escaped uninjured from a plane crash in Tanzania which killed six people.

Nov. 1. A fire at the Sandoz chemical factory in Basle, Switzerland, caused spillage into the Rhine of over 30 tons of agricultural chemicals, including mercury. The chemicals flowed downstream, reaching Amsterdam by Nov. 9 and leaving the upper reaches of the river biologically dead. **6.** Forty-five people died when a Chinook helicopter ferrying oil workers from the Brent oilfield to Sumburgh crashed into the North Sea two miles off the Shetland Islands: there were only two survivors. **13.** Michael Lush, a television viewer undertaking a Houdini-style stunt for the Noel Edmonds' *Late Late Breakfast Show* was killed during rehearsals: the B.B.C. cancelled the show and launched an investigation. **23.** The crew of the *Kowloon Bridge* had to be airlifted to safety after the ship lost her rudder and started to drift in Bantry Bay.

Dec. 12. A Russian airliner crashed in East Berlin, killing 70 people. **25.** Six crewmen died and five were rescued when the cargo ship *Sudurland* sank in heavy seas east of Iceland. Three seamen died and five were missing after a Cypriot tanker, the *Stainless Trader*, sank in heavy seas off Sardinia. **26.** Twelve seamen died when the cargo ship *Syneta* hit rocks and sank off the east coast of Iceland. **31.** Ninety-six people died in a fire at the Dupont Plaza Hotel in San Juan, Puerto Rico, caused by arson.

(1987). Jan. 5. Tower Bridge, London, was closed to traffic after a crane barge crashed into the overhead walkways. **Feb. 27.** Seven British Servicemen were killed in a Chinook helicopter crash in the Falkland Islands.

March 1. Five people were killed when ski lift chairs fell 100 feet to the ground at a French Pyrenees resort. **2.** Forty people were injured when two trains collided at a level crossing near Shrewsbury. An earthquake struck the Bay of Plenty area of New Zealand causing widespread damage but only a few injuries. **6.** A Townsend Thoresen car ferry, the *Herald of Free Enterprise*, capsized just outside the Belgian port of Zeebrugge as it sailed for Dover. 408 passengers and crew were reported safe after an international air and sea rescue operation, but the eventual toll was 189 dead, and three men and a baby missing. Mr. Justice Sheen, an Admiralty judge, was appointed to conduct an inquiry into the disaster.

April 7. The *Herald of Free Enterprise* was righted in an 8¼-hour operation. **27.** The refloated ferry, supported by giant floating cranes, was towed into Zeebrugge harbour. The public inquiry into the disaster opened at Church House, Westminster, concluding on June 12.

May 1. The report of the official inquiry into the loss of the British sailing ship the *Marques* was published. **6.** A forest fire began in north-east China which blazed for nearly a month, destroying vast tracts of forest and towns in a 1,200 square mile area near the Russian border. More than 200 people were killed and over 50,000 were left homeless. **9.** A Polish Airlines airliner attempting an emergency landing crashed in a Warsaw suburb, killing all 183 people aboard. **23.** A tornado destroyed the Texas town of Saragosa, killing 29 people.

June 21. The only airworthy Bristol Blenheim bomber in existence crashed at the annual show of the Guild of Air Pilots.

July 14. A freak storm caused a river to burst its banks near Annecy, France, and flood a crowded camp site, leaving 21 dead and 28 missing. **24.** The report of the inquiry into the *Herald of Free Enterprise* disaster was published. **26.** A heatwave in Greece caused more than 700 deaths.

Aug. 2. A tornado struck Edmonton, Alberta, killing at least 25 people. **13.** Three hundred people were reported dead after floods in Nepal caused by an exceptionally heavy monsoon. **15.** A jet crashed on a highway near Detroit killing 161 people, including five victims on the ground. **21.** An explosion at a grocery store in Balham, south London, caused two deaths. **31.** Seventy miners were missing after an explosion or collapse of a shaft at the St Helena mine, South Africa.

CRIMES, TRIALS, ETC

(1986). Sept. 1. David Bishop, scrum-half for Pontypool and a Welsh international rugby player, was sentenced to a month's imprisonment for assaulting an opponent during a club game. On Sept. 17 the sentence was suspended by the Court of Appeal. **2.** Five people, all members of the same family, were found strangled at a country house near Fordingbridge, Hants., which had been set on fire. **3.** In Florida, Steve Benson, a tobacco heir who killed his mother and adopted brother in a dispute over the family fortune, was sentenced to two consecutive life terms. **11.** About 100 black youths bombarded police with stones and bottles in the St. Paul's district of Bristol during a police raid. **25.** P.C. Richard Johnson, a member of the Cardiff police team, was jailed for six months for biting off part of an ear of P.C. Keith Jones, of Newport police team, during a rugby match. Count Gottfried von Bismarck, who hosted the party at which Olivia Channon died, was fined £80 by Oxford magistrates for possessing amphetamine sulphate. **26.** Rasmi Awad was jailed for 25 years at the Central Criminal Court, London, for his part in a Libyan-backed plot to mount a grenade attack on a British target: Awad's co-defendant Nassar Mohamed was cleared by the jury.

Oct. 2. The first person to be convicted of involvement in last year's Tottenham riots, Simon Macminn, was sentenced to seven years youth custody at the Central Criminal Court, London. **8.** A missing painting by Rembrandt, a portrait of Jacob De Gheyn III which has been stolen four times, was discovered in West Germany and subsequently returned to the Dulwich Picture Gallery. **24.** Nezar Hindawi, a Jordanian terrorist, was sentenced to a record 45 years imprisonment at the Central Criminal Court, London, for the attempted bombing of an El Al airliner: the court was told that Hindawi had Syrian backing for his mission. **27.** A prison officer was seized as a hostage by five prisoners at Saughton jail, Edinburgh, amid demands for an inquiry into claims of staff brutality. The officer was released unharmed on Oct. 31 and the seige ended peacefully on Nov. 2. **28.** Jeremy Bamber was found guilty at Chelmsford Crown Court of murdering his adoptive parents, his sister and her six-year-old twin sons, and was sentenced to life imprisonment.

Nov. 5. Anthony Kelly was jailed for 14 years in Dublin for his part in the kidnap of Mrs. Jennifer Guinness. On Nov. 18 Brian McNicholl was sentenced to 12 years and nine months imprisonment for the kidnap. At his trial at the Central Criminal Court, London, John Steed admitted killing a Mayfair prostitute and raping three other women: on Nov. 10 he was sentenced to four life terms of imprisonment. **6.** A former U.S. Navy radio operator, John Walker, who sold Naval secrets to the Soviet Union, was jailed for life in Baltimore: his son Michael, who helped him, was jailed for 25 years. The Marquess of Blandford received a two-year suspended sentence for possessing cocaine. **9.** A prison officer was taken hostage by prisoners at Peterhead jail, near Aberdeen. The seige ended on Nov. 13 when the prisoners set fire to prison buildings before releasing the officer and surrendering themselves. **11.** A British businessman, Herbert Smith, who smuggled American arms to Iran, was sentenced to 10 years in jail by a New York court. **14.** A fire bomb attack on a house in East Ham, London, killed three Tamils. **20.** The Attorney-General said that Myra Hindley would not be granted immunity from further prosecution in return for helping the search for two more murder victims buried on Saddleworth Moor. **24.** Paul Dye, head of the largest heroin smuggling operation ever broken by Customs officers, was sentenced at the Central Criminal Court, London, to 28 years in prison and fined £200,000: five other members of the gang were jailed for between seven and 17 years. **25.** Patrick McLaughlin was jailed for life at the Central Criminal Court, London, for plotting to plant a bomb outside Chelsea Barracks in 1985. **26.** A West Berlin court found two Jordanians, Ahmed Hazi (brother of Nezar Hindawi) and Farouk Salamek, guilty of attempted murder and of a bomb attack on the offices of the German-Arab Friendship Society on March 29: they were jailed for 14 years and 13 years respectively.

Dec. 3. Two I.R.A. men, Brendan McFarlane and Gerard Kelly, who escaped from the Maze prison and were arrested in Jan. in Amsterdam, were returned to jail in Northern Ireland. **4.** In Grenada, fourteen people were found guilty of murdering Mr. Maurice Bishop, the Prime Minister, whose assassination occurred during a military coup in 1983: on Dec. 5 they were sentenced to death. **5.** Rose Johnston was sentenced to nine months in jail for supplying heroin to Olivia Channon and for possession of drugs: Sebastian Guinness was sentenced to four months in jail for possession of drugs: Paul Dunstan was jailed for four years for supplying heroin to Olivia Channon. The Federal Court of Appeal in Argentina upheld the verdict of a military tribunal acquitting Lt. Alfredo Astiz of involvement in the disappearance of Dagmar Hagelin in 1977. **16.** Myra Hindley visited Saddleworth Moor, near Oldham, to help in the hunt for the graves of two missing children. **17.** A Federal jury in Detroit acquitted John De Lorean of all charges at his trial for embezzlement from his defunct car manufacturing operation in Belfast. **18.** Dr. John Baksh was jailed for life at the Central Criminal Court, London, for murdering his first wife: he was also sentenced to 14 years for the attempted murder of his second wife. **19.** Two Sikhs, Jarnail Ranuana, and Sukhvinder Gill, were found guilty at Birmingham Crown Court of conspiring to murder Mr. Gandhi, the Indian Prime Minister, during his visit to Britain: on Dec. 20 Ranuana was jailed for 16 years and Gill for 14 years. **23.** Twenty-four Belfast men convicted of terrorist crimes on the word of an informer, Harry Kirkpatrick, had their convictions quashed by Belfast's Court of Appeal. Peter Duffy, a drug gang boss, was jailed for 20 years at Mold Crown Court: five confederates received sentences of up to 18 years.

(1987). Jan. 5. Prisoners at Barlinnie jail, Glasgow, held three prison officers hostage, alleging brutality by the warders. On Jan. 8 one prison officer was released in return for food, and on Jan. 9 a second officer was also freed. On Jan. 10 the five-day siege ended after the release of the third officer. **15.** At the Central Criminal Court, London, Inspector Douglas Lovelock was found not guilty of unlawfully and maliciously wounding Mrs. Cherry Groce during an armed police raid on her house in Brixton, London. **16.** Mr. Peter Robinson, Ulster Unionist M.P. for Belfast East, was fined £15,000 in Dublin for his part in a cross-border Loyalist invasion of the Irish village of Clontibret, Co. Monaghan. **20.** Police arrested 26 West Ham and Millwall football supporters suspected of hooliganism in raids in eight counties. **29.** Two Sikhs living in Canada, Kashmir Singh Dhillon and Santokh Singh Khela, were jailed for life by a Quebec court for conspiring to explode a bomb on an Air India jet.

Feb. 2. Three Italian policemen were given prison sentences of between 2½ and four years for raping a British woman but were all released immediately pending an appeal. At the Central Criminal Court, London, Martin McCall and Christopher Byrne, who broke into a vicarage in Ealing, west London, were jailed for, respectively, five years for rape and an additional five years for aggravated burglary, and three years for rape and five years for other offences including burglary. Robert Horscroft, the gang leader who tried to stop the rape, pleaded guilty to aggravated burglary and causing grievous bodily harm, and was jailed for 14 years. **5.** Ten animal rights extremists who attacked businesses with fire bombs were sentenced at Sheffield Crown Court to terms ranging from nine months to 10 years. **9.** Seven armed men who held 23 hostages at gunpoint for nearly 12 hours inside a Marseilles savings bank escaped past a police cordon via a basement exit. The Marquess of Hertford was fined £10,000 at Warwick Crown Court for ploughing a field on his estate covering the first century Roman settlement of Alcester. **11.** An armed man attempted to break into Kensington Palace but was arrested. Mrs. Cynthia Payne was cleared at Inner London Crown Court of controlling prostitutes in sex parties at her home. Two building sub-contractors were each jailed for two years at Belfast Crown Court for a fraud involving tax exemption certificates after they admitted cheating the Inland Revenue of £200,000 tax. **12.** Cecil Gilbert was convicted at the Central Criminal Court, London, of rape and indecent assault: on Feb. 13 Gilbert was jailed for 16 years for raping a 19-year-old girl and for nine years for drugging her: for two years for indecently assaulting a 14-year-old girl: and for four years and nine years for twice drugging a 27-year-old nurse: for the rape of a physiotherapist, he was jailed for 16 years, all the sentences to run concurrently. **16.** Count Otto Lambsdorff, former West German Economics Minister, was convicted by a Bonn court of evading tax on donations to the Free Democratic Party but he was acquitted of charges of corruption arising from the Flick affair. **17.** The last of 15 trials at the Central Criminal Court, London, involving an organised male prostitution racket in Piccadilly, London, ended with the conviction and jailing of a man for living off the immoral earnings of "rent boys". **20.** Jerry Hall, the fashion model, was found not guilty of possessing marijuana by a Barbados court. **23.** The trial opened in Paris of the Lebanese guerrilla leader Georges Abdallah on charges of political violence: the case was heard by seven professional magistrates instead of a jury. On Feb. 28 Abdallah was sentenced to life imprisonment. **24.** Two 15-year-old youths accused of murdering P.C. Keith Blakelock during the Broadwater Farm riots were cleared at the Central Criminal Court, London, on the direction of the judge.

March 6. Derrick Gregory, a 37-year-old Briton, was sentenced to death by the High Court in Penang for attempting to smuggle heroin from Malaysia to the U.S.A. **11.** At the Central Criminal Court, London, four members of the Mafia were jailed for up to 25 years for trafficking in heroin: while in a separate trial an Asian heroin "baron" and eight of his couriers received sentences of up to 16 years. **13.** At Stafford Crown Court Errol Henry admitted five rapes, an attempted rape and an indecent assault and was sentenced to six life sentences. **16.** Official crime figures issued for England and Wales showed a record 3·8 million notifiable offences in 1986, compared with 3·6 million in 1985. **19.** Winston Silcott, ringleader of the mob who murdered P.C. Keith Blakelock during the Tottenham riots in 1985, was sentenced to life imprisonment at the Central Criminal Court, London: it was the fourth time he had stood trial for murder. Engin Raghip and Mark Braithwaite were also found guilty of the police officer's murder and were jailed for life. **26.** John Fleming, wanted for questioning about the Brinks-Mat gold bullion robbery in 1983, arrived in Britain under arrest after being deported from the United States. On March 27 he was charged with dishonestly handling more than £1 million. **27.** It was disclosed that Myra Hindley had returned in secret to the moors outside Oldham to help the police search for the bodies of two missing children. **30.** The trial opened in Madrid of 41 men allegedly involved in the toxic cooking oil scandal in Spain which has killed 586 people and left 24,992 adversely affected since 1981.

April 1. John Palmer, was cleared at the Central Criminal Court, London, of handling gold bullion stolen in the Brinks-Mat robbery; Christopher Weyman was acquitted of the same charge. **3.** Myra Hindley admitted in a signed statement having killed the two children whose bodies police were seeking on the Pennine moors. **10.** John Reed and Peter Mitchell, the leaders of a gang which stole £500,000 from an armoured security van in 1985, were each jailed for 22 years at the Central Criminal Court, London. **14.** Michael McKenny, an I.R.A. terrorist, was jailed for 16 years at the Central Criminal Court, London, for his part in a scheme to bomb London and 12 coastal resorts in 1985. **15.** The I.R.A. claimed responsibility for parcel bombs sent to two of Mrs. Thatcher's advisers: a third device was found at the home of a senior civil servant in London. On April 16 two more I.R.A. letter bombs addressed to civil servants were found in London on April 20 a sixth letter bomb was discovered. **16.** The B.B.C. was fined £2,000 at Aylesbury, Bucks, for failing to take adequate safety precautions for a television stunt in which a volunteer, Michael Lush, died.

25. Sir Maurice Gibson, a Lord Justice of Appeal in Northern Ireland, and his wife Cecily were killed by an I.R.A. car bomb near Newry.

May 11. Two ringleaders of a gang of Chelsea football hooligans responsible for violence at soccer matches over a six-year period were each jailed for 10 years at Inner London Crown Court: three other members of the gang were sentenced to a total of 18 years for their part in the violence. **15.** Nigel Hall was sentenced to life imprisonment for the murder of Kim Carlile, his girlfriend's four-year-old daughter: Kim's mother, Pauline Carlile, was jailed for 12 years for grievous bodily harm. **20.** Harvey Proctor, who resigned as Conservative M.P. for Billericay on May 16, was fined £1,450 at Bow Street Court, London, after admitting four charges of gross indecency with two male prostitutes under the age of 21.

June 2. At the Central Criminal Court, London, Shaun Francis was sentenced to 13 years' youth custody after admitting eight rapes, an attempted rape and two indecent assaults. **9.** At Maidstone Crown Court Kelvin Chapman was jailed for 14 years after pleading guilty to the attempted murder of a 10-year-old girl he stabbed and left for dead in an alleyway. **16.** In New York Bernhard Goetz was found not guilty of attempted murder and assault for the shooting of four teenagers he said had tried to rob him on the New York underground. **22.** Two soldiers, Cpl. David Knighton and Cpl. Kenneth Smith, and two militaria dealers, Paul Barker and Peter Kabluczenko, were jailed at Bristol Crown Court for dealing in anti-tank rockets: the soldiers were sentenced to three years each, Barker to five years and Kabluczenko to six years. A boy of 13, Billy Waugh, convicted 11 months ago of murder was cleared by the Appeal Court and had his conviction quashed. **25.** John Fleming, who was deported from the U.S. to answer charges relating to the Brinks-Mat bullion robbery, was released by the court because of insufficient evidence to support police allegations. Fleming's wife, Lesley, was acquitted on a charge of handling stolen money.

July 1. In the first case brought under the Company Securities (Insider Dealing) Act 1985, Geoffrey Collier, former joint managing director of Morgan Grenfell Securities, was given a suspended sentence and fined £25,000 at the Central Criminal Court after admitting using confidential information for personal gain. A body believed to be that of Pauline Reade, a victim of the Moors murderers, was found on Saddleworth Moor. **3.** Ian Brady visited Saddleworth Moor to help in the search for the graves of his victims. **4.** Klaus Barbie, known as "The Butcher of Lyons," was jailed for life in Lyons for war crimes. **7.** Six former officials and technicians at the Chernobyl power plant went on trial charged with "blatant violation" of security regulations. **9.** Two armed robbers were shot dead and a third seriously wounded in Plumstead, London, when police ambushed them as they attempted to rob a Securicor van making a wages delivery. **10.** Michele Lupo, a homosexual A.I.D.S. carrier who murdered four men and attempted to kill two others, was jailed for life at the Central Criminal Court, London. **13.** Two men tricked their way into the Knightsbridge Safety Deposit Centre and escaped with cash and jewels estimated at millions of pounds. On Aug. 17 the managing director of the Centre, Parvez Latiff, appeared in court charged with the robbery. **16.** At the Central Criminal Court, London, five policemen were jailed for terms ranging from 18 months to four years for an attack on five schoolboys in north London four years ago which they had subsequently conspired to cover up. **17.** Ronald Jenkins, former private secretary to the chairman of the British and Commonwealth Shipping Group, was fined a total of £10,000 at the Central Criminal Court, London, after admitting insider trading. **22.** Mr. Ali Naji Awad Al Adhami, a Palestinian political cartoonist, was seriously injured after being shot in Chelsea, London, outside the office where he worked. **29.** Three former managers of the Chernobyl power station were sentenced to ten years in a labour camp: three other officials found guilty were given jail sentences of between two and five years. **30.** Ian Wood was jailed for life at Sheffield Crown Court for the murders of his mistress, Mrs. Danielle Lloyd, and her two-year-old daughter Stephanie, and sentenced to a concurrent 12 years for the attempted murder of Mrs. Lloyd's five-year-old son, Christopher.

Aug. 10. Capt. Simon Hayward was found guilty of drug smuggling by the district court in Uppsala, Sweden, and was sentenced to five years' imprisonment. **19.** In Hungerford, Berks., fourteen people were shot dead and 16 people wounded by Michael Ryan before he killed himself: two of the injured subsequently died. **24.** At a court martial in Virginia, Sgt. Clayton Lonetree, an American marine, was sentenced to 30 years in jail for disclosing secrets to the K.G.B. while he was a guard at the U.S. Embassy in Moscow. **30.** In South Korea 32 members of a religious sect committed ritual suicide. Special Branch detectives arrested a man and a woman, both from the Irish Republic, found close to the house of Mr. Tom King, Northern Ireland Secretary, at Ford, Wilts. A second Irishman was arrested later at Wookey Hole, Somerset. **31.** The Notting Hill carnival ended in violence after running fights broke out between police and mobs in the Portobello Road area of London: during the carnival one man was stabbed to death.

ECCLESIASTICAL

(1986) Sept. 7. Desmond Tutu was enthroned as Archbishop of Cape Town.

Oct. 4. The Pope arrived at Lyons for a four-day visit to France. **28.** The House of Commons approved by 303 votes to 25 the Deacons (Ordination of Women) Measure, enabling women to be ordained as deacons in the Church of England. **31.** The Bishop of London (Dr. Leonard) confirmed members of the American Episcopal Church, defying the Archbishop of Canterbury, British Bishops and the local Episcopal hierarchy.

Nov. 17. The Pope left Rome to visit Australia, New Zealand, Bangladesh, Singapore, the Fiji Islands, and the Seychelles.

(1987) Feb 17. An ecclesiastical court ruled that Henry Moore's controversial eight ton slab of marble, was an altar and might remain in St. Stephen Walbrook church, London. **25.** The Catholic Media Office announced that 85 Catholics martyred between 1584 and 1679 in England were to be beatified. **26.** The General Synod voted to proceed with legislation to allow the ordination of women priests. **27.** The Archbishop of Canterbury ordained 15 women as deacons.

March 18. Deacon Sylvia Mutch became the first woman to conduct a marriage ceremony in the Church of England.

June 8. The Pope started a seven-day visit to Poland. **18.** A Church of England working group on Freemasonry published a report expressing concern about aspects of Masonic ritual.

July 11. The General Synod, sitting in York, rejected a proposal to abandon the modern version of The Lord's Prayer, and adopted a motion to print both the original and the new forms. **13.** A report critical of the compatibility of Freemasonry with Christianity was endorsed by the General Synod.

EDUCATION

(1986) Oct. 14. The Education Secretary (Mr. Baker) announced the entry requirements, courses and possible locations of the proposed new technology colleges.

Nov. 4. Brent Council's disciplinary subcommittee announced that Miss Maureen McGoldrick, the headmistress accused of racism, would be immediately reinstated.

(1987) Jan. 30. Mr. Baker announced student grants were to be increased by 3·75 per cent from Sept.

Feb. 23. A West Midlands school was designated as the site of the first city technology college. **25.** Mr. Baker announced the establishment of a review of the standards and content of A-level examinations.

April 1. A White Paper on higher education was published, announcing plans to take polytechnics from local authority control. **10.** Mr. Baker announced proposals for a shift of financial control of schools from local education authorities to heads and governors.

May 5. Mr. Baker announced a relaxation of the policy of closing schools with small numbers of pupils.

July 24. Mr. Baker outlined plans for a national curriculum which would require all children to take tests in up to ten basic subjects at four stages during their school career.

ENVIRONMENT AND LOCAL AFFAIRS

(1986) Sept. 11. The Environment Secretary (Mr. Ridley) announced a £600 million ten-year programme to clean up Britain's coal-fired power stations and reduce acid rain.

Nov. 3. Health officials began a project to screen the whole population of Stonehouse, near Stroud, Glos., where the number of meningitis cases is 14 times the national average.

Dec. 8. Mr. Waldegrave, Environment and Countryside Minister, launched a £280 million programme to clean up the sea at more than 350 bathing beaches around Britain and Northern Ireland. **9.** The N.S.P.C.C. published a report on child abuse showing considerable increases in reported cases of mistreatment. **11.** The contract to provide the first British satellite television system was awarded to a consortium including Granada T.V., Anglia T.V., Virgin, Amstrad, and Pearson. **18.** The Government announced plans to provide clean needles for drug addicts to reduce the risk of A.I.D.S. infection, and the grant of an extra £1 million for research into the disease.

(1987) Jan. 26. The report of the four-year public inquiry by Sir Frank Layfield into the plan to build a nuclear pressurised water reactor at Sizewell, Suffolk, was published.

March 25. It was announced that Cape Cornwall, a headland near Land's End, and 65 acres of hinterland had been bought by the

Heinz company and presented to the nation.
30. Hammersmith Hospital, London, was ordered by magistrates to close its cockroach-infested kitchens, the first hospital to be prosecuted since hospitals lost their Crown immunity in Feb. **31.** Mr. Ridley approved a major scheme to redevelop the Royal Docks, London, as a new town.

May 5. British Nuclear Fuels announced a £50 million programme of improvements to the Sellafield nuclear complex in Cumbria. A charity to co-ordinate voluntary efforts against A.I.D.S. was launched.

June 17. British Gas announced cuts in its domestic tariff of 1·7p a therm from July 1, with quarterly standing charges also being cut.

July 17. An agreement to build a £3 billion development at Canary Wharf, Isle of Dogs, east London, was signed by Olympia and York, the Toronto-based developers, and the London Docklands Development Corporation.

Aug. 27. The Central Electricity Generating Board announced plans to build Britain's second pressurized water reactor at the existing nuclear power site at Hinkley Point, near Bridgwater, Somerset.

FINANCE

(1986) Sept. 24. August trade figures showed that Britain had a record deficit of £1,490 million.

Oct. 10. Dealing in T.S.B. shares opened on the stock market. **14.** Bank base rates rose to 11 per cent. **27.** The deregulation of the Stock Exchange ("Big Bang") came into effect.

Nov. 15. Measures to curb improper dealing in shares came into effect.

Dec. 1. The Department of Trade appointed inspectors to inquire into dealings in Guinness shares during the company's takeover bid for the Distillers company. **8.** Dealings in British Gas shares opened on the stock market. **18.** The Trade and Industry Secretary (Mr. Channon) ordered an inquiry into allegations that civil servants were involved in insider share dealings.

(1987) Jan. 9. Guinness announced that Mr. Ernest Saunders, chairman and chief executive of the company, would step down until the outcome of a Department of Trade investigation was known. **14.** Guinness dismissed Mr. Saunders and urged him to resign his directorship. **20.** Mr. Christopher Reeves, chief executive of Morgan Grenfell, the mer-

chant bank advising Guinness during the Distillers takeover bid, and Mr. Graham Walsh, head of corporate finance, resigned after breaches of established procedures and policies came to light during an internal investigation into the bid; both men denied any personal involvement with the breaches. **21.** Mr. Gerald Ronson, the financier, disclosed he had bought Guinness shares to support their price during the takeover battle for Distillers and that he had returned a £5 million fee his company received from Guinness. **22.** An inquiry into Lloyd's practices, chaired by Sir Patrick Neill, recommended tighter regulation of the insurance market.

Feb. 11. Dealings in British Airways shares opened on the stock market. **20.** The indefinite suspension of interest payments on medium and long-term international debts was announced by Brazil.

March 9. Bank base rates were cut to 10½ per cent.

April 9. The Government ordered a D.T.I. inquiry into share dealings during the takeover of the House of Fraser group. Lloyd's of London announced plans to raise £134 million to settle the losses of the P.C.W. insurance syndicates. **28.** Bank base rates were cut to 9½ per cent, and on May 8 to 9 per cent.

May 6. Mr. Saunders was charged with offences arising from the investigation of the Guinness company. **18.** Uganda introduced a new currency as part of an economic recovery package. **20.** Dealings in Rolls Royce shares opened on the stock market. **27.** The Director-General of Fair Trading ordered the Monopolies Commission to investigate Access and Barclaycard as part of an inquiry into the credit card industry.

June 5. Britain and China signed an agreement settling all property claims arising from the 1949 Communist revolution. **30.** News International agreed to buy the *Today* newspaper from the Lonrho group for £38 million.

July 1. The Trade and Industry Secretary (Lord Young) consented to the sale of *Today* to News International. **7.** The Midland Bank announced the sale of three subsidiaries (Clydesdale Bank, Northern Bank and Northern Bank (Ireland)) to cover its losses on loans to Third World countries.

Aug. 6. The Bank of England raised bank base rates by one per cent and more than three per cent was wiped off the value of shares and Government securities in one day's trading. **25.** Eurotunnel concluded loans of £5,000 million with 50 international banks to finance the building of the Channel Tunnel.

LABOUR AND TRADE UNIONS

(1986) Sept. 1. The T.U.C. conference opened at Brighton: delegates voted to support an N.G.A. and SOGAT motion that E.E.T.P.U. members should stop doing print workers jobs at the News International plant at Wapping. Delegates also approved a resolution calling for secret strike ballots. **4.** T.U.C. delegates voted for the next Labour Government to introduce a statutory minimum wage of £80 a week. **18.** The Department of Employment published figures showing that the number of strikes had fallen to the lowest level for 47 years.

Oct. 1. A report by the Electoral Reform Society into the election of Mr. John Macreadie as general secretary of the Civil and Public Services Association, ordered a re-run of the ballot. **16.** Sealink ferry services resumed after a week of industrial action.

Nov. 10. The C.B.I. annual conference opened in Bournemouth. **21.** A deal on teachers' pay and conditions of service was signed by local authority negotiators and four of the six teaching unions. **26.** The Educational Institute for Scotland voted against accepting the 16·4 per cent pay offer.

Dec. 5. The Secondary Heads Association voted unanimously not to endorse the 16·4 per cent staged pay deal agreed with employers.

(1987) Jan. 3. A strike was begun by B.B.C. television electricians, who demanded pay increases of up to 20 per cent. **24.** Police and demonstrators were injured in violent clashes outside the News International printing plant in Wapping, London; there were 67 arrests. **25.** A strike by telephone engineers began.

Feb. 5. Picketing at Wapping was called off by SOGAT's executive to save the union from bankruptcy. **6.** The N.G.A. called off picketing at Wapping after an emergency meeting of union leaders. British Coal announced plans to invest £90 million in a new pit in South Wales on condition miners accepted a six-day working week. **8.** The executive of the National Communications Union agreed with British Telecom a 12·75 per cent pay deal phased over two years. **11.** Telephone engineers voted to resume work.

March 3. The Institution of Professional Civil Servants announced an agreement under which their members would receive pay increases averaging 10 per cent, plus inflation linkage, over two years. **6.** The two largest teachers' unions, the N.U.T. and the N.A.S./U.W.T., announced a renewed programme of

half-day strikes followed by a work-to-rule in protest at the Education Secretary's decision to remove negotiating rights and to impose pay and conditions of service. **8.** Miners in South Wales voted for six-day working at the planned Margam new pit in spite of N.U.M. opposition. **10.** Farm workers accepted a new minimum wage rate for full-time adults of £99·20 a week. **17.** The Assistant Masters and Mistresses Association voted against strike action over the Teachers' Pay and Conditions Act but decided to launch a national advertising campaign outlining its opposition. **30.** Mr. Sammy Thompson was elected to succeed Mr. Mick McGahey as vice-president of the N.U.M.

April 21. Scottish trade unionists voted to withdraw co-operation from the Government's Job Training Scheme. **23.** British Rail stated it was to pay a 4·5 per cent wage increase to staff without an agreed settlement. **26.** The 14-week occupation of the Caterpillar tractor factory, near Glasgow, ended: workers decided to allow a working party to seek alternative uses for the plant.

May 11. The Union of Democratic Mineworkers accepted a 6·3 per cent pay rise backdated to Nov. 14. Prison officers in England and Wales voted in favour of changes to their pay and working conditions. **19.** British Coal imposed an £11·50 a week pay rise for National Union of Mineworkers members.

June 8. The Civil and Public Services Association and the Society of Civil and Public Servants began a two-day national strike in support of their claim for a 15 per cent, or £20 a week, pay rise. **18.** Unemployment figures for May showed under three million unemployed for the first time in three years.

July 8. The N.U.M.'s annual conference voted to reject flexible shift working. **14.** The N.A.S./U.W.T. renewed industrial action to protest at the abolition of their negotiating rights. Equity ended its 12-year ban on the sale of television and radio programmes to South Africa. **15.** The Civil and Public Services Association abandoned its pay campaign after its members rejected all-out strike action.

Aug. 24. Members of the N.U.M. voted for industrial action to be taken if British Coal refused to withdraw their new disciplinary code. **25.** Coastguard members of the Civil Service Union voted on a proposal to hold a 24-hour strike over their pay offer: the proposal just failed to win the necessary two-thirds majority.

LEGAL

(1986) Sept. 11. A High Court judge in London granted an injunction against protestors preventing contractors carrying out tests at three possible dumping sites for nuclear waste.

Oct. 21. Two Conservative M.P.s, Mr. Neil Hamilton and Mr. Gerald Howarth, were each awarded £20,000 damages by the High Court after suing the B.B.C. over allegations in a Panorama programme that they had close links with Right-wing racist groups. **22.** The High Court ordered the lifting of the suspension of Miss Maureen McGoldrick, a Brent headmistress accused of making a racist remark.

Nov. 5. The London boroughs of Camden, Ealing, and Hammersmith and Fulham were ordered by the High Court to stop banning News International newspapers from their public libraries. **17.** The hearing opened in the New South Wales Supreme Court of the British Government's action seeking an injunction to prevent publication of *Spycatcher*, the memoirs of former MI5 officer Mr. Peter Wright. The Australian Government supported the British Government's contention that publication was prejudicial to national security and contravened an officer's obligation of confidentiality. The hearing ended on Dec. 19 but judgement was reserved until the New Year. **19.** Brent Council was given permission by the Court of Appeal to proceed with charges of racism against Miss Maureen McGoldrick, a primary school headmistress, before a council disciplinary committee. On Dec. 15 Miss McGoldrick won a temporary High Court order to stop Brent Council holding disciplinary proceedings against her. On Dec. 16 the Education Secretary (Mr. Baker) ordered Brent Council to drop disciplinary proceedings against her. **21.** A High Court judge ruled that miners who took part in the 1984–5 pit strike should lose pension benefits unless they made up the contributions missed during the dispute. An industrial tribunal ruled that British Gas was not guilty of unlawful sexual discrimination in compulsorily retiring six female employees at the age of 60. **28.** The Government won a High Court injunction preventing the publication or sale of copies of *One Girl's War* by a wartime member of MI5, Miss Joan Miller. The book was published in the Republic of Ireland and the Irish courts had granted the British Government an injunction on Nov. 27.

(1987) Feb. 17. A court order prevented the Home Office from deporting 58 Sri Lankan Tamils who had arrived in the U.K. on Feb. 13 with incomplete documents and had claimed political asylum. **23.** A High Court judge ruled that an Oxford undergraduate father-to-be was not entitled to a court order to prevent the mother-to-be of his child, also an Oxford undergraduate, from having her planned abortion. He was allowed to bring an emergency appeal. On Feb. 24 Court of Appeal judges decided that as the foetus was incapable legally of being born alive, its abortion would not be a criminal offence; they refused the undergraduate leave to appeal to the House of Lords. **24.** The 58 Tamils whom the Home Office tried unsuccessfully to deport won their fight for a judicial review of the Home Secretary's refusal to grant them asylum. **25.** The High Court lifted its injunction preventing Mr. Duncan Campbell, a *New Statesman* journalist, from disclosing information about the Zircon spy satellite project.

March 5. Court of Appeal judges upheld a ruling by the Employment Appeal Tribunal that in assessing whether women were obtaining equal pay for work of equal value, all financial benefits must be taken into account and compared with those of the men. **12.** Forty-seven Liverpool councillors were disqualified from office for five years after their appeals against penalties imposed for failing to set a legal rate in 1985 were dismissed. **13.** The New South Wales' Supreme Court ruled in favour of Mr. Peter Wright and granted permission for his book to be published. **16.** The British Government announced that it would appeal against the Australian court's decision. **26.** A White Paper announced plans for the administration of legal aid in England and Wales to be transferred from the Law Society to an independent legal aid board. **31.** A High Court judge decided that an *Independent* financial journalist had reasonable grounds for refusing to reveal his sources for articles on insider trading.

April 13. The High Court prevented the extradition to Belgium of 26 Liverpool soccer supporters because legal procedures had not been completed satisfactorily. **27.** *The Independent*, followed by the *London Evening Standard* and the *London Daily News*, published details from Mr. Peter Wright's book. The Government announced that it would start contempt proceedings against the three newspapers.

May 6. Appeal Court judges ordered an *Independent* financial journalist to reveal his sources for articles on take-over bids to Department of Trade inspectors investigating insider dealing.

June 2. *The Independent*, the *London Evening Standard* and *London Daily News* were cleared of contempt. In Australia Mrs. Lindy Chamberlain received a pardon, but her conviction for the murder of her daughter Azaria was not quashed.

July 13. The Law Lords allowed an appeal by the Brussels Government, who will now be able to extradite 26 Liverpool soccer supporters arrested after the Heysel Stadium riot. **15.** The Court of Appeal ruled that newspapers which published information attributable to Mr. Peter Wright despite court orders restraining other newspapers could be in contempt of court, and upheld an appeal by the Attorney-General against dismissal of contempt proceedings against *The Independent, London Evening Standard, London Daily News* and their editors. **17.** The High Court ordered Mr. Thomas Ward, a former Guinness director, to repay £5·2 million to Guinness as his agreement with Mr. Ernest Saunders, former chairman and chief executive of Guinness, had not been disclosed to the board of the company during the takeover of Distillers. **24.** Mr. Jeffrey Archer won a record £500,000 in damages in his High Court libel action against Express Newspapers, publishers of *The Star*, and Mr. Lloyd Turner, *The Star*'s editor. *The Star* also had to pay the costs of the case, estimated at about £700,000. The Court of Appeal ruled that newspapers should be allowed to publish summaries in very general terms of the allegations made by Mr. Peter Wright in his book *Spycatcher*, but that there must be no other publication in this country of the book, extracts from it or any statements made by Mr. Wright about the British or any other security service: the Court of Appeal unanimously allowed an appeal by the Attorney-General against a ruling by the Vice-Chancellor on July 22 which lifted injunctions preventing three newspapers from publishing extracts. **28.** The Divisional Court in London upheld the right of police to bring prosecutions for drunken driving based on the back-calculation of the level of alcohol present, even though the motorist might be below the legal limit when tested. **29.** An order that the ferry company Townsend Thoresen should pay £350,000 towards the costs of the public inquiry into the *Herald of Free Enterprise* disaster was made by the inquiry chairman, Mr. Justice Sheen, in the High Court. **30.** The ban on newspapers publishing Mr. Peter Wright's allegations of Secret Service misconduct was reimposed by the Law Lords, who also ruled that the ban should cover reporting of the Government's court case against the book in Australia. **31.** In a test case brought by the Woolwich Building Society against the Inland Revenue, the High Court ruled that the Government had exceeded its powers in imposing a £500 million double tax bill on Britain's building societies last year.

Aug. 4. The British Government won an injunction to stop publication of excerpts from *Spycatcher* in New Zealand.

SPORT

(1986) Sept. 22. Luton Town were expelled from the Littlewoods Challenge Cup by the Football League after refusing to lift a ban on visiting supporters. **23.** Yorkshire County Cricket Club decided not to renew the contract of Geoffrey Boycott.

Oct. 2. The Environment Minister (Mr. Waldegrave) announced that lead weights used by anglers would be banned from the beginning of 1987. **8.** The Football Association allowed Luton Town to compete in this season's F.A. Cup competition. **12.** The Rugby Football Union International Board agreed in principle to changes in regulations governing amateurism. **17.** The International Olympic Committee decided that the 1992 Games should be held in Barcelona and the Winter Olympics in France.

Nov. 8. Members of Somerset County Cricket Club voted against a resolution of no-confidence in the committee following the decision to dismiss Joel Garner and Viv Richards.

Dec. 9. The greyhound Ballyregan Bob set a world record for consecutive victories with his 32nd win. **14.** Bradford City's Valley Parade ground was re-opened.

(1987) Jan. 11. South Africa cricket selectors included in the team for the first time a non-white player, Omar Henry. **19.** The Sports Minister (Mr. Tracey), announced that tobacco firms' sponsorship of sport was to be severely curtailed.

Feb. 1. The rebellion by the Oxford Boat Race crew ended when all but two members agreed to row under President Donald Macdonald. On Feb. 4 a meeting of club captains passed a vote of confidence in the President and the two dissenting crew members were replaced by members of the reserve crew. **4.** In Fremantle the American yacht *Stars & Stripes* beat the Australian yacht *Kookaburra III*, winning the America's Cup. **11.** England's cricketers, on tour in Australia, completed a grand slam by winning the World Series Cup as well as the Ashes and Perth Challenge tournament. **16.** The Department of the Environment announced action to combat soccer thugs on car ferries. **28.** Princess Anne came fourth and last in her steeplechasing debut at Kempton Park.

March 1. The proposed merger of Fulham and Queen's Park Rangers football clubs was called off after being vetoed by the Football League. **9.** The English R.F.U. condemned the English team's behaviour in the game against Wales at Cardiff on March 7. **17.** The English R.F.U. announced that Hill, Dooley, Chilcott, and Dawe would not be selected for the next home international match.

April 6. Alex Higgins was fined £12,000 and banned from tournament play for six months by the World Professional Billiards and Snooker Association for abuse of referees.

May 25. Crowd disturbances at a one-day England–Pakistan cricket international at Edgbaston left a fan with a severed jugular vein and windpipe.

June 1. After the violence at Edgbaston, the Test and County Cricket Board decided that flags and banners, and musical instruments would be banned from Test matches, fans would be prevented from taking excessive amounts of alcohol into the grounds, and more stewards and police would be on duty.

Aug. 8. In the centenary match at Wembley the Football League side beat the Rest of the World team by 3–0. **20.** The M.C.C. bicentennial game between the M.C.C. and the Rest of the World opened at Lord's but was abandoned on the 25th because of heavy rain, and declared a draw.

TRANSPORT

(1986) Oct. 1. The system of fixed penalties for certain types of motoring offences came into force. **27.** The first day of the deregulation of bus services introduced competition on routes outside London. **29.** Mrs. Thatcher opened the last section of the M25 motorway round London.

Dec. 10. The Duke of Kent opened the longest motorway tunnel in Britain, part of the A1 in Herts.

(1987) Jan. 11. British Rail fares increased, some by as much as ten per cent.

March 13. Lord Skelmersdale, Environment Under-Secretary, opened the first "toad tunnel", under the A4155 in Bucks.

May 18. The House of Lords Select Committee on the Channel Tunnel Bill published its report. **31.** A Brymon Airways aircraft made the first landing at the new short take-off and landing airport in London's docklands.

July 16. British Airways and British Caledonian announced that the two airlines were to merge. On Aug. 6 the proposal was referred to the Monopolies and Mergers Commission. **30.** The Queen and the Duke of Edinburgh became the first passengers on London's new £77 million Docklands Light Railway: the line opened to the public on Aug. 31.

AFRICA

(*See also* "Commonwealth")

(1986). Sept. 4. The Natal Supreme Court declared illegal emergency powers restricting the Press in South Africa. **24.** The Togo Government said it had crushed an attack by armed men who entered the country from neighbouring Ghana: clashes with security forces in the capital left 14 dead. Zaire and France subsequently sent troops to Togo to support the government of President Gnassinghe Eyadema. **30.** The South African Appeal Court upheld the Government's powers to detain people without trial under State of Emergency regulations.

Oct. 9. Pres. Botha of South Africa declared the United Democratic Front an affected organisation, effectively cutting all foreign funding to the movement. **19.** Pres. Samora Machel of Mozambique and several members of his government were among 30 people killed when their plane crashed just inside South Africa. **21.** The Dutch Reformed Church in South Africa voted to open membership to people of all races. **23.** Former Emperor Jean-Bedel Bokassa returned from France to the Central African Republic and was arrested for offences including murder, theft and cannibalism. **26.** South Africa ordered the International Committee of the Red Cross to suspend its activities in the country immediately, following a vote by the I.R.C. conference in Geneva on Oct. 25 to suspend a South African Government delegation from its proceedings.

Nov. 3. Mr. Joachim Chissano was elected President of Mozambique. A white South African woman, Marion Sparg, a member of the banned African National Congress, was convicted of treason and arson: on Nov. 6 she was jailed for 25 years. **15.** Two Lesotho ex-Cabinet ministers, Mr. Desmond Sixishe and Mr. Vincent Maliapeng, and Mr. Sixishe's wife, were found murdered by the roadside. On Nov. 17 Government sources said the men were involved in a plot to install a Marxist government in Lesotho. **24.** Barclays Bank announced the sale of its interest in South Africa to the Anglo-American Mining Corporation. **27.** Three people on trial for treason in South Africa were acquitted and six others allowed bail. **30.** After ten months of negotiations, an agreement was announced between black and white regional leaders in Natal to establish a multiracial government elected on a one-man, one-vote system. On Dec. 1 Mr. Stoffel Botha, Minister of Home Affairs, dismissed the agreement.

Dec. 8. South Africa admitted that 256 children under 16 years were being detained under the emergency regulations. **11.** Press restrictions in South Africa were extended to cover non-violent opposition, obliging local newspapers and foreign correspondents to seek official authorisation before articles may be published. **12.** The Chadian Government said that a major offensive in the north of Chad by Libyan forces had been checked. **20.** The Chadian Government said Libyan troops had launched an attack in north-east Chad. **23.** President Barre of Somalia was re-elected unopposed.

(1987). Jan. 2. The Chadian Government said its troops had captured the north-eastern town of Fada from Libyan forces. **4.** Libyan aircraft bombed the town of Arada in southern Chad. **7.** French aircraft destroyed Libyan radar installations at Ouadi-Doum in the north of Chad. On the first day of the school year in South Africa there was large-scale registration of students, after two years of boycotts. **30.** Dennis Worrall announced his resignation as South Africa's Ambassador to Britain: in Feb. it was announced that he intended to stand as an opponent to the Government in the forthcoming elections.

Feb. 1. In a referendum Ethiopians approved a new constitution.

March 9. Chad and Libya began talks about a possible peace agreement but made no progress. **22.** Chadian troops captured Ouadi Doum. **27.** Chadian troops captured Faya Largeau as Libyan troops retreated. **29.** Mr. John Wiley, South Africa's Minister of Environment Affairs and Tourism, was found shot dead at his home near Cape Town: police said his death appeared to be suicide.

April 22. Six striking transport workers were shot dead by police in South Africa. The South African Transport Services announced the dismissal of 16,000 workers who had been on strike for six weeks. **24.** The Natal Supreme Court declared null and void most of the South African Government's emergency restrictions on reporting of violence and unrest.

May 6. South Africa held a General Election to the white House of Assembly: the ruling National party was re-elected. Sixty people received death sentences in Guinea for crimes committed during the late President Toure's rule. **14.** The South African Government refused to renew the work permits of two British television reporters, Mr. Peter Sharp and Mr. Michael Buerk.

June 5. The 16,000 South African railway workers dismissed in April were reinstated. **11.** The state of emergency in South Africa was extended for another year, and the regulations governing Press censorship and detention without trial were tightened. **12.** Jean-Bedel Bokassa, former Emperor of the Central African Republic, was sentenced to death for crimes committed during his 13-year rule. **14.** Ethiopians voted for the 835-member Shengo (Parliament) established under the new constitution. **27.** Members of the Dutch Reformed Church in South Africa who opposed the decision to open the Church to all races announced the formation of the breakaway Afrikaans Gereformeerde Kerk, which is for whites only.

July 9. A 50-strong white Afrikaner group led by Dr Frederick van Zyl Slabbert held three days of talks with the African National Congress in Senegal: a joint communique gave unanimous support to a negotiated settlement in South Africa. **30.** A car bomb in Johannesburg injured 68 people: the African National Congress was believed to be responsible.

Aug. 9. Thousands of black gold miners went on strike in South Africa in a pay dispute. The strike ended on Aug. 30, the miners settling for improved benefits and holiday pay and pay rises of between 15 and 23·4 per cent. During the strike nine men were killed, over 300 injured, and some 45,000 were dismissed. **25.** A British nurse abducted in southern Sudan, Miss Heather Sinclair, and three American aid workers were released after being held for six weeks by the Sudanese People's Liberation Army. **28.** Libya claimed its troops had recaptured the disputed desert strip of Aouzou seized by Chad earlier in the month.

COMMONWEALTH

Oct. 2. An unsuccessful attempt was made to assassinate India's Prime Minister, Rajiv Gandhi, in New Delhi. **15.** President Ershad of Bangladesh was re-elected amid accusations of ballot-rigging. **22.** Mr. Rajiv Gandhi, the Indian Prime Minister, dismissed five ministers and appointed seven new ones.

Nov. 7. President's rule was lifted in the Indian state of Jammu and Kashmir. **10.** Martial law was lifted in Bangladesh. **17.** The Solomon Islands Prime Minister, Sir Peter Kenilorea, resigned following allegations of maladministration of cyclone damage relief funds. **25.** Mr. Gorbachev, the Russian leader, visited India and held talks with Mr. Gandhi, the Indian Prime Minister, on south Asian affairs and arms control. **30.** In India, Sikh extremists killed 24 Hindus in the Punjab.

Dec. 2. There were violent clashes between Hindus and Sikhs in New Delhi and in the Punjab. **23.** The Quebec Court of Appeal declared illegal a law passed by the former separatist government of Quebec requiring signs on shops, etc. to be in French only.

(1987). Jan. 18. The Canadian Transport Minister, Andre Bissonnette, was dismissed after inquiries into a land transaction linked to a government project. **23.** Indian forces were ordered to occupy forward defensive positions along the border with Pakistan as each country accused the other of using exercises as an excuse to mass its forces. On Jan. 30 talks between the two countries began, aimed at defusing the growing tension. **26.** Government troops in Uganda crushed an armed rebellion by forces loyal to ex-President Milton Obote in the eastern district of Soroti.

Feb. 11. Sikh high priests excommunicated the Punjab's Chief Minister, Surjit Singh Barnala, for defying their call for his resignation and appearance before them at Amritsar's Golden Temple. **19.** India and Pakistan completed the withdrawal of their troops from positions along the border. **20.** Canada imposed new immigration regulations to halt the abuse of political refugee status. **27.** Under a Bill passed in Bangladesh, Bengali is to replace English in official work except for communications with other countries.

March 23. An attempted coup in Sierra Leone was suppressed by forces loyal to Pres. Momoh.

April 10. The federal Liberal-National coalition in Australia was badly split when Sir Johannes Bjelke-Petersen announced the formation of a new political party, the New National Party. **12.** In the General Election in Fiji a coalition of the Indian-backed National Party and the Labour Party defeated the ruling Alliance Party. **15.** President Kaunda of Zambia accused businessmen of plotting with South Africa to instigate a military overthrow of his Government. **17.** In Sri Lanka Tamil separatist guerrillas killed 120 people near Trincomalee. On April 21 about 105 people were killed by a bomb explosion in Colombo, and from April 22–27, at least 80 died in the Government's retaliatory air strikes in the Jaffna area. **20.** The Indian Prime Minister, Mr. Gandhi, widened an inquiry into arms deal bribery to include a full investigation of other malpractices. **23.** The Kenyan Government ordered five Libyan diplomats suspected of spying to leave the country. **28.** The Australian federal Liberal-National coalition ended as a result of the formation of the New National Party. **30.** Dr William Herbert, ambassador from St Kitts and Nevis to the United States, resigned five days after American investigators accused him of involvement in international money-laundering rackets.

May 9. Malta's General Election resulted in victory for the Nationalist Party after 16 years of Labour Party government. **11.** The Indian Government imposed direct rule in the state of Punjab because of continued unrest and violence. **13.** Mr. Ian Smith, former Prime Minister of Rhodesia, resigned as leader of the Conservative Alliance party in Zimbabwe. **14.** Fiji's Army seized power in a coup led by Lt.-Col. Sitiveni Rabuka and ousted the Indian-dominated government of Dr. Timoci Bavadra. The Governor General, Ratu Sir Penaia Ganilau, proclaimed a state of emergency and announced that he was assuming Government authority in the name of the Queen. On May 17 the Governor General swore in Rabuka as chairman of a Council of Ministers but on May 19 refused to swear in the other members. The Governor General announced instead the dissolution of Parliament and said he would assume executive power pending an election. On May 21 an Advisory Council, which included Lt.-Col. Rabuka, was appointed to form an interim government and to review the constitution. On June 12 a formula for returning Fiji to parliamentary rule was announced. **26.** The Sri Lankan armed forces launched a major offensive against Tamil guerrillas in the Jaffna peninsula. Five days of clashes between Hindus and Moslems near Delhi ended, leaving 100 dead. **27.** The Indian Government warned Sri Lanka against continuing the offensive in the Jaffna Peninsula.

June 2. Twenty-nine monks were killed by Tamil separatists in Sri Lanka. **3.** India's attempt to provide food and medical supplies to Sri Lankan Tamils was described by the Sri Lankan Government as a violation of their sovereignty. Canada's Federal Government and ten provinces agreed terms under which the province of Quebec would sign the country's constitution. **4.** India airdropped food to the Jaffna Peninsula and Sri Lanka protested at the violation of sovereignty. On June 10 the Sri Lankan Government halted operations against Tamil terrorists and on June 15 Sri Lanka and India reached agreement over the distribution of Indian food aid in Jaffna. **19.** The Bahamas General Election resulted in the Progressive Liberal Party led by Sir Lynden Pindling being re-elected.

July 11. In the Australian General Election the Labour Party was returned for a third term. **25.** Mr. Ramaswamy Venkataraman was sworn in as President of India. **28.** At least 30 people were killed in violent protests in Sri Lanka at the plan agreed between Sri Lanka and India to end the communal bloodshed in the island. **29.** Mr. Rajiv Gandhi, the Indian Prime Minister, and Pres. Jayawardene signed a pact in Sri Lanka to settle the Tamil issue. This provided for a merger of the northern (Tamil) and eastern regions and the surrender of arms by Tamil guerrillas. Indian troops monitored the subsequent ceasefire and surrender of arms.

Aug. 14. New Zealand's General Election resulted in the re-election of the Labour

Government. **18.** A Sri Lankan M.P. was killed and several Ministers and M.P.s injured by a bomb explosion in a parliamentary committee room during a meeting addressed by Pres. Jayawardene. **21.** The official report of the constitutional review committee in Fiji said that Fiji's political framework should be changed without severing links with the British Crown. The Zimbabwe Parliament voted to abolish the 30 seats constitutionally reserved for whites.

EUROPEAN COMMUNITY

(1986). Sept. 16. Foreign ministers of the Community agreed a package of economic sanctions against South Africa which banned new investment in South Africa and stopped its exports to the E.C. of iron, steel and Krugerrands. **25.** The E.C. countries agreed on measures to be taken by their police forces as part of a new campaign against international terrorism. **28.** The U.K. Foreign Secretary (Sir Geoffrey Howe) announced that Britain would block further E.C. financial aid to Syria because of its involvement in the attempted bombing of an Israeli airliner.

Nov. 10. With only Greece dissenting, the E.C. countries supported Britain in its charges of Syrian involvement in terrorism and agreed to introduce an arms ban and other measures against Syria.

Dec. 6. At the two-day summit of E.C. leaders in London a package of measures was agreed, including action against A.I.D.S., drugs and terrorism. **9.** European Justice and Interior Ministers produced a dossier analysing the threat to E.C. countries from international terrorism and proposed a package of intelligence measures: Greece refused to join the other countries in adopting it. **16.** After seven days' negotiations, Ministers secured a deal to reduce the E.C.'s surpluses of unsaleable milk and beef.

(1987). Jan. 15. An £86 million E.C. aid package for British regions was announced. **20.** Sir Henry Plumb, leader of the British Conservatives, was elected the first British President of the European Parliament. In Strasbourg, the European Commission of Human Rights rejected Civil Service trade unions' challenge to the U.K. Government's ban on activities at G.C.H.Q. in Cheltenham: the Commission accepted Government statements that restrictions on workers there were necessary. **27.** An allocation to Britain of regional aid totalling £183 million was announced. **29.** The E.C. and the United States reached a solution to problems raised by U.S.'s loss of agricultural export markets in Spain following Spain's entry to the E.C., averting a trade war.

Feb. 10. Agriculture Ministers of the Community approved the E.C. Commission's plans

to dispose of surplus butter. **16.** The E.C. Commission approved plans for a new tax on oils and fats.

March 12. The European Court of Justice in Brussels ruled that the centuries-old laws stipulating the ingredients of all beer sold in West Germany were a violation of Common Market free trade regulations. **19.** Agreement to negotiate a global reduction in the chemicals believed to damage the ozone layer around the Earth was reached by E.C. Environment Ministers. **25.** The European Community celebrated its 30th birthday with formalities in Rome and other E.C. capitals.

April 14. Turkey formally applied to join the European Community. **28.** European Interior and Justice Ministers agreed to impose penalties on airliners and other carriers which brought immigrants without proper documents into the E.C.

June 30. The E.C. summit meeting in Brussels ended in disarray when Mrs. Thatcher refused to make an advance commitment to provide extra cash for the Community in the forthcoming year.

July 1. An agreement on E.C. farm prices for 1987–88 was reached in Brussels. **8.** In five cases brought against the British Government by parents of children taken into care by local authorities, the European Court of Human Rights in Strasbourg ruled that the care and access procedures followed by the authorities violated the parents' rights under the European Human Rights Convention. **13.** E.C. Foreign Ministers in Copenhagen decided the twelve E.C. countries could resume contacts with Syria in pursuit of their Middle East peace initiative.

Aug. 7. The E.C. began legal proceedings against the U.K. over its failure to observe an E.C. directive on safe drinking water which became effective in 1982.

MIDDLE EAST

(1986). Sept. 6. Gunmen attacked an Istanbul synagogue with automatic weapons and hand grenades during Sabbath prayers: twenty-three people died, including the two assailants. **11.** Mr. Peres, Israel's Prime Minister, and Pres. Mubarak held talks in Alexandria in an effort to revive the spirit of the Israeli-Egypt peace accords. **29.** John Demjanjuk, extradited to Israel from the United States in Feb., was formally charged with war crimes.

Oct. 15. Hand grenades were thrown at a group of Israeli soldiers and their families near Jerusalem's Wailing Wall, causing one death and over 60 casualties. **20.** Mr. Peres,

Israel's Prime Minister, exchanged posts with Mr. Shamir, the Foreign Minister, under a coalition agreement reached in 1984. **24.** Britain broke off diplomatic relations with Syria, accusing the government of supporting terrorism. In response Syria closed its air-space and territorial waters to British craft.

Nov. 2. Mr. Terry Waite, the Archbishop of Canterbury's personal envoy, succeeded in securing the release of Mr. David Jacobsen, an American held hostage in Lebanon. **11.** Two Frenchmen, M. Camille Sontag and M. Marcel Coudari, held hostage in Lebanon, were handed over to the French Ambassador in Syria. **30.** Mordechai Vanunu, the technician who gave details about Israel's nuclear arsenal to *The Sunday Times*, appeared in court in Jerusalem charged with treason and espionage.

Dec. 4. A plot by Islamic fundamentalists to overthrow the Egyptian Government was foiled. **10.** The international committee arbitrating on the Taba border dispute between Egypt and Israel held its first meeting. **24.** A French hostage in Lebanon, M. Aurel Cornea, was released by his captors. **29.** A report released by the Attorney-General of Israel exonerated the Prime Minister, Mr. Yitzhak Shamir, and other officials of responsibility for the killing of two Palestinians after a bus hijack in 1984.

(1987). Jan. 12. Mr. Terry Waite, the Archbishop of Canterbury's personal envoy, returned to Beirut to negotiate the release of Western hostages. **17.** Herr Rudolf Cordes, a West German businessman, was kidnapped in Beirut. On Jan. 21 another West German, Herr Alfred Schmidt, was kidnapped. **24.** Three U.S. citizens and an Indian with an American passport were kidnapped in Beirut. **26.** Reports reached Lambeth Palace that Mr. Terry Waite, was being held in Lebanon: Mr. Waite had not been seen since leaving his Beirut hotel on Jan. 20 for secret negotiations. On Jan. 30 a senior Lebanese militia official in Beirut said that Waite had been kidnapped.

Feb. 12. International relief agencies taking supplies to the Palestinian refugee camp of Bourj al-Barajneh in Beirut were forced to share them with Amal gunmen besieging the camp. On Feb. 13 a relief worker was killed and another wounded when Amal gunmen opened fire on U.N. lorries and ambulances trying to reach the camp. **15.** The Lebanese Druze leader, Mr. Walid Jumblatt, appealed to pro-Iranian militiamen to free Mr. Terry Waite. **16.** The war crimes trial opened in Jerusalem of John Demjanjuk, who denied he was "Ivan the Terrible", a guard at a Nazi death camp. **19.** Four days of battles for control of West Beirut were partially quelled after Syrian pressure and appeals by militia

leaders for a ceasefire. On Feb. 22 Syrian troops entered West Beirut in an effort to control the militiamen and on Feb. 24 took over the main strongholds of the Druze and Amal militias. On Feb. 25 U.N. lorries took food into the besieged Bourj al-Barajneh camp in Beirut.

March 2. The Lebanese Prime Minister, Rashid Karami, announced that the Moslem militia leaders had signed a Syrian-sponsored agreement to re-activate the dormant national reconciliation process. **4.** Amal militia forces in West Beirut freed over 600 Palestinians. Subsequently two Saudi Arabian hostages were also freed, Bakr El Damanhouri on March 18 and Khaled Deeb on March 20. **11.** The Israeli Government agreed to set up a special commission to investigate the Jonathan Jay Pollard spy scandal: Pollard, a U.S. Navy intelligence analyst, was jailed for life on March 4 in the U.S.A. for spying for Israel. **18.** The Israeli Cabinet decided on a number of sanctions against South Africa. **24.** Egypt and the Soviet Union signed an agreement resolving long-standing financial disputes. **26.** Tension rose between Greece and Turkey over Turkey's plan to send a geophysical research ship, accompanied by warships, to the disputed waters of the Aegean to explore for oil. On March 28 tension eased after Turkey announced that its ships would stay within territorial waters, and Greece said that it would not at present explore for oil in the area.

April 5. A Syrian-sponsored ceasefire ended a five-month blockade of two Palestinian refugee camps in Beirut by the Amal militia. On April 6 food supplies were delivered to Chatila camp. Syrian forces entered Chatila on April 7 and Bourj al-Barajneh camp on April 8. **6.** Pres. Mubarak's National Democratic party won the General Election in Egypt.

DIPLOMATIC TENSION WITH IRAN.—**May 9.** The Iranian vice-consul in Manchester, Mr. Ahmed Ghassemi, was accused of shoplifting and given police bail until May 26. **26.** Mr. Ghassemi failed to answer bail. **28.** Mr. Ghassemi was arrested after a police chase and charged with reckless driving, assaulting a police officer and other charges. Mr. Ghassemi appeared in court in Manchester and was released on bail. The First Secretary at the British Interests Section in Tehran, Mr. Edward Chaplin, was arrested and beaten. **29.** Mr. Chaplin was released after 24 hours. **June 4.** Britain ordered the closure of the Iranian vice-consulate in Manchester and told Iran to withdraw its five staff, including Mr. Ghassemi. **5.** Britain withdrew three diplomats from Tehran. **6.** Iran expelled five British diplomats, including Mr. Chaplin. **17.** After the withdrawal of staff and expulsions on both sides, Britain reduced to two its diplomatic staff in Tehran, and on June 18 ordered 15 Iranians to leave the U.K., only one Iranian diplomatic representative remaining in London. **30.** In France, police placed a cordon around the Iranian Embassy in Paris after learning that Mr. Vahid Gordji, an Iranian suspected of involvement in terrorism, had taken refuge there. The Iranians imposed a siege on the French Embassy in Tehran. **July 2.** The Iranian Ambassador in France said that Mr. Gordji would not be given up for questioning. **5.** France broke off negotiations designed to lead to normalization of relations. **13.** An Iranian gunboat attacked a French container vessel in the Gulf. **14.** Pres. Mitterrand denounced the Iranian attack on the French vessel and said that Mr. Gordji should give himself up. The French Consul in Tehran, M. Paul Torri, was accused of espionage, drug-trafficking and other charges. **16.** Iran renewed the blockade of the French Embassy in Tehran and France retaliated with a blockade of the Iranian Embassy in Paris. **17.** France broke off diplomatic relations with Iran.

May 17. A U.S. Navy frigate, the *Stark*, sailing in the Gulf, was hit by an Exocet missile fired by an Iraqi warplane: 28 sailors were killed outright and the death toll eventually rose to 37. On May 18 Pres. Hussein of Iraq admitted that his country was responsible for the "unintentional accident" and on May 19 it was announced that the U.S. and Iraq would carry out a joint investigation of the incident. **19.** The U.S. announced that it had agreed with Kuwait that eleven Kuwaiti oil tankers would be permitted to sail under the U.S. flag, and receive U.S. naval protection in the Gulf. **25.** The Supreme Court in Israel overturned an Army officer's conviction on treason and espionage charges and criticized the interrogation methods of Shin Bet, the Israeli internal security service. On May 29 the Attorney-General, Mr. Yosef Harisah, ordered a police investigation into Shin Bet's conduct during the case, while on May 31 the Cabinet ordered a judicial inquiry into Shin Bet's methods in anti-terrorist operations. **26.** The Israeli Government accepted the recommendations of two inquiries into the Pollard espionage affair, both of which criticized its actions.

June 1. Lebanon's Prime Minister, Mr. Rashid Karami, was killed when a bomb hidden in his helicopter exploded. **18.** Gunmen kidnapped Ali Osseiran, son of Lebanon's Defence Minister, and Charles Glass, an American journalist, in West Beirut: Osseiran was released on June 24.

THE GULF CRISIS.—**July 20.** The U.N. Security Council passed Resolution 598 calling for a ceasefire between Iran and Iraq. **24.** A Kuwaiti tanker reflagged under the U.S. registry, the *Bridgeton*, was holed by a mine in the northern Gulf while sailing to Kuwait under U.S. naval escort. **Aug. 10.** An American-operated tanker, the *Texaco Caribbean*, struck a mine in the Gulf of Oman. Iraq warned that it would not observe the ceasefire unilaterally and resumed air attacks on Iranian oil installations. **15.** A U.A.E. supply ship, the *Anita*, was hit by a mine off the port of Fujairah outside the Gulf. Six people were killed, including the British captain, Mr. Gerry Blackburn. **16.** The U.S. aircraft carrier *Guadalcanal*, with mine-sweeping helicopters on board, arrived off Bahrain to assist in escort duties. **17.** Five Royal Navy minesweepers sailed from Rosyth for the Gulf. **18.** A Liberian tanker was hit by a missile fired from an Iranian gunboat near the mouth of the Gulf, the first Iranian attack outside the Gulf. **29.** The unofficial truce in the "tanker war" ended when Iraqi warplanes attacked an Iranian tanker in the Gulf. **31.** Iran retaliated to three days of Iraqi attacks on its oil installations and tankers with a gunboat attack on a Kuwaiti container ship.

July 31. Over 400 Moslems on pilgrimage to Mecca (Saudi Arabia) were killed and about 650 injured in violent clashes outside the Grand Mosque in Mecca. The Saudis announced that the dead (275 Iranians, 85 Saudi citizens and 42 pilgrims of other nationalities) were crushed in a stampede which occurred when an Iranian demonstration turned violent. In response to Iranian claims that police had opened fire on peaceful marchers, the Saudi authorities said that police had intervened only after Iranians began burning cars and assaulting bystanders. On Aug. 1 the Saudi Arabian and Kuwaiti embassies in Tehran were attacked by demonstrators, and on Aug. 3 Iran warned international shipping to keep clear of its territorial waters in the Gulf while Revolutionary Guards carried out naval manoeuvres in honour of the dead pilgrims.

Aug. 18. Charles Glass, the American journalist kidnapped in Beirut in June escaped from his captors after two months as a hostage. **30.** Israel's Cabinet voted to scrap its Lavi fighter jet project and to buy cheaper U.S. fighter jets.

U.S.A.

(1986). Sept. 1. It was confirmed that Mr. Nicholas Daniloff, a U.S. journalist, had been arrested in Moscow on Sept. 7 he was charged with spying. **17.** The U.S. Government ordered the expulsion of 25 of the 275 employees at the Soviet mission to the United Nations.

The Americans said the mission's size was disproportionate to its U.N. work and claimed the staff were engaged in spying. **22.** Pres. Reagan offered to limit nuclear tests in parallel with weapons reductions when addressing the U.N. General Assembly in New York and called on the Soviet Union to enter into a new treaty which could lead to the sharing of "Star Wars" defences. **29.** Nicholas Daniloff was released and left the Soviet Union. The U.S. imposed new but limited sanctions against South Africa. **30.** A Brooklyn court placed the Soviet spy Gennady Zakharov on probation for five years and ordered him to leave America within 24 hours. In return the Soviet Union agreed that Yuri Orlov, a leading dissident, would be allowed to leave the Soviet Union for the U.S. with his wife.

Oct. 21. The U.S. Government expelled 55 Soviet diplomats accused of spying.

THE IRAN-CONTRA AFFAIR.—**Nov. 3.** The Lebanese magazine *Al Shiraa* revealed that Mr. Robert McFarlane, a former National Security Advisor, had visited Iran on a secret mission connected with the supply of military equipment. **4.** The Speaker of the Iranian Parliament confirmed that Mr. McFarlane had recently visited Tehran. In the next few days speculation grew that the U.S. administration had supplied military spare parts to Iran in return for the release of American hostages held in Lebanon. **10.** Pres. Reagan said that his government's policy of not negotiating with terrorists remained intact and that no U.S. laws had been broken in trying to free American hostages. **13.** Pres. Reagan admitted to Congressional leaders that the administration had supplied arms to Iran: he said it was part of an attempt to forge links with moderate elements in Iran. **19.** In a television press conference Pres. Reagan said that no more arms would be sent to Iran and that no other country was involved. The White House later contradicted the latter assertion, saying that there was a third country involved but did not identify the country; this was subsequently discovered to be Israel. **25.** The Attorney General, Mr. Edwin Meese, announced that the proceeds of the arms sales to Iran (put at between $10 million and $30 million) had been deposited in Swiss bank accounts for the use of Nicaraguan Contra rebels. Vice-Adm. John Poindexter, National Security Advisor, resigned and Lt.-Col. Oliver North, the member of the National Security Council who directed the operation, was sacked. **26.** Pres. Reagan appointed a three-member special review board, under the chairmanship of former Senator John Tower, to examine the role of the National Security Council in the affair. The Attorney General continued with a separate judicial enquiry.

Dec. 1. The Senate intelligence committee began its own investigations into the affair. Lt.-Col. North and Vice-Adm. Poindexter both refused to testify to the committee, invoking their rights against self-incrimination under the Fifth Amendment. **2.** Pres. Reagan announced that an independent special prosecutor was to be appointed to investigate the affair. **4.** Congressional Democratic and Republican leaders agreed on the establishment of special investigating committees. **7.** The Swiss Government confirmed that a bank account had been frozen to allow American officials to inspect transactions. **19.** An independent special prosecutor, Mr. Lawrence Walsh, was appointed to investigate possible criminal violation of U.S. laws by those involved in the arms sales. **26.** Pres. Reagan appointed Mr. David Abshire as a Cabinet-level adviser to co-ordinate White House response to the crisis.

Feb. 2. Mr. William Casey resigned as director of the C.I.A. Pres. Reagan nominated Mr. Robert Gates to replace Mr. Casey as director of the C.I.A.: the nomination was withdrawn on March 3 after criticism of Gates's role in the sale of arms to Iran and Mr. William Webster was nominated to the post instead. **9.** Mr. Robert McFarlane attempted to commit suicide. **26.** The Tower review board's report was published: it attributed failure to exert control over National Security Council officials only indirectly to Pres. Reagan but most directly to Mr. Donald Regan, the White House Chief of Staff. **27.** Mr. Donald Regan resigned and was replaced by Mr. Howard Baker.

March 18. The Congressional committees investigating the Iran-Contra affair decided to grant Vice-Adm. Poindexter and Lt.-Col. North limited immunity from prosecution but this would be delayed until June to allow the independent special prosecutor, Mr. Walsh, to complete his inquiry into whether criminal acts had been committed.

May 5. The select committees of the Senate and the House of Representatives began joint public hearings into the arms deals with Iran and transfer of profits from the deals to Contra rebels. **6.** Mr. William Casey died.

July 7. Lt.-Col. North began six days of testimony before the joint Congressional hearing. **15.** Vice-Adm. Poindexter opened his testimony before the joint Congressional hearing during which he said that he had not told Pres. Reagan that the proceeds of the arms sales to Iran were being diverted to assist the Contra rebels in Nicaragua.

Aug. 12. In a televised speech from the White House, Pres. Reagan confirmed that he had not known of the diversion of profits from the Iran arms sales to the Contra rebels but said that, nevertheless, the ultimate responsibility for the Iran-Contra affair lay with him.

(1986). Nov. 4. In the mid-term elections, the Democrats secured ten-seat majority in the Senate, and in the House of Representatives increased their majority over the Republicans to 23 seats. 14. The U.S. imposed economic sanctions against Syria for its support of terrorism. 16. Mr. Ivan Boesky, a disgraced Wall Street speculator, agreed to forfeit $100 million (about £67 million) for his part in insider trading. 28. The U.S. exceeded the limits of the Salt II Treaty by bringing the 131st B-52 equipped with cruise missiles into service. 30. Mr. Kinnock, the U.K. Labour Party leader, visited the U.S. on a week-long trip.

Dec. 4. Mr. Larry Speakes, Pres. Reagan's spokesman, announced his resignation to join a Wall Street investment firm. 23. Nine days, three minutes and 44 seconds after taking-off, Dick Rutan and Jeana Yeager landed in California after piloting their *Voyager* aircraft on a 25,012 mile non-stop flight round the world without refuelling.

(1987). Feb. 18. The Senate foreign relations committee voted to cut off U.S. aid to the Contra rebels in Nicaragua, including $40 million already approved.

March 4. The U.S. offered a draft treaty on medium-range missile reductions at arms control talks with the Soviet Union in Geneva. Jonathan Jay Pollard, an intelligence analyst for the U.S. Navy who passed top-secret intelligence documents on the Middle East to Israel, was jailed for life: his wife, Anne, was sentenced to five years in prison for unauthorized possession of classified documents. 18. The Senate defeated a move to stop U.S. military aid reaching the Contra rebels in Nicaragua. 26. Mr. Kinnock, the Labour Party leader, arrived in the U.S. on a three-day visit. 30. Two Marine guards at the U.S. Embassy in Moscow, Sgt. Clayton Lonetree and Cpl. Arnold Bracy, were accused of espionage: they had both had affairs with Russian women and had been persuaded into allowing K.G.B. officers to roam the Embassy at night. On March 31 a third Marine who served as a guard at the Embassy was arrested. 31. The "Baby M" trial in New York was won by Mr. and Mrs. Stern, the childless professional couple who had paid Mrs. Mary Beth Whitehead $10,000 to bear a child for them: the contract was declared legal and custody of the one-year-old baby was awarded to Mr. Stern.

April 13. The U.S. Secretary of State, Mr. George Schultz, visited Moscow for two days of talks with the Soviet leader, Mr. Gorbachev, and other senior officials. 21. Karl Linnas was deported from the U.S. to Estonia, where he was sentenced to death 25 years ago

for war crimes. 23. Ivan Boesky, the Wall Street arbitrageur, pleaded guilty in New York to one charge of illegal insider trading. 30. Pres. Reagan welcomed the Japanese Prime Minister, Mr. Nakasone, for talks aimed at solving trade problems between their countries.

May 5. On the day that the Immigration Reform and Control Act came into effect, illegal immigrants were offered an amnesty from deportation. 8. Mr. Gary Hart, a prospective Democrat nominee, announced his withdrawal from the presidential race after allegations of extra-marital affairs. 19. The House of Representatives voted to extend by another year a ban on testing anti-satellite weapons in space. 25. Mr. Raymond Donovan, who resigned as U.S. Labour Secretary in 1985 after fraud charges were brought against him, was acquitted on all charges at his trial.

June 10. The Justice Department said that a lawsuit was being prepared which would replace the president and executive board of the International Brotherhood of Teamsters, the largest trade union, with court-appointed trustees.

July 9. Police staged simultaneous raids on art galleries in more than ten American states after uncovering a £600 million fraud involving fakes of Salvador Dali's works. 25. The U.S. Secretary of Commerce, Mr. Malcolm Baldridge, died in a rodeo accident.

Aug. 28. A new Federal regulation was issued, effective from Dec. 1, which requires A.I.D.S tests for all immigrants and refugees who apply for permanent residence in the U.S.

OTHER COUNTRIES

(1986). Sept. 5. *Pakistani* commandos stormed a Pan Am jet at Karachi airport after gunmen holding nearly 400 hostages opened fire with automatic weapons and threw hand grenades: about 20 people died. 8. Benazir Bhutto, the political leader challenging President Zia of *Pakistan*, was released from detention in Karachi. *Japan*'s Education Minister (Mr. Fujio) was dismissed for publicly trying to vindicate Japan's colonial rule of Korea and excuse atrocities committed by Japan. Bombings in *Paris* on Sept. 8, 12, 14, 15 and 17 killed a total of 10 people. 9. *Denmark* stated it planned to ban all refugees for a year because of a lack of accommodation and would temporarily turn back refugees at the border. 11. Mrs. Thatcher arrived in *Norway* on a two-day visit and faced noisy demonstrations from students protesting at the U.K.'s stand on South African sanctions, Northern Ireland, and trade unions. **14.** After the third bombing in Paris within a week *France* announced new anti-terrorist measures, including the introduction of visas for all visitors to France except those from other E.C. countries and Switzerland. A bomb exploded at Kimpo airport, Seoul, *South Korea*, killing five. **18.** *East Germany* agreed to stop allowing refugees from third world countries to pass into West Germany without valid visas. **21.** An agreement was approved in *Stockholm* by the 35-nation European Security Conference providing for a measure of military disclosure and inspection with measures for verification of compliance with the accord. **28.** Opposition politicians in *Taiwan* formed the Democratic Progress party.

Oct. 6. A transport plane taking supplies to the Contra rebels was shot down in *Nicaragua*, killing two of the crew. The third, an American, Eugene Hasenfus, stood trial on Oct. 20 on charges of terrorism and "violating state security". On Nov. 15 Hasenfus was sentenced to 30 years imprisonment. **10.** Pres. Reagan and Mr. Gorbachev met in Reykjavik, *Iceland*, for two days of talks. On Oct. 12 the talks broke down when Mr. Gorbachev insisted that the U.S. limit its S.D.I. research. It was announced that the *Russian* poet Irina Ratushinskaya had been released from jail halfway through her sentence for anti-Soviet agitation. **12.** The Queen and the Duke of Edinburgh began a six-day State visit to *China*, before travelling to Hong Kong on Oct. 21–23. **15.** The Soviet Union reported the withdrawal of some 8,000 of their troops from *Afghanistan*. **19.** Five U.S. diplomats were ordered to leave the *Soviet Union* because of activities incompatible with their status. **22.** *The Soviet Union* announced the expulsion of another five American diplomats and said that Soviet staff at the U.S. Embassy in Moscow and the U.S. consulate in Leningrad were being withdrawn. **31.** Prince Souphanouvong resigned as Head of State of *Laos* because of failing health. A four-day occupation of Konkuk University in Seoul by students ended when *South Korean* riot police stormed the buildings.

Nov. 2. *Scandinavian* governments ordered searches of their Moscow embassies after Soviet microphones were found hidden in the walls of Sweden's Embassy. **3.** British and Irish nurses, ordered out of *Saudi Arabia* for attending an illegal drinks party, returned to Britain. **9.** Two of *Iceland*'s whaling ships were scuttled in Reykjavik harbour by saboteurs from an environmentalist organization who claimed that the Icelandic whalers were operating in contravention of the moratorium on whaling: on Nov. 10 the whaling station in Hvalurforjdur was

wrecked. **11.** *France* announced that it was prepared to repay to Iran $330 million of a billion-dollar loan but denied any link between the decision and the freeing of two French hostages held in Lebanon. **13.** A report on atrocities in *Afghanistan* resulting from the invasion of Soviet troops was published by the U.N. Human Rights Commission. **15.** Elections for federal and state congresses and state governors took place in *Brazil* with overwhelming wins for the parties of the ruling coalition. The Communist Party newspaper *Pravda* stated that the *Chernobyl* nuclear reactor which caught fire in April had now been buried in reinforced concrete. **17.** M. Georges Besse, chief executive of the Renault car firm, was shot dead outside his *Paris* home. *Argentina* offered to end formally its state of hostilities with Britain in return for "global negotiations" and removal of the protection zone around the Falkland Islands. **19.** The Supreme *Soviet* approved a law permitting individuals to engage privately and on a part-time basis in 29 types of economic activity. **20.** Babrak Karmal resigned as President of the Revolutionary Council in *Afghanistan*. **21.** The *Spanish* Government relaxed the country's rigid abortion law. **24.** Pres. Aquino of the *Philippines* dismissed the Defence Minister, Mr. Juan Ponce Enrile, and asked the rest of the Cabinet to submit their resignations after a reported coup attempt on Nov. 22. *Austria*'s ruling Socialist Party retained its majority in the General Election. **25.** Protests were organized by *French* students against the Government's plan to tighten university entry: on Dec. 5, after ten days of violent clashes between protesters and police, the Government made major concessions to the students but on Dec. 6 renewed rioting occurred after the death of a student. On Dec. 8 the Government withdrew the Universities Bill and announced that controversial secondary school reforms were shelved. **27.** The *West German* Government expelled three Syrian diplomats after Syria was implicated in a bomb attack in Berlin. Violent clashes between demonstrators and police took place in *Brasilia* over recent price increases. **30.** *Spain*'s Socialists won elections to the Basque regional parliament.

Dec. 10. A 60-day ceasefire agreement between Government troops and Communist guerrillas began in the *Philippines*. **14.** Riots in Karachi, *Pakistan*, left 54 dead: on Dec. 15 more clashes between the Pathan and Mahajir communities in Karachi led to 44 deaths. **16.** Dr. Andrei Sakharov, the *Soviet* dissident scientist, was released from seven years exile in Gorky. **17.** *Nicaragua* released the American gun-runner, Eugene Hasenfus as a gesture of peace towards the U.S. Rioters in Alma-Ata, capital of the *Soviet* Republic of Kazakstan, burned cars and fought police in protest at the appointment of a Russian as local Communist Party chief: rioting continued on Dec. 18. **19.** Thousands of *Chinese* students marched on Shanghai's city hall and demanded to speak to the mayor in pro-democracy protests. On Dec. 20 there were larger student demonstrations after the mayor refused to grant their demands. On Dec. 22 unofficial protest marches were banned and key city areas sealed off. On Dec. 23 the protests spread to Peking with students holding street debates. On Dec. 26 the Government took steps to quash the demonstrations.

(1987). Jan. 2. Railway services were halted throughout *France* as the train drivers strike escalated. The Islamic guerrilla groups fighting the Communist regime in *Afghanistan* rejected the offer of a cease-fire. **9.** The new *Nicaraguan* constitution was signed into effect by Pres. Ortega, who immediately formally reintroduced the state of emergency. **11.** The *Soviet Union* replaced Mr. Victor Karpov, head of its arms negotiating team, with Mr. Yuli Vorontsov, First Deputy Foreign Minister, for the Geneva arms control talks. **12.** The official *Chinese* news agency said that senior academics accused of causing nationwide demonstrations in 12 Chinese cities calling for more democracy and freedom, had been dismissed. **16.** Hu Yaobang resigned as General Secretary of the *Chinese* Communist Party: Premier Zhao Ziyang was elected acting General Secretary. Dissident armed forces officers in *Ecuador* seized Pres. Leon Febres Cordero and his Defence Minister, and demanded the release of Gen. Frank Vargas, the leader of a military insurrection in 1986: on Jan. 17 Pres. Cordero submitted to the demands and was released. **22.** Soldiers shot dead at least 15 demonstrators during a march to demand land reform in the *Philippines*. **25.** *West Germany*'s General Election was won by the ruling centre-right coalition with a reduced majority. **27.** There was an attempted coup by rebel troops in the *Philippines*: on Jan. 29 the last rebels surrendered. **29.** The United States and *Poland* restored high-level contacts for the first time since the Solidarity free trade union was suppressed in 1981.

Feb. 2. A referendum was held in the *Philippines* which approved a new constitution. **3.** The *U.S.* conducted nuclear weapons tests on Feb. 3 and 11, whereupon the Soviet Union declared an end to its 18-month unilateral moratorium on testing. **8.** The communist New People's Army broke off ceasefire renewal talks with the *Philippines* Government at the end of a 60-day truce. **10.** *The Soviet Union* released and pardoned 140 political dissenters jailed for anti-State activities. **11.** *Romania* further restricted the use of fuel and power. Pres. Aquino swore alle-

giance to the new *Philippines* constitution. **12.** *Soviet* security police attacked protesters on the fourth day of demonstrations over the jailed Jewish activist, Josef Begun: on Feb. 13 Jewish refuseniks peacefully demonstrating in Moscow were beaten up or arrested: Josef Begun was released on Feb. 20. **17.** At the Geneva conference on disarmament, *the Soviet Union* expressed willingness to accept on-site inspections of declared stockpiles of chemical weapons. **18.** Anatoly Koryagin, the *Soviet* dissident psychiatrist, was released from prison. **23.** It was announced that Boris Pasternak, the author of *Dr. Zhivago*, had been formally rehabilitated by the *Soviet* Writers' Union. **25.** Peace talks between *Pakistan* and *Afghanistan* opened in Geneva: over sixty people were killed when Afghan bombers attacked Pakistani border villages on Feb. 26 and 27. **26.** *The Soviet Union* ended its 18-month freeze on nuclear weapons testing with an underground explosion in central Asia.

March 3. *Italy*'s five-party coalition government led by Bettino Craxi resigned after holding office for 3½ years, a post-war record. **11.** Two leaders of the dissident *Czechoslovakian* Jazz Section were jailed in Prague. Pres. Pinochet of *Chile* promulgated a law allowing political parties to be formed. **15.** *Finland*'s two-day General Election began. A series of strikes in *Yugoslavia* brought workers into open conflict with the Government for the first time, in protest at a partial wage freeze. **17.** Osel Hita, a two-year old from Spain was enthroned in India as the reincarnation of a *Tibetan* lama. **18.** A bomb at the *Philippine* Military Academy killed four people. **20.** Air Force Gen. Licio Giorgieri was shot dead in *Rome* by Red Brigade terrorists. **22.** The prime minister of *Yugoslavia*, Mr. Branko Mikilic, said that the Government was prepared to call on the army to defend the Communist system in the face of an unprecedented series of strikes and growing political tension. On March 24 the Yugoslav Government partially backed down on its wage freeze law and a general return to work followed. **23.** An I.R.A. bomb exploded at a British military base in *West Germany*, injuring 31 people. **28.** Mrs. Thatcher arrived in *the Soviet Union* on a five-day visit, the first by a British Prime Minister for 12 years.

April 2. *France* expelled six Soviet diplomats: on April 5 *Russia* ordered four French diplomats and two businessmen to leave Moscow. **3.** *Chilean* police quelled anti-Government demonstrations during the Pope's visit to Santiago. The *Portuguese* Government was defeated on a censure motion: Parliament was dissolved on April 28. **5.** Tighter laws on refugees and asylum seekers were endorsed by *Swiss* voters in a referendum. **6.** Pres. Herzog of *Israel* made a pilgrimage to the site of the Nazi concentration camp at Bergen-Belsen and unveiled a memorial stone during a five-day German visit. **8.** Pres. Alfredo Stroessner lifted the 40-year-old state of siege in *Paraguay*. *Afghan* rebels launched their first attack on Russian territory in Tadzhikstan. **13.** The U.S. Secretary of State, Mr. Shultz, visited *Moscow* for arms negotiations talks with Mr. Gorbachev and Mr. Shevardnadze. Portugal and China signed an agreement under which *Macao* will revert to China as a Special Administrative Region in 1999. **13.** Pres. Chun Doo Hwan announced that there would be no constitutional reforms in *South Korea* until after the 1988 Olympic Games in Seoul. **17.** President Alfonsin of *Argentina* asked Congress to declare a state of siege to end a rebellion by officers objecting to human rights trials. *Italy*'s 44-day Government crisis ended when Senator Amintore Fanfani announced his Cabinet. **19.** *Argentina*'s three-day military crisis ended when President Alfonsin obtained the surrender of rebel troops. **23.** Mr. Robert Maxwell, the Scottish engineer jailed by the *Libyans* on bribery and industrial espionage charges, was released from prison and returned to Britain on April 29. The *Indonesian* General Election returned the ruling Golkar party to power. **23.** Anatoly Koryagin, the dissident *Soviet* psychiatrist, was granted an exit visa and left Russia accompanied by his family. **25.** In *Iceland's* General Election the ruling centre-right coalition lost its majority and on April 28 the Government resigned. **28.** *Finland's* first Conservative-led Cabinet since 1945, a four-party coalition, was appointed. The *Italian* Government lost a vote of confidence: Parliament was dissolved and a General Election called for June 14.

May 6. The *Dutch* Prime Minister, Mr. Ruud Lubbers, and his wife escaped injury in a petrol bomb attack on their private residence in Rotterdam. **11.** The General Election in the *Philippines* resulted in a large majority for President Aquino's supporters. **23.** *The Soviet Union* decided to halt commercial whaling. **28.** Ministers of Britain, the U.S., Canada, Japan, W. Germany, France, Italy, Belgium and Denmark met to discuss ways of changing their extradition laws to improve the campaign against international terrorism. **28.** Mathias Rust, a 19-year-old West German pilot, flew through Russian air defences without permission to land a light aircraft in Red Square, *Moscow:* on May 30 Marshal Sergei Sokolov, Soviet Defence Minister, and Marshal Alexander Koldunov, commander of the air defence forces, were dismissed and the Politburo condemned the defence forces for their failure to take action. **29.** Rioting occurred in Seoul over the death of a student in police custody in Jan. and

because of the *South Korean* President's refusal to introduce constitutional reforms.

June 4. Chancellor Kohl of *West Germany* announced his Government's support of the proposed withdrawal from Europe of all American and Russian intermediate-range nuclear missiles. **6.** It was revealed that the poet Irina Ratushinskaya, now living in Britain, had been stripped of her *Soviet* citizenship. Yang Zhong, *Chinese* Forestry Minister, was dismissed after disasterous forest fires in the north-east of China over the previous month: he was replaced by Gao Dezhan. **10.** The ruling Democratic Justice Party in *South Korea* endorsed Pres. Chun's choice of Roh Tae Woo as his successor. **11.** *Panama* declared a state of emergency after two days of anti-government riots. Over 400 students occupied Myongdong Catholic Cathedral in *Seoul*, which was then encircled by riot police. **12.** Office workers and the middle classes in *South Korea* joined the cathedral sit-in in Seoul, demanding free elections. The cathedral protest ended peacefully on June 15 but over 60,000 were subsequently involved in fresh street and campus clashes with riot police. **14.** The *Italian* General Election resulted in the Christian Democrats consolidating their position as the largest party. **15.** A *West German* naval vessel was hit by shell fire from a Warsaw Pact ship on exercise in the Baltic Sea: the Defence Ministry in Bonn treated the incident as an accident. **17.** The ruler of *Sharjah*, Sheikh Sultan bin Muhammad Al-Qassimi, was deposed while on a visit to Britain by his brother. On June 20 Sheikh Al-Qassimi was re-instated by the Supreme Council of the United Arab Emirates, who confirmed him as the legitimate ruler. **18.** There was renewed rioting in the centre of *Seoul* and on June 21 riot police arrested 800 protestors in Pusan, South Korea's second city, as demonstrations against the Government continued throughout the country. On June 24 Pres. Chun met the opposition leader Kim Young Sam, to discuss ways of moving to a more democratic form of government, and the other major opposition leader, Kim Dae Jung, was released from house arrest. On June 29, Roh Tae Woo called on the President to accept the will of the people and put forward a number of reforms to move the nation towards democracy. **22.** Herr Hans Rudolf Kurz, a Swiss historian, was named as the head of a commission of inquiry into the wartime record of the *Austrian* President, Dr. Kurt Waldheim.

July 1. Pres. Chun Doo Hwan of *South Korea* declared that he completely accepted demands for direct presidential elections and calls for electoral reforms, press freedom, release of political prisoners, and other civil liberties. **6.** Crimean Tartars began a series of demonstrations in *Moscow* in protest at their expulsion from their homeland in 1944: on July 23 a commission headed by Pres. Gromyko was appointed to investigate their grievances. **9.** Under an amnesty, civil rights were restored to over 2,000 people in *South Korea*. **10.** Pres. Chun Doo Hwan of *South Korea* resigned as chairman of the ruling Democratic Justice party in favour of Roh Tae Woo. **13.** Giovanni Goria, Treasury Minister in the outgoing *Italian* Government, was asked to form a Government, and was was sworn in as Prime Minister on July 29. **14.** President Chiang Ching Kuo of *Taiwan* ordered the lifting of martial law, in force since 1949. **18.** *East Germany* decreed an amnesty for thousands of political and other prisoners, and abolished the death penalty. **19.** In *Portugal's* General Election the ruling Social Democrats won an outright majority of seats, the first party to do so since the 1974 revolution. **27.** Pres. Aquino of the *Philippines* laid down her presidential powers as she inaugurated the new, American-style, Senate and House of Representatives. **29.** Pres. Mitterrand of France and Mrs. Thatcher ratified the Channel Tunnel Treaty. Kakuei Tanaka, former **Japanese** Prime Minister, lost an appeal in Tokyo against a conviction for accepting bribes. **30.** *Norway* announced it had expelled a Soviet diplomat and three Soviet trade officials for spying. *Yugoslavia's* dock strike ended when pay increases were agreed.

Aug. 5. The leaders of Guatemala, El Salvador, Nicaragua, Honduras and Costa Rica met in Guatemala City to discuss regional conflicts and Pres. Reagan's peace plan for *Central America*: on Aug. 8 they signed a preliminary peace plan calling for a ceasefire in areas of conflict, reconciliation between governments and opposition groups, democratic reforms, and an end to foreign aid for rebel forces. On Aug. 23, 13 Latin American countries agreed formally to join a commission to monitor compliance with the plan. **8.** The Western allies in *Berlin* ordered ten Iranians, including diplomats from Iran's embassy in East Berlin, to leave the city. **17.** Rudolf Hess, Hitler's former deputy, died aged 93: on Aug. 19 the Allied authorities in Berlin said Hess had committed suicide. **25.** The Governor and 16 staff of an *Italian* prison on the island of Elba were taken hostage by six prisoners who demanded safe conduct from the jail: they were freed when the prisoners surrendered on Sept. 2. **26.** Chancellor Kohl announced that *West Germany* was prepared to scrap its Pershing missiles if the superpowers agreed on the elimination of medium-range nuclear missiles in Europe. **27.** Rebel troops in the *Philippines* attempted to overthrow Pres. Aquino but were defeated by loyal troops.

MISCELLANEOUS

(1986). Sept. 20. A 2½-month-old boy became the youngest person in the world to receive a new heart and lungs, in an operation at Harefield Hospital, London. **26.** A £55 million rebuilding programme for the Royal Opera House was announced.

Oct. 6. A new national daily newspaper, *The Independent*, was published.

Nov. 2. Britain's first artificial heart transplant operation was performed at Papworth Hospital, near Cambridge.

Dec. 17. The world's first triple transplant patient, Mrs. Davina Thompson, received a new heart, lungs, and liver at Papworth Hospital, Cambridge.

(1987). Jan. 30. Super Channel, the British satellite television channel for Europe, went on the air.

Feb. 24. Mr. Robert Maxwell's new newspaper, *The London Daily News*, was launched. Associated Newspapers re-launched the *London Evening News*, which had merged with the *London Evening Standard* in 1980.

March 30. Van Gogh's *Sunflowers* was sold at Christie's in London for a record £24,750,000. The purchaser of the painting was the Yasuda Fire and Marine Insurance Company of Japan.

April 2 & 3. The Duchess of Windsor's jewels, sold at auction in Geneva, realized £31,380,197. **22.** A baby girl was born to a Staffordshire couple who is biologically the twin of their 18-month old elder daughter. Both children were conceived at the same time but born more than one year apart after embryos were kept deep frozen before implantation in the mother's womb. **25.** A new newspaper, *The News on Sunday*, was launched.

May 13. Eleven square-rigged sailing ships sailed from the Solent for Botany Bay, recreating the voyage of the First Fleet carrying 1,350 settlers as part of the Australian bicentenary celebrations.

June 3. The newspaper *Sunday Today* ceased publication.

July 3. Richard Branson and Per Lindstrand abandoned their hot-air balloon *Virgin Atlantic Flyer* when it ditched in the Irish Sea 60 miles from the Scottish coast. The balloon had travelled 2,820 miles across the Atlantic from Maine, U.S.A., setting a world distance record. **11.** A baby boy born in

Zagreb, Yugoslavia, was symbolically named the world's five billionth resident by the U.N. Secretary-General. **25.** *The London Daily News* closed down five months after it was launched.

Aug. 1. Eve Jackson completed the first Microlight plane flight from Britain to Australia. **16.** Septuplets were born in Liverpool, but none survived for more than two weeks, the last dying on Aug. 31.

OBITUARIES, SEPT. 1, 1986–AUG. 31, 1987

Ackroyd, Dame Elizabeth, D.B.E., civil servant and Director, Consumer Council 1963–71, aged 77—*June* 28.

Allen, Sir Denis, G.C.M.G., C.B., diplomat, aged 76—*May* 20.

Armstrong, *Most Rev.* John, Archbishop of Armagh and Primate of All Ireland 1980–86, aged 71—*July* 21.

Astaire, Fred, dancer and actor, aged 88—*June* 22.

Baldridge, Michael, U.S. Secretary of Commerce since 1981, aged 64—*July* 25.

Barnett, Guy, Labour M.P. for Greenwich since 1971, aged 58—*Dec.* 24, 1986.

Barrow, Rt. Hon. Errol, Prime Minister of Barbados 1966–76 and since 1986, aged 67—*June* 1.

Bass, Alfie, actor, aged 66—*July* 17.

Baster, *Col.* Norman, G.C., aged 95—*June.*

Bearsted, 3rd Viscount, T.D., merchant banker and financier, aged 77—*Oct.* 15, 1986.

Bennett, *Air Vice-Marshal* Donald, C.B., C.B.E., D.S.O., aged 76—*Sept.* 15, 1986.

Beswick, Lord, P.C., Labour M.P. for Uxbridge 1946–59, Labour Chief Whip, House of Lords 1967–70, Minister of State, Industry 1975, aged 75—*Aug.* 17.

Blakely, Colin, actor aged 56—*May* 7.

Braine, John, author, aged 64—*Oct.* 28, 1986.

Brookeborough, 2nd Viscount, P.C. (N.I.), aged 64—*March* 5.

Bull, *Dr.* James, C.B.E., pioneer of neuro-radiology, aged 76—*July* 5.

Burden, Sir Frederick, Conservative M.P. for Gillingham 1950–83, aged 81—*July* 6.

Byng, Douglas, entertainer, aged 94—*Aug.* 24.

Caldwell, Erskine, American writer, aged 83—*April* 11.

Cameron, *Lt.-Gen.* Sir Alexander, K.B.E., C.B., M.C., aged 88—*Dec.* 25, 1986.

Carson, The Hon. Edward, Conservative M.P. for the Isle of Thanet 1945–53, aged 67—*March* 6.

Casey, William, Director of the C.I.A. since 1981, aged 74—*May* 6.

Chamoun, Camille, President of Lebanon 1952–58, aged 87—*Aug.* 7.

Cheney, *Prof.* Christopher, C.B.E., F.B.A., historian, aged 80—*June* 19.

Cherns, *Prof.* Albert, social scientist, aged 65—*May* 14.

Childs, *Most Rev.* Derrick, Archbishop of Wales 1983–86, aged 69—*March* 18.

Clwyd, 2nd Baron, Assistant Secretary of Commissions, Lord Chancellor's Department 1948–61, aged 86—*March* 30.

Cochet, Henri, French tennis player, aged 85—*April* 1.

Coldstream, Sir William, C.B.E, painter and arts administrator, aged 78—*Feb.* 18.

Collier, *Air Vice-Marshal* Sir Conrad, K.C.B., C.B.E., aged 90—*Sept.* 16, 1986.

Collier, Patience, actress, aged 76—*July* 13.

Cooke, Sir Robert (Robin), Conservative M.P. for Bristol West 1957–79, aged 56—*Jan.* 7.

Costain, Sir Albert, Conservative M.P. for Folkestone and Hythe 1959–83, aged 76—*March* 5.

Creasey, *Gen.* Sir Timothy, K.C.B., O.B.E., aged 63—*Oct.* 5, 1986.

Croft, Michael, O.B.E., founder and director of the National Youth Theatre, aged 64—*Nov.* 15, 1986.

Crowther-Hunt, Lord, Ph.D., academic, Minister of State, Education 1974–76, and Privy Council Office 1976, Rector, Exeter College, Oxford, since 1982, aged 66—*Feb.* 16.

Dainty, Billy, comedian, aged 59—*Nov.* 19, 1986.

Daniel, *Prof.* Glynn, F.B.A., archaeologist, aged 72—*Dec.* 13, 1986.

de Broglie, 7th Duc, French physicist and Nobel laureate, aged 94—*March* 19.

Denmark, H.H. Prince Georg of, K.C.V.O., aged 66—*Sept.* 29, 1986.

Donald, *Prof.* Ian, C.B.E., F.R.C.S. (Glas), F.R.C.O.G., obstetrician, aged 76—*June* 19.

Drummond, Dame Margaret, D.B.E., Director of the W.R.N.S. 1964–67, aged 69—*April* 21.

Drury, Paul, etcher and painter, aged 83—*May* 19.

Duncan, *Maj.-Gen.* Nigel, C.B., C.B.E., D.S.O., aged 87—*March* 24.

Dundonald, 14th Earl, aged 67—*Oct.* 4, 1986.

Eaker, *Gen.* Ira, HON. K.C.B., HON. K.B.E., D.S.M., commander of U.S. and Allied air forces in Second World War, aged 91—*Aug.* 6.

Edwardes Jones, *Air Marshal* Sir Humphrey, K.C.B., C.B.E., D.F.C., A.F.C., aged 81—*Jan.* 19.

Elwes, Polly, television broadcaster, aged 59—*July* 15.

Ensor, David, solicitor, braodcaster, Labour M.P. for Bury and Radcliffe 1964–70, aged 80—*Feb.* 5.

Evans, Alfred, Labour M.P. for Caerphilly 1968–79, aged 73—*April* 13.

Finlay, Sir Graeme, Bt., E.R.D., Conservative M.P. for Epping 1951–64 and jurist, aged 69—*Jan.* 21.

Franklin, Olga, C.B.E., Matron-in-Chief, Q.A.R.N.N.S. 1947–50, aged 91—*April* 20.

Fraser, Sir Hugh, Bt. former chairman of House of Fraser stores, aged 50—*May* 5.

Fydenlund, Knut, Norwegian Foreign Minister 1973–81 and since 1986, aged 59—*Feb.* 26.

Gibson, Rt. Hon. Sir Maurice, Lord Justice of Appeal, Supreme Court of Judicature, Northern Ireland, since 1975, *assassinated*, aged 73—*April* 25.

Gingold, Hermoine, actress, aged 89—*May* 24.

Gleason, Jackie, American actor, aged 71–*June* 24.

Goddard, *Air Marshal* Sir Victor, K.C.B., C.B.E., aged 89—*Jan.* 21.

Goode, Sir William, G.C.M.G., Governor of Singapore 1957–59, and of Borneo 1960–63, aged 79—*Sept.* 15, 1986.

Gordon Lennox, *Rear-Adm.* Sir Alexander, K.C.V.O., C.B., D.S.O., Serjeant of Arms, House of Commons 1962–76, aged 76—*July* 4.

Gorell Barnes, Sir William, K.C.M.G., C.B., Deputy Under-Secretary of State, Colonial Office 1959–63, aged 77—*March* 25.

Gourley, Harry, Labour M.P. for Kirkcaldy (formerly Kirkcaldy Burghs) since 1959, aged 70—*April* 20.

Grant, Cary, film actor, aged 82—*Nov.* 29, 1986.

Gray, *Air Vice-Marshal* John, C.B., C.B.E., D.S.O., G.M., aged 87—*June* 6.

Greene, Sir Hugh, K.C.M.G., O.B.E., Director General of the B.B.C. 1960–69, aged 76—*Feb.* 19.

Greenwood, Joan, actress, aged 65—*Feb.* 27.

Grundy, *Air Marshal* Sir Edouard (Bill), K.B.E., C.B., aged 78—*June* 15.

Guthrie-James, David, M.B.E., D.S.C., Conservative M.P. for Brighton Kemptown 1959–64, and Dorset North 1970–79, aged 66—*Dec.* 15, 1986.

Haden-Guest, 3rd Baron, aged 82—*May* 26.

Harland, *Rt. Rev.* Maurice, Bishop of Lincoln 1947–56, Bishop of Durham 1956–66, aged 90—*Sept.* 29, 1986.

Harrowby, 6th Earl, Unionist M.P. (as Lord Sandon) for Shrewsbury 1922–23 and 1924–29, aged 94—*May* 7.

Harvey, Ian, Conservative M.P. for Harrow East 1950–58, aged 72—*Jan.* 10.

Hasler, *Lt. Col.* H. G. ('Blondie'), D.S.O., O.B.E., commander of 'cockleshell heroes' raid 1942, aged 73—*May* 5.

Hayworth, Rita, American film actress, aged 68—*May* 14.

Heinz II, Henry J., HON. K.B.E., aged 78—*Feb.* 23.

Helpmann, Sir Robert, C.B.E., dancer and actor, aged 77—*Sept.* 28, 1986.

Hess, Rudolph, aged 93—*Aug.* 17.

Hirsch, *Prof.* Karl, mathematician, aged 80—*Nov.* 4, 1986.

Hobley, McDonald, broadcaster, aged 70—*July* 30.

Huntly, 12th Marquess of, aged 78—*Jan.* 26.

Huston, John, film director, aged 81—*Aug.* 28.

Jameson, Margaret Storm, writer, aged 95—*Sept.* 30, 1986.

Jinks, *Prof.* John, C.B.E., F.R.S., geneticist, Deputy Chairman and Secretary, Agricultural and Food Research Council since 1985, aged 57—*June* 6.

Jochum, Eugen, German conductor, aged 84—*March* 26.

Jonathan, Chief Leabua, Prime Minister of Lesotho 1965–86, aged 73—*April* 5.

Kaldor, Baron, F.B.A., economist, aged 78—*Sept.* 30, 1986.

Karami, Rashid, Lebanese Prime Minister, *assassinated*, aged 65—*June* 1.

Kaye, Danny, actor and comedian, aged 74—*March* 3.

King, Cecil, newspaper proprietor, aged 86—*April* 17.

Knight, Esmond, actor, aged 80—*Feb.* 23.

Laithwaite, Sir Gilbert, G.C.M.G., K.C.B., K.C.I.E., C.S.I., civil servant and diplomat, aged 92—*Dec.* 21, 1986.

Lanchester, Elsa, actress, aged 84—*Dec.* 26, 1986.

Lartique, Jacques-Henri, French photographer, aged 92—*Sept* 12, 1986.

Latymer, 7th Baron, banker, aged 85—*May* 24.

Leader, Harry, band leader, aged 73—*Jan.*

Le Marchant, Sir Spencer, Kt., Conservative M.P. for High Peak 1970–83, aged 55—*Sept.* 7, 1986.

Levi, Primo, Italian writer, aged 67—*April* 11.

Liberace, entertainer, aged 67—*Feb.* 4.

Lifar, Serge, Russian-born dancer and ballet master, aged 81—*Dec.* 16, 1986.

Linlithgow, 3rd Marquess of, M.C., T.D., Lord Lieutenant of West Lothian 1964–86, aged 75—*April* 7.

Linstead, Sir Hugh, O.B.E., Conservative M.P. for Putney 1942–64, aged 86—*May* 27.

Locke, Bobby, South African golfer, aged 69—*March* 9.

MacDonald, John D., American mystery writer, aged 70—*Dec.* 1986.

MacFarquhar, Sir Alexander, K.B.E., C.I.E., Director of Personnel, U.N. 1962–67, aged 83—*July* 29.

Machel, Samora, President of Mozambique since 1975, *killed accidentally*, aged 53—*Oct.* 19, 1986.

Mackay, Fulton, O.B.E., actor, aged 64—*June* 6.

McKenna, Siobhán, Irish actress, aged 63—*Nov.* 16, 1986.

Maclagan, *Prof.* Noel, F.R.C.P., F.R.C.Path., F.R.I.C., chemical pathologist, aged 82—*July* 16.

Maclean, Alistair, novelist, aged 64—*Feb.* 2.

McLean, *Lt.-Gen.* Sir Kenneth, K.C.B., K.B.E., an Operation Overlord planner, aged 90—*June* 5.

Magill, Sir Ivan, K.C.V.O., F.R.C.S., anaesthetist, aged 98—*Nov.* 25, 1986.

Mahon, Simon, Labour M.P. for Bootle 1955–79, aged 72—*Oct.* 19, 1986.

Marvin, Lee, actor, aged 63—*Aug.* 29.

Mason, Brewster, actor, aged 64—*Aug.* 14.

Mason, *Capt.* Dudley, G.C., captain of the *Ohio* which helped to relieve Malta in 1942, aged 85—*April* 26.

Maybray-King, Baron, P.C., Speaker of the House of Commons 1965–70, aged 85—*Sept.* 3, 1986.

Middleditch, Edward, M.C., R.A., artist, aged 64—*July* 29.

Mikes, George, Hungarian-born author, aged 75—*Aug.* 30.

Molotov, Vyacheslav, former Soviet Foreign Minister, aged 96—*Nov.* 8, 1986.

Moore, Gerald, C.B.E., F.R.C.M., accompanist, aged 87—*March* 13.

Moult, Edward (Ted), television personality, aged 60—*Sept.* 3, 1986.

Murless, Sir Noel, racehorse trainer, aged 76—*May* 9.

Negri, Pola, Polish-born film actress, aged 92—*Aug.* 1.

Neville, Sir Robert, K.C.M.G., C.B.E., Governor of the Bahamas 1950–53, aged 90—*June* 12.

Nicholson, Norman, O.B.E., poet, aged 73—*May* 30.

Noble, Sir Peter, Principal, King's College, London 1952–68, Vice-Chancellor, University of London 1961–64, aged 87—*May* 12.

Page, Geraldine, American actress, aged 62—*June* 13.

Parker Bowles, Dame Anne, D.C.V.O., C.B.E., Chief Commissioner of Girl Guides 1966–75, aged 68—*Jan.* 22.

Penhaligon, David, Liberal M.P. for Truro since 1974, *killed accidentally*, aged 42—*Dec.* 22, 1986.

Phillips, *Prof.* John, F.R.S., Vice-Chancellor of Loughborough University since 1986, aged 53—*March* 14.

Phoenix, Pat, actress, aged 62—*Sept.* 17, 1986.

Pim, *Capt.* Sir Richard, K.B.E., V.R.D., ran Map Room at Downing Street in Second World War, Inspector-General, R.U.C. 1945–61, aged 86—*June* 26.

Pitt, Terence (Terry), Labour M.E.P. for Midlands West since 1984, aged 49—*Oct.* 3, 1986.

Platt, Sir Harry, Bt., orthopaedic surgeon, aged 100—*Dec.* 20, 1986.

Plimsoll, Sir James, A.C., C.B.E., Governor of Tasmania since 1982, aged 70—*May* 8.

Polson, *Prof.* Cyril, forensic scientist, aged 85—*Dec.* 31, 1986.

Poston, Elizabeth, composer, aged 81—*March* 18.

Rich, Buddy, jazz drummer, aged 69—*April* 2.

Richards, Sir Gordon, jockey and trainer, aged 82—*Nov.* 10, 1986.

Rigby, Sir Ivo, Chief Justice of Hong Kong and of Brunei 1970–73, aged 75—*April* 19.

Roberts, Sir David, K.B.E., C.M.G., C.V.O., diplomat, aged 62—June 7.

Robertson, Fyfe, journalist and television reporter, aged 84—*Feb.* 4.

Robinson, Sir David, multi-millionaire and philanthropist, aged 82—*Jan.* 10.

Rundell, Sir Francis, G.C.M.G., O.B.E., diplomat, aged 78—*July* 7.

Saifuddin, Sir Muda Omar Ali, formerly Sultan of Brunei, aged 71—Sept. 7, 1986.

Salomon, Sir Walter, banker, aged 81—*June* 16.

Samuel of Wych Cross, Lord, property developer, aged 75—*Aug.* 28.

Sangster, Vernon, football pools millionaire, aged 87—*Dec.* 17, 1986.

Saunders, *Air Chief Marshal* Sir Hugh, G.C.B., K.B.E., M.C., D.F.C., M.M., aged 92—*May* 8.

Scott, Randolph, American actor, aged 89—*March* 2.

Segovia, Andrés, Spanish classical guitarist, aged 94—*June* 2.

Silkin, *Rt. Hon.*, John, Labour M.P. for Lewisham, Deptford (formerly Deptford) since 1963, Minister of Agriculture, Fisheries and Food 1976–79, aged 64—*April* 26.

Skyrme, *Prof.* Tony, physicist, aged 64—*June* 25.

Smout, *Hon.* Judge (David), Q.C., an Official Referee of the High Court, aged 63—*May* 7.

Snedden, *Rt. Hon.* Sir Billy, K.C.M.G., Speaker, House of Representatives, Australia 1976–83, aged 60—*June* 27.

Stanley, *Dr.* Herbert, F.R.S., researcher in petrochemicals and development of plastics, aged 83—*July* 4.

Stevens, *Air Marshal* Sir Alick, K.B.E., C.B., aged 88—*July* 2.

Steward, Sir William, Conservative M.P. for Woolwich West 1950–59, aged 86—*May*.

Stewart, Hon. Lord (Ewan Stewart), M.C., Senator of the College of Justice in Scotland since 1975, Solicitor General for Scotland 1967–70, aged 63—*March* 31.

Stockton, 1st Earl of, O.M., P.C., F.R.S., Conservative Prime Minister 1957–63, aged 92—*Dec.* 29, 1986.

Stockwell, *Gen.* Sir Hugh, G.C.B., K.B.E., D.S.O., aged 83—*Nov.* 27, 1986.

Stokes, Doris, medium and author, aged 68—*May*.

Strathmore and Kinghorne, 17th Earl, aged 58—*Aug.* 18.

Streatfeild, Noel, author, aged 90—*Sept.* 11, 1986.

Sutherland-Harris, Sir Jack, K.C.V.O., C.B., Under Secretary, Ministry of Agriculture and Fisheries 1950–60, Second Crown Estate Commissioner 1960–68, aged 78—*Dec.* 28, 1986.

Talbot of Malahide, 9th Baron, aged 87—*Feb.* 20.

Tarkovsky, Andrei, Russian film director, aged 54—*Dec.* 29, 1986.

Tate, Phyllis, composer, aged 76—*May* 29.

Taylor, *Gen.* Maxwell, HON. K.B.E., American officer, aged 85—*April* 19.

Thistleton-Smith, *Vice-Adm.* Sir Geoffrey, K.B.E., C.B., G.M., aged 81—*Nov.* 15, 1986.

Thomas, *Dr.* Claudius, C.M.G., Commissioner for the Eastern Caribbean Governments in the U.K. since 1975, aged 58—*April* 6.

Thornton, Dr. Grace, C.B.E., L.V.O., diplomat, aged 73—*June* 23.

Trenchard, 2nd Viscount, M.C., Minister of State, Dept. of Industry 1979–81, Ministry of Defence 1981–83, aged 63—*April* 29.

Trend, Lord, P.C., G.C.B., C.V.O., Cabinet Secretary 1963–73, aged 73—*July* 21.

Troughton, Patrick, actor, aged 67—*March* 28.

Tudor, Anthony, choreographer, aged 79—*April* 19.

Vaughan-Thomas, Wynford, C.B.E., F.R.S.A., broadcaster, author and journalist, aged 78—*Feb.* 4.

Ventry, 7th Baron, aeronaut, aged 88,—*March* 7.

von Trapp, Baroness Maria, aged 82—*March* 28.

Walker, *Air Chief Marshal* Sir Augustus, G.C.B.., C.B.E., D.S.O., D.F.C., A.F.C., aged 74—*Dec.* 11, 1986.

Warhol, Andy, pop artist and film maker, aged 59—*Feb.* 22.

Waring, Eddie, M.B.E., rugby commentator, aged 76—*Oct.* 28, 1986.

Weitzman, David, Q.C., Labour M.P. for Stoke Newington 1945–50, and for Hackney North and Stoke Newington 1950–79, aged 88—*May* 6.

Westminster, Viola, Dowager Duchess of, Lord Lieutenant of Co. Fermanagh 1979–86, *killed accidentally,* aged 74—*May,* 3.

Wharncliffe, 4th Earl of, aged 52—*June* 3.

Whateley, Dame Leslie, D.B.E., T.D., Director of the A.T.S. 1943–46, Director of World Bureau of Girl Guides/Girl Scouts 1951–64, aged 88—*July* 4.

Wilson, Sir Graham, F.R.C.P., F.R.S., Director of Public Health Laboratory Service 1941–63, aged 91—*April* 5.

Wittig, *Prof.* Georg, German chemist and Nobel laureate, aged 90—*Aug.* 26.

Woolley, Sir Richard, O.B.E., F.R.S., Astronomer Royal 1956–71, aged 80—*Dec.* 24, 1986.

Wood, Sir Michael, C.B.E., founder of E. Africa Flying Doctor service and co-founder of African Medical Research Foundation, aged 68—*May* 16.

Worth, Joy, broadcaster, aged 77—*Aug.* 8.

Youde, Sir Edward, G.C.M.G., G.C.V.O., M.B.E., Governor of Hong Kong since 1982, aged 62—*Dec.* 4, 1986.

CENTENARIES

One Hundred Years Ago (1888).—A selection follows of "Remarkable Occurrences" (as "Events of the Year" was then called) as printed in the 1889 and 1890 editions of *Whitaker's Almanack* covering the year 1888. This year saw the start of the Whitechapel murders attributed to Jack the Ripper and the continuation of agitation over home rule for Ireland.

JANUARY.

1. Pope Leo XIII. celebrated a Jubilee mass in St. Peter's, Rome: 20,000 persons present.

9. The remains of Napoleon III. and the Prince Imperial removed from Chislehurst to Farnborough.

— Collision on the Union Pacific Railway; several persons burnt to death and others frostbitten.

17. Colonel Kitchener severely wounded in an attack on Osman Digna at Handoub.

18. Mr. C. Graham, M.P., and Mr. Burns convicted for taking part in an assemblage in Trafalgar Square.

24. Centenary of New South Wales celebrated, and a statue of the Queen unveiled in Sydney.

25. A new reredos unveiled in St. Paul's Cathedral.

30. A "solemn office" in memory of the Young Pretender celebrated in the Anglican church of All Saints, Lambeth.

FEBRUARY.

2. Southwell collegiate church opened as the cathedral of the new diocese.

3. Publication of a Treaty of Alliance concluded between Germany and Austria in 1879.

— Two men sentenced to fifteen years' penal servitude for being in possession of dynamite for a felonious purpose.

9. Tracheotomy successfully performed on the Crown Prince of Germany.

10. Lord Dufferin announced his resignation of the Viceroyalty to the Legislative Council at Calcutta.

— Mr. Pyne, M.P., and Mr. Gilhooly, M.P., arrested at the House of Commons.

16. Four men killed by the collapse of a bridge at the Festiniog slate quarries, North Wales.

22. Terms of the Canadian Fisheries Treaty published.

24. Mr. E. S. Campbell, while rowing in the Clare College boat, killed by the prow of that of Trinity Hall.

28. Panic on the Bourse at St. Petersburg: the rouble declined to a point never before known.

— Convocation of the Province of Canterbury assented to the new canons relating to the hours of marriage.

MARCH.

1. M. Wilson, son-in-law of ex-President Grévy, sentenced to two years' imprisonment and other penalties for trafficking in decorations.
— The Panama Canal shareholders resolved to issue bonds for 340,000,000 francs to complete the canal.
5. The Porte telegraphed to Prince Ferdinand that his presence in Bulgaria is illegal.
9. Prize fight, £100 a side, near Amiens, between John L. Sullivan, American, and Charles Mitchell, English: after 39 rounds, a draw was agreed upon.
12. Lying-in-state of the German Emperor.
15. General Boulanger's dismissal from the French army announced.
— Marriage of Prince Oscar of Sweden to Miss Ebba Munck at Bournemouth.
16. Funeral of William I. of Germany.
21. The Queen left Windsor for Italy.
22. A British expeditionary force captured the Thibetan post of Lingtu.
24. The Queen arrived at Florence.
26. The Appeal Court of Paris quashed the sentence passed on M. Wilson.
27. The *Nile*, the heaviest armoured ship yet built, launched at Pembroke Dockyard.
30. The Emperor Frederick and the Empress enthusiastically received in Berlin.

APRIL.

2. Woman murdered and mutilated in the east end of London—the first of a series.
— During a bull-fight at Mexico the circus caught fire, causing the loss of many lives.
9. Major Templer, accused of betraying official secrets, honourably acquitted by court-martial.
10. Salvation Army meeting at Clapton Hall on the marriage of Miss Booth to "Commissioner" Tucker.
15. The health of the German Emperor stated to be alarming.
— General Boulanger elected for the department of the Nord by over 96,000 votes.
18. Verdict of £300 against Mr. Bradlaugh for a libel on Mr. Peters.
23. Queen Victoria received at Innsbruck by the Emperor of Austria, and next day reached Charlottenburg.
24. A school-board teacher at Dudley committed suicide owing to the difficult nature of the examination he had to undergo.
25. The Queen received Prince Bismarck at a special audience at Berlin, and reached England two days later.
28. The French Chambers agreed to the Panama Canal Loan Bill.

MAY.

1. The Prince of Naples and several Italian officers wounded by the bursting of a shell.
3. Mr. W. O'Brien, M.P., sentenced to three months' imprisonment.
7. The Prince and Princess of Wales arrived at Glasgow, and next day formally opened the International Exhibition.
11. Mr. Dillon, M.P., sentenced to six months' imprisonment.
12. The Italian Exhibition at West Kensington opened by the Lord Mayor.
14. The Anglo-Danish Exhibition opened at South Kensington by the Princess of Wales.
17. The combined European fleets assembled at Barcelona previous to the opening of the Spanish Exhibition.
18. The Scandinavian Exhibition in Copenhagen opened by the King of Denmark.

19. Severe thunderstorms over many parts of England and Scotland: Fifeshire Lunatic Asylum set on fire.
20. International Exhibition opened at Barcelona.
— Meeting in Phoenix Park, Dublin, to protest against Papal interference in the affairs of Ireland.
22. Savage murder of a warder in Manchester Gaol by a convict, Jackson, who afterwards escaped.
23. The Thibetans repulsed with serious loss in an attack upon Gnatong.
24. Marriage of Prince Henry of Prussia and Princess Irene of Hesse at Charlottenburg.
— A young man murdered without provocation by a gang of youths in Regent's Park.
27. Transcaspian Railway opened to Samarcand, a distance of 900 miles, and telegraphic communication with Europe established.

JUNE.

1. The Emperor Frederick of Germany removed from Charlottenburg to Potsdam.
4. Irish Exhibition at Kensington opened by the Lord Mayors of London and Dublin.
11. Lord Stanley of Preston sworn into office at Ottawa as Governor-General of Canada.
12. The French Senate rejected the Government Bill to transfer the financial year from Jan. 1 to July 1.
— Unfavourable reports issued as to the condition of the German Emperor.
13. "Ireland, a Nation," the first toast proposed at a dinner in honour of Mr. Parnell.
16. Statue of General Gordon unveiled at Aberdeen.
— A tablet unveiled in St. Paul's Cathedral in memory of newspaper war correspondents who died in the Soudan.
18. Religious services performed in England contemporaneously with the funeral of the Emperor Frederick at Potsdam.
20. Meeting of licensed victuallers at St. James's Hall, to protest against the retention of the Sunday clause in the Local Government Bill.
23. A School of Handicraft at Toynbee Hall, Whitechapel, opened by Sir W. Hart-Dyke, M.P.
25. The German Reichstag opened by the new Emperor, William II.
27. The Prussian Parliament opened by the Emperor.
29. One farthing damages obtained against the *Licensed Victuallers' Gazette* for libel on Charles Wood, a jockey.

JULY.

2. Opening of the Lambeth Conference at Lambeth Palace.
4. Preparations commenced under the Naval Mobilization Scheme, by commissioning ships carrying 6,000 men and 197 guns.
5. Oxford and Cambridge cricket-match, after four days' play, abandoned owing to rain.
8. Demonstration in Hyde Park against the Sunday Closing Bill.
10. The Gentlemen beat the Players at Lord's Cricket Ground by five runs.
11. Fire in the De Beers Mine, Kimberley, and great loss of life.
12. On the rejection of a motion by General Boulanger in the French Chamber he resigned his seat.
13. Duel between M. Floquet and General Boulanger: the latter seriously wounded.
14. The Cunard steamer *Etruria* reached Queenstown from New York in six days four hours and fifty minutes.

19. Major Barttelot killed by Manyemas when on his way to support Stanley.

— Tercentenary of the defeat of the Spanish Armada celebrated at Plymouth.

20. Four hundred dervishes who attacked a village near Wady Halfa driven off with great loss by Colonel Wodehouse.

25. Mr. and Mrs. Gladstone celebrated their golden wedding.

26. The Emperor William visited Stockholm.

27. The 900th anniversary of the introduction of Christianity into Russia celebrated at Kieff.

— Volcanic eruption in Japan; 1,000 persons and many villages destroyed.

29. The German Empress gave birth to a son.

31. George C. Greenway sentenced to five years' penal servitude and Kelynge Greenway to twelve months' imprisonment for improperly converting securities in their possession as bankers.

AUGUST.

1. International Exhibition opened at Melbourne to celebrate the centenary of the foundation of the colony of New South Wales.

3. Eland's Bank at Kettering suspended payment.

— Explosion at a firework factory at Wandsworth: two women killed and others injured.

6. Robbery of over £500 at the Plymouth station of the Cornwall Railway Company.

7. Second of a series of brutal murders committed in the east end of London.

— Donovan, an expert diver, drowned upon leaping from Charing Cross Bridge.

10. Surrey in an innings against Sussex scored 668 runs.

13. The Italians in Abyssinia defeated with considerable loss.

— Through railway communication being established between Western Europe and Turkey, the first train passed through Bulgaria, and next day reached Constantinople.

19. General Boulanger returned to the French Chamber by three Departments.

20. The Barrack Street Band from Cork refused to play "God Save the Queen" at the Irish Exhibition in Kensington.

24. Germany announced its occupation of Addelah, near Dahomey, West Africa.

27. Mr. Simmons, in descending near Witham, lost his life by the bursting of a balloon.

29. The Duke of Edinburgh received with great honours at Constantinople.

31. The third of a series of murders committed at the east end of London.

SEPTEMBER.

7. The grant of a charter to Lord Brassey and others, under the title of The Imperial British East Africa Company, published in the *London Gazette*.

8. Fourth of a series of murders committed at the east end of London.

11. Lord Stanley of Preston opened an Exhibition at Toronto.

— Marriage of the Duke of Aosta to his niece, Princess Lætitia, daughter of Prince Napoleon.

17. Preliminary meeting of the Special Commission appointed to investigate the charges made by the *Times* in "Parnellism and Crime."

29. The annual Convention of the Irish National League of Great Britain held at Birmingham.

30. Two women murdered, one of them mutilated, in the east end of London.

OCTOBER.

2. Discovery of the mutilated remains of a woman in a vault near the Embankment at Whitehall.

3. The Maori football team played and won their first match in England.

5. The first three columns of the Black Mountain Expedition occupied the ridge after some skirmishing.

10. Terrible railway accident on the Lehigh Valley Railway, U.S.A.: 63 killed and 22 injured.

13. Anniversary of the death of King Edward the Confessor observed in the Roman Catholic churches of London.

14. A statue of Shakspeare unveiled in the Boulevard Haussmann, Paris.

16. Statue of General Gordon unveiled in Trafalgar Square.

19. Great Fire in Well Court, Cheapside.

22. The Special Commission to inquire into the charges against Mr. Parnell opened before the President of the Probate Court and Justices Day and Smith.

24. The dissolution announced of the marriage between King Milan and Queen Natalie.

29. Wreck of a train carrying the Czar and Czarina near Borki: about 20 servants and officials killed.

30. Notice given in the *London Gazette* that certain territories in New Guinea have been annexed to the British dominions.

31. The English publisher of M. Zola's works having pleaded guilty at the Central Criminal Court, was fined £100.

NOVEMBER.

6. General Harrison, new President of the United States, elected.

9. Another woman murdered and mutilated in Whitechapel.

10. The through express train from Paris arrived at Constantinople.

13. Mr. Pyne, M.P., supposed to have fallen from the deck of a Dublin steamer.

17. Seventy-fifth anniversary of the liberation of the Netherlands from French rule.

21. Explosion of 300 barrels of naphtha on board a vessel in Bristol Docks.

DECEMBER.

6. The German factories at Bagamoyo attacked by a native chief with a large force.

8. A farmer near Ennis brutally beaten for refusing to subscribe to the Parnell Indemnity Fund.

11. A deputation had an interview with the Chancellor of the Exchequer to represent the desirability of taking a quinquennial Census.

17. A poacher at King's Lynn killed by the explosion of his own gun.

18. Four men decapitated at Zanzibar by order of the Sultan, who further ordered similar executions for another seven days.

20. Defeat of the Arabs near Suakin by the Black Brigades supported by British and Egyptian troops.

— The dead body of a woman found in a builder's yard at Poplar.

22. The Suez Canal Convention ratified at Constantinople.

29. The master and chief officer of the British barque *Glyfe* sentenced to ten years' penal servitude for scuttling that vessel.

THE CENTENARIES OF 1988

Died 1888

Jan. 30	Edward Lear, writer and artist.
March 6	Louisa M. Alcott, American novelist.
April 15	Matthew Arnold, poet and educationalist.

Born 1888

Jan. 3	Herbert Morrison, Labour statesman.
Feb. 5	Admiral Lord Fraser of North Cape.
Feb. 25	John Foster Dulles, U.S. Secretary of State 1953–59.
May 11	Irving Berlin, American composer.
June*	Sir Lewis Namier, British historian.
July 23	Raymond Chandler, American detective story writer.
Aug. 13	John Logie Baird, pioneer of the television.
Aug. 15	T. E. Lawrence, soldier and writer.
Sept. 12	Maurice Chevalier, French singer and actor.
Sept. 26	T. S. Eliot, poet and playwright.
Sept. 28	Cyril McNeile ("Sapper"), writer.
Oct. 14	Katherine Mansfield, author.
Oct. 16	Eugene O'Neill, American playwright.
Oct 25	Richard Byrd, American admiral, aviator and Polar explorer.
Dec. 6	Will Hay, comedian.
Dec. 7	Joyce Cary, novelist.
Dec. 22	J. Arthur Rank, film magnate.

Died 1788

Jan. 31	Charles Edward Stuart (the Young Pretender).
March 29	Charles Wesley, evangelist and hymn writer.
Aug. 2	Thomas Gainsborough, painter.
Dec. 14	Carl Philipp Emanuel Bach, German musician and composer.

Born 1788

Jan. 22	Lord Byron, poet.
Feb. 5	Sir Robert Peel, Tory statesman and founder of the Metropolitan Police.
Feb. 22	Arthur Schopenhauer, German philosopher.
Sept. 30	Lord Raglan, army officer.

Died 1688

Aug. 31	John Bunyan, religious writer.

Born 1688

Jan. 29	Emanuel Swedenborg, Swedish scientist, philosopher and theologian.
May 21	Alexander Pope, poet.
June 10	James Stuart, the Old Pretender.

Died 1588

*	Paulo Veronese, Italian painter.

Born 1588

April 5	Thomas Hobbes, philosopher.

Died 988

*	St. Dunstan.

Events 1888

March	English Football League formed.
Nov. or Dec.*	Petrol car first run by Karl Benz.
Dec 7	Bicycle tyres (pneumatic) patented by John Boyd Dunlop.

*	Ball-point pen invented by an American, John Loud.
*	Electric motor (AC) invented by Nikola Tesla.
*	Photography, on film, invented by John Carbutt of U.S.A. (also Kodak by George Eastman).

Events 1588

July 29	Spanish Armada defeated.

*Exact date unknown.

THE CENTENARIES OF 1989

Died 1889

March 27	John Bright, statesman and orator.
Sept. 23	Wilkie Collins, novelist.
Oct. 11	James Joule, physicist.
Dec. 12	Robert Browning, poet.

Born 1889

Feb. 22	Olave, Lady Baden-Powell.
April 2	Sir Neville Cardus, music critic and cricket writer.
April 8	Sir Adrian Boult, conductor.
April 14	Arnold Toynbee, writer and historian.
April 16	Sir Charles Chaplin, actor.
April 20	Adolf Hitler.
April 24	Sir Stafford Cripps, Labour statesman.
May 11	Paul Nash, artist.
July 5	Jean Cocteau, French writer.
Nov. 14	Jawaharlal Nehru.
Dec. 25	Humphrey Bogart, American actor.

Born 1789

Sept. 15	James Fenimore Cooper, American novelist.
Nov. 18	Louis Daguerre, French painter and pioneering photographer.

Died 1689

April 18	Judge George Jeffreys.

Died 1589

Jan. 5	Catherine de Medici, Queen of France 1547–1559.

Born 1489

July 2	Archbishop Thomas Cranmer.

Died 1189

July 6	Henry II.

Events 1889

March 31	Eiffel Tower completed.
Nov. 15	Brazil declared a Republic.

Events 1789

April 28	Mutiny on the *Bounty*.
July 14	Storming of the Bastille.

Events 1689

Feb. 13	Accession of William III and Mary II.
Dec.*	Bill of Rights.

PRIME MINISTERS AND SPEAKERS

PRIME MINISTERS SINCE 1782

Marquess of Rockingham, *Whig*, March 27, 1782.
Earl of Shelburne, *Whig*, July 13, 1782.
Duke of Portland, *Coalition*, April 4, 1783.
William Pitt, *Tory*, Dec. 7, 1783.
Henry Addington, *Tory*, March 21, 1801.
William Pitt, *Tory*, May 16, 1804.
Lord Grenville, *Whig*, Feb. 10, 1806.
Duke of Portland, *Tory*, March 31, 1807.
Spencer Perceval, *Tory*, Dec. 6, 1809.
Earl of Liverpool, *Tory*, June 16, 1812.
George Canning, *Tory*, April 30, 1827.
Viscount Goderich, *Tory*, Sept. 8, 1827.
Duke of Wellington, *Tory*, Jan. 26, 1828.
Earl Grey, *Whig*, Nov. 24, 1830.
Viscount Melbourne, *Whig*, July 13, 1834.
Sir Robert Peel, *Tory*, Dec. 26, 1834.
Viscount Melbourne, *Whig*, March 18, 1835.
Sir Robert Peel, *Tory*, Sept. 6, 1841.
Lord John Russell, *Whig*, July 6, 1846.
Earl of Derby, *Tory*, Feb. 28, 1852.
Earl of Aberdeen, *Peelite*, Dec. 28, 1852.
Viscount Palmerston, *Liberal*, Feb. 10, 1855.
Earl of Derby, *Conservative*, Feb. 25, 1858.
Viscount Palmerston, *Liberal*, June 18, 1859.
Earl Russell, *Liberal*, Nov. 6, 1865.
Earl of Derby, *Conservative*, July 6, 1866.
Benjamin Disraeli, *Conservative*, Feb. 27, 1868.
W. E. Gladstone, *Liberal*, Dec. 9, 1868.
Benjamin Disraeli, *Conservative*, Feb. 21, 1874.
W. E. Gladstone, *Liberal*, April 28, 1880.
Marquess of Salisbury, *Conservative*, June 24, 1885.
W. E. Gladstone, *Liberal*, Feb. 6, 1886.
Marquess of Salisbury, *Conservative*, Aug. 3, 1886.
W. E. Gladstone, *Liberal*, Aug. 18, 1892.
Earl of Rosebery, *Liberal*, March 3, 1894.
Marquess of Salisbury, *Conservative*, July 2, 1895.
A. J. Balfour, *Conservative*, July 12, 1902.
Sir H. Campbell-Bannerman, *Liberal*, Dec. 5, 1905.
H. H. Asquith, *Liberal*, April 8, 1908.
H. H. Asquith, *Coalition*, May 26, 1915.
D. Lloyd-George, *Coalition*, Dec. 7, 1916.
A. Bonar Law, *Conservative*, Oct. 23, 1922.
S. Baldwin, *Conservative*, May 22, 1923.
J. R. MacDonald, *Labour*, Jan. 22, 1924.
S. Baldwin, *Conservative*, Nov. 4, 1924.
J. R. MacDonald, *Labour*, June 8, 1929.
J. R. MacDonald, *Coalition*, Aug. 25, 1931.
S. Baldwin, *Coalition*, June 7, 1935.
N. Chamberlain, *Coalition*, May 28, 1937.
W. S. Churchill, *Coalition*, May 11, 1940.
W. S. Churchill, *Conservative*, May 23, 1945.
C. R. Attlee, *Labour*, July 26, 1945.
Sir W. S. Churchill, *Conservative*, Oct. 26, 1951.
Sir A. Eden, *Conservative*, April 6, 1955.
H. Macmillan, *Conservative*, Jan. 13, 1957.
Sir A. Douglas-Home, *Conservative*, Oct. 19, 1963.
J. H. Wilson, *Labour*, Oct. 16, 1964.
E. R. G. Heath, *Conservative*, June 19, 1970.

J. H. Wilson, *Labour*, March 4, 1974.
L. J. Callaghan, *Labour*, April 5, 1976.
Mrs. M. H. Thatcher, *Conservative*, May 4, 1979.

SPEAKERS OF THE COMMONS SINCE 1660

PARLIAMENT OF ENGLAND

1660 Sir Harbottle Grimston.
1661 Sir Edward Turner.
1673 Sir Job Charlton.
1673 Sir Edward Seymour.
1678 Sir Robert Sawyer.
1679 Sir William Gregory.
1680 Sir William Williams.
1685 Sir John Trevor.
1688 Henry Powle.
1694 Paul Foley.
1698 Sir Thomas Lyttelton.
1700 Robert Harley (*Earl of Oxford and Mortimer*).
1702 John Smith.

PARLIAMENT OF GREAT BRITAIN

1708 Sir Richard Onslow (*Lord Onslow*).
1710 William Bromley.
1713 Sir Thomas Hanmer.
1715 Spencer Compton (*Earl of Wilmington*).
1727 Arthur Onslow.
1761 Sir John Cust.
1770 Sir Fletcher Norton.
1780 Charles Cornwall.
1788 Hon. William Grenvill (*Lord Grenville*).
1789 Henry Addington (*Viscount Sidmouth*).

PARLIAMENT OF UNITED KINGDOM

1801 Sir John Mitford (*Lord Redesdale*).
1802 Charles Abbot (*Lord Colchester*).
1817 Charles M. Sutton (*Viscount Canterbury*).
1835 James Abercromby (*Lord Dunfermline*).
1839 Charles Shaw-Lefevre (*Viscount Eversley*).
1857 J. Evelyn Denison (*Viscount Ossington*).
1872 Sir Henry Brand (*Viscount Hampden*).
1884 Arthur Wellesley Peel (*Viscount Peel*).
1895 William Court Gully (*Viscount Selby*).
1905 James W. Lowther (*Viscount Ullswater*).
1921 John Henry Whitley.
1928 Hon. Edward Algernon FitzRoy.
1943 Col. D. Clifton Brown (*Viscount Ruffside*).
1951 William Shepherd Morrison (*Viscount Dunrossil*).
1959 Sir Harry Hylton-Foster.
1965 Horace Maybray King, PH.D. (*Lord Maybray-King*).
1971 (John) Selwyn (Brooke) Lloyd (*Lord Selwyn-Lloyd*).
1976 (Thomas) George Thomas (*Viscount Tonypandy*).
1983 (Bruce) Bernard Weatherill.

HOME FINANCE

Central government financial transactions

£ million

	Consolidated Fund			National Loans Fund				Central government borrowing requirement
					Other transactions			
	Revenue	Expenditure	Consolidated fund deficit	Receipts	Payments	Deficit	Other funds and accounts	
1983	86,610	−96,257	−9,647	11,511	−16,201	−14,337	−165	−14,502
1984	95,194	−103,385	−8,191	12,799	−14,844	−10,236	71	−10,165
1985	104,193	−110,497	−6,304	13,899	−19,226	−11,631	−142	−11,773
1986	110,867	−113,305	−2,438	14,984	−20,397	−7,851	−594	−8,445
Financial years								
1984–85	98,247	−105,608	−7,361	12,916	−15,418	9,863	−237	−10,100
1985–86	106,132	−110,127	−3,995	14,213	−20,592	10,374	−564	−10,938
1986–87	111,211	−116,451	−5,240	15,614	−21,251	10,877	327	−10,550
1987 1st quarter..	32,877	−32,024	853	4,671	−6,861	1,337	72	1,265
2nd quarter .	26,492	−29,068	−2,576	3,377	−5,747	4,946		
1986 July........	10,138	−10,031	107	1,835	−2,038	96	−169	265
August	9,435	−8,433	1,002	1,123	−1,045	−1,080	−2,217	1,137
September ..	6,761	−9,880	−3,119	1,311	−1,554	3,362	791	2,571
October....	10,178	−9,365	813	1,154	−1,146	−821	−656	−165
November ..	8,819	−9,123	−304	1,523	−1,300	81	−440	521
December ..	10,537	−9,506	−1,031	612	−751	−892	538	−1,430
1987 January ...	14,348	−9,688	−4,660	258	−2,086	−2,832	451	−3,283
February ...	8,753	−8,387	366	450	−1,406	590	393	197
March	9,776	−13,949	−4,173	3,963	−3,369	3,579	−772	4,351
April	8,603	−11,177	−2,574	1,075	−2,082	3,581	1,110	2,471
May	8,657	−9,141	−484	1,628	−2,572	1,428	−219	1,647
June	9,232	−8,750	482	674	−1,093	−63		

Public sector borrowing requirement

£ million

	Total		Contributions by			Financed by				
						Non-bank private sector		Monetary sector	Overseas sector	
									External finance	
	Unadjusted	Seasonally adjusted†	Central government*	Local authorities	Public corporations	Notes and coin	Other	Borrowing in sterling from banks	Foreign currency borrowing from banks	Direct external finance
1983	11,628		14,502	−2,449	−425	670	11,529	−2,039	115	1,457
1984	10,213		10,165	−470	518	281	8,067	892	293	1,376
1985	7,522		11,773	−3,378	−873	587	7,870	−2,092	403	1,429
1986	2,210		8,445	−5,227	−1,008	652	4,394	−960	44	555
Financial years										
1984–85........	10,172		10,100	−944	1,016	619	15,024	−4,379	417	−709
1985–86........	5,758		10,938	−4,071	−1,109	467	3,277	1,841	316	751
1986–87........	3,341		10,550	−5,678	−1,518	−297	4,825	712	61	903
1986 1st quarter	−1,885	1,333	−840	−962	−83	310	2,384	−2,164	1	−2,148
2nd quarter	2,171	2,084	6,386	−3,519	−696	−496	1,673	534	−69	2,154
3rd quarter	3,577	2,487	3,973	−82	−314	−66	3,793	481	203	−793
4th quarter	−1,653	−2,514	−1,074	−664	85	904	−3,456	189	−91	1,342
1987 1st quarter	−754	1,361	1,265	−1,413	−593	−639	2,815	−492	18	−1,800

†Financial year constrained.   *An increase in debt is shown positive.

BALANCE OF PAYMENTS OF THE UNITED KINGDOM (£ million)

	1980	1981	1982	1983	1984	1985
Current account						
Visible trade						
Exports (fob)	47,422	50,977	55,565	60,776	70,367	78,051
Imports (fob)	46,061	47,617	52,234	61,611	74,751	80,162
Visible balance	1,361	3,360	2,331	−835	−4,384	−2,111
Invisibles						
Credits	41,008	56,635	64,592	65,224	76,737	80,608
Debits	39,440	53,836	62,986	61,255	71,141	74,895
Invisibles balance	1,568	2,799	1,606	3,969	5,596	5,713
Services balance	*3,868*	*3,826*	*2,607*	*3,652*	*3,744*	*5,812*
Interest, profits and dividends balance	*−222*	*949*	*960*	*2,421*	*4,157*	*3,400*
Transfers balance	*−2,078*	*−1,976*	*−1,961*	*−2,104*	*−2,305*	*−3,499*
Current balance	2,929	6,159	3,937	3,134	1,212	3,602
Transactions in external assets and liabilities*						
Investment overseas by UK residents						
Direct	−4,926	−6,094	−4,322	−5,301	−5,957	−7,307
Portfolio	−3,230	−4,300	−6,720	−6,520	−9,550	−18,220
Total UK investment overseas	−8,156	−10,394	−11,042	−11,821	−15,507	−25,527
Investment in the UK by overseas residents						
Direct	4,355	2,932	2,964	3,438	425	3,370
Portfolio	1,499	323	225	1,888	1,419	7,065
Total overseas investment in U.K.	5,854	3,255	3,189	5,326	1,844	10,435
Foreign currency lending abroad by UK banks	−30,010	−37,164	−16,539	−16,100	−9,135	−20,286
Foreign currency borrowing abroad by UK banks	30,505	36,763	19,904	17,184	18,693	25,402
Net foreign currency transactions of UK banks	495	−401	3,365	1,084	9,558	5,116
Sterling lending abroad by UK banks	−2,810	−2,987	−4,019	−2,232	−4,933	−1,573
Sterling borrowing and deposit liabilities abroad of UK banks	3,044	2,497	4,421	3,946	6,133	4,171
Net sterling transactions of UK banks	234	−490	402	1,174	1,200	2,598
Deposit with and lending to banks abroad by UK non-bank private sector	−1,042	−494	−1,242	−1,279	1,264	−3,760
Borrowing from banks abroad by:						
UK non-bank private sector	107	715	504	372	−2,289	2,283
Public corporations	−15	−178	−35	−35	−47	64
General government	−40	−192	57	77	48	87
Official reserves (additions to − drawings on +)	−291	2,419	1,421	607	908	1,758
Other external assets of:						
UK non-bank private sector and public corporations	−183	−1,054	559	488	−3,110	3,613
General government	351	93	−161	−478	−743	−730
Other external liabilities of:						
UK non-bank private sector and public corporations	301	224	116	−75	634	343
General government	−553	−13	350	−653	−96	−60
Net transactions in assets and liabilities	−2,938	−6,510	−2,517	−4,673	−6,336	−7,296
Allocation of special drawing rights	180	158	—	—	—	—
Balancing item	−171	193	−1,420	1,539	5,124	3,694

* Assets: increase −/decrease +. Liabilities: increase +/decrease−.

GROSS DOMESTIC PRODUCT BY INDUSTRY

(Before depreciation but after stock appreciation) £ million

	1975	1980	1981	1982	1983	1984	1985
Agriculture, forestry and fishing	2,507	4,192	4,696	5,395	5,373	5,971	5,485
Energy and water supply	5,041	20,098	24,081	26,917	30,657	30,952	34,335
Manufacturing (revised definition)	27,638	53,833	54,952	59,433	63,504	69,545	76,800
Construction	6,299	12,343	12,985	13,906	15,507	17,296	18,651
Distribution; hotels and catering; repairs	11,927	24,737	26,804	29,029	32,514	36,014	40,384
Transport	5,263	9,541	10,000	10,499	11,375	12,232	12,913
Communication	2,509	4,728	5,558	6,417	6,521	7,308	8,044
Banking, finance, insurance, business services and leasing	10,010	23,140	25,724	29,478	32,480	36,960	42,473
Ownership of dwellings	5,589	12,118	13,684	15,026	15,735	16,455	17,775
Public administration, national defence and compulsory social security	7,321	14,717	16,467	17,623	18,999	20,291	21,599
Education and health services	9,012	17,530	19,719	20,672	22,961	24,343	26,187
Other services	5,000	10,760	11,926	13,183	14,954	16,363	17,978
Total	98,116	207,737	226,776	247,578	270,580	293,730	322,624
Adjustment for financial services	−3,374	−8,268	−9,788	−10,440	−11,351	−13,601	−16,883
Residual error	1,061	137	826	−1,762	−957	−4,734	−3,276
Gross domestic product at factor cost (income-based)	94,742	199,469	216,988	237,138	259,229	280,129	305,741

GENERAL GOVERNMENT CURRENT ACCOUNT

£ million

	1975	1980	1981	1982	1983	1984	1985
Receipts							
Taxes on income	16,758	30,862	36,022	40,526	43,177	46,940	51,959
Taxes on expenditure	14,036	36,441	42,492	46,641	49,113	52,496	56,812
Social security contributions	6,848	13,944	15,923	18,106	20,767	22,314	24,068
Gross trading surplus	126	171	209	180	36	−81	264
Rent, dividends and interest, etc.	3,538	8,015	8,987	10,190	9,800	10,396	11,733
Miscellaneous current transfers	73	164	164	184	214	223	206
Imputed charge for consumption of non-trading capital	778	1,746	1,945	2,014	2,071	2,167	2,321
Total	42,157	91,343	105,742	117,841	125,178	134,455	147,363
Expenditure							
Final consumption	23,131	48,936	55,358	60,478	65,932	69,886	74,012
Subsidies	3,686	5,718	6,416	5,862	6,333	7,723	7,710
National insurance benefits	6,376	14,405	17,170	18,679	20,008	21,356	22,426
Other current grants to personal sector	3,887	11,111	13,958	17,753	19,628	21,405	23,701
Current grants paid abroad (net)	337	1,782	1,634	1,801	1,956	2,129	3,362
Debt interest	4,127	10,872	12,708	13,985	14,179	15,743	17,526
Total current expenditure	41,544	92,824	107,244	118,558	128,036	138,242	148,737
Balance: current surplus*	613	−1,481	−1,502	−717	−2,858	−3,787	−1,374
Total	42,157	91,343	105,742	117,841	125,178	134,455	147,363

* Before depreciation.

GROSS NATIONAL PRODUCT
By Category of Expenditure
£ million

	1980	1981	1982	1983	1984	1985
Expenditure at market prices						
Consumers' expenditure	137,234	152,544	167,362	182,877	195,711	213,208
General government final consumption	48,936	55,358	60,478	65,932	69,886	74,012
of which: Central government	29,993	33,873	37,126	40,770	43,350	45,975
Local authorities	18,943	21,485	23,352	25,162	26,536	28,037
Gross domestic fixed capital formation	41,774	41,612	44,683	48,775	55,567	60,118
Value of physical increase in stocks and work in progress	−2,844	−2,810	−1,306	651	−356	528
Total domestic expenditure	225,100	246,704	271,217	298,235	320,808	347,866
Exports of goods and services	63,097	67,861	73,060	80,399	91,750	102,304
Total final expenditure	288,197	314,565	344,277	378,634	412,558	450,170
less imports of goods and services[1]	−57,868	−60,675	−68,122	−77,582	−92,390	−98,603
Gross domestic product at market prices[2]	230,329	253,890	276,155	301,052	320,168	351,567
less Taxes on expenditure	−36,441	−42,492	−46,641	−49,113	−52,496	−56,812
plus Subsidies	5,718	6,416	5,862	6,333	7,723	7,710
Gross domestic product at factor cost[2]	199,606	217,814	235,376	258,272	275,395	302,465
Factor incomes						
Income from employment	137,352	148,181	158,415	170,063	180,348	195,350
Income from self-employment[3]	17,900	19,380	21,392	23,932	27,013	29,859
Gross trading profits of companies[3,4]	28,759	29,360	32,470	39,713	48,399	52,977
Gross trading surplus of public corporations[3]	6,162	7,821	9,389	9,948	8,336	7,106
Gross trading surplus of general government enterprises[3]	171	209	180	36	−81	264
Rent[5]	13,836	15,858	17,312	18,143	19,026	20,541
Imputed charge for consumption of non-trading capital	2,015	2,246	2,325	2,392	2,503	2,681
Total domestic income[3]	206,195	223,055	241,483	264,227	285,544	308,778
less Stock appreciation	−6,726	−6,067	−4,345	−4,998	−5,415	−3,037
Gross domestic product (income-based)	199,469	216,988	237,138	259,229	280,129	305,741
Residual error	137	826	−1,762	−957	−4,734	−3,276
Net property income from abroad	−222	949	960	2,421	4,157	3,400
Gross national product at factor cost	199,384	218,763	236,336	260,693	279,552	305,865
less Capital consumption	−28,180	−31,837	−33,813	−36,141	−38,576	−41,846
National income (i.e. net national product)	171,204	186,926	202,523	224,552	240,976	264,019

1. Excluding taxes on expenditure levied on imports. 4. Including financial institutions.
2. Including taxes on expenditure levied on imports. 5. Before providing for depreciation.
3. Before providing for depreciation and stock appreciation.

CONSUMERS' EXPENDITURE

£ million

	Total consu- mers' expen- diture	Durable goods				Other goods								Services	
		Total	Cars, motor cycles and other vehi- cles	Furn- iture and floor cover- ings	Other dur- able goods	Food (house- hold expen- diture)	Beer	Other alco- holic drink	Tobac- co	Cloth- ing other than foot- wear	Foot- wear	Energy prod- ucts	Other goods	Rent, rates and water char- ges	Other ser- vices
At current prices															
1981	152,847	13,983	6,556	3,548	3,879	24,207	5,971	5,181	5,515	8,315	1,844	13,422	15,603	19,445	39,361
1982	167,381	15,341	7,222	3,701	4,418	25,649	6,450	5,553	5,881	8,856	2,068	15,027	16,919	22,422	43,215
1983	182,598	17,880	8,754	3,965	5,161	27,385	7,138	6,232	6,209	9,860	2,314	16,312	18,455	23,535	47,278
1984	195,341	18,638	8,778	4,140	5,720	28,642	7,734	6,696	6,622	10,778	2,548	17,025	20,347	24,805	51,506
1985	213,168	21,026	10,253	4,353	6,420	29,950	8,416	7,367	7,006	12,127	2,767	18,629	22,552	26,989	56,339
1986	232,013	23,251	11,327	4,611	7,313	32,038	8,849	7,625	7,471	13,443	2,946	18,474	24,873	29,133	63,910
Unadjusted															
1986 1st quarter	54,376	5,699	2,952	1,101	1,646	7,529	1,938	1,403	1,759	2,709	575	5,714	5,333	7,023	14,694
2nd quarter	56,250	5,415	2,873	1,035	1,507	7,982	2,268	1,637	1,877	3,036	733	4,121	5,794	7,300	16,087
3rd quarter	59,410	6,486	3,669	1,114	1,703	8,146	2,351	1,747	1,899	3,193	741	3,748	6,081	7,372	17,646
4th quarter	61,977	5,651	1,833	1,361	2,457	8,381	2,292	2,838	1,936	4,505	897	4,891	7,665	7,438	15,483
1987 1st quarter	57,867	6,390	3,443	1,185	1,762	7,720	1,978	1,451	1,876	2,900	596	5,637	5,853	7,641	15,825
Revalued at 1980 prices															
1981	137,211	13,687	6,521	3,386	3,780	22,713	5,000	4,612	4,471	8,101	1,687	11,039	14,465	16,236	35,200
1982	138,277	14,370	6,680	3,427	4,263	22,642	4,825	4,545	4,128	8,333	1,812	11,097	14,712	16,489	35,324
1983	143,603	16,461	7,958	3,559	4,944	23,109	4,913	4,817	4,082	8,940	1,952	11,203	15,065	16,699	36,362
1984	146,657	16,629	7,561	3,535	5,533	22,891	4,943	5,040	3,943	9,496	2,065	11,329	15,849	16,948	37,524
1985	151,986	17,844	8,032	3,594	6,218	23,197	4,934	5,290	3,837	10,250	2,128	11,840	16,465	17,113	39,088
1986	159,715	19,383	8,355	3,671	7,357	23,906	4,935	5,362	3,731	11,094	2,185	12,317	17,448	17,284	42,070
Unadjusted															
1986 1st quarter	37,622	4,720	2,230	894	1,596	5,682	1,094	984	933	2,268	433	3,604	3,764	4,303	9,837
2nd quarter	38,655	4,449	2,134	821	1,494	5,990	1,276	1,157	928	2,532	547	2,831	4,072	4,312	10,561
3rd quarter	40,651	5,285	2,662	892	1,731	6,072	1,308	1,224	928	2,643	549	2,627	4,266	4,326	11,423
4th quarter	42,787	4,929	1,329	1,064	2,536	6,162	1,257	1,997	942	3,651	656	3,255	5,346	4,343	10,249
1987 1st quarter	38,974	5,181	2,451	939	1,791	5,618	1,083	1,002	909	2,379	435	3,601	4,052	4,365	10,349
Seasonally ad- justed															
1986 1st quarter	39,128	4,523	1,957	893	1,673	5,905	1,202	1,311	943	2,686	538	3,108	4,206	4,303	10,403
2nd quarter	39,811	4,832	2,125	902	1,805	5,970	1,253	1,329	942	2,741	548	3,076	4,285	4,312	10,523
3rd quarter	40,396	5,078	2,238	939	1,901	6,066	1,230	1,352	924	2,818	547	3,080	4,452	4,326	10,523
4th quarter	40,380	4,950	2,035	937	1,978	5,965	1,250	1,370	922	2,849	552	3,053	4,505	4,343	10,621
1987 1st quarter	40,513	4,950	2,144	938	1,868	5,857	1,189	1,332	919	2,809	541	3,109	4,526	4,365	10,916

PERSONAL INCOME AND EXPENDITURE (£ million)

	1980	1981	1982	1983	1984	1985
Income before tax						
Income from employment:						
Wages and salaries	116,790	124,996	133,877	143,524	152,908	166,302
Pay in cash and kind of HM Forces	2,436	2,689	2,905	3,121	3,288	3,509
Total............................	119,226	127,685	136,782	146,645	156,196	169,811
Employers' contributions:						
National insurance, etc.	8,210	8,814	9,344	10,523	11,263	12,133
Other	9,916	11,682	12,289	12,895	12,889	13,406
Total income from employment ...	137,352	148,181	158,415	170,063	180,348	195,350
Income from self-employment:						
After deducting stock						
appreciation	17,105	18,747	21,029	23,446	26,663	29,394
Stock appreciation	795	633	363	486	350	465
Total............................	17,900	19,380	21,392	23,932	27,013	29,859
Rent, dividends and net interest:						
Receipts by life assurance and						
pension schemes	7,790	8,758	10,319	11,556	13,840	15,647
Imputed rent of owner-occupied						
dwellings.....................	7,830	9,114	10,173	11,011	11,723	12,778
Other receipts, net	4,811	4,313	4,865	4,016	3,233	2,157
Total............................	20,431	22,185	25,357	26,583	28,796	30,582
Social security benefits and other						
current grants from general						
government	25,516	31,128	36,432	39,636	42,761	46,127
Current transfers from overseas	842	956	1,134	1,315	1,428	1,511
Current transfers to charities from						
companies	52	62	69	86	105	119
Imputed charge for capital consump-						
tion of private non-profit making						
bodies..........................	269	301	311	321	336	360
Total personal income	202,362	222,193	243,110	261,936	280,787	303,908
Deductions from income						
UK taxes on income	25,544	28,738	31,494	32,909	35,006	38,205
Social security contributions	13,944	15,923	18,106	20,767	22,314	24,068
Current transfers abroad	1,138	1,298	1,294	1,463	1,604	1,648
Miscellaneous current transfers	164	164	184	214	223	206
Personal disposable income	161,572	176,070	192,032	206,583	221,640	239,781
Expenditure						
Consumers' expenditure	137,234	152,544	167,362	182,877	195,711	213,208
Balance saving.....................	24,338	23,526	24,670	23,706	25,929	26,573
Total............................	161,572	176,070	192,032	206,583	221,640	239,781
Memorandum items						
Saving ratio (per cent)	*15.1*	*13.4*	*12.8*	*11.5*	*11.7*	*11.1*
Real personal disposable income:						
At 1980 prices	161,572	158,055	158,573	162,430	166,349	170,987
1980 = 100......................	100.0	97.8	98.1	100.5	103.0	105.8

INSOLVENCY

Bankruptcies, etc.

	England and Wales				Northern Ireland			
	1982	1983	1984	1985	1982	1983	1984	1985
Number of bankruptcies, etc.								
Debtors adjudicated bankrupt	5,303	6,555	7,714	6,340	56	76	86	117
Compositions and schemes of arrangement	2	4	3	4	17	12	10	10
Administration orders of deceased debtors' estates	14	17	9	14	—	2	1	2
Liabilities (£ thousand)								
Debtors adjudicated bankrupt	210,615	226,277	556,484	337,090	2,171	4,650	4,010	7,389
Compositions and schemes of arrangement	39	81	149	27	892	533	662	882
Administration orders of deceased debtors' estates	380	709	2,299	364	—	342	54	90
Assets (£ thousand)								
Debtors adjudicated bankrupt	34,464	54,117	102,280	83,910	497	1,376	942	3,197
Compositions and schemes of arrangement	43	47	28	84	352	127	195	395
Administration orders of deceased debtors' estates	135	225	1,350	179	—	244	16	514

Sequestrations (bankruptcies) in Scotland

	1975	1980	1981	1982	1983	1984	1985
Number of sequestrations	89	111	117	144	174	197	160
Liabilities (£ thousand)	3,461	4,843	12,266	9,757	18,434	11,055	13,093
Assets (£ thousand)	1,305	2,060	4,228	3,975	5,601	3,100	2,322

Company Liquidations

Number

	1975	1980	1981	1982	1983	1984	1985
England and Wales							
Compulsory liquidations	2,287	2,935	2,771	3,745	4,807	5,260	5,761
Voluntary liquidations:							
Creditors'	3,111	3,955	5,825	8,322	8,599	8,461	9,137
Members'	3,917	3,970	3,638	3,908	3,808	3,772	3,946
Total liquidations notified (all types)	9,315	10,860	12,234	15,975	17,214	17,493	18,844
Scotland							
Compulsory liquidations	53	135	158	177	263	272	306
Voluntary liquidations:							
Creditors'	151	244	280	326	258	251	231
Members'	276	242	248	253	243	234	233
Total liquidations notified (all types)	480	621	686	756	764	757	770
Northern Ireland							
Compulsory liquidations	3	8	16	10	15	19	36
Voluntary liquidations:							
Creditors'	15	66	83	111	96	64	75
Members'	36	39	39	41	52	60	69
Total liquidations notified (all types)	54	113	138	162	163	143	180

AGRICULTURE

Estimated quantity of crops and grass harvested (thousand tonnes)

	1975	1980	1981	1982	1983	1984	1985*
Cereals							
Wheat	4,490	8,470	8,710	10,320	10,800	14,970	12,050
Barley	8,510	10,325	10,230	10,960	9,980	11,070	9,740
Oats	795	600	620	575	465	515	615
Mixed corn for threshing	120	60	44	39	35	35	31
Rye for threshing	19	24	25	25	24	28	35
Maize for threshing†	3	†	†	†	†	†	†
Potatoes							
Early crop	350	455	375	430	320	395	405
Main crop	4,201	6,650	5,840	6,445	5,565	7,000	6,490
Fodder crops							
Beans for stockfeeding	95	149	123	122	105	125	155
Turnips and swedes‡	6,035	5,065	4,795	4,575	3,655	3,960	3,300
Fodder beet and mangolds‡	411	370	320	370	295	570	815
Maize for threshing or stockfeeding†	884	785	635	635	550	580	770
Rape for stockfeeding	618	} 2,115	2,195	1,985	1,660	1,805	1,555
Kale, cabbage, savoys and kohl rabi	2,607						
Peas harvested dry for stockfeeding	—	—	—	—	85	170	215
Other crops							
Sugar beet	4,864	7,380	7,395	10,005	7,495	9,015	7,715
Rape grown for oilseed	61	300	325	581	565	925	895
Hops	8	10	9	10	9	8	6
Hay							
From all grasses under five years old	3,757	} 6,945	6,780	6,580	5,980	5,700	4,650
From all grasses five years old and over	3,120						
Horticultural crops							
Vegetables grown in the open:							
Brussels sprouts	162	228	197	223	154	169	154
Cabbage (including savoys and							
spring greens)	555	576	546	610	518	671	685
Cauliflowers	293	367	325	353	299	344	367
Carrots	573	553	711	723	554	572	627
Parsnips	45	54	53	55	51	57	62
Turnips and swedes	150	163	109	145	135	143	160
Beetroot	103	109	97	105	94	115	113
Onions, dry bulb	221	224	232	232	175	238	230
Onions, salad	25	26	25	25	25	22	27
Leeks	24	40	40	43	44	53	56
Broad beans	18	18	17	19	17	21	21
Runner beans including French	92	62	69	92	65	77	67
Peas, green for market	34	18	25	28	23	27	22
Peas, green for processing	263	223	277	238	198	241	206
Celery	69	54	50	51	46	57	56
Lettuce	123	135	134	161	155	193	195
Rhubarb	40	43	41	39	29	26	27
Protected crops							
Tomatoes	123	129	125	118	118	129	124
Cucumbers	47	57	54	56	61	59	59
Lettuce	29	36	37	45	49	48	49
Fruit crops							
Total dessert apples	242	178	152	216	186	184	164
Cooking apples	136	179	80	147	126	163	136
Pears	28	44	49	40	54	48	51
Plums	19	47	16	34	36	34	24
Cherries	7	7	3	7	3	5	5
Soft Fruit	100	110	105	109	124	115	109

*Provisional figures.
†From 1979 maize for threshing is included with maize for threshing or stock feeding.
‡Before 1977 fodder beet was included with turnips and swedes for stock feeding.

Cattle, Sheep, Pigs and Poultry on Agricultural Holdings

Thousands

At June	1975	1980	1981	1982	1983	1984	1985
Cattle and calves: total	14,717	13,426	13,138	13,244	13,290	13,213	12,865
Dairy herd	3,242	3,228	3,191	3,250	3,333	3,281	3,150
Beef herd	1,899	1,478	1,420	1,389	1,358	1,351	1,333
Heifers in calf (first calf)	903	838	863	851	847	811	828
Bulls for service	97	86	84	84	83	80	78
Other cattle:							
Two years old and over	987	1,005	963	937	904	905	852
One year old and under two	3,559	3,153	3,041	3,057	3,059	3,069	3,012
Six months old and under one year	2,062	1,866	1,876	1,890	1,924	1,949	1,905
Under six months old	1,968	1,770	1,699	1,786	1,783	1,768	1,707
Sheep and lambs: total	28,270	31,446	32,097	33,067	34,069	34,802	35,628
Breeding ewes	11,279	12,178	12,528	12,909	13,310	13,648	13,893
Rams for service	326	353	358	366	383	393	406
Other sheep	3,442	3,672	3,584	3,748	3,764	3,680	3,763
Lambs under one year old	13,222	15,243	15,628	16,044	16,612	17,080	17,566
Pigs: total	7,532	7,815	7,828	8,023	8,174	7,689	7,865
Breeding herd	814	831	836	864	856	800	828
Boars for service	40	42	43	45	45	42	44
Gilts not yet in pig	87	84	87	89	82	77	80
Barren sows for fattening	14	12	11	12	15	12	12
Other pigs:							
110 kg and over	79	102	90	117	100	91	89
80 kg and under 110 kg	611	657	638	630	605	599	589
50 kg and under 80 kg	1,697	1,772	1,776	1,824	1,868	1,787	1,813
20 kg and under 50 kg	2,255	2,240	2,227	2,281	2,362	2,198	2,260
Under 20 kg	1,935	2,074	2,119	2,163	2,241	2,082	2,151
Poultry: total	136,572	135,105	132,286	135,363	129,598	127,507	128,968
Fowls: total	130,259	127,063	122,639	126,091	119,834	118,846	119,456
Growing pullets	18,195	14,457	14,219	14,766	12,455	12,536	12,503
Laying flock	49,359	46,012	44,473	44,792	42,480	40,573	39,538
Breeding flock	5,997	6,678	6,117	6,457	6,012	6,396	6,104
Table birds	56,708	59,917	57,830	60,075	58,887	59,341	61,311
Ducks	1,201	*1,390	*1,333	*1,443	} 1,566	1,527	1,648
Geese	112	*133	*148	*157			
Turkeys	5,000	6,519	8,167	7,672	8,198	7,134	7,864

* Excludes Scotland.

Agricultural land: area

Thousand hectares

	1975	1980	1981	1982	1983	1984	1985
Total tillage	4,816	5,031	5,071	5,127	5,124	5,196	5,265
All grasses under five years old	2,138	1,965	1,911	1,859	1,846	1,794	1,796
Total arable	6,954	6,996	6,982	6,986	6,970	6,990	7,061
All grasses five years old and over	5,074	5,140	5,103	5,097	5,107	5,105	5,019
Total crops and grass	12,028	12,136	12,085	12,083	12,078	12,095	12,080
Rough grazings							
Sole rights	5,429	5,119	5,021	4,984	4,927	4,895	4,872
Common (estimated)	1,126	1,214	1,214	1,214	1,212	1,212	1,216
Woodland on agricultural holdings	225	271	277	285	292	299	312
All other land on agricultural holdings	171	214	211	217	227	218	223
Total area of agricultural land	18,978	18,953	18,808	18,783	18,735	18,720	18,703
Total area of the United Kingdom	24,105	24,088	24,089	24,088	24,088	24,088	24,085

FISHERIES

Fishing fleet

Number

At 31 December	1975	1980	1981	1982	1983	1984	1985
England and Wales							
Total fishing vessels	3,721	4,047	4,637	4,228	4,325	5,051	6,137
Trawlers	1,489	1,573	1,750	1,755	1,757	1,686	1,894
Drifters	87	87	133	88	111	114	99
Liners	610	697	794	469	499	627	741
Seiners..................................	224	236	231	219	200	184	150
Others	1,311	1,454	1,729	1,697	1,758	2,456	3,253
Scotland							
Total fishing vessels	2,678	2,514	2,370	2,233	2,214	2,180	2,198
Demersal trawl	375	359	339	315	291	244	253
Demersal pair trawl	2	38	72	70	76	104	116
Industrial trawl...........................	22	6	9	19	17	12	10
Seine net	407	320	308	296	302	291	291
Lines	359	235	208	147	112	94	83
Purse seine	23	46	43	45	42	44	45
Pelagic trawl	106	42	35	34	26	23	20
Other nets*	19	15	22	27	43	48	46
Nephrops trawl†	259	306	303	302	317	337	335
Other shellfishing†	1,106	1,147	1,031	978	988	983	999

*Gill and cod nets, drift and ring nets.
† All shellfishing methods except nephrops trawl.

Landings of fish of British taking (Great Britain)

	Landed weight (Thousand tonnes)				Value (£ thousand)			
	1980	1983	1984	1985	1980	1983	1984	1985*
Total all fish	747·6	729·6	715·1	737·7	217,092	271,807	290,220	312,564
Total wet fish	679·0	662·7	647·0	668·4	184,847	224,789	236,334	253,021
Demersal: total	376·2	416·9	383·8	388·3	156,338	198,057	207,829	221,894
Catfish	1·1	1·3	1·3	1·4	358	494	589	755
Cod	102·1	109·7	88·7	87·9	57,429	70,928	63,901	68,216
Dogfish..................	12·2	10·0	10·6	12·2	3,361	3,099	3,240	4,150
Haddock	84·7	122·6	107·4	132·1	34.069	57,351	64,192	67,649
Hake	2·1	2·0	2·3	2·5	1,831	2,162	2,573	3,602
Halibut	0·2	0·2	0·1	0·1	389	360	319	365
Lemon sole	5·4	5·9	5·7	5·7	4,839	5,493	5,970	7,130
Plaice	26·1	20·9	21·3	20·3	12,931	13,714	14,023	13,732
Redfish..................	1·4	0·3	0·4	0·2	266	73	98	75
Saithe (Coalfish)	14·5	12·2	11·7	13·8	4,540	3,387	2,671	3,725
Skate and ray	6·1	6·4	6·7	6·8	2,619	2,852	2,755	2,944
Sole.....................	1·8	2·2	2·4	2·7	4,820	5,826	6,650	9,033
Turbot	0·7	0·5	0·5	0·5	1,402	1,419	1,655	1,946
Whiting.................	52·5	51·8	55·0	41·8	15,774	16,325	21,615	16,953
Livers...................	0·1	—	—	—	4	—	—	1
Roes	0·5	0·4	0·4	0·4	324	261	278	362
Other demersal	64·7	70·5	69·3	59·9	11,383	14,313	17,300	21,256
Pelagic: total	302·8	245·8	263·1	280·1	28,509	26,732	28,505	31,127
Herring	3·1	52·2	69·7	92·1	1,195	6,694	8,812	11,063
Mackerel	253·0	174·5	185·2	172·7	24,068	18,532	18,663	18,522
Other pelagic	46·7	19·1	8·2	15·3	3,246	1,506	1,030	1,542
Total shell fish	68·6	66·9	68·2	69·4	32,245	47,018	53,884	59,542
Cockles	15·2	5·8	5·4	7·8	807	327	311	476
Crab	9·7	11·3	14·0	12·7	3,967	6,372	8,421	8,073
Lobster	0·7	1·0	1·2	1·1	3,295	5,697	7,614	7,616
Mussels	9·1	5·9	4·3	5·8	460	468	314	467
Nephrop (Norway lobster).................	12·1	17·1	18·2	20·4	13,094	20,230	21,442	27,453
Oysters	0·6	0·3	0·4	0·4	1,001	636	770	734
Shrimps	1·2	1·1	0·7	0·8	998	739	562	712
Whelks..................	1·2	1·3	2·2	1·6	259	226	456	355
Other shell fish...........	18·8	23·1	21·8	18·8	8,364	12,323	13,994	13,656

*Contains some provisional information.

MERCHANT SHIPPING

PRINCIPAL MERCHANT FLEETS OF THE WORLD. Source: *Lloyd's Register of Shipping*

Flag	1975 No.	1975 Gross Tonnage	1980 No.	1980 Gross Tonnage	1985 No.	1985 Gross Tonnage	1986 No.	1986 Gross Tonnage
Liberia	2,520	65,820,414	2,401	80,285,176	1,808	58,179,717	1,658	52,649,444
Panama	2,418	13,667,123	4,090	24,190,680	5,512	40,674,201	5,252	41,305,709
Japan	9,932	39,739,598	10,568	40,959,683	10,298	38,040,144	10,011	38,490,773
Greece	2,243	22,527,216	3,922	39,472,000	2,219	31,040,544	2,255	28,390,800
U.S.S.R.	7,652	19,235,973	8,279	23,443,534	7,154	24,745,435	6,726	24,960,888
*U.S.A.	4,346	14,586,616	5,579	18,464,271	6,447	19,517,571	6,263	18,300,337
China, People's Republic of	466	2,828,290	955	6,873,608	1,408	10,568,236	1,562	11,566,974
Taiwan	428	1,449,957	497	2,039,123	583	4,327,487	587	4,272,795
United Kingdom	3,622	33,157,422	3,181	27,135,155	2,378	14,343,512	2,256	11,567,117
Cyprus	735	3,221,070	688	2,007,490	844	8,196,056	940	10,616,809
Norway	2,706	26,153,682	2,501	22,007,490	2,219	15,338,557	2,107	9,234,630
Hong Kong	418	418,512	187	1,717,299	396	6,855,009	416	8,179,670
Italy	1,732	10,136,989	1,739	11,095,694	1,573	8,843,181	1,569	7,896,569
Korea (South)	828	1,623,532	1,428	4,344,114	1,847	7,168,940	1,837	7,932,499
Philippines	413	879,043	623	1,927,999	1,000	4,693,979	1,131	6,540,121
India	471	3,868,187	616	5,917,367	741	6,604,548	736	6,287,627
Singapore	610	3,891,902	988	7,664,229	758	6,504,582	716	6,212,287
Brazil	482	2,691,408	607	4,533,663	702	6,057,364	697	5,986,011
Bahamas	119	189,890	91	87,320	195	3,907,267	302	5,936,268
France	1,393	10,745,999	1,241	11,924,557	1,136	8,237,418	984	5,565,214
Germany, Federal Republic of	1,964	8,516,567	1,906	8,355,638	1,816	6,177,032	1,752	5,422,002
Spain	2,667	5,433,354	2,767	8,112,245	2,477	6,256,188	2,397	4,651,224
Denmark	1,371	4,478,112	1,253	5,390,365	1,070	4,942,175	1,063	4,324,135
Netherlands	1,348	5,679,413	1,263	5,723,845	1,344	4,301,324	1,334	3,657,072
Poland	696	2,817,129	642	3,639,078	781	3,515,365	749	3,423,745
Turkey	387	794,238	508	1,456,038	817	3,023,357	825	3,233,906
Romania	122	797,309	317	1,856,292	410	3,023,770	426	3,160,043
Canada	1,257	2,565,501	1,324	3,180,126	1,286	3,343,823	1,249	2,978,016
Saudi Arabia	55	180,246	214	1,589,668	398	3,137,178	380	2,911,359
Iran	135	479,718	229	1,283,629	347	2,379,967	359	2,872,613
Yugoslavia	414	1,873,482	486	2,466,574	479	2,699,302	490	2,580,924
Kuwait	172	990,857	296	2,529,491	245	2,349,904	239	2,516,614
Sweden	775	7,486,196	700	4,233,977	694	3,161,939	660	2,419,661
Belgium	252	1,368,425	290	1,809,829	344	2,400,292	355	2,388,462
Australia	419	1,205,248	497	1,642,594	652	2,088,349	673	2,117,017
Argentina	374	1,447,165	537	2,546,306	549	2,457,337	454	2,085,635
Indonesia	724	869,678	1,150	1,430,306	1,533	1,855,807	1,707	2,014,947
Malta	31	44,950	60	132,861	235	1,773,115	246	1,743,629
Malaysia	129	358,795	221	702,145	467	1,085,807	498	1,612,948
Gibraltar	11	28,850	5	2,291	79	583,270	100	1,520,246
Mexico	274	534,857	361	1,006,417	638	1,467,191	642	1,518,944
German Democratic Republic	437	1,389,000	451	1,532,197	402	1,434,428	403	1,469,927
Finland	361	2,001,618	354	2,530,091	307	1,974,008	276	1,389,903
Cayman Islands	56	49,320	200	256,715	244	413,752	282	1,385,009
Bulgaria	179	937,458	192	1,233,303	203	1,322,231	205	1,208,276
Bermuda	59	1,450,387	114	1,723,682	79	980,707	97	1,114,444
Portugal	440	1,209,701	350	1,355,989	387	1,436,992	355	1,063,020
Egypt	143	301,933	278	536,989	389	458,644	422	1,043,020
Iraq	56	310,694	142	1,465,949	148	1,011,884	149	1,016,343

* Including ships of the United States Reserve Fleet.

CLASSIFICATION WITH LLOYD'S REGISTER OF SHIPPING

Ships classed or to be classed with Lloyd's Register at 30th June, 1986, totalled 9,301, with an aggregate of over 96 million gross tonnage.

MERCHANT SHIPPING

Merchant Ships Completed in the World During 1986

Source: *Lloyd's Register of Shipping*

Country of Build	No.	Gross Tonnage	For Registration in	No.	Gross Tonnage
Japan	648	8,177,953	Japan	426	3,746,628
Korea (South)	128	3,642,495	Panama	168	2,895,018
*China, People's Republic of	25	258,456	Liberia	45	1,785,197
Taiwan	10	382,995	Hong Kong	16	737,800
Germany, Federal Republic of	79	515,394	China, People's Republic of	40	354,929
Brazil	19	429,855	Taiwan	11	339,677
Poland	43	375,305	U.S.S.R.	131	637,437
German Democratic Republic	55	361,669	Singapore	21	535,024
Denmark	46	361,492	Korea (South)	29	481,059
Yugoslavia	16	232,996	Norway	41	429,208
Finland	21	230,788	Germany, Federal Republic of	73	372,330
U.S.A.	36	223,396	Greece	23	358,589
Spain	71	167,429	Australia	38	332,873
France	23	158,451	U.S.A.	57	328,257
Netherlands	76	150,915	Netherlands	44	295,789
*Romania	10	142,000	India	40	284,699
*U.S.S.R.	30	138,101	Denmark	10	212,937
Bulgaria	9	99,059	Philippines	19	212,736
United Kingdom	36	98,895	Brazil	10	199,953
Belgium	5	90,460	Bahamas	10	191,124
Norway	44	84,639	Poland	12	186,844
Sweden	12	81,073	Iran	7	178,443
Argentina	6	70,452	Belgium	9	138,005
Portugal	13	66,175	Romania	8	120,792
Canada	10	48,085	Finland	17	120,417
India	16	39,377	France	10	116,367
Turkey	25	35,496	German Democratic Republic	11	109,569
Peru	7	34,754	Cyprus	35	94,300
Italy	20	34,388	Spain	8	84,094
Egypt	3	31,056	Sweden	37	83,586
Greece	7	21,362	United Kingdom	23	312,084
Other Countries	85	59,948	Other Countries	205	569,144
WORLD TOTAL	1,634	16,844,909	WORLD TOTAL	1,634	16,844,909

Included in the tables above is 1 steamship of 18,000 gross tonnage to be built in the U.S.S.R.

Of the steamships and motorships completed in the world during the year 3,824,970 gross tonnage (19·7%) is to be classed with Lloyd's Register.

* Information incomplete.

TRANSPORT

Goods transport in Great Britain

	1980	1981	1982	1983	1984	1985
Total tonne kilometres (thousand millions)	161·9	165·8	170·0	172·0	173·2	170·3
Road	92·4	97·1	100·0	100·4	106·9	102·1
Rail (British Rail only)	17·6	17·5	15·9	17·1	12·7	15·3
Water: seagoing*	41·4	41·5	44·4	44·2	42·8	41·3†
Water: internal	0·4	0·4	0·4	0·4	0·4	0·4
Pipelines (except gases)	10·1	9·3	9·3	9·9	10·4	11·2
Total (million tonnes)	1,689	1,634	1,676	1,697	1,674	1,707
Road	1,383	1,339	1,390	1,402	1,444	1,435
Rail (British Rail only)	154	154	142	145	79	122†
Water: seagoing*	58	57	60	60	57	54†
Water: internal	11	9	9	9	7	7
Pipelines (except gases)	83	75	78	82	88	89

*Movements between seaports in Great Britain. Excludes one-port traffic and traffic with Northern Ireland, Isle of Man and Channel Islands.
† Provisional.

Seaport traffic of Great Britain

Million gross tonnes

	1980	1981	1982	1983	1984	1985*
Foreign traffic						
Imports						
Bulk fuel traffic	63·8	53·7	49·5	42·1	60·4	58·8
Other bulk traffic	28·8	32·8	31·8	34·3	34·6	36·7
Container and roll-on traffic	20·4	21·9	23·4	26·0	28·1	29·8
Semi-bulk traffic	13·3	12·3	14·1	14·6	14·7	14·6
Conventional traffic	3·9	3·0	2·3	2·3	2·3	2·1
All imports	130·1	123·7	121·2	119·3	140·2	142·0
Exports						
Bulk fuel traffic	79·9	86·9	92·0	95·8	97·3	103·0
Other bulk traffic	14·7	16·2	15·3	16·3	18·7	17·7
Container and roll-on traffic	16·7	16·5	17·1	18·6	20·2	21·3
Semi-bulk traffic	2·7	3·6	3·0	3·5	3·6	4·1
Conventional traffic	3·3	2·7	2·9	2·1	1·8	1·9
All exports	117·2	125·8	130·3	136·3	141·7	147·9
Domestic traffic						
Bulk fuel traffic	124·5	118·4	127·9	130·7	122·7	118·5
Other bulk traffic	31·6	29·5	30·3	31·7	30·9	31·6
Container and roll-on traffic	4·6	4·5	4·9	5·8	6·2	6·6
Semi-bulk traffic	0·3	0·3	0·2	0·2	0·4	0·3
Conventional traffic	2·9	2·8	0·4	0·3	0·2	0·3
Non-oil traffic with UK offshore installations†	—	—	2·1	2·2	3·2	3·6
All domestic traffic	163·9	155·6	165·7	170·8	163·6	160·9
Total foreign and domestic traffic	411·1	405·1	417·2	426·4	445·6	450·8

*Provisional.
† Previous to 1982 included in conventional traffic.

Passenger transport in Great Britain

Thousand million passenger kilometres

	1980	1981	1982	1983	1984	1985
Total	458	463	473	485	502	519
Air (domestic scheduled services)	3	3	3	3	3	4
Rail*	35	34	31	34	35	36
Road:						
Public service vehicles	45	42	41	42	42	42
Cars and taxis	365	373	386	394	410	426
Motorcycles	6	7	7	7	7	6
Pedal cycles	4	4	5	5	5	5

*Including London Regional Transport and Passenger Transport Executive railway systems.

AIR

Air traffic between the United Kingdom and abroad*

Thousands

	1980	1981	1982	1983	1984	1985
Flights: total	506·9	495·8	511·4	518·5	566·3	579·3
United Kingdom airlines						
Scheduled services	166·1	149·7	143·5	141·9	151·3	170·8
Non-scheduled services	153·9	162.2	176·3	184·9	214·0	196·2
Overseas airlines†						
Scheduled services	157·8	152.0	154·3	155·2	160·9	172·8
Non-scheduled services	29·1	31·9	37·3	36·5	40·2	39·5
Passengers carried: total	42,644·6	43,732·0	44,131·9	46,284·9	51,154·8	52,862·7
United Kingdom airlines						
Scheduled services	13,901·0	13,559·0	12,214·7	12,140·0	13,174·2	14,854·3
Non-scheduled services	11,195·3	12,128·9	13,216·6	14,661·9	16,643·7	15,529·0
Overseas airlines†						
Scheduled services	14,900·9	15,398·8	15,520·5	16,065·6	17,623·0	18,815·6
Non-scheduled services	2,647·4	2,645·4	3,180·1	3,417·4	3,713·9	3,663·8

* Excludes travel to and from the Channel Islands.
† Includes airlines of overseas UK Territories.

Activity at civil aerodromes

	1980	1981	1982	1983	1984	1985
Movement of civil aircraft (thousands)	2,181	2,103	2,113	2,238	2,363	2,354
Commercial: total	1,046	1,028	1,072	1,243	1,179	1,205
Transport	954	927	974	1,019	1,079	1,097
Other	92	101	98	224	100	108
Non-commercial	1,135	1,075	1,041	995	1,184	1,149
Passengers handled (thousands): total	58,942	58,979	60,033	62,301	68,830	71,812
Terminal	57,823	57,771	58,778	61,099	67,572	70,434
Transit	1,119	1,208	1,255	1,202	1,258	1,377
Commercial freight handled (tonnes): total	744,244	723,709	692,693	725,897	860,629	850,268
Set down	352,133	341,932	320,604	332,162	388,292	377,127
Picked up	392,111	381,777	372,088	393,737	472,335	473,140
Mail handled (tonnes): total	98,336	106,497	118,406	124,080	136,640	145,770
Set down	44,978	50,063	55,200	56,943	61,461	64,138
Picked up	53,358	56,434	63,206	67,138	75,179	81,632

BRITISH OIL STATISTICS

(million tonnes)

	1981	1982	1983	1984	1985
Oil production†					
Land	0·2	0·3	0·3	0·3	0·4
Offshore	89·2	103·1	114·6	125·6	127·1
Refinery output	72·0	70·7	70·9	73·2	72·9
Deliveries of petroleum products for inland consumption	66·3	67·2	64·5	81·4	70·1
Exports (including re-exports):					
Crude petroleum	51·4	60·4	68·3	75·9	79·6
Refined petroleum products and process oils	13·1	14·5	15·9	16·4	18·9
Imports:					
Crude petroleum	33·1	28·3	22·8	25·0	26·9
Refined petroleum products and process oils	14·1	17·2	17·3	28·5	25·0

† Crude oil plus condensates and petroleum gases derived at onshore treatment plants.

ROADS

Highway Authorities

The powers and responsibilities of highway authorities in England and Wales are set out in the Highways Acts 1980: for Scotland there is separate legislation.

Responsibility for trunk road motorways and other trunk roads in Great Britain rests in England with the Secretary of State for Transport, in Scotland with the Secretary of State for Scotland and in Wales with the Secretary of State for Wales. The costs of construction, improvement and maintenance are paid for by central government. The highway authority for non-trunk roads in England and Wales is, in general, the county council in whose area the roads lie, and in Scotland the regional or islands council. In Northern Ireland the Northern Ireland Department of the Environment is responsible for public roads and their maintenance and construction.

Expenditure

Transport Supplementary Grant (T.S.G.) is a block grant and was introduced in England and Wales on April 1, 1975, to replace a variety of specific grants paid towards local transport expenditure.

In England grant was paid towards capital and current spending on transport by county councils and the G.L.C. from 1975–76 to 1984–85. From April 1, 1985, T.S.G. has only been paid towards capital spending on highways and the regulation of traffic, current expenditure having been subsumed by Rate Support Grant. With the abolition of the G.L.C. and the Metropolitan County Councils on April 1, 1986, grant has become payable to London Boroughs, the Common Council of the City of London and Metropolitan District Councils. In Wales, grant was also paid to the Welsh County Councils towards current and capital expenditure on transport. Since April 1982, T.S.G. became payable on capital expenditure only; current expenditure having been subsumed into the Rate Support Grant. From April 1, 1985 eligibility of new transport schemes for T.S.G. has been confined to those costing over £5 million.

Grant rates are determined by the respective Secretaries of State; for 1987–88 grant is paid at 50 per cent of expenditure accepted for grant in England and Wales. For the financial year 1987–88 local authorities in England will receive £180 million in T.S.G. In Wales local authorities will receive £21·3 million.

Total expenditure on roads (excluding New Town roads) during the financial year 1985–86 was £2,286 million in England, £397 million in Scotland and £247 million in Wales, a total of £2,930 million. Of this, some £1,029 million was spent on trunk roads and £1,901 million on principal and other roads. The amount spent on new construction and improvement of roads in the same financial year was £1,475 million.

Road Lengths (miles)
(at April 1986)

	Public Roads	Trunk Roads (incl. motorways)	*Trunk Motorways
England	165,896	6,433	1,557
Wales	20,300	1,103	75
Scotland ...	31,536	1,945	135
N. Ireland ..	14,746	369	70
U.K.	232,478	9,850	1,837

*There were in addition 63 miles of local authority motorway in England and 15 miles in Scotland.

Motorways

The network in England and Wales is based on five main routes—London–Yorkshire (M1), London–

South Wales (M4), Birmingham–Bristol–Exeter (M5), Birmingham–Carlisle (M6) and Lancashire–N. Humberside (M62). Other important motorways in use include: Medway Towns (M2); London–Basingstoke (M3); London–Cambridge (M11); Rotherham–Goole (M18); London–Folkestone (M20); London orbital route (M25); London–Oxford (M40); North Cheshire (M56); and South Humberside (M180).

Motorways in use in Scotland include: Edinburgh–Glasgow–Greenock (M8); Edinburgh–Stirling (M9); Maryville–Mollisburn (M73); Millbank–Maryville (M74); Stirling–Haggs (M80); Friarton Bridge–Perth (M85); Inverkeithing–Perth (M90), and (M80)–Kincardine Bridge (M876).

Driving Tests

The number of driving tests conducted in Great Britain in 1986 was 1,999,738, of which 48·61 per cent resulted in a pass. In addition 62,518 H.G.V./P.S.V. tests were undertaken, of which 53·43 per cent were successful. In 1986 4,187 Part I motorcycle tests were also conducted by Departmental examiners (50 per cent successful) and 43,947 by Approved Training Bodies (95 per cent successful).

Motor Vehicles

The number of vehicles in Great Britain with current licences in 1986 was:

Private and light goods	18,752,000
Motor cycles, scooters, mopeds	1,065,000
Public transport vehicles...............	125,000
Heavy goods vehicles	592,000
Agricultural tractors	371,000
Others	73,000
TOTAL	21,699,000

There were 720,000 Crown vehicles and vehicles exempt from licensing.

Buses and Coaches 1985–86
(Great Britain)

No. of vehicles (Dec.)	67,899
Buses and coaches	67,820
Tramcars	79
Vehicle kilometres (millions)	3,324
Passenger journeys (millions)...........	6,177
Passenger receipts (£ million)	2,218·6

Road Accidents 1985

Road accidents	245,645
Vehicles involved:	
Pedal cycles	27,953
Motor vehicles	389,473
Total casualties	317,524
Pedestrians.........................	61,390
Vehicle users	256,134
Killed*	5,165
Pedestrians.........................	1,789
Pedal cycles	286
All two-wheeled motor vehicles	796
Cars & taxis	2,061
Others	233

*Died within 30 days of accident.

Year	Killed	Injured	Year	Killed	Injured
1965	7,952	389,985	1982	5,934	328,362
1970	7,499	355,869	1983	5,445	303,139
1975	6,366	318,584	1984	5,599	318,715
1980	6,010	323,000	1985	5,165	312,359

BRITISH RAILWAYS

The British Railways Board was set up by the Transport Act, 1962, and assumed its responsibilities on January 1, 1963.

The railway business is broken down into five distinct business sectors each with its own Director. The sectors focus on three passenger businesses of Intercity; Network South East; and Provincial; together with the Railfreight and Parcels businesses. In addition for the purposes of management and operation the railways are divided into Regions. They cover the following areas:

London Midland Region—bounded by a line joining Carlisle, Oldham, Nottingham, Bedford, London, Banbury, Kidderminster, Aberystwyth.

Western Region—west of a line joining Yeovil, Westbury, Reading, London and the southern border of the L.M. Region.

Southern Region—south of a line joining Dorchester, Salisbury, London and the Thames.

Eastern Region—east of a line joining London, Peterborough, Sheffield, Bradford and Carlisle.

Scottish Region—north of a line joining Carlisle and Berwick.

Staff.—On March 31, 1987, British Rail employed 140,067 staff (142,740 at March 31, 1986). Including B.R. Property Board, Travellers Fare, Intercity Catering, Freightliners Ltd., B.R. Engineering Ltd., Transmark, British Transport Advertising Ltd., and B.R. Pension Trustee Co. Ltd., the group total at March 31, 1987, was 166,989 (173,760 at March 31, 1986).

Financial Results, 1986–87.—The Profit and Loss Account for 1986–87 showed a group surplus of £73·7 million, £2·4 million after interest, compared with a loss of £11·5 million after interest in 1985–86. The railway working surplus was £71·8 million compared with a surplus of £48·4 million for the previous year.

Railways	£ million 1986–7	
Gross receipts:		
Passenger (including grants) ..	2,213·9	
Freight (inc. parcels and mails)	652·5	
TOTAL....................		2,866·4
Working expenses:		
Train services	1,290·8	
Terminals	292·3	
Miscellaneous traffic expenses .	111·8	
Track and signalling..........	575·0	
General expenses.............	481·6	
Provision for replacement of assets	109·0	
TOTAL.................		2,860·5

	£	
Railway net surplus		21·1
Net income from Operational Property Letting, Advertising and Catering		50·7
OPERATING SURPLUS		71·8

OPERATING STATISTICS

At March 31, 1987, British Rail had 23,645 miles of standard gauge lines and sidings in use, representing 10,358 miles of route of which 2,581 miles were electrified. Standard rail on main line has a weight of 110 lb. per yard. British Rail had 2,441 locomotives (diesel and diesel electric, 2,201 and electric, 240); 2,625 diesel multiple-unit vehicles, 7,034 electric multiple-unit vehicles and 3,276 locomotive-hauled passenger carriages. Loaded train miles run in passenger service totalled 202·8m. 689·4m passenger journeys were made during the year, including 309·2m made by holders of season tickets. The average distance of each passenger journey on ordinary fare was 36·0 miles; and on season ticket, 17·7 miles. Passenger stations in use in 1987 numbered 2,405 and freight stations 123.

Freight.—There were 33,649 freight-vehicles and 1,659 other vehicles in the non-passenger-carrying stock. Train miles run in freight service totalled 31·1m.

Accidents on Railways

	1984	1985
Train accidents: total	1,359	1,240
Persons killed : total	30	6
Passengers	18	—
Railway staff	6	—
Others	6	6
Persons injured : total	475	380
Passengers	386	261
Railway staff	68	88
Others	21	31
Other accidents through movement of railway vehicles		
Persons killed....................	41	55
Persons injured	2,486	2,489
Other accidents on railway premises		
Persons killed....................	5	13
Persons injured	6,267	6,295
Trespassers and suicides		
Persons killed....................	339	310
Persons injured	128	104

UNEMPLOYMENT (Thousands)

	United Kingdom		Great Britain				Northern Ireland			
	Total	Percentage rate	Total	Percentage rate	Males	Females	Total	Percentage rate	Males	Females
1982 ⎫	2,916·9	10·9	2,808·5	10·8	2,055·9	752·6	108·3	16·0	77·3	31·0
1983 ⎪ Annual	3,104·7	11·7	2,987·6	11·5	2,133·5	854·0	117·1	17·2	85·1	32·0
1984 ⎬ averages	3,159·8	11·7	3,038·4	11·5	2,109·6	928·8	121·4	17·7	87·7	33·7
1985 ⎪	3,271·2	11·8	3,149·4	11·7	2,163·7	985·7	121·8	17·6	88·0	33·8
1986 ⎭	3,289·1	11·9	3,161·3	11·7	2,159·6	1,001·7	127·8	18·6	92·9	34·9
1987 January 8	3,297·2	11·9	3,166·0	11·7	2,176·5	989·5	131·2	19·1	95·9	35·3
February 12 ..	3,225·8	11·6	3,096·6	11·4	2,139·2	957·4	129·2	18·8	94·7	34·5
March 12	3,143·4	11·3	3,016·5	11·1	2,088·2	928·4	126·8	18·5	92·9	34·0
April 9	3,107·1	11·2	2,979·9	11·0	2,065·1	914·8	127·2	18·5	93·1	34·1
May 14	2,986·5	10·8	2,860·3	10·6	1,988·0	872·3	126·1	18·4	92·3	33·8
June 11	2,905·3	10·5	2,779·8	10·3	1,931·5	842·3	125·6	18·3	91·5	34·1

EMPLOYMENT

Distribution of total working population

Thousands

At mid-June	1975	1980	1981	1982	1983	1984	1985
United Kingdom							
Total working population	25,877	26,819*	26,718	26,663	26,586†	27,113	27,593
Unemployed	838	1,513*	2,395	2,770	2,984†	3,030	3,179
Employed labour force	25,039	25,306	24,323	23,894	23,602	24,083	24,414
HM Forces	336	323	334	324	322	326	325
Self-employed persons (with or without							
employees)...........................	1,993	2,011	2,118	2,170	2,221	2,515	2,623
Total employees in employment	22,710	22,972	21,870	21,400	21,059	21,242	21,466
of whom:							
Total, index of production industries	9,507	8,918	8,068	7,639	7,280	7,165	7,116
Total, all manufacturing industries	7,524	6,940	6,220	5,897	5,608	5,542	5,532
Great Britain							
Total working population	25,283	26,176*	26,076	26,023	25,946†	26,452	26,930
Unemployed	803	1,444*	2,299	2,664	2,871†	2,911	3,057
Employed labour force	24,481	24,731	23,777	23,360	23,075	23,541	23,873
HM Forces	336	323	334	324	322	326	326
Self-employed persons (with or without							
employees)...........................	1,932	1,950	2,057	2,109	2,160	2,435	2,543
Total employees in employment	22,213	22,458	21,386	20,927	20,593	20,780	21,003
of whom							
Total, index of production industries	9,298	8,737	7,910	7,494	7,143	7,031	6,983
Total, all manufacturing industries	7,365	6,805	6,099	5,788	5,505	5,441	5,431

*The figures are affected by the introduction in Great Britain of fortnightly payment of unemployment benefit.
†From April 1983, the figures of unemployment reflect the effects of the provisions in the Budget for some men aged 60 and over who no longer have to sign on at an unemployment office.

Employees in employment: all industries

At June Industries analysed according to the Standard Industrial Classification 1980 Thousands

	1978	1979	1980	1981	1982	1983	1984	1985	1986
Total employees in employment	22,789	23,173	23,991	21,891	21,414	21,067	21,238	21,509	21,594
Males...........................	13,398	13,487	13,319	12,562	12,205	11,940	11,888	11,967	11,903
Females.........................	9,391	9,686	9,672	9,330	9,209	9,127	9,350	9,542	9,691
of which: Total production and con-									
struction industries.............	9,197	9,213	8,906	8,061	7,610	7,217	7,062	6,976	6,691
Agriculture, forestry and fishing ..	395	380	373	363	358	350	340	341	329
Coal, oil and natural gas extraction									
and processing	358	354	355	344	328	311	289	271	230
Electricity, gas, other energy and									
water supply	359	368	371	366	352	338	328	318	309
Manufacturing industries	7,281	7,253	6,937	6,222	5,863	5,525	5,409	5,365	5,239
Construction	1,199	1,239	1,243	1,130	1,067	1,044	1,037	1,022	992
Wholesale distribution and repairs	1,096	1,138	1,173	1,137	1,140	1,150	1,181	1,194	1,208
Retail distribution	2,102	2,176	2,177	2,092	2,026	2,005	2,054	2,086	2,110
Hotels and catering	892	943	972	943	973	963	1,010	1,061	1,085
Transport	1,051	1,056	1,049	987	943	912	910	911	904
Postal services and									
communications	415	423	437	438	437	433	432	434	437
Banking, finance, insurance	1,569	1,647	1,695	1,738	1,798	1,875	1,969	2,083	2,203
Public administration	1,995	2,002	1,980	1,899	1,881	1,918	1,936	1,962	1,984
Education......................	1,622	1,660	1,642	1,615	1,598	1,592	1,602	1,619	1,656
Medical and other health services,									
veterinary services	1,212	1,233	1,258	1,293	1,304	1,294	1,298	1,312	1,300
Other services	1,242	1,303	1,327	1,324	1,348	1,358	1,446	1,530	1,592

FUEL AND POWER

Coal: supply and demand   Million tonnes

	1980	1981	1982	1983	1984	1985
SUPPLY						
Production of deep-mined coal	112·4	110·5	106·2	101·7	35·2	75·2
Production of opencast coal	15·8	14·8	15·3	14·7	14·3	15·6
Recovered slurry, fines, etc.	1·9	2·2	3·3	2·8	1·6	3·3
Imports	7·3	4·3	4·1	4·5	8·9	12·6
Change in colliery stocks	+5·3	+4·3	+0·2	+1·2	−7·9	−5·3
Change in stocks at opencast sites	+2·4	+0·5	−0·4	+0·8	+4·7	−6·3
Total supply	129·7	127·0	128·9	121·7	63·2	118·2
HOME CONSUMPTION						
Electricity supply industry	89·6	87·2	80·2	81·6	53·4	73·9
Coke ovens	11·6	10·8	10·4	10·4	8·2	11·1
Low temperature carbonization plants	1·9	1·3	1·2	1·2	1·1	1·4
Manufactured fuel plants	1·1	1·1	1·1	0·9	0·2	0·8
Railways	0·1	0·1	0·1	—	—	—
Collieries	0·7	0·6	0·5	0·5	0·2	0·3
Industry (disposals to users)	7·8	7·0	7·1	7·2	6·1	7·4
Domestic (disposals to users)	8·9	8·4	8·6	8·0	6·5	8·6
Public services	1·5	1·4	1·4	1·4	1·3	1·3
Miscellaneous	0·3	0·4	0·5	0·4	0·5	0·4
Total home consumption	123·5	118·4	111·0	111·4	77·3	105·4
Overseas shipments and bunkers	3·8	9·1	7·4	6·6	2·3	2·4
Total consumption and shipments	127·3	127·5	118·4	+118·0	79·6	107·8
Change in distributed stocks*	+2·1	−0·2	+10·3	+3·5	−17·1	+10·0
Balance†	+0·3	−0·3	+0·2	—	+0·7	+0·5

*Stock change excludes industrial and domestic stocks.
† This is the balance between supply and consumption, shipments and changes in known distributed stocks.

Fuel input and gas output; gas sales

	1980	1981	1982	1983	1984	1985
FUEL INPUT TO GAS INDUSTRY:			million tonnes			
Petroleum	0·1	0·1	0·1	0·1	0·1	0·1
			million therms			
Petroleum gases	79	71	52	33	30	28
Natural gas	—	—	—	—	—	—
Coke oven gas	—	—	—	—	—	—
Total to gas works	106	100	85	61	56	57
Natural gas for direct supply	17,012	17,044	16,667	17,153	17,739	18,988
Total fuel input	17,118	17,144	16,752	17,214	17,794	19,046
GAS OUTPUT AND SALES			million therms			
Gas output:						
Town gas	35	31	26	23	21	20
Natural gas supplied direct	17,076	17,108	16,719	17,186	17,764	19,017
Gross total available	17,111	17,139	16,745	17,209	17,785	19,038
Own use	134	139	126	121	129	140
Statistical difference*	−347	−378	+38	−244	−354	−508
Total sales	16,630	16,622	16,657	16,844	17,302	18,390
Analysis of gas sales						
Power stations	140	78	76	77	178	197
Final users:						
Iron and steel industry	451	409	365	342	462	464
Other industries	5,539	5,261	5,319	5,295	5,258	5,319
Domestic	8,439	8,764	8,719	8,871	8,931	9,682
Public administration	948	966	1,003	1,050	1,071	1,183
Miscellaneous	1,113	1,144	1,175	1,210	1,337	1,474

*Supply greater than recorded demand (−). Includes losses in distribution.

FUEL AND POWER

Electricity: production and fuel used

	1980	1981	1982	1983	1984	1985
Electricity generated: total (GWh)	267,087	260,422	256,090	261,082	266,645	280,602
England and Wales	230,940	224,315	220,505	226,324	227,010	242,248
S. Scotland Electricity Board	25,565	25,331	23,276	20,332	22,938	25,771
N. Scotland Hydro-Electric Board	4,205	4,640	6,312	8,395	10,451	6,015
Northern Ireland	5,673	5,445	5,346	5,384	5,591	5,938
Railway and transport authorities	704	691	651	647	655	630
Method of generation (GWh)						
Steam plant, nuclear	33,462	34,043	40,001	45,776	49,498	56,354
Steam plant, other	228,577	220,849	210,545	209,116	209,711	216,830
Gas turbines and oil engines	551	610	580	401	2,012	1,138
Hydro-electric plant other than pumped storage plant	3,309	3,917	3,884	3,892	3,368	3,447
Pumped storage plant	1,188	1,003	1,080	1,897	2,055	2,831
Fuel used (Thousand tonnes)						
Coal	89,348	87,038	79,816	81,439	53,413	73,941
Coke and coke breeze	117	82	69	33	19	—
Oil	6,573	5,075	6,232	4,704	21,282	12,964
Natural gas*	557	313	304	311	712	762
Electricity sales total (GWh)	225,053	221,621	217,096	220,352	224,298	235,379
Domestic and farm premises	87,907	86,201	84,601	84,640	85,520	89,990
Domestic and commercial	2,197	2,129	2,014	1,979	1,984	1,711
Shops, offices, other commercial premises	44,539	45,359	46,134	49,019	51,039	55,420
Factories, other industrial premises	85,539	83,078	79,806	79,967	80,972	83,348
Public lighting	2,252	2,240	2,243	2,259	2,292	2,333
Traction	2,619	2,614	2,298	2,488	2,491	2,577

*Expressed in thousand tonnes of coal equivalent.

Electricity Council Finance 1985–87

	£ million	
	1985–86	1986–87
Turnover		
Electricity Supply	10,092·7	10,385·1
Contracting	168·7	183·8
Appliance Marketing	481·2	549·7
TOTAL	10,742·6	11,118·6
Operating Costs		
Electricity Supply	9,158·7	9,266·7
Contracting	161·4	174·8
Appliance Marketing	449·2	510·9
TOTAL	9,769·3	9,952·4
Operating profit/loss before monetary working capital adjustment		
Electricity Supply	934·0	1,118·4
Contracting	7·3	9·0
Appliance Marketing	32·0	38·8
TOTAL	973·3	1,166·2
Monetary working capital adjustment	29·1	16·5
Profit/loss on ordinary activities before interest ..	944·2	1,149·7
Interest payable	529·8	436·3
Profit/loss before extraordinary charge	414·4	586·9
Extraordinary charge	—	—
Profit/loss for the year transferred to reserves	414·4	586·9

British Gas P.L.C. Finance (£ million)

	1985–86	1986–87
Turnover		
Gas supply	7,109	6,967
Installation and contracting	275	310
Appliance trading	278	300
Exploration subsidiaries	94	189
Other activities	21	28
	7,777	7,794
Less: intra-group sales	(90)	(184)
TOTAL	7,687	7,610
Operating costs		
Gas prime materials	3,376	3,024
Gas levy	520	503
Salaries, wages, associated costs	1,202	1,180
Cost of sales adjustment	5	2
Monetary working capital adjustment	44	(27)
Current cost depreciation	749	773
Lease rentals	48	34
Exploration expenditure	38	24
Research, testing & development	76	74
Auditor's remuneration	0·581	0·558
Current cost operating profit ..	688	1,005
Gearing adjustment	—	8
Net interest receivable	94	49
Current cost profit on ordinary activities before taxation ...	782	1,062
Taxation	(380)	(487)
Current cost profit for the year	402	575
Dividend	—	(166)
Current cost profit retained ...	402	409

British Coal Corporation Finance (£million)

	1985–6	1986–7		1985–6	1986–7
Turnover	5,340	4,515	Turnover	5,340	4,515
Operating results:			Exceptional restructing costs—		
Mining activities	575	285	Social costs, less grants	(170)	(197)
Deep mines	232*	41	Terminal depreciation	(66)	(62)
Opencast	343	244			
Other mining activities	27	26	(Loss) on ordinary activities before taxation	(48)	(276)
Total mining activities	602	311	Taxation—ordinary activities	(1)	—
Non-mining activities	(5)*	5	Minority interests	(1)	—
Income from related companies and partnerships	4	1	(Loss) after taxation—ordinary activities	(50)	(276)
Profit from sales of fixed assets	24	52	Extraordinary items	—	(12)
Operating profit	625*	369	(Loss) for the year	(50)	(288)
Interest charges	(437)	(386)	Government deficit grant	50	288
Profit/(loss) on ordinary activities	188	(17)	Surplus/(deficit) carried to reserves	—	—

*After taking credit of provision of £342 million to cover the post-strike recovery costs.

HOUSING

Stock of dwellings (Great Britain)

	1982	1983	1984	1985
Estimated annual gains and losses (thousands)				
Gains: New construction	174·0	195·0	203·4	188·7
Other	13·9	15·5	17·6	18·9
Losses: Slum clearance	23·1	17·4	12·4	12·1
Other	9·5	9·1	14·2	16·0
Net gain	155·3	183·8	194·4	179·5
Stock at end of year	21,338	21,521	21,716	21,896
Estimated tenure distribution at end of year (percentage)				
Owner occupied	58·6	59·9	60·9	61·9
Rented: From local authorities and new towns	29·5	28·6	27·9	27·3
From housing associations	2·2	2·3	2·4	2·5
From private owners including other tenures	9·6	9·1	8·7	8·3

Permanent dwellings completed

	United Kingdom				England and Wales			
	Total	For local housing authorities	For private owners	Other	Total	For local housing authorities	For private owners	Other
1964	383,192	154,754	221,264	7,174	336,505	119,468	210,432	6,605
1974	279,582	121,017	145,177	13,388	241,173	99,423	129,626	12,124
1979	251,805	88,485	144,055	19,265	220,722	77,192	125,306	18,224
1980	240,906	87,974	131,090	21,842	213,815	70,006	115,280	20,529
1981	205,631	68,139	117,773	19,719	178,859	58,215	103,195	17,449
1982	180,024	39,879	126,531	13,614	157,518	33,349	112,327	11,842
1983	203,003	38,836	147,879	16,294	176,998	31,300	131,242	14,456
1984	212,191	37,176	158,420	16,645	184,798	30,955	139,818	14,025
1985	197,416	30,187	153,973	13,256	170,343	24,143	134,687	11,513

	Scotland				Northern Ireland			
	Total	For local housing authorities	For private owners	Other	Total	For local housing authorities	For private owners	Other
1964	37,171	29,156	7,662	353	9,516	6,130	3,170	216
1974	28,336	16,182	11,239	915	10,073	5,412	4,312	349
1979	23,782	7,857	15,175	750	7,301	3,436	3,574	291
1980	20,611	7,455	12,242	914	6,480	2,513	3,568	399
1981	20,015	7,065	11,021	1,929	6,757	2,859	3,557	341
1982	16,432	3,716	11,532	1,184	6,074	2,814	2,672	588
1983	17,830	3,486	13,067	1,277	8,175	4,044	3,570	561
1984	18,671	2,633	13,992	2,046	8,722	3,588	4,610	574
1985	18,376	2,811	14,449	1,116	8,697	3,233	4,837	627

BIRTHS AND MARRIAGES (Thousands)

	Live births				Marriages				
	United Kingdom	England and Wales		Scotland	Northern Ireland	United King-dom	England and Wales		Scotland	Northern Ireland
		Total	Wales				Total	Wales		
1980	753·7	656·2	37·4	68·9	28·6	418·4	370·0	21·1	38·5	9·9
1981	730·8	634·5	35·8	69·1	27·3	397·8	352·0	19·8	36·2	9·6
1982	719·2	625·9	35·7	66·2	27·0	387·0	342·2	19·0	34·9	9·9
1983	721·5	629·1	35·5	65·1	27·3	389·3	344·3	19·9	35·0	10·0
1984	729·6	636·8	35·9	65·1	27·7	395·8	349·0	19·2	36·3	10·4
1985	750·7	656·4	36·8	66·7	27·6	393·1	346·4	19·1	36·4	10·3
1986	755·0	661·0	37·0	65·8	28·2	394·1	347·9	19·5	35·8	10·4
1986 1st quarter	182·4	160·0	8·9	15·5	6·9	57·3	50·8	3·0	5·0	1·5
2nd quarter	193·7	169·0	9·5	17·2	7·5	111·1	98·1	5·4	10·2	2·9
3rd quarter	194·5	170·8	9·5	16·6	7·1	150·2	132·9	7·4	13·0	4·3
4th quarter	184·4	161·2	9·2	16·5	6·6	75·4	66·2	3·8	7·6	1·7
1987 1st quarter		163·0†			7·0†					

† Provisional.

DIVORCE

	1975	1980	1981	1982	1983	1984	1985
England and Wales							
Decrees absolute granted:							
Number	120,522	148,301	145,713	146,698	147,479	144,501	160,300
Rate per 1,000 married population ...	*9·6*	*12·0*	*11·9*	*12·0*	*12·2*	*12·0*	*13·4*
Scotland							
Decrees absolute, granted:							
Number	7,795	10,528	9,894	11,288	13,238	11,906	13,371
Rate per 1,000 married population ...	*6·2*	*8·6*	*8·0*	*9·2*	*11·0*	*9·9*	*11·2*
Northern Ireland							
Petitions filed							
Nullity of marriage	9	9	9	5	—	6	6
Divorce...........................	572	1,620	1,645	1,734	1,577	1,749	1,986
Judicial separation	—	4	2	2	9	5	15

DEATHS REGISTERED* (Thousands)

	Total					Infants under one year				
	United Kingdom	England and Wales		Scotland	Northern Ireland	United King-dom	England and Wales		Scotland	North-ern Ireland
		Total	Wales				Total	Wales		
1980	661·5	581·4	35·1	63·3	16·8	9·11	7·90	0·43	0·83	0·38
1981	658·0	577·9	35·0	63·8	16·3	8·16	7·02	0·45	0·78	0·36
1982	662·8	581·9	35·2	65·0	15·9	7·90	6·78	0·38	0·75	0·37
1983	659·1	579·6	35·2	63·5	16·0	7·36	6·38	0·38	0·65	0·33
1984	644·9	566·9	33·7	62·3	15·7	7·00	6·04	0·31	0·67	0·29
1985	670·6†	590·7	35·5	64·0	16·0†	7·03†	6·14	0·36	0·62	0·27†
1986		581·2	34·7	63·5†	16·1†		6·31	0·35	0·58†	0·29†
1986 1st quarter	194·3†	171·1	10·1	18·5†	4·8†	2·00†	1·78	0·09	0·15†	0·07†
2nd quarter	160·8†	141·3	8·6	15·6†	4·0†	1·79†	1·56	0·11	0·15†	0·09†
3rd quarter	146·8†	129·0	7·7	14·3†	3·6†	1·61†	1·41	0·07	0·14†	0·06†
4th quarter	158·7†	139·8	8·4	15·1†	3·8†	1·78†	1·56	0·08	0·15†	0·06†

* Excluding stillbirths.   † Provisional.

Deaths Analysed by Cause

	England and Wales		Scotland	
	1984	1985	1984	1985
Total deaths	566,881	580,734	62,345	63,967
Deaths from natural causes	548,046	571,725	59,519	61,148
Infections and parasitic diseases	2,295	2,381	259	278
Cholera	—	1	—	—
Typhoid fever	—	—	—	—
Shigellosis and amoebiasis	3	2	—	—
Enteritis and other diarrhoeal diseases	135	124	11	14
Tuberculosis of respiratory system	376	408	46	47
Other tuberculosis, including late effects	377	366	39	57
Plague	—	—	—	—
Diphtheria	—	—	—	—
Whooping cough	1	4	—	—
Streptococcal sore throat and scarlatina	3	1	—	1
Meningococcal infection	79	97	7	9
Acute poliomyelitis	—	—	—	—
Smallpox	—	—	—	—
Measles	10	11	3	1
Louse-borne typhus and other rickettsioses	2	2	—	—
Malaria	4	5	1	—
Syphilis	68	40	2	2
Neoplasms	140,101	141,618	14,456	14,618
Malignant neoplasm of stomach	10,360	9,971	970	1,010
Malignant neoplasm of trachea, bronchus and lung	35,739	35,792	4,225	4,307
Malignant neoplasm of breast	13,409	13,592	1,248	1,264
Malignant neoplasm of uterus	3,381	3,494	379	353
Leukaemia	3,572	3,696	306	352
Benign and unspecified neoplasms	1,358	1,346	109	113
Endocrine, nutritional and metabolic diseases & immunity disorders	8,499	9,798	669	723
Diabetes mellitus	6,369	7,452	477	534
Nutritional deficiencies	104	130	24	21
Diseases of blood and blood-forming organs	2,100	2,422	149	181
Anaemias	1,363	1,522	89	83
Mental disorders	10,744	12,011	645	965
Diseases of nervous system and sense organs	10,483	11,414	776	810
Meningitis	246	306	25	18
Diseases of the circulatory system	278,849	287,054	31,489	32,319
Acute rheumatic fever	2	6	—	—
Chronic rheumatic heart disease	2,931	2,889	275	252
Hypertensive disease	4,644	4,581	411	391
Ischaemic heart disease	157,506	163,104	18,107	18,758
Diseases of pulmonary circulation & other forms of heart disease	22,425	22,835	2,549	2,620
Cerebrovascular disease	71,470	73,219	8,378	8,505
Diseases of the respiratory system	56,828	64,607	7,099	7,156
Influenza	346	662	59	54
Pneumonia	24,687	27,931	3,974	3,880
Bronchitis, emphysema	14,009	14,255	1,009	969
Asthma	1,764	1,972	157	146
Diseases of the digestive system	16,980	18,148	2,015	2,038
Ulcer of stomach and duodenum	4,483	4,861	475	470
Appendicitis	147	147	13	18
Hernia of abdominal cavity & other intestinal obstruction	1,947	2,001	189	201
Chronic liver disease and cirrhosis	2,280	2,582	423	423
Diseases of the genito-urinary system	7,731	8,012	804	897
Nephritis, nephrotic syndrome and nephrosis	4,391	4,640	513	555
Hyperplasia of prostate	689	668	37	37
Complications of pregnancy, child birth etc.	52	46	8	9
Abortion	6	9	1	1
Diseases of the skin and subcutaneous tissue	601	670	70	89
Diseases of the musculo-skeletal system	4,943	5,452	239	269
Congenital anomalies	3,017	2,909	291	265
Certain conditions originating in the perinatal period	2,289	2,293	278	246
Birth trauma, hypoxia, birth asphyxia & other respiratory conditions	1,243	1,293	160	122
Signs, symptoms and other ill-defined conditions	2,534	2,890	272	285
Deaths by violence	18,835	19,009	2,826	2,819
All accidents	12,603	12,475	2,050	1,981
Motor vehicle accidents	5,090	4,914	612	609
Suicide and self-inflicted injury	4,315	4,419	519	569
All other external causes	1,917	2,115	257	269

THE UNITED KINGDOM

Area.—The land area of the United Kingdom* (England, Wales, Scotland and N. Ireland) is 93,005 sq. miles. The area of inland water in the United Kingdom is 1,242 sq. miles. Total 94,247 sq. miles.

Sq. miles	England	Wales	Scotland	N. Ireland
Land	50,070	7,968	29,761	5,206
Inland Water	293	50	653	246
Total	50,363	8,018	30,414	5,452

* Excludes the Isle of Man (227 sq. miles) and the Channel Islands (75 sq. miles)

POPULATION: CENSUS RESULTS, 1801–1981   Thousands

	United Kingdom			England and Wales			Scotland			Northern Ireland†		
	Total	Male	Female	Total	Male	Female	Total	Male	Female	Total	Male	Female
1801	11,944	5,692	6,252	8,893	4,255	4,638	1,608	739	869	1,443	698	745
1811	13,368	6,368	7,000	10,165	4,874	5,291	1,806	826	980	1,397	668	729
1821	15,472	7,498	7,974	12,000	5,850	6,150	2,092	983	1,109	1,380	665	715
1831	17,835	8,647	9,188	13,897	6,771	7,126	2,364	1,114	1,250	1,574	762	812
1841	20,183	9,819	10,364	15,914	7,778	8,137	2,620	1,242	1,378	1,649	800	849
1851	22,259	10,855	11,404	17,928	8,781	9,146	2,889	1,376	1,513	1,443	698	745
1861	24,525	11,894	12,631	20,066	9,776	10,290	3,062	1,450	1,612	1,396	668	728
1871	27,431	13,309	14,122	22,712	11,059	11,653	3,360	1,603	1,757	1,359	647	712
1881	31,015	15,060	15,955	25,974	12,640	13,335	3,736	1,799	1,936	1,305	621	684
1891	34,264	16,593	17,671	29,003	14,060	14,942	4,026	1,943	2,083	1,236	590	646
1901	38,237	18,492	19,745	32,528	15,729	16,799	4,472	2,174	2,298	1,237	590	647
1911	42,082	20,357	21,725	36,070	17,446	18,625	4,761	2,309	2,452	1,251	603	648
1921	44,027	21,033	22,994	37,887	18,075	19,811	4,882	2,348	2,535	*1,258*	*610*	*648*
1931	46,038	22,060	23,978	39,952	19,133	20,819	4,843	2,326	2,517	*1,243*	*601*	*642*
1951	50,225	24,118	26,107	43,758	21,016	22,742	5,096	2,434	2,662	1,371	668	703
1961	52,709	25,481	27,228	46,105	22,304	23,801	5,179	2,483	2,697	1,425	694	731
1971	55,515	26,952	28,562	48,750	23,683	25,067	5,229	2,515	2,714	1,536	755	781
1981	55,776	27,064	28,701	49,154	23,873	25,281	5,130	2,466	2,664	1,491	725	756

NOTES.—1. Before 1801 there existed no official return of the population of either England or Scotland. Estimates of the population of England at various periods, calculated from the number of baptisms, burials and marriages, are: in 1570, 4,160,221; 1600, 4,811,718; 1630, 5,600,517; 1670, 5,773,646; 1700, 6,045,008; 1750, 6,517,035. Because of the War there was no Census in 1941.

2. The last official Census of Population in respect of England and Wales, Scotland, Northern Ireland, the Isle of Man and Guernsey, was taken on the night of April 5, 1981.

3. † All figures refer to the area which is now Northern Ireland. Figures for N. Ireland in 1921 and 1931 are estimates based on the Censuses held in 1926 and 1937.

ISLANDS.—*The figures given above do not include islands of the British seas.* Populations of these islands at census years since 1900 were:—

	ISLE OF MAN			JERSEY			GUERNSEY		
	Total	Male	Female	Total	Male	Female	Total	Male	Female
1901	54,752	25,496	29,256	52,576	23,940	28,636	43,042	21,140	21,902
1911	52,016	23,937	28,079	51,898	24,014	27,884	45,001	22,215	22,786
1921	60,284	27,329	32,955	49,701	22,438	27,263	40,529	19,303	21,226
1931	49,308	22,443	26,865	50,462	23,424	27,038	42,743	20,675	22,068
1951	55,123	25,749	29,464	57,296	27,282	30,014	45,747	22,094	23,380
1961	48,151	22,060	26,091	57,200	27,200	30,000	47,178	22,890	24,288
1971	56,289	26,461	29,828	72,532	35,423	37,109	52,708	25,382	27,326
1981	64,679	30,901	33,778	77,000	37,000	40,000	56,000	27,000	29,000

INCREASE OF THE PEOPLE, ETC.

In Great Britain 6·3 per cent of the usually resident population was born outside the United Kingdom, and in England and Wales this figure was 6·6 per cent. Some 4·5 per cent of the population of England and Wales lived in households whose head was born in the New Commonwealth or Pakistan. Britain's total population is expected, on 1985 estimates, to be 56·8 million in 1991, 57·7 million in 2001 and 58 million in 2011. The number of live births declined between 1968 and 1978 and has fluctuated since. The average size of family in 1985 was 1·80, below the level of 2·1 required for replacement of the population. The number of live births in 1985 was 752,000 (22,500 more than in 1984), of which 19 per cent were illegitimate.

Although the total population has remained relatively stable in the last decade there have been changes in the age and sex structure. The proportion of people under 16 is about 21 per cent; 16–64 years, 64 per cent; 65 and over, 15 per cent. Some 18 per cent were over normal retirement age (60 for women, 65 for men). There are about 6 per cent more male than female births every year, but the higher mortality of men at all ages, means that at about 51 years of age the number of women begins to exceed the number of men.

LOCAL GOVERNMENT

ENGLAND AND WALES

The London Government Act, 1963, and the Local Government Acts of 1972 and 1985 have brought about the present system of local government in England and Wales. The system is based on two tiers of local authorities, county and district councils, in the non-metropolitan areas; and a single tier, of metropolitan district and London borough councils, in the six metropolitan areas of England and in London respectively.

Structures and Areas in England

England outside Greater London is divided into counties. Each county is divided into districts. Six *metropolitan counties* cover the main conurbations outside Greater London: Tyne and Wear, West Midlands, Merseyside, Greater Manchester, West Yorkshire and South Yorkshire. They are divided into 36 *metropolitan districts*, most of which have a population of over 200,000. There are 39 *non-metropolitan counties*; each of these is divided into *non-metropolitan districts*, of which there are 296. These districts have populations broadly in the range of 60,000 to 100,000: some however, have larger populations, because of the need to avoid dividing large towns, and some in mainly rural areas have smaller populations. Greater London is divided into 32 *London boroughs*, with populations between 134,000 and 390,000, and the *City*, with a daytime population of 340,000 but only 5,400 by night.

There are also about 10,000 parishes, in 219 of the non-metropolitan and 18 of the metropolitan districts.

A Permanent Local Government Boundary Commission keeps the areas and electoral arrangements under review, and makes proposals to the Secretary of State for changes found necessary.

Constitution and Elections

For districts, non-metropolitan counties, London boroughs, the City, and for about 8,000 parishes, there are elected councils, consisting of directly elected councillors. Broadly, county councils range from 60–100 members; metropolitan district councils 50–80 members; non-metropolitan district councils 30–60 members. The councillors elect annually one of their number as chairman.

The general pattern in England is that councillors serve 4 years and there are no elections of district and parish councillors in county elections years. In metropolitan districts one-third of the councillors for each ward are elected each year except in the year of county elections. Non-metropolitan districts can choose whether to have elections by thirds or whole council elections. In the former case, one-third of the council, as nearly as may be, is elected in each year of metropolitan district elections. If whole council elections are chosen, these are held in the year midway between county elections. The London boroughs have whole council elections, in the year immediately following the county council election years. Local elections are normally held on the first Thursday in May.

Generally speaking, all British subjects or citizens of the Republic of Ireland of 18 years or over, resident on the qualifying date in the area for which the election is being held, are entitled to vote at local government elections. A register of electors is prepared and published annually by local electoral registration officers.

A returning officer has the overall responsibility for an election. Voting takes place at polling stations, arranged by the local authority and under the supervision of a presiding officer specially appointed for the purpose. Candidates, who are subject to various statutory qualifications and disqualifications designed to secure that they are suitable persons to hold office, must be nominated by electors for the electoral area concerned.

Internal Organisation

Local authorities increasingly are organised along party political lines and over 80 per cent are now controlled by groups of councillors having allegiance to one of the main political parties. However, the council as a whole are the final decision-making body within any authority. They are free to a great extent to make their own internal organisational arrangements. Normally, questions of major policy are settled by the full council, while the administration of the various services is the responsibility of committees of members. Day to day decisions are delegated to the council's officers, who act within the policies laid down by the members.

Functions

Local authorities are empowered or required by various Acts of Parliament to carry out functions in their areas. The legislation concerned comprises public general Acts and "local" Acts which local authorities have promoted as private bills. In non-metropolitan areas, functions are divided between the districts and counties, those requiring the larger area or population for their efficient performance going to the county. The metropolitan district councils, with the larger population in their areas, already had wider functions than non-metropolitan councils, and following abolition of the metropolitan county councils have now been given most of their functions also. A few functions continue to be exercised over the larger area by joint bodies, made up of councillors from each district.

The allocation of functions is as follows:

county councils: education; strategic planning; traffic, transport and highways; police; fire service; consumer protection; refuse disposal; smallholdings; social services; libraries.

non-metropolitan district councils: local planning; housing; highways (maintenance of certain urban roads and off-street car parks); building regulations; environmental health; refuse collection; cemeteries and crematoria.

metropolitan district and London borough councils: their functions are all those listed above, except that fire, civil defence (and in some cases, refuse disposal) in all areas and police and passenger transport in the metropolitan counties only are exercised by joint bodies. Education in inner London is the responsibility of a special authority.

Functions exercised *concurrently* by county and district councils and London boroughs: recreation (parks, playing fields, swimming pools); museums; encouragement of the arts, tourism and industry.

The sewerage and sewage disposal functions of local authorities have been transferred to 9 water authorities in England and the Welsh Water Authority. Water authorities, however, are expected to make agreements whereby the new district councils discharge sewerage sewage functions on an agency basis. Apart from these functions, the water authorities are responsible for water supply and conservation; river pollution control and river management; fisheries; land drainage; and use of water space for recreation and amenity purposes.

The personal health functions of local authorities were transferred in 1977 to area health authorities, whose areas were the same as non-metropolitan and Welsh counties and metropolitan districts. From April 1982 this two-tier structure was replaced by about 199 District Health Authorities. They work in close collaboration with local education, social services and environment health authorities.

Residuary Bodies

Residuary bodies were set up in 1985 to deal with the business of the Greater London and Metropolitan County Councils which had not already devolved onto other bodies at the time of the Councils' abolition in 1986. Addresses and details of principal officers are given on page 632 (page 659 for Greater London).

Parishes

Parishes with 200 or more electors must generally have parish councils, and about three-quarters of the parishes have councils. A parish council comprises at least 5 members, the number being fixed by the district council. Elections are held every four years, in the year in which the local district councillor is elected. All parishes have parish meetings, comprising the electors of the parish. Where there is no council, the meeting must be held at least twice a year.

Parish council functions include: allotments; encouragement of arts and crafts; community halls, recreational facilities (e.g. open spaces, swimming pools), cemeteries and crematoria; and many minor functions. They must also be given an opportunity to comment on planning applications. They may, like county and district councils, spend limited sums for the general benefit of the parish. They precept on the district councils for their rate funds.

Civic Dignities

District councils may petition for a Royal Charter granting borough status to the district. In boroughs the chairman of the council is the mayor. The status "City" and the right to call the mayor "Lord Mayor" may also be granted by letters patent. Parish councils may call themselves "town councils", in which case their chairman is the "town mayor".

Charter trustees are established for those former boroughs which were too large to have parish councils when local government was reorganised in 1974 and they became part of districts without city or borough status. The charter trustees are the district councillors representing the area of the former borough and they elect a mayor, continue civic tradition, and look after the charters, insignia and civic plate of the former borough.

Local Commissioners for England and Wales

Local Commissioners for England and Wales have been appointed with the duty of investigating complaints of maladministration in aspects of local government; they report to the local council concerned.

Wales

Since 1974 Wales, including the former Monmouthshire, has been divided into eight counties; Gwynedd; Clwyd; Powys; Dyfed; West, Mid and South Glamorgan; and Gwent. There are 37 districts in Wales, many of those in the less populated parts reflecting the areas of former Welsh counties.

The arrangements for Welsh counties and districts are generally similar to those for English nonmetropolitan counties and districts. There are some differences in functions: Welsh district councils have refuse disposal as well as refuse collection functions and they may provide on-street as well as off-street car parks with the consent of the county council. A few districts have also been designated as library authorities.

In Wales parishes have been replaced by communities. Unlike England, where many areas are not in any parish, communities have been established for the whole of Wales; approximately 1,000 communities in all. Community meetings may be convened as and when desired. Community councils exist in about 770 communities and further councils may be established at the request of a community meeting. Community councils have broadly the same range of powers as English parish councils. Community councillors are elected *en bloc* on the same basis as parish councillors in England, i.e. at the same time as a district council election and for a term of four years.

Local Government Finance

Local government is financed from various sources.

(1) *Rates.*—Levied by district councils, and in London by the boroughs and City Corporation. Sums required by county and parish councils, and joint boards for police, fire and transport services in the metropolitan areas are included in the rates levied by the rating authorities. Rates are levied by a poundage tax on the rateable value of property in the area of the rating authority. The General Rate Act 1967 requires rating authorities to charge a lower rate (18½p less) in the pound on dwellings than on property generally in their area. Annual rental values, on certain statutory assumptions are determined as at the date of the current valuation lists prepared by valuation officers of the Board of Inland Revenue and which came into force on April 1, 1973.

New property is added to the list and significant changes to existing property necessitate amendments to the rateable value. The lists remain in force until the next general revaluation. Certain types of property are exempt from rates, e.g. agricultural land and buildings, and places of public religious worship. Some charities and other non-profit-making organizations can receive full or partial exemption. Local authorities can rate specified classes of empty property, though these powers have been suspended in respect of empty industrial properties since April 1984 and empty warehouses since April 1985. The Social Security and Housing Benefits Act 1982 (administered by the D.H.S.S.) makes provision for rate rebates for domestic ratepayers, eligibility depending on income, rates payable and number of people in the household. The Rating (Disabled Persons) Act 1978 provides rate relief in respect of certain facilities needed by disabled persons.

The Rates Act, 1984 gives the Secretary of State for the Environment power to limit by law the rates or precepts some local councils can ask their ratepayers to pay. Twenty authorities are subject to rate limitation in 1987–88, and a further twenty (I.L.E.A. and 19 joint boards set up following the abolition of the G.L.C. and the metropolitan counties in 1986) have their precepts limited.

(2) *Government Grants.*—In addition to specific Government grants-in-aid of revenue expenditure on particular services, from April 1, 1981 grants known as rate support grants have been payable to local authorities. These grants consist of two elements: block grant and domestic rate relief grant. The block grant, which is a single grant payment, is payable to local authorities and joint boards established by the Local Government Act, 1985. The block grant is

intended to enable all authorities to provide comparable standards of service at the same poundage cost to local ratepayers. The domestic rate relief grant is payable to all rating authorities to reimburse them for the cost of giving the domestic rate relief prescribed for the year.

In order to arrive at the total amount of the rate support grants to local authorities in England for any year (the grant system provides for Wales to be administered separately), the aggregate of Exchequer grants to local authorities in respect of their relevant expenditure for the year is determined in advance (housing subsidies and specific grants towards expenditure on rate rebates and mandatory awards to students and trainee teachers are outside this aggregate amount) and from this is deducted the estimated amount of specific grants for the year in aid of revenue expenditure and the supplementary grants for transport purposes and in connection with national parks; the resulting balance is the amount of rate support grant.

Forecasts of local authority relevant expenditure for 1987–88 in England adopted by the Government for rate support grant purposes were as follows. The amounts given are at 1987–88 cash prices.

Service	£M
Education	11,940
School meals and milk	450
Libraries, museums and art galleries ..	453
Personal social services and port health............................	2,847
Police	3,021
Fire	690
Other Home Office services	404
Local transport	1,950
Local environmental services.........	2,850
Agricultural services	120
Consumer protection and trading standards	69
Employment........................	96
Non-Housing Revenue Account housing	135
Housing benefits	186
Unallocated current expenditure	40
Total current expenditure	25,251
Rate fund revenue account contributions to capital outlay	19
Loan charges (including leasing)......	2,560
Rate fund revenue account contributions to Housing Revenue Account..	437
Interest receipts	−521
Total relevant expenditure	27,746

The aggregate amount of Exchequer grants for 1987–88 was determined at £12,842 million. Of this, the specific grants and the transport and National Parks supplementary grants were estimated at £3,293 million, giving a total for rate support grants of £9,549 million, of which £8,832 million was in respect of the block grant and £717 million the domestic rate relief grant.

Rates and Rateable Values.—The total rateable value for England on April 1, 1986 was £7,623·6 million (figure for 1987 not yet available) and an estimate of the amount to be raised in rates, gross of rebates, in 1987–88 is £16,194 million.

Average Rates.—The estimated average rates levied in England in 1987–88 were: Inner London Boroughs, *domestic* rate 173·8p, *non-domestic* rate 184·1p; Outer London, 185·5p and 206·4p; Metropolitan Districts, 254·5p and 275·0p. The average rates levied in England were estimated at 210·4p (domestic)

and 226·6p (non-domestic). In Wales the estimated average rates levied were, *domestic* rate 218·1p, *non-domestic* rate 236·5p.

SCOTLAND

Since 1975, mainland Scotland has been divided into nine regions within which there are 53 districts. Regional and district councils have separate responsibility for specific functions. In the three islands areas, Orkney, Shetland and the Western Isles, there are single tier Islands Councils responsible for most of the functions of both regional and district councils.

Regional Functions—Regional Councils are responsible for education; social work; strategic planning; the provision of infrastructure such as roads, water and sewerage; consumer protection; flood prevention; coast protection; and valuation and rating. They also have responsibility for the police and fire services; civil defence; and electoral registration, and in relation to public transport and registration of births, deaths and marriages.

District Functions—District Councils deal with more local matters such as housing; leisure and recreation, including tourism, parks, libraries, museums and galleries; development control and building control; environmental health, including cleansing, refuse collection and disposal, food hygiene, inspection of shops, offices and factories, clean air, markets and slaughterhouses, burial and crematoria; licensing, including liquor, cinemas and theatres, taxis, street traders, betting and gaming, and charitable collections; allotments; public conveniences; the administration of district courts.

Community Councils—Unlike the parish councils of England or community councils of Wales, Scottish community councils are not local authorities. Their purpose as defined in statute is to ascertain and express the views of the communities which they represent, and to take in the interests of their communities such action as appears to be expedient or practicable. Schemes drawn up by district and islands councils provide for a possible total of 1,342 community councils, of which about 1,130 are in existence.

Local Government Electors.—In 1987 Register shows 3,994,211 electors in Scotland. Elections are next due to take place in 1988 for district councils, and in 1990 for regional and island councils.

Rates and Rateable Values.—In 1983–84, the latest year for which final figures were available, a total of £1,480,800,000 was received from the general rates of local government in Scotland and £45,300,000 from domestic water rates. The rateable value on which rates were leviable was £1,320,800,000 on the general rates and £481,900,000 on the domestic water rates. The average general rate levied was 124·9p and the domestic water rate levied was 9·0p.

Provisional figures for 1986–87 show total receipts from general rates of £1,907,100,000 and £52,421,000 from domestic water rates. The average rate per £ levied for 1986–87 was 67·38p (general) and 3·95p (domestic water rate).

NORTHERN IRELAND

For the purpose of local government Northern Ireland has a system of 26 single-tier district councils. There are 566 members of the councils, elected for periods of four years at a time on the principle of proportional representation.

The district councils all have the same three main roles. These are:

(a) an executive role in which the councils are responsible for a wide range of local services including the provision of recreational, social, community, and cultural facilities; environmental health; consumer protection; the enforcement of building regulations; the promotion of tourist development schemes; gas supply; street cleansing; refuse collection and disposal; litter prevention; and miscellaneous licensing and registration provisions, including dog control;

(b) a representative role in which they nominate representatives to sit as members of the various statutory bodies responsible for the administration of regional services such as education and

libraries, health and personal social services, drainage, fire and electricity; and

(c) a consultative role in which they act as the media through which the views of local people are expressed on the operation in their area of other regional services notably planning, roads, and conservation (including water supply and sewerage services) provided by those departments of central government which have an obligation, either statutorily or otherwise, to consult the district councils about proposals affecting their areas.

PARTY REPRESENTATION IN LOCAL GOVERNMENT

Abbreviations: *A.* = Liberal/S.D.P. Alliance; *C.* = Conservative; *Com.* = Communist; *Ind.* = Independent; *Ind.C.* = Independent Conservative; *Ind.L.* = Independent Liberal; *Ind.Lab.* = Independent Labour; *L.* = Liberal; *Lab.* = Labour; *M.K.* = Mebyon Kernow; *N.P.* = Non-Political/Non-Party; *O.S.M.* = Orkney and Shetland Movement; *P.C.* = Plaid Cymru; *R.A.* = Ratepayers'/Residents' Associations; *S.D.P.* = Social Democratic Party; *S.M.* = Shetland Movement; *S.N.P.* = Scottish National Party.

ENGLAND

Counties (as at end May 1987)

Avon ....*Lab.* 36, *C.* 31, *A.* 9.
Bedford ....*C.* 30, *Lab.* 29, *A.* 11, *L.* 3.
Berkshire ....*C.* 41, *A.* 17, *Lab.* 17, *R.A.* 1
Bucks. ....*C.* 48, *Lab.* 12, *A.* 8, *Ind.* 1, *Ind.* C. 1, *L.* 1.
Cambridge..........*C.* 30, *Lab.* 21, *L.* 19, *S.D.P.* 6, *Ind.* 1.
Cheshire ....*C.* 27, *L.* 32, *A.* 11, *Ind.* 1.
Cleveland ....*Lab.* 51, *C.* 20, *A.* 6.
Cornwall ....*L.* 28, *Ind.* 26, *C.* 16, *Lab.* 5, *S.D.P.* 2, *M.K.* 1, (1 Vac).
Cumbria............*Lab.* 39, *C.* 37, *L.* 5, *Ind.* 2.
Derbyshire ....*Lab.* 54, *C.* 24, *L.* 3, *Ind.* 2, *S.D.P.* 1.
Devon..............*C.* 38, *A.* 35, *Lab.* 10, *Ind.* 2.
Dorset ....*C.* 42, *A.* 26, *Ind.* 4, *Lab.* 4 (1 Vac).
Durham ....*Lab.* 48, *A.* 7, *Ind.* 7, *C.* 6, *N.P.* 2, *Ind.Lab.* 1, (1 Vac).
Essex ....*C.* 45, *Lab.* 29, *A.* 23, *R.A.* 1.
Gloucestershire .....*A.* 23, *C.* 20, *Lab.* 13, *Ind.* C. 4, *Ind.* 1, *Others* 2.
Hampshire ....*C.* 50, *A.* 32, *L.* 18, *Ind.* 2.
Hereford and
    Worcester ....*C.* 40, *Lab.* 18, *A.* 14, *Ind.* 4.
Hertfordshire.......*C.* 36, *Lab.* 27, *A.* 14.
Humberside ....*Lab.* 36, *C.* 35, *A.* 4.

Kent ....*C.* 57, *Lab.* 24, *L.* 16, *S.D.P.* 2.
Lancashire ....*Lab.* 48, *C.* 42, *L.* 9.
Leicestershire ......*C.* 42, *Lab.* 32, *A.* 11.
Lincolnshire........*C.* 39, *A.* 15, *Lab.* 13, *L.* 5, *Ind.* 2, *Others* 2.
Norfolk ....*C.* 43, *Lab.* 25, *A.* 16.
Northampton-
    shire. ....*C.* 34, *Lab.* 29, *L.* 4, *Ind.* 1.
Northumberland ....*Lab.* 31, *A.* 20, *C.* 13, *Ind.* C. 2.
Nottinghamshire. ...*Lab.* 47, *C.* 37, *A.* 4.
Oxfordshire ....*C.* 31, *Lab.* 20, *A.* 18, (1 Vac.).
Shropshire ....*C.* 26, *Lab.* 24, *A.* 9, *Ind.* 7.
Somerset ....*A.* 25, *C.* 25, *Lab.* 6, (1 Vac.).
Staffordshire ....*Lab.* 48, *C.* 30, *L.* 3, *S.D.P.* 1.
Suffolk ....*C.* 50, *Lab.* 22, *Ind.* 4, *A.* 3, (1 Vac.).
Surrey ....*C.* 48, *A.* 14, *Lab.* 7, *Ind.* 3, *R.A.* 2, (2 Vac.).
Sussex, East ....*C.* 35, *L.* 20, *Lab.* 14, *A.* 1.
Sussex, West ....*C.* 47, *A.* 17, *Lab.* 7.
Warwickshire ....*C.* 26, *Lab.* 24, *L.* 6, *S.D.P.* 4, *Ind.* 1, *R.A.* 1.
Wight, I. of ....*L.* 27, *C.* 13, *Ind.* 3.
Wiltshire...........*C.* 31, *A.* 24, *Lab.* 17, *Ind.* 2, *R.A.* 1.
Yorkshire, N. ....*C.* 42, *A.* 28, *Lab.* 19, *Ind.* 6, (1 Vac.).

Metropolitan District Councils (as at end May 1987)

GREATER MANCHESTER

Bolton ....*Lab.* 38, *C.* 15, *A.* 7.
Bury ....*Lab.* 30, *C.* 18.
Manchester.........*Lab.* 77, *C.* 13, *L.* 8, *S.D.P.* 1.
Oldham ....*Lab.* 41, *C.* 10, *L.* 7, *S.D.P.* 2.
Rochdale ....*Lab.* 35, *C.* 12, *L.* 12, *Other* 1.
Salford ....*Lab.* 53, *C.* 5, (2 Vac.).
Stockport ....*A.* 22, *C.* 22, *Lab.* 15, *R.A.* 3, *Other* 1.
Tameside ....*Lab.* 45, *C.* 8, *L.* 4.
Trafford ....*C.* 28, *Lab.* 28, *L.* 7.
Wigan ....*Lab.* 61, *A.* 6, *C.* 3, *Ind.* 1, (1 Vac.).

MERSEYSIDE

Knowsley ....*Lab.* 60, *C.* 4, *A.* 1, *Ind. Lab.* 1.
Liverpool...........*Lab.* 51, *A.* 44, *C.* 4.
St. Helens ....*Lab.* 43, *C.* 9, *A.* 2.
Sefton..............*C.* 27, *Lab.* 24, *A.* 18.
Wirral ....*C.* 29, *Lab.* 27, *A.* 10.

SOUTH YORKSHIRE

Barnsley ....*Lab.* 62, *C.* 2, *Ind.* 1, *R.A.* 1.
Doncaster ....*Lab.* 53, *C.* 9, *L.* 1.
Rotherham ....*Lab.* 62, *A.* 2, *C.* 1, *Ind.* 1.
Sheffield...........*Lab.* 65, *C.* 13, *A.* 9.

TYNE AND WEAR

Gateshead..........*Lab.* 58, *C.* 3, *S.D.P.* 3, *L.* 1, (1 Vac.).
Newcastle upon
    Tyne.............*Lab.* 52, *A.* 13, *C.* 12, (1 Vac.).
North Tyneside .....*Lab.* 31, *C.* 16, *A.* 9, *Ind. Lab.* 1, *Others* 3.
South Tyneside .....*Lab.* 53, *C.* 3, *Others* 4.
Sunderland ....*Lab.* 60, *C.* 10, *A.* 4, (1 Vac.).

WEST MIDLANDS

Birmingham ....*Lab.* 65, *C.* 46, *L.* 3, *S.D.P.* 3.
Coventry ....*Lab.* 41, *C.* 11, *L.* 2.
Dudley ....*Lab.* 41, *C.* 30, (1 Vac.).

Sandwell .... Lab. 56, C. 12, L. 3, Ind. L. 1.
Solihull .... C. 28, Lab. 14, A. 3, Ind. 3, R.A. 3.
Walsall .... Lab. 29, C. 18, A. 9, Ind. 4.
Wolverhampton ..... Lab. 30, C. 23, L. 7.

WEST YORKSHIRE

Bradford .... Lab. 49, C. 38, L. 3.
Calderdale .... Lab. 24, C. 16, A. 14.
Kirklees .... Lab. 33, C. 21, L. 18.
Leeds .... Lab. 58, C. 25, A. 14, Ind. 2.
Wakefield .... Lab. 56, C. 3, L. 3, Ind. 1.

Non-Metropolitan District Councils (as at end May 1987)
(* one-third of councillors of Councils so denoted retire each year, except in those years when County Council elections are held)

*Adur .... L. 22, C. 15, R.A. 2.
Allerdale .... Lab. 24, Ind. 19, C. 12.
Alnwick .... L. 12, N.P. 8, Ind. 4, C. 3, Lab. 2.
*Amber Valley ..... Lab. 21, C. 19, A. 2, Ind. 1.
Arun .... C. 51, A. 4, Lab. 1.
Ashfield .... Lab. 26, C. 4, A. 3.
Ashford .... C. 31, A. 10, Lab. 6, Ind. 1, Ind. L. 1.
Aylesbury Vale .... C. 34, A. 14, Ind. 8, Lab. 2.
Babergh .... C. 18, Ind. 11, A. 4, Lab. 2, Others 7.
*Barrow-in-Furness .... Lab. 24, C. 13, Ind. 1.
*Basildon .... Lab. 20, C. 11, L. 8, S.D.P. 3.
*Basingstoke & Deane .... C. 32, Lab. 14, S.D.P. 5, Ind. 4, L. 3, (1 Vac.).
*Bassetlaw .... Lab. 27, C. 18, Ind. 3, Others 2.
*Bath .... C. 24, A. 16, Lab. 8.
Berwick upon Tweed .... L. 13, C. 5, Ind. 3, Lab. 1, Others 6.
Beverley .... C. 34, L. 16, Lab. 2, Ind. 1.
Blaby .... C. 31, Ind. 4, A. 3, Ind. C. 1.
*Blackburn .... Lab. 30, C. 21, A. 7, R.A. 2.
Blackpool .... C. 22, Lab. 15, A. 6, Ind. C. 1.
Blyth Valley ...... Lab. 24, L. 11, S.D.P. 11, A. 1.
Bolsover .... Lab. 30, A. 2, R.A. 2, C. 1, Ind. 1, Other 1.
Boothferry .... C. 17, Lab. 10, Ind. 8.
Boston .... C. 15, Ind. 7, A. 5, Lab. 5, (2 Vac.).
Bournemouth ...... C. 37, A. 13, Lab. 4, Ind. 3.
Bracknell .... C. 40.
Braintree .... C. 30, Lab. 13, Ind. 8, A. 5, R.A. 4.
Breckland .... C. 33, Lab. 7, Ind. 5, N.P. 5, A. 2, (1 Vac.).
*Brentwood .... C. 24, L. 13, Lab. 2.
Bridgnorth .... C. 11, Ind. 8, N.P. 8, A. 2, Ind. Lab. 2, L. 2.
Brighton .... Lab. 24, C. 20, L. 3, Ind. C. 1.
*Bristol .... Lab. 37, C. 25, L. 6.
*Broadland .... C. 33, A. 10, Ind. 6.
Bromsgrove .... C. 28, Lab. 7, A. 4, R.A. 2.
*Broxbourne ...... C. 34, Lab. 6, A. 2.
Broxtowe .... C. 32, Lab. 10, A. 6, Ind. 1.
*Burnley .... Lab. 39, C. 5, S.D.P. 4, L. 3, Ind. 1, (1 Vac.).
*Cambridge .... Lab. 20, A. 11, C. 11.
*Cannock Chase ... Lab. 23, L. 15, C. 3, (1 Vac.).
Canterbury .... C. 33, A. 8, Lab. 5, L. 3.
Caradon .... Ind. 25, C. 7, A. 5, R.A. 3, Lab. 1.
Carlisle .... Lab. 27, C. 20, L. 3, Ind. 1.
Carrick .... A. 21, C. 15, Ind. 5, Lab. 4.
Castle Morpeth .... A. 9, Ind. 9, C. 5, Lab. 5, L. 3, Others 3.
Castle Point .... C. 39.
Charnwood .... C. 39, Lab. 10, A. 3.
Chelmsford .... A. 29, C. 24, Ind. 3.
*Cheltenham ...... C. 15, L. 14, Lab. 2, R.A. 2.
*Cherwell .... C. 33, Lab. 12, A. 7.
*Chester .... C. 29, Lab. 18, L. 10, Ind. 2, (1 Vac.).
Chesterfield .... Lab. 35, A. 7, C. 5.
Chester-le-Street ... Lab. 24, Ind. 4, L. 4, C. 1.

Chichester .... C. 35, A. 12, Ind. 2, R.A. 1.
Chiltern .... C. 41, A. 6, Lab. 1, R.A. 1, (1 Vac.).
*Chorley .... C. 24, Lab. 20, A. 2, Ind. 1, L. 1.
Christchurch ...... C. 15, Ind. 4, A. 3, Lab. 3.
Cleethorpes .... A. 15, C. 11, Lab. 11, Ind. 4.
*Colchester .... C. 24, A. 23, Lab. 9, R.A. 3, Ind. 1.
*Congleton .... A. 21, C. 18, Lab. 5, Ind. 1.
Copeland .... Lab. 26, C. 20, Ind. 3, R.A. 2.
Corby .... Lab. 23, C. 3, Ind. 1.
Cotswold .... N.P. 26, C. 9, Ind. 6, A. 2, Ind. C. 1, Lab. 1.
*Craven .... C. 14, L. 12, Ind. 5, Lab. 3.
*Crawley .... Lab. 18, C. 13, A. 1.
*Crewe and Nantwich .... C. 26, Lab. 24, A. 5, Ind. C. 1, L. 1.
Dacorum .... C. 40, A. 10, Lab. 8.
Darlington .... C. 24, Lab. 24, Ind. 2, L. 2.
Dartford .... C. 29, Lab. 16, R.A. 2.
*Daventry .... C. 19, Lab. 9, Ind. 5, L. 2.
*Derby .... L. 22, C. 20, (2 Vac.).
Derbyshire Dales .. C. 23, A. 9, Lab. 3, N.P. 2, Ind. 1, Ind. C. 1.
Derwentside .... Lab. 43, Ind. 9, C. 3.
Dover .... C. 33, Ind. 19, A. 4.
Durham .... Lab. 26, A. 14, Ind. 6, Ind. Lab. 3.
Easington .... Lab. 43, Ind. 4, L. 2, A. 1, Ind. Lab. 1.
*Eastbourne .... A. 17, C. 13.
East Cambridgeshire ... N.P. 24, Ind. 4, L. 3, S.D.P. 2, C. 2, Others 2.
*East Devon .... C. 52, A. 7, Lab. 1.
East Hampshire .... C. 26, A. 11, Ind. 5.
East Hertfordshire . C. 32, R.A. 6, A. 5, Ind. 5, Ind. C. 1, Lab. 1.
*Eastleigh .... A. 22, C. 15, Lab. 7.
East Lindsey .... N.P. 25, A. 12, C. 10, Ind. 10, Lab. 3.
East Northamptonshire C. 30, Lab. 5, A. 1.
East Staffordshire .. C. 22, Lab. 21, A. 2, Ind. 1.
East Yorkshire ..... C. 21, Ind. 14, A. 6, Ind. L. 1, Lab. 1.
Eden .... Ind. 36, C. 1.
*Ellesmere Port & Neston .... Lab. 28, C. 12, Ind. Lab, 1.
*Elmbridge .... C. 29, N.P. 18, A. 7, Lab. 6.
*Epping Forest ..... C. 35, Lab. 11, R.A. 6, A. 4, Ind. 2, Ind. C. 1.
Epsom & Ewell ... R.A. 35, Lab. 3, A. 1.
Erewash .... C. 29, Lab. 20, Ind. C. 1, Ind. Lab. 1, N.P. 1.
Exeter .... C. 15, Lab. 13, L. 6, Ind. 1, S.D.P. 1.
*Fareham .... C. 23, A. 7, S.D.P. 6, L. 3, R.A. 3.
Fenland .... C. 25, Ind. 5, Lab. 4, L. 3, A. 3.
Forest Heath ...... C. 14, Ind. 9, Others 2.
Forest of Dean ..... Lab. 13, A. 9, N.P. 9, C. 7, Ind. Lab. 6, Ind. 4, R.A. 1.
Fylde .... C. 29, R.A. 11, Ind. 5, Ind. C. 2, L. 1, Lab. 1.
Gedling .... C. 48, A. 4, Lab. 4, Ind. 1.
*Gillingham .... C. 22, A. 14, Lab. 6.
Glanford .... C. 25, Ind. 13, Lab. 2, A. 1.

*Gloucester.........C. 17, *Lab.* 10, *L.* 5, *Ind.* C. 1.
*Gosport ....C. 19, *L.* 6, *Lab.* 5.
Gravesham ....C. 22, *Lab.* 22.
*Great Grimsby .....*Lab.* 26, C. 12, A. 6, *Ind.* 1.
Great Yarmouth ...C. 24, *Lab.* 22, A. 2.
Guildford..........C. 30, A. 9, *Lab.* 6.
*Halton ....*Lab.* 43, A. 5, C. 4, *Other* 1.
Hambleton ....C. 21, *Ind.* 17, A. 7, *Ind.* C. 1,
   Lab. 1.
Harborough ....C. 17, A. 11, *Ind.* 7, *Lab.* 2.
*Harlow...........*Lab.* 37, A. 3, C. 2.
Harrogate ....C. 32, *L.* 18, A. 5, *Lab.* 3, *Ind.* 2.
*Hart ....A. 16, C. 14, *Ind.* 5.
*Hartlepool ....*Lab.* 33, C. 10, A. 2, *Ind.* 2.
*Hastings ....*L.* 14, C. 11, *Lab.* 7.
*Havant............C. 23, *Lab.* 11, A. 4, *Ind.* 2, *R.A.*
   2.
*Hereford ....A. 19, C. 4, *Lab.* 3, *Ind.* 1.
*Hertsmere ....C. 22, *Lab.* 12, A. 5.
High Peak ....C. 21, *Lab.* 11, A. 7, *Ind.* 5.
Hinckley and
   Bosworth ....C. 21, A. 8, *Lab.* 5.
Holderness ........N.P. 21, A. 5. *Ind.* 4, C. 1.
Horsham ....C. 33, A. 6, *Ind.* 4.
Hove..............C. 22, *Lab.* 4, *L.* 3, *Ind.* 1.
*Huntingdon ....C. 44, *Lab.* 5, *Ind.* 2, A. 1, *Ind.*
   L. 1.
Hyndburn ....*Lab.* 26, C. 14, A. 7.
*Ipswich ....*Lab.* 33, C. 15.
Kennet............C. 14, N.P. 11, A. 8, *Ind.* 7.
Kerrier ...........S.D.P. 19, N.P. 11, *Ind.* 5, C. 4,
   Lab. 4, M.K. 1.
Kettering ....C. 17, *Lab.* 12, A. 9, *Ind.* 7.
King's Lynn &
   W. Norfolk ......C. 47, *Lab.* 11, A. 1, S.D.P. 1.
*Kingston upon Hull *Lab.* 52, C. 4, *L.* 3, (1 Vac.).
Kingswood ....C. 26, *Lab.* 20, *L.* 2, *Ind.* 1,
   S.D.P. 1.
Lancaster ....C. 28, *Lab.* 21, A. 9, R.A. 1,
   Other 1.
Langbaurgh ....*Lab.* 27, C. 24, A. 7, *Ind. Lab.* 2.
*Leicester ....*Lab.* 34, C. 16, A. 6.
*Leominster ....*Ind.* 23, C. 8, A. 3, *L.* 1.
Lewes.............C. 34, A. 11, *Ind.* 3.
Lichfield ....C. 42, *Lab.* 10, *Ind. Lab.* 3, *Ind.*
   1.
*Lincoln ....C. 25, *Lab.* 8.
Luton ....C. 32, *Lab.* 13, *L.* 3.
*Macclesfield ......C. 35, A. 13, *Lab.* 5, *Ind.* 4, R.A.
   3.
*Maidstone ....A. 25, C. 20, *Lab.* 8, *Ind* 2.
Maldon ....C. 14, A. 11, *Ind.* 3, *Ind.* C. 1,
   Lab. 1.
Malvern Hills......A. 17, C. 11, N.P. 11, *Ind.* 10,
   Lab. 1, *Other* 1.
Mansfield..........*Lab.* 36, C. 9, S.D.P. 1.
Medina............C. 20, A. 12, *Ind.* 2, *L.* 1, N.P. 1.
Melton ....C. 15, A. 7, *Ind.* 4.
Mendip............A. 19, C. 18, *Ind.* 4, *Lab.* 2.
Mid Bedfordshire ..C. 42, A. 3, *Ind.* 3, N.P. 3, *Lab.*
   2.
Mid Devon ....*Ind.* 27, A. 9, *L.* 4.
Middlesbrough.....*Lab.* 37, C. 12, A. 3, *Ind.* 1.
Mid Suffolk ....C. 19, *Lab.* 7, *Ind.* 6, A. 4, N.P.
   4.
*Mid Sussex ....C. 36, A. 13, *Ind.* 5.
*Milton Keynes .....*Lab.* 18, A. 14, C. 11, *Ind.* 3.
*Mole Valley ....C. 15, N.P. 14, *L.* 10, *Lab.* 1,
   S.D.P. 1.
Newark ....C. 26, *Lab.* 23, *Ind.* L. 3, A. 2.
Newbury ....C. 34, A. 11.
*Newcastle under
   Lyme ....*Lab.* 36, A. 9, C. 9, *Ind.* 2.
New Forest ....C. 33, A. 18, *Ind.* 3, N.P. 2, R.A.
   1, *Other* 1.
Northampton ......C. 25, *Lab.* 16, *L.* 2.
Northavon ....C. 30, A. 18, *Lab.* 8, *Ind.* 1.

*North Bedfordshire C. 26, A. 14, *Lab.* 12, *Ind.* 1.
North Cornwall ....*Ind.* 9, A. 7, C. 2, *Others* 20.
North Devon ....*Ind.* 17, *L.* 16, C. 9, *Others* 2.
North Dorset ......*Ind.* 24, A. 8, C. 1.
N.-E. Derbyshire ...*Lab.* 32, C. 15, *Ind.* 4, A. 1, *Other*
   1.
*North Hertfordshire C. 26, *Lab.* 13, A. 8, R.A. 3.
North Kesteven ...C. 15, *Ind.* 13, N.P. 5, A. 4, *Lab.*
   2.
North Norfolk .....N.P. 16, *Ind.* 13, C. 11, A. 3,
   Lab. 3.
North Shropshire ..N.P. 27, C. 6, *Ind.* 5, *Lab.* 2.
N. Warwickshire...*Lab.* 19, C. 12, *Ind.* 1, N.P. 1,
   S.D.P. 1.
N.-W. Leicestershire *Lab.* 19, C. 14, *Ind.* 4, A. 3.
North Wiltshire....C. 28, A. 22, *Ind.* 1, *Lab.* 1.
*Norwich ....*Lab.* 36, A. 9, C. 3.
Nottingham ....C. 28, *Lab.* 26, *Com.* 1.
*Nuneaton &
   Bedworth ....*Lab.* 33, C. 11, A. 1.
*Oadby & Wigston ..C. 18, *L.* 8.
Oswestry .........N.P. 14, C. 6, *Lab.* 5, A. 4.
*Oxford ....*Lab.* 28, C. 11, A. 5, (1 Vac.).
*Pendle ....L. 25, *Lab.* 19, C. 5, S.D.P. 1, (1
   Vac.).
*Penwith...........N.P. 13, C. 12, *Lab.* 5, A. 2, *L.* 1,
   M.K. 1.
*Peterborough ......*Lab.* 22, C. 17, *L.* 8, *Ind. L.* 1.
Plymouth ....C. 31, *Lab.* 19, A. 10.
Poole ....C. 21, A. 15.
Portsmouth........C. 21, *Lab.* 9, A. 6, *Ind.* 1, *Ind.*
   C. 1, *Ind. Lab.* 1.
*Preston ....*Lab.* 35, C. 16, *L.* 6.
*Purbeck ....C. 7, *L.* 4, A. 3, *Ind.* 3, N.P. 3,
   R.A. 2.
Reading ....*Lab.* 24, C. 16, A. 5.
*Redditch ....*Lab.* 18, C. 9, A. 2.
*Reigate & Banstead C. 32, *Lab.* 10, *L.* 4, S.D.P. 2,
   Ind. 1.
Restormel ....A. 15, N.P. 11, *Ind.* 7, *L.* 5, C. 4,
   Ind. C. 1, *Lab.* 1.
Ribble Valley ......C. 31, *Ind.* 3, *Lab.* 3, A. 2.
Richmondshire ....*Ind.* 27, A. 7.
Rochester upon
   Medway ....C. 29, *Lab.* 14, A. 6, *Ind.* 1.
*Rochford ....C. 23, *L.* 10, *Lab.* 6, *Ind.* 1.
*Rossendale ....*Lab.* 19, C. 17.
Rother ....C. 29, *Ind.* 7, A. 3, R.A. 3, *Lab.*
   2, *L.* 1.
*Rugby.............C. 25, *Lab.* 16, R.A. 3, A. 1, *Ind.*
   1, *Other* 2.
*Runnymede ....C. 25, *Lab.* 8, *Ind.* 6, *L.* 2, S.D.P.
   1.
Rushcliffe ....C. 46, A. 6, *Lab.* 2.
*Rushmoor ....C. 31, *L.* 6, *Lab.* 6, A. 2.
Rutland ....C. 9, A. 8, *Ind.* 3.
Ryedale ....A. 17, *Ind.* 9, C. 3, *Others* 13.
St. Albans ....C. 25, A. 24, *Lab.* 7, *Ind.* 1.
St. Edmundsbury...C. 31, *Lab.* 8, A. 4, *Ind.* 1.
Salisbury ....C. 32, A. 9, *Ind.* 9, R.A. 5, *Lab.*
   3.
Scarborough ....C. 19, *Ind.* 14, A. 8, *Lab.* 8.
*Scunthorpe ....*Lab.* 30, C. 6, S.D.P. 4.
Sedgefield ....*Lab.* 36, A. 7, C. 2, *Ind.* 2, N.P.
   2.
Sedgemoor ....C. 32, A. 7, *Lab.* 5, *Ind.* 4, *Ind.*
   Lab. 1.
Selby..............C. 26, *Ind.* 10, *Lab.* 9, A. 5.
Sevenoaks ....C. 34, *Ind.* 11, A. 6, *Ind.* C. 1, *L.*
   1.
Shepway ....A. 26, C. 26, *Ind.* 3, S.D.P. 1.
*Shrewsbury &
   Atcham ....C. 21, *Lab.* 16, *L.* 6, S.D.P. 3,
   Ind. 2.
*Slough ....*Lab.* 24, C. 11, *L.* 3, S.D.P. 1.
*Southampton ......*Lab.* 21, C. 19, A. 4, *Ind.* 1.
*South Bedfordshire. C. 39, *Lab.* 8, A. 4, R.A. 2.

South Bucks. ...... *C.* 30, *A.* 4, *R.A.* 4, *N.P.* 2, *Ind.* 1.
*South
  Cambridgeshire ... *Ind.* 30, *C.* 19, *A.* 3, *Lab.* 3.
South Derbyshire ... *Lab.* 18, *C.* 9, *Ind.* 4, *Ind. C.* 2, *L.* 1.
*Southend-on-Sea ... *A.* 19, *C.* 15, *Lab.* 5.
South Hams .... *C.* 27, *N.P.* 7, *Ind.* 6, *A.* 3, *Lab.* 1.
*Sth. Herefordshire .*N.P.* 17, *Ind.* 8, *A.* 5, *C.* 5.
South Holland ..... *N.P.* 17, *C.* 13, *Ind.* 5, *A.* 2, *Lab.* 1.
South Kesteven ..... *C.* 34, *Lab.* 9, *L.* 8, *Others* 6.
*South Lakeland .... *C.* 23, *A.* 12, *Ind.* 7, *N.P.* 5, *Lab.* 4, (1 Vac.).
South Norfolk ...... *C.* 24, *A.* 17, *Ind.* 5, *Ind. C.* 1.
S. Northants. ...... *C.* 28, *Ind.* 8, *Lab.* 2, *Others* 2.
S. Oxfordshire ..... *C.* 38, *Lab.* 8, *Ind.* 6, *A.* 4.
South Ribble ...... *C.* 36, *Lab.* 11, *L.* 7.
S. Shropshire ...... *N.P.* 17, *A.* 6, *C.* 5, *Ind.* 4, *Ind. L.* 1, *Others* 7.
South Somerset .... *A.* 34, *C.* 15, *Ind.* 11.
South Staffordshire *C.* 38, *Lab.* 4, *A.* 3, *Ind.* 2, *Others* 3.
South Wight ...... *C.* 13, *Ind.* 6, *L.* 4, *R.A.* 1.
Spelthorne .... *C.* 38, *Lab.* 2.
Stafford .... *Ind. C.* 31, *L.* 17, *A.* 12.
Staffordshire
  Moorlands .... *C.* 20, *Ind. C.* 14, *Lab.* 9, *R.A.* 6, *Ind.* 4, *A.* 3.
*Stevenage .... *Lab.* 26, *S.D.P.* 7, *L.* 5, *C.* 1.
Stockton-on-Tees . *Lab.* 28, *C.* 18, *A.* 9.
*Stoke-on-Trent .... *Lab.* 54, *C.* 6.
*Stratford-on-
  Avon. .... *C.* 36, *L.* 9, *Ind.* 7, *Lab.* 2, *S.D.P.* 1.
*Stroud .... *C.* 23, *A.* 15, *Lab.* 9, *Ind.* 8, *Other* 1.
Suffolk Coastal ..... *C.* 39, *Ind.* 7, *A.* 6, *N.P.* 2, *Lab.* 1.
Surrey Heath ...... *C.* 36.
*Swale .... *C.* 19, *Lab.* 13, *L.* 12, *S.D.P.* 5.
*Tamworth .... *C.* 16, *Lab.* 14.
*Tandridge .... *C.* 28, *A.* 9, *Lab.* 3, *Ind.* 1, (1 Vac.).
Taunton Deane ... *C.* 28, *A.* 15, *Lab.* 7, *Ind.* 3.
Teesdale .... *Ind.* 21, *Lab.* 5, *C.* 3, *Ind. Lab.* 1, *L.* 1.
Teignbridge ...... *C.* 27, *N.P.* 25, *A.* 3, *Lab.* 2, *Ind. L.* 1.
Tendring .... *C.* 32, *A.* 15, *R.A.* 5, *Lab.* 4, *Ind.* 1, *Ind. C.* 1, *Others* 2.
Test Valley .... *C.* 26, *A.* 14, *Ind.* 2, *N.P.* 2.
Tewkesbury ...... *C.* 17, *Ind.* 10, *N.P.* 8, *A.* 5, *Lab.* 1, *Others* 4.
*Thamesdown ..... *Lab.* 35, *C.* 12, *A.* 6, *Ind.* 1.
Thanet .... *C.* 25, *Ind.* 11, *A.* 10, *Lab.* 7, *N.P.* 1.
*Three Rivers ..... *A.* 24, *C.* 15, *Lab.* 7, (1 Vac.).
*Thurrock .... *Lab.* 28, *C.* 9, *Ind. Lab.* 2.

*Tonbridge &
  Malling .... *C.* 30, *L.* 13, *Lab.* 6, *S.D.P.* 2, *Ind.* 1.
*Torbay .... *C.* 25, *A.* 10, *Ind.* 1.
Torridge .... *N.P.* 16, *C.* 8, *Ind.* 6, *Lab.* 4, *A.* 2.
*Tunbridge Wells ... *C.* 34, *A.* 11, *Ind.* 1, *Lab.* 1, (1 Vac.).
Tynedale .... *C.* 16, *A.* 12, *Ind.* 9, *Lab.* 9, *N.P.* 1.
Uttlesford .... *C.* 24, *A.* 10, *Ind.* 7, *Lab.* 1.
Vale of White
  Horse .... *C.* 41, *A.* 8, *Ind.* 1, *Lab.* 1
Vale Royal .... *C.* 27, *Lab.* 24, *A.* 5, *Ind.* 3, *R.A.* 1.
Wansbeck .... *L.* 38, *A.* 7, (1 Vac.).
Wansdyke .... *C.* 27, *Lab.* 16, *Ind.* 4.
Warrington .... *Lab.* 37, *C.* 15, *A.* 8.
Warwick .... *C.* 28, *Lab.* 7, *A.* 6, *R.A.* 3, *Ind. C.* 1.
*Watford .... *Lab.* 23, *C.* 10, *A.* 3.
Waveney .... *C.* 22, *L.* 21, *A.* 4, *N.P.* 1.
Waverley .... *C.* 42, *A.* 13, *Ind.* 2.
Wealden .... *C.* 49, *A.* 5, *R.A.* 4.
Wear Valley ...... *Lab.* 26, *Ind.* 6, *A.* 3, *C.* 3, *Ind. Lab.* 1, *Other* 1.
Wellingborough ... *C.* 21, *Lab.* 9, *Ind.* 3, *L.* 1.
*Welwyn Hatfield .. *Lab.* 23, *C.* 18, *A.* 2.
*West Devon .... *N.P.* 12, *C.* 10, *Ind.* 6, *A.* 1, *Lab.* 1
*West Dorset .... *N.P.* 18, *C.* 13, *A.* 12, *Ind.* 6, *Lab.* 3, *Ind. C.* 2, *L.* 1.
*W. Lancashire .... *C.* 29, *Lab.* 23, *A.* 3.
*West Lindsey ...... *A.* 19, *Ind.* 9, *C.* 8, *Lab.* 1.
*W. Oxfordshire ... *C.* 25, *Ind.* 11, *A.* 9, *Lab.* 3, *Other* 1.
West Somerset .... *N.P.* 23, *C.* 5, *Ind.* 4.
West Wiltshire .... *C.* 31, *A.* 7, *Lab.* 3, *Ind.* 1, *Ind. C.* 1.
*Weymouth and
  Portland .... *Lab.* 14, *C.* 12, *Ind.* 4, *L.* 3, *A.* 1, *R.A.* 1.
Wimborne .... *C.* 25, *A.* 6, *Ind.* 5.
*Winchester .... *C.* 25, *A.* 23, *Lab.* 5, *Ind.* 2.
Windsor and
  Maidenhead ..... *C.* 42, *A.* 9, *R.A.* 7.
*Woking .... *C.* 15, *A.* 13, *Lab.* 7.
*Wokingham .... *C.* 36, *L.* 13, *S.D.P.* 4, *Lab.* 1.
*Woodspring ...... *C.* 45, *A.* 5, *Lab.* 4, *Ind.* 3, *Ind. C.* 1, *Other* 1.
*Worcester .... *Lab.* 21, *C.* 15.
Worthing .... *C.* 24, *A.* 12.
Wrekin .... *Lab.* 29, *C.* 11, *Ind.* 4, *A.* 2.
Wychavon .... *C.* 21, *A.* 8, *Ind.* 3, *Ind. C.* 3, *Lab.* 3, *Others* 11.
Wycombe .... *C.* 51, *L.* 3, *Lab.* 3, *Ind.* 1, *Ind. Lab.* 1, *S.D.P.* 1.
Wyre .... *C.* 43, *Lab.* 7, *L.* 4, *Ind.* 1, *R.A.* 1.
*Wyre Forest ...... *L.* 16, *C.* 13, *Lab.* 10, *Ind.* 3.
*York .... *Lab.* 26, *C.* 12, *A.* 7.

Greater London Boroughs (as at end May 1987)

Barking .... *Lab.* 36, *A.* 5, *C.* 3, *R.A.* 3, *Ind.* 1.
Barnet .... *C.* 39, *Lab.* 18, *A.* 3.
Bexley .... *C.* 36, *Lab.* 15, *A.* 11.
Brent .... *Lab.* 42, *C.* 21, *L.* 3.
Bromley .... *C.* 44, *Lab.* 10, *A.* 6.
Camden .... *Lab.* 44, *C.* 13, *A.* 2.
Croydon .... *C.* 44, *Lab.* 26.
Ealing .... *Lab.* 47, *C.* 20, *A.* 3.
Enfield .... *C.* 38, *Lab.* 28.
Greenwich .... *Lab.* 43, *C.* 12, *S.D.P.* 5, *L.* 2.
Hackney .... *Lab.* 53, *L.* 5, *C.* 2.

Hammersmith ..... *Lab.* 40, *C.* 9, *L.* 1.
Haringey .... *Lab.* 41, *C.* 16, *L.* 1, (1 Vac.).
Harrow .... *C.* 32, *L.* 18, *Lab.* 9, *R.A.* 4.
Havering .... *C.* 28, *Lab.* 20, *R.A.* 10, *A.* 5.
Hillingdon .... *Lab.* 34, *C.* 28, *A.* 7.
Hounslow .... *Lab.* 40, *C.* 17, *A.* 3.
Islington .... *Lab.* 36, *A.* 16.
Kensington and
  Chelsea .... *C.* 39, *Lab.* 14, *Ind. Lab.* 1.
Kingston-on-Thames *C.* 24, *A.* 21, *Lab.* 4, (1 Vac.).
Lambeth .... *Lab.* 40, *C.* 21, *S.D.P.* 2, *L.* 1.
Lewisham .... *Lab.* 48, *C.* 18, *S.D.P.* 1.

Merton..............*C.* 29, *Lab.* 25, *R.A.* 3.
Newham..............*Lab.* 59, *L.* 1.
Redbridge..........*C.* 45, *Lab.* 17, *A.* 1.
Richmond..........*A.* 49, *C.* 3.
Southwark.........*Lab.* 44, *L.* 13, *C.* 6, *S.D.P.* 1.

Sutton..............*A.* 28, *C.* 21, *Lab.* 7.
Tower Hamlets......*L.* 25, *Lab.* 24, *S.D.P.* 1.
Waltham Forest......*Lab.* 31, *C.* 16, *A.* 10.
Wandsworth........*C.* 31, *Lab.* 30.
Westminster........*C.* 32, *Lab.* 27, *Ind.* 1.

WALES
County Councils (as at end May 1987)

Clwyd..............*Lab.* 26, *Ind.* 22, *C.* 15, *L.* 2, *A.* 1.
Dyfed..............*Ind.* 34, *Lab.* 30, *L.* 7, *P.C.* 5, *Ind. Lab.* 1, *R.A.* 1, *S.D.P.* 1, (1 Vac.).
Gwent.............*Lab.* 67, *C.* 9, *L.* 1, *P.C.* 1.
Gwynedd..........*N.P.* 39, *P.C.* 11, *Lab.* 5, *C.* 3, *A.* 4, *L.* 3, (1 Vac.).

Mid Glamorgan.....*Lab.* 68, *P.C.* 7, *Ind.* 3, *A.* 1, *C.* 1, *Com* 1, *L.* 1, *R.A.* 1, *S.D.P.* 1, *Others* 1.
Powys..............*Ind.* 41, *Lab.* 8, *A.* 2, *L.* 1, (1 Vac.).
S. Glamorgan.......*Lab.* 34, *C.* 18, *A.* 9, *P.C.* 1.
W. Glamorgan.....*Lab.* 54, *C.* 6, *A.* 5, *R.A.* 2, *Ind.* 1, *N.P.* 1, (1 Vac.).

District Councils (as at end May 1987)

Aberconwy.........*N.P.* 12, *A.* 11, *C.* 8, *Ind.* 5, *Lab.* 4, *P.C.* 1.
Alyn & Deeside.....*Lab.* 25, *C.* 8, *Ind.* 6, *A.* 4.
Arfon...............*Ind.* 14, *P.C.* 13, *Lab.* 11, *A.* 1.
Blaenau Gwent.....*Lab.* 33, *R.A.* 4, *Ind.* 2, *Com.* 1, *L.* 1, *P.C.* 1, *Others* 2.
Brecknock..........*Ind.* 30, *Lab.* 13, *L.* 1.
Cardiff..............*L.* 29, *C.* 24, *A.* 12.
Carmarthen........*Ind.* 28, *Lab.* 4, *P.C.* 2, *R.A.* 2, *L.* 1
Ceredigion.........*Ind.* 22, *L.* 9, *A.* 7, *P.C.* 4, *Lab.* 2.
Colwyn............*L.* 15, *Ind.* 10, *C.* 4, *Lab.* 2, *R.A.* 2, *Ind. C.* 1.
Cynon Valley.......*Lab.* 30, *P.C.* 5, *Ind.* 2, *Com.* 1.
Delyn..............*Ind.* 17, *Lab.* 11, *A.* 7, *C.* 3, *Ind. Lab.* 3, *P.C.* 1.
Dinefwr............*Lab.* 18, *Ind.* 11, *P.C.* 2, *Ind. Lab.* 1.
Dwyfor............*N.P.* 22, *P.C.* 6, *Other* 1.
Glyndwr...........*Ind.* 29, *A.* 3, *Lab.* 3.
Islwyn............*Lab.* 24, *P.C.* 10, *A.* 1.
Llanelli...........*Lab.* 19, *Ind. Lab.* 8, *Ind.* 2, *L.* 1, *S.D.P.* 1, *Others* 4.
Lliw Valley........*Lab.* 24, *Ind.* 5, *P.C.* 4.
Meirionnydd.......*N.P.* 22, *P.C.* 7, *Lab.* 5, (3 Vac.).
Merthyr Tydfil......*Lab.* 22, *R.A.* 6, *Ind.* 4, *P.C.* 1.
Monmouth.........*C.* 26, *Lab.* 11, *Ind.* 2, *Ind. Lab.* 1.

Montgomery-
shire.............*N.P.* 39, *Ind.* 3, *L.* 2, *Lab.* 1, *P.C.* 1.
Neath..............*Lab.* 31, *A.* 2, *Com.* 1.
Newport..........*Lab.* 36, *C.* 10, *A.* 1.
Ogwr..............*Lab.* 30, *C.* 17, *Ind.* 2.
Port Talbot.........*Lab.* 23, *R.A.* 5, *Ind.* 1, *L.* 1, *S.D.P.* 1.
Preseli
Pembrokeshire....*Ind.* 36, *A.* 2, *C.* 1, *Lab.* 1.
Radnor............*N.P.* 31, *Lab.* 2.
Rhondda...........*Lab.* 26, *R.A.* 4, *P.C.* 2, *Ind.* 1.
Rhuddlan..........*Ind.* 20, *C.* 6, *Lab.* 6.
Rhymney Valley...*Lab.* 32, *P.C.* 7, *Ind.* 5, *Others* 2.
S. Pembroke........*N.P.* 23, *Ind.* 3, *Lab.* 2, *P.C.* 1, *A.* 1.
Swansea............*Lab.* 30, *C.* 11, *A.* 3, *Ind.* 2, *L.* 2, *R.A.* 2, (1 Vac.).
Taff-Ely............*Lab.* 23, *P.C.* 10, *Ind.* 3, *R.A.* 3, *L.* 2, *A.* 1, *C.* 1.
Torfaen............*Lab.* 33, *Ind.* 6, *A.* 1, *C.* 1, *Com.* 1, *Ind. Lab.* 1, *R.A.* 1.
Vale of Glamorgan ..*C.* 26, *Lab.* 14, *P.C.* 4, *Ind.* 2.
Wrexham Maelor ...*Lab.* 26, *C.* 6, *N.P.* 5, *Ind.* 4, *A.* 2, *L.* 1, *P.C.* 1, (1 Vac.).
Ynys Môn.........*Ind.* 30, *Lab.* 4, *P.C.* 3, *C.* 1, *A.* 1.

SCOTLAND
Scottish Regional Councils (as at end May 1987)

Borders............*Ind.* 11, *C.* 6, *N.P.* 3, *A.* 2, *S.N.P.* 1.
Central ....*Lab.* 23, *S.N.P.* 5, *C.* 4, *Ind.* 1, *A.* 1.
Dumfries &
Galloway........*N.P.* 12, *Ind.* 10, *Lab.* 5, *C.* 4, *S.N.P.* 3, *A.* 1.
Fife.................*Lab.* 30, *A.* 8, *C.* 3, *S.N.P.* 2, *Ind.* 2, *Com.* 1.
Grampian..........*Lab.* 17, *C.* 16, *A.* 13, *S.N.P.* 8, *Ind.* 3.

Highland...........*N.P.* 24, *Ind.* 13, *Lab.* 7, *S.N.P.* 3, *L.* 3, *C.* 2.
Lothian............*Lab.* 32, *C.* 13, *A.* 3, *S.N.P.* 1.
Orkney............*N.P.* 23, *Other* 1.
Shetland...........*N.P.* 16, *Lab.* 4, *S.M.* 4.
Strathclyde.........*Lab.* 86, *C.* 6, *A.* 5, *S.N.P.* 3, *Ind.* 2, (1 Vac.).
Tayside ....*Lab.* 19, *C.* 14, *S.N.P.* 9, *Ind.* 3, *A.* 1.
Western Isles .......*N.P.* 30.

Scottish District Councils (as at end May 1987)

Aberdeen..........*Lab.* 25, *A.* 20, *C.* 7.
Angus..............*S.N.P.* 11, *C.* 8, *Ind.* 2.
Annandale
& Eskdale.......*Ind.* 9, *A.* 5, *N.P.* 2.
Argyll & Bute......*Ind.* 21, *C.* 3, *S.N.P.* 2.
Badenoch and
Strathspey......*N.P.* 10, *S.N.P.* 1.
Banff & Buchan.....*Ind.* 6, *N.P.* 6, *S.N.P.* 3, *A.* 2, *C.* 1.

Bearsden and
Milngavie......*C.* 5, *A.* 3, *Ind.* 1, *Lab.* 1.
Berwickshire.......*C.* 8, *Ind.* 3, *A.* 1.
Caithness..........*Ind.* 15, *Ind. L.* 1.
Clackmannan.......*Lab.* 9, *S.N.P.* 2, *C.* 1.
Clydebank..........*Lab.* 11, *C.* 1.
Clydesdale..........*Lab.* 7, *Ind.* 6, *S.N.P.* 3.
Cumbernauld
& Kilsyth.........*Lab.* 7, *S.N.P.* 5.

Cumnock &
Doon Valley ......*Lab.* 10.
Cunninghame ......*Lab.* 23, *C.* 5, *Ind.* 1, *Other* 1.
Dumbarton ....*Lab.* 10, *C.* 2, *A.* 1, *Ind.* 1, *N.P.* 1, S.N.P. 1.
Dundee ....*Lab.* 25, *C.* 13, *A.* 3, *S.N.P.* 2, *Ind. C.* 1.
Dunfermline ....*Lab.* 23, *A.* 6, *C.* 2, *S.N.P.* 2, *Com.* 1.
East Kilbride ......*Lab.* 14, *C.* 2..
East Lothian.......*Lab.* 11, *C.* 6.
Eastwood ....*C.* 10, *R.A.* 2.
Edinburgh.........*Lab.* 34, *C.* 22, *A.*4, *SNP.* 2.
Ettrick and
Lauderdale ....*Ind.* 13, *C.* 1, *Lab.* 1, *S.N.P.* 1.
Falkirk ....*Lab.* 25, *SNP.* 7, *C.* 2, *Ind.* 1, *Other* 1.
Glasgow...........*Lab.* 59, *C.* 5, *A.* 2.
Gordon............*Ind.* 7, *C.* 3, *A.* 1, *L.* 1.
Hamilton ....*Lab.* 17, *L.* 2, *C.* 1.
Inverclyde.........*Lab.* 11, *L.* 9.
Inverness ....*Ind.* 18, *Lab.* 8, *L.* 2.
Kilmarnock and
Loudoun ....*Lab.* 14, *C.* 3, *S.N.P.* 1.
Kincardine and
Deeside ....*Ind.* 7, *C.* 3, *L.* 1, *S.N.P.* 1.
Kirkcaldy ....*Lab.* 29, *A.* 3, *C.* 3, *Ind.* 2, *S.N.P.* 2, *R.A.* 1.

Kyle & Carrick......*Lab.* 11, *C.* 10, *Ind.* 2, *Ind. C.* 1, *Ind. Lab.* 1.
Lochaber ....*Ind.* 8, *Lab.* 5, *Ind. Lab.* 2.
Midlothian ....*Lab.* 13, *A.* 1, *Ind. Lab.* 1.
Monklands ....*Lab.* 17, *C.* 2, (1 Vac.).
Moray ............*N.P.* 10, *Ind.* 5, *S.N.P.* 2, *Lab.* 1.
Motherwell ....*Lab.* 23, *S.N.P.* 3, *C.* 2, *Com.* 1, *Ind.* 1.
Nairn ....*Ind.* 9, *Lab.* 1.
Nithsdale...........*C.* 7, *S.N.P.* 7, *Lab.* 6, *Ind.* 5, *Ind. Lab.* 1, *Others* 2.
N.E. Fife ....*A.* 11, *C.* 5, *Ind.* 2.
Perth & Kinross.....*C.* 14, *Lab.* 6, *A.* 5, *Ind.* 3, *S.N.P.* 1.
Renfrew............*Lab.* 36, *C.* 5, *A.* 2, *S.N.P.* 2.
Ross &
Cromarty........*Ind.* 19, *Lab.* 2, *C.* 1.
Roxburgh ....*Ind.* 8, *C.* 5, *N.P.* 2, *L.* 1.
Skye & Lochalsh ....*N.P.* 9, *A.* 1, (1 Vac.).
Stewartry .........*N.P.* 9, *Ind.* 3.
Stirling ....*Lab.* 10, *C.* 9, *Ind.* 1.
Strathkelvin.......*Lab.* 11, *C.* 3, *A.* 1.
Sutherland .........*N.P.* 14.
Tweeddale ....*Ind.* 10.
West Lothian ....*Lab.* 18, *Ind.* 3, *S.N.P.* 3.
Wigtown ..........*N.P.* 13, *S.N.P.* 1.

WATER AUTHORITIES

The Water Act 1973, which provided for the reorganization of the water services in England and Wales, resulted in the creation of ten autonomous multipurpose water authorities (nine regional authorities in England and the Welsh Water Authority).

The water authorities are responsible for water supply, water conservation, sewerage and sewage disposal, prevention of river pollution, fisheries, land drainage and the recreational use of their waters. Between them the authorities employ about 50,000 people.

Following the Water Act 1983, the Water Authorities Association was set up by the regional water authorities. The Association enables the water authorities to discuss amongst themselves and with the Government and other bodies matters of common concern, co-ordinates any necessary joint action by the water authorities, and provides press and public relations services.

THE WATER AUTHORITIES ASSOCIATION, 1 Queen Anne's Gate, SW1H 9BT [01-222 8111].—M. Carney.

Regional Water Authorities

THAMES WATER AUTHORITY, Nugent House, Vastern Road, Reading RG1 8DB.—*Managing Director*, W. Harper.

SOUTHERN WATER AUTHORITY, Guildborne House, Worthing, Sussex.—*Chief Executive*, B. R. Thorpe.

SEVERN TRENT WATER AUTHORITY, Abelson House, 2297 Coventry Road, Sheldon, Birmingham.—*Chief Executive*, R. F. O'Brien.

WESSEX WATER AUTHORITY, Wessex House, Passage Street, Bristol.—*Chief Executive*, K. F. Roberts, C.B.E.

ANGLIAN WATER AUTHORITY, Ambury House, Huntingdon.—*Managing Dir.*, A. G. Semple.

SOUTH WEST WATER AUTHORITY, Peninsula House, Rydon Lane, Exeter EX2 7HR.—*Chief Executive*, K. Court.

NORTHUMBRIAN WATER AUTHORITY, Northumbria House, Regent Centre, Gosforth, Newcastle-upon-Tyne.—*Chief Executive*, W. F. Ridley.

NORTH WEST WATER AUTHORITY, Dawson House, Great Sankey, Warrington.—*Chief Executive*, J. B. Oldfield.

YORKSHIRE WATER AUTHORITY, West Riding House, 67 Albion Street, Leeds.—*Director of Water Services*, D. Jeffrey.

WELSH WATER AUTHORITY, Cambrian Way, Brecon, Powys.—*Chief Executive*, (vacant).

The Kingdom of England

Position and Extent.—The Kingdom of England lies between 55° 46' and 49° 57' 30" N. latitude (from a few miles north of the mouth of the Tweed to the Lizard), and between 1° 46' E. and 5° 43' W. (from Lowestoft to Land's End). England is bounded on the north by the Cheviot Hills; on the south by the English Channel; on the east by the Straits of Dover (Pas de Calais) and the North Sea; and on the West by the Atlantic Ocean, Wales and the Irish Sea.

It has a total area of 50,363 sq. miles (land 50,070; inland water 293). The population (1981 Census) was 46,362,836 (males 22,520,723; females 23,842,113). The average density of the population in 1981 was 915 per square mile. The population, mid-1985 estimate, was 47,112,000.

Relief.—There is a marked division between the upland and lowland areas of England. In the extreme north the Cheviot Hills (highest point, *The Cheviot*, 2,674 ft.) form a natural boundary with the Kingdom of Scotland. Running south from the Cheviots, though divided from them by the Tyne Gap, is the Pennine range (highest point, *Cross Fell*, 2,930 ft.), the main orological feature of the country. The Pennines culminate in the Peak District of Derbyshire (*Kinder Scout*, 2,088 ft.). West of the Pennines are the Cumbrian Mountains, which include *Scafell Pike* (3,210 ft.), the highest peak in England, and to the east are the Yorkshire Moors, their highest point being *Urra Moor* (1,490 ft.).

In the west, the foothills of the Welsh mountains extend into the bordering English counties of Shropshire (the *Wrekin*, 1,334 ft.; *Long Mynd*, 1,694 ft.) and Hereford and Worcester (the Malvern Hills—*Worcestershire Beacon*, 1,394 ft.). Extensive areas of high land and moorland are also to be found in the south-western peninsular formed by Somerset, Devon and Cornwall: principally Exmoor (*Dunkery Beacon*, 1,704 ft.), Dartmoor (*High Willhays*, 2,038 ft.) and Bodmin Moor (*Brown Willy*, 1,377 ft.). Ranges of low, undulating hills run across the south of the country, including the Cotswolds in the Midlands and southwest, the Chilterns to the north of Greater London, and the North (Kent) and South (Sussex) Downs of the south-east coastal areas.

The lowlands of England lie in the Vale of York, East Anglia and the area around the Wash, the lowest lying being the Cambridgeshire Fens in the valleys of the Great Ouse and the River Nene, which are below sea-level in places; since the 17th century extensive drainage has brought much of the Fens under cultivation. The North Sea coast between the Thames and the Humber, low-lying and formed of sand and shingle for the most part, is subject to erosion and defences against further incursion have been built along many stretches.

Hydrography.—The *Severn* is the longest river in Great Britain, rising in the north-eastern slopes of Plinlimmon (Wales) and entering England in Shropshire with a total length of 220 miles from its source to its outflow into the Bristol Channel, where it receives on the east the Bristol Avon, and on the west the Wye, its other tributaries being the Vrynwy, Tern, Stour, Teme and Upper (or Warwickshire) Avon. The Severn is tidal below Gloucester, and a high bore or tidal wave sometimes reverses the flow as high as Tewkesbury (13½ miles above Gloucester). The scenery of the greater part of the river is very picturesque and beautiful, and the Severn is a noted salmon river, some of its tributaries being famous for trout. Navigation is assisted by the Gloucester and Berkeley Ship Canal (16¾ miles), which admits vessels of 350 tons to Gloucester. The *Severn Tunnel*, begun

in 1873 and completed in 1886 (at a cost of £2,000,000) after many difficulties from flooding, is 4 miles 628 yards in length (of which 2¼ miles are under the river). The Severn road bridge between Haysgate, Gwent, and Almondsbury, Glos., with a centre span of 3,240 ft. was opened in 1966.

The longest river wholly in England is the *Thames*, with a total length of 215 miles from its source in the Cotswold hills to the Nore, and is navigable by ocean-going ships to London Bridge. The Thames is tidal to Teddington (69 miles from its mouth) and forms county boundaries almost throughout its course; on its banks are situated London, Windsor Castle, the home of the Sovereign, Eton College, the first of the public schools, and Oxford, the oldest university in the kingdom.

Of the remaining English rivers those flowing into the North Sea are the Tyne, Wear, Tees, Ouse and Trent from the Pennine Range, the Great Ouse (160 miles) from Northamptonshire, and the Orwell and Stour from the hills of East Anglia. Flowing into the English Channel are the Sussex Ouse from the Weald, the Itchen from the Hampshire Hills, and the Axe, Teign, Dart, Tamar and Exe from the Devonian Hills; and flowing into the Irish Sea are the Mersey, Ribble and Eden from the western slopes of the Pennines and the Derwent from the Cumbrian Mountains. The *English Lakes*, noteworthy for their picturesque scenery and poetic associations, lie in Cumbria, the largest being Windermere (10 miles long), Ullswater and Derwentwater.

Islands.—The *Isle of Wight* is separated from Hampshire by the Solent; total area 147 sq. miles, population about 120,400. The climate is mild and healthy, making the island a popular holiday resort. Capital, Newport, at the head of the estuary of the Medina, Cowes (at the mouth) being the chief port; other centres are Ryde, Sandown, Shanklin, Ventnor, Freshwater, Yarmouth, Totland Bay, Seaview and Bembridge.

Lundy (= Puffin Island) 11 miles N.W. off Hartland Point, Devon, is about 2 miles long and about ½ mile broad (average), with a total area of about 1,116 acres, and a population of about 20; it became the property of the National Trust in 1969 and is now principally a bird sanctuary.

(*See also* The Isles of Scilly, p. 691.)

Climate.—England has a generally mild and temperate climate. Because of the prevailing south-westerly winds, the weather day to day is variable, being affected mainly by depressions moving eastwards across the Atlantic Ocean. This maritime influence means that the west of the country tends to experience wetter but also milder weather than the east. Rainfall also increases with altitude, the mountainous areas of the north and west having more rain than the lowlands of the south and east. Rain is fairly well-distributed throughout the year in all areas but, on average, the driest months are March to June, and the wettest September to January.

The mean annual temperature reduced to sea-level varies from 11°C in the south-west to 9°C near Berwick-on-Tweed. In winter, temperatures tend to be higher in the south and west than in the east, while the warmest in summer are the south and inland areas. Latitude for latitude the mean annual temperature is lower in the east; the decrease of mean temperature with height is about 0·6°C per 100 metres.

EARLY INHABITANTS

Prehistoric Man.—Archaeological evidence suggests that England has been inhabited since at least the Palaeolithic period, though the extent of the various Palaeolithic cultures was dependent upon the degree of glaciation. The succeeding Neolithic and Bronze Age cultures have left abundant remains throughout the country, the best-known of these being the henges and stone circles of Stonehenge (10 miles north of Salisbury, Wilts.) and Avebury (Wilts.), both of which are believed to have been of religious significance. In the latter part of the Bronze Age the *Goidels*, a people of Celtic race, and in the Iron Age other Celtic races of *Brythons* and *Belgae*, invaded the country and brought with them Celtic civilization and dialects, place names in England bearing witness to the spread of the invasion over the whole kingdom.

The Roman Conquest.—The Roman conquest of Gaul (57–50 B.C.) brought Britain into close contact with Roman civilization, but although Julius Cæsar raided the south of Britain in 55 B.C., and 54 B.C., conquest was not undertaken until nearly 100 years later. In A.D. 42 the Emperor Claudius dispatched Aulus Plautius, with a well-equipped force of 40,000, and himself followed with reinforcements in the same year. Success was delayed by the resistance of *Caratacus* (Caractacus), the British leader from A.D. 48–51, who was finally captured and sent to Rome, and by a great revolt in A.D. 61 led by *Boudicca* (Boadicea), Queen of the Iceni; but the south of Britain was secured by A.D. 70, and Wales and the area north to the Tyne by about A.D. 80.

In A.D. 122, the Emperor Hadrian visited Britain and built a continuous rampart, since known as *Hadrian's Wall*, from Wallsend to Bowness (Tyne to Solway). The work was entrusted by the Emperor Hadrian to Aulus Platorius Nepos, legate of Britain from 122 to 126, and it formed the northern frontier of the Roman Empire in the west for three and a half centuries.

The Romans administered Britain as a Province under a Governor, with a well-defined system of local government, each Roman municipality ruling itself and surrounding territory, while London was the centre of the road system and the seat of the financial officials of the Province of Britain. Colchester, Lincoln, York, Gloucester and St. Albans stand on the sites of five Roman municipalities, and Wroxeter, Caerleon, Chester, Lincoln and York were at various times the sites of legionary fortresses. Well-preserved Roman towns have been uncovered at (or near) *Silchester* (Calleva Atrebatum), 10 miles south of Reading, *Wroxeter* (Viroconium), near Shrewsbury, and *St. Albans* (Verulamium) in Hertfordshire.

Four main groups of roads radiated from London, and a fifth (the Fosse) ran obliquely from Lincoln through Leicester, Cirencester and Bath to Exeter. Of the four groups radiating from London one ran S.E. to Canterbury and the coast of Kent, a second to Silchester and thence to parts of Western Britain and South Wales, a third (later known as *Watling Street*) ran through Verulamium to Chester, with various branches, and the fourth reached Colchester, Lincoln, York and the eastern counties.

In the 4th century Britain was subject to raids along the east coast by Saxon pirates, which led to the establishment of a system of coast defence from the Wash to Southampton Water, with forts at Brancaster, Burgh Castle (Yarmouth), Walton (Felixstowe), Bradwell, Reculver, Richborough, Dover, Lympne, Pevensey and Portchester (Portsmouth). The Irish (Scoti) and Picts in the north were also becoming more aggressive; from about A.D. 350 incursions became more frequent and more formid-able. As the Roman Empire came under attack increasingly towards the end of the 4th century many troops were removed from Britain for service in other parts of the Empire. The island was cut off from Rome by the Teutonic conquest of Gaul early in the 5th century, and with the withdrawal of the last Roman garrison in A.D. 442, the Romano-British were left to themselves.

According to legend, the British King *Vortigern* called in the Saxons to defend him against the Picts, the Saxon chieftains being *Hengist* and *Horsa*, who landed at Ebbsfleet, Kent, and established themselves in the Isle of Thanet; but the events during the 150 years between the final break with Rome and the re-establishment of Christianity are unclear. However, it would appear that in the course of this period the raids turned into large-scale settlement by invaders traditionally known as Angles (England north of the Wash and East Anglia), Saxons (Essex and southern England) and Jutes (Kent and the Weald), which pushed the Romano-British into the mountainous areas of the north and west, Celtic culture outside Wales and Cornwall surviving only in topographical names. Various kingdoms were established at this time which attempted to claim overlordship of the whole country, hegemony finally being achieved by *Wessex* (capital, Winchester) in the 9th century. This century also saw the beginning of raids by the Vikings (Danes), which were resisted by *Alfred the Great* (871–899), the greatest of the Wessex kings, who fixed a limit to the advance of Danish settlement by the Treaty of Wedmore (878), giving them the area north and east of Watling Street, on condition they adopt Christianity.

In the 10th century the Kings of Wessex recovered the whole of England from the Danes, but subsequent rulers were unable to resist a second wave of invaders. England paid tribute (*Danegeld*) for many years, and was invaded in 1013 by the Danes and ruled by Danish Kings from 1016 until 1042, when Edward the Confessor was recalled from exile in Normandy. In 1066 Harold Godwineson (brother-in-law of Edward and son of Earl Godwin of Wessex) was chosen King of England, but after defeating (at Stamford Bridge, Yorkshire, Sept. 25) an invading army under Harald Hadraada, King of Norway (aided by Harold Godwineson's younger brother, the outlawed Earl Tostig of Northumbria), he was himself defeated at the *Battle of Hastings* on Oct. 14, 1066, and the Norman Conquest secured the throne of England for Duke William of Normandy, a cousin of Edward the Confessor.

Christianity reached the Roman province of Britain from Gaul in the 3rd century (or possibly earlier), *Alban*, traditionally Britain's first martyr, being put to death as a Christian during the persecution of Diocletian (June 22, 303), at his native town Verulamium; and the Bishops of Londinium, Eboracum (York), and Lindum (Lincoln) attended the Council of Arles in 314. However, the Anglo-Saxon invasions submerged the Christian religion in England until the 6th century when conversion was undertaken in the north from 563 by Celtic missionaries from Ireland led by St. Columba, and in the south by a mission sent from Rome in 597 which was led by St. Augustine, who became the first archbishop of Canterbury. England appears to have been converted again by the end of the 7th century and followed, after the Council of Whitby in 663, the practices of the Roman Church, which brought the country into the mainstream of European thought and culture.

AREA AND POPULATION OF ENGLISH COUNTIES

County	Administrative Headquarters	Area (*hectares*)	Population	Rateable Value 1987 £	Actual Rateable Value per head £
Avon	Avon House, The Haymarket, Bristol	134,614	946,000	128,561,883	136·00
Bedfordshire......	*Bedford	123,460	523,200	90,734,000	173·40
Berkshire	†Reading	125,890	738,000	140,273,963	190·07
Buckinghamshire .	*Aylesbury	188,284	619,900	111,927,000	180·56
Cambridgeshire ...	†Cambridge	340,892	623,400	97,104,091	152·18
Cheshire	*Chester	232,846	942,400	145,477,223	154·34
Cleveland	Municipal Buildings, Middlesbrough	58,308	558,200	81,111,850	145·44
Cornwall	*Truro	354,792‡	446,200	50,702,060	113·63
Cumbria..........	The Courts, Carlisle	681,012	483,600	52,081,000	107·52
Derbyshire	County Offices, Matlock	263,094	912,000	111,283,577	121·97
Devon............	*Exeter	671,088	999,000	120,171,594	121·63
Dorset	*Dorchester	265,375	638,200	93,728,439	146·86
Durham	*Durham	243,592	594,694	61,297,378	103·07
Essex	*Chelmsford	367,192	1,504,700	250,437,656	166·00
Gloucestershire ...	†Gloucester	264,266	517,105	70,931,041	137·17
Hampshire	The Castle, Winchester	377,698	1,544,100	230,658,903	145·99
Hereford and Worcester	*Worcester	392,650	654,500	93,757,662	143·25
Hertfordshire.....	*Hertford	163,415	994,800	181,154,000	182·10
Humberside	*Beverley, N. Humberside	351,212	850,000	103,464,000	121·72
Kent	*Maidstone	373,060	1,504,200	199,900,000	188·00
Lancashire	*Preston	306,346	1,380,300	151,614,764	109·84
Leicestershire	*Leicester	255,293	872,200	122,584,400	140·55
Lincolnshire......	County Offices, Lincoln	591,485	570,100	68,871,613	120·81
Norfolk	*Norwich	536,776	727,800	99,326,873	136·25
Northamptonshire	*Northampton	236,737	550,700	82,011,911	148·92
Northumberland ..	*Morpeth	503,165	300,600	35,121,914	116·84
Nottinghamshire..	*Nottingham	216,365	1,005,900	128,444,726	127·00
Oxfordshire	*Oxford	260,782	572,000	91,017,500	159·00
Shropshire	†Shrewsbury	349,014	390,300	49,167,228	125·97
Somerset	*Taunton	345,094	455,600	55,861,457	122·61
Staffordshire	County Buildings, Stafford	271,615	1,040,240	133,635,002	130·89
Suffolk	*Ipswich	379,663	628,600	85,353,717	135·78
Surrey	*Kingston upon Thames	167,924	1,011,400	188,359,825	186·24
Sussex, East	Pelham House, St. Andrew's Lane, Lewes	179,512	682,400	104,000,000	147·30
Sussex, West	*Chichester	198,935	691,650	108,788,103	156·35
Warwickshire	†Warwick	198,053	479,700	73,576,632	153·38
Wight, Isle of	*Newport, I.O.W.	38,066	124,100	14,697,961	118·44
Wiltshire.........	*Trowbridge	348,070	550,000	67,839,000	123·34
Yorkshire, North .	*Northallerton	830,865	699,800	84,038,461	120·09

* County Hall.   † Shire Hall.   ‡ Excluding Isles of Scilly.

ENGLISH COUNTIES AND SHIRES
LORD LIEUTENANTS AND HIGH SHERIFFS

County or Shire	Lord Lieutenant	*High Sheriff, 1987–88
Avon	Sir John Wills, Bt., T.D.	R. Chermside
Bedfordshire	Lt. Col. H. C. Hanbury, L.V.O., M.C.	Sir Neville Bowman-Shaw
Berkshire	Col. The Hon. G. W. N. Palmer, O.B.E., T.D.	The Hon. L. H. L. Cohen
Buckinghamshire	Cdr. The Hon. J. T. Fremantle, R.N.(*retd*)	Sir Philip Duncombe, Bt.
Cambridgeshire	M. G. Molesworth	Sir Alexander Reid
Cheshire	The Rt. Hon. The Viscount Leverhulme, T.D.	A. G. Barbour
Cleveland	The Rt. Hon. The Lord Gisborough	Maj. J. M. Catterall, T.D.
Cornwall	The Rt. Hon. The Viscount Falmouth	The Rt. Hon. the Viscountess Boyd of Merton
Cumbria	Maj. Sir Charles Graham, Bt.	M. V. Gubbins
Derbyshire	Col. P. Hilton, M.C.	R. H. Boissier
Devon	Lt. Col. The Rt. Hon. The Earl of Morley	J. R. Trahair
Dorset	The Rt. Hon. The Lord Digby	Lt. Cdr. Crutchley, R.N.(*retd*)
Durham	The Rt. Hon. The Lord Barnard, T.D.	I. G. Bonas
Essex	Adm. Sir Andrew Lewis, K.C.B.	J. A. S. Neave
Gloucestershire	Col. M. St. J. V. Gibbs, C.B., D.S.O., T.D.	D. R. A. Sanford
Hampshire	Lt. Col. Sir James Scott, Bt.	Mrs. P. Wake
Hereford and Worcester	T. R. Dunne	C. C. Harley
Hertfordshire	S. A. Bowes Lyon	C. H. A. Bott
Humberside	R. A. Bethell	P. B. Oughtred
Kent	The Rt. Hon. Robin Leigh-Pemberton	R. Neame
Lancashire	S. Towneley	R. P. Shepherd
Leicestershire	Col. R. A. St. G. Martin, O.B.E.	J. P. A. de Lisle
Lincolnshire	H. N. Nevile	N. E. McCorquodale
Greater London	The Rt. Hon. The Lord Bramall, G.C.B., O.B.E., M.C.	D. G. Steel
Greater Manchester	Sir William Downward	Col. A. Axford, O.B.E., T.D.
Merseyside	Wing Cmdr. K. M. Stoddart, A.E.	Col. Mary Creagh
Norfolk	T. Colman	The Rt. Hon. The Lord FitzRoy
Northamptonshire	J. L. Lowther, C.B.E.	E. C. S. J. G. Brudenell
Northumberland	The Rt. Hon. The Viscount Ridley, T.D.	A. R. Pearson
Nottinghamshire	Sir Gordon Hobday	Sir John Starkey, Bt.
Oxfordshire	Sir Ashley Ponsonby, Bt., M.C.	F. R. Goodenough
Shropshire	J. R. S. Dugdale	A. E. H. Herber-Percy
Somerset	Lt. Col. G. W. F. Luttrell, M.C.	M. J. F. Carter
Staffordshire	Sir Arthur Bryan	N. S. G. Bostock
Suffolk	Sir Joshua Rowley, Bt.	H. L. Philbrick
Surrey	R. E. Thornton, O.B.E.	Dr. J. Johnston
Sussex, East	The Most Hon. The Marquess of Abergavenny, K.G., O.B.E.	T. F. Jones
Sussex, West	Her Grace Lavinia, Duchess of Norfolk, C.B.E.	Lt.-Cdr. D. H. L. Hopkinson, C.B.E., R.D.
Tyne and Wear	Sir Ralph Carr-Ellison, T.D.	M. F. Pyman
Warwickshire	C. M. T. Smith-Ryland	P. R. Doyne
West Midlands	The Rt. Hon. The Earl of Aylesford	P. W. Welch
Wight, Isle of	The Rt. Hon. The Lord Mottistone, C.B.E.	H. A. Bowring
Wiltshire	Col. Sir Hugh Brassey, K.C.V.O., O.B.E., M.C.	T. S. Sykes
Yorkshire, North	Sir Marcus Worsley, Bt.	J. H. V. Sutcliffe
Yorkshire, South	Sir Hugh Neill, C.B.E., T.D.	J. E. Eardley
Yorkshire, West	The Rt. Hon. The Lord Ingrow, O.B.E., T.D.	G. C. Armitage

* High Sheriffs are nominated by the Queen on November 12 and come into office after Hilary Term.

ENGLISH COUNTIES AND SHIRES
CHIEF EXECUTIVES, TREASURERS AND CHAIRMEN OF COUNTY COUNCILS

County or Shire	Chief Executive	County Treasurer	Chairman of C.C.
Avon	N. J. L. Pearce	D. G. Morgan	R. Mullett
Bedfordshire........	J. W. Elven	V. F. Phillips	J. P. B. Kinchella
Berkshire	A. J. Allen	M. Beasley	F. G. R. Gimblett
Buckinghamshire ...	E. M. E. White	H.I.R. Springthorpe	W. Rooke
Cambridgeshire	A. G. Lister	D. Prince	Mrs. B. Wrout
Cheshire	R. G. Wendt	J. E. H. Whiteoak	D. B. Kingston
Cleveland	B. Stevenson	B. Stevenson	R. Waller
Cornwall	G. K. Burgess	C. E. J. Cainey	F. J. Williams, C.B.E.
Cumbria	J. R. Ford	R. Wirth	G. E. Smith
Derbyshire	E. T. Cobb*	R. C. Beard	A. J. Hough
Devon..............	D. D. Macklin	B. J. Weston	Mrs. E. M. Stacey
Dorset	K. A. Abel, C.B.E.	D. M. Gasson	Air Cmmdre. K. J. McIntyre, C.B., C.B.E.
Durham	P. Dawson	K. W. Smith	R. Pendlebury
Essex	R. W. Adcock	K. D. Neale	R. W. Dixon-Smith
Gloucestershire	M. G. Bichard	J. R. Cockroft	E. J. Radley
Hampshire	A. R. Hodgson	J. E. Scotford	J. Maynard
Hereford and Worcester	G. A. Price	J. Rocke	J. T. Arnett
Hertfordshire.......	M. J. Le Fleming	K. S. Cliff	F. Peacock
Humberside	P. R. Wellings*	J. A. Parkes	W. E. Williams
Kent	P. R. Sabin	P. Martin	W. J. McNeill, M.B.E.
Lancashire	B. Hill	D. Morgan	Mrs. N. Orrell
Leicestershire	S. Jones	R. Hale	M. Ryan
Lincolnshire........	R. J. D. Procter	D. G. Barrett	Mrs. Z. Scoley
Norfolk	B. J. Capon	C. A. Boar	H. K. Rose
Northamptonshire ..	A. J. Greenwell	J. Smith	G. Pollard
Northumberland	C. B. Rodger	R. Wolstenholme	R. K. Gilchrist
Nottinghamshire....	A. Sandford	G. S. Luff	Miss F. Price
Oxfordshire	A. T. Brown, C.B.E.	J. T. Vokins	B. H. Duggan
Shropshire	M. Suter	M. N. Davis	J. Turner
Somerset	J. E. Whittaker	B. M. Tanner	R. B. Clark
Staffordshire	B. A. Price	B. Smith	F. A. Cholerton, C.B.E.
Suffolk	C. W. Smith	P. B. Atkinson	D. S. Farthing
Surrey	F. A. Stone	D. J. Thomas	D. Robertson
Sussex, East	R. M. Beechey	M. R. Hancock	N. P. Mackilligin
Sussex, West........	J. R. Hooley	B. Fieldhouse	P. G. Shepherd
Warwickshire	I. G. Caulfield	J. P. Hunt	H. W. De'Ath
Wight, Isle of	J. S. Horsnell	D. A. Tuck	B. H. Drake
Wiltshire...........	I. A. Browning	A. F. Gould	J. B. Ainslie, O.B.E.
Yorkshire, North ...	H. J. Evans	D. Martin	L. Backhouse

* Director of Administration.

Residuary Bodies

GREATER LONDON, (see page 659).

GREATER MANCHESTER, County Hall, Piccadilly Gardens, Manchester M60 3HP (061–247 3111).
Chairman, J. P. B. Hadfield.
Chief Executive, P. D. Quick.
Chief Finance Officer, K. E. Butterworth.

MERSEYSIDE, Metropolitan House (P.O. Box 119), Old Hall Street, Liverpool L69 3LL (051–227 5234).
Chairman, N. G. Brodrick.
Chief Executive, A. A. Thompson.
Treasurer, J. R. Smith.

TYNE AND WEAR, Scottish Life House, Block E, Archbold Terrace, Newcastle-upon-Tyne NE2 1ED (091–281 6144).
Chairman, A. S. Robertson.

General Manager, P. J. Smith.
Chief Finance Officer, I. M. Burns.

WEST MIDLANDS, 1 Lancaster Circus, Queensway, Birmingham B4 7DJ (021–300 5151).
Chairman, Dr. M. Skillicorn.
Chief Executive, K. E. Rose.
Finance Officer, G. J. Walters.

SOUTH YORKSHIRE, Britannic Assurance Building, Regent Street, Barnsley S70 2HG (0226–733222).
Chairman, B. Cotton.
Chief Executive, W. K. Irvine.
Treasurer, P. A. Appleyard.

WEST YORKSHIRE, County Hall, Wakefield, WF1 2QW (0924–367111).
Chairman, T. McDonald.
Chief Executive, P. Lodge.

MUNICIPAL DIRECTORY OF ENGLAND

A list of METROPOLITAN BOROUGH AND CITY COUNCILS. Those accorded CITY status are in SMALL CAPITALS.

Metropolitan Boroughs	Popula-tion	Rateable Value 1987 £	Chief Executive	Mayor †Lord Mayor *Chairman 1987–88
GREATER MANCHESTER				
Bolton	261,800	29,160,401	K. P. Bounds	W. Robinson
Bury...........................	173,300	20,148,814	J. A. McDonald	Mrs. J. Adler
MANCHESTER	451,400	80,085,156	R. M. W. Taylor	*Ms. E. Kelly
Oldham	219,700	23,928,889	C. Smith	A. Tweedale, O.B.E.
Rochdale	206,200	22,124,986	J. F. D. Pierce	J. A. Whitehead
SALFORD	239,300	32,606,527	R. C. Rees	(vacant)
Stockport	288,000	40,490,491	A. L. Wilson	Mrs. W. M. Crook
Tameside	215,300	22,431,793	D. Spiers	J. Fitzpatrick
Trafford	217,800	40,478,929	R. M. C. Shields	W. J. Golding
Wigan	306,700	32,773,308	P. Johnson	J. Jones
MERSEYSIDE				
Knowsley	166,300	21,341,027	R. Penn	C. W. White
LIVERPOOL......................	485,616	70,021,788	C. M. Reddington	†T. McManus
St. Helens	187,600	23,701,321	B. S. Lace	W. R. Crosby
Sefton..........................	298,400	37,493,089	A. G. Corless	E. Storey
Wirral	336,500	43,062,656	C. D. Darley	A. E. Smith
SOUTH YORKSHIRE				
Barnsley	222,226	19,949,471	P. G. Thompson	R. Warden
Doncaster	288,500	30,379,668	C. B. Jeynes	Mrs. G. Ambler
Rotherham	252,500	24,315,065	J. Bell	K. E. Billington
SHEFFIELD	540,500	67,248,144	I. L. Podmore	†P. Horton
TYNE AND WEAR				
Gateshead	209,600	22,397,923	L. N. Elton	J. Hattam
NEWCASTLE UPON TYNE	280,000	42,690,159	G. N. Cook	†S. J. C. Allan
North Tyneside	193,200	21,270,272	E. B. Lincoln	E. Dalziel
South Tyneside	155,900	15,737,378	S. Clark	A. Tate
Sunderland....................	300,000	29,392,294	G. P. Key	J. Mawston
WEST MIDLANDS				
BIRMINGHAM....................	1,007,000	167,493,228	T. Caulcott	†F. J. Grattidge
COVENTRY	310,000	44,812,014	R. J. Tarr	†J. D. White
Dudley	302,300	45,670,413	T. H. Meredith (acting)	J. D. Davies
Sandwell	302,900	50,320,921	G. A. Hadley	R. Handley
Solihull	200,000	31,780,857	J. Scampion	R. Lewis
Walsall	262,900	39,620,318	A. V. Astling	B. S. Powell
Wolverhampton...............	253,600	43,218,897	M. T. Lyons	Mrs. D. M. Seiboth
WEST YORKSHIRE				
BRADFORD	468,700	46,375,094	D. F. Holmes	†L. C. Coughlin
Calderdale......................	191,800	17,697,231	M. Ellison	W. Sharp
Kirklees........................	377,000	34,168,159	(vacant)	G. Speight
LEEDS	705,792	94,070,000	J. Rawnsley‡	†Mrs D. E. Wood
WAKEFIELD	310,200	33,877,759	J. G. Stanbury	W. Inman

‡ Chief Officer.

DISTRICT COUNCILS

A list of non-Metropolitan District Councils in England. Those accorded CITY status are in SMALL CAPITALS, those with Borough status are distinguished by having § prefixed.

District	Popula-tion	Rateable Value 1987 £	Chief Executive (*Clerk)	Chairman 1987–88 (a) Mayor (b) Lord Mayor
Adur, West Sussex	58,570	8,682,211	F. M. G. Staden	A. V. Biggs
Allerdale, Cumbria	95,600	9,433,277	A. G. Perry	J. M. Lister
Alnwick, Northumberland	29,700	3,220,155	A. G. A. Groome	H. W. Philipson
Amber Valley, Derbyshire......	108,900	12,624,074	J. Ragsdale	V. Barber
Arun, West Sussex	126,900	17,724,653	J. V. Midgley	T. Fripp
Ashfield, Nottinghamshire	106,700	10,618,713	S. Beedham	B. Chance
§Ashford, Kent.................	88,500	12,408,411	E. H. W. Mexter	(a) D. Weatherall
Aylesbury Vale, Bucks.	140,000	21,695,736	B. J. Quoroll	B. M. Griffin

District	Population	Rateable Value 1987 £	Chief Executive (*Clerk)	Chairman 1987–88 (a) Mayor (b) Lord Mayor
Babergh, Suffolk	76,710	9,925,206	D. C. Bishop	J. W. Baxter
§Barrow in Furness, Cumbria	74,600	6,793,870	D. G. B. Lyon	(a) J. E. Smith
Basildon, Essex	158,910	26,883,713	R. C. Mitchinson	D. B. Harrison
§Basingstoke and Deane, Hants.	137,000	22,818,259	D. W. Pilkington, R.D.	(a) K. W. D. Morgan
Bassetlaw, Notts.	104,200	17,018,971	R. D. Blair	D. R. Boardman
BATH, Avon	84,300	11,496,836	N. C. Abbott	(a) I. C. Dewey
§Berwick-upon-Tweed, Northumberland	26,300	3,183,470	J. Healy	(a) A. E. Clemit
§Beverley, Humberside	108,300	12,871,445	W. J. H. Thomas	(a) W. L. M. Daunby
Blaby, Leics.	80,300	10,124,925	J. E. Meakin	S. E. Mayne
§Blackburn, Lancs.	141,300	14,408,603	S. M. Jones	(a) Mrs S. Liddle
§Blackpool, Lancs.	145,800	19,005,146	D. Wardman	(a) L. Pomfret
§Blyth Valley, Northumberland	78,300	7,638,627	D. Crawford†	(a) W. Day
§Bolsover, Derbys.	70,880	6,162,764	C. A. Tucker	W. Annable
§Boothferry, Humberside	61,500	5,562,105	J. W. Barber	O. M. Stewart
§Boston, Lincs.	53,669	6,581,595	R. E. Coley	(a) R. F. Harlow
§Bournemouth, Dorset	144,300	25,389,681	K. Lomas	(a) Mrs. B. R. Siberry
Bracknell, Berks.	90,689	16,150,629	A. J. Targett	A. Cheney
Braintree, Essex	117,094	16,430,071	C. R. Daybell	E. J. R. McDowell
Breckland, Norfolk	99,200	12,398,394	J. B. Heath	J. O. C. Birkbeck
Brentwood, Essex	70,731	13,591,476	C. P. Sivell	P. O. Adams
Bridgnorth, Salop	51,500	6,156,908	G. C. Nutley	C. D. Bache
§Brighton, East Sussex	143,100	25,826,977	T. J. Blake	(a) R. J. Blackwood
BRISTOL, Avon	400,000	62,000,000	W. Miller	(b) M. Alderson
Broadland, Norfolk	100,300	11,204,581	B. R. Grayling	A. S. Watts
Bromsgrove, Hereford and Worcs.	88,070	12,364,112	R. P. Bradshaw	M. W. V. Firminger
§Broxbourne, Herts.	81,900	13,265,323	M. J. Walker	F. Dolan
§Broxtowe, Notts.	104,400	12,316,127	A. E. Hodder	(a) J. D. Taylor
§Burnley, Lancs.	88,800	8,464,410	B. Whittle	(a) J. F. Heyes
CAMBRIDGE	98,700	23,188,775	G. G. Datson	(a) (vacant)
Cannock Chase, Staffs.	85,500	11,353,189	B. E. Rastall, M.B.E.	G. Alcott
CANTERBURY, Kent	114,321	15,853,335	C. C. Gay	(a) K. Nicholls
Caradon, Cornwall	72,200	7,275,303	L. J. Gawley	A. Brooking
CARLISLE, Cumbria	101,300	11,716,619	R. Wilson	(a) V. H. G. Davis
Carrick, Cornwall	76,104	9,816,385	P. M. Talbot	F. A. Cheshire
§Castle Morpeth, Northumberland	50,700	6,720,489	M. Cole	(a) I. McConnell-Wood
Castle Point, Essex	81,116	12,014,026	A. R. Neighbour	A. G. Allen
§Charnwood, Leics.	143,500	20,743,570	D. L. Harris	(a) E. R. Greenwood
§Chelmsford, Essex	149,800	25,987,157	R. M. C. Hartley	(a) T. T. Matthews
§Cheltenham, Glos.	86,000	15,489,708	B. N. Wynn	(a) G. J. Wakeley
Cherwell, Oxon.	120,350	17,870,441	A. M. Brace	A. W. A. Tallents
CHESTER, Cheshire	116,600	19,229,684	D. F. G. Burton	(a) J. D. Haynes
§Chesterfield, Derbyshire.	96,800	12,556,849	D. R. Shaw	(a) E. H. Barker
Chester-le-Street, Durham	52,244	4,755,206	A. Golightly	R. H. Suddick
Chichester, West Sussex	101,550	14,913,000	P. G. Lomas	Mrs. J. M. Illius
Chiltern, Bucks.	92,500	16,842,808	D. G. Sainsbury	A. J. H. Tate
§Chorley, Lancs.	93,500	9,602,799	A. B. Webster	(a) Mrs. E. Shere
§Christchurch, Dorset	41,800	6,998,370	C. H. Dewsnap	(a) D. J. Fox
§Cleethorpes, Humberside	68,800	9,067,115	R. W. Bull	(a) D. J. Leam
§Colchester, Essex	145,100	20,467,879	J. Cobley	(a) J. Lampon
§Congleton, Cheshire	84,700	11,039,278	A. Molyneux	(a) W. Vickers
§Copeland, Cumbria	71,800	8,941,548	P. N. Denson	(a) P. Bennett
Corby, Northants.	50,700	9,341,159	D. Hall	J. G. Breen
Cotswold, Glos.	72,700	9,924,767	D. Waring	P. A. Cutts
Craven, North Yorks	48,400	5,317,820	A. Howell*	Miss E. Graham
§Crawley, West Sussex	87,000	19,230,356	M. D. Sander	(a) T. F. Bowden
§Crewe and Nantwich, Cheshire	98,217	13,092,259	R. Mather	(a) C. E. Elson
Dacorum, Herts.	137,000	24,415,061	R. H. Davis	(a) J. Nichols
§Darlington, Durham	98,900	13,497,600	H. R. C. Owen	(a) Mrs. B. Cuthbertson
§Dartford, Kent	79,900	13,207,361	R. J. Duck	(a) P. F. Coleman
Daventry, Northants.	59,800	9,430,903	R. J. Symons	Lady Dent
§DERBY	215,300	31,637,620	F. R. Tagg	(a) Mrs. N. R. Wawman
Derbyshire Dales	66,000	7,269,251	R. Bubb	C. B. Hoole
Derwentside, Durham	86,300	7,732,560	T. M. Hodgson	M. Brough
Dover, Kent	102,500	12,127,812	J. P. Moir, T.D.	Mrs. A. M. Williamson
DURHAM	86,700	9,576,028	C. G. Firmin	(a) Mrs. I. E. Humphries
Easington, Durham	97,100	7,790,513	T. Robinson†	A. Barker

† Principal Chief Officer.

District	Popula-tion	Rateable Value 1987 £	Chief Executive (*Clerk)	Chairman 1987–88 (a) Mayor (b) Lord Mayor
§Eastbourne, East Sussex	80,000	14,502,782	C. A. Bloor	Mrs. J. M. Grist
East Cambridgeshire	56,900	6,335,086	T. T. G. Hardy	H. Rouse
East Devon	112,200	14,162,861	C. A. Moseley	D. E. Dray
East Hampshire	97,000	13,468,218	H. S. Fry	C. O. G. Smith
East Hertfordshire	116,000	17,981,550	D. J. Anstey	F. J. Clay
§Eastleigh, Hants.	100,300	15,366,301	M. C. Brainsby	(a) P. Spearey
East Lindsey, Lincs.	108,700	13,553,020	A. W. Silcox-Crowe	J. A. Amos
East Northamptonshire	64,192	7,316,526	D. B. Adnitt	D. C. Lawson
East Staffordshire	94,000	13,479,278	F. W. Saunders	G. Handley
§East Yorkshire, Humberside	78,300	7,622,688	J. H. Gibson	(a) D. V. Southwell
Eden, Cumbria	43,984	4,979,086	J. D. Brown	J. M. Carlyle
§Ellesmere Port and Neston, Cheshire	80,200	17,038,080	S. Ewbank	(a) Mrs. P. A. Wilson
§Elmbridge, Surrey	111,400	23,741,512	D. W. L. Jenkins	(a) Mrs. R. J. M. Lyon
Epping Forest, Essex	114,609	19,857,731	A. V. Hackman	R. J. Amanet
§Epsom and Ewell, Surrey	67,100	12,263,914	D. J. Smith	(a) C. M. D. Shearly
§Erewash, Derbyshire.	103,000	12,102,924	J. M. Parker	Mrs. M. A. Orchard
Exeter, Devon	102,000	15,111,276	B. Frowd	(a) W. H. J. Rowe
§Fareham, Hants.	95,800	14,138,521	O. D. Ellis	(a) Capt. A. D. Mac-Donald
Fenland, Cambs.	68,900	8,542,975	E. S. Thompson	M. Cotterell
Forest Heath, Suffolk	57,800	6,948,061	J. F. Gale	N. A. Roman
Forest of Dean, Glos.	75,200	7,219,749	P. R. Starling	A. C. Cooper
§Fylde, Lancs.	72,800	9,381,155	B. J. Smith	(a) R. Smith, M.B.E.
§Gedling, Notts.	111,160	12,138,633	W. Brown	(a) Mrs. V. C. Pepper
§Gillingham, Kent	95,200	11,174,415	Dr. R. Chilton	(a) B. P. Heffernan
§Glanford, Humberside	68,300	9,417,803	D. D. H. Cameron	(a) Mrs. V. C. Lockwood
Gloucester	91,100	13,540,700	H. R. T. Shackleton	(a) A. Gravells
§Gosport, Hants.	77,800	9,974,766	W. D. Hooper	G. Rushton
§Gravesham, Kent	94,600	12,984,450	R. D. Dewar	(a) L. J. Glanfield
§Great Grimsby, Humberside	91,900	11,900,661	R. V. Hughes	D. C. Casswell
§Great Yarmouth, Norfolk	84,700	12,084,000	K. G. Ward	(a) G. S. Johnson
§Guildford, Surrey	125,300	23,725,178	D. T. Watts	(a) A. Hodges
§Halton, Cheshire	125,300	17,887,319	R. Turton	(a) R. Eastup
Hambleton, North Yorks.	76,000	8,539,877	C. Spencer	B. Bosomworth
Harborough, Leics.	63,200	8,339,535	F. T. Berry	E. V. Hubbard
Harlow, Essex	75,200	14,356,339	H. Platt	M. R. Danvers
§Harrogate, North Yorks.	144,500	17,417,567	J. V. Lovell	(a) D. H. Muscroft
Hart, Hants.	83,709	11,023,231	M. W. Tyler	J. G. York
§Hartlepool, Cleveland	91,600	11,951,707	N. D. Abram	(a) M. Watson
§Hastings, East Sussex	81,800	10,399,540	R. A. Carrier	(a) Mrs. S. Barr
§Havant, Hants.	116,080	16,332,638	D. E. Ridley	(a) L. T. Dryer
Hereford	48,300	7,078,704	C. E. S. Willis	(a) G. M. Bow
§Hertsmere, Hertfordshire	88,100	16,966,437	J. Pearson	(a) G. A. Nunn
§High Peak, Derbyshire.	83,400	9,421,282	R. P. H. Brady	(a) Mrs M. K. Holtom
§Hinckley and Bosworth, Leics.	93,300	12,388,791	F. Shaw	(a) A. J. Chantrell
§Holderness, Humberside	48,300	5,275,821	D. B. Law	(a) R. J. Garbutt
Horsham, West Sussex	104,330	15,419,554	M. J. Pearson	Gp. Capt. J. K. Burningham, M.B.E.
§Hove, East Sussex	89,500	15,577,102	G. H. Longden	(a) J. N. Broadley
Huntingdon, Cambs.	141,700	17,383,123	T. J. Gee	Mrs. R. L. Mills
§Hyndburn, Lancs.	78,862	6,782,395	N. D. Macgregor	(a) W. Parkinson
§Ipswich, Suffolk	120,200	19,229,671	J. R. Savage	(a) D. Warsop
Kennet, Wilts.	67,000	7,138,802	P. L. Owens	A. V. Gray
Kerrier, Cornwall	85,700	8,887,284	J. G. Millward	Mrs. B. Waters
§Kettering, Northants.	73,200	8,771,681	R. M. Eagland	(a) K. T. Gosland
§King's Lynn and W. Norfolk	128,300	17,380,000	A. Pask	(a) Mrs. I. M. Major
Kingston upon Hull, Humberside	258,200	29,492,269	A. B. Wood*	(b) Miss V. A. Mitchell
Kingswood, Avon	89,732	9,194,527	A. Smith	D. Upjohn
Lancaster, Lancs.	126,800	13,676,000	W. Pearson*	(a) A. Briggs
§Langbaurgh, Cleveland	147,200	23,741,441	K. Abigail	(a) N. Loughran
Leicester	282,900	43,511,398	D. Mellor	(b) G. D. Parmar
Leominster, Hereford and Worcs.	37,800	3,872,927	G. A. Robson	Mrs. P. Housden
Lewes, East Sussex	84,600	13,038,551	C. W. Mann	Mrs. M. E. Benham
Lichfield, Staffs.	91,700	12,911,446	J. T. Thompson	C. McEwan
Lincoln	78,200	11,348,000	C. J. Thomas	(a) C. R. Ireland
§Luton, Beds.	166,000	32,772,358	J. C. Southwell (acting)	(a) Mrs. P. Wolsey
§Macclesfield, Cheshire	151,500	24,640,876	B. W. Longden	(a) C. Allen

District	Population 1987	Rateable Value 1987 £	Chief Executive (*Clerk)	Chairman 1987–88 (a) Mayor (b) Lord Mayor
§Maidstone, Kent	133,700	18,117,647	J. D. Makepeace	(a) D. Milner
Maldon, Essex	51,000	7,586,798	T. K. Griffin	R. L. Bass
Malvern Hills, Hereford and Worcs.	86,900	10,747,130	M. J. Jones	Mrs. L. M. Norfolk
Mansfield, Notts.	100,000	10,433,710	R. P. Goad	R. Wix
§Medina, Isle of Wight	70,700	8,504,931	(vacant)	(a) N. P. J. Butchers
§Melton, Leics.	42,900	5,758,235	P. J. G. Herrick°	(a) B. W. Ludwig
Mendip, Somerset	93,405	10,707,134	G. Jeffs	R. S. G. Hewett
Mid Bedfordshire	110,000	14,836,379	P. A. Freeman	R. O. Bennett
Mid Devon	61,400	5,847,183	R. C. Greensmith	E. F. Champion
§Middlesbrough, Cleveland	145,400	18,100,891	J. R. Foster	(a) M. T. Pritchard
Mid Suffolk	74,420	8,862,522	H. McFarlane	S. R. Hawes
Mid Sussex	119,700	17,717,781	B. J. Grimshaw	C. Snowling
§Milton Keynes, Bucks.	164,370	28,304,512	M. J. Murray	(a) D. W. Taylor
Mole Valley, Surrey	77,300	13,222,205	A. A. Huggins	K. Matts
Newark, Notts.	106,100	11,379,557	V. G. Crawley	R. Marklew
Newbury, Berks.	127,600	21,821,905	B. J. Thetford	P. W. Dolphin
§Newcastle under Lyme, Staffs.	118,500	14,067,832	A. G. Owen	(a) R. Dean
§New Forest, Hants.	156,400	24,982,875	P. A. Bassett	A. Lee
§Northampton	169,800	30,033,817	R. J. B. Morris	(a) T. R. Bailey
Northavon, Avon	125,997	18,202,000	F. Maude	C. Williams
§North Bedfordshire	133,100	21,957,034	J. F. Hayward	(a) W. Astle
North Cornwall	69,200	7,742,891	I. Whiting	W. J. H. Burden
North Devon	80,400	8,553,933	R. D. Hall	H. G. Geen
North Dorset	46,479	5,433,253	A. J. Bridgeman	Mrs. M. E. Cossins
North East Derbyshire	97,200	9,487,774	D. G. Hunt†	R. W. Brunt
North Hertfordshire	111,400	19,548,760	J. S. Philp	A. G. Burrows
North Kesteven, Lincs.	80,292	8,626,251	Dr. G. J. Coady	A. Higgs
North Norfolk	90,200	11,168,762	T. V. Nolan	A. N. G. Duckworth-Chad
North Shropshire	52,040	5,226,469	K. Flood	D. Nagington
§North Warwickshire	60,200	8,830,397	D. Monks	(a) Mrs. M. Hall
North West Leicestershire	78,600	10,755,940	J. E. White	P. Kane
North Wiltshire	108,500	11,454,347	H. Miles	D. C. Hartley
NORWICH, Norfolk	122,300	23,537,240	A. R. H. Glover	(b) G. S. Wheatley
NOTTINGHAM	277,800	43,443,591	M. H. F. Hammond	(b) C. A. Clarke
§Nuneaton and Bedworth, Warwickshire	112,500	14,492,266	I. J. Clarke	(a) W. J. Oliver
§Oadby and Wigston, Leics.	53,100	7,167,133	J. B. Burton	(a) N. G. Reynolds
§Oswestry, Shropshire	32,167	3,269,154	D. A. Towers	(a) K. J. Griffiths
OXFORD	116,200	21,823,414	E. J. Patrick	(b) Mrs. E. M. F. Standingford
§Pendle, Lancs.	84,800	6,526,288	F. Wood	(a) K. Walton
Penwith, Cornwall	55,500	6,268,172	J. C. Moore, M.B.E.	Miss B. Hicks
PETERBOROUGH, Cambs.	146,200	23,685,914	P. B. Sidebottom	R. E. Perkins
PLYMOUTH, Devon	253,400	31,271,092	A. F. Watson	(b) A. H. Parish
§Poole, Dorset	124,500	21,600,006	I. K. D. Andrews	(a) R. C. J. Meech
PORTSMOUTH, Hants.	187,900	28,374,526	R. Trist	(b) J. G. Lodge
§Preston, Lancs.	125,200	15,989,608	A. Owens	(a) G. Walmsley
Purbeck, Dorset	43,300	5,905,910	T. J. Driver††	Mrs. B. S. Debenham
§Reading, Berks.	136,000	29,542,725	W. H. Tee	(a) Mrs. D. Lawrence
§Redditch, Hereford and Worcs.	76,000	12,194,451	Miss A. C. Griffin	(a) R. Passingham
§Reigate and Banstead, Surrey	116,700	19,869,430	C. T. Pollard	(a) J. McFarlane
§Restormel, Cornwall	85,735	10,712,025	D. Brown	(a) T. G. Alexander, O.B.E.
§Ribble Valley, Lancs.	53,300	5,809,657	M. Jackson	(b) L. Nevett
Richmondshire, North Yorks.	48,400	4,632,107	M. F. Tooze	Mrs. A. F. Harris
ROCHESTER UPON MEDWAY, Kent	145,600	23,877,118	R. E. Painter	(a) Mrs. M. C. Fennemore
Rochford, Essex	76,200	10,819,866	A. G. Cooke	W. H. Budge
§Rossendale, Lancs.	64,500	5,414,132	J. S. Hartley‡	(a) P. Navin
Rother, East Sussex	81,000	11,698,053	D. F. Powell	R. Pulford
§Rugby, Warwicks.	85,600	13,113,330	J. S. R. Lawton	(a) R. N. French
§Runnymede, Surrey	75,100	12,548,376	E. W. Andrews	(a) Miss S. Pert, M.B.E.
§Rushcliffe, Notts.	95,600	13,302,560	J. Saxton	(a) L. Cottingham
§Rushmoor, Hants.	79,100	12,826,465	D. Hartley	A. J. Callan
Rutland, Leics.	35,000	4,159,060	A. S. Jowett	B. A. Montgomery
Ryedale, North Yorks.	88,800	8,425,763	D. Cudworth	Mrs. D. M. Stead
ST. ALBANS, Herts.	128,800	23,958,893	R. H. Braddon	(a) C. Gunner
§St. Edmundsbury, Suffolk	89,616	12,847,433	G. R. N. Toft	(a) J. S. Long
Salisbury, Wilts.	102,500	13,641,137	D. R. J. Rawlinson	H. C. Farris
§Scarborough, North Yorks.	103,300	11,477,440	J. M. Trebble	(a) B. H. Bosomworth

† Chief Officer.   ‡ Borough Director.   †† Secretary.   ° Borough Secretary.

District	Population	Rateable Value 1987 £	Chief Executive (*Clerk)	Chairman 1987–88 (a) Mayor (b) Lord Mayor
§Scunthorpe, Humberside	66,047	12,182,439	K. Lescure	(a) D. Keedle
Sedgefield, Durham............	89,300	9,771,677	A. J. Roberts	J. Burton
Sedgemoor, Somerset	90,000	11,457,321	M. V. P. Hart	W. J. D. Roach
Selby, North Yorks.	85,500	14,752,597	J. C. Edwards	R. Wilson
Sevenoaks, Kent	107,900	13,923,000	B. Cova	F. G. Shubert
Shepway, Kent.................	89,300	14,071,284	R. H. Summers	F. D. Raymond
§Shrewsbury and Atcham, Shropshire	91,300	12,718,668	D. M. Clarke	(a) D. T. Preece
§Slough, Berks.	99,092	24,623,666	A. Bhattacharya*	(a) R. W. Prosser
SOUTHAMPTON, Hants.	202,300	32,162,445	E. A. Urquhart	(a) Mrs. I. I. White
South Bedfordshire............	110,000	21,176,061	T. D. Rix	J. A. Pergunas
South Bucks.	62,000	14,413,990	S. R. Jobson	Mrs. R. K. Wingrove
South Cambridgeshire	116,100	18,229,228	B. J. Hancock	Dr. C. M. Attwood
South Derbyshire	67,329	9,825,069	I. F. Baylis	W. Lord
§Southend-on-Sea, Essex	159,900	27,906,435	F. R. Peacock	K. P. Cater, M.B.E.
South Hams, Devon	69,700	8,792,500	F. G. Palmer	Mrs. M. Verniquet
South Herefordshire...........	48,600	5,334,162	D. T. Cole	W. A. Watkins
South Holland, Lincs...........	64,500	7,197,573	J. T. Brindley	J. R. Pearl
South Kesteven, Lincs.........	101,076	12,968,000	K. R. Cann	P. F. Spiegl
South Lakeland, Cumbria	98,500	11,687,001	A. F. Winstanley	G. P. George
South Norfolk	98,800	11,353,080	A. G. T. Kellett	A. W. Cook
South Northamptonshire	67,510	8,194,867	C. M. Major	C. L. Berey
South Oxfordshire	133,000	19,497,536	J. B. Chirnside	J. J. Eyston
§South Ribble, Lancs.	98,300	10,980,820	R. N. L. Hamm	(a) A. F. Bannister
South Shropshire	33,771	3,623,184	G. Kellet, M.B.E.	J. H. Meredith
South Somerset	139,100	16,268,793	D. J. Ashford	Mrs. J. Clarke
South Staffordshire	105,501	13,265,707	G. J. Haywood	D. Bramall
§South Wight, I.O.W.	52,700	6,193,030	D. W. Jaggar	(a) Maj. J. H. Finch
§Spelthorne, Surrey	92,000	22,400,000	G. F. Hilbert	(a) Miss R. E. Fox
§Stafford	117,800	17,044,439	R. E. Humphreys	(a) D. J. James
Staffordshire Moorlands	95,900	10,192,340	A. W. Law	A. S. Forrester
§Stevenage, Herts.	74,400	14,600,000	H. L. Miller	(a) A. G. Campbell
§Stockton-on-Tees, Cleveland ..	174,100	27,338,000	F. F. Theobalds*	(a) Mrs. M. Platts
STOKE-ON-TRENT, Staffs.	249,400	32,884,542	S. W. Titchener	(b) G. Tuck
Stratford-on-Avon, Warwicks...	104,600	16,904,617	T. J. W. Foy	F. W. Parrott
Stroud, Glos...................	104,500	12,680,479	D. F. Collins	Mrs. V. Gardiner
Suffolk Coastal	104,600	15,252,371	D. L. Blay	Cdr. N. A. Woodcock
§Surrey Heath	79,300	14,411,852	M. F. Orlik	(a) I. J. Christmas
§Swale, Kent.................	110,250	13,023,592	H. White, C.B.E., D.F.C., A.F.C.	(a) P. Morgan
§Tamworth, Staffs.	66,700	8,436,247	P. E. Thorpe	(a) P. J. Chesworth
Tandridge, Surrey.............	75,701	10,467,204	C. W. Rockall	C. J. Latilla
§Taunton Deane, Somerset	90,900	11,402,851	P. F. Berman	(a) R. S. Hutchings
Teesdale, Durham	24,700	2,291,299	C. E. Fell	J. Barker
Teignbridge, Devon	97,900	12,098,784	P. B. Young	F. G. Marks
Tendring, Essex	121,200	16,441,404	D. Mitchell-Gears	F. Good
§Test Valley, Hants.	99,300	15,040,788	G. Blythe	(a) Mrs. D. C. P. Bunting
§Tewkesbury, Glos.............	84,100	12,446,895	R. A. Wheeler°	(a) E. L. Western
§Thamesdown, Wilts.	160,000	23,561,583	D. M. Kent	(a) P. Owen
Thanet, Kent	120,300	15,636,297	I. G. Gill	F. A. Twyman
Three Rivers, Herts.	77,800	13,138,077	A. S. Potts	M. Dunstone
§Thurrock, Essex..............	124,400	28,102,155	C. Ennis	(a) J. Dunn
Tonbridge and Malling, Kent ...	100,000	14,245,422	T. J. Shellard	(a) Mrs. J. Hutchinson
§Torbay, Devon	117,900	17,542,648	D. P. Hudson	(a) Mrs. E. J. Armes
Torridge, Devon	47,271	4,244,755	R. K. Brasington	C. Cluick
§Tunbridge Wells, Kent	98,500	12,926,364	R. J. Stone	(a) D. G. G. Kirby
Tynedale, Northumberland	54,900	6,479,461	A. Baty	R. I. Johnson
Uttlesford, Essex	67,000	9,634,360	J. F. Vernon	H. W. Pugh
Vale of White Horse, Oxon......	109,100	18,729,454	J. C. Neville Wood	Mrs. E. Webb
Vale Royal, Cheshire	112,000	15,538,406	W. R. T. Woods	R. L. F. Woodhouse
Wansbeck, Northumberland....	60,400	7,897,908	A. G. White†	Mrs. D. Brown
Wansdyke, Avon	78,500	9,044,984	P. May‡	M. L. Offer
§Warrington, Cheshire	182,000	27,587,321	W. H. Lawton, T.D.	(a) P. H. J. Hetherington
Warwick	116,800	20,192,733	M. J. Ward	J. S. Hammon
§Watford, Herts.	76,500	17,290,580	R. B. McMillan	(a) L. T. Hughes
Waveney, Suffolk	103,200	12,288,399	M. Berridge	R. J. Niblett
Waverley, Surrey	114,300	18,130,600	G. W. Nuttall	(a) Lady Anson
Wealden, East Sussex	127,300	15,000,000	D. R. Holness	Col. J. D. Richards
Wear Valley, Durham	64,700	6,082,724	M. R. Sutcliff	G. Taylor
§Wellingborough, Northants....	65,100	9,074,855	W. B. Veal	(a) C. A. R. Blackmore

† Principal Chief Officer. ‡ General Manager. ° Borough Secretary.

District	Population	Rateable Value 1987 £	Chief Executive (*Clerk)	Chairman 1987–88 (a) Mayor (b) Lord Mayor
Welwyn Hatfield, Herts.	94,000	19,273,678	L. Asquith	Mrs. T. Welham
§West Devon.................	43,900	4,267,482	J. S. Ligo	(a) Mrs. B. M. P. Savage
West Dorset	81,300	9,869,097	M. B. Taylor	E. H. King
West Lancashire	107,500	13,425,799	J. C. Cowdall	C. R. Baily
West Lindsey, Lincs.	76,500	8,360,304	A. W. Hancock	M. French
West Oxfordshire	89,600	11,203,500	N. J. Robson	M. L. Chadwick
West Somerset	30,382	5,935,500	H. Close	V. A. Brewer
West Wiltshire...............	105,000	12,033,995	G. A. F. Garland	Mrs. K. M. Self
§Weymouth and Portland, Dorset	60,900	6,901,351	R. E. F. Norman	(a) R. G. Gainey
Wimborne, Dorset............	76,334	11,063,190	W. G. Press	Mrs. D. J. Harrison
WINCHESTER, Hants.	94,546	14,217,431	D. H. Cowan	(a) Maj. D. F. Covill
§Windsor and Maidenhead, Berks.	133,507	27,151,318	G. B. Blacker	(a) W. W. Cooley
§Woking, Surrey	86,600	17,050,894	P. Russell	(a) Mrs. M. M. Gammon
Wokingham, Berks.	138,400	21,019,720	N. E. Butler	L. F. Southgate
Woodspring, Avon	171,718	20,748,568	R. H. Moon	H. J. Ashman
WORCESTER	77,500	13,835,344	(vacant)	(a) C. W. V. Lord
§Worthing, West Sussex	95,900	15,077,071	T. L. Elliott	(a) E. A. McDonald
Wrekin, Shropshire	131,000	17,553,504	R. E. Paine	M. J. Davies
Wychavon, Hereford	97,200	14,738,647	P. G. Rust, M.B.E.	D. Lawley
Wycombe, Bucks..............	158,500	30,325,060	L. Timms	L. Hampton
§Wyre, Lancs.................	100,100	11,613,632	A. K. B. Boatswain	(a) A. Vink
Wyre Forest, Hereford and Worcs.	93,100	13,602,477	A. S. Dick	A. J. Millington
YORK, North Yorks.	102,500	12,086,043	J. Cairns	(b) M. Heppell

THE PRINCIPAL ENGLISH CITIES

BIRMINGHAM

BIRMINGHAM (West Midlands) is Britain's second city and the largest metropolitan district in the country.

The generally accepted derivation of "Birmingham" is the *ham* or dwelling-place of the *ing* or the family of *Beorma* presumed to have been a Saxon. Between the 11th and 16th centuries the de Berminghams were Lords of the Manor. By 1889 Birmingham had achieved City status.

Despite the decline in manufacturing, it is estimated that there are still 1,500 distinct trades carried on in the City, and Birmingham is still a major hardware trade and motor component industry centre. Recent development includes the National Exhibition Centre (opened in 1976), the Aston Science Park for high technology industries, and a partnership between the City Council, Lloyd's Bank and Aston University to provide risk-capital for such industries. Birmingham is also a regional centre for the media.

The principal buildings are the Town Hall, built in 1832–1834; the Council House (1879); Victoria Law Courts (1891); the University (1909); the 13th century Church of St. Martin (rebuilt 1873); the Cathedral (formerly St. Philip's Church); the Roman Catholic Cathedral of St. Chad (Pugin) and the Methodist Central Hall.

BRADFORD

BRADFORD (West Yorkshire), 192 miles N.N.W. of London, is the administrative centre of the Metropolitan District of Bradford. The District covers an area of 91,444 acres and lies on the southern edge of the Yorkshire Dales National Park, including within its boundaries the village of Haworth, home of the Brontë sisters, and Ilkley Moor.

Originally a Saxon township, Bradford received a market charter in 1251 but developed only slowly until the industrialisation of the textile industry brought rapid growth during the 19th century. The prosperity of that period is reflected in much of the city's architecture, particularly the public buildings—City Hall (1873), Wool Exchange (1867), St George's Hall (Concert Hall, 1853), Cartwright Hall (Art Gallery, 1904) and Technical College (1882). Other chief buildings are the Cathedral (15th century) and Bolling Hall (14th century).

Textiles still play an important part in the city's economy but industry is now more broadly based, including engineering and micro-electronics. The city has a strong banking, insurance and building society sector, and a growing tourism industry.

BRISTOL

BRISTOL (Avon) is the largest non-metropolitan district in population in the country, and lies 119 miles W. of London. The present municipal area is 10,954 hectares.

Bristol's commercial port systems comprise the largest municipally owned port in the country. The Avonmouth dock complex, Royal Portbury Dock and Portishead Dock handle import and export cargoes. Principal imports include cocoa, timber, metals, animal feeding stuffs, oil products, chemicals, vehicles and molasses. The Royal Portbury Dock, opened by H.M. the Queen in Aug. 1977, is capable of accommodating up to six vessels of 70,000 d.w.t.

The chief buildings include the 12th century

Cathedral (with later additions), with Norman Chapter House and gateway, the 14th century Church of St. Mary Redcliffe, Wesley's Chapel, Broadmead, the Merchant Venturers' Almshouses, the Council House (1956), Guildhall, Exchange (erected from the designs of John Wood in 1743), Cabot Tower, the University and Clifton College. The Roman Catholic Cathedral at Clifton was opened in 1973.

The *Clifton Suspension Bridge*, with a span of 702 feet over the Avon, was projected by Brunel in 1836 but was not completed until 1864. Brunel's *SS Great Britain*, the first ocean going propeller driven ship, is now being restored in the City Docks from where she was launched in 1843. The docks themselves have been extensively restored and redeveloped.

Bristol was a Royal Borough before the Norman Conquest. The earliest form of the name is *Bricgstow*. In 1373 it received from Edward III a charter granting it county status.

CAMBRIDGE

CAMBRIDGE, a settlement far older than its ancient University, lies on the Cam or Granta, 51 miles north of London. It has an area of 10,060 acres.

The city is a county town and regional headquarters. Its industries include electronics, flour milling, cement making and the manufacture of scientific instruments. Among its open spaces are Jesus Green, Sheep's Green, Coe Fen, Parker's Piece, Christ's Pieces, the University Botanic Garden, and the Backs, or lawns and gardens through which the Cam winds behind the principal line of college buildings. East of the Cam, King's Parade, upon which stand Great St. Mary's Church, Gibbs' Senate House and King's College Chapel with Wilkins' screen, joins Trumpington Street to form one of the most beautiful throughfares in Europe.

University and College buildings provide the outstanding features of Cambridge architecture but several churches (especially St. Benet's, the oldest building in the City, and St. Sepulchre's the Round Church) also are notable. The modern Guildhall (1939) stands on a site of which at least part has held municipal buildings since 1224.

CANTERBURY

CANTERBURY, the Metropolitan City of the Anglican Communion, has a history going back to prehistoric times. It was the Roman Durovernum and the Saxon Cant-wara-byrig (stronghold of the men of Kent). Here in 597 St. Augustine began the conversion of the English to Christianity, when Ethelbert, King of Kent, was baptized.

Of the Benedictine St. Augustine's Abbey, burial place of the Jutish Kings of Kent (whose capital Canterbury was) only extensive ruins remain. St. Martin's Church, on the eastern outskirts of the City, is stated by Bede to have been the place of worship of Queen Bertha, the Christian wife of King Ethelbert, before the advent of St. Augustine.

In 1170 the rivalry of Church and State culminated in the murder in Canterbury Cathedral, by Henry II's knights, of Archbishop Thomas Becket, whose shrine became a great centre of pilgrimage as described by Chaucer in his *Canterbury Tales*. After the Reformation pilgrimages ceased, but the prosperity of the City was strengthened by an influx of Huguenot refugees, who introduced weaving. The Elizabethan poet and playwright Christopher Marlowe was born and reared in Canterbury, and there are literary associations also with Defoe, Dickens, Joseph Conrad and Somerset Maugham.

The Cathedral, with architecture ranging from the eleventh to the fifteenth centuries, is world famous. Modern pilgrims are attracted particularly to the Martyrdom, The Black Prince's Tomb, the Warriors' Chapel and the many examples of mediæval stained glass.

The medieval City Walls are built on Roman foundations and the fourteenth century West Gate is one of the finest buildings of its kind in the country.

The 1,000 seat Marlowe Theatre is the base for the Canterbury International Festival of the Arts each autumn.

Before the institution of the Mayoralty in 1448 the City was governed by bailiffs and earlier still by prefects or provosts.

CARLISLE

CARLISLE is situated at the confluence of the River Eden and River Caldew, 309 miles north west of London and a few miles from the Scottish border. It has an area of 254,955 acres, and was granted a charter in 1158.

The city stands at the western end of Hadrian's Wall and dates from the original Roman settlement of *Luguvalium*. Granted to Scotland in the 10th century, Carlisle is not included in the Doomsday Book. William Rufus reclaimed the area in 1092 and the Castle and city walls were built to guard Carlisle and the western border; the Citadel is a Tudor addition to protect the south of the city. Until the Union of the Crowns in 1603, Carlisle changed hands several times and was frequently besieged. During the Civil War the city remained Royalist; in 1745 it supported the Young Pretender.

The Cathedral, originally a 12th century Augustinian priory, was enlarged in the 13th and 14th centuries after the diocese was created in 1133. To the south is a restored Tithe Barn and nearby the 18th century church of St. Cuthbert, the third to stand on a site dating from the 7th century.

Carlisle is the major shopping, commercial and agricultural centre for the area, and industries include the manufacture of metal goods, biscuits and textiles. However, the largest employer is the services sector, notably in retailing and transport. The city has an important communications position at the centre of a network of major roads, as an important stage on the main west coast rail services and with its own airport at Crosby.

CHESTER

CHESTER is situated on the River Dee, 189 miles north west of London. The city administers an area of 173 square miles and was granted Borough and City status in 1974.

Chester's recorded history dates from the 1st century when the Romans founded the fortress of *Deva*. The city's name is derived from the Latin *castra* (a camp or encampment). During the Middle Ages, Chester was the principal port of north west England but declined with the silting of the Dee estuary and competition from Liverpool. The city was also an important military centre, notably during Edward I's Welsh campaigns and the Elizabethan Irish campaigns. During Civil War, Chester supported the King and was besieged from 1643–6. Chester's first charter was granted *c* 1175 and the city was incorporated in 1506. The office of Sheriff is the earliest created in the country (c 1120's), and the Mayor also enjoys the title "Admiral of the Dee".

The city's architectural features include the city walls (an almost complete two mile circuit), the unique Rows (covered galleries above the street level shops), the Victorian Gothic Town Hall (1869), the Castle (rebuilt 1788 and 1822) and numerous half-timbered buildings. The Cathedral was a Benedictine abbey until the Dissolution. Remaining monastic buildings include the chapter house, refectory and cloisters and there is a modern free-standing bell tower. The Norman church of St. John the Baptist was a Cathedral church in the early Middle Ages.

Chester's principal industry is tourism, and the city is also a shopping centre for North Wales and the North West. Other industries include light engineering and manufacture of car components. In 1984 the city was awarded Development Area status.

COVENTRY

COVENTRY (West Midlands) is a city 92 miles N.W. of London, and an important industrial centre, producing cars, machine tools, agricultural machinery, man made fibres, composite materials and telecommunications equipment.

The city owes its beginning to Leofric, Earl of Mercia and his wife Godiva who, in 1043, founded a Benedictine monastery. The guildhall of St. Mary dates from the 14th century, three of the city's churches date from the 14th and 15th centuries and 16th century almshouses may still be seen. Coventry's first cathedral was destroyed at the Reformation, its second in the 1940 blitz (its walls and spire remain) and the new cathedral designed by Sir Basil Spence, consecrated in 1962, now draws innumerable visitors.

Coventry is the home of the University of Warwick and its Science Park, the rapidly-expanding Westwood Business Park and the Museum of British Transport.

DERBY

DERBY stands on the banks of the River Derwent, 127 miles N.N.W. of London, and covers an area of 30 square miles. The name Derby dates back to 880 when the Danes settled in the locality and changed the original Saxon name of "Northworthy" to "Deoraby".

Derby has a wide range of industries: its products include the aero engines of Rolls Royce Ltd., lawn mowers, pipework, specialised mechanical engineering equipment, textiles, chemicals, plastics and the Royal Crown Derby porcelain. The city is an established railway centre, the site of British Rail's Technical Centre with its research laboratories.

Buildings of interest include St Peter's Church, (14th century), the Cathedral (1525), St Mary's Roman Catholic Church (1839), the Industrial Museum, formerly the Old Silk Mill (1721), and the Old Abbey Building dating from the 14th century. Two recent developments are the Assembly Rooms in the Market Place and the Eagle Centre, a shopping precinct covering twelve acres, including a market and the new Derby Playhouse.

The first charter granting a Mayor and Aldermen was that of Charles I in 1637. Previous charters date back to 1154. It was granted City status in 1977.

DURHAM

The city of DURHAM is a district in the county of Durham and covers an area of 73 square miles. The city is the major tourist attraction in the county because of its prominent Norman Cathedral and Castle set high on a wooded peninsula overlooking the River Wear. The Cathedral was founded as a shrine for the body of St. Cuthbert in 995. The present building dates from 1093 and among its many treasures is the tomb of the Venerable Bede (673–735). Durham's Prince Bishops had unique powers up to 1836, being lay rulers as well as religious leaders. As a palatinate Durham could have its own army, nobility, coinage and courts. The Castle was the main seat of the Prince Bishops for nearly 800 years; it is now used as a college by the University.

The University, founded on the initiative of Bishop William Van Mildert, is England's third oldest. Its students live in 14 colleges spread across the city.

Among other buildings of interest is the Guildhall in the Market Place which dates originally from the 14th century. Much work has been carried out to conserve this area, forming part of the city's major contribution to the Council of Europe's Urban Renaissance Campaign. Annual events include Durham's Regatta in June (claimed to be the oldest rowing event in Britain) and the Miners' Gala in July.

In the past 20 years the economy of Durham has undergone a significant change with the replacement of mining as the dominant feature by "white collar" employment. Although still a predominantly rural area, the industrial and commercial sector is growing and a wide range of manufacturing and service industries are based on industrial estates on and around the City area.

EXETER

EXETER lies on the River Exe 170 miles S.W. of London and 10 miles from the sea. It covers an area of 11,037 acres and was granted a Royal Charter by Henry II.

The Romans founded *Isca Dumnoniorum* in the 1st century A.D., and in the 3rd century a stone wall (most of which remains) was built, providing protection against Saxon, and then Danish invasions. After the Conquest, the city led resistance to William in the west, until reduced by siege. The Normans built the motte and bailey castle of Rougemont, the gatehouse and one tower of which remain, although the rest was pulled down in 1784. The first bridge across the Exe was built in the 13th century. The city's role as a port declined due to the silting of the river, but was somewhat restored by the construction in the 1560's of the first ship canal in England. Exeter was the Royalist headquarters in the West during the Civil War.

The diocese of Exeter was established by Edward the Confessor in 1050, although a church existed on the Cathedral site in the early 10th century. A new cathedral was built in the 12th century but the present building was begun *c.* 1275 in the Gothic style, although incorporating the Norman towers, and completed about a century later with the West Front. The Guildhall dates from the 12th century and there are many other medieval buildings in the city, as well as architecture in the Georgian and Regency styles (Custom House, The Quay). Damage suffered by bombing in 1942 led to the redevelopment of the city centre.

Exeter's prosperity from medieval times was based on trade in wool and woollen cloth (commemorated by Tuckers Hall), which remained at its height until the late 18th century when export trade was hit by the French Wars. Subsequently Exeter has developed as an administrative and commercial centre, notably in the distributive trades and light manufacturing industries.

KINGSTON UPON HULL

HULL (officially "Kingston upon Hull") lies in the mostly rural County of Humberside, at the junction of the River Hull with the Humber, 22 miles from the North Sea and 205 miles N. of London. The municipal area is 17,535 acres.

Hull is one of the great seaports of the United Kingdom. It has docks covering a water area of 172 acres, equipped to handle cargoes by unit-load techniques, and is a departure point for car ferry services to the continent. There is a great variety of industry and service industries, as well as increasing tourism and conference business.

The city, restored after very heavy air raid damage during World War II, has good office and administrative buildings, its municipal centre being the Guildhall, its educational centre the University of Hull and its religious centre the Parish Church of the Holy Trinity. The old Town area is being renovated and includes a new marina and plans for a shopping complex. Just west of the city is the Humber Bridge, the world's longest single span suspension bridge, which was officially opened by H.M. the Queen in July 1981.

Kingston upon Hull was so named by Edward I. City status was accorded in 1897 and the office of Mayor raised to the dignity of Lord Mayor in 1914.

LEEDS

LEEDS (West Yorkshire), a Metropolitan District from April 1, 1974, is a junction for road, rail, canal and air services and an important commercial centre, situated in the lower Aire Valley, 195 miles by road N.N.W. of London. The metropolitan area is 138,915 acres.

The main manufacturing industries are mechanical engineering, printing, publishing and clothing. However, 65 per cent of employment is in sevices, notably professional and scientific, particularly education and medicine, distributive trades, finance and banking.

The principal buildings are the Civic Hall (1933), the Town Hall (1858), the Municipal Buildings and Art Gallery (1884) with the Henry Moore Gallery (1982), the Corn Exchange (1863) and the University. The Parish Church (St. Peter's) was rebuilt in 1841; the 17th century St. John's Church has a fine interior with a famous English renaissance screen; the last remaining 18th century church is Holy Trinity, Boar Lane (1727). Kirkstall Abbey (about 3 miles from the centre of the city), founded by Henry de Lacy in 1152, is one of the most complete examples of Cistercian houses now remaining. Temple Newsam, birthplace of Lord Darnley, was acquired by the Council in 1922. The present house was largely re-built by Sir Arthur Ingram in about 1620. Adel Church, about 5 miles from the centre of the city, is a fine Norman structure.

Leeds was first incorporated by Charles I in 1626. The earliest forms of the name are *Loidis* or *Ledes*, the origins of which are obscure.

LEICESTER

LEICESTER is situated geographically in the centre of England, 100 miles N. of London. The City dates back to pre-Roman times and was one of the five Danish *Burhs*. In 1589 Queen Elizabeth I granted a Charter to the City and the ancient title was confirmed by Letters Patent in 1919. Under local government reorganization Leicester's area remained unchanged at 18,141 acres, and it retains its designation as a City.

The principal industries of the city are hosiery, and knitwear, footwear manufacturing and engineering. The growth of Leicester as a hosiery centre increased rapidly from the introduction there of the first stocking frame in 1670 and to-day it has some of the largest hosiery factories in the world, with much of the output being exported.

The principal buildings in the city are the Town Hall, the New Walk Centre, the University, Leicester Polytechnic, De Montfort Hall, one of the finest concert halls in the provinces seating over 2,750 persons, and the Granby Halls, a major indoor sports facility. The ancient Churches of St. Martin (now Leicester Cathedral), St. Nicholas, St. Margaret, All Saints, St. Mary de Castro, and buildings such as the Guildhall, the 14th century Newarke Gate, the Castle and the Jewry Wall Roman site still exist. The

Haymarket Theatre, an integral part of a large shopping and car-parking complex, was opened in 1973.

LINCOLN

Situated 143 miles N. of London and 40 miles inland on the River Witham, LINCOLN derives its name from a contraction of *Lindum Colonia*, the settlement founded in A.D. 48 by the Romans to command the crossing of Ermine Street and Fosse Way. Sections of the 3rd century Roman city wall can be seen, including an extant gateway (Newport Arch), and excavations have discovered traces of a sewerage system unique in Britain. The Romans also drained the surrounding fenland and created a canal system, laying the foundations of Lincoln's agricultural prosperity, and also of the city's importance in the medieval wool trade as a port and Staple town. As one of the Five Boroughs of the Danelaw, Lincoln was an important trading centre in the 9th and 10th centuries and medieval prosperity from the wool trade lasted until the 14th century, enabling local merchants to build parish churches (of which three survive), and attracting in the 12th century a Jewish community (Jew's House and Court, Aaron's House). However, the removal of the Staple to Boston in 1369 heralded a decline from which the city only recovered fully in the 19th century when improved fen drainage made Lincoln agriculturally important, and improved canal and rail links led to industrial development, mainly in the manufacture of machinery, components and engineering products.

The Castle was built shortly after the Conquest and is unusual in having two mounds; on one motte stands a Keep (Lucy's Tower) added in the 12th century. The Cathedral was begun c.1073 when the first Norman bishop moved the see of Lindsey to Lincoln, but was mostly destroyed by fire and earthquake in the 12th century. Rebuilding was begun by St. Hugh and completed over a century later. The Wren library contains manuscripts including one of the four surviving originals of the Magna Carta. Other notable architectural features of the city are the 12th century High Bridge, the oldest in Britain still to carry buildings, and the Guildhall situated above the 15–16th century Stonebow gateway.

LIVERPOOL

LIVERPOOL (Merseyside) on the right bank of the river Mersey, 3 miles from the Irish Sea and 210 miles N.W. of London, is one of the greatest trading centres of the world and the principal port in the United Kingdom for the Atlantic trade. The municipal area of 27,852 acres includes 2,840 acres in the bed of the river Mersey.

There are 7 miles of docks on both sides of the river and the Gladstone and Royal Seaforth Docks can accommodate the largest vessels afloat. Annual tonnage of cargo handled is approximately 11,000,000 deadweight tonnes. The main imports are petroleum, grain, ores, edible oils, timber, containers and break bulk cargo. The Royal Seaforth Dock, opened in 1973, is the latest development. It comprises container, timber and grain terminals and is within the Liverpool Free Port, superimposed upon 600 acres of active dockland.

Liverpool was created a borough in 1207 and a city in 1880. From the early eighteenth century it expanded rapidly with the growth of the port. Surviving buildings from this date include the Bluecoat Chambers (1717, formerly the Bluecoat School), the Town Hall (1754, rebuilt to the original design, 1795), and buildings in Rodney Street, Canning Street and the suburbs. Notable from the nineteenth and twentieth centuries are the Anglican

Cathedral, built from the designs of Sir Giles Gilbert Scott (the foundation stone was laid in 1904, and the building was only completed in 1980), the Catholic Metropolitan Cathedral (designed by Sir Frederick Gibberd, consecrated 1967) and St. George's Hall, (1838–1854), regarded as one of the finest modern examples of classical architecture. In 1852 an Act was obtained for establishing a public library, museum and art gallery; as a result Liverpool had one of the first public libraries in the country. The Brown, Picton and Hornby libraries now form one of the country's major libraries. The Victoria Building of Liverpool University, The Royal Liver, Cunard and Mersey Docks & Harbour Company buildings at the Pier Head, the Municipal Buildings and the Philharmonic Hall are other examples of the City's fine buildings.

Constructed between 1925 and 1934, the first Mersey Tunnel was named "Queensway". The second Mersey Tunnel—"Kingsway"—was opened on June 24, 1971, and a similar tunnel adjacent to it was opened on February 14, 1974. In 1969 the Merseyside Passenger Transport Executive was formed to improve and co-ordinate local transport throughout Merseyide, and, in partnership with British Rail, developed the Merseyside Loop/Link system, opened in 1977 to link Southport, Ormskirk, Kirby and Garston with the City Centre stations and lines to the Wirral.

In 1984 a 250 acre area of Liverpool's southern waterfront was cleared and landscaped to accommodate Britain's first International Garden Festival.

MANCHESTER

MANCHESTER (the *Mancunium* of the Romans, who occupied it in A.D. 78) is 189 miles N.W. of London and covers about 43 square miles.

Manchester is a commercial and industrial centre with a population engaged in engineering, chemical, clothing, food processing and textile industries. Banking and insurance are among the prime commercial activities. The city is connected with the sea by the Manchester Ship Canal, opened in 1894, 35½ miles long, and accommodating ships up to 15,000 tons. Manchester Airport handles more than 5 million passengers yearly.

The principal buildings are the Town Hall, erected in 1877 from the designs of Alfred Waterhouse, R.A., together with a large extension of 1938; the Royal Exchange (1869, enlarged 1921) the Central Library (1934); Heaton Hall; the 17th century Chetham Library; the Rylands Library (1899), which includes the Althorp collection; the University precinct; the 15th-century Cathedral (formerly the parish church) and the Free Trade Hall. Manchester is the home of the Hallé Orchestra, the Royal Northern College of Music, the Royal Exchange Theatre and seven public art galleries.

The town received its first charter of incorporation in 1838 and was created a city in 1853. The title of city was retained under local government reorganization.

NEWCASTLE UPON TYNE

NEWCASTLE UPON TYNE (Tyne and Wear) a Metropolitan District on the north bank of the River Tyne, is 8 miles from the North Sea, 272 miles N. of London and has an area of 27,640 acres. A Cathedral and University City, it is the administrative, commercial and cultural centre for north-east England and the principal port. It is an important manufacturing centre with a wide variety of industries.

The principal buildings include the Castle Keep (12th century), Black Gate (13th century), Blackfriars (13th century), West Walls (13th century), St. Nicho-

las's Cathedral (15th century, fine lantern tower), St. Andrew's Church (12th–14th century), St. John's (14th–15th century), All Saints (1786 by Stephenson), St. Mary's Roman Catholic Cathedral (1844), Trinity House (17th century), Sandhill (16th century houses), Guildhall (Georgian), Grey Street (1834–39), Central Station (1846–50), Laing Art Gallery (1904), University of Newcastle Physics Building (1962) and Medical Building (1985), Civic Centre (1963), Central Library (1969) and Eldon Square Development (1976). Open spaces include the Town Moor (927 acres) and Jesmond Dene. Eight bridges span the Tyne at Newcastle.

The City derives its name from the "new castle" (1080) erected as a defence against the Scots. In 1400 it was made a County, and in 1882 a City.

NORWICH

NORWICH (Norfolk) is an ancient City 110 miles N.E. of London. It grew from an early Anglo-Saxon settlement near the confluence of the Rivers Yare and Wensum, and now serves as provincial capital for the predominantly agricultural region of East Anglia. The name is thought to relate to the most northerly of a group of Anglo-Saxon villages or "wics". The present City has an area of 9,655 acres. The City's first known Charter was granted in 1158 by Henry II.

Norwich serves its surrounding area as a market town and commercial centre, banking and insurance being prominent among the City's businesses. From the 14th century until the Industrial Revolution, Norwich was the regional centre of the woollen industry, but now the biggest single industry is the manufacturing of shoes and other principal trades are engineering, printing, and the production of chemicals, clothing, confectionery and other foodstuffs. Norwich is accessible to seagoing vessels by means of the River Yare, entered at Great Yarmouth, 20 miles to the east.

Among many historic buildings are the Cathedral (completed in the twelfth century and surmounted by a fifteenth century spire 315 feet in height), the Keep of the Norman Castle (now a museum and art gallery), the fifteenth century flint-walled Guildhall, some thirty medieval parish churches, St. Andrew's and Blackfriars' Halls, the Tudor houses preserved in Elm Hill and the Georgian Assembly House. The University of East Anglia has been established in Norwich on a spacious site at Earlham on the City's western boundary and received its first students in 1963.

NOTTINGHAM

NOTTINGHAM (Nottinghamshire) stands on the River Trent, 124 miles N.N.W. of London in one of the most valuable coalfields of the country connected by canal with the Atlantic and the North Sea. The municipal area is 18,364 acres.

The principal industries are hosiery, lace, bleaching, dyeing and spinning, tanning, engineering and cycle works, brewing and the manufacture of tobacco, chemicals, furniture, typewriters and mechanical products.

The chief buildings are the 17th century Nottingham Castle (restored in 1878, and now the City Museum and Gallery of Art), Wollaton Hall (1580–88) owned by the City Council and now a Natural History Museum, St. Mary's, St. Peter's, and St. Nicholas's Churches, the Roman Catholic Cathedral (Pugin, 1842–4), the Council House (1929), the Guildhall and Court House (1888), Shire Hall, Albert Hall, the University, Trent Polytechnic, Newstead Abbey, home of Lord Byron, the Theatre Royal (1865), the Playhouse (1963) and the Royal Concert Hall (1982).

Snotingaham or *Notingeham*, "the village or home of the sons of Snot" (the Wise), is the Anglo-Saxon name for the Celtic *Tuigogobauc*, "Cave Homes". The City possesses a Charter of Henry II, and was created a City in 1897. Under local government reorganization, the style of city was reaccorded from April, 1974.

OXFORD

OXFORD is a University City, an important industrial centre, and a market town, with an area of 8,785 acres. Industry played a minor part in Oxford until the motor industry was established in 1912.

It is for its architecture that Oxford is of most interest to the visitor, its oldest specimens being the reputed Saxon tower of St. Michael's church, the remains of the Norman castle and city walls and the Norman church at Iffley. It is chiefly famous however, for its Gothic buildings, such as the Divinity Schools, the Old Library at Merton College, William of Wykeham's New College, Magdalen College and Christ Church and many other college buildings. Later centuries are represented by the Laudian quadrangle at St. John's College, the Renaissance Sheldonian Theatre by Wren, Trinity College Chapel, and All Saints Church; Hawksmoor's mock-Gothic at All Souls College, and the eighteenth century Queens' College. In addition to individual buildings, High Street and Radcliffe Square, just off it, both form architectural compositions of great beauty. Most of the Colleges have gardens, those of Magdalen, New College, St. John's (designed by "Capability" Brown) and Worcester being the largest.

PLYMOUTH

PLYMOUTH is situated on the borders of Devon and Cornwall at the confluence of the Rivers Tamar and Plym, 210 miles from London, with an area of 19,572 acres. The city has a long maritime history; it was the home port of Sir Francis Drake and the starting point for his circumnavigation of the world, as well as the last port of call for the Mayflower when the Pilgrim Fathers sailed for the New World in 1620. Today Plymouth is host to many international yacht races. The Barbican harbour area has many Elizabethan buildings, and on Plymouth Hoe stands the first lighthouse to be built on the Eddystone Rocks, some miles offshore.

Following extensive war damage, the city centre, comprising a large shopping centre, municipal offices, law courts and public buildings, has been re-built. The main employment is provided by H.M.Dockyard, though many new industrial firms and service industries have become established in the post-war period and the city is a growing tourism centre. In 1982 the Theatre Royal was opened. In conjunction with the Cornwall County Council, the Tamar Bridge was constructed linking the City by road with Cornwall.

PORTSMOUTH

PORTSMOUTH occupies Portsea Island, Hampshire, with boundaries extending to the mainland. It has an area of 15½ sq. miles and is 70 miles from London.

Portsmouth is a centre of industry and commerce, including many high technology and manufacturing industries. It is the U.K. headquarters of a major computer company and two insurance companies. H.M. Naval Base still has a substantial work force, although this has decreased in recent years. The commercial port and Continental Ferry Port is owned and run by the City Council, and carries passengers and vehicles to France and the Channel Islands.

A major port since the 16th century, Portsmouth is also a thriving seaside resort catering for thousands of visitors and day-trippers annually. Among many historic attractions are Lord Nelson's flagship, H.M.S. *Victory*, the Tudor warship *Mary Rose*, Britain's first "ironclad", H.M.S. *Warrior*, the D-Day Museum, Charles Dickens' birthplace at 393 Old Commercial Road, the Royal Naval and Royal Marine museums, Southsea Castle (built by Henry VIII), the Round Tower and Point Battery, which for hundreds of years have guarded the entrance to Portsmouth Harbour, Fort Widley on Portsdown Hill and the Sealife Centre.

ST. ALBANS

Twenty-five miles north west of London and situated on the River Ver, ST. ALBANS' origins stem from the major Roman town of *Verulamium*. Named after the first Christian martyr in Britain, who was executed here, St. Albans has developed around the Norman Abbey and Cathedral Church (consecrated 1115), the second longest in Britain, built partly of materials from the old Roman city. The museums house Iron Age and Roman artifacts and the Roman Theatre, unique in Britain, has a stage as opposed to an amphitheatre. Archæological excavations in the city centre continue also to reveal evidence of pre-Roman, Saxon and medieval occupation.

The town's significance grew to the extent that it was a signatory and venue for the drafting of the Magna Carta. It was also the scene of major riots during the Peasants' Revolt; the French King John was imprisoned there after the Battle of Poitiers, and heavy fighting took place during the Wars of the Roses; but it is as a Roman town that it is best recognized.

Previously controlled by the Abbot, the town achieved a Royal Charter in 1553 and City status in 1877. The street market, first established in 1553, is still an important feature of the city, as are many hotels and inns which survive from the days when St. Albans was an important coach stop. Tourist attractions include historic churches and houses, and a fifteenth century clock tower.

The advent of the railway saw the gradual expansion of the city, and the area now contains a wide range of firms, with special emphasis on microtechnology and electronics, particularly in the medical field. In addition, it is the home of the Royal National Rose Society, and of Rothamsted Park, the agricultural research centre.

In 1974 the City and District of St. Albans was formed, taking in the town of Harpenden and many villages, and it now covers an area of 63 square miles.

SHEFFIELD

SHEFFIELD (South Yorkshire), the centre of the special steel and cutlery trades, is situated 159 miles N.N.W. of London, at the junction of the Sheaf, Porter, Rivelin and Loxley with the River Don.

Sheffield has an area of 91,000 acres (nearly 150 square miles), including 4,619 acres of publicly owned parks and woodland. Though its cutlery, silverware and plate have long been famous, Sheffield has other and now more important industries—special and alloy steels, engineering and tool-making. Research in glass, metallurgy, radiotherapy and other fields is carried on.

The parish church of St. Peter and St. Paul, founded in the twelfth century, became the Cathedral Church of the Diocese of Sheffield in 1914. The Roman Catholic Cathedral Church of St. Marie (founded 1847) was created Cathedral for the new diocese of Hallam in 1980. Parts of the present building date from about 1435. The principal buildings are the Town Hall (1897, 1923 and 1977), the Cutlers' Hall

(1832), the University (1905 and recent extensions, including 19-storey Arts Tower), City Hall (1932), Graves Art Gallery (1934), Castle Market Building (1959), the retail market (1973), Mappin Art Gallery and the Crucible Theatre.

Sheffield was created a city in 1893 and on April 1, 1974 became a Metropolitan District Council incorporating Stocksbridge and most of the Wortley Rural area, and retained city status.

Master Cutler (1985–86) 362nd *Master of the Company of Cutlers in Hallamshire*, P. W. Lee.

SOUTHAMPTON

SOUTHAMPTON is the leading British deep sea port on the Channel and is situated on one of the finest natural harbours in the world. In 1984 a Free Trade Zone was established in the port. The first Charter was granted by Henry II and Southampton was created a county of itself in 1447. In February, 1964, Her Majesty the Queen granted city status by Royal Charter. The city has an area of 12,071 acres excluding tidal waters.

There have been Roman and Saxon settlements on the site of the city, which has been an important port since the time of the Conquest due to its natural deep-water harbour. The oldest church is St. Michael's (1070) which has a black tournai marble font and an unusually tall spire built in the eighteenth century as a landmark for navigators of Southampton Water. Other buildings and monuments within the city walls are the Tudor House, God's House Tower, Bargate Museum, the Tudor Merchants Hall, the Weighhouse, West Gate, King John's House, Long House, Wool House, the ruins of Holy Rood Church, St. Julien's Church and the Mayflower Memorial. The medieval town walls, built for artillery, are among the most complete in Europe. Public open spaces total over 1,000 acres in extent and comprise 9 per cent. of the city's area. The Common covers an area of 328 acres in the central district of the city and is mostly natural parkland.

STOKE-ON-TRENT

STOKE-ON-TRENT (Staffordshire), familiarly known as The Potteries, stands on the River Trent 157 miles N. of London. The present municipal area is 22,916 acres (36 square miles) and the city is the main centre of employment for the population of North Staffordshire. It is the largest clayware producer in the world (china, earthenware, sanitary goods, refractories, bricks and tiles) and has a considerable coal mining output drawn from one of the richest coalfields in Western Europe. The city has steelworks, foundries, chemical works, engineering plants, rubber works, paper mills, and a very wide range of manufactures. The city is also the venue for the 1986 National Garden Festival.

Extensive reconstruction has been carried on in recent years. A unique feature of the city is that it has six "centres" and more shops and public halls than other areas of comparable size. The City was formed by the federation in 1910 of the separate municipal authorities of Tunstall, Burslem, Hanley, Stoke-upon-Trent, Fenton, and Longton, all of which are now combined in the present City of Stoke-on-Trent.

WINCHESTER

WINCHESTER, the ancient capital of England, is situated on the River Itchen 65 miles S.W. of London and 12 miles N. of Southampton. Since local government reorganization in 1974, the style of City has been accorded to the whole of the new district of Winchester, which embraces an area of 162,921 acres of mid-Hampshire.

Winchester is rich in architecture of all types but the Cathedral takes pride of place. The longest Gothic cathedral in the world, it was built in 1079–1093 and exhibits examples of Norman, Early English and Perpendicular styles. Winchester College, founded in 1382, is one of the most famous public schools, the original building (of 1393) remaining unaltered. St. Cross Hospital, another great medieval foundation, lies 1 mile south of the city. The Almshouses were founded in 1136 by Bishop Henry de Blois, and Cardinal Henry Beaufort added a new Alms House of "Noble Poverty" in 1446. The Chapel and dwellings are of great architectural interest, and visitors may still receive the "Wayfarer's Dole" of bread and ale.

Recent excavations have done much to clarify the origins and development of Winchester. Part of the forum and several of the streets of the Roman town have been discovered; and excavations in the Cathedral Close have uncovered the entire site of the Anglo-Saxon cathedral (known as the Old Minster) and parts of the New Minster, built by Alfred's son Edward the Elder, and the burial place of the Alfredian dynasty. The original burial place of St. Swithun, before his remains were translated to a site in the present cathedral, was also uncovered.

Excavations in other parts of the City have thrown much light on Norman Winchester, notably on the site of the Royal Castle, adjacent to which the new Law Courts have been built, and in the grounds of Wolvesey Castle, where the great house built by Bishops Giffard and Henry of Blois in the twelfth century has been uncovered.

YORK

The City of YORK is a District in the County of North Yorkshire, and is an archiepiscopal seat. The City has an area of 7,295 acres.

The recorded history of York dates from A.D. 71, when the Roman Ninth Legion established a base under Petilius Cerealis which later became the fortress of Eboracum. In Anglo-Saxon times the city was the royal and ecclesiastical centre of Northumbria, and was captured by a Viking army in A.D. 866, after which it became the capital of the Viking kingdom of Jorvik. By the 14th century the city had become a great mercantile centre, chiefly owing to its control of the wool trade, and was used as the chief base against the Scots. Under the Tudors its fortunes declined, though Henry VIII made it the headquarters of the Council of the North. Recent excavations on many sites, including Coppergate, has greatly expanded knowledge of Roman, Viking and medieval urban life.

With its development as a railway centre in the 19th century the commercial life of York expanded and it is now a flourishing modern city. The principal industries are the manufacture of chocolate, railway coaches, scientific instruments, and sugar. The City is also an important tourist centre.

It is rich in examples of architecture of all periods. The earliest church (built, 627) was succeeded by several others until, in the 12th to the 15th centuries, the present Minster was built in a succession of styles. The finest features are the West front with its two towers, the spacious transepts and the stained glass. Other examples within the city are the medieval city walls and gateways, churches and guildhalls. Domestic architecture includes the Georgian mansions of The Mount, Micklegate and Bootham. Its museums are world-famous and include the Castle Museum, one of the best-known folk museums in Great Britain, the National Railway Museum, and the Jorvik Viking Centre.

THE NATIONAL PARKS

The ten National Parks described below in their order of designation have been established in England and Wales. These areas are not public property and although many public paths exist and some areas of open land are available for walking visitors are not free to wander over private land within the Park boundaries. They have been marked out for special care aimed at two prime purposes: to conserve and enhance their natural beauty, and to promote their enjoyment by the public.

Peak District National Park (542 sq. miles).—Mainly in Derbyshire but extending into Staffordshire, Cheshire, South Yorkshire, West Yorkshire and Greater Manchester. There are information centres at Bakewell, Edale (open all year), Fairholmes and Castleton (April–October and winter weekends), and information points in Goyt Valley and at Hartington (summer weekends and Bank Holidays). An information caravan tours the Park and there is a residential study centre at Losehill Hall.

Lake District National Park (866 sq. miles).—In Cumbria. The area includes England's highest mountains (Scafell Pike, Helvellyn and Skiddaw) and largest lakes. There are information centres at Keswick, Waterhead, Hawkshead, Seatoller, Bowness, Grasmere, Coniston, Glenridding and Pooley Bridge, and an information van at Gosforth. At Brockhole, on the shore of Windermere, there is a National Park centre.

Snowdonia National Park (838 sq. miles).—In Gwynedd, North Wales. There are information centres at Aberdyfi, Bala, Betws y Coed, Blaenau Ffestiniog, Conwy, Harlech, Dolgellau and Llanberis. Plas Tan y Bwlch is a residential study centre.

Dartmoor National Park (365 sq. miles).—In Devon. The Park is rich in prehistoric relics. Information centres are sited at Newbridge, Tavistock, Bovey Tracey, Steps Bridge, Princeton and Postbridge.

Pembrokeshire Coast National Park (225 sq. miles).—In South Wales. In the north is Mynydd Preseli, abounding in prehistoric relics. There are information centres at Tenby, St. David's, Pembroke, Newport, Kilgetty, Haverfordwest and Broad Haven.

North York Moors National Park (553 sq. miles).—In North Yorkshire and Cleveland, stretching from the Hambleton Hills to the coastline above Scarborough. There are information centres at Danby, Pickering, Sutton Bank, Ravenscar, Helmsley and Hutton-le-Hole, and a day study centre at Danby (The Moors Centre).

Yorkshire Dales National Park (680 sq. miles).—Mostly in North Yorkshire but extending into Cumbria. The three peaks of Ingleborough, Whernside and Pen-y-Ghent are included. There are information centres at Clapham, Grassington, Hawes, Aysgarth Falls, Malham and Sedbergh, and an outdoor recreation and study centre at Whernside Manor.

Exmoor National Park (265 sq. miles).—Mainly in Somerset but extending into Devon. There are information centres at Lynmouth, County Gate, Dulverton and Combe Martin.

Northumberland National Park (398 sq. miles).—Stretching from Hadrian's Wall to the Scottish Border. There are information centres at Ingram, Once Brewed, Rothbury, Housesteads, Harbottle and Kielder. An information caravan is sited at Cawfields.

Brecon Beacons National Park (519 sq. miles).—Mostly in southern Powys but extending into Dyfed and Gwent and a small area of Mid Glamorgan. The Park is centred on "The Beacons", Pen y Fan, Corn Du and Cribyn, but includes the Black Mountains to the east and the Black Mountain to the west. There are information centres at Brecon, Craig-y-nos Country Park, Abergavenny, Llandovery, a study centre at Danywenallt and a day visitor centre near Libanus, Brecon.

AREAS OF OUTSTANDING NATURAL BEAUTY

These are designated solely for landscape conservation purposes. They are listed below, in alphabetical order, having been designated between December, 1956 and July, 1985.

Anglesey (83 sq. miles).—The designated area extends along the entire coastline of the island, except for breaks around the urban areas and in the vicinity of Wylfa.

Arnside and Silverdale (29 sq. miles).—The area embraces the upper half of Morecambe Bay, the Kent estuary, and includes extensive tidal flats in the Bay.

Cannock Chase (26 sq. miles).—An area of high heathland in Staffordshire. Deer continue to roam over the Chase.

Chichester Harbour (29 sq. miles).—The area extends from Hayling Island to Apuldram and includes Thorney Island.

Chilterns (309 sq. miles).—Chalk downlands running from South Oxfordshire northeastwards to Bedfordshire, including the outlying group of hills beyond Luton.

Clwydian Range (60 sq. miles).—A prominent ridge extending southwards from Prestatyn on the North Wales coast. Offas's Dyke runs along the crest of the Range.

Cornwall (360 sq. miles).—A number of separate areas including Bodmin Moor; most of the Land's

End peninsula; the coast between St. Michael's Mount and St. Austell (with Falmouth omitted); the Fowey Estuary: in north Cornwall most of the coast to Bedruthan Steps and between Perranporth and Godrevy Towans, plus 10 sq. miles of the Camel Estuary.

Cotswolds (582 sq. miles).—The area of limestone hills above the Vales of Gloucester and Evesham.

Cranborne Chase and West Wiltshire Downs (370 sq. miles).—A chalkland area, covering parts of Wiltshire, Dorset, Hampshire and Somerset, including the wooded remnants of the ancient Chase.

Dedham Vale (28 sq. miles).—The area bordering Essex and Suffolk, where John Constable painted.

East Devon (103 sq. miles).—The coastline between Exmouth and Lyme Regis, with Sidmouth, Beer and Seaton omitted. Inland Gittisham Hill, East Hill and Woodbury and Aylebeare Commons are included.

North Devon (66 sq. miles).—Includes most of the N. Devon coastline, from just north of Bude to the boundary of the Exmoor National Park.

South Devon (128 sq. miles).—Includes the coast between Bolt Head and Bolt Tail, Salcombe, Slapton Sands and Dartmouth, and the estuaries and valleys of the Yealm, Erme, Avon and Dart.

Dorset (400 sq. miles).—The coastline between Lyme Regis and Poole, with the Isle of Portland and

Weymouth omitted, stretching inland to include the Purbeck Hills and the downs, of the Hardy country.

Forest of Bowland (310 sq. miles).—A moorland area mostly in Lancashire running westward from the River Ribble, with a small outlying area east of the Ribble which includes Pendle Hill.

Gower (73 sq. miles).—A peninsula in West Glamorgan, South Wales, known for its coastline.

East Hampshire (151 sq. miles).—A chalkland area stretching from the outskirts of Winchester to the Sussex border at a distance of about 10 miles inland.

South Hampshire Coast (30 sq. miles).—14 miles of coastline between Hurst Castle and Calshot Castle, extending inland up the Beaulieu River for about six miles.

High Weald (560 sq. miles).—The area covers parts of East and West Sussex, Kent and Surrey. It is predominantly wooded, and includes larger heathland areas like Ashdown Forest, the remnants of the old Wealden forests.

Kent Downs (326 sq. miles).—Running east and south-east from the Surrey border near Westerham to the coast near Dover and Folkestone, with a coastal outlier at South Foreland and a narrow strip of the old sea cliff escarpment west of Hythe overlooking Romney Marsh.

Lincolnshire Wolds (216 sq. miles).—The area extends in a south-east direction from Laceby and Caistor in the north to the region of Spilsby, about ten miles west of the coast.

Lleyn (60 sq. miles).—An isolated peninsula in Gwynedd, North Wales.

Malvern Hills (40 sq. miles).—The whole range of the Malvern Hills in the county of Hereford and Worcester, just touching Gloucestershire.

Mendip Hills (78 sq. miles).—Comprising over half of the Mendip Hills, the area stretches from Bleadon Hill to the A39 road north of Wells and includes Cheddar Gorge and Wookey Hole.

Norfolk Coast (174 sq. miles).—An almost continuous coastal strip three to five miles in depth from Hunstanton to Bacton, with a further small strip between Sea Palling and Winterton-on-Sea. The area includes part of the Sandringham Estate.

Northumberland Coast (50 sq. miles).—Stretches from just south of Berwick to Amble and includes Holy Island and the Farne Islands.

Quantock Hills (38 sq. miles).—A range of sandstone hills in Somerset.

Isles of Scilly (6 sq. miles).—About 140 islands and skerries in the Scillies group of which only five are inhabited. There are a number of sites of special scientific interest.

Shropshire Hills (300 sq. miles).—Most of southwest Shropshire between the Welsh border and the boundary with Hereford and Worcester, including the region around Clun, the area of the Stiperstones, the Long Mynd and Wenlock Edge, with the tongues of land running north-east to the Wrekin and south towards Ludlow.

Solway Coast (41 sq. miles).—A stretch of coastline in Cumbria from Maryport to the estuaries of the Rivers Eden and Esk (with Silloth omitted) backed by the Solway Plain.

Suffolk Coast and Heaths (151 sq. miles).—The area includes 38 miles of coastline and parts of the Stour and Orwell estuaries, while the Deben, Alde and Blyth flow through it.

Surrey Hills (160 sq. miles).—An area of hills to the east and south of Guildford, including the Hog's Back and the ridge of the North Downs.

Sussex Downs (379 sq. miles).—The area includes the chalk escarpment of the South Downs from Beachy Head to the Hampshire border, and stretches down to the coast between Eastbourne and Seaford.

North Wessex Downs (671 sq. miles).—An upland area in Hampshire, Wiltshire, Oxfordshire and Berkshire, bounded by the Marlborough and Lambourn Downs in the west and the Chiltern Hills in the east. Salisbury Plain forms the southern limit of what is so far the largest area designated.

Isle of Wight (73 sq. miles).—A number of separate areas comprising stretches of coastline, the Yar Valley, the high downland behind Ventnor and the chalk ridge which runs from Newport to Culver Cliff and Foreland.

Wye Valley (125 sq. miles).—The river valley running through the counties of Gwent, Gloucestershire and Hereford and Worcester.

HISTORIC MONUMENTS

England

A select list of monuments under the control, since its creation in April 1984, of the Historic Buildings and Monuments Commission for England.

Charges for admission represent the figures obtaining in 1987–8. Concessionary rates are available for children etc.

Annual membership passes are available at £10 for adults, £6 for pensioners and £4 for children upon application to P.O. Box 43, Ruislip, Middx., HA4 0XW.

Standard hours of opening (marked *) are as follows:

	Weekdays	Sundays
March 15–Oct. 15	9.30–6.30	2.00–6.30
Oct. 16–March 14	9.30–4.00	2.00–4.00

Monuments not marked * open April–Sept. only.

Those marked † open on Sundays at 9.30 a.m. from April–Sept. inclusive.

All monuments are closed on Christmas Eve, Christmas Day, Boxing Day and New Year's Day. Some smaller sites may close for the lunch-hour, which is normally 1–2 p.m.

BEESTON CASTLE, Cheshire. £1*. Thirteenth-century inner ward with gatehouse and towers, and considerable remains of large outer ward.

BERKHAMSTED CASTLE, Hertfordshire*. Extensive remains of a large 11th century motte-and-bailey castle.

BOLSOVER CASTLE, Derbyshire. £1*. Notable for its exceptionally interesting 17th century buildings.

BOSCOBEL HOUSE, Salop. 75p*. Timber-framed early 17th century hunting lodge with later alterations. Charles II's "Royal Oak" is nearby.

BRINKBURN PRIORY, Northumberland. 75p*. A house of Augustinian canons; the church (c. 1200, repaired in 1858) and parts of the cloister buildings survive.

BROUGHAM CASTLE, Cumbria. 75p†*. Extensive remains of the 13th century keep, and of other buildings of periods up to the 17th century.

BYLAND ABBEY, North Yorkshire. 75p*. Considerable remains of church and conventual buildings date from the abbey's foundation in 1177 by the Cistercians.

CARISBROOKE CASTLE, Isle of Wight. £1·70†*. Norman castle, the prison of Charles I from 1647–1648.

CARLISLE CASTLE, Cumbria. £1†*. The Castle was begun by William Rufus. Inner and outer wards enclosing a 12th century keep.

CASTLE ACRE PRIORY, Norfolk. 75p* (closed Mon. and Tue. in winter). Extensive remains include the 12th century church and the prior's lodgings.

CASTLE RISING, Norfolk. 75p†* (closed Mon. and Tue. in winter). A 12th-century keep standing in a massive earthwork with its gatehouse and bridge.

CHESTERS ROMAN FORT, Northumberland. £1†*. Fine example of a bath house.

CHYSAUSTER ANCIENT VILLAGE, Cornwall, 75p* (closed Thur. and Fri. in winter). 2nd century B.C. Iron Age village of courtyard houses.

CLEEVE ABBEY, Somerset. 75p* Much of the claustral buildings survive including timber-roofed frater, but only foundations of the church.

CORBRIDGE ROMAN SITE, Northumberland. £1*. Excavations have revealed the central area of a Roman town and successive military bases.

DEAL CASTLE, Kent. 75p*. The largest and most complete of the castles erected by Henry VIII for coastal defence.

DOVER CASTLE, Kent. £2†* (Sun. mornings all year). Underground Works closed in Winter. One of the largest and most important English castles.

DUNSTANBURGH CASTLE, Northumberland. 75p†*. The 14th century castle standing on a cliff above the sea, has an unusual gatehouse-keep.

FARLEIGH HUNGERFORD CASTLE, Somerset. 75p* (closed Tues. and Thurs. morning in winter). Late 14th century castle of two courts. The chapel contains fine tomb of Sir Thomas Hungerford.

FARNHAM CASTLE, Surrey. 50p. Built by the Bishops of Winchester, the motte of the castle is enclosed by a large 12th century shell keep. Foundations of a Norman tower.

FINCHALE PRIORY, Durham. 50p* (free in Winter). Benedictine priory on banks of River Wear with considerable 13th century remains.

FRAMLINGHAM CASTLE, Suffolk. 75p†*. Impressive castle (c. 1200) with high curtain-walls enclosing a poor-house of 1639.

FURNESS ABBEY, Cumbria. 75p†*. Founded in 1123 by Stephen, afterwards King of England; extensive remains of church and conventual buildings.

GOODRICH CASTLE, Hereford and Worcester. 75p†*. Extensive remains of beautiful 13th and 14th century castle incorporating 12th century keep.

GRIMES GRAVES, Norfolk. 75p†*. Extensive group of flint mines dating from the Neolithic period. Several shafts can be inspected.

HAILES ABBEY, Gloucestershire. 75p*. Ruins of a Cistercian monastery founded in 1246. Museum contains some fine architectural fragments.

HELMSLEY CASTLE, North Yorkshire. 75p†*. Twelfth century keep and curtain wall with 16th century domestic buildings. Spectacular earthwork defences.

HOUSESTEADS ROMAN FORT, Northumberland. £1†*. Excavation has exposed this infantry fort on Hadrian's Wall with its extra-mural civilian settlement.

KENILWORTH CASTLE, Warwickshire. £1†*. One of the finest and most extensive castles in England, showing many styles of building from 1155 to 1649.

LANERCOST PRIORY, Cumbria. 75p. The nave of the Augustinian priory church, c. 1166, is still used and there are remains of other claustral buildings.

LINDISFARNE PRIORY, Northumberland. 75p†*. The bishopric of the Northumbrian Kingdom destroyed by the Danes; re-established in 11th century as a Benedictine priory, now ruined.

LULLINGSTONE ROMAN VILLA, Kent. £1·20†*. A large villa occupied through much of the Roman period; fine mosaics. (*Closed until Spring 1988 for refurbishment.*)

MIDDLEHAM CASTLE, North Yorkshire. 75p*. The 12th century keep stands within later fortifications and domestic buildings.

MOUNT GRACE PRIORY, North Yorkshire. 75p*. Carthusian monastery, founded 1398, with remains of monastic buildings.

NETLEY ABBEY, Hampshire. 50p* (weekends only in winter). Extensive remains of Cistercian abbey, founded 1239, with remarkable Tudor house.

OLD SARUM, Wiltshire. 75p†*. Large earthworks enclosing the excavated remains of the castle and the first Salisbury cathedral.

ORFORD CASTLE, Suffolk. 75p* (closed all day Thurs. and Fri. mornings in winter). Circular keep of c. 1170 and remains of coastal defence castle built by Henry II.

PENDENNIS CASTLE, Cornwall. 75p†*. Well-preserved castle erected by Henry VIII for coastal defence.

PEVENSEY CASTLE, East Sussex. 75p*. Walls of a 4th century Roman fort enclosing remains of an 11th century castle.

PEVERIL CASTLE, Derbyshire. 50p*. In a picturesque and nearly impregnable position, this 12th century castle is defended on two sides by precipitous rocks.

PORTCHESTER CASTLE, Hampshire. 75p*. Walls of a late-Roman fort enclosing a Norman keep and an Augustinian priory church.

RECULVER TOWERS and ROMAN FORT, Kent. 50p* (June–Aug.). Remains of Saxon and Norman church with 12th century towers, standing in a Roman fort.

RICHBOROUGH CASTLE. Kent. 75p*. The landing-site of the Claudian invasion in 43 A.D., with massive 3rd century stone walls.

RICHMOND CASTLE, North Yorkshire. 75p†*. This 12th century keep, with 11th century curtain-wall and gatehouse, commands Swaledale.

RIEVAULX ABBEY, North Yorkshire. £1†*. Founded c. 1132. Extensive remains include an early Cistercian nave and fine 13th century choir and claustral buildings.

ROCHESTER CASTLE, Kent. 75p*†. Eleventh century wall, partly overlying the Roman city wall, encloses square keep of c. 1130.

ST. AUGUSTINE'S ABBEY, Canterbury, Kent. 75p*. Remains of Benedictine monastry, with Norman church, on site of abbey founded by St. Augustine in 598.

ST. MAWES CASTLE, Cornwall. 75p†*. Coast defence castle built by Henry VIII consisting of central tower and three bastions.

SCARBOROUGH CASTLE, North Yorkshire. 75p†*. Remains of 12th century keep and curtain-walls dominating the town.

STONEHENGE, Wiltshire. £1·30†*. Prehistoric monument consisting of central stone circles surrounded by ditch and bank.

TILBURY FORT, Essex. 75p* (opens 30 mins. late and closes 30 mins. early). One of Henry VIII's coastal ports, extended by Charles II.

TINTAGEL CASTLE, Cornwall. £1†*. 12th century castle on cliff-top Dark Age settlement site.

TYNEMOUTH PRIORY and CASTLE, Tyne and Wear. 75p†* (closed Tues. and alternate Wed. in winter). Remains of a Benedictine priory, founded 1090, on Saxon monastic site. Coastal batteries with reconstructed First World War magazine.

WALMER CASTLE, Kent. £1·20*. (Closed Mon. except Bank Hols and when Lord Warden is in residence.) One of Henry VIII's coast defence castles, it is the residence of the Lord Warden of the Cinque Ports.

WARKWORTH CASTLE, Northumberland. 75p†*. 15th century keep amidst earlier ruins. 14th century hermitage upstream.

WHITBY ABBEY, North Yorkshire. 50p†*. 13th and 14th century Benedictine church on site of monastery founded in 657.

WROXETER ROMAN CITY, Shropshire 75p*. The 2nd century public baths and part of the forum remain of the Roman town of Viroconium.

Wales

A select list of monuments under the control of Cadw: Welsh Historic Monuments. Charges for admission (subject to alteration) are given below. Concessionary rates are available for children, etc.
Standard hours of admission:

	Weekdays	Sundays
March 15–Oct. 15	9.30–6.30	2.00–6.30
Oct. 16–March 14	9.30–4.00	2.00–4.00

All monuments are closed on Christmas Eve, Christmas Day, Boxing Day and New Year's Day.

BEAUMARIS CASTLE, Anglesey, Gwynedd. £1. The finest example of the concentrically planned castle in Britain, it is still almost intact.

CAERLEON ROMAN AMPHITHEATRE, Gwent. 75p. Late 1st-century oval arena surrounded by bank for spectators with entrance passages.

CAERLEON ROMAN FORTRESS BATHS, Gwent. 75p. Rare example of a legionary bath-house.

CAERNARFON CASTLE, Gwynedd. £2., Family Ticket £5. The most important of the Edwardian castles, built together with the town wall between 1283 and 1330.

CAERPHILLY CASTLE, Mid-Glamorgan. £1. Concentrically planned castle (c. 1270) notable for its great scale and use of water defences.

CASTELL COCH, S. Glamorgan. £1. Rebuilt 1875–90 on medieval foundations.

CHEPSTOW CASTLE, Gwent. 75p. Fine rectangular keep in the middle of extensive fortifications.

CONWY CASTLE, Gwynedd. £1. Built by Edward I to guard the Conway ferry, it is a magnificent example of medieval architecture.

CRICCIETH CASTLE, Gwynedd. 75p. A native Welsh castle of the early 13th century, much altered by Edward I.

DENBIGH CASTLE, Clwyd. 75p. The remains of the castle, which dates from 1282–1322, includes an unusual triangular gatehouse.

HARLECH CASTLE, Gwynedd. £1. Well preserved Edwardian castle with a concentric plan sited on rocky outcrop above the former shore-line.

RAGLAN CASTLE, Gwent. 75p. Extensive and imposing remains of 15th-century castle with moated hexagonal keep.

ST. DAVID'S, BISHOP'S PALACE, Dyfed. 75p. Extensive remains of principal residence of Bishop of St. David's dating from 1280–1350.

TINTERN ABBEY, Gwent. £1. Very extensive remains of the fine 13th-century church and conventual buildings of this Cistercian monastery.

Scotland

A select list of monuments under the control of Historic Buildings and Monuments, Scottish Development Department.

Charges for admission are those obtaining in 1987. Except where indicated differently, charges are adults 50p, concessions (con.) 25p.

Standard hours of opening (marked S.) are as follows:

	Weekdays	Sundays
April–Sept.	9.30–7.00	2.00–7.00
Oct.–March	9.30–4.00	2.00–4.00

Monuments open at any reasonable time are indicated by A.

ABERLEMNO, Tayside. Four Pictish stones. A. Closed in winter. Adm. free.

ANTONINE WALL, Central and Strathclyde Regions. A. Adm. free.

ARNOL BLACKHOUSE, Western Isles. S. Closed Sun. Traditional Hebridean dwelling.

BONAWE, Strathclyde. S. Closed in winter. Mid-18th century iron-furnace.

BROUGH OF BIRSAY, Orkney. S. Closed Mon., Tues. a.m. in winter. Remains of the Norse period.

BROWN AND WHITE CATERTHUNS, Tayside. A. Adm. free. Iron Age hill forts.

CAERLAVEROCK CASTLE, Dumfries and Galloway. S.

CAIRNPAPPLE HILL, Lothian. S. Closed in winter. A prehistoric ritual complex and Bronze Age cairn.

CALLANISH, Western Isles. A. Adm. free. Standing Stones.

CAMSTER CAIRNS, Highland. A. Adm. free.

CLAVA CAIRNS, Highland. A. Adm. free.

DRYBURGH ABBEY, Borders. S. £1, con. 50p.

EARLS AND BISHOPS PALACES, Kirkwall, Orkney. S. Closed in winter.

EDINBURGH CASTLE, including Scottish National War Memorial, Scottish United Services Museum and Historic Apartments. Adm. to War Memorial, free; to all other areas, Adm. £2., con. £1., Family Ticket £4. Open winter: Jan. 4–March 31 and Oct. 1–Dec. 31, Mon.–Sat. 9.30–4.20, Sun. 12.30–3.35. Summer: April 1–Sept. 30, Mon.–Sat. 9.30–5.05, Sun. 11–5.05.

Alterations may also be made to opening hours during the Tattoo, State and Military events.

EDZELL CASTLE, Tayside. S. Closed Tues., Thurs. a.m.

ELGIN CATHEDRAL, Grampian. S.

FORT GEORGE, Highland. S. £1, con. 50p.

GLASGOW CATHEDRAL, Strathclyde. S. Adm. free.

GLENELG BROCHS, Highland. A. Adm. free.

HERMITAGE CASTLE, Borders. S.

HUNTLY CASTLE, Grampian. S.

JARLSHOF, Shetland. S. Closed Tues., Wed. p.m. in winter. Remains of villages from Bronze Age to Viking times.

JEDBURGH ABBEY, Borders. S. Closed Thurs. p.m. and Fri. in Winter. £1., con. 50p.

KELSO ABBEY, Borders. S. Adm. free.

LINLITHGOW PALACE, Lothian. S. £1., Con. 50p.

LOANHEAD STONE CIRCLE, Grampian. A. Adm. free.

MAES HOWE, Orkney. S. £1., Con. 50p. Prehistoric tomb.

MEIGLE MUSEUM, Tayside. S. Closed Sun. Pictish stones.

MELROSE ABBEY, Borders. S. £1., Con. 50p.

MOUSA BROCH, Shetland. A. Adm. free.

NETHER LARGIE CAIRNS, Strathclyde. A. Adm. free.

NEW ABBEY CORN MILL, Dumfries and Galloway. S. Closed Wed. p.m., Thurs.

RING OF BROGAR, Orkney. A. Adm. free.

RUTHWELL CROSS, Dumfries and Galloway. A. Adm. free.

ST. ANDREWS' CASTLE AND CATHEDRAL, Fife. S.

SKARA BRAE, Orkney. S. £1. Prehistoric village.

SMAILHOLM TOWER, Borders. S. Closed in winter.

STIRLING CASTLE, Central. Open winter: Jan. 4–March 31 and Oct. 1–Dec. 31, Mon.–Sat. 9.30–4.20, Sun. 12.30–3.35; summer: April 1–Sept. 30, Mon.–Sat. 9.30–5.15, Sun. 10.30–4.45. £1·50, Con. 75p, Family Ticket £3.

TANTALLON CASTLE, Lothian. S. £1. Closed Wed., Thurs. a.m. in Winter.

THREAVE CASTLE, Dumfries and Galloway. S. Adm. free. Ferry charge 50p, con. 25p.

HOUSES OPEN TO THE PUBLIC

Times of summer opening and admission fees shown are those which obtained in 1987, and are subject to modification. Space permits only a selection of some of the more noteworthy houses in the U.K. which are open to the public. (*Property of the National Trust; Adm. admission; con. concessionary rates).

A LA RONDE, Exmouth.—April–Oct., Mon.–Sat. 10–6, Sun. 2–7. Adm. £1.50.

ALNWICK CASTLE, Northumberland. Seat of the Duke of Northumberland.—May 2–Oct. 2 daily (except Sat.) 1–5. Adm. £1.80.

ALTHORP, Northampton.—Daily 1.30–5.30. June, July, Aug., and Bank Hols, 11–6. Adm. £2.50, Weds. £3.50 (Connoisseurs' Day).

*ANGLESEY ABBEY, Cambs.—Easter–Oct. Wed.–Sun. and Bank Hol. Mons. 1.30–5.30. Adm. £2.50. Gardens only April–June, Wed.–Sun., July–Oct. daily. Same times. Adm. £1.

ARUNDEL CASTLE, W. Sussex. Seat of the Duke of Norfolk.—April 1–Oct. 31 daily (not Sat.) 1–5, June–Aug. and Bank Hols. 12–5.

*BASILDON PARK, Berks.—April–Oct. Wed.–Sat. 2–6, Suns. and Bank Hol. Mons. 12–6. Adm. £1.80.

BEAULIEU, Hants.—May–Sept. daily 10–6. Oct.–May, daily 10–5 (see also page 651).

*BELTON HOUSE, Grantham.—April–Oct. Wed.–Sun. and Bank Hol. Mons. 1–5.30. Adm. £2.40.

BELVOIR CASTLE, nr. Grantham. Seat of the Duke of Rutland.—March 21–Oct. 4 Tues., Wed., Thurs., Sat. and Good Friday, 12–6; Bank Hols, 11–7; Sun., 12–7. (Oct. Sun., 2–6.) Adm. £2.40.

BERKELEY CASTLE, Glos.—April, Sept. daily (not Mon.) 2–5; May–Aug. Tues.–Sat. 11–5, Sun. 2–5; Oct. Sun. only 2–4.30.

BLAIR CASTLE, Tayside. Seat of the Duke of Atholl.—April, Sun. and Mon. April 16–Oct. 11. Mon.–Sat. 10–6, Suns. 2–6. Adm. £2.

BLENHEIM PALACE, Oxon. Seat of the Duke of Marlborough.—March 16–Oct. 31 daily 11–6.

BOUGHTON HOUSE, Northants. Seat of the Duke of Buccleuch & Queensberry.—Aug. daily, Grounds 12–6, House 2–5. May 2–Sept. 27 Grounds daily (not Fri.) 12–5. Adm. £2, Grounds only 80p.

BOWHILL, Selkirk.—House July 4–Aug. 16 daily (not Fri.) 1–4.30; Grounds May 2–Aug. 31 Mon.–Sat. (not Fri.) 12–5, Sun. 2–6. Adm. £2, Grounds only 80p.

BROADLANDS, Hants.—April–Sept. daily (closed Mon., except Aug., Sept. and Bank Hols) 10–6. Adm. £3.

BRONTË PARSONAGE, Haworth, West Yorks.—Daily, April–Sept. 11–5.30, Oct.–Mar. 11–4.30. Adm. 50p.

BROUGHTON CASTLE, Oxon.—mid May–mid Sept., Wed., Sun. (also Thurs. in July and Aug.) and Bank Hol. Mons. 2–5. Adm. £1.80.

*BUCKLAND ABBEY, Devon. Closed to visitors until summer 1988.

BURGHLEY HOUSE, Stamford.—Good Friday–Oct. 4 (closed Sept. 12) daily 11–5 (Good Friday 2–5).

*CALKE ABBEY, Derbyshire.—Gardens open all year. House opens April 1989.

CARDIFF CASTLE.—May–Sept. daily 10–6, Nov.–Feb. daily, 10–4.30; March, April, Oct. daily, 10–5.

CARLTON TOWERS, N. Yorks.—May to Sept. Sun. only, Bank Hols (Sat.–Tues.) 1–5. Adm. £1.75.

CASTLE ASHBY, Northants.—Open all year to parties by prior arrangement. Adm. Groups £2.

*CASTLE COOLE, Enniskillen.—Closed for restoration work. Parklands open April–Sept.

*CASTLE DROGO, Devon.—April–Oct. daily 11–6. Adm. £2.50.

CASTLE HOWARD, N. Yorks.—March 25–Oct. daily 11–5.

CAWDOR CASTLE, Inverness.—May–Oct. 4, daily 10–5.30. Adm. £2.20.

*CHARTWELL, Kent. Home of Sir Winston Churchill.—March and Nov. Sat., Sun., Wed. 11–4; April–Oct. 30 Tues., Wed., Thurs. 12–5; Sat., Sun. and Bank Hol. Mons, 11–5. (Closed Good Friday and Tues. after Bank Hols.). Adm. £2.50.

CHATSWORTH, Derbyshire. Seat of the Duke of Devonshire.—April 1–Nov. 1 daily 11.30–4.30.

CHICHELEY HALL, Newport Pagnell.—April 17–Sept. 27 Suns. and Bank Hols 2.30–6. Adm. £2.

*CLIVEDEN, Maidenhead.—Gardens, daily 11–6 (closed Jan. and Feb.); House, April–Oct., Thurs. and Sun. 3–6. Adm. £2, 80p extra for House.

*COMPTON CASTLE, nr. Paignton.—April–Oct. Mon., Wed., Thurs. 10–12.15, 2–5. Adm. £1.30.

*CROFT CASTLE, Herefordshire.—May–Sept. Wed.–Sun. 2–6 (also Bank Hols). April and Oct. weekends and Easter Bank Hol. Mon. 2–5. Adm. £1.60.

DOWN HOUSE, Downe, Kent. Home of Charles Darwin.—March–Jan. 31, 1–6, not Mon. (except Bank Hols.) or Fri. Adm. £1·20.

DRUMLANRIG CASTLE, Dumfries.—May and June, daily (not Fri.) 1.30–5; July and Aug. daily (not Fri.) 11–5; Sun. 2–6. Adm. £2.

GLAMIS CASTLE, Angus.—May–Sept. daily (except Sat.), also Easter, 1–5. Admission, £2.

HADDON HALL, Derbyshire.—Easter–Sept. Tues.–Sat., also Bank Hols., 11–6. Closed Sun. in July and Aug. (except Bank Hol. weekends). Adm. £2.40.

*HARDWICK HALL, Derbyshire.—April–Oct. House Wed., Thurs., Sat., Sun., Bank Hol. Mons. 1–5.30. Garden daily 12–5.30. Adm. £2.40, Garden only £1.20.

HAREWOOD HOUSE, Leeds.—April–Oct. daily from 11. Sun. only, Feb., March, and Nov.

HATFIELD HOUSE, Herts.—March 25–Oct. 11 daily (except Mon. and Good Friday) 12–5, Sun. 2–5.30, Bank Hols 11–5. Adm. £2.75.

HEVER CASTLE, Kent.—April–Oct. daily 12–6.

HOLKER HALL, Cumbria.—Easter Sun.–Oct. daily (not Sat.), 10.30–4.30.

HOLKHAM HALL, Norfolk.—June–Sept. Sun., Mon., Thurs., 1.30–5; also Wed. July–Aug. (and Spring and Summer Bank Hol. Mons. 11.30–5). Adm. £1.70. Also Bygones Collection £1.30.

HOPETOUN HOUSE, nr. Edinburgh.—Easter and May–Sept. 15, daily 11–5.30. Adm. £2.

HOUGHTON HALL, Norfolk.—Easter Sun.–Sept. 27, Sun., Thurs. and Bank Hols 1–5.30. Adm. £2.

*HUGHENDEN MANOR, High Wycombe. Disraeli's home.—April–Oct. Wed.–Sat. 2–6, Sun. and Bank Hol. Mons. 12–6. March weekends 2–6 or dusk. Adm. £1.80.

INVERARAY CASTLE, Argyll. Seat of the Dukes of Argyll.—April 4–Oct. 11 weekdays (not Fri.) 10–6, Sun. 1–6. Woods open all year.

JANE AUSTEN'S HOUSE, Chawton, Hants.—April–Oct. daily; Jan. and Feb. weekends; Nov., Dec. and March, Wed.–Sun. 11–4.30. Adm. 85p.

KELMSCOTT MANOR, nr. Lechlade.—Tues., Wed., Thurs. (on written application). Adm. £2.

*KINGSTON LACY HOUSE, Dorset.—April–Oct. Wed.–Sun. 1–5. Adm. £2.50.

KNEBWORTH HOUSE, Herts.—April–May, Sun., School Hols, Bank Hols.; May 23–Sept. 13 daily (except Mons.) 12–5.

*KNOLE, Kent.—April–Oct. Wed.–Sat. and Bank Hol. Mons. 11–5, Sun. 2–5. Adm. £2.

LEEDS CASTLE, Kent.—April–Oct. daily 11–5. Nov.–March, weekends only, 12–4.

*LITTLE MORETON HALL, Cheshire.—April–Sept. daily (not Tues.), March and Oct. weekends, 1.30–5.30. Adm. £1.60. Weekends and Bank Hols. £2.

LONGLEAT HOUSE, Warminster.—Easter–Sept. daily 10–6, Oct.–Easter 10–4.

LUTON HOO, Beds.—April 16–Oct. 11 daily 2–5.45 (not Mon. except Bank Hols.). Adm. £2.

MELBOURNE HALL, Derbyshire.—June 3–Oct. 7 Wed. 2–6. Adm. £1.50.

MICHELHAM PRIORY, E. Sussex.—March 25–Oct. 31 daily 11–5.30. Adm. £1.50.

*MONTACUTE HOUSE, Yeovil.—April–Oct. daily (not Tues.) 12.30–5.30. Adm. £2.50.

*MOUNT STEWART, Co. Down.—April, Sept., Oct. weekends 2–6; Easter week 2–6; May–June Wed.–Sun. 2–6; July–Aug. daily (not Mon.). Adm. £1.50.

OSBORNE HOUSE, I.O.W. State and Private Apartments.—April 6–Oct. 10 Mon.–Sat. 10–5, Sun. 11–5.

*PENRHYN CASTLE, Bangor.—April 17–Oct. 25 daily (not Tues.) 12–5. (July–Aug. 11–5). Adm. £2.10.

PENSHURST PLACE, Kent.—April 1–Oct. 4 daily (not Mon.) also Bank Hols. 1–5.30. Adm. charge.

*PETWORTH HOUSE, W. Sussex.—April–Oct. Wed., Thurs., Sat., Sun., Bank Hol. Mons. 2–6. Adm. £2.40.

PORTMEIRION, Gwynedd.—April–Oct., Daily, 9.30–5.30. Admission charge.

POWDERHAM CASTLE, Exeter.—May 24–Sept. 10 Sun.–Thurs. 2–5.30.

*POWIS CASTLE, Powys.—April 18–June 30, Wed.–Sun. 11–6; July–Aug. daily (not Mon.) 11–6; Sept.–Oct. Wed.–Sun. 12–5; Bank Hol. Mons. 11–6. Adm. £2.30.

RABY CASTLE, Durham.—Easter (Sat.–Wed.), May 2–June 30 Wed. and Sun., July–Sept. daily (not Sat.) 1–5. Also Bank Hols. Adm. £1.80.

RAGLEY HALL, Warwicks.—April 12–Oct. 4 daily (not Mon., Fri.) April, May, Sept. 1.30–5.30, June–Aug. Tues., Wed., Thurs. 12–5, Sat., Sun. 1.30–5.30. Open Bank Hols. Adm. £2.90.

ROCKINGHAM CASTLE, Corby.—Easter Sunday–Sept. Sun., Thurs.; Tues. in Aug. and Bank Hols. (Mon. and Tues.) 2–6. Adm. £2.

*RUFFORD OLD HALL, Lancashire—April–Oct. daily (not Fri.) 1–6. Adm. £1.40.

SANDRINGHAM, Norfolk.—April 19–Sept. 25 (closed July 24–Aug. 5) 11–4.45 (Sun. 12–4.45).

SCONE PALACE, Perth.—Good Friday–mid Oct. Mon.–Sat. 9.30–5, Sun. 1.30–5 (July and Aug. 10–5). Adm. £2.20.

SHERBORNE CASTLE, Dorset.—Easter Sat.–Sept. Thurs., Sat., Sun. and Bank Hol. Mons. 2–6. Adm. charge.

*SHUGBOROUGH, Staffs.—March 14–Oct. 25 Tues.–Fri. and Bank Hol. Mons. 10.30–5.30, weekends 2–5.30. Adm. £2.50.

*SISSINGHURST, Kent.—Garden open April–Oct. 15 Tues.–Fri. 1–6.30, Sat., Sun. and Good Friday, 10–6.30. Closed Bank Hols. Adm. £2.60 (Sun. £3.20).

SKIPTON CASTLE, N. Yorks.—Mon.–Sat. 10–6, Sun. 2–6. Adm. £1.20.

*SMALLHYTHE PLACE, Kent. Dame Ellen Terry's home.—April–Oct. daily Sat.–Wed. 2–6. Closed Good Friday. Adm. £1.20.

STANFORD HALL, Leics.—Easter Sunday–Sept. Thurs., Sat., Sun., Bank Hols. (Mon. and Tues.) 2.30–6. Adm. £1.80.

STONELEIGH ABBEY, Warwicks.—Easter Sunday and Mon., May Bank Hol. Sun. and Mon., Spring Bank Hol. Sun. and Mon.; June–Aug. Sun., Mon., Wed., Thurs., Fri.; Sept. Sun. only. 1–5.

STONOR PARK, Oxon.—April Sun. & Bank Hols, May–Sept. Wed., Thurs., Sun. (also Sat. in Aug.) 2–5.30. Bank Hol. Mons. 11–5.30. Adm. £1.90.

*STOURHEAD, Wilts.—May–Sept. Sat.–Thurs., April and Oct. Sat.–Wed. 2–6. Adm. £2. Gardens, daily 8–7 or dusk. Adm. £1.50.

STRATFIELD SAYE HOUSE, Reading.—Easter Sat., Sunday and Mon., April weekends, then May–last Sun. in Sept. daily (not Fri.) 11.30–5. Adm. £2.60.

*SUDBURY HALL, Derbys.—April–Oct. Wed.–Sun. and Bank Hol. Mons. 1–5.30. Closed Good Friday. Adm. £2.

SUDELEY CASTLE, Glos.—April–Oct. daily 12–5. Adm. £2.95.

SULGRAVE MANOR, Northants. Home of the Washington family.—Feb.–Dec. daily (not Wed.) 10.30–5.30 (10.30–4 Feb., March, Oct.–Dec.). Adm. £1.

*TRERICE, Cornwall.—April–Oct. daily 11–6. Adm. £2.20.

*THE VYNE, Basingstoke.—April–Oct. 18 daily (not Mon. and Fri.) 2–6, Bank Hol. Mons. 11–6. Adm. £1.80 (Sun. and Bank Hol. Mons. £2.20).

TYN-Y-RHOS HALL, Shropshire—May–Sept. Wed., Thurs., Sat., Sun. and Bank Hol. Mons. 2.30–6. Adm. £1.

*WADDESDON MANOR, Bucks.—March 25–Oct. 25, Wed. (except after Bank Hol.) to Sun. 2–6 (2–5 on weekdays in March, April and Oct.) Bank Hols. 11–6. Adm. £2.50.

WARWICK CASTLE.—March–Oct. daily 10–5.30, Nov.–Feb. daily 10–4.30. Adm. charge.

WILTON HOUSE, Wilts.—April 7–Oct. 11 Tues–Sat. and Bank Hol. Mons. 11–6, Sun. 1–6. Adm. £3.35.

*WIMPOLE HALL, Cambs.—April 11–Oct. 25 daily (not Mon., Fri.) 1–5, Bank Hol. Mons. 11–5. Adm. £2 (weekends £2.30).

WINSLOW HALL, Bucks.—July 15–Sept. 15 daily (not Mon.) 2.30–5.30. July 1–15 and Sept. 15–30 weekends only. Bank Hol. Mons., 2–5.30. Adm. £1.50.

WOBURN ABBEY, Beds. Seat of the Duke of Bedford.—March 30–Nov. 1 daily 11–5.45 (Sun. 11–6.15). Jan. 3–Mar. 29 weekends only 11–4.45. Adm. charge.

MUSEUMS AND ART GALLERIES OUTSIDE LONDON

(For National Art Galleries and Museums outside London see pages 372–3, 417, and 419–20.)

(Adm. admission; con. concessionary rates)

Barnard Castle, Co. Durham.—*The Bowes Museum.* Important collections of British and European fine art, from medieval period to 19th century Fine porcelain and glass, tapestries and furniture. Music and costume galleries. English period rooms from Elizabeth I to Victoria; French decorative arts of 18th and 19th centuries; local antiquities. Temporary exhibitions. Open weekdays: May–Sept., 10–5.30; March, April, Oct., 10–5; Nov.–Feb., 10–4. Sun.: 2–5 (summer); 2–4 (winter). Adm. £1·40, con. 50p.

Bath.—*Roman Baths Museum.* Roman Baths complex including newly excavated Temple precinct. Adm. (including Pump Room), £2, con. £1.15. *Museum of Costume,* Assembly Rooms. Fashion from 16th century to current year. winter: weekdays 10–5, Sun. 11–5. summer: weekdays 9·30–6, Sun. 10–6. Adm. £1.40, con. 85p. *American Museum in Britain,* Claverton Manor. American decorative arts from late 17th to mid 19th centuries. Open April 1–Oct. 30, daily (except Mon.), 2–5; Bank Hol. Mons. and preceding Suns., 11–5. During winter only on application. Adm. charge. *Victoria Art Gallery,* Bridge Street. Open Mon.–Fri. 10–6, Sat. 10–5. Closed Sun., Bank Hols. Adm. free.

Beamish.—*North of England Open Air Museum,* Chester-le-Street, Co. Durham. Re-creates Northern life around the turn of the century. Buildings from the region have been rebuilt and furnished, including a 1920s street with houses, shops, etc., colliery buildings, drift mine, station and steam locomotives, farmhouse, agricultural machinery and farm animals. Open daily: summer 10–6, winter 10–5.

Beaulieu.—*National Motor Museum.* Displays of vehicles dating from 1895 to present day. Open daily 10–6 (winter, 10–5). Adm. charge.

Belfast.—*Ulster Museum,* Botanic Gardens. Collections of Irish antiquities, natural and local history, fine and applied arts. Open Mon.–Fri. 10–5, Sat. 1–5, Sun. 2–5. *Ulster Folk and Transport Museum,* Holywood. Indoor and outdoor exhibits of all aspects of Ulster folklife. Open Oct.–April, weekdays 11–5, Sun. 2–5 (May–Sept. 2–6). May–June (Wed. only) 11–9. Adm. £1, children 30p, other con. 50p. *Transport Museum,* Holywood and Witham Street. History of land, sea and air transport in Ireland and road, rail and sea vehicles. Holywood site—open as for Folk Museum. Witham Street site open weekdays 10–5. Adm. 30p, children 20p, other con. 15p. Special arrangements apply at both museums over Christmas and Easter.

Beverley, N. Humberside.—*Museum of Army Transport.* Exhibits include field workshop, amphibious assault landing, railway section and aircraft. Open daily 10–5. Adm. £1·50, con. 75p.

Birmingham.—*City Museum and Art Gallery.* British and European masters from 14th to 20th centuries (particularly of the Pre-Raphaelite movement), sculpture, European gold, silver and jewellery, metalwork, glass, pottery and porcelain, furniture, textiles and costume, archaeology, local and natural history. Open Mon.–Sat. 9.30–5, Sun. 2–5. Closed Christmas Day, Boxing Day, New Year's Day and Good Friday. Adm. free.
Museum of Science and Industry, Newhall Street. The history of science from the Industrial Revolution to the present; many working machines under steam, gas, etc. Open Mon.–Sat. 9.30–5, Sun. 2–5. Adm. free. Also *Aston Hall, Blakesley Hall, Birmingham Nature Centre, Sarehole Mill,* and *Weoley Castle.*

Bradford.—*Cartwright Hall,* Lister Park. Contains mainly British 19th and 20th century fine art. *Bolling Hall,* off Wakefield Road, a furnished period house, mainly 17th and 18th century. *Industrial Museum,* Moorside Road, illustrates the local wool and worsted industries and transport in an old mill, with mill owner's house. *Cliffe Castle,* Keighley. Natural and local history, period rooms. *Manor House,* Ilkley. Archaeology, local history and contemporary fine art. Open 10–5 (April–Sept. 10–6, except Industrial museum). Closed Good Friday, Christmas Day, Boxing Day and Mons. (except Bank Hols.). Adm. free.

Brighton.—*The Royal Pavilion, Palace of George IV.* Chinoiserie interiors, much of the original furniture returned on loan from H.M. the Queen. Open daily 10–5 (June–Sept. 10–6). Closed Christmas Day and Boxing Day. Adm. £2., con.
Museum and Art Gallery, Church Street (adjacent Royal Pavilion). Old master paintings; Willett pottery and porcelain collection, 20th-century art and furniture, ethnography, archaeology, local history, musical instruments, costume gallery. Open Tues.–Sat. 11–5, Sun. 2–5. Closed Christmas Day, Boxing Day, Good Friday, Mons and Jan. 1. Adm. free.
Preston Manor, Preston Park. (Thomas-Stanford: Macquoid bequests of English period furniture, furnishings, china and silver.) Open Wed.–Sat. 10–5; Tues. and Sun. 10–1, 2–5. Adm. £1., con. parties. Closed Christmas Day, Boxing Day, Good Friday, Mons. Gardens open, free.
The Grange, Art Gallery and Museum, Rottingdean. Sussex Room, Kipling Room and collections of National Toy Museum. Open Mon., Thurs., Sat. 10–5, Tues. and Fri. 10–1, 2–5, Sundays, 2–5. Closed Christmas Day, Boxing Day, Good Friday, Weds. and Jan. 1. Adm. free.
The Booth Museum of Natural History, Dyke Road. Open 10–5, Sun. 2–5. Closed Christmas Day, Boxing Day, Good Friday, Thursdays and Jan. 1. Adm. free.

Bristol.—*City Museum and Art Gallery.* Collections of Egyptology, British archaeology, natural and local history. Collection of Old Masters, 19th century and modern paintings, Chinese ceramics and glass, English silver, glass, porcelain and delftware, English and foreign embroideries. Open weekdays, 10–5. *Bristol Industrial Museum,* Prince's Wharf. Collections of manufacturing equipment and transport, including unique steam carriage and Bristol-built aero-engines. Open daily (except Thurs. and Fri.) 10–1, 2–5. *Maritime Heritage Centre* including *SS Great Britain,* open daily 10–6 (winter 10–5). Closed Christmas Eve and Day. Also *Red Lodge, Blaise Castle House Museum, Kingsweston Roman Villa, Georgian House* and *St. Nicholas Church Museum.*
National Life-boat Museum, Princes Wharf, Wapping Road. Displays of life-boats, models and equipment. Open daily 10.30–4.30. Adm. £1·50p, con. 75p.

Cambridge.—*Fitzwilliam Museum.* Egyptian, Greek, Near Eastern and Roman antiquities, coins and medals, medieval manuscripts, paintings and drawings, prints, sculpture, Oriental and Occidental fans, pottery and porcelain, textiles, arms and armour, medieval and renaissance objects of art, and a library. Open Tues.–Sat., Lower Galleries 10–2, Upper Galleries 2–5; Sun. 2.15–5. Closed Dec. 24–Jan. 1 and Good Friday. Closed Mons. incl. May Day Bank Hol. but not Easter and Bank Hol. Mons. Permanent exhibitions free.

Canterbury.—*Royal Museum and Art Gallery, and Buffs Regimental Museum.* Collections include archaeology, porcelain, prints and pictures. Open free weekdays, 10–5. *Canterbury Heritage*, Poor Priests' Hospital, a time-walk through the city's history. Open Mon.–Sat. 10.30–4. Adm. 70p, con. 30p. *Roman Mosaic Museum.* Roman material from post-war excavations of Canterbury. *West Gate Tower Museum.* Arms and armour and display of city walls and gates. Roman and West Gate Museums open 10–1, 2–5 (Oct.–March, 2–4). Adm. 30p, con. 15p.

Carlisle.—*Carlisle Museum and Art Gallery,* Tullie House, Castle Street. Collections of archæology, natural and social history, fine and decorative arts in Jacobean house. Open Mon.–Fri. 9–6.45, Sat. 9–5 (Oct.—March, Mon.–Sat. 9–5); Spring and Summer Bank Hols and Sun. June–Aug. 2.30–5. *Guildhall,* Greenmarket. Civic and Guild history and artefacts. Contact Tullie House Museum for opening information.

Chester.—*Grosvenor Museum,* Grosvenor Street. Collection of Roman antiquities from legionary fortress; natural history, art and folk-life. Open weekdays 10.30–5, Sun. 2–5. *The Georgian House,* Castle Street. Period room displays, costume and musical instruments. Open weekdays, 10.30–5, Sun., 2–5. *King Charles Tower* on City Walls. Civil War displays. Open daily (summer), weekends (winter), times vary. Adm. charge.

Colchester.—*Colchester and Essex Museum, The Castle* contains local archæological antiquities, especially those from Roman Colchester. The *Holly Trees Mansion* (1718) covers social life of the 18th and 19th centuries. *Natural History Museum,* All Saints Church. Natural history of Essex. *Museum of Social History,* Holy Trinity Church. Domestic life and crafts. Open Mon.–Sat. 10–5 (Oct.–March Sat. 10–4). Castle only, Sundays 2.30–5 (April–Sept.). Adm. 75p, con. 35p.

Coventry.—*Herbert Art Gallery and Museum,* Jordan Well. Archæology, natural and local history, fine and decorative arts. Open weekdays 10–5.30, Sun. 2–5. Closed Good Friday and Christmas period. *Museum of British Road Transport,* St. Agnes Lane, Hales Street. Open April–Sept., Mon.–Fri. 10–4, Sat., Sun. 10–5.30; Oct.–March, Fri., Sat. and Sun. only. Adm. £1., con. 50p. *Lunt Roman Fort,* Baginton. June–Sept., 12–6 (closed Mon. and Thurs.). Adm. 50p, con. 25p. *Whitefriars Museum.* Open Thurs., Fri., Sat., and some Bank Hols, 10–5.30.

Crich, Nr. Matlock, Derbyshire—*National Tramway Museum.* Open air working museum with collection of trams from Britain and abroad. Open April–Nov. weekends and Bank Holidays 10.30–6.30. April–Sept. also open daily (except Fri.) 10–5.30, also Fris. during summer holidays.

Derby.—*Museum and Art Gallery,* Strand. Archaeology, military, social history, natural history, collections of paintings by Joseph Wright of Derby, Derby porcelain, costume, model theatres. Open Tues.–Sat. 10–5. *Industrial Museum,* Silk Mill, Full Street, Rolls Royce collection of aero engines, a railway engineering gallery. Tues.–Fri. 10–5. Sat. 10–4.45. Closed on all Bank Hols.

Dorchester.—*Dorset County Museum.* Geology, archæology, local and natural history and rural crafts of Dorset. Collection of Thomas Hardy's manuscripts, books, notebooks, drawings, etc. Open weekdays 10–5, closed Christmas Day, Boxing Day and Good Friday. Adm. 90p, con. 45p.

Durham.—*Light Infantry Museum and Arts Centre.* County Regiment's 200 year history displayed, arts and crafts exhibitions. Open weekdays (except Mon.) 10–5, Sun. and Bank Hol. Mon. 2–5.

Closed Christmas Day and Boxing Day. Adm. 60p, con. 25p. *Oriental Museum,* The University. Collections ranging from Ancient Egypt to China and Japan. Open weekdays: 9.30–5. Weekends: Nov.–Feb. closed; March–Oct. Sat. 9.30–5, Sun. 2–5. *Cathedral Treasury.* Relics of St. Cuthbert, church plate, medieval seals, manuscripts and vestments. Open weekdays 10–4.30, Sun. 2–4.30. Adm. 60p, con. 10p. *Old Fulling Mill Museum.* Archaeological material from local excavations. Open Nov.–March, daily 2–4, April–Oct., Mon.–Fri. 10–4, Sat. and Sun., 2–4. Adm. free.

Edinburgh.—*City Art Centre,* 2 Market Street. Late 19th and 20th century art, mostly Scottish, and temporary exhibitions. Open weekdays 10–5 (June–Sept. 10–6). Adm. free. *Canongate Tolbooth,* 163 Canongate. Courthouse and prison for 300 years. Open weekdays 10–5 (June–Sept. 10–6). Adm. free. *Huntly House,* 142 Canongate. Local history, collections of Edinburgh silver, glass and Scottish pottery. Open weekdays 10–5 (June–Sept. 10–6). Adm. free. *Lady Stair's House,* Lawnmarket. Mon.–Sat. 10–5 (June–Sept. 10–6). *Lauriston Castle,* Cramond Road South, April–Oct. daily (except Fri.), 11–5; Nov.–March, weekends only. *Museum of Childhood,* 42 High Street. Open weekdays 10–5 (June–Sept. 10–6). Adm. free.

Exeter.—*Royal Albert Memorial Museum and Art Gallery,* Queen Street. Fine art, Exeter silver, ceramics and glass, natural and local history. Open Tues.–Sat. 10–5.15. Adm. free. *Maritime Museum,* The Haven. Collection of working boats. Open daily 10–5 (July–Aug. 10–6). Adm. charge. *Underground Passages,* Princesshay. Medieval aqueducts. Tues.–Sat. 2–4.40. *Rougemont House Museum of Costume and Lace,* Castle Street. Open Mon.–Sat. 10–5.

Fort William.—*West Highland Museum,* Cameron Square. Historical, natural history and folk exhibits, including those of the 1745 Rising. Daily (except Sun.) 10–5; June and Sept. 9.30–5.30; July and Aug. 9.30–9.

Glasgow.—*Art Gallery and Museum,* Kelvingrove. Old Masters, 19th century French paintings; archæology and natural history, collection of armour. *People's Palace,* Glasgow Green. History of city from 1175 to present. *The Burrell Collection,* Pollok Park. Textiles, furniture, ceramics, stained glass, silver and other art objects, paintings, especially 19th century French. *Pollok House,* Pollok Park. Spanish paintings, furniture, silver, ceramics. *Haggs Castle Museum,* St. Andrews Drive. Children's museum. *Provand's Lordship,* Castle Street. Oldest house in Glasgow, period furniture displays. *Rutherglen Museum,* King Street. History of former royal burgh of Rutherglen. All open weekdays 10–5, Sun. 2–5. Adm. free.

Hull.—*Ferens Art Gallery.* European art, especially Dutch 17th century, British portraits of 18th–20th centuries, Humberside marine paintings, contemporary art and changing exhibitions. *Wilberforce House.* Jacobean merchant's house, birthplace of Wilberforce; collection of slavery relics, period furniture, costume and ceramics. *Transport and Archæology Museum.* Veteran cars, trams, coaches and velocipedes; archæological finds from Humberside, including Roman mosaics. *Town Docks Museum.* Whaling, fishing, trawling, ships and shipping. All open Mon.–Sat. 10–5, Sun. 1.30–4.30. *Posterngate Gallery.* Exhibitions and one-man shows. Tues.–Sat. 10–5.30.

Huntingdon.—*Cromwell Museum.* Remaining portion of the 12th century Hospital of St. John housing portraits of Cromwell, his family and Parliamentary notables, and Cromwelliana—documents, armour, coins, etc. Open April–Oct. Tues.–Fri. 11–5,

Sat, Sun. 11–4; Nov.–March, Tues.–Fri. 2–5, Sat. 11–1, 2–4, Sun. 2–4. Closed Bank Hols other than Good Friday. Adm. free.

Ipswich.—*Ipswich Museum.* Collections of Suffolk geology, archæology and natural history and ethnology. Temporary exhibitions. Open Mon.–Sat. 10–5. Closed Bank Hols. *Christchurch Mansion.* Tudor house contains furniture, Suffolk portraits, English porcelain, pottery and glass. *Wolsey Art Gallery,* attached, houses Borough collections of paintings (local artists, Gainsborough, Constable), modern prints, sculpture. Open Mon.–Sat. 10–5, Sun. 2.30–4.30. Closed some Bank Hols.

Leeds.—*City Art Gallery.* English watercolours. British and European painting, modern sculpture, incl. Henry Moore gallery. Print Room contains study collection of drawings and prints. Open weekdays, 10–6, Suns., 2–5.

Temple Newsam House. Tudor/Jacobean house, furnished in style of 17th and 18th centuries, with silver, European porcelain and pottery, pictures, etc. Open daily (except Mon.) 10.30–6.15 or dusk, Weds. (May–Sept.) 10.30–8.30, all Bank Hols (except Christmas). Adm. 65p, con. 30p. *Lotherton Hall,* Gascoigne art and silver collection, oriental gallery, costume collection, 19th century furniture, ceramics, park and gardens. Open daily (except Mon.) 10.30–6.15 or dusk, Thurs. (May–Sept.) 10.30–8.30, all Bank Hols (except Christmas). Adm. 65p, con. 30p. *Abbey House Museum.* Folk museum including three full-sized streets. Open Oct.–March weekdays 10–5, Sun. 2–5 (April–Sept. 2–6). *Industrial Museum.* Open April–Sept. Tues.–Sat. 10–5, Sun. 2–5 (Oct.–March 2–4). Open Bank Hols.

Leicester.—*Leicestershire Museum and Art Gallery,* New Walk. Natural history, geology, Egyptology, 18th–20th century English paintings, ceramics, silver. *Newarke Houses,* The Newarke. Social history of Leicestershire from 1500 A.D., musical instruments, local clocks. *Jewry Wall Museum,* St. Nicholas Circle. Archaeology (prehistoric–1500). Roman Jewry Wall and Baths, mosaics. *Belgrave Hall,* Church Road. A Queen Anne house with furniture and garden of note. Coaches and agricultural collection. *Museum of the Royal Leicestershire Regiment,* The Magazine, Oxford Street. *Museum of Technology,* Corporation Road. Knitting industry and Power galleries. Horse-drawn and motor vehicles, beam engines. *Wygston's House Museum of Costume,* Applegate. Costume from 1789–1924. All museums open weekdays (except Fri.) 10–5.30, Sun. 2–5.30. Closed Christmas Day, Boxing Day and Good Friday.

Lewes.—*Museum of Sussex Archæology,* Barbican House, near Castle. Prehistoric, Roman, Saxon and mediæval collections relating to Sussex; local pictures and prints. Open weekdays, 10–5.30, Sun. (April–Oct.) 11–5.30. Adm. £1., con. 50p.

Anne of Cleves House, Southover. Local history and folk museum. Open weekdays (mid. Feb.–mid. Nov.) 10–5.30. Sun. (April–Oct.) 2–5.30. Adm. 85p, con. 45p.

Lincoln.—*Usher Gallery.* Watches, miniatures, porcelain, silver, etc., Peter de Wint collection of oils and watercolours, Lincolnshire topographical drawings, *personalia* associated with Tennyson family. Open weekdays 10–5.30, Sun. 2.30–5. *City and County Museum,* The Greyfriars. Geology, natural history and archæology of Lincolnshire. Open weekdays 10–5.30, Sun. 2.30–5. *Museum of Lincolnshire Life.* Collections illustrate life and work in Lincolnshire over the last 200 years. Includes large agricultural collection. Open weekdays 10–5.30, Sun. 2–5.30. *National Cycle Museum,* Brayford Wharf North. Collection of vintage cycles. Open Easter to Oct. 10–5 daily; Oct. to Easter Fri., Sat., and Sun. 10–5.

Manchester.—*City Art Gallery,* Mosley Street. Old Masters, Turner, Pre-Raphaelites; sculpture, porcelain, silver. Mon.–Sat. 10–6, Sun. 2–6. *Athenaeum Gallery,* Princess Street. Adm. free. *Whitworth Art Gallery,* University of Manchester, Oxford Road. Watercolours, drawings, prints, textiles and wallpapers collections, and 20th century British art. Mon.–Sat. 10–5 (Thurs. 10–9), closed Suns. *Greater Manchester Museum of Science and Industry,* Liverpool Road Station. Working machinery and displays in world's oldest passenger railway station. Open daily 10–5. *National Paper Museum,* history of papermaking. *Gallery of English Costume,* Platt Hall, Rusholme. Exhibits from 16th century to present. Also *Heaton Hall,* Prestwich, *Wythenshawe Hall,* Northenden and *Fletcher Moss Museum,* Didsbury. Opening times vary.

Newcastle upon Tyne.—*Laing Art Gallery,* Higham Place. Fine art from 17th century, pottery, glass, silver and metalwork. Open Tues.–Fri. 10–5.30, Sat. 10–4.30, Sun. 2.30–5.30. *Keep Museum,* St. Nicholas Street. History of site. Oct.–March, Mon.–Sat. 10–4.30 (April–Sept. 10–5.30). *Trinity Maritime Centre* and *Trinity House,* Broad Chare. Centre open April–Sept. Tues.–Fri. 10.30–4; Oct.–March, Tues.–Thurs. 11–3. Trinity House April–Oct., Tues., Wed., Thurs. 2–4. *Military Vehicle Museum,* Exhibition Park. Open daily 10.15–4.30. *Museum of Science and Engineering,* West Blandford Square. Tues.–Fri. 10–5.30, Sat. 10–4.30. *Newburn Hall Motor Museum,* Townfield Gdns. Tues.–Sat. 10–8.

Newmarket.—*National Horseracing Museum.* Five galleries of displays relating to the development of horseracing and to the horses and people connected with the sport. Equine Tours. Open April 2–Dec. 4, Tues.–Sat. 10–5, Sun. 2–5. Closed Mon. except Aug. and Bank Hols. Adm. £1.60, con. 80p.

Norwich.—*Castle Museum.* Exhibits of art (including Norwich School), local archæology, social and natural history, pottery and glass. Open, Mon.–Sat., 10–5, Sun. 2–5. *Strangers' Hall,* Charing Cross. Late medieval mansion furnished as a museum of urban domestic life, 16th–19th centuries. Open, Mon.–Sat. 10–5. *Bridewell Museum of Local Industries,* Bridewell Alley. Transport, crafts and industries of Norwich. Open Mon.–Sat. 10–5. *St. Peter Hungate Church Museum,* Princes Street. 15th century church used for display of church art and antiquities. Open Mon.–Sat. 10–5.

Nottingham.—*Castle Museum and Art Gallery.* English and Dutch paintings and drawings 17th–20th centuries, special collections of Bonington and Paul Sandby. Ceramics, silver, glass, medieval Nottingham alabaster carvings, local historical and archaeological displays, classical, oriental and ethnographical antiquities, the regimental collection of the Sherwood Foresters. Open Summer, 10–5.45, Winter, 10–4.45. Closed Christmas Day. Adm. free, small charge on Sun. and Bank Hols.

Industrial Museum, Wollaton Park. Industrial, lacemaking machinery, steam engines, transport. Open April–Sept. Mon.–Sat. 10–6, Sun. 2–6; Oct.–April, Thurs., Sat. 10–4.30, Sun. 1.30–4.30. Closed Christmas Day. Adm. free, small charge on Sun. and Bank Hols.

Canal Museum, Canal Street. Open Easter–Oct. Wed.–Sat. 10–5.45, Sun. 1–5.45; Oct.–Easter, Wed.–Sat. 1–5, Sun. 1–5. Adm. free.

Natural History Museum, Wollaton Hall. Open summer 10–7, Sun. 2–5; winter 10 till dusk (Sun. 1.30–4.30). Closed Christmas Day. Adm. free except Sun. and Bank Hols.

Castlegate Museum of Costumes and Textiles. Open daily 10–5. Closed Christmas Day. Adm. free.

Brewhouse Yard Museum, Castle Boulevard. Everyday life from the 17th century to present. Open daily 10–5. Adm. free. Closed Christmas Day.

Green's Mill and Science Centre, Sneinton. Working windmill and museum with models, displays about George Green. Open daily, Wed.–Sun. 10–5. Closed Christmas Day. Adm. free.

Oakham, *Rutland County Museum*, Catmos Street.—Archæology, local history, craft tools and agricultural implements. Open Tues.–Sat. 10–5, Sun. (April–Oct.) 2–5, and Bank Hol. Mons.

Oxford, *Ashmolean Museum*, Beaumont Street.— The University's collections of European and Oriental fine and applied arts, Classical and Near-Eastern archaeology and Numismatics. Open Tues.–Sat. 10–4, Sun. 2–4. Bank Hol. Mons. 2–5. Adm. free.

Plymouth.—*City Museum and Art Gallery*, Drake Circus. Fine art, including Cottonian collection and Reynolds' portraits, Plymouth porcelain, archaeology, local and natural history. Mon.–Fri. 10–5.30, Sat. 10–5. Adm. free. The 16th century *Elizabethan House*, 32 New Street. Also *Merchant's House*, 33 St. Andrew's Street, dating from the 16th and early 17th centuries.

Portsmouth.—*City Museum and Art Gallery*, Museum Road. *Cumberland House Natural Science Museum and Aquarium*, Eastern Parade. *Southsea Castle and Museum*, Clarance Esplanade. *D-Day Museum*, Clarence Esplanade. All open daily 10.30–5.30, except Dec. 24–26. Adm. charge. *Charles Dickens' Birthplace Museum*, Old Commercial Road. Open March 1–Oct. 31, daily 10.30–5.30. Adm. charge. *Eastney Pumping Station*, Henderson Road. Open April–Sept. daily 1.30–5.30; Oct.–March 1st Sun. of month. Adm. charge. *Fort Widley*, Portsdown Hill. Open April–Sept. Sat., Sun., Bank Hols. 1.30–5.50. Adm. charge. *Royal Naval Museum*, H.M. Naval Base. Deals with the history of the Royal Navy from Tudor times to the South Atlantic Campaign of 1982. Open daily, 10.30–5. Adm. charge. *Mary Rose Ship Hall and Exhibition*, H.M. Naval Base. Open daily March 2 to Oct. 31, 10.30–5.30; Nov. 1–March 1, 10.30–5. Closed Christmas Day. Adm. charge. *HMS Victory*, H.M. Naval Base. Open Mon.–Sat. 10.30–5.30, Sun. 1–5.30 (closes Nov. 5–March). Adm. charge.

St. Albans.—*City Museum*, Hatfield Road. Natural history, geology, craft and trade tools. Open weekdays 10–5. Admission free. *Verulamium Museum*, St. Michael's. Roman and Belgic material including mosaics, one *in situ* in Hypercaust annexe. Open weekdays 10–4, Sun. 2–4 (10–5.30 and 2–5.30 in summer). Adm. 70p, con. 40p.

Sheffield.—*City Museum*, Weston Park. Includes the Bateman Collection of antiquities from Peak District Bronze Age barrows, cutlery and old Sheffield plate. Open weekdays 10–5 (June–Aug. 10–8), Sun. 11–5 (Closed Christmas Eve, Christmas Day and Boxing Day). *Mappin Art Gallery*, Weston Park. Paintings and sculpture of 18th–20th centuries (mainly British School) and contemporary works. Open weekdays 10–5 (June–Aug. 10–8) Sun. 2–5. *Abbeydale Industrial Hamlet*, Abbeydale Road South. A late 18th–early 19th century scythe and steel works with associated housing. Open weekdays 10–5, Sun. 11–5. *Kelham Island Industrial Museum*. Open Wed.–Sat. 10–5, Sun. and Bank Hol. Mon. 11–5. *Shepherd Wheel*, Whiteley Wood. Water-powered cutlery grinding establishment. Open Wed.–Sat. 10–5 (11–5 Sun.). *Bishops' House*, Meersbrook Park. Museum of local history in timber-framed domestic building. Open Wed.–Sat. 10–5, Sun. 11–5.

Stoke-on-Trent.—*City Museum and Art Gallery*, Bethesda Street, Hanley. Major ceramic collections. Open daily 10.30–5, Sun. 2–5. *Chatterley Whitfield Mining Museum*, Tunstall. Guided tours underground. *Gladstone Pottery Museum*, Longton. A working Victorian pottery. Adm. £1.50, con. 70p.

Pottery Factory Tours: Tours are available at the following: *Minton*, London Road, Stoke; *Royal Doulton*, Nile Street, Burslem; *Spode*, Church Street, Stoke, *Beswick*, Gold Street, *Melba-Wain*, Heathcote Road, *Healacraft China*, Weston Coyney Road, Longton, *Coalport and Crown Staffordshire*, Park Street, Fenton and *Wedgwood's* at Barlaston.

Stratford-upon-Avon.—*Shakespeare's Birthplace*. Period furniture, rare books, MSS and objects of Shakespearean interest with new Shakespeare Centre nearby. *Anne Hathaway's Cottage*, Shottery, early home of Shakespeare's wife. *Mary Arden's House*, Wilmcote, Tudor farmhouse home of Shakespeare's mother. *New Place*, where Shakespeare died. *Hall's Croft*, half-timbered home of Shakespeare's daughter and her family. *Grammar School* attended by Shakespeare. *Royal Shakespeare Theatre* burnt down 1926, rebuilt 1932. New *Swan Theatre* opened in 1986.

Styal.—*Quarry Bank Mill*, Cheshire. History of the cotton industry, weaving demonstrations. Giant iron waterwheel. Open April, May Tues.–Sun. 11–5; June–Sept. daily 11–5; Oct.–March Tues.–Sun. 11–4. Open Bank Hols. Adm. £2.50, con. £1.75, Family Ticket £7.

Winchester.—*City Museum*. Weekdays 10–5, Sun. 2–5 (closed Mon. in winter). *Cathedral Library*. MSS and other exhibits from 10th century onwards. Open weekdays. Adm. free. *Cathedral Treasury*. Exhibition of church silver and other pieces. Open May–Sept. Adm. charge.

Worcester.—*City Museum and Art Gallery*. Natural history of Worcestershire and temporary art exhibitions; also museum of the Worcestershire Regiment and the Worcester Yeomanry Cavalry. Open Mon.–Wed., Fri. 9.30–6, Sat. 9.30–5. Closed Thurs., Sun. *The Commandery*, Sidbury. Civil War Centre, costume, industrial history. Weekdays 10.30–5, Sun. 2–5. *Tudor House Museum*, Friar Street. Local domestic and social history. Mon.–Wed., Fri., Sat. 10.30–5. *Dyson Perrins Museum of Worcester Porcelain*, Severn Street. Mon. to Fri. 9.30–5, Sat. 10–5.

York.—*Castle Museum*. Museum of everday life of the last four centuries. Open weekdays 9.30–5, Suns. 10–5 (closes 6.30 April–Oct.). Adm. £2.25, con. £1·15.

Jorvik Viking Centre, Coppergate. Reconstruction of Viking York and display of artifacts. Open daily. Adm. £2.50, con. £2/£1.25.

Yorkshire Museum and Gardens, Museum Street, Roman Life gallery, archæology, decorative arts, geology, natural history. Open weekdays 10–5, Sun. 1–5. Adm. £1.50, con. 75p, Family Ticket £4. Gardens, Roman, Anglian and medieval ruins. Open weekdays 7.30–dusk (summer 7.30–8), Sun. 10–dusk. *The York Story*, Castlegate. Open weekdays 10–5, Sun. 1–5. Adm. 80p, con. 40p.

Art Gallery, Exhibition Square. European paintings, 14th–20th century; watercolours and prints of Yorkshire; modern English stoneware pottery. Open weekdays 10–5, Sun. 2.30–5.

Treasurer's House (National Trust). Chapter House Street. Open April–Oct. 10.30–5 (closed Good Friday). Adm. charge.

CLOSE SEASONS AND TIMES

Hunting and Ground Game

There is no statutory close-time for fox-hunting or rabbit-shooting, nor for hares: but by an Act passed in 1892 the *sale* of hares or leverets in Great Britain is prohibited from March 1 to July 31 inclusive under a penalty of a pound. The First of November is the recognized date for the opening of the *fox-hunting* season, which continues till the following April.

Deer

The table below shows the statutory close seasons for deer (all dates inclusive).

Species	Sex	England and Wales	Scotland
Red	M. F.	1 May–31 July 1 Mar.–31 Oct.	21 Oct.–30 June 16 Feb.–20 Oct.
Fallow	M. F.	1 May–31 July 1 Mar.–31 Oct.	1 May–31 July 16 Feb.–20 Oct.
Sika	M. F.	1 May–31 July 1 Mar.–31 Oct.	21 Oct.–30 June 16 Feb.–20 Oct.
Roe	M. F.	1 Nov.–31 Mar. 1 Mar.–31 Oct.	21 Oct.–31 Mar. 1 Apr.–20 Oct.
Red/Sika Hybrids	M. F.		21 Oct.–30 June 16 Feb.–20 Oct.

Wild Birds

The *Wildlife and Countryside Act*, 1981, lays down a close season for wild birds (other than Game Birds) from February 1 to August 31 inclusive, each year. Exceptions to these dates are made for—

Capercaillie and (except Scotland) *Woodcock*, Feb. 1—Sept. 30.

Snipe, Feb. 1—Aug. 11.

Wild Duck and *Wild Goose* (below high water mark), Feb. 21—Aug. 31.

Birds which may be killed or taken outside the close season (except on Sundays and on Christmas Day in Scotland, and on Sundays in prescribed areas of England and Wales) are the above and coot, certain wild duck (gadwall, goldeneye, mallard, pintail, pochard, shoveler, teal, tufted duck, wigeon), certain wild geese (Canada, greylag, pink-footed, white-fronted (in England and Wales only)), moorhen, golden plover and woodcock.

Certain wild birds may be killed or taken at any time by authorized persons—crow, collared dove, gull (great and lesser black-backed or herring), jackdaw, jay, magpie, pigeon (feral or wood), rook, sparrow and starling.

Game Birds

In each case the dates are inclusive:—

Black Game—Dec. 11 to Aug. 19 (Aug. 31 in Somerset, Devon, and New Forest).

*Grouse—Dec. 11 to Aug. 11.

*Partridge—Feb. 2 to Aug. 31.

*Pheasant—Feb. 2 to Sept. 30.

*Ptarmigan—(Scotland only) Dec. 11 to Aug. 11.

It is also unlawful (in *England* and *Wales*) to kill the game marked * above on a Sunday or Christmas Day.

All other British birds are fully protected by law throughout the year.

Angling

Close seasons (dates inclusive) are: *Coarse fishing.*—Yorkshire, last day in Feb. to May 31; South West, none; rest of country, March 15 to June 15. *Game fishing.*—Trout, Oct. 1 to last day of Feb.*; Salmon, Nov. 1 to Jan. 31*.

* The above dates are statutory close times. Particularly with salmon, migratory trout and trout, close seasons vary in accordance with water authority local by-laws. In all cases, it is best to check with the water authority concerned.

PROTECTED SPECIES

The following are protected animals under the provision of the *Wildlife and Countryside Act*, 1981:—

Bat (all species of the horseshoe and the typical bat), rainbow leaf beetle, burbot, butterfly (chequered skipper, heath fritillary, large blue, swallowtail), cricket (field, mole), dolphin (bottle-nosed, common), Norfolk aeshna dragonfly, wart-biter grasshopper, sand lizard, moth (barberry carpet, black-veined, Essex emerald, New Forest burnet, reddish buff), great-crested newt, common otter, harbour porpoise, snail (Carthusian, glutinous, sandbowl), smooth snake, spider (fen raft, ladybird), red squirrel, natterjack toad.

It is illegal to buy or sell the following:—
adder, common frog, viviparous lizard, newt (palmate, smooth), slow-worm, grass snake, common toad.

THE COUNTRY CODE

The following are the points of The Country Code, issued by the Countryside Commission:

(a) Enjoy the countryside and respect its life and work; (b) Guard against all risks of fire; (c) Fasten all gates; (d) Keep your dogs under close control; (e) Keep to public paths across farmland; (f) Use gates and stiles to cross fences, hedges and walls; (g) Leave livestock, crops and machinery alone; (h) Take your litter home; (i) Help to keep all water clean; (j) Protect wildlife, plants and trees; (k) Take special care on country roads; (l) Make no unnecessary noise.

WEATHER INFORMATION AND FORECASTS

Recorded weather forecasts for the areas listed below are available by telephoning the numbers shown:

Herts, Beds and		N.W. England	051–246 8091	Dorset and Hants. Coast	
Inland Essex	Bedford 8091		061–246 8091	(including I.O.W.)	
	Cambridge 8091		Blackburn 8091		Bournemouth 8091
	01–246 8099		Blackpool 8091		Portsmouth 8091
	Luton 8091		Southport 8091		Southampton 8091
Northern Ireland	Belfast 8091	West		Gloucestershire, Hereford	
	Bangor 8091	Yorkshire	Bradford 8091	and Worcester	
West Midlands and	021–246 8091		Huddersfield 8091		Cheltenham 8091
Warwickshire	Coventry 8091		Leeds 8091		Gloucester 8091
Avon and	Bristol 8091	Greater London	01–246 8091		Hereford 8091
Somerset	Swindon 8091		Tunbridge Wells 8091	Sussex and	
Glamorgan, Gwent			Guildford 8091	S. Kent Coast	01–246 8097
and South Dyfed	Cardiff 8091	East Anglia	Cambridge 8092		Brighton 8091
	Newport 8091		Norwich 8091		Hastings 8091
	Swansea 8091		Ipswich 8091		Canterbury 8092
Devon and Cornwall	Exeter 8091		Lowestoft 8091	Oxon, Berks and	
	Plymouth 8091		Peterborough 8091	Bucks	01–246 8090
	Torquay 8091	North East England			High Wycombe 8091
Dundee, Tayside		(incl. N. Yorks)			Oxford 8091
and Fife	Dundee 8091		Middlesbrough 8091		Reading 8091
Edinburgh, S. Fife			Newcastle upon Tyne 8091	North Downs and	
and Borders	031–246 8091	Lincs &		the Weald	01–246 8092
Glasgow area	041–246 8091	Humberside	Grimsby 8091	Staffs and Shropshire	
Grampian	Aberdeen 8091		Lincoln 8091		Stoke-on-Trent 8091
N. Kent and	01–246 8096	East Midlands	Nottingham 8091		Shrewsbury 8091
S. Essex Coast	Canterbury 8091		Leicester 8091	Lake District	Carlisle 8092
	Medway 8091		Derby 8091		Kendal 8092
	Chelmsford 8091		Northampton 8091		Leeds 8092
	Colchester 8091	S. Yorkshire and		Wiltshire, N. Dorset	
	Southend 8091	Peak District	Sheffield 8091	and Hampshire	Swindon 8092
			Doncaster 8091		Andover 8092

H.M. COASTGUARD

Founded in 1822 to guard our coasts against smuggling, H.M. Coastguard's role today is a very different one—that of complete dedication to the guarding and saving of all life at sea. Administered by the Department of Transport, it is responsible for co-ordinating all civil marine search and rescue operations around the 2,500 mile coastline of Great Britain and Northern Ireland, and 1,200 miles into the Atlantic as well as co-operating with search and rescue organizations of neighbouring countries both in Western Europe and around the Atlantic seaboard. In addition the Service maintains a 24-hour watch on the Dover Strait, providing a Channel Navigation Information Service for all shipping in one of the busiest sea lanes in the world.

Since 1978 H.M. Coastguard has been organized into six Regions, each with a Regional Controller operating from a Maritime Rescue Co-ordination Centre. Each Region is subdivided into Districts under District Controllers, operating from Maritime Rescue Sub-Centres. In all there are 24 of these major centres. They are on 24-hour watch and are fitted with a comprehensive range of communications and rescue equipment. They are supported by some 350 smaller stations manned by Auxiliary Coastguards under the direction of Regulars, each of which keeps its parent centre fully informed of day to day casualty risk, particularly on the more remote danger spots around the coast.

Between January 1 and December 31, 1986, the 560 Regular and 7,500 Auxiliary Coastguards co-ordinated 5,300 incidents requiring search and rescue facilities, resulting in assistance being given to 8,960 persons. All distress telephone and radio calls are centralized on the 24 centres, which are particularly on the alert for people or vessels in distress, shipping hazards and oil slicks. Using their modern telecommunications equipment and the facilities provided by British Telecom's Coast Radio Stations, they can alert and co-ordinate the most appropriate rescue facilities: RNLI lifeboats, Royal Navy or RAF helicopters, fixed-wing aircraft, Naval vessels, ships in the vicinity, and Coastguard shore and cliff rescue teams.

For those who regularly sail in local waters, or make longer passages, the Coastguard Yacht and Boat Safety Scheme provides a valuable free service. Its aim is to give the Coastguard a record of the details of craft, their normal operating areas and their passage plans. Yacht and Boat Safety Scheme Cards are available from all Coastguard stations, harbourmasters' offices and most yacht clubs and marinas.

Members of the public who see an accident or a potentially dangerous incident on or around the coast should without hesitation dial '999' and ask for the Coastguard.

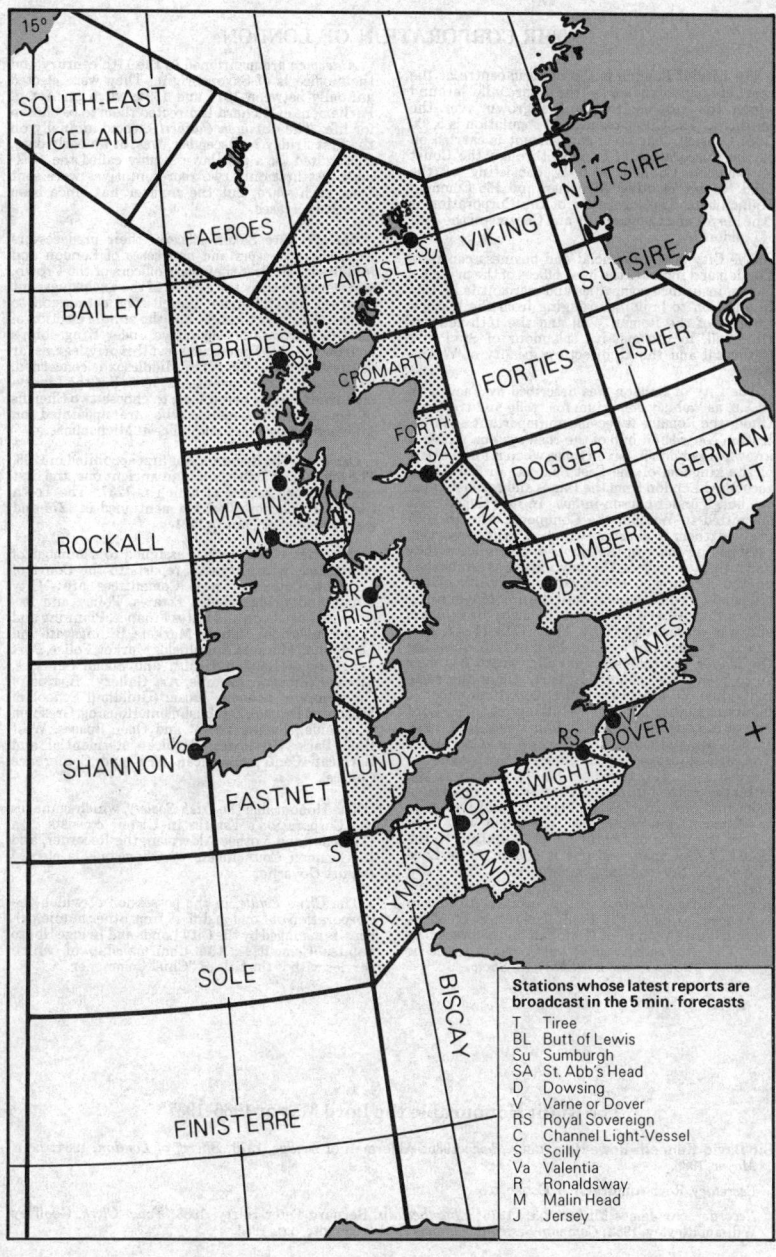

Stations whose latest reports are
broadcast in the 5 min. forecasts

T	Tiree
BL	Butt of Lewis
Su	Sumburgh
SA	St. Abb's Head
D	Dowsing
V	Varne or Dover
RS	Royal Sovereign
C	Channel Light-Vessel
S	Scilly
Va	Valentia
R	Ronaldsway
M	Malin Head
J	Jersey

THE CORPORATION OF LONDON

The City of London is the historic centre at the heart of London known as "the square mile" around which the vast metropolis has grown over the centuries. The City's residential population is 5,300 (1981 Census). The civic government is carried on by the Corporation of London through the Court of Common Council, a body consisting of the Lord Mayor, 24 other Aldermen and 136 Common Councilmen. The legal title of the Corporation is "the Mayor and Commonalty and Citizens of the City of London."

The City is the financial and business centre of London and includes the head offices of the principal banks, insurance companies and mercantile houses, in addition to buildings ranging from the historic interest of the Roman Wall and the 15th century Guildhall, to the massive splendour of St. Paul's Cathedral and the architectural beauty of Wren's spires.

The City of London was described by Tacitus in 62 A.D. as "a busy emporium for trade and traders". Under the Romans it became an important administration centre and hub of the road system. Little is known of London in Saxon times when it formed part of the kingdom of the East Saxons. In 886 Alfred recovered London from the Danes and reconstituted it a burgh under his son-in-law. In 1066 the citizens submitted to William the Conqueror who in 1067 granted them a charter, which is still preserved, establishing them in the rights and privileges they had hitherto enjoyed. The mayoralty was established on the recognition of the corporate unity of the citizens by Prince John in 1191, the first Mayor being Henry Fitz Ailwyn who filled the office for 21 years and was succeeded by Fitz Alan (1212–14). A new charter was granted by King John in 1215, directing the Mayor to be chosen annually, which has ever since been done, though in early times the same individual often held the office more than once. A familiar instance is that of "Whittington, thrice Lord Mayor of London" (in reality four times, 1397, 1398, 1406, 1419); and many modern cases have occurred. The earliest instance of the phrase "Lord Mayor" in English is in 1414. It is used more generally in the latter part of the 15th century and becomes invariable from 1535 onwards. At Michaelmas the Liverymen in Common Hall choose two Aldermen who have served the office of Sheriff for presentation to the Court of Aldermen, and one is chosen to be Lord Mayor for the ensuing mayoral year. The Lord Mayor is presented to the Lord Chief Justice at the Royal Courts of Justice on the second Saturday in November to make the final declaration of office, having been sworn in at Guildhall on the preceding day. The procession to the Royal Courts of Justice is popularly known as the *Lord Mayor's Show*.

Aldermen are mentioned in the 11th century and their office is of Saxon origin. They were elected annually between 1377 and 1394, when an Act of Parliament of Richard II directed them to be chosen for life. The *Common Council*, elected annually on the first Friday in December, was, at an early date, substituted for a popular assembly called the *Folkmote*. At first only two representatives were sent from each ward, but the number has since been greatly increased.

Sheriffs were Saxon officers: their predecessors were the *wic-reeves* and *portreeves* of London and Middlesex. At first they were officers of the Crown, and were named by the Barons of the Exchequer; but Henry I (in 1132) gave the citizens permission to choose their own Sheriffs, and the annual election of Sheriffs became fully operative under King John's charter of 1199. The citizens lost this privilege, as far as the election of Sheriff of Middlesex is concerned, by the Local Government Act, 1888; but the Liverymen continue, as heretofore, to choose two Sheriffs of the City of London, who are appointed on Midsummer Day, and take office at Michaelmas.

Officers.—The Recorder was first appointed in 1298. The office of Chamberlain is an ancient one, the first contemporary record of which is 1237. The Town Clerk (or Common Clerk) is mentioned in 1274 and the Common Serjeant in 1291.

Activities.—The work is assigned to a number of committees which present reports to the Court of Common Council. These Committees are:—City Lands and Bridge House Estates, Policy and Resources, Coal, Corn and Rates Finance, Planning and Communications, Central Markets, Billingsgate and Leadenhall Markets, Spitalfields Market, Police, Port and City of London Health and Social Services, Library (Library, Records, Art Gallery), Boards of Governors of Schools, Music (Guildhall School of Music and Drama), Establishment, Housing, Gresham (City side), Epping Forest and Open Spaces, West Ham Park, Privileges, Barbican Residential and Barbican Centre (Barbican Arts and Conference Centre).

The Honourable the *Irish Society*, which manages the Corporation's Estates in Ulster, consists of a Governor and 5 other Aldermen, the Recorder, and 19 Common Councilmen, of whom one is elected Deputy Governor.

The *City's Estate*, in the possession of which the Corporation of London differs from other municipalities, is managed by the City Lands and Bridge House Estates Committee, the Chairmanship of which carries with it the title of "Chief Commoner."

The Right Honourable the Lord Mayor 1986–1987*

Sir David Kenneth Rowe-Ham, G.B.E., *born* 1935; Alderman of *Bridge*, 1976; *Sheriff of London*, 1984; *Lord Mayor*, 1986.

Secretary, Rear-Admiral A. J. Cooke, C.B.

Recorder, Sir James Miskin, Q.C., 1975; *Chamberlain*, Bernard Peter Harty, 1983; *Town Clerk*, Geoffrey William Rowley, 1982; *Common Serjeant*, Thomas Herbert Pigott, Q.C., 1984.

The Aldermen

Aldermen	Ward	Born	C.C.	Ald.	Shff.	Lord Mayor
Cdr. Sir Robin Danvers Penrose Gillett, Bt., G.B.E., R.D., R.N.R.	Bassishaw	1925	1965	1969	1973	1976
Sir Peter Drury Haggerston Gadsden, G.B.E.	Farringdon Wt.	1929	1969	1971	1970	1979
Sir Christopher Leaver, G.B.E.	Dowgate	1937	1973	1974	1979	1981
Dame Mary Donaldson, G.B.E.	Coleman St.	1921	1966	1975	1981	1983
Sir Alan Towers Traill, G.B.E.	Langbourn	1935	1970	1975	1982	1984
Sir William Allan Davis, G.B.E.	Cripplegate	1921	1971	1976	1982	1985
Sir David Kenneth Rowe-Ham, G.B.E.	Bridge	1935	....	1976	1984	1986

All the above have passed the Civic Chair

Col. Greville Douglas Spratt, T.D.	Castle Baynard	1927	....	1978	1984	....
Christopher Collett	Broad Street	1931	1973	1979	1985	....
Hugh Charles Philip Bidwell	Billingsgate	1934	....	1979	1986	....
Alexander Michael Graham	Queenhithe	1938	1978	1979	1986	....
Brian Garton Jenkins	Cordwainer	1935	....	1980	....	....
Francis McWilliams	Aldersgate	1926	1978	1980	....	....
Paul Henry Newall, T.D.	Walbrook	1934	1980	1981	....	....
Christopher Rupert Walford	Farringdon Wn.	1935	....	1982	....	....
Roderic Neil Young	Bread Street	1933	1980	1982	....	....
Roger William Cork	Tower	1947	1978	1983	....	....
Brian Edward Toye	Lime Street	1938	....	1983	....	....
Richard Everard Nichols	Candlewick	1938	1983	1984	....	....
Peter Anthony Bull	Cheap	1937	1968	1984	....	....
Peter Keith Levene	Portsoken	1941	1983	1984	....	....
Leonard John Chalstrey	Vintry	1931	1981	1984	....	....
Clive Haydn Martin, O.B.E., T.D.	Aldgate	1935	....	1985	....	....
David Howarth Seymour Howard	Cornhill	1945	1972	1985	....	....
James Michael Yorrick Oliver	Bishopsgate	1940	1980	1986	....	....

* The Lord Mayor for 1987–88 was elected on Michaelmas Day (*See* "Occurrences During Printing").

The Sheriffs 1987–1988

Brian Garton Jenkins (*see above*) and Richard Saunders (*see below*), *elected* June 24; *assumed office* September 26, 1987.

THE COMMON COUNCIL OF LONDON

Archibald, W. W. (1986) .... *Cornhill*
Ballard, K. A., M.C. (1969) .... *Castle Baynard*
Balls, *Deputy* H. D. (1970) .... *Cripplegate*
Barker, J. A. (1981) .... *Cripplegate Wt.*
Barnes, H. M. F. (1986) .... *Coleman Street*
Beale, M. J. (1949) .... *Lime Street*
Bird, J. L. (1977) .... *Bridge*
Birkett, *Lt. Col.*, D., M.C. (1983) ...... *Aldersgate*
Block, S. A. A. (1983) .... *Cheap*
Boreham, B. P. (1986) .... *Dowgate*
Bramwell, F. M. (1983) .... *Langbourn*
Brighton, R. L. (1984) .... *Portsoken*
Brooks, W. I. B. (1979) .... *Cripplegate Wn.*
Brown, D. T. (1971) .... *Walbrook*
Cassidy, *Deputy* M. J. (1980) .... *Aldersgate*
Catt, B. F. (1982) .... *Farringdon Wn.*
Challis, G. H. (1978) .... *Langbourn*
Champness, *Deputy* P. H. (1966) .... *Walbrook*
Chandler, *Deputy* E. G., C.B.E. (1982) . *Cornhill*
Clements, *Deputy* G. E. I. (1960) .... *Farringdon Wt.*
Cohen, Mrs. C. M. (1986) .... *Lime Street*
Cohen, *Deputy* S. E., C.B.E. (1951) .... *Farringdon Wt.*
Cole, *Lt.-Col.*, Sir Colin, K.C.V.O., T.D. (1964) .... *Castle Baynard*
Colover, D. (1975) .... *Bishopsgate*
Cope, Dr. J. (1963) .... *Farringdon Wt.*
Coven, *Deputy* Mrs. E. O. (1972) ..... *Dowgate*
Currie, Miss S. E. M. (1985) .... *Cripplegate*
David, C. P. (1984) .... *Aldgate*
Day, M. J. (1986) .... *Aldersgate*
Deith, R. C. (1944) .... *Farringdon Wn.*
Delderfield, D. W. (1982) .... *Aldersgate*
Denny, A. M. (1971) .... *Billingsgate*
de Silva, D., Q.C. (1980) .... *Farringdon Wt.*

Dewhirst, *Deputy* W. (1971) .... *Cripplegate*
Donnelly, T. A., M.B.E. (1982) .... *Bread Street*
Duckworth, *Deputy* H. C.B.E. (1960) . *Lime St.*
Dunitz, A. A. (1984) .... *Portsoken*
Durnin, J. C. (1976) .... *Cordwainer*
Edwards, R. D. K. (1978) .... *Bassishaw*
Eskenzi, A. N. (1971) .... *Farringdon Wn.*
Evans, Mrs. J. (1975) .... *Farringdon Wn.*
Eve, R. A. (1980) .... *Cheap*
Everett, K. M. (1984) .... *Candlewick*
Falk, F. A., T.D. (1984) .... *Farringdon Wt.*
Farthing, R. B. C. (1981) .... *Aldgate*
Fell, J. A. (1982) .... *Queenhithe*
FitzGerald, R. C. A. (1981) .... *Bread Street*
Floyd-Ewin, *Deputy* Sir David, L.V.O., O.B.E. (1963) .... *Castle Baynard*
Frappell, C. E. (1973) .... *Bread St.*
Fraser, W. B. (1981) .... *Vintry*
Frazer, C. M. (1986) .... *Farringdon Wt.*
Galloway, A. D. (1981) .... *Broad Street*
Gass, *Deputy* G. J. (1967) .... *Coleman St.*
Gold, R. (1965) .... *Castle Baynard*
Gordon, Miss C. F. (1978) .... *Cripplegate Wn.*
Graves, A. C. (1985) .... *Bishopsgate*
Gugan, K., Ph.D. (1974) .... *Dowgate*
Harding, N. H. (1970) .... *Farringdon Wn.*
Hart, *Deputy* M. G. (1970) .... *Bridge*
Hatfield, A. F. R. (1968) .... *Bishopsgate*
Haynes, J. E. H. (1986) .... *Cornhill*
Henderson, *Deputy* J. S., O.B.E. (1975) *Langbourn*
Henderson-Begg, M. (1977) .... *Coleman Street*
Holland, *Deputy* J. (1972) .... *Aldgate*
Horlock, *Deputy* H. W. S. (1969) ..... *Farringdon Wn.*
Humphrays, Mrs. R. (1976) .... *Cripplegate*

Ide, W. R. (1972) . . . .*Castle Baynard*
Jackson, L. St. J. T., T.D. (1978) . . . . . .*Bassishaw*
James, A. J. (1973) . . . .*Cordwainer*
James, J. F. (1977) . . . .*Farringdon Wt.*
Kellett, Mrs. M. W. F. (1986) . . . .*Tower*
Kemp, D. L. (1984) . . . .*Coleman St.*
Knowles, S. K. (1984) . . . .*Candlewick*
Langmead, A. D. G., T.D. (1982) . . . . . .*Tower*
Lawrence, D. W. O., T.D. (1979) . . . . . .*Bridge*
Lawson, G. C. H. (1972) . . . .*Portsoken*
McAuley, *Deputy*, C. (1957) . . . .*Bread St.*
McDonald, G. I. (1986) . . . .*Cripplegate Wn.*
McNeil, I. D. (1977) . . . .*Lime Street*
Malins, J. H. (1981) . . . .*Farringdon Wt.*
Martin, R. C. (1986) . . . .*Queenhithe*
Mayhew, Miss J. (1986) . . . .*Queenhithe*
Mills, A. P. (1969) . . . .*Bassishaw*
Minshull-Fogg, J., T.D. (1986) . . . .*Walbrook*
Mitchell, C. R. (1972) . . . .*Castle Baynard*
Mizen, *Deputy* D. H. (1979) . . . .*Broad Street*
Mobsby, D. J. L. (1985) . . . .*Billingsgate*
Morgan, *Deputy* B. L., C.B.E. (1963) . .*Bishopsgate*
Murkin, *Deputy* C. H., O.B.E. (1969) . .*Vintry*
Nash, Mrs. J. C. (1983) . . . .*Aldersgate*
Neary, J. E. (1982) . . . .*Aldgate*
Northall-Laurie, P. D. (1975) . . . .*Walbrook*
Olson, A. H. F. (1972) . . . .*Dowgate*
Owen, Mrs. J. (1975) . . . .*Langbourn*
Owen-Ward, J. R. (1983) . . . .*Bridge*
Packard, Brig. J. J. (1973) . . . .*Cripplegate*
Palmer, D. H. (1985) . . . .*Cripplegate*
Pembroke, *Deputy* Mrs. A. M. F.
(1978) . . . .*Cheap*
Ponsonby of Shulbrede, The Lady
(1981) . . . .*Farringdon Wt.*

Pulman, G. A. (1983) . . . .*Tower*
Ratner, R. A., T.D. (1981) . . . .*Broad Street*
Reed, *Deputy* J. L., M.B.E. (1967) . . . . .*Farringdon Wn.*
Revell-Smith, P. A. (1959) . . . .*Vintry*
Rigby, P. P. (1972) . . . .*Farringdon Wn.*
Rodgers, S. C. (1969) . . . .*Farringdon Wt.*
Rogers, Miss E. H. L. (1982) . . . .*Cornhill*
Roney, *Deputy* E. P. T., C.B.E. (1974) . .*Bishopsgate*
Samuel, *Deputy* Mrs. I. (1972) . . . .*Portsoken*
Saunders, *Deputy* R. (1975) . . . .*Candlewick*
Savory, M. B. (1980) . . . .*Broad Street*
Scriven, R. G. (1984) . . . .*Candlewick*
Scrivener, M. J. H. (1986) . . . .*Cripplegate Wt.*
Shalit, D. M. (1973) . . . .*Farringdon Wn.*
Sharp, *Deputy* Mrs. I. M. (1974) . . . . .*Queenhithe*
Shindler, *Deputy* A. B. (1966) . . . .*Billingsgate*
Smithers, H. J. (1986) . . . .*Billingsgate*
Snyder, M. J. (1986) . . . .*Cordwainer*
Spanner, J. H., T.D. (1984) . . . .*Broad St*
Stevenson, J. L. (1970) . . . .*Coleman Street*
Stitcher, G. M., C.B.E. (1966) . . . .*Farringdon Wt.*
Swan, N. E. B. (1985) . . . .*Coleman Street*
Turner, *Deputy* R. L. (1973) . . . .*Tower*
Webb, C. J. (1986) . . . .*Bishopsgate*
White, J. W. (1986) . . . .*Cornhill*
Williams, G. M. E. (1985) . . . .*Aldersgate*
Willoughby, P. J. (1985) . . . .*Bishopsgate*
Wilmot, *Deputy* R. T. D. (1973) . . . . . .*Cordwainer*
Wilson, A. B. (1960) . . . .*Cheap*
Wixley, *Deputy* G. R. A., C.B.E., T.D.
(1964) . . . .*Bassishaw*
Woodward, C. D. (1972) . . . .*Cripplegate*
Wylie Harris, W. H. (1957) . . . .*Farrington Wn.*

Deputies.—In the preceding list each Common Councilman so described serves as *Deputy* to the Alderman of his Ward.

THE CITY GUILDS (LIVERY COMPANIES)

The Livery Companies of the City of London derive their name from the assumption of a distinctive dress or livery by their members in the 14th century.

The order of precedence (according to 2nd Report of Municipal Corporations' Commissioners, 1837, omitting extinct companies, is given in parentheses after the name of each Company.

About 22,500 Liverymen of the Guilds are entitled to vote at elections in *Common Hall.*

MERCERS *(1). Hall,* Ironmonger Lane, EC2V 8HE. *Livery,* 238.—*Clerk,* G. M. M. Wakeford; *Master,* D. C. Watney.

GROCERS *(2). Hall,* Princes Street, EC2R 8AQ. *Livery,* 300.—*Clerk,* C. P. G. Chavasse; *Master,* W. Martineau.

DRAPERS *(3). Hall,* Throgmorton Street, EC2N 2DQ. *Livery,* 250.—*Clerk,* R. C. G. Strick; *Master,* R. Harris.

FISHMONGERS *(4). Hall,* London Bridge, EC4R 9EL. *Livery,* 296.—*Clerk,* E. S. Earl; *Prime Warden,* G. R. C. Shepard.

GOLDSMITHS *(5). Hall,* Foster Lane, EC2V 6BN. *Livery,* 280.—*Clerk,* C. P. de B. Jenkins, M.B.E., M.C.; *Prime Warden,* Sir Anthony Touch.

SKINNERS *(6* and *7). Hall,* 8 Dowgate Hill, EC4R 2SP. *Livery,* 360.—*Clerk,* M. H. Glover; *Master,* D. A. Emms.

MERCHANT TAYLORS *(6* and *7). Hall,* 30 Threadneedle Street, EC2R 8AY. *Livery* 330.—*Clerk,* Capt. D. A. Wallis, R.N.; *Master,* Sir Edward Studd, Bt.

HABERDASHERS *(8). Hall,* Staining Lane, EC2V 7DD. *Livery,* 320.—*Clerk,* Capt. M. E. Barrow, D.S.O., R.N.; *Master,* O. M. W. Swingland, Q.C.

SALTERS *(9). Hall,* 4 Fore Street, EC2Y 5DE. *Livery,* 150.—*Clerk,* J. M. Montgomery; *Master,* E. J. N. Hicks.

IRONMONGERS *(10). Hall,* Barbican, EC2Y 8AA. *Livery,* 32.—*Clerk,* R. B. Brayne, M.B.E.; *Master,* A. D. Moss.

VINTNERS *(11). Hall,* 68 Upper Thames Street, EC4V 3BE. *Livery,* 333.—*Clerk,* Brig. G. Read, C.B.E. *Master,* M. H. Fairbank.

CLOTHWORKERS *(12). Hall,* Dunster Court, Mincing Lane, EC3R 7AH. *Livery,* 185.—*Clerk,* C. M. Mowll; *Master,* C. St. G. S. Clarke.

The above are the Twelve "Great" London Companies in order of Civic precedence.

ACCOUNTANTS, CHARTERED (86). *Livery*, 320.—*Clerk*, G. H. Kingsmill, The Grove, Hinton Parva, Swindon SN4 0DH; *Master*, D. G. Richards.

ACTUARIES (91). *Livery*, 136.—*Clerk*, A. K. Tudor, 8 Madgeways Close, Great Amwell, Herts., SG12 9RU; *Master*, D. G. Millard.

AIR PILOTS AND AIR NAVIGATORS, GUILD OF (81). *Livery*, 400.—*Grand Master*, H.R.H. the Prince Philip, Duke of Edinburgh, K.G., K.T.; *Clerk*, Capt. P. Wilson, 30 Eccleston Street, SW1W 9PY; *Master*, R. Pooley.

APOTHECARIES, SOCIETY OF (58). *Hall*, Black Friars Lane, EC4V 6EJ. *Livery*, 1,100.—*Clerk*, Maj. J. C. O'Leary; *Master*, Dr J. F. Fisher.

ARBITRATORS (93). *Livery*, 190.—*Clerk*, B. W. Vigrass, O.B.E., V.R.D., 75 Cannon Street, EC4N 5BH; *Master*, A. B. Shindler.

ARMOURERS AND BRASIERS (22). *Hall*, 81 Coleman Street, EC2R 5BJ. *Livery*, 120.—*Clerk*, Lt. Col. R. F. Cowe; *Master*, E. R. J. Hill.

BAKERS (19). *Hall*, Harp Lane, Lower Thames Street, EC3R 6DP. *Livery*, 385.—*Clerk*, Col. P. F. Wilson, D.F.C.; *Master*, J. P. Copeman.

BARBERS (17). *Hall*, Monkwell Square, EC2Y 5BL. *Livery*, 178.—*Clerk*, B. W. Hall, *Master*, J. A. H. Bootes.

BASKETMAKERS (52). *Livery*, 500.—*Clerk*, D. J. Farrier, 5 The Spinney, Warren Road, Purley, Surrey CR2 1AB; *Prime Warden*, Sir Colin Cole, K.C.V.O., T.D., F.S.A.

BLACKSMITHS (40). *Livery*, 250.—*Clerk*, D. T. Dresch, Hill House, Branksome Park Road, Camberley, Surrey GU15 2AE; *Prime Warden*, F. A. Jackman, O.B.E.

BOWYERS (38). *Livery*, 94.—*Clerk*, A. Black, 2 Serjeants' Inn, Fleet Street, EC4Y 1LL; *Master*, J. R. Bickford Smith, T.D.

BREWERS (14). *Hall*, Aldermanbury Square, EC2V 7HR. *Livery*, 119.—*Clerk*, Rr. Adm. M. La T. Wemyss, C.B; *Master*, Sir Derrick Holden-Brown.

BRODERERS (48). *Livery*, 125.—*Clerk*, S. G. B. Underwood, 11A Bridge Road, East Molesey, Surrey KT8 9EY; *Master*, E. J. S. Hannam.

BUILDERS MERCHANTS (88). *Livery*, 230.—*Clerk*, A. G. P. Lincoln, 9 Little Trinity Lane, EC4V 2AD; *Master*, R. E. Silvester.

BUTCHERS (24). *Hall*, 87 Bartholomew Close, EC1A 7EB. *Livery*, 660.—*Clerk*, A. H. Emus; *Master*, R. Pooley.

CARMEN (77). *Livery*, 457.—*Clerk*, Lt. Col. G. T. Pearce, M.B.E., St. Olave's Rectory, 8 Hart Street, EC3R 7NB; *Master*, H.R.H. the Princess Royal, G.C.V.O.

CARPENTERS (26). *Hall*, 1 Throgmorton Avenue, EC2N 2JJ. *Livery*, 150.—*Clerk*, Capt. K. G. Hamon, R.N.; *Master*, Dr W. F. Felton.

CLOCKMAKERS (61). *Livery*, 281.—*Clerk*, Air Cdre. B. G. Frow, D.S.O, D.F.C., 2 Greycoat Place, SW1P 1SD; *Master*, P. M. Vine.

COACHMAKERS AND COACH-HARNESS MAKERS (72). *Livery*, 400.—*Clerk*, Maj. W. H. Wharfe, R.M., 149 Banstead Road, Ewell, Epsom, Surrey KT17 3HL; *Master*, D. M. Shalit.

COOKS (35). *Livery*, 75.—*Clerk*, H. J. Lavington, T.D. 49 Queen Victoria Street, EC4N 4SE; *Master*, Adm. Sir Lindsay Bryson, K.C.B.

COOPERS (36). *Hall*, 13 Devonshire Square, EC2M 4TH. *Livery*, 260.—*Clerk*, J. A. Newton; *Master*, Lt. Col. C. R. Perrin, V.R.D., R.N.R. (retd).

CORDWAINERS (27). *Livery* 143.—*Clerk*, Capt. C. T. Codrington, C.B.E., R.N., 30 Fleet Street, EC4Y 1AA; *Master*, C. A. H. Willcocks.

CURRIERS (29). *Livery*, 92.—*Clerk*, I. R. McNeil, 43 Church Road, Hove, Sussex BN3 2BT; *Master*, D. T. Sparrow.

CUTLERS (18). *Hall*, Warwick Lane, EC4M 7BR.

Livery, 100.—*Clerk*, K. S. G. Hinde, T.D.; *Master*, W. G. Prynne.

DISTILLERS (69). *Livery*, 250.—*Clerk*, B. Dehn, 60 Mountford Place, Kennington Lane, SE11 5DF; *Master*, A. Burrough, C.B.E.

DYERS (13). *Hall*, Dowgate Hill, EC4R 2ST. *Livery*, 130.—*Clerk*, J. R. Chambers; *Prime Warden*, R. M. S. Goodsall.

ENGINEERS (94). *Hall*, 19 Old Broad Street, EC3. *Livery*, 255.—*Clerk*, Cdr. B. D. Gibson, R.N. (retd); *Master*, R. B. Dunn.

ENVIRONMENTAL CLEANERS (97). *Hall*, Mark Lane, EC3. *Livery*, 80.—*Clerk*, S. J. Holt; *Master*, B. Barclay.

FAN MAKERS (76). *Livery*, 215.—*Clerk*, Lt. Col. I. R. P. Green, 28 Commercial Street, E1 6LS; *Master*, R. A. Pollitt.

FARMERS (80). *Hall*, 3 Cloth Street, EC1A 7LD. *Livery*, 300.—*Clerk*, C. M. Taylor; *Master*, S. F. B. Taylor.

FARRIERS (55). *Livery*, 375.—*Clerk*, H. W. H. Ellis, 37 The Uplands, Loughton, Essex IG10 1NQ; *Master*, A. G. W. Scott.

FELTMAKERS (63). *Livery*, 350.—*Clerk*, E. J. P. Elliott, 44 Davies Street, W1Y 2BL; *Master*, C. Simeons.

FLETCHERS (39). *Hall*, 3 Cloth Street, EC1A 7LD. *Livery*, 112.—*Clerk*, J. R. Garnett; *Master*, A. N. Taylor.

FOUNDERS (33). *Hall*, 1 Cloth Fair, EC1. *Livery*, 180.—*Clerk*, A. J. Gillett; *Master*, A. F. Mitchener.

FRAMEWORK KNITTERS (64). *Livery*, 225.—*Clerk*, C. J. Eldridge, Apothecaries' Hall, Black Friars Lane, EC4V 6EL; *Master*, E. G. Harding.

FRUITERERS (45). *Livery*, 240.—*Clerk*, Brig. R. Eccles, D.S.O., Church Leys, Buckland, Aylesbury HP22 5HX; *Master*, A. G. Coster.

FUELLERS (95). *Livery*, 250.—*Clerk*, H. C. F. Squire, 6 Farm Avenue, Horsham, W. Sussex RH12 2JY; *Master*, R. N. Horne.

FURNITURE MAKERS (83). *Livery*, 253.—*Clerk*, Wg. Cdr. G. Acklam, M.B.E., 30 Harcourt Street, W1H 2AA; *Master*, J. D. Radford.

GARDENERS (66). *Livery*, 250.—*Clerk*, A. L. McGeachy, 7/8 Kings Bench Walk, Temple, EC4Y 7DT; *Master*, His Hon. G. F. Leslie.

GIRDLERS (23). *Hall*, Basinghall Avenue, EC2V 5DD. *Livery*, 80.—*Clerk*, T. J. Straker.

GLASS-SELLERS (71). *Livery*, 180.—*Hon. Clerk*, P. J. Willoughby, 25 New Street Square, EC4A 3LN; *Master*, P. J. Willoughby.

GLAZIERS (53). *Hall*, 9 Montague Close, SE1 9DD. *Livery*, 295.—*Clerk*, P. H. Trollope; *Master*, J. Stone.

GLOVERS (62). *Livery*, 300.—*Clerk*, Gp. Capt. D. G. F. Palmer, O.B.E., Glovers, Tismans Common, Rudgwick, W. Sussex RH12 3DU; *Master*, K. D. Smith.

GOLD AND SILVER WYRE DRAWERS (74). *Livery*, 350.—*Clerk*, D. Reid, P.O. Box 153, 40A Ludgate Hill, EC4M 7DE; *Master*, R. M. Thorpe.

GUNMAKERS (73). *Livery*, 220.—*Clerk*, F. B. Brandt, The Proof House, 48/50 Commercial Road, E1 1LP; *Master*, Hon. Sir Peter Vanneck, G.B.E., C.B., A.F.C., A.E.

HORNERS (54). *Livery*, 420.—*Clerk*, Dr. E. M. Hunt, 11 Hobart Place, SW1W 0HL; *Master*, B. Becker, V.R.D.

INNHOLDERS (32). *Hall*, College Street, Dowgate Hill, EC4R 2SY. *Livery*, 120.—*Clerk*, J. R. Edwardes Jones; *Master*, S. Druce.

INSURERS (92). *Livery*, 344.—*Clerk*, V. D. Webb, The Hall, 20 Aldermanbury, EC2V 7HY; *Master*, J. R. Redfern.

JOINERS AND CEILERS (41). *Livery*, 123.—*Clerk*, D. A. Tate, Parkville House, Bridge Street, Pinner, Middx. HA5 3JD; *Master*, A. G. H. Clare.

LAUNDERERS (89). *Livery*, 300.—*Clerk*, W. E. Kingsland, 34 Broadhurst, Ashtead, Surrey KT21 1QD; *Master*, W. H. Davidson, M.B.E.

LEATHERSELLERS (15). *Hall*, 15 St. Helens Place, EC3A 6DQ. *Livery*, 150.—*Clerk*, Capt. C. N. MacEacharn, C.B.E., R.N.; *Master*, N. A. Dove.

LIGHTMONGERS (96). *Livery*, 240.—*Clerk*, S. H. Birch, 53 Leithcote Gardens, SW16 2UX; *Master*, C. A. Castlo.

LORINERS (57). *Livery*, 350.—*Clerk*, J. R. Williams, 2/ 5 Benjamin Street, EC1M 5QL; *Master*, R. H. Furniss.

MARKETORS (90). *Livery*, 150.—*Clerk*, B. F. Catt, 29 Queen Street, EC4R 1BH; *Master*, E. A. G. Morgan.

MASONS (30). *Livery*, 111.—*Clerk*, H. J. Maddocks, 9 New Square, WC2R 3QN; *Master*, C. J. Jeffries.

MASTER MARINERS, HONOURABLE COMPANY OF (78). H.Q.S. *Wellington*, Temple Stairs, WC2R 2PN. *Livery*, 300.—*Clerk*, D. H. W. Field; *Admiral*, H.R.H. the Duke of Edinburgh, K.G., K.T.; *Master*, Capt. J. S. Allen.

MUSICIANS (50). *Livery*, 261.—*Deputy Clerk*, L. J. D. Halcrow, 4 St. Paul's Churchyard, EC4M 8BA; *Master*, W. R. I. Crewdson.

NEEDLEMAKERS (65). *Livery*, 250.—*Clerk*, M. G. Cook, 17 Southampton Place, WC1A 2EH; *Master*, Sir Henry Warner, Bt.

PAINTER STAINERS (28). *Hall*, 9 Little Trinity Lane, EC4V 2AD. *Livery*, 407.—*Clerk*, Col. A. G. P. Lincoln, M.C., T.D.; *Master* D. B. Hobday.

PATTENMAKERS (70). *Livery*, 250.—*Clerk*, P. Merritt, 25 Wellesley Road, W4 4BU; *Master*, W. R. F. Chamberlain.

PAVIORS (56). *Livery*, 250.—*Clerk*, R. F. Coe, Cutlers' Hall, Warwick Lane, EC4M 7BR; *Master*, Sir Kirky Laing.

PEWTERERS. (16). *Hall*, Oat Lane, EC2V 7DE. *Livery*, 110.—*Clerk*, Maj. J. M. Halford, R.M.; *Master*, P. Boggis-Rolfe.

PLAISTERERS (46). *Hall*, 1 London Wall, EC2Y 5JU. *Livery*, 203.—*Clerk*, H. Mott; *Master*, T. C. Spicer.

PLAYING CARD MAKERS (75). *Livery*, 148.—*Clerk*, M. J. Smyth, 6 The Priory, Godstone, Surrey RH9 8NL; *Master*, C. R. Walford.

PLUMBERS (31). *Livery*, 304.—*Clerk*, Col. E. M. P. Hardy, Ironmongers Hall, Barbican, EC2Y 8AA; *Master*, L. Hill.

POULTERS (34). *Livery*, 162.—*Clerk*, I. G. Williamson, 84 Brook Street, Grosvenor Square, W1Y 1YG; *Master*, R. E. Marshall.

SADDLERS (25). *Hall*, Gutter Lane, EC2V 6BR. *Livery*, 70.—*Clerk*, Gp. Capt. K. M. Oliver; *Master*, Maj. J. P. E. Welch.

SCIENTIFIC INSTRUMENT MAKERS (84). *Livery*, 230.— *Clerk*, Gp. Cpt. R. L. Smith, 9 Montague Close, SE1 9DD; *Master*, H. J. Kroch, C.B.E.

SCRIVENERS (44). *Livery*, 183.—*Clerk*, H. J. W. Harman, Chancery House, 53/64 Chancery Lane, WC2A 1QU; *Master*, M. J. Scannall.

SECRETARIES AND ADMINISTRATORS (87). *Livery*, 225.—*Hon. Clerk*, G. H. Challis, The Irish Chamber, Guildhall Yard, EC2V 5AE; *Master*, R. Bounds.

SHIPWRIGHTS (59). *Livery*, 472.—*Clerk*, Gp. Capt. R. C. Olding, C.B.E., D.S.C., Ironmongers' Hall, Barbican, EC2Y 8AA; *Permanent Master*, H.R.H. the Duke of Edinburgh, K.G., K.T.; *Prime Warden*, Rear Adm. Sir Morgan Morgan-Giles, D.S.O., O.B.E., G.M.

SOLICITORS (79). *Livery*, 412.—*Clerk*, Miss S. H. Robinson, T.D., 14 Charterhouse Square, EC1M 6AX; *Master*, M. H. Sheldon.

SPECTACLEMAKERS (60). *Livery*, 316.—*Clerk*, C. J. Eldridge, Apothecaries' Hall, Black Friars Lane, EC4V 6EL; *Master*, Sir Richard Meyjes.

STATIONERS AND NEWSPAPER MAKERS (47). *Hall*, Ave Maria Lane, EC4M 7DD. *Livery*, 450.—*Clerk*, Capt. P. Hames, R.N.; *Master*, M. F. Tollit, M.B.E.

SURVEYORS, CHARTERED (85). *Livery*, 314.—*Clerk*, Mrs. A. L. Jackson, 16 Mary-at-Hill, EC3R 8EE; *Master*, S. K. Knowles.

TALLOW CHANDLERS (21). *Hall*, 4 Dowgate Hill, EC4R 2SH. *Livery*, 175.—*Clerk*, Col. M. ff. Woodhead, O.B.E.; *Master*, M. D. Bridges Webb.

TIN PLATE WORKERS (67). *Livery*, 259.—*Clerk*, A. Hill, 71 Lincolns Inn Fields, WC2A 3JF; *Master*, C. Brough.

TOBACCO PIPE MAKERS AND TOBACCO BLENDERS (82). *Livery*, 190.—*Clerk*, I. J. Kimmins, Bouverie House, 154 Fleet Street, EC4A 2HX; *Master*, R. Dunhill.

TURNERS (51). *Livery*, 170.—*Clerk*, R. G. Woodwark, D.S.C., 33a Hill Avenue, Amersham, Bucks. HP6 5BX; *Master*, Maj. Gen. Sir Leonard Atkinson, K.B.E.

TYLERS AND BRICKLAYERS (37). *Livery*, 130.—*Clerk*, F. A. G. Rider, 6 Martin Lane, Cannon Street, EC4R 0DP; *Master*, M. J. L. Marshall.

UPHOLDERS (49). *Livery*, 200.—*Clerk*, W. R. Wallis, Charrington House, The Causeway, Bishops Stortford CH23 2EW; *Master*, S. A. G. Rust.

WAX CHANDLERS (20). *Hall*, Gresham Street, EC2V 7AD. *Livery*, 100.—*Clerk*, T. Wood; *Master*, A. G. Horton.

WEAVERS (42). *Livery*, 125.—*Clerk*, J. G. Ouvry, 1 The Sanctuary, SW1P 3JT; *Upper Bailiff*, C. J. Bourne.

WHEELWRIGHTS (68). *Livery*, 265.—*Clerk*, M. R. Francis, Greenup, Milton Avenue, Gerrards Cross, Bucks.. SL9 8QW; *Master*, E. J. Macey.

WOOLMEN (43). *Livery*, 150.—*Clerk*, D. R. L. Humble, R.D., Kingsmead House, 250 King's Road, SW3 5UE; *Master*, A. A. Hammond, O.B.E.

PARISH CLERKS (*No livery*) (*Brethren*, 100).—*Clerk*, R. H. Adams, T.D., F.S.A., 14 Dale Close, Oxford OX1 1TU; *Master*, J. A. Prodger, E.R.D.

WATERMEN AND LIGHTERMEN (*No livery. Craft Owning Freemen*, 280).—*Hall*, 16 St. Mary-at-Hill, EC3R 8EE.—*Clerk*, W. A. A. Wells, T.D.; *Master*, R. G. Crouch.

NOTE.—In certain companies the election of Master or Prime Warden for the year does not take place till the autumn. In such cases the Master or Prime Warden for 1986–87 is given.

LONDON BOROUGHS

City or Borough (*Inner London Borough)	Municipal Offices	Population	Rateable Value April 1, 1987	Town Clerk (*Chief Executive)	Mayor or (a) Lord Mayor
			£		
City of Westminster*	City Hall, Victoria St., SW1E 6QP.	179,100	332,646,085	*R. G. Brooke	(a) K. Gardner
Barking	‡Dagenham, RM10 7BN.	147,700	27,037,015	D. C. J. Farr	Mrs. M. Arnold
Barnet	†The Burroughs, Hendon, NW4 4BG.	301,200	62,923,111	E. M. Bennett	M. Lester
Bexley	‡Bexleyheath, DA6 7LB.	218,500	32,257,843	*T. Musgrave	S. J. Carter
Brent	†Forty Lane, Wembley, HA9 9EZ.	254,900	52,325,622	*C. Wood	L. Williams
Bromley	†Bromley, BR1 3UH.	298,400	51,736,809	*N. T. Palk	J. Lewis
Camden*	†Euston Rd., NW1 2RU.	172,014	124,122,367	F. Nickson	J. Williams
Croydon........	†Taberner House, Park Lane, Croydon.	319,300	72,516,335	F. S. H. Birch	A. Carey
Ealing	†Ealing, W5 2BY.	295,500	58,610,490	J. Leadbetter (acting)	R. N. Pathak
Enfield	‡Enfield, EN1 3XA.	260,000	50,300,962	*B. McAndrew	A. J. Young, C.B.E.
Greenwich*	†Wellington St., SE18 6PW.	217,800	33,500,000	*A. Glover	J. Austin-Walker
Hackney*	Mare St., E8 1EA.	187,500	39,095,651	*Ms. P. Gordon	N. Syed
Hammersmith and Fulham* .	†King St., W6 9JU.	153,100	37,404,308	*A. Eddison	Mrs. J. O. Adegoke
Haringey	Wood Green, N22 4LE.	202,650	37,445,477	*R. C. Limb	A. Mikkides
Harrow	‡Harrow, HA1 2UH.	201,700	35,764,012	*A. G. Redmond	M. A. Carmody
Havering	†Romford, RM1 3BD.	234,400	38,907,962	*J. L. Guest	R. Adaire
Hillingdon......	‡Uxbridge, UB8 1JN.	234,610	60,884,815	*P. A. Johnson	F. W. Taylor
Hounslow	‡Lampton Rd., Hounslow, TW3 4DN.	201,300	52,215,016	*R. D. Jefferies	J. Spence
Islington*	†Upper St., N1 2UD.	167,900	54,594,293	*E. W. Dear	T. Herbert
Kensington and Chelsea (Royal Borough)*	†Hornton St., W8 7NX.	136,100	73,686,643	R. S. Webber	Mrs. E. Russell
Kingston upon Thames (Royal Borough)	Guildhall, Kingston upon Thames.	133,900	29,640,790	R. J. McCloy (Co-ordinator)	Mrs. J. Philpott
Lambeth*	Brixton Hill, SW2 1RW.	245,000	62,612,681	A. J. George	B. Hodge
Lewisham*	†Catford, SE6 4RU.	232,400	35,590,000	J. W. Harwood	N. Smith
Merton.........	Crown Ho., London Rd., Morden, SM4 5DX.	164,500	32,449,705	*W. A. McKee	H. C. A. Turner
Newham	†East Ham Rd., E6 2RP.	207,000	36,687,599	*J. Samuel	F. York
Redbridge	Ilford, IG1 1DD.	228,000	37,087,640	*G. U. Price	G. F. Borrott
Richmond upon Thames	York House, Twickenham, TW1 3AA.	160,800	33,710,321	M. J. Honey	M. Emerson
Southwark*	†Peckham Rd., SE5 8UB.	215,000	62,288,726	*Ms. A. Whyatt	Mrs. D. Winters
Sutton	‡St. Nicholas Way, Sutton, SM1 1EA.	170,000	30,377,326	*A. Taylor	K. Bishop
Tower Hamlets*.	†Patriot Square, E2 9LN.	147,100	53,151,104	*C. E. Lea	B. Williams
Waltham Forest .	†Walthamstow, E17.	216,200	32,346,922	*L. G. Knox	W. J. Dearmine
Wandsworth*....	†Wandsworth, SW18.	260,500	44,724,850	*S. K. Jones	W. F. D. Hawkins

† Town Hall.   ‡ Civic Offices.

ABOLITION OF THE G.L.C.

The abolition of the Greater London Council on April 1, 1986, led to the bulk of its work being passed to the London Boroughs, Government Departments and Government-appointed bodies, and to joint boards and committees.

The London Residuary Body (L.R.B.) was established by the Local Government Act, 1985, which abolished the G.L.C. Its function is to wind up the affairs of the G.L.C. within a maximum life of five years. Its tasks fall mainly in three areas:

(i) to clear up functions of the G.L.C. which have not been transferred to other successor bodies. These include debt management, the preparation of the final (i.e. 1985–86) accounts of the G.L.C., and payment of compensation to former G.L.C. staff made redundant.

(ii) to dispose of former G.L.C. properties, other than those such as fire stations, piers and refuse transfer stations passing to other successor bodies.

(iii) to manage former G.L.C. services until new homes have been found for them.

Properties.—One of the L.R.B.'s major duties is the sale of ex-G.L.C. buildings and properties. Amongst the more important are Covent Garden, Feltham shopping centre, Kingsway, Centre Point and County Hall itself. The future of County Hall was undecided at the time of going to press but it still houses the offices of I.L.E.A. and the District Auditor.

Other property including shops, flats, commercial and industrial premises must be disposed of within the L.R.B.'s five year lifespan. With this aim a programme of sales and auctions has been drawn up. A number of options are available for the future of the 35,000 people with G.L.C. mortgages.

Projects.—The L.R.B. has several projects which it is managing with a view to transference at a later date. They include:

(i) Traffic control—Central London's traffic lights are operated by L.R.B. on behalf of the Department of Transport.

(ii) The North–South route, an existing G.L.C. project which will be completed by the L.R.B., although the two Boroughs which it connects, Enfield and Haringey, will bear the expected £73,000,000 cost.

Recreation, Parks, etc.—The G.L.C.'s responsibility for the arts facilities on the South Bank has been taken over by the South Bank Board and the Arts Council. Responsibility for the historic buildings, parks, open spaces, etc. previously run by the G.L.C. has devolved onto the Borough Councils or bodies such as English Heritage.

Land Drainage and Flood Prevention.—These functions are now exercised by the Borough Councils and the Thames Water Authority.

Scientific Services.—London Scientific Services, formerly the G.L.C. Scientific Services Branch, continues its work as an advisory service helping the London Boroughs and other agencies, although at present its future is undecided.

Finance.—The boroughs and successor bodies finance the L.R.B. In Feb. 1987 the budget which was drawn up was £480,000,000, the boroughs meeting a £21,500,000 levy and the remainder coming from grants, mortgage repayments and rents, in addition to G.L.C. balances which were inherited at abolition. Surplus funds have been distributed amongst the boroughs and a further £142,000,000 in capital receipts, mainly from the sale of former G.L.C. properties and land, is being distributed.

LONDON RESIDUARY BODY, St. Vincent House, 30 Orange Street, WC2H 7HH. (01-633 5000).
Chairman, Sir Godfrey Taylor.
Director of Administration, J. Howes.
Director of Finance, C. McArdle.

Education

The local education authority for an area corresponding with the area of the twelve inner London boroughs and the City of London is the Inner London Education Authority. Under the Local Government Act, 1985, I.L.E.A. became a directly-elected body, taking over responsibility for the education service on April 1, 1986. The first elections of the 58 members took place on May 8, 1986, and subsequent elections will be held every four years. The 20 outer London Borough Councils remain the education authorities for their Boroughs.

The total number of pupils on the rolls of the Authority's nursery, primary and secondary schools (including special schools for handicapped children) is 289,372. There are 1,064 schools, staffed by the equivalent of 20,156 full-time teachers. Vocational instruction, cultural studies and recreational activities for persons over compulsory school age are arranged at the various establishments for further education. The Authority maintains 19 colleges and makes grants to 5 polytechnics and 2 other institutions. Part-time classes are offered at 20 adult education and literary institutes, and 82 youth centres, including 2 drama centres.

Since the G.L.C.'s abolition, I.L.E.A. is solely responsible for the Geffrye and Horniman Museums.

I.L.E.A., County Hall, SE1 7PB (01-633 5000).

Transport

The G.L.C.'s responsibility, through the London Transport Executive, for transport services in London was transferred in June 1984 to the London Regional Transport board (*see* p. 411), which is responsible to the Secretary of State for Transport. Former G.L.C. responsibilities, including the maintenance of the Thames bridges, ferries and tunnels, have been passed to the Borough councils and to the Department of Transport.

Solid waste disposal

Responsibility for the disposal of refuse throughout London lies with the London Waste Regulation Authority, operationally organised into eight borough groupings.

There are four statutory bodies—*West London Waste Authority* (Brent, Ealing, Harrow, Hillingdon, Hounslow, Richmond upon Thames), *North London Waste Authority* (Barnet, Camden, Enfield, Hackney, Haringey, Islington, Waltham Forest), *East London Waste Authority* (Barking and Dagenham, Havering, Newham, Redbridge) and *Western Riverside Waste Authority* (Hammersmith and Fulham, Kensington and Chelsea, Lambeth, Wandsworth).

In addition, there are four voluntary groupings— Bromley, Croydon, Kingston upon Thames, Merton, Sutton (*Group 1*), Greenwich, Lewisham, Southwark (*Group 2*), City of London, City of Westminster, Tower Hamlets (*Group 6*), and Bexley.

LONDON WASTE REGULATION AUTHORITY, County Hall, SE1 7PB (01-633 2786/7346).

Fire Services

The successor authority for London's fire service is the London Fire and Civil Defence Authority (L.F.C.D.A.), with effect from April 1, 1986. The Fire Brigade is now organised into five Area Commands, which coincide with Borough boundaries. The L.F.C.D.A.'s responsibilities also include petroleum licensing.

LONDON FIRE AND CIVIL DEFENCE AUTHORITY, London Fire Brigade Headquarters, 8 Albert Embankment, SE1 7SD (01-582 3811).

LONDON AND ITS ENVIRONS

(For National Art Galleries and Museums in London and for London Cathedrals, Churches, etc. see Index.)

Adelphi, Strand, W.C.2.—Adelphi Terrace and district commemorate the four Adam brothers, James, John, Robert and William, who laid out the district (formerly Durham House) at the close of the 18th century, though few 18th century buildings now remain. Four of the streets were formerly called after the brothers but are now Adam Street, John Adam Street, Robert Street and Durham House Street. In the neighbourhood of the Adelphi was York House, built by the Duke of Buckingham in 1625 (the Water Gate of which still stands in Embankment Gardens), the commemorative streets being Charles Street, Villiers Street, Duke Street, Buckingham Street.

Alexandra Palace and Park, Wood Green, N.22.—Set in a park of 200 acres, the second Palace was completed in 1875 at a cost of £400,000. Although it suffered severe damage from fire in July 1980 the redevelopment of the building is well underway for the re-opening in 1988. Alexandra Palace will provide modern facilities for exhibitions, sports, meetings and leisure activities. Meanwhile, events continue in the Alexander Pavilion adjacent to the Palace. Trusteeship of the Palace devolved onto Haringey Council on Jan. 1, 1980.

Baltic Exchange, St. Mary Axe, E.C.3.—The world market for the chartering of cargo ships. The present Exchange was built in 1903 and the new wing opened by H.M. The Queen on Nov. 21, 1956.

Bank of England, Threadneedle Street, E.C.2. (Not open to the public)—The Bank of England, founded in 1694, has always been closely connected with the Government. The present building, completed in 1940 to the designs of Sir Herbert Baker, incorporates features reminiscent of the earlier architects, Sampson (1734), Sir Robert Taylor (1765) and Sir John Soane (1788).

Banqueting House, Whitehall, S.W.1.—The only important building left of the great Palace of Whitehall. The previous banqueting house was burnt down in 1619, and replaced by the present structure designed by Inigo Jones. In 1635 it was enriched with Rubens' ceiling paintings. Charles I was executed on a scaffold set up just in front of the present entrance. Open Tues.–Sat. 10–5, Sun. 2–5. Closed Mon. Admission (1987) 70p, concessions 35p.

Barbican Centre, EC2Y 8DS.—Owned, funded and managed by the Corporation of London, the Barbican Centre was opened on March 3, 1982 by H.M. The Queen, and is the largest complex of its kind in Western Europe. It houses the 1,166 seat Barbican Theatre, now the London base of the Royal Shakespeare Company, along with a smaller 200 seat studio theatre (The Pit), and the 2,026 seat Barbican Hall, the home of the London Symphony Orchestra. There are also three cinemas, an art gallery, a sculpture court, a large lending library, facilities for trade exhibitions and conferences, and bars and restaurants.

Blackheath, S.E.10.—272 acres of parkland. Morden College, founded in 1695 as a home for "decayed Turkey merchants", is near the S.E. corner. The building was designed by Wren and its Chapel doors have carvings attributed to Grinling Gibbons. Concerts and poetry recitals are held at Rangers House, an early 18th century mansion, which houses the Suffolk collection of English portraits from the Elizabethan to the Georgian period. (The house, concerts, etc. are now the responsibility of English Heritage.)

Bridges.—The bridges over the Thames (from East to West) are: *Tower Bridge* (built by the Corporation of London and opened in 1894), with its bascules, operated now by new electrically-run machinery, walkway, opened to the public in 1982, and museum, opened in 1983; *London Bridge* (opened after rebuilding in 1831 by Rennie; the new London Bridge was completed in 1973 and opened by H.M. The Queen on March 16, 1973); *Southwark Bridge* (opened in 1819, also by Rennie; rebuilt by the Corporation of London, 1922); *Blackfriars Bridge* (opened in 1769, rebuilt, 1869, and widened by the Corporation of London in 1909); *Waterloo Bridge* (Rennie), opened in 1817, commanding a fine view of western London, rebuilt by L.C.C. and reopened 1944; *Hungerford Bridge,* 1863 (railway bridge with a footbridge); *Westminster Bridge* (built in 1750 and then presenting a view that inspired Wordsworth's sonnet; rebuilt and re-opened in 1862; width, 84 ft.) with Thomas Thornycroft's *Boadicea* at the north-eastern end; this bridge leads from Westminster Abbey and the Houses of Parliament to the County Hall and St. Thomas' Hospital; *Lambeth Bridge* (built 1862, rebuilt 1932) leading from Lambeth Palace to Millbank; *Vauxhall Bridge* (built in 1811–16, rebuilt in 1906), leading to Kennington Oval; *Chelsea Bridge,* leading from Chelsea Hospital to Battersea Park (reconstructed and widened, 1937) and *Albert Bridge* (1873); *Battersea Bridge* (opened in 1890); *Wandsworth Bridge* (opened in 1873; rebuilt and re-opened in 1940); *Putney Bridge* (built 1729, rebuilt 1884, widened in 1933), where the Oxford and Cambridge Boat Race is started for Mortlake; *Hammersmith Bridge* (rebuilt 1887); *Barnes Bridge* (for pedestrians only, 1933); *Chiswick Bridge* (opened in 1933); *King Edward VII Bridge, Kew* (rebuilt in 1902, opened 1903), leading to the Royal Botanic Gardens, Kew; *Twickenham Lock Bridge; Twickenham Bridge* (opened 1933); *Richmond Bridge* (opened in 1777); *Kingston Bridge* (built 1828 and widened 1914) and *Hampton Court Bridge* (rebuilt, 1933).

Buckingham Palace, St. James's Park, S.W.1. (Not open to the public.)—Purchased by King George III in 1762 from the heir of the Duke of Buckingham, the Palace has been the London home of the Sovereign since Queen Victoria's accession in 1837. It was altered by Nash for King George IV, and refronted in stone (part of the Queen Victoria Memorial) by Sir Aston Webb in 1913.

The Queen's Gallery, containing a changing selection of the finest pictures and works of art from all parts of the royal collection, was opened to the public on July 25, 1962. Open Tues.–Sat. and Bank Holidays 11–5, Sun. 2–5. Admission charges are payable, entering from Buckingham Palace Road.

The Royal Mews is open to visitors on Wed. and Thurs. throughout the year (except in Ascot Week), 2–4. Admission charges, the net proceeds of which are devoted to charities, are payable at the entrance.

Canada House, Trafalgar Square, S.W.1.—Designed by Sir Robert Smirke and built in 1824–7, it underwent major alterations to incorporate the former Royal College of Physicians building, also by Smirke, between 1964–67. Certain interior features of the original building, now housing the Canadian High Commission, are preserved including the spacious, richly furnished room now occupied by the High Commissioner.

Canonbury Tower, N.1.—The largest remaining part of a 16th century house originally built by the Priors of St. Bartholomew, and since 1952 used as the headquarters of a non-professional theatre company. Contains the "Spencer" and "Compton" oak-panelled rooms. Other relics of Canonbury House can be seen nearby.

Carlyle's House, 24 Cheyne Row, Chelsea, S.W.3. The home of Thomas Carlyle for 47 years until his death in 1881, and containing many of his effects. Now the property of the National Trust. Open daily, April–Oct. Wed.–Sun. and Bank Holiday Mondays 11–5. Admission £1·40; concessions 70p.

Catholic Central Library, St. Francis Friary, 47 Francis Street, SW1P 1QR.—Founded as a private library in 1914, it was taken over in 1959 by the Franciscan Friars of the Atonement. It is an up-to-date lending and research library of over 55,000 volumes and 150 periodicals, for the general reader, student and ecumenist. Books are sent by post when required. Open Mon.-Fri. 10–5, Sat. 10–1.30.

Cemeteries.—In *Kensal Green Cemetery*, North Kensington, W.10 (70 acres), are tombs of Thackeray, Trollope, Sydney Smith, Wilkie Collins, Tom Hood, George Cruikshank, John Leech, Leigh Hunt, I. K. Brunel, Charles Kemble (actor). In *Highgate Cemetery*, N.6, are the tombs of George Eliot, Herbert Spencer, Faraday and Marx. In *Abney Park Cemetery*, Stoke Newington, N.16 are the tomb of General Booth, founder of the Salvation Army, and memorials to many Nonconformist Divines. In the *South Metropolitan Cemetery*, Norwood, S.E.27, are the tombs of Sir Henry Bessemer, Sir Hiram Maxim, Mrs. Beeton, Sir Henry Tate and Joseph Whitaker, F.S.A. (*Whitaker's Almanack*). In the churchyard of the former *Marylebone Chapel* are buried Charles Wesley and his son Samuel Wesley (musician). The chapel itself was demolished in 1949. **Crematoria.**—*Ilford* (City of London); *Norwood*; *Hendon*; *Streatham Park*; *Finchley* (St. Marylebone) and *Golders Green* (12 acres), near Hampstead Heath, with "Garden of Rest" and memorials to famous men and women.

Cenotaph, Whitehall, S.W.1.—(Literally "empty tomb"). Monument erected "To the Glorious Dead", as a memorial to all ranks of the Sea, Land and Air Forces who gave their lives in the service of the Empire during the First World War. Designed by Sir Edwin Lutyens. Erected as a temporary memorial in 1919 and replaced by a permament structure in 1920. Unveiled by King George V on Armistice Day, 1920. An additional inscription was added after the 1939-45 War to commemorate those who gave their lives in that conflict.

Charterhouse, Sutton's Hospital, Charterhouse Square, E.C.1. (*Master*, E. E. Harrison, M.A., F.S.A.; *Registrar and Clerk to the Governors*, Lt. Col. I. Macdonald). A Carthusian monastery from 1371–1537, when it came into the possession of Sir Edward (later first Lord) North, who sold it in 1565 to the fourth Duke of Norfolk. After his execution in 1572, following the Ridolfi Plot, hatched at Charterhouse, it was eventually granted by Queen Elizabeth, in 1587, to Norfolk's second son, Thomas Howard, Earl of Suffolk. In 1608 he sold it to Thomas Sutton, who endowed it as a Hospital for aged men "of gentle birth" and a School for Boys (removed to Godalming in 1872). The buildings are partly 14th but mainly 15th and 16th century. The Duke's private palace was destroyed by enemy action in the Second World War, but the Hall, Chapel and Great Chamber are intact or restored and now accommodate some 30 Brothers. Roger Williams, founder and governor of Rhode Island, was a scholar on the Foundation. Among other famous pupils were John Wesley, Lord Baden-Powell, the poets and writers Crashaw, Lovelace and Thackeray, and more recently Lord Beveridge. Visitors are shown round on Wednesdays at 2.45 (April–July). Admission £1.50.

Chelsea Physic Garden, 66 Royal Hospital Road, SW3 4HS.—A garden of general botanical research, maintaining a wide range of rare and unusual plants.

Established in 1673 by the Society of Apothecaries, now administered by the Chelsea Physic Garden Co. Ltd. Open to the public on Wed. and Sun. p.m. during summer months. All enquiries to the Curator at above address.

Chelsea, Royal Hospital, Royal Hospital Road, Chelsea, S.W.3. Founded by Charles II, in 1682, and built by Wren; opened in 1692 for old and disabled soldiers. Great Hall, Chapel and Museum open daily 10–12, 2–4 (Museum closed on Sunday afternoons Oct.–March). The extensive grounds include the former Ranelagh Gardens, and are the venue for the Chelsea Flower Show held each May by the Royal Horticultural Society. *Governor*, General Sir Roland Guy, G.C.B., C.B.E., D.S.O.; *Lieut-Governor and Secretary*, Major-Gen. A. L. Watson, C.B.

City Business Library (Corporation of London), 55 Basinghall Street, EC2V 5BX. Open Mon.-Fri. 9.30-5.00.

College of Arms or Heralds' College, Queen Victoria Street, E.C.4—Her Majesty's Officers of Arms (Kings, Heralds and Pursuivants of Arms) were first incorporated by Richard III, and granted Derby House on the site of the present College building by Philip and Mary. The building now in use dates from 1671–88. The powers vested by the Crown in the Earl Marshal (The Duke of Norfolk) with regard to State ceremonial are largely exercised through the College, which is also the official repository of English pedigrees and all Arms granted to subjects of the Queen (except in Scotland). Enquiry may be made to the Officer on duty in the Public Office, Mon.-Fri. 10–4.

The Heralds Museum at the Tower of London (admission charge included in the Tower's own charge) aims to explain what heraldry is about and traces its development over the centuries to its application and use in modern times. Open April–Sept.

Commonwealth Institute, Kensington High Street, W.8.—A cultural and educational centre opened on Nov. 6, 1962, by Her Majesty the Queen, replacing the former Imperial Institute opened in 1893 in S. Kensington. A distinctive feature of the building is its paraboloid copper-sheathed roof. The Institute contains, in 60,000 square feet arranged in 3 floors of circular galleries, a visual representation of the history, geography and ways of life of the Commonwealth countries and dependencies, as well as art galleries, a cinema, a theatre, a Teachers' Resource Centre, a restaurant and a bookshop.

Open weekdays 10–5.30, Sun. 2–5. Admission free. Closed Christmas Eve, Christmas Day, Boxing Day, New Year's Day, Good Friday and May Day.

County Hall, Westminster Bridge, S.E.1.—Formerly the Headquarters of the Greater London Council, built on the Pedlar's Acre, Bishop's Acre, Four Acres and Float Mead, Lambeth, from the designs of Ralph Knott, with a river façade of 750 ft. The main building was completed in 1933. The North and South blocks were occupied in 1939 but not finally completed until 1963.

Courtauld Institute Galleries, University of London, Woburn Square, WC1.—The galleries of the University of London contain the Lee collection and the Gambier–Parry collections (14th century to 18th century old masters); the important Courtauld collection of Impressionist and Post-Impressionist paintings; the Roger Fry collection and the Witt and Spooner collections (old master drawings and English water-colours). A major new bequest, the Princes Gate collection of old master paintings and drawings, was opened to the public in July 1981. Open weekdays 10–5, Sun. 2–5. Admission £1·50, concessions 50p.

Custom House, Lower Thames Street, E.C.3.—Built 1813–17, with a wide quay on Thames. The Long Room is about 190 ft. long.

Dickens House, 48 Doughty Street, W.C.1.—In this house Charles Dickens lived from 1837 to 1839, and here he completed *Pickwick Papers.* It is the headquarters of the Dickens Fellowship and contains many relics of the novelist. Open daily 10–5 (except Sundays and Bank Holidays). Admission £1·50, concessions 75p/50p, family ticket £3.

Downing Street.—Number 10 Downing Street, S.W.1, is the official town residence of the Prime Minister, No. 11 of the Chancellor of the Exchequer and No. 12 is the office of the Government Whips. The street was named after Sir George Downing, Bt. soldier and diplomatist, who was M.P. for Morpeth from 1660 to 1684.

Chequers, a Tudor mansion in the Chilterns, about 3 miles from Princes Risborough, was presented together with a maintenance endowment by Lord and Lady Lee of Fareham in 1917 to serve, from Jan. 1, 1921, as a country residence for the Prime Minister of the day, the Chequers estate of 700 acres being added to the gift by Lord Lee in 1921. The mansion contains a famous collection of Cromwellian portraits and relics.

Dr. Johnson's House, Gough Square, Fleet Street, E.C.4.—A tall late 17th century house in which Johnson (and his wife) lived between 1748 and 1759. His *Dictionary* was compiled here. The house is furnished with 18th century pieces and there is an excellent collection of Johnsoniana. Open daily (except Sundays and Bank Holidays) 11–5.30 (winter 11–5). Admission £1·30, concessions 80p.

Dulwich, S.E.21.—Contains *Dulwich College* (founded by Edward Alleyn in 1619) and the *Dulwich Picture Gallery,* built by Sir John Soane to house the collection bequeathed by the artist Sir Francis Bourgeois. The gallery was damaged in the Second World War but rebuilt with the aid of a grant from the Pilgrim Trust and reopened in 1953. *Dulwich Village* retains many of the rural characteristics of the pre-suburban period.

Eltham, S.E.9.—Contains remains of 13th–15th century *Eltham Palace,* the birthplace of John of Eltham (1316), son of Edward II. The hall, built by Edward IV, has a hammer-beam roof of chestnut. In the churchyard of St. John the Baptist is the tomb of *Thomas Doggett,* the comedian and founder of the Thames Watermen's championship (Doggett's Coat and Badge).

Ely Place, Holborn Circus, E.C.1.—Previously the site of the London house of the Bishop of Ely, Ely Place is a private street (built in 1773) whose affairs are administered by Commissioners under a special Act of Parliament. The 14th century chapel, now St. Ethelreda's (R.C.) Church, is open daily until dusk.

Eton College.—The most famous of English public schools, founded by Henry VI in 1440. The buildings date from 1442.

Fulham Palace, Bishop's Avenue, Fulham, S.W.6.—The courtyard is 16th century, remainder 18th and 19th century. Former residence of the Bishop of London.

Geffrye Museum, Kingsland Road, E.2.—Open on Tuesdays to Saturdays 10 to 5, Sundays 2 to 5. Closed on Christmas Eve, Christmas Day, Boxing Day and New Year's Day and on Mondays except Bank Holidays. Admission free.

The Museum is housed in a building erected originally as almshouses in 1713. It was eventually purchased by the L.C.C. and opened as a museum in 1914. The exhibits are shown in a series of period rooms dating from 1600 to 1939, each containing furniture and domestic equipment of a middle-class English home. An 18th century woodworker's shop, an openhearth kitchen and the original chapel are also shown, together with a selection of costume. Temporary exhibitions are held in the Exhibition Hall. There is a reference library of books on furniture, social history and art. Special arrangements for children visiting the Museum in school parties (which must be booked in advance) and in their leisure time. *Director,* D. Rodgers.

George Inn, Southwark.—Near London Bridge Station. Given to the National Trust in 1937. Last galleried inn in London, built in 1677. Open during licensed hours.

Greenwich, S.E.10.—*Greenwich Hospital* (since 1873, the Royal Naval College) was built by Charles II, largely from designs by John Webb, and by Queen Anne and William III, from designs by Wren, on the site of an ancient royal palace, and of the more recent *Palace of Placentia,* an enlarged edition of the palace, constructed by Humphrey, Duke of Gloucester (1391–1447), son of Henry IV. Henry VIII, Queen Mary I and Queen Elizabeth I were born in the Royal Palace (which reverted to the Crown in 1447) and King Edward VI died there. In the principal quadrangle is a marble statue of George II, by Rysbraeck. (For *National Maritime Museum,* see Index.) *Painted Hall* and *Chapel* open daily (except Thursdays) 2.30–5. Visitors are also admitted to Sunday Service in the Chapel at 11 a.m., summer and winter, except during College vacations. *Greenwich Park* (196½ acres) was enclosed by Humphrey, Duke of Gloucester, and laid out by Charles II, from the designs of Le Nôtre. *The Queen's House,* begun in 1616, was designed for Anne of Denmark by Inigo Jones (closed for repairs from Oct. 1984). On a hill in Greenwich Park is the former Royal Observatory (founded 1675). Part of its buildings at Greenwich have been taken over by the Maritime Museum and named *Flamsteed House,* after John Flamsteed (1646–1719), first Astronomer Royal. Astronomical and navigational equipment is exhibited, and the time ball and zero meridian of longitude can also be seen. The Parish church of Greenwich (*St. Alfege*) was rebuilt by Hawksmoor (Wren's pupil) in 1728, and restored after severe damage during the Second World War. General Wolfe and Thomas Tallis are buried in the church. Henry VIII was christened in the former church. *Charlton House,* built in the early 17th century (1607–1612) for Adam Newton, tutor to Prince Henry, brother to Charles I, is largely in the Jacobean style of architecture. *Cutty Sark,* the last of the famous tea clippers, which has been preserved as a memorial to ships and men of a past era is fully restored and re-rigged, with a museum of sail on board. Open weekdays 11–5 (summer 11–6), Sundays and Boxing Day 2.30–5. The yacht *Gipsy Moth IV* in which Sir Francis Chichester sailed single-handed round the world, 1966–67, is preserved alongside the *Cutty Sark.*

Guildhall, Gresham Street, City, E.C.2.—Scene of civic government for the City for more than a thousand years. Built *c.* 1440; façade built 1788–9; damaged in the Great Fire, 1666, and by incendiary bombs, 1940. The main hall and crypt (the most extensive medieval crypt in London) have been restored. Events in Guildhall include the annual election of Lord Mayor, election of Sheriffs, receptions in honour of Sovereigns and Heads of State, and the meetings of the Court of Common Council (*see* "Corporation of London"). Open weekdays 10–5, Sun. (May to Sept.) 10–4. Admission free. *Keeper of the Guildhall,* J. H. Lucioni.

The Guildhall (reference) Library and the Library and Museum of the Clockmakers' Company are housed in new premises. Library open Mon.–Sat. 9.30–5, Museum open Mon. to Fri. 9.30–4.45. Admission free (entrance in Aldermanbury). The Library contains Plans of London, 1570; Deed of Sale with Shakespeare's signature; first, second and fourth folios of Shakespeare's plays etc. (*See also* City Business Library).

Ham House, Richmond.—A notable example of 17th century domestic architecture, long the home of the Tollemache family (Earls of Dysart). The contents were purchased for the Victoria and Albert Museum which now administers the house. Open Tues.–Sun. 11–5. Closed Mon. (except Bank Holidays), Christmas Eve, Christmas Day, Boxing Day, New Year's Day, Good Friday and May Day. Admission £2, concessions £1.

Hampton Court.—Sixteenth-century Palace built by Cardinal Wolsey, with additions by Sir Christopher Wren for William and Mary. Beautiful gardens with maze and grape vine (planted in 1769). State Apartments and collection of pictures. Tennis Court, built by King Henry VIII in 1530. Collection of Mantegna paintings. Gardens open daily 7–9 (or dusk), Maze March–Oct. Hours for specific areas of Palace vary. State apartments open April–Sept. Mon.–Sat. 9.30–6, Sun. 11–6; Oct.–March, Mon.–Sat. 9.30–5, Sun. 2–5. Admission prices vary for specific attractions: all-inclusive ticket £2·80. Gardens free.

Harrow.—Public school founded by John Lyon in 1571. The "Fourth Form Room" dates from 1608.

Holland Park, W.8.—55 acres including an open air theatre and concerts; floodlit gardens; King George VI Memorial Youth Hostel; restaurant.

Honourable Artillery Company's Headquarters, City Road, E.C.1.—The H.A.C. (*Chief Exec.* Capt. G. C. Lloyd, C.B.E., R.N.) received its charter of incorporation from Henry VIII in 1537, and has occupied its present ground since 1641. The Armoury House dates from 1735. The present castellated barracks date from 1860. Four of its members who emigrated in the 17th century, founded in 1638 the Ancient and Honorable Artillery Company of Massachusetts. The H.A.C. is the senior regiment of the Territorial Army Volunteer Reserves, and maintains a Headquarters, four squadrons, a gun troop, and two companies of the Home Service Force.

Horniman Museum and Library, London Road, Forest Hill, S.E.23.—The Museum was presented in 1901 to the London County Council by the founder, Mr. F. J. Horniman, M.P. It is now administered by I.L.E.A. The Museum has three main departments, ethnography, musical instruments and natural history. In the ethnography department the large collections include exhibits illustrating man's progress in the arts and crafts from prehistoric times. The natural history department includes an aquarium. Reference library (except Mondays). Education Service (adults and schoolchildren). Free concerts and lectures (autumn and spring). Special exhibitions. *Director,* D. M. Boston, O.B.E. Open Mon.–Sat. 10.30–6, Sun. 2–6. Admission free.

Horse Guards, Whitehall, S.W.1.—Archway and offices built about 1753. The mounting of the guard (Life Guards, or the Blues and Royals) at 11 a.m. (10 a.m. on Sundays) and the dismounted inspection at 4 p.m. are picturesque ceremonies. Only those on the Lord Chamberlain's list may drive through the gates and archway into *Horse Guard's Parade* (230,000 sq. ft.), where the Colour is "trooped" on the Queen's Official Birthday.

The Houses of Parliament, Westminster, S.W.1.—An ordinance issued in the reign of Richard II stated that "Parliament shall be holden or kepid wheresoever it pleaseth the King" and at the present day the Sovereign summons Parliament to meet and prescribes the time and place of meeting. The royal palace of Westminster, originally built by Edward the Confessor (Westminster Hall (*q.v.*) being added by William Rufus), was the normal place of Parliament from about 1340. St. Stephen's Chapel (first mentioned in the reign of John) was used from about 1550 for the meetings of the House of Commons, which had previously been held in the Chapter House or Refectory of Westminster Abbey. The House of Lords met in an apartment of the royal palace.

The fire of 1834 destroyed the whole palace, except Westminster Hall, and the present Houses of Parliament were erected on the site from the designs of Sir Charles Barry and Augustus Welby Pugin between 1840 and 1867, at a cost of £2,198,000. The Chamber of the House of Commons was destroyed by enemy action in 1941 and the foundation stone of a new building, from the designs of Sir Giles Gilbert Scott, was laid by the Speaker on May 26, 1948. The new Chamber was used for the first time on Oct. 26, 1950.

The Victoria Tower of the House of Lords is about 330 ft. high, and when Parliament is sitting the Union Flag flies by day from its flagstaff. *The Clock Tower* of the House of Commons is about 320 ft. high and contains "Big Ben", the hour bell said to be named after Sir Benjamin Hall, First Commissioner of Works when the original bell was cast in 1856. This bell, which weighed 16 tons 11 cwt., was found to be cracked in 1857. The present bell (13½ tons) is a recasting of the original and was first brought into use in July, 1859. The dials of the clock are 23 ft. in diameter, the hands being 9 ft. and 14 ft. long (including balance piece). A light is displayed from the Clock Tower at night when Parliament is sitting.

The Houses of Parliament are not open to the general public. All arrangements for visits must be made through a Member of Parliament.

Admission to the Strangers' Gallery of the House of Lords is arranged by a Peer or by queue *via* the St. Stephen's Entrance. Admission to the Strangers' Gallery of the House of Commons, is by Members' order (Members' orders should be sought well in advance), or by queue *via* St. Stephen's Entrance. Queues are usually shorter after 6 p.m., Mon.–Thurs. Overseas visitors may obtain cards of introduction from their Embassy or High Commission.

Inns of Court.—The *Inner* and *Middle Temple,* S. of Fleet Street, E.C.4, and N. of Victoria Embankment, to which the gardens extend, have occupied (since early 14th century) the site of the buildings of the Order of Knights Templars. *Inner Temple Hall* (rebuilt in 1955 after bomb damage) is open Mon.–Fri. 10.30–11.30 and 3–4 on application to Treasurer's Office during law sittings. *Temple Church*, restored in 1958 after severe damage by bombing, is open on weekdays 9.30–4 and the public is admitted to Sunday services. *Middle Temple Hall* (1562–70) is open when not in use, Mon.–Fri. 10–12 and 3–4, Sat. when staff are available. Closed on Public Holidays. In Middle Temple Gardens (not open to the public) Shakespeare (Henry VI, Part I) places the incident which led to the "Wars of the Roses" (1455–85). *Lincoln's Inn,* from Chancery Lane to Lincoln's Inn Fields, W.C.2, occupies the site of the palace of a former Bishop of Chichester and of a Black Friars monastery. Records show the Society as being in existence in 1422. The Hall and Library Buildings are of 1845, although the Library is first mentioned in 1474, the old Hall early 16th century and the Chapel was rebuilt c. 1619–23. Halls open by appointment, Chapel and Gardens, Mon.–Fri. 12–2.30. Chapel services Sun. 11.30 a.m. during Law Terms. *Lincoln's Inn Fields* (7 acres). The Square, laid out by Inigo Jones, contains many fine old houses with handsome interiors. *Gray's Inn,* Holborn/Gray's Inn Road, W.C.1. Early 14th century. Hall (1556–60). Chapel (largely rebuilt in 1698). Services 11.15 a.m. (during Law Dining Terms only.) Holy Communion 1st Sunday in every month except Aug.–Sept. Public welcome. Library (30,000 vols., mss. and printed books) may be viewed by appointment. Gardens open to the public May–Sept. 12–2.30. The Inn, although badly damaged during the last war, has been completely restored to its former beauty with gracious red brick buildings overlooking grass covered squares and gardens. Strong Elizabethan associations. No other "Inns" are active, but what remains of *Staple Inn* is worth visiting as a relic of Elizabethan London; though heavy damage was done by a flying-bomb, it retains a picturesque gabled front on Holborn (opposite Gray's Inn Road). *Clement's Inn* (near St. Clement Danes' Church), *Clifford's Inn,* Fleet Street, and *Thavies Inn,* Holborn Circus, are all rebuilt. *Serjeant's Inn,* Fleet Street (damaged by bombing) and another (demolished 1910) of the same name in Chancery Lane, were composed of Serjeants-at-Law, the last of whom died in 1922.

Jewish Museum, Woburn House, Tavistock Square, WC1H 0EP.—Opened in 1932, the Museum contains a rich collection of ceremonial art, portraits and antiquities, illustrating Jewish life, history and religion. Open Tues.–Thurs. (and Fri. in summer) 10–4, Sun. (and Fri. in winter) 10–12.45. Closed on Public and Jewish Holidays. Group visits by arrangement with Secretary.

Keats House, Keats Grove, Hampstead, NW3 2RR.—In two houses here, now made into one, John Keats lived at various times between 1818 and 1820. Restored 1974–75. Open weekdays 10–6, Sundays and Bank Holidays 2–5. Closed on Christmas Day, Boxing Day, New Year's Day, Good Friday, Easter Eve and May Day. The Keats Memorial Library contains over 7,000 volumes.

Kensington Palace, W.8.—The original house was bought by William III in 1689 and enlarged by Christoper Wren. The birthplace of Queen Victoria in 1819. The State Apartments contain pictures and furniture from the royal collections. A suite of rooms devoted to the memory of Queen Victoria is also shown. The *Court Dress Collection* is also open, and includes three restored rooms, the Red Saloon, the Teck Saloon and the room where Queen Victoria is said to have been born. Both open weekdays 9–5, Sun. 1–5. Admission £2·50, concessions £1·25.

Kenwood, N.W.3.—The 200 acres forming the northern part of Hampstead Heath. Part purchased in 1922 by public subscription. Open air symphony concerts each summer. The Iveagh Bequest, in an 18th-century mansion (open to the public), includes valuable art treasures. Recitals and poetry readings in the Orangery. (The house, concerts, etc., are now administered by English Heritage.)

Kew, Surrey.—A favourite home of the early Hanoverian monarchs. Kew House, the residence of Frederick, Prince of Wales, and later of his son, George III, was pulled down in 1803, but the earlier Dutch House, now known as Kew Palace, survives. It was built in 1631 and acquired by George III as an annexe to Kew House in 1781. The famous Kew Gardens (*see* Index) were originally laid out as a private garden for Kew House for George III's mother in 1759 and were much enlarged in the 19th century, notably by the inclusion of the grounds of the former Richmond Lodge.

Kneller Hall, Twickenham.—Royal Military School of Music. A band of up to 120 instrumentalists gives concerts in the grounds on Wednesdays throughout the summer, commencing at 8 p.m.

Admission £1 (Grand concerts, £1·50). Season tickets and party bookings available.

Lambeth Palace, S.E.1.—The official residence of the Archbishop of Canterbury, on south bank of Thames; the oldest part is 13th century, the house itself is early 19th century. For leave to visit the historical portions, applications should be made by letter to the Archbishop's Chaplain.

Livery Companies' Halls.—The Principal Companies (*see* Index) have magnificent halls but admission to view them has generally to be arranged beforehand. The following are among the finest or more interesting. *Goldsmiths' Hall,* Foster Lane. The present hall was completed in 1835, and contains some magnificent rooms. Exhibitions of plate have been shown here periodically in recent years. *Fishmongers' Hall,* London Bridge (built 1831–3), now admirably restored after severe bomb damage, also contains fine rooms. *Apothecaries' Hall,* Black Friars Lane, was rebuilt in 1670, after the Great Fire, and has library, hall and kitchen which are good examples of this period, together with a pleasant courtyard. *Vintners' Hall,* Upper Thames Street, was also rebuilt after the Great Fire, and its hall has very fine late 17th century panelling. The Watermen and Lightermen's Company is not, strictly speaking, a Livery Company, but its *Hall,* in St. Mary at Hill, is a good example of a smaller 18th century building, with pilastered façade. It was completed in 1780. *Stationers' Hall,* in Stationers' Hall Court, behind Ludgate Hill, another post-fire Hall, standing in its own court, has a particularly finely carved screen; its façade dates from 1800. *Barbers' Hall,* Monkwell Street, with a Hall attributed to Inigo Jones, was completely destroyed by bombing, but has now been rebuilt. The new hall was built some 30 ft. from the old site to enable one of the bastions and part of the wall of the Roman fort to remain exposed to view.

Lloyd's, Lime Street, EC3M 7HA.—Housed in the Royal Exchange for 150 years and in Leadenhall Street and Lime Street from 1928–1986. The present building was opened for business in May 1986, and houses the Lutine Bell. Underwriting is on four floors with a total area of 114,000 sq. ft. A visitors' gallery is open daily and incorporates an exhibition showing the history of Lloyds.

London Planetarium, Marylebone Road, NW1 5LR.—Open daily (except Christmas Day), star shows 11–4.30. Admission charge.

London Transport Museum, Covent Garden, W.C.2.—Housed in the former Flower Market, the Museum contains a collection of buses, trams, trolleybuses, trains, working displays and London Transport paraphernalia. There is a research library and lecture theatre. Open daily 10–6 (except Christmas Eve, Christmas Day and Boxing Day). Admission £2·40, concessions £1·10.

Lord's Cricket Ground, St. John's Wood Road, N.W.8.—The headquarters (since 1814) of the Marylebone Cricket Club (founded 1787), the premier cricket club in England, the scene of some of the principal matches of the season and Middlesex County headquarters. Real tennis court and squash courts in building behind members' pavilion.

The Cricket Memorial Gallery, a museum of cricket, open on match days (except Sun.) 10.30–5. Admission £1, concessions 50p. In winter and on non-match days admission is by prior arrangement with the Curator.

Madame Tussaud's Exhibition, Marylebone Road NW1 5LR.—Open daily (except Christmas Day) 10–5.30. Admission charge.

Mansion House, City, E.C.4.—(Built 1739–53, reconstructed 1930–31.) The official residence of the Lord Mayor; the Egyptian Hall and Ballroom are the chief attractions. Admission by order from the Lord Mayor's Secretary.

Marble Hill House, Twickenham (English Heritage).—Example of the English Palladian style, built 1724–9 for Henrietta Howard, Countess of Suffolk, mistress of George II. Houses fine collection of early 18th century paintings and furniture including original overmantel and overdoors by Panini. The house is surrounded by a park, running down to the Thames, which includes an open-air theatre. Open daily (except Fri.) 10– 5, Nov.–Jan. 10–4. Admission free.

Markets.—The London markets (administered by the Corporation of the City of London) provide foodstuffs for 8,500,000 to 9,000,000 people. *Central Meat, Fish, Fruit, Vegetable, and Poultry Markets,* Smithfield (present buildings, 1866) the largest meat market in the world and site of St. Bartholomew's Fair from 9th to 19th century; *Leadenhall Market* (meat and poultry), built 1881, part recently demolished; *Billingsgate* (fish), Thames Street, built 1875, part recently demolished, a market site for over 1,000 years (moved to the Isle of Dogs in Jan. 1982); *Spitalfields,* E.1 (vegetables, fruit, etc.), enlarged 1928, and opened by the late Queen Mary; *London Fruit Exchange,* Brushfield Street, built by Corporation of London 1928–29, faces Spitalfields Market; *Covent Garden* (vegetables, fruit, flowers, etc.), (now moved to Nine Elms) established under a charter of Charles II, in 1661; *Borough Market,* S.E.1 (vegetables, fruit, flowers, etc.).

Marlborough House, Pall Mall, S.W.1.—Built by Wren for the first Duke of Marlborough and completed in 1711, the house finally reverted to the Crown in 1835. Prince Leopold lived there until 1831, and Queen Adelaide from 1837 until her death in 1849. In 1863 it became the London house of the Prince of Wales and was the London home of Queen Mary until her death in 1953. The Queen's Chapel, Marlborough Gate, begun in 1623 from the designs of Inigo Jones for the Infanta Maria of Spain, and completed for Queen Henrietta Maria, is open to the public for services on Sundays at 8.30 a.m. and 11.15 a.m. between Easter Day and end July (*see also* St. James's Palace for winter services in The Chapel Royal). In 1959 Marlborough House was given by the Queen as a centre for Commonwealth Government conferences and it was opened as such in March, 1962.

London Monument (commonly called "The Monument"), Monument Street, E.C.3.—Built from designs of Wren, 1671–77, to commemorate the *Great Fire of London,* which broke out in Pudding Lane, Sept. 2, 1666. The fluted Doric column is 120 ft. high (the moulded cylinder above the balcony supporting a flaming vase of gilt bronze is 42 ft. in addition), and is based on a square plinth 40 ft. high, with fine carvings on W. face (making a total height of 202 ft.). Splendid views of London from gallery at top of column (311 steps). Open Mon.–Fri. 9–2, 3–6 (Oct.–March 9–2, 3–4), Sat. 9–2, 3–4 (Oct.–March), Sat. and Sun. 2–6 (April–Sept.) Closed Christmas Day, Boxing Day and Good Friday. Admission charge.

Monuments.—*Albert Memorial,* South Kensington; *Royal Air Force,* Victoria Embankment; *Beaconsfield,* Parliament Square; *Beatty, Jellicoe* and *Cunningham,* Trafalgar Square; *Belgian Gratitude* (Reginald Blomfield), Victoria Embankment; *Boadicea* (or "Boudicca"), Queen of the Iceni, E. Anglia (Thomas Thornycroft), Westminster Bridge; *Brunel* (Marochetti), Victoria Embankment; *Burghers of Calais* (Rodin), Victoria Tower Gardens, Westmins-

ter; *Burns,* Embankment Gardens; *Carlyle* (Boehm), Cheyne Walk, Chelsea; *Cavalry,* Hyde Park; *Cavell* (Frampton), St. Martin's Place; *Cenotaph* (Lutyens), Whitehall; *Charles I,* Trafalgar Square; *Charles II,* inside the Royal Exchange; *Churchill,* Parliament Square; *Cleopatra's Needle* (68½ ft. high c. 1500 B.C. erected on the Thames Embankment in 1877–8)—the Sphinxes are Victorian; *Clive,* Whitehall; *Captain Cook* (Brock), The Mall; *Crimean,* Broad Sanctuary; *Oliver Cromwell* (Thornycroft), outside Westminster Hall; *Duke of Cambridge,* Whitehall; *Duke of York* (124 ft.), Carlton House Terrace; *Edward VII* (Mackennal), Waterloo Place; *Elizabeth I* (1586, oldest outdoor statue in London) (from Ludgate), Fleet Street; *Eros* (Shaftesbury Memorial) (Gilbert), Piccadilly Circus; *Marechal Foch,* Grosvenor Gardens; *Charles James Fox,* Bloomsbury Square; *George III,* Cockspur Street; *George IV* (Chantrey), riding without stirrups, Trafalgar Square; *George V,* Old Palace Yard; *George VI,* Carlton Gardens; *Gladstone,* facing Australia House, Strand; *Guards'* (Crimea), Waterloo Place; (Great War), Horse Guards' Parade; *Haig* (Hardiman), Whitehall; *Irving* (Brock), N. side of National Portrait Gallery; *James II,* Trafalgar Square; *Samuel Johnson,* opposite St. Clement Danes; *Kitchener,* Horse Guards' Parade; *Abraham Lincoln,* Parliament Square; *Milton,* St. Giles, Cripplegate; *Monument, The* (*see above*); *Mountbatten,* Foreign Office Green; *Nelson* (170 ft. 1½ in.), Trafalgar Square, with Lanseer's lions (cast from guns recovered from the wreck of the *Royal George*); *Florence Nightingale,* Waterloo Place; *Palmerston,* Parliament Square; *Peel,* Parliament Square; *Pitt* (Chantrey), Hanover Square; *Portal,* Embankment Gardens; *Prince Consort,* Holborn Circus; *Raleigh,* Whitehall; *Richard Coeur de Lion* (Marochetti), Old Palace Yard; *Roberts,* Horse Guards' Parade; *Franklin D. Roosevelt* (Reid Dick), Grosvenor Square; *Royal Artillery* (South Africa), The Mall; (Great War), Hyde Park Corner; *Captain Scott* (Lady Scott), Waterloo Place; *Shackleton,* Kensington Gore; *Shakespeare,* Leicester Square; *Smuts* (Epstein), Parliament Square; *Sullivan,* Victoria Embankment; *Trenchard,* Victoria Embankment; *Victoria Memorial,* in front of Buckingham Palace; *George Washington* (Houdon copy), Trafalgar Square; *Wellington,* Hyde Park Corner; *Wellington* (Chantrey) riding without stirrups, Royal Exchange; *John Wesley,* City Road; *William III,* St. James's Square; *Wolseley,* Horse Guards' Parade.

Osterley Park, Osterley, Middx.—House and park of 140 acres given to the National Trust by the Earl of Jersey in 1949 and administered by the Victoria and Albert Museum. The Elizabethan house, built in 1577 for Sir Thomas Gresham, was largely remodelled by Robert Adam, and the staterooms are among the best examples of Adam decoration. Open daily (except Mondays) 11–5. Closed Mon. (except Bank Holidays), Christmas Eve, Christmas Day, Boxing Day, New Year's Day, Good Friday and May Day. Admission £2, concessions £1.

Percival David Foundation of Chinese Art, 53 Gordon Square, W.C.1.—Set up in 1951, the Foundation contains the collection of Chinese ceramics formed by Sir Percival David and his important library of books on Chinese art. To these was added a gift from the Hon. Mountstuart Elphinstone of part of his collection of Chinese monochrome porcelains. The Foundation is administered on behalf of the University of London by the School of Oriental and African Studies. Galleries, Mon.–Fri. 10.30–5. Closed weekends and Bank Holidays. Library available to ticket holders only; applications in writing to the Curator, Miss R. Scott.

Port of London.—The Port of London comprises

the tidal portion of the River Thames from Teddington to the seaward limit (Tongue light vessel), a distance of 95 miles, and one operational dock system and land for redevelopment, covering an area of 3,718 acres, of which 512 acres are water. The governing body is the Port of London Authority, whose Head Office is at Europe House, World Trade Centre, E1 9AA. Particulars of the docks are as follows:—*India & Millwall Docks,* E.14—remaining area vested in Docklands Development Corporation. *Royal Albert & King George V Docks,* E.16—area 512 acres. *Tilbury Docks, Essex*—area 1,037 acres, including 155 acres water. These docks are 26 miles below London Bridge and are used principally by vessels plying on the Australian, North American, Indian, other Eastern routes, West Africa and the Continent. Tilbury Passenger Landing Stage provides accommodation for liners at all states of the tide and adjoins Tilbury Riverside Station. A development and extension scheme at Tilbury added nearly 2 miles of deepwater quays, in addition to a £7 million Grain Terminal. With the Northfleet Hope Development, opened in 1978, Tilbury is capable of handling forest products, containers and roll-on/roll-off traffic.

The *St. Katherine Docks* were sold to the G.L.C. in 1969 and the *London Docks* were closed on May 31, 1969 and sold to Tower Hamlets Council in 1976. *Surrey Commercial Docks* were closed in 1970 and were sold to the G.L.C. and Southwark Council in 1976 and 1977.

Prince Henry's Room, 17 Fleet Street, E.C.4.— Early 17th century timber-framed house containing fine room on first floor with panelling and moulded plaster ceiling. Includes an exhibition on Samuel Pepys and the London in which he lived. Open Mon.– Fri. 1.45–5, Sat 1.45–4.30. Closed Christmas Day, Good Friday and Bank Holidays. Admission free. Available for morning or evening lettings on application to The Town Clerk, Guildhall, E.C.2.

Richmond, Surrey. Contains the red brick gateway of *Richmond Palace* (Henry VII, 1485–1509) and buildings of the Jacobean, Queen Anne, and early Georgian periods, including *White Lodge* in Richmond Park, the former home of Queen Mary's mother (the Duke of Windsor was born there, June 23, 1894), and now the home of the Royal Ballet School. The *Star and Garter* Home for Disabled Soldiers, Sailors, and Airmen (the Women's Memorial of the Great War) was opened by Queen Mary in 1924. *Richmond Park* (2,469 acres) contains herds of fallow and red deer.

Roman London.—Although visible remains from this period are few, excavations carried out in the City on sites due for redevelopment often reveal Roman features. Sections of the City Wall are the most striking remains to be seen of Roman *Londinium*, although even these are largely medieval due to the Roman wall being rebuilt during the medieval period. Sections may be seen near the White Tower in the Tower of London; at Tower Hill; at Coopers' Row; at All Hallows, London Wall, its vestry being built on the remains of a semi-circular Roman bastion; at St. Alphage, London Wall, showing a striking succession of building repairs from Roman until the late medieval period, and at St. Giles Cripplegate. Excavations in the Cripplegate area have revealed that a Roman fort was built there in about A.D.100–120. It was later incorporated into the city wall when this was built about A.D.200.

The administrative centre of the Roman city was the great forum and basilica, more than 165 metres square, sections of which have been encountered during excavations in the area of Leadenhall, Gracechurch Street and Lombard Street. Excavations during the past few years have revealed Roman activity along the river. Traces of a massive riverside wall, built in the late Roman period, have been found and a succession of Roman timber quays have been excavated along Lower and Upper Thames Street helping to prove that Roman London was a thriving commercial centre.

Other major buildings found are the Provincial Governor's Palace in Cannon Street; remains of a bath-building, preserved in Lower Thames Street; and the Temple of Mithras in Walbrook. The fine sculptures from this temple are displayed in the Museum of London, where many other relics from the Roman City may be seen. There is also an Ordnance Survey map of Roman London.

Royal Albert Hall, Kensington Gore, SW7 2AP. The elliptical hall, one of the largest in the world, was completed in 1871, and since 1941 has been the venue each summer for the Promenade Concerts founded in 1895 by Sir Henry Wood. Also used for public meetings, concerts, sports and other entertainments. *Gen. Manager,* D. C. McNicol.

Royal Exchange, EC3V 3LS. (founded by Sir Thomas Gresham, 1566, opened as "The Bourse" and proclaimed "The Royal Exchange" by Queen Elizabeth I, 1571, rebuilt 1667–69 and 1842–44). The building is occupied by the Guardian Royal Exchange Assurance Group and by the London International Financial Futures Exchange. It is administered by the Gresham Committee (*Clerk,* Mercers' Hall, Ironmonger Lane, E.C.2.).

Royal Geographical Society, Kensington Gore, SW7 2AR.—Map room open to public, admission free. Advice for scientific expeditions abroad, by appointment only.

Royal Opera House, Covent Garden, W.C.2.— Home of The Royal Ballet (1931) and The Royal Opera (1946) companies, the Royal Opera House is the third theatre to be built on the site, opening May 15, 1858: the first was opened Dec. 7, 1732. The season of the resident companies runs mid Sept.–Aug. *General Administrator,* Sir John Tooley.

Runnymede.—A meadow of about 100 acres, on S. bank of Thames (part of the Crown Lands), between Windsor and Staines. From June 15 to 23, 1215, the hostile Barons encamped on this meadow during negotiations with King John, who rode over each day from Windsor. The 48 "Articles of the Barons" were accepted by the King on June 15, and were subsequently embodied in a charter, since known as *Magna Carta,* of which several copies were sealed on June 19. About half a mile N.E. of the meadow is *Magna Carta Island* (claimed as the actual site of the sealing), presented to the National Trust in 1930.

A memorial at *Cooper's Hill,* near Runnymede, to members of the Commonwealth air forces who lost their lives in the Second World War while serving from bases in the United Kingdom and north-western Europe and have no known grave, was unveiled by the Queen on October 17, 1953. Her Majesty on May 14, 1965, unveiled a memorial to the late President of the United States, John F. Kennedy, on ground nearby.

St. James's Palace, in Pall Mall, S.W.1.—(Closed to the public.) Built by Henry VIII; the Gatehouse and Presence Chamber remain, later alterations by Wren and Kent. The Chapel Royal is open for services on Sundays at 8.30 a.m. and 11.15 a.m. between beginning October and Good Friday (*see also* Marlborough House for summer services in The Queen's Chapel). Representatives of Foreign Powers are still accredited "to the Court of St. James's". *Clarence House* (1825) in the palace precinct is the home of H.M. the Queen Mother.

St. John's Gate, Clerkenwell, E.C.1.—Now the Chancery of the Order of St. John of Jerusalem, and formerly the entrance of the Priory of that Order, of which the gate house (early 16th century) and crypt of Church (12th century) alone survive. They may be inspected on application to the Curator.

Sir John Soane's Museum, 13 Lincoln's Inn Fields, W.C.2. The house and galleries, built 1812–24, are the work of the founder, Sir John Soane (1753–1837) and contain his collections, arranged as he left them, in pursuance of an Act procured by him in 1833. Exhibits include the Sarcophagus of Seti 1 (c. 1290 B.C.), Classical vases and marbles, Hogarth's *Rake's Progress* and *Election* series, paintings by Canaletto, Reynolds, Turner, Lawrence, etc., and sculpture by Chantrey, Flaxman, etc. Soane's library of 8,000 vols, and collection of 40,000 architectural drawings are available for study by appointment. Open Tues.–Sat. 10–5. Closed Bank Holidays. *Curator,* P. Thornton, F.S.A. *Assistant Curator,* Mrs M. Richardson.

Somerset House, Strand, W.C.2, and Victoria Embankment, W.C.2.—The beautiful river façade (600 ft. long) was built in 1776–86 from the designs of Sir W. Chambers; the eastern extension, which houses part of King's College, was built by Smirke in 1829. Somerset House was the property of Lord Protector Somerset, at whose attainder in 1552 the palace passed to the Crown, and it was a royal residence until 1692.

South Bank, S.E.1.—The arts complex on the south bank of the River Thames includes the South Bank Centre, owned and managed by the South Bank Board, and consisting of the 2,903-seat *Royal Festival Hall* (opened in 1951 for the Festival of Britain), a major venue for concert and ballet seasons, with the adjacent 1,056-seat *Queen Elizabeth Hall* and 368-seat *Purcell Room,* accommodating smaller-scale performances.

The *National Film Theatre* (opened 1958), administered by the British Film Institute, has two auditoria showing films, television and video of outstanding historical, artistic or technical merit. The London Film Festival is held here every November.

The *National Theatre* opened in 1976 and stages classical, modern, new and neglected plays in its three auditoria; the 1,160-seat Olivier theatre (apron stage), the 890-seat Lyttleton theatre (proscenium stage) and the experimental Cottesloe theatre, which holds up to 400.

Stock Exchange, E.C.2.—The market floor of the new Stock Exchange building in London opened for trading in June, 1973. A tower, 331 feet high, and the new Market replace the complex of buildings started in 1801 on the same site. The new building is the headquarters of The Stock Exchange, following the amalgamation of all the Stock Exchanges in Great Britain and Ireland on March 25, 1973.

The Visitors Gallery is open between 9.30 a.m. and 5.00 p.m. Monday to Friday. Admission free and without ticket. Film show, advance bookings are advisable via the Public Information Unit (01-588 2355).

Syon House, Brentford.—The summer home of the Duke of Northumberland. The House is built on the remains of the Nunnery of Syon, founded by order of Henry V in 1415. At the Dissolution of the Monasteries the estate reverted to the Crown. In 1594 it was granted to the 9th Earl of Northumberland, who altered and improved the property. In the eight years, 1762–1770, the interior was transformed and furnished by Robert Adam. Open April 1–Sept. 27 (Sun.–Thurs.), Oct. Sun. only, 12–5.

Thames Embankments.—The *Victoria Embankment,* on the N. side (from Westminster to Black-friars), was constructed by Sir J. W. Bazalgette for the Metropolitan Board of Works, 1864–70 (the seats, of which the supports of some are a kneeling camel, laden with spicery, and of others a winged sphinx, were presented by the Grocers' Company, and by Rt. Hon. W. H. Smith, M.P., in 1874); the *Albert Embankment,* on the S. side (from Westminster Bridge to Vauxhall), 1866–69; the *Chelsea Embankment,* 1871–74. The total cost exceeded £2,000,000. Sir J. W. Bazalgette (1819–91) also inaugurated the London main drainage system, 1858–65. A medallion has been placed on a pier of the Victoria Embankment to commemorate the engineer of the Thames waterside improvements ("Flumini vincula posuit"). County Hall includes an embankment on the Surrey side.

Thames Flood Barrier.—Officially opened in May 1984, though first used in Feb. 1983, the Barrier consists of ten rising sector gates which span 570 yards from bank to bank of the Thames at Woolwich Reach. When not in use the gates lie horizontally, allowing shipping to navigate the river normally; when the Barrier is closed, the gates turn through 90 degrees to stand vertically more than 50 feet above the river bed. The Barrier took eight years to complete and can be raised within about 30 minutes.

Thames Tunnels.—The *Rotherhithe Tunnel,* constructed by the L.C.C. and opened in 1908, connects Commercial Road, E.14, with Lower Road, Rother-hithe; the total length is 1 mile 332 yards, of which 474 yards are under the river. The cost of the tunnel and its approaches was £1,506,914. The first *Blackwall Tunnel* (pedestrians and vehicles) was constructed by the L.C.C. and opened in 1897, connecting East India Dock Road, Poplar, with Blackwall Lane, East Greenwich. The cost of the tunnel with its approaches was about £1,323,663. A second tunnel (for southbound vehicles only) was opened in August, 1967, at a cost of about £9,750,000 and the old tunnel was improved at a cost of about £1,350,000 and made one-way northbound. Both tunnels are for vehicles only. The relative lengths of the tunnels measured from East India Dock Road to the Gate House on the south side are 6,215 ft. (old tunnel) and 6,152 feet. *Greenwich Tunnel* (pedestrians only), constructed by the L.C.C. and opened in 1902, connects the Isle of Dogs, Poplar, with Greenwich. The length of the subway is 406 yards, and the cost was about £180,000. The *Woolwich Tunnel* (pedestrians only), constructed by the L.C.C. and opened in 1912, connects North and South Woolwich below the passenger and vehicular ferry from North Woolwich Station, E.16, to High Street, Woolwich, S.E.18. The length of the subway is 552 yards, and its cost was about £86,000. The *Thames Tunnel* (1,300 feet) was opened in 1843 to connect Wapping with Rotherhithe. In 1866 it was closed to the public, and purchased by the East London Railway Company. The *Tower Subway* for pedestrians was opened in 1870, and has long been closed.

Tower Bridge Walkway and Museum, SE1 2UP.—Owned by the Bridge House Trust and open daily April–Oct. 10–6·30, Nov.–March 10–4·45. Admission £2, concessions £1. Attractions include exhibitions, videos, the observation platform and walkway, engine rooms, working models and souvenir gift shop.

Tower Hill, E.C.1 and E.C.3, was formerly the place of execution for condemned prisoners from the Tower, the site of the scaffold being marked in the gardens of Trinity Square.

Tower of London, E.C.3.—Admission to a general view of the Tower, the White Tower (Armouries), the History, Oriental, Ordnance and 18th–19th century Galleries, and the Wall Walk Phases I and II.

The White Tower is the oldest and central building in Her Majesty's Royal Palace and Fortress of the Tower of London. It was built at the order of William I and constructed by Gundulph, Bishop of Rochester, in the years 1078–98. The Inner Wall, with thirteen towers, was constructed by Henry III in the 12th century. The Moat was extended and completed by Richard I and the Wharf first mentioned in 1228. The Outer Wall was completed in the reign of Edward I and now incorporates six towers and two bastions. The last Monarch to reside in the Tower of London was James I. The Crown Jewels came to the Tower in the reign of Henry III. All coinage used in Great Britain was minted in the Outer Ward of the Tower of London until 1810 when the Royal Mint was formed. The Tower of London has had a military garrison since 1078. The Chapel Royal of St. John the Evangelist, within the White Tower (1080–1088) is the oldest Norman church in London. The chapel of St. Peter ad Vincula was built in the early 16th century.

Constable, Field Marshal Sir Roland Gibbs, G.C.B., C.B.E., D.S.O., M.C.; *Lieutenant*, Lieut. Gen. Sir Peter Hudson, K.C.B., C.B.E.; *Resident Governor and Keeper of the Jewel House*, Maj.-Gen. A. P. W. MacLellan, M.B.E.; *Master of the Armouries*, A. V. B. Norman; *Chaplain at the Chapel Royal of St. Peter ad Vincula*, Rev. J. F. M. Llewellyn. Open weekdays March 1–Oct. 31, 9.30–5, Nov. 1–Feb. 28, 9.30–4; Sundays, March–Oct. 2–5. Tower closed Christmas Eve, Christmas Day, Boxing Day, New Year's Day and Good Friday. On Sundays throughout the year (except August) the public is admitted to Holy Communion, 9.15 a.m. and Morning Service, 11 a.m. Admission £4, concessions £2 includes admission to the Jewel House. (The Jewel House is usually closed for cleaning in Feb. Precise dates available from the Receiver of Fees Office at the Tower.)

Waltham Abbey (or **Waltham Holy Cross**), Essex.—The Abbey ruins, Harold's Bridge (14th century), the Nave of the former cruciform Abbey Church c. 1120 and the traditional burial place of King Harold II (1066), and a Guild Chapel of Edward II, with crypt below, which houses a visitors centre with permanent exhibition. New evidence of the position and style of several buildings, which once stood on the site of the Augustinian monastery, were revealed by the prolonged drought in the summer of 1933 and by subsequent excavations. At Waltham Cross, one mile from the Abbey, is one of the crosses (partly restored) erected by Edward I to mark a resting place of the corpse of Queen Eleanor on its way to Westminster Abbey. (Ten crosses were erected, but only those at Geddington, Northampton and Waltham remain; "Charing" Cross originally stood near the spot now occupied by the statue of Charles I at Whitehall.)

Wellington Museum, Apsley House, 149 Piccadilly, at Hyde Park Corner, W.1.—Known as "No. 1 London", Apsley House was designed by Robert Adam for Lord Bathurst and built 1771–8. It was bought in 1817 by the Duke of Wellington, who in 1828–29 employed Benjamin Wyatt to enlarge it, face it with Bath stone and add the Corinthian portico. The museum contains many fine paintings, sculpture, services of porcelain and silver plate and personal relics of the 1st Duke of Wellington (1769–1852). The House was given to the Nation by the 7th Duke and was first opened to the public in 1952, under the administration of the Victoria and Albert Museum. Open daily 11–5. Closed Mon., Christmas Eve, Christmas Day, Boxing Day and New Year's Day. Admission £2, concessions £1.

Westminster Hall, S.W.1.—The only part of the old Palace of Westminster to survive the fire of 1834, Westminster Hall is adjacent to and incorporated in the Houses of Parliament. Westminster Hall was built by William Rufus from 1097–99 and altered by Richard II, 1394–99. It is about 240 ft. long, 68 ft. wide and 92 ft. high; the hammer beam roof of carved oak dates from 1396–98. The Hall was the scene of the trial of Charles I. Westminster Hall is included on the route followed by those who have arranged a visit to the Houses of Parliament with their M.P.

Whitechapel Art Gallery, Whitechapel High Street, E.1.—Opened in 1901; administered by a charitable trust. There is no permanent collection; temporary exhibitions, mainly of modern art, are presented, and community and educational projects are run. Open Tues.–Suns. 11–5; Weds. 11–8.

Wimbledon Lawn Tennis Museum, SW19 5AE.—Exhibits include fashion, trophies, replicas and memorabilia representing the history of lawn tennis and a theatre shows films of great matches. Open Tues.–Sat. 11–5, Sun. 2–5. Admission £1·50, concessions 75p.

Windsor Castle (begun by William the Conqueror, A.D. 1066–87).—The Castle Precincts are open daily. Admission free. When the Queen is not in official residence, the *State Apartments* of Windsor Castle are open on weekdays and Sunday afternoons during the summer months. Admission £1·60, concessions 80p. By the Queen's command, the net proceeds go to charities. *Queen Mary's Doll's House, the Exhibition of Dolls, the Exhibition of Drawings by Holbein, Leonardo da Vinci and other artists and the Royal Mews Exhibition* can be seen on the same days as the State Apartments; admission 70p, concessions 30p. When the State Apartments are closed, Queen Mary's Doll's House, the Exhibition of Drawings and the Royal Mews Exhibition remain open to the public. The *Albert Memorial Chapel* is open throughout the year (closed on Sundays). Admission free. A fee is charged to visit *St. George's Chapel*. The *Curfew Tower* may be seen under the guidance of the Keeper to whom application must be made at the entrance.

The *Royal Mausoleum*, Frogmore Gardens, Home Park, is open annually on two days in early May in conjunction with the opening of Frogmore Gardens in aid of the National Garden Scheme. Also open on the Wednesday nearest to May 24 (Queen Victoria's birthday). Admission free.

Zoological Gardens, Regent's Park, N.W.1.—(Opened in 1828). Open daily (except Christmas Day) March–Oct. 9–6 or dusk (Bank Holidays and associated Suns. Easter–Aug. and Suns. July 12–Sept. 13, 9–7). Oct.–March opens 10. Admission £3·60, concessions £1·80. Aquarium and Children's Zoo free.

[London Tourist Board.—26 Grosvenor Gardens, S.W.1. (01–730 3450.)]

PARKS, SPACES AND GARDENS

The principal Parks and Open Spaces in the Metropolitan area are maintained as under:—

By the Crown

BUSHY PARK (1,099 acres).—Adjoining Hampton Court, contains avenue of horse-chestnuts enclosed in a four-fold avenue of limes planted by William III. "Chestnut Sunday" (when the trees are in full bloom with their "candles") is usually about May 1 to 15.

GREEN PARK (49 acres), W.1.—Between Piccadilly and St. James's Park with Constitution Hill, leading to Hyde Park Corner.

GREENWICH PARK (196½ acres), S.E.10.

HAMPTON COURT GARDENS (54 acres).

HAMPTON COURT GREEN (17 acres).

HAMPTON COURT PARK (622 acres).

HYDE PARK (341 acres).—From Park Lane, W.1, to Kensington Gardens, W.2 containing the Serpentine. Fine gateway at Hyde Park Corner, with Apsley House, the Achilles Statue, Rotten Row and the Ladies' Mile. To the north-east is the Marble Arch, originally erected by George IV at the entrance to Buckingham Palace and re-erected in present position in 1851.

KENSINGTON GARDENS (275 acres), W.2.—From western boundary of Hyde Park to Kensington Palace, containing the Albert Memorial.

KEW, ROYAL BOTANIC GARDENS *see* p. 431–2.

REGENT'S PARK and PRIMROSE HILL (464 acres), N.W.1.—From Marylebone Road to Primrose Hill surrounded by the Outer Circle and divided by the Broad Walk leading to the Zoological Gardens.

RICHMOND PARK (2,469 acres).

ST. JAMES'S PARK (93 acres), S.W.1.—From Whitehall to Buckingham Palace. Ornamental lake of 12 acres. The original suspension bridge built in 1857 was replaced in 1957. The Mall leads from the Admiralty Arch to the Queen Victoria Memorial and Buckingham Palace, Birdcage Walk from Storey's Gate, past Wellington Barracks, to Buckingham Palace.

By the Corporation of London

BURNHAM BEECHES and FLEET WOOD, Bucks. (510 acres).—Purchased by the Corporation for the benefit of the public in 1880, Fleet Wood (65 acres) being presented in 1921.

COULSDON COMMON, Surrey (133 acres).

EPPING FOREST (6,000 acres).—Purchased by the Corporation for £250,000 and thrown open to the public in 1882. The present forest is 12 miles long by 1 to 2 miles wide, about one-tenth of its original area.

FARTHINGDOWN, Surrey (121 acres).

HIGHGATE WOOD (70 acres).

KENLEY COMMON, Surrey (138 acres).

QUEEN'S PARK, Kilburn (30 acres).

RIDDLESDOWN, Surrey (90 acres).

SPRING PARK, West Wickham (51 acres).

WEST HAM PARK (77 acres).

WEST WICKHAM COMMON, Kent (25 acres).

With smaller open spaces within the City of London, including FINSBURY CIRCUS GARDENS.

Temporarily Maintained
by the London Residuary Body

When the G.L.C. was abolished in April 1986 the responsibility for some of its parks and open spaces had already been transferred to other bodies (indicated where known). Negotiating the transfer of the remainder to individual Boroughs has been the responsibility of the London Residuary Body since abolition.

GOLDERS HILL (36 acres), N.W.3, adjoining West Heath, Hampstead.

HAMPSTEAD HEATH and Extension (283 acres), N.W.3.

PARLIAMENT HILL (271 acres), N.W.3.—Part of Hampstead Heath. Lido and swimming bath. Important cross-country events are held here.

SOUTH BANK (10 acres, including Jubilee Gardens), Belvedere Road, S.E.1.

ROMAN NAMES OF ENGLISH TOWNS AND CITIES

Bath	*Aquae Sulis*	Lincoln	*Lindum*
Canterbury	*Durovernum*	London	*Londinium*
Carlisle	*Luguvalium*	Manchester	*Mancunium*
Chelmsford	*Caesaromagus*	Newcastle upon Tyne	*Pons Aelius*
Chester	*Deva*		
Chichester	*Regni/Regnum*	Pevensey	*Anderida*
Cirencester	*Corinium*	Rochester	*Durobrivae*
Colchester	*Camulodunum*	St. Albans	*Verulamium*
Doncaster	*Danum*	Salisbury (Old Sarum)	*Sorbiodunum*
Dorchester	*Durnovaria*		
Dover	*Dubris*	Silchester	*Calleva Atrebatum*
Exeter	*Isca Dumnoniorum*	Winchester	*Venta Belgarum*
Gloucester	*Glevum*	Wroxeter	*Viroconium*
Lancaster	*Lunecastrum*	York	*Eboracum*
Leicester	*Ratae Coritanorum*		

AERODROMES AND AIRPORTS

Aerodromes in Great Britain, Northern Ireland, the Isle of Man and the Channel Islands which are either State owned, operated by the Highlands and Islands Airports Ltd. or licensed for use by civil aircraft. A number of unlicensed airfields not included in this list are also available for private use by permission of the owner or controlling authority.

Aerodromes designated as Customs airports are printed in bold type. Customs facilities are available at certain other aerodromes by special arrangement.

S = Owned and operated by the State.

BAA = Operated by the British Airports Authority PLC.

M = Owned or operated by Municipal Authority.

HIAL = Operated by Highland and Islands Airports Ltd.

J = Military aerodromes available for civil use by prior permission.

H = Licensed helicopter station.

ENGLAND AND WALES

Aberporth, Dyfed. S
Abingdon, Oxon. J
Andrewsfield, Essex.
Barrow (Walney Island), Cumbria.
Bembridge, I.O.W.
Benson, Oxon. J
Biggin Hill, Kent.
Birmingham, W. Midlands. M
Blackbushe, Hants.
Blackpool, Lancs. M
Bodmin, Cornwall.
Bourn, Cambridge.
Bournemouth, (Hurn), Dorset. M
Bridlington, Humberside.
Bristol, Avon. M
Brize Norton, Oxford. J
Caernarfon, Gwynedd.
Cambridge.
Cardiff, S. Glamorgan. M
Carlisle, Cumbria. M
Chichester (Goodwood), Sussex.
Chivenor, Devon. J
Church Fenton, N. Yorks. J
Clacton, Essex.
Compton Abbas, Dorset.
Cosford, Wolverhampton. J
Coventry, W. Midlands. M
Cranfield, Beds.
Cranwell, Lincs. J
Culdrose, Cornwall. J
Denham, Bucks.
Derby/Burnaston, Derby.
Dishforth, N. Yorks. J
Doncaster, S. Yorks.
Dunkeswell, Devon.
Duxford, Cambs. M
Earls Colne, Halstead.
East Midlands, Derbys. M
Elstree, Herts.
Exeter, Devon.
Fairoaks, Surrey.
Farnborough, Hants. S
Fenland, Lincs.
Finningley, S. Yorks. J
Gloucester/Cheltenham
  (Staverton), Glos. M
Great Yarmouth (North Denes), Norfolk.
Halfpenny Green, Staffs.
Halton, Bucks. J
Hatfield, Herts.
Haverfordwest, Dyfed. M
Hawarden, Clwyd.
Hucknall, Notts.
Humberside. M
Ipswich, Suffolk.
Isle of Wight (Sandown).
Kemble, Glos. J
Land's End (St. Just), Cornwall.
Lashenden, Headcorn, Kent.
Leavesden, Herts.

Leeds and Bradford, Yorks. M
Leeming, N. Yorks. J
Lee-on-Solent, Hants. J
Leicester, Leics.
Linton-on-Ouse, Yorks. J
Liverpool, Merseyside. M
Llanbedr, Gwynedd. J.
London (City).
London (Gatwick). BAA
London (Heathrow). BAA
London (Stansted). BAA
London (Westland Heliport). H
Luton, Beds. M
Lydd, Kent.
Lyneham, Wilts. J
Manchester. M
Manchester (Barton).
Manston, Kent. J
Netherthorpe, S. Yorks.
Newcastle, Tyne and Wear. M
Newton, Notts. J
Northampton (Sywell), Northants.
Northolt, Mddx. J
Norwich, Norfolk. M
Nottingham, Notts.
Old Sarum, Wilts.
Oxford (Kidlington), Oxfordshire.
Panshanger, Herts.
Penzance, Cornwall. H
Peterborough (Conington).
Peterborough (Sibson), Cambs.
Plymouth (Roborough), Devon.
Portland Naval, Dorset. JH
Redhill, Surrey.
Retford/Gamston, Notts.
Rochester, Kent.
St. Mawgan, Cornwall. J
Sandtoft, Humberside.
Scilly Isles (St. Mary's).
Seething, Norfolk.
Shawbury, Shropshire. J
Sherburn-in-Elmet, N. Yorks.
Shipdham, Norfolk.
Shobdon, Herefordshire.
Shoreham, W. Sussex. M
Silverstone, Northants.
Skegness (Ingoldmells), Lincs.
Sleap, Shropshire.
Southampton, Eastleigh, Hants.
Southend, Essex. M
Stapleford, Essex.
Sturgate, Lincs.
Swansea, W. Glam. M
Tees-side, Cleveland. M
Thruxton, Hants.
Tresco, Isles of Scilly. H
Valley, Gwynedd. J
Waddington, Lincs. J
Warton, Lancs.
Wattisham, Suffolk. J
Wellesbourne Mountford,
  Warwick.

Weston, Avon. H
White Waltham, Berks.
Wickenby, Lincs.
Woodford, Gtr. Manchester.
Woodvale, Merseyside. J
Wycombe Air Park (Booker),
  Bucks.
Yeovil, Somerset.
Yeovilton, Somerset. J

SCOTLAND

Aberdeen (Dyce). BAA
Barra, Hebrides.
Benbecula, Hebrides. HIAL
Dounreay (Thurso). S
Dundee, Angus. M
Eday. M
Edinburgh. BAA
Fair Isle.
Fetlar, Shetlands.
Fife/Glenrothes.
Flotta, Orkneys.
Glasgow. BAA
Inverness (Dalcross). HIAL
Islay (Port Ellen). HIAL
Isle of Skye. M
Kinloss. J
Kirkwall. HIAL
Lerwick (Tingwall). M
Leuchars. J
Lossiemouth. J
Machrihanish, Kintyre, J
North Ronaldsay, Orkneys. M
Papa Westray, Orkneys. M
Perth (Scone).
Prestwick, BAA
Sanday, Orkneys. M
Scatsta.
Stornoway, Hebrides. HIAL
Stronsay, Orkneys. M
Sumburgh, Shetlands. HIAL
Tiree. HIAL
Unst, Shetland. M
West Freugh, Wigtown. S
Westray, Orkneys. M
Whalsay, Shetlands.
Wick. HIAL

NORTHERN IRELAND

Belfast (Aldergrove). S
Belfast (Harbour).
Enniskillen (St. Angelo). M
Londonderry (Eglinton). M
Newtownards.

ISLE OF MAN

Ronaldsway. S

CHANNEL ISLANDS

Alderney. S
Guernsey. S
Jersey. S

The Principality of Wales

Position and extent.—Wales (Cymru) occupies the extreme west of the central southern portion of the island of Great Britain, with a total area of 8,018 sq. miles (land 7,968; inland water 50); it is bounded on the N. by the Irish Sea, on the S. by the Bristol Channel, on the E. by the English counties of Cheshire, Shropshire, Hereford and Worcester, and Gloucester, and on the W. by St. George's Channel. Across the Menai Straits is the Welsh island of *Anglesey* or Ynys Môn (276 sq. miles), communication with which is facilitated by the Menai Suspension Bridge (1,000 ft. long), built by Telford in 1826 and by the tubular railway bridge (1,100 ft. long) built by Stephenson in 1850. Holyhead harbour, on Holy Isle (N.W. of Anglesey), provides accommodation for ferry services to Dublin (70 miles).

Population.—The population at the Census of 1981 was 2,791,851 (males 1,352,639; females 1,439,212). The average density of population in 1981 was 343 per square mile. The population, mid 1985 estimate, was 2,812,000.

Relief.—Wales is a country of extensive tracts of high plateau and shorter stretches of mountain ranges deeply dissected by river valleys. Lower-lying ground is largely confined to the coastal belt and the lower parts of the valleys. The highest mountains are those of Snowdonia in the north-west (*Snowdon*, 3,559 ft.), Berwyn (*Aran Fawddwy*, 2,971 ft.), Cader Idris (*Pen y Gadair*, 2,928 ft.), Dyfed (*Plynlimon*, 2,467 ft.), and the Black Mountain, Brecon Beacons and Black Forest ranges in the south-east (*Carmarthen Van*, 2,630 ft., *Pen y Fan*, 2,906 ft., *Waun Fâch*, 2,660 ft.).

Hydrography.—The principal river of those rising in Wales is the *Severn (see* England), which flows from the slopes of Plynlimon to the English border. The *Wye* (130 miles) also rises in the slopes of Plynlimon. The *Usk* (56 miles) flows into the Bristol Channel, through Gwent. The *Dee* (70 miles) rises in Bala Lake and flows through the Vale of Llangollen, where an aqueduct (built by Telford in 1805) carries the Pontcysyllte branch of the Shropshire Union Canal across the valley. The estuary of the Dee is the navigable portion, 14 miles in length and about 5 miles in breadth, and the tide rushes in with dangerous speed over the "Sands of Dee." The *Towy* (68 miles), *Teifi* (50 miles), *Taff* (40 miles), *Dovey* (30 miles), *Taf* (25 miles), and *Conway* (24 miles), the last named broad and navigable, are wholly Welsh rivers.

The largest natural lake in Wales is *Bala* (Llyn Tegid) in Gwynedd, 4 miles long and about 1 mile wide; *Lake Vyrnwy* is an artificial reservoir, about the size of Bala, and forms the water supply of Liverpool, and Birmingham is supplied from a chain of reservoirs in the Elan and Clærwen valleys.

The Welsh Language.—According to the 1981 Census results, the percentage of persons of three years and over able to speak Welsh were:

Clwyd	18·7	Powys	20·2
Dyfed	46·3	S. Glamorgan	5·8
Gwent	2·5	W. Glamorgan	16·4
Gwynedd	61·2		
Mid Glamorgan	8·4	**Wales**	18·9

The 1981 figure represents a slight decline from 20·8 per cent in 1971 (1961, 26 per cent; 1951, 28·9 per cent).

Flag.—A red dragon on a green and white field (per fess argent and vert a dragon passant gules). The flag was augmented in 1953 by a royal badge on a shield encircled with a riband bearing the words *Ddraig Goch Ddyry Cychwyn* and imperially crowned. Only the unaugmented flag is flown on Government offices in Wales and, where appropriate, in London. Both flags continue to be used elsewhere.

EARLY HISTORY

Celts and Romans.—The earliest inhabitants of whom there is any record appear to have been subdued or exterminated by the *Goidels* (a people of Celtic race) in the Bronze Age, and a further invasion of Celtic *Brythons* and *Belgae* followed in the ensuing Iron Age. The *Roman* conquest of South Britain and Wales was for some time successfully opposed by *Caratacus* (Caractacus or Caradog), Chieftain of the Catuvellauni and son of *Cunobelinus* (Cymbeline) King of the Trinobantes. In A.D. 78 the conquest of Wales was completed under Julius Frontinus, and communications were opened up by the construction of military roads from Chester to Caerleon-on-Usk and Caerwent, and from Chester to Conway (and thence to Camarthen and Neath). *Christianity* was introduced (during the Roman occupation) in the 4th century.

The Anglo-Saxon Attacks.—The Anglo-Saxon invaders of South Britain drove the Celtic Goidels and Brythons into the mountain fastness of Wales, and into Strathclyde (Cumberland and S.W. Scotland) and Cornwall, giving them the name of *Waelisc*, or Welsh (= Foreign). The West Saxons' victory of Deorham (577) isolated Wales from Cornwall and the battle of Chester (613) cut off communication with Strathclyde. In the 8th century the boundaries of the Welsh were further restricted by the annexations of Offa, King of Mercia, and counter-attacks were largely prevented by the construction of an artificial boundary from the Dee to the Wye (Offa's Dike). In the 9th century Rhodri Mawr united the country against further incursions of the Saxons by land and against the raids of Norse and Danish pirates by sea, but at his death his three provinces of *Gwynedd* (N.), *Powys* (Mid.) and *Deheubarth* (S.) were divided among his three sons—Anarawd, Mervyn and Cadell—the son of the last named being Hywel Dda, who codified the laws of the country, while Llewelyn ap Seisyll (husband of the heiress of Gwynedd) again united the provinces and reigned as Prince from 1018 to 1023.

The Norman Conquest.—After the Norman conquest of England, William I created Palatine counties along the Welsh frontier, and Robert FitzHamon, the Norman Earl of Gloucester, raided South Wales and erected fortresses from the Wye to Milford Haven. Henry I introduced Flemish settlers into South Wales, but after his death the Welsh rose under the leadership of Griffith ap Rhys and routed the Norman-Flemish forces at the fords of the Teifi (Cardigan) in 1136. From the early years of the 13th century the house of Gwynedd, in the north, gained an ascendancy over the whole of Wales, and Llywelyn ap Iorwerth was in constant strife with England for recognition as an independent sovereign. Llywelyn ap Gruffydd (grandson of Llywelyn ap Iorwerth), the last native prince, was killed in 1282 during hostilities between the Welsh and English, allowing Edward I of England to establish his authority over the country. On Feb. 7, 1301, Edward of Caernarvon, son of Edward I, was created *Prince of Wales*, a title which has subsequently been borne by the eldest son of the sovereign. Strong Welsh national feeling continued, expressed in the early 15th century in the rising led by Owain Glyndŵr, but the situation was altered by the accession to the English throne in 1485 of Henry VI of the Welsh House of Tudor. Wales was politically assimilated to England under the Act of Union of 1535, which extended English laws to the

Principality and gave it parliamentary representation for the first time.

Eisteddfod.—The Welsh are a distinct nationality, with a language and literature of their own, and the national bardic festival (Eisteddfod), instituted by Prince Rhys ap Griffith in 1176, is annually maintained. These *Eisteddfodau* (sessions) form part of the *Gorsedd* (assembly), which is believed to date from the time of Prydian, a ruling prince in an age many centuries before the Christian era.

AREA AND POPULATION OF THE WELSH COUNTIES

County	Administrative Headquarters	Area (*hectares*)	Population	Rateable Value 1987 £	Actual Rateable Value per head £
Clwyd	Shire Hall, Mold	242,650	397,900	41,496,000	104·29
Dyfed	*Carmarthen	576,577	335,900	32,345,037	96·29
Gwent	*Cwmbran	137,599	441,800	47,369,019	107·22
Gwynedd	County Offices, Caernarfon	386,708	233,600	26,952,392	115·38
Mid Glamorgan	*Cardiff	101,867	539,300	41,687,956	77·30
Powys	*Llandrindod Wells	507,741	112,373	10,400,169	92·55
South Glamorgan	County Headquarters, Newport Road, Cardiff	41,629	395,700	53,394,720	134·94
West Glamorgan	*Swansea	81,657	363,500	39,510,358	108·69

* County Hall.

COUNTY OFFICIALS AND CHAIRMEN OF COUNTY COUNCILS

County	Chief Executive	County Treasurer	Chairmen of C.C.
Clwyd	M. H. Phillips	A. Dalby	Mrs. E. Jones
Dyfed	D. H. Davies	A. C. Williams	R. E. Morris
Gwent	M. J. Perry	R. Emmott	J. W. G. Turner
Gwynedd	I. B. Rees	J. L. Williams	Cpt. A. Robertson
Mid Glamorgan	D. H. Thomas*	L. D. Heycock	C. Richards
Powys	M. J. Greenwood	M. J. Greenwood	Mrs. R. M. Thomas
South Glamorgan	M. D. Boyce	R. G. Tettenborn	H. J. Gough
West Glamorgan	M. E. J. Rush	S. G. Dunster	D. H. Cox

* County Clerk.

PRINCIPAL WELSH CITIES

CARDIFF

CARDIFF (South Glamorgan), at the mouth of the rivers Taff, Rhymney and Ely, is the capital City of Wales and one of Britain's major administrative, commercial and office centres. It has many industries, including steel works, cigars and a flourishing port with a substantial and varied trade. There are many fine buildings in the civic centre started early this century which includes the City Hall, the National Museum of Wales, University Buildings, Law Courts, Welsh Office, County Hall, Police Headquarters and the Temple of Peace and Health. Also in the city are Llandaff Cathedral, the Welsh National Folk Museum at St. Fagans, Cardiff Castle, the New Theatre, the Sherman Theatre and the Cardiff College of Music and Drama. New buildings include St. David's Hall, a 2,000-seat concert and conference hall.

SWANSEA

SWANSEA (in Welsh, Abertawe) is a City and a seaport of West Glamorgan with its own municipal airport. The beautiful Gower Peninsula was brought within the City boundary under local government reform on April 1, 1974. The trade of the port includes coal, patent fuel, ores, and the import and export of oil. The municipal area is 60,511 acres.

The principal buildings are the Norman Castle (rebuilt in 1330), the Royal Institution of South Wales, founded in 1835 (containing Museum and Library), the University College at Singleton and the Guildhall, containing the Brangwyn panels. New buildings include the Industrial and Maritime Museum, the new Maritime Quarter and Marina and the leisure centre. Swansea was chartered by the Earl of Warwick, *circa* 1158–1184, and further charters were granted by King John, Henry III., Edward II., Edward III. and James II., 2 from Cromwell and 1 Lord Marcher.

LORD LIEUTENANTS AND HIGH SHERIFFS

County	Lord Lieutenant	High Sheriff (1987–88)
Clwyd	Sir William Gladstone, BT.	The Hon. L. Tyrell-Kenyon
Dyfed	D. C. Mansel Lewis	Hon. R. Lewis
Gwent	R. Hanbury-Tenison	Lt.-Col. G. D. Inkin
Gwynedd	The Most Hon. The Marquess of Anglesey	O. G. Thomas
Mid Glamorgan	D. G. Badham, C.B.E.	P. D. Allen
Powys	M. L. Bourdillon	Mrs. R. M. Thomas
South Glamorgan	Mrs. S. E. Williams, M.B.E.	Sir Donald Walters
West Glamorgan	Col. J. V. Williams, D.S.O., O.B.E., T.D.	P. R. V. Watkins

MUNICIPAL DIRECTORY OF WALES

District Councils

Those accorded CITY Status are shown in SMALL CAPITALS; those with
Borough Status are distinguished by having § prefixed.

District	Population	Rateable Value 1987 £	Chief Executive	Chairman 1987–88 (a) Mayor (b) Lord Mayor
§Aberconwy, Gwynedd	52,200	5,682,410	J. E. Davies	(a) V. Williams
Alyn and Deeside, Clwyd	72,900	8,664,427	W. E. Rogers	T. L. Davies
§Arfon, Gwynedd	54,400	6,732,882	D. L. Jones	(a) I. Llewelyn Jones
§Blaenau Gwent, Gwent	79,000	5,874,001	R. Leadbeter	(a) H. Evans
§Brecknock, Powys	41,000	3,563,444	R. O. Doylend	(a) J. A. Pryce
CARDIFF, South Glamorgan	278,900	41,184,853	H. T. Crippin	(b) J. H. Hermer
Carmarthen, Dyfed	53,000	4,300,480	(vacant)	T. W. Davies
Ceredigion, Dyfed	62,000	5,335,851	D. Morgan	I. J. C. Radley
§Colwyn, Clwyd	51,600	5,564,626	O. Morris	(a) J. Jones
§Cynon Valley, Mid Glamorgan	64,500	4,591,169	G. W. Hosgood	(a) P. Jarman
§Delyn, Clwyd	66,300	6,150,118	J. R. Packer	(a) H. O. Clarke
§Dinefwr, Dyfed	36,413	2,345,613	E. W. Harries	(a) G. Davies
Dwyfor, Gwynedd	26,100	2,705,645	E. Davies	R. J. Williams
Glyndwr, Clwyd	40,915	3,657,461	J. H. Parry	J. R. Elgin
§Islwyn, Gwent	64,769	4,685,140	B. Bird	(a) F. G. Perkins
§Llanelli, Dyfed	75,000	6,263,465	A. B. Thomas	(a) G. Jones
§Lliw Valley, West Glamorgan	60,800	4,781,029	J. C. Howells	(a) C. T. Morgan
Meirionnydd, Gwynedd	31,400	4,108,297	G. W. Hughes	D. W. Price
§Merthyr Tydfil, Mid Glamorgan	59,400	4,779,654	S. Jones	(a) Ms. G. Williams
Monmouth, Gwent	71,400	7,970,440	G. Cummings	V. G. Thomas
Montgomeryshire, Powys	49,300	4,504,704	N. J. Bardsley	E. Glyn Davies
§Neath, West Glamorgan	65,200	6,200,226	G. H. Griffiths	(a) H. D. Thomas
§Newport, Gwent	129,800	19,553,999	C. Tapp	(a) R. F. Allen
§Ogwr, Mid Glamorgan	130,400	11,146,775	J. G. Cole	(a) G. Devine
§Port Talbot, West Glamorgan	51,200	8,407,202	C. A. Millward	(a) D. V. Lewis
Preseli Pembrokeshire, Dyfed	70,300	7,012,531	I. W. R. David	J. G. Cawood
Radnor, Powys	21,000	2,332,021	G. C. Read	E. K. Pugh, M.B.E.
§Rhondda, Mid Glamorgan	78,700	3,965,068	G. Evans	(a) G. Rees
§Rhuddlan, Clwyd	55,200	6,221,287	E. O. Lake	(a) G. Roberts
Rhymney Valley, Mid Glamorgan	107,100	7,755,319	P. A. Bennett	C. Hobbs
South Pembrokeshire, Dyfed	38,600	7,327,567	D. R. Jones	W. Hardy
SWANSEA, West Glamorgan	187,400	19,819,092	B. B. Meller (*acting*)	(b) H. W. Ayres
§Taff-Ely, Mid Glamorgan	92,000	9,449,971	D. Gethin	(a) S. G. Flower
§Torfaen, Gwent	90,212	9,208,767	M. B. Mehta	(a) D. J. Lloyd
§Vale of Glamorgan, South Glamorgan	116,100	14,442,542	J. R. Gau	(a) Mrs. E. E. Lloyd
§Wrexham Maelor, Clwyd	114,600	11,881,186	S. F. Tongue	(a) A. Evans
§Ynys Môn (Isle of Anglesey), Gwynedd	69,700	7,732,518	E. L. Gibson	(a) G. I. Thomas

THE KINGDOM OF SCOTLAND

Position and Extent.—The Kingdom of Scotland occupies the northern portion of the main island of Great Britain and includes the Inner and Outer Hebrides, and the Orkney, Shetland, and many other islands. The Kingdom lies between 60° 51′ 30″ and 54° 38′ N. latitude and between 1° 45′ 32″ and 6° 14′ W. longitude, its southern neighbour being the Kingdom of England, with the Atlantic Ocean on the N. and W., and the North Sea on the E. The greatest length of the mainland (Cape Wrath to the Mull of Galloway) is 274 miles, and the greatest breadth (Buchan Ness to Applecross) is 154 miles. The customary measurement of the Island of Great Britain is from the site of John o' Groats house, near Duncansby Head, Caithness (at the N.E. extremity of the island) to Land's End, Cornwall (at the S.W. extremity), a total distance of 603 miles in a straight line and (approximately) 900 by road.

The total area of the Kingdom is 30,414 square miles (land 29,761; inland water 653). The population (1981 Census) was 5,130,735 (males 2,466,437; females 2,664,298). The average density of the population in 1981 was 168 persons per square mile. The population, mid 1985 estimate, was 5,137,000.

Relief.—There are three natural orographic divisions of Scotland. The Southern Uplands have their highest points in Merrick (2,766 feet), Rhinns of Kells (2,669 feet), and Cairnsmuir of Carsphairn (2,614 feet), in the west; and the Tweedsmuir Hills in the east (*Hartfell* 2,651 ft., *Dollar Law* 2,682 ft., *Broad Law* 2,756 ft.). The Central Lowlands, formed by the valleys of the Clyde, Forth and Tay, divide the Southern Uplands from the heather-clad Northern Highlands, which extend almost from the extreme north of the mainland to the central lowlands, and are divided into a northern and southern system by the *Great Glen*. The Grampian Mountains, which entirely cover the southern Highland area, include in the west *Ben Nevis* (4,406 ft.), the highest point in the British Isles, and in the east the Cairngorm Mountains (*Cairn Gorm* 4,084 ft., *Braeriach* 4,248 ft., *Ben Macdui* 4,296 ft.). The north-western Highland area contains in the mountains of Wester and Eastern Ross *Carn Eige* (3,880 ft.) and *Sgurr na Lapaich* (3,775 ft.).

Created, like the Central Lowlands, by a major geological fault, the *Great Glen* (60 miles long) runs between Inverness and Fort William, and contains Loch Ness, Loch Oich and Loch Lochy. These are linked to each other and to the north-east and southwest coasts of Scotland by the Caledonian Canal, providing a navigable passage between the Moray Firth and the Inner Hebrides.

Hydrography.—The western coast of Scotland is fragmented by peninsulas and islands, and indented by fjords (sea-lochs), the longest of which is *Loch Fyne* (42 miles long) in Argyllshire. Although the east coast tends to be less fractured and lower, there are several great drowned inlets (firths), e.g. Firth of Forth, Firth of Tay, Moray Firth, as well as the Firth of Clyde in the west.

The lochs are the principal hydrographic feature of the Kingdom, both on the mainland and in many of the islands. The largest in the Kingdom and in Great Britain is *Loch Lomond* (27 square miles in area), in the Grampian valleys; the longest and deepest is *Loch Ness* (24 miles long and 800 feet deep), in the Great Glen; and Lochs Shin (20 miles) and Maree in the northern Highlands.

The longest river in Scotland is the *Tay* (117 miles), noted for its salmon. It flows into the North Sea, with Dundee on the estuary, which is spanned by the *Tay Bridge* (10,289 ft.) opened in 1887 and the *Tay Road Bridge* (7,365 ft.) opened in 1966. Other noted salmon rivers are the *Dee* (90 miles) which flows into

the North Sea at Aberdeen, and the *Spey* (110 miles), the swiftest flowing river in the British Isles, which flows into Moray Firth. The *Tweed*, which gave its name to the woollen cloth produced along its banks, marks in the lower stretches of its 96-mile course the border between Scotland and England.

The most important river commercially is the *Clyde* (106 miles), formed by the junction of the Daer and Portrail water, which flows through the city and port of Glasgow to the Firth of Clyde. During its course it passes over the picturesque *Falls of Clyde*, Bonnington Linn (30 ft.), Corra Linn (84 ft.), Dundaff Linn (10 ft.) and Stonebyres Linn (80 ft.), above and below Lanark. The *Forth* (66 miles), upon which stands Edinburgh, the capital, is spanned by the *Forth (Railway) Bridge* (1890), which is 5,330 feet long, and the *Forth (Road) Bridge* (1964), which has a total length of 6,156 ft. (over water) and a single span of 3,000 ft.

The highest waterfall in Scotland, and the British Isles, is *Eas a'Chùal Aluinn* with a total height of 658 ft., which falls from Glas Bheinn in Sutherland. The *Falls of Glomach*, on a head-stream of the Elchaig in Wester Ross, have a drop of 370 ft.

Gaelic Language.—According to the 1981 Census, 82,620 people, mainly in the Highlands and western coastal regions, were able to speak, read or write the Scottish form of Gaelic.

THE SCOTTISH ISLANDS

The Hebrides did not become part of the Kingdom of Scotland until 1266, when they were ceded to Alexander III by Magnus of Norway. Orkney and Shetland fell to the Scottish Crown as a pledge for the unpaid dowry of Margaret of Denmark, wife of James III, in 1468, the Danish claims to suzerainty being relinquished in 1590 when James VI married Anne of Denmark.

Orkney.—The Orkney Islands (total area 375½ square miles) lie about six miles north of the mainland, separated from it by the Pentland Firth. Of the 90 islands and islets (holms and skerries) in the group, about one-third are inhabited. The total population at the 1981 Census was 19,040; the 1981 populations of the islands shown here include those of smaller islands forming part of the same civil parish.

Mainland	14,299	Shapinsay	345
Eday	154	South Ronaldsay	1,188
Hoy and Graemsay	80	Stronsay	462
Papa Westray	94	Walls and Flotta	761
Rousay and Egilsay	264	Westray	741
Sanday and North Ronaldsay	652		

The islands are rich in Pictish and Scandinavian remains, the most notable being the Stone Age village of Skara Brae, the burial chamber of Maeshowe, the many brochs (Pictish towers) and St. Magnus Cathedral. Scapa Flow, between the Mainland and Hoy, was the war station of the British Grand Fleet from 1914–19 and the scene of the scuttling of the surrendered German High Seas Fleet (June 21, 1919).

Most of the islands are low-lying and fertile, and farming (principally beef cattle) is the main industry. Flotta, to the south of Scapa Flow, is now the site of the oil terminal for the Piper, Claymore and Tartan fields in the North Sea.

Capital.—Kirkwall (population 6,881) on Mainland.

Shetland.—The Shetland Islands (total area, 551 square miles; population (1981 Census) 27,271) lie about 50 miles north of the Orkneys, with Fair Isle about half way between the two groups. Out Stack, off Muckle Flugga, one mile north of Unst, is the most

northern part of the British Isles (60° 51′ 30″ N. lat.).
There are over 100 islands, of which 16 are inhabited.

Mainland	22,184	Muckle Roe	101
Bressay	335	Out Skerries	79
East and West Burra,		Papa Stour	29
and Trondra	930	Unst	1,206
Fair Isle	69	Whalsay	1,026
Fetlar	102	Yell	1,168
Foula	39		

Shetland's many archaelogical sites include
Jarlshof, Mousa and Clickhimin, and its long connection with Scandinavia has resulted in a strong Norse
influence on its place names and dialect.

Industries include fishing, knitwear and farming.
In addition to the fishing fleet there are fish
processing factories, while the traditional handknitting of Fair Isle and Unst is supplemented now with
machine knitted garments,. Farming is mainly
crofting, with sheep being raised on the moorland
and hills of the islands. Latterly the islands have
become an important centre of the North Sea oil
industry, with pipelines from the Brent and Ninian
fields running to the terminal at Sullom Voe, the
largest of its kind in Europe. Lerwick is the main
centre for supply services for offshore oil exploration
and development.

Capital.—Lerwick (population 7,901) on Mainland.

The Hebrides.—Until the closing years of the 13th
century "The Hebrides" included other Scottish
islands in the Firth of Clyde, the peninsula of Kintyre
(Argyllshire), the Isle of Man, and the (Irish) Isle of
Rathlin. The origin of the name is stated to be the
Greek *Eboudai*, latinized as *Hebudes* by Pliny, and
corrupted to its present form. The Norwegian name
Sudreyjar (Southern Islands) was latinized as *Sodorenses*, a name that survives in the Anglican bishopric
of "Sodor and Man."

There are over 500 islands and islets, of which
about 100 are inhabited, though mountainous terrain
and extensive peat bogs mean that only a fraction of
the total area is under cultivation. Stone, Bronze
and Iron Age settlement has left many remains,
including those at Callanish on Lewis, and Norse
colonization has influenced language, customs and
place-names. Occupations include farming (mostly
crofting and stock-raising), fishing and the manufacture of tweeds and other woollens. Tourism is also
an important factor in the economy.

The **Inner Hebrides** lie off the west coast of
Scotland and relatively close to the mainland. The
largest and best-known is *Skye* (area 643 sq. miles;
pop. 8,139; chief town, Portree), which contains the
Cuillin Hills (*Sgurr Alasdair* 3,257 feet), the Red Hills
(*Beinn na Caillich* 2,403 feet) as well as *Bla Bheinn*
(3,046 feet) and *The Storr* (2,358 feet). Skye is also
famous as the refuge of Prince Charles Edward (The
Young Pretender) in 1746. Other islands in the
Highland Region include *Raasay* (pop. 182) *Rum,
Eigg* and *Muck*. Islands in the Strathclyde Region
include *Arran* (pop. 4,726) containing *Goat Fell* (2,868
feet); *Coll and Tiree* (pop. 933); *Colonsay and Oronsay*
(pop. 137); *Islay* (area 235 sq. miles; pop. 3,997); *Jura*
(area 160 sq. miles; pop. 239) with a range of hills
culminating in the Paps of Jura (*Beinn-an-Oir*, 2,576
feet, and *Beinn Chaolais*, 2,477 feet); *Mull* (area 367
sq. miles; pop. 2,605; chief town Tobermory) containing *Ben More* (3,171 feet).

The **Outer Hebrides**, separated from the mainland
by the Minch, now form the Western Isles Islands
Council area (area 1,119 sq. miles; pop. 31,842) (1981 Census)
31,842). The main islands are *Lewis with Harris* (area
770 sq. miles, pop. 23,390), whose chief town, Stornoway (pop. 13,409), is the administrative headquarters
of the Islands Council; *North Uist* (pop. 1,454); *South
Uist* (pop. 2,223); *Benbecula* (pop. 1,988) and *Barra*

(pop. 1,232). Other inhabited islands include *Bernera*
(292), *Berneray* (134), *Eriskay* (219), *Grimsay* (206),
Scalpay (461) and *Vatersay* (108).

EARLY HISTORY

Prehistoric Man.—The *Picts*, believed to be of
non-Aryan origin, seem to have inhabited the whole
of North Britain and to have spread over the north
of Ireland. Remains are most frequent in Caithness
and Sutherland and the Orkney Islands. Celtic
Goidels, Brythons and *Belgae* arrived from Belgic
Gaul during the latter part of the Bronze Age and in
the early Iron Age, and except in the extreme north
of the mainland and in the islands, the civilization
and speech of the people were definitely Celtic at the
time of the Roman invasion of Britain.

The Roman Invasion.—In A.D. 80 Julius Agricola
extended the Roman conquests in Britain by advancing into *Caledonia*, but after a victory at *Mons
Graupius* he was recalled. About 60 years later the
Roman frontier was carried to the isthmus between
the Forth and Clyde and marked by the *Wall of Pius*,
but before the close of the second century the
northern limit of Roman Britain had receded to
Hadrian's Wall.

The Scots.—*Christianity* was introduced into
Southern Caledonia about 380 by missionaries from
Romanized Britain, who penetrated to the northern
districts and islands. After the withdrawal (or
absorption) of the Roman garrison of Britain there
were many years of tribal warfare between the Picts
and Scots (the Gaelic tribe then dominant in Ireland),
the Brythonic Waelisc (Welsh) of Strathclyde (Southwest Scotland and Cumberland), and the Anglo-
Saxons of the Lothians. The Waelisc were isolated
from their kinsmen in Wales by the victory of the
West Saxons at Chester (613), and towards the close
of the 9th century the Scots under *Kenneth Macalpine*
became the dominant power in Caledonia. In the
reign of Malcolm I (943–954) Strathclyde was brought
into subjection, the English lowland kingdom (Lothian) being conquered by Malcolm II (1005–1034).
From the late 11th century until the middle of the
16th there were constant wars between Scotland and
England, the outstanding figures in the struggle
being *William Wallace*, who defeated the English at
Stirling Bridge (1297) and *Robert Bruce*, who won
the victory of Bannockburn (1314). James IV and
many of his nobles fell at the disastrous battle of
Flodden (1513).

In 1603 James VI of Scotland succeeded Queen
Elizabeth I on the throne of England (his mother,
Mary Queen of Scots, was the great-granddaughter
of Henry VII), his successors reigning as Sovereigns
of Great Britain. After the abdication (by flight) in
1689 of James VII and II, the crown devolved upon
William III (grandson of Charles I) and Mary
(daughter of James VII and II) and then upon Anne
(second daughter of James VII and II). Anne's
children died young, and the throne devolved upon
George I (great-grandson of James VI and I). In 1689
Graham of Claverhouse "roused the Highlands" on
behalf of James VII and II, but died after a military
success at Killiecrankie. In 1715, armed risings led
to the indecisive battle of Sheriffmuir, but the
Jacobite movement died down until 1745, when
Prince Charles Edward defeated the Royalist troops
at Prestonpans and advanced to Derby in England
(1746). From Derby, the adherents of "James VIII
and III" (the title claimed for his father by Prince
Charles Edward) fell back on the defensive, and the
movement was finally crushed by the Royalist troops
under the Duke of Cumberland at *Culloden* (April 16,
1746).

AREA AND POPULATION OF SCOTTISH REGIONS

Region	Administrative Headquarters	Area (acres)	Population	Rateable Value 1987 £	Actual Rateable Value per head £
Borders	Newtown St. Boswells	1,154,366	101,800	50,544,247	496·51
Central	Stirling	1,015†	271,819	179,682,744	661·04
Dumfries and Galloway	Dumfries	1,574,074	146,770	77,561,346	528·46
Fife	Glenrothes, Fife	322,960	343,825	234,260,192	681·34
Grampian	Aberdeen	2,150,731	502,850	355,351,107	706·67
Highland	Inverness	10,091†	200,764	115,904,955	577·33
Lothian	Edinburgh	433,600	741,910	520,836,548	702·02
Orkney	Kirkwall	217,600	19,266	25,104,662	1,297·33
Shetland	Lerwick	551†	23,009	66,248,965	2,879·26
Strathclyde	Glasgow	5,348†	2,344,585	1,357,599,445	579·04
Tayside	Dundee	2,897†	392,346	230,137,688	587·00
Western Isles	Stornoway, Lewis	1,119†	30,680	9,781,548	318·82

† Sq. miles

CHIEF EXECUTIVES, DIRECTORS OF FINANCE AND CHAIRMEN OF REGIONAL AND ISLANDS COUNCILS

Region	Chief Executive	Director of Finance	Convener
Borders	K. J. Clark	P. Jeary	T. Hunter
Central	J. Broadfoot	S. C. Craig	C. Sneddon, O.B.E.
Dumfries and Galloway	N. W. D. McIntosh	J. C. Stewart	J. V. M. Jameson
Fife	Dr. J. A. Markland	A. Taylor	R. Gough
Grampian	J. D. Macnaughton	A. McLean	Dr. G. Hadley
Highland	R. H. Stevenson	J. W. Bremner	A. J. Russell
Lothian	G. M. Bowie	D. B. Chynoweth	J. Cook
Orkney	R. H. Gilbert	R. H. Gilbert	E. R. Eunson, O.B.E.
Shetland	M. A. Gerrard	M. E. Green	E. Thomason
Strathclyde	R. Calderwood	A. Gillespie	J. Jennings
Tayside	J. A. Wallace	I. B. McIver	R. M. Tosh
Western Isles	G. Macleod	D. G. Macleod	A. Matheson

PRECEDENCE IN SCOTLAND

The Sovereign.

The Prince Philip, Duke of Edinburgh.

The Lord High Commissioner to the General Assembly (while that Assembly *is sitting*).

The Duke of Rothesay (eldest son of the Sovereign). The Duke of York. The Prince Edward.

Nephews of the Sovereign.

Lords Lieutenant of Counties, Lord Provosts of Counties of Cities, and Sheriffs Principal (successively—within their own localities and during holding of office).

Lord Chancellor of Great Britain.

Moderator of the General Assembly of the Church of Scotland.

The Prime Minister.

Keepers of the Great Seal and of the Privy Seal (successively—if Peers).

Hereditary Lord High Constable of Scotland. Hereditary Master of the Household.

Dukes (successively) of England, Scotland, Great Britain and United Kingdom (including Ireland since date of Union).

Eldest sons of Dukes of the Blood Royal.

Marquesses, in same order as Dukes.

Dukes' eldest sons.

Earls, in order as Dukes.

Younger sons of Dukes of Blood Royal.

Marquesses' eldest sons.

Dukes' younger sons.

Keepers of the Great Seal and of the Privy Seal (successively—if not Peers).

Lord Justice General.

Lord Clerk Register.

Lord Advocate.

Lord Justice Clerk.

Viscounts, in order as Dukes.

Earls' eldest sons.

Marquesses' younger sons.

Lord-Barons, in order as Dukes.

Viscounts' eldest sons.

Earls' younger sons.

Lord-Barons' eldest sons.

Knights of the Garter.

Privy Councillors not included in above ranks.

Senators of Coll. of Justice (Lords of Session).

Viscounts' younger sons.

Lord-Barons' younger sons.

Sons of Life Peers.

Baronets.

Knights of the Thistle.

Knights of other Orders as in England.

Solicitor-General for Scotland.

Lord Lyon King of Arms.

Sheriffs Principal (except as shown in column 1).

Knights Bachelor.

Sheriffs Substitute.

Companions of Orders as in England.

Commanders of Royal Victorian and British Empire Orders.

Eldest sons of younger sons of Peers.

Companions of Distinguished Service Order.

Members (Class 4) Royal Victorian Order.

Officers of British Empire Order.

Baronets' eldest sons.

Knights' eldest sons successively (from Garter to Bachelor).

Members of Class 5 of Royal Victorian Order.

Members of British Empire Order.

Baronets' younger sons.

Knights' younger sons.

Queen's Counsel.

Barons-feudal.

Esquires.

Gentlemen.

SCOTTISH DISTRICT COUNCILS

District	Administrative Headquarters	Population	Rateable Value 1987 £	Chief Executive	Chairman (a) Convener (b) Provost (c) Lord Provost
Aberdeen City (5)	Aberdeen	214,082	199,968,750	J. M. Wilson	(c) H. E. Rae
Angus (9)	Forfar	93,150	47,225,343	P. B. Regan	(b) B. M. C. Milne
Annandale and Eskdale (3)	Annan	35,945	18,486,460	J. A. Whitecross	(a) R. G. Greenhow
Argyll and Bute (8) ...	Lochgilphead	65,586	35,474,539	M. A. J. Gossip	D. C. Currie
Badenoch and Strathspey (6)	Kingussie	10,000	6,490,000	H. G. McCulloch	J. A. McCook
Banff and Buchan (5) .	Banff	83,180	51,980,064	R. W. Jackson†	(a) N. Cowie, O.B.E.
Bearsden and Milngavie (8)	Bearsden	40,171	24,613,064	I. C. Laurie	(b) R. W. Robinson
Berwickshire (1)	Duns	18,602	8,800,000	R. A. Christie	Capt. J. Evans
Caithness (6)	Wick	27,302	10,979,673	A. Beattie	(a) J. M. Young
Clackmannan (2)	Alloa	47,809	27,796,702	I. F. Smith	(a) J. Millar
Clydebank (8)	Clydebank	49,966	24,931,196	J. T. McNally	(b) D. S. Grainger
Clydesdale (8)	Lanark	58,200	23,236,700	P. W. Daniels	(a) Miss M. T. Hodgson
Cumbernauld and Kilsyth (8)	Cumbernauld	62,970	31,652,000	J. Hutton	(b) J. Pollock
Cumnock and Doon Valley (8)	Cumnock	43,400	15,729,427	D. T. Hemmings	(a) D. Shankland
Cunninghame (8).....	Irvine	138,777	72,039,111	B. Devine	(a) Mrs. T. Beattie
Dumbarton (8)	Dumbarton	79,100	47,989,760	L. MacKinnon	(b) P. McCann
Dundee City (9)	Dundee	176,208	110,785,394	J. F. Hoey	(c) T. Mitchell
Dunfermline (4)	Dunfermline	129,115	97,110,036	G. Brown	(b) R. W. Mill
East Kilbride (8).....	East Kilbride	82,524	43,335,000	W. G. McNay, O.B.E.	(b) G. McKillop
East Lothian (7)	Haddington	82,160	47,946,097	M. Duncan	T. Wilson
Eastwood (8)	Giffnock	56,060	31,761,000	M. D. Henry	(b) Mrs. J. M. Edmondson
Edinburgh City (7) ...	Edinburgh	439,672	356,220,028	A. Hepburn	(c) Rt. Hon. J. H. McKay, PH.D., C.B.E.
Ettrick/Lauderdale (1)	Galashiels	33,000	17,505,114	C. M. Anderson	(b) A. L. Tulley
Falkirk (2)	Falkirk	143,063	98,222,000	J. P. H. Paton	(b) J. D. Docherty
Glasgow City (8)	Glasgow	718,528	480,898,610	S. F. Hamilton	(c) Rt. Hon. R. Gray
Gordon (5)	Inverurie	70,200	30,880,000	M. C. Barrow	J. B. Presly
Hamilton (8)	Hamilton	107,089	52,191,998	A. Baird	(b) S. Casserly
Inverclyde (8)	Greenock	97,932	57,200,000	I. C. Wilson	(b) Sir Simpson Stevenson
Inverness (6)	Inverness	60,773	41,150,000	B. Wilson	(b) A. G. Sellar
Kilmarnock and Loudoun (8)	Kilmarnock	81,058	39,240,281	R. W. Jenner	(b) T. Ferguson
Kincardine and Deeside (5)	Stonehaven	47,822	25,316,822	T. Hyder	(a) D. J. Mackenzie
Kirkcaldy (4)	Kirkcaldy	148,193	98,505,416	{ J. M. Smith { H. Wilson§	(a) R. King
Kyle and Carrick (8)..	Ayr	113,290	65,358,937	I. R. D. Smillie	(b) G. T. Macdonald
Lochaber (6)	Fort William	19,369	10,495,600	D. A. B. Blair	C. Neilson
Midlothian (7)	Dalkeith	81,261	37,130,286	D. W. Duguid	(a) D. Lennie
Monklands (8)	Coatbridge	107,010	50,737,000	J. S. Ness	(b) E. Cairns
Moray (5)	Elgin	85,543	50,020,474	J. P. C. Bell	E. Aldridge
Motherwell (8)	Motherwell	148,016	78,965,843	J. Bonomy	(b) J. McGhee
Nairn (6)	Nairn	10,239	4,578,447	A. M. Kerr†	(b) Lt. Col. H. McLean, M.B.E.
Nithsdale (3)	Dumfries	57,339	32,157,333	W. W. Japp	(b) K. Cameron
North-East Fife (4) ...	Cupar	66,700	38,945,649	R. G. Brotherton	D. A. Barrie
Perth and Kinross (9) .	Perth	122,988	71,065,340	J. E. D. Cormie	(b) J. M. Mathieson, O.B.E.
Renfrew (8)	Paisley	203,963	116,231,006	Ms. C. Thompson*	(b) W. McCready
Ross and Cromarty (6)	Dingwall	48,000	28,531,071	D. Sinclair	(a) G. D. Finlayson
Roxburgh (1)	Hawick	35,091	16,582,000	K. W. Cramond°	J. R. Irvine
Skye and Lochalsh (6).	Portree	11,516	4,197,485	D. H. Noble	J. F. Munro
Stewartry (3)	Kirkcudbright	23,136	11,784,709	W. L. Dick-Smith, O.B.E.	(a) J. Nelson, T.D.
Stirling (2)	Stirling	81,170	52,201,374	R. W. Black	(a) J. Wyles
Strathkelvin (8)	Kirkintilloch	89,274	37,157,900	C. Mallon	(b) R. M. Coyle
Sutherland (6)	Golspie	13,238	4,347,000	D. W. Martin	Mrs. L. Mackenzie
Tweeddale (1)	Peebles	14,513	7,650,623	G. H. T. Garvie	J. P. Campbell
West Lothian (7)	Bathgate	141,532	71,076,000	W. N. Fordyce	(a) D. McCauley
Wigtown (3)	Stranraer	30,150	14,141,601	A. Geddes	D. R. Robinson

° Principal Officer.   † Director of Administration.   § Joint Chief Officers.   * District Administrator.

REGIONS.—(1) Borders; (2) Central; (3) Dumfries and Galloway; (4) Fife; (5) Grampian; (6) Highland; (7) Lothian; (8) Strathclyde; (9) Tayside.

LORD LIEUTENANTS IN SCOTLAND

Region	Title	Name
Borders	Berwickshire	Lt. Col. W. B. Swan, C.B.E., T.D.
	Roxburgh, Ettrick and Lauder-dale	The Duke of Buccleuch and Queensberry, K.T., V.R.D
	Tweeddale	Lt. Col. A. M. Sprot of Haystoun, M.C.
Central	Clackmannan	The Earl of Mar and Kellie
	Stirling and Falkirk	Lt. Col. J. Stirling of Garden, T.D.
Dumfries & Galloway	Dumfries	Lt. Col. A. J. Jardine Paterson, O.B.E., T.D.
	The Stewartry of Kirkcud-bright	The Lord Sinclair, L.V.O.
	Wigtown	Maj. H. J. Brewis
Fife	Fife	The Earl of Elgin and Kincardine, K.T.
Grampian	Aberdeenshire	Capt. C. A. Farquharson
	Banffshire	J. A. S. McPherson
	Kincardineshire	The Viscount of Arbuthnott, D.S.C., F.R.S.E.
	Morayshire	Capt. Sir Iain Tennant, K.T.
Highland	Caithness	The Viscount Thurso
	Inverness	Lt. Comdr. L. R. D. Mackintosh of Mackintosh, O.B.E.
	Nairn	The Earl of Leven and Melville
	Ross and Cromarty	Vice-Adm. Sir John Hayes, K.C.B., O.B.E.
	Sutherland	Col. A. MacD. Gilmour, O.B.E., M.C.
Lothian	East Lothian	Sir Hew Hamilton-Dalrymple, Bt., K.V.C.O.
	Midlothian	Sir John Dutton Clerk of Penicuik, Bt., C.B.E., V.R.D.
	West Lothian	The Earl of Morton
Strathclyde	Argyll and Bute	The Lord Maclean, K.T., P.C., G.C.V.O., K.B.E.
	Ayr and Arran	Col. B. M. Knox, M.C., T.D.
	Dunbartonshire	Brig. A. S. Pearson, C.B., D.S.O., O.B.E., M.C., T.D.
	Lanarkshire	Col. The Lord Clydesmuir, K.T., C.B., M.B.E., T.D.
	Renfrewshire	Maj. J. D. M. Crichton Maitland
Tayside	Angus	The Earl of Dalhousie, K.T., G.C.V.O., G.B.E., M.C.
	Perth and Kinross	Maj. D. H. Butter, M.C.
Orkney	Orkney	Col. R. A. A. S. Macrae, M.B.E.
Shetland	Shetland	M. M. Shearer
Western Isles	Western Isles	The Earl Granville, M.C.

NOTE.—The Lord Provosts of the four city districts of Aberdeen, Dundee, Edinburgh and Glasgow are Lord Lieutenants for those districts *ex officio.*

PRINCIPAL SCOTTISH CITIES

EDINBURGH

EDINBURGH, the Capital of Scotland, has a municipal area of 100·6 sq. miles. The city is built on a group of hills and contains in Princes Street one of the most beautiful thoroughfares in the world. The principal buildings are the Castle, which includes St. Margaret's Chapel, the oldest building in Edinburgh, and near it, the Scottish National War Memorial; the Palace of Holyroodhouse; Parliament House, the present seat of the judicature; two universities (Edinburgh and Heriot-Watt); St. Giles' Cathedral (restored 1879–83); St. Mary's (Scottish Episcopal) Cathedral (Sir Gilbert Scott); the General Register House (Robert Adam): the National and the Signet Libraries; the National Gallery; the Royal Scottish Academy; and the National Portrait Gallery. The city is governed by the City of Edinburgh District Council which includes the area of South Queensferry, Kirkliston, Currie, Ratho and Balerno.

GLASGOW

GLASGOW, a Royal Burgh, City, largest District in the Strathclyde Region, and the principal commercial and industrial centre in Scotland, has a municipal area of 49,743 acres. The city occupies the north and south banks of the Clyde, formerly one of the chief commercial estuaries in the world. The principal industries include engineering, aero and marine engines, chemicals, printing, etc. The city has also developed recently as a tourism and conference centre. The chief buildings are the 13th century Gothic Cathedral, the University (Sir Gilbert Scott), the City Chambers, Pollok House, the School of Art (Mackintosh), Kelvingrove Art Galleries, the Burrell Collection museum and the Mitchell Library. The city is home of the Scottish National Orchestra, Scottish Opera, Scottish Ballet, etc.

ABERDEEN

ABERDEEN, 126 miles N.E. of Edinburgh, received its charter as a Royal Burgh from William the Lion in 1179. Scotland's third largest city, it covers an area of 73·25 square miles. Aberdeen is the principal commercial and administrative centre in the N. of Scotland, the second largest Scottish fishing port and the main European centre for offshore oil exploration. It is also an ancient university town and distinguished research centre. Other industries include engineering, shipbuilding, food processing, textiles, paper manufacturing and chemicals. Places of interest: King's College, St. Machar's Cathedral, Brig o' Balgownie, the Kirk of St. Nicholas, Mercat Cross, Marischal College, Provost Skene's House, Art Gallery, James Dun's House (children's museum) and Provost Ross's House (maritime museum).

DUNDEE

DUNDEE, a Royal Burgh, City, is the administrative centre of Tayside Region. Situated on the north bank of the Tay estuary, it extends over 96 square miles. The city's first class port and dock installations are important to the offshore oil industry and the airport also provides servicing facilities. Principal industries include textiles, watches and clocks, computers and other electronic industries, lasers, healthcare, printing, tyre manufacture, food processing, carpets, heavy electrical and marine engineering and clothing manufacture. Six sites, totalling 210 acres, have Enterprise Zone status. These include the Technology Park, airport and port, as well as city centre commercial sites and general industrial sites. The University of Dundee was established in 1967. The unique City Churches—three churches under one roof, together with the 15th century St. Mary's Tower—are the most prominent architectural feature.

CHIEFS OF CLANS AND NAMES IN SCOTLAND

THE ROYAL HOUSE: H.M. The Queen

AGNEW: Sir Crispin Hamlyn Agnew of Lochnaw, Bt., 6 Palmerston Road, Edinburgh.

ANSTRUTHER: Sir Ralph Anstruther of that Ilk, Bt., K.C.V.O., M.C., Balcaskie, Pittenweem, Fife.

ARBUTHNOTT: The Viscount of Arbuthnott, C.B.E., D.S.C., Arbuthnott House, Laurencekirk, Kincardineshire.

BARCLAY: Peter C. Barclay of that Ilk, Gatemans, Stratford St. Mary, Colchester, Essex.

BORTHWICK: The Lord Borthwick, T.D., Crookston, Heriot, Midlothian.

BOYD: The Lord Kilmarnock, Casa de Mondragon, Ronda (Malaga), Spain.

BOYLE: Rr. Adm. The Earl of Glasgow, C.B., D.S.C., Kelburn, Fairlie, Ayrshire.

BRODIE: Ninian Brodie of Brodie, Brodie Castle, Forres, Moray.

BRUCE: The Earl of Elgin and Kincardine, K.T., Broomhall, Dunfermline, Fife.

BUCHAN: David S. Buchan of Auchmacoy, Auchmacoy, Ellon, Aberdeenshire.

BURNETT: J. C. A. Burnett of Leys, Crathes Castle, Kincardineshire.

CAMERON: Col. Sir Donald Hamish Cameron of Lochiel, K.T., C.V.O., T.D., Achnacarry, Spean Bridge, Inverness.

CAMPBELL: The Duke of Argyll, Inveraray, Argyll.

CARMICHAEL: Richard John Carmichael of Carmichael, Carmichael, Thankerton, Biggar, Lanarkshire.

CARNEGIE: The Earl of Southesk, K.C.V.O., Kinnaird Castle, Brechin.

CATHCART: Maj. Gen. The Earl Cathcart, C.B., D.S.O., M.C., 2 Pembroke Gardens, W.8.

CHARTERIS: The Earl of Wemyss and March, K.T., Gosford House, Longniddry, East Lothian.

CLAN CHATTAN: M. K. Mackintosh of Clan Chattan, Maxwell Park, Gwelo, Zimbabwe.

CHISHOLM: Alastair Chisholm of Chisholm (*The Chisholm*), Silver Willows, Bury St. Edmunds.

COCHRANE: The Earl of Dundonald, Lochnell Castle, Ledaig, Argyllshire.

COLQUHOUN: Sir Ivar Colquhoun of Luss, Bt., Camstraddan, Luss, Dunbartonshire.

CRANSTOUN: Lt. Col. Alastair Cranstoun of that Ilk, M.C., Corehouse, Lanarkshire.

CRICHTON: Charles Crichton of that Ilk, Monzie, Perth.

DARROCH: Captain Duncan Darroch of Gourock. The Red House, Branksome Park Rd., Camberley.

DRUMMOND: The Earl of Perth, P.C., Stobhall, Perth.

DUNBAR: Sir Jean Ivor Dunbar of Mochrum, Bt., 45/55 39th Street, Long Island City, New York.

DUNDAS: David D. Dundas of Dundas, 8 Derna Road, Kenwyn 7700, South Africa.

ELIOTT: Sir Arthur Eliott of Stobs, Bt., Redheugh, Newcastleton, Roxburghshire.

ERSKINE: The Earl of Mar and Kellie, Claremont House, Alloa.

FARQUHARSON: Capt. A. A. C. Farquharson of Invercauld, M.C., Invercauld, Braemar.

FERGUSSON: Sir Charles Fergusson of Kilkerran, Bt., Kilkerran, Maybole, Ayrshire.

FORBES: The Lord Forbes, K.B.E., Balforbes, Alford, Aberdeenshire.

FORSYTH: Alistair Forsyth of that Ilk, Ethie Castle, by Arbroath, Angus.

FRASER: The Lady Saltoun, Cairnbulg Castle, Fraserburgh, Aberdeenshire.

FRASER (OF LOVAT)*: The Lord Lovat, D.S.O., M.C., T.D., Balblair House, Beauly, Inverness-shire.

GAYRE: Lt. Col. Robert Gayre of Gayre and Nigg, 1–3 Gloucester Lane, Edinburgh.

GORDON: The Marquess of Huntly, Aboyne Castle, Aberdeenshire.

GRAHAM: The Duke of Montrose, Auchmar, Drymen, Stirlingshire.

GRANT: The Lord Strathspey, 111 Elms Ride, West Wittering, W. Sussex.

HAIG: The Earl Haig, O.B.E., Bemersyde, Melrose, Roxburgh.

HALDANE: Alexander N. C. Haldane of Gleneagles, Auchterarder, Perthshire.

HANNAY: Ramsey W. R. Hannay of Kirkdale and of that Ilk, Cardoness House, Gatehouse-of-Fleet, Kirkcudbright.

HAY: The Earl of Erroll, Wolverton Farm, Wolverton, Basingstoke, Hants.

HENDERSON: John W. P. Henderson of Fordell, 7 Owen Street, Toowoomba, Queensland, Australia.

HUNTER: Neil A. Hunter of Hunterston, Tour d'Escas, Carretera d'Escas, La Massana, Andorra.

IRVINE OF DRUM: C. F. Irvine of Drum, 29 Forest Road, Hoylake, Wirral, Merseyside.

JARDINE: Sir Alexander Jardine of Applegirth, Bt., Denbie, Lockerbie, Dumfriesshire.

JOHNSTONE: The Earl of Annandale and Hartfell, Raehills, Lockerbie, Dumfriesshire.

KEITH: The Earl of Kintore, Glenton House, Rickarton, Stonehaven, Aberdeenshire.

KENNEDY: The Marquess of Ailsa, O.B.E., Blanefield, Kirkoswald, Ayrshire.

KERR: The Marquess of Lothian, Monteviot, Ancrum, Roxburgh.

KINCAID: (vacant).

LAMONT: Peter N. Lamont of that Ilk, St. Patrick's College, Manley, N.S.W. 2095, Australia.

LEASK: Madam Leask of Leask, 1 Vincent Road, Sheringham, Norfolk.

LENNOX: Dennis P. H. Lennox of that Ilk, Pools Farm, Downton on the Rock, Ludlow, Shropshire.

LESLIE: The Earl of Rothes, Tanglewood, West Tytherley, Salisbury, Wilts.

LINDSAY: The Earl of Crawford and Balcarres, P.C., Balcarres, Colinsburgh, Fife.

LOCKHART: Angus Hew Lockhart of the Lee, Newholme, Dunsyre, Lanark.

LUMSDEN: Gillem Lumsden of that Ilk and Blanerne, Kinderslegh, Bois Avenue, Chesham Bois, Amersham, Bucks.

McBAIN: J. H. McBain of McBain, 7025, North Finger Rock Place, Tucson, Arizona, U.S.A.

MALCOLM (MACCALLUM): Robin N. L. Malcolm of Poltalloch, Duntrune Castle, Lochgilphead, Argyll.

MACDONALD: The Lord Macdonald (*The Macdonald of Macdonald*), Ostaig House, Skye.

MACDONALD OF CLANRANALD*: Ranald A. Macdonald of Clanranald, 55 Compton Road, N.1.

MACDONALD OF SLEAT (CLAN HUSTEAIN)*: Sir Ian Bosville-Macdonald of Sleat, Bt., Thorpe Hall, Rudston, Driffield, Yorks.

MACDONELL OF GLENGARRY*: Air Cdre. Aeneas R. MacDonell of Glengarry, C.B., D.F.C., Elonbank, Castle Street, Fortrose, Ross-shire.

MACDOUGALL: Madam Coline MacDougall of MacDougall, Dunollie, Argyll.

MACGREGOR: Sir Gregor MacGregor of MacGregor, Bt., Bannatyne, Newtyle, Angus.

MACKAY: The Lord Reay, 11 Wilton Crescent, S.W.1.

MACKENZIE: The Earl of Cromartie, M.C., T.D., Castle Leod, Strathpeffer, Ross-shire.

MACKINNON: Madam Anne Mackinnon of Mackinnon, 16 Purleigh Road, Bridgewater, Somerset.

MACKINTOSH: The Mackintosh of Mackintosh, O.B.E., Moy Hall, Inverness.

MACLACHLAN: Madam Marjorie MacLachlan of MacLachlan, Castle Lachlan, Argyll.

MACLAREN: Donald MacLaren of MacLaren and Achleskine, British Military Government, Berlin (B.F.P.O. 45).

MACLEAN: The Lord Maclean, P.C., K.T., G.C.V.O., K.B.E., Duart Castle, Mull.

MACLENNAN: Ronald G. MacLennan of MacLennan, The Old Mill, Dores, Inverness.

MACLEOD: J. MacLeod of MacLeod, Dunvegan Castle, Skye.

MACMILLAN: George MacMillan of MacMillan, Finlaystone, Langbank, Renfrewshire.

MACNAB: J. C. Macnab of Macnab (*The Macnab*), Finlarig, Killin, Perthshire.

MACNAGHTEN: Sir Patrick Macnaghten of Macnaghten and Dundarave, Bt., Dundarave, Bushmills, Co. Antrim.

MACNEIL OF BARRA: Ian R. Macneil of Barra (*The Macneil of Barra*), Kisimul Castle, Barra.

MACPHERSON: Sir William Macpherson of Cluny, T.D., Newtown Castle, Blairgowrie, Perthshire.

MACTHOMAS: Andrew P. C. MacThomas of Finegand, c/o The Clan MacThomas Society, 19 Warriston Avenue, Edinburgh 3.

MAITLAND: The Earl of Lauderdale, 12 St. Vincent Street, Edinburgh.

MAKGILL: The Viscount of Oxfuird, Hill House, St. Mary Bourne, Andover, Hants.

MAR: The Countess of Mar, St. Michael's Farm, Great Witley, Worcs.

MARJORIBANKS: William Marjoribanks of that Ilk, Kirklands of Forglen, Turriff, Aberdeenshire.

MATHESON: Sir Torquhil Matheson of Matheson, Bt., Sanderwick Court, Frome, Somerset.

MENZIES: David R. Menzies of Menzies, 20 Nardina Crescent, Dalkeith, Western Australia.

MOFFAT: Francis Moffat of that Ilk, Redacres, Moffat, Dumfriesshire.

MONCREIFFE: (vacant).

MONTGOMERIE: The Earl of Eglinton and Winton, The Dutch House, West Green, Hartley Wintney, Hants.

MORRISON: Dr. Iain M. Morrison of Ruchdi, Todhurst Farm, Lake Lane, Barnham, Sussex.

MUNRO: Patrick G. Munro of Foulis, T.D., Foulis Castle, Ross.

MURRAY: The Duke of Atholl, Blair Castle, Blair Atholl, Perthshire.

NICOLSON: The Lord Carnock, 90 Whitehall Court, London S.W.1.

NICOLSON OF SCORRYBREAC*: Ian Nicolson of Scorrybreac, P.O. Box 420, Ballina, N.S.W. 2478.

OGILVY: The Earl of Airlie, K.T., Cortachy Castle, Kirriemuir, Angus.

RAMSAY: The Earl of Dalhousie, K.T., G.C.V.O., G.B.E., M.C., Brechin Castle, Angus.

RATTRAY: James S. Rattray of Rattray, Craighall, Rattray, Perthshire.

ROBERTSON: Alexander Gilbert Haldane Robertson of Struan (*Struan-Robertson*), The Breach Farm, Goudhurst Road, Cranbrook, Kent.

ROLLO: The Lord Rollo, Pitcairns, Dunning, Perthshire.

ROSE: Miss Elizabeth Rose of Kilravock, Kilravock Castle, Croy, Inverness-shire.

ROSS: David C. Ross of that Ilk, The Old Schoolhouse, Fettercairn, Kincardineshire.

RUTHVEN: The Earl of Gowrie, Castlemartin, Kilcullen, Co. Kildare, Eire.

SCOTT: The Duke of Buccleuch and Queensberry, K.T., V.R.D., Bowhill, Selkirk.

SCRYMGEOUR: The Earl of Dundee, Birkhill, Cupar, Fife.

SEMPILL: The Lady Sempill, Druminnor Castle, Rhynie, Aberdeenshire.

SHAW: John Shaw of Tordarroch, Newhall, Balblair, By Conon Bridge, Ross-shire.

SINCLAIR: The Earl of Caithness, Finstock Manor, Finstock, Oxon.

STIRLING: Sir Charles Norman Stirling of Cader, K.C.M.G., K.C.V.O., 17 Park Row, Farnham, Surrey.

SUTHERLAND: The Countess of Sutherland, House of Tongue, Brora, Sutherland.

SWINTON: W. F. H. Swinton of that Ilk, 23301 8th Avenue S.S., Calgary, Alberta, Canada.

URQUHART: Kenneth T. Urquhart of that Ilk, 4713 Orleans Blvd., Jefferson, Louisiana, U.S.A.

WALLACE: Lt.-Col. M. R. Wallace of that Ilk, Hilton of Gask, Auchterarder, Perthshire.

WEDDERBURN OF THAT ILK: The Master of Dundee, Birkhill, Cupar, Fife.

WEMYSS: David Wemyss of that Ilk, Gosford House, Longniddry, East Lothian.

Only chiefs of *whole* Names or Clans are included (except certain special instances (marked *), who though not chiefs of a "whole name", were, or are, for some reason, (*e.g.* the Macdonald forfeiture), independent. Under decision (*Campbell-Gray*, 1950) that a bearer of a "double or triple-barrelled" surname cannot be held chief of a part of such, several others cannot be included in the list at present.

NEW TOWNS IN GREAT BRITAIN

Commission for the New Towns. Glen House, Stag Place, SW1E 5AJ.—The Commission was established under the New Towns Act, 1959, its remit is to (a) take over and, with a view to its eventual disposal, to hold, manage and turn to account the property of Development Corporations transferred to the Commission and (b) as soon as it considers it expedient to do so, to dispose of property so transferred and any other property held by it. In carrying out its remit the Commission must have due regard to the convenience and welfare of persons residing, working or carrying on business there and, until disposal, the maintenance and enhancement of the value of the land held and return obtained from it. The Commission has such responsibilities in 13 towns—Basildon, Bracknell, Central Lancashire, Corby, Crawley, Harlow, Hatfield, Hemel Hempstead, Northampton, Redditch, Skelmersdale, Stevenage and Welwyn Garden City.

Chairman, Sir Neil Shields, M.C.

Deputy Chairman, A. Jones.

Members, R. B. Caws, C.B.E.; W. J. Mackenzie, O.B.E.; P. M. Vine, C.B.E.; Sir Gordon Roberts, C.B.E.; The Lord Bellwin; E. G. Barratt; M. H. Mallinson; R. W. P. Luff.

Chief Executive, D. M. Woodhall.

Director of Estates and Technical Services, H. J. M. Thomas.

Director of Finance, Administrative and Legal Services, G. T. C. Probart.

Director of Promotion, J. Grafton.

BASILDON, Essex.—*Executive Manager,* D. Galloway. *Offices,* Gifford House, London Road, Bowers Gifford, Basildon SS13 2EX.

BRACKNELL, Berks.—Glen House, SW1E 5AJ.

CENTRAL LANCASHIRE, Lancs.—*Executive Officer,* B. Birtwistle. *Offices,* Cuerden Pavilion, Shady Lane, Bamber Bridge, Preston PR5 6AZ.

CORBY, Northants.—*Executive Officer,* J. G. Lloyd. *Offices,* Chisholm House, 9 Queen's Square, Corby NN17 1PA.

CRAWLEY, Sussex.—Glen House, SW1E 5AJ.

HARLOW, Essex.—Glen House, SW1E 5AJ.

HATFIELD, Herts.—Glen House, SW1E 5AJ.

HEMEL HEMPSTEAD, Herts.—Glen House, SW1E 5AJ.

NORTHAMPTON.—*Executive Officer,* W. A. Gray. *Offices,* 2/3 Market Square, Northampton NN1 2EN.

REDDITCH,Worcs.—*Executive Officer,* I. McKay. *Offices,* Highfield House, Headless Cross Drive, Redditch B97 5EU.

SKELMERSDALE, Lancs.—*Executive Officer,* J. Leigh. *Offices,* Pennylands, Skelmersdale WN8 8AR.

STEVENAGE, Herts.—Glen House, SW1E 5AJ.

WELWYN GARDEN CITY, Herts.—Glen House, SW1E 5AJ.

DEVELOPMENT CORPORATIONS

England and Wales

AYCLIFFE AND PETERLEE, Co. Durham.—Amalgamated 1985 (Aycliffe formed 1947; Peterlee formed 1948). *Chairman,* Sir Michael Straker, C.B.E. *Chief Executive,* E. Henderson. *Offices,* Thames House, Newton Aycliffe DL5 6AW. Area, Aycliffe 3,161 acres; Peterlee 2,977 acres. Population, Aycliffe 25,500; Peterlee 25,000. Estimated eventual population, Aycliffe 32,000; Peterlee 25,500.

CWMBRAN, Gwent.—Formed 1949, dissolution to take place in March 1988. *Chairman,* J. D. Allen. *Managing Director,* R. W. Howlett, O.B.E. *Offices,* Gwent House, Town Centre, Cwmbran NP44 1XZ. Area, 3,560 acres. Population, 41,600. Estimated eventual population, 50,000.

MILTON KEYNES, Bucks.—Formed 1967. *Chairman,* Sir Henry Chilver, F.R.S. *General Manager,* F. C. Henshaw. *Offices,* Saxon Court, 502 Avebury Boulevard, Central Milton Keynes MK9 3HS. Area, 22,000 acres. Population, 137,000. Estimated eventual population, 200,000.

PETERBOROUGH, Cambs.—Formed 1967. *Chairman,* J. Rowe, C.B.E. *General Manager,* K. Hutton. *Offices,* Stuart House, City Road, Peterborough PE1 1UJ. Area, 15,000 acres. Population, 133,000. Estimated eventual population, 150,000.

TELFORD, Shropshire.—Formed 1963. *Chairman,* (vacant). *General Manager,* M. D. Morgan. *Offices,* Priorslee Hall, Telford TF2 9NT. Area, 19,500 acres. Population, 111,000. Estimated eventual population, 125,000

WARRINGTON AND RUNCORN, Cheshire.—Amalgamated 1981 (Warrington formed 1968; Runcorn formed 1964). *Chairman,* Prof. A. Mercer. *General Manager,* D. J. Binns. *Offices,* New Town House, Buttermarket Street, Warrington WA1 2LF. Area, Warrington 18,612 acres; Runcorn 7,234 acres. Population, Warrington 146,000; Runcorn 68,100.

WASHINGTON, Tyne and Wear.—Formed 1964. *Chairman,* Prof. W. G. McClelland, D.C.L. *Managing Director,* R. G. Tilmouth. *Offices,* Usworth Hall, Stephenson, District 12, Washington NE37 3HS. Area, 5,610 acres. Population, 57,000. Estimated eventual population, 63,000.

DEVELOPMENT BOARD FOR RURAL WALES.—Formed 1977. *Chairman,* F. L. Morgan, M.B.E.. *Offices,* Ladywell House, Newtown, Powys, SY16 1JB.

Scotland

CUMBERNAULD, Strathclyde.—Formed 1956. *Chairman,* D. Mitchell, C.B.E.. *Chief Executive,* D. W. Anderson, C.B.E. *Headquarters,* Cumbernauld House, Cumbernauld G67 3JH. Area, 7,788 acres. Population, 49,000. Estimated eventual population, 70,000.

EAST KILBRIDE, Strathclyde.—Formed 1947. *Chairman,* J. A. Denholm. *Managing Director,* G. B. Young, C.B.E. *Offices,* Atholl House, East Kilbride G74 1LU. Area, 10,250 acres. Population, 70,000. Estimated eventual population, 82,500.

GLENROTHES, Fife.—Formed 1948. *Chairman,* Prof. C. Blake. *Chief Executive,* W. M. Cracknell. *Offices,* Balbirnie House, Glenrothes KY7 6NR. Area, 5,760 acres. Population, 38,400. Estimated eventual population, 48,000.

IRVINE, Ayrshire.—Formed, 1966. *Chairman,* A. R. Belch, C.B.E. *Managing Director,* Brig. R. A. Rickets. *Offices,* Perceton House, Irvine KA11 2AL. Area, 12,409 acres. Population, 58,537. Estimated eventual population, 63,000.

LIVINGSTON, West Lothian.—Formed, 1962. *Chairman,* R. S. Watt. *Chief Executive,* J. A. Pollock. *Offices,* Sidlaw House, Almondvale, Livingston EH54 6QA. Area, 6,868 acres. Population, 40,500. Estimated eventual population, 70,000.

Northern Ireland

(For geographical, historical and judicial notes on Ireland, see Index)

The usually resident population of Northern Ireland, as revised, at the 1981 Census was 1,556,039 (males, 761,882; females, 794,157) compared with a total population of 1,536,065 at the Census of 1971. (N.B. This revised figure takes account of the population effect of non-enumerated households, estimated at 74,000 persons.) In 1981 the number of persons in the various religious denominations (expressed as percentages of the total usually resident population) were: Roman Catholic, 28·0; Presbyterian, 22·9; Church of Ireland, 19·0; Methodist, 4·0; others 7·6; not stated, 18·5. Northern Ireland has a total area of 5,452 sq. miles (land, 5,206 sq. miles; inland water and tideways, 246 sq. miles) with a density of population of 282 persons per sq. mile in 1981. The population, mid 1985 estimate, was 1,558,000.

CONSTITUTION AND GOVERNMENT

A separate parliament and executive Government was established for Northern Ireland in 1921 by the Government of Ireland Act. The Northern Ireland Constitution Act, 1973, abolished the post of Governor and Parliament of Northern Ireland and provided for the transfer of certain legislative functions to a Northern Ireland Assembly and Executive. Devolved Government came into operation with effect from January 1, 1974 but when the Executive collapsed the Northern Ireland Assembly was prorogued on May 29, 1974. The Northern Ireland Constitution Act, 1974, which became law in July 1974, made provision for temporary arrangements for the government of Northern Ireland by the Secretary of State for Northern Ireland and also provided for the holding of elections and a Constitutional Convention. Direct Rule continues in being under the terms of the Northern Ireland Act 1974.

Attempts have been made by successive governments to find a way of restoring devolved government to Northern Ireland. The most recent attempt failed when the Northern Ireland Assembly (elected on October 20, 1982) was dissolved on June 23, 1986, having failed to make proposals for the resumption of devolved government and also to monitor the work of Northern Ireland departments.

FLAG.—The national flag is that of the United Kingdom.

THE PRIVY COUNCIL

R. J. Bailie (1971); D. W. Bleakley (1971); R. H. Bradford (1969); W. Craig (1963); J. Dobson (1969); W. K. Fitzsimmons (1965); Lt. Col. the Lord Glentoran (1953); Sir Edward Jones (1965); Mr. Justice Kelly (1969); H. V. Kirk (1962); Capt. W. J. Long (1966); Lord Lowry (*Lord Chief Justice*) (1971); R. W. B. McConnell (1964); W. B. McIvor (1971); W. J. Morgan (1961); The Lord Moyola (1966); Sir Ivan Neill (1950); The Lord O'Neill of the Maine (1956); Sir Robert Porter, Q.C. (1969); Lord Rathcavan (1969); R. Simpson (1969); J. D. Taylor (1970); H. W. West (1960).

GOVERNMENT OFFICES

Department of Finance and Personnel

Permanent Secretary, Dr. W. G. H. Quigley, C.B.
Under Secretaries, P. Carvill; J. B. C. Lyttle; W. J. Hodges; J. L. Semple; R. B. Spence.
Assistant Secretaries:
    Resources Group, D. W. Alexander, Dr. J. J. M. Harbison; J. G. Hunter; W. G. Purdy; Dr. D. G. Slattery; P. J. Small; R. G. Smartt; J. F. Walker.
    Personnel and Finance Group, J. R. Ingram; J. Maguire; P. J. Tweedale; Mrs. D. A. Brown; H. Moore; Dr. E. M. Power.
    Central Secretariat, N. Hamilton.
Senior Principals, J. E. Henderson; R. J. Jordan; R. E. Templeton; T. Whiteside; K. L. Millar; F. P. Smyth; D. D. Vincent.

Solicitor, R. F. Cole.
Commissioner of Valuation, D. W. M. Deyermond.
First Legislative Draftsman, T. R. Erskine, C.B.

Department of Education

Permanent Secretary, J. H. Parkes, C.B.
Under Secretaries, A. J. Green; E. G. Martin.
Senior Chief Inspector, I. H. N. Wallace.
Assistant Secretaries, A. M. Dodds; D. Woods; R. T. Holmes; K. H. Clark; R. D. Hill; P. S. Holmes; J. S. Smith; T. Johnston.
Deputy Senior Chief Inspector, J. B. S. O'Kelly.
Chief Inspector, N. Morrison.

Department of the Environment

Permanent Secretary, D. Barry.
Under Secretaries, W. E. C. Ford (*Personnel, Information Systems Unit, Solicitors Branch, Central Management, Local Government*), R. H. Mackenzie (*Conservation, Historic Monuments and Buildings, Environmental Protection, Works Service, Ordnance Survey, Land Registry, Registry of Deeds, Rates*); F. McCann (*Housing, Water*); G. F. Loughran (*Planning, Comprehensive Development, Lands Service*); J. A. G. Whitlaw (*Roads, Transport, Public Records Office*).
Director, Town and Country Planning Service, J. B. Davidson.
Director, Water Service, W. N. Smyth.
Director, Roads Service, I. W. Joiner.
Director, Works Services, J. Brennan.
Director, Conservation, J. B. Phillips.
Director, Environmental Protection, I. McQuiston.
Assistant Secretaries, W. Black; W. N. Campbell; H. E. Carson; J. Cowan; F. A. Dillon; T. Pearson; A. Miller; F. R. Rodgers; J. Kirk; J. M. Irvine; J. F. Russell; R. E. Aiken; E. J. Galway; D. B. McIldouh; Mrs. R. Brown.
Chief Local Government Auditor, S. J. Bailie.
Chief Engineer (Roads Service), Dr. W. M. C. Stevenson.
Chief Planning Officer, E. Hayes.
Chief Engineer (Water Service), S. T. Bratty.
Chief Quantity Surveyor, T. O'Hara.
Chief Survey Officer, M. J. D. Brand.
Chief Civil Engineer, C. E. Ronaldson.
Chief Architect, W. B. Sloan.
Chief Structural Engineer, K. Turkington.
Chief Alkali and Radiochemical Inspector, K. J. Ledgerwood.

Department of Health & Social Services

Permanent Secretary, F. A. Elliott.
Under Secretaries, G. Buchanan; R. F. Mills; R. S. Sterling; Miss Z. Davies.
Assistant Secretaries, A. N. Burns; C. McN. Davie; J. R. Kearney; R. J. Minnis; E. H. Elliott; J. Scott; J. A. Wylie; R. McMurray; A. S. Treacy; D. H. McNally; Miss J. Mills; P. Simpson; Dr. R. W. McQuiston; S. J. Peover; S. Quinn.
Chief Medical Officer, Dr. J. F. McKenna.

Deputy Chief Medical Officers, Dr. D. J. Sloan; Dr. W. D. Thornton.

Chief Inspector, Social Services Inspectorate, P. J. Armstrong.

Department of Economic Development

Permanent Secretary, D. Fell.
Under Secretaries, J. Crozier; D. Gibson; E. Mayne.
Chief Engineer and Scientist, Dr. T. B. Copestake.
Assistant Secretaries, R. B. Gamble; R. J. O'Hara; Miss S. Cooper; J. D. M. Thompson; P. S. McDonnell; D. J. Alexander; Miss J. Dixon; M. Warnock; C. Stutt; R. Wilson; J. C. Wolstencroft; R. H. Thompson.
Director of Industrial Science Division, J. T. McCullins.
Economic Adviser, Prof. W. Black.

Industrial Development Board

Chief Executive, J. B. McAllister.
Deputy Chief Executives, A. S. Hopkins; J. M. Dowdall.
Executive Directors, A. I. Devitt; P. T. Bill; J. H. Caldwell; J. J. Monaghan; F. A. Hewitt; D. C. Gowdy; W. B. Robinson; W. J. Alexander; I. Walters; H. G. Thompson.
Corporate Finance, R. D. Lynn.

Department of Agriculture

Permanent Secretary, Dr. W. H. Jack.
Under Secretaries, J. C. Chalmers; J. Murray.
Chief Scientific Officer, Dr. C. E. Wright.
Chief Agriculture Officer, T. A. Larmour.
Chief Veterinary Officer, E. W. Sullivan.
Chief Forest Officer, W. H. Forbes.
Assistant Secretaries, D. A. G. Hirrell; D. M. Carnson; L. Sinclair; S. R. Armstrong; N. E. Morrison; I. C. Henderson; K. E. Brady.

Head of Northern Ireland Civil Service and Central Secretariat

Head of Northern Ireland Civil Service, Sir Kenneth Bloomfield, K.C.B.
Under Secretary, R. Spence.
Assistant Secretary, N. Hamilton.
Director of Information, A. Wood.

Northern Ireland Audit Office

Comptroller and Auditor-General, L. V. D. Calvert, C.B..
Secretary, J. G. W. McComish.
Directors of Audit, D. A. Kerr; K. G. McCormick; B. H. Poulter; S. B. D. McConnell.

Northern Ireland Business Centre
11 Berkeley Street, W.1.

Senior Executive, F. G. Galbraith.
Executive, R. Bennett.

FINANCE

Taxation in Northern Ireland is largely imposed and collected by the United Kingdom Government. After deducting the cost of collections and of Northern Ireland's contributions to the European Economic Community the balance, known as the Attributed Share of Taxation, is paid over to the Northern Ireland Consolidated Fund. Northern Ireland's revenue is insufficient to meet its expenditure and is supplemented by a grant in aid.

	1986–87* £	1987–88** £
Public income	3,500,753,132	3,663,224,953
Public expenditure	3,500,648,309	3,663,124,953

* Outturn   ** Estimate

EXTERNAL TRADE*

	Tonnes ('000)		
	1984	1985	1986
Total imports ...	9,770	10,766	10,808
Total exports ...	2,399	2,688	2,932

* Including cross-Channel trade with Great Britain.

PRODUCTION

Industries.—The total value of the industrial production (manufacturing, gas, electricity and water) in Northern Ireland by firms employing 20 or more persons in 1982 was approximately £3,902 million and the number of persons employed about 107,000. The products of the engineering, shipbuilding and aircraft industries which employed 33,000 persons, were valued at £678 million. The textile industries, employing about 13,000 persons, produced products valued at approximately £263 million. The food and drink industry, employing about 20,000 persons, produced goods valued at £1,774 million. The value of clothing manufactured in 1981 was about £142 million.

Minerals.—1,577 persons were employed in mining and quarrying operations in Northern Ireland in 1984 and the minerals raised (17,276,204 tonnes) were valued at £29,892,396.

COMMUNICATIONS

Seaports.—The total tonnage handled by N. Irish ports in 1986 was 12·8m. Regular ferry, freight and container services operate to ports in Great Britain and the Continent of Europe from Belfast, Larne, Londonderry and Warrenpoint.

Road and Rail Transport.—The Northern Ireland Transport Holding Company is largely responsible for the supervision of the subsidiary companies, Ulsterbus and Citybus (which operate the public road passenger services) and Northern Ireland Railways. A few privately operated bus services are provided in rural areas under licence. Road freight services are also provided by a large number of hauliers operating competitively under licence.

Air Transport.—Belfast International Airport handles some 1·7 million passengers and about 27,000 tonnes of air freight and mail per annum and provides an extensive range of scheduled and chartered services on domestic and international routes. It is run by Northern Ireland Airports Ltd., a subsidiary of the Northern Ireland Transport Holding Company.

Other airport facilities exist in Northern Ireland. Belfast Harbour Airport provides facilities for airlines operating scheduled flights to nine Great Britain destinations. At present there are three airlines using these facilities. Scheduled services also operate from Eglinton, Co. Londonderry to Blackpool, Glasgow and Dublin.

BELFAST

BELFAST, the seat of Government of Northern Ireland, is situated at the mouth of the River Lagan at its entrance to Belfast Lough. It has a municipal area of 16,017 acres, exclusive of tidal water (2,034) and a population (mid-1986) of 303,600. The city received its first charter of incorporation in 1613 and grew, owing to its easy access by sea to Scottish coal and iron, to be a great industrial centre. The chief industries are ship-building and the manufacture of aircraft, aerostructure, heavy and light engineering, textiles, ropes and tobacco.

The principal buildings are of a relatively recent date and include the Parliament Buildings at Stormont, the City Hall, the Law Courts, the Public

Library and the Museum and Art Gallery. The Queen's University (previously Queen's College) was chartered in 1908.

Belfast was created a city in 1888 and the title of Lord Mayor was conferred in 1892.

LONDONDERRY

LONDONDERRY, situated on the River Foyle, has a population (mid-1986) of 95,700 and was reputedly founded in 546 by St. Columba. Londonderry (formerly *Derry*) has important associations with the City of London. The Irish Society, under its royal charter of 1613, fortified the city and was for long closely associated with its administration.

Famous for the great siege of 1688–89, when for 105 days the town held out against the forces of James II until relieved by sea, Londonderry was an important naval base throughout the Second World War. Interesting buildings are the Protestant Cathedral

COUNTIES OF NORTHERN IRELAND

Counties and County Boroughs	Area* sq. miles	Lord Lieutenant	High Sheriff, 1987
Antrim..................	1,093	Capt. R. A. F. Dobbs	Mrs. P. Mackean
Belfast County Borough	25	Sir Robin Kinahan, E.R.D.	(vacant)
Armagh	484	Capt. F. M. A. Torrens-Spence, D.S.O., D.S.C., A.F.C., R.N. (*retd*).	H. N. Armstrong
Down	945	Col. W. N. Brann, O.B.E., E.R.D.	J. Gorman, C.V.O., C.B.E., M.C.
Fermanagh	647	The Earl of Erne	Miss L. E. M. Baird
Londonderry†	798	Col. M. W. McCorkell, O.B.E., T.D.	R. E. Burns, M.B.E.
Londonderry City	3·4	J. T. Eaton, T.D.	Dr. D. H. Sidebottom
Tyrone	1,211	The Duke of Abercorn	Capt. R. M. Lowry

* Excluding inland waters and tideways.   † Excluding the City of Londonderry.

MUNICIPAL DIRECTORY OF NORTHERN IRELAND

District and *Borough Councils	Population (June 1986)	Net Annual Value	Council Clerk	Mayor (†) or Chairman 1987
		£		
*Antrim, Co. Antrim	45,900	5,994,112	S. J. Magee	†J. H. Allen
*Ards, Co. Down	63,000	6,924,571	D. J. Fallows	†H. J. G. Gibson
Armagh, Co. Armagh ...	51,200	4,488,904	N. C. H. Megaw	S. Foster
*Ballymena, Co. Antrim .	55,800	7,228,749	J. S. McIlroy	†A. Spence
*Ballymoney, Co. Antrim	23,800	2,275,208	W. J. Williamson	†J. A. Gaston
Banbridge, Co. Down ...	31,700	3,147,404	R. J. Weatherall	S. J. Cowan
Belfast, Co. Antrim and Co. Down	303,600	49,953,444	C. Ward	J. S. D. Gilmore (*Lord Mayor*)
*Carrickfergus, Co. Antrim...............	29,000	4,258,133	R. Boyd	†J. Brown
*Castlereagh, Co. Down ..	58,000	7,139,971	A. D. Nichol	†D. Vitty
*Coleraine, Co. Londonderry	47,600	6,886,587	W. E. Andrews	†Mrs. G. E. Black
Cookstown, Co. Tyrone .	27,800	2,674,125	W. A. Bownes	A. Kane
*Craigavon, Co Armagh .	76,100	9,636,690	E. A. McKinley	†S. Cairns
Derry, Co Londonderry .	95,700	10,496,041	C. M. Geary	†J. Guy
Down, Co. Down	55,800	5,133,055	S. Byrne	J. Magee
Dungannon, Co. Tyrone	43,800	3,917,281	W. J. Beattie	D. Irwin
Fermanagh, Co. Fermanagh	51,000	4,544,234	G. Burns	P. Corrigan
*Larne, Co. Antrim......	28,600	3,608,122	G. McKinley	†J. W. Fulton
Limavady, Co. Londonderry	29,100	2,496,315	J. K. Stevenson	R. Cartwright
*Lisburn, Co. Antrim and Co. Down	91,900	11,360,776	H. A. Duff	†W. G. Bleakey
Magherafelt, Co. Londonderry	33,200	2,974,285	W. R. S. McMaster	Mrs. M. K. McSorley
Moyle, Co. Antrim	15,100	1,303,200	J. O'Kane	P. McConaghy
Newry and Mourne, Co. Down	86,100	6,851,324	P. J. O'Hagan	E. Markey
*Newtownabbey, Co. Antrim...............	72,200	10,377,191	J. Campbell (*acting*)	†J. Smith
*North Down, Co. Down .	69,800	8,422,604	J. McKimm	†B. R. Mulligan
Omagh, Co. Tyrone	45,100	3,741,905	D. R. D. Mitchell	F. Mackey
Strabane, Co. Tyrone ...	35,900	2,656,999	J. P. McKinney	J. J. O'Kane
Northern Ireland	1,566,800	188,491,230		

Note.—Since the reorganisation of Local Government, rates in Northern Ireland are collected by the Department of Environment and consist of two rates, a regional rate made by the Department of Finance and a district rate made by individual District Councils.

of St. Columb's (1633) and the Guildhall reconstructed in 1912 and containing a number of beautiful stained glass windows, many of which were presented by the livery companies of London. The famous Walls are still intact and form a circuit of almost a mile around the old city. The traditional activity in Londonderry is shirtmaking. Other industries include mechanical engineering, automobile components including rubber tyres, cord and synthetic fibre. New industries include the manufacture of bicycles. A large part of Ulster's agricultural export trade passes through the port.

THE ISLE OF MAN (ELLAN VANNIN)

An island in the Irish Sea, in lat. 54° 3′–54° 25′ N. and long. 4° 18′–4° 47′ W., nearly equidistant from England, Scotland, and Ireland. Although the early inhabitants were of Celtic origin, the Isle of Man was part of the Norwegian Kingdom of the Hebrides until 1266, when this was ceded to Scotland. Subsequently granted to the Stanleys (Earls of Derby) in the 15th century and later to the Dukes of Atholl, it was brought under the direct administration of the Crown in 1765. The island forms the bishopric of Sodor and Man.

The total land area is 141,263 acres (221 sq. miles). The report on the 1986 Census showed a resident population of 64,282 (males, 30,782; females, 33,500). In 1986 births numbered 709 and deaths 951. The main language in use is English. There are no remaining native speakers of Manx Gaelic but around 200 people are able to speak the language.

CAPITAL, ΨDouglas. Population (1986), 20,368; ΨCastletown (3,019) is the ancient capital; the other towns are ΨPeel (3,660), and ΨRamsey (5,778).

FLAG.—Three legs in white and gold armed conjoined on a red ground.

TYNWALD DAY.—July 5.

GOVERNMENT

The Isle of Man is a self-governing Crown dependency, having its own legal and administrative systems. The Lieutenant-Governor is the Queen's personal representative in the Island. The legislature, called the Tynwald, has two branches—the Legislative Council and the House of Keys. The Council consists of the Bishop of Sodor and Man, the Attorney-General and 8 members chosen by the House of Keys, one of whom is appointed President of the Council. The House of Keys, one of the most ancient legislative assemblies in the world, consists of 24 members, elected by the adult male and female population.

ECONOMY

Most of the income generated in the Island is earned in the services sector with financial and business services being considerably larger than the traditional industry of tourism. Manufacturing industry is also a major generator of income whilst the Island's other traditional industries of agriculture and fishing now play a minor role in the economy.

Under the terms of the Island's special relationship with the European Community the Island has free access to E.C. markets.

The development of a Freeport is now under way.

The Island's unemployment rate is approximately 7 per cent and price inflation is around 3 per cent per annum.

FINANCE

The Island's Budget for 1987–88 provided for gross expenditure of £161,500,000. The principal sources of Government revenue are taxes on income and expenditure. Income tax is payable at a flat rate of 20 per cent. of both personal and company income after the deduction of various allowances. By agreement with the United Kingdom Government, the Island keeps most of its rates of indirect taxation (Value Added Tax and duties) the same as those in the United Kingdom, but this agreement may be terminated by either party. The Island has a reciprocal arrangement with the United Kingdom regarding social security benefits and pensions and the basic rates of contribution are the same in the Isle of Man and United Kingdom. Taxes are also charged on property (rates), but these are comparatively low.

The major Government expenditure items are health, social security and education, which account for 62 per cent. of the Government budget. The Island makes a voluntary annual contribution to the United Kingdom for defence and other external services.

Although the Island has a special relationship with the European Community it neither contributes money to nor receives funds from the E.C. Budget.

Lieutenant-Governor, His Excellency Maj.-Gen. Laurence A. W. New, C.B., C.B.E.
A.D.C. to the Lieutenant-Governor, M. M. Wood.
President of the Legislative Council, J. C. Nivison, C.B.E.
Speaker, House of Keys, Sir Charles Kerruish, O.B.E.
His Honour the First Deemster and Clerk of the Rolls, A. C. Luft.
Clerk of Tynwald and Secretary to the House of Keys, Prof. T. St. J. N. Bates.
Attorney-General, T. W. Cain.
Government Secretary, P. J. Hulme.
Chief Financial Officer, W. Dawson.

THE CHANNEL ISLANDS

Situated off the north-west coast of France (at distances of from ten to thirty miles), are the only portions of the *Dukedom of Normandy* now belonging to the Crown, to which they have been attached ever since the Conquest. They consist of Jersey (28,717 acres), Guernsey (15,654 acres), and the dependencies of Guernsey—Alderney (1,962 acres), Brechou (74), Great Sark (1,035) Little Sark (239), Herm (320), Jethou (44) and Lihou (38)—a total of 48,083 acres, or 75 square miles. In 1986 the population of Jersey was 80,212; and of Guernsey, 54,380; Alderney, 2,000 and Sark, 604.

GOVERNMENT

The islands are Crown dependencies with their own legislative assemblies (the States in Jersey, Guernsey and Alderney, and the Court of Chief Pleas in Sark), and systems of local administration and of law, and their own courts. Acts passed by the States require the sanction of The Queen-in-Council. The British Government is responsible for defence and international relations.

In both Bailiwicks the Lieutenant-Governor and Commander-in-Chief, who is appointed by the Crown, is the personal representative of the Queen and the channel of communication between the Crown (via the Privy Council) and the insular government. The Bailiffs of Jersey and Guernsey, also appointed by the

Crown, are President of the States and of the Royal Courts of their respective islands. The government of each Bailiwick is conducted by committees appointed by the States. Justice is administered by the Royal Courts of Jersey and Guernsey, each consisting of the Bailiff and 12 elected Jurats.

Each Bailiwick constitutes a deanery under the jurisdiction of the Bishop of Winchester (*see* Index).

ECONOMY

A mild climate and good soil have led to the development of intensive systems of agriculture and horticulture, which form a significant part of the economy of the Channel Islands. Equally important are invisible earnings, principally from the tourist trade and from banking and finance, the low rate of income tax (20p. in the £ in Jersey and Guernsey; no tax of any kind in Sark) and the absence of super-tax and death duties making the Channel Islands a popular tax-haven. Principal exports are agricultural produce and flowers; imports are chiefly machinery, manufactured goods, food, fuel and chemicals. Trade with the U.K. is regarded as internal trade.

British currency is legal tender in the Channel Islands but each Bailiwick issues its own coins, and some notes, of the same values as those of the U.K. They also issue their own postage stamps; U.K. stamps are not valid.

LANGUAGE

The official languages are English and French, but French is gradually being supplanted by English, which is the language in daily use. In country districts of Jersey and Guernsey and throughout Sark a Norman-French *patois* is also in use, though to a declining extent.

CHIEF TOWNS, Ψ St. Helier on the south coast of Jersey; Ψ St. Peter Port, on the east coast of Guernsey, and St. Anne's on Alderney.

JERSEY

Lieutenant-Governor and Commander-in-Chief of Jersey, His Excellency Adm. Sir William Pillar, G.B.E., K.C.B. (1985).
Secretary and A.D.C., Comdr. D. M. L. Braybrooke, L.V.O., R.N.

Bailiff of Jersey, Sir Peter Crill, C.B.E.
Deputy Bailiff, V. A. Tomes
Attorney-General and Receiver-General, P. M. Bailhache
Solicitor-General, T. C. Snowden.
Greffier of the States, E. J. M. Potter.
States Treasurer, L. May.

Year to Dec. 31:	1985	1986
Revenue	£172,951,614	£200,477,716
Revenue Expenditure	141,349,826	154,065,104
Capital Expenditure ..	17,928,212	27,301,040
Public Debt	−1,042,906	−1,650,055

FLAG.—A white field charged with a red saltire, and coat of arms.

GUERNSEY AND DEPENDENCIES

Lieutenant-Governor and Commander-in-Chief of the Bailiwick of Guernsey and its Dependencies, His Excellency Lt.-Gen. Sir Alexander Boswell, K.C.B., C.B.E. (1985).
Secretary and A.D.C., Capt. D. P. L. Hodgetts.
Bailiff of Guernsey, Sir Charles Frossard.
Deputy Bailiff, G. M. Dorey.
H. M. Procureur and Receiver-General, de Vic G. Carey.
H. M. Comptroller, A. C. K. Day.
States Supervisor, F. N. Le Cheminant.

Year to Dec. 31:	1985	1986
Revenue	£81,200,137	£90,603,226
Expenditure	65,644,466	73,068,154

FLAG.—White, bearing a red cross of St. George, with an argent a cross gules superimposed on the cross.

Alderney

President of the States, J. Kay-Mouat.
Clerk of the States, D. V. Jenkins.
Clerk of the Court, P. Beer.

Sark

Le Seigneur of Sark, J. M. Beaumont.
The Seneschal, L. P. de Carteret.
The Greffier, J. P. Hamon.
Brechou, Lihou and Jethou are leased by the Crown. Herm is leased by the States of Guernsey.

THE ISLES OF SCILLY

There are about 140 islands and skerries in the Scillies group (total area, 6 square miles) situated 28 miles south-west of Land's End, of which only five are inhabited; St. Mary's, St. Agnes, Bryher, Tresco and St. Martin's. The population is 1,951. The entire group has been designated an Area of Outstanding Natural Beauty, and given National Nature Reserve status by the Nature Conservancy Council because of its unique flora and fauna. Tourism and the Winter/Spring flower trade for the home market form the basis of the economy of the Isles. The island group is a recognised rural development area.

The islands are administered by the Council of the Isles of Scilly, a 21-member non-political body, which combines the powers and duties of a County Council and a District Council under the Local Government

Act 1972 and the Isles of Scilly Orders 1978. Legislation is specifically applied to the Isles of Scilly by Special Order. The Council is responsible for education, fire services, highways, planning and social services, and Cornwall County Council provides other services on an agency basis: the police service is administered by the Devon and Cornwall Police Authority, of which the Council is a member. The Isles are part of the St. Ives electoral division.

Administrative Headquarters, Town Hall, St. Mary's, Isles of Scilly, TR21 0LW.
Chairman of the Council, H. R. Duncan.
Clerk and Chief Executive, I. Glover.
Chief Financial Officer, L. W. Michell.
Chief Technical Officer, B. M. Lowen.

PATRON SAINTS

ST. GEORGE
Patron Saint of England

St. George is believed to have been born in Cappadocia, of Christian parents, in the latter part of the 3rd century and to have served with distinction as a soldier under the Emperor Diocletian, including a visit to England on a military mission. When the persecution of Christians was ordered, St. George sought a personal interview to remonstrate with the Emperor and after a profession of faith resigned his military commission. Arrest and torture followed and he was martyred at Nicomedia on April 23, 303, a day ordered to be kept in remembrance as a national festival by the Council of Oxford in 1222, although it was not until the reign of Edward III that he was made patron saint of England.

St. George's connection with a dragon seems to date from the close of the 6th century and to be due to the transfer of his remains from Nicomedia to Lydda, close to the scene of the legendary exploit of Perseus in rescuing Andromeda and slaying the sea monster, credit for which became attached to the Christian martyr.

ST. DAVID
Patron Saint of Wales

St. David is believed to have been born near the beginning and to have died towards the end of the 6th century. St. David was an eloquent preacher, who founded the monastery at Menevia, now St.

David's. He became the patron of Wales, but there is no record of any papal canonization before 1181. His annual festival is observed on March 1.

ST. ANDREW
Patron Saint of Scotland

St. Andrew, one of the Christian Apostles and brother of Simon Peter, was born at Bethsaida on the Sea of Galilee and lived at Capernaum. He preached the Gospel in Asia Minor and in Scythia along the shores of the Black Sea and became the patron saint of Russia. It is believed that he suffered crucifixion at Patras in Achaea, on a *crux decussata* (now known as St. Andrew's Cross) and that his relics were removed from Patras to Constantinople and thence to St. Andrews, probably in the 8th century, since which time he has been the patron saint of Scotland. The festival of St. Andrew is held on November 30.

ST. PATRICK
Patron Saint of Ireland

St. Patrick was born, probably in England, about 389 and was carried off to Ireland as a slave about sixteen years later, escaping to Gaul at the age of 22. He was ordained deacon at Auxerre and having been consecrated Bishop in 432 was despatched to Wicklow to reorganize the Christian communities in Ireland. He founded the see of Armagh and introduced Latin into Ireland as the language of the Church. He died *c.* 461 and his festival is celebrated on March 17.

THE CINQUE PORTS

As their name implies the Cinque Ports were originally five in number, Hastings, New Romney, Hythe, Dover and Sandwich. They were in existence before the Norman Conquest and were the Anglo-Saxon successors to the Roman system of coast defence organized from the Wash to Spithead to resist Saxon onslaughts. William the Conqueror reconstituted them and granted peculiar jurisdiction, most of which was abolished in 1855. Only jurisdiction in Admiralty still survives.

At some time after the Conquest the "antient towns" of Winchelsea and Rye were added with equal privileges. The other members of the Confederation, known as Limbs, are:—Lydd, Faversham, Folkestone, Deal, Tenterden, Margate and Ramsgate.

The Barons of the Cinque Ports have the ancient privilege of attending the Coronation Ceremony and are allotted special places in Westminster Abbey.

Lord Warden of the Cinque Ports, H.M. Queen Elizabeth the Queen Mother.
Judge, Court of Admiralty, Gerald Darling, R.D., Q.C.
Registrar, I. G. Gill, P.O. Box 9, Margate, Kent CT9 1XZ.

Lord Wardens of the Cinque Ports since 1904

Marquess Curzon	1904
The Prince of Wales	1905
Earl Brassey	1908
Earl Beauchamp	1913
Marquess of Reading	1934
Marquess of Willingdon	1936
Sir Winston Churchill	1941
Sir Robert Menzies	1965
H.M. Queen Elizabeth the Queen Mother	1978

THE COMMONWEALTH

The Commonwealth is a free association of the 49 sovereign independent states listed below together with their associated states and dependencies.

ANTIGUA AND BARBUDA
AUSTRALIA
BAHAMAS
BANGLADESH
BARBADOS
BELIZE
BOTSWANA
BRUNEI
CANADA
CYPRUS
DOMINICA
FIJI
GAMBIA, THE
GHANA
GREAT BRITAIN
GRENADA
GUYANA
INDIA
JAMAICA
KENYA
KIRIBATI
LESOTHO
MALAWI
MALAYSIA
MALDIVES

MALTA
MAURITIUS
NAURU
NEW ZEALAND
NIGERIA
PAPUA NEW GUINEA
SAINT KITTS AND NEVIS
SAINT LUCIA
SAINT VINCENT AND THE
  GRENADINES
SEYCHELLES
SIERRA LEONE
SINGAPORE
SOLOMON ISLANDS
SRI LANKA
SWAZILAND
TANZANIA
TONGA
TRINIDAD AND TOBAGO
TUVALU
UGANDA
VANUATU
WESTERN SAMOA
ZAMBIA
ZIMBABWE

Area and Population.—The total area of the independent Commonwealth is estimated at over 19,500,000 sq. miles (50,504,000 sq. km.) (U.N. estimate 1985), over one third of the world total. The total population of the Commonwealth is estimated to be about one quarter of the world total. In 1985 this amounted to over 1,200,000,000 (U.N. estimate). Details of the areas and populations of the Member States and dependencies appear in the following pages.

History and Government.—The status and relationship of member nations was first defined by the Inter-Imperial Relations Committee of the 1926 Imperial Conference, under the chairmanship of Lord Balfour, in what came to be known as the "Balfour Declaration": "They are autonomous communities . . . equal in status, in no way subordinate one to another in any aspect of their domestic or external affairs, though united by a common allegiance to the Crown and freely associated as members of the British Commonwealth of Nations." This formula was given legal substance by the Statute of Westminster, 1931.

The concept of a group of countries owing allegiance to a single Crown changed in 1949 when India decided to become a republic, and her continued membership of the Commonwealth was agreed by the other members on the basis of her "acceptance of the King as the symbol of the free association of its independent member nations and as such the Head of the Commonwealth". Member nations agreed at the time of the accession of Queen Elizabeth II to recognize Her Majesty as the new Head of the Commonwealth. The position is not vested in the British Crown.

Most members of the Commonwealth are parliamentary democracies.

Queen Elizabeth II is Head of State of 18 member countries of the Commonwealth: Antigua and Barbuda, Australia, the Bahamas, Barbados, Belize, Britain, Canada, Fiji, Grenada, Jamaica, Mauritius, New Zealand, Papua New Guinea, St. Kitts and Nevis, Saint Lucia, Saint Vincent and the Grenadines, Solomon Islands and Tuvalu. In each of these countries (except Britain) The Queen is personally represented by a Governor-General, who holds in all essential respects the same position in relation to the

administration of public affairs in the realm as is held by Her Majesty in Britain (with the exception of certain constitutional functions which are performed by The Queen personally). The Governor-General is appointed by The Queen on the advice of the Government of the country concerned.

Twenty-five member countries are republics: Bangladesh, Botswana, Cyprus, Dominica, The Gambia, Ghana, Guyana, India, Kenya, Kiribati, Malawi, The Maldives, Malta, Nauru, Nigeria, Seychelles, Sierra Leone, Singapore, Sri Lanka, Tanzania, Trinidad & Tobago, Uganda, Vanuatu, Zambia and Zimbabwe. In Malaysia, the Head of State is elected from among the nine hereditary Malay rulers and holds office for five years. Brunei, Lesotho, Tonga, and Swaziland have their own monarchs. Western Samoa has a Head of State whose functions are analogous to those of a constitutional monarch.

Membership of the Commonwealth is subject only to the approval of existing members. Two countries, Nauru and Tuvalu, are special members, with the right to participate in all functional Commonwealth meetings and activities, but not to attend Meetings of Commonwealth Heads of Government.

Consultation.—Commonwealth Heads of Government meet every two years to discuss international developments and to consider co-operation among members. These meetings, the successors to the pre-war Imperial Conferences, have grown in importance as they are the only regular forum of leaders from both developed and developing countries, constituting a broad sample of the world community. Decisions are reached by consensus, and the views of the meeting are set out in a communiqué.

In addition, there are annual meetings of Finance Ministers, and frequent meetings of Ministers and officials in the fields of trade, education, health, law, science, agriculture, labour and employment, and youth affairs.

Defence.—The Commonwealth is not a military alliance and members make their own defence arrangements in the light of their particular requirements. Some are parties to multi-lateral treaties, for example A.N.Z.U.S. and N.A.T.O. Various members of the Commonwealth co-operate with each other in combined exercises, joint research organizations and exchanges of personnel and training facilities.

Law.—English common law forms the basis of the legal system in many Commonwealth countries, although in most cases it has been radically adapted by statute to suit the individual needs and aspirations of a country, and there are countries where other systems have been adopted—for example, the law of Quebec Province and of Mauritius is founded on that of France, and Roman Dutch law forms the basis in Sri Lanka and Lesotho. Of the non-realms in the Commonwealth, Brunei, Dominica, The Gambia, Kiribati, Malaysia, Singapore, and Trinidad and Tobago retain the right of appeal to the Judicial Committee of the Privy Council in the United Kingdom, which also hears appeals from a number of realms (Antigua and Barbuda, the Bahamas, Barbados, Belize, Fiji, Jamaica, Mauritius, New Zealand, St. Kitts and Nevis, St. Lucia, St. Vincent and the Grenadines, Tuvalu) and the dependent territories.

Citizenship and Nationality.—Each member of the Commonwealth defines the citizenship and nationality of its own people and determines the status of other Commonwealth nationals within its own boundaries. Members of the Commonwealth differentiate, to a greater or lesser degree, as regards the grant of privileges, between citizens of the Commonwealth and aliens. The Republic of Ireland, which in 1949 ceased to be a member of the Commonwealth, is not regarded by the other Commonwealth nations as a foreign country nor her citizens as foreigners.

Finance and Development.—Complete financial autonomy is enjoyed by all members of the Commonwealth. In some countries, customs tariffs are lower for merchandise of Commonwealth origin than for imports from foreign countries. Developing countries, including those in the Commonwealth, obtain preference for exports of industrial goods and some agricultural exports from the developed countries under the Generalised Scheme of Preferences (G.S.P.). Many smaller Commonwealth countries are also party to the Lomé Convention which accords preferential access to the European Community. Many former Commonwealth preferences have been replaced by these arrangements.

British aid for the development needs of the Commonwealth countries and dependent territories are dealt with under the provisions of the Overseas Aid Act 1966, administered by the Overseas Development Administration. This Act succeeds the former Colonial Development and Welfare Acts. Those countries which are party to the Lomé Convention also receive aid under that Convention from the European Community.

Commonwealth Secretariat. Marlborough House, Pall Mall, SW1Y 5HX [01-839 3411]. —This was established by decision of Commonwealth Heads of Government in 1965, and is the main agency for multi-lateral communication between Commonwealth Governments on issues relating to the Commonwealth as a whole. It promotes consultation and disseminates information on matters of common concern, organizes meetings and conferences, coordinates Commonwealth activities and provides technical assistance for economic and social development through the Commonwealth Fund for Technical Cooperation. *Secretary-General*, Shridath S. Ramphal, Kt., C.M.G., Q.C.

Commonwealth Institute.—See p. 666.

Dependent Territories and Associated States.—Britain, Australia and New Zealand have a number of dependent territories. New Zealand also has two associated states: Cook Islands (since 1965) and Niue (since 1974).

Member States of the Commonwealth
(with dates of independence)

1867* Canada
1901* Australia
1907* New Zealand
1947 India (Republic, 1950)
1948 Sri Lanka (Republic, 1972)
1957 Ghana (Republic, 1960)
    Federation of Malaya (Federation of Malaysia since 1963—indigenous monarchy)
1960 Cyprus (Republic on independence; joined Commonwealth 1961)
    Nigeria (Republic, 1963)

1961 Sierra Leone (Republic, 1971)
    Tanganyika (Republic, 1962; united 1964 with Zanzibar as TANZANIA)
1962 Western Samoa (Republic on independence; joined Commonwealth 1970)
    Jamaica
    Trinidad and Tobago (Republic, 1976)
    Uganda (Republic, 1967)
1963 Kenya (Republic, 1964)
    Singapore (as State in Federation of Malaysia; seceded as Republic, 1965)
1964 Malawi (Republic, 1966)
    Malta (Republic, 1974)
    Zambia (Republic on independence)
1965 The Gambia (Republic, 1970)
    Maldives (Republic, 1968; joined Commonwealth as a Special Member 1982; full member 1985)
1966 Guyana (Republic, 1970)
    Botswana (Republic on independence)
    Lesotho (indigenous monarchy)
    Barbados
1968 Mauritius
    Nauru (Republic on independence—Special Member)
    Swaziland (indigenous monarchy)
1970 Tonga (indigenous monarchy)
    Fiji
1971 Bangladesh (Republic on independence; joined Commonwealth 1972)
1973 Bahamas
1974 Grenada
1975 Papua New Guinea
1976 Seychelles (Republic on independence)
1978 Solomon Islands
    Tuvalu (Special Member)
    Dominica (Republic on independence)
1979 Saint Lucia
    Kiribati (Republic on independence)
    Saint Vincent and the Grenadines (Joined as a Special Member; became a full member 1985)
1980 Zimbabwe (Republic on independence)
    Vanuatu (Republic on independence)
1981 Belize
    Antigua and Barbuda
1983 Saint Kitts and Nevis
1984 Brunei (indigenous monarchy)

* These are the effective dates of independence, given legal effect by the Statute of Westminster, 1931.

(The above member states are Realms of Queen Elizabeth II unless otherwise stated.)

Associated States

The Cook Islands and Niue are self-governing states in association with New Zealand, which likewise remains responsible for their external affairs and defence.

Countries which have left the Commonwealth

1949 Republic of Ireland
1961 South Africa
1972 Pakistan

AREA AND POPULATION

Provinces or Territories and Capitals (with official contractions)	Area (English Sq. Miles). Land and Water	Population	
		Census, 1981	Census, 1986
Alberta, *Alta.* (Edmonton).....................	255,285	2,237,724	2,365,825
British Columbia, *B.C.* (Victoria)	366,255	2,744,467	2,883,365
Manitoba, *Man.* (Winnipeg)	251,000	1,026,241	1,063,015
New Brunswick, *N.B.* (Fredericton)..........	28,354	696,403	709,440
Newfoundland and Labrador, *Nfld.* (St. John's) .	156,185	567,681	568,350
Nova Scotia, *N.S.* (Halifax)	21,425	847,442	973,175
Ontario, *Ont.* (Toronto)	412,582	8,625,107	9,101,690
Prince Edward Island, *P.E.I.* (Charlottetown) ..	2,184	122,506	126,645
Quebec, *Que.* (Quebec)	594,860	6,438,403	6,532,460
Saskatchewan, *Sask.* (Regina)	251,700	968,313	1,009,615
Yukon Territory, *Y.T.* (Whitehorse)	207,076	23,153	23,505
Northwest Territories, *N.W.T.* (Yellowknife) ..	1,304,903	45,741	52,240
Total...............	3,851,809	24,343,181	25,309,330

Land area, 3,560,238 sq. miles (9,220,973 sq. km.); water area, 291,571 sq. miles (755,165 sq. km.).
Of the total immigration of 84,302 in 1985, 6,669 were from the United States, 4,719 from the United Kingdom and Ireland, and 6,132 from the Caribbean.

Mother Tongues of the Population

	1981	1986
Sole Language		
English	14,684,365	15,334,085
French	6,127,530	6,159,740
Non-Official Languages	2,933,305	2,860,570
Native Indian Languages		
Cree	60,845	57,645
Inuktitut..	18,650	21,050
Ojibway..	17,605	16,380
Bi-/Multi-Lingual		
English and French	208,245	332,610
English and non-official language(s)	325,530	525,720
French and non-official language(s)	22,255	36,310
English, French and non-official language(s)	29,475	46,585
Non-official languages	12,485	13,715
Total Population...	24,343,180	25,309,330

PHYSIOGRAPHY

Canada was originally discovered by Cabot in 1497, but its history dates only from 1534, when the French took possession of the country. The first permanent settlement at Port Royal (now Annapolis), Nova Scotia, was founded in 1605, and Quebec was founded in 1608. In 1759 Quebec was captured by the British forces under General Wolfe, and in 1763 the whole territory of Canada became a possession of Great Britain by the Treaty of Paris of that year. Nova Scotia was ceded in 1713 by the Treaty of Utrecht, the Provinces of New Brunswick and Prince Edward Island being subsequently formed out of it. British Columbia was formed into a Crown colony in 1858, having previously been a part of the Hudson Bay Territory, and was united to Vancouver Island in 1866.

Canada occupies the whole of the northern part of the North American Continent (with the exception of Alaska), from 49° North latitude to the North Pole, and from the Pacific to the Atlantic Ocean. In Eastern Canada, the southernmost point is Middle Island in Lake Erie, at 41° 41′.

Relief.—The relief of Canada is dominated by the mountain ranges running north and south on the west side of the Continent, by the pre-Cambrian shield on the east, with, in between, the northern extension of the North American Plain. From the physiographic point of view Canada has six main divisions. These are: (1) Appalachian-Acadian Region, (2) the Canadian Shield, (3) the St. Lawrence-Great Lakes Lowland, (4) the Interior Plains, (5) the Cordilleran Region and (6) the Arctic Archipelago. The first region occupies all that part of Canada lying southeast of the St. Lawrence. In general, the relief is an alternation of highlands and lowlands and is hilly rather than mountainous. The great Canadian Shield comprises more than half the area. The interior as a whole is an undulating, low plateau (general level 1,000 to 1,500 feet), with the more rugged relief lying along the border between Northern Quebec and Labrador. Throughout the whole area water or muskeg-filled depressions separate irregular hills and ridges, 150 to 200 feet in elevation. Newfoundland, an outlying portion of the shield, consists of glaciated, low rolling terrain broken here and there by mountains.

The flat relief of the St. Lawrence-Great Lakes lowland varies from 500 feet in the east to 1,700 feet south of Georgian Bay. The most striking relief is provided by the eastward facing scarp of the Niagara escarpment (elevation 250 to 300 feet). The interior plains, comprising the Pacific Provinces, slope eastward and northward a few feet per mile. The descent from west to east is made from 5,000 feet to less than 1,000 feet in three distinct levels, with each new level being marked by an eastward facing *conteau* or scarp.

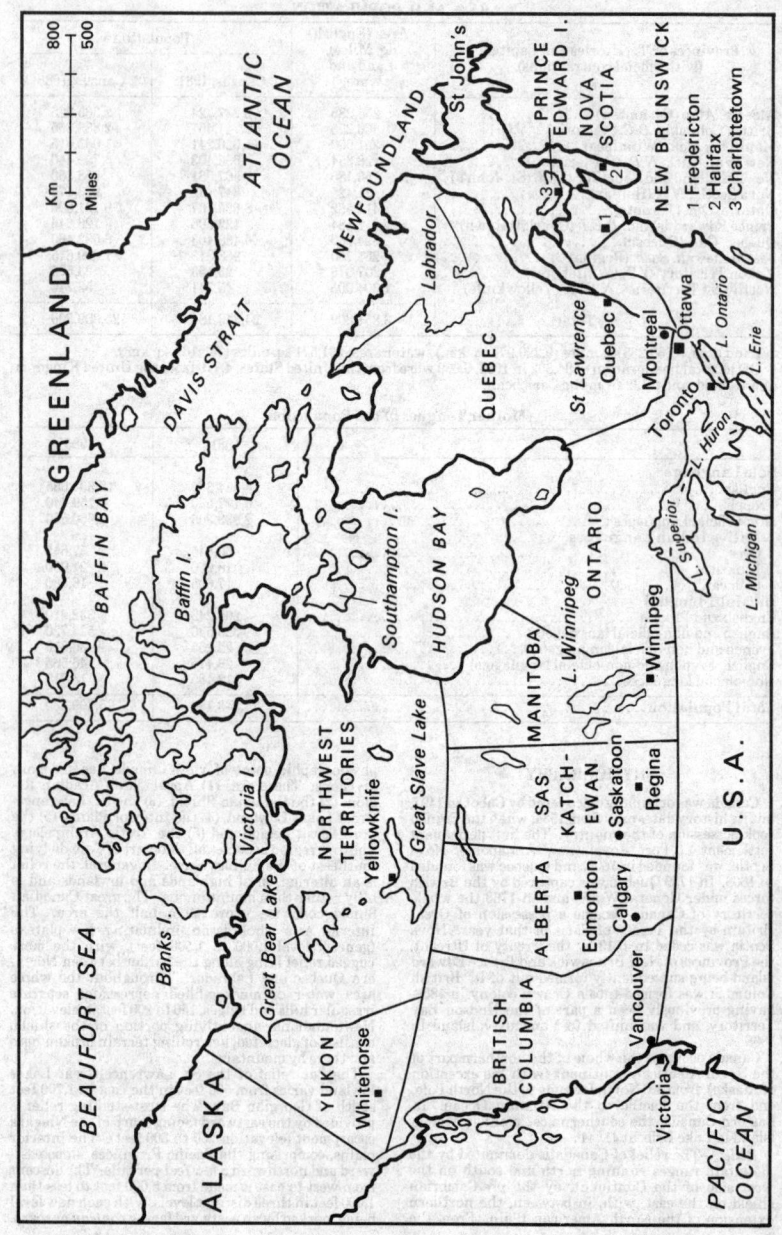

Five fairly well-developed topographic divisions mark out the Cordilleran region of western Canada. These are: (1) coastal ranges, largely above 5,000 feet with deep fiords and glaciated valleys, (2) the interior plateau, around 3,500 feet and comparatively level, (3) the Selkirk ranges, largely above 5,000 feet, (4) the Rocky Mountains with their chain of 10,000 to 12,000 feet peaks, and (5) the Peace River or Tramontane region with its rolling diversified country.

The Arctic Archipelago, with its plateau-like character has an elevation between 500 and 1,000 feet, though in Baffin Land and Ellesmere Island the mountain ranges rise to 8,500 and 9,500 feet. Two tremendous waterway systems, the St. Lawrence and the Mackenzie, providing thousands of miles of water highway, occupy a broad area of lowland with their dominant axis following the edge of the shield.

Climate.—The climate of the eastern and central portions presents greater extremes than in corresponding latitudes in Europe, but in the south-western portion of the Prairie Region and the southern portions of the Pacific slope the climate is milder. Spring, summer, and autumn are of about seven to eight months' duration, and the winter four to five months.

GOVERNMENT

The Constitution of Canada had its source in the British North America Act of 1867 which formed a Dominion, under the name of Canada, of the four provinces: Ontario, Quebec, New Brunswick and Nova Scotia; to this Federation the other Provinces have subsequently been admitted. Under this Act Canada came into being on July 1, 1867 (Dominion Day), and under the Statute of Westminster, which received the royal assent on Dec. 11, 1931, Canada and the Provinces were exempted (in common with other self-governing Dominions of the Commonwealth of Nations) from the operation of the Colonial Laws Validity Act, the Statute of Westminster having removed all limitations with regard to the legislative autonomy of the Dominions, except that the British North America Act could be amended in important respects only by Acts of the British Parliament.

Provinces admitted since 1867 are: Manitoba (1870), British Columbia (1871), Prince Edward Island (1873), Alberta and Saskatchewan (1905) and Newfoundland (1949).

Agreement was reached in Nov. 1981 between the Federal and Provincial Governments (except Quebec) to patriate the Constitution so that it was amendable only in Canada. The inclusion in the Constitution of a Charter of Rights was also agreed. At the request of the Canadian Parliament, legislation was passed at Westminster and the Constitution formally patriated on 17th April 1982.

The Executive power is vested in a Governor-General appointed by the Sovereign on the advice of the Canadian Ministry, and aided by a Privy Council.

FLAG.—Red maple leaf with 11 points on white square, flanked by vertical red bars one half the width of the square.

NATIONAL DAY.—July 1.
NATIONAL ANTHEM.—Oh Canada.

Governor General's Household

Governor-General and Commander-in Chief, Her Excellency The Rt. Hon. Jeanne Sauvé, C.C., C.M.M., C.D.
Secretary to the Governor-General and Sec. Gen. of Honours, L. Amyot.
Deputy Secretaries, A. Smyth; J. M. Sévigny.
Director, Chancellery, R. de C. Nantel, L.V.O., C.D.

Finance, Personnel and Administration Director, G. R. Brunet.
Cultural Advisor, J.-N. Tremblay.
Director, Information Services, Mlle. M. Bender.
Director, Programme Implementation, Health, Safety and Security Programme, C. A. Sangster, C.D.
Policy and Programme Director, Mrs. S. Orr.
Attaché, Miss L. Benoit.
Hospitality Director, Ms. L. D'Ascanio.
Director, Protocol and Ceremonial, L. Lemieux.
Aides-de-Camp, L. Maurice, C.D.; M. Phillips; D. Maybee.
Personal Asst. to the Governor-General, Mlle. R. Langevin.

The Cabinet

Prime Minister, Rt. Hon. M. Brian Mulroney.
Veterans' Affairs, Hon. George H. Hees.
Leader of the Government in the Senate, Hon. Lowell Murray.
External Affairs, Rt. Hon. C. Joseph Clark.
Employment and Immigration, Hon. Benoît Bouchard.
Deputy Prime Minister and President of the Queen's Privy Council, Hon. Donald F. Mazankowski.
Justice and Attorney General, Hon. Ramon J. Hnatyshyn.
Public Works, Hon. Stewart McInnes.
Transport, Hon. John C. Crosbie.
Solicitor General, Hon. James F. Kelleher.
National Health and Welfare, Hon. Jake Epp.
Fisheries and Oceans, Hon. Thomas E. Siddon.
Regional Industrial Expansion, Canada Post, Hon. Harvie André.
Agriculture, Hon. John Wise.
National Defence, Hon. H. Perrin Beatty.
Indian Affairs and Northern Development, Hon. William H. McKnight.
President of the Treasury Board, Hon. Robert R. de Cotret.
National Revenue, Hon. Elmer M. MacKay.
Finance, Hon. Michael H. Wilson.
Supply and Services, Hon. Monique Vézina.
Labour, Hon. Pierre H. Cadieux.
Secretary of State, Hon. David E. Crombie.
Energy, Mines and Resources, Hon. Marcel Masse.
Environment, Hon. Thomas M. McMillan.
Consumer and Corporate Affairs, (vacant).
International Trade, Hon. Patricia Carney.
Communications, Hon. Flora I. MacDonald.
External Relations, Hon. Monique Landry.
Associate Defence Minister, Hon. Paul W. Dick.
Ministers of State, Hon. Otto J. Jelinek (*Fitness and Amateur Sport, and Multiculturalism*); Hon. Frank Oberle (*Science and Technology*); Hon. Charles J. Mayer (*Canadian Wheat Board*); Hon. Gerry. Weiner (*Immigration*); Hon. Bernard Valcourt (*Small Businesses and Tourism*); Hon. Jean J. Charest (*Youth*); Hon. Gerald S. Merrithew (*Forestry and Mines*); Hon. Thomas Hockin (*Finance*); Hon. Barbara J. McDougall (*Privatization*).

The Prime Minister receives remuneration of $142,000; other ministers, each $120,300.

CANADIAN HIGH COMMISSION
Macdonald House, 1 Grosvenor Square, W1X 0AB.
[01–629 9492]

High Commissioner, His Excellency Roy R. McMurtry (1985).
Deputy High Commissioner, L. A. Delvoie.
Ministers, M. Phillips (*Political and Public Affairs*); L. J. Taylor (*Commercial/Economic*).
Minister-Counsellor, J. R. MacLachlan (*Immigration*).

BRITISH HIGH COMMISSION
80 Elgin Street, Ottawa

High Commissioner, His Excellency Sir Derek Day, K.C.M.G.
Deputy High Commissioner, W. N. Wenban-Smith.
Counsellor, Miss C. S. Rycroft (*Economic and Commercial*).
Defence and Military Adviser, Brig. W. M. Addison.
Naval Adviser, Capt. A. K. Potter.
Air Adviser, Gp. Capt. A. C. Tolhurst.
1st Secretaries, D. J. Pugh, M.B.E. (*Administration*); A. N. Foggo; K. W. Kelley, O.B.E. (*Commercial*); J. A. King; D. E. Donald (*Information*).
Cultural Affairs and British Council Representative, C. M. Chadwick, O.B.E.

THE LEGISLATURE

Parliament consists of a Senate and a House of Commons. The *Senate* consists of 104 members, nominated by the Governor-General (age limit 75). They are distributed between the various provinces thus: 24 each for *Ontario* and *Quebec,* 10 each for *Nova Scotia* and *New Brunswick,* 6 each for *Newfoundland, British Columbia, Manitoba, Alberta,* and *Saskatchewan* and 4 for *Prince Edward Island,* 1 for *North West Territories* and 1 for *Yukon*; each Senator must be at least thirty years old, a resident in the province for which he is appointed, a natural-born or naturalized subject of the Queen, and the owner of a property qualification amounting to $4,000. The Speaker of the Senate is chosen by the Government of the day.

The *House of Commons* has 282 members and is elected every five years at longest. Representation by provinces is at present as follows: Newfoundland 7, Prince Edward Island 4, Nova Scotia 11, New Brunswick 10, Quebec 75, Ontario 95, Manitoba 14, Saskatchewan 14, Alberta 21, British Columbia 28, Yukon 1, Northwest Territories 2.

In every case—including the Prime Minister's—a sessional indemnity of $57,400 *per annum* is paid to members of the House of Commons. In addition, Ministers and members of the House of Commons receive an expense allowance. Certain Members of Parliament for large northern constituencies have larger expense allowances.

THE SENATE

The state of the parties in the Senate as of Jan. 28, 1987, was *Liberal* 66, *Conservative* 31, *Independent* 5, *Independent Liberal* 1 (1 vacant).
Speaker of the Senate, Hon. Guy Chapbonneau, Q.C. $98,300
Clerk of the Senate & Clerk of the Parliaments, C. A. Lussier.

THE HOUSE OF COMMONS

The state of parties in the House of Commons as of July 29, 1987, was *Conservative* 208, *Liberals* 40, *N.D.P.* 33, *Independent* 1.
Speaker of the House of Commons, Hon. John A. Fraser.............................. $120,300
Deputy Speaker, Marcel Danis................ $99,500
Clerk of the House of Commons, Dr. C. B. Koester.

THE JUDICATURE

The Judicature is administered by judges following the Civil Law in Quebec Province and Common Law in other Provinces. Each Province has its Court of Appeal. All Superior, County and District Court Judges are appointed by the Governor-General, the others by the Lieutenant-Governors of the Provinces.

The highest federal court is the Supreme Court of Canada, composed of a Chief Justice and eight puisne judges, which exercises general appellate jurisdiction throughout Canada in civil and criminal cases, and which usually holds three sessions each year. There is one other federally constituted Court, the Federal Court of Canada, which has jurisdiction on appeals from its Trial Division, from Federal Tribunals and reviews of decisions and references by Federal Boards and Commissions. The Trial Division has jurisdiction in claims by or against the Crown, its officers or servants or Federal bodies. It also deals with inter-Provincial and Federal-Provincial disputes.

SUPREME COURT OF CANADA

Chief Justice of Canada, Rt. Hon. Brian Dickson, P.C. $143,600
Puisne Judges, Hon. J. Beetz; Hon. W. Z. Estey; Hon. W. R. McIntyre; Hon. A. Lamer; Hon. Bertha Wilson; Hon. G. Le Dain; Hon. G. V. LaForest; Hon. Claire L'Heureux-Dube.................. each $132,000

FEDERAL COURT OF CANADA

Chief Justice, Hon. A. L. Thurlow $121,200
Associate Chief Justice, Hon. J. A. Jerome. $121,200
Appeal Division Judges, Hon. L. Pratte; Hon. D. V. Heald; Hon. J. J. Urie; Hon. J. K. Hugessen; Hon. P. M. Mahoney, P.C.; Hon. L. Marceau; Hon. M. MacGuigan, P.C.; Hon. A. J. Stone; Hon. B. Lacombe; Hon. Alice Desjardins .. each $111,700
Trial Division Judges, Hon. J. E. Dubé; Hon. F. U. Collier; Hon. G. A. Addy; Hon. P. U. C. Rouleau; Hon. J. C. McNair; Hon. F. C. Muldoon; Hon. Barbara J. Reed; Hon. B. L. Strayer; Hon. Y. Pinard; Hon. L. M. Joyal; Hon. P. Denault; Hon. B. Cullen; Hon. L. A. Martin; Hon. M. A. Teitelbaum .... each $111,700

VITAL STATISTICS

BIRTHS, DEATHS AND MARRIAGES, 1985

Province	Births	Deaths	Marriages
Alberta	43,813	13,231	19,750
British Columbia .	43,127	21,302	22,292
Manitoba	17,097	8,756	8,296
New Brunswick ..	10,121	5,230	5,312
Newfoundland ...	8,500	3,557	3,220
Nova Scotia	12,450	7,315	6,807
Ontario	132,208	66,747	72,891
P.E.I.	2,008	1,110	956
Quebec	86,340	45,707	37,026
Saskatchewan ...	18,162	8,031	7,132
Yukon	464	123	185
N. W. Territories	1,437	214	229
Total......	375,727	181,323	184,096

Canada's birth rate per 1,000 population (1985) 14·8; Death Rate 7·2; Marriage Rate 7·3. Divorces 61,980.

FINANCE

Federal Government gross general revenue and expenditure was ($ millions):—

	1985–86	1986–87*
Total Revenue	83,740	90,229
Total Expenditure.........	113,974	116,643

*preliminary.

DEBT ($ millions)

	1985–86	1986–87*
Gross Public Debt	269,286	301,536
Net Public Debt	233,496	263,215

*preliminary.

Banking.—There were 68 chartered banks on March 31, 1987, with assets of $460,252 m. Deposits were $381,197 m. of which $150,294 m. were personal savings.

NATIONAL DEFENCE

The Minister of National Defence has the control and management of the Canadian Armed Forces and all matters relating to National Defence establishments and works for the defence of Canada.

The Canadian Forces are organized on a functional basis to reflect the major commitments assigned by the government and are formed into National Defence Headquarters and five major Commands reporting to the Chief of the Defence Staff. The roles of the five Commands are: *Mobile Command*—Provision of ground forces for the protection of Canadian territory, combat forces in Canada for support of overseas commitments, and forces for support of United Nations or other peace-keeping operations. *Maritime Command*—Provision of sea forces for the defence of Canada, anti-submarine defence in support of NATO. Support to Canadian Military operations and the conduct of search and rescue operations within the Atlantic and Pacific search and rescue areas. Maritime Command also has operational control of Maritime aircraft. *Air Command*—Provision of operationally ready air forces to national, continental and international commitments. *Canadian Forces Communication Command*—Manages, operates and maintains strategic communications for the Canadian Forces. *Canadian Forces Europe*—Canadian Forces allocated to support NATO in Europe consisting of land and air elements.

National Defence expenditure for the fiscal year 1986–87 was estimated at $9,955 million. Canadian Armed Forces strength at April 1987, 87,340 authorized force.

EDUCATION AND LANGUAGE

Education is under the control of the Provincial Governments, the cost of the publicly controlled schools being met by local taxation, aided by provincial grants. In 1986–87 there were 15,595 publicly controlled elementary and secondary schools with 4,943,600 pupils. Of these, 1,331 were private schools with 231,045 pupils; 378 federal schools with 45,200 pupils and 21 special schools for the blind and deaf with 2,790 pupils.

In 1986–87 there were 68 degree-granting universities with a full-time enrolment of 470,330, as well as 319,360 students in 200 other post-secondary, non-university institutions.

CANADIAN PRODUCTION

Agriculture.—About 7 per cent. of the total land area of Canada is classified as farm land and approximately half of this is under cultivation, the remainder being woodland or suitable only for grazing purposes. More than three-quarters of the land now cultivated is found in the prairie region of Western Canada. Farm cash receipts from the sale of farm products in 1986 were $20,578,419,000. Livestock, poultry and eggs contributed $10,197,608,000; field crops $9,373,618,000.

Grain crop production ('000 tonnes)

	1985	1986
Wheat	24,252·3	31,849·8
Oats	2,997·1	3,906·3
Barley	12,443·3	15,025·6
Rye	598·0	670·1
Flaxseed	901·9	1,066·8
Rapeseed	3,507·8	3,886·9
Total	44,700·4	56,405·5

Livestock.—In July 1986 the livestock included 11,464,700 cattle, 721,500 sheep, 10,720,500 hogs and 23,485,000 chickens (layers).

Fur Production.—Canada in 1985–86 produced pelts valued at $99,577,798. Wild life pelts made up 50·4 per cent of the total, with a value of $50,207,693.

Fisheries.—The marketed value of catches in 1986 was $2,881,730,000 (preliminary).

Forestry.—About 44 per cent. of the total land areas is in forests. The shipment value of forest products in 1984 was: newsprint $4,821,195,000; paper (other than newsprint) $2,184,406,000; lumber $4,735,555,000; wood pulp $4,308,786,000.

Minerals.—Canada is the world's largest producer of zinc and the second largest of nickel, asbestos, potash, gypsum, uranium, elemental sulphur and titanium concentrates. The country is also rich in many other minerals, including gold, silver, iron, copper, cobalt and lead.

	1985	1986*
	(tonnes)	
Copper	738·6	768·2
Nickel	169·9	180·6
Lead	268·3	303·5
Molybdenum	7·9	12·9
Zinc	1,049·2	1,055·1
Iron Ore	39,502,000·0	36,096,000·0
Asbestos	750,000·0	640,000·0
Gypsum	8,447,000·0	8,542,000·0
Cement	10,192,000·0	10,058,000·0
Lime	2,212,000·0	1,633,000·0
Salt	10,085,000·0	11,088,000·0
Potash	6,661,000·0	6,969,000·0

*preliminary

Production of gold was 104,655,000 grams in 1986 (87,562,000 in 1985) and of silver was 1,219,000 kg. (1,197,000 kg. in 1985). Uranium production in 1986 was 10,977,000 kilograms (10,441,000 kg. in 1985).

TRADE

Merchandise imports into Canada in 1986 were valued at $112,677,998,000 and merchandise exports (including re-exports) at $120,520,875,000. The main exports in 1986 were motor vehicles and parts, newsprint paper, wheat, crude petroleum, lumber, natural gas, woodpulp, petroleum and coal products, and television and telecommunication equipment. Trade with the U.S.A. accounts for 73 per cent of total trade in merchandise, although efforts are being made to develop alternative markets. Value of trade with Canada's largest trading partners in 1986 was as follows ($'000):

Country	Imports	Domestic Exports
United States	77,336,965	90,297,227
Japan	7,626,298	5,908,225
United Kingdom	3,721,155	2,551,917
West Germany	3,453,227	1,263,535
South Korea	1,749,446	958,753
France	1,585,290	961,663
Italy	1,671,357	692,330
Taiwan	1,744,665	599,358
Republic of China	566,594	1,100,278
Netherlands	694,138	970,021
Mexico	1,179,552	397,438
Brazil	821,641	652,128
Benelux	618,228	820,582

COMMUNICATIONS

Railways.—The total track of railways in operation on Dec. 31, 1985, was 95,670 km.

	1985
Capital	$15,648,278,632
Operating Revenues	7,668,782,000
Operating Expenses	6,845,074,000

In 1985 revenue freight was 242,120,823,078 tonne-kilometres.

Shipping.—The registered shipping on Jan. 1, 1985 including inland vessels, was 36,301 vessels with gross tonnage 5,515,498. The volume of international shipping handled at Canadian ports in 1985 was 143,420,769 metric tonnes loaded and 60,668,828 metric tonnes unloaded.

Canals.—The bulk of canal shipping in Canada is handled through the two sections of the St. Lawrence Seaway, which provide access to the Great Lakes for ocean-going ships. In 1986, transits on the Montreal-Lake Ontario section numbered 3,307 for a total of 37,581,808 cargo tonnes; transits in the Welland Canal section numbered 3,959 for a total of 41,612,770 cargo tonnes. Principal commodities carried were iron ore, wheat, corn, barley, soybeans, fuel oil, manufactured iron and steel, coal and coke.

Civil Aviation.—The number of passengers carried in 1985 (all major Canadian carriers) was 29,055,587. 1,171,810,991 tonne-kms of freight were carried in 1985.

Motor Vehicles.—Total motor vehicle registrations numbered 14,775,000 in 1985.

Post.—There were over 8,000 postal facilities operating in Canada on March 31, 1987. Post office revenue in the fiscal year 1986–87 was $2,970 m.; total expenditure $3,099 m.

FEDERAL CAPITAL

OTTAWA, the federal capital, 111 miles west of Montreal and 247 miles north-east of Toronto, is a city on the south bank of the Ottawa river. The city was chosen as the capital of the Province of Canada in 1857 and was later selected as the site of the Dominion capital. Ottawa contains the Parliamentary Buildings, Royal Mint and the Dominion Observatory.

Manufacturing is also carried on, medical advancement, high technology (communications, defence), printing and publishing being of greatest importance. Ottawa is connected with Lake Ontario by the Rideau Canal. The City population was 300,763 at the Census of 1986; and Metropolitan Ottawa 819,263.

YUKON TERRITORY

The Yukon Act, 1970, as amended, provides for the administration of the Territory by a Commissioner acting under instructions from time to time given by the Governor-in-Council or the Minister of Indian Affairs and Northern Development. Legislative powers, analogous to those of a provincial government, are exercised by a Legislative Assembly of 16 members elected from electoral districts in the Territory. The Executive Council of the Assembly consists of the government leader as chairman and four elected members. The area of the Territory is 207,076 sq. miles (536,324 sq. km.), with a population (1986) of 23,504. Minerals and tourism are the chief industries, followed closely by transport, communications and other utilities industry.

Seat of Government, Whitehorse. Pop. (1986) 15,199.

Commissioner, J. K. McKinnon.

NORTHWEST TERRITORIES

The Northwest Territories Act, 1979, as amended, provides for a Legislative Assembly of 24 elected members, of which the Executive Council under the chairmanship of the government leader is the senior decision-making body of the government in the Territory.

The Northwest Territories are subdivided into the districts of Mackenzie, Keewatin and Franklin.

The area of the Northwest Territories is 1,304,903 sq. miles (3,379,683 sq. km.), with a population (1986 Census) of 52,238. The chief industry is mining, with a total value of $461,200,000 in 1984. Lead, zinc, gold, silver, oil exploration and natural gas contributed about 32 per cent. of the total activities in the Northwest Territories.

Seat of Government, Yellowknife. Pop. (1986) 11,753.

Commissioner, J. H. Parker.

PROVINCES OF CANADA

ALBERTA

Area and Population.—The Province of Alberta has an area of 255,285 sq. miles (661,185 sq. km.), including about 6,485 sq. miles of water (16,796 sq. km.), with a population (April 1987 estimate) of 2,378,100.

Government.—The Government is vested in a Lieutenant-Governor and Legislative Assembly composed of 83 members, elected for five years, representing 83 electoral districts in the Province. At a provincial election held on May 8, 1986, the Progressive Conservative party took 61 seats, the New Democratic Party 16 seats, the Liberal Party 4 seats, and the Representative Party 2 seats.

Lieut.-Governor, Her Honour Helen Hunley.

EXECUTIVE

Premier, President of Executive Council, Hon.
Don Getty $83,418
Deputy Premier and Advanced Education, Hon. David Russell.
Municipal Affairs, Hon. Neil Crawford.
Attorney General and Federal & Intergovernmental Affairs, Hon. Jim Horsman.
Economic Development & Trade, Hon. Larry Shaben.
Provicial Treasurer, Hon. Dick Johnston.
Energy, Hon. Neil Webber.
Technology, Research & Telecommunications, Hon. Les Young.
Transportation and Utilities, Hon. Al Adair.

Hospitals and Medical Care, Hon. Marvin Moore.
Tourism, Hon. LeRoy Fjordbotten.
Labour, Hon. Ian Reid.
Social Services, Hon. Connie Osterman.
Forestry, Lands & Wildlife, Hon. Don Sparrow.
Environment, Hon. Ken Kowalski.
Public Works, Supply & Services, Hon. Ernie Isley.
Agriculture, Hon. Peter Elzinga.
Associate Minister of Agriculture, Hon. Shirley Cripps.
Culture, Hon. Dennis Anderson.
Recreation & Parks, Hon. Norm Weiss.
Career Development and Employment, Hon. Rick Orman.
Education, Hon. Nancy Betkowski.
Solicitor General, Hon. Ken Rostad.
Consumer & Corporate Affairs, Hon. Elain McCoy.
Community & Occupational Health, Hon. Jim Dinning.
Speaker of the Legislative Assembly, Hon. D. Carter $74,545
London Office, Alberta House, 1, Mount Street, W.1.

THE JUDICATURE

Court of Appeal of Alberta, Hon. J. H. Laycraft (*Chief Justice*).
Judges, Hons. S. S. Lieberman; D. C. Prowse, A. F. Moir; W. J. Haddad; J. W. McClung; A. M. Harradence; R. P. Kerans; R. H. Belzil; W. A. Stevenson; M. M. Hetherington; H. L. Irving.

Court of Queen's Bench of Alberta, Hon. W. K. Moore (*Chief Justice*); Hon. T. H. Miller (*Associate Chief Justice*).

ECONOMY

The Gross Domestic Product at factor cost in 1985 was ($ millions):—

Agriculture, fishing and trapping	2,130
Forestry	66
Mining	16,767
Manufacturing	3,947
Construction	3,138
Transportation	4,057
Utilities	2,151
Trade	5,039
Finance	13,116
Services	8,602
Public Administration	3,303
Total G.D.P. at factor cost	62,316

Mineral Production 1986 (preliminary estimates)

	$ '000
Crude oil	7,970,208
Natural gas	6,106,362
Natural gas by-products	1,762,164
Coal	438,000
Sulphur (elemental)	874,186
Sand & gravel	108,000
Cement	124,951
Other	78,860
Total	17,462,731

Manufacturing.—The total value of manufacturing shipments (1986) was $15,473,134,000. Number of industrial establishments 2,482 (1984), total employees 71,451 (1984). The leading industrial products are refined petroleum and coal products, meat and meat products, chemicals and chemical products, fabricated metal products, non-metallic mineral products and primary metals.

GOVERNMENT FINANCE
Budgetary Estimates $ millions

	1986–87	1987–88
Revenue	8,308	8,627
Expenditure	10,807	10,416
Deficit	2,499	1,789

NOTE: The Budgetary revenue figure does not include funds allocated to the Alberta Heritage Savings Trust Fund.

CAPITAL.—Edmonton—city population (1986) 573,982, metropolitan area, 785,465. Other centres are Calgary (636,104), Lethbridge (58,841), Red Deer (54,425), Medicine Hat (41,804), St. Albert (36,710), Fort McMurray (34,949).

BRITISH COLUMBIA

Area and Population.—British Columbia has a total area estimated at 366,255 sq. miles (948,596 sq. km.), with a population of 2,935,000 (April 1987).

Government.—The Government consists of a Lieutenant-Governor and an Executive Council together with a Legislative Assembly of 69 members.

Lieut.-Governor, Hon. Robert Gordon Rogers.

EXECUTIVE COUNCIL

Premier and President of the Council, Hon. William N. Vander Zalm.

Provincial Secretary and Minister of Government Services, Hon. Elwood Veitch.

Attorney-General, Hon. Brian R. D. Smith, Q.C.

Forests and Lands, Hon. David F. H. Parker.

Finance and Corporate Relations, Hon. Melville B. Couvelier.

Agriculture and Fisheries, Hon. John Savage.

Energy, Mines and Petroleum Resources, Hon. John Davis, P.C.

Education, Hon. Anthony J. Brummet.

Labour and Consumer Services, Hon. Lyall Hanson.

Economic Development, Hon. Grace M. McCarthy.

Municipal Affairs, Hon. Rita M. Johnston.

Health, Hon. Peter A. Dueck.

Social Services and Housing, Hon. Claude H. Richmond.

Transportation and Highways, Hon. Clifford C. Michael.

Environment and Parks, Hon. C. Stephen Rogers.

Intergovernmental Relations, Hon. W. Bruce Strachan.

Tourism, Recreation and Culture, Hon. William E. Reid.

Advanced Education and Job Training, Hon. Stanley Hagen.

(The Premier receives a total salary of $76,527: Members of the Executive Council receive a total salary of $71,330).

Speaker, Legislative Assembly, Hon. K. Walter Davidson $64,809

Agent-General in London, A. Hart, Q.C., British Columbia House, 1 Regent Street, S.W.1.

THE JUDICATURE

Court of Appeal—Chief Justice of British Columbia, Hon. N. T. Nemetz.

Justices of Appeal, Hons. J. D. Taggart; P. D. Seaton; A. B. B. Carrothers; E. E. Hinkson; W. A. Craig; J. S. Aikins; J. D. Lambert; J. A. Macdonald; R. P. Anderson; H. E. Hutcheon; A. B. Macfarlane; W. A. Esson; B. M. McLachlin; W. J. Wallace; C. C. Locke.

Supreme Court—Chief Justice, Hon. A. McEachern.

Puisne Judges, Hons. K. E. Meredith; A. A. Mackoff; S. M. Toy; J. C. Bouck; L. G. McKenzie; G. L. Murray; H. P. Legg; W. J. Trainor; P. M. Proudfoot; H. A. Callaghan; A. G. MacKinnon; M. R. Taylor; P. D. Dohm; R. M. P. Paris; D. B. Hinds; A. A. W. Macdonell; J. E. Spencer; W. H. Davies; C. R. Lander; B. D. Macdonald; K. M. Lysyk; L. S. G. Finch; J. Wood; R. J. Gibbs; M. F. Southin; G. S. Cumming; D. B. MacKinnon; W. T. Oppal; M. A. Rowles; B. I. Cohen; C. M. Huddart.

FINANCE

	1986–87	1987–88
Estimated Revenue	$8,578·0 m.	$9,370·0 m.
Estimated Expenditure	9,749·0 m.	10,220·0 m.
Net Guaranteed Debt		10,775·5 m.

ECONOMY

Production and Industry.—Manufacturing activity is based largely on the processing of the output of the logging, mineral, fishing and agriculture industries. The principal manufacturing centres are Vancouver, New Westminster, Victoria, North Vancouver, Kelowna and Prince George. Forestry and forest-based industries form the most important economic activity, accounting for approximately 40 per cent of total production. British Columbia is the leading province of Canada in the quantity and value of its timber and sawmill products. Mining, the second most important non-service economic activity, is based on copper, zinc, lead, iron concentrates, molybdenum, coal, natural gas, crude petroleum, asbestos, gold and silver. Molybdenum production is approximately 99 per cent of the Canadian total.

The production levels for important industries were estimated for 1986 as follows:—

Lumber	31,468,300 cu. metres
Paper	2,601,500 tonnes
Pulp	6,173,500 tonnes
Coal	20,663,300 tonnes
Natural Gas	8,489,800,000 cu. metres

Mineral production for 1986 was valued at $3,236·9 million.

The most important agricultural products are livestock, eggs and poultry, fruits and dairy products. Salmon accounts for approximately 60 per cent of the value of fisheries. Other species include halibut, herring, sole, cod, flounder, perch, tuna and shellfish. In 1986 farm cash receipts were valued at $1,003·1 million.

The economy is dependent upon markets outside the province for the disposal of most of the products of her industry. An estimated 55–60 per cent of production is exported to foreign markets. Manufacturing shipments in 1986 were valued at $20,550·6 million.

Transport.—The Province has deep water harbours which are well serviced by railways and modern highways. Vancouver is the base for regular scheduled air routes to other parts of Canada, the United States, Europe, Mexico, South America, Hawaii, Fiji, Australia, Japan, Hong Kong and the Middle East.

CAPITAL, ΨVICTORIA, Metropolitan population (1986) 265,385. ΨVANCOUVER metropolitan population (1986) 1,266,152, is the western terminus of the Canadian Pacific Railway and the Canadian National Railways (the C.N.R. also has a terminus at Prince Rupert) and the southern terminus of the British Columbia Railway, and possesses one of the finest natural harbours in the world, servicing a variety of vessels, including large bulk cargo carriers. Other principal cities are Prince George, Kamloops, Kelowna and Nanaimo.

MANITOBA

Area and Population.—Manitoba, originally the Red River settlement, is the central province of Canada. The Province has a considerable area of prairie land but is also a land of wide diversity combining 400 miles of sea-coast, large lakes and rivers covering an area of 30,225 square miles and pre-cambrian rock which covers about three-fifths of the Province. The total area is 250,946 sq. miles (649,947 sq. km.), with a population (1987 estimate) of 1,082,800.

Government.—The Government is administered by a Lieutenant-Governor, assisted by an Executive Council of Ministers, who are members of the Legislative Assembly of 57 members. Each member of the Legislative Assembly receives an annual sessional indemnity totalling $37,521 for the year ending July 1, 1987.

The New Democratic Party formed the government of Manitoba in November 1981, and were returned to office in a General Election held on March 18, 1986. The standing in the House at May 1, 1987 was: New Democratic Party 30, Progressive Conservative 26, Liberal 1.

Lieut.-Governor, His Honour George Johnson (1986).

EXECUTIVE

Premier, President of the Council and Minister of Federal-Provincial Relations, Hon. Howard R. Pawley, Q.C.

Health, Hon. Laurent L. Desjardins.
Employment Services and Economic Security, Hon. Leonard S. Evans.
Agriculture, Hon. Billie Uruski.
Co-operative Development, Hon. Jay M. Cowan.
Energy and Mines, Hon. Wilson Parasiuk.

Industry, Trade and Technology, Hon. Victor Schroeder, Q.C.
Business Development and Tourism, and Housing, Hon. Maureen L. Hemphill.
Finance, Hon. Eugene M. Kostyra.
Attorney-General, Hon. Roland Penner, Q.C..
Community Services, Hon. Muriel A. Smith.
Consumer and Corporate Affairs, and Labour, Hon. Alvin H. Mackling Q.C.
Education, Hon. J. T. Storie.
Highways and Transportation, Hon. John S. Plohman.
Municipal Affairs, Hon. John Bucklaschuk.
Environment and Workplace Safety and Health, Hon. Gérard Lécuyer.
Government Services, Hon. Harry M. Harapiak.
Northern and Native Affairs, Hon. Elijah Harper.
Crown Investments and Urban Affairs, Hon. Gary A. Doer.
Natural Resources, Leonard Harapiak.
Culture, Heritage and Recreation, Judy Wasylycia-Leis.

THE JUDICATURE

Court of Appeal:—
Chief Justice of Manitoba, Hon. A. M. Monnin	$117,900
Puisne Judges, Hons. G. C. Hall; J. F. O'Sullivan; C. R. Huband; A. R. Philp; A. K. Twaddle; S. R. Lyon ...	108,700
Queen's Bench, Chief Justice, Q.B.D. Hon. A. S. Dewar	117,900
Associate Chief Justice (Family Division), Hon. A. C. Hamilton	117,900

ECONOMY

Finance.—The revenue of the provincial government, 1987–88, is estimated at $3,773 million and the expenditure $4,188 million.

Agriculture.—The total land area in Manitoba is 135,342,565 acres, of which 19,126,517 acres are in occupied farms. The gross value of agriculture production in 1986 was estimated at $2,200 million.

Manufactures.—Manufacturing enterprises employed about 57,000 persons on average in 1986. The chief manufacturing centres are Winnipeg, Brandon, Selkirk and Portage la Prairie. The largest manufacturing industry is the food and beverage industry, followed by the machinery and metal fabricating industries.

CAPITAL.—Winnipeg, population 595,000. Other cities are Brandon (38,708), Thompson (14,701), Portage la Prairie (13,198) and Flin Flon (7,243).

NEW BRUNSWICK

Area and Population.—New Brunswick is situated between 45°–48° N. lat. and 63° 47′–69° W. long. and comprises an area of 28,354 sq. miles (73,436 sq. km.), with a population (June 1986 Census) of 710,422. It was first colonized by British subjects in 1761, and in 1783 by inhabitants of New England, who had been dispossessed of their property in consequence of their loyalty to the British Crown. New Brunswick entered Confederation in 1867.

Government.—Government is administered by a Lieutenant-Governor, an Executive Council, and a Legislative Assembly of 58 members elected by the people. The last General Election was held October 12, 1982. The composition of the Legislature at June 1987 was 37 Progressive Conservative, 20 Liberal and 1 New Democratic Party members.

Lieutenant-Governor, His Honour Dr. George F. G. Stanley.

EXECUTIVE

Premier, Hon. Richard B. Hatfield.
Justice, Hon. David Clark, Q.C.

Transportation, Hon. Robert McCready.

Agriculture, Hon. Hazen Myers.

Commerce and Technology, Hon. Fernand Dubé, Q.C.

Health and Community Services, Hon. Nancy Clark Teed.

Education, Hon. Jean-Pierre Ouellet.

Advanced Education and Training, Hon. Mabel Deware.

Labour, Hon. Joseph Mombourquette.

Finance, Hon. John Baxter, Q.C.

Municipal Affairs and Environment, Hon. Robert Jackson.

Fisheries, Hon. James Tucker.

Tourism, Recreation and Heritage, Hon. Omer Leger.

Chairman, Board of Management, Hon. Yvon Poitras.

Supply and Services, Hon. William Harmer.

Natural Resources and Energy, Hon. Malcolm Mac-Leod.

Income Assistance, Hon. Paul Dawson.

Housing, Hon. Jean Gauvin.

Speaker of the House, Hon. Charles Gallagher.

THE JUDICATURE

Court of Appeal

Chief Justice, Hon. S. G. Stratton.

Judges of Appeal, Hons. J. C. Angers; W. Hoyt; R. C. Rice; L. C. Ayles; P. A. A. Ryan.

Queen's Bench Division

Chief Justice, Hon. G. A. Richard.

ECONOMY

Finance.—The estimated revenue for the year ending March 31, 1986, was $2,662,864,912 and ordinary expenditure, $2,711,636,827.

Manufactures.—New Brunswick's largest manufacturing group, in terms of shipments, is the paper and allied industries, followed by the food and wood industries. Together these industries accounted in 1986 for 52·7 per cent. of the total value of manufacturing shipments of $4,600·0 million. Saint John has a major ice-free port and is the principal manufacturing centre of the Province.

Agriculture.—Total land area 27,633 sq. miles; farms numbered 3,554 and averaged 284 acres each in 1986. Dairy products and potatoes are the leading agricultural products. Both industries together accounted for 43 per cent of total farm cash receipts in 1986. Farm cash receipts in 1986 totalled $226,430,000.

Fisheries.—Fishing is an important industry, employing about 6,500 fishermen. The chief commercial fish are lobsters, herring, tuna, crab and cod. Landings reached 130,498 tonnes valued at $94,116,000 in 1986.

Minerals.—Extensive zinc, lead and copper deposits are now being mined in the north-eastern part of the Province with New Brunswick being the third largest producer of zinc in Canada. A lead smelter, fertilizer plant and port facilities have been constructed at Belledune. Canada's only primary antimony producer is located at Lake George. There is exploration and development near Sussex and Salt Springs, where potash production continues to escalate. A potash terminal has been built at the port of St. John. Coal is mined at Grand Lake and exploration for other deposits is being undertaken. Total mineral production was valued at $526,000,000 in 1986.

Tourism is of increasing value to the economy.

CAPITAL ΨFREDERICTON: population (1986), 65,768. Other cities are ΨSaint John (121,265); Moncton (102,084); Bathurst (34,895); Edmundston (22,614); Campbellton (17,418).

NEWFOUNDLAND AND LABRADOR

Area and Population.—The Island of Newfoundland is situated between 46° 37′–51° 37′ N. latitude and 52° 44′–59° 30′ W. longitude, on the north-east side of the Gulf of St. Lawrence, and is separated from the North American continent by the Straits of Belle Isle on the N.W. and by Cabot Strait on the S.W. The island is about 317 miles long and 316 miles broad and is triangular in shape. It comprises an area of 43,008 sq. miles (111,390 sq. km.), with a population (1986 Census) (inclusive of Labrador) of 568,349.

Labrador forms the most easterly part of the North American continent, and extends from Point St. Charles, at the northeast entrance to the Straits of Belle Isle, on the south, to Cape Chidley, at the eastern entrance to Hudson's Straits on the north. It has an area of 113,641 sq. miles (294,328 sq. km), with a population (1986 Census) of 28,741. Labrador is noted for its cod fisheries and also possesses valuable salmon, herring, trout and seal fisheries.

Government.—On March 31, 1949 Newfoundland became the 10th Province of the Dominion of Canada. The Government is administered by a Lieutenant-Governor, aided by an Executive Council and a Legislative Assembly of 52 members. A General Election was held on April 12, 1985. The standings in the current House of Assembly are: 35 Progressive Conservatives, 15 Liberals, and 2 New Democrats.

Lieutenant-Governor, Hon. James A. McGrath (Sept. 5, 1986).

EXECUTIVE

Premier and Minister of Intergovernmental Affairs, Hon. A. Brian Peckford.

President of the Council, and Minister of Energy and Government House Leader, Hon. G. Ottenheimer, Q.C.

Finance, Hon. Dr. John Collins.

President of Treasury Board, Hon. H. N. Windsor.

Mines, Hon. J. W. Dinn.

Career Development and Advanced Studies, Hon. C. J. Power.

Public Works and Services, Hon. H. Young.

Justice, and Attorney General, Hon. Lynn Verge.

Transportation, Hon. Ronald Dawe.

Forest Resources and Land, Hon. L. A. Simms.

Municipal Affairs, Hon. N. E. Doyle.

Fisheries, Hon. T. G. Rideout.

Health, Hon. Dr. H. M. Twomey.

Rural, Agricultural and Northern Development, Hon. R. J. Aylward.

Social Services, Hon. R. C. Brett.

Consumer Affairs and Communications, Hon. J. M. Russell.

Development, Hon. H. M. Barrett.

Environment, Hon. J. C. Butt.

Education, Hon. W. L. Hearn.

Culture, Recreation and Youth, Hon. W. B. Matthews.

Labour, Hon. T. A. Blanchard.

Speaker of the House of Assembly, Dr. P. McNicholas.

Clerk of the Executive Council, H. M. Clarke.

ECONOMY

Finance.—The estimated gross capital and current account revenues for 1987–88 were $2,448,824,000 and the gross current and capital account expenditures $2,825,060,000.

Production and Industry.—The main primary industries are fishing, forestry and mining. In 1984 shipments of fish products were valued at $450 million. In 1986 newsprint shipments from the three pulp and paper mills were valued at $328·3 million, mining plus structural materials shipments were estimated at $869·7 million, of which $702·5 million was from the 2 iron ore mines in Labrador. Manufacturing shipments with the exclusion of fish and paper products totalled approximately $562 million in 1986. The hydro-electric plant on the Churchill river is the largest underground plant in the world, with a capacity of 5,225,000 kw.

Petroleum and Natural Gas.—Over 121 wells have been drilled off Newfoundland since 1965. Discovery of oil was made in 1979 on the Grand Banks. Oil production is expected to begin in 1992, with a peak production of 110,000 barrels of oil a day. In 1986, offshore exploration expenditure was approximately $350 million

Transport.—The Province is connected to mainland Canada by a ferry service from North Sydney, Nova Scotia to Port aux Basques and Argentia. The main line of the railway extends from St. John's on the east coast to Port aux Basques on the west coast. Transport between various points on the island is by highway but the south coast and Labrador still rely on the coastal boat service.

CAPITAL, ST. JOHN'S (population 1986 Census, Greater St. John's 161,901) is North America's oldest city, and thus of historical interest and is the seat of the provincial legislature, the site of most provincial and federal government offices and the principal port for the island of Newfoundland. Newfoundland's second city of Corner Brook (population 1986 Census, 22,719) is situated on the west coast, its principal industry being its pulp and paper mill.

NOVA SCOTIA

Area and Population.—Nova Scotia is a peninsula between 43° 25′–47° N. lat. and 59° 40′–66° 25′ W. long., and is connected to New Brunswick by a low fertile isthmus about 17·5 miles wide. It comprises an area of 21,425 sq. miles (55,490 sq. km.), including 1,023 sq. miles of lakes and rivers and 6,479 miles of shoreline. No place is more than 35 miles from the Atlantic Ocean. Population (1986) 865,442.

Government.—The Government consists of a Lieutenant-Governor and a 52-member elected Legislative Assembly, from which the Executive Council (Cabinet) is selected. The Lieutenant-Governor represents the Queen and is appointed by the Governor-in-Council.

Lieutenant-Governor, Hon. Alan R. Abraham.

EXECUTIVE COUNCIL

Premier, Hon. John M. Buchanan, Q.C.
Development, Hon. R. Thornhill.
Agriculture and Marketing, Hon. R. Bacon.
Tourism, Hon. J. MacIsaac.
Lands & Forests, Hon. K. Streatch.
Vocational and Technical Training, Hon. R. Giffin, Q.C.
Attorney General, Hon. T. Donahoe, Q.C.
Education, Hon. T. McInnis.
Mines & Energy, Hon. J. Matheson, Q.C.
Environment, Hon. L. Stirling.
Social Services, Hon. E. Morris.
Health, Hon. R. Russell.
Finance & Culture, Recreation & Fitness, Hon. G. Kerr.
Government Services, Hon. M. Laffin.
Fisheries, Hon. J. Leefe.
Management Board, Hon. G. Moody.
Housing, Hon. M. Pickings.
Municipal Affairs, Hon. D. Nantes.
Consumer Affairs and Culture, Recreation and Fitness, Hon. M. Cochran.
Transportation, Hon. G. LeBlanc.
Labour, Hon. B. Young.

Cabinet Ministers receive $32,950 a year (the Premier receives $42,510), *plus* member's sessional indemnity $27,860 and expense allowance $10,550.

Agent-General in London, Donald M. Smith, 14 Pall Mall, SW1Y 5LU.

THE JUDICATURE

Supreme Court—Appeal Division
Chief Justice, Hon. L. O. Clarke $121,200
Judges, Hons. G. L. S. Hart; I. M. Mackeigan;
A. L. Macdonald; L. L. Pace; M. C. Jones;
L. L. Pace; K. M. Matthews. 111,700

Trial Division
Chief Justice, Hon. Constance R. Glube 121,200
Judges, Hons. A. M. MacIntosh; W. J. Grant;
J. D. Hallett; K. P. Richard; C. Denne
Burchell; R. M. Rogers; H. Nathanson; M.
Nunn; R. B. Macdonald; F. B. W. Kelly; G.
Tidman; J. M. Davison 111,700

ECONOMY

Finance.—The revenue for the fiscal year ending March 31, 1986, was $2,714,566,000 and expenditure was $2,983,588,000. The net direct debt was $3,235,162,000.

Manufacturing.—Manufacturing constitutes the most important goods producing sector of the economy. Shipments were worth $4,745 million in 1986 with a total added value estimated to be more than $1,700 million. Manufacturing plants provide employment for 45,000 or 13 per cent of the labour force. Capital expenditure in the manufacturing sector has increased from $197·2 million in 1986 to $357·8 million in 1987.

Utilities.—Electric power in Nova Scotia is supplied by the Nova Scotia Power Corporation, a Crown corporation. The Corporation's generating stations, which are predominantly coal fired have a nameplate capacity of 1,814,305 kilowatts. The Corporation's generating system is made up of seven thermal plants, three gas turbines, 33 hydro stations scattered throughout the Province and one tidal power station.

Petroleum Activity.—By mid-1987 a total of 123 wells had been completed off-shore since drilling began in 1967, the drilling being done by five major operations. There were no wells drilled onshore in 1985–86.

Mining.—The total value of mineral production in 1986 was estimated at $324,000,000, Dollar value of production for specific minerals was:—

Coal	$179,613,000
Sand, gravel and crushed rock	51,337,000
Salt	47,799,000
Limestone	4,321,000
Barite	565,000

Agriculture.—Farm cash receipts were about $267 million in 1986. About 3 per cent of the total area, or 390,000 acres, is classified as farm land. Dairy, horticulture, cattle, hogs, fur and poultry products form the largest sectors.

Fishing.—The value of fish landed in 1986 was $312,733,000. Products have been diversified and enlarged into a variety of processed foods that are increasing in number. Primary fishing and fish processing employed 20,753 persons in 1986 (13,253 fishermen and 7,500 plant workers).

Forest Products.—The gross value of primary and secondary forestry was $650,000,000 in 1986. Forest lands total 10,800,000 acres or 84 per cent of the land area. About 75 per cent of forest land is privately owned. Forest based industries employ about 8,000.

Tourism.—Between May 15 and October 31, 1985, about 1·2 million visitors spent about $250 million in the Province.

CAPITAL ΨHALIFAX, including the neighbouring city of Dartmouth, has a population of 176,725. In addition to a container-handling terminal in South Halifax a new terminal at the north end of Halifax Harbour was opened in 1981. A 90-acre autoport has been built at Port Halifax to handle both the export and import of motor vehicles. A shipyard, with dry-dock, can build and repair the largest ocean-going liners. The harbour, ice-free the year round, is the main Atlantic winter port of Canada. Other cities and towns include ΨSydney (27,475), ΨGlace Bay (20,292), Amherst (9,576) and New Glasgow (9,941).

Cape Breton Island

This has been part of Nova Scotia since 1819. It is the centre of the steel manufacturing and coal mining industries, and is also noted for its lakes and coastal scenery, making it a tourist attraction in Canada.

ONTARIO

Area and Population.—The Province of Ontario contains a total area of 412,582 sq. miles (1,068,582 sq. km.), with a population (1986 Census) of 9,113,515.

Government.—The Government is vested in a Lieutenant-Governor and a Legislative Assembly of 125 members elected for five years.

After the last election on May 2, 1985, there were 52 Progressive Conservatives, 48 Liberals, 25 New Democrats. The Conservative party formed the Government after the election, but was defeated on a confidence motion in June 1985 and replaced by a Liberal government enjoying New Democrat support.

Lieutenant-Governor, Hon. Lincoln Alexander, P.C., Q.C. (1985).

EXECUTIVE COUNCIL
(as at June 5, 1987)

Premier and Minister of Intergovernmental Affairs, Northern Development and Mines (acting), Hon. David Peterson.
Treasurer and Minister of Economics, Revenue and Chairman of the Management Board of Cabinet (acting), Hon. Robert Nixon.
Education and Government Services, Hon. Sean Conway.
Environment, Hon. James Bradley.
Attorney-General, Hon. Ian Scott.
Agriculture and Food, Hon. Jack Riddell.
Tourism and Recreation, Hon. John Eakins.
Natural Resources and Energy, Hon. Vince Kerrio.
Industry, Trade and Technology, Hon. Hugh O'Neil.
Community and Social Services, Hon. John Sweeney.
Health, Hon. Murray Elston.
Labour, Hon. William Wrye.
Municipal Affairs, Hon. Bernard Grandmaitre.
Housing, Hon. Alvin Curling.
Transportation and Communications, Hon. Ed Fulton.
Solicitor General, Minister of Correctional Services, Hon. Kenneth Keyes.
Consumer and Commercial Relations, Financial Institutions, Hon. Monte Kwinter.
Citizenship and Culture, Hon. Lily Munro.
Colleges and Universities, and Skills Development, Hon. Gregory Sorbara.
Ministers Without Portfolio, Hon. Ronald Van Horne; Hon. Antony Ruprecht.
(N.B. Elections scheduled for September 10, 1987 may lead to changes to the above list.)

Secretary of the Cabinet and Clerk of the Executive Council, R. D. Caraman.
Speaker, Legislative Assembly, Hon. H. Edighoffer.
Agent-General in London, T. Wells, 13 Charles II Street, S.W.1.

JUDICATURE

Chief Justice of Ontario, Hon. W. G. C. Howland.
Chief Justice of the High Court, Hon. W. D. Pucker.

ECONOMY

Agriculture.—Ontario has the highest total of agricultural production in Canada with a gross value of $5,520,000,000 and a total net farm income of $5,460,000,000 in 1986.

Forestry.—Productive forested lands cover 377,000 sq. km. or 35·3 per cent of the land area of the Province. Paper and allied industries are by far the most important sector of Ontario's forest industry.

Minerals.—Ontario's natural resources include 15 basic minerals, such as copper, iron ore, zinc, sulphur, gold and platinum. The province has half the world's supply of nickel and the largest amount of uranium in the western world. Total value of the mineral production in 1986 was estimated at $4,800,000,000.

Energy.—Total electrical energy generated in Ontario in 1985 was 121,000 million kWh (34 per cent hydro, 40 per cent nuclear and 26 per cent other conventional fossil fuels).

Manufacture.—Ontario is the chief manufacturing province in Canada, producing 50 per cent of all manufactured goods. During 1985 Ontario's exports totalled $59,000 million, an increase in value of $4,000 million over 1984. A $4,200 million growth in the value of end products—the sector which contains the bulk of Ontario's manufactured exports—was also achieved.

CAPITAL—ΨTORONTO (metropolitan population 1986, 2,192,721) has a wide range of manufacturing and service industries and is a centre of education, business and finance. Other major urban areas are: Ottawa, the national capital (300,763); ΨHamilton (306,140), with iron and steel industry, metal fabrication, machinery, electrical and chemical industries; London (269,140), a business and manufacturing centre; ΨWindsor (193,111); Kitchener (150,604) and Sudbury (88,717).

PRINCE EDWARD ISLAND

Area and Population.—Prince Edward Island lies in the southern part of the Gulf of St. Lawrence, between 46°–47° N. lat. and 62°–64° 30′ W. long. It is about 140 miles in length, and from 4 to 40 miles in breadth; its area is 2,184 sq. miles (5,656 sq. km.), and its population (1985) 127,400.

Government.—The Government is vested in a Lieutenant-Governor and an Executive Council, and Legislative Assembly of 32 members elected for a term of up to 5 years, 16 as Councillors and 16 as Assemblymen. Party representation at July 1, 1987, was: Liberal 21; Progressive Conservative 10; Vacant 1.

Lieutenant-Governor, His Honour Lloyd G. MacPhail (1985) $69,000
(and expense allowance)

EXECUTIVE

Premier and President of the Executive Council, Hon. Joseph A. Ghiz, Q.C.
Finance and Community and Cultural Affairs, Hon. Gilbert R. Clements.
Energy and Forestry, Hon. Allison Ellis.
Industry, Hon. Leonce Bernard.
Fisheries, Hon. Ross Young.
Transportation and Public Works, Hon. Robert Morrissey.
Education, Hon. Betty Jean Brown.
Agriculture, Hon. Tim Carroll.
Justice and Attorney General, and Labour, Hon. Wayne Cheverie, Q.C.
Tourism and Parks, Hon. Gordon MacInnis.
Health and Social Services, Hon. Keith Milligan.

Speaker of the Legislative Assembly Hon. Edward W. Clark.

Members of the Legislative Assembly receive a salary of $18,000 per annum *plus* $9,000 expense allowance; in addition the Premier receives $43,000 per annum; a Minister, $33,000 per annum; and the Speaker, $9,400 per annum, as at July 1, 1987.

SUPREME COURT

Chief Justice, Hon. Norman H. Carruthers $113,900
Associate Justices, Hon. G. Mitchell; Hon.
    C. R. McQuaid; Hon. K. R. MacDonald;
    Hon. A. B. Campbell; Hon. G. J. Mullally;
    Hon. G. R. McMahon .... each $105,000
Supernumary Justice, Hon. F. A. Large.

Finance.—The ordinary revenue in 1986–87 was
$485·8 million and the expenditure was $511·3 million.

Education.—A university and a college of applied
arts and technology were established in 1969, estimated full- and part-time enrolment for 1986–87 being
2,522 (University of Prince Edward Island), and 881
for the college of applied arts and technology (Holland
College).

CAPITAL, ΨCHARLOTTETOWN (pop. July 1986 Census, 15,776), on the shore of Hillsborough Bay, which
forms a good harbour.

QUEBEC

Area and Population.—The Province of Quebec
contains an area estimated at 594,860 sq. miles
(1,540,668 sq. km.) with a population (June, 1986
Census), of 6,532,461.

Government.—The Government of the Province is
vested in a Lieutenant-Governor, a Council of
ministers and a National Assembly of 122 members
elected for five years. At June, 1987, there were 99
Liberals, 22 Parti Quebecois and 1 Independent.

Lieut.-Governor, The Hon. Gilles Lamontagne.

EXECUTIVE

Prime Minister, Hon. Robert Bourassa.
*Deputy Prime Minister and Minister for Cultural
    Affairs*, Hon. Lise Bacon.
Municipal Affairs, Hon. André Boubeau.
Energy and Resources, Hon. John Ciaccia.
Transport and Regional Development, Hon. Marc-
    Yvan Côté.
Agriculture, Fisheries and Food, Hon. Michel Page.
Finance, Hon. Gérard D. Levesques.
Communications, Hon. Richard French.
Revenue and Electoral Reform, Hon. Michel Gratton.
Industry and Commerce, Hon. Daniel Johnson.
Health and Social Services, Hon. Thérèse Lavoie-
    Roux.
Environment, Hon. Lincoln Clifford.
Foreign Trade and Technological Development, Hon.
    Pierre MacDonald.
Justice, Hon. Herbert Marx.
Manpower and Income Security, and Labour, Hon.
    Pierre Paradis.
Recreation, Fish and Game, Hon. Yvon Picotte.
*International Relations, and Canadian Intergovern-
    mental Affairs*, Hon. Gil Remillard.
Cultural Communities and Immigration, Hon. Louise
    Robic.
Education, Higher Education and Science, Hon.
    Claude Ryan.
Minister-Delegates, Hon. Albert Côté (*Forests*); Hon.
    Raymond Savoie (*Mines*); Hon. Robert Dutil (*Fish-
    eries*); Hon. Pierre Fortier (*Privatisation*); Hon.
    Monique Trembley-Gagnon (*Status of Women*);
    Hon. Paul Gobeil (*Administration/President,
    Treasury Board*); Hon. André Vallerand (*Small
    Businesses*); Hon. Gilles Rocheleau (*Supply and
    Services*).
Solicitor General, Hon. Gérard Latulippe.

Agent-General in London, Patrick Hyndmann, 59
Pall Mall, SW1Y 5JH.

JUDICATURE

Court of Appeal, Chief Justice of Quebec, Hon. Marcel
Crête.

Superior Court, Chief Justice of Quebec (Montreal),
Hon. Alan B. Gold.

ECONOMY

Finance.—The revenue for the year 1985–86
was $24,080,778,000; expenditure amounted to
27,222,178,000. The net debt (March 31, 1986) was
$21,997,000,000.

Production and Industry.—The principal manufacturing centres are Montreal, Montreal East, Quebec,
Trois-Rivières, Sherbrooke, Shawinigan Drummond-
ville and Lachine. Forest lands cover 684,480 sq. km.,
of which 490,693 sq. km. are productive. Forest
products in 1984 included wood pulp, 6,371,393 tonnes.

Total estimated value of shipments in the manufacturing industries in 1986 was $60,729,504,000. Value
of 1986 shipments in the chief industries:—

Food and beverages $9,899,364,000
Paper and allied industries 6,495,361,000
Petroleum and coal products 3,523,799,000
Primary metal industries 4,918,696,000
Transportation equipment industries 5,296,305,000

Agriculture and Fisheries.—In 1986 total farm
receipts were:

Crops $502,430,000
Livestock and livestock products 2,380,162,000
Other farm receipts 852,053,000

In 1986 87,977 tonnes of fish, to the value of
$82,207,000 were landed.

Mineral Production.—Minerals to the value of
$2,244,985,685 were mined in 1985. This included
copper, $146,032,186; zinc, $95,068,414; and asbestos,
$223,622,290.

CAPITAL, ΨQUEBEC. Population (Census 1986),
164,000; Historic city visited annually by thousands
of tourists, and one of the great seaport towns of
Canada. ΨMontreal (1,015,420) is the commercial
metropolis. Other important cities are Laval
(284,164); Verdun (60,246), Sherbrooke (74,436), Mon-
treal-Nord (90,303) and La Salle (75,621).

SASKATCHEWAN

Area and Population.—The Province of Saskatchewan lies between Manitoba on the east and Alberta
on the west and has an area of 251,700 sq. miles
(651,899 sq. km.), (of which the land area is 220,182 sq.
miles), with a population (estimated, 1985) of
1,017,800. Saskatchewan extends along the Canada-
U.S.A. boundary for 393 miles and northwards for
761 miles. Its northern width is 276 miles.

Government.—The Government is vested in the
Lieutenant-Governor, with a Legislative Assembly
of 64 members. There is an Executive Council of 16
members. The Legislative Assembly is elected for 5
years and the state of the parties in June 1987 was:
Progressive Conservative 38; New Democratic Party
25; Liberal 1.

Lieut.-Governor, His Honour F. W. Johnson (1983).

EXECUTIVE COUNCIL

*Premier, President of the Council, and Minister of
    Agriculture*, Hon. G. Devine.
Deputy Premier, Provincial Secretary, Hon. E. Bernt-
    son.
*Attorney-General, Minister of Justice, Economic De-
    velopment and Trade*, Hon. R. Andrew.
Consumer and Commercial Affairs, Hon. Joan Dun-
    can.
Education, Hon. L. Hepworth.
Energy and Mines, Hon. Patricia Smith.
Environment, Hon. H. Swan.
Finance and Telecommunications, Hon. G. Lane.
Health, Hon. G. McLeod.
Highways and Transportation, Hon. G. Hodgins.
Human Resources, Labour and Employment, Hon. G.
    Schmidt.

Parks, Recreation and Culture, Hon. C. Maxwell.
Rural Development, Hon. N. Hardy.
Science and Technology, Hon. R. Meiklejohn.
Tourism, Small Business and Co-operatives, Hon. G. Taylor.
Urban Affairs, Hon. Jack Klein.
Premier, $72,867; Ministers, each $63,538.

Agent-General in London.—P. Rousseau, 21 Pall Mall, S.W.1.

Finance.—Combined* revenue for year ending March 1988 is $3,202,508,000 and combined* expenditure $3,779,743,000 (*Consolidated Fund and Heritage combined).

CAPITAL.—REGINA. Population (Census 1986), 175,064. Other cities: Saskatoon (177,644), Moose Jaw (35,073); Prince Albert (33,686) and Yorkton (15,574).

The Commonwealth of Australia
AREA AND POPULATION

States and Capitals	Area (English Sq. Miles)	Estimated Resident Population		
		June 30, 1976 (a)	June 30, 1981 (a)	June 30, 1985
States				
New South Wales (Sydney)	309,433	4,959,600	5,234,900	5,474,288
Queensland (Brisbane)	667,000	2,092,400	2,345,200	2,546,442
South Australia (Adelaide)	380,070	1,274,100	1,318,800	1,362,876
Tasmania (Hobart)	26,383	412,300	427,200	442,111
Victoria (Melbourne)	87,884	3,810,400	3,946,900	4,121,456
Western Australia (Perth)	975,920	1,178,300	1,300,100	1,407,451
Territories				
Australian Capital Territory (Canberra)	939	207,700	227,600	253,085
Northern Territory (Darwin)	520,280	98,200	122,600	143,801
Total	2,967,909	14,033,100	14,923,300	15,751,510

Population of Aboriginal or Torres Strait Islander Origin (a)

	1976 number			1981 number		
	Aboriginal	T.S.I.	Total	Aboriginal	T.S.I.	Total
States						
New South Wales	37,688	2,763	40,451	33,414	1,953	35,367
Queensland	31,948	9,396	41,344	33,966	10,732	44,698
South Australia	9,940	774	10,714	9,476	349	9,825
Tasmania	2,522	421	2,943	2,334	354	2,688
Victoria	12,415	2,345	14,760	5,283	774	6,057
Western Australia	25,565	560	26,125	30,749	602	31,351
Territories						
Australian Capital Territory	769	59	828	763	60	823
Northern Territory	23,535	215	23,750	28,680	408	29,088
Total	144,382	16,533	160,915	144,665	15,232	159,897

Inter-Censal Increases, 1961–1981

Year of Census	Population at Census			Inter-Censal Increase	Net Immigration during Period	
	Males	Females	Total			
1961	5,333,185	5,215,082	10,548,267	(b) 1,521,656	1954–1961	584,754
1966	5,841,588	5,757,910	11,599,498	1,051,231	1961–1966	395,485
1971 (a)	6,567,936	6,499,329	13,067,265	(c) 1,156,140	1966–1971	521,139
1976 (a)	7,032,034	7,001,049	14,033,083	965,818	1971–1976	281,074
1981 (a)	7,448,267	7,474,993	14,923,260	890,177	1976–1981	370,865

(a) Based on Census counts, place of usual residence, adjusted for under-enumeration, and including an estimate of Australian residents temporarily overseas on Census night.
(b) Excludes full-blood Aboriginals.
(c) Based on 1971 Census figure as enumerated.

Increase of Population

Year	Births	Deaths	Net Overseas Migration (a)	Net Increase (b)	Marriages
1980	225,527	108,695	100,940	204,889	109,240
1981	235,842	109,003	121,785	242,083	113,905
1982	239,895	114,771	102,228	227,352	117,275
1983	242,570	110,084	54,800	187,400	114,860
1984 (p)	234,034	109,965	58,100	184,600	108,655
1985 (p)	247,231	118,957	77,600	203,000	114,616

(a) Net permanent and long-term overseas migration gain with an adjustment for the net effect of category jumping.

(b) Prior to June 30, 1981, differences between the net increase shown and the sum of natural increase and net overseas migration were due to the distribution of intercensal discrepancy.

(p) preliminary.

PHYSICAL FEATURES

Australia, including Tasmania, comprises a land area of 7,682,300 square kilometres lying between latitudes 10°41'S (Cape York) and 43°39'S (South East Cape, Tasmania) and longitudes 113°09'E (Steep Point) and 153°39'E (Cape Byron). The latitudinal distance between Cape York and South East Cape is about 3,680 kilometres and the longitudinal distance between Steep Point and Cape Byron is about 4,000 kilometres. (The latitudinal distance between Cape York and the most southerly point on the mainland South Point, Wilson's Promontory, is about 3,180 kilometres.)

Australia has three major landforms: the western plateau, the interior lowlands and the eastern uplands. The western half of the continent consists mainly of a great plateau of altitude 300–600 metres. The interior lowland includes the channel country of southwest Queensland (drainage to Lake Eyre) and the Murray-Darling river system to the south. The eastern uplands consist of a broad belt of varied width extending from north Queensland to Tasmania and composed largely of tablelands, ranges and ridges with only limited mountain areas above 1,000 metres. The highest point is Mt. Kosciusko (2,228 m.) and the lowest, Lake Eyre (− 15 m.).

Australia's large area and latitudinal range have resulted in climatic conditions ranging from the alpine to the tropical. Two thirds of the continent is arid or semi-arid although good rainfalls (over 800 mm annually) occur in the northern monsoonal belt under the influence of the Australian Asian Monsoon and along the eastern and southern highland regions under the influence of the great atmospheric depressions of the Southern Ocean. The effectiveness of the rainfall is greatly reduced by marked alternations of wet and dry seasons, unreliability from year to year, high temperatures and high potential evaporation.

Fifty per cent of the area of Australia has a medium rainfall of less than 300 mm per year and 80 per cent has less than 600 mm. Extreme minimum temperatures are not as low as those recorded in other continents because of the absence of extensive mountain masses and because of the expanse of ocean to the south. However, extreme maxima are comparatively high, reaching 50 C. over the inland, mainly due to the great east–west extent of the continent in the vicinity of the Tropic of Capricorn.

Only one third of the Australian land mass drains directly to the ocean, mainly on the coastal side of the Main Divide and inland with the Murray-Darling system. With the exception of the Murray-Darling system, most rivers draining to the ocean are comparatively short and account for the majority of the country's average annual discharge.

GOVERNMENT

The Commonwealth of Australia was constituted by an Act of the Imperial Parliament dated July 9, 1900, and was inaugurated Jan. 1, 1901. The Government is that of a Federal Commonwealth within the British Commonwealth of Nations, the executive power being vested in the Sovereign (through the Governor-General), assisted by a Federal Ministry of twenty-seven Ministers of State. Under the Constitution the Federal Government has acquired and may acquire certain defined powers as surrendered by the States, residuary legislative power remaining with the States. The right of a State to legislate on any matter is not abrogated except in connection with matters exclusively under Federal control, but where a State law is inconsistent with a law of the Commonwealth the latter prevails to the extent of the inconsistency.

FLAG.—The British Blue Ensign, consisting of a blue flag, with the Union Jack occupying the upper quarter next the staff, differenced by a large white star (representing the six States of Australia and the Territories of the Commonwealth) in the centre of the lower quarter next the staff and pointing direct to the centre of the St. George's Cross in the Union Jack and five white stars, representing the Southern Cross, in the fly.

NATIONAL DAY.—January 26 (Australia Day).

NATIONAL ANTHEM.—Advance Australia Fair.

Governor-General and Staff

Governor-General, His Excellency the Rt. Hon. Sir Ninian Stephen, A.K., G.C.M.G., G.C.V.O., K.B.E., *born* June 15, 1923; *assumed office* July 29, 1982.

Official Secretary, D. I. Smith, A.O., C.V.O.

Deputy Official Secretary, Mrs L. Lawless.

Cabinet

Prime Minister, Hon. Robert J. L. Hawke, A.C.

Deputy Prime Minister; Attorney-General, Hon. L. F. Bowen.

Special Minister of State, Senator Hon. Susan Ryan.

Industry, Technology and Commerce, Senator Hon. J. N. Button.

Transport and Communications, Senator Hon. G. Evans.

Treasurer, Hon. P. J. Keating.

Immigration, Local Government and Ethnic Affairs, Hon. N. Young.

Finance, Senator Hon. P. A. Walsh.

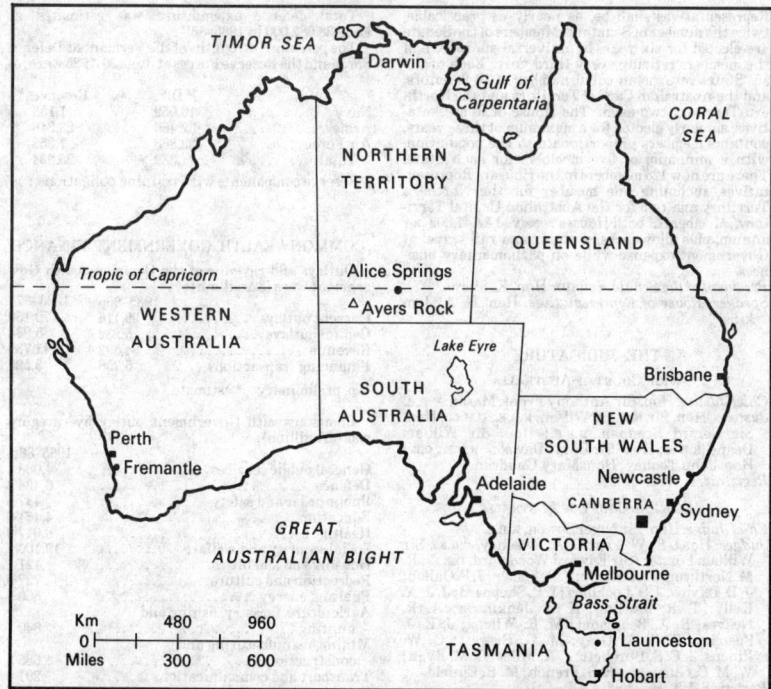

Foreign Affairs and Trade, Hon. W. G. Hayden.
Industrial Relations, Hon. R. Willis.
Employment and Education, Hon. J. S. Dawkins.
Defence, Hon. K. C. Beazley.
Primary Industries and Energy, Hon. J. Kerin.
Social Security, Hon. B. Howe.
Administrative Services, Hon. S. West.
Arts, Sport, Environment, Tourism and Territories, Hon. J. Brown.
Community Services and Health, Hon. N. Blewett.

Junior Ministers

Justice, Senator Hon. M. Tate.
Consumer Affairs, Hon. P. Staples.
Science, Hon. B. Jones.
Land Transports, Hon. P. Duncan.
Local Government, Senator Hon. Margaret Reynolds.
Trade, Hon. M. Duffy.
Employment, Hon. C. Holding.
Resources, Hon. P. Morris.
Home Affairs, Senator Hon. R. Ray.
Environment, Senator Hon. G. Richardson.
Veterans, Hon. B. Humphreys.
Aboriginal Affairs, Hon. G. Hand.
Defence, Hon. R. Kelly.

AUSTRALIAN HIGH COMMISSION
Australia House, Strand, London, WC2B 4LA.
[01–379 4334]

High Commissioner, His Excellency The Hon. Douglas McClelland, A.C.
Deputy High Commissioner, D. W. Evans.
Official Secretary, R. E. Taylor.

Ministers, R. G. Starr; P. J. Sparkes (Commercial); E. F. Delofski (Economic).
Defence Adviser and Head of Defence Staff, Brig. I. J. C. Hearn.

BRITISH HIGH COMMISSION
Commonwealth Avenue, Canberra

High Commissioner, His Excellency Sir John Leahy, K.C.M.G. (1984).
Deputy High Commissioner, Head of Chancery, M. G. Dougal
Defence and Naval Adviser and Head of British Defence Liaison Staff, Cdre. R. M. Lawson.
Counsellors, D. P. R. MacKilligin (Economic and Commercial); C. T. W. Skeate.
First Secretaries, T. E. F. Williams, O.B.E. (Administration); P. Reddicliffe; M. A. Patterson (Commercial, Agriculture); A. N. George; Dr. R. M. Allen (Defence Research); J. Simmons (Passports); W. Talbot.
Military Adviser, Col. G. D. Farrell, M.B.E.
Air Adviser, Group Capt. R. J. Coleman.
Consuls-General, H. J. O. R. Tunnell (Brisbane); M. M. Marshall (Melbourne); Ms S. Darling (Perth); A. J. Sindall (Sydney).
Cultural Adviser and British Council Representative, R. S. Newberry, 203 New South Head Road (P.O. Box 88), Edgecliff, Sydney.

THE LEGISLATURE

Parliament consists of the Queen, the Senate and the House of Representatives. The Constitution provides that the number of members of the House of

Representatives shall be, as nearly as practicable, twice the number of Senators. Members of the Senate are elected for six years by universal suffrage, half the members retiring every third year. Each of the six States returns an equal number of 10 Senators, and the Australian Capital Territory and the Northern Territory two each. The House of Representatives, similarly elected for a maximum of three years, contains members proportionate to the population, with a minimum of five members for each State. There are now 125 members in the House of Representatives, including one member for the Northern Territory and two for the Australian Capital Territory. Members of both Houses received $A41,802 per annum, plus allowances, with air and rail travel at Government expense while on parliamentary business.

President of the Senate, Senator Hon. K. Sibraa.
Speaker, House of Representatives, Hon. H. A. Jenkins.

THE JUDICATURE

HIGH COURT OF AUSTRALIA

Chief Justice, Hon. Sir Anthony Frank Mason, K.B.E.
Justices, Hon. Sir Ronald Wilson, K.B.E., C.M.G.; Hon. Sir Gerard Brennan, K.B.E.; Hon. Sir William Deane, K.B.E.; Hon. Sir Daryl Dawson, K.B.E., C.B.; Hon. John Toohey; Hon. Mary Gaudron.
Registrar, F. W. D. Jones.

FEDERAL COURT OF AUSTRALIA

Chief Judge, Hon. Sir Nigel Bowen, K.B.E.
Judges, Hons. R. W. Fox; C. A. Sweeney, C.B.E.; Sir William Forster; Sir Edward Woodward, O.B.E.; R. M. Northrop; J. A. Keely; F. R. Fisher; J. F. Gallop; J. D. Davies; J. S. Lockhart; I. F. Sheppard; J. J. A. Kelly; T. R. Morling; K. J. Jenkinson; A. R. Neaves; B. A. Beaumont; M. R. Wilcox; J. E. J. Spender; P. R. A. Gray; M. G. Everett; C. W. Pincus; J. C. S. Burchett; J. A. Miles; D. M. Ryan; W. M. C. Gummow; R. S. French; M. R. Einfeld.
Registrar, J. T. Howard, E.D.

SUPREME COURT OF THE AUSTRALIAN CAPITAL TERRITORY

Judges, Hons. J. A. Miles (*Chief Justice*); J. J. A. Kelly; J. F. Gallop (*Resident Judges*); Sir Edward Woodward, O.B.E.; R. M. Northrop; J. D. Davies; J. S. Lockhart; I. F. Sheppard; T. R. Morling; K. J. Jenkinson; B. A. Beaumont; M. R. Wilcox; J. E. J. Spender; C. W. Pincus (*Additional Judges*).
Registrar, P. Dingwall.

SUPREME COURT OF THE NORTHERN TERRITORY

Chief Justice, Hon. K. F. O'Leary.
Judges, Hons. J. A. Nader; Sir William Kearney; M. D. Maurice; P. J. Rice; K. J. A. Asche.
Master, P. G. Lefevre.

DEFENCE

A single Department of Defence was created in 1973, following the abolition of the Departments of the Navy, Army and Air, though the separate identities of the three services have been retained. The defence research and development elements of the former Department of Supply, along with other research groups on the three services, were incorporated in 1978 into the Defence, Science and Technology Organization. The Chief of Defence Force Staff is responsible for command of the Defence Force through the three Service Chiefs of Staff and is also the principal military adviser to the Minister.

The Secretary to the Department of Defence is responsible to the Minister for Defence for advice on policy, resources and organization.

Total defence expenditure was estimated at $A6,838,982,000 in 1985–86.

The personnel strengths of the Permanent Defence Force and the Reserve Forces at June 30, 1985 were:—

	P.D.F.	Reserves*
Navy	16,059	1,135
Army	32,460	23,846
Air Force	22,863	1,353
Total	71,382	26,334

(*Reserve components with training obligations.)

COMMONWEALTH GOVERNMENT FINANCE

Outlays and revenue of the Commonwealth Government were ($Amillion):

	1985–86p	1986–87*
Current outlays	65,116	70,180
Capital outlays	5,232	5,084
Revenue	64,592	71,739
Financing transactions	5,756	3,525

p. preliminary   * estimate

Commonwealth Government outlay by category was ($Amillion):

	1985–86p.
General public services	4,083·4
Defence	6,426·4
Public order and safety	437·0
Education	4,464·6
Health	6,617·0
Social security and welfare	19,106·2
Housing and amenities	121·1
Recreation and culture	727·8
Fuel and energy	360·9
Agriculture, forestry, fishing and hunting	840·1
Mining, manufacturing and construction	685·8
Transport and communications	291·0
Other economic affairs	1,279·4
Other purposes	20,183·7
TOTAL	65,624·5

p. preliminary

STATE GOVERNMENT FINANCE 1984–85(p) ($A million)

State	Outlay (current and capital)	Revenue and grants received	Financing transactions
N.S.W.	13,803·7	11,938·7	1,865·0
Victoria	11,532·5	9,200·0	2,332·5
Queensland	6,626·6	5,996·2	630·4
S. Australia	3,603·8	3,273·6	330·1
W. Australia	4,251·5	3,627·3	624·2
Tasmania	1,545·7	1,298·1	247·5
N.T.	1,059·9	975·8	84·2
Total Six States and N.T.	42,423·6	36,309·8	6,113·8

BANKING

In May 1986 the major trading banks had total liabilities of $A71,458 million including total deposits of $A44,735 million; and total assets of $A77,899 million, including $A7,400 million of liquid assets and Commonwealth Government securities.

PRODUCTION AND INDUSTRY

In 1985, 63·6 per cent of the Australian land area consisted of agricultural establishments, with the remainder being urban areas, State forests, mining leases and unoccupied land. Crop-growing areas constituted up to 4·32 per cent of the total agricultural establishments, emphasizing the relative importance of the livestock industries in Australia (sheep in the warm, temperate, semi-arid lands and beef cattle in the tropics).

The wide range of climatic and soil conditions over the agricultural regions of Australia has resulted in a diversity of crops being grown throughout the country. Generally, cereal crops (excluding rice and sorghum) are grown in all States over wide areas, while other crops are confined to specific locations in a few States. However, scanty or erratic rainfall, limited potential for irrigation and unsuitable soils or topography have restricted intensive agriculture.

The estimated gross values of agricultural commodities ($Am.):—

	1983–84	1984–85p
Crops	8,426·6	7,887·2
Livestock slaughterings ...	3,392·8	3,625·1
Livestock products	3,489·8	3,762·8
Total agriculture	15,309·1	15,276·1
p. provisional.		

AGRICULTURAL PRODUCTION

The principal products (tonnes) were:—

	1984	1985p
Cereal crops		
Barley	4,890,000	5,559,000
Oats	2,296,000	1,395,000
Wheat	21,764,000	18,635,000
Rice	632,000	776,000
Crops for hay		
Barley	45,000	40,000
Oats	994,000	637,000
Wheat	209,000	171,000
Sugar-cane*	24,191,000	25,448,000
Fruit		
Oranges	392,000	439,000
Apples	267,000	n/a
Pears	122,000	n/a
Bananas	146,423,000	151,432,000
Pineapples	115,056,000	135,267,000
Passion fruit	3,714,000	3,149,000
Strawberries	3,890,000	4,092,000
Wool (greasy basis)	728,898	799,961
* Cut for crushing. (p) preliminary.		

In 1984–85 (preliminary figures), gross value of wool production was $A2,398·8 million.

Livestock Numbers at March 31 (in thousands)

	1983	1984	1985p
Sheep and lambs	133,237	139,242	149,248
Cattle and calves	22,478	22,161	22,738
Pigs	2,490	2,527	2,463
Poultry	49,393	48,673	54,833

Mines and Minerals.—Significant mineral resources comprise bauxite, coal, copper, crude petroleum, gems, gold, ilmenite, iron ore, lead, limestone, manganese, nickel, rutile, salt, silver, tin, tungsten, uranium, zinc and zircon. Recently, geological exploration has significantly increased the mineral resources of the nation.

Australia now has fourteen oilfields in production: Alton, Bennett, Conloi, Kincora, Moonie and Trinidad in Queensland; Barracouta, Cobia, Halibut, Kingfish, Mackerel and Tuna in Victoria in the offshore Gippsland Basin and from Dongara and Barrow Island in Western Australia.

In 1983–84, value added by the mining industry was $A8,825·4 million. Mine production of black coal was 116,346,000 tonnes, crude oil (incl. condensate) was 26,826 megalitres and natural gas 12,098 giga-litres. Production of principal metals was:—

Iron ore	76,478,000 tonnes
Copper	249,282 "
Lead-Zinc concentrate	37,932 "
Gold	33,881 kg.

Manufactures.—In 1983–84 there were in Australia 27,470 industrial establishments, employing 1,009,376 persons; wages paid amounted to $A17,461m; purchases, transfers in and selected expenses $A54,666m; value added by manufacture $A34,229m; and turnover $A88,632m.

Trade Unions.—On June 30, 1985, there were 323 reporting trade unions in Australia with a total membership of 3,154,200.

TRADE

Total external trade (including Bullion and Specie.)

	1983–84	1984–85p
Imports	$A24,061,000,000	$A30,022,000,000
Exports	24,808,000,000	30,743,000,000

IMPORTS FROM ALL COUNTRIES, 1985–86
(by commodity classifications)

	$A'000
Food and live animals	1,418,135
Beverages and tobacco	297,582
Crude materials, inedible (except fuels) ..	1,022,713
Crude fertilizers, crude minerals (except coal, petroleum, precious stones)	259,961
Mineral fuels, lubricants, etc	1,927,376
Petroleum, petroleum products, etc ...	1,923,951
Animal and vegetable oils, fats and waxes .	93,612
Chemical and related products, n.e.s.	3,024,400
Organic chemicals	765,610
Manufactured goods	5,619,858
Textile yarn, fabric, made-up articles, n.e.s., etc.	1,678,333
Machinery and transport equipment ...	15,141,493
Road vehicles	3,771,337
Miscellaneous manufactured articles	4,669,068
Imports not classified elsewhere	1,476,959
TOTAL IMPORTS	34,691,197

EXPORTS 1985–86
(by commodity classifications)

	$A'000
Food and live animals	8,102,306
Meat and meat preparations	1,700,615
Cereal grains and preparations	3,940,231
Beverages and tobacco	84,707
Crude materials, inedible (except fuels) ..	9,014,967
Textile fibres and their wastes	3,207,282
Metalliferous ores and metal scrap	4,854,725
Mineral fuels, lubricants, etc	7,989,350
Coal, coke and briquettes	5,252,367
Animal and vegetable oils, fats and waxes	142,302
Chemical and related products, n.e.s.	592,288
Manufactured goods	3,278,293
Non-ferrous metals	1,946,312
Machinery and transport equipment	1,617,623
Miscellaneous manufactured articles	660,063
Exports not classified elsewhere	1,335,683
TOTAL EXPORTS	32,817,583

MAIN TRADING PARTNERS 1985–86

Imports from:—	Value ($Am.)	Percentage of total trade
Japan	8,248·3	23·8
U.S.A.	7,283·7	21·0
Germany, Fed. Rep	2,743·2	7·9

U.K.	2,515·6	7·3
New Zealand	1,454·4	4·2
Taiwan	1,161·1	3·3
Italy	1,094·7	3·2

Exports to:—	Value (\$Am.)	Percentage of total trade
Japan	9,325·7	28·4
U.S.A.	3,249·3	9·9
New Zealand	1,505·2	4·6
China	1,497·4	4·6
Korea, Republic of	1,318·9	4·0
U.K.	1,150·8	3·5
Taiwan	1,063·1	3·2

FOOD EXPORTS TO U.K. 1984–85

	\$A'000
Meat and meat preparations	26,147
Cereal and cereal preparations	1,050
Dairy products and birds' eggs	7,118
Vegetable and fruit	22,643
Sugar, sugar preparations and honey	5,250

COMMUNICATIONS

Railways.—There are six government owned railways systems, operated by the State Rail Authority of N.S.W., Victorian Railways, Queensland Government Railways, Western Australian Government Railways, the State Transport Authority of Southern Australia, and the Australian National Railways Commission. The A.N.R.C. incorporates the former Commonwealth Railways system, and the Tasmanian and non-metropolitan South Australian railways (urban rail services in Southern Australia remain the responsibility of the State Transport Authority). At June 30, 1984 there was a total of 39,251 route-kilometres open.

Gross earnings 1983–84 were:	\$A'000
New South Wales	823,055
Victoria	305,283
Queensland	717,956
South Australia	50,277
Western Australia	228,339
A.N.R.C.	227,063
Total	2,351,973

Figures for all government rail services in the year 1983–84

Passenger journeys	403,456,000
Freight carried (tonnes)	142,183,000
Total gross earnings	\$A2,351,973,000
Coaching	\$A414,999,000
Freight	\$A1,737,347,000
Total working expenses	\$A3,374,398,000
Deficit at June 30, 1984	−754,950,000

Shipping.—Total arrivals and departures (one arrival and one departure per voyage, irrespective of the number of ports visited) of vessels engaged in overseas trade at the various Australian ports in 1985–86 were: arrivals 6,824 (307,406,315 deadweight tonnes); departures 6,622 (304,839,309 deadweight tonnes).

Posts and Telegraphs.—In the year ended June 30, 1984, there were 4,790 post offices dealing with a total of 3,035,060 postal articles. Internal telegrams despatched numbered 3,668,907. At June 30, 1984, there were 53·6 telephones per 100 population.

Broadcasting and Television.—On June 30, 1984, the Australian Broadcasting Corporation operated 144 stations. Privately owned commercial broadcasting stations totalled 137. On June 30, 1984, 276 national and 152 commercial television and translator stations were in operation.

Motor Vehicles.—At June 30, 1985, there were 8,729,100 motor vehicles registered in Australia and 389,200 motor cycles. This represented 561·1 motor vehicles and 25·0 motor cycles per 1,000 population.

Civil Aviation.—At June 30, 1984, there were 441 licensed public aerodromes in the various States and Territories. Aircraft on the Australian Register at June 30, 1984, numbered 6,801.

FEDERAL CAPITAL

CANBERRA is the capital of Australia. It is situated in the Australian Capital Territory which has an area of 939 sq. miles (2,395 sq. km.) and was acquired from New South Wales in 1911. Canberra, which is the seat of the federal government, had a population (estimated) at June 30, 1985, of 273,600. Apart from Parliament House, the city also contains other national institutions, such as the Australian War Memorial, National Library, Royal Australian Mint and the Australian National University. Most Government departments have their headquarters in Canberra. An artificial lake is a central feature of this planned city, based on Walter Burley Griffin's design.

THE NORTHERN TERRITORY

The Northern Territory has a total area of 519,770 sq. miles (1,346,200 sq. km.), and lies between 129°–138° east longitude and 11°–26° south latitude. The estimated population in the Northern Territory at June 1986 was 170,000, of which about a quarter are Aboriginals.

The administration was taken over by the Commonwealth on January 1, 1911, from the government of the State of South Australia.

The Northern Territory (Self-Government) Act 1978 established the Northern Territory as a body politic as from 1 July 1978, with Ministers having control over and responsibility for Territory finances and the administration of the functions of government as specified by the Federal Government by regulations made pursuant to the Act. Proposed laws passed by the Legislative Assembly in relation to a transferred function require the assent of the Administrator. Proposed laws in all other cases may be assented to by the Administrator or reserved by the Administrator for the Governor-General's pleasure. The Governor-General may disallow any laws assented to by the Administrator within six months of the Administrator's assent.

The Northern Territory has federal representation electing one member to the House of Representatives and two members to the Senate.

Administrator, His Hon. Commodore E. E. Johnston, A.M., O.B.E.

THE MINISTRY

Chief Minister, Hon. S. P. Hatton.
Deputy Chief Minister, Minister for Lands and Housing, Conservation and Tourism, Hon. R. A. Hanrahan.
Treasurer and Minister for Local Government, and Mines and Energy, Hon. B. F. Coulter.
Industries and Development, Hon. M. B. Perron.
Attorney-General, Minister for Education, Hon. D. W. Manzie.
Health and Community Services, Hon. D. F. Dale.
Labour and Administrative Services, Hon. T. R. McCarthy.

Various Aboriginal Land Trusts hold title to land previously called Reserves, totalling about one-fifth of the Northern Territory.

The Aboriginal Land Rights (N.T.) Act of 1976 provides for the investigation and determination of Aboriginal traditional claims to vacant Crown land or land already owned by or on behalf of Aboriginals. Successful land claims to date have increased Aboriginal ownership to 34 per cent of the Northern Territory whilst a further 13 per cent is the subject of claims.

A number of major Aboriginal communities previously administered by Church Mission Societies and the Federal Government are now controlled by the Aboriginal people themselves, through local Aboriginal Councils. A recent phenomenon is the voluntary movement of some Aboriginals to their traditional homeland areas where they feel that their culture will be better preserved.

ECONOMY

Northern Territory's economy is based on the exploitation of its natural resources of minerals, land, fisheries and tourist attractions. Following the introduction of a number of government measures designed to expand and diversify primary production, the Territory's agricultural and horticultural industries are also beginning to contribute an increasing amount to Territory rural output.

The beef cattle industry continues to be the major user of pastoral lands and cattle production in the financial year 1985–86 was valued at $109 million.

The buffalo population, estimated at 320,000 head is confined to the Darwin and Gulf districts. Live buffalos and buffalo meat products are an important export, currently valued at $6 million.

The Territory's six main crops are sorghum, maize, mung beans, soybeans, peanuts and rice. A total of 7,764 hectares was harvested in the 1985–86 season.

In 1986, 1,300 hectares were planted for horticulture in the Territory, yielding crops valued at $6 million. Crops include a wide range of temperate and tropical fruit and vegetables.

The annual gross value of production of the Northern Territory's fishing industry was approximately $30 million in 1986. The industry is based on barramundi and prawn fisheries. Other resources, such as mud crab, shark, mackerel and offshore reef fish are becoming increasingly important. A mooring basin for protection of the fleet from cyclonic conditions has been constructed.

Mining has played a major part in the development of the Northern Territory and in the calendar year 1984 the industry produced minerals with a value of $914 million. Four deposits of high-grade uranium have been located in the Alligator Rivers region. Of these, Ranger and Nabarlek are producing uranium oxide: their combined output in 1986 was 4,899 tonnes with a value of about $407 million. In 1986 1·86 million tonnes of manganese was sold, with a total value of about $88 million. Gold production for 1986 was valued at $97 million.

Tourism is of importance to the Territory's economy. It is a major growth industry and generates over $280 million annually.

COMMUNICATIONS

The Northern Territory has three main ports—Darwin, managed by the Darwin Port Authority; and the private mining ports of Gove, operated by Nabalco Pty. Ltd., and Groote Eylandt, operated by Groote Eylandt Mining Co. Pty. Ltd.

The new standard gauge rail link between Southern Australia and Alice Springs was officially opened in October, 1980. The link between Alice Springs and Darwin is provided by a fully co-ordinated rail-road service.

The main population centres are linked by the Stuart Highway, which connects Alice Springs to Darwin via Tennant Creek and Katherine. Of special interest to the Northern Territory is the operation of "road trains". These are basically massive trucks hauling two or three trailers, having a net capacity of about 100 tonnes and measuring up to 45 metres in length.

Darwin is a port of call for international air services between Australia and Asia, and New Zealand. Within Australia, there are flights from Darwin to all Australian capital cities by two major domestic carriers, Australian Airlines and Ansett Airlines of Australia. Internally, the main Territory centres of Katherine, Tennant Creek, Alice Springs, Ayers Rock, Nhulunbuy and Groote Eylandt are linked by Ansett N.T. All the major centres can take jet passenger traffic.

AUSTRALIAN EXTERNAL TERRITORIES

ASHMORE AND CARTIER ISLANDS

Ashmore Islands (known as Middle, East and West Islands) and Cartier Island are situated in the Indian Ocean some 850 km. and Cartier Island are situated in the Indian Ocean some 850 km. and 790 km. west of Darwin respectively. The Islands lie at the outer edge of the continental shelf. They are small and low and are composed of coral and sand. Vegetation consists mainly of grass. Turtles are plentiful at certain times of the year and beche-de-mer is abundant. The Islands are uninhabited.

Great Britain took formal possession of the Ashmores in 1878 and Cartier was annexed in 1909. By Imperial Order in Council of July 23, 1931, the Islands were placed under the authority of the Commonwealth of Australia, and were accepted in 1933 under the name of the Territory of Ashmore and Cartier Islands. The Territory was annexed to the Northern Territory of Australia. With the granting of self-government to the Northern Territory on July 1, 1978, responsibility for the administration of Ashmore and Cartier Islands became a direct responsibility of the Commonwealth Government.

In accordance with an agreement between the governments of Indonesia and Australia, Indonesian fishermen who have traditionally plied the area may fish within the Territory and land to collect water at certain locations.

THE AUSTRALIAN ANTARCTIC TERRITORY

The *Australian Antarctic Territory* was established by an Order in Council, dated February 7, 1933, which placed under the government of the Commonwealth of Australia all the islands and territories, other than Adélie Land, which are situated south of the latitude 60° S. and lying between 160° E. longitude and 45° E. longitude. The Order came into force on August 24, 1936, after the passage of the Australian Antarctic Territory Acceptance Act, 1933. The boundaries of Terre Adélie were definitely fixed by a French Decree of April 1, 1938, as the islands and territories south of 60° S. latitude lying between 136° E. longitude and 142° E. longitude. The Australian Antarctic Territory Act, 1954 declared that the laws in force in the Australian Capital Territory are, so far as they are applicable, in force in the Australian Antarctic Territory. The Territory is administered by the Antarctic Division of the Department of Science, which, since its inception in 1947, has organized yearly expeditions to Antarctica, known as Australian National Antarctic Research Expeditions (ANARE).

On February 13, 1954, ANARE opened Mawson Station in Mac-Robertson Land at latitude 67° 36' S. and longitude 62° 53' E. Scientific research conducted at Mawson includes upper atmosphere physics, cosmic ray physics, meteorology, earth sciences, biology and medical science. Mawson is also a centre for coastal and inland exploration.

Davis Station was opened on the coast of Princess Elizabeth Land on January 13, 1957, at latitude 68° 35′ S. and longitude 77° 58′ E. Scientific programmes carried out at Davis include meteorology, biology, upper atmosphere physics, with field investigations in biology.

In February, 1959, the Australian Government accepted from the U.S. Government custody of Wilkes Station on the Budd Coast, Wilkes Land. The station was closed in February 1969, and activities were transferred to Casey Station. Casey Station is at 66° 17′ S., 110° 32′ E., and scientific programmes carried out there include geophysics, meteorology with field programmes in glaciology, geology, etc.

Each of the stations on continental Antarctica are being replaced by new station buildings of advanced design, in a building programme which is expected to be completed in 1990.

Since 1948 ANARE has operated a station on Macquarie Island, a dependency of Tasmania, situated at 54° 30′ S. and 158° 57′ E., about 900 miles north of the Antarctic Continent.

Summer stations have been established in the Bunger Hills, 200 miles west of Casey, and at Cape Denison in Commonwealth Bay.

CHRISTMAS ISLAND

Until the end of 1957 a part of the then Colony of Singapore, Christmas Island was administered as a separate colony until October 1, 1958, when it became Australian territory. It is situated in the Indian Ocean about 224 miles S. of Java Head. Area 52 sq. miles. Population (estimated, June 30, 1987) is 2,000, consisting of employees of the Phosphate Mining Corporation, the Christmas Island Services Corporation, the Administration, and their families. There is no indigenous population.

The island is densely wooded and has extensive deposits of phosphates, the extraction of which is the major economic activity. An Australian Government company, the Phosphate Mining Corporation of Christmas Island, carries out the mining operations. Resources being limited, alternative economic development is being encouraged. The principal current development is a hotel complex.

The Australian Government administers the Territory through the Department of Territories in Canberra, to which the Administrator is responsible. The second local elections were held in Oct. 1986 and nine members were elected to the Christmas Island Assembly. The Assembly is responsible for directing the operations of the Christmas Islands Services Corporation, which was established in 1984 to provide municipal functions and services.

Administrator, Hon. A. D. Taylor, O.B.E.

COCOS (KEELING) ISLANDS

The Cocos (Keeling) Islands were declared a British possession in 1857. In 1878 they were placed under the control of the Governor of Ceylon and were later annexed to the Straits Settlements and incorporated with the colony of Singapore. On Nov. 23, 1955, their administration was transferred to Australia. The Cocos (Keeling) Islands Act, 1955, provides the legal framework for the present political and administrative arrangements in the Territory. On April 6, 1984, the Cocos community, in an Act of Self-Determination observed by a U.N. mission, chose to integrate with Australia.

The Islands are two separate atolls (North Keeling Island and, 24 km. to the south, the main atoll) comprising some 27 small coral islands with a total area of about 5½ square miles, situated in the Indian Ocean in latitude 12° 5′ South and longitude 96° 53′ East. The main islands of the southern atoll are West

Island (the largest, about 6 miles from north to south) on which are the administrative centre, the aerodrome, and the Australian-based employees of government departments; Home Island, where the Cocos Malay community lives; Direction Island, Horsburgh and South Island.

The main agricultural activity is the production of copra and the export of coconuts. Total production of copra in 1986–87 was 118 tons. The climate is equable and pleasant, being usually under the influence of the south-east trade winds for about three-quarters of the year. An air charter service operates between Perth, the Cocos (Keeling) Islands and Christmas Island. Population (June 30, 1986), 616. The islands are administered by the Australian Government through the Department of Territories in Canberra. All proposed Ordinances, Regulations and By-laws for the Islands must be submitted to the Islands Council (est. 1979) for its consideration.

Administrator, Ms. Carolyn Stuart.

CORAL SEA ISLANDS TERRITORY

The Territory lies east of Queensland between the Great Barrier Reef and longitude 156° 06′ E., and between latitudes 12° and 24° S. It comprises scattered reefs and islands, often little more than sandbanks, spread over a sea area of 780,000 sq. km. The islands (or cays) are formed mainly of coral and sand. Some have grass or scrub cover but most are extremely small, with no permanent fresh water.

There is a manned metereological station in the Willis Group but the remaining islands and cays are uninhabited. Large populations of sea birds nest and breed in the area, and two national nature reserves were designated in the territory in 1982.

The Australian Government bases its claim to the islands on numerous acts of sovereignty since early this century and enacted the Coral Sea Islands Act 1969 which declares the islands a Territory of the Commonwealth of Australia. The Department of Territories, Canberra, is responsible for the administration of the Territory.

HEARD ISLAND AND MCDONALD ISLANDS

The islands, about 4,100 km. south-west of Fremantle, comprise all the islands and rocks lying between 52° 30′ and 53° 30′ S. latitude and 72° and 74° 30′ E. longitude. Sovereignty over the islands was transferred by the U.K. to the Commonwealth of Australia in 1947. The Heard Island and McDonald Islands Act 1953 provides for the government of the islands as one Territory and under this Act the law operating there is that of the Australian Capital Territory. The Islands are administered by the Antarctic Division of the Department of Science.

NORFOLK ISLAND

The island is situated in the South Pacific Ocean at latitude 29° 02′ S. and longitude 167° 57′ E., being about 1,042 miles from Sydney and 400 miles north of New Zealand. It is about five miles in length by three in breadth, with an area of 8,528 acres and circumference of 20 miles. The climate is mild and sub tropical. Resident population at the 1986 Census was 1,977.

The island, discovered by Capt. Cook in 1774, served as a penal colony from 1788 to 1814 and 1825 to 1855. In 1856, 194 descendants of the *Bounty* mutineers accepted an invitation to leave Pitcairn and settle on Norfolk Island, which led to Norfolk Island becoming a separate settlement under the jurisdiction of the Governor of N.S.W. In 1897 Norfolk Island became a dependency of N.S.W., and in 1914, pursuant to the Norfolk Island Act 1913, a territory of Australia. From that date, Norfolk Island has been regarded as an integral part of Australia.

In 1979 Norfolk Island gained a substantial degree of self-government, enabling the island to run its affairs to the greatest practical extent. Wide powers are exercised by a nine-member Legislative Assembly. The Act preserves the Commonwealth's responsibility for Norfolk Island as a Territory under its authority, with the Minister for Territories as the responsible Minister. In 1985, responsibility for a range of matters was transferred, and the transference of more is proceeding.

The island is a popular tourist resort, and a large proportion of the population depends on tourism and its ancillaries for employment. In 1986 there were 29,428 tourist arrivals on the Island. Regular air services operate from mainland Australia and New Zealand.

Seat of Government and Administration Offices, Kingston.

Administrator, Cdre. J. A. Matthew, C.V.O., M.B.E.

STATES OF THE COMMONWEALTH OF AUSTRALIA

NEW SOUTH WALES

The State of New South Wales is situated entirely between the 28th and 38th parallels of S. lat. and 141st and 154th meridians of E. long., and comprises an area of 309,433 sq. miles (801,427 sq. km.) (exclusive of 939 sq. miles of Australian Capital Territory which lies within its borders).

POPULATION.—Preliminary estimated resident population at Dec. 31, 1986 was 5,581,300.

Births, deaths and marriages of usually resident population were:

	1985	1986
Births	87,786	84,530
Deaths	44,264	42,167
Marriages	41,183	41,319

Annual rate per 1,000 of estimated resident population in 1986:—Births, 15·2; Deaths, 7·6; Marriages, 7·5. Deaths under 1 year per 1,000 live births, 9·0.

Religions

The members of the Church of England in New South Wales, according to the Census of 1981, numbered 1,569,374. Roman Catholic (including "Catholic") 1,424,499, Presbyterian 252,725, Uniting 179,271, Orthodox 171,427, Methodist 148,992, Baptist 64,663, Lutheran 31,696, other Christian 239,895, Hebrew 25,176 and Muslim 38,527. The religion of 934,305 persons was either not stated in the census schedules or was stated as "none".

PHYSIOGRAPHY

Natural features divide the State into four main zones extending from north to south, viz., the Coastal Districts; the Tablelands, which form the Great Dividing Range between the coastal districts and the plains; the Western Slopes of the Dividing Range; and the Western Plains. The highest points are Mounts Kosciusko, 7,314 feet, and Townsend, 7,251 feet. The western portion of the State is watered by the rivers of the Murray-Darling system. The Darling, the major part of whose 1,712 miles is in N.S.W., and the Murrumbidgee, 981 miles, are both tributaries of the Murray, part of which forms the boundary between the States of New South Wales and Victoria.

Climate.—New South Wales is situated entirely in the Temperate Zone. The climate is generally mild and mostly free from extremes of heat and cold. At Sydney the average mean shade temperature is 18° C. The mean (shade) temperature ranges for the various divisions of the State are as follows: coastal, 15° C in the south to 20°C in the north; northern and central tableland, 12° C to 16° C; southern tableland, 7° C to 14° C; and for the rest of the State (western slope, central plains, Riverina and western division), 15° C in the south to 20° C in the north.

GOVERNMENT

New South Wales was first colonized as a British possession in 1788, and after progressive settlement a partly elective legislature was established in 1843. In 1855 Responsible Government was granted, the present Constitution being founded on the Constitution Act of 1902. New South Wales federated with the other States of Australia in 1901. The executive authority of the State is vested in a Governor (appointed by the Crown), assisted by a Council of Ministers.

GOVERNOR

Governor of New South Wales, His Excellency Air Marshal Sir James Rowland, A.C., K.B.E., D.F.C., A.F.C., *assumed office* Jan. 20, 1981.

Lt. Governor, Hon. Sir Laurence Whistler Street, K.C.M.G.

THE MINISTRY
(at June 23, 1987)

Premier, Minister for State Development and for Ethnic Affairs, Hon. B. J. Unsworth.

Deputy Premier, Minister for Transport, Hon. R. J. Mulock.

Housing and the Arts, Hon. F. J. Walker, Q.C.

Public Works and Ports, and Roads, Hon. L. J. Brereton.

Industrial Relations, and Employment, Hon. P. D. Hills.

Health, and the Drug Offensive, Hon. P. T. Anderson.

Treasurer, Hon. K. G. Booth.

Attorney-General and Minister Assisting the Premier, Hon. T. W. Sheahan.

Industry and Small Business, and Energy and Technology, Hon. P. F. Cox.

Agriculture, Lands and Forests and Vice-President of the Executive Council, Hon. J. R. Hallam.

Education, Hon. R. M. Cavalier.

Sport and Recreation, Racing, and Tourism, Hon. M. A. Cleary.

Police and Emergency Services, Hon. G. Paciullo.

Local Government, and Water Resources, Hon. J. A. Crosio.

Finance, and Co-operative Societies, Hon. R. J. Debus.

Corrective Services, Hon. J. E. Akister.

Planning and Environment, and Heritage, Hon. R. J. Carr.

Youth and Community Services, Hon. J. J. Aquilina.

Mineral Resources, and Aboriginal Affairs, Hon. K. G. Gabb.

Consumer Affairs, Hon. D. M. Grusovin.

The annual salaries of Ministers are: Premier, $A89,088; Deputy Premier, $A80,257; Leader of the Government members in the Legislative Council, $A81,155; (Deputy $A77,325); other Ministers $A75,808 each. Ministers also receive expense allowances and electoral allowances, and a special expense allowance is paid to Ministers who represent or reside in outlying electorates.

AGENT-GENERAL IN LONDON

Agent-General, Hon. K. J. Stewart, N.S.W. House, 66 Strand, W.C.2.

THE LEGISLATURE

The *Legislative Council* consists of 45 members, elected by popular vote and the *Legislative Assembly* consists of 99 members elected for a maximum period of 4 years. Party representation in the Council at June 30, 1987 was; Labor 24, Liberal 11, National 6, Australian Democrat 1, and Independent 3. Party representation in the Assembly at June 30, 1987 was: Labor 56, Liberal 23, National 16 and Independent 4. The annual salary of members of the Legislative Council and Legislative Asssembly who are not Ministers is $A43,620. Members also receive expense and electoral allowances, and a special expense allowance is paid to members who reside in, or represent outlying electorates.

President of the Legislative Council, Hon. J. R. Johnson.
Speaker, Legislative Assembly, Hon. L. B. Kelly.

THE JUDICATURE

The judicial system includes a Supreme Court, Industrial Commission, District Court, Land and Environment Court, Compensation Court.

Chief Justice, Supreme Court, Hon. Sir Laurence Street, K.C.M.G. (*+ allce.* $A6,435) $A108,921
President, Court of Appeal, Hon. Mr. Justice Kirby, C.M.G. (*+ allce.* $A5,189) $A102,713

GOVERNMENT FINANCES

Consolidated Fund, for year ended June 30th, was:—

	1985	1986
	$A million	$A million
Receipts	8,002·2	8,879·2
Expenditure	8,001·7	8,878·7
Public Debt	5,773·5	5,999·2

Banking, etc.—There were (April 1987) 26 trading banks with deposits of $A24,491 million. Savings bank depositors' balances amounted to $A15,804 million, representing $A2,832 per head of the population.

EDUCATION

Education.—Education is compulsory between the ages of 6 and 15 years. It is non-sectarian and free at all government schools. The enrolment in July 1986 in 2,233 government schools was 755,257. In addition to the government schools there were, in 1986, 848 non-government schools, with an enrolment of 270,793 students. The six universities had an enrolment of 68,107 students at April 30, 1986. In addition, there were 57,580 students enrolled in advanced education courses (predominantly in colleges of advanced education) in 1986. Students enrolled in technical and further education colleges in 1985 numbered 391,721. State Government recurrent expenditure on education was $A3,327 million in the year ended June 30, 1985.

PRODUCTION AND INDUSTRY

Local value of production in 1985–86 was ($A million):—

Agricultural commodities	$A3,991·6
Crops	1,786·0
Livestock products	1,218·9
Slaughterings.....................	986·7
Value added ($A million)	
Mining and Quarrying (1985–86)	$A2,155·0
Manufacturing (1984–85).............	$A14,036·6

Crops.—Production in 1985–86 was (tonnes):

Wheat-grain	5,915,526
Wheat-hay	48,566
Barley	821,394
Oats	538,324
Rice	702,073
Cotton	541,751
Oilseed	208,079
Potatoes...........................	108,568
Sugar-cane, crushed	1,398,183

476,860 kilograms of dried leaf tobacco and 60,867,100 kilograms of bananas were obtained; almost every kind of fruit and vegetable is grown.

Livestock and Livestock Products.—A large area is suitable for sheep-raising, the principal breed of sheep being the merino,.which was introduced in 1797. On March 31, 1986, there were 5,409,262 cattle, 58,001,150 sheep and lambs, and 797,911 pigs. In 1985–86, 280,675,000 kg. of wool (in the grease) were produced, 1,220,000 kg. of butter, 13,048,000 kg. of cheese, and 20,476,000 kg. of bacon and ham.

Mining Industry.—The principal minerals are coal, lead, zinc, gold, rutile, copper and zircon. The total value of minerals extracted in 1985–86 was $A3,030,783,000, of which the value of output of the coal mining industry was $A2,299,591,000 and of the silver-lead-zinc industry, $A265,468,000 and the construction materials industry, including stone, gravel and sand, was $A316,232,704. The average number of persons employed in the mining industry during 1985–86 was 26,649. In 1985–86, 77,186,000 tonnes of coal were produced.

Manufacturing Industry.—At June 30, 1985, there were 10,238 manufacturing establishments (employing four of more persons). The average number of persons employed during 1984–85 was 364,847. Products include iron and steel, pipes, boilers, steel wire and wire netting, copper wire, copper and brass cables and tin-plate. Production of raw steel in 1985–86 was 5,607,000 tonnes.

OVERSEAS TRADE

	1986
Imports f.o.b.....................	$15,129,910,000
Exports f.o.b.....................	7,373,750,000

The chief exports in 1985–86 were coal and coke, wool, meat, iron and steel and wheat. Chief imports were, office machines and data processing equipment, road vehicles and transport equipment, electrical and specialist machinery.

TRANSPORT AND COMMUNICATIONS

Shipping.—2,900 vessels entered the major ports of N.S.W. from overseas during the year ended June 30, 1986, the deadweight tonnage being 96,028,504. The shipping entries at Sydney were 1,379 vessels of 35,712,529 deadweight tonnage.

Roads and Bridges.—Expenditures by the State Government and the local authorities on road systems and regulation in 1984–85 was $A1,272·2 million.

Motor Vehicles.—At Dec. 31, 1986, there were 3,030,561 registered motor vehicles (cars, 1,896,647).

Railways.—The railways of New South Wales are controlled by the State Government. At June 30, 1986, the route kilometres of the State railways open for traffic was 9,909, revenue in the year 1985–86 being $A1,736·5 million.

Aviation.—Sydney is the principal overseas terminal in Australia. Overseas and local traffic at Sydney airport in 1986 were: passengers 9,548,616; freight 195,831 tonnes; aircraft, 107,081 (provisional figs.).

Postal and Telecommunication Services.—The postal and telecommunication services are administered by the Commonwealth Government.

Radio and Television.—At June 30, 1986, there were 24 national radio stations and 44 commercial radio stations operating under licence in N.S.W. There were also 28 licensed non-profit radio stations providing special interest services not catered for by the national and commercial services. At June 30, 1986, there were 28 television stations (14 national, 14 commercial) in operation in the state.

Towns

ΨSYDNEY, the chief city and State capital and the largest city in Australia, stands on the shores of Port Jackson. Sydney Harbour extends inland for 21 km.: the total area of water is about 55 sq. km.

The preliminary estimated resident population at June 30, 1986 of the Sydney Statistical Division was 3,430,550. The Newcastle and Wollongong Statistical Districts contain populations of 429,250 and 237,600 respectively.

The populations of principal municipalities located outside the boundaries of these statistical areas are: Albury 40,400, Dubbo 31,850, Greater Taree 36,850, Hastings 43,500, Lismore 38,750, Orange 32,800, Shoalhaven 61,700, Tamworth 33,900, Wagga Wagga 50,900.

Lord Howe Island

Lord Howe Island, which is part of New South Wales, is situated 702 kilometres north-east of Sydney. Lat. 31° 33′ 4″ S., Long. 159° 4′ 26″ E. Area 6·37 sq. miles (16·5 sq. km.). Pop. June 30, 1986, 300. The island is of volcanic origin with Mount Gower reaching an altitude of 866 m. The affairs of the Island are administered by the Lord Howe Island Board.

QUEENSLAND

This State, situated in lat. 10° 40′–29° S. and long. 138°–153° 30′ E., comprises the whole north-eastern portion of the Australian continent.

Queensland possesses an area of 666,798 sq. miles (1,727,000 sq. km.).

POPULATION.—At June 30, 1986, the estimated resident population numbered 2,592,600.

Births, Deaths and Marriages were:

	1984	1985
Births	40,446	40,437
Deaths	17,405	18,629
Marriages	19,039	17,810

Annual rate per 1,000 of mean population in 1985; Births, 15·9; Deaths, 7·3; Marriages 7·0. Deaths under 1 year, 10·3 per 1,000 live births.

Religions

At the Census of 1981, there were 601,537 Anglican, 554,912 Roman Catholics (including Catholics undefined), 146,898 Uniting Church, 132,525 Presbyterians, 86,750 Methodists, 50,401 Lutherans, 34,323 Baptists, and 166,611 other Christians.

Physiography

The Great Dividing Range on the eastern coast of the continent produces a similar formation to that of New South Wales, the eastern side having a narrow slope to the coast and the western a long and gradual slope to the central plains, where the Selwyn and Kirby Ranges divide the land into a northern and southern watershed.

Government

Queensland was constituted a separate colony with responsible government in 1859, having previously formed part of New South Wales. The executive authority is vested in a Governor (appointed by the Crown), aided by an Executive Council of 18 members.

Governor

Governor of Queensland, His Excellency Sir Walter Benjamin Campbell, Q.C. $A74,000

Executive Council.
(H.E. the Governor presides.)

Premier and Treasurer, Hon. Sir Johannes Bjelke-Petersen, K.C.M.G. $A93,712
Deputy Premier and Minister assisting the Treasurer, and for Police, Hon. W. A. M. Gunn $A80,450
Local Government, Main Roads and Racing, Hon. R. J. Hinze.
Works and Housing, Hon. I. J. Gibbs.
Health and Environment, Hon. M. J. Ahern.
Transport, Hon. D. F. Lane.
Lands, Forestry, Mapping and Surveying, Hon. W. H. Glasson.
Mines, Energy and The Arts, Hon. B. D. Austin.
Education, Hon. L. W. Powell.
Employment, Small Business, and Industrial Affairs, Hon. V. P. Lester.
Water Resources and Maritime Services, Hon. M. J. Tenni.
Primary Industries, Hon. N. J. Harper.
Tourism, National Parks and Sport, Hon. G. H. Muntz.
Industry and Technology, Hon. P. R. McKechnie.
Northern Development and Community Services, Hon. R. C. Katter.
Family Services, Youth and Ethnic Affairs, Hon. Y. A. Chapman.
Corrective and Administrative Services and Valuation, Hon. D. M. Neal.
Justice and Attorney-General, Hon. P. J. Clauson.

Agent-General in London

Agent-General, J. F. S. Brown, A.O., M.C., 392–393 Strand, W.C.2.

The Legislature

Parliament consists of a *Legislative Assembly* of 89 members, elected by all persons aged 18 years and over. Members of the Assembly receive $A45,177 per annum plus an electorate allowance. The Assembly, as elected on Nov. 1,1986, was composed of: National Party, 49; Liberal Party, 10; Australian Labor Party, 30.
Speaker, Hon. K. R. Lingard $A61,841
Chairman of Committees, E. C. Row. $A51,738

The Judicature

There are a Supreme Court; District Courts; Children's Courts; an Industrial Court; a Land Court and a Medical Assessment Tribunal; a Local Government Court; the Industrial Conciliation and Arbitration Commission; Inferior Courts at all the principal towns, presided over by Stipendiary Magistrates; a Small Claims Tribunal; Small Debts Court; and a Licensing Court.
Chief Justice, Supreme Court, Hon. Sir Dormer Andrews $A115,700
Senior Puisne Judge, Hon. J. L. Kelly...... 102,150

Education

Education is compulsory between the ages of 6 and 15 years and is provided free in Government schools. At July 1986 the State administered 1,068 primary, 85 primary/secondary, and 159 secondary schools with 234,926 primary students, and 139,320 secondary students.

Post-secondary education involves technical and further education (TAFE), advanced education, and university education. During 1985, 184,234 students were enrolled in TAFE courses, including 79,936 enrolled in adult education courses. At April 30, 1986, there were 15,708 full-time, 7,896 part-time, and 8,030 external students enrolled in advanced education courses. The three universities had enrolments of 15,102 full-time students, 8,183 part-time, and 2,074 external students at April 30, 1986.

PRODUCTION AND INDUSTRY

Agriculture and Livestock.—The gross value of agricultural commodity production in 1985–86 was $A3,135,382,000 (including crops $A1,670,977,000, livestock disposals $A1,056,712,000, livestock products $A407,693,000).

The most important crops in 1985–86 were (tonnes):

Sugar (raw)	3,208,608
Wheat	1,690,960
Maize	175,777
Sorghum	1,109,312
Barley	809,850

The livestock on March 31, 1986 included 9,662,031 cattle, 358,548 being dairy cattle, 14,310,614 sheep and 584,559 pigs.

Forestry.—Total Australian grown timber processed in 1985–86 amounted to 1,284,873 cubic metres (gross volume measure).

Minerals.—There are rich deposits of both metallic and non-metallic minerals. Coal is mined extensively in Central Queensland and on a lesser scale in North Queensland and Ipswich districts.

Output in 1985–86

	$A'000
Bauxite	161,251
Coal	2,668,465
Copper concentrate	250,219
Crude oil, natural gas, etc.	403,123
Gold (various forms)	173,391
Lead concentrate	145,397
Mineral sands	58,237
Nickel ore	13,604
Scheelite and wolfram concentrate	6,854
Tin concentrate	13,723
Zinc concentrate (incl. middlings)	66,204
Other	231,814
Total	4,192,282

Manufacturing.—In 1984–85 there were 3,392 establishments with four or more workers, employing 109,940 persons, and producing goods and services worth $A12,921 million. The value added was $A4,385 million. Much of the production was the processing of primary products, *e.g.* foodstuffs, timber and minerals. Included in other factory production were the products from engineering, transport equipment, basic and fabricated metal, chemical and fertilizer works, cement, paper and textile mills and oil refineries.

FINANCE

Government finance (Consolidated Revenue Fund) ($A'000) was:—

	1985	1986
Revenue	4,681,674	5,190,941
Expenditure	4,682,431	5,190,727
Gross Debt	2,376,112	2,459,161

Banking.—Advances made by Trading Banks (including the Commonwealth Trading Bank of Australia) at June 30, 1986, totalled $A6,823,816,000. The deposits at the same date amounted to $A7,645,074,000. Depositors' balances in Queensland savings banks at June 30, 1986, $A5,238,364,000, averaged $A2,040 for each inhabitant. There were 3,957,488 operative accounts.

OVERSEAS TRADE

	1984–85	1985–86
Imports	$A2,315,492,000	$A2,649,953,006
Exports	6,602,936,000	7,737,046,078

The chief overseas exports are coal, non-ferrous metals, meat, sugar, wool, and cereal grains.

COMMUNICATIONS

Road and Rail.—The State is served by 10,225 kilometres of railways. During 1985–86, 41,504,000 passengers and 73,599,000 tonnes of goods and livestock were carried. At June 30, 1986, there were 150,188 kilometres of formed roads in the State, and 1,567,400 motor vehicles were on the register.

Aviation.—Regular services operate between Brisbane, the main Queensland coastal and inland towns and the southern capitals. Brisbane, Townsville and Cairns are also ports of call on several international services.

Radio and Television.—On June 30, 1986, 28 national and 29 commercial sound broadcasting and 32 national and 11 commercial television stations were operating in Queensland. There were seven public broadcasting stations.

TOWNS

CAPITAL, ΨBRISBANE, is situated on the Brisbane River, which is navigable by large vessels to the city, over 23 kilometres from Moreton Bay. The estimated resident population of the Brisbane Statistical Division at June 30, 1986 was 1,171,340. This area includes the cities of Brisbane (728,440), Ipswich (73,860), Logan (117,130) and Redcliffe (45,000).

Other cities and towns with population over 30,000 at June 30, 1986, are: ΨTownsville, 81,970; Gold Coast, 120,740; Toowoomba, 75,060; ΨRockhampton, 54,880; ΨCairns, 39,960; ΨBundaberg, 32,980.

SOUTH AUSTRALIA

The State of South Australia is situated between 26° lat. and 38° S. lat. and 129° and 141° E. long., the total area being 380,070 sq. miles (984,376 sq. km.).

POPULATION.—At June 30, 1986, the resident population was estimated to be 1,373,150.

Births, deaths and marriages were:

	1985	1986
Births	19,790	19,826
Deaths	10,496	10,377
Marriages	10,148	9,878

Religions

Religion is free and receives no State aid. At the Census, 1986, the persons belonging to the principal religious denominations were as follows: Catholic, 267,137; Anglican, 242,722; Uniting Church, 176,980; Lutheran, 64,851; Orthodox, 37,149; Baptist, 21,415; Presbyterian, 18,566; Church of Christ, 16,629; and Pentecostal, 14,997.

PHYSIOGRAPHY

The most important physical features of South Australia are broad plains, divided longitudinally by four great secondary features, which form barriers to east-west movement, and which have thus largely determined the direction of roads and railways, the sites of towns and villages and the manner of distribution of the population. These four barriers are Spencer Gulf, Gulf St. Vincent, the Mt. Lofty-Flinders Ranges and the River Murray.

The north-western portion of the State is mostly desert, while north of latitude 32° S. the country is unpromising by comparison with the fertile land which surrounds the hill country of the east. The Murray, which flows for some 400 miles through the south-eastern corner, is the only river of importance.

The lack of rivers and fresh-water lakes in the settled areas has necessitated the building of a number of reservoirs, which are supplemented by pipelines from the River Murray.

Climate.—The mean annual temperature at Adelaide is 17·1°C, the winter temperature (June-August) averaging 11·9°C, and the summer (Nov.-Mar.) 22·3°C. During the summer months the maximum temperature at times exceeds 40°C, but is associated with a relatively low humidity. The average annual rainfall at Adelaide is 21 inches.

GOVERNMENT

South Australia was proclaimed a British Province in 1836, and in 1851 a partially elective legislature was established. The present Constitution rests upon a Law of Oct. 24, 1856, the executive authority being vested in a Governor appointed by the Crown, aided by a Council of 13 Ministers.

GOVERNOR

Governor of South Australia, His Excellency Lt. Gen. Sir Donald B. Dunstan, K.B.E., C.B. (1982).

Lt.-Governor, Hon. Sir Condor Laucke, K.C.M.G. (1982).

THE MINISTRY

Premier, Treasurer, and Minister for the Arts, Hon. J. C. Bannon.

Deputy Premier, Minister for Environment and Planning, Chief Secretary, Minister of Emergency Services and Water Resources, Hon. D. J. Hopgood.

Attorney-General; Minister of Consumer Affairs, Corporate Affairs, and Ethnic Affairs, Hon. C. J. Sumner.

Lands, Marine, Forests and Repatriation, Hon. R. K. Abbott.

Health and Community Welfare, Hon. J. R. Cornwall.

State Development and Technology, Employment, and Further Education, Hon. L. M. F. Arnold.

Transport, Hon. G. F. Keneally.

Mines and Energy, Hon. R. G. Payne.

Education, Children's Services, and Aboriginal Affairs, Hon. G. J. Crafter.

Housing and Construction; Public Works, Hon. T. H. Hemmings.

Labour, Correctional Services, Hon. F. T. Blevins.

Tourism, Local Government and Youth Affairs, Hon. Miss Barbara Wiese.

Agriculture, Fisheries, and Recreation and Sport, Hon. M. K. Mayes.

AGENT-GENERAL IN LONDON

Agent-General, G. Walls, South Australia House, 50 Strand, W.C.2.

THE LEGISLATURE

Parliament consists of a *Legislative Council* of 22 members elected for 8 years, one-half retiring every 4 years; and a *House of Assembly* of 47 members, elected for a maximum duration of 4 years. Election is by ballot, with universal adult suffrage for both the Legislative Council and the House of Assembly.

The representation in the House of Assembly is 27 Labor, 16 Liberals, 1 National Party and 3 Independent.

President of the Legislative Council, Hon. Anne Levy $A75,498

Speaker of the House of Assembly, Hon. J. P. Trainer $A75,498

THE JUDICATURE

Law and Justice.—The Supreme Court is presided over by the Chief Justice and 13 Puisne Judges.

EDUCATION

Education at the primary and secondary level is available at Government schools controlled by the Education Department and at non-government schools, most of which are denominational. In 1986 there were 711 Government schools with 192,489 students, and 178 independent schools with 52,788 students. Tertiary education is available through universities, colleges of advanced education, and technical and further education.

The two universities had, in 1985, a total enrolment of 14,020 full-time students.

FINANCE

Revenue and expenditure of the Consolidated Revenue Account and debt of South Australia (year ended June 30) was:—

	1985	1986
Revenue	3,054,408,000	3,468,164,000
Expenditure	3,040,741,000	3,457,064,000
Debt	1,990,537,000	n/a

Banking.—There are seven trading banks in Adelaide, including the Commonwealth Trading Bank and the State Bank of South Australia, having total average deposits of $A3,749,739,000 in June 1986. The six savings banks had deposits of $A2,970,784,000 at June 30, 1986.

PRODUCTION AND INDUSTRY

The gross value of primary production in 1985–86 was:—

Crops	$A915,462,000
Livestock products	429,932,000
Slaughterings....................	251,596,000
Fisheries	76,017,000

Agriculture.—Wheat harvest 1985–86 1,943,712 tonnes; barley, 1,709,380 tonnes. Oranges, lemons, apples, apricots, peaches, and all stone fruits and olives are successfully grown, and a quantity of this fruit is dried. In 1985–86, 211,770,000 litres of wine and 8,013 tonnes of sultanas, currants and raisins were produced. Considerable quantities of fruits (fresh and dried), wine and brandy, are annually sent to overseas countries, and to other Australian States. Some areas of the State, particularly near Adelaide, are also very suitable for growing all kinds of root crops and vegetables.

Livestock (March 31, 1987).—There were 17,300,000 sheep, 915,000 cattle, 413,000 pigs. Wool production (1986–87), 106,585,000 kg.

Minerals.—Iron, pyrite, gypsum, salt, coal, limestone, clay, oil and gas, etc., are found. The total mineral output was valued at $A962,213,000 in 1984–85, including oil and gas valued at $A765,047,000.

OVERSEAS TRADE

	1984–85	1985–86
Imports	1,603,240,000	1,736,757,000
Exports	1,921,413,000	1,988,233,000

The principal exports are wool, wheat, barley, meat, lead and lead alloys, silver, zinc, iron and steel, petroleum products, rock lobster and prawns.

TRANSPORT AND COMMUNICATIONS

The State Transport Authority operated (in 1986) 153 km. of railway and 1,033 km. of tram and bus routes in the metropolitan area. Australian National operated 5,438 km. of railway in country areas. There are 102,000 km. of roads.

There are a number of excellent harbours, of which Port Adelaide is the most important. The number of vessels (exceeding 200 net tonnage) entering South Australia from overseas during 1985–86 was 891 with 1,701,640 import tonnes and leaving with 5,779,505 export tonnes.

Civil Aviation.—There are 36 Government and licensed airports; the largest of these, Adelaide airport, recorded 1,980,663 passenger movements during 1985–86.

Motor Vehicles.—The registration on June 30, 1986, totalled 835,841.

Radio and Television (June 1987)—Broadcasting stations 31; Television stations 51 (including translator and satellite fed stations).

TOWNS

ΨADELAIDE, the chief city and capital, estimated resident population on June 30, 1986, 993,130, inclusive of suburbs. Other centres (with 1986 populations) are: ΨWhyalla (28,700); ΨMt. Gambier (19,400); ΨPort Pirie (15,720); ΨPort Augusta (16,250); and ΨPort Lincoln (12,670).

TASMANIA

Tasmania is an island state of Australia situated in the Southern ocean off the south-eastern extremity of the mainland. It is separated from the Australian mainland by Bass Strait and incorporates King Island and the Furneaux group of islands which are in the Strait. It lies between 40° 38′–43° 39′ S. lat. and 144° 36′–148° 23′ E. long., and contains an area of 26,383 sq. miles (68,331 sq. km.).

POPULATION.—The estimated resident population at June 30, 1986 was 446,900.

Births, deaths and marriages were:

	1985
Births	7,249
Deaths	3,693
Marriages	3,520

Vital Statistics.—The birth rate in 1985 was 16·4, death rate 8·4, marriage rate 8·0 per 1,000. Infant mortality (1985) 12·0 per 1,000 births.

Religions

In 1986 there were 154,748 members of the Anglican Church of Australia, 80,479 Catholics, 36,724 Uniting Church of Australia, 12,084 Presbyterians and 8,092 Baptists.

PHYSIOGRAPHY

The surface of the country is generally hilly and wooded, with mountains from 1,500 to 5,300 ft. in height, and expanses of level, open plains. There are numerous rivers, the South Esk, Gordon, Derwent and Huon being the largest. At Hobart the mean maximum temperature ranges from about 12°C in winter to 21°C in summer, the mean minimum from 5°C to 11°C. The western side of the island is very wet, the eastern side being much drier.

GOVERNMENT

The island was first settled by a British party from New South Wales in 1803, becoming a separate colony in 1825. In 1851 a partly elective legislature was inaugurated, and in 1856 responsible government was established. In 1901 Tasmania became a State of the Australian Commonwealth. The State executive authority is vested in a Governor (appointed by the Crown), but is exercised by Cabinet Ministers responsible to the Legislature, of which they are members.

GOVERNOR

Governor of Tasmania, (new appointment awaited). *Lt. Governor,* Hon. Sir Guy Green, K.B.E.

THE MINISTRY

Premier, Treasurer, Minister for State Development, Small Business and Energy, Hon. R. T. Gray.

Deputy Premier, Minister for Tourism, Licensing, Police and Emergency Services, Road Safety and Gaming, Hon. G. A. Pearsall.

Attorney-General, Minister for Lands, National Parks, Sport and Recreation, Hon. J. M. Bennett.

Employment and Training, Housing, Labour, and Industry and Consumer Affairs, Hon. R. J. Beswick.

Local Government, Main Roads, Water Resources and Racing, Hon. I. M. Braid.

Public Administration, Primary Industry and Transport, Hon. N. C. K. Evers.

Health, Community Welfare and the Elderly, and Ethnic Affairs, Hon. F. R. Groom.

Forests, Mines, Sea Fisheries and Minister assisting the Premier, Hon. R. G. Groom.

Construction, Administrative Services, Environment and Inland Fisheries, Hon. P. C. L. Hodgman.

Education, the Arts, Industrial Relations, Deregulation and Technology, Hon. P. E. Rae.

THE LEGISLATURE

Parliament consists of two Houses, a *Legislative Council* of 19 members, elected for six years (3 retiring annually, in rotation, except in every sixth year, when four retire) and a *House of Assembly* of 35 members, elected by proportional representation for four years in five 7-member constituencies, the electors for both Houses being all Tasmanians of 18 years and over who have resided continuously in the State for at least 6 months. Elections for the Assembly are held every four years.

The election of Feb. 1986 resulted in the election of the Liberal Government. The state of the parties in the Legislative Council following the election was Independent 19. The state of parties in the House of Assembly in June 1987 was: Liberals 19, Labor 14, Independent 2.

President of the Legislative Council, Hon. A. J. Broadby.

Speaker of the House of Assembly, Hon. R. Cornish.

THE JUDICATURE

The Supreme Court of Tasmania, with civil, criminal ecclesiastical, admiralty and matrimonial jurisdiction, was established by Royal Charter on October 13, 1823.

Local Courts are held before Commissioners who are legal practitioners. Courts of General Sessions, constituted by a chairman who is a Justice of the Peace and at least one other Justice, are established in the municipalities and, Courts of Petty Sessions are constituted by Magistrates sitting alone, or any two or more justices. A single justice may hear and determine certain matters.

Chief Justice, Supreme Court, Hon. Sir Guy Green.

EDUCATION

Government schools are of three main types: primary, secondary and secondary colleges. On July 1, 1986, there were 66,050 students enrolled in 255 Government schools. There were also 69 independent schools with an enrolment of 17,459. The University of Tasmania at Hobart, established 1890, had 3,479 full-time students and 2,289 part-time (including external) students in 1986. The Tasmanian State Institute of Technology, offering degree and diploma courses, was established in 1972. Enrolments in 1986 were 12,780 full-time students and 1,540 part-time students.

FINANCE

Revenue and expenditure of the Consolidated Revenue Fund and debt of Tasmania at current rates of exchange (June 30) was:—

	1985–86
Revenue	\$A1,024,696,665
Expenditure	1,036,954,099
Debt	1,246,273,209

Banking.—The weekly average of depositors' balances at trading banks in March 1987 was \$A766,922,000; the savings bank balances were \$A1,336,180,000.

PRODUCTION AND INDUSTRY

Gross value of agricultural production in 1984–85 was \$A382m. Total value added in manufacturing in 1984–85 was \$A937·9m.; value added in mining was \$A167m. in 1984–85.

Agriculture and Livestock.—The principal crops are apples, potatoes, green peas, oil poppies, hops, barley, beans and onions.

The livestock included (March 31, 1986) 570,000 cattle, 5,083,000 sheep and 45,000 pigs. The shorn wool production (1985–86) was 22,989 tonnes.

Electrical Energy.—Tasmania, the smallest Australian state, ranks fourth as a producer of electrical energy—most of it derived from water power, with a total installed generator capacity of 2,171,400 kW. By reason of its low-cost electrical energy, Tasmania has large plants producing ferro-manganese and newsprint. A large aluminium plant is situated at Bell Bay and Tasmania is the source of the bulk of Australian requirements of zinc and fine papers. The Hydro-Electric Commission has completed a network of 26 stations including a dual machine oil fired station at Bell Bay. Work is continuing on three hydro-electric developments in the remote western region of the State, which will increase the installed generator capacity to 2·54 million kW.

Forestry.—The quantity of timber (excluding firewood) of various species cut in 1985–86 was 4,454,800 cubic metres, including 3,595,900 cubic metres for woodchip and wood-pulp.

Minerals.—The chief ores mined are those containing copper, tin, iron, silver, zinc and lead.

Manufactures.—The chief manufactures for export are: refined metals, preserved fruit and vegetables, butter, cheese, textiles, paper, confectionery, wood chips and sawn timber. In 1984–85, 575 manufacturing establishments employed 24,494 persons, including working proprietors. Salaries and wages paid totalled \$A443·0m.

OVERSEAS TRADE

	1984–85	1985–86
Imports	\$A389,613,000	\$A299,398,000
Exports	841,312,000	902,921,000

The principal overseas exports are ores and concentrates, refined metals, woodchips, greasy wool, meat, abalone, fresh fruit, cheese and hides and skins.

COMMUNICATIONS

Road and Rail.—Tasmania is served by a 1,067 mm gauge Federal Government railway system of 856 route kms. An additional 134 route kms of the same gauge is privately operated. Regular passenger services no longer operate. At June 30, 1985 there were 22,046 kilometres of road normally open to traffic. Of this total 8,603 kilometres were sealed. Motor vehicles on the register at June 30, 1986 were: cars and station wagons, 206,200; commercial vehicles, 60,500 and motor cycles, 6,500.

Aviation.—Regular services operate between Tasmania and the other Australian States. During 1985–86 1,095,367 passengers were carried on these services. The main cities and towns in the State are served by regular internal services.

TOWNS

CAPITAL, ΨHOBART, founded 1804. Population (June 30, 1986), 127,106.

Other towns (with population at June 30, 1986) are ΨLaunceston (66,286), ΨDevonport (22,654), Burnie-Somerset (20,665), Ulverstone (10,055), Kingston-Blackmans Bay (10,932), New Norfolk (6,152).

VICTORIA

The State of Victoria comprises the south-east corner of Australia, at the part where its mainland territory projects farthest into the southern latitudes; it lies between 34°–39° S. latitude and 141°–150° E. longitude. Its extreme length from east to west is about 493 miles, its greatest breadth is about 290 miles, and its extent of coast-line is about 1,043 geographical miles, including the length around Port Phillip Bay, Western Port and Corner Inlet, the entire area being 87,876 sq. miles (227,597 sq. km.).

Population.—The estimated resident population at June 30, 1985 was 4,122,500.

Births, deaths and marriages were:

	1983	1984
Births..........................	60,123	59,763
Deaths	29,320	29,476
Marriages	28,974	28,931

Annual rate per 1,000 of estimated resident population in 1984: Births, 14·65; Deaths, 7·22; Marriages, 7·09. Deaths under 1 year per 1,000 live births, 8·97.

Religions

At the Census in 1981, members of the Catholic Church numbered 1,064,514, Church of England 777,551, Uniting (union of Presbyterian, Congregationalist and Methodist) 213,257, Presbyterian 175,291, Orthodox 171,131, Methodist 90,444 and Baptist 40,790. The number of persons who did not state their religion was 451,550.

PHYSIOGRAPHY

The *Australian Alps* and the *Great Dividing Range* pass through the centre of the State, and divide it into a northern and southern watershed, the latter sloping down to the ocean and containing, especially in the south-east, well-wooded valleys. The length of the Murray River, which forms part of the northern boundary of Victoria, is about 1,196 miles along the Victorian bank. Melbourne, the capital city, stands upon the Yarra River, which rises in the southern slopes of the Dividing Range.

Climate.—The climate of Victoria is characterized by warm to hot summers and rather cold winters. The highest temperature ever recorded in the State is 50·8°C, the lowest being −12·8°C. Normally, rain falls at most places throughout the year, with a maximum in winter or spring. In Melbourne, the mean annual temperature is 14·8°C.

GOVERNMENT

Victoria was originally known as the Port Phillip District of New South Wales and was created a separate colony in 1851, with a partially elective legislature. In 1855 Responsible Government was conferred. The executive authority is vested in a Governor, appointed by the Crown, aided by an Executive Council of Ministers.

Governor of Victoria, His Excellency Rev. Dr. John Davis McCaughey, *assumed office* Feb. 18, 1986.

Lt.-Governor, Hon. Sir John McIntosh Young, K.C.M.G. (1974).

THE MINISTRY

Premier, Hon. J. Cain.
Deputy Premier, and Minister of Industry, Technology and Resources, Hon. R. C. Fordham.
Agriculture and Rural Affairs, Hon. E. Walker.
Health, Hon. D. R. White.
Education, Hon. I. R. Cathie.
Labour, Hon. S. M. Crabb.
Consumer Affairs, and Ethnic Affairs, Hon. P. C. Spyker.
Community Services, Hon. C. J. Hogg.
Treasurer, Hon. R. A. Jolly.
Attorney-General, Planning and Environment, and Minister responsible for the Office of Corrections, Hon. J. H. Kennan.
Conservation, Forests and Lands, Hon. J. E. Kirner.
Arts, and Police and Emergency Services, Hon. C. R. T. Mathews.
Water Resources, and Property and Services, Hon. A. McCutcheon.
Transport, Hon. T. W. Roper.
Local Government, Hon. J. L. Simmonds.
Sport and Recreation, Hon. N. B. Trezise.
Public Works and Minister assisting the Minister for Labour, Hon. R. W. Walsh.
Housing, Hon. F. N. Wilkes.

AGENT-GENERAL IN LONDON

Agent-General, Mr. K. Finnin, Victoria House, Melbourne Place, Strand, WC2B 4LG.

THE LEGISLATURE

Parliament consists of a *Legislative Council* of 44 members, elected for the 22 Provinces for 8 years, one-half retiring every 4 years; and a *Legislative Assembly* of 88 members, elected for a maximum duration of 4 years. Voting is compulsory.

President of the Legislative Council, Hon. R. A. MacKenzie	\$A79,739
Speaker of the Legislative Assembly, Hon. C. T. Edmunds	79,739

THE JUDICATURE

There is a Supreme Court with a Chief Justice and 21 Puisne Judges, a County Court and Magistrates' Courts.

Chief Justice, Supreme Court, Hon. Sir John Young, K.C.M.G.	\$A107,812
Chief Judge, County Court, Hon. G. R. D. Waldron	\$A95,401
Solicitor-General, H. C. Berkeley, Q.C.	\$A95,296

EDUCATION

Primary education is compulsory, secular and free between the ages of 6 and 15. At July 1, 1985, there were 1,609 Government Primary Schools, 22 Primary–Secondary Schools and 408 Secondary Schools attended by 305,040 primary students and 248,303 secondary students. In addition there are technical and further education institutions and Colleges of Advanced Education.

At July 1, 1985, 245,176 pupils attended 734 non-Government schools, 500 of which were Roman Catholic.

There are four State-aided Universities.

FINANCE

Revenue and expenditure from the Consolidated Fund, and the debt of Victoria were:—

	1983–84	1984–85
Revenue	\$A7,780,985,185	\$A8,827,256,489
Expenditure	7,752,858,373	8,827,728,064
Debt	4,204,126,406	5,720,919,563

Banking, etc.—State Savings Bank deposits at June 30, 1985, amounted to \$A6,488,090,000; in addition, deposits in the Commonwealth Savings Bank (in the State of Victoria) amounted to \$A2,708,075,000, and in other savings banks \$A5,074,578,000.

PRODUCTION AND INDUSTRY

The gross value of primary production (excluding mining and quarrying) in 1983–84 was \$A3,273,492,000, crops \$A1,291,548,000, livestock \$A1,981,944,000. The local value of production of primary industries, excluding mining, was \$A2,941,620,000. Wool, wheat, flour, butter, livestock, fruits, milk and cream, meats, poultry and eggs are staple products.

Livestock.—There were on establishments with agricultural activity on 31st March, 1985, 26,471,000 sheep, 3,576,000 cattle, and 410,000 pigs. The quantity of wool produced in 1984–85 was valued at \$A502,300,000.

Minerals.—Minerals raised include oil and natural gas, brown coal, limestone, clays and stone for construction material. Production of brown coal in 1984–85 amounted to 36,369,405 tonnes.

Crude Oil and Natural Gas.—In 1965 natural gas was first discovered in commercial quantities in the offshore waters of the Gippsland Basin in eastern Victoria and in 1966–67, three more valuable oilfields were located in the same general area. These fields are still the largest yet found in Australia. Following the development of the four fields, commercial gas and crude oil came on stream in October, 1969. Production from the Gippsland fields during the financial year 1984–85 was: stabilized crude oil, 26,457,173 cubic metres; treated natural gas, 5,314,157,000 cubic metres; commercial propane, 1,594,150 cubic metres, and commercial ethane, 171,788,557 cubic metres.

Secondary Industry.—In 1984–85 there were 12,229 manufacturing establishments in which 256,230 males and 108,212 females were employed. Value added in the course of manufacture by all manufacturing establishments with four or more persons employed was \$A13,179 million.

OVERSEAS TRADE

The export trade (excluding inter-state trade) consists largely of agricultural and mining products, machinery and transport equipment. The principal overseas imports of the State are apparel and textiles, electrical and other machines and machinery, motor vehicles and tractors, metals and metal manufactures, iron and steel, chemicals, petroleum and petroleum products, artificial resins and plastic materials.

	1983–84	1984–85
Imports	\$A8,186,719,000	\$A10,500,541,000
Exports	5,132,526,000	6,832,277,000

TRANSPORT

Victoria State Railways—At June 30, 1986, there were 5,760 kms of railway open for traffic. The revenue for the year ended June 30, 1984, was \$A219,898,000. Total distance travelled in 1984–85 was 30,288,000 kms and goods and livestock carried amounted to 11,872,000 tonnes.

Shipping.—During the year ended June 30, 1985, 2,171 overseas vessels with dead-weight tonnage of 54,328,942 arrived at Victorian ports and 2,145 overseas vessels with dead-weight tonnage of 53,554,024 departed.

Motor Vehicle Registration.—The number of vehicles on the register at June 30, 1985, was: cars and stationwagons, 1,936,800; utilities and panel vans, 196,800; trucks and omnibuses, 220,600, and motor cycles, 83,400.

Towns

ΨMELBOURNE, the capital city, had a resident population at June 30, 1986, estimated at 2,917,200. Other urban centres are ΨGeelong, 147,140; Ballarat, 77,590; Bendigo, 63,750; Shepparton-Mooroopna, 38,870; ΨWarrnambool, 23,300; Wodonga, 23,040.

WESTERN AUSTRALIA

Includes all that portion of the continent west of 129° E. long., the most westerly point being in 113° 9′ E. long. and from 13° 44′ to 35° 8′ S. lat. Its extreme length is 1,480 miles, and 1,000 miles from east to west; total area 975,920 sq. miles (2,527,621 sq. km.).

POPULATION.—At June 1985, the estimated resident population was 1,407,451.

Births, deaths and marriages were:

	1985	1986p
Births	23,066	24,174
Deaths	8,863	9,302
Marriages	10,398	10,379
p=provisional		

Religions

Census of 1981—Church of England 375,848, Roman Catholics 316,337, Methodists 51,225, Uniting Church 32,592, and Presbyterians 32,033.

Physiography

Large areas of the State, for some hundreds of miles inland, are hilly and even mountainous, although the altitude, so far as ascertained, rises nowhere above that of Mount Meharry (4,097 ft.) in the north-west division or that of Bluff Knoll (3,640 ft.) in the Stirling Range in the south-west. The coastal regions are undulating, with an interior slope to the unsettled central portion of Australia. The Darling and Hamersley ranges of the west have a seaward slope to the Indian Ocean, into which flow many streams, notably the Preston, Collie, Murray, Swan, Murchison, Gascoyne, Ashburton, Fortescue and De Grey. In the north the Fitzroy flows from the King Leopold ranges into the Indian Ocean, and the Drysdale and Ord into the Timor Sea. The greater portion of the State may be described as an immense tableland, with an average elevation of 1,000 to 1,500 ft. above sea-level. The climate is one of the most temperate in the world. Of the total area two-thirds is suitable for pastoral purposes.

Government

Western Australia was first settled by the British in 1829, and in 1870 it was granted a partially elective legislature. In 1890 responsible government was granted, and the Administration vested in a Governor, a Legislative Council, and a Legislative Assembly. The present constitution rests upon the Constitution Act, 1889, the Constitution Acts Amendment Act, 1899, and amending Acts. The Executive is vested in a Governor appointed by the Crown and aided by a Council of responsible Ministers.

The Legislative Assembly (elected February, 1986) is composed of Australian Labor Party 32, Liberal Party 19, National Party of Australia 6.

Governor of Western Australia, His Excellency Prof. Gordon Reid.

Lt.-Governor and Administrator, Hon. Sir Francis Burt, K.C.M.G.

The Ministry

Premier, Treasurer, Minister for Public Sector Management, and Women's Interests, Hon. B. T. Burke $A102,282

Deputy Premier, Minister for Industry, Technology, Communications, Defence Liaison and Parliamentary and Electoral Reform, Hon. M. J. Bryce $A91,023

Attorney-General, Minister for Budget Management, Corrective Services, Leader of the Government in the Legislative Council, Hon. J. M. Berinson.

Community Services, the Family, Youth, the Aged, Minister assisting the Minister for Women's Interests, Hon. E. K. Hallahan.

Local Government and Regional Development, Hon. J. P. Carr.

Education, Planning, Intergovernmental Relations, Leader of the House in the Legislative Assembly, Hon. R. J. Pearce.

Conservation and Land Management, Environment, Hon. B. J. Hodge.

Minerals and Energy, Economic Development, the Arts, Hon. D. C. Parker.

Agriculture, the South-West, Fisheries, Hon. J. F. Grill.

Housing and Lands, Hon. K. J. Wilson.

Works and Services, Labour, Productivity and Employment, Minister assisting the Treasurer and the Minister for Public Sector Management, Hon. P. M. Dowding.

Health, Consumer Affairs, Minister assisting the Minister for Economic Development, Hon. I. F. Taylor.

Tourism, Racing and Gaming, Hon. P. A Beggs.

Transport and Small Business, Hon. G. J. Troy.

Water Resources, the North-West, Aboriginal Affairs, Hon. E. F. Bridge.

Police and Emergency Services, Multicultural and Ethnic Affairs, Hon. G. L. Hill.

Sport and Recreation, Parliamentary Secretary of the Cabinet, Hon. G. J. Edwards.

Ministers, each $A81,803–$A97,114, according to location of electorate.

Agent-General in London, R. Douglas, Western Australia House, 115 Strand, W.C.2.

The Legislature

Parliament consists of a *Legislative Council* and a *Legislative Assembly*, elected by adult suffrage subject to qualifications of residence and registration. The qualifying age for electors for both the Legislative Council and Legislative Assembly is 18 years. There are 34 members in the Legislative Council, two from each Province, for a period of 6 years, one member from each Province retiring triennially. The Legislative Assembly is composed of 57 members, who are elected for a term of 3 years.

President of the Legislative Council, Hon. C. E. Griffiths $A76,056
Speaker of the Legislative Assembly, Hon. M. Barnett 76,056

The Judicature

Chief Justice, Hon. Sir Francis Burt, K.C.M.G. $A111,675
Senior Puisne Judge, Hon. A. R. A. Wallace 102,679
Puisne Judges, Hons. P. F. Brinsden; C. H. Smith; G. A. Kennedy; H. W. Olney; W. P. Pidgeon; B. W. Rowland; E. M. Franklyn .... each 99,484

Education

In 1986 there were 728 government and 233 non-government primary and secondary schools with 207,426 and 60,211 students respectively. The total recurrent and capital outlay expended on education (by State authorities) during the year ended June 30, 1985, was \$A992,700,000, including grants totalling \$A90,639,000 to the University of Western Australia (9,512 enrolments in 1986), and to Murdoch University (4,624 enrolments in 1986). These amounts included Commonwealth monies.

PRODUCTION AND INDUSTRY

The gross value of agricultural production in 1985–86 was: crops \$A1,185,557,000; livestock slaughterings, etc., \$A372,002,000; livestock products \$A656,594,000; fishing and gross value of fisheries was \$A138,689,900.

Crops and Livestock.—The production of wheat for grain in 1985–86 was 4,362,000 tonnes. On March 31, 1986, the livestock included 1,690,000 cattle, 33,212,700 sheep, and 278,200 pigs. Wool production in 1985–86 was 175,500 tonnes in the grease.

Manufacturing Industries.—There were 3,902 manufacturing establishments operating in the State at June 30, 1985. The total number of persons employed (including working proprietors) by these establishments at the end of June, 1985 was 66,342.

Forestry.—The forests contain some of the finest hardwoods in the world. The total quantity of sawn timber produced during 1985–86 was 324,962 cubic metres.

Minerals.—The State has large deposits of a wide range of minerals, many of which are being mined or are under development for production. The ex-mine value of all minerals produced during 1985–86 was \$A4,204,100,000.

Communications.—On June 30, 1986, there were 5,563 km. of State government railway open for general and passenger traffic; and 731 km. (Kalgoorlie-W.A. border) of the Australian National Railway. In the year ended June 30, 1986, 2,600 vessels entered Western Australian ports direct from, and 2,584 were cleared direct to, overseas. The number of registered motor vehicles at June 30, 1986, was 887,357.

FINANCE

	1984–85	1985–86
	\$A	\$A
Revenue	2,843,079,541	3,099,411,391
Expenditure	2,842,267,768	3,099,044,981
Public Debt (June 30)	1,597,996,696	1,589,828,314

OVERSEAS TRADE

	1984–85	1985–86
Imports	\$A2,155,270,699	\$A2,063,186,000
Exports	6,070,016,944	6,513,174,000

Principal overseas exports in 1985–86 included iron ore and concentrates, wheat, wool, live sheep and lambs, petroleum and petroleum products, beef and veal, gold bullion, rock lobster tails.

TOWNS

CAPITAL.—ΨPERTH. Estimated resident population (estimate for June 30, 1986) of Perth Statistical Division, including the port of Fremantle, 1,025,340.

Perth stands on the right bank of the Swan River estuary, 12 miles from Fremantle.

New Zealand

AREA AND POPULATION

Islands	Area (English) Sq. Miles)	Population	
		Census Mar. 24, 1981†	Census Mar. 4, 1986†
(a) Exclusive of Island Territory:			
North Island	44,281	2,322,989	2,441,615
South Island	58,093	852,748	865,469
Stewart Island	670	600*	531*
Chatham Islands	372	751*	755*
Minor Islands:			
Inhabited—			
Kermadec Islands	13	5*	5**
Campbell Island	44	10*	10**
Uninhabited—			
Three Kings	3	..	..
Snares	1	..	..
Solander	½	..	..
Antipodes	24	..	..
Bounty	½	..	..
Auckland	234	..	..
Total exclusive of Island Territory	103,736	3,175,737	3,307,084
(b) Island Territory:			
Tokelau Islands	..	1,572‖	1,595§
(c) Niue island¶	..	3,226§	3,002**
Cook Islands¶	..	18,000‡	17,400**
Ross Dependency	175,000	..	..

* Included in North Island and South Island totals.

† Excluding members of the Armed Forces overseas—979 in 1981; 1,247 in 1986.

¶ The Cook Islands have had complete internal self-government since Aug. 4, 1965, as has Niue since Oct. 19, 1974, but Cook Islanders and Niueans remain New Zealand citizens.

‖ Nov. 2, 1981.   § Oct. 1, 1983.   ‡ Dec. 31, 1980.   ** March 31, 1983.

Vital Statistics

Year	Births	Deaths	Natural Increase	Deaths of Infants under one year	Infant Mortality per 1,000 live births	Marriages
1980	50,542	26,676	23,866	650	12·86	22,981
1981	50,794	25,150	25,644	592	11·65	23,660
1982	49,938	25,532	24,406	587	11·75	25,537
1983	50,474	25,991	24,483	633	12·54	24,678
1984	51,636	25,378	26,258	597	11·56	25,272
1985	51,798	27,480	24,318	560	10·81	24,657
1986	52,826	27,045	25,781	592	11·20	24,037

Inter-Censal Increases

Year	Results of Census			Numerical Increase	Net Inflow or Outflow from Total Migration
	Males	Females	Total		
1966	1,343,743	1,333,176	2,676,919	261,935	+ 12,950
1971	1,430,856	1,431,775	2,862,631	185,712	+ 8,481
1976	1,562,042	1,567,341	3,129,383	266,752	+ 6,567
1981	1,578,927	1,596,810	3,175,737	46,354	− 15,328
1986	1,616,004	1,645,782	3,261,786	131,347	− 18,518

Excluding 1,936 members of the Armed Forces overseas at the time of the 1966 Census, 1,482 at the 1971 Census, 1,333 at the 1976 Census, 979 at the 1981 Census and 1,247 at the 1986 Census.

Races and Religions

Races	1981	1986	Religions	1981	1986
				per cent	per cent
Europeans	2,696,568	2,612,958	Church of England	25·7	24·0
Maoris	279,084	294,201	Presbyterians	16·7	18·0
Chinese	18,480	19,206	Roman Catholics	14·3	15·2
Polynesians (other than N.Z. Maoris)	88,827	90,612	Methodists	4·7	4·7
			Baptists	1·6	2·1

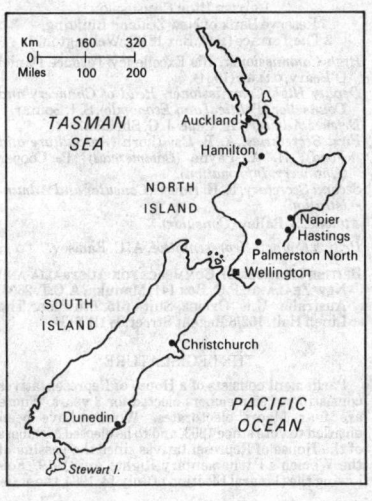

PHYSIOGRAPHY

New Zealand consists of a number of islands of varying size in the South Pacific Ocean, and has also administrative responsibility for a large tract in the Antarctic Ocean. The two larger and most important islands, the North and South Islands of New Zealand, are separated by only a relatively narrow strait. The remaining islands are very much smaller and, in general, are widely dispersed over a considerable expanse of ocean. The boundaries, inclusive of the most outlying islands and dependencies, range from 33° to 53° South latitude, and from 162° East longitude to 173° West longitude.

Geographical Features.—The two principal islands have a total length of 1,040 miles, and a combined area of 102,344 sq. miles, (265,069 sq. km.). A large proportion of the surface is mountainous in character. The principal range is that of the Southern Alps, extending over the entire length of the South Island and having its culminating point in Mount Cook (12,349 ft.). The North Island mountains include several volcanoes, two of which are active, others being dormant or extinct. Mt. Ruapehu (9,175 ft.) and Mt. Ngauruhoe (7,515 ft.) are the most important. Of the numerous glaciers in the South Island, the Tasman (18 miles long by 1¼ wide), the Franz Josef and the Fox are the best known. The North Island is noted for its hot springs and geysers. For the most part the rivers are too short and rapid for navigation.

The more important include the Waikato (270 miles in length), Wanganui (180), and Clutha (210). Lakes (Taupo, 234 sq. miles in area; Wakatipu, 113; and Te Anau, 133) are abundant, many of them of great beauty.

Climate.—New Zealand has a moist-temperate marine climate, but with abundant sunshine. A very important feature is the small annual range of temperature which permits of some growth of vegetation, including pasture, all the year round. Very little snow falls on the low levels even in the South Island. The mean temperature ranges from 15° C. in the North to about 9° C. in the South. Rainfall over the more settled areas in the North Island ranges from 35 to 70 inches and in the South Island from 25 to 45 inches. The total range is from approximately 13 to over 250 inches.

GOVERNMENT

The discoverers and first colonists of New Zealand were Polynesian people, ancestors of the Maoris of today. Whether there was a single colonization, several, or many, is not known. By the 13th or 14th century early exploration was over and there were well established Maori settlements.

The first European to discover New Zealand was a Dutch navigator, Abel Tasman, who sighted the coast on December 13, 1642 but did not land. It was the British explorer James Cook who circumnavigated New Zealand and landed in 1769. Traders, whalers and sealers made up the majority of Europeans in New Zealand during the 18th century and until the late 1830s, when the proportion of permanent European settlers became significant.

Largely as a result of increased British emigration, the country was annexed by the British Government in 1840. The British Governor, William Hobson, RN, proclaimed sovereignty over the North Island by virtue of the Treaty of Waitangi, signed by him and many Maori chiefs, and over the South Island and Stewart Island by right of discovery.

On May 3, 1841, New Zealand was, by letters patent, created a separate colony distinct from New South Wales. Organized colonization on a large scale commenced in 1840 with the New Zealand company's settlement at Wellington. On Sept. 26, 1907, the designation was changed to *The Dominion of New Zealand*. The Constitution rests upon the Imperial Act of 1852, and on the New Zealand Constitution (Amendment) Act of Dec. 10, 1947. The Statute of Westminster was formally adopted by New Zealand in 1947. The executive authority is entrusted to a Governor-General appointed by the Crown and aided by an Executive Council, within a Legislature consisting of one chamber, the House of Representatives.

FLAG: Blue ground, with Union Jack in top left quarter, four five-pointed red stars with white borders on the fly. On June 20, 1968, a naval ensign bearing the Southern Cross was adopted, replacing the British white ensign.

NATIONAL DAY.—February 6 (Wantangi Day).

NATIONAL ANTHEM.—God Save The Queen/God Defend New Zealand.

Governor-General and Staff

Governor-General and Commander-in-Chief of New Zealand, His Excellency The Most Rev. Sir Paul Alfred Reeves, G.C.M.G., *sworn in,* Nov. 20, 1985.
Official Secretary, Paul Canham.

THE EXECUTIVE COUNCIL

His Excellency the GOVERNOR-GENERAL

Prime Minister and Minister of Education, Hon. David Lange.
Deputy P.M., Attorney-General and Minister of Justice, Hon. Geoffrey Palmer.
Overseas Trade and Marketing, Hon. Michael Moore.
Finance, Hon. Roger Douglas.
State-Owned Enterprises, Postmaster General, Works and Development, Hon. Richard Prebble.
Maori Affairs, Hon. Koro Wetere.
Health, Trade and Industry, Hon. David Caygill.
Foreign Affairs, Disarmament and Arms Control, Hon. Russell Marshall.
Internal Affairs, Hon. Dr. Michael Bassett.
Minister of State and Leader of the House, Hon. Jonathan Hunt.
Defence, Hon. Bob Tizard.
Agriculture and Fisheries, Hon. Colin Moyle.
Labour and Immigration, Hon. Stan Rodger.
Employment, Hon. Phil Goff.
Women's Affairs, Consumer Affairs and Statistics, Hon. Mrs. Margaret Shields.
Police, Forestry and Lands, Hon. Peter Tapsell.
Housing and Conservation, Hon. Mrs. Helen Clark.
Social Welfare, Hon. Dr. Michael Cullen.
Transport and Civil Aviation, Hon. Bill Jeffries.
Energy and Regional Development, Hon. David Butcher.

The Prime Minister receives $129,250 per annum with an allowance of $23,400 for expenses of his office and the Ministerial residence. The salary of each Minister holding a portfolio is $90,200 with expense allowance of $9,600 and that of each Minister without portfolio $73,150, with $7,150 expense allowance.

NEW ZEALAND HIGH COMMISSION
New Zealand House, Haymarket, SW1Y 4TQ
[01–930 8422]

High Commissioner, His Excellency Bryce Harland (1985).
Deputy High Commissioner, R. A. Farrell.
Minister (Administration), P. K. Munn.
Minister (Commercial), R. J. Turnbull.
Head, Defence Liaison Staff, Brig. R. J. Andrews, O.B.E.

BRITISH HIGH COMMISSION
Reserve Bank of New Zealand Building,
2 The Terrace (P.O. Box 1812), Wellington, 1

High Commissioner, His Excellency Terence Daniel O'Leary, C.M.G., (1984).
Deputy High Commissioner, Head of Chancery and Counsellor (Political and Economic), S. I. Soutar.
Defence Adviser, Gp. Capt. J. G. Sheldon.
First Secretaries, A. B. Cawthorn (*Agriculture and Food*); H. A. Payne (*Commercial*); P. Cooper (*Chancery, Information*).
Second Secretary, R. H. House (*Consular and Administration*).
Attaché, S. Bailey (*Consular*).

British Council Representative, A. C. Ramsey.

BRITISH CHAMBER OF COMMERCE FOR AUSTRALIA AND NEW ZEALAND, P.O. Box 141, Manuka, A.C.T. 2603, Australia; U.K. OFFICE, Suite 615, 6th Floor The Linen Hall, 162/8 Regent Street, W1R 5TB.

THE LEGISLATURE

Parliament consists of a House of Representatives consisting of 95 members elected for 3 years. There are four Maori electorates. Women have been entitled to vote since 1893, and to be elected Members of the House of Representatives since the passing of the Women's Parliamentary Rights Act, 1919. Following the General Election of July 14, 1984, the state of the parties in Parliament was Labour 56, National Party 37 and Social Credit 2.

Members of the House receive $NZ49,500 *per annum*, with an allowance of $NZ4,800 *per annum* for expenses, plus an electorate allowance. The Leader of the Opposition receives $NZ90,200 *per annum* and $NZ9,600 *per annum* for expenses, plus house and travelling allowances.

Speaker of the House of Representatives,
Dr. G. A. Wall (*plus expense allowance*
and residential quarters in Parlia-
ment House) $NZ83,600

THE JUDICATURE

The judicial system comprises a High Court and a Court of Appeal; also District Courts having both civil and criminal jurisdiction.

Chief Justice, Rt. Hon. Sir Ronald Davison, G.B.E., C.M.G. $NZ132,000
President, Court of Appeal, Rt. Hon. Sir Robin Cooke, K.B.E. 127,600
Judges, Rt. Hons. Sir Ivor Richardson; Sir Duncan McMullin; E. J. Somers; M. E. Casey; G. E. Bisson 123,200
High Court Puisne Judges, Hons. J. P. Quilliam; M. F. Chilwell; J. F. Jeffries; R. I. Barker; J. B. Sinclair; A. D. Holland; T. M. Thorp; L. M. Greig; M. Hardie-Boys; J. H. Wallace; J. T. Eichelbaum; P. G. Hillyer; R. G. Gallen; D. L. Tompkins; J. S. Henry; R. A. Heron; N. W. Williamson; A. A. T. Ellis; R. P. Smellie; R. E. Wylie; R. A. McGechan; J. A. Doogue; A. P. C. Tipping; N. C. Anderson............ 118,800
High Court Administrative Divn., Rt. Hon. Sir Ronald Davison (*Chief Justice*); Hons. M. F. Chilwell; J. F. Jeffries; A. D. Holland; L. M. Greig; D. L. Tompkins.
Judge, Court of Arbitration, Judge J. R. P. Horn.

POLICE

On March 31, 1986 the strength of the New Zealand Police Force was 5,203 of all ranks, equivalent to 1 for every 636 of the population. Total police expenditure for the year 1985–86 was $NZ243,000,000.

DEFENCE

A unified Ministry of Defence which retained the three single services was set up in 1964. The Minister of Defence is responsible for national defence, and, with the other members of the Defence Council, commands and administers the three services:

The *Royal New Zealand Navy* consists of 2,619 officers and ratings as at March 31, 1986, as well as the Volunteer Reserve in four divisions. The strength is four frigates, one survey ship and one research vessel, as well as patrol and inshore survey craft.

The *New Zealand Army* consists of the Regular Force, the Territorial Force and the Army Reserve. The strength of the Regular Force at March 31, 1986 was 5,814, and of the Territorial Force and Army Reserve, 5,821. The Army is structured to provide a Regular Force battalion group which is available for rapid deployment on military operations or civil assistance tasks, as well as a framework of integrated Regular Force/Territorial Force Units as a basis for expansion when required. One infantry battalion is based in Singapore.

The *Royal New Zealand Air Force* had a Regular Force strength of 4,176 at March 31, 1986, with 1,003 Territorial and Reserve Forces. Operational units include fighter ground attack, maritime, medium and short-range transport, and helicopter squadrons, and flying training units. A helicopter support unit is based in Singapore.

FINANCE

Into the Consolidated Account (New Zealand's main public account) are paid the proceeds of income tax, sales tax, customs and excise duties and other taxes, also interest, profits from trading undertakings, and departmental receipts (departmental expenditure is included gross). Revenue from taxation is also paid into the National Roads Fund principally from a tax on motor spirits and registration and licence fees for motor vehicles.

Revenue and expenditure for year ended March 31 ($NZ'000):

	1985	1986
Revenue	16,162,371	18,451,206
Expenditure*	16,162,371	18,451,206

Revenue from taxation was ($NZ'000):

	1985	1986
Total...............	11,913,628	14,235,870
Consolidated Account........	11,579,485	13,812,265
National Roads Fund...........	334,143	423,605

*Includes ($NZ'000):

	1985	1986
Education	1,746,868	2,028,416
Social Welfare	4,386,995	5,363,389
Health	1,914,293	2,312,476
Development of Industry	1,984,750	1,697,287
Defence	756,408	870,456
Debt services	2,781,411	3,622,430
Law and order	358,297	458,872

DEBT

The gross *Public Debt* amounted on March 31, 1986, to $NZ32,002,246,000 of which $NZ5,348,989,000 was domiciled in Europe, $NZ4,362,524,000 in U.S.A. and $NZ4,579,490,000 in Japan; $NZ2,250,000 represented World Bank loans.

BANKING

There are four trading banks, two of which are predominantly New Zealand banks. At Dec. 24, 1985, assets of all trading banks in respect of New Zealand business amounted to $NZ15,464,800,000, liabilities, $NZ13,454,200,000; New Zealand's official overseas reserves at Dec. 1986, amounted to $NZ7,204,900,000. Trading banks' advances in 1986 averaged $NZ10,599,600,000 weekly, and deposits with the trading banks averaged $NZ14,325,900,000

Post-office, trustee and private savings banks had, at March 31, 1986, over 7,731,000 accounts having $NZ27,119,100,000 to their credit.

The Reserve Bank of New Zealand notes are the legal tender. Value of notes in circulation on March 31, 1986 amounted to $NZ981,448,000.

EDUCATION

Schools are free and attendance is compulsory between the ages of 6 and 15. There are opportunities for apt pupils to proceed to university. At July 1985 there were 441,435 pupils attending public primary schools, and 10,991 pupils attending registered private primary schools. The secondary education of boys and girls in the cities and large towns is carried on in 316 state secondary schools, and 16 private secondary schools. The total number of pupils receiving full-time secondary education in July 1985 was 230,970 and in addition there were 128,200 students attending technical classes including 31,949 receiving part-time tuition from the Technical Correspondence School. Almost all the students attending technical classes are part-time. There are six universities; the Lincoln university college of agriculture is associated with the University of Canterbury. The university system is co-ordinated by the University Grants Committee. The Universities had a total of 59,868 students in 1985.

The total expenditure on education out of public funds in 1985–86 is estimated at $NZ2,010,000,000.

PRODUCTION AND INDUSTRY

Gross Agricultural Production (Gross Output)

	Year ended March	
	1983–84	1984–85*
	$NZ(million)	
Sheep	518	792
Wool	935	1,214
Cattle	720	1,063
Pigs	89	102
Dairy products	1,198	1,455
Crops and seeds	286	323
Fruit, nuts, oilseeds	238	346
Vegetables	274	232
Poultry products	143	170
Agricultural services	318	357
Other horticulture	174	204
Other products n.e.c.	94	120
Value of change in livestock	169	314
Sales of live animals	743	887
Gross Output	5,900	7,579

*Provisional

Agricultural and Pastoral Production

	1985	1986
*Wheat, metric tons	309,600	379,700
*Wool, metric tons	373,000	n/a
†Butter, metric tons	293,110	299,600
†Cheese, metric tons	118,450	127,270
‡Stock Slaughtered—		
Lambs, No.	39,961,000	34,669,000
Sheep, No.	10,740,000	6,709,000
Cattle, No.	1,981,000	1,882,000
Calves, No.	836,000	952,000
Pigs, No.	849,000	843,000

* Year ended June 30.
† Year ended May 31.
‡ Year ended Sept. 30. Provisional.

Forestry.—The output of sawn timber for 1986 was 2,398,000 cubic metres, of which 2,265,000 cubic metres represented exotic varieties, mainly radiata pine.

Livestock.—Livestock on farms at June 30, 1986, included 3,371,000 dairy cattle (of which 2,252,000 were dairy cows in milk during season), 4,866,000 beef cattle (of which 1,478,000 were beef breeding cows), and 435,000 pigs. Sheep numbered 68,132,000.

Minerals.—Non-metallic minerals such as coal, clay, limestone and dolomite are both economically and industrially more important than metallic ones. Coal output in 1985 was 2,546,000 tonnes. Of the metals, the most important is ironsand, which is mined for export. Natural gas deposits in Taranaki are being used for electricity generation and as a premium fuel, piped to an increasing number of North Island centres.

TRADE

	1984–85	1985–86
Imports (v.f.d.)	$NZ11,344,200,000	$NZ10,468,300,000
Exports (f.o.b.)	11,315,800,000	10,571,700,000

Trade with U.K.

	1985	1986
Imports from U.K.	$NZ989,700,000	$NZ985,500,000
Exports to U.K.	1,030,100,000	933,900,000

New Zealand produce exported to the U.K. in the 12 months ending June, 1986, included butter, valued at $NZ249,100,000; beef ($NZ257,000); wool ($NZ156,669,000); lamb ($NZ235,200,000).

COMMUNICATIONS

Railways.—The national railway system is owned and operated by the New Zealand Railways Corporation. In March, 1986, there were 4,273 km. of Government railway in operation.

Motor Vehicles.—In the year ended June 30, 1986 there were 2,493,908 licensed motor vehicles. These included 1,558,307 cars and 143,165 motor and power cycles.

Shipping.—During 1986 the vessels entered from overseas ports numbered 2,483 (net tonnage 13,421,000) and those cleared for overseas 2,524 (net tonnage 16,337,000).

Civil Aviation—Figures are for scheduled services in the year to end Dec. 1985:

	Domestic Flights	International Flights
Kilometres flown	37,281	
Passengers carried	3,255	2,061
Freight carried (tonnes)	42,200	92,227
Mail carried (tonnes)	—	3,936

CAPITAL.—ΨWELLINGTON, in the North Island (estimated population March 4, 1986, Wellington statistical division, 352,000).

Other large centres; ΨAuckland, 889,200; ΨChristchurch, 333,200; ΨDunedin, 113,600; Palmerston North, 93,500; Hamilton, 167,700; ΨNapier-Hastings, 115,400.

THE TERRITORIES OF NEW ZEALAND

In addition to North, South, Stewart and Chatham Islands:—

The Three Kings (discovered by Tasman on the Feast of the Epiphany), in 34° 9′ S. lat. and 172° 8′ 8″ E. long. (uninhabited). *Auckland Islands*, about 290 miles south of Bluff Harbour, in 50° 32′ S. lat. and 166° 13′ E. long. *Antipodes Group*, 40° 41′ 15″ S. lat. and 178° 43′ E. long. *Bounty Islands*, 47° 4′ 43″ S. lat., 170° 0′ 30″ E. long. *Snares Islands and Solander*. All these islands are uninhabited.

The Kermadec Group (population normally 9 or 10) between 29° 10′ to 31° 30′ S. lat., and 177° 45′ to 179° W. long., includes Raoul or Sunday, Macaulay, Curtis Islands, L'Esperance, and some islets. All the inhabitants are government employees at a meteorological station. *Campbell Island* (used as a weather station).

TOKELAU (OR UNION ISLANDS)

A group of atolls (Fakaofo, Nukunono and Atafu) (estimated population 1,627 at Oct. 1, 1984), proclaimed part of New Zealand as from Jan. 1, 1948.

THE ROSS DEPENDENCY

The *Ross Dependency*, placed under the jurisdiction of New Zealand by Order in Council dated July 30, 1923, and defined as all the islands and territories between 160° E. and 150° W. longitude which are situated south of the 60° S. parallel. The Ross Dependency includes Edward VII Land and portions of Victoria Land. For some years there have been permanent bases in the area, staffed by survey and scientific personnel.

ASSOCIATED STATES

COOK ISLANDS

Included in the boundaries of New Zealand since June, 1901, the group consists of the islands of Rarotonga, Aitutaki, Mangaia, Atiu, Mauke, Mitiaro, Manuae, Takutea, Palmerston, Penrhyn or Tongareva, Manihiki, Rakahanga, Suwarrow, Pukapuka or Danger and Nassau. The total population of the group was estimated at 18,000 (1985 U. N. estimate). The chief exports of the Cook Islands are fruit juice, clothing, copra, bananas, citrus fruit and pulp, and pearl shell. The trade is chiefly with New Zealand, Australia, Japan, the U.K. and the U.S.A. The New Zealand Government continues to give financial aid to the Cook Islands.

The High Commissioner of the Cook Islands is employed in a dual role, since he represents both the Queen and the New Zealand Government. Since Aug. 4, 1965, the Islands have enjoyed complete internal self-government, executive power being in the hands of a Cabinet consisting of the Premier and five other ministers. The new Constitution Act was passed by the New Zealand Parliament in November 1964, but did not come into force until it had been endorsed by the 22-member Legislative Assembly of the Cook Islands, elected in April 1965.

The New Zealand citizenship of the Cook Islanders is embodied in the Constitution, and assurances have been given that the changed status of the Islands will in no way affect the consideration of subsidies or the right of free entry into New Zealand for exports from the group.

New Zealand Representative, L. A. Beath.

NIUE

Geographically part of Cook Islands, but administered separately. Had a population (1983) of 3,002.

A New Zealand Representative is stationed at Niue, which since October 1974 has been self-governing in free association with New Zealand, which is responsible for external affairs and defence, and continues to give financial aid. Executive power is in the hands of a Premier and a Cabinet of 3 drawn from the Assembly of 20 members.

New Zealand Representative, J. R. Springford.

ANTIGUA AND BARBUDA
(State of Antigua and Barbuda)

AREA, POPULATION, ETC.—Antigua and Barbuda comprises the islands of Antigua (108 sq. miles (279 sq. km.)), Barbuda (62 sq. miles (160 sq. km.)) 25 miles north of Antigua, and Redonda ($\frac{1}{2}$ square mile; 1·2 sq. km.) 25 miles south-west of Antigua. Antigua is part of the Leeward Islands in the Eastern Caribbean and lies 17° 3' N. and 61° 48' W. It is distinguished from the rest of the Leeward group by its absence of high hills and forest, and a drier climate than most of the W. Indies. Barbuda, formerly a possession of the Codrington family, is very flat with a large lagoon and well wooded in the north east. Antigua was first settled by the English in 1632, and was granted to

Lord Willoughby by Charles II. Antigua has a population of 80,000, (1985 U.N. estimate); Barbuda, 1,500, and Redonda is uninhabited.

CAPITAL.—ΨST. JOHN'S. Population, 30,000. The town of Barbuda is Codrington.

FLAG.—Inverted triangle (centred on a red field) divided horizontally into three bands of black over blue over white; rising sun device in gold on black band.

NATIONAL DAY.—November 1 (Independence Day).
NATIONAL ANTHEM.—"Fair Antigua and Barbuda".

GOVERNMENT

Antigua became internally self-governing in 1967 and fully independent on Nov. 1, 1981, as a constitutional monarchy with H.M. The Queen as Head of State, represented by the Governor-General. There is a Senate of 17 appointed members and a House of Representatives elected every 5 years. The Attorney-General may be appointed.

Governor-General, Sir Wilfred Ebenezer Jacobs, G.C.M.G., G.C.V.O., O.B.E., Q.C.

Cabinet

Prime Minister, Rt. Hon. Vere C. Bird, Sr.
Deputy P.M. and Minister for Foreign Affairs, Economic Development, Tourism and Energy, Hon. Lester Bird.
Public Utilities and Aviation, Hon. Robin Yearwood.
Finance, Hon. John E. St. Luce.
Education, Culture and Youth Affairs, Hon. Reuben H. Harris.
Labour, Health and Co-operatives, Hon. Adolphus Freeland.
Home Affairs, Hon. Christopher M. O'Mard.
Agriculture, Fisheries and Lands, Housing, Hon. Hilroy Humphreys.
Attorney General (apptd), Hon. Keith Ford.
Public Works, Hon. V. C. Bird, Jnr.
Ministers within a Ministry:
 Foreign Affairs, Economic Development, Tourism and Energy, Hon. Hugh Marshall.
 Public Utilities and Aviation, Hon. Eustace Cochrane.
 Education, Culture and Youth Affairs, Hon. D. Christian.
 Finance and Port Authority, Hon. Henderson St. Clair Simon.
 Labour, and Health, Hon. Molwyn Joseph.

HIGH COMMISSION FOR
ANTIGUA AND BARBUDA
15 Thayer Street, W1M 5LD
[01–486 7073]

High Commissioner for Eastern Caribbean States, (new appointment awaited).

BRITISH HIGH COMMISSION
38 St. Mary's Street (P.O. 483), St. John's

High Commissioner, (resides at Bridgetown, Barbados).
Resident Representative, B. Taylor (*First Secretary*).

ECONOMY

Tourism is the main feature of the economy, with several hotels (and a number under construction) to take advantage of the many white sand beaches which made Antigua one of the first Caribbean islands to attract tourists.

For many years sugar was the dominant crop but is now produced primarily for local consumption.

Areas of agricultural development include livestock, sea island cotton, corn (for cornmeal production) and improved vegetable and fruit production.

FINANCE

	1984	1985
Revenue	EC$124,550,943	EC$138,212,022
Expenditure (recurrent) ...	107,511,557	129,385,195

Trade with U.K.

	1985	1986
Imports from U.K........	£28,800,000	£17,774,000
Exports to U.K.	1,900,000	2,069,000

THE BAHAMAS
(The Commonwealth of The Bahamas)

AREA, POPULATION, ETC.—The Bahama Islands are an archipelago lying in the North Atlantic Ocean between 20° 55′–25° 22′ N. Lat; 72° 35′–79° 35′ W. Long. They extend from the coast of Florida on the north-west almost to Haiti on the south-east. The group consists of 700 islands, of which 30 are inhabited and 2,400 cays comprising an area of more than 5,380 sq. miles, (19,935 sq. km.). The population, at the census of 1980 was 237,090. The principal islands include: Abaco, Acklins, Andros, Berry Islands, Bimini, Cat Island, Crooked Island, Eleuthera, Exumas, Grand Bahama, Harbour Island, Inagua, Long Island, Mayaguana, New Providence (on which is located the capital, Nassau), Ragged Island, Rum Cay, San Salvador and Spanish Wells. San Salvador was the first landfall in the New World of Christopher Columbus on October 12, 1492.

The Bahamas were settled by British subjects when the islands were deserted. The ownership of The Bahamas was taken over in 1782 by the Spanish, but the Treaty of Versailles in 1783 restored them to the British.

CAPITAL.—ΨNASSAU. Population (1980 census), 135,437.

FLAG.—Horizontal stripes of aquamarine, gold and aquamarine, with a black equilateral triangle on the hoist.

NATIONAL DAY.—July 10 (Independence Day).

NATIONAL ANTHEM.—March on, Bahamaland.

GOVERNMENT

The Bahamas gained independence on July 10, 1973. The Head of State is H.M. Queen Elizabeth II, represented in the islands by a Governor-General. There is a Senate of 16 members and an elected House of Assembly of 49 members.

Governor-General, His Excellency Sir Gerald Cash, G.C.M.G., G.C.V.O., O.B.E.

Cabinet

Prime Minister and Minister of Finance, Rt. Hon. Sir Lynden Pindling, K.C.M.G.

Foreign Affairs, and Tourism, Hon. Clement T. Maynard.

Attorney General, Minister of Education and Government Leader in House of Assembly, Hon. Paul L. Adderley.

Works and Utilities, Hon. Darrell E. Rolle.

Employment and Immigration, Hon. Alfred T. Maycock.

Transport, and Local Government, Hon. Philip M. Bethel.

Health, Hon. Dr. Norman Gay

Housing and National Insurance, Hon. George W. Mackey.

Agriculture, Trade and Industry, Hon. Ervin Knowles.

Youth, Sports and Community Affairs, Hon. Peter J. Bethell.

President of Court of Appeal, (new appointment awaited).

Chief Justice, Hon. Philip Telford-Georges.

BAHAMAS HIGH COMMISSION
Bahamas House, 10 Chesterfield Street, W1X 8AH
[01–408 4488]

High Commissioner, His Excellency Mr. Richard C. Demeritte (1984).

BRITISH HIGH COMMISSION
Bitco Building, East St.
P.O. Box N7516, Nassau.

High Commissioner, His Excellency Colin Garth Mays (1986).

Deputy High Commissioner, P. H. Johnson (*Head of Chancery*).

ECONOMY

Tourism is the economic mainstay of The Bahamas, employing about two-thirds of the labour force. It provides about two-thirds of Government revenue and about half the country's foreign exchange earnings. The second main industry is international banking and trust business, The Bahamas' absence of any direct taxation and internal stability enabling the country to become one of the world's leading financial centres.

Agricultural production is mainly of fresh vegetables, fruit, meat and dairy products for the domestic market, and crawfish, mostly for export. There are large reserves of aragonite, and reserves of limestone and salt, all of which are being commercially exploited. Freeport is the country's leading industrial centre, with a chemicals and a pharmaceutical plant, an oil transhipment and storage terminal, and port and bunkering facilities. There are also a brewery and a rum distillery on New Providence.

EDUCATION

Education is compulsory between the ages of 5 and 14. More than 62,000 students are enrolled in Ministry of Education and Independent schools in New Providence and the Family Islands.

COMMUNICATIONS

The main ports are Nassau (New Providence), Freeport (Grand Bahama), Matthew Town (Inagua). International air services are operated from Abaco, Bimini, Eleuthera, Exuma, Grand Bahama and New Providence. About 50 smaller airports and landing strips facilitate services between the islands, the services being provided by Bahamasair, the national carrier. There are roads on the larger islands, and roads are under construction on the smaller islands. There are no railways. Wireless and telephone services are in operation to all parts of the world. There are 132 radio-telephone channels among the islands.

FINANCE AND TRADE

	1985	1986p.
Public revenue	B$376·8m	B$380·1m
Expenditure	406·1m	399·7m

p. provisional

Trade with U.K.

	1985	1986
Imports from U.K.	£74,059,000	£95,816,000
Exports to U.K.	70,763,000	10,266,000

The imports are chiefly foodstuffs, manufactured articles, building material, vehicles and machinery, chemicals and petroleum. The chief exports are rum, petroleum and petroleum products, hormones, salt, crawfish and aragonite.

BANGLADESH
(Ghana Praja Tantri Bangladesh)

AREA, POPULATION, CLIMATE, ETC.—The People's Republic of Bangladesh consists of the territory which was formerly East Pakistan (the old province of East Bengal and the Sylhet district of Assam), covering an area of 55,598 sq. miles (143,998 sq. km.) in the region of the Gangetic delta, and has a population (1987 estimate) of just over 100 million.

The country is crossed by a network of navigable rivers, including the eastern arms of the Ganges, the Jamuna (Brahmaputra) and the Meghna, flowing into the Bay of Bengal. The climate is tropical and monsoon; hot and extremely humid during the summer, and mild and dry during the short winter. The rainfall is heavy, varying from 50 inches to 135 inches in different districts and the bulk of it falls during monsoon season from June to September.

CAPITAL.—DHAKA. Population (1983 estimate), 4,023,000.

FLAG.—Red circle on a bottle-green ground.

NATIONAL DAY.—March 26 (Independence Day).

NATIONAL ANTHEM.—Sonar Bangla.

GOVERNMENT

Prior to becoming East Pakistan, the territory had been part of British India. It acceded to Pakistan in October, 1947, which became a Republic on March 23, 1956.

By a proclamation of March 26, 1971, Bangladesh purported to secede from the central government, and a government-in-exile was set up in April in Calcutta. The short war between India and Pakistan, in both the East and the West, and India's overwhelming defeat of the Pakistani Army in the East, brought about a *de facto* secession of the East wing. The Indo-Pakistan war was concluded on December 16, 1971, and Mr. Zulfiqar Ali Bhutto became President of Pakistan on December 20. Sheikh Mujib was sworn in as Prime Minister of Bangladesh on January 12, 1972. Pakistan and Bangladesh accorded one another mutual recognition in Feb. 1974 and established diplomatic relations in Jan. 1976.

From 1975 a non-political administration ran the country under martial law. A Presidential election was held on June 3, 1978, and President Zia was elected by a considerable majority. Martial law was subsequently lifted. Zia was assassinated in May 1981 in an unsuccessful coup, but the military, led by Lt.-Gen. Ershad, took over in March 1982 and and martial law was again imposed. Following elections in May 1986 a civilian Cabinet was appointed. Presidential elections were held on Oct. 15, 1986 and Ershad gained a substantial majority. Martial law was subsequently lifted on Nov. 10 and the 1972 Constitution fully restored.

President, Hossain Mohammed Ershad.

Council of Ministers

Vice-President, Minister for Law and Justice, Judge A. K. M. Nurul Islam.

Prime Minister, Posts and Telecommunications, Mizanur Rahman Chowdhury.

Deputy P.M. and Minister of Industry, Moudud Ahmed.

Deputy P.M. and Minister of Interior, Prof. M. A. Matin.

Relief and Rehabilitation, Maj.-Gen. M. Shamsul Huq.

Commerce, Maj.-Gen. M. A. Munem.

Co-operatives, Shah Moazzem Hossain.

Irrigation, Water Development and Flood Control, Anisul Islam Mahmud.

Fisheries and Livestock, Mirza Ruhul Amin.

Social Welfare and Women's Affairs, Begum Rabeya Bhuiyan.

Energy and Mineral Resources, Anwar Hossain.

Foreign Affairs, Humayun Rasheed Chowdhury.

Health and Family Planning, Salauddin Kader Chowdhury.

Ports and Shipping, Mayeedul Islam.

Land Reform and Administration, Sirajul Hussain Khan.

Agriculture, M. Mahbubuzzaman.

Religious Affairs, Moulana M. A. Mannan.

Works, Sawfiqul Ghani.

Textiles, Sunil Kumar Gupta.

Information, Anwar Zahid.

Finance, M. Sayeeduzzaman.

Planning, Air Vice-Marshal A. K. Khondoker.

Education, Mahbubur Rahman.

Jute, Zafar Imam.

Communications, M. Motiur Rahman.

Labour and Manpower, Anwar Zahid.

Minister without portfolio, Maj.-Gen. Mahmudul Hasan.

BANGLADESH HIGH COMMISSION
28 Queen's Gate, SW7 5JA
[01–584 0081–4/589 4842–4]

High Commissioner, His Excellency Maj.-Gen. K. M. Safiullah (1987).

BRITISH HIGH COMMISSION
Abu Bakr House, P.O. Box 6079, Gulshan
Dhaka–12

High Commissioner, His Excellency Terence George Streeton, C.M.G, M.B.E. (1983).

Deputy High Commissioner, A. F. Blake-Pauley.

British Council Representative, W. G. Harvey, 5 Fuller Road, (P.O. Box 161), Ramna, Dhaka 2.

EDUCATION

Primary education is free but not universal. Most primary schools are under government management. The majority of secondary schools and colleges are privately managed, but many receive government grants. There are six Universities. In 1981 literacy was estimated at 23·8 per cent of the whole of Bangladesh and 26 per cent of the male population.

TRANSPORT AND COMMUNICATIONS

Principal seaports are Chittagong and Mongla. The Bangladesh Shipping Corporation has been set up by the Government to operate the Bangladesh merchant fleet. The principal airports are Dhaka, (Zia International) and Chittagong. The international airline, Bangladesh Biman, serves Europe, the Middle East, South and South-East Asia, and an internal network.

There are about 6,880 miles of roads in Bangladesh; 4,724 miles are metalled. There are 2,798 miles of railway track.

Radio Bangladesh is the main national broadcasting service. A television service was introduced in 1965 and colour transmissions began in 1981.

ECONOMY

Bangladesh is a principal producer of raw jute. Other agricultural products are rice, tea, oil seeds, pulses, and sugar cane. The chief industries are jute, cotton, tea, leather, pharmaceuticals, fertilizer, sugar, fishing (prawns), natural gas and garment manufacture.

Aid

Bangladesh is a major recipient of bilateral and multilateral development aid. The total annual development plan for 1985–86 is budgeted at U.S. $1,366 million, of which U.S. $1,146 million will be financed from external sources as follows:

Project aid	U.S. $714 million
Commodity aid	392 million
Food aid	38 million

Trade with U.K.

	1985	1986
Imports from U.K.	£69,420,000	£48,218,000
Exports to U.K.	35,348,000	34,117,000

BARBADOS

AREA, POPULATION, ETC.—Barbados, the most easterly of the Caribbean islands, is situated in latitude 13° 14′ N. and longitude 59° 37′ W. The island has a total area of 166 sq. miles, (430 sq. km.), the land rising in a series of tablelands marked by terraces to the highest point, Mt. Hillaby (1,116 ft.). It is nearly 21 miles long by 14 miles broad. The climate is equable with annual average temperature 26·6°C. (79·8°F.) and rainfall varying from a yearly average of 75 inches in the high central district to 50 inches in some of the low-lying coastal areas.

POPULATION.—The population of Barbados (1985 U.N. estimate) was 253,000. There are eleven administrative areas (parishes); St. Michael; Christ Church; St. Andrews; St. George; St. James; St. John; St. Joseph; St. Lucy; St. Peter; St. Philip, and St. Thomas.

CAPITAL.—ΨBRIDGETOWN (population, estimated April, 1980, 7,466) in the parish of St. Michael. There are three other towns, Oistins in Christ Church, Holetown in St. James and Speightstown in St. Peter.

FLAG.—Three vertical stripes, dark blue, gold and dark blue, with trident devises on gold stripe.

NATIONAL DAY.—Nov. 30 (Independence Day).

NATIONAL ANTHEM.—In Plenty and in Time of Need.

GOVERNMENT

The first inhabitants of Barbados were Arawak Indians but the island was uninhabited when first settled by the British in 1627. It was a Crown Colony from 1652 until it became an independent state within the Commonwealth on November 30, 1966. The Legislature consists of the Governor-General, a Senate and a House of Assembly. The Senate comprises 21 Senators appointed by the Governor-General, of whom 12 are appointed on the advice of the Prime Minister, 2 on the advice of the Leader of the Opposition and 7 by the Governor-General at his discretion to represent religious, economic or social interests in the Island or such other interests as the Governor-General considers ought to be represented. The House of Assembly comprises 27 members elected every five years by adult suffrage. In 1963 the voting age was reduced to 18. The last General Election

took place on May 28, 1986 and, as a result, seats in the House of Assembly were distributed as follows: Democratic Labour Party 24, Barbados Labour Party 3.

Governor-General, Sir Hugh Springer, K.C.M.G., C.B.E., apptd 1984.

Cabinet

Prime Minister, Minister of Economic Affairs, Education and Culture, Hon. L. Erskine Sandiford.
Deputy P.M., Minister of Transport, Works and Telecommunications, and Leader of the House, Hon. Philip M. Greaves, Q.C.
Attorney General and Minister of Legal Affairs, Hon. Maurice A. King, Q.C.
Agriculture, Food and Fisheries, Hon. Warwick O. Franklyn.
Employment, Labour Relations and Community Development, Hon. N. Keith Simmons.
Finance, Dr. Hon. Richard C. Haynes.
Foreign Affairs and Leader of the Senate, Sen. Hon. Sir James Tudor, K.C.M.G.
Health, Hon. Branford M. Taitt.
Housing and Lands, Hon. Harold A. Blackman.
Tourism and Sport, Hon. Wesley W. Hall.
Minister of State for the Civil Service, Hon. L. V. Harcourt Lewis.
Minister of State in the Ministry of Education and Culture, Hon. Cyril V. Walker.

President of the Senate, Senator Hon. Frank Walcott, O.B.E.
Speaker, House of Assembly, Hon. Lawson Weekes.

BARBADOS HIGH COMMISSION
1 Great Russell Street, WC1B 3NH
[01–631 4975]

High Commissioner, His Excellency Vernon O. Smith (1986).

BRITISH HIGH COMMISSION
Lower Collymore Rock, P.O. Box 676,
Bridgetown

High Commissioner, His Excellency Kevin Francis Xavier Burns, C.M.G. (1986).

JUDICATURE

There is a Supreme Court of Judicature consisting of a High Court and a Court of Appeal. In certain cases a further appeal lies to the Judicial Committee of H.M. Privy Council. The Chief Justice and Puisne Judges are appointed by the Governor-General on the recommendation of the Prime Minister and after consultation with the Leader of the Opposition.
Chief Justice, The Hon. Sir Denys Ambrose Williams, K.B.

EDUCATION

Primary and secondary education is free in Government schools. There are 105 primary schools, 21 Government secondary schools and 15 approved Government secondary schools.

COMMUNICATIONS

Barbados has some 965 miles of roads, of which about 917 miles are asphalted. The Grantley Adams International airport is situated at Seawell, 12 miles from Bridgetown, and frequent scheduled services connect Barbados with the major world air routes. Bridgetown, the only port of entry, has a deep-water harbour with berths for 8 ships, but oil is pumped ashore at Spring Gardens and at an Esso installation on the West Coast. Barbados has a colour television service, three radio broadcasting services, and a wired broadcasting service.

FINANCE

	1987–88*
Current revenue	BDS$698,071,077
Current expenditure	711,636,404
Capital expenditure	176,518,229

* estimated.

ECONOMY

The economy of the island is based on tourism, sugar and light manufacturing. In 1986, 369,770 tourists visited Barbados and 145,335 cruise ship passengers. Chief exports are sugar and its by-products (15·7 per cent of exports in 1986), electrical components (52·1 per cent) and clothing (8·4 per cent).

	1985 BDS$	1986 BDS$
Total imports	1,221·5 m	1,181·0 m
Total exports	707·7 m	552·3 m

Trade with U.K.

	1986
Imports from U.K.	BDS$127,582
Exports to U.K.	42,202

BELIZE

AREA, POPULATION, ETC.—Belize lies on the east coast of Central America, bounded on the north and north-west by Mexico, and on the west and south by Guatemala. The total area (including offshore islands) is about 8,867 sq. miles (22,965 sq. km.), with a length and breadth of 174 miles and 68 miles respectively. The climate is sub-tropical, with a mean annual temperature of 79°F, but is tempered by sea breezes. There are two dry seasons, the main one from March to May and the other (the Maugre season) from August to September. The country is occasionally affected by hurricanes.

The coastal areas are mostly flat and swampy but the country rises gradually towards the interior. The northern and western districts are hilly, and in the south the Maya Mountains and the Cockscombs form the backbone of the country, reaching a height of 3,800 feet at Victoria Peak.

The population is 166,000 (1985 U.N. estimate), of which the main racial groups are Creoles, Mestizos (Maya-Spanish) and Caribs, plus a number of East Indian and Spanish descent. The races are now heavily inter-mixed. The majority of the population is Christian, about 60 per cent Catholic and most of the remainder Protestant.

The early history of Belize is little known, although the numerous ruins in the area indicate that it was heavily populated by the Maya Indians. The first British settlement was established in 1638 but was subject to repeated attacks by the Spanish, who claimed sovereignty over the area, until the decline of Spanish power in the Americas in the 19th century. In 1862 the area was recognised by Britain as a Colony and called British Honduras. On June 1, 1973 the colony was officially renamed Belize, and was granted independence on September 21, 1981. The long-standing territorial dispute with Guatemala, which had delayed independence earlier, remains unresolved despite efforts to reach a settlement.

CAPITAL.—BELMOPAN (estimated population, 1980, 2,935). The largest city and the former capital is Ψ Belize City (population, 1980 census, 39,771). Other towns are ΨCorozal (6,899), San Ignacio (5,616), Dangriga (6,661), Orange Walk (8,439), Punta Gorda (2,396).

FLAG.—Blue ground with red band along top and bottom edges, and in centre a white disc containing the coat of arms surrounded by a green garland.

NATIONAL DAY.—September 21 (Independence Day).

NATIONAL ANTHEM.—Land of the Gods.

GOVERNMENT

The Queen is Head of State, represented in Belize by a Governor-General, who is a citizen of the country, appointed in consultation with the Prime Minister of Belize. There is a National Assembly, comprising a House of Representatives (28 members elected for 5 years) and a Senate (8 members appointed by the Governor-General). Executive power is vested in the Cabinet, which is responsible to the National Assembly.

Governor-General, Her Excellency Dame Minita Elvira Gordon, G.C.M.G.

The Cabinet

Prime Minister and Minister of Finance, Hon. Manuel Esquivel.
Deputy Prime Minister and Minister of Home Affairs, Hon. Curl Thompson.
Commerce, Industry and Tourism, Hon. Eduardo Juan Jr.
Education, Youth and Sports, Hon. Elodio Aragon.
Health, Hon. Israel Alpuche.
Natural Resources, Hon. Charles Wagner.
Foreign Affairs and Economic Development, Hon. Dean Barrow.
Electricity, Transport, and Communications, Hon. Derek Aikman.
Works and Housing, Hon. Hubert Elrington.
Agriculture, Hon. Dean Lindo.
Labour and Social Services, Hon. Philip Goldson.

ECONOMY

About 42 per cent of the population is engaged in agriculture. Corn (maize), rice, red kidney beans, root crops and fruit are the main food crops, although main agricultural exports are sugar, bananas and citrus products. The country is more or less self-sufficient in fresh beef, pork and poultry, but processed meat and dairy products are imported. About 25 per cent of timber production (mostly mahogany) is exported, and there is a large U.S. market for lobster, conch and scale fish. Tourism is also a valuable source of income.

FINANCE

	1986–87	1987–88
Revenue	BZ $107·0 m	BZ $114·2 m
Expenditure	116·0 m	134·6 m
Deficit	9·0 m	20·4 m

The Belize dollar (BZ $) is tied to the U.S. dollar: BZ $2=U.S. $1.

TRADE

	1985	1986
Total imports	BZ $256·3 m	BZ $243·9 m
Total exports	180·0 m	185·2 m

Trade with U.K.

	1985	1986
Imports from U.K.	£8,329,000	£8,232,000
Exports to U.K.	15,050,000	17,954,000

EDUCATION

Education is compulsory from 5 to 14 years of age. In 1985 primary education was provided by 225 schools, most of which are government aided. Enrolment totalled 38,512. Secondary education is provided by 29 secondary and post-secondary institutions with an enrolment of 7,441. Plans are underway for Ferris State College of Michigan, U.S.A., to establish an affiliate university in Belize. The Government also offers scholarships for students to go abroad. There is an extra-mural faculty of the University of the West Indies, with a resident tutor.

COMMUNICATIONS

There is a Government-operated radio service but no official television service in the country. An automatic telephone service covers the whole country; internal services are handled by the Belize Telecommunication Authority and external services by Cable and Wireless Ltd. through the earth satellite system (opened 1978).

The principal airport is at Belize City and various airlines operate international flights to U.S. and other Central American states. The main port is also Belize City, where construction of deep water quays was recently completed. There are 1,865 miles of road, including four main highways, but there is no railway system.

BELIZE HIGH COMMISSION
15 Thayer Street,
WIM 5DL
[01–486 8381]
High Commissioner, His Excellency Sir Edney Cain.

BRITISH HIGH COMMISSION
P.O. Box 91, Belmopan.
High Commissioner, His Excellency John M. Crosby, L.V.O.

Deputy High Commissioner, D. R. F. Flanagan.

BOTSWANA
(The Republic of Botswana)

AREA, POPULATION, ETC.—Botswana (formerly the British Protectorate of Bechuanaland) lies between latitudes 18° and 26° S. and longitudes 20° and 28° W. and is bounded by the Cape and Transvaal Provinces of South Africa on the south and east, by Zimbabwe, the Zambesi and Chobe (Linyanti) Rivers on the north and north-east and by South West Africa on the west. Botswana has a total area of 224,607 sq. miles (581,730 sq. km.). The climate of the country is generally sub-tropical, but varies considerably with latitude and altitude. A plateau at a height of about 4,000 feet divides Botswana into two main topographical regions. To the east of the plateau streams flow into the Marico, Notwani and Limpopo Rivers; to the west lies a flat region comprising the Kgalagadi Desert, the Okavango Swamps and the Northern State Lands area. Large areas of the country support only herds of game. Elephant numbers have been estimated at 15–30,000.

POPULATION.—Botswana has an estimated population (1986) of 1,127,880. The eight principal Botswana tribes are Bakgatla, Bakwena, Bangwaketse, Bamalete, Bamangwato, Barolong, Batawana and Bat-

lokwa. The principal languages in use in Botswana are Setswana and English.

CAPITAL.—GABORONE, estimated population 94,700. Other centres are Francistown (43,600), Lobatse (23,700), and Selebi-Phikwe (41,200).

FLAG.—Horizontal bands of blue, white, blue, with a black stripe on the white band.

NATIONAL DAY.—Sept. 30.

NATIONAL ANTHEM.—Fatshe La Rona.

GOVERNMENT

On September 30, 1966, Bechuanaland became a Republic within the Commonwealth under the name Botswana. The President of Botswana is Head of State and appoints as Vice-President a member of the National Assembly who is his principal assistant and leader of Government business in the National Assembly. The Assembly consists of the President, 34 members elected on a basis of universal adult suffrage, 4 specially elected members, the Attorney-General (non-voting) and the Speaker. There is also a House of Chiefs.

President, His Excellency Dr. Q. K. J. Masire.

Cabinet

Vice President, Minister of Finance and Development Planning, Hon. P. S. Mmusi.
External Affairs, Hon. Dr G. K. T. Chiepe, M.B.E.
Presidential Affairs and Public Administration, Hon. P. H. K. Kedikilwe.
Health, Hon. J. T. Mothibamele.
Agriculture, Hon. D. K. Kwelagobe.
Local Government and Lands, Hon. P. K. Balopi.
Works and Communications, Hon. C. Blackbeard.
Commerce and Industry, Hon. M. P. K. Nwako.
Education, Hon. K. P. Morake.
Mineral Resources and Water Affairs, Hon. A. M. Mogwe, M.B.E.
Home Affairs, Hon. E. M. K. Kgabo.
Assistant Minister, Finance and Development Planning, Hon. I. O. Chilume.
Assistant Ministers, Local Government and Lands, Hon. C. T. Butale; Hon. M. R. Tshipinare.
Assistant Minister, Agriculture, Hon. G. M. Oteng.

BOTSWANA HIGH COMMISSION
6 Stratford Place, WIN 9AE
[01–499 0031]

High Commissioner, His Excellency Mr. G. U. S. Matlhabaphiri (1986).

BRITISH HIGH COMMISSION
Private Bag 0023, Gaborone

High Commissioner, His Excellency Peter Albert Raftery, C.V.O., M.B.E. (1986).
British Council Representative, S. Moss, O.B.E.

ECONOMY

Botswana is predominantly a pastoral country. The national herd is normally around 3 million cattle and 1 million sheep and goats but drought conditions during the past 5 years have reduced the number of cattle to around 2·5 million.

Cattle rearing accounts for about 80 per cent of agricultural output and livestock products, particularly beef, are a major source of foreign exchange earnings. The Government has a number of programmes to improve land use and cattle and crop production, and schemes to provide financial assistance for farmers.

Mineral extraction and processing is now the major source of income for the country following the opening of large mines for diamonds and copper-nickel. Botswana is one of the largest producers of diamonds in the world. Large deposits of coal have been discovered and are being mined on a small scale. Much of the country has yet to be fully prospected. Manufacturing industry is growing and will continue to do so as communications improve but it is still a small sector of the economy.

EDUCATION

There are over 500 primary schools (enrolment 229,116), 44 community junior secondary schools (enrolment 29,138) and 23 government and government-aided senior secondary schools (enrolment 4,583). The government embarked on a massive expansion of secondary education in January 1984 aimed at providing universal access to junior secondary education. There are 5 teacher training establishments (total enrolment 1,540) including one for secondary teachers (enrolment 340), one Polytechnic with 635 students and the University of Botswana with 1,544 undergraduates. Further expansion of the technical education system is planned via a network of vocational training centres.

COMMUNICATIONS

The railway from Cape Town to Zimbabwe passes through eastern Botswana. The main roads in the country are the north–south road, which closely follows the railway, and the road running east–west that links Francistown and Maun. A new road from Nata to Kazungula provides a direct link to Zambia from Botswana. Air services are provided on a scheduled basis between the main towns, linking with services from South Africa, Swaziland, Zambia and Zimbabwe.

FINANCE

	1983–84	1984–85
Actual Revenue (Recurrent and development)	P563 m	P803 m
Actual Expenditure	460 m	615 m

Currency: In August 1976 Botswana introduced its own currency, the *pula*, to replace the South African *rand* formerly in use. It is linked to a basket of currencies. P1 = $US0·521 (June, 1986).

TRADE

Principal exports are diamonds, copper-nickel matte, and beef and beef products.

	1984	1985
Imports	P870 m	P1,142 m
Exports	870 m	1,358.2 m

Trade with U.K.

	1985	1986
Imports from U.K.	£6,800,000	£8,629,000
Exports to U.K.	21,000,000	16,652,000

BRUNEI
(Negara Brunei Darussalam)

Brunei is situated on the north-west coast of the island of Borneo, total area of 2,226 sq. miles (5,765 sq. km.), population (1985 U.N. estimate) 224,000 of whom 72 per cent are of Malay or other indigenous race and 20 per cent Chinese. The country has a humid tropical climate.

CAPITAL.—BANDAR SERI BEGAWAN, with a population of 49,902 (1981).

FLAG.—Yellow, with diagonal bands of white over narrow black band (from top by staff), with red device on diagonal bands.

NATIONAL DAY.—February 23.

NATIONAL ANTHEM.—Ya Allah Lanjutkan Lah Usia Duli Tuanku (Oh God, long live our Majesty the Sultan).

GOVERNMENT

In 1959, the Sultan of Brunei promulgated the first written Constitution, which provides for a Privy Council, a Council of Ministers and a Legislative Council. On January 1, 1984 Brunei resumed full independence. A ministerial system of government was established at independence, the seven Ministers being appointed by the Sultan and responsible to him. The Sultan presides over the Privy Council and the Council of Ministers. The Legislative Council was disbanded in Feb. 1984.

Sultan, H.M. Sir Muda Hassanal Bolkiah Mu'izzadin Waddaulah, G.C.M.G., *acceded* 1967, *crowned* Aug. 1, 1968.

The Government

Prime Minister, Minister of Defence, H.M. The Sultan.
Foreign Affairs, H.R.H. Prince Mohammed.
Finance, H.R.H. Prince Jefri.
Special Adviser to the Sultan and Minister for Home Affairs, Pehin Dato Haji Isa.
Communications, Pehin Dato Abdul Aziz.
Law, Pengiran Bahrin.
Education, Pehin Dato Abdul Rahman.
Religious Affairs, Pehin Dato Mohammed Zain.
Development, Pengiran Dato Dr. Ismail.
Culture, Youth and Sports, Pehin Dato Haji Hussein.
Health, Dato Dr. Johar.

BRUNEI HIGH COMMISSION
49 Cromwell Road, SW7 2ED
[01–581 0521]

High Commissioner, His Excellency Pengiran Setia Raja Pengiran Haji Jaya (1984).

BRITISH HIGH COMMISSION
Hong Kong and Shanghai Bank
Building (3rd floor), Bandar
Seri Begawan.

High Commissioner, His Excellency Roger Westbrook (1986).

British Council Representative, D. Elliott, P.O. Box 3049, Bandar Seri Begawan.

FINANCE

	1985 (forecast)
Revenue	B$4,500 million
Expenditure*	2,600 million

*Including development expenditure.

Currency.—The unit of currency is the *Brunei dollar* of 100 *cents,* which is fully interchangeable with the currency of Singapore.

Trade with U.K.

	1985	1986
Imports from U.K.	£71,496,000	£154,146,000
Exports to U.K.	23,346,000	71,624,000

CYPRUS
(Kypriaki Dimokratia/Kibris Cumhuriyeti)

AREA, CLIMATE AND POPULATION.—Cyprus with
an area of 3,572 sq. miles (9,251 sq. km.), is the third
largest island in the Mediterranean Sea. Its greatest
length is 140 miles and greatest breadth 60 miles,
situated at latitude 35°N. and longitude 33° 30′E. It
is about 40 miles distant from the nearest point of
Asia Minor, 60 miles from Syria and 240 miles from
Port Said.

Cyprus has a Mediterranean climate with a hot
dry summer and a variable warm winter, while the
intermediate seasons are short and transitional.

In 1985 the population (estimate) was 673,100.
There are two major communities, Greek Cypriots
(78 per cent) and Turkish Cypriots (18·2 per cent);
and minorities of Armenians, Maronites and others.

CAPITAL.—NICOSIA, near the centre of the island,
with a population of 164,400 (in the Government
controlled area); the other principal towns are Ψ
Limassol, ΨFamagusta, ΨLarnaca, Paphos and Kyr-
enia.

FLAG.—Gold map of Cyprus on a white ground,
surmounting crossed olive branches (green).

NATIONAL DAY.—October 1 (Independence Day).

NATIONAL ANTHEM.—Ode to Freedom.

GOVERNMENT

Cyprus passed under British administration from
1878. Cyprus was formally annexed to Great Britain
on Nov. 5, 1914, on the outbreak of war with Turkey.
From 1925 to 1960 it was a Crown Colony administered by a Governor, assisted by an Executive Council
and also for a time by a partly-elected Legislative
Council. Following the launching in April 1955 of an
armed campaign by EOKA in support of union with
Greece, a state of emergency was declared in November, 1955, which lasted for four years. After a meeting
at Zürich between the Prime Ministers of Greece and
Turkey, a conference was held in London and an
agreement was signed on February 19, 1959, between
the United Kingdom, Greece, Turkey and the Greek
and Turkish Cypriots which provided that Cyprus
would be an independent Republic.

Under the Cyprus Act, 1960, the island became an
independent sovereign republic on August 16, 1960.
The constitution provided for a Greek Cypriot
President and a Turkish Cypriot Vice-President
elected for a five-year term by the Greek and Turkish
communities respectively. The House of Representatives, elected for five years by universal suffrage of
each community separately, was to consist of 35
Greek and 15 Turkish members. The 1960 Constitution proved unworkable in practice and led to
intercommunal troubles. The U.N. Peace Keeping
Force in Cyprus (UNFICYP) was set up in March
1964: its mandate was last renewed on June 13, 1986.

On July 15, 1974, mainland Greek officers of the
Greek Cypriot National Guard launched a *coup d'état*
against President Makarios and installed a former
EOKA member, Nikos Sampson, in his place. Turkey
reserved to itself the right to maintain constitutional
order and the independence and territorial integrity
of the island, invaded Northern Cyprus and occupied
over a third of the island. In Feb. 1975 a "Turkish
Federated State of Cyprus" under Mr. Rauf Denktash
was declared in this area, its constitution being
approved by referendum in July 1975. In Nov. 1983 a
"Declaration of Statehood" was issued which purported to establish the "Turkish Republic of Northern
Cyprus". The declaration was condemned by the
U.N. Security Council and only Turkey has recognized the new "state". In May 1985 a referendum in
the north of Cyprus approved a constitution for the
"Turkish Republic of Northern Cyprus": in June

1985 Mr. Denktash was elected President of the
"state" and a General Election was held.

Since 1974 attempts to reach a settlement have
focused on intercommunal talks under the auspices
of the U.N. The latest talks ended in Jan. 1985
without agreement, but the U.N. Secretary General
has continued his efforts to find a settlement.

A general election was held for the Greek House of
Representatives on Dec. 8, 1985, resulting in the
parties gaining the following number of seats:
Democratic Rally 19; Democratic Party (Centre) 16;
AKEL (Communist) 15; EDEK (Socialist) 6.

President, Spyros Kyprianou, *elected* Feb. 28, 1978,
re-elected, Feb. 13, 1983.

COUNCIL OF MINISTERS

Foreign Affairs, George Iacovou.
Interior, Constantinos Michaelides.
Finance, Christos Mavrellis.
Education, Andreas Christofides.
Justice and Minister to the President, Demetrios
Liveras.
Defence, Elias Eliades.
Communications & Works, Rois Nicolaides.
Health, Christos Pelekanos.
Commerce and Industry, Michalakis Michaelides.
Labour and National Insurance, Andreas Moushiou-
tas.
Agriculture and Natural Resources, Andreas Pana-
solomontos.

CYPRUS HIGH COMMISSION
93 Park Street, W1Y 4ET
[01-499 8272]

High Commissioner, His Excellency Mr. Tasos
Panayides (1979).

BRITISH HIGH COMMISSION
Alexander Pallis Street (P.O. Box 1978)
Nicosia

High Commissioner, His Excellency William John
Antony Wilberforce, C.M.G. (1981).
British Council Representative, C. Mogford, P.O. Box
1995, 3 Museum Street, Nicosia.

ECONOMY

Agriculture still occupies a prime position in the
Cyprus economy but little further growth is expected.
Main products are citrus fruits, grapes and vine
products, potatoes and other vegetables. Manufacturing, construction, distribution and other service
industries are other major employers. Tourism is the
main growth industry with 900,000 long-stay tourists
producing C£256 million in foreign exchange earnings in 1986. Some 4,000 foreign firms and individuals
have registered as "offshore companies" in Cyprus,
which supports Cyprus' claim to be a centre for
Middle East trade.

Britain is still the country's most important
trading partner, taking some 31 per cent of its exports
in 1986 and supplying 13·4 per cent of its imports.
Cyprus is seeking to diversify its export markets and
until recently sold almost half its exports to the
Middle East. However, these traditional markets are
now drying up, and Cyprus is looking more towards
Europe. A Customs Union between Cyprus and the
E.C. was initialled in May 1987.

The trading account continues in deficit and is
offset by invisible earnings, mainly from tourism,
foreign aid and development loans, capital inflows
and income derived from the Sovereign Base Areas
and United Nations personnel.

FINANCE

	1986
Total Revenue	C£401·1 million
Ordinary Expenditure	530·6 million

TRADE

	1985	1986
Imports	C£726·3 m	C£659·1 m
Exports (including re-exports)	290·6 m	260·2 m

Trade with U.K.

	1985	1986
Imports from U.K.	C£103·5 m	C£88·6 m
Exports to U.K.	47·0 m	58·9 m

BRITISH SOVEREIGN AREAS

The United Kingdom retained full sovereignty and jurisdiction over two areas of 99 square miles in all—Akrotiri–Episkopi–Paramali and Dhekelia–Pergamos–Ayios Nicolaos–Xylophagou—and use of roads and other facilities. The British Administrator of these areas is appointed by the Queen and is responsible for the Secretary of State for Defence.

Administrator of the British Sovereign Areas, Air Vice-Marshal Kenneth Hayr.

DOMINICA
(The Commonwealth of Dominica)

AREA, POPULATION, ETC.—Dominica, the loftiest of the Lesser Antilles, lies in the Windward Group, between 15° 20′ and 15° 45′ N. lat. and 61° 13′ and 61° 30′ W. long., 95 miles S. of Antigua. It is about 29 miles long and 15 broad comprising an area of 290 sq. miles (751 sq. km.). The island is of volcanic origin and very mountainous, and the soil is very fertile. The temperature varies, according to the altitude, from 55° to 85°F. The climate is healthy, and during the winter months is very pleasant. The population is 76,000 (1985 U.N. estimate).

CAPITAL.—ΨROSEAU, on the south-west coast, population, 8,346. The other principal town is Portsmouth, population, 2,220.

FLAG.—Green ground with a cross overall of yellow, white and black stripes, and in the centre a red disc charged with a Sisserou parrot in natural colours within a ring of 11 green stars.

NATIONAL DAY.—November 3 (Independence Day).
NATIONAL ANTHEM.—Dominica Day Song.

GOVERNMENT

The island was discovered by Columbus in 1493, when it was a stronghold of the Caribs, who remained virtually the sole inhabitants until the French established settlements in the 18th century. It was captured by the British in 1759 but passed back and forth between France and Britain until 1805, after which British possession was not challenged. From 1871–1939 Dominica was part of the Leeward Islands Colony, then from 1940 the island was a unit of the Windward Islands group. Internal self-government from 1967 was followed on Nov. 3, 1978 by independence as a republic with the name The Commonwealth of Dominica. Executive authority is vested in the President, who is elected by the House of Assembly for not more than two terms of five years. Parliament consists of the President and the House of Assembly (representatives elected by universal adult suffrage) and nine Senators, who may be appointed by the President or elected. Parliament has a life of five years.

President, His Excellency Sir Clarence Seignoret, G.C.B., O.B.E.

Cabinet

Prime Minister and Minister for Finance, Economic Development, and Foreign Affairs, Hon. Mary Eugenia Charles.
Attorney General and Minister for Legal Affairs, and Labour, Hon. Brian Alleyne.
Agriculture, Trade, Industry and Tourism, Hon. Charles Maynard.
Communications and Works, Hon. Alleyne Carbon.
Education and Sports, Hon. Henry George.
Health, Hon. Ronan David.
Community Development, Housing and Social Affairs, Hon. Heskeith Alexander.

DOMINICA HIGH COMMISSION
1, Collingham Gardens, SW5 0HW
[01–370 5194/5]

High Commissioner, His Excellency Mr. Franklin A. Baron (1986).

BRITISH HIGH COMMISSION

High Commissioner, (resides at Bridgetown, Barbados).

FINANCE

	1985–86 revised	1986–87 estimated
Recurrent Revenue	EC$83·6 m	EC$88·2 m
Recurrent Expenditure	81·1 m	91·6 m
Capital Revenue	37·9 m	49·3 m
Capital Expenditure	45·3 m	57·2 m

ECONOMY

Agriculture is the principal occupation, with tropical and citrus fruits the main crops. Products for export are bananas, lime juice, lime oil, bay oil, copra and rum. Forestry and fisheries are being encouraged. The only commercially exploitable mineral is pumice, used chiefly for building purposes. Manufacturing consists largely of the processing of agricultural products.

TRADE

	1985
Imports	EC$149,376,000
Exports	76,766,000

Trade with U.K.

	1985	1986
Imports from U.K.	£10,257,000	£8,780,000
Exports to U.K.	18,110,000	26,612,000

FIJI
(Matanitu Ko Fiti)

AREA, POPULATION, ETC.—Fiji is made up of about 332 islands and over 500 islets (including numerous atolls and reefs) in the South Pacific Ocean, about 1,100 miles north of New Zealand. About 100 islands are permanently inhabited. The gross area of the group, which extends 300 miles from east to west, and 300 north to south, between 15° 45′—21° 10′ S. lat. and 176° E.—178° W. long. is 7,055 sq. miles (18,274 sq. km.). The International Date Line has been diverted to the east of the island group. The largest islands are Viti Levu and Vanua Levu. The main groups of islands are Lomaiviti, Lau and Yasawas. Most of the larger islands are mountainous with sharp peaks and crags, but also have conspicuous areas of flat land and many of the rivers have built extensive deltas. The climate is tropical, without extremes of heat and temperatures rarely exceed 32°C. and seldom fall below 15°C.

The population (1985 U.N. estimate) was 696,000, of which about 44 per cent are indigenous Fijians and about 50 per cent Indians.

CAPITAL.—ᵥSUVA, in the island of Viti Levu. Population (1985) 75,000.

FLAG.—Light blue ground with Union flag in top left quarter and the shield of Fiji in the fly.

NATIONAL DAY.—October 10 (Dominion Day).

NATIONAL ANTHEM.—Hail to Fiji.

GOVERNMENT

Fiji was a British colony from 1874 until October 10, 1970, when it became an independent state and a member of the Commonwealth. Under the Constitution there is a Governor-General appointed by the Queen.

A coalition of the left under Dr. Timoci Bavadra defeated the Alliance Party of Ratu Sir Kamisese Mara in a General Election on April 12, 1987. The new Government, drawing its support mainly from the Indian population, was overthrown in a military coup on May 14 by Lt.-Col. Sitiveni Rabuka. In the wake of the constitutional crisis an Advisory Council of 19 members was set up by the Governor-General as an interim government to consider constitutional reform.

Governor-General, His Excellency Ratu Sir Penaia Ganilau, G.C.M.G., K.C.V.O., K.B.E., D.S.O., E.D.

Advisory Council

Home Affairs and Armed Forces, Col. Sitiveni Rabuka.

Foreign Affairs and Civil Aviation, Ratu Sir Kamisese Mara.

Public Services, William Cruickshank.

Fijian Affairs, Ratu Josua Toganivalu.

Agriculture and Fisheries, Ratu Joshua Cavalevu.

Forestry, Ratu Sir Josaia Tavaiqia.

Co-operatives and Consumer Affairs, Livai Nasilivata.

Finance and Economic Planning, Savenaca Siwatibau.

Health and Social Welfare, Dr. Apenisa Kuruisaqila.

Posts and Telecommunications, Col. Paul Manueli.

Public Works and Road Transport, Villime Gonelevu.

Education, Youth and Sport, Felipe Bole.

Information, Rev. Tomasi Raikivi.

Trade, Industry and Tourism, Mumtaz Ali.

Rural Development, Rehabilitation and Housing, Jone Veisamasama.

Justice and Crown Law Officer, Alipate Qetaki.

(Three members were offered posts but declined them.)

FIJI HIGH COMMISSION
34 Hyde Park Gate, SW7 5BN
[01-584 3661/2]

High Commissioner, His Excellency Mr. Sailosi Wai Kepa (1985).

BRITISH HIGH COMMISSION
Victoria House, 47 Gladstone Road,
P.O. Box 1355, Suva

High Commissioner, His Excellency Roger Arnold Rowlandson Barltrop, C.V.O. (1982).

JUDICIARY

The Constitution guarantees the independence of the judiciary. Judges are appointed by the Governor-General.

Chief Justice of Fiji, Hon. Sir Timoci Tuivaga.

FINANCE

	1983	1984
Public Income	$296,405,000	$337,658,000
Public Expenditure ...	304,100,000	344,407,000

Currency.—Currency is the *Fiji dollar*.

ECONOMY

The economy is primarily agrarian, with about 600,000 acres under cultivation. The principal cash crop is sugar cane, which is the main export, followed by coconuts, ginger and copra. A variety of other fruit, vegetables and root crops are also grown, and self-sufficiency in rice is a major aim. Forestry, fishing and beef production are being encouraged in order to diversify the economy. The processing of agricultural, marine and timber products are the main industries, along with gold mining.

Tourism is also a major factor in the economy, second only to sugar as a money-earner. There were 228,175 visitors in 1985.

TRADE

	1984	1985
Total Imports	$487,105,000	$508,191,000
Total Exports (including Re-exports)	279,418,000	263,887,000

Trade with U.K.

	1986
Imports from U.K.	£8,775,000
Exports to U.K.	66,500,000

The chief imports are foodstuffs, machinery, mineral fuels, chemicals, beverages, tobacco and manufactured articles. Chief exports are sugar, coconut oil, gold, lumber, molasses, ginger and canned fish.

COMMUNICATIONS

Fiji is one of the main aerial crossroads in the Pacific. Air Pacific Ltd. is based at Nausori Airport near Suva and operates scheduled domestic services within the Fiji Islands and from Suva provides services to New Zealand, Australia, Tonga, Western Samoa, Vanuatu, the Solomon Islands, Kiribati, Tuvalu, New Caledonia and American Samoa. Fiji Air Services Ltd. operates charter flights within the Fiji group of islands and South Pacific and provides scheduled services within the Fiji group.

Fiji has three ports of entry, at Suva, Lautoka and Levuka.

THE GAMBIA
(The Republic of the Gambia)

AREA, POPULATION, ETC.—The Gambia takes its name from the Gambia River, which it straddles for over 200 miles inland from the west coast of Africa. It is a narrow strip, surrounded by the Republic of Senegal, except at the coast, lying between 13° 10'–13° 45' N. and 13° 90'–16° 50' W. The area is 4,361 sq. miles (11,295 sq. km.), of which one fifth is the river. The Gambia River basin was part of the region dominated in the 10th–16th centuries by the strong Songhai and Mali kingdoms centred on the upper

Niger. The population comprises mainly Wolof, Mandinka and Fula peoples who originally migrated there from the north and east. Population (1983 Census) was 695,886.

The first recorded Europeans to reach the Gambia River were the Portuguese in 1447. In 1588 Queen Elizabeth I gave the first charter to English merchants to trade along the river. Merchants from France, Courland (now part of Latvia) and the Netherlands also established trading posts there. The English presence was strongly challenged by the French, who were dominant further north up the coast, but in 1783 the Treaty of Versailles acknowledged English rights. In 1816, after the Napoleonic Wars, and in order to enforce abolition of the slave trade, the British stationed a garrison on a low sandy island called Banjul at the river mouth. Renamed Bathurst, this became the capital of a small British-administered colony, initially under the Governor of Sierra Leone. Negotiations with France continued sporadically until 1889 when it was agreed that the British rights along the upper river should extend 10 km on either bank. British administration was extended from the Colony to this Protectorate. The Gambia became independent within the Commonwealth on February 18, 1965, and a Republic on April 24, 1970.

The Gambia's relationship with Senegal has always been an important factor in political and economic policy. Moves towards a closer association were accelerated after an abortive coup in The Gambia in July 1981 was put down with the help of Senegalese troops. In February 1982 the Senegambia Confederation was formally instituted based on certain joint institutions and integration of policies, but each country remains sovereign and independent.

Except during the rainy season from June to October, when it sometimes becomes uncomfortably humid, Banjul's climate is very pleasant. Rainfall is 32–40 inches a year.

CAPITAL.—ΨBANJUL. Population (1983 Census) of island of Banjul was 44,536; and of adjacent Kombo St. Mary district 102,858. Total population of Banjul/Kombo St. Mary, 147,394.

FLAG.—Horizontal stripes of red, blue and green, separated by narrow white stripes.

NATIONAL DAY.—February 18 (Independence Day).

NATIONAL ANTHEM.—For The Gambia, Our Homeland.

GOVERNMENT

The constitution is democratic and Parliamentary, with an executive President elected for five years. The House of Representatives has 35 elected members, 5 elected Chiefs Representatives and up to 8 nominated members plus the Attorney-General (*ex-officio*). The Vice President and other Ministers are appointed by the President. Parliament must be dissolved after five years. The last general elections were held in March 1987. The present state of the parties for elected members is PPP (People's Progressive Party) 31; NCP (National Convention Party) 5.

President and Cabinet

President and Minister of Defence, His Excellency Alhaji Sir Dawda Kairaba Jawara, G.C.M.G.

Vice-President and Minister of Education, Youth, Sports and Culture, Hon. Bakary Bunja Darbo.

Attorney-General and Minister of Justice, Hon. Hassan B. Jallow.

Finance and Trade, Hon. Sheriff Saikouba Sisay.

External Affairs, Hon. Alhaji Omar Baru Sey.

Interior, Hon. Lamin Kiti Jabang.

Agriculture, Hon. Alhaji Saikou S. Sabally.

Local Government and Lands, Hon. Landing Jallow Sonko.

Water Resources, Forestry and Fisheries, Hon. Omar Amadou Jallow.

Health, Environment, Labour and Social Welfare, Hon. Mrs. Louise A. N'Jie.

Works and Commuanications, Hon. Alhaji Muhammadu Cadi Cham.

Economic Planning and Industrial Development, Hon. Mbemba Jatta.

Information and Tourism, Hon. Dr. Lamin Kebba Saho.

Chief Justice, Hon. E. O. Ayoola.

Speaker, Alhaji Hon. M. B. N'Jie.

GAMBIA HIGH COMMISSION
57 Kensington Court, W8 5DG
[01-937 6316–8]

High Commissioner, His Excellency Mr. Samuel J. O. Sarr, M.B.E. (1983).

BRITISH HIGH COMMISSION
48 Atlantic Road, Fajara (P.O. Box 507), Banjul

High Commissioner, His Excellency John Donald Garner, L.V.O., *apptd.* 1984.

COMMUNICATIONS

There is an international airport at Yundum, 17 miles from Banjul, with scheduled services flying to other West African states and to the U.K. Banjul is the main port. Internal communication is by road and river. There is no railway system. There are two broadcasting stations and a U.H.F. telephone service linking Banjul with the principal towns in the provinces. There is no television service.

EDUCATION

There are 24 secondary schools (eight high and 16 technical) with a total enrolment of 15,635 students. Two High Schools provide 'A' level education. Gambia College provides post-secondary courses in education, agriculture, public health and nursing. There are seven vocational training institutions with a total enrolment of 1,400. Higher education and advanced training courses are taken outside The Gambia, currently by over 200 students.

PRODUCTION

Eighty-five per cent of the population depend for their livelihood on agriculture (40 per cent of Gross Domestic Product). The chief product, groundnuts, is also the most important export item, forming over 90 per cent of all domestic exports. Other crops are rice, millet, sorghum, maize and cotton. Fishing and livestock industries are being developed. Thirty per cent of the country's basic food requirements are imported. There are no significant deposits of minerals. Manufactures are limited to groundnut processing, minor metal fabrications, paints, furniture, soap and bottling. Tourism is developing quickly, with 67,000 visitors in 1985–86. The entrepôt trade through The Gambia, re-exporting imported goods to neighbouring countries, is an important element in the national economy.

FINANCE

	1984–85	1985–86
Recurrent Revenue ...	D172,600,000	D218,000,000
Recurrent Expenditure	180,900,000	203,000,000

Over 80 per cent of capital expenditure comes from external aid grants and loans. The Five Year

Development Plan 1981–86 envisaged an annual GDP growth rate of 5·1 per cent or 2·5 per cent per capita (at 1980–81 prices).

Currency.—The unit is the *dalasi* of 100 *butut*.

TRADE

	1983–1984	1984–85
Total imports	D314,300,000	D332,600,000
Total exports	160,500,000	97,500,000

Trade with U.K.

	1985	1986
Imports from U.K.	£11,918,000	£16,707,000
Exports to U.K.	2,823,000	2,273,000

GHANA
(The Republic of Ghana)

AREA AND POPULATION.—Ghana (formerly known as the Gold Coast) is situated on the Gulf of Guinea, between 3° 07′ W. long. and 1° 14′ E. long. (about 334 miles), and extends 441 miles north from Cape Three Points (4° 45′ N.) to 11° 11′ N. It is bounded on the north by Burkina Faso, on the west by the Côte d'Ivoire, on the east by Togo, and on the south by the Atlantic Ocean. Although a tropical country, Ghana is cooler than many countries within similar latitudes.

Ghana has a total area of 92,099 sq. miles (238,537 sq. km.). The population at the Census of 1984 was 12,205,574. A 1985 U.N. estimate gave a figure of 13,588,000. Almost all Ghanaians are Sudanese Negroes, although Hamitic strains are common in Northern Ghana. The official language is English. The principal indigenous language group is Akan, of which Twi and Fanti are the most commonly used. Ga, Ewe and languages of the Mole–Dagbani group are common in certain regions.

CAPITAL.—ΨACCRA. Population of the Greater Accra Region (including Tema) was (1984 Census) 1,420,066. Other towns are Kumasi, Tamale, Sekondi-Takoradi, Cape Coast, Sunyani, Ho, Koforidua, Tarkwa and Winneba.

FLAG.—Equal horizontal bands of red over yellow over green; five-point black star on gold stripe.

NATIONAL DAY.—March 6 (Independence Day).

NATIONAL ANTHEM.—Hail the Name of Ghana.

GOVERNMENT

There is no recorded history of the Gold Coast region before the coming of Europeans in the fifteenth century. The constituent parts of the State came under British administration at various times, the original Gold Coast Colony (the coastal and Southern areas) being first constituted in 1874; Ashanti in 1901; and the Northern Territories Protectorate in 1901. The territory of Trans-Volta-Togoland, part of the former German colony of Togo, was mandated to Britain by the League of Nations after the First World War, and remained under British administration as a United Nations Trusteeship after the Second World War. After a plebiscite in May, 1956, under the auspices of the United Nations, the territory was integrated with the Gold Coast Colony.

The former Gold Coast Colony and associated territories became the independent state of Ghana and a member of the British Commonwealth on March 6, 1957 and adopted a Republican constitution on July 1, 1960. A coup in June 1979 led to the formation of an Armed Forces Revolutionary Council chaired by Flt.-Lt. Jerry Rawlings. Civilian rule was restored in Sept. 1979 but overthrown on Dec. 31,

1981, when another coup brought back into power Flt.-Lt. Rawlings.

Provisional National Defence Council

Chairman, Flt.-Lt. Jerry J. Rawlings.
Acting Vice-Chairman, Justice Daniel Annan.
Members, Mrs. Aanaa Enin; Ebo Tawiah; Alhaji Mahama Iddrisu; P. V. Obeng; Capt. Kojo Tsikata (retd); Maj.-Gen. Arnold Quainoo; Brig W. M. Mensa-Wood.

P.N.D.C. Secretaries

Foreign Affairs, Obed Y. Asamoah.
Internal Affairs, Nii Okaija Adamfio.
Finance and Economic Planning, Dr. Kwesi Botchwey.
Defence, Alhaji Mahama Iddrisu.
Fuel and Power, Ato Ahwoi.
Trade and Tourism, Kofi Djin.
Local Government and Social Welfare, W. H. Yeboah.
Education and Culture, Dr. Mohammed Ben Abdallah.
Youth and Sports, Ato Austin.
Transport and Communications, Yaw Donkor.
Works and Housing, E. Appiah-Korang.
Industries, Science and Technology, Dr. Francis Acquah.
Justice and Attorney-General, G. E. Aikins.
Agriculture, Cdre. Steve Obimpoh.
Information, Kofi Totobi Quakyi.
Lands and Natural Resources, Kwame Peprah.
Roads and Highways, Lt.-Col. Mensah Gbedemah.
Labour and Social Welfare, W. W. Yeboah.
Health, Air Cdre. F. W. K. Klutse (retd).

GHANA HIGH COMMISSION
13 Belgrave Square, SW1 8PR
[01-235 4142]

High Commissioner, His Excellency Dr. J. L. S. Abbey.

BRITISH HIGH COMMISSION
P.O. Box 296, Osu Link, Accra

High Commissioner, His Excellency Arthur Hope Wyatt, C.M.G. (1986).

British Council Representative, A. L. M. Russell, Liberia Road (P.O. Box 771), Accra, and an Office in *Kumasi.*

PRODUCTION, ETC.

Agriculture.—Agriculture forms the basis of Ghana's economy, employing 70 per cent. of the working population. Crops of the Forest Zone include cocoa, which is the largest single source of revenue, rice and a variety of other foodstuff crops grown on mixed-crop farms. Fruits such as avocado pears, oranges and pineapples are grown. Cassava is the most important crop of the Coastal Savannas Zone, of the lower Volta area. Production of pulses such as groundnuts is widespread. Near the Togo border oil palms, yams, maize, cassava, fruit and vegetables are produced. Livestock is raised in the uncultivated areas. The Northern Savanna Zone is Ghana's principal cattle rearing area and other livestock production there is important for home consumption. Corn and millet crops are produced in the far north and maize, yams, rice and groundnut crops in more southerly parts of the Zone.

Attempts are being made to diversify agricultural production, with cash crops produced extensively cultivated for export and to provide raw materials for local industry.

Fisheries.—Fishing is important in coastal areas and in the Volta itself. However production cannot meet demand and there are considerable imports of fish products. About 80 per cent of home supply is obtained from sea fisheries, but production from the Volta Lake and other inland fisheries is increasing.

Mineral Production.—The area within a 60 mile radius of Dunkwa produces 90 per cent of Ghana's mineral exports. Manganese production from Nsuta ranks among the world's highest and gold, industrial diamonds and bauxite are also produced. Some 30,000 persons are employed by the mining companies.

Manufactures.—Examples of the small-scale traditional industries are tailoring, goldsmithing and carpentry. Priority has been given in recent years to the establishment of a number of "Pioneer Industries" including timber products, vehicle and refrigerator assembly, cigarettes, boatbuilding, food processing, cotton textiles, clothing, footwear, printing and other light industries. A modern industrial complex is growing in the Accra-Tema area.

Volta River Project.—From 1966 the Volta Dam at Akosombo has generated hydro-electric power for the processing of bauxite and fed a power transmission network for the Accra-Kumasi-Takoradi area. Electricity is now also sent to Togo and Benin.

COMMUNICATIONS

Accra Airport is an international airport and Ghana Airways Corporation is the national airline. There are also internal airports at Takoradi, Kumasi and Tamale.

There are 20,000 miles of motorable roads, of which 2,335 miles are bitumenized. There are 600 miles of railway, linking Accra and the principal ports of Takoradi and Tema with their hinterlands, and with each other.

Takoradi Harbour consists of seven quay berths—one is leased specially for manganese exports. Tema Harbour has 10 berths for larger ocean going vessels and the largest dry dock on the West African coast. An oil berth has also been built to serve the Ghaip refinery which has been constructed at Tema.

Trade with U.K.

	1985	1986
Imports from U.K.	£116,883,000	£113,218,000
Exports to U.K.	99,410,000	103,480,000

Principal exports are cocoa, timber and gold. Principal imports are road vehicles, manufacturing equipment, petroleum and raw materials.

The currency of Ghana is the *cedi* (¢) of 100 *pesawas*.

GRENADA
(The State of Grenada)

AREA, POPULATION.—Grenada is situated between the parallels of 12° 13'–11° 58' N. lat. and 61° 20'–61° 35' W. long., and is about 80 miles north of Trinidad, 68 miles S.S.W. of St. Vincent, and about 120 miles S.W. of Barbados. The island is about 21 miles in length and 12 miles in breadth, with an area of 133 sq. miles (344 sq. km.). Also included in the territory of Grenada are some of the Grenadines islets, the largest of which is Carriacou, 13 square miles in area. The population was estimated at 112,000 (1985 U.N. estimate). The country is mountainous and very picturesque, and the climate is healthy.

CAPITAL.—ΨST. GEORGE'S (population 7,500) lies on the southwest coast, and possesses a good harbour.

FLAG.—Rectangle formed of yellow triangles top and bottom, and green triangles at side, with yellow five-pointed star on red circle in centre, and a nutmeg in green triangle nearest the fly; all on a red ground with three yellow five-pointed stars at top and bottom.

NATIONAL DAY.—February 7 (Independence Day).

GOVERNMENT

Grenada was discovered by Columbus in 1498, and named Conception. It was originally colonized by the French, and was ceded to Great Britain by the Treaty of Versailles in 1783. It became an Associated State in 1967 and an independent nation on Feb. 7, 1974.

The government of Sir Eric Gairy was overthrown on March 13, 1979 by the New Jewel Movement and a People's Revolutionary Government was set up. Disagreements within the P.R.G. led, in Oct. 1983, to violence and the death of the Prime Minister, whose government was replaced by a Revolutionary Military Council. These events prompted the intervention of Caribbean and U.S. forces. The Governor-General installed an advisory council in Nov. 1983 to act as an interim government until a General Election was held, on Dec. 3, 1984. The New National Party won 14 of the 15 seats in the House of Representatives and, following the dissolution of the advisory council, its leader, Mr. Herbert Blaize, was sworn in as Prime Minister. A phased withdrawal of U.S. forces was completed in June 1985.

Governor-General, Sir Paul Scoon, G.C.M.G., G.C.V.O., O.B.E. *apptd.* 1978.

Cabinet

Prime Minister and Minister of Home Affairs, Security, Energy, Finance, Trade, Planning, Industrial Development and Carriacou and Petit Martinique Affairs, Rt. Hon. Herbert A. Blaize.

Attorney General and Minister of External and Legal Affairs, Agriculture, Tourism, Forestry and Lands, Hon. Benjamin Jones.

Health, Housing, Physical Planning and Women's Affairs, Hon. Daniel Williams.

Education, Culture, Sport and Youth Affairs, Social Services, Labour, Civil Aviation, Local Government, Fisheries and Co-operatives, Hon. George McGuire.

Communications, Works, Public Utilities and Community Development, Hon. Dr. Keith Mitchell.

Ministers of State, Hon. Alleyne Walker (*Works, Communications, Public Utilities and Community Development*); Hon. Felix Alexander (*Education, Social Services, Labour, Sports, Civil Aviation*); Hon. Pauline Andrew (*Legal and External Affairs, Agriculture and Tourism*); Hon. Grace Duncan (*Health, Housing, Women's Affairs and Physical Planning*).

GRENADA HIGH COMMISSION
1 Collingham Gardens, SW5 0HW
[01–373 7808/7800]

High Commissioner, His Excellency Mr. Oswald M. Gibbs, C.M.G. (1984).

BRITISH HIGH COMMISSION
14 Church Street, St. George's.

High Commissioner, (resides at Bridgetown, Barbados).

Resident Representative, G. Roberts (*First Secretary*).

ECONOMY

The economy is principally agrarian, with cocoa, nutmegs and bananas the major crops. Fruit and vegetables are grown and livestock raised for domestic consumption. The fishing industry is being developed. Manufacturing is mostly confined to processing agricultural products.

Tourism has prospered since the opening in 1984 of the Point Salines International Airport. British Airways began regular flights in April 1987. A hotel expansion programme is planned. The number of cruise ships visiting Grenada in 1986–87 was 236.

Total value of imports in 1986 was EC\$225 million. Principal domestic exports for 1986 were cocoa (EC\$10·6m), nutmeg (EC\$26·1m), mace (EC\$5·3m) and fruit (EC\$15·3m).

Trade with U.K.

	1985	1986
Imports from U.K.	£8,820,000	£8,628,000
Exports to U.K.	6,735,000	7,011,000

GUYANA
(The Co-operative Republic of Guyana)

AREA, POPULATION, ETC.—Guyana, the former colony of British Guiana, which includes the Counties of Demerara, Essequibo and Berbice, is situated on the north-east coast of South America, bordering on Venezuela, Brazil and Suriname. It has a total area of 83,000 sq. miles (214,969 sq. km.). The population numbers 790,000 (1985 U.N. estimate). There are three distinct areas. (1) A narrow alluvial coastal belt 10 to 40 miles deep, the eastern part of which is intensively cultivated and contains some 90 per cent of the population. Much of this is below the level of the sea and is drained and irrigated by an intricate system of canals constructed by the Dutch. (2) A mountainous area of dense rain forest behind the coastland, still partly unexplored, which reaches its highest point at *Mount Roraima* (9,000 ft.) on the junction of the Guyana–Brazil–Venezuela borders. (3) The open savannah country of the Rupununi in the south-west where cattle ranching is practised and oil deposits have been discovered.

The entire country is intersected by numerous large rivers, though these are of limited navigational use because of rapids and waterfalls, the most notable of which are the *Kaieteur Fall* on the Potaro River with a sheer drop of 741 ft., the *Horse Shoe Falls* on the Essequibo and the *Marina Fall* on the Ipobe River.

Climate.—The two dry seasons normally last from mid February to end April, and from mid August to end November. In the Aug.–Oct. period it is hot. The mean temperature is 80·3°F., the usual extremes being 70°F. and 90°F. In the interior the mean temperature is higher—82·6°F., its extremes ranging from 66°F. to 103°F. The yearly rainfall is subject to marked variation, its mean on the coast lands averaging about 90 inches with an average of 58 inches on the savannahs.

CAPITAL.—ΨGEORGETOWN. Estimated population, including environs, 185,000. Other towns are: Linden (population 29,000); ΨNew Amsterdam (population 23,000); Corriverton (population 17,000).

FLAG.—Red triangle with black border, pointing from hoist to fly, on a yellow triangle with white border, all on a green field.

NATIONAL DAYS.—May 26 (Independence Day); February 23 (Republic Day).

NATIONAL ANTHEM.—"Dear Land of Guyana".

GOVERNMENT

Guyana became independent on May 26, 1966, with a Governor-General appointed by the Queen. It became a Co-operative Republic on Feb. 23, 1970. Under the Independence Constitution the Prime Minister and Cabinet were responsible to a National Assembly elected by secret ballot every 5 years. The last election under this Constitution was in 1973 and the term of that Assembly was later extended to October 1980.

A new Constitution was passed into law in February 1980 and promulgated in October 1980. It provides for an Executive President, a National Assembly of 65 members, and also for a National Congress of Local Democratic Organs responsible for local government. The Supreme Congress of the People consists of all members of these two assemblies.

The electoral system is a Proportional Representation or "single list" system, each voter casting his vote for a party list of candidates. The voting age is 18.

Executive President, H. Desmond Hoyte, *took office* Aug. 1985, *sworn in* Dec. 12, 1985 for five-year term.

Cabinet

Executive President (with responsibility for Home Affairs, Co-operatives, Regional Development), H. D. Hoyte.
First Vice President and Prime Minister, Hamilton Green.
Vice President, First Deputy P.M. and Attorney General, Dr. Mohamad Shahabuddeen.
Vice President (National Development) and Deputy P.M., Ranji Chandisingh.
Vice President (Education and Social Development) and Deputy P.M., Mrs. Viola Burnham.
Deputy P.M. (Public Utilities), Robert H. O. Corbin.
Deputy P.M. (Planning and Development), William H. Parris.

SENIOR MINISTERS

Foreign Affairs, Rashleigh Jackson.
Finance, Carl Greenidge.
Labour, Seeram Prashad.
Trade and Tourism, Winston Murray.

GUYANA HIGH COMMISSION
3 Palace Court, Bayswater Road, W2 4LP
[01-229 7684]

High Commissioner, His Excellency Mr. Cecil S. Pilgrim.

BRITISH HIGH COMMISSION
44 Main Street (P.O. Box 10849),
Georgetown

High Commissioner, His Excellency David Purvis Small, M.B.E. (1987) (also Ambassador to Suriname).

JUDICATURE

The Supreme Court of Judicature consists of a Court of Appeal and a High Court. There are also Courts of Summary Jurisdiction. The Court of Appeal consists of the Chancellor as President, the Chief Justice and such number of Justices of Appeal as may be prescribed by Parliament.

The High Court consists of the Chief Justice, as President, and nine Puisne Judges. It is a court with unlimited jurisdiction in civil matters and exercises exclusive jurisdiction in probate, divorce and admiralty, and certain other matters.
Chancellor, K. S. Massiah.
Chief Justice, K. M. George.

PRODUCTION, ETC.

The economy is based almost entirely on the main export items of sugar, rice, bauxite and alumina. Diamonds and gold are also mined, timber and rum are produced and there is some cattle ranching. The fishing industry is being expanded. Industry is fairly small-scale.

COMMUNICATIONS

Georgetown and New Amsterdam are the principal ports, though bauxite ships also sail to Linden, on the

R. Demerara, and Everton, on the R. Berbice. There are no public railways and the few roads are confined mainly to the coastal areas. Air transport is the easiest form of communication between the coast and the interior. There is a state-owned radio broadcasting station which operates two channels; there is no television service.

EDUCATION

The Government assumed total control of the education system in September 1976 and made education free from nursery to university level. The Government trains teachers for primary and secondary schools at its own institutions. In 1982 there were 368 nursery schools with 29,958 pupils, 423 primary schools with 130,003 pupils, and 414 secondary schools with 73,762 students.

Approximately 1,800 students were enrolled at the University of Guyana in degree programmes and certificate and diploma courses in 1986.

There are several technical and vocational institutions, as well as some 30 adult education schools (with an enrolment of 13,500). There are also a number of technical and vocational institutions not under the aegis of the Ministry of Education.

Trade with U.K.

	1985	1986
Imports from U.K.	£18,406,000	£13,737,000
Exports to U.K.	52,377,000	55,535,000

INDIA
(The Republic of India)

AREA AND POPULATION.—The Republic of India has an area of 1,269,346 sq. miles (3,287,590 sq. km.), composed of three well-defined regions: the mountain range of the Himalayas; the Indo–Gangetic plain; and the Southern Peninsula. The main mountain ranges are the Himalayas in the north (over 29,000 feet) and the Western and Eastern Ghats (over 8,000 feet). Major rivers include the Ganges, Indus, Krishna, Godavari and Mahanadi.

There are four seasons: the cold season (Dec.–March); the hot season (April–May); the rainy season (June–Sept.); and the season of the retreating S.W. monsoon (Oct.–Nov.). Temperatures vary over the whole country, between averages of about 50° F and 92° F, reaching over 100° F in some parts during the hot season. There are similar variations in rainfall, from only a few inches a year falling in the western Thar Desert to over 400 inches in Meghalaya.

India is the second most populous country in the world. The population at the 1981 Census was 685,184,692, of which slightly more than 20 per cent was urban. A 1985 U.N. estimate gave a figure of 750,900,000. The majority of the population are Hindu (82 per cent), the rest being Muslim (11 per cent), Christian (2·5 per cent), Sikh (1·8 per cent), Buddhist (0·7 per cent) and Jain (0·5 per cent). The official languages are Hindi in the Devanagari script and English, though 14 regional languages also are recognized for adoption as official State languages.

HISTORY.—The Indus civilization was fully developed by c. 2,500 B.C. but collapsed c. 1,750 B.C., subsequently being replaced by an Aryan civilization spread from the west. The first Arabic invasions of the north west began in the seventh century and Moslem, Hindu and Buddhist states developed until the establishment of the Mogul dynasty in 1526. The British East India Company established settlements throughout the 17th century; clashes with the French and native princes led to the British government taking control of the Company in 1784. The separate dominions of India and Pakistan became independent within the Commonwealth in 1947 and India became a Republic in 1950.

FLAG.—The National Flag is a horizontal tricolour with bands of deep saffron, white and dark green in equal proportions. In the centre of the white band appears an Asoka wheel in navy blue.

CAPITAL.—DELHI (population in 1981 was 6,220,000). Populations of other principal cities (1981 figures) were ΨCalcutta, 9,166,000; ΨBombay (Mumbai), 8,202,000; ΨMadras, 4,277,000; Bangalore, 2,914,000; Hyderabad, 2,566,000; Ahmedabad, 2,124,000; Kanpur, 1,685,000; Pune, 1,685,000; Lucknow, 1,007,000.

NATIONAL DAY.—January 26 (Republic Day).

NATIONAL ANTHEM.—Jana-gana-mana.

STATES AND TERRITORIES OF THE UNION

There are 25 States and seven Union Territories. Each State is governed by a Governor appointed by the President who holds office for five years, and a Council of Ministers. All States have a Legislative Assembly, and some have also a Legislative Council, elected directly by adult suffrage for a maximum period of five years. The judges of the High Court of a State are appointed by the President.

The Union Territories are administered, except where otherwise provided by Parliament, by the President acting through an Administrator or Lieutenant Governor, or other authority appointed by him.

GOVERNMENT

The Constitution of India came into force in 1950. Executive power is vested in the President, who is elected for a five year term by an electoral college consisting of the elected members of the Union and State Legislatures. He appoints the Prime Minister and, on the latter's advice, the Ministers, and can dismiss them. The Council of Ministers is collectively responsible to the *Lok Sabha* (Lower House). The Vice President is *ex-officio* chairman of the *Rajya Sabha* (Upper House).

Legislative power rests with the President, the *Rajya Sabha* (which has up to 250 members) and the *Lok Sabha* (which has up to 544 members). Twelve members of the *Rajya Sabha* are nominated by the President, the rest are indirectly elected representatives of the State and Union Territories. They hold office for six years. The 525 members of the *Lok Sabha* representing the States are directly elected by universal adult franchise, and 17 representatives of the Union Territories are chosen, for a maximum term of five years. Subject to the provisons of the Constitution, the Union Parliament can make laws for the whole of India and the State legislatures for their respective units.

The Supreme Court consists of the Chief Justice and not more than 17 other judges, appointed by the President. It is the highest court in respect of all constitutional matters and the final Court of Appeal.

President of the Republic of India, Ramaswami Venkataraman, *elected* July 16, 1987.
Vice-President, Shankar Dayal Sharma.

Cabinet

Prime Minister (also head of Ministries of Foreign Affairs; Personnel; Administrative Reforms; Planning; Science & Technology; Atomic Energy; Electronics; Ocean Development; Space; Water Resources), Rajiv Gandhi.
Urban Development and Transport, Mrs. Mohsina Kidwai.
Home Affairs, Buta Singh.

	Area (sq. km.)	Population (1981 Census)	State Territory Capital	Governor
STATES				
Andhra Pradesh	275,100p	53,549,673	Hyderabad	Miss K. Joshi
Arunachal Pradesh	83,700p	631,839	Itanagar	B. N. Singh
Assam	78,400	19,896,843†	Dispur	B. N. Singh
Bihar	173,900p	69,914,734	Patna	P. Venkatasubbiah
Goa	3,701	1,000,000†	Panaji	Dr. G. Singh
Gujurat	196,000p	34,085,799	Gandhinagar	R. K. Trivedi
Haryana	44,200p	12,922,618	Chandigarh	S. M. H. Burney
Himachal Pradesh	55,700	4,280,818	Shimla	Vice-Adm. (retd) R. K. S. Ghandi
Jammu and Kashmir*	222,200p	5,987,389	Srinagar/ Jammu	Jag Mohan
Karnataka	191,800	37,135,714	Bangalore	A. N. Banerjee
Kerala	38,900p	25,453,680	Trivandrum	P. Ramachandran
Madhya Pradesh	443,500p	52,178,844	Bhopal	K. M. Chandy
Maharashtra	307,700p	62,784,171	Bombay (Mumbai)	S. D. Sharma
Manipur	22,300	1,420,953	Imphal	Gen. K. V. Krishna Rao
Meghalaya	22,400p	1,335,819	Shillong	B. N. Singh
Mizoram	21,100	493,757	Aizawl	H. Saikia
Nagaland	16,600	774,930	Kohima	Gen. K. V. Krishna Rao
Orissa	155,700	26,370,271	Bhubaneswar	B. N. Pande
Punjab	50,400	16,788,915	Chandigarh	S. S. Ray
Rajasthan	342,200	34,261,862	Jaipur	Vasantrao Patil
Sikkim	7,100	316,385	Gangtok	T. V. Rajeshwar
Tamil Nadu	130,100p	48,408,077	Madras	S. L. Khurana
Tripura	10,500	2,053,058	Agartala	Gen. K. V. Krishna Rao
Uttar Pradesh	294,400p	110,862,013	Lucknow	M. Usman Arif
West Bengal	88,800p	54,580,647	Calcutta	S. Nurul Hasan
UNION TERRITORIES				*Lt. Governor*
Andaman and Nicobar Is.	8,200	188,741	Port Blair	Lt.-Gen. T. S. Oberoi
Chandigarh	100	451,610		S. S. Ray‡
Dadra and Nagar Haveli	500	103,676	Silvassa	Dr. Gopal Singh‡
Daman and Diu	112	51,602†		P. P. Srivastava
Delhi	1,500	6,220,406		A.V.M. (retd) H. Lal Kapur
Lakshadweep	30	40,249	Kavaratti	J. Sagar‡
Pondicherry	500	604,471		T. P. Tewary

p provisional figure   † estimated figure   ‡ Administrator

* Jammu and Kashmir is an area disputed between India, Pakistan and China, all three controlling a part of the territory. The area figure includes those parts occupied by Pakistan and China, which are claimed by India, but the population figure excludes the population of these areas, where the census was not taken. The state's capital is at Srinagar in winter and Jammu in summer.

Parliamentary Affairs (and additional charge of Food and Civil Supplies), H. K. L. Bhagat.
Steel and Mines, M. L. Fotedar.
Health and Family Welfare, and Human Resources Development, P. V. Narasimha Rao.
Power, Puroshottam Vasant Sathe.
Finance and Commerce, Narayan Dutt Tiwari.
Agriculture and Rural Development, Gurdial Singh Dhillon.
Tourism, Mufti Mohammed Syed.
Communications, Arjun Singh.
Defence, K. C. Pant.
Environment and Forests, Bhajan Lal.
Industry, J. Vengal Rao.
Petroleum and Natural Gas, Brahm Dutt.
In addition to the members of the Council of Ministers there are six Ministers of State with independent charge, 32 Ministers of State and three Deputy Ministers in the Government.

INDIAN HIGH COMMISSION
India House, Aldwych, WC2B 4NA
[01–836 8484]

High Commissioner, His Excellency Dr. P. C. Alexander (1985).
Deputy High Commissioner, S. S. Haider.

BRITISH HIGH COMMISSION
Chanakyapuri, New Delhi, 21, 1100–21.

High Commissioner, His Excellency Sir David Goodall, K.C.M.G. (1987).
British Council Representative in India, J. G. Hanson, C.B.E., AIFACS Building, Rafi Marg, New Delhi 110 001. Offices also at *Bombay, Madras* and *Calcutta*. There are British Council libraries at these four centres and British libraries at *Ahmedabad, Bangalore, Bhopal, Hyderabad, Lucknow, Patna, Pune, Ranchi* and *Trivandrum*.

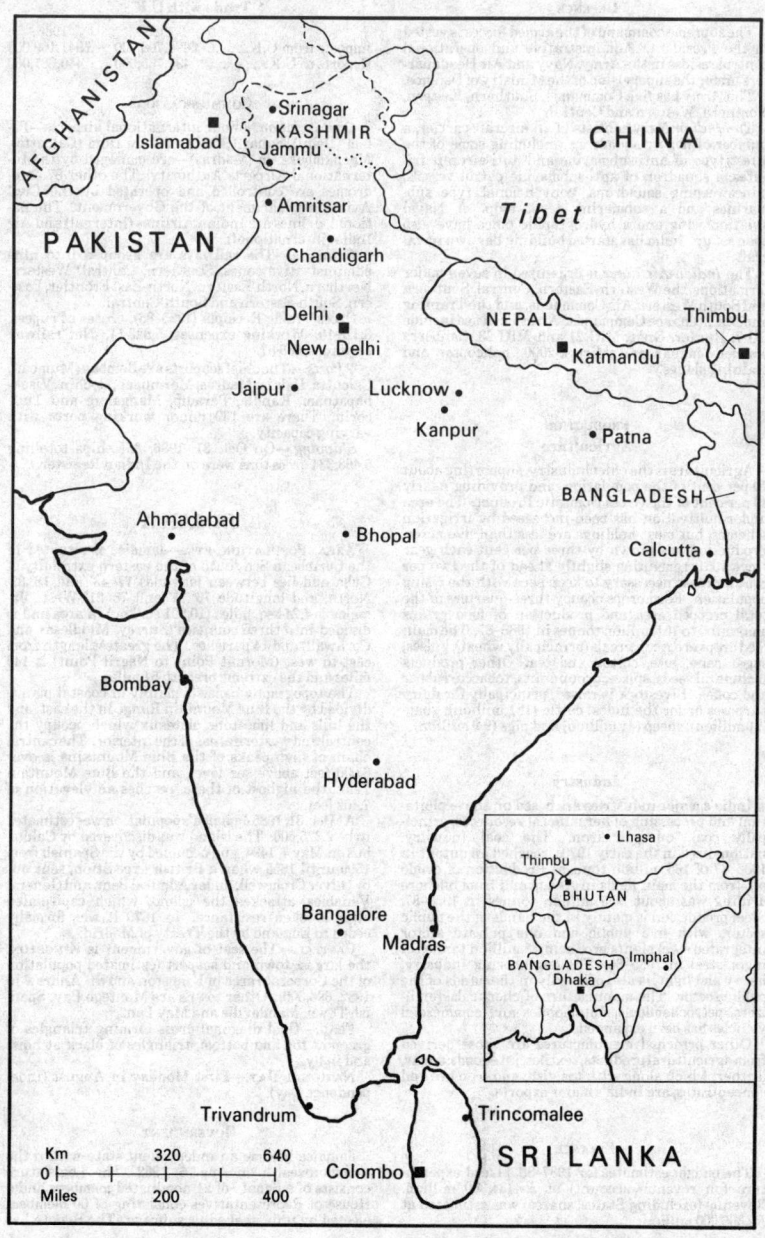

DEFENCE

The supreme command of the armed forces is vested in the President. Administrative and operational control resides in the Army, Navy and Air Headquarters under the supervision of the Ministry of Defence.

The *Army* has five Commands, Southern, Eastern, Northern, Western and Central.

The *Indian Navy* consists of an aircraft-carrier, a number of frigate squadrons, including some of the latest type of anti-submarine and anti-aircraft frigates, a squadron of anti-submarine patrol vessels, minesweeping squadrons, conventional type submarines and a submarine depot ship. A Naval aviation wing and a hydrographic office have also been set up. India has started building her own naval craft.

The *Indian Air Force* is organized in seven major formations, the Western, Eastern, Central, Southern and South Western Air Commands, and the Training and Maintenance Commands. Aircraft in use include SU-7, Hunter, Gnat, MiG 21 and MiG 23, Canberra bomber, Jaguar and Mirage-2000, helicopter and training planes.

PRODUCTION
Agriculture

Agriculture is the chief industry, supporting about 70 per cent of the population, and providing nearly 40 per cent of the Gross Domestic Product. The area under cultivation has been increased by irrigation schemes, but most holdings are less than five acres. Production has grown by three per cent each year since 1951, remaining slightly ahead of the two per cent increase necessary to keep pace with the rising population. Food crops occupy three-quarters of the total cropped area and production of food grains amounted to 151 million tonnes in 1986–87. The main food crops are rice, cereals (principally wheat), pulses, sugar cane, jute, cotton and tea. Other products include oil seeds, spices, groundnuts, tobacco, rubber and coffee. Livestock is raised, principally for dairy purposes or for the hides: cattle (181 million), goats (71 million), sheep (41 million) and pigs (9·9 million).

Industry

India's major industries are based on the exploitation and processing of her mineral resources, principally coal, oil and iron. The coal industry, nationalized in the early 1970s, reached an output in 1986–87 of 166 million tonnes. Production of crude oil, from the main fields in Assam and from offshore drilling was about 30·5 million tonnes in 1986–87. Steel production is mainly in the hands of the public sector, with five public and one private sector integrated steel plants producing 7 million tonnes of ingot steel in 1985–86. The engineering industry, heavy and light, is also primarily in the hands of the public sector. The manufacture of chemicals, fertilizers, petrochemicals, automobiles and commercial vehicles has been expanded.

Other principal manufactures are those derived from agricultural products, textiles, jute goods, sugar, leather, which along with tea, fish, and iron ore and concentrates, are India's major exports.

FINANCE

The budget estimates for 1987–88, placed expenditure (on revenue account) at *Rs.*434,300 million. Revenue (excluding States' shares) was estimated at *Rs.*366,900 million.

Trade with U.K.

	1985	1986
Imports from U.K.	£894,708,000	£941,169,000
Exports to U.K.	431,785,000	440,681,000

COMMUNICATIONS

Civil Aviation.—Four international airports—Palam (Delhi), Sahar (Bombay), Dum Dum (Calcutta), Meenambakkam (Madras)—are managed by the International Airports Authority. The other 87 aerodromes are controlled and operated by the Civil Aviation Department of the Government. The national airlines are Indian Airlines (internal) and Air India (international).

Railways.—The railways are grouped into nine administrative zones, Southern, Central, Western, Northern, North-Eastern, North-East Frontier, Eastern, South-Eastern and South-Central.

Gross Traffic Receipts (1985–86), crores of rupees, 6,428·10. Working expenses, 5,823·14. Net railway revenues, 685·87.

Ψ *Ports.*—The chief seaports are Bombay (Mumbai), Calcutta, Haldia, Madras, Mormugao, Cochin, Visakhapatnam, Kandla, Paradip, Mangalore and Tuticorin. There are 139 minor working ports with varying capacity.

Shipping.—On Oct. 31, 1986, 361 ships totalling 5,463,334 gross tons were on the Indian Register.

JAMAICA

AREA, POPULATION, ETC.—Jamaica is situated in the Caribbean Sea south of the eastern extremity of Cuba and lies between latitudes 17° 43′ and 18° 32′ North, and longitude 76° 11′ and 78° 21′ West. Jamaica is 4,244 sq. miles (10,991 sq. km.) in area and is divided into three counties (Surrey, Middlesex and Cornwall) and 14 parishes. The greatest length from east to west (Morant Point to Negril Point) is 146 miles and the extreme breadth 51 miles.

The topography consists mainly of coastal plains, divided by the Blue Mountain Range in the east, and the hills and limestone plateaux which occupy the central and western areas of the interior. The central chain of high peaks of the Blue Mountains is over 6,000 feet above sea level, and the Blue Mountain Peak, the highest of these, reaches an elevation of 7,402 feet.

At Dec. 31, 1985 Jamaica's population was estimated to be 2,325,500. The island was discovered by Columbus on May 4, 1494, and occupied by the Spanish from 1509 until 1655 when a British expedition, sent out by Oliver Cromwell, under Admiral Penn and General Venables, attacked the island, which capitulated after a token resistance. In 1670 it was formally ceded to England by the Treaty of Madrid.

CAPITAL.—The seat of government is KINGSTON, the largest town and seaport (estimated population of the Corporate area of Kingston and St. Andrew in 1982, 696,300). Other towns are Montego Bay, Spanish Town, Mandeville and May Pen.

FLAG.—Gold diagonal cross forming triangles of green at top and bottom, triangles of black at hoist and in fly.

NATIONAL DAY.—First Monday in August (Independence Day).

GOVERNMENT

Jamaica became an independent state within the Commonwealth on Aug. 6, 1962. The Legislature consists of a Senate of 21 nominated members and a House of Representatives consisting of 60 members elected by universal adult suffrage. The Senate has no power to delay money bills for longer than one month or other bills for longer than seven months against the wishes of the House of Representatives. The Constitution provides for a Leader of the Opposition.

At the General Election of Dec. 15, 1983, the Jamaica Labour Party won all 60 seats after the People's National Party decided not to contest the election.

Governor-General, His Excellency Sir Florizel Glasspole, G.C.M.G., G.C.V.O.

Cabinet

Prime Minister and Minister of Finance and Planning, Rt. Hon. E. Seaga, P.C., M.P.
Deputy Prime Minister, Minister of Foreign Affairs, Trade and Industry, Rt. Hon. H. Shearer.
Construction and Electoral Affairs, Hon. B. Golding.
Agriculture, Hon. Dr. P. Broderick.
Justice and Attorney General, Senator The Hon. O. Harding.
National Security, Hon. E. Anderson.
Local Government, Hon. N. B. Lewis.
Labour, Hon. J. A. G. Smith.
Public Utilities and Transport, Hon. P. Charles.
Education, Hon. Dr. N. Gallimore.
Public Service, Hon. C. Stone.
Youth and Community Development, Hon. E. C. Bartlett.
Mining, Energy and Tourism, Senator Hon. H. Hart.
Social Security and Consumer Affairs, Hon. Dr. Mavis Gilmour.
Ministers of State, Hon. Enid Bennett (*Local Government*); Hon. H. Brown (*Tourism*); Rt. Hon. R. Marsh (*Construction*); Hon. E. Bartlett (*Youth and Community Development*); Hon. K. Samuda (*Industry and Commerce*); Hon. B. Lee, Hon. A. Johnson (*Agriculture*); Hon. M. Henry (*Office of Prime Minister (Information)*).

JAMAICAN HIGH COMMISSION
50 St. James's Street, SW1A 1JS
[01–499 8600]

High Commissioner, His Excellency Mr. H. S. Walker.

BRITISH HIGH COMMISSION
P.O. Box 575, Trafalgar Road, Kingston 10.

High Commissioner, His Excellency Alan Jeffrey Payne (1987).

JUDICATURE

Chief Justice and Keeper of Records, Hon. E. Zacca.
Judges of the Court of Appeal, Hon. I. D. Rowe (*President*); Hons. H. D. Carberry; J. S. Kerr; B. H. Carey; R. O. C. White; M. L. Wright; J. Campbell; D. Bingham.

COMMUNICATIONS

There are several excellent harbours, Kingston being the principal port. The island has 2,944 miles of main roads and over 7,000 miles of subsidiary roads. There are about 204 miles of railway. Telegraph stations and post offices are established in every town and in very many villages.

There are two international airports capable of handling the largest civil jet aircraft, the Norman Manley International Airport on the south coast serving Kingston, and Sangster Airport on the north coast serving the major tourist areas. In addition there are licensed aerodromes at Port Antonio, Ocho Rios, Mandeville and Negril. There are 16 privately owned, seven public and two military airstrips.

Air Jamaica, the national airline, operates international services; Trans-Jamaica Airlines operates scheduled internal services.

PRODUCTION

Agriculture.—Most of the staple products of tropical climates are grown; sugar, bananas, pimento, coffee and citrus fruit. Some of the sugar is used to produce rum and molasses. Main products exported in 1986 were sugar (*US*$62·2 million), bananas (*US*$9·2 million), citrus fruit and citrus products (*US*$6·1 million).

Industry.—Jamaica is the fourth largest producer of bauxite in the world; output for 1985 was 5,975,000 tonnes of which 1,513,000 tonnes were processed into alumina before being exported. In 1986 exports of bauxite and alumina were valued at US$295·54 million. Cement is manufactured locally, the output being 232,800 long tons in 1985.

In the last decade, manufacturing has grown from the processing of a few agricultural products into the production of a whole range of commodities such as textiles, clothing, footwear, and construction materials. Jamaica is a popular tourist resort, attracting visitors mainly from the U.S.A. In 1985 the total number of visitor arrivals was 846,716, and expenditure was estimated at US$406·8 million.

Currency.—Jamaican Dollar (J$). June 1987 £1 = J$8·85; US$1 = J$5·46.

FINANCE

	1985–86*	1986–87**
Revenue	J$3,078·4m	J$3,942·9m
Expenditure	3,830·9m	4,688·5m
*provisional	**estimates	

National External Debt at Dec. 1985 US$1,841·3 million.

TRADE

	1985	1986
Total imports	J$6,146·6m	J$5,322·2m
Total exports	2,958·8m	3,089·2m

Trade with U.K.

	1985	1986
Imports from U.K.	£44,290,000	£43,380,000
Exports to U.K.	89,684,000	87,420,000

KENYA
(Jamhuri ya Kenya)

AREA, POPULATION, ETC.—Kenya is bisected by the equator and extends approximately from latitude 4° N. to latitude 4° S. and from longitude 34° E. to 41° E. From the coast of the Indian Ocean in the east, the borders of Kenya are with Somalia in the east and Ethiopia and Sudan in the north and north-west. To the west lie Uganda and Lake Victoria. On the south is Tanzania. The total area is 224,961 sq. miles (582,646 sq. km.), including 5,171 square miles of water. The country is divided into 7 Provinces (Nyanza, Rift Valley, Central Coast, Western, Eastern and North-Eastern). The population is 20,333,000 (1985 U.N. estimate). The main tribal groups are the Kikuyu, Luhya, Luo, Kamba, Kalenjin and Masai. The official languages are Swahili, which is generally understood throughout Kenya, and English: numerous indigenous languages are also spoken.

CAPITAL.—NAIROBI, population 1,103,554 (1984 estimate).

FLAG.—Three equal horizontal bands of black over red over green; red and white spears and shield device in centre.

NATIONAL DAY.—December 12 (Independence Day).

NATIONAL ANTHEM.—Kenya, Land of the Lion.

GOVERNMENT

Kenya became an independent state and a member of the British Commonwealth on December 12, 1963, after six months of internal self-government. Kenya became a Republic on Dec. 12, 1964. In 1982 the Government introduced amendments to the constitution and election law, making the country a one-party (K.A.N.U.) state. There is a uni-cameral National Assembly of 171 members.

President, Hon. Daniel T. arap Moi, *took office*, Oct. 14, 1978.

Cabinet

The President.

Vice-President and Minister of Home Affairs, Hon. Mwai Kibaki.

Finance and Planning, Hon. Prof. George Saitoti.

Co-operative Development, Hon. Maina Wanjigi.

Agriculture, Hon. Elijah Mwangale.

Livestock, Hon. Paul. J. Ngei.

Culture and Social Services, Hon. Henry Kosgey.

Information and Broadcasting, Hon. Katana Ngala.

Foreign Affairs, Hon. Dr. Zacharia Onyonka.

Lands and Settlements, Hon. P. C. J. O. Nyakiamo.

Water Development, Hon. Kyale Mwendwa.

Local Government, Hon. Moses Mudavadi.

Education, Hon. Oloo Aringo.

Tourism and Wildlife, Hon. George Muhoho.

Energy and Regional Development, Hon. Nicholas Biwott.

Commerce, Hon. Prof. Jonathan K. Ng'eno.

Planning and National Development, Hon. Andrew Omanga.

Health, Hon. Kennetah Matiba.

Works, Housing and Physical Planning, Hon. Eliud Mwamunga.

Labour, Hon. Peter Okondo.

Industry, Hon. Dr. Robert Ouko.

Transport and Communications, Hon. Arthur Magugu.

Research, Science and Technology, Hon. William Odongo Omamo.

Environment and Natural Resources, Hon. Jeremiah Nyagah.

Supplies and Marketing, Hon. Laban Kitele.

Ministers of State in the Office of the President, Hon. Justus ole Tipis; Hon. Jackson Angaine; Hon. Hussein Maalim Mohamed.

Attorney-General, Hon. Matthew Guv Muli.

KENYA HIGH COMMISSION IN LONDON
45 Portland Place, W1N 4AS
[01–636 2371/5]

High Commissioner, Her Excellency Dr. Sally Jemng-'Etich Kosgei (1987).

BRITISH HIGH COMMISSION
Bruce House, Standard Street, P.O. Box 30465
Nairobi

High Commissioner, His Excellency John Rodney Johnson, C.M.G. (1986).

British Council Representative, Miss A. B. Lambert, O.B.E., (P.O. Box 40751) ICEA Building, Kenyatta Avenue, Nairobi. There are offices at *Kisumu* and *Mombasa*.

PRODUCTION

Agriculture provides about 52 per cent of total export earnings (excluding processed oil products). The great variation in altitude and ecology provide conditions under which a wide range of crops can be grown. These include wheat, barley, pyrethrum, coffee, tea, sisal, coconuts, cashew nuts, cotton, maize and a wide variety of tropical and temperate fruits and vegetables. The total area of well-farmed land on which concentrated mixed farming can be practised is small and the remainder is arid or semi-arid country but population pressure and the need to increase agricultural production for export has led to attempts to develop such areas.

Prospecting and mining are carried on in some parts of the country, the principal minerals produced being soda ash, salt and limestone.

Hydro-electric power has been developed, particularly on the Upper Tana River. Kenya is now almost self-sufficient in electric power generation but the connection with Owen Falls in Uganda is still in being.

There has been considerable industrial development over the last 15 years and Kenya has a wide variety of industries processing agricultural produce and manufacturing an increasing range of products from local and imported raw materials. New industries have recently come into being such as steel, textile mills, dehydrated vegetable processing and motor tyre manufacture as well as many smaller schemes which have added to the country's already considerable consumer goods. There is an oil refinery in Mombasa supplying both Kenya and Uganda, and a fuel pipeline now connects Mombasa and Nairobi.

COMMUNICATIONS

The Kenya Railways Corporation has 1,300 miles of railway open to traffic. There are also 31,000 miles of road, of which 2,700 are bitumen surfaced. Trans-border links with Tanzania were re-opened in 1985 with rail services for freight and steamer services for passengers and freight.

The principal port is Mombasa, operated by the Kenya Ports Authority.

International air services operate from airports at Nairobi and Mombasa.

TRADE

Principal exports are coffee and tea, which account for 33 per cent of total export earnings. Also exported are fruit, vegetables, and crude animal and vegetable material. Petroleum products account for about 37 per cent of imports; other imports are manufactured goods, particularly machinery, transport equipment, metals, pharmaceuticals and chemicals.

Trade with U.K.

	1985	1986
Imports from U.K.	£160,651,000	£170,671,000
Exports to U.K.	185,622,000	163,745,000

KIRIBATI
(Ribaberikin Kiribati)

AREA, POPULATION, ETC.—Kiribati, the former Gilbert Islands, became an independent Republic in 1979. Kiribati comprises 33 islands—the Gilberts Group (17) including Banaba, formerly Ocean Island; the Phoenix Islands (8); and the Line Islands (8)—situated in the South West Central Pacific around the point at which the International Date Line cuts the Equator. The total land area of 281 sq. miles (728 sq. km), is spread over some 2 million square miles of ocean. Few of the atolls are more than half a mile in width or more than 12 feet high. The vegetation consists mainly of coconut palms, breadfruit trees and pandanus. The population (1985 Census) was approx. 63,800. The population is predominantly Christian.

CAPITAL.—TARAWA (Population estimated at 24,400).

FLAG.—Red, with blue and white wavy lines in base, and in the centre a gold rising sun and a flying frigate bird.

NATIONAL DAY.—July 12 (Independence Day).

NATIONAL ANTHEM.—Teirake Kain Kiribati (Stand Kiribati).

GOVERNMENT

The President is Head of State as well as Head of Government and is elected nationally. There is an elected House of Assembly (36 members); executive authority is vested in the Cabinet.

President and Minister of Foreign Affairs, Hon. Ieremia Tabai, G.C.M.G.

Vice-President and Minister of Finance, Hon. Teatao Teannaki.

Works and Energy, Hon. Babera Kirata, O.B.E.

Natural Resources Development, Hon. Taomati T. Iuta.

Home Affairs and Decentralization, Hon. Tiwau Awira.

The Line and Phoenix Islands, Hon. Boanereke Boanereke.

Trade, Industry and Labour, Hon. Baitika Toum.

Transport and Communications, Hon. Uera Rabaua.

Health and Family Planning, Hon. Rotaria Ataia.

Education, Hon. Ataraoti Bwebwenibure.

Attorney-General, Hon. Michael N. Takabwebwe.

Chief Justice, Hon. V. Maxwell.

ECONOMY

Most people still practise a semi-subsistence economy, the main staples of their diet being coconuts and fish.

The unit of currency is the Australian dollar. Estimated recurrent revenue for 1987 is $A18,381,940. United Kingdom budgetary assistance ceased in 1985. The principal imports are foodstuffs, consumer goods, machinery and transport equipment. The principal exports are copra, which earned around $A4,718,000, and fish, income from which was around $A1,400,000 in 1985. Total value of exports in 1985 was $A6,057,000.

COMMUNICATIONS

Air communication exists between most of the islands, and is operated by Air Tungaru, a statutory corporation. Air Nauru flies weekly between Tarawa and Nauru. Air Marshall Islands operate a weekly service between Majuro/Tarawa/Funafuti and Nandi. Inter-island shipping is operated by a statutory corporation, the Shipping Corporation of Kiribati.

SOCIAL WELFARE

The Government maintains a teacher training college and a secondary school. Four junior secondary schools are maintained by missions. Throughout the Republic there are about a hundred primary schools. The total enrolment of children of school age is about 14,000. The Marine Training School at Tarawa trains seamen for service with overseas shipping lines. There is a general hospital at Tarawa. The other inhabited islands have dispensaries.

BRITISH HIGH COMMISSION

P.O. Box 61, Bairiki Tarawa

High Commissioner, His Excellency Charles Thompson (1983).

Trade with U.K.

	1985	1986
Imports from U.K.	£775,000	£179,000
Exports to U.K.	209,000	4,000

LESOTHO

('Muso oa Lesotho)

Lesotho is a landlocked mountainous state entirely surrounded by the Republic of South Africa. Of the total area of 11,720 sq. miles, (30,355 sq. km.), a belt between 20 and 40 miles in width lying across the western and southern boundaries and comprising about one-third of the total is classed as Lowlands, being between 5,000 and 6,000 ft. above sea level. The remaining two-thirds are classed as Foothills and Highlands, rising to 11,425 ft. The population was 1,443,853 (1986 Census).

CAPITAL.—MASERU, population, (1986 Census) 288,951.

FLAG.—Diagonally white over blue over green with the white of double width, and an assegai and knobkerrie on a Basotho shield in brown in the upper hoist.

NATIONAL DAY.—October 4 (Independence Day).

NATIONAL ANTHEM.—Pina ea Sechaba.

GOVERNMENT

Lesotho became a constitutional monarchy within the Commonwealth on October 4, 1966. The independence constitution was suspended in January 1970, when the country was governed by a Council of Ministers, until the establishment of a nominated National Assembly in April 1974. The Government was overthrown in Jan. 1986: all legislative and executive authority is now vested in the King acting on advice from a Military Council and a Council of Ministers.

The country is divided into ten administrative districts. In each district there is a District Coordinator who co-ordinates all Government activity in the area, working in co-operation with hereditary chiefs.

Head of State, H.M. King Moshoeshoe II.

Military Council

Chairman, Maj. Gen. Justin Metsing Lekhanya.

Members, Col. Elias P. Ramaema; Col. Aloysieus K. Mosoeunyane; Col. Michael N. Ts'otetsi; Col. Thaabe S. Letsie; Col. J. Sekhobe N. Letsie.

Council of Ministers

Chairman, Minister of Defence and Internal Security, Public Service and Cabinet Office, Maj. Gen. Justin Metsing Lekhanya.

Foreign Affairs, Hon. L. B. Monyake.

Law, Constitutional and Parliamentary Affairs, Hon. K. Sello.

Works, Hon. M. M. Lebotsa.

Justice and Prisons, Hon. B. M. Khaketla.

Information and Broadcasting, Hon. V. M. Malebo.

Employment, Social Welfare and Pensions, Hon. Col. B. R. Nts'ohi.

Planning, Economic and Manpower Development, Hon. Dr. M. M. Sefali.

Finance, Agriculture, Co-operatives and Marketing, Hon. E. R. Sekhonyana.

Transport and Communications, Hon. Col. P. M. Mokhants'o.

Tourism, Sports and Culture, Hon. M. L. Mathealire.

Water, Energy and Mining, Hon. Col. A. L. Jane.

Interior and Chieftainship Affairs, Hon. Morena M. Seeiso.
Education, Hon. M. M. Tiheli.
Trade and Industry, Hon. M. Mokoroane
Health, Hon. Dr. S. T. Makenete.
Ministers of State, Hon. P. L. 'Mabathoana (*Agriculture, Co-operatives and Marketing*); Hon. Mrs. A. 'M. Hlalele (*Youth and Women's Affairs*); Hon. Morena P. J. Molapo (*Interior, Chieftainship Affairs and Rural Development*); Hon. P. M. 'Mabathoana (*Education*).

JUDICIARY

The Lesotho Courts of Law consist of the Court of Appeal, the High Court, Magistrates' Courts, Judicial Commissioners' Court, Central and local Courts. Magistrates' and higher courts administer the laws of Lesotho which are framed on the basis of the Roman–Dutch law. They also adjudicate appeals from the Judicial Commissioner's and Subordinate Courts.

Chief Justice, Hon. B. P. Cullinan.

LESOTHO HIGH COMMISSION
10 Collingham Road, SW5 0NR
[01–373 8581]

High Commissioner, His Excellency Dr. John T. Kolane (1986).

BRITISH HIGH COMMISSION
P.O. Box 521, Maseru

High Commissioner, His Excellency Peter Edward Rosling, C.M.G., L.V.O. (1984).
British Council Representative, A. D. Bates, Hobson's Square, P.O. Box 429, Maseru, 100.

EDUCATION

Most schools are mission-controlled, the Government providing grants for salaries and buildings. There are over 1,000 primary and over 100 secondary schools; few areas lack a school and there is a high literacy rate of about 70 per cent. Increasing emphasis is being laid on agricultural and vocational education. The National University of Lesotho at Roma was established in 1975.

COMMUNICATIONS

A tarred road of 110 miles links Maseru to several of the main lowland towns, and this is being extended in the south of the country. The mountainous areas are linked by 1,300 miles of gravelled and earth roads and tracks. Roads link border towns in South Africa with the main towns in Lesotho. Maseru is connected by rail with the main Bloemfontein–Natal line of the South African Railways. Scheduled international air services are operated daily between Maseru and Johannesburg and other scheduled international flights are to Manzini and Maputo. There are around 30 airstrips. Internal scheduled services are operated by the Lesotho Airways Corporation.

The telephone network is fully automated in all urban centres. Radio telephone communication is used extensively in the remote rural areas.

PRODUCTION

The economy of Lesotho is based on agriculture and animal husbandry, and the adverse balance of trade (mainly consumer and capital goods) is offset by the earnings of the large numbers of the population who work in South Africa. Apart from some diamonds, Lesotho has few natural resources and only small-scale industrial development. The Lesotho National Development Corporation was set up to promote the development of industry, mining, trade and tourism. Work has commenced on the Highlands Water Scheme designed to provide water for the Vaal industrial zone in South Africa and hydro-electricity for Lesotho. Drilling is being carried out for oil. Tourism is being developed and is rapidly playing a major role in the economic progress of the country: a National Park has been established at Sehlabathebe in the Maluti mountains. A number of light manufacturing and processing industries have recently been established.

FINANCE AND TRADE

The main sources of revenue are customs and excise duty. Estimates of expenditure and revenue (1986) are recurrent revenue $M241.2$ million; recurrent expenditure $M265.3$ million; capital revenue $M144$ million; capital expenditure $M198$ million.

On Jan. 19, 1980 the *Maloti* was introduced as Lesotho's currency, on the basis of parity with the S. Africa *rand*.

Trade with U.K.

	1985	1986
Imports from U.K.	£3,023,000	£2,128,000
Exports to U.K.	290,000	277,000

MALAWI
(Mfuko La Malawi)

AREA, POPULATION, ETC.—Malawi comprises Lake Malawi (formerly Lake Nyasa) and its western shore, with the high table-land separating it from the basin of the Luangwa River, the watershed forming the western frontier with Zambia; south of the lake, Malawi reaches almost to the Zambesi and is surrounded by Mozambique, the frontier lying on the west on the watershed of the Zambesi and Shire Rivers, and to the east on the Ruo, a tributary of the Shire, and Lakes Chiuta and Chirwa. This boundary reaches the eastern shore of Lake Malawi and extends up to the mid-point of the lake for about half its length where it returns to the eastern and northern shores to form a frontier with Tanzania.   Malawi has a total area of 45,747 sq. miles (118,484 sq. km). The population, according to the Census held in September 1977, is 5,547,460; a U.N. estimate put the figure at 7,059,000 in 1985. The official languages are Chichewa and English.

CAPITAL.—LILONGWE (population (1977) 102,924). The city of Blantyre in the Southern Region, incorporating Blantyre and Limbe (population (1977) 222,153), is the major commercial and industrial centre. Other main centres are: Mzuzu, Thyolo, Mulanje, Mangochi, Salima, Dedza and Zomba, the former capital.

FLAG.—Horizontal stripes of black, red and green, with rising sun in the centre of the black stripe.

NATIONAL DAY.—July 6 (Independence Day).

NATIONAL ANTHEM.—O God Bless Our Land of Malawi.

GOVERNMENT

Malawi became a republic on July 6, 1966, having assumed internal self-government on February 1, 1963, and achieved independence on July 6, 1964, and is a member of the Commonwealth. There is a Cabinet consisting of the Life President and other Ministers. The Parliament consists of 112 members, each elected by universal suffrage. Under the 1981 Amendment to the Constitution, the Life President has the power to nominate as many Members of Parliament as he wishes. Being a one-party State (the Malawi Congress Party), all elected members are required to be members of the Party. The Parliament, which usually meets three times a year, is presided over by a Speaker.

President, Minister of External Affairs, Agriculture, Justice, Works and Supplies, Dr. H. Kamuzu Banda, *elected* 1966, *sworn in as* President for Life, July 6, 1971.

Cabinet

Minister Without Portfolio, Hon. Robson W. Chirwa.
Trade, Industry and Tourism, Hon. Michael Mlambala.
Transport and Communications, Hon. Dalton Katopola.
Health, Hon. Edward Bwanali.
Finance, Hon. Louis Chimango.
Labour, Wadson Bini Deleza.
Education and Culture, Hon. Maxwell Pashane.
Community Services, Hon. E. C. Katola Phiri.
Forestry and Natural Resources, Hon. Stanford Demba.
Local Government, Hon. R. M. Banda.

JUDICIARY

Chief Justice, Hon. F. L. Makuta.

MALAWI HIGH COMMISSION
33 Grosvenor Street, W1X 0DE
[01-491 4172/7]

High Commissioner, His Excellency Mr. Bernard B. Mtawali (1987).

BRITISH HIGH COMMISSION
Lingadzi House (P.O. Box 30042),
Lilongwe 3

High Commissioner, His Excellency Dr. Denis Osborne (1987).
Deputy High Commissioner, T. W. Abbott.
British Council Representative, C. G. Housden, (P.O. Box 30222), Lilongwe. There is also a library at Blantyre.

EDUCATION

Primary education is the responsibility of local authorities in both urban and rural areas, although policy, curricula and inspection are the responsibility of the Ministry of Education and Culture. The Ministry is also responsible for secondary schools, technical education and primary teacher training. Religious bodies, with Government assistance, still play an important part in these fields. The University of Malawi was opened in 1965 and has four constituent colleges.

COMMUNICATIONS

A single-track railway runs from Mchinji on the Zambian border, through Lilongwe and Salima on Lake Malawi (itself served by two passenger and a number of cargo boats) through Blantyre to the southern frontier into Mozambique, and connecting with the Mozambique port of Beira. In 1970 a 70-mile line was opened to Nayuchi, linking the Malawi rail system with the Mozambique network to the port of Nacala. There are 11,428·5 km. of roads in Malawi of which about 19 per cent are bituminized.

There is an international airport 26 km. from Lilongwe, which handles regional and inter-continental flights.

FINANCE

(excluding Development Account)

	1984–85	1985–86
Revenue	K313m	K483m
Expenditure	367m	657m

The unit of currency is the *kwacha*.

ECONOMY

The economy is largely agricultural, with maize the main subsistence crop. Tobacco, sugar, tea, groundnuts and cotton are the main cash crops and principal exports. There are two sugar mills and total production in 1985 was 143,818 tonnes. A number of light manufacturing industries have been established recently.

TRADE

	1984	1985
Imports	K382m	K492m
Exports	446m	420m

Trade with U.K.

	1985	1986
Imports from U.K.	£20,525,000	£28,557,000
Exports to U.K.	87,218,000	56,983,000

MALAYSIA
(Persekutuan Tanah Malaysia)

AREA, POPULATION, ETC.—Malaysia, comprising the 11 states of peninsular Malaya plus Sabah and Sarawak, forms a crescent well over 1,000 miles long between latitudes 1° and 7° N. and longitudes 100° and 119° E. It occupies two distinct regions—the Malay peninsula which extends from the isthmus of Kra to the Singapore Strait and the north-west coastal area of the island of Borneo. Each is separated from the other by 400 miles of the South China Sea. The total area of Malaysia, including the Federal Territories of Kuala Lumpur and Labuan, is approx. 127,317 sq. miles, (329,749 sq. km.), containing a population of 16,544,000 (1986 Census). The principal racial groups are the Malays, the Chinese and those of Indian and Sri Lankan origin, as well as the indigenous races of Sarawak and Sabah. Bahasa Malaysia (Malay) is the sole official language, but English, various dialects of Chinese, and Tamil are also widely spoken. There are a few indigenous languages widely spoken in Sabah and Sarawak.

RELIGION.—Islam is the official religion of Malaysia, each Ruler being the head of religion in his State, though the Heads of State of Sabah and Sarawak are not heads of the Muslim religion in their States. The Yang di-Pertuan Agung is the head of religion in Malacca and Penang. The Constitution guarantees religious freedom.

CLIMATE.—The year is commonly divided into the Southwest and Northwest monsoon seasons. Rainfall averages about 100 inches throughout the year, though the annual fall varies from place to place. The average daily temperature throughout Malaysia varies from 70° F. to 90° F., though in higher areas temperatures are lower and vary widely.

CAPITAL.—Kuala Lumpur was proclaimed Federal Territory on February 1, 1974. Its population is (1985) 1,103,200.

FLAG.—Equal horizontal stripes of red (7) and white (7); 14 point yellow star and crescent in blue canton.

NATIONAL DAY.—August 31 (*Hari Kebangsaan*).
NATIONAL ANTHEM.—Negara-Ku.

STATES OF THE FEDERATION

The 13 States of the Federation of Malaysia (State capitals in brackets) and their populations at the 1986 Census are:

Johore (Johore Bahru)	1,867,333
Kedah (Alor Setar)	1,263,155
Kelantan (Kota Bahru)	1,048,420
ΨMelaka (Melaka)	524,028
Negri Sembilan (Seremban)	647,159
Pahang (Kuantan)	921,360
ΨPenang (Georgetown)	1,049,282
Perak (Ipoh)	2,020,135
Perlis (Kangar)	166,948
ΨSabah (Kota Kinabalu)	1,222,718
ΨSarawak (Kuching)	1,477,428
Selangor (Shah Alam)	1,731,090
Terengganu (Kuala Terengganu)	638,830
ΨSeaport	

FEDERAL TERRITORIES

The two Federal Territories (capitals in brackets) and their populations at the 1986 Census are:

Kuala Lumpur (Kuala Lumpur)	1,103,200
Labuan (Victoria)	12,219*
* 1980 Census	

GOVERNMENT

The Federation of Malaya became an independent country within the Commonwealth on August 31, 1957, as a result of an agreement between H.M. the Queen and the Rulers of the Malay States. On Sept. 16, 1963, the Federation was enlarged by the accession of the states of Singapore, Sabah (*formerly* British North Borneo) and Sarawak, and the name of MALAYSIA was adopted from that date. On Aug. 9, 1965, Singapore seceded from the Federation.

The Constitution was designed to ensure the existence of a strong Federal Government and also a measure of autonomy for the State Governments. It provides for a constitutional Supreme Head of the Federation (H.M. the *Yang di-Pertuan Agung*) to be elected for a term of five years by the Rulers from among their number, and for a Deputy Supreme Head (H.R.H. *Timbalan Yang di-Pertuan Agung*) to be similarly elected. The Malay Rulers are either chosen or succeed to their position in accordance with the custom of the particular state. In other states of Malaysia choice of the Head of State is at the discretion of the *Yang di-Pertuan Agung* after consultation with the Chief Minister of the State.

The Federal Parliament consists of two houses, the Senate and the House of Representatives. The Senate (*Dewan Negara*) consists of 68 members, under a President (*Yang di-Pertua Dewan Negara*), 26 elected by the Legislative Assemblies of the States (2 from each) and 42 appointed by the *Yang di-Pertuan Agung*. The House of Representatives (*Dewan Rak-yat*), consists of 177 members (Peninsular Malaysia, 134; Sarawak, 24; and Sabah, 20). Members are elected on the principle of universal adult suffrage with a common electoral roll.

The Constitution provides that each State shall have its own Constitution not inconsistent with the Federal Constitution, with the Ruler or Governor acting on the advice of an Executive Council appointed on the advice of the Chief Minister and a single chamber Legislative Assembly. The State Secretary, the State Legal Adviser and the State Financial Officer sit in the Executive Council as *ex-officio* members. The Legislative Assemblies are fully elected on the same basis as the Federal Parliament.

Supreme Head of State, H.M. Sultan Mahmood Iskandar Al-Haj ibni Al-Marhun Sultan Ismail (Sultan of Johore), *assumed office for a term of 5 years*, April 1984, *sworn in* Nov. 15, 1984.

Deputy Supreme Head of State, H.R.H. Raja Tun Azlan Shah (Sultan of Perak).

MINISTRY

Prime Minister and Minister of Home Affairs and Justice, Datuk Seri Dr. Mahathir Mohamed.

Deputy P.M. and Minister of National and Rural Development, Ghafar Baba.

Labour, Datuk Lee Kim Sai.

Welfare Services, Encik Mustaffa Mohamed.

Youth and Sports, Datuk Najib Tun Razak.

Land and Regional Development, Datuk Sulaiman Daud.

Works, Datuk S. Samy Vellu.

Health, Datuk Chan Siang Sun.

Finance, Daim Zainuddin.

Foreign Affairs, Datuk Haji Abu Hassan Omar.

Education, Anwar Ibrahim.

Information, Datuk Mohamed Rahmat.

Transport, Datuk Ling Liong Sik.

Trade and Industry, Datin Paduka Rafidah Aziz.

Defence, Tengku Ahmad Rithaudden.

Agriculture, Datuk Seri Sanusi Junid.

Public Enterprises, Puan Napsiah Omar.

Primary Industries, Datuk Lim Kheng Yaik.

Science, Technology and Environment, Datuk Stephen Yong.

Energy, Telecommunications and Posts, Datuk Leo Moggie.

Housing and Local Government, Encik Ng Cheng Kiat.

Tourism and Culture, Datuk Hj Sabaruddin Chik.

Ministers in Prime Minister's Department, Kasitah Gadam; Datuk Dr. Yusoff Noor.

NOTE.—The words "Tunku/Tengku", "Tun", "Tan Sri", and "Datuk" are titles. The word "Tunku/Tengku" is equivalent to "Prince". "Tun" denotes membership of a high Order of Malaysian Chivalry and "Tan Sri" and "Datuk" ("Datuk Seri" in Perak and "Datu" in Sabah) are each the equivalent of a knighthood. The wife of a "Tun" is styled "Toh Puan", that of a "Tan Sri" is styled "Puan Sri" and of a "Datuk" "Datin". The honorific "Tuan" or "Encik" is equivalent to "Mr." and the honorific "Puan" is equivalent to "Mrs.". The words "Al-Haj" or "Haji" indicate that the person so named has made the pilgrimage to Mecca.

MALAYSIAN HIGH COMMISSION
45 Belgrave Square, SW1X 8QT
[01–235 8033]

High Commissioner, His Excellency Datuk Jamaluddin Abu Bakar (1986).

BRITISH HIGH COMMISSION
Wisma Damansara, Jalan Semantan
(P.O. Box 11030), 50732 Kuala Lumpur

High Commissioner, His Excellency John Nicholas Teague Spreckley, C.M.G. (1986).

British Council Representative, O. R. Siddle, O.B.E., (*representative designate*, A. Johnson), Jalan Bukit Aman, 50480, Kuala Lumpur 10–01; offices at *Kota Kinabalu* (Sabah) and *Kuching* (Sarawak), and a library in Penang.

JUDICATURE

The Judicial System consists of a Supreme Court and two High Courts, one in Peninsular Malaysia and one for Sabah and Sarawak (sitting alternately in Kota Kinabalu and Kuching).

The Supreme Court comprises a President, the two Chief Justices of the High Courts and other judges.

It possesses appellate, original and advisory jurisdiction.

Each of the High Courts consists of a Chief Justice and not less than 4 other judges. The Federal Constitution allows for a maximum of twelve such judges for Malaya and eight for Borneo. In Peninsular Malaysia the Subordinate Courts consist of the Sessions Courts and the Magistrates' Courts. In Sabah/Sarawak the Magistrates' Courts constitute the Subordinate Courts.

DEFENCE

The Malaysian Armed Forces consist of the Army, Navy and Air Force, together with volunteer forces for each arm. The defence of the country is largely borne by the army in its role of providing defence against external threat and counter-insurgency operations and also to assist the police in the performance of public order duties. The *Royal Malaysian Navy* (*RMN*) has the responsibility of defending the 3,000 miles of the country's coastline and maintaining constant patrol of 500 miles of the high seas that separate Sabah and Sarawak from the mainland. The *Royal Malaysian Air Force* (*RMAF*) is capable of providing close strategic and tactical support to the army and police in the defence and internal security of the country.

FINANCE

	M$million	
	1986	1987
Revenue	22,121	18,021
Expenditure	30,812	26,312

PRODUCTION AND TRADE

The agricultural sector continues to be the mainstay of the Malaysian economy. However, diversification of crops and rapid growth in the manufacturing sector has made Malaysia less vulnerable to fluctuations in the price of its primary crop, natural rubber.

Malaysia is the largest exporter of natural rubber, tin, palm oil and tropical hardwoods. Other major export commodities are manufactured and processed products, petroleum, oil, and other minerals, palm kernel oil, tea and pepper.

Exports of major commodities were (percentage of total exports):

	1985	1986
Primary commodities	33·4	27·9
Petroleum	23·5	19·9
Manufactured goods	32·0	40·5

Another commodity which is produced throughout Malaysia is rice, the staple food, and efforts are being made to achieve self-sufficiency.

Imports consist mainly of machinery and transport equipment, manufactured goods, foods, mineral fuels, chemicals and inedible crude materials for her growing population and to accelerate the pace of her economic growth and development.

	M$million	
	1985	1986
Imports	33,250	26,774
Exports	38,007	33,552

Trade with U.K.

	1985	1986
Imports from U.K.	£281,671,000	£226,912,000
Exports to U.K.	383,860,000	350,058,000

THE MALDIVES

(Divehi Jumhuriya)

AREA, POPULATION, ETC.—The Maldives are a chain of coral atolls, some 400 miles to the south-west of Sri Lanka, stretching from just south of the equator for about 600 miles to the north. There are about 20 coral atolls comprising over 1,200 islands, 202 of which are inhabited. Total area of the islands is 115 sq. miles (298 sq. km.). No point in the entire chain of islands is more than 8 feet above sea-level. The population of the islands (1986) is 189,400. The people are Sunni Moslems and the Maldivian language is akin to Elu or old Sinhalese.

CAPITAL.—MALÉ (population, 1985, 46,334). There is an international airport at Malé.

FLAG.—Green field bearing a white crescent, with wide red border.

NATIONAL DAY.—July 26.

NATIONAL ANTHEM.—Qawmee Salaam.

GOVERNMENT

Until 1952 the islands were a Sultanate under the protection of the British Crown. Internal self-government was achieved in 1948 and full independence in 1965. In 1982 the Republic of the Maldives became a special member of the Commonwealth, and a full member in 1985.

The Maldives form a Republic which is elective. There is a Parliament (the *Citizens' Majlis*) with representatives elected from all the atolls. The life of the Majlis is 5 years. The Government consists of a Cabinet, which is responsible to the Majlis.

President, His Excellency Maumoon Abdul Gayoom, *elected* 1978, *re-elected* Sept. 30, 1983 (also *Minister of Defence and National Security*).

Cabinet

Foreign Affairs, Hon. Fathulla Jameel.
Justice, Hon. Abdulla Hameed (*acting*).
Home Affairs and Social Services, Hon. Umar Zahir.
Education, Hon. Mohamed Zahir Hussain.
Health, Hon. Abdulla Jameel.
Fisheries, Hon. Abdul Sattar.
Transport and Shipping, Hon. Ahmed Mujathaba.
Atolls Administration, Hon. Abdulla Hameed.
Trade and Industries, Hon. Ilyas Ibrahim.
Attorney General, Hon. Ahmed Zaki.
Speaker of Majlis, Hon. Ibrahim Shihab.
Chief Justice, Hon. Moosa Sathy.

BRITISH HIGH COMMISSION

High Commissioner, (*resident* at Colombo).

PRODUCTION

The vegetation of the islands is coconut palms with some scrub. Hardly any cultivation of crops is possible and nearly all food to supplement the basic fish diet has to be imported. The principal industry is fishing and considerable quantities of fish are exported to Japan. Dried fish is exported to Sri Lanka, where it is a delicacy. The tourist industry is expanding very rapidly. Maldives Shipping Ltd. has a fleet of some 30 merchant ships.

Trade with U.K.

	1985	1986
Imports from U.K.	£1,243,000	£1,321,000
Exports to U.K.	73,000	276,000

MALTA

(Repubblika Ta'Malta)

AREA, POPULATION, ETC.—Malta lies in the Mediterranean Sea, 58 miles from Sicily and about 180 miles from the African coast, about 17 miles in length and 9 in breadth, and having an area of 94·9 square miles. Malta includes also the adjoining island of *Gozo* (area 25·9 sq. miles); *Comino* and minor islets. The U.N. estimated population at 1985 was 383,000.

Maltese and English are the official languages of administration and Maltese is ordinarily the official language in all the courts of law and the language of general use in the islands.

Malta was in turn held by the Phœnicians, Greeks, Carthaginians, Romans and Arabs. In 1090 it was conquered by Count Roger of Normandy. In 1530 it was handed over to the Knights of St. John, who made of it a stronghold of Christianity. In 1565 it sustained the famous siege, when the last great effort of the Turks was successfully withstood by Grandmaster La Valette. The Knights expended large sums in fortifying the island and carrying out many magnificent works, until they were expelled by Napoleon in 1798. The Maltese rose against the French garrison soon afterwards, and the island was subsequently blockaded by the British fleet. The Maltese people freely requested the protection of the British Crown in 1802 on condition that their rights and privileges would be preserved and respected. The islands were finally annexed to the British Crown by the Treaty of Paris in 1814.

Malta was again closely besieged in the last war. From June, 1940, to the end of the war, 432 members of the garrison and 1,540 civilians were killed by enemy aircraft, and about 35,000 houses were destroyed or damaged. The island was awarded the George Cross in 1942.

CAPITAL.—ΨVALLETTA. Population (estimated 1984), 14,013. Valletta Grand Harbour is one of the finest in the world; it is very deep, and large vessels can anchor alongside the shore. It is an important port of call and ship repairing centre for vessels, being half-way between Gibraltar and Port Said.

FLAG.—Two equal vertical stripes, white at the hoists and red at the fly. A representation of the George Cross is carried edged in red in the top corner of the white stripe.

NATIONAL DAY.—March 31.

GOVERNMENT

On Sept. 21, 1964, under the Malta Independence Order, 1964, Malta became an independent state within the Commonwealth; on December 13, 1974, Malta became a republic within the Commonwealth. In the General Election of May 9, 1987, the Nationalist Party won 50·9 per cent of the vote but only 31 seats in the 65-member parliament compared with 34 by the Labour Party. However, amendments to the Constitution in Jan. 1987 meant that the Nationalist Party gained four "extra" seats on the basis of the size of the popular vote and therefore formed a government on this basis.

Acting President.—Paul Xuereb.

Cabinet

Prime Minister, Hon. Dr. Edward Fenech Adami.
Deputy P.M. and Minister of the Interior and Justice, Hon. Dr. Guido De Marco.
Foreign Affairs, Hon. Dr. Vincent Tabone.
Education, Hon. Dr. Ugo Mifsud Bonnici.
Social Policy, Hon. Dr. Luis Galea.
Finance, Hon. Dr. G. B. Du Puis.
Infrastructure Development, Hon. Michael Falzon.

Productive Development, Hon. Lawrence Gatt.
Tertiary Sector Development, Hon. Dr. Emmanuel Bonnici.
Gozo, Hon. Anton Gabone.
Health, Hon. Dr. George Hyzlar.
Elderly, Hon. Dr. John Rizzo Naudi.
Housing, Hon. Dr. Joe Cassar.
Water, Electricity and Energy, Hon. Anthony Zammit.
Post and Telecommunications, Hon. Pierre Muscat.
Industry, Hon. John Dalli.
Tourism, Hon. Dr. Michael Rasalo.
Maritime Affairs, Hon. Dr. Joe French.

MALTESE HIGH COMMISSION
16 Kensington Square, W8 5HH
[01–938 1712]

High Commissioner, (new appointment awaited).

BRITISH HIGH COMMISSION
7 St. Anne Street, Floriana, Malta

High Commissioner, His Excellency Stanley Frederick St. Clare Duncan, C.M.G., (1985).

EDUCATION

In June 1984 there were 83 Government Primary Schools with 26,130 pupils and 38 Secondary Schools and new Lyceums, with a total of 13,813 pupils.

The Government also runs 4 Technical Institutes and 15 Trade Schools (with an enrolment of 5,275 students). Schools of Art, Music, Secretarial Studies, Catering, Nursing and Dramatic Art are sponsored by the Government. Tertiary education is available at the University of Malta, which has 1,468 students.

A number of private schools offer more or less the same facilities that exist in Government schools. All education is free.

In religion, the Maltese are Roman Catholics. The Maltese language is of Semitic origin and held by some to be derived from the Carthaginian and Phoenician tongues.

AGRICULTURE

Agriculture plays a significant role in the economy. There are 4,332 full time farmers and about 11,026 part time farmers. The yearly crop production is about 99,727 tonnes consisting mainly of tomatoes, potatoes, onions, cabbages and cauliflowers, and some 2,922 tonnes of fruit. Grape is the largest fruit crop. Flowers and cuttings are produced for export markets.

INDUSTRY

The island's leading industry is the state-owned Malta Drydocks, employing about 5,000 people. The main port of Grand Harbour handled traffic (excluding mineral oils) of 1,551,528 tonnes in 1984.

At the end of 1984 manufacturing firms employed some 29,566 people. The wide range of produce includes food processing, textiles and clothing, plastics and chemical products, electronic equipment and components. The gross output of the manufacturing industry in 1984 was £M299·7 million, of which £M160·9 million were export sales.

Tourism has assumed primary importance, with over 479,747 tourists visiting the island in 1984, and there are plans to develop Marsamxett Harbour as a yachting centre. Gross income from this industry stood at £M63·1 million.

FINANCE

	1985	1986
Revenue	£M230,189,000	£M231,500,000
Expenditure	230,189,000	240,000,000

The Maltese pound is divided into 100 *cents* and 1,000 *mils.*

TRADE

The principal imports for home consumption are foodstuffs—mainly wheat, meat and bullocks, milk and fruit—fodder, beverages and tobacco, fuels, chemicals, textiles and machinery (industrial, agricultural and transport). The chief domestic exports are flowers and cuttings, processed food, electronics, textiles, and other manufactures.

	1984	1985
Imports	£M330,000,000	£M354,000,000
Exports	181,000,000	186,000,000

Trade with U.K.

	1985	1986
Imports from U.K.	£101,247,000	£101,877,000
Exports from U.K.	51,794,000	49,197,000

MAURITIUS

AREA, POPULATION, ETC.—Mauritius is an island group lying in the Indian Ocean, 550 miles east of Madagascar, between 57° 17′–57° 46′ E. long. and lat. 19° 58′–20° 33′ S., and comprising with its dependencies an area of 790 square miles (2,045 sq. km.). The population (1985 U.N. estimate) was 1,020,000 made up of Asiatic races (Hindus 52·6 per cent, Muslims 16·5 per cent), and persons of European (mainly French extraction), mixed and African descent (28·3 per cent).

English is the official language but French may be used in the Legislative Assembly and lower law courts. However, Creole is the mostly commonly used language.

CLIMATE.—Mauritius enjoys a sub-tropical maritime climate, with a wide range of rainfall and temperature resulting from the mountainous nature of the island. Humidity is rather high throughout the year and rainfall is sufficient to maintain a green cover of vegetation, except for a brief period in the driest districts.

CAPITAL.—ΨPORT LOUIS, population (1985), 138,272; other centres are Beau Bassin-Rose Hill (93,059); Curepipe (64,072); Vacoas-Phoenix (55,330) and Quatre Bornes (65,405).

FLAG.—Red, blue, yellow and green horizontal stripes.

NATIONAL DAY.—March 12.

NATIONAL ANTHEM.—Glory to the Motherland.

GOVERNMENT

Mauritius was discovered in 1511 by the Portuguese; the Dutch visited it in 1598, and named it Mauritius, after Prince Maurice of Nassau. From 1638 to 1710 it was held as a small Dutch colony and in 1715 the French took possession but did not settle it until 1721. Mauritius was taken by a British Force in 1810. A British garrison remained on the island until June 1960. The French language and French law were preserved under British rule.

A Crown Colony for 158 years, Mauritius became an independent state within the Commonwealth on March 12, 1968. The Constitution defined by Order in Council in 1964 was slightly altered in 1966 on the recommendation of the Banwell Commission, the effect being to increase the membership of the Legislative Assembly to 70, 62 elected by block voting in multi-member constituencies (including 2 members for Rodrigues) and 8 specially-elected members. Of the latter, 4 seats go to the "best loser" of whichever

communities in the island are under-represented in the Assembly after the General Election and the four remaining seats are allocated on the basis of both party and community. The Constitution provides for the appointment of a Governor-General who acts on the advice of the Council of Ministers, collectively responsible to the Legislative Assembly.

In the August 1983 General Election, the Mouvement Socialiste Militant, allied with the Labour Party and the Parti Mauricien Social Democrate, defeated the Mouvement Mauricien Militant and formed the Government, with a majority of 43 seats.

Governor-General, His Excellency Sir Veerasamy Ringadoo, G.C.M.G., Q.C.

Council of Ministers

Prime Minister and Minister of Defence, Internal Security, External Communications, Information, Industry and of the Outer Islands, Rt. Hon. Anerood Jugnauth, Q.C.

Deputy Prime Minister and Minister of Employment and Tourism, Hon. Sir Gaetan Duval, Q.C.

Attorney-General and Minister of Justice, External Affairs and Emigration, Hon. Sir Satcam Boolell, Q.C.

Finance, Hon. Seetanah Lutchmeenaraidoo.

Trade and Shipping, Dr. Hon. Beergoonath Ghurburrun.

Education, Arts and Culture, Hon. Armoogum Parsuramen.

Economic Planning and Development, Hon. Dwarkanath Gungah.

Energy and Internal Communications, Hon. Mahyendrah Utchanah.

Social Security, National Solidarity and Reform Institutions, Hon. Karl Offmann.

Housing, Lands and the Environment, Hon. Joseph Herve Duval.

Women's Rights and Family Affairs, Labour and Industrial Relations, Hon. Mrs. Sheilabai Bappoo.

Youth and Sports, Hon. Michael J. K. Glover.

Rodrigues, Hon. France Felicite.

Co-operatives, Hon. Iswardeo Seetaram.

Health, Hon. Jagdishwar Goburdhun.

Agriculture, Fisheries and Natural Resources, Hon. Murlidas Dulloo.

Local Government, Hon. Babooram Mahadoo.

Works, Dr. Hon. Dineshwur Ramjuttun.

MAURITIUS HIGH COMMISSION
32–33 Elvaston Place, SW7 5NW
[01–581 0294–7]

High Commissioner, His Excellency Mr. Gian Nath (1983).

BRITISH HIGH COMMISSION
King George V Avenue, Floreal.

High Commissioner, His Excellency Richard Borman Crowson, C.M.G. (1985).

EDUCATION

Primary education is free and in 1986 was provided for 138,765 children at 273 primary schools. Although education is not compulsory it is estimated that about 90 per cent of children of primary age attend school. At post-primary level there are a total of 68,604 students attending secondary schools: fees and teachers' salaries in the private secondary schools are paid by government. 168 students attend the Industrial Trade Training Centre. The College of Education trains primary school teachers. The Institute of Education is responsible for training secondary school teachers and for curriculum development. The University of Mauritius consists of

Schools of Agriculture, of Administration and of Industrial Technology. Estimated expenditure on education in 1985–86 was Rs.604,600,000.

COMMUNICATIONS

Port Louis, on the N.W. coast, handles the bulk of the island's external trade. A bulk sugar terminal capable of handling the total crop began operating in 1980. The international airport is located at Plaisance in the southeast of the island about 5 miles from Mahébourg. There are 6 daily newspapers and 5 weeklies, mostly in French, and 2 Chinese daily papers and one weekly paper. The Mauritius Broadcasting Corporation has a monopoly of radio broadcasting in the country: television was introduced in 1965. There is a satellite communications ground station near Port Louis.

PRODUCTION

In 1986 the manufacturing sector employed 84,370, while the sugar industry employed 46,708.

About 55 per cent of the total sugar crop is produced on a plantation scale, while smaller owners (cultivating less than 10 acres) cultivate about 24 per cent of the land under cane. Tea and tobacco are also grown commercially but on a smaller scale than sugar.

	1985	1986
	tonnes	
Sugar	645,797	706,839
Tea (manufactured)	8,115	7,876
Tobacco (leaves)	831	982

In 1986 production of molasses, mainly for export, was 166,000 tonnes. Other products include alcohol, rum, denatured spirits, perfumed spirits and vinegar.

The bulk of the island's requirements in manufactured products still has to be imported. However, the Mauritius Export Processing Zone (M.E.P.Z.) scheme, introduced in 1971, has attracted investment from overseas and the number of export-orientated enterprises has risen from ten in 1971 to 408 at the end of 1986, employing 74,000 people. The biggest firms are in clothing manufacture, particularly woollen knitwear, but the range of goods produced includes toys, plastic products, leather goods, diamond cutting and polishing, watches, television sets and telephones.

Tourism is a major source of income for Mauritius, with 165,000 tourists in 1986. Earnings from tourism in 1986 are estimated to be Rs1,175 million (£56·76 million), compared with Rs840 million (£42 million) in 1985. The neighbouring French island of Réunion is the most important source of tourists, followed closely by South Africa. An increasing number of tourists also come from Europe.

FINANCE

The main sources of Government revenue are private and company income tax, customs and excise duties, mainly on imports, but also on sugar exports.

	1984–85	1985–86
Public revenue	Rs.3,562·1 m	Rs.4,130·5 m
Public expenditure	4,276·5 m	4,504·9 m
Currency—Rs. = Rupee.		

TRADE

Most foodstuffs and raw materials have to be imported from abroad. Apart from local consumption (about 36,500 metric tons per annum), the sugar produced is exported, mainly to Britain.

	1985	1986
Total imports	Rs.8,119·5 m	Rs.9,090·0 m
Total exports	7,017·7 m	9,400·5 m

Trade with U.K.

	1985	1986
Imports from U.K.	Rs.642 m	Rs. 686 m
Exports to U.K.	2,899 m	3,415 m

RODRIGUES AND DEPENDENCIES OF MAURITIUS

Rodrigues, formerly a dependency but now part of Mauritius, is about 350 miles east of Mauritius. Area, 40 square miles. Population (1985) 35,303. Cattle, salt fish, sheep, goats, pigs and onions are the principal exports. The island is administered by an Administrative Secretary.

Administrative Secretary, Maxime Labour.

The islands of Agalega and St. Brandon are dependencies of Mauritius. Other small islands, formerly Mauritian dependencies, have since 1965 constituted the British Indian Ocean Territory (*see* p. 776–7).

REPUBLIC OF NAURU

The Republic of Nauru is an island of 8·2 sq. miles (21 sq. km.) in size, situated in 166° 55′ E. longitude and 0° 32′ S. of the Equator. It has a population (Census May 1983) of 8,042 (Nauruans 4,964; other Pacific Islanders 2,134; Asians 682; Caucasians 262). About 43 per cent of Nauruans are adherents of the Nauruan Protestant Church and there is a Roman Catholic Mission on the island.

FLAG.—Twelve-point star (representing the 12 original Nauruan tribes) below a gold bar (representing the Equator), all on a blue ground.

NATIONAL DAY.—January 31 (Independence Day).

GOVERNMENT

From 1888 until the First World War Nauru was administered by Germany, in 1920 becoming a British mandated territory under the League of Nations administered by Australia. A Trusteeship superceding the Mandate was approved in 1947 by the U.N. and Nauru continued to be administered by Australia until it became an Independent State on February 1, 1968. It was announced in November, 1968, that a limited form of membership of the Commonwealth had been devised for Nauru at the request of its Government.

Parliament has eighteen members including the Cabinet and Speaker. Voting is compulsory for all Nauruans over 20 years of age, except in certain specified instances. Elections are held every three years. The Cabinet is chosen by the President and comprises not fewer than five nor more than six members including the President.

President and Minister for External Affairs, Internal Affairs, Island Development and Industry, Civil Aviation Authority and the Public Service, His Excellency Hon. Hammer DeRoburt, G.C.M.G., O.B.E.

Cabinet

Works and Community Services and Minister Assisting the President, Hon. R. B. Detundamo.
Finance, Hon. K. Clodumar.
Health and Education, Hon. R. Kun.
Justice, Hon. B. Dowiyogo.

JUDICIARY

A Supreme Court of Nauru is presided over by the Chief Justice. The District Court, which is subordinate to the Supreme Court, is presided over by a Resident Magistrate. Both the Supreme Court and the District Court are Courts of Record. The Supreme Court exercises both original and appellate jurisdiction.

Nauru has a hospital service and other medical and dental services. There is also a maternity and child welfare service. Education is available in 9 primary and 2 secondary schools on the island with a total enrolment of about 1,600 pupils receiving primary education and 500 secondary education.

PRODUCTION, ETC.

The only fertile areas are the narrow coastal belt and local requirements of fruit and vegetables are mostly met by imports. The economy is heavily dependent on the extraction of phosphate, of which the island has one of the world's richest deposits. About 2 million tonnes of phosphate are mined each year, providing employment for over 1,000 people. The industry has been run since 1970 by the Nauru Phosphate Corporation. Considerable investments have been made abroad with the royalties on phosphate exports to provide for a time when production declines.

The Nauru Pacific Line owns six ships: the Government-owned Air Nauru operates scheduled air services throughout the Pacific region and to Australia, New Zealand, Japan, Singapore and the Philippines.

Trade with U.K.

	1985	1986
Imports from U.K.	£1,199,000	£1,239,000
Exports to U.K.	479,000	148,000

BRITISH HIGH COMMISSION (*see* Suva, Fiji).

NIGERIA

(Federal Republic of Nigeria)

AREA, POPULATION, ETC.—The Republic of Nigeria is situated on the west coast of Africa. It is bounded on the south by the Gulf of Guinea, on the west by the Republic of Benin, on the north by Niger and on the east by Cameroon. It has an area of 356,669 sq. miles (923,768 sq. km.), with a population presently estimated at around 100,000,000. The population is almost entirely African. The main ethnic groups are Hausa/Fulani, Yoruba and Ibo, and the principal languages are English, Hausa, Yoruba and Ibo. Over half the population are Muslim, these being concentrated in the north and west. In the southern areas in particular there are many Christians.

A belt of mangrove swamp forest 10–60 miles in width lies along the entire coastline. North of this there is a zone 50–100 miles wide of tropical rain forest and oil-palms. North of this the country rises and the vegetation changes to open woodland and savannah. In the extreme north the country is semi-desert. There are few mountains, but in Northern Nigeria the central plateau rises to an average level of 4,000 feet. The Niger, Benue, and Cross are the main rivers.

The climate varies with the types of country described above, but Nigeria lies entirely within the tropics and temperatures are high. The rainy season is from about April to October; rainfall varies from under 25 inches a year in the extreme north to 172 inches on the coast line. During the dry season the *harmattan* wind blows from the desert; it is cool and laden with fine particles of dust.

CAPITAL.—ΨLAGOS, estimated population, 3,000,000. Other important towns are Ibadan, Ka-duna, Kano, Benin City, Enugu and ΨPort Harcourt. Movement of Federal Ministries to a new capital at Abuja has begun.

FLAG.—Three equal vertical bands, green, white and green.

NATIONAL DAY.—October 1 (Republic Day).

NATIONAL ANTHEM.—Arise, O Compatriots.

GOVERNMENT

The Federation of Nigeria attained independence as a member of the Commonwealth on Oct. 1, 1960 and became a republic in 1963. On Jan. 15, 1966 the military took power, suspended the Constitution and dissolved the legislature. In 1979 civil rule was restored under a new constitution similar to that of the United States after elections at National and State level. After similar elections in 1983 the new administration was removed by the military on Dec. 31, this regime itself being overthrown in Aug. 1985. A 28-member Armed Forces Ruling Council was sworn in on Aug. 30. It is the country's most senior decision-making body. The Council of Ministers is the third most senior body after the A.F.R.C. and the National Council of States, which comprises the 19 State Governors.

Originally regional in structure the Federation was divided into 12 states in 1967 and into the present 19 states in 1976.

Head of State, Commander-in-Chief of the Armed Forces, Chairman of the Armed Forces Ruling Council, Maj.-Gen. Ibrahim Babangida.

Armed Forces Ruling Council

Chairman, Maj.-Gen. Ibrahim Babangida.
Members, Maj.-Gen. D. Y. Bali; Maj.-Gen. S. Abacha; Rear-Adm. A. Aikhomu; Air Vice-Marshal I. Alfa; Rear-Adm. P. S. Koshoni; Maj.-Gen. M. G. Nasko; Maj.-Gen. P. Omu; Air Vice-Marshal M. Yahaya; Brig. P. Adomokai; Brig. D. O. Ajayi; Brig. A. B. Mamman; Brig. O. Oni; Brig. G. Duba; Brig. O. Diya; Brig. J. N. Dogonyaro; Cdre. M. A. B. Elegbede; Cdre. N. Kanu; Cdre. S. Aluko; Cdre. A. Nyako; Air Cdre. N. Yusuf; Air Cdre. L. Koinyan; Air Cdre. N. Iman; Col. J. N. Shagaya; Col. H. Akilu; Col. A. T. Ayuba; Col. D. Mark; Brig. Y. Y. Kure.

Council of Ministers

Agriculture, Water Resources and Rural Development, Maj.-Gen. G. Nasko.
Communications, Col. A. T. Ayuba.
Defence, Maj.-Gen. D. Y. Bali.
Education, Prof. J. Aminu.
Employment, Labour and Productivity, Brig. I. Nwa-chukwu.
External Affairs, Prof. B. Akinyemi.
Federal Capital Territory, Abuja, Air Cdre. H. Abdul-lahi.
Finance, Dr. S. P. Okongwu.
Health, Prof. K. Ransome-Kuti.
Information and Culture, Prince Tony Momoh.
Internal Affairs, Col. J. N. Shagaya.
Industry, Lt.-Gen. A. I. Akinrinade.
Justice, Prince Bola Ajibola.
Mines, Power and Steel, Alhaji Buna Sherrif Musa.
National Planning, Dr. K. I. Kalu.
Petroleum Resources, Alhaji Rilwanu Lukman.
Science and Technology, Prof. E. Emovon.
Social Development, Youth and Sports, Air Cdre. B. Lawal.
Trade, Alhaji Samaila Mamman.
Transport and Aviation, Brig. J. T. Useni.
Works and Housing, Alhaji Abubakar Umar.
Special Duties, Air Vice-Marshal A. I. Shekarri.

NIGERIA HIGH COMMISSION
Nigeria House, 9 Northumberland Avenue,
WC2N 5BX
[01–839 1244]

High Commissioner, His Excellency Mr. George Dove-
Edwin (1986).

BRITISH HIGH COMMISSION
Eleke Crescent, Victoria Island, Lagos

High Commissioner, His Excellency Sir Martin
Kenneth Ewans, K.C.M.G. (1987).

British Council Representative, D. M. Waterhouse,
19A, Olosa Street, Opposite Eko Hotel, Victoria
Island (P.O. Box 3702), Lagos. Branch offices
at Kano, Kaduna and Enugu.

EDUCATION

A programme was introduced in September 1976
intended to achieve universal primary education.
Numbers of pupils in 1982–83 were: 15·4 million in
primary schools, 3·5 million in secondary schools,
53,766 in polytechnics and 88,636 in universities.
There are 24 universities.

COMMUNICATIONS

The Nigerian railway system, which is controlled
by the Nigerian Railway Corporation, is the most
extensive in West Africa. There are 2,178 route miles
of lines. The principal international airlines operating from Lagos, Kano and Port Harcourt bring
Nigeria within about six hours of the Western
European capitals. There are also services to other
parts of Africa and to the United States. A network
of internal air services connects the main centres.
The principal seaports are served by a number of
shipping lines, including the Nigerian National Line.
A nationwide television and radio network is being
developed, with each State eventually having its own
television and radio station. There is a network of
meteorological reporting stations.

PRODUCTION AND INDUSTRY

Nigeria was a predominantly agricultural country
until the early 1970s with agriculture contributing
over 60 per cent of export revenue and 45 per cent of
G.N.P. Tin and calumbite mining on the Jos plateau,
textiles and coal mining were also important. The
major exports were ground nuts, palm products, tin,
cocoa, rubber and timber. Recently oil has provided
over 90 per cent of exports revenue and agricultural
exports have greatly declined. Nigeria now imports
wheat, rice and other food. Though agriculture still
employs half the labour force it contributes only 20
per cent of G.N.P., exceeded by trading and oil. The
construction sector is twice as large as the manufacturing sector and industries dependent on imported
raw materials such as vehicle assembly have faltered
recently. Three oil refineries are in operation at Port
Harcourt, Warri and Kaduna. A steel plant has been
opened near Warri and a larger one is being completed
at Ajaokuta. Other projects include natural gas liqui-
faction, petro-chemicals, fertilizers and several power
stations plus the Abuja Federal Capital. Several
large irrigation schemes have been completed and
more are planned.

TRADE

Oil revenues have been falling since 1981 and are
now restricted by an OPEC production quota and
lower prices to half their peak level. In March 1982
imports curbs and payments restrictions were introduced but exchange reserves fell and debts increased.

Austerity measures were introduced, and continue,
while the present Government attempts to stimulate
greater self-reliance in the economy by encouraging
non-oil exports and the use of local rather than
imported raw materials.

The unit of currency is the *Naira.*

Trade with U.K.

	1985	1986
Imports from U.K.	£960,703,000	£566,176,000
Exports to U.K.	660,410,000	329,036,000

PAPUA NEW GUINEA

AREA, POPULATION, ETC.—Papua New Guinea extends from the equator to Cape Baganowa in the
Louisiade Archipelago at 11° S. latitude and from the
border with Irian Jaya to 160° E. longitude. The total
area of Papua New Guinea is 178,260 sq. miles, (461,691
sq. km.), of which approximately 152,420 sq. miles
form the mainland, on the island of New Guinea. The
country has many island groups, principally the
Bismarck Archipelago, a portion of the Solomon
Islands, the Trobriands, the D'Entrecasteaux Islands
and the Louisade Archipelago. The main islands of
the Bismarck Archipelago are New Britain, New
Ireland and Manus. Bougainville is the largest of the
Solomon Islands within Papua New Guinea.

Papua New Guinea lies within the tropics and has
a typically monsoonal climate. Temperature and
humidity are uniformly high throughout the year.
The average rainfall is about 80 inches per year but
there are wide variations—from 47 inches at Port
Moresby to over 200 inches in mountainous western
areas.

The estimated population in 1985 was 3,329,000.
The inhabitants of the country comprise a great
diversity of physical types and a large number of
linguistic groups.

CAPITAL.—PORT MORESBY. Estimated population
(1985), 139,300. Other major towns are Lae, Rabaul,
Madang, Wewak, Goroka and Mount Hagen.

FLAG.—A rectangle divided diagonally from the
top of the hoist to the bottom of the fly, the upper
segment scarlet and containing a soaring yellow bird
of paradise. The lower segment is black charged with
five white five-pointed stars representing the
Southern Cross.

NATIONAL DAY.—September 16 (Independence
Day).

NATIONAL ANTHEM.—Arise All You Sons.

GOVERNMENT

New Guinea was sighted by Portuguese and
Spanish navigators in the early sixteenth century,
but remained largely isolated from the rest of the
world. In 1884, a British Protectorate was proclaimed
over the southern coast of New Guinea (Papua) and
the adjacent islands. British New Guinea, as the
Protectorate was called, was annexed outright in
1888. In 1906 the Territory of British New Guinea
was placed under the authority of the Commonwealth
of Australia. Also in 1884 Germany had formally
taken possession of certain northern areas, which
later came to be known as the Trust Territory of New
Guinea. In 1914 the German areas were occupied by
Australian troops and remained under military
administration until 1921, when the League of
Nations conferred on Australia a mandate for their
government.

New Guinea was administered under the Mandate
and Papua under the Papua Act until the invasion
by the Japanese in 1942 when the civil administration
was suspended until the surrender of the Japanese in
1945.

The first House of Assembly for the whole country met in 1964 and included an elected majority and ten nominated official members. After 1970 there was a gradual assumption of powers by the Papua New Guinea Government, culminating in formal self-government in December 1973. Final reserve powers held by Australia over defence and foreign relations were relinquished to Papua New Guinea in March 1975, and Papua New Guinea achieved full independence on September 16, 1975.

Elections are held every five years. The Parliament comprises 109 elected Members, 20 from Regional electorates, the remainder from Open electorates. There are 19 provinces, which have their own provincial governments with certain legislative and administrative powers.

Governor-General, Sir Kingsford Dibela, G.C.M.G.

National Executive Council
(CABINET)

Prime Minister, Rt. Hon. Paias Wingti, C.M.G.
Deputy P.M. and Minister for Trade and Industry, Sir Julius Chan, K.B.E.
Finance and Planning, Galeva Kwarara.
Public Service, Dennis Young.
Lands and Physical Planning, Kala Swokim.
Housing, Tom Amaiu.
Agriculture and Livestock, Gai Duwabane.
Minerals and Energy, John Kaputin.
Fisheries and Marine Resources, Alan Ebu.
Forests, Tom Horik.
Labour and Employment, Masket Iangalio.
Education and Foreign Affairs (acting), Aruru Matiabe.
Health, Timothy Ward.
Home Affairs and Youth, Eserom Burege.
Environment and Conservation, Perry Zeipi.
Police, Legu Vagi.
Civil Aviation, Culture and Tourism, Hugo Berghuser.
Justice, Albert Kipalan.
Administrative Services, Aron Noaio.
Transport, Roy Yaki.
Works, Aita Ivarato.
Communications, Gabriel Ramoi.
Defence, James Pokasui.
Provincial Affairs, Jacob Lemecki.
Minister without Portfolio, Ted Diro.

PAPUA NEW GUINEA HIGH COMMISSION
3rd Floor, 14 Waterloo Place, SW1R 4AR
[01–930 0922/7]

High Commissioner, His Excellency Mr. Ilinome F. Tarua, O.B.E. (1983).

BRITISH HIGH COMMISSION
P.O. Box 739, Port Moresby

High Commissioner, His Excellency Michael Edward Howell, O.B.E. (1986).

COMMUNICATIONS

Road communications are very limited, the most important road being that linking Lae with the populous Highlands.

Air Niugini (the national airline) and Qantas operate regular air services between Port Moresby and Australia. Air Niugini also operates services to Manila (Philippines), Honiara (Solomon Islands), Jayapura (Indonesia), Honolulu and Singapore. Internal air services are operated by Air Niugini, Douglas Airways, and Talair.

Several shipping companies operate cargo services between Papua New Guinea and Australia, Europe, the Far East and U.S.A. There are very limited cargo and passenger services between Papua New Guinea main ports, outports, plantations and missions.

Papua New Guinea is linked by international cable to Australia, Guam, Hong Kong, Kota Kinabalu, the Far East and U.S.A. Telecommunications are widely available.

ECONOMY

Until the 1970s the Papua New Guinea economy was based almost entirely on agriculture. At the beginning of the 20th century copra plantations formed the basis of the cash economy. Further crops which have been introduced over the years are cocoa, tea, coffee, palm oil, rubber, groundnuts, spices and timber. A variety of commercial agricultural developments now co-exist with the traditional informal rural economy. Government expenditure is still reliant on Australian budgetary support, to the extent of just under 30 per cent in 1983.

In 1972, Bougainville Copper Pty Ltd (BCL) began mining in the North Solomons Province, producing copper, silver and gold. There are extensive mineral deposits throughout Papua New Guinea, including nickel, chromite, bauxite and possibly commercial deposits of oil and gas. The most important new development is the exploitation of large copper and gold deposits on the Ok Tedi, in the Western Province.

In 1984 the Papua New Guinea economy was influenced by good prices for agricultural commodities, offset by low prices for copper and gold. New developments to promote export crops and increase employment, typically involving foreign investment, are planned for the future.

Industry includes processing of primary products, and brewing, bottling and packaging, paint, plywood, and metal manufacturing and the construction industries.

Although the formal economy is still dominated by non-Papua New Guineans, the participation of Papua New Guineans is increasing.

Trade with U.K.

	1985	1986
Imports from U.K.	£12,592,000	£12,084,000
Exports to U.K.	59,642,000	38,474,000

The unit of currency is the *Kina*.

ST. CHRISTOPHER AND NEVIS

(The Federation of St. Christopher and Nevis)

The State of St. Christopher and Nevis is located at the northern end of the Eastern Caribbean. It comprises the islands of St. Christopher (St. Kitts) (65 sq. miles: 168 sq. km.; population about 35,700) and Nevis (36 sq. miles: 93·2 sq. km.; population about 9,400).

St. Christopher, lat. 17° 18′ N. and long. 62° 48′ W. was the first island in the British West Indies to be colonized (1623). The central area of the island is forest-clad and mountainous, rising to the 3,792 ft. Mount Liamuiga.

CAPITAL—ΨBASSETERRE (estimated population, 15,000).

Nevis, lat. 17° 10′ N. and long. 62° 35′ W. is separated from the southern tip of St. Christopher by a strait two miles wide and is dominated by the central Nevis Peak, 3,232 ft. *Chief town*—ΨCharlestown (pop. 1,200), is a port of entry.

FLAG—Three diagonal bands, green, black and red; each colour separated by a stripe of yellow. Two white stars on the black band.

NATIONAL DAY.—September 19 (Independence Day).

NATIONAL ANTHEM.—Our Land of Beauty.

GOVERNMENT

The Territory of St. Kitts and Nevis became a State in Association with Britain on Feb. 27, 1967. The State of St. Kitts and Nevis became an independent nation on Sept. 19, 1983, with a new constitution under which Great Britain relinquished its responsibility for defence and external affairs. Under the new Constitution, H.M. The Queen is Head of State, represented in the islands by the Governor-General. There is a central Cabinet Government with a Ministerial system, the Head of which is the Prime Minister of St. Kitts and Nevis, and a National Assembly located on St. Kitts. On Nevis there is a Nevis Island Administration, the Head being styled Premier of Nevis, and a Nevis Island Assembly.

Governor-General, His Excellency Sir Clement Athelston Arrindell, G.C.M.G. (1981).

Cabinet

Prime Minister and Minister of Finance, Home Affairs and Foreign Affairs,, Rt. Hon. Dr. K. A. Simmonds.
Deputy P.M. and Minister of Labour and Tourism, Rt. Hon. M. O. Powell.
Natural Resources and Environment, Hon. S. Daniel.
Education, Health and Community Affairs, Hon. S. E. Morris.
Communications, Works and Public Utilities, Hon. I. A. W. Stevens.
Agriculture, Lands, Housing and Development, Hon. H. C. Heyliger.
Women's Affairs, Hon. Constance Mitcham.
Trade and Industry, Hon. F. Jones.
In Ministry of Finance, Hon. R. Caines.
Without Portfolio, Hon. U. S. Swanston.
Attorney-General, Hon. S. W. T. Seaton.
Cabinet Secretary, C. Farier.

ST. KITTS HIGH COMMISSION
10 Kensington Court, W8 5DL
[01-937 9522]

Acting High Commissioner for the Eastern Caribbean States, Mr. Charles M. E. Cadet, C.B.E.

FINANCE

	1984	1985
Revenue	EC$65,894,030	EC$58,615,400
Expenditure	54,850,905	56,173,221

ECONOMY

The economy of the islands has been based on sugar for over three centuries. Tourism and light industry are now being developed. The economy of Nevis centres on small peasant farmers, but a sea-island cotton industry is being developed for export.

COMMUNICATIONS

Basseterre is a port of registry and has deep water harbour facilities. Golden Rock airport, on St. Kitts, can take most large jet aircraft; Newcastle airstrip on Nevis can take small aircraft and has night landing facilities.
The sea ferry route from Basseterre to Charlestown is 11 miles.

Trade with U.K.

	1985	1986
Imports from U.K.	£5,256,000	£6,008,000
Exports to U.K.	5,634,000	4,429,000

ST. LUCIA

St. Lucia, the second largest of the Windward group, situated in 13° 54′ N. lat. and 60° 50′ W. long., at a distance of about 21 miles N. of St. Vincent, and 24 miles S. of Martinique, is 27 miles in length, with an extreme breadth of 14 miles. It comprises an area of 238 sq. miles (616 sq. km.), with an estimated population (1985) of 130,000. It possesses perhaps the most interesting history of all the smaller islands. Fights raged hotly around it, and it constantly changed hands between the English and the French. It is mountainous, its highest point being Mt. Gimie (3,145 feet) and for the most part it is covered with forest and tropical vegetation.

CAPITAL.—ΨCASTRIES (estimated population 1984, 50,798) is recognized as being one of the finest ports in the West Indies on account of its reputation as a safe anchorage in the hurricane season.

FLAG.—Blue, bearing in centre a device of yellow over black over white triangles having a common base.

NATIONAL DAY.—February 22 (Independence Day).
NATIONAL ANTHEM.—"Sons and Daughters of Saint Lucia."

GOVERNMENT

St. Lucia became independent within the Commonwealth on Feb. 22, 1979. The Head of State is H.M. The Queen, represented in the island by a St. Lucian Governor-General, and there is a bicameral legislature. The Senate has 11 members, 6 appointed by the ruling party, 3 by the Opposition and 2 by the Governor-General. The House of Assembly, which has a life of five years, has 17 elected Members and a Speaker, who may be elected from outside the House.

Acting Governor-General, His Excellency Sir Vincent Floissac, C.M.G., Q.C.

Cabinet

Prime Minister, Minister of Finance, Foreign Affairs, Development and Home Affairs, Rt. Hon. John G. M. Compton.
Deputy P.M. and Minister of Trade, Industry and Tourism, Hon. George Mallet.
Communications, Works and Transport, Hon. Senator Desmond Fostin.
Health, Housing, Labour, Information and Broadcasting, Hon. Romanus Lansiquot.
Youth, Community Development, Social Affairs, Sport, Hon. Stephenson King.
Attorney General and Minister for Legal Affairs, Hon. Senator Parry Husbands.
Agriculture, Lands, Fisheries and Co-operatives, Hon. Ferdinand Henry.
Education and Culture, Hon. Louis George.

ST. LUCIA HIGH COMMISSION
10 Kensington Court, W8 5DL.
[01-937 9522]

Acting High Commissioner for the Eastern Caribbean States, Mr. Charles M. E. Cadet, C.B.E.

OFFICE OF THE BRITISH HIGH COMMISSION
Columbus Square, P.O. Box 227, Castries.

High Commissioner, (resides at Bridgetown, Barbados).
Resident Representative, C. H. Woodland.

ECONOMY

The economy is mainly agrarian, with manufacturing based on the processing of agricultural products. Principal crops are bananas, coconuts, cocoa, mangoes, avocado pears, breadfruit, spices, root crops such as cassava and yams, and citrus fruit. Attempts are being made to diversify the economy, in particular through greater industrialization; tourism is also of increasing importance, with 96,649 visiting the island in 1985.

The principal exports are bananas, coconut products (copra, edible oils, soap), cardboard boxes, beer, and textile manufactures. The chief imports are flour, meat, machinery, building materials, motor vehicles, cotton piece goods, petroleum and fertilizers.

Trade with U.K.

	1985	1986
Imports from U.K........	£11,550,000	£12,441,000
Exports to U.K.	44,047,000	59,855,000

ST. VINCENT AND THE GRENADINES

The territory of the State of St. Vincent includes certain of the Grenadines, a chain of small islands stretching 40 miles across the Caribbean Sea between Grenada and St. Vincent, some of the larger of which are Bequia, Canouan, Mayreau, Mustique, Union Island, Petit St. Vincent and Prune Island. The whole territory extends 150 sq. miles (388 sq. km.).

The main island, St. Vincent, is situated between 13° 6' and 14° 35' N. latitude and 61° 6' and 61° 20' W. longitude, approximately 21 miles south west of St. Lucia and 100 miles west of Barbados. The island is 18 miles long and 11 miles wide at its extremities comprising an area of 133 sq. miles (344 sq. km.), and a population (1985 U.N. estimate) of 104,000. St. Vincent was discovered by Christopher Columbus in 1498. It was granted by Charles I to the Earl of Carlisle in 1627 and after subsequent grants and a series of occupations alternately by the French and English, it was finally restored to Britain in 1783.

CAPITAL.—ΨKINGSTOWN, population approximately 33,694.

FLAG.—Three vertical bands, of blue, yellow and green, with three green diamonds in the shape of a "V" mounted on the yellow band.

NATIONAL DAY.—October 27 (Independence Day).

NATIONAL ANTHEM.—St. Vincent, Land So Beautiful.

GOVERNMENT

St. Vincent and the Grenadines achieved full independence within the Commonwealth on Oct. 27, 1979.

St. Vincent has a constitution under which there is a Governor-General who is Her Majesty's Representative. Except where otherwise provided, the Governor-General is required to act in accordance with the advice of the Prime Minister.

The House of Assembly consists of 13 elected members and 6 Senators appointed by the Governor-General. It is presided over by a Speaker elected by the House from within or without it.

Governor-General, His Excellency Sir Joseph Lambert Eustace, G.C.M.G., G.C.V.O., *sworn in* Feb. 21, 1985.

Cabinet

Prime Minister, Minister of Finance and Foreign Affairs, Rt. Hon. James Mitchell.

Trade, Industry and Agriculture, Hon. M. P. De-Freitas.

Housing, Labour and Community Development, Hon. J. C. Scott.

Tourism, Aviation, Culture and Women's Affairs, Hon. B. B. Williams.

Education, Hon. J. C. A. Horne.

Health, Hon. D. E. Jack.

Communications and Works, Hon. A. C. Cruickshank.

Attorney General and Minister of Legal Affairs and Information, Hon. P. R. Campbell, C.V.O.

Ministers of State, Hon. H. B. Young (*Trade, Industry and Agriculture*); Hon. L. Jones (*Housing, Labour and Community Development*).

Parliamentary Secretary, Hon. R. S. Nanton (*Office of the Prime Minister*).

ST. VINCENT AND THE GRENADINES
HIGH COMMISSION
10 Kensington Court, W8 5DL
[01-937 9522]

Acting High Commissioner for the Eastern Caribbean States, Mr. Charles M. E. Cadet, C.B.E.

OFFICE OF THE BRITISH HIGH COMMISSION
Granby Street (P.O. Box 132), Kingstown.

High Commissioner, (resides at Bridgetown, Barbados).

Resident Representative, M. S. Hone, M.B.E.

ECONOMY

This is based mainly on agriculture but the tourist and manufacturing industries have been expanding. The main products are bananas, arrowroot, coconuts, sugar, cocoa, spices and various kinds of food crops. The main imports are foodstuffs (meat, rice, beverages), textiles, lumber, cement and other building materials, fertilizers, motor vehicles and fuel.

EDUCATION

Primary and secondary education in Government schools is free but not compulsory. In 1982 there were 24,651 enrolments in state primary schools and 5,501 enrolments in state secondary schools.

Trade with U.K.

	1985	1986
Imports from U.K.	£6,600,000	£8,288,000
Exports to U.K.	22,339,000	21,161,000

SEYCHELLES

(The Republic of Seychelles)

The Republic of Seychelles, in the Indian Ocean, consists of 115 islands with a total land area of 108 sq. miles (280 sq. km.), spread over 400,000 square miles of ocean. There is a relatively compact granitic group, 32 islands in all, with high hills and mountains (highest point about 2,990 ft.), of which Mahé is the largest and most populated (90 per cent of the population live on Mahé): and the outlying coralline group, for the most part, only a little above sea-level. Although only 4° S. of the Equator, the climate is pleasant though tropical. The population was estimated (end 1984) to be 65,032.

CAPITAL.—ΨVICTORIA (population, 1982, 24,733), on the N.E. side of Mahé.

FLAG.—Red over green, divided by wavy white band.

NATIONAL DAY.—June 5.

NATIONAL ANTHEM.—Fyer Seselwa (Proud Seychellois).

GOVERNMENT

Proclaimed as French territory in 1756, the Mahé group began to be settled as a dependency of Mauritius from 1770, was captured by a British ship in 1794, changed hands several times between 1803 and 1814, when it was finally assigned to Great Britain. By Letters Patent of September, 1903, these islands, together with the coralline group, were formed into a separate Colony. On June 29, 1976, the Islands became an independent republic within the Commonwealth. A *coup d'état* took place on June 5, 1977.

A new constitution making Seychelles a one-party state came into force in June 1979. The executive power lies with the President, who is elected by universal suffrage for a five year term. Legislative power lies with the President and the People's Assembly (which has 23 elected members and two nominated by the President), an independent judiciary commission and an integrity commission.

President, France Albert René, *assumed office* June 5, 1977; *elected* June 26, 1979; *re-elected* June 18, 1984.

Council of Ministers

Administration, Finance, Legal Affairs, Planning, External Relations and Defence, The President.
Education, Information and Youth, James Michel.
National Development, Jacques Hodoul.
Health and Social Services, Joseph Belmont.
Political Organization, Esme Jumeau.
Internal Affairs, Mrs. Rita Sinon.
Tourism and Transport, Ralph Adam.
Manpower, Jeremie Bonnelame.

Seychelles High Commission
Box No. 4PE, 50 Conduit Street, W1A 4PE
[01–439 0405]

High Commissioner, Her Excellency Mrs. Danielle de St. Jorre (1983).
Counsellor and Acting High Commissioner, R. F. Delpech.

British High Commission
Victoria House, P.O. Box 161,
Victoria, Mahé.

High Commissioner, His Excellency (Alexander Basil) Peter Smart (1986).

Economy

The economy is based on tourism, agriculture and fishing. The Government has recently been encouraging farmers to diversify from the traditional plantation crops into the growing of food crops and rearing of livestock. However, copra and cinnamon bark remain the principal agricultural exports. Fishing and forestry are also considered to have considerable potential and are being developed.

Tourism has proved a major industry since the opening of an international airport on Mahé. Other industries include brewing and tobacco, plastics, soap and detergent factories are in operation. There is also a range of small-scale manufacturing industries.

Trade

	1984	1985
Imports	Rs.616,682,000	Rs.718,700,000
Exports	21,398,000	19,500,000
Re-exports	160,085,000	177,200,000

The principal imports are foodstuffs, beverages, tobacco, mineral fuels, manufactured items, building materials, machinery and transport equipment. The chief exports are copra, fish (fresh and frozen) and cinnamon bark. Re-exports cover a large proportion of exports from Seychelles and include such items as petroleum products, fuel and services for both aviation and shipping needs.

Trade with U.K.

	1985	1986
Imports from U.K.	£9,561,000	£9,639,000
Exports to U.K.	1,663,000	938,000

SIERRA LEONE

(The Republic of Sierra Leone)

Area, Population, etc.—Sierra Leone, with a total land area of 27,699 sq. miles (71,740 sq. km.), is on the west coast of Africa, between Guinea and Liberia. There was a population at the Census of 1974 of 3,123,000; a U.N. estimate put the population in 1985 at 3,602,000. The origins of the country date back to the late 18th century when a project was begun to settle destitute Africans from England on Freetown peninsula. In 1808 the settlement was declared a Crown Colony and became the main base in West Africa for enforcing the 1807 Act outlawing the slave trade. The Colony was also used as a settlement for Africans from North America and the West Indies, and great numbers of Africans rescued from slave ships, also settled there. Their descendants, known as Creoles, still live on Freetown peninsula. The southern half of Sierra Leone is inhabited by peoples whose languages fall into the Mende group; the northern half by the Temne, and smaller groups such as the Limba, Loko, Koranko and Susu.

Capital.—Freetown (population at 1985 Census, 470,000).

Flag.—Three horizontal stripes of leaf green, white and cobalt blue.

National Day.—April 27 (Independence Day).
National Anthem.—"High We Exalt Thee, Realm of the Free."

Government

Sierra Leone became a fully independent state within the Commonwealth on April 27, 1961. On April 19, 1971 a Republican Constitution was adopted and Dr. Siaka Stevens became the first Executive President. In June 1978 Sierra Leone became a one-Party State, following approval by Parliament and a Referendum. The first General Election under the one party system was held on May 1, 1982. The Parliament now comprises 85 elected members and 12 Paramount Chiefs, plus nine nominated members, two of whom are the Army Commander and the Inspector General of Police.

President, His Excellency Maj.-Gen. Joseph Saidu Momoh, *sworn in* Nov. 28, 1985.

Cabinet

President and Minister of Defence with responsibility for Public Services, His Excellency Maj.-Gen. J. S. Momoh.
First Vice-President and Minister of Lands, Housing and Environment, Hon. A. B. Kamara.
Second Vice-President and Minister of State Enterprises, Hon. S. Jusu Sheriff.
Finance, Hon. H. Gbessay Kanu.
Attorney-General and Minister of Justice, Hon. Dr. Abdulai Conteh.
Foreign Affairs, Hon. Abdul Karim Koroma.
Economic Planning and National Development, Hon. Dr. Sheka Kanu.
Agriculture, Natural Resources and Forestry, Hon. Suffian Kargbo.
Trade and Industry, Hon. J. Amara Bangali.
Education, Cultural Affairs and Sports, Hon. Dr. Moses Dumbuya.
Transport and Communications, Hon. Michael Abdulai.
Mines, Hon. Birch Conteh.
Health, Hon. Dr. Wiltshire Johnson.
Works and Labour, Hon. Prof. V. Mambu.
Energy and Power, Hon. Dr. Sheku Sesay.
Information and Broadcasting, Hon. Eya Mbayo.

Tourism, Hon. Abdul Iscandari.
Internal Affairs, Hon. M. L. Siddique.
Rural Development, Social Services and Youth, Hon. Alhaji Musa Kabia.
Ministers of State, Hon. Harry Williams (*Leader of the House*); Hon. Maj.-Gen. M. S. Tarawallie (*Force Cdr.*); Hon. Bambay Kamara (*Inspector General of Police*); Hon. E. T. Kamara (*Party Affairs*).

SIERRA LEONE HIGH COMMISSION
33 Portland Place, W1N 3AG
[01–636 6483–5]

High Commissioner, His Excellency Mr. Caleb B. Aubee (1987).

BRITISH HIGH COMMISSION
Standard Bank of Sierra Leone Building
Lightfoot Boston Street, Freetown

High Commissioner, His Excellency Derek William Partridge, C.M.G. (1986).
British Council Representative, G. W. Reid, P.O. Box 124, Tower Hill, Freetown.

COMMUNICATIONS

Since the phasing out of the railway system in 1974 the road network has been developed considerably and there are now 5,000 miles of roads in the country, over 2,000 miles being surfaced. A bridge has been constructed over the Mano River linking Sierra Leone and Liberia.

The Freetown international airport is situated at Lungi, across the Sierra Leone River from Freetown. The main port is Freetown, which has one of the largest natural harbours in the world, and where there is a deep water quay providing about six berths for medium sized ships. There are smaller ports at Pepel, Bonthe and Niti.

Radio and television are operated by the Department of Broadcasting of the Sierra Leone Government. There are two shortwave transmitting and receiving stations in Freetown. Broadcasts are made in several of the more important indigenous languages in addition to English. There is also a weekly broadcast in French.

EDUCATION

In 1986 there were 1,289 primary schools in Sierra Leone and 190 secondary schools. Technical education is provided in the two Government Technical Institutes, situated in Freetown and Kenema, in two Trade Centres and in the technical training establishments of the mining companies. Teacher training is carried out at the university, six colleges in the Provinces and in the Milton Margai Training College near Freetown. The University of Sierra Leone (1967), consists of Fourah Bay College (1827) and Njala University College (1964).

PRODUCTION AND TRADE

On the Freetown peninsula, farming is largely confined to the production of cassava and garden crops, such as maize and vegetables, for local consumption. In the hinterland, the principal agricultural product is rice, which is the staple food of the country, and cash crops such as cocoa, coffee, palm kernels, and ginger.

The economy depends largely on mineral exports mainly diamonds, gold, bauxite and rutile. Iron ore production recommenced in 1982. Diamonds provide about 60 per cent of export earnings. Total exports in 1983–84 were estimated at Le102·1 million.

Trade with U.K.

	1985	1986
Imports from U.K.	£23,620,000	£17,403,000
Exports to U.K.	17,435,000	11,599,000

Currency.—The basic unit is the *Leone.*

SINGAPORE

AREA, POPULATION, ETC.—The Republic of Singapore consists of the island of Singapore and 57 smaller islands, covering a total area of 224 sq. miles (581 sq. km.). Singapore island is 26 miles long and 14 miles in breadth and is situated just north of the Equator off the southern extremity of the Malay Peninsula, from which it is separated by the Straits of Johore. A causeway, carrying a road, railway and a water pipeline, crosses the three-quarters of a mile to the mainland. The highest point of the island is 581 feet above sea level. The climate is hot and humid and there are no clearly defined seasons. Rainfall averages 240 cm. a year and temperature ranges from 24°–32° C (76°–89° F).

In June 1986, the population was 2,586,200. (Chinese, 1,972,000; Malays, 387,400; Indians, 166,800; others (Europeans, Eurasians, etc.), 60,000). Malay, Mandarin, Tamil and English are the official languages. At least 8 Chinese dialects are used.

FLAG.—Horizontal bands of red over white; crescent with five five-point stars on red band near staff.
NATIONAL DAY.—August 9.
NATIONAL ANTHEM.—Majulah Singapura.

GOVERNMENT

Singapore, where Sir Stamford Raffles had first established a trading post under the East India Company in 1819, was incorporated with Penang and Malacca to form the Straits Settlements in 1826. The Straits Settlements became a Crown Colony in 1867. Singapore fell into Japanese hands in 1942 and civil government was not restored until 1946, when it became a separate colony. Internal self-government and the title "State of Singapore" were introduced in 1959. Singapore became a state of Malaysia when the Federation was enlarged in September, 1963, but left Malaysia and became an independent sovereign state within the Commonwealth on August 9, 1965. Singapore adopted a Republican constitution from that date, the Yang di-Pertuan Negara being restyled President. There is a Cabinet collectively responsible to a fully-elected Parliament of 79 members.

HEAD OF STATE

President, Wee Kim Wee, *elected* Aug. 30, 1985.

Cabinet

Prime Minister, Lee Kuan Yew, G.C.M.G., C.H.
Senior Minister, S. Rajaratnam.
First Deputy P.M. and Minister for Defence, Goh Chok Tong.
Second Deputy P.M., Ong Teng Cheong.
Law, E. W. Barker.
Foreign Affairs and National Development, S. Dhanabalan.
Education, Dr. Tony Tan Keng Yam.
Environment, Dr. Ahmad Mattar.
Communications and Information, Dr. Yeo Ning Hong.
Home Affairs, Prof. S. Jayakumar.
Finance, Dr. Richard Hu Tsu Tau.
Labour, Lee Yock Suan.
Community Development, Wong Kan Seng.

Trade and Industry, Lee Hsien Loong.
Health (acting), Yeo Cheow Tong.

Speaker of Parliament, Dr. Yeoh Ghim Seng.

SINGAPORE HIGH COMMISSION
2 Wilton Crescent, SW1X 8RW
[01–235 8315–7]

Acting High Commissioner, Mrs. Mary Seet-Cheng.

BRITISH HIGH COMMISSION
Tanglin Road, Singapore 1024

High Commissioner, His Excellency Michael Edmund
Pike, C.M.G. (1987).
British Council Representative, D. R. Howell, O.B.E.,
Rubber House, Collyer Quay, Singapore 0104.

COMMUNICATIONS

Singapore is one of the largest and busiest seaports
in the world, with deep water wharves and ship
repairing facilities. Ships also anchor in the roads,
unloading into lighters. In 1986, 69,760,000 freight
tonnes of seaborne cargo was discharged and
50,460,000 freight tonnes loaded. More than 500
shipping lines use the port, with over 30,000 foreign
flagged ships calling annually. The international
airport is at Changi, in the east of the island. There
are 25·75 km. of metric gauge railway connected to
the Malaysian rail system by the causeway across the
Straits of Johore, and 2,686 kilometres of roads.
There are both wireless and wired broadcasting
services carrying commercial advertising. There are
three television channels. The Singapore Broadcasting Authority Corporation was established in February 1980.

ECONOMY

Historically Singapore's economy was largely based
on the sale and distribution of raw materials from
surrounding countries and on entrepot trade in
finished products. In the last decade, however, new
manufacturing industries have been introduced,
including ship building and repairing, iron and steel,
textiles, footwear, wood products, micro-electronics,
scientific instruments, detergents, confectionery,
pharmaceuticals, petroleum products, etc. Singapore
has also become a financial centre with 134 commercial banks and 58 merchant banks established in the
Republic, and an oil-refining centre.
Projects now being undertaken include the construction of a Mass Rapid Transit Rail system
(opening in December 1987); expansion of Changi
airport; the improvement of public utilities (electricity and gas supply, sewage system) and telecommunications, including a submarine telephone cable
system; building projects; and computerization in
schools and government departments.

Finance (estimates)

	1986–87	1987–88
Revenue	S$14,552,911,000	S$10,804,786,000
Expenditure	22,193,618,230	21,999,157,140

Trade

	1985	1986
Total imports	S$57,817·5m	S$55,545·4m
Total exports	50,179·8m	48,985·5m

Trade with U.K.

	1985	1986
Imports from U.K........	£612,920,000	£547,419,000
Exports to U.K.	441,345,000	462,878,000

SOLOMON ISLANDS

Forming a scattered archipelago of mountainous
islands and low-lying coral atolls, Solomon Islands
stretches about 900 miles in a south-easterly direction
from Bougainville, in Papua New Guinea, to the
Santa Cruz islands. The archipelago covers an area
of about 249,000 square nautical miles while the land
area is 10,938 sq. miles (28,446 sq. km.). Solomon
Islands lies between the east longitudes 155° 30′ and
170° 30′ and between south latitudes 5° 10′ and 12° 45′.
The six biggest islands are: Choiseul, New Georgia,
Santa Isabel, Guadalcanal, Malaita and Makira. They
are characterised by precipitous, thickly-forested
mountain ranges intersected by deep, narrow valleys,
and vary between 90 to 120 miles in length and
between 20 to 30 miles in width.
Distribution of population at the Census of 1976
was: Melanesian 183,665; Polynesian 7,821; Micro-
nesian 2,783; European 1,359; Chinese 452; Others
773. Total 196,823. A 1986 estimate put the total
population at 285,796.
CAPITAL.—HONIARA (population (1986 estimate),
30,499).
FLAG.—Blue over green divided by a diagonal
yellow band, with five white stars in the top left
quarter.
NATIONAL DAY.—July 7 (Independence Day).
NATIONAL ANTHEM.—God Bless our Solomon
Islands.

GOVERNMENT

The origin of the present Melanesian inhabitants
is uncertain. European discovery of the islands began
in the mid-16th century and continued intermittently for about 300 years, when the inauguration of
sugar plantations in Queensland and Fiji (which
created a need for labour) and the arrival of
missionaries and traders led to increased European
interest in the region. Great Britain declared a
Protectorate in 1893 over the Southern Solomons,
adding the Santa Cruz group in 1898 and 1899. The
islands of the Shortland groups were transferred by
treaty from Germany to Great Britain in 1900.
The Solomon Islands achieved internal self-government in 1976, and became independent in July 1978.
The Solomon Islands are a constitutional monarchy,
H.M. The Queen being represented locally by the
Governor-General. Legislative power is vested in a
unicameral National Parliament of 38 members,
elected for a four-year term. The executive authority
is exercised by the Cabinet.
Governor-General, Sir Baddeley Devesi, G.C.M.G,
G.C.V.O. (1978).
Prime Minister, Ezekiel Alebua.

Cabinet

Prime Minister, Ezekiel Alebua.
Deputy P.M. and Minister of Natural Resources, Rt.
Hon. Sir Peter Kenilorea, K.B.E.
Foreign Affairs, Paul Tovua.
Posts and Communications, John Maetia.
Transport, Works and Utilities, Alfred Maetia.
Education and Training, Joini Tutua.
Immigration and Labour, Jason Dorovolomo.
Home Affairs and Provincial Govt., Andrew Nori.
Health and Medical Services, John Tepaika.
Public Service, Ben Foukona.
Trade, Commerce and Industry, Danny Philip.
Economic Planning, Alex Bartlett.
Finance, George Kejoa.
Police and Justice, Swanson Konofilia.
Agriculture and Lands, Daniel Sande.

JUDICIARY

The High Court of Solomon Islands, constituted by the Solomon Islands Independence Order, consists of a Chief Justice and not fewer than two nor more than three Puisne Judges. The Court of Appeal Act was enacted on May 8, 1978.

FINANCE AND TRADE

Revenue (1985), SI$63,567,000.

The main imports are foodstuffs, consumer goods, machinery and transport materials. Principal exports are timber, fish, copra, and palm oil. Other exports include cocoa and marine shells.

Trade with U.K.

	1985	1986
Imports from U.K.	£1,862,000	£1,618,000
Exports to U.K.	7,714,000	4,074,000

COMMUNICATIONS

An internal air service, Solair, serves 28 airstrips throughout the country, four of which are designated international airports. Solair operates international flights to Vanuatu and to Bourgainville (Papua New Guinea), and combined services with Air Pacific making two air connections weekly to Brisbane via Honiara. Air Nauru makes two flights a week, and Air Niugini also provides flights between Honiara/Port Moresby twice a week.

There are about 52 miles of secondary and minor roads in the urban areas of Honiara, Auki and Gizo. About 18 miles of road in and around Honiara and one mile in Auki and Gizo are bitumen sealed, the remainder being coral or gravel surfaced. In the rural areas there are some 800 miles of road, including those in private plantations, forestry areas and roads built and maintained by councils. All main islands have transceivers to maintain communications with Honiara and there is a telephone link between Honiara and Auki, Gizo and Tulagi.

Soltel, a company jointly owned by Cable and Wireless Limited and Solomon Islands Government operates the international telephone circuits from a ground station in Honiara via the Intelsat Pacific Ocean communication satellite.

BRITISH HIGH COMMISSION
Soltel House, Mendana Avenue,
Honiara.
High Commissioner, His Excellency John Bramble Noss (1986).

SRI LANKA

Sri Lanka Prajatantrika Samajawadi Janarajaya)

AREA, POPULATION, ETC.—Sri Lanka (formerly Ceylon) is an island in the Indian Ocean, off the southern tip of the peninsula of India and separated from it by a narrow strip of shallow water, the Palk Strait. Situated between 5° 55′–9° 50′ N. latitude and 79° 42′–81° 52′ E. longitude, it has an area of 25,332 sq. miles (65,610 sq. km.), including 33 square miles of inland water. Its greatest length is from north to south, 270 miles; and its greatest width 140 miles, no point in Sri Lanka being more than 80 miles from the sea.

The population at the 1981 census was 14,800,001. (A 1985 U.N. estimate gave a figure of 15,837,000.) Of these 74 per cent were Sinhalese, 12·6 per cent Sri Lankan Tamils, 5·6 per cent Indian Tamils, 7·1 per cent Sri Lankan Moors and 0·7 per cent Burghers,

Malays and others. The religion of the great majority of inhabitants is Buddhism, introduced from India, according to ancient Sinhalese chronicles, in 247 B.C. Next to Buddhism (69·3 per cent), Hinduism has a large following (15·5 per cent); 7·6 per cent of the population are Muslims and 7·5 per cent Christians. The national languages are Sinhalese, Tamil and English.

Forests, jungle and scrub cover the greater part of the island, often being intermingled. In areas over 2,000 feet above sea level grasslands (*patanas* or *talawas*) are found. One of the highest peaks in the central massif is Adam's Peak (7,360 ft), a place of pilgrimage for Buddhists, Hindus and Moslems.

The climate of Sri Lanka is warm throughout the year, with a high relative humidity. In the hills the climate is more temperate. Temperatures average 80° F. in the lowlands, and 60° F. at elevations over 6,000 ft. Day humidity is over 70 per cent and night humidity over 85 per cent. Rainfall is generally heavy, with marked regional variations. The two main monsoon seasons are mid-May to September (south-west) and November to March (north-east).

CAPITAL.—ΨCOLOMBO, population (1981) 585,776. 1984 estimate 643,000. Other principal towns are Ψ Jaffna (118,215), Kandy (101,281), ΨGalle (77,183), Ψ Negombo (51,376) and ΨTrincomalee (44,913).

FLAG.—On a dark red field, within a golden border, a golden lion passant holding a sword in its right paw, and a representation of a *bo*-leaf, issuing from each corner; and to its right, two vertical stripes of saffron and green also placed within a golden border, to represent the minorities of the country.

NATIONAL DAY.—Feb. 4 (Independence Commemoration Day).

NATIONAL ANTHEM.—Namo Namo Matha (We all stand together).

GOVERNMENT

Early in the sixteenth century the Portuguese landed in Ceylon and founded settlements, eventually conquering much of the country. Portuguese rule in Ceylon lasted 150 years, but in 1658, following a twenty-year period of decline, Portuguese rule gave place to that of the Dutch East India Company which was to exploit Ceylon with varying fortunes until 1796.

The Maritime Provinces of Ceylon were ceded by the Dutch to the British on February 16, 1798, becoming a British Crown Colony in 1802 under the terms of the Treaty of Amiens. With the annexation of the Kingdom of Kandy in 1815, all Ceylon came under British rule.

On February 4, 1948, Ceylon became a self-governing state and a member of the British Commonwealth of Nations. A republican Constitution was adopted on May 22, 1972, providing for a unicameral legislature, the National State Assembly, which has a six year term, and the country was renamed the Republic of Sri Lanka (meaning 'Resplendent Island'). On Sept. 5, 1978 a new Constitution introduced the title the Democratic Socialist Republic of Sri Lanka and a system of proportional representation. Legislative power is exercised by Parliament, the executive power being exercised by the President. A referendum in Dec. 1982 extended the life of the 1977 Parliament by six years from Aug. 1983.

Following increased Tamil guerilla activity throughout 1987 in northern and eastern Sri Lanka, an agreement was signed between President Jayewardene of Sri Lanka and the Prime Minister of India designed to merge the Northern and Eastern provinces. A ceasefire by Tamil guerrillas was agreed and arms surrendered. President Jayewardene promised that a referendum would be held before the end of 1988.

President, His Excellency Junius Jayewardene, *acceded,* Feb. 4, 1978, *elected* Oct. 20, 1982. (*also Minister of Defence, Plan Implementation, Janatha Estates Development, State Plantations, Power and Energy, Manpower Mobilisation*).

Cabinet

Prime Minister, Minister of Local Government, Housing and Construction, Highways and of the Emergency Civil Administration, and Leader of the House of Parliament, Hon. R. Premadasa.
Public Administration and Plantation Industries, Hon. W. G. Montague Jayawickrema.
Social Services, Hon. N. H. Asoka Mahanama Karunaratne.
Cultural Affairs, Hon, E. L. B. Hurulle.
Transport, Transport Boards and Security of Commercial and Industrial Establishments, Hon. M. H. Mohamed.
Rural Development, Hon. Wimala Kannangara.
Textile Industries, Hon. Wijayapala Mendis.
Agricultural Development and Research and Food, Hon. Gamani N. Jayasuriya.
Foreign Affairs, Hon. A. C. S. Hameed.
Home Affairs, Hon. K. W. Devanayagam.
Posts and Telecommunications, Hon. D. B.Wijetunge.
Finance and Planning, Hon. R. J. G. de Mel.
Lands and Land Development and Mahaweli Development, Hon. L. Gamini Dissanayake.
Parliamentary Affairs and Sports, (vacant).
National Security, Hon. Lalith W. Athulathmudali.
Justice, Hon. Nissanka P. Wijeyeratna.
Fisheries, Hon. M. Festus W. Perara.
Rural Industrial Development, Hon. S. Thondaman.
Youth Affairs and Employment and Education, Hon. Ranil Wickremasinghe.
Minister of State, Hon. Anandatissa de Alwis.
Regional Development, Hon. C. Rajadurai.
Health, Hon. Ranjith Atapattu.
Women's Affairs and Teaching Hospitals, Hon. Sunethra Ranasinghe.
Without Portfolio, Hon. M. A. B. M. Bakeer Markar.
Trade and Shipping, Hon. M. S. Amarasiri.
Industries and Scientific Affairs, Hon. Denzil Fernande.
Labour, Hon. P. C. Imbulana.
Co-operatives, Hon. Dr. W. Dahanayake.

SRI LANKA HIGH COMMISSION
13 Hyde Park Gardens, W2 2LX
[01–262 1841]

High Commissioner, His Excellency Mr. Chandra Monerawela (1984).

BRITISH HIGH COMMISSION
Galle Road, Kollupitiya (P.O. Box 1433),
Colombo 3

High Commissioner, His Excellency David Arthur Steuart Gladstone (1987).
British Council Representative, R. A. K. Baker, 47 Alfred House Gardens, Colombo 3. Office also in *Kandy.*

THE JUDICATURE

The Judicial System provides for a Supreme Court, a Court of Appeal, a High Court and other Courts of First Instance.

PRODUCTION

Agriculture.—The staple products of the island are tea, rubber, copra, spices and gems. There is increasing emphasis on local production of food, especially rice, and plans for the large-scale production of sugar cane, cotton and citrus fruits.

Industry.—Factories are established for the manufacture or processing of ceramic ware, vegetable oils and by-products, paper, tobacco, tanning and leather goods, plywood, cement, chemicals, sugar, flour, salt, textiles, ilmenite, tiles, tyres, fertilizers, clothing, jewellery and hardware and there is a petroleum refinery.

Trade with U.K.

	1985	1986
Imports from U.K.	£79,234,000	£83,316,000
Exports to U.K.	73,956,000	51,860,000

COMMUNICATIONS

There are over 15,660 miles of motorable roads in Sri Lanka and a government-run railway system with 984 miles of lines.

There is a satellite earth station at Padukka, in south-west Sri Lanka, which provides telecommunication links *via* satellite with any part of the globe.

The principal airports are at Katunayake, 19 miles north of Colombo, and Ratmalana, nine miles south of the capital. Air Lanka operates on 76 flights weekly to the Gulf States, the Maldives, Western Europe and throughout the Far East.

SWAZILAND

(Umbuso we Swatini)

AREA, POPULATION, ETC.—Surrounded by South Africa on its northern, western and southern borders and by Mozambique to the east, this small land-locked country is geographically and climatically divided into three principal areas. The broken mountainous Highveld along the western border with an average altitude of 4,000 feet is densely forested mainly with conifers and eucalyptus; the Middleveld, averaging about 2,000 feet, is a mixed farming area including cotton and pineapples; and the Lowveld in the east, which was mainly scrubland until the introduction of large sugar cane plantations west of the Lubombo mountain range and the Mozambique border. Four rivers, the Komati, Usutu, Mbuluzi and Ngwavuma, flow from west to east. The total area of Swaziland is 6,704 sq. miles (17,363 sq. km.), and the population is estimated at some 647,000.

CAPITAL.—MBABANE (population, estimated 30,000), the headquarters of the Government, is situated at an average altitude of 3,800 ft. Other main townships are: Manzini (population, estimated, 30,000), Big Bend, Mhlambanyati, Mhlume, Nhlangano, Pigg's Peak and Simunye.

FLAG.—Five horizontal bands, crimson, bearing shield and spears device, bordered by narrow yellow bands; blue bands at top and foot.

NATIONAL DAY.—September 6 (Independence Day).
NATIONAL ANTHEM.—Elwatini.

GOVERNMENT

The Kingdom of Swaziland came into being on April 25, 1967, under a new internal self-government constitution and became an independent kingdom, headed by H.M. Sobhuza II, in membership of the Commonwealth on September 6, 1968.

A new electoral law was introduced in 1978, under which each of the 40 traditional Tinkhundla elect two members to the electoral college who elect 40 members to the House of Assembly. The King nominates 10 members to the House of Assembly, making 50 in all, who then elect 10 members (not of their own number) to the Senate. To these are added 10 senators nominated by the King, bringing the full membership of the Senate to 20. Under the Establishment of the Parliament of Swaziland Order, 1978, the Head of State, advised by the Swazi National Council, continues to reserve a large measure of executive, legislative and judicial authority.

Head of State, H.M. King Mswati III, *inaugurated* April 25, 1986.

Cabinet

Prime Minister, Hon. Sotsha E. Dlamini.
Foreign Affairs, Hon. Senator Shadrack J. S. Sibanyoni.
Labour and Public Service, H.R.H. Prince Phiwokwakhe Dlamini.
Defence and Youth, Hon. Brig. Fonono Gideon Dube.
Justice, Hon. David Jabulani Matse.
Education, H.R.H. Prince Khuzulwandle Dlamini.
Agriculture and Co-operatives, Hon. Sipho Hezekiel Mamba.
Finance, Hon. Barnabas Sibusiso Dlamini.
Commerce, Industry and Tourism, Hon. Derek von Wissell.
Natural Resources, Land Utilisation and Energy, Hon. Moses Mhambi Paul Mnisi.
Interior and Immigration, Hon. Phenyane Mamba.
Health, Hon. Chief Sipho Shongwe.
Works and Communications, Hon. King Mtetwe.

SWAZILAND HIGH COMMISSION
58 Pont Street, SW1X 0AE
[01–581 4976]

High Commissioner, His Excellency Senator the Hon. G. M. Mamba, G.C.V.O. (1978).

BRITISH HIGH COMMISSION
Allister Miller Street, Mbabane

High Commissioner, His Excellency John Gerrard Flynn (1987).

EDUCATION

In 1982, there were 125,303 pupils enrolled at 470 primary schools and 26,576 at 86 secondary schools.

COMMUNICATIONS

Swaziland's railway is about 150 miles long and runs from Ngwenya in the west to the Mozambique border near Goba in the east, and thence to the Mozambique port of Maputo. A southern link from Phuzumoya in central Swaziland joins up with the South African railway network to Richards Bay. A rail link from Mpaka in central Swaziland to the north-west border opened in 1986 and provides a link to Komatipoort.

Most passenger and goods traffic is carried by privately-owned motor transport services. There are daily scheduled air services by Royal Swazi National Airways to Johannesburg and scheduled routes to Durban, Harare, Lusaka, Gaborone, Nairobi and Dares-Salaam. International telecommunications and television services are provided through a satellite earth station opened in 1983. There is also a national telephone network through a series of microwave links.

FINANCE

Government revenue for 1987–88 is estimated at £284,783,000, of which £134,928,000 (or 47·4 per cent) is anticipated revenue from the South African Common Customs Union with South Africa, Botswana and Lesotho. A local sales tax introduced from Sept. 1984 is expected to yield £38,412,000 in 1987–88. Total Government-financed recurrent and capital expenditure in 1987–88 is estimated at £295,857,000.

Swaziland is a member of the Common Monetary Area and its unit of currency *Emalangeni* (singular *Lilangeni*) has a par value with the South African Rand.

Trade with U.K.

	1985	1986
Imports from U.K........	£3,122,000	£3,922,262
Exports to U.K.	41,281,000	48,194,218

TANZANIA

(Jamhuriya Mwungano wa Tanzania)

AREA, POPULATION, ETC.—Tanganyika, the mainland part of the United Republic of Tanzania (Tanganyika and Zanzibar), occupies the east-central portion of the African continent, between 1°–11° 45′ S. lat. and 29° 20′–40° 38′ E. long. It is bounded on the N. by Kenya and Uganda; on the S.W. by Lake Malawi, Malawi and Zambia; on the S. by Mozambique; on the W. it is bounded by Rwanda, Burundi and Zaire; on the E. the boundary is the Indian Ocean. Tanzania has an area of 364,900 sq. miles (945,087 sq. km.). The greater part of the country is occupied by the Central African plateau from which rise, among others, Mt. Kilimanjaro (19,340 ft.), the highest point on the continent of Africa, and Mt. Meru (14,974 ft.). The Serengeti National Park, which covers an area of 6,000 sq. miles in the Arusha, Mwanza and Mara Regions, is famous for its variety and number of species of game.

The African population consists mostly of tribes of mixed Bantu race. The total population of Tanzania at the Census held in August, 1978 was 17,551,925; a 1985 estimate put the figure at 21,733,000. Africans form a very large majority, while Europeans, Asians, and other non-Africans form a small minority. Swahili is the national and official language. The use of English is widespread both for educational and government purposes.

Zanzibar.—Formerly ruled by the Sultan of Zanzibar, and a British Protectorate until Dec. 10, 1963. Zanzibar consists of the islands of Zanzibar, Pemba and Latham.

CAPITAL—ΨDAR ES SALAAM (population 1,096,000 1985 estimate). Other towns (1978 population) are Ψ Tanga (103,409); Mwanza (110,611); Arusha (55,281); Moshi (52,223); Morogoro (61,890); Dodoma (45,703); Tabora (67,392) and ΨMtwara (48,510). Zanzibar (population, 110,669) is the chief town and seaport of the island.

FLAG.—Green (above) and blue; divided by diagonal black stripe bordered by gold, running from bottom (next staff) to top (in fly).

NATIONAL DAY.—April 26 (Union Day).

NATIONAL ANTHEM.—Mungu Ibariki Afrika (God Bless Africa).

GOVERNMENT

Tanganyika became an independent state and a member of the British Commonwealth on December 9, 1961, and a Republic, within the Commonwealth, on December 9, 1962, with an executive President, elected by universal suffrage as the Head of State and Head of the Government. On Dec. 10, 1963, Zanzibar became an independent state within the Commonwealth and on April 26, 1964, Tanganyika united with Zanzibar to form the United Republic of Tanzania.

Tanzania became a one-party state on July 10, 1965 but with the Tanganyika African National Union (TANU) and the Afro-Shirazi Party (ASP) remaining the ruling parties in Tanganyika and Zanzibar respectively. On Feb. 5, 1977 these two parties merged to form the Chama Cha Mapinduzi (CCM) (Revolutionary Party).

A new constitution was introduced on April 26, 1977 and revised in Oct. 1984. There is a President and two Vice-Presidents, one the President of Zanzibar and the other the Prime Minister. The President may only serve two five year terms and if he comes from Zanzibar the Prime Minister will be the First Vice-President and must come from Tanganyika. If the President comes from Tanganyika the President of Zanzibar will be the First Vice President. In a Presidential election a single Presidential candidate nominated by the C.C.M. has to obtain an affirmative majority of the votes cast, failing which a fresh candidate must be nominated. The National Assembly contains 243 members, of whom 118 are elected from mainland constituencies and 50 from Zanzibar, 25 are ex-officio, 15 nominated and 35 indirectly elected. The Speaker may either be elected from among the members or be an additional member. Constituency members are elected by popular vote at a general election held at a maximum of five-yearly intervals in which the C.C.M. nominates two candidates to contest each seat.

A new constitution was also approved in 1984 for Zanzibar providing for an elected President and House of Representatives. Although Zanzibar has its own government and Chief Minister, Tanganyika is governed by the government of the Union. Overall policy is decided by the C.C.M. whose chairman, Julius Nyerere, was elected in 1982 by the Party National Conference for a 5 year term.

President of the United Republic, H.E. Hon. Ali Hassan Mwinyi, *b.* 1925; *elected* Oct. 27, 1985; *sworn in* Nov. 5, 1985.

First Vice-President of the United Republic and Prime Minister, Hon. Joseph Sinde Warioba.

Second Vice-President of the United Republic and President of Zanzibar, H.E. Idris Abdul Wakil.

Cabinet

Deputy Prime Minister and Minister of Defence, Hon. Salim Ahmed Salim.
Without Portfolio, Hon. Rashid Kawawa.
Foreign Affairs, Hon. Benjamin Mkapa.
Finance, Economic Affairs and Planning, Hon. Cleopa Msuya.
Communications and Works, Hon. Mustafa Nyang'anyi.
Local Government Co-operatives, Hon. Kingunge Ngombale-Mwiru.
Agriculture and Livestock Development, Hon. Jackson Makwetta.
Labour and Manpower Development, Hon. Paul Bomani.
Home Affairs, Hon. Brig. Muhidin Kimario.
Energy and Minerals, Hon. Al-Noor Kassum.
Lands, Natural Resources and Tourism, Hon. Gertrude Mongella.
Industry and Trade, Hon. Daudi Mwakawago.
Education, Hon. Kighoma Malima.
Health and Social Welfare, Hon. Aaron Chiduo.
Justice, and Attorney-General, Hon. Damian Lubuva.
Water, Hon. Pius Ng'wandu.
Community Development, Culture, Youth and Sport, Hon. Fatima Saidi Ali.

TANZANIA HIGH COMMISSION
43 Hertford Street, W1Y 7TF
[01–499 8951]

High Commissioner, His Excellency Mr. Anthony B. Nyakyi (1981).

BRITISH HIGH COMMISSION
Hifadhi House, Samora Avenue (P.O. Box 9200), Dar es Salaam.

High Commissioner, His Excellency Colin Henry Imray, C.M.G. (1985).
British Council Representative, J. Mayatt, Samora Avenue, (P.O. Box 9100), Dar es Salaam.

EDUCATION

Education, almost entirely under state control, is characterised by official insistence that education must serve the aims of overall Government policy and planning. All Tanzanian secondary schools are expected to include practical subjects in the basic course. All who receive secondary (or equivalent) education are called up for a period of National Service. The school system is administered in Swahili but the Government is making efforts to improve English standards for the purposes of secondary and higher education. For higher education Tanzanian students go to the University of Dar es Salaam, Sokoine University of Agriculture in Morogoro, other East African universities, or to Universities and Colleges outside East Africa, including Britain.

COMMUNICATIONS

The main port is Dar es Salaam, and there are other ports on the coast at Tanga, Mtwara, Zanzibar, Mkoani and Wete, in addition to Mwanza, Musoma and Bukoba on Lake Victoria and Kigoma on Lake Tanganyika. Coastal shipping services connect the mainland to Zanzibar, and lake services are operated on Lake Tanganyika and Lake Malawi with neighbouring countries.

The principal international airports are Dar es Salaam and Kilimanjaro. Other airports include Zanzibar, Arusha, Mwanza and Tanga.

There are two railway systems; one connecting Dar es Salaam to Zambia; and the second having two main lines running from Dar es Salaam, one to northern Tanzania and Kenya and the other to Lake Tanganyika and Victoria.

PRODUCTION AND TRADE

The economy is based mainly on the production and export of primary produce and the growing of foodstuffs for local consumption. The islands of Zanzibar and Pemba produce a large part of the world's supply of cloves and clove oil; and coconuts, coconut oil and copra are also produced. The mainland's chief export crops are coffee, cotton, sisal, tea, tobacco, cashew nuts and diamonds. The most important minerals are diamonds. Hides and skins are another valuable export. Industry is at present largely concerned with the processing of raw material for either export or local consumption. There are also secondary manufacturing industries, including factories for the manufacture of leather and rubber footwear, knitwear, razor blades, cigarettes and textiles, and a wheat flour mill.

Trade with U.K.

	1985	1986
Imports from U.K.	£88,622,000	£62,870,000
Exports to U.K.	46,640,000	40,270,000

TONGA
(Kingdom of Tonga)

Tonga, or the Friendly Islands, comprises a group of islands situated in the Southern Pacific some 450 miles to the E.S.E. of Fiji, with an area of 270 sq. miles (699 sq. km.), and population (1985 U.N. estimate) of 97,000. The largest island, Tongatapu, was discovered by Tasman in 1643. Most of the islands are of coral formation, but some are volcanic (Tofua, Kao and Niuafoou or "Tin Can" Island). The limits of the group are between 15° and 23° 30′ S., and 173° and 177° W.

CAPITAL.—ΨNUKU'ALOFA (27,815), on Tongatapu.
FLAG.—Truncated red cross on rectangular white ground (next staff) on a red field.
NATIONAL DAY.—June 4 (Independence Day).
NATIONAL ANTHEM.—E, 'Otua Mafimafi (Oh, Almighty God Above).

GOVERNMENT

The Kingdom of Tonga is an independent constitutional monarchy within the Commonwealth. Prior to June 4, 1970 it had been a British-protected state for 70 years. The constitution provides for a Government consisting of the Sovereign, a privy council and cabinet, a legislative assembly and a judiciary. The legislative assembly has 28 members, with a Speaker, and includes the Ministers of the Crown, the two Governors of Island groups, and the representatives of the Nobles and of the people (nine of each), who are elected triennially.

Head of State, H.M. King Taufa'ahau Tupou IV, G.C.M.G., G.C.V.O., K.B.E., *acceded* Dec. 16, 1965.
Heir, H.R.H. Crown Prince Tupouto'a.

Cabinet

Prime Minister and Minister of Agriculture, H.R.H. Prince Fatafehi Tu'ipelehake, K.B.E.
Deputy Prime Minister, Minister of Lands, Hon. Baron Tuita, C.B.E.
Health, Hon. Dr. S. Tapa.
Finance, Hon. J. C. Cocker.
Education, Works and Civil Aviation, Hon. Dr. S. L. Kavaliku.
Police, Hon. 'Akau'ola.
Labour, Commerce and Industries, Baron Vaea.
Foreign Affairs and Defence, H.R.H. Crown Prince Tupouto'a.
Governor of Vava'u, Hon. Dr. Ma'afu Tupou.
Governor of Ha'apai, Hon. Fakafanua.

ECONOMY

The economy is primarily agricultural; the main crops are coconuts, bananas, vanilla, yams, taro, cassava, groundnuts and other fruits. Fish is an important staple food though recent shortfalls have led to canned fish being imported. Industry is based on the processing of agricultural produce, and the manufacture of foodstuffs, clothing and sports equipment. The principal exports are copra, other coconut products, tropical root crops and bananas.

Trade

	1984	1985
Total imports	T$46,614,000	T$58,900,000
Total exports	9,995,000	7,700,000

Trade with U.K.

	1985	1986
Imports from U.K.	£699,000	£936,000
Exports to U.K.	70,000	86,000

The unit of currency is the *Pa'anga* (T$), which is close to parity with the Australian dollar.

TONGA HIGH COMMISSION
New Zealand House, Haymarket, SW1Y 4TE
[01–839 3287/8]

High Commissioner, His Excellency Mr. S. T. 'Aho (1986).

BRITISH HIGH COMMISSION
P.O. Box 56, Nuku'alofa

High Commissioner, His Excellency (Andrew) Paul Fabian.

TRINIDAD AND TOBAGO

(The Republic of Trinidad and Tobago)

AREA, POPULATION, ETC.—*Trinidad,* the most southerly of the West Indian islands, lies close to the north coast of S. America, the nearest point being Venezuela, 7 miles distant. The island is situated between 10° 2′–11° 12′ N. lat. and 60° 30′–61° 56′ W. long., and is about 50 miles in length by 37 miles in width, with an area of 1,864 sq. miles (4,827 sq. km.). Two mountain systems, the Northern and Southern Ranges, stretch across almost its entire width and a third, the Central Range, lies diagonally across its middle portion; otherwise the island is mostly flat. The climate is tropical with temperatures averaging 82° F. (27·8° C) by day and 74° F. (23·3° C) by night, and a rainfall averaging 82 inches a year. There is a well-marked dry season from January to May, and a wet season from June to December broken by a short dry season (the Petite Careme) in September and October. The island was discovered by Columbus in 1498, was colonized in 1532 by the Spaniards, capitulated to the British under Abercromby in 1797, and was ceded to Britain under the Treaty of Amiens (March 25, 1802).

Tobago lies between 11° 9′ and 11° 21′ N. lat. and between 60° 30′ and 60° 50′ W. long., 19 miles northeast of Trinidad. The island is 32 miles long at its widest point, and 11 wide, and has an area of 116 sq. miles (300 sq. km.). It is a popular tourist resort. It was ceded to the British Crown in 1814 and amalgamated with Trinidad in 1888.

In 1985 the population of Trinidad and Tobago was estimated at 1,185,000.

Other Islands.—Corozal Point and Icacos Point, the N.W. and S.W. extremities of Trinidad, enclose the Gulf of Paria. West of Corozal Point lie several islands, of which Chacachacare, Huevos, Monos and Gaspar Grande are the most important.

CAPITAL.—ΨPORT-OF-SPAIN (population approximately 59,649 in 1985) is the administrative centre of the islands. About 33 miles south of the capital is San Fernando (population approximately 34,300 in 1985), a town of growing importance which is emerging as the industrial centre of Trinidad, and which is in close proximity to a number of large industrial plants. The main town of Tobago is ΨScarborough.

FLAG.—Black diagonal stripe bordered with white stripes, running from top by staff, all on a red field.
NATIONAL DAYS.—August 31 (Independence Day); September 24 (Republic Day).

GOVERNMENT

The Territory of Trinidad and Tobago became an independent state and a member of the British Commonwealth on August 31, 1962, and a Republic in 1976. The President is elected for 5 years by all members of the Senate and the House of Representatives. The House of Representatives has 36 members, elected by universal adult suffrage, and the Senate has 31, of whom 16 are appointed on the advice of the Prime Minister, 6 on the advice of the Leader of the

Opposition and 9 at the discretion of the President. Legislation was passed in Sept. 1980 which afforded Tobago a degree of self-administration through the 12-member Tobago House of Assembly.

President, His Excellency Noor Mohammed Hassanali.

Cabinet

Prime Minister and Minister of Finance and The Economy, Hon. A. N. R. Robinson.
External Affairs and International Trade, Hon. B. Panday.
Attorney-General and Minister of Legal Affairs, Hon. S. Richardson.
Planning and Reconstruction, Hon. W. Dookeran.
Health, Welfare and Women's Affairs, Hon. E. Hosein.
Works, Settlements and Infrastructure, Hon. J. Humphrey.
Youth, Sports, Culture and Creative Arts, Hon. J. Johnson.
Energy, Hon. K. Ramnath.
Labour, Employment and Manpower Resources, Hon. A. Richards.
National Security, Hon. C. Pantin.
Industry, Enterprise and Tourism, Hon. K. Gordon.
Food Production, Marine Exploitation, Forestry and the Environment, Hon. L. Myers.

TRINIDAD AND TOBAGO HIGH COMMISSION
42 Belgrave Square, SW1X 8NT
[01–245 9351]

High Commissioner, (new appointment awaited).

BRITISH HIGH COMMISSION
Furness House, 90 Independence Square
(P.O. Box 778) Port of Spain

High Commissioner, His Excellency Martin Seymour Berthoud, C.M.G.

EDUCATION

The education system provides for free education at all state-owned and government-assisted denominational schools and certain faculties at the University of the West Indies. In addition there are various private teaching establishments. Attendance is compulsory for children aged 6–12 years, after which attendance at free secondary schools is determined by success in the common entrance examination at 11 years. There are three technical institutes, two teachers' training colleges, and one of the three branches of the University of the West Indies is located in Trinidad, at the St. Augustine campus. A medical teaching complex was built at Mt. Hope, and operates in collaboration with the University of the West Indies.

COMMUNICATIONS

There are some 6,436 km. of all-weather roads in Trinidad and Tobago. The only general cargo port is Port-of-Spain but there are specialized port facilities elsewhere for landing crude oil, loading refinery products and sugar, and for storing and transmitting bauxite and cement. Regular shipping services call here and many inter-island craft use the port. Another, rapidly growing, port is at Port Lisas where new industries powered by local natural gas are located.

International scheduled airlines, including the national airline, Trinidad and Tobago Airways (BWIA) Corporation, use Piarco International Airport outside Port-of-Spain. The airline also flies between Piarco and Crown Point Airport in Tobago.

Two commercial broadcasting stations and one commercial television station operate in Trinidad

and Tobago. The internal telephone system and the external telephone and telegraph connections are operated by state-owned companies.

PRODUCTION

Trinidad and Tobago's main source of revenue is from oil. Production of domestic crude in 1985 was 10·2 million cu. metres. The two major oil refineries increased production in 1985 to an average throughput of 12,538 cu. metres per day, and refined both local and imported crude. Trinidad has large reserves of natural gas, estimated at 18,000,000 million cu. feet, and in 1985 production was 7,413 million cu. metres. An integrated steel plant, an anhydrous ammonia plant and a methanol plant have been constructed at Point Lisas.

Fertilizers, tyres, clothing, soap, furniture and foodstuffs are manufactured locally while motor vehicles, radios, TV sets, and electro-domestic equipment are assembled from parts, mainly from Japan.

Finance

	1985	1986
Revenue	*TT*$6,766·7m	*TT*$5,239·9m
Expenditure	7,684·1m	8,004·4m
Gross public debt	3,640·7m	3,605·4m

TRADE

	1985	1986
Imports	*TT*$3,739·0m	*TT*$4,027·2m
Exports	5,247·1m	4,249·8m

In Jan. 1987, the exchange rate was unified at *TT*$1·00 = US$0·27778.

Trade with U.K.

	1985	1986
Imports from U.K.	£93,897,000	£79,029,000
Exports to U.K.	81,719,000	41,622,000

TUVALU

Tuvalu, formerly the Ellice islands, formed part of the Gilbert and Ellice Islands Colony until October 1, 1975, when separate constitutions came into force. Separation from the Gilbert Islands was implemented on January 1, 1976.

Tuvalu comprises nine coral atolls situated in the South West Pacific around the point at which the International Date Line cuts the Equator. The total land area is only about 10 square miles. Few of the atolls are more than 12 feet above sea level or more than half a mile in width. The vegetation consists mainly of coconut palms. The resident population in 1985 was 8,229, but it is estimated that about 1,500 Tuvaluans work overseas, mostly in Nauru, or as seamen. The people are almost entirely Polynesian. The principal languages are Tuvaluan and English. The entire population is Christian and is predominantly Protestant.

CAPITAL.—ΨFUNAFUTI. Estimated population 2,856. The capital has a grass strip airfield from which a service operates regularly to Fiji and Kiribati, and is also the only port.

FLAG.—Blue ground with Union Jack in top left quarter and nine five-pointed gold stars in the fly.

NATIONAL DAY.—October 1 (Independence Day).

NATIONAL ANTHEM.—Tuvalu Mo Te Atua (Tuvalu for the Almighty).

GOVERNMENT

On October 1, 1978, Tuvalu became fully independent as a sovereign state within the Commonwealth.

The Constitution provides for a Prime Minister and four other Ministers who must be members of the 12-member elected Parliament. The Prime Minister presides at meetings of the Cabinet, which consists of the five Ministers, and is attended by the Attorney General. Local Government services are provided by elected Island Councils.

Governor-General, His Excellency Sir Tupua Leupena, G.C.M.G., M.B.E., *sworn in* March 1, 1986.

Cabinet

Prime Minister, Rt. Hon. Dr. Tomasi Puapua.
Minister for Finance, Hon. Kitiseni Lopati.
Commerce and Natural Resources, Hon. Lale Seluka.
Works and Communications, Hon. Metia Tealofi.
Social Services, Hon. Telava Tevasa.
Secretary to Government (acting), Silinga Kofe.
Attorney-General, Robin Webster.

ECONOMY

Most people still practise a subsistence economy, the main staples of their diet being coconuts and fish. The main imports are foodstuffs, consumer goods and building materials. The only export is copra (333 tons in 1985), but philatelic sales provide a major source of revenue and handicraft sales are increasing. The unit of currency is the Australian dollar. In addition there are Tuvalu dollar and cent coins in circulation.

Trade

	1984
Imports	A$3,954,000
Exports	307,917

Trade with U.K.

	1985	1986
Imports from U.K.	£87,000	£78,000
Exports to U.K.	—	88,000

EDUCATION AND WELFARE

There are eight primary schools in Tuvalu and a church secondary school run jointly with the Government. The total of enrolled children of school age in 1985 was 1,300. A Maritime Training School started in 1979 now caters for 60 boys per annum.

There is a 30-bed hospital at Funafuti. All islands are served by a dispensary and a primary school.

UGANDA

(Republic of Uganda)

AREA, POPULATION, ETC.—Situated in Eastern Africa, Uganda is flanked by Zaire, the Sudan, Kenya and on the south by Tanzania and Rwanda. Large parts of Lakes Victoria, Edward and Albert (Mobuto) are within its boundaries, as are Lakes Kyoga, Kwania, George and Bisina (formerly Salisbury) and the course of the River Nile from its outlet from Lake Victoria to the Sudan frontier post at Nimule. Uganda has an area of 91,259 sq. miles (236,036 sq. km.) (water and swamp 16,400 sq. miles) and population (1985 U.N. estimate) of 15,477,000. The official language of Uganda is English. The main local vernaculars are of Bantu, Nilotic and Hamitic origins. Ki-Swahili is generally understood in trading centres.

Despite its tropical location, the climate is tempered by its situation some 3,000 ft. above sea level, and well over that altitude in the highlands of the Western and Eastern Regions. In South Uganda, temperatures seldom rise above 85° F. (29° C.) or fall below 60° F. (15° C.). The rainfall averages about 50 inches

a year. Uganda has three National Parks and a fourth (Lake Mburo) has been designated.

CAPITAL.—KAMPALA (population of Greater Kampala, 460,000). Other principal towns are Jinja (45,000), Mbale (28,000) and Masaka (29,000).

FLAG.—Six horizontal stripes of black, yellow and red (repeated) with a crested crane emblem on a white orb in the centre.

NATIONAL DAY.—October 9 (Independence Day).

GOVERNMENT

Uganda became an independent state and a member of the Commonwealth on October 9, 1962, after some 70 years of British rule. A Republic was instituted on September 8, 1967, under an executive President, assisted by a Cabinet of Ministers.

Early in 1971 an army coup took place and Maj.-Gen. Idi Amin, the Army Commander, proclaimed himself Head of State. In 1979, following risings and military intervention by Tanzania, President Amin was overthrown. Following elections in 1980, Dr. Milton Obote became President. A military coup on July 27, 1985 ousted Dr. Obote and installed a military council which attempted to negotiate a power-sharing agreement with the National Resistance Movement led by Yoweri Museveni. However, the National Resistance Army captured Kampala in late Jan. 1986, securing control of the rest of the country in the following few months. Yoweri Museveni was sworn in as President on Jan. 29, 1986; subsequently the Prime Minister and a 24-member National Resistance Council were appointed, and a government was formed.

President, H. E. Yoweri Museveni, *sworn in* Jan. 29, 1986.

Cabinet

President and Minister of Defence, Yoweri Museveni.
Prime Minister, Dr. Samson Kisekka.
Finance, Dr. Crispas Kiyonga.
Co-operatives and Marketing, John Ssebana-Kizito.
Animal Husbandry, Dr. Shebe Musaba.
Health, Dr. Ruhakanu Rugunda.
Public Service and Cabinet Affairs, D. Kibirango.
Industry and Technology, Prof. Stanley Tumwine.
Works, Daniel Kigozi Serwano.
Foreign Affairs, Ibrahim Mukiibi.
Internal Affairs, Paul Ssemogerere.
Information and Broadcasting, Abubakar Mayanja.
Planning and Economic Development, Joseph Okune.
Commerce, Dr. George Kanyeihamba.
Rehabilitation, Dr. Alex Ofumbi.
Lands and Surveys, James Obol Ochola.
Water and Mineral Development, Chango Macho.
Justice and Attorney-General, Joseph Mulenga.
Tourism and Wildlife, Anthony Butele.
Education, Joshua Mayanja Nkangi.
Agriculture and Forestry, Robert Kitariko.
Transport and Communications, Ali Kirunda Kivenjinjiya.
Energy, Jaberi Badandi-Ssali.
Youth, Culture and Sports, Stanley Okurut.
Minister without portfolio, Tom Rubale.

UGANDA HIGH COMMISSION

Uganda House, 58–59 Trafalgar Square, WC2N 5DX
[01–839 5783]
High Commissioner, His Excellency Mr. Ernest Rusita (1986).

BRITISH HIGH COMMISSION

10/12 Parliament Avenue, P.O. Box 7070, Kampala
High Commissioner, His Excellency Derek Maxwell March, C.B.E. (1986).
British Council Representative, K. F. Burd, O.B.E.

EDUCATION

Education is a joint undertaking by the Government, local authorities and, to some extent, voluntary agencies. In 1981 Uganda had 4,276 primary schools with an enrolment of 1,421,615 children. Secondary schools numbered 199 with 78,727 students enrolled; and 4,979 students in various technical training institutions.

The National University is Makerere University, Kampala, founded as a trade school in 1921 and becoming an independent University in 1970.

COMMUNICATIONS

There is an international airport at Entebbe, with direct flights to destinations in Africa, Asia and Europe. There are 8 other airfields in Uganda. Having no sea coast, Uganda is heavily dependent upon rail and road links to Mombasa for her trade. There are 2,226 kilometres of bituminized and 25,310 kilometres of gravel roads. The state of the roads at present is very poor. A railway network joins the capital to the western, eastern and northern centres. National Corporations have been established to provide rail and air services.

TRADE, ETC.

The principal export earner is coffee (over 90 per cent of all exports), which earned $339 million in 1983. Attempts are being made to increase production of cotton and tea for export, and cotton exports earned $11·7 million in 1983. Hydro-electricity is produced from the Owen Falls power station which has a capacity of 150 MW and about 30 MW is exported to Kenya. The principal food crops are plantains, bananas, cassava, sweet potatoes, potatoes and sorghum.

Trade with U.K.

	1985	1986
Imports from U.K.	£39,925,000	£26,046,000
Exports to U.K.	48,571,000	50,870,000

Currency.—In May 1987 Uganda's currency was devalued by 76·6 per cent. A *new* shilling was introduced equal to 100 *old* shillings.

VANUATU

(Ripablik Blang Vanuatu)

AREA, POPULATION, ETC.—Vanuatu, the former Anglo-French Condominium of the New Hebrides, is situated in the South Pacific Ocean, between 13° and 21° S. and 166° and 170° E. It includes 13 large and some 70 small islands, of coral and volcanic origin, including the Banks and Torres Islands in the North, and has a total land area of 5,700 sq. miles (14,763 sq. km.). The principal islands are Vanua Lava and Gaua (Banks), Espiritu Santo, Maewo, Pentecost, Aoba, Malekula, Ambrym, Epi, Efate, Erromango, Tanna and Aneityum. Most islands are mountainous and there are active volcanoes on several. The climate is oceanic tropical, moderated by the south-east trade winds which blow between May and October. At other times winds are variable and cyclones may occur. Temperatures range between 62° F. and 83° F, with annual rainfall averaging 90 in. in the south and 155 in. in the north.

A 1986 estimate showed a population of 140,154. About 95 per cent of the population are Melanesian, the rest being small numbers of Micronesians, Polynesians and Europeans. The national language is Bislama (Pidgin), but English and French are also official languages.

SEAT OF ADMINISTRATION—ΨVILA, Efate, population (1986), 18,796. The only other town is Luganville (population, 1986, 5,621), on Santo.

FLAG.—Red over green with a black triangle in the hoist, the three parts being divided by fimbriations of black and yellow, and in the centre of the black triangle a boar's tusk overlaid by two crossed fern leaves.

NATIONAL DAY.—July 30 (Independence Day).

NATIONAL ANTHEM.—"Nasimal Sing sing long Vanuatu."

GOVERNMENT

The Condominium of the New Hebrides became an independent republic within the Commonwealth under the name of Vanuatu on July 30, 1980.

President, His Excellency Ati George Sokomanu, M.B.E., *elected* 1980, *re-elected* 1984.

Council of Ministers

Prime Minister and Minister of Justice, Hon. Father Walter Lini, C.B.E.

Deputy P.M. and Minister for Home Affairs, Hon. S. J. Regenvanu.

Finance, Commerce, Industry and Tourism, Hon. K. Kalsakau.

Lands, Energy and Water Supply, Hon. D. Kalpokas.

Foreign Affairs and External Trade, Hon. S. Molisa.

Education, Youth and Sports, Hon. O. Tahi.

Transport, Communications and Public Works, Hon. A. Sande.

Health, Hon. N. Natapei.

Agriculture, Fisheries and Forestry, Hon. J. Hopa.

Chief Justice, Hon. Mr. Justice F. G. Cooke.

Attorney-General, S. Hakwa.

BRITISH HIGH COMMISSION
Melitco House, Rue Pasteur, Vila.
High Commissioner, His Excellency Malcolm Lars Creek, L.V.O., O.B.E. (1985).

ECONOMY

Most of the population is employed on plantations or in subsistence agriculture. Subsistence crops include yams, toro, manioc, sweet potato and breadfruit; principal cash crops are copra, cocoa and coffee. Large numbers of cattle are kept on the plantations and an export trade in meat is being developed. On the island of Santo a plant freezes tuna and bonito for export.

Principal exports are copra, meat (frozen, tinned and chilled), fish and cocoa.

Tourism is an increasingly important revenue earner, and the absence of direct taxation has led to some growth in the finance and associated industries. The unit of currency is the *Vatu.*

Trade with U.K.

	1985	1986
Imports from U.K.	£768,000	£1,037,000
Exports to U.K.	174,000	62,000

WESTERN SAMOA

(Malotuto'atasi o Samoa i Sisifo)

Western Samoa consists of the islands of Savai'i (662 sq. miles) and of Upolu, which, with seven other islands, has an area of 435 sq. miles (1,714 sq. km.). All islands are mountainous. Upolu, the most fertile, contains the harbours of ΨApia and ΨSaluafata and Savai'i the harbour of ΨAsau. The population at the 1981 census was 158,130, the largest numbers being on Upolu (114,980) and Savai'i (43,150): a 1985 U.N. estimate put the figure at 163,000. The Samoans are a Polynesian people, though the population also includes other Pacific Islanders, Euronesians, Chinese and Europeans. The main languages spoken are Samoan and English. The islanders are Christians of different denominations.

CAPITAL.—ΨAPIA, on Upolu (population (1981 census) 33,100). Robert Louis Stevenson died and was buried at Apia in 1894.

FLAG.—Five white stars (depicting the Southern Cross) on a quarter royal blue at top next staff, and three quarters red.

NATIONAL DAY.—January 1 (Independence Day).
NATIONAL ANTHEM.—The Banner of Freedom.

GOVERNMENT

Formerly administered by New Zealand (latterly with internal self-government), Western Samoa became, on January 1, 1962, the first fully-independent Polynesian State. The State was treated as a member country of the Commonwealth until its formal admission on August 28, 1970.

The 1962 Constitution provides for a Head of State to be elected by the Legislative Assembly for a five year term. However, it was decided that initially two of the four Paramount chiefs should jointly hold the office of Head of State for life. When one of the chiefs died in April 1963, Malietoa Tanumafili II became the holder of the office of Head of State for life. The Head of State's functions are analogous to those of a constitutional monarch. Executive government is carried out by a Cabinet of Ministers.

Head of State, H. H. Malietoa Tanumafili II, G.C.M.G., C.B.E. (April 15, 1963).
Deputy Head of State, Hon. Mataafa Faasuamaleaui Puela.

Cabinet

Prime Minister and Minister of Foreign Affairs, Internal Affairs, Immigration, Police and Prisons, Hon. Vaai Kolone.
Deputy P.M. and Minister of Public Works, Hon. Tupuola Efi.
Finance, Hon. Faasootauloa Semu Saili.
Agriculture, Forestries and Fisheries, Hon. Fuimaono Mimio.
Economic Development, Telecommunications and Broadcasting, Hon. Le Tagaloa Pita.
Lands and Survey, Parks and Recreation, Hon. Faumuina Anapapa.
Education, Sports, Youth and Culture, Hon. Le Mamea Ropati Mualia.
Health and Transport, Hon. Toeolesulusulu Siueva.
Justice and Labour, Hon. George M. Lober.

ECONOMY

Agriculture is the basis of Western Samoa's economy, the principal cash crops (and exports) being coconuts (copra), cocoa and bananas. Other agricultural exports include coffee, timber, tropical fruits and seeds. Efforts are being made to develop fishing on a commercial scale. Manufacturing is very small in scope and concerned largely with processing agricultural products, but is being encouraged by the Government. Tourism is increasing rapidly.

The unit of currency is the *tala* (WS $).

Trade with U.K.

	1985	1986
Imports from U.K.	£619,000	£433,000
Exports to U.K.	292,000	622,000

BRITISH HIGH COMMISSION (*see* New Zealand)

ZAMBIA

(Republic of Zambia)

AREA, POPULATION, ETC.—The Republic of Zambia lies on the plateau of Central Africa between the longitudes 22° E. and 33° 33′ E. and between the latitudes 8° 15′ S. and 18° S. It has an area of 290,586 sq. miles (752,614 sq. km.) within boundaries 3,515 miles in length and a population (U.N. estimate, 1985) of 6,666,000, including about 50,000 non-Africans.

With the exception of the valleys of the Zambesi, the Luapula, the Kafue and the Luangwa Rivers, and the Luano valley, elevations vary from 3,000 to 5,000 feet above sea level, but in the north-east the plateau rises to occasional altitudes of over 6,000 feet.

Although Zambia lies within the tropics, and fairly centrally in the African land mass, its elevation relieves it from extremely high temperatures and humidity.

CAPITAL.—LUSAKA, situated in the Central Province. Population (estimated, 1980), 641,000. Other centres are Livingstone, Kabwe, Chipata, Mazabuka, Mbala, Kasama, Solwezi, Mongu, Mansa, Ndola, Luanshya, Mufulira, Chingola, Chililabombwe, Kalulushi and Kitwe, the last six towns being the main centres on the Copperbelt.

FLAG.—Green with three small vertical stripes, red, black and orange (next fly); eagle device on green above stripes.

NATIONAL DAY.—October 24 (Independence Day).
NATIONAL ANTHEM.—Stand and Sing of Zambia, Proud and Free.

GOVERNMENT

At the dissolution of the Federation of Rhodesia and Nyasaland, on December 31, 1963, Northern Rhodesia (as Zambia was then known) achieved internal self-government under a new constitution. Zambia became an independent republic within the Commonwealth on October 24, 1964—75 years after coming under British rule and nine months after achieving internal self-government.

In July 1973, a new Constitution was introduced, making the United National Independence Party (U.N.I.P.) the only party.

President, Dr. Kenneth David Kaunda, *assumed office* Oct. 24, 1964; *re-elected*, Dec. 1973, Dec. 1978 and Oct. 1983.

Cabinet

Prime Minister, K. Musokotwane.
Secretary of State, Defence and Security, A. K. Shapi.
Defence, Lt.-Gen. M. Masheke.
Foreign Affairs, L. Mwananshiku.
Finance, and National Commission for Development Planning, G. Chigaga.
Legal Affairs (Attorney-General), F. M. Chomba.
Higher Education, Prof. L. Goma.
Health, R. Sakuhuka.
Commerce and Industry, J. K. M. Kalaluka.
Home Affairs, P. Malukutila.
Mines, P. S. Chitambala.
Agriculture and Water Development, F. Chuula.
Power, Transport and Communications, Gen. G. K. Chinkuli.
Works and Supply, H. Mwale.
Labour and Social Services, U. G. Mwila.

Tourism, L. S. Subulwa.
National Guidance, Information and Broadcasting Services, J. C. M. Punabantu.
Youth and Sports, F. Hapunda.
Lands and Natural Resources, B. Kakoma.
Co-operatives, J. Mukando.
Decentralization, R. Kunda.
General Education and Culture, B. R. Kabwe.
Presidential Affairs, A. K. Simuchimba.

Sec.-Gen., U.N.I.P., A. G. Zulu.

ZAMBIA HIGH COMMISSION
2 Palace Gate, W8 5NG
[01–589 6655]

High Commissioner, His Excellency Mr. Wilted Phiri (1986).

BRITISH HIGH COMMISSION
Independence Avenue (P.O. Box 50050), Lusaka

High Commissioner, His Excellency William Kelvin Kennedy White, C.M.G. (1984).
British Council Representative, R. B. Timms, Heroes Place, Cairo Road, (P.O. Box 34571), Lusaka. There is also a library in Ndola.

JUDICATURE

There is a Chief Justice appointed by the President, all other judges being appointed on the recommendation of the Judicial Service Commission consisting of the Chief Justice, the chairman of the Public Service Commission, a senior Justice of Appeal and one Presidential nominee.

PRODUCTION

Principal products are maize, sugar, groundnuts, cotton, livestock, vegetables and tobacco.
Mineral production was valued at *K*2,646,640,000 in 1985, of which copper production (of 479,900 tonnes) accounted for *K*2,090,580,000.

FINANCE AND TRADE

The unit of currency is the *Kwacha.*
Gross Domestic Product (current prices) was *K*6,332·1m in 1985. G.D.P. per capita (current prices) was *K*942·3.

	1984	1985
Imports	*K*1,107,900,000	*K*2,089,500,000
Exports	1,188,100,000	1,486,073,000

Trade with U.K.

	1985	1986
Imports from U.K.	£85,949,000	£77,840,000
Exports to U.K.	27,879,000	27,260,000

ZIMBABWE

(Republic of Zimbabwe)

AREA, POPULATION, ETC.—Zimbabwe, the former Southern Rhodesia (named after Cecil Rhodes) comprising eight provinces (Manicaland, Masvingo, Matabeleland North, Matabeleland South, Midlands, Mashonaland West, Central and East), lies south of the Zambesi river. The political neighbours are Zambia and Mozambique on the N.: South Africa and Botswana on the S. and W., and Mozambique on the E. It has a total area of 150,804 sq. miles (390,580 sq. km.), and a population (estimated 1987) of 8,660,000.

CAPITAL.—HARARE (Salisbury) situated on the Mashonaland plateau, population (August 1982) 658,364. Bulawayo—the largest town in Matabeleland, population (August 1982) 495,317. Other centres are, Chitungwiza, Mutare, Gweru, Kadoma, Kwe Kwe, Masvingo and Hwange.

FLAG.—Seven horizontal stripes (green, gold, red, black, red, gold, green) with white triangle at the hoist containing the Zimbabwe bird superimposed on red five-point star.

NATIONAL DAY.—April 18 (Independence Day).
NATIONAL ANTHEM.—Ishe Komborerai Africa.

GOVERNMENT

Southern Rhodesia was granted responsible government in 1923. An illegal declaration of independence on November 11, 1965 was finally terminated on December 12, 1979. Following elections in February 1980 the country obtained independence on April 18, 1980 as the Republic of Zimbabwe, a member of the British Commonwealth. The Parliament consists of a House of Assembly of 100 members and a Senate of 40 Senators and has a maximum life of five years. The President is elected by the Members of Parliament and holds office for a period of six years. A Constitutional Amendment Bill designed to replace the 20 reserved white seats with nominated members from any race, was given an unopposed first reading in August 1987.
The first post-independence election was held in June and July 1985. State of the black parties at June 1987 was Zanu (PF) 66, Zapu 14, CAZ 14, IZG 3, Zanu 1, Independents 2.

President, Rev. The Hon. Canaan Banana, *elected* April 11, 1980, *re-elected* April 17, 1986.

Ministry

Prime Minister and Minister of Defence, Robert G. Mugabe.
Deputy Prime Minister, Simon V. Muzenda.
Home Affairs, Enos Nkala.
Transport, Herbert Ushewokunze.
Education, Dzingai Mutumbuka.
Health, Sydney Sekeramayi.
Information, Posts and Telecommunications, Nathan Shamuyarira.
Foreign Affairs, Witness Mangwende.
Finance, Economic Planning and Development, Bernard Chidzero.
Trade and Commerce, Oliver Munyaradzi.
Industry and Technology, Senator Callistus Ndlovu.
Lands, Agriculture and Rural Resettlement, Movan Mahachi.
Mines, Richard Hove.
Local Government, Rural and Urban Development, Enos Chikoware.
Justice, Legal and Parliamentary Affairs, Eddison Zvobgo.
Labour, Manpower Planning and Social Welfare, Frederick Shava.
Energy and Water Resources and Development, Kumbirai Kangai.
Natural Resources and Tourism, Victoria Chitepo.
National Supplies, Simbi Mubako.
Public Construction and National Housing, Simbarashe Mumbengegwi.
Youth, Sport and Culture, David Karimanzira.
Co-operative Development, Maurice Nyagumbo.
Ministers of State, Ernest Kadungure (*Defence*); Emmerson Munangagwa (*Security*); Teurai Ropa Nhongo (*Community Development and Women's Affairs*); Chris Andersen (*Public Service*).

ZIMBABWE HIGH COMMISSION
Zimbabwe House, 429 Strand, WC2R 0SA
[01-836 7755]

High Commissioner, His Excellency Dr. Herbert M. Murerwa (1984).

BRITISH HIGH COMMISSION
Stanley House, Stanley Avenue,
(PO Box 4490), Harare

High Commissioner, His Excellency Michael Ramsay Melhuish, C.M.G. (1985).
British Council Representative, N. M. Ross, 23 Stanley Avenue, (P.O. Box 664), Harare.

EDUCATION

Since independence, a policy of free primary education and accelerated expansion at secondary level has resulted in rapidly expanding enrolment. In 1986 there were 2,260,367 primary school and 545,841 secondary school pupils in both Government and Government aid schools. Over 80 per cent of schools are privately run; they receive grants for materials. Other schools are government-owned and run.

ECONOMY

The country is endowed with minerals, water, forests, wildlife and other resources. The agricultural sector is well developed with both commercial and communal farmers. Tobacco remains the most important crop in terms of export and maize the most important for domestic consumption. Other crops include wheat, cotton, and sugar. Good quality beef is exported to the E.C. Production can be severely affected by drought.

The manufacturing sector has a high degree of inter-dependency and many industries depend on the agricultural sector for their raw materials. Industry is dependent on vital imports e.g. fuel oil, steel products and chemicals, as well as heavy machinery and items of transport. The mining sector, although contributing a relatively small portion to G.D.P. (7.6 per cent in 1984) is important to the economy as a foreign exchange earner (26 per cent of total in 1984). Almost all mineral production is exported. Gold is the most important mineral, others are asbestos, silver, nickel, copper, chrome ore, tin, iron ore and cobalt. There is a successful ferro-chrome industry and a substantial steel works which has been heavily subsidized by Government.

A high domestic budget deficit combining with a high external debt service ratio has put the economy into decline. The 1986–87 drought made this worse.

GOVERNMENT FINANCE

	1984-85	1985–86
Revenue	Z$2,212·3m	Z$2,616·2m
Expenditure	2,923·0m	3,307·8m

Trade with U.K.

	1985	1986
Imports from U.K.	£73,571,000	£61,937,000
Exports to U.K.	90,398,000	80,702,000

Dependent Territories, etc.

ANGUILLA

Anguilla is a flat coralline island, about 16 miles in length, 3¼ miles in breadth at its widest point and its area is about 35 sq. miles (91 sq. km.). It lies approximately 18° N. latitude and 63° W longitude, to the north of the Leeward Islands group.

The island is covered with low scrub and fringed with some of the finest white coral-sand beaches in the Caribbean. The climate is pleasant and healthy with temperatures in the range of 75-85°F. throughout the year. The population (U.N. 1985 estimate) is about 7,000.

CAPITAL.—THE VALLEY (population 500).

GOVERNMENT

Anguilla has been a British colony since 1650. For most of its history it has been linked administratively with St. Kitts, but three months after the Associated State of Saint Christopher (St. Kitts)-Nevis-Anguilla came into being in 1967 the Anguillans repudiated government from St. Kitts. A Commissioner was installed in 1969 and in 1976 Anguilla was given a new status and separate constitution. Final separation from St. Kitts and Nevis was effected on Dec. 19, 1980 and Anguilla reverted to a British Dependency. A new Constitution was introduced in 1982, providing for a Governor, an Executive Council comprising the Governor, four elected Ministers and two *ex-officio* members (Attorney General and Permanent Secretary, Finance), and an 11-member legislative House of Assembly presided over by a Speaker.

Governor, His Excellency Mr. G. O. Whittaker (1987).

Executive Council

President, The Governor.
Chief Minister and Minister of Home Affairs, Tourism and Economic Development, Hon. Emile Gumbs.
Lands, Agriculture and Fisheries, Health and Prisons, Hon. Eric Reid.
Communications, Public Utilities and Works, Hon. Nashville Webster.
Finance, Education, Community Development, Osbourne Fleming.
Permanent Secretary (Finance), Hon. Franklin Connor, O.B.E.
Attorney-General, R. Whitehead.

ECONOMY

Low rainfall limits agricultural output and export earnings are mainly from sales of lobsters and salt. Tourism is being developed. The unit of currency is the East Caribbean dollar (*EC*$).

FINANCE (estimated)

	1985	1986
Revenue	EC$13,600,000	EC$15,900,000
Expenditure	13,300,000	15,200,000

ASCENSION
See ST. HELENA

BERMUDA

The Bermudas, or Somers Islands, are a cluster of about 100 small islands (about 20 only of which are inhabited) situated in the west of the Atlantic Ocean, in 32° 18′ N. lat. and 64° 46′ W. long., the nearest point of the mainland being Cape Hatteras in North Carolina, about 570 miles distant. The colony derives its name from Juan Bermudez, a Spaniard, who sighted it before 1515, but no settlement was made until 1609, when Sir George Somers, who was shipwrecked here on his way to Virginia, colonized the islands.

The total area is approximately 20·59 sq. miles (53 sq. km.), which includes 2·3 sq. miles leased to the U.S.A. The civil population was 56,000 in 1985 (U.N. estimate).

CAPITAL.—HAMILTON (population, 1984, 1,669).

GOVERNMENT

Internal self-government was introduced on June 8, 1968. There is a Senate of 11 Members and an elected House of Assembly of 40 Members. The Governor retains responsibility for external affairs, defence, internal security and the police, although administrative matters for the Police Service have been delegated to the Minister of Home Affairs.

Governor and Commander-in-Chief, His Excellency The Viscount Dunrossil, C.M.G. (1983).
Deputy Governor, B. Canty.

Cabinet

Premier, Hon. J. W. Swan.
Deputy Premier and Minister of Finance, Dr. Hon. C. James.
Tourism, Hon. J. Irving Pearman.
Education, Hon. G. D. E. Simons.
Works and Housing, Hon. Q. L. Edness.
Health and Social Services, Hon. A. F. Cartwright DeCouto.
Transport, Hon. S. Stallard.
Environment, Hon. T. H. Davis.
Labour and Home Affairs, Hon. Sir John Sharpe.
Community and Cultural Affairs, Hon. R. Barritt.
Youth, Sport and Recreation, Hon. M. A. Burgess.
Legislative Affairs, with responsibility for Telecommunications, Sen. Hon. C. T. M. Collis.

President of the Senate, Hon. H. Richardson, C.B.E.
Speaker of the House of Assembly, Hon. F. J. Barritt, C.B.E.
Chief Justice, Hon. Sir James R. Astwood.
Puisne Judges, Hon. G. Collett, C.B.E., Q.C.; Hon. J. Melville; Hon. L. Austin Ward, Q.C.

ECONOMY

Locally manufactured concentrates and pharmaceuticals are now the colony's leading exports. Little food is produced except vegetables and fish, other foodstuffs being imported.

The Islands' economic structure is based on tourism, the major industry, and international company business, attracted by the low level of taxation and sophisticated telecommunications system. In 1986 a total of 591,716 visitors arrived in Bermuda, of which 132,958 arrived by cruise ships. Cruise ships dock at Hamilton, Somerset and St. George's.

Free elementary education was introduced in 1949. Free secondary education was introduced in 1965 for those children in the aided and maintained schools who were below the upper limit of the statutory school age of 16 (from 1969 onwards).

There are 5 radio and one television station, one daily and 2 weekly newspapers and overseas telephone and telegraph services are maintained.

FINANCE

	1986–87	1987–88
Public revenue	$231,508,700	$251,550,300
Public expenditure	231,458,400	220,172,000

Currency.—The unit of currency is the Bermudan dollar (*Bd* $), which has parity with the U.S. $.

Trade with U.K.

	1985	1986
Imports from U.K.	£39,600,000	£26,180,000
Exports to U.K.	2,000,000	1,262,000

THE BRITISH ANTARCTIC TERRITORY

The British Antarctic Territory was designated in 1962 and consists of the areas south of 60°S. latitude which were previously included in the Falkland Islands Dependencies. The territory lies between longitudes 20° and 80°W., south of latitude 60°S. and includes the South Orkney Islands, the South Shetland Islands, the mountainous Antarctic Peninsula (highest point *Mount Jackson*, 13,620ft, in Palmer Land) and all adjacent islands, and the land mass extending to the South Pole. The territory has no indigenous inhabitants and the British population consists of the scientists and technicians who man the British Antarctic Survey stations. The number averages about 60 to 70 in winter, but increases considerably in the summer months with the arrival of field workers; Argentina, Brazil, Chile, China, Poland, U.S.A., U.S.S.R. and Uruguay also have scientific stations in the territory.

The first two British Antarctic Survey stations were established in the South Shetland Islands in 1944, and by 1956 the number of stations had risen to twelve. Due to the completion of field work in some areas and increased mobility, the number has now been reduced to five. These are Signy (Signy Island, S. Orkney Islands), Faraday (Argentine Islands, Graham Coast), Rothera (Adelaide Island), Halley (Caird Coast) and, in summer only, Fossil Bluff (George VI Sound). Fifteen other stations have been established but are at present unoccupied.

The territory is administered by a High Commissioner, resident in the Falkland Islands.

High Commissioner, Gordon Wesley Jewkes, C.M.G. (1985).

(*see index also for* The Antarctic)

THE BRITISH INDIAN OCEAN TERRITORY

The British Indian Ocean Territory was established by an Order in Council in 1965 and included islands formerly administered by Mauritius and the Seychelles. After the independence of both, the territory was redefined in 1976 as comprising only the islands of the Chagos Archipelago.

The Chagos Archipelago consists of six main groups of islands situated on the Great Chagos Bank and covering some 21,000 sq. miles (54,389 sq. km.). The largest and most southerly of the Chagos Islands is *Diego Garcia,* a sand cay with a land area of about 17 square miles approximately 1,100 miles east of Mahe, used as a joint naval support facility by Britain and U.S.A.

The other main island groups of the archipelago, *Peros Banhos* (29 islands with a total land area of 4 sq. miles) and *Salomon* (11 islands with a total land area of 2 sq. miles) are uninhabited. The islands have a typical tropical maritime climate, with average temperatures between 77°F and 84°F in Diego Garcia, and rainfall in the whole archipelago of 90–100 inches a year.

Commissioner, W. Marsden.
Administrator, T. C. S. Stitt.

THE BRITISH VIRGIN ISLANDS

The Virgin Islands are a group of islands at the eastern extremity of the Greater Antilles, divided between Great Britain and the U.S.A. Those of the group which are British number 46, of which 11 are inhabited, and have a total area of about 59 sq. miles, (153 sq. km.). The principal are Tortola, the largest (situated in 18° 27′ N. lat. and 64° 40′ W. long., area, 21 sq. miles), Virgin Gorda (8¼ sq. miles), Anegada (15 sq.miles) and Jost Van Dyke (3½ sq. miles). The 1980 Census showed a total population of 10,985 (Tortola (9,119); Virgin Gorda (1,443); Anegada (169); Jost Van Dyke (136); and other islands (82). A 1985 U.N. estimate gave a figure of 13,000. Apart from Anegada, which is a flat coral island, the British Virgin Islands are hilly, being an extension of the Puerto Rico and the U.S. Virgin Islands archipelago. The highest point is Sage Mountain on Tortola which rises to a height of 1,780 feet. Tourism is the main industry, but there is some cattle raising and fishing. Other products are vegetables, fruit, charcoal and rum.

The islands lie within the Trade Winds belt and possess a pleasant and healthy sub-tropical climate. The average temperature varies from 71°–82° F. in winter and 78°–88° F. in summer. The summer heat is tempered by sea breezes and the temperature usually falls by about 10°F. at night. Average rainfall is 53 inches.

CAPITAL.—ΨROAD TOWN, on the south-east of Tortola. Population, 2,479.

GOVERNMENT

Under the 1977 Constitution, the Governor, appointed by the Crown, remains responsible for defence and internal security, external affairs and the civil service but in other matters acts in accordance with the advice of the Executive Council. The Executive Council consists of the Governor as Chairman, one *ex officio* member (the Attorney-General), the Chief Minister and three other ministers. The Legislative Council consists of a Speaker chosen from outside the Council, one *ex officio* member (the Attorney-General), and nine elected members returned from nine one-member electoral districts.

Governor, His Excellency (John) Mark (Ambrose) Herdman, L.V.O. (1986).
Deputy Governor, E. Georges.
Financial Secretary, R. Mathavious.

The Executive Council

Chairman, The Governor.
Chief Minister and Minister of Finance, Hon. H. Lavity Stoutt.
Deputy Chief Minister and Minister of Natural Resources and Labour, Hon. Omar Hodge.
Communications and Works, Hon. Oliver Cills.
Health, Education and Welfare, Hon. Louis Walters.
Attorney-General, Hon. St. Clair Atterbury.

Puisne Judge (resident), Hon. Miss Sylvia Bertrand.

FINANCE

	1985	1986
Revenue	U.S.$21,370,000	U.S.$23,195,000
Expenditure	20,123,100	21,213,097

ECONOMY

Tourism is the main industry but other industries include a rum distillery, three stone-crushing plants and factories manufacturing concrete blocks and paint. The major export items are fresh fish, gravel, sand, fruits and vegetables: exports are largely confined to the U.S. Virgin Islands. Chief imports are building materials, machinery, cars and beverages.

Trade with U.K.

	1985	1986
Imports from U.K.	£3,522,000	£3,491,000
Exports to U.K.	698,000	267,000

COMMUNICATIONS

The principal airport is on Beef Island, linked by bridge to Tortola, and an extended runway of 3,600 feet enables larger aircraft to call. There is a second airfield on Virgin Gorda and a third on Anegada. There are direct shipping services to the United Kingdom and the United States and fast passenger services connect the main islands by ferry.

THE CAYMAN ISLANDS

The Cayman Islands, between 79° 44′ and 81° 26′ W. and 19° 15′ and 19° 46′ N., consist of three islands, Grand Cayman, Cayman Brac, and Little Cayman, with a total area of 100 sq. miles (259 sq. km.). Population (1986 estimate), 21,600.

CAPITAL.—ΨGEORGE TOWN, in Grand Cayman, population (1981) 8,200.

GOVERNMENT

The constitution provides for a Governor, Legislative Assembly and an Executive Council. The Legislative Assembly consists of the Governor, three official members and 12 elected members. The Governor presides over the Executive Council, which consists of three official members appointed by the Governor, and four elected members, chosen by the elected members of the Assembly from among their own number. The normal life of the Assembly is four years.

Governor, His Excellency Alan James Scott, C.V.O., C.B.E.

Executive Council

President, The Governor.
Financial Secretary, Hon. T. C. Jefferson, O.B.E.
Administrative Secretary, Hon. J. L. Hurlston.
Attorney-General, Hon. R. W. Ground.
Member for Health, Education and Social Services, Hon. B. O. Ebanks.
Member for Communications, Works and District Administration, Hon. Capt. C. Kirkconnell.
Member for Tourism, Aviation and Trade, Hon. W. N. Bodden, M.B.E.
Member for Development, Lands and Natural Resources, Hon. V. Johnson, C.B.E.

LONDON OFFICE

Cayman Islands Government Office,
17B Curzon Street, W1Y 7FE.

Government Representative, T. Russell, C.M.G., C.B.E.

	1986	1987*
Revenue	CI$65·89m	CI$74·1m
Expenditure	61·44m	72·1m
*estimated		

At end 1986, public debt totalled CI$12·95 million, compared to CI$10·7 million at end 1985.

TRADE

	1984	1985
Total imports	CI$116m	CI$120m
Total exports	1m	1·5m

Trade with U.K.

	1985	1986
Imports from U.K........	£6,410,000	£11,403,000
Exports to U.K.	826,000	2,422,000

FALKLAND ISLANDS

The Falkland Islands, the only considerable group in the South Atlantic, lie about 300 miles east of the Straits of Magellan, between 52° 15′–53° S. lat. and 57° 40′–62° W. long. They consist of East Falkland (area 2,610 sq. miles; 6,759 sq. km.), West Falkland (2,090 sq. miles; 5,413 sq. km.) and upwards of 100 small islands in the aggregate. Mount Usborne (E. Falkland), the loftiest peak, rises 2,312 feet above the level of the sea.

The climate is cool. At Stanley the mean monthly temperature varies between 49° F. in January and 35·5° F. in July. The islands are chiefly moorland.

The Falklands were sighted first by Davis in 1592, and by Hawkins in 1594: the first known landing was by Strong in 1690. A settlement was made by France in 1764; this was subsequently sold to Spain, but the latter country recognized Great Britain's title to a part at least of the group in 1771. The settlement was destroyed by the Americans in 1831. In 1833 occupation was resumed by the British for the protection of the seal-fisheries, and the islands were permanently colonized as the most southerly organized colony of the British Empire. Argentina has long claimed sovereignty over the Islands (known to them as las Islas Malvinas), and in pursuance of this claim invaded the Islands on April 2, 1982 and also occupied South Georgia. A Task Force despatched from Great Britain recaptured South Georgia on April 25, and after landing at San Carlos Bay on May 21, recaptured the Islands from the Argentines, who surrendered on June 14, 1982. A British naval and military presence remains in the area.

The population was 1,916 at Dec. 31, 1986 and is almost totally British.

CHIEF TOWN.—ΨSTANLEY, population 1,231 (1986). Stanley is distant from England about 8,103 miles.

GOVERNMENT

Under the 1985 Constitution, the Governor is advised by an Executive Council consisting of three elected members of the Legislative Council and two *ex-officio* members, the Chief Executive and the Financial Secretary. The Legislative Council consists of eight elected members and the same two *ex-officio* members.

Governor, His Excellency Gordon Wesley Jewkes, C.M.G. (1985).
Commander, British Forces, Falkland Islands, Maj.-Gen. A. N. Carlier, O.B.E.
Chief Executive, B. R. Cummings.
Financial Secretary, H. T. Rowlands, O.B.E.
Attorney General, D. G. Lang, Q.C.

	1984–85	1985–86*
Public Revenue	£4,768,948	£5,598,900
Expenditure	4,999,038	5,588,490
	*Estimated.	

ECONOMY

The economy was formerly based solely on agriculture, principally sheep-farming with a little dairy farming for domestic requirements and crops for winter fodder. Since the establishment of an interim conservation and management zone around the Islands and the consequent introduction on Feb. 1, 1987 of a licensing regime for vessels fishing within the zone the economy has diversified and income from the associated fishing activities is now the largest source of revenue. Chief imports are provisions, alcoholic beverages, timber, clothing and hardware.

Trade with U.K.

	1985	1986
Imports from U.K........	£9,502,000	£11,135,000
Exports to U.K.	7,434,000	14,286,000

Dependencies

SOUTH GEORGIA, An island 800 miles east-south-east of the Falkland group, with an area of 1,450 sq. miles. The population comprises an army unit at King Edward Point, and staff of the British Antarctic Survey at Bird Island, in the north-west of S. Georgia.

THE SOUTH SANDWICH ISLANDS lie some 470 miles S.E. of South Georgia. The group is a chain of uninhabited, actively volcanic islands about 150 miles long, with a wholly Antarctic climate.

Commissioner for South Georgia and the South Sandwich Islands, Gordon W. Jewkes, C.M.G.

GIBRALTAR

Gibraltar is a rocky promontory, 2¾ miles in length, three-quarters of a mile in breadth and 1,396 feet high at its greatest elevation, near the southern extremity of Spain, with which it is connected by a low isthmus. It is about 14 miles distant from the opposite coast of Africa. In a total area of 2¼ sq. miles (6 sq. km.), the population at the census of Nov. 1981 was 28,719. At the end of 1986, it stood at 29,166.

Gibraltar is a naval base of strategic importance to Great Britain. It was captured in 1704, during the war of the Spanish Succession, by a combined Dutch and English force, under Sir George Rooke, and was ceded to Great Britain by the Treaty of Utrecht, 1713. Several attempts have been made to retake it, the most celebrated being the great siege in 1779–83, when General Eliott, afterwards Lord Heathfield, held it for 3 years and 7 months against a combined French and Spanish force. The town stands at the foot of the promontory on the W. side.

GOVERNMENT

The Constitution of Gibraltar, approved in 1969, made formal provision for certain domestic matters to devolve on Ministers appointed from among elected members of the House of Assembly then set up to replace the former Legislative Council. The House of Assembly consists of an independent Speaker, 15 elected members, the Attorney-General and the Financial and Development Secretary.

Governor and Commander-in-Chief, His Excellency Air Chief Marshal Sir Peter Terry, G.C.B., A.F.C.

Flag Officer, Gibraltar, and Admiral Supr., H.M. Naval Base, Gibraltar, Rear-Adm. P. G. V. Dingemans, D.S.O.

Deputy Governor, J. K. E. Broadley £32,350
Financial and Development Secretary, B. Traynor
£28,975
Attorney-General, E. Thistlethwaite £28,975
Chief Justice, A. Kneller £32,350
Chief Minister, Sir Joshua Hassan, K.C.M.G., C.B.E., L.V.O., Q.C.
Speaker, A. J. Vasquez, C.B.E.

ECONOMY

Gibraltar enjoys the advantages of an extensive shipping trade and is a popular shopping centre. The chief sources of revenue are the port dues, the rent of the Crown estate in the town, and duties on consumer items. The free port tradition of Gibraltar is still reflected in the low rates of import duty. The gradual change from a fortress city to a holiday centre has led to a flourishing tourist trade.

A total of 2,493 merchant ships (32,662,935 gross registered tons aggregate) entered the port during 1986. Of these 1,692 were deep-sea ships (24,918,579 gross registered tons aggregate). In addition 5,409 yachts (113,088 gross registered tons) called at the port. There are 26·75 miles of roads.

Education is compulsory and free for children between the ages of 4 and 15 whose parents are ordinarily resident in Gibraltar. Scholarships are available for higher education in Britain. The total enrolment in Government schools was 4,496 in Dec. 1986.

Finance and Trade

	1984–85	1985–86
Revenue	£53,846,000	£64,500,000
Expenditure	55,380,000	61,054,000

	1984–85	1985–86
Total imports	£113,163,000	£111,651,000
Total exports	48,348,000	44,323,000

Trade with U.K.

	1985	1986
Imports from U.K.	£47,052,000	£46,200,000
Exports to U.K.	3,582,000	6,021,000

HONG KONG

Hong Kong, consisting of a number of islands and of a portion of the mainland (Kowloon and the New Territories), on the south-eastern coast of China, is situated at the eastern side of the mouth of the Pearl River, between 22° 9′ and 22° 37′ N. lat. and 113° 52′–114° 30′ E. long. The total area of the territory (including recent reclamation) is 403 sq. miles (1,045 sq. km.) with a population which at the end of 1986 was 5,500,000.

The island of *Hong Kong* is about 11 miles long and from 2 to 5 miles broad, with a total area of 29 sq. miles; at the eastern entrance to the harbour it is separated from the mainland by a narrow strait. The island was first occupied by Great Britain in January, 1841, and formally ceded by the Treaty of Nanking in 1842; *Kowloon* was subsequently acquired by the Peking Convention of 1860; and the *New Territories*, consisting of a peninsula in the southern part of the Guangdong province, together with adjacent islands, by a 99-year lease signed June 9, 1898.

Climate.—Hong Kong enjoys unusually varied weather for a tropical area. The mean monthly temperature ranges from 15° C. to 29° C., though summer temperatures can exceed 33° C and winter temperatures drop below 10° C. The average annual rainfall is 2,225 mm., of which nearly 80 per cent falls between May and September. Tropical cyclones passing at various distances from Hong Kong occur between July and September, causing high winds and heavy rain.

CAPITAL.—VICTORIA, situated on the island of Hong Kong, is about 81 miles S.E. of Canton and 40 miles E. of the Portuguese province of Macao at the other side of the Pearl River. It lies along the northern shore of the island and faces the mainland; the harbour (23 sq. miles water area) lies between the city and the mainland.

GOVERNMENT

Hong Kong is administered by the Hong Kong Government, at the head of which is the Governor, and its administration has developed from the basic pattern applied to all British-governed territories overseas. Under the terms of the Joint Declaration of the British and Chinese Governments, which entered into force on May 27, 1985, Hong Kong will become with effect from July 1, 1997, a Special Administrative Region of the People's Republic of China. However, the social and economic systems in the S.A.R. will remain unchanged for 50 years.

The Governor governs aided by an Executive Council, consisting of 4 *ex officio* and 12 nominated members (two official, ten unofficial), and a Legislative Council, which consists of three *ex-officio* and seven official members, 22 appointed members and 24 elected members.

There is also an Urban Council which provides services relating to public health and sanitation, culture and recreation in the urban area. A Regional Council was also set up in 1986 to provide similar services in the New Territories. Both Councils are financially autonomous.

Governor, His Excellency Sir David Wilson, K.C.M.G. (1987).
Chief Secretary, Hon. D. R. Ford, L.V.O., O.B.E.
Commander, British Forces, Maj.-Gen. Hon. A. Boam, C.B.E.
Financial Secretary, Hon. P. Jacobs, O.B.E.
Attorney-General, Hon. M. D. Thomas, C.M.G., Q.C.
Secretary for Trade and Industry, Hon. N. W. H. Macleod.
Secretary for District Administration, Hon. D. Liao, C.B.E.
Secretary for Economic Services, Hon. Mrs. Anson Chan.
Secretary for Security, Hon. D. G. Jeaffreson, C.B.E.
Secretary for Lands and Works, Hon. G. Barnes.
Secretary for Education and Manpower, Hon. J. N. Henderson, O.B.E.
Secretary for Health and Welfare, Hon. J. W. Chambers.
Secretary for Administrative Services and Information, Hon. P. K. Y. Tsao.
Secretary for Housing, Hon. J. R. Todd, C.V.O., O.B.E.
Secretary for Transport, Hon. M. Leung.
Secretary for Monetary Affairs, D. A. C. Nendick.
Secretary for the Civil Service, H. S. Grewal, E.D.
Secretary for Municipal Services, A. K. Chui.
Secretary (General Duties), E. B. Wiggham.
Chief Justice, Hon. Sir Denys Roberts, K.B.E.
British Council Representative, J. Davey, Easey Commercial Building, 225 Hennessy Road, Hong Kong.

HONG KONG GOVERNMENT OFFICE IN LONDON
6 Grafton Street, W1X 3LB
[01-499 9821]
Commissioner, Mr. Selwyn Alleyne, C.B.E.

COMMUNICATIONS

Hong Kong, one of the world's finest natural harbours, possesses excellent wharves. The Kwai Chung container terminal has six berths which can accommodate six "third-generation" container ships simultaneously. An ocean terminal pier with an overall length of 381 m. can accommodate large liners and cargo vessels. Other vessels up to 305 metres length and 14·6 metres draught can be berthed. Mooring buoys in the harbour are available to vessels of up to 11·2 metres draught. Excellent dockyard facilities are available and include five floating drydocks, the largest of which has a lifting capacity of over 100,000 tonnes. In 1986 some 14,100 ocean-going vessels and 81,150 river-trade vessels called at Hong Kong and loaded and discharged more than 62 million tonnes of cargo.

Hong Kong International Airport, Kai Tak, situated on the north shore of Kowloon Bay, is an important link on the main air routes of the Far East. It is regularly used by over 32 international airlines, providing some 1,000 frequent scheduled passenger and cargo services each week between Hong Kong and the United Kingdom, the People's Republic of China, North and South America, Europe, East and South Africa, the Middle East, Australasia, the South Pacific region, and Asian countries. In addition, several other airlines operate about 25 non-scheduled services a week.

During 1986, 64,770 aircraft on international flights arrived and departed, carrying 10·6 million passengers and 536,000 tonnes of freight.

EDUCATION

In 1986 there were 2,668 schools with 1,374,627 pupils. Free education for children up to the age of 15 was made compulsory in 1979. Post-secondary education is provided by two universities, two polytechnics, the Hong Kong Baptist College and two approved post-secondary colleges. The Hong Kong Polytechnic and City Polytechnic of Hong Kong have about 9,145 and 2,205 full-time students respectively. There are also five technical institutes and four teacher-training colleges.

FINANCE

	1984–85	1985–86
Public revenue	HK$38,525m	HK$43,695m
Public expenditure	36,154m	40,692m

TRADE AND INDUSTRY

The manufacturing sector is the mainstay of Hong Kong's economy, contributing about 22 per cent to the G.D.P. and accounting for about 39 per cent of total employment. Up to 90 per cent of Hong Kong's manufacturing output is eventually exported.

Hong Kong's manufacturing industries produce mainly light consumer goods. In the past ten years or so, industries like electronics, plastics, electrical products, and watches and clocks have grown significantly—they accounted for 38 per cent of Hong Kong's total domestic exports in 1986. The corresponding share of textiles and clothing, Hong Kong's traditional leading industries, decreased to 41 per cent in 1986.

Diversification in terms of products and markets continues to be the main feature of recent industrial development, as are industrial partnerships with overseas companies. It is the world's largest exporter of clothing, toys and games and electric hairdressing apparatus in value terms. The economy of Hong Kong is based on export rather than the domestic market. In 1986, the total value of visible trade

(including domestic exports, re-exports and imports) amounted to 189 per cent of the G.D.P. Hong Kong's visible trade account attained in 1986 a surplus of HK$574 million. Taking visible and invisible trade together, there was a combined surplus of HK$13,589 million, compared with HK$15,753 million in 1985. In 1986, Hong Kong's principal customers for its domestic products, in order of value of trade, were U.S.A., China, the Federal Republic of Germany, the United Kingdom, Japan, Canada and Australia. China was its principal supplier.

	1985	1986
	H.K.$	H.K.$
Total Exports	235,152m	276,530m
Total Imports	231,420m	275,955m

Trade with U.K.

	1985	1986
Imports from U.K.	£949,180,000	£960,956,000
Exports to U.K.	1,175,984,000	1,530,786,000

MONTSERRAT

Situated in 16° 45′ N. lat. and 61° 15′ W. long., 27 miles S.W. of Antigua, the island is about 11 miles long and 7 wide, with an area of 38 sq. miles (98 sq. km.), and a population (1986), of 11,888. Discovered by Columbus in 1493, it was settled by Irishmen in 1632, conquered and held by the French for some time, and finally assigned to Great Britain in 1783. Fertile and green, it is volcanic with several hot springs. About two-thirds of the island is mountainous, the rest capable of cultivation.

CHIEF TOWN.—ΨPLYMOUTH. Population 1,660.

GOVERNMENT

A Ministerial system was introduced in Montserrat in 1960. The Executive Council is presided over by the Governor and is composed of 4 elected members (the Chief and 3 other Ministers) and two *ex-officio* members (the Attorney-General and the Financial Secretary). The 4 Ministers are appointed from the members of the political party holding the majority in the Legislative Council. The Legislative Council consists of the Speaker, two *ex officio* members (the Attorney General and the Financial Secretary), two nominated unofficial members and 7 elected members.

Governor, His Excellency Christopher John Turner, O.B.E. (1987).

Executive Council

President, The Governor.
Chief Minister and Minister of Finance, Hon. J. A. Osborne.
Communications and Works, Hon. J. B. Chalmers.
Education, Health and Community Services, Hon. Mrs. M. M. Dyer.
Agriculture, Trade, Lands and Housing, Hon. N. Tuitt.
Attorney-General, Hon. O. Adams.
Financial Secretary, Hon. J. E. Ryan.

Speaker of the Legislative Council, Hon. H. A. Fergus, O.B.E.

ECONOMY

The chief exports are sea island cotton products, live plants, leather goods, plastic bags, hot peppers and other fruits and vegetables. Real estate development and tourism have done much to aid the island's economy.

FINANCE

	1985	1986
Revenue	EC$24,370,900	EC$25,843,338
Expenditure	22,933,700	25,156,090

Trade with U.K.

	1985	1986
Imports from U.K....	EC$7,160,000	EC$8,000,000
Exports to U.K.	184,000	182,000

PITCAIRN ISLANDS

Pitcairn, a small volcanic island, 1·9 sq. miles (5 sq. km.), in area, is the chief of a group of Islands situated about midway between New Zealand and Panama in the South Pacific Ocean at longitude 130° 06′ W. and latitude 25° 04′ S.

The island rises in cliffs to a height of 1,100 feet and access from the sea is possible only at Bounty Bay, a small rocky cove, and then only by surf boats. Mean monthly temperatures vary between 66° F. in August and 75° F. in February and the average annual rainfall is 80 inches. With an equable climate, the island is very fertile and produces both tropical and sub-tropical trees and crops.

The small community, numbering 57 (1986), are descendants of the Bounty mutineers and their Tahitian companions who did not wish to remain on Norfolk Island when the entire community was transferred there in 1856, and returned to Pitcairn three years later.

Pitcairn became a British Settlement under the British Settlement Act, 1887, and was administered by the Governor of Fiji from 1952 until 1970, when the administration was transferred to the British High Commission in New Zealand and the British High Commissioner was appointed Governor. The local Government Ordinance of 1964 provides for a Council of ten members of whom four are elected.

Governor of Pitcairn, Henderson, Ducie and Oeno Islands, His Excellency T. O'Leary, C.M.G. (*British High Commissioner to New Zealand*).

Island Magistrate and Chairman of Island Council, B. Young.

Education Officer and Government Adviser, L. Buckley.

The Islanders live by subsistence gardening and fishing, and their limited monetary needs are satisfied by the manufacture of wood carvings and other handicrafts which are sold to passing ships and to a few overseas customers. Other than small fees charged for gun and driving licences there are no taxes and Government revenue is derived almost solely from the sale of postage stamps. Communication with the outside world is maintained by cargo vessels travelling between New Zealand and Panama which call at irregular intervals; and by means of telephone telegraphic links with New Zealand.

The New Zealand Education Department provides assistance in recruiting a teacher for the sole-charge school. Education is compulsory between the ages of five and fifteen. Secondary education in New Zealand is encouraged by the Administration which provides scholarships and bursaries for the purpose. Medical care is provided by a registered nurse when a doctor is not present. Since 1887 the islanders have all been adherents of the Seventh Day Adventist Church.

The other three islands of the group (Henderson lying 105 miles E.N.E. of Pitcairn, Oeno lying 75 miles N.W. and Ducie lying 293 miles E.) are all uninhabited. Henderson Island is occasionally visited by the Pitcairn Islanders to obtain supplies of "miro" wood which is used for their carvings. Oeno is visited for excursions of about a week's duration every two years or so.

ST. HELENA

Probably the best known of all the solitary islands in the world, St. Helena is situated in the South Atlantic Ocean, 955 miles S. of the Equator, 702 S.E. of Ascension, 1,140 from the nearest point of the African Continent, 1,800 from the coast of S. America, 1,694 from Cape Town and 4,477 from Southampton (transit 5 days and 16 days respectively), in 15° 55′ S. lat. and 5° 42′ W. longitude. It is 10½ miles long, 6½ broad, and encloses an area of 47 sq. miles (122 sq. km.), with a population of 5,564 (end 1987).

St. Helena is of volcanic origin, and consists of numerous rugged mountains, the highest rising to 2,700 feet, interspersed with picturesque ravines. Although within the tropics, the south-east "trades" keep the temperature mild and equable. St. Helena was discovered by the Portuguese navigator, Juan da Nova Castella, in 1502 (probably on St. Helena's Day) and remained unknown to other European nations until 1588. It was used as a port of call for vessels of all nations trading to the East until it was annexed by the Dutch in 1633. It was never occupied by them, however, and the English East India Company seized it in 1659. In 1834 it was ceded to the Crown. During the period 1815 to 1821 the island was lent to the British Government as a place of exile for the Emperor Napoleon Bonaparte who died in St. Helena on May 5, 1821. It was formerly an important station on the route to India, but its prosperity decreased after the construction of the Suez Canal. Since the collapse of the New Zealand flax industry in 1965, there have been no significant exports, but a second five year development plan, launched in 1979, sought primarily to increase the island's productivity in its limited land and sea resources. ΨSt. James's Bay, on the north-west of the Island, possesses a good anchorage. There is no airport or airstrip.

CAPITAL.—ΨJAMESTOWN. Population (1987), 1,330.

GOVERNMENT

The government of St. Helena is administered by a Governor, with the aid of a Legislative Council, consisting of the Governor, two *ex-officio* members (Government Secretary and Treasurer) and twelve elected members. Six committees of the Legislative Council are reponsible for general oversight of the activities of Government Departments and have in addition a wide range of statutory and administrative functions. The Governor is also assisted by an Executive Council of the two *ex-officio* members and the Chairmen of the Council committees.

Governor, His Excellency Francis E. Baker, C.B.E. (1984).

Government Secretary, E. C. Brooks, O.B.E.

Treasurer and Development Secretary, P. C. Knights, M.B.E.

Senior Medical Officer, Dr. S. J. Wooltorton.

Agricultural and Forestry Officer, M. D. Holland.

Education Officer, B. A. George.

FINANCE AND TRADE

	1984	1985
Public revenue	£8,296,154	£8,484,825
Expenditure	7,721,940	7,370,155
Total imports	3,219,960	4,090,516
Imports from U.K.	1,820,782	2,452,129

Figures include development aid, shipping subsidy and grant-in-aid.

ASCENSION

The small island of Ascension lies in the South Atlantic (7° 56′ S., 14° 22′ W.) some 700 miles north-west of the island of St. Helena. It is a rocky peak of purely volcanic origin, the highest point (Green Mountain) some 2,817 ft. is covered with lush vegetation. B.B.C. (Ascension Island Services) operate a farm of some 10 acres on the mountain, permitting the production of vegetables and live-stock. The island is famous for turtles, which land on the beaches from January to May to lay their eggs. It is also a breeding area for the sooty tern, or wideawake, large numbers of which settle on the south-western coastal section every eighth month to hatch their eggs. Other wild life on the island includes feral donkeys and cats, rabbits and francolin partridge. All wild life except rabbits and cats is protected by law. The ocean surrounding the island abounds with shark, barracuda, tuna, bonito and many other fish.

Ascension is said to have been discovered by Juan da Nova Castella, on Ascension Day, 1501, and two years later was visited by Alphonse d'Albuquerque, who gave the island its present name. It was uninhabited until the arrival of Napoleon in St. Helena in 1815 when a small British naval garrison was stationed on the island. It remained under the supervision of the Board of Admiralty until 1922, when it was made a dependency of St. Helena by Royal Letters Patent.

The British Foreign Secretary appoints the Administrator. There is a small Police Force and Post Office. The British organizations provide and operate various common services for the island (school, hospital, public works etc).

Ascension Island is a main relay point of the coaxial submarine cable system laid between South Africa, Portugal and the United Kingdom, which is operated by the South Atlantic Cable Company. Cable & Wireless Ltd operates the international telephone and cable services, maintains an internal telephone service, and also operates an Earth Station on behalf of N.A.S.A. The B.B.C. opened its Atlantic relay station broadcasting to Africa and South America in 1967.

The resident population in March 1987 totalled 1,107, of whom 688 were from St. Helena, 206 from the U.K., 202 from the U.S.A. and 11 from the Republic of South Africa. The residents consist of the employees and families of the British organizations, of the contractors for the U.S. Air Force and N.A.S.A. (Pan American Airways, Radio Corporation of America and Bendix Field Engineering Corporation) and of the St. Helena Government.

British forces returned to the island in April 1982 in support of operations in the Falkland Islands. At present there are about 200 R.A.F. personnel on the island supporting the air link to the Falklands.

Administrator, M. T. Blick.

TRISTAN DA CUNHA

Tristan da Cunha is the chief of a group of islands of volcanic origin lying in lat. 37° 6′ S. and long. 12° 2′ W., discovered in 1506 by a Portuguese admiral (Tristão da Cunha), after whom they are named. They have a total area of 40 sq. miles (104 sq. km.). Population (1985) 310. The main island, with a peak rising to 6,760 ft., is about 1,500 miles W. of the Cape of Good Hope, 3,600 miles N.E. of Cape Horn, and about 1,320 miles S.S.W. of St. Helena. It was the resort of British and American sealers from the middle of the 18th century, and in 1760 a British naval officer visited the group and gave his name to Nightingale Island. On August 14, 1816, the group was annexed to the British Crown and a garrison

was placed on Tristan da Cunha, but this force was withdrawn in 1817, William Glass, a corporal of artillery (*died* 1853), remaining at his own request, with his wife and two children. This party, with five others, formed a settlement. In 1827 five coloured women from St. Helena, and afterwards others from Cape Colony, joined the party.

The islands form a dependency of St. Helena, being administered by the Foreign and Commonwealth Office through a resident Administrator, with head-quarters at the settlement of Edinburgh. Under a new constitution introduced in 1969, he is advised by an elected Island Council of 8 members of whom one must be a woman, and three appointed members, with universal suffrage at 18. The population numbered 294 persons in 1986, plus 5 expatriate Government officers and their families, and a resident chaplain.

In October, 1961, a volcano, believed to have been extinct for thousands of years, erupted and the danger of further volcanic activity led to the evacuation of inhabitants to the United Kingdom. An advance party returned to Tristan da Cunha in the spring of 1963, and subsequently the main body of the islanders returned to the island.

A boat harbour was completed in 1967. The first freezing factory was re-established in 1966. There are no taxes on Tristan, income being derived from royalties paid by the fishing company and from the sale of stamps. The Camogli Hospital was opened early in 1971 and a new school in 1975.

Administrator, R. Perry.

INACCESSIBLE ISLAND is a lofty mass of rock with sides 2 miles in length; the island is the resort of penguins and sea-fowl. Cultivation was started in 1937, but has been abandoned.

THE NIGHTINGALE ISLANDS are three in number, of which the largest is 1 mile long and ½ mile wide, and rises in two peaks, 960 and 1,105 ft. above sea-level respectively. The smaller islands, Stoltenhoff and Middle Isle, are little more than huge rocks. Seals, innumerable penguins, and vast numbers of sea-fowl visit these islands.

GOUGH ISLAND (or Diego Alvarez), in 40° 20′ S. and 9° 44′ W., lies about 250 miles S.S.E. of Tristan da Cunha. The island is about 8 miles long and 4 miles broad, with a total area of 40 square miles, and has been a British possession since 1816. The island is the resort of penguins and sea-elephants and has valuable guano deposits. There is no permanent population, but there is a meteorological station maintained on the island by the South African Government and manned by South Africans.

TURKS AND CAICOS ISLANDS

The Turks and Caicos Islands are situated between 21° and 22° N. latitude and 71° and 72° W. longitude, about 100 miles north of the Dominican Republic and 50 miles south-east of the Bahamas of which they are geographically an extension. There are over 30 islands of which eight are inhabited covering an estimated area of 166 sq. miles (430 sq. km.). The principal is Grand Turk. The population in 1985 was 8,000 (Grand Turk 3,146).

The Islands lie in the Trade Wind but with an excellent climate. The average temperature varies from 75°–80°F. in the winter and 85°–90°F. in the summer and humidity is generally low. Average rainfall is 21 inches per annum.

GOVERNMENT

A new Constitution was introduced in 1976, providing for an Executive Council and Legislative Council. The Executive Council is presided over by the Governor and comprises the Chief Minister and three elected Ministers, together with the Chief Secretary, the Attorney General and the Financial Secretary *ex officio*.

Following the resignation of three ministers in July 1986 and until elections are held in Spring 1988, the Governor will govern with the present Legislative Council, and an Advisory Council which replaces the Executive Council.

Governor, His Excellency Michael John Bradley, Q.C. (1987).

Advisory Executive Council

President, The Governor.
Chief Secretary, Hon. A. N. Hoole.
Acting Attorney-General, Hon. P. R. Ellum.
Acting Financial Secretary, Hon. A. Robinson, M.B.E.
Members, Hon. D. Malcolm; Hon. T. Lightbourne; Hon. H. Ingham.

The principal airports are on the islands of Grand Turk, Providenciales and South Caicos. There are direct shipping services to the U.S.A. (Miami). There is an air service between Miami, Providenciales and Grand Turk, and between South Caicos and the Bahamas. An internal air service provides a twice daily service between the principal islands. A comprehensive telephone and telex service is provided by Cable and Wireless (W.I.) Ltd.

The most important industries are fishing, tourism and offshore finance.

FINANCE

	1986–87*	1987–88*
Local Revenue	U.S.$11,123,000	U.S.$11,593,550
Expenditure	13,106,000	13,616,550
Budgetary Aid	1,983,000	2,022,000
*estimated.		

Trade with U.K.

	1985	1986
Imports	£1,063,000	£1,025,000
Exports	6,000	86,000

VIRGIN ISLANDS,
see BRITISH

UNIVERSITIES OF THE COMMONWEALTH
(outside the United Kingdom)

With date of foundation

Australia

ADELAIDE (1874); AUSTRALIAN NATIONAL (1946), Canberra; CURTIN U. OF TECHNOLOGY (1987), Perth; DEAKIN (1974), Geelong; FLINDERS, SOUTH AUSTRALIA (1966), Adelaide; GRIFFITH (1971), Brisbane; JAMES COOK, NORTH QUEENSLAND (1970), Townsville; LA TROBE (1964), Melbourne; MACQUARIE (1964), Sydney; MELBOURNE (1853); MONASH (1958), Melbourne; MURDOCH (1973), Perth; NEWCASTLE (1965); NEW ENGLAND (1954), Armidale; NEW SOUTH WALES (1949), Sydney; QUEENSLAND (1909), Brisbane, incorporating UNIV. COLLEGE OF THE NORTHERN TERRITORY (1985); SYDNEY (1850); TASMANIA (1890), Hobart; WESTERN AUSTRALIA (1911), Perth; WOLLONGONG (1975).

Bangladesh

BANGLADESH AGRICULTURAL (1961), Mymensingh; BANGLADESH U. OF ENGINEERING AND TECHNOLOGY (1961), Dhaka; CHITTAGONG (1966); DHAKA (1921); JAHANGIRNAGAR (1970), Dhaka; RAJSHAHI (1953).

Botswana

BOTSWANA (1976), Gaborone.

Brunei Darussalam

BRUNEI DARUSSALAM (1985), Gadong.

Canada

ACADIA (1838), Wolfville; ALBERTA (1906), Edmonton; ATHABASCA (1970), Athabasca; BISHOP'S (1843), Lennoxville; BRANDON (1967); BRITISH COLUMBIA (1908), Vancouver; BROCK (1964), St. Catharines; CALGARY (1966); UNIVERSITY COLLEGE OF CAPE BRETON (1982), Sydney; CARLETON (1942), Ottawa; CONCORDIA (1929), Montreal; DALHOUSIE (1818), Halifax, incorporating UNIVERSITY OF KING'S COLLEGE (1789), Halifax; DOMINION COLLEGE OF PHILOSOPHY AND THEOLOGY (1967), Ottawa; GUELPH (1964); LAKEHEAD (1965), Thunder Bay; LAURENTIAN, U. OF SUDBURY (1960), incorporating SUDBURY (1957); LAVAL (1852), Quebec; LETHBRIDGE (1967); McGILL (1821), Montreal; McMASTER (1887), Hamilton; MANITOBA (1877), Winnipeg, incorporating ST. JOHN'S COLL. (1866), Winnipeg and ST. PAUL'S COLL. (1926), Winnipeg; MEMORIAL U. OF NEWFOUNDLAND (1949), St. John's; MONCTON (1963), Moncton, Edmundston and Shippagan; MONTREAL (1876); MOUNT ALLISON (1858), Sackville; MOUNT ST. VINCENT (1925), Halifax; NEW BRUNSWICK (1785), Fredericton and St. John, incorporating ST. THOMAS (1934), Fredericton; NOVA SCOTIA AGRICULTURAL COLLEGE (1905), Truro; NOVA SCOTIA COLLEGE OF ART AND DESIGN (1887), Halifax; OTTAWA (1848), incorporating ST. PAUL (1848), Ottawa; PRINCE EDWARD ISLAND (1969), Charlottetown; QUEBEC (1968), Chicoutimi, Hull, Montreal, Rimouski, Rouyn, Trois-Rivières, and other centres; QUEEN'S U. AT KINGSTON (1841); REDEEMER REFORMED CHRISTIAN COLLEGE (1980), Ancaster; REGINA (1974), incorporating CAMPION COLLEGE. (1918), Regina, LUTHER COLLEGE (1913), Regina, SASKATCHEWAN INDIAN FEDERATED COLLEGE (1976), Regina; ROYAL MILITARY COLLEGE OF CANADA (1876), Kingston; ROYAL ROADS MILITARY COLLEGE (1942), Victoria; RYERSON POLYTECHNICAL INSTITUTE (1963), Toronto; STE.-ANNE (1892), Church Point; ST. FRANCIS XAVIER (1853), Antigonish; ST. MARY'S (1841), Halifax; SASKATCHEWAN (1907), Saskatoon, incorporating ST. THOMAS MORE COLLEGE (1936), Saskatoon; SHERBROOKE (1954); SIMON FRASER (1963), Burnaby; TECHNICAL

U. OF NOVA SCOTIA (1909), Halifax; TORONTO (1827), incorporating UNIV. OF ST. MICHAEL'S COLL. (1852), Toronto, UNIV. OF TRINITY COLL. (1851), Toronto, VICTORIA (1836), Toronto, ONTARIO INSTITUTE FOR STUDIES IN EDUCATION (1965), Toronto; TRENT (1963), Peterborough; TRINITY WESTERN (1962), Langley; VICTORIA (1963), British Columbia; WATERLOO (1959), incorporating ST. JEROME'S COLLEGE, Waterloo; WESTERN ONTARIO (1878), London, incorporating BRESCIA COLLEGE (1919), London, HURON COLLEGE (1863), London, KING'S COLLEGE (1912), London; WILFRED LAURIER (1973), Waterloo; WINDSOR (1857); WINNIPEG (1967); YORK (1959), Toronto.

Ghana

CAPE COAST (1962); GHANA (1961), Legon; UNIVERSITY OF SCIENCE AND TECHNOLOGY (1961), Kumasi.

Guyana

GUYANA (1963), Georgetown.

Hong Kong

CHINESE UNIV. OF HONG KONG (1963); HONG KONG (1911).

India

AGRA (1927); AGRICULTURAL SCIENCES (1964), Bangalore; ALAGAPPA (1985), Karaikudi; ALIGARH MUSLIM (1920); ALLAHABAD (1887); ALL-INDIA INSTITUTE OF MEDICAL SCIENCES (1956), New Delhi; AMRAVATI (1983); ANDHRA (1926), Waltair; ANDHRA PRADESH AGRICULTURAL (1964), Hyderabad; ANDHRA PRADESH OPEN (1982), Hyderabad; ANNA (1978); Madras; ANNAMALAI (1928), Annamalainagar; ASSAM AGRICULTURAL (1969), Jorhat; AVADH (1975), Faizabad; AWADHESH PRATAP SINGH VISHWAVIDYALAYA (1968), Rewa; BANARAS HINDU (1915); BANASTHALI VIDYAPITH (1983); BANGALORE (1964); BARODA (1949); BERHAMPUR (1967); BHAGALPUR (1960); BHARATHIAR (1982), Coimbatore; BHARATHIDASAN (1982), Tiruchirapalli; BHAVNAGAR (1978); BHOPAL (1970); BIDHAN CHANDRA KRISHI VISWAVIDYALAYA (1974), Kalyani; BIHAR (1952), Muzaffarpur; BIRLA INSTITUTE OF TECHNOLOGY (1955), Ranchi; BIRLA INSTITUTE OF TECHNOLOGY AND SCIENCE (1964), Pilani; BIRSA AGRICULTURAL (1980), Ranchi; BOMBAY (1857); BUNDELKHAND (1975), Jhansi; BURDWAN (1960); CALCUTTA (1857); CALICUT (1968); CENTRAL INSTITUTE OF ENGLISH AND FOREIGN LANGUAGES (1958), Hyderabad; CHANDRA SHEKHAR AZAD U. OF AGRICULTURE AND TECHNOLOGY (1975), Kanpur; COCHIN U. OF SCIENCE AND TECHNOLOGY (1971), Tripunithura; DAKSHINA BHARAT HINDI PRACHAR SABHA (1918), Hyderabad; DAYALBAGH EDUCATIONAL INSTITUTE (1981), Agra; DELHI (1922); DEVI AHILYA VISHWAVIDYALAYA (1964), Indore; DIBRUGARH (1965); DOCTOR HARISINGH GOUR VISHWAVIDYALAYA (1964), Sagar; GANDHIGRAM RURAL INSTITUTE (1956), Madurai; GANDHIJI (1983), Kottayam; GARHWAL (1973), Srinagar; GAUHATI (1948); GOA (1985); GORAKHPUR (1956); GOVIND BALLABH PANT U. OF AGRICULTURE AND TECHNOLOGY (1960), Pantnagar; GUJARAT (1949), Ahmedabad; GUJARAT AGRICULTURAL (1969), Ahmedabad; GUJARAT AYURVED (1966), Jamnagar; GUJARAT VIDYAPITH (1920), Ahmedabad; GULBARGA (1980); GURU GHASIDAS (1983), Bilaspur; GURUKULA KANGRI VISHWAVIDYALAYA (1900), Saharahpur; GURU NANAK DEV (1969), Amritsar; HARYANA AGRICULTURAL (1970), Hissar; U. OF HEALTH SCIENCES (1982),

Vijayawada; HIMACHAL PRADESH (1970), Simla; HIMACHAL PRADESH KRISHI VISHVA VIDYALAYA (1978), Palampur; HYDERABAD (1974); INDIAN AGRICULTURAL RESEARCH INSTITUTE (1905), New Delhi; INDIAN INSTITUTE OF SCIENCE (1909), Bangalore; INDIAN INST. OF TECHNOLOGY, BOMBAY (1958); INDIAN INST. OF TECHNOLOGY, DELHI (1961); INDIAN INST. OF TECHNOLOGY, KANPUR (1960); INDIAN INST. OF TECHNOLOGY, KHARAGPUR (1951); INDIAN INST. OF TECHNOLOGY, MADRAS (1959); INDIAN SCHOOL OF MINES (1926), Dhanbad; INDIAN STATISTICAL INST. (1932), Calcutta; INDIAN VETERINARY RESEARCH INST (1889), Izatnagar; INDIRA GANDHI NATIONAL OPEN (1985), Delhi; INDIRA KALA SANGIT VISHAVIDYALAYA (1956), Khairagarh; INTERNATIONAL INSTITUTE FOR POPULATION SCIENCES (1956), Bombay; JADAVPUR (1955), Calcutta; JAMIA MILLIA ISLAMIA (1962), New Delhi; JAMMU (1969); JAWAHARLAL NEHRU KRISHI VISHWA VIDYALAYA (1964), Jabalpur; JAWAHARLAL NEHRU TECHNOLOGICAL (1972), Hyderabad; JAWAHARLAL NEHRU U. (1969), New Delhi; JIWAJI (1964), Gwalior; JODHPUR (1962); KAKATIYA (1976), Warangal; KALYANI (1960); KAMESHWARA SINGH DARBHANGA SANSKRIT VISHWAVIDYALAYA (1961), Darbhanga; KANPUR (1965); KARNATAK (1949), Dharwar; KASHI VIYAPITH (1921), Varanasi; KASHMIR (1969), Srinagar; KERALA (1937), Trivandrum; KERALA AGRICULTURAL (1971), Trichur; KONKAN KRISHI VIDYAPEETH (1972), Ratnagiri; KUMAUN (1973), Nainital; KURUKSHETRA (1956); L. N. MITHILA (1972), Darbhanga; LUCKNOW (1921); MADRAS (1857); MADURAI-KAMARAJ (1966); MAGADH (1962), Gaya; MAHARSHI DAYANAND (1976), Rohtak; MAHATMA PHULE AGRICULTURAL (1967), Ahmednagar; MANGALORE (1980); MANIPUR (1980), Imphal; MARATHWADA (1958), Aurangabad; MARATHWADA AGRICULTURAL (1972), Parbhani; MEERUT (1966); MOHAN LAL SUKHADIA (1962), Udaipur; MOTHER TERESA WOMEN'S (1984), Kodaikanal; MYSORE (1916); NAGARJUNA (1976), Nagarjunanagar; NAGPUR (1923); NARENDRA DEV. U. OF AGRICULTURE AND TECHNOLOGY (1974), Faizabad; NORTH BENGAL (1962), Darjeeling; NORTH-EASTERN HILL (1973), Shillong; ORISSA U. OF AGRICULTURE AND TECHNOLOGY (1962), Bhubaneswar; OSMANIA (1918), Hyderabad; PANJAB (1947), Chandigarh; PATNA (1917); PONDICHERRY (1985); POONA (1948); POSTGRADUATE INSTITUTE OF MEDICAL EDUCATION AND RESEARCH (1962), Chandigarh; PUNJAB AGRICULTURAL (1962), Ludhiana; PUNJABI (1961), Patiala; PUNJABRAO KRISHI VIDYAPEETH (1969), Akola; RABINDRA BHARATI (1962), Calcutta; RAJASTHAN (1947), Jaipur; RAJENDRA AGRICULTURAL (1970), Pusa; RANCHI (1960); RANI DURGAVATI VISHWAVIDYALAYA (1957), Jabalpur; RAVISHANKAR (1963), Raipur; ROHILKHAND (1975), Bareilly; ROORKEE (1949); SAMBALPUR (1967); SAMPURNANAND SANSKRIT VISHWAVIDYALAYA (1958), Varanasi; SARDAR PATEL (1955), Vallabh Vidyanagar; SAURASHTRA (1966), Rajkot; SCHOOL OF PLANNING AND ARCHITECTURE (1955), New Delhi; SHER-E-KASHMIR U. OF AGRICULTURAL SCIENCES AND TECHNOLOGY (1982), Srinagar; SHIVAJI (1962), Kolhapur; SHREEMATI N. D. THACKERSEY WOMEN'S (1951), Bombay.; SHRI JAGANNATH SANSKRIT VISHWAVIDYALAYA (1981), Puri; SOUTH GUJARAT (1966), Surat; SREE CHITRA TIRUNAL INST. FOR MEDICAL SCIENCES AND TECHNOLOGY (1973), Trivandrum; SRI KRISHNADEVARAYA (1981), Anantapur; SRI PADMAVATI MAHILA VISWAVIDYALAYAM (1983), Tirupati; SRI SATHYA SAI INSTITUTE OF HIGHER LEARNING (1981), Anantapur; SRI VENKATESWARA (1954), Tirupati; TAMIL (1981), Thanjavur; TAMIL NADU AGRICULTURAL (1971), Coimbatore; TATA INSTITUTE OF SOCIAL SCIENCES (1936), Bombay; TELUGU (1987), Hyderabad; THAPAR INSTITUTE OF ENGINEERING AND TECHNOLOGY (1956), Patiala; UTKAL (1943), Bhubaneswar; VIDYASAGAR (1981), Midnapore; VIKRAM (1957), Ujjain; VISVA-BHARATI (1951), Santiniketan.

Kenya

KENYATTA (1972), Nairobi; MOI (1984), Eldoret; NAIROBI (1970), incorporating EGERTON UNIV. COLLEGE (1986), Njoro.

Lesotho

NATIONAL U. OF LESOTHO (1975), Roma.

Malawi

MALAWI (1964), Zomba and other centres.

Malaysia

UNIV. OF AGRICULTURE, MALAYSIA (1971), Serdang; MALAYA (1962), Kuala Lumpur; NATIONAL UNIV. OF MALAYSIA (1970), Kuala Lumpur; NORTHERN MALAYSIA (1984), Alor Star; SCIENCE U., MALAYSIA (1969); U. OF TECHNOLOGY (1972), Kuala Lumpur.

Malta

MALTA (1980), Msida.

Mauritius

NATIONAL U., MAURITIUS (1965), Réduit.

New Zealand

AUCKLAND (1882); CANTERBURY (1873), Christchurch, incorporating LINCOLN COLLEGE (1878); MASSEY (1964), Palmerston North; OTAGO (1869), Dunedin; VICTORIA, WELLINGTON (1897); WAIKATO (1964), Hamilton.

Nigeria

AHMADU BELLO (1962), Zaria; ANAMBRA STATE U. OF TECHNOLOGY (1980), Enugu and Awka; BAYERO (1975), Kano; BENDEL STATE (1981), Ekpoma; BENIN (1970); CALABAR (1975); CROSS RIVER STATE (1983), Uyo; FEDERAL U. OF TECHNOLOGY, AKURE (1981); FEDERAL U. OF TECHNOLOGY, MINNA; FEDERAL U. OF TECHNOLOGY, OWERRI (1980); IBADAN (1948); IFE (1961), Ile-Ife; ILORIN (1975); IMO STATE (1981), Etiti; JOS (1975); LAGOS (1962); LAGOS STATE (1983), Ojo; MAIDUGURI (1975); NIGERIA (1960), Nsukka and Enugu; OGUN STATE (1982), Ago-Iwoye; ONDO STATE (1982), Ado-Ekiti; PORT HARCOURT (1975); RIVERS STATE U. OF SCIENCE AND TECHNOLOGY (1980), Port Hartcourt; SOKOTO (1975).

Papua New Guinea

PAPUA NEW GUINEA (1965), Port Moresby; PAPUA NEW GUINEA UNIV. OF TECHNOLOGY (1973), Lae.

Sierra Leone

SIERRA LEONE (1966), with colleges at Freetown and Njala.

Singapore

NATIONAL U. OF SINGAPORE (1980), incorporating NANYANG TECHNOLOGICAL INSTITUTE (1981), Singapore.

South Pacific

SOUTH PACIFIC (1967), Suva and Alafua.

Sri Lanka

BUDDHIST AND PALI (1982), Colombo; COLOMBO (1979); JAFFNA (1979); KELANIYA (1979); MORATUWA (1979), Katubedda; OPEN U. OF SRI LANKA (1980), Nugegoda; PERADENIYA (1979), incorporating BATTICALOA U. COLLEGE (1981); RUHUNA (1979), Matara; SRI JAYEWARDENEPURA (1979), Gangodawila.

Swaziland
SWAZILAND (1976), Kwaluseni.

Tanzania
DAR ES SALAAM (1970); SOKOINE U. OF AGRICULTURE (1984), Morogoro.

Uganda
MAKERERE (1970), Kampala.

West Indies
UNIV. OF THE WEST INDIES (1962), Jamaica, with campuses in Trinidad and Barbados.

Zambia
ZAMBIA (1965), Lusaka and Ndola.

Zimbabwe
ZIMBABWE (1955), Harare.

ELEMENTS

Element	Symbol	Atomic Number	Element	Symbol	Atomic Number	Element	Symbol	Atomic Number
Actinium	Ac	89	Hafnium	Hf	72	Promethium	Pm	61
Aluminium	Al	13	Helium	He	2	Protactinium	Pa	91
Americium	Am	95	Holmium	Ho	67	Radium	Ra	88
Antimony	Sb	51	Hydrogen	H	1	Radon	Rn	86
Argon	A	18	Indium	In	49	Rhenium	Re	75
Arsenic	As	33	Iodine	I	53	Rhodium	Rh	45
Astatine	At	85	Iridium	Ir	77	Rubidium	Rb	37
Barium	Ba	56	Iron	Fe	26	Ruthenium	Ru	44
Berkelium	Bk	97	Krypton	Kr	36	Samarium	Sm	62
Beryllium	Be	4	Lanthanum	La	57	Scandium	Sc	21
Bismuth	Bi	83	Lawrencium	Lr	103	Selenium	Se	34
Boron	B	5	Lead	Pb	82	Silicon	Si	14
Bromine	Br	35	Lithium	Li	3	Silver	Ag	47
Cadmium	Cd	48	Lutetium	Lu	71	Sodium	Na	11
Caesium	Cs	55	Magnesium	Mg	12	Strontium	Sr	38
Calcium	Ca	20	Manganese	Mn	25	Sulphur	S	16
Californium	Cf	98	Mendelevium	Md	101	Tantalum	Ta	73
Carbon	C	6	Mercury	Hg	80	Technetium	Tc	43
Cerium	Ce	58	Molybdenum	Mo	42	Tellurium	Te	52
Chlorine	Cl	17	Neodymium	Nd	60	Terbium	Tb	65
Chromium	Cr	24	Neon	Ne	10	Thallium	Tl	81
Cobalt	Co	27	Neptunium	Np	93	Thorium	Th	90
Copper	Cu	29	Nickel	Ni	28	Thulium	Tm	69
Curium	Cm	96	Niobium	Nb	41	Tin	Sn	50
Dysprosium	Dy	66	Nitrogen	N	7	Titanium	Ti	22
Einsteinium	Es	99	Nobelium	No	102	Tungsten	W	74
Erbium	Er	68	Osmium	Os	76	(Wolfram)		
Europium	Eu	63	Oxygen	O	8	Uranium	U	92
Fermium	Fm	100	Palladium	Pd	46	Vanadium	V	23
Fluorine	F	9	Phosphorus	P	15	Xenon	Xe	54
Francium	Fr	87	Platinum	Pt	78	Ytterbium	Yb	70
Gadolinium	Gd	64	Plutonium	Pu	94	Yttrium	Y	39
Gallium	Ga	31	Polonium	Po	84	Zinc	Zn	30
Germanium	Ge	32	Potassium	K	19	Zirconium	Zr	40
Gold	Au	79	Praseodymium	Pr	59			

U.K. TRADE OVERSEAS (£'000)

	1985		1986	
	Imports	Exports	Imports	Exports
Benelux*	10,567,624	10,692,277	10,699,734	9,275,108
Denmark	1,715,233	1,371,556	1,752,174	1,211,637
France	6,632,410	7,751,751	7,348,574	6,210,216
Germany, Fed. Rep. of	12,601,387	8,947,055	14,139,097	8,542,196
Greece	320,131	335,352	308,644	356,020
Rep. of Ireland	2,816,007	3,642,844	3,053,807	3,558,372
Italy	4,293,941	3,466,495	4,658,036	3,472,364
Portugal	695,744	439,499	768,470	472,078
Spain	1,770,862	1,553,424	1,777,341	1,905,479
E.E.C.—TOTAL	41,413,338	38,200,252	44,505,877	35,003,470
Afghanistan	52,061	13,882	11,913	11,444
Albania	212	5,252	129	2,887
Algeria	251,462	176,596	140,860	129,624
Andorra	198	10,413	40	13,174
Angola	150,639	43,187	43,147	30,896
Anguilla	165	1,754	60	1,136
Antigua	1,877	28,798	2,069	17,774
Argentina	2,032	3,815	28,635	10,115
Aruba	28,386	5,933	576	6,972
Australia	738,986	1,373,184	643,238	1,227,647
Austria	630,586	381,047	705,732	403,000
Bahamas	70,763	74,059	10,266	95,816
Bahrain	45,219	161,560	19,732	130,991
Bangladesh	35,348	69,420	34,117	48,218
Barbados	13,512	36,856	11,661	38,338
Belize	15,050	8,329	17,954	8,232
Benin	7,390	8,362	4,910	6,728
Bermuda	6,394	28,024	1,262	26,180
Bhutan	—	109	—	76
Bolivia	14,434	10,443	10,225	3,663
Botswana	20,998	6,680	16,652	8,629
Brazil	610,624	211,512	552,259	295,152
Brit. Indian Ocean Terr.	412	502	54	817
Brunei	23,346	71,496	71,624	154,146
Bulgaria	22,291	109,970	32,459	80,504
Burkina	557	2,729	1,369	3,104
Burma	9,944	20,221	6,092	10,835
Burundi	3,367	1,592	3,074	2,324
Cameroon	73,746	44,806	7,634	34,368
Canada	1,652,812	1,692,487	1,499,600	1,698,372
Canary Is.	64,625	48,946	63,529	66,949
Cape Verde	370	2,282	426	1,618
Cayman Is.	826	6,410	2,422	11,403
Central African Rep.	1,739	1,151	1,452	787
Ceeta & Melilla	—	2,893	44	2,762
Chad	1,099	1,847	2,806	1,250
Chile	134,750	73,914	128,007	67,459
China	307,963	396,156	327,032	535,943
Colombia	112,486	82,639	94,112	58,084
The Comoros	234	603	—	307
Congo	2,819	12,112	2,444	9,165
Cook Is.	63	183	46	279
Costa Rica	22,646	14,413	30,318	12,007
Côte d'Ivoire	116,699	29,514	117,058	34,266
Cuba	7,273	59,332	8,555	58,760
Curaçao	134,850	13,911	78,509	17,260
Cyprus	93,689	150,921	124,198	140,387
Czechoslovakia	120,017	100,452	125,399	108,841
Djibouti	293	21,546	53	12,537
Dominica	18,110	10,257	26,612	8,780
Dominican Rep.	7,900	14,595	7,599	15,178
Ecuador	19,015	58,628	11,339	46,673
Egypt	162,162	471,091	328,053	371,007
El Salvador	1,662	8,507	1,323	6,917
Equatorial Guinea	—	191	1	633
Ethiopia	13,805	66,089	22,343	50,049
Falkland Is.	7,434	9,502	14,286	11,135
Faroe Islands	21,383	5,605	21,380	5,709

* Belgium, Luxembourg and the Netherlands

	1985		1986	
	Imports	Exports	Imports	Exports
Fiji	36,328	9,843	66,500	8,775
Finland	1,324,792	705,365	1,346,058	664,461
French Guyana	124	1,146	55	1,052
French Polynesia	23	3,961	95	4,890
Gabon	48,292	30,588	36,642	16,627
Gambia	2,823	11,918	2,273	16,707
German Dem. Rep.	204,293	63,797	195,513	81,276
Ghana	99,410	116,883	103,480	113,218
Gibraltar	3,582	47,052	6,021	46,200
Greenland	3,168	348	4,789	452
Grenada	6,735	8,820	7,011	8,628
Guadeloupe	322	3,089	1,711	3,477
Guatemala	5,176	13,397	8,098	9,288
Guinea	9,064	10,301	23,892	10,679
Guinea-Bissau	2	1,209	214	1,319
Guyana	52,377	18,406	55,535	13,737
Haiti	1,512	5,048	899	5,147
Honduras	11,139	9,026	5,280	9,213
Hong Kong	1,175,984	949,180	1,530,786	960,956
Hungary	84,114	107,226	77,228	101,557
Iceland	128,281	76,914	173,140	73,640
India	431,785	894,708	440,681	941,169
Indonesia	155,934	172,818	141,242	196,629
Iran	63,317	525,589	100,303	399,373
Iraq	44,125	444,749	66,129	443,890
Israel	403,952	434,470	385,164	462,407
Jamaica	89,684	44,290	87,416	43,378
Japan	4,117,024	1,012,436	4,932,497	1,193,933
Jordan	86,077	154,270	49,766	130,385
Kampuchea	77	467	58	217
Kenya	185,622	160,651	163,745	170,671
Kiribati	209	775	4	179
Korea, North	1,983	2,608	1,374	3,331
Korea, South	480,448	247,887	661,975	288,421
Kuwait	156,912	347,915	58,517	300,586
Laos	6	523	150	1,460
Lebanon	7,888	52,751	9,845	55,867
Lesotho	290	3,023	277	2,128
Liberia	5,967	15,957	7,574	22,056
Libya	311,764	237,639	136,390	260,529
Macao	36,509	1,595	45,286	6,522
Madagascar	6,236	9,484	6,432	6,872
Malawi	87,218	20,525	56,983	28,557
Malaysia	383,860	281,671	350,058	226,912
Maldives	73	1,243	276	1,321
Mali	4,804	7,294	8,282	4,121
Malta	51,794	101,247	49,197	101,877
Martinique	128	2,776	14	21,230
Mauritania	6,311	2,069	2,184	2,496
Mauritius	122,829	28,512	153,271	32,087
Mayotte	22	2,000	9	506
Mexico	236,811	203,404	116,078	162,328
Mongolia	3,264	142	4,750	1,031
Montserrat	414	2,330	358	3,926
Morocco	74,820	92,658	65,419	84,510
Mozambique	6,908	11,343	1,335	13,175
Namibia	21,920	4,084	6,826	2,915
Nauru	479	1,199	148	1,239
Nepal	9,347	7,835	6,966	4,672
New Caledonia	4	2,109	45	3,520
New Zealand	533,047	396,595	455,694	343,145
Nicaragua	1,324	6,368	1,307	7,349
Niger	399	12,076	848	10,367
Nigeria	660,410	960,703	329,036	566,176
Niue & Tokelau	21	331	236	327
Norway	4,367,154	1,140,376	3,265,157	1,147,790
Oceania, Australian	134	498	524	488
Oceania, U.S.	52	2,948	287	3,154
Oman	69,015	489,926	87,236	399,647
Pakistan	119,006	255,419	131,296	227,064
Panama	14,612	55,424	4,950	44,975
Papua New Guinea	59,642	12,592	38,474	12,084
Paraguay	2,086	15,540	1,455	31,010

	1985		1986	
	Imports	Exports	Imports	Exports
Peru	108,943	40,371	82,141	48,275
Philippines	179,979	94,370	182,852	79,809
Pitcairn	90	513	459	912
Poland	320,276	184,143	309,746	182,841
Polar Regions	1,090	1,510	43	674
Puerto Rico	126,971	117,861	81,131	49,620
Qatar	32,607	142,065	29,587	112,143
La Réunion	1,391	4,081	12,259	4,225
Romania	102,946	78,474	86,730	82,011
Rwanda	3,998	3,565	7,487	1,681
St. Helena	4,515	7,914	380	8,196
St. Kitts-Nevis	5,634	5,256	4,429	6,008
St. Lucia	44,047	11,550	59,855	12,441
St. Pierre & Miquelon	497	370	474	367
St. Vincent	22,339	6,600	21,161	8,288
Sao Tomé & Príncipé	197	824	327	455
Saudi Arabia	483,634	1,256,081	435,930	1,507,062
Senegal	17,671	13,514	13,881	12,328
Seychelles	1,663	9,561	938	9,639
Sierra Leone	17,435	23,620	11,599	17,403
Singapore	441,345	612,920	462,878	547,419
Solomon Is.	7,714	1,862	4,074	1,618
Somalia	1,448	8,646	740	9,139
South Africa	989,757	1,009,629	829,305	849,557
Sri Lanka	73,956	79,234	51,860	83,316
Sudan	21,323	103,635	12,826	83,335
Suriname	15,405	9,398	15,554	9,743
Swaziland	41,281	3,122	48,194	3,922
Sweden	2,465,582	3,006,890	2,756,536	2,307,900
Switzerland	2,371,090	1,306,757	2,989,112	1,575,247
Syria	78,575	80,901	31,298	55,511
Taiwan	582,904	164,776	705,775	192,492
Tanzania	46,640	88,622	40,268	62,869
Thailand	131,806	157,723	182,756	158,195
Tonga	70	699	86	936
Togo	4,597	17,034	5,008	17,488
Trinidad & Tobago	81,719	93,897	41,622	79,029
Tunisia	39,826	43,209	17,292	39,824
Turkey	538,462	460,220	406,605	433,753
Turks & Caicos Is.	6	1,063	86	1,025
Tuvalu	0	87	88	78
Uganda	48,571	39,925	50,870	26,046
U.A.E.	96,554	621,348	74,012	581,762
U.S.A.	9,919,689	11,498,802	8,468,160	10,379,585
U.S.S.R.	724,453	536,555	694,624	539,368
Uruguay	28,824	15,513	41,366	24,465
Vanuatu	174	768	62	1,037
Vatican City	54	839	76	1,099
Venezuela	238,879	165,268	96,339	170,101
Vietnam	1,758	2,077	1,200	1,288
Virgin Is., British	698	3,522	267	3,491
Virgin Is., U.S.	514	4,060	5,455	5,955
Wallis & Futuna	—	13	—	—
Western Samoa	292	619	622	433
Yemen, North	2,312	94,382	2,106	58,149
Yemen, South	7,938	34,827	4,848	23,928
Yugoslavia	122,132	177,530	145,127	188,390
Zaire	35,198	34,975	17,192	34,217
Zambia	27,879	85,949	27,260	77,840
Zimbabwe	90,398	73,571	80,702	61,937

FOREIGN COUNTRIES

The following articles have been revised under the direction of the various Governments or of the British Representatives at foreign capitals and by the Foreign and Commonwealth Office in London, whom the Editor warmly thanks. The Editor is also greatly indebted to the Embassies and Consulates-General in London for various corrections and additions.

AFGHANISTAN
(De Afghanistan Democrateek Jamhuriat)

President of the Revolutionary Council of the Democratic Republic of Afghanistan, Haji Mohammad Tsamkani (*acting*).

COUNCIL OF MINISTERS

Chairman of the Council, Sultan Ali Kishtmand.
President of State Planning Committee, Mohammad Aziz.
Deputy Chairmen, Maj. Gen. Mohammad Rafi; Sayed Amanuddin Amin; Sayed Naseem Mehanparast; Gen. Nazar Mohammed; Abdul Hamid Mohtat; Prof. Guldad.
Foreign Affairs, Abdul Wakil.
Interior, Maj. Gen. Sayed M. Gulabzoi.
Defence, Gen. Mohammad Rafie.
Communications, Lt. Col. M. Aslam Watanjar.
Finance, Muhammad Kabir.
Tribes and Nationalities, Suleiman Laeq.
Transport, Lt. Col. Sher Jan Mazdooryar
Power, Dr. Raz M. Pakteen.
Mines and Industries, Lmar Ahmed Lmar.
Public Works, Nazar Mohammad.
Agriculture and Land Reform, Ghulam Faruk Kobak-iwal.
Commerce, Mohammad Khan Jalalar.
Public Health, Sher Bahadur.
Justice, Mohan Bashir Baghliani.
Education, Abdul Samad Qayumi.
Higher Education, Burhanuddin Ghiasi.
Irrigation, Ahmad Shah Sorkhabi.
State Security, Ghulam Farouq Yaqubi.
Without Portfolio, Dr. Faqir M. Yaqubi.

PEOPLE'S DEMOCRATIC PARTY

General Secretary, Dr. Najib.
Politburo, Sultan Ali Keshtmand; Sulaiman Laeq; Najibullah; Noor Ahmed Noor; Gen. Mohammad Rafie; Abdul Wakil; Sayed Gulabzoi; Abdul Zohor Ramjo; Ghulam Farouq Yaqubi; Mohammad Aslam Watanjar; Saleh Mohammad Zaery (*full members*); Mahmud Baryalai; Mir Saheb Karwal; Nazar Mohammad; Niaz Mohammad Mohmand; Najmuddin Kawyani; Farid Mazdak (*alternate members*).
Secretariat, Mahmud Baryalai; Mir Saheb Karwal; Najmuddin Kawiani; Haider Masoud; Niaz Mohammad Mohmand; Noor Ahmed Noor; Dr. Saleh Mohammed Zeary.

EMBASSY OF THE DEMOCRATIC REPUBLIC OF AFGHANISTAN
31 Prince's Gate, SW7 1QQ.
[01–589 8891/2]

Chargé d'Affaires, Ahmad Sarwar.

Afghanistan lies to the N. and W. of Pakistan. Its ancient name was Aryana, by which title it is referred to by Strabo, the Greek geographer who lived in the 1st century B.C. The estimated area is 250,000 sq. miles (647,497 sq. km.), and the population 18,136,000 (1985 U.N. estimate), although it is estimated that over three million have become refugees in Pakistan

and over one million in Iran since the Soviet invasion. The population is very mixed. The most numerous race is the Pathan which predominates in the South and West, the Tadjiks, an Iranian people mainly cultivators and small traders, Uzbeks and Turkomen in the North, Hazaras in the centre, Baluchis in the South-West and Nuristanis, who live near the Chitral border. All are Sunni Moslems, except the Hazaras and Kizilbashes, who belong to the Shia sect.

Afghanistan is bounded on the W. by Iran, on the S. by Pakistan, on the N. by the U.S.S.R., and on the E. by Pakistan and China.

Mountains, chief among which are the Hindu Kush, cover three-quarters of the country, the elevation being generally over 4,000 feet. There are three great river basins, the Oxus, Helmand, and Kabul. The climate is dry, with extreme temperatures.

Government.—The constitutional monarchy, introduced by the 1964 Constitution, was overthrown by a *coup d'etat* on July 17, 1973. The country was ruled by Presidential decree until February 1977 when a constitution was approved by a Loya Jirgah (Grand Assembly). Mohammad Daoud was elected President of the Republic but was overthrown on April 27, 1978, by the Armed Forces and power handed to the People's Democratic Party of Afghanistan (PDPA). In December 1979 Soviet troops invaded Afghanistan and installed Babrak Karmal as Secretary-General of the PDPA, President of the Revolutionary Council and Head of State. Karmal was replaced as General Secretary of the PDPA by Dr. Najib in May 1986. Haji Mohammad Tsamkani became acting head of the Revolutionary Council in Nov. 1986.

Afghanistan is divided into 26 provinces each under a local Party Secretary.

Judiciary.—The Constitution introduced in 1965 provided for the creation of a legal code, and for a new structure of courts, consisting of a lower court in each *woleswali* (sub province), and a court of appeal in each province, with a Supreme Court in Kabul. The complete separation of executive and judiciary in this constitution was abolished by Presidential Decree in July, 1973. In late 1976 and early 1977 new Penal and Civil Codes were published.

Defence.—The Army, which numbered about 80,000 before the Soviet invasion, has been greatly depleted by desertions. Men between the ages of 18 and 40 are liable to three years' military service. A military academy and military colleges are located in Kabul; some regular officers are trained in the U.S.S.R. A small Air Force is maintained. All military and air force equipment is now of Russian pattern.

Production.—Agriculture and sheep raising are the principal industries. There are generally two crops a year, one of wheat (the staple food), barley, or lentils, the other of rice, millet, maize, and dal. Sugar beet and cotton are grown. Afghanistan is rich in fruits. Sheep, including the Karakuli, and transport animals are bred. Silk, woollen and hair cloths and carpets are manufactured. Salt, silver, copper, coal, iron, lead, rubies, lapis lazuli, gold, chrome, barite, uranium. and talc are found.

Main roads run from Kabul to Kandahar, Herat, Maimana *via* Mazari-Sharif and Faizabad *via* Khanabad. The road from Kabul to the North was shortened by the completion in 1964 of the Salang pass. Roads cross the border with Pakistan at Chaman and *via* the Khyber Pass, and there are roads from Herat to the Russian and Iranian borders. A network of minor roads fit for motor traffic in fine weather links up all important towns and districts.

In 1982 the Afghan and Soviet shores of the River

Oxus were linked by a road and rail bridge which joins the Afghan port of Hairatan and the Soviet port of Termez. A network of internal air services operates between the main towns.

Language and Literature.—The principal languages of the country are Dari (a form of Persian) and Pushtu, although a number of minority languages are also spoken in various provinces. All schoolchildren learn both Persian and Pushtu. Education is free and nominally compulsory, elementary schools having been established in most centres; there are secondary schools in large urban areas and two universities, one in Kabul (established 1932) and one in Jalalabad (established early 1970's).

Trade with U.K.

	1985	1986
Imports from U.K.	£13,882,000	£11,444,000
Exports to U.K.	52,061,000	11,913,000

Exports are mainly Persian lambskins (Karakul), dried fruits, nuts, cotton, raw wool, carpets, spice and natural gas, while the imports are chiefly oil, cotton yarn and piece goods, tea, sugar, machinery and transport equipment.

CAPITAL, Kabul (about 2,000,000). The chief commercial centres are Kabul and Kandahar (185,000). Other provincial capitals are Herat (145,000), Mazar-i-Sharif (105,000), Jalalabad (55,000).

FLAG.—Black, red and green horizontal stripes with a device in top left-hand corner.

NATIONAL DAY.—April 27.

BRITISH EMBASSY
Karte Parwan, Kabul

Chargé d'Affaires a.i., I. W. Mackley.

ALBANIA
(Republika Popullore socialiste e Shqipërisë)

Chairman of the Praesidium of the People's Assembly (i.e. Head of State), Ramiz Alia, *assumed office,* Nov. 22, 1982; *re-elected,* Feb. 19, 1987.

COUNCIL OF MINISTERS

Chairman, Adil Çarçani.
Deputy Chairmen, Manush Myftiu; Besnik Bekteshi; Vangjel Cerrava.
Deputy Chairman, and Minister of the Interior, Hekuran Isai.
Agriculture, Mrs. Themie Thomai.
Transport, Luan Babamento.
Construction, Farudin Hoxha.
People's Defence, Prokop Murra.
Education, Skenda Gjinushi.
Energy, Lavdosh Hametaj.
Finance, Andrea Nako.
Foreign Affairs, Reis Malile.
Foreign Trade, Shane Korbeci.
Health Service, Ahmet Kamberi.
Food Industry, Jovan Bardhi.
Industry and Mining, Llambi Gegprifti.
Chairman of State Planning Commission, Niko Gjyzari.
Chairman of State Control Commission, Enver Halili.
Public Services, Xhemal Tafaj.

Albanian Party of Labour

Politbureau of the Central Committee, R. Alia; M. Asllani; A. Carcani; H. Celiku; H. Isai; R. Marko; P. Miska; M. Myftiu; L. Cuko; S. Stefani; B. Bekteshi; F. Cami; P. Murra *(full members);* L. Gegprifti; Q.

Mihali; K. Mustaqi; P. Kondi; V. Cerava *(candidate members).*
Secretariat of the Central Committee, R. Alia *(First Secretary);* F. Çami; V. Cerava; L. Cuko; S. Stefani.

Situated on the Adriatic Sea, Albania is bounded on the north and east by Yugoslavia and on the south by Greece. The area of the Republic is estimated at 11,099 sq. miles (28,748 sq. km.), with a population (1986 estimate) of about 3 million.

Albania was under Turkish suzerainty from 1468 until 1912, when independence was declared. After a period of unrest, a republic was declared in 1925, and in 1928 a monarchy. The King went into exile in 1939 when the country was occupied by the Italians: Albania was liberated in Nov. 1944. Elections in Dec. 1945 resulted in a Communist-controlled Assembly: the King was deposed *in absentia* and a republic declared in Jan. 1946. United Kingdom diplomatic relations with Albania ceased due to the invasion in 1939 and although U.K. recognised the provisional government of Enver Hoxha in 1945, relations were broken off in 1946 after a mine sunk a British warship in Albanian waters. They have so far not been restored.

Much of the country is mountainous and nearly a half is covered by forest. There are fertile areas along the Adriatic coast and the Koritza Basin and there have been land reclamation and irrigation programmes. The main crops are wheat, maize, sugar-beet, potatoes and fruit.

All industry is nationalised. The principal industries are agricultural product processing, textiles, oil products and cement. Output is small at present but the chemical and engineering industries are being built up and the country's considerable mineral resources are being increasingly exploited.

Exports include crude oil, minerals (bitumen, chrome, nickel, copper), tobacco, fruit and vegetables.

Trade with U.K.

	1985	1986
Imports from U.K.	£5,252,000	£2,887,000
Exports to U.K.	212,000	128,000

CAPITAL, Tirana, pop. 210,757 (1984).
FLAG.—Black-two-headed eagle surmounted by yellow outline star, all on a red field.
NATIONAL DAY.—January 11.

ALGERIA
(Al-Jumhuriya al-Jazairiya ad-Dimuqratiya ash-Shabiya)

President of State, Secretary-General of the Party, Bendjedid Chadli, *elected,* Feb. 1979, *re-elected,* Jan. 1984.

Ministers

Prime Minister, Abdelhamid Brahimi.
Secretary-General of the Government, Mohamed Salah Mohammedi.
Foreign Affairs, Ahmed Taleb Ibrahimi.
Interior, Mohamed Yala.
Finance, Abdelaziz Khellef.
Trade, Mostefa Benamar.
Heavy Industry, Faycal Boudraa.
Light Industry, Zitouni Messaoudi.
Hydraulics, Environment and Forestry, Mohamed Rouighi.
Energy and Petrochemicals, Belkacem Nabi.
Information, Bachir Rouis.
Primary Education, Mme. Z'Hor Ounissi.
Higher Education, Rafik Abdelhak Brerhi.
Vocational Training, Boubaker Belkaid.
Transport, Rachid Benyelles.
Labour, Boubaker Belkaid.

Agriculture and Fisheries, Kasdi Merbah.
Justice, Mohamed Cherif Kharroubi.
Culture and Tourism, Boualem Bessaih.
Youth and Sports, Kamal Bouchama.
Planning and Organization of National Territory,
　Abdelmalek Nourani.
Public Health, Djamel Eddine Houhou.
Posts and Telecommunications, Mostefa Benzaza.
Public Works, Ahmed Benfreha.
Housing and Construction, Abdelmalek Nourani.
Religious Affairs, Abderrahman Chibane.
Social Affairs, Mohamed Nabi.
Ex-Combatants, Mohamed Djeghaba.

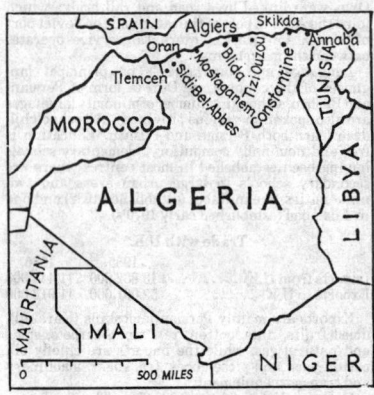

ALGERIAN EMBASSY IN LONDON
54 Holland Park, W11 3RS
[01–221 7800]

Ambassador Extraordinary and Plenipotentiary, His
　Excellency Ahmed Laidi (1984).

Algeria lies between 8° 45′ W. to 12° E. longitude
27° 6′ N. to a southern limit about 19° N. Area, 919,595
sq. miles (U.N. estimate). The population in 1985 was
estimated at 21,718,000.

Government.—Algiers surrendered to a French
force on July 5, 1830, and Algeria was annexed to
France in Feb. 1842. From 1881 the three northern
departments of Algiers, Oran and Constantine formed
an integral part of France. The Southern Territories
of the Sahara, formerly a separate colony, became an
integral part of Algeria on the attainment of independence. An armed rebellion led by the Moslem
Front de Liberation Nationale (*F.L.N.*) against
French rule broke out on Nov. 1, 1954. French control
of Algeria came to an end when President de Gaulle
declared Algeria independent on July 3, 1962; by
October, 1963, all agricultural land held by foreigners
had been expropriated and by 1965 more than 80 per
cent. of the French population had left Algeria.

Ben Bella was elected President of the Republic in
Sept., 1963, but was deposed and a Council of the
Revolution presided over by Col. Boumediène as-
sumed power on June 19,1965.

A new constitution was established by referendum
on Nov. 19, 1976, and on Dec. 10, 1976 President
Boumediène was elected for a six-year term of office.
Elections for a national popular assembly were held
in Feb. 1977. Following President Boumediène's
death in December 1978, M. Bendjedid Chadli was
elected President in February 1979.

Development in Algeria is regulated by a series of
national development plans. The 1970–73 Plan placed
emphasis on industrial development, and the 1974–77
Plan on infrastructure development and social services. The 1980–84 Plan concentrated on housing,
water supply and agriculture. The 1985–89 Plan
continues with these objectives and also includes
food and processing industries.

Algeria's main industry is the hydrocarbons industry. Oil and natural gas are pumped from the Sahara
to terminals on the coast before being exported; the
gas is first liquefied at liquefaction plants at Skikda
and Arzew.

Other major industries being developed include a
steel industry, motor vehicles, building materials,
paper making, chemical products and metal manufactures. All major industrial enterprises are now under
State control.

Trade with U.K.

	1985	1986
Imports from U.K.	£176,596,000	£129,624,000
Exports to U.K.	251,462,000	140,860,000

Algeria's main exports are crude oil and liquefied
natural gas. Principal imports from the United

Kingdom are capital plant, equipment for industrial
use and foodstuffs.

Algeria has a rapidly expanding network of roads
and railways. Considerable sums are also being spent
on the development of the State airline, the national
shipping company and telecommunications.

CAPITAL.—ΨAlgiers, population 3,250,000 (approx).
It is one of the principal ports of the Mediterranean
as well as an important industrial centre. Other
towns include ΨOran; Constantine; ΨAnnaba; Blida;
Setif; Sidi-Bel-Abbès; Tlemcen; Mostaganem; Ψ
Skikda; ΨBejaia and Tizi Ouzou.

FLAG.—Red crescent and star on vertically divided
green and white background.

NATIONAL DAY.—November 1.

BRITISH EMBASSY
Résidence Cassiopée, 7 Chemin de Glycines,
Algiers.

Ambassador Extraordinary and Plenipotentiary, His
　Excellency Patrick Howard Caines Eyers, C.M.G.,
　L.V.O.
Counsellor, Head of Chancery and Consul General,
　J. Illman.
Cultural Attaché, British Council Representative,
　W. M. Jefferson, O.B.E., 6 Avenue Souidani Boudje-
　maa, Algiers. There is a British Council library in
　Algiers.

ANDORRA
(Principat d'Andorra)

Viguier Français, M. Louis Deblé.
Viguier Episcopal, Sr. Francesc Badia.
Head of Government, Sr. Josep Pintat Solens.

A small, neutral principality (formed by a treaty in
1278), situated on the southern slopes of the Pyrenees
between Spain and France, with an approximate area
of 175 sq. miles (453 sq. km.), and population of about
35,000 (1985 U.N. estimate), less than one-fifth of
whom are native Andorrans. It is surrounded by
mountains of 6,500 to 10,000 feet. Andorra is divided
into seven Parishes, each of which has four Councillors elected by vote to the Valleys of Andorra Council
of twenty-eight. The Council appoints the head of
the executive government, who designates the members of his government. Constitutionally, the sovereignty of Andorra is vested in two "Co-Princes", the
President of the French Republic and the Spanish

Bishop of Urgel. These two "co-princes" can veto certain decisions of the Council of the Valleys but cannot impose their own decisions without the consent of the Council. They are represented by Permanent Delegates of whom one is the French Prefect of the Pyrenees Orientales Department at Perpignan and the other is the Spanish Vicar-General of the Diocese of Urgel. They are in turn represented in Andorra la Vella by two resident "Viguiers" known as the Viguier Français and the Viguier Episcopal, who have a joint responsibility for law and order and overall administration policy, together with judicial powers as members of the Supreme Court.

The language of the country is Catalan, but French and Spanish (Castilian) are also spoken. Spanish *pesetas* and French *francs* are the accepted currency and the Budget is expressed in *pesetas*. The estimated national revenue (1984) was US$417 million, with a per capita income of $9,752. The climate is cold for six months, but mild in spring and summer. Potatoes are produced in the highlands and tobacco in the valleys. The mountain slopes have been developed for skiing, and it is estimated that 10,000,000 tourists visit the Valleys during the year. The economy is largely based on tourism, commerce, tobacco, construction and forestry; a third of the country is classified as forest in which pine, fir, oak, birch and box-tree predominate.

A good road into the Valleys from Spain is open all year round, and that from France is closed only occasionally in winter. An airport at Seo d'Urgell just outside Andorra provides daily air connections with Barcelona. There are two radio stations in Andorra, one privately-owned and one operated by a French Government corporation. Both pay dues to the Council of the Valleys.

Trade with U.K.

	1985	1986
Imports from U.K.	£10,413,000	£13,174,000
Exports to U.K.	198,000	40,000

CAPITAL: Andorra la Vella (population 16,000).

FLAG.—Three vertical bands, blue, yellow, red; Andorran coat of arms frequently imposed on central (yellow) band but not essential.

NATIONAL DAY.—September 8.

H.M. Consul-General, J. C. Church, C.M.G., M.B.E. (*Resident at Barcelona*).

ANGOLA
(República Popular de Angola)

President, Jose Eduardo Dos Santos.

COUNCIL OF MINISTERS

Interior, Gen. Manuel Rodrigues.
State Security, (vacant).
Defence, Col. Gen. Pedro Tonha.
Foreign Affairs, Afonso van Dunem.
Planning, Antonio Henriques da Silva.
Internal Trade, Adriano Pereira dos Santos.
External Trade, Ismael Gaspar Martins.
Justice, Fernando França van Dunem.
Petroleum and Energy, Col. Pedro Van Dunen.
Industry, Henrique de Carvalho Santos.
Health, Antonio Ferreira Neto.
Labour and Social Security, Diogo Jorge de Jesus.
Construction and Housing, Joac Garcia de Carvalho.
Fisheries, Emilio Guerra.
Agriculture, Col. Evaristo Domingos.
Transport and Communications, Carlos Antonio Femandes.
Education, Augusto Teixeira.

Finance Augusto Teixeira de Matos.
Ministers of State, Mrs. M. Mambo Café (*Economic and Social Sphere*); K. Paihama (*Inspection and Control*); Pedro van Dumem (*Productive Sector*).

ANGOLAN EMBASSY IN LONDON
87 Jermyn Street, S.W.1.
[01–839 5743]

Ambassador Extraordinary and Plenipotentiary, His Excellency Elisio de Figueiredo (1984).

Angola, which has an area of 481,354 sq. miles (1,246,700 sq. km.), lies on the western coast of Africa; its population in 1985 was estimated at 8,754,000.

After a Portuguese presence of at least four centuries, and an anti-colonial war since 1961, Angola became independent on Nov. 11, 1975 in the midst of civil war. Soviet-Cuban military assistance to the Popular Movement for the Liberation of Angola (M.P.L.A.) enabled it to defeat its rivals early in 1976. However, the M.P.L.A. government remains under pressure from the U.N.I.T.A. guerrilla movement (led by Dr. Jonas Savimbi) which now controls up to one-third of the country and operates freely in another third.

The M.P.L.A., a Marxist-Leninist party, is the sole legal party. The Constitution provides for an executive President, who appoints a Council of Ministers to assist him, and a National People's Assembly.

Angola has valuable oil and diamond deposits and exports of these two commodities account for 70–80 per cent of total exports.

Principal agricultural crops are cassava, maize, bananas, coffee, palm oil and kernals, cotton and sisal. Coffee, sisal, maize and palm oil are exported: exports also include mahogany and other hardwoods from the tropical rain forests in the north of the country.

Trade with U.K.

	1985	1986
Imports from U.K.	£43,187,000	£30,896,000
Exports to U.K.	150,639,000	43,147,000

CAPITAL.—ΨLuanda (Est. over 1 million in 1984).

FLAG.—Red and black with a yellow star, machete and cog-wheel.

NATIONAL DAY.—November 11. (Independence Day).

BRITISH EMBASSY
Rua Diogo Cao 4 (Caixa Postal 1244), Luanda.

Ambassador Extraordinary and Plentipotentiary, His Excellency Patrick Stanislaus Fairweather, C.M.G., (1985).

ARGENTINE REPUBLIC
(República Argentina)

President, Dr. Raúl Alfonsín, *took office* Dec. 10, 1983.

Vice President, Dr. Víctor Martínez.

CABINET

Interior, Dr. Antonio Troccoli.
Foreign Affairs, Sr. Dante Caputo.
Labour, Sr. Carlos Alderette.
Economy, Sr. Juan Sourouille.
Education and Justice, Sr. Julio Rajneri.
Defence, Dr. Horacio Juan Jaunarena.
Health and Social Welfare, Dr. Conrado Storani.
Public Works, Dr. Pedro Augusto Trucco.

The Embassy closed after the Argentine invasion of the Falkland Islands. Argentine interests in Great Britain are currently handled by the Brazilian Embassy.

Argentina is a wedge-shaped country, occupying the greater portion of the southern part of the South American Continent, and extending from Bolivia to Cape Horn, a total distance of nearly 2,300 miles; its greatest breadth is about 930 miles. It is bounded on the north by Bolivia, on the north-east by Paraguay, Brazil and Uruguay, on the south-east and south by the Atlantic, and on the west by Chile, from which Republic it is separated by the Cordillera de los Andes. On the west the mountainous Cordilleras, with their plateaux, extend from the northern to the southern boundaries: on the east are the great plains.

The Republic consists of 22 provinces, one territory (Tierra del Fuego) and one federal district (Buenos Aires), comprising in all an area of 1,068,302 sq. miles (2,766,889 sq. km.), with a population of 30,564,000 (1985, U.N. estimate).

Government.—The estuary of La Plata was discovered in 1515 by Juan Díaz de Solís, but it was not until 1534 that Pedro de Mendoza founded Buenos Aires. This city was abandoned and later re-founded by Don Juan de Garay in 1580. In 1810 (May 25) Spanish rule was defied, and in 1816 (July 9), after a long campaign of liberation conducted by General José de San Martín, the independence of Argentina was declared by the Congress of Tucumán.

In 1946 Juan Domingo Perón became President until overthrown in 1955. There followed eighteen years of political and economic instability, and eventually in 1973, Perón was recalled from exile. Elected President he died within a year and was succeeded by his widow, Vice President María Estela Martínez de Perón. However, warring factions in the Perónist movement and increasing terrorist activity eventually led to a bloodless *coup* by the armed forces on March 24, 1976. A Junta, consisting of the three commanders of the Armed Forces, was established with one of their number as President. Following the Falkland Islands defeat in 1982 the President, Gen. Galtieri, resigned and the Army appointed Gen. Bignone as President. The Navy and Air Force withdrew from the Junta but this was reconstituted shortly afterwards. Elections for a civilian government to replace the military one were held on October 30, 1983 and the Radical Party's candidate, Raúl Alfonsín, was elected President.

Agriculture.—Of a total land area of approximately 700 million acres, farms occupy about 425 million. About 60 per cent. of the farmland is pasture, 10 per cent. annual crops, 5 per cent. permanent crops and the remaining 25 per cent. forest and wasteland. A large proportion of the land is still held in large estates devoted to cattle raising but the number of small farms is increasing. The principal crops are wheat, maize, oats, barley, rye, linseed, sunflower seed, alfalfa, sugar, fruit and cotton. Argentina is pre-eminent in the production of beef, mutton and wool, and pastoral and agricultural products provide about 85 per cent. of Argentina's exports.

Mineral Production.—Oil is found in various parts of the Republic and the production of oil is of first importance to her industries and, to some extent, to her economic and financial development. Total petroleum output for 1984 was 27,900,000 cubic metres. There is a refinery in San Lorenzo (Santa Fé province). Natural gas is also produced in a number of provinces.

Coal, lead, zinc, tungsten, iron ore, sulphur, mica and salt are the other chief minerals being exploited. There are small worked deposits of beryllium, manganese, bismuth, uranium, antimony, copper, kaolin,

arsenate, gold, silver and tin. Coal production in 1984 was 500,000 tonnes; this is produced at the Rio Turbio mine in the province of Santa Cruz. The output of other materials is not large but greater attention is now being paid to the development of these natural resources, especially copper for which the Government and private companies are carrying out exploration.

Industries.—Meat-packing is one of the principal industries; flour-milling, sugar-refining, and the wine industry are also important. In recent years great strides have been made by the textile, plastic and machine tool industries and engineering, especially in the production of motor vehicles and steel manufactures.

Communications.—There are 25,386 miles of railways, which are State property. Plans are in hand for complete re-organization of the railways in order to improve their operating efficiency and reduce a very large financial deficit. The combined national and provincial road network totals approximately 137,000 miles of which 23,180 miles are surfaced. There are air services between Argentina and all the neighbouring republics, Europe, Asia, Canada, the U.S.A. and South Africa. Total tonnage entering Argentine ports in 1979 was 13,879,391.

Defence.—The Army consists of four corps organized into 12 brigades, including mountain, jungle, airborne and armoured troops. It numbers about 5,000 officers, 15,000 N.C.O.s and 35,000 conscripts who serve for between 6 months and 1 year.

The Navy consists of 1 aircraft carrier, 6 destroyers, 6 corvettes, 4 submarines, 6 minesweepers and ancillary craft. Strength is about 3,000 officers and 33,000 ratings, including 16,000 conscripts.

The Air Force consists of 9 brigades and a training force, with a strength of 1,600 officers, 15,000 other ranks and 20,000 civilians.

Education—Primary and Secondary. The government is formulating a new education policy. At the moment, education is compulsory for the 7 grades of primary school (6 to 13). Secondary schools (14 to

17+) are available in and around Buenos Aires and in most of the important towns in the interior of the country. Most secondary schools are administered by the Central Ministry of Education in Buenos Aires, while primary schools are administered by the Central Ministry or by Provincial Ministries of Education. Private schools, of which there are many, are also loosely controlled by the Central Ministry. Teacher-Training now takes place at post school level, courses lasting from 2 to 5 years. Many new universities have been created in recent years. The total is now over 50 with 24 national, 25 private and a small number of provincial universities.

Language and Literature.—Spanish is the language of the Republic and the literature of Spain is accepted as an inheritance by the people. There is little indigenous literature before the break from Spain, but all branches have flourished since the latter half of the nineteenth century. About 450 daily newspapers are published in Argentina, including 7 major ones in the city of Buenos Aires. The English language newspaper is the *Buenos Aires Herald* (daily). There are several other foreign language newspapers.

Trade with U.K.

	1985	1986
Imports from U.K.	£3,815,000	£10,115,000
Exports to U.K.	2,032,000	28,635,000

CAPITAL.—ΨBuenos Aires, Pop. (Dec. 1980), Metropolitan area 2,908,000; with suburbs, 9,677,200. Other large towns are: ΨRosario de Santa Fé (798,292), Córdoba (798,663), ΨLa Plata (408,300), ΨMar del Plata (317,444), San Miguel de Tucuman (326,000), Santa Fé (312,427) and Mendoza (118,568).

FLAG.—Horizontal bands of blue, white, blue; gold sun in centre of white band.

NATIONAL DAY.—May 25.

BRITISH EMBASSY

The British Embassy was closed after the Argentine invasion of the Falkland Islands. British interests are currently handled by a section at the Swiss Embassy, Dr. Luis Agote 2412 52, 1425, Buenos Aires. BRITISH CHAMBER OF COMMERCE, Av. Corrientes 457, 10 piso, 1043 Buenos Aires.

AUSTRIA
(Republik Österreich)

President of the Republic of Austria, Dr. Kurt Waldheim, *born* 1918; *elected* June 8, 1986.

CABINET

Chancellor, Dr. Franz Vranitzky (*SPÖ*).
Vice-Chancellor and Minister for Foreign Affairs, Dr. Alois Mock (*ÖVP*).
Interior, Karl Blecha (*SPÖ*).
Justice, Dr. Egmont Foregger (*Ind.*).
Finance, Ferdinand Lacina (*SPÖ*).
Nationalised Industries and Transport, Dr. Rudolf Streicher (*SPÖ*).
Agriculture and Forestry, Josef Riegler (*ÖVP*).
Defence, Dr. Robert Lichal (*ÖVP*).
Science and Research, Prof. Dr. Hans Tuppy (*ÖVP*).
Employment and Social Affairs, Alfred Dallinger (*SPÖ*).
Education, Arts and Sports, Dr. Hilde Hawlicek (*SPÖ*).
Economic Affairs, Robert Graf (*ÖVP*).
Environment, Youth and Family, Dr. Marilies Flemming (*ÖVP*).
Ministers at Federal Chancellery, Dr. Franz Loweschnack (*SPÖ*) (*Civil Servants and Health*); Dr. Heinrich Neisser (*ÖVP*) (*Reforms, Constitution, Federalism*); Johanna Dohnal (*SPÖ*) (*Women's Affairs*).

SPÖ: Socialists; *ÖVP*: People's Party (Conservatives); *FPÖ*: Freedom Party (Liberals).

AUSTRIAN EMBASSY IN LONDON
18 Belgrave Mews, SW1X 8HU
[01–235 3731]

Ambassador Extraordinary and Plenipotentiary, His Excellency Dr. Reginald Thomas (1982).

Austria is a country of Central Europe bounded on the north by Czechoslovakia, on the south by Italy and Yugoslavia, on the east by Hungary, on the north-west by Germany and on the west by Switzerland and Liechtenstein. Its area is 32,374 sq. miles (83,849, sq. km.), and its population is 7,555,000 (1985, U.N. estimate).

Government.—The Republic of Austria comprises nine provinces (Vienna, Lower Austria, Upper Austria, Salzburg, Tyrol, Vorarlberg, Carinthia, Styria and Burgenland) and was established in 1918 on the break-up of the Austro-Hungarian Empire. In March 13, 1938, as a result of the *Anschluss,* Austria (*Österreich*) was incorporated into the *Deutsches Reich* under the name *Ostmark.* After the liberation of Vienna in 1945, the Republic of Austria was reconstituted within the frontiers of 1937 and a freely-elected Government took office on December 20, 1945. The country was divided at this time into four zones occupied respectively by the U.K., U.S.A., U.S.S.R. and France, while Vienna was jointly occupied by the four Powers. On May 15, 1955, the Austrian State Treaty was signed in Vienna by the Foreign Ministers of the four Powers and of Austria. This Treaty recognized the re-establishment of Austria as a sovereign, independent and democratic state, having the same frontiers as on January 1, 1938.

There is a national assembly of 183 Deputies. After the elections of Nov. 1986, the Socialists formed a coalition with the People's Party.

The state of the parties in the Nationalrat (Lower House) in April 1983, was:

Socialist Party (Social Democrat)	80
People's Party (Conservative)	77
Freedom Party (Liberal)	18
Green Party	8

In the Bundesrat (Upper House) in Nov. 1986 the People's Party held 33 seats and the Socialist Party, 30.

Religion and Education.—The predominant religion is Roman Catholic. Education is free and compulsory between the ages of 6 and 15 and there are good facilities for secondary, technical and professional education. There are 12 state-maintained Universities and six colleges of art.

Language and Literature.—The language of Austria is German, but the rights of the Slovene- and Croat-speaking minorities in Carinthia, Styria and Burgenland are protected. The press is free.

Communications.—Internal communications in Austria are partly restricted because of the mountainous nature of the country, although there has been an extensive programme to increase the number of motorways, many of which are tunnelled through the mountains. There were, in 1985, 37,501 km. of roads, including a network of *autobahn* between major cities which also links up with the West German and Italian networks. The railways in Austria are state-owned and in 1985 had 5,766 km. of track, over half of which is electrified. Of the 425 km. of waterways, 355 km. are navigable and there is considerable trade through the Danube ports by both local and foreign shipping. There are six commercial airports catering for 4,872,922 passengers in 1985.

Tourism.—In 1986, 15,092,200 tourists visited Austria. Foreign exchange receipts from tourism were

101,555 million Schilling—a major contribution to the balance of payments.

PRODUCTION AND INDUSTRY

The origin of Gross Domestic Product in 1986 was as follows (in per cent.):

Agriculture and forestry	4·7
Mining and material goods production	30·8
Energy and water supply	3·2
Construction	6·3
Commerce, hotels, restaurants	16·4
Transport and communications	6·4
Asset management	12·6
Other services and producers	16·7
Import duties and other items	2·9

The value of G.D.P. in 1986 (at current prices) was S1,441,100 million: G.D.P. per capita (at current prices) was S190,627.

Agriculture.—The arable land produces wheat, rye, barley, oats, maize, potatoes, sugar beet, turnips, and miscellaneous crops. Many varieties of fruit trees flourish and the vineyards produce excellent wine. The pastures support horses, cattle and pigs. Timber forms a valuable source of Austria's indigenous wealth, about 40·7 per cent. of the total land area consisting of forest areas. Coniferous species predominate (75 per cent. of afforested area).

Energy.—Energy production in 1986 was:—
Crude oil

—production	1,116,000	tonnes
—imports	6,188,000	„
(from Libya	2,113,202	„)
(from Algeria	838,647	„)

Natural gas

—production	1,112m.	cu. metres
—imports	4,055m.	cu. metres
(from U.S.S.R.	3,956m.	cu. metres)

Electric power

—output	44,652m.	kWh.
—imports	5,962m.	kWh.
—exports	7,426m.	kWh.

A 700 mw nuclear power station had already been constructed when in November 1978 the Austrian people decided by a very small margin in a national referendum not to allow the introduction of nuclear power stations in Austria.

Mining.—Production was (tonnes):—

	1985	1986
Lignite	3,081,071	2,968,978
Iron/manganese ore	3,270,000	3,120,000
Raw magnesite	1,255,043	1,084,360
Lead/zinc ore	643,255	400,246
Crystal salt	437,584	485,513
Graphite	30,764	36,167

In addition 2,306,706 cu. metres of brine was produced in 1985 and 2,335,067 cu. metres in 1986.

Industry.—Heavy industry production in 1986 included pig iron 3,348,600 tonnes, raw steel 4,291,895 tonnes and rolled steel 3,461,545 tonnes. In addition, petroleum, non-ferrous metals and chemicals are processed in quantity and construction materials, industrial machinery, vehicles, paper and textiles are produced.

FINANCE

	1985	1986*
	Schilling, million	
Federal Budget:		
Revenue	372,841	391,321
Expenditure	464,482	498,033
Gross Budget Deficit	91,641	106,712
* estimated.		

Federal Budget expenditure (preliminary figures) (S million):—

	1985	1986*
Agriculture, forestry	12,493·0	13,622·0
Defence	17,147·3	18,495·0
Education	39,733·6	42,452·0
Internal security, justice	14,583·4	15,365·0
Public services	7,892·8	6,479·0
Roads	15,927·8	16,682·0
Science and research	14,110·8	17,166·0
Health and Social welfare	113,686·3	119,949·0
Transportation	89,369·4	97,334·0
Expenditure on debts	69,654·0	75,707·0
Other purposes	69,883·6	74,782·0
*estimated		

TRADE

Main exports are processed goods (iron and steel, textiles, paper and cardboard products), machinery and transport equipment, other finished goods (including clothing) raw materials and foodstuffs. Main imports are machinery and transport equipment, processed goods, chemical products, foodstuffs, fuel and energy.

	1985	1986
	Schilling, million	
Imports	430,969	407,954
Exports	353,962	342,479

Over 80 per cent. of all trade is with other European countries, E.E.C. countries accounting for about 60 per cent., Eastern Europe for about 9 per cent. and E.F.T.A. members for 9 per cent.

Trade with U.K.

	1986
Imports from U.K.	S9,356 million
Exports to U.K.	15,297 million

Currency.—The unit of currency is the *Schilling* (S) of 100 *Groschen* (Gr.) For rate of exchange *see* p. 81.

CAPITAL, Vienna, on the Danube, population 1,531,346. Other towns are Graz (243,166), Linz (199,910), Innsbruck (117,287), Salzburg (139,426), and Klagenfurt (87,321).

FLAG.—Horizontal stripes of red, white, red, with eagle crest on white stripe.

NATIONAL DAY.—October 26.

BRITISH EMBASSY
Reisnerstrasse 40, 1030 Vienna

Ambassador Extraordinary and Plenipotentiary, His Excellency Robert James O'Neill, C.M.G. (1986).
Counsellor, Consul General and Head of Chancery, A. H. Morgan.
Counsellor, D. H. Cecil.
1st Secretaries, R. G. Bowen; Miss D. M. Symes (*Commercial*); A. E. Clarke M.V.O. (*H.M. Consul*); J. McDougall, O.B.E. (*Administration*).
Defence Attaché, Lt.-Col. M. Ledger.
There is a British Consular Office at *Vienna*, and Honorary Consulates at *Bregenz, Innsbruck, Graz and Salzburg*.
British Council Representative, T. Sandell, Schenkenstrasse 4, A-1010 Vienna.

BAHRAIN
(Dawlet al-Bahrein)

Amir, H.H. Shaikh Isa bin Sulman Al Khalifa, G.C.M.G., *born* 1932; *acceded* Dec. 16, 1961.
Crown Prince and C.-in-C., Bahrain Defence Force, H.E. Shaikh Hamad bin Isa Al Khalifa, K.C.M.G.

CABINET

Prime Minister, H.E. Shaikh Khalifa bin Sulman Al-Khalifa.
Minister of Defence, The Crown Prince.

Foreign Affairs, Shaikh Mohammed bin Mubarak Al-Khalifa.
Justice and Islamic Affairs, Shaikh Abdullah bin Khalid Al-Khalifa.
Development and Industry, and Cabinet Affairs, Yusuf Ahmad Shirawi.
Education, Dr. Ali Fakhroo.
Health, Jawad Salim Al-Arayyed.
Transportation, Ibrahim Mohammed Humaidan.
Interior, Shaikh Mohammed bin Khalifa Al-Khalifa.
Information, Tariq Abdulrahman Al Moayed.
Labour and Social Affairs, Shaikh Khalifa bin Sulman bin Mohammed Al-Khalifa.
Works, Power and Water, Majid Jawad Al-Jishi.
Housing, Shaikh Khalid bin Abdullah Al-Khalifa.
Finance and National Economy, Ibrahim Abdulkarim Mohammed.
Commerce and Agriculture, Habib Ahmed Kassim.
Minister of State, Legal Affairs, Dr. Hussain Al-Baharna.

BAHRAIN EMBASSY IN LONDON
98 Gloucester Road, SW7 4AU
[01–370 5132]

Ambassador Extraordinary and Plenipotentiary, His Excellency Salman Abdul Wahab Al Sabbagh (1984).

Area and Population.—Bahrain consists of a group of low-lying islands situated about half-way down the Gulf, some 20 miles off the east coast of Arabia. The largest of these, Bahrain island itself, is about 30 miles long and 10 miles wide at its broadest. The capital, Manama, is situated on the north shore of this island. The next largest, Muharraq, with the town and Bahrain International Airport, is connected to Manama by a causeway 1½ miles long.

The population (1985 estimate) is 417,210, of whom 151,831 are foreign. About 35 per cent. of the Bahrainis are Sunni Moslems, the remaining 65 per cent. being Shias; the ruling family and many of the most prominent merchants are Sunnis.

Climate.—The climate is humid all the year round, with rainfall of about 3 in. concentrated in the mild winter months, December to March; in summer, May to October, temperatures can exceed 110° F. (44°C).

Government.—Bahrain has been a fully independent state since 1971. Government takes the form of a constitutional monarchy, in which traditional consultative procedures continue to play an important role.

Economy.—The largest sources of revenue are oil production and refining. The Bahrain field, discovered in 1932, is wholly owned by the Bahrain National Oil Co. Production in 1986 stood at about 42,000 b.p.d. The Sitra refinery derives about 70 per cent. of its crude oil by submarine pipeline from Saudi Arabia. Bahrain also has a half share with Saudi Arabia in the profits of the offshore Abu Sa'afa field. A reservoir of unassociated gas has recently been developed on Bahrain island.

Heavy industry is currently limited to the Aluminium Bahrain (ALBA) smelter, producing 170,000 tonnes p.a.; the Gulf Petrochemical Industries Co. (GPIC) producing 150,000 tonnes p.a. of ammonia and methanol, the Gulf Aluminium Rolling Mill (GARMCO), and the Arab Shipbuilding and Repair Yard (ASRY), operating dry dock facilities up to 500,000 tons.

There are a number of small to medium sized industrial units.

The state has developed as a financial centre. Apart from commercial banks, led by the National Bank of Bahrain, the Standard Chartered Bank, the British Bank of the Middle East and the Bank of Bahrain and Kuwait, many international banks have been licensed as "offshore banking units"; there are also money brokers and merchant banks.

The currency is the Bahraini Dinar (BD) divided into 1,000 fils.

Trade with U.K.

	1985	1986
Imports from U.K.	£161,560,000	£130,991,000
Exports to U.K.	45,219,000	19,732,000

Communications.—Bahrain International airport is the main air traffic centre of the Gulf; it is the headquarters of Gulf Air, and a stopping point on routes between Europe and Australia and the Far East for other airlines. A causeway linking Bahrain to Saudi Arabia was opened in Nov. 1986.

A world-wide telephone and telex service, by satellite and cable, is operated by Bahrain Telecommunications Company.

CAPITAL.—Manama; population (1981 Census), 121,986.

FLAG.—Red, with vertical serrated white bar next to staff.

NATIONAL DAY.—December 16.

BRITISH EMBASSY
21 Government Avenue,
Manama 306, P.O. Box 114

Ambassador Extraordinary and Plenipotentiary, His Excellency Francis S. E. Trew, C.M.G. (1984).
1st Secretaries, W. I. Rae, M.B.E. (*Commercial and Head of Chancery*); S. P. Muir.
2nd Secretary, D. Leith (*Commercial*).
British Council Representative, D. R. Thomas, 21 Government Avenue (P.O. Box 452), Manama 306.

BELGIUM
(Royaume de Belgique)

King of the Belgians, H.M. King Baudouin, K.G., *born* Sept. 7, 1930; *succeeded* July 17, 1951, on the abdication of his father, King Leopold III, after having acted as Head of the State since August 11, 1950; *married* Dec. 15, 1960, Doña Fabiola de Mora y Aragòn.
Heir Presumptive, H.R.H. Prince Albert, *born* June 6, 1934, *brother* of the King; *married* July 2, 1959, Donna Paola Ruffo di Calabria, and has *issue* Prince Philippe Léopold Louis Marie, *b.* April 15, 1960; Princess Astrid Josephine-Charlotte Fabrizia Elisabeth Paola Marie, *b.* June 5, 1962; Prince Laurent, *b.* Oct. 20, 1963.

CABINET

Prime Minister, Wilfried Martens (*CVP*).
Deputy Prime Minister and Minister for Justice and Institutional Reform, Jean Gol (*PRL*).
Deputy Prime Minister and Minister for Economic Affairs, Philippe Maystadt (*PSC*).
Deputy Prime Minister and Minister of the Budget, of Scientific Policy and of the Plan, Guy Verhofstadt (*PVV*).
External Relations, Leo Tindemans (*CVP*).
Finance, Mark Eyskens (*CVP*).
Public Works, Louis Olivier (*PRL*).
Communications and for Foreign Trade, Herman De Croo (*PVV*).
Employment and Labour, Michel Hansenne (*PSC*).
National Education (Flemish Sector), Daniel Coens (*CVP*).
National Education (French Sector), Antoine Duquesne (*PRL*).
Social Affairs and for Institutional Reform, Jean-Luc Dehaene (*CVP*).
Interior, Civil Service and Decentralization, Joseph Michel (*PSC*).
National Defence, and the Brussels Region, François-Xavier de Donnéa (*PRL*).

The Middle Classes, Jacky Buchmann (*PVV*).

CVP—Christian Democrat Party (Flemish); *PSC*— Christian Democrat Party (Francophone); *PVV*— Liberals (Flemish); *PRL*—Liberals (Francophone).

BELGIAN EMBASSY IN LONDON
103 Eaton Square, SW1W 9AB
(01–235 5422)

Ambassador Extraordinary and Plenipotentiary, His Excellency Jean-Paul van Bellinghen (1984).
Minister Plenipotentiary, M. C. Raulier.
Minister Counsellor, R. Vandemeulebroucke (*Economic*).
Military, Naval and Air Attaché, Capt. W. Cornelis.

A Kingdom of Western Europe, with a total area of 11,781 sq. miles (30,513 sq. km.), and a population, (1986) of 9,858,895 (Greater Brussels, 976,536; Flanders, 5,676,194; Wallonia, 3,206,165, of whom 66,445 are German-speaking). The majority of Belgians are Roman Catholics. The Kingdom of Belgium is bounded on the N. by the Kingdom of the Netherlands, on the S. by France, on the E. by W. Germany and Luxemburg, and on the W. by the North Sea.

Belgium has a frontier of 898 miles, and a seaboard of 41 miles. The Meuse and its tributary, the Sambre, divide it into two distinct regions, that in the west being generally level and fertile, while the table-land of the Ardennes, in the east, has for the most part a poor soil. The "polders" near the coast, which are protected by dykes against floods, cover an area of 193 sq. miles. The highest hill, Signal de Botranges, rises to a height of 2,276 feet, but the mean elevation of the whole country does not exceed 526 feet. The principal rivers are the Scheldt and the Meuse.

Government.—The kingdom formed part of the "Low Countries" (Netherlands) from 1815 until Oct. 14, 1830, when a National Congress proclaimed its independence, and on June 4, 1831, Prince Leopold of Coburg was chosen hereditary king. The separation from the Netherlands and the neutrality and inviolability of Belgium were guaranteed by a Conference of the European Powers, and by the *Treaty of London* (April 19, 1839), the famous "Scrap of Paper," signed by Austria, France, Great Britain, Prussia, The Netherlands, and Russia. On Aug. 4, 1914, the Germans invaded Belgium, in violation of the terms of the treaty. The Kingdom was again invaded by Germany on May 10, 1940. The whole Kingdom eventually fell and was occupied by Nazi troops until liberated by the Allies in September 1944.

According to the Constitution of 1831 the form of government is a constitutional representative and hereditary monarchy with a bicameral legislature, consisting of the King, the Senate and the Chamber of Deputies. The parliamentary term is four years.

The last general election was held on October 13, 1985. The results were as follows (seats):
Chamber of Deputies: CVP, 49; PS (Socialist), 35; SP (Socialist), 32; PRL, 24; PVV, 22; PSC, 20; VU (Flemish Nationalist), 16; Ecologists, 9; FDF (Brussels Francophones), 3; UDRT (Anti-tax), 1; VLAAMS BLOK, 1.
Senate: CVP, 25; PS, 18; SP, 16; PRL, 13; PVV, 11; PSC, 10; VU, 8; Ecologists, 4; FDF, 1. Besides these directly elected representatives the Senate also includes 51 members who are elected by the Provincial Councils and 26 who are co-opted in the proportions of the directly elected seats. H.R.H. Prince Albert is a "sénateur de droit".

Regional Governments.—The 1980 regionalization law made provision for the establishment of three Regional Community Parliaments (Assemblies) with executive councils which were set up in November 1981 and became effective in January 1982. The executives are autonomous from the central government, and their members are elected by the members of the Assemblies to whom they are responsible. They prepare Bills within the limits of their regional/ community competences, and once these Bills have been passed by the regional assembly and published in the *Moniteur Belge*, they have the force of law.

The Flemish Regional Assembly (182 members) and Executive (a President and 8 Regional Ministers) covers the provinces of Antwerp, East and West Flanders, Limbourg and the Flemish *arrondissements* (Halle, Vilvoorde, Leuven) in the province of Brabant, and is also responsible for the Flemish population of Brussels. The Walloon Regional Assembly (106 members) and Executive (a President and 5 Regional Ministers) covers the provinces of Hainaut, Liege, Luxembourg and Namur, and the *arrondissement* of Nivelles in the province of Brabant. The French Community Assembly (137 members) and Executive (a President and 2 Community Ministers) has no fixed territory but is responsbile for the francophone population of Brussels and, in concert with the Walloon Regional Assembly, deals with certain Walloon regional affairs. The German-speaking community (about 66,000) also has an Assembly, which gained autonomy in 1984. It is based in Eupen.

Although the regionalization laws defined the City of Brussels as a region, there is no autonomous regional parliament for the City and its affairs are handled by a Brussels Executive within the national government.

An Arbitration Court was set up in 1984 to resolve conflicts between laws made by the various legislative bodies.

Language and Literature.—Belgium is divided between those who speak Dutch (the Flemings) and those who speak French (the Walloons). Dutch is spoken in the provinces of West Flanders, East Flanders, Antwerp, Limburg, and the northern half of Brabant, and French in the provinces of Hainault, Namur, Luxemburg, Liège and the southern half of Brabant. Dutch is recognized as the official language in the northern areas and French in the southern (Walloon) area and there are guarantees for the respective linguistic minorities. Brussels is officially bi-lingual. There is a small German-speaking area (Eupen and Malmedy) along the German border, east of Liège.

The literature of France and the Netherlands is supplemented by an indigenous Belgian literary activity, in both French and Dutch. Maurice Maeterlinck (1862–1949) was awarded the Nobel Prize for Literature in 1911. Emile Verhaeren (1855–1916) was a poet of international standing. Of contempo-

0   20   40   60 MILES

rary Belgian writers, perhaps the most celebrated is Georges Simenon (*born* at Liège in 1903). There are 39 daily newspapers in Belgium (23 in French, 15 in Dutch and 1 in German).

Education.—The nursery schools provide free education for the 2½ to 6 age group. There are over 8,000 primary schools (6 to 12 years) of which approximately 5,000 are administered by the State, province or commune and the remainder are free institutions (predominantly Roman Catholic). There are more than 1,100 secondary schools offering a general academic education slightly over half of which are free institutions (predominantly Roman Catholic but subsidized by the State) and the remainder official institutions. The official school leaving age is 18.

Production.—Belgium is a manufacturing country. With no natural resources except coal, annual production of which was approximately 6 million tonnes in 1986, industry is based largely on the processing for re-export of imported raw materials. Gross National Product per capita in 1986 was *B.Fr.*439,992. Principal industries are steel and metal products, chemicals and petrochemicals, textiles, glass, and foodstuffs.

FINANCE

Budget	1985	1986
	B. Fr. (millions)	
Consolidated revenue....	2,363,800	2,434,200
Consolidated expenditure	2,918,300	3,007,300

The unit of currency is the Belgian *franc*. (*See also* p. 81). External trade figures relate to Luxembourg as well as Belgium since the two countries formed an Economic Union in 1921.

TRADE

	1985	1986
	B. Fr. (millions)	
Total Imports	3,315,468	2,990,700
Total Exports	3,163,724	3,060,200

Trade with U.K. (Belgium and Luxembourg)

	1985	1986
Imports from U.K...	£3,347,500,000	£3,832,605,000
Exports to U.K.	4,016,800,000	4,083,883,000

Communications.—In 1983, there were 3,920 kilometres of normal gauge railways operated by the Belgian National Railways, of which 1,763 kilometres were electrified. The Belgian National Light Railways (SNCV) also operated 27,671 kilometres of regular bus routes. In 1984 there were 2,930,000 telephone subscribers in Belgium.

Ship canals include *Ghent-Terneuzen* (18 miles, of which half is in Belgium and half in the Netherlands) which permits the passage to Ghent of ships up to 60,000 tons; the Canal of *Willebroek Rupel-Brussels* (20 miles, by which ships drawing 18 ft reach Brussels from the sea; opened in 1922); and *Bruges* (from Zeebrugge on the North Sea to Bruges, 6¼ miles). The *Albert Canal* (79 miles), links Liège with Antwerp; it was completed in 1939 and accommodates barges up to 1,350 tons. The modernization of the port of Antwerp is well advanced. Inland waterway approaches to Antwerp are also to be improved. The river Meuse from the Dutch to the French frontiers, the river Sambre between Namur and Monceau, the river Scheldt from Antwerp-Ghent and the Brussels-Charleroi Canal are being widened or deepened to take barges up to 1,350 tons. Most of the maritime trade of Belgium is carried in foreign shipping.

In 1981 there were 13,093 km. of trunk roads of which about 1,315 km. are motorways.

The Belgian National Airline *Sabena* operates regular services between Brussels and London, and many continental centres, as well as overseas services to Northern and Central America, Africa, Middle East, Far East, etc. Many foreign airlines call at Brussels.

THE CAPITAL, Brussels, has a population (1986) of 976,536. Other towns are ΨAntwerp, the chief port (918,963); ΨGhent (484,295); Liège (592,732); Charleroi (430,767); ΨBruges (258,917); ΨOstend (134,215); Malines (293,050).

FLAG.—Three vertical bands, black, yellow, red.

NATIONAL DAY.—July 21 (Accession of King Leopold I, 1831).

BRITISH EMBASSY.
Britannia House, 28 rue Joseph II,
1040 Brussels.

Ambassador Extraordinary and Plenipotentiary, His Excellency Peter Charles Petrie, C.M.G., (1985).
Counsellors, D. Evans (*Head of Chancery*); M. B. Collins, O.B.E. (*Commercial*).
Defence and Military Attaché, Col. P. M. Beaumont, M.B.E.
Naval and Air Attaché, Wing Cdr. J. N. Landeryou, R.A.F.
There are British Consular Offices at *Brussels, Antwerp* and *Liège.*

British Council Representative to Belgium and Luxemburg, J. P. Harniman, O.B.E., 30 rue Joseph II, 1040 Brussels (Council Library at *Brussels*).
BRITISH CHAMBER OF COMMERCE FOR BELGIUM AND LUXEMBURG (INC.), 30 rue Joseph II, 1040 Brussels.

BENIN
(République Populaire du Benin)

President of the Military Revolutionary Government and Head of State, Brig.-Gen. Ahmed Mathieu Kerekou; *assumed office,* Oct. 26, 1972, *re-elected,* July 31, 1984.

NATIONAL EXECUTIVE COUNCIL
(as at October 1986)

President of the Council and Minister of Defence, Brig.-Gen. Ahmed Mathieu Kerekou.
Minister-Delegate to the Presidency (Interior, Security, Territorial Administration), Maj. Edouard Zodehougan.
Minister-Delegate to the Presidency (Planning, Statistics), Souradjou Ibrahim.
Rural Development and Co-operative Action, Maj. Martin Dohou Azonhiho.
Equipment and Transport, Soule Dankoro.
Finance and Economy, Barnabe Bidouzo.
Commerce, Crafts and Tourism, Girigissou Gado.
Primary Education, Capt. Philippe Akpo.
Secondary and Higher Education, Vincent Guedzodje.
Culture, Youth and Sports, Ousmane Batoko.
Labour and Social Affairs, Lt. Col. Nathanael Mensah.
Public Health, André Atchade.
Information and Communications, Houdou Ali.
Foreign Affairs and Co-operation, Guy Landry Hazoume.
Justice, and Inspection of Parastatal Enterprises, Didier Dassi.

A republic situated in West Africa, between 2° and 3° W. and 6° and 12° N., Benin (formerly known as Dahomey) has a short coastline of 78 miles on the Gulf of Guinea but extends northwards inland for 437 miles. It is flanked on the west by Togo, on the north by Burkina Faso and Niger and on the east by Nigeria. It has an area of 43,484 sq. miles (122,622 sq. km.), and a population of 3,932,000 (1985, U.N.

estimate). Although poor in resources, Benin is one of the most heavily populated areas in West Africa, with a high standard of education. It is divided into four main regions running horizontally: a narrow sandy coastal strip, a succession of inter-communicating lagoons, a clay belt and a sandy plateau in the north.

Government.—The first treaty with France was signed by one of the kings of Abomey in 1851 but the country was not placed under French administration until 1892. Benin became an independent republic within the French Community on Dec. 4, 1958; full independence outside the Community was proclaimed on August 1, 1960. In October, 1963, a popular revolution led to the fall of the government and the Army held power until a civilian government was formed. The government's life was very short, however, and in the subsequent 8–9 years successive governments were overthrown by the military after only a short term in office until a *coup d'état* of October 26, 1972 brought to power a Military Revolutionary Government, headed by Lt.-Col. Kerekou. Although now a one-party state, a general election was held in Nov. 1979, and a new Constitution and National Assembly were established.

Benin is a member of the *Conseil de l'Entente*, the *Organisation Commune Africaine et Malgache* (OCAM), the Organization of African Unity (O.A.U.) and the Economic Community of West African States (ECOWAS). The official language is French.

Finance.—The currency of Benin is the *Franc CFA* of 100 *centimes*.

Trade.—The principal exports are cotton, palm products, ground nuts, shea-nuts, and coffee. Small deposits of gold, iron and chrome have been found; oil production started in 1983.

Trade with U.K.

	1985	1986
Imports from U.K.	£8,362,000	£6,728,000
Exports to U.K.	7,390,000	4,910,000

CAPITAL.—Porto Novo (population (1982 estimate) 208,258). Political capital and principal commercial town and port, ♈Cotonou (popn. (1982) 487,020).

FLAG.—Green, with five pointed red star in the top left corner.

NATIONAL DAY.—November 30.

British Embassy (see Lagos, Nigeria).

BHUTAN
(Druk-yul)

King of Bhutan, H.M. Jigme Singye Wangchuck, *born* Nov. 11, 1955; *succeeded his father*, July, 1972; *crowned*, June 2, 1974.

COUNCIL OF MINISTERS

H.M. Representative in the Ministry of Finance, H.R.H. Ashi S. C. Wangchuk.

H.M. Representative in the Ministry of Agriculture and the Ministry of Communications and Tourism, H.R.H. Ashi D. W. Wangchuk.

Home Affairs, Trade, Industry and Forests, H.R.H. Namgyel Wangchuk.

Foreign Affairs, Lyonpo Dawa Tshering.

Social Services, Lyonpo Sangyen Penjor.

Deputy Minister of Defence, Col. Lam Dorji.

Speaker of the National Assembly, Lyonpo Tamji Jagar.

Bhutan is a small Himalayan Kingdom situated between Tibet (to the north) and India (to the west, south and east). The total area is about 18,147 sq. miles (47,000 sq. km.), with a mountainous northern region which is infertile and sparsely populated, a central zone of upland valleys where most of the population and cultivated land is found, and in the south the densely forested foothills of the Himalayas, which are mainly inhabited by Nepalese settlers and indigenous tribespeople.

The population of Bhutan is estimated at 1,417,000 (1985, U.N. estimate), about three-quarters of whom are Buddhists. The remainder (mostly the Nepali Bhutanese) are Hindu. The official language, for administrative and religious purposes, is Dzongkha, a variant of Tibetan, which functions as a *lingua franca* amongst a variety of languages and dialects. It is government policy to make the study of Dzongkha compulsory in schools, although English is the medium of instruction and has become widely used within the administration.

In 1949, a treaty was concluded with the Government of India under which the Kingdom of Bhutan agreed to be guided by the Government of India in regard to its external relations, but it still retains independence, issues its own passports, has its own diplomatic representatives and is a member of the U.N. and other international and regional organisations. It also receives from the Government of India an annual payment of *Rs.*500,000 as compensation for portions of its territory annexed by the British Government in India in 1864.

Government.—Bhutan has a 150-member National Assembly which meets twice a year. The 8-member Royal Advisory Council, nominated by the King and the National Assembly, acts as a consultative body when the National Assembly is not in session. The King is also assisted by a Council of Ministers.

Economy.—The sixth 5-year Plan (1987–91) has a projected expenditure of 8811·2m. Nu. Economic emphasis is on the infrastructure, especially roads and telecommunications. The economy is based on agriculture and animal husbandry, which engage over 90 per cent of the workforce in what is largely a self-sufficient rural society. The principal food crops are rice, wheat, maize and barley. Vegetables and fruit are also produced. Bhutan is the world's largest producer of cardamom, which forms its principal export to countries other than India. Mineral resources include dolomite and small amounts of coal, which are exported to India. A modest industrial base is being developed. A distillery and cement, chemicals and food processing plants are in production: a forestry industries complex is being expanded. Tourism and postage stamps are increasingly important sources of foreign exchange. Over 90 per cent of foreign trade is with India. Principal exports are agricultural products, timber, cement and coal; main imports are textiles, cereals and consumer goods. Bhutan's airline, Druk Air, flies between Paro and Calcutta.

Currency.—*Ngultrum* (parity with Indian rupee).

Trade with U.K.

	1985	1986
Imports from U.K.	£109,000	£76,000
Exports to U.K.	—	—

CAPITAL.—Thimphu (Population estimate 1977, 8,922).

FLAG.—Saffron yellow and orange-red divided diagonally, with dragon device in centre.

NATIONAL DAY.—December 17.

BOLIVIA
(República de Bolivia)

President of the Republic, Sr. Victor Paz Estenssoro, *inaugurated*, Aug. 6, 1985.

Vice President, Sr. Julio Garret Ayllón.

CABINET

Foreign Affairs, Guillermo Bedregal.
Interior, Dr. Juan Carlos Duran Saucedo.
Defence, Alfonso Revollo Thenier.
Finance, Juan Cariaga Osorio.
Planning, Gonzalo Sanchez de Lozada.
Education, Enrique Ipiña Melgar.
Transport and Communications, Andrés Petricevic.
Industry and Commerce, Fernando Moscoso.
Labour, Dr. Alfredo Franco Guachalla.
Health, Dr. Carlos Perez Guzman.
Mines and Metallurgy, Jaime Villalobos.
Agriculture, José Guillermo Justiniano.
Energy and Hydrocarbons, Carlos Morales Landivar.
Housing, Franklin Anaya.
Information, Herman Antelo Louckling.
Aeronautics, Gen. Antonio Tovar Piérola.
Secretary General, Dr. Walter Zuleta Roncal.
Secretary to the Presidency, Eduardo O. Lopez Muñoz.

BOLIVIAN EMBASSY IN LONDON
106 Eaton Square, SW1W 9AD
[01–235 2257/4248]

Ambassador Extraordinary and Plenipotentiary, His
    Excellency Eduardo Arauco-Paz (1986).
Minister Counsellor, J. Loayza.
1st Secretary, Srta. Marta Bosacoma Bonel.

The land-locked Republic of Bolivia extends between lat. 10° and 23° S. and long. 57° 30' and 69° 45' W.
It has an area estimated at 424,165 sq. miles (1,098,581
sq. km.), with a population (1985 U.N. estimate) of
6,429,000. (*For* MAP, *see* Index.) The Republic derives
its name from its liberator, Simon Bolivar (1783–
1830).

The chief topographical feature is the great central
plateau (65,000 square miles) over 500 miles in length,
at an average altitude of 12,500 feet above sea level,
between the two great chains of the Andes, which
traverse the country from south to north. The total
length of the navigable streams is about 12,000 miles,
the principal rivers being the Itenez, Beni, Mamore
and Madre de Dios.

Language and Literature.—The official language of
the country is Spanish, but many of the Indian
inhabitants (about two-thirds of the population)
speak Quechua or Aymará, the two linguistic groups
being more or less equal in numbers.

The Roman Catholic religion was disestablished in
1961 but relations between it and the State are good.
Elementary education is compulsory and free and
there are secondary schools in urban centres. Provision is also made for higher education; in addition to
St. Francisco Xavier's University at Sucre, founded
in 1624, there are six other universities, the largest
being the University of San Andres at La Paz. There
are nine principal daily newspapers in Bolivia.

Production.—Mining, natural gas, petroleum and
agriculture are the principal industries. The ancient
silver mines of Potosí are now worked chiefly for tin,
but gold, partly dug and partly washed, is obtained
on the Eastern Cordillera of the Andes; the tin
output is one of the largest in the world, and together
with other minerals (copper, antimony, lead, zinc,
asbestos, wolfram, bismuth salt and sulphur), provides
over half of Bolivia's exports.

In 1982 Bolivia produced 1·4 million cubic metres
of oil, sufficient for internal consumption. Gas
(currently providing about a quarter of Bolivia's
export income) is piped to Argentina and there are
plans to build a pipeline to Sao Paulo, Brazil, by 1988.
Bolivia's agricultural produce consists chiefly of rice,
barley, oats, wheat, sugar-cane, maize, cotton, indigo,
rubber, cacao, potatoes, cinchona bark, medicinal
herbs, brazil nuts etc.

Transport and Communications.—There are 2,200
miles of railways in operation including the lines
from Corumbá to Santa Cruz (312 miles). There are
about 10,950 miles of telegraphs, and microwave
telephone communications between La Paz, Santa
Cruz, Cochabamba, Oruro and Sucre. Most other
towns of any size have radio/telephone communication with the main cities. There is direct railway
communication to the sea at Antofagasta (32 hours),
Arica (10 hours), and Mollendo (2 days), and also to
Buenos Aires (3½ days). Communication with Peru is
by road from La Paz *via* Copacabana and thence to
the railhead at Puno.

Commercial aviation in Bolivia is conducted by
the national airline, Lloyd Aereo Boliviano and
Transporte Aereo Militar between the major towns,
and Lloyd Aereo Boliviano and a number of foreign
airlines provide international flights to the U.S.A.,
South and Central America and Europe.

Bolivia is without a coastline, having been deprived
of the ports of Tocopilla, Cobija, Mejillones and
Antofagasta by the "Pacific War" of 1879–1884.

FINANCE

The economy has deteriorated since 1977, with
disappointing petroleum reserves, a large external
debt, and the collapse of world tin prices (Oct. 1985).
The peso was devalued to 2,000 to 1 U.S. dollar in
April 1984. The inflation rate in 1985 was about
11,750 per cent. Total exports (c.i.f.) in 1985 were U.S.
$672·5 million.

Trade with U.K.

	1985	1986
Imports from U.K.	£10,443,000	£3,663,000
Exports to U.K.	14,434,000	10,225,000

Mineral exports represent about 94 per cent of
these totals. A large part of Bolivia's minerals were
shipped to U.K. for smelting and re-export, but
Bolivia is now developing her own smelters and will
in future be exporting metals. The chief imports are
wheat and flour, iron and steel products, machinery,
vehicles and textiles.

CAPITAL.—La Paz (Population, 1,000,000). Other
large centres are Cochabamba (250,000), Oruro
(180,000), Santa Cruz (380,000), Potosí (90,000), Sucre,
the legal capital and seat of the judiciary (80,000) and
Tarija (45,000).

FLAG.—Three horizontal bands; red, yellow, green.
NATIONAL DAY.—August 6 (Independence Day).

BRITISH EMBASSY
Avenida Arce 2732–2754,
(Casilla 694) La Paz.

Ambassador Extraordinary and Plenipotentiary, His
    Excellency Colum John Sharkey, C.M.G., M.B.E.,
    (1987).
First Secretary, T. J. Duggin (*Commercial and Head
    of Chancery*).

BRITISH CONSULAR OFFICES

There is a British Consular Office at *La Paz.*

BRAZIL
(República Federativa do Brasil)

President, José Sarney, *inaugurated*, April 22, 1985.

CABINET

Chief Minister Civil Staff, Ronaldo Costa Couto.
Chief Minister Military Staff, Gen. Rubens Bayma
    Denys.

Justice, Paulo Brossard.
Navy, Adm. Henrique Sabóia.
External Relations, Roberto Abreu Sodré.
Army, Gen. Leônidas Pires.
Finance, Luis Carlos Bresser Pereira.
Transport, José Reinaldo C. Tavares.
Agriculture, Iris Rezende.
Education, Jorge K. Bornhausen.
Labour, Almir Pazzianotto.
Air Force, Brig. Octavio J. Moreira Lima.
Health, Roberto F. Santos.
Industry and Commerce, José Hugo Castello Branco.
Mines and Energy, A. Aureliano Chaves.
Planning, Anibal Teixeira.
Interior, Joaquim F. Cavalcante.
Communications, Antonio Magalhães.
Social Security, Raphael de Almeida Magalhães.
National Information Service, Gen. Ivan de Souza
    Mendes.
Armed Forces General Staff, Gen. Ex. Paulo Campos
    Paiva.
Land Reform and Development, Marcos Freire.
Science and Technology, Renato B. Archer.
Culture, Celso M. Furtado.
Urban Planning and Environment, Deni L. Schwartz.
Administration, Aluízio Alves.

BRAZILIAN EMBASSY IN LONDON
32 Green Street, W1Y 4AT
[01–499 0877]

Ambassador Extraordinary and Plenipotentiary, His
Excellency Senhor Celso de Souza e Silva (1986).
There are also a Brazilian Consulate-General in
London and honorary consular offices at *Cardiff* and
Glasgow.

Area and Population.—Brazil, discovered in 1500
by Pedro Alvares Cabral, Portuguese navigator, is
bounded on the north by the Atlantic Ocean, the
Guianas, Colombia and Venezuela; on the west by
Peru, Bolivia, Paraguay, and Argentina; on the south
by Uruguay; and on the east by the Atlantic Ocean.
Brazil extends between lat. 5° 16′ N. and 33° 45′ S. and
long. 34° 45′ and 73° 59′ 22″ W. The Republic comprises
an area of 3,286,488 sq. miles (8,511,965 sq. km.), with
a population (1985 U.N. estimate) of 135,564,000.
The northern States of Amazonas and Pará are
mainly wide, low-lying, forest-clad plains. The central states of Mato Grosso are principally plateau
land and the eastern and southern States are
traversed by successive mountain ranges interspersed with fertile valleys. The principal ranges are
Serra do Mar, the *Serra da Mantiqueira* and the

Serra do Espinhaço along the east coast. The River *Amazon* with a total length of some 4,000 miles has tributaries which are themselves great rivers, and flows from the Peruvian Andes to the Atlantic. Its principal northern tributaries are the *Rio Branco*, *Rio Negro*, and *Japurá*; its southern tributaries are the *Juruá*, *Purus*, *Madeira* and *Tapajós*, while the *Xingú* meets it within 200 miles of its outflow into the Atlantic. The *Tocantins* and *Araguaia* flow northwards from Mato Grosso and Goiás to the Gulf of Pará. The *Parnaiba* flows from Piaui into the Atlantic. The *São Francisco* rises in the South of Minas Gerais and flows to the eastern coast. The *Paraguai*, rising in the south-west of Mato Grosso, flows through Paraguay to its confluence with the *Paraná*, which rises in the mountains of that name and divides Brazil from Paraguay.

Government.—Brazil was colonized by Portugal in the early part of the sixteenth century, and in 1822 became an independent empire under Dom Pedro, son of the refugee King Joao VI of Portugal. On Nov. 15, 1889, Dom Pedro II, second of the line, was dethroned and a republic was proclaimed.

The Federative Republic of Brazil is made up of the Federal District, 23 States and 3 Territories (the most under-developed frontier regions). The constitution of January 1967 draws on the same conceptual basis as that of the United States, and envisages an equal distribution of power between the executive, the legislature and the judiciary. Under the existing constitutional provisions the President, who heads the executive, is indirectly elected.

The Congress consists of a Senate (3 Senators per State elected for an 8-year term) and a Chamber of Deputies which is re-elected every 4 years. (The number of Deputies per State depends upon the State's population). Each State has a Governor, and a Legislative Assembly with a 4-year term.

The Congress, sitting as the Constituent Assembly, which came into being February 1, 1987, is to determine the length of Sr. Sarney's presidential term and to rewrite the Constitution. The new Brazilian Constitution will be promulgated after its approval by the Constituent Assembly in late 1987 or 1988.

Production.—There are large and valuable mineral deposits including among others, iron ore (hematite), manganese, bauxite, beryllium, chrome, nickel, tungsten, cassiterite, lead, gold, monazite (containing rare earths and thorium) and zirconium. Diamonds and precious and semi-precious stones are also found. The mineral wealth is being exploited to an increasing extent. The iron ore deposits of Minas Gerais are exceeded by those of the Amazon region, principally in the Carajás areas where deposits are estimated at 35,000 million tonnes. Mining operations began in Feb. 1985.

Electric power production in 1986 was 201,618 Gwh. In the same year, the total output of steel was 21,239,825 tonnes. Production of oil was 593,452 b.p.d. Of these 416,124 b.p.d. were produced from offshore fields.

Agriculture production was (tonnes):

	1985	1986
Black Beans	2,547,925	2,221,000
Cassava	23,072,555	25,542,000
Castor Beans	415,884	263,000
Cocoa	419,268	459,000
Coffee	3,753,379	2,007,000
Cotton	2,836,266	2,314,000
Maize	22,017,154	20,510,000
Peanuts	339,335	216,000
Potatoes	1,989,261	1,834,000
Rice	9,019,156	10,399,000
Sisal	290,901	255,000

Soya	18,278,422	13,335,000
Tobacco	410,902	386,000
Wheat	4,247,197	5,433,000

Defence.—The peace-time strength of the Army is 192,000. The Navy consists of 1 aircraft carrier, 7 submarines, 10 destroyers, 6 frigates, 9 patrol vessels, 5 river patrol ships, 1 river monitor, 1 river transport, 6 coastal mine sweepers, 7 survey ships, and 29 other vessels. The strength of the Navy is 49,000. The Air Force, with a strength of 43,000, has 680 aircraft, of which 151 are fast-jet.

Education.—Primary education is compulsory and is the responsibility of State governments and municipalities. At this level approximately 10 per cent. attend private schools. Secondary education is largely the responsibility of State and municipal governments, although a small number of very old foundations (the Pedro II Schools) remain under direct federal control. Over 50 per cent. of all pupils at this level attend private schools. Higher education is available in Federal, State, municipal and private universities and faculties.

Language and Literature.—Portuguese is the language of the country, but Italian, Spanish, German, Japanese and Arabic are spoken by immigrant minorities, and newspapers of considerable circulation are produced in those languages. English and French are currently spoken by educated Brazilians.

Public libraries have been established in urban centres and there is a flourishing national press with widely circulated daily and weekly newspapers.

Communications.—In 1983 there were 1,552,463 km. of highways. The route-length of railways in 1980 was 35,100 km. Internal air services are highly developed. There are 21,944 miles of navigable inland waterways. During 1982, 9,574 vessels entered Rio de Janeiro and Santos, the two leading ports.

Currency.—The new *Cruzado* (CZ$) corresponds to 1,000 old Cruzeiros. The Centavo is re-established to designate one hundredth of the cruzado.

Notes currently in circulation are CZ$500, 100, 50, 10. Also, Cruzeiro notes still in circulation, Cruzeiro 100,000, 10,000, 5,000, 1,000, 500, 200, 100. Coins in circulation are CZ$1; Centavos 50, 20, 10; plus Cruzeiros 200, 100, 50.

FINANCE

	1986
	Cruzados
Revenue	394,036 m.
Expenditure	500,178 m.

At Dec. 1986 Brazil's foreign debt stood at U.S.$110·6 million. Reserves in Dec. 1986 were $5,330 million.

TRADE

	1985	1986
Total imports	US$13,168 m.	US$12·866 m.
Total exports	25,639 m.	22·393 m.

Trade with U.K.

	1985	1986
Imports from U.K.	£211,512,218	£295,152,000
Exports to U.K.	610,623,677	552,259,000

Principal imports are fuel and lubricants, machinery, chemicals, wheat, metals and metal manufactures. Principal exports are coffee, iron ore, soya, meat, steel and orange juice. In 1986 the Brazilian automobile industry produced 1,056,500 vehicles. Of these, 183,300 vehicles were exported.

CAPITAL.—Brasilia (inaugurated on April 21, 1960). Population (1985 estimate), 1,576,657. Other important centres (1980 Census) are São Paulo (8,490,763);

the former capital ΨRio de Janeiro (5,094,396); ΨBelo Horizonte (1,774,712); ΨRecife (1,204,794); ΨSalvador (1,017,591); ΨPorto Alegre (1,125,091); ΨFortaleza (1,308,859); and Belem (934,330).

FLAG.—Green, with yellow lozenge in centre; blue sphere with white band and stars in centre of lozenge.

NATIONAL DAY.—September 7 (Independence Day).

BRITISH EMBASSY
Setor de Embaixadus Sul, Quadra 801, Conjunto K, 70.408 Brasilia, D.F.

Ambassador Extraordinary and Plenipotentiary, His Excellency Sir John Burns Ure, K.C.M.G., L.V.O. (1984).

There are British Consulates-General at Rio de Janeiro and São Paulo.

British Council Representative, J. Lawrence, SCRN 708/9-BLF Nos 1/3 (Caixa Postal 6104), 70,740 Brasilia D.F. Regional Directors in *Rio de Janeiro, Recife* and *São Paulo.*

BRITISH AND COMMONWEALTH CHAMBER OF COMMERCE IN São PAULO, Rua Barão de Itapetininga 275, 7th Floor, 01042, São Paulo (*Postal Address*, P.O. Box 1621, 01000 Sao Paulo) and Rua Real Grandeza 99, 22281 Rio de Janeiro.

BULGARIA
(Narodna Republika Bulgaria)
COUNCIL OF STATE

Chairman of the Council of State, Todor Zhivkov, *elected*, July 7, 1971; *re-elected*, June 1981 and June 1986 (*Head of State*).
First Deputy Chairman, Petur Tanchev.
Deputy Chairman, Georgi Dzhagarov; Mitko Grigorov; Yaroslav Radev.
Secretary, Nikola Manolov.

COUNCIL OF MINISTERS

Chairman (Prime Minister), Georgi Atanasov.
First Deputy Chairman, and Chairman, Committee for Research and Technology, Stoyan Markov.
First Deputy Chairman, Andrey Lukanov.
Deputy Chairmen, Ognyan Doynov; Ivan Iliev; Grigor Stoichkov; Georgi Yordanov; Kiril Zarev.
Chairman, Council for Intellectual Development, Georgi Yordanov.
Chairman, Social Council, Georgi Karamanev.
Chairman, Economic Council, Ognyan Doynov.
Chairman, Council for Agriculture and Forests, Aleksi Ivanov.
Finance, Belcho Belchev.
Foreign Affairs, Petur Mladenov.
Internal Affairs, Col. Gen. Dimitur Stoyanov.
Justice, Mrs. Svetla Daskalova.
National Defence, Gen. Dobri Dzhurov.
National Education, Ilcho Dimitrov.
Public Health, Radoy Popivanov.
Trade, Khristo Khristov.
Transport, Vasil Tsanov.
Without Portfolio, Georgi Pankov.
Chairman, Committee on State and People's Control, Georgi Georgiev.

THE COMMUNIST PARTY

Politbureau of the Central Committee, T. Zhivkov; S. Todorov; P. Kubadinski; G. Filipov; O. Doynov; D. Dzhurov; P. Mladenov; M. Balev; C. Aleksandrov; Y. Yotov; G. Atanasov (*full members*); A. Lukanov; G. Yordanov; P. Dyulgerov; G. Stoichkov; D. Stoyanov; S. Markov (*candidate members*).

Secretariat of the Central Committee, Todor Zhivkov (*Secretary-General*); D. Stanishev; S. Mikhaylov; M. Balev; V. Tsanov; E. Khristov; C. Aleksandrov; G. Filipov; Y. Yotov.

BULGARIAN EMBASSY AND CONSULATE IN LONDON
186–188 Queen's Gate Gardens, SW7 5HL
[01–584 9400/9433]

Ambassador Extraordinary and Plenipotentiary, His Excellency Mr. Dimitar Zhulev (1987).

The Republic of Bulgaria is bounded on the north by Romania, on the west by Yugoslavia, on the east by the Black Sea, and on the south by Greece and Turkey. The total area is 42,823 sq. miles (110,912 sq. km.), with a population at the Dec. 1985 Census of 8,948,388. The largest religion of the Bulgarians is the Bulgarian Orthodox Church.

A Principality of Bulgaria was created by the *Treaty of Berlin* (July 13, 1878) and in 1885 Eastern Roumelia was added to the newly-created principality. In 1908 the country was declared to be an independent kingdom. In 1912–13 a successful war of the *Balkan League* against Turkey increased the size of the kingdom, but in August, 1913, a short campaign against the remaining members of the League reduced the acquired area, and led to the surrender of Southern Dobrudja to Romania. On Oct. 12, 1915, Bulgaria entered the War on the side of the Central Powers by declaring war on Serbia. She thus became involved in the defeats of 1918, and on Sept. 29, 1918, made an unconditional surrender to the Allied Powers. On Nov. 29, 1919, she signed the *Treaty of Neuilly*, which ceded to the Allies her Thracian territories (later handed over to Greece) and some territory on the western frontier to Yugoslavia.

Nazi troops entered the country on March 3, 1941, and occupied Black Sea ports, but Bulgaria was not at war with the Soviet Union. On August 26, 1944, the government declared Bulgaria to be "neutral in the Russo-German war" and sought terms of peace from Great Britain and the United States. The Soviet Union refused to recognize the so-called "neutrality" and called upon Bulgaria to declare war against Germany, and no satisfactory reply being received on Sept. 5, 1944, the U.S.S.R. declared war on Bulgaria. Bulgaria then asked for an armistice and on Sept. 7 declared war on Germany, hostilities with U.S.S.R. ending on Sept. 10. The armistice with the Allies was signed in Moscow, Oct. 28, 1944. The Peace Treaty with Bulgaria was signed on Feb. 22, 1947, and came into force on Sept. 15, 1947. It recognized the return of Southern Dobrudja to Bulgaria.

On Sept. 9, 1944 a *coup d'état* gave power to the Fatherland Front, a coalition of Communists, Agrarians, Social Democrats and officers and intellectuals. In August, 1945, the main body of Agrarians and Social Democrats left the Government. On Sept. 8, 1946, a referendum was held, which led to the abolition of the Monarchy and the setting up of a Republic. On Oct. 27, 1946, a general election to a Grand National Assembly (with power to make a constitution) was held; the Opposition won 101 seats out of 465. The opposition Agrarian Party was suppressed in 1947, but its remnant was later revived as the Agrarian Union which now constitutionally shares power with the Communist Party.

A new Constitution was adopted in 1971 according to which the legislature is a single chamber National Assembly or *Subranie* elected by adult suffrage for a maximum term of 5 years and consisting of 400 deputies representing constituencies of equal size. This Constitution also established the Council of State, being the supreme permanent body of the National Assembly with both legislative and executive functions.

Production.—Until 1939 Bulgaria was a predominantly agricultural country, but has since pursued an elaborate programme of industrialization. About 90 per cent of the country's agriculture has been turned over to co-operatives, and a smaller proportion mechanized. The principal crops are wheat, maize, beet, tomatoes, tobacco, oleaginous seeds, fruit, vegetables and cotton. The livestock includes cattle, sheep, goats, pigs, horses, asses, mules and water buffaloes.

There is now a substantial engineering industry which accounts for about two-thirds of Bulgaria's exports; and considerable production of ferrous and non-ferrous metals. In 1985 production of electricity was 41,621 million kilowatt-hours, of steel 2,926,000 tons and of coal 32,450,000 tons (of which about one-quarter was soft coal).

There are mineral deposits of varying importance. Bulgaria's heavy industry includes the Kremikovtsi Steel Plant near Sofia and the Lenin steel mill at Pernik, the chemical complex at Devnia, the petro-chemical plant at Bourgas and various other chemical and metallurgical works situated around the country. The Soviet-designed nuclear power station at Kozlodui has four reactors, each with a capability of producing 800 million kilowatt/hours.

Defence.—Under the Peace Treaty signed between Bulgaria and the Allies, the Bulgarian Army is limited to 55,000 men, but it is believed at present to be at least 152,000 strong.

Education.—Free basic education is compulsory for children from 7 to 15 years inclusive. The Bulgarian educational system was reorganized on Soviet lines in September, 1950, providing kindergartens and educational establishments for primary and secondary education including vocational, technical and other specialized schools for secondary age pupils. There are three Universities (at Sofia, Plovdiv and Veliko Turnovo) and 21 higher educational establishments.

Language and Literature.—Bulgarian is a Southern Slavonic tongue, closely allied to Serbo-Croat and Russian with local admixtures of modern Greek, Albanian and Turkish words. There is a modern literature, chiefly educational and popular. The alphabet is Cyrillic. In 1983 there were 8 daily newspapers in Sofia.

Finance.—Planned budget revenue for 1987 is 20,672,800,000 *leva*, expenditure 20,662,800,000 *leva*.

TRADE

The principal imports are industrial and agricultural machinery, industrial raw materials, machine tools, chemicals, dyestuffs, pharmaceuticals, rubber, paper. The principal exports are non-ferrous metals, electric trucks and motors, pumps, ships, accumulators and machine tools, cereals, tobacco, fruit, vegetables, oil seeds, fats, textiles, eggs, chemicals and oils including attar of roses. In 1986, 79·2 per cent of Bulgaria's foreign trade was within the C.M.E.A., including 59·2 per cent with the Soviet Union.

Trade with U.K.

	1985	1986
Imports from U.K.	£109,970,000	£80,504,000
Exports to U.K.	22,291,000	32,459,000

CAPITAL.—Sofia, Pop. (1985), 1,114,759, at the foot of the Vitosha Range, the capital and commercial centre is on the main railway line to Istanbul, 338 miles from the Black Sea port of ΨVarna (302,211) and 125 miles from Lom (32,121), on the Danube; ΨBourgas (182,549) is also a Black Sea Port, those on the Danube being ΨRousse (183,746), ΨVidin (62,693). Other important trading and industrial centres are Plovdiv (342,131), Pleven (129,766), Stara Zagora

(150,803), Pernik (94,758), Sliven (102,423), Yambol (90,215), Khaskovo (97,763) and Tolbukhin (109,066).

FLAG.—3 horizontal bands, white, green, red; national emblem on white stripe near hoist.

NATIONAL DAY.—Sept. 9 (Day of Freedom).

BRITISH EMBASSY
Boulevard Marshal Tolbukhin, 65–67, Sofia.

Ambassador Extraordinary and Plenipotentiary, His Excellency John Harold Fawcett C.M.G. (1986).

First Secretaries, E. A. Burner (*Consul and Head of Chancery*); B. W. Cross (*Commercial*); J. B. Macpherson (*Chancery/Information*).

BURKINA
(République Démocratique Populaire de Burkina Faso)

Head of State and Minister of the Interior, Capt. Thomas Sankara, *assumed office,* Aug. 1983.

COUNCIL OF MINISTERS

Minister of State, Delegate to President, and Minister of Justice, Capt. Blaise Compaoré.

Popular Defence, Com. Jean-Baptiste Boukari Lingani.

External Relations and Cooperation, Leonore Bassole.

Economic Promotion, Capt. Henri Zongo.

Planning and Popular Development, Issouf Ouédraogo.

Agriculture and Livestock, Jean-Marie Somda.

Water, Michael Kouda.

Health, Azara Bamba.

Budget, Mme. Adèle Ouédraogo.

Financial Resources, Talata Eugene Dondasse.

Commerce and Supply, Mamadou Touré.

National Education, Sansah Dah.

Higher Education and Scientific Research, Valere Dieudonne Some.

Equipment, Moussa Michel Tapsoba.

Transport and Communications, Alain Koeffe.

Family Development and National Solidarity, Mme. Josephine Ouédraogo.

Culture, Bernadette Sanou.

Environment and Tourism, Mme. Béatrice Damiba.

Security, Fidèle Toé.

Territorial Administration and Security, Ernest Nongma Ouédraogo.

Sport and Leisure, Maj. Abdul Salam Kabore.

Information, Basile Guyissou.

Peasants' Affairs, Leonard Compaore.

Secretary General, Nayatiguingou E. Congo Kaboré.

(The Council above was dissolved in Aug. 1987—no further details were available at the time of going to press.)

Burkina is an inland savannah state in West Africa, situated between 9° and 15°N. and 2°E. and 5°W. with an area of 105,869 sq. miles (274,200 sq. km.), and a population of 6,639,000 (1985 U.N. estimate). It has common boundaries with Mali on the west, Niger and Benin on the east and Togo, Ghana and the Côte d'Ivoire on the south. The largest tribe is the Mossi whose king, the Moro Naba, still wields a certain moral influence.

Burkina was annexed by France in 1896 and between 1932 and 1947 was administered as part of the Colony of the Ivory Coast. It decided on December 11, 1958, to remain an autonomous republic within the French Community; full independence outside the Community was proclaimed on August 5, 1960. The official language is French.

The 1960 constitution provided for a presidential form of government with a single chamber National Assembly, but in January, 1966, the Army assumed power. A new constitution allowing for a partial return to civilian rule but with the Army still in effective control was adopted in 1970, but in 1974 this was suspended. Full legislative and presidential elections were held again in 1978. In a military *coup* in Nov. 1980, Col. Zerbo assumed power. He was overthrown in Nov. 1982 by Maj. Ouedraogo, who was himself overthrown in Aug. 1983 by radical Army officers led by Capt. Sankara.

On 4 Aug. 1984, Upper Volta changed its name to Burkina.

Finance and Trade.—The currency of the Republic is the *Franc CFA* (*Francs CFA* 50 = 1 *French Franc*). The 1985 Budget totalled *Francs CFA* 76,700 million.

The principal industry is the rearing of cattle and sheep and the chief exports are livestock, groundnuts, shea-nuts and cotton. Small deposits of gold, manganese, copper, bauxite and graphite have been found. Trade in 1985 was valued at Imports, *CFA* 95,158 m. Exports, *CFA* 23,065 m.

Trade with U.K.

	1985	1986
Imports from U.K.	£2,729,000	£3,104,000
Exports to U.K.	557,000	1,369,000

CAPITAL.—Ouagadougou (375,001). Other principal towns; Bobo-Dioulasso (211,538) and Kouddougou (52,431).

FLAG.—Equal bands of red over green, with a yellow star in centre.

NATIONAL DAY.—August 4.

BRITISH REPRESENTATION

British Ambassador (*resident in Abidjan,* Côte d'Ivoire).

BURMA
(Pyidaungsu Socialist Thammada Myanma Naingngandaw)
Government of the Union

President, San Yu, *elected* Nov. 9, 1981, *re-elected* Nov 4, 1985.

COUNCIL OF MINISTERS

Prime Minister, Maung Maung Kha.
Deputy Prime Minister and Planning and Finance, Thura Tun Tin.
Deputy Prime Minister and Defence, Thura Kyaw Htin.
Home and Religious Affairs, Min Gaung.
Agriculture and Forests, Than Nyunt.
Industry I, Tint Swe.
Education, Kyaw Nyein.
Industry II, Maung Cho.
Trade, Khin Maung Gyi.
Co-operatives, Than Hlaing.
Livestock and Fisheries, Maung Maung Win.
Labour and Social Welfare, Ohn Kyaw.
Foreign Affairs, Ye Gaung.
Culture and Information, Aung Kyaw Myint.
Construction, Myint Lwin.
Transport and Communications, Thura Saw Pru.
Health, Tun Wai.
Mines, Than Tin.
Energy, Sein Tun.

BURMESE EMBASSY AND CONSULATE
19A Charles St., Berkeley Square, W1X 8ER
[01–499 8841]

Ambassador Extraordinary and Plenipotentiary, His Excellency U Tin Tun (1985).

Area and Population.—Burma forms the western portion of the Indo-Chinese district of the continent of Asia, lying between 9° 58′ and 28° N. latitude and 92° 11′ and 101° 9′ E. longitude, with an extreme length of approximately 1,200 miles and an extreme width of 575 miles. It has a sea coast on the Bay of Bengal to the south and west and a frontier with Bangladesh along the Naaf River (defined in 1964) and India to the north-west (defined in 1967). In the north and east the frontier with China was determined by a treaty with the People's Republic in October, 1960, and has since been demarcated; there is a short frontier with Laos in the east, while the long finger of Tenasserim stretches southward along the west coast of the Malay Peninsula, forming a frontier with Thailand to the east. The total area of the Union is 261,218 sq. miles (676,552 sq. km.), with a population of 37,153,000 (1985 U.N. estimate).

Physical Features.—Burma falls into four natural divisions. Arakan (with the Chin Hills region), the Irrawaddy basin, Tenasserim, including the Salween basin and extending southwards to the Burma-Thailand peninsula, and the elevated plateau on the east. Mountains enclose Burma on three sides, the highest point being Hka-kabo Razi (19,296 ft.) in the northern Kachin hills. Mt. Popa, 4,981 ft., in the Myingyan district is an extinct volcano and a well-known landmark in Central Burma. The principal river systems are the Kaladan-Lemro in Arakan, the Irrawaddy-Chindwin and the Sittang in Central Burma, and the Salween which flows through the Shan Plateau.

Races, Language and Religions.—The indigenous inhabitants who entered Burma from the north and east are of similar racial types and speak languages of the Tibeto-Burman, Mon-Khmer and Thai groups. The three important non-indigenous elements are Indians, Chinese and those from the former East Pakistan. Burmese is the official language, but minority languages include Shan, Karen, Chin, Kayah and the various Kachin dialects. English is spoken in educated circles. Buddhism is the religion of 85 per cent of the people, with 5 per cent Animists, 4 per cent Moslems, 4 per cent Hindus and less than 3 per cent Christians.

Government.—Burma became an independent republic outside the British Commonwealth on January 4, 1948, and remained a parliamentary democracy for 14 years. On March 2, 1962 the army took power, and suspended the parliamentary Constitution. A Revolutionary Council of senior officers under General Ne Win took measures to create a Socialist State.

In January 1974 a new Constitution was adopted under which the highest authority is the People's Assembly (476 representatives) which meets twice a year. When the Assembly is not in session the Council of State (29 members) is vested with wide powers. The senior executive body is the Council of Ministers. The Chairman of the Council of State is also President of the Socialist Republic of the Union of Burma. The Burmese Socialist Programme Party is the only legal political party.

Political Divisions.—Burma is comprised of seven States (Chin, Kachin, Karen, Kayah, Mon, Rakhine, Shan) and seven Divisions (Irrawaddy, Magwe, Mandalay, Pegu, Rangoon, Sagaing, Tenasserim).

Education.—The literacy rate is high compared with other Asian countries, there is no caste system and women engage freely in social intercourse and play an important part in agriculture and retail trade.

Most Burmese children attend primary school, and about four million are currently enrolled; in middle and high schools, 11 million. There are two universities, at Rangoon and Mandalay, and in 1986–87 the numbers graduating were 9,981. A number of autonomous institutes of university standard award their own degrees. Under the two universities are three affiliated Degree Colleges and the Workers' College,

Rangoon. There are also 14 two-year colleges affiliated to the universities, spread throughout the country.

There are three Teachers' Training Institutes for middle and primary schools, and 13 Teachers' Training Schools for primary only. Seven Government Technical Institutes offer post-secondary technical training courses and 14 Technical High Schools train semi-skilled tradesmen. Six Agricultural Institutes offer training courses in agriculture and veterinary science; nine Agricultural High Schools train semi-skilled agriculturists. There are 34 Vocational Schools for weaving, handicrafts, etc.

Finance.—The chief sources of revenue are profits on state trading, income-tax, customs duties, commercial taxes and excise duties; the chief heads of expenditure are general administration, defence, education, police and development. The budget estimates for 1987–88 were: Revenue, K45,421,000,000; Expenditure, K63,226,000,000. The monetary unit is the *Kyat* of 100 *Pyas.*

Production, Industry and Commerce.—Three-quarters of the population depend on agriculture; the chief products are rice, oilseeds (sesamum and groundnut), maize, millet, cotton, beans, wheat, grain, tea, sugarcane, Virginia and Burmese tobacco, jute and rubber. Rice has traditionally been the mainstay of Burma's economy and the quantity of rice and by-products available for export was 900,000 tons in 1986–87. The principal export after rice is teak, of which 190,000 cubic tons was exported in 1986–87.

Burma is rich in minerals, including petroleum, lead, silver, tungsten, zinc, tin, wolfram and gemstones. Of these, petroleum products are the most important. Oil is now being produced from oilfields in Myanaung, Prome and Shwepyitha and at Chauk, Yenangyaung, Mann, and Letpando. Production of crude oil in 1986–87 totalled 10,103,000 U.S. barrels. There is a refinery at the main oilfield, Chauk, another at Syriam near Rangoon and a third is being built at Mann. There has been a slight decline in Burma's oil production in recent years and the country is no longer self-sufficient. Onshore exploration continues. There has also been some offshore oil exploration on a small scale. Major reserves of natural gas have been discovered in the Martaban Gulf, which Burma is hoping to develop.

All industrial activity of any size is in the public sector. Under development plans, projects completed or under construction with overseas financial and technical assistance include the production of cement, bricks and tiles, sheet glass, steel sections, jute bags and twine, cotton yarns, cotton and cotton mixture cloth, pharmaceuticals, sugar, paper, plywood, urea fertilizers, soda ash, tractors and tyres; also a hydro-electric scheme and various irrigation works. Japan continues to be the major individual donor of soft loans and grant aid in the industrial and agricultural sectors. West Germany has also been an important contributor of soft loans.

Loans amounting to US $450 million have been extended by the World Bank. As a member of the Colombo Plan since 1952 Burma continues to receive technical assistance from a number of countries and international agencies. Faced with a serious foreign exchange shortage, Burma has applied for Least Developed Country status (LLDC) at the U.N.

Trade with U.K.

	1985	1986
Imports from U.K.	£20,221,000	£10,835,000
Exports to U.K.	9,944,000	6,092,000

Communications.—The Irrawaddy and its chief tributary, the Chindwin, form important waterways,

the main stream being navigable beyond Bhamo (900 miles from its mouth) and carrying much traffic.

The chief seaports are Rangoon, Moulmein, Akyab and Bassein.

The Burma Railways network covers 2,764 route miles, extending to Myitkyina, on the Upper Irrawaddy. There were 2,452 miles of Union highways and 11,767 miles of other main roads in 1982–83. The airport at Mingaladon, about 13 miles north of Rangoon, only handles limited international air traffic.

CAPITAL.—The chief city of Lower Burma, and the seat of the government of the Union is Rangoon, on the left bank of the Rangoon river, about 21 miles from the sea. The city contains the Shwe Dagon pagoda, much venerated by Burmese Buddhists. Population (1983): Rangoon District, 3,973,872; city population, 2,458,712.

Mandalay is the chief city of Upper Burma, population (1983): Mandalay district, 4,580,923; city, 532,985; Moulmein of 219,991 and Bassein of 144,092. Pagan, on the Irrawaddy, S.W. of Mandalay, contains many sacred buildings.

FLAG.—The Union flag is red, with a canton of dark blue, inside which are a cogwheel and two rice ears surrounded by 14 white stars.

NATIONAL DAY.—January 4.

BRITISH EMBASSY
80 Strand Road (Box No. 638), Rangoon

Ambassador Extraordinary and Plenipotentiary, His Excellency Martin Robert Morland C.M.G. (1986).
First Secretaries, D. G. Alexander, M.B.E. (*Head of Chancery and Consul*); F. A. Wilson, M.B.E. (*Commercial*).
Cultural Attaché and British Council Representative, T. C. White, M.B.E.

BURUNDI
(République de Burundi)

President, Col. Jean-Baptiste Bagaza, *assumed office* Nov. 1, 1976, *elected* Dec. 1979, *re-elected,* Aug. 31, 1984.

COUNCIL OF MINISTERS

Defence, The President.
Foreign Affairs and Co-operation, Egide Nkuriyingoma.
Planning, Mathias Sinamaye.
Presidency in charge of Relations with the National Assembly, Lt.-Col. Stanislas Mandi.
Agriculture and Stockbreeding, Mathias Ntibarikure.
Finance, Isaac Buda Buda.
Justice, Aloys Ndenzako.
Interior, Lt.-Col. Charles Kazatsa.
Trade and Industry, Albert Muganga.
National Education, Isidore Hakizimana.
Transport, Posts and Telecommunications, Remy Nkengurutse.
Public Works, Energy and Mines, Isidore Nyaboya.
Public Health, Dr. Fidèle Bizimana.
Civil Service, Damien Barakamfitye.
Labour and Professional Training, Cyrille Baracira.
Information, Benoit Muyebe.
Youth, Sports and Culture, Balthazar Habonimana.
Rural Development, Jean Kabura.
Women's Affairs, Mme. Euphrasie Kandecke.
Social Affairs, Mme. Caritas Mategeko.

Formerly a Belgian trusteeship under the United Nations, Burundi was proclaimed an independent State on July 1, 1962. Situated on the east side of Lake Tanganyika, the State has an area of 10,747 sq. miles (27,834 sq. km.) and a population (1985 U.N.

estimate) of 4,718,000. The majority of the population are of the Bahutu ethnic group, but power rests in the hands of the minority Batutsi ethnic group.

Burundi became independent as a constitutional monarchy but this was overthrown on November 28, 1966 and the country became a republic. On Nov. 1, 1976, the government of President Micombero was overthrown and a Supreme Revolutionary Council led by Col. Jean-Baptiste Bagaza took power. In 1980 the S.R.C. was replaced by a political bureau and central committee as part of a process of political normalization, which continued with elections to the National Assembly, a 65-member legislature. The most recent elections were in Oct. 1982.

The chief crop is coffee, representing about 80 per cent of Burundi's export earnings. Cotton is the second most important crop. Minerals, tea, hides and skins exports are also important.

Trade with U.K.

	1985	1986
Imports from U.K......	£1,592,000	£2,324,000
Exports to U.K.	3,367,000	3,074,000

The currency is the Burundi *Franc.*

CAPITAL.—Bujumbura (*formerly* Usumbura), with about 150,000 inhabitants. Kitega (18,000 inhabitants) is the only other sizeable town. Official languages are Kirundi, a Bantu language, and French. Kiswahili is also used.

FLAG.—White diagonal cross on green and red quarters, with a circular white panel in the centre.

NATIONAL DAY.—July 1.

British Ambassador (see Kinshasa, Zaire).

CAMBODIA

COALITION GOVERNMENT OF
DEMOCRATIC KAMPUCHEA

President, Prince Norodom Sihanouk (Prince Sihanouk reportedly stepping aside for 12 months from May 1987).
Vice-President responsible for Foreign Affairs, Khieu Samphan.
Prime Minister, Son Sann.

PEOPLE'S REPUBLIC OF KAMPUCHEA

Head of State, Heng Samrin.
Chairman of Council of Ministers, Hun Sen.
Foreign Minister, Kong Korm.

Area and Population.—Situated between Thailand and the south of Vietnam and extending from the border with Laos on the north to the Gulf of Thailand, Cambodia covers an area of 69,898 sq. miles, (181,035 sq. km.). It has a population (1985 U.N. estimate) of 7,284,000. The climate is tropical monsoon with a rainy season from May to October. (*For* MAP, *see* Index.)

Fifty per cent. of the total land area is forest or jungle. Around the Tonlé Sap lake in the centre of the country and along the Mekong river, which traverses the country, there is ample fertile land for the support of the population in times of peace.

History.—Once a powerful kingdom, which, as the Khmer Empire, flourished between the tenth and fourteenth centuries, Cambodia became a French protectorate in 1863 and was granted independence within the French Union as an Associate State in 1949. Full independence was proclaimed on November 9, 1953, and the process was completed when, in January, 1955, the Kingdom of Cambodia became financially and economically independent not only of France but also of Laos and Vietnam. For the next fifteen years the political life of the country was dominated by Prince Norodom Sihanouk, first as

King, then as Head of Government after he had abdicated in favour of his father and finally (following his father's death in 1960) as Head of State.

On March 18, 1970, during his absence from the country, Prince Sihanouk was deposed as Head of State by a vote of the National Assembly. A Republic was declared on October 9, 1970, and the name of the country changed to the Khmer Republic.

In April 1970 widespread fighting developed between communist insurgents and government forces which gradually developed into a general civil war. In April 1975 Phnom-Penh fell to the North Vietnamese-backed Khmer Rouge. Prince Sihanouk returned to Cambodia on September 9, as nominal Head of State. However, a new Constitution was promulgated in Jan. 1976 and elections to a People's Representative Assembly were held in March. Prince Sihanouk resigned as Head of State in April, and Khieu Samphan was elected President of the State Presidium. A Government led by Pol Pot, the leader of the Khmer Rouge (Communist) party, was appointed; during the years of Khmer Rouge rule thousands of Cambodians died or fled into exile. Relations between the Khmer Rouge regime and their Vietnamese backers deteriorated sharply, and on Dec. 25, 1978 Vietnamese troops invaded Cambodia in support of an uprising. The Cambodian capital, Phnom-Penh, fell on Jan. 7, 1979. The following day the Cambodian National United Front for National Salvation established a People's Revolutionary Council, recognized by Vietnam, U.S.S.R. and by other, chiefly Soviet-aligned, countries. The P.R.K. Government, backed by an occupation army of some 150,000 Vietnamese troops, more or less controls Cambodia, but is challenged by the guerrilla forces of the Coalition Government of Democratic Kampuchea, which was formed in June 1982 by the Khmer Rouge and non-communist groups. The C.G.D.K. occupies Cambodia's seat at the U.N.

Economy.—Cambodia has an economy based on agriculture, fishing and forestry, the bulk of its people being rice-growing farmers. In addition to rice, which is the staple crop, the major products are rubber, livestock, maize, timber, pepper, palm sugar, fresh and dried fish, kapok, beans, soya and tobacco. Rice and rubber used to be the main exports though production was brought to a standstill by the hostilities. Following the Khmer Rouge victory, the populations of Phnom-Penh and other towns were forcibly evacuated to the country to work on the land, and re-establish the plantations producing such crops as cotton, rubber and bananas. Following the Vietnamese invasion of 1978 the towns were repopulated and commerce revived; currency was reintroduced. Factories, in particular textile mills, iron smelting works and cement works were put back in production.

Trade with U.K.

	1985	1986
Imports from U.K........	£467,000	£217,000
Exports to U.K.	77,000	58,000

Communications.—The country had over 5,000 kilometres of roads, of which nearly half were hard-surfaced and passable in the rainy season, although now in a state of disrepair. There are two railways, one from Phnom-Penh to the Thai border; the other from Phnom-Penh to Kampot and Kompong Som, but operations and repairs are hindered by the continuing fighting. Phnom-Penh is on a river capable of receiving ships of up to 2,500 tons all the year round. The deep water port at Kompong Som on the Gulf of Thailand can receive ships up to 10,000 tons. The port is linked to Phnom-Penh by a modern highway.

Religion and Education.—The state religion was Buddhism of the "Little Vehicle". The new constitution guaranteed religious freedom, but in practice Buddhism was suppressed by the Khmer Rouge. There has been some revival recently. There were also small Muslim and Christian communities, but many members of them died or fled the country during Khmer Rouge rule. The national language is Khmer. In the years preceding the civil war considerable efforts were devoted to the development of education and new schools, colleges and technical institutes had been established. Until April 1975 there was a Buddhist University in Phnom-Penh, and several residential teachers' training colleges were in operation. However, most of the country's educated elite died under the Khmer Rouge regime, which closed all institutions of higher education.

CAPITAL.—Phnom-Penh.

FLAG.—(C.G.D.K.) Red, with a yellow three-towered temple in the middle. (P.R.K.) Red with a yellow five-towered temple in the middle.

NATIONAL DAY.—April 17.

CAMEROON
(République Unie du Cameroun)

President, Head of State, Government and Commander in Chief of the Armed Forces, Paul Biya, *acceded* Nov. 6, 1982, *elected* Jan. 14, 1984, *sworn in* Jan. 21, 1984.

MINISTRY

Ministers Delegate at the Presidency, Michel Neva M'Eboutou (*Defence*); Joseph Chongwain Awunti (*Relations with the National Assembly*); Paul Kamga Njike (*Computer Services and Public Contracts*); Mohamadou Labarang (*Gen. State Inspectorate and Admin. Reform*).

Justice, Benjamin Itoe.

Planning and Land Development, Sadou Hayatou.

Youth and Sports, Dr. Joseph Fofe.

Foreign Affairs, Philippe Mataga.

Minister Delegate at the Ministry of Foreign Affairs, Mahamat Paba Sale.

Minister Delegate for Territorial Administration, Jerôme-Emilier Abondo.

Finance, André Boto A. Ngon.

Civil Service, René Ze Nguele.

Ministers at the Presidency in charge of Special Missions, Joseph-Charles Doumba; Titus Edzoa.

Higher Education and Scientific Research, Abdoulaye Babale.

Livestock, Animal Industries and Fisheries, Hamadjoda Adjoudi.

Social Affairs, Mrs. Rose Zang Nguele.

Posts and Telecommunications, Léonard-Claude Mpouma.

Housing and Town Planning, Ferdinand Léopold Oyono.

Transport, André Bosco Cheuwa.

Information and Culture, Ibrahim Mbombo Njoya.

Equipment, Herman Maimo.

Agriculture, Jean-Baptiste Yonkeu.

National Education, Prof. George Ngango.

Women's Affairs, Boubakari Yaou Aissatou

Trade and Industry, Edouard Nomo-Ongolo.

Labour and Social Welfare, Adolphe Moudiki.

Public Health, Victor Anomah Ngu.

Mines and Energy, Michael Kima Tabong.

CAMEROON EMBASSY
84 Holland Park, W11 3SB
[01–727 0771]

Ambassador Extraordinary and Plenipotentiary, His Excellency Dr. Gibering Bol-Alima (1987).

The Republic of Cameroon lies on the Gulf of Guinea between Nigeria to the west, Chad and the Central African Republic to the east and Congo and Gabon and Equatorial Guinea to the south. It has an area of 183,569 sq. miles, (475,442 sq. km.) and a population of 10,106,000 (1985 U.N. estimate).

The whole territory was administered by Germany from 1884 to 1916. From 1916 to 1959, the former East Cameroon was administered by France as a League of Nations (later U.N.) trusteeship. On Jan. 1, 1960 it became independent as the Republic of Cameroon. The Republic was joined on October 1, 1961, by the former British administered trust territory of the Southern Cameroons, after a plebiscite held under United Nations auspices. Cameroon became a Federal Republic with separate East and West Cameroon state governments. Subsequently, after plebiscite held in May, 1972, Cameroon became a United Republic.

Cameroon is the only country in Africa where French and English are both official languages enjoying equal status, and the government's declared long-term objective is to achieve complete "bilingualism" and "biculturalism".

The main economic emphasis is on agricultural development, both through encouraging small-scale peasant agriculture, and through the development of large-scale agro-industrial complexes, with the aim of making the country agriculturally self-sufficient and a major food exporter.

Principal products are cocoa, coffee, bananas, cotton, timber, ground-nuts, aluminium, rubber and palm products. There is an aluminium smelting plant at Edéa with an annual capacity of 50,000 tons. Oil is now also one of Cameroon's principal products with an estimated production of 9·2m. tonnes during 1984–5.

TRADE

	1984
Total imports	*FCFA*484,000 m.
Total exports	381,300 m.

Trade with U.K.

	1985	1986
Imports from U.K.	£44,806,000	£34,368,000
Exports to U.K.	73,746,000	7,634,000

CAPITAL.—Yaoundé (1984 estimate, 522,000). Ψ Douala (1984 estimate, 763,000) is the commercial centre.

FLAG.—Vertical stripes of green, red and yellow with single five-pointed yellow star in centre of red stripe.

NATIONAL DAY.—May 20.

BRITISH EMBASSY
Avenue Winston Churchill, B.P. 547
Yaoundé

Ambassador Extraordinary and Plenipotentiary, His Excellency Michael John Carlisle Glaze (1984).

First Secretary, R. P. Osborne (*Head of Chancery and Consul*).

Second Secretaries, R. O. Arrowsmith; W. N. C. Paterson (*Commercial/Aid*); E. M. E. Alexander, B.E.M. (*Administration and Vice Consul*).

British Council Representative, P. Ellwood, Les Galéries, Avenue J. F. Kennedy, (B.P. 818), Yaoundé.

CAPE VERDE ISLANDS
(República de Cabo Verde)

President, Aristides Pereira *born* 1924, *assumed office,* July 5, 1975, *re-elected,* Jan. 13, 1986.

COUNCIL OF MINISTERS

Prime Minister, Minister of Co-operation and Planning, and Minister for Finance, M. Pedro Pires.

Justice, Dr. José E. F. Araujo.
Foreign Affairs, Col. Silvino M. Da Luz.
Transport, Commerce and Tourism, Maj. Osvaldo L. da Silva.
Armed Forces and Security, Maj. Julio de Carvalho.
Agriculture and Fisheries, Maj. João P. Silva.
Education, André C. Tolentino.
Local Government and Town Planning, Tito L. S. de O. Ramos.
Information, Culture and Sport, Dr. David H. Almada.
Health, Labour and Social Services, Dr. Irineu Gomes.
Industry and Energy, Adão Rocha.
Public Works, Adriano de O. Lima.

The Cape Verde Islands, off the west coast of Africa, consist of two groups of islands, *Windward* (Santo Antão, São Vicente, Santa Luzia, São Nicolau, Boa Vista and Sal) and *Leeward* (Maio, São Tiago, Fogo and Brava) with a total area of 1,557 sq. miles, (4,033 sq. km.). The population (1985 U.N. estimate) was 326,000, the majority of whom are Roman Catholic.

The Islands, colonized in *c.* 1460, achieved independence from Portugal on July 5, 1975, under the nationalist party of Guinea Bissau and Cape Verde. A federation of the islands with Guinea Bissau was planned (till 1879 Guinea-Bissau and the Islands were a single administrative unit) but this was dropped following the 1980 coup in Guinea Bissau.

The Republic is a one-party (the P.A.I.C.V.) state with a President elected by the National Assembly. He has a mandate of 5 years, as do Assembly deputies, who are elected by universal adult suffrage.

The islands have had little rain since 1969, and agriculture is mostly confined to irrigated inland valleys, the chief products being bananas and coffee (for export), maize, sugarcane and nuts. Fish and shellfish are important exports. Salt is obtained on Sal, Boa Vista and Maio; volcanic rock is also mined for export. The main ports are Praia and Mindelo, and there is an international airport on Sal.

Trade with U.K.

	1985	1986
Imports from U.K.	£2,282,000	£1,618,000
Exports to U.K.	370,000	426,000

CAPITAL, Ψ Praia (1980, 57,748).

FLAG.—Horizontal band of yellow over green, with a vertical red band in the hoist charged with a black star over a garland of maize sheaves, two corn cobs and a clam shell.

NATIONAL DAY.—July 5. (Independence Day).
British Ambassador (resident at Dakar, Senegal.)

CENTRAL AFRICAN REPUBLIC
(République Centrafricaine)

Head of State, Gen. Andre Kolingba, *assumed office* Sept. 1, 1981, *re-elected* Nov. 21, 1986.

COUNCIL OF MINISTERS

President, Prime Minister, Minister of Defence, Armed Forces and Veteran's Affairs, Gen. André Kolingba.
Economy and Finance, Dieudonné Wazoua.
Foreign Affairs, Jean-Louis Psimhis.
Rural Development and Water, Basil Erepe.
Public Health and Social Affairs, Bernard Belloun.
Interior, Christophe Grelombe.
Justice, Lt.-Col. Jean-Louis Gervil Yambala.
Public Works and Territorial Planning, Jacques Kitte.
Education, Jean-Paul Ngoupande.
Post Office and Telecommunications, Joseph Stanislas Pollagba.

Transport and Civil Aviation, Pierre Gonifei Gaibouanou.
Trade and Industry, Justin Njapou.
Planning Statistics and International Co-operation, Guy Darlan.
Civil Service, Labour and Social Security, Daniel Sehoulia.
Tourism, Water, Forests, Hunting and Fishing, Raymond Mbitikon.
Scientific and Technical Research, Jean-Claude Kazgui.
Energy and Mines, Lt. Michel Salle.
Information, Arts, Culture, Youth, Sport and National Organisations, Joaquim da Silva Nzengue.

The Republic lies just north of the Equator between the Cameroon Republic, the Republic of Chad, the southern part of Sudan and Zaire. The Republic has an area of 240,535 sq. miles, (622,984 sq. km.), and a population (1985 U.N. estimate) of 2,608,000.

On December 1, 1958, the French colony of Ubanghi Shari elected to remain within the French Community and adopted the title of the Central African Republic. It became fully independent on August 17, 1960. The first President of the Central African Republic, M. David Dacko, held office from 1960 until Jan. 1, 1966, when he was replaced by the then Col. Bokassa after a *coup d'état.* On Dec. 4, 1976, President Bokassa proclaimed himself Emperor and a new constitution (Parliamentary Monarchy) was introduced, the country being known as the Central African Empire. On Sept. 20, 1979, Emperor Bokassa was deposed by M. David Dacko in a bloodless *coup* and the country reverted to a Republic. President Dacko surrendered power on 1st September 1981 to army commander Gen. Andre Kolingba in a bloodless *coup.* On Sept. 21, 1985 President Kolingba dissolved the Military Committee for National Recovery (C.M.R.N.) and appointed a civilian-dominated cabinet. Moves towards democratisation have been made and on Nov. 21, 1986, a referendum was held whereby voters approved a new Constitution and the establishment of a one-party state. Legislative elections are to be held in the near future.

Economy.—A programme of economic reconstruction is under way, concentrating on agricultural production and private investment. Cotton, diamonds, coffee and timber are the major exports;

Trade with U.K.

	1985	1986
Imports from U.K.	£1,151,000	£787,000
Exports to U.K.	1,739,000	1,452,000

CAPITAL.—Bangui, near the border with Zaire, 473,817 (1984 est.).

FLAG.—Four horizontal stripes, blue, white, green, yellow, crossed by central vertical red stripe with a yellow five-pointed star in top left-hand corner.

NATIONAL DAY.—December 1.
British Ambassador, (resident at Yaoundé, Cameroon).

CHAD REPUBLIC
(Republique du Tchad)

Head of State, Hissène Habré, *took office* June 1982.

COUNCIL OF MINISTERS

President and Minister of Defence, Veterans and War Victims, Hissène Habré.
Minister of State, Djidingar Dono Ngardoum.
Foreign Affairs and Co-operation, Goura Lassou.
Interior, and Administrative Reform, Ibrahim Mahamat Itno.
Justice, Djibril Négué Djogo.

National Education, Mahamat Senoussir.
Finance and Data Processing, Mbailem Bana Ngarnyal.
Transport and Civil Aviation, Abderramane Ali Abdoul.
Civil Service, Rotouang Yoma.
Livestock and Water Resources, Taher Guinassou.
Agriculture and Rural Development, Yoyama Baniara.
Mines and Energy, Adoum Moussa Seif.
Public Health, Mahamat Nour Malaye.
Public Works, Housing & Town Planning, Moussa Kadam.
Social Affairs & Womens' Advancement, Mme. Yomite Romba.
Labour, Employment and Vocational Training, Odalbaye Naham.
Food, Security and Disaster Relief, Taher Abdeldjelil.
Post and Telecommunications, Assilec Halata.
Tourism and Environment, M'Bailaou Naimbaye Lossimian.
Planning (Minister Delegate at the Presidency), Mahamat Soumaila.
Culture, Youth and Sport, Djibrine Grinky.
Trade and Industry, Haroun Abdoulaye.
Presidential Advisor, Ouang Monching Homsala.

Situated in north-central Africa, the Chad Republic extends from 23° N. latitude to 7° N. latitude and is flanked by the Republics of Niger and Cameroon on the west, by Libya in the north, by the Sudan on the east and by the Central African Republic on the south. It has an area of 495,755 sq. miles, (1,284,000 sq. km.) and a population (1985 U.N. estimate) of 5,018,000.

Chad became a member state of the French Community on Nov. 28, 1958, and was proclaimed fully independent on August 11, 1960. On April 14, 1962, a new Constitution was adopted involving a presidential-type regime. This was suspended on April 13, 1975 when President Tombalbaye was killed in a military coup. The country was run by a Supreme Military Council, under General Felix Malloum until his overthrow in February 1979. A Transitional Government of National Unity, headed by Goukouni Oueddei, was replaced in June 1982 by the government of Hissène Habre. Forces commanded by Oueddei, and supported by Libyan troops, occupied the north of Chad until April 1987, when government-backed Chadian troops forced the Libyans to withdraw to the Aouzou Strip.

About 90 per cent of the workforce is occupied in agriculture, fishing and forestry. There is an oilfield in Kanem and salt is mined around Lake Chad, but the most important activities are cotton growing (mostly in the south) and animal husbandry (in central areas). Raw cotton and meat are the main exports.

Trade with U.K.

	1985	1986
Imports from U.K	£1,847,000	£1,250,000
Exports to U.K.	1,099,000	2,806,000

CAPITAL.—Ndjaména (formerly known as Fort Lamy) south of Lake Chad (402,000).
FLAG.—Vertical stripes, blue, yellow and red.
NATIONAL DAY.— April 13.
British Ambassador (resident in London).

CHILE
(República de Chile)

Head of State, Army Commander-in-Chief and President of the Republic, General Augusto Pinochet (Ugarte), *born*, November 25, 1915.

Junta Members, Adm. José T. Merino, C.-in-C. Navy; Gen. Fernando Matthei, C.-in-C. Air Force; Gen. Rudolfo Strange, Dir.-Gen. of Carabineros; Lt.-Gen. Humberto Gordon (Army).

CABINET
(as at June 30, 1987)

Foreign Affairs, Jaime del Valle Alliende.
Interior, Ricardo García.
Defence, Vice Adm. Patricio Carvajal.
Education, Sergio Gaete.
Mines, Samuel Lira.
Finance, Hernán Büchi.
Justice, Hugo Rosende.
Public Works, Brig.-Gen. Bruno Siebert.
Transport, Gen. Enrique Escobar.
Agriculture, Jorge Prado Aranguiz.
National Patrimony, Gen. René Peri Fagerstrom.
Labour and Social Security, Alfonso Márquez de la Plata.
Health, Winston Chinchon.
Housing, Miguel Angel Poduje.
Economy, Juan Carlos Delano.
Planning, Gen. Sergio Valenzuela.
Energy, Gen. Hernan Brady.
Secretary General of the Government, Francisco Javier Cuadra.

CHILEAN EMBASSY AND CONSULATE IN LONDON
12 Devonshire Street, W1N 2FS
[01–580 6392/4]

Ambassador Extraordinary and Plenipotentiary, His Excellency Mario Silva-Concha (1985).

A State of South America lying between the Andes and the shores of the South Pacific, Chile extends coastwise from just north of Arica to Cape Horn south, between lat. 17° 15′ and 55° 59′ S. and long. 66° 30′ and 75° 48′ W. Extreme length of the country is about 2,800 miles, with an average breadth, north of 41°, of 100 miles. The great chain of the Andes runs along its eastern limit, with a general elevation of 5,000 to 15,000 feet above the level of the sea; but numerous summits attain a greater height. The chain, however, lowers considerably towards its southern extremity. The Andes form a boundary with Argentina, and at the head of the pass where the international road from Chile to Argentina crosses the frontier, has been erected a statue of *Christ the Redeemer*, 26 feet high, made of bronze from old cannon, to commemorate the peaceful settlement of a boundary dispute in 1902. There are no rivers of great size, and none of them is of much service as a navigable highway. In the north the country is arid. The total area of the Republic is 292,258 sq. miles, (756,945 sq. km.), with a population (1985 U.N. estimate) of 12,074,000.

Among the island possessions of Chile are the *Juan Fernandez group* (3 islands) about 360 miles distant from Valparaiso. One of these islands is the reputed scene of Alexander Selkirk's (Robinson Crusoe) shipwreck. *Easter Island* (27° 8′ S. and 109° 28′ W.), about 2,000 miles distant in the South Pacific Ocean, contains stone platforms and hundreds of stone figures, the origin of which has not yet been determined. The area of the island is about 45 sq. miles, (116·5 sq. km.).

Chile is divided into 12 regions and the Metropolitan Area. The disputed boundary with Argentina in the Beagle Channel was settled by a treaty ratified in May 1985.

The Chilean population has four main sources: (a) indigenous Araucanian Indians, Fuegians, and Changos; (b) Spanish settlers and their descendants; (c) mixed Spanish Indians; and (d) European immigrants. Only the few remaining indigenous Indians and some originally Bolivian Indians in the north are racially separate. Following extensive intermarriage there is no effective distinction among the remainder.

Government.—Chile was discovered by Spanish adventurers in the 16th century and remained under Spanish rule until 1810, when a revolutionary war, culminating in the *Battle of Maipu* (April 5, 1818), achieved the independence of the nation.

At a general election held on Sept. 4, 1970, the Marxist candidate Dr. Allende was elected President by a narrow margin. After severe industrial unrest and widespread violent incidents, Allende was overthrown on September 11, 1973, in a *coup* carried out by leaders of the Armed Forces and National Police. President Allende was said to have committed suicide.

After a national plebiscite, the Constitution of 1925 was replaced early in 1981 and Gen. Pinochet was sworn in as President, to serve until 1989. Economically, the regime is pursuing a free-market economy and the level of inflation has been reduced, from 1,000 per cent in 1973 to about 31 per cent in 1985.

Production.—Cereals, legumes, sugar beet, vegetables, fruit, tobacco, hemp and vines are grown extensively (especially in the central zone) and livestock accounts for nearly 40 per cent of agricultural production. Sheep farming predominates in the extreme south (Province of Magallanes). There are large timber tracts in the central and southern zones of Chile, some types of which are exported, along with wood derivatives such as cellulose and pulp. Industrial-scale fishing, which exceeds 4 million tonnes p.a., makes Chile the third largest nation in terms of catch. The principal end product is fish meal.

The mineral wealth is considerable, the country being particularly rich in copper-ore, iron-ore and nitrate. Chile also produces iodine, manganese ore, coal, mercury, molybdenum, zinc, lead and a small quantity of gold. Uranium is also said to have been discovered in small quantities. The rainless north is the scene of the only commercial production of nitrate of soda (Chile saltpetre) from natural resources in the world. The country has also large deposits of high grade sulphur, but mostly around high extinct volcanoes in the Andes Cordillera, difficult of access. Oil was struck in Magallanes (Tierra del Fuego) in December, 1945, and oil and natural gas are produced in the Magallanes area from on- and off-shore wells. This domestic production, which covers approximately 50 per cent of total oil requirement, plus imported crude oil is refined at Concon and San Vicente in the central part of the country. There is a steel plant at Huachipato, near Concepción.

Production figures for 1985 were:

Copper (tonnes)	1,357,070
Potassium and sodium nitrate (tonnes)	785,400
Coal (tonnes)	1,367,665
Steel ingots (tonnes)	695,700
Crude oil (cu. metres)	2,074,400
Natural gas (cu. metres)	4,638,100

Industry is based on the processing of mineral, forestry, fish and agricultural products, and the manufacture of consumer goods.

Communications.—Chilean ships have a virtual monopoly in the coastwide trade, though, with the improvement of the roads, an increasing share of internal transportation is moving by road and rail. The Chilean mercantile marine numbers about 62 vessels (of over 100 tons gross) with a total deadweight tonnage of 841,796 (1984).

There are 6,575 miles of railway track. A metre-gauge line (the *Longitudinál*) runs from La Calera, just north of Santiago, to Iquique: however, road transport has caused a reduction in rail traffic along this route. The wide gauge railway runs from Valparaiso through La Calera, 60 miles inland, and after passing through Santiago ends at Puerto Montt.

With the completion of a section of 435 miles from Corumba, Brazil, to Santa Cruz, Bolivia, the Trans-Continental Line will link the Chilean Pacific port of Arica with Rio de Janeiro on the Atlantic. Another line from Antofagasta to Salta (Argentine) was opened in 1948. Further south, the Trans-Andine Railway connects Valparaiso on the Pacific with Buenos Aires, crossing the Andes at 11,500 ft. However services have now been suspended due to financial difficulties.

Chile is served by about 20 international airlines. The domestic traffic is carried by the State-owned Linea Aerea Nacional and the privately-owned LADECO, which also operate internationally, and smaller regional carriers.

Chile's road system is about 65,000 kilometres in length, but only an estimated 7,000 kilometres are first-class paved highways.

Defence.—Military service is compulsory, but not all those who are liable are required. Recruitment for the Navy is mostly voluntary, but there are some conscripts. The Navy consists of 1 cruiser, 10 destroyers, frigates and escorts, 6 patrol vessels and FPBs and 4 submarines. There is a support force of transports, tankers, 1 submarine depot ship and ancillary small craft. The strength of the Navy is 28,000 (3,000 conscripts) including men of the Marine Force. The Army's total strength is 53,000, which includes 3,000 officers and 30,000 conscripts (2 years). In addition there is a police force of "Carabineros" of 28,000 officers and men. The Air Force total strength is 15,000 with a strength of 120 aircraft.

Education.—Elementary education is free, and has been compulsory since 1920. There are 8 Universities (3 in Santiago, 2 in Valparaiso, 1 in Antofagasta, 1 in Concepción and 1 in Valdivia). The religion is Roman Catholic.

Language and Literature.—Spanish is the language of the country, with admixtures of local words of Indian origin. Recent efforts have reduced illiteracy and have thus afforded access to the literature of Spain, to supplement the vigorous national output. The Nobel Prize for Literature was awarded in 1945 to Señorita Gabriela Mistral, for Chilean verse and prose, and in 1971 to the poet Pablo Neruda. There are over 100 newspapers and a large number of periodicals.

FINANCE

	1984(p)
Total revenue	US$3,241·2 m.
Total expenditure	3,357·2 m.
(p) provisional.	

Foreign debt at December 31, 1985 was provisionally quoted at U.S. $21,000 million.

EXTERNAL TRADE
($U.S. ,000)

	1984	1985
Total imports	3,481,000	2,742,500
Total exports	3,657,500	3,795,700

Trade with U.K.

	1985	1986
Imports from U.K.	£73,914,000	£67,459,000
Exports to U.K.	134,750,000	128,007,000

The principal exports are metallic and non-metallic minerals (copper represented 46 per cent. of total export earnings in 1985), wood derivatives, some metal products, fish products, vegetables, fruit and wool. The principal imports are wheat, sugar and other food products, industrial raw materials, machinery, equipment and spares, oil fuels, lubricants and transportation equipment.

CAPITAL, Santiago, 4,132,293 (Greater Santiago), Other large towns are:—ΨValparaiso (500,000), Concepción (170,000), Temuco (110,000), ΨAntofagasta (110,000), Chillán (79,461), ΨTalcahuano (75,643), Talca (75,354); ΨValdivia (70,000), ΨIquique (50,000), ΨPunta Arenas (50,000). Punta Arenas on the Straits of Magellan, is the southernmost city in the world.

FLAG.—Two horizontal bands, white, red; in top sixth a white star on blue square, next staff.

NATIONAL DAY.—September 18 (National Anniversary).

BRITISH EMBASSY
Avenida La Concepción 177, Santiago 9
(Casilla 72-D)

Ambassador Extraordinary and Plenipotentiary, John Kyrle Hickman, C.M.G. (1977).

Counsellor, Head of Chancery and Consul-General, G. M. Baker.

Defence Attaché, Capt. T. Leland, R.N.

BRITISH CONSULAR OFFICES
There are British Consular Offices at *Santiago, Arica, Valparaiso* and *Punta Arenas.*

BRITISH COUNCIL
Cultural Attaché and British Council Representative, W. Campbell, Eliodoro Yañez 832, Santiago (Casilla 15-T). The Council supplies books to the libraries of the *Instituto Chileno-Britanico* in *Santiago, Viña del Mar/Valparaiso* and *Concepción.*

BRITISH-CHILEAN CHAMBER OF COMMERCE
Agustinas 972 O.F. 1011, Santiago
(*Postal Address,* Casilla 536, Santiago).

CHINA
(Zhonghua Renmin Gongheguo—
The People's Republic of China.)

President of the People's Republic of China, Li Xiannian, *elected* June 1983.

Vice President, Ulanhu.

Chairman of the Standing Committee of the Sixth National People's Congress, Peng Zhen.

Chairman of the Central Military Commission, Deng Xiaoping.

STATE COUNCIL
Premier, Zhao Ziyang.

Vice-Premiers, Wan Li; Yao Yilin; Li Peng; Tian Jiyun; Qiao Shi.

State Councillors, Chen Muhua; Gu Mu; Ji Pengfei; Kang Shien; Song Ping; Wang Bingqian; Wu Xueqian; Zhang Aiping; Song Jian; Fang Yi; Zhang Jingfu.

Ministers:

Agriculture, Animal Husbandry and Fisheries, He Kang.

Aviation Industry, Mo Wenxiang.

Chemical Industry, Qin Zhongda.

Civil Affairs, Cui Naifu.

Coal Industry, Yu Hongen.

Commerce, Lui Yi.

Communications, Qian Yongchang.

Culture, Wang Meng.

Economic Relations and Foreign Trade, Zheng Tuobin.

Electronics Industry, Li Tieying.

Finance, Wang Bingqian.

Foreign Affairs, Wu Xueqian.

Forestry, (vacant).

Geology and Minerals, Zhu Xun.

Justice, Zou Yu.

Labour and Personnel, Zhao Dongwan.

Light Industry, Zeng Xianlin.

Metallurgical Industry, Qi Yuanjing.

National Defence, Zhang Aiping.

Nuclear Industry, Jiang Xinxiong.

Petroleum Industry, Wang Tao.

Posts and Telecommunications, Yang Taifang.

Public Health, Chen Minzhang.

Public Security, Wang Fang.

Radio and Television, Ai Zhisheng.

Railways, Ding Guangen.

Space Industry, Li Xue.

State Security, Jia Chunwang.

Supervision, Wei Jianxing.

Textile Industry, Wu Wenying.

Urban and Rural Construction and Environmental Protection, Ye Rutang.

Water Conservancy and Power, Qian Zhengying.

MINISTERS IN CHARGE OF STATE COMMISSIONS
Economic, Lu Dong.

Education, Li Peng.

Family Planning, Wang Wei.

Machine Building Industry, Zou Jiahua.

Nationalities Affairs, Ismail Amat.

Physical Culture and Sports, Li Menghua.

Planning, Yao Yiling.

Restructuring the Economic System, Li Tieying.

Science, Technology and Industry for National Defence, Ding Henggao.

Scientific and Technological, Song Jian.

Auditor General, Lu Peijian.

Secretary-General, Chen Junsheng.

President of the People's Bank of China, Chen Muhua.

THE CHINESE COMMUNIST PARTY
General Secretary, Zhao Ziyang (*acting*).

The Politburo Standing Committee, Zhao Ziyang; Deng Xiaoping; Li Xiannian; Chen Yun; Hu Yaobang.

The Politburo of the Central Committee, Wan Li; Xi Zhongxun; Fang Yi; Deng Xiaoping; Yang Shangkun; Yang Dezhi; Yu Qiuli; Chen Yun; Zhao Ziyang; Hu Qiaomu; Hu Yaobang; Ni Zhifu; Peng Zhen; Tian Jiyun; Yao Yilin; Li Peng; Wu Xueqian; Hu Qili; Qiao Shi (*full members*); Qin Jiwei; Chen Muhua (*alternate members*).

The Secretariat of the Central Committee, Wan Li; Deng Liqun; Yu Qiuli; Chen Pixian; Hu Qili; Qiao Shi; Tian Jiyun; Li Peng; Hao Jianxiu; Wang Zhaoguo; Qiao Shi (*full members*).

The Advisory Commission, Deng Xiaoping (*Chairman*); Bo Yibo; Song Renqiong; Wang Zhen (*Vice Chairmen*).

The Discipline Inspection Commission, First Secretary, Chen Yun; Second Secretary, Wang Heshou; Standing Secretary, Han Guang.

Membership, 42,000,000.

EMBASSY IN LONDON
49–51 Portland Place, W1N 3AH
[01–636 9375]

Ambassador Extraordinary and Plenipotentiary, His Excellency Ji Chaozhu (1987).

AREA AND POPULATION.—The area of China is 3,705,408 sq. miles, (9,596,961 sq. km.). A nationwide census (the third) was held in July 1982, which recorded a total population of 1,008,175,288. A 1985 U.N. estimate gave the figure as 1,059,521,000. China is anxious to control the growth of the population and has introduced stringent policies intended to result in a population of 1,200 million by the year 2000. About 6 per cent of the population belong to around 55 ethnic minorities. Among the largest are the Zhuang of Guangxi, the Uygurs of Xinjiang, the Tibetans and the Mongols.

THE PROVINCES OF CHINA

1982 census results were:

Anhui	49,665,724
Fujian	25,931,106
Gansu	19,569,261
Guangdong	59,299,220
Guangxi Zhuang Autonomous Region	36,420,960
Guizhou	28,552,997
Hebei	53,005,875
Heilongjiang	32,665,546
Henan	74,422,739
Hubei	47,804,150
Hunan	54,008,851
Jiangsu	60,521,114
Jiangxi	33,184,827
Liaoning	35,721,693
Nei Monggol Autonomous Region	19,274,279
Ningxia Hui Autonomous Region	3,895,578
Peking	9,230,687
Qinghai	3,895,706
Shaanxi	28,904,423
Shandong	74,419,054
Shanghai	11,859,748
Shanxi	25,291,389
Sichuan	99,713,310
(Taiwan	18,270,749)
Tianjin	7,764,141
Tibet Autonomous Region	1,892,392
Xinjiang Uygur Autonomous Region	13,081,681
Yunnan	32,553,817
Zhejiang	38,884,603
Armed Forces	4,238,210

Xinjiang is the largest region or province in area (about one sixth of the whole area of China) and Sichuan the most populous.

Government.—On October 10, 1911, the party of reform forced the Imperial dynasty to a "voluntary" abdication, and a Republic was proclaimed at Wuchang.

On September 30, 1949, the Chinese People's Political Consultative Conference (C.P.P.C.C) met in Peking and appointed the National People's Government Council under the Chairmanship of Mao Zedong (Mao Tse-Tung). On October 1, Mao proclaimed the inauguration of the Chinese People's Republic.

The *régime* was recognized by all the Communist *bloc* countries in quick succession, and soon after by the Asian countries of the Commonwealth, the United Kingdom and by a number of other countries. Others, led by the United States, continued to recognize the Chiang Kai-shek *régime* on Taiwan as the rightful Government of China. In 1971 the People's Republic won acceptance into the United Nations on the expulsion of Taiwan. Since then many more countries have accorded recognition.

A new Constitution was adopted in December 1982, under which the National People's Congress is the highest organ of state power. It is elected for a term of five years and is supposed to hold one session a year. It is empowered to amend the Constitution, make laws, select the President and Vice-President and other leading officials of the state, approve the national economic plan, the state budget and the final state accounts, and to decide on questions of war and peace. The State Council is the highest organ of the state administration. It is composed of the Premier, the Vice Premiers, the State Councillors, heads of Ministries and Commissions, the Auditor General and the Secretary General. Command over the armed forces is vested in the Central Military Commission, of which Deng Xiaoping is the Chairman.

Deputies to congresses at the primary level are "directly elected" by the voters "through a secret ballot after democratic consultation". This is now being extended to county level. These Congresses elect the Deputies to the Congress at the next higher level. Deputies to the National People's Congress are elected by the People's Congresses of the provinces, autonomous regions and municipalities directly under the Central Government, and by the armed forces.

Local government is conducted through People's Governments at provincial, municipal and county levels. Autonomous regions, prefectures and counties exist for national minorities and are described as self-governing. The system prevailing is that found elsewhere, i.e. People's Congresses and People's Governments. Peking, Shanghai and Tianjin continue to come directly under the central government.

Following the deaths of Mao Zedong and Zhou Enlai in 1976 the disgraced Vice-Premier Deng Xiaoping was recalled. At the 11th Congress in 1977 Deng was elected Vice-Chairman and has since become the dominant force within the Party by eliminating leftist influence, rehabilitating fallen leaders and adjusting Maoist policies to meet the needs of a developing economy. Deng's policies were reaffirmed at the 12th Congress in 1982. The Congress also elected a new Party leadership dominated by Deng and his supporters. The post of Chairman of the Party was abolished. The Party leader now holds the post of General Secretary.

Armed Forces.—All three military arms in China are parts of the People's Liberation Army (P.L.A.) The size of this body has not been formally given, but it is estimated that China has approximately 3·5 million men under arms, with a further 12 million (or perhaps many more) reserves who take part in militia activities. In June 1985 a planned reduction of over 1 million in the course of a year was officially announced. In 1955 compulsory military service was introduced for all men between the ages of 18 and 40. This service was on a selective basis. The present length of service for those conscripted is three years in the Army, four years in the Air Force and five years in the Navy. With effect from June 1, 1965, the rank structure was abolished, together with all marks of distinction of branch of service. Both are expected to be reinstated.

China exploded her first experimental nuclear device on Oct. 16, 1964 and made further tests in 1965 and in May, Oct. and Dec., 1966. Her first hydrogen bomb was tested in June, 1967. Further tests of nuclear devices and hydrogen bombs have since been announced, though China no longer conducts atmospheric nuclear tests. China embarked on a programme of earth-satellite launchings in April 1970, the latest being made in January 1978. A long-range I.C.B.M. was tested in 1980, and a submarine-launched ballistic missile in 1982.

Religion.—The indigenous religions of China are Confucianism (which includes ancestor worship), Taoism (originally a philosophy rather than a religion) and, since its introduction in the first century of the Christian era, Buddhism. There are also Chinese Moslems (officially estimated at about 12 million) and Christians (unofficially estimated at about 50 million). Religious freedoms, severely curtailed during the Cultural Revolution, are reviving slightly under more liberal policies.

Education.—The Cultural Revolution caused considerable disruption to the educational system and since 1976 attempts have been made to raise academic standards. Primary education now lasts five years, and has a claimed enrolment of 146,000,000 pupils. Secondary education lasts five years (three years in Junior Middle School and two years in Senior Middle School). There were 47,000,000 Middle School pupils in 1986. The proportion of illiterates and semi-

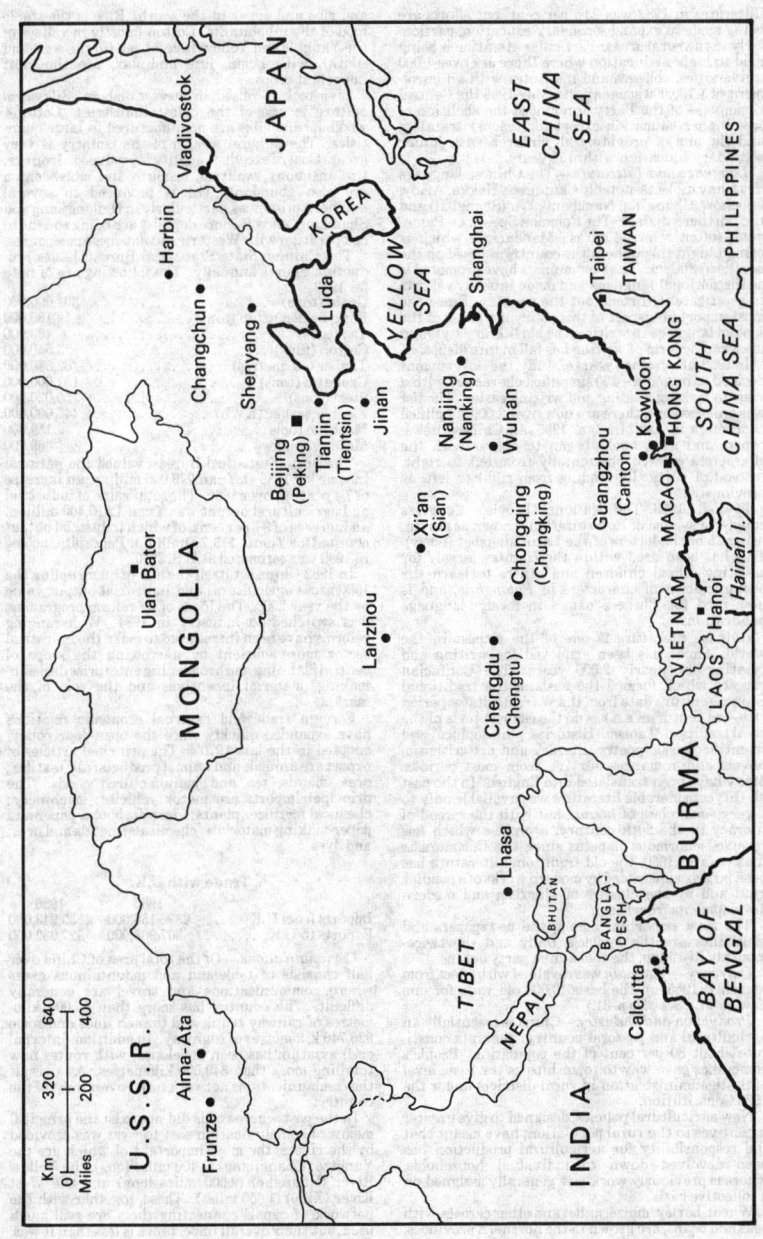

illiterates in 1982 was 23·5 per cent, but efforts are being made to expand secondary education, particularly in the rural areas. Particular attention is being paid to higher education where there are over 1,000 universities, colleges and institutes with an enrolment of 1,700,000 students. In May 1985 the Central Committee of the Party announced the abolition of free higher education except for teacher training, and the aim of providing all children with junior secondary education within 10 years.

Language and Literature.—The Chinese language has many dialects, notably Cantonese, Hakka, Amoy, Foochow, Changsha, Nanchang, Wu (Shanghai) and the northern dialect. The Common Speech or *Putonghua* (often referred to as "Mandarin") which is being taught throughout the country is based on the northern dialect. The Communists have promoted it as the national language and made intensive efforts to propagate it throughout the country. Since the most important aspect of this policy is the use of the spoken language in writing, the old literary style and ideographic form of writing has fallen into disuse.

In 1956, after some 4 years of study, the Government decided to introduce 230 simplified characters with a view to making reading and writing easier. The list was enlarged and there are now over 2,000 simplified characters in use. In Jan. 1956, all Chinese newspapers and most books began to appear with the characters printed horizontally from left to right, instead of vertically reading from right to left, as previously.

In Feb. 1958 The National People's Congress adopted a system of Romanization, known as pinyin, using 25 of the letters of the Latin alphabet (not v). This has been used within the country largely for assisting school children and others to learn the pronunciation of characters in *Putonghua*, and is now used for Chinese names in foreign-language publications.

Chinese literature is one of the richest in the world. Paper has been employed for writing and printing for nearly 2,000 years. The Confucian classics which formed the basis of the traditional Chinese culture date from the Warring States period (4th–3rd centuries B.C.) as do the earliest texts of the rival tradition, Taoism. Histories, philosophical and scientific works, poetry, literary and art criticism, novels and romances survive from most periods. Many have been translated into English. In the past all this considerable literature was available only to a very small class of *literati*, but with the spread of literacy in the 20th century, a process which has received enormous impetus since the Communists took over in 1950, the old traditional literature has been largely superseded by modern works of a popular kind and by the classics of Marxism and modern developments from them.

The most important among the newspapers and magazines are the People's Daily and the twice-monthly Red Flag, the communist party organs.

Currency.—The *yuan* was revalued with effect from March 1, 1955, on the basis 10,000 old *yuan* for one new *yuan*. (*See also* p. 81.)

Production and Industry.—China is essentially an agricultural and pastoral country: peasants constitute about 80 per cent of the population. People's communes gave way to townships as the basic level of State administration in rural districts under the 1982 Constitution.

New agricultural policies, designed to give greater incentives to the rural population, have meant that the responsibility for agricultural production has been devolved down to individual households, whereas previously work was generally assigned on a collective basis.

Wheat, barley, maize, millet and other cereals, with peas and beans, are grown in the northern provinces,

and rice and sugar in the south. Rice is the staple food of the inhabitants. Cotton (mostly in valleys of the Yangtze and Yellow Rivers), tea (in the west and south), with hemp, jute and flax, are the most important crops.

Livestock is raised in large numbers. Silkworm culture is one of the oldest industries. Cottons, woollens and silks are manufactured in large quantities. The mineral wealth of the country is very great. Coal of excellent quality is produced. Iron ore, tin, antimony, wolfram, bismuth and molybdenum are also abundant. Oil is produced in several northern provinces, particularly in Heilongjiang and Shandong, and off-shore deposits are being sought in co-operation with Western and Japanese companies.

The Chinese State Statistical Bureau issues production figures annually. The following are of note for 1986:

Grain (tons)	391,090,000
Pork, beef, mutton (tons)	19,180,000
Tea (tons)	463,000
Cotton (tons)	3,540,000
Timber (cu. metres)	62,880,000
Crude oil (tons)	131,000,000
Steel (tons)	50,020,000
Electric power (KWh)	445,000,000
Machine tools	159,000
Motor vehicles	369,000

The State Statistical Bureau valued the national income for 1986 at Yuan 779,000 million, an increase of 7·4 per cent over 1985. The total value of industrial and agricultural output was Yuan 1,510,400 million, an increase of 9·3 per cent, of which industrial output counted for Yuan 1,115,700 million. Per capita income in 1980 was estimated at U.S. $270.

In 1982 China set itself the aim of quadrupling the 1980 gross agricultural and industrial output value by the year 2000. The focus of its reform programme was switched to industry in 1984. Wide-ranging reforms have been introduced to make the industrial sector more efficient by narrowing the scope of central planning and broadening enterprise decision-making, material incentives and the role of the market.

Foreign trade and external economic relations have expanded quickly since the open-door policy, adopted in the late 1970's. The principal articles of export are animals and animal products; oil; textiles; ores, metals, tea and manufactured goods. The principal imports are motor vehicles; machinery; chemical fertilizer plants; aircraft; books, paper and paper-making materials; chemicals; metals and ores; and dyes.

Trade with U.K.

	1985	1986
Imports from U.K.	£396,156,000	£535,943,000
Exports to U.K.	307,963,000	327,032,000

Communications.—Of the total area of China over half consists of tableland and mountainous areas where communications and travel are generally difficult. The country has more than 52,000 kilometres of railway trunk and branch lines and some 926,746 kilometres of highway. In addition, internal civil aviation has been developed, with routes now totalling more than 340,000 kilometres. As a result the communications network now covers most of the country.

In the past where roads did not exist the principal means of communication east to west was provided by the rivers, the most important of which are the Yangtze (Changjiang) (3,400 miles long), the Yellow River (Huanghe) (2,600 miles long) and the West River (Xihe) (1,650 miles). These, together with the network of canals connecting them are still much used, but their overall importance is less than it was.

Coastal port facilities are being improved and the merchant fleet expanded. In the past 10 years great progress has been made in developing postal services and telecommunications. It is now claimed that 95 per cent of all rural communes are on the telephone and that postal routes reach practically every production brigade headquarters.

CAPITAL.—Beijing (Peking), population (1986), 5,860,000.

Population of major cities in 1985:

Shanghai....	6,980,000	Chengdu	2,580,000
Tianjin......	5,380,000	Xian	2,330,000
Shenyang ...	4,200,000	Nanjing	2,250,000
Wuhan......	3,400,000	Taiyuan.....	1,880,000
Guangzhou ..	3,290,000	Kunming	1,490,000
Harbin	2,630,000	Lanzhou	1,350,000

FLAG.—Red, with large gold five-point star and four small gold stars in crescent, all in upper quarter next staff.

NATIONAL DAY.—October 1 (Founding of People's Republic).

BRITISH EMBASSY
11 Guang Hua Lu,
Jian Guo Men Wai, Peking.

Ambassador, His Excellency Sir Richard Evans, K.C.M.G., K.C.V.O. (1984)
Counsellors, P. Thomson, C.V.O. (*Head of Chancery*); J. K. Chapman (*Commercial*); D. Marler, O.B.E. (*Cultural, and British Council Representative*).
Defence Attaché, Col. W. H. Clements.
First Secretaries, C. W. Parton; A. G. J. Insall, L.V.O.; R. F. Wye; D. Utley; T. A. Craig-Cameron; P. G. Wood.

There is also a Consulate-General in *Shanghai.*

TIBET

Tibet is a plateau seldom lower than 10,000 feet, which forms the northern frontier of India (boundary imperfectly demarcated), from Kashmir to Burma, but is separated therefrom by the Himalayas. The area is estimated at 463,000 square miles with a population of 1,892,392 in 1982.

From 1911 to 1950, Tibet was virtually an independent country though its status was never officially so recognized. In October 1950, Chinese Communist forces invaded Eastern Tibet. On May 23, 1951, an agreement was reached whereby the Chinese army was allowed entry into Tibet. A Communist military and administrative headquarters was set up. In 1954 the Government of India recognized that Tibet was an integral part of China, in return for the right to maintain trade and consular representation there.

A series of revolts against Chinese rule over several years culminated on March 17, 1959, in a rising in Lhasa. Heavy fighting continued for several days before the rebellion was suppressed by Chinese troops and military rule imposed. The Dalai Lama fled to India where he and his followers were granted political asylum. On March 28, 1959, the Chinese Premier issued an order dissolving the Tibetan Government. In its place the 16-member Preparatory Committee for the Tibetan Autonomous Region, originally set up in 1955 with the Dalai Lama as Chairman, was to administer Tibet under the State Council. The Preparatory Committee was to have the Panchen Lama as Acting Chairman and also to include 4 Chinese Officials. Elections were held to choose local People's Congresses in Tibet, thus indicating that the government organization there

no longer differed significantly from that of any ordinary province in China.

In December, 1964, the Dalai Lama was declared to be a traitor, and both he and the Panchen Lama were dismissed. The position of Acting Chairman of the Preparatory Committee was assumed by Ngapoi Ngawang Jigmi, who had long been the most prominent secular figure in Tibet. This move marked the end of the period of co-operation by the Chinese Government with the traditional religious authorities, and the eclipse of the latter. The Preparatory Committee completed its work with the setting up of Tibet as an Autonomous Region of China on Sept. 9, 1965. The Panchen Lama is now rehabilitated as an official of the C.P.P.C.C., and the Chinese have invited the Dalai Lama to return from exile.

TAIWAN
(Ta Chung-Hwa Min-Kwo)

President, Chiang Ching-kuo, *elected,* March, 1978, re-elected, March 21, 1984.
Vice-President, Lee Teng-hui, *elected,* March 22, 1984.
Premier, Yu Kuo-hwa (May 20, 1984).

An island of some 13,800 sq. miles, (35,742 sq. km.), in the China Sea, Taiwan, formerly Formosa, lies 90 miles east of the Chinese mainland in latitude 21° 45′N.—25° 38′N. The population (19,135,254 in 1985), is almost entirely Chinese in origin and includes about 2,000,000 mainlanders who came to the island with Chiang Kai-shek in 1947-49. The territories administered by the Chinese Nationalists include the Pescadores Islands (50 sq. miles), some 35 miles west of Taiwan, as well as Quemoy (68 sq. miles) and Matsu (11 sq. miles) which are only a few miles from the mainland. Settled for centuries by the Chinese, the island was administered by Japan from 1895 to 1945. General Chiang Kai-shek withdrew to Taiwan in 1949, towards the end of the war against the Communist *régime,* accompanied by 500,000 Nationalist troops, after which the territory continued under his presidency until his death on April 5, 1975. A mutual defence treaty between the United States and Taiwan Governments was signed in 1954 but this has been terminated as the United States recognized the People's Republic of China on January 1, 1979. Martial law was lifted in July 1987, after 38 years.

The eastern part of the main island is mountainous and forest covered. Mt. Morrison (Yu Shan) (13,035 ft.) and Mt. Sylvia (Tz'ukaoshan) (12,972 ft.) are the highest peaks. The western plains are watered by many rivers and the soil is very fertile, producing sugar, rice, sweet potatoes, tea, bananas, pineapples and tobacco. Coal, sulphur, iron, petroleum, copper and gold are mined. There are important fisheries. The principal seaports ΨKeelung and ΨKaohsiung are situated in the northern and southern sections of the island.

Trade with U.K.

	1985	1986
Imports from U.K......	£164,776,000	£192,492,000
Exports to U.K.	582,904,000	705,775,000

CAPITAL.—Taipei (population 1985, 2,507,620). Other towns are ΨKaohsiung (1,314,364); Tainan (572,590); Taichung (585,205); and ΨKeelung (345,392).

FLAG.—Red, with blue quarter at top next staff, bearing a twelve-point white sun.

NATIONAL DAY.—October 10.

COLOMBIA
(República de Colombia)

President, Dr. Virgilio Barco Vargas, *assumed office*, August 7, 1986.

CABINET

Interior, César Gaviria.
Foreign Affairs, Col. Julio Londoño.
Justice, Jose Manuel Arias.
Finance, Luis Fernando Alarcon.
Defence, Gen. Rafael Samudio.
Agriculture, Luis Guillermo Parra.
Economic Development, Fuad Char.
Mines and Energy, Guillermo Perry.
Education, Antonio Yepes.
Labour, Diego Younes.
Health, Jose Granada.
Communications, Fernando Cepeda.
Public Works, Luis Fernando Jaramillo.

COLOMBIAN EMBASSY IN LONDON
3 Hans Crescent, SW1X 0LR
[01–589 9177]

Ambassador Extraordinary and Plenipotentiary, new appointment awaited.
Chargé d'Affaires, Dr. Ricardo Samper.
There are *Consulates-General* in *London* and *Liverpool*.

The Republic of Colombia lies in the extreme north-west of South America, having a coastline on both the Caribbean Sea and Pacific Ocean. It is situated between 4° 13′ S. to 12° 30′ N. lat. and 68° to 79° W. long., with an area of 439,737 sq. miles (1,138,914 sq. km.), and a population (census 1985) of 26,525,670.

The country is divided into a narrow coastal strip in the west and extensive plains in the east by the Cordillera de los Andes. The Eastern Cordillera consists of a series of vast tablelands. This temperate region is the most densely peopled portion of the Republic. The principal rivers are the Magdalena, Guaviare, Cauca, Atrato, Caquetá, Putumayo and Patia.

Government.—The Colombian coast was visited in 1502 by Christopher Columbus, and in 1536 a Spanish expedition under Jiménez de Quesada penetrated to the interior and established on the site of the present capital a government which continued under Spanish rule until the revolt of the Spanish–American colonies of 1811–1824. In 1819 Simón Bolívar (1783–1831) established the Republic of Colombia, consisting of the territories now known as Colombia, Panama, Venezuela and Ecuador. In 1829–1830 Venezuela and Ecuador withdrew from the association of provinces, and in 1831 the remaining territories were formed into the Republic of New Granada. In 1858 the name was changed to the Granadine Confederation and in 1861 to the United States of Colombia. In 1866 the present title was adopted. In 1903 Panama seceded from Colombia, and became a separate Republic.

During the early nineteen-fifties Colombia suffered a period of virtual civil war between the supporters of the traditional political parties, the Conservatives and the Liberals. From 1957–1974 the country was governed under the "National Front" agreement with the presidency alternating between the two parties every four years and ministerial posts being shared equally by the parties. The alternation of the presidency was ended in 1974 and parity in appointments in 1978. Thereafter, the constitution lays down that Government portfolios and Administrative appointments shall be divided among the two majority parties in Congress in an "adequate and equitable" manner. However, after a General Election in 1986, the Liberal Party won a large majority. The Liberals are now known as the majority and the Conservatives, the Opposition.

Defence.—The Army peace effective strength is 60,000; war effective, approx. 400,000. The Navy, with 9,000 personnel including approximately 5,000 marines, has four corvettes, one destroyer, one frigate, one sail training ship, two submarines and a number of patrol boats. The Air Force, with 6,000 personnel, is equipped with Mirage fighters, 837B's, C47's and a number of support helicopters.

Production.—Much of Colombia's natural resources in coal, natural gas and hydro-electricity remain largely unexploited. Development of coal is being given priority but no new hydro projects are likely to be started for the next 4–5 years. Annual coal production is increasing from the recent peak of 5·5 million tonnes now that the Cerrejón Norte coalfield is being fully worked. This is essentially for export. Proven coal reserves stand at 16,000 million tonnes. Estimated natural gas reserves are 3,788,000 million cu. ft., with daily use at 381,772 million B.t.u. Proven crude oil reserves stand at 1,300 million barrels. Colombia is again a net exporter of oil. In 1987 exports should average 152,000 b.p.d. rising to 282,000 b.p.d. by 1989.

The hydrocarbon sector accounts for over half of the mining output with precious metals (gold, platinum and silver) and iron ore accounting for the remainder. Iron ore production in 1982 was 450,000 tons. Other mineral deposits include nickel (a processing plant started operating in 1982), bauxite, copper, gypsum, limestone, phosphates, sulphur and uranium. Colombia is also the world's largest producer of emeralds and has deposits of other precious and semi-precious stones.

Because of the range of climate, a wide variety of crops can be grown, and the country is close to self-sufficiency in food. The principal agriculture products are coffee (Colombia is second only to Brazil as the world's largest coffee producer) and other major cash crops are sugar, bananas, cut flowers and cotton. Cattle are raised in large numbers, and meat and cured skins and hides are also exported.

Industry.—The Government has encouraged diversification to reduce dependence on coffee as the major export and this has led to the growth of new export-orientated industries, particularly textiles, paper products and leather goods. Stimulus to the economy has been provided by large loans from the World Bank and IADB for project development, particularly in the power sector (in which hydroelectric projects have predominated) and for telecommunications.

Communications.—The massive ranges of the Andes make surface transport difficult therefore air transport is used extensively. There are daily passenger and cargo air services between Bogotá and all the principal towns, as well as daily services to the U.S.A., frequent services to other countries in South America, and to Europe. The "Atlantic Railway" links the departmental lines running down to the river, and completes the connection between Bogotá and Santa Marta. Although the railways generally are in a poor state there are about 2,600 miles of rail in use at present. The total road network (1985) consists of 105,201 km. of roads of all types, of which 21,800 km. are classified as main trunk and transversal roads.

Large appropriations have been made for modernization of the country's telecommunication system. There are 485 radio stations (1983) and two national television channels with several regional ones.

Language and Literature.—Spanish is the language of the country and education has been free since 1870. Great efforts have been made in reducing illiteracy and estimates (1980) put the literacy rate at 77·6 per cent of those over 10 years of age. In addition to the National University with headquarters at Bogotá there are 26 other universities. There is a flourishing press in urban areas and a national literature supplements the rich inheritance from the time of Spanish rule.

Roman Catholicism is the established religion.

TRADE

Colombia's principal export is still coffee although other products, principally bananas, cut flowers, clothing and textiles, ferro-nickel and coal are important exports.

	1984 $U.S.	1985 $U.S.
Total imports (c.i.f.)	4,492m.	4,688m.
Total exports (f.o.b.)	3,483m.	3,763m.

Trade with U.K.

	1985	1986
Imports from U.K.	£82,639,000	£58,084,000
Exports to U.K.	1120,486,000	94,112,000

CAPITAL, Bogotá, population (census, 1985) 3,967,988. Bogotá is an inland city in the Eastern Cordilleras, at an elevation of 8,600 to 9,000 ft. above sea level. Other centres are Medellin (1,500,000); Cali (1,350,000); Barranquilla (900,000); Ψ Cartagena (530,000); Bucaramanga (350,000); Buenaventura (130,000) is the country's major port.

FLAG.—Broad yellow band in upper half, surmounting equal bands of blue and red.

NATIONAL DAY.—July 20 (National Independence Day).

BRITISH EMBASSY
Calle 98, 9–03, 4th Floor, Bogotá (Apartado Aereo 4508, Bogotá)

Ambassador Extraordinary and Plenipotentiary, His Excellency Richard A. Neilson, C.M.G., L.V.O. (1987). There are British Consular Offices at *Bogotá, Barranquilla* and *Cali*.
British Council Representative, Dr. B. J. Lavercombe, Calle 87, No. 12–79, Bogotá D.E.

COLOMBO-BRITISH CHAMBER OF COMMERCE, Apartado Aereo 54 728, CVA. 13 No. 82-20, Bogotá D.E.

THE COMOROS
(Republique Fédérale Islamique des Comores)

Head of State, President Ahmed Abdallah Abdermane, *took office* May 1978; *elected*, Oct. 22, 1978; *re-elected*, Sept. 30, 1984.
Prime Minister, Ahmed Abdallah Abdermane.
Director of the President's Office, Ali Nassor.
Secretary General of the Presidency and Government, Said Ahmed Cheikh.

MINISTERS

Interior, Information and Press, Omar Tamou.
Vocational Training, Culture, Youth and Sports, Education, Salim Idarousse.
Production, Industry, Economy and Trade, Tourism and Crafts, Mohamed Ali.
Economics and Trade, Management, Control of State Companies, Commercial and Public Organisations, Said Ahmed Said Ali.
Environment, Urban Planning, Housing, Mikidache Abdourahim.
Foreign Affairs and Co-operation, Said Kafe.

Finance and Budget, Said Ahmed Ali.
Public Health and Population, Ali Hassan Ali.
Justice, Civil Service, Employment and Professional Training, Dr. Ben Ali Bacar.

The Comoro archipelago includes the islands of Great Comoro, Anjouan, Mayotte and Moheli and certain islets in the Indian Ocean with an area of 838 sq. miles (2,171 sq. km.) and a population (1985 U.N. estimate) of 444,000, most of whom are Muslim. The islanders voted for independence from France in December 1974 and three islands became independent on July 6, 1975. (The island of Mayotte was against independence and has remained under French administration.) On October 1, 1978 the three islands voted in a referendum to adopt a new Constitution which provides for a President, directly elected for a six year term. The Council of Government, consisting of a Prime Minister and up to nine other Ministers, is appointed by the President. There is a 39-member Federal Assembly elected for 5 years. Each island is administered by a Governor, assisted by up to four Commissioners whom he appoints, and has an elected Legislative Council.

The most important products are vanilla, copra, cloves and essential oils, which are the principal exports; cacao, sisal and coffee are also cultivated. Great Comoro is well forested and produces some timber.

Trade with U.K.

	1985	1986
Imports from U.K.	£603,000	£307,000
Exports to U.K.	234,000	—

CAPITAL.—Moroni, on Great Comoro. (Pop. 17,267).

FLAG.—Green ground with a crescent and four stars all in white in the half by the hoist.

NATIONAL DAY.—July 6. (Independence Day).

British Ambassador, (*resident in* Mauritius).

CONGO
(République Populaire du Congo)

President, Col. Denis Sassou-Nguesso, *appointed* 1979, *re-elected*, July 30, 1984 (also holds *Defence and Security Portfolios*).

COUNCIL OF MINISTERS

Prime Minister, A. E. Poungui.
Finance and Budget, I. Lekoundzou.
Administration and Local Government, R. D. Ngollo.
Rural Development, (vacant).
Foreign Affairs and Co-operation, A. Ndinga-Oba.
Transport and Civil Aviation, H. Monthault.
Public Works, Construction and Housing, B. Moundele-Ngóllo.
Plan and Economy, P. Moussa.
Secondary and Higher Education, Culture and Arts, J.-B. Tati-Loutard.
Industry and Fisheries, A. Noumazalaye.
Mines and Energy, R. Adada.
Scientific Research, C. Bouramoue.
Forestry, O. Douniam.
Employment, Social Security and Justice, D. Kimbembe.
Tourism, Leisure and Sport, J.-C. Ganga.
Trade, and Small and Medium Enterprises, A. Poaty-Souchlaty.
Primary Education and Literacy, P. D. Boussoukou Boumba.

Health and Social Affairs, B. Combo-Matsiona.
Information, Posts and Telecommunications, C.-G. Bembet.

The Republic lies on the Equator between Gabon on the west and Zaire on the east, the River Congo and its tributary the Ubanghi forming most of the eastern boundary of the state. The Congo has a short Atlantic coastline. Area of the Republic of Congo is 132,047 sq. miles (342,000 sq. km.), with a population of 1,740,000 (1985 U.N. estimate). Formerly the French colony of Middle Congo, it became a member state of the French Community on November 28, 1958, and was proclaimed fully independent on August 17, 1960.

In 1968, conduct of affairs was assumed by a National Council of Army officers. The Parti Congolais du Travail (*PCT*) was created by the Congress of December 29–31, 1969 and the People's Republic of the Congo was established. Under the present Constitution, approved by referendum in 1979, executive power is vested in the President, who is elected by the Congress of the P.C.T. (the only legal party). The Council of Ministers is appointed and led by the President.

Congo has its own oil deposits, producing about 6 million tonnes annually. It also produces lead, zinc and gold. The principal agricultural products are timber, cassava, sugar cane and yams. Imports are mainly of machinery.

Trade with U.K.

	1985	1986
Imports from U.K.	£12,111,986	£9,165,243
Exports to U.K.	2,819,004	2,443,964

Currency.—The currency is the CFA Franc.
CAPITAL.—Brazzaville (600,000); Ψ Pointe Noire (350,000).
FLAG.—Red, with hammer and sickle in wreath of leaves in top corner.
NATIONAL DAY.—August 15.

BRITISH EMBASSY

B.P. 1038, Brazzaville

Ambassador Extraordinary and Plenipotentiary, His Excellency Thomas Clive Almond (1987).

COSTA RICA
(República de Costa Rica)

President, Dr. Oscar Arias Sánchez, *took office,* May 8, 1986.

MINISTERS

Vice Presidente, J. Manuel Dengo; Sra. V Garrón de Doryan.
Minister for the Presidency, R. Arias Sánchez.
Foreign Affairs, R. Madrigal Nieto.
Interior and Police, G. Fernández Saborío.
Justice, L. Paulino Mora.
Public Security, H. Garrón Salazar.
Finance, Dr. F. Naranjo Villalobos.
Agriculture, A. Esquivel Volio.
Economy and Commerce, L. D. Escalante Vargus.
Industry, Energy and Mines, C. Chávez Zamora.
Public Works and Transport, Dr. G. Constenla Umaña.
Education, F. Antonio Pacheco.
Health, Dr. E. Mohs Villalta.
Culture, Youth and Sports, C. Echeverría Salgado.
Labour and Social Security, E. León Villalobos.
Planning, O. Solís Fallas.
Housing and Urban Development, Dr. F. Zumbado Jiménez.
Foreign Trade, Sra. M. Figueres de Jiménez.
Science and Technology, R. Zeledón Araya.

COSTA RICAN EMBASSY
93 Star Street, W2 1QF
[01–723 1772/9630]

Ambassador Extraordinary and Plenipotentiary, His Excellency Dr. Marcelo Martén (1986).

The Republic of Costa Rica in Central America extends across the isthmus between 8° 17′ and 11° 10′ N. lat. and from 82° 30′ to 85° 45′ W. long., has an area of 19,575 sq. miles (50,700 sq. km.), and a population (1985 Census) of 2,655,000. The population is basically of European stock, in which Costa Rica differs from most Latin American countries. The Republic lies between Nicaragua and Panama and between the Caribbean Sea and the Pacific Ocean. The coastal lowlands by the Caribbean Sea and Pacific

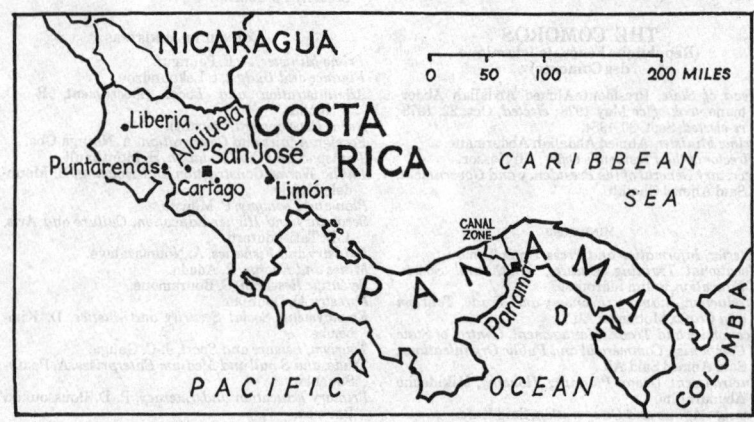

have a tropical climate but the interior plateau, with a mean elevation of 4,000 feet, enjoys a temperate climate.

For nearly three centuries (1530–1821) Costa Rica formed part of the Spanish-American dominions, the seat of government being at Cartago. In 1821 the country obtained its independence, although from 1824 to 1839 it was one of the United States of Central America.

On Dec. 1, 1948, the Army was abolished, the President declaring it unnecessary, as the country loved peace.

Economy.—Agriculture is the chief industry and the principal products are coffee, bananas, sugar and cattle (for meat), all of which are important exports. Other crops are cocoa, rice, maize, potatoes and hemp. Industrial activity is principally in the manufacturing sector and manufactured goods are the largest category of exports. The main goods are foodstuffs, textiles and clothing, plastic goods, pharmaceuticals, fertilizers and electrical equipment.

Communications.—The chief ports are Limón, on the Atlantic coast, through which passes most of the coffee exported, and Puntarenas and Golfito on the Pacific coast. A new Pacific port, Caldera, currently under construction with Japanese aid, is likely to divert traffic from Puntarenas within a few years. In 1981, 1,221 ships entered Costa Rican ports handling imports and exports of approximately 2,393,374 tons of goods. The railway system is nationalized. About 500 miles of railroad are open. LACSA is the national airline, operating flights throughout Central and South America, the Caribbean and U.S.A., besides internal flights to local airports by SANSA.

Language, etc.—Spanish is the language of the country. Education is compulsory and free. The literacy rate is the highest in Latin America.

FINANCE

	1981
	Colones
Revenue	12,355·2m.
Expenditure	12,423·2m.

Currency is the *colon* of 100 *centimos*.

TRADE

The chief exports were manufactured goods and other products, coffee, bananas, cocoa and sugar. The chief imports were machinery, including transport equipment, manufactures, chemicals, fuel and mineral oils and foodstuffs.

	1983	1984
Total imports	$987,826,445	$1,093,739,311
Total exports	$559,951,375	$1,006,389,617

Trade with U.K.

	1985	1986
Imports from U.K.	£14,413,000	£12,007,000
Exports to U.K.	22,646,000	30,318,000

CAPITAL.—San José pop. 890,434; Alajuela (427,962); Cartago (271,671); Heredia (197,575); ΨPuntarenas (265,883); ΨLimón (168,076); Guanacaste (195,208). (Populations shown are of provinces, cantons and districts).

FLAG.—Five horizontal bands, blue, white, red, white, blue (the red band twice the width of the others with emblem near staff).

NATIONAL DAY.—September 15.

BRITISH EMBASSY

Apartado 815, Edificio Centro Colon 1007, San José.

Ambassador Extraordinary and Plenipotentiary and Consul-General, His Excellency Michael Francis Daly (1986).

CÔTE D'IVOIRE
(République de Côte d'Ivoire)

President, Félix Houphouët-Boigny, *elected* for five years in 1960; *re-elected* 1965, 1970, 1975, 1980 and 1985.

CABINET

Ministers of State, A. Denise; M. Ekra; C. Alliali (*Justice*); M. S. Gnoleba (*Planning and Industry*); E. K. Boguinard (*Public Service*); L. N. P. Coulibaly (*Public Health and Population*); A. Thiam (*Information*); P. Gui Bibo (*Mining*); L. Diabaté (*Member of Political Bureau and of Social and Economic Advisory Board*).

Ministers, J. K. Banny (*Defence*); N. Nemin (*Justice*); S. Ake (*Foreign Affairs*); L. K. Koffi (*Interior*); A. Koné (*Economy and Finance*); D. B. Kanon (*Agriculture*); V. P. Lokrou (*Water and Forest Resources*); A. Koffi (*Public Works and Transport*); Dr. B. Keita (*National Education*); A. N'Diayé (*Scientific Research*); V. Bamba (*Construction and Urbanism*); V. Tieko Djédje (*Posts and Telecommunications*); A. Barry-Battesti (*Technical Education and Professional Training*); L. Dona-Folongo (*Information, Culture, Youth and Sport*); A. V. Bi Tra (*Labour*); Y. E. Angoran (*Mining*); Gen. O. N'daw (*Internal Security*); L. Fadika (*Navy*); G. Laubhouet (*Rural Development*); B. Ehui (*Industry*); A. Djédje (*Public Health and Population*); J. J. Béchio (*Commerce*); D. Sadia (*Tourism*); E. Brou (*National Assembly relations*); Y. Ouattara (*Social Affairs*); C. Gboho (*Animal Production*); O. Kouamé N'Guessan (*Education*); M. Kouamé Koffi (*Budget*); O. Diarra (*Planning*); H. Aka Anghi (*Betterment of Women*).

CÔTE D'IVOIRE EMBASSY IN LONDON
2 Upper Belgrave Street, SW1X 8BJ
[01–235 6991]

Ambassador Extraordinary and Plenipotentiary, His Excellency Mr. Theodore de Mel (1986).

First Counsellor, G. G. Ballou.

The Côte d'Ivoire is situated on the Gulf of Guinea between 5° and 10° N. and 3° and 8° W. and is flanked on the west by Guinea and Liberia, on the north by Mali and Burkina and on the east by Ghana. It has an area of 124,503 sq. miles (322,463 sq. km.)—tropical rain forest in the southern half and savannah in the northern—and a population of 10,056,000 (1985 estimate) divided into a large number of ethnic and tribal groups.

Although French contact was made in the first half of the 19th century, the Côte d'Ivoire became a Colony only in 1893 and was finally pacified in 1912. It decided on December 5, 1958 to remain an autonomous republic within the French Community; full independence outside the Community was proclaimed on August 7, 1960. Special agreements with France, covering financial and cultural matters, technical assistance, defence, etc., were signed in Paris on April 24, 1961. The official language is French.

The Côte d'Ivoire has a presidential system of government modelled on that of the United States and the French Fifth Republic. The single Chamber National Assembly of 175 members was elected in 1985. The defence of the Constitution which was promulgated on Nov. 3, 1960, is vested in a Supreme Court.

Finance.—The unit of currency of the Côte d'Ivoire is the *Franc CFA*.

BUDGET

	1986
Current Expenditure	CFA433,620m.
Investment and Equipment	115,740m.

Trade.—The principal exports are coffee, cocoa, timber, palm oil, pineapples, bananas, and cotton. Diamonds are exported. There are a few deposits of minerals including manganese and iron.

TRADE

	1984	1985
Imports	CFA658,569m.	CFA772,987m.
Exorts	1,184,347m.	1,318,059m.

Trade with U.K.

	1985	1986
Imports from U.K..	£29,514,000	£34,270,000
Exports to U.K. ...	116,699,000	117,058,000

CAPITAL, ΨAbidjan (population, 2,000,000) which is also the main port. In March 1983 the National Assembly ratified a decision to transfer the political and administrative capital from Abidjan to Yamoussoukro, but the date of the transfer is not yet known.

FLAG.—3 vertical stripes, orange, white and green.

NATIONAL DAY.—December 7.

BRITISH EMBASSY
Immeuble Les Harmonies, 01 B.P. 2581,
Abidjan 01.

Ambassador Extraordinary and Plenipotentiary, new appointment awaited.

Head of Chancery and Consul, P. W. Chandley.

First Secretary (Education) and British Council Representative, C. Hickey.

BRITISH CHAMBER OF COMMERCE, c/o Price Waterhouse & Co., Boite Postale 2921, Abidjan 01.

CUBA
(Republica de Cuba)

President of Council of State and Head of Government, Dr. Fidel Castro Ruz, *appointed* Nov. 2, 1976.

COUNCIL OF STATE

President, Dr. Fidel Castro Ruz.

First Vice-President, Raúl Castro Ruz.

Vice-Presidents, Juan Almeida Bosque; Osmany Cienfuegos Gorriarán; José Ramón Machado Ventura; Pedro Miret Prieto; Carlos Rafael Rodríguez.

Secretary, José M. Miyar Barrueco.

COUNCIL OF MINISTERS

President, Dr. Fidel Castro Ruz.

First Vice-President, Raúl Castro Ruz.

Vice-Presidents, Dr. Carlos Rafael Rodríguez; Pedro Miret Prieto; Diocles Torralba González; José Ramón Fernández Alvarez; José A. López Moreno; Osmany Cienfuegos Gorriarán; Antonio Esquivel Yedra; Raul Cabrera Nunez; Joel Domenech Benítez; Antonio Rodriguez Maurell.

Secretary, Osmany Cienfuegos Gorriarán.

Presidents of State Committees: Jose A. Lopez Moreno (*Central Planning Board*); Hector Rodriguez Llompart (*National Bank*); Levi Farah Balmaseda (*Construction*); Ernesto Melendez Bachs (*Economic Co-operation*); Rodrigo J. Garcia Leon (*Finance*); Francisco Linares Calvo (*Labour and Social Security*); Sonia Rodriguez Cardona (*Material and Technical Supply*); Arturo Guzman Pascual (*Prices*); Ramón Darias Rodés (*Standardization*); Fidel Emilio Vascos Gonzalez (*Statistics*).

Ministers, Adolfo Diaz Suarez (*Agriculture*); Marcos J. Portal Leon (*Basic Industry*); Manuel Castillo Rabasa (*Communications*); Raul Cabrera Nunez

(*Construction*); Levi Farah Balmaseda (*Construction Materials Industry*); Armando Enrique Hart Davalos (*Culture*); Manuel Vila Sosa (*Domestic Trade*); José Ramon Fernandez Alvarez (*Education*); Jorge A. Fernandez Cuervo-Vinent (*Fishing*); Alejandro Roca Iglesias (*Food Industry*); Isidoro Octavio Malmierca Peoli (*Foreign Relations*); Ricardo Cabrisas Ruiz (*Foreign Trade*); Fernando Vecino Alegret (*Higher Education*); José Abrantes Fernández (*Interior*); Juan Escalona Reguera (*Justice*); Antonio Esquivel Yedra (*Light Industry*); Julio Jesus Teja Pérez (*Public Health*); Raul Castro Ruz (*Revolutionary Armed Forces*); Marcos Lage Coello (*Steel Industry*); Juan Ramon Herrera Machado (*Sugar Industry*); Diocles Torralba Gonzalez (*Transport*); Jose Alberto Naranjo Morales (*Minister without Portfolio*).

CUBAN EMBASSY IN LONDON
167 High Holborn, W.C.1
[01–240 2488]

Ambassador Extraordinary and Plenipotentiary, His Excellency Dr. Oscar Fernández-Mell (1987).

Cuba, the largest island in the Caribbean, lies between 74° and 85° W. long., and 19° and 23° N. lat., with a total area of 42,804 sq. miles (110,861 sq. km.). The country is divided into 14 provinces. The estimated total population in 1986 was 10,200,000.

The island of Cuba was visited by Christopher Columbus during his first voyage, on Oct. 27, 1492, and was then believed to be part of the western mainland of India. Early in the 16th century the island was conquered by the Spanish, to be used later as a base of operations for the conquest of Mexico and Central America, and for almost four centuries Cuba remained under a Spanish Captain-General. [The island was under British rule for one year, 1762–1763, when it was returned to Spain in exchange for Florida.] Separatist agitation culminated in the closing years of the 19th century in open warfare. In 1898 the government of the United States intervened and on April 20, 1898, demanded the evacuation of Cuba by the Spanish forces. A short Spanish-American war led to the abandonment of the island, which was occupied by U.S. troops. Cuba was under U.S. military rule from Jan. 1, 1899 until May 20, 1902, when an autonomous government was inaugurated with an elected President, and a legislature of two houses. The island was, however, again the prey of revolution from Aug. to Sept., 1906, when the U.S. Government resumed control. On Jan. 28, 1909, a republican government was again inaugurated.

A revolution led by Dr. Fidel Castro overthrew the Government of General Batista on January 1, 1959. In October, 1965, the Communist Party of Cuba was formed to succeed the United Party of the Socialist Revolution. It is the only authorized political party. The new Socialist Constitution came into force on February 24, 1976 and indirect elections to the National Assembly of People's Power were subsequently held.

Production.—The Government has carried out programmes of land and urban reform and of nationalization; by March, 1968, virtually all industrial and commercial enterprises were nationalized. About 85 per cent of the cultivated land is in state farms or State-controlled co-operatives. Private smallholders, who own the remainder, have to sell all their produce to the state.

Although efforts are being made to diversify the economy, sugar is still its mainstay and principal source of foreign exchange. In 1985–86 the harvest was 7·1 million tons. Cuba's other main exports are oil, nickel, seafood, citrus fruits, tobacco and rum.

Despite increased trade with Western Europe and Japan, the Communist countries, particularly the

Soviet Union, form Cuba's main trading partners, covering about 86 per cent of imports and exports. In addition, the U.S.S.R. offers substantial aid through a system of subsidies which has recently been estimated to amount to $4,500 million.

There are 12,700 kms. of railway track, of which 5,000 kms. are in public service. In 1986 there were 13,247 kms. of road. At present scheduled international air services run to North, Central and South American countries and Europe.

Language and Literature.—Spanish is the language of the island. English, formerly widely understood, is now spoken less. Education is compulsory and free. In 1964 illiteracy was officially declared to be completely eliminated. The press and broadcasting and television are under the control of the Government.

	1985	1986
	Pesos, million	
Imports	7,983·2	7,569·0
Exports	5,983·0	5,325·0

Trade with U.K.

	1985	1986
Imports from U.K.	£59,332,000	£58,760,000
Exports to U.K.	7,273,000	8,550,000

CAPITAL.—ΨHavana (pop., est. 1986), 2,100,000; other towns are ΨSantiago (429,800), Santa Clara (198,800), Camagüey (279,800), Holguín (254,300), and ΨCienfuegos (124,600).

FLAG.—Five horizontal bands, blue and white (blue at top and bottom) with red triangle, close to staff, charged with 5-point star.

NATIONAL DAY.—January 1 (Day of Liberation).

BRITISH EMBASSY

Edificio Bolívar, Cárcel 101–103
e Morro y Prado, Apartado 1069, Havana.

Ambassador Extraordinary and Plenipotentiary, His Excellency Andrew Eustace Palmer, C.V.O., C.M.G. (1986).
Counsellor, A. R. F. Burgess, C.V.O. (*Head of Chancery*).
First Secretary, G. Livesey, M.B.E. (*Commercial and H.M. Consul*).

CZECHOSLOVAKIA
(Československá Socialistická Republika)

President, Gustáv Husák, *born* Jan. 10, 1913; *elected* May 29, 1975, *re-elected*, May, 1980, 1985.

Federal Government

Prime Minister, Lubomír Štrougal.
First Deputy Prime Minister, Rudolf Rohlíček.
Deputy Prime Ministers, Ladislav Adamec; Peter Colotka; Ladislav Gerle; Pavel Hrivnák; Karol Laco; Matej Lúčan; Svatopluk Potač; Jaromír Obzina; Miroslav Toman.

Ministers

Agriculture and Food, Miroslav Toman.
Finance, Jaromír Zák.
Foreign Affairs, Bohuslav Chňoupek.
Foreign Trade, Bohumil Urban.
Fuel and Power, Vlastimil Ehrenberger.
Interior, Vratislav Vajnar.
Labour and Social Affairs, Miroslav Boďa.
Metallurgy and Heavy Engineering, Eduard Saul.
National Defence, Col. Gen. Milan Václavík.
Communications, Jíří Jíra.
Transport, Vladimir Blažek.
People's Control, František Ondřich.
Prices, Michal Sabolčík.
General Engineering, Ladislav Luhový.

Electrical Engineering, Milan Kubat.
Chairman of State Planning Commission, Svatopluk Potáč.

Prime Minister of the Czech Socialist Republic, Ladislav Adamec.
Prime Minister of the Slovak Socialist Republic, Dr. Peter Colotka.

CZECHOSLOVAK COMMUNIST PARTY

Presidium of the Central Committee, G. Husák; L. Adamec; V. Bilak; P. Colotka; K. Hoffman; A. Indra; M. Jakeš; A. Kapek; J. Kempný; J. Lenárt; L. Štrougal (*full members*); M. Hruškovič; J. Fojtik; J. Haman; V. Herman; I. Janák; F. Pitra (*candidate members*).
Secretariat of the Central Committee, Gustáv Husák (*General Secretary*); M. Jakeš; M. Beňo; J. Haman; V. Bilak; J. Fojtik; J. Havlín; J. Poledník; F. Pitra (*secretaries*); M. Kabrhelová; Z. Hoření; M. Zavadil; K. Hoffman (*members*).

CZECHOSLOVAK EMBASSY

25 Kensington Palace Gardens, W8 4QY
[01–229 1255]

Ambassador Extraordinary and Plenipotentiary, His Excellency Jan Fidler (1986).
Counsellor, R. Hronek.
Commercial Counsellor, S. Žiak.
Military and Air Attaché, Col. Jaromír Široký.
Commercial Attachés, J. Slánský; J. Navara.
Assistant Military and Air Attaché, Maj. B. Kramář.
Press Secretary, J. Pavlíček.

Area and Population.—Czechoslovakia, formerly part of the Austro-Hungarian Empire, declared its independence on Oct. 28, 1918 (Czechoslovak Independence Day). It has an area of 49,370 sq. miles (127,869 sq. km.). The population of Czechoslovakia (1985 U.N. estimate) was 15,500,000.

Government.—The Communist Party came to power in Czechoslovakia in February, 1948, and Communist control of the country is now unqualified. On July 11, 1960, a new constitution was proclaimed, replacing that of 1948 and the official title of the State was accordingly changed to "The Czechoslovak Socialist Republic".

In January, 1968, pressures for reform of the system led to the proposal of new legislation, which envisaged the democratisation of the country's political life, greater guarantees of fundamental liberties and the establishment of a federal system.

The implications for the internal development of the other communist regimes in Eastern Europe and the Soviet Union, as well as for the system of alliances among these countries, alarmed the Soviet Union. On the night of August 20, Czechoslovakia was invaded by Soviet, Polish, East German, Hungarian and Bulgarian troops, the capital and all major towns being occupied. The Czechoslovak leadership was forced to modify its policies and to legalise the presence of Soviet troops on Czechoslovak territory. With the exception of the Federal system of government, the reforms of 1968 were abandoned when Gustáv Husák became leader of the Communist party in April 1969.

Czechoslovakia now consists of the Czech Socialist Republic and the Slovak Socialist Republic, each of which has its own government responsible to its legislative body—the National Council. Areas such as the constitution, defence, foreign affairs, state material reserves and currency are the responsibility of the Federal Administration. The Federal Government is responsible to the Federal Assembly, which is composed of two Chambers, the Chamber of the People, whose deputies are elected throughout the Federation, and the Chamber of the Nations, consisting of an equal number of Czech and Slovak Deputies.

The federal system was not extended to the organization of the Communist Party.

The Economic System.—Under the present political system industry is state-owned, and nearly all agricultural land is cultivated by state or co-operative farms. Economic planning is centralized, and state economic plans have the force of law. In Jan. 1987 a programme of "reconstruction" was announced, aimed at increasing the efficiency of the economy by a measure of decentralization and relaxation of controls.

Czechoslovakia is not rich in minerals, although significant quantities of coal, brown coal and lignite are mined. Principal agricultural products are sugarbeet, potatoes and cereal crops; the timber industry is also very important. The country has long been highly industrialized, and machinery, industrial consumer goods and raw materials are major exports. The 8th Five Year Plan (1986–90) aims to raise national income by 18–19 per cent over the five years.

Language and Literature.—Czech and Slovak are the official languages, each having its own literature. The Reformation gave a wide-spread impulse to Czech literature, the writings of Jan Hus (martyred in 1415 as a religious and social reformer) familiarizing the people with Wyclif's teaching. This impulse endured to the close of the 17th century when Jan Amos Komensky or Comenius (1592–1670) was expelled from the country. Under Austrian rule and with the persistent pursuit of Germanization, there was a period of stagnation until the national revival in the first half of the 19th century. Authors of international reputation include Jaroslav Hašek (1883–1923), Jaroslav Seifert (1901–1986, Nobel Prize for Literature, 1985), Václav Havel (b. 1936) and Milan Kundera (b. 1929). Many of the best Czechoslovak authors are either in exile or in disfavour at home.

Education.—Education is compulsory and free for all children from the ages of 6 to 16. The number of pupils in basic nine-year schools is 1,992,000 (1983). There are 175,198 students in the secondary grammar schools and the number given for technical schools of all kinds is 290,038. There are five universities in Czechoslovakia of which the most famous is Charles University in Prague (founded 1348), the others being situated at Bratislava, Brno, Olomouc and Košice. In addition there are a considerable number of other institutions of university standing, technical colleges, agricultural colleges, etc.

Finance.—The Czechoslovak currency is the Czechoslovak *Koruna* (*Kčs* = Czechoslovak crown) of 100 *heller*.

Trade with U.K.

	1985	1986
Imports from U.K.	£100,452,000	£108,836,000
Exports to U.K.	120,017,000	125,366,000

CAPITAL.—Prague (Praha), on the Vltava (Moldau), the former capital of Bohemia with a population (1985) of 1,190,576. Other towns are Brno (Brünn), capital of Moravia (381,000), Bratislava (Pressburg), capital of Slovakia (401,000), Ostrava (324,000), Košice (214,000) and Plzen (Pilsen) (174,000).

FLAG.—Two equal horizontal stripes, white (above) and red; a blue triangle next to staff.

NATIONAL DAY.—May 9.

BRITISH EMBASSY
Thunovská 14, 11800 Prague 1.

Ambassador Extraordinary and Plenipotentiary, His Excellency Stephen Jeremy Barrett, C.M.G.
Counsellor, J. M. MacGregor (*Head of Chancery*).
Defence and Military Attaché, Col. R. J. M. Drummond, O.B.E.
Air Attaché, Wing-Cdr. C. A. S. Maynard.
Cultural Attaché, J. R. Potts (*British Council Representative*).

DENMARK
(Kongeriget Danmark)

Queen, Margrethe II, eldest daughter of King Frederik IX, *born* April 16, 1940, *succeeded* Jan. 14, 1972, *married* June 10, 1967, Count Henri de Monpezat (Prince Henrik of Denmark) and *has issue* Crown Prince Frederik *born* May 26, 1968; and Prince Joachim, *born* June 7, 1969.

CABINET
(as at end July 1987)

Prime Minister, Poul Schlüter (*C*).
Finance Minister, Palle Simonsen (*C*).
Foreign Affairs, Uffe Ellemann-Jensen (*V*).
Environment and Nordic Affairs, Christian Christensen (*Ch.P.*).
Ecclesiastical Affairs, Mette Madsen (*V*).
Greenland, Tom Høyem (*C.D.*)*.
Culture, Hans Peter Clausen (*C*)*.
Social Affairs, Mimi Stilling Jakobsen (*C.D.*).
Interior, Knud Enggaard (*V*).
Justice, Erik Ninn-Hansen (*C*).
Agriculture, Britta Schall-Holberg (*V*).
Fisheries, Lars P. Gammelgaard (*C*).
Education, Bertel Haarder (*V*).
Economic Affairs, Anders Andersen (*V*)*.
Taxation, Dr. Isi Foighel (*C*).
Defence, Hans Engell (*C*).
Labour, Henning Dyremose (*C*)*
Industry, Nils Wilhjelm (*C*)*.
Housing, Thor Pedersen (*V*).
Transport and Public Works, Frode Noer Christensen.
Energy, Svend Erik Hovmand (*V*).
* Not a member of the folketing.
V, Venstre (Liberals); *C,* Conservatives; *C.D.,* Centre Democrats; *Ch.P.,* Christain Peoples.
A General Election is to be held on Sept. 8, 1987.

ROYAL DANISH EMBASSY IN LONDON
55 Sloane Street, SW1X 9SR
[01–235 1255]

Ambassador Extraordinary and Plenipotentiary, His Excellency Peter Dyvig (1986).
Minister Counsellors, P. Essemann (*Commercial*); J. Anker Nielsen (*Press and Culture*).

Counsellor, Per Poulsen-Hansen (*Economic and Consular Affairs*).
Defence Attaché, Col. F. Tingleff.

Area and Population.—A Kingdom of Northern Europe, consisting of the islands of Zeeland, Funen, Lolland, etc., the peninsula of Jutland, and the outlying island of Bornholm in the Baltic, the Faroes and Greenland. Denmark is situated between 54° 34′–57° 45′ N. lat., 8° 5′–15° E. 12′ long., with an area of 16,629 sq. miles (43,069 sq. km.), and a population estimated (1987) of 5,124,794.

Government.—Under the Constitution of the Kingdom of Denmark Act of June 5, 1953, the legislature consists of one chamber, the *Folketing*, of not more than 179 members, including 2 for the Faröes and 2 for Greenland. The voting age is 18.

The Social Democrat Government of Mr. Jørgensen, formed in January 1982, resigned from office in early September 1982 after failing to obtain approval of Budget proposals and a four-party non-Socialist coalition government was formed, which continued unchanged after an election on January 10, 1984.

Education is free and compulsory. Special schools are numerous, commercial, technical and agricultural predominating. There are Universities at Copenhagen (founded in 1479), Aarhus (1933), Odense (1966), Roskilde (1972) and Aalborg (1974). A further University at Esbjerg is planned.

Language and Literature.—The Danish language is akin to Swedish and Norwegian. Danish literature, ancient and modern, embraces all forms of expression, familiar names being Hans Christian Andersen (1805–1875), Sören Kierkegaard (1813–1855) and Karen Blixen (1885–1962). Some 48 newspapers are published in Denmark; 10 daily papers are published in Copenhagen.

Production and Industry.—Of the labour force, in 1985, 6·9 per cent was engaged in agriculture, fishing, forestry, etc.; 27·3 per cent. in manufacturing, building and construction; 11·3 per cent. in commerce and 53·7 per cent. in administration, transport, financial services, the liberal professions, etc. The chief agricultural products are pigs, cattle, dairy products, poultry and eggs, seeds, cereals and sugar beet; manufactures are mostly based on imported raw material but there are also considerable imports of finished goods.

Communications.—Mercantile marine (ships above 100 gross tonnage) at end of 1985, totalled 598 ships, with a gross tonnage of 4,339,757. In 1984 there was 2,471 km. of railway.

FINANCE (BUDGET ESTIMATES)

	1985	1986
Revenue	*Kr.* 204,100m.	*Kr.* 185,955m.
Expenditure	240,600m.	185,437m.

Denmark's balance of payments on current account showed a deficit for 1986 of *Kr.*34,545 million (1985, *Kr.* 28,400 million).

MERCHANDISE TRADE

The principal imports are petroleum and its products, machinery, raw materials, vehicles and textile products. The chief exports are agricultural and dairy products and machinery.

	1985	1986
	Kr. million	
Total Imports	191,371	185,955
Total Exports	179,339	185,437

Trade with U.K.

	1985	1986
Imports from U.K.	£1,371,556,000	£1,211,637,000
Exports to U.K.	1,715,233,000	1,752,174,000

CAPITAL.—ΨCopenhagen, pop. (1987), 469,706; Greater Copenhagen, 1,716,237. Other centres are: Ψ Aarhus, 255,932; Ψ Odense 173,331; Ψ Aalborg, 154,853; Ψ Esbjerg, 80,825; Ψ Randers, 61,094; Helsingør, 56,618; Ψ Kolding, 57,148; Ψ Horsens, 54,676; Roskilde, 48,862; Ψ Vejle, 50,492; Ψ Fredericia, 45,935.

FLAG.—Red, with white cross.

NATIONAL DAY.—April 16 (The Queen's Birthday).

BRITISH EMBASSY

36–40 Kastelsvej, DK-2100 Copenhagen.

Ambassador Extraordinary and Plenipotentiary, His Excellency Peter William Unwin, C.M.G. (1986).
Counsellors, J. W. Hodge (*Head of Chancery*); P. Longworth (*Commercial*).
Defence Attaché, Cmdr. T. Goetz, R.N.
There are Consulates at *Aabenraa, Aalborg, Aarhus, Esbjerg, Fredericia, Odense* and at *Tórshavn* (Faröe Islands).

British Council Representative and Cultural Attaché, J. A. A. H. Moore, Møntergade 1, Copenhagen.

Outlying Parts of the Kingdom

THE FARÖES, or Sheep Islands (540 sq. miles; 1,399 sq. km.; pop. (1985) 46,000), capital, Tórshavn, are governed by a *Lagting* of 26 members, a *Landsstyre* of 4 members which deals with special Faröes affairs, and send 2 representatives to the *Folketing* at Copenhagen. On Sept. 14, 1946, the *Lagting*, with the consent of the Danish Government, for its own guidance held a plebiscite on the Faröes. About one-third of the electors did not, however, take part in the voting: of the rest a little more than half the votes cast were in favour of separation from Denmark and the establishment of a republic. At subsequent general election for the *Lagting* a great majority voted in favour of remaining part of the Kingdom of Denmark with a certain measure of home rule and in 1948 the Faröes received this. The Faröes are not part of the E.C.
Prime Minister, Atli Dam.

GREENLAND (ice-free portion about 132,000 sq. m., total area about 840,000 sq. m., population (1985) 52,940) is divided into 3 provinces (West, North and East). Greenland (capital, Nuuk (Godthåb)) has a *Landsraad* of 17 members and sends 2 representatives to the *Folketing* at Copenhagen. Greenland attained a status of internal autonomy on May 1, 1979. The trade of Greenland is mainly under the management of the Royal Greenland Trade Department. Following a plebiscite Greenland negotiated its withdrawal from the E.C., but without discontinuing relations with Denmark, and left in Feb. 1, 1985. Mineral and oil prospecting revealed deposits of lead, zinc, iron ore, oil, gas and uranium. Commercial exploitation of these resources has already begun. The United States of America has acquired certain rights to maintain air bases in Greenland.
Premier, Jonathan Motzfeldt.

DJIBOUTI
(Jumhouriyya Djibouti)

President, Hassan Gouled Aptidon.

CABINET

Prime Minister and Minister for Port Affairs, Barkat Gourad Hamadou.
Justice, Omar Kamil Warsama.
Foreign Affairs and Co-operation, Moumin Bahdon Farah.
Interior, Posts and Telecommunications, Youssouf Ali Chirdon.
Defence, Moussa Boúraleh Robleh.

Finance, Mohamed Djaha Elabeh.
Commerce, Transport and Tourism, Moussa Bouraleh Robleh.
Education, Youth and Sports, Souleiman Farah Lodon.
Public Health, Mohamed Adabo Kako.
Labour, Mohamed Del Waiss.
Civil Service and Administrative Reform, Helem Houmed.
Public Works, Town Planning and Housing, Bourhan Ali Warki.
Industry, Salem Abdou Yaya.
Rural Development, Ahmed Hassan Liban.

Formerly known as French Somaliland and then the French Territory of the Afars and the Issas, the country became independent on June 27, 1977. Djibouti is situated on the north-east coast of Africa (i.e. the Horn of Africa) and has an area of 8,494 sq. miles (22,000 sq. km.). It has an estimated population (1985) of 430,000. The climate is harsh and much of the country is semi-arid desert. The French continue to maintain army, navy and air force bases. Djibouti has an excellent port, international airport and a railway line runs to Addis Ababa.

Trade with U.K.

	1985	1986
Imports from U.K.	£21,546,000	£12,537,000
Exports to U.K.	293,000	53,000

CAPITAL.—Ψ Djibouti (1985, 200,000).

FLAG.—Blue over green with white triangle in the hoist containing a red star.

NATIONAL DAY.—June 27 (Independence Day).

BRITISH CONSULATE

P.O. Box 81/9–11, Rue de Geneve, Djibouti.

Honorary Consul, G. G. D. Cattle.

DOMINICAN REPUBLIC
(República Dominicana)

President, Dr. Joaquin Balaguer, took office, 16 Aug. 1986.
Vice-President, Carlos Morales Troncoso.

CABINET

Armed Forces, Gen. Antonio Imbert Barreras.
Interior and Police, Juan Cotes Morales.
Secretary for the Presidency, Rafael Bello Andino.
Secretary of the Presidency (Technical), Guillermo Caram.
External Relations, Dr. Donald Reid Cabral.
Finance, Roberto Saladin.
Education, Pedro C. Pichardo.
Agriculture, Norberto Quezada.
Public Works, Simon Tomas Fernández.
Labour, Juan Aristides Taveras Guzman.
Public Health, Dr. Ney Arias Lora.
Industry and Commerce, Roberto Martinez.
Sport, Andrés Vanderhorst.
Tourism, Fernando Rainieri.
Administrative Secretary of the Presidency, Luis Toral.
Sec. of State without Portfolio, Manuel Guaroa Liranzo.

HONORARY CONSULATE

6 Queen's Mansions, Brook Green, W6 7EB
[01–602 1885]

Honorary Consul, Mrs. J. De Wardener.

There are also Consular Offices at Liverpool, Birmingham, Manchester, Grimsby, Southampton, Cardiff and Plymouth.

The Dominican Republic, formerly the Spanish portion of the island of Hispaniola, is the oldest settlement of European origin in America. The western part of the island forms the Republic of Haiti. The island lies between Cuba on the west and Puerto Rico on the east and the Republic covers an area of 18,816 sq. miles (48,734 sq. km.), with a population (1984 Census) of 6,416,000. The climate is tropical in the lowlands and semi-tropical to temperate in the higher altitudes.

Spanish is the language of the Republic.

Government.—Santo Domingo was discovered by Christopher Columbus in December, 1492, and remained a Spanish Colony until 1821. In 1822 it was subjugated by the neighbouring Haitians who remained in control until 1844 when the Dominican Republic was proclaimed. The country was occupied by American marines from 1916 until the adoption of a new Constitution in 1924. From 1930 until May 30, 1961 (when he was assassinated) Generalissimo Rafael Trujillo ruled the country.

President Juan Bosch held office from Dec. 1962 to Sept. 1963, when he was deposed by a military junta. A revolt in favour of ex-President Bosch in April, 1965, developed into civil war lasting until September the same year when a provisional President was elected. On June 1, 1966, Dr. Joaquin Balaguer was elected President and in Nov. 1966 a new Constitution was introduced.

Executive power is vested in the President, who is elected by direct vote and serves for four years. The President forms his cabinet without reference to the Congress.

Legislative power is exercised by the Congress, which has a term of four years concurrent with the Presidency. The Upper Chamber is the Senate of 27 senators, one for each province and one for Santo Domingo. The lower is the Chamber of Deputies which has 120 members, one for each 50,000 inhabitants in each province, with the provision that no province has less than two members. Judicial power is exercised by the Supreme Court of Justice.

Communications.—According to local classification there are 2,932 miles of first class and 1,392 miles of second class and inter-communal roads in the Republic. There is a direct road from Santo Domingo to Port-au-Prince, the capital of Haiti, but that part of it in the border area has fallen into disuse. The frontier has been closed since Sept., 1967, except for that section crossed by the main road linking the two capitals. A telephone system connects practically all the principal towns of the republic and there is a telegraph service with all parts of the world. There are more than 90 commercial broadcasting stations and six television stations.

The Republic is served by two national and six foreign airlines, and an international airport 18 miles to the east of the capital is in operation. Another has been built near Puerto Plata on the north coast.

Economy.—Sugar, coffee, cocoa, and tobacco are the most important crops. Other products are peanuts, maize, rice, bananas, molasses, salt, cement, ferro-nickel, gold, silver, cattle, sisal products, honey and chocolate. There is a growing number of light industries producing beer, tinned foodstuffs, glass products, textiles, soap, cigarettes, construction materials, plastic articles, shoes, papers, paint, rum, matches, peanut oil and other products.

FINANCE

	1983	1984 (est.)
Budget		
Revenue	RD$999,300,000	RD$1,345,751,270

TRADE

The chief imports are machinery, food stuffs, iron and steel, cotton textiles and yarns, mineral oils (including petrol), cars and other motor vehicles, chemical and pharmaceutical products, electrical equipment and accessories, construction material, paper and paper products, and rubber and rubber products. The chief exports are sugar, coffee, cocoa, tobacco, chocolate, molasses, bauxite, ferro-nickel and gold. Tobacco and tobacco manufactures are the principal exports to the U.K.

	1983	1984
Imports	RD$1,279,019,958	RD$1,459,000,000
Exports	811,054,942	1,211,100,000

Trade with U.K.

	1985	1986
Imports from U.K.	£14,595,000	£15,178,000
Exports to U.K.	7,900,000	7,599,000

CAPITAL.—Ψ Santo Domingo, population of the Capital District (1981 census), 1,313,172. Other centres, with populations (1981 census); Santiago de los Caballeros (550,372); La Vega (385,043); San Francisco De Macoris (235,544); San Juan (239,957); San Cristóbal (446,132).

FLAG.—Red and blue, with white cross bearing an emblem at centre.

NATIONAL DAY.—February 27 (Independence Day, 1844).

BRITISH AMBASSADOR, (resident at Caracas, Venezuela).

ECUADOR
(Republica del Ecuador)

President Léon Febres Cordero, *took office* Aug. 10, 1984.

CABINET

Interior, Luis Robles Plaza.
Foreign Affairs, Rafael Garcia Velasco.
Education, Trajano Naranjo.
Defence, Medardo Salazar.
Finance, Rodrigo Espinosa.
Labour and Human Resources, Dr. Jorge Egas Peñe.
Agriculture and Livestock, (vacant).
Natural Resources, Javier Espinosa Teran.
Industry, Commerce and Integration, (vacant).
Public Information, Marco Lara.
Public Works, Cesar Rodriguez.
Health, Jorge Bracho.
Social Welfare, Ernesto Velázquez.
Sec. Gen. of the Administration, Patricio Quevedo.

EMBASSY AND CONSULATE
Flat 3B, 3 Hans Crescent, SW1X 0LS
[01–584 1367/2648]

Ambassador Extraordinary and Plenipotentiary, new appointment awaited.
Chargé d'Affaires, Mrs. Ximena de Pérez.

Area and Population.—Ecuador is an equatorial state of South America, the mainland extending from lat. 1° 38′ N. to 4° 50′ S., and between 75° 20′ and 81° W. long., comprising an area reduced by boundary settlements with Peru (Jan. 29, 1942) to about 226,000 sq. miles (585,337 sq. km.).

The Republic of Ecuador is divided into 20 provinces. It has a population (1985 U.N. estimate) of approximately 9,378,000, mostly descendants of the Spanish, aboriginal Indians, and Mestizoes. The territory of the Republic extends across the Western Andes, the highest peaks in Ecuador being Chimborazo (20,408 ft.) and Ilinza (17,405 ft.) in the Western Cordillera; and Cotopaxi (19,612 ft.) and Cayambe (19,160 ft.) in the Eastern Cordillera. Ecuador is watered by the Upper Amazon, and by the rivers Guayas, Mira, Santiago, Chone, and Esmeraldas on the Pacific coast. There are extensive forests.

Government.—The former *Kingdom of Quito* was conquered by the Incas of Peru in the latter part of the 15th century. Early in the 16th century Pizarro's conquests led to the inclusion of the present territory of Ecuador in the Spanish Vice-royalty of Peru. The independence of the country was achieved in a revolutionary war which culminated in the battle of Mount Pichincha (May 24, 1822).

After seven years of military rule, Ecuador returned to democracy in 1979. The present constitution, introduced in 1978, provides for an elected President and Vice-President who serve for a four year term. (Neither may stand for re-election.) There is a Chamber of Representatives with 79 members elected every four years, 12 of whom are elected on a national basis and the rest by the provinces. The Chamber meets for two months every year (Aug.–Oct.) but can be convoked at any time for extraordinary sessions. Four Legislative Commissions meet through the year.

Voting is compulsory for all literate and (since 1980) voluntary for all illiterate citizens over the age of 18. Thirteen political groupings are recognized.

Agriculture and Industry.—Agriculture is the most important sector of the economy, supporting nearly 50 per cent of the population (particularly the poorest) and contributing 14·5 per cent of the Gross Domestic Product and 19·5 per cent of exports. The main products for export are fish (mainly shrimps, tuna and sardines), which had become the largest agricultural export by early 1982; bananas, which provide a third of agricultural exports; cocoa and coffee. Other important crops are sugar, corn, soya, rice, cotton, African palm (for oil), vegetables, fruit and timber, the temperate crops being produced mostly in the highlands.

The economy was transformed by the discovery in 1972 of major oil fields in the Oriente area, and oil accounted for two thirds of 1981 export earnings. The economy grew rapidly in the 1970s but is now faced with reduced growth, due mainly to the fall in the price of oil. The oil deposits in the Oriente are estimated at between 10–15,000 million barrels, and further exploration and development is taking place. The oil is evacuated by a trans-Andean pipeline to the port of Balao (near Esmeraldes).

Communications.—There are 23,256 km. of permanent roads and 5,044 km. of roads which are only open during the dry season. There are about 750 miles of railway, including the railway from Quito to Guayaquil. Ten commercial airlines operate international flights, linking Ecuador with major foreign cities and there are internal services between all important towns.

Defence.—The standing Army has a strength of about 38,000. There is an Air Force of some 120 aircraft of various kinds and 4,800 personnel. The Navy is 4,500 strong.

Language, etc.—Spanish is the principal language of the country but Quechua is also a recognized language and is spoken by the majority of the Indian population. As a result of an intensive national education programme more than 75 per cent of the population are now literate. Elementary education is free and compulsory. There are 9 Universities, at Quito (2), Guayaquil (3), Cuenca, Machala, Loja and Portoviejo, Polytechnic Schools at Quito and Guayaquil and 8 technical colleges in other provincial capitals. 2 daily newspapers are published at Quito and 4 at Guayaquil.

Finance.—The estimated government budget at Jan. 1985 was 144,151 million *sucres* (53,600 million *sucres* in 1981). The balance of payments deficit stands at U.S.$25 million, and foreign exchange reserves at U.S.$195 million.

TRADE

Import licences are required for all merchandise and these are issued by the Central Bank of Ecuador.

	1985
Imports	U.S.$1,614·5m.
Exports	2,904·6m.

Trade with U.K.

	1985	1986
Imports from U.K........	£58,628,000	£46,673,000
Exports to U.K.	19,015,000	11,339,000

Manufactured goods and machinery are the main imports.

CAPITAL.—Quito. Population (1985 estimate), 1,003,875; Ψ Guayaquil (1,000,000) is the chief port; Cuenca (110,000).

FLAG.—Three horizontal bands, yellow, blue and red (the yellow band twice the width of the others); emblem in centre.

NATIONAL DAY.—August 10 (*Dia de la Independencia*).

BRITISH EMBASSY
Calle Gonzalez Suarez, 111 (Casilla 314),
Quito.

Ambassador Extraordinary and Plenipotentiary, His Excellency Michael William Atkinson, C.M.G., M.B.E. (1985).

There is a British Consular Office at Guayaquil.

British Council Representative, J. T. Wright, O.B.E., Av. Amazonas 1646 (Casilla 8829), Quito.

The GALÁPAGOS (Giant Tortoise) ISLANDS forming the province of the Archipelago de Colón, were annexed by Ecuador in 1832. The archipelago lies in the Pacific, about 500 miles from Saint Elena peninsula, the most westerly point of the mainland. There are 12 large and several hundred smaller islands with a total area of about 3,000 sq. miles and an estimated population (1982) of 6,119. The capital is San Cristobal, on Chatham Island. Although the archipelago lies on the equator, the temperature of the surrounding water is well below equatorial average owing to the *Antarctic Humboldt Current*. The province consists for the most part of National Park Territory, where unique marine birds, iguanas, and the giant tortoises are conserved. There is some local subsistence farming; the main industry, apart from tourism, is tuna and lobster fishing.

EGYPT
(Al-Jumhuriyat Misr al-Arabiya)

President, Muhammad Hosni Mubarak, *elected*, Oct. 14, 1981 *re-elected*, 1987.

CABINET

Prime Minister, Dr. Alef Mohamed Naguib Sidki.
Deputy P.M., Defence and Military Production, F. M. Muhammad Abdul Halim Abu Ghazala.
Deputy P.M., Foreign Affairs, Dr. Ahmed Esmat Abdul Meguid.
Deputy P.M., Planning and International Co-operation, Dr. Kamal Ahmed el Ganzouri.
Deputy P.M., Agriculture and Land Reclamation, Dr. Youssef Amin Wali.
Social Insurance and Social Affairs, Dr. Mrs. Amal Abdel Rehim Osman.
Housing, New Communities and Public Utilities, Hasaballah al-Kafrawi.
Minister of State, Foreign Affairs, Dr. Boutros Boutros-Ghali.
Justice, Ahmed Mamduh Attia.
Transport, Communications and Maritime Transport, Soliman Metwalli.
Electricity and Energy, Mohamed Maher Abaza.

Ministers of State, People's Assembly and Shura Council Affairs, Muhammad Radwan; Dr. Sayyed Ali Sayyed.
Information, Safwat al-Sharif.
Interior, Gen. Zaki Badr.
Irrigation, Essam Radi.
Industry, Mohamed Abdel Wahab.
Petroleum and Mineral Resources, Abdul Hadi Kandil.
Cabinet Affairs, and Minister of State, Administrative Development, Dr. Atef Ubaid.
Finance, Mohamed Ahmed al Razaz.
Local Government, Dr. Ahmed Salama Mohamed.
Supply and Internal Trade, Dr. Mohamed Galal el Din Abou el Zahab.
Waqfs (Religious Endowments), Dr. Mohamed Ali Mahgoub.
Economy and Foreign Trade, Dr. Youssri Ali Mostafa.
Education, Dr. Ahmed Fathi Sorour.
Culture, Dr. Ahmed Abdel Maksoud Heikal.
Minister of State, Emigration and Expatriate Egyptians, Adly Abdel Shahid Beshay.
Scientific Research, Dr. Adel Abdel Hamid Ezz.
Tourism and Civil Aviation, Dr. Fouad Soltan.
Health, Dr. Mohamed Ragheb Dewidar.
Manpower and Vocational Training, Assem Abdel Haq Saleh.

EGYPTIAN EMBASSY
26 South Street, W1Y 8EL
[01–499 2401]

Ambassador Extraordinary and Plenipotentiary, His Excellency Yousef Sharara (1984).

AREA AND POPULATION.—The total area of Egypt is 386,662 sq. miles (1,001,449 sq. km.), only three per cent of which is cultivated land, with a population now officially estimated (1986) at 49,000,000.

There are three distinct elements in the native population. The largest, or "Egyptian" element, is a Hamito-Semite race, known in the rural districts as *Fellahin* (*fellâh*—ploughman, or tiller of the soil). A second element is the *Bedouin*, or nomadic Arabs of the Western and Arabian deserts, of whom about one-seventh are real nomads, and the remainder semi-sedentary tent-dwellers on the outskirts of the cultivated end of the Nile Valley and the Fayûm. The third element is the *Nubian* of the Nile Valley

between Aswân and Wadi-Halfa of mixed Arab and Negro blood. Over 90 per cent of the population are Moslems of the Sunní denomination, and most of the rest Coptic Christians.

The territory of Egypt comprises (1) *Egypt Proper*, forming the N.E. corner of the African continent, divisible into (a) the valley and delta of the Nile, (b) the Western Desert, and (c) the Arabian or Eastern Desert; (2) *The Peninsula of Sinai*, forming part of the continent of Asia; and (3) a number of *Islands* in the Gulf of Suez and Red Sea, of which the principal are Jubal, Shadwan, Gafatin and Zeberged (or St. John's Island). This territory lies between 22° and 32° N. lat. and 24° and 37° E. long. The northern boundary is the Mediterranean, and in the south Egypt is conterminous with the Sudan. The western boundary runs from a point on the coast 10 kilometres N.W. of Sollûm to the latitude of Siwa and thence due S. along the 25th meridian. The E. boundary follows a line drawn from Rafa on the Mediterranean (34° 15′ E. long.) to the head of the Gulf of 'Aqaba.

Physical Features.—The country is mainly flat but there are mountainous areas in the south-west, along the Red Sea coast and in the south of the Sinai peninsula, rising in some places to peaks of over 6,000 ft. The highest mountain in Egypt is Mt. Catherina (8,668 ft). Most of the land is desert but the Nile valley and delta are covered by silt 20–30 feet deep, and areas of desert are increasingly being reclaimed by irrigation and fertilization.

The *Nile* has a total length of 4,145 miles. In the 960 miles of its course through Egypt it receives not a single tributary stream. The river formerly had a regular yearly rise and fall of about 13 feet at Cairo, but since the completion of the Aswan High Dam in 1965, there has been no flood downstream of the dam and the water level remains almost constant throughout the year. The area of fertile land, a 5–15 mile wide strip in the Nile valley and some 6,000 square miles of the Nile delta, has been increased by the opening of the Aswan Dam. This has allowed the reclamation of about 1,300,000 acres, and a further 700,000 acres have been converted from basin to perennial irrigation. Westward from the Nile Valley stretches the *Western desert*, containing some depressions, whose springs irrigate small areas known as *Oases*, of which the principal, from S.E. to N.W., are known as Kharga, Dakhla, Farafra, Baharia and Siwa.

In the Eastern Desert between the Nile and the mountains along the Red Sea coast, are plateaux of sandstones and limestones, dissected by *wadis* (dry water-courses), often of great length and depth, with some wild vegetation and occasional wells and springs.

History.—The unification of the Kingdoms of Lower and Upper Egypt under the Pharaohs in *c.* 3,100 B.C. marked the establishment of the Egyptian state, with Memphis as its capital. Egypt was ruled for nearly 2,800 years by a succession of Pharaonic dynasties (31 in all), which built the pyramids at Gizeh. The oldest of these is that of Zoser, built *c.* 2,700 B.C., and the highest the Great Pyramid of Cheops, at 451 feet; nearby is the Sphinx, 189 feet long. A period of Hellenic rule began in 332 B.C., after the conquest of Egypt by Alexander the Great, followed by a period of rule by Rome (30 B.C. to A.D. 324) and then by the Byzantine Empire. In A.D. 640 Egypt was subjugated by Arab Muslim invaders, becoming a province of the Eastern Caliphate. In 1517 the country was incorporated in the Ottoman Empire under which it remained until early in the 19th century.

A British Protectorate over Egypt declared on Dec. 18, 1914, lasted until Feb. 28, 1922, when Sultan Ahmed Fuad was proclaimed King of Egypt. In July, 1952, following a military *coup d'état*, King Farouk abdicated in favour of his infant son, who became King Ahmed Fuad II. In June, 1953, however, Gen. Neguib's military council deposed the young king, and Egypt became a Republic.

In 1956, as a result of Egypt's trade agreements with Communist countries, Britain and U.S.A. withdrew offers of financial aid and in retaliation Pres. Nasser seized the assets of the Suez Canal Company. An Egyptian invasion of the Canal Zone while repulsing an Israeli attack provoked military action by Britain and France in support of their Suez Canal Company interests. A ceasefire and Anglo-French withdrawal were negotiated by the U.N.

The Israeli invasion of 1956 overran the Sinai peninsula but six months later Israel withdrew and a U.N. peace-keeping force was established in the area. However, mounting tension culminated in a second invasion of Sinai (the Six Day War of June 1967) and occupation of the peninsula by Israel. Egypt's attempt to recapture the territory (the Yom Kippur War of October 1973) was unsuccessful but Sinai was returned to Egypt in April 1982, under the treaty of 1979 which resulted from the Camp David talks between Pres. Sadat and Mr. Begin and formally terminated a 31-year old state of war between the two countries. Pres. Hosni Mubarak came to power on Oct. 6, 1981 after the assassination of Pres. Sadat by Moslem fundamentalists.

Government.—The Constitution of 1971 provides for an executive President who appoints Ministers to the Cabinet. The President determines policy which the Cabinet implements and Ministers are responsible to him. The Legislature consists of the People's Assembly (458 members, 448 of whom are elected, the remaining 10 nominated by the President); the Shura Council, or Consultative Assembly (210 members) has an advisory role. The Constitution guarantees also the independence of the Judiciary. Religious courts were abolished in 1956 and their functions transferred to the national court system. Freedom of the press is guaranteed under the Constitution.

Agriculture.—Despite increasing industrialisation, agriculture remains the most important economic activity, employing over 45 per cent of the labour force and producing nearly half of the country's exports. Agricultural output has been increased as a result of land reclamation programmes and the introduction of more efficient methods, *e.g.* the change from basin to perennial irrigation which yields 2–3 crops per year instead of one, the pivotal sprinkling irrigation system which uses water more efficiently, and the increasing mechanization and use of fertilizers. Egypt is still a net importer of foodstuffs, especially grain, and a food security programme has been set up with the aim of achieving self-sufficiency through the use of more advanced technology. Estimates suggest that an additional 3 million acres of land could be reclaimed by the end of the century.

The main cash crop is cotton, of which Egypt is one of the world's main producers. Production in 1985 was 443,000 tons. Other important summer crops are (1985 figures) maize 3,982,000 tons, rice 2,312,000 tons, millet 551,000 tons and sugar cane 9,140,000 tons. Important winter crops are wheat 1,874,000 tons, beans 302,000 tons and onions 490,000 tons. Citrus fruit and other fruits and vegetables are also grown.

Energy.—With its considerable reserves of petroleum and natural gas in Sinai, the Nile Delta and the Western Desert, and the hydro-electric power produced by the Aswan and High Dams, Egypt is self-sufficient in energy. Electricity has been provided to almost all of the country and there are plans to extend the natural gas network to all major cities.

Industry.—The production of petroleum provides Egypt with its major export and supports a growing refining industry. Steel production is another important heavy industry. The major manufacturing industries are in food processing, motor cars and electrical goods, chemical products and yarns and textiles.

FINANCE

	1985–86	1986–87
Estimated revenue	L.E.15,000m.	L.E.14,451m.
Total expenditure ...	20,000m.	20,000m.

The fiscal year commences July 1.

The monetary unit of Egypt is the Egyptian *pound* (L.E.) of 100 *piastres*.

TRADE

The main imports are wheat and flour, wood and trucks. The main exports are crude petroleum, cotton, cotton yarn, oranges, rice and cotton textiles.

	1984–5
Imports	L.E.7,734m.
Exports	2,838m.

Trade with U.K.

	1985	1986
Imports from U.K.	£471,091,000	£371,007,000
Exports to U.K.	162,162,000	328,053,000

Communications.—The road and rail networks link the Nile Valley and Delta with the main development areas to east and west of the river.

The Suez Canal was re-opened in 1975 and a two-stage development project begun to widen and deepen the canal to allow the passage of larger shipping and to permit two-way traffic. Port Said and Suez have been reconstructed and the port of Alexandria is being improved.

CAPITAL.—Cairo (population, estimated in 1986 at 14,000,000), stands on the E. bank of the Nile, about 14 miles from the head of the Delta. Its oldest part is the fortress of Babylon in old Cairo, with its Roman bastions and Coptic churches. The earliest Arab building is the Mosque of 'Amr, dating from A.D. 643, and the most conspicuous is the Citadel, built by Saladin towards the end of the 12th century and containing in its walls the Mosque of Mohamed Ali built in the 19th century.

ΨALEXANDRIA (estimated population in 1986 of 5,000,000), founded 332 B.C. by Alexander the Great, was for over 1,000 years the capital of Egypt and a centre of Hellenic culture which vied with Athens herself. Its great *pharos* (lighthouse), 480 feet high, with a lantern burning resinous wood, was one of the "Seven Wonders of the World". Other towns are: Ismailia (400,000); ΨPort Said (285,000); Mansura (120,000); Asyût (300,000); Faiyûm (180,000); Tanta (150,000); Mahalla el Kubra (130,000); ΨSuez; Ψ Damietta (100,000).

FLAG.—Horizontal bands of red, white and black, with an eagle in the centre of the white band.

NATIONAL DAY.—July 23 (Anniversary of Revolution in 1952).

BRITISH EMBASSY
Ahmed Ragheb Street, Garden City, Cairo

Ambassador Extraordinary and Plenipotentiary, His Excellency Sir Alan Urwick, K.C.V.O., C.M.G. (1985).
British Council Representative, G. Tindale, 192 Sharia el Nil, Agouza, Cairo. There is also a library in Alexandria.

EQUATORIAL GUINEA
(República de Guinea Ecuatorial)

President, Col. Teodoro Obiang Nguema Mbasogo, *took office*, Aug. 1979.

MINISTERS

Minister of Defence, Security and Political Affairs, The President.
Prime Minister and Minister for Health, C. Seriche Bioko.
Deputy P.M., Minister of Territorial Administration and National Security, Monsuy Andeme.
Public Works, Housing, Town Planning, Alejandro Envoro Ovono.
Economic Planning, Hilario Nsue Alene.
Education and Sport, Fortunato Nzambi Michinde.
Information and Tourism, Leandro Mbomio Nsue.
Labour, Anacleto Ejapa Bolekia.
Communications and Transport, Demetrio Elo Ndongo Nsefumu.
Agriculture, Alfredo Abero Nvono.
Industry and Commerce, Francisco Pascual Obama Eyegue.
Justice and Religion, Angel Ndong Micha.
Civil Service, Massoko Mecheba Ikaka.
Secretary-General to the Presidency, Martin Mka Esono.
Territorial Administration, Isidoro Eyi Monsuy Andeme.
Energy, Juan Olo Mba Nseng.
Water Resources and Forestry, Angel Alogo Nchama.
Foreign Affairs, Marcelino Nguema Ongueme.
Finance, Felipe Inestroca Ikaka.
Relations ꞏ᷒ith the House of Reps, Eloy Elo Nve Mbengono.
Deputy Minister of Defence, Maj. Melanio Ebendeng Nsomo.

Equatorial Guinea (formerly Spanish Guinea) consists of the island of Biogo (formerly Macias Nguema), in the Bight of Biafra about 20 miles from the west coast of Africa, Pagalu Island (formerly Annobon) in the Gulf of Guinea, the Corisco Islands (Corisco, Elobey Grande and Elobey Chico) and Rio Muni, a mainland area between Cameroon and Gabon. It has a total area of 10,830 sq. miles (28,051 sq. km.), and a population (1985 U.N. estimate) of 392,000.

Government.—Formerly colonies of Spain, the territories now forming the Republic of Equatorial Guinea were constituted as two provinces of Metropolitan Spain, in 1960, became autonomous in 1964 and fully independent in 1968. Serious disorders in Rio Muni early in 1969 caused many of the Spanish community to leave. Following Nigerian allegations of continuing mistreatment, most of the Nigerian labour force, on whom cocoa production largely depended, were repatriated in late 1975 and early 1976.

In Aug. 1979, President Macias was deposed by a revolutionary military council headed by his nephew Col. T. Obiang Nguema. The first parliamentary elections since 1968 were held on Aug. 28, 1983, under a new constitution approved by a referendum in Aug. 1982. Forty-one representatives were elected to the National Assembly for a five-year term.

Economy.—The chief products are cocoa, coffee and wood (which is exported almost entirely from Rio Muni). Production has declined and except for cocoa, there is little commercial agriculture and the economy is now heavily dependent on outside aid, principally from Spain. Equitorial Guinea entered the 'Franc zone' in 1985.

TRADE

	1984
Total Imports	US$18·7m.
Total Exports	30·0m.

Trade with U.K.

	1985	1986
Imports from U.K.	£191,000	£633,000
Exports to U.K.	—	1,000

CAPITAL.—ΨMalabo on the island of Bioco (population 1983 estimate, 34,980). ΨBata is the principal town and port of Rio Muni.

FLAG.—Three horizontal bands, green over white over red; blue triangle next staff; coat of arms in centre of white band.

NATIONAL DAY.—October 12.

British Ambassador, (resides at Yaoundé).

ETHIOPIA
(Hebretesebawit Ityopia)

Head of State, Chairman of the Derg and of the Council of Ministers, Mengistu Haile Mariam.

Secretary General of the Derg and Deputy Chairman of the Council of Ministers, Fikre-Selassie Wogderes.

COUNCIL OF MINISTERS

Agriculture, Dr. Geremew Debele.
Coffee and Tea Development, Tekola Dejene.
Construction, Kassa Gebre.
Culture, Girma Yilma.
Domestic Trade, Mersha Wodajo.
Education, Bililign Mandefro.
Finance, Wolle Chekol.
Foreign Affairs, Berhanu Bayih.
Foreign Trade, Tadesse Gebre Kidan.
Health, Dr. Gizaw Tsehay.
Industry, Fanta Belay.
Information and National Guidance, Dr. Feleke Gedle-Giorgis.
Interior, Endale Tessema.
Labour and Social Affairs, Shimelis Adug.
Law and Justice, Wondayen Mihiretu.
Mines and Energy, Tekize-Shoa Ayitenfisu.
National Defence, Maj.-Gen. Haile-Ghiorgis Habte-Mariam.
Public and National Security, Tesfaye Wolde-Selassie.
State Farm Development, Yoseph Muleta.
Transport and Communications, Youssouf Ahmed.
Urban Development and Housing, Tesfaye Marru.

EMBASSY IN LONDON
17 Prince's Gate, SW7 1PZ
[01–589 7212]

Ambassador Extraordinary and Plenipotentiary, His Excellency Ato Teferra Haile-Selassie (1985).

Position and Extent.—Ethiopia is in North-Eastern Africa, bounded on the north-west by the Sudan; on the south by Kenya; on the east by Djibouti and the Republic of Somalia: and on the north-east by the Red Sea. The area is 471,778 sq. miles (1,221,900 sq. km.), with a population (1985) of 43,350,000. About one-third are of the dominant race of Semitic origin (Amharas and Tigreans) and the remainder mainly Gallas (about 40 per cent of the population), Somalis and Afar.

Ethiopia has a large central plateau (average height, 6,000–7,000 ft.) which rises to nearly 15,000 ft. at Ras Dashan in the north. The plateau drops to the Nile basin in the west and the Red Sea in the east. To the north (Eritrea) and east (Ogaden) the land is mostly desert. The chief river is the Blue Nile, issuing from Lake Tana; the Atbara and many other tributaries of the Nile also rise in the Ethiopian highlands.

Those of Semitic origin (Amharas and Tigreans), and many of the Gallas, are Christians of the Ethiopian Orthodox Church, which was formerly led by the head of the Coptic Church, the Patriarch at Alexandria. Since 1959, however, the Ethiopian Church has been autocephalous and the new Patriarch, Abuna Tekle Haimanot, was enthroned in 1976. The Afar people, who inhabit lowland Eritrea, Wollo, Harargne and Bale provinces, and the Somalis, in the south-east, are Moslem. The Falashas, to be found principally in Gandar and Tigre provinces, practise Judaism. Between autumn 1984 and February 1985 a secret airlift ("Operation Moses") took 7,000 of the estimated 25,000 Falashas to Israel, via Sudan.

History.—The basic Hamitic culture was heavily influenced by Semitic immigration from Arabia in the centuries about the time of Christ. Christianity was introduced in the 4th century. The empire expanded sporadically, attaining a zenith in the 6th century under the Axum rulers, but subsequently checked by Islamic expansion from the east. Modern Ethiopia dates from 1855 when Theodore succeeded in establishing supremacy over the various tribes. The last Emperor was Haile Selassie who reigned from 1930, though in exile from 1936–1941 during the Italian occupation. After considerable military and civil unrest the armed forces assumed power in Sept. 1972 and deposed the Emperor. Pending the promulgation of a new Constitution, expected in September 1987, the country is ruled by a Provisional Military Administration Council (the *Derg*). A Worker's Party on the Soviet model was formed in Sept. 1984, with Mengistu as General-Secretary.

Eritrea was administered by Great Britain from the end of the Second World War until September 15, 1952, when it was federated with Ethiopia. It was incorporated as a province of Ethiopia in 1962. An armed campaign for independence started in 1962 and has intensified since the early 1970's.

Due to the lack of spring rains both the harvests of 1983 and 1984 failed. A famine relief programme launched in October 1984 drew world-wide attention to the problem, and airlifts of food began almost immediately. In two of the worst hit areas, the provinces of Tigre and Eritrea, the situation was exacerbated by the difficulty of supplying food and other aid to areas experiencing guerrilla activity.

In July 1977, Somalia, claiming the Ogaden region of Ethiopia in support of Western Somalia Liberation Front guerrillas, invaded the region. Ethiopia, with

Soviet arms, and the aid of Cuban troops, was able to defeat the Somalis. The Somali regular army withdrew in March 1978, but guerrilla activity by the Western Somalia Liberation Front continues.

The Tigrean province, which lies south of Eritrea, seeks to establish greater autonomy : the activities of the Tigrean People's Liberation Front have escalated since the early 1980s, and the T.P.L.F. claims to control and administer large areas of the province.

Production and Industry.—The principal pursuit is agriculture, which accounts for approximately 50 per cent. of G.D.P., 90 per cent. of exports and 85 per cent. of total employment. Land was nationalized in 1975 and tenants given rights of use to the land they had tilled : large private holdings became state farms. The major food crops are teff, maize, barley, sorghum, wheat, pulses and oil seeds. Coffee, the principal export crop generates over 60 per cent. of the country's export earnings. The country's livestock herd is the largest in Africa.

Manufacturing industry accounts for 10 per cent. of G.D.P. and is heavily dependent on agriculture. Ethiopia's known, but as yet largely unexploited, natural resources include gold, platinum, copper and potash. Traces of oil and natural gas have been found.

Communications.—With the aid of loans from the IBRD and the International Development Agency, a network of roads has been built linking the major cities with each other, and with the Sudanese and Kenyan borders and the Red Sea coast. There is a railway link from Addis Ababa to Djibouti, though this is vulnerable to guerrilla activity. The narrow gauge line in Eritrea has been closed by conflict. The Ethiopian Air Lines maintain regular services from Addis Ababa to many provincial towns. External services are operated throughout Africa and to Europe and the Middle and Far East.

Defence.—Under the Ministry of Defence the armed forces comprise the Army, the Air Force and the Navy. The Army strength totals 210,000 personnel (including a People's Militia) divided into 23 divisions.

The Air Force comprises a transport squadron, a bomber squadron, three fighter squadrons, a training squadron, a jet conversion squadron, and an elementary training unit. There are 120 fighter planes, mostly of Russian manufacture, and a few F.5.s. The Air Force Headquarters is situated at Debre Zeit.

The Navy has a headquarters in Addis Ababa with a main base at Massawa and a smaller one at Assab.

National Military Service was established on May 4, 1983 and came into effect in May 1984.

Education.—Elementary education is provided without religious discrimination by Government schools in the main centres of population ; there are also Mission schools, and cadet-schools for the Army, Navy, Air Force, and Police. Government secondary schools are found mainly in Addis Ababa, but also in most of the provincial capitals. The National University (founded 1961) co-ordinates the institutions of higher education (University College, Engineering, Building and Theological Colleges in Addis Ababa, Agricultural College at Alemaya, near Harar, and Public Health Centre in Gondar, etc.). It is intended to develop the provincial colleges to university level and status. Amharic is the official language of instruction, with English as the first foreign language and main language of instruction from secondary level upwards. Arabic is taught in Koran Schools ; and Ge'ez (the ancient Ethiopic) in Christian Church Schools, which abound.

FINANCE

	1984
Revenue	US$1,062·8m.
Expenditure	1,449·3m.

The Ethiopian unit of currency is the *birr* of 100 cents.

Trade.—The chief imports by value are machinery and transport equipment, manufactured goods and chemicals (from U.K.) ; the principal exports by value being coffee, oilseeds, hides and skins, and pulses.

TRADE

	1984
Total Imports	US$917·8m.
Total Exports	402·8m.

Trade with U.K.

	1985	1986
Imports from U.K.	£66,089,000	£50,049,000
Exports to U.K.	13,805,000	22,343,000

CAPITAL.— Addis Ababa (population, 1985 estimate 1,464,901), also capital of the province of Shoa ; Asmara (population 250,000) is the capital of the Province of Eritrea. Dire Dawa is the most important commercial centre after Addis Ababa and Asmara, ΨMassawa and ΨAssab (recently enlarged) are the two main ports. There are ancient architectural remains at Aksum, Gondar, Lalibela and elsewhere.

FLAG.—Three horizontal bands ; green, yellow, red.

NATIONAL DAY.—September 12 (People's Revolution Day).

BRITISH EMBASSY

Fikre Mariam Abatechan Street (P.O. Box 858), Addis Ababa

Ambassador Extraordinary and Plenipotentiary, His Excellency Harold Berners Walker, C.M.G. (1986).

There is a British Consular Office at *Addis Ababa.*

British Council Representative, N. O. Hudson, O.B.E., Artistic Building, Adwa Avenue (P.O. Box 1043), Addis Ababa. There is also a library in Asmara.

FINLAND
(Suomen Tasavalta)

President, Dr. Mauno Koivisto, *born,* 1923, *elected,* Jan 26, 1982.

CABINET

Prime Minister, Harri Holkeri (*NCP*).
Foreign Affairs, Kalevi Sorsa (*SDP*).
Cabinet, Ilkka Kanerva (*NCP*).
Foreign Trade, Pertti Salolainen (*NCP*).
Justice, Matti Louekoski (*SDP*).
Interior, Jarmo Rantanen (*SDP*).
Defence, Ole Norrback (*SPP*).
Finance, Erkki Liikanen (*SDP*).
Deputy Minister of Finance, Ms. Ulla Puolanne (*NCP*).
Education, Christoffer Taxell (*SPP*).
Deputy Minister of Education, Ms. Anna-Liisa Piipari (*SDP*).
Agriculture and Forestry, Toivo T. Pohjola (*NCP*).
Transport and Communications, Pekka Vennamo (*FRP*).
Trade and Industry, Ilkka Suominen (*NCP*).
Social Affairs and Health, Ms. Helena Pesola (*NCP*).
Deputy Minister of Social Affairs and Health, Ms. Tarja Halonen (*SDP*).
Labour, Matti Puhakka (*SDP*).
Environment, Kaj Bärlund (*SDP*).

(*NCP* = National Coalition Party, *SDP* = Social Democratic Party, *SPP* = Swedish People's Party of Finland, *FRP* = Finnish Rural Party).

FINNISH EMBASSY AND CONSULATE
38 Chesham Place, SW1X 8HW
[01–235 9531]

Ambassador Extraordinary and Plenipotentiary, His Excellency Ilkka Pastinen (1983).
Minister Counsellor, Seppo Kauppila.
Counsellors, Asko Numminen; I. Ström.
Press Counsellor, Lasse Lehtinen.
Defence Attaché, Col. T. Aaltonen.

Area and Population.—A country situated on the Gulfs of Finland and Bothnia, with a total area of 137,851 sq. miles (337,032 sq. km.), of which 65 per cent. is forest, 8 per cent. cultivated, 9 per cent. lakes and 18 per cent. waste and other land. The population (December, 1985) was 4,908,000, of whom 90·3 per cent. are Lutheran, 1·1 per cent. Greek Orthodox and 8·4 per cent. others.

The Aland Archipelago (Ahvenanmaa), a group of small islands at the entrance to the Gulf of Bothnia, covers about 572 square miles, with a population (December, 1984) of 23,595 (95·2 per cent. Swedish-speaking). The islands have a semi-autonomous status.

Government.—Under the Constitution there is a single Chamber (*Eduskunta*) composed of 200 members, elected by universal suffrage. The legislative power is vested in the Chamber and the President. The highest executive power is held by the President who is elected for a period of 6 years.

The present government came into office on April 30, 1987. The four parties in the coalition are the National Coalition Party (conservative), the Social Democratic Party, the Swedish People's Party of Finland, and the Finnish Rural Party.

Defence.—By the terms of the Peace Treaty (Feb. 10, 1947) with U.K. and U.S.S.R., the Army is limited to a force not exceeding 34,400. The Navy is limited to a total of 10,000 tons displacement with personnel not exceeding 4,500. The Air Force, including naval air arm, is limited to 60 machines with a personnel not exceeding 3,000. Bombers or aircraft with bomb-carrying facilities are expressly forbidden. The Defence Forces contain a cadre of regular officers and N.C.O.'s, but their bulk is provided by conscripts who serve for 8–11 months. Total strength of trained and equipped reserves is over 700,000, 16,500 of whom have served in the U.N. peacekeeping force.

Education.—Primary education (co-educational comprehensive school) is compulsory for children from 7 to 16 years, and free of charge. In the autumn of 1985, there were 685,052 in comprehensive schools (374,413 at basic stage and 310,639 at upper stage), and 115,000 in vocational institutions of senior level. There are 21 universities or other schools of academic level, and enrolment was (1984) 88,242.

Language and Literature.—There are two official languages in Finland. 93·5 per cent. of the population speak Finnish as their first language, 6·3 Swedish (1979). The remaining 0·2 per cent. speak other languages (mainly Lapps who number about 2,500 and live in the Far North). Both Finnish and Swedish are used for administration and education; newspapers, books, plays and films appear in both languages. There is a vigorous modern literature. F. E. Sillanpää, who died in 1964, was awarded the Nobel prize for Literature. Best known among the living authors are Väinö Linna, Veijo Meri and Paavo Haavikko. There are 99 daily newspapers in Finland which appear on 4 or more days per week (12 Swedish).

Production and Industry.—Finland is a highly industrialized country producing a wide range of capital and consumer goods. Timber and the products of the forest-based industries remain the backbone of the economy, accounting for 40 per cent. of her export earnings, but the importance of the metal-working, shipbuilding and engineering industries has been growing. This sector in 1981 accounted for 31 per cent. of Finland's exports. The textile industry is well developed and Finland's glass, ceramics and furniture industries enjoy international reputations. Other important industries are rubber, plastics, chemicals and pharmaceuticals, footwear, foodstuffs and electronic equipment.

Communications.—There are 6,976 kilometres of railroad, a railway connection with Sweden and U.S.S.R., passenger boat connection with Sweden, West Germany, Poland and U.S.S.R. Vessels on the London to Leningrad route call at Helsinki. There are also passenger/cargo services between Britain and Helsinki, Kotka and other Finnish ports. External civil air services are maintained by most European airlines. The merchant fleet at the end of Dec. 1985 totalled 439 vessels (1,650,000 tons gross).

FINANCE

	1983	1984
	Finnmarks	Finnmarks
Revenue (*Budget*) ...	64,938,000	75,395,000
Expenditure (*Budget*)	76,590,000	86,095,000

Currency.—The unit of currency is the *markka* of 10 penniä.

TRADE

The principal imports are raw materials, machinery and manufactured goods. The exports are principally the output of the paper and other forest industries, engineering, metal industry (*e.g.* paper-working machinery and ships) and chemicals.

	1983	1984
	Finnmarks	Finnmarks
Total Imports	71,519,000	74,684,000
Total Exports	69,751,000	80,922,000

Trade with U.K.

	1985	1986
Imports from U.K.	£703,365,000	£664,461,000
Exports to U.K.	1,324,792,000	1,346,058,000

CAPITAL.—ΨHelsinki (Helsingfors). Population (Dec. 1984), 484,263; other towns are Tampere (Tammerfors), 166,300; ΨTurku (Åbo), 163,700; Espoo, 137,500; Vantaa, 132,100; Lahti, 94,700; ΨOulu (Uleåborg), 93,800; ΨPori (Björneborg), 79,400; Kuopio, 74,600; Jyväskylä, 64,200.

NATIONAL DAY.—December 6 (Day of Independence).

FLAG.—White with blue cross.

BRITISH EMBASSY
Uudenmaankatu 16–20
00120 Helsinki 12

Ambassador Extraordinary and Plenipotentiary, His Excellency (Hubert Anthony) Justin Staples, C.M.G. (1986).
Counsellor (Commercial), B. Rose.
First Secretaries, G. S. Hand (*Head of Chancery*); A. J. Marlowe; A. R. Powell.
Defence, Naval, Military and Air Attaché, Lt.-Col. W. J. Collings, M.B.E.

There are British Consular offices at *Helsinki, Tampere, Turko, Pori, Kotka, Oulu, Vaasa* and *Kuopio.*

British Council Representative, M. B. L. Nightingale, Etelä esplanadi 22A, 00130 Helsinki 13.

FRANCE
(La République Française)

President of the French Republic, Francois Mitterrand, *elected* May 10, 1981.

CABINET

Prime Minister, Jacques Chirac (*R.P.R.*).
Minister of State, Economy, Finance and Privatization, Edouard Balladur (*R.P.R.*).
Justice, Albin Chalandon (*R.P.R.*).
Defence, André Giraud.
Culture and Communication, François Léotard (*U.D.F.-P.R.*).
Foreign Affairs, Jean-Bernard Raimond.
Interior, Charles Pasqua (*R.P.R.*).
Housing, Transport and Urban Affairs, Pierre Méhaignerie (*U.D.F.-C.D.S.*).
Overseas Departments and Territories, Bernard Pans (*R.P.R.*).
Education, René Monory (*U.D.F.-C.D.S.*).
Employment and Social Affairs, Philippe Séguin (*R.P.R.*).
Industry, Posts and Telecommunications, Tourism, Alain Madelin (*U.D.F.-P.R.*).
Agriculture, Francois Guillaume.
Co-operation, Michel Aurillac (*R.P.R.*).
Relations with Parliament, André Rossinot (*U.D.F.-Radical*).
European Affairs, Bernard Bosson.
(*R.P.R.* = Rally for the Republic; *U.D.F.* = Union for French Democracy; *P.R.* = Republican Party; *C.D.S.* = Centre of Social Democrats; *P.S.D.* = Social Democratic Party).

The French parliamentary elections of March 16, 1986 resulted in a majority of members in the National Assembly from the centre-right alliance of the Rally for the Republic and the Union for French Democracy parties. On March 18, President Mitterrand invited

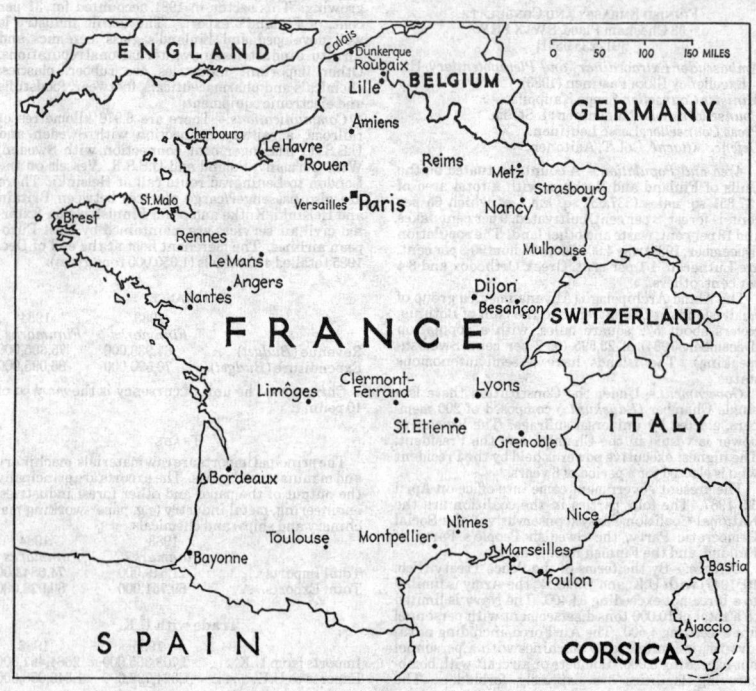

Jacques Chirac, leader of the Rally for the Republic party, to form a government. The composition of the Government is 20 *R.P.R.* members (out of 41), 7 from the *U.D.F.-P.R.*, 7 from the *U.D.F.-C.D.S.*, 2 *U.D.F.-Radicals* and 1 member *U.D.F.-P.S.D.*; the remainder were not formally attached to any political party. Subsequently a new portfolio of European Affairs was created.

FRENCH EMBASSY IN LONDON
58 Knightsbridge, SW1X 7JT
[01–235 8080].

Ambassador Extraordinary and Plenipotentiary, His Excellency Vicomte Luc de La Barre de Nanteuil (1986).

Area and Population.—The largest state in Central Europe, extending from 42° 20' to 51° 5' N. lat., and from 7° 85' E. to 4° 45' W. long. Its area is estimated at 211,208 sq. miles (547,026 sq. km.), divided into 95 departments, including the island of Corsica, in the Mediterranean, off the west coast of Italy. The population of France in 1986 was 55,279,100.

POPULATION OF THE REGIONS 1986 (provisional)
(Names of Departments in brackets)

Alsace (Bas-Rhin, Haut-Rhin)	1,599,800
Aquitaine (Dordogne, Gironde, Landes, Lot-et-Garonne, Pyrénées-Atlantiques)	2,718,200
Auvergne (Allier, Cantal, Haute-Loire, Puy-de-Dôme)	1,334,400
Basse-Normandie (Calvados, Manche, Orne)	1,373,400
Bourgogne (Côte-d'Or, Nièvre, Saône-et-Loire, Yonne)	1,607,200
Bretagne (Côtes-du-Nord, Finistère, Ille-et-Vilaine, Morbihan)	2,764,200
Centre (Cher, Eure-et-Loir, Indre, Indre-et-Loire, Loir-et-Cher, Loiret)	2,324,400
Champagne-Ardenne (Ardennes, Aube, Marne, Haute-Marne)	1,352,500
Corse (Corse-du-Sud, Haute-Corse)	248,700
Franche-Comté (Doubs, Haute-Saône, Jura, Territoire-de-Belfort)	1,085,900
Haute-Normandie (Eure, Seine-Maritime)	1,692,800
Île-de-France (Essone, Haute-de-Seine, Seine-et-Marne, Seine-St. Denis, Val-de Marne, Val-d'Oise, Ville de Paris, Yvelines)	10,250,900
Languedoc-Roussillon (Aude, Gard, Hérault, Lozère, Pyrénées-Orientales)	2,011,900
Limousin (Corrèze, Creuse, Haute-Vienne)	735,800
Lorraine (Meurthe-et-Moselle, Meuse, Moselle, Vosges)	2,313,200
Midi-Pyrénées (Ariège, Aveyron, Haute-Garonne, Gers, Lot, Hautes-Pyrénées, Tarn, Tarn-et-Garonne)	2,355,100
Nord (Nord, Pas-de-Calais)	3,923,200
Pays-de-la Loire (Loire-Atlantique, Maine-et-Loire, Mayenne, Sarthe, Vendée)	3,017,700
Picardie (Aisne, Oise, Somme)	1,774,000
Poitou-Charentes (Charente, Charente-Maritime, Deux-Sèvres, Vienne)	1,583,600
Provence-Alpes-Côte d'Azur (Alpes-de-Haute Provence, Alpes-Maritime, Bouches-du-Rhône, Haute-Alpes, Var, Vaucluse)	4,058,800
Rhône-Alpes (Ain, Ardèche, Drôme, Isère, Loire, Rhône, Savoie, Haute-Savoie)	5,153,600

Archæology, etc.—There are dolmens and menhirs in Brittany, prehistoric remains and cave drawings in Dordogne and Ariège, and throughout France various megalithic monuments erected by primitive tribes, predecessors of Iberian invaders from Spain (now represented by the Basques), Ligurians from northern Italy and Celts or Gauls from the valley of the Danube. Julius Cæsar found Gaul "divided into three parts" and described three political groups—Aquitanians south of the Garonne, Celts between the Garonne and the Seine and Marne, and Belgae from the Seine to the Rhine. Roman remains are plentiful throughout France in the form of aqueducts, arenas, triumphal arches, etc., and the celebrated Norman and Gothic Cathedrals, including Notre Dame in Paris, and those of Chartres, Reims, Amiens (where Peter the Hermit preached the First Crusade for the recovery of the Holy Sepulchre), Bourges, Beauvais, Rouen, etc., have survived invasions and bombardments, with only partial damage, and many of the renaissance and the XVIIth and XVIIIth century châteaux survived the French Revolution.

Language and Literature.—French is the universal language of France and of a large proportion of the people of Belgium, Luxembourg, Switzerland, North and West Africa, and the Province of Quebec, Canada. The work of the *French Academy*, founded by Richelieu in 1635, has established *le bon usage*, equivalent to "The Queen's English" in Great Britain. French authors have been awarded the Nobel Prize for Literature on 11 occasions—R.F.A. Sully-Prudhomme (1901), F. Mistral (1904), Romain Rolland (1915), Anatole France (1921), Henri Bergson (1927), Roger M. du Gard (1937), André Gide (1947), François Mauriac (1952), Albert Camus (1957), St. John Perse (Alexis Léger) (1960) and Jean Paul Sartre (1964).

GOVERNMENT

Parliament consists of the National Assembly and the Senate. The normal session of Parliament is confined to 5½ months each year and it may also meet in extraordinary session for 12 days at the request of the Prime Minister or a majority of the Assembly.

The Prime Minister is appointed by the President, as is the Cabinet on the Prime Minister's recommendation. They are responsible to Parliament, but as the executive is constitutionally separate from the legislature Ministers may not sit in Parliament.

A Constitutional Council is responsible for supervising all elections and referenda and must be consulted on all constitutional matters and before the President of the Republic assumes emergency powers.

DEFENCE

The personnel of the Defence Forces in 1985 totalled 464,000. National nuclear forces include medium-range ballistic missiles, submarine-launched ballistic missiles and *Mirage* IV medium bombers. The Army has a variety of new French-made equipment in service, including medium tanks, field and anti-aircraft SP guns, trucks and radio equipment. Defence Budget for 1986, 158,350 million francs.

EDUCATION

The educational system is highly centralized and is administered by the Ministry of National Education. Local Administration comprises 25 Territorial Academies, with inspecting staff for all grades, and Departmental Councils presided over by the *Préfet*, and charged especially with primary education.

Primary and secondary education are compulsory, free and secular, the school age being from 6 to 16. Schools may be single-sex or co-educational. Primary education is given in nursery schools, primary schools and *collèges d'enseignement général* (4-year secondary modern course); Secondary education in *collèges d'enseignement technique, collèges d'enseignement secondaire* and *lycées* (7-year course leading to one of the five *baccalauréats*). Special schools are numerous.

There are many *Grandes Ecoles* in France which award diplomas in many subjects not taught at university, especially applied science and engineering. Most of them are State institutions but have a competitive system of entry, unlike the universities. There are universities in twenty-four towns in France, two or three in some major provincial towns and thirteen in Paris and the immediate surrounding district.

In 1984–85 enrolment in primary schools was 4,126,435; in secondary schools 5,310,295, and in postsecondary education 1,163,903 (of which university students accounted for 962,080).

COMMUNICATIONS

Roads.—The length of roads in use at the end of 1985 was 34,221 km. of which 5,886 km. were motorways.

Railways.—The system of railroads in France is very extensive. The length of lines open for traffic at the end of 1985 was 34,676 km., of which 11,488 km. were electrified.

Shipping.—The French mercantile marine consisted in Jan. 1986, of 311 ships of over 100 tons gross, of which 27 were passenger vessels (177,000 tons gross), 63 tankers (2,968,000 tons gross) and 221 cargo vessels (2,685,000 tons gross). The principal rivers of France are the Seine, Loire, Garonne, and Rhône.

ECONOMY

Budget.—Government expenditure by function, as provided for in the 1984 general Budget, was:

	F million
Agriculture	2,002
Commerce and the Working Class	57
Culture	2,957
Economy, Finance and Budget	11,106
Education	5,334
Environment	441
Foreign Affairs	1,410
Industry and Research	33,955
Interior	4,260
Justice	515
Leisure, Youth and Sports	323
Overseas Departments and Territories	481
Social Services, Labour, Health and Employment	2,139
Tourism	68
Town Planning and Housing	7,356
Transport	9,402
Other expenditure	2,800
Total general Budget	84,806

Currency.—The unit of currency is the *franc* of 100 *centimes*.

PRODUCTION

Agriculture.—Approximately 31,513,000 hectares of land is used for agricultural purposes, 14,389,000 hectares is forested. Production in 1985 included wheat, 29,011,840 tonnes, and sugar-beet, 28,684,280 tonnes. Value of production in 1983 was crops *F*119,400 million and livestock *F*113,100 million.

The vine is extensively cultivated, regions famous for their wines including Bordeaux, Burgundy and Champagne. Production of wine in 1985 was 15,918,121 hectolitres. Cognac, liqueurs and cider are also important products.

Energy.—France produces its own oil, the greater part coming from fields in the Landes area, but is a net importer of crude oil, for processing by its important oil-refining industry. Natural gas is produced in the foothills of the Pyrenees. Electricity production was 309,805 GWh in 1984, of which 67,298 GWh. was hydro-electric and 181,739 GWh. nuclear power.

Industry.—France's heavy industries include oil-refining and the production of iron and steel, and aluminium. In 1984 production of pig-iron was 14,840,000 tonnes, steel 23,400,000 tonnes, and cement 22,700,000 tonnes. Other important industries produce chemicals, tyres, aluminium, textiles, and processed food. Engineering products include motor vehicles, and television and radio sets.

TRADE

The principal imports are raw materials for the heavy and manufacturing industries (*e.g.* oil, minerals, chemicals), machinery and precision instruments, agricultural products and vehicles. Raw materials, semi-manufactured and manufactured goods are also France's principal exports. Other member countries of the E.E.C. are France's main trading partners.

TOTAL TRADE

	1984 Francs	1985 Francs
Imports	904,118 m.	967,700 m.
Exports	813,829 m.	906,900 m.

Trade with U.K.

	1985	1986
Imports from U.K.	£7,751,751,000	£6,210,216,000
Exports to U.K.	6,632,410,000	7,348,574,000

CAPITAL.—Paris, on the Seine. Population (census, 1982), 2,188,918 (town); 8,707,000 (incl. suburbs).

The largest conurbations (populations, 1982) are ΨMarseilles (1,111,000); Lyons (1,221,000); Toulouse (541,000); ΨLille (936,000) and Bordeaux (640,000).

The chief towns of Corsica are ΨAjaccio (55,279) and ΨBastia (45,081).

FLAG.—The "tricolour", three vertical bands, blue, white, red (blue next to flagstaff).

NATIONAL DAY.—July 14.

BRITISH EMBASSY

35 rue du Faubourg St. Honoré, 75383 Paris Cedex 08

Ambassador Extraordinary and Plenipotentiary, His Excellency Sir Ewan Alastair John Fergusson, K.C.M.G. (1987).

Minister, P. J. Weston, C.M.G.

Defence and Air Attaché, Air Cdre. B. N. J. Speed, O.B.E.

Chancellor and Head of Chancery, J. Q. Greenstock.

Consul-General, J. Daly.

BRITISH CONSULAR OFFICES

There are British Consulates-General in Metropolitan France at *Paris, Bordeaux, Lille, Lyons, Marseilles.*

BRITISH COUNCIL

Representative in Paris, P. J. Prescott, 9 rue de Constantine, 75007 Paris.

There are British Council libraries at *Paris, Bordeaux, Lille, Lyons* and *Marseilles.*

FRANCO-BRITISH CHAMBER OF COMMERCE
8 rue Cimarosa, 75116 Paris

President, R. E. King.

Vice-Presidents, J. Tuby, O.B.E.; R. D. Carrington.

OVERSEAS DEPARTMENTS

Legislation passed in Dec. 1982 by the French Parliament granted greater powers of self-government to four of the five overseas departments—French Guiana, Guadeloupe, Martinique and Réunion. These former colonies had enjoyed departmental status since 1947 and the status of regions of France since 1974. Elections to their new directly-elected Assemblies were held in each department in Feb. 1983 and the Assemblies will operate in parallel with the existing, indirectly constituted Regional Councils.

French Guiana.—Situated on the north-eastern coast of South America, French Guyana is flanked by Suriname on the west and by Brazil on the south and east. Area, 34,749 sq:-miles (90,000 sq. km.). Population (1985 U.N. estimate), 82,000. Capital, ΨCayenne (38,135). Under the administration of French Guyana is a group of islands (St. Joseph, Ile Royal and Ile du Diable), known as Iles du Salut. On Devil's Isle, Captain Dreyfus was imprisoned from 1894 to 1899.

Guadeloupe.—A number of islands in the Leeward Islands group of the West Indies, consisting of the two main islands of Guadeloupe (or Basse-Terre) and Grande-Terre, with the adjacent islands of Marie-Galante, La Désirade and Iles des Saintes, the islands of St. Martin and St. Barthélemy over 150 miles to the north-west. Area, 687 sq. miles (1,779 sq. km.). Population (1985 U.N. estimate), 334,000. Capital ΨBasse Terre (15,778) in Guadeloupe. Other towns are ΨPointe à Pitre (23,889) on Grande-Terre and ΨGrand Bourg (6,611) in Marie Galante.

Martinique.—An island situated in the Windward Islands group of the West Indies, between Dominica in the north and St. Lucia in the south. Area, 425 sq. miles (1,102 sq. km.). Population (1985), 328,566. Capital ΨFort de France (100,576). Other towns are ΨTrinité (11,214) and ΨMarin (6,104).

Mayotte.—Area, 144 sq. miles (372 sq. km.). Population (1980 estimate), 50,400. Capital, Dzaoudzi (4,147). Part of the Comoros Islands group, Mayotte remained a French dependency when the other 3 islands became independent as the Comoros Republic in 1975. Since 1976 the island has been a *collectivité particulière*, an intermediate status between Overseas Department and Overseas Territory.

Réunion.—Réunion, which became a French possession in 1638, lies in the Indian Ocean, about 569 miles east of Madagascar and 110 miles S.W. of Mauritius. Area, 969 sq. miles (2,510 sq. km.). Population (1985 U.N. estimate), 531,000. Capital, St. Denis (109,072).

Also lying in the Indian Ocean adjacent to Madagascar are the smaller, uninhabited islands of Bassas da India, Europa, Iles Glorieuses, Juan de Nova and Tromelin, which are administered from Réunion.

St. Pierre and Miquelon—Area, 93 sq. miles (242 sq. km.). Population (1987), 6,500. Two small groups of Islands off the coast of Newfoundland. Became an Overseas Department in 1976 but this status is under review.

OVERSEAS TERRITORIES

French Polynesia.—Five archipelagos in the south Pacific, comprising the Society Islands (Windward Islands group includes Tahiti, Moorea, Makatea, Mehetia, Tetiaoro, Tubai Manu, etc: Leeward Islands group includes Huahine, Raiatea, Tahaa, Bora-Bora, Maupiti, etc.), the Tuamotu Islands (Rangiroa, Hao, Turéia, etc.), the Gambier Islands (Mangareva, etc.), the Tubuai Islands (Rimatara, Rurutu, Tubuai, Raivavae, Rapa, etc.) and the Marquesas Islands (Nuku-Hiva, Hiva-Oa, Fatu-Hiva, Tahuata, Ua Huka, etc.). Area, 1,544 sq. miles (4,000 sq. km.). Population (1985 estimate) 176,400. Capital, ΨPapeete (22,967) in Tahiti. Economy based on tourism and exports of copra, coffee, vanilla, citrus fruits and cultured pearls.

New Caledonia.—A large island in the Western Pacific, 700 miles E. of Queensland. Dependencies are the Isles of Pines, the Loyalty Islands (Mahé, Lifou, Urea, etc.), the Bélep Archipelago, the Chesterfield Islands, the Huon Islands and Walpole. New Caledonia was discovered in 1774 and annexed by France in 1854; from 1871 to 1896 it was a convict settlement. A referendum is to be held in 1987 on the question of independence for New Caledonia. Area, 7,358 sq. miles (19,058 sq. km.). Population (1985 U.N. estimate), 153,000. Capital ΨNoumea (60,112). It is one of the world's largest producers of nickel.

Southern and Antarctic Territories.—Created in 1955 from the former Réunion dependencies, the territory comprises the islands of New Amsterdam (25 sq. miles) and St. Paul (2·7 sq. miles), the Kerguelen Islands (2,700 sq. miles) and Crozet Islands (116 sq. miles) archipelagos and Adélie Land (116,800 sq. miles) in the Antarctic continent. The only population are members of staff of the scientific stations.

Wallis and Futuna Islands.—Two groups of islands (the Wallis Archipelago and the Îles du Hooru) in the central Pacific, N.E. of Fiji. Area, 106 sq. miles (274 sq. km.). Population (estimate 1985) 13,100. Capital, Mata-Utu on Urea, the main island of the Wallis group.

THE FRENCH COMMUNITY

The Constitution of the fifth French Republic promulgated on Oct. 6, 1958, envisaged the establishment of a French Community of States closely linked with common institutions. A number of the former French States in Africa have seceded from the Community but for all practical purposes continue to enjoy the same close links with France as those that remain formally members of the French Community. The Community Institutions in fact never operated as envisaged. Nevertheless, with the exception of Guinea, which opted out of the Community in the 1958 referendum, all the former French African colonies are closely linked to France by a series of financial, technical and economic agreements.

FRANCOPHONE COUNTRIES

In the following countries French is either the official or national language or the language of instruction; where there is another national language the name of it is shown after the name of the country:—Algeria (*Arabic*); Belgium (*Flemish*); Benin; Burkina Faso; Burundi (*Kirundi*); Cambodia (*Khmer*); Cameroon (*English*); parts of Canada (in Quebec, parts of Ontario and New Brunswick) (*English*); Central African Republic (*Sangho*); Chad; Congo; Côte d'Ivoire; France; Gabon; Guinea; Haiti (*Creole*); Laos (*Laotian*); Lebanon (*Arabic*); Luxembourg (*German and Letzeburgesch*); Madagascar (*Malagasy*); Mali; Morocco (*Arabic*); Mauritania (*Arabic*); Niger; Rwanda (*Kinyarwanda*); Senegal; Switzerland (1,000,000 French speaking); Togo; Tunisia (*Arabic*); Vietnam (*Vietnamese*); Zaire. French is also spoken in the Overseas Departments (*see* above).

GABON
(République Gabonaise)

President, El Hadj Omar Bongo, *assumed office,* Dec. 1967, *re-elected,* Feb. 1973, Dec. 1979 and Nov. 1986.

MINISTERS

Prime Minister, L. Mébiame.
First Deputy P.M., Minister for Transport, Water, Forests and Social Communications, G. Rawiri.
Second Deputy P.M., Minister for Mines and Hydrocarbons, G.-E. Mouvagha.

Third Deputy P.M., Minister for the Civil Service and Administrative Reform, E. Kassa Mapsi.
Fourth Deputy P.M., Minister for Housing and Town Planning, S. Essimengane.
Foreign Affairs and Co-operation, M. Bongo.
Public Lands and Registration, and Law of the Sea, H. Minko.
Secretary General to the Presidency, R. R. Coniquet.
Higher Education and Scientific Research, J. B. Ogouliguende.
Industry and Consumer Affairs, E. Moussirou.
Territorial Administration, Local Collectives and Immigration, R. Nguema Bekale.
Commerce, Technology Transfer and Rationalization, J.-F. Ntoutoume-Emane.
Culture and Arts, F. Owono-Nguema.
Defence, Veterans' Affairs and Public Security, J. Mpouho-Epigat.
Justice, Mrs. S. Ngwamassana.
Information, Post and Telecommunications, Z. Myboto.
Finance, Budget and State Shareholdings, J.-P. Lemboumba-Le-Pandou.
Public Works, Equipment, Construction and Land Development, Gen. J.-B. Assele.
Planning and Economy, P. Nze.
Agriculture, Livestock and Rural Development, M. Anchouey.
Education, A. Sambat.
Labour, Employment and Human Resources, L.-G. Mayila.
Civil and Commercial Aviation, M. Essonghe.
Public Health and Population, J.-P. Okias.
Social Affairs, Natural Disasters and Social Security, S. Oyouomi.
Youth and Sports, V. Afene.
State Control, E. Mbot.
Professional Training and Handicrafts, J.-J. Amiar Nganga.
Energy and Water Resources, D. Di Dinge.
Small and Medium-Sized Enterprises, E. Nze-Bekale.
Environment and Conservation, Dr. H. Moutsinga.

EMBASSY IN LONDON
48 Kensington Court, W8 5DB
[01–937 5285/9]

Ambassador Extraordinary and Plenipotentiary, His Excellency Mr. Charles Mamadou Diop (1986).

Gabon lies on the Atlantic coast of Africa at the Equator and is flanked on the north by Equatorial Guinea and Cameroon and on the east and south by the People's Republic of Congo. It has an area of 103,347 sq. miles (267,667 sq. km.) and a population (1985 U.N. estimate) of 1,151,000. Gabon elected on Nov. 28, 1958, to remain an autonomous republic within the French Community and was proclaimed fully independent on August 17, 1960.

The Constitution provides for an Executive President directly elected for a seven-year term, who appoints the Council of Ministers. There is a unicameral National Assembly comprising 84 members directly elected for a five-year term and nine members nominated by the President. The sole legal party is the *Parti democratique gabonais*.

Gabon's economy remains heavily dependent on oil, and, to a much lesser extent, other mineral resources, including manganese and uranium. Gabon has considerable timber reserves (particularly Okoumé) although production in this industry has stagnated in recent years.

The economy, which experienced considerable growth in real terms from the mid-1970s onwards, has since 1986 been adversely affected by the fall in oil prices. As a result government spending is expected to remain at a reduced level until 1989.

Gabon is a full member of OPEC.

Trade with U.K.

	1985	1986
Imports from U.K.	£30,588,000	£16,627,000
Exports to U.K.	48,292,000	36,642,000

CAPITAL.—ΨLibreville (251,000).
FLAG.—Horizontal bands, green, yellow and blue.
NATIONAL DAY.—August 17.

BRITISH EMBASSY
B.P. 476, Libreville

Ambassador Extraordinary and Plenipotentiary, His Excellency Mark Aubrey Goodfellow (1986).
First Secretary, J. Cummins, M.B.E.

GERMANY
* Deutsches Reich (German Realm)

The term "deutsch" (German) probably began to be used in the 8th century and initially described the language spoken in the eastern part of the Frankish realm which reached its apogee in Charlemagne's reign, subsequently being divided into an eastern and western realm whose political and linguistic borders coincided. Then the term was transferred from the language to its speakers, and ultimately to the region they lived in. The first German realm was the Holy Roman Empire, established in A.D. 962 when Otto I of Saxony was crowned Emperor. The Empire endured until 1806, but from as early as the 12th century the achievement of a national state was prevented by territorial fragmentation into small principalities and dukedoms, the gradually increasing autonomy of their rulers weakening the central power.

The Holy Roman Empire was replaced by a loose association of the individual sovereign states known as the German Confederation, which survived until 1866 when it was dissolved and replaced by the Prussian-dominated North German Federation. Prussia, directed by its Prime Minister (later Chancellor) Otto von Bismarck, had translated its earlier economic predominance amongst the German states into political hegemony by the annexation of the duchies of Schleswig and Holstein from Denmark in 1864 and a decisive defeat of Austria in 1866 (the Seven Weeks' War) which ended Austrian influence over German politics. After the Franco-Prussian War of 1870–71 resulted in the defeat of France and the cession to Prussia of Alsace and Lorraine, the south German principalities united with the northern federation to form a second German Empire, the King of Prussia being proclaimed Emperor at Versailles on Jan. 18, 1871.

Germany's defeat in the 1914–18 War led to the abdication of the Emperor and the princes, and the country became a Republic. The 1919 Treaty of Versailles returned Alsace and Lorraine to France, large areas in the east of the country were lost to the newly created state of Poland, and all German colonies placed under the administration of other countries. The world economic crisis of 1929 led to the collapse of the Weimar Republic and the subsequent rise to power of the National Socialist movement of Adolf Hitler, who became Chancellor in 1933.

THE WAR OF 1939–1945.—After concluding a Treaty of Non-Aggression with Soviet Russia (Aug. 24, 1939), Germany invaded Poland (Sept. 1, 1939), thus precipitating war with France and Great Britain, which had (March 31) given a pledge to support Poland against aggression.

---

* Nazi historians referred to the National Socialist régime as *Drittes Reich*.

Hitler committed suicide on April 30, 1945. On May 8, 1945, the unconditional surrender of all German forces was accepted by representatives of the Western Allied and Soviet Supreme Commanders.

THE POST WAR PERIOD.—After the surrender the Allied Powers exercised supreme authority in Germany on lines laid down in the Potsdam agreement (August 1945) between the U.K., U.S.A. and U.S.S.R. Power was exercised by the Commanders-in-Chief, each in his own zone of occupation and jointly in matters affecting Germany as a whole through a Control Council. Berlin was governed jointly by the four occupying powers. The agreement also provided for the total disarmament and demilitarisation of Germany, the destruction of the National Socialist German Workers' Party, the decentralisation of the economy and the construction of a democratic constitution. No central German government was permitted but central German administration was established in the fields of finance, industry, foreign trade, transport and communications as support organs for the Control Council. The Potsdam agreement was to have been confirmed or revised by a peace treaty but no treaty has been drawn up. Some provisions of the Potsdam agreement were carried out but differences in interpretation among the Allies made it impossible to implement in full and the system of quadripartite control broke down when the Russians withdrew from the Control Council in March 1948.

FEDERAL REPUBLIC OF GERMANY
(Bundesrepublik Deutschland)

Federal President, Dr. Richard von Weizsäcker, *born 1920, elected May 22, 1984, sworn in, July 1, 1984, for five years.*

CABINET

Federal Chancellor, Dr. Helmut Kohl (*CDU*).
Foreign Minister and Vice-Chancellor, Hans Dietrich Genscher (*FDP*).
Interior, Dr. Friedrich Zimmerman (*CSU*).
Justice, Hans Engelhard (*FDP*).
Finance, Dr. Gerhard Stoltenberg (*CDU*).
Economics, Dr. Martin Bangemann (*FDP*).
Food, Agriculture and Forestry, Ignaz Kiechle (*CSU*).
Intra-German Relations, Dr. Dorothee Wilms (*CDU*).
Labour and Social Affairs, Dr. Norbert Blüm (*CDU*).
Defence, Dr. Manfred Wörner (*CDU*).
Youth, Family Affairs, Women and Health, Prof. Dr. Rita Süssmuth (*CDU*).
Transport, Dr. Jürgen Warnke (*CSU*).
Environment, Nature Conservation and Reactor Safety, Dr. Walter Wallmann (*CDU*).
Posts and Telecommunications, Dr. Christian Schwarz-Schilling (*CDU*).
Regional Planning, Building and Urban Development, Dr. Oscar Schneider (*CSU*).
Research and Technology, Dr. Heinz Riesenhuber (*CDU*).
Education and Science, Jürgen Möllemann (*FDP*).
Economic Co-operation, Dr. Hans Klein (*CSU*).
Federal Minister at the Chancellery, Dr. Wolfgang Schäuble (*CDU*)
CDU = Christian Democratic Union; *CSU* = Christian Social Union; FDP = Free Democratic Party.

EMBASSY IN LONDON
23 Belgrave Square, SW1X 8PZ
[01–235 5033]

Ambassador Extraordinary and Plenipotentiary, His Excellency Baron Rüdiger von Wechmar (1984).
Minister Plenipotentiary, Baron Hans von Stein.

Minister-Counsellor, Dr. Eike Bracklo.
1st Counsellors, Oskar Rudolph (*Head of Economic Dept.*); G. H. von Neubronner (*Cultural*); Dr. W. Hoffman (*Scientific Affairs*); Dr. R. Peters (*Agriculture*).

NOTE.—Except where otherwise indicated statistical data on the Federal Republic of Germany include Berlin (West).

Area and Population.—The area of the Federal Republic is approximately 95,976 sq. miles (248,577 sq. km.). Total population of the Federal Republic at end Oct. 1986 was 61,139,000. Distribution of the population among the *Länder* at end 1985 was:

Baden-Württemberg	9,271,000
Bavaria	10,974,000
Berlin (West)	1,860,000
Bremen	660,000
Hamburg	1,580,000
Hesse	5,529,000
Lower Saxony	7,197,000
North Rhine Westphalia	16,674,000
Rhineland Palatinate	3,615,000
Saarland	1,046,000
Schleswig-Holstein	2,614,000

Vital Statistics.—There were 10·3 live births per 1,000 inhabitants in the Federal Republic in 1986.

Government.—The Federal Republic grew out of the fusion of the three western zones. The economic union of the U.K. and U.S. zones was later joined by the French zone and in 1948–49 Parliamentary Council, elected by the parliaments of the *Länder* in the three zones, drafted a provisional democratic federal constitution for Germany. This Basic Law came into force in the three western zones on May 23, 1949. When the Federal Government took office the Allied Military Governors were replaced by High Commissioners. In 1952 a contractual agreement was signed between the Federal Republic and the western Allies, whereby the Republic, in return for certain promises regarding a defence contribution, a foreign debt settlement, and the continuation of allied policies concerning decartelization, democratization, restitution, etc., regained virtual sovereignty in May, 1955, after ratification by all the parties concerned. The High Commissioners then became Ambassadors.

The Basic Law provides for a President, elected for a five-year term, a Lower House (*Bundestag*), with a four-year term of office, elected by direct universal suffrage, and an Upper House (*Bundesrat*) composed of 45 delegates of the *Länder*, without a fixed term of office.

The results of the elections held for the lower House (*Bundestag*) on Jan. 25, 1987, were as follows:

Party	Numbers
Social Democrats	186
Christian Democratic Union	174
Christian Social Union	49
Free Democrats	46
The Greens	42

with an additional 22 representatives of Berlin elected by the House of Representatives of Berlin (CDU 11; SPD 7; FDP 2; Alternative Liste 2).

The Prime Ministers of the *Länder* governments in June, 1987, were:

Ministers-President

Baden-Württemberg.—Lothar Späth.
Bavaria.—Franz Josef Strauss.
Berlin.—Eberhard Diepgen (*Governing Mayor*).
Bremen.—Klaus Wedemeier (*Mayor*).
Hamburg.—Dr. Klaus v. Dohnanyi (*First Mayor*).
Hesse.—Dr. Walter Wallmann.
Lower Saxony.—Dr. Ernst Albrecht.

North Rhine-Westphalia.—Johannes Rau.
Rhineland-Palatinate.—Dr. Bernhard Vogel.
Saarland.—Oskar Lafontaine.
Schleswig-Holstein.—Dr. Dr. Uwe Barschel.

Law and Justice.—Judicial authority is exercised by the Federal Constitutional Court, the Federal courts provided for in the Basic Law and the courts of the Länder.

The death sentence has been abolished.

Economy

Despite the difficulties arising from the division of Germany, which cut off from the Federal Republic the main food producing areas of Eastern Germany and some of the principal centres of light industry, Germany has regained her position as the main industrial power on the Continent, and is the most economically powerful member of the European Community. The Gross National Product at current prices in 1986 was estimated at *DM*1,949,000 million, an increase of 5·5 per cent over 1985. In real terms GNP grew by 2·4 per cent, after a 2·5 per cent growth in 1985. Forecasts for real growth in 1987 range from 1·0 to 2·5 per cent.

Agriculture.—In 1985 total area of farmland was 12,019,000 hectares, of which 7,240,300 hectares were arable land. Forest areas cover 7,360,000 hectares.

Crop yields were (tonnes):

	1984	1985
Rye	1,930,800	1,821,400
Wheat	10,223,300	9,865,900
Maslin	52,000	55,100
Barley	10,284,000	9,690,500
Oats	2,506,900	2,806,500
Potatoes	7,272,300	7,905,300
Sugar beet	20,060,000	20,813,000
Colza and rape	661,800	802,800
Fruit	3,122,665	2,548,515

Milk production in 1984 was 25,674,100 tonnes. Total yield of fisheries was 190,670 tonnes, valued at *DM*.269,084,000.

Industrial Production.—The Federal Republic has a predominantly industrial economy. Principal industries are coal mining, iron and steel production, machine construction, the electrical industry, the manufacture of steel and metal products, chemicals and textiles, and the processing of foodstuffs. The index of industrial net production adjusted for irregularities of the calendar (1980 = 100) is as follows:

	1985	1986
Mining	91·1	86·8
Manufacturing industry	105·1	107·7
(i) Basic materials	99·1	98·5
(ii) Capital goods	112·7	117·7
(iii) Consumer goods	95·1	97·0
(iv) Foodstuffs	104·0	105·3
Power (electricity and gas)	110·5	109·8
Construction	82·7	85·8
Total industry	103·0	105·3

Annual production figures were:

	1985	1986
	Tonnes '000	
Hard coal	82,398	80,801
Brown coal	120,667	114,310
Crude petroleum	4,105	4,017
Pig iron	30,229	27,622
Raw steel	40,081	36,370
Rolled steel	28,887	27,524
Fuel oils	34,851	34,208
Petrol, special and testing benzines	20,037	19,200
Chemical fibres	977	952
Cement	25,574	26,639
	Number	
Passenger cars	3,868,000	3,953,000
Televisions	3,793,000	3,866,000

Labour.—Labour figures, in annual averages, were:

	1985	1986
Employment	25,534,000	25,786,000
Unemployed	2,304,000	2,228,000
Men	1,289,000	1,200,000
Foreign Workers	1,567,500	1,600,200

FINANCE

Receipts.—As from January 1, 1979, the distribution of taxes in the Fed. Rep. of Germany between Federation, Länder, communities and local authorities has been regulated by the Basic Law (Constitution).

Expenditure.—Figures of budgetary expenditure are:

	1986	Draft 1987
	DM million	
Total expenditure	261,600	271,000
Agriculture	6,900	7,800
Defence	49,900	51,300
Social Welfare	76,700	78,600
Transport	25,400	25,600

Currency.—The currency of the Federal Republic is the *Deutsche Mark* of 100 *Pfennig.* (*See also* p. 81.)

TRADE

	1985	1986
	DM million	
Total imports	463,811·0	413,744·4
Total exports	537,164·2	526,363·0

Of imports, 13·2 per cent were foodstuffs and 7·5 per cent industrial raw materials in 1986. Main trading partners in 1986 were (figures shown as percentage of total trade):

	Imports	Exports
Netherlands	11·5	8·6
France	11·4	11·8
U.K.	7·2	8·5
Italy	9·2	8·1
U.S.A.	6·5	10·5
Japan	5·8	1·7

Trade with U.K.

	1985	1986
Imports from U.K	£8,947,055,000	£8,542,196,000
Exports to U.K.	12,601,387,000	14,139,097,000

The U.K. is currently the largest supplier to the Federal Republic of petroleum and petroleum products (1986: £1,236,838,000).

Communications.—At the end of 1984 the state-owned railways of the Federal Republic (*Deutsche Bundesbahn*) measured 27,798 kilometres of which 11,264 kilometres were electrified, and the privately owned railways 2,922 kilometres, a total of 30,720 kilometres. Railway rolling stock included, in 1984, 2,624 electric locomotives, 4,058 diesel locomotives and 261,518 goods waggons; in 1984 the railways handled 316,079,000 tonnes of goods. Classified roads measured 173,045 kilometres in 1985, of which motorways were 8,198 kilometres. On Jan 1, 1987, there were 27,223,810 cars registered, 1,363,738 commercial vehicles and 1,723,797 tractors. Ocean-going shipping under the German flag in Dec., 1984, amounted to 6,304,000 tons gross. Inland waterways handled 236,478,000 tonnes of goods in 1984.

Social Welfare.—There is compulsory insurance against sickness, accident, old age and unemployment. Children's allowances are payable in respect of the second and subsequent children. Pension schemes for widows and orphans of public servants are in operation. Public assistance is given to persons unable to earn their living, or with insufficient income to maintain a decent standard of living.

Education.—School attendance is compulsory for all children and juveniles between the ages of 6 and 18 and comprises 9 years full-time compulsory education at primary and main schools (*Grund und Hauptschulen*) and 3 years of compulsory vocational education on a part-time basis. In autumn, 1984, there were in the Federal Republic 19,325 primary and main schools (*Grund- und Hauptschulen*) with 4,005,638 pupils. Secondary modern schools (*Realschulen*) numbered 2,628 with 1,132,205 pupils. There were 2,788 other general secondary schools (*Gymnasien* including *Gesamtschulen*) with 2,073,571 pupils.

There were also 2,819 special schools (*Sonderschulen*) for retarded, physically and mentally handicapped and socially maladjusted children in the Federal Republic with 284,594 pupils.

The secondary school leaving examination (*Abitur*) entitles the holder to a place of study at a university or another institution of higher education.

Children below the age of 18 who are not attending a general secondary or a full-time vocational school are obliged to take a three-year course (part-time) at a vocational school. In November, 1984, there were 1,548 full and part-time vocational schools (*Berufsschulen*) and 372 vocational extension schools (*Berufsaufbauschulen*) with 1,996,484 pupils, 2,750 full-time vocational schools (*Berufsfachschulen*) with 399,119 pupils, 1,006 schools for secondary technical studies (*Fachoberschulen/Fachgymnasien*) with 140,015 students.

Results for the winter term 1985–86 show a total of 1,338,042 students at institutions of higher education, of whom 912,253 were attending universities. The largest universities were in Munich, Berlin, Hamburg, Bonn and Cologne.

Language and Literature.—Modern (or New High) German has developed from the time of the Reformation to the present day, with differences of dialect in Austria and Alsace and in the German-speaking cantons of Switzerland. The literary language is usually regarded as having become fixed by Luther and Zwingli at the Reformation, since which time many great names occur in all branches, notably philosophy, from Leibnitz (1646–1716) to Kant (1724–1804), Fichte (1762–1814), Schelling (1775–1854) and Hegel (1770–1831); the drama from Goethe (1749–1832) and Schiller (1759–1805) to Gerhart Hauptmann (1862–1946); and in poetry, Heine (1797–1856). German authors have received the Nobel Prize for Literature on seven occasions—Theodor Mommsen (1902), R. Eucken (1908), P. Heyse (1909), Gerhart Hauptmann (1912), Thomas Mann (1929), N. Sachs (1966) and Heinrich Böll (1972). In 1985 there were 382 daily papers.

Religion.—In 1970 there were 29,696,571 Protestants in the Republic, 27,060,826 Roman Catholics, 31,684 Jews and 3,861,518 others.

CAPITAL, Bonn, in North Rhine Westphalia, 15 miles distant from Cologne. Population 291,700 (end June 1983).

The population of the principal cities and towns in the Federal Republic at end June 1985, was:

Berlin (West)	1,852,700	Dortmund	575,200
ΨHamburg...	1,585,900	Düsseldorf	563,000
Munich	1,266,100	Stuttgart	561,200
Cologne	919,300	ΨBremen	528,900
Essen	622,000	Duisburg	520,200
Frankfurt am		Hannover	517,900
Main.......	598,000	Nuremberg ...	466,100

FLAG.—Horizontal bars of black, red and gold.
NATIONAL DAY.—May 23.

BRITISH EMBASSY
Friedrich-Ebert-Allee 77, 5300 Bonn 1

Ambassador Extraordinary and Plenipotentiary, His Excellency Sir Julian Bullard, G.C.M.G. (1984).
Ministers, N. C. R. Williams, C.M.G.; Miss L. P. Neville Jones, C.M.G.
Counsellors, D. K. Haskell, C.V.O. (*Head of Chancery*); G. J. Garrett; R. P. Flower; H. H. Chambers (*Defence Supply*); A. C. Thorpe (*Economic*); Dr. J. K. Duxbury (*Science and Technology*); A. L. Free-Gore (*Administration*); D. J. Young (*Commercial*); Mrs. A. Le Strange (*Labour*).
First Secretaries, D. E. Lyscom; M. A. Arthur; Miss R. M. Marsden; D. M. Bell; C. H. Salvesen; R. Weaver; R. Gwilliams; P. Elliott; M. Uden; I. Woods; E. Jenkinson; M. Evans; A. B. Gundersen; D. J. Skinner; R. Sands.
Legal Advisor, J. O. Hill.
Defence and Military Attaché, Brig. N. M. Pughe.
Asst. Military Attaché, Lt. Col. G. C. Gray.
Naval Attaché, Capt. W. K. Hutchinson, R.N.
Asst. Naval Attaché, Lt.-Cdr. R. Stanton.
Air Attaché, Air Cdre. C. Reineck.
Head of Visa Section (Düsseldorf), P. Faulkner.
Chaplain, Rev. J. Newsome.

There are British Consulates-General at *Berlin, Hamburg, Düsseldorf, Frankfurt* and *Munich.*

BRITISH COUNCIL

Representative, T. Rutter, O.B.E., Hahnenstrasse 6, 5000 Cologne 1. Offices at *Berlin, Hamburg* and *Munich* and British Council libraries at all four centres.

BRITISH CHAMBER OF COMMERCE
Neumarkt 14, D-5000 Cologne 1.
Director, J. Parr.

BERLIN

G.O.C. British Sector, Maj.-General P. G. Brooking, M.B.E.

Minister and Deputy Commandant, M. St. E. Burton, C.V.O.
Counsellor, R. H. Smith (*Political Adviser and Head of Chancery*).

GERMAN DEMOCRATIC REPUBLIC
(Deutsche Demokratische Republik)

COUNCIL OF STATE

Chairman, Erich Honecker.
Deputy Chairmen, Dr. Manfred Gerlach; Ernst Mecklenburg; Gerald Götting; Prof. Heinrich Homann; Horst Sindermann; Willi Stoph; Egon Krenz; Günter Mittag.
Members, E. Aurich; F. Dallmann; W. Felfe; Prof. K. Hager; Frau B. Hanke; L. Helmschrott; F. Kind; Frau E. Klett; Prof. L. Kolditz; P. Moreth; Frau M. Müller; A. Pisnik; B. Quandt; Dr. K. Sorgenicht; P. Strauss; Frau I. Thiele; H. Tisch; Prof. J. Töpfer; P. Verner; Frau R. Walther; Frau M. Werner; H. Eichler.

COUNCIL OF MINISTERS

Chairman, Willi Stoph.
Deputy Chairmen, Werner Krolikowski (*First Deputy Chairman*); M. Flegel; H-J. Heusinger; G. Kleiber; W. Rauchfuss; Dr. H. Reichelt; G. Schürer; R. Schulze; H. Sölle; Dr. H. Weiz.
Total membership of the Council is 45.

SOCIALIST UNITY PARTY OF GERMANY

Politbureau of the Central Committee, H. Axen; H.-J. Böhme; H. Dohlus; W. Eberlein; W. Felfe; Prof. K. Hager; J. Herrmann; E. Honecker; W. Jarowinsky; Gen. H. Kessler; G. Kleiber; E. Krenz; W. Krolikowski; S. Lorenz; E. Mielke; G. Mittag; E. Mückenberger; A. Neumann; G. Schabowski; H. Sindermann; W. Stoph; H. Tisch (*full members*); Frau I. Lange; G. Müller; Frau M. Müller; G. Schürer; W. Walde (*candidate members*).
Secretariat of the Central Committee, E. Honecker (*General Secretary*); H. Axen; H. Dohlus; W. Felfe; Prof. K. Hager; J. Herrmann; W. Jarowinsky; E. Krenz; I. Lange; G. Mittag; G. Schabowski (*secretaries*).

EMBASSY OF THE G.D.R.
34 Belgrave Square, SW1X 8QB
[01–235 9941]

Ambassador Extraordinary and Plenipotentiary, His Excellency Dr. Gerhard Lindner (1984).
Counsellors, H. Bock; H. Vorpahl.
1st Secretaries, H. Kopp; M. Rudolph, Dr. H. Kluge.

Area and Population.—The German Democratic Republic comprises the five former German *Länder* of Brandenburg, Mecklenburg, Saxony, Saxony-Anhalt and Thuringia (an area of 41,768 sq. miles; 108,178 sq. km.). The seat of Government is the Soviet sector of Berlin (eastern part of Berlin) (156 sq. miles). The population of the Republic, including East Berlin (end of 1985) is 16,644,000. In 1952 the former *Länder* were replaced by fourteen *Bezirke* (regions): Potsdam, Cottbus and Frankfurt (*formerly* Brandenburg); Rostock, Schwerin and Neubrandenburg (*formerly* Mecklenburg); Karl-Marx-Stadt, Dresden and Leipzig (*formerly* Saxony); Halle and Magdeburg (*formerly* Saxony-Anhalt); Erfurt, Gera and Suhl (*formerly* Thuringia.)

Government.—The present Constitution, which defines the G.D.R. as a Socialist state, came into force on April 9, 1968 after endorsement by a referendum. It replaced the first Constitution of October 7, 1949. The supreme organ of State power is the *Volkskammer,* which has power to elect and dismiss the Council of State, the Council of Ministers, the Chairman of the National Defence Council, the Supreme Court and the Procurator-General. The Council of State retains the presidential powers which it has exercised since the abolition of the office of President on September 12, 1960, together with responsibility for the organization of defence with the help of the National Defence Council. The Council of Ministers is responsible to the *Volkskammer* for the conduct of State policy. The present *Volkskammer* is that elected in April 1986.

As with other communist countries, effective power lies with the ruling Marxist-Leninist Party, in this case the Socialist Unity Party of Germany (SED). The other parties and mass organizations are members of the SED-controlled National Front.

ECONOMY

The G.D.R. economy, including the control of industry and foreign trade, is centrally planned and administered. The State Planning Commission, which is subordinate to the Council of Ministers, is responsible for drawing up the 5- and 1-Year Plans. The 5-Year Plans determine the future development and structure of the economy; the 1-Year Plans have to achieve these aims. The implementation of these plans is the responsibility of the State Production Enterprises under the supervision of the economic and industrial Ministries. The economy is very closely integrated with those of other member countries of C.M.E.A. and particularly with the U.S.S.R.

The Budget for 1986 was: revenue, *M*263,750·7 million; expenditure, *M*263,590·9 million. The unit of currency is the *Mark of the G.D.R.* (M) of 100 *pfennig*.

Agriculture.—Land is cultivated mostly on state or collective farms, though some is cultivated independently. Crop yields in 1985 were: potatoes 12,350,000 tonnes; sugar-beet 7,397,000 tonnes; corn (green and silage) 12,884,000 tonnes; grain 11,640,000 tonnes, and oilseeds 396,000 tonnes.

Industry.—Almost all industry is nationally or co-operatively owned with less than 2 per cent. of the working population engaged in private enterprise. G.D.R. is the leading world producer of lignite, production in 1985 was 312,000,000 tonnes, and the iron and steel industry is also important. Other highly developed industries include basic chemicals and petro-chemicals, machine tools and industrial plant, ship-building and transport equipment, electronic and engineering equipment, precision tools and optical instruments.

Trade with U.K.

	1985	1986
Imports from U.K.	£63,797,000	£81,276,000
Exports to U.K.	204,293,000	195,513,000

Principal cities and towns (population, 1985): East Berlin (1,202,895); Leipzig (554,595); Dresden (519,860); Karl-Marx-Stadt (316,361); Magdeburg (288,914); Rostock (242,729); Halle (Saale) (235,858); Erfurt (215,499); Potsdam (138,737).

FLAG.—Horizontal bands of black, red, gold; hammer, compasses and corn device at centre.

NATIONAL DAY.—October 7.

BRITISH EMBASSY
108 Berlin, Unter den Linden 32/34

Ambassador Extraordinary and Plenipotentiary, His Excellency Timothy John Everard, C.M.G. (1984).
Counsellor, A. Ford.
First Secretaries, D. B. Merry (*Head of Chancery*); F. T. Cameron (*Information*); J. E. Brook (*Commercial*).

Second Secretaries, D. A. Muat (*Administration and Consul*); J. W. Lawson.
Third Secretary, R. C. Morton.
Cultural Attaché, M. G. Holcroft (*British Council Representative*).

GREECE
(Elliniki Dimokratia)

President of the Hellenic Republic, Christos Sartzetakis, *born* 1927, *elected* March 29, 1985.

CABINET

Prime Minister, Dr. Andreas Papandreou.
Deputy Prime Minister and Minister of National Defence, Ioannis Haralambopoulos.
Minister to the Prime Minister, Apostolos Kaklamanis.
Foreign Affairs, Carolos Papoulias.
Interior, Emmanuel Papastefanakis.
National Economy, Constantine Simitis.
Finance, Dimitrios Tsovolas.
Health, Welfare and Social Security, George–Alexander Mangakis.
Justice, Eleftherios Veryvakis.
Education and Religion, Antonios Tritsis.
Culture, Miss Melina Mercouri.
Public Order, Antonios Drosoyiannis.
Northern Greece, Stylianos Papathemelis.
The Aegean, Petros Valvis.
Agriculture, Ioannis Pottakis.
Environment, Regional Planning and Public Works, Evangelos Kouloumbis.
Industry, Energy and Technology, Markos Natasinas.
Labour, Constantine Papanayotou.
Commerce, Panayotis Roumeliotis.
Transport and Communications, Constantine Bandouvas.
Merchant Marine, Efstathios Alexandris.

GREEK EMBASSY IN LONDON
1a Holland Park, W11 3TP
[01–727 8040]

Ambassador Extraordinary and Plenipotentiary, His Excellency Stephanos G. Stathatos (1986).
Defence Attaché, Capt. H. N. George Beserianos.
Counsellors, Chr. Tsalikis; A. Anninos; E. Clis (*Consular Affairs*); T. Karavias (*Economic and Commercial*); I. Staikos (*Education*); A. Xerikos (*Labour*); T. Chytiris (*Press*).
Tourist Adviser, P. Analytis.

There are Honorary Consulates at *Belfast, Birmingham, Edinburgh, Falmouth, Glasgow, Leeds, Manchester* and *Southampton.*

A maritime State in the south-east of Europe, bounded on the N. by Albania, Yugoslavia and Bulgaria, on the S. and W. by the Ionian and Mediterranean seas, and on the E. by Turkey, with an estimated area of 50,944 sq. miles (131,944 sq. km.). Population (1985 U.N. estimate) is given as 9,935,000.

The main areas of Greece are: *Macedonia* (which includes Mt. Athos and the island of Thasos), *Thrace* (including the island of Samothrace), *Epirus, Thessaly, Continental Greece* (which includes the island of Euboea and the Sporades or "scattered islands" of which the largest is Skyros), the *Peloponnese* (or *Morea*), the *Dodecanese* or *Southern Sporades* (12 islands occupied by Italy in 1911 during the Italo-Turkish War and ceded to Greece by Italy in 1947) consisting of Rhodes, Astypalaia, Karpathos, Kassos, Nisyros, Kalymnos, Leros, Patmos, Kos, Symi, Khalki and Tilos, the *Cyclades* (a circular group numbering about 200, with a total area of 923 sq. miles; the chief islands are Syros, Andros, Tinos, Naxos, Paros, Santorini, Milos and Serifos), the *Ionian Islands*

(Corfu, Paxos, Levkas, Ithaca, Cephalonia, Zante and Cerigo), the *Aegean Islands* (Chios, Lesbos, Limnos and Samos). In *Crete* there was for over 1,500 years (3000 to 1400 B.C.) a flourishing civilization which spread its influence far and wide throughout the Aegean, and the ruins of the palace of Minos at Knossos afford evidence of astonishing comfort and luxury. Greek civilization emerged about 1300 B.C. and the poems of Homer, the blind poet of Chios, which were probably current about 800 B.C., record the 10-year struggle between the Achaeans of Greece and the Phrygians of Troy (1194–1184 B.C.).

Language and Literature.—The spoken language of modern Greece is descended by a process of natural development from the "Common Greek" of Alexander's empire. *Katharevousa*, a conservative literary dialect evolved by Adamantios Corais (Diamant Coray), who lived and died in Paris (1748–1833) and used for official and technical matters, is to be phased out over the next few years. Novels and poetry are mostly composed in *dimotiki*, a progressive literary dialect which owes much to John Psycharis (1854–1929). The poets Solomos, Palamas, Cavafis, Sikelianos, Seferis and Elytis have won a European reputation.

Religion.—Over 97 per cent of the people are adherents of the Greek Orthodox Church, which is the State religion, all others being tolerated and free from interference. The Church of Greece recognizes the spiritual primacy of the Œcumenical Patriarch of Constantinople, but is otherwise a self-governing body administered by the Holy Synod under the Presidency of the Archbishop of Athens and All Greece. It has no jurisdiction over the Church of Crete, which has a degree of autonomy under the Œcumenical Patriarch, nor over the Monastic Community of Mount Athos and the Church in the Dodecanese, both of which come directly under the Œcumenical Patriarch.

Government.—A military coup on April 21, 1967, suspended parliamentary government and, following an unsuccessful royal counter coup on December 13, 1967, King Constantine went into voluntary exile in Rome. On June 1, 1973 the monarchy was abolished and a republic established under the Presidency of Mr. George Papadopoulos.

The overthrow of Archbishop Makarios, President of Cyprus, on July 15, 1974, by a military coup led by Greek officers of the Cypriot National Guard caused an international crisis, in the wake of which the heads of the Greek armed forces decided, on July 23, to relinquish power. Mr. Konstantinos Karamanlis, Prime Minister between 1955 and 1963, returned from his self-imposed exile in Paris to form a provisional Government, and the first elections for ten years were held on November 17, 1974.

The constitutional position of the King, who was still in exile, remained unsettled until December 8, when by a referendum, the Greek people rejected "crowned democracy" by 69·2 per cent to 30·8 per cent and Greece became a republic. A new constitution came into force on June 11, 1975.

The Socialist Movement under Andreas Papandreou came into office following the General Election of Oct. 1981, and remained in power after winning the 1985 General Election.

Defence.—The strength of the Army is 130,000 backed up by some 50,000 in the National Guard. The Navy consists of 19,500 men and is equipped with a fleet of destroyers, submarines, patrol boats and amphibious warfare vessels, mostly of U.S., French, Dutch and German origin. The Air Force consists of 25,000 men and is equipped with aircraft disposed in 14 combat squadrons supported by the necessary transport, training, helicopter and reconnaissance squadrons. National service is 2 years on average.

Communications.—The 2,650 kilometres of Greek railways are State-owned with the exception of the Athens–Piraeus Electric Railway. Greek roads total somewhat over 35,500 kilometres, of which about 25 per cent are classified as national highways and just under 30,000 km. are classified as provincial roads. The road connection with Albania was reopened in 1985.

On Dec. 31, 1986, the Greek Mercantile fleet numbered 2,138 ships with a total tonnage of 24,792,516 tons gross. On the same day Greek-owned ships registered under foreign flags numbered 276 with a total tonnage of 5,176,347 tons gross. (N.B. These figures exclude Greek-owned vessels under 100 tons gross). Athens has direct airline links with Australasia, North America, most countries in Europe, Africa and the Middle East.

Education is free and compulsory from the age of 6 to 15 and is maintained by State grants. There are six Universities, Athens, Salonika, Patras, Thrace, Ioannina and Crete. There are several other institutes of higher learning, mostly in Athens.

Production.—Though there has in recent years been a substantial measure of industrialization, agriculture still employs about a quarter of the working population. The most important agricultural products are tobacco, wheat, cotton, sugar and rice. The most important of the fruit trees are the olive, peach, vine, orange, lemon, fig, almond and currant-vine, and now exports of Greek fresh fruit and vegetables have established themselves as an important contributor to the economy and have considerable growth potential. Currants, grown mainly around Patras, remain one of Greece's main exports, the United Kingdom being the principal purchaser.

The principal minerals mined in Greece are nickel, bauxite, iron ore, iron pyrites, manganese magnesite, chrome, lead, zinc and emery, and prospecting for petroleum is being carried on. Oil refineries are in operation near Athens and at Salonika, where there is also a petro-chemical plant. The chief industries are textiles (cotton, woollen and synthetics), chemicals, cement, glass, metallurgy, shipbuilding, domestic electrical equipment and footwear. In recent years new factories have been opened for the production of aluminium, nickel, iron and steel products, tyres, chemicals fertilizers and sugar (from locally-grown beet). Food processing and ancillary industries have also grown up throughout the country. The development of the country's electric power resources, irrigation and land reclamation schemes and the exploitation of Greece's lignite resources for fuel and industrial purposes are also being carried out. Tourism has developed rapidly, but is now slowing down.

Currency.—The Greek *drachma* has a floating exchange rate.

TRADE

	1985	1986
Total imports ...	Drs 1,412,797·3m.	Drs 1,587,214·0m.
Total exports ...	629,188·3m.	789,994·6m.

Trade with U.K.

	1985	1986
Imports from U.K. ...	£335,352,000	£356,020,000
Exports to U.K.	320,131,000	308,644,000

CAPITAL.—Athens. Population (including ΨPiraeus and suburbs), 3,027,331 (1981 Census). Other large towns are ΨSalonika (706,180); ΨPatras (154,596), ΨVolos (107,407); Larissa (102,426); and ΨKavalla (56,705); in Crete—ΨHeraklion or Candia (102,398), ΨCanea (47,451), and ΨRethymnon (18,190); in the Ionian Islands—ΨCorfu (36,901); in the Dodecanese—ΨRhodes (41,425); in the Cyclades—ΨSyros Hermoupolis (13,877); in Lesbos—ΨMytilene (24,991); in Chios—ΨChios (24,070).

FLAG.—Blue and white stripes with a white cross on a blue field in the canton.

NATIONAL DAY.—March 25 (Independence Day).

BRITISH EMBASSY
1 Ploutarchou Street, 10675 Athens.

Ambassador Extraordinary and Plenipotentiary, His Excellency Sir Jeremy Cashel Thomas, K.C.M.G. (1985).

Counsellors, C. Hulse, O.B.E. (*Political and Consul-General*); B. Eastwood (*Economic and Commercial*).

Defence and Military Attaché, Brig. R. Evans.

Naval and Air Attaché, Capt. R. Evans.

Embassy Chaplain, Rev. S. J. B. Peake.

Hon. Attaché, H. W. Catling, O.B.E., D.Phil. (*Director, British School of Archæology*).

BRITISH CONSULAR OFFICES

There are British Consular Offices at *Athens, Corfu, Samos, Rhodes, Salonika, Heraklion* (Crete) and *Patras.*

BRITISH COUNCIL
17 Plateia Philikis Etairias (P.O. Box 3488), 10673 Athens.

Representative, Dr. R. T. Taylor.

There is also an office at *Salonika* and British Council libraries at both centres.

BRITISH-HELLENIC CHAMBER OF COMMERCE
4 Valaoritou Street, GR-10671 Athens.

GUATEMALA
(República de Guatemala)

Head of State, President Marco Vinicio Cerezo, *inaugurated,* Jan. 14, 1986.

CABINET

Vice President, Roberto Carpio Nicolle.

Minister of Government, Juan Jose Rodil Peralta.

Foreign Affairs, (vacant).

National Defence, Gen. Héctor Alejandro Gramajo.

Finance, Dr. Rudolfo Paiz Andrade.

Communications, Eduardo Goyzeuta Weissbach.

Education, Dr. Eduardo Meyer Maldonado.

Agriculture, Rodolfo Augusto Estrada.

Economy, Lizardo Arturo Sosa Lopez.

Public Health and Social Welfare, Dr. Carlos Armando Soto Gomez.

Labour and Social Insurance, Catalina Soberanis Reyes.

Energy and Mines, Roland Castillo Contoux.

Special Affairs, Alfonso Cabrera Hidalgo.

Urban and Rural Development, Rene Armando De-Léon Schlotter.

Culture and Sport, Elmar Rene Rojas Azurdia.

Guatemala is to establish an Embassy in London in late-1987.

Guatemala, in Central America, is situated in N. lat. from 13° 45′ to 17° 49′, and in W. long. from 88° 12′ 49″ to 92°13′ 43″, and has an area of 42,042 sq. miles (108,889 sq. km.), and a population (1985 U.N. estimate) of 7,963,000.

The Republic is divided into 22 departments, and is traversed from W. to E. by an elevated mountain chain, containing several volcanic summits rising to 13,000 feet above the sea; earthquakes are frequent. The country is well watered by numerous rivers; the climate is hot and malarial near the coast, temperate in the higher regions. The rainfall in the capital is 57 in. per annum. The chief seaports are San José de Guatemala and Champerico on the Pacific and Santo Tomás de Castilla and Puerto Barrios on the Atlantic side.

Language and Literature.—Spanish is the language of the country, but 40 per cent. of the population speak an Indian language. Since the establishment of the University in the capital, education has received a marked impulse and the high figure of illiteracy is being reduced. The National library contains about 80,000 volumes in the Spanish tongue.

Government.—The constitutionally elected president, Gen. Miguel Ydigoras Fuentes, was overthrown on March 31, 1963, by the Army, which handed executive and legislative powers to the Minister of Defence, Col. Enrique Peralta Azurdia. Important changes were included in a new constitution promulgated on Sept. 15, 1965, and elections for a new Congress and for President and Vice-President took place on March 6, 1966. The constitution was suspended "for as long as the situation demands" following a military coup in March 1982. An amnesty for guerrillas was unsuccessful and the Army was fully occupied dealing with the proliferating subversive groups throughout the country.

Elections for a Constituent Assembly were held on July 1, 1984, as promised by Gen. Mejía Victores when he overthrew Gen. Ríos Montt in 1983. The Assembly drew up a new Constitution, promulgated in June 1985, and a new electoral law, paving the way for Presidential, Governmental and Municipal elections which took place on Nov. 3 and Dec. 8, 1985. The elections were won by the Christian Democratic party and Vinicio Cerezo was elected President.

Finance.—The Central Government revenue in 1985 was *Quetzales* 865 million, and expenditure *Quetzales* 1,076 million.

TRADE

	1985	1986
Imports (c.i.f.) ...	U.S.$1,755 m.	U.S.$1,261 m.
Exports (f.o.b.) ..	1,112 m.	1,210 m.

Trade with U.K.

	1985	1986
Imports from U.K.	£13,397,000	£9,288,000
Exports to U.K.	5,176,000	8,098,000

The principal export is coffee, other articles being manufactured goods, sugar, bananas, cotton, beef and essential oils. The chief imports are petroleum, vehicles, machinery and foodstuffs.

CAPITAL.—Guatemala City. Population : 1,300,000.

Quezaltenango has a pop. of over 100,000. Other towns are ΨPuerto Barrios (23,000), Mazatenango (21,000), and Antigua (30,000).

FLAG.—Three vertical bands, blue, white, blue; coat of arms on white stripe.

NATIONAL DAY.—September 15.

BRITISH EMBASSY
Centro Financiero Torre II (7th Floor), Seventh Avenue 5–10 Zone 4, Guatemala City.

Ambassador Extraordinary and Plenipotentiary, His Excellency Bernard Everett.

GUINEA
(République de Guinée)

President, Brig. Gen. Lansana Conté, *took power*, April 3, 1984 (*also holds Defence Portfolio*)

COUNCIL OF MINISTERS

Resident Regional Ministers:
Maritime Guinea (*Kindia*), Maj. Jean Kolipé Lama.
Middle Guinea (*Labé*), Mankan Camara.
Upper Guinea (*Kankan*), Capt. Mamadou Balde.
Forest Region (*N'Zerékoré*), Capt. Facinét Touré.
Ministers delegated to the Presidency:
National Defence, Lt. Col. Sory Doumbouya.
Interior and Decentralization, Maj. Alpha Oumar Diallo.
Planning and International Co-operation, Edouard Benjamin.
Information and Culture, Zainoue Abidine Sanoussi.
Ministers:
Justice, Bassirou Barry.
Foreign Affairs, Maj. Jean Traoré.
Economy and Finance, Lamine Bolivogui.
Rural Development, Maj. Alhoussény Fofana.
Natural Resources, Energy and Environment, Dr. Ousmane Sylla.
Human Resources, Industry, Small and Medium Enterprises, Kemoko Keita.
Equipment and Town Planning, Mbaya Sibidi.
National Education, Dr. Saliou Koumbassa.
Health and Social Affairs, Dr. Pathe Diallo.
Religious Affairs, El-Hadj Abdourahmane Bah.

Formerly part of French West Africa, Guinea has a coastline on the Atlantic Ocean between Guinea-Bissau and Sierra Leone and in the interior is adjacent to Senegal, Mali, Côte d'Ivoire, Liberia and Sierra Leone. Area, 94,926 sq. miles (245,857 sq. km.). The population (1985 U.N. estimate) is 6,075,000, mostly the Fullah, Malinké and Soussou tribes.

Government.—Guinea was separated from Senegal in 1891 and administered by France as a separate colony until 1958. In a referendum held in Sept. 1958, Guinea rejected the new French Constitution and on Oct. 2, 1958, became an independent republic governed by a Constituent Assembly. M. Sékou Touré, Prime Minister in the Territorial Assembly, assumed office as head of the new Government.

Under a provisional constitution, adopted on Nov. 12, 1958, powers of government are exercised by a president assisted by the Cabinet. The President, eligible for a term of 7 years and for re-election, is head of state and of the armed forces. M. Sékou Touré was elected President of the Republic in January, 1961. Pres. Sékou Touré died in March 1984: a few days later there was a military *coup*. Guinea is now ruled by a military government, which is directed by a Military Committee for National Recovery (C.M.R.N.). The country's foreign policy is one of non-alignment.

Guinea withdrew from the Franc Zone on March 1, 1960, and established her own currency. Guinea is in receipt of economic aid and technical assistance from a number of countries, including the United States, Canada, West Germany, Yugoslavia, the Soviet Union and China.

Production, etc.—The principal products of Guinea are bauxite, alumina, iron-ore, palm kernels, millet, rice, coffee, bananas, pineapples and rubber. At Sangaredi in the mountainous hinterland, where the rivers Senegal, Gambia and Niger have their sources, large deposits of bauxite are mined. Deposits of iron ore, gold, diamonds and uranium have also been discovered. Principal imports are cotton goods, manufactured goods, tobacco, petroleum products, sugar, rice, flour and salt; exports, bauxite, alumina, iron-ore, diamonds, coffee, hides, bananas, palm kernels and pineapples.

Trade with U.K.

	1985	1986
Imports from U.K.	£10,301,000	£10,679,000
Exports to U.K.	9,064,000	23,892,000

CAPITAL.—ΨConakry (763,000). Other towns are Kankan, which is connected with Conakry by a railway, Kindia, N'Zérékoré, Mamou, Siguiri and Labé.

FLAG.—Three vertical stripes of red, yellow and green.

NATIONAL DAY.—October 2 (Anniversary of Proclamation of Independence).

BRITISH EMBASSY
British Ambassador (*resident at* Dakar, Senegal).

GUINEA-BISSAU
(República da Guiné-Bissau)

President of the Council of State (*Head of State*), Gen. João Bernardo Vieira, *took power*, Nov. 1980.

COUNCIL OF MINISTERS

Minister of State for the Armed Forces, Col. Iafai Camara.
Minister of State at the Presidency, Tiago Aleluia Lopes.
Rural Development and Fisheries, Carlos Correia.
Education, Culture and Sports, Fidelis Cabral d'Almada.
Commerce and Tourism, Manuel Maria Santos.
National Security and Public Order, José Pereira.
Minister for the Northern Province, Mario Cabral.
Natural Resources and Industry, Filinto Barros.
Foreign Affairs, Julio Semedo.
Public Health, Alexandre Nunes Correia.
Minister for the Eastern Province, Malan Bacai Sanha.
Minister for the Southern Province, Luis Oliveira Sanca.
Justice, Nicandro Pereira Barreto.
Finance, Victor Freire Monteiro.
Governor of the National Bank, Pedro Godinho Gomes.
Information and Telecommunications, Musa Djassi.
Planning, Bartolomeu S. Pereira.
Public Works, Avito José Da Silva.
Civil Service, Labour and Social Security, Henriqueta Godinho Gomes.

Guinea-Bissau, formerly Portuguese Guinea, lies in Western Africa, between Senegal and Guinea; it has an area of 13,948 sq. miles (36,125 sq. km.), and had a population (1985 U.N. estimate) of 890,000. The main ethnic groups are the Balante, Malinké, Fulani, Mandjako and Pepel.

Guinea-Bissau achieved independence on Sept. 10, 1974. Sr. Luis Cabral was ousted in a coup led by Maj.

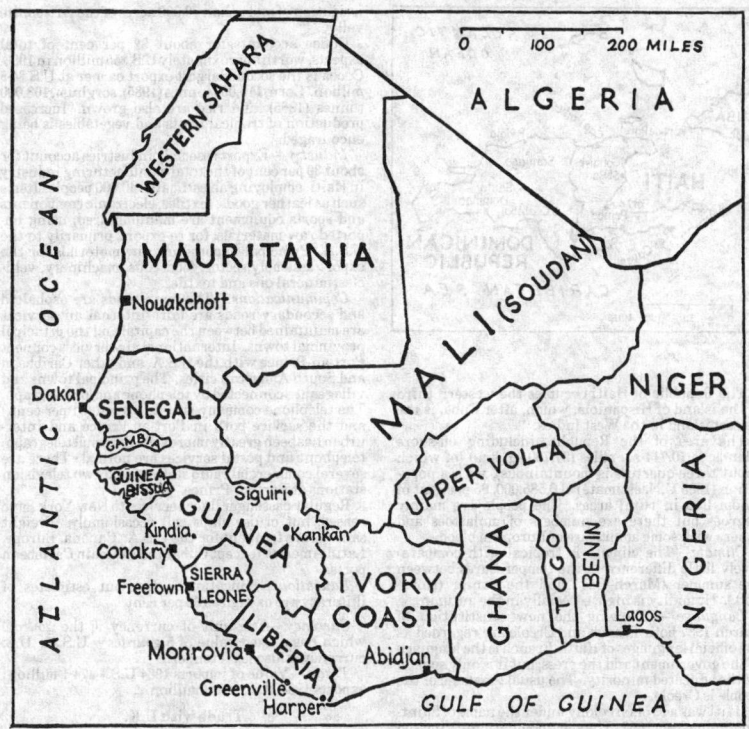

(now Gen.) Vieira in November, 1980. Following the coup the Assembly was suspended, and a Revolutionary Council was established. Under a new constitution adopted in April 1984 the Revolutionary Council became a 15-member Council of State, and a parliament was set up. An attempted coup to overthrow President Vieira was defeated in November 1985.

Currency.—The *escudo* was replaced by the *peso* in March 1976.

Economy.—The country produces rice, coconuts, ground-nuts and palm oil products. Cattle are raised, and there are bauxite deposits in the south.

Trade with U.K.

	1985	1986
Imports from U.K.	£1,209,000	£1,319,000
Exports to U.K.	2,000	214,000

CAPITAL.—ΨBissau (census 1979, 109,486), also the chief port.

FLAG.—Horizontal bands of yellow over green with vertical red band in the hoist charged with a black star.

NATIONAL DAY.—September 24 (Independence Day).

BRITISH EMBASSY

British Ambassador, (resident at Dakar, Senegal).

HAITI
(République d'Haiti)

COUNCIL MEMBERS

President of the Council, Lt. Gen. Henri Namphy.
Members, Brig.-Gen. Williams Regala; Luc Hector.

CABINET

Interior and National Defence, Brig.-Gen. Williams Regala.
Foreign Affairs, Col. Herard Abraham.
Finance and Economy, Dr. Lesly Delatour.
Commerce and Industry, Mario Celestin.
Social Affairs, François Gerard Noel.
National Education, Youth and Sports, Patrice Dalencourt.
Public Works, Transport and Communications, Mines and Energy, Col. Jacques Joachim.
Public Health and Population, Lt.-Col. Jean Verly.
Agriculture, Natural Resources and Rural Development, Gustave Menager.
Information and Public Relations, Jacques Lorthe.
Justice, François St. Fleur.
Minister without Portfolio, Jean Conde.

The London Embassy of the Republic of Haiti closed on March 30, 1987.

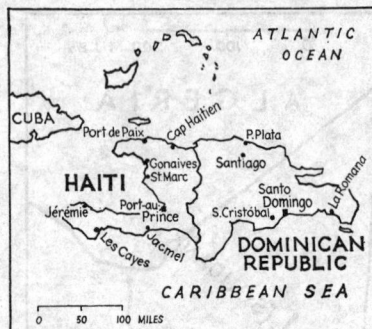

The Republic of Haiti occupies the western third of the island of Hispaniola, which, after Cuba, is the largest island in the West Indies.

The area of the Republic, including off-shore islands, is 10,714 sq. miles (27,750 sq. km.) (of which about three-quarters is mountainous), with a population (1985 U.N. estimate) of 6,585,000, 85 per cent of whom live in rural areas. The people are mainly negroes but there are numbers of mulattoes and others with some admixture of European blood.

Climate.—The climate is tropical with comparatively little difference in the temperatures between the summer (March–Oct.) and the winter (Nov.–Feb.). Humidity is high, especially in the autumn.

Language.—Following the new constitution of March 1987 both French and Creole are the official languages of Haiti. French is the language of the government and the press, but it is only spoken by the educated minority. The usual language of the people is Creole.

Haiti was a French colony under the name of Saint-Domingue from 1697. The slave population, estimated at 500,000, revolted in 1791 under the leadership of Toussaint L'Ouverture, who was born a slave and made himself Governor-General of the colony. He capitulated to the French in 1802 and died in captivity in 1803. Resistance was continued by Jean Jacques Dessalines, also a former negro slave, who, on January 1, 1804, declared the former French colony to be an independent state. It was at this time that the name Haiti, an aboriginal word meaning mountainous, was adopted. Dessalines became Emperor of Haiti, but was assassinated in 1806. In 1915, following a period of political upheaval, the country was occupied by a force of U.S. marines. The occupation came to an end in 1934, and U.S. control of the revenue of Haiti officially ended on October 1, 1947.

Dr. Duvalier was installed as President in 1957 and held the position until his death in 1971. He was succeeded as President for life on the same day by his son, Jean Claude Duvalier, whom he had nominated as his successor. President Duvalier fled to France on Feb. 7, 1986 in the face of sustained popular unrest, and a six-man council headed by Henri Namphy assumed power. In March three ex-Duvalier council members resigned and a new council was formed. Presidential and legislative elections have been promised for November 1987.

Production.—In recent years measures for agricultural rehabilitation have been taken with the aim of a gradual restoration of productivity, which had declined after the ending of the colonial plantation system. The main project is a scheme for the irrigation of more than 70,000 acres of the Artibonite valley.

Coffee accounts for about 32 per cent of total exports, worth approximately U.S.$55 million in 1986. Cocoa is the second largest export earner at U.S.$4·5 million. Corn, 110,000 tonnes (1985), sorghum, 108,000 tonnes (1985), and rice are also grown. Increased production of tropical fruits and vegetables is being encouraged.

Industry.—Export assembly industries account for about 30 per cent of the total manufacturing industry in Haiti, employing an estimated 40,000 people. Items such as leather goods, textiles, electronic components and sports equipment are manufactured, using imported raw materials, for re-export, primarily to the U.S.A. Principal imports are raw materials for the export assembly sector, foodstuffs, machinery, vehicles, mineral oils and textiles.

Communications.—The main roads are asphalted and secondary roads are fair. Internal air services are maintained between the capital and the principal provincial towns. International air-services connect Port-au-Prince with the U.S.A. and other Caribbean and South American cities. The principal towns and villages are connected by telephone and/or telegraph. The telephone company is state owned (51 per cent.) and the service both in Port-au-Prince and Interurban has been greatly improved. External telegraph, telephone and postal services are normal. There are several commercial radio stations and two television stations at Port-au-Prince.

Regular passenger liner services to New York have ceased, but cruise ships call occasionally. Freight sailings are frequent for the U.S.A., Canada, Europe, Latin America (except Cuba) and the main Caribbean ports.

Education.—Education is free but estimates of illiteracy are as high as 85 per cent.

Currency.—The unit of currency is the *gourde*, which has a fixed value of 5 *gourdes* = U.S.$1. U.S. currency is also legal tender.

Trade.—Value of imports 1984 U.S.$ 474·1 million; exports 1984 U.S.$ 219·4 million.

Trade with U.K.

	1985	1986
Imports from U.K.	£5,048,000	£5,147,000
Exports to U.K.	1,512,000	899,000

CAPITAL.—Ψ Port-au-Prince. Population estimated at about 1 million. Other centres are: Ψ Cap Haitien (54,691); Ψ Gonaives (36,736); Ψ Les Cayes (27,222); Jérémie (25,117); Ψ St. Marc (20,504); Ψ Jacmel (16,449); Ψ Port de Paix (21,733).

FLAG.—Horizontal blue over red with national arms on a white square in the centre.

NATIONAL DAY.—January 1.

British Ambassador, (resident at Kingston, Jamaica).

HONDURAS
(Republica de Honduras)

President of the Republic, José Azcona del Hoyo, *assumed office,* 27 Jan. 1986.

CABINET

Interior and Justice, Raúl Elvir Colindres.
Foreign Affairs, Carlos López Contreras.
Defence, Col. Luiz Alonzo Cardona.
Education, Elisa Valle de Martinez.
Finance, Efraín Bú Girón.
Economy, Reginaldo Panting.

Communications, Public Works and Transport, Juan Fernando López.
Health, Dr. Rubén Villeda Bermúdez.
Labour and Social Security, Adalberto Discua.
Natural Resources, Rodrigo Castilla.
Culture and Tourism, Dr. Arturo Rendón Pineda.
Economic Planning, Francisco Figueroa.
Director of National Agrarian Institute, Marlo Espinal Zelaya.
Minister for the Presidency, Celeo Arias Moncada.

HONDURAS EMBASSY IN LONDON
47 Manchester Street, W1M 5PB
[01–486 3380]

Ambassador Extraordinary and Plenipotentiary, His Excellency Sr. Max Velásquez-Diaz (1984).

Honduras, in Central America, lies between lat. 13° and 16° 30′ N. and long. 83° and 89° 41′ W. with a seaboard of about 375 miles on the Caribbean Sea and an outlet, consisting of a small strip of coast 63 miles in length on the Pacific. Its frontiers are contiguous with those of Guatemala, Nicaragua and El Salvador.

The Republic contains a total area of approximately 43,277 sq. miles (112,088 sq. km.) and is very mountainous, being traversed by the Cordilleras, with peaks rising to 1500 and 2400 metres above sea level. Most of the soil is poor and acid, except for the coastal plains of the north and some areas of the interior. Rainfall is seasonal, May to October being wet and November to April dry. Three-quarters of the territory is covered by pine forests which contribute to much of the country's wealth in natural resources.

The population (1985 U.N. estimate) of 4,372,000 is of mixed Spanish and Indian blood. There is a negro (West Indian) element in Northern Honduras who are known as Garifunas.

The language of the country is Spanish, although English is the first language of many in the islands and on the North coast. Primary and secondary education is free, primary education being compulsory, and the Government have launched a campaign to eradicate illiteracy.

Government.—Originally discovered and settled by the Spanish at the beginning of the sixteenth century Honduras formed part of the Spanish American Dominions for nearly three centuries until 1821 when independence was proclaimed. Under military government from 1972–81, the present Liberal government was elected in Nov. 1985 and took office in Jan. 1986.

The Republic is divided into 18 departments, the newest of which, Gracias a Dios, formed in Feb. 1957, is now the home of thousands of Miskito Indian refugees from Nicaragua.

Production.—Agriculture is mainly confined to the large and fertile valleys on the wide Caribbean plain, and the extensive valleys found in the Comayagua and Olancho regions of the interior. Reaching inland from the Caribbean towards the eastern border with Nicaragua a vast tropical forest area called the Mosquitia provides valuable reserves of timber. Lead, zinc and silver are mined on a small scale.

The chief exports are coffee, bananas and timber, the most important woods being pine, mahogany and cedar. Cattle raising and the exporting of frozen meat is an important industry, and exports of shrimps and lobsters are increasing. Other products are tobacco, beans, maize, rice, cotton, palm oil, sugar cane, cement and tropical fruits. There are large tracts of uncultivated land.

Communications.—There are about 1,004 km. of railway in operation, chiefly to serve the banana plantations and the Caribbean ports. There are 15,006 km. of roads, of which 1,809 are paved, excluding some 250 kms of new major highways recently inaugurated. Improvements are being made and new roads built. There are 33 smaller airstrips and three international airports, Tegucigalpa, San Pedro Sula and La Ceiba.

Ψ The chief ports are Puerto Cortes, Tela and La Ceiba on the North Coast, through which passes the bulk of the trade with the United States and Europe. Peurto Castilla is being developed as a deep-water container port, and San Lorenzo is also experiencing rapid growth.

The unit of currency is the *Lempira* of 100 *centavos*.

TRADE

	1983	1984
Imports ....*Lempiras*	1,511·7 m.	1,688·1 m.
Exports .... „	1,360·6 m.	1,531·6 m.

Trade with U.K.

	1985	1986
Imports from U.K.	£9,026,000	£9,213,000
Exports to U.K.	11,139,000	5,280,000

CAPITAL.—Tegucigalpa. Pop. 539,600 (1984 est.); other towns are San Pedro Sula (397,900), Ψ La Ceiba (68,900), Ψ Puerto Cortes (62,300), Choluteca (89,000) and Ψ Tela (61,200).

FLAG.—Three horizontal bands, blue, white, blue (with five white stars on white band).

NATIONAL DAY.—September 15.

BRITISH EMBASSY
Apartado Postal 290, Tegucigalpa.

Ambassador Extraordinary and Plenipotentiary, His Excellency David Joy, C.B.E. (1987).

HUNGARY
(Magyar Népköztársaság)

President of the Presidential Council of the Republic, Karoly Nemeth, *elected* June 1987.

COUNCIL OF MINISTERS

Prime Minister, Karoly Grosz.
Deputy Prime Ministers, Judit Csehák; Lajos Czinege; József Marjai; Frigyes Berecz; László Maróthy.
Foreign Affairs, Peter Várkonyi.
Interior, János Kamara.
Defence, Ferenc Karpati.
Finance, Peter Medgyessy.
Justice, Dr. Imre Markója.
Industry, László Kapolyi.
Foreign Trade, Péter Veress.
Internal Trade, Zoltán Juhar.
Agriculture and Food, Jenö Váncsa.
Health, László Medve.
Culture and Education, Dr. Béla Köpeczi.
Building and Town Planning, László Somogyi.
Transport and Postal Affairs, Lajos Urbán.
President, National Planning Office, László Maróthy.
President, Technical Development Committee, Pál Tétényi.

THE COMMUNIST PARTY

Politbureau of the Central Committee, G. Aczél; S. Gáspár; K. Grósz; Cs. Hámori; F. Havasi; J. Kádár;

G. Lázár; P. Losonczi; L. Maróthy; K. Németh; M. Ovári; I. Sárlos; I. Szabó; J. Berecz; J. Csehak.
Secretariat of the Central Committee, János Kádár (*Gen. Sec.*); G. Lázár (*Deputy Gen. Sec.*); J. Berecz; F. Havasi; I. Horváth; L. Pál; M. Ovári; M. Szürös.

HUNGARIAN EMBASSY AND CONSULATE
35 Eaton Place, S.W.1.
[01–235 4048, 7191; *Consulate:* 01–235 2664]

Ambassador Extraordinary and Plenipotentiary, His Excellency Dr. Mátyás Domokos (1984).
Counsellors, Dr. J. Kalanovics; I. Bene (*Commercial*).
Military and Air Attaché, Col. G. Demeter.
Consul, Dr. L. Mayer.

Area and Population.—The area of Hungary is 35,919 sq. miles (93,030 sq. km.) with a population (1985) of 10,658,000.

Government.—Hungary was reconstituted a kingdom in 1920 after having been declared a republic on Nov. 17, 1918. She joined the Anti-Comintern Pact on Feb. 24, 1939, and entered the 1939–45 War on the side of Germany in 1941. On Jan. 20, 1945, a Hungarian provisional government of liberation, which had been set up during the preceding December, signed an armistice under the terms of which the frontiers of Hungary were withdrawn to the limits existing in 1937.

After the liberation, a coalition of the Smallholder, National Peasant, Social Democrat and Communist parties carried out major land reform and mines, heavy industry, banks and schools were nationalized. By 1949 the Communists had succeeded in gaining a monopoly of power. A campaign was opened to collectivize agriculture and by 1952 practically the entire economy had been "socialized". The Party formulates policy and the function of the Government is mainly executive.

The period from July 1956 to the outbreak of the national revolution on Oct. 23 was marked by growing ferment in intellectual circles and increased discord within the Party. The withdrawal of Soviet troops from the country and free elections were among the demands put forward. Fighting broke out on the night of Oct. 23 between demonstrators, who had been joined by large numbers of factory workers, and the State Security Police (A.V.H.). Soviet forces intervened in strength early the next morning. By Oct. 30 Soviet troops had withdrawn from Budapest and on Nov. 3 an all-party coalition government under Imre Nagy was formed. This government was overthrown and the revolution suppressed as the result of a renewed attack by Soviet forces on Budapest in the early hours of Nov. 4. Simultaneously the formation of a new Hungarian Revolutionary Worker Peasant Government under the leadership of Mr. Kádár was announced.

Economy.—Since 1968 the Hungarian economy has been run according to a system which allows more decentralized decision-making than in some other Eastern European countries, although central control in vital areas such as the allocation of fuels and raw materials has remained. Industrialization has made considerable progress in the last decade and now produces 68 per cent of national income. Industry is mainly based on imported raw materials but Hungary has her own coal (mostly brown), bauxite, considerable deposits of natural gas (some not yet under full exploitation), some iron ore and oil. Output figures in 1985 (1,000 tons), coal, 24,042; bauxite, 2,815; rolled steel 2,860; crude oil, 2,000; cement, 3,678. Natural gas production totalled 7,441 million cubic metres.

Agriculture still occupies an important place in the Hungarian economy. Ten and a half per cent. of the entire land area is owned by State farms and a further 63·8 per cent is within co-operative farms.

Production in 1985 was (tons):

Wheat	6,584,000
Rye	163,000
Barley	1,040,000
Maize	6,613,000
Oats	132,000
Sugar beet	4,024,000
Green and silage maize	6,613,000

In 1983, national income grew by only 0·5 per cent. Consumption and, particularly, investment continued to be squeezed by the adjustment measures necessitated by Hungary's hard currency debts. Retail prices rose by just under 8 per cent, whilst real incomes stagnated.

Religion and Education.—About two-thirds of the population are Roman Catholics, and the remainder mostly Calvinist. There are five types of schools under the Ministry of Education—kindergartens 3–6, general schools 6–14 (compulsory), vocational schools (15–18), secondary schools (15–18), universities and adult training schools (over 18).

Language and Literature.—Magyar, or Hungarian, is one of the Finno-Ugrian languages. Hungarian literature began to flourish in the second half of the sixteenth century. Among the greatest writers of the nineteenth and twentieth centuries are Mihály Vörösmarty (1800–1855), Sándor Petőfi (1823–1849), János Arany (1817–1882), Imre Madach (1823–1864), Kálmán Mikszáth (1847–1910), Endre Ady (1877–1918), Attila József (1905–1937), Mihály Babits (1883–1941) and Dezsö Kosztolányi (1885–1936).

Finance.—The budget estimates for the year 1986 were: Revenue, *Forints* 681,000 million; Expenditure, *Forints* 706,000 million. The unit of currency is the *forint* of 100 *fillér*.

TRADE

	1985	
	Non-convertible trade *(roubles)*	Convertible trade U.S.$
Imports	4,620·8 m.	6,734·8 m.
Exports	4,741·7 m.	7,041·5 m.

(1 *rouble* = 26 forints: 1 U.S.$ = 48·05 forints)

Trade with U.K.

	1985	1986
Imports from U.K.	£107,226,000	£101,557,000
Exports to U.K.	84,114,000	77,228,000

CAPITAL.—Budapest, on the Danube; population (1985), 2,072,000. Other large towns are: Miskolc (212,000); Debrecen (210,000); Szeged (181,000) and Pecs (175,000).

FLAG.—Red, white, green (horizontally).

NATIONAL DAY.—April 4 (Anniversary of Liberation, 1945).

BRITISH EMBASSY
Harmincad Utca 6, Budapest V

Ambassador Extraordinary and Plenipotentiary, His Excellency Leonard Vincent Appleyard, C.M.G. (1986).

Counsellor, D. H. Colvin (*Head of Chancery*).

Defence and Military Attaché, Lt.-Col. F. N. J. Davies.

Air Attaché, Wg.-Cdr. O. J. A. Knight.

First Secretary and British Council Representative, W. K. Dobson.

Consul, J. Bradley

ICELAND
(Island)

President, Vigdís Finnbogadóttir, *born* 1930, *elected* June 29, 1980, *re-elected*, July 1984.

CABINET

Prime Minister, Thorsteinn Palsson (*I.*).
Foreign Affairs, Steingrimur Hermannsson (*Pr.*).
Finance, Jon Baldvin Hannibalsson (*SDP*).
Industry, Fridrik Sophusson (*I.*).
Fisheries, Halldor Asgrimsson (*Pr.*).
Commerce and Justice, Jon Sigurdsson (*SDP*).
Communications, Matthias A. Mathiesen (*I.*).
Health, Gudmundur Bjamason (*Pr.*).
Education, Birgir I. Gunnarsson (*I.*).
Agriculture, Jon Helgason (*Pr.*).
Social Affairs, Johanna Sigurdardottir (*SDP*).

(*I.*—Independence Party; *Pr.*—Progressive Party; *SDP*—Social Democrat Party.)

EMBASSY IN LONDON
1 Eaton Terrace, SW1W 8EY
[01–730 5131]

Ambassador Extraordinary and Plenipotentiary, His Excellency Mr. Ólafur Egilsson (1986).

Counsellors, S. Björnsson; E. Benedikz; S. Gunnlaugsson (*Commercial*).

Iceland is a large volcanic island in the North Atlantic Ocean, extending from 63° 23′ to 66° 33′ N. lat., and from 13° 22′ to 24° 35′ W. long., with an estimated area of 39,768 sq. miles (103,000 sq. km.). The population was 243,698 on Dec. 1, 1986.

Iceland was uninhabited before the ninth century, when settlers came from Norway. For several centuries a form of republican government prevailed, with an annual assembly of leading men called the *Althing*, but in 1241 Iceland became subject to Norway, and later to Denmark. During the colonial period, Iceland maintained its cultural integrity but a deterioration in the climate, together with frequent volcanic eruptions and outbreaks of disease led to a serious fall in the standard of living and to a decline in the population to little more than 40,000. In the nineteenth century a struggle for independence began which led first to home rule for Iceland under the Danish Crown (1918), and later to complete independence under a republican form of rule in 1944.

Government.—The parliamentary (*Althing*) elections in April 1987 gave the Independence Party 18 seats, Progressives 13, Social Democratic Party 10, People's Alliance 8, Citizens' Party 7, Women's Alliance 6 and 1 Independent.

Language and Literature.—The ancient Norraena

(or Northern tongue) presents close affinities to Anglo-Saxon and as spoken and written in Iceland today differs little from that introduced into the island in the ninth century. There is a rich literature with two distinct periods of development, from the mid-11th to the late 13th century and from the early 19th century to the present.

Production.—Iceland has considerable resources of hydro-electric and geothermal energy. It is estimated that exploited water power (4,000 Gigawatt hours/a) represents only about 9 per cent of that economically exploitable, whereas only 5 per cent of the estimated 80,000 Gigawatt hours/a of available geothermal power has so far been harnessed. Energy-intensive heavy industry includes an aluminium smelter, a nitrogen fertilizer factory, a diatomite plant and a ferro-silicone plant.

The principal exports are frozen fish fillets, salt fish, stock fish, fresh fish on ice, frozen scampi, fishmeal and oil, skins and aluminium; the imports consist of almost all the necessities of life, the chief items being petroleum products, transport equipment, textiles, foodstuffs, animal feeds, timber, and alumina.

At January 1, 1987, the mercantile marine consisted of 560 vessels of under 100 gross tons and 391 ships of 100 gross tons and over; a total of 951 vessels (179,005 gross tons), of which 822 (112,391 gross tons) are decked fishing vessels. There are regular shipping services between Reykjavík and Felixstowe, Humber ports and the Continent.

A regular air service is maintained between Glasgow and London and Reykjavík. There are also air services from the island to Scandinavia, U.S.A., Germany, France and Luxembourg.

Road communications are adequate in summer but greatly restricted by snow in winter. Only roads in town centres and key highways are metalled the rest being of gravel, sand and lava dust. The climate and terrain make first-class surfaces for highways out of the question. There are no railways.

FINANCE

	1985	1986
	Krónur (millions)	
Revenue	26,889	38,235
Expenditure	29,260	40,111

TRADE

	1985	1986
	Krónur (millions)	
Exports	33,750	44,968
Imports	37,600	45,910

Trade with U.K.

	1985	1986
Imports from U.K.	£76,914,000	£73,640,000
Exports to U.K.	128,281,000	173,140,000

CAPITAL: ΨReykjavík. Population (Dec. 1, 1986), 91,394.

Other centres in approximate order of importance are Akureyri, Kópavogur, Hafnarfjördur, Keflavík, Westmann Islands, Akranes, Isafjördur and Siglufjördur.

FLAG.—Blue, with white-bordered red cross.
NATIONAL DAY.—June 17.

BRITISH EMBASSY
Laufásvegur 49, Reykjavik

Ambassador Extraordinary and Plenipotentiary and Consul-General, His Excellency Mark Fenger Chapman, C.V.O. (1986).

Second Secretary, Head of Chancery and Consul, S. C. Parris.

Vice Consul and Attaché (Commercial), J. N. L. Burgess.

BRITISH CONSULAR OFFICES

There are Consular Offices at *Reykjavík* and *Akureyri.*

INDONESIA
(Republik Indonesia)

President, General Suharto, *born* June 9, 1921. *Acting President,* March 12, 1967; *confirmed as President,* Mar. 28, 1968, *re-elected for a term of 5 years,* March, 1973, March 1978 and March 1983.

Vice-President, Umar Wirahadi Kusumah, *elected* March 1983.

CABINET

Minister-Co-ordinators, Gen. Surono (*Political and Security Affairs*); Prof. Ali Wardhana (*Economic, Financial and Industrial Affairs and Development Control*); Lt. Gen. A. Ratu Perwiranegara (*People's Welfare*).

Ministers of State, Maj. Gen. Sudharmono (*State Secretary, and Non-departmental Government agencies*); Dr. J. B. Sumarlin (*National Planning and Development*); Dr. B. J. Habibie (*Research and Technology*); Prof. E. Salim (*Demography and Environment*); K. Batubara (*Public Housing*); Dr. A. Gafur (*Youth and Sports*); Dr. S. Afif (*Reform of State Apparatus*); Mrs. L. Sutanto (*Women's Affairs*).

Ministers, Gen. S. Rustam (*Home Affairs*); Prof. M. Kusumaatmadja (*Foreign Affairs*); Gen. Poniman (*Defence and Security*); I. Saleh (*Justice*); Mr. Harmoko (*Information*); Dr. R. Prawiro (*Finance*); R. Saleh (*Trade*); B. Arifin (*Co-operative Affairs*); A. Affandi (*Agriculture*); Mr. Sujarwo (*Forestry*); Mr. Hartato (*Industry*); Prof. Subroto (*Mining and Energy*); S. Sosrodarsoto (*Public Works*); Air Marshal R. Nurjadin (*Communications*); Gen. A. Tahir (*Tourism, Posts and Telecommunications*); Adm. Sudomo (*Manpower*); Mr. Martono (*Transmigration*); Prof. Fuad Hassan (*Education and Culture*); Dr. S. Surjaningrat (*Health*); M. Sjadzali (*Religious Affairs*); Mrs. N. Sudarsono (*Social Affairs*).

INDONESIAN EMBASSY
157 Edgware Road, W2 2HR
[01-499 7661]

Ambassador Extraordinary and Plenipotentiary, His Excellency S. Suhartoyo (1986).

Minister, Hidayat Soemo (*Deputy Chief of Mission*).

Situated between latitudes 6° North and 11° South and between longitudes 95° and 141° East, Indonesia comprises the islands of *Java, Madura,* and *Sumatra,* the *Riouw-Lingga Archipelago* (which with Karimon, Anambas, Natuna Islands, Tambelan, and part of Sumatra, forms the province of Riau), the islands of *Bangka* and *Billiton,* part of the island of *Borneo* (Kalimantan), *Sulawesi (formerly* Celebes) *Island,* the *Molucca Islands* (Ternate, Tidore, Halmahera, Buru, Seram, Banda, Timor-Laut, Larat, Bachiam, Obi, Kei, Aru, Babar, Leti and Wetar), the island of *Bali* and the islands of *Lombok, Sumbawa, Sumba, Flores, Timor* and others comprising the provinces of East and West *Nusa Tenggara* and the western half of the island of New Guinea (*Irian Jaya*), with a total area of 735,358 sq. miles (1,904,569 sq. km.), and a population (1985) of about 165,030,000.

From the early part of the 17th century much of the Indonesian Archipelago was under Netherlands rule. Following the World War 1939–45, during which the Archipelago was occupied by the Japanese, a strong nationalistic movement manifested itself and after sporadic fighting the formal transfer of

sovereignty by the Netherlands of all the former Dutch East Indies except W. New Guinea took place on December 27, 1949.

Western New Guinea became part of Indonesia in 1963 under the name West Irian (now Irian Jaya), this interpretation being confirmed in an "Act of Free Choice" in July, 1969, of which the United Nations took note in November 1969. Following a unilateral declaration of independence by the Fretilin, Indonesia took over the former Portuguese colony of East Timor, which in July 1976 was declared the 27th province of Indonesia.

Following a three-week period of unrest and violent student demonstrations the Minister of the Army, General Suharto, took over effective political power in March, 1966.

General Suharto was made Acting President with full powers, on March 11, 1967, and on March 28, 1968, appointed full President for a period of five years.

In the general election of April 1987, Golkar obtained 299 seats. At the time of going to press the number of seats for the Muslim Development Party and the Christian-Nationalist Democratic Party was not known.

Production.—Nearly 70 per cent. of the population of Indonesia is engaged in agriculture and related production. Copra, kapok, nutmeg, pepper and cloves are produced, mainly by smallholders; palm oil, sugar, fibres and cinchona are produced by large estates. Rubber, tea, coffee and tobacco are also produced by both in large quantities. Rice is a traditional staple food for the people of Indonesia and the islands of Java, Sulawesi and Sumatra are important producers.

Production has risen rapidly in recent years to 25 million tons and the country is now self sufficient.

Oil and LNG are the most important assets, the export of which in 1985–86 earned about U.S. $11,000 million (about 80 per cent. of Indonesia's exports), but more recent developments have underscored the vulnerability of the economy to depressed international markets and weak oil prices. Timber is the second largest foreign exchange earner after oil.

Indonesia is rich in minerals, particularly tin, of which the country is the world's third biggest producer; petroleum, coal, nickel and bauxite are the other principal products; there are also considerable deposits of gold, silver, manganese phosphates and sulphur. Aid to Indonesia is channelled through the Inter-Governmental Group on Indonesia (IGGI), which has pledged U.S. $2,500,000 for 1986–7.

Indonesia's Fourth Development Programme started in 1984 and its main objectives are the elimination of poverty, agricultural and urban problems, and the continued growth of installed power generation.

Finance.—The drop in oil prices led in March 1983 to the rupiah being devalued by 27 per cent, and a rescheduling of major projects was undertaken. More recently an increase in foreign reserves has meant that several of these projects could be re-instated.

Currency.—The unit of currency is the *rupiah* of 100 *sen.*

Trade with U.K.

	1985	1986
Direct Imports from U.K.	£172,818,000	£196,629,000
Exports to U.K.	155,934,000	141,242,000

Principal exports to the United Kingdom are rubber, timber, non-ferrous metals, tea, coffee, spices, and crude oil for refinement. Imports from the United Kingdom are mainly of machinery, transport equipment and electrical equipment.

Transport.—In Java a main line connects Jakarta with Surabaya in the East of Java and there are several branches. In Sumatra the important towns of Medan, Padang and Palembang are the centres of short railway systems.

Sea communications in the archipelago are maintained by the State-run shipping companies Djakarta-Lloyd (ocean-going) and Pelni (coastal and inter-island) and other small concerns. Transport by small craft on the rivers of the larger islands plays an important part in trade. Air services in Indonesia are operated by Garuda Indonesian Airways and other local airlines, and Jakarta is served by various international services. There are approximately 50,000 miles of roads.

CAPITAL.—ΨJakarta (population 6,503,449). Other important centres are: (Java) ΨSurabaya (7,027,913), ΨSemarang (1,026,671), Bandung (1,462,637); (Sumatra) Palembang (787,187), Medan (1,378,955); (Sulawesi), ΨUjung Pandang (*formerly Makassar*) (709,038); (Kalimantan) Banjarmasin (381,286), ΨPontianak (304,778), ΨBalikpapan (280,675); (Moluccas) Ambon (208,898); (Bali) Denpasar, Singaraja (for whole island 2,174,105); (Nusa Tenggara) Kupang (329,371); (Irian Jaya) Jayapura (107,164).

NATIONAL DAY.—August 17 (Anniversary of Proclamation of Independence).

FLAG.—Equal bands of red over white.

BRITISH EMBASSY
Jalan M. H. Thamrin 75, Jakarta

Ambassador Extraordinary and Plenipotentiary, His Excellency Alan Ewen Donald, C.M.G. (1984).

BRITISH CONSULAR OFFICES

There are British Consular Offices at *Jakarta* and *Medan*.

British Council Representative, Dr. J. C. Blackwell, S Widjojo Centre, 57 Jalan Jendral Sudirman, Jakarta. There are also libraries at *Bandung* and *Medan*.

INDONESIA BRITAIN ASSOCIATION

c/o Mr. R. A. M. Ramsay, Sarinah Building, 13th Floor, Jl. M. H. Thamrin 11, Jakarta.

IRAN
(Jomhori-e-Islami-e-Iran)

Leader of the Islamic Revolution, Ayatollah Ruholla Ruhollah Khomeini, *born* 1902; *assumed power*, Feb., 1979.
President, Hojatoleslam Seyed Ali Khamene'i, *elected* Oct. 2, 1981, *re-elected* Aug. 16, 1985.
Prime Minister, Mir Hossein Moussavi.
Foreign Affairs, Dr. Ali Akbar Velayati.
Education, Seyed Kazem Akrami.
Commerce, Hassan Abedi Jaafari.
Health, Dr. Ali Reza Marandi.
Justice, Dr. Hassan Ebrahim Habibi.
Defence, Col. Mohammad Hussein Jalali.
Oil, Gholamreza Aqazadeh.
Energy, (vacant).
Agriculture, Dr. Abbas Ali Zali.
Economics and Finance, Mohammad Javad Iravani.
Interior, Ali Akbar Mohtashami.
Labour, Abol Hassan Sarhadi-Zadeh.
Housing, Serajeddin Kazeruni.
Mining and Metals, Mohammad Reza Ayatollahi.

Industry, Gholamreza Shafei.
Heavy Industry, Behzad Nabavi.
Islamic Guidance, Seyed Mohammed Khatami.
Culture and Higher Education, Mohammad Farhadi.
Intelligence, Mohammad Mohammadi Reyshahri.
Roads and Transport, Mohammad Saeedi Kia.
Construction Crusade, Bijan Namdar Zanganeh.
Islamic Revolutionary Guard, Mohsen Rafiqdust.

IRANIAN EMBASSY IN LONDON
27 Prince's Gate, SW7 1PX
[01–584 8101–8]

Chargé d'Affaires, Mr. Mohammad Mehdi Akhoond Zadeh Basti.

Area and Population.—Iran has an area of 636,296 sq. miles (1,648,000 sq. km.), with a population (1986 estimate) of 49,765,000. It is mostly an arid tableland, encircled, except in the east, by mountains, the highest in the north rising to 18,934 ft. The central and eastern portion is a vast salt desert.

The Iranians are mostly Shi'ah Moslems but among them are Zoroastrians, Bahais, Sunni Moslems and Armenian and Assyrian Christians. Emigration has much reduced the once substantial Jewish community.

Language and Literature.—Persian, or Farsi, the language of Iran, and of some other areas formerly under Persian rule, is an Indo-European tongue with many Arabic elements added; the alphabet is mainly Arabic, with writing from right to left. Among the great names in Persian literature are those of Abu'l Kásim Mansúr, of Firdausi (A.D. 939–1020), Omar Khayyám, the astonomer-poet (died A.D. 1122), Muslihu'd-Din, known as Sa'di (born A.D. 1184) and Shems-ed-Din Muhammad, or Hafiz (died A.D. 1389).

Government.—Iran was ruled from the end of the 18th century by Shahs of the Qajar Dynasty. A nationalist movement became active in Dec., 1905, and in Aug., 1906, the Shah, Muzaffer-ud-Din, admitting the need for reforms, granted a Constitution. After the war of 1914–18, the subsequent troubles and the signature of the Soviet-Iranian Treaty of 1921, a vigorous Prime Minister, Reza Khan re-established general order. On Oct. 31, 1925, the last representative of the Qajar Dynasty, Sultan Ahmed Shah was deposed in his absence by the National Assembly, which handed over the government to the Prime Minister, Reza Khan, who was elected Shah on Dec. 13, 1925, by the Constituent Assembly, and took the title Reza Shah Pahlavi. On September 16, 1941, Reza

Shah abdicated in favour of the Crown Prince, who ascended the throne under the title of Mohammed Reza Shah Pahlavi.

Following widespread and persistent opposition to his regime, the Shah departed from Iran in January, 1979. Ayatollah Khomeini, the main spiritual leader of the Shi'ah Moslems, returned to Iran from exile on February 1. Following a national referendum, Iran was declared an Islamic Republic by Ayatollah Khomeini on April 1, 1979. A new constitution, providing for a President, Prime Minister and Consultative Assembly, and also for overall leadership by Khomeini, was approved by referendum in December 1979. Opposition to the fundamentalist policies of the government and religious leaders led initially to assassination and bombings, but the government's subsequent severe measures suppressed violent opposition. In Dec. 1982 an Assembly of Experts was elected to decide the eventual succession to Ayatollah Khomeini.

Iran has been at war with Iraq since the Iraqi invasion of Iran in Sept. 1980. Following their defeat at Khorramshahr Iraqi forces withdrew from most Iranian territory in June 1982. The Iranians launched a major offensive against Basra in July 1982 and several subsequent minor offensives in which they have gained small areas of territory. After Iraq declared a Maritime Exclusion Zone in August 1982, shipping entering the Iranian port of Bandar Khomeini at the head of the Gulf came under Iraqi attack. Since the summer of 1984 both sides have carried out attacks on neutral shipping further south in the Gulf and in 1987 several foreign navies entered the Gulf to escort neutral merchant shipping.

Defence.—The Army has a strength of about 150,000 men, in 4 armoured divisions, 4 infantry divisions and one airborne division. The Air Force has a strength of about 35,000, with some 70 combat aircraft. The Navy has a strength of about 20,000 and consists of 3 destroyers, 4 frigates, 4 corvettes, 5 minesweepers, and patrol boats, support ships, landing craft and hovercraft. The Islamic Revolutionary Guards Corps numbers about 500,000 men, of whom approximately half are at the front. Total armed forces personnel including paramilitary forces number over one million.

Education.—Since 1943 primary education has been compulsory and free, but there is large scale absenteeism, particularly outside the towns. There are in Iran 22 universities (8 in Tehran, 14 in the provinces). They were closed in July 1981 for "Islamization" but have now reopened. The educational system has been reformed following the revolution.

Finance.—The budget for the Iranian year beginning March 22, 1987, was revenue *Rials.* 3,970,000 million; expenditure *Rials.* 3,970,000 million. The unit of currency is the *Rial* (for rate of exchange, *see* p. 82).

Agriculture.—While petroleum is the principal product and by far the greatest export, Iran is otherwise largely an agricultural and pastoral country. After the 1979 revolution the Provisional Government announced its intention of giving greater emphasis to the development of agriculture with a view to reducing Iran's dependence on food imports. Although half of Iran's area is either mountain or desert, more than half the country's population live in rural areas, depending on the 10 million hectares under crop, sheep, goats and cattle for their livelihood. Wheat is the principal crop; other important crops are barley, rice, cotton, sugar beet, fruit, nuts and vegetables. Wool is also a major product. There are extensive forests in the north and west, the conservation of which is a continuing problem.

Industry.—Under the Shah, great emphasis was given to the development of industry. Apart from oil, the principal industrial products are carpets, textiles, sugar, cement and other construction materials, ginned cotton, vegetable oil and other food products, leather and shoes, metal manufactures, pharmaceuticals, motor vehicles, fertilizers and plastics. Industrial output was severely curtailed by the 1979 revolution, as a result of which many industrialists left the country. In July 1979 the Provisional Government nationalized a wide range of major industrial concerns, having nationalized the banks and the insurance companies the previous month. Foreign trade is controlled by the State, although recently more encouragement has been given to private sector companies.

Energy.—The oilfields, which lie in South Western Iran, were nationalised in 1951. From 1957 until the 1979 revolution a consortium of eight oil companies (one British, one French, one Dutch, and five U.S.) was responsible for the production, refining and sale of oil. In July 1979 the National Iranian Oil Company assumed full control of the oil industry. In addition to that extracted from the onshore wells, oil is also produced from a number of off-shore oilfields. Oil production by June 1979 had reached an average of 3·5 million b.p.d., but is now approximately 2·2 million b.p.d., of which some 1·5 million b.p.d. is exported. Iran is a member of O.P.E.C.

Communications.—Tehran is at the centre of a network of highways linking the capital with other major towns, the ports and the frontiers with Turkey, U.S.S.R., Afghanistan and Pakistan, and with the Caspian Sea. The Trans-Iranian Railway runs from Bandar Turcoman, on the Caspian Sea, via Tehran to Bandar Khomeini, on the Persian Gulf. Other lines link Tehran with Tabriz and with Mashad. There are also railways from Tabriz to Julfa and from Zahedan to Quetta, and a branch line from Ahwaz to Khorramshahr. An extension from Qom to Yazd via Kashan is now in operation, as is one from Bandar Turcoman to Gorgan. An extension from Yazd to Kerman is partially complete. The Iranian rail system is linked to the Turkish system via Van. There is an international airport at Tehran (Mehrabad), and airports at all the major provincial centres. The national airline, Iranair, is government-owned and operates international and domestic routes.

TRADE

Imports to Iran declined dramatically at the beginning of 1979 as a result of the economic disruption caused by the revolution. Iran's aggressive oil sales policy during 1982 enabled foreign exchange reserves to recover from the 1981 low level and made possible increased imports. However, the drop in world oil prices in 1986 again affected Iran's foreign exchange earnings, and her level of imports declined.

Imports into Iran consist mainly of industrial and agricultural machinery, motor vehicles and motor vehicle components for assembly, iron and steel (including manufactures), electrical machinery and goods, meat, various other foods, and certain textile fabrics and yarns. The principal exports, apart from oil, are cotton, carpets, dried fruit, nuts, hides and skins, mineral ores, wool, gums, caviare, cumin seed and spices. West Germany, Japan and the U.K. are Iran's leading suppliers.

	1984	1985
Imports	US$15,343 m.	US$11,145 m.
Exports	15,136 m.	13,952 m.

Trade with U.K.

	1985	1986
Imports from U.K. ...	£525,589,000	£399,373,000
Exports to U.K.	63,317,000	100,303,000

CAPITAL: Tehran, population (1986 estimate) over 6 million. Other large towns are Tabriz (853,296), Isfahan (1,000,000) Meshed (500,000), Shiraz (300,000), Resht (150,000), Kerman (100,000), Hamadan (130,000), Yazd (70,000), Kermanshah (152,000), Ahwaz (175,000).

FLAG.—Equal horizontal bands of green, white and red; with an emblem of the Islamic Republic.

NATIONAL DAY.—February 11.

IRAQ
(Al-Jumhouriya al-'Iraqia)

REVOLUTIONARY COMMAND COUNCIL

Chairman, President of the Republic, and *Supreme Commander of the Armed Forces,* Saddam Hussain, *assumed office* July 16, 1979.

Members, Izzat Ibrahim (*RCC Vice-Chairman*); Taha Muhiddin Ma'aruf (*Vice-President of the Republic*); Taha Yasin Ramadhan (*First Deputy Prime Minister*); Dr. Sa'doun Hammadi (*Speaker of National Assembly*); Tariq 'Aziz (*Deputy Prime Minister and Foreign Minister*); General Adnan Khairallah (*Deputy Prime Minister and Minister of Defence*); Sa'doun Shakir (*Interior*); Hassan Ali (*Trade*); Khalid Abdul Mun'im Rasheed (*acting Secretary-General*).

In addition to those members of the R.C.C. holding departmental portfolios listed above, there are 17 other Ministers and 4 Ministers of State.

Area, etc.—Traversed by the Rivers Euphrates and Tigris, Iraq extends from Turkey on N. and N.E. to the Gulf on the S. and S.E. and from Iran on E. to Syria and Arabian Desert on W., the approximate position being between 37¼° to 48½° E. long., and from 37¼° to 30° N. lat. (*see* MAP, p. 853). The area of Iraq is 167,925 sq. miles (434,924 sq. km.), of which 37 per cent. is desert land. About 35 to 40 per cent. of the remainder is potentially cultivable either by rainfall or by irrigation.

The *Euphrates* (which has a total length of 1,700 miles from its source to its outflow in the Persian Gulf) is formed by two arms, of which the Murad Su (415 miles) rises in eastern Erzurum, and flows westwards to a junction with the Kara Su, or Frat Su (275 miles); the other arm rises in the north-west of Erzurum in the Dumlu Dagh. The *Tigris* has a total length of 1,150 miles from its source to its junction with the Euphrates at Qurna, 70 miles from the Gulf, and rises in two arms south of the Taurus mountains, in Kurdistan, uniting at Til, where the boundaries of the districts of Diarbekir, Van and Bitlis conjoin.

Population.—At the Census of October 1977 Iraq had a total population of 12,171,480. Recent surveys (1985 U.N. estimate) give a figure of 15,898,000.

Language.—The language is mainly Arabic and English is widely used in commerce, science and the arts.

Antiquities.—In 1944 excavations at Tell Hassuna, near Shura (on the Tigris in North Iraq) unearthed abundant traces of culture dating back to 5000 B.C.

Excavations in 1948 at Tel Abu Shahrain, south of "Ur of the Chaldees," confirm Eridu's claim to be the most ancient city of the Sumerian world. Hillah, the ancient city on the left bank of the Shatt el Hillah, a branch of the Euphrates, about 70 miles south of Baghdad, is near the site of Babylon and of the "house of the lofty-head" or "gate of the god" (Tower of Babel). Mosul Governorate covers a great part of the ancient kingdom of *Assyria,* the ruins of Nineveh, the Assyrian capital, being visible on the banks of the Tigris, opposite Mosul. Qurna, at the junction of the Tigris and Euphrates, is traditionally supposed to be the site of the *Garden of Eden.*

Government.—Under the Treaty of Lausanne (1923), Turkey renounced sovereignty over Mesopotamia. A provisional Arab Government was set up in Nov., 1920, and in Aug., 1921, the Emir Faisal was elected King of Iraq. The country was a monarchy until July, 1958, when King Faisal II was assassinated. From 1958 Iraq has been under Presidential rule. The ruling Party is the Arab Ba'ath Socialist Party, which came to power on July 17, 1968.

Iraq has been engaged in hostilities with Iran since September 1980, originally over control of the Shatt-al-Arab waterway. In July 1982 Iranian forces moved across the border into Iraq, and since that time a series of inconclusive battles have been fought along the borders. Iraq declared a Maritime Exclusion Zone in Aug. 1982 and thereafter regularly attacked shipping entering the Iranian port of Bandar Khomeini at the head of the Gulf. The war extended further down the Gulf in the summer of 1984, with both sides attacking neutral shipping, including tankers and in 1985 Iraq launched several attacks on Iran's oil installations. In the summer of 1987 foreign navies entered the Gulf to escort neutral merchant shipping.

Communications and Trade.—New roads are being rapidly built, and communications between Baghdad and the provincial capitals are being improved and secured. Facilities at the port of Basra have been improved but the port has not been used since the outbreak of hostilities with Iran in Sept. 1980. Continuous dredging of the Shatt-al-Arab has also been suspended by hostilities and the channel has seriously silted. The port of Um Qasr near the Kuwaiti border has been developed for freight and sulphur handling and a container terminal is ready for operation but not in use due to the port's proximity to the war zone. Road routes from Turkey and the Mediterranean are well used, and carry through traffic to Kuwait and the south. The border between Syria and Iraq was closed in late 1977, reopened in November, 1978 and closed again in April 1982.

There is an international airport at Baghdad. Iraqi Airways provide flights between Baghdad and London, and other international airlines operate to Europe. Iraqi Republican Railways provide regular passenger and goods services between Basra, Baghdad and Mosul, and links up through Syria and Turkey with the Mediterranean and the Bosphorus, though no through traffic has used the line since the Syrian government cut the rail link in April 1982. There is also a metre gauge line connecting Baghdad with Khanaqin, Kirkuk and Arbil.

Agriculture and Industry.—Apart from the valuable revenues to be derived from oil, agricultural development makes a valuable contribution to the wealth of the country and two harvests can usually be gathered in the year. Production fluctuates from year to year according to rainfall. The Government's concern with agricultural development is shown in the large financial allocations made to the sector. Salinity and soil erosion, caused by a high water table, inadequate irrigation and drainage and traditional farming methods, are the major problems now being addressed by development planners.

Increasing industrialization is taking place, mainly in the public sector. Priority is being given to petrochemicals, food industries, construction industries and engineering. Existing industries include cement, building materials, steel fabrications, food processing and the manufacture of consumer goods, as well as the development of mineral resources.

Iraq's major industry is oil production. It was nationalized on June 1, 1972 and accounts for approximately 98 per cent. of the total government revenue and 45 per cent. of the Gross National Product. Production was some 3·5 million barrels per day in 1979 but the effects of war damage on the Basra terminals and the closure of the trans-Syria pipeline have reduced production to an estimated 1·3–1·5 million barrels per day. Total revenues from oil are believed to be less than $10,000 million following the collapse of oil prices, although they are difficult to calculate due to fluctuations in price.

FINANCE

	1981*
Total revenue	ID19,434,856,809
Total expenditure	19,250,261,450

* Estimates.

TRADE

	1984
Total Imports	$11,260,000
Total Exports	11,720,000

Trade with U.K.

	1985	1986
Imports from U.K.	£444,749,000	£443,890,000
Exports to U.K.	44,125,000	66,129,000

The principal imports are iron and steel, cement and other building materials, mechanical and electrical machinery, motor vehicles, textiles and clothing, essential foodstuffs, grain, tinned foods and raw industrial materials. The chief exports are crude petroleum, dates, raw wool, raw hides and skins and raw cotton.

CAPITAL.—Baghdad. Population of the governorate (Census 1977) 3,205,645. Other towns of importance are Ψ Basra, Mosul and Kirkuk.

FLAG.—Horizontal stripes of red, white and black, with three green stars on the white stripe.

NATIONAL DAY.—July 17 (Revolution Day).

BRITISH EMBASSY
Sharia Salah Ud-Din,
Karkh, Baghdad

Ambassador Extraordinary and Plenipotentiary, His Excellency Terence Joseph Clark, C.M.G., C.V.O. (1985).

Counsellor, R. A. Kealy (*Consul General*).
First Secretary, A. Brown (*Commercial*).
Defence Attaché, Col. B. Aldridge.

British Council Representative, P. Elborn, Waziriya, 301, Street 3, (P.O. Box 298), Baghdad.

IRELAND

Position and Extent.—Ireland lies in the Atlantic Ocean, to the W. of Great Britain, and is separated from Scotland by the North Channel and from Wales by the Irish Sea and St. George's Channel. The area of the island is 32,588 sq. miles (84,402 sq. km.), and its geographical position between 51° 26′ and 55° 21′ N. latitude and from 5° 25′ to 10° 30′ W. longitude. The greatest length of the island, from N.E. to S.W. (Torr Head to Mizen Head), is 302 miles, and the greatest breadth, from E. to W. (Dundrum Bay to Annagh

Head), is 174 miles. On the N. Coast of *Achill Island* (Co. Mayo) are the highest cliffs in the British Isles, 2,000 feet sheer above the sea. Ireland is occupied for the greater part of its area by the *Central Plain*, with an elevation 50 to 350 ft. above mean sea level, with isolated mountain ranges near the coastline. The principal mountains, with their highest points, are the *Sperrin Mountains* (Sawel 2,240 ft.) of County Tyrone; the *Mountains of Mourne* (Slieve Donard 2,796 ft.) of County Down, and the *Wicklow Mountains* (Lugnaquilla 3,039 ft.); the *Derryveagh Mountains* (Errigal 2,466 ft.) of County Donegal; the *Connemara Mountains* (Twelve Pins 2,695 ft.) of County Galway; *Macgillicuddy's Reeks* (Carrantuohill 3,414 ft., the highest point in Ireland); and the *Galtee Mountains* (3,018 ft.) of County Tipperary, and the *Knockmealdown* (2,609 ft.) and *Comeragh Mountains* (2,470 ft.) of County Waterford. The principal river of Ireland (and the longest in the British Isles) is the *Shannon* (240 miles), rising in County Cavan and draining the central plain; the Shannon flows through a chain of loughs to the city of Limerick, and thence to an estuary on the western Atlantic seaboard. The *Slaney* flows into Wexford Harbour, the *Liffey* to Dublin Bay, the *Boyne* to Drogheda, the *Lee* to Cork Harbour, the *Blackwater* to Youghal Harbour, and the *Suir, Barrow* and *Nore,* to Waterford Harbour. As in Scotland, the principal hydrographic feature is the *Loughs*, of which Lough *Neagh* (150 sq. miles) in the north-east is the largest in Ireland and the British Isles, others being the Shannon Chain of *Allen, Boderg, Forbes, Ree* and *Derg,* and the Erne Chain of *Gowna, Oughter, Lower Erne,* and *Erne*; *Melvin, Gill, Gara* and *Conn* in the north-west; and *Corrib* and *Mask* (joined by a hidden channel) in the west. In County Kerry, to the east of Macgillicuddy's Reeks, are the famous *lakes of Killarney.*

Primitive Man.—Although little is known concerning the earliest inhabitants of Ireland, there are many traces of neolithic man throughout the island; a grave containing a polished stone axehead assigned to 2,500 B.C. was found at Linkardstown, Co. Carlow, in 1944, and the use of bronze implements appears to have become known about the middle of the 17th century B.C. In the later Bronze Age a Celtic race of *Goidels* appears to have invaded the island, and in the early Iron Age *Brythons* from South Britain are believed to have effected settlements in the southeast, while *Picts* from North Britain established similar settlements in the north. Towards the close of the Roman occupation of Britain, the dominant tribe in the island was that of the *Scoti,* who afterwards established themselves in Scotland.

History.—According to Irish legends, the island of Ierne was settled by a Milesian race, who came from Scythia by way of Spain, and established the *Kingdom of Tara,* about 500 B.C. The supremacy of the *Ardri* (high king) of Tara was acknowledged by eight lesser kingdoms (Munster, Connaught, Ailech, Oriel, Ulidia, Meath, Leinster and Ossory) ruled by descendants of the eight sons of Miled. The basalt columns on the coast of Antrim, eight miles from Portrush, known as the *Giant's Causeway,* are connected with the legendary history of Ireland as the remnants of a bridge built in the time of Finn M'Coul (Fingal) to connect Antrim with Scotland (Staffa).

Hibernia was visited by Roman merchants but never by Roman legions, and little is known of the history of the country until the invasions of *Northmen* (Norwegians and Danes) towards the close of the 8th century A.D. The Norwegians were distinguished as Findgaill (White Strangers) and the Danes as Dubgaill (Black Strangers), names which survive in "Fingall," "MacDougall" and "MacDowell," while the name of the island itself is held to be derived from the Scandinavian *Ira-land* (land of the Irish), the names of the Provinces being survivals of Norse dialect forms (Ulaids-tir, Laiginstir, Mumans-tir and Kunnak-tir). The outstanding events in the encounters with the Northmen are the *Battle of Tara* (980), at which the Hy Neill king Maelsechlainn II defeated the Scandinavians of Dublin and the Hebrides under the king Amlaib Cuarán; and the *Battle of Clontarf* (1014) by which the Scandinavian power was completely broken. After Clontarf the supreme power was disputed by the O'Briens of Munster, the O'Neills of Ulster, and the O'Connors of Connaught, with varying fortunes. In 1152 Dermod MacMurrough (Diarmit MacMurchada), the deposed king of Leinster, sought assistance in his struggle with Rauidhri O'Connor (the high king of Ireland), and visited Henry II, the Norman king of England. Henry authorized him to obtain armed support in England for the recovery of his kingdom, and Dermod enlisted the services of Richard de Clare, the Norman Earl of Pembroke, afterwards known as *Strongbow*, who landed at Waterford (Aug. 23, 1170) with 200 knights and 1,000 other troops for the reconquest of Leinster, where he eventually settled, after marriage with Dermod's daughter. In 1172 (Oct. 18) Henry II himself landed in Ireland. He received homage from the Irish kings and established his capital at Dublin. The invaders subsequently conquered most of the island and a feudal government was created. In the 14th and 15th centuries, the Irish recovered most of their lands, while many Anglo-Irish lords became virtually independent, royal authority being confined to the "Pale," a small district round Dublin. Though, under Henry VII, Sir Edward Poynings, as Lord Deputy, had passed at the *Parliament of Drogheda* (1494) the act later known as *Poynings' Law*, subordinating the Irish Legislature to the Crown, the Earls of Kildare retained effective power until, in 1534, Henry VIII began the reconquest of Ireland. Parliament in 1541 recognized him as King of Ireland and by 1603 English authority was supreme.

Christianity.—Christianity did not become general until the advent of St. Patrick. *St. Patrick* was born in Britain about 389, and was taken to Ireland as a slave about sixteen years later escaping to Gaul at the age of 22. In 432 he was consecrated Bishop of Auxerre and landed in Wicklow to establish and organize the Christian religion throughout the island.

REPUBLIC OF IRELAND
(Poblacht Na L'Eireann)

Uachtarán-na-hÉireann (*President*), Patrick J. Hillery, *born* 1923, *assumed office*, Dec. 3, 1976, *sworn in for 2nd term,* Dec. 3, 1983.

MEMBERS OF THE GOVERNMENT

Taoiseach and Minister for the Gaeltacht, Charles J. Haughey.
Tánaiste and Minister for Foreign Affairs, Brian Lenihan.
Finance, Ray MacSharny.
Justice, Gerard Collins.
Tourism and Transport, John P. Wilson.
Agriculture and Food, Michael O'Kennedy.
Social Welfare, Michael Woods.
Industry and Commerce, Albert Reynolds.
Energy and Communications, Ray Burke.
Marine, Brendan Daly.
Environment, Pádraig Flynn.
Labour, Bertie Ahern.
Health, Rory O'Hanlon.
Defence, Michael J. Noonan.
Education, Mary O'Rourke.

The present Government was formed by the Fianna Fail Party following a general election on Feb. 17, 1987.

EMBASSY IN LONDON

17 Grosvenor Place, SW1X 7HR
[01-235 2171]

Ambassador Extraordinary and Plenipotentiary, His Excellency Andrew O'Rourke (1987).

Area and Population.—The Republic has a land area of 27,136 sq. miles (70,283 sq. km.), divided into the four Provinces of *Leinster* (Carlow, Dublin, Kildare, Kilkenny, Laoighis, Longford, Louth, Meath, Offaly, Westmeath, Wexford and Wicklow); *Munster* (Clare, Cork, Kerry, Limerick, Tipperary and Waterford); *Connacht* (Galway, Leitrim, Mayo, Roscommon and Sligo); and part of *Ulster* (Cavan, Donegal and Monaghan).

Total population of the Republic at the Census held on April 13, 1986, was 3,537,195 (preliminary). Provisional figures showed 62,250 births, 18,552 marriages and 33,222 deaths in the year 1985.

GOVERNMENT

The Constitution.—The constitution, approved by a plebiscite on July 1, 1937, came into operation on December 29, 1937. The Constitution declares the national territory to be the whole island of Ireland, its islands and the territorial seas. Pending the reintegration of the national territory, and without prejudice to the right of the Parliament and the Government established by the Constitution to exercise jurisdiction over the whole of the national territory, the laws enacted by that Parliament shall have the like area and extent of application as those of the Irish Free State, which did not include the six counties of Northern Ireland.

The Irish language, being the national language, is the first official language. The English language is recognized as a second official language.

The President (*Uachtarán na hEireann*) is elected by direct vote of the people for a period of seven years. A former or retiring President is eligible for a second term. The President summons and dissolves Dáil Éireann on the advice of the *Taoiseach* (Head of the Government). He signs and promulgates laws. The supreme command of the Defence forces is vested in him, its exercise being regulated by law. He has the power of pardon. The President, in the exercise and performance of certain of his constitutional powers and functions, is aided and advised by a Council of State.

The National Parliament (*Oireachtas*) consists of the President and two Houses: a House of Representatives (*Dáil Éireann*) and a Senate (*Seanad Éireann*). Dáil Éireann is composed of 166 members elected by adult suffrage on a basis of proportional representation by means of the single transferable vote. All citizens, and such other persons in the state as may be determined by law, who have reached the age of 18 years and are not disqualified by law have the right to vote. Each Dáil may continue for a period not exceeding five years from the date of election.

Seanad Éireann is composed of 60 members, of whom 11 are nominated by the Taoiseach and 49 are elected; six by institutions of higher education, and 43 from panels of candidates, established on a vocational basis.

Members of Dáil Éireann are paid an allowance of IR£19,265 per annum (and members of Seanad Éireann IR£10,714). They are allowed travelling facilities between Dublin and their constituencies and are, subject to certain restrictions, granted free telephone and postal facilities from Leinster House and allowances for overnight stays in Dublin.

The executive authority is exercised by the Government subject to the Constitution. The Government is responsible to Dáil Éireann, meets and acts as a collective authority, and is collectively responsible for the Departments of State administered by the Ministers.

The Taoiseach is appointed by the President on the nomination of Dáil Éireann. The other members of the government are appointed by the President on the nomination of the Taoiseach with the previous approval of Dáil Éireann. The Taoiseach appoints a member of the Government to be the *Tánaiste* who acts for all purposes in the place of the Taoiseach in the event of the death, permanent incapacitation, or temporary absence of the Taoiseach. The Taoiseach, the Tánaiste and the Minister for Finance must be members of Dáil Éireann. The other members of the Goverment must be members of Dáil Éireann or Seanad Éireann, but not more than two may be members of Seanad Éireann.

The result of the general election on Feb. 17, 1987 was as follows: *Fianna Fáil*, 81; *Fine Gael*, 51; *Progressive Democrats*, 14; *Labour*, 12; *Workers' Party*, 4; *Independent*, 4. Total membership including the *Ceann Comhairle* (Chairman), 166.

JUDICIAL SYSTEM

The Judicial system comprises Courts of First Instance and a Court of Final Appeal called the Supreme Court (*Cúirt Uachtarach*). The Courts of First Instance include a High Court (*Ard-Chúirt*) and Courts of local and limited jurisdiction, with a right of appeal as determined by law. The High Court alone has original jurisdiction to consider the question of the validity of any law having regard to the provisions of the Constitution. The Supreme Court has appellate jurisdiction from all decisions of the High Court, with such exceptions and subject to such regulations as may be prescribed by law.

Chief Justice, Hon. Thomas A. Finlay .... IR£52,067
President of the High Court, Hon. Liam
  Hamilton .... IR£45,164
Judges, Supreme Court, Hon. Brian
  Walsh; Hon. Seamus Henchy; Hon.
  Francis Griffin; Hon. Anthony Heder-
  man; Hon. Niall J. McCarthy .... IR£42,575
Judges, High Court, Hon. Donal Barring-
  ton; Hon. John M. Gannon; Hon. Rory
  O'Hanlon; Hon. Declan Costello; Hon.
  Ronan Keane; Hon. Ms. Mella Carroll;
  Hon. Henry D. Barron; Hon. Francis D.
  Murphy; Hon. Kevin Lynch; Hon. Sea-
  mus Egan; Hon. Robert Barr; Hon.
  Gerard Lardner; Hon. John J. Blayney;
  Hon. John P. McKenzie; Hon. Richard
  Johnson; Hon. Thomas F. Roe (*ex
  officio*) .... IR£38,261
Attorney-General, John Murray.

RELIGION
(Census of 1981)

Catholic	3,204,476
Church of Ireland	95,366
Presbyterians	14,255
Methodists	5,790
Others	123,518
Total	3,443,405

DEFENCE

Establishments provide at present for a Permanent Defence Force of approximately 17,974 all ranks, including the Air Corps and the Naval Service. Recruitment is on a voluntary basis. Minimum term of enlistment is three years in the Permanent Defence Force followed by six years in the Reserve Defence Force. Establishment also provide for a Reserve Defence Force of 22,214 all ranks. Recruitment is

also on a voluntary basis; minimum term of enlistment is three years. The Defence Estimate for the year ending Dec. 31, 1987 provides for an expenditure of IR£260,270,000.

FINANCE

	1986 (*Provisional*)	1987 (*Estimated*)
Revenue	IR£6,709·3 m.	IR£7,216·9 m.
Expenditure	8,124·0 m.	8,417·0 m.

The estimated revenue includes:

	IR£m.	IR£m.
Customs Duties	81·5	85·0
Excise Duties	1,380·3	1,449·0
Capital Taxes	33·8	36·0
Stamp Duties	158·6	142·4
Income Tax	2,388·5	2,721·7
Income Levy	32·9	2·0
Corporation Tax	258·0	261·8
Value-Added Tax	1,527·1	1,631·0
Agricultural Levies (E.E.C.)	12·8	13·0
Motor Vehicle Duties	130·8	132·0
Youth Employment Levy	91·3	95·0
Total (including other non-tax items)	6,709·3	7,216·9

The principal items of expenditure in the Budget:

	IR£m.	IR£m.
Debt Service	1,989	2,146
Industry and Labour	248	255
Agriculture	340	295
Fisheries	13	13
Forestry	16	11
Tourism	26	23
Roads	31	31
Sanitary Services	45	57
Transport	2	2
Health	1,049	1,044
Education	956	1,062
Welfare	1,612	1,660
Housing	199	241
Subsidies	264	213
Defence	295	295
Garda	268	266
Prisons	54	53
Legal, etc.	50	42
Other	667	708
Total	8,124	8,417

The Gross Debt at end 1985 was IR£20,417,000,000 and capital assets were IR£4,971,684,868.

EDUCATION

Primary education is directed by the State, with the exception of 64 private primary schools with an enrolment of 9,512 in 1985–86.

There were 3,384 State-aided primary schools with an enrolment of 567,110.

In 1985-86 there were 504 recognized secondary schools with 214,275 pupils under private management (mainly religious orders), and 247 vocational schools with 81,828 pupils. Vocational schools are controlled by 38 statutory local Vocational Education Committees. There were 15 State comprehensive schools in 1985–86 with a total enrolment of 8,959 students, and 44 community schools with an enrolment of 29,662 students. There were also other miscellaneous second-level schools and the total full-time enrolment at second-level for 1985–86 was 338,207.

Third-level education is catered for by five University Colleges, two National Institutes for Higher Education, and also by third-level courses offered by the Technical Colleges and Regional Technical Colleges and other miscellaneous third-level institutions. There were 55,523 full-time third-level students in 1985–86, of whom 26,581 were attending university courses.

The estimated State expenditure on education in 1987, excluding administration and inspection, is Primary IR£444,015,000; Post-Primary IR£498,558,000. The vote for Universities and third-level Colleges amounted to IR£124,644,000.

MINERALS AND FISHERIES

Minerals.—275 persons were employed in the coal mines in 1986 and 53,500 tons of coal was produced.

Sea Fisheries.—7,778 persons were employed in the fisheries in 1985. Total value of all fish landed in 1985 was IR£59,900,000.

COMMUNICATIONS

Railways.—In the year ended Dec. 31, 1985, there were 1,944 kms of railway; 20,090,000 passengers and 3,379,000 tonnes of merchandise were conveyed; the receipts were IR£131,865,000 and expenditure IR£132,127,000. These figures are in respect of railway working by *Coras Iompair Eireann.*

Road Motor Services.—In 1985 road motor vehicles carried 226,144,234 passengers, the gross receipts being IR£123,014,942.

Shipping.—In 1985 the number of ships with cargo which arrived at Irish ports was 11,335 (20,455,000 net registered tons); of these 2,577 (6,029,000 net registered tons) were of Irish nationality.

CIVIL AVIATION

Shannon Airport, 15 miles W. of Limerick, is on the main transatlantic air route. In 1986 the airport handled 1,140,459 passengers.

Dublin Airport, 6 miles N. of Dublin, serves the cross-channel and European services operated by the Irish national airline *Aer Lingus* and other airlines. In 1986 the airport handled 2,925,573 passengers.

Cork Airport, 5 miles S. of Cork serves the cross Channel and European services operated by *Aer Lingus* and other airlines. In 1986 the airport handled 357,710 passengers.

Trade with U.K.

	1985	1986
	IR£	IR£
Imports from U.K.	4,026,046,392	3,586,791,823
Exports to U.K.	3,211,476,648	3,201,343,278

OVERSEAS TRADE

	1985	1986
	IR£	IR£
Imports	9,428,197,691	8,629,706,444
Exports	9,743,037,929	9,388,206,370
Trade balance	− 314,840,238	− 758,499,926

PRINCIPAL ARTICLES

Principal imports in 1986 were:

	IR£
Live animals	66,730,077
Food, drink and tobacco	1,012,696,048
Petrol and petroleum products	554,169,891
Chemicals	1,047,719,864
Machinery	2,252,904,844
Transport equipment	460,688,878
Metal and manufactures	524,177,133
Textiles and clothing	766,923,460
Paper, paperboard and manufactures	265,695,379
Professional, scientific etc. goods	196,782,165

Principal exports in 1986 were:

	IR£
Live animals	255,392,746
Meat and meat preparations	659,142,910
Other food, drink and tobacco	1,508,153,539
Machinery and transport equipment	2,860,527,213
Clothing, headgear and footwear . . .	211,127,636
Textiles	354,833,567
Metal ores and scrap	137,297,237
Metal and manufactures	277,832,297
Non-metallic mineral manufactures .	138,600,048
Chemicals	1,251,001,477
Professional, scientific etc., goods . . .	387,430,569

CAPITAL.—Dublin (*Baile Atha Cliath*) is a City and County Borough on the River Liffey at the head of Dublin Bay. In April, 1981, its population (1981 Census) was 525,882. A 1985 U.N. estimate gave a figure of 915,115.

Other cities and towns, with their populations at the Census of 1981 are ΨCork (136,344); ΨLimerick (60,736); ΨDun Laoghaire (54,496); ΨWaterford (38,473); ΨGalway (37,835); ΨDundalk (25,663).

FLAG.—Equal vertical stripes of green, white and orange.

NATIONAL DAY.—March 17 (St. Patrick's Day).

BRITISH EMBASSY
31 Merrion Road, Dublin 4

Ambassador Extraordinary and Plenipotentiary, His Excellency Nicholas Maxted Fenn, C.M.G. (1986).
Counsellor and Head of Chancery, R. F. Stimson.
First Secretaries, D. L. S. Coombe (*Commercial*); W. M. L. Dickinson; J. C. Radcliffe, M.V.O.; J. D. F. Holt; Miss B. M. Pugh; P. M. Innes.

ISRAEL
(Medinat Israel)

President of Israel, Chaim Herzog, *born* 1918, *elected* Mar. 22, 1983, *inaugurated,* May 5, 1983.

CABINET

**Prime Minister,* Yitzhak Shamir (*L.H.*).
**Vice-Premier and Foreign Minister,* Shimon Peres (*Lab.*).
**Deputy P.M. and Education and Culture,* Yitzhak Navon (*Lab.*).
**Deputy P.M. and Construction and Housing,* David Levy (*L.H.*).
Agriculture, Arieh Nehamkin (*Lab.*).
**Commerce and Industry,* Ariel Sharon (*L.H.*).
Communications, (vacant).
**Defence,* Yitzhak Rabin (*Lab.*).
Economy and Planning, Gad Yaacobi (*Lab.*).
Energy and Infrastructure, Moshe Shahal (*Lab.*).
Justice, Avraham Sharir (*L.L.*).
Health, Shoshana Arbeli Almoslino (*Lab.*).
Immigration and Absorption, Yaakov Tsur (*Lab.*).
**Finance,* Moshe Nissim (*L.L.*).
Labour and Social Affairs, Moshe Katzav (*L.H.*).
**Police,* Haim Bar-Lev (*Lab.*).
Science and Development, Gideon Patt (*L.L.*).
Tourism, Avraham Sharir (*L.L.*).
Transportation, Haim Corfu (*L.H.*).
Interior, Yitzhak Shamir (*acting*).
Religious Affairs, Zevulun Hammer (*National Religious Party*).
* *In Prime Minister's Office,* Ezer Weizman (*Lab.*).
Without Portfolio, *Moshe Arens (*L.H.*); Yosef Shapira (*Morasha*); Yigal Hurwitz (*Ometz*); Rabbi Yitzak Peretz (*Shas*).

= Labour Party; *L.H.* = Likud Party—Herut
faction; *L.L.* = Likud Party—Liberal faction.
*Member of Inner Cabinet.
(Under the agreement by which the Government of
National Unity was formed, Mr. Peres gave up the
Premiership in Oct. 1986 to Mr. Shamir.)

EMBASSY IN LONDON
2 Palace Green, Kensington, W8 4QB
[01–937 8050]

Ambassador Extraordinary and Plenipotentiary, His
Excellency Yehuda Avner (1983).

Area and Population.—Israel lies on the western
edge of the continent of Asia at the eastern extremity
of the Mediterranean Sea, between lat. 29° 30′–33° 15′
N. and longitude 34° 15′–35° 40′ E. Its political
neighbours are Lebanon on the North, Syria on the
North and East, Jordan on the East and the Egyptian
province of Sinai on the South-West.

The area is estimated at 8,019 sq. miles (20,770 sq.
km.). The population was estimated at the end of
1985 at 4,266,600. During the upheavals of 1948–49 a
large number of Arabs left the country as refugees
and settled in neighbouring countries.

Hebrew and Arabic are the official languages of
Israel. Arabs are entitled to transact all official
business with Government Departments in Arabic,
and provision is made in the *Knesset* for the

simultaneous translation of all speeches into Arabic.

Physical Features.—Israel comprises four main
regions: (*a*) the hill country of Galilee and Judea and
Samaria, rising in places to heights of nearly 4,000
feet; (*b*) the coastal plain from the Gaza strip to North
of Acre, including the plain of Esdraelon
running from Haifa Bay to the south-east, and
cutting in two the hill region; (*c*) the Negev, a semi-
desert triangular-shaped region, extending from a
base south of Beersheba, to an apex at the head of the
Gulf of 'Aqaba; and (*d*) parts of the Jordan valley,
including the Hula Region, Tiberias and the south-
western extremity of the Dead Sea. The principal
river is the Jordan, which rises from three main
sources in Israel, the Lebanon and Syria, and flows
through the Hula valley and the canals which have
replaced Lake Hula, drained in 1958. Between Hulata
and Tiberias (Sea of Galilee) the river falls 926 ft. in
11 miles and becomes a turbulent stream. Lake
Tiberias is 696 ft. below sea-level and liable to sudden
storms. Between it and the Dead Sea the Jordan falls
591 ft. The other principal rivers are the Yarkon and
Kishon. The largest lake is the *Dead Sea* (shared
between Israel and Jordan); area 393 sq. miles, 1,286
feet below sea-level, 51·5 miles long, with a maximum
width of 11 miles and a maximum depth of 1,309 ft.; it
receives the waters of the Jordan and of six other
streams, and has no outlet, the surplus being carried
off by evaporation. The water contains an extraor-

dinarily high concentration of mineral substances. The highest mountain peak is Mount Meron, 3,962 feet above sea-level, near Safad, Upper Galilee.

Climate.—The climate is variable, similar to that of Lower Egypt, but modified by altitude and distance from the sea. The summer is hot but tempered in most parts by daily winds from the Mediterranean. The winter is the rainy season lasting from November to April, the period of maximum rainfall being January and February.

Antiquities.—The following are among the principal historic sites in Israel: *Jerusalem*: the Church of the Holy Sepulchre: the Al Aqsa Mosque and Dome of the Rock, standing on the remains of the Temple Mount of Herod the Great, of which the Western (wailing) Wall is a fragment; the Church of the Dormition and the Cœnaculum on Mount Zion; Ein Karem: Church of the Visitation, Church of St. John the Baptist. *Galilee*: The Sea; Church and Mount of the Beatitudes, ruins of Capernaum and other sites connected with the life of Christ. *Mount Tabor*: Church of the Transfiguration. *Nazareth*: Church of the Annunciation and other Christian shrines associated with the childhood of Christ. There are also numerous sites dating from biblical and medieval days, such as Ascalon, Cæsarea, Atlit, Massada, Megiddo and Hazor. Other antiquities in the West Bank of Jordan and the Golan Heights at present occupied by Israel can now be visited from Israel. In accordance with the terms of the peace treaty signed between Egypt and Israel on March 26, 1979, Israel withdrew in April 1982 to the pre-1967 boundary, returning the Sinai area to Egyptian sovereignty.

Government.—There is a Cabinet and a single-chamber Parliament (*Knesset*) of 120 members. A general election is held at least once every four years. The last General Election was held on July 23, 1984; the result was inconclusive. After about six weeks of negotiations between political parties a Government of National Unity was formed.

Immigration.—The Declaration of Independence of May 14, 1948, laid down that "the State of Israel will be open to the immigration of Jews from all countries of their dispersion.". The Law of Return, passed by the *Knesset* on July 5, 1950, provides that an immigrant visa shall be granted to every Jew who expresses his desire to settle in Israel. From the establishment of the State until April 1978, about 1·7 million immigrants had entered Israel from over 100 different countries.

Education.—Elementary education for all children from 5 to 15 years is free, though secondary education is not compulsory. The law also provides for working youth, age 15–18 who for some reason have not completed their primary education, to be exempted from work in order to do so.

In 1985–86 enrolment in all educational establishments was 1,383,838: kindergartens 277,200; elementary education, 622,056; secondary education, 348,262; post-secondary, 98,420.

Finance.—Government expenditure in 1986 was 25,399,234,000 new Shekels at market prices. GNP at market prices was 40,354,955,000 new Shekels.

The unit of currency, the Shekel (of 100 agorot), has been revalued and 1,000 old Shekels=1 new Shekel. Exchange rate, *see* p. 82.

COMMUNICATIONS

Railways and Roads.—Israel State Railways started operating in August 1949. Towns now served are Haifa, Tel Aviv, Jerusalem, Lod, Nahariya, Beersheba, Dimona, Ashdod and intermediate stations. In 1985 the total railway network amounted to 852 km. There were 12,760 km. of paved road and in 1985 776,217 licensed vehicles.

Shipping.—Israel's merchant marine had reached

a total of 2,805,000 tons deadweight by December, 1985.

The chief ports are Haifa, a modern harbour, with a depth of 30 ft. alongside the main quay; the harbour on the Red Sea at Eilat, inaugurated in September 1965, has a capacity of 10,000 tons a day; Acre has an anchorage for small vessels; the deep-water port at Ashdod, 20 miles south of Tel Aviv, which started operations at the end of 1965, handled 7,252,000 tons of cargo in 1985. In the same year Israel's three main ports handled 16,294,000 tons of cargo.

Civil Aviation.—In 1985, 3,114,000 passengers passed through Ben Gurion airport, of which 356,945 arrived by charter flight.

PRODUCTION AND INDUSTRY

Agriculture.—The country is generally fertile and climatic conditions vary so widely that a large variety of crops can be grown, ranging from temperate crops, such as wheat and cherries, to subtropical crops such as sorghum, millet and mangoes. The famous "Jaffa" orange is produced in large quantities mostly in the coastal plain for export: high-profit export crops such as strawberries and cut flowers are increasingly important. The citrus yield during the 1985–86 season was 1,242,903 tons. Specialized glass-house crops for export, such as flowers, tomatoes and strawberries, are becoming increasingly popular and exports of flowers in 1985 earned U.S.$75,454,000. Olives are cultivated, mainly for the production of oil used for edible purposes and for the manufacture of soap. The main winter crops are wheat and barley and various kinds of pulses, while in summer sorghum, millet, maize, sesame and summer pulses are grown. Large areas of seasonal vegetables are planted. Beef, cattle and poultry farming have been developed and the production of mixed vegetables and dairy produce has greatly increased. Tobacco and medium staple cotton are now grown. Fishing production (mostly from fish farms) was 14,958 tons in 1985–86. All kinds of summer fruits such as figs, grapes, plums and apples are produced in increasing quantities for local consumption. Water supply for irrigation is the principal limiting factor to greater production. The area under cultivation is 4,370,000 dunams, of which 2,370,000 is under irrigation. The Israel land measure is the *dunam*, equivalent to 1,000 square metres (approximately a quarter of an acre).

Industry.—In value polished diamonds account for about one quarter of Israel's total exports. Amongst the most important of her exporting industries are textiles, foodstuffs, chemicals (mainly fertilisers and pharmaceuticals). Her metal-working and science-based industries are highly sophisticated and technologically advanced. These include the aircraft and military industries. Other important manufacturing industries include plastics, rubber, cement, glass, paper and oil refining.

TRADE

The principal imports are foodstuffs, crude oil, machinery and vehicles, iron, steel and manufactures thereof, and chemicals. The principal exports are citrus fruits and by-products, polished diamonds, plywood, cement, tyres, minerals, finished and semi-finished textiles.

	1985	1986
Imports	U.S.$8,020·9 m.	U.S.$9,275·4 m.
Exports	6,080·4 m.	6,914·2 m.

Trade with U.K.

	1985	1986
Imports from U.K.	U.S.$753·9 m.	U.S.$985·0 m.
Exports to U.K.	477·0 m.	511·5 m.

CAPITAL.—Most of the Government departments are in Jerusalem (population, 1984, 506,200). A resolution proclaiming Jerusalem as the capital of Israel was adopted by the Israel parliament on Jan. 23, 1950. It is not, however, recognized as the capital by the United Nations. Other principal towns are ΨTel Aviv and district (1,904,400); ΨHaifa and district (592,700) and Beersheba and district (296,200).

FLAG.—White, with two horizontal blue stripes. the Shield of David in the centre.

JERUSALEM

Until 1967 Jerusalem was divided between Israel and Jordan, two of the 36 recognized Christian Holy Places (in the New City) being under Jewish administration, the remainder under Arab administration in the Old City. At the conclusion of hostilities between Israel and the surrounding Arab countries in 1967 the entire city was under Israeli control.

BRITISH EMBASSY

192 Hayarkon Street, Tel Aviv.

Ambassador Extraordinary and Plenipotentiary, His Excellency C. W. Squire, C.M.G., L.V.O. (1984).

Counsellor, S. W. J. Fuller (*Head of Chancery, Consul-General and Counsellor, Commercial*).

Defence Attaché, Col. R. McCrum.

British Council Representative, P. Sandiford, 140 Hayarkon Street, (P.O. Box 3302), Tel Aviv. There is a library in *Tel Aviv* and in *Jerusalem.*

ISRAEL-BRITISH CHAMBER OF COMMERCE, 76 IBN Guirol Street, Tel Aviv 64162.

ITALY
(Repubblica Italiana)

President of the Italian Republic, Francesco Cossiga, *born* 1928, *sworn in,* July 3, 1985.

COUNCIL OF MINISTERS

Prime Minister and Southern Affairs, Giovanni Goria (*CD*).
Deputy P.M. and Treasury, Giuliano Amato (*S*).
Foreign Affairs, Giulio Andreotti (*CD*).
Interior, Amintore Fanfani (*CD*).
Justice, Giuliano Vassalli (*S*).
Finance, Antonio Gava (*CD*).
Budget and Economic Planning, Emilio Colombo (*CD*).
Defence, Valerio Zanone (*Lib*).
Agriculture and Forests, Filippo Maria Pandolfi (*CD*).
Labour, Salvatore Formica (*S*).
Regional Affairs, Aristide Gunnella (*Rep*).
Civil Protection, Remo Gaspari (*CD*).
Education, Giovanni Galloni (*CD*).
Public Works, Emilio de Rose (*SD*).
Transport, Calogero Mannino (*CD*).
Posts, Oscar Mammi (*Rep*).
Industry, Adolfo Battaglia (*Rep*).
State Participation, Luigi Granelli (*CD*).
Foreign Trade, Renato Ruggiero (*S*).
Health, Carlo Donat-Cattin (*CD*).
Culture, Carlo Vizzini (*SD*).
Tourism, Franco Carraro (*S*).
Merchant Navy, Giovanni Prandini (*CD*).
Relations with Parliament, Sergio Mattarella (*CD*).
Public Administration, Giorgio Santuz (*CD*).
EC Affairs, Antonio La Pergola (*SD*).
Scientific Research, Antonio Ruberti (*S*).
Environment, Giorgio Ruffolo (*S*).
Urban Problems, Carlo Tognoli (*S*).
Special Affairs, Rosa Russo Jervolino (*CD*).

S = Socialist; *CD* = Christian Democrat; *SD* = Social Democrat; *Rep* = Republican; *Lib* = Liberal.

ITALIAN EMBASSY IN LONDON

14 Three Kings Yard, Davies Street, W1Y 2EH [01–629 8200]

Ambassador Extraordinary and Plenipotentiary, (new appointment awaited).

Minister-Counsellor, Sig. Umberto Vattani.

First Counsellors, Sig. Mario Fugazzola; Sig. Enrico Augelli; Sig. Giancarlo Aragona; Sig. Gianfranco Varvesi; Sig. Roberto Di Leo (*Consular Affairs*).

Italy is a Republic in the south of Europe, consisting of a peninsula, the large islands of Sicily and Sardinia, the island of Elba and about 70 other small islands. Italy is bounded on the N. by Switzerland and Austria, on the S. by the Mediterranean, on the E. by the Adriatic and Yugoslavia, and on the W. by France and the Ligurian and Tyrrhenian Seas. The total area is about 116,304 sq. miles (301,225 sq. km.).

The peninsula is for the most part mountainous, but between the Apennines, which form its spine, and the East coastline are two large fertile plains; of Emilia/Romagna in the north and of Apulia in the south. The Alps form the northern limit of Italy, dividing it from France, Switzerland, Austria and Yugoslavia. *Mont Blanc* (15,771 feet), the highest peak, is in the French Pennine Alps, but partly within the Italian borders are Monte Rosa (15,217 feet), Matterhorn (14,780 feet) and several peaks from 12,000 to 14,000 feet.

The chief rivers are the Po (405 miles), which flows through Piedmont, Lombardy and the Veneto, and the Adige (Trentino and Veneto) in the north, the Arno (Florentine Plain) and the Tiber (flowing through Rome to Ostia). The *Rubicon,* a small stream flowing into the Adriatic near Rimini formed the boundary between Italy and Cisalpine Gaul: "crossing the Rubicon" (as Caesar did in 49 B.C., thus "invading" Italy in arms) is used to indicate definite committal to some course of action.

Population.—In Feb. 1986 Italy's population was 57,193,708. The annual rate of population increase between 1981 and 1985 was 0·3 per cent.

Government.—Italian unity was accomplished under the House of Savoy, after a struggle from 1848 to 1870, in which Mazzini (1805–72), Garibaldi (1807–82) and Cavour (1810–61) were the principal figures. It was completed when Lombardy was ceded by Austria in 1859 and Venice in 1866, and through the evacuation of Rome by the French in 1870. In 1871 the King of Italy entered Rome, and that city was declared to be the capital.

Benito Mussolini, known as *Il Duce* (The Leader) was continuously in office as Prime Minister from Oct. 30, 1922, until July 25, 1943, when the Fascist *régime* was abolished. He was captured by Italian partisans while attempting to escape across the Swiss frontier and was put to death on April 28, 1945.

In fulfilment of a promise given in April, 1944, that he would retire when the Allies entered Rome a decree was signed on June 5, 1944, by the late King Victor Emmanuel III under which Prince Umberto, the King's son, became "Lieutenant-General of the Realm." The King remained head of the House of Savoy and retained the title King of Italy until his abdication on May 9, 1946, when he was succeeded by the Crown Prince.

A general election was held on June 2, 1946, together with a referendum on the future of the monarchy. The result showed a majority in favour of replacing the monarchy with a Republic. The Royal Family left the country on June 13, and on June 28, 1946, a Provisional President was elected.

Constitution.—The constitution of the Republic of Italy, approved by the Constituent Assembly on December 22, 1947, provides for the election of the President by an electoral college which consists of the two Houses of Parliament (the Chamber of

Deputies and the Senate) sitting in joint session together with three delegates from each region (one in the case of the Valle d'Aosta). The President, who must be over 50 years of age, holds office for 7 years. He has numerous carefully defined powers, the main one of which is the right to dissolve one or both Houses of Parliament, after consultation with the Speakers.

Defence.—The Armed Forces are largely manned by conscripts, who serve for 12 months. The Army has approx. 295,000 men, of whom 40,000 are regular officers and N.C.O.s. In addition, the elite paramilitary *Carabinieri* force, which is part of the Army, has over 96,000 men, most of whom are regulars. The Army, which has three Corps concentrated in the North, is equipped with Leopard 1 and M60 tanks and M113 armoured personnel carriers. There is also a parachute brigade, 5 alpine brigades, a missile brigade, and a Light Aviation Arm with over 300 helicopters. The Navy consists of one helicopter carrier, 3 cruisers, 4 destroyers, 9 submarines, 24 frigates and corvettes and 24 mine warfare ships. Manpower strength is approx. 45,000. The Air Force has 70,000 men and 347 combat aircraft. It is largely a tactical airforce, equipped with Tornado, F104 and G91 aircraft, but also has transport, anti-submarine and helicopter search and rescue units. There is a large Reserve Force of ex-conscripts under the age of 35.

REGIONS OF ITALY

Rome and Central Italy.—Rome was founded, according to legend, by Romulus in the year now known as 753 B.C. It was the focal point of Latin civilization and dominion under the Republic and afterwards under the Roman Empire, and became the capital of Italy when the Kingdom was established in 1871. The capital is concerned mainly with tourism and government, but its importance as a business centre is steadily increasing, and it is reportedly the third largest industrial centre in the country.

Lombardy and Milan.—In the Lombardy region are to be found some 15·7 per cent of Italy's commercial and banking services and some 21·9 per cent of her manufacturing industry. The whole range of Italian industry is represented, most important being the steel, machine tool and motor car factories.

Turin and Piedmont.—Turin between 1861 and 1865 was Italy's first capital as the home of the Piedmontese Royal Family. Now it is the headquarters of Europe's largest manufacturer of motor cars, produces 75 per cent. of Italy's motor vehicles and over 80 per cent. of its roller bearings. Turin is also Italy's second largest steel producing city. Piedmont is the centre of the Italian textile industry based mainly on Biella.

Genoa and the Ligurian Riviera.—Genoa has been one of Europe's major ports since the Middle Ages, and handles one-third of Italy's foreign trade. About 80 per cent. of the goods handled are imports.

Venice and the North-East.—Venice is primarily a tourist attraction of unique beauty. It was founded in the middle of the 5th century by refugees from the mainland fleeing attacks, and by the 16th century it was one of the strongest and richest states of Europe, dominating Eastern Mediterranean trade. It lost its independence in 1797 when Napoleon handed it over to Austria. Industry (paper and stationery, mechanical equipment, consumer goods, electrical appliances, woollens) is now developing in the Venice area, particularly on the autostrada linking Venice with her historical and now developing rivals, Verona, Vicenza, Padua and in the areas around Treviso and Pordenone. Near Trieste, is the modern Monfalcone shipyard.

Tuscany, Emilia and Romagna.—Florence, the capital of Tuscany, was one of the greatest cities in Europe from the 11th to the 16th centuries, and the cradle of the Renaissance. Under the Medici family in the 15th century flourished many of the greatest names in Italian art, including Filippo Lippi, Botticelli, Donatello and Brunelleschi and in the 16th century great Florentine artists like Michelangelo and Leonardo da Vinci. These regions were the agricultural centre of Italy but the post-war period has seen the development of large industrial centres at Bologna, Florence, Modena, Pistoia and Ravenna. Most of the new firms are small or medium-sized. The footwear industry is based on Florence, textiles in Prato, reproduction furniture at Cascina and Poggibonsi, ceramics at Sassuolo, and glass and pottery at Empoli and Montelupo. Bologna is an important centre for the food industry.

Naples and the Toe of Italy.—Naples, formerly the capital and administrative centre of the Kingdom of Naples and Sicily, remains the dominant city in the area, but it is beset with great problems of unemployment and the need for modernization. Around it, however, helped by Government incentives, industry is slowly developing, northwards to Caserta, southwards to Salerno and eastwards to Benevento.

Puglia.—Bari has always been a commercial centre and now industrial development is also taking place in the areas of Taranto, Brindisi and Foggia. At Taranto there are a highly-mechanized steel-works and a modern oil refinery. The Bari industrial zone has factories producing electronic and pneumatic valves, specialized vehicle bodies and tyres, etc. The main industry of Brindisi is a petro-chemical plant. At Foggia there is a textile factory.

Sicily.—The main source of income is agriculture, particularly citrus fruits, almonds and tomatoes, but this faces severe competition. Oil in small quantities has been found off the southern shore of the island and drilling continues, while onshore there are growing oil-refining, natural gas and petrochemical industries. Small and medium sized industries, benefiting from the Government's incentives, are developing, and tourism is bringing an increasing amount of revenue to the island.

Sardinia.—Sardinia is an autonomous region, with its capital at Cagliari. Six main industrial development areas have been officially designated. The major industries are aluminium production (there is a smelting plant at Porto Vesme), petrochemicals, lead and zinc mining; and the tourist industry is flourishing.

THE ECONOMY

Italian gross domestic product in 1986 was L894,362,000 million. The economy has recovered from the setbacks of the early seventies, reversing the balance of payments and halving inflation, but this was accompanied by stagnation and increasing unemployment. The rate of inflation for 1985–86 was 5·9 per cent.

Currency.—The unit of currency is the *lira*. (*see* also p. 81).

Industry.—The general index of industrial production (1980 = 100) stood at +2·7 per cent in 1985–86. The State-owned sector of Italian industry is important, dominated by the holding companies IRI (mechanical, steel, airlines), ENI (petro-chemicals) and ENEL (electricity).

Mineral Production.—Italy is generally poor in mineral resources but since the war deposits of natural methane gas and small deposits of oil have been discovered and rapidly exploited. Production of lignite has also increased. Other minerals produced in significant quantities include iron ores and pyrites, mercury (over one-quarter of the world production), lead, zinc and aluminium. Marble is a traditional product of the Massa Carrara district.

Agriculture.—Agriculture accounted for 5·2 per cent. of gross domestic product in 1984. The agricultural labour force was 2,242,000 in 1986.

Tourist Traffic.—In 1986 an estimated 18 million foreign tourists visited Italy, and in 1986 foreigners spent an estimated L14,691,000 million. The net balance on tourism was about L10,579,000 million.

Communications.—The main railway system is State-run by the *Ferrovia dello Stato.* A network of motorways (*autostrade*) covers the country, built and operated mainly by the IRI State-holding company and ANAS the State highway authority. The autostrada network covered 5,176 kms. in 1974. *Alitalia*, the principal international and domestic airline, is also State-controlled by the IRI group. Other smaller companies, including ATI (an *Alitalia* subsidiary) and Air Mediterranea operate on domestic routes. The Italian mercantile marine totalled 7,587,117 tons in December, 1985.

FOREIGN TRADE

The balance of trade in 1986 showed a deficit of 26,745 billion lire, 3,722 billion lire above the 1985 total.

The main markets for Italian exports in 1986 were the E.C. countries, which accounted for almost half of the total, and the U.S.A. Imports came principally from West Germany, France, U.S.A., the Netherlands, the U.S.S.R. and the U.K. The E.C. provided about 55 per cent. of imports.

Trade with U.K.

	1985	1986
Imports from U.K. .	£3,466,495,000	£3,472,364,000
Exports to U.K. ...	4,293,941,000	4,658,036,000

Language and Literature.—Italian is a Romance language derived from Latin. It is spoken in its purest form in Tuscany, but there are numerous dialects, showing various ly French, German, Spanish and Arabic influences. Sard, the dialect of Sardinia, is accorded by some authorities the status of a distinct Romance language. Italian literature (in addition to Latin literature, which is the common inheritance of Western Europe) is one of the richest in Europe, particularly in its golden age (Dante, 1265–1321; Petrarch, 1304–1374; Boccaccio, 1313–1375) and in the renaissance (Ariosto, 1474–1533; Machiavelli, 1469–1527; Tasso, 1544–1595). Modern Italian literature has many noted names in prose and verse, notably Manzoni (1785–1873), Carducci (1835–1907) and Gabriele d'Annunzio (1864–1938). The Nobel

Prize for Literature has been awarded to Italian authors on four occasions—G. Carducci (1906), Signora G. Deledda (1926), Luigi Pirandello (1934) and Salvatore Quasimodo (1959). In 1985, there were 48 daily newspapers published in Italy, of which 6 were published in Rome and 7 in Milan.

Education.—Education is free and compulsory between the ages of 6 and 14; this comprises five years at primary school and three in the "middle school", of which there are about 8,000. Pupils who obtain the middle school certificate may seek admission to any "senior secondary school", which may be a lyceum with a classical or scientific or artistic bias, or an institute directed at technology (of which there are eight different types), trade or industry (including vocational schools), or teacher-training. Courses at the lyceums and technical institutes usually last for five years and success in the final examination qualifies for admission to university. There are 35 State and 14 private universities, some of ancient foundation; those at Bologna, Modena, Parma and Padua were started in the 12th century. University education is not free, but entrants with higher qualifications are charged reduced fees according to a sliding scale. In general, schools, lyceums and universities are financed by local taxation and central government grants.

CAPITAL.—Rome. Population of the commune (1986) 2,821,420.

1986 estimates of the population of the communes of the principal cities and towns are Milan, 1,511,193; ΨNaples, 1,204,959; Turin, 1,034,007; ΨGenoa, 733,990; Bologna, 436,570; Florence, 429,865; Sicily, Palermo, 719,960; *Sardinia*, ΨCagliari, 223,021.

ISLANDS.—*Pantelleria Island* (part of Trapani Province) in the Sicilian Narrows, has an area of 31 sq. miles and a population of 9,601. The *Pelagian Islands* (Lampedusa, Linosa and Lampione) are part of the Province of Agrigento and have an area of 8 sq. miles, pop. 4,811. The Tuscan Archipelago (including Elba), area 293 sq. km., pop. 31,861; Pontine Archipelago (including Ponza, area 10 sq. km., pop. 2,515); Flegrean Islands (including Ischia, area 60 sq. km., pop. 51,883); Capri; Eolian Islands (including Lipari, area 116 sq. km., pop. 18,636); Tremiti Islands (area 3 sq. km., pop. 426).

FLAG.—Vertical stripes of green, white and red.
NATIONAL DAY.—June 2.

British Embassy
Via XX Settembre 80a, 00187 Rome

Ambassador Extraordinary and Plenipotentiary, His Excellency Sir Derek Morison David Thomas, K.C.M.G. (1987).
Minister, G. E. Fitzherbert, C.M.G..
Minister, R. F. R. Deare (*FAO*).
Defence and Military Attaché, Brig. M. J. Hague.
Naval Attaché, Capt. R. F. Channon, R.N.
Air Attaché, Group-Capt. R. J. M. David, R.A.F.
Counsellors, M. J. Williams, C.V.O., O.B.E. (*Head of Chancery*); G. Tantum, O.B.E.; M. Perceval (*Commercial*).
First Secretaries, A. McGuffog (*Labour*); J. Easton, O.B.E. (*Administration*); Miss C. M. T. Elmes (*Economic*); R. Godfrey (*Consul*); M. Adams (*Commercial*); D. B. A. Evans (*Agriculture*); Miss K. Coombs (*Information*); S. M. J. Lamport; R. J. Northern, M.B.E.; A. C. Tutton; N. Martin.
Chaplain, Rev. B. Wardrobe.
There are British Consular Offices at *Milan, Rome, Naples, Genoa, Florence, Venice, Trieste* and *Cagliari* and a trade representative at *Turin.*

British Council Representative, D. T. Ricks, O.B.E., Palazzo del Drago, Via Quattro Fontane 20, 00184, Rome.

There are *British Council Offices* at Milan and Naples, each with a library.

BRITISH CHAMBER OF COMMERCE, Via San Paolo 7, 20121 Milan.

JAPAN
(Nihon Koku—Land of the Rising Sun)

Emperor of Japan, His Majesty Hirohito, *born* April 29, 1901; *succeeded* Dec. 25, 1926; *married* (1924) Princess Nagako (*born* March 6, 1903), daughter of the late Prince Kuniyoshi Kuni, and has issue two sons and four daughters.
Heir-Apparent, His Imperial Highness Prince Akihito, *Crown Prince*, *born* Dec. 23, 1933; *married* April 10, 1959, Miss Michiko Shoda and has issue Prince Naruhito Hironomiya, *born* Feb. 23, 1960, Prince Fumihito, *born* Nov. 30, 1965 and Princess Sayako, *born* April 18, 1969.

THE CABINET

Prime Minister, Yasuhiro Nakasone.
Justice, Kaname Endo.
Foreign Affairs, Tadashi Kuranari.
Finance, Kiichi Miyazawa.
Education, Masajuro Shiokawa.
Health and Welfare, Juro Saito.
Agriculture, Forestry and Fisheries, Mutsuki Kato.
International Trade and Industry, Hajime Tamura.
Transport, Ryutaro Hashimoto.
Posts and Telecommunications, Shunjiro Karasawa.
Labour, Takushi Hirai.
Construction, Kosei Amano.
Home Affairs, Nobuyuki Hanashi.
Management and Co-ordination, Tokuo Yamashita.
Hokkaido Development Agency and National Land Agency, Tamisuke Watanuki.
Defence, Yuko Kurihara.
Economic Planning, Tetsuo Kondo.
Science and Technology, Yataro Mitsubayashi.
Environment, Toshiyuki Inamura.
Okinawa Development Agency, Tamisuke Watanuki.
Chief Cabinet Secretary, Masaharu Gotoda.

JAPANESE EMBASSY AND CONSULATE
46 Grosvenor Street, W1X 0BA
Information Centre: 9 Grosvenor Square, W1X 9LB
[01–493 6030]

Ambassador Extraordinary and Plenipotentiary, His Excellency Toshio Yamazaki (1985).
Ministers, Katsuhisa Uchida; Yuichi Ezawa (*Financial*); Mikio Shibata (*Commercial*).
Counsellors, Y. Kawashima (*Head of Chancery*); S. Tanaka (*Information*); T. Nakamoto (*Political*); T. Ito (*Economic*); K. Fukushima (*Agriculture*); Y. Masuhara (*Financial*); S. Shutoh (*Political*).
Defence Attaché, Capt. Isamu Kyoda.

Area and Population.—Japan consists of 4 large and many small islands situated in the North Pacific Ocean between longitude 128° 6′ East and 145° 49′ East and between latitude 26° 59′ and 45° 31′ N., with a total area of 145,834 sq. miles (377,708 sq. km.), and a population (1986) of 121,740,000. In 1985 the birth rate was 11·9 per 1,000, and the death rate 6·3 per 1,000.

Japan Proper consists of *Honshū* (or Mainland), 230,448 sq. km. (88,839 sq. m.), *Shikoku*, 18,757 sq. km. (7,231 sq. m.), *Kyūshū*, 42,079 sq. km. (16,170 sq. m.), *Hokkaido*, 78,508 sq. km. (30,265 sq. m.).

Physiography.—The coastline exceeds 17,000 miles and is deeply indented, so that few places are far from the sea. The interior is very mountainous, and crossing the mainland from the Sea of Japan to the Pacific is a group of volcanoes, mainly extinct or dormant. Mount Fuji, the loftiest and most sacred

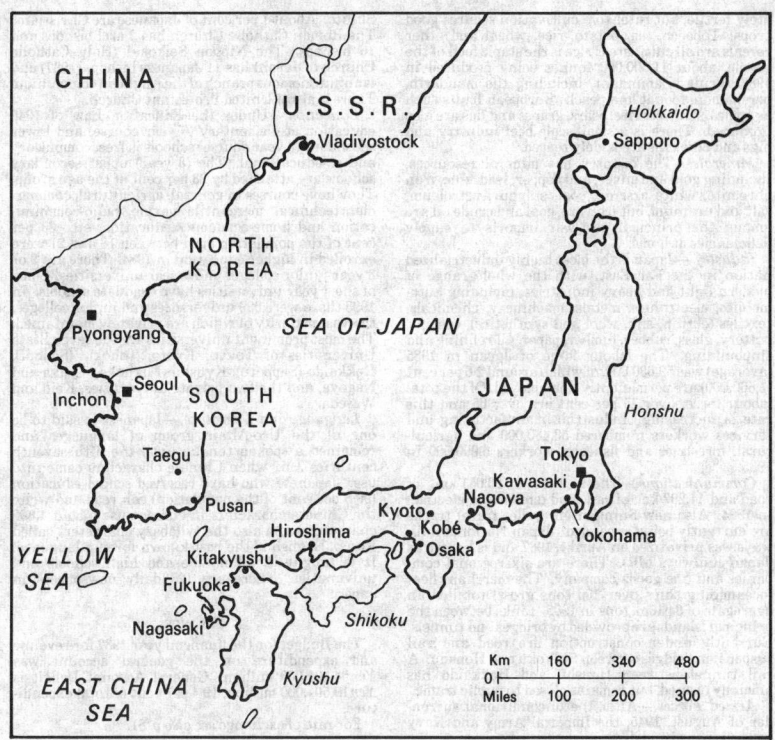

mountain of Japan, about 60 miles from Tokyo, is 12,370 ft. high and has been dormant since 1707, but there are other volcanoes which are active, including Mount Aso in Kyūshū. There are frequent earthquakes, mainly along the Pacific coast near the Bay of Tokyo. Japan proper extends from sub-tropical in the south to cool temperate in the north. Heavy snowfalls are frequent on the western slopes of Hokkaidō and Honshū, but the Pacific coasts are warmed by the Japan current. There is a plentiful rainfall and the rivers are short and swift-flowing offering abundant opportunities for the supply of hydro-electric power.

Government.—According to Japanese tradition, Jimmu, the First Emperor of Japan, ascended the throne on Feb. 11, 660 B.C. Under the *Meiji* constitution of Feb. 11, 1889, the monarchy was hereditary in the male heirs of the Imperial house.

After the unconditional surrender to the Allied Nations (Aug. 14, 1945), Japan was occupied by Allied forces under General MacArthur (Sept. 15, 1945). A Japanese peace treaty conference opened at San Francisco on Sept. 4, 1951, and on Sept. 8, 48 nations signed the treaty, which became effective on April 28, 1952. Japan then resumed her status as an independent power.

A new constitution came into force on May 3, 1947. Legislative authority rests with *The Diet*, which is bicameral, consisting of a *House of Representatives* and a *House of Councillors*, both Houses being composed of elected members. Executive authority is vested in the Cabinet which is responsible to the Legislature.

The conservatives have governed Japan almost without interruption since World War II. Since 1955, when it was formed, the Liberal Democratic Party has maintained an absolute majority in the House of Representatives. In June 1987 the strength of the Parties was: Liberal Democratic Party, 303; Japan Socialist Party, 87; Komeito, 57; Democratic Socialist, 29; Japan Communist Party, 27; Independents, 5. (Four vacant seats).

The House of Councillors whose powers are subordinate to the House of Representatives, re-elects half of its members every three years. In June, 1987, the strength of the Parties was: Liberal Democratic Party, 142; Japan Socialist Party, 42; Komeito, 24; Japan Communist Party, 16; Democratic Socialist Party, 12; Shimsei Club, 4; Niim Club, 4; Salaryman Party, 3; Independents, 4. (Two vacant seats).

Agriculture and Livestock.—Owing to the mountainous nature of the country not more than one-sixth of its area is available for cultivation. The forest land includes Cryptomeria japonica, Pinus massoniana, Zeikowaskeaki, and Paulownia imperialis, in addition to camphor trees, mulberry, vegetable wax tree and a lacquer tree which furnishes the celebrated lacquer of Japan. The soil is only moderately fertile, but intensive cultivation secures good crops. Tobacco, tea, potato, rice, wheat and other cereals are all cultivated: rice is the staple food of the people, about 11,500,000 tonnes being produced in 1986. Fruit is abundant, including the mandarin, persimmon, loquat and peach; European fruits such as apples, strawberries, pears, grapes and figs are also produced. There is a small-scale beef industry and pigs and chickens are widely reared.

Minerals.—The country has mineral resources, including gold and silver, and copper, lead, zinc, iron chromite, white arsenic, coal, sulphur, petroleum, salt and uranium, but iron ore, coal and crude oil are among the principal post-war imports to supply deficiencies at home.

Industry.—Japan is the most highly industrialized nation in the Far East, with the whole range of modern light and heavy industries, including auto-mobiles, electronics, metals, machinery, chemicals, textiles (cotton, silk, wool and synthetics), cement, pottery, glass, rubber, lumber, paper, oil refining and shipbuilding. The labour force of Japan in 1985 (average) was 59,630,000, of which around 2·6 per cent (1,560,000) are permanently unemployed. Of the total labour force, over 15 per cent are over 65 and this rate is increasing. Industrial, manufacturing and services workers numbered 53,430,000 and agricul-tural, forestries and fisheries workers 5,090,000 in 1985.

Communications.—There were 1,120,051 km. of road and 44,297 km. of rail road (steam and electric) in 1984. Also new Shinkansen (bullet train) tracks are currently being expanded. Japan National Rail-ways was privatized on April 1, 1987 and is known as Japan Railways (JR). There are six regional com-panies and one goods company. The merchant fleet (oceangoing ships over 100 tons gross) totalled an aggregate of 64·16m. tons in 1985. Links between the principal islands are provided by bridges and tunnels. Currently under construction are road and rail suspension bridges between Shikoku and Honshu. A rail tunnel between Honshū and Hokkaido has officially opened, but remains closed to public traffic.

Armed Forces.—After the unconditional surren-der of August, 1945, the Imperial Army and Navy were disarmed and disbanded.

Although the Constitution of Japan prohibits the maintenance of armed forces, internal security forces came into being in 1950, and 1952. In July, 1954, the mission of the forces was extended to include the defence of Japan against direct and indirect aggres-sion.

The defence budget allocated for the fiscal year 1986–87 amounted to *Yen* 3,343,549 million, equiva-lent to 6·18 per cent of the General Account budget. The authorized uniformed strength was: Ground Self-Defence Force (GSDF) 180,000 (Reserve 43,000); Maritime Self-Defence Force (MSDF) 43,897 (Reserve 600); Air Self-Defence Force (ASDF) 46,204. Actual strengths of all three services are slightly below their authorised figure.

The GSDF is organized into five regional Armies, totalling thirteen Divisions, one of which is an Armoured Division. Major equipment includes tanks, APC's, towed and SP guns and rocket launch-ers, Hawk AA missiles, and 425 aircraft. Equipment is now largely manufactured in Japan.

The MSDF has 164 warships and auxiliaries including four DDH, four TARTAR-equipped GMDs, 42 destroyers, 14 submarines and 99 others, 205 fixed-wing aircraft and 97 helicopters.

The ASDF has 820 aircraft including 375 trainers; 43 transports and 75 support aircraft including helicopters). There are 6 groups of Nike SAM missiles and one training unit of Patriot.

Religion.—All religions are tolerated. The princi-pal religions of Japan are Mahayana Buddhism and Shinto. About 1 per cent of Japanese are Christians. The Roman Catholic Church has 2 archbishops and 16 bishops. The Nippon Seikokai (Holy Catholic Church of Japan) has 11 Japanese bishops (1987) and is an autonomous branch of the Anglican communion. There is also a United Protestant Church.

Education.—Under the Education Law of 1948 education at elementary (6 year course) and lower secondary (3 year course) schools is free, compulsory and co-educational. The (3 year) upper secondary schools are attended by 93 per cent of the age group. They have courses in general, agricultural, commer-cial, technical, mercantile marine, radio-communi-cation and home-economics education, etc. 33 per cent of the population aged between 18 and 21 were enrolled in higher education in 1984. There are 2 or 3 year junior colleges and 4 year universities. Some of the 4 year universities have graduate schools. In 1983 there were 989 universities and junior colleges, the vast majority of which are privately maintained. The most prominent universities are the seven State Universities of Tokyo, Kyoto, Tohoku (Sendai), Hokkaido (Sapporo), Kyushu (Fukuoka), Osaka and Nagoya, and the two private universities, Keio and Waseda.

Language and Literature.—Japanese is said to be one of the Uro-Altaic group of languages and remained a spoken tongue until the fifth–seventh centuries A.D., when Chinese characters came into use. Japanese who have received school education (99·8 per cent of the population) can read and write the Chinese characters in current use (about 1,800 characters) and also the syllabary characters called Kana. English is the best known foreign language. It is taught in all middle and high schools and universities. There are 125 daily newspapers in Japan.

FINANCE

The Budget for the financial year 1987 for revenue and expenditure on the general account was Yen54,101,000 million. General Account Deficit is Yen10,501,000 million, 19·4 per cent of total expendi-ture.

For rate of exchange *see also* p. 81.

PRODUCTION AND TRADE

Being deficient in natural resources, Japan has had to develop a complex foreign trade. Principal imports in 1984 consisted of mineral oils (44·4 per cent), raw materials (14·3 per cent) e.g. metal ores and scrap, 4·8 per cent, timber, 2·9 per cent, foodstuffs (11·7 per cent) (e.g. wheat and sugar), machinery (8·8 per cent), chemicals (6·1 per cent) and textiles (2·8 per cent).

Principal exports consist of steel (8·1 per cent), ships (4·3 per cent), automobiles (17·5 per cent), electric machinery and appliances (17·2 per cent), non-electric machinery (16·4 per cent), chemicals (4·5 per cent) and textile goods (4·0 per cent).

FOREIGN TRADE

	1985	1986
	($1,000)	($1,000)
Total imports	129,538,747	126,407,786
Total exports	175,637,772	209,151,151

Trade with U.K.

	1985	1986
Imports from U.K..	£1,012,436,000	£1,193,933,000
Exports to U.K. ...	4,117,024,000	4,932,497,000

CAPITAL.—TOKYO. Population, 11,806,729. The other chief cities had the following populations: ΨOsaka (2,629,135); ΨNagoya (2,103,460); ΨYoko-hama (2,925,877); Kyoto, the ancient capital (1,486,873); ΨKobé (1,401,928); Kita-Kyushu

(1,060,470); ΨSapporo (1,515,582); ΨKawasaki (1,076,673); ΨFukuoka (1,144,802).

FLAG.—White, charged with sun (red).
NATIONAL DAY.—April 29.

BRITISH EMBASSY
No. 1 Ichiban-cho, Chiyoda-ku, Tokyo 102

Ambassador Extraordinary and Plenipotentiary, His Excellency Sir John Stainton Whitehead, K.C.M.G., C.V.O. (1986).

Minister, B. Hitch, C.M.G., C.V.O.

Counsellors, S. J. Gomersall (*Economic*); M. R. J. Guest (*Commercial*); D. G. Raikes (*Financial*); J. A. Barnett, C.B.E., (*Cultural*); A. N. R. Millington (*Head of Chancery*); Dr. C. C. Bradley (*Science and Technology*); A. A. Huggard (*Atomic Energy*); J. R. H. Walker.

First Secretaries, S. D. M. Jack; R. R. Hoggard; D. J. Fitton; D. F. Middleton (*Economic*); D. L. Brown (*Administration*); J. Ivins, N. K. Hook (*Commercial*); K. J. Pocknell (*Science and Technology*); C. E. A. Ripley (*Consul*); C. E. J. Wilton; S. E. Bradley; J. B. Roberts.

Defence and Military Attaché, Col. N. G Gray.
Naval Attaché, Capt. R. H. S. Thompson, R.N.
Air Attaché, Gp. Capt. D. I. Oakden, R.A.F.
There is a British Consulate-General at *Osaka* and an Honorary Consulate at *Fukuoka.*

British Council Representative, J. A. Barnett, C.B.E., 2 Kagurazaka, 1-Chome, Shinjuku-ku, Tokyo 162. There is also an office and library in Kyoto.

BRITISH CHAMBER OF COMMERCE
World Import Mart Branch 7th Floor, 1–3 Higashi-Ikebukuro 3-Chome, Toshima-ku, Tokyo 170; (*Postal Address,* P.O. Box 2145, World Import Mart Branch, Toshima-ku, Tokyo 170).

JORDAN
(Al-Mamlaka al Urduniya al-Hashemiyah)

King of the Jordan, Hussein, G.C.V.O., *born* November 14, 1935, *succeeded* on the deposition of his father, King Talal, Aug. 11, 1952, *assumed constitutional powers,* May 2, 1953, on coming of age.

Crown Prince, Prince Hassan, third son of King Talal of Jordan, *born* 1948, *appointed Crown Prince,* April 1, 1965.

CABINET

Prime Minister and Minister for Defence, Zaid Rifa'i.
Deputy P.M. and Minister of Prime Ministry Affairs, Abdul Wahab Majali.
Education, Thugan Hindawi.
Foreign Affairs, Taher Masri.
Communications, Muhieddin Al-Husseini.
Supply, Trade and Industry, Dr. Raja'i Mu'asher.
Higher Education, Dr. Nasreddin Al-Asad.
Information, Culture, Tourism and Antiquities, Mohammed Khatib.
Finance, Dr. Hanna Odeh.
Municipal and Rural Affairs and the Environment, Yousef Hamdan.
Awqaf and Islamic Affairs, Sheikh Aboul Aziz Al-Khayyat.
Agriculture, Marwan al-Hammoud.
Labour and Social Development, Khaled Al Haj Hassan.
Occupied Territory Affairs, Marwan Dudin.
Health, Dr. Zaid Hamzi.
Public Works, Mahmoud Hawamdeh.
Transport, Ahmed Dakhqan.
Planning, Dr. Taher Kanlan.
Energy and Natural Resources, Dr. Hisham Khatib.
Youth, Dr. Eid Dahiyet.

Minister of State, Parliamentary Affairs, Dr. Sami Joudeh.
Interior, Raja'i Dajani.
Justice, Riyadh Shaka'a.

JORDANIAN EMBASSY
6 Upper Phillimore Gardens, W8 7HB
[01-937 3685]

Ambassador Extraordinary and Plenipotentiary, His Excellency Dr. Albert Butrous.

Counsellor, Dr. Issa Dabbah.
Defence Attaché, Brig. Shafic Yacoub Ajeilat.
Service Office: 16 Upper Phillimore Gardens, W.8. (01–937–9611).

Area and Population.—The Hashemite Kingdom of the Jordan, which covers 37,738 sq. miles (97,740 sq. km.), is bounded on the north by Syria, on the west by Israel, on the south by Saudi Arabia and on the east by Iraq. Since the hostilities of June, 1967, that part of the country lying to the west of the Jordan River has been under Israeli occupation. The majority of the population are Sunni Moslems and Islam is the religion of the State, freedom of belief is, however, guaranteed by the Constitution. Total population on the East Bank of the Jordan was estimated (1985) to be 3,515,000.

History.—After the defeat of Turkey in the First World War the Amirate of Transjordan was established in the area east of the River Jordan as a state under British mandate. The mandate was terminated after the Second World War and the Amirate, still ruled by its founder, the Amir Abdullah, became the Hashemite Kingdom of Jordan. Following the 1948 war between Israel and the Arab States, that part of Palestine remaining in Arab hands (but excluding Gaza) was incorporated into the Hashemite Kingdom. King Abdullah was assassinated in 1951; his son Talal ruled briefly but abdicated in favour of the present King, Hussein, in 1952. All of Jordan west of the River has been under Israeli occupation since 1967. As a result of the wars of 1948 and 1967 there are about 991,000 refugees and displaced persons living in East Jordan, about 200,000 of whom live in refugee and displaced persons camps established by the U.N. Relief and Works Agency (UNRWA). In addition there are some 300,000 entirely self-supporting Palestinian members of the East Jordanian community.

Government.—The present constitution of the Kingdom came into force in 1952. It provides for a senate of 30 members (all appointed by the King) and an elected House of Representatives of 60 persons. (New legislation has been passed to more than double the size of both houses at the next general election). Half of the constituencies of the latter are on the West Bank and since the Israeli occupation of this area in 1967 it has not been possible to hold elections there. For a time membership of the House continued on the basis of pre-1967 membership but was eventually suspended in 1974. The Lower House was recalled in January 1984. By-elections were held in March 1984 to fill East Bank seats which had become vacant as a result of the death of deputies elected in 1967, and the House appointed new West Bank members to bring itself up to full strength. The King himself appoints the members of the Council of Ministers. Crown Prince Hassan normally acts as Regent when King Hussein is away from Jordan. Following the Arab summit meeting at Rabat in October 1974, and the U.N. General Assembly in November, at which the Palestinian Liberation Organization achieved recognition as the sole legitimate representative of the Palestinian people, King Hussein took measures to amend the 1952 constitution to take account of the resultant change in the status of the West Bank in relation to the administration of Jordan east of the river.

Production and Industry.—West Jordan is fertile, though many areas have suffered from soil erosion. In East Jordan the main agricultural areas are the east part of the Jordan Valley, the hills overlooking the Valley and the flatter country to the south of Amman and around Madaba and Irbid. The rest of the country is desert and semi-desert. The principal crops are wheat, barley, vegetables, olives and fruit (mainly grapes and citrus fruits). Agricultural production in the Jordan Valley has increased considerably in recent years due to the extension of the East Ghor Canal and the King Talal Dam. The only important industrial products are raw phosphates (production 1986: 6,249,200 tons) and potash, most of which is exported. There are schemes under construction for the production of potash and phosphate fertilizers. The Trans-Arabian oil pipeline (Tapline) runs through North Jordan on its way from the eastern province of Saudi Arabia to the Lebanese coast of Sidon. A branch pipeline feeds a refinery at Zerqa (production 1986: 2,257,000 tons) which meets most of Jordan's requirements for refined petroleum products.

Tourism has recovered fast since the Israeli occupation of the West Bank in 1967. International-class hotels have been built to cater for businessmen, and for tourists visiting the archaeological sites of East Jordan and the resort of Aqaba.

Communications.—The trunk road system is good. Amman is linked to Damascus, Baghdad and Jeddah by tarred roads which are of considerable importance in the overland trade of the Middle East. The former Hejaz Railway enters Jordan east of Ramtha and runs through Zerqa and Amman to Ma'an with a spur to the top of the Ras al-Naqb escarpment. The formerly abandoned section from Ma'an to Medina in Saudi Arabia is being studied and redesigned by consultants. A total of 2,677 vessels called at Aqaba in 1986 and 16,849,700 tons of cargo were handled. Much of Jordan's trade moves overland to and from the ports in Syria and Lebanon. The Royal Jordanian Airline operates from Amman Airport to other cities in the Middle East and Gulf area, to most major European cities, to New York, and to Bangkok in the Far East. There is also a service to the airport at Aqaba.

FINANCE

	1985	1986
	JD (Thousands)	
Revenue	860,629	937,100
Expenditure	812,848	1,002,600
Surplus/Deficit...........	+47,780	−65,500

Trade with U.K.

	1985	1986
Imports from U.K.	£154,270,000	£130,385,000
Exports to U.K.	86,077,000	49,766,000

CAPITAL.—Amman. Population, 777,500 (1984 estimate).

FLAG.—Black, white and green horizontal stripes, surcharged with white seven-point star on red triangle.

NATIONAL DAY.—May 25 (Independence Day).

BRITISH EMBASSY
Third Circle, Jebel Amman (P.O. Box 87), Amman

Ambassador Extraordinary and Plenipotentiary, His Excellency Arthur John Coles, C.M.G. (1984).

Counsellors, H. N. H. Synnott (*Head of Chancery and Consul-General*); P. J. F. Mansley.

Defence Attaché, Col. D. C. Whitten.

Air Attaché, Wing-Cdr. P. W. Mayes.

First Secretaries, D. J. Hawkes, M.B.E. (*Commercial*); D. H. Whitbread (*Information*); R. Kay M.B.E. (*Consul and Administration*).

Second Secretaries, L. B. Evans (*Development*); Miss S. C. Rowland Jones; N. S. Archer; P. J. Sullivan (*Works*); A. Reynolds (*Works*); W. Hamilton (*Commercial*).

British Council Representative, D. A. M. Latta, Amman Centre, Rainbow Street, (P.O. Box 634), Jebel Amman, Amman.

KOREA

Korea is situated between 124° 11″ and 130° 57′ E. long., and between 33° 7′ and 43° 1″ N. lat. It has an area of 84,565 sq. miles (219,022 sq. km.), with an estimated population of approx. 62 million, of whom about 42 million live south of the present dividing line. The southern and western coasts are fringed with innumerable islands, of which the largest, forming a province of its own, is Cheju.

History.—The last native dynasty (Yi) ruled from 1392 until 1910, in which year Japan formally annexed Korea. The country remained an integral part of the Japanese Empire until the defeat of Japan in 1945, when it was occupied by troops of the U.S.A. and the U.S.S.R., the 38th parallel being fixed as the boundary between the two zones of occupation. The U.S. Government endeavoured to reach agreement with the Soviet Government for the creation of a Korean Government for the whole country and the withdrawal of all Russian and American troops. These efforts met with no success, and in September, 1947, the U.S. Government laid the whole question of the future of Korea before the General Assembly of the United Nations. The Assembly in November, 1947, resolved that elections should be held in Korea for a National Assembly under the supervision of a temporary Commission formed for that purpose by the United Nations and that the National Assembly when elected should set up a Government. The Soviet Government refused to allow the Commission to visit the Russian Occupied Zone and in consequence it was only able to discharge its function in that part of Korea which lies to the south of the 38th parallel.

A general election was held on May 10, 1948, and the first National Assembly met in Seoul on May 31. The Assembly passed a constitution on July 12, and on July 20 elected Dr. Syngman Rhee as the first President of the Republic of Korea. On August 15, 1948, the Republic was formerly inaugurated and American Military Government came to an end.

Meanwhile in the Russian-occupied zone north of the 38th parallel the Democratic People's Republic had been set up with its capital at Pyongyang; a Supreme People's Soviet was elected in September 1948, and a Soviet-style Constitution adopted.

The Korean War.—The country remained effectively divided into two along the line of 38th parallel until the aggression of June 25, 1950, when the North Korean forces invaded South Korea. An emergency meeting of the U.N. Security Council adopted a Resolution calling for an immediate cease fire and the withdrawal of North Korean forces. This was ignored and the communist advance continued. In response to Security Council recommendations that United Nations members should furnish assistance to repel the attack, 16 nations including the U.S.A. and the U.K. came to the aid of the Republic of Korea. However the communist advance could not be contained until eventually a front was established around Pusan. Later, following a successful U.S. marine landing at Inchon, the communist forces were driven beyond the 38th parallel. At this point the Chinese "volunteers" joined the campaign and although the U.N. forces were initially driven back beyond Seoul they regrouped and threw the communist forces back to approximately the old dividing line. The fighting was ended by an Armistice Agreement signed by the U.N. Commander-in-Chief and the Commander of the North Korean army and the Chinese People's "volunteers" on July 27, 1953. By this Agreement (which was not signed by the representatives of the Republic of Korea) the line of division between North and South Korea remained in the neighbourhood of the 38th parallel. The Geneva Conference discussed Korea in 1954, but failed to agree on measures for re-unifying the country. Talks between North and South Korea on the reunification of the country have taken place intermittently.

Language and Literature.—Despite the great cultural influence of the Chinese, Koreans have developed and preserved their own cultural heritage. The Korean language is of the Ural-Altaic Group. Its script, Hangul, was invented in the 15th century; prior to this Chinese characters alone were used. Also invented around this time was the first metal movable printing type. The first works translated into Hangul were Buddhist, Confucian and other classics and it was only in the late 19th century that the European influence first began to be felt.

Republic of Korea
(Han Kook)

President, Chun Doo Hwan (August, 1980).

CABINET

Prime Minister, Kim Chung Yul.
Home Affairs, Chung Kwan Yong.
Defence, Chung Ho Yong.
Education, Suh Myung Won.
Sports, Cho Sang Ho.
Communications, Oh Myung.
Government Administration, Chang Ki-oh.
Science, Park Kung Shik.
Political Affairs, Lee Chong Yul.
Foreign Affairs, Choi Kwang Soo.
Finance, Sakong Il.
Justice, Chung Hae Chang.
Agriculture, Forestry and Fisheries, Kim Joo Hu.
Trade and Industry, Rha Woong Bae.
Energy and Resources, Choi Chang Nak.
Construction, Lee Kyu Hyo.
Health and Social Affairs, Rhee Hai Won.
Labour, Lee Heun Ki.
Transportation, Cha Kyu Hun.
Culture and Information, Lee Woong Hee.
National Unification, Huh Moon Do.
Office of Legislation, Kim Chong Keon.
Patriots and Veteran's Agency, Kim Keun Soo.
Dir. of National Security Planning Agency, Ahn Moo Hyuk.

KOREAN EMBASSY
4 Palace Gate, W8 5NF
[01–581 0247]

Ambassador Extraordinary and Plenipotentiary, His Excellency Mr. Young Choo Kim (1984).
Minister, Ri Hoon Hur.

The Republic of Korea has been officially recognized by the Governments of the United States, France, Great Britain, and most other countries except the communist bloc.

President Syngman Rhee was overthrown by a popular rising in 1960. After a year of unstable government a new regime was set up on May 16, 1961 by an army officers' *coup* led by Major General Park Chung Hee. On March 22, 1962 he took over as acting President. He was elected President in December 1963 and again in 1967, 1971, 1972 and 1978, but was assassinated on October 26, 1979. The country was placed under partial martial law. The then Prime Minister Choi Kyu Hah was elected President that December but resigned in August 1980 to be succeeded by Gen. Chun Doo Hwan. The constitution was revised and new elections held. President Chun was re-elected and his Democratic Justice Party gained a majority in the National Assembly after elections in March 1981. It retained its majority in the Feb. 1985 elections but now faces stronger opposition.

Constitution.—The President, who is Head of State, Chief of the Executive and Commander-in-Chief of the Armed Forces, is indirectly elected for a single term of seven years by an electoral college of over 5,000 members, who are directly elected. He appoints the Prime Minister with the consent of the National Assembly, and members of the State Council on the recommendation of the Prime Minister. The President is also empowered to take wide-ranging measures in an emergency, including the declaration of martial law, but must obtain the agreement of the National Assembly. The National Assembly is directly elected for a four-year term, one third by proportional representation, two thirds from constituencies.

By Sept. 1987 a draft constitution had been agreed upon by both ruling and opposition groups to provide for direct elections for the presidency. The new constitution is to be the subject of a national referendum.

Armed Forces.—The Republic of Korea has an army of about 520,000, a small navy mostly for coastal patrol and protection duties, an air force with over 500 combat aircraft and a marine corps which is incorporated in the navy. About six per cent of the nation's G.N.P. is currently spent on defence.

Education and Religion.—Primary education is compulsory for six years from the age of seven. Secondary and higher education is extensive. The national illiteracy rate is among the lowest in Asia. There is freedom of religion. Buddhism has the most followers (13 million) followed by Protestantism (8 million) and Confucianism (4·7 million). Catholics number 2·2 million.

Agriculture and Fisheries.—The soil is fertile but the arable land is limited by the mountainous nature of the country. Staple agricultural products are rice, barley and other cereals, beans, tobacco and hemp. Fruit growing and sericulture are also practised. Ginseng, a medicinal root much used by both the Chinese and Koreans, forms a useful source of revenue. The Korean fishing industry is a major contributor to both food supply and exports.

Minerals.—The Republic of Korea is deficient in mineral resources, except for deposits of coal on the East Coast and tungsten. There are some prospects of discovering oil in the sea between Korea and Japan.

Finance.—The budget for 1986 totals about U.S.$15,500 million.

Trade and Industry.—Since the beginning of 1962 a series of successful five-year plans resulted in real economic growth averaging around 10 per cent a year. The 6th economic development plan (1987–91) envisages a growth rate of 7·5 per cent. Annual per capita G.N.P. is U.S.$2,094.

Since the 1960s the Republic of Korea has industrialised rapidly on the basis of greatly expanded exports. Important exports include cars, electrical and electronic equipment, footwear, ships, railway rolling stock and iron and steel products.

TRADE

	1984	1985
Imports	U.S.$30,796 m.	U.S.$31,132 m.
Exports	28,090 m.	30,273 m.

Currency.—The unit of currency is the *won.*

Trade with U.K.

	1985	1986
Imports from U.K......	£247,887,000	£288,421,000
Exports to U.K.	£480,448,000	661,975,000

Communications and Transport.—In 1980 there were 15,599 km. of paved road. Seoul has a subway system and there are national railway and airline systems. Korean Air Lines operates regular flights to Europe, the United States, the Middle East and South East Asia. Pusan and Inchon are the major ports with Pusan serving the industrial areas of the southeast. Inchon, 28 miles from Seoul, serves the capital, but development and operation at Inchon are hampered by a tidal variation of 9–10 metres.

CAPITAL.—Seoul, population (1980), 9,200,000. Other main centres are ΨPusan (pop. 3,160,000), Taegu (pop. 1,607,000) and ΨInchon (pop. 1,084,000).

FLAG.—White, with red over blue device in centre, three black parallel bars, some broken, in each quarter.

NATIONAL DAY.—August 15 (Independence Day).

BRITISH EMBASSY
No. 4, Chung-Dong, Chung-Ku, Seoul 100

Ambassador Extraordinary and Plenipotentiary, His Excellency Lawrence John Middleton, C.M.G. (1986).

Counsellor, R. M. Jackson, C.V.O. *(Commercial).*

Defence and Military Attaché, Brig. T. W. Hackworth, O.B.E.

First Secretaries, W. B. McCleary (*Head of Chancery and Consul*); A. V. Hill (*Commercial/ Information*).

Cultural Attaché and British Council Representative, D. G. Rogers, Room 401 Anglican Church Annex, 3/7 Chung Dong, Chung-ku, Seoul.

There is an Honorary British Consul at Pusan.

BRITISH CHAMBER OF COMMERCE, c/o Chartered Bank, 1st and 2nd Floors, Samsung Building, 50, 1-Ka Ulchi Ro, Chung-Ku, Seoul.

Democratic People's Republic of Korea
(Chosun Minchu-chui Inmin Kongwa-guk)

Politburo of the Central Committee, Kim Il-sung; Kim Chong-il; O Chin-u (*full members and members of the presidium*); Pak Song-chol; Yim Chun-chu; So Chol; Kim Yong-nam; Yon Hyong-muk; O Kuk-yol; Kang Song-san; So Yun-sok; Ho Tam; Yi Chong-ok; Yi Kun-mo; Hong Song-nam (*full members*). Choe Kwang; Cho Se-ung; Chong Chun-ki; Hyon Mu-kwang; Kye Ung-tae; Kang Huiwon; Chon Pyong-ho; Kim Pok-sin; Hong Si-hak; Yi Son-sil (*alternate members*).

Secretariat of the Central Committee, Kim Il-sung (*General Secretary*); Kim Chong-il; Yon Hyong-muk; Hwang Chang-yop; Ho Chong-suk; So Kwan-hui; Ho Tam; Kye Ung-tae; Kang Song-san; Chon Pyong-ho; Choe Tae-pok.

The area of North Korea is 46,540 sq. miles (120,538 sq. km.), with a population of about 20,385,000 (1985 U.N. estimate). North Korea is rich in minerals and industry has been developed, but the economy has stagnated in recent years because of poor planning and a shortage of foreign exchange. The armed forces are believed to number about 750,000 men.

Government.—The Constitution of the Democratic People's Republic of Korea provides for a Supreme People's Assembly, presently consisting of 615 deputies, which is elected every four years by universal suffrage. The Assembly elects a President, and the Central People's Committee. In turn, the Central People's Committee directs the Administrative Council which implements the policy formulated by the Committee. The Administrative Council (31 members), formally the government of N. Korea, includes the Prime Minister and various ministers. In practice, however, the country is ruled by the Communist Party which elects a Central Committee; this in turn appoints a Politburo. The Senior Ministers of the Administrative Council are all members of the Communist Central Committee and the majority are also members of the Politburo.

Trade with U.K.

	1985	1986
Imports from U.K........	£2,608,000	£3,331,000
Exports to U.K.	1,983,000	1,374,000

CAPITAL.—Pyongyang (population, approx. 1,500,000).

FLAG.—Broad red horizontal band bordered by white lines bearing a five-point red star on a white disc in centre; blue horizontal bands at top and bottom.

NATIONAL DAY.—September 8.

KUWAIT
(Dowlat al- Kuwait)

Amir, H. H. Shaikh Jaber Al Ahmad Al Sabah, *born* 1928; acceded Jan. 1, 1978.

CABINET

Prime Minister, H.H. Crown Prince, Sheikh Saad Al-Abdullah.

Deputy Premier and Minister of Foreign Affairs, Sheikh Sabah Al-Ahmed Al Jaber.

Education, Anwar Abdulla Al Nouri.

Social Affairs, and Labour, Sheikh Jaber Mubarak Al Hamad.

Finance, Jasem Mohammed Al Khorafi.

Awqaf and Islamic Affairs, Khalid Ahmed Al Jassar.

Communications, Khalid Salem Al Jumeian.

Minister of State for Cabinet, Rashed Abdul Aziz Al Rashed.

Defence, Sheikh Salem Sabah Al Salem.

Minister of State for Foreign Affairs, Saoud Mohammed Al Osaimi.

Justice and Legal Affairs, Dhari Abdulla Al Othman.

Public Works, Abdul Rahman Ibrahim Al Houti.

Minister of State for Municipality Affairs, Abdul Rahman Khalid Al Ghunaim.

Public Health, Abdul Rahman Abdulla Al Awadi.

Oil, Sheikh Ali Al-Khalifa Al-Athbi.

Minister of State for Services Affairs, Issa Mohammed Al Mazeidi.

Commerce and Industry, Faisal Abdul Razaq Al Khalid.

Planning, Mohammed Soleiman Sayed Ali.

Electricity and Water, Mohammed Abdul Mohsen Al Rifai.

Interior, Sheikh Nawaf Al Ahmed Al Jaber.

Minister of State for Housing Affairs, Naser Abdulla Al Rodhan.

Information, Sheikh Nasser Mohammed Al Ahmed.

KUWAIT EMBASSY IN LONDON
45–46 Queen's Gate, S.W.7.
[01–589 4533]

Ambassador Extraordinary and Plenipotentiary, His Excellency Ghazi M. A. Al-Rayes (1980).

Area and Population.—Kuwait extends along the shore of the Persian Gulf from Iraq to Saudi Arabia, with an area of 6,880 sq. miles (17,818 sq. km.). Kuwait has a dry, desert climate with a summer season extending from April to September. The mean temperature varies between 84° and 113° F. in summer, and 46° and 64° F. in winter. Humidity rarely exceeds 60 per cent except in July and August. The population is 1,695,128 (census 1985), of which about 42 per cent are Kuwaiti citizens, the remainder being large numbers of other Arab peoples, Iranians, Indians and Pakistanis. The total European and American population is about 12,500. The gross population growth rate is 6·4 per cent, a growth rate of 3·5 per cent for Kuwaiti citizens.

The official language is Arabic, and English is widely spoken as a second language. Islam is the official religion, though religious freedom is constitutionally guaranteed.

Government.—Although Kuwait had been independent for some years, the "exclusive agreement" of 1899 between the Shaikh of Kuwait and the British Government was formally abrogated by an exchange of letters dated June 19, 1961. This exchange was immediately followed by Iraqi claims to sovereignty over Kuwait, but on Oct. 4, 1963, Iraq recognized Kuwait's independence although the Kuwait-Iraqi border has not yet been determined formally. Under the Constitution legislative power is vested in the Amir and the 50-member National Assembly, and executive power in the Amir and the Cabinet. The sixth National Assembly was elected for a four year term in March 1985.

Education, etc.—As a result of the very considerable oil revenues, the Kuwait Government embarked on a large scale development scheme and plans for social services. Education and medical treatment are free. New hospitals and schools continue to be built. Kuwait University was opened in 1966, and in 1985 had 16,000 students. In 1983 there were over 433,000 pupils at government and private schools.

Public Utilities.—Kuwait has a domestic water supply from water distillation plants which operate on natural gas from the oil fields. These plants can produce over 118,000,000 gallons of fresh water daily. Total water storage capacity, in reservoirs and water towers, amounts to over 1,201 million gallons. A natural source of fresh water, discovered at Raudhatain in the north of the State, has been developed to produce up to 3,000,000 gallons per day for at least 20 years and a pipeline has been built to carry the water to Kuwait town.

Electricity is produced by four power stations in Kuwait. Production in 1985 was 18,694 million Kwh.

Communications.—Ships of British, Dutch, Kuwaiti and other lines make regular calls at Kuwait. Several international and Middle Eastern airlines operate regular air services, and other companies make non-scheduled flights to Kuwait under charter. There is a network of dual-carriageway roads and more are under construction. Telecommunications, and postal services are conducted by the Kuwait Government, which has built an earth satellite station.

Finance.— Revenue for the financial year 1983–84 was budgeted at *KD*3,038 million. Oil revenues constitute 91·8 per cent. of total revenue. Estimated total expenditure for the same year was *KD*3,376·3 million. There are a large number of investment banks in some of which the Government holds equity. The banking system is controlled by the Central Bank of Kuwait.

Production.—The G.N.P. of Kuwait in 1983 was estimated at *KD*7,593 million.

Despite the desert terrain, 8·4 per cent of land is under cultivation, fruit and vegetables being the main crops. Shrimp fishing is becoming important.

The Government of Kuwait began to participate in the ownership of the British- and American-owned Kuwait Oil Company in 1974 and an agreement was signed in November 1975 which brought 100 per cent government ownership. After a reorganisation of the national oil industry in 1980, all the business was taken over by the Kuwait Petroleum Corporation.

The centre of Kuwait oil production is at Burgan, south of Kuwait City. Oil is also lifted in the Kuwait/Saudi Arabia Partitioned Zone (Wafra) south of the State. Oil is exported through a specially constructed port at Mina al Ahmadi. Production of crude oil in 1984 was approximately 1,115 million barrels per day. About 3,000 people are employed, including Kuwaitis, British, Americans, Indians, Pakistanis and citizens of other Arab countries.

Trade.—Oil exports constitute about 88 per cent. of Kuwait's total exports. Non-oil exports include chemical fertilizers, ammonia and other chemicals, metal pipes, shrimps and building materials; re-exports accounted for 73 per cent. of non-oil exports in 1982. Major trading partners are Asian countries, followed by E.C. countries and Arab states.

	1982
Imports	*KD*2,098·0m
Exports	3,261·7m

Trade with U.K.

	1985	1986
Imports from U.K.	£347,915,000	£300,586,000
Exports to U.K.	156,912,000	58,517,000

CAPITAL.— Ψ Kuwait (population, excluding suburbs, 400,000).

FLAG.—Three horizontal stripes of green, white and red, with black trapezoid next to staff.

NATIONAL DAY.—February 25.

BRITISH EMBASSY
P.O. Box Safat 2,
Arabian Gulf Street, Kuwait

Ambassador Extraordinary and Plenipotentiary, His Excellency Peter Robert Mossom Hinchcliffe, C.V.O. (1987).

Counsellor, D. R. MacLennan.

First Secretaries, R. Bland, O.B.E.; A. Heath (*Financial and Economic, and Head of Chancery*); B. R. R. Rainbow (*Consul*); A. R. Michael (*Commercial*); J. Brand.

British Council Representative, D. Brown, P.O. Box 345, 2 al Arabi Street, Mansouriyah. There is a library in *Kuwait.*

LAOS
(Sathalamalid Pasathu' Paait)

President, Phoumi Vongvichit (*acting*).
President of the Supreme People's Assembly, Sisomphone Lovansay (*acting*).
Deputy President, Khamsouk Keola.

COUNCIL OF MINISTERS

Prime Minister, Kaysone Phomvihane.
First Deputy P.M., Nouhak Phoumsavan (*responsibility for economic matters*).
Deputy P.M.s, Phoun Sipaseut (*Minister, Foreign Affairs*); Khamtai Siphandone (*Minister of Defence*); Sali Vongkhamsao (*Chairman, State Planning Committee*).
Ministers attached to the P.M.'s Office, Ma Khaikhamphithoun. (*Special Affairs*); Souli Nanthavong

(*Chairman, State Commission for Science and Technology*); Thongchanh Ouplavan (*Prices*); Soth Phetrasi (*Mapping and Frontiers*).

Agriculture, Irrigation and Agricultural Co-operatives, Inkong Mahavong.

Construction, Khemphon Phouipaseut.

Culture, Thongsing Thammavong.

Education, Bountiam Phitsamai.

Finance, Yao Phonvantha.

Health, Khamlien Pholsena.

Industry, Handicrafts and Forestry, Maysouk Saysompheng.

Chairman, Information, Press, Radio and Television Committee, Interior, Sisavath Keobounphan.

Justice, Kou Souvannamethi.

Materials and Technology, Thongsouk Saisangkhi.

Chairman, National Bank, Bousbong Souvannavong.

Chairman, Nationalities Committee, Nhiaveu Lobliayao.

Chairman, Social Welfare and Veterans Committee, Meun Somvichit.

Trade, Vanthong Sengmuong.

Transport, Posts and Telecommunications, Phao Bounnaphon.

Position and Extent.—The People's Democratic Republic of Laos is in the northerly part of Indo-China, lying between China and Vietnam, on the north and east, and Burma and Thailand on the west. Laos has a common boundary with Cambodia to the south. The area of the country is 91,429 sq. miles (231,800 sq. km.), with a population (1985 U.N. estimate) of 4,117,000.

History.—The Kingdom of Lane Xang, the Land of a Million Elephants, was founded in the 14th century, but broke up at the beginning of the 15th century into the separate kingdoms of Luang Prabang and Vientiane and the Principality of Champassac, which together came under French protection in 1893. In 1945 the Japanese executed a coup and suppressed the French administration. Under a Constitution of 1947 Laos became a constitutional monarchy under King Sisvang Vong of the House of Luang Prabang, and an independent sovereign state in 1949. The next twenty-five years in Laos were marked by power struggles and civil war.

After the fall of Saigon in April 1975, internal resistance to the *Pathet Lao* (communists) crumbled; Communist troops occupied the whole country and, though still paying lip-service to the 1973 ceasefire agreement and maintaining a façade of coalition, the *Pathet Lao* took over the government and began to implement an authoritarian régime with policies of austerity and economic self-sufficiency. On December 2, 1975, following the abdication of the King, Laos was declared a People's Democratic Republic and the *Pathet Lao* assumed full charge of the country.

Economy.—There is no significant industrial base in Laos, an estimated 85 per cent. of the work force being engaged in agriculture, largely concerned with rice cultivation. Rice production in 1984 amounted to 1·3 million tonnes, thus rendering the country theoretically self-sufficient in this staple food. In 1983, however, the authorities stated that due to late rains there was an overall shortfall of about 100,000 tons.

In 1984, exports amounted to US$36·2 m. and imports to US$98·4 m. Hydro-electric power was 88·3 per cent. of exports, timber 8·5 per cent. and coffee 1·2 per cent. Clearing agreements have been signed with certain socialist countries and the trade gap is largely financed by foreign aid, of which some 60 per cent. is provided by socialist countries.

Laos' economic performance so far has been poor and shows no signs of early recovery, the free market rate for the dollar is much higher than the official rate and prices of consumer items continue to increase.

Currency.—In January 1980 a "new" *Kip* replaced the former currency. In July 1983 the non-commercial rate of exchange was rectified by the State Bank.

Trade with U.K.

	1985	1986
Imports from U.K.	£523,000	£1,460,000
Exports to U.K.	6,000	150,000

CAPITAL.—Vientiane, population (estimated 1984) 120,000.

FLAG.—Blue background with a central white circle, framed by 2 horizontal red stripes.

NATIONAL DAY.—December 2.

BRITISH AMBASSADOR, *resides at* Bangkok, Thailand.

LEBANON
(Al-Jumhouriya al-Lubnaniya)

President of the Republic of Lebanon, Amin Gemayel, *elected*, Sept. 21, 1982.

Prime Minister, Selim Hoss (*acting*).

LEBANESE EMBASSY IN LONDON
21 Kensington Palace Gardens, W8 4QM
[01–229 7265/8485]

Ambassador Extraordinary and Plenipotentiary, His Excellency Gen. Ahmed El-Hajj (1983).

First Secretary, Farid Abboud.

Second Secretaries, Michel El-Khoury; Mohammed Dib.

Consular Section, 15 Palace Gardens Mews, W.8 (01–727 6696)

Area and Population.—Lebanon forms a strip about 120 miles in length and varying in width from 30 to 35 miles, along the Mediterranean littoral, and extending from the Israel frontier on the south to the Nahr al Kebir (15 miles north of Tripoli) on the north; its eastern boundary runs down the Anti-Lebanon range and then down the Great Central depression, the *Beqaa*, from which flow the rivers Orontes and Litani. It is divided into 5 districts, North Lebanon, Mount Lebanon, Beirut, South Lebanon and Beqaa. The seaward slopes of the mountains have a Mediterranean climate and vegetation. The inland range of Anti-Lebanon has the characteristics of steppe country. There is a mixed Arabic-speaking population of Christians, Moslems and Druses. The total area of Lebanon is 4,015 sq. miles, (10,400 sq. km.), population (1985 U.N. estimate), 2,668,000.

Government.—Lebanon became an independent State on Sept. 1, 1920, administered under French Mandate until Nov. 22, 1943. Powers were transferred to the Lebanese Government from Jan. 1, 1944, and French troops were withdrawn in 1946.

In April 1975, serious fighting broke out in Beirut between members of the predominantly Christian Phalangist Party and mainly Moslem militias later supported by Palestinian guerrillas based in Lebanon. The fighting continued and increased throughout 1975 and 1976. In the autumn of 1976 the Arab Deterrent Forces composed mainly of Syrian troops, imposed an effective ceasefire. In March 1978, Israeli forces invaded but withdrew some months later, handing over their positions, except for a belt in the south, to the U.N. Interim Force in Lebanon (UNIFIL). Major bouts of fighting took place in October 1978 and April/May 1981, interspersed with regular clashes on a smaller scale. In the summer of 1982 Israeli forces again invaded the country, penetrating as far as Beirut. Following negotiations, Palestine Liberation Organisation guerrillas left Beirut for various Arab countries.

The north-east of the country is currently occupied by Syrian and Palestinian forces. Although the bulk of Israeli troops withdrew from southern Lebanon in 1985, a buffer zone controlled by Israeli-backed Christian militias has been established along the Israeli-Lebanon border.

Reconciliation talks in Geneva and Lausanne, Switzerland, in March 1984, failed to produce any lasting agreement. Attempts to impose a Syrian-brokered accord in December 1985 failed when the main Christian militia overthrew the leadership which had signed it.

Production.—Fruits are the most important products and include citrus fruit, apples, grapes, bananas and olives. There is some light industry, mostly for the production of consumer goods, but most factories have been adversely affected by the instability of the past 10 years. There is little remaining of the famous cedars of Lebanon.

Communications.—A railway runs from Beirut to Damascus, connecting at Rayak with a branch line which runs from Tripoli through Homs, Hama and Aleppo to the Turkish frontier, from Nusaybin to the Iraq frontier at Tel Kotchek. A railway also runs up the coast from Nakowia to Tripoli. The railways are not functioning as a result of the civil war. There is an international airport at Beirut, served by the national carrier MEA and a few others from East Europe. Operations can be disrupted by fighting in the city.

Archaeology, etc.—Lebanon has some important historical remains, notably Baalbek (Heliopolis) which contains the ruins of first to third century Roman temples and Jubail (Biblos), one of the oldest continuously inhabited towns in the world, and ancient Tyre.

Language and Literature.—Arabic is the official language, and French and English are also widely used.

Education.—There are six universities in Beirut, the American and the French (R.C.) Universities established in the last century, and the Lebanese National University, the Beirut University College, the Kaskik Saint Esprit University and the Arab University which are recent foundations in the early stages of development. There are several institutions for vocational training, some of which have been rendered inoperative by the civil war, and there is a good provision throughout the country of primary and secondary schools, among which are a great number of private schools.

Finance.—No reliable statistics have been published for some time. The country is known to have a deficit, and the Lebanese £ has lost much of its value against foreign currencies. (*See also* p. 82.)

Trade.—Principal imports are gold and precious metals, machinery and electrical equipment, textiles and yarns, vegetable products, iron and steel goods, and motor vehicles. There has been a gradual decline in the overall amount of imports, as a result of continued instability.

Principal exports include gold and precious metals, fruits and vegetables, textiles, building materials, furniture, plastic goods, foodstuffs, tobacco and wine.

At one time there was a considerable transit trade through Beirut into the Arab hinterland. Lebanon is the terminal for two oil pipe lines, one formerly belonging to the Iraq Petroleum Company, debouching at Tripoli, the other belonging to the Trans Arabian Pipeline Company, at Sidon. These lines have not functioned for some years, for political/security considerations.

Trade with U.K.

	1985	1986
Imports from U.K.	£52,751,000	£55,867,000
Exports to U.K.	7,888,000	9,845,000

CAPITAL.— ΨBeirut (population, 702,000). Other towns are ΨTripoli (175,000), Zahlé (46,800), ΨSidon (24,740), ΨTyre (14,000).

FLAG.—Horizontal bands of red, white and red with a green cedar of Lebanon in the centre of the white band.

NATIONAL DAY.—November 22.

BRITISH EMBASSY
Shamma Building, Raouché, Ras Beirut, Beirut

Ambassador Extraordinary and Plenipotentiary, His Excellency John Walton David Gray, C.M.G. (1986).

LIBERIA
(Republic of Liberia)

President and Commander-in-Chief, Samuel K. Doe.

Rural Development, Samuel D. Brownell.
Agriculture, S. Gblorzuo Toweh.
Commerce, Industry and Transportation, Emmanuel S. Shaw.
Education, Othello Gongar.
Finance, John Bestman.
Foreign Affairs, Dr. Bernard Blamo.
Health and Social Affairs, Mrs. M. S. Belleh.
Information, Cultural Affairs and Tourism, Emmanuel Z. Bowier.
Justice, J. K. Z. B. Scott.
Labour, Manpower and Development, Robert Tubman.
Lands, Mines and Energy, William Freeman.
Internal Affairs, Col. E. K. Sackor.
National Defence, Maj. Gen. Gray D. Allison.
Planning and Economic Affairs, Rudolph Johnson.
Postal Affairs, Mrs. McLeod Darpoh.
Public Works, Yudu S. Gray.
State for Presidential Affairs, G. Alvin Jones.
Minister of State without Portfolio, Dr. Peter Naigow.

LIBERIAN EMBASSY IN LONDON
2 Pembridge Place, W2 4XB
[01–221 1036]

Ambassador Extraordinary and Plenipotentiary, His Excellency Willie A. Givens (1985).

An independent republic of West Africa, occupying that part of the coast between Sierra Leone and the Côte d'Ivoire, which is between the rivers Mano in the N.W. and Cavalla in the S.E., a distance of about 350 miles, with an area of about 43,000 sq. miles (111,369 sq. km.), and extending to the interior to latitude 8° 50′, a distance of 150 miles from the seaboard. It was founded by the American Colonization Society in 1822, and has been recognized since 1847 as an independent State. The population at the Census of 1974 was 1,481,524; a 1985 U.N. estimate put the figure at 2,189,000.

William V. S. Tubman, President of Liberia since 1944, died on July 23, 1971, and was succeeded by Dr. Tolbert. The Constitution was suspended following a military coup on April 12, 1980 led by M/Sgt. Samuel K. Doe, who then became Head of State. Executive power is now vested in the Head of State assisted by an appointed Cabinet of 18. A new Constitution was endorsed by a referendum on July 3, 1984 and on July 22 the People's Redemptive Council was dissolved and replaced by an interim National Assembly, comprising the Council and 35 civilian members, which will oversee the country's return to civilian rule. Presidential and legislative elections were held in Oct. 1985; and on Jan. 6, 1986 the Interim Assembly was dissolved and replaced by a legislative Assembly.

The Army of Liberia consists of one division of 2 brigades of militia, three regular infantry battalions, one engineer battalion and a small coastguard.

The artificial harbour and free port of Monrovia was opened on July 26, 1948. There are 9 ports of entry, including 3 river ports. International and African airlines call at Robertsfield, 35 miles from Monrovia. Spriggs Payne airfield, on the outskirts of Monrovia, is used by Air Liberia for internal flights.

Liberia is receiving assistance from a number of countries, including the United Kingdom, and from the E.C. and various international agencies. This aid is mainly directed towards the implementation of Liberia's National Socio-Economic Development Plan.

FINANCE

	1984	1985
Revenue	$183,000,000	$192,000,000
Expenditure	241,600,000	172,000,000

$ = U.S. Dollar

TRADE

The principal exports are iron ore, crude rubber, timber, uncut diamonds, palm kernels, cocoa and coffee. The chief imports are manufactured goods of all kinds, transport and iron-ore mining equipment and foodstuffs.

	1985	1986
Imports	$284,377,000	$259,037,900
Exports	435,570,000	408,374,099

Trade with U.K.

	1985	1986
Imports from U.K.	£15,957,000	£225,056,000
Exports to U.K.	5,967,000	7,574,000

The language of the Republic is English. American weights and measures are used.

CAPITAL, Ψ Monrovia. Est. Pop. (1984) 425,000. Other ports are Ψ Buchanan, Ψ Greenville (Sinoe) and Ψ Harper (Cape Palmas).

FLAG.—Alternate horizontal stripes (5 white, 6 red), with 5-pointed white star on blue field in upper corner next to flagstaff.

NATIONAL DAY.—July 26.

BRITISH EMBASSY

Mamba Point (P.O. Box 120), Monrovia

Ambassador Extraordinary and Plenipotentiary, and Consul-General, His Excellency Alec Ibbott, (1985).
Second Secretary and Consul, R. Daly.

LIBYA
(Al-Jamahiriya Al-Arabiya Al-Libya Al-Shabiya Al-Ishtirakiya)

Leader of the Revolution, Col. Muammar al-Qadhafi.
Secretary of the General People's Committee, Umar al-Muntasir.

GENERAL PEOPLE'S COMMITTEE

Sec. of Public Service, Fawzi al-Shakshuki.
Sec. of Planning, Muhammad Lufti Farhat.
Sec. of Treasury, Muhammad al-Madani al-Bukhari.
Sec. of Communications and Maritime Transport, Mubarak al-Shamikh.
Sec. of Information and Culture, Rajab Miftah Abu Dabbus.
Sec. of Economy and Commerce, Farhat Sharnana.
Sec. of External Relations, Jadallah Azzuz al-Talhi.
Sec. of Industry, Ahmad Fathi bin Shatwan.
Sec. of Health, Mustafa Muhammad al-Zaydi.
Sec. of Education and Scientific Research, Ahmad Ibrahim.

LIBYAN DIPLOMATIC MISSION IN LONDON

Following the break of diplomatic relations with Libya in April 1984, the Royal Embassy of Saudi Arabia has handled Libyan interests in Britain.

Libya, on the Mediterranean coast of Africa, is bounded on the East by Egypt and the Sudan, on the South by the Republics of Chad and Niger, and on the West by Algeria and Tunisia. It consists of the three former provinces of Tripolitania, Cyrenaica and the Fezzan, with a combined area of 679,362 sq. miles (1,759,540 sq. km) and a population (1985 estimate) of 3,800,000. The people of Libya are principally Arab with some Berbers in the West and aboriginal tribes in the Fezzan. Islam is the official religion of Libya, but other religions are tolerated. The official language is Arabic.

Vast sand and rock deserts, almost completely barren, occupy the greater part of Libya. The Southern part of the country lies within the Sahara Desert. There are no rivers, and, as rainfall is irregular good harvests are rare. The ancient ruins in Cyrenaica, at Cyrene, Ptolemais (Tolmeta) and Apollonia, are outstanding, as are those at Leptis Magna near Homs, 70 miles from Tripoli and at Sabratha, 40 miles west of Tripoli. An Italian expedition found in the S.W. of the Fezzan a series of rock-paintings more than 5,000 years old.

Production and Industry.—Agriculture is confined mainly to the coastal areas of Tripolitania and Cyrenaica, where barley, wheat, olives, almonds, citrus fruits and dates are produced, and to the areas of the oases, many of which are well supplied with springs supporting small fertile areas. Among the important oases are Jaghbub, Ghadames, Jofra, Sebha, Murzuq, Brak, Ghat, Jalo and the Kufra group in the South-East. The main industry is oil and gas production. There are pipelines from Zelten to the terminal at Mersa Brega, from Dahra to Ras-es-Sider, from Amal to Ras Lanuf and from the Intisar field to Zuetina. Since 1984 average production of crude oil has been about 1 million barrels per day. A major petrochemical complex is under construction at Ras Lanuf where a refinery and ethylene plant began operations in early 1985. The construction of an iron and steel plant at Misurata is well under way, with production expected to start in 1987. However, economic constraints have slowed some projects, particularly since Libya decided in 1983 to go ahead with a major irrigation scheme, the "Great Man-Made River".

Exports from Libya are dominated by crude oil, but some wool, cattle, sheep and horses, olive oil, and hides and skins are also exported. Principal imports are foodstuffs, including sugar, tea and coffee and most constructional materials and consumer goods. In recent years the private sector has been virtually eliminated and Libya is now a state trading country with imports controlled by state monopolies.

Communications in Libya are good. Besides the coastal road running from the Tunisian frontier through Tripoli to Benghazi, Tobruk and the Egyptian border, which serves the main population centres, main roads now link the provincial centres, and the oil-producing areas of the south with the coastal towns. There are airports at Tripoli and Benghazi (Benina), Tobruk, Mersa Brega, Sebha, Ghadames and Kufra regularly used by commercial airlines, and military airfields near Tobruk, near Tripoli and at Al Watiya, south of Zuara.

Government.—Libya was occupied by Italy in 1911–12 in the course of the Italo-Turkish War, and under the Treaty of Ouchy (Oct. 1912) the sovereignty of the province was transferred by Turkey to Italy. In 1939 the four Provinces of Libya (Tripoli, Misurata, Benghazi and Derna) were incorporated in the national territory of Italy as *Libia Italiana*. After the Second World War Tripolitania and Cyrenaica were placed provisionally under British and the Fezzan under French administration, and in conformity with a resolution of the U.N. General Assembly on Nov. 21, 1949, Libya became on Dec. 24, 1951, the first independent state to be created by the United Nations. The monarchy was overthrown by a revolution on Sept. 1, 1969, and the country was declared a republic. It was ruled by the Revolutionary Command Council (RCC) under the leadership of Colonel Muammar Qadhafi.

In March 1977 a new form of direct democracy, the "Jamahiriya" (state of the masses) was promulgated and the official name of the country was changed to Socialist People's Libyan Arab Jamahiriya. At local level authority is now vested in about 1,500 Basic and 25 Municipal People's Congresses which appoint Popular Committees to execute policy. Officials of these Congresses and Committees, together with representatives from unions and other organisations, form the General People's Congress, which normally meets for about a week early each year. This is the highest policy-making body in the country. The General People's Congress appoints its own General Secretariat and the General People's Committee, whose members head the 10 government departments which execute policy at national level. The Secretary of the General People's Committee has functions similar to those of a Prime Minister.

Since a reorganization in March 1979 neither Col. Qadhafi nor his former RCC colleagues have held formal posts in the administration. Qadhafi continues to hold the ceremonial title "Leader of the Revolution".

Currency.—The unit of currency is the Libyan *dinar* of 1,000 *dirham*. (*See also* p. 81.)

Libya has technical assistance agreements with a number of countries, and also employs large numbers of foreign labourers and experts.

Trade with U.K.

	1985	1986
Imports from U.K....	£237,639,000	£260,529,000
Exports to U.K.	311,764,000	136,390,000

CAPITAL.—Tripoli, pop. 1981, about 1,000,000.

The principal towns are: ΨBenghazi (500,000); Ψ Misurata (194,047).

FLAG.—Libya uses a plain emerald green flag.
NATIONAL DAY.—Sept. 1.

BRITISH EMBASSY

Diplomatic relations between the U.K. and Libya were broken in April 1984. British interests are currently handled by a section at the Italian Embassy, 1 Sharia Oran, Tripoli.

LIECHTENSTEIN
(Fürstentum Liechtenstein)

Prince, Franz Josef II., *b.* Aug. 16, 1906; *suc.* July 26, 1938; *married* March 7, 1943, Countess Gina von Wilczek.
Heir, Crown Prince Hans Adam, *b.* Feb. 14, 1945; *married* July 30, 1967, Countess Marie Kinsky; and has issue, Prince Alois, *b.* June 11, 1968; Prince Maximilian, *b.* May 16, 1969; Prince Constantin, *b.* March 15, 1972; Princess Tatjana, *b.* April 10, 1973.

From Aug. 26, 1984, Prince Hans Adam took over official duties and executive authority; Prince Franz Josef II remains titular Head of State.

MINISTRY

Prime Minister, Hans Brunhart (*Foreign Affairs, Education, Finance, Construction*).
Deputy Prime Minister, Dr. Herbert Wille (*Interior, Agriculture, Forestry and Environment, Culture, Youth and Sport, Justice*).
Government Councillors, René Ritter (*Economy*), Dr. Peter Wolff (*Social and Health Services*), Wilfried Büchel (*Communications*).

Liechtenstein is represented in diplomatic and consular matters in the United Kingdom by the Swiss Embassy, *q.v.*

Liechtenstein is a Principality on the Upper Rhine, between Vorarlberg (Austria) and Switzerland, with an area of 61 sq. miles (157 sq. km.), and a population in 1986 of 27,400. The language of the Principality is German.

At the General Election on Feb. 2, 1986, the Patriotic Union Party won 8 seats and Progressive Citizens Party 7.

The main industries are high and ultra-high vacuum engineering, semi-conductor industry, roller bearings, fastenings and securing systems, artificial teeth, heating and hot water equipment, synthetic fibres, woollen and homespun fabrics.

FINANCE

	1985	1986
Revenue	F318,091,262	F337,257,584
Expenditure	305,265,193	311,604,845
	(F = Swiss *francs*)	

CAPITAL, Vaduz. Pop. (1986), 4,920.
FLAG.—Equal horizontal bands of blue over red; gold crown on blue band near staff.
NATIONAL DAY.—August 15.

British Consul General, Gordon Aldridge Duggan (*office* at Dufourstrasse 56, 8008 Zürich).

LUXEMBOURG
(Grand-Duché de Luxembourg)

Grand Duke, H.R.H. Jean, *b.* Jan. 5, 1921, *married*, April 9, 1953, Princess Joséphine-Charlotte of Belgium, and has issue, 3 sons and 2 daughters; *succeeded* (on the abdication of his mother) Nov. 12, 1964.
Heir Apparent, Prince Henri, *b.* April 16, 1955, *married* February 14, 1981, Maria Teresa Mestre, and *has issue*, Prince Guillaume, *b.* Nov. 11, 1981; Prince Felix, *b.* June 3, 1984; Prince Louis, *b.* Aug. 1986.

CABINET

Christian Socialists:
Minister of State, President of the Government, Minister of Finance, National Development, Posts, Telecommunications and Information Technology, M. Jacques Santer.
Interior, the Family, Housing, Social Solidarity, M. Jean Spautz.
Education and Tourism, M. Fernand Boden.
Labour and Minister-Delegate for Finance, M. Jean-Claude Juncker.
Defence, Agriculture, Sport and the Civil Service, M. Marc Fischbach.
State Sec. for Agriculture and Viticulture, M. Rene Steichen.

Social Democrats:
Vice-President of the Government, Minister of the Economy, Foreign Affairs, Foreign Trade and Co-operation, Middle Classes and Treasury, M. Jacques Poos.
Public Health and Social Security, M. Benny Berg.
Justice, Cultural Affairs and the Environment, M. Robert Krieps.
Energy, Transport and Public Works, M. Marcel Schlechter.
State Secretary for Foreign Affairs, Foreign Trade and Co-operation and the Middle Classes, M. Robert Goebbels.
State Secretary for the Economy, M. Johny Lahure.

EMBASSY AND CONSULATE
27 Wilton Crescent, SW1X 8SD
[01–235 6961]

Ambassador Extraordinary and Plenipotentiary, His
Excellency Jean Wagner (1986).

Luxembourg is a Grand Duchy in Western Europe,
bounded by Germany, Belgium, and France. The
area is 998 sq. miles (2,586 sq. km.), the population
(Dec. 1984) 365,900, nearly all Roman Catholics. The
country is well wooded, with many deer and wild
boar. The language is Letzeburgesch but French is
the official language; most speak German and many
English.

Established as an independent State under the
sovereignty of the King of the Netherlands as Grand
Duke by the Congress of Vienna in 1815, it formed
part of the Germanic Confederation, 1815–66, and
was included in the German "Zollverein". In 1867
the Treaty of London declared it a neutral territory.
On the death of the King of the Netherlands in 1890
it passed to the Duke of Nassau. The territory was
invaded and overrun by the Germans at the beginning
of the war in 1914, but was liberated in 1918. By the
Treaty of Versailles, 1919, Germany renounced her
former agreements with Luxembourg in respect of
the customs union, etc., and in 1921 an economic
union was made with Belgium. The Grand Duchy
was again invaded and occupied by Germany on May
10, 1940. The constitution of the Grand Duchy was
modified on April 28, 1948, and the stipulation of
permanent neutrality was then abandoned. Luxembourg is now a fully effective member of the Western
association of powers and a signatory of the Brussels
and North Atlantic Treaties, and also a member of
the European Communities. Luxembourg is a member of the Belgium–Netherlands–Luxembourg Customs Union (Benelux, 1960).

The Court of the European Communities has its
seat in Luxembourg, as does the Secretariat of the
European Parliament, the European Investment
Bank, the European Audit Court and the European
Monetary Co-operation fund.

There is a Chamber of 64 Deputies, elected by
universal suffrage for 5 years. Legislation is submitted to the Council of State.

The Grand Duchy was rich in iron-ore and possesses
an important iron and steel industry with an annual
productive capacity over 5,700,000 tons. Government
revenue for 1986 was estimated at *L.F.* 78,625·9
million, expenditure *L.F.* 78,280·4 million. The Luxembourg *franc* has at present the same value as the
Belgian *franc* and the latter is legal tender in the
Grand Duchy.

There are 170 miles of railway.

Trade with U.K.

	1984	1985
Imports from U.K.	£42,335,000	£62,217,000
Exports to U.K.	93,612,000	133,450,000

CAPITAL.—Luxembourg, pop. (1987), 77,500, is a
dismantled fortress.

FLAG.—Three horizontal bands, red, white and
blue.

NATIONAL DAY.—June 23.

BRITISH EMBASSY
14 Boulevard F. D. Roosevelt, L-2450, Luxembourg

Ambassador Extraordinary and Plenipotentiary, His
Excellency Richard Oliver Miles, C.M.G., (1985).

MADAGASCAR
(Repoblika Demokratika n'i Madagaskar)

President, Didier Ratsiraka, *took office* 1975, *re-elected*
Nov. 7, 1982 for a seven-year term.

COUNCIL OF MINISTERS
Prime Minister, Col. Désiré Rakotoarijaona.
Finance and Economy, Pascal Rakotomavo.
Agricultural Production, Jose Michel Andrianoeli-
son.
Animal Production, Water and Forests, Joseph Ran-
drianasolo.
Trade, Georges Solofoson.
Industry, Energy and Mines, Jose Rakotomavo.
Population and Social Condition, Youth and Sports,
Jean André Ndremanjary.
Revolutionary Art and Culture, Gisèle Rabesahala,
Posts and Telecommunications, Rakotovoa Andrian-
tiana.
Justice, Gilbert Sambson.
Transport, Meteorology and Tourism, Joseph Bedo.
Civil Service and Labour, Georges Ruphin.
Defence, Gen. Mahasampa Raveloson.
Health, Dr. Jean-Jacques Séraphin.
Interior, Ampy Portos.
Primary and Secondary Education, Charles Zeny.
Higher Education, Ignace Rakoto.
Scientific Research, Antoine Zafera.
Information, Pierre Simon.
Foreign Affairs, Jean Bemananjara.
Public Works, Lt. Col. Victor Ramahatra.

Madagascar lies 240 miles off the east coast of
Africa and is the fourth largest island in the world.
It has an area of 226,669 sq. miles (587,041 sq. km.),
and a population (1985 U.N. estimate) of 9,985,000.
The people are of mixed Polynesian, Arab and Negro
origin. The languages spoken are Malagasy and
French. There are sizeable French, Chinese and
Indian communities.

Government.—It became a French protectorate in
1895, and a French colony in 1896 when the former
queen was exiled. Republican status was adopted on
October 14, 1958, and independence was proclaimed
on June 26, 1960.

The post-independence civilian government was
replaced by a military government in Jan. 1975 and
the following month martial law was declared. A
Supreme Council of the Revolution of 18 members
under Capitaine de Frégate (now Admiral) Didier
Ratsiraka was established on June 15, 1975.

In December 1975 a new constitution was approved
in a referendum, which vested executive power in
the President. He appoints a Council of Ministers to
assist him, with the guidance of the Revolutionary
Supreme Council. There is a 137-member National
People's Assembly elected for a 5-year term by
universal suffrage,

Revised agreements with France, signed on June
4, 1973, provided for the withdrawal of the French
forces stationed in the country after independence.
The French naval base at Diégo Suarez was turned
into a civilian ship repair yard. Madagascar also
withdrew from the Franc Zone and announced a
claim to the Islands of Juan de Nova, Glorieuses, Isle
de l'Europe, Bassa da India and Tromelin which had
remained integral parts of the French Republic after
independence.

The island's economy is still largely based on
agriculture, which accounts for three-quarters of its
exports. Development plans have placed emphasis on
increasing agricultural and livestock production, the
improvement of communications, the exploitation of
mineral deposits and the creation of small industries.

TRADE

	1983
Imports	$U.S.522,000,000
Exports	432,000,000

The unit of currency is the Malagasy *franc* (FMG).

Trade with U.K.

	1985	1986
Imports from U.K.	£9,484,000	£6,872,000
Exports to U.K.	6,236,000	6,432,000

CAPITAL.—Antananarivo (population about 1,000,000). Other main towns are the chief port Toamasina (55,000); Mahajanga (50,000); Fianarantsoa (47,000); Antsiranana (41,000).

FLAG.—Equal horizontal bands of red (above) and green, with vertical white band by staff.

NATIONAL DAY.—June 26 (Independence Day).

BRITISH EMBASSY
(BP 167, Antananarivo)

Ambassador Extraordinary and Plenipotentiary, His Excellency David Malcolm McBain, L.V.O. (1984).
Second Secretary, R. W. Hyde, M.B.E.
Vice-Consul (Commercial), A. J. Marcelin.

MALI
(République du Mali)

Secretary-General of the U.D.P.M. and President of the Government, Gen. Moussa Traore, *born* 1937, *assumed office* Nov. 20, 1968, *elected* June 19, 1979, re-elected June 9, 1985.

GOVERNMENT MINISTERS

Prime Minister, Dr. Mamadou Dembélé.
Transport and Public Works, Cheick Oumar Doumbia.
Defence, Gen. Sékou Ly.
Foreign Affairs and International Co-operation, Modibo Keita.
Information and Telecommunications, Mme. Fatou Gakou Niang.
Agriculture, Lt. Issa Ongoiba.
Territorial Administration and Basic Development, Lt. Col. Abdourahmane Maiga.
Finance and Trade, Zoumane Sacko.
Justice, Diango Sissoko.
Industrial Development and Tourism, Drissa Keita.
Natural Resources and Stock Farming, El Hadj Oumar Tall.
Planning, Ousmane Mohamed Diallo.
Minister in Charge of State Corporations, Anthioumane N'Diaye.
National Education, Oumar Isslaka Bah.
Public Health and Social Affairs, Mme. Sidibé Aissata Cisse.
Sports, Art and Culture, Bakari Traoré.
Employment and Civil Service, Hama Ag Mahamoud.

The Republic of Mali, an inland state in north-west Africa has an area of 478,791 sq. miles (1,240,000 sq. km.), and a population (1985 U.N. estimate) of 8,206,000. The principal rivers are the Niger and the Senegal.

Formerly the French colony of Soudan, the territory elected on Nov. 24, 1958, to remain as an autonomous republic within the French Community. It associated with Senegal in the Federation of Mali which was granted full independence on June 20, 1960. The Federation was effectively dissolved on August 22 by the secession of Senegal. The title of the Republic of Mali was adopted on Sept. 22, 1960.

Government.—The régime of Modibo Keita was overthrown on Nov. 19, 1968, by a group of Army officers who formed a National Liberation Committee and appointed a Prime Minister. Moussa Traore assumed the functions of Head of State. A new civil constitution came into being in 1979. The new government formed on May 4, 1978 contained a majority of civilians. On June 19, 1979, elections were held for an 82-member National Assembly.

Presidential elections held on the same day confirmed Traore as President.

Economy.—Mali's principal exports are groundnuts (raw and processed), cotton fibres, meat and dried fish. The Republic rejoined the CFA franc zone on June 1, 1984 when measures were taken to convert the *Franc Malien* at the rate of 2*FM* : 1 *Franc CFA*.

Trade with UK

	1985	1986
Imports from UK	£7,294,000	£4,121,000
Exports to UK	4,804,000	8,282,000

CAPITAL.—Bamako (600,000). Other towns are Gao, Kayes, Mopti, Sikasso, Segou and Timbuktu (all regional capitals).

FLAG.—Vertical stripes of green (by staff), yellow and red.

NATIONAL DAY.—September 22.

BRITISH EMBASSY
British Ambassador (resident at Dakar, Senegal).

MAURITANIA
(République Islamique de Mauritanie)

President, Col. Moaouia Ould Sidi Mohamed Taya, took power Dec. 12, 1984 (*also holds portfolios of Prime Minister and Defence*).
Foreign Affairs, Lemine Ould N'Diayane.
Interior, Lt.-Col. Djibril Ould Abdallahi.
Justice and Islamic Affairs, Hamdi Samba Diop.
Economy and Finance, Cdr. Mohamed Salem Ould Lekhal.
Fisheries and Maritime Economy, Sidi Ould Cheikh Abdallahi.
Mines and Economy, Mahfoud Ould Lemrabott.
Trade and Transport, Capt. Dia Elhadj Abderahmane.
Equipment, Lt.-Col. Brahim Ould Alioune Ndiaye.
National Education, Hasni Ould Didi.
Civil Service, Administrative Training, Labour, Youth and Sports, Lt.-Col. Mohammed Mamoud Ould Den.
Energy and Water, Soumare Oumar.
Rural Development, Messoud Ould Belkheir.
Public Health and Social Affairs, Maj. N'Daye Kane.
Information, Posts and Telecommunications, Culture, Mohamed Mahmoud Ould Weddadi.
Deputy Minister of the Interior, N'Gam Lirwane.
Sec.-Gen. to the Government, Barou Abdallah.

Mauritania lies on the north-west coast of Africa immediately to the north of Senegal. It is bounded on the east by the Republic of Mali. To the north it is bounded by Morocco and the Western Sahara. Mauritania and Morocco took possession of that territory in February 1976 when Spain formally relinquished all right to it and in April 1976 agreed on a new frontier dividing the territory between them. In August 1979, Mauritania relinquished all claim to the southern sector of the Western Sahara after a three-year war against the Polisario front guerrilla army. Area 397,955 sq. miles (1,030,700 sq. km.). The population was estimated at 1,888,000 in 1985. The Republic of Mauritania elected on November 28, 1958, to remain within the French Community as an autonomous republic. It became fully independent on Nov. 28, 1960. In 1972 Mauritania broke with the franc zone and established its own unit of currency, the *Ouguiya*, equal in value to 5 *francs CFA*.

Mauritania's main source of potential wealth lies in rich deposits of iron ore around Zouérate, in the north of the country. Exports began in 1963, via a railway laid for the purpose from the mine to the port of Nouadhibou. The deposits are being exploited under the aegis of the *Société Nationale Industrielle Miniere* following the nationalization in 1974 of the internationally based company MIFERMA. There are copper deposits at Akjoujt which are being exploited by SOMIMA, a company nationalized on Feb. 25, 1975; the mine was closed in 1978, but reopened in 1981.

Trade with U.K.

	1985	1986
Imports from U.K.	£2,069,000	£2,496,000
Exports to U.K.	6,311,000	2,184,000

CAPITAL.—Nouakchott (500,000).
FLAG.—Yellow star and crescent on green ground.
NATIONAL DAY.—November 28.
British Ambassador, (Resident at *Dakar, Senegal*).

MEXICO
(Estados Unidos Mexicanos)

President (1982–88), Lic. Miguel de la Madrid Hurtado, *elected*, 4 July 1982, *took office*, 1 Dec. 1982.

THE CABINET

Interior, Sr. Manuel Bartlett Diaz.
Foreign Affairs, Sr. Bernardo Sepúlveda Amor.
Finance and Public Credit, Sr. Gustavo Petricioli Iturbide.
Defence, Gen. Juan José Arévalo Gardoqui.
Navy, Adm. Miguel Angel Gómez Ortega.
Budget and Planning, Sr. Carlos Salinas de Gortari.
Energy, Mines and Parastatal Industries, Sr. Alfredo del Mazo González.
Trade and Industrial Development, Sr. Héctor Hernández Cervantes.
Agriculture and Water Resources, Sr. Eduardo Pesqueira Olea.
Communications and Transport, Sr. Daniel Diaz Diaz.
Education, Sr. José Miguel González Avelar.
Urban Development and Ecology, Sr. Manuel Camacho Solis.
Health, Dr. Guillermo Soberón Acevedo.
Labour and Social Security, Sr. Arsenio Farell Cubillas.
Agrarian Reform, Sr. Rafael Rodríguez Barrera.
Tourism, Sr. Antonio Enríquez Savignac.
Fisheries, Sr. Pedro Ojeda Paullada.
Attorney-General, Sr. Sergio García Ramírez.
Attorney-General of Federal District, Sr. Renato Sales Gasque.
Comptroller-General, Sr. Ignacio Pichardo Pegaza.
Mayor of Mexico City, Sr. C. P. Ramón Aguirre Velázquez.

MEXICAN EMBASSY IN LONDON
8 Halkin St., SW1X 7DW
[01–235 6393]
Ambassador Extraordinary and Plenipotentiary, His Excellency Jorge Eduardo Navarrete (1986).

Area and Population.—Mexico occupies the southern part of the continent of North America, with an extensive seaboard to both the Atlantic and Pacific Oceans, extending from 14° 33′ to 32° 43′ N. lat. and 86° 46′ to 117° 08′ W. long., and comprising one of the most varied zones in the world. It contains 31 states and the federal district of Mexico, making in all 32 political divisions, covering an area of 761,605 sq. miles (1,972,547 sq. km.). At the 1980 Mexican General Census, the total population was 67,383,000, but a 1985 U.N. estimate gives a figure of 78,524,000.

The two great ranges of North America, the Sierra Nevada and Rocky Mountains, are prolonged from the north to a convergence towards the narrowing isthmus of Tehuantepec, their course being parallel to the west and east coasts. The surface of the interior consists of an elevated plateau between the two ranges, with steep slopes both to the Pacific and Atlantic (Gulf of Mexico). In the west is the peninsula of Lower California, with a mountainous surface, separated from the mainland by the Gulf of California. The Sierra Nevada, known in Mexico as the *Sierra Madre*, terminates in a transverse series of volcanic peaks, from Colima on the west to Citlaltepetl ("El Pico de Orizaba") on the east. The low-lying lands of the coasts form the *Tierra Caliente*, or tropical regions (below 3,000 ft.), the higher levels form the *Tierra Templada*, or temperate region (from 3,000 to 6,000 ft.), and the summit of the plateau with its peaks is known as *Tierra Fria*, or cold region (above 6,000 ft.). The only considerable rivers are the *Rio Grande del Norte* which forms part of the northern boundary, and is navigable for about 70 miles from its mouth in the Gulf of Mexico, and the *Rio Grande de Santiago*, the *Rio Balsas* and *Rio Papaloapan*. The largest fresh-water lakes are *Chapala* (70 miles long and 20 miles wide), and *Pátzcuaro*.

History and Archaeology.—The present Mexico and Guatemala were once the centre of a remarkable indigenous civilization, which had unknown beginnings in the centuries before Christ, flowered in the periods from A.D. 500 to 1100 and A.D. 1300 to 1500 and collapsed before the little army of Spanish adventurers under Hernán Cortés in the years following 1519. Pre-Columbian Mexico was divided between different but connected Indian cultures, each of which has left distinctive archaeological remains: the best-known of these are Chichén Itzá, Uxmal, Bonampak and Palenque, in Yucatán and Chiapas (Maya); Teotihuacon, renowned for the Pyramid of the Sun (216 feet high) in the Valley of Mexico (Teotihuacáno); Monte Albán and Mitla, near Oaxaca (Zapotec); El Tajín in the State of Veracruz (Totonac); and Tula in the State of Hidalgo (Toltec). The last and most famous Indian culture of all, the Aztec, based on Tenochitlán suffered more than the others from the Spanish and only very few Aztec monuments remain.

A few years after the Conquest, the Spanish built Mexico City on the ruins of Tenochitlán, and appointed a Viceroy to rule their new dominions, which they called New Spain. The country was largely converted to Christianity, and a distinctive colonial civilization, representing a marriage of Indian and Spanish traditions, developed and flourished, notably in architecture and sculpture. In 1810 a revolt began against Spanish rule. This was finally successful in 1821, when a precarious independence was proclaimed. Friction with the United States in Texas led to the war of 1845–48, at the end of which Mexico was forced to cede the northern provinces of Texas, California and New Mexico. In 1862 Mexican insolvency led to invasion by French forces which installed Archduke Maximilian of Austria as Emperor. The empire collapsed with the execution of the Emperor in 1867 and the austere reformer, Juárez, restored the republic. Juárez's death was followed by the dictatorship of Porfirio Diaz, which saw an enormous increase of foreign, particularly British and United States, investment in the country. In 1910 began the Mexican Revolution which reformed the social structure and the land system, curbed the power of foreign companies and ushered in the independent industrial Mexico of today.

Government.—Under the Constitution of Feb. 5, 1917 (as subsequently amended), Congress consists of a Senate of 64 members, elected for six years, and of a Chamber of Deputies, at present numbering 400, elected for three years. Presidents, who wield full executive powers, are elected for six years; they cannot be re-elected.

There are nine political parties registered in Mexico, of which by far the largest and most influential is the *Partido Revolucionario Institucional* (P.R.I.) which has for many years constituted the governing party. The Mexican Communists allied with several like-minded smaller parties to form the Mexican United Socialist Party (P.S.U.M.) in 1982.

Communications.—Veracruz, Tampico and Coatzacoalcos are the chief ports of the Atlantic, and Guaymas, Mazatlán, Puerto Lázaro Cárdenas, Acapulco, Salina Cruz and Puerto Madero on the Pacific. Work is proceeding on the reorganization and re-equipment of the whole system; help in this has been forthcoming from the World Bank, the Export-Import Bank and private sources in the United States. The railways were completely nationalized in 1970.

Mexico City may be reached by at least three highways (with 14 entry points) from the United States, and work is complete on roads southward from Mexico City to Yucatán as well as on two principal highways to the Guatemalan border (with three entry points).

International telegraph services to the United States frontier are provided by the government-owned Mexican Telegraph Company and then through the United States to Canada and Europe.

Teléfonos de México, a state-controlled company, controls about 98 per cent of all telephone services. Satélite Latinoamericano, S.A. (SATELAT) is a joint government/private sector venture disseminating television programmes to Latin America through Intelstat IV satellite facilities leased by the Mexican Government.

There is a good national and international network of air services. There are 1,113 airports and landing fields in Mexico, of which eighteen are equipped to handle long-distance flights. There are 166 airline companies, including two of the major national airlines—*Mexicana de Aviación* and *Aeroméxico.* Passenger traffic is growing by about 14 per cent yearly, while cargo is increasing by a similar percentage.

Production.—The principal agricultural crops are maize, beans, rice, wheat, sugar cane, coffee, cotton, tomatoes, chili, tobacco, chick-peas, groundnuts, sesame, alfalfa, vanilla, cocoa and many kinds of fruit, both tropical and temperate. The maguey, or Mexican cactus, yields several fermented drinks, mezcal and tequila (distilled) and pulque (undistilled). Another species of the same plant supplies sisal-hemp (henequen). The forests abound in mahogany, rosewood, ebony and chicle trees. Agriculture employs an estimated 30 per cent of the working population.

The principal industries are mining and petroleum, but over the last twenty years there has been very considerable expansion of both light and heavy industries. Exports of manufactured goods now average about 20 per cent of total exports. The steel

industry expanded steadily until recently and current production is around 6·5 m. tons. The mineral wealth is great, and principal minerals are gold, silver, copper, lead, zinc, quicksilver, iron and sulphur. Substantial reserves of uranium have been found. In the non-metals sector, Mexico continues to produce 25 per cent of the world's supply of fluorspar.

The total proven petroleum reserves were 72 billion barrels in 1983. Crude oil production is currently about 2,600,000 barrels. Daily production of natural gas is approximately 3 billion cubic feet. Oil reserves have increased substantially due to important discoveries in the Gulf of Campeche. A new refinery at Tula, State of Hidalgo is the nation's largest; and new refineries in Monterrey, State of Nuevo Leon, and Salina Cruz, State of Oaxaca, are under construction.

Textile production is led by the artificial fibres sector, which comprised 66 per cent. of the industry's output in 1983.

Defence.—Supreme command is vested in the President, exercised through the Ministries of Defence (for Army and Air Force) and Marine.

The country is divided into 36 zones in which the regular army (106,000) and part-time conscripts (250,000) are trained. The Army in 1985 had three HQ Brigades, five Artillery Regiments, 26 mechanized and one Horse Cavalry Regiments, Transport, Engineering and Signals Regiments, and 78 Infantry Battalions. In addition, there is a Rural Defence Militia of some 12,000 men.

The Navy has a strength of about 38,500 officers and men including the Naval Air Force and Marines. It is equipped with three destroyers, five frigates, six OPVs, 19 corvettes, 17 minesweepers, 31 coastal craft patrol, 12 inshore and river patrol boats, 13 transports and tugs, and one sail training ship. Many vessels are non-operational. The Marine Infantry has 10 battalions (4,300 officers and men). The Naval Air Force consists of four squadrons and 49 aircraft.

The Air Force has an approximate strength of 5,500 officers and men and 298 aircraft, including tactical/training aircraft, reconnaissance aircraft/helicopters and transport aircraft. There is a Parachute Brigade consisting of three Parachute battalions (approx. 2,000 men).

Language and Literature.—Spanish is the official language of Mexico and is spoken by about 95 per cent of the population. In addition to Spanish, there are five basic groups of Indian languages spoken in Mexico. The 1970 Census showed that of the 3,111,415 inhabitants speaking an Indian language, 25·7 per cent spoke Náhuatl; 14·6 per cent Maya; 9·1 per cent Zapotec; 7·1 per cent Otomí; 7·5 per cent Mixtec and 36 per cent one or other of the 59 dialects derived from these basic languages.

Education.—Education is divided into primary, secondary, preparatory and university. Primary education is free, secular and nominally compulsory.

Trade with U.K.

	1985	1986
Imports from U.K.	£203,403,689	£162,328,000
Exports to U.K.	236,810,854	116,078,000

Imports consist largely of transport, sound-recording and power-generating equipment, chemicals, industrial machinery, pharmaceuticals and specialized appliances. Principal exports are oil, fertilizers, minerals, metallic ores and scrap, sugar, honey, textiles and power-generating equipment.

CAPITAL.—Mexico City, metropolitan area 18,748,000 (est. pop. 1986). Other cities (est. pop. 1986) are:

Guadalajara .	2,587,000	Puebla	1,217,600
Monterrey...	2,335,000	León	946,800

Torréon 729,800
San Luis
Potosí 601,900
Ciudad
Juarez 595,700
Mérida 580,300

FLAG.—Three vertical bands in green, white, red, with the Mexican emblem (an eagle on a cactus devouring a snake) in the centre.

NATIONAL DAY.—September 16 (Proclamation of Independence).

BRITISH EMBASSY

Calle Río Lerma 71, Colonia Cuauhtémoc, 06500 Mexico City, D.F.

Ambassador Extraordinary and Plenipotentiary, His Excellency John Albert Leigh Morgan, C.M.G. (1986).

There are British Consular Offices at *Mexico City, Acapulco, Guadalajara, Mérida, Monterrey, Tampico* and *Cuidad Juarez.*

British Council Representative.—R.Watkins, Maestro Antonio Caso 127, Col. San Rafael (P.O. Box 30-588), Mexico 06470, D.F.

BRITISH CHAMBER OF COMMERCE, British Trade Centre, Rio Tiber 103–60, Mexico 5 D.F.—*Manager,* J. Carral.

MONACO
(Principauté de Monaco)

Sovereign Prince, H.S.H. Rainier III-Louis-Henri-Maxence Bertrand, *born* May 31, 1923, *succeeded his grandfather* (H.S.H. Prince Louis II), May 9, 1949; *married* April 19, 1956, Miss Grace Patricia Kelly (died Sept. 14, 1982) and *has issue* Prince Albert Alexandre Louis Pierre, *born* March 14, 1958, Princess Caroline Louise Marguerite, *born* January 23, 1957; and Princess Stephanie Marie Elisabeth, *born* Feb. 1, 1965.

President of the Crown Council, M. Jean-Charles Marquet.

President of the National Council, M. Jean-Charles Rey.

Minister of State, Jean Ausseil, *appointed* 1985.

CONSULATE-GENERAL IN LONDON
4 Audley Square, W1Y 5DR
[01–629 0734]

Consul-General, I. S. Ivanovic.

A small Principality on the Mediterranean, with land frontiers joining France at every point, and consisting of the old town of Monaco, La Condamine, Fontvielle and Monte Carlo, where is the famous casino. The Principality comprises a narrow strip of country about 2 miles long (area approx. 467 acres), with approximately 28,000 inhabitants (1983) and a yearly average of over 250,000 visitors.

The principality, ruled by the Grimaldi family since the late 13th century, was abolished during the French Revolution and re-established in 1815 under the protection of the Kingdom of Sardinia. In 1861 Monaco came under French protection. The 1962 Constitution, which can be modified only with the approval of the National Council, maintains the traditional hereditary monarchy and guarantees freedom of association, trade union freedom and the right to strike. Legislative power is held jointly by the Prince and a uni-cameral, 18 member National Council elected by universal suffrage. Executive power is exercised by the Prince and a four-member Council of Government, headed by a Minister of State. The judicial code is based on that of France.

The whole available ground is built over, so that there is no cultivation, though there are some notable public and private gardens. Monaco has a small harbour (30 ft. alongside quay) and the import duties are the same as in France.

CAPITAL.—Monaco-ville (1,443).

FLAG.—Two equal horizontal stripes, red over white.

NATIONAL DAY.—November 19.

H.M. Consul-General, T. E. J. Mound, O.B.E. (*Resident at Marseilles*).

MONGOLIA
(Mongolian People's Republic— Bugd Nairamdakh Mongol Ard Uls)

President: J. Batmunkh.
Prime Minister: D. Sodnom.

Mongolian People's Revolutionary
(= *Communist*) Party

Politburo of the Central Committee, J. Batmunkh; D. Sodnom; D. Molomjamts; B. Dejid; B. Altangerel; B. Lamjav (*full members*); N. Jagaval; S. Luvsangombo; P. Damdin (*candidate members*).

Secretariat of the Central Committee, J. Batmunkh (*General Secretary*); D. Molomjamts; Ts. Namsrai; B. Dejid; P. Damdin; Ts. Balkhaajav.

Chairman, Council of Ministers, D. Sodnom.

First Deputy Chairman, (vacant).

Deputy Chairmen, B. Altangerel; S. Luvsangombo; Ch. Suren; M. Peljee; P. Jasrai.

MONGOLIAN EMBASSY
7 Kensington Court, W8 5DL
[01–937 0150]

Ambassador Extraordinary and Plenipotentiary, His Excellency Ishetsogyin Ochirbal (1987).

Third Secretary, C. Battomor.

Attaché, T. O. Munkhsaikhan.

Area and Population.—The Mongolian People's Republic (Mongolia) is a large and sparsely populated country to the north of China. Its area is 604,250 sq. miles (1,565,000 sq. km.). Its population (Dec. 1985) is about 1,900,000. However, this total constitutes only part of the Mongolians of Asia, a number of whom are to be found in China and in the neighbouring regions of the Soviet Union (especially the Mongolian Buryat Autonomous Region). This country, which is almost nowhere below 1,000 metres above sea level, forms part of the Central Asiatic Plateau and rises towards the west in the high mountains of the Mongolian Altai and Khanggai Ranges. The Khentai Mountain Range, situated to the north-east of the capital Ulan Bator, is less high. The Gobi region covers much of the southern half of the country. It contains some sand deserts, but between these less hospitable areas there is semi-desert which provides pasture for great numbers of sheep, goats, camels and horses (the latter is still the characteristic means of transport for the rural population) and some cattle. In the steppe areas to the north pasturage is better and livestock more abundant. Even further north, in the better watered provinces, grain, fodder and vegetable crops are increasingly grown. There are several long rivers and many lakes, but good water is scarce since much of the lake water is salty. The climate is harsh, with a short mild summer giving way to a long winter when temperatures can drop as low as minus 50° C.

History.—Mongolia, under Genghis Khan the conqueror of China and much of Asia, was for many years a buffer state between Tsarist Russia and China, although it was under general Chinese suzerainty. The outbreak of the Chinese Revolution in 1911 led to a declaration of autonomy under Chinese suzerainty which was confirmed by the Sino-Russian Treaty of Kiakhta (1915), but cancelled by a unilateral Chinese declaration in 1919. Later the country became a battleground of the Russian Civil

War, and Soviet and Mongolian troops occupied Ulan Bator in 1921: this was followed by another declaration of independence. However, in 1924 the Soviet Union in a Treaty with China again recognized the latter's sovereignty over Mongolia; but this was never properly exercised because of China's pre-occupation with internal affairs, and later by the anti-Japanese war. The Mongolian People's Republic was formally established in 1924. Under the Yalta Agreement, Chiang Kai-shek agreed to a plebiscite, held in 1945, in which the Mongolians declared their desire for independence and this was formally recognized by Nationalist China. The country entered the United Nations in 1961. The heroes of Mongolian history during the earlier part of the century were Sukhebator, who died in 1923, and the Communist Choibalsan (died 1952), who did much to turn the country into the Communist state it is today, and carried out a systematic destruction of the power of the Lamas and the old princely houses which had previously been the dominant force in both the economy and the government.

Production, etc.—The total of Mongolia's livestock was 23 million in 1984. Traditionally the Mongolian is a herdsman, tending his flock of sheep, goats and horses, cows and camels and leading a totally nomadic life. With the coming of the Communist régime (under the Mongolian People's Revolutionary Party) and especially since 1952, great efforts have been made to settle the population, but a large proportion still live nomadically or semi-nomadically in the traditional *ger* (circular tent). The pastoral population was collectivized at the end of the 1950s into huge *negdels* (co-operatives) and State farms which have hastened the process of settlement, but within these the herdsmen and their families still move with their *gers* from pasture to pasture as the seasons change. The country, and three city districts (Ulan Bator, Darkhan and Erdenet), is today divided into 18 *aimaks* (provinces) and beneath these into 258 *somons* (districts), and these form the basis of the State organization of the country, parallel with which runs the apparatus of the Revolutionary Party.

Membership of the Communist bloc has brought Mongolia considerable quantities of aid from other Socialist countries, especially Czech, Polish and East German aid to supplement the massive assistance from the Soviet Union. Soviet and Bloc aid is hastening the process of industrialization; for although the economy remains predominantly based on the herds of animals, and the principal exports of the country are still animal by-products (especially wool, hides and furs) and cattle, factories serving the needs of the country have been started up and the coal and electricity industries are being developed to provide an industrial base. A joint Mongolian/Soviet enterprise for copper and molybdenum mining was opened in 1978, at Erdenet in northern Mongolia. It is now in full production and processes 16 million tonnes of ore annually. A major geological survey is being carried out by the CMEA countries, in order to prepare for the extraction of the considerable mineral deposits known to exist in Mongolia. Coal production in 1980 was 4·5 million tons and was expected to rise to 6·8 million tons by 1985.

Ulan Bator, which contains over a quarter of the country's population, is the main seat of industry. The second largest industrial centre is at Darkhan (pop. 60,000), north of the capital, near the Soviet frontier. Its industries include lime, cement and building materials, a flour mill and a power station. Choibalsan, in the east, is also being developed industrially. Agriculture, formerly little practised, is now being extended. Average cereal production for 1976–80 was 347,000 tons, but by 1983 had risen to 800,000 tonnes. Communication is still difficult in the country as there are very few tarmac roads. The trans-Mongolian railway, following the line of the old north-south trade route, was opened in 1955 and links Mongolia with both China and Russia. Mongolia's fundamental difficulty is its very small population and labour force.

Foreign trade is dominated by the Soviet Union, with the eastern European countries taking most of what is left. Trade with western countries and Japan is developing slowly.

Trade with U.K.

	1985	1986
Imports from U.K.	£142,000	£1,031,000
Exports to U.K.	3,264,000	4,750,000

CAPITAL.—Ulan Bator. (Pop. 480,000.)

FLAG.—Vertical tri-colour red, blue, red and in the hoist the traditional Soyombo symbol in gold.

NATIONAL DAY.—July 11 (Anniversary of the Mongolian People's Republic).

BRITISH EMBASSY
30 Enkh Taivny Gudamzh (P.O. Box 703)
Ulan Bator 13

Ambassador Extraordinary and Plenipotentiary, His Excellency Guy William Pulbrook Hart, O.B.E. (1987).
Second Secretary, D. A. Slinn (*Head of Chancery*).
Attachés, P. Pickthorn; S. G. McDonald.

MOROCCO
(Al-Mamlaka Al-Maghrebia)

King, H.M. King Hassan II (Moulay Hassan Ben Mohammed), *born* July 9, 1929; *acceded* February 26, 1961, *on the death of his father,* King Mohammad V. *Heir,* Crown Prince Sidi Mohamed, *b.* August 21, 1963.

MINISTERS

Prime Minister, Kazeddine Laraki
Ministers of State, Hadj M'hamid Bahnini; Moulay Ahmed Alaoui.
Justice, Moulay Mustapha Belarbi Alaoui.
Interior and Information, Driss Basri.
Foreign Affairs and Co-operation, Abdellatif Filali.
National Education, Mohamed Hilali.
Health, Tayeb Bencheikh.
Religious Endowments and Islamic Affairs, Abdelke-bir Alaoui M'Daghri.
Equipment, Training of Cadres and Professional Training, Mohamed Kabbaj.
Finance, Mohamed Berrada.
Tourism, Moussa Saadi.
Traditional Industry and Social Affairs, Mohamed Labied.
Transport, Mohamed Bouamoud.
Energy and Mines, Mohamed Fettah.
Youth and Sport, Abdellatif Semlali.
Fisheries and Merchant Shipping, Bensalem Smili.
Secretary General of the Government, Abbès Kaissi.
Culture, Mohamed Benaissa.
Environment, Abderrahmane Boufettass.
Posts and Telecommunications, Mohamed Laensar.
Agriculture and Agricultural Reform, Othman Demnati.
Trade and Industry, Abdellah Al Azmani.
Employment, Hassan Abbadi.
Prime Minister's Office, Moulay Zine Zahidi (*Economic Affairs*); Khali Hanna Ould Errachid (*Development of the Sahara Provinces*); Rachidi Ghazouani (*the Plan*); Abdeslem Baraka (*Relations with Parliament*); Abderrahim Ben Abdeljalil (*Administrative Affairs*).

EMBASSY OF THE KINGDOM OF MOROCCO AND
CONSULATE
49 Queen's Gate Gardens, SW7 5NE
[01–581 50014]

Ambassador Extraordinary and Plenipotentiary, His
Excellency Mr. Abdeslam Zenined (1981).
Military, Naval and Air Attaché, Col. Mustapha
Jabrane.

Area and Population.—Morocco is situated in the
north-western corner of the African continent between latitude 27° 40′–36° N. and longitude 1°–13° W.
with an area estimated at 172,414 sq. miles (446,550 sq.
km.), and a population (1985 U.N. estimate) of
21,941,000. It is traversed in the north by the Rif
mountains and in a general S.W. to N.E. direction,
by the Middle Atlas, the High Atlas, the Anti-Atlas
and the Sarrho ranges. The northern flanks of the
Middle and High Atlas mountains are well wooded
but their southern slopes, exposed to the dry desert
winds, are generally arid and desolate. The northwesterly point of Morocco is the peninsula of Tangier
which is separated from the continent of Europe by
the narrow strait of Gibraltar. The Jebel Mousa
dominates the promontory and, with the rocky
eminence of Gibraltar, was known to the ancients as
the *Pillars of Hercules*, the western gateway of the
Mediterranean.

Western Sahara.—Formerly the Spanish Sahara,
the territory was split between Morocco and Mauritania in 1976 after Spain withdrew in Dec. 1975. In
1979 Mauritania renounced its claim to its share of
the territory, which was added by Morocco to its
area. Morocco's annexation is being opposed by
Polisario guerrillas, who want the territory to become
an independent state.

Climate.—The climate of Morocco is generally good
and healthy, especially on the Atlantic coast, (where
a high degree of humidity is, however, prevalent) the
country being partially sheltered by the Atlas mountains from the hot winds of the Sahara. The rainy
season may last from November to April. The plains
of the interior are intensely hot in summer. Average
summer and winter temperatures for Rabat are 81°
F. and 45° F.

Government.—Morocco became an independent
sovereign state in 1956, following joint declarations
made with France on March 2, 1956, and with Spain
on April 7, 1956. The Sultan of Morocco, Sidi
Mohammad ben Youssef, adopted the title of King
Mohammad V.

Following serious disturbances in Casablanca in
March, 1965, attempts were made by King Hassan, in
consultation with all political parties, to form a
government of national union. These efforts were
unsuccessful and on June 7, 1965, the King proclaimed
a "state of exception" and suspended Parliament.
Assuming himself the office of Prime Minister, he
announced the formation of a new government and
indicated that constitutional changes were to follow.
A revised Constitution was approved by a national
referendum on July 24, 1970 and brought into effect
soon after. It was superseded by another constitution,
also approved by a national referendum, on March 1,
1972. This provides that not only political parties,
but trade unions, chambers of commerce and professional bodies will participate in the organization of
the State and representation of the people; specifies
that the King is the supreme representative of the
people; makes changes in the composition of the
Regency Council and the Sovereign's rights and
establishes a unicameral legislature. The Chamber
has 306 members, 204 elected by direct universal
suffrage (including 5 representing overseas workers)
and 102 members elected by electoral colleges representing local government, industry, agriculture and
working class groups. There were elections in Sept.-
Oct 1984 and the new Parliament began its 6 year
term on Oct. 12. A new government was named in
April 1985 which included members of three political
parties, though over half the portfolios went to non-
political appointees.

Defence.—The Moroccan army, formed in 1956, is
about 140,000 strong. A Moroccan air force was
formed in 1959 and a navy in 1960. Their strengths
are about 13,000 and 6,000 respectively. The armed
forces possess quantities of French and American
equipment, including aircraft, as well as Soviet-
supplied hardware.

Production and Trade.—Morocco's main sources
of wealth are agricultural and mineral. The Five
Year Plan (1981–85) for economic development placed
particular emphasis on social improvement. Other
priority sectors were industrial development, fisheries, agriculture and tourism. The next development
plan (1987 onwards) is expected to be similar to the
last. The world recession and high energy prices,
coupled with a fall in the price of phosphates and
poor harvests due to low rainfall have created
problems for the economy since the end of the 1970's.
However, rains in the winter of 1985–6 ended the
long drought and the 1986 harvest was expected to be
good. Similarly the fall in oil prices, the value of the
dollar and interest rates have helped.

Agriculture employs more than 40 per cent. of the
working population and accounts for about 36 per
cent. of Morocco's exports. The main agricultural
exports are fruit and vegetables. Cork and wood-pulp
are the most important commercial forest products.
Esparto grass is also produced. There is a fishing
industry and substantial quantities of canned fish,
mainly sardines and fishmeal, are exported. Manufacturing industries are centred in Casablanca, Fez,
Tangier and Safi.

Morocco's mineral exports are phosphates, fluorite,
barite, manganese, iron ore, lead, zinc, cobalt, copper
and antimony. Morocco possesses nearly three-
quarters of the world's estimated reserves of phosphates. There are oil refineries at Mohammedia and
Sidi Kacem handling about 4 million tonnes of crude
oil per year, but no significant quantities of hydrocarbons have been found.

Tourism is of increasing importance to the Moroccan economy with development concentrated in
Agadir and Marrakesh.

Morocco's main import requirements are petroleum products, motor vehicles, building materials,
agricultural and other machinery, chemical products,
sugar, green tea and other foodstuffs.

The trade of Morocco is chiefly with France,
U.S.A., Saudi Arabia, W. Germany, Italy, the United
Kingdom and Spain.

	1985
Imports	*DH*38,675 million
Exports	21,740 million

Trade with U.K.

	1985	1986
Imports from U.K.	£92,657,867	£84,510,000
Exports to U.K.	74,820,377	65,419,000

Currency.—The unit of currency is the *dirham*.
Exchange rate (*see* p. 82).

Communications.—The railway runs south from
Tangier to Sidi Kacem. From this junction, one line
runs eastwards through Fez to Oujda, and another
continues southwards, through Rabat and Casablanca, to Marrakesh. A line running due south from
Oujda skirts the Morocco-Algeria frontier and
reaches Bouarfa. Moroccan railroads cover 1,250
miles and traction is electric or diesel. An extensive
network of well-surfaced roads covers all the main
towns in the kingdom.

British Airways and Royal-Air-Maroc operates services between Casablanca and London. There are air services between Tangier, Agadir (seasonal), Marrakesh and London, and also between Tangier and Gibraltar connecting with London. Royal Air Inter operates internal services. There are also regular services by many airlines with many parts of the world.

Language.—Arabic is the official language. Berber is the vernacular mainly in the mountain regions. French and Spanish are also spoken mainly in the towns. The national daily press consists of 6 Arabic and 5 French newspapers.

Education.—There are government primary, secondary and technical schools. At Fez there is a theological university of great repute in the Moslem world. There is a secular university at Rabat. Schools for special denominations, Jewish and Catholic, are permitted and may receive government grants.

CAPITAL.—ΨRabat (population 893,402). Regional capitals, with municipal population figures as at 1982, are: ΨCasablanca (2,139,204); Marrakesh (439,728); Fez (448,823); Oujda (260,082); Meknes (319,783); Agadir (110,479). The towns of Fez, Marrakesh and Meknes were capitals at various times in Morocco's history.

FLAG.—Red, with green pentagram (the Seal of Solomon).

NATIONAL DAY.—March 3 (Anniversary of the Throne).

BRITISH EMBASSY
17 Boulevard de la Tour Hassan (B.P. 45), Rabat

Ambassador Extraordinary and Plenipotentiary, His Excellency Ronald Archer Campbell Byatt, C.M.G. (1985).
First Secretary, R. Kinchen, M.V.O. (*Head of Chancery/ Commercial, and Consul*).
Defence Attaché, Lt.-Col. G. Latham.
Vice Consul (Tangier), W. A. T. Pulleyblank, M.B.E.

There is a British Consular/Commercial Office at Casablanca.

British Council Representative, J. W. Edmundson, (P.O. Box 427), 22 Avenue Moulay Youssef, Rabat.

BRITISH CHAMBER OF COMMERCE, 291 Boulevard Mohamed V, Casablanca.

MOZAMBIQUE
(República Popular de Moçambique)

President, Joaquim Alberto Chissano, *sworn in,* November 1986.

COUNCIL OF MINISTERS

Prime Minister, Mario da Graca Machung.
Foreign Affairs, Pascoal Mocumbi.
National Defence, Alberto Joaquim Chipande.
Chief of Staff of the Armed Forces, Sebastiao Marcos Mabote.
Co-operation, Jacinto Veloso.
Planning, Mario Machungo.
Minister in the Presidency for State Administration, Jose Oscar Monteiro.
Education, Graca Machel.
Interior, Manuel Antonio.
Security, Mariano de Araujo Matsinha.
Transport and Communications, Armando Emilio Guebuza.
Finance, Abdul Magid Osman.
Health, Fernando Everard do Rosario Vaz.
Information, Teodato Hunguana.
Construction and Water, Joao Salomao.
Trade, Aranda da Silva.

Agriculture, Joao Ferreira.
Industry and Energy, Antonio Branco.
Mineral Resources, John Kachamila.
Justice, Ossumane Ali Dauto.

Area and Population.—The People's Republic of Mozambique lies on the east coast of Africa, and is bounded by Swaziland in the south, South Africa in the south and west, Zimbabwe in the west, Zambia and Malawi in the north-west and Tanzania in the north. It has an area of 309,495 sq. miles (801,590 sq. km.), with a population estimated at 14,000,000 (1986). The official language is Portuguese.

Government.—Mozambique, discovered by Vasco de Gama in 1498, and colonized by Portugal, achieved complete independence from Portugal on June 25, 1975. The date had been agreed in September 1974 by Portugal and *Frelimo (Frente de Libertação de Moçambique)*, the Marxist liberation movement.

Constitution.—The country is governed by a Council of Ministers and by the Permanent Political Committee of the *Frelimo* Party; membership of these two bodies virtually overlaps. No other political parties are permitted. The principal legislative body, the People's Assembly, consists of 216 members nominated by *Frelimo.*

The basis of the economy is subsistence agriculture, but there is an industrial sector based mainly in Beira and Maputo. After giving priority to the development of collective farms and state enterprises in all sectors, the government is now encouraging the private sector and foreign investment, particularly in agriculture and consumer goods production. Main exports are sugar, cashew nuts, copra, cotton, tea and sisal. There are substantial coal deposits in Tete province. Mozambique has a range of aid and co-operation agreements with a number of countries in Eastern Europe and in the West. An agreement of non-aggression and good neighbourliness with South Africa was signed on March 16, 1984 (the Nkomati Accord).

Trade with U.K.

	1985	1986
Imports from U.K.	£11,343,000	£13,175,000
Exports to U.K.	6,908,000	1,335,000

CAPITAL.—Ψ Maputo (pop. 850,000). Other main ports are Beira and Nacala.

FLAG.—From top, three lateral bands of green, black and yellow separated by white stripes, and red half diamond pointing to centre of flag over which is superimposed a yellow star, book, and crossed rifle and hoe.

NATIONAL DAY.—June 25 (Independence Day).

BRITISH EMBASSY
C.P. 55, Av. V. I. Lenine, 310, Maputo.

Ambassador Extraordinary and Plenipotentiary, His Excellency James Nicholas Allan, C.B.E. (1986).
First Secretary, John W. Guy, O.B.E. (*Head of Chancery and Consul*).
Second Secretaries, B. McIntyre; R. F. Terry.

NEPAL
(Sri Nepala Sarkar)

Sovereign, H.M. King Birendra Bir Bikram Shah Dev, *born* Dec. 28, 1945; *succeeded* Jan. 31, 1972; *crowned* Feb. 24, 1975; *married,* Feb. 1970, H.M. Queen Aishwara Rajya Laxmi Devi Shah. *Heir,* H.R.H. Crown Prince Dipendra Bir Bikram Shah Dev, *born,* June 27, 1971.

COUNCIL OF MINISTERS

Prime Minister for Royal Palace Affairs, Defence and General Administration, Marich Man Singh Shrestha.

Foreign Affairs and Land Reforms, Shailendra Kumar Upadhaya.

Works, Tranport and Communications, Hari Bahadur Basnet.

Panchayat and Local Development, Pashupati Shumsher J. B. Rana.

Agriculture, Law and Justice, Hari Narayan Rajauriya.

Forests and Soil Conservation, Hem Bahadur Malla.

Commerce, Bijaya Prakash Thebe.

Water Resources, Yadav Prasad Pant.

Supplies, Parsu Narayan Chaudhari.

Health, Gunjeshwari Prasad Singh.

ROYAL NEPALESE EMBASSY IN LONDON
12A, Kensington Palace Gardens, W8 4QU
[01–229 1594/6231]

Ambassador Extraordinary and Plenipotentiary, His Excellency Ishwari Raj Pandey, G.C.V.O. (1983).

Counsellor, Prabal S. J. B. Rana, C.V.O.

Military Attaché, Lt.-Col. C. B. Gurung.

Attachés, Baikuntha Prasad Aryal; Ghanashyam Lall Joshi.

Area and Population.—Nepal lies between India and the Tibet Autonomous Region of China on the slopes of the Himalayas, and includes Mount Everest (29,028 feet). It has a total area of 54,342 sq. miles (140,747 sq. km.), and a population estimated (1987) at about 17·5 million. The country comprises three distinct horizontal formations. In the south, joining the Indian plains, is the Terai, a fair proportion of which was covered with jungle. It has recently been more widely cultivated but wild life is preserved in parts. The region represents 10 per cent of the total land area and nearly 40 per cent of the population live there. The central belt of the country is hilly, but with many fertile valleys, leading up to the snowline at about 14,000 feet. The hills account for 60 per cent of the area of the country and about 50 per cent of the population. The remainder of the country consists of high mountains which are sparsely inhabited. The country is drained by three great river systems rising within and beyond the Himalayan mountain ranges and eventually flowing into the Ganges in India.

The inhabitants are of mixed stock, with Mongolian characteristics prevailing in the North and Indian in the south. The official religion is Hinduism but there is also a strong Buddhist adherence. Gautama Buddha was born in Nepal.

History and Government.—The country was originally divided into numerous hill clans and petty principalities, but Nepal emerged as a nation in the middle of the 18th Century when its component parts were unified by the warrior Raja of Gorkha, Prithvi Narayan Shah, who founded the present Nepalese dynasty. In 1846 power was seized by Jung Bahadur Rana after a massacre of nobles, and he was the first of a line of hereditary Rana Prime Ministers who ruled Nepal for 104 years. During this time the role of the Monarchs was mainly ceremonial.

In 1950–51 a revolutionary movement achieved its aim of breaking the hereditary power of the Ranas and restoring the Monarchy to its former position. After 10 years, during which various parties and individuals tried their hand at government, the late King Mahendra proscribed all political parties and assumed direct powers on December 16, 1960, with the object of leading a united country to democracy. In 1962 he introduced a new Constitution embodying a tiered, partyless system of panchayat (council) democracy, under which there were elected councils at village level which in turn elect members to district council and thence to zonal councils; a referendum in May 1980 decided in favour of retaining the panchayat system, with some reforms; namely, election to the Rastriaya Panchayat (National Parliament) by universal adult franchise (over 21 years old); selection of the Prime Minister by the Rastriaya Panchayat and responsibility of his government to that body. The King retains certain reserve powers. In a general election in May 1986, 112 members were elected from the 75 districts of Nepal. The King appoints 28 other members, making a total of 140.

Economy.—Nepal exports carpets, textile yarn, fabrics, clothing, jute, rice and other grains, hides, oil seeds, ghi, cattle, timber, etc., and imports cotton goods and yarns, sugar, salt, spices, petrol, metals, etc. Foreign aid supports 60 per cent of the development budget of the Kingdom and tourism is the single largest commercial earner of foreign exchange (U.S.$40·4 million in 1984–85).

Revenue for the fiscal year 1985–86 is estimated at *N Rps.* 4,624·6m; foreign aid *N Rps.* 3,605·6m; and internal borrowing *N Rps.* 1,364·9m.

Trade with U.K.

	1985	1986
Imports from U.K.	£7,395,000	£4,670,000
Exports to U.K.	9,347,000	6,960,000

A State Bank was inaugurated on April 26, 1956, to issue bank notes, regulate the Nepalese currency, fix foreign exchange rates and help in the preparation of a national budget. There are three commercial banks with branches throughout Nepal and three further banks, based only in Kathmandu, established since 1984 with approximately 49 per cent foreign bank participation.

Communications.—Kathmandu is connected with India by a road, the mountain section of which was built by India under the Colombo Plan, and to Tibet by a road to Kodari on the border which was built by the Chinese and opened on May 26, 1967. The Indian-aided Sunauli-Pokhara road (128 miles) was inaugurated in April 1972, and a road between Pokhara and Kathmandu, constructed by the Chinese, was opened in 1973. A link road between Mugling and Naryanghat, completed by the Chinese in 1981, has further improved communications between Kathmandu and the Terai. The East–West Highway (Mahendra Raj Marg) to run the length of the country, is almost complete. Work is in progress from Butwal westwards. Sections of the highway have been built, with aid from India, Great Britain, U.S.S.R., U.S.A. and the Asian Development Bank. British assistance has included the building of an external communications satellite, improving telex and telephone services, and the completion in 1984 of the mountainous Dharan–Dhankuta highway.

There are daily flights from Kathmandu to New Delhi, and frequent flights to Calcutta and Patna. There are also daily flights to Bangkok, a twice weekly direct flight to Dhaka, and regular flights to to Rangoon, Colombo, Hong Kong, Karachi and Dubai. A weekly flight to Frankfurt is scheduled to start in Autumn 1987.

CAPITAL.—Kathmandu, population (1981) 235,000. Other towns of importance are Biratnagar (94,000), Lalitpur (81,000) and Bhaktapur (50,500) and Pokhara (48,500).

FLAG.—Double pennant of crimson with blue border on peaks; white moon with rays in centre of top peak; white quarter sun, recumbent in centre of bottom peak.

NATIONAL DAY.—December 28.

BRITISH EMBASSY
(Lainchaur Kathmandu, P.O. Box 106)

Ambassador Extraordinary and Plenipotentiary, His Excellency Richard Eagleson Gordon Burges Watson, C.M.G. (1987).

First Secretary, M. Hickson, L.V.O. (*Head of Chancery and Consul*).

Defence and Military Attaché, Lt.-Col. F. D. Scotson.

Vice-Consul, N. J. K. Stucley-Houghton.

British Council Representative, P. Moss, (P.O. Box 640), Kanti Path, Kathmandu.

NETHERLANDS (or HOLLAND)
(Koninkrijk der Nederlanden)

Queen of the Netherlands, Her Majesty Queen Beatrix Wilhelmina Armgard, G.C.V.O., *born* Jan. 31, 1938; *married* March 10, 1966, H.R.H. Prince Claus George Willem Otto Frederik Geert of the Netherlands, Jonkheer van Amsberg; *and has issue*, Prince Willem Alexander, *b.* April 27, 1967; Prince Johan Friso, *b.* Sept, 25, 1968; Prince Constantijn Christof, *b.* Oct. 11, 1969; *succeeded*, April 30, 1980, upon the abdication of her mother Queen Juliana.

CABINET

Prime Minister and Minister of General Affairs, Ruud Lubbers (*C.D.A.*).

Deputy P.M. and Minister for Economic Affairs, Dr. Rudolf de Korte (*V.V.D.*).

Social Affairs and Employment, and Netherlands Antillean and Aruban Affairs, Dr. Jan de Koning (*C.D.A.*).

Defence, Dr. Wim van Eekelen (*V.V.D.*).

Finance, Dr. Herman Ruding (*C.D.A.*).

Transport and Waterways, Mrs. Neelie Smit-Kroes (*V.V.D.*).

Education and Science, Dr. Wim Deetman (C.D.A.).

Welfare, Public Health and Culture, Elco Brinkman (*C.D.A.*).

Development Co-operation, Piet Buckman (*C.D.A.*).

Agriculture and Fisheries, Gerrit Braks (*C.D.A.*).

Housing, Physical Planning and Environment, Ed Nijpels (*V.V.D.*).

Justice, Frits Korthals Altes, (*V.V.D.*).

Home Affairs, Cees van Dijk, (*C.D.A.*).

Foreign Affairs, Hans van den Broek (*C.D.A.*).

(*C.D.A.* = Christian Democrats; *V.V.D.* = Liberals.)

ROYAL NETHERLANDS EMBASSY IN LONDON
38 Hyde Park Gate, SW7 5DP
[01–584 5040]

Ambassador Extraordinary and Plenipotentiary, His Excellency Hans Jonkman, G.C.V.O.

Ministers Plenipotentiary, L. W. Veenendaal; R. R. Smit.

Counsellors, A. J. van der Stadt; D. Vries; A. D. H. Simonsz; A. E. Moses.

1st Secretaries, Baroness H. J. C. M. van Lynden; A. C. Brouwer; R. G. de Vos.

Defence, Naval and Air Attaché, Capt. A. H. A. G. Remmen.

Military Attaché, Col. J. Smit.

Area and Population.—The Kingdom of the Netherlands is a maritime country of Western Europe, situated on the North Sea, in lat. 50° 46′–53° 34′ N. and long. 3° 22′–7° 14′ E., consisting of 12 provinces (Eastern and Southern Flevoland being amalgamated to form the twelfth province) and containing a total area of 15,770 sq. miles (40,844 sq. km). The population (1985 U.N. estimate) is 14,484,000. The live birth rate in Jan., 1984 was 12·1 per 1,000 of the population, and the death-rate was 8·3.

The land is generally flat and low, intersected by numerous canals and connecting rivers—in fact, a

NETHERLANDS

network of water courses. The principal rivers are the Rhine, Maas, Yssel and Scheldt.

Language and Literature.—Dutch is a West-Germanic language of Saxon origin, closely akin to Old English and Low German. It is spoken in the Netherlands and the northern part of Belgium. It is also used in the Netherlands Antilles. Afrikaans, one of the two South African languages, has Dutch as its origin, but differs from it in grammar and pronunciation. There are six national papers, four of which are morning papers, and there are many regional daily papers.

Government.—In 1815 the Netherlands became a constitutional Kingdom under King William I, a Prince of Orange-Nassau, a descendant of the house which had taken a leading part in the destiny of the nation since the 16th century. The States-General consists of the *Eerste Kamer* (First Chamber) of 75 members, elected for 4 years by the Provincial Council; and the *Tweede Kamer* (Second Chamber) of 150 members, elected for 4 years by men and women voters of 18 years and upwards. Members of the *Tweede Kamer* are paid.

Production.—The chief agricultural products are potatoes, wheat, rye, barley, sugar beet, cattle, pigs, milk and milk products, cheese, butter, poultry, eggs, beans, peas, vegetables, fruit, flower bulbs, plants and cut flowers and there is an important fishing industry. Among the principal industries are engineering, both mechanical and electrical, electronics, nuclear energy, petro-chemicals and plastics, road vehicles, aircraft and defence equipment, shipbuilding repair, steel, textiles of all types, electrical appliances, metal ware, furniture, paper, cigars, sugar, liqueurs, beer, clothing etc.

In 1985 the production of crude oil was 3,729 million kgs and refined oil products 61,000 million kgs; steel (1984) 5,739 million kgs, and natural gas 80,721 million cubic metres.

Defence.—The armed forces are almost entirely committed to NATO. All ground and air units are assigned to the NATO Central Region, and naval forces to the Atlantic and Channel commands. Total armed forces number 106,183, which includes 48,720 conscripts and 1,495 women. In addition there are over 176,000 reservists. There is compulsory military service of 14–17 months.

Education.—Primary and secondary education is given in both denominational and State schools, the denominational schools being eligible for State assistance on equal terms with the State schools. Attendance at primary school is compulsory. The principal Universities are at Leiden, Utrecht, Groningen, Amsterdam (2), Nijmegen (R.C.) and Rotterdam, and there are technical Universities at Delft (polytechnic); Eindhoven (polytechnic), Enschede (polytechnic) Wageningen (agriculture). Illiteracy is practically non-existent.

Communications.—The total extent of navigable rivers including canals, was 4,845 km. at Jan. 1, 1985, and of metalled roads 97,189 km. In 1985 the total length of the railway system amounted to 2,867 km., of which 1,810 km. were electrified. The mercantile marine in January 1985 consisted of 550 ships of total 3,461,000 gross registered tons. The total length of air routes covered by K.L.M. (Royal Dutch Airlines) in 1985 was 370,640 km.

FINANCE

	1986
Budget Revenue	D.fl. 175,610 m.
Budget Expenditure	194,493 m.

TRADE

The Dutch are traditionally a trading nation. Entrepôt trade, banking and shipping are of particular importance to the economy. The geographical position of the Netherlands, at the mouths of the Rhine, Meuse and Scheldt, brings a large volume of transit trade to and from the interior of Europe to Dutch ports.

Principal trading partners are the Federal Republic of Germany and Belgium/Luxembourg. U.K. supplied 10 per cent of Netherlands imports in 1985 and took 9·5 per cent of Netherlands exports.

Excluding the building industry, the index of industrial production in the Netherlands (1980 = 100) was 101 in 1984 and the index of industrial production per worker (1980 = 100) was 122 in 1984.

	1984	1985
Imports	D.fl. 198,922 m.	D.fl. 215,467 m.
Exports	210,691 m.	225,568 m.

Trade with U.K.

	1985	1986
Imports from U.K.	£7,344,681,000	£5,442,503,000
Exports to U.K.	6,550,735,000	6,615,581,000

SEAT OF GOVERNMENT, The Hague (Den Haag or, in full, 's-Gravenhage). Pop. 443,456.

CAPITAL.—ΨAmsterdam, 996,096 (urban agglomeration). Other principal cities; ΨRotterdam, 571,081; Utrecht, 229,969; Eindhoven, 191,675; Haarlem, 151,025; Groningen, 168,119; Tilburg, 153,812.

FLAG.—Three horizontal bands of red, white and blue.

BRITISH EMBASSY
Lange Voorhout, 10, The Hague, 2514 ED

Ambassador Extraordinary and Plenipotentiary, His Excellency Sir John Margetson, K.C.M.G. (1984).
Counsellors, G. Archer; L. G. Faulkner (*Commercial/Agriculture*).
Defence and Naval Attaché, Capt. R. N. Blair, R.N.
Military and Air Attaché, Lt. Col. R. H. Paterson, O.B.E.
Head of Chancery, A. R. Paul.
H. M. Consul-General, T. W. Sharp.

British Council Representative, J. Andrews, Keizersgracht 343, Amsterdam (Library).
NETHERLANDS-BRITISH CHAMBER OF COMMERCE, The Dutch House, 307–308 High Holborn, WC1V 7LS; U.K. OFFICE, Holland Trade House, Bezuidenhoutseweg 181, 2594 AH The Hague.

OVERSEAS TERRITORY

The Netherlands Antilles comprise certain islands in the West Indies (Curaçao, Bonaire, part of St. Martin, St. Eustatius, and Saba). On January 1, 1986 the neighbouring island of Aruba became a separate territory within the Kingdom of the Netherlands. Both the Netherland Antilles (which have a federal parliament) and Aruba are largely self-governing under the terms of the Realm Statute which took effect on December 29, 1954. The 1983 Constitutional Conference which agreed that Aruba's separate status would begin in 1986 also stated that it would last for about 10 years, after which the island would become fully independent.

The economy of Aruba is based largely upon tourism. The economy of the Netherlands Antilles is based almost entirely on the refining of oil. There are, however, some manufacturing industries in both territories. The soil is too poor to permit large-scale agriculture and most products for consumption, and industrial raw materials must be imported.

Governor, Dr. R. A. Römer (1983).
Prime Minister, Don Martina.
Governor of Aruba, F. B. Tromp.
Prime Minister, J. Henny Eman.

Trade with U.K.

Netherlands Antilles	1985	1986
Imports from U.K.	£19,844,000	£24,232,000
Exports to U.K.	163,236,000	79,085,000

The capital of Curaçao is ΨWillemstad (pop. over 100,000), of Aruba, ΨOranjestad; of Bonaire, Ψ Kralendijk; of St. Martin, Philipsburg; of Statius (St. Eustatius), Oranjestad; and of Saba, Bottom.

NICARAGUA
(República de Nicaragua)

President, Sr. Daniel Ortega Saavedra, *inaugurated,* Jan. 10, 1985.
Vice-President, Sr. Sergio Ramírez Mercado.

MINISTERS

Foreign, Fr. Miguel d'Escoto.
Defence, Humberto Ortega.
Minister of the Interior, Tomás Borge.
External Co-operation, Henry Ruiz.
Agriculture, Jaime Wheelock.
Industry, Emilio Baltodano.
Minister of the Presidency, René Núñez.
Foreign Trade, Dr. Alejandro Martínez.
Trade, Ramón Cabrales.
Transport, William Ramírez.
Finance, William Hupper.
Housing, Mauricio Valenzuala.
Health, Dora María Téllez.
Education, Fr. Fernando Cardenal.
Justice, Dr. Rodrigo Reyes.
Culture, Fr. Ernesto Cardenal.
Environment, Miguel E. Vigil.
Labour, Benedicto Meneses.
First Vice-Minister of the Presidency, Luis Carrión.

NICARAGUAN EMBASSY IN LONDON
8 Gloucester Road, SW7 4PP
[01–584 4365]

Ambassador Extraordinary and Plenipotentiary, His Excellency Señor Francisco José d'Escoto (1981).
First Secretary, Sr. Patricio Cranshaw.

Nicaragua is the largest State of Central America, with a long seaboard on both the Atlantic and Pacific Oceans, situated between 10° 45′–15° N. lat. and 83° 40′–87° 38′ W. long., containing an area of 50,193 sq. miles (130,000 sq. km.). It has a population (1985 U.N. estimate) of 3,272,000, of whom about three-quarters are of mixed blood. Another 15 per cent are white, mostly of pure Spanish descent and the remaining 10 per cent are Indians or negroes. The latter group includes the Mosquitos, who live on the Atlantic coast and were formerly under British protection.

Government.—The eastern coast of Nicaragua was touched by Columbus in 1502, and in 1518 was overrun by Spanish forces under Davila, and formed part of the Spanish Captaincy-General of Guatemala until 1821, when its independence was secured. In 1927, Augusto Cesar Sandino began a guerrilla war against the occupation of Nicaragua by U.S. Marines, which continued until they were expelled in 1933. Sandino was assassinated by Anastasio Somoza, Director of the National Guard, and in 1936 Somoza assumed the Presidency. He was succeeded in power by his sons Luis and Anastasio Somoza, until 1979 when the family and the National Guard were overthrown by guerrillas of the Sandinista National Liberation Front. A Junta of National Reconstruction subsequently took power.

Elections for President, Vice-President and a National Assembly were held on Nov. 4, 1984, and on Jan. 10, 1985 replaced the Junta and the Council of State. Distribution of seats in the National Assembly was: Sandinista National Liberation Front 61; Democratic Conservative Party 14; Independent Liberal Party 9; People's Christian Social Party 6; Communist Party 2; Socialist Party 2; Marxist–Leninist Popular Action Movement 2.

On Jan. 9, 1987, President Ortega signed the new constitution but almost immediately re-introduced the state of emergency.

Agriculture and Industry.—The country is mainly agricultural. The major crops are cotton, coffee (30 per cent of total export earnings), sugar cane, tobacco, sesame and bananas. Beans, rice, maize and ipecacuanha, livestock and timber production are also important. However, fishing, forestry, grain and cattle production have been hit by the civil war in the main growing areas. Nicaragua possesses deposits of gold and silver.

Communications.—There are 252 miles of railway, all on the Pacific side and approximately 5,500 miles of telegraph. There are 51 radio stations and two television stations in Managua. An automatic telephone system has been installed in the capital and extended to all major cities. A ground station for satellite communication was inaugurated in 1973. Transport except on the Pacific slope, is still attended with difficulty but many new roads have either been opened or are under construction. The Inter-American Highway runs from the Honduras frontier in the north to the Costa Rican border in the south; the interoceanic highway runs from the Corinto on the Pacific coast via Managua to Rama, where there is a natural waterway to Bluefields on the Atlantic. The country's main airport is at Managua. The chief port is Corinto on the Pacific.

Language and Literature.—The official language of the country is Spanish and the majority profess Catholicism, although the English language and the Moravian Church are widespread on the Atlantic coast. There are 3 daily newspapers published at Managua, apart from the official Gazette (*La Gaceta*). A national literacy campaign in 1980 has reduced illiteracy to 12 per cent. There are universities at León and Managua.

Trade with U.K.

	1985	1986
Imports from U.K.	£6,368,000	£7,349,000
Exports to U.K.	1,324,000	1,307,000

Considerable quantities of foodstuffs are imported as well as cotton goods, jute, iron and steel, machinery and petroleum products. The chief exports are cotton, coffee, beef, gold, sugar, cottonseed and bananas.

CAPITAL.—Managua, population 615,000. The centre was almost totally destroyed in the earthquake of December 1972. León, 158,577; Granada, 72,640; Masaya, 78,308; Chinandega, 144,291.

FLAG.—Horizontal stripes of blue, white and blue, with the Nicaraguan coats of arms in the centre of the white stripe.

NATIONAL DAY.—September 15.

British Ambassador, (resident at San José, Costa Rica).

NIGER
(République du Niger)

President, Maj. Gen. Seyni Kountché, *assumed power*, April 15, 1974 (*also holds Defence and Interior portfolios*).

MINISTERS

Prime Minister, Hamid Algabid.
Civil Service and Labour, Quartermaster Mamadou Beidari.
Youth and Sports, Maj. Toumba Boubacar.
Culture and Communications, Daouda Diallo.
National and Higher Education and Research, Illa Maikassoua.
Public Works and Housing, Yacouba Moumouni.
Minister Delegate for Interior, Amadou Fiti Maiga.
Public Health and Social Affairs, Abdou Moudi.
Agriculture, Allele Elhadji Habibou.
Finance, Boukary Adji.
Mines and Energy, Sani Koutoubi.
Justice, Hadj Nadjir.
Commerce, Industry and Transport, Amadou Nouhou.
Hydrology and Environment, Attaher Darkoye.
Planning, Almoustapha Soumaila.
Foreign Affairs and Co-operation, Mahamane Sani Bako.
Animal Resources, Salha Haladou.
Minister Delegate to the P.M., Public Establishments, State Enterprises and Parastatals, Maina Moussa Ooukar.
Sec. of State for National Education, Amadou Madougou.
Sec. of State for Interior, Khamed Abdoulaye.

Situated in West Central Africa, between 12° and 24° N. and 0° and 16° E., Niger has common boundaries with Algeria and Libya in the north, Chad, Nigeria, Benin, Mali and Burkina.

It has an area of about 489,191 sq. miles (1,267,000 sq. km.), with a population (estimate, 1985) of 6,475,000. Apart from a small region along the Niger Valley in the south-west near the capital the country is entirely savannah or desert. The main ethnic groups are the Hausa (54 per cent.) in the south, the Songhai and Djerma in the south-west, the Fulani, the Beriberi-Manga, and the nomadic Tuareg in the north. The official language is French.

The first French expedition arrived in 1891 and the country was fully occupied by 1914. It decided on

December 18, 1958, to remain an autonomous republic within the French Community; full independence outside the Community was proclaimed on August 3, 1960. Special agreements with France, covering financial and cultural matters, technical assistance, defence, etc., were signed in Paris on April 24, 1961. These are now being revised.

The constitution of Niger, adopted on November 8, 1960, provided for a presidential system of government, modelled on that of the United States and the French Fifth Republic, and a single Chamber National Assembly. In April 1974 Lt.-Col. Seyni Kountché seized power, suspended the Constitution, dissolved the National Assembly, and suppressed all political organizations. He then set up a Supreme Military Council with himself as President.

Finance.—The currency of Niger is the *Franc CFA*. The 1986 General Budget allocation was *CFA* 87,930 million.

Trade.—The cultivation of ground-nuts and the production of livestock are the main industries and provide two of the main exports. A company formed by the Government, the French Atomic Energy Authority and private interests is exploiting uranium deposits at Arlit, and this is the main export. Value of imports in 1985 was *CFA* 123,977 m.; exports was *CFA* 77,940 m.

Trade with U.K.

	1985	1986
Imports from U.K.	£12,076,000	£10,370,000
Exports to U.K.	399,000	850,000

CAPITAL.—Niamey (399,100).

FLAG.—Three horizontal stripes, orange, white and green with an orange disc in the middle of the white stripe.

NATIONAL DAY.—December 18.

British Ambassador, (resident at Abidjan, Côte d'Ivoire).

NORWAY
(Kongeriket Norge)

King, Olav V, K.G., K.T., G.C.B., G.C.V.O., *b.* July 2, 1903; *succeeded,* Sept. 21, 1957, on death of his father King Haakon VII; *married* March 21, 1929, Princess Märtha of Sweden (*born* March 28, 1901; *died* April 5, 1954); having issue, Harald (*see below*) and two daughters.

Heir-Apparent, H.R.H. Prince Harald, G.C.V.O., *b.* Feb. 21, 1937; *m.* Aug. 29, 1968, Sonja Haraldsen, and has issue Princess Märtha Louise, *b.*Sept. 22, 1971; and Prince Haakon Magnus, *b.* July 20, 1973.

CABINET

Prime Minister, Ms. Gro Harlem Brundtland.
Foreign Affairs, Thorvald Stoltenberg.
Cultural and Scientific Affairs, Hallvard Bakke.
Environment, Ms. Sissel Rønbeck.
Industry, Finn Kristensen.
Petroleum and Energy, Arne Øien.
Local Government and Labour, William Engseth.
Development Co-operation, Ms. Vesla Vetlesen.
Trade, Kurt Mosbakk.
Fisheries, Bjarne Mørk Eidem.
Defence, Johan Jørgen Holst.
Transport and Communications, Kjell Borgen.
Justice, Ms. Helen Bøsterud.
Finance, Gunnar Berge.
Church and Education, Ms. Kirsti Kolle Grøndahl.
Health and Social Affairs, Ms. Tove Strand Gerhardsen.
Agriculture, Ms. Gunhild Øyangen.
Consumer Affairs and Government Administration, Ms. Anne-Lise Bakken.

ROYAL NORWEGIAN EMBASSY IN LONDON
Offices: 25 Belgrave Square, SW1X 8QD
[01–235 7151]

Ambassador Extraordinary and Plenipotentiary, His Excellency Rolf Busch (1982).
Minister-Counsellor, Kai Lie.
Counsellors, Jan Flatla (*Press and Cultural*); Viggo Jan Olsen (*Fisheries*); Eva Bugge (*Economic*); Jan Enger (*Commercial*).
First Secretaries, Kjell Harald Dalen (*Political*); Øistein Bergh (*Consul*).
Second Secretaries, Pål Gretland (*Economic*); Anna Rikter-Svendsen (*Press, Information and Cultural*).

Area and Population.—Norway ("The Northern Way"), a kingdom in the northern and western portion of the Scandinavian peninsula, was founded in 872. It is 1,752 km. in length, its greatest width about 430 km. The length of the coastline is 2,542 km., and the frontier between Norway and the neighbouring countries is 2,542 km. (Sweden 1,619 km., Finland 727 km. and U.S.S.R. 196 km.). It is divided into 19 counties (*fylker*) and comprises an area of 149,282 sq. miles (386,638 sq. km.), of which Svalbard and Jan Mayen have a combined area of 24,101 sq. km., with a population (estimated, Jan. 1986) of 4,159,335.

The Norwegian coastline is extensive, deeply indented with numerous fjords, and fringed with an immense number of rocky islands. The surface is mountainous, consisting of elevated and barren tablelands, separated by deep and narrow valleys. At the North Cape the sun does not appear to set from the second week in May to the last week in July, causing the phenomenon known as the *Midnight Sun*; conversely, there is no apparent sunrise from about Nov. 18 to Jan. 23. During the long winter nights are seen the multiple coloured *Northern Lights* or *Aurora Borealis*, which have a maximum intensity in a line crossing North America from Alaska to Labrador and Northern Europe to the Arctic coast and Siberia.

Language and Literature.—Old Norse literature is among the most ancient and richest in Europe. Norwegian in both its present forms is closely related to other Scandinavian languages. Independence from Denmark (1814) and resurgent nationalism led to the development of "new Norwegian" based on dialects, which now has equal official standing with "bokmål", in which Danish influence is more obvious. This was formed in the time of the Reformation, and Ludvig Holberg (1684–1754) is regarded as the father of Norwegian literature, though the modern period begins with the patriotic and romantic writings of Henrik Wergeland (1808–1845). Some of the famous names are Henrik Ibsen (1828–1906), Bjørnstjerne Bjørnson (1832–1910), Nobel Prizewinner in 1903, and the novelists Jonas Lie (1833–1908), Alexander Kielland (1849–1906), Knut Hamsun (1859–1952) and Sigrid Undset (1882–1949), the latter two both Nobel Prizewinners, and the latter a champion of Norwegian womanhood. In 1987 there were 161 daily newspapers.

Government.—From 1397 to 1814 Norway was united with Denmark, and from Nov. 4, 1814, with Sweden, under a personal union which was dissolved on June 7, 1905, when Norway regained complete independence. Under the constitution of May 17, 1814, the *Storting* (Parliament) itself elects one-quarter of its members to constitute the *Lagting* (Upper Chamber), the other three-quarters forming the *Odelsting* (Lower Chamber). Legislative questions alone are dealt with by both parts in separate sittings.

The three-party coalition government fell on May 1, 1986, when it lost a vote of confidence, and was succeeded by a minority Labour government which took office on May 9, 1986.

Production.—The cultivated area is about 8,636 sq. km. (2·3 per cent of total surface area); forests cover nearly 25 per cent; the rest consists of highland pastures or uninhabitable mountains.

The *Gulf Stream* pours from 140 to 170 million cubic feet of warm water per second into the sea around Norway and causes the temperature to be higher than the average for the latitude. It brings shoals of herring and cod into the fishing grounds and causes a warm current of air over the west coast, making it possible to cultivate potatoes and barley in latitudes which in other countries are perpetually frozen. In normal years the quantity of fish caught by Norwegian fishing vessels is greater than that of any other European country except U.S.S.R. In 1986 the total catch amounted to 1,960,759 tonnes.

The chief industries are manufactures, agriculture and forestry, fisheries, mining, production of metals and ferro-alloys and shipping. Also in recent years industries providing both manufactured products and services for the development of North Sea oil and gas resources have assumed growing importance. In 1986, the total workforce was 2,071,000 of which 371,000 persons were employed in Norwegian industry. Manufactures are aided by great resources of hydro-electric power. Actual production in 1986 amounted to 97,156 Gwh.

Defence.—Norway is a member of the North Atlantic Treaty Organization, and the Headquarters of Allied Forces, Northern Europe, is situated near Oslo. The period of compulsory national service is 15 months (without refresher training) in the Navy and Air Force, and 12 months (with refresher training) in the Army. In March 1978 Norway committed an infantry battalion with additional support to the U.N. Interim Force in the Lebanon.

Education from 7 to 16 is free and compulsory in the "basic schools" maintained by the municipalities with State grants-in-aid. The majority of the pupils receive post-compulsory schooling at "upper secondary" schools, colleges of education (19) regional colleges akin to polytechnics (12), universities (4) and other university-level specialist institutions.

Communications.—The total length of railways open at the end of 1986 was 4,219 km., excluding private lines. There are 86,147 km. of public roads in Norway (including urban streets). At the end of 1986, 2,780,311 road motor vehicles were registered.

Scheduled internal air services are operated by Scandinavian Airlines System (SAS) on behalf of Det Norske Luftfartselskap (DNL), by Braathens South American and Far East Airtransport (SAFE), and by Widerόes Flyveselskap A.S.

The Mercantile Marine, 1986, consisted of 1,355 vessels of 7,197,036 gross tons (vessels above 100 gross tons, excluding fishing boats, floating whaling factories, tugs, salvage vessels, icebreakers and similar types of vessel). The fleet ranks seventh among the merchant navies of the world.

FINANCE, 1986

Total Revenue	*K*240,905,920
Total Expenditure..........	228,340,220

TRADE

	1985	1986
	million *Kroner*	
Total imports	194,308	211,054
Total exports	235,383	194,047

Trade with U.K.

	1985	1986
Imports from U.K.	£1,140,680	£1,147,790
Exports to U.K.	4,444,292	3,265,157

The chief imports are raw materials, motor vehicles, chemicals, motor spirit, fuel and other oils; coal, ships and machinery; together with manufactures of silk, cotton and wool. The exports consist chiefly of crude oil and gas, manufactured goods, fish and products of fish (as canned fish, whale oils), pulp, paper, iron ore and pyrites, nitrate of lime, stone, calcium carbide, aluminium, ferro-alloys, zinc, nickel, cyanamide, etc.

CAPITAL.—ΨOslo (incl. Aker). Pop. (Jan. 1986), 449,337. Other towns are ΨTrondheim, 134,426; ΨBergen, 207,916; ΨStavanger, 95,089; ΨKristiansand, 62,640; ΨDrammen, 50,855; ΨTromsø, 48,109.

FLAG.—Red, with white-bordered blue cross.

NATIONAL DAY.—May 17 (Constitution Day).

BRITISH EMBASSY
Thomas Heftyesgate 8,0264 Oslo 2.

Ambassador Extraordinary and Plenipotentiary, His Excellency John Adam Robson, C.M.G. (1987).

Counsellors, R. G. Short, M.V.O. (*Head of Chancery and Consul General*); C. P. Burdess, (*Economic*).

First Secretaries, J. Venning; D. O. Hay-Edie.

Defence and Air Attaché, Wg. Cdr. J. S. Cresswell, R.A.F.

Naval Attaché, Cdr. H. L. Foxworthy, R.N.

Military Attaché, Lt. Col. R. A. Gamble.

BRITISH CONSULAR OFFICES

There is a British Consular Office at *Oslo* and Honorary Consulates at *Bergen, Tromsø, Alesund, Kristiansund N., Stavanger, Trondheim, Kristiansund S., Haugesund* and *Harstad.*

British Council Representative, P. A. Thompson, Fridtjof Nansens Plass 5,0160, Oslo 1.

SVALBARD
(Spitsbergen and Bear Island)

By Treaty (Feb. 9, 1920) the sovereignty of Norway over the Spitsbergen ("Pointed Mountain") Archipelago was recognized by the Great Powers and other interested nations, and on Aug. 14, 1925, Norway assumed sovereignty. In September, 1941, Allied forces (British, Canadian and Norwegian) landed on the main island. After destruction of the accumulated stocks of coal and dismantling of mining machinery and the wireless installation, the Norwegian inhabitants (about 600) were evacuated to a British port and the Russians (about 1,500) to the U.S.S.R. After the war the Norwegian mining plants were rebuilt. 288,000 metric tons of coal were extracted from Norwegian mines in Svalbard in 1980.

The Svalbard Archipelago lies between 74°–81° N. lat. and between 10°–35° E. long., with an estimated area of 24,295 square miles. The archipelago consists of a main island, known as Spitsbergen (15,200 sq. miles); North East Land, closely adjoining and separated by Hinlopen Strait; the Wiche Islands, separated from the mainland by Olga Strait; Barents and Edge Islands, separated from the mainland by Stor Fjord (or Wybe Jansz Water); Prince Charles Foreland, to the W.; Hope Island, to the S.E.; Bear Island (68 square miles) 127 miles to the S.; with many similar islands in the neighbourhood of the main group. In addition to those engaged in coal-mining, the archipelago is also visited by hunters for seals, foxes and polar bears.

South Cape is 355 miles from the Norwegian Coast. Ice Fjord is 520 miles from Tromsø, 650 miles from Murmansk, and 1,300 miles from Aberdeen. Transit from Tromsø to Green Harbour 2 to 3 days; from Aberdeen 5 to 6 days.

JAN MAYEN, an island in the Arctic Ocean (70° 49′–71° 9′ N. lat. and 7° 53′–9° 5′ W. long.) was joined to Norway by law of Feb. 27, 1930.

Norwegian Antarctic

BOUVET ISLAND (54° 26′ S. lat. and 3° 24′ E. long.) was declared a dependency of Norway by law of Feb. 27, 1930.

PETER THE FIRST ISLAND (68° 48′ S. lat. and 90° 35′ W. long.), was declared a dependency of Norway by resolution of Government, May 1, 1931.

PRINCESS RAGNHILD LAND (from 70° 30′ to 68° 40′ S. lat. and 24° 15′ to 33° 30′ E. long.) has been claimed as Norwegian since Feb. 17, 1931.

QUEEN MAUD LAND.—On Jan. 14, 1939, the Norwegian Government declared the area between 20° W. and 45° E., adjacent to Australian Antarctica, to be Norwegian territory.

OMAN
(The Sultanate of Oman)

Sultan, Qaboos Bin-Said, *succeeded* on deposition of Sultan Said bin Taimur, July 23, 1970.

(The Sultan acts as his own Prime Minister, Minister of Foreign Affairs, Defence and Finance.)

COUNCIL OF MINISTERS

Agriculture and Fisheries, H.E. Muhammad bin Abdullah bin Zahir al Hinai.

Commerce and Industry, H.E. Col. Salim bin Abdullah al Ghazali.

Communications, H.E. Hamoud bin Abdullah al Harthi.

Deputy P.M., Security and Defence, H.H. Sayyid Fahr bin Taimur Al Said.

Minister of State for Defence, H.E. Brig. Sayyid al Mutassim bin Hamoud Al Bu Saidi.

Office of the Personal Representative of H.M. The Sultan, H.H. Sayyid Thuwaini bin Shihab Al Said.

Education and Youth Affairs, H.E. Yahya bin Mahfuth al Manthari.

Electricity and Water, H.E. Khalfan bin Nasr al Wahaibi.

Environment, H.H. Sayyid Shabib bin Taimur Al Said.

Deputy P.M., Financial and Economic Affairs, H.E. Qais bin Abdul Munim al Zawawi.

Minister of State for Foreign Affairs, H.E. Yusuf bin Alawi bin Abdullah.

Health, H.E. Dr. Mubarak bin Salih al Khaduri.

Housing, H.E. Abdullah bin Hamad bin Saif Al Busaidi.

Information, H.E. Abdul Aziz bin Muhammad al Rowas.

Interior, H.E. Sayyid Badr bin Saud bin Harib al Bu Saidi.

Justice, Awqaf and Islamic Affairs, H.E. Sayyid Hilal bin Hamad Al Bu Saidi.

Office of the Deputy Prime Minister for Legal Affairs, H.H. Sayyid Fahd bin Mahmoud Al Said.

National Heritage and Culture, H.H. Sayyid Faisal bin Ali Al Said.

Petroleum and Minerals, H.E. Said bin Ahmad bin Said al Shanfari.

Posts, Telegraphs and Telephones, H.E. Ahmid bin Suwaidan al Balushi.

Regional Municipalities, H.E. Sheikh Muhammad bin Ali al Qutbi.

Special Adviser to H.M. The Sultan, H.E. Sayyid Hamad bin Hamoud.

Social Affairs and Labour, H.E. Shaikh Mustahail bin Ahmad al Mashani.

President, Consultative Council of the State, H.E. Salim bin Nasr Al Busaidi.

Office of the Minister of State and Wali of Dhofar, H.E. Sayyid Hilal bin Saud bin Harib al Bu Saidi.

President, Diwan of Royal Court Affairs, H.E. Sayyid Saif bin Hamad bin Saud.

First ADC to H.M. The Sultan and President of the Palace Office, H.E. Maj. Gen. Ali bin Majid al Mamari.

Secretary to the Council of Ministers, H.E. Sayyid Hamoud bin Faisal Al Bu Saidi.

OMAN EMBASSY IN LONDON
44a/b Montpelier Square, SW7 1JJ
[01–584 6782/3/4]

Ambassador, His Excellency Hussain bin Mohamed bin Ali (1984).

The independent Sultanate of Oman lies at the eastern corner of the Arabian Peninsula. Its seaboard is nearly 1,000 miles long and extends from near Tibat on the west coast of the Musandam Peninsula round to Ras Darbat Ali, with the exception of the stretch between Dibba and Kalba on the east coast which belongs to Sharjah and Fujairah of the United Arab Emirates. Ras Darbat Ali marks the boundary between the Sultanate and the People's Democratic Republic of Yemen. The Sultanate extends inland to the borders of the Rub al Khali, or "Empty Quarter" of the Arabian Desert.

The area of Oman has been estimated at 82,030 sq. miles (212,457 sq. km.), and the population at 1,500,000 (1986). The inhabitants of the North are for the most part Arab but along the coast there is a strong infusion of negro blood, while in the Capital Area which stretches from Muscat to Seeb there are large communities of Hindus, Khojas and Baluch, in addition to Zanzibaris of Omani origin. In Dhofar there is also an infusion of negro blood around Salalah, but in the mountains the inhabitants are either of pure Arab descent or belong to tribes of pre-Arab origin, the Qarra and Mahra, who speak their own dialects of semitic origin.

Physically and historically modern Oman can be split into two main parts, the North and the South, divided by a large tract of desert. *Northern Oman* has three main sections. The *Batinah*, the coastal plain, varies in width from 30 miles in the neighbourhood of Suwaiq to almost nothing at Muscat where the mountains descend abruptly to the sea. The plain is fertile, with date gardens extending over its full length of 150 miles. The *Hajjar*, a mountain spine running from north east to south west, reaching nearly 10,000 feet in height on Jebal Akhdar. For the most part the mountains are barren, but numerous valleys penetrate the central massif of Jabal Akhdar and in these there is considerable cultivation irrigated by wells or a system of underground canals called *falajs* which tap the water table. The two plateaus leading from the western slopes of the mountains, the *Dhahirah*, in the north and the *Sharqia* in the south east also have centres of settlements and cultivation. They fall from an average height of 1,000 feet into the sands of the Empty Quarter. The north is separated from the south by nearly 400 miles of inhospitable country crossed by one trunk road, the only land link. *Dhofar*, the southern province, is the only part of the Arabian Peninsula to be touched by the south west monsoon. Temperatures are more moderate than in the north and sugar cane and coconuts are grown on the coastal plain, while cattle are bred on the mountains.

Government.—A Consultative Council for the State was established by Sultanic decree on October 18, 1981. The Council is a nominated body consisting of 55 members (36 representing the public and 19 representing the government). The Council's jurisdiction is confined to economic affairs and social development.

Finance.—The main unit is the *Rial Omani* of 1,000 *baiza*.

Commerce and Trade.—Trade is mainly with the United Kingdom, Japan, the Netherlands, U.S., West Germany, France and India. Total imports for the year 1985 were *OR*1,088,900,000. Chief imports were machinery, cars, building materials, refined petroleum and food and telecommunications equipment.

Trade with U.K.

	1985	1986
Imports from U.K.	£489,900,000	£399,600,000
Exports to U.K.	69,000,000	87,200,000

Production.—Petroleum Development (Oman) Ltd. (owned 60 per cent by Oman Government and 34 per cent by Shell) began exporting oil in 1967. Concessions (off and on shore) are held by several major international companies. The current level of oil production is over 520,000 barrels per day.

Development.—For many years the Sultanate was a poor country with a total annual income of less than £1,000,000. The advent of oil revenues since 1967 and the change of régime in 1970 led to the initiation of a wide-ranging development programme, especially concerned with health, education and communications. New hospitals have been completed in the main provincial centres and there are now 40 hospitals with 2,861 beds, and 668 schools, with 247,546 pupils, were in operation in 1986. A gas turbine power station operates at Rusail, where there is also a 200 plot industrial estate. There is a desalination plant near Muscat and flour, animal feed, cement and copper production facilities.

Communications.—Since 1972 ships have been using Port Qaboos at Matrah, where eight deep water berths have been constructed as part of the new harbour facilities.

The telegraph office, an automatic telephone service in Muscat and Matrah and an international telephone service are operated by the General Telecommunications Organisation. There are now good tarmac roads linking most main population centres of the country with the coast and with the towns of the U.A.E. There is now 3,800 km. of asphalted road in the Sultanate.

CAPITAL.—Ψ Muscat, population (estimated), 200,000. The commercial centre has grown around Mutrah, 3 miles away and the main port, and Ruwi. The main towns on the northern coast are Sur, Barka and Sohar, all ports. The main town of Dhofar is Salalah, and Raysut and Murbat are the ports.

FLAG.—Red, green and white with crossed daggers in red sector.

NATIONAL DAY.—November 18.

BRITISH EMBASSY
P.O. Box 300, Muscat

Ambassador Extraordinary and Plenipotentiary, His Excellency Robert John Alston, C.M.G. (1986).
Counsellor, A. M. Layden (*Head of Chancery*).
Defence Attaché, Brig. M. J. Smith.
Naval and Air Attaché, Cdr. A. R. W. Ogilvy, A.F.C., R.N
First Secretaries, D. S. Watson; R. French.
British Council Representative, E. K. Jones, P.O. Box 7090, Jibroo, Oman.

PAKISTAN
(Islami Jamhuriya-e-Pakistan)

President, Gen. Mohammad Zia-ul-Haq, *assumed power*, July 1977; *elected*, Dec. 19, 1984.

CABINET MINISTERS

Prime Minister, Mohammad Khan Junejo (*also responsible for Cabinet Division, Establishment, Political, Science and Technology, Population, Defence, Culture and Tourism*).
Chairman of the Senate, Sen. Ghulam Ishaq Khan.
Speaker, National Assembly, Sardar Wazir Ahmad Jogezai.
Education, Health, Special Education and Social Welfare, Sen. Naseem Ahmad Aheer.
Finance and Economic Affairs, Petroleum and Natural Resources, Mohammad Yasin Khan Wattoo.
Commerce, Planning and Development, Sen. Dr. Mahbubul Haq.
Food, Agriculture and Co-operatives, Sen. Mir Mohammad Ibrahim.
Foreign Affairs, Sen. Sahabzada Yaqub Khan.
Housing and Works, Haji Mohammad Hanif Tayyab.
Information, Broadcasting, Water and Power, Kazi Abdul Majid Abid.
Industries and Production, Chaudhry Shujaat Hussain.
Communications and Railways, Mohammad Aslam Khan Khattak.
Justice, Parliamentary Affairs and Interior, Sen. Wasim Ahmad Sajjad.
Labour, Manpower and Overseas Pakistanis, Shah Mohammad Pasha Khuro.
Religious and Minority Affairs, Haji Mohammad Saifullah Khan.
State and Frontier Regions, Kashmir Affairs, Syed Qasim Shah.
Federal Minister, Local Government and Rural Development, Iqbal Ahmad Khan.

PAKISTAN EMBASSY
35 Lowndes Square, SW1X 9JN
[01–235 2044]

Ambassador Extraordinary and Plenipotentiary, His Excellency Mr. Shaharyar M. Khan (1987).
Ministers, Karam Elahi; Nawabzada Mehboob Ali Khan (*Political*); Raziuddin Shaikh (*Information*).
Defence Attaché, Cdre N. M. Siddiqui.

Area and Population.—The Islamic Republic of Pakistan consists of country situated to the north-west of the Indian sub-continent, bordered by Iran, Afghanistan, the disputed territory of Kashmir, and India. It covers a total area of 307,374 sq. miles (746,045 sq. km.). The Government of Pakistan census in 1981 showed a population figure of 83,780,000 (1985 U.N. estimate, 96,180,000). Of these, about 95 per cent are Moslems, about 1 per cent Hindus, 3·5 per cent Christians, and 0·5 per cent Buddhists.

Running through Pakistan are five great rivers, the Indus, Jhelum, Chenab, Ravi and Sutlej. The upper reaches of these rivers are in Kashmir, and their sources in the Himalayas.

Government.—Pakistan was constituted as a Dominion under the Indian Independence Act, 1947, which received Royal Assent on July 18, 1947. In terms of the Act the Dominion of Pakistan consisted of former territories of British India. The States of Bahawalpur and Khairpur (in Punjab and Sind), with a Muslim population of almost 80 per cent and with Muslim rulers, acceded to Pakistan in October, 1947. The following States also acceded to Pakistan: the Baluchistan States of Kalat, Mekran, Las Bela and Kharan, and the North-West Frontier States of Amb, Chitral, Dir and Swat. (The States of Junagadh and Manavadar which had acceded to Pakistan were occupied by India on November 8, 1947.) Boundaries of the Provinces of East Bengal and of Punjab (West Punjab) were defined by a Boundary Commission. Thus, until 1972, when East Pakistan seceded Pakistan consisted of two geographical units, West and East Pakistan, which were separated by about 1,100 miles of Indian territory.

Pakistan became a Republic on March 23, 1956, when a Parliamentary Constitution came into force. On October 7, 1958, however, this Constitution was abrogated and Pakistan came under martial law.

The first general elections ever held in Pakistan on a basis of "one man, one vote", were held in Dec. 1970 and Jan. 1971. The Awami League in East Pakistan, led by Shiekh Mujibur Rahman, and the Pakistan People's Party in West Pakistan, led by Zulfikar Ali Bhutto, won large majorities. Following the elections there was total disagreement between the two main parties on the question of a new Constitution for Pakistan, Sheikh Mujib insisting on complete autonomy for East Pakistan. The proposed opening of the National Assembly at Dacca on March 25, 1971, was postponed and civil war broke out. East Pakistan seceded by unilateral declaration the following day. Fighting continued until Dec. 1971 when a ceasefire was arranged, and "The Democratic Government of Bangladesh" was formally proclaimed on April 17, 1972.

Following general elections in March 1977 and allegations of vote-rigging the Armed Forces under Gen. Zia-ul-Haq assumed power on July 5, 1977 and imposed martial law throughout the country. The military government scheduled new general elections for October 1977, but these were postponed. Gen. Zia declared himself President on Sept. 16, 1978. In Dec. 1984 Gen Zia got a five-year mandate as a civilian President through a national referendum. There was a general election to a National Assembly on Feb. 25, 1985. In March 1985 President Zia nominated Mohammad Khan Junejo as Prime Minister who received a vote of confidence by the National Assembly. Martial law was lifted on Dec. 30, 1985.

Education.—Formal education in Pakistan is organized into five stages. These are five years of primary education (5–9 years), three years of middle or lower secondary (general or vocational), two years of upper secondary, two years of higher secondary (intermediate) and two to five years of higher education in colleges and universities. Education is free to upper secondary level. It is anticipated that primary education will become universal for boys by mid-1985 and for girls by mid-1988.

At primary level enrolment has increased to 6·5 million in 1984–85, and the number of schools to 75,000. At the middle level enrolment has increased to 1·7 million in 1984–85, and the number of schools to 6,200. At the upper secondary level enrolment increased to 570,000 in 1984–85.

Provincial Governments are responsible for the total financial support of the government institutions and for grants to non-government institutions. But policy making is authorized by the national Government, which makes annual grants. In 1986, 24 per cent of adults were estimated as being literate.

Production.—Pakistan's economy is chiefly based on agriculture. The principal crops are cotton, rice, wheat, sugar cane, maize and tobacco. There are large deposits of rock salt. Pakistan has one of the longest irrigation systems in the world. The total area irrigated is 33 million acres.

Pakistan also produces hides and skins, leather, wool, fertilizers, paints and varnishes, soda ash, paper, cement, fish, carpets, sports goods, surgical appliances and engineering goods, including switch-gear, transformers, cables and wires.

Trade.—Pakistan imported manufactured goods and raw materials to the value of *Rupees* 89,778 million in 1984–85 and exported mainly agricultural products valued at *Rupees* 38,039 million. Principal imports are listed as: petroleum products, machinery, fertilizers, transport equipment, edible oils, chemicals and ferrous metals. Principal exports are raw cotton, cotton yarn and cloth, carpets, rice, petroleum products, synthetic textiles, leather, and fish.

Trade with U.K.

	1985	1986
Imports from U.K.	£255,419,000	£228,384,000
Exports to U.K.	119,006,000	131,333,000

Finance.—The unit of currency is the *Rupee* of 100 *Paisa* (1 *crore = 10 million Rupees*). For rate of exchange, see p. 81.

The 1986–87 Budget anticipated net federal revenues of *Rs.*92,889·8 million and current expenditure (excluding development expenditure) of some *Rs.*100,371·8 million.

Communications.—The main seaport is Karachi. The main airport at Karachi occupies an important position on international trunk routes and is equipped with modern facilities and equipment. Pakistan International Airlines (P.I.A.) operates air services between the principal cities within the country as well as abroad.

Post and telegraph facilities are available to every country in the world.

CAPITAL.—Islamabad, pop. 350,000. ΨKarachi (pop. est. 6,500,000) is the largest city and seaport; Lahore has a population of about 3,500,000.

FLAG.—Dark green ground, with white vertical stripes at the mast, the green portion bearing a white crescent in the centre and a five-pointed heraldic star.

NATIONAL DAYS.—March 23 (Pakistan Day), August 14 (Independence Day).

BRITISH EMBASSY
Diplomatic Enclave, Ramna 5,
P.O. Box 1122, Islamabad.

Ambassador Extraordinary and Plenipotentiary, His Excellency Nicholas John Barnington, C.M.G., C.V.O. (1987).

There is a British Consulate-General at *Karachi.*

British Council Representative, R. F. Budd, P.O. Box 1135, Islamabad. There are regional offices at Karachi and Lahore, and a library in Peshawar.

PANAMA
(República de Panama)

President of the Republic, Eric Arturo Delvalle, *took office,* Sept. 1985.
Vice President, Dr. Roderick Esquivel.

MINISTERS OF STATE

Government and Justice, Rodolfo Chiari de León.
Foreign Affairs, Dr. Jorge Abadía Arias.
Treasury and Finance, Dr. Héctor Alexander.
Agricultural Development, Dr. Hirisnel Sucre.
Public Works, Rogelio Dumanoir.
Commerce and Industry, José Bernardo Cárdenas.
Labour and Social Welfare, Jorge Federico Lee.
Health, Dr. Francisco Sánchez Cárdenas.
Housing, Ricardo Bermúdez.
Planning and Economic Policy, Dr. Ricaurte Vásquez.
Education, Manuel Solís Palma.
Presidency, Nander Pitti Velásquez.

PANAMANIAN EMBASSY IN LONDON
Eagle House, 109–110 Jermyn Street, S.W.1
[01–930 1591]

Ambassador Extraordinary and Plenipotentiary, His Excellency Lic. Guillermo Vega (1984).
Minister-Counsellor, Prof. Dionisio Johnson.

CONSULATE
24 Tudor Street, EC4Y 0JD
[01–353 4792/3].

There are also Consular Offices of the Republic at *Glasgow* and *Liverpool.*

Panama lies on the isthmus of that name which connects N. and S. America (*for* MAP, *see* INDEX). The area of the Republic is 29,762 sq. miles (77,082 sq. km.), the population (1985 U.N. estimate) 2,180,500. After a revolt (Nov. 3, 1903) it declared its independence from Colombia and established a separate Government.

After 1968 control of Panama was increasingly taken over by Gen. Omar Torrijos, Commander of the National Guard, following a military coup. On October 11, 1972, at an assembly of representatives from the 505 electoral districts, the President and Vice-President were installed for a six-year term, and General Torrijos was designated as "Leader of the Revolution" with wide overriding powers. In October 1978 he withdrew from government, and Dr. Aristides Royo was elected President by the Assembly of Representatives. In a Presidential election in May 1984, Sr. Nicolas Barletta was elected president and took office in Nov. 1984. However, he resigned in Sept. 1985 after disagreements with military leaders and was succeeded by his Vice-President.

The Panama Canal Zone.—With effect from Oct. 1, 1979 the Canal Zone (647 sq. miles) was disestablished, with all areas of land and water within the Zone reverting to Panama. By the 1977 treaty with the U.S.A., the U.S.A. is allowed the use of operating bases for the Panama Canal, together with several military bases, but the Republic of Panama is sovereign in all such areas. Control of the Canal will revert to Panama in the year 2000.

The soil is moderately fertile, but nearly one-half of the land is uncultivated. The chief crops are bananas, sugar, coconuts, cacao, coffee and cereals. The shrimping industry plays an important role in the Panamanian economy. A railway 47 miles in length joins the Atlantic and Pacific oceans.

Education is compulsory and free from 7 to 15 years.

Language and Literature.—The official language is Spanish. There are five Spanish language and one English language newspaper published daily in the capital.

Currency.—The monetary unit is the *Balboa* (= $1 U.S.); no Panamanian paper currency is issued, and U.S. dollar bills of all values are in circulation in the Republic.

TRADE

Republic of Panama	1985 (provisional)
Imports	U.S.$1,391 million
Exports	301 million

Colon Free Zone	1985
Imports	U.S.$1,589 million
Exports	1,793 million

Trade with U.K.†

	1985	1986
Imports from U.K.	£55,424,000	£44,975,000
Exports to U.K.	14,612,000	4,950,000

† Including Colon Free Zone.

The imports are mostly manufactured goods, machinery, lubricants, chemicals and foodstuffs; exports are bananas, petroleum products, shrimps, sugar, meat and fishmeal.

CAPITAL, ΨPanama City. Population (1985 est.), 608,890.

FLAG.—Four quarters; white with blue star (top, next staff), red (in fly), blue (below, next staff) and white with red star.

NATIONAL DAY.—November 3.

Dependencies of Panama.—Taboga Island (area 4 sq. miles) is a popular tourist resort of some 12 miles from the Pacific entrance to the Panama Canal. Tourist facilities are also being developed in the Las Perlas Archipelago in the Gulf of Panama. There is a penal settlement at Guardia on the island of Coiba (area 19 sq. miles) in the Gulf of Chiriqui.

BRITISH EMBASSY
(120 Via España, Panama)

Ambassador Extraordinary and Plenipotentiary, Her Excellency Mrs. Margaret Bryan (1986).
First Secretary and Consul, N. J. Bown.

There is a British consular office at *Panama City.*

PARAGUAY
(República del Paraguay)

President, General Alfredo Stroessner, *inaugurated* Aug. 15, 1954, *re-elected* 1958, 1963, 1968, 1973, 1978 and 1983.
Foreign Affairs, Dr. Carlos Augustus Saldívar.
Finance, General César Barrientos (*ret.*).
Interior, Dr. Sabino A. Montanero.
Defence, General Gaspar Germán Martínez.
Justice and Labour, Dr. José Eugenio Jacquet.
Education and Worship, Dr. Carlos Ortiz Ramirez.
Public Works and Communications, General de División Juan A. Cáceres.
Agriculture and Livestock, Ing. Hernando Bertoni.
Industry and Commerce, Dr. Delfin Ugarte Centurión.
Public Health and Social Welfare, Dr. Adán Godoy Jiménez.
President of Central Bank, Dr. César Romero Acosta.

PARAGUAYAN EMBASSY AND CONSULATE IN LONDON
Braemer Lodge, Cornwall Gardens, SW7 4AQ
[01–937 1253; *Consulate*: 01-937 6629]

Ambassador Extraordinary and Plenipotentiary, His Excellency Antonio Zuccolillo (1981).
Counsellor and Consul General, Rubén Alvarenga-Cabañas.

Area and Population.—Paraguay is an inland subtropical state of South America, situated between Argentina, Bolivia and Brazil.

The area is estimated at 157,048 sq. miles (406,752 sq. km.), with a population (1985 U.N. estimate) of 3,681,000.

Paraguay is a country of grassy plains and dense forest, the soil being marshy in many parts and liable to floods; while the hills are covered for the most part with immense forests. The streams flowing into the Alto Paraná descend precipitously into that river. In the angle formed by the Paraná-Paraguay confluence are extensive marshes, one of which, known as "Neembucú," or "endless," is drained by *Lake Ypoa*, a large lagoon, south-east of the capital. The *Chaco*, lying between the rivers Paraguay and Pilcomayo and bounded on the north by Bolivia, formed the subject of a long-standing dispute with that country and led to war between Paraguay and Bolivia from 1932 to 1935. The Chaco is a flat plain, rising uniformly towards its western boundary to a height of 1,140 feet; it suffers much from floods and still more from drought, but the building of dams and reservoirs has converted part of it into good pasture for cattle raising.

Government.—In 1535 Paraguay was settled as a Spanish possession. In 1811 it declared its independence of Spain.

The 1967 constitution provides for a two-chamber parliament consisting of a 30-member Senate and a 60-member Chamber of Deputies. Two-thirds of the seats in each chamber are allocated to the majority party and the remaining one-third shared among the minority parties in proportion to the votes cast. Voting is compulsory for all citizens over 18.

The President is elected for 5 years and may be re-elected for a further term. He appoints the Cabinet, which exercises all the functions of government. During parliamentary recess it can govern by decree through the Council of State, the members of which are representative of the Government, the armed forces and various other bodies. The state of siege, in force since 1947, was lifted on April 8, 1987.

Production.—About three-quarters of the population are engaged in agriculture and cattle raising. Cotton, soya beans, tobacco, edible and essential oils, sugar, coffee and timber are the main exports. The forests contain many varieties of timber which find a good market abroad. Paraguay's hydroelectric power station at Acaray produced in 1985, 1,118 Kwh. of which a surplus is exported to Argentina and Brazil.

At Itaipú the largest hydroelectric dam in the world, a joint project by Paraguay and Brazil, was inaugurated in 1982. It is expected to be completed in 1990 when it will have a capacity of over 12 million k.w. Work is also under way on a hydroelectric project with Argentina at Yacyretá which it is hoped will be in operation by the end of the decade.

Communications.—A railway, 985 miles in length, connects Asunción with Buenos Aires. The journey takes 55 hours. Train ferries enable the run to be accomplished without break of bulk. River steamers also connect Buenos Aires and Asunción (3 to 5 days). This service is liable to cancellation without warning when the river is low or in flood. There are direct shipping services to Asunción from England, Western Europe and the U.S.A. Eight airlines operate services from Asunción.

There are 1,176 km. of asphalted roads in Paraguay, connecting Asunción with São Paulo (26 hrs.) *via* the Bridge of Friendship and Foz de Yguazú and with Buenos Aires (24 hrs.) *via* Puerto Pilcomayo, and about 4,050 miles of earth roads in fairly good condition, but liable to be closed or to become impassable in wet weather. A 1,000 km. road, of which 300 km. are paved, links Asunción with the Bolivian border. There are services to Buenos Aires, São Paulo and Paranagua, a port on the Brazilian coast.

Defence.—There is a permanent military force of about 25,000 all ranks, most of whom are conscripts doing their military service; and about 6,500 armed police (again mostly conscripts). Three gunboats and a number of small armed launches patrol inland waters.

Language and Literature.—Spanish is the official language of the country but outside the larger towns *Guarani*, the language of the largest single unit of original Indian inhabitants, is widely spoken. Four daily, one weekly and one bi-weekly newspapers are published in Asunción. There are 48 AM, 15 FM and three TV stations in the country.

Education.—Education is free and compulsory. In 1984 there were 3,209 government primary schools and 587 private schools with 559,080 pupils and 22,091 teachers. There are 713 secondary schools with 149,019 pupils and 2,448 teachers. The National University in Asunción had in 1984 20,343 students. The Catholic University had 10,971 students.

BUDGET 1986
(in million guaranies)

Central Government	*Decentralized Bodies*
Expenditure . . . . 142·2	321·3

Currency.—The unit is the *guarani* of 100 *céntimos*. (*See also* p. 82.)

Trade.—The imports are chiefly articles of food and drink, consumer goods, textiles, vehicles and machinery. Main exports: Soja, cotton, tobacco, meat, timber, seeds, maize, fruit and vegetable oils.

Trade with U.K.

	1985	1986
Imports from U.K.	£15,540,000	£31,010,000
Exports to U.K.	2,086,000	1,455,000

CAPITAL, ΨAsunción, about 1,000 miles up the River Paraguay from Buenos Aires. Pop. (census, 1985), 729,307; other centres being Ciudad Presidente Stroessner, 98,491; ΨEncarnación, 31,445; Concepción, 25,607; P. Juan Caballero, 41,475.

FLAG.—Three horizontal bands, red, white, blue with the National seal on the obverse white band and the Treasury seal on the reverse white band.

NATIONAL DAY.—May 14.

BRITISH EMBASSY
Calle Presidente Franco 706,
(PO Box 404)

Ambassador Extraordinary and Plenipotentiary and Consul-General, His Excellency John Grant Macdonald, C.M.G., M.B.E. (1986).

PERU
(República del Peru)

President, Sr. Alan García Pérez, *assumed office*, July 28, 1985.

CABINET

Prime Minister and Minister of the Presidency, Guillermo Larco Cox.
Foreign Affairs, Dr. Allan Wagner Tizon.
Interior, Jose Barsallo Burga.
Economy and Finance, Gustavo Saberbein Chevalier.
Industry, Commerce, Tourism and Integration, Manuel Romero Caro.
Agriculture, Remigio Morales Bermudez.
Energy and Mines, Abel Salinas Izaguirre
Education, Mercedes Cabanillas de Llanos de la Mata.
Health, Hilda Urizar Peroni de Arias.
Transport and Communications, Gen. German Parra Herrera.
Justice, Carlos Blancas Bustamante.
Labour, Orestes Rodriguez Campos.

Housing, Luis Bedoya Velez.
Fisheries, Javier Labarthe.
Defence, Jorge Torres Flores (*Army*); Vice-Adm. Willy Harm Esparza (*Navy*); Lt-Gen. Jose Guerra Lorenzetti.

PERUVIAN EMBASSY AND CONSULATE
52 Sloane Street, SW1X 9SP
[01–235 1917/2545]

Ambassador Extraordinary and Plenipotentiary, Dr. Carlos A. Raffo (1986).
Minister, Counsellor, Jose Augusto Tenorio.
Naval Attaché, Rear Adm. Hector de Romano.
Air and Military Attaché, Maj. Gen. Justo Pastor Raminez.

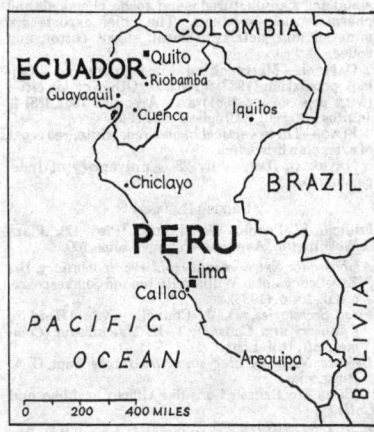

Area and Population.—Peru is a maritime Republic of South America, situated between 0° 00′ 48″ and 18° 21′ 00″ S. latitude and between 68° 39′ 27″ and 81° 20′ 13″ W. longitude. The area of the Republic is 496,225 sq. miles (1,285,216 sq. km.), with a population estimated (1985) at 19,700,000.

Physical Features.—The country is traversed throughout its length by the Andes, running parallel to the Pacific coast, the highest points in Peru being *Huascaran* (22,211 feet), *Huandoy* (20,855 feet), *Ausangate* (20,235 feet), *Misti* volcano (18,364 feet), *Hualcan* (20,000 feet), *Chachani* (19,037 feet), *Antajasha* (18,020 feet), *Pichupichu* (17,724 feet), and *Mount Meiggs* (17,583 feet).

There are three main regions, the *Costa,* west of the Andes, the *Sierra* or mountain ranges of the Andes, which include the *Punas* or mountainous wastes below the region of perpetual snow and the *Montaña,* or *Selva,* which is the vast area of jungle stretching from the eastern foothills of the Andes to the eastern frontiers of Peru. The coastal area, lying upon and near the Pacific, is not tropical, though close to the Equator, being cooled by the Humboldt Current. It contains the capital, Lima, and most of the white population.

In the mountains, where most of the Indians live, are to be found minerals in great richness and variety, and cattle, sheep, llamas and alpacas are bred there.

Language and Literature.—Spanish, the language of the original Spanish stock from which the governing and professional classes are mainly recruited, was formerly the only official language of the country. However, in May 1975, the Quechua language was declared the second official tongue. Quechua and Aymará are widely spoken by more than half the population of the country. Before the arrival of Pizarro, the Incas had attained a high state of culture, some traces of which survived three centuries of Spanish rule. Modern Peruvian literature includes a national drama in the Spanish tongue and many Peruvian writers have attained international fame.

Government.—Peru was conquered in the early 16th century by Francisco Pizarro (born 1478, died 1541). He subjugated the Incas (the ruling caste of the Quechua Indians), who had started their rise to power some 500 years earlier, and for nearly three centuries Peru remained under Spanish rule. A revolutionary war of 1821–1824 established its independence, declared on July 28, 1821. The constitution rests upon the fundamental law of Oct. 18, 1856, and is that of a democratic Republic. A new constitution was drawn up and approved in July 1979.

Production.—The chief products of the coastal belt are cotton, sugar and petroleum. There are large tracts of land suitable for cultivation and stock raising on the eastern slopes of the Andes, and in the mountain valleys maize, potatoes and wheat are grown. The jungle area is a source of timber and petroleum. Other major crops are fruit, vegetables, rice, barley, grapes and coffee. Mineral exports include lead, zinc, copper, iron ore and silver. Peru is normally the world's largest exporter of fishmeal.

Communications.—In recent years the coastal and sierra zones have been opened up by means of roads and air routes and there is air communication, as well as communication by protracted land routes, with the tropical and little known eastern zones, which lie east of the Andes towards the borders of Brazil. The completion in 1944 of the trunk road of the Andean Highway from the Pacific port of Callao, *via* Lima to Pucallpa, the river port on the Ucayali, forms a link between the Pacific, the Amazon and the Atlantic.

The first railway was opened in 1850 and the 2,400 miles of track are now administered by the Government. There is also steam navigation on the Ucayali and Huallaga, and in the south on Lake Titicaca. Air services are maintained throughout Peru, and many international services call at Lima.

Defence.—The Army is recruited by voluntary enlistment, supplemented by conscription (2 years), and numbers about 45,000 of all ranks. Armoured units are equipped with American, Russian and French vehicles. Engineer units are employed on the construction of roadways in Peru using American equipment. The main Naval base is in Callao and supports all ships of the Fleet. There are training establishments in Callao and La Punta. The Naval Air Arm consists of U.S. and French helicopters; U.S. anti-submarine aircraft and DC3's. The Air Force is equipped with British, U.S. and French aircraft and U.S. and French helicopters. There are military airfields at Talara, Piura, Chiclayo, Lima, Pisco, Joya, Iquitos and Arequipa plus a seaplane base at Iquitos. There are also a Civil Guard and a Republican Guard whose members number respectively 30,000 and 5,000.

Education.—Education is compulsory and free for both sexes between the ages of 6 and 15.

Finance.—The unit of currency is the *Sol* of 100 *centavos.* For rate of exchange, *see* p. 82.

Trade.—Import trade of Peru in 1984 totalled U.S.$2,140 million and exports U.S.$3,147 million.

Trade with U.K.

	1985	1986
Imports from U.K.	£40,371,000	£48,275,000
Exports to U.K.	108,943,000	82,141,000

The principal imports are machinery, foodstuffs,

metal and manufactured metal goods, chemicals and pharmaceutical products. The chief exports are minerals and metals, fishmeal, sugar, cotton and coffee.

CAPITAL.—Metropolitan Lima (including ΨCallao), population (1983) 5,258,600. Other major cities (with pop census, 1981) are: Arequipa (561,338) Ψ Iquitos (540,560), ΨChiclayo (533,266).

FLAG.—Three vertical bands, red, white, red; coat of arms on white band.

NATIONAL DAY.—July 28 (Anniversary of Independence).

BRITISH EMBASSY

Edificio El Pacifico-Washington (Piso 12), Plaza Washington, Avenida Arequipa, Lima 100.

Ambassador Extraordinary and Plenipotentiary, His Excellency John William Richmond Shakespeare, C.M.G., L.V.O. (1983).

First Secretaries, D. J. Couvell, L.V.O. (*Head of Chancery and Consul*); T. H. Malcolmson (*Commercial*); D. J. Logan.

Defence, Naval, Military and Air Attaché, Capt. G. A. Hogg, R.N.

There are British Consular Offices at *Lima* and *Callao.*

British Council Representative, J. England, P.O. Box No. 14.0114, Calle Alberto Lynch 110, San Isidro, Lima 1.

THE PHILIPPINES
(Repúblika ng Pilipinas)

President, Corazon C. Aquino *b.* 1933, *elected* Feb. 7, 1986, *assumed office* Feb. 25, 1986.

CABINET SECRETARIES

Foreign Affairs, Salvador Laurel.
Finance, Jaime Ongpin.
Justice, Sedfrey Ordonez.
Agriculture, Carlos Dominguez.
Public Works and Highways, Vicente Jayne.
Education, Culture and Sports, Lourdes Quisumbing.
Labour, Franklin Drilon.
Health, Alfredo Bengzon.
Trade and Industry, Jose Concepcion.
Social Services and Development, Mita Pardo de Tavera.
Economic Planning, Solita Monsod.
Agrarian Reform, (vacant).
Special Counsel, Teodoro Locsin Jr.
Local Government, (vacant).
Tourism, Jose Antonio Gonzalez.
Natural Resources, Fulgenio Factóran.
Budget, Guillermo Caragne.
Transportation and Communications, Reinero Reyes.
National Defence, Rafael Ileto.
Executive Secretary, Joker Arroyo.
Muslim Affairs and Cultural Communities, Jiamil Dianalan.
Chairman, Presidential Commission on Good Government, Ramon Diaz.
Science and Technology, Antonio Arrizabal.
Presidential Press Secretary, Teodoro Benigno.
Presidential Adviser on National Security, Emanuel Soriano.
Cabinet Secretary, Jose de Jesus.

PHILIPPINE EMBASSY
9a Palace Green, W8 4QE
[01–937 1600/9]

Ambassador Extraordinary and Plenipotentiary, His Excellency Juan T. Quimson (1986).

Minister-Counsellor and Consul General, Edmundo Libid.
Commercial Counsellor, Peregrino Sales.

Area and Population.—The Philippines are situated between 21° 20′–4° 30′ N. Lat. and 116° 55′–126° 36′ E. long., and are distant about 500 miles from the south-east coast of the continent of Asia. (For MAP, see p. 853).

The total land area of the country is 115,831 sq. miles (300,000 sq. km.). There are eleven larger islands and 7,079 other islands.

The principal islands are:—

Name	sq. miles	Name	sq. miles
Luzon	40,422	Mindoro	3,759
Mindanao	36,538	Leyte	2,786
Samar	5,050	Cebu	1,703
Negros	4,906	Bohol	1,492
Palawan	4,550	Masbate	1,262
Panay	4,446		

Other groups in the Republic are the Sulu islands (Capital, Jolo), Babuyanes and Batanes; the Catanduanes; and Culion Islands.

The population of the Philippines was estimated (1987) at 57,000,000.

The inhabitants, known as Filipinos, are basically all of Malay stock, with a considerable admixture of Spanish and Chinese blood in many localities, and about 90 per cent of them are Christians, predominantly Roman Catholics. Most of the remainder are Moslems, in the south, and animists and pagans, mainly in the north. There is a Chinese minority estimated at 500,000, and other much smaller foreign communities, notably Spanish, American and Indian.

History.—The Portuguese navigator Magellan came to the Philippines in 1521 and was slain by the natives of Mactan, a small island near Cebu. In 1565 Spain undertook the conquest of the country which was named "Filipinas", after the son of the King of Spain, and in 1571 the city of Manila was founded by the conquistador Legaspi, who subdued the inhabitants of almost all the islands, their conversion being undertaken by the Augustinian friars in Legaspi's train. In 1762 Manila was occupied by a British force, but in 1764 it was restored to Spain. In the Spanish–American War of 1898, Manila was captured by American troops with the help of Filipinos and the Islands were ceded to the United States by the *Treaty of Paris* of Dec. 10, 1898. Despite a rebellion against the U.S. government between 1899 and 1902, the Americans remained in control of the country until 1946.

The Republic of the Philippines came into existence on July 4, 1946 with a presidential form of government based on the American system.

Martial law was imposed on September 21, 1972. This was lifted, except in two southern provinces, on January 17, 1981.

The assassination on Aug. 21, 1983 of Marcos' main political opponent, Benigno Aquino, and a subsequent financial crisis caused a weakening in Marcos' position. Although Marcos gained a majority of votes in the official count of a Presidential election in Feb. 1986, the election was marred by widespread electoral abuse and his rival, Mrs Corazon Aquino, launched a series of non-violent civil disturbance actions.

On Feb. 22, Defence Minister Enrile and Vice Chief of Staff Ramos broke away from the Marcos government and declared their support for Mrs. Aquino. Thousands of people took to the streets to support their revolt and they were joined by a large section of the Armed Forces. On Feb. 25, Marcos, his family and aides left for Hawaii. Mrs Aquino took over as President. On March 25, she abolished the Batasan (legislature) and promulgated a Freedom (Provisional) Constitution.

An appointed Constitutional Convention drafted a new Constitution with a Congressional system of government, having a senate of 24 members and a House of Representatives with 250 members. This was overwhelmingly approved by a referendum in Feb. 1987. Elections to the Congress were held in May and the new Constitution came into force on July 27, 1987.

There is unrest in many of the islands due to insurgency. Muslim insurgents, the Moro National Liberation Front, operate in western Mindanao and the Sula archipelago. Most of the current activity is due to the Communist New People's Army, which is strongest in eastern Mindanao, Negros, Samar, Bicol, the mountains of northern Luzon, and Bataan. As of June 1987 the ceasefire agreed between the Government and the Moro National Liberation Front was still holding, unlike the ceasefire with the Communists which ended in Feb. 1987.

Language and Literature.—The official languages are Filipino and English. Filipino, the national language, is based on Tagalog, one of the Malay-Polynesian languages and the language of the part of Luzon surrounding Metro Manilla. Filipino is spoken by 29·66 per cent of the total number of households, but local languages and dialects are strong and Cebuano is spoken by 24·20 per cent. of total households. English, which is the language of government and of instruction in secondary and university education, is spoken by at least 44 per cent of the population. Spanish, which ceased to be an official language in 1973, is now spoken by a very small minority. 89 per cent of the population are literate.

Education.—Secondary and higher education is extensive and there are 37 private universities recognized by the Government, including the Dominican University of Santo Tomas (founded in 1611); there are also 296 State-supported colleges and universities, including the University of the Philippines, founded 1908. Students at private and state colleges and universities in 1984–85 numbered 13,814,359.

Roads and Railways.—The highway system covered 161,709 kilometres in 1985 and there was a total of 1,120,172 registered road vehicles. The Philippine National Railway operate 740 km. of track on Luzon Island.

Shipping.—There are 94 ports of entry in the Philippines and 164,404 vessels of various types totalling 50,467,000 tons, are engaged in inter-island traffic.

Civil Aviation.—There 82 national airports and 137 privately operated airports. Philippine Air Lines have regular flights throughout the Far East, to the U.S.A. and Europe, in addition to inter-island services.

TRADE

	1985	1986
Total imports	$5,110,673,000	$5,043,597,000
Total exports	4,628,954,000	4,841,780,000

Trade with U.K.

	1985	1986
Imports from U.K.	£94,370,000	£79,809,000
Exports to U.K.	197,979,000	182,852,000

The Philippines is a predominantly agricultural country, the chief products being rice, coconuts, maize, sugar-cane, abaca (manila hemp), fruits, tobacco and lumber. There is, however, an increasing number of manufacturing industries and it is the policy of the Government to diversify its economy.

Principal exports are sugar, coconut oil, copper concentrate, lumber and copra.

CAPITAL.—ΨManila, in the island of Luzon: population (1980): City area, 1,630,485; Manila with suburbs (incl. Quezon City, Pasay City, Caloocan City, Makati, Parañaque, San Juan Mandaluyong and Navotas), 6,720,050. The next largest cities are ΨCebu (490,281), ΨDavao (610,375), ΨIloilo (244,027), ΨZamboanga (343,722), and Bacolod (262,415).

FLAG.—Equal horizontal bands of blue (above) and red; gold sun with three stars on a white triangle next staff.

NATIONAL DAY.—June 12 (Independence Day).

BRITISH EMBASSY
(P.O. Box 1970 MCC), Manila

Ambassador Extraordinary and Plenipotentiary, His Excellency Keith Gordon MacInnes, C.M.G. (1987).
Counsellor, P. J. Priestley.
Defence Attaché, Col. P. D. Pettigrew.
First Secretaries, A. E. Huckle (*Head of Chancery*); K. R. Gosling.
Second Secretaries, C. T. Imrie; J. R. Albright (*Commercial*); P. J. Karmy (*Consul*).
Cultural Attaché, H. Salmon (*British Council Representative.*

POLAND
(Polska Rzeczpospolita Ludowa)

COUNCIL OF STATE

Chairman (i.e. Head of State), Gen. Wojciech Jaruzelski.
Deputy Chairmen, T. Mlynczak; K. Barcikowski; Z. Komender; T. Szelachowski.

COUNCIL OF MINISTERS

Prime Minister, Zbigniew Messner.
Deputy Prime Minister and Chairman, Planning Commission, Manfred Gorywoda.
Deputy Prime Ministers, Zbigniew Gertych; Manfred Gorywoda; Nladyslaw Gwiazda; Josef Kozix; Zbigniew Szalajda.
Chairman, Supreme Chamber of Control, Tadeusz Hupalowski.
Interior, Lt.-Gen. Czeslaw Kiszczak.
Foreign Affairs, Marian Orzechowski.
Defence, Gen. Florian Siwicki.
Finance, Bazyli Samojlik.
Foreign Trade, Andrzej Wojcik.
Justice, Lech Domeradzki.
Higher Education, Science and Technology, Prof. Benon Miskiewicz.
Health and Social Welfare, Miroslaw Cybulko.
Labour, Stanislaw Gebala.
Culture and Art, Alexsander Krawczuk.
Metallurgical and Engineering Industries, Janusz Maciejewicz.
Agriculture, Forestry and Food Industry, Stanislaw Zieba.
Internal Trade and Services, Jerzy Jozwiak.
Transport, Jan Kaminski.
Raw Materials and Fuels Management, Jerzy Wozniak.
Education, Joanna Michalowska-Gumowska.
Chemical and Light Industries, Edward Grzywa.
Communications, Wladyslaw Majewski.
Mining and Energy, Jan Szlachta.
Religious Affairs, Wladyslaw Loranc.
Maritime Economy, Adam Nowotnik.
Environmental Protection and Water Economy, Stefan Jarzebski.

Construction, Territorial and Communal Management, Jerzy Bajszczak.
Head of Office for Scientific and Technical Progress, Konrad Tott.
Government Spokesman, Jerzy Urban.
Head of Office of Council of Ministers, Michal Janiszewski.
Youth Affairs, Aleksander Kwasniewski.

POLISH UNITED WORKERS' PARTY

Politburo, K. Barcikowski; J. Baryla; J. Czyrek; J. Glowczyk; W. Jaruzelski; C. Kiszczak; Z. Messner; A. Miodowicz; W. Mokrzyszczak; Z. Muranski; M. Orzechowski; T. Porebski; F. Siwicki; Z. Stepien; M. Wozniak *(full Members)*; S. Bejger; B. Ferensztajn; J. Kubasiewicz; Z. Michalek; G. Rembisz *(candidate members).*
Secretariat, J. Baryla; H. Bednarski; S. Ciosek; K. Cypryniak; J. Czyrek; J. Glowczyk; Z. Porebski; A. Wasilewski; M. Wozniak.

POLISH EMBASSY IN LONDON
47 Portland Place, W1N 3AG
[01–580 4324]

Ambassador Extraordinary and Plenipotentiary, His Excellency Dr. Zbigniew Gertych (1987).

Area and Population.—Poland adjoins East Germany in the west, the boundary being formed by the rivers Oder and Neisse, Czechoslavakia in the south, and the U.S.S.R. in the east. (The present frontiers were established at the end of the Second World War.) To the north is the Baltic Sea. The country has an area of 120,725 sq. miles (312,677 sq. km.), and a population (1985 U.N. estimate) of 37,203,000. Roman Catholicism is the religion of 95 per cent. of the inhabitants.

Government.—The Polish Commonwealth had ceased to exist in 1795 after three successive partitions in 1772, 1793 and 1795, in which Prussia, Russia and Austria shared. The Republic of Poland (reconstituted within the limits of the old Polish Commonwealth) was proclaimed at Warsaw in November, 1918, and its independence guaranteed by the signatories of the Treaty of Versailles.

German forces invaded Poland on Sept. 1, 1939; on Sept. 17, Russian forces invaded eastern Poland, and on September 21, 1939, Poland was declared by Germany and Russia to have ceased to exist. A line of demarcation was established between the areas occupied by German and Russian forces. At the end of the war a Coalition Government was formed in which the Polish Workers' Party played a large part. In December, 1948, the Polish Workers' Party and the Polish Socialist Party fused in the new Polish United Workers' Party. This is a Communist Party which closely controls every branch of State activity. A new Constitution modelled on the Soviet Constitution of 1936 was adopted on July 22, 1952, and was modified in February 1976. It changed the title of the country to the Polish People's Republic (*Polska Rzeczpospolita Ludowa*). It made no provision for a President of the Republic, whose functions were to be jointly exercised by a Council of State. Private ownership of land and freedom of religion were recognized. Church and State were to be separate.

Despite the guarantee of religious freedom in the Constitution, a campaign of encroachment in 1953 culminated in the arrest of the Primate of the Roman Catholic Church, and dissatisfaction with the *régime* and conditions of life have led periodically to unrest. The expression of severe popular discontent in December 1970 led to the ousting of Gomulka, and substantial Government and Party changes followed. In July 1980 steep rises in food prices but static wages led to widespread strikes. The strikes continued throughout August, causing a major government reshuffle and obliging the government to agree to allow independent trade unions, the right to strike, the easing of censorship and other political and economic demands. The independent trade union movement, Solidarity, led by Lech Walesa, became a powerful force but many of its leaders, including Walesa, were detained and union activity suspended when martial law was declared on Dec. 13, 1981. Initially there was some passive resistance to martial law, which was suspended on Dec. 31, 1982, and finally lifted in July 1983.

Education.—Elementary education (ages 7–15) is compulsory and free. Secondary education is optional and free. There are universities at Kraków, Warsaw, Poznan, Lódź, Wroclaw, Lublin and Toruń and a considerable number of other towns.

Language and Literature.—Polish is a western Slavonic tongue (*see* U.S.S.R.), the Latin alphabet being used. Polish literature developed rapidly after the foundation of the University of Krakow (a printing press was established there in 1474 and there Copernicus died in 1543). A national school of poetry and drama survived the dismemberment and the former era of romanticism, whose chief Polish exponent was Adam Mickiewicz, was followed by realistic and historical fiction, including the works of Henryk Sienkiewicz (1846–1916), Nobel Prize-winner for Literature in 1905, Boleslaw Prus (1847–1912), and Stanislaw Reymont (1868–1925), Nobel Prize-winner in 1924.

Production and Industry.—On January 3, 1946, a decree was issued to provide for the nationalization of mines, petroleum resources, water, gas and electricity services, banks, textile factories and large retail stores. At present over 99 per cent of Polish industry is stated to be "socialized", but 68 per cent of agricultural land is privately farmed.

Trade with U.K.

	1985	1986
Imports from U.K.	£184,100,000	£182,841,000
Exports to U.K.	320,300,000	309,746,000

CAPITAL.—Warsaw, on the Vistula, pop. (1984) 1,644,626. Other large towns are Lódz (849,000); Kraków (735,000); Wroclaw (632,000); Poznan (571,000); Gdansk (464,000); Szczecin (389,000); Katowice (361,000); Bydgoszcz (358,000).

FLAG.—Equal horizontal stripes of white (above) and red.

NATIONAL DAY.—July 22.

BRITISH EMBASSY

No. 1 Aleja Róz, 00-556 Warsaw

Ambassador Extraordinary and Plenipotentiary, His Excellency Brian Leon Barder (1986).
Counsellor, N. J. Thorpe (*Head of Chancery*).
Defence and Air Attaché, Gp.-Capt. M. R. Killick.
Naval and Military Attaché, Lt.-Col. R. C. Eyres.
British Council Representative, R. H. Alford, Al. Jerozolimskie 59, 00-697 Warsaw.

PORTUGAL
(República Portuguesa)

President of the Republic, Dr. Mario A. Nombre Lopes Soares, *elected*, February 16, 1986.

Prime Minister, Dr. Anibal Cavaco Silva.
Deputy P.M. and Defence, Eurico de Melo.
State and Justice, Fernando Nogueira.
Parliamentary Affairs, Antonio Capucho.
Finance, Miguel Ribeiro Cadilhe.
Planning and Territorial Administration, Luis Valente de Oliveira.
Interior, José Silveira Godinho.
Foreign, João de Deus Pinheiro.
Agriculture, Fisheries and Food, Alvaro Barreto.
Industry and Energy, Luis Mira Amaral.
Education, Roberto Carneiro.
Public Works and Communications, João Oliveira Martins.
Health, Leonor Beleza.
Labour and Social Security, José Silva Peneda.
Trade and Tourism, Joaquim Ferreira do Amaral.
Youth, Antonio Couto dos Santos.

EMBASSY IN LONDON

11 Belgrave Square, SW1X 8PP

[01–235 5331]

Ambassador Extraordinary and Plenipotentiary, His Excellency João Hall Themido, G.C.V.O. (1984).
Counsellors, Sr. Manuel Corte Real, C.B.E.; Sra. Ana Barata, O.B.E.

Area and Population.—Continental Portugal occupies the western part of the Iberian Peninsula, covering an area of 34,317 sq. miles (88,880 sq. km.). It lies between 36° 58′–42° 12″ N. lat. and 6° 11′ 48″–9° 29′ 45″ W. long., being 362 miles in length from N. to S., and averaging about 117 in breadth from E. to W. The population (including the Azores and Madeira) was estimated at 10,229,000 in 1985.

Language and Literature.—Portuguese is a Romance language with admixtures of Arabic and other idioms. It is the language of Portugal and Brazil, and is the *lingua franca* of Angola, Mozambique and Guinea-Bissau.

Portuguese language and literature reached the culminating point of their development in the *Lusiadas* (dealing with the voyage of Vasco da Gama) and other works of Camoens (Camões) (1524–1580).

Government.—From the eleventh century until 1910 the government of Portugal was a monarchy, and for many centuries included the Vice-Royalty of Brazil, which declared its independence in 1822. In 1910 an armed rising in Lisbon drove King Manuel II and the Royal family into exile, and the National Assembly of Aug. 21, 1911, sanctioned a Republican form of government. A period of great political instability ensued until eventually the military stepped in. The Constitution of 1933 gave formal expression to the corporative "Estado Novo" (New State) which was personified by Dr. Salazar, Prime Minister from 1932–68. Dr. Caetano succeeded Salazar as Prime Minister in 1968 but his failure to liberalize the régime or to conclude the wars in the African colonies resulted in his government's overthrow by a military coup on April 25, 1974. The next two years were characterized by great political turmoil with no fewer than 6 provisional governments between April 1974 and July 1976 but with the failure of an attempted coup by the extreme left in November 1975 the situation began to become more stable.

Constitutional reforms introduced in Aug. 1982 have reduced the President's scope for day-to-day intervention in government but the decision to dissolve the Assembly is still largely the President's. The revisions also ended the military's capacity for political interference, and created two new organs of state, the Constitutional Tribunal and the Council of State, to advise the President.

In the General Election held on July 19, 1987, the Social Democratic Party (*P.S.D.*) won 148 of the 250 seats; the Socialist Party (*P.S.*) 60 seats; the Communist Party (*P.C.P.*) 31 seats, The Democratic Renewal Party (*PRD*) 7 seats and the Christian Democrats (*PCD*) 4 seats.

Defence.—Most physically fit males are liable for military service but conscription is becoming increasingly selective as the armed forces were greatly reduced following the end of the colonial wars, and reorganized and re-equipped for a conventional national defence role. The present strength of the Army is about 41,000. One brigade is earmarked for N.A.T.O. service. The Navy consists of about 14,800 officers and men, including 2,500 marines, manning about 60 craft of various types, many of which are obsolete. The present serving strength of the Air Force is about 12,600, (including 2,200 paratroops) and about 80 combat aircraft plus helicopters and transport and training aircraft.

Education is free and compulsory for eight years from the age of 7. Secondary education is mainly conducted in State lyceums, commercial and industrial schools, but there are also private schools. There are also military, naval, technical and other special schools. There are old established Universities at Coimbra (founded in 1290), Oporto and Lisbon. New Universities have been established at Lisbon, Braga, Aveiro and in the Azores; a University at Faro is expected to open in 1987.

Newspapers and Broadcasting.—There are now five morning and three evening daily newspapers in Lisbon and 3 morning papers in Oporto, and 4 main weekly newspapers. There are 2 TV channels (broadcasting in colour) and 4 radio stations (3 state controlled) broadcasting nationwide.

Civil aviation is controlled by the Administração Nacional Aeronaútica. There is an international airport at Portela, about 5 miles from Lisbon, and the airport of Pedras Rubras near Oporto is also used for scheduled international services. There are direct flights between London and Faro in the Algarve.

Agriculture.—The chief agricultural products are cork, cereals, rice, vegetables, olives, figs, citrus fruits, almonds, timber, port wine and table wines. There are extensive forests of pine, cork, eucalyptus and chestnut covering about 20 per cent of the total area of the country.

Minerals.—The principal mineral products are pyrites, wolfram, tin, iron ores, copper and sodium and calcium minerals.

Industry.—The country is so far only moderately industrialized, but is fairly rapidly extending its industries. The principal manufactures, some of which are still protected by high tariffs, are textiles, clothing and footwear, machinery (including electric machinery and transport equipment), foodstuffs (tomato concentrates and canned fish), chemicals, fertilizers, wood, cork, furniture, cement, glassware and pottery. There is a modern steelworks, and two modern and very large shipbuilding and repair yards at Lisbon and Setúbal working mainly for foreign ship-owners. There are several hydro-electric power stations and a new thermal power station.

Finance.—Portugal is a member of the European Monetary Agreement, the World Bank, the International Monetary Fund and the International Finance Corporation. The country has substantial, but declining, gold and foreign exchange reserves.

Currency.—Escudos (of 100 *Centavos*). A *Conto* consists of 1,000 *Escudos*.

Trade.—Portugal joined the E.E.C. on January 1, 1986.

The principal imports are cereals, meat, raw and semi-manufactured iron and steel, industrial machinery, chemicals, crude oil, motor vehicles and raw materials for textiles.

The principal exports are textiles, footwear, timber, cork, electrical and other machinery, and chemicals.

	1985	1986
Total imports	*E*1,326,528 m.	*E*1,412,579 m.
Total exports	971,747 m.	1,076,079 m.

Trade with U.K.

	1985	1986
Imports from U.K..	*E*100,007 m	*E*106,209 m
Exports to U.K. ...	141,454 m	153,522 m

The British share of the Portuguese market was 7 per cent in 1984 and the U.K. was the largest market for Portuguese exports (15·4 per cent).

CAPITAL.—ΨLisbon. Population (estimated, 1984) 807,937. ΨOporto 327,368; ΨSetubal 77,885.

FLAG.—Vertical band of green (next staff) and square of red, bearing arms of the Republic, framed.
NATIONAL DAY.—June 10.

BRITISH EMBASSY
35–37 Rua de S. Domingos à Lapa,
1296 Lisbon

Ambassador Extraordinary and Plenipotentiary, His Excellency Michael Keith Orlebar Simpson-Orlebar, C.M.G. (1986).

There are British Consulates in *Oporto, Portimão, Funchal* (Madeira) and *Ponta Delgada* (Azores).

British Council Representative, J. Mallon, O.B.E., The British Institute, Rua de Cecilio de Sousa 65, 1294.

BRITISH PORTUGUESE CHAMBER OF COMMERCE, Rua da Estrela 8, 1200 Lisbon and Rua Sa de Bandeira 784–20E, Frente, 4000 Oporto.

MADEIRA AND THE AZORES

Madeira and The Azores are two administratively autonomous regions of Portugal, having locally elected Assemblies and Governments.

Madeira is a group of islands in the Atlantic Ocean about 520 miles south-west of Lisbon, and consist of Madeira, Porto, Santo and 3 uninhabited islands (Desertas). The total area is 314 sq. miles (813 sq. km.), with a population of 264,800 (1984). ΨFunchal in Madeira, the largest island (270 square miles), is the capital, with a population of 44,111; Machico (10,905).

The Azores are a group of 9 islands (Flores, Corvo, Terceira, São Jorge, Pico, Faial, Graciosa, São Miguel and Santa Maria) in the Atlantic Ocean, with a total area of 922 sq. miles (2,387 sq. km.), and a population of 250,700 (1984). ΨPonta Delgada, on São Miguel, is the capital of the group; population is 21,347. Other ports are ΨAngra, in Terceira, (16,476) and ΨHorta (2,509).

MACAO

Macao, situated at the mouth of the Pearl River, comprises a peninsula and the islands of Coloane and Taipa, having an area of six sq. miles (15·5 sq. km.), with a population 1984 estimate of 343,000. Portuguese trade with China began early in the 16th century and Macao became a Portuguese colony in 1557: in a Sino-Portuguese treaty of Dec. 1887 China recognised Portugal's sovereignty over, and government of, Macao. In 1974 Portugal changed Macao's status from that of an Overseas Province to "a territory under Portuguese administration". Following the Sino-British Joint Declaration on Hong Kong in 1984, Sino-Portuguese negotiations on the transfer of administration began on June 30, 1986. The agreement on the transfer of the Administration of Macao to the Chinese authorities was signed on April 13, 1987. Macao will become a 'special administrative region' of China when transferred on Dec. 20, 1999.

Macao is subject to Portuguese constitutional law but otherwise enjoys administrative, economic and financial autonomy. The Governor is appointed by the Portuguese President and since 1976 there has been a 17 member legislative assembly, which has a three year term. The assembly comprises 12 elected deputies appointed by the Governor. A new electoral system which came into effect February 28th 1984, gave equal voting rights to all residents, thus enfranchising the Chinese population.

Macao's major industry is textile manufacturing which accounts for 62 per cent. of all exports. Port Macao is served by British, Portuguese and Dutch shipping lines and has regular services to Hong Kong, some 35 miles away.

Governor, Carlos Melancia.

Trade with U.K.

	1985	1986
Imports from U.K. ...	£1,595,000	£9,109,131
Exports to U.K.	36,509,000	52,981,000

QATAR
(Dawlat al-Qatar)

Amir of Qatar, H.H. Sheikh Khalifa Bin Hamad Al-Thani, G.C.M.G.; *assumed power* February 22, 1972 *(also Prime Minister).*

COUNCIL OF MINISTERS

Heir Apparent, Minister of Defence and Commander-in Chief of the Qatar Armed Forces, H.H. Sheikh Hamad Bin Khalifa Al-Thani, K.C.M.G.
Education, H.E. Shaikh Mohammad Bin Hamad Al-Thani.
Foreign, (vacant).
Finance and Petroleum Affairs, H.E. Shaikh Abdul Aziz Bin Khalifa Al-Thani.
Municipal Affairs, (vacant).
Economy and Commerce, (vacant).
Justice (vacant).
Electricity and Water, H.E. Shaikh Jasem Bin Moh'd Al-Thani.
Interior, H.E. Shaikh Khalid Bin Hamad Al-Thani.
Industry and Agriculture, H.E. Shaikh Faisal Bin Thani Al-Thani.
Public Health, H.E. Sayed Khalid Bin Mohammed al-Mana.
Public Works, H.E. Sayed Khaled Bin Abdullah Al-Attiyah.
Labour and Social Welfare Affairs, H.E. Sayed Ali Bin Ahmed Al-Ansari.
Communications and Transport, H.E. Sayed Abdullah Bin Naser al-Suwaidi.
Information, H.E. Sayed Issa Ghanim al-Kawari.

Minister of State for Foreign Affairs, H.E. Shaikh Ahmed bin Saif Al-Thani.
Adviser to H.H. The Amir, Dr. Hassan Kamel.

EMBASSY IN LONDON
27 Chesham Place, SW1X 8HG
[01–235 0851/4]

Ambassador Extraordinary and Plenipotentiary, His Excellency Sherida Sa'ad Jubran Al-Ka'abi, G.C.V.O. (1981).

The state of Qatar covers the peninsula of Qatar from approximately the northern shore of Khor al Odaid to the eastern shore of Khor al Salwa. The area is about 4,247 sq. miles (11,000 sq. km.), with a population estimated in 1985 at about 315,000. The great majority of the population is concentrated in the urban district of the capital Doha. Only a small minority still pursue the traditional life of the semi-nomadic tribesmen and fisherfolk.

Until 1971, Qatar was one of the nine independent Emirates in the Arabian Gulf in special treaty relations with the U.K. In that year, with the withdrawal of H.M. Forces from the area, these special treaty relations were terminated. On April 2, 1970 a Provisional Constitution for Qatar was proclaimed, providing for the establishment of a Council of Ministers and for the formation of a Consultative Council to assist the Council of Ministers in running the affairs of the State. The first Cabinet was formed of 10 members on May 29, 1970. Qatar is a member of the Arab League as well as of the United Nations.

Production.—Although Qatar is a desert country, there are gardens and smallholdings near Doha and to the north and encouragement is being given to the development of agriculture.

The Qatar General Petroleum Corporation is the state-owned company controlling Qatar's interests in oil, gas and petrochemicals. The corporation is responsible for Qatar's oil production onshore and offshore. The production level for Qatar agreed in O.P.E.C. is currently 285,000 b.p.d. Explorations continue for further oil. The large reserves of natural gas in the North Field are expected to come into production by 1990. A new 50,000 b.p.d. oil refinery was commissioned in 1984 to increase domestic refinery capacity.

Current industries include a steel mill, a fertiliser plant, a cement factory, a petrochemical complex and two natural gas liquids plants. With the exception of the cement works, which is at Umm Bab, all these industries are at Umm Said, about 30 miles south of Doha. Qatar is also expanding its infrastructure including electrical generation and water distillation, roads, houses, and Government buildings, although reduced demand for crude oil in international markets has led to a downturn in the economy and a slower rate of development than hitherto.

Communications.—Doha is an expanding town with an airport built to international standards. Regular air services connect Qatar with Bahrain and the United Arab Emirates, Kuwait, Muscat, Saudi Arabia, Jordan, Syria, Lebanon, Egypt, the Indian sub-continent and Europe. The Qatar Broadcasting Service transmits on medium, shortwave, and V.H.F. Regular television transmissions in colour began in 1974 and a second channel opened in 1982.

Trade with U.K.

	1985	1986
Imports from U.K.	£142,065,000	£112,000,000
Exports to U.K.	32,607,000	30,000,000

CAPITAL.—Doha. Population (estimated) 220,000. Other towns include Khor, Dukhan, Wakra and Umm Said.

FLAG.—White and maroon, white portion nearer the mast; vertical indented line comprising 17 angles divides the colours.

NATIONAL DAY.—September 3.

BRITISH EMBASSY
P.O. Box 3, Doha

Ambassador Extraordinary and Plenipotentiary, His Excellency Patrick Michael Nixon, O.B.E. (1987).
First Secretary, K. N. Johnson, M.B.E. (*Commercial*).
Second Secretary, G. Fairhurst (*Consul and Administration*).
Third Secretary, C. A. R. Forrester-Bennett.
Attaché, C. D. Wright (*Commercial*).
Vice Consul, R. J. Clark.
British Council Representative, W. S. Beniston, Ras Abu Aboud Road (P.O. Box 2992), Doha.

ROMANIA
(Republica Socialistă România)

President of the Republic, Nicolae Ceausescu, *first elected*, 1967; *latest re-election*, March 28, 1985.
State Council, N. Ceausescu (*President*); Manea Mănescu; Gheorghe Rădulescu; Petru Enache; Maria Ghitulica; Arpád Páll (*Vice-Presidents*).

COUNCIL OF MINISTERS
Prime Minister, Constantin Dascalescu.
1st Deputy Prime Ministers, Elena Ceaușescu; Ion Dinca; Gheorghe Oprea.
Deputy Prime Ministers, Ion Petre; Gheorghe Petrescu; Ludovic Fazekas; Dimitrie Ancuta; Neculai Ibanescu, Cornel Pacoste; Aneta Spornic.
Secretary, (vacant).
Agriculture and Food Industry, Gheorghe David.
Chemical Industry, Gheorghe Dinu.
Education and Instruction, Ion Teoreanu.
Electric Power, Ioan Avram.
Finance, Alexandru Babe.
Food Industry and Agricultural Produce Acquisition, Paula Prioteasa.
Foreign Affairs, Ioan Totu.
Foreign Trade, Ilie Vaduva.
Forestry Administration, Eugen Tarhon.
Mining, Oil and Geology, Ioan Folea.
Health, Victor Ciobanu.
Industrial Construction, Alexandru Dimitriu.
Internal Affairs, George Homostean.
Internal Trade, Ana Muresan.
Justice, Gheorghe Chivulescu.
Labour, Maxim Berghianu.
Light Industry, Lina Ciobanu.
Heavy Equipment Industry, Mihai Moraru.
Machine-Building Industry, Serban Teodorescu.
Electrical Engineering Industry, Alexandru Necula.
Metallurgical Industry, Marin Enache.
National Defence, Col. Gen. Vasile Milea.
Petrochemical Industry, Adrian Stoica.
Technical and Material Supply, Petre Preoteasa.
Tourism and Sports, Ion Stanescu.
Transportation and Communications, Pavel Aron.
Timber and Building Materials, Richard Winter.
Youth, Nicu Ceausescu.
Minister, Chairmen of Central Bodies, Gheorghe Pana(*Committee of People's Councils' Affairs*); Ion Patan (*State Prices Committee*); Cornel Mihulecea (*State Committee for Nuclear Power*); Stefan Birlea (*State Planning Committee*); Miu Dobrescu (*Central Council of General Confederation of Trade Unions*); Ion Bucur (*1st Vice-Chairman, Council of Economic and Social Organisations*); Suzana Gadea (*Council for Socialist Culture and Education*); Elena Ceausescu (*National Council of Science and Technology*); Ioan Ursu (*1st Vice-Chairman,*

National Council of Science and Technology); Ion Badea (*National Council for Water Resources*); Ana Muresan (*National Council of Women*); Traidu Girba (*National Union of Agricultural Production Co-operatives*).

Minister, Secretaries of State, T. Postelnicu (*Internal Affairs, and Chief of State Security Dept.*); A. Duma (*Foreign Affairs*); I. Ceausescu (*1st Vice-Chair, State Planning Committee*); I. Constantinescu (*State Planning Committee*); D. Bejan (*Technical and Material Supply and Control of Fixed Assets*); T. Dudas; G. Cazan (*Foreign Trade*); F. Nagy; F. Gruia (*Agriculture*); M. Florescu, E. Dobrescu (*National Council for Science and Technology*).

THE COMMUNIST PARTY

Political Executive Committee, N. Ceauşescu; E. Bobu; V. Cazacu; E. Ceauşescu; L. Ciobanu; I. Coman; N. Constantin; C. Dascalescu; I. Dinca; M. Dobrescu; L. Fazekąs; M. Mănescu; P. Niculescu; C. Olteanu; G. Oprea; G. Pana; I. Pătan; D. Popescu; G. Rădulescu (*full members*); S. Andrei; S. Birlea; N. Ceausescu; L. Constantin; G. David; P. Enache; S. Gadea; M. Gere; M. Ghitulica; N. Giosan; I. Moga; A. Mureşan; E. Nae; M. Nedelcu; C. Pacoste; T. Postelnicu; I. Radu; I. Stoian; I. Szasz; I. Totu; I. Ursu; R. Winter; M. Marina; I. Matei; V. Milea; G. Stoica (*candidate members*).

Permanent Bureau of the Political Executive Committee, N. Ceauşescu; E. Bobu; E. Ceauşescu; C. Dascalescu; M. Mănescu; G. Oprea; G. Rădulescu.

Secretariat of the Central Committee, N. Ceauşescu (*Secretary General*); I. Coman; P. Enache; E. Bobu; S. Curticeanu; C. Radu; I. Stoian; S. Andrei; V. Barbulescu.

ROMANIAN EMBASSY IN LONDON
4 Palace Green, W8 4QD
[01–937 9666]

Ambassador Extraordinary and Plenipotentiary, His Excellency Mr. Stan Soare (1986).

Area and Population.—Romania is a republic of South-Eastern Europe, formerly the classical *Dacia* and *Scythia Pontica*, having its origin in the union of the Danubian principalities of *Wallachia* and *Moldavia* under the *Treaty of Paris* (April, 1856). The area of Romania is 91,699 sq. miles (237,500 sq. km.) and the population (1985 U.N. estimate) is 23,017,000.

Government.—The principalities remained separate entities under Turkish suzerainty until 1859, when Prince Alexandru Ion Cuza was elected Prince of both, still under the suzerainty of Turkey. Prince Cuza abdicated in 1866 and was succeeded by Prince Charles of Hohenzollern-Sigmaringen, in whose successors the crown was vested. By the *Treaty of Berlin* (July 13, 1878) the Principality was recognized as an independent State, and part of the *Dobrudja* (which had been occupied by the Romanians) was incorporated. On March 27, 1881, it was recognized as a Kingdom.

The outcome of the War of 1914–18 added Bessarabia, the Bukovina, Transylvania, The Banat and Crisana-Maramures, these additions of territory being confirmed in the Treaty of St. Germain, 1919, and the Treaty of Petit Trianon, 1920.

On June 27, 1940, in compliance with an ultimatum from U.S.S.R., Bessarabia and Northern Bukovina were ceded to the Soviet Government, and in August, 1940, Romania ceded to Bulgaria the portion of Southern Dobrudja taken from Bulgaria in 1913.

Romania became "The Romanian People's Republic" in December, 1947, on the abdication of King Michael. A new Constitution, modelled on the Soviet Constitution of 1936, was adopted unanimously on September 24, 1952, by the Grand National Assembly. The Assembly was later dissolved and elections were held for a new Grand National Assembly on November 30, 1952; in each constituency there was only one candidate for election, representing the People's Democratic Front, now the Socialist and Democratic Unity Front (S.D.U.F.) A new Constitution was approved by the Grand National Assembly in 1965 when the name of the state was changed to The Socialist Republic of Romania. The Constitution states (Art. 3) that the leading political force of the whole society is the Romanian Communist Party. The Constitution was modified in March, 1974.

Agriculture.—Wallachia, Moldavia and Transylvania are among the most fertile areas in Europe, and agriculture and sheep and cattle raising are the principal industries of Romania, although the intense winter cold and summer heat, and fierce summer drought sometimes have adverse effects on crops. These are principally cereal crops, legumes and other vegetables, flax and hemp. Vines and fruits are also grown. The forests of the mountainous regions are extensive, and the timber industry is important.

Socialization of agriculture was completed when collectivization was achieved in the spring of 1962.

Natural Resources and Industry.—Before the war petroleum and agriculture were the backbone of the Romanian economy but rapid industrialisation since 1948 has meant that they no longer hold the same dominant position. There are plentiful supplies of natural gas, together with various mineral deposits including coal, iron ore, bauxite, lead, zinc, copper and uranium in quantities which allow a substantial part of the requirements of industry to be met from local resources. Production of crude oil was put at about 11,600,000 tonnes in 1985.

The economy has faced increasing problems since the late 1970s, the result of over investment in energy-intensive heavy industry and neglect of agriculture, which has led to food shortages. The effects of these policies were aggravated by the international recession and by high interest rates, and Romania was severely in debt by the early 1980s. The government has sought to alleviate the situation by reducing borrowing and cutting imports. The economy is centrally organized on the basis of Five-Year Plans which cover all branches of national activity including investment and production.

Language and Literature.—Romanian is a Romance language with many archaic forms and with admixtures of Slavonic, Turkish, Magyar and French words. The folk-songs and folklore, transmitted orally through many centuries and collected in the 19th century, form one of the most interesting of such collections. The publication of all books and reviews is controlled and authorized by the Council for Socialist Culture and Education, which has the status of a Ministry. The leading religion is that of the Romanian Orthodox Church; the Roman Catholics and some Protestant denominations are of importance numerically. The Jewish community has declined through emigration.

Education is free and nominally compulsory. There are Universities at Bucharest, Iasi, Cluj, Timisoara, Craiova and Brasov, polytechnics at Bucharest, Timisoara, Cluj, Brasov, Galati and Iasi, two commercial academies at Bucharest and Brasov, and agricultural colleges at Bucharest, Iasi, Cluj, Craiova and Timisoara.

Communications.—In 1979 there were 11,113 km. of railway open for traffic. The mercantile marine had a gross tonnage of 13,220,000 tons in 1979. The principal ports are Constanta (on the Black Sea), Sulina (on the Danube Estuary), Galati, Braila, Giurgiu and Turnu Severin. The Danube and the Black Sea are linked by a canal completed in 1984. Romania is a member of the Danube Commission whose seat is at Budapest.

FINANCE

	1984	1985
Revenue	Leu 308,917m.	Leu 362,645m.
Expenditure	308,917m.	362,600m.

The unit of currency is the *Leu* of 100 *Bani* (*see also* p. 82).

TRADE

	1983	1984
Imports	Leu 130,370m.	Leu 160,816m.
Exports	173,324m.	228,123m.

Imports are chiefly semi-manufactured goods, raw materials, machinery and metals; export consists principally of maize, wheat, barley, oats, petroleum, timber, cattle, machines and industrial equipment. External trade with Communist countries dropped from 80 per cent. in 1960 to 45 per cent. in 1978.

Trade with U.K.

	1985	1986
Imports from U.K.	£78,474,000	£81,986,000
Exports to U.K.	102,946,000	86,730,000

CAPITAL, Bucharest, on the Dimbovita, population 1,961,189. Other large towns are:

Brașov 290,722		ΨGalati 254,636
Constanța 284,801		Craiova 243,117
Cluj-Napoca ...270,820		Ploiești......215,500
Iasi 265,176		ΨBrăila 214,561
Timișoara 261,950		

FLAG.—Three vertical bands, blue, yellow, red, with the emblem of the Republic in the centre band.
NATIONAL DAY.—August 23 (Liberation Day, 1944).

BRITISH EMBASSY
24 Strada Jules Michelet, Bucharest

Ambassador Extraordinary and Plenipotentiary, His Excellency Hugh James Arbuthnott, C.M.G. (1987).
Counsellor, A. R. Clark (*Head of Chancery*).
Defence, Naval and Military Attaché, Lt.-Col. G. M. Longdon, O.B.E.
Cultural Attaché and British Council Representative, K. McGuinness.

RWANDA
(Republika y'u Rwanda)

President, Maj. Gen. Juvénal Habyarimana, *assumed office*, July 5, 1973, *elected*, Dec. 24, 1978, *re-elected*, Dec. 19, 1983.

MINISTERS

Minister of Defence, The President.
Sec. Gen. of the National Revolutionary Movement for Development, Bonaventure Habimana.
President of the National Council for Development, Maurice Ntahobari.
Minister at the Presidency, Simeon Nteziryayo.
Institutional Relations, Edouard Karemera.
Interior and Community Development, Thomas Habanabakize.
Justice, Jean-Marie-Vianney Mugemana.
Civil Service, François Habiyakare.
Finance and Economy, Vincent Ruhamanya.
Mines and Industry, Juvenal Uwilingiyimana.
Agriculture, Husbandry and Forests, Anastase Nteziryayo.
Planning, Ambroise Mulindangabo.
Public Works and Energy, Joseph Nzirorera.
Transport and Communications, Andre Ntageruru.
Primary and Secondary Education, Col. Aloys Nsekalije.
Higher Education and Scientific Research, Charles Nyandwi.
Youth, Lt-Col. Augustin Ndindiliyimana.

Foreign Affairs and Co-operation, François Ngarukiyintwali.
Public Health and Social Welfare, Dr. Casimir Bizimungu.

Rwanda, formerly part of the Belgian-administered trusteeship of Ruanda-Urundi, has an area of 10,169 sq. miles (26,338 sq. km.), and a population (1985 U.N. estimate) of 6,070,000, mainly of the Bahutu tribe, with Batutsi and Batwa minorities.

A referendum held in September, 1961, showed the majority of the population were opposed to the retention of the monarchy which was accordingly abolished on Oct. 2, 1961. Rwanda became an independent Republic on July 1, 1962, with Gregoire Kayibanda as Head of State and Head of the Government. He was deposed in 1973, and replaced by a military government under Maj.-Gen. Juvénal Habyarimana.

Coffee (the chief cash crop), tea and sugar are grown. Tin, hides, bark of quinine and extract of pyrethrum flowers are also exported.

The National University of Rwanda is situated at two campuses, Butare and Ruhengeri.

The currency is the *Rwanda franc*. In 1983 total imports were valued at *Rw.Fr.*25,267 m.; total exports, *Rw.Fr.*7,427 m.

Trade with U.K.

	1985	1986
Imports from U.K.	£3,565,000	£1,681,000
Exports to U.K.	3,998,000	7,487,000

CAPITAL.—Kigali (156,000).
FLAG.—Three vertical bands, red, yellow and green with letter R on yellow band.
NATIONAL DAY.—July 1.

British Ambassador (resident at *Kinshasa*, Zaire).

EL SALVADOR
(República de El Salvador)

President, José Napoleon Duarte, *elected* March 25, 1984, *assumed office*, June 1, 1984.

CABINET

Vice-President and Foreign Minister, Ricardo Acebeoto Peralta.
Minister of the Presidency, Dr. Jorge E. Tenorio.
Culture and Communications, Julio A. Rey Prendes.
Planning and Co-ordination of Economic and Social Development, Dr. Fidel Chávez Mena.
Justice, Dr. Julio A. Samayoa.
Finance, Ricardo J. López.
Trade, Julio Rivas Gallont.
Economy, Dr. Ricardo Gonzalez Camacho.
Education, Prof. Alberto Buendía Flores.
Defence and Public Security, Gen. Carlos E. Vides Casanova.
Labour and Social Security, Dr. Miguel A. Gallegos.
Agriculture, Carlos A. Duarte Funes.
Public Works, Roberto Mueza.
Health, Dr. Benjamin Valdés.

SALVADOREAN EMBASSY AND CONSULATE
9 Welbeck House, 62 Welbeck Street, W.1
[01-486 8182/3]

Ambassador Extraordinary and Plenipotentiary, His Excellency Dr. Maurico Rosales-Rivera.
First Secretary and Consul, Snrta Carolina Calderón.

Area and Population.—The Republic of El Salvador extends along the Pacific coast of Central America for 160 miles with a general breadth of about 50 miles, and contains an area of 8,124 sq. miles (21,041 sq. km.), with a population (1985 estimate) of 5,480,000. It is divided into 14 Departments.

The surface of the country is very mountainous, many of the peaks being extinct volcanoes. The highest are the Santa Ana volcano (7,700 ft.) and the San Vicente volcano (7,200 ft.). Much of the interior has an average altitude of 2,000 feet. The lowlands along the coast are generally hot, but towards the interior the altitude tempers the severity of the heat. There is a wet season from May to October, and a dry season from November to April. Earthquakes have been frequent in the history of El Salvador, the most recent being that of May 3, 1965, when considerable damage was done to San Salvador.

The principal river is the Rio Lempa. There is a large volcanic lake (Ilopango) a few miles to the east of the capital, while farther away and to the west lies the smaller lake of Coatepeque, which appears to have been formed in a vast crater flanked by the Santa Ana volcano.

Government.—El Salvador was conquered in 1526 by Pedro de Alvarado, and formed part of the Spanish vice-royalty of Guatemala until 1821.

After two years of government by a Junta headed by José Napoleon Duarte, elections for a Constituent Assembly were held in March 1982. The Assembly has completed its principal task of adopting a new Constitution. Presidential elections, although boycotted by the guerrilla movement, were held in March 1984 and in the run-off between the two largest parties, Sr. Duarte, the Christian Democrat leader, won with a 54 per cent. majority over the ARENA candidate, Roberto d'Aubuisson. Assembly and municipal elections took place in March 1985.

Despite the new government, guerrilla warfare continues.

Agriculture.—The principal cash crops are coffee, which is grown principally on the slopes of the volcanoes, cotton, which is cultivated on the coastal plains, and sugarcane. (However, cotton and sugar production have decreased as a result of the civil war.) Also cultivated are maize, sesame, indigo, rice, balsam, etc. In the lower altitudes towards the east, sisal is produced and used in the manufacture of coffee and cereal bags. Land reforms, announced in March 1980, are being undertaken. The Salvadorean Coffee Company, sugar exports and the banking system are nationalised.

Industry.—Existing factories make textiles, constructional steel, furniture, cement and household items. El Salvador is a member of the Central American Common Market. The first trade zone was inaugurated in November 1974 and the National Assembly approved a new Export Development Law.

Education.—The illiteracy rate is about 30·5 per cent (1980). Primary education is nominally compulsory, but the number of schools and teachers available is too small to enable education to be given to all children of school age. In recent Budgets, however, a high percentage of the national revenue has been devoted to education and great efforts are being made to eliminate the existing shortage of schools and teachers.

Language and Literature.—The language of the country is Spanish. Indigenous literature has not yet produced work of international repute. There are 4 daily newspapers published at the capital, and 4 in the provinces.

Communications.—The Executive Autonomous Port Commission (CEPA) which administers the previously foreign-owned port of Cutuco, at La Union and the principal port of Acajutla, and the railways under the new railroad organization, FENADESAL. There is continuous railway communication between San Salvador and Guatemala City and Puerto Barrios on the Caribbean coast. The roads are paved and in good condition but bridges are frequently dynamited. There are good roads between Port Acajutla and the capital (60 miles), and between the capital and Guatemala City. The Pan-American Highway from the Guatemalan frontier follows this route and continues to the Honduran frontier. The El Salvador international airport can receive jet aircraft and many international airlines fly to San Salvador.

There are post and telegraph offices throughout the country. There are 40 broadcasting stations and six television stations.

BUDGET

	1984	1985
	Colones '000	
Revenue	2,817,730	2,391,010
Expenditure	2,685,009	2,276,052

TRADE

	1983	1984
	Colones '000	
Imports	2,230,000	2,420,000
Exports	1,838,500	1,902,200

Trade with U.K.

	1985	1986
Imports from U.K.	£8,507,000	£6,917,000
Exports to U.K.	1,662,000	1,323,000

There is strict foreign exchange control (*see also* p. 82).

Other exports are sugar, shrimps, sisal (in the form of bags used for exporting coffee, sugar, etc.), balsam, meat, towels, hides and skins. The chief imports are chemicals, fertilizers, pharmaceutical goods, petroleum, manufactured goods, industrial and electronic machinery and equipment.

CAPITAL.—San Salvador. Population, (est. 1980) 425,119. Other towns are Santa Ana (204,570), San Miguel (157,838), Ψ La Union (Cutuco), Ψ La Libertad and Ψ Acajutia.

FLAG.—Three horizontal bands light blue, white, light blue; coat of arms on white band.

NATIONAL DAY.—September 15.

BRITISH EMBASSY
P.O. Box 1591, San Salvador

British Ambassador, (*resident at* Tegucigalpa, Honduras).

Chargé d'Affaires a.i., D. F. C. Ridgway (*First Secretary*).

SAN MARINO
(Repubblica di San Marino)

Regents, Two "Capitani Reggenti".

CONSULATE GENERAL IN LONDON
86 Park Lane, W1A 3AA
[01-493 4090]
Consul-General, The Lord Forte.

A small Republic in the hills near Rimini, on the Adriatic, founded, it is stated, by a pious stonecutter of Dalmatia in the 4th century. The Republic always resisted the Papal claims, and those of neighbouring dukedoms, during the 15th–18th centuries, and its integrity and sovereignty is recognized and respected by Italy. The Republic is governed by a State Congress of 10 members, under the Presidency of two Heads of State, who are elected at six-monthly intervals. The Great and General Council, a legislative body of 60 members, is elected by a universal suffrage for a term of 5 years. A Council of Twelve forms in certain cases a Supreme Court of Justice. The area is approximately 23 sq. miles (61 sq. km.), the population (April 30, 1985) is 22,361. The city of San Marino, on the slope of Monte Titano, has three towers, a fine church and Government palace, a theatre and museums. The principal products are wine, cereals, and cattle, and the main industries are tourism, ceramics, lime, concrete, cotton yarns, colour and paints. A Treaty of Extradition between the Governments of Great Britain and the Republic of San Marino has been in force since 1899.

FLAG.—Two horizontal bands, white, blue (with coat of arms of the Republic in centre).
NATIONAL DAY.—September 3.

BRITISH CONSULATE-GENERAL

Consul-General, I. J. Rawlinson (resides at Florence).

SÃO TOMÉ AND PRÍNCIPE
(República Democrática de São Tomé e Príncipe)

President, Dr. Manuel Pinto da Costa.

COUNCIL OF MINISTERS

Foreign Affairs, Guillermo Posser da Costa.
Defence and Security, Raoul Branqanca Neto.
Planning and Internal Trade, Agostinho Silveira Rita.
Co-operation, Frederiquo Bandeira Minezes.
Trade, Industry and Fishing, Carlos Brangaca Gomes.
Transport and Communications, Tomé Dias da Costa.
Agriculture, Oscar Aguiar do Sacramento e Souza.
Justice and Public Affairs, Francesco Fortunato Pires.
Information, Barbosa Reto.
Education, Labour and Welfare, Celestino Rocha da Costa.
Health, Frederico Jose Henriques Sequeira.

The islands of São Tomé and Príncipe are situated in the gulf of Guinea, off the west coast of Africa. They have an area of 372 sq. miles (964 sq. km.), and a population (1985 U.N. estimate) of 108,000.

Following Portugal's decision to grant independence, a transitional government was installed on Dec. 21, 1974, and the islands became an independent democratic republic on July 12, 1975.

Cacao is the main product.

Trade with U.K.

	1985	1986
Imports from U.K........	£824,000	£455,000
Exports to U.K.	197,000	327,000

CAPITAL.—ΨSão Tomé (25,000).

FLAG.—Horizontal stripes of green, yellow, green, the yellow of double width and bearing two black stars; and a red triangle in the hoist.
NATIONAL DAY.—July 12 (Independence Day).

British Ambassador (resident in *Luanda*, Angola).

SAUDI ARABIA
(Al Mamlaka al Arabiya as-Sa'udiyya)

Custodian of the Two Holy Mosques and King of Saudi Arabia, H.M. King Fahd bin Abdul Aziz, born, 1921, ascended the throne June 1, 1982.
Crown Prince, H.R.H. Amir Abdullah bin Abdul Aziz.

COUNCIL OF MINISTERS

Prime Minister, H.M. King Fahd bin Abdul Aziz.
First Deputy Prime Minister and Commander of the National Guard, H.R.H. Prince Abdullah bin Abdul Aziz.
Second Deputy Prime Minister, Defence and Aviation, H.R.H. Prince Sultan bin Abdul Aziz.

Public Works and Housing, H.R.H. Prince Mit'ab bin Abdul Aziz.
Interior, H.R.H. Prince Naif bin Abdul Aziz.
Foreign Affairs, H.R.H. Prince Saud al-Faisal bin Abdul Aziz.
Finance and National Economy, Muhammad Aba al-Khail.
Agriculture and Water, Dr. Abdul Rahman bin Abdul Aziz bin Hassan Al al-Shaikh.
Municipal and Rural Affairs, Ibrahim bin Abdullah al-Angari.
Commerce, Dr Sulaiman al-Solaim.
Communications, Dr. Hussain Mansouri.
Petroleum and Mineral Resources, Hisham Nazer (*and acting Minister of Planning*).
Justice, Ibrahim bin Mohammed Al al-Shaikh.
Labour and Social Affairs, Dr. Mohamed Ali al-Faiz.
Information, Ali Sha'er.
Health, Faisal bin Abdul Aziz al Hejailan.
Pilgrimage and Endowments, Abdul Wahhab Ahmed Abdul Wasi.
Education, Dr. Abdul Aziz Al-Abdullah al-Khuwaiter (*and acting Minister of Higher Education*).
Posts, Telegraphs and Telephones, Dr. Alawi Darwish Kayyal.
Industry and Electricity, Abdul Aziz al-Zamil.
Ministers of State, Muhammad Ibrahim Mas'oud; Dr. Muhammad Abdul Latif al-Melhem; Omar Abdul Qader Faqih; Dr. Fayez Ibrahim Badr; Turki bin Khalid Al Sudairi; Mohammed bin Abdulaziz Bin Zar'a; Mohammed bin Ibrahim Bin Jubeir.

ROYAL SAUDI ARABIAN EMBASSY
30 Belgrave Square, SW1X 8QB
[01–235 0831]

Ambassador Extraordinary and Plenipotentiary, His Excellency Sheikh Nasser Almanqour, G.C.V.O. (1980).

Minister Plenipotentiary, Ibrahim M. Mosly.

The Kingdom of Saudi Arabia is a personal union of two countries, the Sultan of Nejd becoming also King of the Hejaz. Great Britain recognized Abdul Aziz Ibn Saud as an independent ruler, King of the Hejaz and of Nejd and its Dependencies, by the Treaty of Jeddah (May 20, 1927). The name was changed to the Kingdom of Saudi Arabia in Sept 1932.

The total area of the Kingdom is about 830,000 sq. miles (2,149,640 sq. km.), with a population (1985 est.) of 12,400,000, of whom perhaps 3 million are non-Saudis. Islam is the established and only permitted religion.

In the 18th century Nejd was an independent state

governed from Diriya (now in ruins, 25 km. from Riyadh) and the stronghold of the Wahhabis, a puritanical Islamic sect. It subsequently fell under the Turkish yoke, but in 1913 Abdul Aziz Ibn Saud threw off Turkish rule and captured the Turkish province of Al Hasa. In 1920 he captured the Asir, and in 1921, by force of arms, he added to his dominions the Jebel Shammar territory of the Rashid family. In 1925 he completed the conquest of the Hejaz.

Saudi Arabia comprises almost the whole of the Arabian peninsula, with the exception of the small states in the extreme south (N. and S. Yemen), south-east (Oman and the U.A.E.) and east (Qatar). In the north-west it borders Jordan and in the north-east Iraq and Kuwait, while to the west lies the Red Sea and to the east the Gulf. The Nejd ("Plateau"), now the Central Province, extends over the centre of the peninsula, including the Nafud and Dahna deserts. The Hejaz ("the Boundary") now the Western Province, extends along the Red Sea coast to Asir and contains the holy towns of Mecca and Medina. The former, about 60 km. east of Jeddah, is the birthplace of the Prophet Mohammed, and contains the Great Mosque, within which is the Kaaba or sacred shrine of the Muslim religion. This is the focus of the annual Hajj ("Pilgrimage") performed by 3·4 million in 1986. The latter, Medina Al Munawwarah ("The City of Light") some 300 km. north of Mecca, is celebrated as the first city to embrace Islam and as the Prophet Mohammed's burial place (he died there on Rabia 12, 11 AH, corresponding to June 7, 632 AD).

Asir ("Inaccessible") is named for its mountainous terrain, and, with the coastal plain of the Tihama, lies along the southern Red Sea coast from Hejaz to the border with Yemen. It is the only region to enjoy substantial rainfall. Water supplies are, however, supplemented by dams and irrigation. The east and south-east of the country are lower-lying and largely desert. Outside the manufacturing centres which have grown up around some of the towns, most of the population are engaged in agriculture. The productivity of traditional dryland farming is increasingly supplemented by irrigation.

Industry.—Oil was first found in commercial quantities in Dhahran, near Dammam, in 1938. Total production of crude oil peaked at 9·9 m.b.d. in 1980, and in 1986 was 4·8 m.b.d. About 97 per cent of the total is extracted by the Arabian–American Oil Company. Recoverable reserves stood at about 167 billion barrels at the end of 1986, equivalent to about 95 years' production at the 1986 rate. Aramco's 66-year lease will terminate in 1999 but the company was effectively nationalized in 1980. Aramco operates a deepwater oil terminal at Ras Tanura.

The Government actively encourages the establishment of manufacturing industries in the country. The policy includes the provision of industrial estates and loans covering 50 per cent of capital investment. By the end of 1984 3,310 private industrial licences had been granted, and 650 were in production. These establishments were concentrated in the fields of construction materials, metal fabrication, simple machinery and electrical equipment, food and beverages, chemicals and plastics. The Government is trying to encourage future investment in industrial gases, intermediate petrochemicals, light engineering, machinery and all kinds of spare parts. A new pharmaceutical plant is scheduled for completion by 1989.

The Government has also established two industrial poles at Jubail and Yanbu, financed by the state agency Saudi Arabian Basic Industries Corp., to be the focus of heavy industrial development. Linked by gas and oil pipelines, both are to have petrochemical complexes producing, initially, ethylene and methanol, six of the seven plants now on-stream are joint ventures with American and Japanese companies. In addition an integrated steel complex and a urea fertilizer factory are in production in Jubail with West German and Taiwanese partners. Complete new cities are being built at each pole: Jubail will eventually house 300,000 and Yanbu 190,000. The state agency Petromin operates three domestic refineries and two lubricant plants and the last of three joint-venture export refineries came on-stream in 1986. Total refining capacity is now approximately 1,950,000 b.p.d.

Communications.—The railway from the port of Dammam to the oilfields at Abqaiq and through Hofuf to Riyadh was opened in 1951, and a direct Dammam-Riyadh line opened in 1985. An extension to Jeddah via Medina and the reopening of the Hejaz railway are planned. Metalled roads connect all the cities and main towns: the network consisted of 28,500 km. in 1985. The principal port of the Gulf is Dammam which has 39 berths and an annual capacity of 9·1 million tons. Jeddah is the centre of commercial traffic on the Red Sea and has 51 piers, giving an annual capacity of 17 million tons. The Government-owned Saudi Arabian Airlines (Saudia) operate scheduled services to 19 domestic airports. There are international class airports at Dhahran, Jeddah and Riyadh. Work has begun on the new King Fahd International Airport in Eastern Province, due to be completed in 1990. Saudia have an extensive overseas operation, and a large number of international airlines operate into the country. Telecommunications are being rapidly expanded. By the end of 1985 60,000 telex and 1,216,000 telephone lines were installed; telephone and telex exchanges will be able to handle 2·25 million lines by 1990. The Government is a major participant in the Arab Satellite Communications Organisation.

Education.—With the exception of a few schools for expatriate children, all schools are government supervised and segregated for boys and girls. By mid-1985 there were a total of 1,692,300 schoolchildren in 5,323 primary and 1,219 intermediate and 418 secondary schools. There are Universities in Jeddah, Mecca, Riyadh (branches in Abha and Qassim), Dammam (branch at Hofuf) and Dhahran, and there are Islamic universities in Medina and Riyadh. In addition there is great emphasis on vocational training, provided at 24 literacy and artisan skill training centres and 21 more advanced industrial, commercial and agricultural education institutes. Education in government-owned institutes is free at all levels.

Finance and Trade.—Oil remains the main source of receipts in the balance of payments. As a result, Government revenues have been markedly affected by oil prices and volume of production, and fell away from a peak of SR368,000 million in 1981–82 to SR133,600 million in 1985–86. The 1987 budget provided for expenditure of SR170,000 million. There is no public debt. There are no restrictions on foreign exchange transactions. The currency is strong, backed by gold and foreign exchange reserves, and maintained on a close parity to the U.S. dollar.

There is a total ban on the importation of alcohol, pork products, firearms and items regarded as non-Islamic or pornographic. The Arab boycott list also applies. In addition, certain chemicals now require import licences and fresh food items require radiation-free certificates. The leading suppliers of imports are U.S.A., Japan, West Germany, the U.K., Italy and France and the chief customers for exports are Japan, France, U.S.A. and Singapore.

	1985	1986
Total imports	*SR*99,645m.	*SR*75,000m.
Total exports	85,500m.	70,800m.

Trade with U.K.

	1985	1986
Imports from U.K....	£1,256,081,000	£1,507,000,000
Exports to U.K.	483,634,000	435,000,000

CAPITAL.—Riyadh, population about 1 million. Other major centres are Jeddah (pop. approx. 1 million), Damman, Buraydah, Hofuf and Tabuk.

FLAG.—Green oblong, white Arabic device in centre: "There is no God but God, Muhammad is the Prophet of God," and a white scimitar beneath the lettering.

BRITISH EMBASSY
P.O. Box 94351, Riyadh 11693.

Ambassador Extraordinary and Plenipotentiary, His Excellency Stephen Loftus Egerton, C.M.G. (1986).
Counsellors, A. F. Green (*Head of Chancery and Consul-General*); P. W. Ford (*Commercial*).
Defence and Military Attaché, Brig. T. Walcot.
Air Attaché, Wing-Cdr. R. Springett.
Naval Attaché, Cdr. N. Kerr.
First Secretaries, M. J. Crawford (*Chancery*); R. D. Lamb (*Economic*); J. R. Moore (*Deputy Consul-General*); R. J. Newell (*Commercial*); J. B. Midgley; (*Administration*); S. R. Bonde (*Commercial*).

Consul General, Jeddah, G. P. Lockton, M.B.E., P.O. Box 393, Jeddah 21411.
British Council Representative, W. L. Radford, Mura'aba, P.O. Box 2701, Riyadh 11461. There is also an office in Jeddah.

SENEGAL
(République du Sénégal)

President and Head of Government, Abdou Diouf, *installed,* Jan. 1, 1981, *elected for 5-year term,* Feb. 27, 1983.

MINISTERS

Armed Forces, Médoune Fall.
Justice, Seydou Madani Sy.
Foreign Affairs, Ibrahima Fall.
Interior, Jean Collin.
Economy and Finance, Mamoudou Touré.
Planning and Co-operation, Cheikh Hamidou Kane.
National Education, Iba der Thiam.
Equipment, Robert Sagna.
Communication, Djibo Ka.
Rural Development, Famara Ibrahima Sagna.
Industrial Development and Handicrafts, Serigne Lamine Diop.
Public Health, Mme. Marie Sarr Mbodj.
Commerce, Abdourahmane Touré.
Civil Service, Employment and Labour, André Sonko.
Tourism, Momar Talla Cissé.
Housing and Urban Affairs, Alioune Diagne Coumba Aïta.
Social Development, Mme. Mantoulaye Guéne.
Water Resources, Samba Yéla Diop.
Culture, Makhily Gassama.
Youth and Sports, Landing Sané.
Conservation, Cheikh Cissokho.
Ministers Delegate, Thierno Ba (*Relations with National Assembly*); Mme Fambaye Fal Diop (*Emigration*).
Secretaries of State, Moussa Ndoye (*Decentralization*); Moussa Touré (*Economy and Finance*); Mbaye Diouf (*Rural Development, Animal Resources*).

SENEGAL EMBASSY IN LONDON
11 Phillimore Gardens, W8 7QG
[01–937 0925/6, 3139]

Ambassador Extraordinary and Plenipotentiary, His Excellency Gen. Idrissa Fall, M.B.E. (1984).

Senegal lies on the west coast of Africa between Mauritania in the north, Mali in the east, and Guinea-Bissau and Guinea in the south. The Gambia lies entirely within Senegal, except for its sea-coast. (*For* MAP, *see* index.) It has an area of 75,750 sq. miles (196,192 sq. km.), and a population (1985 estimate) of 6,540,000.

Formerly a French colony, Senegal elected on Nov. 25, 1958, to remain within the French Community as an autonomous republic. In March, 1963 (after an attempted *coup d'état* by the then Prime Minister in the previous December) a new constitution was approved giving executive powers to the President, on the lines of the present French constitution. The process of political liberalisation continued; there are now 16 political parties officially recognised. Eight parties contested the General Election in Feb. 1983. The P.S. took 111 seats, the P.D.S. 8, and the R.N.D. 1.

In Feb. 1982, after an attempted coup in The Gambia in July 1981 had been put down with the aid of Senegalese troops, the Senegambia Confederation was established, based on certain joint institutions and the integration of defence, security and some other matters. Each country remains sovereign and independent. The President of Senegal is President of the Confederation and the President of The Gambia is Confederal Vice-President.

Senegal's principal exports are groundnuts (raw and processed) and phosphates. Tourism is also of growing importance as a revenue earner.

Trade with U.K.

	1985	1986
Imports from U.K.	£13,514,000	£12,328,000
Exports to U.K.	17,671,000	13,881,000

CAPITAL—ΨDakar (1,000,000).
FLAG.—Three vertical bands, green, yellow and red; a green star on the yellow band.
NATIONAL DAY.—April 4.

BRITISH EMBASSY
B.P. 6025, Dakar.

Ambassador Extraordinary and Plenipotentiary, His Excellency John Esmond Campbell Macrae, C.M.G. (1985).
First Secretary, S. F. Howarth (*Head of Chancery*).
Second Secretaries, B. Williams (*Consul*); R. D. Fitchett.
Cultural Attaché (*British Council Representative*), J. M. Tod, O.B.E.

SOMALIA
(Jamhuriyadda Dimugradiga Somaliya)

President and Sec. Gen. of Council, Maj.-Gen. Mohamed Siad Barre, *assumed office* Oct. 21, 1969.
First Vice-President and Prime Minister, Lt. Gen. M. A. Samantar.
Second Vice-President and Minister of Planning, Maj. Gen. H. K. Afrah.
Commerce, M. S. Mohamed.
Industry, H. A. Alasow.
Interior, Brig. Gen. A. S. Abdalla.
Finance, Dr. M. S. Osman.
Mineral Resources, Col. A. M. Farah.
Information, A. S. Ahmed.
Public Works, Col. M. R. Ghod.
Livestock, Col. B. R. Guleid.
Labour and Sports, Col. M. A. Jama.
Minister of State for Political Affairs in the Presidency, A. M. Fadil.
Chairman, Central Committee, Somali Revolutionary Socialist Party, A. A. Botan.
Chairman, People's Assembly, Brig. Gen. M. I. Ahmed.

SOMALI EMBASSY
60 Portland Place, W1N 3DG
[01–580 7148]

Ambassador Extraordinary and Plenipotentiary, His
Excellency Salah Mohamed Ali (1985).

The Somali Democratic Republic occupies part of
the north-east horn of Africa, with a coast-line on
the Indian Ocean extending from the boundary with
Kenya (2° South latitude) to Cape Guardafui (12° N.);
and on the Gulf of Aden to the boundary with
Djibouti. Somalia is bounded on the west by Djibouti,
Ethiopia and Kenya and covers an area of approximately 246,201 sq. miles (637,657 sq. km.). The population, of which a large proportion is nomadic, is
estimated (1987) at 5,800,000.

Government.—The Somali Democratic Republic,
consisting of the former British Somaliland Protectorate and the former Italian trust territory of
Somalia, was established on July 1, 1960. British rule
in Somaliland lasted from 1887 until 1960 except for a
short period in 1940–41 when the Protectorate was
occupied by Italian forces. Somalia, formerly an
Italian colony, was occupied by British forces in 1941.
In 1950 it was placed under Italian administration by
a resolution of the U.N.; this trusteeship lasted until
independence. Following the assassination of President Shermake on October 15, 1969, the armed forces,
assisted by the police, took over the Government
without resistance and a Revolutionary Council
under Siad Barre assumed control of the country. A
new constitution was introduced following a referendum in 1979. This provides for an elected People's
Assembly of 171 seats. The Assembly met for the first
time in January 1980. There is an outstanding
territorial dispute with Ethiopia and incursions by
Ethiopian-backed Somali rebels have occurred from
time to time.

Livestock raising is the main occupation in Somalia
and there is a modest export trade in livestock on the
hoof, skins and hides. Italy, the Gulf States and
Saudi Arabia import the bulk of the banana crop, the
second biggest export.

Trade with U.K.

	1985	1986
Imports from U.K.	£8,646,000	£9,140,000
Exports to U.K.	1,448,000	740,000

CAPITAL.—ΨMogadishu, population (estimated
1987), 1,000,000. Other towns are Hargeisa (150,000),
Kisimayu (30,000), ΨBerbera (60,000) and Burao
(15,000).

FLAG.—Five-pointed white star on blue ground.
NATIONAL DAY.—October 21.

BRITISH EMBASSY
(PO Box No. 1036) Mogadishu

Ambassador Extraordinary and Plenipotentiary, His
Excellency Jeremy Richard Lovering Grosvenor
Varcoe (1987).
First Secretary and Consul, R. C. Huxley (*Head of
Chancery*).

SOUTH AFRICA
(Republiek van Suid-Afrika)

State President, Pieter Willem Botha, *sworn in*, Sept.
14, 1984.

CABINET

Defence, Gen. M. Malan.
Manpower and Public Works, P. T. du Plessis.
*Co-operation and Development and (Black) Educa-
tion*, Dr. G. van N. Viljoen.
Agriculture, J. J. G. Wentzel.
Industries and Commerce, Dr. David J. de Villiers.

Finance, B. J. du Plessis.
Transport, E. Van der M. Louw.
*National Education, and Chairman, Ministers Coun-
cil for White Own Affairs*, F. W. De. Klerk.
Education and Development Aid, Dr. G. van N.
Viljoen.
Interior, S. Botha.
Justice, H. J. Coetzee.
Environment and Water Affairs, G. Kotze.
Home Affairs, Posts and Communications, J. C. G.
Botha.
Foreign Affairs, R. F. Botha.
Economic Affairs and Technology, D. W. Steyn.
Law and Order, A. Vlok.
National Health and Population Planning, Dr. W.
Van Niekerk.
Constitutional Development and Planning, S. Van
der Merwe.
*Administration and Advisory Services to the Office of
the State President*, E. Louw.
Chairman, Ministers Council for Indian Own Affairs,
A. Rajbansi.

EMBASSY AND CONSULATE
South Africa House, Trafalgar Square, WC2N 5DP
[01–930 4488]

Ambassador Extraordinary and Plenipotentiary, His
Excellency Mr Ray Killen (1987).
Minister, J. De Goede.
Armed Forces Attaché, Col. R. F. Crowther.
Counsellor (Press & Information), A. K. Dwyer.
Minister (Commercial), E. A. Erasmus.

There is a consulate-general at Golden Cross House,
8 Duncannon Street, W.C.2. [01–839 2211]

Area and Population.—The Republic, comprising
the Provinces of the Cape of Good Hope, Natal, the
Transvaal and the Orange Free State, occupies the
southernmost part of the African continent from the
courses of the Limpopo, Molopo and Orange Rivers
(34° 50′ 22″ South latitude) to the Cape of Good Hope,
with the exception of Lesotho, Botswana and Swaziland, and part of Mozambique. It has a total area of
471,445 sq. miles (1,221,031 sq. km.) and a total population (U.N. estimate, 1985) of 32,392,000 (of which
approx. 18 per cent are white).

The southernmost province contains many parallel
ranges, which rise in steps towards the interior. The
south-western peninsula contains the famous *Table
Mountain* (3,582 feet), while the *Great Swartberg* and
Langeberg run in parallel lines from west to east of
the Cape Province. Between these two ranges and
the *Roggeveld* and *Nuweveld* ranges to the north is
the Great Karoo Plateau, which is bounded on the
east by the *Sneeuberg*, containing the highest summit
in the province (Kompasberg, 7,800 feet). In the east

are ranges which join the *Drakensberg* (11,000 feet) between Natal and the Orange Free State.

The Orange Free State presents a succession of undulating grassy plains with occasional hills or kopjes. The Transvaal is also mainly an elevated plateau with parallel ridges in the *Magaliesberg* and *Waterberg* ranges of no great height. The eastern province of Natal has pastoral lowlands and rich agriculture land between the slopes of the Drakensberg and the coast, the interior rising in terraces as in the southern provinces. The *Orange*, with its tributary the *Vaal*, is the principal river of the south, rising in the Drakensberg and flowing into the Atlantic between Namibia and the Cape Province. The *Limpopo*, or Crocodile River, in the north, rises in the Transvaal and flows into the Indian Ocean through Mozambique. Most of the remaining rivers are furious torrents after rain, with partially dry beds at other seasons.

Government.—The self-governing colonies of the Cape of Good Hope, Natal, the Transvaal and the Orange River Colony became united on May 31, 1910, under the South Africa Act, 1909, in a legislative union under the name of the Union of South Africa, the four colonies becoming Provinces of the Union. The Union of South Africa continued as a member of the British Commonwealth until 1961. After a referendum held among white voters on October 5, 1960, the Union of South Africa became a republic on May 31, 1961, and withdrew from the Commonwealth.

A new Constitution came into effect on Sept. 30, 1984, which provided for an executive President and a three-chamber Parliament; the House of Assembly (178 members) representing Whites, the House of Representatives (85 members) representing Coloureds, and the House of Delegates (45 members) representing Indians. The black population has no representation. There is joint parliamentary responsibility for "general" affairs (foreign policy, defence, finance, law and order, justice, transport, manpower, commerce and industry, agriculture), and each chamber has separate responsibility for the "own" affairs of the population group it represents (housing, social welfare, health, education, local government and some aspects of agriculture). Disputes between the chambers may be referred by the President to the President's Council (60 members—20 White, 10 Coloured, 5 Indian elected by their respective chambers, 15 nominated by the President, 10 nominated by Opposition parties).

The President is chosen by an 88-member electoral college (in the proportion 4 White : 2 Coloured : 1 Indian) of the majority parties of the three chambers. The President appoints the Cabinet, which he chairs, from all three communities, and also appoints each community's ministerial council for "own" affairs.

Elections to the House of Representatives and House of Delegates took place in Aug. 1984. The turnout for the Coloured assembly election was estimated at 29·6 per cent of registered voters (18 per cent of those eligible) and for the Indian assembly election at 20·3 per cent of registered voters (16·6 per cent of those eligible).

Elections to the House of Assembly took place on May 6, 1987 and the results were: National Party, 133 seats; Conservative Party, 23; Progressive Federal Party, 20; New Republic Party, 1; Independent, 1.

The promulgation of the new Constitution on Sept. 3, 1984 coincided with rioting in the black townships and the continuing unrest led to the declaration on July 20, 1985 of a State of Emergency in 36 districts. This was lifted in most districts in the course of the next few months, and suspended throughout the country in March 1986. However, a nationwide State of Emergency was declared June 12, 1986 and was extended indefinitely from June 1987.

The Black Homelands.—The homelands are areas

set aside for occupation by blacks. Six areas—Gazankulu, Lebowa, KwaNdebele, KaNgwane, Qwaqwa and KwaZulu—are designated self-governing "national states". A further four areas—Bophuthatswana, Ciskei, Transkei and Venda—are regarded as independent republics by the South African government but they are not recognised as such by the United Nations.

Education.—The Provinces have been relieved of all vocational education (technical and industrial), and the Department of National Education under the Minister is concerned with universities, technical colleges, schools of industries, reformatories and State technical, housecraft and commercial high schools, State-aided vocational schools and State and State-aided special schools for the physically handicapped.

Communications.—The State-owned and controlled South African Transport Services operates the national railway system, the principal harbours, most long-distance passenger and freight road transport services, the South African Airways airline and a network of pipelines for petroleum products.

There are international airports at Johannesburg (Jan Smuts), Durban (Louis Botha) and Cape Town (D. F. Malan), with another under construction at La Mercy, Natal. South African Airways operates international services to Europe, North and South America, Australia, the Far East and the Middle East, as well as to neighbouring countries, and it is the principal operator of domestic flights.

The largest sea-port is Durban, Natal. Other major ports are Cape Town, Port Elizabeth, East London, Saldanha Bay and Mossel Bay in Cape Province and Richards Bay, Natal.

Production.—Mining is of the greatest importance to the South African economy, contributing 14·3 per cent to G.D.P. in 1982 (of which gold mining accounted for 10 per cent). Principal minerals produced are: gold, coal, iron ore, diamonds, copper, manganese, lime and limestone and asbestos.

Agriculture, forestry and fishing accounts for 6·2 per cent of G.D.P. Over 50 per cent of land is pasture so livestock farming is widespread with meat and wool important products. Principal crops are maize, sugar-cane, fruits and vegetables, wheat, sorghum, sunflower seed and groundnuts. Cotton is widely grown because of its suitability to the climate, and viticulture is also widespread.

Industries, concentrated most heavily around Johannesburg, Pretoria and the major ports, process foodstuffs, metals and non-metallic mineral products, and also produce beverages and tobacco, motor vehicles, chemicals and chemical products, machinery, textiles and clothing, and paper and paper products.

Trade.—Principal exports are: gold, base metals and metal products, diamonds, food (especially fruit), chemicals, machinery and transport equipment, and wool. Principal imports are: machinery, chemicals, motor vehicles, metals and metal products, food, inedible raw materials and textiles.

Trade with U.K.

	1985	1986
Imports from U.K.	£1,009,629,000	£849,557,000
Exports to U.K.	989,757,000	829,305,000

Currency.—The unit of currency is the *Rand* of 100 cents. For exchange rate, *see* p. 81.

Finance.—Estimated revenue for 1985–86 was R29,851 million, and estimated expenditure was R33,026 million.

CAPITAL.—The administrative seat of the Government is Pretoria, Transvaal; population (1985 estimate), 822,925; the seat of the Legislature is ΨCape Town, population (1985) 1,911,521. Other large towns

(1985 figures) are Johannesburg, Transvaal (1,609,408); Ψ Durban, Natal, the largest seaport (634,301); Ψ Port Elizabeth, Cape (651,993); Bloemfontein, capital of Orange Free State (232,984); Ψ East London, Cape (167,992); and Pietermaritzburg, capital of Natal (192,417).

FLAG.—Three horizontal stripes of equal width; from top to bottom, orange, white, blue; in the centre of the white stripe, the old Orange Free State flag hanging vertical, towards the pole the Union Jack horizontal, away from the pole the old Transvaal Vierkleur, all spread full.

NATIONAL DAY.—May 31.

BRITISH EMBASSY
6 Hill Street, Pretoria
91 Parliament Street, Cape Town (Jan.–June)

Ambassador Extraordinary and Plenipotentiary, His Excellency Robin William Renwick, C.M.G. (1987).

Minister, Miss T. A. H. Solesby, C.M.G.

Counsellors, J. R. James (*Head of Chancery*); M. G. Thickett.

First Secretaries, A. J. Gooch (*Labour*); D. J. White (*Internal*); A. E. Lewis (*Economic*); G. W. W. Charlton, M.B.E. (*Administration*); M. J. Griffiths (*Press*).

Cultural Attaché and British Council Representative, R. E. Underwood, 4th Flr. Federated Building, 38 Ameshoff St., (P.O. Box 30637), Braamfontein 2017, Johannesburg.

There are British Consular Offices at *Cape Town, Johannesburg* and *Durban*; and Honorary Consuls at *Port Elizabeth* and *East London*.

NAMIBIA

Administrator General, Louis Pienaar.

COUNCIL OF MINISTERS

Mining, Conservation, Tourism and Commerce, Andreas Zack Shipanga.

Agriculture, Water Affairs, and Sea Fisheries, Ebenezer van Zijl.

Justice, Information, Posts and Telecommunications, Fanuel Jariretundu Kozonguizi.

National Health, Welfare and Manpower, Moses Ngesuako Katjiuongua.

Local Government and Civic Affairs, Hans Diergaardt.

Education, Andrew Nick Matjila.

Finance and Governmental Affairs, Dirk Frederik Mudge.

Transport Services, Dawid Bezuidenhout.

Namibia (South West Africa) stretches from the southern border of Angola (lat. 17° 23′ S.) to part of the northern (Orange River) and north-western borders of the Cape Province of the Republic of South Africa; and from the Atlantic Ocean in the west to Botswana in the east.

The territory has an area of 318,261 sq. miles (824,292 sq. km.), including the area of Walvis Bay (434 sq. miles) which is claimed by South Africa. The population was estimated at 1,184,000 in 1986 and the main population groups are: Ovambo (587,000), Whites (78,000), Damara (89,000), Kavango (110,000), Herero (89,000), Nama (57,000), Coloured (48,000), Caprivians (44,000), Bushmen (34,000), Rehoboth Baster (29,000), Tswana (7,000).

Government.—A German protectorate from 1880 to 1915, South West Africa was administered until the end of 1920 by the Union of South Africa. In terms of the Treaty of Versailles the Territory was entrusted to South Africa with full powers of administration and legislation over the Territory. After the dissolution of the League of Nations and in the absence of a trusteeship agreement, South Africa

informed the United Nations that she would continue to administer South West Africa in the spirit of the Mandate. Since the establishment of the United Nations, South West Africa has been the subject of dispute.

On June 21, 1971, the International Court of Justice at The Hague delivered an advisory opinion as requested by the U.N. Security Council on the legal consequences for States of the continued presence of South Africa in "Namibia" (South West Africa). The Court decided by 13 votes to 2, that (*inter alia*) "the continued presence of South Africa being illegal, South Africa is under obligation to withdraw its administration from Namibia immediately and thus put an end to its occupation of the Territory". The South African Government rejected this opinion, but accepted the principle that the territory should attain independence. In September 1975 constitutional talks (known as the Turnhalle Conference) were begun in Windhoek between delegates from the 11 ethnic groups of the territory in order to determine the future of South West Africa. But their representative nature was contested by, *inter alia*, SWAPO, a liberation movement with substantial international support and when, in April 1977, it became clear that independence based on the Turnhalle would not solve the problem, the Five Western members of the U.N. Security Council at that time drew up a plan, later incorporated into Security Council Resolution 435, for a peaceful settlement. The plan involves free and fair elections under U.N. supervision leading to independence. The plan has been accepted by all the parties to the Namibia question and attempts to implement the plan are continuing.

Meanwhile, the South African Government appointed an Administrator-General in 1977 to establish a central administration there for those functions previously administered from Pretoria. In December 1978, the South Africans organized an election for a constituent assembly which SWAPO and most of the internal political parties boycotted. The resultant assembly was transformed into a National Assembly with legislative powers in May 1979, and a Council of Ministers was established in 1980 but both were abolished in Jan. 1983 and the territory again came under direct rule. However, in May 1985 legislative powers and executive authority were restored under a Transitional Government of National Utility intended to hold office while South Africa and the U.N. negotiate Namibia's independence. The 62-member National Assembly, made up of members proposed by Namibian political parties, appointed a speaker and an eight member cabinet which is to draw up plans for a new constitution.

Production.—Mining, agriculture and fisheries are important. Animal husbandry accounts for 99 per cent of the total gross output of commercial agriculture. The average rainfall over 70 per cent of the Territory is below 400 mm. per annum.

Trade with U.K.

	1985	1986
Imports from U.K.	£4,084,000	£2,915,000
Exports to U.K.	21,920,000	6,826,000

CAPITAL.—Windhoek (population, 1970 census, 61,260). The only port of any size is Ψ Walvis Bay.

SPAIN
(España)

Head of the Spanish State, King Juan Carlos I de Borbón y Borbón, *born* Jan. 5, 1938, *acceded to the throne*, Nov. 22, 1975, *married* May 14, 1962, Princess Sophie of Greece *and has issue*, Infante Felipe Juan Pablo Alfonso Todos Los Santos (Prince of Asturias, *and heir to the throne) born* Jan. 30, 1968; Infanta Elena Maria Isabel Dominica, *born* Dec. 20, 1963; and Infanta Christina Frederica Victoria, *born* June 13, 1965.

CABINET

Prime Minister (President of the Government), Felipe González Márquez.
Deputy P.M. (Vice-President), Alfonso Guerra González.
Foreign Affairs, Francisco-José Fernández Ordoñez.
Defence, Narcis Serra Serra.
Education and Science, José María Maravall Herrero.
Labour and Social Security, Manuel Chaves González.
Health and Consumption, Julián García Vargas.
Economy and Finance, Carlos Solchaga Catalán.
Public Works and Urbanisation, Javier Sáenz de Cosculluela.
Agriculture, Fisheries and Food, Carlos Romero Herrera.
Industry and Energy, Luis Carlos Croissier Batista.
Justice, Fernando Ledesma Bartret.
Culture and Government Spokesman, Javier Solana Madariaga.
Interior, José Barrionuevo Peña.
Transport, Tourism and Communications, Abel Caballero Alvarez.
Relations with Parliament, Virgilio Zapatero Gómez.
Public Administration, José Joaquín Almunia Amann.

SPANISH EMBASSY IN LONDON
24 Belgrave Square, SW1X 8QA
[01-235 5555]

Ambassador Extraordinary and Plenipotentiary, His Excellency José Joaquin Puig de la Bellacasa, G.C.V.O. (1983).
Minister-Counsellor, Sr. D. J. I. Benavides, K.C.V.O.

Area and Population.—Situated in the south-west of Europe, between 36°–43° 45′ N. lat. and 4° 25′ E.–9° 20′ W. long., Spain is bounded on the south and east by the Mediterranean, on the west by the Atlantic and Portugal, and on the north by the Bay of Biscay and France, from which it is separated by the Pyrenees. Continental Spain occupies about eleven-thirteenths of the Iberian peninsula, the remaining portion forming the Republic of Portugal. Its coast-line extends 1,317 miles—712 formed by the Mediterranean and 605 by the Atlantic—and it comprises a total area of 194,897 sq. miles (504,782 sq. km.), with a population (1986 estimate) of 38,818,355.

Physical Features.—The interior of the Iberian Peninsula consists of an elevated tableland surrounded and traversed by mountain ranges—the Pyrenees, the Cantabrian Mountains, the Sierra Guadarrama, Sierra Morena, Sierra Nevada, Montes de Toledo, etc. The principal rivers are the Duero, the Tajo, the Guadiana, the Guadalquivir, the Ebro and the Miño.

Government.—Spain was a monarchy until April 1931, when King Alfonso XIII left the country and a Republic was proclaimed and a Provisional Government, drawn from the various Republican and Socialist parties, was formed. On July 18, 1936, a counter-revolution broke out in many military garrisons in Spanish Morocco and spread rapidly throughout Spain. The principal leader was General Francisco Franco Bahamonde, formerly Governor of the Canary Islands. The struggle, in its later phases, threatened to embroil other European countries, those of Nazi-Fascist tendency lending aid to General Franco (leader of the Military-Fascist fusion, or *Falange*) while those of Communist views supported the Azaña (*Popular Front*) government. In October, 1938, many of the supporting troops were withdrawn, and on March 29, 1939, the Civil War was declared to have ended, the Popular Front Governments in Madrid and Barcelona surrendering to the *Nationalists* (as General Franco's followers were then named). On June 5, 1939, the Grand Council of the *Falange Española Tradicionalista y de las Juntas Ofensivas Nacional-Sindicalistas,* met at Burgos to legislate for the reorganization of the country under the Presidency of General Franco, who had assumed the title of *Caudillo (Leader) of Spain and Chief of the State.* In the Civil War of 1936–39 over 1,000,000 lives were lost.

On July 22, 1969, General Franco nominated Prince Juan Carlos (Alfonso) of Bourbon (grandson of the late King Alfonso XIII) to succeed him as head of state at his death or retirement. The nomination was approved in the *Cortes* by a large majority. Following the death of General Franco, on November 20, 1975, Juan Carlos acceded to the throne on Nov. 22, 1975.

Under the Constitution drawn up in 1977–78 there is a bi-cameral *Cortes* comprising a 350-member Congress of Deputies elected for 4 years by universal adult suffrage, and a Senate consisting of directly elected representatives of the provinces, islands, autonomous regions and Ceuta and Melilla.

In the regional and municipal elections of May 1983, the P.S.O.E. won the majority of the votes. In elections held in the Basque country in February, and in Cataluña in April 1984, local nationalist parties (P.N.V. and C.I.U.) retained their majorities and formed autonomous governments. At the General Election on June 22, 1986, P.S.O.E. won 184 seats; C.P., 105; C.D.S., 19; and I.U., 7 seats.

Regions.—Since the promulgation of the 1978 Constitution, 17 autonomous regions have been established, with their own parliaments and governments. These are Andalucia, Aragon, Asturias, Balaerics, the Basque country, Canaries, Castilla-La Mancha, Castilla-Leon, Cantabria, Cataluña, Extremadura, Galicia, Madrid, Murcia, Navarre, La Rioja and Valencia.

Defence.—*Army:* There are in Spain 1 armoured, 1 mechanized, 1 motorized and 2 mountain divisions; 1 artillery brigade, 2 cavalry brigades, 1 air-transportable brigade, 1 helicopter brigade, 1 coastal artillery brigade. The *Guardia Civil* operates as a gendarmerie in the rural areas under the control of the Ministry of Defence.

The active Spanish *Navy* consists of 1 aircraft carrier, 9 destroyers, 12 frigates and corvettes, 12 minesweepers, 6 major amphibious vessels, 8 submarines, 12 fast patrol craft, 6 hydrographic vessels, 1 tanker, and many smaller patrol craft and auxiliaries.

The Navy also has 50 helicopters and 10 Harrier aircraft.

The *Air Force* is divided geographically into 3 Regions covering Spain plus an Air Zone for the Canaries. There are also separate functional Combat, Tactical and Transport Commands. The Air Force consists of 4 attack squadrons, 6 air defence squadrons, 1 maritime squadron, 9 transport squadrons, 3 search and rescue squadrons, 9 training squadrons and 1 firefighting squadron.

Spain became a member of N.A.T.O. in May 1982. Her continued membership (linked to non-military integration) was confirmed in a referendum in March 1986. The present government has also initiated reorganization of the military structure. •

Education.—Under the Education Law 1985 free education for all children aged 6 to 15 is guaranteed. Under the new law, private schools (30 per cent of primary and 60 per cent of secondary schools) will have to fulfill certain criteria to receive government maintenance grants.

There are 29 state universities, the oldest of which, Salamanca, was founded in 1230. Other ancient foundations are Valencia (1245), Oviedo (1317), Valladolid (1346), Barcelona (1450), Zaragoza (1474), Santiago (1501), Seville (1502), Granada (1526), and Madrid (1590). Private universities are Deusto in Bilbao, and Navarra in Pamplona. Student numbers in the universities have risen to over 700,000.

Language and Literature.—Castilian is the language of more than three-quarters of the population of Spain. Basque, reported to have been the original language of Iberia, is spoken in the rural districts of Vizcaya, Guipuzcoa and Alava. Catalan is spoken in Provençal Spain, and Galician, spoken in the northwestern provinces, is akin to Portuguese; the governments of these regions actively encourage use of their local languages.

The literature of Spain is one of the oldest and richest in the world, the *Poem of the Cid,* the earliest and best of the heroic songs of Spain, having been written about A.D. 1140. The outstanding writings of its golden age are those of Miguel de Cervantes Saavedra (1547–1616), Lope Felix de Vega Carpio (1562–1635) and Pedro Calderón de la Barca (1600–1681). The Nobel Prize for Literature has four times been awarded to Spanish authors—J. Echegaray (1904), J. Benavente (1922), Juan Ramón Jimenez (1956) and Vicente Aleixandre (1977).

Currency.—The *peseta* = 100 *céntimos. (See also* p. 81.)

Production and Industry.—The country is generally fertile, and well adapted to agriculture and the cultivation of heat-loving fruits—olives, oranges, lemons, almonds, pomegranates, bananas, apricots, tomatoes, peppers, cucumbers and grapes. The agricultural products include wheat, barley, oats, rice, hemp and flax. The orange crop is exported mainly to Germany, France and the United Kingdom. The vine is cultivated widely; in the south-west, Jerez, the well-known sherry and tent wines are produced. The fishing industry is important.

Spain's mineral resources of coal, iron, wolfram, copper, zinc, lead and iron ores are variously exploited. Many of the richer and more easily worked deposits have been exhausted, but the authorities are actively engaged in stimulating the exploitation of hitherto unworked or lower grade deposits. Output of coal in 1985 was 29·4 million tonnes; output of iron ore (1985) was 6·5 million tonnes and of steel (1986) 13 million tonnes.

The principal goods produced are cars, steel, ships, manufactured goods, textiles, chemical products, footwear and other leather goods, ceramics, sewing machines and bicycles. In 1985 tourism contributed (net) an estimated 1,374,682 m. *pesetas* to the balance of payments.

TRADE

	1984	1985
	million pesetas	
Imports	4,628,991·1	5,073,239·1
Exports	3,734,487·1	4,093,208·6

The balance of payments on current account showed a surplus of $4,963m. in 1986 and reserves stood at $17,327 million at the end of the year.

Trade with U.K.
(inc. Canary Islands)

	1985	1986
Imports from U.K.	£1,605,200,000	£1,975,200,000
Exports to U.K.	1,835,500,000	1,840,800,000

The principal imports are cotton, tobacco, cellulose, timber, coffee and cocoa, food products, fertilizers, dyes, machinery, motor vehicles and agricultural tractors, wool and petroleum products. The principal exports include cars, petroleum products, iron ore, cork, salt, vegetables, fruits, wines, olive oil, potash, mercury, pyrites, tinned fruit and fish, tomatoes and footwear.

CAPITAL, Madrid. Population (1982) 3,188,297. Other large cities are ΨBarcelona (1,754,900), Valencia (751,734), ΨSeville (653,833), Zaragoza (590,750), ΨMálaga (503,251), Bilbao (433,030); Murcia (288,631).

FLAG.—Three horizontal bands, red, yellow and red, with coat of arms on yellow band.

NATIONAL DAY.—October 12.

BRITISH EMBASSY
Calle Fernando el Santo, 16, Madrid 4

Ambassador Extraordinary and Plenipotentiary, His Excellency Lord Nicholas Gordon Lennox, K.C.M.G., L.V.O. (1984).
Minister, D. C. Walker, L.V.O.
Counsellor, D. R. Christopher.
Defence and Military Attaché, Brig. A. D. Morland.
Head of Chancery, R. H. T. Gozney.
Second Secretary, A. Smith.
There are Consulates General in *Barcelona, Bilbao;* Consulates in *Tenerife, Alicante, Seville, Malaga, Palma de Mallorca* and *Las Palmas,* and Vice Consulates in *Algeciras* and *Ibiza.*
British Council Representative, R. T. Joscelyne, Plaza de Santa Barbara 10, Madrid 28004. There is also a regional office in Seville and offices with English language institutes in Bilbao, Granada, Palma de Mallorca, Las Palmas and Vigo.

BRITISH CHAMBER OF COMMERCE, Marques de Valdeiglesias 3, Madrid 4 also Paseo de Gracia 11, Barcelona 7 and Alameda de Mazarredo 5, Bilbao 1.

The BALEARIC ISLES form an archipelago off the east coast of Spain. There are four large islands (Majorca, Minorca, Ibiza and Formentera), and seven smaller (Aire, Aucanada, Botafoch, Cabrera, Dragonera, Pinto and El Rey). The islands were occupied by the Romans after the destruction of Carthage and provided contingents of the celebrated Balearic slingers. The total area is 1,935 sq. miles (5,011 sq. km.), with a population of 685,088. The archipelago forms a province of Spain, the capital being ΨPalma in Majorca, pop. 304,422; ΨMahon (Minorca), pop. 22,926.

The CANARY ISLANDS are an archipelago in the Atlantic, off the African coast, consisting of 7 islands and 6 mostly uninhabited islets. The total area is 2,807 sq. miles (7,270 sq. km.), with a population of 1,444,626. The Canary Islands form two Provinces of Spain.—*Las Palmas* (Gran Canaria, Lanzarote (38,500), Fuerteventura (19,500) and the islets of Alegranza, Roque del Este, Roque del Oeste, Graciosa, Montaña Clara and Lobos), with seat of administration at ΨLas Palmas (pop. 366,454) in Gran Canaria, where major oil companies have installations for refueling shipping; and *Santa Cruz de Tenerife* (Tenerife, La Palma (76,000), Gomera (31,829), and Hierro (10,000)), with seat of administration at ΨSanta Cruz in Tenerife, pop. 190,784.

ISLA DE FAISANES is an uninhabited Franco-Spanish condominium, at the mouth of the Bidassoa in La Higuera bay.

ΨCEUTA is a fortified post on the Moroccan coast, opposite Gibraltar. The total area is 5 sq. miles (13 sq. km.), with a population of 70,864.

ΨMELILLA is a town on a rocky promontory of the Rif coast, connected with the mainland by a narrow isthmus. Melilla has been in Spanish possession since 1492. Population 58,449. Ceuta and Melilla are parts of Metropolitan Spain.

OVERSEAS TERRITORIES

Spanish settlements on the Moroccan seaboard are:—

Peñon de Alhucemas, the bay of that name includes six islands: population 366.

Peñon de la Gomera (or *Peñon de Velez*) is a fortified rocky islet about 40 miles west of Alhucemas Bay; population 450.

The Chaffarinas (or Zaffarines) are a group of three islands near the Algerian frontier, about 2 miles north of Cape del Agua; population 610.

The former provinces of Spanish Guinea, Fernando Póo and Rio Muni achieved independence on October 12, 1968, under the title of Equatorial Guinea.

The protectorate of Spanish Morocco was incorporated in Morocco on the latter's independence in 1956. Ifni, the former enclave in Morocco, was incorporated by treaty, on June 30, 1969, and the Spanish Sahara came under joint Moroccan and Mauritanian control in November 1975.

SUDAN
(Al-Jamhuryat es-Sudan Al-Democratia)

President, Ahmed Ali Al Mirghani (D.U.P.).

SOVEREIGNTY COUNCIL

The President; Mohammed Al Hassan Abdalla Yassin (D.U.P.); Idris Abdalla Al Banna (Umma); Ali Al Hassan Taj Al Din (Umma); Pacifico Lado Lolik (S.A.P.C.O.).

CABINET

Prime Minister and Minister of Defence, Sadiq El Mahdi (Umma).
Agriculture, Omer Nur El Daim (Umma).
Finance and Planning, Beshir Omer Fadl (Umma).
Education, Bakri Ahmed Adil (Umma).
Energy and Mining, Adam Musa Madibou (Umma).
Industry, Mubarak Abdalla Al Fadl (Umma).
Cabinet Affairs, Sahaheddin Abdel Salam (Umma).
Attorney General, Abdul Mahmoud Salih (Umma).
Irrigation and Hydro-Electric Power, Mahmoud Beshir Gamaa (Umma).
Social Affairs and Zakat, Rashida Ibrahim Abdul Karim (Umma).
Youth and Sports, Hassan Mohammed Mustafa (Umma).
Foreign Affairs, Mohammed Tawfiq Ahmed (D.U.P.).
Interior, Sid Ahmed El Hussein (D.U.P.).
Commerce, Ibrahim Hassan Abdel Galil (D.U.P.).
Health, Hussein Abu Salih (D.U.P.).
Culture and Information, Mamoon Sinada (D.U.P.).
Housing, Works and Public Utilities, Mohammed Tahir Gailani (D.U.P.).
Local Government, Reit Cuol Jok (S.P.F.P.).
Transport and Communications, Aldo Ajou Deng (S.S.P.A.).

Labour and Public Service, Lawrence Modi Tode (P.P.P.).
Public Service, (vacant).
Religious Affairs, (vacant).
Unity and Peace, (vacant).
Animal Resources, (vacant).
Following the dismissal of the entire Cabinet by the Prime Minister on May 13, 1987 a new Cabinet was formed on June 2.

SUDANESE EMBASSY IN LONDON
3 Cleveland Row, SW1A 1DD
[01-839 8080]

Ambassador Extraordinary and Plenipotentiary, His Excellency Sayed Ibrahim Mohamed Ali (1985).

Area and Population.—The Sudan extends from the southern boundary of Egypt, 22° N. lat., to the northern boundary of Uganda, 3° 36′ N. lat., and reaches from the Republic of Chad about 21° 49′ E. (at 12° 45′ N.) to the north-west boundary of Ethiopia in 38° 35′ E. (at 18° N.). On the east lie the Red Sea and Ethiopia; on the south lie Kenya, Uganda and Zaire; and on the west the Central African Republic, Chad, and Libya. The greatest length from north to south is approximately 1,300 miles, and east to west 950 miles.

The *White Nile* enters from Uganda at Nimule as the *Bahr el Jebel*, and leaves the Sudan at Wadi Halfa. The *Blue Nile* flows from Lake Tana on the Ethiopian Plateau. Its course in the Sudan is nearly 500 miles long, before it joins the White Nile at Khartoum. The next confluence of importance is at Atbara where the main Nile is joined by the River Atbara. Between Khartoum and Wadi Halfa lie five of the six *Cataracts*.

The estimated area is about 967,500 sq. miles (2,505,813 sq. km.), with a population of 21,550,000, partly Arabs, partly Negros, and partly of mixed Arab-Negro blood, with a small foreign element. The Arabs are mostly Moslems. The Nilotics of the Bahr el Ghazal and Upper Nile Valleys are generally animists, but some have been converted to Christianity and others are Moslems. There are some 1 million refugees in the Sudan.

Government.—The Anglo-Egyptian Condominium over the Sudan which had been established in 1899 ended when the Sudan House of Representatives, on Dec. 19, 1955, voted unanimously a declaration that the Sudan was a fully independent sovereign state.

A Republic was proclaimed on Jan. 1, 1956, and was recognized by Great Britain and Egypt, a Supreme Commission being sworn in to take over sovereignty. The Sudan was under military rule from Nov., 1958, until 1964 when a new civilian Cabinet was appointed. Government of the country was taken over on May 25, 1969, by a ten-man revolutionary council headed by Col. Gaafar Mohamed El Nimeri. In February 1972 an agreement was signed at Addis Ababa which brought to an end nearly 17 years of insurrection and civil war in the six southern provinces, and which recognized southern regional autonomy within a unified Sudanese State. Insurrection broke out again in 1983. In April 1985 the Army command assumed power after popular demonstrations, deposed Nimeiri and appointed transitional government which undertook to hand over power to a democratically elected government. Elections were held in April 1986 and a new government formed, a coalition of Umma and D.U.P. members. The Umma party won 100 seats, the Democratic Unionist Party, 63 seats, and National Islamic Front, 51 seats; Progressive Peoples' Party, 10 seats; S. Sudanese Political Association, 8 seats; Sudanese National Party 8 seats; Sudan African Peoples Congress, 7 seats and others 13.

Education.—School education is free for most children, but not compulsory, beginning with six years primary education, followed by three years secondary education at general secondary schools, the more academic higher secondary schools or vocational schools. The medium of instruction is Arabic. English is taught as the principal foreign language in all schools.

Khartoum University has 10 faculties. There is a branch of Cairo University in Khartoum, an Islamic University at Omdurman and a University at Juba.

In addition to the four universities there are various technical post-secondary institutes as well as professional and vocational training establishments.

Production.—The principal grain crops are *dura* (great millet) and wheat, the staple food of the people in the Sudan. Sesame and ground-nuts are other important food crops, which also yield an exportable surplus and a promising start has been made with castor seed. The principal export crop is cotton. Traditionally a major producer of long-staple cotton, Sudan has in recent years grown more short and medium-staple cotton. These grades now account for more than half total production. Production in 1986–87 is estimated to have been around 906,000 bales. The Sudan also produces the bulk of the world's supply of gum arabic. Sugar is an increasingly important crop. The Sudan aims to become self-sufficient in sugar production in 1987. Livestock is the mainstay of the nomadic Arab tribes of the desert and the negro tribes of the swamp and wooded grassland country in the South. Production has, however, been affected by drought and famine.

Much of Sudan's agriculture production, which comprised 31·8 per cent. of gross domestic product in 1985–86, is based on large and medium sized public sector irrigation projects with small scale private irrigation schemes providing mostly fruit and vegetables. Mechanised and traditional agriculture is practiced in areas of sufficient rainfall.

Communications.—The railway system has a route length of about 3,200 miles, linking Khartoum with Wadi Halfa, Karima, Port Sudan, Wad Medani, Sennar, El Damazin, Kosti, El Obeid and Nyala. A line branches out southwards to Wau from the Sennar/Nyala western line. Nile river services between Khartoum and Juba have been interrupted by the southern insurrection. ΨPort Sudan is a well-equipped modern seaport. Sudan Airways fly services from Khartoum to many parts of the Sudan and to other African states, Europe and the Middle East.

FINANCE

	1986–87*
Revenue	£S 2,683 m.
Expenditure	5,542 m.
Deficit	2,859 m.
Estimated deficit financing	2,859 m.

*Estimates

£S = Sudanese *Pound* of 100 *Piastres*.

TRADE

	1984–85*	1985-86*
Total Imports ...	US$1,237 m.	US$1,055 m.
Total Exports ...	544 m.	497 m.

*Estimates

Trade with U.K.

	1985	1986
Imports from U.K.	£103,635,000	£83,300,000
Exports to U.K.	21,323,000	12,800,000

The principal exports are cotton, livestock, gum arabic and other agricultural produce. The chief imports are petroleum goods and other raw materials, machinery and equipment, transport and equipment, medicines and chemicals.

CAPITAL, Khartoum. The town contains many mosques, a Catholic cathedral and an Anglican cathedral, and the University with extensive government buildings. The combined population of Khartoum, Khartoum North and Omdurman is just over 2,000,000.

FLAG.—Three horizontal stripes of red, white and black with a green triangle next to the hoist.

NATIONAL DAY.—January 1 (Independence Day).

BRITISH EMBASSY
Khartoum

Ambassador Extraordinary and Plenipotentiary, His Excellency John Lewis Beaven, C.M.G., C.V.O. (1987).
Counsellor, D. I. Lewty (*Head of Chancery*).
Defence and Military Attaché, Col. R.J.M. Carson, O.B.E.
British Council Representative, R. A. Jarvis, O.B.E., P.O. Box 1253, Khartoum. The British Council has a sub-office in Juba and there are libraries at *El Obeid,* and *Omdurman.*

SURINAME
(Nieuwe Republick van Suriname)

Head of the National Military Council, Lt.-Col. Desi Bouterse.

CABINET

Prime Minister and Minister of Home Affairs, Jules Wijdenbosch.
Foreign Affairs, Henricus A. F. Heidweiller.

Suriname is situated on the north coast of South America and is bounded by French Guyana in the east, Brazil in the south and Guyana in the west. It has an area of 63,037 sq. miles (163,265 sq. km.), with a population (1985 U.N. estimate) of 375,000.

Formerly known as Dutch Guiana, Suriname remained part of the Netherlands West Indies until November 25, 1975, when it achieved complete independence. Suriname had received autonomy in domestic affairs under the Realm Statute which took effect on December 29, 1954. The civilian government was ousted by the military in Feb. 1980, who appointed the predominantly civilian Cabinet. A National Assembly of 31 members was appointed on Jan. 1, 1985 to draft a new constitution. A referendum on this constitution is set for Sept. 30, 1987 with elections to follow on Nov. 25.

Suriname has large timber resources. Rice and sugar cane are the main crops. Bauxite is mined, and is the principal export.

TRADE

	1985
Imports	U.S.$ 359·5 m
Exports	337·3 m

Trade with U.K.

	1985	1986
Imports from U.K.	£9,398,000	£9,743,000
Exports to U.K.	15,405,000	15,554,000

CAPITAL.—ΨParamaribo (population, 1971, 110,000).

FLAG.—Horizontal stripes of green, white, red, white, green, with a five pointed yellow star in the centre.

NATIONAL DAY.—November 25.

British Ambassador (resides at *Georgetown*, Guyana). There is a *British Consulate* at Paramaribo.
Honorary Consul, J. J. Healy, M.B.E.

SWEDEN
(Konungariket Sverige)

King of Sweden, Carl XVI Gustaf, *born* April 30, 1946, *succeeded* September 15, 1973, *married* June 19, 1976 Fräulein Silvia Renate Sommerlath *and has issue*, Crown Princess Victoria Ingrid Alice Désirée, Duchess of Västergötland, *born* July 14, 1977; Prince Carl Philip Edmund Bertil, Duke of Värmland, *born* May 13, 1979; Princess Madeleine Thérèse Amelie Josephine, Duchess of Hälsingland and Gästrikland, *born* June 10, 1982.

COUNCIL OF MINISTERS

Prime Minister, Ingvar Carlsson.
Justice, Sten Wickbom.
Foreign Affairs, Sten Andersson.
Agriculture, Mats Hellström.
Finance, Kjell-Olof Feldt.
Housing, Hans Gustafsson.
Labour, Anna-Greta Leijon.
Education, Lennart Bodström.
Industry, Thage Peterson.
Health and Social Affairs, Gertrud Sigurdsen.
Culture, Bengt Göransson.
Equality and Immigration, Georg Andersson.
Energy and the Environment, Birgitta Dahl.
Public Sector, Bo Holmberg.
Foreign Trade, Anita Gradin.
Defence, Roine Carlsson.
Health and Social Affairs (Deputy Minister), Bengt Lindqvist.
Communications, Sven Hulterström.
Aid, Lena Hjelm-Wallén.
Wages and Salaries, Bengt Johansson.
Sport, Youth and Tourism, Ulf Lönnqvist.

SWEDISH EMBASSY IN LONDON
11 Montagu Place, W1H 2AL
[01-724 2101]

Ambassador Extraordinary and Plenipotentiary, His Excellency Leif Leifland, G.C.V.O. (1982).
Minister Plenipotentiary, H. Granqvist.
Counsellors, A. A. E. Alsterdal (*Press*); P. Bruce (*Commodities*); H. Leo. (*Consular and Administration*); N. Daag (*Political*).
Defence and Air Attaché, Gp. Capt. B. Lennhammar.
Military and Naval Attaché, Col. G. De Geer.
Trade Commissioner, M. Nilsson (73 Welbeck Street, W1M 8AN.)

Area and Population.—Sweden occupies the eastern area of the Scandinavian peninsula in N.W.

Europe and comprises 24 local government districts, "*Län*", with a total area of 173,732 sq. miles (449,964 sq. km.), and population Dec. 31, 1985 of 8,358,139. In 1985 the birth rate was 11·79 per 1,000 inhabitants, the death rate 11·26 per 1,000 inhabitants and infant mortality rate was 6·8 per 1,000 live births.

Government.—Under the Act of Succession of June 6, 1809 (with amendments) the throne is hereditary in the House of Bernadotte. (A 1979 amendment vested the succession in the monarch's eldest child, irrespective of sex.) Jean-Baptiste Jules Bernadotte, Prince of Ponte Corvo, a Marshal of France, was invited to accept the title of Crown Prince, with succession to the throne. He succeeded Charles XIII in 1818. There is a unicameral Diet (*Riksdag*) of 349 members elected for 3 years. The Council of Ministers (*Statsråd*) is responsible to the *Riksdag*.

Production and Industry.—The country's industrial prosperity is based on an abundance of natural resources in the form of forests, mineral deposits and water power. The forests are extensive, covering about half the total land surface, and sustain flourishing timber, pulp and paper milling industries. The mineral resources include iron ore, lead, zinc, sulphur, granite, marble, precious and heavy metals (the latter not exploited) and extensive deposits of low grade uranium ore. Industries based on mining, principally iron and steel, aluminium and copper are important but it is the general engineering industry that provides the basis of Sweden's exports. Growth areas are largely in the specialised machinery and systems and chemical industries. The relative importance of agriculture has declined and in 1983 only 5·4 per cent of the population was engaged in farming.

Apart from water power Sweden has no significant indigenous resources of conventional hydrocarbon fuels and relies to a high degree upon imported oil. Much of Sweden's electricity is generated by nuclear power but as a result of a referendum in 1980 the nuclear programme is to be discontinued by 2010. Small supplies of natural gas are imported from Denmark into southern Sweden, with the pipeline being extended to Gothenburg.

Communications.—The total length of Swedish railroads is 11,745 km. The number of passenger cars in use on December 31, 1985 was 3,151,195.

The Mercantile Marine amounted on December 31, 1985 to 2,619,625 gross tonnage. The Board of Civil Aviation under the control of the Ministry of Communications handles civil aviation matters. Regular domestic air traffic is maintained by the Scandinavian Airlines System and by A. B. Linjeflyg. Regular European and inter-continental air traffic is maintained by the Scandinavian Airlines System.

Defence.—Based on the policy of non-alignment in peace leading to neutrality in war Sweden maintains a Total Defence intended to make any attack on her costly. Total Defence includes peacetime organizations for civil, economic and psychological defence as well as compulsory national service for all acceptable males. Some 50,000 National Servicemen are called up for 7–15 months training each year and all are recalled every fourth year for refresher training. On mobilization the Army strength totals 4 armoured brigades, 1 mechanised brigade and 23 infantry and winter warfare brigades. The Navy has 12 submarines, 48 fast attack craft, a number of minor craft and auxiliaries and 5 coast artillery units. The Air Force has modern supersonic aircraft of Swedish manufacture forming a standing force of 220 air defence, 150 attack and 55 reconnaissance with support aircraft and a modern air defence radar system. Facilities exist for rapid dispersal from main bases in war.

Religion.—The State religion is Lutheran Protestant, to which over 95 per cent of the people officially adhere.

Language and Literature.—Swedish belongs, with Danish and Norwegian, to the North Germanic language group. Swedish literature dates back to King Magnus Eriksson, who codified the old Swedish provincial laws in 1350. With his translation of the Bible, Olaus Petri (1493–1552) formed the basis for the modern Swedish language. Literature flourished during the reign of Gustavus III, who founded the Swedish Academy in 1786. Swedish literature is studded with names such as Almquist (1795–1866), Strindberg (1849–1912) and Lagerlöf (1858–1940), Nobel Prize Winner in 1909. Contemporary authors include Lagerquist (1891–1974), Nobel Laureate in 1951, Martinson (1904–1978) and Johnson (1900–1976), Nobel Laureates jointly in 1974. The Swedish scientist Alfred Nobel (1833–1896) founded the Nobel Prizes for Literature, Science and Peace.

Education.—Tuition within the State system, which is maintained by the State and by local taxation, is free. It provides 9 years' compulsory schooling from the age of 7 to 16 in the comprehensive elementary schools; further education of 2, 3 or 4 years in the upper secondary schools; a unified higher education system administered in 6 regional areas containing one of the universities—Uppsala (founded 1477); Lund (1668); Stockholm (1878); Gothenburg (1887); Umeå (1963) and Linköping (1967). At present there are 33 institutions of higher education including three technical universities in Stockholm, Gothenburg and Luleå, and the Karolinska Institute in Stockholm, which specializes in medicine and dentistry.

FINANCE

	1985–86	1986–87
	Kronor million	*Kronor* million
Revenue	275,638	293,190
Expenditure	327,177	336,392

The currency is the Swedish *Krona* of 100 *Öre*. (*See also* p. 81.)

TRADE

	1985	1986
	Kronor million	*Kronor* million
Imports	243,974·4	231,444·9
Exports	259,985·1	265,039·7

Trade with U.K.

	1985	1986
Imports from U.K.	£3,006,890,000	£2,307,900
Exports to U.K.	2,465,582,000	2,756,536

Sweden's main imports from Britain are crude oil and petroleum products, machinery and parts, road vehicles and components, clothing and textiles and steel. Britain's main imports from Sweden are paper and board, road vehicles, machinery, wood, steel and pulp.

CAPITAL.—ΨStockholm. Population (1985): City 659,030; Greater Stockholm, 1,435,474; ΨGothenburg (Göteborg) (425,495); ΨMalmö (229,936); Uppsala (154,859)

FLAG.—Yellow cross on a blue ground.

NATIONAL DAY.—June 6 (Day of the Swedish Flag).

BRITISH EMBASSY
Skarpögatan 6–8, 115 27 Stockholm

Ambassador Extraordinary and Plenipotentiary, His Excellency Sir Richard Parsons, K.C.M.G., *apptd.*, 1984.

British Council Representative, J. R. Day.

BRITISH CONSULAR OFFICES

There is a British Consular Office at *Stockholm*.
BRITISH-SWEDISH CHAMBER OF COMMERCE: Grevgatan 34, 11453 Stockholm.

SWITZERLAND
(Schweizerische Eidgenossenschaft— Confédération Suisse—Confederazione Svizzera.)

FEDERAL COUNCIL

President of the Swiss Confederation (1987) *and Head of Foreign Affairs*, Pierre Aubert.
Vice-President (1987) *and Head of Finance*, Otto Stich.
Military, Arnold Koller.
Justice and Police, Mrs. Elizabeth Kopp.
Transport, Energy and Communications, Leon Schlumpf.
Public Economy, Jean-Pascal Delamuraz.
Interior, Flavio Cotti.

SWISS EMBASSY IN LONDON
16–18 Montagu Place, W1H 2BQ
[01–723 0701]

Ambassador Extraordinary and Plenipotentiary, His Excellency F. C. Pictet (1984).
Ministers, Willy Hold ; Milan J. A. Lusser (*Economic and Financial*).
Counsellor, H. Hofer (*Commodities and Agriculture*).
Defence, Military, Naval and Air Attaché, Maj.-Gen. G. de Loës.
Consul and Head of Administration, A. Mehr.

There is a Swiss Consulate-General in *Manchester*.

Area and Population.—The Helvetia of the Romans, a Federal Republic of Central Europe, situated between 45° 50′–47° 48′ N. lat. and 5° 58′–10° 3′ E. long. It is composed of 23 Cantons, 3 subdivided, making 26 in all, and comprises a total area of 15,943 sq. miles (23,623 sq. km.), with a population (estimated January, 1986) of 6,484,800. In 1985 there were 74,684 live births, 59,583 deaths and 38,776 marriages. Of the total population in 1980, 44·3 per cent of the population was Protestant, 47·6 per cent Roman Catholic and 0·3 per cent Jewish.

Physical Features.—Switzerland is the most mountainous country in all Europe. The Alps, covered with perennial snow and from 5,000 to 15,217 feet in height, occupy its southern and eastern frontiers, and the chief part of its interior; and the Jura mountains rise in the north-west. The Alps occupy 61 per cent, and the Jura mountains 12 per cent, of the country. The *Alps* are a crescent-shaped mountain system situated in France, Italy, Switzerland, Bavaria and Austria, covering an area of 80,000 square miles from the Mediterranean to the Danube (600 miles). The highest peak, Mont Blanc, Pennine Alps (15,782 feet) is partly in France and Italy ; Monte Rosa (15,217 feet) and Matterhorn (14,780 feet) are partly in Switzerland and partly in Italy. The highest wholly Swiss peaks are Dufourspitze (15,203 ft.), Finsteraarhorn (14,026), Aletschhorn (13,711), Jungfrau (13,671), Mönch (13,456), Eiger (13,040), Schreckhorn (13,385), and Wetterhorn (12,150) in the Bernese Alps, and Dom (14,918), Weisshorn (14,803) and Breithorn (13,685).

The Swiss lakes are famous for their beauty and include Lakes Maggiore, Zürich, Lucerne, Neuchâtel, Geneva, Constance, Thun, Zug, Lugano, Brienz and the Walensee. There are also many artificial lakes.

Government.—The legislative power is vested in a Parliament, consisting of two Chambers, a National Council (*Nationalrat*) of 200 members, and a States Council (*Ständerat*) of 46 members; both Chambers united are called the Federal Assembly, and the members of the National Council are elected for four years, an election taking place in October. The executive power is in the hands of a Federal Council (*Bundesrat*) of seven members, elected for four years by the Federal Assembly and presided over by the President of the Confederation. Each year the

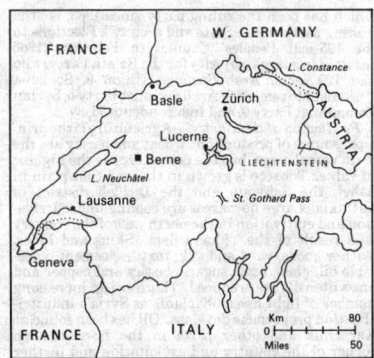

School age varies, generally 7 to 14. (ii) *Secondary*: Age 12–15 for boys and girls. Schools numerous and well-attended, and there are many private institutions. (iii) *Special schools* make a feature of commercial and technical instruction. (iv) *Universities*: Basle (founded 1460), Berne (1834), Fribourg (1889), Geneva (1873), Lausanne (1890), Zürich (1832), and Neuchâtel (1909), and the technical Universities of Lausanne and Zürich and commercial University of St. Gall.

Language and Literature.—There are three official languages: French, German and Italian. In addition Romansch is recognized as a national, but not an official language. German is the dominating language in 19 of the 26 cantons; French in Fribourg, Jura, Geneva, Neuchâtel, Valais and Vaud; Italian in Ticino, and Romansch in parts of the Grisons.

Many modern authors, alike in the German school and in the Suisse Romande, have achieved international fame. Karl Spitteler (1845–1924) and Hermann Hesse (1877–1962) were awarded the Nobel Prize for Literature, the former in 1919, the latter in 1946.

Federal Assembly elects from the Federal Council the President and the Vice-President. Not more than one of the same canton may be elected member of the Federal Council; on the other hand, there is a tradition that Italian and French-speaking areas should between them be represented on the Federal Council by at least two members.

Defence.—All Swiss males must undertake military service in the Army or the Air Force, which is part of the Army. Swiss Army equipment includes some British items, such as Centurion tanks, Bloodhound missiles, Vampire and Hunter aircraft and the Medium Girder Bridge. The Rapier guided missile system is being delivered.

Production and Industry.—Agriculture is followed chiefly in the valleys and all over the Mittelland, where cereals, flax, hemp, and tobacco are produced, and nearly all temperate zone fruits and vegetables as well as grapes are grown. Dairying and stock-raising are the principal industries, about 3,000,000 acres being under grass for hay and 2,000,000 acres pasturage. The forests cover about one-quarter of the whole surface. The chief manufacturing industries comprise engineering and electrical engineering, metal-working, chemicals and pharmaceuticals, textiles, watchmaking, woodworking, foodstuffs and footwear. Banking, insurance and tourism are major industries.

Communications.—There are 4,997 km of railway tracks (Swiss Federal Railways, 2,946 km; Swiss privately owned railways 2,951 km). At the end of 1985 the number of telephones amounted to 5,435,800 and the network was fully automatic throughout the country. At the same time there were 2,467,200 licensed radio receivers and 2,186,500 television receivers.

At the end of 1982 the total length of motorways was 1,288 km. The number of motor vehicles licensed in 1983 was 2,887,117.

A merchant marine, established in 1940, consisted at the end of 1985 of 39 vessels with a total gross tonnage of 225,434 tonnes. In 1982, goods handled at Basle Rhine ports amounted to 9,423,093 tonnes. In 1982 151 lake vessels transported 9,146,000 passengers and 2,640 tonnes of freight. Swiss airlines have a network covering 314,762 km and in 1983 carried 7,281,328 passengers. Swissair, the State airline, which owned 51 aircraft in 1983, flies to and from the Swiss airports at Zürich, Geneva and Basle.

Education.—Control by cantonal and communal authorities. No central organization. Illiteracy practically unknown. (i) *Primary*: Free and compulsory.

FINANCE

	1986	1987
	Sw. Frs.	Sw. Frs.
Revenue	25,144m.	24,396m.
Expenditure	23,176m.	24,225m.

TRADE

	1985	1986
	Sw. Frs.	Sw. Frs.
Total Imports	74,785m.	73,512m.
Total Exports	66,624m.	67,004m.

Trade with U.K.
(including Liechtenstein)

	1985	1986
Imports from U.K.	£1,306,757,000	£1,575,247,000
Exports to U.K.	2,371,090,000	2,989,112,000

The principal imports are machinery, electrical and electronic equipment, textiles, motor vehicles, non-ferrous metals, chemical elements, clothing, food, medicinal and pharmaceutical products. The principal exports are machinery, chemical elements, non-ferrous metals, watches, electrical and electronic equipment, textiles, dyeing, tanning and colouring equipment. Switzerland is a member of E.F.T.A.

CAPITAL.—Berne. Population, 301,100 (urban agglomeration). Other large towns are Zürich (840,000), Basle (363,600), Geneva (382,000), Lausanne (260,200), Winterthur (107,400), St. Gallen (125,400), Lucerne (160,000).

FLAG.—Red, with white cross.

NATIONAL DAY.—August 1.

BRITISH EMBASSY
Thunstrasse 50, 3000 Berne 15

Ambassador Extraordinary and Plenipotentiary, His Excellency John Rowland Rich, C.M.G. (1985).

Counsellor, M. L. H. Hope.

First Secretaries, G. C. Duncan; B. England; Miss M. A. Savill.

Second Secretary, A. M. M. McDermott.

Defence, Naval and Military Attaché, Lt.-Col. T. H. G. Duke.

Air Attaché, Wing. Cdr. T. N. King.

Attaché, P. C. Albrecht (*Commercial*).

BRITISH CONSULAR OFFICES

There is a Consular Section at H.M. Embassy, Berne; *Consulates-General* at *Zürich* and *Geneva* and Consular offices at *Lugano* and *Montreux*. The Directorate of British Export Promotion in Switzerland is in the Consulate-General Office in *Zürich*.

BRITISH-SWISS CHAMBER OF COMMERCE, Freiestrasse 155, 8032 Zürich.

SWISS-BRITISH SOCIETIES:

Berne.—*President*, Dr. H. Beriger.
Zürich.—*President*, Dr. R. J. Schneebeli.
Basle.—*President*, G. Simons.

SYRIA
(Al-Jamhouriya Al-Arabia as-Souriya)

President, Lt.-Gen. Hafez el Assad, *b.* 1930, *assumed office* March 14, 1971, *re-elected*, Feb. 1978, March 13, 1985.

Vice-Presidents, Abdul Halim Khaddam, Rifaat Al Assad, Zuhair Mashariqa.

Prime Minister, Abdul-Raouf Al-Kasam.

Deputy Prime Minister and Minister for Defence, Gen. Mustafa Tlass.

Deputy Prime Minister for Public Services, Mahmoud Qaddur.

Deputy Prime Minister for Economic Affairs, Dr. Salim Yassin.

SYRIAN EMBASSY IN LONDON

The Syrian Embassy has been closed since Oct. 31, 1986, when Syria and the U.K. broke off diplomatic relations.

Area and Population.—Syria is in the Levant, covering a portion of the former Ottoman Empire, with an estimated area of 71,498 sq. miles (185,180 sq. km.), and a population (1985 U.N. estimate) of 10,267,000, most of whom are Arabic-speaking and Muslim. (*For* Map, *see* index.) The Orontes flows northwards from the Lebanon range across the northern boundary to Antakya (Antioch, Turkey). The Euphrates crosses the northern boundary near Jerablus and flows through north-eastern Syria to the boundary of Iraq.

Archaeology, etc.—The region is rich in historical remains. Damascus (*Dimishq ash-Sham*) is said to be the oldest continuously inhabited city in the world (although Aleppo disputes this claim), having an existence as a city for over 4,000 years. It is situated on the river Barada, in an oasis at the eastern foot of the Anti-Lebanon, and at the edge of the wide sandy desert which stretches to the Euphrates. The city contains the Omayed Mosque, the Tomb of Saladin, and the "Street Called Straight" (Acts ix. 11), while to the North-East is the Roman outpost of Dmeir and further east is Palmyra.

On the Mediterranean coast at Amrit are ruins of the Phoenician town of Marath, where the well has been found and is being excavated and also ruins of Crusaders' fortresses at Markab, Sahyoun, and Krak des Chevaliers. At Tartous (also on the coast) the cathedral of Our Lady of Syria, built by the Knights Templars in the 12th and 13th centuries has been restored as a museum. One of the oldest alphabets in the world has been discovered at Ugarit (Ras Shamra), a Phoenician village near the port of Latakia.

Hittite cities dating from 2,000 to 1,500 B.C., have recently been explored on the west bank of the Euphrates at Jerablus and Kadesh.

Government.—Syria, which had been under French mandate since the 1914–18 war, became an independent Republic during the 1939–45 war. The first independently elected Parliament met on August 17, 1943, but foreign troops were in part occupation until April, 1946. Syria remained an independent Republic until February, 1958, when it became part of the United Arab Republic. It seceded from the United Arab Republic on Sept. 28, 1961.

A new Constitution was promulgated in March 1973; this declared that Syria is a "democratic, popular socialist State", and that the Ba'ath Party,

which has been the ruling party since 1963, is "the leading party in the State and society". Elections to the 195-seat Peoples' Council in February 1986 resulted in a large majority for the Ba'ath Party, who had 129 seats, Arab Socialist Union 9, Socialist Unionist Movement 8, Arab Socialist Party 5, Syrian Communist Party 9, and Independents 35.

Production and Industry.—Agriculture is the principal source of production; wheat and barley are the main cereal crops, but the cotton crop is the highest in value. Tobacco is grown in the maritime plain in Sahel, the Sahyoun and the Djebleh district of Lattakia. Large new areas are coming under irrigation and cultivation in the north-east of the country as a result of the Thawra dam. Skins and hides, leather goods, wool and silk, textiles, cement, vegetable oil, glass, soap, sugar, plastics and copper and brass utensils are produced. There are an increasing number of light assembly plants as Syria's industrialisation programme develops. Oil has been found at Karachuk and other parts in the north-eastern corner of the country and exploitation and further excavations have recently discovered considerable high quality reserves in the region of Deir ez Zor. Syria produces about 8·2 million tons of oil per year at present. A pipeline has been built to the Mediterranean port of Banias, *viâ* Homs. Two oil refineries are in production at Homs and Banias. Revenue is derived from the pipeline from the oilfields of Saudi Arabia to Sidon in Lebanon (Tapline). Another pipeline from the Iraq oilfields was closed in April 1982. Syria also has deposits of phosphate and rock salt, and produces asphalt.

Language and Literature.—Arabic is the principal language, but Kurdish, Turkish and Armenian are spoken among significant minorities and a few villages still speak Aramaic, the language spoken by Christ and the Apostles. There are 3 daily newspapers and several periodicals in Arabic published in Damascus, and also a daily newspaper in English. English has taken over from French as the main foreign language, especially among the young.

Education.—Education in Syria is under State control and, although a few of the schools are privately owned, they all follow a common system and syllabus. Elementary education is free at State Schools, and is compulsory from the age of seven. Secondary education is not compulsory and is free only at the State Schools. Because of the shortage of places, entry to these State Schools is competitive. Damascus University, founded in 1924, has nine faculties and a Higher Teachers' Training College. The number of students has risen to over 60,000. There are also about 20,000 students at Aleppo University (founded 1961), over 10,000 at Tishrin University, Latakia (founded 1975) and 6,000 at Ba'ath University, Homs. Approximately 10 per cent of all students receive scholarships, and at the present time Palestinian refugees are admitted free. The rest pay fees.

Communications.—Although railway lines run from Damascus to both Beirut and Amman, train services go only as far as the border towns. A track has been opened connecting Homs with Damascus but is not yet open to passengers. A track links Homs, Hamah, Aleppo and Qamishliye to the Iraq frontier. Branch lines connect the ports of Tartous and Latakia to the system and another line runs from Aleppo down Euphrates valley to Deir ez Zor and thence north to Qamishliye, with a branch going to the Euphrates Dam. All the principal towns in the country are connected by roads which vary from modern dual carriageways to narrow country lanes. An internal air service operates between all major towns. The main International Airport is at Damascus and there are also flights to Eastern Europe, Turkey, Greece and Armenia from Aleppo.

Currency.—The monetary unit is the Syrian pound (£*Syr.*). Exchange rate, *see* p. 82.

Trade.—The principal imports are foodstuffs (fruit, vegetables, cereals, meat and dairy products, tea, coffee and sugar), mineral and petroleum products, yarn and textiles, iron and steel manufactures, machinery, chemicals, pharmaceuticals, fertilizers and timber. Raw cotton, oil, cereals, fruit, phosphates, livestock and dairy products, other foodstuffs, textiles and raw wool.

Trade with U.K.

	1985	1986
Imports from U.K.	£80,901,000	£55,511,000
Exports to U.K.	78,575,000	31,298,000

CAPITAL.—Damascus (population (estimated) 2,250,000). Other important towns are Aleppo, Homs and Hama, and the principal port is Latakia.

FLAG.—Red over white over black horizontal bands, with two green stars on central white band.

NATIONAL DAY.—April 17.

BRITISH INTERESTS SECTION
Quartier Malki, 11 rue Mohammad Kurd Ali,
Imm. Kotob, Damascus.

Following the break in diplomatic relations with Syria in October 1986, Australia has been protecting British interests in Syria.

THAILAND
(Prathes Thai)

King, His Majesty Bhumibol Adulyadej, *born* 1927; *succeeded his brother,* June 9, 1946; *married* Princess Sirikit Kitiyakara, April 28, 1950; *crowned* May 5, 1950; *and has issue,* Princess Ubolratana, *born,* April 6, 1951; Crown Prince Vajiralongkorn, *born,* July 28, 1952; Princess Sirindhorn, *born,* April 2, 1955; Princess Chulabhorn *born,* July 4, 1957.

CABINET

Prime Minister, Gen. Prem Tinsulanonda.
Deputy Prime Ministers, Bhichai Rattakul; Maj.-Gen. Chatichai Choonhavan; Pong Sarasin; Gen. Thienchai Sirisamphan; Adm. Sontee Boonyachai.
Ministers attached to the Prime Minister's Office, Vichit Saengtong; Amnuay Suwankhiri; Chaisiri Ruangkarnchanaset; Meechai Ruchupan; Ft.-Lt. Suli Mahasantana; Chirayu Isarangkun Na Ayuthaya.
Defence, Air Chief Marshal Panieng Kantarat.
Foreign Affairs, Air Chief Marshal Panieng Siddhi Savetsila.
Finance, Suthee Singhasaneh.
Interior, Gen. Prachuab Suntrangkoon.
Agriculture and Co-operatives, Gen. Harn Leenanonda.
Commerce, Montri Pongpanit.
Industry, Pramual Sapavasu.
Communications, Banharn Silpa-archa.
Education, Marut Bunnag.
Public Health, Tirdpong Jayanandana.
Science, Technology and Energy, Banyat Bantadtan.
Justice, Sa-ard Piyawan.
University Affairs, Subin Pinkayan.

ROYAL THAI EMBASSY IN LONDON
30 Queen's Gate, SW7 5JB
[01–589 0173]

Ambassador Extraordinary and Plenipotentiary, His Excellency Mr. Sudhee Prasasvinitchai (1986).

Area and Population.—The Kingdom of Thailand, formerly known as Siam, has an area of 198,457 sq. miles (514,000 sq. km.), with a population (estimated 1986) of 52,970,000. The population growth rate averages 2·4 per cent. per year. It has a common boundary with Malaysia in the south, is bounded on the west by Burma and on the north-east and east by Laos and Cambodia. (For MAP, *see* INDEX.) Although there is no common boundary between Thailand and China, the Chinese province of Yunnan is separated from the Thai northern border only by a narrow stretch of Burmese and Laotian territory.

The capital, Bangkok, is situated in the south of the central plain area. To the north-east there is a plateau area and to the north-west mountains. The south of Thailand consists of a narrow mountainous peninsula. The principal rivers are the Chao Phraya in the central plains, and the Mekong on the northern and north-eastern borders.

Language and Religion.—Thai is basically a monosyllabic, tonal language, a branch of the Indo-Chinese linguistic family, but its vocabulary especially has been strongly influenced by Sanskrit and Pali. It is written in an alphabetic script derived from ancient Indian scripts. The principal religion is Buddhism. In 1985 94·95 per cent of the population were Buddhists, 3·91 per cent Moslems, 0·53 per cent Christians and 0·61 per cent other religions.

Government.—Thailand became a Constitutional Monarchy in 1932. The Constitution promulgated in December 1978 provides for a National Assembly consisting of a Senate appointed by the King and a House of Representatives elected by universal adult suffrage. There are 260 Senate seats and 347 House seats. Each senator is appointed for six years and each M.P. for four years.

A General Election was held in July 1986, following the dissolution of the House after three years. Sixteen political parties entered the contest. The results were: Democrat, 100 seats; Chart Thai, 63; Social Action 51; United Democracy, 38; Prachakorn Thai, 24; Ruam Thai, 19; Rassadorn, 18; Community Action, 15; Progessive, 9; Chart Prachatipatai, 3; Mass, 3; Puang Chon Chao Thai, 1; New Force, 1; Democratic Labour, 1; Liberal, 1; and Rak Thai, 0. The present Government is a coalition of Democrats, Chart Thai, Social Action and Rassadorn.

Education.—Primary education is compulsory and free and secondary education in Government Schools is free. In 1983 there were 35,846 schools and training colleges, with a total of 10,058,295 pupils and 539,680 teachers. Private universities and colleges are playing an increasing role in higher education. In 1984 the Government agreed to upgrade four private colleges to universities. Out of 29 universities and other similar higher institutes of learning, 11 are private and attended by some 25,000 students. In 1984 their total enrolment was 668,810 students. The two open universities, Ramkamhaeng and Sukhothaithammathirat, had an enrolment of 409,686 and 73,000 students respectively.

Agriculture and Industry.—The agricultural sector provides just under half the national income and employs 67·5 per cent of the labour force, which in 1985 was estimated at 26·8 million. Rice remains the most important crop, accounting for 60 per cent of the area planted. After rice the main crops are sugar, maize, rubber, tobacco, kenaf and jute. In recent years the production of livestock and poultry, especially pigs and chickens for export, has gained importance. There is a large fishing industry with more than 20,000 vessels registered. Fish farming is popular in many inland areas. A ban on hardwood export has resulted in the decline of the forestry industry.

The discovery of onshore oil and offshore gas in the late 1970s ushered in a new economic era. Crude production which began in 1983 stood at around

20,000 barrels per day in mid-1985, or about 10 per cent of the country's need. At the same time gas and condensate output stood at over 350 million cubic feet per day. It was estimated that by the end of 1985 indigenous oil and gas supplies should account for about half of Thailand's petroleum demand. The predicted surplus of natural gas has led the Government to designate an area on the east coast as the future centre of the petrochemical industry. Another energy resource becoming more important is lignite which is found mainly in the north and is being used increasingly for electricity production.

Mineral resources are mainly tin, tungsten, lead, antimony and iron. Among these, tin is the most important, with exports totalling 18,455 tons in 1984. In addition, about 60,000 tons of zinc ingots a year are expected to be produced by a zinc refinery which was opened in early 1984.

Industry is divided into two main categories: service and manufacturing. Since 1982 tourism has replaced rice as the country's top foreign exchange earner. There were 2·4 million tourists in 1985, an increase of 3·3 per cent on 1984. Total tourism income was estimated at between £675–750 million. The banking system is large and contributes much to the economy, especially employment. There are over 1,800 bank branches in the country employing some 72,000 workers.

Since 1960 the Government has actively promoted industrial investments by means of tax relief and other incentives to local and foreign investors; in 1985, 74·6 per cent. of this investment was in Thai projects. Most of the industries established under this scheme in early years were import-substituting. However, there has been an increasing shift to export-oriented industries, taking advantages of low-wage labour and available domestic resources. Manufacturing now accounts for about 20 per cent of the national income. Crops contribute 12·6 per cent. of G.D.P., and industries 19·8 per cent.

Communications.—The importance of rivers and canals as the traditional mode of transportation has been replaced by highways and roads. The existing road and highway network, totalling 34,701 kilometres in 1984, reaches all parts of the country. Most of the smaller towns and bigger villages are now served by paved roads.

Navigable waterways have a length of about 1,100 km. in the dry season and 1,600 km. in the wet season. About 3,825 km of State-owned railways were open to traffic in 1984. Main lines run from Bangkok to Aranya Prathet on the Cambodian border *via* Korat to Ubon and to Nong Khai, the ferry terminal on the River Mekong opposite Vientiane, capital of Laos; to Chiang Mai and to Hat Yai, whence lines go down the eastern and western sides of the Malay peninsula, *via* Sungei Galok and Penang respectively, to Singapore. A new line to Sattahip on the east coast is being constructed.

Bangkok is an important international air centre and has direct flights to most of the world's major cities. The airports at Chiang Mai and Hat Yai also receive international flights. Most major provincial towns have airports. Thai International, founded in 1960, operates international routes. Domestic routes are operated by Thai Airways. Both are state-owned.

Thailand has an extensive network of telecommunications services, and the telephone service though still poor is being improved. Most major cities and towns are linked by direct long-distance calls.

There are two important ports in the country. Bangkok, which is a river port, can serve vessels up to 27 ft. draught. The deep-sea port at Sattahip caters for larger vessels. Many existing ports in the south are being upgraded to allow more direct cargo shipments. All are owned and operated by a state enterprise.

TRADE

Thailand's main exports are rice, tapioca and tapioca products, garments, rubber, integrated circuit boards, precious stones, pearls and other ornaments, maize, canned sea food, fabrics, sugar and tin. Main imports are crude oil, chemicals and pharmaceuticals, electrical and non-electrical machinery and spare parts, industrial machinery, iron and steel, diesel oil and other fuel oil, vehicle and transport equipment.

	1985	1986
	millions of *Baht*	
Total imports	253,340	246,570
Total exports	191,710	229,340

Trade with U.K.

	1985	1986
Imports from U.K.	£157,723,000	£182,756,079
Exports to U.K.	131,806,000	158,194,823

The Baht currency was unpegged from the U.S. dollar in Nov. 1984. The 'managed floating' is done daily by the central bank. (See also p. 82.)

CAPITAL.—ΨBangkok (population 5,400,000 (1985)); at the mouth of the River Chao Phraya. Other centres are Chiang Mai, Phitsanuloke, Chon Buri, Korat, Khon Kaen, Surat Thani, Hat Yai and Phuket but none approaches Bangkok in size or importance.

FLAG.—Five horizontal bands, red, white, dark blue, white, red (the blue band twice the width of the others).

NATIONAL DAY.—December 5 (The King's Birthday).

BRITISH EMBASSY
Wireless Road, Bangkok

Ambassador Extraordinary and Plenipotentiary, His Excellency Derek Tonkin, C.M.G. (1985).

British Council Representative, E. C. Pugh, 428 Rama 1 Road, Siam Square, Bangkok 10500.

BRITISH CHAMBER OF COMMERCE,
302 Silom Road, Bangkok 10500

TOGO
(République Togolaise)

President and Minister of Defence, Gen. Gnassingbé Eyadéma, *born* 1937, *assumed office*, April 14, 1967; *re-elected for seven-year term*, Dec. 23, 1986.
Interior, Komla Agbetiafa.
Planning and Mines, Barry Moussa Barque.
Rural Development, Koffi Walla.
Minister Delegate to the Presidency (Information), Gbegnon Amegboh.
Equipment, Posts and Telecommunications, Nassirou Ayeva.
National Education and Scientific Research, Tchaa-Kozah Tchalim.
Public Health, Social and Women's Affairs, Aissah Agbetra.
Commerce and Transport, N'Souwoudji Kawo Ehe.
Youth, Sports and Culture, Komla Dometo Nyemenya.
Foreign Affairs and Co-operation, Yaovi Adodo.
Industry and State Enterprises, Koffi Djondo.
Technical Instruction and Professional Training, Koffi Edoh.
Economy and Finance, Komla Alipui.
Planning and Industry, Yaovi Adodo.
Labour and Public Works, Bitokotipou Yagninim.
Justice, Kpotivi Tevi Djidjogbe Lacle.

EMBASSY IN LONDON
30 Sloane Street, S.W.1.
[01–235 0147/9]

Ambassador Extraordinary and Plenipotentiary, His Excellency Mr. Assiongbon Agbenou (1986).
Counsellor, Noglo Kodzo Senanu.

The Republic is situated in West Africa between 0°–2° W. and 6°–11° N., with a coastline only 35 miles long on the Gulf of Guinea, and extends northward inland for 350 miles. It is flanked on the west by Ghana, on the north by Burkina Faso and in the east by Benin. It has an area of 21,925 sq. miles (56,785 sq. km.), and a population (estimate, 1985) of 3,030,000, including people of several African races. The official language is French.

The first President of Togo, Sylvanus Olympio, assassinated on January 13, 1963, was succeeded by Nicolas Grunitzky, who was himself overthrown by an army coup d'état on January 13, 1967. On April 14, 1967, the Commander-in-Chief of the Togolese army, Lt. Colonel (later promoted General) Eyadéma named himself President.

Finance.—The currency of Togo is the *Franc C.F.A.*

Production and Trade.—Although the economy of Togo remains largely agricultural, exports of phosphates have superseded agricultural products as the main source of export earnings. Other exports include palm kernels, copra and manioc. The production of phosphates entirely for export was taken over completely by the government in February 1974.

Trade with U.K.

	1985	1986
Imports from U.K.	£17,034,000	£17,490,000
Exports to U.K.	4,597,000	5,001,000

CAPITAL.—ΨLomé, population (1983), 366,476.

FLAG.—Five alternating green and yellow horizontal stripes; a quarter in red at top next staff bearing a white star.

NATIONAL DAY.—April 27 (Independence Day).

BRITISH EMBASSY
British Ambassador, (resides at *Accra, Ghana*).

TUNISIA
(Al-Djoumhouria Attunusia)

President, Habib Bourguiba, *elected* July 25, 1957; *re-elected* 1959, 1964, 1969 and 1974. Proclaimed President for life March 1975.
Prime Minister, Rachid Sfar.
Justice, Mohamed Salah Ayari.
Foreign Affairs, Hédi Mabrouk.
National Defence, Slaheddine Baly.
Planning and Finance, Ismail Khelil.

TUNISIAN EMBASSY IN LONDON
29 Prince's Gate, SW7 1QG
[01–584 8117]

Ambassador Extraordinary and Plenipotentiary, His Excellency Hamadi Khouini (1987).

Area and Population.—Tunisia lies between Algeria and Libya and extends southwards to the Sahara Desert, with a total area of 63,170 sq. miles (163,610 sq. km.), and an estimated population in 1985 of 7,205,106.

Government.—A French Protectorate from 1881 to 1956, Tunisia became an independent sovereign State with the signing on March 20, 1956, of an agreement whereby France recognized Tunisia's independence and right to conduct her own foreign policy and to form a Tunisian Army.

Following a first general election held on March 25, 1956, a Constituent Assembly met for the first time on April 8. On July 25, 1957, the Constituent Assembly deposed the Bey, abolished the monarchy and elected M. Bourguiba first President of the Republic. On June 1, 1959, the Constitution was promulgated and on December 7, 1959, the National Assembly held its first session. In March 1975 the National Assembly proclaimed M. Bourguiba as President for life.

The country is divided into 22 regions (*gouvernorats*) each administered by a Governor.

Production, Trade, etc.—The valleys of the northern region support large flocks and herds, and contain rich agricultural areas, in which wheat, barley, and oats are grown. The vine and olive are extensively cultivated.

The chief exports are crude oil, phosphates, olive oil, finished textiles, and fruit. The chief imports are machinery and equipment, foodstuffs, petroleum products, and textiles. Some oil has been discovered and production reached an annual rate of 5·4 million tons in 1985. Gas has also been discovered off the east coast but exploitation is not viable at present. Tourists numbered 2,000,000 in 1985.

	1985	1986
Total Imports ...	TD2,287,000	TD2,294,400
Total Exports ...	1,443,000	1,403,600

France remains the main trading partner, supplying 27·6 per cent of the country's imports and purchasing 22·9 per cent of Tunisia's exports.

Trade with U.K.

	1985	1986
Imports from U.K.	£43,209,000	£39,824,358
Exports to U.K.	39,826,000	17,291,779

Currency.—The unit of currency is the *dinar* of 1,000 *millimes*.

Tunisia became an associate member of the E.C. early in 1969, and signed a new agreement with the E.C. in 1976. In 1977 the introduction of import quota measures by the E.C. on some textile goods resulted in a reduction of growth in this important sector of the Tunisian market. The quotas for some textile products was renegotiated and increased in 1982.

CAPITAL.—Ψ Tunis, connected by canal with La Goulette on the coast, has a population (1984) of 1,394,749. The ruins of ancient Carthage lie a few miles from the city. Other towns of importance are: Ψ Sfax (577,992); Ψ Sousse (322,491); Ψ Bizerta (394,670); Kairouan; Gabes; Menzel Bourguiba.

FLAG.—Red crescent and star in a white orb, all on a red ground.

NATIONAL DAY.—June 1.

BRITISH EMBASSY
Place de la Victoire, Tunis

Ambassador Extraordinary and Plenipotentiary and Consul-General, His Excellency William James Adams, C.M.G. (1984).
First Secretary, B. E. Stewart (*Head of Chancery*).
Second Secretary, J. F. Larner (*Commercial and Consul*).
British Council Representative, Dr. P. J. A. Clark. There is a British Council Library in *Tunis*.

TURKEY
(Türkiye Cumhuriyeti)

President, Gen. Kenan Evren, *assumed power*, Sept. 12, 1980; *elected for 7-year term*, Nov. 1982.

GOVERNMENT

Prime Minister, Turgut Özal.
Deputy Prime Minister, Kaya Erdem.

Ministers of State, Kazim Oksay; Hasan Celal Guzel; Mustafa Tinaz Titiz; Abdullah Tenekeci; M. Vehbi Dinçerler; Ahmet Karaevli; Prof. Ali Bozer.
Justice, Mahmut Oltan Sungurlu.
National Defence, Zeki Yavuztürk.
Interior, Yildirim Akbulut.
Foreign Affairs, Vahit Halefoğlu.*
Finance and Customs, A. Kurtcebe Alptemoçin.
National Education, Youth and Sport, Metin Emiroğlu.
Public Works and Construction, I. Safa Giray.
Health and Social Welfare, Mustafa Kalemli.
Communications, Veysel Atasoy.
Agriculture, Forestry and Rural Affairs, Hüsnü Doğan.*
Labour and Social Security, Mukurrem Taşcioğlu.
Industry and Commerce, Cahit Aral.
Energy and Natural Resources, Sudi Neşet Turel.
Culture and Tourism, Mesut Yilmaz.
Presidential Council, Pres. Kenan Evren; Gen. Nurettin Ersin; Gen. Tahsin Sahinkaya; Adm. Nejat Tumer; Gen. Sedat Celasun.
(* not an M.P.)
(A General Election is due to take place in November 1987.)

TURKISH EMBASSY IN LONDON
Chancery: 43 Belgrave Square, SW1X 8PA
[01–235 52525]

Ambassador Extraordinary and Plenipotentiary, His Excellency Rahmi Gümrükcüoğlu (1981).

Area and Population.—People of Turkic stock are to be found scattered throughout a wide belt extending from China through the Soviet Union, Afghanistan and Iran to the present day Turkish State, and into Bulgaria.

Turkey itself extends from Edirne (Adrianople) to Transcaucasia and Iran, and from the Black Sea to the Mediterranean, Syria and Iraq. Total population at the Census of 1985 was 51,428,514, of which 6,942,780 were in Europe and 44,485,734 in Asia.

Turkey in Europe consists of Eastern Thrace, including the cities of Istanbul and Edirne, and is separated from Asia by the Bosphorus at Istanbul and by the Dardanelles—about 40 miles in length with a width varying from 1 to 4 miles—the political neighbours being Greece and Bulgaria on the west.

Turkey in Asia comprises the whole of Asia Minor or Anatolia and extends from the Aegean Sea to the western boundaries of Georgia, Soviet Armenia and Iran, and from the Black Sea to the Mediterranean and the northern boundaries of Syria and Iraq. Population (est. 1980), 40,500,000.

Government.—On October 29, 1923, the National Assembly declared Turkey a Republic and elected Gazi Mustafa Kemal (later known as Kemal Atatürk) President. In 1945 a multi-party system was introduced but in 1960 the government was overthrown by the Turkish Armed Forces which ruled through the Committee of National Union, a body of military officers. A new constitution was adopted in July 1961 and in Oct., after a general election, a civilian government took office. Civilian governments remained in power until Sept. 1980 when mounting problems with the economy and terrorism led the military to assume legislative powers. A civilian technocratic government was appointed later that month.

A new Constitution, extending the powers of the President, was approved by a referendum on Nov. 7, 1982. It provided for the separation of powers between the legislature, executive and judiciary, and the holding of free elections to the unicameral Grand National Assembly, which has 400 members elected every five years. Following the General Election on Nov. 6, 1983 the military leadership handed over power to a newly elected civilian government.

Party representation in the Assembly May 11, 1987 was: Motherland Party, 255 seats; Social Democrat Populist Party, 63; Correct Way Party, 40; Democratic Left Party, 23; Independents, 17. (Two seats are empty, awaiting by-elections).

Since the General Election of Nov. 6, 1983, the Populist Party has merged with the extra-parliamentary S.O.D.E.P. to form the Social Democrat Populist Party. The National Democracy Party has dissolved itself and several new parties have formed.

Turkey is divided for administrative purposes into 67 *il* with subdivisions into *kaza* and *nahiye*. Each *il* has a governor (*vali*) and elective council.

Religion and Education.—On April 10, 1928, the Grand National Assembly passed a law in virtue of which Islam ceased to be the State religion of the Republic. However, 98·99 per cent of the population are Moslems. The main religious minorities, which are concentrated in Istanbul and on the Syrian frontier, are: Greek Orthodox, 10,000; Armenians, 42,000; Syriani Christians, 42,000; Others, 6,000. (Total Christians, 100,000); Jewish, 44,000. Education is free, secular and compulsory at primary level. There are elementary, secondary and vocational schools.

There are 27 universities in Turkey, including four in Istanbul, four in Ankara, two in Izmir, and one each in Erzurum and Trabzon.

The expenditure allocated to education in the 4th Five Year Plan (1979–83) was *TL*76,000,000,000, compared with *TL*14,000,000,000 in the 3rd Five Year Plan (1973–77).

Language and Literature.—Until 1926, Turkish was written in Arabic script, but in that year the Roman alphabet was substituted for use in official correspondence and in 1928 for universal use, with Arabic numerals as used throughout Europe. Ancient Turkish literature aped the Arabic manner, but the revolution of 1908 led to the introduction of a native literature free from foreign influences and adapted to the understanding of the people. The leading Turkish newspapers are centred in Istanbul and Ankara, although most provincial towns have their own daily papers. There are foreign language papers in French, Greek, Armenian and English and numerous magazines and weeklies on various subjects, but few trade commercial publications.

Agricultural Production.—In 1985 agricultural production accounted for some 16 per cent of the gross domestic product at constant factor prices. About 50 per cent of the working population are in the rural sector. Estimated production figures for the principal crops in 1985 were ('000 tons):

Wheat	17,000	Olives	600
Barley	6,500	Tea (wet leaves)	625
Rice	162	Hazlenuts	180
Tobacco	170	Oranges	505
Sugar	1,429	Grapes	3,308

With the important exception of wheat, which is mostly grown on the arid Central Anatolian Plateau, most of the crops are grown on the fertile littoral. Tobacco, sultana and fig cultivation is centred around Izmir, where substantial quantities of cotton are also grown. The main cotton area is in the Cukurova Plain around Adana. The forests which lie between the littoral plain and the Anatolian Plateau, contain beech, pine, oak, elm, chestnut, lime, plane, alder, box, poplar and maple. During recent years the Government has attempted, so far not altogether successfully, to combat the depredations of peasant and goat which threaten to destroy the existing forests within the next 25 years.

Industry.—After agriculture, Turkey's second most important industry is based on her considerable mineral wealth which is, however, as yet comparatively unexploited. The main export minerals are chromite and boron. Production in 1984 was (tons):

Coal	7,103,000
Lignite	27,199,000
Iron ore	4,049,000
Chrome ore	689,000
Copper	2,466,000
Boron minerals	1,411,000

The progress made in the manufacture of sugar, cotton, woollen and silk textiles, and cement, has been such that the bulk of the country's requirements can now be produced locally, while other industries contributing substantially to local needs include vehicle assembly, paper, glass and glassware, iron and steel, leather and leather goods, sulphur refining, canning and rubber goods, soaps and cosmetics, pharmaceutical products, prepared foodstuffs and a host of minor industries.

In common with other developing countries, Turkey's economy was adversely affected by the steep rises in oil prices from 1973 onwards. This led to a succession of economic crises and high inflation culminating in Jan. 1980 in the introduction of an economic stability programme. Exports have since risen dramatically, topping $8,000 million in 1985. Inflation, however, remains high (43 per cent. in 1985) and as a result investment is low. Turkey's current account deficit has been reduced to about $1,000 million. G.N.P. growth for 1985 was about 5 per cent. and unemployment remains high.

COMMUNICATIONS

Railways.—The complete network became the property of the State Railways Administration in 1948. The total length of lines in operation is 8,193 kilometres.

Roads.—At the end of 1985 there were 59,300 km. of national roads (55,296 of which were macadamized). The estimated number of vehicles in 1984 was 2,159,417.

The Bosporus is spanned by a single bridge, opened in 1973. Work on a second bridge began in 1985 and plans are being drawn up for a third fixed link between the two continents.

Shipping.—In August 1980 there were 343 merchants ships over 300 gross tons, 79 passenger ships and 73 tankers, giving a total draft weight of 1,545,062 tons.

Civil Aviation.—The State airlines (T.H.Y.) operate all internal services and have services to Europe and the Middle East. Most of the leading European airlines, including British Airways, operate services to Istanbul and some also to Ankara.

FINANCE

	1983–84 TL million
Estimated Expenditure	2,512,420
Estimated Revenue	2,783,141

Currency.—The Turkish *Lira (TL)* is divided into 100 *Kurus*. For rate of exchange *see also* p. 82.

TRADE

	1985
Total imports	$11,343,600,000
Total exports	7,558,100,000

Most imports are no longer subject to licence. The main imports are machinery, crude oil and petroleum products, iron and steel, vehicles, medicines and dyes, chemicals, fertilizers and electrical appliances. Agricultural commodities (cotton, tobacco, fruits, nuts, livestock) represent 47 per cent of total exports. Other exports are minerals, textiles, glass and cement.

Trade with U.K.

	1985	1986
Imports from U.K.	£460,220,000	£433,753,000
Exports to U.K.	538,462,000	406,605,000

CAPITAL.—Ankara (Angora), an inland town of Asia Minor, about 275 miles E.S.E. of Istanbul, with a population (1980) of 3,196,460. Ankara (or Ancyra) was the capital of the Roman Province of *Galatia Prima*, and a marble temple (now in ruins), dedicated to Augustus, contains the *Monumentum (Marmor) Ancyranum*, inscribed with a record of the reign of Augustus Cæsar. ΨIstanbul (4,870,747), the former capital, was the Roman city of Byzantium. It was selected by Constantine the Great as the capital of the Roman Empire about A.D. 328 and renamed Constantinople. Istanbul contains the celebrated church of St. Sophia, which, after becoming a mosque, was made a museum in 1934; it also contains Topkapi, former Palace of the Ottoman Sultans, which is also a museum. Other cities are ΨIzmir (1,968,614); Adana (1,467,346); Bursa (1,161,553); Gaziantep (387,093); and Eskişehir (543,733).

FLAG.—Red, with white crescent and star.
NATIONAL DAY.—October 29 (Republic Day).

BRITISH EMBASSY
(Ankara)

Ambassador Extraordinary and Plenipotentiary, His Excellency Timothy Lewis Achilles Daunt, C.M.G. (1986).

Counsellor, A. P. F. Bache; Dr. F. H. Taylor (*Cultural Affairs*).

First Secretaries, K. R. Tebbitt (*Head of Chancery*); N. J. Morley (*Consul*); I. C. Sloan (*Economic and Commercial*); Ms. C. M. Street (*Cultural Affairs*); H. K. Gilmour (*Cultural Affairs*); M. R. Willson (*Cultural and Science Affairs*); D. J. Ray (*Administration*).

Defence and Military Attaché, Brig. C. W. G. Bullocke, O.B.E.

Naval and Air Attaché, Wing Cdr. A. J. Raley, M.B.E.

BRITISH CONSULAR OFFICES

There is a British Consulate-General at *Istanbul*, a Vice-Consulate at *Izmir* and an Hon. British Consulate at *Iskenderun*.

British Council Representative, Dr. F. H. Taylor, 50–52 Güniz Sokak, Kavaklidere, Ankara..—There is also a centre and library at *Istanbul* and a library at *Ankara*.

BRITISH CHAMBER OF COMMERCE OF TURKEY INC., Mesrutiyet Caddessi No. 34, Tepebasi Beyoğlu, Istanbul (Postal Address, P.O. Box 190 Karaköy, Istanbul).

UNION OF SOVIET SOCIALIST REPUBLICS
(Soyuz Sovetskikh Sotsialisticheskikh Respublik)

THE COMMUNIST PARTY OF THE SOVIET UNION
(K.P.S.S. = Kommunisticheskaya Partiya Sovetskogo Soyuza)

Politbureau, G. A. Aliev; V. M. Chebrikov; M. S. Gorbachev; A. A. Gromyko; E. K. Ligachev; V. P. Nikonov; N. I. Ryzhkov; V. V. Shcherbitsky; E. A. Shevardnadze; N. N. Slyunkov; M. S. Solomentsev; V. I. Vorotnikov; A. N. Yakovlev; L. N. Zaikov (*full members*); P. N. Demichev; V. I. Dolgikh; B. N.

Eltsin; Yu. F. Soloviev; N. V. Talyzin (*candidate members*).

Secretariat, Mikhail Sergevich Gorbachev (*General Secretary since* March 11, 1985); A. P. Biryukova; A. F. Dobrynin; V. I. Dolgikh; E. K. Ligachev; A. I. Lukyanov; V. A. Medvedev; V. P. Nikonov; G. P. Razumovsky; N . N. Slyunkov; A. N. Yakovlev; L. N. Zaikov.

Committee of Party Control, M. S. Solomentsev (*Chairman*).

Komsomol (*Young Communist League*). I. Mironenko (1st *Secretary*).

GOVERNMENT OF THE U.S.S.R.

The Presidium of the Supreme Soviet of the U.S.S.R.

Chairman (= *President of the U.S.S.R.*), Andrei A. Gromyko, *since* July 2, 1985.

Secretary,T. N. Menteshashvili.

The Supreme Soviet (= Parliament) consists of two chambers.

Chairman (= *Speaker*) *of the Council of the Union*, L. N. Tolkunov.

Chairman (= *Speaker*) *of the Council of Nationalities*, A. E. Voss.

The Council of Ministers of the U.S.S.R.

Chairman (= *Prime Minister*), Nikolai Ryzhkov *since* Sept. 27, 1985.

First Vice-Chairmen, G. A. Aliev; V. S. Murakhovsky; N. V. Talyzin.

Vice-Chairmen, A. K. Antonov; B. E. Shcherbina; Yu. P. Batalin; V. K. Gusev; V. M. Kamentsev; Yu. D. Maslyukov; I. S. Silaev; B. L. Tolstykh; G. G. Vedernikov; L. A. Voronin.

Four Buros/State Commissions of the Council of Ministers have been set up since March 1985:

Fuel and Energy Complex, B. E. Shcherbina.

Machine Building, I. S. Silaev.

Social Development, G. A. Aliev.

State Foreign Economic Commission, V. M. Kamentsev.

Ministries.—There are three groups of departmental ministries, with a total of 84 ministers—37 All Union Ministries, *i.e.* federal ministries, 23 Union Republican Ministries (co-ordinating ministries of individual republics) and 24 State Committees whose Chairmen rank as Ministers. The Prime Ministers of the 15 constituent republics belong to the Council *ex officio*.

Atomic Energy, N. F. Lukonin.

Automobile Industry, N. A. Pugin.

Aviation Industry, A. S. Systov.

Chemical Industry, Yu. A. Bespalov.

Chemical and Oil Machine Building, V. M. Lukyanenko.

Civil Aviation, A. N. Volkov.

Communications Equipment Industry, E. K. Pervyshin.

Construction, Road and Municipal Machine Building, E. A. Varnachev.

Construction in Eastern Regions, A. A. Babenko.

Construction in Northern and Western Regions, V. I.Reshetilov.

Construction in Southern Regions, A. N. Shchepetilnikov.

Construction in Regions of Urals and Western Siberia, S. V. Bashilov.

Defence, Marshal D. T. Yazov.

Defence Industry, P. V. Finogenov.

Electronics Industry, V. G. Kolesnikov.

Electrical Engineering Industry, O. G. Anfimov.

Foreign Trade, B. I. Aristov.

Gas Industry, V. S. Chernomyrdin.

General Machine Building, O. D. Baklanov.

Heavy, and Transport, Machine Building, (vacant).

Instrument-Making, Automation and Control Systems, M. S. Shkabardnya.

Machine Building, B. Belousov.

Machine Building, Light, Food and Domestic Appliances, L. B. Vasiliev.

Machine Building, Livestock Farming and Animal Foods Production, (vacant).

Machine-Tool Building and Tool Industry, N. A. Panichev.

Medical and Micro-biological Industry, V. A. Bykov.

Medium Machine Building, L. D. Ryabev.

Merchant Marine, Yu. M. Volmer.

Oil Industry, V. A. Dinkov.

Petroleum and Gas Industry Enterprises Construction, V. G. Chirskov.

Power Machine Building, V. M. Velichko.

Production of Mineral Fertilizers, N. M. Olshansky.

Radio Industry, P. S. Pleshakov.

Railways, N. S. Konarev.

Ship Building Industry, I. S. Belousov.

Tractor and Agricultural Machine Building, A. A. Ezhevsky.

Transport Construction, V. A. Brezhnev.

Among the more important Union Republican Ministries are:

Education, S. Scherbakov.

Finance, B. I. Gostev.

Foreign Affairs, E. A. Shevardnadze.

Health, E. I. Chazov.

Higher and Specialized Secondary Education, G. Yagodin.

Internal Affairs, A. V. Vlasov.

Justice, B. Kravtsov.

Computer and Information Technology, N. V. Gorshkov.

Foreign Economic Relations, K. F. Katushev.

Hydrometeorology and Monitoring of the Environment, Yu. A. Izrael.

Inventions and Discoveries, I. S. Nayashkov.

Material Reserves, F. I. Loshchenkov.

Science and Technology, B. L. Tolstykh.

Standards, G. D. Kolmogorov.

Supervision of Atomic Energy Industry Safety, V. M. Malyshev.

13 Kensington Palace Gardens, W8 4QX
[01–229 3628]

Ambassador Extraordinary and Plenipotentiary, His Excellency Leonid M. Zamyatin (1986).

The total area of the U.S.S.R. is 8,649,461 sq. miles (22,402,000 sq. km.); the total population: (Jan. 1, 1986) 278,784,000.

Area and population (January, 1986) of the constituent Republics of the U.S.S.R. with their capitals:—

Republic (Capital)	Sq. miles	Population
I. R.S.F.S.R.		
(Moscow)	6,593,391	144,080,000
II. Ukraine (Kiev)	252,046	50,994,000
III. Belorussia (Minsk)	80,300	10,008,000
IV. Uzbekistan		
(Tashkent)	157,181*	18,487,000
V. Kazakhstan		
(Alma-Ata)	1,064,980*	16,028,000
VI. Georgia (Tbilisi)	26,911	5,234,000
VII. Azerbaidjan (Baku)	33,436	6,708,000
VIII. Lithuania (Vilnius)	26,173	3,603,000

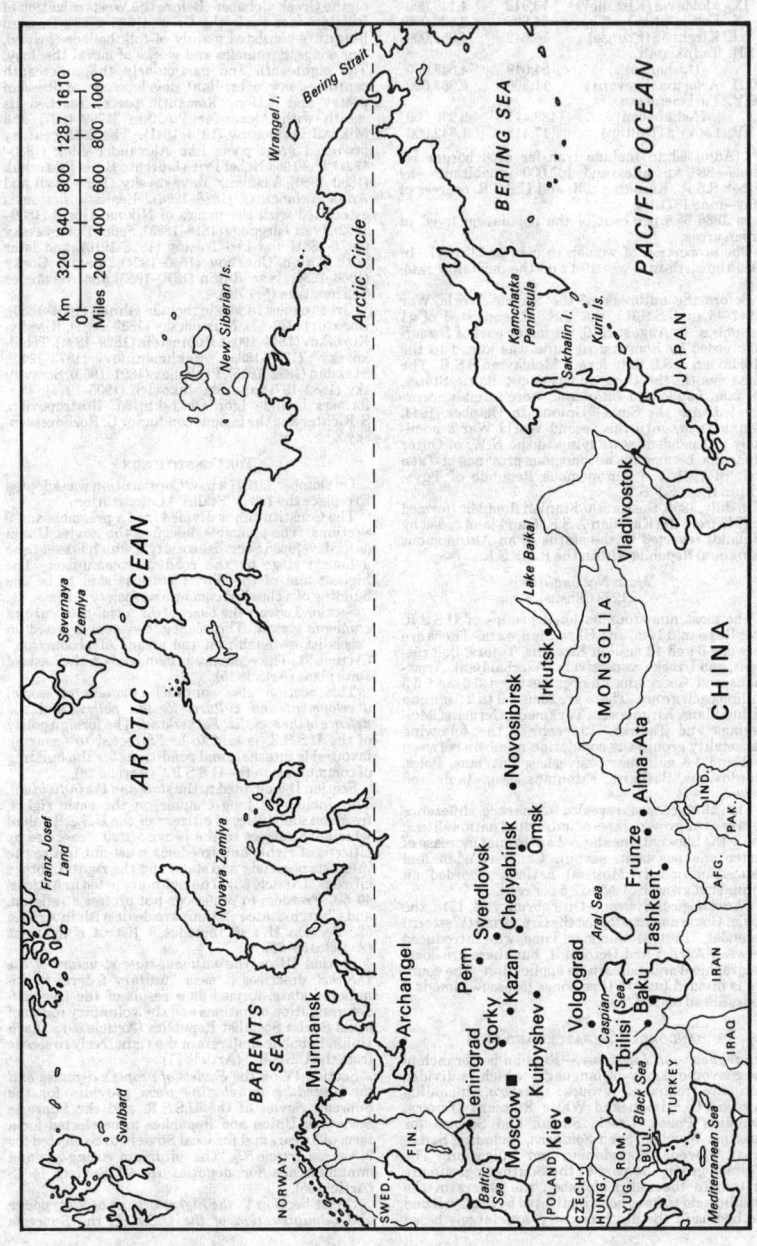

IX. Moldavia (Kishinev)	13,912	4,147,000
X. Latvia (Riga)	24,695	2,622,000
XI. Kirghizia (Frunze) .	76,642	4,051,000
XII. Tadjikistan (Dushanbe)	54,019	4,648,000
XIII. Armenia (Erevan)..	11,306	3,362,000
XIV. Turkmenistan (Ashkhabad).....	188,417	3,270,000
XV. Estonia (Tallinn) ...	17,413	1,542,000

* (Adjusted to include transfer of 3 border regions—888 sq. miles and 162,000 inhabitants—by Uzbek S.S.R., Kazakh S.S.R. and U.S.S.R. decrees of May–June 1971.)

In 1986 65·6 per cent of the population lived in urban areas.

The proportion of women to men is 53 to 47. In 1985 the birth-rate was 19·4 and the mortality rate, 10·6.

Before the outbreak of the Second World War (1941–45 in U.S.S.R.), the U.S.S.R. consisted of 11 Republics. In August 1940, the major part of *Bessarabia* ceded by Romania in June was joined to the Moldavian A.S.S.R. to form a Moldavian S.S.R. The same month, the three independent Baltic States, *Estonia, Latvia* and *Lithuania*, were forcibly incorporated into the Soviet Union. In October, 1944, *Tannu-Tuva*, until the Second World War a nominally independent state lying to the N.W. of Outer Mongolia, became the autonomous province of *Tuva* and, in 1961, the Autonomous Republic of Tuva, within the R.S.F.S.R.

In July, 1956, the Karelo-Finnish Republic (formed in 1940 from the Karelian A.S.S.R. and land ceded by Finland) reverted to the status of an Autonomous (*Karelian*) Republic within the R.S.F.S.R.

Main Nationalities
(1979 Census)

The most numerous national groups of U.S.S.R. are: Russian, 137 m. and Ukrainian, 42 m. There are between 6 and 12 million Kazakhs, Tatars, Belorussians, and Uzbeks respectively. Azerbaidjani, Armenians and Georgians number between 3·5 and 5·5 million each group. There are some 1·9 to 2·9 million Lithuanians, Kirghizians, Turkmens, Germans, Moldavians and Tadjiks. In each of the following nationality groups the population numbers between 1·02 and 1·8 millions: Chuvashes, Latvians, Poles, Mordovians, Bashkirs, Estonians, Dagestanis and Jews.

The 1979 census revealed a marked difference between the growth rates of individual nationalities: while the Slav nations showed an annual increase of under one per cent, certain Central Asian and Caucasian (mostly Moslem) nations recorded an annual net growth of 2·5 to 3·5 per cent.

Chronological System.—On February 14, 1918, the Soviet Government adopted the Gregorian (Western) Calendar. In 1981 Summer Time was introduced between April 1 and October 1, but there are some geographical anomalies in its application. The country is divided into 11 time zones (Moscow time is 3 hours ahead of G.M.T.).

LANGUAGE, LITERATURE AND ARTS

Language and Literature.—Russian is a branch of the Slavonic family of languages which is divided into the following groups: *Eastern,* including Russian, Ukrainian and White Russian; *Western,* including Polish, Czech, Slovak and Sorbish (or Lusatian Wendish); and *Southern,* including Serbo-Croat, Slovene, Macedonian and Bulgarian. The Western group and part of the Southern group are written in the Latin alphabet, the others in the Cyrillic, said to have been instituted by SS. Cyril and Methodius in the ninth century, and largely based

on the Greek alphabet. Before the Westernization of Russia under Peter the Great (1682–1725), Russian literature consisted mainly of folk ballads (*byliny*), epic songs, chronicles and works of moral theology. The eighteenth and particularly the nineteenth centuries saw a brilliant development of Russian poetry and fiction. Romantic poetry reached its zenith with Alexander Pushkin (1799–1837) and Mikhail Lermontov (1814–1841). The 20th century produced great poets like Alexander Blok (1880–1921), the 1958 Nobel Prize laureate Boris Pasternak (1890–1960), Vladimir Mayakovsky (1893–1930) and Anna Akhmatova (1888–1966). Realistic fiction is associated with the names of Nikolai Gogol (1809–1852), Ivan Turgenev (1818–1883), Fedor Dostoyevsky (1821–1881) and Leo Tolstoy (1828–1910), and later with Anton Chekhov (1860–1904), Maxim Gorky (1868–1936), Ivan Bunin (1870–1953) and Alexander Solzhenitsyn (*b.* 1918).

Great names in music include Glinka (1804–1857), Borodin (1833–87), Mussorgsky (1839–1881), Rimsky-Korsakov (1844–1908), Rubinstein (1829–1894), Tchaikovsky (1840–1893), Rakhmaninov (1873–1943), Skriabin (1872–1915), Prokofiev (1891–1953), Stravinsky (1882–1971) and Shostakovich (1906–1975). Performers include Igor Oistrakh, M. Rostropovich, S. Richter and the famous conductor G. Rozhdestvensky.

THE CONSTITUTION

On October 7, 1977 a new Constitution was adopted to replace the 1936 ("Stalin") Constitution.

The Constitution is divided into a preamble and 9 Sections. The preamble describes the Soviet Union as a "developed Socialist society", which is said to be a logical stage on the road to communism. The highest aim of the Soviet state is said to be the building of a classless communist society.

Section I covers the *bases of the social-political and economic system.* The economic system is based on "socialist ownership of the means of production" (Article 9). The economy is managed on the basis of state plans (Article 15).

This section also contains chapters on *social development and culture, foreign policy,* and the *defence of the socialist Fatherland.* The foreign policy of the U.S.S.R. is said to be "directed to ensuring favourable international conditions for the building of communism in the U.S.S.R." (Article 28).

Section II is devoted to the *state and the individual.* This includes a long chapter on the basic rights, freedoms and duties of citizens of the U.S.S.R., all of which are subject to the proviso that "exercise by citizens of rights and freedoms must not injure the interests of society and state, and the rights of other citizens" (Article 39). The rights are listed in Articles 40–50. Freedom to profess or not profess a religion, and Church-State relations are dealt with in Article 52. Section II also includes a list of obligations (Articles 59–68).

Section III on the *national-state structure of the U.S.S.R.* describes it as a "unitary federal multinational state, formed as a result of the free self-determination of nations and the voluntary union of equal Soviet Socialist Republics (Article 69). "Each Union Republic shall retain the right freely to secede from the U.S.S.R." (Article 71).

Section IV on the *Soviets of people's deputies and the procedure for electing them* provides for the Supreme Soviet of the U.S.S.R. and the Supreme Soviets of Union and Republics to be elected for a term of 5 years and for local Soviets to be elected for 2½ years (Article 89). The minimum voting age and minimum age for deputies in all Soviets is 18 (Article 95).

Under Section V, *the higher organs of State power and administration of the U.S.S.R.,* the Supreme

Soviet of the U.S.S.R. is the highest organ of State power (Article 106). It consists of two chambers, a Council of the Union and Council of Nationalities, which consist of the same number of deputies (Articles 107 and 108). Sessions of the Supreme Soviet are convoked twice a year (Article 110); between sessions the Supreme Soviet is represented by its Presidium, (Articles 117 and 118).

The highest executive organ of the State is the Council of Ministers of the U.S.S.R. (Article 127), consisting of the Chairman, his Deputies, U.S.S.R. Ministers and Chairmen of State Committees, Chairmen of the Councils of Ministers of Union Republics *ex officio* and others (Article 128). The Council of Ministers is accountable to the Supreme Soviet (Article 129). A smaller body, the Presidium of the Council of Ministers, acts as the permanent organ of the Council of Ministers (Article 131).

Section VI covers the bases of the structure of organs of state power and administration in Union Republics. Section VII deals with justice, arbitration and supervision by the Procuracy. Section VIII deals with the arms, flag, anthem and capital of the U.S.S.R. Section IX is on the procedure for bringing the Constitution into effect and amending it.

Constitutionally, the highest executive organ of the C.P.S.U. is its *Central Committee*, as elected by the *Party Congress*. The Central Committee elected at the XXVIIth Party Congress in March, 1986 consisted of 307 full members and 170 candidate members with a consultative voice; another 83 were elected members of the *Central Revision Commission*. The real power in the Party is vested, however, in the *Politbureau*, the *Secretariat* and the permanent Departments of the Central Committee.

FINANCE

A new "heavy" Rouble was introduced on January 1, 1961. Prices and wages were changed accordingly at the rate of 10 old Roubles = 1 new Rouble. The official exchange rate bears little relation to the actual purchasing power of the currency.

DEFENCE

Defence expenditure in the U.S.S.R. for 1986 is put officially at 19,063,000 million roubles (or 4·7 per cent of total budget). It is believed, however, that this does not represent the total spent on defence in the U.S.S.R. Much of this is concealed in estimates for other ministries. The general trend is a continuing emphasis on nuclear weapons while improving the levels and capabilities of conventional arms.

The basic military service is two years in the Army and Air Force and two to three years in the Navy and Border Guards.

The total size of the Soviet regular forces is now estimated to be about 5,130,000, excluding some 1,135,000 Border Guard, internal security, railway and construction troops (mainly uniformed civilians), but including some 1,500,000 command and general support troops not otherwise listed.

Operational ICBMs, i.e. Inter-Continental Ballistic Missiles, now total about 1,400. SLBMs number 983. The number of MRBMs and IRBMs deployed is 553. The operational personnel of the Strategic Rocket Forces totals 298,000 (not including 112,000 assigned from Air and Navy).

The total strength of all Soviet air elements (including helicopters) is some 19,000. Of these, 10,000 can be classified as combat aircraft. The total strength of the Air Forces, excluding the Naval Air Force (68,000) and the bomber forces of the Aviation Armies (100,000), is about 450,000 men. The total personnel of the separate Air Defence Command, now merged with the Air Defence Troops of the Ground Forces, is estimated at 630,000 men.

The total size of the Soviet Army is estimated at 1,991,000. It is thought to be organized in 194 divisions, distributed as follows: 30 divisions in Central and Eastern Europe, 63 in European U.S.S.R., 30 in Southern Theatre (includes 4 in Afghanistan), 53 in Far Eastern Theatre, and 18 in the Central Strategic Reserve.

The total strength of the Soviet Navy and Naval Air Force is 451,000 men. In total tonnage, it is the second largest navy in the world, and its main strength lies in the submarine fleet. There are now 277 cruise missile and attack submarines, (118 nuclear-powered, 145 diesel-powered submarines), with a further 114 converting to other roles including SSN, and 84 attack submarines in reserve.

The Soviet Navy now has 269 major surface combat vessels, including five aircraft carriers, 36 cruisers and 61 destroyers and some 180 frigates. The landbased Naval Air Force comprises about 915 combat aircraft, 395 of which are bombers, and some 300 helicopters.

The para-military forces number 570,000, including 230,000 border troops and 340,000 internal security troops. There are also DOSAAF members (claimed active membership, 80 million) who participate in such activities as athletics, flight training, shooting, parachuting and pre-military training.

Minister of Defence, D. T. Yazov (with rank of Marshal of the Soviet Union).

Chief of General Staff, Marshal S. F. Akhromeyev.

Chief, Political Administration, Soviet Army and Navy, Army Gen. A. D. Lizichev.

On May 14, 1955, a Treaty of Friendship, Mutual Assistance and Co-operation was signed in Warsaw between the Soviet Union and its European associates (Bulgaria, East Germany, Hungary, Poland, Romania, and Czechoslovakia) (and Albania which left the Pact in Sept. 1968) to serve as a counterpoise to NATO. A united military command was set up in Moscow, *C.-in-C.,* Marshal V. G. Kulikov; *Chief of Staff,* Army General A. I. Gribkov. The Treaty (Warsaw Pact), due to have expired in June 1985, was extended by Protocol in its existing form for a further 20 years, with provision for a further 10 year extension thereafter, at a meeting of Pact leaders in Warsaw on April 26, 1985. The Pact came into force on May 31, 1985.

INDUSTRY AND AGRICULTURE

One of the most remarkable aspects of the Soviet economy has been the transformation of an essentially agricultural country into the second-strongest industrial power in the world. The 1986 output amounted to 161 million tonnes of steel, 112 million tonnes of rolled metal, 751 million tonnes of coal, 615 million tonnes of crude oil, 135 million tonnes of cement, 1,599,000 million kW/h of electricity and 1,300,000 cars.

Agricultural development has been slower, mainly owing to lack of incentives among peasants organized in *kolkhozy* (collective farms). Repeated droughts, such as in 1980-81, were a contributing factor to a shortage of grain. The 1986 harvest was 210 million tonnes. Stock breeding has also suffered from the general mismanagement of farming, and from shortages of fodder in recent years. The livestock at Jan. 1, 1986 included 42,900,000 cows, 77,800,000 pigs and 147,300,000 sheep and goats. Besides *kolkhozy* (collective farms) and *sovkhozy* (state farms) a significant contribution to agricultural production is made by the private plots cultivated by individual peasants. The cultivation of these plots is encouraged by the Soviet authorities. The level of productivity remains very low. *Forests* cover nearly 40 per cent of the whole area of the Union and form a considerable source of wealth.

Trade with U.K.

	1985	1986
Imports from U.K.	£536,555,000	£539,368,000
Exports to U.K.	724,453,000	694,624,000

COMMUNICATIONS

European Russia is relatively well served by railways, Leningrad and Moscow being the two main focal points of rail routes. The centre and south have a good system of north-south and east-west lines, but the eastern part (the Volga lands), traversed as it is by trunk lines between Europe and Asia which enter Siberia *via* Sverdlovsk, Chelyabinsk, Magnitogorsk and Ufa, lacks north-south routes. In Asia, there are still large areas of the U.S.S.R., notably in the Far North and Siberia, with few or no railways. Railways built since 1928 include the Turkestan-Siberian line (*Turksib*) which has made possible a large-scale industrial exploitation of Kazakhstan, a number of lines within the system of the *Trans-Siberian Railway* (Magnitogorsk-Kartaly-Troitsk, Sverdlovsk-Kurgan, Novosibirsk-Proyektnaya, etc.), which are of great importance for the industrial development in the east, the Petropavlovsk-Karaganda-Balkhash line which has made possible the development of the Karaganda coal basin and of the Balkhash copper mines, and the Moscow-Donbass trunk line. In the northern part of European Russia, the North Pechora Railway has been completed, while in the Far East a recently completed second Trans-Siberian line (the Baikal-Amur Railway) is partially in use; it follows a more northerly alignment than the earlier Trans-Siberian and terminates in the Pacific port of Sovetskaya Gavan.

Sea Ports and Inland Waterways.—The most important ports (Odessa, Nikolayev, Batumi, Taganrog, Rostov, Kerch, Sevastopol and Novorossiisk) lie around the Black Sea and the Sea of Azov. The northern ports (Leningrad, Murmansk and Archangel) are, with the exception of Murmansk, icebound during winter. Several ports have been built along the Arctic Sea route between Murmansk and Vladivostok and are in regular use every summer. The great Far Eastern port of Vladivostok, the Pacific naval base of the U.S.S.R., is kept open by icebreakers all the year round. Inland waterways, both natural and artificial, are of great importance in the country, although some of them are icebound in winter (from 2½ months in the south to 6 months in the north). The great rivers of European Russia flow outwards from the centre, linking all parts of the plain with the chief ports, an immense system of navigable waterways which carried about 632,600,000 tons of freight in 1985. They are supplemented by a system of canals which provide a through traffic between the White, Baltic, Black and Caspian Seas. The most notable of them are the *White Sea-Baltic Canal*, the *Moscow-Volga Canal* and the *Volga-Don Canal* linking the Baltic and the White Seas in the north to the Caspian, the Black Sea and the Sea of Azov in the south.

FLAG.—Red, with five-pointed star above hammer and sickle.

NATIONAL DAY.—November 7 (Commemorating the October Bolshevist Revolution of 1917).

BRITISH EMBASSY
(Naberezhnaya Morisa Toreza 14, Moscow)

Ambassador Extraordinary and Plenipotentiary, His Excellency Sir Bryan Cartledge, K.C.M.G., *apptd.* 1985.
Minister, N. H. Marshall, C.M.G.

There is a Consular Section attached to the Embassy.

I.—R.S.F.S.R.

(The Russian Soviet Federal Socialist Republic)

Chairman of the Presidium of the Supreme Soviet, V. P. Orlov.
Chairman of the Council of Ministers, V. I. Vorotnikov.

The R.S.F.S.R. has no central Communist Party organization of its own.

The R.S.F.S.R., the largest and the most important of the Republics, occupies the major half of the European part of the U.S.S.R. and the major northern portion of its Asiatic part and makes up 77 per cent of the total territory of the U.S.S.R. with 53 per cent of the total population. (About 83 per cent of the population are Russians.) It consists of 16 Autonomous Republics (the Bashkir, Buryat, Checheno-Ingush, Chuvash, Daghestan, Kabardin-Balkar, Kalmyk, Karelian, Komi, Mari, Mordovian, North-Osetian, Tatar, Tuva, Udmurt and Yakut, A.S.S.R.s); 6 regions (Altai, Khabarovsk, Krasnodar, Krasnoyarsk, Maritime and Stavropol) containing in their turn 5 autonomous provinces; 49 provinces (Amur, Archangel, Astrakhan, Belgorod, Bryansk, Chelyabinsk, Chita, Gorky, Irkutsk, Ivanovo, Kalinin, Kaliningrad, Kaluga, Kamchatka, Kemerovo, Kirov, Kostroma, Kuibyshev, Kurgan, Kursk, Leningrad, Lipetsk, Magadan, Moscow, Murmansk, Novgorod, Novosibirsk, Omsk, Orel, Orenburg, Penza, Perm, Pskov, Rostov, Ryazan, Sakhalin, Saratov, Smolensk, Sverdlovsk, Tambov, Tomsk, Tula, Tyumen, Ulyanovsk, Vladimir, Volgograd, Vologda, Voronezh and Yaroslavl).

There are three principal geographic areas: a lowlying flat Western part stretching eastwards up to the Yenisei and divided in two by the Ural ridge; an eastern part, between the Yenisei and the Pacific, consisting of a number of tablelands and ridges, and a southern mountainous part. Climatically, the R.S.F.S.R. extends from arctic and tundra belts to the sub-tropical in the south. It has a very long coast-line, including the longest Arctic coast-line in the world (about 17,000 miles). The most important rivers are the Volga, the Northern Dvina and the Pechora, the Neva, the Don and the Kuban in the European part, and in the Asiatic part, the Ob, the Irtysh, the Yenisei, the Lena and the Amur, and, further north, Khatanga, Olenek, Yana, Indigirka, Kolyma and Anadyr. Lakes are abundant, particularly in the north-west. The huge Baikal Lake in Eastern Siberia is the deepest lake in the world. There are also two large artificial water reservoirs within the Greater Volga canal system, the Moscow and Rybinsk "Seas".

Minerals.—The Republic has some of the richest mineral deposits in the world. Coal is mined in the Kuznetsk area, in the Urals, south of Moscow, in the Donets basin (its Eastern part lies in the R.S.F.S.R.) and in the Pechora area in the North. Oil is produced in the Northern Caucasus, in the area between the Volga and the Ural and in Western Siberia, which also has large deposits of natural gas. Coal and gas deposits in Siberia and the Far East (especially Yakutia) are currently being developed, now that some deposits in the western parts of the U.S.S.R. are approaching exhaustion. The Ural mountains contain a unique assortment of minerals—high-quality iron ore, manganese, copper, aluminium, gold, platinum, precious stones, salt, asbestos, pyrites, coal, oil, etc. Iron ore is also mined near Kursk, Tula, Lipetsk, in several areas in Siberia and in the Kola Peninsula. Non-ferrous metals are found in the Altai, in Eastern Siberia, in the Northern Caucasus, in the Kuznetsk-Basin, in the Far East and in the Far North. Nine-tenths of all U.S.S.R. forests are located in the R.S.F.S.R.

Production and Industry.—The vastness of the territory of the Republic and the great variety in climatic conditions cause great differences in the structure of agriculture from north to south and from west to east. In the far north reindeer breeding, hunting and fishing are predominant. Further south, timber industry is combined with grain growing. In the southern half of the forest zone and in the adjacent forest-steppe zone, the acreage under grain crops is far larger and the structure of agriculture more complex. An extensive programme of land improvement mainly involving this zone aims to double its total agricultural output by 1990. In the eastern part of this zone, between the Volga and the Urals, cericulture is predominant (particularly summer wheat), with cattle breeding next. Beyond the Urals is another important grain-growing and stock-breeding area in the southern part of the Western-Siberian plain. The southern steppe zone is the main wheat granary of the U.S.S.R., containing also large acreages under barley, maize and sunflower. In the extreme south cotton is now cultivated. Vine, tobacco and other southern crops are grown on the Black Sea shore of the Caucasus.

Industrially, the R.S.F.S.R. occupies the first place among the Soviet Republics. Moscow and Leningrad are still the two largest industrial centres in the country, but new industrial areas are being developed in the Urals, the Kuznetsk basin, and more recently in Siberia and the Far East. Most of the oil produced in the U.S.S.R. now comes from the R.S.F.S.R., half annual output comes from Tyumen Oblast in Western Siberia. All industries are represented in the R.S.F.S.R., including iron and steel and engineering.

CAPITAL.—Moscow. Population 8,714,000 (Jan. 1, 1986). Moscow, founded about A.D. 1147 by Yuri Dolgoruki, became first the centre of the rising Moscow principality and in the 15th century, the capital of the whole of Russia (Muscovy). In 1325, it became the seat of the Metropolitan of Russia. In 1703 Peter the Great transferred the capital to the newly built St. Petersburg, but on March 14, 1918, Moscow was again designated as the capital. ΨLeningrad (before the First World War "St. Petersburg" and from 1914–1924 "Petrograd") has a population of 4,904,000 (Jan. 1, 1986).

Other towns with populations exceeding 1,000,000 are:—

Gorky (Nizhny-Novogorod)	1,409,000
Novosibirsk (Novonikolayevsk)	1,405,000
Sverdlovsk (Yekaterinburg)	1,315,000
Kuibyshev (Samara)	1,267,000
Omsk	1,122,000
Chelyabinsk	1,107,000
Ufa	1,077,000
Perm (Molotov)	1,065,000
Kazan	1,057,000

II.—UKRAINE

First Secretary of the Party Central Committee, V. V. Shcherbitsky.
Chairman of the Presidium of the Supreme Soviet, V. S. Shevchenko.
Chairman of the Council of Ministers, (vacant).

This Republic, second largest in population, lying in the south-western part of the European half of the U.S.S.R., was formed in December, 1917. It consists of 25 provinces—Cherkassy, Chernigov, Chernovtsy, Crimea, Dnepropetrovsk, Donetsk, Ivano-Frankovsk, Kharkov, Kherson, Khmelnitsky, Kiev, Kirovograd, Lvov, Nikolayev, Odessa, Poltava, Rovno, Sumy, Ternopol, Transcarpathia, Vinnitsa, Volhynia, Voroshilovgrad, Zaporozhye and Zhitomir.

Physical Features.—The larger part of the Ukraine forms a plain with small elevations. The Carpathian

mountains lie in the south-western part of the Republic. The climate is moderate, with relatively mild winters (particularly in the south-west) and hot summers. The main rivers are the Dnieper with its tributaries, the Southern Bug and the Northern Donets (a tributary of the Don).

Production and Industry.—The main centre of Soviet coal mining and iron and steel industry is situated in the southern part of the Ukraine. In 1980, the Ukraine provided 36 per cent of the total Soviet steel, 51 per cent of iron ore and 27 per cent of coal. The engineering and chemical industries are also of importance. The central forest-steppe region (mainly on the right bank of the Dnieper) is the greatest sugar-producing area in the U.S.S.R. The Ukraine also leads in grain-growing and stock-raising.

There are large deposits of coal and salt in the Donets Basin, of iron ore in Krivoy Rog and near Kerch in the Crimea, of manganese in Nikopol, and of quicksilver in Nikitovka.

CAPITAL (since 1934), Kiev, one of the oldest cities in the U.S.S.R., founded in the 6th–7th century A.D., was the capital of the Russian State from 865 to 1240. Population (Jan. 1, 1986), 2,495,000. Other towns are:—

Kharkov	1,567,000
Dnepropetrovsk (Yekaterinoslav)	1,166,000
Ψ Odessa	1,132,000
Donetsk (Stalino; Yuzovka, *i.e.* Hughesovka)	1,081,000

III.—BELORUSSIA
(White Russia)

First Secretary of the Party Central Committee, E. E. Sokolov.
Chairman of the Presidium of the Supreme Soviet, G. S. Tarazevich.
Chairman of the Council of Ministers, M. V. Kovalev.

The Belorussian S.S.R., lying in the western part of the European area of the U.S.S.R., was formed early in 1919. It now consists of six provinces (Brest, Gomel, Grodno, Minsk, Mogilev and Vitebsk). Belorussians make up four-fifths of the population, with Russians and Poles coming next. It is largely a plain with many lakes, swamps and marshy land. Before the revolution of 1917 the area was one of the most backward parts of European Russia. Since then, agriculture has been greatly developed, thanks to draining of swamps. Most of the Republic's industry is also of recent growth. Woodworking is of great importance, but engineering has also been greatly extended with several major plants built in Gomel and Minsk.

The main rivers are the upper reaches of the Dnieper, of the Niemen and of the Western Dvina.

CAPITAL, Minsk. Population 1,510,000 (Jan. 1, 1986).

IV.—UZBEKISTAN

First Secretary of the Party Central Committee, I. B. Usmankhodzhaev.
Chairman of the Presidium of the Supreme Soviet, R. N. Nishanov.
Chairman of the Council of Ministers, G. Kh. Kadyrov.

The Uzbek S.S.R. was formed in 1924 and consists of the Kara-Kalpak A.S.S.R. and of 12 provinces (Andizhan, Bokhara, Dzhizak, Ferghana, Kashkadarya, Khorezm, Namangan, Navoi, Samarkand, Surkhan-darya, Syr-darya and Tashkent). It lies between the high Tienshan Mountains and the Pamir highlands in the east and south-east and sandy lowlands in the west and north-west. The major part of the territory is a plain with huge waterless deserts and several large oases, which form the main centres of population and economic life. The largest is the Ferghana valley, watered by the Syr-Darya. Other oases include Tashkent, Samarkand, Bokhara and Khorezm. The climate is continental and dry. Minerals include gold, natural gas, oil, copper, lead, zinc and coal.

The Uzbeks, a Turkic people, make up 68·7 per cent of the population, the Russians (10·8 per cent), Tatars (4·2 per cent) and Kazakhs (4 per cent) come next.

There are major agricultural and textile machinery plants and several chemical combines. Uzbekistan is the main cotton-growing area of the U.S.S.R. producing more than 60 per cent of all Soviet cotton. Irrigation has always been of decisive importance in this area, and the Soviet Government has done much in this field, including the construction of the Great Ferghana Canal (230 miles).

CAPITAL, Tashkent. Population 2,077,000 (Jan. 1, 1986). Samarkand (population (1986), 380,000) contains the Gur-Emir (Tamerlane's Mausoleum), completed A.D. 1400 by Ulugbek, Tamerlane's astronomer-grandson, and a 15th-century observatory.

V.—KAZAKHSTAN

First Secretary of the Party Central Committee, G. V. Kolbin.

Chairman of the Presidium of Supreme Soviet, S. Mukashev.

Chairman of the Council of Ministers, N. A. Nazarbaev.

The Kazakh S.S.R., the second-largest Union-Republic, stretching from the lower reaches of the Volga and the Caspian in the west to the Altai and Tienshan in the east, and bordering on China, was formed in 1920 as an autonomous republic (under the name of the Kirghiz A.S.S.R.) within the R.S.F.S.R., and was constituted a Union Republic in 1936. It consists of 19 Provinces: Aktyubinsk, Alma-Ata, Chimkent, Dzhambul, Dzhezkazgan, East-Kazakhstan, Guryev, Karaganda, Kokchetav, Kustanay, Kzyl-Orda, Mangyshlak, North-Kazakhstan, Pavlodar, Semipalatinsk, Taldy-Kurgan, Tselinograd, Turgay and Uralsk.

Kazakhstan is a country of arid steppes and semi-deserts, flat in the west, hilly in the east and mountainous in the south-east (Southern Altai and Tienshan). The climate is continental and very dry. The main rivers are the (Upper) Irtysh, the Ural, the Syr-Darya and the Ili. Kazakhstan is very rich in minerals: copper in Kounrad and Dzhezkazgan, lead and zinc in the Altai and Karatau mountains, iron ore in Radryg and Lisakovsk, coal in Ekibastuz and Karaganda and oil and natural gas in the Mangyshlak peninsula. Major centres of metal industry exist in the Altai Mountains, in Chimkent, north of the Balkhash Lake and in Central Kazakhstan. Stock-raising is highly developed, particularly in the central and south-western parts of the Republic. Grain is grown in the north and north-east and cotton in the south and south-east.

The Kazakhs (a Turkic people) are in a minority in the Republic named after them; they constitute only 36 per cent of its population, Russian settlers make up 41 per cent and Ukrainians 6 per cent.

CAPITAL, Alma-Ata (formerly Verny). Population 1,088,000 (Jan. 1, 1986). Karaganda, a major mining centre, has a population of 624,000 (Jan. 1, 1986).

VI.—GEORGIA

First Secretary of the Party Central Committee, Dzh. I. Patiashvili.

Chairman of the Presidium of the Supreme Soviet, P. G. Gilashvili.

Chairman of the Council of Ministers, O. E. Cherkeziya.

The Georgian, S.S.R., occupying the north-western part of Transcaucasia, lies on the shore of the Black Sea and borders in the south-east on Turkey. It was formed in 1921; in 1922 it joined the Transcaucasian Federation which, in its turn, adhered to the U.S.S.R. in the same year. After the liquidation of the Transcaucasian S.F.S.R. in 1936 Georgia became a Union Republic. It contains two Autonomous Republics (Abkhazia and Adjaria) and the South-Osetian Autonomous Province. Georgia is a country of mountains, with the Greater Caucasus in the north and the Lesser Caucasus in the south. A relatively low-lying land between these two ridges is divided into two parts by the Surz Ridge: Western Georgia with a mild and damp climate and Eastern Georgia with a more continental and dry climate. The Black Sea shore and the Rioni lowland are subtropical in their climatic character. The most important mineral deposits are manganese (Chiatura), coal (Tkibuli and Tkvarcheli) and oil (Kakhetia). Georgia is a leading producer of manganese in the U.S.S.R. There are also many oil refineries. viniculture, tea and tobacco-growing are the three main agricultural industries. The Black Sea harbours many famous holiday resorts. Georgians make up 68·8 per cent of the population, the remainder being largely composed of Armenians, Russians, Azerbaidjanis and Osetians.

CAPITAL, Tbilisi (Tiflis), population 1,174,000 (Jan. 1, 1986).

VII.—AZERBAIDJAN

First Secretary of the Party Central Committee, K. M. Bagirov.

Chairman of the Presidium of the Supreme Soviet, S. B. Tatliev.

Chairman of the Council of Ministers, G. N. Seidov.

The Azerbaidjan S.S.R. occupies the eastern part of Transcaucasia, on the shore of the Caspian Sea, and borders on Iran. It was formed in 1920. Between 1922 and 1936 it formed part of the Transcaucasian Federation. In 1936 it became a Union Republic. It contains the Nakhichevan Autonomous Republic and the Nagorno-Karabakh Autonomous Province.

The north-eastern part of the Republic is taken up by the south-eastern end of the main Caucasus ridge, its south-western part by the smaller Caucasus hills, and its south-eastern corner by the spurs of the Talysh Ridge. Its central part is a depression irrigated by the Kura and by the lower reaches of its tributary Araks. Sheltered by the mountains from the humid west winds blowing from the Black Sea, Azerbaidjan has a continental climate. The land requires artificial irrigation. Industry is dominated by oil and natural gas extraction and related chemical and engineering industries centred on Baku and Sumgait. A large power station on the Araks was completed in 1969, in conjunction with Iran. Azerbaidjan is also important as a cotton growing area. The Azerbaidjani (Turkic) make up more than three-quarters of the population of the Republic, Armenians, about 8 per cent, and Russians, 8 per cent.

CAPITAL, Ψ Baku. Population 1,722,000 (Jan. 1, 1986).

VIII.—LITHUANIA

First Secretary of the Party Central Committee, P. P. Grishkyavichus.

Chairman of the Presidium of the Supreme Soviet, R.-B. I. Songaila.

Chairman of the Council of Ministers, V. V. Sakalauskas.

Lithuania, formerly a Province of the Russian Empire, was declared an independent Republic at Vilna in 1918 and was incorporated into the U.S.S.R. in August, 1940. The Republic forms a plain with a large number of lakes and swamps. The forests occupy 19 per cent of the whole area. The main river is the Niemen with its tributaries.

The chief industries are agriculture and forestry, the chief products being rye, oats, wheat, barley, flax, sugar-beet and potatoes.

The Lithuanians make up four-fifths of the population, Russians and Poles, 7–9 per cent each.

CAPITAL, Vilnius (Vilna). Population 555,000 (Jan. 1, 1986).

IX.—MOLDAVIA

First Secretary of the Party Central Committee, S. K. Grossu.

Chairman of the Presidium of the Supreme Soviet, A. A. Mokanu.

Chairman of the Council of Ministers, I. P. Kalin.

Moldavia, occupying the south-western corner of the U.S.S.R., borders in the west on Romania with the Pruth forming the frontier. In 1918, Romania seized the Russian Province of Bessarabia, but in 1940 the U.S.S.R. forced Romania to give back Bessarabia, the major part of which was merged with the Moldavian A.S.S.R. (formed in 1924) to create the Moldavian S.S.R.

The northern part of the Republic consists of flat steppe lands, now all under plough. Some forests skirt the Dniester. Further south, around Kishinev, there are woody hills and further south again, low-lying steppe lands. The climate is moderate. The main river is the Dniester, navigable along the whole course.

The main industry is agriculture (viniculture, fruit-growing and market-gardening). Industry is insignificant in both parts of Moldavia, but the Republic has the densest population in the U.S.S.R. Moldavians make up 64 per cent of the population, with Ukrainians, and Russians next.

CAPITAL, Kishinev (Chisinau). Population, 643,000 (Jan. 1, 1986).

X.—LATVIA

First Secretary of the Party Central Committee, B. K. Pugo.

Chairman of the Presidium of the Supreme Soviet, Ya. Ya. Vagris.

Chairman of the Council of Ministers, Yu. Ya. Ruben.

The Latvian S.S.R., lying on the shores of the Baltic and of the Gulf of Riga, was formerly a Baltic Province of the Russian Empire. It was proclaimed an independent state in 1918 and was forcibly incorporated into the U.S.S.R. in August 1940.

The surface of the country is generally flat, interspersed by occasional chains of hills. The climate is moderately continental. The main rivers are the lower reaches of the Western Dvina and its tributaries. Forests occupy 20 per cent of the total territory.

The Latvians make up 53·7 per cent of the Republic's population, Russians 32·8 per cent.

Latvian industry was always highly developed, with shipbuilding, engineering, chemical industry, textile industry, wood-working and dairying being the chief occupations. Both Riga and Liepaja (Libava, Libau) are important sea-ports.

CAPITAL, Ψ Riga. Population, 890,000 (Jan. 1, 1986).

XI.—KIRGHIZIA

First Secretary of the Party Central Committee, A. M. Masaliev.

Chairman of the Presidium of the Supreme Soviet, T. Kh. Koshoev.

Chairman of the Council of Ministers, A. Dzhumagulov.

The Kirghiz S.S.R. occupies the north-eastern part of Soviet Central Asia and borders in the south-east on China. In 1924, a Kara-Kirghiz Autonomous Province was formed within the R.S.F.S.R. In 1926 it became a Kirghiz Autonomous Republic, and in 1936 a Union Republic. It contains three provinces, Issyk-Kul, Naryn and Osh. The Kirghiz Republic is a mountainous country, the major part being covered by the ridge of the Central Tienshan, while mountains of the Pamir-Altai system occupy its southern part. There are a number of spacious mountain valleys, the Alai, Susamyr, the Issyk-Kul lake and others. The majority of the population is concentrated in plains, lying at the foot of mountains—Chu, Talass, part of the Ferghana Valley where agriculture prospers. Crops include sugar beet and cotton, and sheep are important in the mountains. Industry is being developed and some mining is done. The Kirghiz constitute 47·9 per cent of the population, the Russians 25·9 per cent. The Uzbeks (in Eastern Ferghana) amount to 12·1 per cent.

CAPITAL, Frunze (formerly Pishpek). Population, 617,000 (Jan. 1, 1986).

XII.—TADJIKSTAN

First Secretary of the Party Central Committee, K. Makhkamov.

Chairman of the Presidium of the Supreme Soviet, G. Pallaev.

Chairman of the Council of Ministers, I. Khaeev.

The Tadjik S.S.R. lies in the extreme south-east of Soviet Central Asia and borders in the south on Afghanistan and in the east on China. It was originally formed in 1924 as an Autonomous Republic within the Uzbek S.S.R. and became a Union Republic in 1929. It includes the Gorno-Badakhshan Autonomous Province and the Kulyab and Leninabad Provinces.

The country is mountainous: in the east lie the Pamir highlands with the highest point in the U.S.S.R., Pik Kommunizma (24,500 feet), in the centre the high ridges of the Pamir-Altai system. Plains are formed by wide stretches of the Syr-Darya valley in the north and of the Amu-Darya in the south.

Like the other Central-Asiatic Republics, Tadjikistan is a cotton-growing country. Its climatic conditions favour the cultivation of Egyptian cotton. Irrigation is of great importance. Of the population 58·8 per cent are Tadjiks (linguistically and culturally akin to the Persians), 23 per cent Uzbeks, the rest Russians and others.

CAPITAL, Dushanbe (formerly Stalinabad; Dyushambe). Population, 567,000 (Jan. 1, 1986).

XIII.—ARMENIA

First Secretary of the Party Central Committee, K. S. Demirchyan.

Chairman of the Presidium of the Supreme Soviet, G. M. Voskanyan.

Chairman of the Council of Ministers, F. T. Sarkisyan.

The Armenian S.S.R. occupies the south-western part of Transcaucasia: it was formed in 1920. In 1922 it joined the Transcaucasian Federation, and on its liquidation in 1936 became a Union Republic. In the south it borders on Turkey. It is a mountainous country consisting of several vast table lands surrounded by ridges. The population and the economic life are concentrated in the low-lying part of Armenia, the Aras valley and the Erevan hollow; the climate is continental, dry and cold, but the Araks valley has a long, hot and dry summer. Irrigation is essential for agriculture. In Turkey, at the junction of the former Turkish, Persian and Russian boundaries, is *Mount Ararat* (17,160 ft.), the traditional resting place of "Noah's Ark." Industrial and fruit crops are grown in the low-lying districts, grain in the hills. Armenia is traditionally noted for her wine. There are large copper ore and molybdenum deposits and other minerals. The Armenian Church centred in Etchmiadzin is the oldest established Christian Church, Christianity having been recognized as the State religion in A.D. 300.

Nearly 90 per cent of the population is Armenian.

CAPITAL, Erevan. Population, 1,148,000 (Jan. 1, 1986).

XIV.—TURKMENISTAN

First Secretary of the Party Committee, S. A. Niyazov.
Chairman of the Presidium of the Supreme Soviet, B. Yazkuliev.
Chairman of the Council of Ministers, A. Khodzhamuradov.

Turkmenia occupies the extreme south of Soviet Central Asia, between the Caspian and the Amu-Darya, and borders in the south on Iran and Afghanistan. It was formed in 1924 and contains five Provinces: Ashkhabad, Chardjou, Krasnovodsk, Mary and Tashauz. The country is a low-lying plain, fringed by hills in the south. Ninety per cent of the plain is taken up by the arid Kara-Kum desert. Of all Central-Asiatic Republics, Turkmenia is the lowest and driest. The cultivation of cotton, stock-raising and mineral extraction are the principal industries. The republic produces about 16 per cent of the Soviet Union's natural gas, as well as astrakhan furs and carpets. Most of the land under plough is artificially irrigated. The oil and silk industries are of old standing. There are also some fisheries in the Caspian.

Turkmens make up 68·4 per cent of the population, Russians 12·6 per cent, and Uzbeks 8·5 per cent.

CAPITAL, Ashkhabad (formerly Askhabad, Poltoratsk). Population, 366,000 (Jan. 1, 1986).

XV.—ESTONIA

First Secretary of the Party Central Committee, K. G. Vaino.
Chairman of the Presidium of the Supreme Soviet, A. F. Ryuitel.
Chairman of the Council of Ministers, B. E. Saul.

Estonia, formerly a Baltic province of the Russian Empire, was proclaimed an independent Republic in 1918. In 1940, it was forcibly incorporated into the U.S.S.R. It lies on the shores of the Baltic and of the Finnish Gulf in the north and of the Gulf of Riga in the south-west. Some 800 islands, among them Dagö and Ösel, form part of Estonian territory.

The country forms a low-lying plain with many lakes, among them the Chud (or Pskov) Lake, on the border with the R.S.F.S.R. Forests take up about one-fifth of the territory. Agriculture and dairy-farming are the chief industries, rye, oats, barley, flax and potatoes being the chief crops, and butter, bacon and eggs the chief products of dairy farming. There are important manufactures, including textiles, engineering, shipbuilding, woodworking, etc.

The population consists of Estonians (64·7 per cent) and Russians (27·9 per cent).

CAPITAL, Ψ Tallinn (formerly Reval). Population, 472,000 (Jan. 1, 1986).

UNITED ARAB EMIRATES
(Al-Imarat Al-Arabiya Al-Muttahida)

President, Shaikh Zaid bin Sultan al Nahayyan (*Abu Dhabi*).
Vice-President and Prime Minister, Shaikh Rashid bin Said al Maktum.
Deputy Prime Ministers, Shaikh Maktum bin Rashid al Maktum; Shaikh Hamdan bin Muhammad al Nahayyan.
Interior, Shaikh Mubarak bin Muhammad al Nahayyan.
Finance and Industry, Shaikh Hamdan bin Rashid al Maktum.
Defence, Shaikh Muhammad bin Rashid al Maktum.
Minister of State for Foreign Affairs, Sayyid Rashid Abdullah al Nu'aimi.
Petroleum and Mineral Resources, Dr. Mana Said al Otaiba.
Economy and Commerce, Sayyid Saif al Jarwan.
Information and Culture, Shaikh Ahmad bin Hamid bin Butti.
Communications, Sayyid Muhammad Said al Mulla.
Public Works and Housing, Sayyid Muhammad Khalifa al Kindi.
Education, Sayyid Faraj Fadel al Mazroui.
Planning, (vacant).
Justice, Sayyid Abdullah Humaid al Mazroni.
Islamic Affairs and Awqaf, Shaikh Mohammad bin Hassan al Khazraji.
Agriculture and Fisheries, Sayyid Said al Raqabani.
Water and Electricity, Sayyid Humaid Nasser al Owais.
Labour and Social Affairs, Sayyid Khalfan al Roumi.
Health, Sayyid Hamad Abdul Rahman al Madfa.

EMBASSY IN LONDON
30 Prince's Gate, SW7 1PT
[01–581 1281]

Ambassador Extraordinary and Plenipotentiary, new appointment awaited.
Chargé d'Affaires, Ali Mubarak Ahmed Al Mansoori.

Area and Population.—The approximate area of the U.A.E. is 32,278 sq. miles (83,600 sq. km.), and the population in 1985 was estimated at about 1·6 million.

The United Arab Emirates (formerly the Trucial States) is composed of seven Emirates (Abu Dhabi, Ajman, Dubai, Fujeirah, Ras al Khaimah, Sharjah and Umm al Qaiwain) which came together as an independent state on December 2, 1971, when they ended their individual special treaty relationships with the British Government (Ras al Khaimah joined the other six on February 10, 1972).

The British Government, by virtue of a treaty made in 1892, had been responsible for the external affairs of the states through the British Political Resident in the Persian Gulf and the British Political Agents in each state, but on independence the Union Government assumed full responsibility for all internal and external affairs apart from some internal matters that remained the prerogative of the individual Emirates. Six of the Emirates lie on the shore of the Gulf between the Musandam peninsula in the East and the Qatar peninsula in the West while the seventh, Fujeirah, lies on the gulf of Oman.

Security in the area is maintained by the U.A.E. Armed Forces. The Ministry of Defence is located in Dubai with a General Headquarters in Abu Dhabi. Most of the separate police forces have also been merged.

Revenue is chiefly derived from oil, re-exports and customs dues on imports. A substantial amount is spent on overseas aid, where commitments in 1980 totalled £154·8 million, doubling those of 1979.

Trade with U.K.

	1985	1986
Imports from U.K.	£621,400,000	£581,762,000
Exports to U.K.	96,600,000	74,012,000

FLAG.—Horizontal stripes of green over white over black with vertical red stripe in the hoist.

NATIONAL DAY.—December 2.

Abu Dhabi

Abu Dhabi is the largest Emirate of t' ; U.A.E. in area, stretching from Khor al Odaid in the west to the borders with Dubai in the Jebel Ali area. It includes six villages in the Buraimi oasis, the other three being part of the Sultanate of Oman, and a number of settlements in the Liwa Oasis system. Following negotiations with Saudi Arabia, some adjustment of the border has now been made in the Khor al Odaid region, but the agreement has not yet been ratified. The population of the Emirate is now about 670,000

The Abu Dhabi Government controls oil, gas and petrochemical operations in the Emirate through the Abu Dhabi National Oil Company (ADNOC) which has majority shareholdings in the several oil operating and gas treatment companies. ADNOC also has majority shareholdings in oil industry-related companies covering drilling, refining, distribution, chemical manufacture and investment. Offshore production began in 1962, the most important fields being Umm Shaif and Lower Zakum, near Das Island, site of a large associated gas liquefaction plant. The Upper Zakum field came on stream in late 1982, and four other offshore fields are being developed, one near Abu Dhabi city and three near Delma. Production of oil onshore began in 1963 from the Murban field. A large onshore associated gas liquefaction project based at Ruwais started production in 1981. Other large natural gas finds in recent years will consolidate Abu Dhabi's position as a holder of some of the largest reserves of natural gas in the world. Abu Dhabi's crude oil production in 1985 was 732,000 barrels per day.

With its oil wealth the Emirate has seen a decade of growth (which is currently slowing down), not only at Abu Dhabi, now a modern city of about 450,000 people, but also at Al Ain in the Buraimi Oasis and at the new petro-chemical city at Ruwais. An international airport opened in 1982 at Abu Dhabi and another is under construction at Al Ain. There are airfields at Das Island and Jebel Dhanna. The port and harbour on Abu Dhabi island are now completed and there are port facilities at Ruwais.

Dubai

Dubai is the second largest Emirate both in size and in population, which is now about 419,000. The town of Dubai is the main port for the import of goods into the U.A.E. and has a wide re-export trade to the other Gulf States. Dubai's prosperity was established by this trade long before the discovery of oil. Oil was discovered in 1966 and production began in September 1969. The producer in Dubai's offshore oilfields is Dubai Petroleum Company, operated by CONOCO. Production is in excess of 350,000 b.p.d. In 1982 an ARCO-Britoil joint venture discovered an extensive gas and condensate field onshore. Production of condensate is about 22,000 b.p.d.

Oil income has been used to finance Dubai's infrastructure and major construction projects include an international airport, a dry dock complex and an international trade and exhibition centre. There is also a 66 berth port at Jebel Ali, forming the heart of an industrial complex which includes an aluminium smelter with an associated de-salination plant and a gas processing plant. The port and its immediate area is a free trade zone which is expected to attract more industry.

Sharjah

Sharjah, with a present population of approx. 269,000, has declined from its position 50 years ago as principal town in the area. It became the third oil producing Emirate in the summer of 1974, following the discovery of oil offshore. The field declined over the years and by 1982 was yielding less than 6,000 b.p.d. However, new oil and gas discoveries were made in 1982 in the northern emirates and production now stands at about 50,000 b.p.d. Sharjah is well connected by metalled roads to all the other Northern Emirates. It experienced a construction boom in the mid-1970's including an ambitious layout of roads and flyovers within the town. A new container port has been constructed on the Gulf of Oman at Khor Fakkan. The international airport was officially opened in 1979.

Ras al Khaimah

Ras al Khaimah has a population of 116,000 of whom more than half live in the town. An ancient sea-port, near to which archaeological remains have been found, Ras al Khaimah is developing as the most agricultural of the Emirates, producing vegetables, dates, fruit and tobacco. In 1982 Ras al Khaimah announced the discovery of oil and gas offshore and this field currently produces 12,500 b.p.d. An industrial area has been developed to the north of the Emirate, which includes 2 cement works. Ras al-Khaimah has an international airport and has also expanded its port. A new international airport is nearing completion. A new trade centre has just been completed and it is hoped that more industry will be attracted to the emirate.

Fujeirah

Fujeirah, with a population of 40,000, is the poorest and most remote of the seven Emirates lying on the Gulf of Oman coast, and only connected by a metal road to the rest of the country since the end of 1975. Largely agricultural, its population is spread between the slopes of the inland Hajar mountain range and the town of Fujeirah itself, together with a number of smaller settlements on the comparatively fertile plain on the coast. Although exploration work continues, there have been no hydrocarbon discoveries in the Emirate. However, there are some chrome and other mineral deposits. Fujeirah has a new general cargo port.

Ajman and Umm al Qaiwain

Ajman and Umm al Qaiwain are the smallest Emirates, having populations of approx. 64,000 and 29,000 respectively. Both lie on the Gulf coast although Ajman has two inland enclaves at Manama and Masfut. Exploration work continues in both Emirates for oil and gas but so far only Umm Al Qaiwain has experienced any success, with the offshore discovery of natural gas, but the field has yet to be commercially developed. The discovery of onshore gas in nearby Sharjah has increased hopes of similar discoveries in both Ajman and Umm Al Qaiwain.

BRITISH EMBASSY
P.O. Box 248, Abu Dhabi
Ambassador Extraordinary and Plenipotentiary, His
Excellency Michael Logan Tait, C.M.G., L.V.O. (1986).
British Council Representative, Dr. B. H. G. McAdam,
P.O. Box 6523, Abu Dhabi.

(Dubai)
Counsellor and Consul General, J. C. Kay.
British Council Representative, J. D. Ewart, P.O. Box
1636, Dubai.

UNITED STATES OF AMERICA

AREA AND POPULATION

	Area, 1980 (sq. miles)		Population	
	Total	Land	Census 1970	Census 1980
The United States (a)	3,618,770	3,539,289	203,302,031*	226,545,805
Puerto Rico........................	3,515	3,459	2,712,033	3,196,520
Outlying areas under U.S. jurisdiction	1,176	1,176	314,657*	368,856
Territories	459	459	179,519**	235,927
Guam	209	209	84,996	105,979
Virgin Islands of U.S.	132	132	62,468	96,569
American Samoa	77	77	27,159	32,297
Midway Islands	2	2	2,220	453
Wake Island	3	3	1,647	302
Canton Island and Enderbury Island	27	27	—	—
Johnston Atoll (b)	0·5	0·5	1,007	327
Other (c)	9	9	—	—
Pacific Islands Trust Territory (excluding N. Mariana Is.)........	533	533	81,300	116,149
N. Mariana Islands	184	184	9,640	16,780
Population abroad (d)			1,737,836†	995,546
Armed Forces.....................			1,057,776	515,408
Total	**3,543,924**	**3,623,461**	**208,066,557**	**231,106,727**

(a) The 50 States and the Federal *District of Columbia (see* pp. 941).
(b) Formerly listed as Johnston and Sand Island. Sand Island uninhabited at time of enumeration.
(c) Navassa, Baker, Howland and Jarvis Islands, Kingman Reef, and Palmyra Atoll.
(d) Excludes U.S. citizens temporarily abroad on private business.
* Includes population of Swan Islands (22) and Panama Canal Zone (44,198). Jurisdiction over the Swan Islands was transferrred to Honduras in 1972. Due to the 1978 Treaty, the Census is no longer conducted in the Canal Zone.
** Includes population of Swan Islands (22).
† Includes U.S. citizens abroad for long periods who were not connected with the U.S. government (236,336) and crews of U.S. merchant vessels (15,910).

Resident Population by Race 1980
(in thousands)

White 188,372	Filipino .... 774·7	Vietnamese .... 261·7	Puerto Rican .. 2,014
Black.......... 26,495	Japanese 701	Spanish origin** 14,609	Other Spanish . 3,051
American Indian*....... 1,420·4	Asian Indian ...... 361·5	Cuban 803	All other races ... 6,999·2
Chinese 806	Korean .... 354·6	Mexican 8,740	TOTAL 226,546

*Includes Eskimo and Aleut.
**Persons of Spanish origin may be of any race.

PHYSIOGRAPHY

The conterminous States of the Republic occupy nearly all that portion of the North American Continent between the Atlantic and Pacific Oceans, in latitude 25° 07'–49° 23' North and longitude 66° 57'–124° 44' West, its northern boundary being Canada and the southern boundary Mexico. The separate State of Alaska reaches a latitude of 71' 23° N., at Point Barrow (2,502 miles from the U.S. geographic centre).

The general coastline of the 50 States has a length of about 2,069 miles on the Atlantic, 7,623 miles on the Pacific, 1,060 miles on the Arctic, and 1,631 miles on the Gulf of Mexico.

The principal river is the mighty Mississippi-Missouri-Red, traversing the whole country from north to south, and having a course of 3,710 miles to its mouth in the Gulf of Mexico, with many large affluents, the chief of which are the Yellowstone, Platte, Arkansas, and Ohio, Rivers. The rivers flowing into the Atlantic and Pacific Oceans are

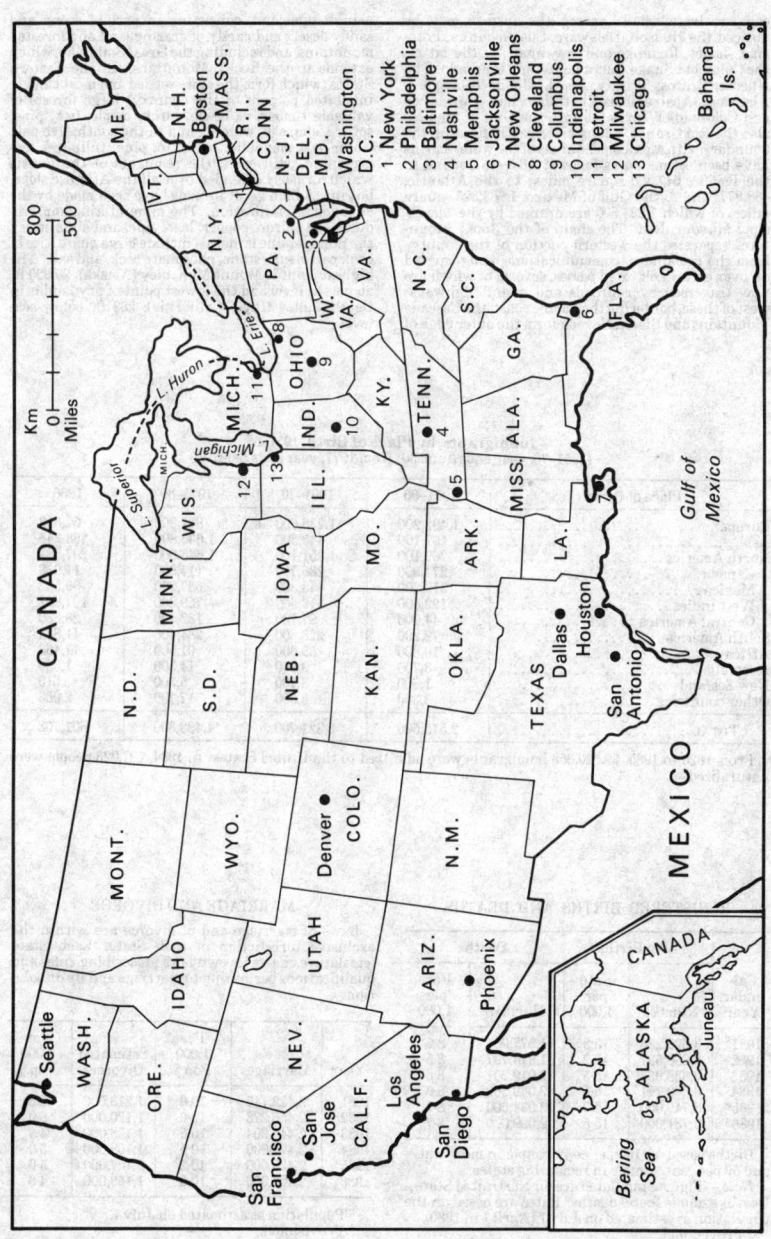

comparatively small; among the former may be noticed the Hudson, Delaware, Susquehanna, Potomac, James, Roanoke and Savannah; of the latter, the Columbia-Snake, Sacramento, and Colorado. The Nueces, Brazos, Trinity, Pearl, Mobile-Tombigbee-Alabama, Apalachicola-Chattahoochee, Suwannee and Colorado of Texas fall into the Gulf of Mexico, also the Rio Grande, a long river partly forming the boundary with Mexico. The areas of the water-basins have been estimated as follows:—Rivers flowing to the Pacific, 647,300 square miles; to the Atlantic, 488,877; and to the Gulf of Mexico, 1,683,325 square miles, of which 1,234,600 are drained by the Mississippi-Missouri-Red. The chain of the Rocky Mountains separates the western portion of the country from the remainder, communications being carried on over certain elevated passes, several of which are now traversed by railroads and major highways; west of these, bordering the Pacific coast, the Cascade Mountains and Sierra Nevada form the outer edge of a high tableland, consisting in part of stony and sandy desert and partly of grazing land and forested mountains, and including the Great Salt Lake, which extends to the Rocky Mountains. In the Eastern States (which form the more settled and most thickly inhabited portion of the country) large forests of valuable timber, as beech, birch, maple, oak, pine, spruce, elm, ash, walnut; and in the south, live oak, water-oak, magnolia, palmetto, pine, tulip-tree, cypress, etc., still exist, the remnants of the forests which formerly extended over all the Atlantic slope, but into which great inroads have been made by the advance of civilization. The mineral kingdom produces ore of iron, copper, lead, zinc, and aluminium, the non-metallic minerals include large quantities of coal, petroleum, stone, phosphate rock, and salt. The highest point is Mount McKinley (Alaska), 20,320 ft. above sea level and the lowest point of dry land is in Death Valley (Inyo, California), 282 ft. below sea-level.

Immigrants, by Place of Birth, 1951–86
(1951–76, year ends June 30: from 1977, year ends Sept. 30)

Place of Birth	1951–60	1961–70	1971–80	1986
Europe	1,492,200	1,238,600	801,300	62,512
Asia	157,100	445,300	1,633,800	268,248
North America	769,100	1,351,100	1,645,000	207,584
Canada	274,900	286,700	114,800	11,039
Mexico	319,300	443,300	637,200	66,533
West Indies	122,800	519,500	759,800	101,632
Central America	44,600	97,700	132,400	28,380
South America	72,200	228,300	284,400	41,874
Africa	16,600	39,300	91,500	17,463
Australia	3,700	9,900	14,300	1,354
New Zealand	1,300	3,700	5,300	610
Other countries	3,300	5,500	17,700	2,063
TOTAL	2,515,500	3,321,700	4,493,300	601,708

From 1820 to 1985, 52,520,358 immigrants were admitted to the United States: in 1984, 197,023 people were naturalized.

REGISTERED BIRTHS AND DEATHS

Calendar Year	Live Births		Deaths	
	Number	Rate per 1,000	Number	Rate per 1,000
1981	3,629,238	15·8	1,977,981	8·6
1982	3,680,537	15·9	1,974,797	8·5
1983	3,638,933	15·5	2,019,201	8·6
1984	3,669,141	15·5	2,039,369	8·6
1985*	3,749,000	15·7	2,084,000	8·7
1986*	3,731,000	15·5	2,099,000	8·7

Births based on 100 per cent sample in most states and 50 per cent. sample in remaining states.

Note.—Figures tabulated are for the United States. Deaths exclude foetal deaths. Rates are based on the population as estimated on July 1 (April 1 in 1980).
* Provisional.

MARRIAGE AND DIVORCE

Laws of marriage and of divorce are within the exclusive jurisdiction of each State. Each State legislature enacts its own laws prescribing rules and qualifications pertaining to marriage and its dissolution.

Year	Marriages	Per 1,000 Pop.§	Estimated Divorces	Per 1,000 Pop.§
1981	2,422,145	10·6	1,213,000	5·3
1982	2,456,278	10·6	1,170,000	5·0
1983	2,445,604	10·5	1,158,000	4·9
1984	2,477,000	10·5	1,169,000	5·0
1985*	2,425,000	10·2	1,187,000	5·0
1986	2,400,000	10·0	1,159,000	4·8

§ Population as estimated on July 1.
* Provisional.

THE UNITED STATES

State (with date and *order* of admission)	Land Area Sq. M.	Population, (1984 estimates)	Capital	Governor (term of office in years, and expiry year)
Alabama (Ala.) (1819) *(22)*	50,767	3,989,000	Montgomery	Harold G. Hunt *(R)* (4—1991)
Alaska (1959) *(49)*	570,833	505,000	Juneau	Steven Cooper *(D)* (4—1990)
Arizona (Ariz.) (1912) *(48)*	113,508	3,072,000	Phoenix	Evan Mecham *(R)* (4—1991)
Arkansas (Ark.) (1836) *(25)*	52,078	2,346,000	Little Rock	Bill Clinton *(D)* (4—1991)
California (Calif.) (1850) *(31)*	156,299	25,795,000	Sacramento	George Deukmejian *(R)* (4—1991)
Colorado (Colo.) (1876) *(38)*	103,595	3,190,000	Denver	Roy Romer *(D)* (4—1991)
Connecticut (Conn.)§(1788) *(5)*	4,872	3,155,000	Hartford	William O'Neill *(D)* (4—1991)
Delaware (Del.) § (1787) *(1)*	1,932	614,000	Dover	Michael N. Castle *(R)* (4—1989)
Florida (Fla.) (1845) *(27)*	54,153	11,050,000	Tallahassee	Bob Martinez *(R)* (4—1991)
Georgia (Ga.) § (1788) *(4)*	58,056	5,842,000	Atlanta	Joe F. Harris *(D)* (4—1991)
Hawaii (1959) *(50)*	6,425	1,037,000	Honolulu	John D. Waihee III *(D)* (4—1990)
Idaho (1890) *(43)*	82,412	999,000	Boise	Cecil D. Andrus *(D)* (4—1991)
Illinois (Ill.) (1818) *(21)*	55,645	11,522,000	Springfield	James R. Thompson *(R)* (4—1991)
Indiana (Ind.) (1816) *(19)*	35,932	5,492,000	Indianapolis	Robert D. Orr *(R)* (4—1989)
Iowa (1846) *(29)*	55,965	2,903,000	Des Moines	Terry Branstad *(R)* (4—1991)
Kansas (Kan.) (1861) *(34)*	81,778	2,440,000	Topeka	Mike Hayden *(R)* (4—1991)
Kentucky (Ky.) (1792) *(15)*	39,669	3,720,000	Frankfort	Martha L. Collins *(D)* (4—1987)
Louisiana (La.) (1812) *(18)*	44,521	4,461,000	Baton Rouge	Edwin W. Edwards *(D)* (4—1988)
Maine (Me.) (1820) *(23)*	30,995	1,156,000	Augusta	John R. McKernan, Jr. *(R)* (4—1991)
Maryland (Md.)§ (1788) *(7)*	9,837	4,349,000	Annapolis	William D. Schaefer *(D)* (4—1991)
Massachusetts (Mass.)§ (1788) *(6)*	7,824	5,798,000	Boston	Michael S. Dukakis *(D)* (4—1991)
Michigan (Mich.) (1837) *(26)*	56,954	9,058,000	Lansing	James J. Blanchard *(D)* (4—1991)
Minnesota (Minn.) (1858) *(32)*	79,548	4,163,000	St. Paul	Rudy Perpich *(D)* (4—1991)
Mississippi (Miss.) (1817) *(20)*	47,233	2,598,000	Jackson	William A. Allain *(D)* (4—1988)
Missouri (Mo.) (1821) *(24)*	68,945	5,001,000	Jefferson City	John Ashcroft *(R)* (4—1989)
Montana (Mont.) (1889) *(41)*	145,388	823,000	Helena	Ted Schwinden *(D)* (4—1989)
Nebraska (Neb.) (1867) *(37)*	76,644	1,605,000	Lincoln	Kay A. Orr *(R)* (4—1991)
Nevada (Nev.) (1864) *(36)*	109,894	917,000	Carson City	Richard H. Bryan *(D)* (4—1991)
New Hampshire (N.H.)§ (1788) *(9)*	8,993	978,000	Concord	John H. Sununu *(R)* (2—1989)
New Jersey (N.J.)§ (1787) *(3)*	7,468	7,517,000	Trenton	Thomas H. Kean *(R)* (4—1990)
New Mexico (N.M.) (1912) *(47)*	121,335	1,426,000	Santa Fé	Garrey E. Carruthers *(R)* (4—1991)
New York (N.Y.)§ (1788) *(11)*	47,377	17,746,000	Albany	Mario M. Cuomo *(D)* (4—1991)
North Carolina (N.C.)§ (1789) *(12)*	48,843	6,166,000	Raleigh	James G. Martin *(R)* (4—1989)
North Dakota (N.D.) (1889) *(39)*	69,300	687,000	Bismarck	George A. Sinner *(D)* (4—1989)
Ohio (1803) *(17)*	41,004	10,740,000	Columbus	Richard F. Celeste *(D)* (4—1991)
Oklahoma (Okla.) (1907) *(46)*	68,655	3,310,000	Oklahoma City	Henry Bellmon *(R)* (4—1991)
Oregon (Ore.) (1859) *(33)*	96,184	2,676,000	Salem	Neil Goldschmidt *(D)* (4—1991)
Pennsylvania (Pa.)§ (1787) *(2)*	44,888	11,887,000	Harrisburg	Robert P. Casey *(D)* (4—1991)
Rhode Island (R.I.)§ (1790) *(13)*	1,055	962,000	Providence	Edward D. Di Prete *(R)* (2—1989)
South Carolina (S.C.)§ (1788) *(8)*	30,203	3,302,000	Columbia	Carroll A. Campbell, Jr. *(R)* (4—1991)
South Dakota (S.D.) (1889) *(40)*	75,952	705,000	Pierre	George S. Mickelson *(R)* (4—1991)
Tennessee (Tenn.) (1796) *(16)*	41,155	4,726,000	Nashville	Ned R. McWherter *(D)* (4—1991)
Texas (1845) *(28)*	262,017	16,083,000	Austin	William P. Clements, Jr. *(R)* (4—1991)
Utah (1896) *(45)*	82,073	1,623,000	Salt Lake City	Norman H. Bangerter *(R)* (4—1989)
Vermont (Vt.) (1791) *(14)*	9,273	530,000	Montpelier	Madeleine M. Kunin *(D)* (2—1989)
Virginia (Va.)§ (1788) *(10)*	39,704	5,636,000	Richmond	Gerald L. Baliles *(D)* (4—1990)
Washington (Wash.) (1889) *(42)*	66,511	4,349,000	Olympia	Booth Gardner *(D)* (4—1989)
West Virginia (W. Va.) (1863) *(35)*	24,119	1,951,000	Charleston	Arch A. Moore, Jr. *(R)* (4—1989)
Wisconsin (Wis.) (1848) *(30)*	54,426	4,762,000	Madison	Tommy Thompson *(R)* (4—1991)
Wyoming (Wyo.) (1890) *(44)*	96,989	513,000	Cheyenne	Michael Sullivan *(D)* (4—1991)
Dist. of Columbia (D.C.) (1791)	63	625,000	..	†
OUTLYING TERRITORIES AND POSSESSIONS				
American Samoa	76	34,500	Pago Pago	A. P. Lutali *(D)* (4—1989)
Guam	209	120,977	Agaña	Joseph Ada *(D)* (4—1991)
Northern Mariana Is.	183	20,000	Saipan	Pedro P. Tenorio *(R)* (4—1990)
Puerto Rico	3,421	3,451,000	San Juan	Rafael Hernández Colón *(PDP)* (4—1989)
Virgin Islands	132	101,000	Charlotte Amalie	Alexander Farrelly *(D)* (4—1991)

D.—Democratic Party.   *R.*—Republican Party.   *I.*—Independent.   *PDP.*—Popular Democratic party.   § The 13 Original States.
† The capital territory is governed by Congress through a Commissioner and City Council.

Largest Cities 1984 (estimated populations)

Ψ New York, NY	7,164,742	San Jose, California	686,178
Ψ Los Angeles, California	3,096,721	Memphis, Tennessee	648,399
Ψ Chicago, Illinois	2,992,472	Washington, D.C.	622,823
Ψ Houston, Texas	1,705,697	Ψ Milwaukee, Wisconsin	620,811
Ψ Philadelphia, Pennsylvania	1,646,713	Jacksonville	577,971
Ψ Detroit, Michigan	1,088,973	Ψ Boston, Massachusetts	570,719
Dallas, Texas	974,234	Columbus	566,114
Ψ San Diego, California	960,452	Ψ New Orleans	559,101
Phoenix, Arizona	853,266	Ψ Cleveland	546,543
San Antonio, Texas	842,779	Denver, Colorado	504,588
Ψ Baltimore, Maryland	763,570	Ψ Seattle, Washington	488,474
Ψ San Francisco, California	712,753	Nashville-Davidson, Tennessee	462,450
Ψ Indianapolis	710,280	Ψ Seaport	

THE PRESIDENTS OF THE UNITED STATES OF AMERICA

Name *(with Native State)*	Party	Born	Inaug.	Died	Age
1. GEORGE WASHINGTON, *Va*	Fed.	1732, Feb. 22	1789	1799, Dec. 14	67
2. John Adams, *Mass.*	,,	1735, Oct. 30	1797	1826, July 4	90
3. Thomas Jefferson, *Va*...................	Rep.	1743, April 13	1801	1826, July 4	83
4. James Madison, *Va*.....................	,,	1751, Mar. 16	1809	1836, June 28	85
5. James Monroe, *Va*......................	,,	1758, April 28	1817	1831, July 4	73
6. John Quincy Adams, *Mass.*	,,	1767, July 11	1825	1848, Feb 23	80
7. Andrew Jackson, *S.C.*	Dem.	1767, Mar. 15	1829	1845, June, 8	78
8. Martin Van Buren, *N.Y.*	,,	1782, Dec. 5	1837	1862, July 24	79
9. William Henry Harrison†, *Va.*	Whig.	1773, Feb. 9	1841	1841, April 4	68
10. John Tyler (*a*), *Va.*	,,	1790, Mar. 29	1841	1862, Jan. 17	71
11. James Knox Polk, *N.C.*	Dem.	1795, Nov. 2	1845	1849, June 15	53
12. Zachary Taylor† *Va.*	Whig.	1784, Nov. 24	1849	1850, July 9	65
13. Millard Fillmore (*a*), *N.Y.*	,,	1800, Jan. 7	1850	1874, Mar. 8	74
14. Franklin Pierce, *N.H.*	Dem.	1804, Nov. 23	1853	1869, Oct. 8	64
15. James Buchanan, *Pa.*	,,	1791, April 23	1857	1868, June 1	77
16. Abraham Lincoln†§, *Ky.*	Rep.	1809, Feb. 12	1861	1865, April 15	56
17. Andrew Johnson (*a*), *N.C.*	,,	1808, Dec. 29	1865	1875, July 31	66
18. Ulysses Simpson Grant, *Ohio*	,,	1822, April 27	1869	1885, July 23	63
19. Rutherford Birchard Hayes, *Ohio*	,,	1822, Oct. 4	1877	1893, Jan. 17	70
20. James Abram Garfield†§, *Ohio*	,,	1831, Nov. 19	1881	1881, Sept. 19	49
21. Chester Alan Arthur (*a*), *Vt.*	,,	1830, Oct. 5	1881	1886, Nov. 18	56
22. Grover Cleveland, *N.J.*	Dem.	1837, Mar. 18	1885	1908, June 24	71
23. Benjamin Harrison, *Ohio*	Rep.	1833, Aug. 20	1889	1901, Mar. 13	67
Grover Cleveland, *N.J.*	Dem.	1837, Mar. 18	1893	1908, June 24	71
24. William McKinley†§, *Ohio*..............	Rep.	1843, Jan. 29	1897	1901, Sept. 14	58
25. Theodore Roosevelt (*a*), *N.Y.*	,,	1858, Oct. 27	1901	1919, Jan. 6	60
26. William Howard Taft, *Ohio*	,,	1857, Sept. 15	1909	1930, Mar. 8	72
27. Woodrow Wilson, *Va.*	Dem.	1856, Dec. 28	1913	1924, Feb. 3	67
28. Warren Gamaliel Harding†, *Ohio*	Rep.	1865, Nov. 2	1921	1923, Aug. 2	57
29. Calvin Coolidge (*a*), *Vt.*	,,	1872, July 4	1923	1933, Jan. 5	60
30. Herbert Clark Hoover, *Iowa*............	,,	1874, Aug. 10	1929	1964, Oct. 20	90
31. Franklin Delano Roosevelt†‡, *N.Y.*	Dem.	1882, Jan. 30	1933	1945, April 12	63
32. Harry S. Truman (*a*), *Missouri*	,,	1884, May 8	1945	1972, Dec. 26	88
33. Dwight David Eisenhower, *Texas*	Rep.	1890, Oct. 14	1953	1969, Mar. 28	78
34. John Fitzgerald Kennedy, *Mass.*†§	Dem.	1917, May 29	1961	1963, Nov. 22	46
35. Lyndon Baines Johnson (*a*), *Texas*	,,	1908, Aug. 27	1963	1973, Jan. 22	64
36. Richard Milhous Nixon, *California*	Rep.	1913, Jan. 9	1969	..	..
37. Gerald Rudolph Ford (*a*), *Nebraska*	,,	1913, July 14	1974	..	..
38. James Earl Carter, *Georgia*	Dem.	1924, Oct. 1	1977	..	..
39. Ronald Wilson Reagan, *Illinois*...........	Rep.	1911, Feb. 6	1981	..	..

† Died in office.   § Assassinated.   (*a*) Elected as Vice-President.
‡ Re-elected Nov. 5, 1940, the first case of a third term; re-elected for a fourth term Nov. 7. 1944.

GOVERNMENT

The United States of America is a Federal Republic consisting of 50 States and 1 Federal District (of which 13 are Original States, 7 were admitted without previous organization as Territories, and 30 were admitted after such organization), and of organized Territories. Hawaii formally entered the Union as the 50th State on Aug. 21, 1959, from which date the flag of the United States has 13 stripes and 50 stars in 9 horizontal rows of six and five alternatively. July 4 (Independence Day) is observed as the National Day.

THE CONSTITUTION.—By the Constitution of Sept. 17, 1787 (to which ten amendments were added on Dec. 15, 1791 and eleventh to twenty-sixth, Jan. 8, 1798, Sept. 25, 1804, Dec. 18, 1865, July 28, 1868, March 30, 1870, Feb. 25, 1913, May 31, 1913, Jan. 16, 1920, Aug. 26, 1920, Feb. 6, 1933, Dec. 5, 1933, Feb. 26, 1951, March 29, 1961, Jan. 23, 1964, Feb. 10, 1967 and June 30, 1971), the government of the United States is entrusted to three separate authorities—the Executive, the Legislative, and the Judicial.

THE EXECUTIVE

THE *Executive* power is vested in a President, who is elected every four years. The mode of electing the President is as follows:—Each State elects (on the *first Tuesday after the first Monday in November* of the year preceding the year in which the Presidential term expires), a number of electors, equal to the whole number of Senators and Representatives to which the State may be entitled in the Congress; but no Senator or Representative, or anyone holding office under Government, shall be appointed an elector. The electors for each State meet in their respective States on the *first Monday after the second Wednesday in December* following, and there vote for a President by ballot. The ballots are then sent to Washington, and opened on the *sixth day of January* by the President of Senate in presence of Congress, and the candidate who has received a majority of the whole number of electoral votes cast is declared President for the ensuing term. If no one has a majority, then from the highest on the list (not exceeding three) the House of Representatives elects a President, the votes being taken by States, the representation from each State having one vote. There is also a Vice-President, who, on the death of the President, becomes President for the remainder of the term. Under the XXth Amendment to the Constitution the terms of the President and Vice-President end at noon on the 20th day of January of the years in which such terms would have ended if the Amendment had not been ratified, and the terms of their successors then begin.

In case of the removal or death of both President and Vice-President, a statute provides for the succession. Under the XXIInd Amendment to the Constitution, the tenure of the Presidency is limited to two terms.

Executive duties:—(1) He is Commander-in-Chief of the Army and of the Navy (and of the Militias when they are in Federal service), and he commissions all officers therein. (2) With the consent of the Senate, he appoints the Cabinet officers and all the chief (and many minor) officials. (3) He exercises a general supervision over the whole Federal Administration and sees that the Federal Laws are duly carried out. Should disorder arise in any state which the authorities thereof are unable to suppress, the aid of the President is invoked. (4) He conducts the foreign policy of the Republic, and has power, "by and with the Advice and Consent of the Senate, to make Treaties, provided two thirds of the senators present concur." The declaration of war rests with Congress. (5) He makes recommendation of a general nature to Congress, and when laws are passed by Congress he may return them to Congress with a veto. But if a measure so vetoed is again passed by both Houses of Congress by two-thirds majority in each House, it becomes law, notwithstanding the objection of the President. The President must be at least 35 years of age and a native citizen of the United States. He receives a taxable salary of $200,000 with a taxable expense allowance of $50,000 and a non-taxable travelling allowance not exceeding $100,000.

President of the United States, RONALD WILSON REAGAN, *born* Feb. 6, 1911, *sworn in* January 20, 1981; *for a second term* January 20, 1985. Republican.

Vice-President, George Herbert Walker Bush, *born* June 12, 1924, *sworn in* Jan. 20, 1981; *for a second term* Jan. 20, 1985.

THE CABINET

Secretary of State, George Shultz.
Secretary of the Treasury, James A. Baker III.
Secretary of Defence, Caspar W. Weinberger.
Attorney-General, Edwin Meese III.
Secretary of the Interior, Donald P. Hodel.
Secretary of Agriculture, Richard E. Lyng.
Secretary of Commerce, William Verity.
Secretary of Labour, William E. Brock.
Secretary of Health and Human Services, Otis R. Bowen.
Secretary of Housing and Urban Development, Samuel J. Pierce, Jr.
Secretary of Transportation, Mrs. Elizabeth Dole.
Secretary of Energy, John S. Herrington.
Secretary of Education, William J. Bennett.

UNITED STATES EMBASSY
Grosvenor Square W1A 1AE
[01-499 9000]

Ambassador Extraordinary and Plenipotentiary, His Excellency Charles H. Price II (1983).
Minister, Hon. Raymond G. H. Seitz.
Minister for Economic Affairs, Michael Calingaert.
Counsellors, Edward Kreuser (*Consular Affairs*); Lawrence D. Russell (*Administrative Affairs*); David K. Diebold (*Commercial Affairs*); James B. Devine (*Scientific and Technological Affairs*); Robert J. Korengold (*Public Affairs*); Rolland E. Anderson (*Agricultural Affairs*); Miles S. Pendleton (*Political Affairs*); Richard M. Ogden (*Economic Affairs*); William J. Graver (*Programme Coordinator*).
Defence Attaché, Col. Keith N. Lacey II.
Army Attaché, Col. James T. Hennessey, Jr.
Naval Attaché, Cpt. Joseph R. McCleary.

CAPITAL OF THE UNITED STATES

In 1790 Congress ratified the cession of 100 sq. miles by the States of Maryland and Virginia as a site for a Federal City to be the national capital of the United States. In 1791 it was decided to name the capital *Washington* and in 1793 the foundation-stone of the Capitol building was laid. In 1800 the seat of Government was removed to Washington, which was chartered as a city in 1802. In 1846 the Virginia portion was retroceded and the present area of the *District of Columbia* (with which the City of Washington is considered co-extensive) is 63 sq. miles (163 sq. km.), with a resident population (mid-1985 estimate) of 626,000.

The District of Columbia is governed by an elected mayor and City Council.

The *City of Washington* is situated on the west central edge of Maryland, opposite the State of Virginia, on the left bank of the Potomac at its confluence with the Anacostia. The population of the metropolitan area in 1985 was estimated at 3,490,000.

THE CONGRESS

The Legislative power is vested in two Houses, the Senate and the House of Representatives, the President having a *veto* power, which may be overcome by a two-thirds vote of each House. The Senate is composed of two Senators from each State, elected by the people thereof for the term of six years, and each Senator has one vote. Representatives are chosen in each State, by popular vote, for two years. The average number of persons represented by each Congressman is 1 for 550,000. The *Senate* consists of 100 members. The salary of a Senator is $89,500 per annum. The *House of Representatives* consists of 435 Representatives, a resident commissioner from Puerto Rico and a delegate from American Samoa, the District of Columbia, Guam and the Virgin Islands. The salary of a Representative is $89,500 per annum. By the XIXth Amendment, sex is no disqualification for the franchise. The Bureau of the Census estimated on July 1, 1986 there were 178,300,000 persons of voting age, excluding members of the armed forces overseas.

THE HUNDRETH CONGRESS

President of the Senate, George Bush (*Vice President of the United States*).
Speaker of the House of Representatives, James C. Wright, Jr., *Texas*.
Secretary of the Senate, Walter J. Stewart, *Dist. of Columbia*.
Clerk of the House of Representatives, Donald K. Anderson, *California*.

Members of the 100th Congress were elected on Nov. 4, 1986.

The 100th Congress is constituted as follows:
Senate.—Democrats 54; Republicans, 46; Total, 100.
House of Representatives.—Democrats, 258; Republicans, 177. Total, 435.

THE JUDICATURE

The *Federal Judiciary* consists of three sets of Federal Courts: (1) The *Supreme Court* at Washington, D.C., consisting of a Chief Justice and eight Associate Justices, with original jurisdiction in cases affecting Ambassadors, etc., or where a State is a party to the suit, and with appellate jurisdiction from inferior Federal Courts and from the judgments of the highest Courts of the States. (2) The *United States Courts of Appeals*, dealing with appeals from District Courts and from certain federal administrative agencies, and consisting of all the Circuit Judges within the circuit. (3) The 94 *United States District Courts* served by 700 District Court Judges.

THE SUPREME COURT
(U.S. Supreme Court Building, Washington, D.C., 20543)

Chief Justice, William R. Rehnquist, *Ariz., born* Oct. 1, 1924, *appointed* 1986.

ASSOCIATE JUSTICES

Name	Born	Apptd
William J. Brennan, Jr., *N.J.*	1906	1956
Byron R. White, *Colo.*	1917	1962
Thurgood Marshall, *N.Y.*	1908	1967
Harry Blackmun, *Minn.*	1908	1970
John Paul Stevens, *Ill.*	1920	1975
Sandra Day O'Connor, *Ariz.*	1930	1981
Antonin Scalia	1936	1986

Clerk of the Supreme Court, Joseph F. Spaniol, Jr.

The appointment of Robert Bork to the Supreme Court was awaiting confirmation in September 1987.

CRIMINAL STATISTICS, U.S.

	No. of offences	
Crime	1985	1986
Murder and Non-negligent Manslaughter	18,976	20,613
Rape	87,340	90,434
Robbery	497,874	542,775
Aggravated Assault	723,246	834,322
Burglary	3,073,348	3,241,410
Larceny—Theft	6,926,380	7,257,153
Thefts of Motor Vehicles	1,102,862	1,224,137
Total	12,430,026	13,210,844

DEFENCE

Department of Defence

Secretary of Defence (in the Cabinet), Caspar W. Weinberger.
Secretary of the Army, John O. Marsh, Jr.
Secretary of the Navy, James H. Webb, Jr.
Secretary of the Air Force, Edward Aldridge.
Chairman, Joint Chief of Staff, Adm. William Crowe.

The Department of Defence includes the Secretary of Defence as its head, the Deputy Secretary of Defence, the Defence staff offices, the Joint Chiefs of Staff and the Joint Staff, the three military departments and the military services within those departments, the unified and specified commands, and other Department of Defence agencies as the Secretary of Defence establishes to meet specific requirements. The Defence staff offices and the joint Chiefs of Staff, although separately organized, function in full coordination and cooperation. They include the offices of the Director of Defence Research and Engineering, the Assistant Secretaries of Defence, the General Counsel of the Department of Defence and such other staff offices as the Secretary of Defence may establish. The Joint Chiefs of Staff, as a group, are directly responsible to the Secretary of Defence for the functions assigned to them. Each member of the Joint Chiefs of Staff, other than the Chairman, is responsible for keeping the Secretary of his military department fully informed on matters considered or acted upon by the Joint Chiefs of Staff.

Each military department is separately organized under its own Secretary and functions under the direction, authority and control of the Secretary of Defence.

The Department of Defence maintains and employs armed forces: (1) to support and defend the Constitution of the United States against all enemies, foreign and domestic; (2) to insure, by timely and effective military action, the security of the United States, its possessions, and areas vital to its interests; (3) to uphold and advance the national policies and

interest of the United States; and (4) to safeguard the internal security of the United States. All functions in the Department of Defence and its component agencies are performed under the direction, authority and control of the Secretary of Defence.

Commanders of unified and specified commands are responsible to the President and the Secretary of Defence for the accomplishment of military missions assigned to them.

Unified Defence Commands

COMMANDERS-IN-CHIEF

U.S. European Command, Brussels.—Gen. John R. Galvin (*U.S. Army*) (concurrently *N.A.T.O. Supreme Allied Commander*).
U.S. Southern Command, Quarry Heights, Panama Canal Zone.—Lt.-Gen. Frederick F. Woerner (*U.S. Army*).
Atlantic, Norfolk, Virginia.—Adm. Lee Baggett, Jr. (*U.S. Navy*) (concurrently *N.A.T.O. Supreme Allied Commander, Atlantic*).
Pacific, Hawaii.—Adm. Ronald J. Hays (*U.S. Navy*).
U.S. Space Command, Gen. John L. Piotrowski (*U.S.A.F.*).
*Strategic Air Command, Omaha.—Gen. John T. Chain (*U.S.A.F.*).
* Military Air Lift Command, Gen. Duane H. Cassidy (*U.S.A.F.*).
U.S. Readiness Command, Gen. James J. Lindsey (*U.S. Army*).
* U.S. Central Command, Gen. George B. Crist (*U.S. Marine Corps*).
Military Sea Lift Command, Rear Adm. Walter T. Piotti, Jr. (*U.S. Navy*).
* A Specified Command.

Army.—The U.S. Army had a strength on March 30, 1986, of 777,518. Stationed in Germany were four divisions.
Chief of the Staff of the Army, Gen. John A. Wickham, Jr.

Navy.—The strength of the Navy (including Marine Corps) on March 31, 1987 was 782,494 active duty personnel.

The U.S. Navy had in service in 1986, 555 active fleet ships (Surface vessels, 454; Submarines, 101).
Chief of Naval Operations, Adm. Carlisle A. H. Trost.

Marine Corps.—Established 1775. Strength on March 31, 1987 was 198,940 active duty personnel.
Commandant, Gen. Paul X. Kelley.

Air.—The United States Air Force was established as a separate organization on September 18, 1947. On Sept. 30, 1985, there were 597,003 officers and airmen on active duty, with 250,400 civilian employees. Air Force Reserve and Air National Guard numbered 226,983.

The Air Force has up to 30 per cent of the strategic bomber and tanker forces maintaining constant alert as well as 1,009 inter-continental ballistic missiles in silos. In addition, the Air Force maintains the capability to carry out limited war and special warfare operations, with more than 5,500 strategic, tactical and support aircraft. In March, 1961, the Air Force was assigned primary responsibility for the Department of Defence space development programmes and projects. In September 1982, Air Force Space Command was established to support and direct operational space activities. On May 29, 1986, the United States had a total of 1,540 spacecraft tracked in near earth or deep space orbits. These included military, other government agency and commercial equipment. The U.S. also has 489 space objects in near earth or deep space orbits.
Chief of Staff of the U.S. Air Force, Larry D. Welch.

THE UNITED STATES BUDGET
(fiscal year; in millions of dollars)

Receipts by Source	1986 (actual)	1987 (estimated)
Individual income taxes	349,000	364,000
Corporation income taxes	63,100	104,800
Social insurance taxes and contributions	283,900	301,500
Excise taxes	32,900	32,600
Estate and gift taxes	7,000	6,000
Customs duties	13,300	14,400
Miscellaneous	19,900	19,100
Total	769,100	842,400
Outlays by Function		
National defence	273,400	282,200
International affairs	14,200	14,600
General science, space, and technology	9,000	9,500
Energy	4,700	3,800
Natural resources and environment	13,600	13,900
Agriculture	31,400	31,100
Commerce and housing credit	4,400	9,300
Transportation	28,100	27,000
Community and regional development	7,200	6,200
Education, training, employment, and social services	30,600	29,800
Health	35,900	39,700
Social security and medicare	269,000	279,500
Income security	119,800	124,900
Veterans' benefits and services	26,400	26,700
Admininstration of justice	6,600	8,300
General government	6,100	6,800
General purpose fiscal assistance	6,400	1,900
Interest	136,000	137,500
Undistributed offsetting receipts	−33,000	−37,100
Total	989,800	1,015,600

FINANCE

SOCIAL WELFARE EXPENDITURE

Total expenditure by programme was:

	1983	1984
Social insurance	331,058	342,264
Education	141,813	152,025
Public aid	85,830	89,871
Health and medical	35,976	37,864
Veterans' programmes	25,826	26,127
Other social welfare	12,484	13,445
Housing	9,090	10,374
TOTAL	642,077	671,972

Expenditure per capita was ($):

Social insurance	1,389·93	1,424·20
Education	597·73	635·14
Public aid	361·91	375·50
Health and medical	151·70	158·21
Veterans' programmes	108·04	108·33
Other social welfare	52·64	56·18
Housing	38·33	43·35
TOTAL	2,700·27	2,800·91

PUBLIC DEBT

At the end of 1986 the total gross *Federal Debt* of the United States stood at $2,132,900 million.

COST OF LIVING IN U.S.A.

The Consumer Price Index (for city wage-earner and clerical workers—single persons and families—in 50 cities representative of all cities in the United States) showed an annual average during the calendar year 1985 of 322 (1967 = 100), a rise of 3·5 per cent over the 1984 figure.

GROSS NATIONAL PRODUCT

Gross National Product by industry in 1985 was ($ million):—

All industries, total	3,957,000
Agriculture, forestry, fisheries	91,500
Mining	122,800
Construction	182,200
Manufacturing	795,800
Transportation and public utilities	374,400
Communications	108,500
Electric, gas, sanitary services	121,400
Trade	652,500
Finance, insurance, real estate	626,600
Services	639,400
Government enterprises	477,400
Rest of the world	41,200

G.N.P., national and personal income in 1985 were ($ million):—

Gross national product	3,998,100
Net national product	3,560,900
National income	3,222,300

Corporate profits	280,700
Net interest	311,400
Personal income	3,314,500
Personal tax and non-tax payments .	486,500
Disposable personal income..........	2,828,000
Personal outlays	2,684,700
Personal saving	143,300

Personal consumption expenditure in 1985 was $2,601,000 million, of which durable goods accounted for $359,000 million, non-durable goods $905,000 million and services $1,336,000 million. Gross private domestic investment in 1985 was $661,000 million.

UNITED STATES STOCK OF CURRENCY AND COIN

U.S. stock of currency and coin at Sept. 30, 1984 was:—

	$ million
Gold*	11,097·2
Dollars†	2,024·7
Subsidiary Coin	10,408·3
Minor Coin	3,208·5
Silver Certificates§	202·5
U.S. Notes	322·5
Federal Reserve Notes	189,882·3
TOTAL‡	217,216·6

*Held by U.S. Treasury only.

† Figures consist of $481·8 m in standard silver and the balance in cupro-nickel clad dollars.

‡ Totals include value of early issue notes in process of withdrawal, not separately shown. Value, September 1984, $70·6 m.

§In process of withdrawal. Not redeemable in silver.

AGRICULTURE AND LIVESTOCK

The total number of farms in 1986 was 2,214,420, with a total area of land in farms of 1,007,363,000 acres, and an average acreage per farm of 455 acres. The total number of people employed on farms during the week of July 6–12, 1986 was 3,469,000, of whom 1,971,000 were unpaid workers, 1,233,000 hired workers and 265,000 agricultural service workers.

Principal crops are corn for grain, soybeans, wheat hay, cotton, tobacco, grain sorghums, potatoes, oranges and barley.

Livestock on farms on Jan. 1, 1986 and 1987 (*Dec. 1985 and 1986) was:—

	1986 (000's)	1987 (000's)
All cattle	105,468	102,031
Milk cows.............	11,177	10,547
Sheep and lambs	9,983	10,328
Hogs and pigs*	52,313	51,160
Chickens*	386,548	368,681

Gross income from farming in 1985 was $166,566 million, of which cash receipts from marketing were $142,103 million and Government payments $7,704 million. Cash income from all crops in 1985 was $72,702 million and from livestock and livestock products $69,400 million.

NONFUEL MINERALS

The value of nonfuel raw mineral production in the United States in 1986 totalled an estimated $23,480 million compared with $23,233 million in 1985.

Trading Figures

	1984	1985
Imports	$31,500 m	$29,500 m
Exports	14,000 m	13,000 m

Production Figures
('000 tonnes)

	1985	1986p
Aluminium*	3,858	3,300
Iron Ore†	48,751	40,034
Phosphate rock	50,835	38,710
Zinc Ore	252	216
Refined Copper	1,436	1,500
Refined Lead	1,082	960

* measured in short tons
† measured in long tons
p = preliminary.

ENERGY

Energy Summary
(Quadrillion (10^{15}) Btu)

	1984	1985	1986
Production	65·81	64·78	64·25
Consumption	74·06	73·96	73·93
Imports	12·76	12·10	14·07
Exports	3·80	4·23	4·01

Breakdown of Production and Consumption
(Quadrillion (10^{15}) Btu)

	1985	1986
Production		
Crude Oil	18·99	18·35
Coal	19·33	19·48
Natural Gas (dry)	16·92	16·49
Natural Gas Plant Liquids .	2·24	2·17
Hydroelectric..............	2·94	3·04
Nuclear	4·15	4·48
Other*	0·21	0·22
Total..................	64·78	64·25
Consumption		
Petroleum	30·92	31·89
Natural Gas (dry)	17·85	16·53
Coal	17·48	17·32
Hydroelectric..............	3·36	3·50
Nuclear	4·15	4·48
Other*	0·20	0·22
Total..................	73·96	73·93

* Includes geothermal power, solar power and electricity produced from wood and waste.

During 1986 oil and gas drilling rigs in operation averaged 964 and the number of well completions in 1986 totalled 37,530. Seismic exploration work in progress involved a total of 200 crews, 24 in offshore areas and 176 on shore. Domestic crude oil production in 1986 averaged 8,668,000 barrels per day and total petroleum imports averaged 5,290,000 barrels per day. Production of dry natural gas in 1986 was 15,970 billion cubic feet (Bcf): together with imports it supplied 16,000 Bcf required for domestic consumption. Stocks of gas available for withdrawal were estimated at 2,747 Bcf in 1986. Production of coal in 1986 was 888,200,000 short tons with domestic consumption requiring 806,200,000 short tons. In 1986 U.S. nuclear power generators produced 414,000 million net kilowatt-hours of electricity, accounting for 16·6 per cent of domestic electricity generation.

Operable reactors at end Dec. 1986 totalled 100, with a net summer capacity of 85·2 million net kilowatts.

LABOUR

Organized Labour.—Approximately 17·5 per cent. of the employed wage and salary workers in the United States were members of labour organizations in 1986.

Work Stoppages.—There were 69 stoppages involving 1,000 or more workers in 1986. They resulted in 11,861,000 man-days of idleness, representing 0·05 per cent. of estimated working time of all non-agricultural workers.

Employment and Unemployment.—The civilian labour force (working population) was 119,993,000 in May 1987. This includes self-employed wage and salary-earners, and unpaid family workers, employed and unemployed. Unemployment was estimated at 7,546,000 in May 1987 (6·3 per cent.) (it was 7·2 per cent. in May 1986).

Wages.—In March 1987, gross average weekly earnings in industry ranged from $692·62 per week in malt beverage industry (41·8 hours and $16·57 average hourly earnings) to $112·38 in eating and drinking places (25·6 hours and $4·39 average hourly earnings). The average for all manufacturing was $402·87 compared with $396·01 in March 1986.

On Jan. 1, 1981, the minimum wage set by federal law became $3·35. The law requires at least time and a half of an employee's regular rate of pay for all hours over 40 a week for most covered workers.

The Fair Labour Standards Act covers all employees of certain enterprises having workers engaged in interstate commerce, producing goods for interstate commerce, or handling, selling, or otherwise working on goods or materials that have been moved in or produced for such commerce by any person.

There are certain exemptions from these requirements in specific occupations and industries.

In addition to cash wages, almost all workers are covered by legally required social security, unemployment insurance and workers' compensation insurance. Also though not required by law, most workers receive some type of "fringe" benefits—the most common forms being paid vacations, and public holidays, various types of retirement plans, insurance and health benefits financed by the employer or by employer and employees jointly.

EXTERNAL TRADE OF THE UNITED STATES

	1985	1986
	$ million	
General Imports:		
c.i.f. value	361,626·3	387,082·0
customs value	345,275·5	369,961·0
Exports and re-exports:		
f.a.s. value†	213,133·0	217,292·0
Trade balance:		
f.a.s. exports : c.i.f. imports	−148,493·3	−169,790·0
f.a.s. exports : customs imports	−132,142·5	−152,669·0

† Excluding military aid.

EXPORTS BY PRINCIPAL COMMODITIES OF DOMESTIC ORIGIN, 1986

Commodity	Value
	$ (million)
Food and Live Animals	17,302·6
Grain and cereal preparations	7,367·9
Beverages and Tobacco	2,920·2
Crude materials (inedible) except fuel .	17,323·8
Raw cotton	773·3
Metal ores, concentrates, scrap	2,801·6

Mineral fuels, lubricants, etc..........	8,114·5
Coal (bituminous)	3,861·9
Petroleum and products	3,639·5
Oils and Fats (animal and vegetable) ..	1,014·9
Chemicals and products	22,765·8
Machinery and Transport Equipment .	95,289·5
Electronic computers, parts, etc.	14,514·0
Electrical machinery, appliances, etc.	13,629·6
Motor vehicles and parts	18,575·0
Other Manufactured Goods	16,629·3
Unclassified Commodities	11,010·7

U.S. IMPORTS BY PRINCIPAL COMMODITIES, 1986

Commodity	Value
	$ (million)
Food and Live Animals	20,802·5
Fish and fish preparations	3,929·6
Vegetables and fruit	4,200·2
Coffee–crude......................	4,293·2
Beverages and Tobacco	3,866·1
Crude materials (inedible), except fuels	10,431·5
Mineral fuels, lubricants, etc..........	37,309·9
Crude petroleum	22,720·5
Petroleum products	11,420·0
Oils and Fats (animal and vegetable) ..	515·9
Chemicals and products	15,000·7
Machinery and Transport Equipment .	161,561·6
Telecommunications, sound recording apparatus	20,720·1
Electrical machinery, parts.........	20,155·1
Motor vehicles	54,660·6
Other Manufactured Goods	56,732·9
Unclassified Commodities	14,914·3

U.S. FOREIGN TRADE BY ECONOMIC CLASS 1986

	$ million	
Class	Imports	Exports*
Crude Materials...	36,287	10,729
Crude Foodstuffs ..	11,125	9,120
Manufactured Foods	13,058	9,303
Semi-manufactures	41,395	36,335
Finished Manufactures...	268,096	140,889
Total..........	369,961	206,376

*Excluding the total military grant-aid of $206,364 million.

U.S. FOREIGN TRADE BY PRINCIPAL AREAS AND COUNTRIES, 1986

Area/Country	Exports and Re-exports to	General Imports from
	$ million	
Africa...................	5,978·2	11,056·8
Asia	64,531·8	162,667·8
Japan	26,881·6	85,456·7
Saudi Arabia	3,448·8	4,054·3
Taiwan	5,524·2	21,251·5
Korea, Rep. of	6,354·9	13,497·0
Hong Kong	3,030·1	9,473·6
Oceania	6,658·5	4,080·3
Australia.............	5,551·2	2,872·6
Europe	64,269·8	97,267·5
West Germany	10,560·5	26,128·1
U.K.	11,418·2	16,032·5
Other E.C.	31,175·3	79,520·2
Other O.E.C.D.........	7,849·4	14,011·2
Communist bloc	1,989·2	2,205·6

N. & Central America....	121,004·0	92,664·2
Canada..............	45,332·6	68,662·4
Mexico.............	12,391·6	17,558·3
S. America	11,788·1	19,803·9

COMMUNICATIONS
RAILWAYS

Data on Class I line-haul railroads (*dollars in thousands*)

	1984	1985
Operating Revenues		
Freight	28,077,394	26,468,797
Passenger	101,189	103,205
Total.......	29,040,737	27,361,093
Total operating expenses	25,445,005	24,997,912
Net working capital	1,858,590	1,083,524
Average number of employees	319,081	297,985

ROADS

In 1985 there were 3·86 million miles of public roads and streets in the United States, of which 3·17 million miles were in rural areas and 691,000 miles were in urban areas. Surfaced roads and streets account for 3·48 million miles, or 87·8 per cent, of the total; 382,000 miles, or 9·9 per cent, were unimproved or graded and drained.

An estimated total of $54,725 million was spent in 1985 for roads and streets in the United States. Capital outlay accounts for 49·6 per cent of the total expenditure; 29·3 per cent was spent for maintenance, and 7·4 per cent for administration; 9·7 per cent for highway police and safety; and 4·0 per cent for interest on highway bonds.

Motor Vehicles and Taxation.—The number of motor vehicles registered in 1985 in the United States was 171,690,733, an increase of 3·3 per cent over the 1984 total of 166,248,816. In 1985 the State governments received $23,283,000,000 in State Highway-User Tax Receipts, including road and crossing tolls, and $12,751,000,000 in Federal Highway-User Tax Receipts.

Accidents.—In 1985 there were 43,795 deaths caused by motor vehicle accidents. The death rate per 100,000,000 vehicle-miles of travel was 2·47 in 1985 compared with 2·58 in 1984.

SHIPPING

The ocean-going Merchant Marine of the U.S. on June 1, 1986, consisted of 736 vessels of 1,000 gross tons and over, of which 471 were privately owned and 265 were government-owned ships. Of the 471 privately owned vessels, 371 were active including 2 combination passenger and cargo ships, 29 freighters, 18 bulk carriers, 168 tankers, 12 tug-barge units, 7 liquefied natural gas carriers and 135 intermodal ships. There were 212 ships in the National Defence Reserve Fleet of inactive government-owned vessels, of which 7 were to be sold for scrap.

AIR TRANSPORT

United States domestic and international scheduled airlines in 1984 carried 344,460,600 passengers over 304,987,288,000 revenue passenger miles. Cargo revenue ton-miles totalled 8,200,000,000, an increase of 8·0 per cent over 1983. Air cargo ton-miles were distributed as follows: freight 6,500,000,000 (up 7·7 per cent); express 64,400,000 (up 2·8 per cent); and air mail 1,600,000,000 (up 9·3 per cent).

Total operating revenues of all U.S. scheduled airlines were $43,800,000,000 in 1984, an increase of 13·5 per cent from 1983.

Total operating expenses rose to $41,700,000,000 in 1984, a 9·0 per cent increase over 1983. Scheduled operations showed a net operating profit of $2,100,000,000 in 1984, compared with a net operating profit of $361,700,000 in 1983.

Three principal classes of commercial air carriers have been established in the United States based on annual operating revenues. They are: Majors, with annual operating revenues of over $1,000 million; Nationals, with annual operating revenues of $75–1,000 million; and Regionals, with annual operating revenues of up to $75,999,000.

U.S. Scheduled Airline Industry Statistics, 1984 (Thousands)

	Majors	Nationals	Regionals	System
Revenue Passenger Carried	250,150	80,337	13,974	344,461
Revenue Passengers Miles	252,295,400	43,820,182	8,871,706	304,987,288
Air Mail Ton Miles	1,402,063	199,028	15,841	1,616,932
Express Ton Miles	60,255	2,024	131	62,410
Freight Ton Miles	3,905,550	2,445,897	145,714	6,497,161
Revenue Ton Miles	30,597,429	7,028,968	1,048,857	38,675,254
Revenue Plane Miles	2,391,806	579,533	159,890	3,131,229

EDUCATION
State School Systems

All the 50 States and the District of Columbia have compulsory school attendance laws. In general, children are obliged to attend school from 7 to 16 years of age. Officers of local administrative units, usually known as truant or attendance officers, are charged with enforcing the compulsory attendance laws.

In the autumn of 1985, 45,113,000 children were enrolled in regular elementary and secondary day schools in the United States, of whom 5·6 million or 12·4 per cent attended private schools.

The following percentages of the school-age population were estimated to be enrolled in school in the autumn of 1985; of 5- and 6-year-olds, 95 per cent; of 7- to 13-year-olds, 99 per cent; of 14- to 17-year-olds, 95 per cent; and of 18- to 24-year-olds, 32 per cent.

During the 1985–86 school year, the average daily attendance in regular public elementary and secondary day schools was 36,642,000. In the 1985–86 school year 2,378,000 students graduated from regular public high schools, 265,000 graduated from private high school. In addition some 25,000 graduated from evening schools and adult education programmes, and an estimated 500,000 received high school equivalency certificates. Public school teachers numbered 2,210,000, with an average salary of $25,206.

Most of the revenue for public elementary and secondary school purposes comes from the Federal, State, and local governments. Less than ½ per cent comes from gifts from tuition and transportation fees. Estimated revenue receipts during 1985–86 amounted to $151,333,000,000; 6·5 per cent from the Federal Government, 49·8 per cent from State governments, and 43·8 per cent from local sources. Estimated current expenditure in the 1985–86 school year was $139,782 million; for sites, buildings, furniture and equipment expenditures, $8,555 million; for interest in school debt $2,577 million.

Institutions of Higher Education

In the autumn of 1985, total enrolment in universities, colleges, professional schools, and two-year schools numbered 12,247,000.

Degrees conferred during the academic year 1985–86 were:—

Degree	
Bachelor's	987,823
First-Professional	73,910
Master's	288,567
Doctorates	33,653

During 1985–86 the major fields for bachelor's degrees were business and management (238,160), engineering (95,953) and social sciences (93,703). First-profession degrees in law (35,844) and medicine (15,938) predominated. Master's degrees were heavily concentrated in education (76,353) and business and management (67,137). The most popular fields of study for doctorates were education (7,110) and life sciences (3,358).

During the 1985–86 academic year, the 3,340 colleges and universities employed about 710,000 (full-time equivalent) instructional faculty. Total expenditures for colleges and universities during the 1985–86 academic year were $107,685,000,000.

Particulars of some of the Universities (with opening autumn enrolment figures, 1985) are: *Harvard* (20,711 students, including 7,747 women), founded at Cambridge, Mass. on Oct. 28, 1636, and named after John Harvard of Emmanuel College, Cambridge, England, who bequeathed to it his library and a sum of money in 1638; *Yale* (10,809 students, including 4,740 women), founded at New Haven, Connecticut, in 1701; *Bowdoin*, Brunswick, Me. (founded 1794; 1,446 students including 626 women); *Brown*, Providence, R.I. (founded 1764; 7,277 students, including 3,398 women); *Columbia*, New York, N.Y. (founded 1754; 23,556 students, including 12,393

women); *Cornell* (founded at Ithaca, N.Y., 1865; 19,680 students, including 8,626 women); *Dartmouth*, Hanover, N.H. (founded 1769, 4,519 students, including 1,826 women); *Georgetown*, Washington, D.C. (founded 1789; 11,985 students, including 5,484 women); *North Carolina*, Chapel Hill, N.C. (founded in 1789; 22,066 students, including 12,504 women); *Pennsylvania*, Philadelphia, Pa. (founded 1740; 21,870 students, including 9,926 women); *Princeton*, N.J. (founded 1746; 6,293 students and 2,215 women); and *William and Mary*, Williamsburg, Va. (founded 1693; 6,676 students, including 3,448 women).

WEIGHTS AND MEASURES

The weights and measures in common use in the United States are of British origin, and date back to the American Revolution when practically all the standards were intended to be equivalent to those used in England at that period. Divergencies in these weights and measures were, however, quite common, due no doubt to the fact that the system of weights and measures in England was not itself well established, and hence the copies brought to the United States were often adjusted to different standards. Because of these discrepancies, the system of weights and measures in the United States (U.S. inch-pound system) is not identical with the British system.

The U.S. ton (short) = 2,000 pounds (British Imperial ton = 2,240 pounds, or 1 U.S. long ton). The U.S. gallon = 231 cubic inches (277·42 cubic inches in U.K.) or 128 fluid ounces (160 fluid ounces in U.K.). In the British system the units of dry measure are the same as those of liquid measure. In the United States these two are not the same, the gallon and its subdivisions being used in the measurement of liquids, while the bushel, with its subdivisions, is used in the measurement of certain dry commodities. The U.S. gallon is divided into 4 liquid quarts and the U.S. bushel into 32 dry quarts.

The International System of Units—officially abbreviated SI—is a modernized version of the metric system. It was established by international agreement to provide a logical and interconnected framework for all measurements in science, industry and commerce.

In 1971, a study recommended a concerted, coordinated, but voluntary national effort to make the SI the predominant form of measurement in the United States. In December 1975, legislation was passed which established the United States Metric Board to coordinate voluntary conversion to the metric system. Since 1982 this function has been assumed by the Office of Metric Programmes of the U.S. Department of Commerce.

TERRITORIES, ETC. OF THE UNITED STATES

The territories and the principal islands and island groups under the sovereignty of the United States of America comprise the Commonwealth of Puerto Rico, the Commonwealth of the Northern Mariana Islands, and the following territories: Guam; American Samoa; U.S. Virgin Islands; Jarvis Island, Palmyra Island and Kingman Reef; Johnston Atoll; Midway Islands; Wake Islands.

Jarvis Island, Palmyra Island and Kingman Reef are uninhabited islands in the Line Island group. Johnston Atoll (formerly Johnston and Sand Islands) comprises two small islands, less than 1 sq. mile in area, to the south-west of Hawaii which are administered by the U.S. Air Force. The two Midway Islands (area, 2 sq. miles; population (1970), 2,200), at the western end of the Hawaiian chain, are administered

by the U.S. Navy. The Wake Islands have an area of about 3 sq. miles and a population (1979) of 300. They lie about 2,300 miles west of Hawaii and are administered by the U.S. Air Force.

Under the terms of a Treaty of Friendship between the United States and Kiribati, signed in 1979 and subsequently ratified by the U.S. Senate, the United States renounced its claim to Canton and Enderbury Islands.

There are certain small guano islands, rocks, or keys which, in pursuance of action taken under the Act of Congress, August 18, 1856, subsequently embodied in Sections 5570–5578 of the Revised Statutes are considered as appertaining to the United States. Responsibility for territorial affairs generally is centred in the Office of the Assistant Secretary,

Territorial and International Affairs, Dept. of the Interior, Washington, D.C. Puerto Rico was removed from the Department of the Interior's administrative jurisdiction with the acquisition of Commonwealth status in 1952.

The Trust Territory of the Pacific Islands is under the jurisdiction of the United States pursuant to a trusteeship agreement between the U.S. Government and the Security Council of the United Nations. It consists of the Mariana (except Guam), Caroline and Marshall Islands: the Northern Mariana Islands voted in 1975 to become a Commonwealth of the U.S. and the Covenant Agreement became effective on Nov. 3, 1986.

As a result of the Panama Canal Treaty of 1977 the Canal Zone was placed under Panamanian jurisdiction. The Panama Canal Commission, an arm of the U.S. Government, will continue to operate the canal until the year 2000.

THE COMMONWEALTH OF PUERTO RICO

Puerto Rico (Rich Port) is an island of the Greater Antilles group in the West Indies, and lies between 17° 50′–18° 30′ N. lat. and 65° 30′–67° 15′ W. long., with a total area of 3,435 sq. miles (8,897 sq. km.), and an estimated population (1985) of 3,451,000. The majority of the inhabitants are of Spanish descent and Spanish and English are the official languages. The island is about 111 miles from west to east, and 36 miles from north to south. The capital is 1,600 miles distant from New York, and 1,000 miles from Miami.

Puerto Rico was discovered in 1493 by Christopher Columbus and explored by Ponce de Léon in 1508. It continued as a Spanish possession until Oct. 18, 1898, when the United States took formal possession as a result of the Spanish-American War. It was ceded by Spain to the United States by the Treaty ratified on April 11, 1899.

The Constitution approved by the Congress and the President of the United States, which came into force on July 25, 1952, establishes the Commonwealth of Puerto Rico with full powers of local government. Legislative functions are vested in the Legislative Assembly, which consists of 2 elected houses; the Senate of 27 members (2 from each of 8 senatorial districts and 11 at large) and the House of Representatives of 51 members (1 from each of 40 representative districts and 11 at large). Membership of each house may be increased slightly to accommodate minority representatives. The term of the Legislative Assembly is 4 years. The selection of the Secretary of State must be approved also by the House of Representatives.

The Governor is popularly elected for a term of 4 years. A Supreme Court of 7 members is appointed by the Governor, with the advice and consent of the Senate. The Governor appoints all Judges. Residents of Puerto Rico are U.S. citizens. Puerto Rico is represented in Congress by a Resident Commissioner, elected for a term of 4 years, who has a seat in the House of Representatives, but not a vote, although he has a right to vote on those committees of which he is a member.

Preliminary 1983 figures for the Commonwealth Government's budget were Receipts, $4,948 million (of which $1,180 million were transfers from the Federal Government) and Expenditures, $4,111 million (including payments of $135 million to the Federal Government). Manufacturing added $5,765 million to net Commonwealth income in 1983 (preliminary figures), trade $1,743 million, finance, insurance and real estate $1,841 million and agriculture $435 million. Principal crops are sugar cane, coffee, vegetables, fruits and tobacco. Most valuable areas of manufacturing are chemicals and allied products,

metal products and machinery. Public and private schools are established throughout—enrolment in 1985–86 was 686,914. Enrolment in private colleges and universities for 1985–86 was 98,402.

CAPITAL.—ΨSan Juan, population of the municipality, 1,816,300; Other major towns are: ΨPonce (188,500); Bayamón (205,800); ΨMayagüez (99,800); and ΨArecibo (83,300).

Governor, Rafael Hernández Colón.
Secretary of State, Hector Luis Acevedo.
Resident Commissioner, Jaime Fuster.
Chief Justice, Victor Pons.

TRADE

	1985	1986
Total Imports	$10,113 m.	$10,108 m.
Total Exports	10,543 m.	11,588 m.

Trade with U.K.

	1985	1986
Imports from U.K.	£117,861,000	£49,620,000
Exports to U.K.	126,971,000	81,131,000

GUAM

Guam, the largest of the Ladrone or Mariana Islands in the North Pacific Ocean, lies in 13° 26′ N. lat. and 144° 39′ E. long., at a distance of about 1,506 miles east of Manila. The area of the island is estimated at 212 sq. miles (549 sq. km.), with an estimated population (1985) of 120,977.

The Guamanians are of Chamorro stock mingled with Filipino and Spanish blood. The Chamorro language belongs to the Malayo-Polynesian family, but has had considerable admixture of Spanish. English is the language used throughout the island, although Chamorro is also used in Guamanian homes.

Guam was occupied by Japanese in Dec. 1941 but was recaptured and occupied throughout by U.S. forces before the end of July, 1944. Under the Organic Act of Guam of August 1, 1950 (Public Law 630 of the 81st Congress), Guam has statutory powers of self-government, and Guamanians are United States citizens. A 21-member unicameral legislature is elected biennially. The Governor and Lieutenant Governor are popularly elected. A non-voting Delegate is elected to serve in the U.S. House of Representatives. There is also a District Court of Guam, with original jurisdiction in cases under federal law.

CAPITAL.—Agaña. Port of entry, ΨApra.

Governor, Ricardo J. Bordallo, *elected* Nov. 1982.
Lt. Governor, Edward D. Reyes, *elected* Nov. 1982.

AMERICAN SAMOA

American Samoa consists of the island of Tutuila, Anu'u, Ofu, Olesega, Ta'u, Rose and Swains Islands, with a total area of 76 sq. miles (197 sq. km.) and an estimated population of 35,000 in 1985.

Tutuila, the largest of the group, has an area of 52 square miles and contains a magnificent harbour at ΨPago Pago. The remaining islands have an area of about 24 square miles. Tuna and copra are the chief exports.

American Samoans are U.S. nationals, but some have acquired citizenship through service in the United States armed forces or other naturalization procedure.

The 1960 Constitution grants American Samoa a measure of self-government, with certain powers reserved to the U.S. Secretary of the Interior. There is a bicameral legislature with popularly elected Representatives and Governors, and a popularly-elected Governor. A non-voting Delegate is elected to serve in the U.S. House of Representatives.

The constitution of American Samoa designates the village of Fagatogo as the seat of government.

Governor, A. P. Lutali, *elected* Nov. 1984.
Lt.-Governor, Eni F. Hunkin, Jr.

VIRGIN ISLANDS

Purchased by the United States from Denmark for the sum of $25 million, and proclaimed, January 25, 1917. The total area of the islands is 132 sq. miles (342 sq. km.), with an estimated population (1984) of 108,000. There are three main islands, *St. Thomas* (28 sq. miles), *St. Croix* (84 sq. miles), *St. John* (20 sq. miles) and about 50 small islets or cays, mostly uninhabited.

The government of the Virgin Islands is organized under the provisions of the Revised Organic Act of the Virgin Islands, enacted by the Congress of the United States on July 22, 1954. Legislative power is vested in the Legislature of the Virgin Islands, a unicameral body composed of 15 senators popularly elected for two-year terms. Virgin Islanders are citizens of the United States. From the elections of November, 1970, the Governor has been popularly elected. A non-voting Delegate is elected to serve in the U.S. House of Representatives. The Virgin Islands are now a favourite tourist area in the Caribbean. The climate of the islands is delightful at all times, and particularly so during the winter months.

CAPITAL.—ψCharlotte Amalie on St. Thomas.

Governor, Juan F. Luis.
Lt.-Governor, Julio Bradley.

FORMER TRUST TERRITORY OF THE PACIFIC ISLANDS

The former Trust Territory of the Pacific Islands consists of the Mariana (excluding Guam), Caroline and Marshall Islands which extend from latitude 1° to 20° N. and from longitude 130° to 172° E. They cover an ocean area of 3,000,000 square miles but have a total land area of only 687 sq. miles (1,779 sq. km.). There are 96 separate islands and island groups in the Trust Territory. The population in 1980 was 116,662. The inhabitants of the Trust Territory are broadly classed as Micronesians. The native cultures vary considerably among island groups and even more among islands and atolls in the same geographic area. Nine different languages are spoken in the territory. Copra is the principal export.

The former Trust Territory is administered by the United States pursuant to a Trusteeship Agreement with the Security Council of the United Nations of July 18, 1947, administration being under the general jurisdiction of the Secretary of the Interior.

The former Trust Territory has been divided into three separate and distinct governments. In May, 1979, duly constituted governments were inaugurated in the Marshall Islands and the Federated States of Micronesia (comprising Yap, Truk, Pohnpei (Ponape), and Kosrae), and in January, 1981 a constitutional government was established in Palau.

A compact of Free Association with the Marshall Islands and the Federated States of Micronesia, which recognizes the States as having emerged from the Trust Territory, became law in January 1986. It was followed by a separate compact which the citizens of Palau approved in a plebiscite held in December 1986, but the requisite majority was not achieved. Under the C.F.A. the three states will invest in the U.S. Full responsibility for defence, (for a period of fifteen years for Marshall Islands and the Federated States of Micronesia, and fifty years for Palau) although enjoying full self government. This rela-

tionship, detailed in the Compact of Free Association, must be approved by the people of the Trust Territory, the U.S. Congress and the United Nations. The Trusteeship Agreement will be terminated by the United Nations.

CAPITAL.—Saipan, Mariana Islands.

High Commissioner, Janet J. McCoy.
President of Palau, Sen. Lazarus Salii.
President of the Federated States of Micronesia, Tosiwo Nakayama.
President of the Marshall Islands, Amata Kabua.

NORTHERN MARIANA ISLANDS

The land area of the Northern Mariana Islands is 184 sq. miles (476 sq. km.) with an estimated population (1984) of 16,800.

A law enacted by Congress on March 24, 1976 provides a Covenant to establish a Commonwealth of the Northern Mariana Islands. The provisions of the Covenant became fully effective upon termination of the Trusteeship Agreement on Nov. 3, 1986. There is a popularly elected bicameral legislature and a popularly elected Governor.

Governor, Pedro P. Tenorio.
Lt.-Governor, Pedro A. Tenario.

THE PANAMA CANAL

With effect from October 1, 1979 the Canal Zone was disestablished, with all areas of land and water within the former Canal Zone reverting to Panama. By treaty, the United States is allowed the use of operating areas for the Panama Canal, together with several military bases, although the Republic of Panama is sovereign in all such areas.

TOTAL OCEAN GOING TRAFFIC

Fiscal Year	No. of Transits	Canal, Net Tons	Cargo Tons
1980	13,507	182,063,175	167,214,955
1981	13,884	188,656,491	171,221,762
1982	14,009	202,884,207	185,452,332
1983	11,707	169,503,918	145,590,759
1984	11,384	163,469,927	140,800,425
1985	11,654	170,091,933	138,903,287
1986	12,023	183,750,972	140,125,818

The canal is fifty statute miles long (44·08 nautical miles), and the channel is from 500 to 1,000 feet wide at the bottom. It contains 12 locks in twin flights; 3 steps at Gatun on the Atlantic side, 1 step at Pedro Miguel and 2 at Miraflores on the Pacific side. Each lock chamber is 1,000 feet long and 110 feet wide. Transit from sea to sea takes on average 8 to 10 hours. The least width is in Gaillard Cut, and the greatest in Gatun Lake.

BRITISH EMBASSY
3100 Massachusetts Avenue, N.W.
Washington, D.C. 20008

Ambassador Extraordinary and Plenipotentiary, His Excellency Sir Antony Acland, G.C.M.G., G.C.V.O., (1986).
Ministers, T. Lankester (*Economic*); J. S. Shrimplin (*Defence Equipment*); B. L. Crowe, C.M.G. (*Commercial*); M. Jenkins, C.M.G.
Head of British Defence Staff and Defence Attaché, Air Vice-Marshal R. Dick.
Naval Attaché, Rear Adm. M. C. Cole.
Military Attaché, Brig. T. K. Thompson, M.B.E.
Air Attaché, Air Cdre. L. Swart, C.B.E., A.D.C.

ψSeaport.

Counsellors and Attachés, R. B. Bone (*Head of Chancery*); A. Pover (*Admin. and H.M. Consul-General*); R. I. Allen (*Economic*); T. G. Harris (*Commercial*); J. A. L. Faint (*Overseas Development*); P. Lo (*Hong Kong Commercial Affairs*); A. J. Hunt (*Civil Aviation and Shipping*); M. Parkes (*Civil Aviation Air Traffic Systems*); P. Meiklem (*Civil Aviation, Safety*); Dr. A. R. Cox (*Science and Technology*); N. A. Hirst (*Energy*); P. H. West (*Defence*); R. J. Harding, C.M.G. (*Defence Supply*); M. Hall (*Technical Works Group*); D. Wilson (*Crown Suppliers Area Officer*); J. D. Gutteridge (*Defence Supply*); Dr. D. I. Kirkpatrick (*Defence Equipment*); D. Johnson (*Defence Equipment*); J. Platt (*Defence Equipment*); H. J. Muir (*Defence Equipment*); I. Frater (*Education*); R. F. Cornish (*Information*); Capt. B. Burns (*Assistant Naval*); Col. C. H. Howgill (*Assistant Defence*); Col. R. Ffrench-Blake (*Assistant Military*); Gp. Capt. R. Sweatman (*Assistant Air*); M. E. Pellew, M.V.O.; D. Stuart; M. L. H. Doyle; R. D. Lord; S. Band.

Cultural Attaché and British Council Representative, J. W. Daniel.

There are British Consulates in Atlanta, Boston, Chicago, Cleveland, Dallas, Houston, Los Angeles, Miami, New York, San Francisco and Seattle.

BRITISH-AMERICAN CHAMBER OF COMMERCE, 275 Madison Avenue, New York 10016; U.K. OFFICE, Suite 201, High Holborn, WCIV 6RR.

URUGUAY
(República Oriental del Uruguay)

President, Dr. Julio María Sanguinetti, *took office*, March 1, 1985.
Vice President, Sr. Enrique Tarigo.

CABINET

Interior, Dr. Antonio Marchesano.
Foreign Affairs, Cr. Enrique Iglesias.
Economy and Finance, Cr. Ricardo Zerbino.
Transport and Public Works, Sr. Jorge Sanguinetti.
Public Health, Dr. Raúl M. Ugarte.
Labour and Social Security, Sr. Hugo Fernández Faingold.
Agriculture and Fisheries, Sr. Pedro Bonino.
Education, Culture and Justice, Dra. Adela Reta.
National Defence, Dr. Juan Vicente Chiarino.
Industry and Energy, Dr. Jorge Presno.
Planning and Budget Office, Cr. Ariel Davrieux.
Tourism, Sr. José Villar.

URUGUAYAN EMBASSY AND CONSULATE
48 Lennox Gardens, SW1X 0DL
[01–589 8835; *Consulate* 01–589 8835]

Ambassador Extraordinary and Plenipotentiary, His Excellency Dr. Luis Alberto Solé-Romeo (1987).

Area and Population.—The smallest Republic in South America, on the east coast of the Rio de la Plata situated in lat. 30°–35° S. and long. 53° 15′–57° 42′ W., with an area of 68,037 sq. miles (176,215 sq. km.), and an estimated population (1985) of 3,012,000, almost entirely white and predominantly of Spanish and Italian descent. Many Uruguayans are Roman Catholics. There is complete freedom of religion and no church is established by the State.

Physical Features.—The country consists mainly of undulating grassy plains. The principal chains of hills are the Cuchilla del Haedo, which cross the Brazilian boundary and extend southwards to the Cuchilla Grande of the south and east. In no case do the peaks exceed 2,000 feet.

The principal river is the *Rio Negro* (with its tributary the Yi), flowing from north-east to south-

west into the *Rio Uruguay*. The boundary river *Uruguay* is navigable from its estuary to Salto, about 200 miles north, and the Negro is also navigable for a considerable distance. Smaller rivers are the Cuareim, Yaguaron, Santa Lucia, Queguay and the Cebollati.

The climate is reasonably healthy. The summer is warm, but the heat is often tempered by the breezes of the Atlantic. The winter is, on the whole, mild, but cold spells, characterized by winds from the South Polar regions, are experienced in June, July and August. Rainfall is regular throughout the year, but there are occasional droughts. Floods also occur.

Government.—Uruguay—or the *Banda Oriental*, as this territory lying on the eastern bank of the Uruguay River was then called—resisted all attempted invasions of the Portuguese and Spanish until the beginning of the 17th century, and 100 years later the Portuguese settlements were captured by the Spanish. From 1726 to 1814 the country formed part of Spanish South America and underwent many vicissitudes during the Wars of Independence. In 1814 the armies of the Argentine Confederation captured the capital and annexed the province, and it was afterwards annexed by Portugal and became a province of Brazil. In 1825, the country threw off the Brazilian yoke. This action led to war between Argentina and Brazil which was settled by the mediation of the United Kingdom, Uruguay being declared an independent state in 1828. In 1830 a Republic was inaugurated.

According to the Constitution the President appoints a council of 11 ministers and a Secretary (Planning and Budget Office), and the Vice-President presides over Congress. The legislature consists of a Chamber of 99 deputies and a Senate of 30 members (plus the Vice-President), elected for five years by a system of proportional representation. Voting is obligatory and extends to all citizens of good repute and certain long standing residents who are not citizens, from the age of 18. General elections held in Nov. 1984 marked the return to democracy after 11 years of presidential rule with military support. The new government took office on March 1, 1985 and the provisions of the 1967 Constitution now prevail.

The Republic is divided into 19 Departments each with a chief of police and a Departmental Council.

Production and Industry.—Wheat, barley, maize, linseed, sunflower seed and rice are cultivated. The wealth of the country is obtained from its pasturage, which supports large herds of cattle and sheep, the wool of which is of excellent quality. There are just over 9 million cattle and just under 24 million sheep. In addition to meat packing, other foodstuffs, (citrus, wine, beer), fishing and textile industries are of importance.

The development of local industry continues and, in addition to the greatly augmented textile industry, marked expansion in local production is notable in respect of tyres, sheet-glass, three-ply wood, cement, leather-curing, beet-sugar, plastics, household consumer goods, edible oils and the refining of petroleum and petroleum products.

Mineral Deposits.—There are some ferrous minerals, not extracted at present. Non-ferrous exploited minerals include clinker, dolomite, marble and granite.

Communications.—There are about 9,899 km. of national highways, and about 12,083 km. of telegraph, with 48,375 miles of telephones.

There are about 2,987 km. of standard gauge railway in use in Uruguay. A State Autonomous Entity was formed to administer the railway systems purchased by the Government from four British companies in 1948.

An airline, PLUNA, which is owned by the State, runs daily services to southern Brazil, Paraguay and

Argentina, and two flights a week to Madrid. The principal capitals of the interior and a limited freight service are connected to Montevideo by TAMU, another State owned airline, using principally military aircraft and personnel. International passenger and freight services are maintained by American, South American and European airlines. The international airport of Carrasco lies 12 miles outside Montevideo.

Education and Social Services.—Uruguay is one of the most advanced of the South American states, with old-age pensions, maternity and child welfare centres, accident insurance, etc. Primary education is compulsory and free, and technical and trade schools and evening courses for adult education are state controlled. There are about 322,053 pupils in the 2,362 state schools. The University at Montevideo (founded in 1849) has about 18,000 students enrolled in its ten faculties.

Language and Literature.—Spanish is the language of the Republic. Modern literature has provided some authors with international reputations and the literature of Spain is accessible in all public libraries. Five daily newspapers are published in Montevideo with an estimated total circulation of 150,000. Most of them are distributed throughout the country.

FINANCE

	1985	1986
Revenue	N$76,786·9 m.	N$149,851·6 m.
Expenditure	91,425·2 m.	161,170·4 m.

The external debt at Dec. 1986 was U.S.$5,193 million. Central Bank reserves (Dec., 1986) were US$786·5 million.

Currency.—The monetary unit is the *peso* (N$). For sterling exchange see p. 82.

TRADE

	1985	1986
Total exports	US$853,600,000	US$1,087,600,000
Total imports	707,100,000	838,800,000

The major exports are meat and by-products, wool and by-products, hides and bristle and agricultural products. The principal imports are raw materials, construction materials, oils and lubricants, automotive vehicles, kits and machinery.

Trade with U.K.

	1985	1986
Imports from U.K.	£15,513,000	£24,465,000
Exports to U.K.	28,824,000	41,366,000

The principal export items to the U.K. are wool and beef, the main imports are chemicals, kits, machinery, raw materials and metals.

CAPITAL.—ΨMontevideo. Population (1984) 1,355,312. Other centres (with 1967 estimates) are ΨSalto (60,000), ΨPaysandu (60,000), ΨMercedes (34,000), Minas (34,000), Melo (30,000), and Rivera (40,000).

FLAG.—Four blue and five white horizontal stripes surcharged with sun on a white ground in the top corner, next flagstaff.

NATIONAL DAY.—August 25 (Declaration of Independence, 1825).

BRITISH EMBASSY
Calle Marco Bruto 1073 Montevideo

Ambassador Extraordinary and Plenipotentiary, His Excellency Eric Victor Vines, C.M.G., O.B.E. (1986)
First Secretary, P. Hunt (*Head of Chancery and Consul*).
Second Secretaries, G. O'Neil (*Commercial*); W. A. Allan; N. J. Fish; N. J. A. Langman.
Defence Attaché, Col. R. Garnett, M.B.E.

BRITISH CONSULAR OFFICES
There is a British Consular Office at *Montevideo*.

ANGLO-URUGUAYAN CULTURAL INSTITUTE, San José 1426, Montevideo. There are branch Institutes throughout Uruguay.

BRITISH-URUGUAYAN CHAMBER OF COMMERCE, Avenida Labertador Brig. Gen., Lavalleja 1641, P2-OF 201, Montevideo.

THE VATICAN CITY STATE
(Stato della Città del Vaticano)

Sovereign Pontiff, His Holiness Pope John Paul II (Karol Wojtyla), *born* at Wadowice (Krakow, Poland), May 18, 1920, *elected* Pope (in succession to Pope John Paul I), Oct. 16, 1978.
Secretary of State, Cardinal Agostino Casaroli, *appointed* April, 1979.

APOSTOLIC NUNCIATURE IN LONDON
54 Parkside, SW19 5NF
[01–946 1410]

Apostolic Pro Nuncio, His Excellency Archbishop Luigi Barbarito (1986).
Counsellor, Mons. Rino Passigato.

The office of the ecclesiastical head of the Roman Catholic Church (Holy See) is vested in the Pope, the Sovereign Pontiff. For many centuries the Sovereign Pontiff exercised temporal power, but by 1870 the Papal States had become part of unified Italy. The temporal power of the Pope was in suspense until the treaty of Feb. 11, 1929, which recognized the full and independent sovereignty of the Holy See in the City of the Vatican. The area of the Vatican City is 108 acres and its population in 1985 was 1,000.

FLAG.—Square flag; equal vertical bands of yellow (next staff), and white; crossed keys and triple crown device on white band.

NATIONAL DAY.—October 22 (Inauguration of present Pontiff).

BRITISH EMBASSY TO THE HOLY SEE
91 Via Condotti, 00187 Rome

Ambassador Extraordinary and Plenipotentiary, His Excellency David Neil Lane, C.M.G., *apptd.* 1985.
First Secretary, M. J. Long.

VENEZUELA
(La Republica de Venezuela)

President, Dr. Jaime Lusinchi, *elected* Dec. 4, 1983, *assumed office* Feb. 2, 1984.

COUNCIL OF MINISTERS

Interior, Jose Angel Ciliberto.
Foreign Affairs, Dr. Simon Alberto Consalvi.
Finance, Dr. Manuel Azpúrua Arreaza.
Defence, Gen. Jose Rafael Cardozo Grimaldi.
Development, Augusto Mirabel Bustillos.
Education, Luis Carbonell.
Health and Social Welfare, Otto Hernandez Pieretti.
Agriculture and Livestock, Dr. Felipe Gómez Alvarez.
Labour, Dr. Simón Antoni Paván.
Transport and Communications, Dr. Juan Pedro del Moral.
Justice, Sr. José Manzo González.
Mines and Energy, Dr. Arturo Hernández Grisanti.
Environment and Natural Resources, Guillermo Colmenares Fimol.
Urban Development, Cesar Quintana.
Youth, Dra. Virginia Olivo de Celli.

Secretariat of the Presidency, Dr. Carmello Lauria Lesseur.

Ministers of State, Leopoldo Carnevalli (*Co-ordination and Planning*); Hector Hurtado (*Pres., Venezuelan Investment Fund*); Dra. Paulina Gamus (*Culture*); Tulio Arends (*Science and Technology*); Leopoldo Sucre Figarella (*Pres., Venezuelan Corporation of Guyana*); Hernan Anzola Jimenez (*Three Year Plan*); Miguel A. Contreras Laguado (*Governor of Federal District*).

VENEZUELAN EMBASSY IN LONDON
1 Cromwell Road, SW7 2HW
[01–584 4206/7]

Ambassador Extraordinary and Plenipotentiary, (new appointment awaited).

Minister Counsellor, E. González Urrutia.

There is also a Consulate-General at *Liverpool*.

Area and Population.—A South American Republic, situated approximately between 0° 45′ S. lat. and 12° 12′ N. lat. and 59° 45′–73° 09′ W. long. It consists of one Federal District, 20 states and 2 territories. Venezuela has a total area of 352,144 sq. miles (912,050 sq. km.) and a population (1985) of 17,323,000.

Venezuela lies on the north of the South American continent, and is bounded on the north by the Caribbean Sea, west by the Republic of Colombia, east by Guyana, and south by Brazil. Included in the area of the Republic are 72 islands off the coast, with a total area of about 14,650 square miles, the largest being *Margarita*, which is politically associated with Tortuga, Cubagua and Coche to form the State of *Nueva Esparta*. Margarita has an area of about 400 square miles.

Physical Features.—The Eastern Andes from the south-west cross the border and reach to the Caribbean Coast, where they are prolonged by the Maritime Andes of Venezuela to the Gulf of Paria on the north-east. The main range is known as the Sierra Nevada de Merida, and contains the highest peaks in the country in Pico Bolivar (16,411 feet) and Picacho de la Sierra (15,420 feet). Near the Brazilian border the Sierras Parima and Pacaraima, and on the eastern border the Sierras de Rincote and de Usupamo, enclose the republic with parallel northward spurs, between which are valleys of the Orinoco tributaries. The slopes of the mountains and foothills are covered with dense forests, but the basin of the Orinoco is mainly *llanos*, or level stretches of open prairie, with occasional woods.

The principal river is the *Orinoco*, with innumerable affluents, the main river exceeding 1,600 miles in length from its rise in the southern highlands of the republic to its outflow in the deltaic region of the north-east. The Orinoco is navigable for large steamers from its mouth for 700 miles, and by smaller vessels as far as the Maipures Cataract, some 200 miles farther up-stream. Dredging operations have opened the Orinoco to ocean-going ships, of up to 40 ft. draft, as far as Ciudad Guayana (about 150 miles up-stream). Among the many tributaries of the main stream are the Ventuari, Apure (with its tributary the Portuguesa), Arauca, Meta, and Guaviare from the west, the Meta and Guaviare being principally Colombian rivers. The upper waters of the Orinoco are united with those of the Rio Negro (a Brazilian tributary of the Amazon) by a natural river or canal, known as the *Casiquiare*.

The coastal regions of Venezuela are much indented and contain many lagoons and lakes, of which *Maracaibo*, with an area of 8,296 square miles, is the largest lake in South America. Other lakes are Zulia (290 square miles), south-west of Maracaibo, and Valencia (216 square miles) about 1,400 ft. above sea-level in the Maritime Andes.

The climate is tropical and, except where modified by altitude or tempered by sea breezes, is unhealthy, particularly in the coastal regions and in the neighbourhood of lowland streams and lagoons. The hot, wet season lasts from April to October, the dry, cooler season from November to March.

Language and Literature.—Spanish is the language of the country. There are 61 daily newspapers in Venezuela, of which ten are published in Caracas, and about 60 to 70 weekly news magazines. There are also a large number of fortnightly, monthly and quarterly publications.

Education is free and compulsory between the ages of 7 and 13. There are ten universities in Venezuela, five in Caracas and the others in Maracaibo, Mérida, Valencia, Cumaná and Barquisimeto.

Production and Industry.—Products of the tropical forest region include: orchids, wild rubber, timber, mangrove bark, balata gum and tonka beans: of agricultural areas, cocoa beans, coffee, cotton, rice, maize, sugar, sesame, groundnuts, potatoes, tomatoes, other vegetables, sisal and tobacco. There is an extensive beef and dairy farming industry. Despite substantial improvements in agriculture, Venezuela is heavily reliant upon food imports, which constitute about 60 per cent of total consumption.

The principal industry is that of petroleum, which in 1986 contributed 83 per cent of Venezuela's foreign exchange income. Daily production in the oilfields (nationalized 1976) has steadily declined since 1973 in line with Venezuela's conservation policies, reaching 1·7 mbd in 1986 (1973—3·366 mbd). There are refineries at Punta Cardon, Amuay, Caripitó, San Lorenzo, Puerto La Cruz, Tucupeido, El Chaure and El Palito. Development of the Orinoco heavy oil belt is now moving ahead with the inauguration of the Lagovén continuous steam injection pilot plant at El Jobo in southern Monagas. It has been estimated conservatively that there might exist recoverable resources of 70,000 million barrels in the Orinoco region, but the initial aim of the Lagovén project is the production of 125,000 and 500,000 bpd of upgraded crude by 1988 and 2000 respectively.

Aluminium is the second highest source of foreign exchange after petroleum. The Venezuelan state now holds the majority stake in both the principal producing companies, Venalum and Alcasa, and is moving towards a consolidation of the aluminium industry, with both companies sharing their resources and adopting general policies of marketing and procurement of supplies. Output in 1980 was 222,100 tons, with 151,250 tons exported.

Rich iron ore deposits in Eastern Venezuela have been developed. Secondary processes for pelletizing and briqueting ore for export have been installed. The government-owned steel mill at Matanzas in the Guayana uses local iron ore and obtains its electric power from hydro-electric installations on the Caroni River. It produces seamless steel tubes, billets, wire and profiles. The production of more steel products is planned over the next few years. A mill at Ciudad Guayana for the production of centrifugally-cast iron pipe came into operation at the end of 1970, with an annual capacity of 30,000 tons.

Other industries include petrochemicals, gold, diamonds and asbestos; textiles, clothing and footwear; plastics; manufacture or preparation of foodstuffs, alcoholic and non-alcoholic beverages; manufacture of paper, cement, glass, tyres, cigarettes, soap, animal feeding concentrates, simple steel products, tins, jewellery, rope, furniture, sacks, paint and motor-vehicle assembly; preparation of pharmaceutical goods; pearl fishing, sanitary ware, electric home appliances, pumps, toys, agricultural machinery, bicycles, electronic components, cosmetics and many others.

Communications.—There are about 62,449 km. of roads, 22,975 km. of them paved. The State has now

acquired all but a very few of the railway lines, whose total length is only some 372 kilometres. Road and river communications have made railways of negligibile importance in Venezuela except for carrying iron ore in the south-east. However, the government is restoring the Puerto Cabello-Barquisimeto line and expanding it to Turén in the agricultural heartland of Venezuela. A new line connecting Caracas with La Guaira is planned, and in 1983 the Caracas Metro came into operation. British, U.S. and European airlines provide Venezuela with a wide range of services. There are three Venezuelan airlines (two of them state-owned) which between them have a comprehensive network of internal lines and also connect Caracas with the United States, Central and South America, the Caribbean and Europe. Foreign vessels are not permitted to engage in the coast trade. The telegraph, radio-telegraph and radio-telephone services are state-owned. There are two government-controlled, 150 commercial and one cultural, FM, broadcasting stations. There are four television stations in Venezuela, all in Caracas. Two are government controlled.

TRADE

	1985	1986
Total imports	US$7,388 m	US$7,600 m
Total exports	14,178 m	8,880 m

Trade with U.K.

	1985	1986
Imports from U.K.	£165,268,000	£170,101,000
Exports to U.K.	238,879,000	96,339,000

CAPITAL.—Caracas (3,000 ft.). Population (1981), 1,816,901. Other principal towns are ΨMaracaibo (870,000), Barquisimeto (495,000), Valencia (495,000), Maracay (322,000), San Cristobal (164,000), Cumaná (135,000) and Ciudad Guayana (250,000).

FLAG.—Three horizontal bands, yellow, blue, red (with seven white stars on blue band and coat of arms next staff on yellow band).

NATIONAL DAY.—July 5.

BRITISH EMBASSY
Apartado 1246, Caracas 1010-A.

Ambassador Extraordinary and Plenipotentiary, His Excellency Giles Eden FiztHerbert, C.M.G., *apptd.* 1987.

Counsellor, W. Quantrill *(Head of Chancery)*.
Defence Attaché, Capt. J. B. Lean, R.N.

BRITISH CONSULAR OFFICES
There are British Consular Offices at *Caracas, Maracaibo, Puerto La Cruz* and *Valencia.*

British Council Representative, J. W. Daniel, Aparto 1246, Caracas 1010-A.

BRITISH-VENEZUELAN CHAMBER OF COMMERCE, Apartado 5713 Edificio Blandin, Piso I Oficina I-C, Plaza Chacaito, Caracas.

VIETNAM
(Công Hòa Xã Hôi Chu Nghĩa Viêt Nam)

COUNCIL OF STATE

Chairman, Vo Chi Cong.
Deputy Chairmen, Huynh Tan Phat; Nguyen Huu Tho; Le Quang Dao; Nguyen Quyet; Dam Quang Trung; Mrs. Nguyen Thi Dinh.
Members, Y Ngong Niet Dam; Pham The Duyet; Tran Do; Nguyen Xuan Huu; Vu Mao; Hoang Bich Son; Nguyen Dinh Tu.

COUNCIL OF MINISTERS

Chairman, Pham Hung.
Vice Chairmen, Vo Van Kiet; Nguyen Co Thach; Dong Sy Nguyen; Vo Nguyen Giap; Nguyen Khanh; Nguyen Ngoc Trin; Nguyen Van Chinh; Doan Duy Thanh; Tran Duc Luong.
Members, all Ministers, and Chairmen of most State Committees (around 35 in all).

VIETNAMESE COMMUNIST PARTY

Politburo of the Central Committee, Nguyen Van Linh *(General Secretary)*; Pham Hung; Vo Chi Cong; Do Muoi; Vo Van Kiet; Le Duc Anh; Nguyen Duc Tam; Nguyen Co Thach; Dong Sy Nguyen; Tran Xuan Bach; Nguyen Thanh Binh; Doan Khue; Mai Chi Tho *(full members)*; Dao Duy Tung *(alternate member)*.

EMBASSY IN LONDON
12–14 Victoria Road, W8 5RD
[01–937 1912–8564]

Ambassador Extraordinary and Plenipotentiary, His Excellency Tran Van Hung (1986).
Third Secretaries, Phiec Ngo Ngoc; Phuc Nguyen Ba.

Vietnam, with an area of 127,242 sq. miles (329,556 sq. km.), and an estimated population (1986) of 62,000,000, is bordered on the north by China and the west by Laos and Cambodia.

Government.—Following the end of the war in Vietnam in 1975, and the establishment of a Provisional Revolutionary Government to administer South Vietnam, a National Assembly representing the whole of Vietnam was elected on April 25, 1976. The Assembly met in Hanoi on June 24, and on July 2 approved the reunification of North and South Vietnam under the name of the Socialist Republic of Vietnam. The national flag, anthem and capital of North Vietnam were unanimously adopted for the Socialist Republic, and Saigon was renamed Ho Chi Minh City.

Effective power lies with the ruling Party, the Vietnamese Communist Party (*V.C.P.*), its highest executive body being the Central Committee, elected by a Party Congress on a national basis.

The Sixth Party Congress of the V.C.P. in December 1986 elected a new Central Committee. It is the Politburo and the Secretariat of the Central Committee which exercises real power and rules Vietnam.

INDO-CHINA

Economy.—During the last five years, Vietnam's economy has faced considerable problems. These include serious agricultural losses because of adverse weather, major reductions in Western aid (as a result of Vietnam's invasion and occupation of neighbouring Cambodia), border hostilities with China, and the continued allocation of resources to military expenditure. Efforts to integrate the economies of the North and South have not been very successful.

Although food production has substantially increased (over 18 million tonnes of grain in 1985) as has G.D.P. in general, Vietnam's overall economic position at the end of 1985 was not good. There was little foreign exchange because of minimal exports to hard currency areas. Vietnam was in default of repayments to the international banking world from the I.M.F. to major commercial and merchant banks and therefore received very few long term credits.

Some attempted reforms of the economic system in 1985, including devaluation and a currency change, were implemented disastrously and inflation increased rapidly in late 1985 and early 1986. Despite massive assistance from the Soviet Union (estimated at over 1,000 million dollars p.a.) and other member countries of C.M.E.A. (of which Vietnam is a member), Vietnam's economy continued to decline.

Trade with U.K.

	1985	1986
Imports from U.K.	£2,077,000	£1,288,000
Exports to U.K.	1,758,000	1,200,000

CAPITAL.—Hanoi (population (1984), City, 925,000; Province, 2,800,000).

FLAG.—Red, with yellow five-point star in centre.

NATIONAL DAY.—September 2.

BRITISH EMBASSY
16 Pho Ly Thuong Kiet, Hanoi

Ambassador Extraordinary and Plenipotentiary, His Excellency Emrys Thomas Davies, *apptd.* 1987.
First Secretary, C. D. Partridge.

YEMEN (North)
(Al-Jamhuriya Al-Arabiya Al-Yamaniya)

President and Commander of the Armed Forces, Col. Ali Abdullah Saleh, *elected* July 19, 1978, *re-elected* May 23, 1983.
Prime Minister, Abdul Aziz Abdul Ghani.
Deputy Prime Ministers, Col. Mujahid Abu Shuwarib; Dr. Abdul Karim Al Iryani *(Foreign Affairs)*; Dr. Hassan Mohammed Makki.
Minister of Development, Chairman of C.P.O., Dr. Mohammed Said Al Attar.
Public Works and President of Supreme Council for Reconstruction of Earthquake Affected Areas, Abdullah Al Kurshumi.
Awqaf and Guidance, Qadi Ali Al Samman.
Economy, Supply and Trade, Mohammed Al Khadim Al Wajih.
Social Affairs and Labour, Lt. Col. Mohsin Mohammed al Ulafi.
Agriculture and Fisheries, Dr. Hussein Abdullah Al Amri.
Civil Service & Administrative Reform, Ismail Ahmed Al Wazir.
Finance, Alwi Saleh as Salami.
Communications and Transport, Ahmed Al Anisi.
Interior, Lt. Col. Abdullah Hussein Barakat.
Information and Culture, Hassan Al Lawzi.
Municipalities and Planning, Mohammed Ahmed Luqman.
Oil and Mineral Resources, Ahmed Ali Al Mohanni.
Health, Dr. Mohammed Al Kabab.
Electricity, Water and Sewerage, Mohammed Hassan Sabra.
Minister of State and Sec. Gen. of Council for Youth and Sports, Abdullah Nasir Al Dhorafi.
Education, Mohammed Abdullah Al Jaifi.
Justice, Qadi Ahmed Mohammed Al Jawbi.
Minister of State for Prime Ministerial Affairs, Ahmed Saleh Al Roueni.
Minister of State for Unity Affairs, Yahya Hussein Al Arashi.

YEMEN EMBASSY
41 South Street, W1Y 5PD
[01–629 9905/8]

Ambassador Extraordinary and Plenipotentiary, His Excellency Ahmed Daifellah Alazeib (1981).

Yemen, the *Arabia Felix* of the ancients, occupies the S.W. corner of Arabia between the kingdom of Saudi Arabia and the People's Democratic Republic of Yemen, with an estimated area of 75,290 sq. miles (195,000 sq. km.). The highlands and central plateau of Yemen, and the highest portions of the maritime range, form the most fertile part of Arabia, with an abundant but irregular rainfall. The ruins of Marib, the ancient Sabæan capital, and its dam are in the Yemen.

The population is (1985 U.N. estimate) 6,849,000.

Government.—A General Popular Conference was established in Aug. 1982, consisting of 700 elected members and 300 appointed members. It agreed a new National Charter and elected a Permanent Council of 75 members (50 elected, 25 appointed), with a General Council and four sub-committees (economic; political; administrative and public works; cultural and reform).

The General Popular Conference meets every two years and is re-elected every four. The Permanent Council meets regularly for two months, followed by a two-month break. The General Council and sub-committees meet regularly. In 1986 the total membership of the General Popular Conference was expanded to 22,250, comprising elected and appointed members.

Trade.—The main exports are cotton, coffee, hides and skins.

Trade with U.K.

	1985	1986
Imports from U.K.	£94,382,000	£58,149,000
Exports to U.K.	2,312,000	2,106,000

CAPITAL.—Sana'a (pop. 427,185). Other main cities are Taiz (178,043), Hodeida (155,110), Ibb (48,806) and Dhamar (47,733).

FLAG.—Horizontal bands of red, white and black, with 5-point green star in centre of white band.
NATIONAL DAY.—September 26.

BRITISH EMBASSY
P.O. Box 1287, Sana'a

Ambassador Extraordinary and Plenipotentiary, His Excellency David Everard Tatham (1984).
First Secretaries, B. C. Seddon *(Head of Chancery and Aid)*; J. D. Orr *(Commercial)*.
British Council Representative, P. J. Chenery, Beit Al-Mottahar, Harat Handhal (P.O. Box 2157), Sana'a.

YEMEN (South)
(Al-Jumhurijah Al-Yemen Al-Dimugratiyah Al Sha'abiyah)

President, Haider Abubaker Al-Attas, *assumed power* January 1986, *elected* Nov. 6, 1986 *for a 5-year term.*
Prime Minister, Dr. Yassin Saeed No'man.

EMBASSY
57 Cromwell Road, SW7 2ED
[01–584 6607/9]

Ambassador Extraordinary and Plenipotentiary, His Excellency Ahmed Abdo Rageh (1987).

Area and Population.—The Democratic Republic of Yemen lies at the southern end of the Arabian peninsula, having a frontier with the Yemen Arab Republic, Saudi Arabia and the Sultanate of Oman, and a coastline extending 700 miles from the Red Sea eastwards along the Gulf of Aden. The area is largely composed of mountains and desert. Rainfall is generally scarce and unpredictable. The population outside Aden is concentrated in the fertile districts. In the more extensive desert and near-desert areas nomadic communities depend on their livestock for a livelihood.

Included in the State are the offshore islands of Perim (in the Bab al-Mandeb Straits) and Socotra. Sovereignty over the island of Kamaran (area 70 sq. miles) in the Red Sea is under dispute following its occupation by forces of the Yemen Arab Republic during border conflicts in October, 1972. The area of the People's Democratic Republic is 128,560 sq. miles (332,968 sq. km.), with a population (1985 estimate) of 2,500,000.

Government.—The People's Republic of South Yemen was set up on Nov. 30, 1967 when the British government ceded power to the National Liberation Front, thus bringing to an end 129 years of British rule in Aden and some years of protectorate status in the hinterland. Its name was changed to People's Democratic Republic of Yemen on Nov. 30, 1970. Territory of the Republic is that of the former Federation of South Arabia and the Aden Protectorates, consisting of the State of Aden and some 17 sultanates and emirates. It is now divided into six Governorates. Under a constitution promulgated on Nov. 30, 1970, there is a Supreme People's Council of 101 members and an 11-member Presidium. The Chairman of the Presidium is head of state.

In Jan. 1986, severe rivalries within the régime led to a fierce outbreak of fighting in Aden and the temporary evacuation of the foreign community. The President, Ali Nasser Mohammed, escaped abroad and a new government was set up continuing the existing Marxist régime.

The Government receives substantial development from the World Bank, Kuwait and Abu Dhabi (Arab Development Funds). Other aid is provided by China, the E.C., U.S.S.R. (including military aid) and other Socialist Bloc countries.

Production.—Agriculture is the main occupation of the inhabitants outside Aden town. This is largely of a subsistence nature, sorghum, sesame and millets being the chief crops, with wheat and barley widely grown at the higher elevations. Disastrous floods in 1983 caused major damage to the principal agricultural areas.

Yemen is not an oil producing country but significant traces of hydrocarbons were found during exploration activities offshore in 1982. The Aden Refinery Company has a refining capacity of 8 m. tons per annum but for a number of years output has not exceeded a rate equivalent to 5 m. tons annually.

Under the Five Year Development Plan 1974–79 much importance was attached to the development of agricultural and fisheries projects. Under the second Five Year Plan (1981–85) emphasis shifted to industrial development, which was allocated 29 per cent of the total investment budget (YD508m); agricultural development was allocated 12 per cent. Light industries are being established which will replace imports and use locally produced raw materials.

Expenditure in 1986 was severely affected by the January fighting and had to be diverted to repair the considerable material damage.

Communications.—Following the closure of the Suez Canal in 1967 the once prosperous trading economy of Aden fell into a steady decline, which has not been reversed by the re-opening of the Canal. In the main harbour, cargo handling for larger vessels is by lighter, but wharves at Maalla can accommodate alongside vessels up to 300 feet in length and 18 feet in draught.

There are no railways in the Republic. Yemen has 760 miles of good roads and construction of a further 300 miles is in hand. A system of undeveloped but motorable roads links the towns and villages outside Aden. There is an international airport at Aden (Khormaksar) into which a limited number of international airlines operate.

Finance and Currency.—During 1977 revenue was estimated at about £51,000,000 and expenditure £68,000,000. Currency is the South Yemen *dinar* (YD).

Trade with U.K.

	1985	1986
Imports from U.K.	£34,827,000	£23,928,000
Exports to U.K.	7,938,000	4,848,000

CAPITAL.—Aden (population, 270,000). Other towns are Mukalla, Seiyoun, Shabwa, Beihan, Lawdar, Shuqra, Dhala and Lahes.

FLAG.—A tricolour, red, white and black horizontal bands, with a triangle of light blue at the hoist pointing towards the fly and charged with a five pointed red star.

NATIONAL DAYS.—Independence Day, Nov. 30; Revolution Day, Oct. 14.

BRITISH EMBASSY
Khormaksar, Aden.

Ambassador Extraordinary and Plenipotentiary, His Excellency Arthur Stirling-Maxwell Marshall, C.B.E. (1986).
Second Secretary, D. P. Spencer (*Vice-Consul*).

YUGOSLAVIA
(Socijalistička Federativna Republika Jugoslavije)

President of the Presidency (1987–88), Lazar Mojsov (*Macedonia*).
Vice-President of the Presidency (1987–88), Hamdija Pozderac (*Bosnia/Hercogovina*).
Members of the Presidency, Hamdija Pozdernc (*Bosnia/Hercegovina*); Stane Dolanc (*Slovenia*); Nikola Ljubičić (*Serbia*); Josip Vrhovec (*Croatia*); Veselin Djuranović (*Montenegro*); Radovan Vlajković (*Vojvodina*); Bösko Krunić (*L.C.Y.*).

FEDERAL EXECUTIVE COUNCIL

President, Branko Mikulić.
Vice-Presidents, Miloš Milosavijević; Janez Zemljarič.
Foreign Affairs, Raif Dizdarević.
National Defence, Branko Mamula.
Internal Affairs, Dobroslav Čulafić.
Finance, Svetozar Rikanović.
Foreign Trade, Nenad Krekić.
Trade and General Economic Affairs, Aleksandar Donev.
Justice and Organization of Federal Administration, Petar Vajović.
Information, Svetozar Durutović.
    Federal Committee Presidents:—
Energy and Industry, Andrej Ocvirk.
Agriculture, Savoc Vujkov.
Transport and Communications, Mustafa Pljakić.
Labour, Health and Social Security, Janko Obočki.
Questions concerning War Veterans and Disabled Veterans, Ilija Vakić.
Legislature, Lojze Ude.
Scientific and Technological Development, Božidar Matić.
Tourism, Miodrag Mirović.
Other F.E.C. members, Dragi Danev; Francka Herga; Oskar Kovač; Radoje Kontić; Radovan Makić; Nevenka Meralić-Milivojević; Muhamet Mustafa; Tibor Salma; Ibrahim Tabaković; Momcílo Vučinić; Egon Padovan; Mito Pejovski.

President of the SFRY Assembly, Marjan Rožič.
President of the Socialist Alliance of the Working People, Milojko Drulović.

LEAGUE OF COMMUNISTS OF YUGOSLAVIA

Presidency of the Central Committee
President of the Presidency, Boško Krunić (*elected for one year in June* 1987).
Secretary, Radiša Gačic (*elected for two years in June* 1986).
Members, Ivan Brigić; Dušan Čkrebić; Štefan Korošec; Ivica Račan; Milanko Renovica; FrancŠetinc; Stipe Šuvar; V. Tupurkovski; V. Žarković.

YUGOSLAV EMBASSY IN LONDON
5–7 Lexham Gardens W8 5JJ
[01–370 6105]

Ambassador Extraordinary and Plenipotentiary, His Excellency Mitko Čalovski (1985).
Minister Counsellors, Branko Brankovic; Predrag Mitic (*Economic*).
Counsellor, Mario Mikolic (*Press and Culture*).
Defence Attaché, Col. Dragoljub Milovanovic.

Area and Population.—Yugoslavia is a Federation comprising the Socialist Republics of Serbia, Croatia, Slovenia, Montenegro, Bosnia and Herzegovina, and Macedonia. Serbia includes the Socialist Autonomous Provinces of Vojvodina and Kosovo. The area of Yugoslavia is estimated at 98,766 sq. miles (255,804 sq. km.). The population was estimated (1985) at 23,123,000; the latest Census (April 1981) broke down the population into 8,140,000 Serbs, 4,430,000 Croats, 1,750,000 Slovenes, 1,730,000 Albanians, 1,341,000 Macedonians and 1,220,000 "Yugoslavs", as well as a variety of other minorities.

Government.—On Nov. 29, 1945, the Constituent Assembly of Yugoslavia at a joint session of the Skupština and the House of Nationalities, proclaimed Yugoslavia a Republic.

The official name of the country, "The Socialist Federal Republic of Yugoslavia", was adopted by the 1963 Constitution.

Several amendments to the Constitution were made in 1971. The most important formed a new ruling body called the Presidency, which has 8 members, one from each Republic and Autonomous Province. Since the death of President Tito in May 1980, its members take it in turns according to a fixed order of succession to become President of the Presidency of the Republic for a period of 12 months each. A new Constitution was proclaimed in 1974 followed by the reconstitution of the Federal Assembly into two chambers consisting of the Federal Chamber (220 delegates) and the Republican/Provincial Chamber (88 delegates). A new Federal Executive Council (i.e. government) was also formed. The current Council was elected in May 1986 with a 2 year renewable mandate. The first election of the S.F.R.Y. Presidency since Pres. Tito's death took place in May 1984; each new member has a five-year mandate.

There is only one political party in Yugoslavia, the "League of Communists of Yugoslavia" (within which each Republic and Province has its own separate L.C.Y. organization) but there is a formal separation of State and Party; no-one may hold a post in the Federal or Republican/Provincial governments and a paid L.C.Y. post simultaneously. Political and economic decisions on many issues are devolved from Federal to Republican/Provincial level. Yugoslavia has a "self-management" form of industrial organization under which the workforce have the constitutional right to own and control their own enterprises.

Defence.—The Army, Navy and Air Force on a peace footing consist of 250,000 officers and men.

Religion and Education.—The three main religions are the Orthodox, Catholic and Islamic, and freedom to practice is constitutionally guaranteed. Religion is separated from the State and no religious instruction is allowed in state schools.

Education.—Eight years' elementary education is compulsory and all education is free. There are 18 universities.

Language and Literature.—The language mainly used throughout Yugoslavia and in the Federal Government is Serbo-Croat but Slovenian and Macedonian (also South-Slav tongues) and Albanian, Bulgarian, Romanian, Italian, Slovak, Ruthenian, Hungarian and Turkish are also spoken in certain areas. There is, however, no official language since all are constitutionally equal, except in the Armed Forces where Serbo Croat is obligatory. In Serbia, Macedonia and Montenegro the Cyrillic script is used and in the rest of the country the Latin. There are 4 Serbian daily newspapers in Belgrade, 2 Slovene dailies in Ljubljana, 2 Croat dailies in Zagreb, and many other dailies published in other towns. There are also many local newspapers and radio programmes in the different "minority" languages.

Production and Industry.—The share of industry in Gross Domestic Product (average annual rate in real terms of 6·5 per cent in 1981) is now 40 per cent, while agriculture is 14 per cent. In industry the high level of investment of recent years is being cut back and present efforts are directed towards development of high priority areas such as mining, energy resources and transport and communications. Agricultural policy is directed towards substantially increased production, to make the country self-sufficient and to provide significant exports of foodstuffs. Some 80 per cent of land is still privately owned.

The main crops are wheat, maize, sugar beet, sunflower and soya. Yields in 1985 were (tons): wheat, 4·9 m; maize, 9·9 m; sugar beet, 6·2 m. According to Yugoslav official estimates, the livestock population in 1985 was approximately as follows: cattle, 5,199,000; sheep, 7,678,000; pigs, 8,673,000; poultry, 70,453,000.

Minerals are an important source of wealth particularly in the central and south eastern regions. Production in 1983 included the following (tons):—

Coal	57,900,000
Coke	3,440,000
Iron ore	5,090,000
Pig iron	2,870,000
Steel	4,165,000
Crude oil	4,130,000

Smaller quantities of copper, zinc and mercury are produced.

Communications.—In 1984 there were 9,279 kms of standard and narrow gauge railway and approximately 116,600 kms of classified roads. In 1984 there were 3,031,000 telephones in use in the country. The principal ports on the long Adriatic seaboard of Yugoslavia are Rijeka, Bakar, Šibenik, Split, Zadar, Kardeljeva (formerly Ploče), Dubrovnik, Bar, Kotor (Cattaro) and Koper. The Danube forms a great commercial highway and the tributary rivers Sava and Tisa provide other shipping routes.

FINANCE

	1983	1984
	million *Dinars*	million *Dinars*
Revenue	1,140,000	374,000
Expenditure	1,140,000	374,000

The rate of exchange is variable. On June 6, 1980 the *dinar* was devalued against all convertible currencies and there have been several devaluations since then. (*See also* p. 82.)

Trade with U.K.

	1985	1986
Imports from U.K.	£177,530,000	£188,330,000
Exports to U.K.	122,132,000	144,800,000

CAPITAL.—Belgrade, population (1981) 1,455,000. Other towns are Zagreb (763,000); Skopje (503,000); Ljubljana (253,000); Sarajevo (447,000); Novi Sad (169,000); Priština (1971) (153,000); Ψ Split (152,000); Ψ Rijeka (133,000); Titograd (95,000).

FLAG.—Five-point red star outlined by narrow yellow stripe, on a ground of three horizontal bars, blue, white and red.

NATIONAL DAY.—November 29.

BRITISH EMBASSY
General Ždanova 46, Belgrade.

Ambassador Extraordinary and Plenipotentiary, His Excellency Andrew Marley Wood, C.M.G., (1985).

Counsellor, D. C. A. Madden.

Defence and Military Attaché, Col. A. E. F. Cowan, O.B.E.

Naval and Air Attaché, Wg. Cdr. E. A. Harris, M.B.E.

First Secretaries, R. J. Campbell (_Economic_); F. B. Holroyd, O.B.E. (_Admin. and Consular_); G. M. Johnston (_Commercial_).
Second Secretary, R. J. A. Huxter (_Chancery and Information_).

BRITISH CONSULAR OFFICES

There are British Consular Offices at _Belgrade, Zagreb_ and _Split_.

British Council Representative, D. Gunton, O.B.E. Generala Ždanova 34, (P.O. Box 248), 11001 Belgrade. British Council Reading Room, Knez Mihajlova 45, Belgrade. There are also a centre and library at _Zagreb_.

ZAIRE
(République du Zaïre)

President of the Republic and National Security, Marshal Mobuto Sésé Séko, _born_ Oct. 30, 1930; _assumed office_ November 25, 1965; _elected_ Nov. 5, 1970; _re-elected for third term_, July 28, 1984.

EXECUTIVE COUNCIL

Prime Minister, Mabi Mulumba.
Justice, N'Singa Udjuu Ongwakebi Untube.
Planning, Sambwa Pida N'Bangui.
Territorial Administration and Decentralisation, Duga Kugbe Toro.
Foreign Affairs and International Co-operation, Ekila Liyonda.
Citizen's Rights and Freedoms, Nimy Mayidika Ngimbi.
Information and Press, Mandungu Bula Nyati.
Finance and Budget, Nyembo Shabani.
National Economy and Industry, Tshiunza Mbiye.
Portfolio, Thambwe Mwamba.
Foreign Trade, Kasereka Kasai.
Agriculture, Kayinga Osindal.
Rural Development, D'Zbo Kalogi.
Mines and Energy, Ileo Itambala.
Public Works and Territorial Development, Mokolo wa Mpombo.
Transport and Communications, Sampassa Kaweta Milombe.
Land Management, Environment and Conservation, Pendje Demodetdo.
Higher Education, Universities and Scientific Research, Mokanda Bonza.
Primary and Secondary Education, Nzege Alaziambina.
Youth, Sports and Leisure, Tshimbombo Mukuna.
Women's and Family Affairs, Mayuma Kala.
Public Health and Social Welfare, Dr. Ngandu Kabeya.
Civil Service, Mwando Nsimba.
Post and Telecommunications, Tokwaulu Bolamba.
Culture, Arts and Tourism, Beyeye Djema.

ZAIRE EMBASSY
26 Chesham Place, SW1X 8HH
[01–235 6137]

Ambassador Extraordinary and Plenipotentiary, (new appointment awaited).

The State of the Congo, founded in 1885, became a Belgian Colony on Nov. 15, 1908, and was administered by Belgium until 1960, when it became the Democratic Republic of the Congo. In October 1971 the name changed to the Republic of Zaire. Situated between long. 12°–31° E. and lat. 5° N.–13° S., the Republic of Zaire comprises an area of 905,567 sq. miles (2,345,409 sq. km.), with a population (1985 estimate) of 34,671,607.

Climate.—Apart from the coastal district in the West which is fairly dry, the rainfall averages

between 60 and 80 inches. The average temperature is about 80° F., but in the South the winter temperature can fall nearly to freezing point. Extensive forest covers the central districts.

Government.—On June 30, 1960, the Belgian Congo became an independent unitary state under the Presidency of M. Kasavubu with a provisional constitution drawn up by the metropolitan Belgian Parliament. On July 11, M. Moise Tshombe announced the independence of the State of Katanga although he failed to obtain international recognition. Katanga did not come under the Government at Leopoldville until January 14, 1963.

The constitutional and political situation remained unsettled, the United Nations having mixed forces in the country until 1964. By the middle of 1965, the Congolese Government formed by M. Tshombe in July, 1964, had succeeded in gaining control of all the towns from the rebels and depriving them of military aid from outside the Congo. Gen. Joseph-Désiré Mobutu, Commander-in-Chief of the Congolese National Army, announced on November 25, 1965 that he had assumed the Presidency.

A Presidential régime was instituted by the 1967 Constitution, subsequently amended in 1974 and totally revised in Feb. 1978. The Mouvement Populaire de la Révolution is the sole political party. The President changed his name to Mobutu Sésé Séko Kuku Ngbendu Wa Za Banga in 1972, but is usually known by the first three of these names only.

Provinces.—There are 8 regions, each under a Governor and provincial administration (names of capitals in brackets) Bas-Zaire _(Matadi)_; Bandundu _(Bandundu)_; Equateur _(Mbandaka)_; Haut-Zaire _(Kisangani)_; Kivu _(Bukavu)_; Shaba, _formerly_ Katanga _(Lubumbashi)_; East Kasai _(Mbuji-Mayi)_; West Kasai _(Kananga)_.

Language, Religion and Education.—The people are mainly of Bantu-Negro stock, divided into semi-autonomous tribes, each speaking a Bantu tongue. Swahili, a Bantu dialect with an admixture of Arabic, is the nearest approach to a common language in the East and South, while Lingala is the language of a large area along the river and in the north, and Kikongo of the region between Kinshasa and the sea. French is the language of administration. It is estimated there are 9,500,000 African Christians in the Republic (Roman Catholic 5,800,000, Protestant 1,600,000). The local Kimbanguist religion has over two million adherents. The National University of Zaire has campuses in Kinshasa, Kisangani and Lubumbashi, with approximately 28,000 students (1978–79).

Production.—The cultivation of oil palms is widespread, palm oil being the most important agricultural cash product though it is no longer exported. Coffee, rubber, cocoa and timber are the most important agricultural exports. The production of cotton, pyrethrum and copal fell sharply on independence but is now increasing. The country is rich in minerals, particularly Shaba (_ex_-Katanga) province. Copper is widely exploited, and industrial diamonds and cobalt are also produced. Oil deposits are exploited off the Zaire estuary and reef-gold is mined in the north-east of the country.

There is a wide variety of small secondary industries, the main products being: cotton fabrics, blankets, sacks, footwear, beer, cigarettes, cement, paint, sugar, furniture, metal goods and tyres, and local assembly of motor vehicles. There are very large reserves of hydro-electric power and the huge Inga dam on the river Zaire is now supplying electricity to Matadi, Kinshasa and Shaba.

The chief exports are copper, crude oil, coffee, diamonds, rubber, cobalt, gold, cassiterite, zinc and other metals.

Communications. There are approximately

20,500 km of roads (earth-surfaced) of national importance, and 6,000 km of railways. The country has two international and 40 principal airports.

Currency.—The unit of currency is the *Zaire.*

Trade with U.K.

	1985	1986
Imports from U.K.....	£34,975,000	£34,220,000
Exports to U.K.	35,198,000	17,190,000

CAPITAL.—Kinshasa (*formerly* Leopoldville), population (estimated, 1985) 2,778,281. Principal towns, Lubumbashi (*formerly* Elisabethville) (403,623); Kisangani (*formerly* Stanleyville) (310,705); Likasi

(146,394); Kananga (601,239); Ψ Matadi (143,598); and Mbandaka (134,495).

FLAG.—Dark brown hand and torch with red flame in yellow roundel on green background.

NATIONAL DAY.—November 24.

BRITISH EMBASSY
B.P. 8049, Kinshasa.

Ambassador Extraordinary and Plenipotentiary, His Excellency Robert Linklater Burke Cormack (1987).

First Secretaries, T. I. Hay-Campbell; A. Godson (*Commercial and H.M. Consul*).

Second Secretary, A. D. B. Newton.

ROMAN EMPERORS

[The *First Triumvirate* (Julius Cæsar, Pompey and Crassus) 60–53 B.C.]

The Twelve Cæsars

I. Caius JULIUS CÆSAR, *born* A.U.C. 651 (102 B.C.); *Dictator* A.U.C. 705 (48 B.C.); *Assassinated* A.U.C. 709 (44 B.C.).

[The *Second Triumvirate* (Octavian, Antony and Lepidus) 44–31 B.C.]

II. Caius Julius Cæsar Octavianus AUGUSTUS, *born* 63 B.C.; *Emperor* 27 B.C.; *Died* A.D. 14.
III. Claudius Nero Cæsar TIBERIUS, *born* 24 B.C.; *Emperor* A.D. 14; *Died* A.D. 37.
IV. Caius Cæsar CALIGULA, *born* A.D. 12; *Emperor* A.D. 37; *Assassinated* A.D. 41.
V. Tiberius Drusus CLAUDIUS, *born* 10 B.C.; *Emperor* A.D. 41; *Assassinated* A.D. 54.
VI. Claudius NERO, *born* A.D. 37; *Emperor* A.D. 54; *Suicide* A.D. 68.
VII. Servius Sulpicius GALBA, *born* 3 B.C.; *Emperor* A.D. 68; *Assassinated* A.D. 69.
VIII. Marcus Salvius OTHO, *born* A.D. 32; *Emperor* A.D. 69; *Suicide* A.D. 69.
IX. AULUS VITELLIUS, *born* A.D. 15; *Emperor* A.D. 69; *Assassinated* A.D. 69.
X. Titus Flavius VESPASIAN, *born* A.D. 9; *Emperor* A.D. 69; *Died* A.D.79.
XI. Flavius Sabinus Vespasianus TITUS, *born* A.D. 48; *Emperor* A.D. 79; *Died* A.D. 81.
XII. Titus Flavius DOMITIAN, *born* A.D. 52; *Emperor* A.D. 81; *Assassinated* A.D. 96.

PARLIAMENTS SINCE 1945

Assembled	Dissolved	Duration yrs. m. d.	Assembled	Dissolved	Duration yrs. m. d.
1945 Aug. 1	1950 Feb. 3	4 6 2	1970 June 29	1974 Feb. 8	3 7 10
1950 March 1	1951 Oct. 5	1 7 4	1974 March 6	1974 Sept. 20	0 6 14
1951 Oct. 31	1955 May 6	3 6 6	1974 Oct. 22	1979 April 7	4 5 16
1955 June 7	1959 Sept. 18	4 3 11	1979 May 9	1983 May 13	4 0 4
1959 Oct. 20	1964 Sept. 25	4 11 5	1983 June 15	1987 May 18	3 11 3
1964 Oct. 27	1966 March 10	1 4 11	1987 June 17		
1966 April 18	1970 May 29	4 1 11			

THE ANTARCTIC

THE ANTARCTIC is generally defined as the area lying within the Antarctic Convergence—the zone where cold northward-flowing Antarctic sea water sinks below warmer southward-flowing water. This zone is at about lat. 50° S. in the Atlantic Ocean and lat. 55°–62° S. in the Pacific Ocean. The continent itself lies almost entirely within the Antarctic Circle, an area of about 5·5 million square miles, 99 per cent of which is permanently ice-covered. The average thickness of the ice is 7,100 ft. but in places exceeds 14,500 ft., submerging entire mountain ranges; some mountains protrude—the highest being Vinson Massif, 16,066 ft. The ice amounts to some 7·2 million cubic miles and represents more than 90 per cent of the world's fresh water.

Along one-third of the Antarctic coastline, land-ice flowing outwards forms extensive ice shelves, fragments of which break off to form tabular icebergs, leaving ice cliffs up to 150 ft. high. Much of the sea freezes in winter, forming fast ice which breaks up in summer and drifts north as pack ice. The presence of ice and continuous darkness in winter restrict access to the coastline by sea to the summer months.

The most conspicuous physical features of the continent are its high inland plateau (much of it over 10,000 ft.), the Transantarctic Mountains (which together with the large embayments of the Weddell Sea and Ross Sea mark the approximate boundary between Greater and Lesser Antarctica), and the mountainous Antarctic Peninsula and off-lying islands (which extend northwards towards South America). The continental shelf averages about 20 miles in width (half the global mean, and in places it is non-existent) and reaches exceptional depths (1,300–2,600 ft., which is 3–6 times the global mean).

Climate.—On land, summer temperatures range from just below freezing around the coast to −30° F. (about −34° C.) on the plateau, and in winter −5° F. (−20° C.) on the coast to −85° F. (−65° C.) inland. Over a large area the maxima do not exceed +5° F. (−15° C.).

Precipitation is scanty over the plateau but amounts to 10–30 ins. (water equivalent) along the coast and some scientific stations are permanently buried by snow. Some rain falls over the more northerly areas in summer. Gravity winds on the plateau slopes and cyclonic storms further north can both exceed 100 m.p.h. and gusts have been known to reach 150 m.p.h. Visibility can be reduced to zero in blizzards.

Flora and Fauna.—Although a small number of flowering plants, ferns and clubmosses occur on the sub-Antarctic islands, only two (a grass and a pearlwort) extend south of 60° S. Antarctic vegetation is dominated by lichens and mosses, with a few liverworts, algae, and fungi. Most of these occur around the coast or on islands, but lichens and some mosses also occur inland.

The only land animals are tiny insects and mites with nematodes, rotifers, and tardigrades in the mosses, but large numbers of seals, penguins, and other sea-birds go ashore to breed in the summer. The emperor penguin is the only species which breeds ashore throughout the winter. In contrast, the Antarctic seas abound with life—a wide variety of invertebrates (including krill) and fish providing food for the seals, penguins, and other birds and a residual population of whales.

Exploration and Antarctic Treaty.—In the 180 years from Captain James Cook's circumnavigation of the Antarctic in 1772–75 to the mid-1950's, about half of all expeditions to the Antarctic were British and a number of these made major contributions to geographical and scientific knowledge of the area. Notable, were the expeditions of Sir James Clark Ross, Captain Robert Scott, and Sir Ernest Shackleton.

Apart from four years during World War II, British Antarctic research has been continuous since 1925, and most of it is now organized and carried out by the British Antarctic Survey (a component of the Natural Environment Research Council).

The world-wide International Geophysical Year, 1957–58, gave great impetus to Antarctic research. Prior to the mid-1950's, only 17 stations were operated in the Antarctic by four nations and vast areas of the continent were still unknown. By 1957, 44 stations had been established by 12 nations. The co-operative scientific effort proved so fruitful that the 12 nations involved pledged themselves to continue to promote scientific and technical co-operation unhampered by politics (territorial claims being left in abeyance) and agreed that the continent should be used for peaceful purposes only. These aims were embodied in the Antarctic Treaty (covering the area south of lat. 60° S., excluding the high seas but including the ice shelves), which came into force in 1961. It has since been signed by a further 32 acceding nations, 19 of which are active in the Antarctic and have therefore been accorded consultative status.

Potential resources.—Increasing pressure on the world's food and mineral supplies has stimulated the search for new sources even in the extremely hostile polar environment. Minerals have been found in great variety but not in commercially exploitable concentrations in accessible localities. (For example, coal seams occur in the Theron Mountains and Horlick Mountains.)

There are indications that off-shore hydrocarbons could be present but mostly below great depths of stormy, ice-infested seas. However, the Antarctic Treaty nations and their scientific advisors are already considering the environmental implications of possible mineral exploration and exploitation.

Currently, the chief interest is in marine protein, including the shrimp-like krill already fished commercially by Japan, Poland and U.S.S.R. Basic research to ensure rational management of stocks of this key organism is being continued by international groups, but it is estimated that they could sustain a yield equal to the present total annual world fish catch.

Scientific research.—At present, five British stations are maintained in the British Antarctic Territory and at South Georgia. Two are biological stations, two geophysical observatories, and one is the centre for airborne earth sciences.

There are a number of permanently occupied stations operated by other nations including one maintained at the South Pole by the U.S.A.

The staff of these stations and summer field-workers are the only people present on the continent and off-lying islands. There are no indigenous inhabitants.

(British Antarctic Survey, *see* entry on p. 422).

The Nobel Prizes are awarded each year from the income of a trust fund established by the Swedish scientist Alfred Nobel, the inventor of dynamite, who died on December 10, 1896, leaving a fortune of £1,750,000. They are awarded to those who have contributed most to the common good in the domain of (a) Physics; (b) Chemistry; (c) Physiology and Medicine; (d) Literature; (e) Peace. The first awards were made in 1901 on the fifth anniversary of Nobel's death. The awarding authorities are the Royal Swedish Academy of Sciences: (a) Physics—(b) Chemistry; the Royal Caroline Institute, Stockholm—(c) Physiology and Medicine; the Karolinska Institute —(d) Literature; a committee of five persons elected by the Norwegian Storting—(e) Peace. The Trust is administered by the Board of Directors of the Nobel Foundation, Stockholm. The Board consists of five members and three deputy members. The Swedish Government appoints a chairman and a deputy chairman, the remaining members being appointed by the awarding authorities.

The nationality of prizewinners is indicated as follows: (a) United Kingdom; (b) U.S.A.; (c) France; (d) Sweden; (e) Germany; (f) U.S.S.R.; (g) Germany; (h) Netherlands; (i) Switzerland; (k) Denmark; (l) Norway; (m) Spain; (n) Poland; (o) Austria; (p) Italy; (q) India; (r) Hungary; (s) Finland; (t) Canada; (u) Chile; (v) Argentina; (w) Japan; (x) Portugal; (y) Irish Free State; (z) Republic of Ireland; (aa) South Africa; (bb) Iceland; (cc) China; (dd) Czechoslovakia; (ee) Australia; (ff) Yugoslavia; (gg) Greece; (hh) Israel; (ii) Guatemala; (kk) Egypt; (ll) Pakistan; (mm) West Indies; (nn) Bulgaria; (oo) Colombia; (pp) Mexico; (qq) Nigeria. The distribution by nationalities is shown at foot of table.

For prize winners for the years 1901–1979, *see* earlier editions of WHITAKER'S ALMANACK.

Year	(a) PHYSICS	(b) CHEMISTRY	(c) PHYSIOLOGY AND MEDICINE	(d) LITERATURE	(e) PEACE
1980	Prof. J. Cronin (b) Prof. V. Fitch (b)	Prof. P. Berg (b) Prof. W. Gilbert (b) Prof. F. Sanger (a)	G. Snell (b) J. Dausset (c) B. Benacerraf (b)	Prof. C. Milosz (n)	A. P. Esquivel (v)
1981	Prof. K. Siegbahn (d) Prof. N. Bloembergen (b) Prof. A. Schawlow (b)	Prof. K. Fukui (w) Prof. R. Hoffmann (n)	Prof. R. Sperry (b) Prof. D. Hubel (b) Prof. T. Wiesel (d)	E. Canetti (nn)	Office of the U.N. High Commission for Refugees
1982	Prof. K. G. Wilson (b)	Dr. A. Klug (a)	Prof. S. K. Bergstrom (d) Prof. B. I. Samuelson (d) Dr. J. R. Vane (a)	G. Garcia Marquez (oo)	A. Garcia Robles (pp) Mrs. A. Myrdal (d)
1983	Prof. S. Chandrasekhar (b) Prof. W. Fowler (b)	Prof. H. Taube (b)	Dr. B. McClintock (b)	W. Golding (a)	L. Walesa (n)
1984	Prof. C. Rubbia (p) Dr. S. van der Meer (h)	Prof. R. B. Merrifield (b)	Dr. N. K. Jerne (k) Dr. G. J. F. Köhler (g) Dr. C. Milstein (a)	J. Seifert (dd)	Bishop D. Tutu (aa)
1985	Prof. K. von Klitzing (g)	Prof. H. Hauptman (b) Prof. J. Karle (b)	Dr. J. Goldstein (b) Dr. M. Brown (b)	C. Simon (c)	International Physicians for the Prevention of Nuclear War
1986	Prof. E. Ruska (g) Dr. G. Binnig (g) Dr. H. Rohrer (i)	Prof. D. Herschbach (b) Prof. Y. Tseh Lee (b) Prof. J. Polanyi (t)	Prof. S. Cohen (b) Prof. R. Levi-Montalcini (p)	Prof. Wole Soyinka (qq)	Prof. E. Wiesel (b)

The awards have been distributed as follows: PHYSICS.—*U.S.A.*, 47; *U.K.*, 20; *Germany*, 17; *France*, 9; *U.S.S.R.*, 7; *Netherlands*, 6; *Sweden*, 4; *Austria*, 3; *Denmark*, 3; *Italy*, 3; *Japan*, 3; *China*, 2; *India*, 1; *Ireland*, 1; *Pakistan*, 1; *Switzerland*, 1.

CHEMISTRY.—*U.S.A.*, 30; *Germany*, 24; *U.K.*, 22; *France*, 6; *Sweden*, 4; *Switzerland*, 4; *Canada*, 2; *Netherlands*, 2; *Argentina*, 1; *Australia*, 1; *Austria*, 1; *Belgium*, 1; *Czechoslovakia*, 1; *Finland*, 1; *Hungary*, 1; *Italy*, 1; *Japan*, 1; *Norway*, 1; *Poland*, 1; *U.S.S.R.*, 1.

PHYSIOLOGY AND MEDICINE.—*U.S.A.*, 58; *U.K.*, 20; *Germany*, 11; *France*, 7; *Sweden*, 6; *Austria*, 5; *Denmark*, 5; *Switzerland*, 5; *Belgium*, 4; *Italy*, 3; *Netherlands*, 3; *Australia*, 2; *Canada*, 2; *Hungary*, 2; *U.S.S.R.*, 2; *Argentina*, 1; *Portugal*, 1; *South Africa*, 1; *Spain*, 1.

LITERATURE.—*France*, 12; *U.S.A.*, 8; *Germany*, 7; *U.K.*, 7; *Sweden*, 6; *Italy*, 5; *Spain*, 4; *U.S.S.R.*, 4; *Denmark*, 3; *Norway*, 3; *Poland*, 3; *Chile*, 2; *Greece*, 2; *Ireland*, 2; *Switzerland*, 2; *Australia*, 1; *Belgium*, 1; *Bulgaria*, 1; *Colombia*, 1; *Czechoslovakia*, 1; *Finland*, 1; *Guatemala*, 1; *Iceland*, 1; *India*, 1; *Israel*, 1; *Japan*, 1; *Nigeria*, 1; *Yugoslavia*, 1.

PEACE.—*U.S.A.*, 17; *Institutions*, 13; *France*, 9; *U.K.*, 8; *Sweden*, 5; *Germany*, 4; *Belgium*, 3; *Switzerland*, 3; *Argentina*, 2; *Austria*, 2; *Norway*, 2; *South Africa*, 2; *Canada*, 1; *Denmark*, 1; *Egypt*, 1; *Ireland*, 1; *Israel*, 1; *Italy*, 1; *Japan*, 1; *Mexico*, 1; *Netherlands*, 1; *Poland*, 1; *U.S.S.R.*, 1; *Yugoslavia*, 1.

In 1969 a Nobel Prize for Economic Sciences was instituted, to be awarded by the Royal Swedish Academy of Sciences. Prize-winners have been: 1969, J. Tintergen (h) and R. Frisch (l); 1970, P. A. Samuelson (b); 1971, S. Kuznets (b); 1972, Sir John Hicks (a) and K. J. Arrow (b); 1973, W. Leontief (b); 1974, F. von Hayek (a) and G. Myrdal (d); 1975, Prof. L. V. Kantorovich (f) and Prof. T. C. Koopmans (b); 1976, Prof. M. Friedman (b); 1977, Prof. J. E. Meade (a) and Prof. B. Ohlin (d); 1978, Prof. H. A. Simon (b); 1979, Prof. T. W. Shultz (b) and Prof. Sir Arthur Lewis (mm); 1980, Prof. L. Klein (b); 1981, Prof. J. Tobin (b); 1982, Prof. G. Stigler (b); 1983, Prof. G. Debreu (b); 1984, Sir Richard Stone (a); 1985, F. Modigliani (b); 1986, Prof. J. M. Buchanan (b).

THE UNITED NATIONS

The foundations of the Charter of the United Nations were laid at the Conference of Foreign Ministers in Moscow in 1943, and upon those foundations a structure was built at the meetings at Dumbarton Oaks, Washington, D.C., Aug. 21–Oct. 7, 1944. The design was discussed and criticized at San Francisco from April 25 to June 26, 1945, on which date representatives of 50 Allied Nations appended their signatures to the Charter.

The United Nations formally came into existence on October 24, 1945. It was later decided that its seat should be in the United States. Permanent headquarters have been erected at Manhattan, New York. October 24 has been designated "United Nations Day".

The following 159 states are members of the United Nations:—

Afghanistan, Albania, Algeria, Angola, Antigua and Barbuda, Argentina,* Australia,* Austria, Bahamas, Bahrain, Bangladesh, Barbados, Belgium, Belize,* Benin, Bhutan, Bolivia,* Botswana, Brazil,* Brunei, Bulgaria, Burkina Faso, Burma, Burundi, Byelorussian Soviet Socialist Republic,* Cambodia, Cameroon, Canada,* Cape Verde, Central African Rep., Chad, Chile,* China,* Colombia,* Comoros, Congo (Pop. Repub.), Costa Rica,* Côte d'Ivoire, Cuba,* Cyprus, Czechoslovakia,* Denmark,* Djibouti, Dominica, Dominican Republic,* Ecuador,* Egypt,* Equatorial Guinea, Ethiopia,* Fiji, Finland, France,* Gabon, Gambia, Germany (East), Germany (West), Ghana, Greece,* Grenada, Guatemala,* Guinea, Guinea-Bissau, Guyana, Haiti,* Honduras,* Hungary, Iceland, India,* Indonesia, Iran,* Iraq,* Republic of Ireland, Israel, Italy, Jamaica, Japan, Jordan, Kenya, Kuwait, Laos, Lebanon,* Lesotho, Liberia,* Libya, Luxembourg,* Madagascar, Malawi, Malaysia, Maldive Islands, Mali, Malta, Mauritania, Mauritius, Mexico,* Mongolia, Morocco, Mozambique, Nepal, Netherlands,* New Zealand,* Nicaragua,* Niger, Nigeria, Norway,* Oman, Pakistan, Panama,* Papua New Guinea, Paraguay,* Peru,* Philippines,* Poland,* Portugal, Qatar, Romania, Rwanda, St. Christopher and Nevis, St. Lucia, St. Vincent and the Grenadines, El Salvador,* Sao Tome and Principe, Saudi Arabia,* Senegal, Seychelles, Sierra Leone, Singapore, Solomon Islands, Somalia, South Africa,* Spain, Sri Lanka, Sudan, Suriname, Swaziland, Sweden, Syria,* Tanzania, Thailand, Togo, Trinidad and Tobago, Tunisia, Turkey,* Uganda, Ukrainian Soviet Socialist Republic,* Union of Soviet Socialist Republics,* United Arab Emirates, United Kingdom,* United States of America,* Uruguay, Vanuatu,* Venezuela,* Vietnam, Western Samoa, Yemen (Arab Repub.), Yemen (P.D.R.), Yugoslavia,* Zaire, Zambia, Zimbabwe.

*Original member (i.e. from 1945). (From October 25, 1971, "China" was taken to mean the People's Republic of China.)

The principal organs of the United Nations are:—
(1) The General Assembly; (2) The Security Council; (3) The Economic and Social Council; (4) The Trusteeship Council; (5) The International Court of Justice; (6) The Secretariat.

1. The General Assembly

The General Assembly consists of all the Members of the United Nations. Each Member is entitled to be represented at its meetings by five representatives, but has only one vote. The General Assembly meets once a year in regular session beginning on the third Tuesday in September. A new President is elected by the General Assembly at the start of every annual session. Special Sessions may also be held.

The work of the General Assembly is divided among seven Main Committees, on each of which every Member has the right to be represented :—(1) Disarmament and related security questions; (2) Economic and Financial; (3) Social, Humanitarian and Cul-

tural; (4) Decolonization (including Non-Self Governing Territories); (5) Administrative and Budgetary; (6) Legal. There is also a Special Political Committee, to relieve the burden on the first Committee.

The Main Committees consider items referred to them by the General Assembly and recommend draft resolutions for submission to the Assembly's plenary meetings.

The Assembly has two procedural committees—a General Committee and a Credentials Committee; and three standing committees—an Advisory Committee on Administrative and Budgetary Questions, a Committee on Contributions and a Disarmament Commission.

The General Assembly appoints such *ad hoc* committees as may be required from time to time for special purposes. The Assembly is also assisted in its work by subsidiary bodies such as the Board of Auditors, the Committee on Conferences, the International Law Commission, etc. In 1964 the General Assembly set up the United Nations Conference on Trade and Development (UNCTAD) as a permanent body.

The United Nations Industrial Development Organization was set up on Jan. 1, 1967, to promote industrialization and co-ordinate United Nations activities in this field.

President of the United Nations General Assembly, Humayan Rashid Chowdhury (*Bangladesh*) (1986).

2. The Security Council

The Security Council consists of fifteen Members, each of which has one representative and one vote. There are five permanent Members and ten non-permanent Members elected for a two-year term.

The Security Council bears the primary responsibility for the maintenance of peace and security. Decisions on procedural questions are made by an affirmative vote of nine Members. On all other matters the affirmative vote of nine Members must include the concurring votes of the permanent Members, and it is this clause which makes the Veto possible.

The General Assembly, any member of the United Nations, or the Secretary-General, can bring to the Council's attention any matter considered to threaten international peace and security. A non-member State can bring a dispute before the Council provided it accepts in advance the U.N. Charter obligations for peaceful settlement.

The Security Council also establishes *ad hoc* committees and commissions which may be required from time to time for special purposes.

The five permanent Members are China, France, U.K., U.S.A., and U.S.S.R. The present ten non-permanent Members are: Bulgaria, Congo, Ghana, U.A.E. and Venezuela (*elected in 1985*): Federal Republic of Germany, Italy, Japan, Argentina and Zambia (*elected in 1986*).

3. The Economic and Social Council

This body is responsible under the General Assembly for carrying out the functions of the United Nations with regard to international economic, social, cultural, educational, health and related matters.

It has established the following Commissions: Statistical, Human Rights, Social Development, Status of Women, Narcotic Drugs, Population, Regional

Economic Commissions for Europe, Asia and the Pacific, Western Asia, Latin America and Africa. The Council also makes recommendations for the co-ordination of the policies and activities of 15 specialized agencies and other organizations in the U.N. system.

4. Trusteeship Council

The Trusteeship Council now consists of five members: the U.S.A. (administering authority of Micronesia, the only remaining trust Territory of the original 11), and the other four permanent members of the Security Council, China, France, U.K. and U.S.S.R.

The Trusteeship Council considers reports from administering authorities; examines petitions in consultation with the administering authority; makes periodic inspection visits; and checks conditions with an annual questionnaire on the political, economic, social, and educational advancement of the inhabitants of trust territories.

5. International Court of Justice

The International Court of Justice is the principal judicial organ of the United Nations. The Statute of the court is an integral part of the Charter and all Members of the United Nations are *ipso facto* parties to it. The Court is composed of 15 judges, no two of whom may be nationals of the same State, and is based at The Hague.

If any party to a case fails to adhere to the judgment of the Court, the other party may have recourse to the Security Council.

President, Nagendra Singh *(India)*.

THE SECRETARIAT

Secretary-General, Javier Pérez de Cuellar *(Peru)*.
Director-General, Development and International Economic Co-operation, Jean Ripert *(France)*.

U.N. Office and Information Centre, Ship House, 20 Buckingham Gate, S.W.1.

OTHER ORGANS

The U.N. Centre for Human Settlements (Habitat), Nairobi; U.N. Children's Fund (UNICEF), New York; U.N. Conference on Trade and Development (UNCTAD), Geneva; U.N. Development Programme (UNDP), New York; U.N. Disaster Relief Office (UNDRO), Geneva; U.N. Environment Programme (UNEP), Nairobi; U.N. Fund for Population Activities (UNFPA), New York; U.N. High Commissioner for Refugees (UNHCR), Geneva; U.N. Institute for Training and Research (UNITAR), New York; International Research and Training Institute for the Advancement of Women (INSTRAW); U.N. Relief and Works Agency for Palestine Refugees in the Near East (UNRWA), Vienna; U.N. University (UNU), Tokyo; World Food Council (WFC), Rome; World Food Programme (WFP), Rome.

These programmes are supported by voluntary contributions from governments, non-governmental organizations and individuals. The U.N. programmes receiving the largest total contributions in 1983 were: the U.N. Development Programme (U.N.D.P.— $714m); the U.N. Children's Fund (U.N.I.C.E.F.— $297m), and the U.N. Fund for Population Activities (U.N.F.P.A.—$310m). The World Food Programme (W.F.P.), jointly administered by the U.N. and F.A.O., provided aid worth $900m in 1983.

BUDGET OF THE UNITED NATIONS

The budget is now approved for periods of two years, and the appropriation for the biennium 1986–87 is U.S.$1,663,341,600 *(gross)*. The scale of assess-

ment contributions of 78 U.N. members is set at 0·01 per cent., that of a further 11 at 0·02 per cent., and a further five at 0·03 per cent. The ten largest assessments are as follows: U.S.A., 25 per cent.; U.S.S.R., 11·82 per cent.; Japan, 10·84 per cent.; West Germany, 8·26 per cent.; France, 6·37 per cent.; U.K., 4·67 per cent.; Italy, 3·79 per cent.; Canada, 3·06 per cent.; Spain, 2·03 per cent. and Netherlands, 1·74 per cent.

U.K. MISSION TO THE UNITED NATIONS
845 Third Avenue, New York

Permanent Representative to the United Nations and Representative on the Security Council, Sir Crispin Tickell, K.C.V.O. (1987).
Deputy Permanent Representative, J. A. Birch, C.M.G.
Counsellors, D. E. S. Blatherwick *(Head of Chancery)*; D. M. Edwards *(Legal Adviser)*; E. J. Field *(Economic and Social Affairs)*; R. C. Tutt; J. R. Leeland *(Administration)*.

U.K. MISSION TO THE U.N. AND OTHER INTERNATIONAL ORGANIZATIONS IN GENEVA
37–39 rue de Vermont, 1211 Geneva 20

Ambassador, Permanent U.K. Representative, John Anthony Sankey, C.M.G. (1985).
Deputy Permanent Representative, D. J. Moss.

SPECIALIZED AGENCIES

Fifteen other independent international organizations, each with its own membership, budget and headquarters, carry out their responsibilities in co-ordination with the U.N. under agreements made with the Economic and Social Council. These agencies set standards and provide technical assistance in economic, social and cultural and technical fields.

Food and Agriculture Organization of the United Nations (FAO), Via delle Terme di Caracalla, 00100 Rome.—Established on October 16, 1945, to raise levels of nutrition and standards of living, to secure improvements in the efficiency of the production and distribution of all food and agricultural products and to better the condition of rural populations, thus contributing to the expansion of world economy and ensuring man's freedom from hunger. Among its many activities the Organization promotes the global exchange of information in the fields of agriculture, forestry and fisheries, facilitates international agreement in these fields and provides technical assistance in such subjects as nutrition and food management, soil erosion control, re-afforestation, the establishment of paper industries, irrigation engineering, control of infestation of stored foods, production of fertilizers, control of crop pests and diseases, and improvement of fishing vessels, fish distribution and marketing. Jointly with the United Nations it administers the World Food Programme, which since 1964 has committed nearly $10,000,000 in cash and commodities to low-income countries. The 1985 session of the FAO governing Conference approved a budget of $437,000,000 for the two years 1986–87. In addition FAO is carrying out field programmes involving annual expenditure of about $280,000,000 under the U.N. Development Programme and other aid programmes including trust funds. Through its co-operative programme with the World Bank it is helping to increase international investment in agriculture and allied fields.

The policy of the Organization is directed by a two-yearly Conference of the 158 member countries. A council (49 members) acts for the Conference between its sessions.

Director-General, Edouard Saouma (*Lebanon*).
Permanent U.K. Representative, R. F. R. Deare.

International Bank for Reconstruction and Development (IBRD), Washington, D.C. 20433; *European office*, 66 Ave. d'Iéna, 75116, Paris, France; *Tokyo office*, Kokusai Building 1–1, Marunouchi 3-Chome, Chiyoda-ku, Tokyo 100.—Established on Dec. 27, 1945, to help raise standards of living in developing countries by the provision of financial resources through loans made for productive purposes to a government, or guaranteed by the government concerned. Loans are directed towards developing countries at more advanced stages of economic and social growth.

The Bank, which is owned by the governments of 151 countries and whose capital is subscribed by its member countries, finances its lending operations primarily from its own borrowing in the world capital markets, and derives a substantial contribution to its resources from its retained earnings and the repayment of loans. The interest rate on its loans is calculated in relation to its cost of borrowing; loans generally have a grace period of five years and are repayable over 20 years or less. The loans made by the Bank since its inception to June 30, 1986, totalled $126,098,600,000 to 110 countries. Subscribed capital, $77,526,969,000.

The Board of Governors consists of one Governor and one alternate appointed by each of the member countries. Twenty-two Executive Directors exercise all powers of the Bank except those reserved to the Board of Governors. The President, selected by the Executive Directors, conducts the business of the Bank, with the assistance of an international staff.
President, B. B. Conable (*U.S.A.*).
U.K. Executive Director, T. P. Lankester.

International Development Association (IDA), Washington, D.C. 20433; *European office*, 66 Ave. d'Iéna, 75116 Paris, France; *Tokyo office*, Kokusai Building 1–1, Marunouchi 3-Chome, Chiyoda-ku, Tokyo 100.—The IDA is an affiliate of the IBRD (the two together comprising the World Bank) and was established in September 1960 to provide assistance for the same purposes as the IBRD but primarily in the poorer developing countries and on terms that bear less heavily on their balance of payments than IBRD loans. Assistance is concentrated on the very poor countries, i.e. those with an annual per capita GNP of less than $791 (in 1984 dollars); more than 50 countries are eligible.

Membership is open to all members of IBRD and 135 have joined to date. Funds, called credits to distinguish them from IBRD loans, come mostly in the form of subscriptions, general replenishments and special contributions by IDA's richer members, and transfers from the net earnings of the IBRD. The term of IDA credits, which are made to governments only, are ten-year grace periods, 50-year maturities, and no interest. By June 30, 1986, IDA had extended development credits totalling $39,822,000,000 in 95 countries.

Although legally and financially distinct from the IBRD, IDA is administered by the same staff, and the Board of Governors and Executive Directors are the same as those holding equivalent positions in the IBRD.

International Civil Aviation Organization (ICAO), 1,000 Sherbrooke Street, W., Montreal, Quebec, Canada.—The ICAO was established on April 4, 1947, to study problems of international civil aviation to establish international standards and regulations for civil aviation in areas such as airworthiness, personnel licensing, aeronautical charts, rules of the air, etc., ICAO encourages the use of safety measures, uniform regulations or operation, and simpler procedures at international airports. It promotes the use of new technical methods and equipment. With the co-operation of members, it has evolved a pattern for meteorological services, traffic control, telecommunications, search and rescue organization, and other facilities required for safe international flight. It has secured much simplification of government customs, immigration, and public health regulations as they apply to international air transport. 157 states are now members of ICAO.

An Assembly of delegates from member states meets at least once every three years. A Council of 33 members is elected by the Assembly, taking into account the countries of chief importance in air transport: countries which make the largest contribution to the provision of facilities for international civil air transport and those ensuring representation of the main geographical areas of the world. The Council is the executive body, working through subsidiary committees.
President of Council, Dr. Assad Kotaite (*Lebanon*).
Secretary-General, Yves Lambert (*France*).

International Finance Corporation (IFC), 1818 H Street, Washington, D.C. 20433; *European representative*, New Zealand House, Haymarket, S.W.1.—The IFC was established in 1956 as an affiliate of the World Bank to assist less developed member countries by promoting the growth in the private sector of their economies and helping to mobilize domestic and foreign capital for this purpose. Membership of the IBRD is a prerequisite for membership in the IFC, which has 128 members. Legally and financially the IFC and IBRD are separate entities; and the Corporation has its own operating and legal staff, but draws upon the Bank for administrative and other services. IFC's share capital was $601,755,000 at June 30, 1986, and it is also empowered to borrow up to approximately $3,542,404,000 from the World Bank for use in its lending programme. At the end of June 1986, IFC had made approvals totalling more than $8,309,000 in 87 countries.
President, B. B. Conable (*U.S.A*).

International Fund for Agricultural Development (IFAD), 107 Via del Serafico, 00142 Rome, Italy.—The establishment of the Fund was proposed by the 1974 World Food Conference and it began operations in December 1977. The Fund's purpose is to mobilize additional funds for agricultural and rural development in developing countries through projects and programmes directly benefiting the poorest rural populations.

The Fund's operations are directed by the Governing Council, consisting of the entire membership. It has an 18-member Executive Board. Its governing structure provides for equal voting rights among the three groups of member countries, namely, the developed, the oil-exporting developing countries and other developing countries.
President, Idriss Jazairy (*Algeria*).

International Labour Organization (ILO) Geneva (*London Branch Office*, 96–98 Marsham Street, SW1P 4LY). Established with the League of Nations in 1919 under the Treaty of Versailles, the ILO became in 1946 the first specialized agency associated with the United Nations. In May, 1986 the Organization had 150 member States. The aim of the ILO is to promote lasting peace through social justice, and to this end it works for better economic

and social conditions everywhere. It was awarded the Nobel Peace Prize in 1969.

The ILO establishes international labour standards, which set guidelines for improving working conditions and protecting basic human rights; runs a world-wide programme of technical assistance to developing countries; conducts research and disseminates information on the human aspects of economic activity, with a view to improving social and economic well-being. Through its World Employment Programme, the ILO is attacking unemployment and its associated ills by aiding national and international efforts to provide productive work for the world's fast-growing population. It is also developing an international programme for the improvement of working conditions and the working environment.

The ILO is financed by contributions from its member states. A proportion of its budget is devoted to its technical assistance programme, but this is financed mainly by funds from UNDP and other sources. The I.L.O. budget for 1986–87 amounted to U.S.$253,000,000.

The International Labour Conference, composed of national delegations of two government delegates, one worker delegate and one employer delegate, meets at least once a year. It formulates international labour standards and broad policies of the Organization, provides a forum for discussion of world labour and social problems, and approves the ILO's work programme and budget, which is financed by member States.

A 56-member Governing Body, composed of 28 government members, 14 worker members and 14 employer members, acts as the Organization's executive council. Ten governments hold seats on the Governing Body because of their industrial importance.

The International Labour Office, the secretariat of the Organization, collects and distributes information, assists governments on request in drafting legislation on the basis of international labour standards, directs technical co-operation activities, and issues publications.

Director-General, Francis Blanchard *(France).*

International Maritime Organization (IMO),

Albert Embankment, S.E.1. A United Nations Specialized Agency established on March 17, 1958, to provide means for co-operation and exchange of information among governments on technical matters related to international shipping, especially with regard to safety at sea and preventing marine pollution caused by ships. IMO is responsible for calling maritime conferences and drafting maritime agreements. It has produced numerous technical codes relating to the carriage of various types of cargo such as chemicals, ores, and dangerous goods and to the construction and equipment of ships, e.g., gas and chemical carriers. In June, 1987, 130 nations were in membership. Budget, 1986–87, $30,059,000. (The Organization changed its name from the Inter-Governmental Maritime Consultative Organization (IMCO) on May 22, 1982.)

Secretary-General, C. P. Srivastava *(India).*

International Monetary Fund (IMF), 700 19th

Street, N.W. Washington, D.C.—Established on Dec. 27, 1945, the Fund exists to promote international monetary co-operation and the expansion of international trade; to promote exchange stability, maintain orderly exchange arrangements and avoid competitive exchange depreciations; and to assist in the establishment of a multilateral system of payments in respect of current transactions between members and in the elimination of foreign exchange restrictions which hamper world trade. 151 countries were in membership of the Fund in June, 1987.

The Fund's financial assistance takes the form of a foreign exchange transaction. The member pays to the Fund an amount of its own money equivalent to the amount of foreign currency it wishes to purchase. The member is expected to "repurchase" its own currency from the Fund, usually within three to five years, with a payment of SDR or dollars or usable currency acceptable to the Fund. These arrangements are subject to certain charges.

Currencies drawn from the Fund may be used in a flexible way to relieve the member's payments difficulty, and usually the member is expected to undertake policy changes, where needed, to correct the payment imbalance.

Each member of the Fund is assigned a quota which determines its voting power and the amount of resources that it may draw from the Fund. The subscription of each member is equal to its quota, and is payable in the member's own currency and SDRs.

Managing Director, Michel Camdessus *(France).*
U.K. Executive Director, T. P. Lankester.

International Telecommunication Union

(ITU), Place des Nations, Geneva.—Founded at Paris in 1865 as the International Telegraph Union. ITU became a U.N. Specialized Agency in 1947 and as from Jan. 1, 1984, is governed by the Convention adopted by the Torremolinos Conference held in Nairobi in 1982. ITU exists to set up international regulations for telegraph, telephone and radio services to further their development and extend their utilization by the public, at the lowest possible rates; to promote international co-operation for the improvement and rational use of telecommunications of all kinds; the development of technical facilities and their most efficient operation. ITU allocates the radio frequency spectrum and registers radio frequency assignments. It studies, recommends, collects and publishes information on telecommunication matters, including space radio communications. The Budget for 1987 is 128,000,000 *Swiss Francs.*

Secretary-General, R. E. Butler *(Australia).*

United Nations Educational, Scientific and Cultural Organization (UNESCO), 7 Place de

Fontenoy, Paris 75700.—Under its constitution, the Organization makes its contribution to peace and security by promoting collaboration among its Member States in the fields of education, science, culture and communication. It aims at furthering a universal respect for justice, for the rule of law and for human rights, without distinction of race, sex, language or religion, in accordance with the Charter of the United Nations.

The Organization is composed of three organs: (i) the *General Conference,* consisting of representatives of Member States, which meets biennially to decide the programme and budget; (ii) the *Executive Board,* composed of 51 members elected by the General Conference to supervise the execution of the approved programme and (iii) the *Secretariat,* which is responsible for Unesco's day-to-day functioning and the execution of the programme. In most Member States National Commissions serve as a link with Unesco and help to carry out the programme. Member States in June 1986, 158 and three Associate Members (British Eastern Caribbean group, Netherlands Antilles and the British Virgin Islands).

The U.K. withdrew from Unesco on Dec. 31, 1985. At its 124th session the Executive Board of Unesco decided to grant to the U.K. the observer facilities requested.

Director-General, Amadou-Mahtar M'Bow *(Senegal).*

United Nations Industrial Development Organization (UNIDO), Wagramerstrasse 5, P.O. Box 300, 1400 Vienna, Austria.—Established as an organ of the U.N. General Assembly in Nov. 1966, as an action-oriented body, replacing the Centre for Industrial Development, which had been operating since July 1961. It became a U.N. specialized agency on Jan. 1, 1986, with the aim of promoting the industrialization of developing countries, with special emphasis upon the mobilization of the manufacturing sector. U.N.I.D.O. provides help on formulation of planning policies, and technical advice and assistance to Third World countries. U.N.I.D.O.'s principal policy-making body is the Industrial Development Board, with 53 members each serving a four year term.
Director-General, Domingo Siazon (*Philippines*).

Universal Postal Union (UPU), Weltpostrasse 4, 3000 Berne 15.—Established on October 9, 1874, by the postal Convention of Berne and in operation from July 1, 1875, UPU exists to form a single postal territory of all the countries, members of the Union, for the reciprocal exchange of correspondence in order to secure the organization and improvement of the various postal services and to promote in this sphere the development of international collaboration. Every member agrees to transmit the mail of all other members by the best means used for its own mail. The Union includes almost all the countries of the world. Budget, 1987, S.Fr. 24,761,900. A Universal Postal Congress meets at five-yearly intervals. The last was held in Hamburg in June-July 1984, and the next is scheduled to take place in Washington in the autumn of 1989.
Director-General, A.C. Botto de Barros (*Brazil*).

World Health Organization (WHO), 1211 Geneva 27. Established on April 7, 1948, the aim of the World Health Organization is the attainment by all peoples of the highest possible level of health. It co-operates with its member governments in their efforts to develop health manpower, streamline health services, control communicable diseases, promote family health—including mother and child care, family planning, nutrition and health education—and strengthen environmental health. It promotes biomedical and health services research through some 850 collaborating research centres in different parts of the world. Its other services include the International Pharmacopoeia, drug evaluation and monitoring, biological standardization, epidemiological surveillance and scientific publications. Approved budget for 1988 and 1989, $633,980,000. Membership (May 1987), 166.

Organs are a World Health Assembly meeting annually to frame policy, an Executive Board (31 members), meeting at least twice a year, and a Secretariat.
Director-General, Dr. H. T. Mahler (*Denmark*).

World Intellectual Property Organization (WIPO), 34 chemin des Colombettes, 1211 Geneva 20, Switzerland.—Established by a 1967 convention to succeed the United International Bureau for the Protection of Intellectual Property. Became a specialized agency of the United Nations in 1974, and has 117 members. WIPO promotes the protection of intellectual property throughout the world through co-operation among states and, where appropriate, in collaboration with other international organizations; and ensures administrative co-operation among states in the development of various international agreements on such matters as industrial property (chiefly patents and other rights in technological inventions, rights in trademarks, industrial designs, appellations of origin, etc.) and copyright and neighbouring rights (chiefly in industrial design,

the classification of goods and services, the protection of appellations of origin, of literary and artistic works, of performers, producers of phonograms and broadcasting organizations).

The Conference and the General Assembly control the International Bureau (or secretariat). The Bureau provides the necessary documentation and other services for meetings and carries out projects for the promotion of increased international co-operation among member states.
Director-General: Arpad Bogsch (*United States*)

World Meteorological Organization (WMO), Geneva.—Came into existence in 1951. The present membership is 155 States and 5 Territories. WMO exists to facilitate world-wide co-operation in establishing networks of stations making observations related to meteorology and hydrology, and to promote the establishment and maintenance of centres providing meteorological and related services; to promote the establishment of systems for the rapid exchange of weather information; to promote standardization of meteorological observations and to ensure their uniform publication; to further the application of meteorology to aviation, shipping, water problems, agriculture, and other human activities; to promote activities in operational hydrology and to further close co-operation between meteorological and hydrological services; to encourage research and training in meteorology and to co-ordinate their international aspects. Budget (1988–91), 170,000,000 *Swiss Francs.* A World Meteorological Congress meets at least once every four years. An Executive Council (36 members), meeting at least annually, carries out the resolutions of the Congress, initiates studies and makes recommendations on matters requiring international action. Other organs are six Regional Meteorological Associations (Africa, Asia, S. America, N. and Central America, Europe and South-West Pacific), eight technical commissions and a Secretariat.
Secretary-General, G. O. P. Obasi (*Nigeria*).

RELATED ORGANISATIONS

International Atomic Energy Agency, Vienna International Centre, P.O. Box 100, A–1400, Vienna. Set up on July 29, 1957, to accelerate and enlarge the contribution of atomic energy to peace, health and prosperity throughout the world and to ensure that assistance provided by it or under its supervision is not used to further any military purpose. Agreements have been reached concerning the Agency's working relationship with the United Nations and some of the specialized agencies. In June, 1987, 112 states were members.

A General Conference of all members meets in regular annual session and in such special session as may be necessary. A Board of Governors (35 members) carries out the functions of the Agency and meets usually four times a year. The Regular Budget for 1987 amounted to $100,389,000.
Director-General, Hans Blix (*Sweden*).
Permanent U.K. Representative, M. J. Wilmshurst.

General Agreement on Tariffs and Trade (GATT), Centre William Rappard, Rue de Lausanne 154, CH-1211 Geneva 21. A multilateral treaty, in operation since 1948, to which 94 countries are parties, and one acceded provisionally; a further 30 countries apply GATT *de facto.* Its rules thus govern over four-fifths of world trade. Objectives of GATT are to expand international trade and promote economic development. GATT provides a permanent forum for discussion and solution of particular international trade problems, and for multilateral negotiations to reduce tariffs and other obstacles to the expansion of international trade. Special attention is given to trade problems of developing countries. In November 1979, participating countries concluded the Tokyo Round of multilateral trade negotiations (launched in Tokyo in September 1973) with agreements covering tariff reductions, non-tariff measures, an improved framework for the conduct of international trade, bovine meat, dairy products, tropical products, civil aircraft, and a revised GATT anti-dumping code. More recently, the GATT's work has been covering areas such as agriculture, textiles, quantitative restrictions and services. The Uruguay Round of multilateral trade negotiations was launched in October 1986 and is expected to last four years. An International Trade Centre, set up by GATT in 1964 to aid developing countries in export promotion, is now operated jointly by GATT and UNCTAD. *Director-General*, A. Dunkel (*Switzerland*).

EUROPEAN COMMUNITY

The twelve member states: Belgium, Denmark, France, Federal Republic of Germany, Greece, Ireland, Italy, Luxembourg, The Netherlands, Portugal, Spain, the United Kingdom.

The beginnings of the European Community date from May 9, 1950, when Robert Schuman, France's Foreign Minister, proposed that France and Germany should pool their coal and steel industries under an independent ("supranational") High Authority, in a Community open to the membership of any other European country wishing to join. Not only West Germany, but also Italy, Belgium, the Netherlands, and Luxembourg accepted this invitation.

The Coal and Steel Community (E.C.S.C.), European Economic Community and Euratom share a single institutional framework: a Commission, Council of Ministers, Parliament and Court of Justice. The core of the Community policymaking process is the "dialogue" between the Commission, which initiates and implements policy, and the Council of Ministers, which takes major policy decisions. The beginnings of democratic control are exercised by the European Parliament, while the Court of Justice ensures the rule of law and is the final arbiter in all matters arising from the Community Treaties.

Since the start of the European Economic Community and Euratom in 1958, the Parliament and Court of Justice have been common to all three Communities. Up to July, 1967, each Community had its own executive body (the E.E.C. and Euratom Commissions, and the E.C.S.C. High Authority) and its own Council of Ministers.

In April, 1965, the Six signed a treaty providing for the merger of the three executive bodies in a single Commission and the three Councils in a single Council, with a view to the eventual merger of the three Communities themselves. The merger treaty came into force on July 1, 1967; the single Commission and single Council then took office. They enjoy the same powers under the three Community Treaties as did their predecessors.

On December 1 and 2, 1969, the Heads of State or Government of the Six met at the Hague and decided on the completion, strengthening, and, provided that other European countries wished to accept the Treaties of Rome, enlargement of the Community. They instructed the Commission to draw up a plan for economic and monetary union, and the Foreign Ministers to report by the end of July on possible moves towards political unification. They also resolved to intensify the co-ordination of research and development programmes.

In accordance with the Hague decisions the Council of Ministers agreed in April, 1970, that as from 1975 the Community would have its own revenue, independent of national contributions. The Foreign Ministers agreed (May, 1970) to hold formal political consultations twice a year.

In June, 1970, the Six invited Britain, the Irish Republic, Denmark and Norway to open negotiations on June 30 at Luxembourg on their applications to join the Community. Negotiations continued in 1971 and were concluded with the United Kingdom Government for all major questions by the end of June; on July 8, H.M. Government issued a White Paper on the results. On Jan. 22, 1972, the four applicant countries signed the Treaty of Accession in Brussels. Norway conducted a referendum on its Common Market entry and as a result withdrew its application. The enlarged Community of the Nine came into existence on Jan. 1, 1973.

With the advent of a Labour Government in the U.K. in 1974, there followed a period of renegotiation of the terms of Britain's entry into the Community, culminating in a referendum on June 5, 1975, as to whether or not the country should remain a member of the E.C. The result of the referendum showed two to one in favour of staying in. British Labour Party representatives who had hitherto boycotted the European Parliament then took up their 18 allotted seats.

In January 1976 the European Parliament approved a Report urging direct elections to the Parliament in 1978. On July 12–13, 1976, the Heads of Government or State, meeting in European Council, decided to approve a 410 member Parliament with Britain, France, West Germany and Italy allocated 81 seats each; the Netherlands 25, Belgium 24, Denmark 16, Ireland 15 and Luxembourg 6. Because some countries (including Britain) had not passed the relevant legislation in time, the date of European Elections was postponed until June 1979. When Greece joined the E.C. in January 1981, she was allocated 24 seats in the Parliament, bringing the total number to 434. When Spain and Portugal became members in 1986, they took an additional 84 seats; Spain taking 60 and Portugal 24 making the total 518.

The "European Council", an addition to the institutionalized meetings provided under the Treaties, evolved from the "summit" conference of December 1974, when the Heads of Government decided to meet at least three times a year in order to discuss Community problems and matters requiring political co-operation.

OFFICE OF THE UNITED KINGDOM PERMANENT
REPRESENTATIVE TO THE EUROPEAN COMMUNITIES
Rond-point Robert Schuman 6, 1040 Brussels

Ambassador and U.K. Permanent Representative, Sir
David Hannay, K.C.M.G. (1985).

The Commission

On July 1, 1970, the Commission was reduced from
14 members to nine, two each from France, France
and Italy, and one each from Belgium, the Netherlands and Luxembourg. Following the 1973 enlargement, the number rose to 13, with two seats each
from Britain, France, Germany, and Italy and one
each for the other members. The admission of Greece
in 1981, with 1 seat, brought the total to 14
Commissioners. When the Community was again
enlarged in 1986, the total number of Commissioners
grew to 17, two being appointed from Spain and one
from Portugal.

The members of the Commission are appointed by
agreement among the twelve member governments
for a four-year renewable term; the president and
vice-presidents are appointed from among the members for a two-year term, also renewable.

The members of the Commission are pledged to
independence of the governments and of national or
other particular interests. They accept joint responsibility for their decisions, which are taken by
majority vote.

In addition to being the initiator of Community
action and having specific powers, the Commission
acts as a mediator between the member governments
in Community affairs and is the guardian of the
Community Treaties.

Commission of the European Communities
200 Rue de la Loi, 1049 Brussels

President, Jacques Delors (France) (from 1985).
Vice-Presidents, Frans Andriessen (Netherlands),
Henning Christophersen (Denmark), Lord Cock-
field (U.K.), Manuel Marin (Spain), Karl-Heinz
Narjes (Federal Republic of Germany), Lorenzo
Natali (Italy).
Members, Claude Cheysson (France), Antonio José
Baptista Cardoso e Cunha (Portugal), Stanley
Clinton Davis (U.K.), Willy de Clercq (Belgium),
Abel Matutes (Spain), Nicolas Mosar (Luxem-
bourg), Alois Pfeiffer (Federal Republic of Ger-
many), Carlo Ripa di Meana (Italy), Peter
Sutherland (Ireland), Grigoris Varfis (Greece).

The Commission maintains information offices in
London (8 Storey's Gate, SWIP 3AT), Edinburgh (7
Alva Street EH2 4PH), Cardiff (4 Cathedral Road),
Belfast (Windsor House, 9/15 Bedford Street), Dublin
(39 Molesworth Street), Washington (2100 M. Street,
N.W. (Suite 707), Washington, D.C. 20037, New York
(1 Dag Hammarskjöld Plaza, 245 East 47th Street,
New York, N.Y. 10017), Ottawa (Inn of the Provinces,
Office Tower (Suite 1110), 350 Sparks Street, Ontario,
KIR 7S8), and other cities.

The Council of Ministers
170 Rue de la Loi, 1048 Brussels

This consists of ministers from the governments of
each of the twelve member states, the ministers
concerned depending on the subject under discussion.
A single Council exists for the three European
Communities. It is the main decision-taking body
within the Community legislative process. The
Council acts, in almost all cases, on the basis of
proposals submitted by the Commission, which is
present at Council sessions to participate in the
shaping of the measures taken. Before examining
Commission proposals the Council normally obtains
the opinions of the European Parliament and the
Economic and Social Committee on them.

As prescribed by the E.C. treaty, under which the
great majority of the Council's business falls, decisions are taken by majority vote, qualified majority
vote (a system in which the members' votes are
weighted) or by unanimity. The Council acts under
the E.C. treaty by issuing (a) "regulations" which
are binding in their entirety and directly applicable
in all member states; (b) "directives" which are
binding as to the result to be achieved but leave open
to national governments the method of attaining this
result; (c) "decisions" which bind those addressed;
(d) "recommendations" and (e) "opinions", which
have no binding force. The Euratom treaty has the
same system of voting and taking action; the E.C.S.C.
system differs in certain respects.

The Presidency of the Council is held in rotation
for periods of six months. The sessions of the Council
are prepared by a Committee of Permanent Representatives of the member states. The Council and its
committees are serviced by a general secretariat.

European Parliament

Secretariat: Centre Européen, Kirchberg, Luxem-
bourg.
U.K. Information Office, 2 Queen Anne's Gate,
SW1H 9AA.

The first direct elections to the European Parliament were held in mid-1979, the second five years
later. Of 518 seats, the United Kingdom, France,
Germany and Italy have 81 each, Spain 60, the
Netherlands 25, Belgium, Greece, and Portugal 24,
Denmark 16, Ireland 15 and Luxembourg 6. The
Parliament meets in Strasbourg and its Committees
in Brussels. The pre-1979 Parliament consisted of 198
members nominated by their national Parliaments—
the United Kingdom, France, Germany and Italy had
36 seats each, Belgium and the Netherlands 14 each,
Denmark and Ireland 10 each and Luxembourg 6. Set
up in 1952 under the European Coal and Steel
Community Treaty of 1951, the Parliament's authority was extended by the 1957 Convention on Common
Institutions to cover the European Economic Community and Euratom. It must be consulted on all
major issues and has the right to dismiss the
Commission by a vote of censure. Apart from general
powers of supervision and consultation, it questions
the Commission and the Council of Ministers and has
a measure of control over the Community's annual
budget including its final adoption. It can reject the
budget as a whole and can amend items of non-
obligatory expenditure (i.e. expenditure not specified
in the original treaties or derived legislation—
amounting to some 27 per cent. of the total budget).

The Members of the Parliament serve on specialized committees and sit in political groups—Socialists, Christian Democrats, Liberals and Democrats, European Democrats, European Progressive Democrats and Communists. There are also a number of Independents in the Parliament.

President, Lord Plumb (*U.K.*).

European Court of Justice
L–2925 Luxembourg

The European Court superseded the Court of Justice of E.C.S.C. and is common to the three European Communities. It exists to safeguard the law in the interpretation and application of the Community treaties, to decide on the legality of decisions of the Council of Ministers or the Commission and to determine violations of the Treaties. Cases may be brought to it by the member States, the Community institutions, firms or individuals. Its decisions are directly binding in the member countries. The thirteen judges and six advocates-general of the Court are appointed for renewable six-year terms by the member Governments in concert. During 1986, 328 new cases were lodged at the court and 174 judgments were delivered.

Judges, Hon. Lord Mackenzie Stuart (*President*); Y. Galmot (*President of 3rd and 5th Chambers*); C. N. Kakouris (*President of 4th and 6th Chambers*); T. F. O'Higgins (*President of 2nd Chamber*); F. A. Schockweiler (*President of 1st Chamber*); G. Bosco; T. Koopmans; O. Due; U. Everling; K. Bahlmann; R. Joliet; J. C. de Carvalho Moitinho de Almeida; G. C. Rodriguez Iglesias.

Advocates-General, C. O. Lenz (1st *Advocate-General*); Sir Gordon Slynn; G. F. Mancini; M. Darmon; J. Mischo; J. L. da Cruz Vilaça.

Registrar, P. E. Heim.

The European Investment Bank
100 Boulevard Konrad Adenauer,
L–2950 Luxembourg

The European Investment Bank (E.I.B.) was set up in 1958 under the terms of the Treaty of Rome to finance capital investments promoting the balanced development of the European Community.

It grants long-term loans to enterprises, public authorities and financial institutions, to finance projects which assist: the development of less advanced regions, the attainment of the Community's energy policy objective, the modernisation or conversion of undertakings, development and introduction of advanced technology to improve the competitiveness of Community industry, fostering of cooperation between undertakings in different member countries, improvement of communications between member states, and other Community objectives such as protection of the environment.

E.I.B. activities have also been extended outside member countries under the terms of different association or cooperation agreements which more than 78 countries have signed with the Community.

The Bank's total financing operations in 1986 amounted to 7,545 million E.C.U.,* of which 7,071 million (including 393 million from the resources of the New Community Instrument for borrowing and lending) were for investments in the European Community and 474 million for outside the Community. Between 1973 and 1986 the E.I.B. had made available a total of £5,044 million E.C.U. for investment in the U.K.

The members of the European Investment Bank are the twelve member countries of the Community, who have all subscribed to the Bank's capital, which the Bank's Board of Governors doubled to 28,800 million E.C.U., with effect from January 1, 1986. The funds required by the Bank to carry out its tasks are borrowed on the capital markets of the Community and non-member countries, and on the international market.

As it operates on a non-profit-making basis, the interest rates charged by the E.I.B. therefore closely reflect conditions on world capital markets.

The Board of Governors of the European Investment Bank consists of Ministers nominated by the member countries, usually the Finance Minister, who lay down general directives on the policy of the Bank and appoint members to the Board of Directors (21 nominated by the member states, 1 by the Commission of the European Communities), which takes decisions on the granting and raising of loans and the fixing of interest rates. A Management Committee, also appointed by the Board of Governors, is responsible for the day-to-day operations of the Bank.

President, Ernst-Günther Bröder.

Vice-Presidents, C. Richard Ross; Arie Pais; Lucio Izzo; Noel Whelan; Alain Prate; Miguel A. Arnedo Orbañanos.

(The President and Vice-Presidents also preside as Chairman and Vice-Chairmen at meetings of the Board of Directors.)

U.K. Office: 68 Pall Mall, SW1Y 5ES.

EUROPEAN COAL AND STEEL COMMUNITY

This, the first of the European Communities, was established in 1952. Since then, for coal, iron ore and scrap, it has abolished customs duties, quantitative restrictions, the dual pricing system whereby prices charged on exported coal or steel differed from those charged to home consumers, currency restrictions and discrimination in transport rates based on the nationality of customers and the special frontier charges which made international transport of these goods within the Community dearer than transport within national frontiers. It has applied rules for fair competition and a harmonized external tariff for the whole Community.

---

* The financial statements of the European Investment Bank are drawn up in E.C.U. which at March 31, 1987 equalled ± £0·72, U.S.$1·15.

THE TREATY OF ROME

Discussions were held at Messina, Sicily, in 1955 between the foreign ministers of the six member states of E.C.S.C. (Belgium, France, Germany, Italy, Luxembourg and The Netherlands) on proposals for further advances towards economic integration in Europe, and after intensive study of these proposals, a treaty was signed at Rome on March 25, 1957, setting up the European Economic Community.

The Treaty aimed to lay the foundations of an enduring and closer union between the European peoples by gradually removing the economic effects of their political frontiers. The Treaty provides for the elimination of customs duties and quotas in trade between member states; the establishment of a common customs tariff and a common trade policy towards third countries; the abolition of the obstacles to free movement of persons, services and capital between member states; the inauguration of common policies for agriculture and transport; the establishment of a system ensuring that competition shall not be distorted in the Common Market; the co-ordination of economic policies; the harmonization of social and economic legislation to the extent necessary in order to enable the Common Market to work; the creation of a European Social Fund in order to improve the possibilities of employment for workers and to contribute to the raising of their standard of living; the establishment of an Economic and Social Committee which must be consulted on major proposals, consisting of representatives of employers, workers, consumers and other groups; the establishment of a European Investment Bank intended to aid investment in underdeveloped areas and help to finance modernization; and the association of overseas countries and territories with the Community with a view to increasing trade and to pursuing jointly their effort towards economic and social development.

ENLARGEMENT OF THE COMMUNITY

The question of possible enlargement of the Community played an important part in its development from the autumn of 1961 when Britain, the Irish Republic, Denmark and Norway first sought membership, and Austria, Sweden, Switzerland, Spain and Cyprus sought association with the Community. The negotiations were vetoed by France in January, 1963. In May, 1967, Britain, the Irish Republic and Denmark formally submitted applications for Community membership. In July Norway followed suit and Sweden announced that it would seek to participate in the enlargement of the Community on terms compatible with its neutrality. These applications made very slow progress and appeared to come to a standstill when in December, 1967, France declared that Britain's economy would have to be strengthened before negotiations could begin. But shortly after taking office as President of France, Georges Pompidou stated in July, 1969, that there was no objection in principle to the admission of Britain to the Community. At the Hague "summit" meeting in December, 1969, the Six decided that provided that the completion of the Community was not prejudiced, and provided that the Community

was strengthened to provide for enlargement, then the entry of other European countries would be desirable. After deciding on a common negotiating position, the Six invited Britain and the other applicants to begin negotiations for membership.

A single overall transitional period of five years, during which the Three were to adopt Community rules and regulations, started on January 1, 1973, giving time for the gradual integration of the economies of the Three with the Six by the end of 1977.

The first 40 per cent alignment on the Community's Common External Tariff (C.E.T.)—i.e. 40 per cent of the difference between the new members' tariffs and the C.E.T.—was made at the beginning of 1974, and three further alignments of 20 per cent each followed.

Negotiations with Greece were concluded and the Treaty of Accession signed on May 28, 1979. Greece became the tenth member of the Community on January 1, 1981. Portugal and Spain applied to join the Community and became the eleventh and twelfth members on January 1, 1986.

Following a plebiscite, Greenland negotiated its withdrawal from the E.C. (but without discontinuing relations with Denmark) formally left on February 1, 1986.

EUROPEAN ATOMIC ENERGY COMMUNITY (EURATOM)

A second treaty, arising from the Messina discussions between the E.C.S.C. powers on additional means of co-operation, was signed in Rome on March 25, 1957, setting up the European Atomic Energy Community. The task of *Euratom*, defined in detail in the Treaty, is to create within a short period the technical and industrial conditions necessary to utilize nuclear discoveries and especially to produce nuclear energy on a large scale. The United Kingdom, Denmark and Ireland joined Euratom on Jan. 1, 1973, Greece on Jan. 1, 1981, and Spain and Portugal on Jan. 1, 1986.

EUROPEAN PARLIAMENT SUMMARY, 1986–87

The European Parliament set up an all-party committee of inquiry on Sept. 11 to investigate surplus butter production in the Common Market. James Elles (Con., Oxford and Buckinghamshire), one of the M.E.P.s who pushed for the establishment of the committee, said that the Commission and the member Governments had neglected their responsibilities despite growing public concern about food "mountains".

Some M.E.P.s were embarrassed when it was announced that the second World Whores Congress was to meet at the Parliament's headquarters in Brussels on Oct. 1. The Parliament's executive committee agreed that the prostitutes could meet there as long as the Congress was clearly dissociated from the Parliament.

M.E.P.s voted 301 to 39 on Oct. 31 to block £65 million of Common Market aid to Syria in response to Britain's plea for solidarity against terrorism following the Heathrow bomb plot trial in London.

On Nov. 27 Budget Ministers of the 12 member countries set the Common Market's 1987 Budget at £22,450 million. Following an all-night session chaired by Peter Brooke, U.K. Minister of State at the Treasury, they decided on small increases in regional and social aid as proposed by the European Parliament, although the final figure was £1,560 million less than the overall spending demanded by the Parliament. The Budget Ministers rejected the M.E.P.s' proposal for a £1,500 million one-off contribution to finance the disposal of surplus food: they felt that money should not be made available for this purpose until Agriculture Ministers had decided on measures to reduce present over-production.

On Dec. 12 the Parliament voted a 1987 spending total exceeding the levels laid down by the Budget. Peter Brooke said the Parliament's decision was illegal and accused the Parliament of not having observed the proper budget procedures laid down by the European Court of Justice earlier in the year. The dispute was settled on Feb. 19 when the Parliament and the member Governments agreed on a figure of £23,600 million.

Mrs. Thatcher spoke to the European Parliament on Dec. 9 about Britain's presidency of the E.C. and of her Government's commitment to the community, pointing out that the U.K. had been among the first to ratify the Single European Act. The Prime Minister praised the agreements reached on jobs, terrorism, drugs, cancer and A.I.D.S. and she stressed the importance of the E.C. taking action to check farm spending in the months ahead, warning that the "money will soon run out". During Mrs. Thatcher's speech, Ian Paisley (D.U.P., N. Ireland) interrupted her to protest at the Anglo-Irish agreement and was suspended from the assembly.

On Jan. 20 M.E.P.s elected Sir Henry Plumb (later Lord Plumb) president of the Parliament; he is the first Briton to hold the position.

On Feb. 22 E.C. Foreign Ministers began talks on the programme for overhauling the Budget system proposed the previous week by Jacques Delors, president of the E.C. Commission. The plan aimed to end the lengthy annual battles with the European Parliament over E.C. spending, to increase Community resources through a fairer system of contributions, to reduce the large proportion of the Budget going to farmers, and to increase spending on social and regional development programmes.

In the European Parliament by-election on March 6 John Bird held the Midland West seat for Labour but the 1984 majority of over 19,500 was cut to 4,025.

On March 13 the Parliament asked for E.C. funds to build cycle paths and urged the E.C. Commission to study the causes of accidents involving cyclists. It also called on the Commission to adopt safety standards for bicycle construction similar to those in force in the United States.

30 Years Old

The European Community celebrated its 30th anniversary on March 25, with formalities in Rome and ceremonies in other E.C. capitals. However, the idea of holding a ceremonial session of the Parliament in Rome came to nought. The proposal provoked vigorous opposition because of the expense involved

and the vote on the proposal failed to win an absolute majority.

Guy Guermeur, a French M.E.P., alleged to the Parliament on April 7 that fictitious claims for distilling surplus wine were costing the Common Market tens of millions of pounds every year, some of this money going into the hands of the Mafia. M. Guermeur also claimed that about 10 per cent of the slaughter subsidies paid to farmers to reduce milk production had been obtained fraudulently and cost the E.C. Budget about £45 million, while inadequate checks at Common Market intervention stores where surplus grain was stored had resulted in low-quality cereals being bought. John Tomlinson (Lab., Birmingham West) called for the E.C. Commission to set up its own "Flying Squad" to investigate reports of fraud and to carry out spot checks.

Despite objections from all the U.K. M.E.P.s, the Parliament on May 14 voted by 148 to 76 to approve a new tax on oil and fats sold and imported into the Community. The resolution carried by the Assembly said, however, that costs should be absorbed by industry and not passed on to the consumer. The E.C. Commission stressed that the yield from the proposed tax was necessary to help balance the E.C. Budget and to correct imbalances in the oils and fats sector. Britain, West Germany, Holland, Denmark and Portugal strenuously opposed the tax and together formed a blocking minority to prevent the plan being voted through. The proposed tax on oil and fats was one of a number of measures proposed by the E.C. Commissioners to further the harmonization of V.A.T. throughout the Community. The proposals proved controversial, bringing protests from many member countries. Though the measures were scheduled to be formally approved by the Commission in July, the session was cancelled and on July 8 it emerged that the proposals were under revision.

The E.C.'s financial crisis came to the fore again on June 18 when the Parliament in Strasbourg unanimously rejected any temporary measures to deal with the 1987 Budget deficit and demanded additional funds from member Governments. The crisis arose from the failure of Agriculture Ministers to agree on savings or new taxes in the farm sector. The U.K. Government refused to make extra funds available, taking the view that the deficit could be virtually eliminated by delaying for two months reimbursements to governments for farm payments. The European Parliament's response was that it was no longer possible to accept a Budget in which real expenditure was not covered by revenue. However, an agreement on E.C. farm prices for 1987 was reached at top ministerial level on July 1. It was decided to meet the £4,000 million deficit by postponing two months of farm spending from 1987 to 1988.

On July 30 Henning Christophersen, an E.C. Budget Commissioner, stated that member governments would be given greater control over E.C. spending to ensure Budget discipline under new rules, which he outlined. He also said that the European Parliament would be assigned a larger role in fixing spending levels, pointing out that the parliament had traditionally taken a more expansionist line than Budget Ministers of the member countries.

OTHER INTERNATIONAL ORGANIZATIONS

ASSOCIATION OF SOUTH EAST ASIAN NATIONS (A.S.E.A.N.)

Central Secretariat: Jakarta, Indonesia

Formed in 1967, the main aims of the Association are the acceleration of economic growth, social progress and cultural development, the promotion of collaboration and mutual assistance in matters of common interest, and the continuing stability of the South East Asian region.

The Heads of Government of the member countries are the highest authority and give directions to A.S.E.A.N. as and when necessary. The main policy-making body is the annual meeting of Foreign Ministers of the member countries. The members of the Association are Brunei, Indonesia, Malaysia, the Philippines, Singapore and Thailand.

Sec. Gen., Roderick Yong (*Brunei*).

BANK FOR INTERNATIONAL SETTLEMENTS

(1930), Centrebahnplatz 2, 4002 Basle, Switzerland.

The objectives of the Bank are to promote the co-operation of central banks; to provide facilities for international financial operations; and to act as trustee or agent in international financial settlements entrusted to it. The London agent is the Bank of England, and the Governor of the Bank of England is a member of the Board of Directors, in which administrative control is vested.

Chairman of the Board of Directors and President of the Bank for International Settlement, Jean Godeaux (*Belgium*), from Jan. 1, 1985.

C.A.B. INTERNATIONAL
Wallingford, Oxon. OX10 8DE
[0491-32111]

C.A.B. International (formerly the Commonwealth Agricultural Bureaux) was founded in 1929. It consists of four Institutes and ten Bureaux under the control of an Executive Council comprising representatives of the countries which contribute to its funds. The functions of C.A.B.I. are to provide a scientific information service, identification of pests; biological control services and mutual assistance. Each Institute and Bureau acts as an effective clearing house for the collection, collation and dissemination of information in its particular branch of agricultural science.

Chairman, K. Tavola (*Fiji*).
Vice-Chairman, F. Madzima (*Zimbabwe*).
Director General, D. Mentz.

CARIBBEAN COMMUNITY AND COMMON MARKET (CARICOM)

P.O. Box 10827, Georgetown, Guyana

CARICOM was established on 1973 with three objectives: economic co-operation through the Caribbean Common Market; the co-ordination of foreign policy among the independent member states; the provision of common services and co-operation in functional matters such as health, education and culture, communications and industrial relations. The principal organs are the Conference of Heads of Government, which determines policy, and the Common Market Council of Ministers, consisting of Ministers of Government (usually Ministers of Trade) designated by each member state, which is responsible for the development and smooth running of the Common Market and for the settlement of any problems arising out of its functioning. The principal administrative arm is the Secretariat, based in Guyana.

The 13 member states are Antigua and Barbuda, The Bahamas, Barbados, Belize, Dominica, Grenada, Guyana, Jamaica, Montserrat, St. Christopher and Nevis, St. Lucia, St. Vincent and the Grenadines and Trinidad and Tobago. The Dominican Republic and Haiti have observer status.

Sec. Gen., Roderick Rainford (*Jamaica*).

COUNCIL FOR MUTUAL ECONOMIC ASSISTANCE (C.M.E.A. OR COMECON)

56 Kalinin Avenue, Moscow G–205, U.S.S.R

Established in 1949, the Council's aim is to promote the development of the national economies of the member states and the development of socialist economic integration, through the co-operation of members in the most rational use of resources and the acceleration of economic and technical progress, industrialisation and productivity. The highest body is the Session of the Council, which consists of delegations from all member states, usually led by the heads of government. The Executive Committee consists of representatives of member states at the level of deputy heads of government, and is responsible for the implementation of the tasks set by the Session of the Council and for directing the work of the Committees, Standing Commissions, Secretariat and other bodies.

The member countries are Bulgaria, Cuba, Czechoslovakia, German Democratic Republic, Hungary, Mongolia, Poland, Romania, U.S.S.R. and Vietnam. Yugoslavia participates in the work of some C.M.E.A. bodies and representatives from Angola, Afghanistan, Yemen, Laos, Mozambique, Nicaragua and Ethiopia take part in the work of some C.M.E.A. bodies in the capacity of observers. There are also co-operation agreements with Finland, Iraq, Mexico, Mozambique and Nicaragua.

THE COUNCIL OF EUROPE

Headquarters: 67006 Strasbourg, France.

A European organization founded in 1949 whose aim is to achieve greater unity between its members to safeguard their European heritage and to facilitate their economic and social progress through discussion and common action in economic, social, cultural, educational, scientific, legal and administrative matters and in the maintenance and furtherance of human rights and fundamental freedoms.

The 21 members are Austria, Belgium, Cyprus, Denmark, France, the Federal Republic of Germany, Greece, Iceland, the Republic of Ireland, Italy, Liechtenstein, Luxembourg, Malta, Netherlands, Norway, Portugal, Spain, Sweden, Switzerland, Turkey and the U.K.

The organs are the Committee of Ministers, consisting of the Foreign Ministers of member countries, who meet twice yearly, and the Parliamentary Assembly of 170 members, elected or chosen by the national parliaments of member countries in proportion to the relative strength of political parties. There is also a Joint Committee of Ministers and Representatives of the Parliamentary Assembly.

The Committee of Ministers is the executive organ of the Council. The majority of its conclusions take the form of international agreements (known as European Conventions) or recommendations to governments. Decisions of the Ministers may also be embodied in partial agreements to which a limited number of member governments are party. Member governments accredit Permanent Representatives to the Council in Strasbourg, who are also the Ministers' Deputies. The Committee of Deputies meets every month to transact business and to take decisions on behalf of Ministers.

The Parliamentary Assembly holds three week-long sessions a year. It debates reports on, *inter alia*, political, economic, agricultural, social, educational, legal and regional planning affairs, and also reports received annually from the O.E.C.D., other European organisations and certain specialised agencies of the United Nations. Its 13 permanent committees meet, normally in private, once or twice between each public plenary session of the Assembly. The Standing Conference of Local and Regional Authorities of Europe each year brings together mayors and municipal councillors in the same numbers as the members of the Parliamentary Assembly.

One of the principal achievements of the Council of Europe is the European Convention of Human Rights (1950) under which was established the European Commission and the European Court of Human Rights. 124 other conventions and agreements have now been concluded. They include the European Social Security Code, and conventions on extradition, the legal status of migrant workers, conservation, and the transfer of sentenced prisoners.

Non-member states take part in certain Council of Europe activities on a regular or ad hoc basis; thus Finland, San Marino and the Holy See participate in all the educational, cultural and sports activities. The European Youth Foundation funds events in both Eastern and Western European countries and in some outside Europe, while nationals of these countries attend courses and seminars at the European Youth Centre.

Secretary General, Marcelino Oreja (*Spain*).

Permanent U.K. Representative, His Excellency Colin McLean, C.M.G., M.B.E.

EUROPEAN FREE TRADE ASSOCIATION (E.F.T.A.)

The members of the European Free Trade Association, which was established on May 3, 1960, are Austria, Finland (an associate from 1960 to 1985 and a member since Jan. 1, 1986), Iceland (since March 1, 1970), Norway, Sweden and Switzerland.

In 1973 all the E.F.T.A. Member States entered into a new relationship with the E.C. Two—Denmark and the United Kingdom—withdrew from E.F.T.A. at the end of December 1972 to become members of the E.C. on January 1, 1973. Agreements establishing industrial free trade between all other E.F.T.A. Member States and the enlarged E.C. came into force on that same date. Similar agreements with Norway and Finland came into force on July 1, 1973, and Jan. 1, 1974, respectively. On Jan. 1, 1986 Portugal became a member of the E.C. The free trade agreements therefore now apply to trade between the six countries remaining in E.F.T.A. and Portugal.

E.F.T.A.'s first objective was free trade between its original members and this was realized at the end of 1966. Its second objective was the creation of a single market to include all Western European countries, achieved through the free trade agreements.

The final abolition of tariffs on E.F.T.A.–E.C. trade was marked by a meeting in Luxembourg in April 1984 when ministers from all E.F.T.A. and E.C. countries met. They agreed on general guidelines for greatly increased co-operation between their countries. The emphasis was on the removal of technical barriers to trade and the simplification of the origin rules which determine which products may be traded free of duty. A start was made towards multilateral co-operation in research and development as a means of strengthening the industrial potential of Western Europe, and multilateral efforts to protect the environment are under discussion.

All E.F.T.A. and E.C. countries have co-operated in a successful attempt to simplify border formalities for trade in goods in Western Europe: new multilateral conventions provide for the use of a single administrative document for customs purposes and for the introduction of a common transit procedure.

The Council of E.F.T.A. meets every two weeks at the level of the heads of the permanent national delegations to E.F.T.A. and usually twice a year at the level of ministers. Each state has a single vote and recommendations must normally be unanimous. Decisions of the Council are binding on member countries.

Secretary-General, Per Kleppe (Norway) 9–11 Rue de Varembé, 1211 Geneva 20 (*Secretary General from April 16, 1988,* Georg Reisch (*Austria*)).

LEAGUE OF ARAB STATES

37 Av. Khereddine Pacha, Tunis, Tunisia

The purpose of the League of Arab States (founded 1945) is to ensure co-operation among member states and protect their independence and sovereignty, to supervise the affairs and interests of Arab countries and to control the execution of agreements concluded among the member states. The League considers itself a regional organization and is an observer at the United Nations.

Member states are Algeria, Bahrain, Djibouti, Iraq, Jordan, Kuwait, Lebanon, Libya, Mauritania, Morocco, Oman, Palestine, Qatar, Saudi Arabia, Somalia, Sudan, Syria, Tunisia, United Arab Emirates, Arab Republic of Yemen and Democratic Republic of Yemen. (The membership of Egypt, a founder state, was suspended in 1979.)

Secretary-General, Chedli Klibi (*Tunisia*).

U.K. OFFICE.—Arab Information Centre, 52 Green Street, WIY 3RH.

NORTH ATLANTIC TREATY ORGANIZATION

Headquarters: Brussels 1110, Belgium.
Secretary General, Lord Carrington (*United Kingdom*).

The North Atlantic Treaty was signed on April 4, 1949, by the Foreign Ministers of twelve nations. The twelve are Belgium, Canada, Denmark, France, Iceland, Italy, Luxembourg, the Netherlands, Norway, Portugal, the United Kingdom and United States. Greece and Turkey acceded to the Treaty in 1952, the Federal Republic of Germany in 1955, and Spain in 1982. The North Atlantic Council, chaired by the Secretary General, is the highest authority of the Alliance and is composed of permanent representatives of the sixteen member countries. It meets at ministerial level (Foreign Ministers) at least twice per year. The permanent representatives (Ambassadors) head national delegations of advisers and experts.

Defence matters are dealt with in the Defence Planning Committee (D.P.C.), composed of representatives of all member countries, except France. Within the specialized field of defence, the D.P.C. has the same functions and authority as the Council. Like the Council it meets regularly at ambassador level and twice a year in ministerial sessions, when the nations are represented by their Defence Ministers.

The Council/D.P.C., as a unique forum for confidential and constant inter-governmental consultation and as the main decision-making body within the

North Atlantic Alliance, is assisted by an International Staff, divided into five divisions: Political Affairs; Defence Planning and Policy; Defence Support; Infrastructure, Logistics and Civil Emergency Planning; Scientific Affairs.

U.K. Permanent Representative, His Excellency Michael O'D. B. Alexander, c.m.g.

The senior military authority in N.A.T.O., under the Council and D.P.C., is the Military Committee composed of the Chief of Defence of each member country except France and Iceland. The Military Committee, which is assisted by an international military staff, functions in permanent session with permanent military representatives and is responsible for making recommendations to the Council and Defence Planning Committee on measures considered necessary for the common defence of the N.A.T.O. area and for supplying guidance on military matters to the major N.A.T.O. Commanders.

Chairman of the Military Committee, Gen. Wolfgang Altenburg (*Federal Republic of Germany*).

The strategic area covered by the North Atlantic Treaty is divided among three Commands (European, Atlantic and Channel) and a Regional Planning Group (Canada and the United States).

The Major N.A.T.O Commanders are responsible for the development of defence plans for their respective areas, for the determination of force requirements and for the deployment and exercise of the forces under their command. The Major N.A.T.O. Commanders report to the Military Committee.

The three Major N.A.T.O Commanders are:

Supreme Allied Commander, Europe, Gen. John R. Galvin (*U.S.*).

Supreme Allied Commander, Atlantic, Adm. Lee Baggett, Jr. (*U.S.*).

Commander-in-Chief, Channel, Adm. Sir Julian Oswald (*U.K.*).

ORGANIZATION FOR ECONOMIC CO-OPERATION AND DEVELOPMENT

Headquarters: 2, rue André-Pascal, 75116 Paris.
Secretary-General, Jean-Claude Paye (*France*).

Formed on September 30, 1961, the O.E.C.D. replaced the Organization for European Economic Co-operation (O.E.E.C). The O.E.C.D. is the instrument for international co-operation among industrialized member countries on economic and social policies. Its objectives are to assist its member governments in the formulation and co-ordination of policies designed to achieve high, sustained economic growth while maintaining financial stability, to contribute to world trade on a multilateral basis and to stimulate members' aid to developing countries.

The following countries belong to the O.E.C.D.: Australia, Austria, Belgium, Canada, Denmark, Federal Republic of Germany, Finland, France, Greece, Iceland, Irish Republic, Italy, Japan, Luxembourg, the Netherlands, New Zealand, Norway, Portugal, Spain, Sweden, Switzerland, Turkey, U.K. and U.S.A. (Yugoslavia participates with a special status).

The Council is the supreme body of the Organization. Composed of one representative for each member country, it meets at Permanent Representative level under the Chairmanship of the Secretary General, or at Ministerial level (usually once a year) under the Chairmanship of a Minister elected annually. Decisions and Recommendations are adopted by mutual agreement of all members of the Council. Fourteen members of the Council are chosen annually to form an Executive Committee to assist the Council. However, most of the O.E.C.D.'s work is undertaken in over 200 specialized committees and working parties. Five autonomous or semi-autonomous bodies are related in varying degrees to the Organization:

the Nuclear Energy Agency, the International Energy Agency, the Development Centre, the Centre for Educational Research and Innovation, and the European Conference of Ministers of Transport. These bodies, the committees and the Council are serviced by an international Secretariat headed by the Secretary-General of the Organization.

U.K. Permanent Representative, Nicholas Peter Bayne, c.m.g., 19 rue de Franqueville, Paris 75116.

ORGANIZATION OF AFRICAN UNITY (O.A.U.)

P.O. Box 3243, Addis Ababa, Ethiopia

The Organization of African Unity was established in 1963 and has 50 members. It aims to further African unity and solidarity, to co-ordinate political, economic, social and defence policies, and to eliminate colonialism in Africa.

The chief organs are the Assembly of heads of state or government and the Council of Foreign Ministers. The main administrative body is the Secretariat, based in Addis Ababa.

Sec. Gen., Ide Oumarou (Niger).

ORGANIZATION OF AMERICAN STATES (O.A.S.)

17th Street and Constitution Ave. N.W., Washington D.C. 20006, U.S.A.

Originally founded in 1890 for largely commercial purposes, the O.A.S adopted its present name and charter in 1948. Its aims are to strengthen the peace and security of the continent; to prevent possible causes of difficulties and to ensure the pacific settlement of disputes that may arise among the member states; to provide for common action on the part of those states in the event of aggression; to seek the solution of political, judicial and economic problems that may arise among them; and to promote, by co-operative action, their economic, social and cultural development. The O.A.S. is a regional organization within the United Nations.

Policy is determined by the annual General Assembly. Meetings of Ministers of Foreign Affairs consider urgent problems, and advise in cases of armed attack and threats to peace.

The 32 member states are Antigua and Barbuda, Argentina, Bahamas, Barbados, Bolivia, Brazil, Chile, Colombia, Costa Rica, Cuba, Dominica, Dominican Republic, Ecuador, El Salvador, Grenada, Guatemala, Haiti, Honduras, Jamaica, Mexico, Nicaragua, Panama, Paraguay, Peru, St. Christopher and Nevis, St. Lucia, St. Vincent and the Grenadines, Suriname, Trinidad and Tobago, U.S.A., Uruguay and Venezuela.

Secretary-General, João Clemente Baena Soares (*Brazil*).

ORGANIZATION OF THE PETROLEUM EXPORTING COUNTRIES (O.P.E.C.)

Obere Donaustrasse 93, A-1020 Vienna, Austria

The Organization of the Petroleum Exporting Countries was created in 1960 as a permanent intergovernmental organization with the aims of unifying and co-ordinating the petroleum policies of members and determining the best means of protecting their interests, individually and collectively.

The supreme authority is the Conference of Ministers of Oil, Mines and Energy of member countries hich meets at least twice a year and formulates policy. The Board of Governors, nominated by member countries, directs the management of

O.P.E.C. and implements Conference resolutions. The Secretariat, based in Vienna, carries out executive functions under the direction of the Board of Governors.

The 13 member countries are Algeria, Ecuador, Gabon, Indonesia, Iran, Iraq, Kuwait, Libya, Nigeria, Qatar, Saudi Arabia, U.A.E. and Venezuela.

THE WORLD COUNCIL OF CHURCHES

150 route de Ferney, CH–1211 Geneva 20, Switzerland

General-Secretary, Dr. Emilio Castro (*Uruguay*).

The World Council of Churches was constituted in Amsterdam in 1948 to promote unity between the many different Christian churches. The 307 member churches of the W.C.C. have adherents in more than 100 countries. With the exception of Roman Catholicism, virtually all Christian traditions are included in the W.C.C. membership.

The policies of the Council are determined by delegates of the member churches meeting in Assembly, about every 10 years, the last Assembly being in Vancouver in 1983. More detailed decisions are taken by a 150-member Central Committee which is elected by the Assembly and meets, with the seven W.C.C. Presidents, annually. The Central Committee in turn appoints a smaller Executive Committee and also nominates commissions and working groups, and guides the various programmes. The implementation of the policies laid down by the churches and the coordination of the 14 programmes are the responsibility of the General Secretariat.

British Council of Churches, 2 Eaton Gate, SW1N 9BL.

CURRENCIES OF THE WORLD

Country	Monetary Unit	Denomination in Circulation	
		Notes	Coins
Afghanistan	Afghani of 100 Puls	Afghanis 1,000, 500, 100, 50, 20, 10	Afghanis 5, 2, 1; Puls 50, 25
Albania	Lek of 100 Qindarka	Leks 100, 50, 25, 10, 5, 3, 1	Lek 1: Qindarka 50, 20, 10, 5
Algeria...........	Dinar of 100 Centimes	Dinars 200, 100, 50, 20, 10, 5	Dinars 5, 1; Centimes 50, 20, 10, 5, 2, 1
Angola	Kwanza of 100 Lweis	Kwanzas 1,000, 500, 100, 50, 20	Kwanzas 20, 10, 5, 2, 1; Lweis 50
Argentina	Austral of 100 Centavos or 1,000 Pesos	Australes 100, 50, 10, 5, 1	Centavos 50, 10, 5, 1
Australia	Dollar of 100 Cents	$A 100, 50, 20, 10, 5, 2, 1	$A200, 10; Cents 50, 20, 10, 5, 2, 1
Austria	Schilling of 100 Groschen	Schilling 1,000, 500, 100, 50, 20	Schilling 1,000, 500, 100, 50, 25, 20, 10, 5, 1; Groschen 50, 10, 5, 2, 1
Bahamas	Bahamian Dollar of 100 Cents	B$ 100, 50, 20, 10, 5, 3, 1; Cents 50	B$ 5, 2, 1; Cents 50, 25, 15, 5, 1
Bahrain	Dinar of 1,000 Fils	Dinars 20, 10, 5, 1, ½	Fils 100, 50, 25, 10, 5
Bangladesh	Taka of 100 Poisha	Taka 500, 100, 50, 20, 10, 5, 1	Taka 1; Poisha 50, 25, 10, 5, 2, 1
Barbados	Barbados Dollar of 100 Cents	BDS$100, 20, 10, 5, 2, 1	BDS$1; Cents 25, 10, 5, 1
Belgium	Belgian Franc of 100 Centimes	Frs. 5,000, 1,000, 500, 100, 50	Frs. 500, 20, 5, 1; Centimes 50
Belize	Dollar of 100 Cents	$100, 20, 10, 5, 1	Cents 50, 25, 10, 5, 1
Benin	Franc C.F.A.	Frs. 10,000, 5,000, 1,000, 500, 100, 50	Frs. 100, 50, 25, 10, 5, 2, 1
Bermuda	Bermuda Dollar of 100 Cents	$100, 50, 20, 10, 5, 1	$5, 1; Cents 50, 25, 10, 5, 1
Bolivia	Peso of 100 Centavos	Pesos 100,000, 50,000, 10,000, 5,000, 1,000, 500, 100, 50, 20, 10, 5, 1	Peso 1; Centavos 50, 25, 20, 10, 5
Botswana	Pula of 100 Thebe	Pula 20, 10, 5, 2, 1	Pula 1; Thebe 50, 25, 10, 5, 2, 1
Brazil	Cruzado (= 1,000 old Cruzeiros)	(see p. 803)	
Brunei	Brunei Dollar of 100 Sen	$1,000, 500, 100, 50, 10, 5, 1	Sen 50, 20, 10, 5, 1
Bulgaria	Lev of 100 Stotinki	Léva 20, 10, 5, 2, 1	Léva 2, 1; Stotinki 50, 20, 10, 5, 2, 1
Burkina	Franc C.F.A.	Frs. 10,000, 5,000, 1,000, 500, 100, 50	Frs. 100, 50, 25, 10, 5, 2, 1
Burma	Kyat of 100 Pyas	Kyats 100, 25, 10, 5, 1	Kyat 1; Pyas 50, 25, 10, 5, 1
Burundi..........	Burundi Franc	Frs. 5,000, 1,000, 500, 100, 50, 20, 10	Frs. 10, 5, 1
Cameroon	Franc C.F.A.	Frs. 10,000, 5,000, 1,000, 500, 100	Frs. 500, 100, 50, 25, 10, 5, 2, 1
Canada...........	Dollar of 100 Cents	$1,000, 100, 50, 20, 10, 5, 2, 1	$1; Cents 50, 25, 10, 5, 1
Cape Verde Is.	Escudo of 100 Centavos	Esc 1,000$00, 500$00, 100$00	Esc 50$00, 20$00, 10$00, 2$50, 1$00, Centavos $50, $20
Cayman Islands ...	Cayman Is. Dollar of 100 Cents	$100, 40, 25, 10, 5, 1	Cents 25, 10, 5, 1
Central African Republic	Franc C.F.A.	Frs. 10,000, 5,000, 1,000, 500, 100	Frs. 500, 100, 50, 25, 10, 5, 2, 1
Chad	Franc C.F.A.	Frs. 10,000, 5,000, 1,000, 500, 100	Frs. 500, 100, 50, 25, 10, 5, 2, 1
Chile.............	New Peso of 100 Centavos	Pesos 5,000, 1,000, 500	Pesos 100, 50, 10, 5, 1
China	Renminbi or Yuan of 10 Jiao or 100 Fen	Yuan 10, 5, 2, 1; Jiao 5, 2, 1	Fen 5, 2, 1
Colombia	Peso of 100 Centavos	Pesos 2,000, 1,000, 500, 200, 100, 50, 20, 10, 5, 2, 1	Pesos 10, 5, 2, 1; Centavos 50, 25, 20, 10
Comoros..........	Franc KMF	Frs. 5,000, 1,000, 500	
Congo............	Franc C.F.A.	Frs. 10,000, 5,000, 1,000, 500, 100	Frs. 500, 100, 50, 25, 10, 5, 2, 1
Costa Rica	Colon of 100 Céntimos	Colones 1,000, 500, 100, 50, 20, 10, 5	Colones 25, 20, 10, 5, 2, 1; Céntimos 50, 25, 10, 5
Côte d'Ivoire......	Franc C.F.A.	Frs. 10,000, 5,000, 1,000, 500, 100, 50	Frs. 100, 50, 25, 10, 5, 2, 1
Cuba	Peso of 100 Centavos	Pesos $100, 50, 20, 10, 5, 1	Centavos 40, 20, 5, 3, 2, 1
Cyprus	Cyprus Pound of 100 Cents	£10, 5, 1; Cents 50	Cents 20, 10, 5, 2, 1, ½
Czechoslovakia ...	Koruna (Crown) of 100 Haléru (Heller)	Kcs 1,000, 500, 100, 50, 20, 10	Kcs 5, 2, 1; Heller 50, 20, 10, 5, 1

Country	Monetary Unit	Denomination in Circulation	
		Notes	Coins
Denmark	*Krone* of 100 *Öre*	*Kroner* 1,000, 500, 100, 50, 20	*Kroner* 10, 5, 1; *Öre* 25, 10, 5
Dominican Republic	*Peso* of 100 *Centavos*	*RD*$1,000, 500, 100, 50, 20, 10, 5, 1	*Peso* 1; *Centavos* 50, 25, 10, 5, 1
East Caribbean Territory	*East Caribbean Dollar* of 100 *Cents*	$100, 20, 5, 1	*Cents* 50, 25, 10, 5, 2, 1
Ecuador	*Sucre* of 100 *Centavos*	*Sucres* 1,000, 500, 100, 50, 20, 10, 5	*Sucre* 1; *Centavos* 50, 20, 10
Egypt	*Egyptian Pound* of 100 *Piastres* or 1,000 *Millièmes*	*£E.*100, 20, 10, 5, 1, ½, ¼; *Piastres* 10, 5	*£E.*5, 1; *Piastres* 20, 10, 5, 2, 1; *Millièmes* 10, 5
El Salvador	*Colon* of 100 *Centavos*	*Colones* 100, 50, 25, 10, 5, 2, 1	*Centavos* 50, 25, 10, 5, 3, 2, 1
Equatorial Guinea	*Franc C.F.A.*	*Frs.* 10,000, 5,000, 1000, 500, 100	*Frs.* 500, 100, 50, 25, 10, 5, 1
Ethiopia..........	*Ethiopian Birr* of 100 *Cents*	*Eth. Birr* 100, 50, 10, 5, 1	*Cents* 50, 25, 10, 5, 1
Falkland Islands ..	*Pound* of 100 *Pence*	£20, 10, 5, 1	*Pence* 50, 20, 10, 5, 2, 1 U.K. coins are also in circulation except the £1, 50p, 20p
Faröe Islands	*Kronur* of 100 *Öre*	*Kr.* 1,000, 500, 100, 50, 10	As in Denmark
Fiji	*Fiji Dollar* of 100 *Cents*	$20, 10, 5, 2, 1	*Cents* 50, 20, 10, 5, 2, 1
Finland	*Markka* of 100 *Penniä*	*Mk.* 500, 100, 50, 10, 5, 1	*Mk.* 5, 1; *P.* 50, 20, 10, 5, 1
France	*Franc* of 100 *Centimes*	*Francs* 500, 200, 100, 50, 20, 10	*Francs* 10, 5, 2, 1, ½; *Centimes* 20, 10, 5
Gabon............	*Franc C.F.A.*	*Frs.* 10,000, 5,000, 1,000, 500, 100	*Frs.* 500, 100, 50, 25, 10, 5, 2, 1
Gambia	*Dalasi* of 100 *Bututs*	*Dalasis* 25, 10, 5, 1	*Dalasi* 1; *Bututs* 50, 25, 10, 5, 1
Germany (Democratic Republic of)	*Mark der Deutschen Demokratischen Republik* of 100 *Pfennig*	*M* 100, 50, 20, 10, 5	*M* 20, 10, 5, 2, 1; *Pfennig* 50, 20, 10, 5, 1
Germany (Federal Republic of)	*Deutsche Mark* of 100 *Pfennig*	*DM* 1,000, 500, 100, 50, 20, 10, 5	*DM* 10, 5, 2, 1; *Pfennig* 50, 10, 5, 2, 1
Ghana	*Cedi* of 100 *Pesewas*	*Cedis* 200, 100, 50, 20, 10, 5, 2, 1	*Cedis* 1; *Pesewas* 50, 20, 10, 5, 2½, 1, ½
Gibraltar	*Pound* of 100 *Pence*	£20, 10, 5, 1	As in U.K.
Greece	*Drachma* of 100 *Lepta*	*Drachmae* 5,000, 1,000, 500, 100, 50	*Drachmae* 20, 10, 5, 2, 1; *Lepta* 50, 20, 10
Guatemala	*Quetzal* of 100 *Centavos*	*Quetzales* 100, 50, 20, 10, 5, 1; *Centavos* 50	*Centavos* 25, 10, 5, 1
Guinea	*Franc Guineen* of 100 *Centimes*	*Francs Guineen* 5,000, 1,000, 500, 100, 50, 25	—
Guinea-Bissau	*Escudos* of 100 *Centavos*	*Esc.* 1,000$00, 500$00, 100$00, 50$00	*Esc.* 20$00, 5$00, 2$50, 1$00 *Centavos* $50
Guyana	*Guyana Dollar* of 100 *Cents*	*Dollars* 20, 10, 5, 1	*Cents* 100, 50, 25, 10, 5, 1
Haiti.............	*Gourde* of 100 *Centimes**	*Gourdes* 500, 250, 100, 50, 10, 5, 2, 1	*Gourdes* 1,000, 200, 100, 50, 25, 20, 10, 5; *Centimes* 50, 20, 10, 5
Honduras	*Lempira* of 100 *Centavos*	*Lempiras* 100, 50, 20, 10, 5, 2, 1	*Centavos* 50, 20, 10, 5, 2, 1
Hong Kong	*Hong Kong Dollar* of 100 *Cents*	*HK Dollars* 1,000, 500, 100, 50, 20, 10; *Cents* 1	*HK Dollars* 5, 2, 1; *Cents* 50, 20, 10, 5
Hungary	*Forint* of 100 *Fillér*	*Forints* 500, 100, 50, 20, 10	*Forints* 100, 20, 10, 5, 2, 1; *Fillér* 50, 20, 10, 5, 2
Iceland...........	*Króna* of 100 *Aurar*	*Kr.* 5,000, 1,000, 500, 100, 50, 10	*Kr.* 5, 1; *Aurar* 50, 10, 5
India.............	*Rupee* of 100 *Paise*	*Rs.* 100, 50, 20, 10, 5, 2, 1	*Rs.* 2, 1; *Paise* 50, 25, 20, 10, 5
Indonesia	*Rupiah* of 100 *Sen*	*Rupiahs* 10,000, 5,000, 1,000, 500, 100; *Sen* 50, 25, 10, 5, 1	*Rupiahs* 100, 50, 25, 10, 5, 2, 1
Iran	*Rial* of 100 *Dinars*	*Rials* 10,000, 5,000, 1,000, 500, 200, 100	*Rials* 50, 20, 10, 5, 2, 1
Iraq..............	*Iraqi Dinar* of 1000 *Fils*	*Dinars* 25, 10, 5, 1, ½, ¼	*Fils* 100, 50, 25, 10, 5, 1
Ireland (Republic of)	*Pound* of 100 *Pence*	£20, 10, 5, 1	*New Pence* 50, 10, 5, 2, 1, ½
Israel	*New Israel Shekel* of 100 *Agora*	*NIS* 50, 10, 5, 1	*Agora* 10, 5, 1
Italy	*Lira* of 100 *Centesimi*	*Lire* 100,000, 50,000, 20,000, 10,000, 5,000, 2,000, 1,000	*Lire* 1,000, 500, 200, 100, 50, 20, 10, 5, 2, 1
Jamaica	*Jamaican Dollar* of 100 *Cents*	$20, 10, 5, 2, 1	$1, *Cents* 50, 25, 20, 10, 5, 1
Japan	*Yen*	*Yen* 10,000, 5,000, 1,000, 500	*Yen* 500, 100, 50, 10, 5, 1
Jordan (Hashemite Kingdom of)	*Jordanian Dinar* of 1,000 *Fils*	*J. D.* 20, 10, 5, 1; *Fils* 500	*Fils* 250, 100, 50, 25, 20, 10, 5, 1

Country	Monetary Unit	Denomination in Circulation	
		Notes	Coins
Kenya	*Kenya Shilling* of 100 *Cents*	*Shillings* 100, 50, 20, 10, 5	*Shillings* 1; *Cents* 50, 10, 5
Korea, North (Democratic People's Republic of)	*Won* of 100 *Chon*	*Won* 100, 50, 10, 5, 1	*Chon* 50, 10, 5, 1
Korea, South (Republic of)	*Won* of 100 *Jeon*	*Won* 10,000, 5,000, 1,000, 500	*Won* 500, 100, 50, 10, 5, 1
Kuwait	*Kuwaiti Dinar* of 1,000 *Fils*	*Dinars* 20, 10, 5, 1, ½, ¼	*Fils* 100, 50, 20, 10, 5, 1
Laos	*Kip* of 100 *Ats*	*Kips* 500, 200, 50, 20, 10	—
Lebanon	*Lebanese Pound* of 100 *Piastres*	*LL.* 250, 100, 50, 25, 10, 5, 1	*LL.* 1; *Piastres* 50, 25, 10, 5, 2½, 1
Liberia	*Liberian* $ of 100 *Cents*	$20, 10, 5, 1 (U.S. notes)	$5, 1; *Cents* 50, 25, 10, 5, 1*
Libya	*Libyan Dinar* of 1,000 *Dirhams*	*LD.* 10, 5, 1, ½, ¼	*Dirham* 100, 50, 20, 10, 5, 1
Luxembourg	*Franc*†	*Francs* 100, 50, 20	*Francs* 250, 100, 20, 10, 5, 1, ½
Macao	*Pataca* of 100 *Avos*	*Patacas* 500, 100, 50, 10, 5	*Patacas* 5, 1; *Avos* 50, 20, 10
Madagascar	*Franc Malgache* (*F.M.G.*)	*Frs.* 10,000, 5,000, 1,000, 500, 100, 50	*Frs.* 100, 50, 20, 10, 5, 2, 1
Malawi	*Kwacha* of 100 *Tambala*	*K.* 20, 10, 5, 1; *Tambala* 50	*Tambala* 20, 10, 5, 2, 1
Malaysia	*Malaysian Dollar* (*Ringgit*) of 100 *Cents* (*Sen*)	*Dollars* 1,000, 500, 100, 20, 10, 5, 1	*Dollar* 1; *Cents* 50, 20, 10, 5, 1
Maldive Islands	*Rufiyaa* of 100 *Laris*	*Rupees* 100, 50, 10, 5, 2, 1, ½	—
Mali	*Franc C.F.A.*	*Frs.* 10,000, 5,000, 1,000, 500, 100, 50	*Frs.* 100, 50, 25, 10, 5, 2, 1
Malta	*Maltese Lira* of 100 *Cents* or 1,000 *Mils*	*Lm* 20, 10, 5, 2	*Lm* 100, 50, 25, 20, 10, 5, 4, 2, 1; *Cents* 50, 25, 10, 5, 2, 1; *Mils* 5
Mauritania	*Ouguiya* of 5 *Khoums*	*UM* 1,000, 500, 200, 100	*UM* 20, 10, 5, 1, ⅕
Mauritius	*Rupee* of 100 *Cents*	*Rs.* 50, 25, 10, 5	*Rupee* 1; *Cents* 50, 25, 10, 5, 2, 1
Mexico	*Peso* (*$*) of 100 *Centavos*	*Pesos* 10,000, 5,000, 2,000, 1,000, 500, 100, 50, 20	*Pesos* 10, 5, 1; *Centavos* 50, 20, 10
Monaco	*Franc* of 100 *Centimes*	As in France	*Francs* 50, 10, 5, 1, ½; *Centimes* 20, 10
Mongolian People's Republic	*Tugrik* of 100 *Mongo*	*Tugriks* 100, 50, 25, 20, 10, 5, 3, 1	*Tugrik* 1; *Mongo* 50, 20, 15, 10, 5, 2, 1
Morocco	*Dirham* of 100 *Centimes*	*DH.* 100, 50, 10, 5	*DH.* 5, 1, ½; *Centimes* 20, 10, 5, 2, 1
Mozambique	*Metical* of 100 *Centavos*	*MT.* 1,000, 500, 100, 50	*MT.* 20, 10, 5, 2½, 1, ½
Nepal	*Rupee* of 100 *Paisa*	*Rupees* 1,000, 500, 100, 50, 20, 10, 5, 2, 1	*Rupee* 100, 50, 25, 20, 10, 5, 2, 1; *Paisa* 50, 25, 20, 10, 5, 2, 1
Netherlands	*Florin* (*Guilder*) of 100 *Cents*	*Florins* 1,000, 250, 100, 50, 25, 10, 5, 2½, 1	*Florins* 10, 2½, 1; *Cents* 25, 10, 5
Netherlands Antilles	*Netherlands Antilles Guilder* of 100 *Cents*	*Guilders* 250, 100, 50, 25, 10, 5, 2½, 1	*Guilders* 2½, 1, ¼, $\frac{1}{10}$; *Cents* 5, 2½, 1
New Zealand	*New Zealand Dollar* of 100 *Cents*	N.Z.$ 100, 50, 20, 10, 5, 2, 1	*Cents* 50, 20, 10, 5, 2, 1
Nicaragua	*Córdoba* of 100 *Centavos*	*Córdobas* 1,000, 500, 100, 50, 20, 10, 5, 2, 1	*Cordobas* 5, 1; *Centavos* 50, 25, 10, 5
Niger	*Franc C.F.A.*	*Frs. C.F.A.* 10,000, 5,000, 1,000, 500, 100, 50	*Frs. C.F.A.* 100, 50, 25, 10, 5, 2, 1
Nigeria	*Naira* of 100 *Kobo*	N 20, 10, 5, 1	*k* 25, 10, 5, 1, ½
Norway	*Krone* of 100 *Öre*	*Kroner* 1,000, 500, 100, 50	*Kroner* 10, 5, 1; *Öre* 50, 10
Oman	*Rial Omani* of 1,000 *Baisa*	*Rial Omani* 50, 20, 10, 5, 1, ½, ¼; *Baisa* 100	*Baisa* 500, 250, 100, 50, 25, 10, 5, 2
Pakistan	*Rupee* of 100 *Paisa*	*Rs.* 100, 50, 10, 5, 2, 1	*Re.* 1, ½, ¼; *Paisa* 50, 25, 10, 5, 2, 1
Panama	*Balboa* of 100 *Cents* (= *U.S.$*)	As in U.S.A.	*Balboa* 500, 150, 100, 5, 1, ½, ¼, $\frac{1}{10}$, $\frac{1}{20}$; *Cent* 1*.
Papua New Guinea	*Kina* = 100 *Toea*	*K.* 20, 10, 5, 2	*K.* 1; *T.* 50, 20, 10, 5, 2, 1
Paraguay	*Guarani* of 100 *Céntimos*	*Guaraníes* 10,000, 5,000, 1,000, 500, 100, 50, 10, 5, 1	—
Peru	*Inti* of 100 *Centimos*	*Intis* 100, 50, 10, 5	—
Philippines	*Philippine Peso* of 100 *Centavos*	*Pesos* 100, 50, 20, 10, 5, 2	*Peso* 1; *Centavos* 50, 25, 10, 5, 1
Poland	*Zloty* of 100 *Groszy*	*Zlotys* 5,000, 2,000, 1,000, 500, 200, 100, 50, 20, 10	*Zlotys* 2,000, 1,000, 500, 200, 100, 50, 20, 10, 5, 2, 1; *Groszy* 50, 20, 10, 5, 2
Portugal	*Escudo* of 100 *Centavos*	*Esc.* 5,000$00, 1,000$00, 500$00, 100$00	*Esc.* 25$00, 5$00, 2$50, 1$00; *Centavos* $50

* U.S. coins also circulate. † Belgian currency is also legal tender.

Country	Monetary Unit	Denomination in Circulation	
		Notes	Coins
Portuguese Timor	*Escudo* of 100 *Centavos*	*Esc.* 1,000$00, 500$00, 100$00, 50$00, 20$00	*Esc.* 10$00, 5$00, 2$50, 1$00; *Centavos* $50, $20, $10
Qatar	*Qatar Riyal* of 100 *Dirhams*	*Qatar Riyals* 500, 100, 50, 10, 5, 1	*Dirhams* 50, 25, 10, 5, 1
Romania	*Leu* of 100 *Bani*	*Lei* 100, 50, 25, 10, 5, 3, 1	*Lei* 5, 3, 1; *Bani* 25, 15, 10, 5, 3, 1
Rwanda	*Rwanda Franc*	*Frs.* 5,000, 1,000, 500, 100	*Frs.* 50, 20, 10, 5, 1
St. Helena	*St. Helena Pound* of 100 *Pence*	£10, 5	£1; *Pence* 50, 10, 5, 2, 1
Sao Tomé and Principé	*Dobra* of 100 *Centimos*	*Dobras* 1,000, 500, 100, 50	*Dobras* 20, 10, 5, 2, 1; *Centimos* 50
Saudi Arabia	*Riyal* of 20 *Qursh* or 100 *Halalas*	*Riyals* 500, 100, 50, 10, 5, 1	*Halala* 100, 50, 25, 10, 5, 1
Senegal	*Franc C.F.A.*	*Frs.* 10,000, 5,000, 1,000, 500, 100, 50	*Frs.* 100, 50, 25, 10, 5, 2, 1
Seychelles	*Rupee* of 100 *Cents*	*SR* 100, 50, 25, 10	*Rupees* 1,500, 1,000, 100, 50, 25, 20, 10, 5, 1; *Cents* 25, 10, 5
Sierra Leone	*Leone* of 100 *Cents*	*Le.* 20, 10, 5, 2, 1; *Cents* 50	*Cents* 50, 20, 10, 5, 1, ½
Singapore	*Singapore Dollar* of 100 *Cents*	*Dollars* 10,000, 1,000, 500, 100, 50, 20, 10, 5, 1	*Dollar* 1; *Cents* 50, 20, 10, 5, 1
Solomon Islands	*Solomon Islands Dollar* of 100 *Cents*	*SI.$* 20, 10, 5, 2	*SI.$* 1; *Cents* 20, 10, 5, 2, 1
Somali Democratic Republic	*Somali Shilling* of 100 *Cents*	*S. Shillings* 100, 20, 10, 5	*Shillings* 1, ½; *Cents* 10, 5, 1
South Africa	*Rand* of 100 *Cents*	*R* 50, 20, 10, 5, 2	*R* 1; *Cents* 50, 20, 10, 5, 2, 1
Spain	*Peseta* of 100 *Céntimos*	*Pesetas* 5,000, 2,000, 1,000, 500, 200, 100	*Pesetas* 100, 50, 25, 5, 1; *Céntimos* 50
Sri Lanka	*Rupee* of 100 *Cents*	*Rs.* 1,000, 500, 100, 50, 20, 10, 5, 2	*Rs.* 1; *Cents* 50, 25, 10, 5, 2, 1
Sudan	*Sudanese Pound* of 100 *Piastres* or 1,000 *Milliemes*	*£S.* 20, 10, 5, 1; *Piastres* 50, 25	*Piastres* 50, 10, 5, 2; *Milliemes* 10, 5, 2, 1
Suriname	*Guilder* (*Sf.*) of 100 *Cents*	*Sf.* 500, 100, 25, 10, 5, 2½, 1	*Guilder* 1; *Cents* 25, 10, 5, 1
Swaziland	*Lilangeni* (plural *Emalangeni*) of 100 *Cents*	*E* 20, 10, 5, 2, 1	*E* 2, 1; *Cents* 50, 20, 10, 5, 2, 1*
Sweden	*Krona* of 100 *Öre*	*Kronor* 10,000, 1,000, 500, 100, 50, 10, 2½	*Kronor* 5, 2, 1; *Öre* 50, 10
Switzerland	*Franc* of 100 *Centimes*	*Francs* 1,000, 500, 100, 50, 20, 10	*Francs* 5, 2, 1; *Centimes* 50, 20, 10, 5, 1
Syria	*Syrian Pound* of 100 *Piastres*	*S. Pounds* 500, 100, 50, 25, 10, 5, 1	*Pound* 1, ½; *Piastres* 50, 25, 10, 5, 2½
Taiwan	*New Taiwan Dollar* of 100 *Cents*	*NT$* 1,000, 500, 100, 50, 10, 5, 1	*NT$*10, 5, 1; *Cents* 50, 10
Tanzania	*Tanzanian Shilling* of 100 *Cents*	*Shillings* 100, 20, 10	*Shilling* 5, 1; *Cents* 50, 20, 10, 5
Thailand	*Baht* of 100 *Stangs*	*Bahts* 500, 100, 20, 10, 5, 1; *Stangs* 50	*Baht* 5, 1; *Stangs* 50, 25, 10, 5, 1
Togo	*Franc C.F.A.*	*Frs.* 10,000, 5,000, 1,000, 500, 100, 50	*Frs.* 500, 100, 50, 25, 10, 5, 2, 1
Tonga	*Pa'anga* (*T$*) of 100 *Seniti*	*T$* 10, 5, 2, 1, ½	*T$* 2, 1; *Seniti* 50, 20, 10, 5, 2, 1
Trinidad and Tobago	*Trinidad and Tobago Dollar* of 100 *Cents*	*Dollars* 100, 20, 10, 5, 1	*Dollar* 1; *Cents* 50, 25, 10, 5, 1
Tunisia	*Tunisian Dinar* of 1,000 *Millimes*	*Dinars* 10, 5, 1, ½	*Dinars* 5, 1, ½; *Millimes* 100, 50, 20, 10, 5, 2, 1
Turkey	*Turkish Lira* of 100 *Kurus*	*TL.* 10,000, 5,000, 1,000, 500, 100, 50, 20, 10	*TL.* 100, 50, 20, 10, 5, 1
Uganda	*U. Shilling* of 100 *Cents*	*Shillings* 100, 50, 20, 10	*Shillings* 5, 2, 1; *Cents* 50, 20, 10, 5
U.S.S.R.	*Rouble* of 100 *Copecks*	*Roubles* 100, 50, 25, 10, 5, 3, 1	*Rouble* 1; *Copecks* 50, 20, 15, 10, 5, 3, 2, 1
United Arab Emirates	*Dirham* of 100 *Fils*	*Dirhams* 1,000, 100, 50, 10, 5, 1	*Dirham* 1; *Fils* 50, 25, 10, 5, 1
United Kingdom	*Pound Sterling* of 100 *Pence*	£50, £20, £10, £5, £1	£1; *Pence* 50, 20, 10, 5, 2, 1; 2*s.* (10p). 1*s* (5p)
U.S.A.	*Dollar* of 100 *Cents*	$100, 50, 20, 10, 5, 2, 1	$1; *Cents* 50, 25, 10, 5, 1
Uruguay	*Peso* of 100 *Centésimos* and *New Peso* of 1,000 *Pesos*	*New Pesos* 10,000, 5,000, 1,000, 500, 100, 50	*Pesos* 10,000, 5,000, 1,000, 500, 100, 50; *New Pesos* 10, 5, 2, 1; *Centésimos* 50, 20, 10
Venezuela	*Bolivar*	*Bolivares* 500, 100, 50, 20, 10, 5	*Bolivares* 100, 20, 10, 5, 2, 1, ½, ¼, $\frac{1}{10}$, $\frac{1}{20}$

Country	Monetary Unit	Denomination in Circulation	
		Notes	Coins
Vietnam	*Dông* of 10 *Hào* or 100 *Xu*	*Dông* 10, 5, 2, 1; *Hào* 5, 2, 1; *Xu* 5	*Xu* 5, 2, 1
Western Samoa ...	*Tala (WS$)* of 100 *Sene*	*Tala* 20, 10, 5, 2	*Sene* 50, 20, 10, 5, 2, 1
Yemen, North (Arab Republic)	*Riyal* of 100 *Fils*	*Riyals* 100, 50, 20, 10, 5, 1	*Fils* 50, 25, 10, 5, 1
Yemen, South (People's Democratic Republic)	*Yemeni Dinar (YD)* of 1,000 *Fils*	*YD* 10, 5, 1; *Fils* 500, 250	*Fils* 50, 25, 5, 2½, 1
Yugoslavia	*Dinar* of 100 *Paras*	*Dinars* 5,000, 1,000, 500, 100, 50, 20, 10, 5	*Dinar* 10, 5, 2, 1; *Paras* 50, 20, 10, 5, 2, 1
Zaire	*Zaïre* of 100 *Makuta* or 10,000 *Sengi*	*Zaïres* 50, 10, 5, 1; *Makuta* 50	*Makuta* 20, 10, 5, 1; *Sengi* 10
Zambia	*Kwacha* of 100 *Ngwee*	*Kwacha* 20, 10, 5, 2, 1	*Ngwee* 50, 20, 10, 5, 2, 1
Zimbabwe	*Dollar* of 100 *Cents*	Z.$ 20, 10, 5, 2, 1	Z.$ 1, *Cents* 50, 20, 10, 5, 1

SERVICES SOUND AND VISION CORPORATION
(Incorporating B.F.B.S.)
Bridge House, 63/65 North Wharf Road, W2 1LA

The British Forces Broadcasting Service came into existence during the middle of the Second World War to provide radio programmes of entertainment and information, and a link with home. No exact date can be given for the inception of the service because it began in many different places almost simultaneously during 1943.

In 1960 B.F.B.S. was reorganized: a Director was appointed and a Head Office was created in London to co-ordinate the activities of the service and to provide programme material specifically aimed at H.M. Forces, and their dependents overseas, and featuring leading personalities in all walks of life which the stations cannot produce themselves. These programmes are recorded in London and flown to B.F.B.S. stations abroad, as well as to H.M. Ships in many parts of the world, and for the benefit of personnel serving in places such as Belize and Dhahran.

Over the years output has increased considerably and the stations in Germany, Cyprus and Gibraltar are now on the air round the clock. In Cyprus and Gibraltar a second channel for minority tastes is also available on medium wave. In Hong Kong and Brunei, B.F.B.S. stations provide services in Gurkhali and in English. B.F.B.S. operates a service in the Falkland Islands in collaboration with the Falkland Islands Broadcasting Station. A 24-hour live news and sports service is provided by B.F.B.S. London, via satellite and line, for most overseas stations.

On April 1, 1983, B.F.B.S. was merged with the Services Kinema Corporation to form the Services Sound & Vision Corporation (S.S.V.C.). B.F.B.S. now forms the radio division of S.S.V.C., still transmitting under its original title.

S.S.V.C. Television, a service combining programmes from B.B.C. and I.T.V., with some specially produced, started at Celle, near Hanover on September 18, 1975. S.S.V.C. Television now serves virtually the whole of the British military community in Germany. There are also in-vision services in Cyprus and the Falkland Islands providing four hours per day of recorded programmes and S.S.V.C. provides a service of V.H.S. cassettes containing recorded programmes which are sent to a variety of British military locations overseas.

The Combined Services Entertainment section of S.S.V.C. (previously part of B.F.B.S.) arranges stage and cabaret shows, as well as solo artistes, to tour Northern Ireland and Commands overseas.

The staff of B.F.B.S. are all civilian, professional broadcasters and engineers. The Service is sponsored by the Army on behalf of the other two Services, and is financed from Ministry of Defence funds.

Managing Director, S.S.V.C., J. Grist.

SUMMARY OF SPORT 1986–87

ATHLETICS
WORLD RECORDS

(All the world records given below have been accepted by the International Amateur Athletic Federation except those marked with an asterisk* which are awaiting homologation.)

Fully automatic timing to 1/100th second is mandatory up to and including 400 metres. For distances up to and including 10,000 metres records will be accepted to 1/100th second if timed automatically, and to 1/10th if hand timing is used.

MEN'S EVENTS
Running

Distances	hr.	min.	Time sec.	Name	Nation	Year
100 metres			9·83*	B. Johnson	Canada	1987
200 metres (turn)			19·72	P. Mennea	Italy	1979
400 metres			43·86	L. Evans	U.S.A.	1968
800 metres		1	41·73	S. Coe	G.B.	1981
1,000 metres		2	12·18	S. Coe	G.B.	1981
1,500 metres		3	29·46	S. Aouita	Morocco	1985
1 mile		3	46·32	S. Cram	G.B.	1985
2,000 metres		4	50·81*	S. Aouita	Morocco	1987
3,000 metres		7	32·1	H. Rono	Kenya	1978
5,000 metres		12	58·39	S. Aouita	Morocco	1987
10,000 metres		27	13·81	F. Mamede	Portugal	1984
20,000 metres		57	24·2	J. Hermens	Netherlands	1976
20,944 metres (13 miles 24 yards 2 feet)	1	00	00·0	J. Hermens	Netherlands	1976
25,000 metres	1	13	55·8	T. Seko	Japan	1981
30,000 metres	1	29	18·8	T. Seko	Japan	1981
110 metres hurdles			12·93	R. Nehemiah	U.S.A.	1981
400 metres hurdles			47·02	E. Moses	U.S.A.	1983
3,000 metres steeplechase		8	05·4	H. Rono	Kenya	1978

Relay Racing

Distance	min.	Time sec.	Nation	Year
4 × 100 metres		37·83	U.S.A.	1984
4 × 200 metres	1	20·26	Univ. of S. Calif.	1978
4 × 400 metres	2	56·16	U.S.A.	1977
4 × 800 metres	7	03·89	G.B.	1982
4 × 1,500 metres	14	38·8	F.R.G.	1977

Jumping and Throwing

	ft.	in.	metres	Name	Nation	Year
High Jump	7	11½	2·42*	P. Sjöberg	Sweden	1987
Pole Vault	19	9¼	6·03*	S. Bubka	U.S.S.R.	1987
Long Jump	29	2½	8·90	R. Beamon	U.S.A.	1968
Triple Jump	58	11½	17·97	W. Banks	U.S.A.	1985
Shot	75	1	22·91*	A. Andrei	Italy	1987
Discus	243	0	74·08	J. Schult	G.D.R.	1986
Hammer	284	7	86·74	Y. Sedykh	U.S.S.R.	1986
Javelin†	343	9	104·80	U. Hohn	G.D.R.	1984
Decathlon			8,847 pts.°	D. Thompson	G.B.	1984

° Scored with new scoring tables.
† New type of javelin now in force

Walking (Track)

Distance	hr.	min.	Time sec.	Name	Nation	Year
20,000 metres	1	18	40	E. Canto	Mexico	1984
28,565 metres (17 miles 1319 yards)	2	00	00·0	M. Damilano	Italy	1985
30,000 metres	2	06	27·3	M. Damilano	Italy	1985
50,000 metres	3	41	39·00	R. Gonzalez	Mexico	1979

WOMEN'S EVENTS
Running

Distance	Time min. sec.		Name	Nation	Year
100 metres		10·76	E. Ashford	U.S.A.	1984
200 metres		21·71	M. Koch	G.D.R.	1979
		21·71	H. Drechsler	G.D.R.	1986
400 metres		47·60	M. Koch	G.D.R.	1985
800 metres	1	53·28	J. Kratochvilova	Czechoslovakia	1983
1,500 metres	3	52·47	T. Kazankina	U.S.S.R.	1980
1 mile	4	16·71	M. Slaney	U.S.A.	1985
3,000 metres	8	22·62	T. Kazankina	U.S.S.R.	1984
5,000 metres	14	37·33	I. Kristiansen	Norway	1986
10,000 metres	30	13·74	I. Kristiansen	Norway	1986
100 metres hurdles (2 ft. 9 in.)		12·25*	G. Zagorcheva	Bulgaria	1987
400 metres hurdles		52·94*	M. Stepanova	U.S.S.R.	1986

Relays

Distance	Time min. sec.		Nation	Year
4 × 100 metres		41·37	G.D.R.	1985
4 × 200 metres	1	28·15	G.D.R.	1980
4 × 400 metres	3	15·92	G.D.R.	1984
4 × 800 metres	7	50·17	U.S.S.R.	1984

Women's Jumping and Throwing

	ft.	in.	metres	Name	Nation	Year
High Jump	6	10½	2·09	S. Kostadinova	Bulgaria	1987
Long Jump	24	5½	7·45	H. Drechsler	G.D.R.	1986
	24	5½	7·45*	J. Joyner	U.S.A.	1987
Shot Putt	74	3	22·63*	N. Lisovskaya	(U.S.S.R.)	1987
Discus	244	7	74·56	Z. Silhava	Czechoslovakia	1984
Javelin	258	10	78·90*	P. Felke	G.D.R.	1987
Heptathlon†	7,158* pts.			J. Joyner	U.S.A.	1986

† Seven events comprising 100 m hurdles, shot, high jump, 200 m, long jump, javelin, 800 m.

UNITED KINGDOM (NATIONAL) RECORDS
(Records made anywhere by athletes eligible to represent Great Britain and Northern Ireland)

Men

100 *metres*—10·03 sec. (L. Christie, 1987).
200 *metres*—20·18 sec. (J. Regis, 1987).
400 *metres*—44·50 sec. (D. Redmond, 1987).
800 *metres*—1 min. 41·73 (S. Coe, 1981).
1,000 *metres*—2 min. 12·18 sec. (S. Coe, 1981).
1,500 *metres*—3 min. 29·67 sec. (S. Cram, 1985).
1 *mile*—3 min. 46·32 sec. (S. Cram, 1985).
2,000 *metres*—4 min. 51·39 sec. (S. Cram, 1985).
3,000 *metres*—7 min. 32·79 sec. (D. Moorcroft, 1982).
5,000 *metres*—13 min. 00·41 sec. (D. Moorcroft, 1982).
10,000 *metres*—27 min. 30·3 sec. (B. Foster, 1978).
20,000 *metres*—58 min. 39·0 sec. (R. Hill, 1968).
12 *miles* 1,268 *yards*—1 hr. (R. Hill, 1968).
25,000 *metres*—1 hr. 15 min. 22·6 sec. (R. Hill, 1965).
30,000 *metres*—1 hr. 31 min. 30·4 sec. (J. Alder, 1970).
3,000 *metres Steeplechase*—8 min. 12·11 sec. (C. Reitz, 1986).
110 *metres Hurdles*—13·29 sec. (J. Ridgeon, 1982).
400 *metres Hurdles*—48·12 sec. (D. P. Hemery, 1968).
4 × 100 *metres Relay*—38·62 (G.B. Team, 1980)
4 × 200 *metres*—1 min. 24·1 sec. (G.B. Team, 1971).
4 × 400 *metres*—2 min. 58·86 sec. (G.B. Team, 1987).
4 × 800 *metres*—7 min. 03·89 sec. (G.B. Team, 1982).
4 × 1,500 *metres*—14 min. 56·8 sec. (G.B. Team, 1979).
High Jump—2·28 m., 7 ft. 5¼ in. (G. Parsons, 1986).
Pole Vault—5·65 m., 18 ft. 6½ in. (K. Stock, 1981).
Long Jump—8·23 m., 27 ft. 0 in. (L. Davies, 1968).
Triple Jump—17·57 m., 57 ft. 7¼ in. (K. Connor, 1982).
Shot—21·68 m., 71 ft. 1½ in. (G. Capes, 1980).
Discus—64·32 m., 211 ft. 0 in. (W. Tancred, 1974).
Hammer—77·54 m., 254 ft. 5 in. (M. Girvan, 1984).

Javelin—91·40 m., 299 ft. 10 in. (R. Bradstock, 1985).
Decathlon—8,847 pts.° (D. Thompson, 1984).
° Scored with new scoring tables.
Walking (Track)
20,000 *metres*—1 hr. 26 min. 22 sec. (S. Barry, 1981).
2 *Hours*—16 miles 315 yds. (R. Wallwork, 1971).
30,000 *metres*—2 hr. 19 min. 18 sec. (C. Maddocks, 1984).
50,000 *metres*—4 hr. 05 min. 48 sec. (C. Maddocks, 1984).

Women

100 *metres*—11·10 sec. (K. Cook, 1981).
200 *metres*—22·10 sec. (K. Cook, 1984).
400 *metres*—49·43 sec. (K. Cook, 1984).
800 *metres*—1 min. 57·42 sec. (K. McDermott, 1985).
1,500 *metres*—3 min. 59·96 sec. (Z. Budd, 1985).
1 *mile*—4 min. 17·57 sec. (Z. Budd, 1985).
3,000 *metres*—8 min. 28·83 sec. (Z. Budd, 1985).
5,000 *metres*—14 min. 48·07 sec. (Z. Budd, 1985)
10,000 *metres*—31 min. 19·82 sec. (E. Lynch, 1987).
100 *metres Hurdles*—12·87 sec. (S. Strong, 1983).
400 *metres Hurdles*—56·04 sec. (S. Morley, 1983).
4 × 100 *metres Relay*—42·43 sec. (G.B. Team, 1980).
4 × 200 *metres Relay*—1 min. 31·57 sec. (G.B. Team, 1977).
4 × 400 *metres Relay*—3 min. 25·51 sec. (G.B. Team, 1984).
4 × 800 *metres Relay*—8 min. 23·8 sec. (G.B. Team, 1971).
High Jump—1·95 m., 6 ft. 4¼ in. (D. Elliott, 1982).
Long Jump—6·90 m., 22 ft. 7¼ in. (B. Kinch, 1983).

Shot—19·00 m., 62 ft. 4 in. (J. Oakes, 1986).
Discus—67·48 m., 221 ft. 5 in. (M. Ritchie, 1981).
Javelin—77·44 m., 254 ft. 1 in. (F. Whitbread, 1986).
Heptathlon—6,623 pts. (J. Livermore, 1986).

	metres
High Jump—K. Sterk (Hungary)	1·91
Long Jump—M. Berkeley (U.K.)	6·36
Shot—M. Augee (U.K.)	17·94

U.K. beat Hungary by 67 pts. to 50.

A.A.A. Indoor Championships

Held at Cosford, January 23–24, 1987

Metres	min.	sec.
60—E. Bunney (Edinburgh S.H.)		6·62
200—L. Christie (T.V.H.)		21·23
400—T. Bennett (Team Solent)		47·12
800—A. Morrell (Wolverhampton)	1	48·66
1,500—M. Edwards (Army)	3	47·52
3,000—A. Passey (Bromsgrove)	7	52·87
60 *Hurdles*—J. Ridgeon (Haringey) ...		7·66

	metres
High Jump—H. Pierre (Haringey) ...	2·15
Pole Vault—J. Gutteridge (Windsor) ..	5·30
Long Jump—B. Williams (Sheffield) ...	7·64
Triple Jump—A. Holm (Sweden)	16·38
Shot—G. Savory (Blackheath)	17·52

W.A.A.A. Indoor Championships

Held at Cosford, January 23–24, 1987

Metres	min.	sec.
60—B. Kinch (Hounslow)		7·27
200—S. Gunnell (Essex Ladies)		24·37
400—D. Gandy (Hounslow)		55·67
800—J. Prictoe (Exeter)	2	04·18
1,500—K. Wade (Blaydon)	4	09·26
60 *Hurdles*—L. Skeete (Swindon)		8·21

	metres
High Jump—J. Boyle (Belfast)	1·90
Long Jump—M. Berkeley (Croydon) ..	6·38
Shot—J. Oakes (Croydon)	18·05

Held at Cosford, January 10, 1987

Metres	min.	sec.
3,000—K. McLeod (Edinburgh A.C.) ..	9	30·98

United Kingdom v. Hungary

Held at Budapest, February 7–8, 1987

Men's Events

Metres	min.	sec.
60—E. Obeng (U.K.)		6·63
200—J. Regis (U.K.)		20·85
400—S. Heard (U.K.)		46·83
800—A. Morrell (U.K.)	1	48·08
1,500—G. Szabo (Hungary)	3	44·17
3,000—M. Howland (U.K.)	7	50·63
60 *Hurdles*—C. Jackson (U.K.)		7·57
4 × 400 *Relay*—United Kingdom	3	09·07

	metres
High Jump—D. Grant (U.K.)	2·24
Pole Vault—G. Molnar (Hungary)	5·20
Long Jump—L. Szalma (Hungary)	8·00
Triple Jump—F. Abejide (U.K.)	15·67
Shot—L. Szabo (Hungary)	18·28

U.K. beat Hungary by 73½ pts. to 63½.

Women's Events

Metres	min.	sec.
60—P. Dunn (U.K.)		7·38
200—C. Smart (U.K.)		24·27
400—J. Forgacs (Hungary)		52·29
800—J. Bell (U.K.)	2	02·79
1,500—Y. Murray (U.K.)	4	11·21
3,000—Z. Agoston (Hungary)	9	22·82
60 *Hurdles*—L-A. Skeete (U.K.)		8·13
4 × 200 *Relay*—United Kingdom	1	35·87

National Cross-Country Championships (Women)

Held at Bexley, February 14, 1987

Senior Race (5,500 m)	min.	sec.
1. J. Shields (Sheffield)	21	03
2. S. Ellis (Worcester)	21	13
3. A. Wyeth (Southampton)	21	25
Team result		
1. Sale (10, 17, 18, 39)		84 pts.
2. Southampton & Eastleigh (3, 5, 36, 68)		112 pts.
3. Aldershot, Farnham & District (23,30,40,47)..................		140 pts.
Intermediate Race (4,000 m)	min.	sec.
1. A. Holmes (Liverpool)	16	27
2. M. Newman (Leicester)........	16	33
3. L. Hollick (Luton)	16	38
Team result		
1. Leicester (2, 11, 14, 20)		47 pts.
2. Liverpool (1, 9, 25, 58)........		93 pts.
3. Mid Hants (12, 23, 29, 33)......		97 pts.
Junior Race (3,500 m)	min.	sec.
1. C. Nicholson (Darlington)	12	38
2. N. Ashe (Hounslow)...........	12	43
3. J. Adkin (Tonbridge)	12	51
Team result		
1. Liverpool (4, 19, 41, 43)		107 pts.
2. Oldham & Rochdale (8, 21, 33, 54)........................		116 pts.
3. City of Stoke (18, 30, 49, 73)		170 pts.
Girl's Race (3,000 m)	min.	sec.
1. C. Mayock (Rockingham)	11	47
2. K. Foster (Bedford)	11	55
3. N. Pearce (Thurrock)	12	02
Team result		
1. Bedford (2, 4, 17, 31)		54 pts.
2. Liverpool (9, 18, 33, 42)		102 pts.
3. Manchester (19, 22, 37, 83)		161 pts.

National Cross-Country Championships (Men)

Held at Luton, February 21, 1987

Senior Race (9 miles)	min.	sec.
1. D. Clarke (Hercules-Wimbledon)	47	04
2. S. Binns (Bingley)	47	18
3. R. Hackney (Aldershot)	47	46
Team result		
1. Gateshead (6, 9, 13, 32, 33, 78) ...		171 pts.
2. Bingley (2, 17, 27, 48, 79, 96)		269 pts.
3. Tipton (18, 37, 56, 64, 67, 84)		326 pts.
Junior Race (6 miles)	min.	sec.
1. R. Findlow (Airedale)	30	05
2. S. Mugglestone (Westbury)	30	38
3. N. O'Brien (Stretford).........	30	39
Team result		
1. Newham & Essex (11, 57, 60, 102)		230 pts.
2. Westbury (2, 65, 78, 110)		255 pts.
3. Wolverhampton & Bilston (27, 48, 55, 146)		276 pts.
Youth Race (4 miles)	min.	sec.
1. J. Dennis (Camberley)	21	53
2. S. Brooks (Bingley)	21	56
3. A. Juby (G.E.C. Avionics)......	21	59
Team result		
1. G.E.C. Avionics (3, 15, 27, 37) ...		82 pts.
2. Stretford (10, 17, 35, 58)		120 pts.
3. Leicester (13, 18, 63, 108)		202 pts.

European Indoor Championships

Held at Lievin, France, February 21–22, 1987

Men's Events

Metres	min.	sec.
60—M. Woronin (Poland)		6·51
200—B. Marie-Rose (France)		20·36
400—T. Bennett (U.K.)		46·81
800—R. Druppers (Holland)	1	48·12
1,500—H. Kulker (Holland)	3	44·79
3,000—J-L. Gonzalez (Spain)	7	52·27
60 *Hurdles*—A. Bryggare (Finland)		7·59
5,000 *Walk*—J. Pribilinec (Czech.)	19	08·44

	metres
High Jump—P. Sjöberg (Sweden)	2·38
Pole Vault—T. Vigneron (France)	5·85
Long Jump—R. Emmiyan (U.S.S.R.)	8·49
Triple Jump—S. Helan (France)	17·15
Shot—U. Timmermann (G.D.R.)	22·19

Women's Events

Metres	min.	sec.
60—N. Cooman (Holland)		7·01
200—K. Emmelmann (G.D.R.)		23·10
400—M. Pinigina (U.S.S.R.)		51·27
800—C. Wachtel (G.D.R.)	1	59·89
1,500—S. Gasser (Switzerland)	4	08·76
3,000—Y. Murray (U.K.)	8	46·06
60 *Hurdles*—Y. Donkova (Bulgaria)		7·79
3,000 *Walk*—N. Dmitrochenko (U.S.S.R.)	12	57·59

	metres
High Jump—S. Kostadinova (Bulgaria)	1·97
Long Jump—H. Drechsler (G.D.R.)	7·12
Shot—N. Akhrimenko (U.S.S.R.)	20·84

World Indoor Championships

Held at Indianapolis, USA, March 6–8, 1987

Men's Events

Metres	min.	sec.
60—B. Johnson (Canada)		6·41
200—K. Baptiste (U.S.A.)		20·73
400—A. McKay (U.S.A.)		45·98
800—J. Barbara (Brazil)	1	47·49
1,500—M. O'Sullivan (Ireland)	3	39·04
3,000—F. O'Mara (Ireland)	8	03·32
60 *Hurdles*—T. Campbell (U.S.A.)		7·51
5,000 *Walk*—M. Schennilov (U.S.S.R.)	18	27·79

	metres
High Jump—I. Paklin (U.S.S.R.)	2·38
Pole Vault—S. Bubka (U.S.S.R.)	5·05
Long Jump—L. Myricks (U.S.A.)	8·23
Triple Jump—M. Conley (U.S.A.)	17·54
Shot—U. Timmermann (G.D.R.)	22·24

Women's Events

Metres	min.	sec.
60—N. Cooman (Holland)		7·08
200—H. Drechsler (G.D.R.)		22·27
400—S. Busch (G.D.R.)		51·66
800—C. Wachtel (G.D.R.)	2	01·32
1,500—D. Melinte (Romania)	4	05·68
3,000—T. Samolenko (U.S.S.R.)	8	46·52
60 *Hurdles*—C. Oschkenat (G.D.R.)		7·82
3,000 *Walk*—O. Krishtop (U.S.S.R.)	12	05·49

	metres
High Jump—S. Kostadinova (Bulgaria)	2·05
Long Jump—H. Drechsler (G.D.R.)	7·10
Shot—N. Lisovskaya (U.S.S.R.)	20·52

World Cross-Country Championships

Held at Warsaw, Poland, March 22, 1987

Men (11,950 m)	min.	sec.
1. J. Ngugi (Kenya)	36	07
2. P. Kipkoech (Kenya)	36	07
3. P. Arpin (France)	36	51

Team result
1. Kenya (1,2,5,6,18,21) ... 53 pts.
2. England (10,20,22,23,33,38) ... 146 pts.
3. Ethiopia (4,17,27,29,39,45) ... 161 pts.

Women (5,050 m)	min.	sec.
1. A. Sergent (France)	16	46
2. E. Lynch (Scotland)	16	48
3. I. Kristiansen (Norway)	16	51

Team result
1. United States (4,5,14,23) ... 46 pts.
2. France (1,12,18,19) ... 50 pts.
3. Soviet Union (10,13,15,17) ... 55 pts.

Juniors (7,050 m)	min.	sec.
1. O. Kirochi (Kenya)	22	18
2. D. Bekele (Ethiopia)	22	18
3. D. Demisse (Ethiopia)	22	20

Team result
1. Ethiopia (2,3,6,8) ... 19 pts.
2. Kenya (1,4,5,10) ... 20 pts.
3. Japan (14,18,20,21) ... 73 pts.

A.A.A. 10,000 metres Road Championship

Held at Hemel Hempstead, April 4, 1987

	min.	sec.
1. J. Gregorek (U.S.A.)	28	14·0
2. A. Barrios (Mexico)	28	16·0
3. J. Buckner (U.K.)	28	18·0

Team result: Gateshead.

National 20 km. Walk

Held at Birmingham, April 18, 1987

	hr.	min.	sec.
1. L. Morton (Sheffield)	1	31	17
2. D. Jackson (York Postal)	1	33	50
3. C. Smith (Leicester)	1	33	51
Team result: Leicester		51 pts.	

A.A.A./London Marathon

Held May 10, 1987

Men	hr.	min.	sec.
1. H. Taniguchi (Japan)	2	09	50
2. N. El Mostapha (Morocco)	2	10	09
3. H. Jones (U.K.)	2	10	11

Women	hr.	min.	sec.
1. I. Kristiansen (Norway)	2	22	48
2. P. Welch (U.K.)	2	26	51
3. V. Marot (U.K.)	2	30	15

United Kingdom Championships

Held at Derby, May 24–25, 1987

Men's Events

Metres	min.	sec.
100—L. Christie (T.V.H.)		10·35
200—R. Black (Team Solent)		20·80
400—S. Heard (Wolverhampton)		46·96
800—J. Gladwin (Belgrave)	1	47·66
1,500—N. Horsfield (Newport)	3	43·69
5,000—S. Mugglestone (Westbury)	13	43·82
3,000 *Steeplechase*—C. Walker (Gateshead)	8	33·28
110 *Hurdles*—A. Jarrett (Haringey)		13·72
400 *Hurdles*—K. Akabusi (Army) M. Robertson (Wolverhampton)	}	49·56
10,000 *Walk*—I. McCombie (Cambridge H.)	40	45·87

	metres
High Jump—F. Manderson (Wolverhampton)	2·18
Pole Vault—J. Gutteridge (Windsor)	5·10
Long Jump—S. Faulkner (Birchfield)	7·68
Triple Jump—E. McCalla (Birchfield)	16·46
Shot—C. Jennings (Hull Spartan)	17·37
Discus—P. Mardle (Wolverhampton)	59·96
Hammer—D. Smith (Hull Spartan)	74·50
Javelin—M. Hill (Leeds)	81·02

Women's Events

Metres	min.	sec.
100—P. Dunn (Stretford)		11·31
200—P. Dunn (Stretford)		23·41
400—C. Finley (Liverpool)		53·47
800—D. Edwards (Sale)	2	01·68
1,500—C. Benning (Southampton)	4	07·37
3,000—Y. Murray (Edinburgh A.C.)	8	53·89
100 *Hurdles*—L.-A. Skeete (Swindon)		13·29
400 *Hurdles*—E. McLaughlin (Edinburgh W.M.S.H.)		57·91
5,000 *Walk*—L. Langford (Wolverhampton)	22	19·04

	metres
High Jump—D. Davies (Leicester)	1·85
Long Jump—M. Berkeley (Croydon)	6·44
Shot—J. Oakes (Croydon)	18·43
Discus—K. Farr (Southport)	55·42
Javelin—F. Whitbread (Thurrock)	75·62

Held at Gateshead, June 13, 1987

Men:

Metres	min.	sec.
10,000—N. Rose (Bristol)	28	22·05

Held at Stoke, May 31, 1987

Women:

Metres	min.	sec.
10,000—S. Crehan (Wigan)	33	22·28

United Kingdom v. Poland v. Canada

Held at Gateshead, June 13, 1987

Men's Events

Metres	min.	sec.
100—B. Johnson (Canada)		10·42
200—L. Christie (U.K.)		20·98
400—M. Sira (Poland)		46·98
800—P. Elliott (U.K.)	1	50·12
1,500—D. Campbell (Canada)	3	43·64
3,000—S. Ovett (U.K.)	7	51·22
2,000 *Steeplechase*—T. Hanlon (U.K.)	5	28·34
110 *Hurdles*—N. Walker (U.K.)		14·01
400 *Hurdles*—M. Robertson (U.K.)		49·93
4 × 100 *Relay*—United Kingdom		39·71
4 × 400 *Relay*—United Kingdom	3	04·81

	metres
High Jump—K. Krawczyk (Poland)	2·25
Pole Vault—R. Kolasa (Poland)	5·40
Long Jump—I. James (Canada)	7·92
Triple Jump—J. Herbert (U.K.)	16·94
Shot—J. Gassowski (Poland)	18·61
Discus—D. Juzyszyn (Poland)	61·60
Hammer—D. Smith (U.K.)	72·92
Javelin—M. Hill (U.K.)	83·00

U.K. 169 pts. beat Poland 103 and Canada 101.

Women's Events

Metres	min.	sec.
100—A. Issajenko (Canada)		11·41
200—A. Phipps (Canada)		23·46
400—C. Crooks (Canada)		52·30
800—D. Edwards (U.K.)	2	01·73
1,500—K. Wade (U.K.)	4	02·13

100 *Hurdles*—J. Rocheleau (Canada)		13·93
400 *Hurdles*—J. Pearson (U.K.)		58·39
4 × 100 *Relay*—Canada		45·17
4 × 400 *Relay*—Canada	3	33·49

	metres
High Jump—U. Kielan (Poland)	1·86
Long Jump—M. Berkeley (U.K.)	6·29
Shot—J. Oakes (U.K.)	18·72
Discus—E. Siepsiak (Poland)	58·68
Javelin—F. Whitbread (U.K.)	71·38

U.K. 119 pts. beat Canada 83 and Poland 74.

EUROPEAN CUP

Held in Prague, June 27–28, 1987

Men's Events

Metres	min.	sec.
100—L. Christie (U.K.)		10·23
200—L. Christie (U.K.)		20·63
400—T. Schönlebe (G.D.R.)		44·96
800—T. McKean (U.K.)	1	45·96
1,500—J.-L. Gonzalez (Spain)	3	45·49
5,000—J. Abascal (Spain)	13	32·87
10,000—A. Anton (Spain)	28	46·65
3,000 *Steeplechase*—F. Panetta (Italy)	8	13·47
110 *Hurdles*—I. Kazanov (U.S.S.R.)		13·48
400 *Hurdles*—H. Schmid (F.R.G.)		48·67
4 × 100 *Relay* U.S.S.R.		38·42
4 × 400 *Relay*—G.D.R.	3	00·80

	metres
High Jump—I. Paklin (U.S.S.R.)	2·32
Pole Vault—G. Yegorov (U.S.S.R.)	5·70
Long Jump—R. Emmiyan (U.S.S.R.)	8·38
Triple Jump—O. Protsenko (U.S.S.R.)	17·61
Shot—U. Timmermann (G.D.R.)	22·01
Discus—V. Kidikas (U.S.S.R.)	66·80
Hammer—S. Litvinov (U.S.S.R.)	82·28
Javelin—V. Yevsyukov (U.S.S.R.)	84·86

U.S.S.R. 117 pts., G.D.R. 114½, U.K. 99, F.R.G. 88, Italy 87, Czechoslovakia 73, Spain 72, Poland 58½.

Women's Events

Metres	min.	sec.
100—M. Göhr (G.D.R.)		10·95
200—S. Gladisch (G.D.R.)		21·99
400—P. Müller (G.D.R.)		49·91
800—T. Samolenko (U.S.S.R.)	1	59·26
1,500—K. Wade (U.K.)	4	09·03
3,000—U. Bruns (G.D.R.)	8	44·48
10,000—K. Ulrich (G.D.R.)	32	32·05
100 *Hurdles*—C. Oschkenat (G.D.R.)		12·47
400 *Hurdles*—S. Busch (G.D.R.)		54·23
4 × 100 *Relay*—G.D.R.		41·94
4 × 400 *Relay*—U.S.S.R.	3	20·41

	metres
High Jump—S. Kostadinova (Bulgaria)	2·00
Long Jump—H. Drechsler (G.D.R.)	7·26
Shot—N. Lisovskaya (U.S.S.R.)	21·56
Discus—D. Gansky (G.D.R.)	73·90
Javelin—P. Felke (G.D.R.)	71·26

G.D.R. 119 pts., U.S.S.R. 92, Bulgaria 86, F.R.G. 77, U.K. 59½, Czechoslovakia 51½, Poland 45, France 45.

National 50 km. Walk

Held at Sheffield, July 11, 1987

	hr.	min.	sec.
1. L. Morton (Sheffield)	4	23	40
2. C. Berwick (Leicester)	4	34	02
3. I. Harvey (Coventry)	4	34	04

W.A.A.A. Championships

Held at Birmingham, July 24–25, 1987.

Metres	min.	sec
100—P. Dunn (Stretford)		11·28
200—J. Baptiste (Essex Ladies)		23·24
400—L. Keough (Basingstoke)		53·17
800—D. Edwards (Sale)	2	03·39
1,500—B. Nicholson (Sale)	4	14·48
3,000—W. Sly (Hounslow)	9	04·23
5,000—C. Newman (Exeter)	16	14·62
100 *Hurdles*—S. Gunnell (Essex Ladies)		13·01
400 *Hurdles*—S. Flemming (Australia)		57·62
5,000 *Walk*—L. Langford (Wolverhampton)	22	35·04

	metres
High Jump—H. Haugland (Norway)	1·88
Long Jump—M. Berkeley (Croydon)	6·52
Shot—J. Oakes (Croydon)	18·44
Discus—E. Mulvihill (Greenwich)	52·56
Javelin—F. Whitbread (Thurrock)	72·96

A.A.A. Championships

Held at Crystal Palace, August 1–2, 1987

Metres	min.	sec.
100—D. Evans (U.S.A.)		10·33
200—J. Regis (Belgrave)		20·25
400—G. Tiacoh (Côte d'Ivoire)		45·10
800—P. Elliot (Rotherham)	1	48·71
1,500—S. Crabb (Enfield)	3	41·23
5,000—J. Buckner (Charnwood)	13	25·02
10,000—S. Harris (Haringey)	28	35·07
3,000 *Steeplechase*—E. Wedderburn (Tipton)	8	24·78
110 *Hurdles*—J. Ridgeon (Haringey)		13·36
400 *Hurdles*—M. Robertson (Wolverhampton)		49·51
10,000 *Walk*—I. McCombie (Cambridge H.)	41	16·14

	metres
High Jump—G. Parsons (London)	2·24
Pole Vault—J. Gutteridge (Windsor)	5·35
Long Jump—M. Powell (U.S.A.)	7·94
Triple Jump—E. McCalla (Birchfield)	16·86
Shot—P. Edwards (Wolverhampton)	17·26
Discus—P. Mardle (Wolverhampton)	57·34
Hammer—D. Smith (Hull Spartan)	70·60
Javelin—M. Hill (Leeds City)	81·68

EUROPEAN JUNIOR CHAMPIONSHIPS

Held at Birmingham, August 6–9, 1987

Men's Events

Metres	hr.	min.	sec.
100—J. Henderson (U.K.)			10·21
200—M. Adam (U.K.)			20·95
400—P. Crampton (U.K.)			46·03
800—T. de Teresa (Spain)		1	49·37
1,500—G. Di Napoli (Italy)		3	52·10
5,000—S. Mugglestone (U.K.)		14	12·83
10,000—J. Karrass (G.D.R.)		29	19·38
20,000 *Road Race*—Z. Holba (Hungary)	1	03	22
3,000 *Steeplechase*—A. Fischer (F.R.G.)		8	54·83
110 *Hurdles*—A. Jarrett (U.K.)			13·72
400 *Hurdles*—N. Wallenlind (Sweden)			50·65
4 × 100 *Relay*—United Kingdom			40·20
4 × 400 *Relay*—United Kingdom		3	07·89
10,000 *Walk*—G. Di Benedictis (Italy)		39	44·71

	metres
High Jump—A. Partyka (Poland)	2·19
Pole Vault—R. Barabachov (U.S.S.R.)	5·40
Long Jump—V. Otchkan (U.S.S.R.)	8·17
Triple Jump—G. Schumann (G.D.R.)	16·45
Shot—P. Pogorelyi (U.S.S.R.)	18·48
Discus—S. Patchine (U.S.S.R.)	59·96
Hammer—J. Hubner (G.D.R.)	72·10
Javelin—S. Backley (U.K.)	75·14
Decathlon—P. Esiemokumoh (G.D.R.)	7,614 pts.

Women's Events

Metres	min.	sec.
100—D. Dietz (G.D.R.)		11·39
200—D. Dietz (G.D.R.)		23·18
400—U. Rohlander (G.D.R.)		52·46
800—B. Bruhns (G.D.R.)	2	00·56
1,500—S. Pajkic (Yugoslavia)	4	16·09
3,000—F. Ribiero (Portugal)	8	56·33
10,000—B. Jerschabek (G.D.R.)	33	44·37
100 *Hurdles*—B. Wolf (F.R.G.)		13·34
400 *Hurdles*—S. Rieger (F.R.G.)		57·44
4 × 100 *Relay*—G.D.R.		44·62
4 × 400 *Relay*—G.D.R.	3	32·17
5,000 *Walk*—O. Stchastnia (U.S.S.R.)	21	30·92

	metres
High Jump—K. Scholz (G.D.R.)	1·88
Long Jump—F. May (U.K.)	6·64
Shot—I. Wyludda (G.D.R.)	19·45
Discus—I. Wyludda (G.D.R.)	70·58
Javelin—A. Reiter (G.D.R.)	64·88
Heptathlon—P. Beer (G.D.R.)	6,068 pts.

WORLD CHAMPIONSHIPS

Held at Rome, Aug. 29–Sept. 7, 1987

Men's Events

Metres	hr.	min.	sec.
100—B. Johnson (Canada)			9·83
200—C. Smith (U.S.A.)			20·16
400—T. Schoenlebe (G.D.R.)			44·33
800—B. Konchellah (Kenya)		1	43·06
1,500—A. Bile (Somalia)		3	36·80
5,000—S. Aouita (Morocco)		13	26·44
10,000—P. Kipkoech (Kenya)		27	38·63
3,000 *Steeplechase*—F. Panetta (Italy)		8	08·57
110 *Hurdles*—G. Foster (U.S.A.)			13·21
400 *Hurdles*—E. Moses (U.S.A.)			47·46
4 × 100 *Relay*—United States			37·90
4 × 400 *Relay*—United States		2	57·29
20,000 *Walk*—M. Damilano (Italy)	1	20	45
50,000 *Walk*—H. Gauder (G.D.R.)	3	40	53
Marathon—D. Wakihuru (Kenya)	2	11	48

	metres
High Jump—P. Sjöberg (Sweden)	2·38
Pole Vault—S. Bubka (U.S.S.R.)	5·85
Long Jump—C. Lewis (U.S.A.)	8·67
Triple Jump—K. Markov (Bulgaria)	17·92

		metres
Shot—W. Günther		
(Switzerland)		22·23
Discus—J. Schult (G.D.R.) ...		68·74
Hammer—S. Litvinov		
(U.S.S.R.).................		83·06
Javelin—S. Raty (Finland) ...		83·54
Decathlon—T. Voss (G.D.R.)..		8,680 pts.

Women's Events

Metres	hr.	min.	sec.
100—S. Gladisch (G.D.R.) ...			10·90
200—S. Gladisch (G.D.R.)			21·74
400—O. Bryzgina (U.S.S.R.) ..			49·38
800—S. Wodars (G.D.R.)		1	55·26
1,500—T. Samolenko			
(U.S.S.R.).................		3	58·56
3,000—T. Samolenko			
(U.S.S.R.).................		8	38·73
10,000—I. Kristiansen			
(Norway).................		31	05·85

	hr.	min.	sec.
100 *Hurdles*—G. Zagorcheva			
(Bulgaria)			12·34
400 *Hurdles*—S. Busch			
(G.D.R.)			53·62
4 × 100 *Relay*—United States .			41·58
4 × 400 *Relay*—G.D.R.		3	18·63
10,000 *Walk*—I. Strakhova			
(U.S.S.R.).................		44	12
Marathon—R. Mota			
(Portugal)	2	25	17

	metres
High Jump—S. Kostadinova	
(Bulgaria)	2·09
Long Jump—J. Joyner-Kersee	
(U.S.A.)	7·36
Shot—N. Lisovskaya	
(U.S.S.R.).................	21·24
Discus—M. Hellmann	
(G.D.R.)	71·62
Javelin—F. Whitbread (U.K.).	76·64
Heptathlon—J. Joyner-Kersee	
(U.S.A.)	7,128 pts.

GYMNASTICS, 1986

MEN'S

British Men's Champion, A. Morris.
British Men's Individual Apparatus Champions:
   Floor, N. Thomas.
   Pommel Horse, A. Morris.
   Rings, A. Morris.
   Vault, P. Bowler; N. Thomas.
   Parallel Bars, A. Morris.
   High Bar, N. Thomas.
British Men's Team Champions (Adam Shield), Bush Harlow 'A'.

WOMEN'S

British Women's Champion, L. Elliott.
British Women's Individual Apparatus Champions:
   Vault, K. Kennedy.
   Asymmetric Bars, L. Elliott.
   Beam, K. Williams.
   Floor, L. Elliott.
British Women's Open Club Team Champions, Heathrow.

WEIGHTLIFTING

WORLD WEIGHTLIFTING RECORDS (TOTALS)
(as at Sept. 15, 1987)

Class	Kg		
52 kg	262·5	N. Terziski (Bulgaria)	1984
56 kg	300	N. Shalamanov (Bulgaria)	1984
60 kg	335	N. Shalamanov (Bulgaria)	1986
67·5 kg	352·5	A.Behm (G.D.R.)	1984
75 kg	377·5	Z. Stoichkov (Bulgaria)	1984
82·5 kg	405	Y. Vardanyan (U.S.S.R.)	1984
90 kg	422·5	V. Solodov (U.S.S.R.)	1984
100 kg	440	Y. Zakharevich (U.S.S.R.)	1983
110 kg	447·5	Y. Zakharevich (U.S.S.R.)	1986
Over			
110 kg	472·5	L. Taranenko (U.S.S.R.)	1987

BASKETBALL, 1986–7

MEN'S

Prudential National Cup, Team Polycell Kingston.
Carlsberg National League, H.F.S. Portsmouth.
Carlsberg National Championship, B.C.P. London.

WOMEN'S

National Cup, B.C.P. London.
National League, Avon Northampton.
Carlsberg National Championship, Avon Northampton.

NETBALL, 1986–7

Test Matches

1986					
Nov. 22	*Gateshead*	*England*	*39*	*Australia*	*40*
Nov. 29	*Wembley*	*England*	*35*	*Australia*	*44*

Internationals

1987					
Feb. 21	*Gravesend*	*England*	*48*	*Scotland*	*22*
Mar. 21	*Cardiff*	*Wales*	*18*	*England*	*49*

Inter-County Champions, Kent.
National Clubs Champions, New Campbell.
World Championships (Final).—New Zealand beat Trinidad and Tobago, 49–37.

THE TURF

Horseracing in Great Britain is under the control of THE JOCKEY CLUB.

The Jockey Club (incorporating the National Hunt Committee), 42 Portman Square, London, W1H 0EN. Stewards are: The Lord Fairhaven (*Senior Steward*); Viscount Chelsea (*Deputy Senior Steward*); Gen. Sir Cecil Blacker; C. R. Saunders; A. T. A. Wates; Lord Vestey.

Winning Owners, 1986

Sheikh Mohammed	£830,532
K. Abdulla	803,137
H. H. Aga Khan	676,873
H. Ranier	221,196
Maktoum Al Maktoum ...	204,745
R. E. Sangster .	204,395
Hamdan Al-Maktoum ...	201,396
F. Salman	190,653
Lavinia Duchess of Norfolk	174,934
P. Mellon	152,317

Winning Trainers, 1986

M. Stoute...	£1,269,933
G. Harwood ...	942,002
H. Cecil	612,479
J. Dunlop	529,515
B. Hills	347,439
L. Cumani	346,977
W. Hern	339,010
B. Hanbury...	286,566
C. Brittain	273,829
P. Cole	263,529

Leading Breeders, 1986

	Value
H. H. Aga Khan	£677,876
Glen Oak Farm	423,601
J. Allan Mactier	226,171
Edward A. Seltzer & Shadowlawn Farm .	221,196
Lavinia Duchess of Norfolk	175,847
Kilfrush Stud Ltd......................	159,789
Paul Mellon	155,109
Pillar Stud Inc.	120,532
Eaton Farms Inc. & Red Bull Stable	119,976
R. D. Hollingsworth	112,253

Winning Sires, 1986

	Horses	Races won	Value
Lyphard (USA) by Northern Dancer..................	8	18	£458,697
Nijinsky (Can) (1967), by Northern Dancer........	8	11	355,246

Alleged (USA) (1974), by Hoist The Flag	13	24	332,368
Nureyev (USA) (1977), by Northern Dancer........	4	8	249,033
Top Ville (1976), by High Top	3	4	199,714
Try My Best (USA) (1975), by Northern Dancer	16	29	180,399
Vitiges (Fr) (1973) by Phaeton	7	17	180,257
Bustino (1971), by Busted ..	16	29	174,545
Kris (1976), by Sharpen Up .	18	29	169,563
Mill Reef (USA) (1968), by Never Bend.............	17	25	167,783
Ahonoora (1975) by Lorenzaccio	9	18	158,298
Mummy's Pet (1968) by Sing Sing	27	43	153,895

Winning Flat Jockeys, 1986

	1st	2nd	3rd	Unpl.	Total Mts.
P. Eddery	176	118	97	415	808
S. Cauthen.....	149	132	96	402	779
W. Carson	130	115	109	477	831
G. Starkey	102	57	42	304	505
G. Duffield	94	79	69	431	673
R. Cochrane....	89	106	72	462	729
W. Swinburn...	83	79	79	324	565
T. Ives.........	72	105	74	379	630

Winning National Hunt Jockeys 1986–87

	1st	2nd	3rd	Unpl.	Total Mts.
P. Scudamore ..	123	87	66	302	578
M. Dwyer......	81	54	35	167	337
R. Dunwoody ...	70	70	74	344	558
S. Sherwood ...	64	45	37	140	286
C. Grant	63	75	72	259	469
P. Tuck	59	50	42	187	338
S. Smith Eccles .	56	33	35	135	259
G. Bradley	53	32	21	126	232

(The above statistics are the copyright of *The Sporting Life*.)

THE DERBY, 1984–87

For particulars of the Derby from 1780–1983 see 1921–87 editions.

The *Distance* of the Derby course at Epsom is 1½ miles. First winner was Sir Charles Bunbury's Diomed in 1780. Lord Egremont won the Derby in 1782, 1804, 5, 7, 26 (also, 5 Oaks); Duke of Grafton, 1802, 9, 10, 15 (also, 9 Oaks); Mr. Bowes, 1835, 43, 52, 3; Sir J. Hawley, 1851, 58, 59, 68; the 1st Duke of Westminster, 1880, 82, 86, 99; Sir Victor Sassoon, 1953, 57, 58, 60. By winning his 5th Derby, in 1952, the late Aga Khan equalled Lord Egremont's record. He also won 2 Oaks. The Derby was run at Newmarket from 1915–18 and again from 1940–45.

Year	Owner and Name of Winner	Betting	Jockey	Trainer	No. of Run'rs
1984	Mr. L. Miglitti's Secreto	14–1	C. Roche	D. O'Brien....	17
1985	Lord H. de Walden's Slip Anchor	9–4 F.	S. Cauthen	H. Cecil	14
1986	H. H. Aga Khan's Shahrastani	11–2	W. Swinburn ...	M. Stoute....	17
1987	Mr. L. Freedman's Reference Point	6–4 F.	S. Cauthen	H. Cecil	19

Record times: 2 min. 33·8 sec. by Mahmoud in 1936; 2 min. 33·9 sec. by Reference Point in 1987; 2 min. 34 sec. by Hyperion in 1933, and Windsor Lad in 1934.

TWO THOUSAND GUINEAS. First Run, 1809. Rowley Mile. Newmarket. 9st.

Year	Owner and Name of Winner	Betting	Jockey	Trainer	No. of Run'rs
1983	Mr. R. Sangster's Lomond	9 to 1	P. Eddery	M. V. O'Brien	16
1984	Mr. R. Sangster's El Gran Senor	15 to 8 F.	P. Eddery	M. V. O'Brien	9
1985	Maktoum Al Maktoum's Shadeed	4 to 5 F.	L. Piggott	M. Stoute	14
1986	K. Abdulla's Dancing Brave	15 to 8 F.	G. Starkey	G. Harwood	15
1987	Mr. J. Horgan's Don't Forget Me	9 to 1	W. Carson	R. Hannon	13

ONE THOUSAND GUINEAS. 1814. Rowley Mile. Newmarket. Fillies. 9st.

Year	Owner and Name of Winner	Betting	Jockey	Trainer	No. of Run'rs
1983	Maktoum Al Maktoum's Ma Biche	5 to 2 F.	F. Head	Miss C. Head	18
1984	Capt. M. Lemos's Pebbles	8 to 1	P. Robinson	C. Brittain	15
1985	Sheikh Mohammed's Oh So Sharp	2 to 1 F.	S. Cauthen	H. Cecil	17
1986	H. Ranier's Midway Lady	10 to 1	R. Cochrane	B. Hanbury	15
1987	Mr. S. Niarchos's Miesque	15 to 8 F.	F. Head	F. Boutin	14

OAKS. 1779. Epsom. 1½ Mile. Fillies. 9 st.

Year	Owner and Name of Winner	Betting	Jockey	Trainer	No. of Run'rs
1983	Sir Michael Sobell's Sun Princess	6 to 1	W. Carson	W. R. Hern	15
1984	Sir Robin McAlpine's Circus Plume	4 to 1	L. Piggott	J. Dunlop	15
1985	Sheikh Mohammed's Oh So Sharp	6 to 4 F.	S. Cauthen	H. Cecil	12
1986	H. Ranier's Midway Lady	15 to 8 F.	R. Cochrane	B. Hanbury	15
1987	Sheikh Mohammed's Unite	11 to 1	W. Swinburn	M. Stoute	11

ST. LEGER. 1776(8). Doncaster. 1¾ mile, 127 yards.

Year	Owner and Name of Winner	Betting	Jockey	Trainer	No. of Run'rs
1983	Sir Michael Sobell's Sun Princess	11 to 8F.	W. Carson	W. R. Hern	10
1984	Mr. I. Allan's Commanche Run	7 to 4 F.	L. Piggott	L. Cumani	11
1985	Sheikh Mohammed's Oh So Sharp	8 to 11 F.	S. Cauthen	H. Cecil	6
1986	Lavinia Duchess of Norfolk's Moon Madness	9 to 2	P. Eddery	J. Dunlop	8
1987	Mr. L. Freedman's Reference Point	4 to 11 F.	S. Cauthen	H. Cecil	7

	Cheltenham Gold Cup* abt. 3¼ m.	**Lincoln Handicap** Doncaster—1 mile	**Grand National*** Liverpool—4½ m.	**European Free Handicap** Newmarket—3 yrs.—7 f.
1984	Burrough Hill Lad 8y 12st	Saving Mercy 4y 8st 9lb	Hallo Dandy 10y 10st 2lb	Cutting Wind 8st 8lb
1985	Forgive 'N Forget 8y 12st	Cataldi 4y 9st 10lb	Last Suspect 11y 10st 5lb	Over the Ocean 8st 11lb
1986	Dawn Run 8y 11st 9lb	K-Battery 5y 8st 4lb	West Tip 9y 10st 11lb	Green Desert 9st 7lb
1987	The Thinker 9y 12st	Star of a Gunner 7y 8st 8lb	Maori Venture 11y 10st 13lb	Noble Minstrel 9st 7lb

	Irish Grand National Fairyhouse—3 miles	**Jockey Club Stakes** Newmarket—1½ miles.	**Chester Cup** Chester—2¼ m. 77 yd.	**Coronation Cup** Epsom—1½ miles.
1984	Bentom Boy 9y 9st 9lb	Gay Lemur 4y 8st 7lb	Contester 4y 8st 2lb	Time Charter 5y 8st 11lb
1985	Rhyme 'N' Reason 6y 10st 6lb	Kirmann 4y 8st 7lb	Morgan's Choice 8y 7st 11lb.	Rainbow Quest 4y 9st
1986	Insure 8y 9st 11lb	Phardante 4y 8st 7lb	Western Dancer 5y 9st	Saint Estephe 4y 9st
1987	Brittany Boy 8y 10st 10lb	Phardante 5y 8st 12lb	Just David 4y 9st 8lb	Triptych 5y 8st 11lb

	Coventry Stakes Ascot—2 yrs—5 furlongs	**Gold Cup** Ascot—2½ miles	**Irish Sweeps Derby** Curragh—3 yrs—1½ miles	**Eclipse Stakes** Sandown Park—1¼m.
1984	Primo Dominie 8st 11lb	Gildoran 4y 9st	El Gran Senor	Sadler's Wells 3y 8st 8lb
1985	Sure Blade 8st 11lb	Gildoran 5y 9st	Law Society	Pebbles 4y 9st 4lb
1986	Cuttinb Blade 8st 11lb	Longboat 5y 9st	Shahrastani	Dancing Brave 3y 8st 8lb
1987	Always Fair 8st 13lb	Paean 4y 9st	Sir Harry Lewis	Mtoto 4y 9st 7lb

	King George VI and Queen Elizabeth Stakes Ascot—1½ miles	**Goodwood Cup** 2 m. 5 f.	**Gimcrack Stakes** York—2 yrs.—6 Furlongs.	**Middle Park Stakes** Newmarket—2 yrs.—6 f.
1984	Teenoso 4y 9st 7lb	Gildoran 4y 9st 7lb	Doulab 9st	Bassenthwaite 9st
1985	Petoski 3y 8st 8lv	Valuable Witness 5y 9st	Stalker 9st	Stalker 9st
1986	Dancing Brave 3y 8st 8lb	Longboat 5y 9st 7lb	Rich Charlie 9st 5lb	Mister Majestic 9st
1987	Reference Point 3y 8st 8lb	Sergeyevich 3y 7st	Reprimand 9st	Gallic League 9st

	Cambridgeshire Handicap Newmarket—9 f.	**Prix de L'Arc de Triomphe** Longchamp—1½ m.	**Champion Stakes** Newmarket—1¼ m.	**Cesarewitch** Newmarket—2¼ m.
1984	Leysh 3y 8st 7lb	Sagace 4y 9st 4lb	Palace Music	Tom Sharp 4y 7st 5lb
1985	Tremblant	Rainbow Quest 4y 9st 4lb	Pebbles 4y 9st	Kayudee 5y 7st 11lb
1986	Dallas 9st 6lb	Dancing Brave 3y 8st 11lb	Triptych 4y 9st	Orange Hill 4y 7st 9lb
1987	Balthus 8st 1lb	Trempolino 3y 8st 11lb	Triptych 5y 9st	Private Audition 5y 7st 7lb

*National Hunt

CRICKET

TEST MATCHES

Pakistan v. West Indies, 1986

First Test.—(Faisalabad, Oct. 24–29). Pakistan won by 186 runs. Pakistan 159 and 328; West Indies 248 and 53.

Second Test.—(Lahore, Nov. 7–9). West Indies won by an innings and 10 runs. Pakistan 131 and 77; West Indies 218.

Third Test.—(Karachi, Nov. 20–25). Drawn. West Indies 240 and 211; Pakistan 239 and 125 for 7.

Australia v. England, 1986–87

First Test.—(Brisbane, Nov. 14–19). England won by seven wickets. England 456 and 77 for 3; Australia 248 and 282.

Second Test.—(Perth, Nov. 28–Dec. 3). Drawn. England 592 for 8 dec. and 199 for 8 dec.; Australia 401 and 197 for 4.

Third Test.—(Adelaide, Dec. 12–16). Drawn. Australia 514 for 5 dec. and 201 for 3 dec.; England 455 and 39 for 2.

Fourth Test.—(Melbourne, Dec. 26–28). England won by an innings and 14 runs. Australia 141 and 194; England 349.

Fifth Test.—(Sydney, Jan. 10–15). Australia won by 55 runs. Australia 343 and 251; England 275 and 264.

India v. Sri Lanka, 1986–87

First Test.—(Kanpur, Dec. 17–22). Drawn. Sri Lanka 420. India 676 for 7.

Second Test.—(Nagpur, Dec. 27–31). India won by an innings and 106 runs. Sri Lanka 204 and 141; India 451 for 6 dec.

Third Test.—(Cuttack, Jan. 4–7). India won by an innings and 67 runs. India 400; Sri Lanka 191 and 142.

India v. Pakistan, 1987

First Test.—(Madras, Feb. 3–8). Drawn. Pakistan 487 for 9 dec. and 182 for 3; India 527 for 9 dec.

Second Test.—(Calcutta, Feb. 11–16). Drawn. India 403 and 181 for 3 dec.; Pakistan 229 and 179 for 5.

Third Test.—(Jaipur, Feb. 21–26). Drawn. India 465 for 8 dec. and 114 for 2; Pakistan 341.

Fourth Test.—(Ahmedabad, March 4–9). Drawn. Pakistan 395 and 136 for 2; India 323.

Fifth Test.—(Bangalore, March 13–18). Pakistan won by 16 runs. Pakistan 116 and 249; India 145 and 204.

New Zealand v. West Indies, 1987

First Test.—(Wellington, Feb. 20–25). Drawn. New Zealand 228 and 386 for 5 dec.; West Indies 345 and 50 for 2.

Second Test.—(Auckland, Feb. 26–March 3). West Indies won by ten wickets. West Indies 418 for 9 dec. and 16 for no wicket; New Zealand 157 and 273.

Third Test.—(Canterbury, March 13–15). New Zealand won by five wickets. West Indies 100 and 264; New Zealand 332 for 9 dec. and 33 for 5.

Sri Lanka v. New Zealand, 1987

First Test.—(Colombo, April 16–21). Drawn. Sri Lanka 397 for 9 dec.; New Zealand 406 for 5.
(Series abandoned)

England v. Pakistan, 1987

First Test.—(Old Trafford, June 4–9). Drawn. England 447; Pakistan 140 for 5.

Second Test.—(Lord's, June 18–23). Drawn. England 368 all out; (match abandoned).

Third Test.—(Headingley, July 2–6). Pakistan won by an innings and 18 runs. England 136 and 199; Pakistan 353 all out.

Fourth Test.—(Edgbaston, July 23–28). Drawn. Pakistan 439 and 205; England 521 and 109 for 7.

Fifth Test.—(The Oval, Aug. 6–11). Drawn. Pakistan 708; England 232 and 315 for 4.

OTHER INTERNATIONAL MATCHES

M.C.C. Bicentenary Test

Lords, Aug. 20–25.—Drawn. M.C.C. 455 for 7 dec. and 318 for 6 dec.; Rest of World XI 421 for 7 dec. and 13 for 1.

Texaco Trophy

Oval, May 21.—England bt. Pakistan by seven wkts. Pakistan 232 for 6; England 233 for 3.

Trent Bridge, May 23.—Pakistan bt. England by six wkts. England 157 all out; Pakistan 158 for 4.

Edgbaston, May 25.—England bt. Pakistan by one wkt. Pakistan 213 for 9; England 217 for 9.

World Series Cup

Final.—1st Match (Melbourne, Feb. 8). England beat Australia by six wickets.

2nd Match (Sydney, Feb. 11). England beat Australia by 8 runs.

Benson and Hedges Challenge

Final.—(Perth, Australia, Jan. 7). England beat Pakistan by five wickets.

Sharjah Cup

Winners, England; *Runners-Up,* Pakistan.

Australia v. England, 1986–7 (Averages)

ENGLAND BATTING

Batsmen	I	NO	R	HS	Av.
B. C. Broad	9	2	487	162	67.57
D. I. Gower	8	1	404	136	57.71
M. W. Gatting	9	0	393	100	43.66
C. J. Richards	7	0	264	133	37.71
J. E. Emburey	7	2	179	69	35.80
C. W. J. Athey	9	0	303	96	33.66
I. T. Botham	6	0	189	138	31.50
P. A. J. DeFreitas	5	1	77	40	19.25
A. J. Lamb	9	1	144	43	18.00
G. C. Small	3	1	35	21*	17.50
P. H. Edmonds	5	1	44	19	11.00
G. R. Dilley	4	2	6	4*	3.00

Also batted: J. J. Whitaker, 11.
* Not Out.

AUSTRALIA BATTING

Batsmen	I	NO	R	HS	Av.
D. M. Jones	10	1	511	184*	56.77
G. R. J. Matthews .	7	3	215	73*	53.75
A. R. Border	10	1	473	125	52.55
S. R. Waugh	8	1	310	79*	44.28
G. R. Marsh	10	0	429	110	42.90
G. M. Ritchie	8	2	244	46*	40.66
D. C. Boon	8	0	144	103	18.00
T. M. Zoehrer	7	1	102	38*	17.00
C. D. Matthews ...	3	0	21	11	7.00
P. R. Sleep	4	0	25	10	6.25
M. G. Hughes	6	0	31	16	5.16
B. A. Reid	7	4	14	4	4.66

Also batted: G. F. Lawson 13*; C. J. McDermott, 0, 1*; P. L. Taylor, 11, 42; D. M. Wellham, 17, 1.
* Not Out.

BOWLING

Bowlers	O	M	R	W	Av.
G. C. Small	78.4	23	180	12	15.00
G. R. Dilley	176.1	38	511	16	31.93
I. T. Botham	106.2	24	296	9	32.88
P. H. Edmonds	261.4	78	538	15	35.86
J. E. Emburey	315.5	86	663	18	36.83
P. A. J. DeFreitas	141.4	24	446	9	49.55

Also bowled: M. W. Gatting, 23-7-39-0; A. J. Lamb, 1-1-0-0.

BOWLING

Bowlers	O	M	R	W	Av.
P. L. Taylor	55	17	154	8	19.25
C. J. McDermott ..	26.5	4	83	4	20.75
B. A. Reid	198.4	44	527	20	26.35
P. R. Sleep	136	43	316	10	31.60
A. R. Border	16	6	32	1	32.00
S. R. Waugh	108.3	26	336	10	33.60
C. D. Matthews ...	70.1	14	233	6	38.83
M. G. Hughes	136.3	26	444	10	44.40
G. R. J. Matthews .	83	11	295	2	147.50

Also bowled: G. F. Lawson, 50-9-170-0.

England v. Pakistan, 1987 (Averages)

ENGLAND BATTING

Batsmen	I	NO	R	HS	Av.
M. W. Gatting	8	1	445	151*	63.57
D. J. Capel	2	0	81	53	40.50
R. T. Robinson ...	8	0	299	166	37.37
C. W. J. Athey	6	1	186	123	37.20
I. T. Botham	8	1	232	51*	33.14
J. E. Emburey	5	0	162	58	32.40
D. I. Gower	8	0	236	61	29.50
B. C. Broad	7	0	193	55	27.57
B. N. French	5	1	103	59	25.75
P. H. Edmonds	7	4	66	24*	22.00
N. A. Foster	6	0	93	29	15.50
M. D. Moxon	2	0	23	15	11.50
P. A. J. DeFreitas .	1	0	11	11	11.00
C. J. Richards.....	2	0	8	6	4.00

Also batted: N. H. Fairbrother, 0.
* Not Out.

PAKISTAN BATTING

Batsmen	I	NO	R	HS	Av.
Javed Miandad ...	5	0	360	260	72.00
Salim Yousef.....	4	1	187	91*	62.33
Mudassar Nazar ..	5	1	231	124	57.75
Salim Malik	5	0	248	102	49.60
Imran Khan	5	1	191	118	47.75
Ijaz Ahmed	4	0	150	69	37.50
Mansoor Akhtar ..	5	0	152	75	30.40
S. Mohammad.....	4	0	84	50	21.00
Wasim Akram	4	0	80	43	20.00
Ramiz Raja	2	0	29	15	14.50
Mohsin Kamal ...	3	2	13	10	13.00
Abdul Qadir	4	0	28	20	7.00

Also batted: Tansif Ahmed, 0*.
* Not out.

BOWLING

Bowlers	O	M	R	W	Av.
N. A. Foster	137.2	36	339	15	22.60
G. R. Dilley	133.3	26	388	14	27.71
P. A. J. DeFreitas .	12	4	36	1	36.00
P. H. Edmonds	92.3	36	219	4	54.75
I. T. Botham	134.3	30	433	7	61.85

Also bowled: D. J. Capel, 18-1-64-0; J. E. Emburey, 107-21-222-0; M. W. Gatting, 22-5-40-0; M. D. Moxon, 6-2-27-0.

BOWLING

Bowlers	O	M	R	W	Av.
Imran Khan	168.2	33	455	21	21.66
Wasim Akram	180.4	38	464	16	29.00
Mohsin Kamal ...	94.4	14	332	9	36.88
Tansif Ahmed.....	91.1	28	203	5	40.60
Abdul Qadir	175.4	46	450	11	40.90
Mudassar Nazar ..	110	26	303	3	101.00

Also bowled: Javed Miandad, 4-2-10-0.

English Batting Averages, 1987†
(Qualification, 8 Innings)

Batsmen	I	NO	R	HS	Av.
M. D. Crowe	29	5	1627	206*	67·79
K. D. James	16	6	620	142*	62·00
M. W. Gatting	29	2	1646	196	60·96
R. K. Illingworth	19	11	448	120*	56·00
R. J. Hadlee	28	7	1111	133*	52·90
G. A. Hick	38	2	1879	173	52·19
P. M. Roebuck	29	5	1199	165*	49·95
C. G. Greenidge	18	0	899	163	49·94
D. R. Turner	35	8	1328	184*	49·18
R. A. Smith	25	7	869	209*	48·27
R. A. Harper	9	5	193	127*	48·25
G. Fowler	43	5	1800	169*	47·36
T. S. Curtis	40	6	1601	138*	47·08
C. L. Smith	42	9	1519	217	46·03
C. E. B. Rice	32	8	1103	138	45·95
C. M. Wells	39	7	1456	148*	45·50
R. G. Williams	27	7	898	104	44·90
N. E. Briers	32	4	1257	104	44·89
C. W. J. Athey	34	5	1295	160	44·65
D. I. Gower	31	4	1197	125	44·33
M. R. Benson	39	0	1725	131	44·23
J. W. Lloyds	32	4	1213	130	43·32
B. Roberts	41	3	1643	184	43·23
V. P. Terry	37	5	1382	122	43·18
K. M. Curran	33	6	1142	119	42·29

* Denotes not out.

English Bowling Averages, 1987†
(Qualification, 10 Wickets)

Bowlers	O	M	R	W	Av.
R. J. Hadlee	591·0	189	1227	97	12·64
A. H. Gray	291·1	59	748	48	15·58
K. J. Barnett	88·2	27	225	13	17·30
S. T. Clarke	456·4	114	1160	67	17·31
N. G. Cowans	341·3	77	958	51	18·78
T. M. Tremlett	547·0	153	1407	72	19·54
O. H. Mortensen ..	432·5	111	1084	55	19·70
M. D. Marshall....	594·1	152	1508	76	19·84
P. J. W. Allott ...	535·2	166	1222	59	20·71
N. V. Radford.....	741·5	125	2269	109	20·81
A. Walker	390·2	104	1011	48	21·06
T. E. Jesty........	72·4	11	212	10	21·20
J. Simmons.......	640·3	196	1425	67	21·26
S. J. W. Andrew ..	316·1	61	1022	48	21·29
G. J. F. Ferris....	359·1	69	1143	52	21·98
N. A. Foster	674·5	147	1892	86	22·00
G. R. Dilley	265·3	52	817	35	23·34
M. Watkinson	318·0	66	986	42	23·47
S. J. Base........	202·1	38	660	28	23·57
M. P. Bicknell ...	363·2	94	997	42	23·73
G. S. Le Roux	266·5	54	768	32	24·00
K. W. McLeod	126·4	24	409	17	24·05
E. E. Hemmings...	872·4	295	2119	88	24·07
J. P. Agnew	777·0	144	2451	101	24·26
R. G. Newman	364·0	75	1093	45	24·28

† Figures do not include averages for the Pakistani tourists.

County Championship Table, 1987

Order for 1986 in brackets	Played	Won	Lost	Drawn	Bonus Btg.	Bonus Blng.	Points
Nottinghamshire (4) ...	24	9	1	14	68	80	292
Lancashire (15)	24	10	4	10	55	73	288
Leicestershire (7)	24	8	3	13	57	75	260
Surrey (3)	24	7	4	13	65	73	250
Hampshire (6)	24	7	3	14	59	73	244
Derbyshire (11)	24	6	5	12	51	70	225
Northamptonshire (9) ..	24	7	4	13	48	68	224
Yorkshire (9)	24	7	3	14	52	58	222
Worcestershire (10)	24	5	4	15	58	68	206
Gloucestershire (2)	24	5	8	10	62	50	200
Somerset (16)	24	2	3	19	61	70	163
Essex (1)	24	2	4	18	45	77	162
Glamorgan (17)	24	3	9	12	40	70	158
Kent (8)...............	24	2	7	15	53	66	151
Warwickshire (12)	24	2	7	15	48	67	147
Middlesex (12)	24	2	8	14	47	60	139
Sussex (14)	24	1	8	15	47	56	119

(Essex total includes eight points for drawn match in which the scores finished level. Northants total includes 12 points for win in one innings match. Derbyshire and Gloucestershire were involved in a tied match.)

Other Results, 1987

NatWest Trophy.—Nottinghamshire beat Northamptonshire by three wickets. Northamptonshire 228 for 3; Nottinghamshire 231 for 7.

Benson and Hedges Cup Final.—Yorkshire beat Northamptonshire by losing fewer wickets. Northamptonshire 244 for 7; Yorkshire 244 for 6.

Refuge Assurance Sunday League Champions.—Worcestershire.

Universities.—Match drawn. Cambridge 207 and 367 for 5 dec.; Oxford 347 for 7 dec. and 29 for 1.

Eton v. Harrow.—Match drawn. Harrow 196 for 8 dec.; Eton 169 for 5.

BOWLS, 1987

National Championships
(Worthing)

Fours.—*Final:* Aylesbury Town (Bucks.) beat Temple (Surrey) 20–17.

Triples.—*Final:* Worcester County Ground (Worcs.) beat Stroud (Glos.) 24–10.

Pairs.—*Final:* Bolton (Lancs.) beat Uxbridge (Middx.) 23–21.

Singles.—*Final:* D. A. Holt (Bolton, Lancs.) beat A. Allcock (Cheltenham, Glos.) 21–5.

World Indoor Championship, A. Allcock.
National Indoor Singles Championship, A. Allcock.
County Championship, Norfolk.
Inter-County Championship (Middleton Cup).—*Final:* Kent beat Essex 142–89.

RUGBY FOOTBALL

RUGBY UNION

World Cup

Quarter-Finals: Australia beat Ireland 33–15 pts.;
New Zealand beat Scotland 30–3 pts.; France beat
Fiji 31–16 pts.; Wales beat England 16–3 pts.
Semi-Finals: France beat Australia 30–24 pts.; New
Zealand beat Wales 49–6 pts.
3rd place play-off: Wales beat Australia 22–21 pts.
Final: New Zealand beat France 29–9 pts.

International Matches 1986–87

1986					
Sept. 27	Edinburgh:	Scotland	33	Japan	18
Oct. 11	Twickenham:	England	39	Japan	12
Nov. 1	Dublin:	Ireland	60	Romania	0
1987					
Feb. 7	Paris:	France	16	Wales	9
	Dublin:	Ireland	17	England	0
Feb. 21	Twickenham:	England	15	France	19
	Edinburgh:	Scotland	16	Ireland	12
Mar. 7	Cardiff:	Wales	19	England	12
	Paris:	France	28	Scotland	22
Mar. 21	Dublin:	Ireland	13	France	19
	Edinburgh:	Scotland	21	Wales	15
Apr. 1	Cardiff:	Barbarians		New	
			16	Zealand	68
4	Twickenham:	England	21	Scotland	12
	Cardiff:	Wales	11	Ireland	15

International Union Table, 1987

	P	W	D	L	Pts.		Total
					F	A	
France	4	4	0	0	82	59	8
Ireland	4	2	0	2	57	46	4
Scotland	4	2	0	2	71	76	4
Wales	4	1	0	3	54	64	2
England	4	1	0	3	48	67	2

County Championship Final

Warwickshire beat Kent 16–6

Other Chief Matches, 1986–87

Universities. 1986. Oxford beat Cambridge by 15–10
pts.
Services Championship.—Royal Navy beat Army 21–
10; R.A.F. drew with the Army 12–12; Royal Navy
beat R.A.F. 13–6.
John Player Special Cup Final.—Bath beat Wasps
19–12 at Twickenham on May 2.
Hospitals' Cup Final.—St. Mary's beat Charing
Cross/Westminster 22–3.
Middlesex Sevens.—Harlequins.

RUGBY FOOTBALL LEAGUE
(Est. 1895)

International Matches

1986					
Oct. 25	Manchester:	Gt. Britain 16	Australia	38
Nov. 8	Leeds:	Gt. Britain 4	Australia	34
Nov. 22	Wigan:	Gt. Britain 15	Australia	24
1987					
Feb. 8	Carcassone:	France	10	Gt. Britain 20

Rugby League Challenge Cup Final.—Halifax beat
St. Helens 19–18 pts. at Wembley on May 2, 1987.
Premiership Trophy Final.—Wigan beat Warrington
8–0 pts. at Old Trafford on May 17, 1987.
Stones Bitter Champions.—Wigan.
Second Division Champions.—Hunslet.
Yorkshire Cup.—Castleford beat Hull 31–5 pts.
Lancashire Cup.—Wigan beat Oldham 27–6 pts.
John Player Special Trophy Final.—Wigan beat
Warrington 18–4 pts.

HOCKEY, 1986–87

MEN'S HOCKEY

World Cup (Willesden, London)

Semi-Finals: England beat West Germany, 3–2
(a.e.t.); Australia beat U.S.S.R. 5–0.
Final: Australia beat England 2–1.
European Championships Final. Netherlands and
England drew 1–1 (a.e.t.). Netherlands won 3–0 on
penalty strokes.
Champions Trophy. West Germany.
Home Countries Tournament. England.
County Championship Final. Worcestershire beat
Devon 2–1.
National Club Championship Final. Southgate beat
Slough 3–2.
National Indoor Club Championship Final. East
Grinstead and St. Albans drew 3–3. East Grinstead
won 3–2 on penalty strokes.
Universities. Oxford drew with Cambridge 0–0.

WOMEN'S HOCKEY

European Championships Final. Netherlands and
England drew 2–2 (a.e.t.). Netherlands won 3–1 on
penalty strokes.
Champions Trophy. Netherlands.
Home Countries Championship. Wales beat Scotland
3–0; Ireland beat England 2–1; Ireland beat Wales
2–0; England drew with Scotland 1–1.
County Championship Final. Staffordshire beat Lancashire 1–0.

CHESS, 1987

British Championship. N. Short.
Ladies. C. Forbes.
Under-18 (Men). R. Tozer.
Under-18 (Women). J. Harwar.

ASSOCIATION FOOTBALL

LEAGUE COMPETITIONS, 1986–87

Div. I.—Champions: Everton, 86 pts. Runners-up: Liverpool, 77 pts. *Relegated:* Leicester City, 42 pts.; Manchester City, 39 pts.; Aston Villa, 36 pts.

Div. II.—Champions: Derby County, 84 pts.; *Promoted:* Portsmouth, 78 pts. *Relegated:* Grimsby, 44 pts.; Brighton, 39 pts.

Div. III.—Champions: Bournemouth, 97 pts. *Promoted:* Middlesbrough, 94 pts. *Relegated:* Carlisle, 38 pts.; Darlington, 37 pts.; Newport County, 37 pts.

Div. IV.—Champions: Northampton, 99 pts. *Promoted:* Preston, 90 pts.; Southend, 80 pts. *Relegated to G.M. Vauxhall Conference:* Lincoln City, 48 pts.

G.M. Vauxhall Conference.—Champions and Promoted: Scarborough, 91 pts.

END OF SEASON PLAY-OFFS

Divisions 1 and 2: S.F.—Charlton beat *Ipswich 2–1 on agg.; *Leeds beat Oldham, agg. 2–2, on away goals.

Final.—*Charlton 1 Leeds 1 on agg. Charlton won 2–1 after replay.

Divisions 2 and 3: S.F.—*Gillingham beat Sunderland, agg. 6–6, on away goals; Swindon beat *Wigan 3–2 on agg.

Final—Swindon 2 *Gillingham 2 on agg. Swindon won 2–0 after replay.

Divisions 3 and 4: S.F.—*Aldershot beat Bolton 3–2 on agg.; Wolves beat *Colchester 2–0 on agg.

Final—*Aldershot beat Wolves 3–0 on agg.

*Indicates home team in first match.

As a result of the end-of-season play-offs Charlton remained in Division 1, Swindon were promoted to Division 2 and Aldershot to Division 3.

SCOTTISH LEAGUE

Premier Div.—Rangers, 69 pts.
Div. I.—Morton, 57 pts.
Div. II.—Meadowbank, 55 pts.

CUP COMPETITIONS, 1986–87

F.A. CUP.—*S.F.:* (Villa Park), Tottenham Hotspur beat Watford, 4–1; (Hillsborough), Coventry City beat Leeds United, 3–2.
Final: May 16 (Wembley Stadium), Coventry City beat Tottenham Hotspur 3–2 a.e.t.

LITTLEWOODS CUP (formerly the *Milk Cup*).—*Final:* Arsenal beat Liverpool 2–1.

FULL MEMBERS' CUP.—*Final:* Blackburn Rovers beat Charlton Athletic 1–0.

FREIGHT ROVER TROPHY.—*Final:* Bristol City 1 Mansfield 1 a.e.t. Mansfield won 5–4 on penalties.

F.A. VASE.—*Final:* St. Helens Town beat Warrington Town 3–2.

F.A. TROPHY.—*Final:* Burton Albion 0 Kidderminster Harriers 0 a.e.t. Kidderminster won 2–1 after a replay.

F.A. YOUTH CUP.—*Winners:* Coventry City.

ARTHUR DUNN CUP.—*Final:* Old Cholmeleians 2 Old Reptonians 2. Old Reptonians won 3–2 after a replay.

SCOTTISH F.A. CUP.—*Final:* May 16 (Hampden Park), St. Mirren beat Dundee United 1–0 a.e.t.

SKOL CUP.—*Final:* Rangers beat Celtic 2–1.

ROUS CUP.—*Winners:* Brazil.

England 1	Brazil 1		
Scotland 0	England 0		
Scotland 0	Brazil 2		

EUROPEAN CUP.—*Final:* Porto beat Bayern Munich 2–1 in Vienna.

EUROPEAN CUP-WINNERS' CUP.—*Final:* Ajax Amsterdam beat Lokomotiv Leipzig 1–0 in Athens.

U.E.F.A. CUP.—*Final:* I.F.K. Gothenburg beat Dundee United 2–1 (on aggregate).

INTERNATIONALS

1986				
Sept. 10	Stockholm:	Sweden	1 England	0
1987				
Feb. 18	Madrid:	Spain	2 England	4

EUROPEAN FOOTBALL CHAMPIONSHIP

(*Qualifying*)
England, Northern Ireland (*Group 4*); Wales (*Group 6*); Scotland (*Group 7*).

1986				
Oct. 15	Wembley:	England	3 N. Ireland	0
	Dublin:	Rep. Ireland	0 Scotland	0
Nov. 12	Wembley:	England	2 Yugoslavia	0
	Izmir:	Turkey	0 N. Ireland	0
	Hampden:	Scotland	3 Luxembourg	0
1987				
Feb. 18	Hampden:	Scotland	0 Rep. Ireland	1
Apr. 1	Belfast:	N. Ireland	0 England	2
	Wrexham:	Wales	4 Finland	0
	Brussels:	Belgium	4 Scotland	1
Apr. 29	Belfast:	N. Ireland	1 Yugoslavia	2
	Izmir:	Turkey	0 England	0
	Cardiff:	Wales	1 Czechoslovakia	1

PAST WORLD CUP WINNERS

1930 (*Played in Uruguay*)	Uruguay
1934 (*Italy*)	Italy
1938 (*France*)	Italy
1950 (*Brazil*)	Uruguay
1954 (*Switzerland*)	West Germany
1958 (*Sweden*)	Brazil
1962 (*Chile*)	Brazil
1966 (*England*)	England
1970 (*Mexico*)	Brazil
1974 (*West Germany*)	West Germany
1978 (*Argentina*)	Argentina
1982 (*Spain*)	Italy
1986 (*Mexico*)	Argentina

GOLF, 1986–87

MAJOR CHAMPIONSHIPS 1987

THE OPEN (Muirfield, July 16–19)
N. Faldo, (*G.B.*) 279.

THE U.S. OPEN (San Francisco, June 18–21)
S. Simpson, (*U.S.*) 277.

THE MASTERS (Augusta, Georgia, April 9–12)
L. Mize, (*U.S.*) 285.

THE U.S. P.G.A. (Palm Beach, Florida, Aug. 6–9)
L. Nelson, (*U.S.*) 287.

TEAM EVENTS

RYDER CUP (Muirfield Village, Ohio, Sept. 25–27)
Great Britain and Europe beat U.S.A. by 15 to 13.

WALKER CUP (Sunningdale, May 27–28)
U.S.A. beat Great Britain and Ireland by 16½ to 7½.

CURTIS CUP (Prairie Dunes, Aug. 1986)
Great Britain and Ireland beat U.S.A. by 13 to 5.

EUROPEAN P.G.A. TOUR, 1987

Moroccan Open.—H. Clark (G.B.).

Jersey Open.—I. Woosnam (G.B.).

Suze Open.—S. Ballesteros (Spain).

Madrid Open.—I. Woosnam (G.B.).

Italian Open.—S. Torrance (G.B.).

Epson Grand Prix.—M. Lanner (Sweden).

Spanish Open.—N. Faldo (G.B.).

Whyte and Mackay P.G.A.—B. Langer (W. Germany).

London Standard Four Stars Pro-Celebrity Tournament.—M. McNulty (S.A.).

Dunhill British Masters.—M. McNulty (S.A.).

French Open.—J. Rivero (Spain).

Belgian Open.—E. Darcy (Ireland).

Monte Carlo Open.—P. Senior (Australia).

Irish Open.—B. Langer (W. Germany).

Scottish Open.—I. Woosnam (G.B.).

Dutch Open.—G. Brand, Jr. (G.B.).

Scandinavian Open.—G. Brand, Jr. (G.B.).

P.L.M. Open.—H. Clark (G.B.).

Benson and Hedges International.—N. Ratcliffe (Australia).

Lawrence Batley International.—M. O'Meara (U.S.).

German Open.—M. McNulty (S.A.).

European Masters—Swiss Open.—A. Forsbrand (Sweden).

European Open.—P. Way (G.B.).

WOMEN'S CHAMPIONSHIPS

U.S. Women's Open.—L. Davies (G.B.).

European Women's Open.—D. Reid (G.B.).

British Women's Open.—A. Nicholas (G.B.).

English Ladies Amateur Championship.—J. Furby.

European Ladies Amateur Team Championship.—Sweden.

English Girls Open Championship.—S. Shapcott.

British Girls Open Championship.—H. Dobson.

MEN'S AMATEUR CHAMPIONSHIPS

Amateur Championship.—P. Mayo.

English Championship.—K. Weeks.

British Youths Open Championship.—J. Cook.

Boys Amateur Championship.—J. Cook.

Halford Hewitt (for schools).—Merchiston.

Lytham Trophy.—D. Wood.

Brabazon Trophy.—J. Robinson.

Berkshire Trophy.—J. Robinson.

Carris Trophy.—D. Bathgate.

Championships

OPEN (Instituted 1860)	
1980 T. Watson (U.S.A.), 271.	1982 M. Thompson.
1981 W. Rogers (U.S.A.), 276.	1983 P. Parkin.
1982 T. Watson (U.S.A.), 284.	1984 J.-M. Olazabal (Spain).
1983 T. Watson (U.S.A.), 275.	1985 G. McGimpsey.
1984 S. Ballesteros (Spain), 276.	1986 D. Curry.
1985 S. Lyle (G.B.), 282.	1987 P. Mayo.
1986 G. Norman (Australia), 280.	
1987 N. Faldo (G.B.), 279.	

AMATEUR (1885)	LADIES (1893)
1980 D. Evans.	1980 Mrs. A. Sander (U.S.A.).
1981 P. Ploujoux (France).	1981 Mrs. B. Robertson.
	1982 Miss K. Douglas.
	1983 Mrs. J. Thornhill.
	1984 Miss J. Rosenthal (U.S.A.).
	1985 Miss L. Behan.
	1986 Miss M. McGuire (N.Z.)
	1987 J. Furby.

POLO, 1987

Queen's Cup.—Southfield beat Cowdray Park, 8–3.

Cowdray Park Gold Cup.—Tramontana beat Windsor Park, 9–5.

Royal Windsor Cup.—Brent Walker beat Sladmore, 5–4.

Coronation Cup.—N. America beat England, 8–5.

Silver Jubilee Cup.—The Prince of Wales' Team beat Peru, 7–5.

Universities.—Cambridge beat Oxford, 3–2.

Warwickshire Cup.—Southfield beat Cowdray Park, 8–5.

LAWN TENNIS, 1986–87

THE ALL ENGLAND CHAMPIONSHIPS (WIMBLEDON)
1987

Men's Singles.—P. Cash (Australia) beat I. Lendl (Czechoslovakia), 7–6, 6–2, 7–5.

Women's Singles.—Miss M. Navratilova (U.S.A.) beat Miss S. Graf (W. Germany), 7–5, 6–3.

Men's Doubles.—K. Flach and R. Seguso (U.S.A.) beat S. Casal and E. Sanchez (Spain), 3–6, 6–7, 7–6, 6–1, 6–4.

Women's Doubles.—Miss C. Kohde-Kilsch (W. Germany) and Miss H. Sukova (Czechoslovakia) beat Miss B. Nagelsen and Miss P. Smylie (U.S.A.), 7–5, 7–5.

Mixed Doubles.—M. J. Bates and Miss J. M. Durie (G.B.) beat D. Cahill and Miss N. Provis (Australia), 7–6, 6–3.

Australian Championships:
Men's Singles.—S. Edberg (Sweden).
Women's Singles.—Miss H. Mandlikova (Czechoslovakia).
Men's Doubles.—S. Edberg and A. Jarryd (Sweden).
Women's Doubles.—Miss M. Navratilova and Miss P. Shriver (U.S.A.).
Mixed Doubles.—S. Stewart and Miss Z. Garrison (U.S.A.).

U.S.A. Championships:
Men's Singles.—I. Lendl (Czechoslovakia).
Women's Singles.—Miss M. Navratilova (U.S.A.).
Men's Doubles.—S. Edberg and A. Jarryd (Sweden).
Women's Doubles.—Miss M. Navratilova and Miss P. Shriver (U.S.A.).
Mixed Doubles.—E. Sanchez (Spain) and Miss M. Navratilova (U.S.A.).

French Championships:
Men's Singles.—I. Lendl (Czechoslovakia).
Women's Singles.—Miss S. Graf (W. Germany).
Men's Doubles.—A. Jarryd (Sweden) and R. Seguso (U.S.A.).
Women's Doubles.—Miss M. Navratilova and Miss P. Shriver (U.S.A.).
Mixed Doubles.—E. Sanchez (Spain) and Miss P. Shriver (U.S.A.).

DAVIS CUP, 1986–7
(Founder—Dwight Filley Davis (1879–1945))

Australia beat Sweden by 3 matches to 2.

WIGHTMAN CUP, 1986
(Royal Albert Hall, London)

U.S.A. beat G.B. by 7 matches to 0.

Federation Cup.—West Germany.
Youll Cup.—St. Paul's.
Clark Cup.—Repton.

Prudential County Cup—Men: Kent; *Women:* Surrey.

REAL TENNIS, 1986–87

Amateur Singles Championship.—J. Snow beat H. Angus, 3–0.

Amateur Doubles Championship.—J. Snow and J. Male beat A. Lovell and M. Dean, 3–1.

British Open Singles Championship.—C. Ronaldson beat P. Brake, 3–0.

British Open Doubles Championship.—K. Fletcher and L. Deuchar beat C. and S. Ronaldson, 2–0.

Women's Open Doubles.—S. Jones and A. Warren-Piper beat L. Ronaldson and G. Dean, 2–0.

Henry Leaf Cup.—Radley beat Winchester, 2–1.

Universities.—Cambridge beat Oxford, 3–1.

BADMINTON, 1987

ENGLISH NATIONAL CHAMPIONSHIPS

Men's Singles.—S. Baddeley.

Women's Singles.—Miss F. Elliott.

Men's Doubles.—A. Goode and S. Baddeley.

Women's Doubles.—Miss G. Clark and Miss G. Gowers.

Mixed Doubles.—A. Goode and Miss F. Elliott.

ALL-ENGLAND CHAMPIONSHIPS (WEMBLEY)

Men's Singles.—M. Frost (Denmark).

Women's Singles.—K. Larsen (Denmark).

Men's Doubles.—L. Yongbo and T. Hingyi (China).

Women's Doubles.—C. Myung-Hee and H. Hye-Young (S. Korea).

Mixed Doubles.—L. Deuk-Choon and C. Myung-Hee (S. Korea).

RACKETS, 1986–87

Celestion Amateur Singles Championship.—W. Boone beat M. Nicholls, 3–0.
Celestion Amateur Doubles Championship.—J. Male and R. Owen-Browne beat M. and P. Nicholls, 4–3.
Celestion Professional Singles Championship.—N. Smith beat S. Hazell, 3–0.
Celestion British Open Singles Championship.—J. Male beat N. Smith, 4–1.
Celestion British Open Doubles Championship.—J. Prenn and J. Male beat W. Boone and R. Crawley, 4–3.
Noel Bruce Cup.—Eton (W. Boone and T. Pugh) beat Malvern (M. and P. Nicholls), 4–2.
Public Schools Doubles Championship.—Tonbridge beat Marlborough, 4–2.
Universities.—Cambridge beat Oxford, 2–1.

SQUASH RACKETS, 1986–87

World Open Championship.—R. Norman (N.Z.) beat Jahangir Khan (Pakistan), 3–1.
British Open Championship.—Jahangir Khan (Pakistan) beat Jansher Khan (Pakistan), 3–0.
British Women's Open Championship.—Miss S. Devoy (N.Z.) beat Miss L. Soutter (England), 3–2.
National Men's Championship.—B. Beeson beat M. Maclean, 3–1.
National Women's Championship.—Miss L. Opie beat Miss M. Le Moignan, 3–0.
British Under-23 Open.—R. Martin (Australia) beat Z. Jahan (Pakistan), 3–1.
Home International Championships.—*Men:* England; *Women:* England.
Inter-County.—Yorkshire.
Drysdale Cup.—D. Harris beat D. Walker, 3–0.
Universities.—Oxford beat Cambridge, 4–1.

SKI-ING 1986–87

WORLD CHAMPIONSHIPS
(Crans Montana, Switzerland 1987)

Men's:
  Downhill.—P. Mueller (Switz.).
  Slalom.—F. Woerndl (F.R.G.).
  Giant Slalom.—P. Zurbriggen (Switz.).
Women's:
  Downhill.—M. Walliser (Switz.).
  Slalom.—C. Schmidhauser (Switz.).
  Giant Slalom.—V. Schneider (Switz.).

WORLD CUP 1986–87

Men's:
  Downhill.—P. Zurbriggen (Switz.).
  Slalom.—B. Krizaj (Yugo.).
  Giant Slalom.—R. Pramotton (Italy).
Women's:
  Downhill.—M. Figini (Switz.).
  Slalom.—C. Schmidhauser (Switz.).
  Giant Slalom.—V. Schneider (Switz.).

British National Alpine Championships, 1987.
Men.—M. Bell.
Women.—L. Beck.

ICE SKATING, 1986–87

WORLD CHAMPIONSHIPS
(Cincinnati)

Men's Figure.—B. Orser (Canada).
Ladies' Figure.—Miss K. Witt (East Germany).
Pairs.—E. Gordeyeva and S. Grinkov (U.S.S.R.).
Ice Dancing.—A. Bukin and N. Bestemianova (U.S.S.R.).

EUROPEAN CHAMPIONSHIPS
(Sarajevo)

Men's Figure.—A. Fadeyev (U.S.S.R.).
Ladies' Figure.—Miss K. Witt (East Germany).
Pairs.—O. Maharov and L. Selezneva (U.S.S.R.).
Ice Dancing.—A. Bukin and N. Bestemianova (U.S.S.R.).

BRITISH CHAMPIONSHIPS

Men's Figure.—P. Robinson.
Ladies' Figure.—Miss J. Conway.
Pairs.—A. Naylor and Miss C. Peake.
Ice Dancing.—P. Askham and Miss S. Jones.

FENCING, 1986–87

British Championships:
  Foil.—P. Harper (Salle Goodall).
  Epée.—R. Johnson (Salle Boston).
  Ladies' Foil.—Mrs. L. Thurley (Salle Paul).
Sporting Record Cup.—Salle Paul.
Magrini Cup.—Polytechnic.
Savage Shield.—Salle Boston.
Martin Edmunds Cup.—Salle Paul.
Eden Cup.—Weidner (W. Germany).
Challenge Martini International Epée.—A. Schmitt (West Germany).

ETON FIVES, 1987

Amateur Championship (Kinnaird Cup).—B. C. Matthews and J. W. Reynolds.
Nat West County Championship.—Warwickshire.

Holmwoods Schools Championships.—Wolverhampton G.S.
Alan Barber Cup.—Old Cholmeleians.
League Championship (Douglas Keeble Cup).—Old Salopians.

RUGBY FIVES, 1986–87

Amateur Singles Championship.—G. W. Enstone beat A. R. Wynn.
Amateur Doubles Championship.—I. P. Fuller and D. J. Hebden beat D. Parlby and J. Schroeter.
National Schools' Championships.—*Singles:* D. Mellor (St. Dunstan's).
  Doubles: St. Dunstan's.

TABLE TENNIS, 1987

ENGLISH NATIONAL CHAMPIONSHIPS
(Crawley)

Men's Singles: D. Douglas.
Women's Singles: Miss F. Elliot.
Men's Doubles: S. Andrew and N. Mason.
Women's Doubles: Miss L. Bellinger and Miss J. Bellinger.
Mixed Doubles: S. Andrew and Miss F. Elliot.

CYCLING, 1987

Tour de France.—S. Roche (Ireland).
Milk Race.—M. Elliott.
World Professional Road Race Championship.—S. Roche (Ireland).
British Professional Road Race Championship.—P. Sherwen.
British Amateur Road Race Championship.—P. Curran.
Tour of Britain.—J. McLoughlin.

OXFORD AND CAMBRIDGE

PRINCIPAL EVENTS AND WINNERS, 1986–87

Event (with date of first meeting)	Summary of Results			Results 1986–87
	Ox.	Camb.	Drawn	
Athletics (1864)	57	49	7	Oxford
Boat Race (1829)	63	69	1	Oxford
Cricket (1827)	46	54	43	Draw
Football—				
Association (1873–4)	38	44	21	Camb.
Rugby (1871–2)	45	47	13	Oxford
Golf (1878)	39	52	5	Camb.
Hockey (1890)	28	40	16	Draw

OTHER UNIVERSITY EVENTS AND WINNERS, 1986–87

Cross Country	Oxford
Rackets	Cambridge
Polo	Cambridge
Real Tennis	Cambridge
Boxing	Cambridge
Yachting	Cambridge
Squash Rackets	Oxford

ANGLING

NATIONAL COARSE CHAMPIONSHIPS

Year	Venue	No. of teams	Individual Winner	Weight	Team Winners	Points	Division
				k.　g.			
1985	Leeds & Liverpool Canal	79	B. Oliver (Northwich)	4　120	A.B.C.	734	1
	R. Witham	79	M. Hukin (Darnall)	6　320	Kirkstead	734	2
	R. Thames	78	M. O'Neill (Manchester)	27　70	Letchworth	833	3
	R. Trent	75	I. Bristow (Long Eaton)	14　650	Cove	691	4
	R. Trent	43	D. Weston (Royal Oak)	22　650	Trevs	372	5
	R. Trent	60	C. Chesters (Leicester A.S.)	9　130	Leic.	602	Jr. Ch.
1986	Oxford Canal	78	M. Stabler (Provincial)	3　820	I. Walton Stafford	815	1
	R. Trent	76	J. Howard (Bawtry)	18　110	Hull	813	2
	Royal Military Canal	74	P. Barber (Reddish A.C.)	34　270	Starlets	742	3
	R. Witham	75	P. Stanton (Wadsley Bridge)	7　790	Trevs	779	4
	Lancaster Canal	57	A. Holdsworth (Pendle)	5　400	Lansil	589	5
	Grand Union Canal	56	R. Stimpson (Oxford)	5　610	Milton Keynes	594	Jr. Ch.

SWIMMING

NATIONAL SWIMMING CHAMPIONSHIPS
1987 (Crystal Palace)

Men:

50 metres Freestyle.—M. Foster.
100 metres Freestyle.—R. Lee.
200 metres Freestyle.—J. Broughton.
400 metres Freestyle.—K. Boyd.
1,500 metres Freestyle.—K. Boyd.
100 metres Breaststroke.—A. Moorhouse.
200 metres Breaststroke.—N. Gillingham.
100 metres Butterfly.—N. Cochran.
200 metres Butterfly.—S. Poulter.
100 metres Backstroke.—G. Binfield.
200 metres Backstroke.—J. Davey.
200 metres Medley.—G. Binfield.
400 metres Medley.—J. Davey.
4 × 100 metres Freestyle Relay.—City of Birmingham.
4 × 100 metres Medley Relay.—City of Birmingham.

Women:

50 metres Freestyle.—N. Kennedy.
100 metres Freestyle.—Z. Long.
200 metres Freestyle.—R. Gilfillan.
400 metres Freestyle.—R. Gilfillan.
800 metres Freestyle.—K. Mellor.
100 metres Breaststroke.—S. Brownsdon.
200 metres Breaststroke.—S. Brownsdon.
100 metres Butterfly.—S. Purvis.
200 metres Butterfly.—H. Bewley.
100 metres Backstroke.—K. Read.
200 metres Backstroke.—K. Read.
200 metres Medley.—Z. Long.
400 metres Medley.—G. Stanley.
4 × 100 metres Freestyle Relay.—Wigan Wasps.
4 × 100 metres Medley Relay.—Stockport Metro.

WORLD SWIMMING RECORDS
(*As at 15 Sept. 1987*)

Men:

100 metres Freestyle.—M. Biondi (U.S.A.), 48·74 s.
200 metres Freestyle.—M. Gross (F.R.G.), 1 m. 47·44 s.
400 metres Freestyle.—M. Gross (F.R.G.), 3 m. 47·80 s.
800 metres Freestyle.—V. Salnikov (U.S.S.R.), 7 m. 50·64 s.
1,500 metres Freestyle.—V. Salnikov (U.S.S.R.), 14 m. 54·76 s.
100 metres Breaststroke.—S. Lundquist (U.S.A.), 1 m. 01·65 s.
200 metres Breaststroke.—V. Davis (Canada), 2 m. 13·34 s.
100 metres Butterfly.—P. Morales (U.S.A.), 52·84 s.
200 metres Butterfly.—M. Gross (F.R.G.), 1 m. 56·24 s.
100 metres Backstroke.—R. Carey (U.S.A.), 55·19 s.
200 metres Backstroke.—I. Polyanski (U.S.S.R.), 1 m. 58·14 s.
200 metres Medley.—T. Darnyi (Hungary), 2 m.00·56 s.
400 metres Medley.—T. Darnyi (Hungary) 4 m.15·42 s.
4 × 100 metres Freestyle Relay.—U.S.A., 3 m. 17·08 s.
4 × 200 metres Freestyle Relay.—F.R.G., 7 m. 13·10 s.
4 × 100 metres Medley Relay.—U.S.A., 3 m. 38·28 s.

Women:

100 metres Freestyle.—K. Otto (G.D.R.), 54·73 s.
200 metres Freestyle.—H. Friedrich (G.D.R.), 1 m. 57·55 s.
400 metres Freestyle.—T. Wickham (Australia), 4 m. 06·28 s.
800 metres Freestyle.—A. Möhring (G.D.R.), 8 m.19·53 s.
1,500 metres Freestyle.—J. Evans (U.S.A.), 16 m.00·73 s.
100 metres Breaststroke.—S. Hörner (G.D.R.), 1 m.07·91 s.
200 metres Breaststroke.—S. Hörner (G.D.R.), 2 m. 27·40 s.
100 metres Butterfly.—M. Meagher (U.S.A.), 57·93 s.
200 metres Butterfly.—M. Meagher (U.S.A), 2 m. 05·96 s.
100 metres Backstroke.—I. Kleber (G.D.R.), 1 m. 00·59 s.
200 metres Backstroke.—B. Mitchell (U.S.A.), 2 m. 08·60 s.
200 metres Medley.—U. Geweniger (G.D.R.), 2 m. 11·73 s.
400 metres Medley.—P. Schneider (G.D.R.), 4 m. 36·10 s.
4 × 100 metres Freestyle Relay.—G.D.R., 3 m. 40·57 s.
4 × 200 metres Freestyle Relay.—G.D.R., 7 m. 55·47 s.
4 × 100 metres Medley Relay.—G.D.R., 4 m. 03·69 s.

ROWING

HENLEY ROYAL REGATTA, 1987

Grand Challenge Cup.—Soviet Army beat Ridley (Canada) by 1½ lengths.

Ladies Challenge Plate.—University of London beat Tideway Scullers by ¼ length.

Princess Elizabeth Cup.—Belmont Hill School (U.S.A.) beat Hampton School by ⅓ length.

Thames Cup.—University College, Galway, beat Neptune (Ire.) by 2½ lengths.

Prince Philip Cup.—Soviet Army beat Szczecin and Wroclaw by 1½ lengths.

Queen Mother Cup.—Ridley (Canada) beat Soviet Army by ¼ length.

Visitors' Cup.—Imperial College beat University of London "A" by ¾ length.

Wyfold Cup.—Nottinghamshire County beat Lea "A" by 3¼ lengths.

Britannia Challenge Cup.—Lea beat Kingston by 1¼ lengths.

Silver Goblets and Nickall's Cup.—A. Holmes and S. Redgrave (Leander & Marlow) beat Y. and N. Pimenov (Dinamo Moscow), not rowed out.

Double Sculls Cup.—N. Chouprina and V. Dosenko (Dinamo Moscow) beat J. Scrivener and R. Henderson (Lea).

Diamond Sculls.—P.-M. Kolbe (Hamburg) beat V. Jakusha (Soviet Army) by 2¾ lengths.

Special Schools Race.—Radley beat King's, Canterbury by 1¼ lengths.

NATIONAL CHAMPIONSHIPS

(Holme Pierrepont)

Men's:
Eights.—Leander.
Coxed Fours.—Lea.
Coxless Fours.—Lea.
Coxed Pairs.—Tideway Scullers "A".
Coxless Pairs.—Bedford Star.
Quad Sculls.—Tideway Scullers School.
Double Sculls.—Lea.
Single Sculls.—Notts County "B".
Coastal Fours.—Christchurch.
Coastal Pairs.—Southsea.
Coastal Singles.—Southsea.

Women's:
Eights.—Lea/Rob Roy/Sons of Thames/Tideway Scullers School/Walbrook/Weybridge.
Coxed Fours.—Kingston/Oxford Univ./Oxford ULWBC/Wallingford.
Coxless Pairs.—Kingston/Weybridge.
Quad Sculls.—Clyde/Glasgow/Staines/Marlow.
Double Sculls.—Tideway Scullers School.
Single Sculls.—Notts County "A".
Coastal Fours.—Southsea.

THE 133RD UNIVERSITY BOAT RACE

(Putney-Mortlake, 4 m. 1 f. 180 yds.)

Oxford beat Cambridge by 4 lengths, 19 m 59 s. (Cambridge have won 69 times, Oxford 63 and there has been 1 dead-heat. The record time is the 16 m 45 s rowed by Oxford in 1984.)

OTHER ROWING EVENTS

Oxford Summer Eights.—Oriel.
Oxford Torpids.—Oriel.
Cambridge Lents.—Downing.
Cambridge Mays.—Caius.
Doggett's Coat and Badge (Estab. 1715, 273rd race, London Bridge-Chelsea, 4½ miles).—C. Spencer.
Head of the River.—A.R.A. National Squad.

SHOOTING

BISLEY, 118th N.R.A., 1987

Queen's Prize.—1. A. St. G. Tucker, 290 pts.; 2. T. P. Clarke, 289 pts.; 3, A. Marion, 288 pts.

Prince of Wales Prize.—S. Belither, 75pts.

St. George's Challenge Vase.—1. J. P. S. Bloomfield, 148 pts.; 2. R. P. Rosling, 147 pts; 3. B. I. J. Gilson, 147 pts.

Grand Aggregate.—1. Lt. N. C. Crawshaw, 594 pts.; 2. D. B. Lumby, 591 pts.; 3. A. St. J. Tucker, 589 pts.

Elcho Challenge Shield.—1. England, 1,633; 2. Scotland, 1,574; 3. Ireland, 1,559.

National Match.—1. England, 2,050; 2. Scotland, 2,017; 3. Wales, 2,012; 4. Ireland, 1,979.

Kolapore.—1. Canada, 1,170; 2. Great Britain, 1,160; 3. Guernsey, 1,150; 4. Jersey, 1,149.

International Service Rifle Match.—1. Great Britain, 2,568; 2. S.O.L.F., 2,480; 3. Canadian Forces, 2,334; 4. Zimbabwe, 2,158.

Chancellor's Challenge Plate.—1. Cambridge Univ., 1,131; 2. Oxford Univ., 1,099.

Inter-Services Long Range.—1. R.A.F., 844; 2. Regular Army, 842; 3. Territorial Army, 828.

Inter-Services Short Range.—1. Territorial Army, 1,142; 2. Canadian Cadets, 1,130; 3. Regular Army, 1,130.

United Service.—1. Regular Army, 1,425; 2. Royal Marines, 1,333; 3. Canadian Forces, 1,308.

Ashburton Shield.—1. Oakham School, 535; 2. Bradfield Coll., 523; 3. Kimbolton School, 519.

CLAY PIGEON SHOOTING, 1986

International Cup (Down-the-Line).—1. England, 7,206; 2, Scotland, 7,135; 3, Ireland, 7,119; 4, Wales, 7,010.

British Open Down-the-Line Championship.—N. Bailey, 299/300.

Mackintosh Trophy.—Australia, 7,382/7,500.

British Open Skeet Championship.—P. Theobald, 100/100.

British Open Sporting Championship.—T. Booth, 90/100.

Coronation Cup.—A. Harvison, 378/400.

Grand Prix of Great Britain (International Skeet).—K. Harman, 199/200.

Grand Prix of Great Britain (International Sporting).—P. Howe, 135/150.

EQUESTRIANISM, 1987

European 3-day Event:
1. Mrs. V. Leng—Night Cap (G.B.).
2. I. Stark—Sir Wattie (G.B.).
3. C. Erhorn—Justin Thyme (W. Germany).

Team: 1. Great Britain, 146 pts.
2. West Germany, 187 pts.
3. France, 291 pts.

British Open Championship.—Mrs. V. Leng (Night Cap).

Burghley Horse Trials:
1. M. Todd—Wilton Fair (N.Z.).
2. M. Todd—Charisma (N.Z.).
3. Miss D. Clapham—Colonel (G.B.).

Hickstead Derby.—N. Skelton (Raffles J. Nick).

YACHTING, 1986-87

AMERICA'S CUP

Final.—The challenger *Stars and Stripes* (U.S.A.) beat the defender *Kookaburra III* (Australia) by 4-0.

Admiral's Cup.—New Zealand.
Fastnet Race.—M. Peacock's *Juno.*

BOXING, 1986–87

A.B.A. Championships (Winners)

Light-Flyweight.—M. Epton; *Flyweight.*—J. Lyon; *Bantam.*—J. Sillitoe; *Feather.*—P. English; *Light.*—M. Ayers; *Light-Welter.*—A. Holligan; *Welter.*—M. Elliott; *Light-Middle.*—N. Browne; *Middle.*—R. Douglas; *Light-Heavy.*—J. Beckles; *Heavy.*—J. Moran; *Super Heavy.*—J. Oyebola.

PROFESSIONAL BOXING

World (W.B.C.) Champions

Heavy.—M. Tyson (U.S.A.); *Cruiser.*—C. de Leon (Puerto Rico); *Light-Heavy.*—(vacant); *Middle.*—S. R. Leonard (U.S.A.); *Light-Middle.*—L. Aquino (Mexico); *Welter.*—L. Honeyghan (G.B.); *Light-Welter.*—T. Hamada (Japan); *Light.*—H. Camacho (U.S.A.); *Super-Feather.*—J. C. Chavez (Mexico); *Feather.*—A. Nelson (Ghana); *Super-Bantam.*—S. Payakarum (Thailand); *Bantam.*—M. Lora (Colombia); *Super-Fly.*—S. Laciar (Mexico); *Fly.*—S. Chitilada (Thailand); *Light-Fly.*—J. Chang (Korea).

World (W.B.A.) Champions

Heavy.—M. Tyson (U.S.A.); *Cruiser.*—E. Holyfield (U.S.A.); *Light-Heavy.*—V. Hill (U.S.A.); *Middle.*—(vacant); *Light-Middle.*—M. McCallum (Jamaica); *Welter.*—M. Breland (U.S.A.); *Light-Welter.*—P. Oliva (Italy); *Light.*—E. Rosario (U.S.A.); *Super-Feather.*—(vacant); *Feather.*—A. Esparagoza (Venezuela); *Super-Bantam.*—V. C. Jas (Puerto Rico); *Bantam.*—B. Pinango (Venezuela); *Super-Fly.*—K. Galexi (Thailand); *Fly.*—F. Bassa (Colombia); *Light-Fly.*—M. W. Yuh (Korea).

International Boxing Federation (I.B.F.) Champions

Heavy.—M. Tyson (U.S.A.); *Cruiser.*—R. Parky (U.S.A.); *Light-Heavy.*—B. Czyz (U.S.A.); *Middle.*—(vacant); *Light-Middle.*—B. Drayton (U.S.A.); *Welter.*—L. Honeyghan (G.B.); *Light-Welter.*—T. Marsh (G.B.); *Light.*—G. Haugen (U.S.A.); *Super-Feather.*—B. Michael (Australia); *Feather.*—A. Rivera (Puerto Rico); *Super-Bantam.*—(vacant); *Bantam.*—K. Seabrook (U.S.A.); *Super-Fly.*—(vacant); *Fly.*—D. Penalosa (Philippines); *Light-Fly.*—J. Choi (Korea).

British Champions

Heavy.—H. Notice; *Cruiser.*—T. Jay; *Light-Heavy.*—T. Collins; *Middle.*—B. Anderson; *Light-Middle.*—L. Hibbert; *Welter.*—K. Laing; *Light-Welter.*—L. Christie; *Light.*—T. Willis; *Super-Feather.*—N. Daho; *Feather.*—R. Dickie; *Bantam.*—B. Hardy; *Fly.*—D. McAuley.

Commonwealth Champions

Heavy.—H. Notice (G.B.); *Cruiser.*—G. McCrory (G.B.); *Light-Heavy.*—(vacant); *Middle.*—T. Sibson (G.B.); *Light-Middle.*—T. Waters (Australia); *Welter.*—B. Jannsen (Australia); *Light-Welter.*—(vacant); *Light.*—M. Hussein (G.B.); *Super-Feather.*—S. Akroman (Ghana); *Feather.*—T. Downes (Trinidad); *Bantam.*—R. Minus (Bahamas); *Fly.*—R. Clarke (Jamaica).

European Champions

Heavy.—A. Eklund (Sweden); *Cruiser.*—S. Reeson (G.B.); *Light-Heavy.*—A. Blanchard (Netherlands); *Middle.*—S. Kalambay (Italy); *Light-Middle.*—G. Rosi (Italy); *Welter.*—A. Redondo (Spain); *Light-Welter.*—T. N'Kalankete (France); *Light.*—G. B. Jacobsen (Netherlands); *Super-Feather.*—S. Curcetti (Italy); *Feather.*—V. Nati (Italy); *Bantam.*—L. Gomis (France); *Fly.*—D. McKenzie (G.B.).

SNOOKER AND BILLIARDS, 1986–87

World Professional Snooker Championship.—S. Davis beat J. Johnson by 18–14.
Benson and Hedges Masters Snooker Tournament.—D. Taylor beat A. Higgins by 9–8.
U.K. Professional Snooker Championship.—S. Davis beat N. Foulds by 16–7.
World Doubles Snooker Championship.—S. Davis and A. Meo beat M. Hallett and S. Hendry by 12–3.
English Professional Snooker Championship.—A. Meo beat L. Dodd by 9–5.
British Open Snooker Championship.—J. White beat N. Foulds by 13–9.
World Team Cup.—Ireland beat Canada, 9–2.
Rothmans Matchroom League.—S. Davis.
World Professional Billiards Championship.—N. Dagley beat R. Foldvari, 3–1.

MOTOR CYCLING, 1987

Senior Manx Grand Prix.—J. Dunlop (Honda).
Senior T.T., Isle of Man.—J. Dunlop (Honda).
Junior T.T., Isle of Man.—E. Laycock (EMC)
British 500 c.c. Grand Prix (Donnington).—E. Lawson (Yamaha)
Transatlantic Trophy.—U.S.A.

MOTOR SPORT, 1987

Formula One Motor Racing

Grand Prix 1986:
Australian (Adelaide)—1. A. Prost (McLaren); 2. N. Piquet (Williams); 3. S. Johansson (Ferrari).
Formula One Champion, 1986.—A. Prost (McLaren) 72 pts.
Grand Prix 1987:
Brazilian (Rio)—1. A. Prost (McLaren); 2. N. Piquet (Williams); 3. S. Johansson (McLaren).
San Marino (Imola)—1. N. Mansell (Williams); 2. A. Senna (Lotus); 3. M. Alboreto (Ferrari).
Belgian (Spa Francorchamps)—1. A. Prost (McLaren); 2. S. Johansson (McLaren); 3. A. de Cesaris (Brabham).
Monaco—1. A. Senna (Lotus); 2. N. Piquet (Williams); 3. M. Alboreto (Ferrari).
Detroit—1. A. Senna (Lotus); 2. N. Piquet (Williams); 3. A. Prost (McLaren).
French (Le Castellet)—1. N. Mansell (Williams); 2. N. Piquet (Williams); 3. A. Prost (McLaren).
British (Silverstone)—1. N. Mansell (Williams); 2. N. Piquet (Williams); 3. A. Senna (Lotus).
West German (Hockenheim)—1. N. Piquet (Williams); 2. S. Johansson (McLaren); 3. A. Senna (Lotus).
Hungarian (Budapest)—1. N. Piquet (Williams); 2. A. Senna (Lotus); 3. A. Prost (McLaren).
Austrian (Zeltweg)—1. N. Mansell (Williams); 2. N. Piquet (Williams); 3. T. Fabi (Benetton Ford).
Italian (Monza)—1. N. Piquet (Williams); 2. A. Senna (Lotus); 3. N. Mansell (Williams).
Portuguese (Estoril)—1. A. Prost (McLaren); 2. G. Berger (Ferrari); 3. N. Piquet (Williams).
Spanish (Jerez)—1. N. Mansell (Williams); 2. A. Prost (McLaren); 3. S. Johansson (McLaren).

Other Events

Le Mans (24-hour).—D. Bell, H. Stuck and A. Holbert (Porsche).
Lombard R.A.C. Rally, 1986.—T. Salonen (Peugeot).
Monte Carlo Rally.—M. Biasion (Lancia Delta).
Paris/Dakar Trans-Sahara Rally.—A. Vatanen (Peugeot).
Safari Rally.—H. Mikkola (Audi 200 Quattro).
Circuit of Ireland Rally.—J. McRae (Sierra Cosworth).
Indianapolis 500.—A. Unser.

CRICKET
County Championship

1977 {	Kent	1982	Middlesex
	Middlesex	1983	Essex
1978	Kent	1984	Essex
1979	Essex	1985	Middlesex
1980	Middlesex	1986	Essex
1981	Nottinghamshire	1987	Nottinghamshire

ASSOCIATION FOOTBALL

	League Championship	Football Association Cup
1977	Liverpool	Man. U. b. Liverpool 2–1
1978	Nottingham F.	Ipswich b. Arsenal 1–0
1979	Liverpool	Arsenal b. Man. U. 3–2
1980	Liverpool	West Ham U. b. Arsenal 1–0
1981	Aston Villa	Tottenham H. b. Man. C. 3–2
1982	Liverpool	Tottenham H. b. Q.P.R. 1–0
1983	Liverpool	Man. U. b. Brighton 4–0
1984	Liverpool	Everton b. Watford 2–0
1985	Everton	Man. U. b. Everton 1–0
1986	Liverpool	Liverpool b. Everton 3–1
1987	Everton	Coventry b. Tottenham H. 3–2

GOLF
Ryder Cup

1971	U.S.A. beat G.B. by 18½–13½
1973	U.S.A. beat G.B. and Ire. by 19–13
1975	U.S.A. beat G.B. and Ire. by 21–11
1977	U.S.A. beat G.B. and Ire. by 12½–7½
1979	U.S.A. beat G.B. and Europe by 17–11
1981	U.S.A. beat G.B. and Europe by 18½–9½
1983	U.S.A. beat G.B. and Europe by 14½–13½
1985	G.B. and Europe beat U.S.A. by 16½–11½
1987	G.B. and Europe beat U.S.A. by 15–13

HORSE-RACING
The Derby

1977	The Minstrel	L. Piggott
1978	Shirley Heights	G. Starkey
1979	Troy	W. Carson
1980	Henbit	W. Carson
1981	Shergar	W. Swinburn
1982	Golden Fleece	P. Eddery
1983	Teenoso	L. Piggott
1984	Secreto	C. Roche
1985	Slip Anchor	S. Cauthen
1986	Shahrastani	W. Swinburn
1987	Reference Point	S. Cauthen

The Grand National

1977	Red Rum	T. Stack
1978	Lucius	B. Davis
1979	Rubstic	M. Barnes
1980	Ben Nevis	C. Fenwick
1981	Aldaniti	R. Champion
1982	Grittar	C. Saunders
1983	Corbiere	B. de Haan
1984	Hallo Dandy	N. Doughty
1985	Last Suspect	H. Davies
1986	West Tip	R. Dunwoody
1987	Maori Venture	S. Knight

MOTOR RACING
Formula 1 Champions

1977	N. Lauda (Austria)
1978	M. Andretti (U.S.A.)
1979	J. Schecker (S. Africa)
1980	A. Jones (Australia)
1981	N. Piquet (Brazil)
1982	K. Rosberg (Finland)
1983	N. Piquet (Brazil)
1984	N. Lauda (Austria)
1985	A. Prost (France)
1986	A. Prost (France)

ROWING
The University Boat Race

		m.	s.	Won by
1977	Oxford	19	28	7 lengths
1978	Oxford	19		Camb. sank
1979	Oxford	20	33	3½ lengths
1980	Oxford	19	20	A canvas
1981	Oxford	18	11	8 lengths
1982	Oxford	18	21	3½ lengths
1983	Oxford	19	7	4½ lengths
1984	Oxford	16	45	3½ lengths
1985	Oxford	17	11	4½ lengths
1986	Cambridge	17	58	7 lengths
1987	Oxford	19	59	4 lengths

SNOOKER
World Championships

1977	J. Spencer (England)
1978	R. Reardon (Wales)
1979	T. Griffiths (Wales)
1980	C. Thorburn (Canada)
1981	S. Davis (England)
1982	A. Higgins (N. Ireland)
1983	S. Davis (England)
1984	S. Davis (England)
1985	D. Taylor (N. Ireland)
1986	J. Johnson (England)
1987	S. Davis (England)

TENNIS
Wimbledon Singles Champions

Men

1977	B. Borg (Sweden)
1978	B. Borg (Sweden)
1979	B. Borg (Sweden)
1980	B. Borg (Sweden)
1981	J. McEnroe (U.S.A.)
1982	J. Connors (U.S.A.)
1983	J. McEnroe (U.S.A.)
1984	J. McEnroe (U.S.A.)
1985	B. Becker (W. Germany)
1986	B. Becker (W. Germany)
1987	P. Cash (Australia)

Women

1977	S. V. Wade (G.B.)
1978	M. Navratilova (Czechoslovakia)
1979	M. Navratilova (U.S.A.)
1980	E. Cawley (Australia)
1981	C. Lloyd (U.S.A.)
1982	M. Navratilova (U.S.A.)
1983	M. Navratilova (U.S.A.)
1984	M. Navratilova (U.S.A.)
1985	M. Navratilova (U.S.A.)
1986	M. Navratilova (U.S.A.)
1987	M. Navratilova (U.S.A.)

Davis Cup

1977	Australia beat Italy ... 3–1
1978	U.S.A. beat Great Britain ... 4–1
1979	U.S.A. beat Italy ... 5–0
1980	Czechoslovakia beat Italy ... 4–1
1981	U.S.A. beat Argentina ... 3–1
1982	U.S.A. beat France ... 4–1
1983	Australia beat Sweden ... 3–2
1984	Sweden beat U.S.A. ... 4–1
1985	Sweden beat W. Germany ... 3–2
1986	Australia beat Sweden ... 3–2

SPORTS REPRESENTATIVE BODIES

ANGLING.—National Anglers' Council, 11 Cowgate, Peterborough PE1 1LZ. *Exec. Dir.*, P. H. Tombleson, O.B.E.

ASSOCIATION FOOTBALL.—The Football Association. *Gen. Sec.*, E. A. Croker, 16 Lancaster Gate, W2 3LW.

ATHLETICS.—Amateur Athletic Association. *Gen. Sec.*, M. A. Farrell, Francis House, Francis Street, SW1P 1DL.

— Women's Amateur Athletic Association, Francis House, Francis Street, SW1P 1DE. *Hon. Sec.*, Miss M. Hartman, C.B.E.

BADMINTON.—Badminton Association of England, National Badminton Centre, Loughton Lodge, Bradwell Road, Milton Keynes MK8 9LA. *Chief Exec.*, Air Vice-Marshal G. C. Lamb, C.B., C.B.E., A.F.C.

BASKET BALL.—English Basket Ball Association. Calomax House, Lupton Avenue, Leeds LS9 6EE. *Sec.*, M. D. Welch.

BILLIARDS.—Billiards and Snooker Control Council. *Chair.*, S. Brooke, Coronet House, Queen Street, Leeds LS1 2TN.

BOBSLEIGH.—British Bobsleigh Association, 118 Eaton Square, SW1W 9AF. *Sec.*, S. D. M. Strong.

BOWLS.—English Bowling Association, Lyndhurst Rd., Worthing, W. Sussex BN11 2AZ. *Sec.*, D. W. Johnson.

BOXING.—Amateur Boxing Association of England, Francis House, Francis Street, SW1P 1DE.—*Exec. Dir.*, C. J. Howe.

— British Boxing Board of Control, 70 Vauxhall Bridge Road, SW1V 2RP.—*Gen. Sec.*, J. Morris.

CANOEING.—British Canoe Union, Flexel House, 45–47 High Street, Addlestone, Weybridge, Surrey KT15 1JV.—*Dir.*, T. J. Bailey.

CRICKET.—M.C.C., Lord's, NW8 8QN. *Pres.* J. J. Warr; *Sec.*, Lt.-Col. J. R. Stephenson, O.B.E.

—T.C.C.B., Lord's, NW8 8QN. *Chairman* (1987–88), R. Subba Row; *Chief Exec.*, A. C. Smith.

—Cricket Council, Lord's, NW8 8QN. *Chairman*, R. Subba Row; *Sec.*, A. C. Smith.

CYCLING.—British Cycling Federation, 16 Upper Woburn Place, WC1H 0QE.—*Sec.*, L. A. Unwin.

ETON FIVES.—Eton Fives Association.—*Hon. Sec.*, R. M. Knight, Saintbury Close, Saintbury, nr. Broadway, Worcs. WR12 7PX.

FENCING.—Amateur Fencing Association, 83 Perham Road, W. Kensington, W14 9SP. *Sec.*, Mrs. J. Pienne.

GLIDING.—British Gliding Association, Kimberley House, Vaughan Way, Leicester. *Sec.*, B. Rolfe.

GOLF.—Royal and Ancient Golf Club, St. Andrews, Fife KY16 9JD. *Sec.*, M. F. Bonallack, O.B.E.

— English Golf Union. 1–3 Upper King Street, Leicester LE1 6XF. *Sec.*, K. Wright.

— Ladies' Golf Union, The Scores, St. Andrews, Fife KY16 9AT.—*Gen. Administrator*, Mrs A. White.

GYMNASTICS.—British Amateur Gymnastics Association, 2 Buckingham Avenue East, Slough, Berks. SL1 3EA. *Development Dir.*, A. L. Murdock.

HOCKEY.—Hockey Association, 16 Upper Woburn Place, WC1H 0QD. *Chief Exec.*, S. P. Baines.

— All England Women's Hockey Association, 3rd Flr, Argyle House, 29–31 Euston Road, NW1 2SD. *Sec.*, Miss T. Morris.

JUDO.—British Judo Association, 16 Upper Woburn Place, WC1H 0QH. *Gen. Sec.*, Miss G. M. Kenneally.

LACROSSE.—English Lacrosse Union. *Hon. Sec.*, R. Balls, 70 High Road, Rayleigh, Essex SS6 7AD.

— All England Women's Lacrosse Association, Francis House, Francis Street, SW1P 1DE.

LAWN TENNIS.—Lawn Tennis Association, The Queen's Club, W. Kensington, W14 9EG. *Sec.*, J. C. U. James.

— International Tennis Federation, Palliser Rd., Barons Court, W14 9EN. *Gen. Sec.*, Miss S. Woodhead.

MOTOR CYCLING.—Auto-Cycle Union, Miller House, Corporation Street, Rugby, Warwicks. CV21 2DN. *Sec. Gen.*, D. G. Coleman.

NETBALL.—All England Netball Association Ltd., Francis House, Francis Street, SW1P 1DE. *Chief Exec.*, Mrs. E. Nicholl.

ORIENTEERING.—British Orienteering Federation, "Riversdale", Dale Road North, Darley Dale, Derbys. DE4 2HX. *Gen. Sec.*, R. Mason.

POLO.—The Hurlingham Polo Association, Ambersham Farm, Ambersham, Midhurst, W. Sussex GU29 0BX. *Hon. Sec.*, Lt.-Col. A. F. Harper, D.S.O.

RACING.—The Jockey Club (incorporating National Hunt Committee), 42 Portman Square, W1H 0EN *Sec.*, C. N. Foster.

RIFLE SHOOTING.—National Rifle Association. *Sec.*, Brig. P. G. A. Prescott, M.C., Bisley Camp, Brookwood, Woking, Surrey GU24 0PB.

ROWING.—Amateur Rowing Association. *Exec. Sec.*, D. C. Lunn-Rockliffe, 6 Lower Mall, W6 9DJ.

RUGBY FIVES.—Rugby Fives Association. *Hon. Sec.*, P. J. Reeder, 12 Alexandra Cottages, Hardings Lane, SE20 7JJ.

RUGBY FOOTBALL.—The Rugby Football Union, Whitton Road, Twickenham, Middx. TW1 1DZ. *Sec.*, D. E. Wood.

— The Rugby Football League, 180 Chapeltown Road, Leeds LS7 4HT. *Sec.-Gen.*, D. S. Oxley.

SKATING.—National Skating Association of Great Britain. *Gen. Administrator*, E. Waughray, 15–27 Gee Street, EC1V 2RU.

SKI-ING.—British Ski Federation. *Chairman*, T. Fitzpatrick, 118 Eaton Square, SW1W 9AF.

SQUASH RACKETS.—Squash Rackets Association. *Chief Executive*, R. I. Morris, Francis House, Francis Street, SW1P 1DE.

— Women's Squash Rackets Association. *Sec.*, Miss C. Myers, 345 Upper Richmond Road West, SW14 8QN.

SWIMMING.—Amateur Swimming Association, Harold Fern House, Derby Square, Loughborough, Leics. LE11 0AL. *Sec.*, D. A. Reeves.

TABLE TENNIS.—English Table Tennis Association, 21 Claremont, Hastings TN34 1HF. *Chief Exec.*, E. J. Wallbutton.

VOLLEYBALL.—English Volleyball Association, 13 Rectory Road, W. Bridgford, Nottingham NG2 6BE. *National Dir.*, G. Bulman.

WALKING.—Race Walking Association. *Gen. Sec.*, R. Wells, 1 Rye Hill Flats, Cromwell Hill, Luton, Beds. LU1 7PZ.

WATER SKI-ING.—British Water Ski Federation, 390 City Road, EC1V 2QA. *Sec.*, Ms. G. Hill.

WEIGHTLIFTING.—British Amateur Weightlifters Association. *Hon. Sec.*, W. Holland, O.B.E., 3 Iffley Turn, Oxford OX4 4DU.

WRESTLING.—English Olympic Wrestling Association, 16 Choir Street, Cambridge Industrial Estate, Salford M7 9ZD; *Sec.*, H. I. Jacob, O.B.E.

YACHTING.—Royal Yachting Association, Victoria Way, Woking, Surrey GU21 1EQ. *Sec.-Gen.*, R. Duchesne, O.B.E.

Value of United Kingdom imports (cif) (£ million)
Analysis by sections and divisions

	1982	1983	1984	1985*
Total UK imports	56,978·2	66,101·1	78,967·4	84,789·6
Food and live animals chiefly for food	6,414·1	6,907·2	7,820·4	8,043·1
Live animals chiefly for food	133·1	170·3	196·8	238·4
Meat and meat preparations	1,370·9	1,313·4	1,342·2	1,401·0
Dairy products and birds' eggs	567·9	629·2	604·6	606·1
Fish, crustaceans and molluscs, and preparations thereof	404·2	505·2	537·8	600·8
Cereals and cereal preparations	549·9	593·5	629·0	713·3
Vegetables and fruit	1,608·3	1,718·5	1,930·3	2,037·0
Sugar, sugar preparations and honey	429·5	443·2	524·3	443·4
Coffee, tea, cocoa, spices, and manufactures thereof	722·4	799·9	1,291·4	1,205·7
Feeding stuff for animals (not including un-milled cereals)	446·6	523·6	501·5	488·6
Miscellaneous edible products and preparations	181·1	210·4	262·6	309·0
Beverages and tobacco	836·7	962·0	1,112·5	1,230·6
Beverages	517·5	617·4	705·5	843·8
Tobacco and tobacco manufactures	319·2	344·6	407·1	386·8
Crude materials, inedible, except fuels	3,612·9	4,416·1	4,884·9	4,857·1
Hides, skins and furskins, raw	189·5	184·9	235·3	238·9
Oil seeds and oleaginous fruit	259·6	268·6	234·8	238·8
Crude rubber (including synthetic and re-claimed)	182·9	197·4	223·5	228·5
Cork and wood	673·8	937·8	1,009·3	895·3
Pulp and waste paper	412·0	428·0	611·7	505·7
Textile fibres (other than wool tops) and their wastes (not manufactured into yarn or fabric)	410·8	475·9	596·7	663·1
Crude fertilisers and crude minerals (excluding coal, petroleum and precious stones)	263·5	285·8	312·6	354·1
Metalliferous ores and metal scrap	977·5	1,357·8	1,343·8	1,371·1
Crude animal and vegetable materials	243·3	279·7	317·3	361·0
Mineral fuels, lubricants and related materials	7,408·6	7,076·1	10,333·8	10,517·1
Petroleum, petroleum products and related materials	6,276·9	5,743·3	8,219·8	8,173·7
Coal, coke, gas and electric current	1,131·6	1,333·1	2,114·0	2,343·4
Animal and vegetable oils, fats and waxes	317·0	358·8	533·2	531·7
Total manufactured goods	37,114·2	44,936·5	53,010·7	58,288·0
Chemicals and related products	4,179·1	5,118·9	6,322·1	6,903·0
Organic chemicals	1,171·9	1,456·3	1,874·4	1,893·6
Inorganic chemicals	539·3	560·8	709·8	897·3
Dyeing, tanning and colouring materials	198·0	235·1	269·7	310·9
Medicinal and pharmaceutical products	374·6	470·2	542·3	590·4
Essential oils and perfume materials; toilet, polishing and cleansing materials	242·2	305·3	377·1	443·3
Fertilisers, manufactured	127·1	171·1	219·4	217·3
Explosives and pyrotechnic products	10·9	14·1	19·0	20·0
Artificial resins and plastic materials, and cellulose esters and ethers	1,017·7	1,323·5	1,609·4	1,764·5
Chemical materials and products, not elsewhere specified	497·4	581·9	700·8	765·4

* Provisional figures.

Value of United Kingdom imports (cif) (£ million)—*Continued*

	1982	1983	1984	1985*
Total UK imports	56,978·2	66,101·1	78,967·4	84,789·6
Manufactured goods classified chiefly by material	9,852·5	11,846·6	13,447·4	14,347·9
Leather, leather manufactures, nes, and dressed furskins	154·6	183·9	245·1	250·3
Rubber manufactures, nes	362·2	419·6	457·1	527·4
Cork and wood manufactures (excluding furniture)	436·3	578·5	622·1	632·6
Paper, paperboard, and articles of paper pulp, of paper or of paperboard	1,675·1	1,905·8	2,280·4	2,533·2
Textile yarn, fabrics, made-up articles, nes, and related products	1,927·6	2,320·2	2,705·4	3,032·2
Non-metallic mineral manufactures, nes	1,520·3	2,085·4	2,269·3	2,243·6
Iron and steel	1,367·3	1,260·3	1,487·2	1,716·4
Non-ferrous metals	1,495·7	1,985·0	1,996·2	1,904·0
Manufactures of metal, nes	949·5	1,107·8	1,384·4	1,508·1
Machinery and transport equipment	16,464·2	20,260·7	23,781·7	26,899·3
Power generating machinery and equipment	1,482·7	1,568·7	1,782·4	1,996·0
Machinery specialised for particular industries	1,485·9	1,735·6	2,078·6	2,327·0
Metalworking machinery	380·6	342·3	432·7	525·7
General industrial machinery and equipment, nes, and machine parts, nes	1,634·4	1,845·2	2,249·9	2,604·8
Office machines and automatic data processing equipment	2,121·9	3,017·5	4,102·7	4,511·6
Telecommunications, sound recording and reproducing apparatus and equipment	1,586·2	1,915·9	1,848·3	2,129·5
Electrical machinery, apparatus and appliances, nes, and electrical parts thereof (including non-electrical counterparts, nes, of electrical household type equipment)	2,179·1	2,805·8	3,846·7	4,281·2
Road vehicles (including air cushion vehicles)	4,489·6	5,753·8	5,957·6	6,802·0
Other transport equipment	1,103·8	1,275·9	1,482·9	1,721·5
Miscellaneous manufactured articles	6,618·4	7,710·4	9,459·5	10,137·7
Sanitary, plumbing, heating and lighting fixtures and fittings, nes	103·5	126·7	151·2	177·4
Furniture and parts thereof	400·1	490·4	591·6	662·8
Travel goods, handbags and similar containers	108·6	131·1	161·9	174·9
Articles of apparel and clothing accessories	1,500·0	1,601·3	2,011·7	2,094·7
Footwear	468·3	542·0	642·0	671·6
Professional, scientific and controlling instruments and apparatus, nes	1,052·1	1,301·3	1,593·8	1,764·3
Photographic apparatus, equipment and supplies and optical goods, nes, watches and clocks	761·0	862·2	1,068·7	1,173·2
Miscellaneous manufactured articles, nes	2,224·9	2,655·5	3,238·7	3,418·9
Commodities and transactions not classified elsewhere	1,274·8	1,444·3	1,271·8	1,322·0

* Provisional figures.

Value of United Kingdom exports (fob) (£ million)
Analysis by sections and divisions

	1982	1983	1984	1985*
Total UK exports	55,557·8	60,684·3	70,488·3	78,331·4
Food and live animals chiefly for food	2,508·3	2,754·6	3,114·8	3,251·0
Live animals chiefly for food	179·1	187·4	191·0	262·0
Meat and meat preparations	347·5	495·7	491·1	495·0
Dairy products and birds' eggs	325·6	308·1	246·6	281·1
Fish, crustaceans and molluscs, and preparations thereof	162·3	203·2	224·4	260·3
Cereals and cereal preparations	773·9	740·9	992·7	834·2
Vegetables and fruit	154·0	163·2	190·8	205·3
Sugar, sugar preparations and honey	121·1	145·1	165·7	220·8
Coffee, tea, cocoa, spices and manufactures thereof	252·2	291·4	363·4	390·8
Feeding stuff for animals (not including un-milled cereals)	69·0	78·9	96·8	121·8
Miscellaneous edible products and preparations	123·8	140·8	152·3	179·7
Beverages and tobacco	1,451·5	1,486·2	1,577·9	1,719·1
Beverages	1,060·1	1,051·2	1,157·0	1,253·7
Tobacco and tobacco manufactures	391·4	435·0	420·9	465·4
Crude materials, inedible, except fuels	1,293·7	1,527·7	1,898·1	2,048·9
Hides, skins and furskins, raw	180·5	200·2	280·3	288·3
Oil seeds and oleaginous fruit	7·9	37·8	54·0	90·6
Crude rubber (including synthetic and re-claimed)	122·8	141·7	166·9	173·5
Cork and wood	28·6	24·1	25·5	25·7
Pulp and waste paper	11·6	15·8	27·2	24·7
Textile fibres (other than wool tops) and their wastes (not manufactured into yarn or fabric)	314·2	375·1	427·9	428·3
Crude fertilisers and crude minerals (excluding coal, petroleum and precious stones)	224·2	223·8	249·1	278·9
Metalliferous ores and metal scrap	346·6	444·2	591·4	644·8
Crude animal and vegetable materials	57·3	64·9	75·6	94·3
Mineral fuels, lubricants and related materials	11,237·1	13,102·7	15,308·4	16,711·6
Petroleum, petroleum products and related materials	10,685·7	12,501·2	14,851·8	16,049·8
Coal, coke, gas and electric current	551·4	601·4	456·8	661·8
Animal and vegetable oils, fats and waxes	46·5	59·1	91·0	95·9
Total manufactured goods	37,312·6	40,087·2	46,703·0	52,513·9
Chemicals and related products	6,119·3	6,933·0	8,216·8	9,411·0
Organic chemicals	1,592·3	1,930·2	2,381·7	2,743·2
Inorganic chemicals	694·9	699·6	811·1	979·7
Dyeing, tanning and colouring materials	464·1	568·8	633·3	692·0
Medicinal and pharmaceutical products	978·0	1,073·4	1,222·4	1,425·9
Essential oils and perfume materials; toilet, polishing and cleansing materials	525·1	574·5	690·5	767·9
Fertilisers, manufactured	48·8	69·7	64·4	74·8
Explosives and pyrotechnic products	36·8	40·1	47·6	45·7
Artificial resins and plastic materials, and cellu-lose esters and ethers	875·3	980·5	1,179·8	1,330·8
Chemical materials and products, not elsewhere specified	904·1	996·4	1,186·0	1,351·0

* Provisional figures.

Value of United Kingdom exports (fob) (£ million)—*Continued*

	1982	1983	1984	1985*
Total UK exports	55,557·8	60,533·7	70,488·3	78,331·4
Manufactured goods classified chiefly by material	7,940·5	9,016·4	10,010·6	10,422·3
Leather, leather manufactures, nes, and dressed furskins	202·1	233·3	312·5	295·2
Rubber manufactures, nes	417·9	451·6	481·8	554·2
Cork and wood manufactures (excluding furniture)	83·2	85·5	104·6	84·1
Paper, paperboard, and articles of paper pulp, of paper or of paperboard	503·1	543·1	678·6	767·4
Textile yarn, fabrics, made-up articles, nes, and related products	1,192·0	1,285·0	1,484·8	1,701·3
Non-metallic mineral manufactures, nes	1,609·9	1,995·5	2,298·7	2,163·3
Iron and steel	1,291·8	1,330·7	1,528·9	1,856·8
Non-ferrous metals	1,244·7	1,766·6	1,656·7	1,379·6
Manufactures of metal, nes	1,395·6	1,325·1	1,464·1	1,620·3
Machinery and transport equipment	18,100·9	18,324·8	21,520·5	24,684·1
Power generating machinery and equipment	2,809·1	2,472·7	2,709·0	3,076·1
Machinery specialised for particular industries	2,601·3	2,335·0	2,676·8	3,078·9
Metalworking machinery	522·4	416·2	503·8	521·3
General industrial machinery and equipment, nes, and machine parts, nes	2,411·8	2,334·2	2,577·1	2,937·3
Office machines and automatic data processing equipment	1,599·5	2,048·8	3,046·6	3,746·7
Telecommunications and sound recording and reproducing apparatus and equipment	897·2	991·6	1,117·0	1,295·4
Electrical machinery, apparatus and appliances, nes, and electrical parts thereof (including non-electrical counterparts, nes, of electrical household type equipment)	2,117·0	2,292·3	2,805·3	3,381·9
Road vehicles (including air cushion vehicles)	3,109·0	3,092·2	3,318·8	3,910·6
Other transport equipment	2,033·5	2,341·9	2,766·1	2,736·0
Miscellaneous manufactured articles	5,151·8	5,813·0	6,955·0	7,996·4
Sanitary, plumbing, heating and lighting fixtures and fittings, nes	107·0	108·4	118·9	134·7
Furniture and parts thereof	240·9	257·9	282·0	357·6
Travel goods, handbags and similar containers	19·1	19·3	22·4	29·4
Articles of apparel and clothing accessories	840·0	865·2	996·3	1,171·9
Footwear	114·9	123·4	142·7	159·2
Professional, scientific and controlling instruments and apparatus, nes	1,255·4	1,472·1	1,777·6	2,151·1
Photographic apparatus, equipment and supplies and optical goods, nes, watches and clocks	551·9	573·4	694·2	817·3
Miscellaneous manufactured articles, nes	2,022·7	2,393·4	2,920·8	3,175·2
Commodities and transactions not classified elsewhere	1,708·2	1,666·9	1,795·3	1,990·9

* Provisional figures.

WHITE PAPERS

THE LAW ON CHILD CARE AND FAMILY SERVICES

In July 1984, the Government set up a working party to make proposals for codification and amendment of child care law. The working party's report *Review of Child Care Law* was published in September 1985. At that time the D.H.S.S. circulated a consultative document on the law relating to registration of nurseries and childminders. In 1986 the Government drew up proposals for child care law in England and Wales and for day care, which were published in January 1987 in the White Paper *The Law on Child Care and Family Services* (Cm. 62).

The intention of the proposals is to achieve greater clarity and consistency in the laws under which the State, primarily through the social services departments of local authorities:

(a) provides child care services to families with children;

(b) concerns itself with the standard of private care facilities for children in the interests of their protection;

(c) takes steps to protect children at risk;

(d) may intervene to remove children from their natural families;

(e) discharges its responsibilities to children in its care.

The powers and duties of local authorities to support families with children come from two main streams of law: health and welfare legislation and child care legislation. At present the interests of the individual child are better protected under child care law than under welfare legislation although their needs may be similar. Also in need of rationalisation are the separate provisions, more than twenty, leading to compulsory admission of a child into the care of a local authority, with several different sets of criteria for the court to apply, and different legal effects on parental powers and responsibilities.

SERVICES TO FAMILIES

Two main streams of law set out the responsibilities of local authority social services departments towards families with children. Child care law provides for children to be supported in the family, or to be received voluntarily into the local authority's care in specified circumstances. Health and welfare legislation enables the provision of services to children as part of the local authority's responsibilities to particular groups of all ages, such as those who are mentally handicapped or physically disabled. The Government propose the unification of these two sets of legislation, as recommended by the Review.

It is proposed to give local authorities a broad "umbrella" power to provide services to promote the care and upbringing of children, and to help prevent the breakdown of family relationships which might eventually lead to a court order committing the child to the local authority's care. Within this power the local authority will be able to provide services to a child at home, *e.g.* a family aide to assist within the home; at a day centre, *e.g.* a day nursery for pre-school children, an after school scheme for school age children or placement with a childminder; or residential facilities allowing a child to stay for short or long periods away from home, *e.g.* with a foster family or in a children's home. The local authority will also be able to offer financial assistance in exceptional circumstances. Broadly speaking, all existing powers and duties to provide services to children will be maintained and amalgamated, though with some modifications. In all cases the local authority will have discretion to waive or levy a charge.

Local authorities have a duty under current legislation to receive children into their care in specified circumstances, generally where there is a need to care for the child away from home because of the absence or incapacity of parents. This duty will be maintained broadly as at present. So will the duty to return the child to his family where this is consistent with his welfare.

However, proposed modifications to the law as it presently relates to reception of children into care by local authorities include:

(a) local authorities will no longer have an obligation to diminish the need to receive children into care. (The duty to diminish the need to take children into care compulsorily by court order will, however, continue.)

(b) in line with the concept of partnership between the local authority and parents, local authorities should no longer have power to set a period of notice of 28 days or more before a parent wishing to take back a child from their care could do so where the child had been in care for more than six months.

Where the local authority provide for the care of a child away from home with the voluntary agreement of the parents, matters such as initial placement, schooling and access, and subsequent changes to these arrangements should be settled by mutual agreement. An arrangement under which parents will give notice that they wish to take the child back should also normally be settled by mutual agreement between the parents and the local authority in order to prepare a child for returning home. Where action to delay or prevent a return home is thought essential to protect the child from harm, the local authority will be able to apply for an emergency protection order from a magistrate or ask the police to exercise their emergency protection powers.

When the child appears to have been abandoned the local authority will be under a duty to provide accommodation and maintenance, to search out the parents and investigate the possibility of returning the child to them if it is in his best interests. If it is confirmed that the child has been abandoned it will be possible for the local authority to apply for guardianship. Where the child is older his part in the making of agreements and arrangements for his care should be recognised. In particular, provision should be made where a 16 or 17 year old is capable of making his own agreement with the local authority, for both sides to be able to withdraw from any such arrangement.

The local authority's responsibilities in respect of children cared for away from home require statutory definition. At present the respective responsibilities of the parents and the local authority are unclear and can lead to a blurring of the very real distinction between the position of parents of children in care under a voluntary arrangement and those whose children are committed to care following a court order transferring parental powers and responsibilities to the local authority.

LOCAL AUTHORITY RESPONSIBILITIES

The local authority's responsibilities are as relevant to children cared for under voluntary arrangements as to children committed to care by means of a court order. Under voluntary arrangements, however, the manner in which local authorities exercise their responsibilities may be different because of the need for partnership with the parents who have retained parental powers and responsibilities.

Local authorities' existing statutory responsibilities towards children they are caring for away from home will be recast. The local authority will be under an obligation to safeguard and promote the health, development, education and welfare of the child and in particular to afford him opportunities for the proper development of his character and abilities. In addition the authority will continue to be under a duty to review the child's position every six months and at that point to consider the discharge of any court order.

There will be occasions when a child is unhappy with the arrangements made for his care, or when the parents are similarly concerned. The Government propose that local authorities should be required to provide a procedure, with an independent element, to resolve disputes and complaints. The detailed elements of such a procedure will be for local authorities to decide in the light of local requirements but it must be well publicised and easily accessible.

Two changes are proposed to local authorities' duties in respect of children and young people leaving care who may face difficulties in adjusting to the change in their circumstances. First, they will be required to advise and assist children and young people for whom they are caring so as to promote their welfare when that care ends. Secondly, the previous duty to advise and befriend all those who leave care after leaving school provided that their welfare requires it and that they request it, which lasts up to 18, will be extended to cover those up to 21 as well.

The Secretary of State's statutory powers to ensure the quality and effectiveness of local authority services to children and their families will be extended to cover voluntary care arrangements.

Although local authorities have parental powers and responsibilities for children in care subject to a court order, they will be required to inform and consult parents on major decisions such as where a child lives (except when to do so would not be in the child's best interest), and on arrangements for contact between the child and his family.

Where a child is committed to care in "family proceedings" (commonly divorce), local authorities do not at present have full parental authority, and their precise powers and duties vary according to the particular proceedings in which an order is made. The grounds for and legal effects of such orders will, therefore, be harmonised with care orders made in care proceedings. Where a local authority has obtained an emergency protection order the local authority's responsibilities will apply so far as appropriate for the period of the order.

Voluntary organisations can themselves provide care for children at the request of parents, in addition to those children they care for as agents for the local authority. Such organisations will have largely the same responsibilities for children in their care, placed by parents, as a local authority. Local authorities' powers to vest parental rights and duties in voluntary organisations by administrative resolutions will be discontinued.

There are a number of children who may be cared for away from home for fairly long periods in health establishments or schools. Social services departments at present have no clear responsibilities for these children. The Government believe that where a child has been for three months in a N.H.S. establishment a duty should rest upon the health authority to notify the social services department in whose area the child originally lived; or, if this cannot be ascertained, the social services department in whose area the hospital is situated should then satisfy themselves of the child's welfare. Where the child is in a private hospital or nursing home receiving long-term care, the Government propose that such hospitals and nursing homes should also be under a duty to inform local authorities after a child

has been three months in their care. The local authority would be expected to satisfy themselves as to the child's welfare and to consider whether any further help is necessary.

In the case of children placed in residential schools, the local education authority responsible for making the placement should inform their local social services department, who will then satisfy themselves of the child's welfare and consider what help would be most appropriate. Likewise, where a social services department wish to place a child in a residential school or a home where education is provided on site, they should consult the local education authority.

PROTECTION OF CHILDREN AT RISK

There has been particular public concern, derived from some recent tragic cases of child abuse, that the law may be inadequate to provide the protection that children at risk may require. Under existing legislation the local authority have a duty to investigate cases where information is received which suggests that there are grounds for care proceedings. The Review proposed that this should be replaced by a more active duty to investigate in any case where it is suspected that the child is suffering harm or is likely to do so. The Government endorse that proposal and accept that the enquiries made should be such as are necessary to enable the local authority to decide what action, if any, to take. The Government also intend to make legal provision for co-operation between statutory and voluntary agencies in the investigation of harm and the protection of children at risk.

The Government accept the Review's recommendation that, save for the N.S.P.C.C., only local social services authorities should be able to bring care proceedings since they will be responsible for the child if a care or supervision order is made. The exception for the N.S.P.C.C. reflects their specialist role in child abuse cases and they will be expected to act in concert with the local authority. Thus the present powers of the police and local education authorities to initiate care proceedings will be removed. In cases of school non-attendance where care proceedings are not appropriate the local education authority will be able to apply for a supervision order relating to educational need and the legislation will provide for a suitable means of enforcement.

Under existing statutory provisions any person may apply to a magistrate for removal of a child to a "place of safety". The "place of safety order" is unsatisfactory in various ways and it is proposed to replace it by an "emergency protection order". The new order will deal with circumstances where there is reasonable cause to believe that damage to the child's health or well-being is likely unless he can immediately be removed to or detained in a place of protection for a period up to the duration of the order. The responsibility for the child during this period, which is not defined in the present place of safety order, will be the applicant for the order. It will be explicit that he will have the responsibilities of a person with actual custody of the child in the interests of the child's well being. The order will include a specific requirement to notify parents of the making of an order. There will be presumption of reasonable access to the child unless specified otherwise by the magistrate. If the applicant for the order is other than a local authority, he will have to inform the relevant local authority of the order giving details of the child's address and who has charge of the child. The local authority will then be able to apply for the emergency order to be transferred to them if it would be in the child's interest.

A place of safety order may last up to 28 days. The Review proposed that an emergency protection order should last for eight days only and the Government accept the proposal. In exceptional circumstances the local authority will be permitted to apply for an extension of an emergency protection order for a further period of up to seven days to provide continued protection for the child. On this occasion the parents or child may challenge the extension, such a challenge being based on the ground that there is no risk to the child which justifies an extension of the emergency protection order. Within 15 days it should always be possible for the court to decide the case for an interim care order.

A new type of order appropriate in circumstances where removing the child would be too drastic a step, but there is serious, although not urgent, concern about the health and well-being of the child, will be considered in the context of the new proposals for emergency protection orders. These will allow for the child not to be removed if, when seen, this proves not to be necessary. Provision will also be made to require the disclosure of the whereabouts of the child. As at present a search warrant will be necessary if entry cannot be obtained by agreement.

The police will retain their existing power to detain a child in a place of protection without recourse to a magistrate, but this will in future be limited to 72 hours not eight days as at present. There will be provision for a single magistrate or court to allow an extension of up to eight days from the beginning of the initial detention provided that there is satisfactory evidence of the grounds. The parents and the child, if of sufficient age to understand the implication, would be notified of the application and could attend if they wished. The police should endeavour to hand over the child, and responsibility for applying for any further order, to the local authority if possible.

The present law relating to children who abscond or who are unlawfully taken away or detained is complicated and applies only to certain children in care. The Government propose that there should be a single offence consisting of knowingly and without reasonable excuse or lawful authority:

(a) taking the child or;

(b) detaining or harbouring him or;

(c) assisting, inducing or inciting him or her to run away.

The new proposals would apply to children in care under a care order or an emergency protection order, but not children in a local authority's care as part of a voluntary arrangement. It is proposed that the agencies who look after children who have run away for short periods until alternative arrangements can be made could be specified and exempted from liability for the offence in defined circumstances.

Present powers for recovery of children who abscond or are abducted also need to be rationalised. The Government agree with the Review that the current power to arrest such a child without warrant should be discontinued in respect of children committed to care in civil proceedings. The authority should be able to seek an order authorizing a constable, an officer of the court or a person specified by the authority to take charge of a child subject to a care order who has absconded. The Government also intend to adopt a power for the local authority to apply to the court to compel disclosure by a person who there is reason to believe may have relevant information concerning the child's welfare.

Additionally, the court will be able to authorize a constable or an officer of the court to enter and search any named premises where there are grounds to believe that the child may be found. The current power to order a person, reasonably believed to be able to do so, to produce an absent child will be retained. The Government also accept the Review proposal that the court should be able to order any person who it has reasonable grounds to believe

intends to remove or detain a child without permission, not to do so.

Consideration will be given to permitting court orders for the recovery of children to be served and enforced throughout the U.K., Isle of Man, and Channel Islands. The Islands Authorities will be consulted about this.

THE ROLE OF THE COURT

The Government recognise the advantages of involving in care proceedings anyone who has a proper interest in the child's future and his welfare. Anyone whose legal position could be affected by the proceedings will be entitled to be made a party to proceedings. Hence, those who already have legal responsibility for the child, normally parents or the child's legal guardian, will be parties. In addition, anyone who establishes he has a proper interest in the child and who wishes to have custody of the child will be able to be a party.

The Review made a number of recommendations on procedure and participation. The aim was to move care proceedings away from the quasi-criminal model towards a civil model with more advance disclosure, so that the respondents—i.e. the child or the child and his parents—know the elements of the case for an order; and also to allow the use of hearsay evidence. It is also proposed that the use of guardians *ad litem* should no longer be restricted to those care proceedings where a conflict of interest between the parents and the child is identified. The Review recommended that the court should be under a duty to appoint a guardian *ad litem* in all cases except where it appears unnecessary to do so in order to safeguard the child's interests. The Government accept these proposals, with two modifications:

(a) it proposes to require the respondents, as a minimum, to give an outline of their reasons for contesting the application, when practicable.

(b) it will provide that the guardian *ad litem* for the child has access as a statutory right to other parties' records (even though they may not be produced in court). All documents on which each party is to rely in court should be disclosed in advance.

The Review drew attention to the fact that most of the records relevant in care proceedings would be those of the local authority and would be covered by privilege in respect of local authority files on children. The Government recognise the need for confidentiality in this area but nonetheless believe that the partial relaxation of the privilege rule for care proceedings only would be desirable.

A major proposal in the Review which will be implemented is a re-casting of the grounds for an order in care proceedings and an assimilation to them of the grounds in family proceedings other than wardship. There will be three elements in the grounds, each of which must be satisfied for an order to be made. These are:

(a) evidence of harm or likely harm to the child; and that

(b) this is attributable to the absence of a reasonable standard of parental care or the child being beyond parental control; and

(c) that the order proposed is the most effective means available to the court of safeguarding the child's welfare.

It is intended that the inclusion of likely harm in the new grounds should allow those cases to be heard in juvenile courts, and will cover children who are being cared for by the local authority on a voluntary basis where a return home is likely to harm them.

The Government accept the Review's proposal that the court should have the power to make an interim care order only after care proceedings have been initiated and under strict rules as to grounds and duration. It would be necessary for there to be reasonable cause to believe that only the first two elements of the grounds for a full order may exist and, secondly, that the power to remove or detain the child is necessary in order to safeguard his or her welfare during the interim period. The maximum duration of an interim care order will be eight weeks, though it will be possible to apply for extensions of up to 14 days in exceptional circumstances. The local authority will be expected to say how they intend to manage the care of the child during this period.

An important recommendation of the Review was that in care proceedings the court should be able to make custody orders as between parents or spouses, or in favour of a third party, such as a grandparent, if *either* the party is qualified to apply for custodianship *or* the first two elements of the new grounds are satisfied and a custody order is the most effective means of protecting the child's welfare. In cases where the court has found that the first two elements of the new grounds are satisfied, it is intended to couple a supervision order with the custody order unless the court decides that it is unnecessary to do so. In those cases where a supervision order is also made, the local authority could work with the family and supervise the child's care and progress, returning to the court if it is unsatisfactory.

The Government propose that local authorities should be encouraged to agree on access with the parents at an early stage, so that in the few cases where agreement cannot be reached the dispute can be dealt with by the court at the time the care order is made. The court will also have the power to determine subsequent disputes about what is "reasonable" access. Thereafter, the local authority will be able to propose variations in access arrangements specified in an order, but if a parent or child objects the local authority will either have to refer the matter to a court or maintain the previous arrangements.

The Government intend that before a care order may be discharged, the court should be satisfied that discharge of the order would be in the best interests of the child. In reaching its decision the court should satisfy itself that if control is needed (which may be to protect the public as well as the child) it would be provided.

The Government propose that appeals from care and related proceedings should be to the same court. This means that those appeals which are not at present heard in the High Court should be referred to that court, not to the Crown Court. The Government intend to give all parties to the original proceedings the right to appeal against decisions of the court; thus parents and local authorities (amongst others) will enjoy that right, and the latter will no longer need to seek to resort to wardship where a care order is refused.

A decision such as a refusal to make a care order would not prevent an application for an emergency protection order if there appeared to be an immediate risk to the child: in addition, the appellate court will have a power to grant an interim care order. However, where a court of first instance reaches a decision which would result in a child who is already subject to a care order, or interim order, leaving care pending an appeal, it is proposed that the court should have power to stay its decision. That power will be exercised only where it is in the child's best interests and its purpose will be to avoid unnecessary interruptions in the continuity of his care. There will be a time limit governing such stays.

REGULATION OF PRIVATE AND VOLUNTARY FACILITIES

In addition to providing services themselves local authorities have a role in ensuring that minimum standards of care and supervision are maintained in private facilities for children. This area is governed by three separate sets of statutes. The legislation, which is complex and not well understood, is in need of rationalisation. In this area, the opportunity will be taken to amend Scottish legislation.

The functions of local authorities in registering and inspecting facilities for children under five will remain broadly as at present but with more emphasis on the support and training which they could give to childminders and other providers of services.

The present system of registration provides for two registers to be kept by the local authority, one of persons providing care in their own homes for reward (*i.e.* childminders), and one for non-domestic premises where care is provided (usually day-nurseries and play groups). The Government intend to replace this system of registration by a single register of responsible persons providing care at special premises.

The Government intend to remove a number of exemptions provided for under current legislation. These include private day care facilities run on school or hospital premises, and childminders who are also foster parents. Exemptions for maintained nursery schools and nursery classes in independent schools will remain. However, one-off care arrangements such as conference creches, which are registerable at present, will be specifically exempted. The Government will make provision to enable extension of these arrangements to other categories of carers if it is found to be desirable.

The Government intend to include a duty on local authorities to impose appropriate "requirements" in connection with registration, *e.g.* the maximum number of children to be cared for, and to provide for the frequency of inspections. Provision will be made to cover the way in which the registration scheme is operated by the local authority.

The Government propose that the registration requirements should not extend to private arrangements whereby people look after children over the age of five, thus accepting the *de facto* position in many areas.

The present legislation applies to arrangements lasting for continuous periods of two hours up to six days. When an arrangement lasts for a longer period the registration requirements of the Nurseries and Childminders Regulation Act, 1948, give way to the provisions of the Foster Children Acts. However, the definition of a regular foster parent is complex and it is not easy to identify the legal requirements in a particular case. The Government intend to simplify the law by separating the provisions relating to day care and holiday arrangements, *i.e.* the standard of care and facilities for a group of children, from the private foster care law which is directed at securing the welfare needs of individual children notified to local authorities. The Government propose that the registration requirements for day care and holiday activities for children under five should apply to continuous periods of up to twenty-seven days.

The distinguishing feature of private fostering arrangements is that, unlike voluntary care placements arranged by the local authority in consultation with the parents, they are generally not paid for or arranged by the local authority. Under the Foster Children Acts the local authority are required to satisfy themselves as to the well-being of the child. Notification is required by the private fosterers. There is a power to require notification also by the parents and to make regulations concerning the type of supervision provided by the local authority. These powers and duties will be maintained in new legislation. However, the exclusions from the requirements are over-complex. The Government intend to simplify them and restrict the provisions to those placements lasting or intended to last for more than twenty-seven days, or aggregated periods of more than twenty-seven days. This legislation will continue to apply to children up to the age of sixteen. The exemptions covering residential schools, hospitals and other institutions will be maintained.

MINOR MATTERS

The Government also intend to take the opportunity of legislation on the matters included in the White Paper to make minor adjustments to existing legislation, including:

(a) it is proposed to amend Section 44 of the Child Care Act, 1980, to provide that, when premises or parts of premises used for the purposes of a controlled or assisted community home are disposed of or put to alternative use before the home's designation as a community home has been withdrawn, that proportion of the value of the premises or parts disposed of which is attributable to the expenditure of public money will be repaid by the voluntary organisation providing the home (or the trustees in whom the home is vested).

(b) provisions relating to general matters such as research and training and the giving of grants to voluntary organisations will be brought together in child care legislation. A general power will be included for the Secretary of State, through the Social Services Inspectorate, to inspect the work that local authority social services departments carry out for families with children. This will include the inspection of records.

HIGHER EDUCATION: MEETING THE CHALLENGE

The White Paper *Higher Education: Meeting the Challenge* (Cm. 114) was presented to Parliament in April 1987 by the Secretary of State for Education (Mr. Baker), the Secretary of State for Wales (Mr. Edwards), the Secretary of State for Northern Ireland (Mr. King) and the Secretary of State for Scotland (Mr. Rifkind). The proposals in the White Paper were based on those published in the Green Paper *The Development of Higher Education into the 1990s* (Cmnd. 9524).

The introduction to the White Paper makes clear that the Government takes a wide view of the aims and purposes of higher education and that it adheres to the Robbins Committee's definition: instruction in skills, the promotion of the general powers of the mind, the advancement of learning, and the transmission of a common culture and common standards of citizenship. The Government fully recognises the value of research, and especially basic research, together with those areas of learning and scholarship which have at most an indirect relationship to the world of work. The Government also states that higher education should serve the economy more effectively, and have closer links with industry and commerce. The Government believes that higher education has a vital role to play in providing the highly qualified work force that the country needs for technological and economic development. In order to meet this demand, the Government proposes to improve access to higher education.

ACCESS TO HIGHER EDUCATION

Since 1979 the number of full-time home students in higher education in Great Britain has risen by more than 85,000. The size of the 18–19 year-old age group peaked in 1982; the continuing increase in student numbers reflects higher rates of participation in higher education both by 18–19 year olds and by mature entrants (aged 21 and over) whose numbers have grown by a quarter since 1979. The increases in participation have been particularly marked for women who now account for about 44 per cent of full-time students in higher education compared with less than 40 per cent seven years ago. Virtually all of this major increase in full-time student numbers has taken place in the polytechnics and colleges sector of higher education. The polytechnics and colleges have also accommodated over three-quarters of the 27 per cent increase since 1979 in part-time student numbers.

The Government remains committed to the principle that places should be available for all who have the necessary intellectual competence, motivation and maturity to benefit from higher education and who wish to do so. However, in a period when student numbers could decline sharply for demographic reasons, the Government considers student demand alone to be an insufficient basis for the planning of higher education. A major determinant must also be the demands for a highly qualified work force.

For the present, the Government's best judgment is that it should plan for a 5 per cent increase in student numbers between 1985 and 1990, followed by a return to current intake levels in the mid-1990s when the young entrant age group will be at its smallest, and then renewed growth. But the actual numbers will be critically dependent on, *inter alia*, the commitment by universities, polytechnics and colleges to opening up higher education to more mature entrants and to more who do not possess traditional entry qualifications.

Three routes into higher education are generally recognised: traditional sixth form qualifications; vocational qualifications; and "access courses". Although the majority of young students in higher education will continue to gain entrance through holding traditional sixth form qualifications, a growing number of students will enter higher education with vocational qualifications. The polytechnics and colleges already have substantial experience of providing for such students; the Government believes that the universities should also move in this direction.

The third recognised route into higher education is through "access courses". Some access courses are geared to a particular receiving institution; others are designed to offer access to higher education more widely. The responsibilities of validating bodies extend to access provision in all styles, and the Government invites them to give attention, in consultation with the providers, to developing a comprehensive framework within which the availability of well-devised access courses can be increased.

The Government will propose to the validating and planning bodies a programme for monitoring progress in the admission of students with vocational qualifications and from access courses.

Credit transfer schemes are another means of extending access to higher education. Schemes can operate within consortia of institutions, or more widely through such means as the Council for National Academic Awards' Credit Accumulation and Transfer Scheme. The wider range of entrants will increasingly be able to seek academic credit for prior learning, whether gained through formal qualifications or through experience, and to pursue programmes of study tailored to their particular needs but within established academic standards. The National Council for Vocational Qualification is making a priority of arrangements for earning awards by credit accumulation.

Continuing Education

The importance of adult continuing education is now widely accepted. Many individuals want or need education in middle life, and many others need updating, retraining or new skills for employment purposes. The Government intends to encourage developments in this area. The Department of Education and Science and the Welsh Office through the Professional, Industrial and Commercial Updating Programme (PICKUP), the Manpower Services Commission and the Department of Trade and Industry will jointly provide pump-priming finance for a national network of Technology Centres. These are intended to encourage greater collaboration between industry and education and provide a flexible response to the training and related processes of technology transfer.

In continuing education, though not there alone, new technology may allow a larger market to be reached, ultimately at no greater effort. Distance learning is itself not new, but new dimensions have been added in recent years. The Government sees great potential here and will facilitate the extension and development of distance learning provision across a wide range of institutions, covering both learning materials and delivery systems, and building on the excellent foundations laid by the Open University and the newly developing Open College.

QUALITY AND EFFICIENCY

The Government is also committed to improving the quality and efficiency of higher education. It feels that quality would be enhanced by improvements in the design and content of courses, and in validation procedures.

The Lindop Report (1985) found that quality in higher education was best assured when polytechnics and colleges accepted maximum responsibility for their own standards. The Government therefore asked the Council for National Academic Awards: to give "accreditation", and therefore the task of approving individual courses, to those institutions judged ready; to increase delegation to other institutions as far as practicable; and to pay more attention to the quality of teaching and learning and to the achievements of students in both academic and employment terms.

The C.N.A.A. has now agreed a strategy for its future relations with the institutions which will result in virtual self-validation for many. The Council is also strengthening the external examiner system as a further safeguard of academic standards. The Government welcomes the C.N.A.A.'s change of direction and looks to its early implementation.

The Government's proposals for maintaining the quality of teaching include systematic arrangements for: staff training and development; staff appraisal; evaluation of the results achieved, including analysis of external examiners' reports and students' employment patterns; involvement of professional practitioners in vocational courses; and feedback from students themselves.

The Government is committed to maintaining and enhancing the strength and quality of academic research; and accepts its responsibility to provide the main funding. But pressure on resources and the increasing cost of undertaking world-class research mean that a high priority must be given to areas which are likely to lead to useful applications. Overall, the Government is confident that the approaches now being adopted are yielding much increased value for money and it is considering what help it can give to encouraging increased investment by industry in research and development, including research in collaboration with higher education.

The Government is concerned both with the efficiency of individual institutions and with that of the national system of higher education as a whole. The pursuit of efficiency is not just about saving money. It is about helping institutions and individuals to achieve more of what they should achieve with the money that is available.

The universities are currently examining their improvements in efficiency and their financial management, and the use of performance indicators is to be introduced. Initial studies of the management of polytechnics and colleges, however, suggest that the good management of these institutions is inhibited by the excessive engagement in their affairs of local authorities in their role as formal employer of staff and the overseer of budgetary and purchasing matters. The White Paper sets out the Government's plans for providing polytechnics and colleges with the opportunity for self-management.

CHANGES IN STRUCTURE AND NATIONAL PLANNING FOR HIGHER EDUCATION

POLYTECHNICS AND COLLEGES IN ENGLAND

In England 405 institutions outside the universities provide higher education: 29 polytechnics and 346 other colleges under local education authority (L.E.A.) control, plus 30 voluntary and other colleges directly funded by the Department of Education and Science. Most of these institutions are provided and maintained by L.E.A.s and are, in effect, part of them: their land, buildings and equipment belong to the authority and their staff are its employees. Others—generally known as assisted institutions—are separately established, some as corporate bodies, but with constitutions linking them to the L.E.A. on whose financial assistance they substantially depend. Most of the expenditure of the local authority colleges is pooled between all authorities.

The Government acknowledges the contribution which local government has made to the development of higher education. It has, however, concluded that it is no longer appropriate for polytechnics and other colleges predominantly offering higher education to be controlled by individual local authorities.

Polytechnics have strong national, as well as regional and local, roles. They recruit students nationally and meet the needs of employers nationwide. This calls for an effective lead from the centre and the reward of success and enterprise in meeting new national needs, in place of a system giving undue weight to local interests.

It is widely acknowledged that the present relationship between local authorities and their polytechnics and colleges can and often does inhibit good institutional management. The governors, directors/principals and other senior staff of many polytechnics and colleges are prevented from managing their financial and staffing resources to best effect, and from developing to the full the maturity and responsibility appropriate to higher education institutions. Yet progress in educational planning will be even more necessary if the polytechnics and other colleges are to meet the changing needs of industry and commerce in the 1990s and provide in new ways for a wider range of students.

It has been suggested that the simple grant of corporate status to polytechnics and other local authority colleges would satisfactorily resolve these management difficulties. But local authorities would still be able to impose financial and staffing constraints by attaching conditions to their funding. And the grant of corporate status would not remedy deficiencies in the present national planning arrangements. The Government therefore intends to secure the re-establishment of the polytechnics and other institutions of substantial size (with 350 or more full-time equivalent higher education students) engaged predominantly in higher education (more than 55 per cent of their activity) as free-standing outside local authority control. Those predominantly higher education institutions with fewer than 350 students will have the choice to opt in to the new arrangements. Those colleges whose main concern is non-advanced further education will remain with local government.

The Government intends that the new arrangements should also apply to the voluntary and other grant-aided colleges providing higher education, which are already free-standing institutions funded by the Department of Education and Science. The Open University, Cranfield Institute of Technology and the Royal College of Art are currently planned and funded separately from the rest of higher education, with direct funding from the Department of Education and Science on the advice of Visiting Committees appointed by the Secretary of State. The Government recognises that these institutions each have certain features which may continue to justify special arrangements, but will be discussing with each the possibility of its coming within the ambit of one of the proposed new planning and funding bodies.

The New Sector

The polytechnics and other colleges transferred from local authorities will each:

(a) be established with corporate status;

(b) have governing bodies with strong representation from local and regional industry, commerce and the professions, and on which dominance by local authority representatives is no longer possible;

(c) employ their own staff; and

(d) own their land, buildings and equipment.

The Board of Governors of each institution will comprise 20–25 people, of whom about half will be local and regional employers or representatives of the professions. Other members will be appointed by named constituencies in stated proportions or co-opted. Each Board will elect its own Chairman. The Governors will have wide powers to determine the affairs of the institution. The Director of each institution will report only to the Governors.

The academic work of all the institutions in the new sector will continue to be validated by the Council for National Academic Awards, universities or the Business and Technician Education Council as appropriate, and will be subject to inspection by H.M. Inspectorate.

The provision of public money on the appropriate scale for the colleges transferred from local government will become the responsibility of central Government. The equivalent of pooled expenditure will be transferred out of Aggregate Exchequer Grant (A.E.G.) and capital expenditure in the transferred colleges will be deducted from provision for local authority capital expenditure.

Polytechnics and colleges are at present almost wholly dependent on public funds for their recurrent and capital expenditure. The funds they receive have usually been described as "allocations" or "grants", paid by a local authority or central Government. The Government proposes, in place of grants, a system of contracting between institutions and the new planning and funding body.

The P.C.F.C.

The planning of the new polytechnics and colleges sector of higher education and the allocation of resources within it will require the establishment of a new body, which it is proposed to call the Polytechnics and Colleges Funding Council (P.C.F.C.). The National Advisory Body for Public Sector Higher Education with its local authority

majority will cease to be an appropriate planning body and will go out of existence. The Government will consult the voluntary colleges about whether the Voluntary Sector Consultative Council should continue and, if so, about its relationship to the P.C.F.C.

The P.C.F.C. will be an independent non-departmental body appointed by the Secretary of State for Education and Science. It will have a small membership with a strong industrial and commercial element, as well as members from higher education institutions. The Secretary of State will provide general guidance to the P.C.F.C. on its work and will have reserve powers of direction. The Council will be expected to consult the local authorities about their residual interest in higher education and about the small amount of non-advanced further education in the transferred colleges.

The main tasks of the P.C.F.C. will be to:

(a) contract with institutions, using the recurrent funds supplied by Government, for the provision of higher education including, where appropriate, the development of new courses and selective initiatives and research activities;

(b) make funds available for capital expenditure by institutions, from those supplied by Government and from any money available from disposals by institutions of property acquired with public funds.

(c) plan the educational provision in the sector (subject to the powers of the Secretary of State for Education and Science with regard to initial teacher training);

(d) encourage institutions to co-operate in the development of good management practice; and

(e) have power to contract for provision of some of the higher education in colleges which remain under the control of local authorities.

The Government will consult further on the P.C.F.C.'s precise terms of reference.

For colleges remaining under local authority control, the Government intends that:

(a) for all degree and postgraduate work, full-time higher diploma courses, and for some courses of in-service teacher training: the P.C.F.C. will be responsible for planning and funding. In this situation it will, to the extent it judges appropriate, enter into contracts with local authorities for the purchase of provision from their colleges;

(b) for other courses: the local authorities will no longer be guided by a central planning agency. The present pooled funding arrangements will end and L.E.A.s will instead receive credit for students on such courses in the assessment of their Grant Related Expenditure for Rate Support Grant purposes.

As part of their continuing responsibility for non-advanced further education, it will be open to L.E.A.s to make contractual arrangements for it to be provided in colleges transferred from their control.

Assets

A Polytechnics and Colleges Assets Board will be set up for a limited period to resolve any difficulties in the apportionment of assets to transferred institutions and to assist them to make arrangements as quickly as possible for the holding of their own assets. It will also make available to the P.C.F.C. any surplus assets or the proceeds of any sale of assets.

The assets now used in local authority higher education were acquired in most cases under arrangements which shared the cost between ratepayers and taxpayers. The local education authorities will not be compensated for the transfer of the assets now in their ownership. The institutions themselves will become responsible for servicing the debt attributable to past capital expenditure once ownership has transferred to them.

Wales

It is not at present the Government's intention to establish a Polytechnic and Colleges Funding Council for Wales. However the legislation which will be brought forward to establish a P.C.F.C. in England will provide for the same arrangements to be extended to Wales if the Government subsequently considers that to be necessary.

UNIVERSITY FUNDING

The forty-seven universities in England, Scotland, Wales and Northern Ireland are, except for the University of Buckingham, funded by central Government; and, the Open University apart, they receive the greater part of their public funding effectively by decision of the University Grants Committee.

The Croham Report (Feb. 1987) suggested that the U.G.C. should be reconstituted as a University Grants Council, an independent body under the sponsorship of the Secretary of State for Education and Science, with revised terms of reference. The Government accepts the broad thrust of these recommendations. However, the Government proposes for the university sector also that payment of grants to institutions should be replaced by a system of contracting between them and the body to succeed the U.G.C. That body will be named the Universities Funding Council (U.F.C.). The Government will be giving further consideration to the precise terms of reference of the U.F.C.

The Government welcomes and endorses the following other recommendations of the Report:

(a) The Government should provide guidelines at appropriate intervals to set the framework for the planning process which the U.F.C. and the universities should conduct.

(b) The Government should play no part in the distribution of general funding between individual universities in Great Britain.

(c) The U.F.C. for its part should have the power to require that funding is or is not spent for a particular purpose.

(d) Financial relations between the Government and the U.F.C., and between the U.F.C. and universities, should be governed by financial memoranda.

(e) Arrangements for the flow of management information and for accountability from the universities to the U.F.C. and onwards to Government should be much improved.

Higher Education in Scotland

The Government believes that there is scope for improvement in the co-ordination and planning of the university and colleges sectors of higher education in Scotland. Equally, however, it is concerned to ensure that the planning and funding of the eight Scottish universities is not divorced from that of universities elsewhere in the United Kingdom. The Government has therefore decided that the remit of the new Universities Funding Council should cover all the universities currently funded on the advice of the U.G.C. The Council should, however, appoint a Scottish Committee after consultation with the Secretary of State for Scotland and in the development of its policies take account of advice from this Committee. The U.F.C. would have regard to the views of the Secretary of State for Scotland on Scottish needs and plans for the colleges sector of higher education in Scotland, consistent with the national guidelines provided by the Secretary of State for Education and Science.

Northern Ireland

The Government accepts the Croham Committee's recommendation that the U.F.C. should advise the Department of Education for Northern Ireland on the funding of the universities in Northern Ireland. In formulating its advice, the U.F.C. will take account of the views of a Northern Ireland working party which, as now, will consider and report on particular circumstances bearing on higher education provision in the Province.

TO COME WITHIN THE AMBIT OF THE P.C.F.C.

Transferred from Local Authorities

Polytechnics

Portsmouth; North East London; Sheffield; Trent; Leicester; Wolverhampton; Hatfield; Oxford; Newcastle; Liverpool; Middlesex; Bristol; Kingston; Coventry (Lanchester); North London; Leeds; Birmingham; Brighton; North Staffordshire; Lancashire; Thames; Huddersfield; Plymouth; Sunderland; Teesside; Manchester; South Bank; Central London; City of London.

Other L.E.A. Institutions

Edge Hill C.H.E.; Worcester C.H.E.; Bulmershe C.H.E.; North Riding College; West Midlands C.H.E.; Garnett College; Royal Northern College of Music; Charlotte Mason College of Education; Crewe & Alsager C.H.E.; Rolle College; West Sussex I.H.E.; Bretton Hall College; Dorset I.H.E.; Bath C.H.E.; Bolton I.H.E.; West London I.H.E.; Humberside C.H.E.; Ealing C.H.E.; Derbyshire C.H.E.; Essex I.H.E.; West Surrey College of Art and Design; Ravensbourne College of Design and Communication; Southampton I.H.E.; Loughborough College of Art and Design; Slough C.H.E.; Kent Art Institute; Nene College; South West London College.

Voluntary and Other Grant-Aided Colleges

Voluntary Colleges

Bishop Grosseteste College, Lincoln; Chester C.H.E.; Christ Church College, Canterbury; College of Ripon & York St John; College of St Mark & St John, Plymouth; College of St Paul & St Mary, Cheltenham; Homerton College, Cambridge; King Alfred's College, Winchester; La Sainte Union C.H.E., Southampton; Liverpool I.H.E.; Newman College, Birmingham; Roehampton I.H.E.; S. Martin's College, Lancaster; St Mary's College, Twickenham; Trinity and All Saints College, Leeds; Westhill College, Birmingham; Westminster College, Oxford.

Other Grant-Aided Colleges

Goldsmiths' College; Harper Adams Agricultural College; Royal Academy of Music; Royal College of Music; Royal College of Nursing; Seale Hayne College; Shuttleworth Agricultural College; Trinity College of Music.

(C./I.H.E.—College/Institute of Higher Education)

INSTITUTIONS WITH THE CHOICE TO TRANSFER FROM LOCAL AUTHORITIES

Camborne School of Mines; Rose Bruford College of Speech and Drama; Kent College for the Careers Service; Dartington College of Arts; Norwich School of Art; Exeter College of Art and Design; Central School of Speech and Drama; Winchester School of Art; Wimbledon School of Art; Falmouth School of Art; Writtle Agricultural College.

FILM AND CINEMA, 1986–87

1986 was a poor year for British cinema, with only 37 films made in Britain compared with 55 the previous year. The decline had been marked since the Cannon take-over of Thorn-EMI. However, one encouraging note was sounded by J. Paul Getty's donation of £17 million towards film projects, including the establishment of the Museum of the Moving Image, and provision of a new headquarters for the British Film Institute.

Cannon Group's purchase of Thorn-EMI's Screen Entertainment received a mixed reaction in the industry. It subsequently ran into difficulty, and Warner Communications, the Hollywood film group, had to assist Cannon in meeting its obligations to the Bond Corporation of Australia. Bond had originally purchased Thorn-EMI for £125 million, selling it on to Cannon soon afterwards for £175 million, which was considered an inflated price by many people. By helping Cannon to pay its debts to Bond, Warner was granted rights to buy, for $50 million, half of Cannon's European cinema circuit of over 500 screens and its U.S. subsidiary, Warner Brothers, bought video distribution rights.

Cannon's troubles multiplied in 1987. Its new auditors, concerned at Cannon's financial estimates and its previous accounting practices, which led to a Securities and Exchange Commission investigation and shareholders' lawsuits, expressed concern at Cannon's ability to continue operations as a going concern. The group reported a loss of $60 million for the year ending in December 1986. To resolve its parlous financial state, Cannon was forced to dispose of Thorn-EMI assets, with the film archive sold off overseas and Elstree studios also on the market. The worst fears of those such as David Puttnam who resented such a substantial portion of the British film industry falling under foreign control were beginning to be realized.

Goldcrest, the company behind such major successes of recent years as *Chariots of Fire* and *Gandhi*, also came near to collapse after the departure in 1983 of its founder and main inspiration, Jake Eberts. With the expensive and disastrous flops *Revolution* and *Absolute Beginners*, the company lost its magic touch and its sense of direction. However, Eberts returned and succeeded in restructuring the company. With the success of *The Mission* and *The Name of the Rose*, which Goldcrest helped market, it appears that the company will survive.

Oscars

The Mission greatly boosted Goldcrest's morale when, although shown in a barely finished state, it won the Golden Palm at the 1986 Cannes Film Festival. *The Mission* received little reward at the B.A.F.T.A. ceremony but its nomination as one of the five candidates for best picture in the American Academy awards was further confirmation of its international appeal. The film received seven nominations in all. Also prominent in the nominations were the latest Ivory/Merchant collaboration *A Room with a View* and *Platoon*, each of which received eight nominations.

However, *A Room with a View* won only three Oscars on the night; best screen play adaptation from another medium (Ruth Prawer Jhabvala from E. M. Forster's novel), best costume design (Jenny Beavan and John Bright), and best art direction (Gianni Quaranta, Brian Ackland-Snow, Brian Savegar and Elio Altramura). *Platoon* won the premier awards of best film and best director for Oliver Stone, who had spent over ten years trying to raise finance to make a film based on his Vietnam experiences. Rejected by the major Hollywood studios, the film was eventually made with English backing from Hemdale Pictures. It was a huge box office success in America, belying the studios' claim that the "truth" about Vietnam was not commercial. *Platoon* obviously struck a chord, its vivid recreation of the horrors of war providing a necessary corrective after the comic-book excesses of Sylvester Stallone's *Rambo* films. Written and directed by Stone, and made for only $6.5 million, the film featured no major film stars. The cast included Tom Berenger, Charlie Sheen and William Dafoe, and Stone achieved the degree of realism which made *Platoon* so convincing by making the actors live in the jungle for a fortnight under military combat conditions. *Platoon* also won Oscars for best film editing (Claire Simpson) and best achievement in sound (John Wilkinson, Richard Rogers, Charles Grenzbach and Simon Kaye).

The award for best actor went to Paul Newman for his recreation of the character of "Fast Eddie" Felson in *The Color of Money*. Newman was nominated when he first played Felson in the 1961 classic *The Hustler*; in total, he had received six previous nominations without winning, although he did receive an honorary award the previous year. An element of chauvinism and the sympathy vote determined Newman's success; although Newman's was another fine performance in a distinguished career, Bob Hoskins gave what many judged the best performance of the year in *Mona Lisa*. *The Color of Money* was directed by Martin Scorsese, with a script by Richard Price based loosely on another novel by the author of *The Hustler*, Walter Tevis. The film also featured Tom Cruise as Vincent Lauria, the young pool player Newman takes under his wing, with his girlfriend played by Mary Elizabeth Mastrantonio. Also nominated for best actor were Dexter Gordon, veteran jazz saxophonist, in his first acting role in *Round Midnight*; William Hurt, the previous year's winner, in *Children of a Lesser God*; and James Woods in *Salvador*, Oliver Stone's directorial debut.

The best actress was Marlee Matlin, a deaf actress, in her first film role. She played a deaf girl who refuses to speak in *Children of a Lesser God*, an adaptation of the successful stage play. The other nominations for best actress were Jane Fonda in *The Morning After*; Sissy Spacek in *Crimes of the Heart*; Kathleen Turner in *Peggy Sue Got Married*; and Sigourney Weaver in *Aliens*.

Somewhat surprisingly, Michael Caine was voted best supporting actor for his part in Woody Allen's *Hannah and Her Sisters*. Caine has been nominated three times as best actor, for *Alfie*, *Sleuth* and *Educating Rita*, so it was ironic that he should be given the minor award for a cameo role. The award has become more of a compensatory prize than the first recognition of the up-and-coming or previously unrecognised talent. Best supporting actress was Dianne Wiest in *Hannah and Her Sisters*.

Of *The Mission*'s seven nominations, only one was converted into an award. That went to Chris Menges for his stunning cinematography. He also won the award in 1985 for *The Killing Fields*. Woody Allen won the Oscar for best original screenplay for *Hannah and Her Sisters*, and the best foreign language film was *The Assault* (Netherlands). Best sound effects editing was won by Don Sharpe for *Aliens*, and best original score by Herbie Hancock for *Round Midnight*. Best short subject documentary was Vivienne Verdon-Roe's *Women—for America, for the World*, and best documentary feature was shared between *Artie Shaw: Time is All You've Got*, produced by Brigitte Berman, and *Down and Out in America*, produced by Joseph Feury and Milton Justice. Best make-up award was presented to Chris Walas and Stephen Dupuis for *The Fly*; best animated short film was *A Greek Tragedy*; and best live action short film, *Precious Images*.

B.A.F.T.A. Awards

At the British Academy of Film and Television Arts Awards for 1986, presented in March 1987, Ismail Merchant's and James Ivory's *A Room with a View* was judged best film, and Maggie Smith won best actress in a leading role for her part in it: the same part for which she had been nominated for an Oscar in the supporting role category. Judi Dench was best supporting actress in the same film. Woody Allen's *Hannah and Her Sisters* won for him the award for best director and best original screenplay. Best adapted screenplay was Kurt Luedtke's *Out of Africa*. Bob Hoskins was voted best actor for his role as the small-time crook in *Mona Lisa*. Neil Jordan's third film, following the much-praised *Angel* and *The Company of Wolves*, *Mona Lisa* was an atmospheric story of life in London's underworld, brilliantly filmed by Roger Pratt. Apart from Hoskins's powerful performance in the leading role, Cathy Tyson was impressive as the black call-girl whom Hoskins chauffeurs around London and with whom he falls in love, and Michael Caine gave good support as a Soho night club boss. Hoskins also shared best actor award at Cannes in 1986 for his part in the film.

The Academy presented a fellowship to the distinguished Italian director, Federico Fellini. *The Mission* won two awards: best supporting actor for Ray McAnally and best musical score for Ennio Morricone. Best foreign language film was *Ran*, Kurosawa's Japanese version of *King Lear*, and best short film was Simon Shore's *La Boule*. The Flaherty Documentary Award was presented to Claude Lanzmann for his nine and a half hour account of the Holocaust, *Shoah*. Painstakingly assembled from first-hand interviews with survivors, and without the archive pictures that usually accompany film accounts of the concentration camps in the Second World War, *Shoah* was widely praised. Lanzmann, a French Jew who was a leader of the Resistance in central France at the age of 18, took twelve years to make the documentary, which was distilled from some 350 hours of interviews.

In the *London Evening Standard* Film Awards, *A Room with a View* was judged best film, and Tony Pierce-Roberts received the award for outstanding technical achievement for his work on it. Best actor was Ray McAnally for *The Mission* and *No Surrender*, and best actress was Coral Browne for *Dreamchild*. Robert Bolt received the award for best screenplay for *The Mission*, and John Cleese received the Peter Sellers Award for Comedy for *Clockwise*. Most promising newcomer was Gary Oldman in *Sid and Nancy*. A Special Award was presented to Jake Eberts for his contribution to British cinema. The Critics' Circle Film Section chose *A Room with a View* as best film, and *Ran* as best foreign-language film, with Kurosawa as best director. Woody Allen received the award for best screenplay for *Hannah and Her Sisters*. The best actor award was shared by Bob Hoskins for *Mona Lisa* and *Sweet Liberty*, and William Hurt for *Kiss of the Spider Woman*.

Festival of Film

At the 30th London Film Festival a retrospective of the first festival was held. Conceived by Derek Prouse and Dilys Powell, the first festival had featured 15 films, including Kurosawa's *Throne of Blood* and Bergman's *The Seventh Seal*. The 30th Festival, guided by *Guardian* film critic Derek Malcolm in his third and final year as artistic director, included some 150 films from around the world and opened and closed with world premieres "from two of the leading, most controversial and often undervalued British directors, Nicolas Roeg and Ken Russell". An innovation, continuing Malcolm's bold policy of taking the festival out of the confines of the National Film Theatre to the public, was the "Festival on the Square", which used the "flagship cinemas in Leicester Square, the heart of West End movie-going" to show festival films.

Roeg's premiered film, *Castaway*, was based on the best-selling account of her year on a tropical island off Australia by Lucy Irvine. She had responded to an advertisement by writer Gerald Kingsland, who was played by Oliver Reed in the film, with Lucy played by Amanda Donohoe. Ken Russell's *Gothic* was based on the events of the night of June 16, 1816, at the Villa Diodati in Switzerland, when, in response to a challenge from Byron, Mary Shelley had been inspired by a half-waking nightmare to write *Frankenstein, or the Modern Prometheus*. The script was written by Stephen Voir, who described *Gothic* as "a psychological maelstrom of fears, lusts and jealousies". Also featured were Andrei Tarkowsky's final film, *The Sacrifice*, a dark, brooding masterpiece about a writer on an island retreat; and Bill Douglas's worthy but over-long epic on the Tolpuddle Martyrs, *Comrades*.

The Festival also included more new productions from India and the East and Latin America than any other major festival. Another regular, and popular, feature is the restoration of old and lost classics and this time it was Erich von Stroheim's *Greed* which was rescued by Kevin Brownlow and Thames Television. Called by one critic "the filthiest, vilest, most putrid picture in the history of the motion picture business", *Greed* had shocked and outraged a public not used to its innovatory realism. The ten hours of the original cut have long been lost but the two and a half hours that were first released have been restored. Also shown was Murnau's expressionist classic, *Nosferatu*, from the Munich Film Archive, and Grierson's *Man of Africa*, filmed with a black cast in Africa, which belatedly received its English premiere.

The surprise winner of the Golden Lion at the Venice Film Festival was Eric Rohmer's *Le Rayon Vert (The Green Ray)*. Largely improvised, it featured Mary Riviere, and was charming and effective; it also received the International Critics Association and Catholic Jury prizes. However, many felt that the undoubted star of the Festival was Bertrand Tavernier's *Round Midnight*, for which Dexter Gordon had received an Oscar nomination. The Jury's Special Prize was presented to Sergei Soloviev's *The Wild White Pigeon* and Francesco Maselli's *Storia d'Amore*. Best actor was Carlo delle Piane in *Christmas Present*, and Valeria Golino in *Storia d'Amore* was best actress. The Silver Lion was won by Carlos Sorin for *The Film of the King*.

At Locarno, the Polish film *Jezioro Bodenskie (Lake Constance)*, directed by Janusz Zaorski, won the Golden Leopard to muted acclaim. However, the British film *Lamb*, directed by Colin Gregg, was very well received and picked up the Bronze Leopard. The second Dublin Film Festival, on a budget of £40,000, included nearly one hundred feature films and 22 shorts, and opened with a Gala European Premiere of the Australian epic *Burke and Wills*. The Berlin Golden Bear was won by a seven-year-old Russian film, Gleb Panfilov's *Theme*, which also won the International Critics Prize. Oliver Stone's *Platoon* received the Silver Bear, and the Special Jury Prize went to the Japanese film, *The Sea and Prison*, directed by Kei Kumai.

At the 40th Cannes Film Festival, the Golden Palm was awarded to a rank outsider, Maurice Pialat's *Sous le Soleil de Satan*, adapted from the novel by Georges Bernanos which also inspired Robert Bresson's *Diary of a Country Priest*. More popular, and expected, was the award of the Special Grand Prize to Tenghiz Abouladze's *Repentence*, a 1984 Georgian film which powerfully satirises the Stalinist era with a caricature portrayal of a tyrant. Abouladze was inspired to make the film by Eisenstein's words "the truth will triumph, though we may not live long enough to see it do so". Thanks to the new Soviet policy of *glasnost* the film was screened in Moscow in late 1986 and has now been screened abroad to much acclaim. Wim Wenders won the best director prize for the beautifully filmed (by Henri Alekan), but pretentious and overrated, *Wings of Desire*. The best actor was Italian veteran Marcello Mastroianni in *Black Eyes*, directed by Nikita Mikhalkov. Best actress was Barbara Hershey in *Shy People*. Stanley Myers received the award for best artistic contribution for the music in *Prick Up Your Ears*, the story of playwright Joe Orton, directed by Stephen Frears from Alan Bennett's script. The Special Jury Prize was shared between *Light* (directed by Souleymane Cisse of Mali) and *Shinran* (Rentaro Mikuni, Japan). Federico Fellini received a 40th Anniversary prize for *Fellini Intervista*, an account of 50 years of Cinecitta, Rome's "Hollywood on the Tiber". Jean-

Luc Goddard's *King Lear*, commissioned by Cannon, which featured Burgess Meredith in a Shakespearian travesty, was not well received.

The 32nd Moscow Film Festival was notable for its demonstration of *glasnost* in action. Following a protest by the director Askoldov, his 20-year-old film *The Commissar* was at last screened. It had been suppressed when originally made, forcing him out of film-making. Also notable was the choice as jury president of Robert de Niro, the first foreigner to be so honoured. The International Critics Prize was awarded to the Polish film, *Hero of the Year*, directed by Feliks Falk.

Crocs of Gold

Paul Hogan starred in *Crocodile Dundee*, for which he also wrote the script. This tale of an Australian innocent at large in New York, directed by Peter Faiman, was a box office success in America and Britain. Linda Kozlowski plays the American journalist who discovers Dundee in the Australian outback and takes him to New York, with humorous results.

84 Charing Cross Road, Helene Hanff's charming and sentimental tale of her long-distance love affair with a London bookshop and its staff, was adapted by Hugh Whitemore for the screen. Producer Mel Brooks bought the film rights as a present for his wife, actress Anne Bancroft, who starred as the New York writer. The film also featured Anthony Hopkins, and Judi Dench, but some of the innate simplicity of the tale, so well captured in a B.B.C. television adaptation some years ago, was missing from the production.

David Cronenberg's *The Fly* was a modern remake of a classic horror story first filmed in 1958. Featuring Jeff Goldblum as the scientist who experiments with the transmission of matter only to find himself gradually transmuted into a fly, the film persuaded some critics that here was a modern parable on the A.I.D.S. virus. Although this may have been stretching a point too far, the film had a macabre and gruesome charm, helped by Goldblum's impressive leading performance. The excellent special effects were rightly rewarded with an Oscar. *The Fly* also featured Geena Davis, John Getz and Joy Boushel.

Ivan Reitman directed *Legal Eagles*, an amusing comedy on the law which served as a star vehicle for Robert Redford and Debra Winger, with support from Darryl Hannah and Terence Stamp. The film recalled, without ever equalling, the pairing of Spencer Tracy and Katharine Hepburn. James Bond was reincarnated in the shape of Timothy Dalton, who brought to the role more acting ability than his predecessor Roger Moore; accordingly, *The Living Daylights* reinvigorated a formula which had become very tired and stale, with jokes and gimmicks substituted for plot and acting.

Meanwhile, the first James Bond, Sean Connery, starred in a medieval whodunnit. *The Name of the Rose* was "a palimpsest of Umberto Eco's novel", in which the murder mystery was about all that remained of the book. Directed by Jean-Jacques Annaud, with script by Gerard Brach, it also featured F. Murray Abraham and Christian Slater.

Terry Jones directed *Personal Services*, based on

the story of Cynthia Payne. The famous "Madam Cyn" of Streatham had been convicted of keeping a disorderly house in 1980 but was acquitted of a similar charge in 1986 at the time the film was about to be released. Featuring Julie Walters, Alec McCowen, Danny Schiller and Shirley Stelfox, this richly comic slice of English eccentricity was well received.

Roman Polanski's *Pirates* was a spectacular but misguided and self-indulgent send-up of pirate films which featured Walter Matthau, Roy Kinnear, Chris Camion and Charlotte Lewis. Franco Zeffirelli presented a musically impeccable version of Verdi's *Otello*, through which he hoped to attract a new audience to opera. However, the sumptuous staging and at times obvious and heavy-handed approach to the plot detracted from the overall effect. The leading roles were taken by Placido Domingo, Katia Ricci-arelli, Justino Diaz and Urbano Barberini.

Oliver Stone's first film as director gave an impressive evocation of war. Shot on a low budget in some seven weeks, *Salvador* conveyed an impressive sense of urgency and contained fine performances from James Wood and James Belushi. However, the film was too determinedly anti-American throughout to be judged a complete success. Madonna, currently the most successful American female singer, was praised for her performance in *Desperately Seeking Susan* but her much publicised first film with husband Sean Penn, *Shanghai Surprise*, was an unmitigated disaster.

Swimming to Cambodia consisted of a monologue by Spalding Gray. Directed by Jonathan Demme, it provided compulsive viewing, and was a surprising but well-deserved success.

The top box office hit in America was *Top Gun*, a celebration of the U.S. Navy's Air Force fighter weapons school in California where pilots are trained to fly the F-14 fighter plane. It featured Tom Cruise and Kelly McGillis and had good action sequences, but the anti-Soviet theme was somewhat disturbing, with its climax of Eastern bloc MiGs being shot down over the Indian Ocean.

The Mosquito Coast featured Harrison Ford and Helen Mirren in an adaptation of Paul Theroux's novel directed by Peter Weir. *Captive* was based on the Patti Hearst kidnap; directed by Paul Mayersberg, it starred Oliver Reed and Irina Brook. *Tough Guys* paired Kirk Douglas and Burt Lancaster as two ageing robbers trying to relive former successes. Nicholas Gage's powerful novel about his search for the killer of his mother in a Greece riven by civil war transferred unhappily to the screen. Kate Nelligan took the title role in *Eleni*, with support from John Malkovich and Linda Hunt, and Peter Yates directed.

Dust was based on J. M. Coetzee's novel *In the Heart of the Country*, and directed by Marion Hänsel. Jane Birkin was praised for her performance as Magda; Trevor Howard provided support. A Soviet curiosity was Sergei Paradjanov's *The Legend of Suram Fortress*, set in medieval times and with Georgian dialogue. Based on the legend that a new fortress would collapse unless a handsome young man was bricked up alive in its foundations, the film was immaculately staged and filmed. The director, known in the West for his previous film *The Colour of Pomegranates*, has survived being out of favour with the authorities and a spell in jail.

Other notable productions included Alan Rudolph's *Trouble in Mind*, featuring Kris Kristofferson, Lori Singer, Keith Carradine and Divine; David Lynch's imaginative and horrific exposé of life in a small town, *Blue Velvet*, which starred Isabella Rossellini, Laura Dern, Kyle MacLachlan and Dennis Hopper; Federico Fellini's *Ginger and Fred*, a touching and nostalgic comedy, with Marcello Mastroianni and Giuletta Masina; Claude Chabrol's *Inspector Lavardin*, with Jean-Claude Brialy, Jean Poiret and Hermine Claire; Jim Henson's *Labyrinth*, with Jennifer Connelly and David Bowie; *Ruthless People*, with Danny DeVito and Bette Midler; Karl Francis's Welsh-language film *Soldier Boy*; and *Sweet Liberty*, written and directed by Alan Alda, and starring Alda with Bob Hoskins, Michael Caine, Michelle Pfeiffer and Lillian Gish.

TELEVISION, 1986–87

The Peacock report on public service broadcasting was published in July 1986 and its recommendations, particularly on licence fees and franchises, came in for much consideration in the following year. In September 1986, at the annual conference of the International Institute of Communications, Giles Shaw, then Minister of State for Broadcasting, announced that the Government would be commissioning a study to establish whether it was feasible to replace the licence fee by a subscription service, as recommended by Peacock. The report on subscription television was published the following July. It stated that the scheme should not replace the licence fee and advertising as sources of revenue but could be used to meet the extra cost of premium viewing, such as major sporting events or films.

The Government expressed its intention of responding to Peacock within six months. It was also confirmed that the Government does not wish to award new eight-year franchises to I.T.V. companies when the current contracts expire in 1990 because that would prevent any changes being made to the system before 1998. The I.B.A. suggested interim four-year extensions while the Government formulated a policy on broadcasting. However, the I.B.A. suggested that after the four-year automatic extensions, franchises should then be of twelve years duration and automatically renewed.

In a Commons debate on the future of broadcasting, on November 20, 1986, the Home Secretary, Douglas Hurd, stated that the television licence fee would remain at £58 until April 1988. "Since the main questions raised by the Peacock report have yet to be resolved", he said, "I have decided that the present settlement should run for the full three years." He also stated that the Government would introduce legislation to permit the extension of I.T.V. franchises by three years. This would allow the Government time to consider Peacock's proposal that the contracts should be put out to competitive tender. Mr. Hurd also expressed support for Peacock's recommendation of an increase in independent production in broadcast services.

The second reading of a private member's Bill, the Free Television Licences for Pensioners Bill, was defeated in the Commons on January 16 by 21 votes, after a large, and almost unprecedented, turn-out by Government ministers. The Home Secretary announced two days before the debate that the Government had already decided to reject Peacock's proposal that pensioners on supplementary benefit should be exempt from licence fees. He also confirmed that the licence fee would rise in relation to the retail price index after April 1988 and that the B.B.C. would have a greater role in its collection. These arrangements would last for at least three years from 1988. Current differentials between black and white and colour licence fees would be retained.

Sponsorship

The B.B.C. expressed interest in commercial organizations funding programmes made by independent producers; such support would be openly acknowledged but companies would not be allowed to mention particular products or lines of business. Such a move would require a change in the B.B.C.'s charter, which prohibits "any sponsored programme". At a Council of Europe Conference in Vienna, the director-general opposed the Government's plan to permit 25 per cent of television programmes to be made by independent producers, stating that "it would undo the B.B.C.". The question of sponsored production was brought into prominence in December when the B.B.C. withdrew an *Arena* programme, "Night Moves", about the road haulage industry. The programme was made by an independent company in association with the B.B.C., but it was revealed in a newspaper that the B.B.C. had been paid £62,250 by road haulage firms, 21 of which were credited with helping in the production of the film.

The Broadcasting Bill received its second reading in the Commons on February 16. The main provision of the Bill was to give the Government time to consider whether changes in I.T.V. franchises should be made. The period of the franchises would be extended from twelve to 15 years, but if changes to the present system were necessary, they could be implemented in time for the renewal of existing contracts in 1993. In Committee stage the Bill was amended, with all-party support, to call for a substantial proportion of I.T.V.'s output to be supplied by independent production companies: the Government was opposed to the amendment. The B.B.C. said that it wished to increase the amount of airtime commissioned from independent companies from less than 100 hours to 600 hours a year by 1990. The director-general, Mr. Checkland, said that the B.B.C. would offer independent producers access to B.B.C. production resources and to services such as finance, legal resources and libraries. However, the Government felt that this did not go far enough.

In August 1987 the I.B.A. informed the Home Office that it had requested the I.T.V. companies to commission more programmes from independent producers, so that some 400 to 600 hours of programmes should be produced outside the companies by 1989. Companies that failed to comply would have a clause to this effect inserted in their contracts on renewal. The I.B.A. were unhappy with the Government's proposed allocation of 25 per cent of airtime to independents, however, and said that this would be dependent on the necessary talent being available. The director-general, John Whitney, said that the I.B.A. did "not believe that a quota is appropriate to producing good public service broadcasting".

Channel 4, which has seen its audience share grow as it achieved economic and critical acceptability, was forced to consider its future *post* Peacock. Professor Alan Budd of the London Business School was commissioned to consider the implications of Channel 4 becoming an independent self-financing company. He concluded that it could sell enough advertising on its own to operate profitably. Revenue for 1985–86 was 10·9 per cent of the total generated and was rising to 14·5 per cent of revenue, the figure Professor Budd estimated would make independence advantageous. He said "It is reasonable to expect that it can raise this share if it sold its own time, mainly by raising the price of Channel 4's advertising time relative to the price of I.T.V. advertising time, though there could be difficulties in reaching a share of 14·5 per cent". Nevertheless, "the buoyant growth of advertising revenue should ensure that Channel 4 is financially viable with self-financing should it wish to make the change on other grounds (or be required to do so)". The Channel 4 Board was overwhelmingly opposed to the move and a second survey, commissioned by Channel 4 from Coopers and Lybrand, concluded that the station could not survive independently of the other I.T.V. companies.

The B.B.C.'s Year

Having apparently seen off Peacock, the B.B.C. might reasonably have expected to have put the troubles of recent years behind it. However, the corporation lurched from catastrophe to disaster, and yet again found itself in the unfortunate position of making the news instead of reporting it.

The B.B.C.'s Annual Report and Handbook for 1987, incorporating the report and accounts for the year 1985–86, contained a tribute to Stuart Young, who died in August 1986. He had, wrote Alasdair Milne, "led us through times of great difficulty with commitment and courage all the more remarkable in the light of his fatal illness". In his last Foreword, Mr. Young, noting that it was the B.B.C.'s 50th anniversary in television, wrote: "It is hard to equate the vitality which has produced *East Enders*, *Yes, Minister* and *Crimewatch* with an institution venerable enough to have been responsible for the world's first national television transmission 50 years ago. Yet looked at another way, B.B.C. Television has been around long enough to prove that today's popular programmes are part of a tradition of excellence on which the British public can rely, whether in drama, comedy, and factual programming or, indeed, in sport, music, entertainment, education, news or current affairs ... what the B.B.C. has to offer amounts to more than the sum of its constituent parts. Its service to the nation depends not only on excellence in specific fields but also on its commitment to offer services of wide appeal and something special to meet the tastes of every licence payer."

In its review of the year, the Board commented that 1985–86 had been significant "for a series of events and issues that have attracted to the B.B.C.'s affairs over the year a degree of scrutiny, both public and internal, rarely matched in its existence. It has undoubtedly been a year of reappraisal and controversy. This however should not obscure the fact that it has also been a year of remarkable achievement."

The Board's review also commented on a topic which was raised several times in the course of the following year, the portrayal of violence and sexual activity on television. In a statement following a discussion on sex and violence, the Board of Governors stressed its commitment to the highest programme standards but asserted its belief that the application of internal guidelines was a better means of ensuring high standards than Mr. Churchill's proposed legislation (the Bill to bring broadcasting within the scope of the Obscene Publications Act).

With reference to the problems arising from the coverage of sponsored events, particularly events sponsored by tobacco firms, the B.B.C. Annual Report said that it was increasingly difficult to apply the guidelines on advertising issued to programme staff. The Corporation faced pressure from medical and other quarters to cease covering events sponsored by cigarette companies which, it was argued, were by this means effectively advertising their wares on television in defiance of the will of Parliament. The Board felt that it was being looked to "for initiatives in an area of public policy that is properly a matter for Parliament's attention". However, in response to the criticism the B.B.C. announced in October 1986 that tobacco company brand colours would be banned from the sets of televised snooker tournaments, and that government health warnings would be broadcast if those on tournament boards were not clearly visible.

Bias and Balance

The new chairman of the B.B.C., appointed on October 1, 1986, is Mr. Marmaduke Hussey, former managing director of *The Times*. The choice was described as "outrageous and provocative" by Labour's Shadow Home Secretary, and there was a general feeling that the Prime Minister was trying to reassert control over the B.B.C. in response to backbench pressure to curb the Corporation's bureaucracy and to ensure that editorial control was tightened.

Editorial control and evenhandedness were at the centre of several disputes involving the B.B.C. The Corporation was criticised in the Spring by Ian Curteis, who had been commissioned to write a play about the Falklands war. This was scheduled for transmission in April 1987, the fifth anniversary of the Argentinian invasion. The author claimed that he had been asked to rewrite his script to show Government ministers taking military decisions that were politically motivated, and that when he refused the production was cancelled. After much acrimonious public debate about the affair in newspaper columns, Michael Grade, director of B.B.C. Television, made the reasonable point that the B.B.C.'s decision not to broadcast the play was due to the likelihood that a General Election campaign was imminent. It would be, he said, "wholly unacceptable for the B.B.C. to put on a play the central character of which was one of the leaders of the main political parties—presented either positively or negatively— while the country was going to the polls. This is not censorship—this is common sense." Bill Cotton, managing director of B.B.C. Television, said that it would have been "an improper subject ... to undertake".

Further bad publicity was generated by the libel action provoked by a 1984 *Panorama* programme entitled "Maggie's Militant Tendency". Having at first defended the action, the B.B.C. subsequently accepted that allegations against Neil Hamilton and Gerald Howarth, M.P.s for Tatton and Cannock and Burntwood, respectively, in the last Parliament, were "false and should not have been included in the programme". The M.P.s received "unreserved apologies", damages of £20,000 each, and legal bills estimated at nearly £250,000. The Prime Minister commented in the Commons that "the Chairman-designate will wish to do everything possible to achieve the highest standards for the B.B.C.", while Sir Peter Hordern, M.P., commented that "The responsibility rests on the Chairman and Governors to root out those responsible and improve standards". It would seem that the Board of Governors, concerned at the adverse publicity generated by the opening of the case, had instructed the management board to seek a settlement before B.B.C. lawyers were able to put their defence before the court. (The decision was taken by vice-chairman Lord Barnett, as Mr. Hussey had not assumed his new position.)

Political Sensitivity

Yet more accusations of editorial bias involved the B.B.C. in an acrimonious dispute with the Conservative Party chairman Norman Tebbit over the Corporation's coverage of the American bombing raid on Libya in April 1986. Mr. Tebbit published a 21-page dossier which alleged anti-Government and anti-American bias and incompetence in two news broadcasts, which were "riddled with inaccuracy, innuendo and imbalance". Alasdair Milne accused the Conservatives of "attempting to intimidate the B.B.C." and was supported by the Labour Party, which alleged that the Conservatives were seeking to undermine the B.B.C.'s independence.

In fact, Mr. Tebbit's attacks on the B.B.C. were largely self-defeating, for they brought about a concerted defence of the Corporation in what degenerated into a party political issue rather than a debate on editorial standards. At the Commonwealth Broadcasting Association conference in Edinburgh, Lord Barnett warned "friends and colleagues on all sides of the House of Commons that they are bringing the kind of pressure to bear that could have a serious and unintended impact on a great institution. Whichever political party happens to be in power at any given time, the Government feels the B.B.C. is unfair to them ... unfair and thoughtless criticism ... could seriously undermine the morale of the many excellent professionals we are fortunate to be able to employ in the B.B.C. The effect could be very far-reaching indeed. It could damage permanently the ability of the B.B.C. to continue to provide ... good, original programmes. All I ask of the politicians and public figures of this country is that they for their part should ensure their criticism is fair and balanced. For if they are not careful they could destroy a truly independent institution: one which ... plays a vital role in preserving the very democratic society which all of us care so passionately about."

In November, the B.B.C. published its detailed rebuttal of Mr. Tebbitt's charges. It admitted one error in its reports on the Libyan bombings but in general defended its coverage, in particular the reports from Tripoli of journalist Kate Adie. (Kate Adie later received the Royal Television Society's award for international news coverage for her reports from Libya.) In a covering letter, the Governors told Mr. Tebbit that they were charged with reviewing the B.B.C.'s work and its impartiality: "You may rest assured that we intend to discharge these responsi-

bilities as we think proper, in accordance not only with the letter but with the spirit of our charter, which, you will appreciate, requires us to resist undue influence from any political party, and in no way to be swayed from those standards by the imminence or otherwise of a general election."

However, the Corporation was not helped in its defence against Government accusations of left-wing bias by simultaneous publicity about a six-part series entitled *Secret Society* made by journalist Duncan Campbell. Commissioned by B.B.C. Scotland, the programmes were originally scheduled for transmission on B.B.C. 2 in November but at the end of October it was announced that the series had been postponed. The *Secret Society* series included a programme on a highly sensitive British spy satellite project codenamed Zircon. The programme, having been delayed already, was banned on grounds of national security by Mr. Milne but an article on the subject in the *New Statesman* disclosed that Parliament had not been informed about the satellite project. The Attorney-General tried, unsuccessfully, to obtain a High Court injunction to prevent screening of the film, and the Speaker of the House of Commons ordered that the film should not be shown in the precincts of Parliament.

The row continued after Special Branch officers raided the B.B.C.'s Glasgow headquarters and seized all film and documents relating to the series. B.B.C. chairman Mr. Hussey, in a letter to the Home Secretary and the Secretary of State for Scotland, protested "most vigorously at the way in which the Special Branch sought to obtain a wide range of material relating to the B.B.C.'s series *Secret Society* ... it is a matter of grave concern that the warrants should have been drafted in such wide terms as apparently to authorize the seizure of all the material relating to the entire series... We shall of course take whatever legal action may be appropriate." Mr. Rifkind, Secretary of State for Scotland, denied that the Government had initiated the raids or had sought or granted the warrants. This was confirmed by the Prime Minister in the Commons in an emergency debate on the raid.

Violence and Sex

The B.B.C. issued new guidelines on the portrayal of violence on television, particularly in news reports. Gratuitous violence should be avoided and grief shown with restraint. In drama and films in which it was necessary to include scenes of violence, producers should prepare the audience for what was in store, "so that viewers are not ambushed by offensive material". The B.B.C. also wanted to make the public more aware of its policy of a 9 p.m. watershed, after which time it is considered that programmes more suitable for an adult audience can be screened. Programme makers are required to alert heads of department if they feel programmes are wrongly placed. "Scenes of violence may well make a programme unsuitable for early placing, and so too may sex scenes, bad language, blasphemy or scenes of great distress".

There was a certain grim irony in the death of a young man taking part in a stunt for the Noel Edmonds *Late Late Breakfast Show* in the same week that the new guidelines were announced. The programme was cancelled and no further editions appeared. Equity complained about "the growing tendency to use ordinary members of the public for this kind of entertainment".

The question of extending the Obscene Publications Act to include television and sound broadcasting was revived when the Obscene Publications Bill, a private member's Bill, received a second reading in the Commons in April. The Bill proposed to extend the definition of obscenity to include material that was "grossly offensive" to a "reasonable person". The Bill was talked out in Committee, but with Government support it seemed likely that it might resurface.

Complaints

In its annual report for 1987, the Broadcasting Complaints Commission recommended that people or organizations that were criticised on radio or television should be given the opportunity to reply to the criticism before the programmes were broadcast. The Commission considered 53 complaints and gave full adjudications in 21, of which twelve were upheld.

In December, the B.B.C. was criticized by the Comptroller and Auditor General for refusing to allow him to investigate the finances of External Services, which are funded by Government direct grants. The B.B.C. claimed that it was not covered by the National Audit Act, and further, "that if ever the External Services were or were perceived abroad to be controlled by the Foreign Office rather than the B.B.C. Board of Governors then our credibility would be fatally undermined."

On January 29, the director-general of the B.B.C., Alasdair Milne, unexpectedly announced his resignation "for personal reasons". The Board of Governors and senior journalists and staff appeared to have lost confidence in his leadership, making his position increasingly untenable. The shortlist of seven candidates for the post included Mr. Jeremy Isaacs, head of Channel 4, but the job went to Michael Checkland, the deputy director-general. John Birt, director of programmes at London Weekend Television, was appointed as the new deputy director-general. These changes led to a wider reorganization of the Corporation's structure and personnel. In July 1987 plans were announced for the merging of radio news, television news and current affairs to form one directorate. John Birt said that "the formation of the new directorate is a ringing declaration on the part of the B.B.C. that authoritative journalism of quality is one of its main priorities." Lime Grove studios will be closed and all news and current affairs staff will work from one purpose-built headquarters.

I.B.A.

In its annual report, the I.B.A. reported a new morality in television, with an increasing number of programmes on A.I.D.S., and a consequent decline in the depiction of promiscuous behaviour on the screen. The Authority also criticized TV-AM, now midway through its eight-year contract, for its coverage of news, sport and religious affairs. It said that the company should exercise more discretion in the use of material related to advertisements, and in drawing the line between news and public relations material.

It was announced that independent television would launch a daytime schedule in September 1987 to compete with the B.B.C.'s new daytime programmes, which have seriously dented I.T.V.'s viewing figures. By moving schools programmes to Channel 4, I.T.V. hoped to be able to compete on equal terms. Moves were also made by some companies to introduce all-night viewing. Negotiations with the relevant unions delayed introduction of the service but in April Channel 4 began broadcasting until 3 a.m. three nights a week. Two months later Thames introduced continuous broadcasting until 6 a.m., 15 minutes before TV-AM goes on the air, for three nights a week.

In February the I.B.A. approved an increase in the amount of advertising shown on television by 14 minutes a day, with effect from the summer. However, no increase in peak time advertising was permitted.

A study commissioned by the I.B.A. during the year, *Behind and in Front of the Screen: Television's involvement with Family Life*, revealed that television has become "part of the family household", assuming the place that the wireless held in family life 40 years ago. Television has not killed the art of conversation, but gives families something to talk about.

Programmes

The outstanding programme of the year was Dennis Potter's *The Singing Detective*, a six-part drama shown on B.B.C. 1. This was the multi-layered story of a failed middle-aged writer of detective fiction in hospital with psoriatic arthropathy who relived a story he had written in 1945. Michael Gambon was outstanding in the leading role, with support from Janet Suzman, Alison Steadman and Joanne Whalley. Controversy arose over one scene in the series which, taken out of context, detracted from its undoubted overall merits: the episode in question was preceded by a warning that it might cause offence. Michael Grade said that "there are very few people in television drama you are prepared to trust with scenes like this. Dennis Potter is one of them." (Ironically, the B.B.C's retrospective of Potter's work in August 1987 included *Brimstone and Treacle*, filmed in 1976 but banned by the Corporation.)

The Singing Detective was voted best drama series at the Broadcasting Press Guild's Annual Awards, with Michael Gambon winning the best actor award. Dennis Potter was presented with a special award for outstanding personal contribution to television "for his imaginative and pioneering use of the medium as a writer".

The British Academy of Film and Television Arts, however, made the surprising decision to award their prize for best series to B.B.C. 2's *The Life and Loves of a She-Devil*, a two dimensional adaptation of a Fay Weldon novel, featuring Dennis Waterman, Patricia Hodge and newcomer Julie T. Wallace. Michael Gambon was at least rewarded with the prize of best actor. The best single drama was *Hotel du Lac* (B.B.C. 2), for which Anna Massey received the award for best actress. Best factual series was Granada's *World in Action*, and best light entertainment was *Victoria Wood as Seen on TV*. Best comedy series was B.B.C. 1's *Just Good Friends*, best news or outside broadcast coverage, *Channel 4 News*; best light entertainment performance, Nigel Hawthorne in *Yes, Prime Minister*. The Special Foreign Television Award was presented to Edgar Reitz for *Heimat*. *The Singing Detective* was named B.B.C. television programme of the year at the Television and Radio Industries Club awards.

Alan Bleasdale's *The Monocled Mutineer*, a four-part series on B.B.C. 1 featuring Paul McGann, also aroused widespread controversy: the B.B.C. advertised the series in the national press as an "enthralling true-life story", which it demonstrably was not, being only loosely based on the career of Percy Toplis. *The Theban Plays* (B.B.C. 2), adapted by Don Taylor, starring Claire Bloom, John Gielgud, Cyril Cusack, Anthony Quayle and Juliet Stevenson, was widely praised. On I.T.V. Thames T.V.'s 11-part series *Paradise Postponed*, featuring Michael Hordern and David Threlfall, took as its theme the "brave new world we were offered after the Second World War". It was well acted and worthy without ever achieving great heights. John Mortimer had written the novel and screenplay together and the programme fell unhappily between the two stools, the novel reading like a television screenplay, and the programmes giving the impression of a novel adaptation.

Central T.V.'s *Hardwicke House*, a 7-part comedy set in a comprehensive school, was widely slated by the critics and withdrawn by the I.B.A. after one episode. More successful was B.B.C. 2's adaptation by Malcolm Bradbury of Tom Sharpe's *Porterhouse Blue*, which featured David Jason and Ian Richardson.

B.B.C. 1's *East Enders* continued to dominate the ratings and also introduced innovations into the traditional twice-weekly soap format. Two episodes were devoted to two-handers (episodes featuring only two characters), showing that effective drama could still be produced within the constraints of the format. In October 1986, the B.B.C. relaunched its Breakfast Time programme, with more emphasis on news coverage.

In February, both B.B.C. and I.T.V. channels devoted a week to programmes about A.I.D.S.; Anthony Newton, the Minister for Health, welcomed "this co-ordinated effort by the broadcasting authorities to support the public education on A.I.D.S., and in particular to get the message across to young people". I.T.V. later showed a drama series on the topic, *Intimate Contact*, which featured Daniel Massey and Claire Bloom.

Channel 4 experimented with a red-bordered triangle, displayed continuously throughout films which might offend some viewers. The first film to be broadcast was the anarchic French comedy *Themroc*. The device was eventually dropped as it was felt that it only drew attention unnecessarily to controversial material.

Following the success of its *Trial of Richard III*, Channel 4 produced *The Trial of Lee Harvey Oswald*. Recreated according to U.S. judicial procedures and featuring contemporary witnesses, American lawyers and presiding judge, and a jury of American citizens, the programme did not quite manage to repeat the success of the earlier "trial". (The jury found Oswald guilty of the assassination of President Kennedy.)

Satellite T.V.

In December 1986 the I.B.A. awarded the contract to provide a satellite television service to British Satellite Broadcasting, a consortium including Granada and Anglia T.V., the Virgin Group, Amstrad and Pearson (Amstrad later withdrew from the group). The direct broadcasting by satellite service is scheduled to commence in 1990 offering four channels and is to be financed through subscription and advertising. The franchise is for a term of 15 years and will be the world's first privately financed national television service by D.B.S. However, the huge investment required to launch the system raised doubts about its long-term profitability. The contract to build the two satellites required was awarded to the Hughes Aircraft Company of the U.S.A.

BROADCASTING

BRITISH BROADCASTING CORPORATION
(*see also* entry on page 374)

Radio

BBC Radio broadcasts four national services to the United Kingdom, Isle of Man and the Channel Islands plus a fifth tier consisting of national regional services in Wales, Scotland and Northern Ireland and local radio services in England and the Channel Islands. In Wales there are two regional services based on the Welsh and English languages respectively.

The four national services are:

Radio 1: ("Pop" and "rock" network)—Mon. to Fri. 5.30 a.m.–12 midnight. Sat. and Sun. 6 a.m.–12 midnight. Frequencies: MW 1053 kHz/285m and 1089 kHz/275m, plus two local fillers giving population coverage 96% (day) and 57% (night); VHF-FM 88–91 MHz (shared with Radio 2), coverage 97%.

Radio 2: (Light music, entertainment and sport)—24 hours a day. Frequencies: MW 693 kHz/433m and 909 kHz/330m, plus three local fillers giving population coverage 98% (day) and 65% (night); VHF-FM 88–91 MHz (shared with Radio 1), coverage 97%.

Radio 3: (Serious music, drama and documentaries, poetry, and cricket in season)—6.55 a.m.–12 midnight daily. Frequencies: VHF-FM 90.2–92.5 MHz, population coverage 97%. MW (Main centres of population only), 1215 kHz/247m, plus four local fillers on 1197 kHz/251m, coverage 87% (day) and 38% (night).

Radio 4: (News, documentaries, drama and entertainment)—6 a.m. to 12.15 a.m. daily. Frequencies: LW 200 kHz/1500m (from Feb. 1988, 198kHz/1515m), plus eight local fillers on MW giving population coverage 98% (day) and 91% (night): VHF-FM (England, C.I. and I.O.M. plus part of South Wales, S.W. Scotland) 92–95 MHz, coverage 97%.

The national regional services are:

Radio Scotland: Frequencies: MW 810 kHz/370m plus two local fillers, coverage 95% (day) and 87% (night); VHF-FM 92–95 MHz, coverage 94%.

Local programmes on VHF-FM 92–95 MHz: *Radio Aberdeen* (also MW 990 kHz/303m); *Radio Highland; Radio nan Eilean; Radio nan Gaidheal; Radio Orkney; Radio Shetland; Radio Solway* (also MW 585 kHz/513m); *Radio Tweed.*

Radio Ulster: Frequencies: MW 1341 kHz/224m, plus one local filler, coverage 96% (day) and 80% (night); VHF-FM 92–95 MHz, coverage 97%.

Radio Foyle: Frequencies: MW 792 kHz/379m; VHF-FM 92–95 MHz.

Radio Wales: Frequency: MW 882 kHz/340m plus two local fillers giving coverage 96% (day) and 63% (night).

Radio Clwyd: Frequency: MW 657 kHz/457m.

Radio Cymru (Welsh-language): Frequencies: VHF-FM 92–95 MHz, coverage 91%.

Local Radio: There are 32 local stations serving England and the Channel Islands (*see* below).

Television

The BBC's experiments in television broadcasting started in 1929 and in 1936 the BBC began the world's first public service of high-definition television from Alexandra Palace.

The BBC broadcasts two national television services, BBC 1 (BBC Wales in Wales, BBC Scotland in Scotland, BBC Northern Ireland in Northern Ireland) and BBC 2. These are broadcast in colour on 625-lines and UHF from a network of transmitting stations planned and built jointly with the Independent Broadcasting Authority. All stations (with a few exceptions) carry four channels including the two IBA channels.

Transmissions from 50 main stations and more than 800 relays are available to more than 99 per cent of the population.

External Services

The External Services broadcast over 700 hours of programmes a week in 37 languages including the English language BBC World Service. Ninety-eight transmitters are used, 49 of them in the U.K. and 49 at relay stations overseas. In addition the External Services supply many recorded programmes to other radio stations.

World Service, on the air in English for 24 hours a day, directed to all parts of the world, and with additional streams of programmes specially designated for audiences in Africa and South Asia at appropriate peak listening times.

African Service, which broadcasts in Swahili, Somali and Hausa.

Arabic Service, on the air for 9 hours a day to Middle East and North Africa.

Eastern Service, which broadcasts in Bengali, Burmese, Hindi, Nepali, Pashto, Persian, Tamil and Urdu.

Far Eastern Service, in Chinese (Cantonese and Standard Chinese), Indonesian, Japanese, Malay, Thai and Vietnamese.

Latin American Service, in Spanish and Portuguese.

French Service, directed to Europe and Africa.

German Service, directed to West and East Germany and Austria.

Central European Service, in Czech and Slovak, Hungarian, Polish and Finnish.

Russian Service, on the air for 6½ hours a day in Russian to the U.S.S.R.

South-East European Service, in Bulgarian, Romanian, Serbo-Croat and Slovene.

South European Service, in Greek, Portuguese to Europe and Africa, and Turkish.

Topical Tapes provides a variety of programmes on tape for overseas radio stations and produces the twice-weekly 'Calling the Falklands' programme.

BBC English by Radio and Television teaches English to learners outside Britain through radio, television and a wide range of published courses.

Transcription Service produces and sells to overseas radio stations recorded programmes drawn from the whole range of BBC Radio.

Monitoring Service provides regional summaries and a teleprinted news service from the output of overseas radio stations.

BBC Local Radio Stations

BEDFORDSHIRE, P.O. Box 476, Hastings Street, Luton LU1 5BA. (Tel: 0582 459111). *Wavelengths:* 258/476m, 1161/630 kHz, 95·5/103·8 VHF-FM.

BRISTOL, 3 Tyndalls Park Road, Bristol BS8 1PP. (Tel: 0272 741111). *Wavelengths:* 194/227m, 1548/1323 kHz, 94·9/95·5/104·6 VHF-FM.

CAMBRIDGESHIRE, Broadcasting House, Hills Road, Cambridge CB2 1LD. (Tel: 0223 315970). *Wavelengths:* 207/292m, 1449/1026 kHz, 96·0/95·7 VHF-FM.

CLEVELAND, PO Box 1548, Broadcasting House, Newport Road, Middlesbrough, Cleveland TS1 5DG. (Tel: 0642 225211). *Wavelengths:* 194m, 1548 kHz, 95·0/95·8 VHF-FM.

CORNWALL, Phoenix Wharf, Truro, Cornwall TR1 1UA. (Tel: 0872 75421). *Wavelengths:* 476/457m, 630/657 kHz, 95·2/96·0/103·9 VHF-FM.

CUMBRIA, Hilltop Heights, London Road, Carlisle, Cumbria CA1 2NA. (Tel: 0228 31661). *Wavelengths:* 397/206/358m, 756/1458/837 kHz, 95·2/95·6/96·1/104·2 VHF-FM.

DERBY, 56 St. Helen's Street, Derby DE1 3HY. (Tel: 0332 361111). *Wavelengths:* 269m, 1116 kHz, 104·5/94·2/95·3 VHF-FM.

DEVON, P.O. Box 100, St. David's Hill, Exeter, Devon EX4 4DB. (Tel: 0392 215651). *Wavelengths:* 351/303/206/375m, 855/990/1458/801 kHz, 103·4/97·0/96·0/94·8 VHF-FM.

ESSEX, 198 New London Road, Chelmsford, Essex CM2 9AB. (Tel: 0245 262393). *Wavelengths:* 392/196/412m, 765/729/1530 kHz, 103·5/95·3 VHF-FM.

HUMBERSIDE, 63 Jameson Street, Hull HU1 3NU. (Tel: 0482 23232). *Wavelengths:* 202m, 1485 kHz, 95·9 VHF-FM.

KENT, Sun Pier, Chatham, Kent ME4 4EZ. (Tel: 0634 46284). *Wavelengths:* 290/388/187m, 1035/774/1602 kHz, 96·7/104·2 VHF-FM.

LANCASHIRE, King Street, Blackburn, Lancs. BB2 2EA. (Tel: 0254 62411). *Wavelengths:* 351/193m, 855/1557 kHz, 95·5/104·5/103·9 VHF-FM.

LEEDS, Broadcasting House, Woodhouse Lane, Leeds LS2 9PN. (Tel: 0532 442131). *Wavelengths:* 388m, 774 kHz, 92·4/195·3 VHF-FM.

LEICESTER, Epic House, Charles Street, Leicester LE1 3SH. (Tel: 0533 27113). *Wavelengths:* 358m, 837 kHz, 95·1 VHF-FM.

LINCOLNSHIRE, Radion Buildings, P.O. Box 219, Newport, Lincoln LN1 3DF. (Tel: 0522 40011). *Wavelengths:* 219m, 1368 kHz, 94·9 VHF-FM.

LONDON, 35a Marylebone High Street, London W1A 4LG. (Tel: 01-486 7611). *Wavelengths*: 206m, 1458 kHz, 94·9 VHF-FM.

MANCHESTER, New Broadcasting House, Oxford Road, Manchester M60 1SJ. (Tel: 061-228 3434). *Wavelengths*: 206m, 1458 kHz, 95·1 VHF-FM.

MERSEYSIDE, 55 Paradise Street, Liverpool L1 3BP. (Tel: 051-708 5500). *Wavelengths*: 202m, 1485 kHz, 95·8 VHF-FM.

NEWCASTLE, Broadcasting Centre, Barrack Road, Fenham, Newcastle upon Tyne NE99 1RN. (Tel: 091-232 4141). *Wavelengths*: 206m, 1458 kHz, 95·4/ 104·4/96·0 VHF-FM.

NORFOLK, Norfolk Tower, Surrey Street, Norwich NR1 3PA. (Tel: 0603 617411). *Wavelengths*: 351/ 344m, 855/873 kHz, 95·1/104·4 VHF-FM.

NORTHAMPTON, PO Box 1107, Abington Street, Northampton NN1 2BE. (Tel: 0604 20621). *Wavelengths:* 271m, 1107 kHz, 104·2/103·6 VHF-FM.

NOTTINGHAM, York House, Mansfield Road, Nottingham NG1 3JB. (Tel: 0602 415161). *Wavelengths*: 197/189m, 1521/1584 kHz, 103·8/95·5 VHF-FM.

OXFORD, 242/254 Banbury Road, Oxford OX2 7DW. (Tel: 0865 53411). *Wavelengths*: 202m, 1485 kHz, 95·2 VHF-FM.

SHEFFIELD, Ashdell Grove, 60 Westbourne Road, Sheffield S10 2QU. (Tel: 0742 686185). *Wavelengths*: 290m, 1035 kHz, 104·1/88·6 VHF-FM.

SHROPSHIRE, 2–4 Boscobel Drive, Shrewsbury, Shropshire SY1 3TT. (Tel: 0743 248484). *Wavelengths*: 189/397m, 1584/756 kHz, 95·0/96·0 VHF-FM.

SOLENT, South Western House, Canute Road, Southampton SO9 4PJ. (Tel: 0703 631311). *Wavelengths:* 300m, 999 kHz, 96·1 VHF-FM, 221m, 1359 kHz.

STOKE ON TRENT, Conway House, Cheapside, Hanley, Stoke-on-Trent, Staffs. ST1 1JJ. (Tel: 0782 208080). *Wavelengths*: 200m, 1503 kHz, 94·6 VHF-FM.

SUSSEX, Marlborough Place, Brighton, Sussex BN1 1TU (Tel: 0273 680231). *Wavelengths*: 202/258/219m, 1485/1161/1368 kHz, 95·3/104·5/104·0 VHF-FM.

WM (WEST MIDLANDS), PO Box 206, Pebble Mill Road, Birmingham B5 7SD. (Tel: 021-472 5141). *Wavelengths*: 206/362m, 1458/828 kHz, 95·6 VHF-FM.

YORK, 20 Bootham Row, York YO3 7BR. (Tel: 0904 641351). *Wavelengths*: 450/238m, 666/1260 kHz, 103·7/104·3/95·5 VHF-FM.

Two Stations outside the UK :—

GUERNSEY, Commerce House, Les Banques, St. Peter Port, Guernsey. (Tel: 0481 28977). *Wavelengths*: 269m, 1116 kHz, 93·2 VHF-FM.

JERSEY, Broadcasting House, Rouge Bouillon, St. Helier, Jersey. (Tel: 0534 70000). *Wavelengths*: 292m, 1026 kHz, 88·8 VHF-FM.

INDEPENDENT BROADCASTING AUTHORITY

(*see also* entry on pages 404–5)

Independent Television Programme Companies, etc.

ANGLIA TELEVISION (*East of England*), Anglia House, Norwich. (Tel: 0603 615151).

BORDER TELEVISION (*The Borders*), Television Centre, Carlisle. (Tel: 0228 25101).

CENTRAL INDEPENDENT TELEVISION (*East and West Midlands*), Central House, Broad Street, Birmingham. (Tel: 021-643 9898).

CHANNEL TELEVISION (*Channel Islands*), The Television Centre, St. Helier, Jersey. (Tel: 0534 73999).

GRAMPIAN TELEVISION (*North Scotland*), Queen's Cross, Aberdeen. (Tel: 0224 646464).

GRANADA TELEVISION (*North-West England*), Granada TV Centre, Manchester. (Tel: 061-832 7211).

HTV (*Wales and West of England*), HTV Wales, Television Centre, Cardiff CF5 6XJ. (Tel: 0222 590590).

LONDON WEEKEND TELEVISION (*London* [*weekends*]), South Bank Television Centre, Kent House, Upper Ground, London S.E.1. (Tel: 01-261 3434).

SCOTTISH TELEVISION (*Central Scotland*), Cowcaddens, Glasgow. (Tel: 041-332 9999).

THAMES TELEVISION (*London* [*weekdays*]), Thames Television House, 306–316 Euston Road, London N.W.1. (Tel: 01-387 9494).

TSW (TELEVISION SOUTH WEST) (*South-West England*), Derry's Cross, Plymouth. (Tel: 0752 663322).

TVS (TELEVISION SOUTH) (*South and South-East England*), Television Centre, Southampton. (Tel: 0703 34211).

TYNE TEES TELEVISION (*North-East England*), The Television Centre, City Road, Newcastle upon Tyne. (Tel: 091-261 0181).

ULSTER TELEVISION (*Northern Ireland*), Havelock House, Ormeau Road, Belfast. (Tel: 0232 228122).

YORKSHIRE TELEVISION (*Yorkshire*), The Television Centre, Leeds. (Tel: 0532 438283).

TV-AM, Hawley Crescent, London N.W.1. (Tel: 01-267 4300).

CHANNEL FOUR TELEVISION COMPANY LTD, 60 Charlotte Street, London W.1. (Tel: 01-631 4444).

INDEPENDENT TELEVISION COMPANIES ASSOCIATION LTD., Knighton House, 56 Mortimer Street, London W.1. (Tel: 01-636 6866).

INDEPENDENT TELEVISION NEWS LTD, ITN House, 48 Wells Street, London W.1. (Tel: 01-637 2424).

ORACLE TELETEXT LTD., Craven House, 25–32 Marshall Street, London W.1. (Tel: 01-434 3121).

[NOTE: It has only been possible to give one address for each of the Programme Companies].

Independent Local Radio Stations

LBC (London Broadcasting Company Ltd.), Communications House, Gough Square, London E.C.4. (Tel: 01-353 1010). *Wavelengths*: 261m, 1152 kHz, 97·3 VHF-FM.

CAPITAL RADIO P.L.C., Euston Tower, London NW1. (Tel: 01-388 1288). *Wavelengths*: 194m, 1548 kHz, 95·8 VHF-FM.

RADIO CLYDE LTD., Clydebank Business Park, Clydebank, Glasgow. (Tel: 041-941 1111). *Wavelengths*: 261m, 1152 kHz, 95·1 VHF-FM.

BRMB RADIO, (Birmingham Broadcasting Ltd.), PO Box 555, Radio House, Aston Road North, Aston, Birmingham. (Tel: 021-359 4481/9). *Wavelengths*: 261m, 1152 kHz, 96·4 VHF-FM.

PICCADILLY RADIO LTD., 127/131 The Piazza, Piccadilly Plaza, Manchester. (Tel: 061-236 9913). *Wavelengths:* 261m, 1152 kHz, 103·0 VHF-FM.

METRO RADIO (North East Broadcasting Company Ltd.), Radio House, Long Rigg, Swalwell, Newcastle upon Tyne. (Tel: 091-488 3131). *Wavelengths*: 261m, 1152 kHz, 97·1 VHF-FM.

SWANSEA SOUND LTD., Victoria Road, Gowerton, Swansea. (Tel: 0792 893751). *Wavelengths*: 257m, 1170 kHz, 95·1 VHF-FM.

RADIO HALLAM LTD., PO Box 194, Hartshead, Sheffield. (Tel: 0742 71188). *Wavelengths*: 194m, 1548 kHz, 96·1 VHF-FM (Rotherham), 97·4 VHF-FM (Sheffield), 302m, 990 kHz, 103·4 VHF-FM. (Doncaster).

RADIO CITY (Sound of Merseyside Ltd.), PO Box 194, 8–10 Stanley Street, Liverpool. (Tel: 051-227 5100). *Wavelengths*: 194m, 1548 kHz, 96·7 VHF-FM.

RADIO FORTH LTD., Forth House, Forth Street, Edinburgh. (Tel: 031-556 9255). *Wavelengths*: 194m, 1548 kHz, 97·3 VHF-FM.

PLYMOUTH SOUND LTD., Earl's Acre, Alma Road, Plymouth. (Tel: 0752 27272). *Wavelengths*: 261m, 1152 kHz, 96·0 VHF-FM.

RADIO TEES (Sound Broadcasting (Teesside) Ltd.), 74 Dovecot Street, Stockton-on-Tees, Cleveland. (Tel: 0642 615111). *Wavelengths*: 257m, 1170 kHz, 96·6 VHF-FM.

RADIO TRENT LTD., 29–31 Castle Gate, Nottingham. (Tel: 0602 581731). *Wavelengths*: 301m, 999 kHz, 96·2 VHF-FM.

PENNINE RADIO, (Bradford Community Radio Ltd.), PO Box 235, Pennine House, Forster Square, Bradford. (Tel: 0274 731521). *Wavelengths*: 235/196m, 1278/1530 kHz, 97·5 VHF-FM (Bradford, Huddersfield, Halifax) 102·5 VHF-FM.

OCEAN SOUND LTD., 43–44 Bedford Place, Southampton. *Wavelengths*: 257m, 1170 kHz, 103·2 VHF-FM (Southampton), 97·5 VHF-FM (Portsmouth).

RADIO ORWELL LTD., Electric House, Lloyds Avenue, Ipswich. (Tel: 0473 216971). *Wavelengths*: 257m, 1170 kHz, 97·1 VHF-FM.

RADIO 210 THAMES VALLEY (Thames Valley Broadcasting Ltd.), PO Box 210, Reading, Berkshire. (Tel: 0734 413131). *Wavelengths*: 210m, 1431 kHz, 97·0 VHF-FM.

DOWNTOWN RADIO (Community Radio Services Ltd.), PO Box 293, Kiltonga Industrial Estate, Newtownards, Northern Ireland. (Tel: 0247 815555). *Wavelengths*: 293m, 1026 kHz, 97·4 VHF-FM.

BEACON RADIO (Beacon Broadcasting Ltd.), PO Box 303, 267 Tettenhall Road, Wolverhampton. (Tel: 0902 757211). *Wavelengths*: 303m, 990 kHz, 97·2 VHF-FM.

MERCIA SOUND (Midland Community Radio Ltd.), Hertford Place, Coventry. (Tel: 0203 28451). *Wavelengths*: 220m, 1359 kHz, 95·9 VHF-FM.

HEREWARD RADIO LTD., PO Box 225. 114 Bridge Street, Peterborough. (Tel: 0733 46225). *Wavelengths*: 225m, 1332 kHz, 102·7 VHF-FM.

TWO COUNTIES RADIO LTD., 5–7 Southcote Road, Bournemouth. (Tel: 0202 294881). *Wavelengths*: 362m, 828 kHz, 97·2 VHF-FM.

RADIO TAY (Tay Sound Broadcasting Ltd.), PO Box 123, Dundee. (Tel: 0382 29551). *Wavelengths*: 258m, 1161 kHz, 95·8 VHF-FM (Dundee); 189m, 1584 kHz, 96·4 VHF-FM (Perth).

SEVERN SOUND (Gloucestershire Broadcasting Company Ltd.), PO Box 388, Old Talbot House, 67 Southgate Street, Gloucester. (Tel: 0452 423791). *Wavelengths*: 388m, 774 kHz, 102·4 VHF-FM.

NORTH SOUND (North of Scotland Radio Ltd.), 45 Kings Gate, Aberdeen. (Tel: 0224 632234). *Wavelengths*: 290m, 1035 kHz, 96·9 VHF-FM.

RADIO AIRE (West Yorkshire Broadcasting P.L.C.), PO Box 362, 51 Burley Road, Leeds. (Tel: 0532 452299). *Wavelengths*: 362m, 828 kHz, 96·3 VHF-FM.

ESSEX RADIO P.L.C., Radio House, Clifftown Road, Southend-on-Sea, Essex. (Tel: 0702 333711). *Wavelengths*: 210m, 1431 kHz, 96·3 VHF-FM (Southend), 220m, 1359 kHz, 102·6 VHF-FM (Chelmsford).

CHILTERN RADIO P.L.C., Chiltern Radio, Dunstable, Bedfordshire. (Tel: 0582 666001). *Wavelengths*: 362m, 828 kHz, 97·6 VHF-FM (Luton), 379m, 792 kHz, 96·9 VHF-FM (Bedford).

WEST SOUND (Radio Ayrshire Limited), Radio House, 54 Holmston Road, Ayr. (Tel: 0292 283662). *Wavelengths*: 290m, 1035 kHz, 96·7 VHF-FM (Ayr), 97·1 97·5 VHF-FM (Girvan).

GWR RADIO WEST P.L.C., PO Box 963, Watershed, Canons Road, Bristol. (Tel: 0272 279900). *Wavelengths*: 238m, 1260 kHz, 96·3 VHF-FM.

MORAY FIRTH RADIO LTD., PO Box 271, Inverness. (Tel: 0463 224433). *Wavelengths*: 271m, 1107 kHz, 97·4 VHF-FM.

RADIO WYVERN P.L.C., 5/6 Barbourne Terrace, Worcester. (Tel: 0905 612212). *Wavelengths*: 314m, 954 kHz, 97·6 VHF-FM (Hereford), 196m, 1530 kHz, 102·8 VHF-FM (Worcester).

RED ROSE RADIO P.L.C., PO Box 301, St. Paul's Square, Preston, Lancashire. (Tel: 0772 556301). *Wavelengths*: 301m, 999 kHz, 97·3 VHF-FM.

GWR (Wiltshire Radio) P.L.C., Old Lime Kiln, High Street, Wootton Bassett, Swindon, Wiltshire. (Tel: 0793 853222). *Wavelengths*: 258m, 1161 kHz, 97·2 VHF-FM (Swindon), 321m, 936 kHz, 102·6 VHF-FM (West Wiltshire).

SAXON RADIO LTD. IN ASSOCIATION WITH RADIO ORWELL LTD., Long Brackland, Bury St. Edmunds, Suffolk. (Tel: 0284 701511). *Wavelengths*: 240m, 1251 kHz, 96·4 VHF-FM.

COUNTY SOUND P.L.C., The Friary, Guildford. (Tel: 0483 505566). *Wavelengths*: 203m, 1476 kHz, 96·4 VHF-FM.

RED DRAGON RADIO, Radio House, West Canal Wharf, Cardiff. (Tel: 0222 384041). *Wavelengths*: 230m, 1305 kHz, 97·4 VHF-FM.

SOUTHERN SOUND P.L.C., Radio House, Franklin Road, Portslade. (Tel: 0273 422288). *Wavelengths*: 225m, 1332 kHz, 103·4 MHz.

MARCHER SOUND/SAIN-Y-GORORAU, The Studios, Mold Road, Gwersyllt, Wrexham, Clwyd. (Tel: 0978 752202). *Wavelengths*: 238m, 1260 kHz, 95·4 VHF-FM.

SIGNAL RADIO, 67–73 Stoke Road, Stoke-on-Trent, Staffordshire. (Tel: 0782 417111). *Wavelengths*: 257m, 1170 kHz, 102·6 VHF-FM.

VIKING RADIO LTD., Commercial Road, Hull. (Tel: 0482 25141). *Wavelengths*: 258m, 1161 kHz, 96·9 VHF-FM.

RADIO MERCURY, Broadfield House, Brighton Road, Crawley, W. Sussex. (Tel: 0293 519161). *Wavelengths*: 197m, 1521 kHz, 102·7, 97·5 VHF-FM (Horsham).

INVICTA RADIO P.L.C. (incorporating Northdown Radio), 15 Station Road East, Canterbury, Kent. (Tel: 0227 58761). *Wavelengths*: 242m, 1242 kHz, 103·1 VHF-FM.

INVICTA RADIO P.L.C. (incorporating Network East Kent), 15 Station Road East, Canterbury, Kent. (Tel: 0227 58761). *Wavelengths*: 497m, 603 kHz, 97·0 VHF-FM (Dover), 95·9 VHF-FM (Thanet), 102·8 VHF-FM (Canterbury), 96·1 MHz (Ashford).

RADIO BROADLAND, PO Box 260, Norwich. (Tel: 0603 660926). *Wavelengths*: 260m, 1152 kHz, 97·6 MHz.

NORTHANTS 96 (Hereward Radio) P.L.C., PO Box 193, 73 Abington Street, Northampton. (Tel: 0733 46225). *Wavelengths*: 193m, 1557 kHz, 96·6 VHF-FM.

LITERATURE 1986-87

The Booker Prize for Fiction, the "Miss World of the literary world which many people affect to despise" according to Anthony Thwaite, the chairman of the judging panel in 1986, produced a shortlist of six excellent novels and a popular winner. In his speech at the presentation ceremony Mr. Thwaite condemned the "razzamatazz" that had built up around the Booker Prize, with arts reporters and gossip columnists "sniffing out supposed scandals" and inventing stories when they could not find any. "Don't believe in dissension among the judges, public or private", he warned, adding that there had in fact been a remarkable degree of consensus.

Whatever the methodology of the judging process, Mr. Thwaite was entitled to feel aggrieved at the publication of a letter he had written to Julian Barnes expressing sympathy that his novel had been excluded from the shortlist, and about allegations of dictatorial chairmanship. For any group of people to read conscientiously 127 novels, as the Booker judges must, and arrive at a shortlist of six from which one must be singled out is perhaps an unnatural process: no-one can read so many works in so short a space of time for pleasure, and if novel reading becomes a burden the whole exercise becomes self-defeating. Nevertheless, accepting the *caveat* that to treat works of art as participants in a competition is an artificial exercise, it must be said that the Booker Prize is good for fiction and especially for writers. That it also produced a worthy winner in 1986 was an added bonus.

Lucky Old Devil

Kingsley Amis had featured on the Booker shortlist twice before without winning but his 16th novel, *The Old Devils*, deservedly carried off the prize. Amis's first novel, *Lucky Jim*, was inspired by his teaching experiences at Swansea University after the war and he returned to the locality in *That Uncertain Feeling*. *The Old Devils* concerns, in Amis's own words, "a group of old friends, somewhere in South Wales, all in their 60s or worse", who were "old enough to know better". The mainspring of the novel is the return to South Wales of Alun Weaver and his wife Rhiannon and their effect on the people they had known years before. Weaver, a celebrity and "a bit of a charlatan", the "up-market media Welshman", had made a career out of being Welsh and out of his relationship with a Dylan Thomas-like bard called Brydan. Amis's observation of the minutiae of growing old and the obsessions of advancing years are brilliantly described, from "the faint stirring in his entrails" that signals triumph to one character to the descriptions of lives which revolve around drinking and aversion to the modern world. The novel is sharp, funny but imbued with a sense of sadness, of lost opportunities and of pathos. Amis captures perfectly Weaver's stage Welshness, put on for the benefit of the media, such as when he is interviewed about his thoughts on returning home: "Many things, grave and gay and multi-coloured but one above all: I'm coming home. That short rich resounding word means one simple thing to a

Welshman such as I, born and bred in this land of river and hill". Amis is also acute in his perception of what Welshness means to the natives: "a sign used to say Taxi and now said Taxi/Tacsi for the benefit of Welsh people who had never seen a letter x before". Amis said that the book's moral is "that life doesn't stop at 60, but perhaps it should"; a modest description of one of his finest novels, which encompasses much larger themes and ends on a note of hope.

Anthony Thwaite, announcing the judges' decision, said "In the end it became a very hard-fought combat between Robertson Davies's *What's Bred in the Bone*, which has profound significance, and Kingsley Amis's *The Old Devils*, which has a brilliant comic insight". Robertson Davies, a distinguished Canadian writer whose best-known works are "The Salterton Trilogy" and "The Deptford Trilogy", wrote about themes he considered to be very Canadian. *What's Bred in the Bone* is the story of Francis Cornish, an art collector of mixed religious upbringing. Faced with a crucial decision about his future which will affect his reputation, Cornish finds he cannot escape the conscience that is bred into his very bones.

Timothy Mo's *An Insular Possession*, noted in *Whitaker 1987*, is a sprawling epic set in South China between 1834 and 1842, at the time of the Opium Wars. Mo said that he was attempting to combine the methods of the English and American novel simultaneously—to address major issues but in a less serious or apocalyptic fashion than American writers adopt, relying instead on English understatement. Although undoubtedly a fine novel the wealth of historical detail tended to impede the narrative flow.

Paul Bailey's *Gabriel's Lament* was an episodic work full of grotesque characters, notably Gabriel's father, a bullying Edwardian toff living in a vanished feudal England. *Gabriel's Lament* is the son's story of his life, dominated by the disappearance of his mother when he was aged 12. The lament is provoked by his discovery 27 years later, after his father's death, of what actually happened to her. "When I began this lament for my numb life three years ago, I meant to polish you off for ever", Gabriel writes of his father; "and I think I have failed. You are still here, curse you, in these pages." Having learned the truth about his parents, he realises that he cannot cast off his father's memory completely and that his mother was not the innocent victim he had imagined in the years following her disappearance.

The Handmaid's Tale by Margaret Atwood was set in the imaginary Republic of Gilead, a 21st century American republic under totalitarian rule. Government is based on a literal reading of the Book of Genesis in which Jacob used women as intermediaries, or handmaids, to give birth to the twelve tribes of Israel. This distopia, a negative view of a future society, would be a particularly humourless fable were it not for the skill with which the author controls the narrative. The narrator is Offred, a woman who is a national resource because she is able to breed, and so is matched in a loveless relationship with one of the ruling class, the Commanders, to increase the birthrate. In this well-realised allegory, "there are only women who are fruitful and women who are barren, that's the law".

The sixth novel on the Booker shortlist was Kazuo Ishiguro's *An Artist of the Floating World*. The floating world of the title is the decadent world where things that "are put together in the night . . . vanish with the morning". It is the story of artist Masuji Ono who, evaluating his career in later life, after the Second World War, comes gradually to the realisation that his major works are deeply flawed, tainted by propaganda. His "narrow artist's perspective" has led him to contribute to something intrinsically evil, the rise of militarism in Japan, and his career has been wasted. Ishiguro's first novel, *A Pale View of Hills*, was widely praised, and although *An Artist of the Floating World* did not win the Booker Prize, it was judged the best novel and best of the five category winners shortlisted for the Whitbread Prize.

In financial terms the Whitbread surpasses the Booker, but its new format, in which the best novel, best first novel, best children's novel, best poetry and best biography then compete for the £17,500 first prize (as against the Booker's £15,000), seems increasingly eccentric, if not perverse. That each of the five finalists receives £1,000 is no doubt some consolation, but for a panel to decide between such disparate works is clearly a nonsense. The impression is given, whether justified or not, that the "Buggin's turn" principle applies: if poetry (Douglas Dunn's *Elegies*) won last year then it could have little chance this year. Few would complain that Ishiguro's novel was unworthy of the prize, only that the judging process is misguided. The Whitbread judges described the work as "a little masterpiece. Though clearly set in an alien culture, there's much about the place of an artist in any society".

The winner of the Whitbread's first novel category was Jim Crace's *Continent*, an allegorical fantasy set in a mythical seventh continent, a new landmass within contemporary time and geography. The book consists of seven narratives related only by time and place, and is an ambitious and original work, "a debate about the old and new ways of mankind". *Continent* also won the *Guardian* Fiction Prize and the David Higham Prize for a first work of fiction.

The other Whitbread finalists were Peter Reading's *Stet*, a collection of funny and clever verses about contemporary Britain which approaches "things that are difficult to take", Richard Mabey's *Gilbert White, A Biography of the Author of "The Natural History of Selborne"*, and Andrew Taylor's *The Coal House*, a novel for children.

The Smarties Prize for Children's Books, worth £7,000, was awarded to Jenny Nimmo for *The Snow Spider*, illustrated by Joanna Carey. It was described by the judges as "mystical and lyrical and at the same time a gripping and exciting fantasy".

The W. H. Smith Literary Award, established in 1959, was won by Elizabeth Jennings for *Collected Poems 1953–1985*. The award is worth £4,000. The £6,000 British Airways Commonwealth Poetry Prize was shared by Niyi Osundare for *The Eye of the Earth* and Vikran Seth for his verse novel *The Golden Gate*. The £2,000 prize for the best first-time published collection went to Vicki Raymond for *Holiday Girls*. The John Llewellyn Rhys Memorial Prize for an author under 35 years of age (worth £500) was won by Tim Parks for his novel *Loving Roger*.

During the year it was announced that a new literary prize, the NCR Book Award for Non-Fiction, would be endowed. The prize of £25,000 for the winner will be supplemented by awards worth £1,500 for each of three runners-up. The judging panel is to be chaired by Jeremy Isaacs, head of Channel 4, and the judges will be looking for "originality of thought, elegance of expression, and the ability of the author to express his or her knowledge of the subject to the widest possible readership".

An interesting reflection on the merry-go-round nature of the literary prize-giving circuit was provided by the award of the prestigious French Medicis Essai prize (a non-fiction award) to Julian Barnes's *Flaubert's Parrot*, a Booker finalist in 1984.

African Laureate

In terms of financial reward and international publicity, no literary award can hope to compete with the Nobel Prize for Literature. The 1986 award went to the Nigerian writer Wole Soyinka, the first black writer and the first African to win the prize. Whether or not there was an element of political expediency in his selection, Soyinka was a worthy winner. His ability had already been recognised by his election to the American Academy of Arts and Letters, only the third African writer to be so honoured. According to the Swedish Academy Soyinka has "a wide cultural perspective, and with poetic overtones, (he) fashions the drama of existence". In his prime, his writings are "vivid, often harrowing, but also marked by an evocative, poetically intensified diction". Soyinka's best-known work is the journal of his two years' political imprisonment in the 1960s, *The Man Died*, which contains his political credo: "The man dies in all who keep silent in the face of tyranny". Among his plays, poetry and novels are *The Trial of Brother Jero*, *Ake: The Years of Childhood* and *Poems of Black Africa*. Of his Nobel Prize Soyinka said: "This prize is recognition of our culture and our traditions in Africa and I am very glad about it. African culture has not always been understood by other cultures, for instance in Europe." He said the award was "for all the others who laid the basis and were the source from which I could draw. It is the African world which can now be recognised".

Travelling Hopefully

William Golding was awarded the Nobel Prize for Literature in 1983 for his novels which "illuminate the human condition in the world today". This well-deserved tribute was followed by the publication of one of his least successful novels. *The Paper Men* was provoked by Golding's experiences as "the raw material of an academic light industry" but was a disappointment after his masterly *Rites of Passage*, which won the Booker Prize in 1980. *Rites of Passage* was the story of a young colonial administrator, Edmund Talbot, setting out for Australia on an ancient ship of the line. His narrow viewpoint of the events he has recorded in his journal is totally altered when he reads a letter written by the Reverend Colley, who died of shame.

Talbot, still journeying, now reappears in a sequel,

Close Quarters, which, it transpires, is the middle volume in a trilogy. However, according to Talbot "This is not a continuation, but a new venture." Talbot is in search of "A hero for my new journal, a new heroine, a new villain and some comic relief to ameliorate my deep, deep boredom". Although the ship becomes becalmed in the doldrums, there is plenty of incident in Golding's microcosmic world on board, from a near capsize to a near engagement with another ship. This ship turns out not to be hostile but His Majesty's frigate *Alcyone*, with news that "the war with the French is over. Boney is beat and abdicated. He is to be King of Elba". "This tropical nowhere was the whole world—the whole *imaginable* world. This was a neck of history, the end of the greatest war, was the middle of the longest journey, a . . . a nothing!" Talbot falls in love with Marion Chumley when his ship is tied alongside the *Alcyone*, and grows in stature as the voyage continues. When he heard the "painfully thin" Mrs. East sing a song called "Bonnie at Morn", "it changed everything. It admitted us—it admitted *me* to halls, caverns, open spaces, new palaces of feeling—how foolish and impossible! Those tears which I had been able to restrain at my introduction to a new life now fell. I could not help it. They were neither tears of sorrow nor of joy. They were tears—and I do not know how this is possible—they were tears of *understanding*!"

In the *Postscriptum* Talbot promises "a plain narrative at some later date which will see the voyage ended", and hopes the reader "may be mollified and excited as much as I can contrive by this 'puff' for a third volume!" Golding's many admirers will eagerly await the conclusion of the saga.

A tribute to Golding was paid in *William Golding: The Man and His Books. A Tribute on His 75th Birthday*. Edited by John Carey, the volume includes an interview with Golding, who told Carey "There is nothing to a writer but his books". The fifteen pieces are divided between five writers, five literary critics and five friends or acquaintances, ranging from a poem by Seamus Heaney dedicated to Golding to a portrait of Golding's father by Peter Moss, and Ian McEwan recalling the impression that reading *Lord of the Flies* made on him as a schoolboy. Critic John Bayley writes in his essay "Satisfaction and the Novel" that Golding is unusual in that "he admits no intimacy between himself and his reader", while Stephen Medcalf's personal memoir, "Bill and Mr. Golding's Daimon", identifies "the point where the imagination confronts what it is to do before the face of God" which Golding describes so well. Other contributors include Ted Hughes, Craig Raine, John Fowles and Charles Monteith, who relates how he supported the publication of *Lord of the Flies* after a publisher's reader had recommended its rejection.

Anita Brookner continues to produce an exquisitely crafted novel each year, following *Family and Friends* with *A Misalliance*, the story of Blanche Vernon, "a woman of limited appeal", who "occupied her time most usefully in keeping feelings at bay". Divorced from her husband Bertie, who left her for his secretary, she finds the "frightful emptiness of each day" is nevertheless only relieved by his visits. The "misalliance" of the title is the relationship that Blanche forms with Sally Beamish and her autistic

young daughter. Though demonstrating Anita Brookner's usual skill the story seems a step backwards after *Family and Friends* to the lonely middle-aged women she described so well in her Booker-winning *Hotel du Lac*.

The prolific Anthony Burgess in his amusing but indulgent *The Pianoplayers* features Ellen Henshaw. Retired to Provence, Ellen is dictating her memoirs, from her life in Manchester during and after the First World War to her life as a *poule de luxe* on the continent, setting up an international chain of schools for love. Men are the pianoplayers but they are amateurs who need practice and instruction, for women's bodies are like pianos, in need of tuning for variations to be played. Also published was *Little Wilson and Big God, being the First Part of the Confessions of Anthony Burgess*. Author of some thirty novels, Burgess did not start writing until he was 42 years old, when he believed himself to be dying of a brain tumour. In his foreword Burgess writes that "The book is about somebody else, connected by the ligature of a common tract of time and space to the writer of this last segment of it."

Malcolm Bradbury's brief new novella, *Cuts*, was inspired by the cancellation of a television series based on his *Rates of Exchange*, but the unrelenting satire diminishes the overall effect. Jeremy Cooper's first published novel, *Ruth*, attracted favourable notices for its perceptive study of a young woman who never fully recovers from a nervous breakdown at the age of 17 and becomes suicidal in her 30s. It is never established whether there is anything physically or mentally wrong with her but the descriptions of genius and insanity are sensitively handled. For his latest novel, Melvyn Bragg has taken the true story of Mary Robinson, daughter of a Lakeland innkeeper and a celebrated beauty who was a romantic ideal for Coleridge and Wordsworth. *The Maid of Buttermere*, set in 1802–3, relates her surprising marriage to the Hon. Alexander Augustus Hope, whom Coleridge subsequently exposed as a fraud and an impostor.

Dennis Potter, a master of television drama, once said in an interview that the novel form "hasn't the guts, the bravado to be of its time", a remark Paul Theroux condemned as ignorant and offensive. Potter was thus persuaded to explore the novel once more as a vehicle for his ideas. His second novel, *Ticket to Ride*, begins with a man crying on a train. From this moment Potter constructs an original, well-written story detailing the man's life up to the opening incident, from his lost job to marital trouble, all the while exploring the darker recesses of the mind. Paul Theroux, who prompted Potter back into print, has written a novel set in a future when parts of the planet are poisoned by nuclear waste. *The O-Zone* was inspired by a visit he made to Belfast in 1982 when writing *The Kingdom by the Sea*: he imagined a "wilderness in which most people lived hand-to-mouth, and the rich would live like princes". The world of the Outer Zone is convincingly worked out and described, although sentimentality intrudes with the love story that develops.

Martin Amis writes of the "four carefree days, which is more than my juniors ever had", that were his because of being born four days before the

Russians tested their first atomic bomb, at which point "deterrence was in place". *Einstein's Monsters* consists of a collection of five stories written over two years "with the usual purpose in mind: that is to say, with no purpose at all—except, I suppose, to give pleasure, various kinds of complicated pleasure". After he had completed them Amis recognised a unifying strain and a deep preoccupation. The title refers to nuclear weapons "but also to ourselves. We are Einstein's monsters, not fully human, not for now." Also published was a selection of Amis's American journalism, *The Moronic Inferno: and Other Visits to America*, a curiously uncritical account of his American trips, acute in observation but lacking in analysis or any consistent moral standpoint.

Stink of Success

Patrick Süskind's *Perfume* was an international bestseller. The story concerned Jean-Baptiste Grenouille, born with an odourless body but amazing olfactory powers. His only pleasure was in "unravelling the knot of vapour and stench into single strands of unitary odours that could not be unthreaded further". He becomes a famous perfumier, but to create his "angel scent", the greatest perfume ever known, he resorts to the murder of young women to capture the essence. A darkly symbolic thriller, the novel reveals minute research and a vivid imagination.

Christopher Hope's *The Hottentot Room* is an ironic and touching tale about a down-at-heel drinking club for expatriate Africans and political refugees in Earls Court. The curtains are drawn to protect the members from "the greyish, penny-pinching island of antheads", *i.e.* England. No one but South Africans can understand South Africa is their message: the whites there are like the Jews in Europe or the Hottentots, a bush tribe wiped out by early immigrants. The club is dominated by Frau Katie, an elderly, wild-eyed Berliner who suffers from rectal cancer, and the vividly-drawn members include Caleb Looper, a reporter deported for being too radical who has to suffer the English weather he hates, "the cold which gives that lugubrious and characteristically damp texture to the English soul". Janice Elliott's *Dr. Gruber's Daughter* is a witty well-written story of illegal German immigrants lodging in an ancient English university town in 1953 and hiding a dark secret from their neighbours. Howard Jacobson's *Redback* is a funny, frenetic, but ill-disciplined, Antipodean romp in which the hero has to contend with the attentions of a pair of female synchronised swimmers and also the redback (poisonous spider) of the title.

A curiosity was the publication after 50 years of Malcolm Muggeridge's *Picture Palace*. This "barely disguised autobiography" (*per* Richard Ingrams, who wrote the introduction) was written in 1934 and satirised the *Manchester Guardian*, for which Muggeridge had worked. Called the "Accringthorpe Courier" in the novel, it is suggested that the lofty *Guardian* lived off the profits of its lowly companion, the *Manchester Evening News*. Muggeridge was threatened with a libel action which he could not afford to defend and the book was withdrawn.

Another oddity was *Filthy Lucre, or The Tragedy of Andrew Ledwhistle and Richard Soleway* written by Beryl Bainbridge in 1946 at the age of 13. This lively work shows much early promise and includes charming illustrations by the author.

Another previously unpublished work by Hemingway has now been pushed into print. *The Garden of Eden* was begun in 1946 but never finished. His biographer, Carlos Baker, said that Hemingway was rewriting it in 1958, at which time it had reached 48 chapters and some 200,000 words. He was still revising it in 1961 just before his death. The version now issued consists of 30 chapters and 70,000 words. Autobiographical in parts, the story concerns a writer, David Bourne, on honeymoon in the Camargue and Spain with his young wife Catherine. They become involved with a young woman called Marita who falls in love with both of them, sending Catherine mad. There are echoes of Hemingway's desertion of his first wife Hadley for Pauline Pfeiffer but the novel is of minor interest and no great addition to the oeuvre.

John Updike has been accused of writing novels "without ideas". His response, *Roger's Version*, is a brilliantly accomplished and original work based on the supposition that science, in the form of computers, could be used to prove the existence of God. Roger Lambert, a Professor of Divinity at a New England university, is plagued by Dale Kohler who is attempting to establish the mathematical structure of the universe to that end. The novel, influenced by Hawthorne's *The Scarlet Letter*, presents only the perspective of the wronged husband but it is apparent that there are many sides to this enthralling and complex story.

Joseph Heller's *No Laughing Matter*, co-written with Speed Vogel, is an account of his affliction with Guillain-Barré syndrome, which affects the peripheral nervous system and causes paralysis. Heller does not emerge sympathetically from the book, being obsessed with food, celebrities and his own status, and proving that there are few less interesting topics than a person's account of his own illness.

Former Booker winner J. M. Coetzee has written a complex reworking of the Robinson Crusoe story in *Foe*. By including characters called Robinson Crusoe, Friday and a novelist Daniel Foe, Coetzee has written more than a simple satire on Defoe whilst risking alienating readers by the inevitable parallels. However, his main concerns in *Foe* would appear to be the conflict between those who live life and those who record it, the "foes" who embroider the events for their own purposes.

Vladimir Nabokov's *The Enchanter* was "the first little throb" of *Lolita*. Written in Russian when he was living in Paris in 1939, Nabokov thought the work lost when he went to America. Apparently he rediscovered the manuscript in 1959 and thought it "a beautiful piece of Russian writing", but it was put aside again and has only now been translated by his son Dmitri. Only 75 pages long, it is a disturbing and powerful piece about the corruption of children.

Down Under

The Fatal Shore by Robert Hughes is a brilliant and compelling account of "the most successful form of penal rehabilitation that had ever been tried in English, American or European history", the transportation of some 140,000 convicts, ex-convicts and their children to Australia between 1787 and 1868. The scheme was unique in its creation of one nation from the rejects of another. Hughes began the book in 1974 and dedicates it to Alan Moorehead, who inspired him to write it. Thoroughly researched, it includes first-hand accounts gleaned from the Public Record Office and extracts from manuscripts that had not been opened since they were written.

Colombian writer Gabriel Garcia Marquez, who won the Nobel Literature Prize in 1982, has published *The Story of a Shipwrecked Sailor*, the account of Luis Alejandro Velasco's survival for ten days on a raft without food or water, after being washed overboard from a destroyer. The official version of the tale made Velasco a national hero. He then sold his own account to the Bogota daily newspaper *El Espectador*, where Marquez ghosted the memoirs. The publication of this account caused the Government acute embarrassment, for the destroyer from which Velasco had been washed overboard was overloaded at the time with smuggled goods which the sailors were bringing home. As a result of disclosing the suppressed facts Marquez lost his job and the paper was shut down.

Martin Gilbert's magisterial biography of Churchill has now reached the crucial war years. *The Road to Victory: Winston S. Churchill, 1941–1945* opens with the Japanese attack on Pearl Harbor and closes with the German surrender. Although covering well-trodden ground, this authorised life is excellent on Churchill's military strategy and his obsessions, and on his relationship with Stalin. Gilbert demonstrates masterly control of his wealth of source material.

The Harvest of Sorrow by Robert Conquest is a harrowing account of the famine in the Ukraine in the 1930s. In July 1932 Stalin ordered that the Ukraine, the main Soviet grain-producing region, should export nearly all its harvest to the rest of the U.S.S.R. In the famine that followed in the Ukraine an estimated 14 million people starved to death. The purpose of this brutal order was to enable the collective farming system to be imposed on a reluctant peasantry.

Robert Rhodes James's life of *Anthony Eden* is a sympathetic account after David Carlton's more hostile biography. Eden once told his wife "I'm not really a Conservative. I have more sympathy with the Opposition", and it is clear that he was not really suitable to occupy the office of Prime Minister. There was no question of his personal courage, demonstrated when he won the Military Cross in hand-to-hand combat on the Somme, but in office Eden interfered too much at all levels. He "seemed to be two men; the one was charming, kind and deeply impressive—the other impossible". Rhodes James attempts to excuse the Suez debacle by blaming the inadequate military preparation on Monckton and Mountbatten and claiming that Eden's war experiences had forged in him a hatred of war and those who broke treaties. But his weakness becomes only too apparent: he set out to topple Nasser and to conceal that intent.

Enigma: the Life of Knut Hamsun is an excellent study by Robert Ferguson of the Norwegian novelist who won the Nobel Prize for Literature in 1920 for his idealistic work *The Growth of the Soil* and his earlier novel, *Hunger*. Hamsun was a fine novelist but a misguided racist who supported Hitler and Quisling and in 1943 gave his Nobel medal to Goebbels.

Richard Perceval Graves has published the first volume of the biography of his uncle, *Robert Graves: The Assault Heroic, 1895–1926*. However, although he has had access to "a treasured collection of family letters and diaries", he has used them indiscriminately and produced a worthy but dull work. Graves's war service in particular is much better described in his own account, *Goodbye to All That*.

The Oxford University Press have issued the first *Complete Works of Shakespeare* to be published in the U.K. since 1954, the fruits of eight years' work and an investment of £1.2 million. The editors, Stanley Wells and Gary Taylor, have taken some controversial decisions; the volume includes *The Two Noble Kinsmen*, attributed to Shakespeare and John Fletcher in collaboration, and states that *Macbeth* is "adapted by Thomas Middleton". *King Lear* is published in two versions, and Falstaff is renamed Oldcastle on the grounds that that was Shakespeare's original choice, changed only at the request of Oldcastle's relatives. However, the change is not preserved in *Henry IV, Part 2*, or in *The Merry Wives of Windsor*. Most controversial of all is the inclusion of the poem "Shall I die?" discovered by Gary Taylor in the Bodleian Library in 1985. "There is no strong reason to doubt the ascription", he writes, but many scholars do. Such an undistinguished piece can add nothing to Shakespeare's reputation, though it cannot detract much from it either.

The Dictionary of National Biography (1971–1980), edited by Lord Blake and C. S. Nicholls, is the latest decennial supplement to the great work initiated by George Smith in 1882 and first edited by Sir Leslie Stephen and Sir Sidney Lee. This volume includes P. G. Wodehouse, Charlie Chaplin, Edward VIII, John Lennon, W. H. Auden and Terence Rattigan. Of particular note are Sir Edgar Williams' biography of Montgomery, whom he sees as a brilliant general but a weak, self-important man; Philip Ziegler's condensation of his life of Mountbatten to some 12 pages; and Lord Blake on Anthony Eden.

Christopher Ricks's edition of *The New Oxford Book of Victorian verse* is an excellent selection that brings to life the rich variety of poetry in the Victorian age. *The Oxford Book of English Ghost Stories* contains over forty examples of the genre written between 1829 and 1968, chosen by Michael Cox and R. A. Gilbert. Paul Johnson's *The Oxford Book of Political Anecdotes* mines a rich seam, from Richard Crookback to Richard Crossman. Also published was *The Compact Edition of the Oxford English Dictionary, Vol III—A Supplement to the Oxford English Dictionary Volumes 1–4*. Edited by R. W. Burchfield, this volume complements the 1933 supplement and has 62,000 main words and half a million illustrative quotations.

Other books of note published during the year included: *Flowers and Insects* by Ted Hughes, illustrated by Leonard Baskin; *The Enigma of Arrival* by

V. S. Naipaul; *Rebecca West* by Victoria Glendinning; *The Counterlife* by Philip Roth; *The Collected Poems of Vernon Watkins*; *The Free Frenchman* by Piers Paul Read; *Colombo Heat* by Christopher Hudson; *Seasonal Tribal Feasts* by Stuart Evans; *The Radiant Way* by Margaret Drabble; *Bolt* by Dick Francis; *The Oxford Illustrated History of English Literature*; *After a Fashion* by Stanley Middleton; *A History of The Jews* by Paul Johnson; *Beloved Emma* by Flora Fraser; *Innocence* by Penelope Fitzgerald; and *Love Unknown* by A. N. Wilson.

Public Lending Right

The latest payments to writers under the Public Lending Right Scheme were announced at the beginning of 1987. The total sum available for distribution was £2·75 million, which was also fixed as the total for the following year. The maximum pay-out of £5,000 was received by 59 authors. Of the top 100 most borrowed books, Catherine Cookson had 29 novels in the list, followed by Dick Francis and Wilbur Smith with ten each, and Jeffrey Archer and Alistair Maclean with six each. £272,000 was redistributed from those on the maximum amount. 12,990 authors were registered, with 1,995 receiving no payment: the average for the remainder totalled £250. The additional 1,725 authors registered included 86 from West Germany, where a reciprocal scheme is in existence. 188 authors received between £2,500 and £5,000 and 47 per cent of the fund was paid to authors earning less than £1,000 each from it. The payments were based on 8·4 million loans from 20 sampling libraries.

BOOKER PRIZEWINNERS

1969   *Something to Answer For*—P. H. Newby (Faber).
1970   *The Elected Member*—Bernice Rubens (Eyre & Spottiswoode).
1971   *In A Free State*—V. S. Naipaul (Andre Deutsch).
1972   *G*—John Berger (Weidenfeld).
1973   *The Siege of Krishnapur*—J. G. Farrell (Weidenfeld).
1974   *The Conservationist*—Nadine Gordimer (Cape).
        Holiday—Stanley Middleton (Hutchinson).
1975   *Heat and Dust*—Ruth Prawer Jhabvala (Murray).
1976   *Saville*—David Storey (Cape).
1977   *Staying On*—Paul Scott (Heinemann).
1978   *The Sea, The Sea*—Iris Murdoch (Chatto & Windus).
1979   *Offshore*—Penelope Fitzgerald (Collins).
1980   *Rites of Passage*—William Golding (Faber).
1981   *Midnight's Children*—Salman Rushdie (Cape).
1982   *Schindler's Ark*—Thomas Keneally (Hodder & Stoughton).
1983   *Life & Times of Michael K*—J. M. Coetzee (Secker & Warburg).
1984   *Hôtel du Lac*—Anita Brookner (Cape).
1985   *The Bone People*—Keri Hulme (Hodder & Stoughton).
1986   *The Old Devils*—Kingsley Amis (Hutchinson).

The finalists for the 1987 prize are:
Anthills of the Savannah—Chinua Achebe (Heinemann), *The Book and the Brotherhood*—Iris Murdoch (Chatto), *Chatterton*—Peter Ackroyd (Hamish Hamilton), *Circles of Deceit*—Nina Bawden (Macmillan), *The Colour of Blood*—Brian Moore (Cape), *Moon Tiger*—Penelope Lively (Deutsch).

OPERA AND DANCE 1986–87

Recent years have been for the arts world times of increasing financial strain as a central government support has steadily decreased, and the prospect for the future is no brighter. The Arts Council announced grants for 1987–88 which gave most opera and dance companies support at the same level as 1986–87 or an increase of a percentage below the rate of inflation: in either case, a cut in real terms.

As in past years the drop in the subsidy in real terms has obliged companies to cut back on their planned productions. English National Opera has a long tradition of bringing new and neglected work to the public: *Rusalka, Osud,* the British premieres of *Akhnaten,* Busoni's *Dr. Faust, The Stone Guest* (*see* below for production details) and *Lady Macbeth of Mtsensk* (*see* below), and the world premiere of Birtwhistle's *The Mask of Orpheus.* But although the 1987–88 season will see the British premiere of Sondheim's *Pacific Overtures,* the company has had to abandon its plans to stage the rarely-seen Donizetti opera *Anna Bolena* or to revive *Boris Godunov* and *The Valkyrie.* Because it could not find a sponsor and its grant would not cover the cost, Scottish Ballet had to cancel the production of two new works this season, making 1986–87 the second successive season in which the company has had no new productions.

One of the means by which companies have dealt with their declining incomes and rising costs is through co-production deals. This method of spreading production costs has enabled Welsh National Opera and Scottish Opera over the past twelve years to mount a cycle of Janáček works which, taken with works in the E.N.O. repertoire, has led to a reassessment of Janáček's work and recognition of his greatness as a composer. A current project involving W.N.O. and Scottish Opera, the staging of Berlioz's epic five-act opera *Les Troyens,* seems likely to produce a similar reassessment of a neglected masterpiece. The first two acts, *The Capture of Troy,* were given by Opera North in September 1986, and the complete work by W.N.O. in February 1987, to great acclaim by audiences and critics alike. However, completion of the project is in some doubt: the financial stringencies which have affected every company's production plans might also deprive W.N.O. of their home theatre in Cardiff.

The most common means of supplementary public subsidy in recent years has been through sponsorship of specific productions by businesses or individuals. This has produced some sponsors willing to back the innovative: I.B.M. are supporting the *Troyens* project, and their sponsorship deal with Norwest/Holst was specifically intended to allow E.N.O. to mount lesser-known works of famous composers e.g. Wagner's *Rienzi,* Tchaikovsky's *Mazeppa.* However, many sponsors are not attracted to new or little-known works, so an increase in funding through sponsorship might ultimately have implications for the breadth of a company's repertoire.

Penalties for Success

Even renewed efforts to increase funding from alternative sources seems likely to bring problems. In July 1987 the Minister for the Arts attacked the "welfare state mentality" of the arts world and announced that in future public subsidy would be withdrawn from companies which fail to raise specified amounts from other sources (a policy *Opera* magazine described as "the interesting new concept of 'subsidy-capping'"). It would seem that companies will in the future be in the Catch-22 situation of being punished if they fail to obtain sufficient sponsorship and having their subsidy reduced if they succeed.

The purpose of public subsidy is to keep seat prices at a level which is affordable for most members of the public. As government subsidy drops the pressure on companies to increase seat prices becomes increasingly difficult to resist. Covent Garden, always the first target of accusations of elitism, has been obliged to put up all seat prices for the forthcoming season, following the lead of the E.N.O. Yet, ironically, the past season saw all the major opera companies playing to houses filled to over 80 per cent of capacity.

Chinese Capers

A further irony is that Kent Opera, which was threatened with withdrawal of its Arts Council funding this year and has been reprieved only until 1988, was the sole company to mount a new opera this season. *A Night at the Chinese Opera* (*see* below for production details) was commissioned by the B.B.C. from Judith Weir while she was Kent Opera's composer-in-residence under a regional arts council scheme. The composer prepared her own libretto and the choice of subject was influenced by her interest in Chinese musical plays of the 13th and 14th centuries. The second act of this three-act opera is Miss Weir's version of one such Chinese play. The first act, set in modern China, introduces the protagonist, Chao Lin, and describes his background. The third act shows the tragic consequences for him of identifying too closely with the events depicted in the ancient play (the second act) enacted during his "night at the opera". The contemporary setting of the outer acts and the stylized form of the Chinese play are well distinguished musically and dramatically, and the work was a great success with audience and critics.

The Royal Opera continued its policy of introducing modern continental works with the British premiere of Sallinen's *The King Goes Forth to France* (*see* below for production details), first performed at Savonlinna in 1984. A grimly humorous opera, the comic effect was greatly helped at Covent Garden by the use of satirically phrased surtitles.

Popular Novelties

Surtitles, an English translation of the libretto projecting a few lines at a time onto a screen above the proscenium arch, were introduced at Covent Garden for the first time in the 1986–87 season. Although opposed by purists, an audience survey showed widespread support for them, with 80 per cent. of respondents favouring their use at least for some performances.

Another Royal Opera innovation this season was the live relay of a performance in the Opera House to a big screen in the Covent Garden piazza. The performance on June 9, 1987, was a promenade performance of *La Bohème* starring Ilona Tokody and Placido Domingo, who led the cast outside afterwards to take a second "curtain" call from the audience in the piazza. Despite intermittent showers over 2,000 people gathered to watch the free transmission and responded with great enjoyment and enthusiasm. There are hopes that the experiment will be repeated, giving more people the opportunity to see international opera stars in live performances.

Losses

The dance world suffered a number of losses in the past year. Robert Helpmann died in his native Australia on September 28, 1986, aged 77. Helpmann began his career dancing and acting in shows in Australia before coming in 1933 to Britain where he joined Ninette de Valois's Vic-Wells Ballet. Within a year he had taken over leading roles and had his first created part, in *Les Rendezvous*. His technique as a dancer was never strong but his stage presence was striking and he had notable successes in a series of roles created for him by Ashton and de Valois, including the poet in *Apparitions* and the Red King in *Checkmate*. He took over, and made very much his own, the title part in *The Rake's Progress* and during Ashton's absence on war service choreographed roles for himself in *Hamlet* and *Miracle in the Gorbals*.

Helpmann's abilities as a choreographer were not exceptional but he was an imaginative producer and director, bringing to bear in these capacities the experience gained in other areas of the arts, for his activities were not confined to dance. He turned his talents to acting on stage and on film, and to directing opera as well as ballet. It is, however, for his work in ballet that Helpmann is best known. His 17 years at Sadler's Wells, and in particular his partnership with Fonteyn, helped to make the company known to a wider audience and the long period he spent as co-director did much to establish the fledgling Australian Ballet.

Another personality with a varied career was Serge Lifar, dancer, choreographer and director who died on December 16, 1986 at the age of 81. Lifar was born in Kiev and was taught by Nijinska before joining Diaghilev's company. Here he had success in leading roles in ballets by Massine and Balanchine, and his beauty, flair and stage presence inspired the creation of Balanchine's *Apollo* and *Prodigal Son*. After Diaghilev's death, Lifar obtained the post of ballet master with the Paris Opéra where he set about restoring the standards of the company as well as creating some 60 ballets for it.

In the course of his varied career Lifar built up an incomparable personal and professional archive of costumes, scores, designs, posters and other memorabilia. Just before his death he granted trusteeship of the archive to the city of Lausanne and an exhibition of artefacts from the archive was mounted during the winter.

Antony Tudor

The greatest creative loss was the death on April 19 of Antony Tudor, at the age of 79. Tudor started his working life as a clerk at London's Smithfield Market. Attracted to ballet after seeing performances in a music hall and by Pavlova's and Diaghilev's companies, he began in 1928, at the age of 20, to take ballet lessons. He made his dance debut with Marie Rambert's company but his ambition was always to be a choreographer and Rambert gave him employment and encouragement. His first work, performed in 1931, was *Cross-Garter'd*, based on *Twelfth Night*, which showed from the start his originality and inventiveness. This choreographic promise developed in the half-dozen works Tudor created for the Rambert company in the next five years. It reached its fulfilment in 1936 in his first enduring masterpiece *Jardin aux lilas* and his achievement was confirmed with *Dark Elegies* a year later. These two works broke away from the tendency in ballet to conceal emotional tension and gave expression to powerful emotions; in the first ballet the despair of parted lovers and in the second, an abstract work, the grief of bereaved parents.

Tudor left the Rambert company in 1937 and supported himself for the next few years by teaching and undertaking commissions, one of which produced the ironic *Judgement of Paris*. In 1939 he was invited to join the new Ballet Theatre (later American Ballet Theatre) in New York, and his ballets formed the core of the company's repertoire. With *Pillar of Fire* in 1942 Tudor again broke new ground, taking the steps of classical ballet and using them in new ways to reveal the psychology of the characters.

Second Flowering

Throughout the 1940s and 1950s Tudor worked with American Ballet Theatre and the New York City Ballet but in the early 1950s he ended his connections with both companies and devoted the next decade to teaching. It seemed as if his creative career was over but in 1963 he created for the Royal Swedish Ballet *Echoings of Trumpets*, a ballet about wartime resistance which is as powerful and moving as the best of his early work. This was followed in 1967 by *Shadowplay* for the Royal Ballet, and the following decade saw a second period of creativity culminating in *The Leaves are Fading* (1975) and *The Tiller in the Field* (1978) for American Ballet Theatre: subsequently Tudor worked on revivals of his ballets.

His works are popular pieces in the repertoires of companies throughout Europe and in the U.S.A., though sadly not in this country where they have scarcely been seen in the past twenty years. The best of his works are modern classics and as a choreographer Tudor ranks alongside Ashton and Balanchine in the originality of his work and its influence on the form and development of modern ballet.

More widely known than any of the above and supreme master of a different form of dance was Fred Astaire, who died on June 22, aged 88. A star of musical comedies before breaking into films, Astaire was quick to realise the possibilities of dance on film if it were properly handled. He felt that close-ups and trick shots should be abandoned and the whole body kept in the picture to retain the flow of the dance sequence and achieve maximum impact. He also saw the opportunity that film provided for presenting more intricate steps than could be followed by a theatre audience.

Astaire's appreciation of the technical possibilities of film was allied to originality as a choreographer and perfectionism as a performer. He would start work on dance sequences some months before filming began, creating and painstakingly honing routines with his partner. This care was apparent in the polish and seeming effortlessness of his performances, especially with Ginger Rogers; his genius in the freshness and musicality of choreography and dancing.

Lost Voices

The opera world suffered its losses too this season. The bass-baritone Forbes Robinson died on May 13 at the age of 60. Robinson began his career in 1953 with the Royal Opera and remained there for over 30 seasons, many of them as principal bass. He took a wide repertoire of roles including Swallow (*Peter Grimes*) and Bottom (*A Midsummer Night's Dream*), and he was the first British Don Giovanni this century at Covent garden. Among his most memorable roles were those he created: the vocally-taxing title role in Tippett's *King Priam*, the evil Claggart in *Billy Budd*, and the speaking part of Moses in *Moses und Aron* (Schoenberg). Robinson also made frequent appearances with Welsh National Opera and was a popular figure in oratorio and concert performances. Robinson's was a voice of uncommon agility and extensive range: allied to masterly characterisation and an imposing stature, he had a magnetic stage presence.

Another familiar face lost to the opera scene was that of Harold Rosenthal who died, aged 69, on March 19. As co-founder, with Lord Harewood, of *Opera* and editor of the journal for 33 years, Harold Rosenthal made an invaluable contribution to the development of opera in post-war Britain. His encyclopaedic knowledge and his devotion to the art of opera made his views respected and welcomed by performers and administrators all over the world. He was particularly dedicated to the idea that opera should be widely accessible and through his editorship of *Opera*, his other writing, and lecturing at home and overseas he helped to promote knowledge and appreciation of opera throughout the English-speaking world.

OPERA PRODUCTIONS

In the summaries of company activities shown below, the dates in brackets indicate the year in which the current production entered that company's repertoire.

ROYAL OPERA (1946)

Royal Opera House, Covent Garden, W.C.2.

Productions from the repertoire were *La traviata* (1967), *Die Zauberflöte* (1979), *Samson* (1985), *Lucia di Lammermoor* (1959), *Der Rosenkavalier* (1984), *Ariadne auf Naxos* (1985), *The Nightingale* (1983)/*L'enfant et les sortilèges* (1983) double bill, *Turandot* (1984), *Werther* (1979), *La Bohème* (1974), *Il barbiere di Siviglia* (1985), *Die Frau ohne Schatten* (1969), *Fidelio* (1986).

New productions were:

Nov. 17, 1986. **Jenufa** (Janáček). *Conductor*, Bernard Haitink; *producer*, Yuri Lyubimov; *set design*, Paul Hernon; *costume design*, Clare Mitchell.

Jenufa, Ashley Putnam; *The Kostelnička*, Eva Randová; *Grandmother Buryja*, Elizabeth Bainbridge; *Steva*, Neil Rosenshein; *Laca*, Philip Langridge.

Jan. 13, 1987. **Otello** (Verdi). *Conductor*, Carlos Kleiber; *producer*, Elijah Moshinsky; *set design*, Timothy O'Brien; *costume design*, Peter J. Hall.

Otello, Placido Domingo; *Desdemona*, Katia Ricciarelli; *Iago*, Justino Diaz; *Emilia*, Anne Mason.

Feb. 10, 1987. **Norma** (Bellini). *Conductor*, John Pritchard; *producer*, John Copley; *designers*, Robin Don, Bob Ringwood.

Norma, Margaret Price; *Pollione*, Giuseppe Giacomini; *Adalgisa*, Alicia Nafé: *Oroveso*, Gwynne Howell; *Clotilde*, Anne-Marie Owens; *Flavio*, Paul Crook.

April 1, 1987. **The King Goes Forth to France** (Aulis Sallinen), the British premiere. *Conductor*, Okku Kamu; *producer*, Nicholas Hytner; *designer*, Bob Crowley; *choreography*, Anthony van Laast.

The Prince, later the King, Mikael Melbye; *The Nice Caroline*, Eilene Hannan; *The Anne who Steals*, Valerie Masterson; *The Caroline with the Thick Mane*, Sarah Walker; *The Anne who Strips*, Jane Turner; *The Queen*, Nuala Willis; *Prime Minister/ Young Prime Minister*, Stafford Dean; *Guide*, Kim Begley; *English Archer*, Donald Maxwell; *Sir Burghers of Calais*, John Dobson, Paul Crook, Stuart Harling, Gordon Sandison, Eric Garrett, Roderick Earle; *Froissart*, Ian McDiarmid.

June 2, 1987. **Manon** (Massenet). *Conductor*, Jeffrey Tate; *producer*, Rudolf Noelte; *designer*, Peter Rice.

Manon, Julia Migenes; *Des Grieux*, Neil Shicoff; *Lescaut*, J. Patrick Raftery; *De Brétigny*, William Dooley; *Comte Des Grieux*, Robert Lloyd.

The premiere was a Royal Gala performance in the presence of the Duchess of York.

The Royal Opera began the 1986–87 season with a tour of the Far East. After a week in Seoul, S. Korea, where it performed *Turandot, Carmen* and *Samson et Dalila*, the company went on to Japan. The three productions presented in Korea were supplemented by *Così fan tutte* during a month of performances in Tokyo, Osaka and Yokohama.

ENGLISH NATIONAL OPERA (1931)
London Coliseum, St. Martin's Lane, W.C.2.

Productions from the repertoire were *Il trovatore* (1972), *The Marriage of Figaro* (1978), *Madam Butterfly* (1984), *Aida* (1980), *The Rape of Lucretia* (1983), *Die Fledermaus* (1979), *Osud* (1984), *The Queen of Spades* (1983), *Faust* (1985), *Akhnaten* (1985), *Don Giovanni* (1985), *Orpheus in the Underworld* (1985).

New productions were:

Sept. 27, 1986. **The Mikado** (Sullivan). *Conductor*, Peter Robinson; *producer*, Jonathan Miller; *set design*, Stefanos Lazaridis; *costume design*, Sue Blane; *choreography*, Anthony van Laast.

Yum-Yum, Lesley Garrett; *Peep-Bo*, Susan Bullock; *Pitti-Sing*, Jean Rigby; *Katisha*, Felicity Palmer; *Nanki-Poo*, Bonaventura Bottone; *Ko-Ko*, Eric Idle; *Pooh-Ba*, Richard Van Allen; *The Mikado*, Richard Angas; *Pish-Tush*, Mark Richardson.

Oct. 29, 1986. **Cavalleria Rusticana** (Mascagni). *Santuzza*, Jane Eaglen; *Lola*, Fiona Kimm; *Mamma Lucia*, Shelagh Squires; *Turiddu*, Edmund Barham; *Alfio*, Malcolm Rivers.

and **I Pagliacci** (Leoncavallo). *Nedda*, Helen Field; *Canio*, Rowland Sidwell; *Beppe*, Bonaventura Bottone; *Tonio*, Nicholas Folwell; *Silvio*, Christopher Booth-Jones.

Conductor, Jacques Delacôte; *producer,* Ian Judge; *set design,* Gerard Howland; *constume design,* Deirdre Clancy.

Nov. 27, 1986. **Carmen** (Bizet). *Conductor,* Mark Elder; *producer,* David Pountney; *designer,* Maria Bjørnson.

Carmen, Sally Burgess; *Don José,* John Treleaven; *Escamillo,* David Arnold; *Zuniga,* Richard Angas; *Micaëla,* Rosamund Illing.

Dec. 19, 1986. **The Diary of One Who Disappeared** (Janáček). *Conductor,* Mark Elder; *solo piano,* Paul Crossley; *producer,* David Pountney; *designer,* Stefanos Lazaridis.

The Man, Arthur Davies; *The Gypsy,* Jean Rigby; *Three Voices,* Susan Bullock, Shelagh Squires, Ethna Robinson. (This work was performed with *Osud* as a double bill).

Jan 28, 1987. **Tosca** (Puccini). *Conductor,* Jan Latham-Koenig; *producer,* Jonathan Miller; *designer,* Stefanos Lazaridis.

Tosca, Josephine Barstow; *Cavaradossi,* Eduardo Alvares; *Scarpia,* Neil Howlett.

April 2, 1987. **Simon Boccanegra** (Verdi). *Conductor,* Mark Elder; *producer,* David Alden; *designer,* David Fielding.

Simon Boccanegra, Jonathan Summers; *Amelia,* Janice Cairns; *Fiesco,* Gwynne Howell; *Gabriele Adorno,* Arthur Davies; *Paolo Albiani,* Alan Opie; *Pietro,* Clive Bayley.

April 23. **The Stone Guest** (Dargomyzhsky), the British stage premiere. *Conductor,* Paul Daniel; *producer,* Keith Warner; *designer,* Marie-Jeanne Lecca.

Don Juan, Graham Clark; *Leporello;* John Connell; *Donna Anna,* Kathryn Harries; *Don Carlos,* Neil Howlett; *Laura,* Sally Burgess; *The Monk,* Rodney Macann; *The Statue,* Anthony Cunningham; *Laura's Guests,* Terry Jenkins, John Kitchiner, Michael Sadler, Mike Worsley.

May 22, 1987. **Lady Macbeth of Mtsensk** (Shostakovich), the British stage premiere. *Conductor,* Mark Elder; *Producer,* David Poutney; *designer,* Stefanos Lazaridis.

Katerina, Josephine Barstow; *Sergei,* Jacque Trussel; *Boris,* Willard White; *Zinovy,* Stuart Kale; *Sonyetka,* Sally Burgess.

NEW SADLER'S WELLS OPERA (1982)
Sadler's Wells Theatre, Rosebery Ave., E.C.1.

A three-week season at Sadler's Wells Theatre included a revival of *The Count of Luxembourg* (1983), and a new production of *Ruddigore* which was subsequently performed on tour at Sunderland, Wolverhampton, Norwich, Brighton, Northampton, Manchester and Canterbury.

Feb. 19, 1987. **Ruddigore** (Sullivan). *Conductor,* Simon Phipps; *producer,* Ian Judge; *set design,* Gerard Howland; *costume design,* Dierdre Clancy.

Rose, Marilyn Hill Smith; *Dame Hannah,* Joan Davies; *Margaret,* Linda Ormiston; *Robin,* Gordon Sandison; *Richard,* David Hillman; *Despard,* Harold Innocent; *Sir Roderick,* Thomas Lawlor.

WELSH NATIONAL OPERA (1946)
John Sreet, Cardiff CF1 4SP.

The company opened the 1986–87 season with performances of *The Rhinegold* (1983), *The Valkyrie* (1984), *Siegfried* (1985) and *Götterdämmerung* (1985), *The Magic Flute* (1979), *Un Ballo in Maschera* (1982) and a new production of *Lucia di Lammermoor.* The *Ring* cycle was presented for one week at the Royal Opera House, London, and then on tour with the other operas at Birmingham, Liverpool and Bristol.

Other productions from the repertoire during the season were *The Barber of Seville* (1986), *La Bohème* (1984), *Carmen* (1983).

New productions were:
Oct. 18, 1986. **Lucia di Lammermoor** (Donizetti). *Conductor,* Julian Smith; *producer, William Gaskill; designer,* Ultz.

Lucia, Suzanne Murphy; *Edgardo,* Dennis O'Neill; *Enrico,* Mark Holland; *Arturo,* Peter Bronder.

Feb. 28, 1987. **The Trojans** (Berlioz), a co-production with Opera North and Scottish Opera. *Conductor,* Charles Mackerras; *producer,* Tim Albery; *designers,* Tom Cairns, Anthony McDonald.

Cassandra, Kristine Ciesinski; *Anna,* Penelope Walker; *Ascanius,* Yolande Jones; *Hecuba,* Deborah Stuart-Roberts; *Dido,* Della Jones; *Cassandra's Ghost,* Caroline Baker; *Andromache,* Lucy Burge; *Aeneas,* Jeffrey Lawton; *Helenus,* Michael Clifton-Thompson; *Iopas,* Peter Bronder; *Hylas,* Timothy German; *Narbal,* Sean Rea; *Chorobeus,* Philip Joll; *Pantheus,* Mark Holland; *Hector's Ghost,* Peter Rose; *Priam,* Stephen Richardson.

May 20, 1987. **Le nozze di Figaro** (Mozart). *Conductor,* Charles Mackerras; *producer,* Giles Havergal; *designer,* Sue Blane.

Countess Almaviva, Elaine Woods; *Susanna,* Anne Dawson; *Count Almaviva,* Donald Maxwell; *Figaro,* Robert Hayward; *Cherubino,* Beverley Mills.

All new productions were premiered at Cardiff. Performances of the season's repertoire were given at smaller venues throughout Wales, Oxford, Liverpool, Birmingham, Southampton, Bristol, Mold, Swansea, and *Le nozze di Figaro* was performed at the Wiesbaden Festival.

SCOTTISH OPERA (1962)
Theatre Royal, Hope Street, Glasgow 2.

Productions from the repertoire were *The Marriage of Figaro* (1986) and *The Barber of Seville* (1985).

New productions were:
Sept. 30, 1986. **Carmen** (Bizet). *Conductor,* John Mauceri; *producer,* Graham Vick; *designer,* Michael Yeargan.

Carmen, Emily Golden; *Don José,* Gary Bachlund; *Escamillo,* Sergei Leiferkus; *Micaëla,* Jane Leslie McKenzie; *Zuniga,* Jonathan Best.

Oct. 10, 1986. **Intermezzo** (R. Strauss), a 1974 Glyndebourne production. *Conductor,* Stephen Barlow; *producer,* John Cox; *designer,* Martin Battersby.

Christine, Beverly Morgan; *Anna,* Kate Flowers; *Storch,* Alan Opie; *Baron Lummer,* Ian Caley.

Oct. 21, 1986. **Iolanthe** (Sullivan). *Conductor,* Wyn Davies; *producer,* Keith Warner; *designer,* Marie-Jeanne Lecca.

Iolanthe, Christine Boates; *Phyllis,* Patricia O'Neill; *Fairy Queen,* Gillian Knight; *Strephon,* Omar Ebrahim; *Lord Chancellor,* Thomas Hemsley; *Private Willis,* Stephen Richardson; *The Earls,* Hugh Hetherington, Eric Roberts.

Jan. 27, 1987. **Der fliegende Holländer** (Wagner). *Conductor,* Alexander Gibson; *producer,* John Cox; *designer,* Eugene Lee.

Senta, Kathryn Harries; *Dutchman,* Norman Bailey; *Daland,* Oddbjørn Tennfjord; *Mary,* Claire Livingstone; *Erik,* John Treleaven: *Steersman,* Patrick Power.

Feb. 28, 1987. **From the House of the Dead** (Janáček), a co-production with Welsh National Opera. *Conductor,* Richard Armstrong; *producer,* David Pountney; *designer,* Maria Bjørnson.

Goryanchikov, Robert Carpenter Turner; *Luka*

Kuzmich, John Mitchinson; *Skuratov,* Graham Clark; *Shapkin,* Nigel Douglas; *Shishkov,* Donald Maxwell; *Governor,* William McCue.

April 28, 1987. **Madama Butterfly** (Puccini). *Conductor,* Alexander Gibson; *producer,* Nuria Espent; *designers,* Ezio Frigerio, Franca Squarciapino.

Cio-Cio-San, Yoko Watanabe; *Suzuki,* Anne-Marie Owens; *Pinkerton,* Seppo Ruohonen; *Sharpless,* Norman Bailey; *Yamadori,* Henry Newman; *Bonze,* John Tranter; *Kate Pinkerton,* Clare Shearer.

May 21, 1987. **Billy Budd** (Britten). *Conductor,* John Mauceri; *producer,* Graham Vick; *designer,* Chris Dyer.

Billy Budd, Mark Tinkler; *Capt. Vere,* Philip Langridge; *Claggart,* John Tomlinson.

Scottish Opera was inaugurated with a performance of *Madama Butterfly* and a gala performance of this season's new production was given on June 5, 1987, to mark the company's Silver Jubilee.

All new productions were premiered in Glasgow. Performances were given on tour at Liverpool, Edinburgh, Aberdeen and Newcastle. Scottish Opera-Go-Round toured adaptations of *Jenufa, Macbeth* and *La Bohème* to smaller venues throughout Scotland during the 1986–87 season.

OPERA NORTH (1978)
Grand Theatre, New Briggate, Leeds LS1 6NZ

Productions from the repertoire were *Madama Butterfly* (1982), *Oedipus Rex* (1981) and *La traviata* (1985).

New productions were:

Sept. 27, 1986. **The Capture of Troy** (Berlioz) a co-production with Welsh National Opera and Scottish Opera. *Conductor,* David Lloyd-Jones; *producer,* Tim Albery; *designers,* Tom Cairns, Antony McDonald.

Cassandra, Kristine Ciesinski; *Ascanius,* Nicola Sharkey; *Hecuba,* Pauline Thulborn; *Andromache,* Lucy Burge; *Aeneas,* Ronald Hamilton; *Sinon,* David Hillman; *Chorebus,* Richard Salter; *Hector's Ghost,* Clive Bayley; *Priam,* John Hall; *Pantheus,* John Cashmore.

Oct. 10, 1986. **The Barber of Seville** (Rossini), a co-production with Vancouver Opera and Welsh National Opera. *Conductor,* Clive Timms; *producer,* Giles Havergal; *designer,* Russell Craig.

Rosina, Beverley Mills; *Almaviva,* Harry Nicoll; *Figaro,* Peter Savidge; *Berta,* Maria Moll; *Bartolo,* David Wilson-Johnson; *Basilio,* Clive Bayley.

Dec. 18, 1986. **La Bohème** (Puccini). *Conductor,* Elgar Howarth; *producer,* David Freeman; *designer,* David Roger.

Mimi, Eirian Davies; *Rodolfo,* Adrian Martin; *Musetta,* Anna Steiger; *Marcello,* William Shimell; *Colline,* Clive Bayley; *Schaunard,* Richard Suart.

Dec. 20, 1986. **Norma** (Bellini), a co-production with Welsh National Opera and Houston Grand Opera. *Conductor,* Clive Timms; *producer,* Andrei Serban; *designer,* Michael Yeargan.

Norma, Monica Pick-Hieronimi; *Pollione,* Frederick Donaldson; *Adalgisa,* Eiddwen Harrhy; *Oroveso,* John Tranter; *Clotilde,* Shirley Thomas; *Flavio,* Stephen Briggs.

Jan. 13, 1987. Opera North revived *Oedipus Rex* (1981) and presented the opera in a double bill with Ballet Rambert's new production of *Pulcinella* (see below for dance details).

April 2, 1987. **The Seraglio** (Mozart), a co-production with Opera Theatre of St. Louis. *Conductor,* Tomasz Bugaj; *producer,* Graham Vick; *designer,* Kevin Rupnick.

Constanze, Sally Wolf; *Blonde,* Elizabeth Gale;

Belmonte, Laurence Dale; *Pedrillo,* Bonaventura Bottone; *Osmin,* Tom Haenen; *Pasha Selim,* Ewart James Walters.

May 2, 1987. **Daphne** (R. Strauss), the British stage premiere. *Conductor,* David Lloyd-Jones; *producer,* Philip Prowse; *design,* Philip Prowse; *choreography,* Geoffrey Cauley.

Daphne, Helen Field; *Apollo,* Willaim Lewis; *Gaea,* Patricia Payne; *Peneios,* Sean Rea; *Leukippos,* Peter Jeffes; *Maids,* Carol Smith, Elizabeth Woollett; *Shepherds,* Keith Latham, Philip Mills, Anthony Baines-Davis, Galloway Bell.

All new productions were premiered in Leeds. Performances of the repertoire were given on tour in Nottingham, Manchester, Hull and York.

KENT OPERA (1969)
Pembles Cross, Egerton, Ashford, Kent.

Productions from the repertoire were *The Marriage of Figaro* (1981), L'incoronazione di Poppaea (1986) and a revised double bill of *Dido and Aeneas* and *Pygmalion.*

New productions were:

Oct. 1, 1986. **Carmen** (Bizet). *Conductor,* Ivan Fischer; *producer,* Robin Lefèvre; *designer,* Grant Hicks.

Carmen, Anne-Marie Mühle; *Don José,* Howard Haskin; *Micaëla,* Meryl Drower; *Escamillo,* Alan Oke; *Zuniga,* Steven Page.

April 1, 1987. **The Magic Flute** (Mozart). *Conductor,* Ivan Fischer; *producer,* Michael Knights; *designer,* Roger Butlin.

Pamina, Patricia Rozario; *Tamino,* Neill Archer; *Queen of the Night,* Eileen Hulse; *Papageno,* Andrew Shore; *Sarastro,* Ulrik Cold; *Speaker,* Thomas Hemsley.

July 8, 1987. **A Night at the Chinese Opera** (Weir). *Conductor,* Andrew Parrott; *producer,* Richard Jones; *designer,* Richard Hudson.

Little Moon/Actor, Meryl Drower; *Mrs. Chin/Old Crone,* Enid Hartle; *Actor,* Frances Lynch; *Chao Lin as a boy,* Diccon Cooper; *Military Governor,* Michael Chance; *Old P'eng/Mountain Dweller,* David Johnston; *Nighwatchman/Marco Polo,* Tomos Ellis; *Chao Lin,* Gwion Thomas; *Actor,* Alan Oke; *Chao Sun/ Fireman,* Stewart Buchanan; *Mongolian Soldier,* Jonathan Best.

The company visited Canterbury, Tunbridge Wells, Bath, Northampton, Cambridge, Dartford, Southsea, Eastbourne, Norwich and Plymouth.

GLYNDEBOURNE FESTIVAL OPERA (1934)
Glyndebourne, Lewes, Sussex BN8 5UU

The 1987 Festival ran from May 24 to August 22, and the orchestra was the London Philharmonic. Seven operas (including a double bill) were presented, of which four were revivals: *Carmen* (Peter Hall production, 1985); *Così fan tutte* (Peter Hall production, 1978); *Capriccio* (John Cox production, 1976); and *Porgy and Bess* (Trevor Nunn production, 1986).

The three new productions were:
May 24, 1987. **La traviata** (Verdi). *Conductor,* Bernard Haitink; *director,* Peter Hall; *designer,* John Gunter; *choreographer,* Elizabeth Keen.

Violetta, Marie McLaughlin; *Alfredo,* Walter MacNeil; *Germont,* Brent Ellis.

July 22, 1986. **L'heure espagnole** (Ravel). *Conductor,* Simon Rattle; *director,* Frank Corsaro, *designer,* Maurice Sendak; *animation,* Ron Chase; *choreography,* Jenny Weston.

Concepcion, Mariana Cioromila; *Torquemada,* Remy Corazza; *Ramiro,* François Le Roux; *Gonsalve,*

Philip Langridge; *Don Inigo Gomez*, François Loup. and **L'enfant et les sortilèges** (Ravel). Production details, as above.

The Child, Cynthia Buchan; *Mother*, Fiona Kimm. The touring company's repertoire included *Così fan tutte*, *L'heure espagnole*/*L'enfant et les sortilèges* and the premiers of *The Electrification of the Soviet Union* (Nigel Osborne). Performances were given at Glyndebourne, Oxford, Southampton, Manchester and Birmingham.

DANCE PRODUCTIONS

THE ROYAL BALLET (1931)
Royal Opera House, Covent Garden, W.C.2

Full-length ballets from the repertoire performed in the 1986–87 season were *Mayerling* (MacMillan: 1978) *The Sleeping Beauty* (Sergeyev after Petipa, additional choreography by Ashton: 1977), *The Nutcracker* (Ivanov: Wright, 1984), *La Fille mal gardée* (Ashton: 1960).

Programmes also included the following shorter ballets from the repertoire: *La Valse* (Ashton), *The Concert* (Robbins), *The Dream* (Ashton), *Symphonic Variations* (Ashton), *A Month in the Country* (Ashton), *Young Apollo* (Bintley), *Le Baiser de la fée* (MacMillan), and *Gloria* (MacMillan).

New productions were:
Oct. 8, 1986. **Opus 19/The Dreamer**, the British premiere of a short work by Robbins; *music*, Prokofiev; *design*, Ben Benson; *conductor*, Isaiah Jackson; *cast* led by Cynthia Harvey and Jonathan Cope.

March 12, 1987. **Swan Lake**. *Choreography*, Petipa/Ivanov; *music*, Tchaikovsky; *producer*, Anthony Dowell; *designer*, Yolanda Sonnabend. The cast at the premiere was led by Cynthia Harvey and Jonathan Cope; *conductor*, Mark Ermler.

New ballets were:
Oct. 8, 1986. **Galanteries**, the London premiere of a work created for the EXPO 1986 World Festival in Vancouver. *Choreography*, David Bintley; *music*, Mozart; *designer*, Jan Blake; *conductor*, Isaiah Jackson. The cast included Lesley Collier, Deirdre Eyden, Fiona Chadwick, Karen Paisley, Antony Dowson, Mark Silver, Jonathan Cope and Bruce Sansom.

Dec. 2, 1986. **Beauty and the Beast**. *Choreography*, Wayne Eagling; *music*, Vangelis; *design*, Jan Pieńkowski; *conductor*, Ashley Lawrence; *cast* at the premiere included Maria Almeida, Jonathan Cope and Michael Coleman.

July 22, 1987. **Pursuit**, for twelve dancers. *Choreography*, Ashley Page; *music*, Colin Matthew's *Suns Dance*; *designer*, Jack Smith; *cast* led by Fiona Chadwick and Jonathan Cope.

In January 1987 the company spent a week in the Netherlands, where they performed *Mayerling*, *Young Apollo*, *A Month in the Country* and *Gloria*. A month-long trip to Korea and Japan took place from mid-April to mid-May when the works given were *The Sleeping Beauty* and *Mayerling*. The most prestigious of the company's overseas tours was the month spent in Leningrad and Moscow in June performing *Manon* (MacMillan), *Consort Lessons*, *A Month in the Country*, *Gloria*, *The Dream*, *Symphonic Variations* and *Elite Syncopations*.

SADLER'S WELLS ROYAL BALLET (1931)
Sadler's Wells Theatre, Rosebery Avenue, EC1R 4TN.

Full-length ballets from the repertoire were *The Sleeping Beauty* (Petipa/Wright, 1984), *Coppelia* (Petipa/Cecchetti: Wright, 1979), *Swan Lake* (Petipa/Ivanov: Wright, 1980), *The Snow Queen* (Bintley, 1986).

Programmes also included the following shorter ballets: *Quartet* (MacMillan), *The Wand of Youth* (Corder), *Tchaikovsky pas-de-deux* (Balanchine), *Flowers of the Forest* (Bintley), *Prodigal Son* (Balanchine), *Pineapple Poll* (Cranko), *Solitaire* (MacMillan), *Checkmate* (de Valois), *Paquita* (Petipa) and *Elite Syncopations* (MacMillan).

During the company's 40th anniversary season at Sadler's Wells Theatre in January two Ashton ballets, *Valse nobles et sentimentales* and *Capriol Suite*, were revived.

New ballets were:
Dec. 5, 1986. **Peter and The Wolf**, a Ballet Rambert work entering the S.W.R.B. repertoire. *Choreography*, Frank Staff; *music*, Prokofiev; *producer*, Elisabeth Schooling, in collaboration with Sally Gilmour; *designer*, Guy Sheppard; *cast* led by Marion Tait (*Peter*) and Christopher Gable (*Narrator*).

Jan. 15, 1987. **One by Nine**. *Choreography*, Jennifer Jackson; *music*, Vivaldi; *designer*, Deanne Petherbridge; *cast* led by Marion Tait, June Highwood and Joseph Cipolla.

and **Allegri Diversi**. *Choreography*, David Bintley; *music*, Rossini; *designer*, Terry Bartlett; *cast* led by Karen Donovan and Petter Jacobssen.

March 19, 1987. **Paramour**. *Choreography*, Graham Lustig; *music*, Poulenc; *designer*, Nadine Baylis; *cast* led by Galina Samsova, Marion Tait, Petter Jacobssen and David Yow.

also **Private City**. *Choreography*, Susan Crow; *music*, commissioned score by John Surman; *designer*, Tim Shortall.

and **The Picture of Dorian Gray**. *Choreography*, Derek Deane; *music*, commissioned score by Carl Davis; *designer*, Peter Farmer; *cast* led by Roland Price and Samira Saidi.

In addition to their 40th anniversary season at Sadler's Wells Theatre and two two-week seasons at the Royal Opera House, the company also performed at Cambridge (a Big Top season), Sunderland, North ampton, Cardiff, Oxford, Eastbourne, Birmingham, Glasgow, Aberdeen, Manchester, Leeds, Plymouth and the Isle of Wight (a Big Top season). From early-May to mid-June the company spent five weeks on tour in Czechoslovakia, Poland, East Germany and Bulgaria, performing *The Snow Queen* and a triple bill comprising *Flowers of the Forest*, *Checkmate* and *Elite Syncopations*.

LONDON FESTIVAL BALLET (1950)
Festival Ballet House, 39 Jay Mews, SW7 2ES

Performances of full-length ballets from the repertoire included both the Ashton (revived 1985) and Nureyev (1977) versions of *Romeo and Juliet*, *Coppelia* (Hind, after Petipa/Cecchetti: 1985) and *Onegin* (Cranko: 1983).

On Dec. 10, 1986 a new production was premiered of **The Nutcracker**: *choreography*, Peter Schaufuss; *music*, Tchaikovsky; *designer*, David Walker.

Programmes of shorter ballets performed by the company or by the offshoot group LFB2 included *Petrushka Variations* (Neumeier), *Song of a Wayfarer* (Béjart), *Land* (Bruce), *Drop Your Pearls* (Clark), *Carmen* (Petit), *Night Creature* (Ailey), *The World Again* (Bruce), *Symphony in C* (Balanchine) and *La Bayadère* (Makarova after Petipa).

Works introduced into the company's repertoire were *Désir* (Nov. 4, 1986: choreographer, John Neumeier), *Nocturne* (Nov. 7, 1986: choreographer, Kevin Haigen), a revival of Ashton's 1936 ballet *Apparitions* (July 13, 1987) and *Bolero* (July 15, 1987: choreographer, Maurice Béjart).

New works included:
April 3, 1987. **Episodes**. *Choreography*, Ulysses Dove; *music*, Robert Ruggieri.

April 24, 1987. *The Dream is over. Choreography,* Christopher Bruce; *music,* John Lennon; *cast* led by Matz Skoog.

July 13, 1987. **A 'Winged.** *Choreography,* Kevin Haigen; *music,* Britten; *costumes,* John Cowell.

July 15, 1987. **Pas de deux** created by Kevin Haigen for Natalia Makarova with Martin James.

The company performed in London, at the Royal Festival Hall, Sadler's Wells Theatre and the London Coliseum, and on tour at Hull, Manchester, Bradford, Leeds, Canterbury, Plymouth, Norwich, Nottingham, Liverpool, Bristol, Oxford and Birmingham. In addition the LFB2 company performed at a number of smaller venues. The company visited Hong Kong in February 1987 and performed *Romeo and Juliet* (Ashton) at the Arts Festival there.

BALLET RAMBERT (1926)
94 Chiswick High Road, W4 1SH

Repertoire works performed during the year were *Swamp* (Clark), *Soda Lake* (Alston), *Dangerous Liaisons* (Alston), *Ceremonies* (Bruce), *Dipping Wings* (Evelyn), *Mercure* (Spink), *Zansa* (Alston), *Carmen Arcadiae Mechanicae Perpetuum* (Page), *Night with Waning Moon* (Bruce), *Java* (Alston), *Ricercare* (Tetley), *Pierrot Lunaire* (Tetley) and *Dancing Day* (Bruce).

Among the new works were:

Oct. 11, 1986. **Dutiful Ducks,** for four dancers. *Choreography,* Richard Alston; *score,* Charles Amirkhanian.

Jan. 13, 1987. **Pulcinella,** presented in a double bill with Opera North's *Oedipus Rex. Choreography,* Richard Alston; *music,* Stravinsky; *designer,* Howard Hodgkin; *conductor,* David Lloyd-Jones. *Cast* led by Ben Craft (*Pulcinella*) and Cathrine Price (*Pimpinella*). The singers were Della Jones, Mark Tucker and John Tranter.

May 6, 1987. **Rushes,** for six dancers. *Choreography,* Siobhan Davies; *score,* Michael Finnissy; *designer,* David Buckland.

Aug. 6, 1987. **Strong Language.** *Choreography,* Richard Alston; *score,* John-Marc Gowans; *costumes,* Katharine Hamnett; *cast* led by Mary Evelyn and Mark Baldwin.

Aug. 11, 1987. **Wolfy.** *Choreography,* Lynn Seymour; *music,* Mozart's *Piano Concerto in C major* (K467); *designer,* Andrew Logan.

During the 1986–87 season the company performed on tour at Canterbury, Oxford, Plymouth, Bath, Nottingham, Glasgow, Leeds, Mold, Birmingham, Leicester, Manchester and in London at Sadler's Wells Theatre and the Big Top, Battersea Park.

Overseas tours were to Greece in September 1986 and to North America in January 1987.

LONDON CONTEMPORARY DANCE THEATRE (1967)
The Place, 16 Flaxman Terrace, WC1H 9AT

Performances from the repertoire were *Troy Game* (North), *Ceremony* (Cohan), *The Run to Earth* (Davies), *Moves* (Robbins), *Liquid Assets* (Jobe); *Rainbow Bandit* (Alston), *Songs and Dances* (North), and *Class* (Cohan).

New works were:

Sept. 24, 1986. **Unfolding Field.** *Choreography,* Christopher Bannerman; *music,* Man Jumping; *design,* Andrew Storer.

and **Interrogations.** *Choreography,* Robert Cohan; *music,* Barrington Pheloung; *design,* Antonio Lagarto.

Nov. 25, 1986. **And Do They Do.** *Choreography,* Siobhan Davies; *music,* commissioned score by Michael Nyman; *design,* David Buckland.

Feb. 17, 1987. **Irma Vep.** *Choreography,* Daniel Ezralow; *music,* Bartok's *Sonata for Two Pianos and Percussion*; *design,* Daniel Ezralow.

Feb. 19, 1987. **Red Steps.** *Choreography,* Siobhan Davies; *music,* John Adams's *Shaker Loops*; *design,* David Buckland.

March 6, 1987. **Video Life.** *Choreography,* Robert Cohan; *music,* Barry Guy.

June 30, 1987. **Fabrications.** *Choreography,* Robert North; *costumes,* Elizabeth Emanuel.

The company performed on tour at Edinburgh, Sunderland, Norwich, Manchester, Leeds, Leicester, London (Sadler's Wells Theatre and the Queen Elizabeth Hall), Canterbury, Oxford, Southampton, Glasgow, Aberdeen, Hull, Swansea, Eastbourne and Plymouth.

THE SCOTTISH BALLET (1969)
261 West Princes Street, Glasgow G4 9EE.

Productions from the repertoire were *Giselle* (Graeme, after Petipa and Corelli: 1971), *Cinderella* (Darrell: 1979), *Tales of Hoffmann* (Darrell: 1972) and the shorter works *Catulli Carmina* (Lopes), *Five Ruckert Songs* (Darrell), *Nutcracker* excerpts (Darrell, after Ivanov), *Othello* (Darrell), *Napoli Act III* (Bournonville) and *Vespri* (Prokovsky).

In addition to appearing at the Theatre Royal, Glasgow, the company also performed on tour at Bath, Liverpool, Aberdeen, Inverness, Edinburgh, Hull, Belfast, Newcastle and Perth, and in February–March 1987 at a number of smaller venues in Ireland and Scotland.

CLORE GALLERY AT THE TATE, MILLBANK, LONDON

Architects: Stirling, Wilford and Associates

J. M. W. Turner (1775–1851) is widely regarded as our greatest painter, and the vast collection of his works bequeathed to the nation after his death is one of the major treasures of our artistic heritage. The artist had originally wanted a hundred of his best pictures to be hung together in the National Gallery, but in the end difficulties in settling his will resulted in the entire contents of his studio going to the nation, and the Gallery therefore found itself entrusted with some 290 oil paintings and almost 20,000 works on paper, including many sketchbooks. Unfortunately, housing and displaying such a collection proved for many decades to be an insurmountable problem and the situation became a minor national scandal. In 1897, the collection was transferred to the Tate Gallery, but after a flood in 1928 part of the collection was again transferred to the British Museum print room and the Turner Bequest, as it was known, then became divided. There the collection remained through yet more decades of indecision and neglect, until the Turner Exhibition of 1975, jointly presented by the Tate and the Royal Academy, rekindled public demand for a suitable permanent gallery in which to house and display the complete collection.

Sir Charles Clore was among those concerned to see a resolution to this interminable saga, and following his death in 1979, the Clore Foundation offered to sponsor a purpose-built gallery in memory of Sir Charles specifically to accommodate the Turner collection. The offer came just at the time when the area of land to the north-east of the gallery occupied by the old military hospital had become available for the gallery's use. Also in 1979, Stirling Wilford and Associates had been appointed as architects to the Gallery, and from 1980 onwards they became directly involved with the Trustees in developing the brief for the new gallery. This was to comprise a series of interlinked galleries where a selection of the hundred best paintings could be permanently exhibited, together with reserve galleries for the rest of the oil paintings, a print room for all the sketchbooks and works on paper, a conservation studio and framing repair workshop, a reading room and an auditorium, together with the usual back-up facilities. The new gallery was intended to function both as an extension of the Tate and also as a complete building with its own separate rationale and identity, and would form the first phase of a planned substantial expansion of the Tate, which if completed would double the size of the gallery. Parts of the old hospital building are being retained and incorporated in the master plan for the proposed extensions, further phases of which are already being designed. Of immediate relevance to the Clore Gallery is the old Lodge, fronting the riverside roadway, with its red brick and stucco neo-Georgian elevations.

Given its location immediately adjacent to the old Tate building, an immediate question for the architect to address was how the new gallery should relate to the old. The Tate building, designed by Sidney Smith and dating from 1897, is a rugged and forceful essay in the classical Beaux Arts manner with a heavily rusticated plinth and a grand portico with pilasters in the Corinthian order. Such a self-assured and independent building is almost impossible to extend in similar manner without corrupting the symmetry and dominating presence of the original design. The architect has chosen therefore to treat the new extension as a garden wing, rather like an annexe to a large country house such as an Orangery

or summer house, an image which is assisted by its landscaped setting of grass, tall mature trees and gravel paths. The resulting building is L-shaped on plan and attached to the side elevation of the existing gallery immediately to the rear of the north-east corner pavilion.

Although accessible from the interior of the Tate, the new wing is designed to be approached via its own main entrance, situated at the far end of a slightly sunken pedestrian terrace and aligned on the central axis of the old corner pavilion's classical pedimented elevation. Despite the obvious subservience of the new building to the old, emphasised by the lower height and quieter skyline of the new wing as well as the storey-height difference in entry levels between new and old, the architect has nevertheless been at great pains to create an interactive relationship with the dominant mass of the earlier building and particular features of its elevations find their way into the new building. Some are consciously retained in their entirety, others in modified form, while some features are deliberately continued and then abruptly terminated as though they are no longer considered useful or relevant.

The main gallery wing of the new extension grows out from the corner of the classical pavilion. A direct relationship between new and old is achieved by the continuation of Smith's elaborate cornice moulding into the new elevation and right around the two arms of the building fronting the terraced approach. This is surmounted by a low parapet that, with the exception of a short length of projecting attic storey at the far end from the existing gallery, maintains a smooth, level skyline in contrast to the exuberant projections of Smith's elevations.

The principal characteristic of these main elevations is the large square grid picked out in bands of Portland Stone, enclosing either red brick or bright buff-yellow rendered infill panels, which dominates the front elevations either side of the main entrance screen. This, by way of contrast, is clad for its full height in smooth ashlared Portland stone. Out of this solid masonry screen has been cut a simple but dramatic gable-shaped void, its sharp profile echoing the pediments of the classical porticos and enclosing a griddled glazed screen with bright green mullions and transoms and a bright green revolving entrance door. The blank expanse of stonework is relieved by a semi-circular recessed lunette placed over the centre of the gabled entrance void. The external grid of the elevations is, however, quite arbitrary and the bands bear no relation to the structure or floor levels behind. This is demonstrated by the idiosyncratic treatment of the façade where matching red brick filled panels rise diagonally in contextual sympathy at the corner nearest the old Lodge. Here a large corner window lighting the double height reading room features more of the bright green window framing. This slices through the grid with the horizontal bands stopping short while the verticals, together with their brick panels, hang in mid-air, apparently unsupported. The central bay of the gallery wing is projected forward, and features a small glazed gazebo-like enclosure projecting back into one of the upstairs gallery rooms, where visitors can gain relief from the exhibition and enjoy views out over the river. This is centred on the long rectangular pool in the middle of the stone-paved terrace below and sits over a gap in the massive bright red timber pergola placed against the stone-faced base of the building.

Once past the green revolving door, the visitor immediately enters a large and spatially complex entrance hall. A large curved reception desk to the left occupies the internal corner of the building, to the right a pair of doors, with a triangular window at high level, lead to the reading room, and straight ahead the raking pure white solid balustrade of the main staircase climbs from left to right. Behind the sloping soffits of the gabled entrance screen the ceiling is flat until it disappears into the huge toplit void directly over the flights of the main stairs and the front part of an upper level balcony defining the rear wall of the staircase. Daylight floods down from above, giving an outdoor feeling which is reinforced by the reappearance on the back wall of the same decorative square grid that appears on the outside. The most intriguing aspect of the staircase is not its relatively simple design, nor even the bright pink handrail, but that it leads away from the Turner galleries, not towards them. The visitor has to make a U-turn at the head of the staircase and proceed back along its length to get access to the galleries. A balcony-like corridor appears to lead one towards a round-arched opening in the end wall picked out in lurid blue and violet stripes. This is offset from the pedestrian route and set on the axis of the stairs at the end of the toplit space, so that one does not pass through the arch as expected but instead passes round the side and through a pair of swing doors.

The reward for successfuly negotiating this bizarre layout is to gain entrance to a world far removed from the formal mannerisms and aggressive hues of the architect's creation, dominated instead by the great painter's finest works. The main suite of galleries contains nine rooms. The first to be entered is the largest room, the visitor entering either side of a central column supporting a projecting semi-circular mezzanine balcony. To one side on the central cross-axis of this room runs a long "spine" room, with two secondary galleries placed to each side, accessible only from the long gallery, not interlinked. The route concludes with another large room, its main axis at right-angles to the gallery. The colour scheme in these rooms, in which the gallery not the architect had the final say, is subdued and non-committal. Buff carpets, off-white paint and the warm, natural colours of timber in the floors and skirtings give due prominence to the rich and varied palette of Turner's paintings. Even this has caused considerable controversy, however, among those who would opt for a period style of rich and sombre background colours, such as the Indian Red used by Turner in his own gallery. Advocates of this approach may feel happier in the reserve galleries and the room reserved for watercolours, which are decorated in darker colours and have a denser hanging of pictures, though not to the crowded extremes of the Academy walls of old. The lighting of the gallery spaces combines natural and artificial lighting, with computer-controlled external sun blinds which adjust automatically and a central reflective spine that acts as a light scoop, bathing the pictures and wall surfaces with daylight. In normal conditions the centre of the room is slightly darker than the perimeter, producing an ideal atmosphere for viewing the paintings.

Attendances at the new gallery certainly owe something to the controversial nature of the architect's design for the gallery building, but whether this rather than Turner's paintings is the real attraction for most visitors is more difficult to divine. Certainly there is an increasing tendency for the museum as a building to become a cultural and art object in its own right and an excuse for all manner of self-indulgent architectural exploits of doubtful relevance to its actual contents. However, there can be no doubt that, at a cost of £7·7 million (the price of some single paintings these days) the Tate and London have acquired a valuable new cultural venue and Turner a worthy showplace for his genius.

RESIDENTIAL BUILDING, FITZWILLIAM COLLEGE, CAMBRIDGE

Architects: MacCormac, Jamieson, Prichard & Wright

In comparison with some of its more historic sister colleges, Fitzwilliam College is a relative newcomer to the Cambridge scene, having started life as Fitzwilliam House, in Trumpington Street, as recently as 1889. The college moved from there to its present site on the Huntingdon Road in the early 1960s, into a new building designed as the first phase of a larger development, by the architect Denys Lasdun. In the planning of this new college, a number of the long established traditions inherent in the physical arrangement and usage of the older established central colleges were deliberately ignored. However, old habits die hard and over the years the occupants gradually re-asserted their preferences for more convenient routes of entry and departure over the original design intentions. It was for this and other practical reasons related to the usage of the site, as much as a desire to return to traditional patterns of accommodation, that prompted the governing body of the College in 1983 to commission MacCormac, Jamieson, Prichard & Wright to prepare a new master plan for the completion of the college and to undertake the detailed design of the new phase of student accommodation.

The scheme proposed by the architect entailed a rethinking of two of the key elements of the original design and master plan. Firstly, the main entrance to the college was repositioned to coincide with the point which had by general usage become established as such, though not as originally designed, on the main street frontage instead of tucked away down an unimportant side road. Secondly, the original development concept of an expanding spiral of growth was abandoned and the original layout of buildings was extended instead into a more formal and controlled geometric arrangement of interlinked and partly cloistered courtyards, on the traditional model. The first phase of the College's expansion has now opened, housing some 85 undergraduates and two resident and four non-resident fellows out of the projected number of 430 students. It is expected that the rooms will double up for use during vacation conferences and by visiting professors.

A substantial part of the college site is not currently available for development, being the site of a large Regency period villa, The Grove, and its exotically planted garden, which boasts a number of large mature trees. When the college is able to take over The Grove and its garden the new building will be extended with further residential wings, and it is proposed to link all the buildings together by means of a cloister forming a sheltered circulation route around the college. This would be single sided, although punctuated by further small buildings such as a Chapel, so as to preserve the peaceful garden ambience of The Grove, which will provide secluded accommodation for masters and visiting professors.

The layout of the new building returns to the time honoured Oxford and Cambridge tradition of student rooms arranged in groups around a communal staircase. In this instance the rooms are stacked two to each side, front and back, and each staircase therefore serves eight rooms per floor, generating a very economical section and use of space. The staircases are one of the key elements of the design not only because of their traditional social function in linking groups of rooms, thereby generating a feeling of community among the students, but also because of the opportunity that they present for the exploitation of a multitude of spatial, structural and compositional possibilities. Where the standard college staircase often presents a dark and rather forbidding space, the staircases at Fitzwilliam have been developed around the concept of vertical shafts of light penetrating deep into the interior from high level rooflights running down the spine of the building. The staircase spaces have been given further social importance by their close and subtle relationship with the only other truly communal spaces, the student kitchens. These are the vital social centres of student life, each kitchen being a semi-private yet semi-public domain where one can carry out private tasks or fish for company.

Each flight of stairs rises to a first floor landing three steps lower than the actual first floor level. Here it divides into two flights climbing to right and left within a tall cruciform top-lit light-well. Two small flights beyond the landing lead to a lobby for each of the groups of four rooms to left and right. On the other side, suspended over the lower flight and overlooking the branching of the staircase flights, is perched the communal kitchen, behind a gridded glazed timber screen. This reinforces the semi-private/public nature of the room, providing a degree of privacy from the cirulation routes, yet permitting the occupants to observe all who come and go. From the main landing, the pairs of flights diverge in opposite directions to give access to further groups of eight rooms. The subtlety of the planning here is that each second floor group of eight rooms exactly bridges the two opposite halves of groups on the lower floor and is therefore served by two communal staircases, the ascending flights of each being linked to the other by a corridor. The use of glazed doors within this uppermost corridor presents the visitor with a stunning vista along the complete length of the axis of the building, though to journey along this vista would require an athletic series of ascents and descents to and from the first floor landings.

The complex and varying arrangement of the staircase cores has a knock-on effect in the complexity of the room profiles. The arrangement of the rooms differs on each floor, although there is the background discipline of a 1·5 metre structural grid running through all floors. The rooms have been laid out to provide as many alternative furniture arrangements as possible, the length of a bed being the critical dimension in the planning of the individual spaces, so students may imprint their own personality on their room. Much of the furniture has been designed by the architect to be completely movable, the only fixed elements in the room being the wardrobe, the wash-hand basin and a bay window seat.

Coupled with the formal geometry of the staircases and the organization of groups of rooms, the bay window in each of the rooms serves as a major determinant of the architectural form and treatment of the exterior façades. The windows are a means of imparting a particular quality of daylight to each of the rooms, and offer a range of both oblique and direct views over the courtyard and gardens. An attempt has been made to create the feel of a balcony by eliminating as much of the intervening structure between floor and ceiling as possible. This is assisted by the framing of the lower part of the window to look like a glazed "balustrade", and by the introduction of a glass frieze above the normal lintel/string course level to flood light directly on to the ceiling plane from the perimeter. The effect is somewhat mitigated by the continuous curtain rail but nevertheless produces a pleasant enough feature. Each frieze is capped by a shallow, leaded roof projecting out beyond the general building line.

The staggering of the bay windows on plan, and the displacement of the rooms floor to floor generated by the staircase planning, gives rise to a complex and strongly modelled elevational treatment. The building is strongly layered horizontally, with panels of purple/grey brickwork supported at each floor level

on exposed precast concrete elements which form a prominent double string course to each storey at cill and window head levels. The precast concrete elements are given a warm pale buff colour and lightly textured by careful sand-blasting with a mixture of Somerford Keynes aggregate in white Portland cement, and they create a crisp yet sympathetic colour contrast to the warm darker colours of the brickwork. The staircases are entered through a recessed, double-height, glazed opening in the centre of a projecting stepped "portico" formed from each articulated group of six stepped rooms and balconies on the courtyard side.

Internally, the fitting-out features the extensive use of ash and the predominant gridded geometry of glazed timber screens. These are stained a deep Chinese red, contrasting with the black and grey in the joinery of the doors, architraves and staircase flights and panelling. The central high-level rooflights are also framed in red metal sections, and are made to appear continuous down the length of the building, though they are not, by the judicious placing of mirrors in the apex of the roof. The interior spaces are impressive, both in the sombre dignified use of colour and the three-dimensional complexity generated by the unusual staircase planning, and the outward appearance is certainly packed with incident. The building as a whole has a considerable presence and is a most distinguished and cleverly crafted addition to the post-war architecture of the city.

THE WAVES LEISURE CENTRE, BLACKBURN

Architect: Faulkner Browns

In the last ten years the concept of the municipal swimming pool has undergone a radical transformation, and the new generation of leisure pools now embraces a fantasy world of glamour and excitement far removed from the traditional eight-lane, 50 metres length of the competitive swimming fraternity. The Waves Leisure Centre in Blackburn opened in August 1986 with a full array of the latest water features and leisure activities. Geysers, waterfalls, spa pools, tropical plants, fitness training areas, and the now obligatory wave machine and flume ride are all housed in an architectural enclosure of appropriate dramatic quality and popular appeal.

The building is situated in the centre of the town on what was a derelict urban site opposite the Victorian College of Technology and Design. With the King George's Hall, a library, and the old swimming pool in close proximity, The Waves forms a new heart in the town's cultural centre. Its three-dimensional form is basically that of a wedge-shaped square approximately 48 metres long on each side with a monopitch sloping roof. Out of this simple shape a large triangular bite has been taken opposite a similarly shaped open area fronting the Technical College, and both these areas have been paved and landscaped to create an outdoor piazza. The entrance to the Centre is located at the apex of the triangular "bite" and the two angled sides thus created face the new square and receive the most dramatic elevational treatment. The visitor is left in no doubt as to the function of the building, and is offered enticing glimpses of the fantasy world within.

The flume and the wave machine, those essential ingredients of the modern fun pool, have each in their own way inspired the architectural form and treatment of the entrance elevation. The tubular water chute of the flume, constructed in bright pink double-skin glass reinforced plastic, actually breaks free of the building. It emerges at a high level from its glazed staircase tower near the "prow" of the building and meanders in mid-air over the paved entrance area before re-entering through a long, glazed, wavy curtain wall overlooking the main pool area. The rippling waves of glass are an obvious reference to the machine housed within, as well as the name chosen for the building. They aslo lend a fairground feel with their distorting reflections of the outside world, while the apparent simplicity of their sensuous curves conceals a high degree of technological expertise.

The sense of excitement and expectation engendered by the architectural treatment of the exterior is further enhanced by the view through the serpentine glazing which reveals the improbable delights of a tropical lagoon glinting below. The gentle curves lead enticingly on under the flume slide, through the main entrance and into the glazed balustrade of an open balcony foyer from which the full drama of the pool and its many features can be observed before one reaches the control point and payment desk. This dramatic viewpoint is made possible by the architect's successful exploitation of the fall in levels across the site and the placing of the entrance foyer at the highest level. From here the visitor proceeds downwards past a central circular cafeteria through three levels of open terracing, with seating and tables under special lighting "sunshades" and palm tree planting, to the shallow end of the pool referred to as "the beach", or via the circular staircase tower to the basement changing room which is directly alongside and open to the pool. The changing room is designed for mixed usage and has shoulder-high coloured glass changing cubicles, together with separate lockers, arranged in an open plan style with direct access to the "beach" end of the pool. By this means the leisure atmosphere and close relationship of visitors with the pool is maintained throughout all areas of the building, even within the changing area, traditionally a rather grim and unpleasant environment hidden away from view.

The pool itself adopts a free-form shape but with faceted straight sides rather than curvilinear shapes, an alternative to both the normal rectangular pool and the equally overplayed kidney-shape layout which makes an interesting contrast with the long curves of the curtain wall. It is a broad expanse of water, with the raised splash pool at the end of the spiralling water chute of the flume projecting into it and marking the transition from the shallow to the deep end. The pool is arranged diagonally across the square plan shape, starting with the deep end at the corner formed by the curved glazing and the "fitness area" situated over the wavemaking equipment. Then come the shallower pool areas, into which projects an underwater ledge forming a shallow lagoon terminating in the cluster of four geysers and containing further water fountains. At the terrace end the pools terminate in the shallow "beach" end on one side and on the other a high-level 20-seater spa pool with a surrounding moat which overflows as a waterfall into the main lagoon. The interior colour scheme is in gentle hues of pink and blue set against the white of the steel structure and service ducts and highlighted by the vivid red and blue terrace seats. This, together with an imaginative use of lighting techniques—small fluorescent lights within the cafe "umbrellas", backlighting to the planted areas, uplighting of the roof from column-mounted luminaires, underwater spotlights around the pool perimeter—creates an interior of great vigour, variety and excitement, and what must appear to many to be a rather surreal fantasyland in the centre of Blackburn.

Because of the overall construction time and the sequence of building operations a structural steel frame was used. This enabled the main frame and roof to progress ahead of more time-consuming operations such as the complicated concretework involved in forming the irregularly shaped pool. High yield steel has been used to minimise steel section sizes and the entire structural system is exposed internally. The roof is supported on seven 4 metre wide triangulated steel V-trusses, which vary in length up to a maximum of 44 metres. These are supported in turn on internal steel columns on an 8 metre spacing between centrelines, the columns being located at varying points within the overall 4 metre grid to suit the planning of the various internal elements. Being set orthogonal with the grid within the square profile of the building, the trusses pass diagonally over the pool and meet the principal diagonal axis of the curving glazed entrance wall at 45°. At the junction of the two elements, the main trusses stop short of the perimeter and a continuous tubular steel truss follows the curving line of the curtain wall.

The sophisticated curved curtain wall is some 7 metres in height and employs a system of composite aluminium trussed mullions. Lightness of structure was achieved by incorporating a standard box section into a vertical truss to provide vertical bracing against wind loads, and by organizing the curved double-glazed units in such a way that they act structurally and transmit their weight downwards, rather than, as usual with curtain walling, sideways via the transoms onto the mullions. The vertical mullion trusses are in turn braced to the transoms, which here act only as spacer members, by means of steel outriggers, which provide sufficient stiffening over their 7 metre length to prevent buckling.

The same basic curtain wall system, without the trussed bracing, is used in all the external glazing, both in the perimeter high-level clerestory, which steps down at intervals to provide daylight to internal rooms and the main pool area, and in the prominent glazed staircase tower. The tower, half inside and half outside the building, utilizes a faceted series of glazed curtain wall units to enclose the stunning stainless steel spiral flume access stair.

The quality of materials and detailing, if not the same degree of incident, is maintained in the elevations of the three remaining sides of the building. The perimeter walls are of cavity blockwork construction, utilizing on the interior shot blasted blocks with a false perpendicular joint, and on the exterior reconstituted coloured Bath stone blocks, again with a false perpendicular joint. Although laid in stretcher bond, the false joints in the blocks give the finished walls the appearance of being built in smaller, unbonded, square blocks. A string course of polished reconstituted granite follows the stepped profile of the glazing line above and encloses a lower plinth area faced in the same blocks, though these have a ribbed finish with alternate faces polished. These subtle variations in texture and colour, heavy at the bottom, plainer and lighter at the top, serve to impart a degree of character and interest to what would otherwise be plain and unrelieved expanses of wall.

Above all else, the most memorable feature of this memorable building is the 60 metre long flume in its flamingo pink translucent tube, which carries adventurous bathers on a running stream of water through twists and turns, eventually spiralling down into its own splash pool. Despite the fact that their main attraction is the sense of potential danger and the latest designs favour longer, more complex and steeper inclines, safety is of course still of prime importance. Great attention was paid to its design and testing by a team of specialists, to the extent that modifications simplifying the original design were subsequently implemented.

The people of Blackburn can surely be envied for their new, exciting and adventurous tropical playground, while both the architect and the client,

Blackburn Borough Council, must be commended for their enthusiastic commitment to quality in design and finish. The Waves is an outstanding and original contribution to the civic centre of Blackburn.

THE MOUND STAND, LORD'S CRICKET GROUND, LONDON

Architects: Michael Hopkins & Partners

Early in 1985 the M.C.C. invited a limited number of architectural practices to submit proposals for a new stand to replace the old Mound Stand, designed by Frank Verity and built in 1898–99; the project to be completed in time for the 200th anniversary of Lord's and the M.C.C. in 1987. Verity's original stand occupied the easternmost corner of the ground, extending part way along the St. John's Wood Road frontage. One of the earliest of the more steeply raked stands, it was noted for its excellent sightlines, if for little else. The curved eastern section of the stand had been commenced to a design which incorporated a brick arched colonnade at the rear of the raked concrete terracing. However, after seven arches had been completed in this manner the remainder of the structure was completed with a second rate *ad hoc* steel structure which by the early 1980s was clearly in need of attention. A prime requirement of any proposal was the need to resolve and programme the design and construction work not only to meet the 1987 deadline but also to satisfy the M.C.C.'s stipulation that construction work would be permitted only outside the cricket season.

This latter consideration proved to be a determining factor in the selection of the winning scheme, as Hopkins' proposal was the only one to recommend the retention of the existing terraces. Hovering over the solid base of the retained stand, the architect proposed an elegant, lightweight, and to all intents totally independent, steel superstructure designed to replace the existing roof. It would provide shading to the terraces and at the same time house the additional accommodation required. This particular solution matched the needs of the tight building schedule most satisfactorily and enabled the construction programme to be organized into two distinct phases. Phase 1, completed in the winter of 1985–86, comprised the restoration of and alterations to the original Mound Stand. The addition of private boxes, debenture seating, and new restaurants, bars and cloakroom facilities in the independent superstructure followed in Phase 2, completed the following winter. The retention of the majority of the existing Mound Stand was further justified on economic grounds: when no additional terraced seating capacity had been requested, it could be considered excessively extravagant to rebuild totally a stand which, surprisingly, is only filled to capacity for some eight days a year, during Test Matches and Cup Finals.

Having made the decision to retain the basic elements of Verity's stand, it was only logical that Verity's original design intentions should be completed with the extension of the brick arched colonnade for the full length of the stand. This has been faithfully carried out in accordance with the principles of traditional brick construction, to the extent that the external voussoirs were constructed in rubbed bricks (hand rubbed to a template) using London stock bricks salvaged from a demolished Victorian factory building in Camberwell. It is a pity that the pointing of the brickwork has not received the same dedicated attention to detail, being coarse and heavy where, particularly within the rubbed voussoirs, it should be neat and unobtrusive to unify the curved lines of the arches as they spring from the contrasting reconstituted stone abutments at the heads of the columns.

Where the new colonnade fronts St John's Wood Road, the arched openings are filled with simple but handsome new tubular steel railings. This gives passers-by a glimpse of activities within the enclosure and the street a magnificent elevation, while allowing plenty of daylight to penetrate into the open concourse and the accommodation slotted in beneath the terracing. With accommodation for shops, first aid, lavatories, police room and a bar, this area has been extensively replanned and refurbished, with new work and detailing carried out in the manner and style of Verity to reinforce the feeling of an older structure brought sympathetically up-to-date.

The massive and simply detailed brick arches form a most satisfying and convincing base for the bravura display of engineering skills which floats over the top. The new superstructure is essentially a three-storey addition: a layer of private boxes and dining rooms, with catering facilities; on the top level, a raking layer of debenture and private seating backed by open-planned restaurant and bar areas; and an intermediate mezzanine floor housing lavatories, water tanks and services as well as a caterers' store and staff locker room. This large mass of accommodation hovers over the old terrace supported by a single row of six slender columns that penetrate the roofline and act as masts supporting the roof.

The structural solution displays considerable daring as well as ingenuity, and is set out on a module derived from the spacing of the brick arches in Verity's extended colonnade. The principal columns, which are in fireproofed tubular steel and only 406 mm. in diameter, are spaced at 18·3 metre centres and thus align with every fifth pier of the arcade, the arch module being 3·66 metres. It was fortunate that this dimension corresponds very closely with that required for the private boxes, which are therefore organised on the same module. This enables a consistent geometry to run through the entire building from layer to layer despite the radically different forms of construction used in the different layers.

At mezzanine level, the principal columns support a series of huge storey-height plate girders that act as the spine of the building. From this central spine projects a series of ribs, in a mixture of plate and lattice girder construction, which are cantilevered forwards to support the seating and boxes on the pitch side and backwards towards the road. The lowest tier, comprising the 27 private boxes, eight dining rooms and a kitchen, is then suspended from this level with 76 mm. diameter solid steel hangers supporting steel floor beams on the 3·66 metre grid. The rib beams and suspended structure are placed asymmetrically about the central row of columns to produce a slight imbalance. A second storey-height plate girder running continuously along the rear (outer side) of the building picks up the out-of-balance loads. The whole structure is prevented from toppling in towards the ground by means of vertical steel ties in 110 mm. diameter solid steel, with an additional grout-filled steel sleeve for fire protection, attached to the girder on each of the principal column lines. Being coincident with the piers of the brick arcade beneath, the ties run down the centre of the piers to concrete pile foundations and are housed within vertical recesses in the brickwork. However, in certain conditions, for instance in a northerly wind, the ties can go into compression rather than tension, so to avoid buckling they are tied back to the load-bearing masonry structure with straps.

To support the roof, the six columns of the superstructure project upwards as masts supporting, via an array of struts, spars and catenary cables, a series of cone-shaped tent-like peaks formed in translucent P.V.C.-coated woven polyester fibre fabric. From each of the six masts is suspended a circular frame to which the cable tensioned roof fabric rises in a cone-shape from horizontal booms projecting forwards and backwards from the masts out beyond the line of the fabric roof edge. Further steel cable rigging connects adjacent masts with each other and the tips of the projecting booms, and between each pair of masts is slung a secondary, but larger, fabric cone. These rise higher than the mast cones and give the roof profile added variety and interest. It is a dramatic, festive and apt reinterpretation of the village green marquee theme and has also a strong nautical flavour, with the whiteness and openness of the spaces and the somewhat spartan quality of the finishes.

In many respects, and particularly with regard to detailing, finishes and servicing standards, it must be remembered that this building is designed as an open-air and predominantly fair-weather structure; a shelter (for some) from the worst excesses of sun as well as rain rather than an enclosed building with a controlled internal environment in the normal sense. This explains the simplicity, almost crudeness, of a lot of the detailing, the general robustness of the finishes, and the absence of normal comforts such as heating, insulation, draft lobbies, weather seals and even, in places, rainwater gutters. For instance, the glass folding doors to the front of the private boxes have no seals and are open all round, while the glass wind barrier to the upper deck promenade is merely a freestanding head-high glass screen. Elsewhere, the plate girders forming the central core of the structure are used to form the external walls of the lavatories and service areas, exposed both inside and out as a single uninsulated sheet of steel. The walls at the rear of the private boxes are of a single skin of 200 mm. square glass blocks, which allows borrowed light to penetrate the internal spine corridor, and the external roadside elevation presents a similar full-height glazed block wall treatment for the private dining room and kitchen areas.

The topmost floor, with obstructions kept deliberately low under the soaring canopy, is a magnificent space affording excellent views out over the pitch and the surrounding streets, and the quality of the light filtering down through the translucent fabric cones is superb. The lightness and elegance of the structure generates an appropriately festive atmosphere, and the exploitation of the curved plan heightens the sense of involvement of the audience not only with the game but with other spectators. The M.C.C. must be applauded for their obvious commitment to architectural quality and the architect has certainly repaid their patronage with an unusual building of the highest calibre.

SCHOOL OF ART AND DESIGN, NEWCASTLE UPON TYNE

Architects: Newcastle City Architects Department

Schools of art and design are traditionally associated with the tall, naturally lit spaces and resilient but battered finishes typical of our heritage of Victorian and Edwardian educational institutions. Bright, new, well-designed buildings do not often come the way of the students of these disciplines. However, the recently completed Newcastle School of Art and Design is a refreshing exception, presenting staff and students with a bold, intelligently-designed environment.

The new school encompasses a wide range of disciplines, from graphics, photography, fashion, advertising and printing, to ceramics, sculpture, painting and three-dimensional studies. It includes areas specifically designed for exhibition and display of students' work, as well as the usual range of back-up facilities such as tutorial rooms, staff rooms,

canteen, library and resources centre, workshops and plant rooms. The task of creating a new home for all these disciplines was not made any easier by the requirements of central government financing and city council politics, which determined that the entire procurement process through briefing, consultation, design and construction phases should take no more than 30 months from start to finish.

Given these restrictions the architects decided upon a structural system using prefabricated factory-produced components and a steel frame form construction. With the rapid progress made possible by using a large number of separate subcontract packages, the structure and weatherproofing elements were completed in the surprisingly short time of 11 months, and fitting-out of the interior started much earlier than would have been the case using traditional techniques.

The building is planned on three floors, and the sloping site is exploited by the location of the main entrance at the upper end to give access to the middle level. The upper two floors are planned around a central spine of circulation and seminar/tutorial rooms defined by the spacing of the 12·5 metre clear span structural bays of the studio accommodation on either side, with a full height galleried hall running almost half the length of the building. The lowest floor, cut into the slope and not as large as the upper floors, is, apart from two staircases, totally separated from the upper floors. With its internal race-track corridor planning and absence of natural light or dramatic spatial focus, it is totally different in atmosphere from the upper levels, and noticeably cut off from the mainstream of social activity centred on the galleried hall. Though substantially at ground level because of the fall of the site and benefiting from daylight on the three external elevations, the students have taken to calling this area 'the basement', and there can be no doubt that activities consigned to this part of the building miss out on the crossfertilization of ideas that arises from the communal use of the central space on the upper levels.

The 4 metre grid of the structural frame is expressed in the cladding to the external elevations, which are faced with proprietary cladding panels spanning between the steel stanchions. These have an exterior face P.V.F.-coated in a silver colour, and an internal acrylic-coated face with a polyurethane core. The column lines are picked out with 400 mm. cover panels of the same construction in white, with 300 mm. panels positioned horizontally at floor levels. Glazing is continuous between the columns, with an extruded aluminium double-glazed window system and glazing bars dividing the windows into square panes. Projecting outwards from the upper two storeys and suspended from the outer edge of the deep roof overhang, is a combined *brise-soleil* and maintenance catwalk with a galvanised steel open mesh floor, its supporting steel hangers and diagonal bracing picked out in bright blue paint. The roof covering is a profiled steel composite panel acrylic-coated in blue or silver, maintaining the principle of prefabricated and dry forms of construction for the most of the building's external envelope. The upper level studio spaces are spanned by steel lattice trusses which are exposed to view beneath the white acrylic-coated and profiled steel liner panels of the roof construction. These continue into a sharper pitched profile over the central spine supporting the extensive rooflights which bring daylight to flood down into the hall below. Being an institution dedicated to art and design, it is appropriate that the architectural framework for these activities should embrace some works of art and fitting that a contribution should have been made by artist-in-residence, Susan Bradbury. This takes the form of a number of stained glass windows, which light the large seminar room projecting out over the main entrance. These incorporate an abstract design, combining linear and freeform elements, which flow through the regular geometric patterns framing each of the square window panels. It is a subtle and decorative piece of work, its colours echoing the silver and blue of the elevations, its flowing abstract character a welcome contrast to the crisp modelling and simple geometry of the exterior. It is displayed to great advantage at night, particularly when seen in conjunction with the illuminated shopfront-type showcases placed around the main entrance.

Once past the main entrance, one enters a cool and disciplined interior, and a foyer less suggestive of an art school than of an up-market and glamorous shopping centre, with shopfront display windows, a brilliant white tiled floor and polished chrome slatted ceiling. A glazed enclosure to the staircase at the far end of the foyer contains further window display areas with glazed doors to either side, and projects like a ship's prow into the double-height space beyond, giving glimpses of the light and airy interior of the exhibition hall and galleries.

The major architectural feature of the building is unquestionably this central galleried hall. This stunning space has dramatic stage-set staircases at each end, sinuous runs of exposed ductwork, futuristic shining white floor and multiple triangular windows giving glimpses of the adjacent studio spaces. It functions as circulation, meeting and exhibition space, and must be used by all who pass through the building, be they students, staff or visitors. The triangular motif is paramount not only in the studio windows overlooking the hall but also in the bracing of the steeply pitched steel roof trusses and the space frame system used to support the balustrades and exposed air handling ducts at the level of the gallery. This doubles up as a support system for exhibition stands in the main hall. Despite the onerous requirements of the fire regulations, which determined that the central hall must be designed to a one hour fire compartment rating, the architects have achieved the maximum possible degree of transparency and lightness with the glazing of the enclosing walls. The whiteness, the cleanliness, and the smooth hard quality of the prominent and extensive metal finishes generate an image in keeping with a brave new world of nuclear power and space exploration. It will no doubt strike a suitably impressive chord in the minds of students arriving for interview, and ensures that the Newcastle School now possesses a memorable image to back up the reputation it has earned for its courses.

The £4 million building was officially opened in April 1987, although construction work was completed in August 1986 after a 19 month construction period. The standard of finishes is, predictably, rather rudimentary, although carefully detailed, and will require rigorous attention to maintenance and cleaning. The occupants may at times feel cramped for space as a result of economies imposed by the cost targets, but the building provides students with the opportunity to benefit from the easy interaction of a great many creative activities.

PERIODS OF GESTATION AND INCUBATION

The table shows approximate periods of gestation or incubation for some common animals and birds. In some cases the periods may vary and where doubt arises professional advice should be sought.

Species	Shortest Period. Days	Usual Period. Days	Longest Period. Days	Species	Shortest Period. Days	Usual Period. Days	Longest Period. Days
Human	240	273	313	Duck	28	28	32
Mare	305	336	340	Goose	28	30	32
Ass	365	—	374	Pigeon	17	18	19
Cow	273	280	294	Canary	12	14	14
Ewe	140	147–50	160	Guinea Pig	63	—	70
Goat	147	151	155	Mouse	18	—	19
Sow	109	112	125	Rat	21	—	24
Bitch	55	63	70	Elephant		21–22 months	
Cat	53	56	63				
Rabbit	30	32	35	Camel		45 weeks	
Hen	20	21	22	Zebra		56 weeks	
Turkey	25	28	28				

ARCHITECTURAL CONSERVATION: 1986–87

The twelve months under review brought changes in the laws that affect historic buildings. In November 1986 the Housing and Planning Bill received the royal assent, after some bumpy final stages in the House of Lords. Among the changes it introduces is a strengthening of the power of local authorities to insist on repairs at listed buildings in a state of neglect, a circumscription in the powers of District Surveyors to demolish "dangerous" historic buildings without consent, and some rationalization of the legal exemption enjoyed by ecclesiastical buildings. The situation as it affects the Church of England remains largely unaltered but the Secretary of State took to himself permissive powers to limit exemption by particular denomination, to specified parts of the building, or according to the nature of the works proposed. The Government has made it clear that it intends to use these powers only in respect of non-Anglican places of worship and of exteriors rather than interiors. An attempt at the report stage in the Lords to introduce a statutory appeal against listing was defeated by 35 votes to 14.

The report of the Environment Committee of the House of Commons on "Historic Buildings and Ancient Monuments" was published on January 21: it made 42 recommendations. Some of them, particularly the introduction of a rolling cut-off date whereby all buildings over 30 years old would be eligible for listing in England, were accepted almost immediately by the Government. This development brings England into line with the current provisions for Scotland and Wales, although the English policy goes further in permitting the listing of buildings of outstanding quality "in very exceptional circumstances" when they are only 10 years old.

Other recommendations included more power for English Heritage (giving it executive roles in listing historic buildings and scheduling ancient monuments, and the power to serve Building Preservation Notices and Repair Notices) and more money. The latter was proposed for the specific purposes of speeding up the schedule enhancement programme by which the number of scheduled sites would increase from 13,000 to 60,000, and to facilitate grant-aiding of historic gardens. The Committee was opposed to a right of appeal against listing, favouring tougher controls within Conservation Areas, greater delegation to local authorities in the allocation of grants in such Areas, and the extension of grants offered by the National Heritage Memorial Fund to cathedrals "in cases of exceptional need". The recommendation that hit the headlines was that cathedrals should introduce a recommended, but not compulsory, admission charge of at least £1 per head to finance programmes of repair and maintenance and to create a common fund upon which poor cathedrals could draw: it received a frosty response from most Deans and Chapters. The Committee also lent its voice to the chorus of criticism at the levying of V.A.T. on repair work to historic buildings.

1986 witnessed applications to demolish in their entirety 557 listed buildings in England and Wales. These applications, including those submitted in the first three quarters of 1987, threatened: The White House in Gilwell Park, Waltham Abbey, Essex, a 16th and 19th century structure in the middle of a camping and adventure site; a number of mostly Georgian properties in the way of an inner ring road in Darlington; Highhead Castle, Ivegill, Cumbria, a ruined early Georgian mansion designed by James Gibbs; Dee House, Little St. John Street, Chester, an 18th century townhouse and former Ursuline convent with a fine interior; Netherwitton Mill, Northumberland (1794); the Catholic Apostolic Church, Canning Street, Liverpool, a remarkable design of c. 1848; the Town Hall (1831 and 1882), Stalybridge, Greater Manchester; Glebe Farmhouse, Nettleton, Lincs., which has 15th century origins; Belgrave Chapel, Darwen, Lancs., a highly individual design of 1847 by Edward Walters; the Italianate-style Mechanics Institute, Huddersfield (1859); the late medieval aisled barn at Wadlands Hall Farm, Pudsey, Leeds; a barn of slightly later date with seven pairs of cruck blades at Burgh-by-Sands, Cumbria; one of the turn-of-the-century model houses constructed at Letchworth, the first Garden City; a chapel at Sudbury Hill, Harrow, designed by Sir Giles Gilbert Scott in 1906; the Dunlop Rubber Factory, Brynmawr, Gwent, constructed 1945–1951 and regarded as one of the most impressive post-war structures in Wales; the former railway station, Louth, Lincs. (1854); the Friends Meeting House, Malton, N. Yorks. (1823); the surviving stables and kitchen of the great Baroque house at Stoke Edith, Herefordshire, otherwise destroyed by fire in 1927; Stanley Farmhouse, Filton, Avon, a model farm designed by George Godwin in 1860 for the Duke of Beaufort; the late 18th century stables, probably by James Wyatt, at Belmont House, Herefordshire; St. George's Church, Barnsley, S. Yorks., by Rickman and Hutchinson (1821); Lintzford Mill, Rowlands Gill, Co. Durham, a paper mill of c. 1840; The Mill House and Stone Farm, Newington, Kent, threatened by the approach road to the Channel Tunnel; a number of early 19th century buildings in Lower Bond Street, Weymouth, threatened by a scheme for a shopping centre and multi-storey car park; Doublebois House, Dobwalls, Cornwall (c. 1885); Hilltop Methodist Church, Burslem, Stoke-on-Trent (1837), where Arnold Bennett's grandfather was Superintendent; and a mid-18th century pigeon cote at Cawood, N. Yorks.

In the same period public inquiries were convened to consider proposals to demolish two substantial warehouses designed by John Dobson at Hudson Dock, Sunderland (permission granted); St. Alban's Church, Teddington, Middx., an unfinished church of the 1880s (permission refused); the stable block and ice house of the late 18th century Eaton Hall, Cheshire; two Georgian terraces in Upper Parliament Street, Liverpool (permission refused); the Square Chapel, Halifax (inquiry cancelled on submission of a proposal to convert); the mid-19th century Shore Baptist Chapel, Todmorden, W. Yorks.; Robinwood Mill, near Todmorden, designed c. 1830 by Sir William Fairbairn (both applications refused); 20–24 North Street, Bourne, Lincs., of the 17th and 18th centuries, properties now almost wholly demolished; the 1919 Grahame-White Hangar at R.A.F. Hendon, location of one of the first schools of aviation; Bournemouth Station (1880s); a "catalogue house" of c. 1910 constructed at Barrow-upon-Soar, Leics., to show off the potential of Portland cement (permission refused); three blast houses at the military complex known as Weedon Depot, Northants., designed in the 19th century during the threat of a Napoleonic invasion; and Castle Farm, Eardisley, Herefordshire, a 17th century domestic building converted to farm use.

But not all is gloom and threats: there are also success stories. In the same twelve months, decisions were announced to repair long-derelict structures at: Congreaves Hall, Cradley Heath, West Midlands (c. 1780); the 16th century house at Plas Teg, near Mold, Clwyd; Branthwaite Hall, Dean, Cumbria, dating from the late 14th century, to be used as offices by British Coal; St. Thomas's Church, Ryde, Isle of Wight (1827), to be a museum and heritage centre; Melton Constable Hall, Norfolk (1664), part of a £3,000,000 scheme that will encompass the reinstatement of the gardens; and one of the most celebrated of Georgian garden buildings, "The Museum" at Enville Hall, Staffordshire. A conference centre and craft workshop costing £1,500,000 was opened in November 1986 in the late Georgian Holy Trinity Church, Halifax. The former gaol and courthouse (1788 and 1844) at Little Dean in the Forest of Dean, Glos., was proposed for conversion to office and computer space.

The longstanding project by Save Britain's Heritage to repair and convert Sir Robert Taylor's outstanding villa of 1756 at Barlaston Hall, Staffs., received a great fillip in the course of 1986 when British Coal agreed to carry out work to prevent further subsidence beneath the Hall and to pay the cost of repairing damage caused by mining in the past. Save Britain's Heritage acquired the Hall from the Wedgwood company in 1981 for £1 during a public inquiry called to consider an application to demolish. The Venezuelan Government's ambitious and painstaking restoration scheme at 58 Grafton Way, London W.1., built in 1792, was completed late in 1986. The interior has been furnished as it would have been in 1805 when the principal occupant was General Francisco di Miranda, who fought alongside Simon Bolivar for the liberation of several South American countries from Spanish domination. Walton Hall, former home of the Greenall brewing family, was opened to the public in July 1986 as a branch museum of Warrington Museum and Art Gallery. Hertfordshire County Council prepared plans for the sensitive reinstatement of the Shire Hall at Hertford, a James Adam design of 1762 somewhat maltreated in the 19th century. The unique Museum of Chimney Pots run by the Rev. Valentine Fletcher was resited off the Market Place in Blandford Forum, Dorset. The late 18th century Countess of Huntingdon's Chapel in Worcester, a Grade II* listed building narrowly saved from demolition, was opened in August 1987 as a concert hall and Elgar Music Centre. At King's College Chapel, Cambridge, a permanent exhibition on the Chapel's history opened to the public in August: it includes a scale model of the fan vaulting. Belford Hall, Northumberland, designed in 1756 by James Paine, was restored and converted to multiple

residential use by the Northern Heritage Trust and the Monument Historic Buildings Trust: it was opened by the Duke of Gloucester in the summer of 1987.

Plans were announced to create museums within the Grade II* listed Manorial Barn at Whiston near Rotherham, in No. 4 High Street and the adjoining warehouse in Paradise Street, Poole, Dorset, and in the Shire Hall (1822) at Norwich. Hereford and Worcester County Council announced their intention to reconstruct an historic tannery building, formerly off Bridge Street in Leominster, to form a new visitors centre in Queenswood. An Historical and Cultural Centre for Pontypridd was opened in the former Welsh Baptist Chapel of 1861. Plans were announced for the creation of a new Museum of Medieval Art in the triforium of the south transept of Winchester Cathedral: the Cathedral hopes that it will prove "one of the most significant displays of medieval art in Europe". An appeal to restore the former church of St. Agatha's, Landport, Portsmouth, was launched on July 18, 1987. The ambitious trustees, who have just saved the church from demolition, want to create a stained glass gallery and museum of ecclesiology. One of the largest cruck buildings in the world, the Leigh Court Barn near Worcester of c. 1300, was taken into guardianship by English Heritage. An Historic Churches Trust was announced for the county of Berkshire, and a study group mooted for historic stables.

It is hard to predict which cases will make the headlines and one of the more unusual to do so in the past year was the proposal to convert St. John's Lodge in Regents Park. Originally designed in 1817 by the relatively unknown John Raffield, its interest increased due to alterations and additions executed throughout the 19th century by the less obscure Decimus Burton, David Mocatta, Charles Barry, Ambrose Poynter and Robert Weir Schultz. A particularly outstanding embellishment is a series of murals by Horatio Lonsdale. Mr. Fred Koch, the American art collector, proposed to lease the building from the Crown Estate Commissioners to house a largely private collection of 19th century art. He chose as his architect Mr. Michael Manser, a former president of the Royal Institute of British Architects. But the project foundered on the problems inherent in trying to reconcile the display of works of art in suitably self-effacing surroundings with the retention of the character of a building which is a work of art in its own right. Following months of controversy Mr. Koch withdrew and purchased instead Sutton Place in Surrey, the outstanding 16th century mansion formerly owned by Paul Getty I.

1988 will see the conclusion of the resurvey of the lists of buildings of special architectural and historic interest protected by law. By that time the total in England alone will be over 400,000. The eligibility of structures for listing is almost inexhaustible. If stone has been placed purposely on stone, or brick on brick, the structure can be listed. Lists already published have included garden walls, sun dials, ice houses, bridges, canal locks, statues, war memorials, horse troughs, bandstands, pillar boxes, lime kilns, turnstiles, milestones and lampposts. The most photographed lampposts in London, those outside No. 10

Downing Street, are listed Grade II. The Department of the Environment recently announced that yet another "building type" is to be eligible. This was the telephone box. British Telecom propose the eventual replacement of all 55,000 of the traditional red boxes or booths. Although there are a number of types running from K2's to K6's (of 1935), nearly all examples were designed for the then General Post Office by Sir Giles Gilbert Scott. The design was celebrated in contemporary and subsequent literature as a telling and thoughtful combination of modern and classical. Particularly distinctive were the "handkerchief domes", some topped with crowns, that owed a great deal to the architecture of Sir John Soane. The Department have set a limit of 700 listings throughout the country: as this allows protection of

only a fraction, the lucky candidates were picked on the basis of their siting, particularly where they were in groups, in Conservation Areas, or adjacent to listed and inter-war buildings. Multiple London listings included examples at Smithfield Market and adjacent to the Sadlers Wells Theatre. Most of the listings were accepted but one application to demolish (refused) was submitted in respect of a box at Avebury, Wilts. Many hundreds of the disused booths were bought by a company established for the express purpose of selling them abroad where they are regarded as symbols, along with the double decker bus, of all that is best about England. Many seem destined to survive in America and Japan as shower booths.

THE NATIONAL HERITAGE MEMORIAL FUND

The National Heritage Memorial Fund spent £6·4 million in 1985–1986, compared with £12·6 million in 1984–1985 and almost £15 million in 1983–1984. This startling variation reflects not a fluctuation in demand but the capriciousness of Government funding. The Fund has been operating under an erratic financial regime since its earliest days, relying on a "topping up" towards the end of the financial year, the certainty of which and the size of which can never be guaranteed. £10·5 million was provided in this way in March 1986.

In 1985–86 the Fund received 210 applications, of which only a quarter were successful. Those projects that received grants included: the conservation of Anglo-Saxon sculpture at St. Paul's Church, Jarrow; the restoration of colliery buildings at the North of England Open Air Museum, Beamish; the purchase for the National Portrait Gallery of the portrait of Admiral Lord Nelson by Beechey; the purchase for the Scott Polar Research Institute, Cambridge, of the papers of Lt. Henry ("Birdie") Bowers, one of the men who died on Captain Scott's last polar expedition; feasibility studies for the establishment of a Ruskin Centre at Brantwood in the Lake District; the purchase for the Walker Art Gallery, Liverpool, of Ford Maddox Brown's "Waiting"; the rehabilitation of four cottages on the island of Canna by the National Trust for Scotland; the purchase for Leeds City Art Gallery of a particularly important late 18th century writing cabinet by Channon; the purchase of the Deer Park at Chatelherault, Scotland, by Hamilton District Council; repair work to the Victorian piers of Bangor, Clevedon and Brighton (West Pier); the purchase of a letter from Captain Cook, written in November 1776, by the National Maritime Museum; the purchase for the Museum of London of probably the earliest surviving engraved copperplate for a map of the City of London of c. 1560; the purchase for Suffolk County Record Office of the Elveden Hall papers; the purchase of the Exminster Marshes, Devon, by the Royal Society for the Protection of Birds; the purchase of the photographic collecton compiled by Francis Frith, with more than 300,000 named negatives dating from 1860–1970, by Birmingham Public Libraries; the repair of the

Grange Farm Barn, Coggeshall, Essex, one of the oldest timber framed buildings in the country dating from c. 1180; the purchase for the Ulster Museum of the Great Seal of Northern Ireland; the safeguarding of the Guesten Hall roof at the Avoncroft Museum of Buildings, Worcs.; the purchase for York Castle Museum of an 18th century longcase clock by Henry Hindley; the purchase of the papers of Leslie Hore-Belisha (1893–1957) by Churchill College, Cambridge; the safeguarding of the Civil War collection of armour at Littlecote House, Wilts.; the purchase by the National Motor Museum of the Lotus "R3" racing car of 1967; a further grant towards the conservation work on the "Mary Rose"; the purchase of Monks Woods by the Worcestershire Trust for Nature Conservation; the continuing programme of repair to the 18th century landscaped garden at Painshill Park, Cobham, Surrey; the purchase on behalf of the R.A.O.C. Museum of the George Cross awarded to Staff Sgt. Sidney Rogerson in 1946; the purchase for the National Portrait Gallery of the bust by Roubiliac of the fourth Lord Chesterfield and the bust of Alexander Pope by Rysbrack; the continued conservation of the 18th century wall paintings at St. Lawrence's Church, Little Stanmore, Middx.; the purchase of 7,000 12th and 13th century coins by Aberdeen Art Gallery; the purchase for the National Library of Scotland of important manuscripts of Sir Walter Scott; the conservation of historic film by the National Film Archive; the purchase of Tintoretto's "Christ Washing the Disciples' Feet" by the Shipley Art Gallery, Newcastle upon Tyne; the recovery of a Wellington Bomber that crashed into Loch Ness in 1940, now on display at the Brooklands Museum; and the purchase of a voice flute (recorder) by Joseph Bradbury of c. 1720 and two natural horns by Nicholas Winkings of c. 1740 by the University of Edinburgh. A substantial payment of £1,544,990 towards the purchase of chattels at Belton House, Lincs., on behalf of the National Trust brought the total N.H.M.F. contribution to that house to £8,954,190. In late 1986 the N.H.M.F. also played a crucial role in securing the long-term future of two outstanding houses, Kedleston Hall in Derbyshire and Nostell Priory in Yorkshire.

THEATRE MUSEUM

The Theatre Museum opened to the public in 1987 in the former Flower Market in Covent Garden, London. With a gestation period almost as long as that for the National Theatre, the story of its growth from gleam in the eye to reality has at times come dangerously close to Greek melodrama, or French farce, as personality fought personality, Governments repeatedly ate their words, and decisions were no sooner taken than undone.

The idea for a theatre museum was first mooted in 1911 in two newspapers "The Referee" and, most appropriately, "The Stage". The prime mover on that occasion was Mrs. Gabrielle Enthoven, who left her considerable private collection of theatre memorabilia to the Victoria and Albert Museum in 1924. The British Theatre Museum Association took up the torch after its foundation in May 1957 and itself became the focus for generous donations, in particular the archives relating to Sir Henry Irving, and the Ivor Novello collection.

The need to find a place to display the collections became imperative and seemed to be answered in 1963 when the Association rented a former children's library in Leighton House, Kensington. The interior was fitted out by Sir Hugh Casson and the Museum opened by Vanessa Redgrave. Within four years, however, funds ran out and closure loomed. The Museum struggled on until 1970 when the V. & A. agreed to take the lead in the establishment of a new museum under its own auspices but in a separate location. The appointment of Alexander Schouvaloff as Curator in 1974 brought to the campaign one of its doughtiest champions. Soon afterwards the premises at Leighton House were closed and the collections transferred to the V. & A. Rooms at Somerset House were offered as accommodation and the autumn of 1976 was set for the opening ceremony but doubts set in over the suitability of the rooms. Museum walls should not compete with exhibits and important critics began to question whether a building as fine as Somerset House had a sufficiently self-effacing interior.

An alternative venue already favourably regarded by some was the former Flower Market in Covent Garden, an exuberant Edwardian Baroque design at the entrance to the piazza. In 1977 the Government and the Greater London Council, which then owned the building, agreed terms and it seemed that at last the Museum had found a home. 1980 was set as a new target for opening, although this was subsequently put back to 1982. By that time a Government report on the future of the Science Museum and the V. & A. had suggested the closure of two museums, one established, the other putative, as a relatively easy way of saving money. The long-established museum was the Bethnal Green Museum of Childhood: that yet to be born was the Theatre Museum. This move to close the Museum before it even opened was reversed by Mr. Paul Channon, then Arts Minister, who announced a reprieve in August 1982 following an indignant hullabaloo from supporters and public—a petition presented to the Minister contained 32,000 signatures. Even this reprieve proved temporary, for less than a year later Government cuts in public expenditure forced the V. & A. to put the whole project on ice. Fortunately, in the best theatrical tradition, an anonymous "angel" donated £250,000 and the G.L.C. also stepped in. A lease for the Flower Market was signed on September 1, 1983 and work on the building began. The building was completed in two and a half years and the installation of the collection took nine months: the overall cost was £3 million. The architect was John Patterson and the designer Anthony Holland. The Museum was opened by Princess Margaret on April 23, 1987, a date chosen for its symbolic significance, being the 423rd anniversary of the birth of Shakespeare.

The word "theatre" is interpreted in its widest sense, the performing arts, and exhibits cover ballet, the circus, mime, opera and pop music as well as theatre. Major developments, events and personalities are illustrated and the atmosphere of theatre created with the help of stage models, costumes, prints and drawings, posters, puppets, props, a variety of memorabilia, and even architecture and sculpture. The most striking feature of the entrance foyer is the giant "Spirit of Gaiety" statue which adorned the Gaiety Theatre, Aldwych, until its demolition in 1957. Entrance tickets to the museum are sold from the old Duke of York's Theatre box office.

As well as its own collections the Museum will draw upon loan material to mount temporary exhibitions and these will be displayed in the two exhibition galleries, named in honour of Sir John Gielgud and Sir Henry Irving. The Museum also provides research facilities through its library, and these will be greatly enhanced when the Museum's archive has moved into the accommodation currently being prepared for it.

(For details of opening times, etc., *see* page 418.)

ARCHAEOLOGY 1986–87

Most archaeologists would agree that the laws protecting ancient monuments and archaeological sites leave something to be desired. Occasionally this professional concern excites more general public interest, as in the case of the Donhead St. Mary Treasure Trove Hoard. A quantity of Durotrigian silver staters, Iron Age coins, was found within the rampart of Castle Rings hill-fort at Donhead St. Mary, Wilts., in October 1985 and a Coroner's inquest declared the hoard to be treasure trove in February 1986. However, the hill-fort was a Scheduled Ancient Monument and the finder was prosecuted under sections 42(1) and 42(3) of the Ancient Monuments and Archaeological Areas Act 1979 for having used a metal detector in a protected place and for removing objects therefrom. The defendant was found guilty and fined £100 for this offence, having also to bear the costs of the case.

The normal practice when treasure trove is discovered is to reward the finder in order to encourage finders of putative hoards to report their discoveries to the appropriate authorities. In this case the Treasure Trove Reviewing Committee, in full knowledge of the court case, made an *ex gratia* payment of £2,000 to the finder. Also following the usual custom, the hoard was offered to a local museum, the Salisbury and South Wiltshire Museum, which would have to find the sum awarded by the Reviewing Committee. Failure to do so would allow the hoard to be returned to the finder, who could then sell it on the open market, either as a complete entity or coin by coin.

The view taken by the Management Committee and staff of the Salisbury and South Wiltshire Museum was that, as hoard had been found in a way which is illegal, it would be quite wrong for the Museum to make available the sum required: such an action would contravene the Museums Association's Code of Practice for Museum Authorities. The Musuem's stand was endorsed by the local M.P., the Museums and Galleries Commission and the Museums Association. Widespread public interest in the matter stemmed from the fact that this is thought to be the first occasion upon which the Treasure Trove Reviewing Committee has recommended an *ex gratia* payment to a person convicted under the 1979 Act and many people were persuaded that a precedent should not be set. Because of the concern expressed, Treasury Ministers in the Spring of 1987 commissioned officials: "To review, within the framework of existing law, the practice and procedures relating to treasure trove, including the payment of *ex gratia* awards to finders; and to report to Treasury Ministers." The results of the review are still awaited but in the meantime the Museums Association has stated that in its view the Treasure Trove Reviewing Committee should at the very least take into account court decisions in circumstances which are adjudged to contravene the provisions of the Ancient Monuments and Archaeological Areas Act 1979. The Association also suggested that the reward for finding and reporting treasure trove should never exceed the amount of any fine imposed on an individual under the relevant legislation in a court of law. It remains to be seen what, if anything, will be done as a result

of the review, but archaeologists cannot be alone in thinking that it must be contrary to public interests to reward people who have been convicted of committing a crime.

Museum of the Iron Age

While many museums have archaeological galleries, it is not often that a new museum is devoted entirely to a particular period rather than to the history of a particular site. 1986 saw the opening of the Museum of the Iron Age in a cleverly converted school building in Andover, Hants. It adjoins the Andover Museum and is part of the Hampshire County Museum Service. A sign of the times is that certain aspects of the new displays have been financed through the generosity of local commercial enterprises.

The reason for siting the Museum of the Iron Age in Andover is the proximity, some six miles to the south-west, of the Iron Age hill-fort of Danebury Ring. Planned archaeological investigations have been undertaken at Danebury Ring since 1969 and over half of the thirteen acre interior has now been investigated. As the handbook to the Museum explains: "The Central West landscape around Danebury presents one of the densest concentrations of Iron Age sites in Europe". The Museum's displays deal with all aspects of Iron Age life including the warrior tradition, settlement within hill-forts, an exposition of the Iron Age round house, and detailed information on farming methods and diet.

During the eighteen years of the project some 200,000 bones have been found at Danebury and from these archaeozoologists have been able to discover what the inhabitants of Danebury ate and how they managed their flocks and herds. The impression is gained of a tough, hierarchically-organised society with a clear belief in the afterlife. Head-hunting was a common practice among the Celtic peoples of Europe and a number of severed heads have been found at Danebury, possibly the remains of enemies. All in all, the Museum of the Iron Age is a successful addition to those museums catering particularly for the archaeologist.

Rescue Archaeology

In August 1987 the Historic Buildings and Monuments Commission for England (English Heritage) published *Rescue Archaeology Funding in 1987–88*. The publication gives details of the way in which money is allocated for the investigation of those sites of archaeological interest which are under threat, whether it be by redevelopment, new roads, or by the activities of public utilities or farming. The planned expenditure for 1987–88 is £7,094,000, which, significantly, includes an extra £100,000 made available by the Department of Transport for archaeological investigations made necessary by trunk road schemes. Of the total sum, about £5·78 million is for grant-aid to archaeological projects by local authorities and other bodies, and of this £750,000 has been allocated as a contingency reserve for the funding of emergency projects during the year.

In 1986–87 the contingency reserve demonstrated

its flexibility by funding projects which ranged in date from the Stone Age to more recent times. One example is the evaluation of the Dorchester bypass route; work was also done at Stansted, Essex, in advance of the building of the new international airport. The Palaeolithic site at Clacton, Essex, was also investigated in advance of building development, and a Neolithic longbarrow at Haddenham, Cambs., was investigated before drainage schemes were carried out. The latter, described as a "notable excavation", yielded the following: "The mound was found to cover a wooden mortuary structure with a roof of oak planks, a lining of oak logs and planks, and massive oak uprights. A banked façade and posts had been placed in front of the eastern end of the mound outside which was a gravel forecourt."

Grants from the reserve were also made to facilitate the excavation of Bronze Age cairns and settlements in Cumbria at Hardendale and Ewen Rigg, work at the settlement at Brean Down in Somerset "revealed a unique series of five Bronze Age occupation horizons and an Early Christian cemetery, stratified in wind-blown sand." Money was also needed to deal with the threat posed to Hadrian's Wall by the Newcastle western bypass and that to Fishbourne Roman Villa in Sussex by the A27 road improvement scheme: this has now destroyed Roman buildings associated with the villa complex.

The majority of the projects funded from the reserve were of medieval date and in towns: contributions were made towards excavations in Newcastle, Kendal, Hartlepool, York, Beverley, Northampton, Ipswich, Chelmsford, Oxford, Shrewsbury, Ware, Canterbury, London, Trowbridge, Poole and Barnstaple. The report notes that: "At Poole, ship-timbers from a medieval boat yard were found. In the countryside, grants were made to Burton Dassett (Warwicks.) medieval village in advance of its destruction by the M40 Oxford–Birmingham motorway. Burton Dassett is a substantially deserted example of a medieval settlement which in the early fourteenth century was one of the most prosperous places in Warwickshire."

The report is important to anyone concerned with the administration and funding of rescue archaeology in England. Important sections deal with the financing of sites in Greater London, and there is an analysis of the various kinds of threat to which the archaeologist is responding. Particularly helpful is that not only successful applications for grants are listed but also those for which financial provision could not be made, indicating the extent to which the provision of money for rescue archaeology falls short of the actual need.

Roman Britain

A comprehensive account of recent work concerned with the Roman period may be found in *Britannia*, Vol. XVII for 1986. Work continues at the major centres of Roman activity such as Hadrian's Wall and the City of London, and from these come fascinating pieces of information. For instance, in 1983 in St. Clare Street, which would have lain outside the City wall of London, two cremations and four inhumations were noted, "together with the base of a possible mausoleum and a ritual pit containing the bones of a heron and over 100 frogs." Another unusual discovery was at Caerleon, Gwent, in 1985 where, in the Museum garden, five fragments of a wooden ink writing-tablet dating to about A.D. 75–85 were found in the filling of a well. Although fragmentary, the surviving part is of an Old Roman Cursive text written across the grain and "characterised by exaggerated descenders for *A* and *N*". Although too much is missing for the text to be translated, it "is clearly part of a military document, of a type hitherto unknown, since it records the future movements of soldiers. These movements seemed to have involved the escort of pay and the supply of building-timbers."

Across in Lincolnshire an excavation at Old Sleaford yielded about 100 fragments of Iron Age coin-moulds together with pottery and four Iron Age coins, as well as Roman pits, gullies and ditches. From one ditch came 280 coins of third and fourth century date, while at Owmby in the same county a hoard of about 50,000 radiates was recorded.

At the important Roman site at Wroxeter, Shropshire, excavations at the Basilica were completed. It is noted that: "The Basilica went out of use *c*.300 when the accompanying baths were disused; it appears to have been dismantled, for there was no debris of columns or architectural fragments. The herringbone floor in the western three-quarters of the nave was replaced with pebbled surfaces, but the remainder survived apparently protected by an open-ended structure. A coin of *c*.375 was found in one of the lowest pebble surfaces. In the south aisle the herringbone floor remained intact, being presumably protected by a roof. In the northern portico the flags have been removed but erosion had later been made good with dumps of rubble and a plank surface was laid. The western portico, perhaps also originally flagged, yielded many pebble floors of timber buildings. One hearth there associated with a coin of 367 yielded a remanent magnetic date of 400 ± 100. After an uncertain period the whole area was replanned with large timber-framed buildings still of Roman pattern laid out on rubble brought from elsewhere; and further north the E.–W. street was flanked by booths. The site appears to have been abandoned by the early sixth." In neighbouring Hereford and Worcester excavations of a building complex at Brandom Camp revealed "a rich collection of Neronian Samian . . ., an almost complete Spanish wine amphora, sherds of Lyon and Italian eggshell ware and a pottery lamp, together with a complete dolabra head. These finds suggested the quarters of the commanding-officer."

At Laxton, Northants., roadworks on the A43 "revealed a major industrial site. The exposed features included 12 iron-smelting furnaces, an inhumation cemetery of at least 100 graves, and the stone foundations of several buildings." At Baldock, Herts., it was possible to record "the complete layout of a small late Roman inhumation cemetery". About sixty graves produced a total of some 100 inhumations. "Adults, children and infants were represented, many in coffins and many accompanied by one or sometimes two pottery vessels, hob nails and occasional finger-rings; several decapitated skeletons and one prone one were present. Orientation was with the cemetery boundaries." In Colchester excavations at Culver Street allowed the investigations of "parts of the east (centurion's) end of all six barracks of the first cohort . . . and all were found to have remained standing until A.D. 60. The northern three were well preserved, but the others had been damaged by Flavian cultivation".

At Alington Avenue in Fordington, Dorset, some interesting discoveries were made. The report notes that "a D-shaped Iron Age enclosure continued in being as indicated by the peripheral distribution of late Roman burials. There were 4 cremations in Black-burnished jars and 58 extended inhumations, mostly in wooden coffins but one in a Ham-stone sarcophagus and one in a lead-lined coffin (both of them gypsum burials); 30 per cent had grave-goods. One supine skeleton lacked the skull as did another which was accompanied by a dog; one decapitated body lay prone with the skull replaced supine; one prone burial with dog showed wounds, and one burial was that of a dwarf. There were traces of three buildings with stone footing; two were semi-basements, one with an entrance-ramp and oven. A Roman road, presumably from Dorchester to Purbeck, crossed the N. edge of the site and a milestone of Postumus was found re-used in an oven." In the neighbouring county of Hampshire a hoard of 3,502 radiates ending with the Emperor Probus was found at Appleshaw. In the same county, at Silchester, the work at the Roman Amphitheatre was finished and it was demonstrated that "The building had had two timber periods before being rebuilt in stone in the early third century. In the first dated to c.50 to 70, the arena was almost circular, measuring c.43 by 39·7 m., being defined by large posts over a metre apart and with entrances at north and south. Timber recesses existed close to the positions of the later masonry ones. In Period II, probably of second-century date, the arena wall was of close-set small posts, diverging slightly inside the earlier line to form a more oval arena (c.44 by 35·5 m.)."

A sorry state of affairs is reported at the Green Lane temple site at Wanborough, Surrey, where "excavation has uncovered a Romano–Celtic temple after treasure-hunters had systematically looted an area of 300 sq. m. Over 1,000 coins have been recovered, many by the police; but many more have been disposed of. They appear to represent a scattered hoard mainly of Atrebatic silver and gold, but with some Republican and early Imperial issues; it was perhaps deposited c.60. The hoard seems to have lain on the weathered surface of the London Clay; above this was a black layer dated c.50–150 containing pottery, burnt bone and elements of priestly regalia. The temple overlay this deposit; it had flint rubble walls over greensand foundations, with greensand quoins and a tiled roof. The cella, floored with ironstone tesserae, measured c.8 by 7 m. and the surrounding portice was c.15 sq. m. The regalia consisted of (a) 17 sceptre-handles (two of them connected by a wooden shaft), two others remain in the hands of looters; and (b) at least four head-dresses of the type with central bronze disc and dependent chains. Three had standing wheels on the disc, perhaps indicating the cult of Taranis."

The Medieval Period

Recent investigations relating to the medieval period are recorded in *Medieval Archaeology* Vol. XXX for 1986. Among these is the excavation of part of a Scheduled Ancient Monument at Butler's Field in Lechlade, Glos., in advance of building development. It is noted that "In addition to prehistoric material indicated by aerial photographs, a major Anglo-Saxon cemetery was excavated from which almost 250 burials were recovered, some richly furnished. There were 217 bodies in 202 graves and 32 cremations. These are calculated as comprising 50 to 75 per cent of the whole cemetery. Burials date from about A.D. 500 to the 670s. Many 6th-century burials were laid out in rows, the graves lying N.–S. Female burials were grouped together in the N.W. The 6th-century graves did not disturb each other and were probably marked; similarities suggest family groupings. Cremations, two with timber superstructures, were concentrated further East. Grave 57 contained an 18-year old woman buried in a coffin, with a hair ornament, a pair of saucer brooches, a great square-headed brooch, three strings of glass and amber beads, finger-rings, a purse with beads and a chatelaine, as well as a metal-mounted wooden bowl, a bone comb, and a spindle whorl. 7th-century burials lay E.–W. and often cut into earlier graves. Female 7th-century burials were furnished with gold pendants, silver and garnet pins and necklaces, and also weaving equipment. Male graves contained seaxes. Aerial photographs indicate a possible settlement site 250 m. E. of the cemetery."

An unusual site was at Pinner Park Farm in Harrow where a medieval deer park and related earthworks were recorded. "Almost the entire circuit of the former park survived with some sections showing a well-preserved, broad, low bank between two ditches. Depredations had been made by local householders with gardens backing onto the boundary earthwork and representation was made to the local Council to prevent this continuing. Within the park a number of medieval features were noted, including a fine fishpond complete with dam, flood banks, and diversion channels. The dam, up to 2 m. high in places, still exhibited the original sluice exits although modern cuts through the dam had damaged other features. Also identified within the park was the site of a moated lodge, now built over by modern farm buildings. However, linear hollows of a slight nature were observed N. of the moat site and these were attributed to stew ponds associated with the lodge."

Amongst the many other excavations in the London area, mention should be made of the investigation at the Jubilee Hall site in Convent Garden. The east part of the site disclosed archaeological deposits up to 2 metres in depth. "Saxon features showed evidence for buildings: beam-slots with associated post-holes, and an extensive clay floor with a hearth. Industrial use of the site was suggested by various fireplaces, and circular pits of unknown function whose backfill contained slag and horncores. Other features included pits and at least one well. A human burial, probably adult, lying prone with the hands possibly tied together and pushed to the right side of the body, was found sealed by the earlier

Saxon occupation levels and is tentatively dated to the same period. The most conspicuous finds were animal bones, and shells, mostly oyster and mussel. Pottery was relatively sparse; it includes Ipswich ware, probable German and N. French imports as well as local wares. Circular 'doughnut' shaped loomweight fragments were quite common. Quern stone fragments, probably German, were also found. Small finds included a 'sceatta' of *c.*720, associated with Ipswich-ware pottery, a late Roman coin, a possible bronze strap end, a bronze pin, a bone pin, fragments of a bone comb, two pieces of curved iron possibly from frying pans, and fragments of whetstones including an unworked one. The significance of the site is that it fills a gap in the middle Saxon period (mid 7th to mid 9th centuries) during which few signs of occupation are apparent within the walls of the City of London. Chance finds are however known from the area of the Strand and Covent Garden, and these excavated features seem to support the suggestion that a mid Saxon settlement was established on the bank of the Thames along and above the Strand foreshore."

Among the excavations carried out in Canterbury were those in advance of redevelopment at the rear of 41 St. George's Street, where "Roman pits were overlain by a series of Anglo-Saxon levels which included a 6th- or 7th-century sunken-featured building and later Anglo-Saxon industrial structures; at least one may have been associated with iron smelting. These structures were cut by late Saxon and early medieval rubbish pits containing a fine sequence of pottery spanning the mid 10th-century to *c.*1275, and a fine early Norman mace-head of bronze openwork with a silver wash. A late 13th-century feature associated with bronze casting was constructed over the backfilled pits, and was in turn overlain by post-medieval deposits."

A different kind of site was that of the ruined church of St. Michael at Bowthorpe, Norwich, Norfolk. "The church was in ruins by the 16th century although the chancel was restored and used as a chapel between the 1630s and *c.*1790. The earliest uncovered, probably 11th-century, consisted of a twin-celled building of flint and carstone with a round west tower. Most of the chancel had been robbed away, as had much of the S. wall of the nave, but the tower stood over 1 m. high in places. Before construction the site had been levelled with a thick deposit of sandy loam. This necessitated the excavation of deep foundation trenches packed with alternating layers of rammed chalk and flint (that below the S. nave wall was over 2 m. deep). Regrettably all floor surfaces had been destroyed although the soakaway for the font was located, as was a single intra-mural burial in the nave, the grave fill of which contained a penny of Edward III. In the early 14th century the chancel was demolished and a much larger one rebuilt. A N. porch was added to the nave (a large fragment of a 12th to 13th-century grave slab being re-used as part of the threshold) and, perhaps somewhat later, the S. nave doorway was blocked. No other structural changes preceded ruination. By the 1630s it is clear that only the chancel and tower remained standing."

At the "Goblin Works" in Leatherhead, Surrey,

excavations revealed traces of at least 30 interments. "The burials fall into two groups. Firstly there was a series of 17 burials, normally oriented E.–W., with well-defined, if generally shallow, grave cuts into solid chalk. They included men, women, and children, all either supine and extended, or in a sleeping ('foetal') position. Almost all the adult burials contained grave goods, including two spearheads, various knives, bronze buckles and clasps, a bone comb, a necklace of beads, and a cowrie shell (this far-travelled item was, perhaps, an amulet). These are clearly pagan Saxon burials of the 6th to 7th century. The second group of burials was distinct in a number of respects. They were varied in orientation, but tending towards a N.–S. axis, and in general were carelessly interred in very shallow graves which normally did not penetrate solid chalk. Some had their hands behind their backs (presumably tied), others were buried face down, while two were decapitated. All appeared to be adult males. All these facts indicate an execution site, chosen as such because of its pagan connotations after the conversion to Christianity. The possible date range is *c.*700–1200. A large pit containing two small sherds of (?) 12th-century pottery might represent the emplacement for the gallows tree."

The Post-Medieval Period

Post-Medieval Archaeology Vol. 19 for 1985 contains useful summaries of investigations relating to more recent centuries. Among the work noted was the excavation at Dudley Castle in the West Midlands. After removing rubble from the demolition of the Keep in 1647, following the Castle's surrender to Parliamentary forces in 1646, "a large assemblage of 17th-century pottery, including Cistercian type wares, yellow wares, slip wares and vessels of coarser fabrics was recovered from below the rubble, along with a quantity of glass and some worked bone. The group includes an almost complete slipware dish and another dish with impressed decoration. Finds of a military nature are cannon balls, lead shot and a ceramic grenade."

In Lincoln at St. Paul in the Bail the 17th–18th century backfill of a well was investigated. "The sump had apparently been re-cut in the 15th–16th century, possibly at the same time as the construction of a circular well head. The backfill contained some 1,500 artefacts, almost all of 17th-century date. These include three wooden buckets, a cask, over three dozen small leather-covered wooden balls, two bowling balls, bone dice, a wooden chess-piece, a possible spinning top, a small wooden bat, and fragments of shoes."

Investigations at Pottingers Entry in Antrim, Belfast, showed that brick houses had been built, following the creation of the street in the late 18th century, on rubbish pits deriving from the 17th century High Street frontage nearby. "A later 17th-century rubbish pit contained British and Continental ceramics, the remains of two dogs and a range of butchered bones from native and introduced animal species. A sawn pig tibia from an 18th-century context is the earliest known indication from Ireland of the use of this tool for carcass Butchery." Still in Northern Ireland, in Coleraine, Co. Londonderry, the dismantling of a town house built in 1674 for re-erection in the Ulster Folk and Transport Museum led to the discovery of a stone-lined rubbish pit associated with the building. The pit contained "quantities of early 18th-century Staffordshire slip-wares and stonewares, sgraffito dishes from an unknown manufacturing source, local earthenwares, glass bottles and drinking vessels. The period of deposition appears to have been of short duration, and the dump may be associated with a re-leasing of the property in 1738. Beneath the 1674 house were stone footings for part of the terrace of timber-framed houses erected in the 1611 'plantation' of Coleraine. To the rear of the site, and parallel with 17th-century frontage line, a large medieval ditch was sectioned; its alignment suggests that the early 17th-century town plan of Coleraine was influenced by medieval property boundaries."

At Jackfield in Shropshire excavations revealed 18th-century wasters from the Jackfield potteries. "At least three potteries are shown on an estate plan of *c.*1728. The main products during the mid 18th century seem to have been white salt-glazed stone-ware, which is usually ascribed exclusively to Stoke. Many developed forms, with cut, moulded, sprigged or scratch-blue decoration have been recovered, and at least one fragment has traces of overglaze enamel-ling. A waster sherd of red stoneware with white sprigged decoration has also been recovered. Cream-ware wasters, some with a Whieldon-type glaze, as well as the more common slip-trailed earthenwares, were recovered from the waste dumps, one of which is sealed by an ironworks of 1767. The advance production here (contemporary and comparable with developments at Stoke) subsequently gave rise to the development of 'Jackfield ware' and the establish-ment of porcelain manufactures. The potteries are situated by riverside wharves with trade connections to Bristol and America."

In the south-west, at 9–13 Cowick Street in Exeter, excavations revealed part of a bronze foundry which was in use between about 1520 and 1625, probably operated by three generations of the Birdall family. "The manufacture of cauldrons and skillets formed the mainstay of the business. Clay for the moulds was dug from quarry pits both within the tenement and in closes nearby. The pits were backfilled with large quantities of discarded mould. Bell founding probably started in the 1560s following the closure of Exeter's principal late-medieval foundry at Preston Street. Churchwardens' accounts suggest that much of the bell founding was done on an itinerant basis." The foundry closed in 1625, on the death of John Birdall II: in the same year Thomas Pennington came to Exeter from Barnstaple to establish the Paul Street foundry.

Tailpiece

Archaeologists excavating the famous Iron Age hill-fort of Maiden Castle near Dorchester found, amongst other important material, a stuffed alligator! A spokesman for English Heritage said that the alligator was believed to have been buried as a joke on future generations by the archaeologist Sir Mortimer Wheeler, who excavated there in the 1930s.

BRASS BAND CHAMPIONS

The British Open Brass Band Championships 1987 (Sept.)

Test Piece—*Freedom* (H. Bath).

1. Williams Fairey Engineering Works (R. New-some)—194 pts.
2. Britannia Building Society Fodden (H. Snell)—192 pts.
3. Grimethorpe Colliery (D. James)—191 pts.
4. Ever Ready (E. Cunningham)—190 pts.
5. Brighouse and Rastrick (D. Broadbent)—189 pts.
6. Desford Colliery Dowty (G. Whitam)—188 pts.

The National Brass Band Championship of Great Britain 1987 (Oct.)

Championship.—Desford Colliery (J. Watson)—197 pts.
Second Section.—Wakefield Metropolitan (L. Hep-pleston)—189 pts.
Third Section.—Drighlington (C. Hardy)—191 pts.
Fourth Section.—Besses Boys (B. Chappell)—187 pts.
Youth Section.—Desford Youth (K. J. Steward)—185 pts.

European Championships 1987 (May) Black Dyke Mills (Maj. P. Parkes).

SCIENCE AND DISCOVERY, 1986–87

The Ability to see Colours.—Colour blindness has been known for a long time, and scientists have suspected that even the colour perception of people thought to have normal colour vision is by no means uniform. New research carried out by Jay Neitz and Gerald Jacobs of the University of California at Santa Barbara has confirmed these suspicions.

The ability to see colour depends on the activities of three light-sensitive pigments housed in the cone cells of the eye. In the Rayleigh match test, invented over a century ago, an observer adjusts a mixture of red and green lights until the emitted light resembles a standard orange light. Using a more sensitive extension of this principle, the investigators asked each of 200 young adults with normal colour vision whether combinations of red and green light were redder than, greener than, or the same as an orange standard. The results showed that men fall into two distinct categories depending on the amount of red needed to make the match. Before it could be claimed that this was due to differing red-sensitive pigments many external possibilities had to be excluded: all investigations showed that these could not satisfactorily explain the results. It was therefore concluded that two varieties of red-sensitive pigments were widely distributed among the population.

The two pigments, sensitive to light of wavelengths 556 and 559 nm. respectively, spring from two versions of the relevant gene, which sits on the X-chromosome. Men have only one X-chromosome per cell and their vision depends on which of the genes happens to be present. Women, on the other hand, have two X-chromosomes per cell, only one of which is operational. Women fall into three groups depending on the performance of the genes. The important point is that different X-chromosomes could be operational in different cells. Those that carry identical versions of the gene give two groups, as is the case with men. If, however, there is a mixture, a woman's performance will occupy the middle ground of the Rayleigh test. About half the women tested were in this group.

Ancient Observations of Sirius.—Sirius, the Dog Star, is the brightest star in the sky and is clearly white in colour. One of the big mysteries involving ancient records is that Greek and Roman astronomers classed it as a red star. Its colour was compared with that of Mars, which certainly has a ruddy tint, and also the red giant Arcturus. No satisfactory explanation had been put forward for this discrepancy, but now a team of American astronomers have suggested a possible solution.

Sirius is a double star, the bright component being responsible for the light we see with the naked eye. Its companion, Sirius B, is currently a white dwarf, a star which has more or less completed its life cycle. Before it reached the white dwarf stage, it would have been a red giant far outshining Sirius A. Unfortunately, this does not explain the red colour reported a few centuries ago because according to current stellar theories it takes about 10 million years to evolve from a red giant to a white dwarf. This is supported by the data obtained from the *International Ultraviolet Explorer* satellite, which failed to identify any of the ejected gases which would have been present if the change had taken place recently. However, recent work on the behaviour of white dwarves has produced some interesting results. The dwarf consists of a mixture of highly compressed carbon and oxygen surrounded by a thin layer of helium. This is itself surrounded by a thin layer of hydrogen. The American astronomers have suggested that if a small amount of the hydrogen diffused downwards, the carbon-oxygen nuclei would act as a catalyst to convert the hydrogen to helium. This would produce a pulse of heat which would make the hydrogen envelope expand. In doing so its temperature would drop, producing a red colour. This would only be a temporary feature and after about 250 years the situation would revert to the normal condition. This process may be repetitive, so if the explanation is correct Sirius could become a red star again in the future.

The Biggest Objects in the Universe.—Size and distances commonly quoted in astronomical literature cannot be visualized directly: it is only with the use of scale models that one is able to appreciate the relative distances involved. However, the recent discovery of what are thought to be the largest objects in the universe can stun even the most hardened astronomer.

Astronomers from Stanford University and Kitt Peak National Observatory using the 4 metre Mayall telescope at Kitt Peak have identified huge arcs of light forming 110 degrees of a circle. These smoothly curved arcs have lengths of 300,000 light years and they are about 5 thousand million light years away: if they were situated locally they would almost span the gap between our own Milky Way galaxy and the one in Andromeda. Although the arcs were first observed about ten years ago it is only within the last year, using the latest electronic light-gathering techniques, that they have been studied in detail.

Several theories have been put forward to explain the arcs but much more work is required before a firm explanation can be formulated. It is thought that they are young by astronomical standards, less than 100 thousand million years old. It is also thought that they will eventually break up to form separate galaxies due to gravitational forces from nearby galaxies and intergalactic matter. One theory suggests that they were formed by the explosion from galaxies colliding, producing a shock wave that spread out uniformly to form a mass of prestellar material. But to do this would require energy equivalent to 100 million supernovae exploding at once. A further idea is that they are long tails of stars drawn out of a galaxy by gravitational forces, but this explanation cannot account for the brightness of the arcs, each of which is emitting as much light as 100 thousand million Suns.

It is expected that more of these arcs may be found in the outer regions of the observable universe. The next stage of investigation is to carry out a spectral analysis to determine their chemical composition.

Caged Metals.—Placing a metallic ion in a cage of atoms of carbon and nitrogen extends the time the ions remain electronically excited when light falls on them and is open to a number of possible applications.

Jean-Marie Lehn and colleagues from the University of Strasbourg have made a luminescent europium cryptate which shines with a strong red light when irradiated with ultraviolet light. The term cryptate is used to describe a cage of carbon and nitrogen atoms surrounding a metal ion. Jean-Pierre Sauvage and Jean-Marc Kern, also from Strasbourg, have replaced europium by copper and they found that when these molecules were excited by light they behaved as a catalyst to oxidize organic molecules or to link them together *via* the carbon atoms.

If light of the appropriate wavelength is allowed to fall on an atom or molecule, an electron is excited and jumps into a higher energy level. Under normal circumstances when the light source is switched off, the electron falls back to its original state, radiating the released energy as light, a process known as luminescence. In some cases other atoms or molecules, such as those of a solvent, can absorb the energy, thereby shortening the time the atom luminesces or in some cases preventing luminescence completely. This is the case when europium is quenched in water but if the europium atom is surrounded with carbon and nitrogen atoms, the solvent is kept at bay. At the same time, by using a cage which is itself sensitive to ultraviolet light, the cage passes this excitation directly to the europium ion which then shines with its normal powerful red light. An important application of this would be the tagging of the europium cryptate to proteins, thereby causing the luminescence of the protein to last some 10,000 times longer than normal, a technique which would be very useful in protein identification. In the case of the caged copper ion, the copper ion transfers an electron to the surrounding cage. This produces a very reactive copper complex which is very useful in synthesising larger organic molecules and, if air is allowed into the reaction, in producing industrially-useful aldehydes.

Conodonts Identified.—Conodonts, tiny fossilized toothlike objects, were identified first about 130 years ago but it was not known what type of animal was responsible. They have been used by geologists in the oil industry as an indicator of the age of the rocks in which they are found. It is known that they became extinct some 200 million years ago. A wide range of ideas have been put forward about the identity of the animal responsible for the fossils, ranging from worms, molluscs and primitive fish to algae and plants.

Fossil animals have, from time to time, been found with conodonts in them and it was assumed that they were the remains of predators which had eaten the conodonts. Three years ago, however, Euan Clarkson of Edinburgh University found a fossil about 40 mm. long with the conodont in the region of its mouth. The shape, size and tail fins indicated that it belonged to one of two phyla, the chordates (vertibrates) or chaetognaths (arrow worms) but on the strength of one example it was impossible to draw any firm conclusions.

Recently, Clarkson and Richard Aldridge of Nottingham University examined three more specimens found in rocks which are 300 million years old. These fossils have no lateral fins and the body is flattened from side to side, a characteristic of the chordates. The animal rsponsible had small tail fins and hence must have swum with wavelike motions along its ribbon-shaped body. The fossils also showed chevron-shaped body segments. The scientists have suggested that the nearest living relative is the hagfish, a jawless vertebrate with a skeleton made of cartilage rather than bone, although there are important differences. The teeth of the hagfish are not mineralized like the conodonts, which explains why the hagfish has no fossil record like that of the conodonts.

Before any positive identification can be made, further fossils will have to be studied. Such features as the presence or absence of a true tail, the exact arrangements of the caudal fins and the position of the anus are some of the points that need to be clarified.

Cosmic Strings.—Our knowledge of the universe is advancing at such a rate that a need frequently arises for completely new theories to explain the new knowledge. One of the latest theories is that of the cosmic string.

The so-called Big Bang theory postulates how all matter and energy came into existence at a single point in time and then expanded. The theory explains quite readily the observed recession of the galaxies and the existence of low background radiation left over from the Big Bang. However, this does not explain why the universe is so lumpy. Apart from the grouping of galaxies, observations have shown the existence of huge empty regions (voids) and chains of galaxies (filaments). These features could have originated from ripples in the distribution of primordial matter-energy but the problem is, how did the ripples form? A new theory involving elementary particles which could explain this unevenness is the theory of cosmic strings.

A cosmic string is a one-dimensional strand of space-time in the state of the universe at the time of the Big Bang. Physicists have developed many theories to explain the very high temperatures and pressures that existed at that time, most of which depend on the concept of symmetry. These Grand Unified Theories assume that at the beginning there was no difference between the four fundamental forces—gravity, electromagnetism, weak interaction and strong interaction—but just one uniform field. Subsequently this symmetry broke and energy settled into particles such as the proton and electron. But frozen bits of unified field became trapped in long strings containing remnants of the high energy that existed just after the Bang. The existence of such strings is pure speculation, but they provide nevertheless a tool which could answer some of the problems troubling cosmologists at present.

Cosmic strings would have enormous mass, and either have infinite length stretching across the whole universe or form small closed loops. They would not be straight but wander randomly, and when two strings cross they would break and join the other way. This would cause long strings to break and form loops. As these move, they would lose energy by radiating gravitational waves and hence shrink in size until nothing was left but radiation. Some recent ideas have suggested that the strings may be superconducting, with electrons and protons travelling along the string at the speed of light. But interesting as these theories are, much more work needs to be carried out before cosmic strings are generally accepted.

Drilling in the Antarctic.—In 1973 the research vessel *Glomar Challenger* discovered gaseous hydrocarbons in the Ross Sea during a deep sea drilling project, which led to suggestions that petroleum deposits may exist in the area. Recent work has shown that although these existed in the past they are now dissipated. This conclusion is one of the results obtained from drill holes sunk recently in the McMurdo Sound. One of these, called Ciros-1, reached a depth of 99 metres below the sea level. The drill was set up on ice two metres thick which overlay about 200 metres of water. A near-continuous core was obtained through the 700 metres of rock, providing a record of the history of the ice sheet and the rise of the nearby Transantarctic Mountains. And the core at a depth of 632 metres contained dark stained sand 2 metres thick, a residue of a pre-existing petroleum deposit.

It is thought that the drill penetrated the whole of the layer of sedimentary rocks because the lowest parts of the core contained fragments of dolerite, a coarse-grained igneous rock. The upper regions consisted mainly of sandstone and mudstone with poorly sorted gravel beds, providing evidence for the successive advances of glacial ice from the East Antarctic ice sheet. Although detailed examination of the microscopic fossils has yet to be completed, preliminary results point to the base of the core being early Oligocene, thereby pushing back by several millions of years the oldest record of Antarctic deposits. It is hoped that more detailed study of the fossils and study of the magnetic reversals will give accurate data about the start of the extensive ice fields and subsequent glaciations. The core also contained larger fossils, mainly bivalve molluscs, but of particular interest was that of a leaf of the southern beech in the late Oligocene mudstone between two gravel beds deposited from grounded ice. This indicates that trees grew in the area and were able to establish themselves in the periods between glaciations.

Early Man in Asia.—Theories about the development of early man from his ancestors are difficult to establish as each year brings new evidence to contradict previously-held ideas. Both fossil and archaeological evidence from sites in Asia appeared to indicate that *Homo erectus* was the first hominid to leave Africa, about one million years ago, but recent discoveries have cast doubt on this. Members of the British Archaeological Mission to Pakistan have identified stone artefacts near Rawalpindi which are two million years old. These suggest that *Homo habilis*, the first hominid to make stone tools, lived in the area 2·5 to 1·6 million years ago, earlier than they are thought to have lived in eastern and southern Africa.

In the past archaeological finds with ages greater than a million years have been found and, by implication, the presence of hominids suspected at several sites in Asia but their age has been questioned because of the difficulties of obtaining accurate datings of the material. Such difficulties do not exist with this latest find as the artefacts are firmly embedded in deposits of conglomerate and gritstone of the Upper Siwalik series. The ages of these have been determined by palaeomagnetic techniques, which use knowledge of the changes which have taken place in the direction of the Earth's magnetic field.

This discovery opens up several possibilities. It could indicate that the migration to Asia took place a million years earlier than believed or it could revive the theory that the birthplace of the Asian line of *Homo erectus* was Asia. However, neither theory is likely to gain general acceptance until palaeoanthropologists discover hominid fossils with ages comparable to those of the newly discovered artefacts: teams from Britain and Pakistan are currently searching the surrounding area for fossils of this early man.

Early Life on Earth.—The generally accepted time-scale for the development of life on this planet may need to be revised in the light of a recent discovery. This provides evidence suggesting that the time-scale may have been overestimated by as much as 700 million years.

By noting successions of rock strata and their fossils, it is possible to obtain relative ages but not absolute ones. The use of radio isotope techniques has enabled geologists to estimate absolute ages but unfortunately the method is not very precise. Nevertheless, this work led to the belief that the Precambrian era ended about 570 million years ago, when fossils suddenly became very abundant. Earlier rocks tend to be very deformed and their distribution patchy. Such a patch is the Mushandike stromatolitic limestone which occurs in southern Zimbabwe. Although it had never been dated directly, isotopic measurements of a granite body thought to cross it had suggested an age of 3,500 million years. Recent work has shown that the granite did not cut across the limestone but that the limestone was actually deposited on the granite's eroded surface. Further, more refined methods have shown that the granite has an age of only 2,900 million years.

Research carried out by teams from Oxford University, Oxford Polytechnic and Zimbabwe University on the limestone has confirmed that the stromatolites are in fact 700 million years younger than originally thought. Sediments such as limestone are notoriously difficult to date but the Mushandike limestone is rich in lead and this has enabled the scientists to compare the amounts of the radioactive isotopes of lead with the stable isotope and to obtain a reasonably accurate figure. If similar results are obtained elsewhere then there will have to be a major revision of views on the ages of primitive life on the Earth.

Earthquakes and the Moon.—Many theories have been put forward to explain the causes of earthquakes, quite a few involving the Moon. The main purpose of this speculation is to enable major events to be forecast and so reduce the loss of life which frequently occurs.

Many studies have tried to link tremors with the times when the Moon is at perigee, i.e. when it is nearest to the Earth, but none have been conclusive. Recent work carried out by Jim Shirley of Canoga Park, California, shows that at least some of the major events are caused by the gravitational pull of the Moon. In the analysis of 45 large tremors which have occurred in Chile since 1570, there is a statistically significant chance that an earthquake will occur either when the Moon is approaching its highest point in the sky or when it is 180° away. Although not so pronounced, there is also a tendency for these events to occur when the Sun is low on the horizon, a tendency noticed with tremors in California.

Shirley has found also that there is a correlation between the timing of shallow earthquakes on the Moon, monitored by the seismometers left on the Moon's surface during the *Apollo* spaceflights, and some events on the Earth. No explanation for this link has yet been found although it is assumed that there is a common gravitational cause.

The results from the major tremors that have taken place in Chile will not help directly in the forecasting of a major event in that area because tremors do not occur each time the Moon rises high in the sky. It may be beneficial in the long run, however, in helping geologists to understand the processes which take place in earthquake-prone areas.

Fossil Jelly.—One of the weaknesses of studying the past using fossils is that one is likely to obtain a highly distorted picture of the conditions existing at any one time. This is because only the bony or hard parts of animals are normally preserved, so fossil records tell us very little about soft-bodied animals. Recently, however, more evidence about soft-bodied animals has come to light, mainly due to the use of X-rays.

George Stanley of the University of Montana and a West German palaeontologist Wilhelm Sturmer used X-rays to examine the Lower Devonian Hunsruck slate of West Germany and found what have been described as the rarest fossils in the world. This 400 million year old slate is famous for its spectacular fossils, some of which show traces of tissue and soft organs. In 1983 the geologists discovered a fossil of a comb jelly belonging to the phylum *Ctenophora*. These are tiny marine animals bearing eight bands of cilia that propel them through the water. A later discovery has shown more of the delicate comb structure, enabling comb jellies to be assigned to a separate phylum and not lumped together with the *Cnidaria*, the phylum that contains jelly fish and sea anemones. The comb jellies have a more advanced anatomy and the age of the fossils has pushed back the age of the ctenophores to establish them as an independent phylum.

The fossils were located by X-rays and the slate containing the comb jelly was then ground down to a 2 mm. section and X-rayed again. The fossil, like many in the Hunsruck slate, are flattened but by using stereographic radiographs a better shape has been obtained. The fossil is 23 mm. long, and has a mouth and eight comb rows, with the plates of delicate cilia still visible. Basically, neither specimen looks very different from the ctenophores living today. Biologists who have studied the deep oceans in submersibles have found that deep waters contain large quantities of jelly animals but very few are successfully brought to the surface because they are so delicate that they usually disintegrate. If more of these fossil creatures are found it may suggest that conditions in the early seas were not so different from those existing today.

Genetic Engineering of Cereals.—Recent work carried out by teams from the Friedrich Miescher Institute in Switzerland and the John Innes Institute in the U.K. has shown that it is possible to use genetic engineering techniques to implant foreign genes into maize. One of the key techniques in this type of work is based on the bacterium *Agrobacterium tumefaciens*, which causes an infection known as crown-gall disease. Under normal conditions the bacterium injects a part of its genetic material into the cells of a plant, these genes causing the cells to become cancerous and to produce food for the bacterium. When genetic engineers wish to introduce a new gene into a plant they splice the gene into the bacterium's genes and then let the bacterium do its normal work.

Until recently it had not been possible to exploit this with cereal because members of the grass family, which includes many of the important food plants such as wheat, maize, rice, barley and sugar cane, are not susceptible to crown-gall disease. But although it does not normally attack maize, the researchers argued that a limited genetic transfer would take place if suitably doctored. In such cases the bacterium can even be used to inject the genes of an infectious virus into a plant. Once introduced the viral genes will escape, multiply and produce symptoms in the plant which are characteristic of the virus. The teams used a virus known as maize streak virus which is normally only transmitted by insects. The results of their experiments were highly successful, the experiment working within two weeks. The next stage is the introduction of useful foreign genes into the maize. If these are successful, and if the method can be extended to other cereals, this will open up possibilities which could have far-reaching consequences.

Ice Ages and Fossil Beetles.—Much has been learned of the movements of the ice which covered the British Isles some 10,000 to 20,000 years ago by analysing beetle fossils found in peat bogs, dried lake beds and other sedimentary deposits. Teams of investigators from the Universities of East Anglia and Birmingham used for their studies fossils from about 350 species which are still in existence today and whose climatic tolerances are well documented. Differences in the temperatures at which the beetles exist provide good indicators of the temperatures existing at a particular time.

The withdrawal of the ice from northern Europe was not a straightforward affair: the ice receded and then came south again before finally withdrawing to give the conditions existing at present. The evidence from the study of the beetle fossils has modified the time-scale and put fairly firm dates on the movement of the ice. (These dates were obtained from carbon-dating the fossilized plants found with the beetles.) It is now thought that the first warming took place about 13,000 B.P. (before present), the average temperature rising from $-8°C$. to $10°C$. in as short a period as 300–800 years. Over the next 2,000 years the temperatures gradually fell again to sub-zero values. Then, about 10,000 years B.P. the temperature rose again quite rapidly and has remained in the region of $+10°C$. since. The method of dating the movements of the ice sheets using beetles has proved to be of great value and similar investigations are currently being carried out by other countries.

Impact Crater under the Sea.—Meteoritic impact craters in the Earth's land surface have been identified in most parts of the world although the distribution is by no means regular (*see* Meteorite Crater in China). Most of the Earth's surface, however, is covered with water and no underwater impact crater had been identified until recently when Canadian geologists located such a structure in the Atlantic Ocean, about 200 km. south-east of Nova Scotia.

The discovery was made during seismic surveys off the east coast of Canada when a circular structure of about 45 km. in diameter was identified. In the centre lay an irregularly-shaped central uplift 1·8 km. in height and 2·8 km. in diameter. The projected depth of the crater is about 2·8 km. at the centre, but shallower at the edges. The crater is partially infilled with breccia, up to 850 metres thick in places and surrounding the central uplift to a radius of 8·5 km. This breccia exhibits shock deformation features. It is estimated that the impact took place about 54 million years ago in the early Eocene period. The geologists, Lubomir F. Jansa of the Geological Survey of Canada and Georgia Pe-Piper of St Mary's University, Halifax, have supplemented their knowledge of the rocks from the cores obtained when a single oil exploratory well was sunk over the centre of the structure in 1974. They claim that the almost continuous sedimentary record in the surrounding shelf area will, if proper samples are taken, provide a unique opportunity to investigate the effects of a major impact on the marine ecosystems and the sedimentary record. This would help to solve the problem of the so-called mass extinctions suggested by some investigators.

The Lake Nyos Disaster.—Late in the evening of August 21, 1986, a huge volume of gas was released from within the waters of Lake Nyos in the western province of Cameroon. The gas mixed with the water to create an aerosol effect and this poisonous mist swept down the valleys north of the lake killing more than 1,700 people. As relief teams arrived to help the survivors a scientific investigation was set up to establish what had happened and why. Teams from many countries visited the area, talking to survivors and examining the destruction.

Although Lake Nyos lies in the heart of a volcanic region which has been active in the geologically recent past, it is about 300 km. from the nearest known active volcano. The lake does not lie in the crater of a volcano and is only about 200 metres deep. When the waters were examined in September 1986 the lake was highly charged with carbon dioxide. Samples collected from depth revealed no trace of normal volcanic gases except for a small amount of methane. Survivors, however, had commented on the smell of bad eggs and gunpowder, the smell persisting for some time. The conclusion drawn by the investigators is that prior to the explosion the waters of the lake were saturated with carbon dioxide and on August 21 a pulse of volcanic gases, predominantly carbon dioxide but with some hydrogen sulphide, was discharged from a volcanic vent under the north-east corner of the lake. The rising gases drew up the lake water charged with carbon dioxide. As the water rose the carbon dioxide came out of solution, thereby increasing the gas flow. At the surface the mixture was transformed into an aerosol of water in gas which travelled down the nearby valleys. It has been estimated that 200,000 tons of water was lost from the lake and the volume of gas released, at atmospheric pressure, amounted to about 3 million cubic metres.

Meteorite Crater in China.—Most members of the solar system with a rocky surface are scarred by craters which may be up to tens of kilometres in diameter. Most of these are thought to have been caused by meteoritic impact. The high concentration of such features on the Moon has been explained by the fact that erosion forces are relatively small compared to the conditions existing on the Earth. Consequently, although the Earth has been subjected to a similar bombardment, the number of craters identifiable today is relatively small (though the number has increased dramatically as a result of the scanning of the Earth's surface by satellite).

The huge landmass of Asia has revealed far fewer craters than elsewhere but a recent discovery by Chinese geologists has helped to redress the balance. Wu Siben, of the Wuhan College of Geology in Beijing (Peking) has discovered a huge crater about 70 km. in diameter on the border of Hei Province and Inner Mongolia, near to the Luam river. The crater, known as the Duolun crater, is thought to be about 136 million years old. Its size rivals that of the Manicouagan crater in Quebec which is often illustrated in astronomical literature. The impact of cosmic bodies capable of producing craters of such a size must have had a marked effect on the history of our planet. Much has been written on this over the last few years, especially in relation to the possible cause of the extinction of the dinosaurs. Major changes in geological history are often associated with changes in climate, day length, sea level and biological populations. The Duolun crater was formed at a critical geological stage, the end of the Jurassic and beginning of the Cretaceous periods, so one of the principal lines of research will be to investigate whether the event contributed to any major change in the environment.

Millisecond Pulsar in Globular Cluster.—Globular clusters were once thought to be collections of old and dying stars and relatively inactive, but recent work has caused this idea to be completely revised. In support of the new ideas comes the discovery of a millisecond pulsar in the globular cluster M28, in the constellation of Sagittarius. It rotates 327 times every second and is the first pulsar to be discovered in a globular cluster.

Pulsars are believed to be spinning neutron stars formed at the time of a supernova. They gradually slow down as they radiate energy. The pulsar in the Crab nebula, formed at the time of the supernova of A.D. 1054, rotates at 30 times per second whilst those thought to be about a million years old rotate about once every second. This would suggest that a millisecond pulsar is an exceedingly young object but such an idea conflicts with the basic properties of stars in globular clusters. It is possible that these fast rotating objects are in fact older stars which have speeded up due to a gradual accumulation of material from a companion star when they existed as a binary system. Stars in globular clusters are over 100,000 times more closely packed than stars in the vicinity of the Sun and it would be possible for the companion star to be pulled away during its journey through the dense cluster of stars, or for the pulsar gradually to consume all of the star.

Globular clusters contain more X-ray stars in binary systems than exist in the general population of the galaxy. Such binaries contain neutron stars in just the condition to account for millisecond pulsars. Consequently in 1986 a search was carried out for such objects in twelve nearby globular clusters. Astronomers successfully identified the pulsar in M28 using the 250 ft. radio telescope at Jodrell Bank. Finding a periodic signal from the mass of data collected was no easy task: the astronomers compared it to finding a needle in ten tons of hay by examining straws one at a time.

The Most Abundant Mineral.—The Earth's crust consists of a wide range of silicate minerals some of which, such as olivine and pyroxene, are exceedingly common. The core is known to consist of iron and nickel and associated alloys but a lack of detailed knowledge of the constitution and structure of the mantle has been of much concern to the geophysicist. However, recent work has provided a fundamental clue to understanding of this region.

Scientists from the University of California at Berkeley claim that the principal mineral existing in the mantle is magnesium silicate ($Mg SiO_3$), known as perovskite. This mineral was discovered some ten years ago by John Liu at the University of Canberra, Australia. He subjected olivine, pyroxene and garnet to enormous pressures such as those which exist in the mantle and found that the atoms in the molecules rearranged to form perovskite. It was therefore suspected that this mineral played an important part in the mantle but no-one knew whether or not the mineral was stable in the conditions existing within the mantle.

The Californian scientists subjected the mineral to immense pressure and heated samples to temperatures of about 2,000 K. The pressures reached were

similar to those existing just above the core-mantle boundary but the mineral did not change its structure or composition even after the pressure was eased. This showed that the mineral could exist all the way through the mantle down to the core. The density and elasticity at different pressures were also compatible with seismic data.

X-ray analysis showed that the mineral has a cubic structure with the magnesium atom at the centre and silicon atoms at each corner. Each silicon atom is surrounded by six oxygen atoms situated half way along the sides of the cube.

(The name perovskite, used widely in connection with this type of silicate mineral, should not be confused with another mineral known by this name, calcium titanate, which also has a similar structure.)

New Family of Dinosaur.—In 1983 an amateur geologist, William Walker, found a huge clawbone in the Smokejacks brickworks near Dorking. The Natural History Museum in London was informed and Alan Charig and a team from the Museum found more than half of the disarticulated skeleton. Since then they have removed most of the bones from the hard siltstone nodules encasing them and have joined them together to obtain the best skeleton in the world of a flesh-eating dinosaur. In fact it is unlike any other known dinosaur and it has been given the formal classification *Baryonyx walkeri.* (*Baryonyx* means "heavy claw" and *walkeri* acknowledges the part played by William Walker.) In addition, a new family of dinosaurs, Baryonychidae, has been created to accommodate this new type.

The dinosaur had an unusual jaw. The animal is thought to have had a narrow snout about a metre long with a downturned spoonlike end, similar to that of a crocodile. It had 32 teeth on each side of the lower jaw, twice the normal number for therapods, and each tooth shows very fine serrations. Its arms were exceptionally large. Compared with the Tyrannosaurus, which had arms about one tenth of the length of its hindlegs, this new dinosaur's forelimbs were two thirds the size of its hindlegs. This suggests that Baryonyx sometimes walked on all four legs.

The claws of the Baryonyx are disproportionately large: the one discovered had a claw 31 cm. long. Normally, clawed hands and feet have roughly equal-sized claws but in this case two claws were much larger than the others. This feature, and the fact that the teeth are finely serrated, suggests that the animal was a fish eater which would stand in shallow water to hook fish in a manner similar to the way bears catch salmon. An alternative explanation is that it could have been a scavenger.

The Nucleus of Halley's Comet.—The information sent back by the European spaceprobe *Giotto* and the Soviet *Vega* spacecraft as they approached and passed the nucleus of Halley's comet presented astronomers with the problems of putting a logical interpretation on the data. Until the fly-by very little was known about the shape and behaviour of cometary nuclei but on this occasion it was discovered that the nucleus was roughly cigar-shaped, about 16 km. long and 8 km. across. The preliminary analysis showed that there were spin periods of about two and seven days.

A German astronomer, Klaus Wilhelm, subsequently analysed the data more carefully and has put forward the theory that the periodic changes in the appearance of the nucleus arise from the superposition of two rotations. Wilhelm says that the difficulties of interpretation lie in the irregular shape of the nucleus. He believes that the nucleus is spinning about its minor axis, i.e. at right angles to the long axis, with a period of 2·2 days. This spin axis is, however, not orientated in a fixed direction but precessing, i.e. wobbling, with a period of 14·8 days. He claims that this precession is due to two factors: firstly, it is common to most rotating bodies. For example, the Earth's spin axis precesses with a period of about 26,000 years. The other factor is a forced precession caused by jets of gas boiling off from the nucleus.

The periods of 2·2 and 14·8 days are based on variations of the brightness of the comet and interpreted as the rotation of the nucleus. The earlier results, involving a 7·4 day rotation about the long and short axes of the nucleus, could not be substantiated because of the conflict with ground-based and other spacecraft observations.

Observing a Solar Eclipse at Night.—Interesting discoveries are often made by observers making routine observations who are puzzled by a deviation from what was expected. This was the case when Russell Eberst, the world's leading artificial satellite observer, started his observing programme on the evening of October 3, 1986. The sky was clear and so he expected to make a purely routine set of observations. As reported in *Space* (Nov. 7), Eberst located his first satellite, *Cosmos 1682*, at 18.34 U.T. (Universal Time) and noticed that it was much fainter than expected. Satellites are notorious for not having the predicted brightness and he put the discrepancy down to possibly seeing the satellite head-on. But when the second and subsequent satellites were all fainter, averaging about 1·5 magnitudes fainter than expected, he looked for an explanation. He realized that a solar eclipse was occurring which was visible from America. The times of the satellite observations from 18.34 to 19.36 coincided approximately with the times of the maximum phase of the eclipse. Although the umbra of the Moon's shadow was confined to areas well clear of the British Isles, the penumbra would have been visible from a height frequented by the satellites. A fall in brightness of 1·5 magnitudes indicated that the satellites were only about one quarter as bright as they should have been. Eberst had, in fact, observed one aspect of the eclipse.

Observing the Coelocanth.—Much interest was shown by the scientific community when in 1938 a coelocanth, long assumed to be extinct, was brought up in the net of a Comorain fisherman. The coelocanth is the only known survivor of a group of fish which are related to the lobe-finned ancestors of modern four-legged animals. The sea around the Comoros Islands in the Indian Ocean is the only area in which the coelocanth has been found and since 1938 many specimens have been brought to the surface. In every case they have either been dead or have died soon after, due it is thought to rapid changes in temperature, pressure and oxygen levels. Information gained from the fishermen seemed to indicate that the fish were normally found at depths between 180 and 200 metres.

Hans Fricke, of the Max Planck Institute for Animal Behaviour in Munich, constructed a submersible which he used in December 1986 to observe the coelocanths in their natural surroundings at a depth of 180 metres. He is currently analysing the films taken of the way they move through the water. Fricke describes their movements as very sluggish but has not yet published full details. The rather restricted data available suggests that the fish sculls with its fins in contrast with the normal method of using its tail.

Fricke suggests that the fish could have survived because of the very cold water at the depths at which they are found and relates their distribution to the slope of the ocean bed and the cover this provides from predators. He thinks that more information on their ecology might reveal why these strange fish have survived yet their descendants, like the dinosaurs, have long been extinct. There is a danger, however, that the coelocanth will soon be extinct. It exists only in small numbers but due to more efficient fishing methods 10–15 coelocanths are being brought to the surface each year. There is evidence of overfishing in the area and Fricke wants to launch an international campaign to conserve this relic of the past.

Ozone and the Upper Atmosphere.—For some years concern has been expressed about the depletion of ozone, the layer above the biosphere which protects the lower regions of the atmosphere from the damaging effects of the ultraviolet radiation of the sun. Recent research has revealed further cause for concern. Measurements since 1979 have shown a considerable drop in ozone concentration. The concentration of ozone in 1985 was less than 40 per cent of that existing in 1979, although there was a slight increase in 1986, and in southern mid-latitudes it has fallen by as much as 18 per cent. Also, studies have shown the formation of a hole in the ozone layer over the Antarctic during the spring months: a similar hole has been found in the Arctic regions. The hole fills up each summer, but every subsequent spring it becomes larger.

There is no general agreement about the causes for these depletions. One widely-held belief blames the extensive use of chlorofluorocarbons in aerosol propellants, refrigerants, etc. Ultraviolet light breaks down these compounds to produce chlorine, which catalyses the breakdown of the ozone into oxygen. The concentration of these compounds is rising over the Antarctic by at least 5 per cent per year. Their use as a propellant has been banned in the U.S.A. since 1978 but elsewhere there is little restriction. However, some investigators do not believe that these compounds are responsible and lay the blame on naturally-occurring nitrogen oxides, the concentrations of which in the lower stratosphere vary with the eleven-year solar cycle. Winds concentrate the oxides in the Antarctic during the winter and with the advent of spring the oxides gradually spread to lower latitudes, attacking the ozone as they do so. Supporters of this theory believe, therefore, that the fluctuations in the ozone concentration are cyclical; other researchers suspect that the general depletion and the polar holes are two distinct phenomena, caused by winds and not chemical activity; and recent work seems to reject both theories. Nevertheless, chlorofluorocarbons are still high on the list of causes of the depletions.

Other Planetary Systems.—There have been claims in the last few decades of the discovery of planetary systems round stars other than the Sun but subsequent data in some of these cases have shown this to be unlikely. The strongest case to date comes from work carried out by Canadian astronomers from the University of British Columbia using the 3·6 metre telescope at Mauna Kea, Hawaii.

Based on observations over six years, the astronomers claim that of the 14 stars which are similar to the Sun and also relatively nearby, half seem to be accompanied by bodies up to ten times the mass of Jupiter. The planets themselves cannot be seen but their presence is postulated because of the periodic variations in the speed at which the stars approach the Earth. A new method of measurement enables this to be calculated to an accuracy of 40 km. per second. The Canadians examined the small shifts in the wavelength of light from the star to measure changes in the motion along the line of sight. The technique cannot detect planets with orbital planes at right angles to the line of sight, and even with line of sight orbits only planets having masses equal to or greater than that of Jupiter can be detected. Smaller planets may exist, as in our own solar system, but there is no information as to whether or not they are present.

Not all the suspected stars have been identified by the Canadians but the team have said that the strongest evidence points to two stars, Epsilon Eridani and Gamma Cephei. The former lies about 11 light years away and has a mass 0·75 that of the Sun. It is an orange-coloured 4th magnitude star. Gamma Cephei, on the other hand, is eight times brighter than the Sun but it is 48 light years away. It can be seen as a 3rd magnitude star near to the Pole Star.

Astrometric work is also being carried out at the University of Pittsburgh's Alleghany Observatory using a technique which will detect planets as small as that of Saturn. But it is realized that to identify Earth-sized planets, it will require an orbiting instrument making observations for at least ten years.

Pest Control Side Effects.—The widespread use of drugs to control the effects of pests and diseases in domestic stock sometimes creates problems which have far wider implications. Such is the case with the anti-parasitic drug Ivermectin which is commonly administered to cattle, horses, sheep and pigs to control problems associated with warble fly, mites, lice and ticks. The danger lies not in the drug's effect on the herbivores but on the detrivores which feed on their dung. Throughout the world there are some 14,000 species of dung beetles and they fulfil an important role as removal agents of both herbivore and carnivore dung. In addition to simply removing the dung from the surface, the burrowing activities of these creatures, especially in arid and semi-arid regions, help in soil aeration and water percolation.

Biologists from the University of Bristol conducted controlled experiments to examine the rate at which dung was degraded, comparing the drug-contaminated faeces with uncontaminated dung. This latter group were virtually degraded within 100 days, while the contaminated dung failed to degrade in the normal way due to the absence of dung-degrading insects. The Invermectin-contaminated dung attracted only 17 adult beetles, 35 dipterous larvae and 44 earthworms after 100 days, whereas the uncontaminated controls yielded 780 dung beetles, 267 dipterous larvae and 46 earthworms in the same period.

In the mid 1960s Australian biologists encountered a similar problem. They found that endemic species of dung beetle were only adapted to the pelleted dung of marsupials and could not remove the dung from introduced cattle. The introduction of species of dung beetle from elsewhere has more or less cured the problem, and at the same time considerably reduced the fly population.

The rapid removal of dung from the surface has important ecological implications. Dung beetles take the digested material into the soil where much of it is decomposed by bacteria and fungi and its nutrients made available for future plant growth. If this process is stopped or restricted the effects may be catastrophic.

Scheiner's Halo: An Explanation.—The case for the existence of octahedral ice crystals in nature has been considerably strengthened by the recent success of two Austrian scientists, Erwin Mayer and Andreas Hallbrucker of the University of Innsbruck, in forming stable octahedral ice crystals. The existence of these diamond-shaped crystals has been suspected for some time because they are thought to be responsible for the rare form of halo known as Scheiner's halo.

Cirrus cloud, the very high cloud which exists at heights of 9,000 metres or more, consists of ice crystals which have a hexagonal structure. When light passes through these crystals it is refracted through the 60° prism formed by alternate faces of the hexagon to produce a halo known as the 22° halo, a circle of light having a radius of 22° from the Sun or Moon at the centre. A far less common halo at 46° is formed when light is refracted through the 90° formed by the base and side of the crystal. It is not possible to orientate the crystals so that a halo having a radius of 27·5° can be generated but such a halo, named after the Jesuit astronomer Christophe Scheiner who first recorded it in 1629, has been seen on a few occasions.

In 1981 Edward Whalley of the National Research Council of Canada suggested that the halo was caused by octahedral crystals. He claimed that refraction of sunlight through the 71·5° prism would produce the 27·5° angle. Unfortunately, although such crystals could be generated at very low temperatures, they reverted to the standard hexagonal shape at atmospheric temperatures. Mayer and Hallbrucker achieved stability of the octahedral crystals by freezing water droplets of a few microns in diameter, the size found in cirrus cloud. A very low temperature was required but many of the crystals survived for over half an hour when raised to a temperature of −40°C, the normal temperature of cirrus cloud. It is therefore possible that under rare conditions octahedral crystals are formed and it is these that produce the Scheiner's halo.

The Strange World of Pluto.—Ever since its discovery just over 50 years ago there has been much controversy about the precise size and mass of the outermost planet Pluto, although it was generally accepted that it is a relatively small body. Confusion was increased considerably when in 1978 the planet was found to possess a moon far larger than would have been expected for a planet of that size. However, the moon, Charon, has provided information which has enabled astronomers to calculate precise values for the planet's diameter and mass.

The orbit of Charon around Pluto is inclined at a large angle to the ecliptic and so, as seen from the Earth, Charon passes in front of the planet for a few years in every 124 years. Such a sequence started in 1985 and will end in 1989. Manfred Pakull and Klaus Reinsch of the Technical University of West Berlin, using observations made from the European Southern Observatory in Chile, examined the way the light changed as Charon moved in front of Pluto. They concluded that Pluto is 2,200 km. in diameter, with a maximum error of 140 km., i.e. it is about two thirds the size of our Moon.

From this data it was possible to calculate the overall density of Pluto, a value about twice the density of water being obtained. This suggests that the planet contains dense rock with considerable amounts of water ice. The density is much higher than that of Saturn's satellites but roughly the same as that of the moons of Uranus. This has strengthened the views of some astronomers that Pluto is an escaped satellite of either Uranus or Neptune. Although Pluto is quite small, Charon is thought to be about 1,160 km. in diameter, half that of the planet, a value which is far different from any other planet–satellite ratio. There seems to be a good case for referring to the system as a double planet.

Superconductivity.—Kammerlingh Onnes discovered in 1911 that when mercury was cooled to 4·3 Kelvin (K.), it lost its electrical resistance. Over the years many substances have been found to be superconducting when cooled below what is called the critical temperature. The main drive has been to find substances with high critical temperatures and by 1973 a temperature of 23·3 K. had been reached with an alloy of germanium and niobium. A major breakthrough took place in September 1986 when Muller and Bedorz, using a mixture of barium, lanthanum, copper and oxygen produced a superconductor with a critical temperature of 35 K. The pace of development quickened when it was announced that a team of workers at the University of Houston had produced a ceramic with a critical temperature of above 90 K. Since then many ceramics have been made with critical temperatures in the same range.

This temperature is very useful because the ceramics can be cooled with liquid nitrogen instead of by the costlier process using liquid hydrogen.

Within a few days of learning the composition of an yttrium ceramic, I.B.M.'s Amaden Research Centre published its structure, showing it to be one of a family of "oxygen-defect perovskites". The worldwide interest in these compounds meant that by May 1987 a barium, yttrium, copper and oxygen compound had been made with a critical temperature of just above 240 K. More recently claims have been made for ceramics which are superconducting at room temperatures: in one case, however, the ceramic was unstable and lasted only for a few days. Indian scientists also claim to have produced stable room temperature superconductors.

The applications of such superconductors are immense. They range from the light electronic industries making very fast computers and medical equipment to the heavy electrical industries. Much work still needs to be done, mainly in the purification of the materials used, and a better understanding must be reached of molecular structure and reliability in reproduction.

Supernova (SN 1978 A).—Much has been written about supernovae erupting in other galaxies and the role these play in steller evolution, but most of these events take place in the far reaches of the universe and can only be observed by telescope. The last recorded supernova explosion visible to the naked eye was in 1604, so it was with great excitement that astronomers turned their attention to a naked-eye explosion which occurred in the nearby Large Magellanic Cloud (L.M.C.), visible from the southern hemisphere as a large patch of light.

On February 24, 1987, Ian Shelton at the Las Campanas Observatory in Chile found a 5th magnitude object on a photograph he had taken with a 25 cm. telescope. During the exposure Oscar Duhalde walked outside and noticed the unusual appearance of the L.M.C. Later, as night fell in New Zealand, Albert Jones, an amateur variable star observer and member of the British Astronomical Association, immediately noticed the bright object in the L.M.C. and telephoned Robert McNaught, another B.A.A. member stationed at Siding Spring Observatory in New South Wales, who confirmed the supernova. McNaught contacted Brian Marsden of the I.A.U. Circulars Office in Massachusetts, U.S.A., who in turn alerted the professional observatories. As such events cannot be predicted it is usually only possible to study supernovae explosions some time after they have occurred. In this case, however, prediscovery observations provided valuable information. Both Ian Shelton and Robert McNaught had taken photographs the previous night. Shelton's photograph, taken at 0225 U.T., showed no sign of the supernova but McNaught's photograph, taken at 1038 U.T., showed the supernova at magnitude 6. Only 75 minutes earlier, Albert Jones had been looking at the L.M.C. visually and did not record anything unusual, suggesting that the star was fainter than magnitude 7·5.

As the first few days passed it was realized that this supernova was not behaving in the expected manner. It reached maximum brightness of magnitude 4·4 on the night of February 27/28 and fell to 4·6 by March 5. It brightened again to 4·1 by March 20 and since then its brightness has been fluctuating on time scales of 20 minutes to several hours. These magnitudes, however, do not give any guide to the size of the explosion. In the initial surge the star burst forth to shine about 50 million times brighter than the Sun, with gas being ejected at speeds greater than 100,000 km. per second.

The major problem that arose was determining which star had actually exploded. Careful measuring showed the position of the supernova was coincident with the brighter component of a pair of blue giants known as Sanduleak − 69°202 (the name originates from the astronomer who determined the accurate positions of the pair). This created some confusion because it was thought that supernovae originated from red supergiants. Nevertheless, the brighter of the original pair no longer exists.

Most of the information about supernovae come from a study of their spectra. Type I are thought to originate from the total destruction of a white dwarf with little hydrogen, whereas Type II are caused by the collapse of the iron core in the interior of a star at least eight times more massive than the Sun. In the case of SN 1987 A, before the explosion it was a hot blue star thought to be about 20 times more massive than the Sun and the early identification of the presence of hydrogen indicated it to be a Type II supernova.

The early stages of the eruption have also been monitored at wavelengths other than the visual. In infrared, the supernova has been continuously brightening because the gas shell cools as it expands, becoming a more efficient emitter at infrared wavelengths. At ultraviolet wavelengths the intensity peaked very early. The brightness was falling when the I.U.E. satellite examined the supernova only a few hours after the discovery and by the beginning in March no ultraviolet emission could be detected. The southern hemisphere radio observatories are also monitoring the event.

The monitoring of the explosion over the next few years will provide much data on the mechanisms involved. Eventually, the expanding gas shell will become sufficiently transparent to reveal the core of the star. Current theories expect this to be a rapidly rotating pulsar, though the possibility of a black hole has been suggested.

Neutrinos associated with the Supernova.— The supernova explosion in the Large Magellanic Cloud (L.M.C.) on February 24, 1987 has provided vital information about neutrinos, the highly energetic particles with very little mass. Over the last few decades there has been much controversy in scientific circles about these particles. According to current theories an event such as a supernova should have produced a flood of neutrinos and their anti-matter equivalent, antineutrinos.

A team of Italian and Soviet scientists working in a laboratory near Mont Blanc reported a burst of five neutrinos in only five seconds on the morning of February 23. However the event was not confirmed by two other laboratories. The first of these, at Kamioka in Japan, houses the world's most sensitive detector. Records there show a burst of neutrinos at 07.35 U.T., about 18 hours before the supernova was identified. The burst consisted of 11 events spread over 13 seconds, the first five arriving in a pulse lasting less than a second. Although most of the particles were antineutrinos with no information as to their source, the first two events detected were neutrinos and the Japanese were able to show that they had come from the direction of the L.M.C. Detectors located in Ohio, U.S.A., recorded one burst of activity at roughly the same time as that reported by the Japanese. The Americans recorded eight events in six seconds, with the first five occurring in the first two seconds. They had energies of between 30 and 100 MeV.

The similarities between the American and Japanese results have convinced most workers that these actually recorded the initial explosion of the star. The tightness of the initial surge has enabled physicists to put an upper limit to the mass of a neutrino. If it had travelled with the speed of light, it would have no mass. If it had mass, its speed would depend on the energy of the particle. The fact that neutrinos with different energies arrived within a second indicates that their mass must be less than 15 eV, confirming earlier results obtained by workers at the University of Zurich. This mass is not sufficient to make up the suspected missing mass which astronomers think fills the universe.

Tectonic Activity on Venus.— For a long time Venus was considered to be a sister planet to the Earth. This idea was based on the fact that they occupy adjacent orbits round the Sun and are approximately the same size. However, the results from space probes have shown that they are completely different. The very high temperatures and pressures at the surface of Venus, together with the highly corrosive atmosphere virtually excludes all possibility of the existence of life on the planet. Nevertheless, recent work has shown that, like the Earth, Venus is tectonically active with moving crustal plates.

One of the large features on the planet's surface, Aphrodite Terra, is a ridge a few kilometres high which stretches some 4,000 km. in an east–west direction. This has been the subject of research by Jim Head and colleagues at Brown University, Rhode Island. They have analysed data from the *Pioneer Venus* space probe and the Arecibo Radio Observatory and found a series of parallel discontinuities 100–200 km. wide cutting across the ridge. These features, labelled cross-strike discontinuities (C.S.D.s), are very similar to the fracture zones which cut across the mid-oceanic ridges on the Earth. The topology on either side of the axis of the ridge is identical, possibly indicating that new crustal material is being formed in the centre. Another similarity with the mid-Atlantic ridge is the way the Aphrodite ridge is offset laterally along the C.S.D.s. The team estimate that the ridge is spreading at a rate of about 2 cm. per year.

If there is spreading at this point, there must also be compression or subduction elsewhere. Soviet workers using data supplied by *Venera 15* and *16* have indicated the possibility of fold mountains in the Ishtar Terra area north of Aphrodite. Other evidence that Venus is tectonically active at present includes crater counts in the Aphrodite area which point to an age of about 250–500 million years. This age is also suggested by the young appearance of the crests and troughs which exist in that region.

Valleys in the Earth's Core.—It has long been known that the Earth is far from being a perfect sphere but it is the study of the behaviour of artificial satellites whilst orbiting the Earth that has revealed a true picture of the shape of the planet. In addition to being flattened at the poles (the southern hemisphere being flattened more than the northern), there are irregularities superimposed on the large-scale deviations. These deviations have little to do with surface features such as mountain ranges and oceans.

Recent work has concentrated on the coincidences between large-scale sagging of the crust and anomalies in the gravitational and magnetic fields. The American satellites *Geos*-3 and *Seasat* were launched in 1975 and 1978 respectively for the purpose of determining the shape of the Earth to a greater accuracy than hitherto possible. Observations of their courses have revealed a bulge in the shape of the orbit when the satellites passed over the Indian Ocean, indicating a weaker gravitational pull in that area. It has also been discovered that the level of the water in the ocean forms a shallow saucer-shaped depression about 200 km. across and 130 km. deep. This depression is also mirrored in the rocks below the water. The feature was thought at the time to be due to missing mass within the crust or upper mantle. Subsequent work using satellites to map the intensity of the Earth's magnetic field showed that there was a marked magnetic anomaly in that area. Quite often such an anomaly can be explained by magnetism within the surface or near rocks but in this case spectral analysis of the vertical component of the field showed that the anomaly was still present in the long wavelengths. These are associated with currents flowing within the Earth's core.

Janardan Negi of the Geophysical Research Institute in Hyderabad has suggested that the anomaly could be explained by a valley some five to ten km. deep in the Earth's core. Confirmation of this theory will have to wait for the launching of the *Grav-* *Magsat* satellite, still some years away. This satellite is planned to provide in much greater detail maps of the Earth's gravitational and magnetic fields.

Volcanic Eruption Puzzle.—Major eruptions eject into the atmosphere huge quantities of gas and dust which absorb sunlight and so cool the Earth. The dust particles usually settle within a few weeks but the gas, mainly sulphur dioxide, is converted into droplets of sulphuric acid which remain in the atmosphere for many months. Eventually these droplets reach the Earth's surface and records of such falls are preserved in the ice of Antarctica. Study of deposits in Antarctic ice provided evidence of two major volcanic events early in the 19th century. Until now these two events were believed to have been the eruptions in Indonesia of Tambora in 1815 and Galunggung in 1822 but analysis of ice cores from the East Antarctic Plateau conflicts with these ideas.

Michel Legrand and Robert Delmas of the Glaciology Laboratory of Grenoble, who analysed the deposits, found that the first peak of sulphuric acid fallout was not caused by the 1815 eruption because microscopic particles of glass in the core did not match the material known to have been ejected by Tambora. They have shown that the second peak in acid concentration should be attributed to Tambora and the earlier peak to some unknown major eruption which took place six years earlier.

This new evidence seems to sort out the problem of the very cold winters and bad summers reported after 1810, in contrast with the warmer period from 1790 to 1809. It had been suggested that the cold spell was due to Tambora but this eruption occurred in the middle of the cold spell. The occurrence of an earlier event would better explain the weather pattern, with Tambora adding to the effect of the previous eruption and producing the "year without a summer" in 1816. (It is interesting to note that the gardens at Trengwainton, near Penzance in Cornwall, constructed about 1820, incline southwards at an angle of 15° so as to gain heat from the Sun.)

Confirmation of the earlier unknown event is awaited from the core studies being made by the British Antarctic Survey, who are analysing a 200 year core from Dolleman Island, off the Antarctic Peninsula.

EDUCATION IN THE UNITED KINGDOM

ENGLAND AND WALES

Aims

The Government's main aims in education are to raise standards all round and to get the best possible value for money. To achieve these aims, major changes are being made in many aspects of education provision at all levels, or are planned. The Government's intention is to maximize the benefits of decentralization while meeting the requirements of a national system in a modern society by providing strong leadership and direction.

A major Education Bill is likely to be presented in the 1987–88 session of Parliament.

Fall and rise in numbers

In primary education and, increasingly, in secondary education pupil numbers in England have continued to decline. However, for primary schools where pupil numbers peaked at around 4·9 million in the early 1970s and reached their lowest figure of 3·7 million in 1985, numbers are expected to increase gradually year by year until by the year 1991 they reach about 3·9 million. For secondary schools, where pupil numbers have fallen from 3·9 million in 1979 to 3·5 million in 1985 and will decline further to an expected 2·8 million in 1991, it is not expected that they will exceed about 3·1 million for the rest of the century.

Expenditure

In real terms (i.e. cash figures adjusted to 1985–86 price levels), expenditure on education was as follows (£billion): 1984–85, 14·8; 1985–86, 14·5; 1986–87 (estimated), 15·5: and planned spending in 1987–88 is 15·6; 1988–89, 15·7; 1989–90, 15·7. In cash terms, the estimated expenditure on education in 1986–87 was £16 billion; of which (£million), 9,823 was spent on schools, 4,592 on higher and further education, 924 on miscellaneous education services, and 615 on the research councils and related bodies.

The unit cost, in real terms (1979–80=100), for maintained primary and secondary schools in England went up from 107 in 1980–81 to 120 in 1984–85, and to an estimated 124 in 1985–86.

Department of Education and Science

The Department of Education and Science (D.E.S.) is responsible for all aspects of education in England and for government policy and support for universities in England, Scotland and Wales. Responsibility in Wales for nursery, primary and secondary education, and for all non-university institutions of higher and further education, the youth and community services, and adult education lies with the Secretary of State for Wales.

The Department's main concern is the formulation of national policies for education. It is responsible for the broad allocation of resources for education, for the rate and distribution of educational building and for the supply, training and superannuation of teachers. It is concerned with basic educational standards. The Department does not run any schools or colleges or engage any teachers.

The D.E.S. is also responsible for government support for civil science.

It acts within a framework of estimates approved by Parliament. The money which the Department itself spends is a small part of the total public expenditure on education, the major part being expenditure by local authorities (*see below*). This expenditure by local authorities is financed from rates and from the rate support grant payable from the national Exchequer.

The Department commissions research, related to policy interests of the D.E.S. and the L.E.A.s, from universities and other bodies such as the National Foundation for Educational Research.

H.M. Inspectorate

Her Majesty's Inspectors inspect schools and other educational establishments apart from universities. H.M.I.s assess standards and trends and advise the Secretaries of State on the performance of the system nationally. They identify and make more widely known good practice and promising developments and draw attention to weaknesses needing consideration. They provide advice and help to those with responsibilities for, or in, the institutions in the system through the H.M.I.s' day-to-day contacts, their contributions to training, and their publications. Inspection visits are the main, though not the only, way by which the H.M.I.s perform these functions. There were, in 1985, 458 H.M.I.s in England and 46 in Wales. In 1985 in England H.M.I.s visited about 15 per cent of primary schools, 23 per cent of middle schools, and 56 per cent of secondary schools in the maintained sector; and 22 per cent of independent schools. Nearly 90 per cent of public sector institutions of further and higher education (including those providing initial teacher training) also had inspection visits.

Local Education Authorities

The educational service is a national service locally administered. Among its main features are:—

(a) its administration is still largely decentralized, the day-to-day responsibility for providing state primary, secondary and further education (but not university education) to meet the needs of their areas being that of the local education authorities (L.E.A.s). However, subject to guidelines issued by the central education departments in England and Wales and the requirements of examination syllabuses, at present each educational establishment still has freedom to determine its own curriculum and the content of its courses.

These local authorities appoint education committees consisting of some of their own members (a majority of the committee) and other people with experience in education and knowledge of the local education situation. The L.E.A.s own and maintain schools and colleges and build new ones, employ teachers and provide equipment. Most of the public money spent on education is disbursed by the local authorities. L.E.A.'s are financed largely by rate support grants from the Department of the Environment and from the rates; teachers' salaries account for about half of local authority expenditure on education and related services.

Voluntary Agencies

(b) Voluntary agencies play an important part in educational provision often in co-operation with the State. Some indication of its nature and extent is given below.

SCHOOLS AND PUPILS

Schooling is compulsory for all children between 5 and 16 years. Some provision is made for children under 5 and many pupils remain at school after the minimum leaving age. No fees are charged in any publicly maintained school.

There are two main categories of school: (a) those *maintained* by local education authorities, the authorities meeting their expenditure partly from local rates and partly from grants made by the Department of the Environment; (b) *independent* schools (which are liable to inspection by H.M. Inspectorate).

County and Voluntary Schools

Maintained schools are of two types: (i) *county schools* (16,157 in 1986 in England) which are built, maintained and staffed by local education authorities. They are non-denominational and provide primary and secondary education. Their managers (primary schools) and governors (secondary schools) are appointed by the L.E.A.s. (ii) *voluntary schools* (7,678 in 1986 in England) also provide primary and secondary education. Although built by voluntary bodies (mainly religious denominations) they are financially maintained by an L.E.A. Voluntary schools are of three kinds: controlled (3,175), aided (4,415), and special agreement (88). In *controlled* schools the L.E.A. nominates a majority of the managers or governors (the rest are nominated by the voluntary body), bears all costs and appoints the teachers.

In *aided* schools the managers or governors (the majority appointed by the voluntary interest and the rest by the L.E.A.) are responsible for repairs to the outside of the school building and for improvements and alterations to it though the Department of Education and Science may reimburse part of approved capital expenditure. The L.E.A. pays for internal maintenance and other running costs. The managers or governors control the appointment of teachers. *Special agreement* schools are those where the L.E.A. may, by special agreement, pay between one-half and three-quarters of the cost of building a new, or extending an existing, voluntary school, almost always a secondary school. A majority of the governors are appointed by the voluntary body and the remainder by the L.E.A. Expenditure is normally apportioned between the authority and the voluntary body.

New government policies were set out in 1985 in an important White Paper, *Better Schools*. It described in detail the government's plans to raise standards for children of all abilities and to secure the best possible return from the resources invested in the schools. Recent government initiatives are covered and the next steps are described in the process of reform. These steps include: the promotion of national agreement on the purposes and content of the curriculum; the encouragement of schools to do more to prepare young people for work; the completion of the reform of the public examination system at age 16; the introduction of a national system of records of achievement; and the improvement of the training, deployment and management of the more than 400,000 teachers in England and Wales. The White Paper also sets out government decisions to: legislate to reform school governing bodies; introduce a new grant to make in-service teacher training more effective; extend the Secretary of State's powers to regulate the employment of teachers to cover the appraisal of their performance; to introduce the new AS-level examination for sixth-formers (*see below*); to set new guidelines for the minimum size of schools; and tackle truancy.

In November 1986, a new *Education Act* received royal assent. It gives effect to certain of these new policies. In particular it aims to raise standards by improving the management of schools and promoting teaching quality. Among other things, it gives parents a greater say in the running of their children's schools, provides for more effective in-service training of teachers and a new framework for the appraisal of teachers' performance, abolishes corporal punishment in the maintained sector, provides safeguards in the teaching of sex education and political issues, and protects freedom of speech in universities, polytechnics and colleges.

Public Schools

By the term *public schools* is usually meant the independent schools in the membership of the Headmasters' Conference, the Governing Bodies Association or the Governing Bodies of Girls' Schools Association. Most public schools are for one sex (about half of them for girls) but there are some mixed schools and certain boys' schools admit girls to their sixth forms.

Independent schools charge fees and do not receive grants from public funds. *Preparatory schools* are mainly for boys from about 7 to 13 years who wish to enter public schools. All independent schools are open to inspection by H.M. Inspectors (*see above*) and must register with the Department of Education and Science which lays down certain minimum standards and can make schools remedy any unacceptable features of their building or instruction and exclude any unsuitable teacher or proprietor. In 1986 there were in England 2,272 independent schools with 502,456 full-time pupils and a pupil–teacher ratio of 11·3 (which compares with 18·6 for maintained schools). The number of schools was 39 fewer than the previous year but full-time pupil numbers went up by 1,000. The arrangements by which independent schools could be "recognized as efficient", *i.e.* could satisfy the D.E.S. that their standards were broadly comparable with those of grant-aided schools, were discontinued in 1978.

Assisted places.—The Assisted Places Scheme enables bright children to benefit from attendance at good independent secondary schools which their parents could not otherwise afford. The take-up rate for places available at the 226 participating schools, at age 11 to 13, has risen to more than 98 per cent and the proportion of pupils receiving full fee remission to 42 per cent. Some 33,200 places are offered.

The State System

Nursery Education is for children under 5 years who may attend a nursery school or a primary school. 508,600 pupils under 5 years of age were receiving education in maintained nursery and primary schools in January 1986, a decrease of 4,000 on the previous year. However, expressed as a percentage of the population aged 3 and 4 years, the 508,600 represented 43·3 per cent, compared to 43·2 in the previous year and 33·5 in 1977. 236,100 were in infant classes, 223,100 in nursery classes and 49,400 in nursery schools.

Primary Stage.—This begins at 5 years and the transfer to secondary school is generally made at 11 years. Primary schools consist mainly of *infants' schools* for children aged 5 to 7, *junior schools* for those aged 7 to 11 and *junior and infant schools* for both age groups. In addition *first schools* in some areas cater for ages from 5 to 8, 9 or 10. (They are the first stage of a three-tier system: first, middle and secondary.) Many primary schools provide nursery classes for children under 5 (*see above*).

Middle Schools.—Middle schools (which take children from first schools) cover varying age ranges between 8 and 14 and usually lead on to comprehensive upper schools.

Secondary Stage.—Secondary schools are for children aged 11 to 16 and over. The largest have over 2,000 pupils but 82 per cent of the schools take between 400 and 1,500 pupils. In January, 1986, when there were in England 3,388,500 pupils in maintained secondary schools the main types were: (a) *comprehensive* schools (85·4 per cent of pupils), whose admission arrangements are without reference to ability or aptitude; (b) *middle deemed secondary* schools (6·6 per cent); (c) *secondary modern* schools (4·2 per cent) providing mainly a general education with a practical bias; (d) *secondary grammar* schools

(3 per cent) providing an academic course from 11 to 16–18 years; and (e) *technical* schools (0·7 per cent) providing an integrated academic and technical course.

Tertiary Colleges provide normal sixth form school courses as well as a range of courses for further education students over the age of 16.

Special Education is provided for children who require it because of physical or mental disability. In January 1986 there were 111,940 full-time pupils in special schools (of whom 4,265 were in hospital schools). Numbers have been going down since 1978 (131,500).

City Technology Colleges.—The Government plans to provide for the setting up of City Technology Colleges. These schools will be state-aided but independent of L.E.A.s. Their aim is to widen the choice of secondary school for families in disadvantaged urban areas and to provide models for the effective teaching of a broad curriculum with an emphasis on science, technology and business understanding in a disciplined learning environment. Their sponsors will be expected to meet all, or a substantial part, of the capital costs. The schools will receive a grant related to the number of pupils and enough to meet all items of recurrent spending which would fall on an L.E.A. for a comparable school which it maintains.

Primary and Secondary Schools

In 1986 there were 28,162 maintained and non-maintained schools in England, 357 fewer than in 1985. The total number of full-time pupils in them fell by 133,100 over the year to 7,563,000 in 1986. The number of maintained secondary schools (4,286 in 1986) fell slightly for the ninth successive year since the peak in 1977. Over the same period the number of primary schools has also fallen; in 1986 the total of 19,549 was 185 below the total for 1985.

Of the 7,563,000 full-time pupils in 1986, 11,800 were in maintained nursery schools, 3,548,300 in maintained primary schools (including 440,100 under 5 years), 3,388,500 in maintained secondary schools (including 304,700 who were 16 or over), 502,500 in independent schools, and 111,900 in special schools.

Between 1984–85 and 1989–90 primary school pupil numbers are projected to rise by 5·2 per cent and secondary school pupil numbers by 19·5 per cent.

Boys and girls are taught together in almost all maintained primary schools. Most pupils in maintained secondary schools in England and Wales attend mixed schools.

Parents.—Parental involvement in publicly maintained schools is growing through parent/teacher associations and in other ways. There is now statutory provision for elected parent and teacher governors on school governing bodies and for parents to express a preference as to the school they would like their child to attend.

Pupil–teacher ratios.—In both maintained primary and secondary schools the steady year-by-year improvement continued, from 23·9 in primary schools in 1977 to 22·1 in 1986 (following an uncharacteristic jump to 22·2 in 1985) and from 17·0 in secondary schools in 1977 to 15·9 in 1986. In independent schools, there was also a gradual improvement: from 13·2 in 1977 to 11·3 in 1986.

Class sizes.—The average size of classes "as taught" in maintained primary schools rose in 1986 as compared to 1985—from 25·2 to 25·9. This was the second rise in recent years: between 1977 and 1984 there had been a steady year-by-year improvement from 27·5 to 25·0. In secondary schools a steady annual improvement resumed after a rise in 1985 (to 21·4): 22·4 in 1977 to 20·9 in 1984 and 21·3 in 1986.

School meals.—Under the Social Security Act 1986, the duty of L.E.A.s to provide free school meals will from April 1988 be restricted to provision for children of families in receipt of income support.

Advanced levels.—In 1986 the number of pupils in A-level courses was 231,500, almost equally divided between boys and girls. 27·3 per cent of them were studying maths/science subjects only, compared to 28·6 per cent in 1985 and 29·5 in each year from 1981 to 1984.

In 1984–85, 20·8 per cent (proportion of 17 year old age group) achieved 1 or more passes at A level compared to 17·7 per cent ten years before; and 10·8 per cent achieved 3 or more passes compared to 8·6 per cent.

School-leavers.—Three-quarters of those who left school in 1984–85 had achieved five or more graded G.C.E. O-level or C.S.E. results, a substantial increase over the figure for 10 years before.

Examinations.—Secondary school pupils (and others) until the end of 1987 took the General Certificate of Education (G.C.E.) or the Certificate of Secondary Education (C.S.E.). The G.C.E. was introduced in 1951 (it replaced the School Certificate and Higher School Certificate) and the C.S.E. in 1965.

However, after 1987 there will be no G.C.E. or C.S.E. Instead, there will be a new single system of examinations—the *General Certificate of Secondary Education (G.C.S.E.) examinations.* The last O-level, C.S.E. and joint 16+ examinations were held in summer and winter 1987, and the first G.C.S.E. courses started in the autumn of 1986 with the first examinations to be held in summer 1988. National Criteria for the G.C.S.E. were approved by the Secretaries of State in 1985.

The purpose of the change is to improve the examination courses and to raise the standard of performance of all candidates. To achieve this, there will be: fewer examining groups; syllabuses based on national criteria covering course objectives, content and assessment methods; differentiated assessment (i.e. different papers or questions for different ranges of ability); and grade-related criteria (i.e. grades to be awarded on absolute rather than relative performance). The G.C.S.E. is to be a single system of examinations, not a single examination.

The G.C.S.E. certificates will be awarded with a seven-point scale: A to G. Grades A to C will be the equivalent of the corresponding O-level grades A to C or C.S.E. grade 1. Grades D, E, F and G will record achievement at least as high as that represented by C.S.E. grades 2, 3, 4 and 5. There will be no restrictions on entry to any examination. The G.C.S.E. examination is to be administered by six groups of examining boards in England, Wales and Northern Ireland. All G.C.S.E. syllabuses, assessment and grading procedures will be monitored by the Secondary Examinations Council (*see below*) to ensure that they conform to the National Criteria. The National Criteria have two parts: the *General Criteria* which sets out the rules and principles for all courses and examinations; and *Subject Criteria* which set out the aims for the content and teaching of individual subjects.

The Secretary of State has said that the new examinations will: do more than O-levels to stretch the ablest pupils; do more than C.S.E. to motivate other pupils; promote more effectively worthwhile knowledge, understanding and skills; grade candidates by what they know, understand and can do; be clearer to candidates, their parents and employers than the present system; and be more cost effective.

A-level examinations, taken two years after G.C.S.E., will continue though there are changes to the grading system. The Government set up, in February 1987, a small independent committee to review A-levels.

In addition to A-level examinations, new *Advanced Supplementary level (AS-level) examinations* are being introduced. Their purpose is to broaden the curriculum for A-level students but without diluting academic standards. AS-levels are seen by the D.E.S. as "making a useful, if limited, contribution to the problems associated with overspecialisation." Courses leading to AS-level started in September 1987 and the first examinations will be held in summer 1989.

AS-levels will be for full-time A-level students but others can take them too. An AS-level syllabus will cover not less than half the amount of ground covered by the corresponding A-level syllabus and, where possible, will be related to it. An AS-level course will last two years and require not less than half the teaching time of the corresponding A-level course. It is envisaged that students hoping to go on to higher education would continue (where they do so now) to take A-level courses in the subjects they want to specialize in. AS-level courses will supplement and broaden these studies and examinations will be held at the same time as A-levels.

Technical and Vocational Education Initiative.— T.V.E.I., within a framework of general education, aims to give teenagers a curriculum more relevant to adult life and work. Following pilot projects, it is now a national scheme, with newly established curricular criteria, open to all maintained schools and colleges providing for young people, of all abilities, aged 14–18. T.V.E.I. is not an examination or a qualification.

The *Certificate of Pre-Vocational Education* is a one-year full-time (or two years part-time) course intended for a wide ability range at 16+ including pupils who do not intend to go on to A-levels but would like to continue their education on completion of their secondary schooling. This new national qualification is offered by the Business and Technician Education Council and the City and Guilds of London Institute operating together as the Joint Board for Pre-Vocational Education. Within guidelines laid down by that Board, schools and colleges design their own courses, which stress activity-based learning, basic numeracy and work-experience. The C.P.V.E. is mainly for those who want to find out more about what work they may be good at and to prepare themselves for adult work, but who are not yet committed to a particular occupation.

In 1983 two new bodies were set up to replace the Schools Council. They are the *Secondary Examinations Council* (S.E.C.) and the *School Curriculum Development Committee* (S.C.D.C.). The purpose of the S.E.C. (*see also above*) is to co-ordinate and try to improve the school examination system and other forms of school-based assessment in England and Wales; and to advise the Government on these policy areas. The S.C.D.C.'s task is to inform itself of school curriculum development work being done by others in England and Wales; to identify any important gaps; to undertake appropriate work in such areas or to stimulate others to do so; and to promote the dissemination of curriculum development. The S.E.C. is wholly funded by central government but the S.C.D.C. is jointly funded by the Department of Education and Science and the local authorities.

TEACHERS
(*see also* p. 530)

Although it is the duty of each Local Education Authority to ensure that there is efficient education to meet the needs of the local population, what is taught in the schools is normally decided on their behalf by the head teachers of schools, and is subject to guidelines issued by the central education departments and to the requirements of examination syllabuses.

Teachers are appointed by local education author-

ities, school governing bodies or managers. Those in publicly maintained schools must be approved as "qualified" by the Department of Education and Science. To become a qualified teacher it is necessary to have successfully completed an initial course of teacher training. Teacher training is largely integrated with the rest of higher education with training places concentrated in polytechnics, institutes or colleges of higher education, and universities. Nongraduates usually qualify by way of a three- or four-year course leading to a B.Ed. degree while graduates take a one-year postgraduate certificate of education.

Entry requirements are high with a reduced number of training places available. On entry to a course of initial teacher training leading to qualified teacher status (whether at undergraduate or postgraduate level) students are expected to provide evidence of, inter alia, a level of competence in English and mathematics at least equivalent to passes at a minimum of Grade C at G.C.E. "O" level or Grade 1 in C.S.E.

For entry at undergraduate level candidates must also normally have five passes in the G.C.E. (two of which should be at "A" level) or four passes (three of which should be at "A" level).

With certain exceptions, the profession now has an all-graduate entry. Teachers in further education, however, are not required to have qualified teacher status but roughly half have a teaching qualification and most have industrial, commercial or professional experience.

The Government-established Council for the Accreditation of Teacher Education (CATE) has been reviewing all initial teacher training courses to ensure that they meet stringent conditions.

*Newly-Trained Teachers.—*Of teachers who in 1985 had successfully completed initial training courses in public sector institutions in England and Wales, 85 per cent had obtained teaching posts in the U.K. (compared with 80 per cent in 1984 and 77 per cent in 1983), 7 per cent had taken up non-teaching employment in the U.K. or were working abroad, and 6 per cent were unemployed but seeking a teaching post (compared with 10 per cent in 1984 and 12 per cent in 1983). 86 per cent of all successful leavers had a postgraduate certificate in education or a bachelor's degree in education; 14 per cent had taken a one-year specialist certificate in education courses for mature students, or had trained on a special further education course.

*New Intake.—*In the year to January 1986, 10,800 teachers took up first full-time appointments either permanent or for at least one term's duration, in maintained nursery, primary and secondary schools in England and Wales.

*Shortage Subjects.—*In recent years there have been shortages of teachers in a number of secondary subjects, particularly mathematics, the physical sciences and craft, design and technology (C.D.T.). There is a bursary scheme for trainee teachers in these three shortage areas for one- or two-year courses.

*Serving Teachers.—*In 1986 there were 520,163 teachers (full-time and full-time equivalent) in service with L.E.A.s. Of these, 402,932 (down from 414,621 in 1983) were in maintained schools and 117,231 (down from 117,877 in 1985) in further education, special schools, etc. 1,690 were in nursery schools, 174,834 in primary schools, and 225,795 in secondary schools. 97,715 were in maintained and assisted further education, adult education centres and youth clubs and centres (16,322 of these in polytechnics), 17,302 in maintained special schools, and 2,149 provided out of school education.

A new £200 million scheme has been launched for the in-service training of teachers and others employed in the education service.

HIGHER EDUCATION

Higher Education consists of the education provided in universities and in advanced courses in polytechnics and colleges of higher education.

In funding higher education, the Government's stated aims are: to enable scholarship and research of high quality to be undertaken; the effective provision of general intellectual training and specific preparation for employment; and meeting the many specific needs of firms, the Government itself, and other agencies for knowledge and advice. In particular, the Government is concerned to make sure that (a) places are available for all who have the necessary intellectual competence, motivation and maturity to benefit from higher education and who wish to do so; (b) the highly qualified manpower needed by employers is available; (c) the maintenance and improvement of quality, particularly in teaching, is the subject of continuing appraisal; and (d) the quality of institutional management is improved in pursuit of greater economy, efficiency and value for money.

Students.—In 1985–86, the (provisional) number of home full-time and sandwich-course students in universities in Great Britain was 255,000 and in non-university higher education (including polytechnics) in England was 229,000. The university figure was the lowest in recent years (in 1981–82 it was 266,000) and the non-university figure was the highest (in 1981–82 it was 187,000). To these figures must be added the number of overseas students (36,000 in 1985–86 in universities and 13,000 elsewhere) and 301,000 part-time students, including those studying at the Open University.

Between 1979 and 1986, the number of home students in higher education increased by almost 140,000, including an increase of 80,000 in the number of full-time students. The proportion of 18- and 19-year olds entering full-time higher education rose from 12·4 per cent to 14·2 per cent; and the number of mature entrants to full-time higher education is up by over 15 per cent. The proportion of home students on science courses increased from 44 per cent to 47 per cent and the proportion who are women from 42 per cent to 44 per cent. Further increases in numbers over the next few years are envisaged.

Academic Staff.—In 1984–85 there were 42,500 full-time academic staff at universities in Great Britain and 26,200 (full-time equivalent) in local authority higher education in England. Student–staff ratios in 1984–85 were 10·3 in universities in Great Britain and 10·8 in local authority higher education in England, but these ratios are not comparable because of different methods of calculation.

New Technology Centres.—A national network of regional new technology centres is being set up. They will build on existing successful schemes to transfer technological innovations from the laboratory into new products for business and industry.

Universities

Universities are self-governing institutions, usually established by Royal Charter, which are responsible for academic appointments, curriculum and student admissions. They depend on the State for much of their income.

There are 46 universities in the United Kingdom (*see* pp. 504–9). Of these, 35 are in England, eight in Scotland, two in Northern Ireland and one (a federal institution) in Wales.

The non-residential *"Open University"* provides courses leading to degrees by a combination of television, radio, correspondence, tutorials, short residential courses and local audio-visual centres. The Open University offers undergraduate (no qualifications needed for entry), post-experience and post-graduate courses. It is grant-aided directly by the Department of Education and Science and does not come within the University Grants Committee system.

The independent University at Buckingham provides a two-year course leading to a bachelor's degree and its tuition fees are £5,700 for 1988. It receives no capital or recurrent income from the government but its students are eligible for mandatory awards from L.E.A.s. Its academic year consists of four terms of 10 weeks each.

Admission.—Students applying for admission to a first degree course at a university do so through the Universities Central Council on Admissions (U.C.C.A.) which was set up by the universities in 1961 on the initiative of the Committee of Vice-Chancellors and Principals. All universities participate in the U.C.C.A. scheme except the Open University and the University of Buckingham, which conduct their own admissions direct. The U.C.C.A. office is in Cheltenham.

The requirements for entry to first degree courses vary somewhat from one university to another, but the universities publish co-operatively an annual handbook, *University Entrance: the Official Guide,* which describes these requirements.

Fees.—Students with mandatory awards (*see* pp. 513) do not pay tuition fees. Students from outside the E.C. pay fees that are meant to cover the cost of their education.

The *University Grants Committee* advises the Secretary of State for Education and Science on university matters. Most of its members are academics or businessmen. The U.G.C. acts as a buffer between the Government from which it receives a block grant of money and the universities to which it allocates this grant.

Although the universities have freedom in academic matters, the government, through the U.G.C., determines the total size of the university student population, its distribution between arts, science, medicine, etc., and the part which the university sector plays in the whole higher education system.

In February 1987, the Croham Committee, which had been set up by Government to review the work of the U.G.C., recommended that the U.G.C. should be replaced by a smaller body chaired by an eminent industrialist and with roughly equal numbers of academic and non-academic members. The Government subsequently announced that the new body would be called the Universities Funding Council and that its primary responsibility will be to allocate funds to the individual universities under new contractual arrangements.

Finance.—In 1985–86, the total recurrent income of universities in Great Britain was £2,295 million. Exchequer grants as a percentage of total income have dropped from 76·2 in 1975–76 to 57·2 in 1985–86. Income in 1985–86 from contracts with industry, commerce and public corporations rose by 23 per cent compared with the previous year. The exchequer grant of £1,312 million was, in real terms, 1 per cent lower than in 1984–85. The total *non*-recurrent exchequer grant for 1985–86 was £111,353,000.

Polytechnics, Colleges, etc.

Polytechnics and colleges of higher education provide both advanced and non-advanced courses. An *advanced course*—full-time, sandwich or part-time—is one that is of a standard higher than G.C.E. "A" level. It thus includes research, degree-level courses, higher diploma and higher certificate courses, and courses leading to a wide variety of professional qualifications. All other courses are regarded as *non-advanced.* Advanced courses are offered in some 400 institutions outside the universities, most of them maintained by L.E.A.s which are responsible for providing full-time and part-time courses of post-secondary education (other than university education) in their areas.

The Government announced in April 1987 that the polytechnics and 28 other higher education colleges in England would be re-established as free-standing institutions independent of local authority control. There will be a new Polytechnic and Colleges Funding Council which will succeed the National Advisory Body for Public Sector Higher Education (*see below*) and will contract with individual institutions for the provision of higher education.

An important body is the *Council for National Academic Awards* (C.N.A.A.) which awards degrees to students taking courses approved by it in non-university institutions. Following a recommendation of the Robbins Committee it was established by Royal Charter in 1964 as a self-governing body. More than 100 colleges in Britain conduct courses leading to its degrees: B.A., B.Ed., B.Sc., and the higher degrees of M.A. and M.Sc. (for post-graduate course work) and M.Phil. and Ph.D. (for research which may be undertaken jointly in industry and college).

The *Diploma of Higher Education* (Dip.H.E.) is a two-year diploma intended to serve as either a terminal qualification or as a stepping stone to a degree or other further study; it has a normal entry requirement of two "A" levels. The Dip. H.E. is usually awarded by the Council for National Academic Awards (*see above*).

A *National Advisory Body for Public Sector Higher Education* advises the Secretary of State on a co-ordinated approach to the academic provision and the allocation of funds in polytechnics and other local authority and voluntary colleges in respect of courses leading to qualifications higher than A-level. It is to be succeeded by a new body, the Polytechnic and Colleges Funding Council.

Regional Advisory Councils. Responsibility for coordinating further education provision in different areas of England and Wales rests with 10 Regional Advisory Councils (*see* p. 531) set up by the local education authorities in each region. The councils bring together representatives of the L.E.A.s, colleges, universities, industry and commerce.

The 3,112 institutions other than universities in England may be grouped in the following main categories. All three are grant-aided and were in 1985 attended by a total of 3,404,052 students of whom 424,350 were on advanced courses and 582,233 were taking full-time or sandwich courses:—

1. *Polytechnics* (*see also* p. 510).—Twenty-nine major centres in England in which a wide range of full-time, sandwich and part-time courses are provided for students at all levels of higher education, and entirely or almost entirely for those of 18 years or more. They have governing bodies with a large measure of autonomy and are mainly teaching institutions though provision is made for certain research where it is essential to the proper fulfilment of teaching functions and the maintenance of close links with industry. A Polytechnics Central Admissions System (P.C.A.S.) was set up in 1984 in Cheltenham. It deals with admissions to full-time and sandwich first degree and Dip.H.E. courses in all polytechnics and in eight colleges and institutes of higher education in England and Wales, excluding art and design, and teacher training courses. In England in November 1985 there was a total of 241,252 students enrolled at polytechnics; of these 225,610 were on advanced courses (40 per cent of them women) and 15,642 on non-advanced courses; of those on advanced courses 155,067 were full-time or sandwich (42 per cent of them women).

2. *Other Major Establishments* (467).—Including all major establishments (maintained, assisted by

L.E.A.s, direct grant from D.E.S. or voluntary), other than polytechnics, providing courses in teacher training, art, agricultural, commercial, technical and other subjects. In England there were 198,740 on advanced courses including 87,106 on full-time or sandwich; and 1,545,901 on non-advanced courses.

3. *Adult Education Centres* (2,616).—Establishments maintained by local education authorities and offering a wide range of courses, many of them recreational, mainly for evening students, and often housed in premises used by day for other educational purposes. 1,418,159 students in England; 73 per cent were women. *See also* p. 515–17.

In 1983, the *Business and Technician Education Council* (B.T.E.C.) was set up by the Secretary of State for Education and Science to replace the Business Education Council (1974) and the Technician Education Council (1973) and to continue their work of developing a national system of non-degree vocational courses in these fields.

Vocational qualifications.—Following the report in 1986 of a working group, set up by Government, vocational qualifications in England and Wales will be brought within a new national framework to be called the National Vocational Qualification (N.V.Q.). A new National Council for Vocational Qualifications will develop the framework and secure change. The N.V.Q. framework, which will initially consist of four levels, is intended to come into operation in 1991.

The *Youth Service* provides for the spare-time activities of young people. The Local Education Authorities co-operate with voluntary bodies in their areas and may maintain their own youth clubs. There are various national voluntary youth organizations. There are some 3,500 full-time youth workers in England and Wales who are employed by local education authorities and voluntary youth organizations. In addition there are many thousands of part-time paid and unpaid workers. In 1985–86 the D.E.S. grant towards the headquarters' costs of national voluntary youth organizations was £3·5 million. There is a National Advisory Council for the Youth Service.

TRAINING

The main responsibility for carrying out industrial and commercial training lies with individual employers, but the Manpower Services Commission (M.S.C.), which is separate from government but responsible to the Secretary of State for Employment, provides, with government support, opportunities for individuals to acquire new skills and helps to improve the effectiveness of training generally.

The *Youth Training Scheme* (Y.T.S.) is a major development. When it began in 1983, it offered a *one*-year programme of training and planned work experience for employed and unemployed 16-year old school-leavers and some unemployed 17-year old school-leavers.

From 1986 the Y.T.S. was expanded and developed to give 16-year old school-leavers *two* years of training and 17-year olds one year, with special arrangements for disabled young people. The two-year programme involves at least 20 weeks off-the-job training in a college or training centre, in addition to on-the-job training and planned work experience. The second year builds on the first year's foundations by providing specific skill training, leading to vocational qualifications. Entrants receive a tax-free weekly allowance. Since 1983 more than one million young people have joined the scheme. Two-thirds of leavers go into work or further education/training.

The Y.T.S. is meant not just as an alternative to unemployment but as a permanent training scheme to help equip young people for working life. It is part of an overall Government policy whose aim is to ensure that all young people under 18 have a better opportunity than in the past either to continue in full-time education or to enter upon a period of planned work-experience combined with work-related training and education.

Other training programmes offered, under the aegis of the Department of Employment and the Manpower Services Commission, include: the *New Job Training Scheme* which is a programme of training to help people aged 18 or over who have been unable to get a job after six months' unemployment, with priority given to the under-25s; the *Access to Information Technology* scheme which provides evening and week-end training giving an introduction to information technology to employed or unemployed people; and the *Open Tech Programme* which aims to improve the skills, by open learning and training, of employed or unemployed people and thus to widen adult career and jobs opportunities at technician and supervisory management levels of skill.

Building on the experience of the Open Tech Programme, the Government has set up an *Open College* using radio and TV to support and deliver open-learning courses in all areas of vocational competence. It began broadcasting in September 1987, and it is planned that within 5 years it will give up to a million students a chance to progress towards vocational and technical qualifications, and that it will be self-financing as soon as practicable. Wherever appropriate, Open College courses will lead to nationally recognized qualifications or credits towards them.

SCOTLAND

The educational system of Scotland has developed independently to that of England and has a number of distinctive features. The general supervision of the national system of education, except for the universities, is the responsibility of the Secretary of State for Scotland acting through the Scottish Education Department. The duty of providing education locally rests with the nine regional councils and three island councils. Educational facilities of various kinds are also provided by the governing bodies of grant-aided schools, central institutions, colleges of education, and national voluntary organizations in the field of informal further education.

Schools.—Schools in Scotland fall into three main categories: *education authority schools* which are financed and managed by the regional and islands councils; *grant-aided schools*, conducted by voluntary managers who receive grants direct from the department; and *independent schools* which receive no direct grant, but which are subject to inspection and registration.

In 1985–86, there were 3,766 education authority and grant-aided schools and departments, of which 560 were nursery, 2,426 primary, 441 secondary and 339 special. There were also 103 registered independent schools. The total number of pupils in education authority and grant-aided schools and departments (including special) was 845,228 of which 38,210 received nursery education. There were a further 31,899 pupils in independent schools.

Schooling normally starts at the age of 5, and the primary school course lasts for 7 years. Primary schools usually take both boys and girls. Pupils transfer from the primary course to secondary courses about the age of 12.

Over 99 per cent of pupils in education authority secondary schools attend schools with a comprehensive intake. Most of these schools provide a full range of courses appropriate to all levels of ability from first to sixth year.

The Scottish Certificate of Education Examination is conducted by the Scottish Examination Board. Pupils may attempt as many of a wide range of subjects as they are capable of, on either the Ordinary grade which corresponds to the Ordinary level of the General Certificate of Education, or on the Higher grade which is normally taken one year after Ordinary grade. The shorter length of course inevitably means that Higher grades are normally studied to a lesser depth than Advanced levels; on the other hand it is common for pupils to be presented for four or more Higher grades at a single diet of the examination. The Board grants a Certificate of Sixth Year Studies designed to give direction and purpose to sixth-year work by encouraging pupils who have completed their main subjects at Higher grade to study a maximum of three such subjects in depth. Pupils may also use the sixth year to gain improved or additional Higher grades or Ordinary grades.

Further Education.—Facilities for further education are provided by 13 Central Institutions (grant-aided colleges administered by independent Boards of Governors) and by 50 further education colleges managed by education authorities. The Central Institutions provide mainly advanced courses in science and technology, commerce, art, music, domestic science, and other subjects, leading to their own diplomas, to professional qualifications or to degrees validated by C.N.A.A. or universities.

The further education colleges normally provide less advanced courses which are mainly part-time covering vocational and non-vocational subjects, but a few offer courses of degree level. Courses are offered in a wide variety of subjects but to make the most economic use of resources, provision of certain courses is made on a regional or even a national basis.

Teachers.—All teachers in public or grant-aided schools in Scotland are required to be registered with the General Teaching Council for Scotland (which is independent of the Scottish Education Department) and normally to hold a teaching qualification awarded by a Scottish College of Education. There are five of these colleges, four of which provide both one and four year courses leading to a Teaching Qualification (Primary Education), and a one year course leading to a Teaching Qualification (Secondary Education). The remaining college provides only courses leading to a Teaching Qualification (Primary Education). Physical education courses are provided at the Scottish Centre for Physical Education, Movement and Leisure Studies, which is incorporated in Moray House College of Education.

Unpromoted teachers in primary and secondary schools are paid on a single basic scale, while those in promoted posts receive higher salaries in recognition of their additional responsibilities.

NORTHERN IRELAND

Education in Northern Ireland is administered centrally by the Department of Education and locally by five Education and Library Boards. There are two main categories of school: controlled schools which are controlled by the Education and Library Boards with all costs paid from public funds; and voluntary schools which get grants towards capital costs and running costs in whole or in part.

Nursery education for under-fives is provided in nursery schools or nursery classes in primary schools. Primary education is for children up to 11–12 years and is free, though children educated in preparatory departments of grammar schools pay fees. Entry, at 11–12 years, to a secondary (intermediate) school or grammar school is selective in most areas but children can subsequently transfer from one to the other. Grammar schools provide an academic type of secondary education with A-levels at the end of the seventh year, while secondary (intermediate) schools follow a curriculum suited to aptitudes and abilities leading to G.C.S.E. examinations. There are also 8 independent schools. Northern Ireland has 26 institutions of further education (with 231 out-centres), two colleges of education, and two universities.

In January 1986 the total number of pupils enrolled in the 1,363 grant-aided schools was 345,198, of whom 4,681 were in nursery schools, 181,087 in primary schools, 156,872 in secondary schools and 2,558 in special schools. Between 1981 and 1986, primary school enrolments went down by 10,600 and secondary school enrolments by 7,400, pupil–teacher ratios improved from 23·6 to 23·4 (primary) and from 15·5 to 15·2 (secondary) and the staying-on rates for 16-year

olds increased from 37·9 per cent to 40·7 per cent.

There were 18,562 full-time equivalent teachers (78 down on 1985) of whom 156 were in nursery schools, 7,740 in primary, 10,349 in secondary, and 317 in special.

In 1984–85, there were 1,924 students on advanced courses of whom 23 per cent were full-time. In addition, there were 52,311 students on non-advanced vocational courses of further education of whom 26 per cent were full-time; 46,886 non-vocational students and 15,784 adult education students. In colleges of education there were 1,016 students.

Public expenditure on education and related services in 1984–85 was: current—£549,427,000; capital £33,902,000.

DUKE OF EDINBURGH'S AWARD SCHEME

The Duke of Edinburgh's Award Scheme, which operates under a variety of titles in over forty countries around the world, provides an incentive and a challenge to young people to take up sporting, skilful, adventurous and caring activities with the voluntary help of adults. Entrants must be between their 14th and 23rd birthdays, and can enter through their school, their firm, a youth organization, or on their own. Bronze, Silver and Gold Awards can be gained by those who qualify in the four sections of the Scheme: Service, Expeditions, Skills and Physical Recreation. The qualifying standards are expressed in terms of proficiency, perseverance or sustained effort, participants being assessed on the use they make of their personal abilities and aptitudes, and not in competition with others.

In 1986, there were 65,584 new entrants from the United Kingdom and 45,989 from overseas; a total of 50,439 Awards were gained world-wide. Since the Scheme began in 1956, over two and a quarter million young people have taken part.

Head Office: 5 Prince of Wales Terrace, W8 5PG.   Director: Maj.-Gen. M. Hobbs, C.B.E.

DRAMA 1986–87

Sir Kenneth Cork's inquiry into the state of the theatre in England, commissioned by the Arts Council in January 1986, was published in September of that year. The inquiry was intended to determine the criteria that the Council should use for deciding where grants should be applied, and to examine how subsidised theatres could become more productive and gain better rewards when their work transferred successfully to the commercial sector.

The report recommended that a Drama Board should be established to take responsibility for both the subsidised and commercial theatre, and that there should be continuing devolution to regional arts associations. The report, which was intended to form "a blueprint for a radical reconstruction of the provision of publicly-funded theatre in England", also included guidelines on the extent to which artistic directors should benefit personally from the transfer to the commercial theatre of productions which had originated in the subsidised theatre. Controversy had been provoked by allegations, strenuously denied, that Sir Peter Hall, director of the National Theatre, and Mr. Trevor Nunn, co-director of the Royal Shakespeare Company, had amassed private fortunes from the transfer of works from their theatres. The report recommended that a theatre's share of the combined earnings of the originators, other than playwrights, should be at least half, and that the negotiations of exploitation income should be carried out by both the company and its directors.

Further recommendations were that the B.B.C. should pay a levy of 1 per cent of its licence fee income, this sum to be matched by the independent television companies, in recognition of the benefits television derives from live theatre, such as training, experience and the development of new writing talent. This would raise an estimated £14 million which would enable most of the report to be implemented. The money should be administered by the Arts Council. The Government should support new theatrical projects through a £5 million a year development fund. The National Theatre and the R.S.C. should take more responsibility for touring and for hosting regional and foreign theatre companies. Six companies should be declared national theatre companies in the regions. Customers purchasing tickets through booking agencies should be informed of the face value of their tickets and the service charges levied. Charitable donations and sponsorship should be tax-deductible.

Commenting on the report, Sir Kenneth said: "For too long the theatre in England has suffered from a loony system where commercial, touring and publicly-funded theatres have each travelled in their own little carriage without helping one another. We hope that the national importance of theatre to England will be properly recognised as a result of the recommendations in our report, and that every sector will work together to make live theatre move healthily into the next decade." The report was implemented in one respect: Mr. Richard Luce, Minister for the Arts, announced in December that the subsidised theatre companies would in future receive at least half the earnings from the transfer of their productions to the commercial sector. In addition, constraints would be placed on the amount of time that artistic directors of such subsidised companies could work outside those institutions. Sabatical leave should be restricted to six months in any three-year period, and they would be expected to work for at least 40 weeks each year at their base.

In October 1986 Sir Peter Hall served notice that he intended to leave the National Theatre when his contract expired in 1988. He recommended that Richard Eyre should succeed him. Sir Peter's announcement coincided with the tenth anniversary of the South Bank complex, which has established itself as a major force in the theatre, its qualities recognised both in the United Kingdom and abroad. In February 1987 Sir Peter announced that he would establish a transatlantic theatre company when he left the National Theatre. The company would be a production company rather than a permanent ensemble, with a London base. The company was created by the theatrical impresarios Duncan C. Weldon and Jerome Minskoff. Sir Peter intends, however, to retain his links with the National Theatre and the Royal Shakespeare Company. Sir Peter said that he would produce four shows a year, three of which he would direct personally.

Big Freeze

In October 1986 Trevor Nunn announced that he was standing down as the R.S.C.'s chief executive after having served ten years in the post. He was succeeded by his deputy Terry Hands.

Both the National Theatre and the Royal Shakespeare Company were severely affected by the Arts Council's decision, announced in December 1986, to keep their grants at the same level for the following year; with no increase allowed for inflation, this meant a substantial cut in real terms. The National Theatre received £7.8 million and the R.S.C. £5·1 million. Mr. Luke Rittner, secretary-general of the Arts Council, acknowledged that many arts organisations were already working at peak efficiency and would have to use all their ingenuity and skills to remain in business. He admitted that some companies face the prospect of alarming deficits if, on diminishing incomes, they continue to meet the demand for their activities.

The Royal Shakespeare Company staged a record number of 36 productions during the year, including 14 new plays and adaptations, but suffered a year of crises. At one point the company threatened to close either its London or Stratford base. In his annual report for 1985–86, Chairman Geoffrey Cass said that the company had no financial reserves to meet a crisis. A surplus of £5,000 had been produced through the transfer of four productions to the West End, but contingency planning was difficult when they were trying to absorb a significant reduction in the real value of their subsidy. The R.S.C. was also forced to reject a sponsorship deal worth approximately £60,000 from Barclays Bank because of its South African interests. The grant was blocked following pressure from members of the cast of *Macbeth*. The sponsorship would have meant that 1,000 schoolchildren would have been able to see *Macbeth* at reduced prices.

At its London base, the Barbican, the company suffered from poor attendances, with audiences down to 50 per cent capacity, and Feydeau's *Scenes from a Marriage* attracting barely one-third capacity audiences. By June 1987 a deficit of more than £1 million was reported, which prompted the closure threat. The crisis was aggravated by the shortfall in the Arts Council grant, estimated at £600,000 in real terms. Mr Cass admitted that the company would be in breach of its Charter if either base was closed, but he said that the company had no means of eliminating its deficit. The crisis was blamed on a shortfall in American tourists but this ignores the fact that some of its productions are just not appealing to theatregoers. Performances of quality, such as Sher's *Richard III* or Jacobi's *Cyrano de Bergerac*, are sold out to a home-grown audience with no difficulty.

Lifeline

In August 1987 the Royal Insurance Company averted disaster with a sponsorship deal worth £1.5 million to the R.S.C. over three years, commencing in January 1988. The Royal Insurance Company also called on the Government to provide greater support for the arts. Mr Hands described the deal as the R.S.C's "lifeline to the future". The R.S.C. had had little success in resolving its financial difficulties prior to the sponsorship announcement. In an attempt to make some money, the company had attempted to repeat the success of its U.S. tour with *Nicholas Nickleby* five years previously. However, the production lost $700,000 during a nine-week run in Los Angeles, and its 14-week season on Broadway was forced to close early with only 42 per cent of tickets sold.

Get Up and Go

A new touring company appeared on the scene in September 1986 with the formation of the English Shakespeare Company. Founded by director Michael Bogdanov and actor Michael Pennington, with backing from Canadian entrepreneurs Ed and David Mirvish, who were behind the Old Vic's recent restoration, the company consists of a troupe of 25 actors. It spent four and a half months on tour to eleven leading repertory theatres before a season at the Old Vic in London. The first productions were *Henry IV Parts 1 and 2* and *Henry V*, and the tour opened in Plymouth. The productions received widespread acclaim, particularly John Woodvine's outstanding Falstaff. The English Shakespeare Company has followed Sir Anthony Quayle's Compass Theatre Company in taking large-scale classical theatre on tour, a function in which the National Theatre and the Royal Shakespeare Company are considered somewhat deficient.

Another new company set up in the past twelve months is the Renaissance Theatre Company formed by Kenneth Branagh and David Parfitt. Renaissance's first production was *Public Enemy*, with Branagh starring in a play he both wrote and produced. This was followed by a virtuoso performance by John Sessions in *The Life of Napoleon*, directed by Branagh, at the Riverside Studios.

In a mixed year in the theatre one bizarre theatrical saga concerned the production of *Cabaret* at the Strand. This opened in July 1986 and had cost £1.5 million to stage. A dispute between the musicians and the cast, which culminated in five members of the orchestra being sacked for allegedly being out of tune, intoxicated or ill-disciplined, brought the other musicians out on strike. The cast valiantly gave a performance without music to an almost empty house but the show was forced to close down completely.

At the Shaftesbury, Anton Rodgers was replaced by Ray Cooney as director of *An Italian Straw Hat*. "It was felt, after the first preview, and Tom Conti felt particularly, that a farce ought to be greeted with some laughs, but there weren't any at all", said Mr. Cooney. Some critics felt that Mr. Conti's performance showed an idiosyncratic interpretation, his timing and delivery unsuited to the farce: whether this was the cause of the friction with Mr. Rodgers was not clear. In May a combination of circumstances brought about the theatrical shut-down of Shaftesbury Avenue, an event that was thought to be unprecedented in modern times. There was not considered to be a general malaise in London theatreland but it was perhaps significant that production costs were continuing to rise dramatically. With new musicals costing about £2 million to stage and a consequent rise in seat prices, theatregoers are not willing to spend money on shows unless they are established successes.

The year saw the close of the record-breaking hit comedy *No Sex Please, We're British* after a 16-year run in the West End: a phenomenon of sorts. It survived the crucial first few months thanks in no small measure to the performance of Michael Crawford, and its risqué title proved a magnet for foreign tourists. Its success then became self-generating, like that of the other hardy perennial, *The Mousetrap*. At the London Palladium *La Cage aux Folles*, which opened in May 1986 at a cost of £2.5 million, failed to survive a major cast change in January 1987 when Denis Quilley was replaced by James Smillie. It was alleged, however, that its closure was caused by public disquiet over AIDS rather than the change of cast.

Serious Money

But all was not darkness and gloom on the London theatre scene. It was announced that £3 million would be spent on improvements at five London theatres, including the installation of air-conditioning at the Palladium. And the Cambridge, after its brief and disastrous conversion to the Theatre of Magic, is to be reconverted to a musical theatre at a cost of £1.4 million. A grandiose scheme to build a £12 million theatre in Battersea Park was also unveiled. The Theatre in the Park would seat 3,400 people and, if planning permission is granted, could be open by 1989.

The London Festival of Theatre, the brainchild of Lucy Neal and Rose de Wend Fenton and now in its fourth year, has a growing reputation. Lasting for three weeks, it involved some 15 companies, including Joseph Papp's New York Shakespeare Festival production of *The Colored Museum*, directed by Kenneth Richardson, and *The Dragon's Trilogy*, directed by Robert Lepage, by the French Canadian Theatre Reperé from Quebec.

The Royal Court Theatre achieved one of the season's surprise successes with Caryl Churchill's *Serious Money*. This satire on post-"Big Bang" practices and ethics in the City of London was deservedly popular and achieved a West End transfer. The surprising aspect of the play's success was that the majority of its audience were the very people in the City whom the play attacked: many firms took block bookings for staff outings. The Royal Court was less fortunate with *Perdition*, a new play by Jim Allen which was cancelled the day before its scheduled opening in response to widespread public concern and a press campaign, complaining that the play was anti-semitic in alleging Jewish complicity in the Holocaust. It was reported that the cancellation was deeply resented by the cast and the director, Ken Loach, but the president of the Board of Deputies of British Jews said the decision was a "victory for common sense, clear judgment and justice".

Andrew Lloyd Webber confirmed his position as one of the dominant forces in British—and American—theatre, with the triumphant opening of *The Phantom of the Opera* at Her Majesty's in October 1986. The story is well known from the popular film versions of Gaston Leroux's 1911 story and one of the major weaknesses of the production was the absence of any suspense or element of mystery about the unusual happenings in the Paris Opera House. Another criticism was levelled at the weakness of many of the lyrics: a prevailing air of blandness with too much repetition of the better ones. These criticisms apart the £2 million production was brilliantly staged, with some impressive special effects. Michael Crawford threw himself as wholeheartedly into the title role as he had into *Barnum* and confirmed his reputation as one of the major assets of the British stage. Added to his acting talent and his versatility was a marvellously expressive voice which he projected powerfully through his masked face, bringing real pathos to the role. Michael Crawford, whose professionalism is well known, had at one stage to leave the production to receive hospital treatment for a hernia. His understudy then damaged his knee, which brought Crawford from his sickbed to resume the role until the second understudy was able to take over. Not surprisingly, American Equity have granted him permission to repeat the role on Broadway. Less fortunate was Sarah Brightman, who took the part of Christine. Her fine voice will be lost to Broadway in spite of protestations from the producers that there was no one more suitable to play the role in America.

Awards

In the 32nd London Standard Drama Awards, presented in November 1986, the best play was *Les Liaisons Dangereuses*, Christopher Hampton's adaptation of Choderlos de Laclos's epistolary novel; after successful runs at the Other Place, Stratford, and the Barbican Pit this transferred to the Ambassadors. Best musical was *The Phantom of the Opera*, and best

comedy Bob Larbey's *A Month of Sundays*, which featured George Cole in a comedy about an old people's home. Albert Finney won the best actor award for his performance in Lyle Kessler's *Orphans*. Best actress was Julia McKenzie for her part as the frustrated housewife, Susan, in *Woman in Mind*. On stage throughout the play, Julia McKenzie gave a brilliant portrayal of Susan's gradual mental disintegration and collapse in Ayckbourn's 32nd play, one of his best, both funny and disturbing. The most promising playwright was Frank McGuinness, for *Observe the Sons of Ulster Marching Towards the Somme* which was performed at the Hampstead. The Sydney Edwards Award for best director was awarded to Nuria Espert for her production of Lorca's *The House of Bernarda Alba*. Regarded as a leading exponent of Lorca's work, her cast included Joan Plowright and Glenda Jackson in a widely praised drama, the last of Lorca's three great tragedies.

In the 1986 Laurence Olivier Awards *The Phantom of the Opera* was judged best musical, with Michael Crawford taking the prize for best actor in a musical. Albert Finney received further recognition for his performance in *Orphans* with his second best actor award, and Lindsay Duncan won best actress for her part in *Les Liaisons Dangereuses*. Best director was Bill Alexander for *The Merry Wives of Windsor*, and designer of the year William Dudley. Comedy performance of the year was awarded to Bill Fraser in *When We Are Married*, the play also winning the award for best comedy production. The Observer Award for outstanding achievement was presented to the Lyric Theatre, Hammersmith, for Lorca's *The House of Bernarda Alba*, and the B.B.C. Award for the West End Play of the Year to *Les Liaisons Dangereuses*.

In *Drama* magazine's Awards, the best new play was Jim Cartwright's *Road*, which was produced at the Royal Court by Simon Curtis. Best actor was shared by Bill Fraser in *When We Are Married* and Hugh Quarshie in *The Great White Hope*. Best actress was Joan Plowright for her performance in *The House of Bernarda Alba*. *Drama* magazine's Special Award was presented to Nicky Pallot, Simon Stokes and Jenny Topper, directors of the Bush Theatre, for "their continued high standard of production of new plays". Best supporting actor and actress were Tom Wilkinson in Ibsen's *Ghosts* and Alison Steadman in Alan Bennett's *Kafka's Dick*.

A notable success abroad was *Les Miserables* which won eight Tony awards on Broadway, for best musical, best book, best score, best featured actor and actress, best direction of a musical, scenic design, and lighting design. Robert Lindsay was named best actor in a musical for *Me and My Girl*.

New Productions

Notable new productions included Alan Bennett's second play about Franz Kafka, *Kafka's Dick*, which was witty, full of good ideas, but considered too clever by some. However, in its examination of the relationship between a biographer and his subject and a writer and his reputation, some pertinent points were made in Bennett's customary humorous fashion. Hugh Whitemore's *Breaking the Code* featured Derek Jacobi as the brilliant mathematician Alan Turing.

Turing was credited with breaking Germany's complex Enigma code during the Second World War, and laid the foundations of computer science with his theoretical studies in the 1930s. However, he also broke society's code of acceptable behaviour by his avowed homosexuality, for which he was prosecuted and forced to take hormones, leading to his suicide in 1954. Whitemore's play bravely and sympathetically attempted to explore this complex character, and paid the audience the compliment of assuming them intelligent by including a brilliant and complex speech which examined Turing's mathematical theories.

Less successful was Rupert Holmes's 'solve-it-yourself' musical *The Mystery of Edwin Drood*, based on Dickens' unfinished novel. The gimmick of the audience deciding by vote how the musical should end reaped 19 awards for the Broadway production, but London audiences were less receptive. Clare Boothe Luce's *The Women* received its first major revival in 50 years, its 44 female parts providing a vehicle for some of the country's leading actresses: the cast included Susannah York, Maria Aitken, Diana Quick and Georgina Hale. The Young Vic's revival of Ibsen's *Ghosts* was deservedly acclaimed and merited its transfer to Wyndham's. Vanessa Redgrave gave a particularly fine performance as Mrs Alving, and Peter Watt's translation was intelligently adapted by the cast.

Steven Berkoff's parody of *Henry V, Sink the Belgrano!*, which covered the sinking of the Argentinian cruiser in 1982 with the loss of 368 lives, opened at the Half Moon and later transferred to the Mermaid. The Victorian Palace featured the world stage premiere of *High Society*. The story has been through various stages: from Philip Barry's play *Philadelphia Story*, which was filmed, and then filmed again as a musical called *High Society*, to its return to the stage in musical form. Dylan Thomas's *Under Milk Wood* was revived at Greenwich to muted applause, but Brian Abbott's *Milk Wood Blues* at the Lyric Studio was much better received. The story was based on a real incident, which arose when Thomas lost the original manuscript of his classic play about life in Llaregub and promised the manuscript to whoever found it, provoking a court case when his widow tried to recover it from a B.B.C. producer who had taken him at his world. At Soho's Boulevard, Jim McManus gave a fine impersonation of the tragic comedian in Colin Bennett's *Hancock's Finest Hour*, but Griff Rhys Jones struggled to save Brecht's *The Resistible Rise of Arturo Ui* from appearing dated and simplistic.

National Theatre

At the National Theatre, the major productions were David Hare's first Shakespeare's production, and the National's first *King Lear*, featuring Anthony Hopkins. Hare said that *King Lear* was "the only classical play I want to do; I think it's the most profound play ever written". It was also Hopkins's first Shakespeare role since walking out on a production of *Macbeth* in 1973, after which he was lost to the classical stage for many years. The production was a popular success and generally

favourably received by the critics, the main criticisms being directed at the bare stage and the eccentric costumes. Hopkins later starred with Judi Dench in Peter Hall's production of *Antony and Cleopatra*.

In the Lyttelton, Michael Rudman's production of *The Magistrate* by Pinero showed that farce needs to be controlled and taken seriously to be truly funny. Nigel Hawthorne in the leading role contributed especially to a marvellous staging of one of the all-time classic comedies. The Rudman group's first production was a revival of Pirandello's 1921 masterpiece of theatre and psychology, *Six Characters in Search of an Author*. Stephen Poliakoff's new play, *Coming in to Land*, featured Maggie Smith in her National Theatre debut as a Polish woman trying to gain a residence permit. Alan Ayckbourn's *A Small Family Business* was the sixth of his plays to be produced at the National Theatre but the first to be premiered there rather than at Scarborough. It featured Michael Gambon as Jake McCracken, who takes over a furniture business, and gradually becomes as corrupt as the company. Ayckbourn also directed *Tons of Money*, Will Evans' and Valentine's first Aldwych farce, which was of historical rather than artistic interest.

The National also featured the Market Theatre Company from Johannesburg in Percy Mtwo's *Bopha!*, a study of black members of the South African police force, and the Stockholm Royal Dramatic Theatre, under Ingmar Bergman's direction, in *Hamlet* and Strindberg's *Miss Julie*.

Royal Shakespeare Company

In spite of financial problems and some critical hostility the R.S.C. presented a large and varied programme at its London and Stratford bases. Jeremy Irons portrayed *Richard II* as a Christ-like figure, while Jonathan Pryce was a curiously passive *Macbeth*. Antony Sher, whose *Richard III* was one of the great interpretations of modern times, gave another stunning performance as Shylock in *The Merchant of Venice*, directed by Bill Alexander, and also impressed as Malvolio in *Twelfth Night*.

The Swan, which had opened in April 1986, was officially opened by H.M. the Queen in November. Productions in the first season included Thomas Heywood's *The Fair Maid of the West*, a three-hour conflation of his two plays about Bess Bridges with Imelda Staunton in the title role. Directed by Trevor Nunn, this lively and imaginative extravaganza showed that the Swan has added a new dimension to the Stratford programme. In March 1987 the Mermaid became the London base for Swan productions, thanks to the American producers Frank and Woji Gero, and was transformed under the guidance of Ron Daniels to recapture the Swan's "wooden O" atmosphere. Healthy advance bookings appeared to justify the move.

The R.S.C. also staged the first major British revival of Cole Porter's *Kiss Me Kate* for 35 years, jointly produced with private management, not in repertory but for commercial tour. At the Barbican notable productions included Bernard Shaw's "debate in one sitting", *Misalliance*, Richard Nelson's *Principia Scriptoriae*, and Arthur Miller's *The Arch-*

bishop's Ceiling. John Whiting's gentle comedy on "the finer lunacies of the English at war", *A Penny for a Song,* was first performed by the R.S.C. in 1962 but was rather a slight piece for the main auditorium. Peter Barnes's adaptation of *Scenes from a Marriage,* written by Feydeau at the time of the collapse of his marriage, before his descent into insanity, opened with a blood-curdling scream which made laughter difficult to raise thereafter. The three pieces were originally unconnected but were here given as three scenes from the same marriage, which diluted their individual impact. Deborah Levy's *Heresies,* developed from improvisation workshops with the actors, was one result of initiatives taken by the R.S.C's women's group in 1985. Vladimir Gubaryev's *Sarcophagus* was a recent product of Soviet glasnost; as science editor of *Pravda,* Gubaryev had been given carte blanche by the authorities to produce a drama about the Chernobyl nuclear disaster. When the play was completed it was quickly given official approval and received performances in Russia before being produced by the R.S.C.

PRODUCTIONS

London productions between September 1, 1986 and August 31, 1987 included the following:

ALBERY: St. Martin's Lane, WC2. (1986) Dec. 16. *The Old Man of Lochnagar* by H.R.H. the Prince of Wales. (1987) March 25. *March of the Falsettos* by William Finn, with Simon Green, Barry James and Martin Smith, directed by Roger Haines, designed by Chris Kinman. April 27. *Canaries Sometimes Sing* by Frederick Lonsdale, with Peter Bowles, Liz Robertson, Neil Stacy and Sylvia Sims, dir. by Patrick Garland, des. by Saul Radomsky. (Yvonne Arnaud Theatre, Guildford prodn.). June 3. *Three Sisters* by Chekhov, with Francesca Annis, Hywel Bennett, Sara Kestelman, Ian Ogilvy, Susan Penhaligon and Katherine Schlesinger (trans. from Greenwich Theatre).

ALDWYCH: WC2. (1986) Oct. 15. *The Secret Life of Cartoons* by Clive Barker, with Una Stubbs, Derek Griffiths, Geoffrey Hughes and James Warwick, dir. by Tudor Davies, des. by Martin Johns. Nov. 27. *Brighton Beach Memoirs,* with Dorothy Tutin, Susan Engel, Harry Towb, Steven Mackintosh and Robert Glenister (National Theatre prodn.).

ALMEIDA: Almeida St., N1. (1986) Sept. 19. Shakespeare's *Coriolanus,* with Douglas Hodge, Charon Bourke and Hilary Townley, dir. by Deborah Warner (Kick Theatre Co. prodn.). Nov. 25. *The Great Hunger* by Tom MacIntyre, with Tom Hickey, Vincent O'Neill and Michele Forbes, dir. by Patrick Mason, des. by Bronwen Casson (Dublin Abbey Theatre prodn.). (1987) April 8. *The Tourist Guide* by Botho Strauss, with Paul Freeman and Tilda Swinton, dir. by Pierre Audi, des. by Hildegard Bechtler.

AMBASSADORS: West St., Cambridge Circus, WC2. (1986) Oct. 2. *Les Liaisons Dangereuses* (R.S.C prodn.).

APOLLO: Shaftesbury Ave., W1. (1987) Feb. *Siegfried Sassoon* (Hampstead Theatre prodn.). April 1. *A Piece of My Mind* by Peter Nichols, with George Cole, Anna Carteret, Jerome Wills and Gwyneth Strong, dir. by Justin Greene, des. by Martin Johns (Nuffield Theatre, Southampton prodn.).

BARBICAN: EC2. (1986) Oct. 2. *Misalliance* by George Bernard Shaw, with Brian Cox, Mick Ford, Jane Lapotaire, Richard McCabe, Elizabeth Spriggs and Caroline Goodall, dir. by John Caird, des. by Roger Butlin.. Oct. 23. *Scenes from a Marriage* by Feydeau (adapted by Peter Barnes), with Susan Colverd, Janet Dale, Peter Jones, Miriam Karlin and Lila Kaye, dir. by Terry Hands, des. by Gerard Howland. Dec. 17. *A Penny for a Song* by John Whiting, with David Bradley, Brian Cox, Mick Ford, Stephen Moore and Rudi Davies, dir. by Howard Davies, des. by Bob Crowley. 1987) April 1. Shakespeare's *Macbeth,* with Jonathan Pryce, Sinead Cussack, Hugh Quarshie, Peter Guinness and Dilys Laye, dir. by Adrian Noble, des. by Bob Crowley. April 9. Shakespeare's *Romeo and Juliet,* with Sean Bean, Niamh Cusack, Robert Demeger, Dilys Laye, Hugh Quarshie and Michael Kitchen, dir. by Michael Bogdanov, des. by Chris Dyer. May 5. Shakespeare's *Richard II,* with Jeremy Irons, Michael Kitchen and Brewster Mason, dir. by Barry Kyle, des. by William Dudley. July 16. *The Balcony* by Jean Genet (trans. by Terry Hands and Barbara Wright), with Joe Melia, Dilys Laye, Robert Demeger and Jim Carter, dir. by Terry Hands, des. by Farrah. Aug. 13. Shakespeare's *A Midsummer Night's Dream,* with Amanda Harris, Kathryn Pogson, Frances Tomelty, Max Gold, David Haig, Gerard Murphy, Nathaniel Parker, Nicholas Woodeson, dir. by Bill Alexander.

BARBICAN PIT: (1986) Oct. 1. *Principia Scriptoriae* by Richard Nelson, with Sean Baker, Anton Lesser, Clive Merrison and David de Keyser, dir. by David Jones, des. by Bob Crowley. Oct. 29. *The Archbishop's Ceiling* by Arthur Miller, with Roger Allam, David de Keyser, Jane Lapotaire and John Shrapnel, dir. by Nick Hamm, des. by Fotini Dimou. Dec. 10. *Heresies* by Deborah Levy, with Roger Allam, Susan Colverd, Paola Dionisotti, Miriam Karlin, Clive Russell and Susan Tracy, dir. by Susan Todd, des. by Iona McCleish. (1987) March 25. *Country Dancing* by Nigel Williams, with Richard Easton, Stuart Richman and Gerard Murphy, dir. by Bill Alexander, des. by William Dudley. April 16. *Sarcophagus* by Vladimir Gubaryev (trans. by Michael Glenny), with Carol Gillies, Nicholas Woodeson and Geraldine Fitzgerald, dir. by Jude Kelly, des. by Michael Minas. May 8. *Worlds Apart* by Jose Triana (adapted by Peter Whelan from trans. by Kate Littlewood), with Janet McTeer, Henry Goodman, Philip Franks and Anna Patrick, dir. by Nick Hamm, des. by Chris Dyer, music by Ilona Sekacz. July 17. *The Storm* by Alexander Ostrovsky (adapted by Stephen Lowe), with Janet McTeer, Philip Franks, Martin Jacobs and Carole Gillies, dir. by Nick Hamm, des. by Fotini Dimou. July 28. *Flight* by David Lan, with Joe Melia, Geraldine Fitzgerald, Nicholas Woodeson, and Gillian Barge, dir. by Howard Davies. Aug. 13. *The Art of Success* by Nick Dear, with Philip Franks, Michael Kitchen, Niamh Cusack, Penny Downie, Dilys Laye and Dinah Stabb, dir. by Adrian Noble.

BOULEVARD: Walker's Court, W1. (1987) Jan. 26. *Hancock's Finest Hour* by Colin Bennett, with Jim McManus, Alec Bregonzi and Ann Penfold.

BUSH: Shepherd's Bush Green, W12. (1986) Nov. 21. *Ashes* by David Rudkin, with Sheila Gish, Denis Lawson, Sally Watts and Richard Kane, dir. by Rob Walker, des. by Peter Avery.

COMEDY: Panton St., W1. (1986) Sept. 1. *The Maintenance Man* by Richard Harris, with John Alderton, Gwen Taylor, Susan Penhaligon, dir. by Roger Clissold, des. by Tim Bickerton. (1987) April 7. *Spin of the Wheel* by Timothy Prager and Geoff

Morrow, with Maria Friedman, Neil McCaul and Teddy Kempner, dir. by Timothy Prager (Palace Theatre, Watford prodn.). July 2. *Breaking the Code* by Hugh Whitemore, with John Castle, Paul Bigley and Dean Winters (trans. from Theatre Royal, Haymarket).

DONMAR WAREHOUSE: Earlham St., Covent Gdn., WC2. (1987) Jan. *The Cid* by Corneille (trans. by David Bryer), with Aden Gillett, Patricia Kerrigan, dir. by Declan Donnellan (Cheek by Jowl Co. prodn.). Shakespeare's *Twelfth Night*, with Timothy Walker, Anne White, Keith Bartlett, Aden Gillett, Hugh Ross and Patricia Kerrigan, dir. by Declan Donnellan (Cheek by Jowl Co. prodn.). Feb 23. *Lady Day* written and dir. by Stephen Stahl, with Dee Dee Bridgewater, des. by Michael Fresnay, music by Bill Jolly. April 7. *The Heat of the Day* by Elizabeth Bowen (adapted by Giles Havergal and Felicity Brown), with Charon Bourke, Patricia Lawrence, Kate Kitovitz, Mark Lewis and Christian Burgess (Shared Experience Co. prodn.). July. *Mystery of the Rose Bouquet* by Manuel Puig, with Brenda Bruce and Gemma Jones, dir. by Robert Allan Ackerman.

FORTUNE: Russell St., WC2. (1987) March 23. *Nunsense* by Dan Goggin, with Bronwen Stanway, Anna Sharkey, Pip Hinton, Honor Blackman and Louise Gold. dir. by Richard Digby Day, des. by Lee Dean, choreography by Stephanie Carter.

GARRICK: Charing Cross Rd., WC2. (1986) Nov. 17. *Mr and Mrs Nobody* by Keith Waterhouse, with Judi Dench, Michael Williams and Penny Ryder, dir. by Ned Sherrin, des. by Julia Trevelyan Oman. (1987) April 14. *When Did You Last See Your Trousers?* by Ray Galton and John Antrobus, with William Gaunt, Susie Blake, Michael Sharvell-Martin and Terence Longdon, dir. by Roger Smith, des. by Sean Cavanagh.

GLOBE: Shaftesbury Ave., W1. (1987) Jan. 16. *The House of Bernarda Alba* by Lorca (trans. from Lyric, Hammersmith). July 28. *Light Up the Sky* by Moss Hart, with Keith Baxter, Gwen Taylor, Kate O'Mara, Art Metrano, Maxine Audley and Sandra Dickinson, dir. by Elijah Moshinsky, des. by Michael Levine.

GREENWICH: Croom's Hill, SE10. (1986) Oct. 20. *Under Milk Wood* by Dylan Thomas, with Rachel Bell, Denys Graham and Gilbert Wynne, dir. by Anthony Cornish, des. by Belinda Ackermann. Dec. 15. *Night Must Fall* by Emlyn Williams, with Daniel Webb, Margaret Tyzack and Julia McCarthy, dir. by John Dove. (1987) Feb. 2. *The Viewing* by David Pownall, with Jonathan Newth, Graeme Garden, Greg Cruttwell, Lavinia Bertram and Priscilla Morgan, dir. by Alan Strachan. March 23. *Three Sisters* by Chekhov (trans. by Michael Frayn), with Sara Kestelman, Katharine Schlesinger, Joanne Whalley, Ian Ogilvy and Peter Sallis, dir. by Elijah Moshinsky (Royal Exchange, Manchester prodn.). May 11. *Desire Under the Elms* by Eugene O'Neill, with Carmen du Sautoy, Colin Firth and Tom Hickey, dir. by Patrick Mason. Aug. *Mary Rose* by J. M. Barrie, with Amanda Waring, Michael Burrell, Paul Imbusch, Neil Duncan and Patrick Pearson, dir. by Matthew Francis.

HALF MOON: 213 Mile End Rd., E1. (1986) Sept. 9. *Sink the Belgrano!* written and dir. by Steven Berkoff, with Maggie Steed, Rory Edwards, Barry Stanton, Bill Stewart and Edward Tudor Pole. (1987) May 20. *Chicken Soup with Barley* by Arnold Wesker, dir. by Rebecca Wolman (Eastend Theatre Co. prodn.).

HAMPSTEAD: Swiss Cottage, NW3. (1986) Sept. 17. *Ask for the Moon* by Shirley Gee, with Brenda Bruce,

Mona Hammond, Shireen Shah, Jane Horrocks, Victoria Burton, Gaylie Runciman and Brian Hall, dir. by John Dove, des. by John McMurray. Nov. 26. *Selling the Sizzle* by Peter Gibbs, with David Threlfall, Dinsdale Landen, Caroline Bliss and Ann Beach, dir. by Robert Chetwyn, des. by Sue Plummer. (1987) Jan. 6. *Siegfried Sassoon* with Peter Barkworth. Feb. 11. *This Story of Yours* by John Hopkins, with David Suchet, Jane Wood, James Hazeldine and Bryan Pringle, dir. by Jack Gold. April 22. *Spookhouse* by Harvey Fierstein, with Joanne Ridley, Chris Jury and Gwen Taylor, dir. by Robin Lefevre, des. by Robin Don. May 28. *My Sister in this House* by Wendy Kesselman, with Tilly Vosburgh, Maggie Steed, Suzanna Hamilton and Maggie O'Neill, dir. by Nancy Meckler. July 11. *That Summer* by David Edgar, with Edward Rawle-Hicks, Mick Ford, Caroline Berry, Catherine Tregenna, Jessica Turner and Oliver Cotton, dir. by Michael Attenborough, des. by Sue Plummer.

HER MAJESTY'S: Haymarket, SW1. (1986) Oct. 9. *The Phantom of the Opera*, music by Andrew Lloyd Webber, libretto by Richard Stilgoe and Charles Hart, with Michael Crawford, Sarah Brightman and Steve Barton, dir. by Hal Prince, des. by Maria Bjornson, choreog. by Gillian Lynne.

KING'S HEAD: Upper St., N1. (1986) Dec. 8. *Candida* by George Bernard Shaw, with Maureen O'Brien, Rupert Graves, David Rintoul and Nicholas Amer, dir. by Frank Hauser. (1987) June 19. *Hard Times* by Charles Dickens (adapted by Stephen Jeffrey), with Jonathan Stephens, Susan Bovell, John Curry and Helen Bourne, dir. by Dilys Hamlett, des. by Hugh Durrant.

LYRIC: Hammersmith, W6. (1986) Sept. 8. *The House of Bernarda Alba* by Lorca (trans. by Robert David Macdonald), with Patricia Hayes, Glenda Jackson, Joan Plowright, Amanda Root, Deborah Findlay and Julie Legrand, dir. by Nuria Espert, des. by Ezio Frigerio. Nov. 8. *The Infernal Machine* by Jean Cocteau, with Maggie Smith, Robert Eddison, Veronica Smart and Lambert Wilson, dir. and trans. by Simon Callow, des. by Bruno Santini. (1987) Feb. 9. *Scout's Honour* by Christopher Douglas, with John Fortune, Nigel Planer and Steven O'Donnell, dir. by Mike Bradwell. July 10. *Public Enemy* written, dir. and with Kenneth Branagh, and Ethna Roddy, Brenda Peters and John Rogan, des. by Geoff Rose (Renaissance Theatre Co. prodn.). Aug. 26. *Infidelities* by Marivaux, adapted and dir. by William Gaskill, with John Lynch, Eleanor Bron, Saskai Reeves, David Rintoul and Moira Brooker, des. by Rene Allio.

LYRIC STUDIO: Hammersmith, W6. (1986) Dec. 10. *The Bijers Sunbird* by Robert Kirby, with Sean Taylor, Jon Maytham. (1987) Jan. 19. *Milk Wood Blues* by Brian Abbott, with Allan Corduner, and Michael Bertenshaw, dir. by Keith Boak, des. by Paul Dart (One World Arts Co. prodn.). Feb. 17. *Yardsdale and Whatever Happened to Betty Lemon?* by Arnold Wesker, with Brenda Bruce.

LYRIC: Shaftesbury Ave., W1. (1986) Oct. 12. *Lillian* by William Luce, with Frances de la Tour, dir. by Corin Redgrave. (1987) March 17. *The Amen Corner* by James Baldwin (Carib Theatre prodn., trans. from the Tricycle). June 20. *Let Us Go Then, You and I* by Peter Ackroyd, with Eileen Atkins, Edward Fox and Michael Gough, narrated by Joan Bakewell.

MAN IN THE MOON: 392, King's Rd., Chelsea, SW3. (1986) Sept. 26. *A Bethrothal* by Lanford Wilson, with Ben Kingsley and Geraldine James, dir. by Alison Sutcliffe, des. by Martin Tilley.

MERMAID: Puddle Dock, Blackfriars, EC4. (1986) Oct. 21. *Sink the Belgrano!* by Steven Berkoff (Half Moon prodn.)). (1987) April 1. *The Fair Maid of the West* by Thomas Heywood, with Joe Melia, Imelda Staunton, Sean Bean, Paul Greenwood and Pete Postlethwaite, dir. by Trevor Nunn, des. by John Napier (R.S.C. Swan prodn.). April 8. *Every Man in his Humour* by Ben Jonson, with Henry Goodman, Jim Carter, Simon Russell Beale and Philip Franks, dir. by John Caird, des. by Sue Blane (R.S.C. Swan prodn.). May 26. *The Two Noble Kinsmen* by Shakespeare and Fletcher, with Imogen Stubbs, Amanda Harris, Hugh Quarshie, Gerard Murphy and Peter Guinness, dir. by Barry Kyle, des. by Bob Crowley (R.S.C. Swan prodn.). July 16. *They Shoot Horses, Don't They?* by Horace McCoy (adapted by Ray Herman), with Imelda Staunton, Paul Greenwood and Henry Goodman, dir. by Ron Daniels, des. by Ralph Koltai. Aug. 20. *The Great White Hope* by Howard Sackler, with Hugh Quarshie and Jill Baker, dir. by Nicholas Kent.

NATIONAL THEATRE: South Bank, SE1. COTTESLOE: (1986) Sept. 9. *The Bay at Nice* and *Wrecked Eggs* by David Hare, with Irene Worth, Zoe Wannamaker, Philip Locke, Colin Stinton and Kate Buffery, dir. by David Hare, des. by John Gunter. (1987) Jan. 22. *Three Men on a Horse* by George Abbott and John Cecil Holm, with Geoffrey Hutchings, Gemma Craven, Alison Fiske, Claire Parker, Nicholas le Prevost and Ken Stott, dir. by Jonathan Lynn, des. by Saul Radomsky. Jan. 9. *Bopha!* by Percy Mtwa, with Sidney Khumalo, Aubrey Maolosi Molefe and Aubrey Radebe, dir. by Percy Mtwa, lighting by Mannie Manim (the Earth Players, presented by Market Theatre Co., Johannesburg). Feb. 12. *A View from the Bridge* by Arthur Miller, with Michael Gambon, Lewis George, James Hayes, Suzan Sylvester, Elizabeth Bell, Adrian Rawlins and Michael Simkins, dir. by Alan Ayckbourn, des. by Alan Tagg. March 26. *Yerma* by Lorca (trans. by Peter Luke), with Juliet Stevenson, Celia Imrie and Roger Lloyd Pack, dir. by Di Trevis, des. by Pamela Howard. May 6, *Rosmersholm* by Ibsen (trans. by Frank McGuinness), with Roger Lloyd Pack, David Ryall, Ken Drury, Robert Eddison and Suzanne Bertish, dir. by Sarah Pia Anderson, des. by Roger Glossop. July 21. *Mean Tears* written and dir. by Peter Gill, with Karl Johnson, Bill Nighy and Garry Cooper, des. by Alison Chitty.

LYTTELTON: (1986) Sept. 24. *The Magistrate* by Pinero, with Nigel Hawthorne, Gemma Craven, Claire Parker, Graeme Henderson, Alison Fiske and Ken Stott, dir. by Michael Rudman, des. by Carl Toms. Nov. 6. *Tons of Money* by Will Evans and Valentine, with Simon Cadell, Michael Gambon, Polly Adams, Diane Bull and Russell Dixon, dir. by Alan Ayckbourn, des. by Alan Tagg. (1987) Jan. 7. *Coming into Land* by Stephen Poliakoff, with Maggie Smith, Anthony Andrews and Tim Pigott-Smith, dir. by Peter Hall, des. by Alison Chitty. Jan. 29. *School for Wives* by Molière (trans. by Robert David MacDonald), with Celia Imrie, Roger Lloyd Pack, David Ryall, Anthony Trent and Julia Ford, dir. by Di Trevis, des. by Pamela Howard. May. *The Hairy Ape* by Eugene O'Neill, with Ronald Schafer, dir. by Peter Stein. May 23, *La Critique de l'Ecole des Femmes* by Molière (trans. by John Watts), with Celia Imrie, Shona Morris, Christine Absalom and Richard Bonneville. June 11. Shakespeare's *Hamlet*, with Peter Stormare and Pernilla Ostergren, dir. by Ingmar Bergman (Stockholm Royal Dramatic Theatre prodn.). June 18. *Miss Julie* by Strindberg, with Peter Stormare, Gerthi Kulle and Marie Goranzon, dir. by Ingmar Bergman (Stockholm Royal Dramatic Theatre prodn.). July 9. *Fathers and Sons* by Turgenev (adapted by Brian Friel), with Alec McCowen, Robert Glenister, Richard Pasco, Robin Bailey and Joyce Grant, dir. by Michael Rudman, des. by Carl Toms. Aug. 8. *The Wandering Jew* by Michelene Wardor, with Philip Voss, Pip Donaghy, Russell Enoch, and Sylvestra le Touzel, dir. by Mike Alfreds.

OLIVIER: (1986) Dec. 11. Shakespeare's *King Lear*, with Anthony Hopkins, Anna Massey, Suzanne Bertish, Miranda Foster, Roshan Seth, Bill Nighy, Douglas Hodge, Michael Bryant and Basil Henson, dir. by David Hare, des. by Hayden Griffin. Dec. 18. *The American Clock* by Arthur Miller (trans. from Cottesloe). (1987) March 18. *Six Characters in Search of an Author* by Pirandello (adapted by Nicholas Wright), with Robin Bailey, Barbara Jefford, Richard Pasco, Leslie Sands and Lesley Sharp, dir. by Michael Rudman, des. by Carl Toms. April 9. Shakespeare's *Antony and Cleopatra*, with Judi Dench, Anthony Hopkins, Michael Bryant, Miranda Foster, John Bluthal, Tim Pigott-Smith, David Schofield, dir. by Peter Hall, des. by Alison Chitty. May 21. *A Small Family Business*, written and dir. by Alan Ayckbourn, with Michael Gambon, John Arthur, Marcia Warren, Simon Cadell, Elizabeth Bell and Polly Adams, des. by Alan Tagg.

OLD RED LION: St. John St., N1. (1987) Aug. 6 *Mr Bennett and Miss Smith* by Marion Baraitser, with Peter Meakin and Josephine Banham, dir. by Richard Hansom, des. by John Jenkins.

OLD VIC: The Cut, SE1. (1986) Nov. 19. *The Women* by Clare Boothe Luce, with Susannah York, Maria Aitken, Diana Quick, Georgina Hale and Patti Love, dir. by Keith Hack, des. by Voytek. (1987) Jan. 19. *Holiday* by Philip Barry, with Don Fellows, Cherie Lunghi, Frank Grimes, Malcolm McDowell, Mary Steenburgen and Geoffrey Burridge, dir. by Lindsay Anderson, des. by Michael Pavelka. March 16. Shakespeare's *Henry IV, Parts 1 and 2*, and *Henry V*, with Michael Pennington, John Woodvine, Patrick O'Connell, John Price, and Jenny Quayle, dir. by Michael Bogdanov, des. by Chris Dyer (English Shakespeare Company prodn.). May 18. *Kiss Me Kate*, music and lyrics by Cole Porter, book by Sam and Bella Spewack, with Tim Flavin, Fiona Hendley, Nichola McAuliffe, and Paul Jones, dir. by Adrian Noble, des. by John Gunter, choreog. Ron Field (R.S.C. prodn.).

OPEN AIR: Regent's Park, W1. (1987) June 1. *Bartholomew Fair* by Ben Jonson, with Peggy Mount, Christopher Biggins, Peter Bayliss and Christopher Ryan, dir. by Peter Barnes. Aug. Shakespeare's *A Midsummer Night's Dream*. Aug. 4. Shakespeare's *Two Gentlemen of Verona*, with Richard Bain, Paul Kirk, Juliette Crosby and Tom Mannion, dir. by Ian Talbot.

PARAMOUNT CITY: Gt. Windmill St., W1. (1986) Sept. 18. *The News* by Paul Pulse, with Richard O'Brien, Peter Straker, Marcia Johnson, Bee Jaye, dir. by Kevin Williams.

PHOENIX: Charing Cross Rd., WC2. (1986) Nov. 18. *Wildfire* by N. Richard Nash, with Diana Rigg, Kevin McNally, David Healy, Carmen Rodrigues and Mark Wing-Davey, dir. by Peter Wood, des. by Carl Toms. (1987) April 21. *Court in the Act* by Maurice Hennequin and Pierre Veber, with Gabrielle Drake, Michael Denison, Lee Montague, Terence Wilton and Derek Smith, dir. by Braham Murray, des. by Stephen Doncaster (Royal Exchange, Manchester prodn.).

PICCADILLY: Denman St., W1. (1986) Nov. 14. *A*

Funny Thing Happened on the Way to the Forum
(Chichester Festival Theatre prodn.). (1987) June 16.
Rosencrantz and Guildenstern are Dead by Tom
Stoppard, with Mark Arden, Stephen Frost and
Lionel Blair, dir. by Peter Wilson (Nottingham
Playhouse/Mobil Touring Theatre prodn.). April 21.
Lady Day (Donmar Warehouse prodn.).

PRINCE OF WALES: Coventry St., W1. (1986) Nov.
4. *'Allo 'Allo* by Jeremy Lloyd and David Croft, with
Gordon Kaye and Carmen Silvera, dir. by Peter
Farago, des. by Bill Pinner.

QUEENS: Shaftesbury Ave., W1. (1987) April 6. *The
Resistible Rise of Arturo Ui* by Bertold Brecht (trans.
by George Tabori), with Griff Rhys Jones, Brian
Glover, Hugh Paddick, Linal Haft and Ken Bones,
dir. by David Gilmore, des. by Roger Glossop.

RIVERSIDE STUDIOS: Hammersmith, W6. (1986)
Nov. 6. *Too True to be Good* by George Bernard Shaw,
with Sheila Reid, David Beames, Selina Cadell and
Sian Thomas, dir. by Mike Alfreds, des. by Paul Dart.
(1987) Aug. 24. *The Life of Napoleon*, devised, written
and performed by John Sessions, dir. by Kenneth
Branagh (Renaissance Co. prodn.).

ROYAL COURT: Sloane Sq., SW1. (1986) Sept. 23.
Kafka's Dick by Alan Bennett, with Roger Lloyd
Pack, Andrew Sachs, Jim Broadbent, Geoffrey Pal-
mer, Alison Steadman and Charles Lamb, dir. by
Richard Eyre, des. by William Dudley. Nov. 27. *A
Mouthful of Birds* by Caryl Churchill and David Lan,
with Stephen Goff, Philippe Giraudeau, Christian
Burgess and Tricia Kelly, dir. by Ian Spink and Les
Waters (Joint Stock and Birmingham Rep. prodn.).
(1987) Jan. 26. *Road* by Jim Cartwright, with Ian
Dury, Jane Horrocks, Mossie Smith and Susan
Brown, dir. by Simon Curtis, des. by Paul Brown.
March 27. *Serious Money* by Caryl Churchill, with
Gary Oldman, Alfred Molina, Lesley Manville, Linda
Bassett, Allan Corduner and Meera Syal, dir. by Max
Stafford-Clark, music by Colin Sell. June 17. *Jenkin's
Ear* by Dusty Hughes, with Robert Urquhart, Alfred
Molina and Phyllida Law. Aug. 4. *The Colored
Museum* by George C. Wolfe, with Danitra Vance
and Loretta Devine, dir. by Kenneth Richardson
(New York Shakespeare Festival Prodn.).

ROYAL COURT UPSTAIRS: (1987) March 16. *The
Emperor* by Jonathan Miller and Michael Hastings,
with Nabil Shaban, dir. by Jonathan Miller, des. by
Richard Hudson.

SADLER'S WELLS: Rosebery Ave., EC1. (1987) Aug.
11. *Bless the Bride* by Vivian Ellis and A. P. Herbert,
with Ruth Madoc, Simon Williams, Jan Hartley and
Bernard Alane, dir. by Christopher Renshaw, des. by
Tim Goodchild.

SAVOY: Strand, WC2. (1986) Nov. 19. *Killing
Jessica* by Richard Levinson and William Link
(adapted by David Rogers), with Patrick Macnee, Liz
Robertson, David Langton and Jennie Linden, dir.
by Bryan Forbes, des. by Tim Goodchild. (1987) May
7. *The Mystery of Edwin Drood* by Rupert Holmes,
with Ernie Wise, Paul Bentley, David Burt, Lulu,
Mark Ryan and Julia Hills, dir. by Wilford Leach,
choreog. by Gracie la Daniele. Aug. 11. *Portraits* by
William Douglas Home, with Keith Michell, Simon
Ward, Pamela Lane, Stephen Boxer and Richard
Wordsworth, dir. by John Dexter, des. by Brien
Vahey.

SHAFTESBURY: Shaftesbury Ave., WC2. (1986) Sept.
2. *Rookery Nook* by Ben Travers, with Tom Courtenay, Ian Ogilvy, Peggy Mount, Lionel Jeffries,

Derek Smith, Nichola McAuliffe and Georgia Allen,
dir. by Mark Kingston, des. by Alan Pickford.
(Theatre of Comedy prodn.). Dec. 19. *An Italian
Straw Hat* by Eugene Labiche (adapted by Simon
Moore), with Tom Conti, Clive Dunn, Stratford
Johns, Deborah Morton and Sheila Keith, dir. by Ray
Cooney, des. by Saul Radomsky. (1987) July 21.
Follies by Stephen Sondheim, with Julia McKenzie,
Daniel Massey, Diana Rigg, David Healy and Leonard
Sachs, dir. by Mike Ockrent, des. by Maria Bjornson,
choreog. by Bob Avian.

THEATRE ROYAL: Haymarket, SW1. (1986) Oct. 21.
Breaking the Code by Hugh Whitemore, with Derek
Jacobi, Michael Gough, Joanna David, and Isabel
Dean, dir. by Clifford Williams, des. by Liz da Costa.
(1987) June 23. *Melon* by Simon Gray, with Alan
Bates, William Squire, Carole Nimmons and Tim
Hardy, dir. by Christopher Morahan, des. by Liz da
Costa.

THEATRE ROYAL: Stratford East, E15. (1986) Sept.
11. *Tuesday's Child* by Terry Johnson and Kate
Lock, with Michael Angelis, and Eileen Atkins, dir.
by Mike Bradwell. (1987) March 26. *This is My
Dream* by Henry Livings, with Joanne Campbell, dir.
by Philip Hedley.

TRICYCLE: 269 Kilburn High Rd., NW6. (1986) Oct.
14. *The Hostage* by Brendan Behan, with Eric
Richard, Eileen Pollock, P. G. Stephens, Catherine
Cusack and Heather Tobias, dir. by Nicholas Kent,
des. by Saul Radomsky. (1987) April 13. *The Greatest
Story Ever Told* by Patrick Barlow, with Jim Broadbent and Patrick Barlow (National Theatre of Brent
prodn.).

VAUDEVILLE: Strand, WC2. (1986) Sept 3. *Woman
in Mind*, written and dir. by Alan Ayckbourn, with
Julia McKenzie, Martin Jarvis, Peter Blythe and
Josephine Tewson, des. by Roger Glossop. 1987) July
15. *Three Men on a Horse* (National Theatre prodn.).

VICTORIA PALACE: SW1. Feb. 25. *High Society* by
Cole Porter, with Trevor Eve, Stephen Rae, Natasha
Richardson, Angela Richards and Ronald Fraser, dir.
by Richard Eyre, des. by John Gunter, choreog. by
David Toguri (Leicester Haymarket prodn.).

WESTMINSTER: Palace St., SW1. (1987) May 6. *An
Inspector Calls* by J. B. Priestley, with Tom Baker,
Pauline Jameson, Peter Baldwin, Adam Godley,
Charlotte Attenborough and Simon Shepherd, dir.
by Peter Dews, des. by Daphne Dare (Theatre Clwyd
prodn.).

WHITEHALL: SW1. (1986) Dec. 9 *When I Was a Girl
I Used to Scream and Shout* by Sharman Macdonald,
with Julie Walters, Geraldine James, Sheila Reid and
John Gordon Sinclair, dir. by Simon Stokes, des. by
Robin Don.

WYNDHAM'S: Charing Cross Rd., WC2. (1986) Oct.
7. *The Petition* by Brian Clark, with John Mills and
Rosemary Harris, dir. by Peter Hall (National Theatre
prodn.). Nov. 19. *Ghost* by Ibsen (Young Vic prodn.).
(1987) March 4. *Decadence* written and dir. by Steven
Berkoff, with Linda Marlowe and Steven Berkoff.
April. *Jeeves Takes Charge* by P. G. Wodehouse, with
Edward Duke, dir. by Gillian Lynne. July 7. *Serious
Money* by Caryl Churchill (Royal Court prodn.).

YOUNG VIC: 66 The Cut, SE 1. (1986) Oct. 2. *Ghosts*
by Henrick Ibsen (trans. by Peter Watts), with
Vanessa Redgrave, Tom Wilkinson and Adrian
Dunbar, dir. by David Thacker. (1987) Feb. 18 *Who's*

Afraid of Virginia Woolf? by Edward Albee, with Billie Whitelaw and Patrick Stewart, dir. by David Thacker.

Productions outside London included the following:

ROYAL SHAKESPEARE COMPANY, Stratford: (1986) Sept. 10. *Richard II* with Jeremy Irons, Michael Kitchen, Brewster Mason, Imogen Stubbs and Bernard Horsfall, dir. by Barry Kyle, des. by William Dudley. Nov. 11. *Macbeth*, with Jonathan Pryce, Sinead Cusack, Peter Guinness, Hugh Quarshie and David Troughton, dir. by Adrian Noble. (1987) Feb. 10. *Kiss Me Kate* by Cole Porter, with Paul Jones, Nichola McAuliffe, Tim Flavin, Fiona Hendley, Emile Wolk and John Bardon, dir. by Adrian Noble, des. by William Dudley, choreog. by Ron Field. April 2. *Julius Caesar*, with Roger Allam, Sean Baker, Nicholas Farrell and David Waller, dir. by Terry Hands, des. by Farrah. April 23. *The Merchant of Venice*, with Antony Sher, Deborah Findlay, Phil Daniels, John Carlisle and Nicholas Farrell, dir. by Bill Alexander. July 8. *Twelfth Night*, with Antony Sher, Bruce Alexander, Harriet Walter, Paul Spence, Donald Sumpter, Deborah Findlay, David Bradley and Roger Allam, dir. by Bill Alexander, des. by Kit Surrey.

OTHER PLACE:(1986) Sept. 12. *Worlds Apart* by Jose Triana, with Henry Goodman, Janet McTeer, Joely Richardson and Philip Franks, dir. by Nick Hamm, des. by Chris Dyer, music by Ilona Sekacz. Nov. 12. *Country Dancing* by Nigel Williams, with Richard Easton, Stuart Richman, Christopher Ashley, Amanda Harris, Niamh Cusack, and Gerard Murphy, dir. by Bill Alexander. (1987) April 1. *Fashion* by Doug Lucie, with Alun Armstrong, Brian Cox, Estelle Kohler and Clive Russell, dir. by Nick Hamm. April 22. *Temptation* by Vaclav Havel (trans. by George

Theiner), with David Bradley and John Shrapnel, dir. by Roger Michell. July 8. *Indigo* by Heidi Thomas, with Sean Baker and Hakeem Kae-Kazim, dir. by Sarah Pia Anderson.

SWAN: (1986) Sept. 23. *The Fair Maid of the West* by Thomas Heywood, with Imelda Staunton, Simon Russell Beale, Paul Greenwood, Trevor Gordon, Joe Melia, Pete Postlethwaite and Donald McBride, dir. by Trevor Nunn, des. by John Napier. (1987) April 7. *Hyde Park* by James Shirley, with John Carlisle, Fiona Shaw and Alex Jennings, dir. by Barry Kyle, des. by Gerard Howland. April 28. *Titus Andronicus* with Brian Cox, Estelle Kohler, Jim Hooper, Peter Polycarpou and Sonia Ritter, dir. by Deborah Warner, des. by Isabella Bywater. July 14.*The Jew of Malta* by Christopher Marlow, with Alun Armstrong, John Carlisle and Phil Daniels, dir. by Barry Kyle, des. by Bob Crowley.

CHICHESTER FESTIVAL THEATRE: (1987) April 24. *Robert and Elizabeth* by Ronald Miller and Ron Grainer, with John Savident, Gaynor Miles and Mark Wynter, dir. by Stewart Trotter. May 11. *An Ideal Husband* by Oscar Wilde, with David Gwillim, Joanna Lumley, Clive Francis and Lucy Fleming, dir. by Tony Britton. July 6. *A Man for All Seasons* by Robert Bolt, with Tony Britton, Gordon Chater, Martin Chamberlain, Benjamin Whitrow, Roy Kinnear, Gwen Watford and Adrienne Thomas, dir. by Frank Hauser. July 27. *Miranda* by Beverley Cross (after Carlo Goldoni), with Penelope Keith, Milton Johns and John Harding, dir. by Wendy Toye.

MANCHESTER ROYAL EXCHANGE: (1986) Oct. 24, *Edward II* by Christopher Marlowe, with Ian Mc-Diarmid, Michael Grandage, Iain Glen, Brid Brennan and Duncan Bell, des. by Thomas Cairns, dir. by Nicholas Hytner.

THE ACADEMY AWARDS, 1983–86

1983 Best Picture: *Terms of Endearment*.
    Best Director: James L. Brooks, *Terms of Endearment*.
    Best Actor: Robert Duvall, *Tender Mercies*.
    Best Actress: Shirley Maclaine, *Terms of Endearment*.
1984 Best Picture: *Amadeus*.
    Best Director: Milos Forman, *Amadeus*.
    Best Actor: F. Murray Abraham, *Amadeus*.
    Best Actress: Sally Field, *Places in the Heart*.
1985 Best Picture: *Out of Africa*.

    Best Director: Sydney Pollack, *Out of Africa*.
    Best Actor: William Hurt, *Kiss of the Spider Woman*.
    Best Actress: Geraldine Page, *The Trip to Bountiful*.
1986 Best Picture: *Platoon*.
    Best Director: Oliver Stone, *Platoon*.
    Best Actor: Paul Newman, *The Color of Money*.
    Best Actress: Marlee Matlin, *Children of a Lesser God*.

PRINCIPAL LONDON CLUBS

ALPINE (1857), 74 South Audley Street, W1Y 5FF.—
Hon. Sec., S. W. Town.

AMERICAN (1919), 95 Piccadilly, W1V 0BS.—
Sec., A. M. Cook.

AMERICAN WOMEN'S (1899), 95 Piccadilly, W1V 0BS.—
Sec., Ms. M. Dougan.

ANGLO-BELGIAN (1955), 60 Knightsbridge, SW1X
7LF.—*Hon. Sec.*, Baron de Gerlache de Gomery,
M.V.O.

ARMY AND NAVY (1837), 36–39 Pall Mall, SW1Y 5JN.—
Sec., Col. D. O. O'Reilly.

ARTS (1863), 40 Dover Street, W1X 3RB.—*Sec.*, C.
Miers.

ARTS THEATRE (1927), 7 Great Newport Street,
W.C.2.—*Sec.*, Miss C. Dowling.

THE ATHENAEUM (1824), 107 Pall Mall, SW1Y 5ER.—
Sec., R. R. T. Smith.

AUTHOR'S (1892), 40 Dover Street, W1X 3RB.—*Sec.*,
Mrs. H. Ridgway.

BEEFSTEAK (1876), 9 Irving Street, WC2H 7AT.—*Sec.*,
E. Pool, M.C.

BOODLE'S (1762), 28 St. James's Street, S.W.1.—*Sec.*,
R. J. Edmonds.

BROOKS'S (1764), St. James's Street, SW1A 1LN.—
Sec., M. A. Roberts.

BUCK'S (1919), 18 Clifford Street, W1R 1RG.—*Sec.*,
A. G. Fairbrass.

CALEDONIAN (1891), 9 Halkin Street, SW1X 7DR.—
Sec., Cdr. C. M. Bagguley, R.N.

CANNING (1910), 42 Half Moon Street, W1Y 8DS.—
Sec., T. M. Harrington.

CARLTON (1832), 69 St. James's Street, SW1A 1PJ.—
Sec., R. N. Linsley.

CAVALRY AND GUARDS (1893), 127 Piccadilly,
W1V 0PX.—*Sec.*, L. D. de Pinna.

CHALLONER (1949), 59/61 Pont Street, SW1 0BG—
Hon. Sec., J. S. Tosh.

CHELSEA ARTS (1891), 143 Old Church Street,
SW3 6EB.—*Sec.*, Hon. D. Winterbottom.

CITY LIVERY (1914), Sion College, Victoria Embankment, EC4Y 0DN.—*Hon. Sec.*, B. L. Morgan, C.B.E.

CITY OF LONDON (1832), 19 Old Broad Street, EC2N
1DS.—*Sec.*, G. S. Chisholm.

CITY UNIVERSITY (1895), 50 Cornhill, EC3V 3PD.—
Sec., Miss R. Graham.

EAST INDIA (1849), 16 St. James's Square, SW1Y
4LH.—*Sec.*, J. G. F. Stoy.

ECCENTRIC (1890), 9 Ryder Street, SW1Y 6PZ.—*Sec.*,
J. F. W. Hawkins.

FARMERS (1842), 3 Whitehall Court, SW1A 2EL.—
Sec., Lt. Col. J. L. S. Andrews, O.B.E.

FLYFISHERS' (1884), 24A Old Burlington Street, W1X
1RG.—*Sec.*, Cdr. N. T. Fuller, R.N. (*retd.*).

GARRICK (1831), 15 Garrick Street, WC2E 9AY.—*Sec.*,
M. J. Harvey.

GREEN ROOM (1877), 9 Adam Street, WC2N 6AA.—
Hon. Sec., P. Corneille.

GRESHAM (1843), 15 Abchurch Lane, EC4N 7BB.—
Sec., Mrs. J. Downing.

GROUCHO (1985), 45 Dean Street, W1V 5AP.—*Membership Sec.*, Ms. C. Palmer.

HURLINGHAM (1869), Ranelagh Gardens, SW6 3PR.—
Chief Exec., P. H. Covell.

KEMPTON PARK (1878), Sunbury-on-Thames, Middx.,
TW16 5AQ.—*Sec.*, Miss S. Bainbridge.

KENNEL (1873), 1 Clarges Street, W1Y 8AB.—*Sec.*,
Maj. Gen. M. H. Sinnatt, C.B.

LANSDOWNE (1934), 9 Fitzmaurice Place, Berkeley
Square, W1X 6JD.—*Sec.*, Lt. Cdr. T. P. Havers.

LONDON ROWING (1856), Embankment, Putney, SW15
1LB.—*Hon. Sec.*, N. A. Smith.

LONDON THAMES FENCING (1848), 83 Perham Road,
W14 9SY.—*Hon. Sec.*, G. Morrison.

MARYLEBONE CRICKET CLUB (M.C.C.) (1787), Lord's
Cricket Ground, NW8 8QN.—*Sec.*, Lt.-Col. J. R.
Stephenson, O.B.E.

MINING (1910), 3 London Wall Buildings, E.C.2.—
Sec., Miss P. Warner.

NATIONAL (1845), c/o Carlton Club (*q.v.*).—*Sec.*, I. E.
Nash.

NATIONAL LIBERAL (1882), Whitehall Place,
SW1A 2HE.—*Hon. Sec.*, M. J. Cook.

NAVAL (1946), 38 Hill Street, W1X 8DP.—*Sec.*, Cdr.
C. R. Parkes, R.D., R.N.R.

NAVAL AND MILITARY (1862), 94 Piccadilly, W1V
0BP.—*Sec.*, R. B. Raworth, V.R.D.

ORIENTAL (1824), Stratford House, Stratford Place,
W1N 0ES.—*Sec.*, R. N. Rapson, M.V.O.

PORTLAND (1816), 42 Half Moon Street, W1Y 7RD.—
Sec., R. B. Little.

PRATT'S (1841), 14 Park Place, SW1A 1LP.—*Sec.*,
Capt. P. W. E. Parry, M.B.E.

QUEEN'S (1886), Palliser Road, W. Kensington, W14
9EQ.—*Sec.*, J. A. S. Edwardes.

RAILWAY (1899), Keen House, 4 Calshot Street, N1
9DA.—*Hon. Sec.*, N. C. Farebrother.

REFORM (1836), 104–5 Pall Mall, SW1Y 5EW.—*Sec.*,
R. A. M. Forrest.

ROEHAMPTON (1901), Roehampton Lane, SW15 5LR.—
Sec., R. W. Varley.

ROYAL AIR FORCE (1918), 128 Piccadilly, W1V 0PY.—
Sec., Sqn. Ldr. J. Swaffield.

ROYAL AUTOMOBILE (1897), 89–91 Pall Mall, S.W.1.—
Sec., J. N. Cranfield.

ROYAL COMMONWEALTH SOCIETY (1868), 18 Northumberland Avenue, WC2N 5BJ.—*Sec. Gen.*, Sir Michael Scott, K.C.V.O., C.M.G.

ROYAL OCEAN RACING (1925), 20 St. James's Place,
SW1A 1NN.—*Sec.*, E. A. Green.

ROYAL OVER-SEAS LEAGUE (1910), Over-Seas House,
Park Place, St. James's Street, SW1A 1LR.—*Dir.
Gen.*, Capt. J. B. Rumble.

ROYAL THAMES YACHT (1775), 60 Knightsbridge,
SW1X 7LF.—*Sec.*, Capt. A. R. Ward, C.B.E., R.N.

ST. STEPHEN'S CONSTITUTIONAL (1870), 34 Queen
Anne's Gate, SW1H 9AB.—*Sec.*, L. D. Mawby.

SAVAGE (1857), 9 Fitzmaurice Place, W1X 5DE.—
Hon. Sec., D. Coomber, O.B.E.

SAVILE (1868), 69 Brook Street, W1Y 2ER.—*Sec.*, P.
Aldersley.

SKI CLUB OF GREAT BRITAIN (1903), 118 Eaton Square,
SW1W 9AF.—*Sec.*, C. J. Dixon.

THAMES ROWING (1860), Embankment, Putney, SW15
1LB.—*Hon. Sec.*, F. S. Beardmore.

TRAVELLERS' (1819), 106 Pall Mall, SW1Y 5EP.—*Sec.*,
B. J. Scambler.

TURF (1868), 5 Carlton House Terrace, SW1Y 5AQ.—
Sec., P. A. Chandler.

UNITED NURSING SERVICES (1921), 40 South Street,
W.1.—*Sec.*, W. Oakes.

UNITED OXFORD AND CAMBRIDGE UNIVERSITY (1972), 71 Pall Mall, SW1Y 5HD.—*Sec.*, D. J. McDougall.

UNIVERSITY WOMEN'S (1886), 2 Audley Square, W1Y 6DB.—*Sec.*, Mrs. E. Hord.

V.A.D. (1920), 44 Great Cumberland Place, W1H 8BS.—*Sec.*, G. Maylett.

VICTORIA (1863), 150–162 Edgware Road, W.2.—*Sec.*, L. A. Holland.

VICTORY SERVICES (1907), 63–79 Seymour Street, W2 2HL.—*Gen. Manager*, D. G. Stovey.

WHITE'S (1693), 37–38 St. James's Street, SW1A 1JG.—*Sec.*, W. H. West.

WIG AND PEN (1908), 229–230 Strand, WC2R 1BA.— *Sec.*, J. Reynolds.

PRINCIPAL CLUBS OUTSIDE LONDON

Aldershot.—ROYAL ALDERSHOT OFFICERS CLUB (1856), Farnborough Road, Aldershot, Hants.— *Sec.*, Lt. Col. A. F. J. Channon, M.B.E.

Bath.—BATH AND COUNTY CLUB (1865), Queen's Parade, Bath, BA1 2NJ.—*Sec.*, Mrs. G. M. Jones.

Birmingham.—THE BIRMINGHAM CLUB (1872), Winston Churchill House, 8 Ethel Street, Birmingham B2 4BG.—*Hon. Sec.*, R. M. Woodgate, R.D.

  ST. PAUL'S CLUB (1859), 34 St. Paul's Square, Birmingham B3 1QZ.—*Hon. Sec.*, J. S. Scott, T.D.

Bishop Auckland.—THE CLUB (1868), 1 Victoria Avenue, Bishop Auckland, Co. Durham DL14 7JH.—*Hon. Sec.*, L. Cooke.

Bristol.—THE BEAUFORT CLUB (1885), Marsh Street, Bristol BS1 4BG.—*Sec.*, M. Lansdell.

  THE CLIFTON CLUB (1882), 22 The Mall, Bristol BS8 4DS.—*Hon. Sec.*, H. Walder.

Cambridge.—THE AMATEUR DRAMATIC CLUB (1855), A.D.C. Theatre, Park Street, Cambridge.—*Hon. Sec.*, B. Ball.

  HAWKS CLUB (1874), Jesus Lane, Cambridge.— *Hon. Sec.*, J. D. Barton.

  THE UNION (1815), Bridge Street, Cambridge CB2 1UB.—*Chief Clerk*, B. Thoday.

Canterbury.—KENT AND CANTERBURY CLUB (1868), 17 Old Dover Road, Canterbury CT1 3JB.—*Sec.*, P. L. Wood.

Cardiff.—CARDIFF AND COUNTY CLUB (1866), Westgate Street, Cardiff CF1 1DA.—*Hon. Sec.*, A. G. Robertson.

Cheltenham.—THE NEW CLUB (1874), Montpellier Parade, Cheltenham GL5O 1UD.—*Hon. Sec.*, J. A. Warhurst, O.B.E.

Chester.—THE CITY CLUB (1807), St. Peter's Churchyard, Chester CH1 2AG.—*Sec.*, C. Hodkinson.

  GROSVENOR CLUB (1866), Vicars Lane, Chester CH1 1QX.—*Hon. Sec.*, Maj. U. C. E. Farr.

Chichester.—WEST SUSSEX COUNTY CLUB (1872), 5 Stirling Road, Chichester, W. Sussex.—*Sec.*, J. S. Winny.

Colchester.—THE CLUB (1874), 3–5 Culver Street West, Colchester, Essex.—*Sec.*, N. Duncan.

Devizes.—DEVIZES AND DISTRICT CLUB (1932), 27 St. John Street, Devizes, Wilts SN10 1BN.—*Sec.*, D. J. J. Cox.

Durham.—COUNTY CLUB (1890), 52 Old Elvet, Durham.—*Sec.*, Mrs. C. Arnot.

Eastbourne.—THE DEVONSHIRE CLUB (1872), Hartington Place, Eastbourne, Sussex BN21 3RN.—*Hon. Sec.*, D. G. Matthews.

Exeter.—EXETER AND COUNTY CLUB (1871), 5 Cathedral Close, Exeter, Devon EX1 1EZ.—*Sec.*, S. F. Hodge, M.B.E.

Guildford.—THE COUNTY CLUB, 158 High Street, Guildford GU1 3HF.—*Hon. Sec.*, R. M. Pritchett.

Harrogate.—THE CLUB (1857), 36 Victoria Avenue, Harrogate, N. Yorks.—*Hon. Sec.*, C. L. Leslie.

Henley-on-Thames.—LEANDER CLUB (1818), Henley, Oxon. RG9 2LP.—*Hon. Sec.*, J. D. Randall.

  PHYLLIS COURT CLUB (1906), Marlow Road, Henley, Oxon. RG9 2HT.—*Sec.*, R. I. Bulloch.

Hove.—THE HOVE CLUB (1882), 28 Fourth Avenue, Hove, Sussex BN3 2PJ.—*Sec.*, Sqn. Ldr. G. A. Inverarity, D.F.C.

Jersey.—THE VICTORIA CLUB (1853), Beresford Street, St. Helier, Jersey.—*Sec.*, Gp. Capt. J. W. E. Holmes, D.F.C., A.F.C.

Leamington.—TENNIS COURT CLUB (1846), 50 Bedford Street, Leamington, Warwicks. CV32 5DT.—*Hon. Sec.*, O. D. R. Dixon.

Leeds.—THE LEEDS CLUB (1850), 3 Albion Place, Leeds LS1 6JL.—*Manager*, M. J. C. Reynolds.

Leicester.—LEICESTERSHIRE CLUB (1873), 9 Welford Place, Leicester LE1 6ZH.—*Manager*, J. A. Evans.

Liverpool.—THE ATHENAEUM (1797), Church Alley, Liverpool L1 3DD.—*Hon. Sec.*, D. Gee, T.D.

Manchester.—THE MANCHESTER CLUB (1867), 50 Spring Gardens, Manchester M2 1EN.—*Hon. Sec.*, S. P. Jennings.

  THE ST. JAMES'S CLUB—St. James's House, Charlotte Street, Manchester M1 4DZ.—*Hon. Sec.*, C. A. Hadfield.

Newcastle upon Tyne.—THE NORTHERN CONSTITUTIONAL CLUB (1882), 37 Pilgrim Street, Newcastle upon Tyne NE1 6QE.—*Hon. Sec.*, J. L. Browne.

Northampton.—NORTHAMPTON AND COUNTY CLUB (1873), George Row, Northampton NN1 1DF.—*Sec.*, Maj. G. D. Denholm, B.E.M.

Norwich.—THE NORFOLK CLUB (1770), 17 Upper King Street, Norwich NR3 1RB.—*Sec.*, A. J. M. Williamson.

Nottingham.—NOTTINGHAM AND NOTTS. UNITED SERVICES CLUB (1920), Newdigate House, Castle Gate, Nottingham NG1 6AF.—*Hon. Sec.*, A. C. Ready.

Oxford.—THE FREWEN CLUB (1869), 98 St. Aldate's, Oxford OX1 1BT.—*Hon. Sec.*, W. H. Miller, B.E.M.

  OXFORD UNION SOCIETY (1823), Frewin Court, Oxford OX1 3JB.—*Office Manager.*, Mrs. E. R. Clarke.

  VINCENT CLUB (1863), 1A King Edward Street, Oxford OX1 4HS.—*Sec.*, M. Lawson-Statham.

Paignton.—THE PAIGNTON CLUB (1882), The Esplanade, Paignton, Devon TQ4 6ED.—*Hon. Sec.* P. Grafton.

Peterborough.—CITY AND COUNTIES CLUB (1867), Priestgate, Peterborough PE6 7LT.—*Sec.*, J. R. Fillingham.

Reading.—BERKSHIRE ATHENAEUM CLUB (1972), 53 Blagrave Street, Reading, Berks.—*Hon. Sec.*, W. J. Stuck.

Rye.—DORMY HOUSE CLUB (1896), Rye, Sussex TN31 7LD.—*Hon. Sec.*, D. W. Guest.

St. Leonards on Sea.—EAST SUSSEX CLUB (1893), 1 Warrior Square, St. Leonards on Sea, E. Sussex.—*Hon. Sec.*, E. J. Morris.

Shrewsbury.—THE SALOP CLUB (1974), The Old House, Dogpole, Shrewsbury SY1 1EP.—*Hon. Sec.*, T. P. Roberts.

Teddington.—ROYAL CANOE CLUB (1866), Trowlock Island, Teddington, Middx.—*Hon. Sec.*, Mrs. G. V. Barnard.

Worcester.—UNION AND COUNTY CLUB (1861), 40 Foregate Street, Worcester.—*Sec.*, M. G. Maton.

York.—YORKSHIRE CLUB (1839), 17 Museum Street, York YO1 2DW.—*Hon. Sec.*, D. Laughton.

CITY CLUB (1976), 4 Museum Street, York.—*Hon. Sec.*, C. H. Copeland.

Scotland

Ayr.—THE COUNTY CLUB (1872), Savoy Park Hotel, Ayr, Strathclyde.—*Hon. Sec.*, W. W. McHarg.

Edinburgh.—THE CALEDONIAN CLUB (1825), 32 Abercromby Place, Edinburgh EH3 6QE.—*Manager*, I. B. Harvey.

THE NEW CLUB (1787), 86 Princes Street, Edinburgh EH2 2BB.—*Sec.*, Cdr. G. J. T. Creedy, L.V.O., R.N.

Glasgow.—ART CLUB (1867), 185 Bath Street, Glasgow G2 4HU.—*Sec.*, L. J. McIntyre.

ROYAL SCOTTISH AUTOMOBILE CLUB (1899), 11 Blythswood Square, Glasgow G2 4AG.—*Sec.*, H. Dewar.

THE WESTERN CLUB (1825), 32 Royal Exchange Square, Glasgow G1 3AB.—*Sec.*, D. H. Gifford.

Ireland

Belfast.—THE ULSTER REFORM CLUB (1885), 4 Royal Avenue, Belfast BT1 1DA.—*Hon. Sec.*, I. M. S. Agar.

Dublin.—THE STEPHEN'S GREEN CLUB (1840), 9 St. Stephen's Green, Dublin 2.—*Hon. Sec.*, D. H. O'Neill.

Enniskillen.—FERMANAGH COUNTY CLUB (1883), 20 Church Street, Enniskillen, N. Ireland BT74 6DF.—*Sec.*, Lt. Col. G. E. Liddle, C.B.E.

YACHT CLUBS

Beaumaris.—ROYAL ANGLESEY YACHT CLUB (1802), 6–7 Green Edge, Beaumaris, Gwynedd LL58 8AL.—*Hon. Sec.*, V. G. Keep.

Bembridge.—THE BEMBRIDGE SAILING CLUB (1886), Embankment Road, Bembridge, I.o.W. PO35 5NR.—*Sec.*, J. N. McLean.

Birkenhead.—ROYAL MERSEY YACHT CLUB (1844), Bedford Road East, Rock Ferry, Birkenhead, Merseyside L42 1LS.—*Hon. Sec.*, H. H. Browne.

Bridlington.—ROYAL YORKSHIRE YACHT CLUB (1847), 1 Windsor Crescent, Bridlington, Yorks. YO15 3HX.—*Sec.*, I. Harness.

Burnham-on-Crouch.—ROYAL CORINTHIAN YACHT CLUB (1872), Burnham-on-Crouch, Essex CM0 8AX.—*Hon. Sec.*, N. R. Wynn.

Caernarvon.—ROYAL WELSH YACHT CLUB (1847), Porth-Yr-Aur, Caernarvon.—*Hon. Sec.*, J. N. L. Thomas.

Cowes.—ROYAL YACHT SQUADRON (1815), The Castle, Cowes, I.o.W. PO31 7QT.—*Sec.*, Maj. R. P. Rising, R.M.

ROYAL LONDON YACHT CLUB (1838), The Parade, Cowes, I. o. W. PO31 7QS.—*Sec.*, A. J. Clarke.

Dover.—ROYAL CINQUE PORTS YACHT CLUB (1872), 5 Waterloo Crescent, Dover CT16 1LA.—*Hon. Sec.*, G. M. Cartwright.

Fishbourne.—ROYAL VICTORIA YACHT CLUB (1844), Fishbourne Lane, Fishbourne, I. o. W.—*Sec.*, B. Bowers.

Fowey.—ROYAL FOWEY YACHT CLUB (1881), Fowey, Cornwall PL23 1BH.—*Hon. Sec.*, E. P. Warren.

Harwich.—ROYAL HARWICH YACHT CLUB (1843), Woolverstone, Ipswich IP9 1AT.—*Sec.*, Col. C. H. Bavin.

Jersey.—ROYAL CHANNEL ISLANDS YACHT CLUB (1862), The Bulwarks, St. Aubin, Jersey.—*Hon. Sec.*, A. K. Jackson.

Kingswear.—ROYAL DART YACHT CLUB (1866), Priory Street, Kingswear, S. Devon TQ6 0AB.—*Hon. Sec.*, P. Youd.

Leigh-on-Sea.—ESSEX YACHT CLUB (1890), H.Q.S. Bembridge, Foreshore, Leigh-on-Sea, Essex.—*Hon. Sec.*, A. Manning.

London.—THE CRUISING ASSOCIATION (1908), Ivory House, St. Katharine Dock, E1 9AT.—*Gen. Sec.*, Miss L. Nunn.

ROYAL CRUISING CLUB (1880), c/o Naval and Military Club.—*Hon. Sec.*, E. Bourne.

Lowestoft.—ROYAL NORFOLK AND SUFFOLK YACHT CLUB (1859), Royal Plain, Lowestoft, Suffolk NR33 0AQ.—*Sec.*, Lt. Cdr. M. Dowsett (*retd.*).

Lymington.—ROYAL LYMINGTON YACHT CLUB (1922), Bath Road, Lymington, Hants SO41 9SE.—*Sec.*, Gp. Capt. J. D. Hutchinson (*retd.*).

Penarth.—PENARTH YACHT CLUB (1880). The Esplanade, Penarth, S. Glamorgan CF6 2AU.—*Hon. Sec.*, W. H. Jones.

Plymouth.—ROYAL WESTERN YACHT CLUB (1827), 9 Grand Parade, West Hoe, Plymouth PL1 3DG.—*Sec.*, A. Miller.

ROYAL PLYMOUTH CORINTHIAN YACHT CLUB (1877), Madeira Road, Plymouth PL1 2NY.—*Hon. Sec.*, A. R. Trim.

Poole.—EAST DORSET SAILING CLUB (1875), 352 Sandbanks Road, Poole, Dorset BH14 8HY.—*Hon. Sec.*, R. W. Howard.

PARKSTONE YACHT CLUB (1895), Pearce Avenue, Parkstone, Poole, Dorset BH14 8EH.—*Sec.*, Brig. H. J. Goodson.

POOLE HARBOUR YACHT CLUB (1949), 38 Salterns Way, Lilliput, Poole, Dorset BH14 8JR.—*Club Manager*, R. Kelly-Wiseman.

POOLE YACHT CLUB (1865), Harbour Road West, Hamworthy, Poole, Dorset BH15 4AQ.—*Sec.*, Miss L. Clark.

Portsmouth.—ROYAL NAVAL CLUB AND ROYAL ALBERT YACHT CLUB (1867), 17 Pembroke Road, Portsmouth, Hants. PO1 2NT.—*Hon. Sec.*, Cdr. T. C. C. Greaves, O.B.E., RN.

Ramsgate.—ROYAL TEMPLE YACHT CLUB (1857), 6 Westcliff Mansions, Ramsgate, Kent CT11 9HY.—*Flag Officer*, O. Fisher.

Southampton.—ROYAL AIR FORCE YACHT CLUB (1932), Riverside House, Rope Walk, Hamble, Southampton SO3 5HD.—*Sec.*, Mrs. J. D. Hill.

ROYAL SOUTHAMPTON YACHT CLUB, Ocean Village, Southampton, SO1 1JS.—*Sec.*, Mrs. J. Cox.

ROYAL SOUTHERN YACHT CLUB (1837), Hamble, Hants. SO3 5HB.—*Sec.*, Mrs. W. J. F. Clampett.

Southend.—ALEXANDRA YACHT CLUB (1873), Clifton Terrace, Southend, Essex.—*Hon. Sec.*, Mrs. P. Spacey.

Swansea.—BRISTOL CHANNEL YACHT CLUB (1875), 744 Mumbles Road, Mumbles, Swansea SA3 4EL.—*Hon. Sec.*, R. L. Burrell.

Westcliff-on-Sea.—THAMES ESTUARY YACHT CLUB (1895), 3 The Leas, Westcliff-on-Sea, Essex SS0 7ST.—*Hon. Sec.*, J. G. Davison.

Weymouth.—ROYAL DORSET YACHT CLUB (1875), 11 Custom House Quay, Weymouth, Dorset DT4 8BG.—*Acting Sec.*, Mrs. J. B. Cannon.

Windermere.—ROYAL WINDERMERE YACHT CLUB (1860), Lowside, Bowness-on-Windermere, Cumbria LA23 3DH.—*Hon. Sec.*, C. H. Peters.

Yarmouth.—ROYAL SOLENT YACHT CLUB (1878), Yarmouth, I. o. W. PO41 0NS.—*Sec.*, Maj. F. R. Sillitoe, R.M.

Scotland

Dundee.—ROYAL TAY YACHT CLUB (1885), 34 Dundee Road, Broughty Ferry, Dundee DD5 1LX.—*Hon. Sec.*, T. Black.

Edinburgh.—ROYAL FORTH YACHT CLUB (1868), Middle Pier, Granton Harbour, Edinburgh, EH5 1HF.—*Hon. Sec.*, A. R. Woods.

Glasgow.—ROYAL WESTERN YACHT CLUB (1875), 42 Methil Street, Glasgow G14 0AN.—*Hon. Sec.*, Mrs. N. Simpson.

Oban.—ROYAL HIGHLAND YACHT CLUB (1881), 'Whins', 8 Grianach Gardens, Oban, Argyll PA34 4LZ.—*Sec.*, M. Bolton.

Rhu.—ROYAL NORTHERN AND CLYDE YACHT CLUB (1978), Rhu, By Helensburgh, Dunbartonshire G84 8NG.—*Hon. Sec.*, Dr. J. A. Ritchie.

Northern Ireland

Bangor.—ROYAL ULSTER YACHT CLUB (1866), 101 Clifton Road, Bangor, Co. Down BT20 5HY.—*Hon. Sec.*, T. O'Hara.

PRINCIPAL BRITISH AND IRISH SOCIETIES AND INSTITUTIONS

THE ROYAL ACADEMY OF ARTS (1768), Burlington House W1V 0DS—*President*, Roger de Grey, P.R.A., (1984); *Keeper*, Prof. N. Adams, R.A.; *Treas.*, Sir Philip Powell, C.H., O.B.E., R.A.; *Sec.* Piers Rodgers; *Comptroller*, K. J. Tanner, L.V.O.

Royal Academicians

1972 Adams, Norman
1986*Arup, Sir Ove, C.B.E.
1956*Bawden, Edward, C.B.E.
1976 Blackadder, Elizabeth, O.B.E.
1981 Blake, Peter, C.B.E.
1975 Blamey, Norman
1978 Blow, Sandra
1975 Bowey, Olwyn
1981 Bowyer, William
1971 Bratby, John R.
1972 Brown, Ralph
1956 Buhler, Robert
1972 Butler, James
1975 Cadbury-Brown, H. T., O.B.E.
1984 Camp, Jeffery
1970*Casson, Sir Hugh, C.H., K.C.V.O.
1976 Clarke, Geoffrey
1973 Clatworthy, Robert
1972 Coker, Peter
1972 Cooke, Jean E.
1974 Cuming, Frederick
1983 Dannatt, Trevor
1969 de Grey, Roger
1976 Dickson, Jennifer
1985 Dowson, Sir Philip, C.B.E.
1955*Dring, William
1968 Dunstan, Bernard
1953*Eurich, Richard, O.B.E.
1986 Eyton, Anthony
1985 Fraser, Donald Hamilton
1977 Frink, Dame Elisabeth, D.B.E.
1972*Fry, E. Maxwell, C.B.E.
1975*Goldfinger, Ernö
1972 Gore, Frederick, C.B.E.
1977 Green, Anthony
1960*Greenham, Peter, C.B.E.

1970 Hayes, Colin
1961*Hepple, Norman
1984 Hogarth, Paul
1986 Jones, Allen
1986 Kenny, Michael
1974 Kneale, Bryan
1986*Lessore, Helen
1986 Levene, Ben
1963 McFall, David
1956 Machin, Arnold, O.B.E.
1979 Manasseh, Leonard, O.B.E.
1985*Martin, Sir Leslie
1985*Medley, Robert
1979*Moynihan, Rodrigo, C.B.E.
1979 Paolozzi, Eduardo, C.B.E.
1983*Pasmore, Victor, C.H., C.B.E.
1981 Philipson, Sir Robin
1977 Powell, Sir Philip, C.H., O.B.E.
1973 Roberts-Jones, Ivor, C.B.E.
1984 Rogers, Richard
1969 Rosoman, Leonard, O.B.E.
1983*Rothenstein, Michael
1961*Sanders, Christopher C.
1984 Scott, William, C.B.E.
1969*Soukop, Willi
1954*Spear, Ruskin, C.B.E.
1986 Stephenson, Ian
1979 Swanwick, Betty
1979 Tindle, David
1986*Trevelyan, Julian
1965 Ward, John S., C.B.E.
1965*Weight, Carel, C.B.E.
1974 Williams, Kyffin, O.B.E.

1982 Sandle, Michael
1983 Stevens, Norman
1985 Stirling, James
1977 Sutton, Philip
1983 Symons, Patrick

1985 Tilson, Joe
1986 Titchell, John
1980 Whishaw, Anthony
1983 Wragg, John

Former Presidents of the Royal Academy

Sir J. Reynolds, 1768
Benjamin West, 1792
James Wyatt, 1805
Benjamin West, 1806
Sir T. Lawrence, 1820
Sir M. A. Shee, 1830
Sir C. Eastlake, 1850
Sir F. Grant, 1866
Lord Leighton, 1878
Sir J. Millais, 1896
Sir E. Poynter, 1896
Sir A. Webb, 1919

Sir F. Dicksee, 1924
Sir W. Llewellyn, 1928
Sir E. Lutyens, 1938
Sir A. J. Munnings, 1944
Sir G. F. Kelly, 1949
Sir A. E. Richardson, 1954
Sir C. Wheeler, 1956
Sir T. Monnington, 1966
Sir Hugh Casson, 1976

THE ROYAL CAMBRIAN ACADEMY OF ART (1882), Plas Mawr, High Street, Conwy, Gwynedd LL32 8DE—*Pres.*, R. Fields; *Hon. Sec.*, Ms. A. Hind; *Curator and Sec.*, L. H. S. Mercer.

THE ROYAL SCOTTISH ACADEMY (1826), Princes Street, Edinburgh EH2 2EL—*Pres.*, H. A. Wheeler, O.B.E., R.S.A.; *Sec.*, R. R. Steedman, R.S.A.; *Treas.*, W. J. L. Baillie, R.S.A.; *Librarian*, A. Campbell, R.S.A.; *Admin. Sec.*, W. T. Meikle.

Hon. Retired Academicians:

1958 Armour, Mrs. M.
1956 Kininmonth, Sir William
1966 Johnston, Ninian
1967 Lorimer, Hew

1977 Whiston, Peter
1981 Glover, J. Hardie, O.B.E.
1966 Peploe, Denis

Royal Scottish Academicians

1979 Baillie, W. J. L.
1972 Blackadder, Elizabeth
1986 Bushe, Fred
1977 Butler, Vincent
1971 Cameron, Gordon S.
1981 Campbell, Alex
1974 Collins, Peter
1974 Crosbie, William
1970 Cumming, James
1962 Donaldson, David A.
1956 Fleming, Ian
1967 Gordon, Esmé
1972 Houston, John
1979 Knox, John
1973 Littlejohn, W.
1971 McClure, David
1976 Malcolm, Ellen

1972 Michie, David
1963 Morocco, Alberto
1957 Patrick, J. McIntosh
1962 Philipson, Sir Robin
1976 Reeves, Philip
1986 Reiach, Alan
1977 Robertson, R. Ross
1984 Scott, Bill
1987 Smith, Ian McKenzie
1985 Snowden, Michael (*elect.*)
1979 Steedman, R. R.
1975 Wheeler, H. Anthony, O.B.E.
1982 Walker, Frances

Associates

1978 Aitchison, Craigie
1982 Ayres, Gillian, O.B.E.
1986 Bellany, John
1980 Christopher, Ann
1982 Crosby, Theo
1987 Flanagan, Barry
1983 Foster, Norman
1978 Gowing, Sir Lawrence, C.B.E.
1985 Hockney, David
1983 Howard, Ken

1983 Hoyland, John
1987 Huxley, Paul
1977 King, Phillip, C.B.E.
1984 Kitaj, R. B.
1986 Koralek, Paul
1982 Lawson, Sonia
1987 McComb, Leonard
1987 Nolan, Sir Sidney
1980 Partridge, John, C.B.E.
1984 Phillips, Tom

Associates

Arnott, Ian
Balmer, Barbara
Boys, John
Brotherston, William
Brown, Neil Dallas
Bryce, Gordon
Buchan, Dennis
Busby, John
Cairns, Joyce
Campbell, A. Buchanan
Clifford, J. G.
Cocker, Douglas
Crowe, Victoria

Docherty, Michael
Donald, George
Evans, David
Fairgrieve, James
Fraser, Alexander
Gasson, Barry
Harvey, Jake
Howard, Ian
Johnstone, John
Law, Graham C.
McIntosh, Iain R.
Maclean, William J.
MacMillan, Andrew

* Senior.

MacPherson, George
Main, Kirkland
Merrylees, Andrew
Metzstein, Isi
Mooney, John
Morris, James
Morrison, James
Onwin, Glen
Pelly, Frances
Pottinger, Frank
Rae, Barbara

Renton, James S., O.B.E.
Richards, John, C.B.E.
Robertson, James D.
Ross, Alastair
Shanks, Duncan F.
Smart, Alastair
Squire, Geoffrey
Stenhouse, Andrew
Stiven, Fred
Watson, Arthur
Wedgwood, Roland

Non-Resident Associates, Charles Pulsford; Peter Womersley, Leon Morrocco.

ROYAL IRISH ACADEMY (1786), 19 Dawson Street, Dublin 2.—*Pres.,* Prof. J. C. I. Dooge; *Treas.,* Prof. T. D. Spearman; *Sec.,* Prof. J. O. Scanlan.

ABBEYFIELD SOCIETY, 186–192 Darkes Lane, Potters Bar, Herts. EN6 1AB—'Supportive' housing for elderly people, including 'extra care' houses for the frail.—*Gen. Sec.,* D. A. L. Charles.

ACCOUNTANTS, INSTITUTE OF CHARTERED, in England and Wales (1880), P.O. Box 433, Chartered Accountants' Hall, Moorgate Place, EC2P 2BJ—*Sec.,* E. J. D. Warne, C.B.

ACCOUNTANTS, CHARTERED ASSOCIATION OF CERTIFIED (1904), 29 Lincoln's Inn Fields, WC2A 3EE—*Sec.,* Ms. S. J. Small.

ACCOUNTANTS OF SCOTLAND, THE INSTITUTE OF CHARTERED (1854), 27 Queen Street, Edinburgh EH2 1LA—*Sec.,* E. Tait, M.B.E.

ACCOUNTANTS IN IRELAND, INSTITUTE OF CHARTERED (1888), Chartered Accountants House, 87–89 Pembroke Road, Dublin 4.—*Dir.,* R. F. Hussey.

ACCOUNTANTS, SOCIETY OF COMPANY AND COMMERCIAL (1974), 40 Tyndalls Park Road, Bristol BS8 1PL—*Sec. Gen.,* B. T. Banks.

ACCOUNTING TECHNICIANS, ASSOCIATION OF (1980), 21 Jockey's Fields, WC1R 4BN—*Sec.,* J. Hanson.

ACTION RESEARCH FOR THE CRIPPLED CHILD (1952), Vincent House, North Parade, Horsham, West Sussex RH12 2DA—*Dir.,* Col. A. N. Brearley-Smith, O.B.E.

ACTORS' BENEVOLENT FUND (1882), 6 Adam Street, WC2N 6AA—*Gen. Sec.,* Mrs. R. Stevens.

ACTORS' CHARITABLE TRUST, 19–20 Euston Centre, NW1 3JH.—*Admin. Sec.,* Ms. A. Stewart.

ACTORS' CHURCH UNION (1899), St. Paul's Church, Bedford Street, WC2E 9ED—*Senior Chaplain,* Rev. M. Hurst-Bannister.

ACTUARIES IN SCOTLAND, THE FACULTY OF (1856), 23 St. Andrew Square, Edinburgh EH2 1AQ—*Sec.,* W. W. Mair.

ACTUARIES, INSTITUTE OF (1848), Staple Inn Hall, High Holborn, WC1V 7QJ—*Sec.-Gen.,* C. D. A. Mackie.

ADDICTION (TO ALCOHOL AND OTHER DRUGS), SOCIETY FOR THE STUDY OF (1884).—*Sec.,* Mrs. N. C. Blackburn, 3 Oakfield Gardens, Dulwich Wood Avenue, SE19 1HF.

ADMINISTRATIVE ACCOUNTANTS, INSTITUTE OF (1916), Burford House, 44 London Road, Sevenoaks, Kent TN13 1AS.—*Dir.-Gen.,* D. W. Bradley, F.C.I.S.

ADMINISTRATIVE MANAGEMENT, INSTITUTE OF (1915), 40 Chatsworth Parade, Petts Wood, Orpington, Kent BR5 1RW—*Sec.,* M. J. Ainsworth.

ADVERTISING BENEVOLENT SOCIETY, NATIONAL (1913), 3 Crawford Place, W1H 1JB—*Gen. Sec.,* Mrs. D. Larkin.

ADVERTISING, INSTITUTE OF PRACTITIONERS IN, 44 Belgrave Square, SW1X 8QS—*Dir. Gen.,* D. Wheeler.

ADVERTISING STANDARDS AUTHORITY (1962), Brook House, 2–16 Torrington Place, WC1E 7HN—*Director General,* P. Thomson.

AERONAUTICAL SOCIETY, ROYAL (1866) (incorporating the Institution of Aeronautical Engineers and the Helicopter Association of Great Britain), 4 Hamilton Place, W1V 0BQ—*Pres.* Prof. J. L. Stollery; *Sec.,* G. C. May.

AFRICAN INSTITUTE, INTERNATIONAL (1926), Lionel Robbins Building, 10 Portugal Street, WC2A 2HD—*Hon. Dir.,* Prof. I. M. Lewis.

AFRICAN MEDICAL AND RESEARCH FOUNDATION, London House, 68 Upper Richmond Road, SW15 2RP—*Exec. Dir.,* Mrs. E. Young.

AGE CONCERN ENGLAND, Bernard Sunley House, 60 Pitcairn Road, Mitcham, Surrey, CR4 3LL.—*Dir.,* Ms. S. Greengross.

AGE CONCERN NORTHERN IRELAND, 6 Lower Crescent, Belfast, BT2 7BG—*Dir.,* J. O'Neill.

AGE CONCERN SCOTLAND, 33 Castle Street, Edinburgh EH2 3DN—*Dir.,* Ms. M. Marshall.

AGE CONCERN WALES, 1 Cathedral Road, Cardiff, CF1 9SD—*Chief Officer,* D. Haydn-Thomas.

AGED POOR SOCIETY (1708) AND ST. JOSEPH'S HOUSE, 42 Brook Green, W6 7BW—*Sec.,* Flt. Lt. W. Watson (retd).

AGEING, CENTRE FOR POLICY ON, 25–31 Ironmonger Row, EC1V 3QP—*Dir.,* Dr. E. Midwinter.

AGE RESEARCH, FOUNDATION FOR (1978), 49 Queen Victoria Street, EC4N 4SA—*Dir.,* J. Allfrey.

AGRICULTURAL BENEVOLENT INSTITUTION, ROYAL, Shaw House, 27 West Way, Oxford OX2 0QH—*Chairman,* T. C. N. Ransom; *Chief Exec.,* Maj. Gen. P. L. Spurgeon, C.B.

AGRICULTURAL BENEVOLENT INSTITUTION, ROYAL SCOTTISH (1897), Ingliston, Edinburgh, EH28 8NB—*Org. Sec.,* I. G. Cumming, T.D.

AGRICULTURAL SOCIETY, EAST OF ENGLAND, East of England Showground, Peterborough PE2 0XE—*Sec. and Chief Exec.,* R. W. Bird, M.B.E..

AGRICULTURAL SOCIETY, ROYAL ULSTER (1826), The King's Hall, Balmoral, Belfast BT9 6GW—*Chief Exec.,* W. H. Yarr.

AGRICULTURE, ASSOCIATION OF (1947), Victoria Chambers, 16–20 Strutton Ground, SW1P 2HP—*Gen. Sec.,* Miss J. H. D. Bostock, M.B.E.

AIR LEAGUE, THE (1909), 4 Hamilton Place, W1V 0BQ—*Chairman,* Air Marshal Sir Charles Ness, K.C.B., C.B.E.; *Sec. Gen.,* Air Comm. C. A. Alldis, C.B.E., D.F.C., A.F.C.

ALEXANDRA ROSE DAY FUND, 1 Castelnau, Barnes, SW13 9RP—*Nat. Organiser and Administrator,* Mrs. L. Weston.

ALLOTMENT AND LEISURE GARDENERS LIMITED, NATIONAL SOCIETY OF, Hunters Road, Corby, Northants., NN17 1JE—*Sec.,* Ms. P. Grice.

ALMSHOUSES, NATIONAL ASSOCIATION OF, Billingbear Lodge, Wokingham, Berks RG11 5RU—*Dir.,* D. M. Scott.

ANAESTHETISTS OF GREAT BRITAIN AND IRELAND, ASSOCIATION OF (1932), 9 Bedford Square, WC1B 3RA—*Hon. Sec.,* Dr. P. Morris.

ANCIENT BUILDINGS, SOCIETY FOR THE PROTECTION OF (1877), 37 Spital Square, E1 6DY—*Sec.,* P. Venning.

ANCIENT MONUMENTS SOCIETY (1924).—*Sec.*, M. Saunders, St. Andrew-by-the-Wardrobe, Queen Victoria Street, EC4V 5DE.

ANGLO-ARAB ASSOCIATION (1961), The Arab British Centre, 21 Collingham Road, SW5 0NU.—*Exec. Dir.*, D. R. Collard, O.B.E.

ANGLO-BELGIAN SOCIETY (incorporating the Anglo-Belgian Union (1918) and the Cercle Royal Belge de Londres (1922)).—*Hon. Sec.*, Mrs. S. G. Ault, 46 Belgrave Manor, Brooklyn Road, Woking, Surrey GU22 7TW.

ANGLO-BRAZILIAN SOCIETY (1943), 35 Dover Street, W1X 3RA—*Sec.*, Mrs. M. J. Fyfe.

ANGLO-DANISH SOCIETY (1924), 25 New Street Square, EC4A 3LN—*Chairman*, Sir Andrew Stark, K.C.M.G., C.V.O.

ANGLO-NORSE SOCIETY, 25 Belgrave Square, SW1X 8QD—*Chairman*, Sir Peter Scott, K.B.E., C.M.G.

ANGLO-POLISH SOCIETY (1832), London H.Q., c/o S.P.K., 238–246 King Street, W6 0RF—*Hon. Sec.*, C. Roberts.

ANGLO-SWEDISH SOCIETY, 5 Mansfield Street, W1M 9FH—*Sec.*, Mrs. H. E. Wolff.

ANGLO-THAI SOCIETY (1962).—*Hon. Sec.*, Lt. Col. H. Docherty, O.B.E., 22 Ulster Court, Albany Park Road, Kingston, Surrey KT2 5SS.

ANIMAL HEALTH TRUST, Lanwades Hall, Kennett, Newmarket, Suffolk CB8 7PN—*Dir.*, A. J. Higgins, PH.D.

ANTHROPOLOGICAL INSTITUTE, ROYAL (1843), 56 Queen Anne Street, W1M 9LA—*Dir.*, J. Benthall.

ANTHROPOSOPHICAL SOCIETY IN GREAT BRITAIN, Rudolf Steiner House, 35 Park Road, NW1 6XT—*Gen. Sec.*, N. C. Thomas.

ANTIQUARIES, SOCIETY OF (1717), Burlington House, W1V 0HS—*Pres.*, R. M. Robbins, C.B.E.; *Treas.*, D. W. Phillipson, PH.D.; *Dir.*, G. J. Wainwright, PH.D.; *Sec.*, J. Cherry.

ANTIQUARIES OF SCOTLAND, SOCIETY OF (1780), Royal Museum of Scotland, Queen Street, Edinburgh EH2 1JD—*Sec.*, Dr. Anna Ritchie; *Treas.*, R. J. Mercer.

ANTI-SLAVERY SOCIETY FOR THE PROTECTION OF HUMAN RIGHTS (1839), 180 Brixton Road, SW9 6AT—*Dir.*, R. P. H. Davies, O.B.E.

ANTI-VIVISECTION: BRITISH UNION FOR THE ABOLITION OF VIVISECTION (INC.) (1898), 16A Crane Grove, N7 8LB—*Acting Gen.-Sec.*, K. Stallwood.

ANTI-VIVISECTION SOCIETY, THE NATIONAL (1875), 51 Harley Street, W1N 1DD—*Gen. Sec.*, Ms. J. Creamer.

ANTI-VIVISECTION SOCIETY, SCOTTISH, 121 West Regent Street, Glasgow G2 2SD—*Organising Sec.*, J. F. Robins.

APOSTLESHIP OF THE SEA (1920), Stella Maris, Atlantic House, New Strand, Bootle, Merseyside L20 4TQ—For active seafarers. *Nat. Dir.*, Very Rev. Mgr. A. Stringfellow.

APOTHECARIES, SOCIETY OF (1617), Black Friars Lane, EC4V 6EJ—*Clerk*, Maj. J. C. O'Leary; *Registrar*, D. H. C. Barrie.

APPLIED BIOLOGISTS, ASSOCIATION OF, Hill Farming Research Organisation, Bush Estate, Penicuik, Midlothian EH26 0PY—*Hon. Gen. Sec.*, Dr. P. Newbould.

ARBITRATORS, THE CHARTERED INSTITUTE OF, 75 Cannon Street, EC4N 5BH—*Sec.*, K. R. K. Harding.

ARCHÆOLOGICAL ASSOCIATION, BRITISH (1843), 61 Old Park Ridings, Winchmore Hill, N21 2ET—*Hon. Asst. Treas. and Sec.*, Miss I. B. McClure.

ARCHÆOLOGICAL ASSOCIATION, CAMBRIAN (1846).—*Pres.*, Prof. J. G. Williams; *Gen. Sec.*, G. L. Jones, Lleifior, 60 Dan-y-Coed, Aberystwyth, Dyfed SY23 2HD.

ARCHÆOLOGICAL INSTITUTE, ROYAL (1843), c/o Society of Antiquaries, Burlington House, Piccadilly, W1V 0HS.—*Hon. Sec.*, J. G. Coad, F.S.A.

ARCHÆOLOGY, COUNCIL FOR BRITISH (1944), 112 Kennington Road, SE11 6RE—*President*, Prof. P. A. Rahtz, F.S.A.; *Sec.*, Dr. P. W. Dixon, F.S.A.; *Dir.*, Dr. H. F. Cleere, F.S.A., F.B.I.M.

ARCHITECTS, THE ROYAL INSTITUTE OF BRITISH (1834), 66 Portland Place, W1N 4AD—*Pres.*, R. Hackney; *Sec.*, P. K. Harrison, C.B.E.

ARCHITECTS REGISTRATION COUNCIL OF THE UNITED KINGDOM, 73 Hallam Street, W1N 6EE—*Chairman*, Prof. J. Tarn; *Registrar*, K. J. Forder.

ARCHITECTS AND SURVEYORS, INCORPORATED ASSOCIATION OF (1925), Jubilee House, Billing Brook Road, Weston Favell, Northampton NN3 4NW—*Hon. Sec.*, W. A. Black.

ARCHITECTS AND SURVEYORS, THE FACULTY OF, LTD, 15 St. Mary Street, Chippenham SN15 3JN—*Sec.*, A. D. G. Webb.

ARCHITECTS BENEVOLENT SOCIETY (1850), 66 Portland Place, W1N 4AD—*Sec.*, R. J. Double.

ARCHITECTS IN SCOTLAND, ROYAL INCORPORATION OF (1922), 15 Rutland Square, Edinburgh EH1 2BE—*Sec. and Treasurer*, C. A. McKean, F.R.S.A., F.S.A.

ARCHITECTURAL ASSOCIATION (INC.) (1847), 34–36 Bedford Square, W.C.1.—*Sec.*, E. Le Maistre.

ARCHIVISTS, SOCIETY OF (1947), Suffolk Record Office, County Hall, Ipswich IP4 2JS—*Hon. Sec.*, Ms. A. J. E. Arrowsmith.

ARMY BENEVOLENT FUND (1944), 41 Queen's Gate, SW7 5HR—*Controller*, Maj. Gen. G. M. G. Swindells, C.B.

ARMY CADET FORCE ASSOCIATION (1930), Cheltenham Terrace, SW3 4RR—*Gen. Sec.*, Brigadier R. B. MacGregor-Oakford, O.B.E., M.C.

ART-COLLECTIONS FUND, NATIONAL (1903), 20 John Islip Street, SW1P 4LL—*Dir.*, Sir Peter Wakefield, K.B.E., C.M.G.

ART LIBRARIES SOCIETY (ARLIS) (1969).—Central School of Art and Design, Southampton Row WC1B 4AP—*Sec.*, S. M. Price.

ART WORKERS GUILD (1884), 6 Queen Square, Bloomsbury, WC1N 3AR—*Master*, C. Dolmetsche, C.B.E.; *Sec.*, D. G. Pullen.

ARTHRITIS AND RHEUMATISM COUNCIL FOR RESEARCH, 41 Eagle Street, WC1R 4AR—*Gen. Sec.*, J. Norton.

ARTHRITIS CARE, 6 Grosvenor Crescent, SW1X 7ER—*Sec.*, R. M. Sorsbie.

ARTISTS, FEDERATION OF BRITISH, 17 Carlton House Terrace, SW1Y 5BD—*Pres.*, P. J. Garrard; *Vice Pres.*, T. Coates.

ARTISTS' GENERAL BENEVOLENT INSTITUTION (1814) AND ARTISTS' ORPHAN FUND (1871), Burlington House, Piccadilly, W1V 0DJ—*Sec.*, T. Miles.

ASLIB (1924). (The Association for Information Management), Information House, 26–27 Boswell Street, WC1N 3JZ—*Dir.*, Dr. D. A. Lewis.

ASSISTANT MASTERS AND MISTRESSES ASSOCIATION, 7 Northumberland Street, WC2N 5DA—*Secs.*, E. G. Beynon, Miss J. E. L. Baird.

ASTHMA RESEARCH COUNCIL, 300 Upper Street, N1 2XX—*Chairman*, D. M. Walters, M.B.E., M.P.

ASTRONOMICAL ASSOCIATION, BRITISH.—*Office*, Burlington House, Piccadilly, W1V 0NL. Meetings at 23 Savile Row, W.1.—*President*, S. R. Dunlop; *Sec.*, M. de Faubert Maunder; *Asst. Sec.*, E. Watson Jones.

ASTRONOMICAL SOCIETY, ROYAL (Founded 1820), Burlington House, W1V 0NL—*Pres.*, Prof. R. D. Davies; *Sec.*, Dr. B. A. Hobbs.

A.T.S. and W.R.A.C. BENEVOLENT FUNDS (1964), Queen Elizabeth Park, Guildford, Surrey GU2 6QH—*Sec.*, Mrs. K. E. Laurence-Smith.

AUDIT BUREAU OF CIRCULATIONS LTD., 13 Wimpole Street, W1M 7AB—*Dir.*, J. G. Holmes.

AUTHORS, THE SOCIETY OF, 84 Drayton Gardens, SW10 9SB—*Gen. Sec.*, M. Le Fanu.

AUTOMOBILE ASSOCIATION (1905), Fanum House, Basingstoke, Hants.,—*Chairman*, Sir Ralph Carr-Ellison, T.D.; *Dir. Gen.*, S. Dyer.

AVICULTURAL SOCIETY (1894), Warren Hill, Hulford's Lane, Hartley Wintney, Hampshire RG27 8AG.—*Hon. Sec.*, H. J. Horswell.

AYRSHIRE CATTLE SOCIETY OF GREAT BRITAIN AND IRELAND (1877), P.O. Box 8, 1 Racecourse Road, Ayr.—*Gen. Sec.*, S. J. Thomson.

BALTIC AIR CHARTER ASSOCIATION, The Baltic Exchange, 24 St. Mary Axe, EC3A 8BU—*Hon. Exec.*, D. Shepherd.

BALTIC EXCHANGE LTD. (1903), 14–20 St. Mary Axe, EC3A 8BU—*Chairman*, W. Frame; *Sec.*, D. J. Walker.

BALTIC EXCHANGE CHARITABLE SOCIETY (1978), 14–20 St. Mary Axe, EC3A 8BU—*Sec.*, R. T. Wheelans.

BALZAN FOUNDATION 'PRIZE' (1956), Piazzetta U. Giordano 4, Milan, Italy. (Awards prizes for Literature; Moral Sciences and the Arts; Physical, Mathematical and Natural Sciences; Medicine, Humanity, Peace and Brotherhood).—*Sec. Gen.*, F. M. Tedeschi.

BANKERS, THE CHARTERED INSTITUTE OF (1879), 10 Lombard Street, EC3V 9AS—*Sec.-Gen.*, E. Glover.

BANKERS IN SCOTLAND, THE INSTITUTE OF (1875), 20 Rutland Square, Edinburgh EH1 2DE—*Sec.*, B. McKenna.

BAPTIST MISSIONARY SOCIETY (1792), 93–97 Gloucester Place, W1H 4AA—*Gen. Sec.*, Rev. R. G. S. Harvey.

BAR ASSOCIATION FOR LOCAL GOVERNMENT AND THE PUBLIC SERVICE.—23 Wentworth Way, Bletchley, Milton Keynes MK3 7RW. *Chairman*, P. G. Stivadoros.

(DR.) BARNARDO'S (1866), *Head Offices:* Tanners Lane, Barkingside, Essex IG6 1QG. Almost 17,000 handicapped or deprived children, young people and families are helped each year in more than 180 projects throughout the United Kingdom, Republic of Ireland, Australia and New Zealand.—*Senior Dir.*, R. Singleton.

BARONETAGE, STANDING COUNCIL OF THE (1898), *Sec.*, H. Bedingfeld, Rouge Croix Pursuivant, The College of Arms, Queen Victoria Street, EC4V 4BT.

BARRISTERS' BENEVOLENT ASSOCIATION, THE (1873), 14 Gray's Inn Square, WC1R 5JP—*Hon. Treasurers*, T. P. E. Curry, Q.C.; J. R. Reid, Q.C.; *Sec.*, Miss K. M. Hopper.

BIBLE CHURCHMEN'S MISSIONARY SOCIETY (1922), 251 Lewisham Way, SE4 1XF—*Gen. Sec.*, Rev. J. M. Ball.

BIBLE SOCIETY, BRITISH AND FOREIGN (1804), Stonehill Green, Westlea, Swindon SN5 7DG—*Exec. Dir.*, R. Worthing-Davies.

BIBLIOGRAPHICAL SOCIETY (1892), c/o British Library, Humanities and Social Sciences, Great Russell Street, WC1B 3DG—*Hon. Sec.*, Dr. M. M. Foot.

BIBLIOGRAPHICAL SOCIETY, EDINBURGH (1890), c/o National Library of Scotland, George IV Bridge, Edinburgh EH1 1EW—*Hon. Sec.*, I. C. Cunningham.

BIOCHEMICAL SOCIETY, THE (1911), 7 Warwick Court, WC1R 5DP—*Exec. Sec.*, G. D. Jones.

BIOLOGICAL COUNCIL, THE, c/o Institute of Biology, 20 Queensberry Place, SW7 2DZ—*Hon. Sec.*, Prof. M. Sandler.

BIOLOGICAL ENGINEERING SOCIETY.—c/o Royal College of Surgeons, Lincoln's Inn Fields, WC2A 3PN—*Hon. Sec.*, Dr. R. E. Trotman.

BIOLOGY, THE INSTITUTE OF, 20 Queensberry Place, SW7 2DZ—*Gen. Sec.*, P. N. O'Donoghue.

BIRD PRESERVATION, INTERNATIONAL COUNCIL FOR (BRITISH SECTION), Flora and Fauna Preservation Society, 8–12 Camden High Street, NW1 0JH—*Exec. Sec.* J. R. Wilson.

BIRMINGHAM AND MIDLAND INSTITUTE (1854) and PRIESTLEY LIBRARY (1779), Margaret Street, Birmingham B3 3BS—*Admin. and Lib.* J. Hunt.

BLIND, GREATER LONDON FUND FOR THE, (*Sightline*) 2 Wyndham Place, W1H 2AQ—*Pres.*, The Lord Mayor of London; *Gen. Sec.*, Group Capt. J. S. Goodwin, M.B.E.

BLIND, GUIDE DOGS FOR THE, ASSOCIATION, Alexandra House, 9 Park Street, Windsor, Berks., SL4 1JR—*Dir.-Gen.*, Maj. Gen. J. P. Groom, C.B., C.B.E.

BLIND, INCORPORATED ASSOCIATION FOR PROMOTING THE GENERAL WELFARE OF THE (1854), 37–55 Ashburton Grove, N7 7DW—*Chief Exec.*, G. P. Robinson; *Sec.*, A. W. Cairns.

BLIND, LONDON ASSOCIATION FOR THE (1857), 14–16 Verney Road, SE16 3DZ. A national charity helping blind and partially-sighted people throughout the country.—*Dir.*, P. Holland.

BLIND, ROYAL COMMONWEALTH SOCIETY FOR THE (1950), Commonwealth House, Heath Road, Haywards Heath, West Sussex RH16 3AZ—*Exec. Dir.*, A. W. Johns, O.B.E.

BLIND, ROYAL NATIONAL INSTITUTE FOR THE (1868), 224 Great Portland Street, W1N 6AA—Provides an education advisory service; schools; further education college for school leavers; Commercial College and a school of Physiotherapy; a rehabilitation centre; residential homes for the elderly; hotels and a hostel; a conference centre; shops selling equipment for the blind; careers advice and employment services; advice services on social security benefits and monitoring of legislation, etc. affecting the interests of visually handicapped people; braille and tape libraries and the Talking Book Library; information in print, braille, Moon and on tape; advice and practical help for blind people and their families, teachers, social workers, health care staff, etc.; funds research into the prevention of blindness, and the needs of visually handicapped people.—*Dir. Gen.*, I. Bruce.

BLIND, NATIONAL LIBRARY FOR THE (1882), Cromwell Road, Bredbury, Stockport, Cheshire SK6 2SG—Free library service in embossed types for the blind and partially-sighted, and large-print service. Over 400,000 volumes available.—*Dir. Gen.*, A. Leach, F.L.A.

BLIND, THE ROYAL LONDON SOCIETY FOR THE (1838), *Head Office and Workshops*, 105–9 Salusbury Road, Kilburn, NW6 6RH; *School*, Dorton House, Seal, nr. Sevenoaks, Kent TN15 0EB; *Home Workers' Scheme*.—*Sec.-Gen.*, R. J. Pocock.

BLIND, ROYAL NATIONAL COLLEGE (1872), College Road, Hereford HR1 1EB—Further education and training for open employment for visually-handicapped.—*Principal*, L. Marshall.

BLIND, ROYAL SCHOOL FOR THE (1799), Leatherhead, Surrey KT22 8NR—*Dir.*, Rev. B. A. E. Coote.

BLUE CROSS, THE (Incorporating Our Dumb Friends' League) (1897), Animals' Hospital, Hugh Street, Victoria, SW1V 1QQ—*Sec.*, P. Hannon.

BMMF INTERSERVE (formerly Bible and Medical Missionary Fellowship) (1852), 186 Kennington Park Road, SE11 4BT—*Gen. Sec.*, A. M. S. Pont.

BODLEIAN, FRIENDS OF THE, Bodleian Library, Oxford OX1 3BG—*Sec.*, G. Groom.

BOOK-KEEPERS, INSTITUTE OF (1916), (see under Administrative Accounting, Institute of).

BOOKSELLERS ASSOCIATION OF GREAT BRITAIN AND IRELAND (1895), 154 Buckingham Palace Road, SW1W 9TZ—*Dir.*, T. E. Godfray.

BOOK TRADE BENEVOLENT SOCIETY (1967), Dillon Lodge, The Booksellers Retreat, Kings Langley, Herts., WD4 8LT—*Pres.*, G. R. Davies, O.B.E.; *Exec. Sec.*, Mrs. A. R. Brown.

BOOK TRUST (formerly The National Book League), Book House, 45 East Hill, SW18 2QZ—*Chief Exec.*, M. Goff, O.B.E.

BOTANICAL SOCIETY OF THE BRITISH ISLES (1836), c/o British Museum (Natural History), Cromwell Road, SW7 5BD—*Hon. Gen. Sec.*, Mrs. M. Briggs, M.B.E.

BOTANICAL SOCIETY OF EDINBURGH, Royal Botanic Garden, Inverleith Row, Edinburgh EH3 5LR—*Hon. Gen. Sec.*, Dr. I. Edwards.

BOY SCOUTS ASSOCIATION, *see* SCOUT ASSOCIATION, THE.

BOYS' BRIGADE, THE (1883), Brigade House, Parsons Green, SW6 4TH. Membership worldwide: 400,000 in 60 countries—*Brigade Sec.*, G. H. Walker.

BOYS' CLUBS, NATIONAL ASSOCIATION OF (1925), 24 Highbury Grove, N5 2EA. Has affiliated to it 1,954 clubs—*Nat. Dir.*, D. P. Harris.

BOYS' CLUBS, NORTHERN IRELAND ASSOCIATION OF (1940), Bryson House, 28 Bedford Street, Belfast BT2 7FE—*Gen. Sec.*, C. E. Larmour, M.B.E.

BREWING, INSTITUTE OF (1886), 33 Clarges Street, W1Y 8EE—*Sec.*, Capt. K. A. Leppard, C.B.E., R.N.

BRIDEWELL ROYAL HOSPITAL (1553), Witley, Surrey GU8 5SG—*Treas.*, I. Allan; *Clerk to the Governors*, Mrs. A. C. R. Mitchell.

BRITISH ACADEMY, THE (1901), 20–21 Cornwall Terrace, NW1 4QP—*President*, Sir Randolph Quirk, C.B.E.; *Treas.*, Prof. P. Mathias, C.B.E.; *Sec.*, P. W. H. Brown; *Foreign Sec.*, Prof. E. W. Handley, C.B.E.

BRITISH AND FOREIGN SCHOOL SOCIETY (1808). Richard Mayo Hall, Eden Street, Kingston upon Thames, Surrey KT1 1HZ—*Sec.*, S. M. A. Banister.

BRITISH ANTI-COMMON MARKET CAMPAIGN (1976), 52 Fulham High Street, SW6 3LQ—*Hon. Sec.*, Sir Robin Williams, Bt.

BRITISH ARTISTS, FEDERATION OF (1959), 17 Carlton House Terrace, SW1Y 5BD—*Sec. Gen.*, O. B. Warman.

BRITISH ASSOCIATION FOR THE ADVANCEMENT OF SCIENCE (1831), Fortress House, 23 Savile Row, W1X 1AB—*Pres.*, Sir Walter Bodmer, F.R.S.; *Exec. Sec.*, Dr. D. Morley.

BRITISH ASSOCIATION FOR COMMERCIAL AND INDUSTRIAL EDUCATION (BACIE), 16 Park Crescent, W1N 4AP—*Dir.*, B. V. Murphy.

BRITISH ASSOCIATION FOR EARLY CHILDHOOD EDUCATION, Studio 3:2, 140 Tabernacle Street, EC2A 4SD—*Sec.*, Mrs. B. Boon.

BRITISH ASSOCIATION OF THE HARD OF HEARING, 7–11 Armstrong Road W3 7JL—*Chairman*, E. Trinder.

BRITISH ATLANTIC COMMITTEE, 30A St. James's Square, Whitehall, SW1Y 4JH—*Dir.*, Maj. Gen. C. J. Popham, C.B.

BRITISH BEE-KEEPERS' ASSOCIATION (1874). National Agricultural Centre, Stoneleigh, Kenilworth, Warwicks. CV8 2LZ—*Gen. Sec.*, M. H. Solley.

BRITISH BOARD OF FILM CLASSIFICATION, 3 Soho Square, W1V 5DE—*Dir.*, J. Ferman.

BRITISH BUTTERFLY CONSERVATION SOCIETY (1968), Tudor House, Quorn, Nr. Loughborough, Leics. LE12 8AD—*Chairman*, C. J. Tatham, M.B.E.

BRITISH COLLEGE OF OPTOMETRISTS, 10 Knaresborough Place, SW5 0TG—*Gen. Sec.*, T. H. Collingridge.

BRITISH COMMONWEALTH EX-SERVICES LEAGUE, 48 Pall Mall, SW1Y 5JG—*Sec. Gen.*, Col. G. Stocker, C.B.E.

BRITISH COMPUTER SOCIETY (1957), 13 Mansfield Street, W1M 0BP—*Chief Exec.*, J. R. Brookes.

BRITISH COTTON GROWING ASSOCIATION LTD. (1904), 3 Shortlands, Hammersmith, W6 8RT—*Man. Dir.*, M. T. G. Davies.

BRITISH CYCLING FEDERATION (1878), 16 Upper Woburn Place, WC1H 0QE—*Sec.*, L. Unwin.

BRITISH DENTAL ASSOCIATION (1880), 64 Wimpole Street, W1M 8AL—*Sec.*, N. H. Whitehouse.

BRITISH DIABETIC ASSOCIATION (1934), 10 Queen Anne Street, W1M 0BD—*Sec.-Gen.*, D. G. Armytage, C.B.E.

BRITISH DRIVING SOCIETY, 27 Dugard Place, Barford, Nr. Warwick CV35 8DX—*Sec.*, Mrs. J. M. Dillon.

BRITISH EDUCATIONAL MANAGEMENT AND ADMINISTRATION SOCIETY (1971).—*Sec.*, Miss M. E. Hewitt, Buxton Girls' School, Derbys. SK17 6RB.

BRITISH EQUESTRIAN FEDERATION, British Equestrian Centre, Kenilworth, Warwicks. CV8 2LR—*Dir. Gen.*, Maj. M. C. R. Wallace.

BRITISH EXPORT-FINANCE ADVISORY COUNCIL (1981), 1 Grosvenor Place, SW1X 7JB—*Chairman*, C. D. Hankes-Drielsma.

BRITISH FIELD SPORTS SOCIETY (1930), 59 Kennington Road, SE1 7PZ—*Dir.*, Maj. Gen. J. Hopkinson, C.B.

BRITISH FILM INSTITUTE (1933), 127 Charing Cross Road, WC2H 0EA—*Dir.*, A. Smith; *Controller, National Film Theatre*, L. Hardcastle, O.B.E.

BRITISH FOUNDRYMEN, THE INSTITUTE OF (1904), Bridge House, 121 Smallbrook Queensway, Birmingham B5 4JP—*Sec.*, G. A. Schofield.

BRITISH GLIDING ASSOCIATION (1930), affiliated to Royal Aero Club. Kimberley House, Vaughan Way, Leicester LE1 4SE—*Gen. Sec.*, B. Rolfe.

BRITISH GOAT SOCIETY (1879), Moreton House, Moretonhampstead, Devon TQ13 8NF.

BRITISH HEART FOUNDATION (1963), 102 Gloucester Place, W1H 4DH—*Dir. Gen.*, Brig. P. G. S. Tower, C.B.E.

BRITISH HEDGEHOG PRESERVATION SOCIETY, THE (1982), Knowbury House, Knowbury, Ludlow, Shropshire SY8 3LQ—*Sec.* Mrs. A. Jenkins.

BRITISH HOMŒOPATHIC ASSOCIATION, THE (1902), 27A Devonshire Street, W1N 1RJ—*Gen. Sec.*, (vacant).

BRITISH HORSE SOCIETY (incorporating THE PONY CLUB), British Equestrian Centre, Kenilworth, Warwicks. CV8 2LR—*Dir.*, Col. N. Grove-White.

BRITISH INSTITUTE IN EASTERN AFRICA, 1 Kensington Gore, SW7 2AR—*London Sec.*, Mrs. J. Moyo.

BRITISH INSTITUTE OF ARCHÆOLOGY AT ANKARA, THE, c/o British Academy, 20–21 Cornwall Terrace, NW1 4QP—*London Sec.*, Ms. F. Chapman-Purchas.

BRITISH INSTITUTE OF INTERIOR DESIGN (1899), 1C Devonshire Avenue, Beeston, Nottingham NG9 1BS—*Sec.*, N. Parker.

BRITISH INSTITUTE OF PERSIAN STUDIES (1961), *Sec.*, Mrs. M. E. Gueritz, M.B.E., 13 Cambrian Road, Richmond, Surrey TW10 6JQ.

BRITISH INSTITUTE OF RADIOLOGY, 36 Portland Place, W1N 3DG—*Gen. Sec.*, Miss. S. M. Johnstone.

BRITISH INSURANCE BROKERS ASSOCIATION, BIBA House, 14 Bevis Marks, EC3A 7NT—*Dir. Gen.*, J. C. T. Hackett.

BRITISH INTERPLANETARY SOCIETY (1933), 27–29 South Lambeth Road, SW8 1SZ—*Exec. Sec.*, L. J. Carter.

BRITISH INVISIBLE EXPORTS COUNCIL (1983), Dunster House, 37 Mincing Lane, EC3R 7BQ—*Dir. Gen.*, D. P. Thomson.

BRITISH ISRAEL WORLD FEDERATION (1919), 6 Buckingham Gate, SW1E 6JP—*Sec.*, R. B. H. Hall.

BRITISH LEGION, ROYAL, 48 Pall Mall, SW1Y 5JY—*Gen. Sec.*, Maj. R. Tomlins, O.B.E.

BRITISH LEGION SCOTLAND, ROYAL, New Haig House, Logie Green Road, Edinburgh EH7 4HR.

BRITISH MEDICAL ASSOCIATION (1832), B.M.A. House, Tavistock Square, WC1H 9JP—*President*, D. Bolt, C.B.E., F.R.C.S.; *Sec.*, J. D. J. Havard, M.D.

BRITISH MIGRAINE ASSOCIATION, 178A, High Road, Byfleet, Weybridge, Surrey KT14 7ED—*Hon. Sec.*, Mrs. J. Liddell.

BRITISH MUSIC HALL SOCIETY (1963), 68 Drury Lane, WC2B 5SP—*Hon. Sec.*, Mrs. D. Masterton.

BRITISH MUSIC INFORMATION CENTRE, 10 Stratford Place, W1N 9AE—*Centre Man.s*, T. Morgan, M. Greenall.

BRITISH NATURALISTS' ASSOCIATION (1905).—*Hon. Mem. Sec.*, Mrs. Y. H. Griffiths, 23 Oak Hill Close, Woodford Green, Essex IG8 9PH

BRITAIN–NEPAL SOCIETY (1960)—*Hon. Sec.*, Mrs. C. Brown, 1 Allen Mansions, Allen Street, W8 6UY.

BRITISH NUTRITION FOUNDATION (1967), 15 Belgrave Square, SW1X 8PS—*Dir. Gen.*, Prof. D. M. Conning.

BRITISH POLIO FELLOWSHIP (1939), Bell Close, West End Road, Ruislip, Middx. HA4 6LP—*Gen. Sec.*, L. P. Jackson.

BRITISH RECORDS ASSOCIATION (1932), The Charterhouse, Charterhouse Square, EC1M 6AU—*Pres.*, Rt. Hon. Sir John Donaldson, Master of the Rolls; *Hon. Sec.*, T. R. Padfield.

BRITISH RED CROSS SOCIETY (1870).—9 Grosvenor Crescent, SW1X 7EJ—*Dir. Gen.*, J. C. Burke-Gaffney.

BRITISH SAILORS' SOCIETY (1818), 406/410 Eastern Avenue, Ilford, Essex IG2 6NG—*Gen. Sec.*, G. Chambers.

BRITISH SCHOOL AT ATHENS.—*Chairman of the Managing Committee*, Prof. J. N. Coldstream, F.B.A., F.S.A.; *Dir.*, H. W. Catling, O.B.E., D.Phil, F.S.A.; *Sec.*, Mrs. S. E. Waywell, PH.D., 31–34 Gordon Square, WC1H 0PY.

BRITISH SCHOOL AT ROME (1901).—Tuke Building, Regent's College, Inner Circle, Regent's Park, NW1 4NS. *Chairman of Executive Committee*, Sir Alan Campbell; *Director*, Dr. G. Barker, F.S.A.; *Sec.*, Miss A. M. Tighe.

BRITISH SCHOOL OF ARCHÆOLOGY IN JERUSALEM (1919), The British Academy, 20 Cornwall Terrace, N.W.1.—*Pres.*, The Rev. Prof. H. Chadwick, D.D., F.B.A.; *Dir.*, Dr. R. Harper, F.S.A.

BRITISH SEAMEN'S BOYS HOME, Grenville House, Brixham, Devon TQ5 9AF—*Supt.*, Capt. E. M. Marks, R.D., R.N.R.

BRITISH THEATRE ASSOCIATION (1919), Darwin Infill Building, Regent's College, Inner Circle, Regent's Park, NW1 4NS—*Dir.*, Ms. J. Hackworth-Young.

BRITISH TRAVEL AGENTS, THE ASSOCIATION OF (1950), 55–57 Newman Street, W1P 4AH—*Dir. Gen.*, C. McLelland.

BRITISH VETERINARY ASSOCIATION (1881), 7 Mansfield Street, W1M 0AT—*Chief Exec.*, (vacant).

BRUSH MANUFACTURERS' ASSOCIATION, BRITISH, 6A East Street, Epsom, Surrey KT17 1HH—*Sec.*, J. A. Snellgrove.

BUDDHIST SOCIETY, THE (1924), 58 Eccleston Square, SW1V 1PH—*Gen. Sec.*, R. C. Maddox.

BUDGERIGAR SOCIETY, THE (1925), 49–53 Hazelwood Road, Northampton NN1 1LG—*Gen. Sec.*, A. C. Crook.

BUILDING, CHARTERED INSTITUTE OF (1834), Englemere, Kings Ride, Ascot, Berks. SL5 8BJ—*Chief Exec.*, Dr. J. D. Hooper.

BUILDING SERVICES ENGINEERS, CHARTERED INSTITUTION OF (1897), Delta House, 222 Balham High Road, SW12 9BS—*Sec.*, A. V. Ramsay.

BUILDING SOCIETIES ASSOCIATION, 3 Savile Row, W1X 1AF—*Dir.-Gen.*, M. J. Boleat.

BUILDING SOCIETIES INSTITUTE, THE CHARTERED, 19 Baldock Street, Ware, Herts., SG12 9DH—*Sec.*, R. D. Crerar.

BULWER LYTTON CIRCLE, 125 Markyate Road, Dagenham, Essex.—*Sec.*, E. Ford.

BUSINESS AND PROFESSIONAL WOMEN, UNITED KINGDOM FEDERATION OF (1938), 23 Ansdell Street, W8 5BN—*Sec.*, Mrs. R. Bangle.

BUSINESS ARCHIVES COUNCIL, 185 Tower Bridge Road, SE1 2UF—*Chairman*, S. H. G. Twining, O.B.E.; *Sec. Gen.*, Ms. S. Kelly.

BUTCHERS' AND DROVERS' CHARITABLE INSTITUTION (1828).—*Sec.*, J. A. Fordyce, 61 West Smithfield, EC1A 9EA.

CALOUSTE GULBENKIAN FOUNDATION, (1956), 98 Portland Place, W1N 4ET—*Dir.*, L. C. Taylor.

CAMBRIDGE PRESERVATION SOCIETY (1929).—*Chairman*, Mrs. R. G. Johnson; *Sec.*, M. R. Francis, Wandlebury Ring, Gog Magog Hills, Brabraham, Cambridge CB2 4AE.

CAMERA CLUB, THE (1885), 8 Great Newport Street, WC2H 7JA—*Sec.*, D. Pincham.

CAMERON FUND, THE, (1971), Tavistock House North, Tavistock Square, WC1H 9JP—*Sec.*, Miss H. C. Pullen.

CAMPAIGN FOR NUCLEAR DISARMAMENT (CND) (1958), 22–24 Underwood Street, N1 7JG—*Gen. Sec.*, Meg Beresford.

CANADA UNITED KINGDOM CHAMBER OF COMMERCE, 3 Regent Street, SW1Y 4NZ—*Exec. Dir.*, G. F. Bacon.

CANCER RESEARCH CAMPAIGN, 2 Carlton House Terrace, SW1Y 5AR—*Dir. Gen.*, D. de Peyer.

CANCER RELIEF, NATIONAL SOCIETY FOR (MACMILLAN FUND) (1911), Anchor House, 15–19 Britten Street, SW3 3TZ—*Dir. and Gen. Sec.*, D. Scott.

CANCER RESEARCH FUND, IMPERIAL (1902), P.O. Box 123, Lincoln's Inn Fields, WC2A 3PX—*Sec.*, Maj. Gen. A. W. Dennis, C.B., O.B.E.

CANCER RESEARCH, THE INSTITUTE OF: Royal Cancer Hospital, 17A Onslow Gardens, SW7 3AL—*Sec.*, J. Defries.

CAREER TEACHERS, ASSOCIATION OF, Hillsboro., Castledine Street, Loughborough, Leics. LE11 2DX—*Gen. Sec.*, Miss R. Yaffé.

CARNEGIE DUNFERMLINE TRUST (1903). (Social and cultural purposes in Dunfermline). *Sec.*, F. Mann, Abbey Park House, Dunfermline KY12 7PB.

CARNEGIE HERO FUND TRUST (1908). Income £90,000. Makes grants and allowances to people injured or the dependants of people killed in saving human life within the British Isles and territorial waters.—*Sec.*, F. Mann, Abbey Park House, Dunfermline KY12 7PB.

CARNEGIE UNITED KINGDOM TRUST (1913). Comely Park House, Dunfermline, KY12 7EJ—*Sec.*, G. Lord.

CATHEDRALS ADVISORY COMMISSION FOR ENGLAND, 83 London Wall, EC2M 5NA—*Sec.*, P. A. T. Burman.

CATHOLIC MARRIAGE ADVISORY COUNCIL, 15 Lansdowne Road, W11 3AJ; *Chief Exec.*, Mrs. J. Judge.

CATHOLIC RECORD SOCIETY (1904). c/o 114 Mount Street, W1Y 6AH—*Hon. Sec.*, Miss R. Rendel.

CATHOLIC TRUTH SOCIETY (1868), P.O. Box 422, 38–40 Eccleston Square, SW1V 1PD—*Gen. Sec.*, D. Murphy.

CATHOLIC UNION OF GREAT BRITAIN, St. Maximilian Kolbe House, 63 Jeddo Road, W12 9EE—*Pres.*, The Duke of Norfolk, K.G., G.C.V.O., C.B., C.B.E., M.C.; *Hon. Sec.*, Mrs. J. Stuyt, M.B.E.

CATTLE BREEDER'S CLUB, LTD., BRITISH, Lavenders, Isfield, Uckfield, Sussex TN22 5TX—*Sec.*, C. R. Stains.

CECIL HOUSES (Inc.) (Housing Association, Charity), 2 Priory Road, Kew, Richmond, Surrey TW9 3DG—*Sec.*, A. G. Wilmot.

CENTRAL BUREAU (for educational visits and exchanges), Seymour Mews House, Seymour Mews, W1H 9PE—*Dir.* A. H. Male.

CERAMIC SOCIETY, BRITISH (1900), Shelton House, Stoke Road, Shelton, Stoke-on-Trent, Staffs. ST4 2DR—*Pres.*, E. M. Briscoe, O.B.E..

CERAMICS, INSTITUTE OF (1955), Shelton House, Stoke Road, Stoke-on-Trent, Staffs., ST4 2DR—*Pres.*, Dr. G. J. Gittens.

CHADWICK TRUST (1895) (for the promotion of health and prevention of disease).—Chadwick Professor of Civil Engineering, University College London, Gower Street, WC1E 6BT—*Sec.*, D. Kasher.

CHAMBERS OF COMMERCE.—*See* COMMERCE.

CHANTREY BEQUEST (1875).—*Sec.*, P. Rodgers, Royal Academy of Arts, Burlington House, Piccadilly, W1V 0DS.

CHARTERED SECRETARIES AND ADMINISTRATORS, INSTITUTE OF (1891), 16 Park Crescent, W1N 4AH—*Sec.*, B. Barker, M.B.E.

CHEMICAL ENGINEERS, INSTITUTION OF (1922), George E. Davis Building, 165–171 Railway Terrace, Rugby, Warks. CV21 3HQ—*Gen. Sec.*, T. J. Evans.

CHEMICAL INDUSTRY, SOCIETY OF, 14–15 Belgrave Square, SW1X 8PS—*Pres.*, Dr. L. Fernandez; *Gen. Sec.*, Dr. P. P. King, F.R.S.C.

CHEMISTRY, THE ROYAL SOCIETY OF, Burlington House, Piccadilly, W1V 0BN—*Pres.*, Prof. Sir Jack Lewis, F.R.S.; *Sec.-Gen.*, Dr. J. S. Gow.

(LEONARD) CHESHIRE FOUNDATION (1955), 26–29 Maunsel Street, SW1P 2QN. Over 76 homes and 21 family support services in U.K. and affiliated to a further 150 world-wide.—*Dir.*, A. L. Bennett.

CHESS FEDERATION, BRITISH, 9A Grand Parade, St. Leonards-on-Sea, East Sussex TN38 0DD—*Gen. Sec.*, G. Lee.

CHEST, HEART AND STROKE ASSOCIATION (1899), Tavistock House North, Tavistock Square, WC1H 9JE—*Dir. Gen.*, Sir David Atkinson, K.B.E.

CHILDREN'S AID & ADOPTION, MISSION OF HOPE FOR, 14 South Park Hill Road, Croydon, Surrey CR2 7YB—*Gen. Sec.*, R. F. Smith.

CHINA ASSOCIATION (1889), Regis House, 43–46 King William Street, EC4R 9BE—*Exec. Dir.*, Brig. B. G. Hickey, O.B.E., M.C.

CHIROPODISTS, THE SOCIETY OF, 53 Welbeck Street, W1M 7HE—*Sec.*, G. C. Jenkins.

CHOIRS SCHOOLS ASSOCIATION (1921).—*Hon. Sec.*, P. Hannigan, Westminster Cathedral Choir School, Ambrosden Avenue, SW1P 1QH.

CHRISTIAN ACTION—, St. Peter's House, 308, Kennington Lane, SE11 5HY—*Dir.*, Canon E. James.

CHRISTIAN AID (1945), P.O. Box 100, SE1 7RT—*Dir.*, Rev. M. H. Taylor.

CHRISTIAN EDUCATION MOVEMENT (1965), Lancaster House, Borough Road, Isleworth, Middx. TW7 5DU. *Acting Gen. Sec.*, Rev. Dr. S. Orchard.

CHRISTIAN EVIDENCE SOCIETY (1870), St. Stephen's House, St. Stephen's Crescent, Brentwood, Essex CM13 2AT—*Hon. Sec.*, Mrs. G. M. Ryeland.

CHRISTIAN KNOWLEDGE, SOCIETY FOR PROMOTING (S.P.C.K.) (1698), Holy Trinity Church, Marylebone Road, NW1 4DU—*Gen. Sec.*, P. N. G. Gilbert.

CHRISTIANS AND JEWS, COUNCIL OF (1942), 1 Denningston Park Road, West End Lane, NW6 1AX—*Exec. Dir.*, Rev. M. Braybrooke.

CHURCH ARMY, Independents Road, Blackheath, SE3 9LG. *Chief Sec.*, Rev. M. Rees.

CHURCH BUILDING SOCIETY, INCORPORATED (1818), Fulham Palace, SW6 6EA—*Sec.*, Maj. R. I. Radford, M.B.E.

CHURCH EDUCATION CORPORATION, Bedgebury School, Goudhurst, Kent TN17 2SH—*Sec.*, R. P. Gilbert.

CHURCH HOUSE, THE CORPORATION OF (1888), Dean's Yard, SW1P 3NZ—*Sec.*, Capt. P. W. E. Parry, M.B.E.

CHURCH LADS' AND CHURCH GIRLS' BRIGADE, Claude Hardy House, 15 Etchingham Park Road, N3 2DU—*Gen. Sec.*, Rev. C. Grice, M.B.E.

CHURCH MISSIONARY SOCIETY (1799), 157 Waterloo Road, SE1 8UU. Income, 1986, £3,755,000.—*Secs.*, Rt. Rev. H. W. Moore (*General*); Miss E. A. E. Pointon (*Britain*); P. A. Dowsett (*Financial*).

CHURCH OF ENGLAND CHILDREN'S SOCIETY (1881) (The Children's Society), Edward Rudolf House, Margery Street, WC1X 0JL—*Dir.*, I. Sparks.

CHURCH OF ENGLAND PENSIONS BOARD (1926), 53 Tufton Street, SW1P 3QP—*Sec.*, R. G. Radford.

CHURCH OF ENGLAND SOLDIERS', SAILORS' AND AIRMEN'S CLUBS (1891), and CHURCH OF ENGLAND SOLDIERS', SAILORS' AND AIRMEN'S HOUSING ASSOCIATION LTD. (1974), 126 High Street, Portsmouth PO1 2RH. *Chairman*, Rear-Adm. A. G. Watson, C.B.

CHURCH UNION (1859), Faith House, 7 Tufton Street, SW1P 3QN—*Gen. Sec.*, Rev. R. E. Thompson.

CHURCHES, BRITISH COUNCIL OF (1942), Inter-Church House, 35–41 Lower Marsh, SE1 7RL—*Gen. Sec.*, Rev. Dr. P. Morgan.

CHURCHES, COUNCIL FOR CARE OF, 83 London Wall, EC2M 5NA.—*Sec.*, P. A. T. Burman.

CHURCHES, FRIENDLESS, FRIENDS OF (1957), 12 Edwardes Square, W8 6HG—*Hon. Dir.*, I. Bulmer-Thomas; *Hon. Sec.*, L. E. Jones.

CHURCHES MAIN COMMITTEE (1941), Fielden House, Little College Street, SW1P 3JZ—*Sec.*, B. M. Thimont, C.B.

CITIZENS' ADVICE BUREAUX, NATIONAL ASSOCIATION OF (1931), Myddelton House, 115–123 Pentonville Road, N1 9LZ—*Chief Exec. Officer*, Ms. E. Filkin.

CITY PAROCHIAL FOUNDATION, 10 Fleet Street, EC4Y 1AU—*Clerk*, T. Cook.

CIVIL DEFENCE, INSTITUTE OF (1938), Bell Court House, 11 Bloomfield Street, EC2M 7AY—*Hon. Gen. Sec.*, P. B. Bodycombe, M.B.E.

CIVIL ENGINEERS, INSTITUTION OF (1818) (*Amalgamated with* Municipal Engineers, Institution of), 1–7 Great George Street, SW1P 3AA—*Sec.*, J. M. Sutherland.

CIVIL LIBERTIES, NATIONAL COUNCIL FOR (1934), 21 Tabard Street, SE1 4LA—*Gen. Sec.*, Ms. S. Spencer.

CLASSICAL ASSOCIATION (1903).—*Hon. Treas.*, R. Wallace, Dept. of Classics, University of Keele, Keele, Staffs. ST5 5BG.

CLASSICAL TEACHERS, JOINT ASSOCIATION OF (1962), 31–34 Gordon Square, WC1H 0PY—*Exec. Sec.*, J. Murrell.

CLERGY ORPHAN CORPORATION (1749), 57B Tufton Street, Westminster, SW1P 3QL—*Sec.*, Miss J. Buncher.

CLERKS OF WORKS OF GREAT BRITAIN, INSTITUTE OF (1882), 41 The Mall, Ealing, W5 3TJ—*Sec.*, A. P. Macnamara.

COACHING CLUB (1871), 8 Parthenia Road, SW6 4BD.—*Sec.*, D. H. Clarke.

COMBINED CADET FORCE ASSOCIATION (1952), Cheltenham Terrace, SW3 4RR—*Sec.*, Brig. R. B. MacGregor-Oakford, O.B.E., M.C.

COMMERCE, ASSOCIATION OF BRITISH CHAMBERS OF (1860).—*Dir. Gen.*, R. G. Taylor, Sovereign House, 212A Shaftesbury Avenue, WC2H 8EW.

COMMERCE, ASSOCIATION OF SCOTTISH CHAMBERS OF, 30 George Square, Glasgow G2 1EQ—*Sec.*, E. Marwick.

COMMERCE AND INDUSTRY, LONDON CHAMBER OF (1881), 69 Cannon Street, EC4N 5AB—*Pres.*, Sir Andrew Jolliffe, G.B.E.; *Dir.*, A. M. W. Platt.

COMMERCE AND MANUFACTURES, EDINBURGH CHAMBER OF (1786), 3 Randolph Crescent, Edinburgh EH3 7UD—*Chief Exec.*, D. M. Mowat, J.P.

COMMERCE AND MANUFACTURES, GLASGOW CHAMBER OF (1783), 30 George Square, Glasgow G2 1EQ—*Sec.*, E. Marwick.

COMMERCIAL TRAVELLERS' BENEVOLENT INSTITUTION (1849),*Chief Exec.,* E. B. Auger, 49 Lawrie Park Avenue, SE26 6HA.

COMMISSIONAIRES, THE CORPS OF (1859), provides employment for ex-Soldiers, Sailors and Airmen and ex-police, fire service and merchant navy servicemen, *Headquarters,* 3 Crane Court, Fleet Street, EC4A 2EJ. *Outquarters*in Belfast, Birmingham, Bristol, Edinburgh, Glasgow, Leeds, Liverpool, Manchester, Newcastle upon Tyne. Total strength, 2,800—*Commandant,* Col. R. B. Robertson; *Deputy Commandant,* Brig. The Hon. H. E. C. Willoughby.

COMMONWEALTH ASSOCIATION OF PLANNERS (1971), *Hon. Sec.,* G. Franklin, 24 Oakleigh Park North, N20 9AR.

COMMONWEALTH PRESS UNION (1909), Studio House, 184 Fleet Street, EC4A 2DU—*Dir.,* J. C. Rajepakse.

COMMONWEALTH SOCIETY FOR THE DEAF (1959), 105 Gower Street, WC1E 6AH—*Chairman,* C. Holborow, T.D., M.D., F.R.C.S.

COMPLEMENTARY MEDICINE, INSTITUTE FOR (1856), 21 Portland Place, W1N 4AF—*Dir.,* A. Baird.

COMPOSERS' GUILD OF GREAT BRITAIN, THE (1945), 10 Stratford Place, W1N 9AE—*Gen. Sec.,* Miss E. Yeoman.

CONSERVATION OF HISTORIC AND ARTISTIC WORKS, INTERNATIONAL INSTITUTE FOR, 6 Buckingham Street, WC2N 6BA—*Pres.,* Ms. S. P. Sack; *Sec. Gen.,* N. S. Brommelle.

CONSERVATION VOLUNTEERS, BRITISH TRUST FOR (1970), 36 St. Mary's Street, Wallingford, Oxon OX10 0EU—*Dir.,* I. Branton, O.B.E.

CONSERVATIVE AND UNIONIST ASSOCIATIONS, NATIONAL UNION OF (1867), 32 Smith Square, SW1P 3HH—*Sec.,* R. Nelder.

CONSERVATIVE CLUBS, LTD., THE ASSOCIATION OF (1894), 32 Smith Square, SW1P 3HH—*Sec.,* P. Perry.

CONSTRUCTION SURVEYORS' INSTITUTE (1952), Wellington House, 203 Lordship Lane, SE22 8HA—*Exec. Officer,* B. A. Hunt.

CONSULTING ENGINEERS, ASSOCIATION OF (1913), Alliance House, 12 Caxton Street, SW1H 0QL—*Sec.,* Brig. H. Woodrow.

CONSULTING SCIENTISTS, ASSOCIATION OF, 11 Rosemont Road, NW3 6NG—*Pres. and Chairman,* J. H. Edwards.

CONTEMPORARY APPLIED ARTS, 43 Earlham Street, WC2H 9LD—Ms. T. Marsden.

CONVEYANCERS, COUNCIL FOR LICENSED (1986), Golden Cross House, Duncannon Street, WC2N 4JF—*Chairman,* Mrs. R. Waterhouse; *Sec.,* N. R. Osner.

CO-OPERATIVE SOCIETIES AND ASSOCIATIONS:—

Co-operative Party, 158 Buckingham Palace Road, SW1W 9UB—*Sec.,* D. Wise, O.B.E.

Co-operative Union Ltd. (1869), Holyoake House, Hanover Street, Manchester M60 0AS—*Chief Exec.,* D. L. Wilkinson.

Co-operative Wholesale Society (C.W.S.) (1863), P.O. Box 53, New Century House, Manchester M60 4ES—*Chief Exec. Officer,* D. M. Landau; *Sec.,* G. J. Melmoth.

Co-operative Women's Guild, 342 Hoe Street, Walthamstow, E17 9PX—*Nat. Officer.,* Miss D. Paskin.

Fisheries Organization Society, Ltd. (1914), New Fish Quay, Brixham, Devon.—*Sec.,* A. H. Dobbie.

International Co-operative Alliance (1895), 15 route des Morillons, 1218 Grand-Saconnex, Geneva, Switzerland—*Dir.,* R. L. Beasley.

Plunkett Foundation for Co-operative Studies (1919), 31 St. Giles, Oxford OX1 3LF—*Dir.,* E. Parnell.

COPYRIGHT COUNCIL, BRITISH (1953), 29–33 Berners Street, W1P 4AA—*Sec.,* G. V. Adams.

CORONERS' SOCIETY OF ENGLAND AND WALES (1846).—*Hon. Sec.,* Dr. J. D. K. Burton, 7 Orchard Rise, Richmond, Surrey TW10 5BX.

CORPORATE TREASURERS, ASSOCIATION OF, 16 Park Crescent, W1N 4AH—*Sec.,* Mrs. R. Miller.

CORPORATE TRUSTEES, ASSOCIATION OF, 2 Withdean Rise, Brighton BN1 6YN.—*Sec.,* L. C. Howes.

CORRESPONDENCE COLLEGES, ASSOCIATION OF BRITISH (1955), 6 Francis Grove, SW19 4DT—*Sec.,* Mrs. M. Coren.

COUNCIL FOR SMALL INDUSTRIES IN RURAL AREAS (COSIRA), 141 Castle Street, Salisbury, Wilts. SP1 3TP—*Chief Exec.,* A. D. Scott.

COUNSEL AND CARE FOR THE ELDERLY, 131 Middlesex Street, E1 7JF—*Gen. Sec.,* J. H. Hobart.

COUNTRY HOUSES ASSOCIATION LTD. (1955), 41 Kingsway, WC2B 6UB—*Chief Exec.,* R. D. Bratby.

COUNTRY LANDOWNERS' ASSOCIATION (1907), 16 Belgrave Square, SW1X 8PQ—*Dir. Gen.,* J. M. Douglas, C.B.E.

COUNTY CHIEF EXECUTIVES, ASSOCIATION OF—*Hon. Sec.,* R. W. Adcock, County Hall, Chelmsford, Essex CM1 1LX.

COUNTY COUNCILS, ASSOCIATION OF, Eaton House, 66A Eaton Square, SW1W 9BH—*Sec.,* Sir P. Newsam.

COUNTY EMERGENCY PLANNING OFFICERS' SOCIETY, County Hall, Spetchley Road, Worcester WR5 2NP—*Hon. Sec.,* D. Moses.

COUNTY SECRETARIES, SOCIETY OF—*Hon. Sec.,* J. R. Gregory, P.O. Box 11, County Buildings, Martin Street, Stafford, ST16 2LH.

COUNTY SURVEYORS' SOCIETY (1884).—*President,* M. R. Hawkins; *Hon. Sec.,* K. B. Madelin, Shropshire County Council, The Shirehall, Abbey Foregate, Shrewsbury, Shropshire SY2 6ND.

COUNTY TREASURERS, SOCIETY OF (1903)—*President,* J. A. Parkes; *Hon. Sec.,* D. G. Barrett, County Offices, Newland, Lincoln, Lincolnshire LN1 1YG.

CRUELTY TO ANIMALS, ROYAL SOCIETY FOR THE PREVENTION OF. See "ROYAL."

CRUELTY TO ANIMALS, THE SCOTTISH SOCIETY FOR THE PREVENTION OF (1950), 19 Melville Street, Edinburgh EH3 7PL—*Chief Exec.,* Sir Cameron Rusby, K.C.B., L.V.O.

CRUELTY TO CHILDREN. See "NATIONAL" and "ROYAL SCOTTISH."

CULTURAL EXCHANGE, ASSOCIATION FOR (1958), Babraham, Cambridge CB2 4AP—*Gen. Sec.,* P. B. Barnes.

CWMNI URDD GOBAITH CYMRU, Swyddfa'r Urdd, Aberystwyth, Dyfed SY23 1EN—*Dir.,* J. E. Williams.

CYCLISTS' TOURING CLUB (1878), Cotterell House, 69 Meadrow, Godalming, Surrey GU7 3HS—*Sec.,* A. J. Leng.

CYMMRODORION, THE HONOURABLE SOCIETY OF (1751).—*Hon. Sec.,* Mrs. J. Gruffydd, 30 Eastcastle Street, W1N 7PD.

CYSTIC FIBROSIS RESEARCH TRUST (1964), Alexandra House, 5 Blyth Road, Bromley, Kent BR1 3RS—*Dir.,* Mrs. B. Bentley.

DAIRY ASSOCIATION, UNITED KINGDOM (1950), Giggs Hill Green, Thames Ditton, Surrey KT7 0EL—*Sec.*, Mrs. J. M. Newton.

DAIRY TECHNOLOGY, SOCIETY OF (1943), 72 Ermine Street, Huntingdon, Cambs. PE18 6EZ—*Nat. Sec.*, P. H. F. Lee.

D-DAY AND NORMANDY FELLOWSHIP.—*Hon. Secs.*, Mr. and Mrs. L. R. Reed, 9 South Parade, Southsea, Hants. PO5 2JB.

DEAF ASSOCIATION, BRITISH (1890 *formerly* BRITISH DEAF AND DUMB ASSOCIATION), 38 Victoria Place, Carlisle CA1 1HU.—*Gen. Sec.*, A. W. Verney.

DEAF, ROYAL NATIONAL INSTITUTE FOR THE (1911), 105 Gower Street, WC1E 6AH—*Chief Exec.*, M. Whitlam.

DEAF AND DUMB, ROYAL ASSOCIATION IN AID OF, To promote the welfare of deaf and blind/deaf people in Greater London, Essex, Surrey and Kent. 27 Old Oak Road, W3 7HN—*Dir. of Admin.*, Mrs. V. Giles.

DEAF CHILDREN, MARGATE, ROYAL SCHOOL FOR (1792), Victoria Road, Margate, Kent CT9 1NB—*Sec.*, D. E. Downs.

DEAF WOMEN, FOLEY HOUSE RESIDENTIAL HOME FOR, Foley House, 115 High Garrett, Braintree, Essex CM7 5NU—*Dir.*, Mrs. N. Hartard.

DEER MANAGEMENT SOCIETIES, THE FEDERATION OF (1975)—*Hon. Sec.*, R. Young, Easters, Sandhills, Cattistock, Dorchester DT2 0HQ.

DEER SOCIETY, BRITISH, Church Farm, Lower Basildon, Reading, Berks. RG8 9NH.

DENTAL COUNCIL, GENERAL, 37 Wimpole Street W1M 8DQ—*Registrar*, N. T. Davies, M.B.E.

DENTAL HOSPITALS OF THE UNITED KINGDOM, ASSOCIATION OF (1942).—*Hon. Sec.*, Mrs. P. Harrington, Dental Hospital, St. Chad's Queensway, Birmingham B4 6NN.

DESIGN AND INDUSTRIES ASSOCIATION (1915), 29 Bedford Square, WC1B 3EG—*Hon. Dir.*, R. Plummer.

DESIGNERS, THE CHARTERED SOCIETY OF (1930), 29 Bedford Square, WC1B 3EG—*Dir.*, M. Sadler-Forster.

DEVON AND CORNWALL RECORD SOCIETY (1904).—c/o Devon and Exeter Institution, 7 The Close, Exeter EX1 1EZ.—*Hon. Sec.*, J. D. Brunton.

DICKENS FELLOWSHIP, Dickens House, 48 Doughty Street, WC1N 2LF—*Hon. Gen. Sec.*, A. S. Watts.

DIRECTORS, INSTITUTE OF, 116 Pall Mall, SW1Y 5ED—*Dir. Gen.*, Sir John Hoskyns.

DISABILITY AND REHABILITATION, THE ROYAL ASSOCIATION FOR, 25 Mortimer Street, W1N 8AB—*Dir.*, G. Wilson, C.B.E.

DISPENSING OPTICIANS, ASSOCIATION OF BRITISH (1925), 22 Nottingham Place, W1M 4AT—*Sec. Gen.*, A. P. D. Westhead.

DISTRESSED GENTLEFOLK'S AID ASSOCIATION (1897), Vicarage Gate House, Vicarage Gate, W8 4AQ—*Gen. Sec.*, J. A. Marshall, C.B.

DISTRICT COUNCILS, ASSOCIATION OF (1974), 9 Buckingham Gate, SW1E 6LE—*Sec.*, G. McCartney.

DISTRICT MEDICAL OFFICERS, ASSOCIATION OF (1982). *Hon. Sec.*, Dr. P. W. Briggs, Ealing Hospital, St. Bernard's Wing, Uxbridge Road, Southall, Middx.

DISTRICT SECRETARIES ASSOCIATION OF, 9 Margaret Road, Bishopworth, Bristol BS13 9DQ.—*Hon. Sec.*, D. C. Lunn.

DITCHLEY FOUNDATION, Ditchley Park, Enstone, Oxford OX7 4ER—*Dir.*, Sir John Graham, Bt., G.C.M.G.

DOCKLAND SETTLEMENTS, Headquarters and office at 197 East Ferry Road, Isle of Dogs, E14 9AB. Branches at Rotherhithe S.E.16; Stratford, E.15; Hainault, Essex. *Chief Exec.*, M. S. Stribling.

DOMESTIC SERVANTS' BENEVOLENT INSTITUTION (1846), Royal Bank of Scotland P.L.C., 7 Burlington Gardens, W1A 3DD—*Sec.*, D. C. F. Small.

DOWSERS, BRITISH SOCIETY OF.—*Sec.*, M. D. Rust, Sycamore Cottage, Tamley Lane, Hastingleigh, Ashford, Kent TN25 5HW.

DRAINAGE AUTHORITIES, ASSOCIATION OF (1937).—*Sec.*, D. Noble, Ambury Road, Huntingdon, Cambs. PE18 6NZ.

DRINKING FOUNTAIN ASSOCIATION (Metropolitan Drinking Fountain and Cattle Trough Association) (1859)—*Sec.* D. R. W. Randall, 105 Wansunt Road, Bexley, Kent DA5 2DN.

DRUG DEPENDENCE, INSTITUTE FOR THE STUDY OF, 1–4 Hatton Place, EC1N 8ND—*Dir.*, J. Woodcock, O.B.E.

DYERS AND COLOURISTS, SOCIETY OF (1884), Perkin House, P.O. Box 244, 82 Grattan Road, Bradford BD1 2JB—*Gen. Sec.*, M. Tordoff, PH.D.

EARL HAIG'S (BRITISH LEGION) APPEAL FUND. *See* "BRITISH LEGION."

ECCLESIASTICAL HISTORY SOCIETY.—*Sec.*, Dr. Judith Champ, Department of Christian Doctrine and History, King's College, Strand, WC2R 2LS.

ECCLESIOLOGICAL SOCIETY.—*Hon. Sec.*, S. C. Humphrey, 1 Cornish House, Otto Street, SE17 3PE.

EDUCATION IN ART AND DESIGN, NATIONAL SOCIETY FOR (1888), 7A High Street, Corsham, Wilts. SN13 0ES—*Gen. Sec.*, J. Steers.

EDUCATION OFFICERS, SOCIETY OF.—*Gen. Sec.*, R. P. Harding, C.B.E., 21–27 Lambs Conduit Street, WC1N 3NJ.

EDUCATION OFFICERS' SOCIETY, COUNTY—*Hon. Sec.*, N. J. Fitton, County Hall, Chester CH1 1SQ.

EDUCATIONAL CENTRES ASSOCIATION, Chequer Centre, Chequer Street, EC1Y 8PL—*Sec.*, D. J. Delahunt.

EDUCATIONAL FOUNDATION FOR VISUAL AIDS, Paxton Place, Gipsy Road, SE27 9SR—*Chief Exec.*, G. C. Marchant.

EDUCATIONAL INSTITUTE OF DESIGN, CRAFT AND TECHNOLOGY—*Administrator*, F. Willmore, 34 Burton Street, Melton Mowbray, Leicestershire LE13 1AF.

EDUCATIONAL RESEARCH IN ENGLAND AND WALES, NATIONAL FOUNDATION FOR, The Mere, Upton Park, Slough, Berks. SL1 2DQ—*Dir.*, Dr. Clare Burstall.

EDUCATIONAL VISITS AND EXCHANGES, CENTRAL BUREAU FOR (1948), Seymour Mews House, Seymour Mews, W1H 9PE—*Dir.*, A. H. Male.

EGYPT EXPLORATION SOCIETY (1882), 3 Doughty Mews, WC1N 2PG—*Chairman*, T. G. H. James, C.B.E., F.B.A.; *Sec.*, Dr. Patricia A. Spencer.

ELECTORAL REFORM SOCIETY OF GREAT BRITAIN AND IRELAND (founded 1884 as Proportional Representation Society), 6 Chancel Street, SE1 0UU—*Pres.*, Lord Blake, F.B.A..

ELECTRICAL ENGINEERS, INSTITUTION OF (1871), Savoy Place, WC2R 0BL—*Sec.*, H. H. W. Losty.

ELECTRICITY CONSUMERS' COUNCIL, Brook House, 2–16 Torrington Place, WC1E 7LL—*Dir.*, Jennifer Kirkpatrick.

ELECTRONIC AND RADIO ENGINEERS, INSTITUTION OF (1925), 99 Gower Street, WC1E 6AZ—*Sec.*, D. D. Duffett.

ELGAR FOUNDATION, Elgar's Birthplace, Crown East Lane, Lower Broadheath, Worcester WR2 6RH—*Hon. Sec.*, B. Edgington.

ELGAR SOCIETY (1951).—*Sec.*, Mrs. C. Holt, 20 Geraldine Road, Malvern, Worcs. WR14 3PA.

ENERGY, INSTITUTE OF (1927), 18 Devonshire Street, Portland Place, W.1—*Sec.*, H. M. Lodge.

ENGINEERING COUNCIL, THE, 10 Maltravers Street, WC2R 3ER—*Sec.*, J. Carlill, O.B.E.

ENGINEERING DESIGNERS, INSTITUTION OF (1945), Courtleigh, Westbury Leigh, Westbury, Wilts. BA13 3TA—*Gen. Sec.*, P. J. Booker.

ENGINEERING, FELLOWSHIP OF (1976), 2 Little Smith Street, SW1P 3DL—*Exec. Sec.*, V. J. Osola, C.B.E.

ENGINEERING INDUSTRIES ASSOCIATION, 16 Dartmouth Street, SW1H 9BL—*Dir.*, Col. W. T. Williams.

ENGINEERS AND SHIPBUILDERS IN SCOTLAND, INSTITUTION OF (1857), Charing Cross Tower, 10 Elmbank Gardens, Glasgow, G2 4HT—*Pres.*, J. D. Leith; *Sec.*, G. V. Dare.

ENGINEERS AND SHIPBUILDERS, N.E. COAST INSTITUTION OF (1884), 12 Windsor Terrace, Jesmond, Newcastle upon Tyne, NE2 4HE—*Sec.*, Mrs. A. Rainsford.

ENGINEERS, INSTITUTION OF BRITISH (1928), Royal Liver Buildings, 6 Hampton Place, Brighton, BN1 3DD—*Sec.*, Mrs. D. Henry.

ENGINEERS, SOCIETY OF (1854), Parsifal College, 527 Finchley Road, NW3 7BG—*Sec.*, P. A. Lancaster.

ENGLISH ASSOCIATION, THE (1906), The Vicarage, Priory Gardens, W4 1TT—*Sec.*, Dr. Ruth Fairbanks-Joseph.

ENGLISH FOLK DANCE AND SONG SOCIETY (1932), Cecil Sharp House, 2 Regent's Park Road, NW1 7AY—*Hon. Dir.*, S. A. Mathews.

ENGLISH PLACE-NAME SURVEY (1923)—*Hon. Director,* Prof. K. Cameron, C.B.E., F.B.A., The University, Nottingham NG7 2RD.

ENGLISH-SPEAKING UNION OF THE COMMONWEALTH (1918), 37 Charles Street, W1X 8AB—*Chairman,* Sir Donald Tebbit, G.C.M.G.; *Dir. Gen.*, Rear-Adm. R. Heaslip, C.B

ENTOMOLOGICAL SOCIETY OF LONDON, ROYAL (1833), 41 Queen's Gate, SW7 5HU—*Registrar,* G. G. Bentley.

ENVIRONMENTAL CONSERVATION, COUNCIL FOR (1969), London Ecology Centre, 80 York Way, N1 9AG—*Pres.*, The Duke of Wellington, M.V.O., O.B.E., M.C.; *Chairman,* G. England; *Sec.*, D. Hughes.

ENVIRONMENTAL HEALTH OFFICERS, INSTITUTION OF, Chadwick House, Rushworth Street, SE1 0QT—*Sec.*, A. M. Tanner.

EPILEPSY ASSOCIATION, BRITISH, Anstey House, 40 Hanover Square, Leeds LS3 1BE—*Sec.*, T. J. O'-Leary.

EPILEPSY, THE NATIONAL SOCIETY FOR (1892), Chalfont Centre for Epilepsy, Chalfont St. Peter, Gerrards Cross, Bucks. SL9 0RJ—*Chief Exec.*, Col. D. W. Eking.

ESPERANTO ASSOCIATION OF BRITAIN (1977), 140 Holland Park Avenue, W11 4UF—*Hon. Sec.*, J. Brownlee.

EUGENICS SOCIETY (1907), 69 Eccleston Square, SW1V 1PJ—*Gen. Sec.*, Mrs. L. Brooks.

EUROPEAN SCHOOL (1978), Culham, Abingdon, Oxon. OX14 3DZ—*Head*, T. Høyem.

EVANGELICAL ALLIANCE (1846), 186 Kennington Park Road, SE11 4BT—*Gen. Sec.*, Rev. C. Calver.

EVANGELICAL LIBRARY, THE, 78A Chiltern Street, W1M 2HB—*Deputy Librarian,* Miss F. S. Wright.

EXAMINERS UNDER SOLICITORS (SCOTLAND) ACT (1980), Law Society's Hall, 26 Drumsheugh Gardens, Edinburgh EH3 7YR—*Clerk*, K. W. Pritchard.

EXECUTIVES ASSOCIATION OF GREAT BRITAIN, Suite 7, The Hop Exchange, 24 Southwark Street, SE1 1TY—*Sec.*, C. E. Nicholson.

EXPORT, INSTITUTE OF, Export House, 64 Clifton Street, EC2A 4HB—*Sec.*, J. R. Wilson.

EX-SERVICES MENTAL WELFARE SOCIETY, Broadway House, The Broadway, Wimbledon, SW19 1RL—*Gen. Sec.*, J. S. Le Blanc Smith, R.N.

FABIAN SOCIETY (1884), 11 Dartmouth Street, SW1H 9BN—*Gen. Sec.*, J. William.

FAIRBRIDGE SOCIETY (1909), 119–126 Bush House (N.E.), Aldwych, WC2B 4PY—*Dir. and Sec.*, Mrs. C. P. MacGregor.

FAIR ISLE BIRD OBSERVATORY TRUST, 21 Regent Terrace, Edinburgh EH7 5BT—*Hon. Sec.*, R. A. Broad.

FAMILY CONCILIATION COUNCIL, NATIONAL (1982), 34 Milton Road, Swindon, Wilts. SN1 5JA—*Chairman,* Mrs. T. Fisher.

FAMILY HISTORY SOCIETIES, FEDERATION OF (1974)—*Administrator*, Mrs. P. A. Saul, 31 Seven Star Road, Solihull, West Midlands B91 2BZ.

FAMILY PLANNING ASSOCIATION, 27–35 Mortimer Street, W1N 7RJ—*Gen. Sec.*, A. Service.

FAMILY WELFARE ASSOCIATION (Founded 1869 as CHARITY ORGANIZATION SOCIETY), 501–5 Kingsland Road, E8 4AU—*Dir.*, R. E. Morley; *Sec.*, Mrs. A. Weare.

FAUNA AND FLORA PRESERVATION SOCIETY (1903)—c/o Zoological Society of London, Regent's Park, NW1 4RY—*Exec. Sec.*, J. A. Burton.

FELLOWSHIP HOUSES TRUST (Flatlets for the elderly) (1937), Clock House, Byfleet, Weybridge, Surrey KT14 7RN—*Sec.*, L. P. Leech.

FIELD STUDIES COUNCIL (1943), Preston Montford, Montford Bridge, Shrewsbury SY4 1HW—*Dir.*, A. D. Thomas.

FIRE ENGINEERS, INSTITUTION OF, 148 New Walk, Leicester LE1 7QB—*Gen. Sec.*, Mrs. C. E. Mackwood.

FIRE PROTECTION ASSOCIATION, 140 Aldersgate Street, EC1A 4HX—*Dir.*, C. D. Woodward.

FIRE SERVICES ASSOCIATION, THE BRITISH, 86 London Road, Leicester LE2 0QR—*Gen. Sec.*, T. A. Plummer.

FIRE SERVICES NATIONAL BENEVOLENT FUND (1943), Marine Court, Fitzalan Road, Littlehampton, W. Sussex BN17 5NF—*Gen. Man.*, R. A. Spackman.

FLEET AIR ARM OFFICERS ASSOCIATION (1957), 94 Piccadilly, W1V 0BP—*Chairman*, W. J. Hanks.

FOLKLORE SOCIETY, c/o University College London, Gower Street, WC1E 6BT—*Hon. Sec.*, A. R. Vickery.

FOOD SCIENCE AND TECHNOLOGY, INSTITUTE OF, 20 Queensberry Place, SW7 2DR—*Chief Exec.*, Ms. H. G. Wild.

FOOD FROM BRITAIN, 301–344 Market Towers, New Covent Garden Market, SW8 5NQ—*Chairman,* B. Law.

FORCES HELP SOCIETY AND LORD ROBERTS WORKSHOPS (1899), 122 Brompton Road, SW3 1JE—*Comptroller and Sec.*, Col. A. W. Davis, M.B.E.

FOREIGN BONDHOLDERS, COUNCIL OF (1873), 35 High Street, Bromley, Kent BR1 1LE—*Dir.*, M. Gough.

FOREIGN PRESS ASSOCIATION IN LONDON, 11 Carlton House Terrace, SW1Y 5AJ—*Pres.*, A. Bahaijoub; *Sec.* Miss D. Fergusson.

FORENSIC SCIENCES, BRITISH ACADEMY OF (1959).—*Sec. Gen.*, Dr. P. J. Lincoln, Dept. of Haematology, The London Hospital Medical College, Turner Street, E1 2AD.

FORESTERS, INSTITUTE OF CHARTERED (1982), 22 Walker Street, Edinburgh EH3 7HR—*Sec.*, Mrs. M. W. Dick.

FORESTRY ASSOCIATION, COMMONWEALTH (1921), c/o Oxford Forestry Institute, South Parks Road, Oxford OX1 3RB.

FORESTRY SOCIETY OF ENGLAND, WALES AND NORTHERN IRELAND, ROYAL (1882), 102 High Street, Tring, Herts. HP23 4AH—*Dir.*, E. H. M. Harris.

FORESTRY SOCIETY, ROYAL SCOTTISH (1854), 11 Atholl Crescent, Edinburgh EH3 8HE—*Sec.* W. B. C. Walker.

FRANCO-BRITISH SOCIETY, Room 636, Linen Hall, 162–168 Regent Street, W1R 5TB—*Exec. Sec.*, Mrs. M. Clarke.

FREE CHURCH FEDERAL COUNCIL, 27 Tavistock Square, WC1H 9HH—*Moderator*, Rev. B. Green; *Gen. Sec.*, Rev. D. Staple.

FREEDOM ASSOCIATION (1975), Avon House, 360–366 Oxford Street, W1N 0AA—*Executive Officer* J. F. Fletcher.

FREEMASONS, GRAND LODGE OF ANTIENT FREE AND ACCEPTED MASONS OF SCOTLAND (1736), Freemasons' Hall, 96 George Street, Edinburgh EH2 3DH—*Grand Master Mason of Scotland*, J. M. Marcus Humphrey of Dinnet; *Grand Sec.*, A. O. Hazel.

FREEMASONS, UNITED GRAND LODGE OF ENGLAND, Freemasons' Hall, Great Queen Street, WC2B 5AZ—*Grand Master*, H.R.H. the Duke of Kent, K.G., G.C.M.G., G.C.V.O.; *Pro Grand Master*, The Lord Cornwallis, O.B.E.; *Deputy Grand Master*, Hon. E. L. Baillieu; *Asst. Grand Master*, The Lord Farnham; *Grand Wardens*, J. M. Marcus Humphrey of Dinnet; The Rev. Preb. C. E. Leighton Thomson; *Grand Chaplain*, Rev. N. Barker-Cryer; *Grand Sec.*, Cdr. M. B. S. Higham, R.N.

FREEMEN OF ENGLAND (1966), *Sec.*, E. T. Ellis, Gardener's Cottage, Saxby All Saints, Brigg, S. Humberside DN20 0QF.

FREEMEN'S GUILDS:—

Freemen's Guild of Berwick-upon-Tweed, 9 Church Street, Berwick-upon-Tweed TD15 1EF—*Clerk*, J. R. Reay.

Freemen and Guilds of the City of Chester, The Guildhall, Chester.

City of Coventry Freemen's Guild—*Hon. Sec.*, H. J. McCranor, 89 Brinklow Road, Binley, Coventry CV3 2JB—*Clerk*, H. J. McCranor.

Guild of Freemen of the City of London, Suite 1, 2 Cloth Court, St. Bartholomews, EC1A 7LS—*Clerk*, Col. D. Ivy.

Gild of Freemen of the City of Newcastle upon Tyne—*Hon. Sec.*, 8 Leyburn Drive, High Heaton, Newcastle upon Tyne NE7 7AP.

Gild of Freemen of the City of York—*Hon. Clerk*, R. Lee, 29 Albemarle Road, York YO2 1EW.

FRESHWATER BIOLOGICAL ASSOCIATION (1929), The Ferry House, Ambleside, Cumbria LA22 0LP—*Sec. and Director of Laboratories*, Dr. R. T. Clarke.

FRIENDLY SOCIETIES, NATIONAL CONFERENCE OF—*Sec.*, P. M. Madders, Room 313, Victoria House, Vernon Place, WC1B 4DP.

FRIENDS OF CATHEDRAL MUSIC (1956), c/o Addington Palace, Croydon, Surrey CR9 5AD.—*Hon. Gen. Sec.*, N. T. Barnes.

FRIENDS OF THE CLERGY CORPORATION, THE. (incorporating the Friend of the Clergy Corp., the Poor Clergy Relief Corp. and the Curates Augmentation Fund), 27 Medway Street, SW1P 2BD—*Sec.*, J. M. Greany.

FRIENDS OF THE NATIONAL LIBRARIES, The British Library, WC1B 3DG—*Chairman*, The Lord Egremont; *Hon. Sec.*, J. F. Fuggles.

FRIENDS OF THE ELDERLY & GENTLEFOLK'S HELP, 42 Ebury Street, SW1W 0LZ—*Gen. Sec.*, Rev. J. Schofield.

FURNITURE HISTORY SOCIETY (1964).—*Hon. Sec.*, Mrs. H. Hayward, c/o Dept. of Furniture and Interior Design, Victoria and Albert Museum, SW7 2RL.

GALLIPOLI ASSOCIATION (1915).—*Hon. Sec.*, K. Tranmer, 100 Ramsgill Drive, Ilford, Essex IG2 7TP.

GAME CONSERVANCY, THE, Fordingbridge, Hants. SP6 1EF—*Dir.*, R. M. Van Oss.

GARDEN HISTORY SOCIETY (1965), 5 The Knoll, Hereford HR1 1RU—*Hon. Membership Sec.*, Mrs. A. Richards.

GARDENERS' ASSOCIATION, THE GOOD, Two Mile Lane, Higham, Glos. GL2 8DW—*Hon. Dir.*, J. D. Wilkin.

GARDENERS' ROYAL BENEVOLENT SOCIETY (1839), Bridge House, 139 Kingston Road, Leatherhead, Surrey KT22 7NT—*Sec.*, C. R. C. Bunce.

GAS CONSUMERS' COUNCIL, 6th Floor, Abford House, 15 Wilton Road, SW1V 1LT—*Dir.*, I. W. Powe.

GAS ENGINEERS, INSTITUTION OF (1863), 17 Grosvenor Crescent, SW1X 7ES—*Sec.*, D. J. Chapman.

GEMMOLOGICAL ASSOCIATION OF GREAT BRITAIN (1931), St. Dunstan's House, Carey Lane, EC2V 8AB—*Sec.*, J. P. Brown.

GENEALOGICAL RESEARCH SOCIETY, IRISH—*Sec.*, Miss Z. A. M. Kelly, 11 Lyric Road, SW13 9QA.

GENEALOGISTS AND RECORD AGENTS, ASSOCIATION OF (1968), 1 Woodside Close, Caterham, Surrey CR3 6AU—*Sec.*, Mrs. J. Tooke.

GENEALOGISTS, SOCIETY OF (1911), 14 Charterhouse Buildings, Goswell Road, EC1M 7BA—*Dir.*, A. J. Camp.

GENERAL PRACTITIONERS, ROYAL COLLEGE OF (1952), 14–15 Princes Gate, Hyde Park, SW7 1PU—*Gen. Administrator.*, Mrs. S. Irvine.

GENTLEPEOPLE, GUILD OF AID FOR (1904), 10 St. Christopher's Place, W1M 6HY—*Sec.*, Mrs. G. A. Burgess.

GEOGRAPHICAL ASSOCIATION, 343 Fulwood Road, Sheffield S10 3BP.—*Joint Hon. Secs.*, Dr. J. A. Binns; P. S. Fox.

GEOGRAPHICAL SOCIETY, ROYAL (1830), 1 Kensington Gore, SW7 2AR—*Pres.*, Lord Chorley; *Hon. Secs.*, Prof. A. S. Goudie, Dr. R. A. French; *Hon. Foreign Sec.*, Col. S. R. Gilbert; *Hon. Treas.*, A. Tritton; *Director and Sec.*, Dr. J. Hemming; *Keeper of the Map Room*, Brig. G. R. Gathercole; *Librarian*, D. Wileman.

GEOGRAPHICAL SOCIETY, MANCHESTER (1884), 274 The Corn Exchange Buildings, Manchester M4 3EY—*Sec.*, Miss E. Whalley.

GEOGRAPHICAL SOCIETY, ROYAL SCOTTISH (1884), 10 Randolph Crescent, Edinburgh EH3 7TU—*Sec.*, A. B. Cruickshank.

GEOLOGICAL SOCIETY (1807), Burlington House, Piccadilly, W1V 0JU—*Pres.*, Prof. B. E. Leake; *Secs.*, Dr. A. J. Martin, Dr. L. R. M. Cocks, Dr. J. Brooks, W. J. French, PH.D.; *Foreign Sec.*, Prof. J. B. Dawson; *Exec. Sec.*, R. M. Bateman.

GEOLOGISTS' ASSOCIATION, Burlington House, Piccadilly, W1V 9AG—*Hon. Gen. Sec.*, Dr. R. B. Stokes.

GEOLOGISTS, THE INSTITUTION OF (1977), Burlington House, Piccadilly, W1V 9AG—*Pres.*, C. M. Bristow; *Sec.*, J. A. Seymour.

GEORGIAN GROUP (1937), 37 Spital Square, E1 6DY—*Sec.*, R. White.

GIFTED CHILDREN, NATIONAL ASSOCIATION FOR (1966), 1 South Audley Street, W1Y 5DQ—*Dir.*, J. Welch.

GILBERT AND SULLIVAN SOCIETY, 273 Northfield Avenue, W5 4UA.

GIRL GUIDES ASSOCIATION.—An organization founded by the first Lord Baden-Powell as a sister movement to the Scouts and incorporated by Royal Charter in 1922. In 1986 the total membership in the United Kingdom was 778,131. *Commonwealth Headquarters*, 17–19 Buckingham Palace Road, SW1W 0PT.

GIRLS' BRIGADE, THE, Brigade House, Parsons Green, SW6 4TH—*Brigade Sec. for Eng. & Wales*, Miss D. M. Cosser.

GIRLS' FRIENDLY SOCIETY AND TOWNSEND FELLOWSHIP (1875), 126 Queens Gate, SW7 5LQ—*Gen. Sec.*, Miss H. G. Smith.

GIRLS OF THE REALM GUILD (1900).—Small educational grants, loans towards professional training of women. Applications before March for ensuing academic year to: *Sec.*, Mrs. B. Hayward, 2

Watchoak, Blackham, Tunbridge Wells, Kent TN3 9TP.

GIRLS' VENTURE CORPS AIR CADETS, Redhill Aerodrome, Kings Mill Lane, Redhill, Surrey RH1 5JY. A uniformed youth movement for girls between 13 and 20.—*Sec. Gen.*, Miss H. Prosper.

GLASS TECHNOLOGY, SOCIETY OF (1916), 20 Hallam Gate Road, Sheffield S10 5BT—*Hon. Sec.*, W. Simpson.

GRAPHIC ARTISTS, SOCIETY OF (1919), 9 Newburgh Street, W1V 1LH—*Pres.*, Mrs. L. B. Kell; *Sec.*, Miss L. A. Robinson.

GREATER LONDON PLAYING FIELDS ASSOCIATION (1926), 147 Church Street, W2 1NA—*Sec.*, Capt. D. N. Forbes, D.S.C., R.N. (*retd*).

GREEK INSTITUTE (1969) (for the promotion of modern Greek studies), 34 Bush Hill Road, N21 2DS—*Dir.*, Dr. K. Tofallis.

GREEN PARTY, THE (1973), 10 Station Parade, Balham High Road, SW12 9AZ—*Gen. Manager*, J. Bishop.

GROCERS ASSOCIATION, BRITISH INDEPENDENT, 17 Farnborough Street, Farnborough, Hants. GU14 8AG—*Nat. Sec.*, I. A. McKee.

GULBENKIAN FOUNDATION, *see* CALOUSTE.

HAKLUYT SOCIETY (1846), c/o Map Library, The British Library, Great Russell Street, WC1B 3DG—*Joint Hon. Secs.*, Dr. T. E. Armstrong; Mrs. S. Tyacke.

HANSARD SOCIETY FOR PARLIAMENTARY GOVERNMENT (1944), 16 Gower Street, WC1E 6DP—*Sec.*, Mrs. M. T. Goudie.

HARVEIAN SOCIETY OF EDINBURGH (1782), Dept. of Medicine, The Royal Infirmary, Edinburgh EH3 9YW—*Joint Secs.*, Dr. A. D. Toft, I. F. MacLaren.

HARVEIAN SOCIETY OF LONDON.—*Exec. Sec.*, Maj. T. Tudor-Williams, 11 Chandos Street, Cavendish Square, W1M 0EB

HEAD TEACHERS, NATIONAL ASSOCIATION OF—*Gen. Sec.*, D. M. Hart, Holly House, 6 Paddockhall Road, Haywards Heath, West Sussex RH16 1RG.

HEALTH AUTHORITIES, THE NATIONAL ASSOCIATION OF (1974), Garth House, 47 Edgbaston Park Road, Birmingham B15 2RS—*Dir.*, P. A. Hunt.

HEALTH EDUCATION, INSTITUTE OF—*Hon. Sec.*, Dr. L. Baric, 14 High Elm Road, Hale Barns, Altrincham, Cheshire WA15 0HS.

HEALTH, GUILD OF (1904), Edward Wilson House, 26 Queen Anne Street, W1M 9LB—*Sec.*, Ms. T. F. Parker.

HEALTH SERVICES MANAGEMENT, INSTITUTE OF (1902), 75 Portland Place, W1N 4AN—*Dir.*, Ms. M. Dixon, PH.D.

HELLENIC STUDIES, SOCIETY FOR THE PROMOTION OF (1879), 31–34 Gordon Square, WC1H 0PP—*Pres.*, Sir David Hunt, K.C.M.G., O.B.E. *Hon. Sec.*, Prof. J. P. Barron.

HENRY GEORGE FOUNDATION, 177 Vauxhall Bridge Road, SW1V 1EU—*Company Sec.*, Mrs. B. P. Sobrielo.

HERALDIC AND GENEALOGICAL STUDIES, INSTITUTE OF (1961), 79–82 Northgate, Canterbury, Kent CT1 1BA—*Sec.*, C. H. Schofield.

HERALDRY SOCIETY, THE (1947), 44–45 Museum Street, WC1A 1LY—*Sec.*, E. H. Taylor.

HERALDRY SOCIETY OF SCOTLAND (1977)—*Sec.*, Dr. M. C. Stanton, 9 Priestden Park, St. Andrews, Fife KY16 8DL.

HERPETOLOGICAL SOCIETY, BRITISH (1947), c/o Zoological Society of London, Regent's Park, NW1 4RY—*Pres.*, The Earl of Cranbrook.

HIGHWAYS AND TRANSPORTATION, INSTITUTION OF (1930), 3 Lygon Place, Ebury Street, SW1W 0JS—*Sec.*, Miss P. A. Steel.

HISPANIC AND LUSO BRAZILIAN COUNCIL, Canning House, 2 Belgrave Square, SW1X 8PJ—*Dir. Gen.*, Sir Kenneth James, K.C.M.G.

HISTORICAL ASSOCIATION, THE (1906), 59A Kennington Park Road, SE11 4JH—*Sec.*, Mrs. M. Stiles.

HISTORICAL SOCIETY, ROYAL (1868), University College London, Gower Street, WC1E 6BT—*Pres.*, Dr. G. E. Aylmer; *Exec. Sec.*, Mrs. J. Chapman.

HONG KONG ASSOCIATION, THE (1961), Regis House, 43–46 King William Street, EC4R 9BE—*Exec. Dir.*, Brig. B. G. Hickey, O.B.E., M.C.

HORATIAN SOCIETY (1933).—*Hon. Sec.*, C. P. Sydenham, 4 Stone Buildings, Lincolns Inn, WC2A 3XT.

HOROLOGICAL INSTITUTE, BRITISH (1858), Upton Hall, Upton, Newark, Notts. NG23 5TE—*Sec.*, W. M. G. Evans.

HOROLOGICAL SOCIETY, ANTIQUARIAN (1953), New House, High Street, Ticehurst, Wadhurst, E. Sussex TN5 7AL—*Sec.*, R. V. Glazebrook.

HOSPITAL FEDERATION, INTERNATIONAL (1947), 2 St. Andrew's Place, NW1 4LB—*Dir. Gen.*, Dr. E. N. Pickering.

HOSPITALS CONTRIBUTORY SCHEMES ASSOCIATION, BRITISH (1948), 4th Floor, Refuge Building, Baldwin Street, Bristol BS1 1SE—*Exec. Sec.*, C. D. M. Kerr.

HOSPITAL SATURDAY FUND, THE (1873).—*Head Office*, 192–198 Vauxhall Bridge Road, SW1V 1EE *Sec.*, J. R. Yates.

HOSPITAL SAVING ASSOCIATION, THE, Hambleden House, Andover, Hants. SP10 1LQ—*Gen. Sec.*, J. A. Young.

HOTEL CATERING AND INSTITUTIONAL MANAGEMENT ASSOCIATION, 191 Trinity Road, SW17 7HN—*Dir.*, Miss E. Gadsby.

HOTELS, RESTAURANTS AND CATERERS ASSOCIATION, BRITISH (1907), 40 Duke Street, W1M 6HR—*Chief Exec.*, R. Lees, C.B., M.B.E.

HOUSE OF HOSPITALITY LTD., Holy Cross Priory, Cross-in-Hand, Heathfield, Sussex. 28 homes for old people.—*Dir.*, Mother Mary Garson.

HOUSE OF ST. BARNABAS IN SOHO (for Homeless Women in London) (1846), 1 Greek Street, W1V 6NQ—*Dir.*, Gp. Capt. H. A. Lax.

HOUSING, INSTITUTE OF, 9 White Lion Street, Islington, N1 9XJ—*Dir.*, P. McGurk.

HOUSING AID SOCIETY, CATHOLIC (1956), 189A Old Brompton Road, SW5 0AR—*Dir.*, Ms. R. Rafferty.

HOUSING AND TOWN PLANNING COUNCIL, NATIONAL (1900), 14–18 Old Street, EC1V 9AB—*Dir.*, R. Walker.

HOUSING ASSOCIATION FOR OFFICERS' FAMILIES (1916), Alban Dobson House, Green Lane, Morden, Surrey SM4 5NS—*Gen. Sec.*, J. B. Holt.

HOVERCRAFT SOCIETY, THE (1971), 24 Jellicoe Avenue, Alverstoke, Gosport, Hants. PO12 2PE.

HOWARD LEAGUE FOR PENAL REFORM, THE (1866), 322 Kennington Park Road, SE11 4PP—*Dir.*, Ms. F. Crook.

HUGUENOT SOCIETY OF GREAT BRITAIN AND IRELAND (1885), The Huguenot Library, University College, Gower Street, WC1E 6BT—*Sec.*, Mrs. M. Bayliss.

HYDROGRAPHIC SOCIETY, THE (1972), North East London Polytechnic, Dagenham, Essex RM8 2AS—*Hon. Sec.*, Dr. R. C. Britton.

HYMN SOCIETY OF GREAT BRITAIN AND IRELAND, THE (1936), *Sec.*, Rev. M. Garland, The Vicarage, 51 Overgreen Drive, Birmingham B37 6EY.

INDEPENDENT SCHOOL BURSARS' ASSOCIATION, *Sec.*, D. J. Bird, Woodlands, Closewood Road, Denmead, Hants, PO7 6JD.

INDEPENDENT SCHOOLS CAREERS ORGANIZATION, 12A–18A Princess Way, Camberley, Surrey GU15 3SP—*Dir. and Chief Exec.*, R. N. Exton.

INDEPENDENT SCHOOLS INFORMATION SERVICE (I.S.I.S.) (1972), 56 Buckingham Gate, SW1E 6AG—*Dir.*, D. J. Woodhead.

INDEPENDENT SCHOOLS JOINT COUNCIL, 25 Victoria Street SW1H 0EX—*Gen. Sec.*, Dr. A. G. Hearnden.

INDEXERS, SOCIETY OF—*Sec.*, Mrs. H. C. Troughton, 16 Green Road, Birchington, Kent CT7 9JZ.

INDUSTRIAL CHRISTIAN FELLOWSHIP (1877), St. Katharine Cree Church, 86 Leadenhall Street EC3A 3DH—*Dir.*, D. Arthur.

INDUSTRIAL MANAGERS, INSTITUTION OF, Rochester House, 66 Little Ealing Lane, W5 4XX—*Chief Exec.*, P. V. Crooks.

INDUSTRIAL MARKETING RESEARCH ASSOCIATION.—*Dir. Gen.*, E. Barnsley, 11 Bird Street, Lichfield, Staffs. WS13 6PW.

INDUSTRIAL PARTICIPATION ASSOCIATION (1884), 85 Tooley Street, SE1 2QZ—*Dir.*, B. S. Stevens.

INDUSTRIAL SOCIETY, THE (1918), 3 Carlton House Terrace, SW1Y 5DG—*Dir.*, J. A. Graham; *Sec.*, M. R. Hyde.

INDUSTRY AND PARLIAMENT TRUST, 25 Victoria Street, SW1H 0EX. Aims to provide practical ways for parliamentarians and industrialists to bridge the gap between industry and parliament.—*Dir.*, F. R. Hyde-Chambers.

INFANT DEATHS, THE FOUNDATION FOR THE STUDY OF (1971), 15 Belgrave Square, SW1X 8PS—*Administrative Sec.*, Mrs. S. Band.

INFORMATION SCIENTISTS, INSTITUTE OF (1958), 44 Museum Street, WC1A 1LY—*Exec. Sec.*, Mrs. S. A. Carter.

INNER WHEEL CLUBS IN GREAT BRITAIN AND IRELAND, ASSOCIATION OF (1934), 51 Warwick Square, SW1V 2AT—*Gen. Sec.*, Miss J. Dobson.

INSTITUTE OF MASTERS OF WINE, (1955), Black Swan House, Kennet Wharf Lane, EC4V 3BE—*Sec.*, Mrs. B. H. Andrews.

INSURANCE BROKERS REGISTRATION COUNCIL, 15 St. Helen's Place, EC3A 6DS—*Registrar and Sec.*, Miss E. J. Rees.

INSURANCE INSTITUTE, CHARTERED (1897), 20 Aldermanbury, EC2V 7HY—*Sec.-Gen.*, P. V. Saxton.

INTERCONTINENTAL CHURCH SOCIETY, 175 Tower Bridge Road, SE1 2AQ—*Gen. Sec.*, Rev. Canon D. R. Irving.

INTERNATIONAL FRIENDSHIP LEAGUE (1931), 3 Creswick Road, W3 9HE—*Sec.*, Mrs. B. Macdonald.

INTERNATIONAL LAW ASSOCIATION (1873), 3 Paper Buildings, Temple, EC4Y 7EU—*Hon. Sec. Gen.*, B. Mauleverer, Q.C..

INTERNATIONAL POLICE ASSOCIATION (British Section)—1 Fox Road, West Bridgford, Nottingham NG2 6AJ—*Chief Exec. Officer*, K. H. Robinson.

INTERNATIONAL SHIPPING FEDERATION (1909), 30–32 St. Mary Axe, EC3A 8ET—*Pres.*, W. N. Menzies-Wilson; *Sec.*, D. A. Dearsley.

INTERNATIONAL STUDENTS TRUST (1962), 229 Great Portland Street, W1N 5HD—*President*, The Duke of Grafton, K.G.; *Sec.*, G. D. Rates.

INTERNATIONAL TIN RESEARCH INSTITUTE (1932)—*Dir.*, B. T. K. Barry, Kingston Lane, Uxbridge, Middx. UB8 3PJ.

INTERNATIONAL UNION FOR LAND VALUE TAXATION AND FREE TRADE, 177 Vauxhall Bridge Road, SW1V 1EU—*Sec.*, Mrs. B. P. Sobrielo.

INTERNATIONAL VOLUNTARY SERVICE (1920), Ceresole House, 53 Regent Road, Leicester LE1 6YL—*Sec.*, M. C. Goldsmith.

INTER-VARSITY CLUBS, ASSOCIATION OF (1946), 26 Chesswood Road, Worthing, W. Sussex BN11 2AD—*Sec.*, M. Rooke-Matthews.

INVALID CHILDREN'S AID NATIONWIDE (I CAN) (1888), Information service on all aspects of handicap; family social work in parts of London and Surrey; residential special schools. Allen Graham House, 198 City Road, EC1V 2PH—*Dir.*, J. McKinnon.

INVALIDS-AT-HOME (1966). Helps seriously disabled people living at home—*Hon. Sec.*, Mrs. E. Pierce, 23 Farm Avenue, NW2 2BJ.

IRAN SOCIETY (1936), 2 Belgrave Square, SW1X 8PJ—*Hon. Sec.*, K. Bradford.

IRISH SOCIETY, THE HONOURABLE THE (1613), Irish Chamber, Guildhall Yard, EC2V 5AE—*Sec.*, B. E. Manning; *Representative (Ireland)*, Cmdr. P. C. D. Campbell, M.V.O.

JAPAN ASSOCIATION (1950), Regis House, 43–46 King William Street, EC4R 9BE—*Exec. Dir.*, Brig. B. G. Hickey, O.B.E., M.C.

JERUSALEM AND THE MIDDLE EAST CHURCH ASSOCIATION, THE (1887)—*Gen. Sec.*, Ven. R. H. Roberts, C.B., The Old Gatehouse, Castle Hill, Farnham, Surrey GU9 0AE.

JEWISH WELFARE BOARD (1859).—*Exec. Dir.*, M. I. Carlowe, 221 Golders Green Road, NW11 9DW.

JEWISH HISTORICAL SOCIETY OF ENGLAND—*Hon. Sec.*, C. M. Drukker, 33 Seymour Place, W1H 5AP.

JEWISH YOUTH, ASSOCIATION FOR (1899), A.J.Y. House, 50 Lindley Street, E1 3AX.—*Exec. Dir.*, A. Greenbat.

JEWS, CHURCH'S MINISTRY AMONG THE, 30c Clarence Road, St. Albans, Herts. AL1 4JJ—*Gen. Dir.*, Rev. J. M. V. Drummond.

JEWS AND CHRISTIANS, LONDON SOCIETY OF (1927), 28 St. John's Wood Road, NW8 7HA—*Pres.*, Rev. Prof. G. Parrinder, D.D., ph.D., D.Litt.; *Joint Chairmen*, Very Rev. Edward F. Carpenter, ph. D., Rabbi Dr. John D. Rayner, D.D.; The Dean of Westminster; *Sec.*, Mrs. E. Nathan.

JOHN INNES INSTITUTE (1910), Colney Lane, Norwich NR4 7UH—*Acting Dir.*, Prof. D. R. Davies.

JOURNALISTS, THE INSTITUTE OF, Bedford Chambers, Covent Garden, WC2E 8HA—*Gen. Sec.*, J. Hart.

JUSTICE (British Section of the International Commission of Jurists) (1957), 95A Chancery Lane, WC2A 1DT—*Dir.*, Ms. L. Levin.

JUSTICES' CLERKS' SOCIETY (1839).—*Hon. Sec.*, B. H. Forster, Magistrates' Court, Cwmbran, Gwent NP44 3YA.

KEEP BRITAIN TIDY GROUP, Bostel House, 37 West Street, Brighton, Sussex BN1 2RE—*Dir. Gen.*, D. J. Lewis.

KING EDWARD'S HOSPITAL FUND FOR LONDON (1897), 14 Palace Court, W2 4HT—Divides its income between: making grants to hospitals and related organizations both within and outside the N.H.S. but confined to those in or serving the Greater London area; developing health services management through the King's Fund College; promoting standards of care and assisting in the formulation of health policy.—*Chairman of Management Committee*, The Hon. H. Astor; *Treasurer*, R. Dent; *Secretary*, R. J. Maxwell, ph.D.

KING GEORGE'S FUND FOR SAILORS (1917), 1 Chesham Street, SW1X 8NF. Supports all seafarers or their dependants in need. Distributes over £100,000 in grants annually.—*Gen. Sec.*, K. Sutherland, R.N.

KIPLING SOCIETY, THE (1927), 18 Northumberland Avenue, WC2N 5BJ—*Hon. Sec.*, N. Entract.

LADIES IN REDUCED CIRCUMSTANCES, SOCIETY FOR THE ASSISTANCE OF (1886), Lancaster House, 25 Hornyold Road, Malvern, Worcs. WR14 1QQ.

LANCASTRIANS IN LONDON, ASSOCIATION OF (1892), Burnley House, 129 Kingsway, WC2B 6NJ—*Hon. Sec.*, J. D. Dwyer.

LANDSCAPE INSTITUTE (Professional Institute for Landscape Architects, Managers and Scientists), 12 Carlton House Terrace, SW1Y 5AH.

LAND-VALUE TAXATION LEAGUE, 177 Vauxhall Bridge Road, SW1V 1EU—*Pres.*, V. G. Saldji.

LAW REPORTING FOR ENGLAND AND WALES, INCORPORATED COUNCIL OF (1865), 3 Stone Buildings, Lincoln's Inn, WC2A 3XN—*Sec.* R. H. Pettit.

LEAGUE OF THE HELPING HAND, Baileys, Church Street, Charlbury, Oxford OX7 3PR.—*Sec.*, Mrs. D. R. Colvin.

LEAGUE OF WELLDOERS (incorporated) (1893), 119–121 Limekiln Lane, Liverpool L5 8SN—*Warden and Sec.*, K. H. Stanton.

LEATHER AND HIDE TRADES' BENEVOLENT INSTITUTION (1860), 60 Wickham Hill, Hurstpierpoint, Sussex BN6 9NP—*Sec.*, Mrs. G. M. Stapleton, M.B.E.

LEGAL EXECUTIVES, INSTITUTE OF, Kempston Manor, Kempston, Bedford MK42 7AB—*Sec. and Chief Exec.*, L. A. Evans.

LEPROSY MISSION, THE (England and Wales) (1874), 50 Portland Place, W1N 3DG—*Chairman*, D. G. Selley; *Exec. Dir.*, The Rev. R. J. Findlay.

LEUKAEMIA RESEARCH FUND (1962), 43 Great Ormond Street, WC1N 3JJ—*Dir.*, G. J. Piller, O.B.E.

LIBRARY ASSOCIATION (1877), 7 Ridgmount Street, WC1E 7AE—*Chief Exec.*, G. Cunningham.

LIFEBOATS. *See* "ROYAL NATIONAL."

LINGUISTS, INSTITUTE OF (1910), 24A Highbury Grove, N5 2EA—*Gen. Sec.*, A. Bell.

LINNEAN SOCIETY OF LONDON (1788), Burlington House, W1V 0LQ—*Exec. Sec.*, Cdr. J. H. Fiddian-Green.

LIONS CLUBS INTERNATIONAL (British Isles & Ireland) (1949).—*Gen. Sec.*, T. L. Packer, 22 Craddock Street, Swansea SA1 3HE.

LIVERPOOL COTTON ASSOCIATION LTD., 620 Cotton Exchange Building, Edmund Street, Liverpool L3 9LH.—*Dir. Gen. and Sec.*, J. Wilson-Smith.

LLOYD'S, Lime Street, EC3M 7HL—*Chairman*, P. N. Miller; *Deputy Chairmen*, W. N. M. Lawrence, A. Parry; *Chief Exec.*, A. Lord, C.B.

LLOYD'S PATRIOTIC FUND (1803), Lloyd's, Lime Street, EC3M 7HA—*Sec.*, Mrs. J. H. Bright.

LLOYD'S REGISTER OF SHIPPING (1760), 71 Fenchurch Street, EC3M 4BS—Office of *Lloyd's Register of Shipping, Rules for the Classification of Ships, Marine and Industrial Inspection Services, Offshore Certification.*—*Secretary*, W. T. Leadbetter.

LOCAL AUTHORITIES, INTERNATIONAL UNION OF (British Section) (1913), (*also* COUNCIL OF EUROPEAN MUNICIPALITIES AND REGIONS (British Section) (1951)), 35 Great Smith Street, SW1P 3BJ—*Exec. Sec.*, P. N. Bongers.

LOCAL AUTHORITY CHIEF EXECUTIVES, SOCIETY OF—*Hon. Sec.*, A. J. Greenwell, County Hall, Northampton, NN1 1DN—*Hon. Sec.*, J. Greenwell.

LONDON APPRECIATION SOCIETY (1932), 17 Manson Mews, SW7 5AF—*Hon. Sec.*, B. Peers.

LONDON BOROUGHS ASSOCIATION (1964), Westminster City Hall, Victoria Street, SW1E 6QP—*Hon. Sec.*, R. G. Brooke.

LONDON CITY MISSION (1835), 175 Tower Bridge Road, SE1 2AH—*Gen. Sec.*, Rev. D. M. Whyte.

LONDON CORNISH ASSOCIATION (1898), *Hon. Gen. Sec.*, N. S. Bunney, 119 Warwick Road, N11 2SR.

LONDON COURT OF INTERNATIONAL ARBITRATION (1892), 75 Cannon Street, EC4N 5BH—*Pres.*, The Rt. Hon. Sir Michael Kerr; *Registrar*, B. W. Vigrass, O.B.E., V.R.D.

LONDON FLOTILLA (Association of Reserve and Retired Officers of The Royal Navy).—*Hon. Sec.*, Lt. Cdr. P. A. G. Norman R.D., R.N.R., Marden Rise, 81 Lower Road, Fetcham, Surrey KT22 9HG.

LONDON LIBRARY, THE (1841), 14 St. James's Square, SW1Y 4LG—*Librarian*, D. Matthews.

LONDON MAGISTRATES' CLERKS' ASSOCIATION (1889), *Hon. Sec.*, Miss C. Glenn, Hampstead Magistrates' Court, Downshire Hill, Hampstead, NW3 1PA.

"LONDON OVER THE BORDER" CHURCH FUND (1878), 53 New Street, Chelmsford, Essex CM1 1NG—*Sec.*, J. C. Reddington.

LONDON PLAYING FIELDS SOCIETY, THE (1890), Boston Manor Playing Field, Boston Gardens, Brentford, Middx. TW8 9LR—*Sec.*, D. C. Northwood.

LONDON SOCIETY, THE, Room U722, The City University, Northampton Square, EC1V 0HB—*Hon. Sec.*, Mrs. J. Vernau.

LORD MAYOR TRELOAR COLLEGE, for education and care of physically handicapped boys and girls. Administered by the Treloar Trust. Holybourne, Nr. Alton, Hants. GU34 4JX—*Headmaster*, A. M. MacPherson.

LORD'S DAY OBSERVANCE SOCIETY (1831), 5 Victory Avenue, Morden, Surrey SM4 6DL—*Gen. Sec.*, J. G. Roberts.

LORD'S TAVERNERS, THE, 1 Chester Street, SW1X 7HP—*Dir.*, Capt. J. A. R. Swainson, O.B.E.

LOTTERIES COUNCIL, THE, 81 Mansel Street, Swansea SA1 5TT—*Hon. Sec.* J. H. Solly.

MAGISTRATES' ASSOCIATION, THE (1920), 28 Fitzroy Square, W1P 6DD—*Sec.*, T. R. P. Rudin.

MAIL USERS' ASSOCIATION, 6 Whitgift Street, Croydon, Surrey CR0 1DH—*Exec. Dir.*, (vacant).

MALAYSIA, SINGAPORE AND BRUNEI ASSOCIATION (1955), 90 Fenchurch Street, EC3M 4BY—*Sec.*, Mrs. J. Taylor.

MALAYSIAN RUBBER PRODUCERS' RESEARCH ASSOCIATION (1938), Tun Abdul Razak Laboratory, Brickendonbury, Hertford SG13 8NL—*Dir.*, Dr. D. Barnard.

MALCOLM SARGENT CANCER FUND FOR CHILDREN.—*Gen. Administrator*, Miss S. Darley, O.B.E., 14 Abingdon Road, W8 6AF.

MALONE SOCIETY (for the publication of scholarly editions and facsimiles of early English dramatic texts and records).—*Hon. Sec.*, Dr. Lois Potter, Dept. of English, University of Leicester LE1 7RH.

MANAGEMENT, BRITISH INSTITUTE OF, Management House, Parker Street, WC2B 5PT—*Dir. Gen.*, Dr. J. Constable.

MANAGEMENT CONSULTANCIES ASSOCIATION (1956), 11 West Halkin Street, SW1X 8JL.—*Exec. Dir.*, B. O'Rorke.

MANAGEMENT AND PROFESSIONAL STAFFS, ASSOCIATION OF, Parkgates, Bury New Road, Prestwich, Manchester M25 8JX—*Exec. Sec.*, Mr. A. J. Casey.

MANAGEMENT SERVICES, INSTITUTE OF, 1 Cecil Court, London Road, Enfield, Middx. EN2 6DD—*Dir. and Gen. Sec.*, E. A. King.

MANORIAL SOCIETY OF GREAT BRITAIN (1906), 104 Kennington Road, SE11 6RE—*Hon. Chairman*, R. A. Smith.

MANPOWER SOCIETY, THE, Freepost, Headington, Oxford OX3 0BR—*Hon. Sec.*, Mrs. B. Hurley.

MARIE CURIE MEMORIAL FOUNDATION (for the welfare of cancer patients), 28 Belgrave Square, SW1X 8QG—*Dir. Gen.*, Maj. Gen. M. E. Carleton-Smith, C.B.E. *Scottish Office*, 21 Rutland Street, Edinburgh EH1 2AH.

MARINE ARTISTS, ROYAL SOCIETY OF (1939), 17 Carlton House Terrace, SW1Y 5BD—*Sec.*, M. Myers.

MARINE BIOLOGICAL ASSOCIATION OF THE UK (1884), The Laboratory, Citadel Hill, Plymouth PL1 2PB—*Sec. to Council and Director of Plymouth Laboratory*, Dr. M. Whitfield.

MARINE ENGINEERS, INSTITUTE OF (1889), 76 Mark Lane, EC3R 7JN—*Sec.*, J. E. Sloggett.

MARINE SOCIETY, THE (1756), 202 Lambeth Road, SE1 7JW—*Gen. Sec.*, Lt. Cdr. R. M. Frampton, R.N.

MARIO LANZA EDUCATIONAL FOUNDATION (for singers)—*Hon. Sec.*, Miss P. Franklin, Flat 21, Chiswick House, 210 Bell Barn Road, Edgbaston, Birmingham B15 2AB.

MARKET AUTHORITIES, NATIONAL ASSOCIATION OF BRITISH.—*Sec.*, B. Ormshaw, 19 Derwent Avenue, Milnrow, Rochdale, Lancs. OL16 3UD.

MARKETING, INSTITUTE OF (1911), Moor Hall, Cookham, Maidenhead, Berks. SL6 9QH—*Dir. Gen.*, T. McBurnie; *Sec.*, W. E. Hinder.

MARK MASTER MASONS, GRAND LODGE OF (1856), Mark Masons' Hall, 86 St. James's Street, SW1A 1PL—*Grand Master*, H.R.H. Prince Michael of Kent; *Grand Sec.*, P. G. Williams.

MASONIC BENEVOLENT INSTITUTION, ROYAL (1842), 20 Great Queen Street, WC2B 5BG—*Sec.*, N. A. Grout.

MASONIC BENEVOLENT INSTITUTIONS IN IRELAND; *Masonic Girls' Benefit Fund* (1792); *Masonic Boys' Benefit Fund* (1867); *Victoria Jubilee Masonic Annuity Fund* (1887).—*Sec.*, R. J. Clinton, 17–19 Molesworth Street, Dublin 2.

MASONIC TRUST FOR GIRLS AND BOYS (1985), 31 Great Queen Street, WC2B 5AG—*Sec.*, Col. R. K. Hind.

MASTER BUILDERS, FEDERATION OF, Gordon Fisher House, 33 John Street, WC1 2BB—*Dir. Gen.*, W. S. Hilton.

MASTERS OF FOXHOUNDS ASSOCIATION (1881)—*Sec.*, A. H. B. Hart, Parsloes Cottage, Bagendon, Cirencester, Glos. GL7 7DU.

MATERNAL AND CHILD WELFARE, NATIONAL ASSOCIATION FOR (1911), 1 South Audley Street, W1Y 6JS—*Gen. Sec.*, W. Rice.

MATHEMATICAL ASSOCIATION (1871), 259 London Road, Leicester LE2 3BE—*Pres.*, Mrs. A. Straker; *Hon. Secs.*, Miss M. M. Lawton; J. A. Goodwin.

MATHEMATICS AND ITS APPLICATIONS, INSTITUTE OF (1964), Maitland House, Warrior Square, Southend-on-Sea, Essex SS1 2JY—*Sec. and Registrar*, Miss C. M. Richards.

MEASUREMENT AND CONTROL, INSTITUTE OF (1944), 87 Gower Street, WC1E 6AA—*Sec. and Chief Exec.*, M. J. Yates.

MECHANICAL ENGINEERS, INSTITUTION OF, 1 Birdcage Walk, S.W.1.—*Sec.*, A. McKay, C.B.

MEDIC-ALERT FOUNDATION. For the protection, in emergencies, of those with a medical disability; to prevent mistakes. 11–13 Clifton Terrace, N4 3JP—*Sec. Gen.*, Mrs. M. L. Stanton.

MEDICAL COUNCIL, GENERAL, 44 Hallam Street, W1N 6AE. *Registrar*, P. L. Towers.

MEDICAL SOCIETY OF LONDON (1773), 11 Chandos Street, W1M 0EB—*Pres.*, J. F. Newcombe, F.R.C.S.; *Hon. Secs.*, R. D. Illingworth, F.R.C.S.; G. Rettie, M.D.; *Registrar*, Maj. T. Tudor-Williams.

MEDICAL WOMEN'S FEDERATION (1917), Tavistock House North, Tavistock Square, WC1H 9HX—*Pres.*, Dr. L. Newman; *Hon. Sec.*, Dr. P. Price.

MEDIEVAL ARCHAEOLOGY, SOCIETY FOR (1957), University College, Gower Street, WC1E 6BT—*Hon. Sec.*, Dr. Helen Clarke.

MEN OF THE TREES (1922), Turners Hill Road, Crawley Down, Crawley, Sussex RH10 4HL—*Exec. Sec.*, Mrs. E. Sandwell.

MENTAL AFTER CARE ASSOCIATION (1879), Eagle House, 110 Jermyn Street, SW1Y 6HB—*Dir.*, B. G. Garner.

MENTAL HEALTH FOUNDATION, THE (1949), 8 Hallam Street, W1N 6DH—*Dir.*, Maj. Gen. R. B. Loudoun, C.B., O.B.E.

MERCHANT NAVY WELFARE BOARD, 19–21 Lancaster Gate, W2 3LN—*Gen. Sec.*, J. I. K. Walker.

METALS, THE INSTITUTE OF (1985), 1 Carlton House Terrace, SW1Y 5DB—*Sec.*, Sir Geoffrey Ford, K.B.E., C.B.

METEOROLOGICAL SOCIETY, ROYAL (1850), James Glaisher House, Grenville Place, Bracknell, Berks., RG12 1BX—*Pres.*, Prof. R. S. Scorer; *Hon. Secs.*, D. N. Axford, PH.D.; I. N. James, PH.D.; G. J. Jenkins, PH.D.

METROPOLITAN AND CITY POLICE ORPHANS FUND (1870), 30 Hazlewell Road, SW15 6LH—*Sec.*, R. Duff-Cole, B.E.M.

METROPOLITAN AUTHORITIES, ASSOCIATION OF (1974), 35 Great Smith Street, SW1P 3BJ—*Sec.*, A. Gronow.

METROPOLITAN HOSPITAL-SUNDAY FUND (1872), 40 High Street, Teddington, Middx., TW11 8EW. In 1986, £35,816 was distributed to N.H.S. hospitals in the form of Samaritan Fund grants, special grants and long stay/geriatric patient holiday grants through hospital social workers. £158,780 was distributed to hospitals outside the N.H.S., and £40,900 to other medical charities for specific purposes.—*Sec.*, D. A. B. Lynch.

METROPOLITAN PUBLIC GARDENS ASSOCIATION (1882)—*Sec.*, Mrs. J. Bellamy, 3 Mayfield Road, Thornton Heath, Croydon CR4 6DN.

MIDDLE EAST ASSOCIATION, THE (1961), 33 Bury Street, SW1Y 6AX—*Dir.-Gen.*, Sir James Craig, G.C.M.G.; *Sec.*, Miss L. V. Marsh-Smith.

MIDWIVES, ROYAL COLLEGE OF (1881), 15 Mansfield Street, W1M 0BE—*Gen. Sec.*, Miss R. M. Ashton.

MIGRAINE TRUST (1965), 45 Great Ormond Street, WC1N 3HD—*Dir.*, Cdr. O. Wright.

MILITARY HISTORICAL SOCIETY, National Army Museum, Royal Hospital Road, SW3 4HT, *Hon. Sec.*, J. Gaylor.

MIND (National Association for Mental Health), 22 Harley Street, W1N 2ED—*Dir.*, C. Heginbotham.

MINERALOGICAL SOCIETY (1876)—*Pres.*, Dr. D. J. Vaughan; *Hon. Gen. Sec.*, Dr. M. G. Bown, 41 Queen's Gate, SW7 5HR.

MINES OF GREAT BRITAIN, FEDERATION OF SMALL, Northcote Chambers, 13A King Street, Newcastle-under-Lyme, Staffs. ST5 1ER—*Sec.*, R. W. Bladen.

MINIATURE PAINTERS, SCULPTORS AND GRAVERS, ROYAL SOCIETY OF (1895), Westminster Gallery, Westminster Central Hall, SW1H 9NU—*Pres.*, Mrs. S. Lucas; *Sec.*, Ms. P. Gyles.

MINIATURISTS, SOCIETY OF (1895), Castle Gallery, Castle Hill, Ilkley, West Yorks. LS29 9DT—*Dir.*, L. Simpson.

MINING AND METALLURGY, INSTITUTION OF (1892), 44 Portland Place, W1N 4BR—*Sec.* M. J. Jones.

MINING ENGINEERS, THE INSTITUTION OF (1889), 6A South Parade, Doncaster DN1 2DY—*Sec.*, W. J. W. Bourne.

MINING INSTITUTE OF SCOTLAND, c/o British Coal Corporation, Green Park, Greenend, Edinburgh, EH17 7PZ—*Sec.*, E. R. Rodger.

MISSIONS TO SEAMEN, THE, St. Michael Paternoster Royal, College Hill EC4R 2RL—*Gen. Sec.*, Canon W. J. D. Down.

MODERN CHURCHPEOPLE'S UNION (1898), for the advancement of liberal religious thought—*Pres.*, Rev. E. Carpenter; *Hon. Sec.*, Very Rev. R. C. Truss, The Rectory, Church Square, Shepperton, Middx. TW17 9JY.

MODERN LANGUAGE ASSOCIATION, Regent's College, Inner Circle, Regent's Park, NW1 4NS—*Gen. Sec.*, Miss E. Ingham.

MONUMENTAL BRASS SOCIETY (1887), *Hon. Sec.*, W. Mendelsson, 57 Leeside Crescent, NW11 0HA.

MORAVIAN MISSIONS, LONDON ASSOCIATION IN AID OF (1817), Moravian Church House, 5–7 Muswell Hill, N10 3TJ—*Sec.*, Rev. F. J. C. Smith.

MOTOR INDUSTRY, THE INSTITUTE OF THE, Fanshaws, Brickendon, Hertford SG13 8PQ—*Sec.*, F. W. Janes.

MOUNTBATTEN MEMORIAL TRUST (1979), 18 Northumberland Avenue, WC2N 5BJ—*Dir. and Sec.*, Mrs. S. Barnett, O.B.E.

MOUNTBATTEN TRUST, THE EDWINA 1 Grosvenor Crescent, SW1X 7EF—*Sec.*, J. Boyd-Brent.

MULTIPLE SCLEROSIS SOCIETY, 25 Effie Road, SW6 1EE—*Gen. Sec.*, J. Walford.

MUSEUMS ASSOCIATION (1889), 34 Bloomsbury Way, WC1A 2SF—*Dir. Gen.*, G. Farnell.

MUSICIANS BENEVOLENT FUND, 16 Ogle Street W1P 7LG—*Sec.*, M. B. M. Williams.

MUSICIANS, INCORPORATED SOCIETY OF (1882) 10 Stratford Place, W1N 9AE—*Gen. Sec.*, D. E. Padgett-Chandler.

MUSICIANS OF GREAT BRITAIN, ROYAL SOCIETY OF (1738), 10 Stratford Place, W1N 9AE—*Sec.*, Mrs. M. E. Gleed, M.B.E.

MUSIC SOCIETIES, NATIONAL FEDERATION OF (1935), Francis House, Francis Street, SW1P 1DE—*Administrator*, R. Jones.

NATIONAL ADULT SCHOOL ORGANISATION (1899), Norfolk House, Smallbrook Queensway, Birmingham B5 4LJ—*Sec.*, W. J. Scarle.

NATIONAL AND UNIVERSITY LIBRARIES, STANDING CONFERENCE OF (SCONUL) (1950), 102 Euston Street, NW1 2HA—*Sec.*, A. J. Loveday.

NATIONAL ASSOCIATION OF ESTATE AGENTS (1962), Arbon House, 21 Jury Street, Warwick CV34 4EH—*Sec.*, A. B. Clark.

NATIONAL ASSOCIATION OF LOCAL COUNCILS (1947), 108 Great Russell Street, WC1B 3LD—*Gen. Sec.*, J. Clark.

NATIONAL BENEVOLENT INSTITUTION (1812), 61 Bayswater Road, W2 3PG—*Sec.*, Air Cmdre, D. C. Saunders, C.B.E., A.F.C.

NATIONAL BIRTHDAY TRUST FUND (1928), 57 Lower Belgrave Street, SW1W 0LR. For extension of maternity services.—*Sec.*, Mrs. M. C. Matthews.

NATIONAL CATTLE BREEDERS' ASSOCIATION, 106 High Street, Tring, Herts. HP23 4AF—*Sec.*, M. L. Keeble.

NATIONAL CHILDBIRTH TRUST, THE, (1956), 9 Queensborough Terrace, W2 3TB—*Nat. Sec.*, Mrs. H. Corbishley.

NATIONAL CHILDREN'S HOME (1869), 85 Highbury Park, N5 1UD. Supports over 10,000 able and disabled children and their parents annually in residential and day centres, special schools, foster homes and alternative-to-custody centres, and through counselling services in Great Britain and the third world.—*Principal*, Rev. M. Newman.

NATIONAL CHRISTIAN EDUCATION COUNCIL, Robert Denholm House, Nutfield, Redhill, Surrey RH1 4HW—*Exec. Officer*, E. A. Thorn.

NATIONAL COUNCIL FOR VOLUNTARY ORGANISATIONS, 26 Bedford Square, WC1B 3HU—*Dir.*, Ms. U. Prashar.

NATIONAL COUNCIL OF WOMEN OF GREAT BRITAIN (1895), 34 Lower Sloane Street, SW1W 8BP—*Sec.*, Mrs. J. D. Norman; *Pres.*, Mrs. E. Martin.

NATIONAL FEDERATION OF RETIREMENT PENSIONS ASSOCIATIONS, (PENSIONERS' VOICE), 91 Preston New Road, Blackburn, Lancs. BB2 6BD—*Sec.*, G. Dunn.

NATIONAL FEDERATION OF SELF EMPLOYED AND SMALL BUSINESSES LTD. (1974), 32 St. Annes Road West,

Lytham St. Annes, Lancs. FY8 1NY—*National Chairman*, B. A. Prime.

NATIONAL FEDERATION OF YOUNG FARMERS' CLUBS, THE, Y.F.C. Centre, National Agricultural Centre, Kenilworth, Warwicks. CV8 2LG—*Gen. Sec. and Treasurer*, F. E. Shields, M.B.E.

NATIONAL LIGHT HORSE BREEDING SOCIETY (1885), 96 High Street, Edenbridge, Kent TN8 5AR—*Sec.*, G. W. Evans.

NATIONAL MARKET TRADERS' FEDERATION (1899), Hampton House, Hawshaw Lane, Hoyland, Barnsley S74 0HA—*Gen. Sec.*, R. J. Toller.

NATIONAL MARRIAGE GUIDANCE COUNCIL, Herbert Gray College, Little Church Street, Rugby, Warwicks CV21 3AP—*Dir.*, D. French.

NATIONAL MONUMENTS RECORD (1941), Royal Commission on Historical Monuments of England, 23 Savile Row, W1X 1AB—*Sec.*, T. G. Hassall, F.S.A.

NATIONAL OPERATIC AND DRAMATIC ASSOCIATION (1899), 1 Crestfield Street, WC1H 8AU—*Gen. Administrator*, B. Clarke.

NATIONAL PEACE COUNCIL (1908), 29 Great James Street, WC1N 3ES—*Coordinator*, A. McLeod.

NATIONAL PURE WATER ASSOCIATION.—*Sec.*, N. Brugge, Bank Farm, Aston Pigott, Westbury, Shrewsbury SY5 9HH.

NATIONAL SECULAR SOCIETY (1866), 702 Holloway Road, N19 3NL—*Gen. Sec.*, T. Mullins.

NATIONAL SOCIETY FOR CLEAN AIR (1899), 136 North Street, Brighton, E. Sussex BN1 1RG—*Sec.-Gen.*, Air Cmdre. J. Langston, C.B.E.

NATIONAL SOCIETY, THE, (1811), for promoting religious education (Church of England). Church House, Great Smith Street, SW1P 3NZ—*Gen. Sec.*, C. Alves.

NATIONAL SOCIETY FOR THE PREVENTION OF CRUELTY TO CHILDREN (1884), 67 Saffron Hill, EC1N 8RS—*Chairman*, M. R. N. Moore; *Hon. Treas.*, Sir Mark Weinberg; *Dir.*, Dr. A. Gilmour, C.B.E.; *Sec.*, P. R. Fish.

NATIONAL UNION OF STUDENTS, 461 Holloway Road N7 6LJ—*Nat. Sec.*, A. Long.

NATIONAL VIEWERS' AND LISTENERS' ASSOCIATION.—*President*, Mrs. M. Whitehouse, C.B.E, Ardleigh, Colchester, Essex CO7 7RH.

NATION'S FUND FOR NURSES, 57 Lower Belgrave Street, SW1W 0LR—*Administrator*, P. E. Starr.

NATURE CONSERVATION, ROYAL SOCIETY FOR (1912).—*Gen. Sec.*, Dr. F. H. Perring, The Green, Nettleham, Lincoln LN2 2NR.

NAUTICAL RESEARCH, SOCIETY FOR (1911), c/o National Maritime Museum, Greenwich, SE10 9NF—*Hon. Sec.*, Lt. Cdr. L. Phillipps.

NAVAL, MILITARY AND AIR FORCE BIBLE SOCIETY (1780), Radstock House, 3 Eccleston Street, SW1W 9LZ Copies and portions of the Scriptures circulated to the Forces (1986), 214,372—*Gen. Sec.*, R. Kennedy.

NAVAL ARCHITECTS, ROYAL INSTITUTION OF (1860), 10 Upper Belgrave Street, SW1X 8BQ—*Sec.*, P. W. Ayling.

NAVIGATION, ROYAL INSTITUTE OF, c/o The Royal Geographical Society, 1 Kensington Gore, SW7 2AT. *Dir.*, Rear Adm. R. M. Burgoyne, C.B.

NAVY RECORDS SOCIETY, Public Record Office, Chancery Lane, WC2A 1LR. Publishes editions of historical documents relating to the Royal Navy.—*Hon. Sec.*, Dr. N. A. M. Rodger.

NEWCOMEN SOCIETY (1920), for the study of the history of engineering and technology, Science Museum, SW7 2DD—*Exec. Sec.*, I. McNeil.

NEW ENGLISH ART CLUB (1886), 17 Carlton House Terrace, SW1Y 5BD—*Sec.*, W. Bowyer, R.A.

NEWSAGENTS, NATIONAL FEDERATION OF RETAIL, Yeoman House, Sekforde Street, Clerkenwell Green, EC1R 0HD—*Chief Exec.*, K. E. J. Peters.

NEWSPAPER EDITORS, GUILD OF BRITISH (1946),

Bloomsbury House, Bloomsbury Square, 74–77 Great Russell Street, WC1B 3DA—*Pres.*, K. Parker; *Sec.-Treas.*, C. Gordon Page.

NEWSPAPER PRESS FUND (1864), Dickens House, 35 Wathen Road, Dorking, Surrey RH4 1JY.—*Dir. and Sec.*, P. W. Evans.

NEWSPAPER SOCIETY (1836), Whitefriars House, 6 Carmelite Street, EC4Y 0BL—*Pres.*, D. R. Thomas (*North Wales Newspapers Ltd., Oswestry*); *Dir.*, D. Nisbet-Smith.

NEWSVENDORS' BENEVOLENT INSTITUTION (1839), P.O. Box 306, Dunmow, Essex CM6 1HY.—*Sec.*, (vacant).

NOISE ABATEMENT SOCIETY, P.O. Box 8, Bromley, Kent BR2 0UH.—*Chairman*, J. Connell.

NON-SMOKERS, NATIONAL SOCIETY OF (1926), Latimer House, 40–48 Hanson Street, W1P 7DE—*Hon. Sec.*, T. Hurst.

NORTHERN IRELAND TOURIST BOARD, River House, 48 High Street, Belfast BT1 2DS—*Chief Exec.*, S. Belford.

NORWOOD CHILD CARE (Jewish Welfare Organization for Jewish children), 221 Golders Green Road, NW11 9DL—*Exec. Dir.*, S. Brier.

NUCLEAR ENERGY SOCIETY, BRITISH (1962), 1—7 Great George Street, SW1P 3AA—*Exec. Officer*, P. Bacos.

NUFFIELD FOUNDATION (1943), 28 Bedford Square, WC1B 3EG—*Dir.*, J. P. Cornford.

NUFFIELD PROVINCIAL HOSPITALS TRUST (1939), 3 Prince Albert Road, NW1 7SP—*Gen. Sec.*, Dr. M. Ashley-Miller.

NUMISMATIC SOCIETY, BRITISH.—*Hon. Sec.*, W. Slayter, 63 West Way, Edgware, Middx. HA8 9LA.

NUMISMATIC SOCIETY, ROYAL, c/o Dept. of Coins and Medals, The British Museum, Great Russell Street, WC1B 3DG—*Pres.*, J. P. C. Kent, PH.D., F.B.A., F.S.A.; *Hon. Secs.*, A. Burnett, PH.D., F.S.A.; J. E. Cribb.

NURSES', RETIRED, NATIONAL HOME, Riverside Avenue, Bournemouth BH7 7EE—*Chairman*, Dr. R. E. Chaplin.

NURSES, ROYAL NATIONAL PENSION FUND FOR, 15 Buckingham Street, WC2—*General Manager and Actuary*, V. G. West.

NURSING, MIDWIFERY AND HEALTH VISITING, U.K. CENTRAL COUNCIL FOR, 23 Portland Place, W1N 3AF—*Registrar and Chief Exec.*, C. Ralph.
England.—Victory House, 170 Tottenham Court Road, W1P 0HA.
Wales.—Floor 13 Pearl Assurance House, Greyfriars Road, Cardiff CF1 3AG.
Scotland.—22 Queen Street, Edinburgh EH2 1JX.
N.Ireland—RAC House, 79 Chichester Street, Belfast BT1 4JE.

NURSING, ROYAL COLLEGE OF, 20 Cavendish Square, W1M 0AB—*Gen. Sec.*, T. Clay.

NUTRITION SOCIETY (1941).—*Hon. Sec.*, Dr. Margaret Ashwell, Grosvenor Gardens House, 35–37 Grosvenor Gardens, SW1W 0BS.

OBSTETRICIANS AND GYNAECOLOGISTS, ROYAL COLLEGE OF (1929), 27 Sussex Place, NW1 4RG—*Pres.*, G. Pinker; *College Administrator*, P. Barnett.

OCCUPATIONAL SAFETY AND HEALTH, INSTITUTION OF, 222 Uppingham Road, Leicester LE5 0QG—*Sec.*, J. R. Barrell.

OFFICERS' ASSOCIATION, THE (1920), 48 Pall Mall, SW1Y 5JY. Affords relief to ex-officers of the Royal Navy, Army and R.A.F. and their widows and dependants in distress; helps unemployed ex-officers to find employment.—*Gen. Sec.*, Brig. P. D. Johnson.

OFFICERS' FAMILIES FUND (1899), 48 Pall Mall, SW1Y 5JY—*Sec.*, Mrs. I. C. Riley.

OFFICERS' PENSIONS SOCIETY, LTD., 15 Buckingham Gate, SW1E 6NS—*Gen. Sec.*, Maj. Gen. L. W. A. Gingell, C.B., O.B.E.

OIL PAINTERS, ROYAL INSTITUTE OF (1883), 18 Upper Ashlyns Road, Berkhamsted, Herts. HP4 3BW—*Sec.*, Ms. J. Easterling.

OILSEED, OIL AND FEEDINGSTUFFS TRADES BENEVOLENT ASSOCIATION, THE, 14–20 St. Mary Axe, EC3A 8BU—*Sec.*, R. T. Wheelans.

ONE PARENT FAMILIES, NATIONAL COUNCIL FOR, 255 Kentish Town Road, NW5 2LX—*Dir.*, Miss S. Slipman.

OPEN-AIR MISSION, THE (1853), 19 John Street, WC1N 2DL—*Sec.*, A. J. Greenbank.

OPEN SPACES SOCIETY (COMMONS, OPEN SPACES AND FOOTPATHS PRESERVATION SOCIETY) (1865), 25A Bell Street, Henley-on-Thames, Oxon RG9 2BA—*Gen. Sec.*, Miss K. Ashbrook.

OPTICAL COUNCIL, GENERAL, 41 Harley Street, W1N 2DJ—*Registrar*, R. D. Wilshin.

ORDERS AND MEDALS RESEARCH SOCIETY.—*Gen. Sec.*, N. G. Gooding, 123 Turnpike Link, Croydon CR0 5NU.

ORIENTAL CERAMIC SOCIETY (1921), 31B Torrington Square, WC1E 7LJ—*Sec.*, Vice Admiral Sir John Gray, K.B.E., C.B.

ORNITHOLOGISTS' CLUB, THE SCOTTISH, 21 Regent Terrace, Edinburgh EH7 5BT.—*Sec.*, J. C. Davies.

ORNITHOLOGISTS' UNION, BRITISH, c/o Zoological Society of London, Regent's Park, NW1 4RY—*Hon. Sec.*, Dr. D. C. Houston.

ORNITHOLOGY, BRITISH TRUST FOR (1932), Beech Grove, Tring, Herts. HP23 5NR—*Administrator*, J. C. G. Wolf.

ORTHOPÆDIC ASSOCIATION, BRITISH (1918), at the Royal College of Surgeons, 35–43 Lincoln's Inn Fields, WC2A 3PN—*Hon. Sec.*, C. E. Ackroyd.

OSTEOPATHIC MEDICINE, LONDON COLLEGE OF, 8–10 Boston Place, NW1 6QH.

OUTWARD BOUND TRUST, Chestnut Field, Regent Place, Rugby CV21 2PJ—*Dir.*, I. L. Fothergill.

OVERSEAS DEVELOPMENT INSTITUTE (1960), Regent's College, Inner Circle, Regent's Park, NW1 4NS.

OVERSEAS SERVICE PENSIONERS' ASSOCIATION (1960), 63 Church Road, Hove, Sussex BN3 2BD—*Sec.*, C. D. Stenton.

OVERSEAS SETTLEMENT, CHURCH OF ENGLAND BOARD FOR SOCIAL RESPONSIBILITY (1925), Church House, Dean's Yard, SW1P 3NZ—*Admin.-Sec.*, Miss P. J. Hallett.

OXFAM (1942), 274 Banbury Road, Oxford OX2 7DZ—*Dir.*, F. Judd.

OXFORD PRESERVATION TRUST (1927), 10 Turn Again Lane, St. Ebbes, Oxford OX1 1QL—*Sec.*, Mrs. H. E. Turner.

OXFORD SOCIETY (1932), 8 Wellington Square, Oxford OX1 2HY—*Sec.*, Dr. H. A. Hurren.

PAEDIATRIC ASSOCIATION, BRITISH, 5 St. Andrews Place, NW1 4LB—*Hon. Sec.*, Dr. T. L. Chambers.

PAINTER-ETCHERS AND ENGRAVERS, ROYAL SOCIETY OF (1880), Bankside Gallery, 48 Hopton Street, SE1 9JH—*Pres.*, H. N. Eccleston, O.B.E.; *Sec.*, M. Spender.

PAINTERS IN WATER COLOURS, ROYAL INSTITUTE OF (1831), 17 Carlton House Terrace, S.W.1.—*Pres.*, C. Bone.

PAINTERS IN WATER COLOURS, ROYAL SOCIETY OF (1804), Bankside Gallery, 48 Hopton Street, SE1 9JH—*Pres.*, C. Bartlett; *Sec.*, M. Spender.

PALÆONTOGRAPHICAL SOCIETY (1847). *Sec.*, F. G. Dimes, c/o British Geological Survey, Keyworth, Nottingham NG12 5GG—*Sec.*, S. P. Tunnicliff.

PALÆONTOLOGICAL ASSOCIATION (1957).—*Sec.*, Dr. P. W. Skelton, Dept. of Earth Sciences, Open University, Milton Keynes MK7 6AA.

PARKINSON'S DISEASE SOCIETY (1969), 36 Portland Place, W1N 3DG—*Exec. Dir.*, C. A. A. Kilmister.

PARLIAMENTARY AND SCIENTIFIC COMMITTEE, 30 Farringdon Street, EC4A 4EA—*Sec.*, A. Butler.

PASTORAL PSYCHOLOGY, GUILD OF (1936).—*Hon. Sec.*, Mrs. M. Ditchfield, 37 Hogarth Hill, NW11 6AY.

PATENT AGENTS, CHARTERED INSTITUTE OF (1882), Staple Inn Buildings, High Holborn, WC1V 7PZ—*Sec. and Registrar*, Miss M. E. Poole.

PATENTEES AND INVENTORS, INSTITUTE OF (1919), Triumph House, 189 Regent Street, W1R 7WF—*Sec.*, J. R. Kay.

PATHOLOGISTS, ROYAL COLLEGE OF, 2 Carlton House Terrace, SW1Y 5AF—*Sec.*, Miss B. A. Prideaux.

PATIENTS ASSOCIATION (1963), Room 33, 18 Charing Cross Road, WC2H 0HR—*Chairman*, Dame Elizabeth Ackroyd, D.B.E.

PEAK AND NORTHERN FOOTPATHS SOCIETY (1894)—*Chairman*, L. G. Meadowcroft; *Hon. Gen. Sec.*, D. Taylor, 15 Parkfield Drive, Tyldesley, Manchester M29 8NR.

PEARSON'S HOLIDAY FUND, 2A Amity Grove, Raynes Park, SW20 0LH—*Gen. Sec.*, G. P. Holloway.

PEDESTRIANS' ASSOCIATION, 1–5 Wandsworth Road, SW8 2XX—*Chairman*, C. Myerscough.

P.E.N., INTERNATIONAL (1921), 38 King Street, WC2E 8JT. World association of writers.—*International Sec.*, A. Blokh.

PENSION FUNDS, NATIONAL ASSOCIATION OF, LTD (1923), 12–18 Grosvenor Gardens, SW1W 0DH—*Dir. Gen.*, M. Elton; *Sec.*, B. W. Lofthouse.

PEOPLE'S DISPENSARY FOR SICK ANIMALS (1917), PDSA House, South Street, Dorking, Surrey RH4 2LB—*Gen. Sec.*, M. R. Curtis, M.B.E.

PERFORMING RIGHT SOCIETY LTD. (1914), 29–33 Berners Street, W1P 4AA—*Chief Exec.*, M. J. Freegard; *Sec.*, Ms. R. Beltram.

PERIODICAL PUBLISHERS ASSOCATION LTD., Imperial House, 15–19 Kingsway, WC2B 6UN—*Exec. Dir.*, M. J. Finley.

PESTALOZZI CHILDREN'S VILLAGE TRUST, Sedlescombe, Battle, E. Sussex TN33 0RR—*Warden*, A. G. Hatter.

PHARMACEUTICAL SOCIETY OF GREAT BRITAIN, 1 Lambeth High Street, S.E.1.—*Sec. and Registrar*, D. F. Lewis, O.B.E.

PHARMACOLOGICAL SOCIETY, BRITISH.—*Hon. Gen. Sec.*, Dr. G. N. Woodruff, Merck Sharp and Dohme Research Laboratories, Neuroscience Research Centre, Terlings Park, Eastwick Road, Harlow, Essex CM20 2QR.

PHILOLOGICAL SOCIETY (1842).—*Hon. Sec.*, Prof. R. H. Robins, School of Oriental and African Studies, Malet Street, WC1E 7HP.

PHILOSOPHY, ROYAL INSTITUTE OF, 14 Gordon Square, WC1H 0AG—*Director*, Prof. A. Phillips Griffiths.

PHOTOGRAMMETRIC SOCIETY (1952)—*Hon. Sec.*, Dr. A. S. Walker., Survey and General Instrument Co. Ltd., Fircroft Way, Edenbridge, Kent TN8 6HA.

PHOTOGRAPHY, BRITISH INSTITUTE OF PROFESSIONAL (1901), Amwell End, Ware, Herts. SG12 9HN—*Sec.*, P. A. Large.

PHYSICAL EDUCATION ASSOCIATION OF GREAT BRITAIN AND N. IRELAND, 162 King's Cross Road, WC1X 9DH—*Gen. Sec.*, (vacant).

PHYSICAL RECREATION, CENTRAL COUNCIL OF (1935), Francis House, Francis Street, SW1P 1DE—*Gen. Sec.*, P. Lawson.

PHYSICIANS, ROYAL COLLEGE OF (1518), 11 St. Andrew's Place, NW1 4LE—*Pres.*, Sir Raymond Hoffenberg, K.B.E., M.D., Ph.D., F.R.C.P.; *Treas.*, A. M. Dawson, M.D., F.R.C.P.; *Registrar*, D. A. Pyke, C.B.E., M.D., F.R.C.P.; *Sec.*, D. B. Lloyd.

PHYSICIANS AND SURGEONS, ROYAL COLLEGE OF (Glasgow) (1599), 234–242 St. Vincent Street, Glasgow G2 5RJ—*Pres.*, Prof. A. C. Kennedy, M.D.; *Hon. Sec.*, Dr. A. D. Beattie.

PHYSICIANS OF EDINBURGH, ROYAL COLLEGE OF (1681),

9 Queen Street, Edinburgh EH2 1JQ—*Pres.*, Prof. M. F. Oliver, C.B.E.; *Sec.*, Dr. J. L. Anderton.

PHYSICS, INSTITUTE OF (1874), 47 Belgrave Square, SW1X 8QX—*Sec.*, L. Cohen, Ph.D.

PHYSIOLOGICAL SOCIETY (1876)—*Hon. Sec.*, Prof. A. Angel, Dept. of Physiology, The University, Sheffield S10 2TN.

PHYSIOTHERAPY, THE CHARTERED SOCIETY OF (1894), 14 Bedford Row, WC1R 4ED—*Sec.*, T. Simon.

PIG BREEDERS ASSOCIATION, NATIONAL (1884), 7 Rickmansworth Road, Watford, Herts. WD1 7HE—*Chief Exec.*, G. E. Welsh.

PILGRIM TRUST, THE (1930), Fielden House, Little College Street, SW1P 3SH—*Sec.*, Hon. A. H. Millar.

PILGRIMS OF GREAT BRITAIN, THE (1902), Savoy Hotel WC2—*Pres.*, The Rt. Hon. Lord Carrington, K.G., C.H., K.C.M.G., M.C.; *Hon. Sec.*, Lt. Col. S. W. Chant-Sempill, O.B.E., M.C.

PLANT ENGINEERS, INSTITUTION OF, 138 Buckingham Palace Road, SW1W 9SG—*Sec. Gen.*, J. K. Bennett.

PLASTICS AND RUBBER INSTITUTE, THE (1921), 11 Hobart Place, SW1W 0HL—*Sec.-Gen.* G. W. Stockdale.

PLAYING CARD SOCIETY, THE INTERNATIONAL (1972), 188 Sheen Lane, SW14 8LF—*Sec.*, F. M. Collett.

PLAYING FIELDS ASSOCIATION, NATIONAL (1925), 25 Ovington Square, SW3 1LQ—*Chairman*, A. C. Gilmour; *Director Gen.*, C. W. McFadyean.

P.N.E.U., WORLD-WIDE EDUCATION SERVICE OF THE (1888), Strode House, 44/50 Osnaburgh Street, NW1 3NN—*Dir.*, H. Boulter.

POETRY SOCIETY (1909), 21 Earl's Court Square, SW5 9DE—*Dir. and Gen. Sec.*, P. Ralph.

POLICY STUDIES INSTITUTE, 100 Park Village East, NW1 3SR—*Dir.*, W. W. Daniel

POLYTECHNICS, COMMITTEE OF DIRECTORS OF, Kirkman House, 12–14 Whitfield Street, W1P 5RD—*Chairman*, Dr. R. M. W. Rickett, C.B.E.; *Sec.*, Dr. M. S. Lewis.

POLYTECHNIC TEACHERS, ASSOCIATION OF (1973), Caxton Chambers, 81 Albert Road, Southsea, Hants. PO5 2SG—*Chief Exec.*, M. Douglass.

POST OFFICE USERS' NATIONAL COUNCIL (1970), Waterloo Bridge House, Waterloo Road, SE1 8UA—*Sec.*, J. F. Heath.

POULTRY CLUB OF GREAT BRITAIN, THE (1877) *Sec.*, Mrs. M. A. Carefoot, Cliveden, Sandy Bank Farm, Chipping, Preston, Lancs. PR3 2GA.

PRAYER BOOK SOCIETY, THE (1975), 40 Great Smith Street, SW1P 3BU—*Hon. Sec.*, Miss E. M. Gwyer.

PRECEPTORS, COLLEGE OF, Coppice Row, Theydon Bois, Epping, Essex CM16 7DN. Membership is admitted to practising educationalists; Fellowships are reserved for those who have made an outstanding contribution to education.—*Chief Admin. Officer*, P. R. Daniels.

PREPARATORY SCHOOLS, INCORPORATED ASSOCIATION OF, 138 Kensington Church Street, W8 4BN—*Sec.*, J. M. C. Coates.

PRE-SCHOOL PLAYGROUPS ASSOCIATION.—61–63 Kings Cross Road, WC1X 9LL—*Gen. Sec.*, Ms. M. Marshall.

PRESS ASSOCIATION (1868), 85 Fleet Street EC4P 4BE—*Chairman*, J. Evans (*Thompson Regional Newspapers Ltd.*); *General Manager*, I. H. N. Yates; *Sec.*, E. G. Rhodes.

PRINCESS LOUISE SCOTTISH HOSPITAL (Erskine Hospital) for disabled ex-servicemen and women (1916), Bishopton, Renfrewshire PA7 5PU—*Commandant*, Col. W. K. Shepherd; *Treasurer*, I. W. Grimmond.

PRINTERS' CHARITABLE CORPORATION (1827), 20 West Street, Reigate, Surrey RH2 9BS. Homes for elderly printers and widows at Basildon and Bletchley, holidays and convalescence, and direct benefits for those of the printing and allied trades who are in need following retirement, and help for one parent children throughout schooling.—*Dir. & Sec.*, Cpt. D. J. Bradby, R.N. (*retd*).

PRINTING HISTORICAL SOCIETY (1964), St. Bride Institute, Bride Lane, EC4Y 8EE—*Hon. Sec.*, C. L. Hicks.

PRINTING, INSTITUTE OF (1961), 8 Lonsdale Gardens, Tunbridge Wells, Kent TN1 1NU—*Sec.*, C. F. Partridge.

PRISON VISITORS, NATIONAL ASSOCIATION OF (1922), 46B Hartington Street, Bedford MK41 7RP—*Gen. Sec.*, Mrs. A. G. McKenna.

PRIVATE LIBRARIES ASSOCIATION (1957)—*Hon. Sec.*, F. Broomhead, Ravelston, South View Road, Pinner, Middx. HA5 3YD.

PROCURATORS IN GLASGOW, ROYAL FACULTY OF (1600).—*Treas., Clerk and Fiscal*, J. H. Sinclair, 12 Nelson Mandela Place, Glasgow G2 1BT.

PRODUCTION CONTROL, INSTITUTE OF, National Westminster House, Wood Street, Stratford-upon-Avon, Warks. CV37 6JF—*Gen. Sec.*, K. Roberts.

PRODUCTION ENGINEERS, INSTITUTION OF, Rochester House, 66 Little Ealing Lane, W5 4XX—*Sec.*, R. J. Miskin.

PROFESSIONAL CLASSES AID COUNCIL, 10 St. Christopher's Place, W1M 6HY—*Sec.*, Mrs. G. A. Burgess.

PROFESSIONAL ENGINEERS, U.K. ASSOCIATION OF, Hayes Court, West Common Road, Bromley, Kent BR2 7AU—*Sec.*, C. K. Hickling.

PROFESSIONAL FOOTBALLERS' ASSOCIATION, 2 Oxford Court, Bishopsgate, Lower Mosely Street, Manchester M2 3WQ—*Sec.*, G. Taylor.

PROFESSIONS SUPPLEMENTARY TO MEDICINE, COUNCIL FOR, Park House, 184 Kennington Park Road, SE11 4BU—*Registrar*, F. Whitehill.

PROPAGATION OF THE GOSPEL, UNITED SOCIETY FOR THE (U.S.P.G.), Partnership House, 157 Waterloo Road, SE1 8XA—*Sec.*, Rev. Canon H. V. Taylor.

PROTECTION OF LIFE FROM FIRE, SOCIETY FOR THE (1836), 140 Aldersgate Street, EC1A 4HX—*Sec.*, E. H. Gledhill.

PROTESTANT ALLIANCE, THE (1845), 112 Colin Gardens, NW9 6ER—*Gen. Sec.*, Rev. A. G. Ashdown.

PROVINCIAL NOTARIES SOCIETY (1907), P.O. Box 102, Amersham, Bucks. HP7 0QB—*Sec.*, P. D. Leonard.

PSORIASIS ASSOCIATION, THE (1968), 7 Milton Street, Northampton NN2 7JG—*Nat. Sec.*, Mrs. L. A. Henley.

PSYCHIATRISTS, ROYAL COLLEGE OF (1971) 17 Belgrave Square, SW1X 8PG—*Registrar*, Prof. R. G. Priest.

PSYCHICAL RESEARCH, SOCIETY FOR (1882), 1 Adam and Eve Mews, W8 6UG—*Pres.*, Prof. D. J. West.

PSYCHOLOGICAL SOCIETY, THE BRITISH (1901), St. Andrew's House, 48 Princess Road East, Leicester LE1 7DR—*Pres.*, Mrs. L. S. Pearson; *Exec. Sec.*, C. V. Newman, PH.D.

PUBLIC ADMINISTRATION, ROYAL INSTITUTE OF (1922), 3 Birdcage Walk, SW1H 9JH—*Dir. Gen.*, W. Plowden.

PUBLIC FINANCE AND ACCOUNTANCY, CHARTERED INSTITUTE OF (1885), 3 Robert Street WC2N 6BH—*Dir.*, N. P. Hepworth, O.B.E.

PUBLIC HEALTH AND HYGIENE, THE ROYAL INSTITUTE OF (1937), 28 Portland Place, W1N 4DE—*Sec.*, Rear-Adm. W. A. Waddell, C.B., O.B.E.

PUBLIC HEALTH ENGINEERS, INSTITUTION OF (1895), *see* WATER AND ENVIRONMENTAL MANAGEMENT.

PUBLIC RELATIONS, INSTITUTE OF (1948), Gate House, St. John's Square, EC1M 4DH—*Exec. Dir.*, J. B. Lavelle.

PUBLIC TEACHERS OF LAW, SOCIETY OF (1908).—*Pres.*, Prof. J. A. Jolowicz, Trinity College, Cambridge; *Hon. Sec.*, Prof. D. B. Casson, University of Buckingham.

PURCHASING AND SUPPLY, INSTITUTE OF (1967), Easton House, Easton on the Hill, Stamford, Lincs. PE9 3NZ—*Dir.-Gen.*, I. G. S. Groundwater.

QUALITY ASSURANCE, INSTITUTE OF, 10 Grosvenor Gardens, SW1 0DQ—*Sec.-Gen.*, R. Knowles, C.B.E.

QUARRIER'S HOMES (1871), Bridge of Weir, Renfrewshire PA11 3SA—*Chief Exec.*, Dr. J. R. Minto.

QUARRYING, INSTITUTE OF (1917), 7 Regent Street, Nottingham NG1 5BY—*Sec.*, R. Oates.

QUEEN ELIZABETH'S FOUNDATION FOR THE DISABLED (1967), Leatherhead, Surrey KT22 0BN—*Dir.*, M. B. Clark, PH.D.

QUEEN VICTORIA CLERGY FUND (1897), Church House, Dean's Yard, SW1P 3NZ—*Sec.*, Capt. P. W. E. Parry, M.B.E.

QUEEN VICTORIA SCHOOL, Dunblane, Perthshire FK15 0JY—*Commandant*, Brig. O. R. Tweedy (*retd*); *Headmaster*, J. D. Hankinson.

QUEEN'S ENGLISH SOCIETY, THE—*Hon. Sec.*, A. I. Thompson, 2 South Side, Pulborough, Sussex RH20 2DH.

QUEEN'S NURSING INSTITUTE (1887), 57 Lower Belgrave Street, SW1W 0LP—*Dir.*, P. E. Starr.

QUEKETT MICROSCOPICAL CLUB—*Hon. Business Sec.*, A. V. Dodge, 61 Pewley Way, Guildford GU1 3PZ.

RADIOLOGISTS, ROYAL COLLEGE OF (1934), 38 Portland Place, W1N 3DG—*Sec.*, A. J. Cowles.

RAILWAY AND CANAL HISTORICAL SOCIETY, THE.—*Hon. Sec.*, R. E. Kilsby, Banestree, Jacobs Well Road, Guildford, Surrey GU4 7PA.

RAILWAY BENEVOLENT INSTITUTION (1858), 67 Ashbourne Road, Derby DE3 3FY. Railway children's and old people's home at Derby; financial assistance given.—*Exec. Officer and Gen. Sec.*, W. W. K. Humphreys.

RAINER FOUNDATION, 227–239 Tooley Street (2nd Floor), SE1 2JX. Direct help through the provision of community-based schemes for young people at risk or in need: administers the national Intermediate Treatment Fund on behalf of the D.H.S.S.—*Dir.*, R. Kay.

RAMBLERS' ASSOCIATION (1935), 1–5 Wandsworth Road, SW8 2XX—*Dir.*, A. Mattingly.

RATEPAYERS' ASSOCIATIONS, NATIONAL UNION OF, 4 Eysham Court, Station Road, New Barnet, Herts. EN5 1PS—*Hon. Gen. Sec.*, Mrs. D. E. Pannell.

RATING AND VALUATION ASSOCIATION (1882), 115 Ebury Street, SW1W 9QT—*Sec.*, B. L. Hill.

RED CROSS SOCIETY, BRITISH. *See* BRITISH.

RED POLL CATTLE SOCIETY, 6 Church Street, Woodbridge, Suffolk IP12 1DH—*Sec.*, P. Ryder-Davies.

REFRIGERATION, INSTITUTE OF (1899), Kelvin House, 76 Mill Lane, Carshalton, Surrey SM5 2JR—*Sec.*, M. J. Horlick.

REFUGEE COUNCIL, BRITISH (1981), Bondway House, 3–9 Bondway, SW8 1SJ—*Dir.*, M. Barber, PH.D.

REGIONAL STUDIES ASSOCIATION, 29 Great James Street, WC1N 3ES—*Exec. Sec.*, Ms. S. J. Parkinson.

REGULAR FORCES EMPLOYMENT ASSOCIATION (1885), 25 Bloomsbury Square, WC1A 2LN. Finds employment for non-commissioned ex-Regulars.—*General Manager*, Maj. Gen. D. T. Crabtree, C.B.

REINDEER COUNCIL OF THE UNITED KINGDOM (1949), Newton Road, Harston, Cambridge CB2 5NZ—*Hon. Sec.*, Dr. E. J. Lindgren.

RELIGION AND MEDICINE, INSTITUTE OF (1964).—

Organising Sec., C. H. Sinclair, St. Marylebone Parish Church, Marylebone Road, NW1 5LT.

RENT OFFICERS, INSTITUTE OF.—*Hon. Sec.*, M. R. Webber, Musgrave House, Musgrave Row, Exeter, EX4 3TW.

RESEARCH DEFENCE SOCIETY, Grosvenor Gardens House, Grosvenor Gardens, SW1W 0BS—*Hon. Sec.*, Prof. K. M. Spyer.

RETAIL BOOK, STATIONERY AND ALLIED TRADES EMPLOYEES' ASSOCIATION, 8–9 Commercial Road, Swindon, Wilts. SN1 5RB—*Gen. Sec.*, D. A. Williamson.

RICHARD III SOCIETY.—*Sec.*, Miss E. M. Nokes, 4 Oakley Street, SW3 5NN.

ROAD SAFETY OFFICERS, INSTITUTE OF (1971)—*Sec.*, E. M. Marsh, 31 Dyers Close, West Buckland, Somerset TA21 9JU.

ROAD TRANSPORT ENGINEERS, INSTITUTE OF (1945), 1 Cromwell Place, SW7 2JF—*Sec. and Chief Exec.*, D. M. Ivison.

ROMAN STUDIES, SOCIETY FOR PROMOTION OF, 31–34 Gordon Square, WC1H 0PP—*Pres.*, Miss J. M. Reynolds, F.B.A., F.S.A.; *Sec.*, Mrs. P. Gilbert.

ROTARY INTERNATIONAL IN GREAT BRITAIN AND IRELAND (1914), Kinwarton Road, Alcester, Warwickshire B49 6BP—*Sec.*, J. H. Jackson.

ROUND TABLES OF GREAT BRITAIN AND IRELAND, NATIONAL ASSOCIATION OF (1927), Marchesi House, 15 Park Road, N.W.1.—*Gen. Sec.*, P. W. Tipton.

ROYAL AFRICAN SOCIETY (1901), 18 Northumberland Avenue, WC2N 5BJ—*Sec.*, Mrs. M. L. Allan.

ROYAL AGRICULTURAL SOCIETY OF ENGLAND (1838), National Agricultural Centre, Stoneleigh, Kenilworth, Warwicks. CV8 2LZ.—*Chief Exec.*, J. D. M. Hearth C.B.E.

ROYAL AGRICULTURAL SOCIETY OF THE COMMONWEALTH (1957)—*Hon. Sec.*, F. R. Francis, L.V.O., M.B.E., 55 Sleaford Street, SW8 5AB.

ROYAL AIR FORCE BENEVOLENT FUND (1919), 67 Portland Place, W1N 4AR—*Controller*, Air Chief Marshal Sir Alasdair Steedman, G.C.B., C.B.E., D.F.C.

ROYAL AIR FORCES ASSOCIATION, 43 Grove Park Road, W4 3RX—*Sec. Gen.*, M. G. Tomkins, M.B.E.

ROYAL ALEXANDRA AND ALBERT SCHOOL (1758), Foundation Office, Gatton Park, Reigate, Surrey RH2 0TW—*Sec.*, Capt. A. J. Walsh, R.N.

ROYAL ALFRED SEAFARERS' SOCIETY (1865), Weston Acres, Woodmansterne Lane, Banstead, Surrey SM7 3HB—*Gen. Sec.*, J. H. Moore.

ROYAL ARMOURED CORPS BENEVOLENT FUND, H.Q. R.A.C. Centre, Bovington Camp, Dorset BH20 6JA; *Sec.*, Maj. R. Clooney (*retd*).

ROYAL ARTILLERY ASSOCIATION, Artillery House, Connaught Barracks, Grand Depot Road, SE18 6SL—*Gen. Sec.*, Col. R. H. Haynes, M.B.E.

ROYAL ASIATIC SOCIETY OF GREAT BRITAIN AND IRELAND (1823), 56 Queen Anne Street, W1M 9LA—*Dir.*, Dr. D. J. Duncanson, O.B.E.

ROYAL ASSOCIATION OF BRITISH DAIRY FARMERS (1876), 55 Sleaford Street, SW8 5AB—*Chief Exec.*, F. R. Francis, L.V.O., M.B.E.

ROYAL BRITISH NURSES ASSOCIATION, 94 Upper Tollington Park, N4 4NB—*Hon. Sec.*, Mrs. H. M. Vorstermans, M.B.E.

ROYAL CALEDONIAN SCHOOLS (1815), Bushey, Herts. WD2 3TS—*The Master*, Capt. R. E. Wilson, C.B.E., D.F.C., R.N.

ROYAL CAMBRIDGE HOME FOR SOLDIERS' WIDOWS, 82–84 Hurst Road, East Molesey, Surrey KT8 9AH—*Superintendent*, Mrs. A. M. Webb.

ROYAL CELTIC SOCIETY (1820), 23 Rutland Street, Edinburgh EH1 2RN—*Sec.*, J. G. S. Cameron.

ROYAL CHORAL SOCIETY (1871), Royal Albert Hall, SW7 2AP—*Gen. Man.*, M. Heyland.

ROYAL COLLEGE OF VETERINARY SURGEONS, 32 Belgrave Square, SW1X 8QP—*Pres.*, Prof. L. C. Vaughan; *Registrar*, A. R. W. Porter, C.B.E.

ROYAL COMMONWEALTH SOCIETY (1868), Northumberland Avenue, WC2N 5BJ—(21,000 members).—*Sec.-Gen.*, Sir Michael Scott, K.C.V.O., C.M.G.

ROYAL DESIGNERS FOR INDUSTRY, FACULTY OF (1936) (Royal Society of Arts), John Adam Street, WC2N 6EZ—*Master*, Ms. L. Day; *Sec.*, C. T. Lucas.

ROYAL ENGINEERS ASSOCIATION, R.H.Q. Royal Engineers, Brompton Barracks, Chatham, Kent ME4 4UG—*Controller*, Col. G. S. Harris.

ROYAL ENGINEERS, THE INSTITUTION OF (1875), Brompton Barracks, Chatham, Kent ME4 4UG.

ROYAL HIGHLAND AND AGRICULTURAL SOCIETY OF SCOTLAND (1784), Ingliston, Midlothian EH28 8NF—*Sec.*, J. R. Good.

ROYAL HORTICULTURAL SOCIETY (1804).—*Offices*, 80 Vincent Square, S.W.1. *Garden*, Wisley, Woking, Surrey.—*Dir. Gen.*, C. D. Brickell.

ROYAL HOSPITAL AND HOME FOR INCURABLES, PUTNEY (1854), West Hill, Putney, SW15 3SW—*Chief Exec.*, Col. B. E. Blunt.

ROYAL HUMANE SOCIETY (1774).—Gives bravery awards for saving and attempting to save human life. Brettenham House, Lancaster Place, WC2E 7EP—*Sec.*, Maj. A. J. Dickinson.

ROYAL INSTITUTE OF INTERNATIONAL AFFAIRS (1920), Chatham House, 10 St. James's Square, SW1Y 4LE—*Dir.*, Adm. Sir James Eberle.

ROYAL INSTITUTION, THE (1799), 21 Albemarle Street, W1X 4BS—*Pres.*, H.R.H. The Duke of Kent, G.C.M.G., G.C.V.O.; *Dir.*, Prof. J. M. Thomas, F.R.S.; *Sec.*, Prof. E. A. Ash, C.B.E., F.R.S.

ROYAL LIFE SAVING SOCIETY, THE (1891), Mountbatten House, Studley, Warks. B80 7NN—*Dir.*, K. H. Sach.

ROYAL LITERARY FUND (1790), 144 Temple Chambers, Temple Avenue, EC4Y 0DT Grants to necessitous authors of some published work of approved literary merit or to their immediate dependants.—*Pres.*, A. Crook; *Sec.*, Mrs. F. M. Clark.

ROYAL MEDICAL BENEVOLENT FUND (1836), 24 King's Road, Wimbledon, SW19 8QN—*Sec.*, P. G. Gordon-Smith.

ROYAL MEDICAL SOCIETY (1737), Students Centre, 5/5 Bristo Square, Edinburgh EH8 9AL—*Senior Sec.*, E. Sim.

ROYAL METAL TRADES BENEVOLENT SOCIETY (1843), 1 Totteridge Avenue, High Wycombe, Bucks. HP13 6XG—*Sec.*, A. Whittle.

ROYAL MICROSCOPICAL SOCIETY, 37–38 St. Clements, Oxford OX4 1AJ—*Administrator*, Lt. Col. P. G. Fleming.

ROYAL MILITARY POLICE ASSOCIATION (1946), Regimental Headquarters, Corps of Royal Military Police, Roussillon Barracks, Chichester, Sussex PO19 4BN—*Sec.*, Major P. N. Ross (*retd.*).

ROYAL MUSICAL ASSOCIATION—*Sec.*, P. Owens, 41 Burrows Road, NW10 5SL.

ROYAL NATIONAL LIFEBOAT INSTITUTION, (1824)—*Income* (1986) £30,600,000, expenditure £25,171,000; rescued in 1986, 1,398. 260 lifeboats are maintained on the coasts of Great Britain and Ireland. *Offices*, West Quay Road, Poole, Dorset BH15 1HZ—*Chairman*, The Duke of Atholl.

ROYAL NATIONAL MISSION TO DEEP SEA FISHERMEN (1881), 43 Nottingham Place, W1M 4BX—*Sec.*, B. O. Clampton.

ROYAL NAVAL AND ROYAL MARINES CHILDREN'S TRUST (1834), H.M.S. *Nelson*, Portsmouth PO1 3HH—*Sec.*, Mrs. M. Bateman.

ROYAL NAVAL ASSOCIATION (1950), 82 Chelsea Manor Street, SW3 5QJ—*Gen. Sec.*, Capt. J. W. Rayner.

ROYAL NAVAL BENEVOLENT SOCIETY (1739), 1 Fleet Street, EC4Y 1BD—*Sec.*, Capt. M. Murray, R.N., *(retd)*.

ROYAL NAVAL BENEVOLENT TRUST (Grand Fleet and Kindred Funds) (1922), 1 High Street, Brompton, Gillingham, Kent ME7 5QZ (Local Committees at Chatham, Devonport, Portsmouth and Rosyth).—*Gen. Sec.*, Lt. Cdr. D. C. Lawrence, R.N. *(retd.)*.

ROYAL NAVY OFFICERS, ASSOCIATION OF (Trafalgar Day, 1925), 70 Porchester Terrace, W2 6BL—*Sec.-Treas.*, Lt.-Cdr. J. V. Watson, M.B.E., R.N.

ROYAL OVER-SEAS LEAGUE (1910), Over-Seas House, Park Place, St. James's Street, SW1A 1LR—*Chairman*, M. A. S. Dalal; *Dir. Gen.*, Capt. J. B. Rumble, R.N.

ROYAL PATRIOTIC FUND CORPORATION (1854), Golden Cross House, Duncannon Street, WC2 4JR. Administers funds for the benefit of widows, children and other dependants of deceased officers and servicemen of the Armed Forces.—*Sec.*, Brig. D. C. Blomfield-Smith, M.B.E.

ROYAL PHILHARMONIC SOCIETY (1813), 10 Stratford Place, W1N 9AE—*Hon. Sec.*, E. Thompson, O.B.E.

ROYAL PHOTOGRAPHIC SOCIETY (1853), The Octagon, Milsom Street, Bath BA1 1DN—*Sec.*, K. R. Warr.

ROYAL PINNER SCHOOL FOUNDATION, 110 Old Brompton Road, SW7 3RB. (Trustee: The Royal Commercial Travellers' School Trust Ltd.) Assists in the education of children of sales representatives where families have suffered some adversity.—*Sec.*, S. Thurtell.

"ROYAL SAILORS' RESTS" (1876), 2A South Street, Gosport, Hants. PO12 1ES. Centres for naval personnel at Devonport, St. Budeaux, Portland, Gosport, Portsmouth, and Rosyth.—*Sec.*, A. A. Lockwood.

ROYAL SCHOOL OF NEEDLEWORK (1872), 25 Princes Gate, SW7 1QE—*Principal*, Mrs. J. Field.

ROYAL SCOTTISH COUNTRY DANCE SOCIETY (1923), 12 Coates Crescent, Edinburgh EH3 7AF—*Sec.*, Miss M. M. Gibson.

ROYAL SCOTTISH SOCIETY FOR PREVENTION OF CRUELTY TO CHILDREN (1884), Melville House, 41 Polwarth Terrace, Edinburgh EH11 1NU—*Gen. Sec.*, A. M. M. Wood, O.B.E.

ROYAL SEAMEN'S PENSION FUND (1919), P.O. Box 62, 58 High Street, Sutton, Surrey SM1 1HD—*Sec.*, R. F. Van Houten.

ROYAL SIGNALS INSTITUTION (1950), 56 Regency Street, SW1P 4AD—*Sec.*, Col. A. N. de Bretton-Gordon.

ROYAL SOCIETY, THE (1660), 6 Carlton House Terrace, SW1Y 5AG—*Pres.*, Sir George Porter; *Treas. and Vice-Pres.*, Prof. R. W. K. Honeycombe; *Secretaries and Vice-Presidents*, Prof. R. J. Elliott, Prof. B. K. Follett, Prof. M. A. Epstein; *Executive Sec.*, Dr. P. T. Warren.

ROYAL SOCIETY FOR ASIAN AFFAIRS (1901), 2 Belgrave Square, SW1X 8PJ—*Pres.*, The Lord Denman, M.C., C.B.E., T.D.; *Sec.*, Miss M. FitzSimons.

ROYAL SOCIETY FOR THE ENCOURAGEMENT OF ARTS MANUFACTURES AND COMMERCE (Royal Society of Arts) (1754), 8 John Adam Street, WC2N 6EZ—*Chairman*, Prof. C. B. Handy; *Sec.*, C. T. Lucas.

ROYAL SOCIETY FOR THE PREVENTION OF ACCIDENTS, Cannon House, Priory Queensway, Birmingham B4 6BS—*Dir. Gen.*, R. M. Warburton.

ROYAL SOCIETY FOR THE PREVENTION OF CRUELTY TO ANIMALS (1824), Causeway, Horsham, Sussex RH12 1HG—*Exec. Dir.*, A. Richmond, C.B.

ROYAL SOCIETY FOR THE PROTECTION OF BIRDS (1889), The Lodge, Sandy, Beds. SG19 2DL—*Dir. Gen.*, I. Prestt, C.B.E.

ROYAL SOCIETY OF BRITISH SCULPTORS (1904), 108 Old Brompton Road, SW7 3RA—*Pres.*, J. E. Ravera; *Sec.*, Miss M. O'Connor.

ROYAL SOCIETY OF EDINBURGH (1783), 22–24 George Street, Edinburgh EH2 2PQ—*Pres.*, Sir Alwyn Williams, C.B.E.; *Gen. Sec.*, Dr. C. D. Waterston; *Treas.*, Prof. C. Blake; *Curator*, Prof. D. M. Henderson.

ROYAL SOCIETY OF HEALTH, THE (1876), R.S.H. House, 38A St. Georges Drive, SW1V 4BH—*Sec.*, D. Goad.

ROYAL SOCIETY OF LITERATURE (1823), 1 Hyde Park Gardens, W2 2LT—*Sec.*, Mrs. P. M. Schute.

ROYAL SOCIETY OF MEDICINE (1805), 1 Wimpole Street, W1M 8AE—*Exec. Dir.*, R. N. Thomson.

ROYAL SOCIETY OF PORTRAIT PAINTERS (1891), 17 Carlton House Terrace, SW1Y 5BD—*Pres.*, D. Poole.

ROYAL SOCIETY OF ST. GEORGE, THE (1894), 4 Wilton Mews, SW1X 8BD—*Gen. Sec.*, Lt. Col. J. A. Williams *(retd)*.

ROYAL STAR AND GARTER HOME FOR DISABLED EX-SERVICEMEN (1916), Richmond, Surrey TW10 6RR—*Commandant*, Col. R. N. Harris, M.B.E.

ROYAL STATISTICAL SOCIETY (1834), 25 Enford Street, W1H 2BH—*Pres.*, Sir John Kingman, F.R.S.; *Exec. Sec.*, D. W. Harding.

ROYAL TANK REGIMENT ASSOCIATION and BENEVOLENT FUND, H.Q. R.A.C. Centre, Bovington Camp, Dorset BH20 6JA—*Regimental Sec.*, Maj. R. Clooney *(retd)*.

ROYAL TELEVISION SOCIETY, Tavistock House East, Tavistock Square, WC1H 9HR—*Hon. Sec.*, A. Pilgrim.

ROYAL UNITED KINGDOM BENEFICENT ASSOCIATION (1863), 6 Avonmore Road, W14 8RL—*Gen. Sec.*, Rear Adm. B. C. Perowne, C.B.

ROYAL UNITED SERVICES INSTITUTE FOR DEFENCE STUDIES, Whitehall, SW1A 2ET—*Dir.*, Gp. Capt. D. Bolton, R.A.F. *(retd)*.

RUBBER GROWERS' ASSOCIATION LTD., 90 Fenchurch Street, EC3M 4BY—*Sec.*, Mrs. J. Taylor.

RURAL ENGLAND, COUNCIL FOR THE PROTECTION OF (1926), 4 Hobart Place, SW1W 0HY—*Dir.*, A. Purkis.

RURAL SCOTLAND, ASSOCIATION FOR THE PROTECTION OF (1926), 14a Napier Road, Edinburgh EH10 5AY—*Dir.*, R. L. Smith, O.B.E.

RURAL WALES, COUNCIL FOR THE PROTECTION OF, Ty Gwyn, 31 High Street, Welshpool, Powys SY21 7JP—*Dir.*, S. R. J. Meade.

SAILORS' CHILDREN'S SOCIETY, THE (1821), Newland, Hull HU6 7RJ. Cares for British seamen's children who have lost a parent and for short periods during a mother's illness if father is at sea. Provides welfare facilities for seamen in Humber area, and Homes for aged seafarers at Hull and S. Shields.—*Sec.*, Lt. Cdr. C. G. R. Streatfeild-James, R.N.

ST. DEINIOL'S RESIDENTIAL LIBRARY (1902), Hawarden, Deeside, Clwyd CH5 3DF—*Warden and Chief Librarian*, Rev. P. J. Jagger, F.R.Hist.S.

ST. DUNSTAN'S, for men and women blinded on War

Service, 12–14 Harcourt Street, W1A 4XB. In March 1986, the number of blinded men and women in the care of the organization was 1,228.—*Pres.*, Col. Beaumont-Edmonds, M.C.; *Chairman*, Adm. of the Fleet Sir Henry Leach, G.C.B.; *Sec.*, W. C. Weisblatt.

ST. JOHN AMBULANCE ASSOCIATION AND BRIGADE, 1 Grosvenor Crescent, SW1X 7EF. Voluntary unpaid body providing first-aid cover at public gatherings.—*Chief Commander*, Maj.-Gen. P. R. Leuchars, C.B.E.; *Commissioner-in-Chief*, A. J. Sunderland. *Brigade Strength* (U.K. 1986), 59,660.—*Chief Sec.*, Brig. R. C. Middleton, O.B.E.

SALES AND MARKETING MANAGEMENT, INSTITUTE OF—*Chief Exec.*, D. Waller, Georgian House, 31 Upper George Street, Luton, Beds. LU1 2RD.

SALMON AND TROUT ASSOCIATION (1903), Fishmongers' Hall, EC4R 9EL—*Dir.*, J. Ferguson.

SALTIRE SOCIETY (1936), Saltire House, 13 Atholl Crescent, Edinburgh EH3 8HA—*Organising Sec.*, Miss K. Austin.

SAMARITANS, THE (to help the suicidal and despairing).—*Gen. Sec.*, D. Evans, 17 Uxbridge Road, Slough, Berks. SL1 1SN.

SAMUEL PEPYS CLUB—*Sec.*, R. H. Adams, T.D., F.S.A., 14 Dale Close, Oxford OX1 1TU.

SAVE THE CHILDREN FUND, THE (1919), 17 Grove Lane, SE5 8RD—*Dir. Gen.*, N. Hinton, C.B.E.

SCHOOL LIBRARY ASSOCIATION, Liden Library, Barrington Close, Liden, Swindon, Wilts. SN3 6HF—*Exec. Sec.*, Ms. V. Fea.

SCHOOL NATURAL SCIENCE SOCIETY—*Hon. Gen. Sec.*, Miss D. S. Jackson, 29 The Alders, Heston, Middx. TW5 0HP.

SCHOOLMASTERS, SOCIETY OF (1798) (for the relief of necessitous schoolmasters and of their widows and orphans)—*Sec.*, Mrs. M. S. Freeburn, Hall Farm Dairy, Wood Norton, Dereham, Norfolk NR20.

SCHOOLMISTRESSES AND GOVERNESSES BENEVOLENT INSTITUTION, Queen Mary House, Manor Park Road, Chislehurst, Kent BR7 5PY. Helps schoolmistresses, matrons and women administrators employed in independent schools, as well as governesses and self-employed women teachers—*Dir. and Sec.*, R. W. Hayward.

SCIENCE AND LEARNING, SOCIETY FOR THE PROTECTION OF, 20–21 Compton Terrace, NI 2UN—*Sec.*, Ms. E. Fraser.

SCIENCE EDUCATION, ASSOCIATION FOR, College Lane, Hatfield, Herts. AL10 9AA—*Gen. Sec.*, B. G. Atwood, O.B.E.

SCOTCH WHISKY ASSOCIATION, 20 Atholl Crescent, Edinburgh EH3 8HF.—*Dir. Gen. and Sec.*, Col. H. F. O. Bewsher, O.B.E.; *Information and Development Office*, 17 Half Moon Street W1Y 7RB.

SCOTTISH CHURCH HISTORY SOCIETY (1922)—*Hon. Sec.*, Rev. C. G. F. Brockie, Grange Manse, 51 Portland Road, Kilmarnock KA1 2EQ.

SCOTTISH CORPORATION, THE ROYAL (1611), 37 King Street, Covent Garden, WC2E 8JS—*Chief Exec.*, I. S. MacLeod.

SCOTTISH GENEALOGY SOCIETY (1953)—*Hon. Sec.*, Miss J. P. S. Ferguson, 21 Howard Place, Edinburgh EH3 5JY.

SCOTTISH HISTORY SOCIETY (1886)—*Hon. Sec.*, Dr. A. M. Smith, Dept. of Modern History, University of Dundee DD1 4HN.

SCOTTISH LANDOWNERS' FEDERATION (1906), 18 Abercromby Place, Edinburgh EH3 6TY—*Dir.*, D. J. Hughes Hallett.

SCOTTISH LAW AGENTS SOCIETY, 33–34 Charlotte Square, Edinburgh EH2 4HF—*Sec.*, G. F. Davidson.

SCOTTISH LIFE OFFICES, ASSOCIATED (1841), 23 St. Andrew Square, Edinburgh EH2 1AQ—*Sec.*, W. W. Mair.

SCOTTISH MARINE BIOLOGICAL ASSOCIATION (1914),

Dunstaffnage Marine Research Laboratory, P.O. Box 3, Oban, Argyll PA34 4AD—*Dir. and Sec.*, Prof. R. I. Currie, C.B.E., F.R.S.E.

SCOTTISH NATIONAL BLOOD TRANSFUSION ASSOCIATION (1940), 29 Abercromby Place, Edinburgh EH3 6UE—*Sec.*, P. C. Taylor.

SCOTTISH NATIONAL INSTITUTION FOR THE WAR BLINDED (Newington House). Workshops at Glasgow and Linburn.—*Sec. and Treas.*, J. B. M. Munro, Gillespie Crescent, Edinburgh EH10 4HZ.

SCOTTISH NATIONAL WAR MEMORIAL (1927), The Castle, Edinburgh EH1 2YT—*Sec.*, J. D. M. Watson; *Curator*, T. C. Barker.

SCOTTISH RECORD SOCIETY, Scottish History Dept., Univ. of Glasgow G12 8QQ—*Hon. Sec.*, Dr. J. Kirk.

SCOTTISH SECONDARY TEACHERS' ASSOCIATION, 15 Dundas Street, Edinburgh EH3 6QG—*Gen. Sec.*, A. A. Stanley.

SCOTTISH SOCIETY FOR THE PROTECTION OF WILD BIRDS (1927), Foremount House, Kilbarchan, Renfrewshire PA10 2EZ—*Hon. Treas. and Sec.*, Dr. J. A. Gibson.

SCOTTISH TOURIST BOARD (1969), 23 Ravelston Terrace, Edinburgh EH4 3EU—*Chief Exec.*, T. M. Band.

SCOTTISH WILDLIFE TRUST (1964), 25 Johnston Terrace, Edinburgh EH1 2NH—*Chief Exec.*, J. R. Baldwin.

SCOTTISH WOMEN'S RURAL INSTITUTES (1917), 42 Heriot Row, Edinburgh EH3 6ES—*Gen. Sec.*, Mrs. E. Nicol.

SCOUT ASSOCIATION, THE, Baden-Powell House, Queen's Gate, SW7 5JS—*Chief Scout*, Maj.-Gen. M. J. H. Walsh, C.B., D.S.O.; *Chief Exec. Commissioner*, A. E. N. Black, O.B.E. Membership in U.K. (1987), 658,499; World Membership over 16,000,000 in over 150 countries and territories.

SCRIBES AND ILLUMINATORS, THE SOCIETY OF.—*Hon. Sec.*, Mrs. S. Cavendish, 54 Boileau Road, SW13 9BL.

SCRIPTURE GIFT MISSION INCORPORATED (1888), Radstock House, 3 Eccleston Street, SW1W 9LZ Copies and selections of the Scriptures circulated (1986), 16,181,308.—*Gen. Sec.*, R. Kennedy.

SCRIPTURE UNION (1867), 130 City Road, EC1V 2NJ—*Gen. Dir.*, Rev. D. M. S. Cohen.

SEA CADET ASSOCIATION, 202 Lambeth Road, SE1 7JF—*Pres.*, Admiral of the Fleet Sir Henry Leach, G.C.B.; *Gen. Sec.*, Cmdr. P. J. Everett, O.B.E., R.N.

SEAMEN'S CHRISTIAN FRIEND SOCIETY (1846), 26 Davyhulme Road East, Stretford, Manchester M32 0DW—*Gen. Sec.*, G. D. Cartwright.

SECONDARY HEADS ASSOCIATION, 107 St. Paul's Road, N1 2NB—*Gen. Sec.*, T. P. Snape.

SELDEN SOCIETY (1887), Faculty of Laws, Queen Mary College, Mile End Road, E1 4NS To encourage the study and advance the knowledge of the history of English Law.—*Pres.*, Prof. S. F. C. Milsom, Q.C., F.B.A.; *Sec.*, V. Tunkel.

SHAFTESBURY HOMES AND *Arethusa* (1843), 3 Rectory Grove, SW4 0EG—*Gen. Sec.*, Maj. R. P. A. de Berniere-Smart.

SHAFTESBURY SOCIETY, THE (1844), Shaftesbury House, 2A Amity Grove, Raynes Park, SW20 0LJ. Engaged in caring for physically and mentally handicapped, the elderly and socially deprived. Maintains residential schools and hostels, further education centres and holiday centres, and mission centres in Greater London.—*Sec.*, G. P. Holloway.

SHEEP ASSOCIATION, NATIONAL, 106 High Street, Tring, Herts. HP23 4AF—*Sec.*, J. Thorley.

SHELLFISH ASSOCIATION OF GREAT BRITAIN, Fishmongers' Hall, London Bridge, EC4R 9EL—*Dir.*, Dr. E. Edwards.

SHELTER (National Campaign for the Homeless), 88

Old Street, EC1V 9HU—*Pres.*, H.E. Cardinal Archbishop Basil Hume; *Dir.*, Miss S. McKechnie.

SHERLOCK HOLMES SOCIETY OF LONDON (1951)—*Hon. Sec.*, Capt. W. R. Michell, R.N. (*retd*), The Old Crown Inn, Lopen, Nr. S. Petherton, Somerset TA13 5JX.

SHIPBROKERS, INSTITUTE OF CHARTERED (1911), 24 St. Mary Axe, EC3A 8DE—*Sec.*, J. H. Parker.

SHIPWRECKED FISHERMEN AND MARINERS' ROYAL BENEVOLENT SOCIETY (1839), 1 North Pallant, Chichester, West Sussex PO19 1TL—*Gen. Sec.*, Miss V. G. Austin.

SHIRE HORSE SOCIETY (1878), East of England Showground, Peterborough PE2 0XE.—*Sec. and Chief Exec.*, R. W. Bird, M.B.E.

SHRIEVALTY ASSOCIATION, 14 Clumber Street, Nottingham NG1 3DS—*Sec. and Treas.*, R. Bullock.

SIMPLIFIED SPELLING SOCIETY (1908).—*Chairman*, C. J. H. Jolly, Clare Hall, Chapel Lane, Chigwell, Essex IG7 6JJ.

SIR OSWALD STOLL FOUNDATION, 446 Fulham Road, SW6 1DT—*Dir. and Sec.*, R. Brunwin.

SMALL FARMERS ASSOCIATION, THE (1979), Freepost, EC3B 3EH—*Hon. Sec.*, Mrs. R. B. Weiss.

SOCIAL RESPONSIBILITY AND EDUCATION, QUAKER, Friends House, Euston Road, NW1 2BJ.—*Gen. Sec.*, T. Jaggar.

SOCIAL WORKERS, BRITISH ASSOCIATION OF (1970), 16 Kent Street, Birmingham B5 6RD—*Gen. Sec.*, D. N. Jones.

SOCIALIST PARTY OF GREAT BRITAIN (1904), 52 Clapham High Street, SW4 7UN—*Gen. Sec.*, P. Hope.

SOLDIERS' AND AIRMEN'S SCRIPTURE READERS ASSOCIATION, THE (1838), Havelock House, Barrack Road, Aldershot, Hants. GU11 3NP—*Gen. Sec.*, Lt. Col. K. W. Sear (*retd*).

SOLDIERS' DAUGHTERS' SCHOOL, ROYAL (1855), 65 Rosslyn Hill, Hampstead, NW3 5UD—*Bursar*, Brig. N. Roberts, C.B.E.

SOLDIERS', SAILORS' AND AIRMEN'S FAMILIES ASSOCIATION (1885), 16–18 Old Queen Street, SW1H 9HP—*Chairman*, Adm. Sir Peter Herbert, K.C.E., O.B.E.; *Controller*, Maj. Gen. C. R. Grey, C.B.E.; *Sec.*, Capt. W. Stuart.

SOLDIERS, SAILORS AND AIRMEN'S HELP SOCIETY (Incorporated) (1899), *See* FORCES HELP SOCIETY.

SOLICITORS BENEVOLENT ASSOCIATION (1858), Lonsdale Chambers, 27 Chancery Lane, WC2A 1NF—*Sec.*, Lt. Col. D. G. Martin, O.B.E.

SOLICITORS IN THE SUPREME COURTS OF SCOTLAND, SOCIETY OF—*Sec.*, A. R. Brownlie, 2 Abercromby Place, Edinburgh EH3 6JZ—*Treas.*, D. A. Lamb.

SOROPTIMIST INTERNATIONAL OF GREAT BRITAIN AND IRELAND (1923), 63 Bayswater Road, W2 3PJ—*Administrative Officer*, Ms. J. Tuson.

S.O.S. SOCIETY, THE (1929), 38 Kensington Park Road, W11 3BU. Old people's homes (5), Mental Rehabilitation homes (3).—*Chief Exec.*, Lt.-Col. P. Rew.

SOUTH AMERICAN MISSIONARY SOCIETY, Allen Gardiner House, Pembury Road, Tunbridge Wells, Kent TN2 3QU—*Gen. Sec.*, Rt. Rev. J. W. H. Flagg.

SOUTH WALES INSTITUTE OF ENGINEERS (1857), Coal House, Ty Glas Avenue, Llanishen, Cardiff CF4 5YS—*Hon. Sec.*, R. E. Lindsay.

SPASTICS SOCIETY, THE (1952), 12 Park Crescent, W1N 4EQ—*Sec.*, Sir John Cox, K.C.B.

SPEAKERS CLUBS, THE ASSOCIATION OF (1971), 93, Revidge Road, Blackburn BB2 6JH—*Sec.*, B. A. Driscoll.

SPINA BIFIDA AND HYDROCEPHALUS, ASSOCIATION FOR (ASBAH), 22 Upper Woburn Place, WC1H 0EP—*Exec. Dir.*, Miss M. P. Gilbertson.

SPORTS MEDICINE, INSTITUTE OF (1963), c/o Faculty of Engineering & Science, Polytechnic of Central London, 115 New Cavendish Street, W1M 8JS—*Hon. Sec.*, P. Sebastian.

SPURGEON'S CHILD CARE (1867), 30 Mill Street, Bedford MK40 3HD—*Dir.*, J. W. Honey.

STATISTICIANS, INSTITUTE OF (1948), 36 Churchgate Street, Bury St. Edmunds, Suffolk IP33 1RD—*Sec.*, D. A. Holland.

STATUTE LAW SOCIETY (1968), 186 City Road, EC1V 2NU—*Hon. Sec.*, C. E. Shanbury.

STEWART SOCIETY (1899), 48 Castle Street, Edinburgh EH2 3LX—*Hon. Sec.*, D. F. Stewart.

STRATEGIC STUDIES, THE INTERNATIONAL INSTITUTE FOR (1958), 23 Tavistock Street, WC2E 7NQ—*Dir.*, F. Heisbourg.

STRUCTURAL ENGINEERS, INSTITUTION OF (1908), 11 Upper Belgrave Street, SW1X 8BH—*Sec.*, D. J. Clark.

STUDENT CHRISTIAN MOVEMENT (1889), 186 St. Paul's Road, Balsall Heath, Birmingham B12 8LZ—*Gen. Sec.*, Rev. T. E. McClure.

SUFFOLK HORSE SOCIETY, 6 Church Street, Woodbridge, Suffolk IP12 1DH—*Sec.*, P. Ryder-Davies.

SURGEONS OF ENGLAND, ROYAL COLLEGE OF (1800), Lincoln's Inn Fields, WC2A 3PN—*Pres.*, I. P. Todd, M.D.; *Sec.*, R. S. Johnson-Gilbert, O.B.E.

SURGEONS OF EDINBURGH, ROYAL COLLEGE OF (1505), Nicolson Street, Edinburgh EH8 9DW—*Pres.*, T. J. McNair; *Sec.*, P. Edmond, C.B.E., T.D.

SURVEYORS, ROYAL INSTITUTION OF CHARTERED (incorporating the Institute of Quantity Surveyors) (1868), 12 Great George Street, SW1P 3AD—*Sec. Gen.*, M. Pattison.

SUSSEX CATTLE SOCIETY (1887), Station Road, Robertsbridge, E. Sussex TN32 5DG—*Manager*, Miss S. G. Kennedy.

SUTTON HOUSING TRUST (1901), Sutton Court, Tring, Herts. HP23 5BB—*Dir.*, I. C. F. Butcher.

SWEDENBORG SOCIETY (1810), 20–21 Bloomsbury Way WC1A 2TH—*Sec.*, Ms. M. G. Waters.

TALKING BOOKS FOR THE HANDICAPPED (National Listening Library), 12 Lant Street, SE1 1QH—*Exec. Dir.*, D. J. Roskilly.

TAVISTOCK INSTITUTE OF HUMAN RELATIONS, Tavistock Centre, Belsize Lane, NW3 5BA.

TAXATION, INSTITUTE OF (1930), 12 Upper Belgrave Street, SW1X 8BB—*Sec.*, R. J. Ison.

TAX PAYERS' SOCIETY, 22 Wheatsheaf House, 4 Carmelite Street, EC4Y 0BN—*Dir.*, D. J. Bryant.

TEACHERS IN COMMERCE LTD., FACULTY OF, 141 Bedford Road, Sutton Coldfield, West Midlands B75 6DB—*Sec.*, J. Snowdon.

TEACHERS OF HOME ECONOMICS LTD., NATIONAL ASSOCIATION OF, Hamilton House, Mabledon Place, WC1H 9BJ—*Gen. Man.*, P. G. Higgins.

TEACHERS OF MATHEMATICS, ASSOCIATION OF, Kings Chambers, Queen Street, Derby DE1 3DA—*Hon. Sec.*, Ms. G. M. Hatch.

TEACHERS OF THE DEAF, BRITISH ASSOCIATION OF—99 Hertford Road, Stevenage, Herts. SG2 8SE—*Sec.*, P. Robson.

TEACHERS' UNION, ULSTER (1919), 94 Malone Road, Belfast BT9 5HP—*Gen. Sec.*, D. Allen.

TELECOMMUNICATIONS USERS' ASSOCIATION, 34 Grand Avenue, N10 3BP—*Dirs.*, M. Elwes; Ms. V. Peters.

TEMPERANCE SOCIETIES:—

British National Temperance League (1834), Livesey-Clegg House, 44 Union Street, Sheffield S1 2JP—*Hon. Sec.*, Miss. M. Daniel.

British Women's Temperance Association (1876), 8 North Bank Street, Edinburgh EH1 2LP—*Hon. Sec.*, Miss J. E. H. Gillon.

Church of England National Council for Social Aid, 38 Ebury Street, SW1W 0LU—*Gen. Sec.*, Rev. E. W. F. Agar.

Churches Council on Alcohol and Drugs (1915), 4 Southampton Row, WC1B 4AA—*Gen. Sec.*, Mrs. B. Smith.

Division of Social Responsibility of the Methodist

Church, 1 Central Buildings, Westminster, SW1H 9NH—*Gen. Sec.,* Rev. B. Duckworth.

International Christian Federation for the Prevention of Alcoholism and Drug Addiction, 27 Tavistock Square, WC1H 9HH—*Gen. Sec.,* Rev. J. K. Lawton.

Order of the Sons of Temperance, 5 Ashbourne Road, Derby, DE3 3FQ—*Sec.,* D. Newbury.

Royal Naval Temperance Society (auxiliary of Royal Sailors' Rests), 2a South Street, Gosport, Hants. PO12 1ES—*Sec.,* A. A. Lockwood.

Social Responsibility Dept., General Assembly of Unitarian and Free Christian Churches, Essex Hall, 1–6 Essex Street, WC2R 3HY—*Hon. Sec.,* C. Shute.

United Kingdom Alliance, Alliance House, 123 Regent Street W1R 7HA—*Gen. Sec.,* Rev. B. Kinman.

TEMPLETON FOUNDATION, 16 Kingfisher Lane, Turners Hill, Crawley, Sussex RH10 4QP.—*U.K. Rep.,* Rev. J. H. E. Pearse.

TERRITORIAL, AUXILIARY AND VOLUNTEER RESERVE ASSOCIATIONS, COUNCIL OF (1908), Centre Block, Duke of York's Headquarters, Chelsea, SW3 4SG—*Sec.,* Maj. Gen. M. Matthews, C.B.

TEXTILE INSTITUTE, THE (1910), 10 Blackfriars Street, Manchester M3 5DR—*Gen. Sec.,* R. G. Denyer.

THEATRE RESEARCH, SOCIETY FOR (1948), 77 Kinnerton Street SW1X 8ED—*Hon. Sec.,* D. Forbes.

THEATRICAL FUND ASSOCIATION, ROYAL GENERAL (1839), 11 Garrick Street, WC2E 9AR—*Sec.,* J. Berkeley.

THEATRICAL LADIES' GUILD OF CHARITY (1892)—*Admin. Sec.,* Mrs. K. Nichols, 60 York Way, N1 9AB.

THEOSOPHICAL SOCIETY IN ENGLAND (1875), 50 Gloucester Place, W1H 3HJ—*Gen. Sec.,* Dr. H. Gray.

THISTLE FOUNDATION, THE (1945), 27a Walker Street, Edinburgh EH3 7HX—*Dir.,* P. Croft.

THOMAS CORAM FOUNDATION FOR CHILDREN (1739), 40 Brunswick Square, WC1N 1AZ—*Dir. and Sec.,* C. P. Masters.

TOC H (1915), 1 Forest Close, Wendover, Aylesbury, Bucks. HP22 6BT—*Gen. Sec.,* Dr. J. M. A. Kilburn.

TOWN AND COUNTRY PLANNING ASSOCIATION, 17 Carlton House Terrace, SW1Y 5AS—*Dir.,* D. Hall.

TOWN PLANNING INSTITUTE, ROYAL (1914), 26 Portland Place, W1N 4BE.

TOWNSWOMEN'S GUILDS, NATIONAL UNION OF (1929), 75 Harborne Road, Edgbaston, Birmingham B15 3DA—*Nat. Sec.,* Mrs. R. Campbell-Tanner.

TOYNBEE HALL, The Universities' Settlement in East London, 28 Commercial Street, Whitechapel, E1 6LS—*Warden and Chief Exec.,* A. L. Williams, O.B.E.

TRADE MARK AGENTS, INSTITUTE OF (1934), Canterbury House, 2–6 Sydenham Road, Croydon, Surrey CR0 9XE—*Sec.,* Mrs. M. J. Tyler.

TRADE, NATIONAL CHAMBER OF (1897), Enterprise House, Henley-on-Thames, Oxon. RG9 1TU—*Chief Exec.,* B. Tennant.

TRADING STANDARDS ADMINISTRATION, THE INSTITUTE OF, Thamesgate House, 37 Victoria Avenue, Southend-on-Sea, Essex SS2 6DA—*Admin. Officer,* Mrs. G. Jordan.

TRANSPORT ADMINISTRATION, INSTITUTE OF (1944), 32 Palmerston Road, Southampton SO1 1LL—*Nat. Sec.,* Wg. Cdr. P. F. Green.

TRANSPORT, CHARTERED INSTITUTE OF (1919), 80 Portland Place, W1N 4DP—*Dir.-Gen.,* J. C. F. Cameron.

TRANSPORT CONSULTATIVE COMMITTEE, CENTRAL (1948), 1st Floor, Golden Cross House, Duncannon Street, WC2N 4JF—*Sec.,* L. A. Dumelow.

TROPICAL MEDICINE AND HYGIENE, ROYAL SOCIETY OF (1907), Manson House, 26 Portland Place, W1N 4EY.

TURNER SOCIETY, BCM Box Turner, WC1N 3XX—*Chairman,* S. Warburton.

UFAW (Universities Federation for Animal Welfare) (1926), 8 Hamilton Close, South Mimms, Potters Bar, Herts. EN6 3QD—*Sec.,* Lt. Col. T. J. Reynolds.

UNIT TRUST ASSOCIATION (1959), Park House, 16 Finsbury Circus, EC2M 7JP—*Sec.,* A. C. Smith.

UNITED NATIONS ASSOCIATION (1945), 3 Whitehall Court, SW1A 2EL—*Dir.,* M. Harper.

UNITED REFORMED CHURCH HISTORY SOCIETY, 86 Tavistock Place, WC1H 9RT—*Hon. Sec.,* Rev. Dr. S. Orchard.

UNITED SOCIETY FOR CHRISTIAN LITERATURE, Robertson House, Leas Road, Guildford, Surrey GU14 4QW—*Gen. Sec.,* Rev. A. Gilmore.

UNITED SYNAGOGUE (1870).—*Pres.,* V. Lucas; *Sec.,* J. J. Julius, Woburn House, Upper Woburn Place, WC1H 0EZ.

UNIVERSITIES CENTRAL COUNCIL ON ADMISSIONS (1961), P.O. Box 28, Cheltenham, Glos. GL50 1HY—*Gen. Sec.,* P. A. Oakley, M.B.E.

UNIVERSITY WOMEN, BRITISH FEDERATION OF (1907), Crosby Hall, Cheyne Walk, S.W.3.—*Sec.,* Mrs. C. Ellis.

VALUERS AND AUCTIONEERS, INCORPORATED SOCIETY OF, 3 Cadogan Gate, SW1X 0AS—*Sec.,* M. Astbury.

VEGAN SOCIETY, THE (1944), 33–35 George Street, Oxford OX1 2AY—*Gen. Sec.,* B. Kew.

VEGETARIAN SOCIETY OF THE UNITED KINGDOM LTD., Parkdale, Dunham Road, Altrincham, Cheshire WA14 4QG—*Gen. Manager,* Ms. P. McGlashan.

VENEREAL DISEASES, MEDICAL SOCIETY FOR THE STUDY OF—*Hon. Sec.,* Dr. M. A. Waugh, Dept. of Genito-Urinary Medicine, Leeds General Infirmary, Great George Street, Leeds LS1 3EX.

VERNACULAR ARCHITECTURE GROUP (1953), 18 Portland Place, Leamington Spa, Warwicks. CV32 5EU—*Hon. Sec.,* Dr. N. W. Alcock.

VICE-CHANCELLORS AND PRINCIPALS OF THE UNIVERSITIES OF THE UNITED KINGDOM, COMMITTEE OF, 29 Tavistock Square, WC1H 9EZ—*Chairman,* Prof. Sir Mark Richmond, F.R.S.; *Sec. Gen.,* B. H. Taylor.

VICTORIA CROSS AND GEORGE CROSS ASSOCIATION, THE, Room 04, Archway Block South, Old Admiralty Building, SW1A 2BE—*Chairman,* Rear Adm. B. C. G. Place, V.C., C.B., D.S.C.

VICTORIA INSTITUTE, THE (Philosophical Society of Great Britain)—*Pres.,* Dr. D. J. E. Ingram; *Asst. Sec.,* B. H. T. Weller, 29 Queen Street, EC4R 1BH.

VICTORIAN SOCIETY (1958), 1 Priory Gardens, Bedford Park, W4 1TT—*Sec.,* Ms. T. Sladen.

VICTORY (SERVICES) ASSOCIATION LTD. AND CLUB, THE, 63–79 Seymour Street, W2 2HF—*General Manager,* D. G. Stovey.

VIKING SOCIETY FOR NORTHERN RESEARCH, University College, Gower Street, WC1E 6BT—*Hon. Secs.,* Mrs. U. Dronke; Prof. M. P. Barnes.

VITREOUS ENAMELLERS, INSTITUTE OF, Ripley, Derby DE5 3EB.—*Sec.,* J. D. Gardom.

VOLUNTARY SERVICE OVERSEAS (1958), 9 Belgrave Square, SW1X 8PW—*Dir.,* N. McIntosh.

WAR ON WANT (1952), 37–39 Great Guildford Street, SE1 0ES—*Gen. Sec.* (vacant).

WATER AND ENVIRONMENTAL MANAGEMENT, INSTITUTION OF, 15 John Street, WC1N 2EB—*Pres.,* Prof. R. F. Packham, PH.D, F.R.S.C. *Sec. and Exec. Dir.,* H. R. Evans.

WELDING INSTITUTE, THE, Abington Hall, Cambridge CB1 6AL, and 11–12 Pall Mall, SW1Y 5LU—*Dir. Gen.,* Dr. A. A. Wells, O.B.E., F.R.S.

1112 *Societies and Institutions* [1988

WELLCOME TRUST (1936), 1 Park Square West, NW1 4LJ—*Dir.*, P. O. Williams, F.R.C.P.

WELLS (H. G.) SOCIETY, Dept. of Language and Literature, Polytechnic of North London, Prince of Wales Road, NW5 3LB—*Sec.*, C. Rolfe.

WESLEY HISTORICAL SOCIETY (1893)—*Gen. Sec.*, Dr. E. D. Graham, 34 Spiceland Road, Northfield, Birmingham B31 1NJ.

WEST AFRICA COMMITTEE (1956), 315 Oxford Street, W1R 2BQ—*Secs.*, L. J. Walters; G. W. House.

WEST INDIA COMMITTEE (1750), 48 Albemarle Street, 3rd Floor, W1X 4AR—*Dir.*, D. A. Jessop.

WEST LONDON MISSION (1887), 19 Thayer Street, W1M 5LJ—*Supt.*, Rev. L. J. Griffiths, PH.D.

WHICH? CONSUMERS' ASSOCIATION (1957), 14 Buckingham Street, WC2N 6DS—*Dir.*, P. Goldman, C.B.E.

WILDLIFE ARTISTS, SOCIETY OF (1962), 17 Carlton House Terrace, S.W.1.—*Pres.*, R. Gillmor.

WILLIAM MORRIS SOCIETY AND KELMSCOTT FELLOWSHIP (1918), Kelmscott House, 26 Upper Mall, W6 9TA—*Hon. Sec.*, P. Preston.

WINE AND SPIRIT ASSOCIATION OF GREAT BRITAIN AND NORTHERN IRELAND, Five Kings House, Kennet Wharf Lane, Upper Thames Street, EC4V 3BH—*Dir.*, R. H. Insoll, E.R.D.

WOMEN ARTISTS, SOCIETY OF (1855), Westminster Gallery, Westminster Central Hall, SW1H 9NU—*Pres.*, Ms. B. Tate.

WOMEN, NATIONAL ADVISORY CENTRE ON CAREERS FOR (1933), 8th Floor, Artillery House, Artillery Row, SW1P 1RT—*Dir.*, Miss K. M. Menon.

WOMEN PILOTS' ASSOCIATION, BRITISH (1955), 25 Foubert's Place, W1V 2AL; *Hon. Sec.*, Mrs. L. J. McRobert.

WOMEN, SOCIETY FOR PROMOTING THE TRAINING OF (1859), The Dean Cottages, Hedgerley, Bucks. SL2 3UY. Interest-free loan training fund for women students in higher education—*Sec.*, Mrs. W. M. Golding.

WOMEN'S ENGINEERING SOCIETY (1920), Imperial College of Science and Technology, Dept. of Civil Engineering, Imperial College Road, SW7 2BU—*Sec.*, Mrs. B. Hunt.

WOMEN'S INSTITUTES, NATIONAL FEDERATION OF (1915), 39 Eccleston Street, SW1W 9NT—*Gen. Sec.*, Mrs. A. Ballard.

WOMEN'S INTERNATIONAL LEAGUE FOR PEACE AND FREEDOM (1915) British Section, 29 Great James Street, WC1N 3ES—*Chair*, Ms. E. Goffe.

WOMEN'S NATIONAL CANCER CONTROL CAMPAIGN, 1 South Audley Street, W1Y 5DQ—*Dir.*, Alice Burns.

WOMEN'S ROYAL NAVAL SERVICE BENEVOLENT TRUST, 1A Chesham Street, SW1X 8NL—*Sec.*, Mrs. J. Y. Ellis.

WOMEN'S ROYAL VOLUNTARY SERVICE (WRVS) (1938), 234–244 Stockwell Road, SW9 9SP—*National Chairman*, Dame Barbara Shenfield, D.B.E.

WOMEN'S TRANSPORT SERVICE (FANY) (1907), Duke of York's H.Q., Chelsea, SW3 4SJ—*Corps Commander*, Mrs. S. Y. Parkinson, O.B.E.

WOODLAND TRUST, THE (1972), Autumn Park, Dysart Road, Grantham, Lincs. NG31 6LL—*Exec. Dir.*, J. D. James.

WOOD PRESERVING ASSOCIATION, BRITISH, Premier House, 150 Southampton Row, WC1B 5AL—*Dir.*, C. J. Butler.

WORCESTERSHIRE ASSOCIATION (1926).—*Hon. Sec.*, D. M. Alexander, 8 Sansome Walk, Worcester WR1 1LW.

WORKERS' EDUCATIONAL ASSOCIATION, Temple House, 9 Upper Berkeley Street, W1H 8BY—*Gen. Sec.*, R. Lochrie.

WORLD EDUCATION FELLOWSHIP (1921), 33 Kinnaird Avenue, W4 3SH—*Gen. Sec.*, Mrs. R. Crommelin.

WORLD ENERGY CONFERENCE (1924), 34 St. James's Street, SW1A 1HD—*Sec. Gen.*, I. D. Lindsay.

WORLD MISSION, COUNCIL FOR (1977), Livingstone House, 11 Carteret Street, SW1H 9DL—Successor to the Congregational Council for World Mission, the London Missionary Society, the Commonwealth Missionary Society and the Presbyterian Church of England Overseas Mission.—*Gen. Sec.*, Rev. Dr. C. Duraisingh.

WORLD SHIP SOCIETY (1946).—*Sec.*, S. J. F. Miller, 35 Wickham Way, Haywards Heath, W. Sussex RH16 1UJ.

WORLD SOCIETY FOR THE PROTECTION OF ANIMALS, 106 Jermyn Street, SW1Y 6EE—*Dir. Gen.*, T. H. Scott.

WORLD WILDLIFE FUND—U.K. (1961), Panda House, 11–13 Ockford Road, Godalming, Surrey GU7 1QU—*Dir.*, G. J. Medley.

WRITERS TO H.M. SIGNET, SOCIETY OF, 16 Hill Street, Edinburgh EH2 3LD—*Deputy Keeper of the Signet*, P. C. Millar, O.B.E.; *Sub-Keeper and Clerk*, A. M. Kerr.

YEOMANRY BENEVOLENT FUND, 10 Stone Buildings, Lincoln's Inn, WC2A 3TG—*Sec.*, Mrs. C. W. Chrystie.

YORKSHIRE AGRICULTURAL SOCIETY (1837), Great Yorkshire Showground, Hookstone Oval, Harrogate HG2 8PW—*Sec.-Gen.*, Lt. Col. M. G. A. Young.

YORKSHIRE SOCIETY, THE (1812), 18 Broom Lock, Teddington, Middx. TW11 9QP. Educational trust fund making grants to students of all ages.—*Sec.*, G. G. Prince, T.D.

YOUNG MEN'S CHRISTIAN ASSOCIATION, *National Council*, 640 Forest Road, E17 3DZ—*Nat. Sec.*, C. J. Naylor.

YOUNG WOMEN'S CHRISTIAN ASSOCIATION (1855), Clarendon House, 52 Cornmarket Street, Oxford OX1 3EJ—*Exec. Dir.*, Miss F. E. Sharples.

YOUTH CLUBS, NATIONAL ASSOCIATION OF, 30 Peacock Lane, Leicester LE1 5NY.—*Chief Exec.*, J. Holt.

YOUTH CLUBS, NORTHERN IRELAND ASSOCIATION OF, Hampton, Glenmachan Park, Belfast BT4 2PJ—*Dir.*, G. Johnston.

YOUTH HOSTELS ASSOCIATION (ENGLAND AND WALES) (1930), *National Office*, Trevelyan House, 8 St. Stephens Hill, St. Albans, Herts. AL1 2DY—*Chief Exec.*, A. G. F. Chinneck.

YOUTH HOSTELS ASSOCIATION (SCOTTISH) (1931), *National Office*, 7 Glebe Crescent, Stirling FK8 2JA—*Gen. Sec.*, J. Martin.

YOUTH HOSTELS ASSOCIATION OF NORTHERN IRELAND (1931), Bradbury Buildings, 56 Bradbury Place, Belfast BT7 1RU—*Hon. Sec.*, E. R. Henderson.

ZOOLOGICAL SOCIETY OF LONDON, Regent's Park, NW1 4RY—*Pres.*, Sir William Henderson, F.R.S.; *Chief Exec.*, J. L. Boyer, O.B.E.; *Sec.*, Dr. R. M. Laws, C.B.E., F.R.S. Attendances (1986), Regent's Park, 1,190,248, and Whipsnade Park, 352,732.

ZOOLOGICAL SOCIETY OF SCOTLAND, ROYAL, Scottish National Zoological Park, Murrayfield, Edinburgh EH12 6TS—*Dir.*, R. J. Wheater, F.R.S.E.

LOCAL HISTORY AND ARCHÆOLOGICAL SOCIETIES

England and Wales

Bedfordshire.—SOUTH BEDFORDSHIRE ARCHÆOLOGICAL SOCIETY. Hon. Sec. D. H. Kennett, 27 Lords Lane, Bradwell, Great Yarmouth, Norfolk NR31 8NY.

Berkshire.—BERKSHIRE ARCHÆOLOGICAL SOCIETY. Hon. Sec., L. J. Over, 43 Laburnham Road, Maidenhead, Berks. SL6 4DE.

NEWBURY DISTRICT FIELD CLUB. Hon. Sec., Mrs. D. E. Hawkes, 22 Westgate Road, Newbury, Berks. RG14 6AX.

Buckinghamshire.—BUCKS ARCHÆOLOGICAL SOCIETY. Hon. Sec., Dr. R. P. Hagerty, County Museum, Church Street, Aylesbury, Bucks. HP20 2QP.

Cambridgeshire.—CAMBRIDGE ANTIQUARIAN SOCIETY. Sec., Miss A. S. Bendall, Emmanuel College, Cambridge CB2 3AP.

Cheshire.—CHESTER ARCHÆOLOGICAL SOCIETY. Sec., G. R. Coppack, Chamonix, Station Lane, Mickle Trafford, Chester CH2 4EH. See also under *Lancashire.*

Cornwall.—CORNWALL ARCHAEOLOGICAL SOCIETY, County Museum and Art Gallery, Truro TR1 2SJ. Hon. Sec., Mrs. A. Cooke.

Cumberland and Westmorland.—CUMBERLAND AND WESTMORLAND ANTIQUARIAN AND ARCHÆOLOGICAL SOCIETY. Hon. Sec., R. Hall, 2 High Tenterfell, Kendal, Cumbria LA9 4PG.

Derbyshire.—DERBYSHIRE ARCHÆOLOGICAL SOCIETY. Hon. Sec., M. E. Burrows, 12 Wilne Road, Draycott, Derby DE7 3NG.

Devonshire.—DEVON ARCHÆOLOGICAL SOCIETY. Hon. Sec., Miss M. Bird, c/o R.A.M. Museum, Queen Street, Exeter EX4 3RX.

Dorset.—DORSET NATURAL HISTORY AND ARCHÆOLOGICAL SOCIETY, Dorset County Museum, Dorchester DT1 1XA. Curator and Sec., R. N. R. Peers.

Durham.—DURHAM AND NORTHUMBERLAND ARCHITECTURAL AND ARCHÆOLOGICAL SOCIETY. Hon. Sec., Dr. M. J. Millett, 46 Saddler Street, Durham DH1 3NU.

Dyfed.—CEREDIGION ANTIQUARIAN SOCIETY. Hon. Sec., D. M. Jones, Tal-y-werydd, Aberarth, Aberaeron, Dyfed SA46 0LX.

Essex.—ESSEX SOCIETY FOR ARCHÆOLOGY AND HISTORY, Hollytrees Museum, High Street, Colchester CO1 1UG. Sec., Mrs. E. Sellars.

Gloucestershire.—BRISTOL AND GLOUCESTERSHIRE ARCHÆOLOGICAL SOCIETY, Hon. Sec., D. J. H. Smith, 22 Beaumont Road, Gloucester GL2 0EJ.

Hampshire.—HAMPSHIRE FIELD CLUB AND ARCHÆOLOGICAL SOCIETY. Hon. Sec., Dr. M. A. Hicks, King Alfred's College, Winchester, Hants. SO22 4NR.

Herefordshire.—WOOLHOPE NATURALISTS' FIELD CLUB. Hon. Sec., J. W. Tonkin, F.S.A., Chy an Whyloryon, Wigmore, Leominster, Herefordshire HR6 9UD.

Hertfordshire.—EAST HERTFORDSHIRE ARCHÆOLOGICAL SOCIETY. Hon. Sec., Mrs. M. C. Readman, 1 Marsh Lane, Stanstead Abbots, Ware, Herts. SG12 8HH.

ST. ALBANS AND HERTFORDSHIRE ARCHITECTURAL AND ARCHÆOLOGICAL SOCIETY. Hon. Sec., F. I. Kilvington, 122 Marshalswick Lane, St. Albans AL1 4XD.

Kent.—KENT ARCHÆOLOGICAL SOCIETY. Gen. Sec., A. C. Harrison, F.S.A., Prings Cottage, Pilgrims Road, Upper Halling, Rochester ME2 1HR.

Lancashire.— HISTORIC SOCIETY OF LANCASHIRE AND CHESHIRE. Hon. Sec., Dr. J. E. Hollinshead, Liverpool Institute of H.E., Stand Park Road, Liverpool LI6 9JD.

Leicestershire.—LEICESTERSHIRE ARCHAEOLOGICAL AND HISTORICAL SOCIETY. Hon. Sec., Dr. A. D. McWhirr.

London and Middlesex.—CITY OF LONDON ARCHÆOLOGICAL SOCIETY. Hon. Sec., D. R. Lewis, 28 Rothesay Avenue SW20 8JU.

LONDON AND MIDDLESEX ARCHÆOLOGICAL SOCIETY. Hon. Sec., Miss J. Macdonald, 3 Cedar Drive, Pinner, Middx. HA5 4DD.

Norfolk.—NORFOLK AND NORWICH ARCHÆOLOGICAL SOCIETY. Hon. Gen. Sec., R. Bellinger, 30 Brettingham Avenue, Cringleford, Norwich NR4 6XG.

Northumberland and Tyne and Wear.—SOCIETY OF ANTIQUARIES OF NEWCASTLE UPON TYNE. Sec., Dr. C. M. Fraser, c/o Centre for Continuing Education, University of Newcastle upon Tyne NE1 7RU.

SUNDERLAND ANTIQUARIAN SOCIETY. Hon. Sec., G. Patterson, 8 Humbledon View, Sunderland SR2 7RX.

Nottinghamshire.—THOROTON SOCIETY OF NOTTINGHAMSHIRE, Bromley House, Angel Row, Nottingham NG1 6HL. Hon. Sec., J. S. Childs, F.R.S.A.

Oxfordshire.—OXFORDSHIRE ARCHITECTURAL AND HISTORICAL SOCIETY. Hon. Sec., Miss J. M. Cook, Ashmolean Museum, Oxford OX1 2PH.

Powys.—POWYSLAND CLUB. Hon. Sec., W. G. J. Hughes, The Library, Brook Street, Welshpool, Powys SY21 7PH.

RADNORSHIRE SOCIETY. Hon. Sec., A. Batley, c/o Radnor College of F.E., Llandrindod Wells, Powys LD1 5ES.

Shropshire.—SHROPSHIRE ARCHÆOLOGICAL SOCIETY. Chairman, J. B. Lawson, Westcott Farm, Habberley, Pontesbury, Shropshire SY5 0SQ.

Somerset.—SOMERSET ARCHÆOLOGICAL AND NATURAL HISTORY SOCIETY, Taunton Castle, Taunton TA1 4AD. Hon. Sec., J. Reynolds.

Staffordshire.—CITY OF STOKE-ON-TRENT MUSEUM ARCHÆOLOGICAL SOCIETY, City Museum and Art Gallery, Hanley, Stoke-on-Trent. Chairman, E. E. Royle.

Suffolk.—SUFFOLK INSTITUTE OF ARCHÆOLOGY AND HISTORY. Hon. Sec., E. A. Martin, Oak Tree Farm, Finborough Road, Hitcham, Ipswich IP7 7LS.

Surrey.—SURREY ARCHÆOLOGICAL SOCIETY, Castle Arch, Guildford GU1 3SX. Hon. Secs., Mr. and Mrs. K. D. Graham.

Sussex.—SUSSEX ARCHÆOLOGICAL SOCIETY, Barbican House, High Street, Lewes, E. Sussex BN7 1YE. Sec. and Gen. Administrator, J. Houghton.

Warwickshire.—BIRMINGHAM AND WARWICKSHIRE ARCHÆOLOGICAL SOCIETY, c/o Birmingham and Midland Institute, Margaret Street, Birmingham B3 3BS. Hon. Sec., A. J. Wilson.

Wight.—ISLE OF WIGHT NATURAL HISTORY AND ARCHÆOLOGICAL SOCIETY. Hon. Sec., Mrs. T. Goodley, Ivy Cottage, New Barn Lane, Shorwell, Isle of Wight PO30 3JQ.

Wiltshire.—WILTSHIRE ARCHÆOLOGICAL AND NATURAL HISTORY SOCIETY, The Secretary, The Museum, 41 Long Street, Devizes SN10 1NS.

Worcestershire.—WORCESTERSHIRE ARCHÆOLOGICAL SOCIETY. *Hon. Sec.*, Mrs. G. Grice, 91 Hallow Road, Worcester WR2 6DF.

Yorkshire.—YORKSHIRE ARCHÆOLOGICAL SOCIETY. *Hon. Sec.*, P. B. Davidson, Claremont, 23 Clarendon Road, Leeds LS2 9NZ.

HALIFAX ANTIQUARIAN SOCIETY. *Hon. Sec.*, J. Hargreaves, 7 Hyde Park Gardens, Halifax HX1 3AH.

THORESBY SOCIETY. *Hon. Sec.*, D. M. Watson. Claremont, 23 Clarendon Road, Leeds LS2 9NZ.

Channel Islands

SOCIETE JERSIAISE, Archaeological Section, The Jersey Museum, Pier Road, St. Helier, Jersey. *Hon. Sec.*, Ms. T. Tilling.

Scotland

AYRSHIRE ARCHÆOLOGICAL AND NATURAL HISTORY SOCIETY. *Hon. Sec.*, G. E. Sleight, 1 Portmark Avenue, Ayr KA7 4DD.

DUMFRIES AND GALLOWAY NATURAL HISTORY AND ANTIQUARIAN SOCIETY. *Hon. Sec.*, R. H. McEwen, Seaforth, 13 Douglas Terrace, Lockerbie, Dumfries DG11 2DZ.

HAWICK ARCHÆOLOGICAL SOCIETY. *Hon. Sec.*, I. W. Landles, Orrock House, Stirches Road, Hawick, Borders TD9 7HF.

INVERNESS FIELD CLUB. *Hon. Sec.*, Mrs. E. H. L. Macaskill, 9 Dores Road, Inverness IV2 4QX.

THE CIVIC TRUST
17 Carlton House Terrace, SW1Y 5AW
[01–930 0914]

The Civic Trust is a registered charity whose object is to stimulate interest in, and action for, the improvement of the environment throughout the U.K. It was founded in 1957 by Lord Duncan-Sandys. The Trust is supported by voluntary contributions. It has no individual membership and owns no land but works in close co-operation with over a 1,000 local amenity societies. It acts as a spokesman on issues of national concern.

The Trust fosters high standards in planning, design, restoration and new building. It makes annual awards for good development of all kinds. As a result of initiatives where successful programmes of environmental improvement, economic growth and community involvement have been implemented, the Urban Regeneration Unit has been set up to extend the experience gained and to act as a consultancy in other areas.

The Trust is regularly consulted by Government about new legislation concerning the environment. (It inspired the Civic Amenities Act, 1967 which created Conservation Areas.) Frequent published reports focus attention on important issues.

The Trust works in close co-operation with the Architectural Heritage Fund, which operates a national "revolving fund" to help local charities preserve worthwhile old properties which the market deems too difficult to tackle.

On behalf of the Department of the Environment, the Trust runs the Heritage Education Group which aims to stimulate environmental education at all levels, but particularly in schools. The Trust is also a founder member of the Government's UK2000 initiative. It organizes annually National Environment Week.

There are Associate Trusts in the North East and North West of England, in Scotland and in Wales.— *Dir.*, M. C. Bradshaw.

NATIONAL TRUST
36 Queen Anne's Gate, SW1H 9AS
[01–222 9251]

The National Trust was founded in 1895 by Miss Octavia Hill, Sir Robert Hunter and Canon Rawnsley, their object being to preserve as much as possible the history and beauty of their country for its people. It became an organization incorporated by Act of Parliament (1907) to ensure the preservation of lands and buildings of historic interest or natural beauty for public access and benefit. It is independent of the State and relies on the voluntary support of private individuals for working funds. The Trust has now some 1,500,000 members paying an annual subscription. Rents, admission fees, legacies and gifts are other important sources of support and income.

The Trust protects more than 610,000 acres, much of it in the Lake District, Snowdonia, the Peak District and other National Parks. The Trust also owns and opens to the public some 291 country houses, other buildings and gardens and preserves villages, nature reserves, archæological sites and many farms.

In 1965 the Trust launched Enterprise Neptune, a campaign to acquire as much as possible of the most beautiful stretches of coastline which were under threat from development. The Trust now protects more than 475 miles of coastline.

The policy of the Trust is determined by the governing body, the Council. Half of its members are appointed by national institutions, such as the British Museum, the National Gallery, the Ramblers' Association and the Royal Horticultural Society; the other half are elected by Trust members at the annual general meeting. The Council appoints the Executive Committee, which in turn has established Regional Committees responsible for the management of the Trust's properties.

Chairman, Dame Jennifer Jenkins; *Dir. Gen.*, A. Stirling.

NATIONAL TRUST FOR SCOTLAND
5 Charlotte Square, Edinburgh EH2 4DU

The National Trust for Scotland was founded in 1931, and its objects are similar to those of the National Trust. Like that organization, it is incorporated by Act of Parliament and is dependent for finance upon legacies, donations and the subscriptions of its members.

The Trust administers over 100 properties covering over 100,000 acres.

In the Trust's care are also several noteworthy gardens, some associated with the great houses.

Among the mountainous country owned by the Trust is the Pass of Glen Coe and the mountain group "The Five Sisters of Kintail" and the estate of Torridon in Wester Ross, and Ben Lomond.

Islands in the Trust's care include the St. Kilda group, Staffa, Fair Isle, Iona and Canna. At Bannockburn, Killiecrankie, Glenfinnan and Culloden, the Trust owns sites associated with Scottish history.

At Culross, in other Fife coastal villages, and at Dunkeld, Perthshire, the restoration of architecturally attractive groups of houses led to the creation of the Little Houses Improvement Scheme, under which properties are bought, restored and re-sold. Since its inception over 200 houses reflecting the vernacular architecture of Scotland have been restored throughout the country. In addition to its other activities, the Little Houses Improvement Scheme operates a property marketing service.

THE COST OF LIVING

The first cost-of-living index to be calculated in Great Britain was the one which took July, 1914, as 100 and was based on the pattern of expenditure of working class families in 1904. Since 1947 the Index of Retail Prices has superseded the cost-of-living index, although the older term is still often popularly applied to it. This index is designed to reflect the month-by-month changes in the average level of retail prices of goods and services purchased by the "majority" of households in the United Kingdom, including practically all wage-earners and most small and medium salary-earners. For spending coming within the scope of the index, a representative list of items is selected and the prices actually charged for these items are collected at regular intervals. In working out the index figure, the price changes are "weighted"—that is, given different degrees of importance—in accordance with the pattern of consumption of the average family.

A more widely used guide when considering changes in the average level of prices of all consumer goods and services, particularly over a number of years, is the consumer price index, now renamed the consumers' expenditure deflator. This index, which has been calculated back to 1938, covers the expenditure of all consumers as defined for national income purposes, and compares the price of goods and services actually purchased in a given year with the prices of the same goods and services in a base year.

During 1973 the Central Statistical Office constructed an annual index of prices of consumer goods and services over the period 1914 to 1972. This index has been constructed by linking together the pre-war cost of living index for the period 1914–1938, the consumers' expenditure deflator for the period 1938 and 1946–62* and the General Index of Retail Prices for the period 1962–1972.

In August 1979, the tax and price index (TPI) was introduced in order to provide a statistic which incorporates the effects of direct and indirect taxation, as well as prices, on taxpayers. The TPI is not directly concerned with the purchasing power of money, however, but with the purchasing power of pre-tax income. The General Index of Retail Prices thus retains its function of measuring the changes in the prices of goods and services purchased by households (from their post-tax income), and therefore as an indicator of the purchasing power of money.

In 1974 the General Index of Retail Prices was rebased taking January 1974 = 100. Using this index the following table has been constructed:

	General Index of Retail Prices (all items) Jan. 1974 = 100	Comparable Purchasing Power of £1 in 1986
	Annual averages	
1914............	11·1	34·76
1915............	13·7	28·16
1920............	27·7	13·93
1925............	19·6	19·68
1930............	17·6	21·92
1935............	15·9	24·27
1940............	24·4	15·81
1945............	29·3	13·17
1950............	35·6	10·83
1955............	44·1	8·75
1960............	49·6	7·78
1965............	58·4	6·60
1970............	73·1	5·27
1971............	80·0	4·82
1972............	85·7	4·50
1973............	93·5	4·12
1974............	108·5	3·55
1975............	134·8	2·86
1976............	157·1	2·45
1977............	182·0	2·12
1978............	197·1	1·95
1979............	223·5	1·72
1980............	263·7	1·46
1981............	295·0	1·30
1982............	320·4	1·20
1983............	335·1	1·15
1984............	351·8	1·09
1985............	373·2	1·03
1986............	385·9	1·00

By employing this table an annual purchasing power of the pound index may be derived by taking the inverse of the price index. So, for example, if the purchasing power of the pound is taken to be 100p in 1972, then its comparable purchasing power in 1986 would be:

$$100 \times \frac{85 \cdot 7}{385 \cdot 9} = 22 \cdot 2p$$

It should be noted that these figures can only be approximate.

* There are no official figures for 1939–45.

CONFEDERATION OF BRITISH INDUSTRY

Centre Point, 103 New Oxford Street, London WC1A 1DU

[01-379 7400]

The Confederation of British Industry was founded in August 1965 and is an independent non-party political body financed by industry and commerce. It exists primarily to ensure that the Government understands the intentions, needs and problems of British business. It is the recognized spokesman for the business viewpoint and is consulted as such by the Government.

The C.B.I. represents, directly and indirectly, some 250,000 companies. All the nationalized industries are in membership and thereby able to work with the C.B.I. on problems that are the concern of all management.

The governing body of the C.B.I. is the 400-strong Council, which meets monthly in London under the chairmanship of the President. It is assisted by some 27 expert standing committees which advise on the main aspects of policy. There are 13 Regional Councils and offices covering the administrative regions of England, Scotland, Wales and Northern Ireland.

President, Sir David Nickson, K.B.E.
Director-General, J. Banham.
Secretary, M. W. Hunt.

NATIONAL ASSOCIATION OF INDUSTRIES FOR THE BLIND AND DISABLED INC.

Triton House, 43A High Street South,
Dunstable, Beds. LU6 3RZ
[0582–606796]

The National Association of Industries for the Blind and Disabled Inc. was established in 1929 and incorporated in 1936; it is registered as a charity.

The Association acts in the nature of a trade association providing facilities for consultation and co-operation between its members who operate workshops employing blind and disabled people and it represents their interests in discussions with, and

representations to, other organisations (e.g. government departments and local authorities) concerned with sheltered employment. It does not own or operate any of the workshops, which are run by local authorities or voluntary organisations acting as their agents.

Chairman (1987–88), D. D. Cawthorn.
Hon. Secretary, G. J. Entwistle.

EMPLOYERS' AND TRADE BODIES

ADVERTISING ASSOCIATION, Abford House, 15 Wilton Road, SW1V 1NJ.—*Dir. Gen.,* R. Underhill, O.B.E.

AEROSPACE COMPANIES LTD., SOCIETY OF BRITISH (1926), 29 King Street, SW1Y 6RD.—*Dir.,* Air Marshal Sir John Curtiss, K.C.B., K.B.E.

AGRICULTURAL EXPORT COUNCIL, BRITISH, 35 Belgrave Square, SW1X 8QN.—*Chief Exec.,* P. N. Sillars.

BAKERS, FEDERATION OF, 20 Bedford Square, WC1B 3HF.—*Dir.,* A. Casdagli, C.B.E.

BANKERS' ASSOCIATION, BRITISH, 10 Lombard Street, EC3V 9EL.—*Sec.-Gen.,* J. B. Atherton.

BREWERS' SOCIETY, 42 Portman Square, W1H 0BB.—*Dir.,* Maj. Gen. W. D. Mangham, C.B.

BUILDING EMPLOYERS' CONFEDERATION, 82 New Cavendish Street, W1M 8AD.—*Dir. Gen.,* J. A. Newby.

BUILDING MATERIAL PRODUCERS, NATIONAL COUNCIL OF, 10 Great George Street, SW1P 3AE.—*Dir. Gen.,* N. M. Chaldecott.

BUS AND COACH COUNCIL, Sardinia House, 52 Lincoln's Inn Fields, WC2A 3LZ.—*Dir. Gen.,* D. R. Quin.

CHEMICAL INDUSTRIES ASSOCIATION LTD., Alembic House, 93 Albert Embankment, SE1 7TU.—*Dir. Gen.,* J. C. L. Cox.

CLOTHING INDUSTRY ASSOCIATION LTD., BRITISH, British Apparel Centre, 7 Swallow Place, W1R 7AA.—*Dir.* J. R. Wilson.

DAIRY TRADE FEDERATION, 19 Cornwall Terrace, NW1 4QP.—*Dir. Gen.,* J. P. Price.

ELECTROTECHNICAL AND ALLIED MANUFACTURERS' ASSOCIATION, FEDERATION OF BRITISH (BEAMA), Leicester House, 8 Leicester Street, WC2H 7BN.—*Dir. Gen.,* G. Gaddes.

ENGINEERING EMPLOYERS' FEDERATION, Broadway House, Tothill Street, SW1H 9NQ.—*Dir. Gen.,* Dr. J. McFarlane, C.B.E.

FARMERS' UNION, THE NATIONAL, Agriculture House, Knightsbridge, SW1X 7NJ.—*Dir. Gen.,* D. Evans.

FARMERS' UNION OF SCOTLAND, NATIONAL, 17 Grosvenor Crescent, Edinburgh EH12 5EN.—*Dir.,* D. S. Johnston.

FARMERS' UNION, ULSTER, Dunedin, 475–477 Antrim Road, Belfast BT15 3DA.—*Gen. Sec.,* J. V. Smyth.

FOOD AND DRINK FEDERATION, 6 Catherine Street, WC2B 5JJ.—*Dir. Gen.,* M. P. Mackenzie.

FREIGHT TRANSPORT ASSOCIATION LTD., Hermes House, 157 St. John's Road, Tunbridge Wells, Kent TN4 9UZ.—*Dir. Gen.,* G. Turvey.

INSURERS, ASSOCIATION OF BRITISH, Aldermary House, Queen Street, EC4N 1TT.—*Chief Exec.,* M. A. Jones.

KNITTING INDUSTRIES FEDERATION LTD., 7 Gregory Boulevard, Nottingham NG7 6NB.—*Dir.,* J. P. Harrisson.

LEATHER CONFEDERATION, BRITISH, Leather Trade House, Kings Park Road, Moulton Park, Northampton NN3 1JD.—*Dir.,* Dr. R. L. Sykes, O.B.E.

LEATHER PRODUCERS' ASSOCIATION, Leather Trade House, Kings Park Road, Moulton Park, Northampton NN3 1JD.—*Nat. Sec.*, J. Purvis.

MAN-MADE FIBRES FEDERATION, BRITISH, 24 Buckingham Gate, SW1E 6LB.

MARINE INDUSTRIES FEDERATION, BRITISH, Boating Industry House, Vale Road, Oatlands Park, Weybridge, Surrey KT13 9NS.—*Chief Exec.*, P. V. Wagstaffe.

MOTOR MANUFACTURERS AND TRADERS LTD., SOCIETY OF, Forbes House, Halkin Street, SW1X 7DS—*Dir.*, A. W. Fraser.

NEWSPAPER PUBLISHERS ASSOCIATION LTD., 6 Bouverie Street, EC4Y 8AY.—*Dir.*, J. E. Lepage.

OFFICE SYSTEMS AND STATIONERY FEDERATION, BRITISH, 6 Wimpole Street, W1M 8AS.—*Dir.*, D. F. Hall.

PAPER AND BOARD INDUSTRY FEDERATION, BRITISH, 3 Plough Place, Fetter Lane, EC4A 1AL.—*Dir. Gen.*, W. J. Bartlett.

PLASTICS FEDERATION, BRITISH, 5 Belgrave Square, SW1X 8PH.—*Dir.*, R. Lewis, O.B.E.

PORT EMPLOYERS, NATIONAL ASSOCIATION OF, Commonwealth House, 1–19 New Oxford Street, WC1A 1DZ.—*Dir.*, N. H. Finney.

PORTS ASSOCIATION, BRITISH, Commonwealth House, 1–19 New Oxford Street, WC1A 1DZ.—*Dir.* N. H. Finney.

PRINTING INDUSTRIES FEDERATION, BRITISH, 11 Bedford Row, WC1R 4DX.—*Dir. Gen.*, S. W. Bradley.

PUBLISHERS ASSOCIATION, THE, 19 Bedford Square, WC1B 3HJ.—*Chief Exec.*, C. Bradley.

RADIO CONTRACTORS LTD., ASSOCIATION OF INDEPENDENT, Regina House, 259–269 Old Marylebone Road, NW1 5RA.—*Dir.*, B. West.

RETAIL CONSORTIUM, THE, Commonwealth House, 1–19 New Oxford Street, WC1A 1PA.—*Dir. Gen.*, R. Weir.

ROAD FEDERATION LTD., BRITISH, Cowdray House, 6 Portugal Street, WC2A 2HG.—*Dir.*, P. Witt.

ROAD HAULAGE ASSOCIATION LTD., Roadway House, 104 New Kings Road, SW6 4LN.—*Dir. Gen.*, F. J. Plaskett, C.B., M.B.E.

RUBBER MANUFACTURERS' ASSOCIATION LTD., BRITISH, 90–91 Tottenham Court Road, W1P 0BR.—*Dir.*, G. C. Gullan.

SHIPPING, GENERAL COUNCIL OF BRITISH, 30–32 St. Mary Axe, EC3A 8ET.—*Pres.*, (1987–88), K. St. Johnston; *Dir. Gen.*, P. Le Cheminant, C.B.

SPORT AND ALLIED INDUSTRIES FEDERATION LTD., BRITISH, Prudential House, Wellesley Road, Croydon, Surrey CR0 9XY.—*Chief Exec.*, L. F. Standen.

TELEVISION COMPANIES ASSOCIATION LTD., INDEPENDENT, Knighton House, 56 Mortimer Street, W1N 8AN.—*Gen Sec.*, D. Shaw.

TEXTILE CONFEDERATION, BRITISH, 24 Buckingham Gate, SW1E 6LB.—*Dir.*, I. MacArthur.

TIMBER GROWERS' UNITED KINGDOM, Agriculture House, Knightsbridge, SW1X 7NJ.—*Chief Exec.*, A. R. Williams.

TIMBER MERCHANTS' ASSOCIATION, BRITISH, Ridgeway House, 6 Ridgeway Road, Long Ashton, Bristol BS18 9EU.—*Sec.*, H. B. Roberts.

TIMBER TRADE FEDERATION, THE, Clareville House, 26–27 Oxenden Street, SW1Y 4EL. *Dir. Gen.*, A. A. Lockyer, L.V.O.

U.K. OFFSHORE OPERATORS ASSOCIATION LTD., 3 Hans Crescent, SW1X 0LN.—*Dir.*, G. C. Band.

U.K. PETROLEUM INDUSTRY ASSOCIATION LTD., 9 Kingsway, WC2B 6XH.—*Dir. Gen.*, Dr. I. D. G. Berwick.

WHOLESALE AND INDUSTRIAL DISTRIBUTORS, FEDERATION OF, The Old Post Office, Dunchideock, Exeter EX2 9TU.—*Dir.*, J. Hussey.

CAR PRODUCTION IN MAIN PRODUCING COUNTRIES (thousands)

	1977	1978	1979	1980	1981	1982	1983	1984	1985	1986
United Kingdom	1,328	1,223	1,070	924	955	888	1,045	909	1,048	1,019
France	3,092	3,111	3,220	2,939	2,612	2,777	2,961	2,713	2,632	2,773
W. Germany	3,790	3,890	3,933	3,521	3,578	3,761	3,878	3,790	4,167	4,311
Italy	1,440	1,509	1,481	1,445	1,257	1,297	1,396	1,439	1,389	1,652
Sweden	235	254	297	235	258	295	345	353	401	421
Japan	5,431	5,748	6,176	7,038	6,974	6,882	7,152	7,073	7,647	7,810
U.S.A.	9,214	9,176	8,434	6,376	6,253	5,073	6,781	7,774	8,185	7,829
Canada	1,162	1,143	988	847	803	808	969	1,021	1,078	1,061
Total	25,692	26,054	25,599	23,325	22,690	21,785	24,527	25,072	26,547	26,876
UK % of total	5	5	4	4	4	4	4	4	4	4

BRITISH MOTOR VEHICLE PRODUCTION AND EXPORTS

Year	Weeks	Passenger Cars (including taxis)			Commercial Road Vehicles		
		For Export*	Total	Weekly average	For Export*	Total	Weekly average
1980......	...52...	349,592	923,744	17,764	156,270	387,359	7,484
1981......	...52...	304,678	954,650	18,359	113,862	229,555	4,416
1982......	...52...	225,865	887,679	17,070	92,510	268,798	5,169
1983......	...53...	237,376	1,044,597	19,709	62,801	244,514	4,613
1984......	...52...	192,213	908,906	17,479	49,808	224,825	4,323
1985......	...52...	207,671	1,047,973	20,153	65,756	265,973	5,115
1986......	...52...	187,556	1,018,962	19,595	49,776	228,685	4,398

*Export Allocation

TRADES UNION CONGRESS (T.U.C.)

Congress House, 23–28 Great Russell Street, WC1B 3LS
[01–636–4030]

The Trades Union Congress, founded in 1868, is a voluntary association of Trade Unions, the representatives of which meet annually to consider matters of common concern to their members. The Congress has met annually since 1871 and in recent years has met normally on the first Monday in September, its sessions extending through the succeeding four days. Congress is constituted by delegates of the affiliated unions on the basis of one delegate for every 5,000 members, or fraction thereof, on whose behalf affiliation fees are paid. Affiliated unions (in 1986–87) totalled 88 with an aggregate membership of 9,585,729.

The main business of the annual Congress is to consider the report of its General Council dealing with the activities of the Congress year, along with motions from affiliated societies on questions of policy and organization.

The Standing Committees of the General Council are serviced by a full time staff appointed by the General Secretary, who is himself elected by Congress and who remains in office until the age of 65, subject to decision of Congress or the General Council.

Through the General Council and its committees the trade union movement maintains systematic relations with the Government and Government Departments, with the Confederation of British Industry and with a large number of other bodies. It is represented on the National Economic Development Council, the Manpower Services Commission, the Health and Safety Commission, the Council of the Advisory Conciliation and Arbitration Service and a number of other bodies.

Among powers vested in the General Council by consent of the unions in Congress is the responsibility of intervening in disputes and differences between affiliated organizations; if possible this is done through informal conciliation meetings under T.U.C. auspices but where necessary a Disputes Committee is formed consisting of one member of the General Council and two senior officials of unions not involved in the dispute. This investigates the matter concerned and issues its findings.

Unions retain full control of their own affairs and the only sanctions which Congress can apply are suspension or exclusion from membership.

Chairman (1987–88), C. Jenkins (*Association of Scientific, Technical and Managerial Staffs*).
General Secretary, N. D. Willis.

SCOTTISH TRADES UNION CONGRESS

16 Woodlands Terrace, Glasgow G3 6DF
[041-332 4946]

The Congress was formed in 1897 and acts as a national centre for the trade union movement in Scotland. In 1987 it consisted of 63 unions with a membership of 913,186 and 49 directly affiliated Trades Councils. The majority of the unions organize throughout Britain and affiliate on their membership in Scotland.

The Annual Congress in April elects a 26-member General Council on the basis of 13 industrial sections. Congress has been prominent in pressing for economic expansion and full employment in Scotland and the development of the social services, most of which are separately organized in Scotland.

Chairperson C. Gallacher.
General Secretary, C. Christie.

TRADES UNIONS AFFILIATED TO T.U.C.

A list of the Trades Unions affiliated to the Trades Union Congress in September, 1987. The number of members of each Union is shown in parenthesis.

AMALGAMATED ASSOCIATION OF BEAMERS, TWISTERS AND DRAWERS, THE (550), 27 Every Street, Nelson, Lancs. BB9 7NE—*Gen. Sec.*, A. H. Edmondson.

AMALGAMATED ENGINEERING UNION (A.E.U.) (857,559), 110 Peckham Road, SE15 5EL—*Gen. Sec.*, G. H. Laird.

AMALGAMATED SOCIETY OF TEXTILE WORKERS AND KINDRED TRADES (3,100), Foxlowe, Market Place, Leek, Staffs. ST13 6AD—*Gen. Sec.*, A. Hitchmough.

AMALGAMATED UNION OF ASPHALT WORKERS, THE (1,662), Jenkin House, 173a Queens Road, SE15 2NF—*Acting Gen. Sec.*, D. A. McCann.

ASSOCIATED METALWORKERS' UNION, THE (1,900), 92 Deansgate, Manchester M3 2QG—*Gen. Sec.*, R. Marron.

ASSOCIATED SOCIETY OF LOCOMOTIVE ENGINEERS AND FIREMEN (A.S.L.E.F.) (21,446), 9 Arkwright Road, Hampstead, NW3 6AB—*Sec.*, N. Milligan.

ASSOCIATION OF CINEMATOGRAPH, TELEVISION AND ALLIED TECHNICIANS (27,000), 111 Wardour Street, W1V 4AY—*Gen. Sec.*, A. Sapper.

ASSOCIATION OF FIRST DIVISION CIVIL SERVANTS (9,500), 2 Caxton Street, SW1H 0QH—*Gen. Sec.*, J. Ward.

ASSOCIATION OF PROFESSIONAL, EXECUTIVE, CLERICAL AND COMPUTER STAFF (APEX) (90,000), 22 Worple Road, SW19 4DF—*Gen. Sec.*, R. Grantham.

ASSOCIATION OF SCIENTIFIC, TECHNICAL AND MANAGERIAL STAFFS (A.S.T.M.S.) (390,000), 79 Camden Road, NW1 9ES—*Gen. Sec.*, C. Jenkins.

ASSOCIATION OF UNIVERSITY TEACHERS (30,000), United House, 1 Pembridge Road, W11 3HJ—*Gen. Sec.*, Ms. D. Warwick.

BAKERS, FOOD AND ALLIED WORKERS' UNION (36,000), Stanborough House, Great North Road, Stanborough, Welwyn Garden City, Herts. AL8 7TA—*Gen. Sec.*, J. R. Marino.

BANKING, INSURANCE AND FINANCE UNION, THE (157,000), Sheffield House, 1b Amity Grove, SW20 0LG—*Gen. Sec.*, L. Mills.

BRITISH ACTORS' EQUITY ASSOCIATION (35,000), 8 Harley Street, W1N 2AB—*Gen. Sec.*, P. Plouviez.

BRITISH AIR LINE PILOTS ASSOCIATION, THE (3,700), 81 New Road, Harlington, Hayes, Middlesex UB3 5BG—*Gen. Sec.*, M. Young.

BRITISH ASSOCIATION OF COLLIERY MANAGEMENT, THE (13,908), 317 Nottingham Road, Old Basford, Nottingham NG7 7DP—*Gen. Sec.*, A. Wilson.

BROADCASTING AND ENTERTAINMENT TRADES ALLIANCE (42,501), 181–185 Wardour Street, W1V 4BE—*Gen. Sec.*, D. A. Hearn.

CARD SETTING MACHINE TENTERS' SOCIETY (102), 36 Greenton Avenue, Scholes, Cleckheaton, W. Yorks. BD19 6DT—*Sec.*, G. Priestley.

CERAMIC AND ALLIED TRADES UNION, THE (30,470), Hillcrest House, Garth Street, Hanley, Stoke-on-Trent ST1 2AB—*Gen. Sec.*, A. W. Clowes.

CIVIL AND PUBLIC SERVICES ASSOCIATION, THE (152,000), 215 Balham High Road, SW17 7BN—*Gen. Sec.*, J. N. Ellis.

CIVIL SERVICE UNION (29,768), 5 Praed Street, W2 1NJ—*Sec.*, J. D. Sheldon.

COMMUNICATION MANAGERS' ASSOCIATION (19,500), Hughes House, Ruscombe Business Park, Twyford, Reading RG10 9JD—*Gen. Sec.*, R. J. Cowley.

CONFEDERATION OF HEALTH SERVICE EMPLOYEES (C.O.H.S.E.) (214,000), Glen House, High Street, Banstead, Surrey SM7 2LH—*Gen. Sec.*, H. Mackenzie.

EDUCATIONAL INSTITUTE OF SCOTLAND, THE (43,552), 46 Moray Place, Edinburgh EH3 6BH—*Gen. Sec.*, J. D. Pollock.

ELECTRICAL, ELECTRONIC, TELECOMMUNICATION AND PLUMBING UNION (E.E.T.P.U.) (369,469), Hayes Court, West Common Road, Bromley, Kent BR2 7AU—*Gen. Sec.*, E. A. B. Hammond, O.B.E.

ENGINEERS' AND MANAGERS' ASSOCIATION (40,324), Station House, Fox Lane North, Chertsey, Surrey KT16 9HW—*Gen. Sec.*, J. Lyons.

FILM ARTISTES' ASSOCIATION (2,283), 61 Marloes Road, W8 6LE—*Sec.*, S. Brannigan.

FIRE BRIGADES UNION, THE (45,000), Bradley House, 68 Coombe Road, Kingston upon Thames, Surrey KT2 7AE—*Gen. Sec.*, K. Cameron.

FURNITURE, TIMBER AND ALLIED TRADES UNION (47,000), Fairfields, Roe Green, Kingsbury, NW9 0PT—*Gen. Sec.*, C. A. Christopher.

GENERAL, MUNICIPAL BOILERMAKERS AND ALLIED TRADES UNION (G.M.W.) (839,920), Thorne House, Claygate, Esher, Surrey KT10 0TL—*Gen. Sec.*, J. Edmonds.

GENERAL UNION OF ASSOCIATIONS OF LOOM OVER-LOOKERS, THE (1,175), Overlookers Institute, Jude Street, Nelson, Lancs. BB9 7NP—*Pres.*, E. Macro.

GREATER LONDON STAFF ASSOCIATION, THE (12,240), 150 Waterloo Road, SE1 8SB—*Gen. Sec.*, A. Capelin.

HEALTH VISITORS' ASSOCIATION (16,250), 50 Southwark Street, SE1 1UN—*Gen. Sec.*, Ms. S. Goodwin.

HOSPITAL CONSULTANTS AND SPECIALISTS ASSOCIATION, THE (2,374), The Old Court House, London Road, Ascot, Berks. SL5 7EN—*Chief Exec.*, R. B. Martin.

INLAND REVENUE STAFF FEDERATION (55,000), Douglas Houghton House, 231 Vauxhall Bridge Road, SW1V 1EH—*Gen. Sec.*, A. M. G. Christopher, C.B.E.

INSTITUTION OF PROFESSIONAL CIVIL SERVANTS, THE (88,782), 75–79 York Road, SE1 7AQ—*Gen. Sec.*, W. McCall.

IRON AND STEEL TRADES CONFEDERATION, THE (45,300), Swinton House, 324 Gray's Inn Road, WC1X 8DD—*Gen. Sec.*, R. L. Evans.

MILITARY AND ORCHESTRAL MUSICAL INSTRUMENT MAKERS' TRADE SOCIETY (36), 2 Whitehorse Avenue, Boreham Wood, Herts. WD6 1HD—*Gen. Sec.*, F. McKenzie.

MUSICIANS' UNION (38,365), 60–62 Clapham Road, SW9 0JJ—*Gen. Sec.*, J. Morton.

NATIONAL AND LOCAL GOVERNMENT OFFICERS' ASSOCIATION (N.A.L.G.O.) (750,430), 1 Mabledon Place, WC1H 9AJ—*Gen. Sec.*, J. D. Daly.

NATIONAL ASSOCIATION OF COLLIERY OVERMEN, DEPUTIES AND SHOTFIRERS (14,614), Simpson House, 48 Nether Hall Road, Doncaster, S. Yorks. DN1 2PZ—*Sec.*, P. McNestry.

NATIONAL ASSOCIATION OF CO-OPERATIVE OFFICIALS (4,550), Saxone House, 56 Market Street, Manchester M1 1PW—*Gen. Sec.*, L. W. Ewing.

NATIONAL ASSOCIATION OF LICENSED HOUSE MANAGERS (15,400), 9 Coombe Lane, Raynes Park, SW20 8NE—*Gen. Sec.*, D. G. Smith.

NATIONAL ASSOCIATION OF PROBATION OFFICERS (6,088), 3–4 Chivalry Road, Battersea, SW11 1HT—*Sec.*, W. L. Beaumont.

NATIONAL ASSOCIATION OF SCHOOLMASTERS/UNION OF WOMEN TEACHERS (N.A.S./U.W.T.) (124,000), Hillscourt Education Centre, Rose Hill, Rednal, Birmingham B45 8RS—*Gen. Sec.*, F. A. Smithies.

NATIONAL ASSOCIATION OF TEACHERS IN FURTHER AND HIGHER EDUCATION (76,342), 27 Britannia Street, WC1X 9JP—*Gen. Sec.*, J. P. Dawson.

NATIONAL COMMUNICATIONS UNION (150,000), Greystoke House, 150 Brunswick Road, W5 1AW—*Gen. Sec.*, J. Golding.

NATIONAL GRAPHICAL ASSOCIATION 1982 (N.G.A. '82) (131,000), Graphic House, 63–67 Bromham Road, Bedford MK40 2AG—*Sec.*, A. D. Dubbins.

NATIONAL LEAGUE OF THE BLIND AND DISABLED, THE (3,000), 2 Tenterden Road, N17 8BE—*Sec.*, M. A. Barrett.

NATIONAL UNION OF DOMESTIC APPLIANCES AND GENERAL OPERATIVES, THE (3,100), 6–8 Imperial Buildings, Corporation Street, Rotherham, S. Yorks. S60 1PB—*Gen. Sec.*, R. D. Preston.

NATIONAL UNION OF HOSIERY AND KNITWEAR WORKERS, THE (48,973), 55 New Walk, Leicester LE1 7EB—*Gen. Sec.*, T. Kirk.

NATIONAL UNION OF INSURANCE WORKERS (18,280), 27 Old Gloucester Street, WC1N 3AF—*Gen. Sec.*, R. Main.

NATIONAL UNION OF JOURNALISTS (N.U.J.) (33,337), Acorn House, 314–320 Gray's Inn Road, WC1X 8DP—*Gen. Sec.*, H. Conroy.

NATIONAL UNION OF LOCK AND METAL WORKERS (5,118), Bellamy House, Wilkes Street, Willenhall, West Midlands WV13 2BS—*Sec.*, J. Martin, M.B.E.

NATIONAL UNION OF MARINE, AVIATION AND SHIPPING TRANSPORT OFFICERS, THE (23,803), Oceanair House, 750–760 High Road, Leytonstone, E11 3BB—*Gen. Sec.*, E. Nevin.

NATIONAL UNION OF MINEWORKERS (N.U.M.) (105,000), St. James' House, Vicar Lane, Sheffield S1 2EX—*Sec.*, P. E. Heathfield.

NATIONAL UNION OF PUBLIC EMPLOYEES (N.U.P.E.) (650,000), Civic House, 20 Grand Depot Road, SE18 6SF—*Sec.*, R. K. Bickerstaffe.

NATIONAL UNION OF RAILWAYMEN (N.U.R.) (124,991), Unity House, Euston Road, NW1 2BL—*Gen. Sec.*, J. Knapp.

NATIONAL UNION OF SCALEMAKERS (997), Queensway House, 57 Livery Street, Birmingham B3 1HA—*Gen. Sec.*, A. F. Smith.

NATIONAL UNION OF SEAMEN (N.U.S.) (25,000), Maritime House, Old Town, Clapham, SW4 0JP—*Gen. Sec.*, S. McCluskie.

NATIONAL UNION OF TAILORS AND GARMENT WORKERS (75,063), 16 Charles Square, N1 6HP—*Gen. Sec.*, A. Smith.

NATIONAL UNION OF TEACHERS (N.U.T.) (184,455), Hamilton House, Mabledon Place, WC1H 9BD—*Gen. Sec.*, F. F. Jarvis.

NATIONAL UNION OF THE FOOTWEAR, LEATHER AND ALLIED TRADES (36,800), The Grange, 108 Northampton Road, Earls Barton, Northampton NN6 0JH—*Gen. Sec.*, G. Stewart.

NORTHERN CARPET TRADES' UNION (830), 22 Clare Road, Halifax HX1 2HX—*Gen. Sec.*, K. Edmondson.

PATTERN WEAVERS' SOCIETY (60), 38, St. Paul's Road, Kirkheaton, Huddersfield HD5 0EY—*Gen. Sec.*, K. K. Bradley.

POWER LOOM CARPET WEAVERS' AND TEXTILE WORKERS' UNION, THE (3,500), Callows Lane, Kidderminster, Worcs. DY10 2JG—*Gen. Sec.*, B. C. Moule.

PRISON OFFICERS' ASSOCIATION, THE (23,857), Cronin House, 245 Church Street, Edmonton, N9 9HW—*Gen. Sec.*, D. Evans.

ROSSENDALE UNION OF BOOT, SHOE AND SLIPPER OPERATIVES, THE (4,063), Taylor House, 7 Tenterfield Street, Waterfoot, Rossendale, Lancs. BB4 7BA.—*Gen. Sec.*, M. Murray.

SCOTTISH PRISON OFFICERS' ASSOCIATION (3,181), 21 Calder Road, Edinburgh EH11 3PF—*Gen. Sec.*, J. Renton, M.B.E.

SCOTTISH UNION OF POWER-LOOM OVERLOOKERS (71), 3 Napier Terrace, Dundee, Tayside.—*Sec.*, J. Reilly.

SCREW, NUT, BOLT AND RIVET TRADE UNION (400), 368 Dudley Road, Birmingham B18 4HH—*Gen. Sec.*, W. J. Redmond.

SHEFFIELD WOOL SHEAR WORKERS' UNION (17), 50 Bankfield Road, Malin Bridge, Sheffield S6 4RD—*Sec.*, J. H. R. Cutler.

SOCIETY OF CIVIL AND PUBLIC SERVANTS (85,000), 124–130 Southwark Street, SE1 0TU—*Gen. Sec.*, L. Christie.

SOCIETY OF GRAPHICAL AND ALLIED TRADES 1982 (SOGAT '82) (200,000), Sogat House, 274–288 London Road, Hadleigh, Benfleet, Essex SS7 2DE—*Gen. Sec.*, Ms. B. Dean.

SOCIETY OF SHUTTLEMAKERS (46), 31 Moorside Avenue, Blackburn, Lancs. BB1 2BA.—*Gen. Sec.*, H. Bell.

SOCIETY OF TELECOM EXECUTIVES (30,000), 102–104 Sheen Road, Richmond, Surrey TW9 1UF—*Gen. Sec.*, S. Petch.

SPRING TRAPMAKERS' SOCIETY (90), Bellamy House, Wilkes Street, Willenhall, West Midlands WV13 2BS—*Sec.*, J. Martin.

TECHNICAL, ADMINISTRATIVE AND SUPERVISORY SECTION (T.A.S.S.) (240,000), Park House, 64–66 Wandsworth Common North Side, SW18 2SH—*Gen. Sec.*, K. Gill.

TOBACCO MECHANICS ASSOCIATION (106), 30 Battson Road, Stockswood, Bristol BS14 8FN—*Sec.*, G. Dart.

TRANSPORT AND GENERAL WORKERS' UNION (T.G.W.U.) (1,377,944), Transport House, Smith Square, Westminster, SW1P 3JB—*Gen. Sec.*, R. Todd.

TRANSPORT SALARIED STAFFS' ASSOCIATION (45,216), Walkden House, 10 Melton Street, NW1 2EJ—*Gen. Sec.*, C. A. Lyons.

UNION OF COMMUNICATION WORKERS, THE (192,540), U.C.W. House, Crescent Lane, SW4 9RN—*Gen. Sec.*, A. D. Tuffin.

UNION OF CONSTRUCTION, ALLIED TRADES AND TECHNICIANS (U.C.A.T.T.) (265,000), UCATT House, 177 Abbeville Road, Clapham, SW4 9RL—*Sec.*, A. Williams.

UNION OF SHOP, DISTRIBUTIVE AND ALLIED WORKERS (U.S.D.A.W.) (381,984), Oakley, 188 Wilmslow Road, Fallowfield, Manchester M14 6LJ—*Sec.*, G. Davies.

UNITED ROAD TRANSPORT UNION (19,825), 76 High Lane, Manchester M21 1FD—*Gen. Sec.*, F. Griffin.

WIRE WORKERS' UNION (5,142), Prospect House, Alma Street, Sheffield S3 8SA—*Gen. Sec.*, A. M. Ardron.

WRITERS' GUILD OF GREAT BRITAIN, THE (1,700), 430 Edgware Road, W2 1EH—*Gen. Sec.*, W. J. Jeffrey.

YORKSHIRE ASSOCIATION OF POWER LOOM OVERLOOKERS (576), 20 Hallfield Road, Bradford, BD1 3RQ—*Gen. Sec.*, A. D. Barrow.

LABOUR STATISTICS
Industrial Stoppages (thousands)

	Workers beginning in period	Total working days lost						
		All industries and services	Coal, coke, mineral oil and natural gas	Metals, engineering and vehicles	Textiles, footwear and clothing	Construction	Transport and communication	All other industries and services
1982	2,101	5,313	380	1,457	61	41	1,675	1,699
1983	573	3,754	591	1,420	32	68	295	1,348
1984	1,436	27,135	22,484	2,055	66	334	666	1,530
1985	643	6,402	4,143	590	31	50	197	1,391
1986	538	1,920	143	895	38	33	190	622
1987 January	167	891	9	55	2	—	785	41
February	47	924	24	64	17	5	778	37
March	209	252	20	53	3	—	8	167
April	114	307	17	43	3	1	10	233
May	78	203	11	25	—	1	12	155

INDUSTRIAL RESEARCH ASSOCIATIONS

The following are members of the Association of Independent Research and Technology Organizations (A.I.R.T.O.), c/o Helliar & Co., 15 Church Street, Ilchester, Yeovil, Somerset BA22 8LN.

AIRCRAFT RESEARCH ASSOCIATION LTD., Manton Lane, Bedford MK41 7PF.

ADVANCED MANUFACTURING TECHNOLOGY RESEARCH INSTITUTE (*Machine tools and other machinery*), Hulley Road, Macclesfield, Cheshire SK10 2NE.

BCIRA (*Foundry and associated industries*), Alvechurch, Birmingham B48 7QB.

BHRA (BRITISH HYDROMECHANICS RESEARCH ASSOCIATION), The Fluid Engineering Centre, Wharley End, Cranfield, Bedford MK43 0AJ.

BICERI (THE BRITISH INTERNAL COMBUSTION ENGINE RESEARCH INSTITUTE LTD.), 111–112 Buckingham Avenue, Slough SL1 4PH.

BNF METALS TECHNOLOGY CENTRE, Denchworth Road, Wantage, Oxon., OX12 9BJ.

BRITISH CERAMIC RESEARCH LTD., Queen's Road, Penkhull, Stoke-on-Trent ST4 7LQ.

BRITISH CLOTHING CENTRE, Wira House, Clayton Wood Rise, Leeds LS16 6RF.

BRITISH GLASS INDUSTRY RESEARCH ASSOCIATION, Northumberland Road, Sheffield S10 2UA.

BRITISH LEATHER CONFEDERATION, Leather Trade House, Kings Park Road, Moulton Park, Northampton NN3 1JD.

BRITISH MARITIME TECHNOLOGY LTD., Faggs Road, Feltham, Middx., TW14 0LQ.

BUILDING SERVICES RESEARCH AND INFORMATION ASSOCIATION, Old Bracknell Lane West, Bracknell, Berks., RG12 4AH.

CAMBRIDGE CONSULTANTS LTD. (*Product design and process development*), Science Park, Milton Road, Cambridge CB4 4DW.

CIRIA (CONSTRUCTION INDUSTRY RESEARCH AND INFORMATION ASSOCIATION), 6 Storey's Gate, SW1P 3AU.

CUTLERY AND ALLIED TRADES RESEARCH ASSOCIATION, Henry Street, Sheffield S3 7EQ.

ERA TECHNOLOGY LTD. (*Electronic and electrical engineering*), Cleeve Road, Leatherhead, Surrey KT22 7SA.

FABRIC CARE RESEARCH ASSOCIATION, Forest House Laboratories, Knaresborough Road, Harrogate, N. Yorks., HG2 7LZ.

FULMER RESEARCH INSTITUTE LTD. (*New materials development*), Hollybush Hill, Stoke Poges, Slough SL2 4QD.

FURNITURE INDUSTRY RESEARCH ASSOCIATION, Maxwell Road, Stevenage, Herts., SG1 2EW.

HAZLETON UK (*Life sciences*), Otley Road, Harrogate, N. Yorks., HG3 1PY.

HOSIERY AND ALLIED TRADES RESEARCH ASSOCIATION, 7 Gregory Boulevard, Nottingham NG7 6NB.

HYDRAULICS RESEARCH LTD., Howbery Park, Wallingford, Oxon., OX10 8BA.

INVERESK RESEARCH INTERNATIONAL LTD. (*Toxicology, mutagenicity and biotechnology.*), Musselburgh EH21 7UB.

LAMBEG INDUSTRIAL RESEARCH ASSOCIATION (*Linen textiles*), The Research Institute, Lisburn, Co. Antrim, N. Ireland.

LIFE SCIENCE RESEARCH LTD., Eye, Suffolk IP23 7PX.

MOTOR INDUSTRY RESEARCH ASSOCIATION, Watling Street, Nuneaton, Warwicks., CV10 0TU.

NATIONAL COMPUTING CENTRE, Oxford Road, Manchester M1 7ED.

NEI INTERNATIONAL RESEARCH AND DEVELOPMENT COMPANY LTD., (*Electronics and control engineering*), Fossway, Newcastle upon Tyne NE6 2YD.

PAINT RESEARCH ASSOCIATION, 8 Waldegrave Road, Teddington, Middx., TW11 8LD.

PERA (PRODUCTION ENGINEERING RESEARCH ASSOCIATION) (*Advanced manufacturing technology*), Melton Mowbray LE13 0PB.

PIRA (PAPER AND BOARD, PRINTING AND PACKAGING INDUSTRIES RESEARCH ASSOCIATION), Randalls Road, Leatherhead, Surrey KT22 7RU.

RAPRA TECHNOLOGY LTD. (*Rubber and plastics industries*), Shawbury, Shrewsbury, Shropshire SY4 4NR.

RICARDO CONSULTING ENGINEERS P.L.C., Bridge Works, Shoreham by Sea, W. Sussex BN4 5FG.

SATRA FOOTWEAR TECHNOLOGY CENTRE, Satra House, Rockingham Road, Kettering, Northants., NN16 9JH.

SHIPOWNERS REFRIGERATED CARGO RESEARCH ASSOCIATION, 140 Newmarket Road, Cambridge CB5 8HE.

SHIRLEY INSTITUTE (*Textiles and related industries*), Didsbury, Manchester M20 8RX.

SIRA LTD. (*Instrumentation and information technology*), South Hill, Chislehurst, Kent BR7 5EH.

SMITH ASSOCIATES LTD., (*Electronic, optical, mechanical and software systems*), Surrey Research Park, Guildford GU2 5YP.

SPRING RESEARCH AND MANUFACTURERS' ASSOCIATION, Henry Street, Sheffield S3 7EQ.

STEEL CASTINGS RESEARCH AND TRADE ASSOCIATION (SCRATA), 5 East Bank Road, Sheffield S2 3PT.

TIMBER RESEARCH AND DEVELOPMENT ASSOCIATION (TRADA), Stocking Lane, Hughenden Valley, High Wycombe, Bucks., HP14 4ND.

TOXICOL LABORATORIES LTD., Bromyard Road, Ledbury, Hereford., HR8 1LG.

WATER RESEARCH CENTRE, Henley Road, Medmenham, Marlow, Bucks., SL7 2HD.

THE WELDING INSTITUTE, Abington Hall, Abington, Cambridge CB1 6AL.

WIRA TECHNOLOGY GROUP (*Wool textile processes and products*), Wira House, West Park Ring Road, Leeds LS16 6QL.

AGRICULTURAL AND FOOD RESEARCH INSTITUTES AND UNITS

Institute for Animal Disease Research (I.A.D.R.)
Director of Research: Prof. P. M. Biggs, D.SC., D.V.M., F.R.S., Compton, Nr. Newbury, Berks., RG16 0NN.

Pirbright Laboratory, Ash Road, Woking, Surrey GU24 0NF.—*Head of Lab.,* B. W. J. Mahy, PH.D., SC.D.

Houghton Laboratory, Houghton, Huntingdon, Cambs., PE17 2DA.—*Head of Lab. (Acting),* L. N. Payne, PH.D., D.SC.

Institute for Animal Disease Research, Compton, Nr. Newbury, Berks., RG16 0NN.—*Head of Lab. (Acting),* J. M. Rutter, PH.D.

AFRC and MRC Neuropathogenesis Unit, Ogston Building, West Mains Road, Edinburgh EH9 3JF.—*Dir.,* A. G. Dickinson, PH.D.

Institute of Animal Physiology and Genetics Research
Dir. of Research, B. A. Cross, C.B.E., PH.D., SC.D., F.R.S., Babraham Hall, Babraham, Cambridge CB2 4AT.

Cambridge Research Station, Babraham, Cambridge CB2 4AT.—*Deputy Dir. (Acting),* R. B. Heap, PH.D., SC.D.

Edinburgh Research Station, Roslin, Midlothian EH25 9PS.—*Deputy Dir. (Acting),* R. B. Land, PH.D.

Edinburgh Research Station, King's Buildings, West Mains Road, Edinburgh EH9 3JQ.

Dryden Laboratory, Roslin, Midlothian EH25 9PS.

Institute of Arable Crops Research
Dir. of Research, Sir Leslie Fowden, PH.D., F.R.S., Rothamsted Experimental Station, Harpenden, Herts., AL5 2JQ.

Long Ashton Research Station, Long Ashton, Bristol BS18 9AF.—*Dir.,* Prof. K. J. Treharne.

Rothamsted Experimental Station, Harpenden, Herts., AL5 2JQ.—*Head (Acting),* T. Lewis, PH.D., D.SC.

Broom's Barn Experimental Station, Higham, Bury St. Edmunds, Suffolk IP28 6NP.—*Head,* R. K. Scott, PH.D.

Unit of Insect Neurophysiology and Pharmacology, Department of Zoology, University of Cambridge, Downing Street, Cambridge CB2 3EJ.—*Hon. Dir.,* J. E. Treherne, PH.D., SC.D.

Institute of Engineering Research
Director of Research, J. Matthews, Wrest Park, Silsoe, Bedford MK45 4HS.

Institute of Food Research
Director of Research, Prof. R. F. Curtis, C.B.E., PH.D., D.SC., Shinfield, Reading RG2 9AT.

Bristol Laboratory, Langford, Bristol BS18 7DY.—*Head of Lab.* Prof. A. J. Bailey, SC.D.

Norwich Laboratory, Colney Lane, Norwich NR4 7UA.—*Head of Lab.,* P. Richmond, D.SC.

Reading Laboratory, Shinfield, Reading RG2 9AT.—*Head of Lab.,* (vacant).

Institute for Grassland and Animal Production
Director of Research, Prof. J. H. D. Prescott, Hurley, Maidenhead, Berks., SL6 5LR.

Welsh Plant Breeding Station, Plas Gogerddan, Aberystwyth, Dyfed SY23 3EB.—*Dir.,* Prof. R. Q. Cannell.

Animal and Grassland Research Stations:
Hurley Station, Maidenhead, Berks., SL6 5LR.—*Asst. Dir. (Acting),* R. D. Hartley, PH.D., D.SC.

North Wyke Station (Grassland Division), Okehampton, Devon EX20 2SB.—*Assistant Dir. (Acting),* R. J. Wilkins, PH.D.

Reading Station (Pigs Division), Church Lane, Shinfield, Reading RG2 9AQ.—*Asst. Dir. (Acting),* D. Lister, PH.D.

Edinburgh Station (Poultry Division), Roslin, Midlothian EH25 9PS.—*Asst. Dir. (Acting),* C. Fisher, PH.D.

Institute of Horticultural Research
Director of Research, T. R. Swinburne, D.SC., PH.D. Bradbourne House, East Malling, Maidstone, Kent ME19 6BJ.

I.H.R. East Malling, East Malling, Maidstone, Kent ME19 6BJ.—*Head of Station,* C. C. Payne.

I.H.R. Department of Hop Research, Wye College, Wye, Ashford, Kent TN25 5AH.—*Head of Station,* R. E. Gunn.

I.H.R. Littlehampton, Worthing Road, Littlehampton, West Sussex BN17 6LP.—*Head of Station,* R. S. Fraser, PH.D., D.SC.

I.H.R. Wellesbourne, Wellesbourne, Warwick CV35 9EF.—*Head of Station,* Prof. J. K. A. Bleasdale.

Institute of Plant Science Research
Dir. of Research, Prof. H. W. Woolhouse, John Innes Institute, Colney Lane, Norwich NR4 7UH.

Division of Cellular and Molecular Biology, John Innes Institute, Colney Lane, Norwich NR4 7UH.—*Dir.,* Prof. H. W. Woolhouse.

Division of Cytogenetics and Plant Breeding, Plant Breeding Institute, Maris Lane, Trumpington, Cambridge CB2 2LQ.—*Head of Divn.,* C. Law, PH.D.

Division of Nitrogen Fixation Research, University of Sussex, Brighton BN1 9RQ.—*Head of Divn.,* B. E. Smith, PH.D.

Computing Centre, West Common, Harpenden, Herts., AL5 2JE.—*Dir.,* P. Chandler.

Scottish Agricultural Research Institutes
Hannah Research Institute, Ayr KA6 5HL.—*Dir.,* Prof. M. Peaker.

Macaulay Land Use Research Institute, Craigiebuckler, Aberdeen AB9 2QJ; Bush Estate, Penicuik, Midlothian EH26 0PY.—*Dir.,* T. J. Maxwell, PH.D.

Moredun Research Institute, 408 Gilmerton Road, Edinburgh EH17 7JH.—*Dir.,* I. D. Aitken, PH.D.

Rowett Research Institute, Greenburn Road, Bucksburn, Aberdeen AB2 9SB.—*Dir.,* Prof. W. P. T. James.

Scottish Crop Research Institute, Invergowrie, Dundee DD2 5DA.—*Dir.,* Prof. J. Hillman.

Scottish Agricultural Statistics Service, University of Edinburgh, James Clerk Maxwell Building, The King's Buildings, Mayfield Road, Edinburgh EH9 3JZ.—*Dir.,* R. A. Kempton.

C.A.B. INTERNATIONAL

Each Institute and Bureau acts as a clearing house for the collection, collation and dissemination of information.

Institutes

C.A.B.I. Institute of Entomology, 56 Queen's Gate, S.W.7. *Director*, K. M. Harris, Ph.D.

C.A.B.I. Mycological Institute, Ferry Lane, Kew, Richmond, Surrey. *Director*, D. L. Hawksworth, Ph.D.

C.A.B.I. Institute of Biological Control, Imperial College, Silwood Park, Ascot, Berks., SL5 7PY. *Director*, D. J. Greathead, Ph.D.

C.A.B.I. Institute of Parasitology, 395A Hatfield Road, St. Albans, Herts. *Director*, R. L. J. Muller, Ph.D.

Bureaux

Agricultural Economics, Wallingford, Oxon., OX10 8DE.

Animal Breeding and Genetics, Animal Breeding Research Organization, The King's Buildings, West Mains Road, Edinburgh, Scotland.

Animal Health, Central Veterinary Laboratory, New Haw, Weybridge, Surrey.

Dairy Science and Technology, Wallingford, Oxon., OX10 8DE.

Forestry, Commonwealth Forestry Institute, Wallingford, Oxon., OX10 8DE.

Horticulture and Plantation Crops, East Malling Research Station, Maidstone, Kent.

Nutrition, Rowett Research Institute, Bucksburn, Aberdeen, Scotland.

Pastures and Field Crops, Wallingford, Oxon., OX10 8DE.

Plant Breeding and Genetics, Department of Applied Biology, Pembroke Street, Cambridge.

Soils, Rothamsted Experimental Station, Harpenden, Herts.

COST OF RESEARCH AND DEVELOPMENT

(excluding social science research)

Work performed within each sector

	1975		1978		1981		1983	
	£ million	Per cent	£ million	Per cent	£ million	Per cent	£ million	Per cent
Sector carrying out the work								
Central government								
Defence	252·3	*11·7*	331·0	*9·4*	557·7	*9·4*	654·9	*9·9*
Civil:								
Research councils	108·2	*5·0*	152·3	*4·3*	250·2	*4·2*	279·0	*4·2*
Other	203·7	*9·5*	271·8	*7·7*	526·5	*8·9*	552·9	*8·4*
Local government	2·1	*0·1*	3·0	*0·1*	5·0	*0·1*	7·0	*0·1*
Total	566·3	*26·3*	758·1	*21·6*	1,339·4	*22·6*	1,493·8	*22·7*
Universities and further education establishments	179·2	*8·3*	317·3	*9·0*	629·6	*10·6*	749·5	*11·4*
Public corporations	124·0	*5·8*	212·5	*6·1*	384·8	*6·5*	526·2	*8·0*
Research associations	31·1	*1·4*	50·8	*1·4*	88·1	*1·5*		
Private industry	1,185·1	*55·1*	2,061·0	*58·7*	3,319·5	*56·1*	3,637·1	*55·2*
Other	65·6	*3·1*	110·6	*3·2*	159·6	*2·7*	176·4	*2·7*
Total cost of research and development performed	2,151·3	*100·0*	3,510·3	*100·0*	5,921·1	*100·0*	6,583·0	*100·0*

Finance provided by each sector

	1975		1978		1981		1983	
	£ million	Per cent	£ million	Per cent	£ million	Per cent	£ million	Per cent
Sector providing the funds								
Central government								
Defence	611·2	*25·3*	949·8	*25·4*	1,666·7	*24·8*	1,884·3	*25·7*
Civil:								
Research councils	131·1	*5·4*	186·2	*4·9*	363·5	*5·4*	408·3	*5·6*
Other	499·9	*20·8*	610·9	*16·4*	1,161·3	*17·3*	1,265·4	*17·3*
Local government	9·0	*0·4*	10·0	*0·3*	20·0	*0·3*	25·5	*0·3*
Total as returned by Government	1,251·2	*51·9*	1,756·9	*47·0*	3,211·5	*47·7*	3,583·5	*48·9*
Total as returned by sectors carrying out work	1,117·4	*51·9*	1,651·4	*47·0*	2,825·9	*47·7*	3,217·9	*48·9*
Universities	15·5	*0·7*	28·4	*0·8*	58·0	*1·0*	25·0	*0·4*
Public corporations	137·1	*6·4*	259·7	*7·4*	449·2	*7·6*	2,869·4	*43·6*
Private industry*	739·5	*34·4*	1,292·4	*36·8*	2,080·1	*35·1*		
Overseas	107·8	*5·0*	222·6	*6·3*	411·4	*6·9*	347·9	*5·3*
Other	34·0	*1·6*	55·8	*1·6*	96·6	*1·6*	122·8	*1·9*
Total	2,151·3	*100·0*	3,510·3	*100·0*	5,921·1	*100·0*	6,583·0	*100·0*

*Including research associations.

PRINCIPAL CHARITABLE BEQUESTS OF THE YEAR

The alphabetical list below represents some of the principal charitable bequests from wills published since the last edition. The amount available for residuary bequests is not known exactly, as prior legacies, testamentary expenses and Inheritance Tax have to be deducted from the net value in most instances.

The largest charitable beneficiaries were the Imperial Cancer Research Fund, who received the residue of the estate of London widow Barbara Burns, and the R.N.L.I., who received the residue of the estate of retired company director Kenneth Thelwall of Walkington, North Humberside. Both left over £3 million. Dorothy Garside of Elland left the residue of her estate equally between the R.N.L.I. and a local care society; Thomas Lumb of Harrogate left his residue equally between a local disabled association and five other charities; ten charities shared the residue of Phyllis Maybank of Epsom; Sybil Morley of Stanford in the Vale left £100,000 to a local animal sanctuary, and the residue to six other animal charities; Annie Sherr from Manchester left the residue to no less than 26 charities (mostly Jewish and for animals); and Alexandrina Bartlett of Ponteland, Northumberland, left the residue equally between the Fitzwilliam Museum, Cambridge, a local Masonic charity, a local home and a Newcastle upon Tyne mission. They all left over £1 million. Joyce Hole from Dorset left the residue of her £2 million estate to the Victoria and Albert Museum, and the British Library and British Museum shared the residue of the £667,357 estate of Dr. Eric Dingwall, a Sussex librarian and an authority on ghosts and spiritualism.

Retired Yorkshire company director, Norman Sharpe, left the bulk of his £2·1 million estate to Giggleswick School. Three Cambridge colleges received large bequests—Queens' College being remembered by one of its former scholars, Alfred Binnie, who left them virtually all his £919,571 estate. Dorothy Richards of Cambridge left the residue of her £1 million estate to Magdalene College, and Alice White, also of Cambridge, left the residue of her £541,058 estate to Newnham College. Three Oxford colleges also appear in the list—St. Hilda's College was left the residue of the £479,747 estate of Lorna Howell of Bognor Regis, Nuffield College was remembered by its former Warden Sir Norman Chester, who left them the residue of his £350,550 estate, and Trinity College received the residue of the £291,944 estate of former Ambassador, Sir Gilbert Laithwaite. Aberystwyth's Dr. Elwyn Davies left £597,880 and the residue to found a Centre for Advanced Welsh and Celtic Studies at the University of Wales.

A number of churches received large bequests including four in Avon—the Church of St. Quiricus and St. Julietta in Tickenham, which received nearly all Alice Withey's £673,996 estate; Westbury on Trym and Horfield Baptist Churches, who shared the residue of the £401,918 estate of Dr. Winifred Nott, along with Ashley Baptist Church in Hants.; and the Sacred Heart Church, also in Westbury on Trym, which shared the bulk of the £382,669 estate of Lilian Bartlett with nearby St. Joseph's Home in Cotham. Irene Muller left the residue of her £285,209 estate to her local Catholic Church in Hampton, Middx., and Ethel Baines from Wetherby, West Yorks., left her £504,407 estate mostly to Ripon Diocesan Board of Finance. Two Gwent churches are also included— the Ebenezer Baptist Church at Magor receiving nearly all the £284,829 estate of Herbert Williams, and churches in Machen and Pontymister sharing the residue of the £738,764 estate of Olive Sutton of Bournemouth, with four other charities.

No less than six estates in the list include residuary bequests for charities to be decided by their executors or trustees—Londoner Arthur Davis, who left over £3 million, asked that Jewish charities be particularly remembered; Samuel Strauss of Bottisham, Cambs., who left £2·9 million; Philip Henman of Rustington, West Sussex, founder of the Transport Development Group, who left £1·2 million; Irene Halley, of Crowthorne, Berks., who left £535,191; Monica Partridge, of London, who left £386,986; and Percy Evans, of Knighton, Powys, who left £286,977.

The National Trust received the bulk of the £1 million estate of retired solicitor Ivan Parker, a Life member. Alan Keet of Budleigh Salterton also left the Trust £300,000 to purchase coastline in Devon or Cornwall, while Joyce Spence from Aislaby in North Yorks. left half the residue of her £399,925 estate to the Trust for land in Fylingdales, particularly coastland. Harry Ings from Eastbourne left three quarters of the residue of his £550,595 estate to the Men of the Trees and the other quarter to the Tree Council. Mary Cleugh of Whittington, Salop, left the residue of her £670,875 estate equally between Christian Aid and C.N.D., and Cecil Marshall, of Exmouth, left his entire £220,495 estate to the National Council for Civil Liberties.

Aileen Marjorie Allen, of South Mimms, Herts....................................£291,204
(The residue to the Animal Health Trust)

Hon. Mrs. Margaret Judith Sandeman-Allen, of Whiteheads Grove, London S.W.3. .... £2,348,001
(£50,000 to the Woolton Charitable Trust)

Miss Marion Angus, of Gosforth, Tyne and Wear..................................£325,219
(The residue in such proportions as her trustees select to the Abbeyfield Society, Nuffield Nursing Home, Prudhoe Street Mission and St. Oswald's Hospice, all in Newcastle upon Tyne, the Northumberland Scout Association, R.S.P.C.A., Help the Aged Housing Association, Oxford, and Salvation Army)

Miss Gwendoline Mary Artrick, of Horndean, Hants....................................£306,917
(Her entire estate equally between the Police Dependents Trust, Fire Services National Benevolent Fund, P.D.S.A., Salvation Army, Wildfowl Trust and Woodland Trust)

Ethel Marion Baines, of Wetherby, West Yorks...................................£504,407
(The residue to Ripon Diocesan Board of Finance)

Mr. Hubert Stanton Ballard, of Iffley, Oxon....................................£1,042,426
(Half the residue to the Stanton Ballard Charitable Trust)

Mrs. Doris Forshaw Barrie, of Southport, Merseyside..............................£371,024
(The residue equally between the P.D.S.A., Cats Protection League, National Canine Defence League, National Equine Defence League, Blue Cross, and Donkey Sanctuary, Sidmouth)

Mrs. Alexandrina Dewar Wight Bartlett, of Ponteland, Northumberland..............£1,266,952
(The residue equally between Fitzwilliam Museum, Cambridge, Northumberland Masonic Charity Association, the Scarborough Court Homes, Cramlington, and the Prudhoe Street Mission, Newcastle upon Tyne)

Lilian May Bartlett, of Westbury on Trym, Avon..................................£382,669
(The residue equally between the Sacred Heart Church, Westbury on Trym, and St. Joseph's Home, Cotham, Bristol)

Mr. Alfred Maurice Binnie, F.R.S., of Cambridge................................£919,571
(The residue to Queens' College, Cambridge)

Hilda Marie Bisshopp, of Colchester, Essex . £375,847
(The residue to St. Luke's Hospital, London)

Ellen Elizabeth Brawn, of Golders Green, London N.W.11 ....£301,529
(The residue to the Cancer Research Campaign)

Mrs. Annie Broad, of Cranleigh, Surrey £324,019
(The residue equally between the National Fund for Research into Crippling Diseases and the R.N.L.I.)

Mr. William John Bullock, of Wokingham, Berks................................£463,231
(£5,000 and one quarter of the residue to the Imperial Cancer Research Fund, and one quarter of the residue each to the Sue Ryder Foundation, the London Association for the Blind and Age Concern)

Mrs. Barbara Burns, of Kensington Gore, London S.W.7 ....£3,236,317
(The residue to the Imperial Cancer Research Fund)

Mildred Margaret Caird, of Hull, North Humberside £519,477
(The residue to the R.N.L.I. Bridlington Branch)

Sir Daniel Norman Chester, C.B.E., of Oxford................................£350,550
(£50,000 to Manchester University, £30,000 to Oxford University, and the residue to Nuffield College, Oxford)

Lady Frances Audrey Chetwynd, of Lymington, Hants. £364,452
(The residue equally between the R.S.P.C.A. Isle of Wight Branch, the Distressed Gentlefolk's Aid Association, R.N.L.I. and Missions to Seamen)

Miss Mary Frances Cleugh, of Whittington, Salop................................£670,875
(The residue equally between C.N.D. and Christian Aid)

Miss Joan Constance Clifford, of Exmouth, Devon................................£546,642
(The residue to the Distressed Gentlefolk's Aid Association)

Mrs. Annie Ida Lilian Cobb, of Winchester, Hants. £872,307
(The residue equally between the League of Friends of Royal Hampshire County Hospital, Winchester, the Imperial Cancer Research Fund and the Brendon Care Foundation)

Miss Dorothy Violet Crisp, of Newnham, Cambridge................................£431,418
(The residue equally between the Cambridge and District Spastics Society, Cambridge Housing Society, the Edmund House Mentally Handicapped Children's Home, Milton, L.E.P.R.A., Dr. Barnardo's, Children's Society, Institute of Cancer Research, London Association for the Blind, Missions to Seamen, Oxfam, R.N.L.I., R.S.P.C.A. and the Save the Children Fund)

Mr. Leonard Hurworth Dale, C.B.E., of Gristhorpe, North Yorks. £1,971,863
(£50,000 each to St. Catherine's Hospice, Scarborough, and Scarborough District Flower Fund Homes)

Dr. Elwyn Davies, of Aberystwyth, Dyfed .. £597,880
(The residue to the University of Wales, for the establishment of a Centre for Advanced Welsh and Celtic Studies)

Mr. Arthur Felix Davis, of Hill Street, London W.1. ....£3,046,201
(The residue for such charities as his trustees determine, particularly well-established Jewish charities)

Mr. John Denholm, of Ongar, Essex £2,082,701
(£250,000 to be known as the Jessie Denholm Memorial Bequest, £100,000 to the Royal Agricultural Benevolent Institution and £30,000 each to Age Concern England, Help the Aged, Distressed Gentlefolk's Aid Association, Save the Children Fund and the Abbeyfield Society)

Dr. Eric John Dingwall, of St. Leonards on Sea, East Sussex £667,357
(Some books and half the residue to the British Library and a clock and half the residue to the British Museum)

Mrs. Blanche Yvonne Doming, of Worthing, West Sussex £610,328
(The residue to Help the Aged, Oxford)

Mr. Kenneth Mackenzie Duncan, of Garstang, Lancs................................£418,333
(The residue equally between the R.A.F. Association, Imperial Cancer Research Fund, Sue Ryder Foundation, Dr. Barnardo's, British Heart Foundation and Salvation Army)

Hon. Juliet Elizabeth Dutton, of Windrush, Burford, Oxon. £609,292
(The residue equally between the Cancer Research Campaign and R.S.P.C.A.)

Mrs. Mary Dyson, of Dunnington, North York £644,264
(The residue equally between the National Society for Cancer Relief and National Heart Research Fund)

Mrs. Violet Douglas Elliott, of West Lavington, West Sussex £901,791
(The residue to the National Art Collections Fund)

Mr. Percy Wilfred Lloyd Evans, of Knighton, Powys................................£286,977
(The residue to such charities as his trustee thinks fit)

Mr David Finnie, of Burwood Place, London W.2 ....£457,465
(The residue to the David Finnie Charitable Settlement)

Dorothy Garside, of Elland, West Yorks. . £1,031,588
(The residue equally between the R.N.L.I., and the Calderdale Society for Continuing Care, Elland)

Mr. Leslie Tom Gilley, of Torquay, Devon .. £619,578
(The residue to form the L. and R. Gilley Charitable Trust)

Miss Doris Irene Gilmore, of Northwick Terrace, London N.W.8 ....£388,479
(The residue equally between the League of Friends of Middlesex Hospital, London, the Hospital for Sick Children, Great Ormond Street, London, and the Jewish Blind Society)

Mr. Lewis Thomas Green, of Caenby, Lincs................................£543,294
(His farm and land to Lincolnshire and South Humberside Trust for Nature Conservation, and half the residue equally between the Lincoln Association for the Care of the Elderly, Help the Aged, Methodist Homes for the Aged and Imperial Cancer Research Fund)

Miss Irene Gladys Halley, of Crowthorne, Berks................................£535,191
(The residue for such charities as her executor selects)

Marjorie Elizabeth Hammond, of Rugby, Warwickshire £682,587
(£100,000 to the National Trust)

Mr. John Frederick Charles Harvey, of Torquay, Devon................................£2,751,842
(£100,000 to the Rowcroft House Foundation, Torquay, and £50,000 to St. Mary Magdalene Parish Church, Upton, Torquay)

Mrs. Muriel Adelaide Harvey, of Beaconsfield, Bucks. £611,262
(The residue equally between the Imperial Cancer Research Fund, the Crusade of Rescue and the Distressed Gentlefolk's Aid Association)

Miss Eileen Muriel Heard, of Goring, West Sussex..£322,023
(20 per cent. of the residue each to Chichester Diocesan Board of Finance and the Imperial Cancer Research Fund, 10 per cent. each to St. Barnabas Home, Worthing, Gifford House, Worthing, St. Dunstan's, for the Brighton area, Guide Dogs for the Blind Association and U.S.P.G., and 5 per cent. each to the Children's Society and Dr. Barnardo's)

Mr. Philip Sydney Henman, of Rustington, West Sussex..............................£1,287,446
(Half the residue for such charitable purposes as his trustees think fit)

Mrs. Florence Edith Gwendolen Heny, of Alcombe, Minehead, Somerset....................£385,840
(The residue equally between the R.S.P.C.A., Taunton, P.D.S.A., Blue Cross, League Against Cruel Sports, R.S.P.B., the International League for the Protection of Horses, National Anti-Vivisection Society, World Wildlife Fund, Friends of Bristol Horses Society, Donkey Sanctuary, Sidmouth, and the Society for the Protection of Animals in North Africa)

Mr. Alfred Clifford Hitvhon, of Kempley, Dymock, Glos..................................£537,512
(£100,000 to the R.N.L.I.)

Mr. Douglas Harold Hodson, of Ramsey, Isle of Man......................................£454,481
(The residue to the Abbeyfield Society, to erect dwellings for the elderly within six miles of Newport, Gwent)

Mrs. Joyce Margaret Hole, of Iwerne Minster, Dorset................................£2,054,753
(£50,000 to the Strathallan Hospital, Boscombe, and the residue to the Victoria and Albert Museum, London)

Miss Jessie Hope, of Knaresborough, North Yorks....................................£638,733
(The residue equally between the Princess Louise Scottish Hospital for Limbless Sailors and Soldiers, Bishopton, Renfrewshire, the Scottish Institution for the War-Blinded, the Eastpark Home for Infirm Children, Glasgow, Scottish Council for Spastics, R.A.F. Benevolent Fund, R.N.L.I., and Dr. Barnardo's)

Miss Lorna Margaret Berthon Howell, of Bognor Regis, West Sussex....................£479,747
(The residue to St. Hilda's College, Oxford)

Mr. Harry Victor Ings, of Eastbourne, East Sussex..................................£550,595
(Three quarters of the residue to the Men of the Trees and one quarter of the residue to the Tree Council)

Miss Muriel Johns, of Tunbridge Wells, Kent......................................£435,316
(The residue equally between the Friends of Canterbury Cathedral, National Trust and R.N.L.I.)

Anneliese Katz, of Greencroft Gardens, London N.W.6................................£383,959
(The residue equally between the Jewish Welfare Board, the Children and Youth Aliyah Committee for Great Britain, Save the Children Fund, Help the Aged and Oxfam)

Mr. Alan Livingstone Keet, of Budleigh Salterton, Devon...............................£1,193,054
(£300,000 to the National Trust, to purchase attractive unspoilt Devon and/or Cornish coastline and to provide some strong seats)

Mr Joseph Cubitt Frederick Kerry, of Great Ryburgh, Norfolk.................................£887,549
(The residue equally between the Norwich Institution for the Blind, Age Concern, Cancer Research Campaign, Arthritis Care, R.N.L.I., British Kidney Patient Association, British

Heart Foundation, Dr. Barnardo's and the Friends of Norwich Hospitals)

Mr. Martin John Eyles Knowlden, of Holland Park, London W.14...........................£626,391
(His entire estate equally between the Mothercraft Training Society, Highgate, London, Royal Cancer Hospital, London, Salvation Army, Dr. Barnardo's and R.N.L.I.)

Sir (John) Gilbert Laithwaite, G.C.M.G., K.C.B., of Twyford Abbey, London W.10..........£291,944
(The residue to Trinity College, Oxford)

Mrs. Lilian Violet Lawson, of Eastbourne, East Sussex..............................£307,424
(The residue to the Spread Eagle Foundation—a charity for Barclays Bank pensioners and their dependents)

Dorothy Irene Leah, of Selston, Notts......£722,542
(The residue equally between the Cancer Research Campaign and National Society for Cancer Relief)

Kittie Lewis, of Llandybie, Dyfed.........£326,216
(The residue to Tenovus, Cardiff)

Mrs. Babine Florence Marie Lion, of Brighton, East Sussex..............................£1,926,956
(One twelfth of her entire estate each to the Catholic Enquiry Centre, Society for the Protection of the Unborn Child, St. Mary's Abbey, London N.W.7., St. Joseph's Hospice, London E.8., St. Vincent de Paul Society, Patcham, the Little Way Association, the National Crusade, Westminster Cathedral, Guild of Our Lady of Ransom, St. Augustine's Convent, Kemp Town, Brighton, and the Little Sisters of the Poor, Hove)

Mr. George Arthur Longhorn, of Osterley, Middx................................£301,439
(The residue equally between L.E.P.R.A. and the Royal Commonwealth Society for the Blind)

Mr. Edwin Stanley Luff, of Tockington, Avon................................£321,431
(The residue to the General Cancer Fund at Frenchay Hospital, Bristol)

Mr. Thomas John Lumb, of Harrogate, North Yorks................................£1,335,108
(The residue equally between the Yorkshire Association for the Disabled, Sue Ryder Foundation, R.N.L.I., R.N.I.B., Salvation Army and Cheshire Foundation)

Mr. Cecil Roberts Marshall, of Exmouth, Devon................................£220,495
(His entire estate to the National Council for Civil Liberties)

Mrs. Phyllis Jane Maybank, of Epsom, Surrey................................£1,208,047
(The residue equally between the National Canine Defence League, Guide Dogs for the Blind Association, Cancer Research Campaign, British Heart Foundation, Dr. Barnardo's, Age Concern England, Wood Green Animal Shelter, R.N.L.I., N.S.P.C.C., and Royal Hospital and Home for Incurables, Putney)

Sybil Marion Morley, of Stanford in the Vale, Oxon................................£1,084,875
(£100,000 to the Oxfordshire Animal Sanctuary Society, half the residue to the R.S.P.C.A., and half the residue equally between the National Anti-Vivisection Society, Battersea Dogs Home, Wood Green Animal Shelter, National Canine Defence League and P.D.S.A.)

Irene Selina Muller, of Hampton, Middlesex................................£285,209
(The residue to St. Theodore Roman Catholic Church, Hampton, for the building fund)

Mr. Ernest Edward Willie Mullett, of West Clandon, Surrey................................£965,132
(The residue equally between the R.N.L.I., National Trust, Cancer Research Campaign, Dis-

tressed Gentlefolk's Aid Association, Gardeners' Royal Benevolent Society and Royal British Legion)

Dr. Winifred Grace Nott, of Westbury Park, Bristol .... £401,918 (£2,000 and one third of the residue each to Westbury on Trym Baptist Church, Bristol, and Ashley Baptist Church, New Milton, Hants., and one third of the residue to Horfield Baptist Church, Bristol)

Mr. Ivan Felix Brownfield Parker, of Tankerton, Kent .... £1,079,621 (£50,000 and some silver to the Merchant Taylors Company Alms Houses Charity, £10,000 to the Pestalozzi Children's Village Trust, East Sussex, and the residue to the National Trust)

Monica Guendolen Partridge, of Kings Road, London S.W.19 .... £386,986 (The residue for such charities in England as her trustees select)

Mrs. Emmeline Radcliffe, of Bramley, Surrey .... £496,294 (£40,000 each to the Aeronautical Trust and the Institution of Mechanical Engineers, and the residue equally between the Royal College of Nursing, R.N.L.I., Police Dependents Trust, Chest, Heart and Stroke Association, R.A.F. Benevolent Fund and Arthritis Care)

Mrs. Dorothy Eleanor Richards, of Cambridge .... £1,113,054 (The residue to Magdalene College, Cambridge)

Mrs. Minnie Lee-Richardson, of Poole, Dorset .... £988,961 (Three quarters of the residue to the National Society for Cancer Relief and one quarter of the residue to Action Aid, London)

Mr. Norman Harold Sharpe, of Menston, West Yorks. .... £2,159,569 (The residue to Giggleswick School, Settle)

Mrs. Annie Sherr, of Prestwich, Greater Manchester .... £1,231,024 (The residue equally between the Jewish Blind Society, Jewish Welfare Board, J.N.F. Charitable Trust, Joint Palestine Appeal, Heathlands Home for Aged Jews, Manchester, Jewish Philanthropic Association, Shaare Zedek Hospital, Jerusalem, "Jewish Social Services", "World Jewish Relief", Age Concern England, National Old People's Welfare Council, Counsel and Care for the Elderly, Cripples Help Society, Arthritis and Rheumatism Council, Salvation Army, Shelter, Royal Commonwealth Society for the Blind, Lady Hoare Fund, R.S.P.C.A., Animal Defence Society, Animal Health Trust, Blue Cross, Bransby Home of Rest for Horses, Lincoln, Battersea Dogs Home, P.D.S.A. and R.S.P.B.)

Mr. John Ashley Slocock, of Tilford, Farnham, Surrey .... £1,281,156 (Two fifths of the residue to the Nature Conservancy Council, and three tenths of the residue each to the Phyllis Tuckwell Memorial Hospice, Farnham, and the Hamamelis Trust)

Mrs. Muriel Doreen Charter Sparrow, of Kirby le Soken, Essex .... £466,303 (Her entire estate equally between the Animal Health Trust, Royal College of Surgeons and Royal College of Veterinary Surgeons)

Mrs. Joyce Coggin Spence, of Aislaby, Whitby, North Yorks. .... £399,925 (The residue equally between the Cancer Research Campaign, and the National Trust, for the acquisition of an area in Fylingdales, preferably coastal)

Mr. Samuel George Strauss, of Bottisham, Cambs. .... £2,964,524 (The residue for such U.K. charities as his trustees select)

Miss Olive Veen Irene Sutton, of Bournemouth, Dorset .... £738,764 (The residue equally between the Guide Dogs for the Blind Association, Imperial Cancer Research Fund, Salvation Army, MacMillan Cancer Trust at Christchurch Hospital, St. Michael's Church, Machen, Gwent, and St. Margaret's Church, Pontymister, Gwent)

Lilian Maud Elsey Taylor, of Bexhill on Sea, East Sussex .... £484,842 (The residue equally between the Children's Society and Institute of Cancer Research)

Mr. Kenneth Thelwall, of Walkington, Beverley, North Humberside .... £3,050,358 (The residue to the R.N.L.I., for a new lifeboat)

Mrs. Eileen Marguerite Tapster Thwaites, of Cyprus Avenue, London N.3 .... £317,943 (One eighth of the residue to the P.D.S.A., and one sixteenth each to the R.N.I.D., Hostel of God, London S.W.4, Chartered Accountants Benevolent Association, Friends of the Poor and Gentlefolk's Help, Guide Dogs for the Blind Association, R.S.P.C.A., Battersea Dogs Home, St. Dunstan's, Distressed Gentlefolk's Aid Association, British Red Cross Society, Queen Elizabeth's Training College for the Disabled, Leatherhead, Musicians Benevolent Fund, National Canine Defence League, and Guy's Hospital, London)

Mrs. Gladys Florence Wayne, of Denham, Bucks. .... £553,752 (The residue to the Arthritis and Rheumatic Council)

Mr. Walter Weir, of Quendon, Essex .... £543,951 (The residue to the R.S.P.B.)

Mrs. Alice Barbara White, of Cambridge ... £541,058 (£10,000 to New Hall, Cambridge, and the residue to Newnham College, Cambridge)

Nora Gwendoline Wild, of Rhos on Sea, Clwyd .... £334,600 (The residue equally between the Abbeyfield Colwyn Bay Society, Guide Dogs for the Blind Association, Cancer Research Campaign, and the Fund for Aiding Christian Scientists to enter Christian Science Houses)

Mr. Herbert John Thomas Williams, of Redwick, Gwent .... £284,829 (The residue to Ebenezer Baptist Church, Magor)

Mrs. Alice Maud Withey, of Nailsea, Avon. .... £673,996 (The residue to the Church of St. Quiricus and St. Julietta, Tickenham)

Mrs. Mary Woodhead, of Noctorum, Merseyside .... £859,789 (Two thirds of the residue equally between the Clatterbridge Cancer Research Trust, Bebington, and the R.N.L.I.)

Dulcibel Valerie Florence Wright, of Edgbaston, Birmingham .... £435,548 (£200,000 to establish the Arthur and Dulcie Wright Trust, for the welfare of people in need, especially employees of Davenport's Brewery, Birmingham Police Force and for aged people in their own homes)

Olive Melven Wright, of Elsworthy Road, London N.W.3 .... £414,321 (The residue equally between the Sunshine Fund for Blind Babies and the Mouth and Foot Painting Artists)

Mrs. Edith Zenner, of Grove End Road, London N.W.8. .... £779,335 (The residue equally between St. John and St. Elizabeth Hospital, London N.W.8., for medical equipment, the Guide Dogs for the Blind Association, Institute for Research into Mental and Multiple Handicap and Age Concern)

THE STOCK EXCHANGE

The International Stock Exchange of the United Kingdom and Republic of Ireland serves the needs of government, industry and investors by providing facilities for raising capital and a central market place for securities trading. There are over 7,000 securities listed on the International Stock Exchange, which have a value of over £1,547,000,000 million. Last year, shares worth some £570,300,000 million changed hands. This central market place covers not only government stocks (called gilts) and U.K. and overseas company shares (called equities and fixed interest stocks) but other investment instruments such as traded options on equities, currencies and indices.

During 1986 the International Stock Exchange went through the greatest period of change in its two hundred year history. In March 1986 it opened its doors for the first time to overseas and corporate membership of the Exchange, allowing banks, insurance companies and overseas securities houses to become Members of The Exchange and to buy existing Member Firms. On October 27, 1986, three major reforms took place, changes which became known as "Big Bang":

(i) abolition of scales of minimum commissions, allowing clients to negotiate freely with their brokers about the charge for their services

(ii) abolition of the separation of Member Firms into brokers and jobbers. Under the new system, Firms are broker/dealers, able to act as agents on behalf of clients; to act as principals buying and selling shares for their own account; and to become registered market makers, making continuous buying and selling prices in specific securities

(iii) the introduction of the Stock Exchange Automated Quotations (S.E.A.Q.) system. Market makers input their buying and selling prices into S.E.A.Q., which displays the competing quotations on a composite page on-screen. For the largest and most frequently traded company shares ("Alpha"), e.g. Marks and Spencer or BP, volumes and last trade prices are also updated continuously throughout the day.

Of all these changes, the implementation of S.E.A.Q. has had perhaps the most visible effect. Dealing in stocks and shares now takes place *via* the telephone in the Firms' own dealing rooms, rather than face to face on the floor of the Exchange. The new systems also provide increased investor protection. All deals taking place *via* the Exchange's S.E.A.Q. system are recorded on a database which can be used to resolve disputes or to carry out investigations.

Members of the International Stock Exchange buy and sell shares on behalf of the public, as well as institutions such as pension funds or insurance companies. In return for transacting the deal, the broker will charge a commission, which is usually based upon the value of the transaction. The market makers, or wholesalers, in each security do not charge a commission for their services, but will quote the broker two prices, a price at which they will buy and a price at which they will sell. It is the middle of these two prices which is published in lists of Stock Exchange prices in newspapers.

On November 12, 1986 Members of the Exchange agreed to merge with members of the international broking community in London, based outside the Exchange, in order to form two new bodies—the International Stock Exchange of the United Kingdom and Republic of Ireland Ltd. and the Securities Association Ltd. These two regulatory bodies have been formed under the provisions of the Financial Services Act, which requires investment businesses to be authorised and regulated by a Self Regulating Organisation (S.R.O.) of which the Securities Association is one. The Act also requires business to be conducted through a Registered Investment Exchange (R.I.E.). The International Stock Exchange will be an R.I.E., regulating four main markets: U.K. equities, foreign equities, gilts and options.

As well as advising and dealing on behalf of investors, stockbrokers provide a range of services to industry from the raising of initial capital and future, additional, funds to advice on mergers and acquisitions. For a company entering the market for the first time there are three possible Stock Exchange markets, depending upon the size, history and requirements of the company. The first is the listed market, on which the shares of over 2,500 companies are traded. For entry to this market, the company must have an audited trading history of at least five years, and place 25 per cent of its shares in public hands. The second type of market is for smaller, less established companies and is called the Unlisted Securities Market (U.S.M.). In January, 1986, the International Stock Exchange established a third tier called simply the Third Market. This is for very new and small companies incorporated in the U.K. or Ireland. Once admitted to the Exchange, all companies are obliged to keep their shareholders informed of their progress, making announcements of a price-sensitive nature through the Exchange's company announcements department.

The International Stock Exchange has its headquarters in London, and also administrative centres around the U.K. and the Republic of Ireland. At present there are some 5,300 individual Members grouped into about 350 Member Firms.

Chairman, Sir Nicholas Goodison.

LIFE ASSURANCE AND GENERAL INSURANCE

BRITISH INSURANCE COMPANIES IN 1986

The following Insurance Company figures refer to members of the Association of British Insurers, and also to certain non-members who represent about 4 per cent of the total long-term business and about 6 per cent of the general business figures given.

Worldwide General Business Trading Result

	1985 £m	1986 £m
Net Written Premiums	15,795	18,817
Underwriting Profit/Loss for 1 year Account Business		
Motor	−736	−638
Fire & Accident	−1,054	−524
Transfer to Profit and Loss Account for Other Business		
Marine, Aviation, Transport	−56	−6
Other	−366	−252
Total Underwriting Result	−2,212	−1,420
Investment Income	2,213	2,514
Overall Trading Profit	1	1,094
Profit as a % of Premium Income	0·0	+5·8

Worldwide General Business Underwriting Result

	1985				1986			
	UK	USA	Other	Total	UK	USA	Other	Total
Fire & Accident								
Premiums (£m)	4,298	1,737	2,174	8,209	5,328	2,059	2,557	9,944
Profit/Loss (£m)	−381·2	−395·9	−276·5	−1,053·6	−161·8	−132·8	−229·7	−524·3
% of Premiums	−8·9	−22·8	−12·7	−12·8	−3·0	−6·4	−9·0	−5·3
Motor								
Premiums (£m)	2,179	1,140	1,259	4,578	2,666	1,258	1,594	5,518
Profit/Loss (£m)	−370·9	−174·0	−191·1	−736·0	−369·7	−76·6	−191·7	−638·0
% of Premiums	−17·0	−15·3	−15·2	−16·1	−13·9	−6·1	−12·0	−11·6

Net Premium Income by Territory 1986

	UK £m	Other EEC countries £m	USA £m	Other overseas £m	Total (world-wide) £m
Fire and Accident (non-motor)	5,700 (+22·6%)	979 (+33·4%)	2,128 (+10·3%)	2,945 (+13·6%)	11,752 (+18·6%)
Motor	2,692 (+22·4%)	692 (+33·3%)	1,263 (+10·4%)	919 (+21·2%)	5,566 (+20·5%)
Marine, Aviation and Transport	1,139 (+21·4%)	—	—	360 (+9·1%)	1,499 (+18·2%)
Total General Business	9,531 (+22·4%)	1,671 (+33·4%)	3,391 (+10·3%)	4,224 (+14·8%)	18,817 (+19·1%)
Ordinary Long-Term	17,030 (+24·2%)	1,193 (+28·1%)	201 (+41·5%)	1,788 (+41·1%)	20,212 (+25·9%)
Industrial Long-Term	1,248 (+4·2%)	—	—	—	1,248 (+4·2%)
Total Long-Term Business	18,278 (+22·6%)	1,193 (+28·1%)	201 (+41·5%)	1,788 (+41·1%)	21,460 (+24·4%)
TOTAL	27,809 (+22·5%)	2,864 (+31·1%)	3,592 (+11·7%)	6,012 (+21·5%)	40,277 (+21·9%)

(The figures in brackets show the percentage increases of the 1986 figures over those for 1985).

Insurance Company Investments

	1985 £m	1986 £m
Invested Funds		
Long-Term	142,596	174,612
General	28,805	36,699
Net Income from Investments		
Long-Term	8,854	10,088
General	2,213	2,514

Premium Income for World-Wide Long-Term Insurance Business

	1985 £m	1986 £m
Ordinary Branch:		
Yearly premiums for life insurances, annuities and pensions in the UK	8,570	9,509 (+11·0%)
Single premiums for life insurances, annuities and pensions in the UK	4,998	7,352 (+47·1%)
Premiums for permanent health and other long-term insurances in the UK	143	169 (+18·2%)
Overseas Premium Income	2,341	3,182 (+35·9%)
Industrial Branch:		
Premium Income (UK only)	1,198	1,248 (+4·2%)

World-Wide Long-Term Insurance Business—Outgo 1985 & 1986

	1985 £m	1986 £m
Ordinary Branch:		
Total payments made to UK policyholders	9,019	11,189
Total payments made to overseas policyholders	1,399	1,973
Industrial Branch:		
Total payments made to UK policyholders	1,071	1,178

NOTE: Payments to policyholders includes death claims, maturities, annuities, surrenders (including planned cashing in of linked and other similar savings policies and surrenders of bonus and bonuses in cash), refunds under pension schemes and payments under P.H.I. and other long-term contracts.

LLOYD'S OF LONDON

Lloyd's of London is an incorporated society of private underwriters who provide an international market for almost any type of insurance. Ships, aircraft, oil rigs, cargo of all descriptions, motor cars, civil engineering projects, fire, personal accident and third party liability are a few random examples of the everyday risks placed at Lloyd's which currently bring some £8,000 million of premiums to underwriters each year. Three-quarters of this business comes from outside Great Britain and makes a valuable contribution to the country's balance of payments.

Today, as it was three centuries ago, a policy is subscribed at Lloyd's by private individuals with unlimited liability. Now that Lloyd's members are numbered in their thousands, however, the method of underwriting is the same only in principle. The merchant of the past, signing policies in a coffee house as a sideline to his main business, has long since given way to the specialist underwriter who accepts risks at Lloyd's on behalf of members (often referred to as "names") grouped in a syndicate. There are currently over 30,000 members in some 370 syndicates of varying sizes, some with over two thousand names and each managed by an underwriting agent approved by the Council of Lloyd's.

Lloyd's membership today is drawn from many sources. Industry, commerce and the professions are strongly represented while many members work at Lloyd's either for brokerage firms or for underwriting agencies.

Underwriting membership of Lloyd's is open to men and women of any nationality provided that they meet the stringent financial requirements of the Society, or Corporation, of Lloyd's. Assets of up to £500,000 have to be shown and a deposit lodged with the Corporation as security for underwriting liabilities. This deposit, which must be in the form of approved securities, is determined at a percentage of the member's annual premium income, ranging from 25 per cent for an "external" member resident in the United Kingdom, to 50 per cent for a name working in the Lloyd's market and showing nominal means.

Lloyd's is incorporated by Act of Parliament (Lloyd's Acts 1871–1982) and governed by a Council of 28 members, 12 of whom are elected from and by underwriting members working at Lloyd's and 8 from and by the external membership. Eight Council members are nominated by the Council subject to confirmation by the Governor of the Bank of England.

The Council is a legislative body responsible for deciding on major policy matters, for regulating the Lloyd's market, for the election of new underwriting members, and for establishing the requirements of membership and the rules governing the financial security to be provided by those doing business at Lloyd's.

The Council's "working" members form the Committee of Lloyd's, an executive body which is responsible for putting the Council's directives into effect, managing the Society's affairs, and administering the Lloyd's market on a day-to-day basis.

The Corporation is a non-profit-making body chiefly financed by its members' subscriptions. It provides the premises, administrative staff and services enabling Lloyd's underwriting syndicates to conduct their business. It does not, however, assume corporate liability for the risks accepted by its members, who remain responsible to the full extent of their personal means for their underwriting affairs.

Lloyd's syndicates have no direct contact with the public. All business is transacted through some 260 firms of insurance brokers accredited by the Corporation of Lloyd's. In addition, non-Lloyd's brokers

in the United Kingdom when guaranteed by Lloyd's brokers, are able to deal directly with Lloyd's motor syndicates, a facility which has made the Lloyd's market more accessible to the insuring public.

Lloyd's also provides the most comprehensive shipping intelligence service available in the world. The enormous volume of shipping and other information received from Lloyd's Agents, shipowners, news agencies and other sources throughout the world, is collated and distributed to newspapers, radio and television services, as well as to the maritime and commercial communities in general.

This information is compiled, edited and published by a subsidiary company, Lloyd's of London Press Ltd., and distributed worldwide. "Lloyd's List" is London's oldest daily newspaper and contains news of general commercial interest as well as shipping information. "Lloyd's Shipping Index" also published daily, lists some 20,000 ocean-going vessels in alphabetical order and gives the latest known report of each.

LLOYD'S THREE YEAR BUSINESS SUMMARY

	Premiums	Underwriting profit	Investment income and appreciation
	£m	£m	£m
Short Term Life			
1981	1·95	0·50	0·27
1982	2·23	0·68	0·25
1983	2·89	1·03	0·26
Accident & Health			
1981	108·35	11·06	11·63
1982	169·75	(6·20)	13·96
1983	188·38	13·06	14·00
Motor Vehicle Damage & Liability			
1981	265·21	52·06	33·42
1982	273·59	40·13	29·29
1983	283·44	34·60	25·51
Ships, Aircraft Damage & Liability & Transit			
1981	1,110·89	7·48	141·04
1982	1,446·75	138·81	191·95
1983	1,211·42	187·79	184·25
All Other Insurance Business		(loss)	
1981	771·85	(114·62)	175·04
1982	1,000·16	(361·36)	206·53
1983	883·51	(351·17)	192·87

LLOYD'S MEMBERSHIP SYNDICATES AND BROKERS 1981–1987

	1981	1982	1983	1984	1985	1986	1987
Membership	19,136	20,145	21,601	23,438	26,050	28,944	31,484
Including: Brokers	270	266	272	265	261	258	258

LLOYD'S GLOBAL UNDERWRITING ACCOUNTS

Net Premium Income			
	1983 A/C	1984 A/C	1985 A/C
	£m	£m	£m
Life	2·886	4·030	3·833
Accident & Health	188·383	155·452	86·009
Motor Vehicle Damage & Liability	283·439	325·868	346·313
Ships, Aircraft Damage & Liability and Transit	1,211·427	1,372·845	1,085·716
All Other Insurance Business	883·502	1,106·419	988·491
TOTAL	2,569·637	2,964·614	2,310·362

LIFE ASSURANCE IN 1986

Total new premiums for life assurances and annuities increased in 1986 by 32 per cent to £9,752 million. New sums assured rose by 22 per cent to £114,465 million while new annuities per annum declined by 6·1 per cent to £2,317 million. The following figures include all forms of life assurance and annuities, including linked-life assurance and occupational pension and life assurance schemes in the United Kingdom.

	1986 £m	1985 £m
Total new premiums— annual and single	9,752	7,410
Benefits secured by these premiums—		
New sums assured	114,465	93,793
New annuities per annum, deferred and immediate	2,317	2,466

HOME SERVICE INSURANCE IN 1986

The following figures are based on returns from 15 "home service" insurance offices, which together transact over 99 per cent of industrial (collected premium) life business. While they, unlike all other insurers, transact industrial life business, they also carry on a very substantial volume of ordinary life and general insurance, much of it in policyholders' homes through the field staffs.

The following figures show the U.K. business, excluding group pension business.

	1986 £m	1985 £m
Industrial Life Business		
1. Premium Income	1,248	1,198·2
2. Payments to policyholders:		
(a) On death	240·4	219·5
(b) On maturity	567·5	483·6
(c) On surrender	357·2	343·4
(d) Other	12·1	26·0
TOTAL	1,177·3	1,072·5

NEW LINKED LIFE ASSURANCE BUSINESS ANNUAL STATISTICS

	Year ended Dec. 31, 1983	Year ended Dec. 31, 1984	Year ended Dec. 31, 1985	Year ended Dec. 31, 1986
	£m	£m	£m	£m
1. *New Annual Premiums:*				
(a) Assurances & Annuities	302	295	303	395
(b) Personal Pensions (See note below)	73	128	199	148
Total new annual premiums:	375	423	502	543
2. *New Single Premiums:*				
(a) Assurances & Annuities	1,440	1,790	2,465	4,296
(b) Personal Pensions (See note below)	71	106	139	153
Total new single premiums:	1,511	1,896	2,604	4,449

NOTE: Personal pensions are contracts available to the self-employed and those not in pensionable employment.

THE LIFE ASSURANCE COMPANIES

The list on the following pages contains the names of all the more important British life offices, and of Commonwealth offices (marked C) which transact life business in this country.

Class of business. The second column shows whether the company is conducted on the mutual system whereby the whole of the divisible profit is allotted to participating policyholders (M), or whether the company has proprietors by whom part (usually a very small proportion) of such profits received (P). Life offices transacting other business are marked (O) in this column. In such cases the life funds are kept separately, and are not liable for the claims of other departments. The share capital is usually liable for the claims of all branches. Those having an industrial branch are indicated by letter (I).

Figures. These are taken from the latest annual accounts available at date of going to press and in the

majority of cases refer to annual reports for the financial year ended December 31, 1986.

Life funds. The amounts of these funds, though of interest, are not in themselves a sufficient indication of the financial stability of a company, which cannot be judged unless liabilities are actually compared with assets.

Premium income. The annual premium income is in all cases stated after deduction of the amount paid to other companies for reassuring parts of the risk.

Consideration for annuities.—These are the amounts received to provide various types of annuities.

Interest.—The rate of interest earned is important for comparison with the rate assumed in valuing liabilities, since the greater the margin between these rates the greater is the surplus available from this source bonus declaration. The rate of interest given is before deduction of Income Tax except where marked (N)—net.

Valuation.—The valuation returns which are required to be made by the companies to the Department of Trade and Industry indicate liability under existing policies, after making allowance for the amounts to be paid and received. It is assumed that deaths will occur in accordance with a mortality table (various tables are used) and that interest will be earned at a certain rate. If a company assumes that it will earn a high rate of interest in the future the net liability will appear less than if it assumes a low rate, while the liability on account of mortality appears greater by some tables than by others. The position of an office is most satisfactory when a stringent basis of valuation is adopted, because the margin between the calculated and experienced liability is larger and the surplus available for bonuses is greater. The lower the rate of interest assumed the more stringent is the valuation. The foregoing remarks, however, do not apply in the case of an office which has adopted a Bonus Reserve Valuation.

Types of policy.—Although there are scores of life offices in Britain each offering their own particular products under a wide variety of labels, there are really only four basic types of contract. These are:

1. "Term" assurance (sometimes called "temporary" assurance). With this type of policy the assurer, in return for a regular premium agrees to pay the sum assured if the person assured should die within the term of years stated by the policy.

Such policies take care of the temporary need for protection of the family while the children are growing up, and the family is therefore most vulnerable. The commonest and most popular forms are to cover the mortgage on the family home or to assure a regular tax-free income for the family over so many years should the breadwinner die. This is much the cheapest form of life assurance because the majority of policies invariably do not result in claims.

2. "Whole-life" assurance is one under which the assurer undertakes to keep the assurance in force provided the premiums are paid for the whole life of the assured. They will then pay the agreed sum whenever death takes place. This costs a good deal more than term, naturally. All policies end in claims.

3. "Endowment" assurance. This contract really is one which uses a fund for saving to a particular target sum by a particular future date and at the same time secures payment of the sum assured should the saver die before that date arrives. In return for the continued payment of a regular premium over a fixed number of years, the assurer agrees to pay the sum assured at the end of that time, or earlier if the assured person should die. The bulk of an endowment assurance premium is savings; consequently the premium of such a contract is a lot higher than that for a whole life assurance.

4. "Annuities". Life assurance can be divided broadly speaking into death or survival benefits. Death benefits are paid to a policyholder's dependants if and when he dies. Survival benefits are paid to the policyholder himself either in the form of a cash sum when he reaches a certain age or in the form of a guaranteed annual income for life, which is known as an annuity. Pensions are annuities of a kind and a very large proportion of the pensions due to people are being and will be paid by funds run by life offices.

INDUSTRIAL COMPANIES

Established	Class	Name of Office	Life funds	Life premium income	Rate of interest % earned	Interest % assumed at valuation
			£m	£m		
1866	PO	Britannic	609·3	99·5	13·34	—
1862	M	City of Glasgow	29·4	2·8	12·79	3·0
1867	MIO	Co-operative	1,211·7	189·4	10·4	3·0
1939	P	Irish Life	126·1	16·8	7·0	3·0–4·0
1843	M	Liverpool Victoria	814·0	81·9	11·5	3·5
1869	PO	London and Manchester†	208·8	31·1	—	3·0
1864	PO	Pearl	1,136·3	192·8	12·16	3·0–3·5
1891	M	Pioneer Mutual	34·0	1·9	9·48	3·0
1848	PO	Prudential†	2,427·7	355·3	11·10	3·0–4·5
1911	MI	Reliance Mutual†	17·5	2·4	—	2·5–3·75
1850	M	Royal Liver	331·3	51·9	12·17	3·75
1861	MO	Royal London	690·0	55·9	10·4	2·5
1908	P	United Friendly	426·4	88·2	13·4	3·0
1841	MO	Wesleyan and General	187·4	27·0	12·32	3·0

INDUSTRIAL LIFE NEW BUSINESS 1986

Name of Office	No. of policies issued	Net sums assured	Net annual premiums
		£m	£m
Britannic	414,000	384·7	24·4
City of Glasgow	14,149	9·4	0·77
Co-operative	406,673	749·7	30·5
Irish Life	38,548	125·8	2·8
Liverpool Victoria	190,494	150·0	12·1
London and Manchester†	228,178	98·4	6·8
Pearl	414,958	400·4	32·2
Pioneer Mutual	—	—	—
Prudential†	747,177	2,061·6	78·5
Reliance Mutual†	10,664	—	0·72
Royal Liver	118,767	101·5	8·2
Royal London	113,603	162·3	10·5
United Friendly	301,767	196·2	14·2
Wesleyan and General	76,387	111·2	5·0

† 1985 figures.

PRINCIPAL LIFE ASSURANCE COMPANIES

Estab-lished	Class	Name of Office	Life and annuity funds	Life premium income	Considera-tion for annuities	Rate of interest % earned	Interest % assumed at valuation
			£m	£m	£m		
1961	P	Abbey Life	1,849·7	223·8	11·3	—	4·55–10·1
1965	P	Allied Dunbar	3,830·0	259·2	310·3	—	—
1849	M	Australian Mutual Prov. (C)	189·8	20·9	28·4	10·39	2·75
1925	PO	Avon†	44·2	3·5	0·9	11·30	Various
1965	P	Barclays Life	669·0	102·1	30·9	5·35	—
1866	PIO	Britannic (Ord.)	312·0	35·6	0·2	13·34	—
1920	PO	British National†	31·6	8·5	—	—	Various
1847	M	Canada Life	3,879·1	205·3	452·1	12·3	Various
1963	P	Cannon Assurance	292·4	70·1	0·16	—	—
1862	MI	City of Glasgow (Ord.)	23·9	2·2	—	12·79	3·0
1824	M	Clerical, Medical Group	2,177·5	169·7	239·8	6·30	—
1873	M	Colonial Mutual (C)	675·0	88·6	13·0	—	3·5–7·0
1861	PO	Commercial Union	5,734·4	481·4	241·4	9·53	3·0–9·0
1871	M	Confederation Life	3,371·0	205·7	22·8		
1867	MIO	Co-operative (Ord.)	1,125·5	141·9	21·3	10·4	2·75–5·0
1900	M	Crown Financial†	285·7	67·0	54·1		
1899	PO	Crusader	574·4	89·2	31·4	8·43	3·0–10·0
1904	PO	Eagle Star	2,637·0	246·0	107·0	9·00	1·5–7·0
1887	MO	Ecclesiastical	61·4	17·5	5·5	4·96	3·5
1901	P	Economic†	15·8	1·4	0·2	10·4	Various
1762	M	Equitable Life†	1,810·6	303·7		9·9	Various
1832	M	Friends' Provident	2,115·0	350·0	13·0	10·24	2·75
1899	M	FS Assurance	95·3	14·9	15·0	6·62	2·5–10·0
1837	P	General Accident Life	917·0	84·2	49·2	12·26	3·0–5·5
1848	P	Gresham Life	206·4	27·1	0·04	9·5	3·50–4·5
1821	PO	Guardian Royal Exchange	4,444·7	404·1	222·8	6·4	Various
1960	P	Hill Samuel	612·4	104·0	11·8	6·5	4·5–9·75
1896	P	Imperial Life of Canada (C)†	2,152·3	317·8		12·18	Various
1935	P	Insurance Corp. Life	206·6	57·5	7·3	—	4·5
1939	PI	Irish Life (Ord.)	2,068·4	432·9	139·7	10·1	2·5–4·0
1838	P	LAS Group	503·4	101·1	13·0	7·85	Various
1836	PO	Legal and General	3,681·0	429·0	23·0	11·0	Various
1843	MI	Liverpool Victoria (Ord.)	176·9	21·7	—	11·51	3·5
1971	P	Lloyd's Life—see Royal Heritage					
1869	PIO	London and Manchester (Ord.)†	579·2	101,501			Various
1806	M	London Life	1,400·4	129·1	18·0	7·78	Various
1961	P	M & G Assurance†	301·7	67·9	—	4·2	6·0
1852	M	MGM Assurance	455·2	38·5	20·3	Various	Various
1884	M	Medical, Sickness	77·0	8·6	0·4	11·56	3·5–10·0
1970	P	Merchant Investors†	205·3	26·9	9·8	9·5	6·5
1890	M	Nalgo Insurance	27·5	1·9	—	6·2	2·5
1910	MO	National Farmers Union	441·1	21·9	15·7	10·8	Various
1869	M	National Mut. Life of Australasia	253·0	21·8	68·0	—	Various
1830	M	National Mutual	406·4	30·4	36·7	9·25	3·0–8·0
1835	M	National Provident	1,710·7	240·9	2·1	8·6	3·25–9·0
1924	PIO	New Ireland*	245·7	29·0	27·6	11·6	Various
1808	M	Norwich Union	7,097·4	1,340·0	—	10·48	3·5–9·0
1864	PIO	Pearl (Ord.)	1,565·3	236·3	27·0	12·08	2·5–9·0
1891	MI	Pioneer Mutual (Ord.)	98·7	24·1	—	8·97	3·0
1877	P	Provident Life Assoc.	214·5	38·3	1·2	8·34	3·5–7·5
1840	M	Provident Mutual	1,788·8	102·7	116·7	—	Various
1848	PIO	Prudential Group (Ord.)†	8,246·5	999·7	87·6	10·3	Various
1911	MI	Reliance Mutual (Ord.)†	74·4	24·2	—	—	2·75–4·25
1971	P	Royal Heritage†	258·1	77·3	3·8	6·6	Various
1845	PO	Royal Life	2,971·9	256·8	146·3	9·84	2·5–3·75
1850	MI	Royal Liver (Ord.)	138·8	15·7	—	12·17	3·75
1861	MIO	Royal London	458·5	64·1	0·06	9·04	3·0
1887	M	Royal Nat. Pen. Fund for Nurses	223·6	24·6	1·6	10·27	
1963	P	Save & Prosper	869·8	61·7	38·7	4·5	3·5–12·0
1965	P	Schroder	485·1	102·7	47·2	5·6	Various
1826	M	Scottish Amicable	4,057·0	560·0	—	—	Various
1831	M	Scottish Equitable	1,993·1	216·8	170·9	8·6	2·5–8·5
1881	M	Scottish Life	1,057·9	142·7	38·5	8·28(N)	2·5–4·0
1883	MO	Scottish Mutual	1,064·4	273·7	—	7·23	3·0–8·0
1837	M	Scottish Provident	1,784·0	110·0		9·3	Various
1815	M	Scottish Widows'	5,244·6	189·6	282·0	7·3	Various
1825	M	Standard Life	8,482·8	1,305·5		8·9	2·75–10·0
1710	PO	Sun Alliance†	3,758·2	392·2	41·3	10·88	Various
1810	P	Sun Life Ass. Group	3,675·0	518·5	244·2	11·4	3·75–10·25
1865	M	Sun Life of Canada (C)†	8,399·8	424·3	451·3	11·49(N)	Various
1936	P	Teachers'	86·6	36·1	—	8·98	2·25–2·50
1969	P	Trident Life	337·9	87·4	—	15·9	4·0–12·0
1908	P	United Friendly (Ord.)	126·1	16·7	—	12·7	3·0
1841	MIO	Wesleyan & General (Ord.)	137·1	15·8	1·4	13·49	2·75
1963	P	Windsor Life	65·1	9,399·0	398·0	10·0	Various
1960	P	Zurich Life	110·1	30·1	1·0	9·9	3·75

† 1985 figures   (C) Commonwealth Office   (N) Net
* Irish Punts.

LIFE ASSURANCE NEW BUSINESS 1986

Name of Office	No. of policies issued	Net sums assured	Net annual premiums	Net single premiums
		£m	£m	£m
Abbey Life	252,860	3,642·9	66·5	109·2
Allied Dunbar	142,987	3,310·0	106·8	157·0
Australian Mutual Provident (C)	12,930	172·8	3·6	3·2
Avon†	2,257	22·4	0·44	0·06
Barclays Life	83,083	675·4	18·1	62·2
Britannic (Ord.)	45,000	236·6	7·6	0·5
British National†	33,330	70·8	1·6	6·7
Canada Life	35,694	6,202·5	42·8	419·5
Cannon Assurance	39,113	382·1	5·5	23·3
City of Glasgow (Ord.)	1,730	8·2	0·3	0·9
Clerical, Medical Group	124,434	3,022·8	54·4	177·0
Colonial Mutual (C)	72,900	570·0	11·9	8·9
Commercial Union	250,787	6,605·2	58·0	158·9
Confederation Life	73,857	6,210·2	421·5	51·7
Co-operative (Ord.)	127,093	1,368·8	29·6	53·1
Crown Financial†	52,700	275·8	21·4	53·1
Crusader	33,000	1,981·0	15·7	58·4
Eagle Star	58,068	3,063·1	26·4	193·9
Ecclesiastical	2,390	15·0	0·65	0·003
Economic†	2,085	39·0	0·2	0·1
Equitable Life†	51,445	1,111·0	85·0	52·2
Friends' Provident	193,546	4,572·8	74·3	118·4
FS Assurance	8,315	260·0	3·2	14·5
General Accident Life	91,000	3,942·0	23·9	16·6
Gresham Life	20,528	474·9	4·1	0·45
Guardian Royal Exchange	365,010	6,478·4	80·1	334·3
Hill Samuel	65,792	1,253·1	8·2	71·2
Imperial Life of Canada (C)†	54,851	2,687·3	56·4	87·6
Insurance Corp. Life	10,605	—	5·9 (gross)	50·7 (gross)
Irish Life (Ord.)	95,119	2,130·5	54·5	238·8
LAS Group	29,633	528·4	11·1	69·5
Legal & General†	199,000	5,797·0	62·0	12·0
Liverpool Victoria (Ord.)	28,300	130·2	5·0	—
Lloyd's Life—see Royal Heritage				
London & Manchester (Ord.)†	78,765	515·0	16·9	47·7
London Life	41,000	500·6	15·8	79·8
M & G Assurance†	31,088	109·6	2·4	36·6
MGM Assurance	78,676	300·7	9·7	14·3
Medical, Sickness	7,575	99·5	1·4	0·4
Merchant Investors†	16,846	171·5	4·9	16·6
Nalgo Insurance	2,326	40·7	0·3	—
National Farmers Union	13,441	394·3	8·8	3·1
National Mut. Life of Australasia	16,566	256·0	3·8	2·1
National Mutual	20,369	321·3	10·2	15·2
National Provident	76,741	583·6	25·4	94·1
New Ireland*	19,170	297·6	5·8	21·9
Norwich Union	482,735	8,234·4	155·8	783·5
Pearl (Ord.)	121,323	801·4	27·8	126·6
Pioneer Mutual (Ord.)	26,129	504·2	6·3	8·6
Provident Life Association	20,006	370·0	6·7	13·0
Provident Mutual	133,251	1,435·7	41·7	73·2
Prudential Group (Ord.)†	454,122	7,608·0	183·5	218·6
Reliance Mutual (Ord.)†	11,389	—	2·6	—
Royal Heritage†	73,084	459·8	8·0	46·3
Royal Life	163,000	3,116·8	64·4	157·6
Royal Liver (Ord.)	14,984	86·5	2·8	0·07
Royal London	41,673	374·3	10·3	17·6
Royal Nat. Pen. Fund for Nurses	23,996	38·6	5·8	1·8
Save & Prosper	31,237	272·3	9·5	39·5
Schroder	76,611	243·6	14·0	94·9
Scottish Amicable	267,000	5,122·0	114·0	151·0
Scottish Equitable	67,000	1,078·4	36·1	256·7
Scottish Life	54,927	1,408·1	33·4	87·7
Scottish Mutual	60,025	990·1	25·3	184·0
Scottish Provident	93,203	1,157·0	20·5	17·1
Scottish Widows'	108,000	—	84·3	0·26
Standard Life	388,661	not available	196·8	534·6
Sun Alliance†	—	—	45·4	82·9
Sun Life Assurance Group	—	—	53·4	244·2
Sun Life of Canada (C)†	316,188	12,991·2	228·1	182·8
Teachers'	11,119	81·1	1·8	32·0
Trident Life	27,733	23·7	5·3	29·4
United Friendly (Ord.)	21,509	177·3	2·7	—
Wesleyan & General (Ord.)	11,603	98·9	2·1	4·2
Windsor Life	12,928	221·8	3·4	3·3
Zurich Life	24,906	769·6	3·6	0·2

† 1985 figures   (C) Commonwealth Office
* Irish Punts.

DIRECTORY OF INSURANCE COMPANIES

The class of Insurance undertaken is shown in the second column as follows: A—Accident (which includes Motor, Employers' Liability, etc.); F—Fire (including Burglary); L—Life; and M—Marine. A number of offices are now included in a Group—the initials of which appear after the name. The main Groups are as follows—E.S.—Eagle Star; C.U.—Commercial Union; G.R.E.—Guardian Royal Exchange; G.A.—General Accident; N.U.—Norwich Union; R—Royal; S.A.—Sun Alliance & London.

Est'd.	Nature of Business	Name of Company	Address
1961	L	Abbey Life	Holdenhurst Rd., Bournemouth.
1951	AFM	Albion	Plantation House, 31/35 Fenchurch St., E.C.3.
1824	AFM	Alliance .................S.A.	1 Bartholomew Lane, E.C.2.
1965	L	Allied Dunbar	Allied Dunbar Centre, Swindon.
1921	L	American Life	2–8 Altyre Road, Croydon.
1960	AFLM	Ansvar	St. Leonards Rd., Eastbourne.
1808	ALFM	Atlas..................G.R.E.	Royal Exchange, E.C.3.
1849	L	Australian Mutual Provident ..	A.M.P. Ho., Dingwall Rd., Croydon.
1925	AFL	Avon	Tiddington Road, Stratford-upon-Avon.
1905	AFM	Baptist	4 Southampton Row, W.C.1.
1965	L	Barclays	94 St Paul's Churchyard, E.C.4.
1883	AFM	Beacon...............S.A.	1 Bartholomew Lane, E.C.2.
1894	AFM	Bedford General	Zurich House, Stanhope Rd., Portsmouth.
1925	AFM	Black Sea and Baltic	65 Fenchurch St., E.C.3.
1959	AFLM	Bradford	North Park, Halifax.
1866	AFL	Britannic	Moor Green, Moseley, Birmingham.
1863	M	British & Foreign Marine ....R.	New Hall Place, Liverpool.
1878	Machinery	British Engine, &c ....R.	Longbridge House, Manchester 4.
1854	AFL	British Equitable........G.R.E.	Royal Exchange, E.C.3.
1904	AFM	British General .... C.U.	St. Helen's, 1 Undershaft, E.C.3.
1888	AFM	British Law .............S.A.	1 Bartholomew Lane, E.C.2.
1896	L	British Life	Reliance House, Tunbridge Wells, Kent.
1920	AFL	British Nat. Life	Perrymount Rd., Haywards Heath, W. Sussex.
1908	AFM	British Oak...........G.R.E.	Royal Exchange, E.C.3.
1881	A	Builders' Accident	31 & 32 Bedford St., Strand, W.C.2.
1805	AFLM	Caledonian ...........G.R.E.	Royal Exchange, E.C.3.
1934	AFM	Cambrian .............G.R.E.	Royal Exchange, E.C.3.
1847	AL	Canada Life	Canada Life House, Potters Bar, Herts.
1963	L	Cannon	1 Olympic Way, Wembley.
1903	AFM	Car & General .........G.R.E.	Royal Exchange, E.C.3.
1885	AFM	Century	4–5 King William St., E.C.4.
1922	AFMex-motor	Chemists' Mutual	321 Chase Rd., Southgate, N.14.
1862	L	City of Glasgow Friendly	200 Bath Street, Glasgow G.2.
1824	L	Clerical, Medical & Gen.	Narrow Plain, Bristol.
1873	L & Pers. Acc.	Colonial Mutual	24 Ludgate Hill, E.C.4.
1919	AFM	Comrcl. Ins. Co. of Ireland	5 Donegall Square, S., Belfast.
1861	AFLM	Commercial Union	St. Helen's, 1 Undershaft, E.C.3.
1871	L	Confederation	50/52 Chancery Lane, W.C.2.
1891	AF	Congregational	21–22 Apsley Crescent, Bradford 8.
1867	AFLM	Co-operative	Miller St., Manchester.
1905	AFM	Cornhill	32 Cornhill, E.C.3.
1900	L	Crown Financial Management .	Crown House, Woking, Surrey.
1899	AFLM	Crusader	Woodhatch, Reigate, Surrey.
1908	AFM	Dominion	92/94 Gracechurch St., E.C.3.
1904	AFLM	Eagle Star	1 Threadneedle St., E.C.2.
1887	AFL	Ecclesiastical	Beaufort House, Brunswick Rd., Gloucester.
1901	AFLM	Economic	Economic House, London Road, Sittingbourne.
1823	AFM	Edinburgh.............. C.U.	St. Helen's, 1 Undershaft, E.C.3.
1880	AFM	Employers' Liability ...... C.U.	St. Helen's, 1 Undershaft, E.C.3.
1932	Animal Ins.	Equine and Livestock	610–616 Chiswick High Rd, W.4.
1762	L	Equitable Life	4 Coleman St., E.C.2.
1844	L	Equity & Law	20 Lincoln's Inn Fields, W.C.2.
1802	AF	Essex & Suffolk .........G.R.E.	Royal Exchange, E.C.3.
1894	AFM	Excess	13 Fenchurch Avenue, E.C.3.
1925	AFL	Federation Mutual	29 Linkfield Lane, Redhill, Surrey.
1890	AF	Fine Art & General....... C.U.	St. Helen's, 1 Undershaft, E.C.3.
1832	L	Friends' Prov	Pixham End, Dorking, Surrey.
1899	L	FS Assurance	190 West George St., Glasgow.
1885	AFM	General Accident	General Buildings, Perth, Scotland.
1837	L	General Accident Life	2 Rougier St., York.
1848	L	Gresham Life	2–6 Prince of Wales Rd., Bournemouth.
1910	AFM	Gresham Fire & Accident	11 Queen Victoria St., E.C.4.
1840	AFM	Guarantee Society .... G.A.	36–37 Old Jewry, E.C.2.
1821	ALFM	Guardian...............G.R.E.	68 King William Street, E.C.4.

Est'd.	Nature of Business	Name of Company	Address
1908	AFM	Hibernian	Haddington Road, Dublin, 4.
1960	L	Hill Samuel	NLA Tower, Addiscombe Rd., Croydon.
1966	AF	Household & General ......S.A.	1 Bartholomew Lane, E.C.2.
1932	FL	Ideal	Pitmaston, Birmingham, 13.
1896	L	Imperial Life of Canada	Petrofina House, London Road, Gloucester.
1935	L	Insurance Corporation of Ireland (Life)	Burlington Road, Dublin 4.
1939	L	Irish Life	Lr. Abbey St., Dublin 2.
1880	A	Iron Trades Employers'	Iron Trades Ho., 21–24 Grosvenor Pl., S.W.1.
1838	L	LAS Group	10 George St., Edinburgh.
1845	AF	Law Fire .................S.A.	1 Bartholomew Lane, E.C.2.
1806	AFM	Law Union & Rock ....R.	1 North John St., Liverpool, 2.
1907	AFM	Legal ....R.	1 North John St., Liverpool, 2.
1836	AFLM	Legal and General	Temple Court, 11 Queen Victoria St., E.C.4.
1970	L	Liberty Life	Kingmaker House, Station Rd., New Barnet.
1890	AFLM	Licenses & General	14 Bonhill Street, E.C.2.
1836	AFM	L'pool & London & Globe. ....R.	New Hall Place, Liverpool.
1918	AFM	Liverpool Marine & General....	4–5 King William St., E.C.4.
1843	L	Liverpool Victoria Friendly	Victoria House, Southampton Row., W.C.1.
1890	AFM	Local Government Guarantee G.R.E.	Royal Exchange, E.C.3
1836	AFM	Lombard Insurance............	31–35 Fenchurch St., E.C.3.
1720	AFLM	London Assurance ........S.A.	1 Bartholomew Lane, E.C.2.
1869	AFM	London Guar. & Reinsurance...	4 King William St., E.C.4.
1919	AFM	London & Lancashire..........	New Hall Place, Liverpool.
1806	L	London Life	100 Temple St., Bristol.
1869	AFL	London & Manchester	Winslade Park, Exeter, Devon.
1860	AFM	London & Provincial Marine G.A.	Lloyd's Building, Lime St., E.C.3.
1862	AFM	London & Scottish .... C.U.	St. Helen's, 1 Undershaft, E.C.3.
1961	L	M & G Assurance	M & G House, Victoria Rd., Chelmsford
1887	L	Manufacturers Life	St. George's Way, Stevenage.
1836	M	Marine....................R.	34–36 Lime St., E.C.3.
1852	L	Marine & General	MGM House, Heene Rd., Worthing.
1864	M	Maritime .................N.U.	Surrey St., Norwich.
1884	L Sickness A	Med., Sickness, Ann. and Life. ..	7–10 Chandos St., Cavendish Sq., W.1.
1907	Reinsurance	Mercantile & General..........	Moorfields House, Moorfields, E.C.2.
1970	L	Merchant Investors	High Street, Croydon.
1871	M	Merchants' Marine .... C.U.	St. Helen's, 1 Undershaft, E.C.3.
1872	AF	Methodist	Brazennose House, Brazennose St., Manchester.
1940	AFM	Minster	Minster House, Arthur St., E.C.4.
1906	AFM	Motor Union ............G.R.E.	Royal Exchange, E.C.3.
1903	AF	Municipal Mutual	22 Old Queen St., Westminster, S.W.1.
1890	AFL	Nalgo Insurance Association ...	1 Mabledon Place, W.C.1.
1935	L	National Employers' Life	Milton Court, Dorking, Surrey.
1914	AFM	National Employers' Mutual ...	N.E.M. House, Mitre Sq., E.C.3.
1910	AFL	National Farmers' Union	Tiddington Rd., Stratford-upon-Avon.
1863	Fidelity Guar.	Natl. Guaran. & Suretyship C.U.	St. Helen's, 1 Undershaft, E.C.3.
1894	AF	National Ins. & Guarantee Cor. .	Heron House, 145 City Rd., E.C.1.
1830	L	National Mutual Life	5 Bow Churchyard (off Cheapside), E.C.4.
1869	L	National Mutual of Australasia .	N.M. House, Serpentine Rd., Poole, Dorset
1835	L	National Provident............	48 Gracechurch St., E.C.3.
1854	Plate Glass	National Provincial .....G.R.E.	Royal Exchange, E.C.3.
1864	Machinery	National Vulcan Eng. Ins. Group.................S.A.	Empire House, St. Martin's-le-Grand, E.C.1.
1921	Naval Officers risks, etc.	Navigators & General ..... E.S.	1 Threadneedle St., E.C.2.
1924	L	New Ireland	11/12 Dawson St., Dublin, 2.
1809	AFLM	North British & Mercantile C.U.	St. Helen's, 1 Undershaft, E.C.3.
1862	FM	North Pacific ...........G.R.E.	Royal Exchange, E.C.3.
1836	AFLM	Northern................ C.U.	St. Helen's, 1 Undershaft, E.C.3.
1797	AFM	Norwich Union Fire...........	Surrey Street, Norwich.
1808	L	Norwich Union Life	Surrey Street, Norwich.
1871	AFM	Ocean Accident .... C.U.	St. Helen's, 1 Undershaft, E.C.3.
1859	M	Ocean Marine .... C.U.	4 Fenchurch Ave., E.C.3.
1931	AFM	Orion	70–72 King William St., E.C.4.
1886	AF	Palatine......................	108 Cannon St., E.C.4.
1864	AFLM	Pearl.........................	High Holborn, W.C.1.
1958	Sickness A	Permanent	7–10 Chandos Street, Cavendish Sq., W.1.
1782	AFLM	Phoenix	see Sun Alliance

Est'd.	Nature of Business	Name of Company	Address
1891	L	Pioneer Mutual	16 Crosby Rd. N., Liverpool.
1920	AFM	Planet Assurance . . . . .S.A.	1 Bartholomew Lane, E.C.2.
1969	L	Property Growth	Leon House, High St., Croydon
1877	L	Prov. Life Assocn.	Provident Way, Basingstoke, Hampshire.
1840	L	Provident Mutual Life	25/31 Moorgate, London E.C.2.
1903	AFM	Provincial	Stramongate, Kendal, Cumbria.
1848	AFLM	Prudential	Holborn Bars, E.C.1.
1849	AF	Railway Passengers . . . . . . C.U.	St. Helen's, 1 Undershaft, E.C.3.
1864	AFL	Refuge	Oxford St., Manchester M60.
1911	L	Reliance Mutual	Reliance House, Tunbridge Wells, Kent.
1906	AF	Reliance Fire & Accident	Reliance House, Tunbridge Wells, Kent.
1881	AFM	Reliance Marine . . . . . . .G.R.E.	Royal Exchange, E.C.3.
1823	Reversions	Reversionary Interest Society. .	4 Coleman St., E.C.2.
1918	AF	Road Transport & General G.A.	77 Upper Richmond Rd., S.W.15.
1845	L	Royal Life	New Hall Place, Liverpool.
1720	AFL	Royal Exchange	Royal Exchange, E.C.3.
1971	L	Royal Heritage Life	Bretton Way, Peterborough.
1850	L	Royal Liver Friendly	Royal Liver Building, Liverpool 3.
1861	AFL	Royal London	Royal London House, Middleborough, Colchester.
1887	L	Royal Nat. Pensions (Nurses) . . .	15 Buckingham St., W.C.2.
1909	AFM	Salvation Army	101 Queen Victoria St., E.C.4.
1963	L	Save and Prosper	1 Finsbury Ave., London E.C.2.
1965	L	Schroder	Enterprise House, Isambard Brunel Rd., Portsmouth.
1826	L	Scottish Amicable	150 St. Vincent St., Glasgow.
1881	FM	Scottish Boiler . . . . G.A.	250 St. Vincent St., Glasgow.
1831	L	Scottish Equitable	28 St. Andrew Square, Edinburgh.
1919	AFM	Scottish General . . . . G.A.	100 West Nile St., Glasgow, G.2.
1852	L	Scottish Legal	95 Bothwell St., Glasgow, G.2.
1881	L	Scottish Life	19 St. Andrew Square, Edinburgh, 2.
1876	AF	Scottish Metropolitan . . . . C.U.	St. Helen's, 1 Undershaft, E.C.3.
1883	AL	Scottish Mutual	109 St. Vincent Street, Glasgow, G.2.
1837	L	Scottish Provident	6 St. Andrew Square, Edinburgh.
1824	AFLM	Scottish Union & National N.U.	Surrey St., Norwich.
1815	L	Scottish Widows'	15 Dalkeith Rd., Edinburgh.
1875	AFM	Sea . . . . .S.A.	1 Bartholomew Lane, E.C.2.
1904	AFL	Sentinel	2 Eyre Street Hill, E.C.1.
1964	L	Stalwart Assurance	Tuition Hse., St. George's Rd., Wimbledon.
1825	L	Standard Life	3 George Street, Edinburgh.
1891	AFM	State . . . . .G.R.E.	Royal Exchange, E.C.3.
1710	AFM	Sun . . . . .S.A.	1 Bartholomew Lane, E.C.2.
*	AFLM	Sun Alliance & London and Phoenix	1 Bartholomew Lane, E.C.2.
1810	L	Sun Life Assurance Group	107 Cheapside, E.C.2.
1865	L	Sun Life of Canada	2, 3 & 4 Cockspur St., S.W.1.
1936	FL	Teacher's Assurance	12 Christchurch Rd., Bournemouth.
1969	L	Trident	London Road, Gloucester.
1869	L	Tunstall & District	Station Chambers, Tunstall, Stoke on Trent.
1867	M	Ulster Marine . . . . G.A.	5 Donegall Sq., S., Belfast.
1714	AFM	Union Assurance . . . . C.U.	St. Helen's, 1 Undershaft, E.C.3.
1835	AFM	Union Ins. Soc. of Canton G.R.E.	Royal Exchange, E.C.3.
1863	M	Union Marine	4–5 King William St., E.C.4.
1915	AFM	United British . . . . .G.R.E.	Royal Exchange, E.C.3.
1908	AFL	United Friendly	42 Southwark Bridge Road, S.E.1.
1963	L	UK Life Assurance	Royal Albert House, Windsor.
1825	L	University	4 Coleman St., E.C.2.
1974	L	Vanbrugh	41–43 Maddox St., W.1.
1919	Reinsurance	Victory Reinsurance	Castle Hill Ave., Folkestone, Kent
1875	AFM	Warden . . . . .R.	1 North John St., Liverpool.
1911	AF	Welsh Insurance Corpn. . . C.U.	St. Helen's, 1 Undershaft, E.C.3.
1841	AFL	Wesleyan & General	Colmore Circus, Queensway, Birmingham 4.
1886	AF	West of Scotland . . . . C.U.	26 George St., Edinburgh 2.
1851	AFM	Western Assurance . . . . .R.	New Hall Place, Liverpool.
1912	AFLM	Western Australian	Swan Court, Mansel Rd., Wimbledon, S.W.19.
1717	AF	Westminster Fire . . . . .S.A.	1 Bartholomew Lane, E.C.2.
1865	AF	White Cross . . . . C.U.	St. Helen's, 1 Undershaft, E.C.3.
1963	L	Windsor Life	Royal Albert House, Windsor.
1894	AFM	World Marine & General . . C.U.	Dunster House, Mark Lane, E.C.3.
1872	AF	Zurich	11 Guildhall Walk, Portsmouth.

* Sun Alliance & London—Incorporating Funds established 1710, 1720, 1782 and 1824.

BRITISH MONETARY UNITS

COIN	
GOLD COINS	NICKEL-BRASS (COPPER/ NICKEL/ZINC)
Five Pound £5	
Two Pound £2	Two Pound £2
Sovereign £1	One Pound £1
Half-Sovereign 10s.	
SILVER COINS	CUPRO-NICKEL (SILVER)
Crown 25p	Crown 5s. (25p)
Maundy Money‡	Florin 2s. (10p)
Fourpence 4p	Shilling 1s. (5p)
Threepence 3p	*50 Pence 50p
Twopence 2p	*Crown 25p
Penny 1p	*20 Pence 20p
BRONZE COINS	*10 Pence 10p
*2 Pence 2p	*5 Pence 5p
*1 Penny 1p	

‡Gifts of special money distributed by the Sovereign annually on Maundy Thursday to the number of aged poor persons corresponding to the Sovereign's own age.
*For further details of decimal coins, see next page.

Gold Coin.—Gold ceased to circulate during the First World War. An Order of April 27, 1966, made it illegal for U.K. residents to continue holding more than four gold coins minted after 1837, or to acquire such coins unless they had been licensed as genuine collectors by the Bank of England. This Order was revoked on April 1, 1971, by the Exchange Control (Gold Coins Exemption) Order, 1971, whereby residents of the United Kingdom, Channel Islands and the Isle of Man may freely buy and sell and hold gold coins.

The 1971 Order was revoked on April 15, 1975, by the Exchange Control (Gold Coins Exemption) Order, 1975. Under this Order Section 1 of the Exchange Control Act 1947 (which prohibits dealings in gold or foreign currency except with Treasury permission) was exempted for gold coins minted in or before 1837. The import of gold coins minted after 1837 was prohibited except by authorised dealers in gold with individual import licences from the Department of Trade, and dealing between other U.K. residents was restricted to coins already held in the U.K.

Under an amendment, dated December 16, 1977, the exemptions contained in the 1975 Order were extended to cover gold coins minted in or before 1937.

The 1975 controls over the import of and dealing in gold coins were abolished on June 13, 1979 under the Exchange Control (Gold Coins Exemption) Order 1979, and gold coins, with certain exceptions,* may now be imported and exported without restriction.

On April 1, 1982 the Government introduced VAT (currently 15 per cent) on sales of all gold coin.

Silver Coin.—Prior to 1920 our silver coins were struck from standard silver—an alloy of which 925 parts in 1,000 were silver. In 1920 the proportion of silver was reduced to 500 parts. From January 1, 1947 all "silver" coins, except Maundy money, have been struck from cupro-nickel—an alloy of copper 75 parts and nickel 25 parts, except for the 20p, composed of copper 84 parts, nickel 16 parts. Maundy coins since 1947 have been struck from standard silver.

Bronze, introduced in 1860 to replace copper, is currently an alloy of copper 97 parts, zinc 2½ parts and tin ½ part. These proportions have been subject to slight variations in the past.

The "Remedy" is the amount of variation from

standard permitted in weight and fineness of coins when first issued from the Mint.

Legal tender of coin.—Gold, dated 1838 onwards, if not below least current weight, is legal tender to any amount. The £1 coin introduced on April 21, 1983 is legal tender to any amount. 50p and 20p coins are legal tender up to £10; 10p and 5p coins are legal tender up to £5 and bronze coins are legal tender for amounts up to 20p. Farthings ceased to be legal tender on December 31, 1960, the halfpenny on August 1, 1969, the halfcrown on January 1, 1970, the threepence and penny on August 31, 1971, the sixpence on June 30, 1980 and the decimal ½ penny on December 31, 1984.

Since 1982 the word "new" in "new pence" displayed on decimal coins has been dropped.

BANK NOTES

Bank of England notes are currently issued in denominations of £5, £10, £20 and £50 for the amount of the Fiduciary Note Issue, and are legal tender in England and Wales.

The old white notes for £10, £20, £50, £100, £500 and £1,000, which were issued until April 22, 1943, ceased to be legal tender in May 1945.

The old white £5 notes dated up to September 20, 1956, the £5 notes issued between 1957 and 1963, bearing a portrait of Britannia and the first series to bear a portrait of the Queen, issued between 1963 and 1971, ceased to be legal tender on March 14, 1961, June 27, 1967 and September 1, 1973 respectively. The series of £1 notes issued during the years 1928 to 1960 and the 10s. notes of the same type issued from 1928 to 1961—those without the royal portrait—ceased to be legal tender on May 29 and October 30, 1962 respectively. The £1 note first issued in March 1960 (bearing on the back a representation of Britannia) and the £10 note first issued in February 1964 (bearing a lion on the back) both bearing a portrait of the Queen on the front ceased to be legal tender on June 1, 1979. The 10s. note was replaced by the 50p coin in October 1969, and ceased to be legal tender on November 21, 1970. Bank notes which are no longer legal tender are payable when presented at the Head Office of the Bank of England in London.

The first of the current series of Bank notes was a £20 note issued on July 9, 1970. This was followed by the £5 note on November 11, 1971, £10 note on February 20, 1975, £1 note on February 9, 1978 and £50 note on March 20, 1981. The £1 coin was introduced on April 21, 1983 and the £1 denomination note ceased to be issued on December 31, 1984. The predominant identifying feature of each note is the portrayal on the back of a prominent figure from Britain's history namely, £5: The Duke of Wellington; £10: Florence Nightingale; £20: William Shakespeare; and £50: Sir Christopher Wren.

Note Circulation.—Note circulation is highest at the two peak spending periods of the year—around Christmas and during the summer holiday period. A peak of £14,702 million was reached immediately prior to Christmas 1986, a 4·5 per cent increase on the previous year.

The proportion of the total value of notes in circulation of £1 and £5 notes at end-February 1987 compared with the previous year, fell from 1·1 per cent and 18·0 per cent to 0·9 per cent and 15·8 per cent respectively. £10 notes fell from 44·3 per cent to 43·9 per cent, but £20 notes increased from 18·8 per cent to 20·3 per cent and £50 from 10·0 per cent to 11·5 per cent.

On February 28, 1987 the values of notes in

---

*Gold coins which are more than fifty years old and valued at a sum in excess of £8,000 cannot be exported without specific authorization from the Department of Trade.

circulation were: £1: £116,629,303; £5: £2,029,530,690; £10: £5,633,471,990; £20: £2,607,933,480; £50: £1,474,944,700.

Other Bank Notes.—Bank notes are issued by three Scottish banks. The Royal Bank of Scotland and the Bank of Scotland issue notes for £1, £5, £10, £20 and £100. The Clydesdale Bank issues notes for £1, £5, £10, £20, £50, £100. Scottish notes are not legal tender, but in Scotland they enjoy a status equal to that of the Bank of England note.

Channel Islands and the Isle of Man.—The states of Jersey and Guernsey issue notes for £1, £5, £10 and £20. The Government of the Isle of Man issues

notes for 50p, £1, £5, £10 and £20. These are legal tender only in their respective islands.

Although none of the series of notes specified above is legal tender in the United Kingdom they are generally accepted by the banks irrespective of their place of issue. At one time the banks made a commission charge for handling Scottish and Irish notes but this was abolished some years ago.

The Channel Islands and the Isle of Man also issue their own coinage. The states of Jersey and Guernsey issue coins for ½p, 1p, 2p, 5p, 10p, 20p, 50p and £1. The Isle of Man issues coins for ½p, 1p, 2p, 5p, 10p, 20p, 50p and £1.

Denomination	Metal	Standard Weight (grams)	Standard Diameter (centimetres)
Penny	bronze	3·56400	2·0320
2 pence	bronze	7·12800	2·5910
5 pence	cupro-nickel	5·65518	2·3595
10 pence	cupro-nickel	11·31036	2·8500
20 pence	cupro-nickel	5·0	2·14
25p Crown	silver	28·27590	3·8608
25p Crown	cupro-nickel	28·27590	3·8608
50 pence	cupro-nickel	13·5	3·0
£1	copper/nickel/zinc	9·5	2·25
£2	copper/nickel/zinc	15·98	2·84

EXPECTATION OF LIFE

Age	England and Wales Life Table, 1982–84		Scotland Life Table, 1982–84		Northern Ireland Life Table, 1982–84	
	Males	Females	Males	Females	Males	Females
0	71·6	77·4	69·6	75·6	70·2	76·2
5	67·5	73·2	65·6	71·4	66·3	72·2
10	62·6	68·3	60·7	66·5	61·4	67·3
15	57·7	63·4	55·8	61·6	56·4	62·3
20	52·9	58·5	51·0	56·7	51·7	57·4
25	48·1	53·6	46·2	51·7	47·0	52·5
30	43·3	48·7	41·5	46·9	42·2	47·7
35	38·5	43·8	36·7	42·0	37·5	42·8
40	33·7	39·0	32·0	37·2	32·8	38·0
45	29·1	34·2	27·4	32·6	28·2	33·3
50	24·6	29·7	23·1	28·1	23·8	28·7
55	20·4	25·3	19·1	23·8	19·8	24·3
60	16·6	21·1	15·6	19·9	16·0	20·2
65	13·2	17·2	12·4	16·2	12·8	16·4
70	10·3	13·6	9·7	12·8	9·9	12·8
75	7·9	10·4	7·4	9·8	7·4	9·7
80	5·9	7·7	5·6	7·2	5·5	7·1
85	4·4	5·5	4·3	5·2	4·2	5·1

FRIENDLY SOCIETIES—GREAT BRITAIN

Acts 1974–1984

Friendly societies are voluntary mutual organizations the main purposes of which are the provision of relief or maintenance during sickness, unemployment or retirement, and the provision of life assurance. Many of the older traditional societies complement their business activities by social activity and a general care for individual members in ways normally outside the scope of a purely commercial organization. There are three main categories of friendly societies—societies with separately registered branches, commonly called orders, centralized societies, which conduct business directly with members (having no separately registered branches), and collecting societies. Collecting societies conduct industrial assurance business and are subject to the requirements of the Industrial Assurance Acts in addition to the Friendly Societies Acts. Industrial assurance is life assurance, the premiums in respect of which are payable at intervals of less than two months and are received by means of collectors who make house to house visits for the purpose.

At the end of 1986 there were 24 orders with 2,962 branches, 364 centralized societies, and 36 collecting societies.

Long before the term "Friendly Society" came into use, the seeds of voluntary mutual insurance had been sown in the ancient religious and trade "Guilds". As is evident from the many extant parchment returns detailing their rules and possessions under a decree of Richard II, Guilds had become widespread in Britain by the 14th century. By then, the purely charitable character of the original Guilds had largely changed with the emergence of numerous small institutions adopting primitive mutual insurance methods of a regular flat rate contribution to insure relief when sick or in old age and a payment to the widow in the event of death.

The present register of Friendly Societies includes several societies which have been in existence for upwards of 200 years, the oldest, operating in Scotland, being the "Incorporation of Carters in Leith" established as long ago as 1555.

The first Act for the encouragement and protection of "Friendly Societies" in this country was not passed until 1793, but various amending Acts were put on the Statute Book during the next century as the result of the recommendations of successive Select Committees (including a Royal Commission in 1871). For example, it was not until the 1829 Act that all registered Friendly Societies were required to keep proper records of individual sickness and mortality amongst their members, which data enabled the construction of standard actuarial tables showing the expected (average) duration of sickness at successive ages, and also (with data from the Census) the corresponding mortality rates.

The rules and other documents of societies deposited with local justices passed into the custody of the Registrar following the Act of 1846 and are of considerable interest to social historians. Those relating to some societies no longer on the register have been transferred to the Public Record Office for permanent preservation.

The Friendly Societies Act 1974, which came into force in April, 1975, consolidated the nine Acts which comprised the Friendly Societies Acts 1896 to 1971 and a few other minor enactments relating to societies to which those Acts applied. The Act allows various specific classes other than "Friendly Societies" to be registered thereunder, but tax exemption (irrespective of the extent of interest income) is enjoyed only by registered "Friendly Societies". Removal of the £750 sum assured limit for tax exempt business was announced in the March 1987 Budget and enacted in the Finance (No 2) Act 1987. It was replaced by a more flexible limit applied to premiums—up to £100 per annum.

The Friendly Societies Act 1984 abolished the limits on the size of taxable life and annuity business societies could write.

In addition to Friendly Societies there are three other main classes of society which may be registered under the Friendly Societies Act 1974: benevolent societies, working men's clubs and specially authorized societies. Benevolent societies are established for any charitable or benevolent purpose, to provide the same type of benefits as would be permissible for a friendly society, but in contrast the benefits must be for persons who are not members instead of, or in addition to, members. Working men's clubs provide social and recreational facilities for members. Specially authorized societies are registered for any purpose authorized by the Treasury as a purpose to which some or all of the provisions of the 1974 Act ought to be extended. Examples are societies for the promotion of science, literature and the fine arts, or to enable members to pursue an interest in sports and games. At the end of 1986 there were 88 benevolent societies, 2,427 working men's clubs, and 151 specially authorized societies.

The principal statistics at the end of 1985 are given in the table below.

	Friendly Societies (a)	Collecting Societies	Benevolent Societies	Working Men's Clubs	Special Authorized Societies		Other
					Loan	Others	
Number of Societies	3,478	36	89	2,450	9	144	2
Number of Members 000's	3,095	17,005 (b)	327	2,331 (c)	13	115	3
Total Benefits Paid £000's	93,022	122,013	5,326	Not applicable	Not applicable	27	45
Total Funds £000's	1,227,190	1,470,102	16,986	122,912 (c)	488	12,582	462

(a) Centralized societies, orders and branches of orders   (c) 1980 figures
(b) Assurances

INDUSTRIAL AND PROVIDENT SOCIETIES—GREAT BRITAIN

Acts 1965–1979

The familiar "Co-op" societies are amongst the wide variety which are registered under the Industrial and Provident Societies Act 1965. This consolidating Act, which like the Friendly and the Building Societies Act is administered by the Chief Registrar of Friendly Societies, provides for the registration of societies and lays down the broad framework within which they must operate. Internal relations of societies are governed by their registered rules.

Registration under the Act confers upon a society corporate status by its registered name with perpetual succession and a common seal, and limited liability. A society qualifies for registration if it is carrying on an industry, business or trade, and it satisfies the Registrar that either (a) it is a bona fide co-operative society or (b) in view of the fact that its business is being, or is intended to be, conducted for the benefit of the community there are special reasons why it

should be registered under the Act rather than as a company under the Companies Act.

The Credit Unions Act 1979 added a new class of society registerable under the 1965 Act. The Act also lays down provision for supervision of these savings and loan bodies. A similar framework of law for credit unions has existed in Northern Ireland since 1969.

During 1986 the number of registered societies increased by 267 to 10,207. The largest single group was the 3,757 social and recreational clubs. The largest group in terms of turnover was that consisting of the retail societies which includes those trading under the familiar "Co-op" sign, with sales (in 1985) of £3,995 million. Sales of wholesale and productive societies amounted to £2,944 million in 1985. The principal statistics at the end of 1985 are given in the table below.

	Retail	Wholesale and Productive	Agricultural	Fishing	Social and Recreational Clubs	General Service	Housing	Credit Unions	Total
Number of Societies	217	227	1,071	111	3,745	972	3,515	82	9,940
Number of Members 000's	7,186	54	390	8	2,948	513	148	20	11,267
Funds of Members £000's	561,414	352,933	191,311	4,027	171,866	2,522,165	5,951,741	4,337	9,759,794
Total Assets £000's	1,327,267	873,690	460,334	13,263	344,260	2,948,075	8,971,497	4,556	14,942,941

BUILDING SOCIETIES—UNITED KINGDOM

Act 1986

The most significant event for the building societies in recent times was the passage of the Building Societies Act 1986, which received the Royal Assent on July 25, 1986. Most of the provisions of the Act came into effect on January 1, 1987. The Act gives building societies a completely new legal framework, the first since the initial comprehensive building society legislation in 1874. The new Act replaces both the 1962 Act and the 1967 Act covering Northern Ireland, and therefore applies to societies based throughout the United Kingdom.

The number of building societies in Great Britain declined from 167 at the end of 1985 to 148 at the end of 1986. There were, in addition, 3 building societies in Northern Ireland to be brought into the reckoning since the 1986 Act covers the whole of the U.K. During 1986 there were 16 mergers and 3 very small societies had their registrations cancelled.

The 1986 Act makes provision for a Building Societies Commission to promote the protection of shareholders and depositors, the financial stability of societies, and to administer the system of regulation of building societies provided under the Act. Much of the Act is concerned with the powers of control of the Commission and provision in relation to the management of societies, accounts, audit and so on. But the greatest impact and the most visible changes

so far as the general public is concerned flow from the new powers which societies may adopt, leading to an increased range of services which they may provide. There are also some interesting changes in relation to members' rights.

Under the 1962 Act raising funds to make loans was the only purpose for which a building society could exist. Under the 1986 Act that has only to be its principal purpose. The constitutional provisions include the right of members to have access to the register of members, entitlement to have notices of meetings and to vote, and the right of members to have a resolution circulated.

In addition to traditional mortgage business, the power of societies to lend in respect of shared ownership, index-linked and equity-linked schemes is given. Societies may also lend the deposit, lend on registered land before the borrower is registered as the owner and on other equitable interests which may be prescribed by order. Provision is also made for power to be given, by statutory instrument, for societies to make advances secured on land outside the United Kingdom. Larger societies may, for the first time, make unsecured loans. The power to lend on overdraft is specifically provided for. These societies may also make loans of up to £10,000 on mobile homes.

BUILDING SOCIETIES, GREAT BRITAIN, 1976–1986

Year	1 Number of Societies	2 Number of Share Holders 000's	3 Number of Depositors 000's	4 Number of Borrowers 000's	5 Share Balances £m	6 Deposit Balances £m
1976	364	19,991	712	4,609	25,760	848
1977	339	22,536	760	4,836	31,110	1,224
1978	316	24,999	781	5,108	36,186	1,254
1979	287	27,878	797	5,251	42,023	1,281
1980	273	30,636	915	5,383	48,915	1,742
1981	253	33,388	995	5,490	55,463	2,539
1982	227	36,609	1,094	5,643	64,977	3,447
1983	206	37,713	1,202	5,928	75,180	5,610
1984	190	39,385	1,550	6,317	88,078	8,426
1985	167	39,997	2,150	6,659	102,331	10,751
1986	151	40,563	2,850	7,025	115,538	16,864

Year	7 Mortgage Balances £m	8 Total Assets £m	Advances during year 9 Number 000's	10 Amount £m	11 Average Mortgage Rate %	12 Average Share Rate %
1976	22,565	28,202	913	6,183	11·06	7·02
1977	26,427	34,288	946	6,745	11·05	6·98
1978	31,598	39,538	1,184	8,808	9·55	6·46
1979	36,801	45,789	1,040	9,002	11·94	8·45
1980	42,437	53,793	936	9,503	14·92	10·34
1981	48,875	61,815	1,096	12,005	14·01	9·19
1982	56,691	73,033	1,320	14,971	13·32	8·77
1983	67,490	85,868	1,513	19,357	11·05	7·26
1984	81,879	102,688	1,657	23,767	11·83	7·71
1985	96,751	120,764	1,678	26,508	13·46	8·65
1986	115,644	140,603	2,058	35,885	12·07	7·75

Under the 1962 Act building societies could only hold land for the purposes of running their business. Section 17 of the 1986 Act gives building societies power to hold and develop land as a commercial asset. However, the land has to be primarily for residential purposes, or adjoining land, or for purposes incidental to the holding of residential land.

Detailed provisions are contained in the Act for an Investor Protection Scheme similar to those in the Banking Act of 1979. The level of protection given is 90 per cent of accounts up to £10,000.

Of particular interest are the services which societies are, again for the first time, empowered to provide. These are:—

(a) Money transmission services
(b) Foreign exchange services
(c) Making or receiving of payments as agents
(d) Management, as agents, of mortgage investments
(e) Management, as agents, of land (larger societies only)
(f) Arranging for the provision of services relating to the acquisition or disposal of investments for individuals.
(g) Establishment and management of personal equity plans.
(h) Arranging for the provision of credit to individuals.
(i) Establishment and management of unit trust schemes for the provision of pensions (through a subsidiary).
(j) Establishment and administration of pension schemes.
(k) Arranging for the provision of insurance of any description.
(l) Giving advice on insurance of any description.

(m) Estate agency service (through a subsidiary).
(n) Surveys and valuations of land.
(o) Conveyancing services.

Where a society provides a service of any of these descriptions it must not offer to make an advance subject to a condition that any services shall be provided by the society or its subsidiary.

Societies must belong to an "Ombudsman" scheme for the investigation of complaints. Matters to be covered by the scheme include operation of share and deposit accounts, loans (but not the making of new loans), money transmission services, foreign exchange services, agency payments and receipts, and the provision of credit. Grounds for complaint include breach of the Act or contract, unfair treatment or maladministration, and where the complainant has suffered pecuniary loss or expense or inconvenience. A society must agree to be bound by decisions of the adjudicator unless it agrees to give notice to its members and the public of its reasons for not doing so. For address of the Building Societies Ombudsman Scheme, *see* Index.

On mergers, the main difference is that borrowers will have a vote. For a merger to be approved at least 50 per cent of borrowers who exercise their right to vote must vote in favour, as well as 75 per cent of qualifying share investors who vote. Provision is also made for a society to convert to company status.

The 1986 Act replaced two important pieces of secondary legislation:

(a) the Designation Regulations made under The House Purchase and Housing Act 1959 (for trustee status). Under the Act all authorised societies will be able to accept investments from trustees.

(b) the Building Societies Authorization Regulations 1981, which set up a scheme for authorization of societies under European Community requirements. Existing societies authorized under the 1981 regulations were deemed to be authorized under the new legislation.

At the end of 1986 the six largest societies again accounted for about 62 per cent. of the assets of all building societies. The 16 largest societies accounted for about 82 per cent. Details of all societies with assets exceeding £1m. at the end of 1986 are given in the following list.

SOCIETIES WITH TOTAL ASSETS EXCEEDING £1 MILLION AT END OF FINANCIAL YEAR 1986

Year Estab-lished	* Name of Society (abbreviated) Head Office	Share Investors	Assets Total £'000
1849	Abbey National, Abbey House, 27 Baker St., London NW1 6XL	7,705,900	23,041,372
1885	Aid to Thrift, 38 Finsbury Sq., London EC2	937	3,175
1863	Alliance and Leicester, 49 Park Lane, London W1Y 4EQ	2,140,934	8,101,035
1848	Anglia, Moulton Park, Northampton	1,859,214	6,314,432
1853	Barnsley, Regent St., Barnsley, South Yorks	19,251	95,249
1953	Bath Investment and Bldg. Soc., 20 Charles St., Bath	10,555	22,883
1879	Bedford, 65 Midland Rd., Bedford	10,460	35,504
1881	Bedford Crown, 117 Midland Rd., Bedford	3,017	9,773
1866	Beverley, 57 Market Place, Beverley, Yorks	5,742	13,783
1914	Bexhill-on-Sea, 2 Devonshire Sq., Bexhill-on-Sea, Sussex	3,667	9,578
1889	Birmingham Midshires, 42/44 Waterloo Street, Birmingham	664,852	1,858,799
1864	Bolton, 235–237 Baker St., London NW1	6,504	84,162
1851	Bradford and Bingley, P.O. Box 2, Bingley, West Yorks.	1,684,713	4,416,531
1850	Bristol and West, Broad Quay, Bristol	689,347	2,539,583
1856	Britannia, P.O. Box 20, Newton House, Leek, Staffs.	1,052,666	4,211,945
1907	Buckinghamshire, High St., Chalfont St. Giles, Bucks.	5,318	21,971
1866	Bury St. Edmunds, 8 Guildhall St., Bury St. Edmunds	3,961	16,115
1850	Cambridge, 32 St. Andrew's St., Cambridge	32,992	139,161
1865	Cardiff, 92 St. Mary St., Cardiff	4,192	23,784
1960	Catholic, 7 Strutton Ground, London SW1	2,749	11,640
1899	Century, 21–23 Albany St., Edinburgh	1,291	6,249
1875	Chelsea, Chelsea House, 255 Kensington High St., London W8	145,896	764,668
1850	Cheltenham and Gloucester, 37–43 Clarence St., Cheltenham, Glos.	760,386	3,853,805
1845	Chesham, 12 Market Sq., Chesham, Bucks.	8,172	29,718
1870	Cheshire, Castle St., Macclesfield	174,738	476,906
1861	Cheshunt, 100 Crossbrook St., Waltham Cross, Herts.	46,155	188,305
1888	Chilterns, Norfolk House, Station Rd., Chesham, Bucks.	2,576	6,832
1859	Chorley and Dt., 51 St. Thomas's Rd., Chorley, Lancs.	6,294	24,604
1946	City and Metropolitan, 37 Ludgate Hill, London EC4	11,337	50,303
1862	City of London, 54/60 Gresham Street, London EC2V 7LL	27,251	163,475
1931	Civil Service, 5 Brighton Road, South Croydon, Surrey	6,388	44,415
1859	Clay Cross Benefit, 42 Thanet St., Clay Cross, Chesterfield	3,329	8,190
1869	Colchester, 42–48 North Station Road, Colchester	14,398	53,616
1884	Coventry, P.O. Box 9, High Street, Coventry	328,119	966,692
1850	Cumberland, 38 Fisher St., Carlisle	80,661	223,661
1946	Darlington, Tubwell Row, Market Pl., Darlington, Co. Durham	39,007	126,921
1859	Derbyshire, Duffield Hall, Duffield, Derby	256,539	704,555
1858	Dudley, Dudley Hse., Stone St., Dudley, Worcs.	14,215	39,503
1869	Dunfermline, 12 East Port, Dunfermline, Fife.	84,000	312,059
1857	Earl Shilton, 22 The Hollow, Earl Shilton, Leicester	8,922	27,234
1877	Eastbourne Mut., Eastbourne Hse., 22 Gildredge Rd., Eastbourne, Sussex .	53,821	208,691
1980	Ecology, 8A Main St., Cross Hills, Keighley, West Yorks BD20 8TT	897	1,702
1847	Essex Eq., 5 Brooke Road, Grays, Essex	5,021	25,003
1860	Frome Selwood P., 3 Market Pl., Frome, Som.	12,943	23,210
1865	Furness, 51–55 Duke Street, Barrow-in-Furness	52,114	146,646
1911	Gainsborough, 26 Lord St., Gainsborough, Lincs.	3,601	8,970
1924	Gateway, P.O. Box 18, Worthing, W. Sussex	447,510	1,756,926
1852	Greenwich, 279–283 Greenwich High Rd., London SE10	29,531	90,612
1871	Guardian, Guardian Hse., 120 High Holborn, London WC1	65,955	809,479
1853	Halifax, P.O. Box 60, Trinity Rd., Halifax, West Yorks.	7,980,380	28,693,638
1866	Hampshire, Anchor Hse., Kingston Crescent, Portsmouth	14,905	61,008
1854	Hanley Econ., 42 Cheapside, Hanley, Stoke-on-Trent, Staffs.	28,860	80,744
1953	Harpenden, 14 Station Rd., Harpenden, Herts.	6,500	21,931
1882	Harrow, Cunningham Hse., Bessborough Rd., Harrow, Middx.	8,213	47,079
1890	Haywards Heath and Dt., 33 The Broadway, Haywards Heath, West Sussex	19,171	74,792
1863	Heart of England, 22–26 Jury St., Warwick	133,756	370,146
1884	Hemel Hempstead, 43 Marlowes, Hemel Hempstead, Herts.	10,437	54,430

* P. = Permanent; B. = Benefit. The words "Building Society" are the last words in every society's name.

Year Established	Name of Society (abbreviated) Head Office	Share Investors	Assets Total £'000
1926	Hendon, 9 Central Circus, Hendon, London NW4	3,735	21,374
1888	Herts. and Essex, 4 Market Sq., Bishop's Stortford, Herts.	4,085	15,810
1865	Hinckley, and Rugby, Upper Bond St., Hinckley, Leics.	35,385	117,375
1855	Holmesdale B., 43 Church St., Reigate, Surrey	7,152	30,922
1853	Ilkeston P., 24–26 South Street, Ilkeston, Derby	3,959	9,725
1849	Ipswich, 44 Upper Brook St., Ipswich	29,567	83,480
	Kent Reliance, Reliance Hse, Manor Rd, Chatham, Kent	47,552	126,550
1961	Kidderminster Eq., 17 Church St., Kidderminster.....................	918	3,550
1852	Lambeth, 118–120 Westminster Bridge Rd., London SE1	56,675	348,881
	Lancastrian, Sadler St., Middleton, Manchester	49,057	145,839
1853	Leamington Spa, Leamington House, Milverton Hill, Leamington Spa, Warws.	131,000	723,119
1875	Leeds and Holbeck, 105 Albion St., Leeds..............................	212,445	763,331
1848	Leeds P., Permanent Hse., The Headrow, Leeds.........................	2,670,214	7,774,695
1863	Leek United and Midlands, 50 St. Edward St., Leek, Staffs.	45,012	146,645
1876	Londonderry Provident, 7 Castle Street, Londonderry BT48 6HQ	908	3,141
1848	London P., 12 Broadway, St James's Park, London SW1	2,050	9,509
1867	Loughborough P., 6 High St., Loughborough, Leics.	9,212	37,507
1877	Louth, Mablethorpe and Sutton P.B., 3 Eastgate, Louth, Lincs...........	1,352	4,397
1922	Manchester, 18–20 Bridge St., Manchester	5,864	35,207
1870	Mansfield, Regent Hse., Regent St., Mansfield, Notts.	14,802	53,050
1870	Market Harborough, Welland Hse., The Sq., Market Harborough, Leics. ..	28,044	85,696
1860	Marsden, 6–20 Russell St., Nelson, Lancs.	30,300	121,159
1874	Melton Mowbray, 39 Nottingham St., Melton Mowbray, Leics.	27,338	95,566
1966	Mercantile, 75 Howard St., North Shields, Tyne and Wear	16,628	61,115
1880	Mid-Sussex, Mid-Sussex Hse., 66 Church Rd., Burgess Hill, Sussex	5,964	15,204
1869	Monmouthshire, John Frost Sq., Newport, Gwent	12,700	58,609
1866	Mornington, 158 Kentish Town Rd., London NW5	18,929	117,004
1869	National and Provincial, Provincial Hse., Bradford	1,047,045	6,047,574
1896	National Counties, Waterloo Hse., 147–153 High St., Epsom, Surrey	27,254	205,338
1884	Nationwide, New Oxford Hse., High Holborn, London WC1	3,422,662	12,201,708
1856	Newbury, 17–20 Bartholomew St., Newbury, Berks......................	26,268	98,139
1863	Newcastle, Grainger Chambers, Hood Street, Newcastle upon Tyne	105,315	454,928
1877	North of England, 57 Fawcett St., Sunderland	200,071	472,127
1983	North Wilts Ridgeway, 18 and 19 Commercial Rd., Swindon, Wilts.	8,631	43,899
1850	Northern Rock, Northern Rock Hse., P.O. Box No. 2, Gosforth, Newcastle upon Tyne	578,441	1,811,035
1852	Norwich and Peterborough, St. Andrew's Hse., St. Andrew St., Norwich, Norfolk	154,230	474,303
1850	Nottingham, 5–13 Upper Parliament St., Nottingham	122,618	276,502
1935	Nottingham Imperial, Imperial Bldg., 29 Bridgeford Rd., West Bridgeford, Nottingham	4,414	13,580
1879	Paddington, 125 Westbourne Grove, London W2	10,497	38,901
1879	Peckham Graylaw Hse., 1 Copers Cope Rd, Beckenham, Kent BR3 1MB ...	9,995	42,246
1877	Penrith, 7 King St., Penrith, Cumb.	7,948	26,457
1881	Portman, 40 Portman Sq., London W1	138,367	522,142
1896	Portsmouth, Churchill Hse., Winston Churchill Ave., Portsmouth	71,229	404,793
1860	Principality, Principality Bldgs., Queen St., Cardiff	184,978	462,863
1914	Progressive, 33–37 Wellington Place, Belfast BT1 6HH	22,068	107,203
1872	Regency, 130 Western Road, Hove, East Sussex BN3 1DR	73,644	366,390
1888	Rowley Regis, 223 Halesowen Rd., Crawley Heath, Warley, Worcs	29,397	74,538
1849	Saffron Walden and Essex, Market Place, Saffron Walden, Essex	28,255	87,942
1937	St. Pancras, 200 Finchley Rd., London NW3	9,663	59,372
1955	St. Stephens, 70 Chepstow Road, London W2	394	1,599
1846	Scarborough, Prospect House, 442/444 Scalby Road, Scarborough, Yorks...	41,371	140,208
1848	Scottish, 2 York Place, Edinburgh...................................	13,106	44,680
1935	Sheffield, 66 Campo Lane, Sheffield, Yorks.	4,810	12,704
1879	Shepshed, Bull Ring, Shepshed, Loughborough, Leics.	5,931	15,982
1853	Skipton, 59 High St., Skipton, Yorks.	155,522	801,505
1877	Stafford Railway, 4 Market Sq., Stafford	7,574	23,402
1902	Staffordshire, Jubilee Hse., P.O. Box 66, 84 Salop St., Wolverhampton	141,496	404,382
1875	Standard, 64 Church Way, North Shields, Tyne and Wear	2,235	8,525
1850	Stroud and Swindon, 7 Russell St., Stroud, Glos.	51,575	145,075
1903	Surrey, 54 Station Rd., Redhill, Surrey RH1 1PH	9,726	54,756
1870	Sussex County, 40/42 Friars Walk, Lewes, East Sussex	83,069	322,171
1923	Swansea, 11 Cradock St., Swansea	3,249	13,281
1966	Teachers, Allenview Hse., Wimborne, Dorset..........................	9,266	64,333
1886	Thrift, 3/4 Turnpike Parade, Green Lanes, London N15	4,039	9,162
1901	Tipton and Coseley, 57–60 High St., Tipton, Staffs.	13,780	36,270
1853	Town and Country, 215 Strand, London WC2	197,693	1,234,420
1855	Tynemouth, 53–55 Howard St., North Shields, Tyne and Wear	5,867	23,478

Year Established	Name of Society (abbreviated) Head Office	Share Investors	Assets Total £'000
1863	Universal, 41 Pilgrim St., Newcastle upon Tyne	23,367	91,328
1924	Vernon, 26 St. Petersgate, Stockport, Chesh.	15,493	47,995
1877	Walthamstow, 869 Forest Rd., Walthamstow, London E17	36,289	161,945
1949	Wessex, 115 Old Christchurch Rd., Bournemouth, Hants.	32,564	152,580
1849	West Bromwich, 374 High St., West Bromwich, Staffs.	282,192	521,463
1882	West Cumbria, Cumbria Hse., Murray Rd., Workington	6,383	21,846
1846	West of England, 25 High Street, Marlborough, Wilts SN8 1NF	135,010	407,830
1847	Woolwich Eq., Equitable Hse., London SE18	2,101,230	7,827,107
1885	Yorkshire, Yorkshire House, Westgate, Bradford	578,778	2,075,575

INTEREST RATES – MORTGAGE AND SHARE

The interest rates prevailing on mortgage lending and share investment vary to a degree from society to society and in relation to the type or amount of loan or investment. The system whereby the Building Societies Association advised specific rates ceased in November 1984 and in April 1986 collective discussion, leading to a statement that a reduction or increase of a certain order was appropriate, was discontinued. General rate changes, however, continue in response to market conditions and the predominant rates in each of the last 3 years, with the dates of change, are given below.

	Jan. 1985	March 1985	Aug. 1985	March 1986	June 1986	Nov. 1986	May 1987
Mortgages Ordinary	12·75–13·00	13·75–14·00	12·75	12·00	11·00	12·25–12·375	11·25
Shares	7·50	8·25	7·00	6·00	5·25	6·00	5·00

BANKING IN BRITAIN

The main institutions within the British banking system are the Bank of England (the central bank, *see* p. 373), the clearing banks (the major retail banks), the merchant banks, the overseas banks and the discount houses.

The clearing banks are Bank of Scotland, Barclays, Clydesdale, Co-operative, Coutts, Girobank, Lloyds, Midland, National Westminster, Royal Bank of Scotland, the Trustee Savings Bank and the Yorkshire Bank.

Under the Banking Act 1979 deposit-taking businesses require authorization from the Bank of England unless they are specifically exempted from the authorization provisions of the Act. Institutions may be authorized either as recognized banks or as licensed deposit-takers and are subject to the Bank of England's supervision. There follows a list of these recognized banks and licensed deposit-taking institutions (as at August 27, 1987):—

Recognized Banks

ANZ Merchant Bank Ltd.
A P Bank Ltd.
Alexanders Discount P.L.C.
Algemene Bank Nederland N.V.
Allied Arab Bank Ltd.
Allied Bank of Pakistan Ltd.
Allied Irish Banks P.L.C.
Allied Irish Investment Bank P.L.C.
American Express Bank Ltd.
Amsterdam-Rotterdam Bank N.V.
Anglo-Romanian Bank Ltd.
Henry Ansbacher & Co. Ltd.
Arab Bank Ltd.
Arab Banking Corporation B.S.C.
Arbuthnot Latham Bank Ltd.
Associated Japanese Bank (International) Ltd.
Atlantic International Bank Ltd.
Australia & New Zealand Banking Group Ltd.

B.A.I.I. P.L.C.
Banca Commerciale Italiana
Banca Nazionale dell'Agricoltura S.p.A.
Banca Nazionale del Lavoro
Banco Central, S.A.
Banco de Bilbao, S.A.
Banco de la Nación Argentina
Banco de Santander, S.A.
Banco de Vizcaya, S.A.
Banco di Roma S.p.A.
Banco di Santo Spirito
Banco di Sicilia
Banco do Brasil S.A.
Banco do Estado de São Paulo S.A.
Banco Espirito Santo e Comercial de Lisboa
Banco Exterior-U.K. S.A.
Banco Hispano Americano Ltd.
Banco Mercantil de São Paulo S.A.
Banco Nacional de Mexico S.N.C.
Banco Português do Atlântico
Banco Real S.A.
Banco Totta & Açores E.P.
Bancomer, S.N.C.
Bangkok Bank Ltd.
Bank Julius Baer & Co. Ltd.
Bank Bumiputra Malaysia Berhad
Bank für Gemeinwirtschaft A.G.
Bank Hapoalim B.M.
Bank Leumi (U.K.) P.L.C.
Bank Mees & Hope N.V.
Bank Mellat
Bank Melli Iran
Bank of America International Ltd.
Bank of America N.T. & S.A.
Bank of Baroda
The Bank of California N.A.
Bank of Ceylon
Bank of China
Bank of Cyprus (London) Ltd.
Bank of India
The Bank of Ireland
Bank of London & South America Ltd.
Bank of Montreal

The Bank of New York
Bank of New Zealand
The Bank of Nova Scotia
Bank of Scotland
The Bank of Tokyo, Ltd.
Bank of Tokyo International Ltd.
Bank of Wales P.L.C.
The Bank of Yokohama Ltd.
Bank Saderat Iran
Bank Sepah
Bankers Trust Company
Banque Belge Ltd.
Banque Belgo-Zairoise S.A.
Banque Bruxelles Lambert S.A.
Banque Française du Commerce Extérieur
Banque Indosuez
Banque Internationale à Luxembourg S.A.
Banque Internationale pour L'Afrique
   Occidentale S.A.
Banque Nationale de Paris P.L.C.
Banque Nationale de Paris S.A.
Banque Paribas
Barclays Bank P.L.C.
Barclays de Zoete Wedd Ltd.
Baring Brothers & Co. Ltd.
Bayerische Hypotheken-und Wechsel-Bank A.G.
Bayerische Landesbank Girozentrale
Bayerische Vereinsbank
Berliner Bank A.G.
The British Bank of the Middle East
The British Linen Bank Ltd.
Brown, Shipley & Co. Ltd.

CIC—Union Européenne, International et Cie
Caisse Nationale de Crédit Agricole
Canadian Imperial Bank of Commerce
James Capel Bankers Ltd.
Carolina Bank Ltd.
Cassa di Risparmio delle Provincie Lombarde
Cater Allen Ltd.
Charterhouse Bank Ltd.
Chase Investment Bank Ltd.
The Chase Manhattan Bank, N.A.
Chemical Bank
Chemical Bank International Ltd.
The Cho Hung Bank
Christiania Bank og Kreditkasse.
The Chuo Trust & Banking Co. Ltd.
Citibank N.A.
Citicorp Investment Bank Ltd.
City Merchants Bank Ltd.
Clive Discount Company Ltd.
Clydesdale Bank P.L.C.
Commercial Bank of Korea Ltd.
The Commercial Bank of the Near East P.L.C.
Commerzbank A.G.
Commonwealth Bank of Australia
Continental Illinois National Bank and Trust Company of Chicago
Co-operative Bank P.L.C.
Copenhagen Handelsbank A/S
Coutts & Co.

Crédit Commercial de France
Crédit du Nord
Crédit Lyonnais
Credit Lyonnais Bank Nederland N.V.
Crédit Suisse
Credit Suisse First Boston Ltd.
Creditanstalt-Bankverein
Credito Italiano
The Cyprus Popular Bank

The Dai-Ichi Kangyo Bank, Ltd.
The Daiwa Bank, Ltd.
Den Danske Bank af 1871 Aktieselskab.
Den norske Creditbank P.L.C.
Deutsche Bank A.G.
Deutsche Genossenschaftsbank
Discount Bank and Trust Company
Dresdner Bank A.G.

EBC Amro Bank Ltd.
Enskilda Securities—Skandinaviska Enskilda Ltd.
Euro-Latinamerican Bank P.L.C.
European Brazilian Bank P.L.C.

Fidelity Bank N.A.
First City National Bank of Houston
First Interstate Bank of California
First Interstate Capital Markets Ltd.
The First National Bank of Boston
The First National Bank of Chicago
First National Bank of Maryland
First National Bank of Minneapolis
First RepublicBank Dallas, N.A.
First Wisconsin National Bank of Milwaukee
Robert Fleming & Co. Ltd.
French Bank of Southern Africa Ltd.
The Fuji Bank, Ltd.

Gerrard & National Ltd.
Ghana Commercial Bank
Girobank P.L.C.
Girozentrale und Bank der österreichischen Sparkassen A.G.
Grindlays Bank P.L.C.
Guinness Mahon & Co. Ltd.
Gulf International Bank B.S.C.

Habib Bank A.G. Zurich
Habib Bank Ltd.
Hambros Bank Ltd.
Hanil Bank
Havana International Bank Ltd.
Hessische Landesbank-Girozentrale
Hill Samuel & Co. Ltd.
C. Hoare & Co.
The Hokkaido Takushoku Bank, Ltd.
The Hongkong and Shanghai Banking Corporation
Hungarian International Bank Ltd.

The Industrial Bank of Japan, Ltd.
International Commercial Bank P.L.C.
International Mexican Bank Ltd.
International Westminster Bank P.L.C.
Irving Trust Company
Istituto Bancario San Paolo di Torino
ItaB Group Ltd.
Italian International Bank P.L.C.

Japan International Bank Ltd.
Leopold Joseph & Sons Ltd.

Kansallis-Osake-Pankki
King & Shaxson P.L.C.
Kleinwort Benson Ltd.
Korea Exchange Bank
Korea First Bank
The Kyowa Bank, Ltd.

Lazard Brothers & Co., Ltd.
Libra Bank P.L.C.
Lloyds Bank P.L.C.

Lloyds Bank (France) Ltd.
Lloyds Merchant Bank Ltd.
London & Continental Bankers Ltd.
London Interstate Bank Ltd.
The Long-Term Credit Bank of Japan, Ltd.

Malayan Banking Berhad
Manufacturers Hanover Ltd.
Manufacturers Hanover Trust Company
Marine Midland Bank N.A.
Mase Westpac Ltd.
Mellon Bank, N.A.
Merrill Lynch International Bank Ltd.
Midland Bank P.L.C.
The Mitsubishi Bank, Ltd.
The Mitsubishi Trust and Banking Corporation
The Mitsui Bank, Ltd.
The Mitsui Trust & Banking Co. Ltd.
Samuel Montagu & Co. Ltd.
Morgan Grenfell & Co. Ltd.
Morgan Guaranty Trust Company of New York
Moscow Narodny Bank Ltd.

NCNB National Bank of North Carolina
National Australia Bank Ltd.
National Bank of Abu Dhabi
National Bank of Canada
National Bank of Detroit
National Bank of Greece S.A.
The National Bank of Kuwait S.A.K.
The National Bank of New Zealand Ltd.
National Bank of Pakistan
National Westminster Bank P.L.C.
NatWest Investment Bank Ltd.
Nedbank Ltd.
Nederlandsche Middenstandsbank N.V.
The Nippon Credit Bank, Ltd.
Noble Grossart Ltd.
Northern Bank Ltd.
The Northern Trust Company

Orion Royal Bank Ltd.
Oversea-Chinese Banking Corporation Ltd.
Overseas Union Bank Ltd.

P.K. English Trust Company Ltd.
Philadelphia National Bank
Philippine National Bank
Postipankki (UK) Ltd.
Privatbanken Ltd.
Punjab National Bank

Qatar National Bank S.A.Q.
Quin Cope Ltd.

Rafidain Bank
Rea Brothers Ltd.
Republic National Bank of New York
Reserve Bank of Australia
The Riggs National Bank of Washington D.C.
N. M. Rothschild & Sons Ltd.
The Royal Bank of Canada
The Royal Bank of Scotland P.L.C.
Royal Trust Bank

S.F.E. Bank Ltd.
The Saitama Bank, Ltd.
The Sanwa Bank, Ltd.
Saudi International Bank (Al-Bank Al-Saudi Al-Alami Ltd.)
Scandinavian Bank Group P.L.C.
J. Henry Schroder Wagg & Co. Ltd.
Seccombe Marshall & Campion P.L.C.
Security Pacific National Bank
Shanghai Commercial Bank Ltd.
Singer & Friedlander Ltd.
Société Générale
Société Générale Merchant Bank P.L.C.
Sonali Bank
Standard Chartered Bank

Standard Chartered Bank Africa P.L.C.
Standard Chartered Merchant Bank Ltd.
State Bank of India
The Sumitomo Bank, Ltd.
The Sumitomo Trust and Banking Co. Ltd.
Svenska Handelsbanken P.L.C.
Swiss Bank Corporation
Swiss Bank Corporation International Ltd.
Swiss Volksbank
Syndicate Bank

TSB England & Wales P.L.C.
TSB Northern Ireland P.L.C.
TSB Scotland P.L.C.
The Taiyo Kobe Bank, Ltd.
Texas Commerce Bank N.A.
The Thai Farmers Bank Ltd.
The Tokai Bank, Ltd.
The Toronto-Dominion Bank
The Toyo Trust & Banking Company Ltd.

UBAF Bank Ltd.
Uco Bank
Ulster Bank Ltd.
Ulster Investment Bank Ltd.
Union Bank of Finland Ltd.
Union Bank of Switzerland
Union Discount Company Ltd.
United Bank Ltd.
The United Bank of Kuwait P.L.C.
United Overseas Bank Ltd.

S. G. Warburg & Co. Ltd.
Westdeutsche Landesbank Girozentrale
Westpac Banking Corporation
Wintrust Securities Ltd.

The Yasuda Trust and Banking Co. Ltd.
Yorkshire Bank P.L.C.

Zambia National Commercial Bank Ltd.
Zivnostenská Banka National Corporation

Licensed Deposit-taking Institutions

A1 Credit P.L.C.
ANZ Finance Ltd.
Adam & Company P.L.C.
Afghan National Credit & Finance Ltd.
African Continental Bank Ltd.
Airdrie Savings Bank
Aitken Hume Ltd.
Ak International Ltd.
Al Baraka International Ltd.
Al Saudi Banque S.A.
Alliance Trust (Finance) Ltd.
Allied Banking Corporation
Allied Dunbar & Co. P.L.C.
Allied Irish Finance Co. Ltd.
Anglo-Yugoslav (LDT) Ltd.
Arab African International Bank
Arab Bank Investment Co. Ltd.
Argonaut Securities Ltd.
Assemblies of God Property Trust
Associated Credits Ltd.
Associates Capital Corporation Ltd.
Auban Finance Ltd.
Authority & Co. Ltd.
Avco Trust Ltd.

B.C. Finance Ltd.
BMI (Hampshire) Ltd.
BNL (U.K.) P.L.C.
Badische Kommunale Landesbank Girozentrale
Banca Serfin S.N.C.
Banco de Sabadell
Banco di Napoli
Bank Handlowy w Warszawie S.A.
Bank of Credit and Commerce International S.A.
Bank of New England N.A.
The Bank of Nova Scotia Trust Company (United
  Kingdom) Ltd.
Bank of Oman Ltd.
Bank of Seoul
Bank Tejarat
Bankers Trust International Ltd.
Banque du Liban et d'Outre-Mer
Banque Worms
The Baptist Union Corporation Ltd.
Barbados National Bank
Barclays Bank Trust Company Ltd.
Barclays Bank UK Ltd.
Thomas Barlow & Bro. Ltd.
Barrie Vanger & Co. Ltd.
Beirut Riyad Bank S.A.L.
Benchmark Trust Ltd.
Beneficial Trust Ltd.
Berliner Handels-und-Frankfurter Bank
Bradford Investments P.L.C.

British Credit Trust Ltd.
British Railways Savings Company Ltd.
Bunge Finance Ltd.
Burns-Anderson Trust Company Ltd.
Business Mortgages Trust P.L.C.
Byblos Bank S.A.L.

Canada Permanent Mortgage Corporation (U.K.)
  Ltd.
Canara Bank
Carlyle Finance Ltd.
Castle Phillips Finance Co. Ltd.
Cayzer Ltd.
Central Bank of India.
Chancery Securities P.L.C.
The Charities Aid Foundation Money Management
  Company Ltd.
Charter Consolidated Financial Services Ltd.
Chartered Trust P.L.C.
Charterhouse Japhet Credit Ltd.
Chesterfield Street Trust Ltd.
Citibank Trust Ltd.
City Trust Ltd.
Close Brothers Ltd.
Clydesdale Bank Finance Corporation Ltd.
Combined Capital Ltd.
Commercial Financial Services Ltd.
Consolidated Credits & Discounts Ltd.
Coutts Finance Co.
Craneheath Securities Ltd.
Credito Italiano International Ltd.
Cue & Co.
Cyprus Credit Bank Ltd.
Cyprus Finance Corporation (London) Ltd.

Daiwa Europe Finance P.L.C.
Dalbeattie Finance Co. Ltd.
Darlington Merchant Credits Ltd.
Dartington & Co. Ltd.
The Development Bank of Singapore Ltd.
The Dorset, Somerset & Wilts. Investment Society
  Ltd.
Dryfield Finance Ltd.
Duncan Lawrie Ltd.
Dunsterville Allen P.L.C.

E. T. Trust Ltd.
Eagil Trust Co. Ltd.
East Anglian Securities Trust Ltd.
East Midlands Finance Co. Ltd.
Eccles Savings and Loans Ltd.
Edington P.L.C.
Ensign Finance Ltd.
Equatorial Trust Corporation P.L.C.
Euromed Fundings Ltd.

Everett Chettle Associates
Exeter Trust Ltd.

FIBI Financial Trust Ltd.
Fairmount Trust Ltd.
Family Finance Ltd.
Federated Trust Corporation Ltd.
FennoScandia Ltd.
Financial and General Securities Ltd.
James Finlay Corporation Ltd.
Finova Finance Ltd.
First Bank of Nigeria Ltd.
First Commercial Bank
First Indemnity Credit Ltd.
First National Boston Ltd.
First National Securities Ltd.
Fleet National Bank
Ford Financial Trust Ltd.
Ford Motor Credit Co. Ltd.
Foreign & Colonial Management Ltd.
Forward Trust Ltd.
Robert Fraser & Partners Ltd.

Goldman Sachs Ltd.
Goode Durrant Trust P.L.C.
Gota (U.K.) Ltd.
Granville Trust Ltd.
H. T. Greenwood Ltd.
Gresham Trust P.L.C.
Greyhound Guaranty Ltd.
Grosvenor Acceptances Ltd.
Gulf Guarantee Trust Ltd.

HFC Trust & Savings Ltd.
Habibsons Trust and Finance Ltd.
The Hardware Federation Finance Co. Ltd.
Harris Trust and Savings Bank
Harrods Trust Ltd.
Harton Securities Ltd.
The Heritable & General Trust Ltd.
Hill Samuel Personal Finance Ltd.
Holdenhurst Securities P.L.C.

IBJ International Ltd.
Industrial Funding Trust Ltd.
The Investment Bank of Ireland Ltd.
Investors in Industry P.L.C.
Investors in Industry Group P.L.C.
Iran Overseas Investment Corporation Ltd.

Jabac Finances Ltd.
Jordan Finance Consortium P.L.C.
Jyske Bank

Keesler Federal Credit Union
Kredietbank N.V.

Laurentian Financial Services Ltd.
Legal & General (Money Managers) Ltd.
Liechtenstein (U.K.) Ltd.
Little Lakes Finance Ltd.
Lloyds Bowmaker Ltd.
Lloyds Bowmaker Finance Ltd.
Lombard Acceptances Ltd.
Lombard & Ulster Ltd.
Lombard North Central P.L.C.
Lombard Street Investment Trust Co. Ltd.
London and Arab Investments Ltd.
London Law Securities Ltd.
London Scottish Finance Corporation P.L.C.
Lordsvale Finance Ltd.

MLA Finance Ltd.
McNeill Pearson Ltd.
Manchester Exchange Trust Ltd.
W. M. Mann & Co. (Investments) Ltd.
Manufacturers Hanover Finance Ltd.
The Mardun Investment Co. Ltd.
Matheson Trust Co. Ltd.
Medens Trust Ltd.
Meghraj & Sons Ltd.

Mercantile Credit Company Ltd.
Mercury Provident P.L.C.
The Methodist Chapel Aid Association Ltd.
Middle East Bank Ltd.
Midland Bank Finance Corporation Ltd.
Midland Bank Trust Company Ltd.
Milford Mutual Facilities Ltd.
Minories Finance Ltd.
Minster Trust Ltd.
Moneycare Ltd.
Moorgate Mercantile Holdings P.L.C.
Mount Credit Corporation Ltd.
Multibanco Comermex S.N.C.
Muslim Commercial Bank Ltd.
Mutual Trust and Savings Ltd.
Mynshul Trust Ltd.

N.I.I.B. Group Ltd.
National Bank of Dubai
National Bank of Egypt
National Bank of Fort Sam Houston
National Bank of Nigeria Ltd.
The National Commercial Bank
National Guardian Finance Corporation Ltd.
New Nigeria Bank Ltd.
Nomura International Finance P.L.C.
Norddeutsche Landesbank Girozentrale
North West Securities Ltd.
Northern Bank Development Corporation Ltd.
Northern Bank Executor & Trustee Company Ltd.
Norwich General Trust Ltd.

Omega Trust Co. Ltd.
Oppenheimer Money Management Ltd.
Osterreichische Länderbank A.G.
Overseas Trust Bank Ltd.

PKFinans International (U.K.) Ltd.
Paine Webber International Trust Ltd.
The People's Trust & Savings Ltd.
Philadelphia National Ltd.
Phillips & Drew Trust Ltd.
Pointon York Ltd.
Prestwick Investment Trust P.L.C.
Provincial Trust Ltd.
Punjab National Bank

Rabobank Nederland (Coöperatieve Centrale Raiffei-
　　sen-Boerenleenbank B.A.)
Ralli Investment Company Ltd.
R. Raphael & Sons P.L.C.
Rathbone Bros. & Co.
Reliance Trust Ltd.
Riyad Bank
Roxburghe Guarantee Corporation Ltd.
RoyScot Trust Ltd.
The Rural and Industries Bank of Western Australia

S.P. Finance Ltd.
St. Michael's Financial Services Ltd.
Saudi American Bank
Schroder Leasing Ltd.
Scottish Amicable Money Managers Ltd.
Seattle-First National Bank
Secure Homes Ltd.
Security Pacific Trust Ltd.
Shawlands Securities Ltd.
Shire Trust Ltd.
The Siam Commercial Bank, Ltd.
Smith & Williamson Securities
Southsea Mortgage & Investment Co. Ltd.
Spry Finance Ltd.
Standard Property Investment P.L.C.
State Bank of New South Wales
State Bank of South Australia
State Bank of Victoria
State Street Bank and Trust Company
Sterling Trust Ltd.
Swiss Cantobank (International)

TCB Ltd.
TC Ziraat Bankasi
The Teachers & General Investment Co. Ltd.
Thames Trust Ltd.
Thorncliffe Finance Ltd.
Trade Development Bank
Treloan Ltd.
Trucanda Trusts Ltd.
The Trust Bank of Africa Ltd.
Tullett and Riley Money Management Ltd.
Turkish Bank Ltd.
Türkiye İş Bankasi A.Ş.
Tyndall & Co.

Ulster Bank Trust Company
Union Bank of India
Union Bank of Nigeria Ltd.

United Dominions Trust Ltd.
United Mizrahi Bank Ltd.
United Overseas Bank (Banque Unie pour les Pays d'Outre Mer)
Unity Trust P.L.C.

Venture Finance Ltd.
Vernons Trust Corporation
Volkskas Ltd.

Wagon Finance Ltd.
Wallace, Smith Trust Co. Ltd.
Welbeck Finance P.L.C.
Western Trust & Savings Ltd.
Whiteaway Laidlaw & Co. Ltd.
Wimbledon & South West Finance Co. Ltd.

H. F. Young & Co. Ltd.

Banking Hours: England and Wales, Mon.–Fri. 9.30–3.30*; *City of London town clearers,* 9.30–3.00; Saturdays (selected branches open); Barclays, 9.30–12.00; Lloyds, 9.30–12.30 or 10.00–3.00; Midland and National Westminster, 9.30–12.30; Trustee Savings Bank, 9.30–4.00.

Scotland.—Banking hours in Scotland are: Mon.–Wed., 9.30–12.30; 1.30–3.30; Thursday, 9.30–12.30; 1.30–3.30; 4.30–6 p.m.; Fri. 9.30–3.30; Saturday, *closed. Northern Ireland;* Mon.–Fri. 10.00–3.30; 9.30 opening two mornings per week. Open until 5.00 one summer evening per week.

* Still the minimum banking hours but many banks are experimenting with longer hours (usually 9.15–4.30). The Co-operative Bank remains open until 5.00.

FINANCIAL FIGURES, ETC. FOR THE "BIG FOUR" BANKS, 1986

Bank Group	Profit before taxation £m	Profit after taxation £m	Total Asssets £m	Number of U.K. branches
Barclays	895 (855)	618 (449)	78,952 (65,193)	3,000
Lloyds	700 (561)	470 (331)	47,829 (43,808)	2,600
Midland	434 (351)	262 (144)	53,169 (58,074)	2,149
National Westminster	1,011 (804)	614 (442)	83,325 (72,607)	3,200

1985 figures in parentheses.

GIROBANK

Girobank provides a broad range of corporate and personal banking facilities. It operates through 20,0000 U.K. post offices.

OPERATING STATISTICS	1985–86	1986–87
Number of accounts at year end, thousands	1,946	2,005
Average customer balances for year, £m	1,019	1,080
Number of transactions (including social security payments), millions	420	442

BANKING SERVICES

Association for Payment Clearing Services (APACS)
Mercury House, Triton Court, 14 Finsbury Square, EC2A 1BR.

APACS was set up by the banks in 1985 to manage the payment clearing systems and oversee money transmission in the U.K.

Three operational clearing companies operate under the aegis of APACS. They are:

BANKERS' AUTOMATED CLEARING SERVICES LTD. (BACS), De Havilland Road, Edgware, Middx. HA8 5QA.—Provides an automated service for interbank clearing of payment and collection transactions in the U.K. (e.g. standing orders, direct debits). *Chief Exec.,* G. R. Simpson.

CHEQUE AND CREDIT CLEARING CO. LTD., Mercury House, Triton Court, 14 Finsbury Square, EC2A 1BR.—Operates bulk clearing systems for interbank cheques and paper credit items. *Chief Inspector,* E. W. Stubbs.

CLEARING HOUSE AUTOMATED PAYMENT SYSTEM (CHAPS) AND TOWN CLEARING CO. LTD., Mercury House, Triton Court, 14 Finsbury Square, EC2A 1BR.—Provides same-day clearing for high value cheques and electronic funds transfer. *Chief Inspector,* E. W. Stubbs.

In addition, EftPos U.K. Ltd. is a company within the APACS structure set up to develop a national scheme for electronic funds transfer at the point of sale. APACS also oversees the London Dollar Clearing, the London Currency Settlement Scheme and the Cheque Card and eurocheque schemes.

Membership of APACS and the operational clearing companies is open to any appropriately regulated institution providing payment services and meeting the relevant membership criteria.

Committee of London and Scottish Bankers
10 Lombard Street, EC3V 9AP

The Committee is the successor to the Committee of London Clearing Bankers. It consists of the Chairmen of Barclays, Lloyds, Midland, National Westminster, Standard Chartered, Bank of Scotland, Royal Bank of Scotland and the Trustee Savings Bank Group, and meets regularly to discuss matters of common interest. It is the body through which the Bank of England communicates official policy to the banks and through which the banks may present their views to the Bank of England and the Treasury. *Secretary-General,* K. S. Lucas.

British Bankers' Association
10 Lombard Street, EC3V 9EL

The Association provides a means of communication and consultation for the banking industry in this country. Membership is open to institutions accepted as recognized banks by the Bank of England—nearly 300. The Association is a member of the E.C. Banking Federation. *Secretary-General,* K. S. Lucas.

Finance Houses Association
18 Upper Grosvenor Street, W1X 9PB

Director-Secretary, J. B. Damer, O.B.E.

FINANCIAL OMBUDSMEN

The following Ombudsmen schemes are non-statutory.

The Office of the Banking Ombudsman
Citadel House, 5–11 Fetter Lane, EC4A 1BR
[01-583 1395]

The purpose of the Banking Ombudsman Scheme is to investigate complaints from bank customers dissatisfied with the banking services of member banks. The Scheme was set up in 1985, becoming operational on Jan. 1, 1986, by 19 banks and it is funded by contributions from the member banks (19 banks and 17 designated associates). There is a seven-member Council who appoint the Ombudsman, give guidance in the performance of his duties, monitor his terms of reference, prepare the budget and approve the annual report. The Ombudsman and his staff are responsible to the Council.
The Banking Ombudsman, I. Edwards-Jones, Q.C.

The Office of the Building Societies Ombudsman
Grosvenor Gardens House, 35–37 Grosvenor Gardens, SW1X 7AW
[01-931 0044]

The purpose of the Building Societies Ombudsman Scheme, which came into operation on July 1, 1987, it to investigate complaints from building society customers about the services of building societies belonging to the Scheme. About 130 authorised building societies are required to belong to the Scheme and it is funded by contributions from the members. The Ombudsman is appointed by and responsible to an independent Ombudsman Council. *The Building Society Ombudsman,* S. Edell.

The Insurance Ombudsman Bureau
31 Southampton Row, WC1B 5HJ
[01-242 8613]

The purpose of the Insurance Ombudsman Scheme is to settle disputes between insurance policyholders and member insurance companies. The Scheme came into operation in March 1981 and is funded by contributions from the member companies. About 190 companies are members of the Scheme. An independent Council appoints and supervises the work of the Ombudsman.
The Insurance Ombudsman, J. Haswell, O.B.E.

THE NATIONAL DEBT

Net central government borrowing each year represents an addition to the National Debt. At the end of March 1986 the National Debt amounted to some £172,000 million of which £4,000 million was in currencies other than sterling. Of the £168,000 million sterling debt, £130,000 million consisted of gilt-edged stock; of this, 34 per cent had a maturity of up to five years, 39 per cent a maturity of over five years and up to 15 years and 27 per cent a maturity of over 15 years or undated. The remaining sterling debt was made up mainly of national savings (£24,000 million), certificates of tax deposits, Treasury bills, and Ways and Means advances (very short-term internal government borrowing).

SAVINGS

PREMIUM BONDS

These bonds are a United Kingdom Government security and were first introduced on November 1, 1956. Instead of earning interest, however, each bond offers to its holder the chance of winning a money prize in a prize draw. Bonds are issued in values ranging from £10 (the minimum purchase) to £10,000, and may be purchased in multiples of £5; each £1 buys one bond unit, which has one chance in each prize draw. Individual holdings are limited to £10,000.

Prizes are paid from a fund formed by the interest, at present 7 per cent *per annum*, on each bond eligible for the draw. A bond becomes eligible for the draw three clear calendar months following the month of purchase and goes into every subsequent draw whether or not it has won a prize until the end of the month in which it is repaid.

Bonds belonging to a deceased bondholder will remain eligible for all Prize Draws held in the month of death and in the following 12 calendar months, provided they have not been repaid earlier. They will then become ineligible for all further draws. These terms also apply to bonds purchased before August 1, 1960 (Series "A").

The winning numbers are selected by the electronic random number indicator equipment—usually called "ERNIE". Winning numbers are printed monthly in the *London Gazette*.

It is estimated that by the end of April 1987, bonds to the value of £3,904,403,542 had been sold. Of these £1,969,049,113 had been cashed, leaving £1,935,354,429 still invested. After the draws in April 1987, 27,958,827 prizes, totalling £1,610,632,700 had been distributed since the inception of the Premium Savings Bond Scheme.

INCOME BONDS

National Savings Income Bonds were introduced in 1982. They are particularly suitable for those who want to receive regular monthly payments of interest while preserving the full cash value of their capital. The Bonds are sold in multiples of £1,000. The minimum holding is £2,000 and the maximum £100,000.

Interest is calculated on a day-to-day basis and paid monthly. Interest is taxable, but is paid without deduction of tax at source. The Bonds have a guaranteed life of ten years, but may be repaid at par before maturity on giving three months' notice. No formal period of notice for repayment is required if the holder dies.

Net investment in National Savings Income Bonds was £5,684,100,000 at the end of April 1987.

INDEXED INCOME BONDS

Indexed Income Bonds were introduced in 1985 and provide an inflation-proof income. The minimum investment of £5,000 can be increased, in multiples of £1,000, to a £100,000 maximum.

The interest rate is 8% in the first year and this remains the guaranteed minimum. In the second and subsequent years the interest rate increases to reflect the movement in the Retail Price Index. The Bonds have a guaranteed life of ten years but can be repaid at par before maturity on giving three months notice. No formal period of notice is required if the holder dies. Issues of Indexed Income Bonds can be withdrawn from sale without notice and new issues introduced.

Net investment in Indexed Income Bonds was £23,700,000 at the end of April 1987.

ORDINARY AND INVESTMENT ACCOUNTS

National Savings Bank.—On May 31, 1987, there were 15,427,292 active accounts with the sum of approximately £1,685,059,000 due to depositors in Ordinary accounts and 3,699,331 active accounts with the sum of approximately £6,460,639,000 due to depositors in Investment accounts.

Interest is earned at 6 per cent per year on each Ordinary account for every complete calendar month in which the balance is £500 or more provided the account is kept open for the whole of 1987 (December 31, 1986—January 1, 1988); and at 3 per cent per year for all other Ordinary accounts. The minimum deposit is £1; maximum balance £10,000 plus interest credited. On May 31, 1987 the average amount held in Ordinary accounts was approximately £109.

The Investment account pays a higher rate of interest (the current rate can be ascertained at any Savings Bank Post Office). The minimum deposit is £5; maximum balance £100,000 plus interest credited. On May 31, 1987 the average amount held in Investment accounts was approximately £1,746.

Trustee Savings Banks.—There are 4 Trustee Savings Banks with more than 1,620 branches in the United Kingdom. On November 20, 1984, the Banks operated nearly 13,000,000 active accounts and total customer balances exceeded £9,000,600,000. *T.S.B. Group Central Executive*, P.O. Box 33, 25 Milk Street, EC2V 8LU.

DEPOSIT BONDS

National Savings Deposit Bonds were introduced on October 17, 1983. They offer a premium rate of interest on lump sum savings and are best suited for money not needed in less than a year. The minimum purchase is £100, larger purchases can be made in multiples of £50 and the maximum holding is £100,000 plus interest credited.

Interest is taxable, but tax is not deducted at source. The interest rate is variable but is kept competitive. Interest is calculated on a daily basis and credited on the anniversary of purchase. Minimum amount of repayment is £50 and three months notice is required. Any amount repaid within a year of purchase earns interest at half the published rate. No interest is lost once a Bond has been held for a full year. Net investment in National Savings Deposit Bonds was £646,500,000 at May 31, 1987.

YEARLY PLAN

The National Savings "Yearly Plan" was introduced on July 2, 1984, following the withdrawal of Third Issue Save As You Earn. It offers a guaranteed tax-free return. Applicants agree to make 12 monthly payments, leading to the issue of a Yearly Plan Certificate. The maximum guaranteed rate of interest is earned if the Certificate is held for a full four years. Applications may be made by any individuals aged 7 or over; in the name of children under 7; and by not more than two trustees for a sole beneficiary.

Payments must be made on the same date every month by standing order from a bank or other acceptable account. Only one payment may be made in any one month and must be in multiples of £5. Minimum monthly contribution is £20, maximum £200. Net investment in National Savings Yearly Plan was £289,130,993 at May 31, 1987.

On receipt of an application the applicant is sent an Offer Letter telling him the interest rates he will receive on his agreement if he accepts. The Certificate is sent at the end of the first year. It shows the total value of the payments made and the value of the Certificate if held for four years. The Certificate earns interest compounded annually on the anniversaries of the Certificate Date. Maximum interest is earned if the Certificate is held for the full four years. At the end of each year, providing at least seven payments have been made during that year, the applicant is given the option to take up a subsequent agreement, leading to the issue of a further Certificate.

NATIONAL SAVINGS CERTIFICATES

The amount, including accrued interest, index-linked increase or bonus remaining to the credit of investors in National Savings Certificates on March 31, 1987 was approximately £17,481·4m. In 1986–87, approx. £11,731·1m was subscribed and £1,571·1m (excluding interest, index-linked increase or bonus) was repaid. Interest, index-linked increase, bonus or other sum payable is free of United Kingdom income tax (including investment income surcharge) and capital gains tax. The 1st–14th issues continue to attract interest.

Issue and Maximum Holding (in units)	Unit Cost £	Value after		Interest Per Unit
		Years	£ p	
Index-Linked Retirement Issue (June 2, 1975–Nov. 15, 1980) (120)	10			Unlike conventional issues where interest is accrued periodically the repayment value of Index-Linked Certificates, subject to their being held a year, is related to the movement of the U.K. General Index of Retail Prices.** N.B. Certificates of the Retirement Issue were on sale only to men aged 65 years and over and women aged 60 years and over, but may now be transferred to anyone.
Sixteenth .... (Dec. 13, 1976 to Mar. 31, 1977) (300)	5	6	8·51½	After 1st year, 20p is added, during 2nd year, 10p per completed 4 months, during 3rd year, 20p per completed 4 months, during 4th year, 20p per completed 4 months plus 30p bonus at year end, during 5th year, 24p per completed 4 months, during 6th year, 26½p per completed 4 months.†
Eighteenth .... (Jan. 29, 1979–Feb. 2, 1980) (150)	10	5	15·00	After 1 year, 50p is added, during 2nd year, 25p per completed 4 months, during 3rd year, 33p per completed 4 months, during 4th year, 42p per completed 4 months, during 5th year, 50p per completed 4 months.†
Nineteenth .... (Feb. 4, 1980–May 9, 1981) (500)	10	5	16·35	After 1 year 50p is added, during 2nd year 30p per completed 4 months, during 3rd year 35p per completed 4 months, during 4th year 55p per completed 4 months and during 5th year 75p per completed 4 months.†
2nd Index-Linked Issue (Nov. 17, 1980–June 26, 1985) (1,000)	10			Like Retirement Issue, the repayment value of 2nd Index-Linked Issue Certificates, subject to their being held a year, is related to the movement of the U.K. General Index of Retail Prices.** N.B. Certificates of the 2nd Index-Linked Issue were made available to anyone, regardless of age, from September 7, 1981.
Twenty-First .... Issue (May 11, 1981–Nov. 7, 1981) (500)	10	5	15·40	After 1 year, 75p is added, during 2nd year, 28p per completed 4 months, during 3rd year, 33p per completed 4 months, during 4th year, 40p per completed 4 months and during 5th year 54p per completed 4 months.†
Twenty-Third ...... (Nov. 9, 1981–March 10, 1982) (200)	25	5	41·20	After 1 year, £2·25 is added, during 2nd year, 87p per completed 4 months, during 3rd year, £1·02 per completed 4 months, during 4th year, £1·23 per completed 4 months and during 5th year £1·53 per completed 4 months.†
Twenty-Fourth ..... (April 19, 1982–Nov. 4, 1982) (200)	25	5	38·32	After 1 year, £1·80 is added, during 2nd year, 53p per completed 3 months, during 3rd year, 63p per completed 3 months, during 4th year, 77p per completed 3 months and during 5th year 95p per completed 3 months.†*
Twenty-Fifth .... (Nov. 17, 1982–Aug. 13, 1983) (200)	25	5	35·90	After 1 year, £1·50 is added, during 2nd year, 43p per completed 3 months, during 3rd year, 51p per completed 3 months, during 4th year, 62p per completed 3 months and during 5th year 79p per completed 3 months.*
Twenty-Sixth .... (Aug. 15, 1983–Mar. 19, 1984) (200)	25	5	37·17	After 1 year, £1·53 is added, during 2nd year, 47p per completed 3 months, during 3rd year, 58p per completed 3 months, during 4th year, 72p per completed 3 months and during 5th year 89p per completed 3 months.*
Twenty-Seventh .... (April 5, 1984–Aug. 7, 1984) (200)	25	5	35·48	After 1 year, £1·32 is added, during 2nd year, 41p per completed 3 months, during 3rd year, 50p per completed 3 months, during 4th year, 62p per completed 3 months and during 5th year 76p per completed 3 months.*

Issue and Maximum Holding (in units)	Unit Cost £	Value after		Interest Per Unit
		Years	£ p	
Twenty-Eighth ..... (Aug. 8, 1984–Sept. 11, 1984) (200)	25	5	38·47	After 1 year, £1·63 is added, during 2nd year, 51p per completed 3 months, during 3rd year, 64p per completed 3 months, during 4th year, 80p per completed 3 months and during 5th year £1·01 per completed 3 months.*
Twenty-Ninth ...... (Oct. 15, 1984–Feb. 12, 1985) (200)	25	5	36·74	After 1 year, £1·50 is added, during 2nd year, 46p per completed 3 months, during 3rd year, 56p per completed 3 months, during 4th year, 69p per completed 3 months and during 5th year 85p per completed 3 months.*
Thirtieth .... (Feb. 13, 1985–Sept. 9, 1985) (200)	25	5	38·21	After 1 year, £1·69 is added, during 2nd year, 50p per completed 3 months, during 3rd year, 62p per completed 3 months, during 4th year, 78p per completed 3 months and during 5th year 98p per completed 3 months.*
3rd Index-Linked Issue (July 1, 1985–July 31, 1986) (200)	25			Like 2nd Issue Index-Linked Certificates, the repayment value of 3rd Issue Index-Linked Certificates, subject to their being held for one year, is related to the movement of the U.K. General Index of Retail Prices.** In addition, there is guaranteed extra interest of 2·5 per cent for the 1st year, 2·75 per cent for the 2nd year, 3·25 per cent for the 3rd year, 4·0 per cent for the 4th year and 5·25 per cent for the 5th year. This interest is worth 3·54 per cent compound over a full five years.
Thirty-First .... (Sept. 26, 1985–Nov. 11, 1986) (200)	25	5	36·48	After 1 year, £1·44 is added, during 2nd year, 44p per completed 3 months, during 3rd year, 55p per completed 3 months, during 4th year, 68p per completed 3 months and during 5th year, 84p per completed 3 months.*
4th Index-Linked Issue (Aug. 1, 1986–) (200)	25			Like 3rd Issue Index-Linked Certificates, the repayment value of 4th Issue Index-Linked Certificates, subject to their being held for one year, is related to the movement of the U.K. General Index of Retail Prices.** In addition, there is guaranteed extra interest of 3·0 per cent for the 1st year, 3·25 per cent for the 2nd year, 3·5 per cent for the 3rd year, 4·5 per cent for the 4th year, and 6·0 per cent for the 5th year. This interest is worth 4·04 per cent compound over a full five years.
Thirty-Second ...... (Nov. 12, 1986– March 10, 1987) (200)	25	5	38·03	After 1 year, £1·63 is added, during 2nd year, 50p per completed 3 months, during 3rd year, 62p per completed 3 months, during 4th year, 77p per completed 3 months and during 5th year, 96p per completed 3 months.*
Thirty-Third .... (May 1, 1987–) (40, plus special facilities to hold up to a further 200)	25	5	35·06	After 1 year, the repayment value increases by 5·5 per cent for ordinarily held 33rd Issue. However, 33rd Reinvestment Certificates earn interest during the 1st year at the rate of 5·5 per cent per annum for each 3 month period. Thereafter all 33rd Issue earn 5·75 per cent after 2 years, 6·0 per cent after 3 years, 6·5 per cent after 4 years and 7·0 per cent after 5 years.*

* As announced by the Treasury.

† From June 1982, savings certificates of the 7th to 14th, 16th, 18th, 19th, 21st, 23rd and 24th Issues will be extended on General Extension Rates as they reach the end of their existing extension periods. The percentage interest rate is determined by the Treasury and any change in this General Extension Rate will be applicable from the 1st of the month following its announcement.

Under the new system, a certificate earns interest for each complete period of three months beyond the expiry of the previous extension terms. Within each three month period interest is calculated separately for each month at the rate applicable from the beginning of that month. The interest for each month is 1/12 of the annual rate (*i.e.* it does not vary with the number of days in the month) and is capitalised annually on the anniversary of the date of purchase. The current rate of interest under the General Extension Rate is displayed on special posters at most post offices.

** Index-linked certificates are eligible for an annual supplement of 3 per cent for the year to August 1, 1987. There have been four previous annual supplements of 2·4 per cent for 1982–83 and 1983–84 and 3 per cent for 1984–85 and 1985–86. At the 5th anniversary there is a bonus of 4 per cent of the purchase price and at the 10th anniversary there is a second bonus of 4 per cent of the full 5th anniversary value. All supplements and bonuses are fully index-linked once earned.

1156 [1988]

LEGAL NOTES

IMPORTANT

The Purpose of these notes is to outline some of the more common parts of the law as they may affect the average person, and they are, of course, believed to be correct at the time of going to press. The law is constantly developing and changing, however, and it is dangerous for the layman to seek to be his own lawyer—he may not have access to completely up to date books and his case may, because of its special facts, come within an exception to the general rules set out herein.

It is always best to take expert advice, and if you have a Solicitor who has acted for you in the past you should take any legal problems you have to him. If you do not have a Solicitor a friend may be able to recommend one. Failing this your local Citizens' Advice Bureau (whose address can be obtained from the Telephone Directory or from any Post Office or Town Hall) has a list of Solicitors in your area who deal with that particular type of problem which you have. If you are not able to find a Solicitor in any of these ways you should ask for help in doing so from The Law Society, 113 Chancery Lane, London, W.C.2 or The Law Society of Scotland at 26 Drumsheugh Gardens, Edinburgh.

The Legal Aid and Legal Advice and Assistance schemes exist to make the help of the trained lawyer available to everyone whatever their means as of right. The best policy is if in doubt go to a Solicitor without delay—timely advice will set your mind at rest but sitting on your rights can mean that you lose them.

Remember also that it is not necessary for a dispute to have arisen before you go to a Solicitor—the Legal Advice and Assistance Scheme enables him to advise you on your rights say under a tenancy agreement, the estate of a deceased person or in connection with matrimonial and consumer matters, and to write letters or take other steps on your behalf. He can also act for you where there is no question of a dispute at all, e.g. in the making of a will.

Your entitlement to take advantage of the Scheme depends on your means (see below) but a Solicitor or Citizens' Advice Bureau will be able to tell you whether you are covered by it.

BRITISH CITIZENSHIP

Types of citizenship.—There are three types of citizenship known as "British Citizenship", "Citizenship of the British Dependent Territories", and "British Overseas Citizenship".

Acquisition of citizenship on change of law.—The British Nationality Act 1981 which came into force on 1st January 1983 made substantial changes to the law of citizenship (which before that date did not distinguish between the three types of citizenship referred to above). Almost all persons who were then both citizens of the U.K. and Colonies and who had a right of abode in the U.K. became British Citizens when the Act came into force. Most U.K. and Colonies Citizens who did not have a right of abode in the U.K. became Citizens of the British Dependent Territories. This type of citizenship was, broadly speaking, conferred on citizens of the U.K. and Colonies by birth naturalization or registration in dependent territories. Dependent territories include Hong Kong, Gibraltar, the Falkland Islands, St Christopher and Nevis and St Helena and its dependencies. Any U.K. and Colonies Citizen who, on 1st Jan. 1983, did not acquire either British or British Dependent Territories' Citizenship became a British Overseas Citizen.

Later acquisition of British Citizenship.—British Citizenship is acquired automatically by those born in the U.K. (including, for this purpose, the Channel Islands and the Isle of Man) who have a parent who is a British Citizen or a parent who is settled in the U.K. Certain other categories of children born in the U.K. also acquire this type of citizenship i.e. foundlings, those whose parents subsequently settle in the U.K., those who live in the U.K. for 10 years from birth and those adopted in the U.K.

A person born outside the U.K. may acquire British Citizenship in the following ways:—
- (i) if one of his parents is a British Citizen otherwise than by descent (e.g. parent was born in the U.K.).
- (ii) if one of his parents is a British Citizen serving the Crown overseas.
- (iii) if the Secretary of State consents to his registration while he is a minor.
- (iv) if he is a Citizen of the British Dependent Territories, a British Overseas Citizen, a British Subject or a British Protected Person (these last two are residual categories of people who have not acquired one of the 3 new types of citizenship) and has been lawfully resident in the U.K. for 5 years without any time restriction.
- (v) if he is a British Dependent Territories Citizen who is a national of the U.K. for the purposes of the E.C. (i.e. a Gibraltarian).
- (vi) if he is naturalized. Naturalization may be applied for only by adults and the Secretary of State has a discretion whether to permit it. The basic requirements are five years' residence, good character, sufficient knowledge of the English or Welsh language, and an intention to reside in the U.K. permanently. The requirements are somewhat less restrictive in the case of an applicant who is married to a British Citizen.
- (vii) various rights to Citizenship given under the old law are perserved for a period of five years in respect of Commonwealth Citizens settled in the U.K. before 1973, wives of Citizens of the U.K. and Colonies, persons descended from U.K. Citizens and persons who have previously renounced citizenship.

Acquisition of British Dependent Territories and British Overseas Citizenship after the Act.—These citizenships are intended for persons connected with certain Commonwealth countries other than the U.K. In the case of Dependent Territories the rules are very similar to those for acquiring British Citizenship except that the connection is with the Dependent Territory rather than with the U.K. British Overseas Citizenship may be acquired by the minor children and wives of British Overseas Citizens in certain circumstances.

Retention of nationality by persons born in or who are citizens of the Republic of Ireland.—By the Ireland Act 1949, a person who was born before December 6th, 1922, in what is now the Republic of Ireland (Eire) and was a British subject immediately before January 1st, 1949, is not deemed to have ceased to be a British subject unless either (i) he was domiciled in the Irish Free State on December 6th, 1922 or (ii) was on or after April 10th, 1935, and before January 1st, 1949, permanently resident there, or (iii) had before January 1st, 1949, been registered as a citizen of Eire under the laws of that country.

In addition by the British Nationality Act 1948, any citizen of Eire who immediately before January 1st, 1949, was also a British subject can retain that status by submitting at any time a claim to the Home Secretary on any of the following grounds:

(a) he has been in the service of the United Kingdom Government;

(b) he holds a British passport issued in the United Kingdom or in any colony, protectorate, United Kingdom mandated or trust territory;

(c) he has associations by way of descent, residence or otherwise with any such place; or on complying with similar legislation in any of the "Dominions".

The British Nationality Act 1981 provides that persons who have made a claim may continue to be British subjects. Any citizen of Eire who was a British subject before January 1st, 1949, who has not yet made a claim may do so provided:

(a) that he is or has been in Crown Service under the government of the United Kingdom; or

(b) he has associations by way of descent, residence or otherwise with the United Kingdom or any dependent territory.

Renunciation and Resumption.—A person may cease to be a British Citizen by renouncing his citizenship (with the consent of the Secretary of State in wartime). The renunciation will be required to be registered with the Secretary of State and will be revoked if no new citizenship or nationality is acquired within six months. Once renounced, citizenship may be reacquired if the renunciation was necessary to retain or acquire some other citizenship or nationality. Similar rules as to renunciation and reacquisition apply in the case of British Dependent Territories Citizenships and of renunciation (but not reacquisition) in the case of British Overseas Citizenship.

Status of Aliens.—Property may be held by an alien in the same manner as by a natural-born British subject, but he may not hold public office, exercise the franchise or own a British ship or aircraft. The Republic of Ireland Act 1949 declares that the Republic, though not part of H.M. Dominions, is not a foreign country, and any reference in an Act of Parliament to foreigners, aliens, foreign countries, etc., shall be construed accordingly.

CONSUMER LAW

1. THE SUPPLY OF GOODS AND SERVICES

(a) The Sale of Goods Act 1979 provides protection to the purchaser of goods, by implying certain terms into every contract for the Sale of Goods. These implied terms are:

(i) A condition that the seller will pass good title to the buyer (unless the seller agrees to transfer only such title as he or his principal has) and warranties that the goods will be free from undisclosed encumbrances, and that the buyer will enjoy quiet possession of the goods.

(ii) Where there is a sale of goods by description, a condition that the goods will correspond with that description, and where the sale is by sample and description, a condition that the bulk of the goods shall correspond with both sample and description.

(iii) Where the seller sells goods in the course of a business, a condition that the goods will be of merchantable quality, unless before the contract is made, the buyer has examined the goods and ought to have noticed the defect, bearing in mind the purchaser's knowledge of the goods and the extent of the examination, or the seller has specifically drawn the attention of the buyer to the defect. Merchantable quality means fit for the purpose for which goods of the kind are commonly bought, taking into account any description applied to them, the price and other relevant circumstances.

(iv) A condition that where the seller sells goods in the course of a business, the goods are reasonably fit for any purpose made known to the seller by the buyer, unless the buyer does not rely on the seller's skill and judgment, or it would be unreasonable for him to do so.

(v) Where there is a sale of goods by sample, conditions that the bulk of the goods shall correspond with the sample in quality, that the buyer will have a reasonable opportunity of comparing the bulk with the sample, and that the goods are free from any defect rendering them unmerchantable, which would not be apparent from the sample.

For these purposes, the broad difference between a condition and a warranty is that the remedy for a breach of an implied condition may enable the buyer to reject the goods and recover damages if he has suffered loss whereas the remedy for a breach of warranty will only enable the buyer to recover damages.

It is possible for a seller to exclude some of the above terms from a contract, subject to restrictions imposed by the Unfair Contract Terms Act 1977 as given below. These restrictions give more protection ... where the buyer "deals as consumer". In a contract of sale of goods, a buyer "deals as consumer" where there is ... a sale by a seller in the course of a business, the goods are of a type ordinarily bought for private use or consumption, and are sold to a person who does not buy or hold himself out as buying them in the course of a business. A buyer in a sale by auction or competitive tender never "deals as consumer".

The 1977 Act prohibits the exclusion of the implied terms given in (ii) to (v) above, where the buyer "deals as consumer". In sales where the buyer does not "deal as consumer", terms purporting to exclude these implied terms, may be relied upon only to the extent that it would be reasonable to allow reliance. The Act provides guidelines for determining whether it would be reasonable to allow reliance. The implied terms in (i) above cannot be excluded whether the buyer "deals as consumer" or not.

(b) Similar terms to those implied in contracts of sale of goods are implied into contracts of hire-purchase by the Supply of Goods (Implied Terms) Act, 1973 and the 1977 Act limits the exclusion of these implied terms in a similar manner.

(c) Under the Supply of Goods and Services Act 1982, terms similar to those in the Sale of Goods Act relating to quiet possession, compliance with description, merchantable quality, fitness for purpose and correspondence with sample are implied into other types of contract under which ownership of goods passes (e.g. a contract for "work and materials" such as a supply of new parts during the servicing of a motor car) and also into contracts for the hire of goods. In the case of contracts under which ownership of goods is to pass, there is also an implied condition as to title.

The 1977 Act limits the exclusion of these implied terms in a similar manner to the implied terms in the Sale of Goods Act.

(d) The Supply of Goods and Services Act 1982 also implies into a contract for the supply of services, terms that the supplier will use reasonable care and skill, carry out the service within a reasonable time (unless the time is agreed) and charge a reasonable charge (unless the charge is agreed).

(e) The Trade Descriptions Act 1968 provides that it is a criminal offence for a trader or business-man to apply a false trade description to any goods, or to supply or offer to supply any goods to which a false trade description has been applied. A trade description includes a description as to quantity, size, method, place and date of manufacture, other history, composition, other physical characteristics, fitness for purpose, behaviour or accuracy, testing or approval. It is also an offence to give a false indication as to the price of goods. Prosecutions are brought by trading standards inspectors.

(f) The Fair Trading Act 1973 is also designed to protect the consumer. It provides for the appointment of a Director General of Fair Trading, whose duties include keeping under review commercial activities in the U.K. relating to the supply of goods or services to consumers, and to collect information to discover practices that may adversely affect the economic interests of the consumer. He may refer certain consumer trade practices to the Consumer Protection Advisory Committee, or, of his own initiative take proceedings against firms that are trading unfairly. He may also publish information and advice to consumers. Examples of practices which have been prohibited by virtue of references made under this Act, include the use of certain void exclusion clauses in contracts for the sale of goods and hire-purchase, and advertisements by traders appearing to sell as private persons.

(g) The Consumer Protection Act 1987 makes the producer of a product liable for any damage caused by a defect in that product, subject to certain defences. (This provision is expected to be brought into force during 1988).

Scotland

The Sale of Goods Act, 1979, a consolidating Act, applies with some modification to Scotland. For example, it is not necessary in Scotland to distinguish between the words condition and warranty. The remedies of the buyer in both cases are the same, that is, he can either within a reasonable time reject the goods and treat the contract as repudiated, or retain the goods and treat the failure to perform such material part as a breach which may give rise to a claim for compensation or damages.

2. CONSUMER CREDIT

England and Wales

The Consumer Credit Act 1974 is now fully in force. It provides a system for the protection of the consumer, of licensing and control of all matters relating to the provision of credit, or the supply of goods on hire or hire-purchase, administered by the Director-General of Fair Trading. A licence is required to carry on a consumer credit or consumer hire business, or to deal in credit brokerage, debt adjusting, counselling or collecting, for which group licences are available. Any "fit person" may apply to the Director of Fair Trading for a licence which is normally renewable after 10 years. A licence is not

necessary if such types of business are only transacted "occasionally" or if exempt agreements only are involved.

For the Act's provisions to apply the agreement must be "regulated", *i.e.* be to individuals or partnerships only; must not be exempt, *e.g.* certain loans by local authorities or building societies; and the total credit must not exceed £15,000. The terms of a regulated agreement can be varied by the creditor, but only if the agreement gives him the right to do so, and the debtor receives notice in the prescribed form.

To be enforceable the agreement must be properly executed, and the specified information must be given during the antecedent negotiations for the contract. These are conducted by the creditor, credit broker or supplier (these being the creditor's agents) and begin when the parties first begin discussions.

The agreement must state certain information such as the amount of credit, the annual percentage rate of interest and the amount and timing of repayments.

An agreement is cancellable under the Act if oral representations were made in the debtor's presence during antecedent negotiations and the debtor signed the agreement other than at the creditor's (or credit-broker's or negotiator's) place of business. Time for cancellation expires five clear days after the debtor receives a second copy of the agreement. The agreement must inform the debtor of his right to cancel and how to cancel.

Where there are arrangements or connections between the creditor and supplier the former is generally liable for any misrepresentation or breach of contract by the latter, and will thus be liable to indemnify the debtor.

If the debtor is in arrears or is otherwise in breach of the agreement, the creditor may not enforce the agreement, e.g. by repossessing goods, without serving a default notice on the debtor. This notice will give the debtor a chance to remedy the default. Even if the default is not remedied by the debtor, if the agreement is a hire-purchase or conditional sale agreement, the creditor cannot repossess the goods without an order of the court, if the debtor has paid one-third of the total price of the goods.

Where the agreement requires the debtor to make grossly exorbitant payments or is contrary to the ordinary principles of fair dealing the Court can reopen it either at the debtor's request or during enforcement proceedings and (*inter alia*) alter the terms of the contract or set aside any obligations it imposes so as to do justice between the parties. Whether an agreement is such an extortionate credit bargain is decided by reference (*inter alia*) to interest rates prevailing at the date of agreement, the pressure for finance the debtor was under, etc.

If a credit reference agency was used to check the debtor's financial standing the creditor must give the agency's name to the debtor who is entitled to see the agency's file on him on payment of a fee of £1.

Scotland

The Consumer Credit Act (*see* above) also extends to Scotland and goes far in assimilating the Scots Law on this topic with English Law. The Supply of Goods (Implied Terms) Act 1973 also applies to Scotland. Parts II and III only of the Unfair Contract Terms Act 1977 apply to Scotland. The Sale of Goods Act, 1979, applies with some modification to Scotland.

3. RECEIPTS

The law on receipts in Scotland is governed by the Prescription and Limitations (Scotland) Act 1973, which for this purpose came into force on July 25, 1976. Now, receipts need only be kept for a period of five years and if a creditor does not make a relevant claim within that period no action can be raised.

CROWN—PROCEEDINGS AGAINST

Before 1947 proceedings against the Crown were generally possible only by a procedure known as a petition of right, which placed the litigant at a considerable disadvantage and which was not normally available at all in cases of tort (i.e., civil wrongs other than breach of contract). Thus, no proceedings would normally lie against the Government if a subject were injured by the negligent driving of a Government vehicle (although the driver could be sued) or if a Government employee were injured by the defective condition of the Crown premises on which he worked. Now however, by the Crown Proceedings Act 1947, which came into operation on Jan. 1, 1948, the Crown, in its public capacity, is largely placed in the same position as a subject, although some procedural disadvantages remain. Exceptions to the Act include the immunity of the Crown and any member of the armed forces when on duty from liability in tort in respect of death of, or personal injury to, another member of the armed forces on duty (or even if not on duty, on any land, ship or vehicle being used for the purposes of the Armed Forces of the Crown), provided that the death or injury is certified as attributable to service for purposes of pension. This provision, contained in section 10 of the 1947 Act, is however affected by the Crown Proceedings (Armed Forces) Act 1987, which provides that section 10 (exclusion from liability in tort) shall cease to have effect except in relation to anything suffered by a person in consequence of an act or omission committed before May 15, 1987. Power is however reserved to revive section 10 in certain circumstances.

Scotland.—The Act as amended extends to Scotland and has the effect of bringing the practice of the two countries as closely together as the different legal systems will permit. While formerly actions against the Crown, when permissible, were confined to the Court of Session, proceedings may now be brought in the Sheriff Court.

The Act lays down that arrestment of money in the hands of the Crown or of a Government Department is competent in any case where arrestment in the hands of a subject would have been competent, but an exception is made in respect of National Savings Bank deposits. Section 2 (1) of the Law Reform (Miscellaneous Provisions) (Scotland) Act 1966 removes the privilege whereby the wages of Crown servants, other than serving members of the armed forces, are exempt from arrestment in execution.

DEATHS

REGISTRATION, BURIAL AND CREMATION

REGISTRATION

(For Certificates, *see* under FAMILY LAW–CERTIFICATES)

In England and Wales.—When a death takes place, personal information of it must be given to the local Registrar of Births and Deaths, and the register signed in his presence, by one of the following persons: (1) A relative of the deceased present at the death, or in attendance during the last illness. If they fail (2) some other relative of the deceased. In default of any relatives (3) a person present at the death; or, the occupier of the house in which the death happened. If all the above-named fail (4) an inmate of the house. A person (other than a relative) registering the death must be causing the disposal of the body. Relatives present or in attendance are first required to attend to the registration. The registration must be made within five days of the death, or within the same time written notice of the death sent to the Registrar. If the deceased was attended during his last illness by a registered medical practitioner, a certificate of cause of death must be sent by the doctor to the Registrar. The doctor must give to the informant of the death a written notice of the signing of the certificate, which must be delivered to the Registrar. It is essential that a certificate for disposal should be obtained from the Registrar before the funeral and delivered to the clergyman or other person in charge of the churchyard or cemetery. No fee is chargeable for this certificate. If the death is not registered within five days (or fourteen days if written notice of the occurrence of the death is sent to him) the Registrar may require any one of the above-mentioned persons to attend to register at a stated time and place. Failure to comply involves a penalty of ten pounds. The registration of a death is free of charge. After twelve months no death can be registered without the Registrar General's consent.

Whenever the death of a child is registered, particulars of the name and occupation of the mother are to be entered in the register.

A body must not be disposed of until (1) either the Registrar has given a certificate to the effect that he has registered or received notice of the death, or (2) until the Coroner has made a disposal order (*Births and Deaths Registration Act 1926*, s. 1).

A person disposing of a body must within ninety-six hours deliver to the Registrar a notification as to the date, place, and means of the disposal of the body (*ib.*, S. 3).

"Still-born" child (*see* under Births (Registration) *below*).

Death at Sea.—The master of a British ship must record any death on board and send particulars to the Registrar General of Shipping.

Death Abroad.—Consular Officers are authorized to register deaths of British subjects occurring abroad. Certificates are procurable at the Registrar General's Office, London. If the deceased was of *Scottish* domicile, particulars are sent to the Registrar General for Scotland.

With regard to the registration of deaths of members of the armed forces, and deaths occurring on H.M. ships and aircraft, *see* the Registration of Births, etc. Act 1957.

Deaths (Registration) in Scotland.—The Registration of Births, Deaths and Marriages (Scotland) Act 1965 supersedes provisions in former Acts.

Personal notification within 8 days must be given to the registrar of (*a*) the registration district in which the death took place or (*b*) any registration district in which the deceased was ordinarily resident immediately before his death, and (*c*) when a body is found and the place of death is not known, either the registration district in which the body was found or any other registration district appropriate by virtue of the preceding paragraph. When a person dies (in or out of Scotland) in a ship, aircraft or land vehicle during a journey and the body is conveyed therein to any place in Scotland the death shall, unless the Registrar General otherwise directs, be deemed to have occurred at that place.

The register must be signed in the presence of the registrar by one of the following: (a) any relative of the deceased; (b) any person present at the death; (c) the deceased's executor or other legal representative; (d) the occupier, at the time of the death, of the premises where the death took place; (e) if these fail, any other person having knowledge of the particulars to be registered. Failure to comply involves a penalty not exceeding £50.

The medical practitioner who attended the deceased during the last illness must sign a certificate of the cause of death within 7 days. If there is no such medical practitioner, any medical practitioner who is able to do so, may sign the certificate. At the time of registering the death the registrar shall, without charge, give the informant a certificate of registration, and the person to whom the certificate is given must hand it to the undertaker previous to cremation. A body may, however, be interred before the death is registered, in which case the undertaker must deliver a certificate of burial to the Registrar within three days.

The mandatory death grant was abolished in April 1987 but assistance may be obtained from the Department of Health and Social Security by those who are unable to meet funeral expenses.

BURIAL

The duty of burial is incumbent on the deceased person's executors (if any appointed); it is also a recognized obligation of the husband of a woman, and the parent of a child, also of a householder where the body lies. Funeral expenses of a reasonable amount will be repayable out of deceased's estate in priority to any other claims. Directions as to place and mode of burial are frequently contained in the deceased's will or in some memorandum placed with private papers, or may have been communicated verbally to a relative. Consequently steps should immediately be taken to ascertain the deceased's wishes from the above sources. If the wishes are considered objectionable, they are not necessarily enforceable; legal advice should be taken. A person may legally leave directions for the anatomical examination of his body. As to the place of burial—unless closed by Order in Council—the parish churchyard is the normal burying place for parishioners, or any person dying in the Parish, but nowadays this will apply only in villages and the smaller towns. In populous districts cemeteries and crematoria have been established either by the local council, or a private company, and burials will take place there in accordance with the regulations. For an exclusive right to a burial space in the churchyard a faculty is required from the Ecclesiastical Court. Poor persons may be buried at the public expense by the local authority. As to the necessity for obtaining a registrar's certificate or authority from the Coroner for disposal, *see* above.

CREMATION

Under the Cremation Acts, 1902 and 1952, regulations are made by the Home Secretary dealing fully with the cremation of a body, disposal of ashes, etc., and containing numerous essential safeguards.

If Cremation is desired it is advisable for instructions to be left in writing to that effect. However, in Scotland, even if the deceased wished his body to be cremated or anatomically dissected, relatives can still veto his or her wishes.

To arrange for Cremation the Executor or near relative should instruct the undertaker to that effect

and obtain from him the Statutory Forms required as given in the Cremation Regulations issued in 1930 (Statutory Rules and Orders, 1930, No. 1016), as amended by the Cremation Regulations 1965 (No. 1146) and the Cremation (Amendment) Regulations 1985 (No. 153).

INTESTACY

ENGLAND AND WALES

As regards deaths on or after March 15, 1977, the position is governed by the Administration of Estates Act, 1925, as amended by the Intestates' Estates Act, 1952, the Family Provision Act, 1966 and Orders made thereunder. If the intestate leaves a spouse and issue, the spouse takes (i) the "personal chattels"; (ii) £75,000 with interest at 6 per cent. from death until payment; and (iii) a life interest in half of the rest of the estate. This life interest can be capitalized at the option of the spouse. "Personal chattels" are articles of household use or ornament (including motor-cars), not used for business purposes. The rest of the estate goes to the issue. If the intestate leaves a spouse and no issue, but leaves a parent or brother or sister of the whole blood or issue of such brothers and sisters the spouse takes (i) the "personal chattels"; (ii) £125,000 with interest at 6 per cent. from death until payment, and (iii) half of the rest of the estate absolutely. The other half of the rest of the estate goes to the parents, equally if more than one, or, if none, to the brothers and sisters of the whole blood or issue of such brothers and sisters. If the intestate leaves a spouse, but no issue, no parents and no brothers or sisters of the whole blood or their issue, the spouse takes the whole estate absolutely. If resident therein at the intestate's death, the surviving spouse may generally require the personal representatives to appropriate the interest of the intestate in the matrimonial home in or towards satisfaction of any absolute interest of the spouse, including the capitalized value of a life interest. In certain cases, leave of Court is required. On a partial intestacy any benefit (other than personal chattels specifically bequeathed) received by the surviving spouse under the will must be brought into account against the statutory legacy of £75,000 or £125,000, as the case may be. If there is no surviving spouse, the estate is distributed among those who survive the intestate in the following order (those entitled under earlier numbers taking to the exclusion of those entitled under later numbers):—(1) children; (2) father or mother (equally, if both alive); (3) brothers and sisters of the whole blood; (4) brothers and sisters of the half blood; (5) grandparents (equally, if more than one alive); (6) uncles and aunts of the whole blood; (7) uncles and aunts of the half blood; (8) the Crown.

In cases (1), (3), (4), (6) and (7) the persons entitled lose their interests unless they or their issue not only survive the intestate, but also attain eighteen or marry under that age, their shares going to the persons (if any) within the same group who do attain eighteen or marry. Moreover, in the same cases, succession is not *per capita*, but *per stirpes, i.e.,* by stocks or families. Thus, if the intestate leaves one child and two grandchildren, being the children of a child of the intestate, who pre-deceased the intestate, the two grandchildren represent their deceased parent and take between them one-half of the issue's share, the remaining half going to the surviving child. Similarly, nephews and nieces represent a deceased brother, and so on.

When the deceased died partially intestate (*i.e.,* leaving a will which disposed of only part of his property), the above rules apply to the intestate part.

Children must bring into account (hotchpot) any substantial advances received from the intestate during his lifetime before claiming any further share under the intestacy. Special hotchpot provisions apply to partial intestacy.

By the Family Law Reform Act, 1969, the position of an illegitimate child is equated with that of a legitimate child in respect of all deaths occurring on or after January 1, 1970. However, when section 18 of the Family Law Reform Act 1987 is brought into operation, these provisions of the 1969 Act will be replaced by the general provision of the 1987 Act that references to any relationship between two persons shall, unless the contrary intention appears, be construed without regard to whether or not the father and mother of either of them, or the father and mother of any person through whom the relationship is deduced, have or had been married to each other at any time.

In respect of deaths after March 1976 the provisions of the Inheritance (Provision for Family and Dependants) Act 1975 may allow other persons to claim provision out of the estate. See *post* under "Wills".

For personal application for Letters of Administration—*see below*.

SCOTLAND

The Succession (Scotland) Act, 1964, provides that the whole estate of any person dying intestate shall devolve without distinction between heritable and moveable property. By that Act the surviving spouse of an intestate may, as a prior right (in addition to legal rights, *see* below), claim the matrimonial home to a maximum of £50,000, or a choice of one matrimonial home if more than one (or in certain circumstances the value thereof), with its furniture and plenishings not exceeding £10,000 in value, plus the sum of £15,000 if the deceased left issue or, if no issue, the sum of £25,000. These figures apply from 1st August 1981 and may be increased from time to time by order of the Secretary of State.

The Act has been modified by the Law Reform (Miscellaneous Provisions) (Scotland) Act, 1968, which provided that an illegitimate child had exactly the same rights of succession in the estate of his parents as a legitimate child. However, the position still remains that an illegitimate child has no succession rights in the estate of a grandparent even though such would have fallen to his predeceasing parent.

Legal rights, referred to above, are:—

Jus relicti (æ): the right of a surviving spouse to one half of the deceased's net moveable estate after satisfaction of prior rights if there are no surviving children, or to one third if there are any surviving children.

Legitim: right of surviving children to one-half of the net moveable estate of deceased parents if no surviving spouse, or one-third of the net moveable estate of deceased parents after satisfaction of prior rights where there is a surviving spouse.

There are no legal rights in heritage.

In general, the lines of succession are: (1) descendants; (2) collaterals; (3) ascendants and their collaterals, and so on in the ascending scale. The Crown is ultimus haeres. The right of representation, *i.e.*, the right of the issue of a person, who would have succeeded if he had survived the intestate, is open to any line of succession where previously it was limited to apply only when there were next of kin or the issue of predeceasing next of kin. The surviving mother of an intestate now has equal rights of succession with the surviving father, where formerly these were restricted. The intestate's maternal relations, who prior to the Act had no rights of succession, are now on an equal footing with his paternal relations. Where the intestate is survived only by parents, and by brothers and sisters (collaterals) half of the estate is taken by the parents and the other half by the brothers and sisters, those of the whole blood being preferred to those of the half blood; where, however, succession opens to collaterals—(which expression can include the brothers and sisters of an ancestor of the intestate)—of the half blood, they shall rank equally amongst themselves, whether related to the intestate (or his ancestor) through their father or their mother.

WILLS

IMPORTANT NOTE.—The following notes and those on Intestacy must be read subject to the provisions of the Inheritance (Provision for Family and Dependants) Act 1975 which can affect the estate of anyone dying domiciled in England and Wales after March 1976. Very broadly a spouse, former spouse who has not remarried, a child of the deceased himself or one treated by him as a child of his family, or any person maintained by him at his death may apply to the Court under the Act. If the Court thinks that the will or the law of intestacy or both do not make reasonable provision for the applicant it may order payment out of the net estate of maintenance or a lump sum. It may also order the transfer of property, vary certain trusts and the powers can affect property disposed of by the deceased in his lifetime intending to defeat the Act. It is up to the applicant to take the initiative, and the application must generally be made within six months of the grant of Probate or Letters of Administration.

REASONS FOR MAKING A WILL.—Every person over the age of 18 should make a will. However small the estate the rules of Intestacy (see above) may not reflect a person's wishes as to his property; in any case a will can do more than just deal with property—it can in particular appoint executors, give directions as to the disposal of the body and appoint guardians to take care of children in the event of the parents' death. For the wealthier person an appropriately drawn will can operate to reduce the burden of Inheritance Tax.

It is considered desirable for a will to be properly drawn up by a Solicitor, and the making of a will is one of the services which he can provide under the Legal Advice and Assistance Scheme (see below).

In no circumstances should one person prepare a Will for another person where the former is to take any benefit under it—this can easily lead to a suggestion of undue influence which may cause the will to be held bad.

Assuming a lawyer is not employed, a person having resolved to make a will must remember that it is only after a person is dead, and cannot explain his meaning, that his will can be open to dispute. It is the more necessary, therefore, to express what is meant in language of the utmost clearness, avoiding the use of any word or expression that admits of another meaning than the one intended. Avoid the use of "legal terms," such as "heirs" and "issue," when the same thing may be expressed in plain language. If in writing the will a mistake be made, it is better to rewrite the whole. Before a will is executed (*see below*) an alteration *may* be made by striking through the words with a pen, but opposite to such alteration the testator and witnesses should write their names or place their initials. Never scratch out a word with a knife or other instrument, and no alteration *of any kind whatever* must be made after the will is executed. If the testator afterwards wishes to change the disposition of his estate, it is best to make a new will, revoking the old one. The use of *codicils* should be left to the lawyer. *A will should be written in ink and very legibly, on a single sheet of paper.* Although, of course, forms of wills must vary to suit different cases, the following forms may be found useful to those who, in cases of emergency, are called upon to draw up wills, either for themselves or others.

Nothing more complicated should be attempted. The forms should be studied in conjunction with the notes following.

This is the last will and testament of me [*Thomas Smith*] of [*Vine Cottage, Silver Street, Reading, Berks*] which I make this [*thirteenth*] day of [*February*, 1988] and whereby I revoke all previous wills and testamentary dispositions.

1. I hereby appoint [*John Green of —— and Richard Brown of ——*] to be the executor(s) of this my will.

2. I give all my property real and personal to [*my wife Mary* or *my sons Raymond and David equally* or as the case may be].

Signed by the testator in the presence of us both present at the same time who, at his request, in his presence and in the presence of each other have hereunto set our names as witnesses.	Thomas Smith *Signature of Testator;*

William Jones (*signed*) of Green Gables, South Street, Reading, tailor.

Henry Morgan (*signed*) of 16, North Street, Reading, butcher.

Should it be desired to give legacies and/or gifts of specific property, instead of giving the whole estate to one or more persons, the form above should be used with the substitution for clause 2 of the following clauses:— •

2. I give to —— of —— the sum of £—— and to —— of —— the sum of £—— and to —— of —— all my books (*or as the case may require*).

3. All the residue of my property real and personal I give to —— of ——.

TERMS.—Real property includes freehold land and houses; while personal property includes debts due, arrears of rents, money, leasehold property, house furniture, goods, assurance policies, stocks and shares in companies, and the like. The words "my money," apart from the context, will normally only include actual real money. The expression "goods and chattels" should not be used. In giving *particular* property, ordinary language is sufficient, *e.g.*, "my house, Vine Cottage, Silver Street, Reading, Berks." Such specific gifts fail if not owned by the testator at his death.

RESIDUARY LEGATEES.—It is well in all cases where legacies or specific gifts are made, to leave to some person or persons "the residue of my property," although it may be thought that the whole of the property has been disposed of in legacies, etc., already mentioned in the will. *It should be remembered that a will operates on property owned at the time it is made or acquired after it has been made.*

EXECUTION OF A WILL, AND WITNESSES.—The testator should sign his name at the foot or end of the will, in the presence of two witnesses, who will immediately afterwards sign their names in his and in each other's presence. A person who has been left any gift or share of residue in the will, or whose wife or husband has been left such a gift, should not be an attesting witness. Their attestation would be good, but they would forfeit the gift. It is better that a

person named as executor should not be a witness. Husband and wife may both be witnesses, provided neither is a legatee. If a solicitor be appointed executor, it is lawful to direct that his ordinary fees and charges shall be paid; but in this case he (as an interested party) must not be a witness to the will.

It is desirable that the witnesses should be fully described, as they may possibly be wanted at some future time. If the testator should be too ill to sign, even by a mark, another person may sign the testator's name to the will for him, in his presence and by his direction, and in this case it should be shown that the testator knew the contents of the document. The attestation clause should therefore be worded: "Signed by Thomas Brown, by the direction and in the presence of the testator, Thomas Smith, in the joint presence of us, who thereupon signed our names in his presence and in the presence of each other, the will having been first read over to the testator, who appeared fully to understand the same."

Where there is any suspicion that the Testator is not, by reason of age or infirmity, fully in command of his faculties it is desirable to ask his Doctor to act as a witness (see Testamentary capacity below).

A *blind person* may make a will in Braille. If the testator be blind the will should be read aloud to him in the presence of the witnesses, and the fact mentioned in the attestation clause. A blind person cannot witness a will.

If by inadvertance the testator should have signed his will without the witnesses being present, then the attestation should be:—"The testator acknowledged his signature already made as his signature to his last will and testament, in the joint presence," etc. Any omission in the observance of these details may invalidate the will. *The stringency of the law as to signature and witnessing of a will is only relaxed in favour of soldiers, sailors and airmen in certain circumstances.*

EXECUTORS.—It is usual to appoint two executors, although one is sufficient; any number up to and including four may be appointed. The name and address of each executor should be given in full. An executor may be a legatee. Thus a child of full age or wife to whom the whole or a portion of the estate is left may be appointed sole executor, or one of two executors. The addresses of the executors are not essential; but it is desirable here as elsewhere, to avoid ambiguity or vagueness.

LAPSED LEGACIES.—If a legatee dies in the lifetime of the testator, the legacy generally lapses and falls into the residue. Where a residuary legatee predeceases the testator, his share of the residuary estate will not generally pass to the other residuary legatees, but will pass to the persons entitled on the deceased's intestacy. In all such cases it is desirable to make a new will.

An important exception to the general rule of lapse stated above is contained in the Administration of Justice Act 1982, where there is a gift to a child or remoter issue of the testator who dies before the testator leaving issue who survive the testator.

TESTAMENTARY CAPACITY.—A person under the age of 18 cannot make a will (except for soldiers, sailors and airmen and then only in exceptional circumstances).

So far as mental capacity is concerned the Testator must be able to understand and appreciate the nature and effect of making a will, the property of which he can dispose and the claims to which he ought to give effect. If a person is not mentally able to make a will provision exists (under the Mental Health Act, 1983) for the Court to do this for him.

REVOCATION.—A later will revokes an earlier will if it expressly says so, or is completely inconsistent with it. Otherwise the earlier one is only revoked insofar as it is inconsistent with the later one. A will may also be revoked by burning, tearing or otherwise *destroying* the will with the intention of revoking it. Such destruction must either be by the testator or by some other person in his presence and at his direction. *It is not sufficient to obliterate the will with a pen.* Marriage in every case acts as the revocation of a will, except that under the Administration of Justice Act 1982, there is a provision to the effect that if it appears from a will that at the time it was made the testator was expecting to be married to a particular person and that he intended that the will (or a disposition in the will) should not be revoked by the marriage to that person, the will will not be revoked by marriage to that person. The Act also provides that where after a testator has made a will the testator's marriage is terminated by a decree of divorce or nullity, any gift to a spouse shall lapse and any appointment of the spouse as executor shall be omitted from the will unless the will shows a contrary intention.

PERSONAL APPLICATION FOR PROBATE OR LETTERS OF ADMINISTRATION

Application for probate or for letters of administration may be made *in person* at the Personal Application Dept. of the Principal Registry of the Family Division, a district probate registry or sub-registry, or a probate office by the executors or persons entitled to a grant of administration. Applicants should bring (1) the will, if any; (2) a certificate of death; (3) particulars of all property and assets left by the deceased; and (4) a list of debts and funeral expenses.

Intending applicants, before attending at a registry or probate office, should write or telephone to the nearest probate registry or sub-registry for the necessary forms. Postal or telephone applications cannot be dealt with at the local probate offices, which are part-time only.

Certain property can be disposed of on death without a grant of probate or administration, or in pursuance of a nomination made by the deceased, provided the amount involved does not exceed £5,000. *See* the Administration of Estates (Small Payments) Act, 1965.

WHERE TO FIND A PROVED WILL

A will proved since 1858 must have been proved either at the Principal Registry at Somerset House, or a District Registry. In the former case the original will itself is carefully preserved at Somerset House, the copy of which probate has been granted is in the hands of the executors who proved the will, and another copy for Parliament is bound up in a folio volume of wills made by testators of that initial and date; the indices to these volumes fill a room of considerable size at Somerset House, where the indices may be examined and a copy of any will read. In the latter case, the original will proved in the District Registry, is kept there, and may be seen or a *copy* obtained, but a copy is sent to and filed at Somerset House, where also it may be seen. A general index of grants, both probates and administrations, is prepared and printed annually in lexicographical form, and may be seen at either the Principal or a District Registry. This index is usually ready by about October of the following year.

RECENT DEATHS.—A system introduced in 1975 enables a person to discover when a grant of Probate or Letters of Administration is made which may be invaluable to a creditor of the deceased or applicant under the Inheritance (Provision for Family and Dependants) Act 1975—*see above.* A "standing search" may be made by sending a request in the form set out below to the Record Keeper at the Principal Registry of the Family Division with a small fee. The searcher will receive particulars of any grant made in the previous 12 months or the following 6 months, including names and addresses of the executors or administrators and the Registry in which the grant was made.

FORM OF SEARCH

In the High Court of Justice
Family Division
The Principal Registry (Probate)
I/We apply for the entry of a standing search so that there shall be sent to me/us an office copy of every grant of representation in England & Wales in the estate of:—
Full name of deceased:
Alternative or alias name
Full address
Exact date of death

Which either has issued not more than 12 months before the entry of this application or issues within 6 months hereafter
Sgd.—(full address).

SCOTS LAW OF WILLS

A domiciled Scotsman, unlike a domiciled Englishman, cannot in certain circumstances dispose effectively of the entirety of his estate. If he leave a widow and children, the widow is entitled to a one-third share in the whole of the moveable estate (her *jus relictae*), and the children are entitled to another one-third share equally between them (their *legitim*). If he leave a widow but no children—or children but no widow—the *jus relictae* or *legitim* is increased to a one-half share of the net moveable estate. The remaining portion is known as the *dead's part.* A surviving husband and children have comparable rights (*jus relicti* and *legitim*) in the wife's estate. The *dead's part* is the only portion of which the testator can freely dispose. Legacies and bequests are payable only out of the *dead's part.* All debts are payable out of the whole estate before any division. Pupils, *i.e.* a girl up to the age of twelve or a boy up to the age of fourteen, cannot make wills. Formerly a minor could dispose only of movables but since the passing of the Succession (Scotland) Act, 1964 he has a like capacity to test on heritable property. A will must be in writing and may be typewritten or even in pencil. A will may be either (1) *holograph, i.e.* written, dated and subscribed by the testator himself, in which case no witnesses are necessary; a printed form filled up by the testator or a typewritten document is not necessarily a *holograph* but may become so if the testator writes, in hand, at the foot of the form or document the words "*adopted as holograph*" followed by his signature and the date. Words written on erasure or marginal additions or interlineations in *holograph* writings, if proved to be in the handwriting of the maker of the deed, are valid; (2) *attested,* i.e. signed in presence of two witnesses. It is not necessary that these witnesses should sign in presence of one another, or even that they should see the testator signing so long as the testator acknowledges his signature to the witnesses. The Conveyancing and Feudal Reform (Scotland) Act, 1970 whilst altering generally the rules for the subscription of deeds, specifically (s. 44 (2)) makes no change in the rules applying to wills which must still be signed by the testator on every page. If the testator cannot write, or is blind, his will may be authenticated by a law agent, notary public or justice of the peace and two witnesses. It is better that the will be not witnessed by a beneficiary thereunder, although this circumstance will not invalidate the attestation of the will or (as it would in England) the gift. A parish minister may act as a notary for the purpose of subscribing a will in his own parish. Wills may be registered in the Books of the Sheriffdom in which the deceased died domiciled, or in the Books of Council and Session, H.M. General Register House, Edinburgh. The original deed may be inspected on payment of a small fee and a certified official copy may be obtained. A Scottish will is not revoked by the subsequent marriage of the testator. The subsequent birth of a child, no testamentary provision having been made for him, may revoke a will. A will may be revoked by a subsequent will, either expressly or by implication; but in so far as the two can be read together both wills have effect. If a subsequent will is revoked, the earlier will is revived.

"Confirmation", the Scottish equivalent of Probate, is obtained in the Sheriff Court of the Sheriffdom in which the deceased was domiciled at the date of his death or, where he had no fixed domicile or died abroad, in the commissariot of Edinburgh. Executors are either "nominate" or "dative". An Executor nominate is one nominated by the deceased in his will or, where such person has predeceased the testator, by the residuary beneficiary. An Executor dative is one appointed by the Court in the case of intestacy or where the deceased had failed to name an executor in his will and there is no residuary beneficiary. In the former case the deceased's next-of-kin are all entitled to be declared executors dative. An inventory of the deceased's estate and a schedule of debts, together with an affidavit, must first be given up. In estates under £13,000 gross, confirmation is obtained under a simplified procedure at reduced fees.

Presumption of Survivorship.—The Succession (Scotland) Act, 1964, referred to above provides, by s. 31, that where two persons die in circumstances indicating that they died simultaneously or if it is uncertain which was the survivor, the younger will be deemed to have survived the elder unless the elder person left testamentary provision in favour of the younger, whom failing in favour of a third person, the younger person having died intestate (partially or wholly); but if the persons so dying were husband and wife, neither shall be presumed to have survived the other.

EMPLOYMENT

WAGES AND SICK PAY

The Wages Act 1986 has repealed the Truck Acts. Under this Act, subject to certain exceptions, employers may not make deductions from an employee's wages unless authorised by statute or contract or with the employee's prior written consent. There is an upper limit of one-tenth of gross pay for deductions from retail workers' wages on account of cash or stock shortages.

Under the Social Security and Housing Benefits Act 1982 as amended, an employee absent from work due to illness or injury is entitled to receive Statutory Sick Pay from the employer for a maximum period of 28 weeks in any year. No payment is made for the first three days of any period of illness. The employer can recoup the payments from his National Insurance contributions.

The Equal Pay Act 1970, which extends to Scotland, and which came into force on December 29, 1975, prevents discrimination, as regards terms and conditions of employment between men and women employed on like work in the same employment.

PARTICULARS OF TERMS OF EMPLOYMENT

Under the Employment Protection (Consolidation) Act 1978, an employer must give each full-time employee within 13 weeks of the beginning of the employment a written statement containing the following particulars of the contract between them:

(1) the date when the employment began (when continuous employment began if previous work counts as continuous with this job);
(2) the rate of remuneration (or how it is calculated);
(3) the intervals at which wages are paid;
(4) the hours of work;
(5) the employee's entitlement to holidays (including public holidays) and holiday pay;
(6) the title of the employee's job;
(7) terms relating to sickness, injury and sick pay;
(8) details of any pension scheme;
(9) the length of notice which the employee should give and receive in order to terminate the contract.

In addition, the written particulars must specify any disciplinary rules; and also must identify the person to whom the employee can apply if he is dissatisfied with any disciplinary decision or to seek redress of any grievance and what further steps may ensue.

TERMINATION OF EMPLOYMENT

An employee may be dismissed without notice if he is guilty of gross breach of contract, such as disobedience to a lawful order or dishonesty. He is then only entitled to wages accrued due at the date of dismissal.

In other cases, the employee is entitled to reasonable notice which, under the Employment Protection (Consolidation) Act 1978, must not be less than one week if he has been continuously employed for four weeks, but less than two years; after two years it is two weeks' notice increasing by one week's notice for each further full year worked up to a maximum of 12 weeks' notice after 12 years' service.

An employer who wrongfully dismisses an employee (i.e. with less than the length of notice to which he is entitled) is generally liable to pay wages for the period of proper notice.

An employee who has a fixed term contract has no claim against his employer for wrongful dismissal if his contract is not renewed when it expires. He may, however, have a claim for a redundancy payment or compensation for unfair dismissal. If he is wrongfully dismissed before his contract expires, he is generally entitled to remuneration payable over the full period of the contract.

An employee may be entitled to a redundancy payment or to compensation for unfair dismissal if the employment has been terminated by the employer (with or without proper notice) or he has a fixed term contract which expires without being renewed or the employment has been terminated by the employee by reason of the employer's breach of contract.

Under the Employment Protection (Consolidation) Act 1978, an employee who satisfies the foregoing conditions and has been continuously employed for two years and who is dismissed by reason of redundancy may be entitled to a redundancy payment calculated by reference to his age, pay and length of service.

The Employment Protection (Consolidation) Act 1978 also enables an employee who is unfairly dismissed to complain to an Industrial Tribunal (generally within 3 months of dismissal). The onus will then be on the employer to prove that the dismissal was due to capability, conduct, redundancy, illegality or some other substantial reason justifying dismissal. The tribunal must then decide whether the employer acted reasonably in dismissing the employee. If the employer fails to prove that the dismissal was due to one or more of the above five reasons, or the tribunal decides that the employer did not act reasonably in dismissing the employee, the dismissal will be unfair, in which case the tribunal can

- (a) order re-engagement or reinstatement or
- (b) award compensation consisting of a basic and a compensatory award.

For an employee to bring himself within the unfair dismissal provisions, he must have been continuously employed for a period of two years.

All complaints of unfair dismissal are referred to a conciliation officer or the Department of Employment and a very high proportion of complaints are disposed of in this way.

FAMILY LAW
ADOPTION OF CHILDREN

In England and Wales this is now mainly governed by the Children Act 1975 and the Adoption Act 1976. A court order is necessary to legalise the adoption, which, when completed, has the effect of making the adopted child the child of the adopter as if he or she had been born to the adopter in lawful wedlock, and the original rights and duties of the natural parents are thereby cut. The adopter has full rights as to custody, education etc. and the child is treated as his for the purpose of any devolution of property on an intestacy occurring or under any disposition made after the adoption order. The application may be made to the High Court (Family Division) or to a County Court or Magistrates' Court.

Orders may be made in favour of married couples, single, widowed or divorced persons, but not of one party to a marriage alone unless the other spouse cannot be found, is physically or mentally incapable of making an application, or they are separated in circumstances likely to be permanent. A person aged under 21 cannot adopt.

The child's parents or guardians must consent unconditionally to the making of the order unless the court dispenses with the consent, which it may do if the parent cannot be found or is incapable of giving his consent, is withholding his consent unreasonably, or has neglected or ill-treated the child.

Restrictions are placed on societies which may arrange adoptions.

An adopted person aged over 18 may apply to the Registrar General for information to enable him to obtain a full certificate of his birth, but before being supplied with the information he will be informed that counselling services are available to him.

An adopter and the adopted child are within the prohibited degrees for the purposes of marriage to one another.

All Adoptions in Great Britain are registered in the Registers of Adopted Children kept by the Registrars General in London and Edinburgh respectively. Certificates from these registers including short certificates which contain no reference to adoptions, can be obtained on conditions similar to those relating to birth certificates, (See below.)

Scotland.—The Law is consolidated in the Adoption (Scotland) Act 1978 which is now fully in force.

The Law relating to fostering is consolidated in the Foster Children(s) Act 1984. A petition for adoption is presented either to the Sheriff Court or the Court of Session. As in England the petitioner(s) must be 21 or over and may be a married couple or one person who, if married, is living apart permanently from his or her spouse. The consent of the child's natural parents/guardians is required unless dispensed with, or the child is already free for adoption.

The Succession (Scotland) Act 1964, gives the adopted child the same rights of succession as a child born to the adopter in wedlock but deprives him of any such rights in the estates of his natural parents.

BIRTHS (REGISTRATION)

When a birth takes place, personal information of it must be given to the Registrar of Births and Deaths for the sub-district in which the birth occurred, and the register signed in his presence, by one of the following persons:—

1. The father or mother of the child. If they fail; 2. the occupier of the house in which the birth happened; 3. a person present at the birth; or, 4. the person having charge of the child. The duty of attending to the registration therefore rests firstly on the parents. The mother is responsible for the registration of the birth of an illegitimate child. The registration is required to be made within 42 days of the birth. Failure to do this, without reasonable cause, involves liability to a penalty of twenty pounds. The registration of a birth is free. In England or Wales, the informant, instead of attending before the registrar of the sub-district where the birth occurred, may make a declaration of the particulars required to be registered in the presence of any registrar. Under the Public Health Act 1936, notice of every birth must be given by the father, or person in attendance on the mother, to the district medical officer of health by post within 36 hours of the birth. *This is in addition to the registration already mentioned.*

A "Stillbirth" must be registered and a certificate signed by the doctor or midwife who was present at the birth or has examined the body of the child must be produced to the registrar. The certificate must, where possible, state the cause of death and the estimated duration of the pregnancy. A stillbirth may only be registered within 3 months of the birth.

The re-registration of the birth of a person legitimated by the subsequent marriage of the parents is provided for in the Births and Deaths Registration Act 1953. Special provisions apply to the registration and re-registration of births of abandoned children, and the re-registration of births of illegitimate children showing the father's name; the mother must normally be party to the latter application.

Birth at Sea: The master of a British ship must record any birth on board and send particulars to the Registrar General of Shipping.

Birth Abroad: Consular Officers are authorized to register births of British subjects occurring abroad. Certificates are procurable in due course at Registrar General's Office, London.

The registration of births occurring out of the United Kingdom among members of the armed forces, or occurring on board H.M. ships and aircraft, is provided for by the Registration of Births, Deaths and Marriages (Special Provisions) Act 1957, applicable also to Scotland.

SCOTLAND

The Registration of Births, Deaths and Marriages (Scotland) Act 1965, supersedes former Acts. Personal notification within 21 days of any birth, must be given to the registrar of (a) the registration district in which the birth took place, or (b) any registration district in which the mother of the child was ordinarily resident at the time of the birth and (c) in the case of a foundling child, dead or alive, when the place of birth is not known, the registration district in which the child, or the body, was found, within two months from the date on which the child was found. When a child is born (in or out of Scotland) in a ship, aircraft or land vehicle during a journey and the child is conveyed therein to any place in Scotland, the birth shall, unless the Registrar General otherwise directs, be deemed to have occurred at that place.

The register must be signed in the presence of the registrar by the father or mother of the child, and if they fail, by one of the following: (a) any relative of either parent who has knowledge of the birth; (b) the occupier of the premises in which the child was, to the knowledge of that occupier, born; (c) any person present at the birth; (d) any person having charge of the child. Failure without reasonable cause involves a penalty not exceeding £50.

The name of the father of a child born out of wedlock may be entered in the register of births at the time of registration if jointly requested by the mother and father, and the latter's name may also be recorded at a later date on declaration by both parents. A free abbreviated certificate of birth will be issued to the informant at the time of registration. Provision is made for the re-registration of the birth of a person made legitimate by the subsequent marriage of the parents or whose birth entry is affected by any matter respecting status or paternity, or has been so made as to imply that he is a foundling.

A still-birth must be registered and a certificate, signed by the doctor or certified midwife present at the birth or who has examined the body of the child, must be produced.

CERTIFICATES OF BIRTHS, MARRIAGES, OR DEATHS

England and Wales.—Certificates of Births, Deaths, or Marriages can be obtained at the Office of Population Censuses and Surveys, St. Catherine's House, 10, Kingsway, W.C.2 or from the Superintendent Registrar having the legal custody of the register containing the entry of which a certificate is required. Certificates of marriage can also be obtained from the incumbent of the church in which the marriage took place; or from the Nonconformist minister (or other "authorized person") where the marriage takes place in a registered building (*see, post,* under Marriage).

It is considered desirable when a certificate is required to consult the nearest Register Office who, if told the exact or approximate date and place of registration, will be able to advise on the best way of obtaining it, and any fees payable, which vary according to the type of certificate required and other factors.

English Registers.—Records of births, deaths and marriages registered in England and Wales since 1837 are kept at the Office of Population Censuses and Surveys, St. Catherine's House, 10, Kingsway, W.C.2. *The Society of Genealogists,* 37 Harrington Gardens, S.W.7, possess many records of Baptisms, Marriages and Deaths prior to 1837, including copies, in whole or in part of about 4,000 Parish Registers.

Scottish Registers of Births, Deaths, Marriages and Divorces.—Certificates of births, deaths or marriages registered from 1855 when compulsory registration

commenced in Scotland can be obtained personally at the General Register Office, New Register House, Edinburgh, or from the appropriate local Registrar, on payment of the fee of £5·00 for a full extract entry of birth, death, or marriage, and £3·00 for an abbreviated certificate of birth. An abbreviated certificate of registration of deaths is issued free of charge for National Insurance purposes in certain cases. A Register of Divorces (which includes decrees of declaration of nullity of marriage) is kept by the Registrar General at the General Register Office. The fee for an extract decree is £5.

There are also available at the General Register Office old parish registers of the date prior to 1855, which were formerly kept under the administration of the Established Church of Scotland. An extract of an entry in these registers may be obtained on payment of the appropriate fee. A fee of £7·50 per day is payable for a general search of all the Scottish registers.

Registration of Presumed Deaths. (Prescription of Particulars) (Scotland) Regulations 1978 as read with Presumption of Death (Scotland) Act 1977 prescribe the particulars to be notified by the Clerk of Court to the Registrar General after a decree or variation order has been granted in an action of declarator of death of a missing person.

DIVORCE, SEPARATION AND ANCILLARY MATTERS

Preliminary—Matrimonial Suits may be conveniently divided into two classes, viz. (1) those in which it is sought to annul the marriage because of some defect; and (2) those in which, the marriage being admitted, it is sought to end the marriage or the duties arising from it. By virtue of the Matrimonial and Family Proceedings Act 1984, all matrimonial causes are commenced in one of the divorce county courts designated by the Lord Chancellor or in the Divorce Registry in London. If the suit becomes defended, it may be transferred to the High Court.

(1) *Nullity of Marriage.*—This is now mainly governed as to England and Wales by the Matrimonial Causes Act 1973. A marriage is void *ab initio* if the parties were within the prohibited degrees of affinity, or were not male and female, or if it was bigamous or if one of the parties was under the age of consent, i.e. 16, or in the case of a polygamous marriage entered into outside England and Wales, that either party was at the time of the marriage domiciled in England and Wales. Where the *formalities* of the marriage were defective, the marriage is generally void if *both* parties knew of the defect (*e.g.,* where marriage took place otherwise than in an authorized building). But absence of the consent of parents or guardians (or of the Court or other authority, in lieu thereof) in the case of minors does not invalidate the marriage.

A marriage is voidable (i.e. a decree of nullity may be obtained but until such time the marriage remains valid) on the following grounds—(a) incapacity of either party to consummate; (b) respondent's wilful refusal to consummate; (c) that either party did not validly consent to the marriage, whether in consequence of duress, mistake, unsoundness of mind or otherwise, (d) that either party at the time of marriage was a mentally disordered person; (e) that at the time of marriage the respondent was suffering from communicable venereal disease; (f) that at the time of the marriage the respondent was pregnant by another man. In cases (e) and (f) the petitioner must have been ignorant of the grounds at the date of the marriage and in (c), (d), (e) and (f) proceedings must be instituted within 3 years of the marriage, although leave may be obtained to petition outside this period in the case of certain persons suffering from mental illness. In all cases the court shall not grant a decree where the petitioner has led the respondent to believe that he would not seek a decree and it would be unjust for it to be granted.

The 1973 Act provides that a decree of nullity in a voidable marriage only annuls the marriage from the date of the decree. The marriage remains valid until the decree, and any children of the marriage are legitimate. Children of a void marriage are illegitimate unless the father was domiciled in England and Wales at the child's birth (or father's death, if earlier) and at the time of conception (or marriage if later) both or either of the parents reasonably believed the marriage was valid.

A spouse's insistence upon the use of contraceptives will not constitute wilful refusal to consummate within (b) above, even though there has been no normal intercourse, but it may in certain circumstances constitute unreasonable behaviour for the purpose of divorce (as to which *see below*). Further it has been allowed as a *defence* to a charge of desertion against the aggrieved party.

(2) *Judicial Separation and Divorce.*—The second class of suit includes a suit for judicial separation (which does not dissolve a marriage) and a suit for divorce (which, if successful, dissolves the marriage altogether and leaves the parties at liberty to marry again). Either spouse may petition for judicial separation. It is not necessary to prove that the marriage has broken down irretrievably and the five facts listed (a) to (e) under divorce (below) are grounds for judicial separation.

Divorce.—The sole ground on which a divorce is obtained by either husband or wife is the irretrievable breakdown of the marriage. However, the court is precluded from holding that a marriage has irretrievably broken down unless it is satisfied of one or more of the following facts: (a) that the respondent has committed adultery since the marriage and the petitioner finds it intolerable to live with the respondent; (b) that the respondent has behaved in such a way that the petitioner cannot reasonably be expected to continue co-habitation; (c) desertion by the respondent for 2 years immediately before the petition; (d) 5 years separation immediately before the petition (but only 2 years where the respondent consents to the decree). Matrimonial Causes Act 1973.

The foregoing is subject to a clause prohibiting any petition for divorce (but not for judicial separation) before the lapse of one year from the date of the marriage.

Desertion may be defined as a voluntary withdrawal from cohabitation by one spouse without just cause and against the wishes of the other. Where one spouse is guilty of conduct of a serious nature which forces the other to leave, the party at fault is said to be guilty of constructive desertion.

Provisions designed to encourage reconciliation.—The 1973 Act requires the solicitor for the petitioner to certify whether he has or has not discussed the possibility of a reconciliation and whether or not he has given the petitioner the names and addresses of persons qualified to help effect a reconciliation.

A total period of less than six months during which the parties have resumed living together is to be disregarded in determining whether the prescribed period of desertion or separation has been continuous. Similar provision for effecting a reconciliation exists in relation to the other proofs of break-down, but a petitioner cannot rely on an act of adultery by the other party if they have lived together for more than six months after discovery of that act of adultery.

Obtaining the Decree Nisi. Where the suit is defended, *i.e.* the respondent opposes the dissolution or the fact/ground on which the petitioner seeks it—the petition will be heard by a Judge in open court, the parties giving oral evidence. Where the suit is undefended, the evidence will normally take the form of a sworn written statement made by the petitioner which will be sent to the Court and read over by the Registrar. If he is satisfied that he or she has proved the contents of the petition, he will simply fix a date for a Judge to pronounce the decree nisi, it being unnecessary for either party to attend. Only if the Registrar is not satisfied as above will he order that the petition be heard formally by the Judge.

Children.—Subject to exceptions, the decree nisi cannot be made absolute unless a Judge by order declares that he is satisfied with the proposed arrangements for the welfare of any child of the family who is under 16 or under 18 and receiving education or vocational training. If there is no dispute as to the children between the parties and the proposed arrangements for residence, education etc. are specific, an appointment will be made for the Judge to interview one or both parents informally and if satisfied he will make an order to that effect (this will usually be on the same day as the decree nisi is pronounced). If not the Registrar may inform the parties that it is up to them to seek a hearing before the Judge to resolve the matters in dispute.

Decree Absolute.—Every decree of divorce or nullity is in the first instance a decree nisi, and the marriage subsists until the decree is made absolute, usually six weeks after decree nisi on the petitioner's application. After the decree absolute either party is free to remarry.

Maintenance, etc.—The court has wide powers to order either party to the marriage to make financial provision (*e.g.* periodical payments, a lump sum, the transfer of property) for the other party or any child of the family, having regard to the party's means, the recipient's needs and all the important aspects of the case. These so-called 'ancillary matters' often present more difficulty than the divorce itself especially affecting the home, and may go on long after the marriage is dissolved. There is, however, nothing to stop financial matters being negotiated by the parties through their solicitors before the divorce goes through.

The court may, where the husband has wilfully neglected to provide reasonable maintenance for the wife or children, order the husband to make provision for them, *even though* no matrimonial suit is pending between the parties to the marriage, and while such an order is in force the court may also deal with custody of and access to the children.

CUSTODY OF CHILDREN ETC.

The Court may make orders in respect of access to and the custody, maintenance and education of children in connection with a suit for divorce, nullity or judicial separation (above) or with an application to the Magistrates (below) whether the suit succeeds or not. In addition, if there is no other matrimonial suit involved a parent may apply for custody under the Guardianship of Minors Acts 1971, and any person may apply to the High Court for the child to be made a ward of court.

In all cases the welfare of the child is the first and paramount consideration. The categories of child who may be covered by any particular type of proceedings differ according to the nature of those proceedings and to the nature of the particular relief sought, but it should be borne in mind that in connection with divorce, nullity and judicial separation a child which has been *treated* by the spouses as a child of the family may be included as a 'child of the family' as well as the children of the spouses themselves. This also applies to most maintenance cases in the magistrate's court—*see below*.

Under the Children Act 1975 a new procedure called "Custodianship" has been introduced, basically allowing long term foster parents to apply for custody of the foster child.

Any dispute relating to the above matters should be placed in the hands of a Solicitor without delay (see Legal Aid, etc. below) and in particular it should be borne in mind that where there is financial need (because of, *e.g.* continuing education or disability) maintenance may be ordered for children even beyond the age of majority.

SEPARATION BY AGREEMENT

Husband and wife may enter into an agreement to separate and live apart, but the agreement, to be valid, must be followed by an immediate separation. It is most desirable to consult a solicitor in every such case, who will often advise obtaining a court order by consent to reduce the burden of tax.

MAGISTRATES' CUSTODY AND MAINTENANCE ORDERS

For many years the law relating to domestic proceedings in magistrates' courts was out of line with the divorce law which was reformed in 1969. The Domestic Proceedings and Magistrates' Courts Act 1978 took effect in early 1981 and now contains the relevant law.

A husband or wife can apply to a magistrates' court for a matrimonial order on the grounds that the other spouse (a) has failed to pay reasonable maintenance for the applicant or (b) has failed to make a proper contribution towards the reasonable maintenance of a child of the family or (c) has deserted the applicant or (d) has behaved in such a way that the applicant cannot reasonably be expected to live with the respondent. If the case is proved the court can order (a) periodical payments for the applicant (b) periodical payments for a child of the family (c) a lump sum (not exceeding £500) for the benefit of the applicant and for any child of the family. In deciding what orders (if any) to make the magistrates must consider a number of guidelines which are similar to those governing financial orders on divorce. There are also special provisions relating to consent orders and separation by agreement. The court also has powers to make orders relating to the legal custody of a child of the family and these orders together with orders for child maintenance can be made even though the court makes no order for spouse maintenance. Legal custody can only be granted to one person but the court may order that the other party shall retain certain parental rights and exercise them jointly with the person who is awarded legal custody. Other provisions of the Act relate to access by grandparents, interim orders, and variation, discharge and revival of orders. An order may be enforceable even though the parties are living together, but in some cases it will cease to have effect if they continue to do so for six months. The hearing of matrimonial disputes is separate from ordinary court business, and the public are not admitted.

DOMESTIC VIOLENCE

The Domestic Violence and Matrimonial Proceedings Act 1976, the Domestic Proceedings and Magistrates' Courts Act 1978 (the former not being applicable to Scotland and the latter only to a limited extent; but see note below) and the Matrimonial

Homes Act 1983 have made it easier for one spouse who has been subjected to violence by the other to obtain an order to restrain further violence and if need be to have the other excluded from the home. Such orders can be obtained very quickly, and a person disobeying them is liable to be imprisoned for contempt of court. There are some differences of detail between the three Acts; in particular the 1976 Act also applies to unmarried couples. Such orders may also be obtained in the course of suits for divorce and judicial separation.

SCOTLAND
Divorce

Actions of divorce could formerly only be raised in the Court of Session, having jurisdiction to entertain such actions only if either of the parties to the marriage in question (a) is domiciled in Scotland on the date when the action is begun; or (b) was habitually resident in Scotland throughout the period of one year ending with that date. As from May 1, 1984, however, when the Divorce Jurisdiction, Court Fees and Legal Aid (Scotland) Act 1983 came into force, actions of divorce may also be raised in the Sheriff Courts provided the above conditions (a) and (b) are complied with, and provided either party to the marriage was resident in the Sheriffdom for a period of forty days ending with the date the action was begun, or was resident in the Sheriffdom for a period of not less than forty days ending not more than forty days before the date the action was begun.

The Scots Law of Divorce is now governed by the Divorce (Scotland) Act 1976, which for the purposes of divorce came into force on January 1, 1977. The sole ground of divorce is now irretrievable breakdown of the marriage. This can only be established in one of the following ways:

(a) The defending spouse has committed adultery since the date of the marriage. Here it is not necessary for the pursuing spouse to prove that the fact of adultery made it intolerable to live with the defending spouse.

(b) The defending spouse has behaved in such a way that the pursuing spouse cannot reasonably be expected to cohabit with him or her. It is immaterial whether or not the conduct founded upon is active or passive.

(c) The defending spouse has deserted the pursuing spouse for a continuous period of two years. There must be no question of the pursuing spouse having refused a genuine and reasonable offer to adhere. Nor is irretrievable breakdown established if cohabitation is resumed for a period of more than three months, after the two year period has expired.

(d) There has been no cohabitation at any time during a continuous period of two years immediately preceding the action between the parties to the action, and the defending spouse consents to the divorce being granted.

(e) There has been no cohabitation at any time during a continuous period of five years, as in (d) *supra*, except that on the expiry of the five year period, the consent of the defending spouse is not required.

The facts of desertion and separation are not interrupted by the parties cohabiting for a period or periods not exceeding six months. However such a period or periods of cohabitation would not be included in the calculation of the two-year or five-year periods.

Encouragement of Reconciliation: The burden of promoting a reconciliation between spouses in a divorce action in Scotland falls upon the Court by virtue of the 1976 Act. Where an action of divorce has been raised, it may be postponed by the Court to enable the parties to seek to effect a reconciliation, if the Court feels that there may be a reasonable prospect of such reconciliation. If the parties do cohabit during such postponement, no account shall be taken of such cohabitation if the action later proceeds.

Maintenance, etc.: The 1976 Act also provides that either party to a marriage can apply to the Court at any time prior to decree being granted for (a) an order for interim custody of all or some of the children of the marriage under 16 years of age (b) an order for access to all or some of the children of the marriage under 16 years of age in the custody of the other party.

The financial provisions on divorce in the 1976 Act have been superseded by the Family Law (Scotland) Act 1985 which allows either party to the marriage to apply to the court for an order for payment of a capital sum or for a periodical allowance or for an incidental order. The Act sets out principles to be applied by the Court, one of these being that the financial provisions awarded to a party who has been dependant for financial support on the other party should be given over a period of not more than three years.

The Act also defines the rights and obligations of aliment between parents and children thereby excluding aliment between grandparents and grandchildren and of children to parents and provides that a child is entitled to aliment up to the age of eighteen or to twenty five if in full time further education and for the claiming of aliment whether in connection with an action of divorce etc. or independently.

Nullity of Marriage.—A declaration of nullity of marriage may be obtained on the ground of any impediment, viz., consanguinity and affinity, subsistence of a previous marriage, non-age of one of the parties, incapacity or insanity of one of the parties, or by the absence of genuine consent. The financial provisions on divorce contained in the Family Law (Scotland) Act 1985 also apply to an action for declaration of nullity of marriage.

Procedure.—Appearance in Court at a Proof in an undefended Divorce Action has been rendered unnecessary since April, 1978. A full Proof is still necessary if the action is defended in any respect. In place of court appearance Affidavits (Statements sworn before a Notary Public) by the pursuer and any witnesses are lodged in the Court together with a Minute by Counsel craving Decree.

A new Simplified Procedure for "do-it-yourself divorce" was introduced in January 1983 for certain divorces. Thus, if the action is based on (d) or (e) above and will not be opposed, there are no children under 16 and no financial claims, then the applicant can write directly to the Court of Session, Divorce Section (SP), Parliament House, Edinburgh or the local Sheriff Court for the appropriate forms to enable him or her to proceed. The fee is £40 unless the applicant receives supplementary benefit, family income supplement or legal advice and assistance in which case there is no fee.

Separation

Under the Divorce (Scotland) Act 1976 *supra,* a decree of Judicial Separation can be obtained by proof of the same facts necessary to obtain decree of divorce—except that for the principle of irretrievable breakdown there is substituted that of grounds justifying separation. This type of action is competent in both the Court of Session and the Sheriff Court.

Custody of Children

In actions for divorce and separation, the Court has a discretion in awarding the custody of the children of the parties. The welfare of the children is the paramount consideration, and the mere fact that a spouse, by reason of his or her behaviour, brought about the breakdown of the marriage does not of itself preclude him or her from being awarded custody. The Children Act 1975 (*supra*) also applies to Scotland.

Domestic Violence

The Matrimonial Homes (Family Protection) (Scotland) Act 1981 introduces a provision where one spouse—whether or not he or she has title to the matrimonial home—can obtain an exclusion order suspending the other spouse's occupancy rights in the matrimonial home. The Court (either Court of Session or Sheriff Court) is empowered to make such an order if satisfied that it is necessary to protect the applicant or any child of the family from any conduct, actual or threatened or reasonably apprehended of the other spouse which would be injurious to the physical or mental health of the applicant or child. In making the order the Court may include a warrant for the summary ejection of the non-applicant spouse from the matrimonial home and for an interdict prohibiting him/her from entering it.

ILLEGITIMACY AND LEGITIMATION
ENGLAND AND WALES

The former provisions of the Affiliation Proceedings Act 1957, under which a man could be summoned to petty sessions on the application of the mother of an illegitimate child, or by the Supplementary Benefits Commission where benefit has been paid for the requirements of the child, and the Justices, on his being proved to be the father of the child, could make an order requiring him to pay for its maintenance and education a sum in their discretion, have been replaced by extensive provisions relating to parental rights and duties in Part II of the Family Law Reform Act 1987. *Prima facie* every child born of a married woman during a marriage is legitimate; and this presumption can only be rebutted by strong evidence. However, under the Family Law Reform Act 1969, any presumption of law as to the legitimacy (or illegitimacy) of any person may in civil proceedings be rebutted by evidence showing that it is more probable than not that the person is illegitimate (or legitimate) and in any proceedings where paternity is in question, blood tests may be ordered. If however the husband and wife are separated under an Order of the Court, a child conceived by the wife during such separation is presumed not to be the husband's child.

LEGITIMATION.—The Legitimacy Act 1976 consolidates earlier legislation dating back to January 1, 1927. Where the parents of an illegitimate person marry, or have married, whether before or after that date, the marriage, if the father is at the date thereof domiciled in England or Wales, renders that person, if living, legitimate as from Jan. 1, 1927, or from the date of the marriage, whichever last happens. Marriage legitimates a person even though the father or mother was married to a third person at the time when the illegitimate person was born. It is the duty of the parents to supply to the Registrar-General information for re-registration of the birth of a legitimate child.

Declarations of Legitimacy.—A person claiming that he, his parents, or any remoter ancestor has become legitimated, may petition the High Court or the County Court for the necessary declaration.

Rights and Duties of Legitimated Persons.—A legitimated person, his spouse or issue may take property under an intestacy occurring after the date of legitimation, or under any disposition (*e.g.*, a will) coming into operation after such date, as if he had been legitimate.

He must maintain all persons whom he would be bound to maintain had he been born legitimate, and he is entitled to the benefit of any Act of Parliament which confers rights on legitimate persons to recover damages or compensation. The Act specially provides that nothing therein contained is to render any person capable of succeeding to or transmitting a right to any dignity or title.

Property Rights of Illegitimate Children.—By the Family Law Reform Act 1969 the rights of an illegitimate child on an intestacy were broadly equated with those of a legitimate child, and in any disposition made after December 31, 1969, any reference to "children" or other relatives was, unless the contrary intention appears, to be construed as including any person who is illegitimate or who is related through another person who is illegitimate. However, these provisions of the 1969 Act have been replaced by the general provision of the Family Law Reform Act 1987 (*see* pp. 1160–1).

SCOTLAND

The Law Reform (Parent & Child) Scotland Act 1986 implements the Scottish Law Commission's Report on Illegitimacy. The act contains a general provision granting equality status to all persons whatever the marital status of their parents. The mother of an illegitimate child may raise an action of affiliation and aliment against the father, either in the Court of Session or, more usually, in the Sheriff Court. Where in any such action the Court finds that the defender is the father of the child, the Court shall, in awarding inlying expenses, or aliment, have regard to the means of the parties, and the whole circumstances of the case. The Court may, upon application by the mother or by the father of any illegitimate child, or in any action for aliment for an illegitimate child, make such order as it may think fit regarding the custody of such child and the right of access thereto of either parent, having regard to the welfare of the child and to the conduct of the parents and to the wishes as well of the mother as of the father and may on the application of either parent recall or vary such order. The obligation of the mother and of the father of an illegitimate child to provide aliment for such child shall (without prejudice to any obligation attaching at common law) endure until the child attains the age of sixteen.

By Scots Law an illegitimate child is legitimated by and on the date of the subsequent marriage of its parents and there is no objection to there having been an impediment to the marriage of the parents at the time of the child's conception—*see* the Legitimation (Scotland) Act 1968, which came into operation on June 8, 1968, on which date thousands of existing illegitimate children were regarded as legitimated. By the Registration of Births, Deaths and Marriages (Scotland) Act 1965, a child so legitimated, who has already been registered as illegitimate, may be re-registered as legitimate. The consent of the father of an illegitimate child to its adoption is not required unless he has been awarded parental rights by the court.

The Law Reform (Miscellaneous Provisions) (Scotland) Act 1968, gives an illegitimate child full rights of succession (including legitim) in the estate of both parents, while the father and mother share equally in the estate of their illegitimate child. Unless expressly excluded, a reference in a deed executed on or after November 25, 1968, to a relationship, *e.g.*, "issue" or "children" is presumed to include illegitimate children.

MARRIAGE
A.—MARRIAGE ACCORDING TO RITES OF THE CHURCH OF ENGLAND

1. MARRIAGE BY BANNS.—The Marriage Act 1949, prescribes audible publication according to the rubric, on three Sundays preceding the ceremony during morning service or, if there is no morning service on a Sunday on which the banns are to be published, during evening service. Where the parties reside in different parishes, the banns must be published in both. Under the Act, banns may be published and the marriage solemnized in the parish church, *which is the usual place of worship* of the persons to be married or either of them, although neither of such persons dwells in such parish; but this publication of banns is *in addition* to any other publication required by law and does not apply if the church or the residence of either party is in Wales. The Act provides specially for the case where one of the parties resides in Scotland and the other in England, the publication being then in the parish in England in which one party resides, and, according to the law and custom in Scotland, in the place where the other party resides. After the lapse of three months from the last time of publication, the banns become useless, and the parties must either obtain a licence (*see below*), or submit to the republication of banns.

2. MARRIAGE BY LICENCE.—Marriage licences are of two kinds:—

(i) *A Common Licence*, dispensing with the necessity for banns, granted by the Archbishops and Bishops through their Surrogates, for marriages in any church or chapel duly licensed for marriages. A Common Licence can be obtained in London by application at the Faculty Office (1 The Sanctuary, Westminster, S.W.1) and (for marriages in London) at the Bishop of London's Diocesan Registry (1 The Sanctuary, S.W.1), by one of the parties about to be married. In the country they may be obtained at the offices of the Bishop's Registrars, but licences obtained at the Bishop's Diocesan Registry only enable the parties to be married in the diocese in which they are issued; those procured at the Faculty Office are available for *all* England and Wales. No instructions, either verbal or in writing, can be received, except from one of the parties. Affidavits are prepared from the personal instructions of one of the parties about to be married, and the licence is delivered to the party upon payment of fees amounting to six pounds. *No previous notice is required and the licence is available as soon as it is issued.* Before a licence can be granted one of the parties must make an affidavit that there is no legal impediment to the intended marriage; and also that one of such parties has had his or her usual place of abode for the space of fifteen days immediately preceding the issuing of the licence within the parish or ecclesiastical district of the church in which the marriage is to be solemnized, *or* the church in which the marriage is to be solemnized is the usual place of worship of the parties or one of them. In the country there may generally be found a parochial clergyman (Surrogate) before whom the affidavit may be taken, and whose office it is to deliver the licence personally to the applicant. (In some dioceses it is necessary for the Surrogate to procure the licence from the

Bishop's Registry.) The licence continues in force for three months from its date.

(ii) *A Special Licence* granted by the Archbishop of Canterbury, under special circumstances, for marriage at any place with or without previous residence in the district, or at any time, etc.; but the reasons assigned must meet with his Grace's approval. Application must be made to the Faculty Office. Fees for licence, etc., £25.

3. MARRIAGE UNDER SUPERINTENDENT REGISTRAR'S CERTIFICATE.—A marriage may be performed in church on the Superintendent Registrar's Certificate (as to which see below) without banns, provided that the incumbent's consent is obtained. One of the parties must be resident within the ecclesiastical parish of the church in which the marriage is to take place unless the church is the usual place of worship of the parties or one of them.

MARRIAGE FEES.—The Church Commissioners settle tables of fees for all parishes. The usual fees are paid although a stranger-clergyman may be invited to perform the service.

B.—MARRIAGE UNDER SUPERINTENDENT REGISTRAR'S CERTIFICATE

The following marriages may be solemnized on the authority of a Superintendent Registrar's Certificate (either with or without a licence):—

(a) A marriage in a registered building (e.g., a nonconformist church registered for the solemnization of marriages therein).
(b) A marriage in a register office.
(c) A marriage according to the usages of the Society of Friends (commonly called Quakers).
(d) A marriage between two persons professing the Jewish religion according to the usages of the Jews.
(e) A marriage according to the rites of the Church of England (see above—in this case the marriage can only be *without* licence).

NOTICE.—Notice of the intended marriage must be given as follows:—

(i) Marriage by certificate (*without* licence)—if both parties reside in the same registration district, they must both have resided there for seven days before the notice can be given. It may then be given by either party. If the parties reside in different registration districts, notice must be given by each to the Superintendent Registrar of the district in which he or she resides, and the preliminary residential qualification of seven days must be fulfilled by each before either notice can be given.

(ii) Marriage by certificate (*with* licence)—one notice only is necessary, whether the parties live in the same or in different registration districts. Either party may give the notice, which must be given to the Superintendent Registrar of any registration district in which one of the parties has resided for the period of fifteen days immediately preceding the giving of notice, but both parties must be resident in England or Wales on the day notice is given.

The notice (in either case) must be in the prescribed form and must contain particulars as to names, marital status, occupation, residence, length of residence, and the building in which the marriage is to take place. The notice must also contain or have added at the foot thereof a solemn declaration that there is no legal impediment to the marriage, and, in the case of minors, that the consent of the person whose consent to the marriage is required by law (*see below*) has been duly given, and that the residential qualifications (mentioned above) have been complied with. A person making a false declaration renders himself or herself liable to prosecution for perjury. The notice is entered in the marriage notice book.

ISSUE OF CERTIFICATE:

(i) *Without licence.*—The notice (or an exact copy thereof) is affixed in some conspicuous place in the Superintendent Registrar's office for 21 days next after the notice was entered in the marriage notice book. After the lapse of this period the Superintendent Registrar may, provided no impediment is shown, issue his certificate for the marriage which can then take place at any time within three months from the date of the entry of the notice.

(ii) *With licence.*—The notice in this case is not affixed in the office of the Superintendent Registrar. After the lapse of one whole day (other than a Sunday, Christmas Day or Good Friday) from the date of entry of the notice, the Superintendent Registrar may, provided no impediment is shown, issue his certificate and licence for the marriage, which can then take place on any day within three months from the date of entry of the notice.

SOLEMNIZATION OF THE MARRIAGE:

(i) *In a Registered Building.*—The marriage must generally take place at a building within the district of residence of one of the parties, but if the usual place of worship of either is outside the district of his or her residence, it may take place in such usual place of worship. Further, if there is not within the district of residence of one of the parties a registered building within which marriages are solemnized according to the rites and ceremonies which the parties desire to adopt in solemnizing their marriage, it may take place in an appropriate registered building in the nearest district.

The presence of a Registrar of Marriages is not necessary at marriages at registered buildings which have adopted the provisions of section 43 of the Marriage Act 1949. This section provides for the appointment of an "authorized person" (a person, usually the minister or an official of the building, certified by the trustees or governing body as having been duly authorized for the purpose) who must be present and must register the marriage.

The marriage must be solemnized between the hours of 8 a.m. and 6 p.m., with open doors in the presence of two or more witnesses. The parties must at some time during the ceremony make the following declaration—"I do solemnly declare that I know not of any lawful impediment why I, A. B., may not be joined in matrimony to C. D." Also each of the parties must say to the other: "I call upon these persons here present to witness that I, A. B., do take thee, C. D., to be my lawful wedded wife [or husband]," *or*, if the marriage is solemnized in the presence of an authorized person without the presence of a Registrar, each party may say in lieu thereof: "I, A. B., do take thee, C. D., to be my wedded wife [or husband]."

(ii) *In a Register Office.*—The marriage may be solemnized in the office of the Superintendent Registrar to whom notice of the marriage has been given. The marriage must be solemnized between the hours of 8 a.m. and 6 p.m., with open doors in the presence of the Superintendent Registrar or a Registrar of the registration district of that Superintendent Registrar, and in the presence of two witnesses. The parties must make the following declaration: "I do solemnly declare that I know not of any lawful impediment why I, A. B., may not be joined in matrimony to C. D.," and each party must say to the other: "I call upon these persons here present to witness that I, A. B., do take thee, C. D., to be my lawful wedded wife [or husband]." No religious ceremony may take place in the Register Office,though the parties may, on production of their marriage certificate, go through a subsequent religious ceremony in any church or persuasion of which they are members.

(iii) *Other Cases.*—If both parties are members of the Society of Friends (Quakers), or if, not being in membership, they have been authorized by the Society of Friends to solemnize their marriage in accordance with its usages, they may be married in a Friends' meeting-house. The marriage must be registered by the registering officer of the Society appointed to act for the district in which the meeting house is situated. The presence of a Registrar of Marriages is not necessary.

If both parties are Jews they may marry according to their usages in a synagogue, which has a certified marriage secretary, or private dwelling-house at any hour; the building may be situated within or without the district of residence. The marriage must be registered by the secretary of the synagogue of which the man is a member. The presence of a Registrar of Marriages is not necessary.

C.—MARRIAGE UNDER REGISTRAR GENERAL'S LICENCE

The main purpose of the Marriage (Registrar General's Licence) Act 1970, which came into force on January 1, 1971, is to enable non-Anglicans to be married in unregistered premises where one of the persons to be married is seriously ill, is not expected to recover and cannot be moved to registered premises. A fee of £15 is payable to the Registrar General for the licence, though he has power to remit this in whole or in part to avoid hardship.

D.—DETAINED AND HOUSE-BOUND PERSONS

The Marriage Act 1983 (which does not extend to Scotland) enables marriages of detained persons and house-bound persons to be solemnized at their place of residence. The Act came into operation on May 1, 1984.

Miscellaneous Notes

Consanguinity and Affinity.—A marriage between persons within the prohibited degrees of consanguinity or affinity is void. Relaxations have, however, been made by various statutes which have now been replaced by the Marriage Act 1949 (see the 1st Schedule to the Act) and the Marriage (Enabling) Act 1960. It is now permitted to contract a marriage with:—

Sister, aunt or niece of a former wife (whether living or not). Former wife of brother, uncle or nephew (whether living or not).

No clergyman can be compelled to solemnize any of the foregoing marriages, but he may allow his church to be used for the purpose by another minister.

The Marriage (Prohibited Degrees of Relationship) Act 1986 makes further provision with regard to the marriage of persons related by affinity e.g. after section 1 of the Act comes into force a marriage between a man and the daughter or grand-daughter of his former wife will not be void by reason only of that relationship if both parties have attained 21 at the time of the marriage and the younger party has not at any time before attaining 18 been a child of the family in relation to the other party.

Minors.—Persons under 18 years of age are generally required to obtain the consent of certain persons (see Marriage Act 1949, section 3 and 2nd Schedule as amended by the Family Law Reform Act 1969). Where both parents are living, both must consent, where one is dead, the survivor, or, if there is a guardian appointed by the deceased parent, the guardian and the survivor. (For the position where the parents of the child were not married to each other at the time of the birth, see section 9 of the Family Law Reform Act 1987.) No consent is required in the case of an infant's second marriage. In certain exceptional cases consent may be dispensed with, *e.g.*, the insanity of a parent. If consent is refused the Court may, on application being made, consent to the marriage; application can be made for this purpose to the High Court, the County Court, or a Court of Summary Jurisdiction. The Act *prohibits* any marriage where either party is under 16 years of age.

E.—MARRIAGE IN ENGLAND OR WALES WHEN ONE PARTY LIVES IN SCOTLAND OR NORTHERN IRELAND

Notice for a marriage by a Superintendent Registrar's certificate in a register office or registered building may be given in the usual way by the party resident in England. As regards Scotland, the party there should give notice of intention to marry to the registrar; as regards Northern Ireland, the party there, after a residence of seven days, must give notice to the District Registrar of Marriages. Notice cannot be given for such marriages to take place by Certificate *with* licence of the Superintendent Registrar.

Marriage of such parties may take place in a church of the Church of England after the publication of banns, or by Ecclesiastical licence.

MARRIAGES IN SCOTLAND

According to the law of Scotland, marriage is a contract which is completed by the mutual consent of parties. The Marriage (Scotland) Act 1977, which came into force on January 1, 1978, states or restates the law in convenient form. References in this section are to that Act.

Impediments to Marriage: These are (a) nonage, *i.e.*, where either party is under the age of 16. (b) forbidden degrees of relationship (Section 2) as amended by the Marriage Prohibited Degrees of Relationship Act 1986. (c) subsisting previous marriage. (d) incapacity to understand the nature of the contract. (e) both parties of the same sex. (f) non-residence, *i.e.*, if the requirements of prior residence of one or other of the parties in Scotland have not been complied with. The Act also states the grounds on which certain marriages may be declared void but this is amended by the Law Reform (Miscellaneous Provisions) (Scotland) Act 1980 which prevents a marriage being rendered void solely due to the failure to comply with certain formalities, provided the particulars of that marriage are entered in a register of marriages by or at the behest of an appropriate registrar.

Marriages may be regular or irregular, thus:—

REGULAR MARRIAGES

A regular marriage is one which is celebrated by a Minister of Religion or authorised Registrar or other celebrant specified in the Act. The parties must submit to the District Registrar a statutory notice of intention to marry the fee for which is £6·50. The Registrar will then enter the parties' names and particulars in the Marriage Notice Book which must also show the intended date of the marriage. He must then display the notice of intention to marry in a prominent public place until the intended date, and any person claiming an interest may lodge written objections thereto with the Registrar (Section 5). The Registrar, after fourteen days of receipt of the Marriage Notice and on being satisfied that there are no legal impediments to the marriage, will issue to either or both parties a Marriage Schedule. The fourteen day period may be shortened under exceptional circumstances. The Marriage Schedule must be produced to the celebrant of the marriage. The fee for the solemnization ceremony in a Registry Office is £10. After the ceremony the marriage must be registered with the Registrar General for inclusion in the Register of Births, Deaths and Marriages, within three days. Within one month of the ceremony, the fee for an extract marriage certificate is £2; thereafter it is £5.

IRREGULAR MARRIAGES

Since the Marriage (Scotland) Act 1939 the only form of irregular marriage to be recognised by law—viz., marriage by habit and repute, remains competent under the 1977 Act. If the parties live together constantly as husband and wife and are held to be such by the general repute of the neighbourhood and among their friends and relations, then there may arise a presumption from which marriage can be inferred. Before such a marriage can be registered, however, a decree of declarator of marriage must be obtained from the Deputy Principal Clerk of the Court of Session. It is the duty of the Deputy Principal Clerk to register the decree as soon as it is granted.

JURY SERVICE

Every local or parliamentary elector between the ages of eighteen and sixty-five who has resided in the United Kingdom, Channel Islands or Isle of Man for at least five years since he attained the age of thirteen will be qualified to serve on a jury unless he is "ineligible" or "disqualified".

Ineligible persons include those who have at any time been judges, magistrates and certain senior court officials, those who within the previous ten years have been concerned with the law (such as barristers and solicitors and their clerks, court officers, coroners, police, prison and probation officers); priests of any religion and vowed members of religious communities; and certain sufferers from mental illness.

Disqualified persons are those who have at any time been sentenced by a Court in the United Kingdom, Channel Islands or Isle of Man, to a term of imprisonment of five years, or more, or a person who in the last ten years has (a) served any part of a sentence of imprisonment, youth custody or dentention; or (b) been detained in a Borstal institution, or (c) had passed on him or made in respect of him a suspended sentence of imprisonment or order for detention; or (d) had made in respect of him a community service order. A person who at any time in the last five years has been placed on probation is also disqualified.

Some others are excusable as of right. These include members and officers of the Houses of Parliament, full-time serving members of the forces (including Women's forces) and registered and practising members of the medical, dental, nursing, veterinary and pharmaceutical professions and any person who has served on a jury in the two years before he is summoned. In other cases the court may excuse a juror at its discretion (e.g., where the service would be a hardship to the juror).

If a person serves on a jury knowing himself to be disqualified or ineligible he is liable to be fined up to £400 or £100 respectively.

A juror is entitled to subsistence and travelling expenses, compensation for other expenses incurred in consequence of attendance for jury service, loss of earnings and loss of national insurance benefits, but certain maximum figures (which are revised from time to time) are laid down.

A verdict of a jury must normally be unanimous but after two hours consideration (or such longer period as the Court thinks reasonable), a majority verdict is acceptable if ten jurors agree to it (or nine if the size of the jury has been reduced to ten, e.g., by illness during the trial).

Jury trial is now very unusual in civil cases but a person charged with any but the least serious crimes is entitled to be tried by a jury. The defendant may object to any juror if he can show that that juror ought not to be on the jury (e.g., because he is ineligible or is biased against him) and may object to three jurors without giving any reason.

The Coroners' Juries Act 1983 (which does not extend to Scotland) makes new provision in relation to qualification to serve on coroners' juries.

JURY SERVICE IN SCOTLAND

It is the duty of the sheriff principal of each sheriffdom, in respect of each sheriff court district in his sheriffdom, to maintain a book, known as the "general jury book", containing the names and designations of persons within the district who are qualified and liable to serve as jurors. The book, which is compiled from information which every householder is required to provide, is kept open for the inspection by any person, upon payment of a nominal fee, at the sheriff clerk's office for the district. Part II of the Juries Act 1949 (amended by regulations following thereon and by the Law Reform (Miscellaneous Provisions) (Scotland) Act 1980) applies only to Scotland and provides, *inter alia*, for the payment of travelling expenses and subsistence allowances to jurors and for loss of earnings.

The number of a jury in a civil cause in the Court of Session is twelve and in the Sheriff Court seven. In a criminal trial the number is fifteen.

QUALIFICATIONS

Under S.1 of the Law Reform (Miscellaneous Provisions) (Scotland) Act 1980, every man or woman between the ages of 18 and 65 who is for the time being registered as a parliamentary or local government elector and who has been ordinarily resident in the United Kingdom, the Channel Islands or the Isle of Man for any period of at least five years since attaining the age of 13 years, is qualified to serve on a jury.

Ineligible persons include those who at any time within the past ten years have been judges of the supreme courts, sheriffs and certain other senior court officials, those who at any time within the past five years have been concerned with the administration of justice (such as advocates and their clerks, solicitors, court staff, police officers, prison officers, sheriff officers, procurator fiscals, and members of parole boards and children's panels), and certain sufferers from mental illness.

The same rules for disqualified persons operate in Scotland as in England. Those excusable as of right are members and officers of the Houses of Parliament, full time serving members of H.M. naval, army and air forces, registered and practising members of the medical, dental, nursing, veterinary and pharmaceutical professions, ministers of religion and other persons in holy orders, and any person who has attended for jury service in the past five years.

If a person serves on a jury knowing himself to be disqualified or ineligible, he is liable to be fined up to £1,000 or £200 respectively. Jurors failing to attend without good cause are liable to a maximum fine of £200.

LANDLORD AND TENANT
ENGLAND AND WALES

Although basically the relationship between the parties to the lease is governed by the lease itself, the position is complicated by numerous statutory provisions. The few points dealt with may show the desirability of seeking professional assistance in these matters. Important provisions include:—

(1) As to agricultural holdings—the Agricultural Holdings Act 1986. Among other things, the Act regulates the length of notice necessary to determine an agricultural tenancy, the tenant's right to remove fixtures on the land, his right to compensation for damage done by game, for improvements and for disturbance, and his right to require the consent of the Agricultural Land Tribunal to the operation of a notice to quit.

(2) As to business premises—the Landlord and Tenant Acts 1927 and 1954, and the Law of Property Act 1969, Pt. I. Part II of the 1954 Act gives security of tenure to the tenant of most business premises, and in effect he can only be ousted on one or more of the seven grounds set out in the Act. In some cases, where the landlord can resume possession, the tenant is entitled to compensation.

(3) As to dwelling houses. The complicated mass of legislation is now mainly embodied in the Rent Act 1977, which does not extend to Scotland or Northern Ireland. If the house is within the Act, a tenant has a personal right to reside there, and he may only be ousted on certain grounds.

A number of amendments to the 1977 Act have been made by the Housing Act 1980.

Tenancies with full Rent Act protection are known as regulated tenancies. The maximum rent recoverable under such a tenancy is the rent agreed between the landlord and tenant, unless a fair rent has been registered, in which case that is the maximum rent recoverable. Application for the registration of a fair rent may be made by either the landlord or tenant, to the Local Rent Officer, and appeal against his decision lies to the Rent Assessment Committee.

(4) As to dwelling houses with resident landlords. The Rent Act 1974 gave tenants of dwellings let furnished the same security of tenure as those of unfurnished dwellings unless the landlord lived in part of the house. In the latter case, and in the case of a tenancy of a dwelling granted by a resident landlord after August 13, 1974, the tenancy will

usually be outside full Rent Act protection, but may fall within the restricted contract provisions of the Rent Act 1977. In this event, the landlord or the tenant may apply to the Rent Tribunal for a reasonable rent to be registered, and once registered, this is the maximum rent recoverable.

(5) The Protection from Eviction Act 1977 provides that if any person with intent to cause the residential occupier of any premises to give up the occupation thereof does any act calculated to interfere with the peace or comfort of the residential occupier or members of his household, he shall be guilty of an offence. A further provision prevents a landlord enforcing a right to possession against a tenant (who is not protected by any security of tenure legislation) without a court order, and there are special rules in such cases relating to agricultural employees.

(6) A notice to quit *any* dwellinghouse must be given at least four weeks before it is to take effect, and must be in writing and in the prescribed statutory form.

(7) Part I of the Landlord and Tenant Act 1954, applies to most tenancies of houses for over twenty-one years at a ground rent. Where it applies, the contractual tenancy is continued until brought to an end in the manner prescribed by the Act, and in effect the landlord can only get possession on limited grounds.

Further, under the Leasehold Reform Act 1967, tenants of houses under leases for over twenty-one years at a rent less than two-thirds of the rateable value of the house are in most cases given a right to purchase the freehold or to take an extended lease for a term of fifty years, provided the tenant at the time when he seeks to exercise the right has been occupying the house as his residence for the last three years or for periods amounting to three years in the last ten years.

(8) Full Rent Act protection is available only if a house is let on a tenancy, so that if the occupier of a house has a mere licence to occupy, he does not have Rent Act protection. Further, even if he has a tenancy, he will not be Rent Act protected if the rent payable is less than two-thirds of the rateable value of the house. For these reasons, many occupants of houses owned by farmers and occupied by farm workers did not enjoy full security of tenure. The Rent (Agriculture) Act 1976 contains detailed provisions conferring security of tenure on certain agricultural workers housed by their employers and on their successors on death.

(9) Under the Landlord and Tenant Act 1985 (which does not extend to Scotland), in a lease of a dwelling-house granted after October 24, 1961, for a term of less than 7 years, there is implied a covenant by the landlord (a) to keep in repair the structure and exterior of the house and (b) to keep in repair and proper working order the installations in the house (i) for the supply of water, gas and electricity, and for sanitation, and (ii) for space heating or heating water.

(10) The Housing Act 1985 gives security of tenure to many tenants of local authorities and certain other bodies. Further, and subject to certain conditions, such tenants may have the right to purchase their houses or to take a long lease of their flats.

(11) Tenants of flats are given a number of special rights by the Landlord and Tenant Act 1987.

SCOTLAND

A Lease is a Contract, the relationship of the parties being governed by the terms thereof. As is also the case in England (see the foregoing Section) legislation has played an important part in regulating that relationship. Thus, what at Common Law was an Agreement binding only the parties to the deed, becomes in virtue of the Leases Act 1449, a contract binding the landlord's successors, as purchasers or creditors, provided the following four conditions are observed; (1) the lease, if for more than one year, must be in writing, (2) there must be a rent, (3) there must be a term of expiry, and (4) the tenant must have entered into possession.

It would be impracticable in a brief section of these Notes to enter upon a general discussion of this branch of the law and, accordingly, the plan adopted in the preceding Section of quoting a few important Statutes is followed here.

The Agricultural Holdings (Scotland) Act 1949 (amended by the Agriculture Act 1958), which is a consolidating Act applicable to Scotland, contains provisions similar to those in the English Act, alluded to in the preceding Section. It cannot here be analysed in detail.

It is of interest to note that the Small Landholders Act, 1911, provided for the setting up of the Land Court which has jurisdiction over a large proportion of agricultural and pastoral land in Scotland.

In Scotland business premises are not controlled by Statute to so great an extent as in England, but the Tenancy of Shops (Scotland) Act, 1949 gives a measure of security to tenants of shops. This Act enables the tenant of a shop who is threatened with eviction to apply to the Sheriff for a renewal of the tenancy. If the landlord has offered to sell the subjects to the tenant at an agreed price the application for a renewal of the tenancy may be dismissed. Reference should be made to Section 1 (3) of the 1949 Act for particulars of other circumstances under which the Sheriff has a discretion to dismiss an application. The Act extends to premises held by the Crown or Government Departments, either as landlord or tenant.

The Housing (Scotland) Act 1969 and the Rent (Scotland) Act 1971, as amended by the Rent Act 1974, define controlled tenancies and regulated tenancies, both furnished and unfurnished, and lay down the system by which a landlord or tenant may obtain from the Rent Officer registration of a fair rent. The Acts also give to the tenants either of furnished or unfurnished lets a substantial degree of security of tenure. There are, however, certain exceptions; thus, they do not apply to tenancies where the interest belongs to the Crown or to a Government Department or to a local authority, a development corporation of a new town or a Housing Corporation. There must be a true tenancy for the Acts to apply. They do not apply to licensees such as lodgers or persons allowed to occupy houses on a grace and favour basis or to service occupiers. The Acts define the circumstances under which a landlord may apply for increased rent as a consequence of having carried out improvements to his property and also lay down the system of phasing of such rent increases. On the death of a statutory successor to a tenancy the tenancy may pass for a second time to a member of the family or a relative who has been in residence in the house for a period of at least six months. The Acts also lay down the duties and functions of Rent Officers and Rent Assessment Committees with regard to unfurnished accommodation and of Rent Tribunals for furnished accommodation.

The Rent(s) Act 1984, consolidates in relation to Scotland, the Rent Act 1965, the Rent(s) Act 1971, the Rent Act 1974 and the provisions relating to rent and tenant's rights of the Housing(s) Act 1972, the Tenant's Rights Etc(s) Act 1980 and other enact-

ments. The Rent (Amendment) Act 1985 contains further provisions.

The Tenants Rights, Etc. (Scotland) Act 1980 as amended by Tenant's Rights Etc(s) Amendment Act 1984, contains a number of important provisions and deals mainly with the rights of public sector tenants to purchase the houses which they occupy. S. 46 converts all remaining controlled tenancies into regulated tenancies and s. 34 creates a particular type of protected tenancy known as a "short tenancy."

It also makes provisions in relation to housing rents and connected tenancies; the Act makes provision for a tenant's right to security of tenure and to a written lease. It also allows for amendment to the Housing Bill by introducing a landlord's right, in certain circumstances, to refuse to sell a house designed or adapted for occupation by the elderly to a tenant who would otherwise have the right to buy.

LEGAL AID

LEGAL AID IN CIVIL PROCEEDINGS

The Legal Aid Act 1974 (as amended) is designed to make legal aid and advice more readily available for persons of small and moderate means. The main structure of the service is contained in the Act itself and the Regulations made thereunder, administered by the Law Society.

Legal aid is available for proceedings (including matrimonial causes) in the House of Lords, Court of Appeal, High Court, County Courts, Lands Tribunal, Restrictive Practices Court, before the Commons Commissioners, and civil proceedings in Magistrates' Courts. In any event, an application for legal aid will not be approved if it appears that the applicant would gain only a trivial advantage from the proceedings. Further, proceedings wholly or partly in respect of defamation are excepted from the scheme, as are also relator actions and election petitions. It is generally not available for obtaining the decree in undefended divorce and judicial separation, although the Legal Advice and Assistance Scheme (*see* below) will be, and Legal Aid is still available to deal with property, custody disputes etc., arising in the suit.

Where a person is concerned in proceedings only in a representative, fiduciary or official capacity, his personal resources are not to be taken into account in considering eligibility for legal aid. Apart from this, eligibility in civil proceedings depends upon an applicant's "disposable income" and "disposable capital". The figures change frequently; particulars can be obtained from a solicitor, the Law Society or a Citizens' Advice Bureau. Disposable income is calculated by making deductions from gross income in respect of certain matters such as dependants, interest on loans, income tax, rates, rent and other matters for which the applicant must or reasonably may provide. Disposable capital is calculated by excluding from gross capital part of the value of the house in which the applicant resides, of furniture and household possessions; allowances are made in respect of dependants. Except in cases where the spouses are living apart, or have a contrary interest, any resources of a person's wife or husband are to be treated as that person's resources. These figures will be assessed by the Department of Health and Social Security, and will be referred to The Law Society, who will determine whether reasonable grounds exist for the grant of a civil aid certificate. Appeal from refusal of a certificate lies to an Area Committee. A person resident in England or Wales desiring legal aid should apply for a certificate to the appropriate Area Director for the area in which s/he resides; if resident elsewhere application should be made to an

Area Director in London. If a certificate is granted, the applicant may select his solicitor, and, if necessary, counsel from a panel. The costs of the assisted person's solicitor and counsel will be paid out of the legal aid fund. When, however, damages or property are recovered or preserved by the assisted person the legal aid fund has a charge over them in respect of these costs less any contribution towards costs recovered from the unsuccessful party. In matrimonial cases, maintenance is exempt, as is the first £2,500 of any property settlement. The court may order that the costs of a successful unassisted party shall be paid out of the legal aid fund.

In an urgent case, say of domestic violence, or to restrain the kidnapping abroad of a child, Legal Aid may be granted without the applicant's means being fully investigated beforehand. If on a full examination later he is found financially ineligible he is liable to pay all the costs incurred on his behalf, if he does not attend for an examination.

LEGAL ADVICE AND ASSISTANCE

The Scheme is governed by the Legal Aid Act 1974 (as amended).

Under this legal advice and assistance scheme a client may obtain such advice or assistance as is normally provided by a solicitor and if necessary the advice of a barrister may be obtained, but, with the exception of domestic proceedings in a magistrates' court and certain other proceedings (see below) the scheme does not extend to taking any step in any proceedings before any court or tribunal. Where legal aid is available for civil proceedings (see above) or in criminal cases (see below) the scheme covers work done in making application for such legal aid.

A person (other than one receiving advice and assistance at a police station or from a Duty Solicitor) is eligible for advice or assistance under the scheme provided his disposable capital and his disposable income do not exceed limits in force from time to time or if he receives Supplementary Benefit or Family Income Supplement. For a married man or person with children or other dependants deductions will be made from gross income and capital and allowances are made in respect of income tax, National Insurance contributions, etc. It is intended that the financial limits shall approximate to those applying for legal aid in civil proceedings (see above). Except when they are separated or have conflicting interests the means of husband and wife will be aggregated for the purpose of determining financial eligibility. As in the case of Legal Aid, depending on his means, a person may be called upon to pay a contribution towards the costs of work done for him. Particulars may again be obtained from a solicitor, the Law Society or a Citizens' Advice Bureau.

Solicitor's costs and expenses, which should not together exceed £50 (V.A.T. exclusive), or £90 in the case of divorce etc. (not applicable to Scotland, where the £50 limit still applies) without leave of the Area Legal Aid Committee, will be paid out of the client's contribution and any monies recovered in respect of costs or damages from another party (although this may be waived by leave of the Area Committee in cases of hardship) and the balance will be paid by the Legal Aid Fund.

The Act also extends the scheme to cover the costs of a solicitor who is present within the precincts of a magistrates' court or county court and is requested by the court to advise or represent a person who is in need of help.

In April 1980 the Scheme was enlarged to cover the cost of representation in domestic proceedings in a magistrates' court. It has since been extended to cover the representation of parents and children in proceedings under the Child Care Act, 1980, and of patients before Mental Health Review Tribunals. Subject to financial eligibility limits, application is made to the area or local committee for "approval of assistance by way of representation" which will replace legal aid for such proceedings. However the £50 costs limit referred to above will not apply. An applicant who is outside the financial limits but eligible for legal aid will still have to apply for a legal aid certificate as before. Free advice and assistance, and assistance by way of representation from a Duty Solicitor is also available in limited circumstances to persons appearing before a magistrates' court charged with a criminal offence.

In January, 1986 the scheme was further extended to provide free advice and assistance to all suspects detained at a police station whether arrested or merely "helping police with their enquiries", and free representation for all arrested persons who are the subject of an application for a warrant of further detention under the Police and Criminal Evidence Act, 1984. Such persons may instruct a solicitor of their choice or take advantage of the Duty Solicitor Scheme which has now been extended to cover police stations.

LEGAL AID IN CRIMINAL CASES

The Legal Aid Act 1974 Part II and Legal Aid Act 1982 provide for legal aid in criminal proceedings, and for children and parents in care proceedings and related applications under the Children and Young Persons Act, 1969. A criminal court (*e.g.* magistrates' court, Crown Court) has power to order legal aid to be granted where it appears desirable to do so in the interests of justice. The court shall make an order in certain cases, *e.g.*, where a person is committed for trial on a charge of murder. However, the court may not make an order unless it appears to the court that the person's disposable income and capital are such that he requires assistance in meeting the costs of the particular proceedings in question. Application should be made to the appropriate court where proceedings are to take place.

An applicant shall be required to make a contribution towards the costs of his case if his disposable income and capital exceed certain prescribed limits. Persons in receipt of Supplementary Benefit are automatically exempt. In order to ascertain the amount of this contribution he will have to produce written evidence of his means. Investigation of means will be carried out by the court. Any person who falls into arrears with the payment of contribution is liable to have the order revoked.

Any practising barrister or solicitor may act for a legally aided person in criminal proceedings unless excluded by reason of misconduct. In general where legal aid is given it will normally include representation by both counsel and solicitor. However, in connection with magistrates' courts, representation will be by solicitor alone unless it is a serious offence.

Where any doubt arises about the grant of a legal aid order that doubt is to be resolved in favour of the applicant. The court also has power to amend or revoke a legal aid order. Legal aid may also be granted in connection with appellate proceedings, *e.g.*, on appeal to the Criminal Division of the Court of Appeal under the Criminal Appeal Act 1968.

SCOTLAND
CIVIL PROCEEDINGS

Legal Aid in Scotland is now governed by the Legal Aid (Scotland) Act 1986 and the Regulations made thereunder. This Act established the Scottish Legal Board which has the general function of securing that Legal Aid and Legal Advice and Assistance are available in accordance with the Act, and of administering the Scottish Legal Aid Fund. The Board comprises not less than eleven and not more than fifteen members with one member appointed as Chairman. The members are appointed by the Secretary of State for Scotland. Civil Legal Aid is available in relation to civil proceedings in the House of Lords in Appeals from the Court of Session, in the Court of Session, the Lands Valuation Appeal Court, the Scottish Land Court, the Sheriff Court, the Lands Tribunal for Scotland, the Employment Appeals Tribunal and to the European Court of Human Rights. Civil Legal Aid is granted if on application to the Board, the Board is satisfied that there is *probalilis causa litigendi* and it is reasonable on the particular circumstances of the case that Legal Aid should be awarded. As in England eligibility and any contribution required from an applicant is dependent on their disposable income and disposable capital. Information on current financial limits can be obtained from the Scottish Legal Board (44 Drumsheugh Gardens, Edinburgh), a solicitor, or a Citizens Advice Bureau. A person believing himself to be eligible may instruct any solicitor of his own choice. If a court action is not immediately contemplated application will be made for Legal Advice & Assistance which operates in a similar manner to the Legal Advice Assistance Scheme in England. If proceedings are contemplated then a formal application for Civil Legal Aid will be made and there are special provisions for emergency applications in appropriate circumstances.

If proceedings are decided against a person in receipt of Legal Aid the court shall determine a reasonable sum in the circumstances as an appropriate award of expenses to be made against the applicant. The court may only make an award out of the fund if proceedings were instituted by the legally assisted person and the court is satisfied that the resisting party would suffer severe financial hardship unless the order is made and the court is satisfied that in all the circumstances it is just and equitable that an award be made. If monies are recovered by a legally assisted person these fall to be paid to the Scottish Legal Board who will then determine the appropriate level of contribution from the sums received which should be made to the expenses of their litigation.

CRIMINAL PROCEEDINGS

Legal Aid in criminal causes is also administered under the Legal Aid (Scotland) Act 1986. The procedure for application for Criminal Legal Aid is dependent on the circumstances of each case. In serious cases heard before a jury under solemn procedure it is for the court to decide whether to grant Legal Aid. Applications for Legal Aid must normally be made on the prescribed forms to the clerk of court in question and an applicant is required to provide therein particulars of the merits of his case and his financial circumstances. In summary criminal causes however the procedure is dependent on whether the applicant is in custody: if so then he is entitled to automatic free Legal Aid from the Duty Solicitor. If the applicant is not in custody and wishes to plead guilty he is ineligible for full Legal Aid but may be entitled to Criminal Legal Advice & Assistance and in some circumstances may qualify for Assistance by way of Representation which will enable his solicitor to appear and make a plea in mitigation on his behalf. If he is not in custody and wishes to plead not guilty he can apply to the Scottish Legal Aid Board for Criminal Legal Aid on the prescribed form not later than fourteen days after the first court appearance at which he made the plea and Legal Aid shall only be granted if the Board is satisfied that the accused cannot meet the expenses of the case without undue hardship and that it is in the interest of justice as defined by the 1986 Act.

TOWN AND COUNTRY PLANNING

The Town and Country Planning Act 1971 (consolidating earlier Acts) contains very far-reaching provisions affecting the liberty of an owner of land to develop and use it as he will. A person has generally to get planning permission before carrying out any development on his land from the Local Planning Authority.

What is Development:—
(a) Carrying out of building, engineering, mining or other operations.

(b) Making a material change in use.

It is expressly provided that if one dwelling-house is converted into two or more dwelling-houses, this involves a material change in use.

Examples of what is not deemed Development:—

(a) Maintaining, improving or altering the interior of a building (except works for making good war damage), provided there is no material change to the exterior, with the exception that since December 5, 1968, any expansion, or works begun for the expansion, of a building below ground level constitutes development.

(b) Change of use of property within the curtilage of a dwelling-house for a purpose incidental to the use of the dwelling-house as such. (It will, however, be development if building operations are carried out.)

Application can be made to the Local Planning Authority to determine whether or not an operation or change of use constitutes development.

Planning Permission.—Application for such permission is not always necessary, as the Secretary of State may make Development Orders giving general permission for a specified type of development. Thus a General Development Order of 1987 specifies a number of types of development for which no permission is usually required, *e.g.*, enlargement of a dwelling-house (including erection of a garage), so long as the cubic content of the original dwelling (external measurement) is not exceeded by more than 70 cubic metres or 15 per cent, whichever is greater, subject to a maximum of 115 cubic metres. However, in the case of a terraced house, the limitation is 50 cubic metres or 10 per cent, whichever is the greater, subject to the maximum of 115 cubic metres.

Appeal against refusal of permission lies to the Secretary of State and from his decision, in limited circumstances, to the High Court. If the result of the appeal is unsatisfactory, an applicant may in certain circumstances require the Council to purchase the land.

SCOTLAND

The Town and Country Planning (Scotland) Act 1972 consolidates the statute law relating to town and country planning in Scotland.

The Act contains provisions for an appeal to the Secretary of State against the refusal of planning permission. The decision of the Secretary of State is final.

Sections 87 and 92 of the Local Government, Planning and Land Act 1980 contain important provisions on planning applications and, unlike certain parts of this Act, extend to Scotland.

VOTERS' QUALIFICATIONS

The franchise is governed by the Representation of the People Acts 1983 and 1985. Those entitled to vote as electors at a parliamentary election in any constituency are all persons resident there on the qualifying date who, at that date and on the date of the poll are Commonwealth citizens or citizens of the Republic of Ireland and not subject to any legal incapacity to vote and who on the date of the poll are at least 18 years of age. However, a person is not entitled to vote at a parliamentary election in any constituency in Northern Ireland unless he was resident in Northern Ireland during the whole of the period of three months ending on the qualifying date for that election. Also, no person can use his vote unless he is on the Register of electors kept for the constituency. A person who is of voting age on the date of the poll at a parliamentary or local government election is entitled to vote, whether or not he is of voting age on the qualifying date. Accordingly, a qualified person will be entitled to be registered in a register of parliamentary electors or a register of local government electors if he will attain voting age within twelve months from the date on which the register is required to be published. Subject to certain conditions, the 1985 Act extends the franchise to British citizens overseas.

The Register is prepared by the Registration Officer in each constituency in Great Britain. It is the registration officer's duty to have a house to house or other official inquiry made as to the persons entitled to be registered and to publish preliminary electors lists showing the persons appearing to him to be entitled to be registered. Any person whose name is omitted may claim registration, and any person on the list may object to the inclusion therein of other persons' names: the registration officer determines the claims and objections.

Voters at a parliamentary or local government election must generally vote in person at the allotted polling station, except for those entitled to vote by post or at any polling station, and those for whom proxies have been appointed. Certain people can apply to be treated as absent voters at a parliamentary election and thus able to vote by post—among these are registered service voters, those unable by reason of blindness or other physical incapacity to go in person to the polling station, and those unable to go in person from their qualifying address to the polling station without making a journey by air or sea.

Unless entitled to vote by post, a person registered as a service voter may vote by proxy at a parliamentary or local government election. A proxy may also be appointed by a registered elector, where the registration officer is satisfied that the applicant's circumstances on the date of the poll are likely to be such that he cannot reasonably be expected to vote in person at the polling station allotted to him. The appointment of a person to vote as proxy at parliamentary elections has effect also for the purposes of local government elections.

THE PROBATION SERVICE

The Probation Service is employed in each county by an independent committee of justices and it provides a professional social work agency in the courts, with responsibility for a wide range of duties which include: (a) a social enquiry service for the criminal courts; (b) provision of a range of non-custodial measures involving the supervision of offenders in the community; (c) supervisory aftercare for offenders released from custody, together with social work in penal establishments and help for the families of those serving sentences; (d) an enquiry, conciliation and supervision service in the divorce and domestic courts; (e) support for and promotion of preventive and containment measures in the community designed to reduce the level of crime and domestic breakdown. It is a direct grant service funded 80 per cent from the Home Office and 20 per cent from the relevant local authority.

Its national representative bodies are: (i) The Central Council of Probation Committees, 38 Belgrave Square, London SW1X 8NT—Tel: 01-245-9364 (*Secretary*, I. Miles); (ii) The Association of Chief Officers of Probation, 20-30 Lawefield Lane, Wakefield WF2 8SP—Tel: 0924 361156 (*Secretary*, W. R. Weston); (iii) The National Association of Probation Officers, 3/4 Chivalry Road, Battersea, London SW11 1HT—Tel: 01-223-4887 (*Gen. Secretary*, W. Beaumont).

INCOME TAX 1987-88

INTRODUCTION

Income tax is charged on the total income of individuals for a year of assessment commencing on April 6 and ending on the following April 5. The rates of tax and the calculation of liability will frequently differ as between one year of assessment and another. The following information is confined to the year of assessment 1987-88, ending on April 5, 1988.

Liability is determined by establishing the taxable income for a year of assessment. The income may be reduced by an individual's personal allowances and other reliefs. The first slice of taxable income remaining is assessable to income tax at the basic rate of 27 per cent. The rates of tax progressively increase and eventually reach 60 per cent on the slice of income exceeding £41,200. The full rates of income tax chargeable are as follows:

£	%
1–17,900	27
17,901–20,400	40
20,401–25,400	45
25,401–33,300	50
33,301–41,200	55
over 41,200	60

These rates apply to the assessment of both earned and investment income. Indeed there is now little distinction between the two classes, although the receipt of earned income may produce an entitlement to some allowances not available against investment income.

The tables on the following pages show the income tax payable for 1987-88 by an individual on the amount of income specified, after deducting the personal allowance and age allowance. Elderly persons over the age of eighty years may suffer less tax. The taxpayer may also be entitled to further reliefs and allowances which reduce the tax payable below the amount shown in the tables.

The special rules for taxing income derived by a husband and wife are examined later.

Trustees administering settled property are chargeable to income tax at the basic rate of 27 per cent. Where the trustees retain discretionary powers, or income is accumulated, there will also be liability to the additional rate of 18 per cent. Companies residing in the United Kingdom are not liable to income tax but suffer corporation tax on income, profits and gains.

The charge to income tax broadly arises on all taxable income accruing from sources in the United Kingdom. Individuals who are resident in this territory may also become liable on income arising overseas. An individual is resident in the United Kingdom if he or she normally resides here. Persons not normally residing in the United Kingdom may become resident if they visit this territory for periods which average three months or more throughout a period of years, or are present for at least 183 days in a particular year. The existence of a place of abode in the United Kingdom may be sufficient to indicate residence if visits of any duration are made during the year of assessment.

Income arising overseas will often incur liability to foreign taxation. If that income is also chargeable to United Kingdom income tax, excessive liability may well arise. The United Kingdom has concluded Double Taxation Agreements with many overseas territories which ensure that the same slice of income is not doubly assessed. In the absence of such an agreement, foreign tax suffered can usually be relieved when calculating liability to United Kingdom income tax.

INCOME TAXABLE

Income tax is assessed and collected under several Schedules. Each Schedule determines the extent of liability and establishes the amount to be included in taxable income. In some instances the actual income arising in a year of assessment will be charged to income tax for that year. A different basis of assessment may arise for income taxable under Cases I to V of Schedule D. Frequently, income assessable under these Cases will be that arising in a previous year or period but there are special rules where a new source is acquired or an existing source discontinued. The contents of the various Schedules are shown below:

Schedule A.—Tax is charged on annual profits from the ownership or occupation of land in the United Kingdom. This will include rents, ground rents and other income arising from land. Expenditure incurred by the landlord on maintenance, repairs, insurance and management can be subtracted from the annual profits. This Schedule does not include profits from farming, market gardening or woodlands, nor does it extend to mineral rents and royalties. Premiums arising on the grant of a lease for a period not exceeding fifty years are assessed to income tax. However, the amount of the taxable premium may be reduced by 2 per cent for each complete year, after the first year, of the leasing period. Income from furnished lettings is assessable under Case VI of Schedule D, unless an option is exercised for such income to be assessed under Schedule A. Where income arises from furnished holiday lettings additional expenditure may be included in calculating income chargeable to tax. Income of this nature is treated as earned income.

Schedule B.—Assessment is confined to woodlands in the United Kingdom managed on a commercial basis and with a view to the realisation of profits. The assessment will be based on one-third of the annual value. The occupier of woodlands retains the option of being assessed under Case I of Schedule D on profits arising from management.

Schedule C.—This Schedule is confined to interest or dividends on Government or public authority funds and certain payments made out of the public revenues of overseas countries.

Schedule D.—This Schedule is divided into six Cases as follows:

Cases I and II.—Profits arising from trades, professions and vocations, including farming and market gardening. Capital expenditure incurred on assets used for business purposes will often produce an entitlement to capital allowances which reduce the profits chargeable. These profits may also be reduced following the submission of claims for loss relief and other matters.

Case III.—Interest on Government Stocks not taxed at source (e.g. War Loan and British Savings Bonds), interest on National Savings Bank deposits and discounts. Interest up to £70 on ordinary National Savings Bank deposits is exempt from income tax. The exemption applies to both husband and wife separately. Interest on National Savings Bank Special Investment Accounts is not exempt.

Cases IV and V.—Interest from overseas securities, rents, dividends and all other income accruing

. (1) SINGLE PERSONS

Income	Persons under 65		Persons 65 or over*	
	Income Tax	Average Rate	Income Tax	Average Rate
£	£	per cent	£	per cent
2,500	20	0·8	—	—
3,000	155	5·2	11	0·4
4,000	425	10·6	281	7·0
5,000	695	13·9	551	11·0
6,000	965	16·1	821	13·7
7,000	1,235	17·6	1,091	15·6
8,000	1,505	18·8	1,361	17·0
9,000	1,775	19·7	1,631	18·1
10,000	2,045	20·4	1,937	19·4
12,000	2,585	21·5	2,585	21·5
14,000	3,125	22·3	3,125	22·3
16,000	3,665	22·9	3,665	22·9
18,000	4,205	23·4	4,205	23·4
20,000	4,745	23·7	4,745	23·7
25,000	6,812	27·2	6,812	27·2
30,000	9,170	30·6	9,170	30·6
50,000	20,203	40·4	20,203	40·4
100,000	50,203	50·2	50,203	50·2

* Persons aged 80 or over suffer rather less tax on income falling below £12,000.

outside the United Kingdom. Assessment is based on the full amount arising, whether remitted to the United Kingdom or retained overseas, but individuals who are either not domiciled in the United Kingdom or who are ordinarily resident overseas may apply the remittance basis. Overseas pensions are taxable but the amount arising may be reduced by 10 per cent for assessment purposes.

Case VI.—Sundry profits and annual receipts not assessed under any other Case or Schedule. These may include insurance commissions, post-cessation receipts and numerous other receipts specifically charged under Case VI.

Schedule E.—All emoluments from an office or employment are assessable under this Schedule. There are three Cases as follows:

Case I.—This applies to all emoluments of an individual resident and ordinarily resident in the United Kingdom.

Case II.—Of application where the individual is not resident or not ordinarily resident and extends to emoluments for duties undertaken in the United Kingdom.

Case III.—Applies in rare situations to other emoluments remitted to the United Kingdom.

N.B. A part, not exceeding one half, of earnings received from an approved profit-related pay scheme is exempt from income tax.

Special rules apply to emoluments received by non-domiciled employees employed by non-resident employers. In general, where the duties are performed in the United Kingdom such earnings will be assessable subject to a percentage deduction. This deduction, which is gradually being withdrawn, applies at different rates which are governed by personal circumstances.

Although foreign earnings may be assessable under Case I where the employee is resident and ordinarily resident in the United Kingdom, a deduction of 100 per cent may be available for 1987–88. This deduction can be obtained where duties are performed overseas for a continuous period reaching or exceeding 365

days and is confined to earnings from the overseas activity.

The emoluments assessable under Schedule E include all salaries, wages, director's fees and other money sums. In addition, there are a wide range of benefits which must also be added to taxable emoluments. These include the provision of living accommodation on advantageous terms and advantages arising from the use of vouchers.

Further taxable benefits accrue to directors and employees receiving emoluments of £8,500 or more in the year of assessment. These benefits include the reimbursement of expenses, the availability of motor cars for private motoring, the provision of petrol or other fuel for private motoring, the provision of interest free loans, and other benefits provided at the employer's expense.

In arriving at the amount to be assessed under Schedule E all expenses incurred wholly, exclusively and necessarily in the performance of the duties may be deducted. This includes fees and subscriptions paid to certain professional bodies and learned societies.

Compensation for loss of office and other sums received on the termination of an office or employment are assessable to tax. However, the first £25,000 may be excluded and only the balance remains chargeable, subject to some reduction in the amount of tax payable.

Schedule F.—This Schedule is concerned with company dividends and distributions. A United Kingdom resident company paying a dividend or distribution must account to the Inland Revenue for advance corporation tax on the amount paid at the rate of twenty-seven seventy-thirds. A shareholder residing in the United Kingdom receives the dividend or distribution, together with a tax credit equal to the amount of advance corporation tax. The dividend or distribution is regarded as having suffered income tax, equal to the tax credit, at the basic rate, and where the shareholder is not liable, or fully liable, at this rate a repayment can be obtained. Individuals liable at rates in excess of the basic rate will incur further liability. Some payments made by an un-

(2) MARRIED COUPLES

Income	Couples under 65		Couples 65 or over*	
	Income Tax	Average Rate	Income Tax	Average Rate
£	£	per cent	£	per cent
4,000	55	1·4	—	—
5,000	325	6·5	88	1·8
6,000	595	9·9	358	6·0
7,000	865	12·4	628	9·0
8,000	1,135	14·2	898	11·2
9,000	1,405	15·6	1,168	13·0
10,000	1,675	16·8	1,474	14·7
12,000	2,215	18·5	2,215	18·5
14,000	2,755	19·7	2,755	19·7
16,000	3,295	20·6	3,295	20·6
18,000	3,835	21·3	3,835	21·3
20,000	4,375	21·9	4,375	21·9
25,000	6,195	24·8	6,195	24·8
30,000	8,485	28·3	8,485	28·3
50,000	19,381	38·8	19,381	38·8
100,000	49,381	49·4	49,381	49·4

* Persons aged 80 or over suffer rather less tax on income falling below £12,000.

quoted trading company to redeem or purchase its own shares will not be treated as distributions.

Building society interest and bank interest. A special composite rate tax scheme applies to payments of building society interest and most payments of bank interest made to individuals. Interest of this nature incurs no liability to basic rate income tax in the hands of the depositor, nor can tax be recovered by a depositor not liable to income tax. The actual interest received must be "grossed up" at the rate of twenty-seven seventy-thirds to establish the amount of total income received by a depositor liable at rates in excess of the basic rate.

INCOME NOT TAXABLE

This includes interest on National Savings Certificates, most scholarship income, bounty payments to members of the armed services and annuities payable to the holders of certain awards. Dividend income arising from investments in personal equity plans may be exempt from tax, if the investment is not withdrawn for a complete calendar year.

SOCIAL SECURITY BENEFITS

Many Social Security benefits are not liable to income tax. These include the maternity allowance, long term sickness benefit, child benefit, war widow's pension, death grant, mobility allowance and numerous others. Among the limited range of benefits which are taxable is the retirement pension, widow's allowance, widowed mother's allowance, and most unemployment benefit and supplementary benefit paid to the unemployed. Short-term sickness benefit payable by an employer is also chargeable to tax.

PAY AS YOU EARN

The Pay As You Earn system is not an independent form of taxation but has been designed to collect income tax by deduction from most emoluments. When paying emoluments to employees an employer is usually required to deduct income tax and account for that tax to the Inland Revenue. In many cases this deduction procedure will fully exhaust the individual's liability to income tax, unless there is other income.

PERSONAL ALLOWANCES

The following personal allowances are available to individuals and may be subtracted when calculating income chargeable to income tax:

Personal Allowance.—A single person is entitled to a personal allowance of £2,425. This is increased to £3,795 for a married man whose wife is living with or maintained by him. For the year of marriage the increased allowance will only be available if marriage occurs before May 6. The increased allowance is then reduced by one-twelfth of £1,370 (£3,795 less £2,425) for each complete month preceding the marriage date.

The increased married man's allowance may be withdrawn where a wife's earning election is made (see "Husband and Wife" below).

Age Allowance.—A single person who has attained the age of 65 years and is in receipt of income not exceeding £9,800 receives an age allowance of £2,960. This is increased to £4,675 where a married man, or his wife living with him, has reached 65. If the income exceeds £9,800 the allowance is reduced by two-thirds of the amount of the excess. This reduction continues until the age allowance is reduced to the amount of the normal personal allowance. The age allowance is increased to £3,070, or £4,845 for a married couple, where the taxpayer or his wife has reached the age of 80 years. These increased amounts are also subject to restriction where income exceeds £9,800. Age allowance is in substitution for, and not in addition to, the personal allowance.

Wife's Earned Income Allowance.—An allowance equal to the wife's earned income, but limited to a maximum of £2,425, may be obtained. This allowance is not granted in the year of marriage or where a wife's earnings election is made (see "Husband and Wife" below).

Additional Personal Allowance.—An allowance of £1,370 is available to a single person who has a qualifying child resident with him or her in the year of assessment. The allowance can also be obtained by a married man whose wife is totally incapacitated by physical or mental infirmity throughout the year and a child is similarly resident.

A "qualifying child" for 1987–88 must be born during the year, be under the age of 16 years at the commencement of the year, or over the age of 16 years at the commencement of the year and either receiving full-time instruction at a university, college, school or other educational establishment or undergoing training for a trade, profession or vocation throughout a minimum period of two years. It is also necessary that the child is the claimant's own or, if not such a child, was either born during 1987–88 or under the age of 18 years at the commencement of the year and maintained by the claimant at his or her own expense during the whole of the succeeding twelve month period.

Housekeeper Allowance.—An allowance of £100 is available to a widow or widower having a relative residing to act as a housekeeper. This allowance may also be obtained where a housekeeper is employed for a similar purpose.

Son's or Daughter's Services Allowance.—A person who, by reason of his or his wife's old age or infirmity, has to retain the services of a son or daughter is entitled to an allowance of £55.

Dependent Relative Allowance.—The maximum deduction for each dependent relative is normally £100 but an increased allowance of £145 may be claimed where the claimant is a woman (other than a married woman living with her husband). The allowance is reduced by £1 for every £1 by which the relative's own taxable income exceeds the basic Social Security Retirement Pension. The relative must be incapacitated by old age or infirmity from maintaining himself or herself, except in the case of the claimant's, or the claimant's wife's, mother who may be widowed, living apart from her husband or divorced. Additionally, the relative must be maintained by the claimant. If more than one person provides support to the dependent relative the allowance must be apportioned between them.

Blind Person's Allowance.—An allowance of £540 is available to a single person if at any time during the year ending on April 5, 1988, that person was registered as blind on a register maintained by a local authority. The allowance will also be available to a married man if either he or his wife living with him is similarly registered. An increased allowance of £1,080 will be available if both husband and wife are registered blind persons.

Widow's Bereavement Allowance.—For the year of assessment in which a husband dies his surviving widow may obtain a widow's bereavement allowance of £1,370. It is a necessary requirement that the parties were living together immediately before death. A similar allowance will be available in the year following death, unless the widow remarried in the year of death. The special widow's bereavement allowance is available only for the year of death and the following year. It cannot be obtained in subsequent years.

Life Assurance Relief.—Life assurance deduction relief is limited to premiums paid on policies made before March 14, 1984. No relief is available for policies issued after this date. Where the terms of a policy made before March 14, 1984 are subsequently varied or extended to produce increased benefits, future premiums paid may no longer qualify for relief.

When paying premiums under a qualifying policy made before March 14, 1984 the payer will deduct and retain income tax at the rate of 15 per cent. The ability to retain deductions made in this manner is not affected by the payer's liability to income tax on taxable income. No restriction to the deduction procedure arises if aggregate premiums paid during a year of assessment do not exceed £1,500 (calculated before deducting tax). Should premiums exceed this amount, relief will be confined to £1,500 or one-sixth of total income, whichever is the greater. Where sums deducted exceed the maximum limit, the excess must be accounted for to the Inland Revenue.

OTHER DEDUCTIONS

In addition to personal allowances, which reduce taxable income, other eligible deductions may be available to an individual. These include payments of interest.

In some instances interest paid by a business proprietor may be relieved when calculating profits chargeable to income tax under Case I or Case II of Schedule D. Many private individuals cannot obtain relief in this manner and must satisfy stringent requirements before relief will be forthcoming. In general terms, before interest can qualify for relief it must be annual, as opposed to short, interest or paid to a bank, stockbroker or discount house. Relief will not be available to the extent that interest exceeds a reasonable commercial rate and no relief will be forthcoming for interest on an overdraft.

For 1987–88 relief will be available on the following payments:

(i) Interest on a loan to purchase, develop or improve an interest in land owned by the individual and used as his only or main residence or similarly used by a dependent relative or a former or separated spouse, "Land" includes large houseboats and also caravans used for a similar purpose. If the loan or aggregate of several loans, exceeds £30,000 relief is restricted to interest on that amount. Relief may also be forthcoming for interest on a loan used to acquire some other property, perhaps to be used as the only or main residence on retirement, by an individual who is compelled to occupy property by reason of his or her work.

(ii) Interest on a loan to purchase or improve an interest in land which is let or available for letting at a commercial rent. This interest is only capable of being deducted from rental income.

(iii) Interest on a loan made to acquire an interest in a close company or in a partnership.

(iv) Interest on a loan to a member of a partnership to acquire machinery or plant for use in the partnership business.

(v) Interest on a loan to an employed person to acquire machinery or plant for the purposes of his employment.

(vi) Interest on a loan made for the purpose of contributing capital to an industrial co-operative.

(vii) Interest on a loan applied for investment in an employee-controlled company.

(viii) Interest on a loan made to elderly persons for the purchase of an annuity where the loan is secured on land. If the loan exceeds £30,000 relief is limited to interest on this amount.

(ix) Interest on a loan to personal representatives for the payment of capital transfer tax or inheritance tax.

Relief for many payments of mortgage interest is obtained through a special scheme known as MIRAS (mortgage interest relief at source). This applies to interest paid to a building society, bank, insurance company and certain other persons. When making payments of this nature the payer will deduct and retain income tax at the basic rate. This will provide the payer with full relief at the basic rate and no other relief will be necessary, unless the payer is liable at rates in excess of the basic rate. Qualifying payments of interest outside the MIRAS scheme continue to produce relief by deduction from income chargeable to income tax.

Many individuals pay contributions to approved pension schemes. The amount of their contributions may be deducted when establishing emoluments assessable under Schedule E.

Self-employed individuals and those who are not in pensionable employment may pay premiums on qualifying retirement annuity policies. The amount of these premiums may usually be relieved in calculating taxable income but limitations are placed on the maximum amount available for relief. Although existing policies continue, no new retirement annuity arrangements may be entered into after July 1, 1988. The withdrawal of these arrangements is explained by the introduction of wide-ranging personal pension schemes. Premiums payable under these schemes may be deducted from earned income, subject to maximum limits.

Subject to a maximum of £40,000 in any one year the cost of subscribing for shares in an unquoted company may qualify as a deduction from taxable income under the Business Expansion Scheme. Many requirements must be satisfied before this relief can be obtained.

HUSBAND AND WIFE

It is a general rule that the income of a married woman living with her husband must be aggregated with his income for the purpose of charging income tax. Aggregation does not, however, apply for the year of assessment in which the parties marry. For that year the husband will receive the personal allowance appropriate to a married man, although the amount of this allowance may require some restriction if marriage takes place after May 5. The wife will be taxed for the year of marriage as if she were a single person and no wife's earned income allowance can be obtained by the husband.

For subsequent years of assessment the incomes of husband and wife will be aggregated and if the husband does not satisfy the total tax liability the Inland Revenue may require the wife to pay the tax appropriate to her income.

Husband and wife may, however, claim to be separately assessed. This claim does not affect the total amount of income tax payable but allocates the liability between the parties. A quite different election may be made for separate assessment of wife's earnings. The effect of such an election is that the husband will be assessed on his income and on the wife's investment income and will receive the personal allowance appropriate to a single man. The wife will be separately assessed on her earned income and receive allowances as a single person. The wife's earnings election may be of advantage where the saving in higher rates of tax on the wife's income is greater than the increased tax resulting from the loss of the married personal allowance.

CAPITAL GAINS TAX

INTRODUCTION

A person is chargeable to capital gains tax on chargeable gains which accrue to him or her during a year of assessment ending on April 5. The application of the tax has been amended substantially in recent years and the following information is confined to the year of assessment 1987–88, ending on April 5 1988.

Liability extends to persons who are either resident or ordinarily resident for the year but special rules apply where a person permanently leaves the United Kingdom or comes to this territory for the purpose of acquiring residence. Non-residents are not liable to capital gains tax unless, exceptionally, they carry on a business in the United Kingdom through a branch or agency.

Chargeable gains accruing to companies are assessable to corporation tax and not to capital gains tax.

Capital gains tax is chargeable on the total of chargeable gains which accrue to a person in a year of assessment, after subtracting allowable losses arising in the same year. Unused allowable losses brought forward from some earlier year may be offset against current chargeable gains but in the case of individuals this must not reduce the net chargeable gains for 1987–88 below £6,600.

RATE OF TAX

Where the net chargeable gains accruing to an individual during 1987–88 do not exceed £6,600 there will be no liability to capital gains tax. If the net gains exceed £6,600 the excess is chargeable at the flat rate of 30 per cent.

Capital gains tax for 1987–88 normally falls due for payment on or before December 1, 1988. If the return or other information recording chargeable gains is delayed, interest may become chargeable.

HUSBAND AND WIFE

In the year of marriage chargeable gains accruing to husband and wife are separately assessed. Each party may independently obtain the £6,600 exemption for 1987–88 and there is no aggregation. For subsequent years, however, chargeable gains arising to a married woman living with her husband are assessed and charged on the husband, unless an election for separate assessment is made. This election will not reduce the aggregate tax payable but merely apportions liability between the spouses on an equitable basis.

DISPOSAL OF ASSETS

Before liability to capital gains tax can arise a disposal, or deemed disposal, of an asset must take place. This occurs not only where assets are sold or exchanged but applies on the making of a gift. There is also a disposal of assets where any capital sum is derived from assets, for example, where compensation is received for loss or damage to an asset.

The date on which a disposal must be treated as having taken place will determine the year of assessment in which the chargeable gain or allowable loss falls. In those cases where a disposal is made under an unconditional contract, the time of disposal will be that when the contract was entered into and not the subsequent date of conveyance or transfer. A disposal under a conditional contract or option is treated as taking place when the contract becomes unconditional or the option is exercised. Disposals by way of gift are undertaken when the gift becomes effective.

VALUATION OF ASSETS

The amount actually received as consideration for the disposal of an asset will be the sum from which very limited outgoings must be deducted for the purpose of establishing the gain or loss. In some cases, however, the consideration passing will not accurately reflect the value of the asset and a different basis must be used. This applies, in particular, where an asset is transferred by way of gift or otherwise than by a bargain made at arm's length. Such transactions are deemed to take place for a consideration representing market value, which will determine both the disposal proceeds accruing to the transferor and the cost of acquisition to the transferee.

Market value represents the price which an asset might reasonably be expected to fetch on a sale in the open market. In the case of unquoted shares or securities it is to be assumed that the hypothetical purchaser in the open market would have available all the information which a prudent prospective purchaser of shares or securities might reasonably require if he were proposing to purchase them from a willing vendor by private treaty and at arm's length. This is an important consideration as the amount of information deemed to be available to a hypothetical purchaser may materially affect the price "reasonably" offered in an open market situation. The market value of unquoted shares or securities will usually be established following negotiations with the Shares Valuation Division of the Capital Taxes Office.

Special rules apply to determine the market value of shares quoted on the Stock Exchange.

DEDUCTION FOR OUTGOINGS

Once the actual or notional disposal proceeds have been determined it only remains to subtract eligible outgoings for the purpose of computing the gain or loss. There is the general rule that any outgoings deducted, or which are available to be deducted, when calculating income tax liability must be ignored. Subject to this, deductions will usually be limited to—

(a) the cost of acquiring the asset, together with incidental costs wholly and exclusively incurred in connection with the acquisition;

(b) expenditure incurred wholly and exclusively on the asset in enhancing its value, being expenditure reflected in the state or nature of the asset at the time of the disposal, and any other expenditure wholly and exclusively incurred in establishing, preserving or defending title to, or a right over, the asset; and

(c) the incidental costs of making the disposal.

Where the disposal concerns a leasehold interest having less than 50 years to run, any expenditure falling under (a) and (b) must be written off throughout the duration of the lease. This recognises that a lease is a wasting asset which, at the termination of the leasing period, will retain no value.

INDEXATION ALLOWANCE

An indexation allowance will be available when calculating the chargeable gain or allowable loss. For disposals made after April 5, 1985 this allowance is based on percentage increases in the retail prices index between the month of March 1982, or if later the month in which expenditure is incurred, and the month of disposal. The increase is applied to the items of expenditure in (a) and (b) above to determine the amount of the indexation allowance. However, if the asset was acquired before March 31, 1982 a claim may be made to base the indexation allowance on market value at this date.

The amount of the indexation allowance will be subtracted from the gain, or added to the loss, to calculate the chargeable gain or allowable loss arising on disposal.

Different rules applied when calculating the indexation allowance for disposals made before April 6, 1985.

EXEMPTIONS

There is a general exemption from liability to capital gains tax where the net gains of an individual for 1987–88 do not exceed £6,600.

The disposal of many assets will not give rise to chargeable gains or allowable losses and these include—

(a) private motor cars;

(b) Government securities.

(c) Loan stock and other securities (but not shares) quoted on a United Kingdom stock exchange or dealt in on the Unlisted Securities Market.

(d) Options and contracts relating to securities within (b) and (c).

(e) National Savings Certificates, Premium Bonds, Defence Bonds and National Development Bonds;

(f) currency of any description acquired for personal expenditure outside the United Kingdom;

(g) decorations awarded for valour;

(h) betting wins and pools, lottery or games prizes;

(i) compensation or damages for any wrong or injury suffered by an individual in his person or in his profession or vocation;

(j) life assurance and deferred annuity contracts where the person making the disposal is the original beneficial owner;

(k) dwelling-houses and land enjoyed with the residence which is an individual's only or main residence;

(l) tangible movable property, the consideration for the disposal of which does not exceed £3,000;

(m) certain tangible movable property which is a wasting asset having a life not exceeding 50 years;

(n) assets transferred to charities and other bodies;

(o) works of art, historic buildings and similar assets;

(p) assets used to provide maintenance funds for historic buildings;

(q) assets transferred to trustees for the benefit of employees.

DWELLING-HOUSES

Exemption from capital gains tax will usually be available for any gain which accrues to an individual from the disposal of, or of an interest in, a dwelling-house or part of a dwelling-house which has been his only or main residence. The exemption extends to land which has been occupied and enjoyed with the residence as its garden or grounds. Some restriction may be necessary where the land exceeds one acre.

The gain will not be chargeable to capital gains tax if the dwelling-house, or part, has been the individual's only or main residence throughout the period of ownership, or throughout the entire period except for all or any part of the last two years. A proportionate part of the gain will be exempt if the dwelling-house has been the individual's only or main residence for part only of the period of ownership.

Where part of the dwelling-house has been used exclusively for business purposes, part of the gain arising on disposal will not be exempt. It will be comparatively unusual for any part to be used exclusively for such a purpose, except perhaps in the case of doctors' or dentists' surgeries.

In those cases where part of a qualifying dwelling-house has been used to provide rented accommodation this non-personal use may frequently be ignored when calculating exemption from capital gains tax, unless relatively substantial sums are involved.

Dwellings occupied by dependent relatives, separated or divorced former spouses, and also by beneficiaries under trusts, may also qualify for the exemption.

ROLL-OVER RELIEF

Persons carrying on business will often undertake the disposal of an asset and use the proceeds to finance the acquisition of a replacement asset. Where this situation arises a claim for roll-over relief may be made. The broad effect of such a claim is that all or part of the gain arising on the disposal of the old assset may be disregarded. The gain or part is then subtracted from the cost of acquiring the replacement asset. As this cost is reduced, any gain arising from the future disposal of the replacement asset will be correspondingly increased, unless of course a further roll-over situation then develops.

It remains a requirement that both the old and the replacement asset must be used for the purpose of the taxpayer's business. Relief will only be available if the acquisition of the replacement asset takes place within a period commencing twelve months before, and ending three years after, the disposal of the old asset, although the Board of Inland Revenue retain a discretion to extend this period where the circumstances were such that it was impossible for the taxpayer to acquire the replacement asset before the expiration of the normal time limit.

Whilst many business assets qualify for roll-over relief there are exceptions.

GIFTS

Although the gift of an asset is deemed to be a disposal made for a consideration representing market value, a claim can frequently be made to avoid capital gains tax liability. This claim applies to the gift of all assets by one individual to a second individual, by an individual to trustees, by trustees to an individual, or between trustees, residing in the United Kingdom. The effect of the claim is similar to that arising following a claim for roll-over relief and

the cost to the transferee will be reduced. Adjustments will be necessary where a transaction undertaken, otherwise than by way of bargain made at arm's length, involves some inadequate consideration.

A limited claim may also be made on the disposal of assets by an individual to some other person, perhaps a company. This claim is confined to the disposal of business assets, including shares in certain companies.

RETIREMENT RELIEF

Retirement relief is available to an individual who disposes by way of sale or gift of the whole or part of a business. It does not necessarily follow that the isolated disposal of assets will represent the disposal of the whole or part of a business. The main condition for granting this relief is that throughout a period of at least one year the business has been owned either by the individual or by a trading company in which the individual retained a sufficient shareholding interest. The relief extends also to cases where an individual disposes by way of sale or gift of shares or securities of a company. It must be demonstrated that the company was a trading company, the individual retained a sufficient shareholding interest, and he was engaged as a full-time working director.

An individual who has attained the age of 60 years at the time of a disposal may obtain maximum retirement relief of £125,000 for disposals taking place after April 5, 1987. The amount of this relief must be reduced if the conditions have not been satisfied throughout a ten year period. With a single exception no retirement relief can be obtained if the disposal occurs before the individuals 60th birthday. This exception arises where an individual is compelled to retire early on the grounds of ill-health. The normal retirement relief may then be obtained. Any retirement relief must be subtracted from the net gains arising on disposal, leaving the balance remaining, if any, chargeable to capital gains tax in the normal manner.

ASSETS HELD ON APRIL 6, 1965

Capital gains tax is chargeable on gains which accrue from disposals undertaken after April 6, 1965. Special rules must therefore be applied to calculate gains and losses arising from the disposal of assets acquired before this date.

This is often achieved by computing the overall gain and apportioning that gain rateably throughout the period of ownership. Only that part of the gain attributable to the period commencing on April 6, 1965, and ending at the time of disposal will be chargeable to capital gains tax.

This time apportionment procedure may be withdrawn in certain circumstances. It cannot apply to the disposal of quoted shares or securities, unit trust holdings or land retaining development value which are deemed to be acquired for a consideration representing market value on April 6, 1965. Where time apportionment is otherwise available, an election can be made to treat the asset as having been acquired at market value on April 6, 1965. A comparison between this notional cost of acquisition and the eventual disposal proceeds will usually disclose the chargeable gain, subject to an adjustment for the indexation allowance. Restrictions may have to be applied where the calculation produces a loss.

DEATH

No capital gains tax is chargeable on the value of assets retained at the time of death. However, the personal representatives administering the deceased's estate are deemed to acquire those assets for a consideration representing market value on death. This ensures that any increase in value occurring before the date of death will not be chargeable to capital gains tax. If a legatee or other person acquires an asset under a will or intestacy no chargeable gain will accrue to the personal representatives, and the person taking the asset will also be treated as having acquired it at the time of death for its then market value.

INHERITANCE TAX

INTRODUCTION

Throughout a period of some 90 years estate duty was payable on the value of an individual's estate at the time of death. Liability did not extend to lifetime gifts other than those made shortly before death and a limited range of further gifts where the donor continued to retain some benefit from the assets gifted. Estate duty ceased to apply for deaths occurring after March 12, 1975 following the introduction of capital transfer tax. This tax was not limited to the value of an estate at the time of death but applied to many gifts made during lifetime. Although the broad framework of capital transfer tax remains, very substantial changes were introduced for events occurring after March 17, 1986. In recognition of these changes the tax was renamed inheritance tax and now bears many characteristics of the former estate duty.

The nature and scope of inheritance tax is outlined below, but the comments made have little application to events occurring before 18 March 1986 when capital transfer tax applied.

Liability to inheritance tax may arise on a limited range of lifetime dispositions and other dispositions and also on the value of assets retained, or deemed to be retained, at the time of death. An individual's domicile at the time of any gift or on death is an important matter. Domicile will generally be determined by applying normal rules, but special considerations may be necessary where an individual was previously domiciled in the United Kingdom but subsequently acquired a domicile of choice overseas. Where a person was domiciled in the United Kingdom at the time of a disposition or on death the location of assets is immaterial and full liability to inheritance tax arises. Individuals domiciled outside the United Kindom are, however, chargeable to inheritance tax only on transactions affecting assets located in the United Kingdom.

The assets of husband and wife are not merged for inheritance tax purposes. Each spouse is treated as a separate individual entitled to receive the benefit of his or her exemptions, reliefs and rates of tax. Where husband and wife retain similar assets, special "related property" provisions may require the merger of those assets for valuation purposes only.

LIFETIME GIFTS AND DISPOSITIONS

Gifts and dispositions made during lifetime fall under four broad headings, namely:

(a) dispositions which are not transfers of value;
(b) exempt transfers;
(c) potentially exempt transfers; and
(d) chargeable transfers.

Dispositions which are not transfers of value.—Several lifetime transactions are not treated as transfers of value and may be entirely disregarded for inheritance tax purposes. These include transactions not undertaken to confer gratuitous benefit, the provision of family maintenance, the waiver of the right to receive remuneration or dividends, and the grant of agricultural tenancies for full consideration.

Exempt transfers.—Certain other transfers are treated as "exempt transfers" and incur no liability to inheritance tax. The main exempt transfers are listed below:

Transfers Between Spouses.—Transfers between husband and wife are usually exempt. However, if the transferor is, but the transferee spouse is not, domiciled in the United Kingdom transfers will be exempt only to the extent that the total does not exceed £55,000. Unlike the requirement used for income tax and capital gains tax purposes, it is immaterial whether husband and wife are "living together".

Annual exemption.—The first £3,000 of gifts and other dispositions made in a year ending on April 5 is exempt. If the exemption is not used, or not wholly used, in any year the balance may be carried forward to the following year only. The annual exemption will only be available for a potentially exempt transfer (see below) if that transfer subsequently becomes chargeable by reason of the donor's death.

Small Gifts.—Outright gifts of £250 or less to any person in one year ending April 5 are exempt.

Normal Expenditure.—A transfer made during lifetime and comprising normal expenditure is exempt. To obtain this exemption it must be shown that:

(a) the transfer was made as part of the normal expenditure of the transferor;
(b) taking one year with another, the transfer was made out of income; and
(c) after allowing for all transfers of value forming part of normal expenditure the transferor was left with sufficient income to maintain his or her usual standard of living.

Gifts in Consideration of Marriage.—These are exempt if they satisfy certain requirements. The amount allowed will be governed by the relationship between the donor and a party to the marriage. The allowable amounts comprise—

(a) gifts by a parent—£5,000
(b) gifts by a grandparent—£2,500
(c) gifts by a party to the marriage—£2,500
(d) gifts by other persons—£1,000

Gifts to Charities.—Gifts to charities are exempt from liability.

Gifts to Political Parties.—Gifts to political parties which satisfy certain requirements are generally exempt. However, a limit of £100,000 is placed on gifts made within a period of one year before the date of death.

Gifts for National Purposes.—Gifts made to an extensive list of bodies are exempt from liability. These include, among others,—

(a) The National Gallery;
(b) The British Museum;
(c) The National Trust for Places of Historic Interest or Natural Beauty;
(d) The National Art Collections Fund;

(e) The Nature Conservancy Council;
(f) The Historic Buildings and Monuments Commission for England;
(g) Any local authority;
(h) Any university or university college in the United Kingdom.

A number of other gifts made for the public benefit are also exempt.

Potentially Exempt Transfers.—Lifetime gifts and dispositions which are neither to be ignored nor comprise exempt transfers incur possible liability to inheritance tax. However, relief is available for a range of potentially exempt transfers. These comprise gifts made by an individual to—

(a) a second individual;
(b) trustees administering an accumulation and maintenance trust; or
(c) trustees administering a disabled person's trust.

The accumulation and maintenance trust mentioned in (b) must provide that on reaching a specified age, not exceeding twenty-five years, a beneficiary will become absolutely entitled to trust assets or obtain an interest in possession in those assets.

N.B. Further additions were made to the list of potentially exempt transfers for transactions taking place after March 16, 1987. These affect settled property administered by trustees where an individual, or individuals, retain an interest in possession. The transfer of assets to, the removal of assets from, or the rearrangement of interests in such property now comprise potentially exempt transfers if the person transferring an interest and the person benefitting from the transfer are both individuals.

No immediate liability to inheritance tax will arise on the making of a potentially exempt transfer. Should the donor survive for a period of seven years, immunity from liability will be confirmed. However, the donor's death within the seven-year *inter vivos* period produces liability, as explained later, if the amounts involved are sufficiently substantial.

Chargeable Transfers.—Any remaining lifetime gifts or dispositions which are neither to be ignored, represent exempt transfers or potentially exempt transfers incur liability to inheritance tax. The range of such chargeable transfers is severely limited and is broadly confined to transfers made to or affecting certain trusts, transfers to non-individuals and transfers involving companies.

GIFTS WITH RESERVATION

A lifetime gift of assets made at any time after March 17, 1986, may incur additional liability to inheritance tax if the donor retains some interest in the subject matter of the gift. This may arise, for example, where a parent transfers a dwelling-house to a son or daughter and continues to occupy the property or to enjoy some benefit from that property. The retention of a benefit may be ignored where it is enjoyed in return for full consideration, perhaps a commercial rent, or the benefit arises from changed circumstances which could not have been foreseen at the time of the original gift. The gift with reservation provisions will not usually apply to most exempt transfers.

There are three possibilities which may arise where the donor reserves or enjoys some benefit from the subject matter of a previous gift and subsequently dies, namely:

(a) If no benefit is enjoyed within a period of seven years before death there can be no further liability.

(b) If the benefit ceased to be enjoyed within a period of seven years before the date of death the original donor is deemed to have made a potentially exempt transfer representing the value of the asset at the time of cessation.

(c) If the benefit is enjoyed at the time of death the value of the asset must be included in the value of the deceased's estate on death.

It must be emphasised that the existence of a benefit enjoyed at any time within a period of seven years before death will establish liability on gifts with reservation, notwithstanding that the gift may have been made many years earlier, providing it was undertaken after March 17, 1986.

DEATH

Immediately before the time of death an individual is deemed to make a transfer of value. This transfer will comprise the value of assets forming part of the deceased's estate after subtracting most liabilities. Any exempt transfers may, however, be excluded. These include transfers for the benefit of a surviving spouse, a charity and a qualifying political party up to £100,000, together with bequests to approved bodies and for national purposes.

Death may also trigger three additional liabilities, namely:

(a) A potentially exempt transfer made within the period of seven years ending on death loses its potential status and becomes chargeable to inheritance tax.

(b) The value of gifts made with reservation may incur liability if any benefit was enjoyed within a period of seven years preceding death.

(c) Additional tax may become payable for chargeable lifetime transfers made within seven years before death.

VALUATIONS

The valuation of assets is an important matter as this will establish the value transferred for lifetime dispositions and also the value of a person's estate at the time of death. The value of property will represent the price which might reasonably be expected from a sale in the open market. This price cannot be reduced on the grounds that the whole property is placed on the market simultaneously and may therefore depress values.

In some cases it may be necessary to incorporate the value of "related property". This will include property comprised in the estate of the transferor's spouse and certain property previously transferred to charities. The purpose of the related property valuation rules is not to add the value of the property to the estate of the transferor. Related property must be merged to establish the aggregate value of the respective interests and this value is then apportioned, usually on a *pro rata* basis, to the separate interests.

The value of shares and securities quoted on the Stock Exchange will be determined by extracting figures from the daily list of official prices.

Where quoted shares and securities are sold within a period of twelve months following the date of death a claim may be made to substitute the proceeds for the value on death. This claim will only be beneficial if the gross proceeds realized are lower than market value on death. A similar claim may be available for interests in land sold within a period of three years following death.

RELIEF FOR ASSETS

Special relief is made available for certain assets, notably woodlands, agricultural property and business property. The effect of this relief is summarized below:

Woodlands.—Where woodlands pass on death the value will usually be included in the deceased's estate. However, an election may be made in respect of land in the United Kingdom on which trees or underwood is growing to delete the value of those assets. Relief is confined to the value of trees or underwood and does not extend to the land on which they are growing. Liability to inheritance tax will arise if and when the trees or underwood are sold on a future occasion.

Agricultural Property.—Relief is available for the agricultural value of agricultural property. Such property must be occupied and used for agricultural purposes and relief is confined to the agricultural value.

The value transferred, either on a lifetime gift or on death, must be determined. This value may then be reduced by a percentage. A higher 50 per cent deduction will be available if the transferor retained vacant possession or could have obtained that possession within a period of twelve months following the transfer. The increased deduction of 50 per cent may also be available for certain agricultural property held on March 9, 1981. In other cases, notably including land let to tenants, a lower deduction of 30 per cent is available.

It remains a requirement that the agricultural property was either occupied by the transferor for the purposes of agriculture throughout a two-year period ending on the date of the transfer, or was owned by him throughout a period of seven years ending on that date and occupied for agricultural purposes.

Business Property.—Where value transferred is attributable to relevant business property that value may be reduced by a percentage. The reduction in value applies to—

    (a) property consisting of a business or an interest in a business;

    (b) shares or securities of a company which, either by themselves or together with other shares or securities owned by the transferor, provided the transferor with control of the company immediately before the transfer. Control for this purpose may include that created by related property;

    (c) shares in a company which do not fall within (b) and are not quoted on a recognized stock exchange or dealt in on the Unlisted Securities Market;

    (d) any land, building, machinery or plant which, immediately before the transfer, was used wholly or mainly for the purposes of a business carried on by a company of which the transferor had control;

    (e) any land, building, machinery or plant which, immediately before the transfer, was used wholly or mainly for the purposes of a business carried on by a partnership of which the transferor was a partner; and

    (f) any land, building, machinery or plant which, immediately before the transfer, was used wholly or mainly for the purposes of a business carried on by the transferor and was then settled property in which he retained an interest in possession.

For property falling within (a) or (b) the deduction is 50 per cent. A reduced deduction of 30 per cent generally applies to property in (c) to (f). However, the deduction for property under (c) is increased to 50 per cent if the shareholding exceeds 25 per cent and the event occurs after March 16, 1987.

It is a general requirement that the property must have been retained for a period of two years before the transfer or death and restrictions may be necessary if the property has not been used wholly for business purposes. The same slice of property cannot obtain both business property relief and the relief available for agricultural property.

CALCULATION OF TAX PAYABLE

The calculation of inheritance tax payable adopts the use of a cumulative total. Each chargeable lifetime transfer is added to the total with a final addition made on death. The top slice added to the total for the current event determines the rate at which inheritance tax must be paid. However, the cumulative total will only include transfers made within a period of seven years before the current event and those undertaken outside this period must be excluded. Although inheritance tax was only introduced on March 18, 1986, the seven-year cumulative total will include chargeable lifetime gifts made before that date, subject to the seven-year limitation.

Lifetime transfers.—The limited range of lifetime transfers must be added to the seven-year cumulative total to calculate the amount of inheritance tax due. The tax is imposed at one-half of the rates shown by the table below. However, if the donor dies within a period of seven years from the date of the chargeable lifetime transfer, additional tax may be due. This is calculated by applying tax at the full rate (in substitution for the one-half rate previously used). The amount of tax is then reduced to a percentage by applying tapering relief. This percentage is governed by the number of years from the date of the lifetime gift to the date of death and is as follows:

Period of years before death	Percentage
Not more than 3	100
More than 3 but not more than 4	80
More than 4 but not more than 5	60
More than 5 but not more than 6	40
More than 6 but not more than 7	20

Should this exercise produce liability greater than that previously paid at the one-half rate on the lifetime transfer, additional tax, representing the difference, must be paid. Where the calculation shows an amount falling below tax paid on the lifetime transfer, no additional liability can arise nor will the deficiency become repayable.

Potentially exempt transfers.—Where a potentially exempt transfer loses immunity from liability, due to the donor's death within the seven-year *inter vivos* period, the value transferred becomes liable to inheritance tax. Liability is calculated by applying the full rates shown on the table below, reduced to the percentage governed by tapering relief if the original transfer occured more than three years before death.

Death.—The final addition to the seven-year cumulative total will comprise the value of an estate on death. Inheritance tax will be calculated by applying the full rates shown by the table below. No tapering relief can be obtained.

RATES OF TAX

The full rates of inheritance tax, which apply for events taking place after March 16, 1987, are shown by the following table:

For events after March 16, 1987

Portion of value	Rate of tax
£ £	%
0– 90,000	Nil
90,001–140,000	30
140,001–220,000	40
220,001–330,000	50
330,001 and above	60

Only one-half of these rates will be applicable for chargeable lifetime transfers.

It must be anticipated that the above rates and ratebands will be amended on future occasions.

PAYMENT OF TAX

Inheritance tax usually falls due for payment six months after the end of the month in which the chargeable transaction takes place. Where a transfer, other than that made on death, occurs after April 5 and before the folllowing October 1, tax falls due on the following April 30, although there are some exceptions to this general rule.

Inheritance tax attributable to the transfer of certain land, controlling shareholding interests, unquoted shares, businesses and interests in businesses, together with agricultural property, may usually be satisfied by instalments spread over ten years. No liability to interest arises where tax is paid

on the due date. In other cases, delay in the payment of tax may incur liability to interest.

SETTLED PROPERTY

Complex rules apply to establish inheritance tax liability on settled property. Where a person is beneficially entitled to an interest in possession, that person is effectively deemed to "own" the property in which the interest subsists. It follows that where the interest comes to an end during the beneficiary's lifetime and some other person becomes entitled to the property or interest, the beneficiary is treated as having made a transfer of value. However, for events taking place after March 16, 1987 this will usually comprise a potentially exempt transfer. No liability will arise, however, where the property vests in the absolute ownership of the previous beneficiary. The death of a person entitled to an interest in possession will require the value of the underlying property to be added to the value of the deceased's estate.

In the case of other settled property where there is no interest in possession (e.g. discretionary trusts), liability to tax will arise on each ten-year anniversary of the trust. There will also be liability if property ceases to be held on discretionary trusts before the first ten-year anniversary date is reached or between anniversaries. The rate of tax suffered will be governed by several considerations, including previous dispositions made by the settlor, transactions concluded by the trustees, and the period throughout which property has been held in trust.

Accumulation and maintenance settlements which require assets to be distributed not later than a beneficiary's twenty-fifth birthday may be exempt from any liability to inheritance tax.

CORPORATION TAX

INTRODUCTION

Profits, gains and income accruing to companies resident in the United Kingdom incur liability to corporation tax. Non-resident companies are immune from this tax unless they carry on a trade in the United Kingdom through a permanent establishment, branch or office. Companies residing outside the United Kingdom may be liable to income tax at the basic rate on other income arising in the United Kingdom, perhaps from letting property. The following comments are confined to companies resident in the United Kingdom and have little application to those residing overseas.

Liability to corporation tax is governed by the profits, gains or income for an accounting period. This is the period for which financial accounts are made up, and in the case of companies preparing accounts to the same accounting date annually will comprise successive periods of twelve months.

RATE OF TAX

The amount of profits or income for an accounting period must be determined on normal taxation principles. The special rules which apply to individuals where a source of income is acquired or discontinued are ignored and consideration is confined to the actual profits or income for an accounting period.

The rate of corporation tax is fixed for a financial year ending on March 31. Where the accounting period of a company overlaps this date and there is a change in the rate of corporation tax, profits and income must be apportioned.

For earlier years the full rate of corporation tax was 52 per cent but this rate was progressively reduced as follows:

Financial year	Per cent
12 months ending March 31, 1984	50
12 months ending March 31, 1985	45
12 months ending March 31, 1986	40
12 months ending March 31, 1987 and 1988	35

The progressive reduction in the rate of corporation tax was made to compensate companies for the loss of stock relief and the withdrawal of certain allowances for capital expenditure which increased the amount of profits and income chargeable to that tax.

SMALL COMPANIES RATE

Where the profits of a company do not exceed stated limits corporation tax becomes payable at the small companies rate. It is the amount of profits and not the size of the company which governs the application of this rate.

The level of profits which a company may derive without losing the benefit of the small companies rate has been frequently changed. However, for financial years commencing on and after April 1, 1983, the following small companies rate applies where profits do not exceed £100,000:

Financial year	Per cent
12 months ending March 31, 1984	38
12 months ending March 31, 1985 and 1986	30
12 months ending March 31, 1987	29
12 months ending March 31, 1988	27

If profits do exceed £100,000 but fall below £500,000 marginal small companies rate relief applies. The broad effect of marginal relief is that the first £100,000 of profits is taxed at the appropriate small companies rate. Profits falling in the margin exceeding £100,000 then incur liability at the following marginal rates:

Financial year	Per cent
12 months ending March 31, 1984	55
12 months ending March 31, 1985	48·75
12 months ending March 31, 1986	42·5
12 months ending March 31, 1987	36·5
12 months ending March 31, 1988	37

If the accounting period of a company overlaps March 31, profits must be apportioned to establish the appropriate rate for each part of those profits.

The lower limit of £100,000 and the upper limit of £500,000 applies for a period of twelve months in duration and must be proportionately reduced for shorter periods. Some restriction in the small companies rate and the marginal rate may be necessary if there are two or more "associated companies", namely companies under common control.

CAPITAL GAINS

Chargeable gains arising to a company are calculated in a manner similar to that used for individuals. However, companies cannot obtain the annual exemption of £6,300, nor are they assessed to capital gains tax. In place of this tax companies suffer liability to corporation tax on chargeable gains.

N.B. For disposals taking place before March 17, 1987 only a fraction of the chargeable gain was assessable to corporation tax at the full rate. The fraction selected ensured that companies effectively suffered corporation tax at the rate of 30 per cent on the full chargeable gain. A different approach is adopted for disposals taking place after this date. The full chargeable gain, and not a fraction, is assessable to corporation tax. However, unlike the previous system, the chargeable gain is treated as ordinary profit, thereby obtaining the benefit of the small companies rate where figures are sufficiently low.

DISTRIBUTIONS

Dividends and other qualifying distributions made by a United Kingdom resident company are not satisfied after deduction of income tax. However, when making a distribution a company is required to account to the Inland Revenue for an amount of advance corporation tax. For distributions made in the year ending April 5, 1988, the amount of advance corporation tax will represent twenty-seven seventy-thirds of the distribution. Thus a cash dividend of £73 paid to a shareholder will also require satisfaction of advance corporation tax amounting to £27.

Advance corporation tax accounted for in this manner for distributions made in an accounting period may usually be set against a company's corporation tax liability for the same period. Some restrictions are imposed on the amount which can be offset but any surplus can be carried forward, or carried backwards, and set against corporation tax due for other accounting periods.

A United Kingdom resident shareholder receiving a qualifying distribution also obtains a tax credit, which for the year ending April 5, 1988, is equal to twenty-seven seventy-thirds of the distribution made. Therefore the total income of the individual comprises the aggregate of the distribution and the tax credit. If the individual is not liable, or not fully liable, to income tax at the basic rate, all or part of the tax credit can be refunded by the Inland Revenue. Individuals with substantial income incur liability to income tax at the higher rates exceeding 27 per cent on the aggregate of the distribution and the tax credit.

PAYMENT OF TAX

Corporation tax, less any relief for advance corporation tax, usually falls due for payment nine months following the end of the accounting period to which the tax relates. Companies who were carrying on business before 1966 may have a later due and payable date, but this is gradually being amended to achieve a common nine month period for all companies.

INTEREST

On making many payments of interest a company is required to deduct income tax at the basic rate and account for the tax deducted to the Inland Revenue. The gross amount of interest paid will usually comprise a charge on income to be offset against profits on which corporation tax becomes payable.

GROUPS OF COMPANIES

Each company within a group is separately charged to corporation tax on profits, gains and income. However, where one group member realizes a loss, other than a capital loss, a claim may be made to offset the deficiency against profits of some other member of the same group.

Claims are also available to avoid the payment of advance corporation tax on distributions, or the deduction of income tax on the payment of interest, for transactions between members of a group of companies. The transfer of capital assets from one member of a group to a fellow member will incur no liability to tax on chargeable gains.

VALUE ADDED TAX

INTRODUCTION

Unlike income tax, capital gains tax, inheritance tax and corporation tax, which are collected and administered by the Inland Revenue, value added tax is the responsibility of Customs and Excise. Value added tax is charged on the value of supplies made in the United Kingdom by a registered trader and extends both to the supply of goods and to the supply of services. Liability also arises on the value of goods imported into the United Kingdom.

REGISTRATION

All traders, including professional men and women, together with companies, making taxable supplies of a value exceeding stated limits are required to register for value added tax purposes. Taxable supplies represent the supply of goods and services potentially chargeable with value added tax. The limits which govern mandatory registration are amended annually but from March 17, 1987, an unregistered trader must register—

(a) at any time, if there are reasonable grounds for believing that the value of taxable supplies in the year then beginning will exceed £21,300, or

(b) at the end of any quarter, namely March 31, June 30, September 30 or December 31, if the total amount of taxable supplies has exceeded either £7,250 in the last quarter or £21,300 in the last four quarters. Registration will not be mandatory if it can be shown that the value of taxable supplies in the last quarter and the next three quarters is not expected to exceed £21,300.

Where the limits governing mandatory registration have been exceeded it is necessary for the trader to notify Customs and Excise. Failure to provide prompt notification may have unfortunate results as the person concerned will be required to account for value added tax from the proper registration date. In some situations a trader whose taxable supplies do not reach the mandatory registration limits may apply for voluntary registration.

A registered trader may submit an application for de-registration if the value of taxable supplies subsequently falls. From June 1, 1987, an application for de-registration can be made if the value of taxable supplies for the year beginning on the application date is not expected to exceed £20,300. De-registration can also be achieved if the value of taxable supplies in each of the two previous years did not exceed £21,300 and is unlikely to exceed this threshold in the following twelve-month period.

INPUT TAX

A registered trader will both suffer tax (input tax) when obtaining goods or services for the purposes of his business and also become liable to account for tax (output tax) on the value of goods and services which he supplies. Relief can usually be obtained for input tax suffered, either by setting that tax against output tax due or by repayment. Most items of input tax can be relieved in this manner but there are exceptions including the prohibition of relief for the cost of business entertaining. Where a registered trader makes both exempt supplies and also taxable supplies to his customers or clients there may be some restriction in the amount of input tax which can be recovered.

OUTPUT TAX

When making a taxable supply of goods or services a registered trader must account for output tax, if any, on the value of the supply. Usually the price charged by the registered trader will be increased by adding value added tax but failure to make the required addition will not remove liability to account for output tax.

EXEMPT SUPPLIES

No value added tax is chargeable on the supply of goods or services which are treated as exempt supplies. These include the provision of burial and cremation facilities, insurance, finance and education. The granting of a lease to occupy land will usually comprise an exempt supply, but there are numerous exceptions.

Exempt supplies do not enter into the value of taxable supplies which governs liability to mandatory registration. Such supplies made by a registered trader may however limit the amount of input tax which can be relieved.

RATES OF TAX

Two rates of value added tax have applied since June 18, 1979, namely:

(a) a zero, or nil, rate; and

(b) a standard rate of 15 per cent.

Although no tax is due on a zero-rated supply, this does comprise a taxable supply which must be included in the calculation governing liability to register.

ZERO-RATING

A large number of supplies are zero-rated, including the following, among others—

(a) the supply of many items of food and drink for human consumption. This does not include ice creams, chocolates, sweets, potato crisps and alcoholic drinks. Nor does it extend to supplies made in the course of catering, for example, at a wedding reception or other social function, or to items supplied for consumption in a restaurant or cafe. Whilst the supply of "cold" items, for example sandwiches, for consumption away from the suppliers premises, is zero rated, the supply of "hot" food, for example fish and chips, is not.

(b) animal feeding stuffs;

(c) sewerage and water;

(d) books, brochures, pamphlets, leaflets, newspapers, maps and charts;

(e) talking books for the blind and handicapped and wireless sets for the blind;

(f) electricity, gas and coal;

(g) supplies made in the construction of a building. Zero-rating extends to the construction of a new building, the construction of a garage in conjunction with the construction of a new dwelling and the installation of working surfaces in the kitchen of a new building. Alterations to our existing building are not zero-rated, unless they relate to a listed building.

(h) the transportation of persons in a vehicle, ship or aircraft designed to carry not less than twelve persons;

(i) supplies of drugs, medicines and other aids for the handicapped;

(j) supplies of clothing and footwear for young persons;

(k) exports.

This list is not exhaustive but indicates the wide range of supplies which may be zero-rated.

COLLECTION OF TAX

Registered traders submit value added tax returns for accounting periods. Each accounting period is for three months in duration but arrangements can be made to submit returns on a monthly basis. The return will show both the output tax due for supplies made by the trader in the accounting period and also the input tax for which relief is claimed. If the output tax exceeds input tax the balance must be remitted with the value added tax return. Where input tax suffered exceeds the output tax due the registered trader may claim recovery of the excess from Customs and Excise.

This basis for collecting tax explains the structure of value added tax. Where supplies are made between registered traders the supplier will account for an amount of tax which will usually be identical to the tax recovered by the person to whom the supply is made. However, where the supply is made to a person who is not a registered trader there can be no recovery of input tax and it is on this person that the final burden of value added tax eventually falls.

Tax on imports into the United Kingdom must be satisfied at the time of importation or perhaps later where special arrangements have been agreed.

It is anticipated that during the summer of 1988 a new optional scheme will be made available for registered traders having an annual turnover of taxable supplies not exceeding £250,000. Such traders may, if they wish, render returns annually. Nine equal payments of value added tax will be paid on account, with a final balancing payment accompanying submission of the return.

BAD DEBTS

Many retailers operate special retail schemes for calculating the amount of value added tax due. These schemes are, broadly, based on the volume of consideration received in an accounting period. Should a customer fail to pay for goods or services supplied, there will be no consideration on which value added tax falls to be calculated. In other cases, where the special retailers' schemes do not apply, output tax falls due on the value of the supply and liability is not affected by failure to receive consideration. This implies that there will be no relief for the value added tax element in bad debts. However, relief for this element may be obtained where the debtor becomes insolvent.

To avoid the problem of bad debts incurred by traders not operating a special retail scheme, a new optional system of cash accounting was introduced on October 1, 1987. This scheme, confined to traders with annual taxable supplies not exceeding £250,000, enables returns to be made on a cash basis, in substitution for the normal supply basis. Traders using such a scheme will not, of course, include bad debts in the calculation of cash receipts.

OTHER SPECIAL SCHEMES

In addition to the schemes for retailers, there are several special schemes applied to calculate the amount of value added tax due and which also limit the ability to recover input tax. These schemes apply to the supply of second-hand motor cars, motor cycles, caravans, boats, electronic organs, aircraft and firearms, together with works of art, antiques and collectors' pieces.

OTHER TAXES AND STAMP DUTIES

The Commissioners as a general rule allow deeds, etc., to be stamped after execution:—

WITHOUT PENALTY, ON PAYMENT OF DUTY ONLY.
Deeds and instruments not otherwise excepted, within 30 days of *first* execution.
NOTE.—Where wholly executed *abroad,* the period begins to run from the date of arrival here.

PENALTIES ENFORCEABLE ON STAMPING IN ADDITION
  TO DUTY:—
Instruments presented after the proper time (subject to special provisions in some cases and subject to the commissioner's power to mitigate) a penalty equal to the duty   .   £10

AGREEMENT for Lease, *see* LEASES.
AGREEMENT FOR SALE OF PROPERTY—charged with *ad val.* duty as if an actual conveyance on sale with certain exceptions, *e.g.* agreements for the sale of land, stocks and shares, goods, wares or merchandise, or a ship (*see* s. 59 (1), Stamp Act 1891). If *ad val.* duty is paid on an agreement in accordance with this provision, the subsequent conveyance or transfer is not chargeable with any *ad val.* duty and the Commissioners will upon application either place a denoting stamp on such conveyance or transfer or will transfer the *ad val.* duty thereto. Further, if such an agreement is rescinded, not performed, etc., the Commissioners will return the *ad val.* duty paid.
AGREEMENT under seal subject to exemptions.   50p
ASSIGNMENT:
By way of sale—*see* Conveyance.
By way of gift—*see* Voluntary Disposition.
ASSURANCE—*see* Insurance Policies.
BEARER INSTRUMENT:
Inland bearer instrument, *i.e.* share warrant, stock certificate to bearer or any other instrument to bearer by which stock can be transferred, issued by a company or body formed or established in U.K. ......   1½%.

Overseas bearer instrument, *i.e.,* such an instrument issued in G.B. by a company formed out of the U.K. ....   1½%.
BILL OF SALE, Absolute, *see* CONVEYANCE ON SALE.
CAPITAL DUTY.—Where a *chargeable transaction* of a *capital company* takes place after July 31, 1973, duty of £1 is payable on every £100 or fraction of £100 of the actual value of the assets contributed by the members (as opposed to the previous duty of 50p per £100 of the nominal capital), provided the place of effective management of the company is in G.B. or its registered office is in G.B. but the place of its effective management is outside the E.E.C. (Finance Act 1973).

A statement containing prescribed particulars must be delivered to the Commissioners within one month of the transaction unless there is an obligation under the Companies Act 1948 (*e.g.,* on the formation of a limited liability company) or the Limited Partnerships Act 1907 (*e.g.,* on the registration of a limited partnership) to send a statement to the registrar of companies as a result of the transaction.
Capital company includes a company incorporated with limited liability under U.K. law, a limited partnership under the Limited Partnerships Act 1907, a company incorporated according to the law of any other member of the E.E.C. and any other corporation or body of persons whose members have the right freely to dispose of their shares and whose liability for debts is limited.
Chargeable transactions includes the formation of a capital company, an increase in its capital by the contribution of assets of any kind, the transfer to G.B. of its place of effective management from a country outside the E.E.C. if its registered office is

in such a country, and the transfer to G.B. of its registered office from a country outside the E.E.C. if its place of effective management is in such a country.

INHERITANCE TAX

The new Inheritance Tax was introduced by the Finance Act, 1986, to replace Capital Transfer Tax. The most radical change is to take outside the charge to tax many (but not all) lifetime gifts made more than seven years before the death of the donor.

Lifetime transfers made before March 18, 1986, may be subject to capital transfer tax and are broadly unaffected by the new regime. Thus, subject to exemptions and rate bands, capital transfer tax is payable on such tranfers at the lifetime rate with an additional charge to tax at the death rate if the donor dies within three years of the transfer, but no additional charge if the donor survives three years but dies within seven years of the gift.

If the gift is made on or after March 18, 1986, and comes within the definition of what is known as a potentially exempt transfer (for details, see page 1187), tax is not payable at the time of the gift and will not be payable if the donor survives the gift for seven years. If the donor does not survive for three years, the rate of tax payable on death for the year 1987–88 (based on the value of the property at the date of the gift) is shown in the following table—

Value transferred		Rate of tax
Lower limit £	Upper limit £	Per cent
0	90,000	*Nil*
90,000	140,000	30
140,000	220,000	40
220,000	330,000	50
over 330,000	—	60

If the donor survives the gift by more than three but less than seven years, tapering relief is given as follows.

Years between gift and death	*Percentage of full charge*
0–3	100
3–4	80
4–5	60
5–6	40
6–7	20

If the gift does not come within the definition of a potentially exempt transfer e.g., the creation of a new trust for a person for life, it is taxed at the time of transfer at half the full rate, with an additional charge to tax if the donor dies within seven years. Among the exemptions and reliefs given are the following.

(a) Transfers between spouses.
(b) The first £3,000 of gifts made in each tax year. There is provision for carry forward of this relief for one year only, in so far as it has not been used in the previous year.
(c) Gifts which are normal expenditure out of income.
(d) Gifts in consideration of marriage are exempt up to £5,000 if made by a parent; £2,000 if made by a grandparent or some other lineal ancestor, or by one party to another; and £1,000 in any other case.
(e) Gifts to charities and certain other bodies.
(f) Certain relief is given for agricultural and business property where a charge to inheritance tax arises on the donor's death within

seven years, to the extent that the recipient still owns the property transferred or it has been replaced by similar property qualifying for relief.

CONTRACT, *see* AGREEMENT.

CONTRACT OR GRANT FOR PAYMENT OF A
SUPERANNUATION ANNUITY: for every £10
or fractional part of £10 .... 5p

CONVEYANCE OR TRANSFER ON SALE (in the case of a Voluntary Disposition, *see* below) of any property (*except* stock or marketable securities), where the Conveyance or Transfer contains a certificate of value certifying that the transaction does not form part of a larger transaction or a series of transactions in respect of which the aggregate amount or value of the consideration exceeds £30,000.. *nil*
Exceeds £30,000 (for every £100 or fraction of £100) £1
If the Conveyance or Transfer on Sale does not contain the appropriate statement duty at the full rate of £1 for every £100 or fraction of £100 will be payable whatever the amount of the consideration.
However, if the consideration does not exceed £500, and the instrument does not contain a certificate of value, there are graduated duties ranging from 50p to £5.
Conveyances to charities are exempt from duty under this head provided the instrument is stamped with a denoting stamp.

CONVEYANCE OR TRANSFER of any other kind
.... fixed duty 50p
However, under the Stamp Duty (Exempt Instruments) Regulations, 1987, instruments which would otherwise fall under this head are exempt from stamp duty provided that the document is duly certified. The certificate must contain a sufficient description of the category into which the instrument falls, and must be signed by the transferor, his solicitor or agent. "I/We hereby certify that this instrument falls within category ... in the Schedule to the Stamp Duty (Exempt Instruments) Regulations, 1987."

COVENANT—For original creation and sale of any annuity, *see* CONVEYANCE.

DECLARATION OF TRUST, not being a Will or
Settlement 50p

DEMISE, *see* LEASE

DUPLICATE OR COUNTERPART
Same duty as original, but not to exceed ... 50p

GIFT (*see* VOLUNTARY DISPOSITION).

GUARANTEE:
If under seal 50p

INSURANCE POLICIES:
Life:—
Exc. £50 and not exc. £1,000, for every £100 or part of £100 .... 5p
Exc. £1,000, for every £1,000 or any fractional part of £1,000 .... 50p
Made after 1 August 1966 for period not exceeding 2 years..................... 5p

LEASES:—Lease or tack for any definite term less than a year of any furnished dwelling-house or apartments where the rent for such term exceeds £500, £1; of any lands, tenements, etc., in consideration of any rent, according to the following table:—

Annual rent not exceeding	*Term not exceeding			Term exceeding 100 years
	7 years	35 years	100 years	
£	£ p	£ p	£ p	£ p
5	*Nil*	0·10	0·60	1·20
10	*Nil*	0·20	1·20	2·40
15	*Nil*	0·30	1·80	3·60
20	*Nil*	0·40	2·40	4·80
25	*Nil*	0·50	3·00	6·00
50	*Nil*	1·00	6·00	12·00
75	*Nil*	1·50	9·00	18·00
100	*Nil*	2·00	12·00	24·00
150	*Nil*	3·00	18·00	36·00
200	*Nil*	4·00	24·00	48·00
250	*Nil*	5·00	30·00	60·00
300	*Nil*	6·00	36·00	72·00
350	*Nil*	7·00	42·00	84·00
400	*Nil*	8·00	48·00	96·00
450	*Nil*	9·00	54·00	108·00
500	*Nil*	10·00	60·00	120·00
Exceeding £500 for every £50 or fraction of £50	0·50	1·00	6·00	12·00

*If the term is indefinite the same duty is payable as if the term did not exceed 7 years.

Agreement for lease, same as actual lease.

Where a consideration other than rent is payable, the same rule applies where the consideration does not exceed £30,000 as under Conveyance or Transfer on Sale (except stock or marketable securities), provided that any rent payable does not exceed £300 a year and a certificate of value is included in the Conveyance or Transfer.

Leases to charities are exempt from duty under this head provided the instrument is stamped with a denoting stamp.

MORTGAGES are exempt.

RECEIPTS FOR SALARIES, Wages and Superannuation, and other like allowances are exempt.

TRANSFER OF STOCK AND SHARES by way of gift or sale.................................. ½%

UNIT TRUST INSTRUMENT—Any trust instrument of a unit trust scheme—For every £100, and also for any fractional part of £100, of the amount or value of the property subject to the trusts created or recorded by the instrument........................... 25p

VOLUNTARY DISPOSITION *inter vivos*:— 50p

PRINCIPAL BOOK PUBLISHERS AND THEIR ADDRESSES

More than 10,000 firms, individuals and societies have published one or more books in recent years. The list which follows is a selective one comprising, in the main, those firms whose names are most familiar to the general public. An interleaved list containing some 2,500 names and addresses is issued annually in April by the publishers of "Whitaker".

Abelard-Schumann, 7 Leicester Place, W.C.2.
Allan (Ian), Coombelands Ho., Addlestone, Weybridge, Surrey.
Allen (J. A.), 1 Lower Grosvenor Pl., S.W.1.
Allen (W. H.), 44 Hill St., W.1.
Allen & Unwin, 40 Museum St., W.C.1.
Angus & Robertson, 16 Golden Square, W.1.
Apple Press, Unit 3, Ashville Trading Estate, Ashville Way, Baldock, Herts.
Architectural Press, 9 Queen Anne's Gate, S.W.1.
Argus Books, 1 Golden Sq., W.1.
Arlington Books, 15 King St., S.W.1.
Armada Books, 8 Grafton St., W.1.
Arms & Armour Press, 25 West St., Poole, Dorset.
Arnold (Edward), 41 Bedford Sq., W.C.1.
Arnold (E. J.) & Son, Parkside Lane, Leeds.
Arrow Books, 62 Chandos Pl., W.C.2.
Athlone Press, 44 Bedford Row, W.C.1.
B.B.C. Books, 80 Wood Lane, W.12.
Baillière, Tindall, 24 Oval Rd., N.W.1.
Bantam Bks., 61 Uxbridge Rd., W.5.
Barker (Arthur), 91 Clapham High St., S.W.4.
Barrie & Jenkins, 62 Chandos Pl., W.C.2.
Bartholomew & Son, 12 Duncan St., Edinburgh.
Batsford, 4 Fitzhardinge St., Portman Square, W.1.
Bell & Hyman, 37 Queen Elizabeth St., S.E.1.
Benn (Ernest), 35 Bedford Row, W.C.1.
Bingley (Clive), 7 Ridgmount St., W.C.1.
Black (A. & C.), 35 Bedford Row, W.C.1.
Blackie, Bishopbriggs, Glasgow, and 7 Leicester Place, W.C.2.
Blackwell (Basil), 108 Cowley Rd., Oxford.
Blackwood Pillans & Wilson, 162 Leith Walk, Edinburgh.
Blandford Press, Link Ho., West St., Poole, Dorset.
Blond (Anthony), 62 Chandos Pl., W.C.2.
Bloomsbury Publishing, 2 Soho Sq., W.1.
Bodley Head, 32 Bedford Sq., W.C.1.
Boxtree, 25 Floral St., W.C.2.
Boyars (Marion), 24 Lacy Rd., S.W.15.
Bracken Books, 50 Eastcastle St., W.1.
British Museum, 46 Bloomsbury St., W.C.1.
Brown, Son & Ferguson, 4 Darnley St., Glasgow.
Burke Pub. Co., 116 Golden Lane, E.C.1.
Butterworth & Co., Borough Green, Sevenoaks, Kent.
Calder (John), 18 Brewer St., W.1.
Cambridge Univ. Press, Shaftesbury Rd., Cambridge.
Cape (Jonathan), 32 Bedford Sq., W.C.1.
Cassell, Artillery Ho., Artillery Row, S.W.1.
Centaur Press, Fontwell, Arundel, Sx.
Century Hutchinson, 62 Chandos Pl., W.C.2.
Century Publishing Co., see Century Hutchinson
Chambers (W. & R.), 43 Annandale St., Edinburgh.
Chapman & Hall, 11 New Fetter Lane, E.C.4.
Chapman (Geoffrey), Artillery Ho., Artillery Row, S.W.1.
Chatto & Windus, 30 Bedford Sq., W.C.1.
Church House Publishing, Dean's Yard, S.W.1.
Churchill Livingstone, 1–3 Baxter's Place, Leith Walk, Edinburgh.
Collins (William), 8 Grafton St., W.1.
Constable & Co., 10 Orange St., W.C.2.
Consumers' Assn., 14 Buckingham St., W.C.2.
Corgi Books, 61 Uxbridge Road, W.5.
Croom Helm, Provident Ho., Burrell Row, Beckenham, Kent.
Darton, Longman & Todd, 89 Lillie Rd., S.W.6.
David & Charles, Brunel House, Newton Abbot, Devon.

Dean & Son, 69 London Rd., Twickenham.
Dent (J. M.) & Sons, 33 Welbeck St., W.1.
Deutsch (A.), 105 Gt. Russell St., W.C.1.
Dobson Books, Brancepeth Castle, Durham.
Dorling Kindersley, 9 Henrietta St., W.C.2.
Duckworth & Co., 43 Gloucester Crescent, N.W.1.
Elliot Right Way Books, Kingswood Bldg., Kingswood, Tadworth, Surrey.
Encyclopædia Britannica, Carew Ho., Station Approach, Wallington, Surrey.
Epworth Press, 1 Central Bldgs., S.W.1
Evans Bros., 2A Portman Mans., Chiltern St., W.1.
Eyre & Spottiswoode, North Way, Andover, Hants.
Faber & Faber, 3 Queen Square, W.C.1.
Fontana, 8 Grafton St., W.1.
Foulis (G. T.), Sparkford, Yeovil, Som.
Foulsham & Co., Yeovil Rd., Slough, Berks.
Fountain Press, 45 The Broadway, Tolworth, Surbiton, Surrey.
French (Samuel), 52 Fitzroy St., W.1.
Futura, see Macdonald & Co.
Gee & Co., 7 Swallow Pl., W.1.
Geographia, 105 Bath Rd., Cheltenham, Glos.
Gibbons (Stanley), 5 Parkside, Christchurch Rd., Ringwood, Hants.
Gibson (Robert), 17 Fitzroy Place, Glasgow.
Ginn & Co., Prebendal Ho., Parson's Fee, Aylesbury, Bucks.
Glasgow (Mary), 131 Holland Park Ave., W.11.
Gollancz (Victor), 14 Henrietta St., W.C.2.
Gower Publishing Co., Croft Rd., Aldershot, Hants.
Grafton Books, 8 Grafton St., W.1.
Graham (Frank), 6 Queen's Terrace, Newcastle.
Green (W.), 2 St. Giles St., Edinburgh.
Griffin (Charles), 16 Pembridge Rd., W.11.
Guinness Superlatives, 33 London Rd., Enfield, Middx.
H.M. Stationery Office, 51 Nine Elms Lane, S.W.8.
Hale (Robert), 45 Clerkenwell Green, E.C.1.
Hamilton (Hamish), 27 Wright's Lane, W.8.
Hamlyn, 69 London Rd., Twickenham.
Harlequin, 18 Paradise Rd., Richmond, Surrey.
Harper & Row, 34 Cleveland St., W.1.
Harrap, 19 Ludgate Hill, E.C.4.
Hart-Davis, 8 Grafton St., W.1.
Harvester Press, 16 Ship St., Brighton, Sussex.
Haynes (J. H.), Sparkford, Yeovil, Som.
Headline Book Publishing, 79 Great Titchfield St., W.1.
Heinemann (Wm.), 10 Upper Grosvenor St., W.1.
Hodder & Stoughton, 47 Bedford Sq., W.C.1.
Hodge & Co., 34 N. Frederick St., Glasgow.
Hogarth Press, 30 Bedford Sq., W.C.1.
Hollis & Carter, 32 Bedford Sq., W.C.1.
Holmes McDougall, 137 Leith Walk, Edinburgh.
Hutchinson, 62 Chandos Pl., W.C.2.
Jane's Publishing Co., 238 City Rd., E.C.1.
Jarrold Colour, Barrack Street, Norwich.
Jarrolds, 62 Chandos Pl., W.C.2.
Johnston & Bacon, P. O. Box 1, Stirling.
Jordan & Sons, 21 St. Thomas St., Bristol.
Joseph (Michael), 27 Wright's Lane, W.8.
Kaye & Ward, 10 Upper Grosvenor St., W.1.
Kegan Paul Internat., 11 New Fetter Lane, E.C.4.
Kelly's Directories, East Grinstead House, East Grinstead, Sussex.
Kimber (Wm.), 100 Jermyn St., S.W.1.
Kimpton Medical, 205 Gt. Portland St., W.1.
Ladybird, Beeches Rd., Loughborough.
Lawrence & Wishart, 39 Museum St., W.C.1.

Lewis (H. K.), 136 Gower St., W.C.1.
Lion Publishing, Icknield Way, Tring, Herts.
Longman Group, Burnt Mill, Harlow, Essex.
Lund Humphries, 16 Pembridge Rd., W.11.
Lutterworth Press, 7 All Saints Passage, Cambridge.
Macdonald & Co., Greater London House, Hampstead Rd., N.W.1.
Macdonald & Evans, 128 Long Acre, W.C.2.
McGraw-Hill, Shoppenhangers Rd., Maidenhead, Berks.
Macmillan Publishers, 4 Little Essex St., W.C.2.
Marshall Cavendish, 58 Old Compton St., W.1.
Marshall, Morgan & Scott, 3 Beggarwood Lane, Basingstoke, Hants.
Mayflower, 8 Grafton St., W.1.
Methodist Publishing, Wellington Rd., S.W.19.
Methuen & Co., 11 New Fetter Lane, E.C.4.
Mills & Boon, 18 Paradise Rd., Richmond, Surrey.
Mitchell Beazley, 14 Manette St., W.1.
Mowbray, St. Thomas Ho., Becket St., Oxford.
Muller, Blond & White, 62 Chandos Pl., W.C.2.
Murray (John), 50 Albemarle St., W.1.
National Christian Education Council, Robert Denholm Ho., Nutfield, Redhill, Sy.
Nelson (T.), Mayfield Rd., Walton-on-Thames, Sy.
New English Library, 47 Bedford Sq., W.C.1.
Nisbet & Co., 78 Tilehouse St., Hitchin, Herts.
Nonesuch Library, 32 Bedford Sq., W.C.1.
Novello & Co., Borough Green, Sevenoaks, Kent.
Octopus Books, 59 Grosvenor St., W.1.
Oliver & Boyd, 1–3 Baxter's Place, Leith Walk, Edinburgh.
O'Mara (Michael) Books, 20 Queen Anne St., W.1.
Owen (Peter), 73 Kenway Rd., S.W.5.
Oxford Univ. Press, Walton St., Oxford.
Paladin Bks., 8 Grafton St., W.1.
Pan Books, 18 Cavaye Place, S.W.10.
Panther, 8 Grafton St., W.1.
Paul (Stanley), 62 Chandos Pl., W.C.2.
Pelham Books, 27 Wright's Lane, W.8.
Penguin Books, Harmondsworth, Mddx.
Pergamon Press, Headington Hill Hall, Oxford.
Phaidon Press, St. Ebbes St., Oxford.
Pharmaceutical Press, 1 Lambeth High St., S.E.1.
Philip (George), 27A Floral St., W.C.2.
Piatkus Books, 5 Windmill St., W.1.
Piccadilly Press, 15 Golders Green Crescent, N.W.11.
Pickering & Inglis, 3 Beggarwood Lane, Basingstoke, Hants.
Pitkins, North Way, Andover, Hants.
Pitman Publishing, 128 Long Acre, W.C.2.
Putnam & Co., 24 Bride La., E.C.4.
Quartet Books, 27 Goodge St., W.1.
Quiller Press, 50 Albemarle St., W.1.
Reader's Digest, 25 Berkeley Sq., W.1.
Reinhardt (Max), 32 Bedford Sq., W.C.1.
Religious & Moral Education Press, Hennock Rd., Exeter.
Rider & Co., 62 Chandos Pl., W.C.2.

Routledge & Kegan Paul, 11 New Fetter Lane, E.C.4.
S.C.M. Press, 26 Tottenham Rd., N.1.
S.P.C.K., Holy Trinity Church, Marylebone Rd., N.W.1.
St. Andrew Press, 121 George St., Edinburgh.
Saunders (W.B.), 24 Oval Rd., N.W.1.
Scripture Union, 130 City Rd., E.C.1.
Secker & Warburg, 54 Poland St., W.1.
Severn House, 40 William IV St., W.C.2.
Sheed & Ward, 2 Creechurch Lane, E.C.3.
Sheldon Press, Holy Trinity Church, Marylebone Rd., N.W.1.
Sidgwick & Jackson, 1 Tavistock Chambers, W.C.1.
Smith (M. Temple), Gower Ho., Croft Rd., Aldershot, Hants.
Smythe (Colin), P.O. Box 6, Gerrards Cross, Bucks.
Souvenir Press, 43 Gt. Russell St., W.C.1.
Sphere Books, 27 Wright's Lane, W.8.
Spon (E. & F. N.), 11 New Fetter Lane, E.C.4.
Stanford Maritime, 27A Floral St., W.C.2.
Stephens (Patrick), Denington Estate, Wellingborough, Northants.
Stevens & Sons, 11 New Fetter Lane, E.C.4.
Sunshine Books, 12 Little Newport St., W.C.2.
Sweet & Maxwell, 11 New Fetter Lane, E.C.4.
Tavistock Publications, 11 New Fetter Lane, E.C.4.
Technical Press, Gower Ho., Croft Rd., Aldershot, Hants.
Thames & Hudson, 30 Bloomsbury St., W.C.1.
Thorsons, Denington Estate, Wellingborough, Northants.
Times Books, 16 Golden Sq., W.1.
Turnstone Books, Denington Estate, Wellingborough, Northants.
University of Wales Press, Gwennyth St., Cardiff.
University Tutorial Press, 37 Queen Elizabeth St., S.E.1.
Unwin Hyman, 37 Queen Elizabeth St., S.E.1.
Vallentine Mitchell, 11 Gainsborough Rd., E.11.
Viking, 27 Wright's Lane, W.8.
Virago Press, 41 William IV St., W.C.2.
Walker Books, 184 Drummond St., N.W.1.
Ward Lock, 8 Clifford St., W.1.
Ward Lock Educational Co., 47 Marylebone Lane, W.1.
Warne, 27 Wright's Lane, W.8.
Webb & Bower, 9 Colleton Cres., Exeter.
Weidenfeld & Nicolson, 91 Clapham High St., S.W.4.
Wheaton (A.), Hennock Rd., Exeter.
"Whitaker," 12 Dyott St., W.C.1.
Wildwood House, Gower Ho., Croft Rd., Aldershot, Hants.
Wisden (John), 6 Warwick Court, W.C.1.
Witherby (H. F. & G.), 14 Henrietta St., W.C.2.
Wolfe Medical Publications, 3 Conway St., W.1.
World's Work, see Heinemann (Wm.).
Wright (John), Techno Ho., Redcliffe Way, Bristol 1.
Zomba Books, 165 Willesden High Rd., N.W.10.

Most of the principal book publishers are members of The Publishers Association (*see* Index).

BOOK PRODUCTION AND BOOK EXPORTS

These figures for book production and exports are issued by the Department of Trade and Industry. The totals for the years 1971 to 1986 are shown below:

Year	Total value of Books produced in U.K. £ million	Total value of Books exported from U.K. £ million	Year	Total value of Books produced in U.K. £ million	Total value of Books exported from U.K. £ million
1971	179·1	77·9	1979	580·4	215·3
1972	205·3	81·2	1980	666·9	213·7
1973	230·1	95·9	1981	738·0	234·5
1974	281·5	119·4	1982	759·1	232·8
1975	342·4	138·6	1983	831·9	261·1
1976	408·3	175·8	1984	937·2	307·3
1977	467·0	203·9	1985	1044·0	340·9
1978	521·4	211·8	1986 (provisional)	1065·7	314·7

BOOKS PUBLISHED IN GREAT BRITAIN IN 1986

This table shows the books published in 1986 with the number of new editions, translations and limited editions. Books and pamphlets priced at less than 12p have been omitted, as are also all Government publications except the more important issued by H.M. Stationery Office.

Classification	Total	Reprints and New Editions	Translations	Limited Editions
Aeronautics	213	57	—	—
Agriculture and Forestry	448	85	5	—
Architecture	383	76	4	—
Art	1,505	194	28	7
Astronomy	120	26	2	—
Bibliography	747	136	3	1
Biography	1,842	556	65	4
Chemistry and Physics	811	169	11	—
Children's Books	4,510	930	119	4
Commerce	1,683	465	—	1
Customs, Costumes, Folklore	182	53	16	1
Domestic Science	866	175	7	2
Education	1,093	145	7	—
Engineering	1,649	390	43	—
Entertainment	589	99	26	—
Fiction	6,002	2,806	288	11
General	1,087	149	11	1
Geography and Archaeology	585	144	3	1
Geology and Meteorology	253	34	10	—
History	1,947	388	76	5
Humour	293	46	2	—
Industry	414	93	9	—
Language	732	147	4	—
Law and Public Administration	1,678	418	10	2
Literature	1,546	282	83	1
Mathematics	722	132	6	—
Medical Science	3,374	646	18	—
Military Science	238	51	2	1
Music	437	87	9	—
Natural Sciences	1,369	175	22	1
Occultism	548	298	32	—
Philosophy	660	165	55	—
Photography	165	17	1	—
Plays	315	93	35	—
Poetry	751	94	85	30
Political Science and Economy	3,822	730	91	—
Psychology	818	180	14	—
Religion and Theology	2,268	411	190	—
School Textbooks	1,836	258	—	—
Science, General	99	18	1	—
Sociology	1,132	128	20	—
Sports	713	169	8	—
Stockbreeding	295	76	3	1
Trade	512	147	1	—
Travel and Guidebooks	1,113	457	11	—
Wireless and Television	131	46	—	—
Totals	52,496	12,441	1,436	74

COPYRIGHT

The Government Department dealing with Copyright is the *Industrial Property and Copyright Dept., Department of Trade and Industry*, Patent Office, State House, 66–71 High Holborn, WC1R 4TP.

Subject to the provisions of the Copyright Act, 1956, copyright subsists automatically in every original literary, dramatic, musical and artistic work and continues to subsist until the end of the period of fifty years from the end of the calendar year in which the author died, and shall then expire. *No registration nor other formalities are required in order to obtain the protection of the Act.* Protection is conferred not only against reproduction but also against the public performance of a work without permission. Copyright may also subsist in sound recordings, cinematograph films (including video recordings) and television, sound broadcasts and cable programmes. Libraries entitled, under a provision still in force of the Copyright Act, 1911, to receive free copies of books published in the United Kingdom are the British Library, the Bodleian Library, Oxford, University Library, Cambridge, the National Library of Wales, the National Library of Scotland and Trinity College, Dublin.

As the U.K. is a party to both the Berne Copyright Convention and the Universal Copyright Convention, a work originating in this country is automatically protected in all the other countries which are members of these Conventions.

Voluntary Registration at Stationers' Hall.—Compulsory registration at Stationers' Hall was terminated by the Copyright Act of 1911, but in 1924 the Stationers' Company established a *new* Register, in which Books and Fine Arts can be registered, to help establish ownership of copyright.

ANNUAL REFERENCE BOOKS

Advertiser's Annual.—East Grinstead House, East Grinstead, W. Sussex. £47·50.

Aircraft Illustrated Annual.—Terminal House, Shepperton, Middx. £6·00.

Allied Dunbar Investment Guide.—Fourth Avenue, Harlow, Essex. £13·50.

Allied Dunbar Tax Guide.—Fourth Avenue, Harlow, Essex. £12·95.

Annual Register of World Events.—Fourth Avenue, Harlow, Essex. £48·00.

Antique Shops of Britain, Guide to the.—5 Church St., Woodbridge, Suffolk. £8·95.

Art Sales Index.—1 Thames St., Weybridge, Surrey. £85·00.

Astronomical Almanac.—H.M. Stationery Office, Atlantic House, Holborn Viaduct, E.C.1. (Jan.) £18·00.

Automobile Year.—Unit 6, Pilton Estate, Croydon, Surrey. £19·95.

B.B.C. Annual Report & Handbook.—144 Bermondsey St., S.E.1. £8·00.

Baily's Hunting Directory.—1 Lower Grosvenor Place, S.W.1. (Oct.) £20·00.

Banker's Almanac & Year Book.—East Grinstead House, East Grinstead, W. Sussex. (Feb.) 2 v. £102·00.

Bar List of the U.K.—11 New Fetter Lane, E.C.4. (May) £22·50.

Benedictine Year Book.—Ampleforth Abbey, York. £0·70.

Benn's Direct Marketing Services.—P.O. Box 20, Sovereign Way, Tonbridge, Kent. 2 v. each £50·00.

Benn's Hardware & Do-it-Yourself Buyer's Guide.—P.O. Box 20, Sovereign Way, Tonbridge, Kent. £26·00.

Benn's Media Directory.—P.O. Box 20, Sovereign Way, Tonbridge, Kent. 2v. ea £60·00.

"Birmingham Post & Mail" Year Book & Who's Who.—Colmore Circus, Birmingham B4 6AX. (July) £12·75.

Boat World.—39 East St., Epsom, Surrey. £6·00.

British Art & Antiques Directory.—72 Broadwick St., W.1. £9·50.

British Books in Print.—12 Dyott St., W.C.1. £104·00.

British Clothing Industry Year Book.—1–5 Bath St., E.C.1. £21·50.

British Music Year Book.—234/241 Shaftesbury Ave., W.C.2. £9·95.

Brown's Nautical Almanack.—4–10 Darnley St., Glasgow. (Sept.) £20·00.

Building Societies Who's Who.—7 Swallow Pl., WIR 8AB. £32·00.

Building Societies Year Book.—7 Swallow Pl., WIR 8AB. £32·00.

Buses Annual.—Terminal Ho., Shepperton, Middx. £6·00.

Carpet Annual.—P.O. Box 20, Sovereign Way, Tonbridge, Kent. £45·00.

Catholic Directory.—18 Crosby Road North, Liverpool. £14·50.

Charities Digest.—501–5 Kingsland Rd., E.8. £7·65.

Chemical Industry Directory.—P.O. Box 20, Sovereign Way, Tonbridge, Kent. £55·00.

"Chemist & Druggist" Directory.—P.O. Box 20, Sovereign Way, Tonbridge, Kent. £55·00.

Christies' Review of the Season.—Littlegate House, Oxford. (Dec.) £30·00.

Church of England Year Book.—Church House, Dean's Yard, Westminster, S.W.1. (Jan.) £13·50.

Church of Scotland Year Book.—121 George St., Edinburgh 2. (Apr.) £7·95.

City of London Directory.—Fairfax Ho., Colchester. £16·25, £14·25.

Commonwealth Universities Year Book.—36 Gordon Square, W.C.1. (Sept.) £75·00.

Computer Users' Year Book.—32–34 Broadwick St., W.1. £85·00.

Concrete Year Book.—11 Grosvenor Cres., S.W.1. £32·00.

Consulting Engineers Who's Who & Year Book.—178–202 Gt. Portland St., W.1. £19·50.

"Containerization International" Year Book.—72 Broadwick St., W.1. (Mar.) £82·00.

Contractors and Public Works, Annual Directory of.—Beauchamp Clark Garden Centre, Willesborough, Ashford, Kent. £9·90.

Coventry Evening Telegraph Year Book and Who's Who.—Coventry Newspapers Ltd., Corporation St., Coventry. (Nov.) £8·25.

Current Law Year Book.—11 New Fetter La., E.C.4. £45·00.

"Daily Mail" Year Book.—Carmelite House, Fleet St., E.C.4. (Dec.) £2·75.

Decorating Contractor Annual Directory.—2 Queensway, Redhill, Surrey. £5·50.

Decorative Art & Modern Interiors.—35 Red Lion Sq., W.C.1. £19·95.

Diplomatic Service List.—H.M.S.O., Atlantic House, Holborn Viaduct, E.C.1. (April) £16·95.

Directory of Directors.—East Grinstead House, East Grinstead, W. Sussex. (Apr.) £64·00.

Directory of Official Architecture & Planning.—Fourth Avenue, Harlow, Essex. £38·00.

Directory of Opportunities for Graduates.—76 Dean St., W.1. 4v. each £7·95.

Do-it-Yourself Annual.—Link House, Dingwall Ave., Croydon. (Jan.) 85p.

Dod's Parliamentary Companion.—Hurst Green, E. Sussex TN19 7PX. £40.

Education Authorities' Directory and Annual.—Derby House, Bletchingley Rd., Merstham, Surrey. (Jan.) £33·00.

Education Year Book.—Fourth Avenue, Harlow, Essex. £35·00.

Electrical & Electronic Trader Year Book.—40 Bowling Green Lane, E.C.1. £10·00.

Electrical & Electronics Trades Directory.—P.O. Box 26, Station House, Hitchin, Herts. (Feb.) £45·00.

Electrical Contractor's Yearbook.—34 Palace Court, W.2. £2·50.

Electricity Supply Handbook.—40 Bowling Green Lane, E.C.1. (Apr.) £9·00.

"Engineer" Buyers' Guide, 30 Calderwood St., S.E.18. £24·00.

Europa Year Book.—18 Bedford Square, W.C.1. 2 v. £130·00.

European Chemical Buyers' Guide.—40 Bowling Green Lane, E.C.1. £25·00.

European Glass Directory & Buyer's Guide.—2 Queensway, Redhill, Surrey. £32·00.

European Plastics Buyers' Guide.—40 Bowling Green Lane, E.C.1. £25·00.

Export Data: Exporter's Year Book.—Sovereign Way, Tonbridge, Kent. (Dec./Jan.) £20·00.

Fairplay World Shipping Year Book.—52–54 Southwark St., S.E.1. £20·00.

Farm and Garden Equipment Guide.—40 Bowling Green Lane, E.C.1. £5·50.

Finishing Diary.—4 Local Board Rd., Watford. £6·00.

Fire Protection Directory.—Sovereign Way, Tonbridge, Kent. (Nov.) £15·00.

"Flight" Directory of British Aviation.—40 Bowling Green Lane, E.C.1. £20·00.

Food Industry Directory.—48 Poland St., WIV 4PP. £29·00.

Frozen & Chilled Foods Year Book.—2 Queensway, Redhill, Surrey. £22·00.

Fruit Trades World Directory.—1–5 Bath St., E.C.1. (Jan.) £5·00.

Furnishing Trade, Directory to the.—P.O. Box 20, Sovereign Way, Tonbridge, Kent. £60·00.

Gas Directory.—P.O. Box 20, Sovereign Way, Tonbridge, Kent. (Jan.) £45·00.

Gibbons' Stamps of the World Catalogue.—5 Parkside, Christchurch Rd., Ringwood, Hants.(Oct.) 2v. each £15·50.

Good Food Guide.—P.O. Box 6, Mill Rd., Dunton Green, Sevenoaks, Kent. £10·95.

Good Hotel Guide.—P.O. Box 6, Mill Rd., Dunton Green, Sevenoaks, Kent. £10·95.

Government & Municipal Contractors Register.—39 East St., Epsom, Surrey. (Jan.) £30·00.

Guinness Book of Records.—2 Cecil Court, London Rd., Enfield. (Oct.) £8·95.

Hi-fi Year Book.—40 Bowling Green Lane, E.C.1. £3·00.

Hollis Press and P.R. Annual.—Contact House, Lower Hampton Rd., Sunbury-on-Thames. (Oct.) £31·50.

Horse & Hound Hunter Chasers & Point to Pointers.—King's Reach Tower, Stamford St., S.E.1. £5·45.

Hospitals & Health Services Yearbook.—75 Portland Place, W.1. £48·90.

Hotel, Restaurant & Catering Supplies.—39 East St., Epsom, Sy. £30·00.

Hutchins' Priced Schedules.—33 Station Rd., Bexhill-on-Sea. £22·00.

Independent Schools Year Book.—35 Bedford Row, W.C.1. 2v. £12·95, £8·50.

Insurance Directory & Yearbook.—The Butts, Half Acre, Brentford, Middx. £12·50.

International Art & Antiques Yearbook.—72 Broadwick St., W.1. (Jan.) £12·00.

International Film & Television Year Book.—142 Wardour St., W.1. (Jan./Feb.) £18·00.

International Shipping & Shipbuilding Directory.—Sovereign Way, Tonbridge, Kent. £29·00.

International Yearbook & Statesman's Who's Who.—East Grinstead House, East Grinstead, W. Sussex. (Apr.) £75·00.

Jane's All The World's Aircraft.—238 City Rd., E.C.1. (Oct.) £79·00.

Jane's Armour & Artillery.—238 City Rd., E.C.1. (Nov.) £80·00.

Jane's Fighting Ships.—238 City Rd., E.C.1. (Aug.) £77·00.

Jane's Freight Containers.—238 City Rd., E.C.1. (Nov.) £80·00.

Jane's High Speed Marine Craft & Air Cushion Vehicles.—238 City Rd., E.C.1. £72·00.

Jane's Infantry Weapons.—238 City Rd., E.C.1. (May) £77·00.

Jane's Weapon Systems.—238 City Rd., E.C.1. £83·00.

Jane's World Railways.—238 City Rd., E.C.1. £78·00.

Jewish Year Book.—25 Furnival St., E.C.4. (Jan.) £10·50.

Kelly's Business Directory.—East Grinstead House, East Grinstead, W. Sussex. £70·00.

Kelly's Handbook to the Titled, Landed and Official Classes.—East Grinstead House, East Grinstead, W. Sussex. £18·00.

Kelly's Post Office London Business Directory.—East Grinstead House, East Grinstead, W. Sussex. 2v. £75·00.

Kelly's U.K. Exports.—East Grinstead House, East Grinstead, W. Sussex. £45·00.

Kempe's Engineers Year Book.—30 Calderwood St., S.E.18. £45·00.

Kemp's International Film & T.V. Directory.—1–5 Bath St., E.C.1. (May) £28·00.

Kemp's International Music & Recording Industry Year Book.—1–5 Bath St., E.C.1. £15·00.

Kemp's Property Industry Year Book.—1–5 Bath St., E.C.1. (Feb.) £17·50.

Kime's International Law Directory.—170 Sloane St., S.W.1. (June) £18·50.

Laxton's National Building Price Book.—East Grinstead House, East Grinstead, W. Sussex. £33·00.

Library Association Yearbook.—7 Ridgmount St., Store St., W.C.1. (May) £17·50.

Lloyd's List of Shipowners.—71 Fenchurch St., EC3M 4BS. (Sept.) £55·00.

Lloyd's Maritime Guide.—71 Fenchurch St., EC3M 4BS. (Jan.) £50·00.

Lloyd's Nautical Year Book.—Sheepen Pl., Colchester CO3 3LP. (Sept.) £17·50.

Lloyd's Register of Ships.—71 Fenchurch St., EC3M 4BS. (July). £250·00.

London Chamber of Commerce and Industry Directory.—2 Queensway, Redhill, Surrey. (Nov.) £40·00.

Lyle's Official Antiques Review, Glenmayne, Galashiels TD1 3NR. £12·95.

Lyle's Official Arts Review, Glenmayne, Galashiels TD1 3NR. £12·95.

Macmillan & Silk Cut Nautical Almanack.—Little Essex St., W.C.2. £13·95.

Magistrates' Court Guide.—Borough Green, Sevenoaks, Kent. £15·95.

Manufacturers & Merchants Directory.—East Grinstead House, East Grinstead, W. Sussex. £60·00.

"Mechanical World" Electrical Year Book.—14 St. James Rd., Watford. £3·95.

"Mechanical World" Year Book.—14 St. James Rd., Watford. £4·50.

Medical Annual.—Techno House, Redcliffe Way, Bristol. (Sept.). £22·50.

Medical Directory.—Fourth Avenue, Harlow, Essex. (Apr.) 2v, £85·00.

Medical Register.—44 Hallam St., W.1. (Mar.) £57·00.

Middle East & North Africa.—18 Bedford Sq., W.C.1. (Oct.) £52·00.

Miller's Antiques Price Guide.—Sissinghurst Court, Sissinghurst, Kent. £14·95.

"Mining" Annual Review.—P.O. Box 10, Edenbridge, Kent. £30·00.

Mining International Year Book.—Fourth Avenue, Harlow, Essex. (June) £59·00.

Modern Publicity.—35 Red Lion Sq., W.C.1. (Sept.) £29·95.

Motor Industry of Great Britain.—Forbes House, Halkin St., S.W.1. (Oct.) £34·00.

Municipal Yearbook & Public Services Directory, 178 Gt. Portland St., W.1. (Dec.) £42·50.

Music Guide, International.—136 Tooley St., S.E.1. £6·95.

National Trust Year Book.—18 Bedford Sq., W.C.1. £7·00.

Nautical Almanac.—H.M.S.O., Atlantic House, Holborn Viaduct, E.C.1. (Oct.) £9·95.

North Sea & Europe Offshore Yearbook.—Minster Ho., Arthur St., E.C.4. £25·00.

Off Licence News Directory.—5 Southwark St., S.E.1. £6·00.

Offshore Oil & Gas Year Book.—126 Pentonville Rd., N.1. £50·00.

Old Moore's Almanac.—Yeovil Rd., Slough, Bucks. (July) 50p.

Owen's Business Directory and Travel Guide.—22 Mount Pleasant, Alperton, Middx. (Mar.) £52·00.

Packaging Review Directory.—40 Bowling Green Lane, E.C.1. £28·00.

Paper Trade Directory of the World, Phillips'.—P.O. Box 20, Sovereign Way, Tonbridge, Kent. £65·00.

Pears Cyclopedia.—44 Bedford Square, W.C.1. £10·95.

Penrose Annual.—10–16 Elm St., W.C.1. (Apr.) £21·00.

Personnel Yearbook.—120 Pentonville Rd. N.1. £25·00.

Photography Year Book.—45 The Broadway, Tolworth, Surbiton, Surrey. £14·95.

Polymers, Paint & Colour Year Book.—2 Queensway, Redhill, Surrey. £30·50.

Ports of the World.—Sheepen Pl., Colchester, Essex. £75·00.

Printing Industries Annual.—11 Bedford Row, W.C.1. £20·00.

Printing Trades Directory.—P. O. Box 20, Sovereign Way, Tonbridge, Kent. £60·00.

Publishing, Directory of.—35 Red Lion Square, W.C.1. (Oct.) £26·00.

R.A.C. Continental Hotel Guide.—P.O. Box 100, RAC House, Lansdowne Rd., Croydon. (Mar.) £4·95.

R.A.C. Hotel & Touring Guide.—P.O. Box 100, RAC House, Lansdowne Rd., Croydon. (Apr.) £6·00.

R.U.S.I. & Brassey's Defence Year Book.—Headington Hill Hall, Oxford. £32·00, £15·95.

Raceform Up-to-date Form Book: Flat Racing.—2 York Rd., S.W.11. (Dec.) £14·00.

Raceform Up-to-date Form Book: National Hunt.—2 York Rd., S.W.11. (Aug.) £14·00.

Railway Directory & Year Book.—40 Bowling Green Lane, E.C.1. (Dec.) £30·00.

Railway World Annual.—Terminal House, Shepperton, Middx. £6·00.

Reed's Nautical Almanac & Tide Tables.—36–37 Cock Lane, E.C.1. (Oct.) £13·25.

RIBA Directory of Practices.—Royal Institute of British Architects, 35–37 Moreland St., E.C.1. (Oct.) £32·50.

Royal Society Year Book.—6 Carlton Ho. Terr., S.W.1. (Feb.) £10·50.

Ruff's Guide to the Turf & "Sporting Life" Annual.—Paulton, Bristol BS18 5LQ. (Dec.) £47·50.

Salvation Army Year Book.—117–121 Judd St., W.C.1. (Nov.) £2·75, £5·50.

Scottish Current Law Year Book.—St. Giles St., Edinburgh. £21·00.

Scottish Law Directory.—34–36 North Frederick St., Glasgow. £21·50.

Screen World.—55–57 Gt. Ormond St., W.C.1. £12·95.

Sell's Aviation Europe.—39 East St., Epsom, Surrey. £35·00.

Sell's British Exporters.—39 East St., Epsom, Surrey. £30·00.

Sell's Building Index.—39 East St., Epsom, Surrey. £30·00.

Sell's Directory of Products and Services.—39 East St., Epsom, Surrey. (July) £40·00.

Sell's Health Service Buyers Guide.—39 East St., Epsom, Surrey. £30·00.

Sheet Metal Industries Year Book.—2 Queensway, Redhill, Surrey. £29·50.

Shipowners, Shipbuilders & Marine Engineers, Directory of.—40 Bowling Green Lane, E.C.1. £45·00.

Specification.—9–13 Queen Anne's Gate, S.W.1. (May) 5v. £45·00.

Spon's Architects' & Builders' Price Book.—11 New Fetter La., E.C.4. £32·00.

Spon's Mechanical & Electrical Services Prices Book.—11 New Fetter La., E.C.4. £32·00.

Statesman's Yearbook.—Little Essex St., W.C.2. (Aug.) £25·00.

Stock Exchange Official Year Book.—Houndmills Estate, Basingstoke, Hants. £115·00.

Stone's Justices' Manual.—Borough Green, Sevenoaks, Kent. 3v. (May) £96·00.

Stores, Shops, Hypermarkets Retail Directory.—48 Poland St., W.1. £64·00.

T.V. & Radio: Guide to Independent Television.—247 Tottenham Court Rd., W.1. £5·90.

Tanker Register.—12 Camomile St., E.C.3. (May) £80·00.

"Timber Trades Journal" Telephone Address Book.—Sovereign Way, Tonbridge, Kent. £29·00.

Trades Register of London.—1–5 Bath St., E.C.1. (Jan.) £4·50.

Travel Trade Directory.—30 Calderwood St., S.E.18. (July) £18·00.

U.K. Kompass Register of British Industry & Commerce.—East Grinstead House, East Grinstead, W. Sussex. v. 1–3, £120·00, v. 4, £90·00.

Unit Trust Year Book.—Greystoke Pl., Fetter Lane, E.C.4. (Mar.) £24·00.

United Reformed Church Year Book.—86 Tavistock Pl., W.C.1. (Sept.) £6·50.

Veterinary Annual.—42–44 Triangle West, Bristol. (Dec.) £25·00.

"Watchmaker, Jeweller & Silversmith" Directory.—40 Bowling Green Lane, E.C.1. £5·00.

Water Services Year Book.—2 Queensway, Redhill, Surrey. (Oct.) £25·00.

Which Degree?—53 Frith St., W.1. 5v. £34·75.

Whitaker's Almanack.—12 Dyott St., W.C.1. (Nov.) £25·50, £15·25, £7·50.

Whitaker's Publishers in the United Kingdom and their Addresses.—12 Dyott St., W.C.1. (Mar.) £4·00.

Who Owns Whom?—6–8 Bonhill St., E.C.2. 2v. £79·00.

Who's Who.—35 Bedford Row, W.C.1. £55·00.

Who's Who, International.—18 Bedford Sq., W.C.1. (Sept.) £65·00.

Willing's Press Guide.—East Grinstead House, East Grinstead, W. Sussex. (Feb.) £46·00.

Wine & Spirit Trade International Year Book.—76 Dean St., W.1. £18·50.

Wisden Cricketers' Almanack.—13–14 Eldon Way, Lineside Estate, Littlehampton. £15·95; £13·95.

World Hotel Directory.—Fourth Avenue, Harlow, Essex. £45·00.

World Insurance Year Book.—Fourth Avenue, Harlow, Essex. £75.00.

World of Learning.—18 Bedford Square, W.C.1. (Jan.) 2v. £80·00.

World Shipping Year Book.—Minster House, Arthur St., E.C.4. £27·00.

Writers' & Artists' Year Book.—35 Bedford Row, W.C.1. (Jan.) £5·95.

THE PRESS COUNCIL
1 Salisbury Square, EC4Y 8AE
[01–353 1248]

In April, 1947, a Royal Commission was appointed to enquire into the control, management and ownership, etc., of the Press and news agencies and to make recommendations thereon. The Commission, in its report of June, 1949, recommended *inter alia* that a voluntary Press Council be formed.

A constitution ultimately set up provided for the establishment of such a council on July 1, 1953. This constitution was materially amended in 1963 by the introduction of an independent chairman and up to 20 per cent. lay membership. In 1973, the Council was increased to 30 (excluding the Chairman) of whom one-third were lay members. Following a recommendation of the third Royal Commission on the Press made in 1977, the size of the Council was increased in 1978 to 36 (excluding the Chairman) of which half are press members and half non-press members. The objects of the Council are (1) to preserve the established freedom of the British Press; (2) to maintain the character of the British Press in accordance with the highest professional and commercial standards; (3) to consider complaints about the conduct of the Press or the conduct of persons and organizations towards the Press; to deal with these complaints in whatever manner might seem practical and appropriate and record resultant action; (4) to keep under review developments likely to restrict the supply of information of public interest and importance; (5) to report publicly on developments that may tend towards greater concentration or monopoly in the Press (including changes in ownership, control and growth of Press undertakings) and to publish statistical information relating thereto; (6) to make representations on appropriate occasions to the Government, organs of the United Nations and Press organizations abroad; and (7) to publish periodical reports recording the Council's work and to review, from time to time, developments in the Press and the factors affecting them.

The constitution of the Council provides for 18 Press members who are editorial and managerial nominees of The Newspaper Publishers Association Ltd. (3), The Newspaper Society (3), The Periodical Publishers Association Ltd. (2), The Scottish Daily Newspaper Society (1), Scottish Newspaper Proprietors' Association (1), The Guild of British Newspaper Editors (2), The National Union of Journalists (4), The Institute of Journalists (2) plus 18 public members appointed by the Press Council Appointments Commission. In addition each constituent body nominates one official as a non-voting member.

Chairman, Rt. Hon. Sir Zelman Cowen, G.C.M.G., G.C.V.O., Q.C.
Director, K. Morgan, O.B.E.

THE QUEEN'S AWARDS FOR EXPORT AND TECHNOLOGY

The Queen's Award for Export Achievement and The Queen's Award for Technological Achievement were instituted by Royal Warrant in 1976, the two separate Awards taking the place of The Queen's Award to Industry which had been instituted in 1965.

The Awards are designed to recognize and encourage outstanding achievements in exporting goods or services from the United Kingdom and in advancing process or product technology. They differ from a personal Royal honour in that they are given to a unit as a whole—management and employees working as a team.

They may be applied for by any organization within the United Kingdom, the Channel Islands or the Isle of Man producing goods or services which meet the criteria for the Awards. Eligibility is not influenced in any way by the particular activities of the unit applying, its location, or size. Units or agencies of central and local government with industrial functions, as well as research associations, educational institutions and bodies of a similar character, are also eligible, provided that they can show they have contributed to industrial efficiency.

The criteria on which recommendations for the Awards are based are:

1. Export Achievement

A substantial and sustained increase in export earnings to a level which is outstanding for the products or services concerned and for the size of the applicant unit's operations. Account will be taken of any special market factors described in the application. Applicants for the Award will be expected to explain the basis of the achievement (e.g. improved marketing organization or new initiative to cater for export markets) and this will be taken into consideration. Export earnings considered will include receipts by the applicant unit in this country from the export of goods produced in this country, and the provision of services to non-residents. Account will be taken of the overseas expenses incurred other than marketing expenses. Income from profits (after overseas tax) remitted to this country from the applicant unit's direct investments in its overseas branches, subsidiaries or associates in the same general line of business will be taken into account, but not receipts from profits on other overseas investments or by interest on overseas loans or credits.

2. Technological Achievement

A significant advance, leading to increased efficiency, in the application of technology to a production or development process in British industry or the production for sale of goods which incorporate new and advanced technological qualities.

Each award is formally conferred by a Grant of Appointment and is symbolized by a representation of its emblem cast in stainless steel and encapsulated in a transparent acrylic block.

Awards are held for five years and holders are entitled to fly the appropriate Award flag and to display the emblem on the packaging of goods produced in this country, on the goods themselves, on the unit's stationery, in advertising and on certain articles used by employees: units may also display the emblem of any previous current Awards during the 5 years.

Awards are announced on April 21 (the actual birthday of Her Majesty the Queen) and published formally in a special supplement to the London Gazette. All enquiries about the scheme and requests for application forms—completed forms must be returned by October 31—should be made to: The Secretary, The Queen's Awards Office, Dean Bradley House, 52 Horseferry Road, London SW1P 2AG. Telephone: 01-222 2277.

Export Achievement Awards

In 1987, the Queen's Award was conferred on the following concerns for export achievement:

Abekas Video Systems Ltd., Reading; The Process Systems Division of Air Products Ltd., Walton-on-Thames, Surrey; Ajax Magnethermic (UK) Ltd., Oxted, Surrey; The Scunthorpe Rod Mill Division of Allied Steel and Wire Ltd., Scunthorpe, Humberside; Ambassador Press Ltd., St. Albans; Amersham International PLC, Little Chalfont, Bucks.; Anson Ltd., Gateshead, Tyne and Wear; Apollo Fire Detectors Ltd., Havant, Hants.; Ayala-Abbott and Butters Ltd., Needham Market, Suffolk; Babydiner Ltd., Dunfermline; BEC Mobility Ltd., Brierley Hill, W. Midlands; "Bermuda" by Espeshal Ltd., London W.1; Birchwood Boat International Ltd, Sutton-in-Ashfield, Notts.; Bridport-Gundry PLC, Bridport, Dorset; The Hatfield Unit of The Civil Aircraft Division of British Aerospace PLC, Hatfield, Herts.; The Prestwick Unit of The Civil Aircraft Division of British Aerospace PLC, Prestwick, Ayrshire; Buro Happold, Bath; Cambridge University Press, Cambridge; Camtec Ltd. t/a Wild Country, Eyam, Sheffield; Central Independent Television PLC, Birmingham; Chadwyck-Healey Ltd., Cambridge; Claridge Mills Ltd., Selkirk; J. Comfort and Co. Ltd., London S.E.1; Conoco Ltd., London S.E.1; Cunard Line Ltd., London S.W.1; Dean Warburg Ltd., London W.1; Dearden Davies Associates Ltd., Hounslow, Middx.; Domino Amjet Ltd., Cambridge; Dowlish Developments Ltd., Ilminster, Somerset; Druck Ltd., Leicester; The Engineering Department of Dussek Campbell Ltd., Crayford, Kent; Ellison Circlips Ltd., Bingley, W. Yorks.; Envelopes International Ltd., Woodford, Essex; Eurocast Bar Ltd., Loughborough, Leics.; Femcare Ltd., Basford, Notts.; Ferrymasters Ltd. Altrincham, Cheshire; The Airborne Display Division of GEC Avionics Ltd., Rochester, Kent; GEC Turbine Generators Ltd., Rugby; GR-Stein Refractories Ltd., Sheffield; Gandalf Digital Communications Ltd., Warrington; Gracefern Ltd. t/a The Oakwood Design, Letchworth, Herts.; H & S Aviation Ltd., Portsmouth; J. M. Heaford Ltd., Altrincham; Heat Trace Ltd., Stockport; Henri-Lloyd Ltd., Worsley, Manchester; Hewlett-Packard Ltd., Wokingham, Berks.; Historic House Hotels Ltd., London S.W.1; Hozelock-ASL Ltd., Aylesbury, Bucks.; Domnick Hunter Filters Ltd., Birtley, Co. Durham; The Healthcare Division of Huntleigh Technology PLC, Luton, Beds.; IAD (UK) Ltd., Worthing, W. Sussex; IBM (United Kingdom) Holdings Ltd., Portsmouth; The Catalysts and Technology Licensing Business Group of The Chemicals and Polymers Group of ICI PLC, Billingham, Cleveland; IMI Radiators Ltd., Shipley, W. Yorks.; L K Tool Co. Ltd., Castle Donington, Derby; Link Analytical Ltd., High Wycombe, Bucks.; Lydiastar Ltd., London E.C.2; Mabey and Johnson Ltd., Reading; Peter MacArthur & Co. Ltd., Hamilton, Strathclyde; Manesty Machines Ltd., Speke, Liverpool; Marchem Ltd., Stockton-on-Tees, Cleveland; Marconi Instruments Ltd., St. Albans; Masterfil Ltd., Aylesbury, Bucks.; Mediscus Products Ltd., Wareham, Dorset; Metabrasive Ltd., Bilston, W. Midlands; Mitchell Cotts Mining Equipment Ltd., Penkridge, Staffs.; The Monotype International Division of Monotype Corporation PLC, Redhill, Surrey; David Nagli Ltd. t/a Artistic Treasures of Richmond, Richmond, Surrey; Neotronics Technology Ltd., Bishops Stortford, Herts.; Norbrook Laboratories Ltd., Newry, N. Ireland; Norris Biomedical (1980) Ltd., Basingstoke, Hants.; Ometron Ltd., London S.E.26; Osprey Electronics Ltd., Wick, Caithness; Oxford Instruments Ltd., Oxford; Oxford Lasers Ltd., Oxford; Page Aerospace Ltd., Sunbury-on-Thames, Middx.; Pall Europe Ltd., Portsmouth; Paxman Diesels Ltd., Colchester, Essex; W. Pearce & Co. (Northampton) Ltd., Northampton; Penn Fabrication Ltd., High Wycombe, Bucks.; Perkin-Elmer Ltd., Beaconsfield, Bucks.; Pilkington Communication Systems Ltd., Rhyl, Clwyd; Pink Soda (UK) Ltd., London W.1; Polymer Laboratories Ltd., Church Stretton, Salop; R S R Ltd., Cardiff; The Grass Machinery Division of Ransomes Sims and Jefferies PLC, Ipswich; Randall-Woolcott Services Ltd., Gerrards Cross, Bucks.; The Really Useful Group PLC, London W.1; Renishaw Metrology Ltd., Wotton under Edge, Gloucs.; J. A. Robertson & Sons (Dumfries) Ltd., Dumfries; Roche Products Ltd., Welwyn Garden City, Herts.; Romil Chemicals Ltd., Loughborough, Leics.; Derek Rose Pyjamas Ltd., Congleton, Cheshire; Ross Breeders Ltd., Newbridge, Midlothian; Royal Mint, Pontyclun, Mid Glamorgan; S A C International PLC, Bristol; Self-Changing Gears Ltd., Coventry; The Silver Crane Company, Suckley, Worcs.; Solid State Logic Holdings Ltd., Begbroke, Oxon.; The Bridgend Plant of Sony (UK) Ltd., Bridgend, Mid Glamorgan; Soundtracs PLC, Surbiton, Surrey; Spong Manufacturing Ltd., Leatherhead, Surrey; Stannah Lifts (Domestic Products) Ltd., Andover, Hants.; Strayfield International Ltd., Reading, Berks.; Sunseeker International (Boats) Ltd., Poole, Dorset; TI Stainless Tubes Ltd., Walsall; John Tams Ltd., Longton, Stoke-on-Trent; Thermomax Ltd., Bangor, N. Ireland; Thistle Hotels Ltd., London W.1; Total Audio Concepts Ltd., Basford, Notts.; Turbosound Ltd., London N.1; Turners Turkeys Ltd., Spalding, Lincs.; V G Instruments PLC, Crawley, Sussex; V S W Scientific Instruments Ltd., Old Trafford, Manchester; The Vapormatic Company (Exeter) Ltd., Exeter; Varn Products Co. Ltd., Irlam, Manchester; Viking (PTI) Ltd., Stockport; Vista Optics Ltd., Loughborough, Leics.; D. W. Windsor Ltd., Hoddesden, Herts.; Zed Instruments Ltd., Hersham, Surrey.

Awards for Technological Achievement 1987

In 1987, the following concerns received the Queen's Award for technological achievement:

A B Automotive Electronics Ltd., Cardiff (*Development of a microprocessor switching system used in the Jaguar XJ40 cars*); Amersham International PLC, Little Chalfont, Bucks. (*Development of the Amertech II device for hospital preparation of radioactive isotopes for organ scanning*); Baker Perkins Bakery Ltd., Peterborough (*Development of horizontal fixed bowl automatic dough mixing systems for bread dough production*); BICC Data Networks Ltd., Hemel Hempstead, Herts. (*Development of the ISOLAN range of equipment for connecting computers into local area networks*); Bonas Machine Co. Ltd., Sunderland (*Development of an electronic jacquard to control looms for high speed weaving of garment labels*); The Engineering Directorate of The BBC, London W.1 (*Use of the BBC's medium and long wave broadcasting channels for remote switching of electricity consumers'*

time-switches (*jointly with the Electricity Council*)); British Ceramic Research Ltd., Stoke-on-Trent (*Development of the "Total Colour Transfer System" for high quality automatic decoration of tableware*); Cambrian Plastics Ltd., Bridgend, Mid Glamorgan (*Development of the "Camplas" Fibreplacement Process for manufacture of glass reinforced plastic storage tanks for liquid fertilisers*); The Detector Research Division of The Royal Signals and Radar Establishment of The Ministry of Defence, Great Malvern, Worcs. (*Development of the "pyroelectric vidicon" infra-red sensitive TV camera tube used in Fire Service thermal imaging cameras (jointly with EEV)*); The Detector Research Division of The Royal Signals and Radar Establishment of The Ministry of Defence, Great Malvern, Worcs. (*Development of gallium arsenide photo-cathodes to amplify very low levels of light to provide night vision for aircraft pilots, gunsights and security surveillance (jointly with EEV)*); The Flight Systems (Farnborough) Department of The Royal Aircraft Establishment of The Ministry of Defence, Farnborough, Hants. (*Development of night vision systems for high speed ground attack aircraft (jointly with GEC Avionics)*); Dynapert Precima Ltd., Colchester, Essex (*Development of the MPS 500 microplacement system for automatic locating and epoxy-bonding of electronic components*); The Working Party on Energy Management and The Radio Teleswitching Project Group of The Electricity Council, London S.W.1 (*Use of the BBC's medium and long wave broadcasting channels for remote switching of electricity consumers' time-switches (jointly with The BBC)*); The Electronics Division of EEV, Chelmsford, Essex (*Development of the Thermal Imaging Camera Type P4428, applying the pyroelectric vidicon for Fire Service use (jointly with The Ministry of Defence)*); The Light Conversion Devices Division of EEV, Chelmsford, Essex (*Development of image intensifiers using gallium arsenide photocathodes to amplify very low levels of light to provide night vision for aircraft pilots, gunsights, and security surveillance (jointly with The Ministry of Defence)*); Exploration Consultants Ltd., Henley-on-Thames, Oxon. (*Development of the ECLIPSE computer software for accurate simulation of oil and gas reservoirs to assist in development and production decisions*); The Printed Circuit Group of The Bracknell Division of Ferranti Computer Systems Ltd., Bracknell, Berks. (*Development of METLAM metal cored laminated printed circuit boards for electronic assemblies*); The Airborne Display Division Rochester and Electro-Optical Surveillance Division Basildon, of GEC Avionics Ltd., Rochester, Kent and Basildon, Essex (*Development of night vision systems for high speed ground attack aircraft (jointly with The Ministry of Defence)*); The Engineering Division (Large Steam Turbines) of GEC Turbine Generators Ltd., Rugby, Warwicks. (*Development of new families of high efficiency steam turbines for power generation*); ICI Advanced Materials Group of Imperial Chemical Industries PLC, Welwyn Garden City, Herts. (*Development of the "Victrex" PEEK high temperature plastics*); Jaguar Cars Ltd., Coventry (*Design and development of the Jaguar XJ40 models*); The Landis Lund Division of Litton UK Ltd., Keighley, W. Yorks. (*Development of a computer controlled machine for grinding camshaft lobes for motor vehicle engines*); Nimbus Records Ltd., Monmouth, Gwent (*Development of an advanced system for making compact discs*); The Plant Breeding Institute, Trumpington, Cambs. (*The breeding of high yielding winter wheats for milling and bread making*);

Racal Marine Radar Ltd., New Malden, Surrey (*Development of a Digital Scan Converter for colour TV-type display of marine radar*); Racal Recorders Ltd., Southampton (*Development of the "Storehorse" self-calibrating tape recorder for data recording*); The Engineering and Manufacturing Team for The Wide Chord Fan Blades of Rolls-Royce PLC, Derby and Barnoldswick, London S.W.1 (*Development of the wide chord fan blades for the RB211-535E4 engines used on the Boeing 757 airliners*); The Optical Devices Division of STC Defence Systems, Paignton, Devon (*Development of advanced laser devices for fibre optic telecommunications*); Singer Link-Miles Ltd., Lancing, W. Sussex (*Development of aircraft simulators using multiple linked microprocessors*); The Cryogenics Group of Sulzer Bros. (UK) Ltd., Aldershot, Hants. (*Development of the "LINIT" range of small liquid*

nitrogen generators for clinical, agricultural and laboratory use in developing countries); Tech-Nel Data Products Ltd., Banbury, Oxon. (*Development of the NMX "Network Management Engine" for fault detection, restoral and diagnosis of computer networks*); VG Analytical Ltd., Manchester (*Development of laminated magnets for fast scanning mass spectrometers for clinical and environmental biochemical analysis*); The Wellcome Diagnostics Division of The Wellcome Foundation Ltd., Dartford, Kent (*Development of the "Wellcozyme" kit for the testing of blood for antibodies to the AIDS virus*); Wendstone Chemicals PLC, Billingham, Cleveland (*Development of a new, environmentally safe process for producing fluoroaromatic chemicals used as intermediate in the production of new plastics, pharmaceuticals and agricultural chemicals*).

LAND AND WATER SPEED RECORDS

PROGRESSIVE LAND SPEED RECORD

Due to disagreements between various governing bodies in the early days of racing and speed attempts a number of apparently authentic performances were never officially acknowledged. From 1911, the AIACR (Association Internationale des Automobile Clubs Reconnus), the fore-runner of the FIA (Fédération Internationale de l'Automobile), required that for record purposes only the average of two runs, in opposite directions over the course, would be accepted. The AAA (American Automobile Association) accepted one-way records until 1920. Where unofficial performances have been considered authentic, albeit unofficial, they have been included chronologically in the list but within brackets.

km/h	mph	Car	Driver	Venue	Year
63·16	39·24	Jeantaud	Comte Gaston de Chasseloup-Laubat	Achères, France	1898
66·66	41·42	Jenatzy	Camille Jenatzy	Achères, France	1899
70·31	43·69	Jeantaud	Comte Gaston de Chasseloup-Laubat	Achères, France	1899
80·34	49·62	Jenatzy	Camille Jenatzy	Achères, France	1899
92·78	57·65	Jeantaud	Comte Gaston de Chasseloup-Laubat	Achères, France	1899
105·88	65·79	Jenatzy	Camille Jenatzy	Achères, France	1899
(105·88	65·79)	Mercedes-Simplex	William Vanderbilt jr	Achères, France	1899)
120·80	75·06	Serpollet	Leon Serpollet	Nice, France	1902
(120·80	75·06	Mors	Baron de Caters	Bruges, Belgium	1902)
122·44	76·08	Mors	William Vanderbilt jr	Ablis, France	1902
123·28	76·60	Mors	Henri Fournier	Dourdan, France	1902
124·13	77·13	Mors	M Augieres	Dourdan, France	1902
(133·32	82·84	Mors	Charles Rolls	Clipstone, UK	1903)
134·33	83·47	Gobron-Brillié	Arthur Duray	Ostend, Belgium	1903
(135·33	84·09	Mors	Baron de Forest	Dublin, Ireland	1903)
(136·36	84·73	Mors	Charles Rolls	Clipstone, UK	1903)
136·36	84·73	Gobron-Brillié	Arthur Duray	Dourdan, France	1903
147·03	91·37	Ford Arrow	Henry Ford	Lake St Clair, USA	1904
148·52	92·30	Mercedes	William Vanderbilt jr	Daytona, USA	1904
152·54	94·78	Gobron-Brillié	Louis Rigolly	Nice, France	1904
156·25	97·25	Mercedes	Baron de Caters	Ostend, Belgium	1904
166·65	103·55	Gobron-Brillié	Louis Rigolly	Ostend, Belgium	1904
168·21	104·52	Darracq	Paul Baras	Ostend, Belgium	1904
168·42	104·65	Napier	A Macdonald	Daytona, USA	1905
(176·62	109·75	Mercedes	Herbert Bowden	Daytona, USA	1905)
174·46	109·65	Darracq	Victor Héméry	Arles, France	1905
195·65	121·57	Stanley Steamer	Fred Marriott	Daytona, USA	1906
202·69	125·95	Benz	Victor Héméry	Brooklands, UK	1909
211·98	131·72	Benz	Barney Oldfield	Daytona, USA	1910
(228·09	141·73	Benz	Bob Burman	Daytona, USA	1911)
199·72*	124·10	Benz	L. Hornsted	Brooklands, UK	1914
(241·20	149·87	Packard	Ralph de Palma	Daytona, USA	1919)
(251·11	156·03	Duesenberg	Tommy Milton	Daytona, USA	1920)
215·25	133·75	Sunbeam	Lee Guinness	Brooklands, UK	1922
230·64	143·31	Delage	Rene Thomas	Arpajon, France	1924
234·98	146·01	Fiat	Ernest Eldridge	Arpajon, France	1924
235·22	146·16	Sunbeam	Malcolm Campbell	Pendine, UK	1924
242·80	150·87	Sunbeam	Malcolm Campbell	Pendine, UK	1925
245·15	152·33	Sunbeam	Henry Segrave	Southport, UK	1926

km/h	mph	Car	Driver	Venue	Year
272·46	169·30	Thomas Special	Parry Thomas	Pendine, UK	1926
275·23	171·02	Thomas Special	Parry Thomas	Pendine, UK	1926
281·45	174·88	Napier-Campbell	Malcolm Campbell	Pendine, UK	1927
327·97	203·79	Sunbeam	Henry Segrave	Daytona, USA	1927
330·06	206·96	Napier-Campbell	Malcolm Campbell	Daytona, USA	1928
334·02	207·55	White-Triplex	Ray Keech	Daytona, USA	1928
372·48	231·44	Irving-Napier	Henry Segrave	Daytona, USA	1929
396·04	246·09	Napier-Campbell	Malcolm Campbell	Daytona, USA	1931
408·73	253·97	Napier-Campbell	Sir Malcolm Campbell	Daytona, USA	1932
438·48	272·46	Campbell Special	Sir Malcolm Campbell	Daytona, USA	1933
445·49	276·82	Campbell Special	Sir Malcolm Campbell	Daytona, USA	1935
484·62	301·13	Campbell Special	Sir Malcolm Campbell	Bonneville, USA	1935
502·12	312·00	Thunderbolt	George Eyston	Bonneville, USA	1937
556·01	345·49	Thunderbolt	George Eyston	Bonneville, USA	1938
563·59	350·20	Railton	John Cobb	Bonneville, USA	1938
575·34	357·50	Thunderbolt	George Eyston	Bonneville, USA	1938
595·04	369·74	Railton	John Cobb	Bonneville, USA	1939
634·39	394·20	Railton-Mobil	John Cobb	Bonneville, USA	1947
(654·3	406·6	Challenger	Micky Thompson	Bonneville, USA	1960)
(655·72	407·45	Spirit of America	Craig Breedlove	Bonneville, USA	1963)
648·73**	403·10	Bluebird-Proteus	Donald Campbell	Lake Eyre, Australia	1964
664·98	413·20	Wingfoot Express	Tom Green	Bonneville, USA	1964
698·49	434·02	Green Monster	Art Arfons	Bonneville, USA	1964
754·33	468·72	Spirit of America	Craig Breedlove	Bonneville, USA	1964
846·97	526·28	Spirit of America	Craig Breedlove	Bonneville, USA	1964
863·75	536·71	Green Monster	Art Arfons	Bonneville, USA	1964
893·96	555·48	Spirit of America-Sonic I	Craig Breedlove	Bonneville, USA	1965
927·87	576·55	Green Monster	Art Arfons	Bonneville, USA	1965
966·67	600·60	Spirit of America-Sonic I	Craig Breedlove	Bonneville, USA	1965
1014·51	630·38	The Blue Flame	Gary Gabelich	Bonneville, USA	1970
1019·46***	633·46	Thrust	Richard Noble	Black Rock Desert, USA	1983

* The first official two-way run record.

** The last time that a wheel-driven car has held the record. The current best by such a car is 658·67 km/h (409·27 mph) by Robert Summers in "Goldenrod" at Bonneville in 1965. However in 1964 at Lake Eyre, Donald Campbell in Bluebird attained a speed of 690·90 km/h (429·31 mph).

*** In 1979 at Rogers Dry Lake, USA, Stan Barrett in "The Budweiser Special" reached a speed of 1190·37 km/h (739·66 mph) over a short distance.

PROGRESSIVE WATER SPEED RECORD

(as homologated by the Union Internationale Motonautique)

km/h	mph	Boat	Pilot	Venue	Year
149·40	92·83	Miss America VII	George Wood	Detroit	1928
149·86	93·12	Miss America VII	Gar Wood	Indian Creek, Miami	1929
158·94	98·76	Miss England II	Sir Henry Segrave	Lake Windermere	1930
164·56	102·25	Miss America IX	Gar Wood	Indian Creek, Miami	1931
166·55	103·49	Miss England II	Kaye Don	Parana River	1931
177·38	110·22	Miss England II	Kaye Don	Lake Garda	1931
179·78	111·71	Miss America IX	Gar Wood	Indian Creek, Miami	1932
188·98	117·43	Miss England III	Kaye Don	Loch Lomond	1932
192·81	119·81	Miss England III	Kaye Don	Loch Lomond	1932
201·02	124·91	Miss America X	Gar Wood	Revier Canal	1932
203·31	126·33	Bluebird K3	Sir Malcolm Campbell	Lake Maggiore	1937
208·4	129·5	Bluebird K3	Sir Malcolm Campbell	Lake Maggiore	1937
210·73	130·94	Bluebird K3	Sir Malcolm Campbell	Lake Hallwyl	1938
228·10	141·74	Bluebird K4	Sir Malcolm Campbell	Coniston Water	1939
258·01	160·32	Slo-Mo-Shun IV	Stan Sayres	Lake Washington	1950
287·26	178·49	Slo-Mo-Shun IV	Stan Sayres	Lake Washington	1952
325·60	202·32	Bluebird K7	Donald Campbell	Ullswater	1955
347·9	216·2	Bluebird K7	Donald Campbell	Lake Mead	1955
363·12	225·63	Bluebird K7	Donald Campbell	Coniston Water	1956
384·75	239·07	Bluebird K7	Donald Campbell	Coniston Water	1957
400·12	248·62	Bluebird K7	Donald Campbell	Coniston Water	1958
418·99	260·35	Bluebird K7	Donald Campbell	Coniston Water	1959
444·71*	276·33	Bluebird K7	Donald Campbell	Lake Dumbleyung	1964
459·00	285·21	Hustler	Lee Taylor jr	Lake Guntersville	1967
464·45**	288·60	Spirit of Australia	Ken Warby	Blowering Dam	1977
514·39	319·627	Spirit of Australia	Ken Warby	Blowering Dam	1978

* Prior to his fatal crash on Coniston Water in 1967, Donald Campbell reached a speed of 528 km/h (328 mph).

** Warby reached an estimated speed of 555·9 km/h (345·4 mph) on one run.

NATIONAL HEALTH SERVICE

(and Local Authority Personal Social Services)

The National Health Service came into being on July 5, 1948, as a result of the National Health Service Act 1946. The Act placed a duty on the Secretary of State for Social Services to promote the establishment in England and Wales of a comprehensive Health Service designed to secure improvement in the mental and physical health of the people and the prevention, diagnosis and treatment of illness. The Secretary of State for Wales administers the National Health Service in Wales. There are separate Acts for Scotland and Northern Ireland, where the Health Services are run on very similar lines and the respective Secretaries of State are responsible to Parliament.

The National Health Service covers a comprehensive range of hospital, specialist, family practitioner (medical, dental, ophthalmic and pharmaceutical), artificial limb and appliance, ambulance, and community health services. Everyone normally resident in this country is entitled to use any of these services, there are no contribution conditions and the charges made (except those for amenity beds) are reduced or waived in cases of hardship. In addition the Secretary of State for Social Services is responsible under the Local Authority Social Services Act 1970 for the provision by local authorities of social services for the elderly, the disabled, those with mental disorders and for families and children.

The 1980 Health Services Act led to major changes in the structure of the Health Service. Since April 1982, District Health Authorities (DHAs) are responsible for the operational management of health services and for planning within regional and national strategic guidelines. There are 191 DHAs in England and nine in Wales and they are generally coterminous with the local authorities, which provide complementary personal social services. Each DHA is required to arrange its services into units of management at hospital and community services level, and as many decisions as possible are delegated to unit level. Four of the postgraduate teaching hospitals are now managed by DHAs (and eight are managed by special health authorities). Arrangements for the Family Practitioner Service are administered by Family Practitioner Committees (FPCs)—90 in England and eight in Wales. FPCs also contribute to the planning of health services.

The 14 Regional Health Authorities (RHAs) in England are responsible for regional planning, the allocation of resources to District Authorities, and the promotion of national policies and priorities. Performance review meetings are held annually between each hospital unit and its DHA, each DHA and its RHA, and between each RHA and Department of Health and Social Security Ministers, thereby strengthening Authorities' accountability to Parliament, whilst respecting the essentially locally-based nature of decision making. Professional advisory machinery incorporated within the structure ensures that Health Authorities and their staffs make decisions in the full knowledge of expert opinion.

The NHS is financed mainly from taxation and the cost met from moneys voted by Parliament. In Great Britain this amounts to more than £12 billion a year. The Department of Health and Social Security makes capital and revenue allocations to the RHAs and from these the RHAs meet the cost of their own services and make allocations to DHAs as well as funding Community Health Councils.

THE HEALTH SERVICES

Family Doctor Service

In England and Wales the Family Doctor Service (or General Medical Services) is organized by 98 Family Practitioner Committees which also organize the general dental, pharmaceutical and ophthalmic services for their areas. There is a Family Practitioner Committee for one or more District Health Authorities. Under the Health and Social Security Act 1984, FPCs became employing authorities in their own right on April 1, 1985, and all the members and the chairmen (31 in all) are appointed by the Secretary of State. Fifteen of the appointments are made from nominations received from committees, representing local doctors (8), dentists (3), pharmacists (2), ophthalmic opticians (1) and from among all four professions (1). Of the fifteen lay members, four each are appointed from nominations received from District Health Authorities and Local Authorities. The remainder (7) are appointed after such consultations as the Secretary of State considers appropriate. One member must be a qualified district nurse, midwife or health visitor with recent community nursing experience.

Any doctor may take part in the Family Doctor Scheme, provided the area in which he wishes to practise has not already an adequate number of doctors, and about 25,000 general practitioners in England and Wales do so. They may at the same time have private fee-paying patients. Family doctors are paid for their Health Service work in accordance with a scheme of remuneration which includes *inter alia* a basic practice allowance, capitation fees, reimbursement of certain practice expenses and payments for "out of hours" work.

Everyone aged 16 or over can choose his doctor (parents or guardians choose for children under 16) and the doctor is also free to accept a person or not as he chooses. A person may change his doctor if he wishes, either at once if he has changed his address or obtained permission from the doctor on whose list he is, or by informing the Family Practitioner Committee (in which case 14 days must elapse before the other doctor can accept him). When people are away from home they can still use the Family Doctor Service if they ask to be treated as "temporary residents", and in an emergency, if a person's own doctor is not available, any doctor in the service will give treatment and advice.

Patients are treated either in the Doctor's surgery or, when necessary, at home. Doctors may prescribe for their patients all drugs and medicines which are medically necessary for their treatment and also a certain number of surgical appliances (the more elaborate being provided through the hospitals).

Dental Service

Dentists, like doctors, may take part in the Service and may also have private patients. About 14,500 of the dentists available for general practice in England provide NHS general dental services. They are responsible to the Family Practitioner Committees in whose areas they provide services.

Patients are free to go to any dentist taking part in the Service and willing to accept them. Dentists receive payment for items of treatment for individual patients, instead of the capitation fee received by doctors. All treatment and dentures considered by the dentist to be necessary for dental fitness are available under the NHS. But for certain more expensive items such as metal dentures, bridges and gold fillings, it is necessary for the dentist to obtain the prior approval of the Dental Estimates Board.

A dentist may, with the approval of the Dental Estimates Board, charge his patients a prescribed sum for such types of treatment as crowns, inlays or metal dentures where these are not clinically necessary, if the patient wishes to have them. Where a denture supplied under the Service has to be replaced because of loss or damage, the whole or part of the cost may be charged to the patient if he has been careless. Under the current system of charges a patient pays the full cost of each item of treatment (excluding dentures), with a maximum charge for one course of treatment. The most recent revision of charges was introduced on April 1, 1985. They are as follows:—

1. The patient pays the full cost of each item of treatment (except dentures, bridges, crowns, inlays, pinlays and gold fillings) up to £17. If the total cost exceeds £17 the patient pays £17 plus 40 per cent of the excess.

2. For a denture or a bridge—

	Synthetic resin	Metal or Porcelain
(a) 1, 2 or 3 teeth	£26	£50
(b) 4–8 teeth	£28	£52
(c) More than 8 teeth	£30	£55
Maximum for more than one denture (or bridge)	£47	£98

3. For crowns, inlays, pinlays and gold fillings—
   (a) per tooth restored   £33 or £63 depending on the percentage of gold used (these charges include any other restorations in the same tooth, apart from root fillings)
   (b) maximum if more than one tooth restored £115

The maximum charge for a single course of treatment (including crowns, bridges and dentures) is £115.

No charge is made for clinical examination of a patient's mouth, arrest of bleeding, repairs to dentures, the cost of travelling if the dentist has to visit the patient at home or re-opening of the surgery in an emergency. Expectant mothers who were pregnant at the start of treatment, or women who have had a child during the preceding twelve months, children under 18 (except that you have to pay for dentures and bridges if you are over 16 and not in full-time education), or up to 19, but still in full-time attendance at school, do not pay charges. Full remission of charges is automatically available to people in receipt of supplementary benefit or F.I.S., and those entitled to free prescriptions and milk and vitamins on income grounds. Full or partial remission may also be available to those with incomes somewhat above supplementary benefits if they claim.

Pharmaceutical Service

Patients may obtain medicines, appliances and oral contraceptives prescribed under the NHS from any pharmacy whose owner has entered into arrangements with the Family Practitioner Committee to provide this service. Almost all pharmacy owners have done so and display notices that they dispense under the NHS: the number of these pharmacies in England and Wales at the end of 1986 was about 10,400. There are also some appliance suppliers who only provide special appliances. In country areas where access to a pharmacy may be difficult patients may be able to obtain medicines etc. from their doctor.

Except for contraceptives (for which there is no charge), a charge of £2·40 is payable for each item supplied unless the patient is exempt and the declaration on the back of the prescription form is completed. Exemptions cover children under 16, men aged 65 and over and women aged 60 and over, pregnant women and mothers who have had a baby within the last 12 months, people suffering from certain medical conditions, people who receive F.I.S. or supplementary benefit, people on low income and war pensioners (for their accepted disablements). In addition, prepayment certificates may be purchased by those patients not entitled to exemption who require frequent prescriptions. Further information about the exemption and prepayment arrangements is given in leaflet P.11.

General Ophthalmic Services

General Ophthalmic Services, which are administered by Family Practitioner Committees, form part of the ophthalmic services available under the National Health Service and provide for the testing of sight and, for children, full-time students under the age of 19 and people on a low income, help towards the cost of glasses under the NHS voucher scheme. Diagnosis and specialist treatment of eye conditions is available through the Hospital Eye Service as well as the provision of glasses of a special type. Testing of sight may be carried out by any ophthalmic medical practitioner or ophthalmic optician. The optician must hand the prescription, and a voucher if eligible, to the patient who can take this to any supplier of glasses of his choice to have dispensed. However, only registered opticians can supply glasses to children, and people registered as blind or partially sighted.

From July 1, 1986 children, those on a low income and people who require high powered lenses are eligible to have an NHS voucher to help pay for the glasses of their choice. All others must obtain their glasses privately. An NHS sight test remains free. People on a low income may claim help with the voucher scheme on form F1. People in receipt of supplementary benefit, F.I.S., free milk or vitamins, or free prescriptions because of low income are automatically entitled to the full value of the voucher towards the cost of their glasses. Those who are entitled may put it towards more expensive glasses and pay the extra cost themselves. Leaflet G11 gives further details.

Primary Health Care Services

Primary health care services include the general medical, dental, ophthalmic and pharmaceutical services, health centres and clinics, family planning outside the hospital service and preventive activities in the community including vaccination, immunisation and fluoridation. The district nursing and health visiting services include community psychiatric nursing for mentally ill people living outside hospital, and school nursing for the health surveillance of school children of all ages; much ante- and post-natal care and chiropody are also an integral part of the primary health care service.

Community Child Health Services

Pre-school services, usually at child health clinics, provide regular surveillance of children's physical, mental and emotional health and development, and advice to parents on their children's health and welfare. The School Health Service provides for the medical and dental examination of school-children, and advises the local education authority, the school, the parents and the pupil of any health factors which may require special consideration during the pupil's school life.

Hospitals and Other Services

The Secretary of State for Social Services has a duty to provide, to such extent as he/she considers necessary to meet all reasonable requirements, hospital and other accommodation; medical, dental, nursing and ambulance services; other facilities for the care of expectant and nursing mothers and young children, facilities for the prevention of illness, and the care and after-care of persons suffering from illness and such other services as are required for the diagnosis and treatment of illness. Rehabilitation services (occupational therapy, physiotherapy and speech therapy) may also be provided for those who need it and surgical and medical appliances are supplied in appropriate cases.

Specialists and consultants who take part in the Service can engage in private practice, including the treatment of their private patients in NHS hospitals.

In a number of hospitals accommodation is available for the treatment of private in-patients who undertake to pay full hospital maintenance costs and (usually) separate medical fees to a specialist as well. The amount of the medical fees is a matter for agreement between doctor and patient. Hospital charges for private resident patients are determined on a local basis by District Health Authorities.

Certain hospitals have accommodation in single rooms or small wards which, if not required for patients who need privacy for medical reasons, may be made available to patients who desire it as an amenity. In such cases the patients are treated in every other respect as National Health patients.

There is no charge for drugs supplied to National Health hospital in-patients but out-patients pay £1 per item unless they are exempt.

With certain exceptions, hospital out-patients have to pay fixed charges for dentures, glasses and certain appliances. The charge for glasses will be related to the type of lens prescribed; and for dentures will be up to a maximum charge of £60·00.

Local Authority Personal Social Services

Local authorities are responsible for the organization, management and administration of the personal social services and each authority has a Director of Social Services and a Social Services Committee responsible for the social services functions placed upon them by the Local Authority Social Services Act 1970.

NATIONAL INSURANCE AND RELATED CASH BENEFITS

The State insurance and assistance schemes, comprising schemes of national insurance and industrial injuries insurance, national assistance, and non-contributory old age pensions came into force from July 5, 1948. The Ministry of Social Security Act, 1966, replaced national assistance and non-contributory old age pensions with a scheme of non-contributory benefits, termed supplementary allowances and pensions. These, and subsequent measures relating to social security provision in Great Britain, were consolidated by the Social Security Act, 1975; the Social Security (Consequential Provisions) Act, 1975; and the Industrial Injuries and Diseases (Old Cases) Act, 1975: corresponding measures were passed for Northern Ireland. The Social Security Pensions Act, 1975, introduced a new State pensions scheme, which came into force on April 6, 1978, and the graduated pension scheme 1961–1975 has been wound up, existing rights being preserved. The Pensioners' Payments and Social Security Act, 1979, provided for a £10 bonus for pensioners in 1979 and also for the payment of a bonus in succeeding years at levels then to be determined. The Child Benefit Act, 1975, replaced family allowances (introduced 1946) with child benefit and one parent benefit.

Some of the above legislation has been superceded by the provisions of the Social Security Act, 1986, passed in July 1986 and introduced at various dates since.

NATIONAL INSURANCE SCHEME

The National Insurance scheme operates under the Social Security Acts, 1975 to 1980, and orders and regulations made thereunder. The scheme is financed by contributions payable by earners, employers and others (such as non-employed persons, paying voluntary contributions), together with the Treasury supplement. It provides the funds required for paying benefits payable under the Social Security Acts out of the National Insurance Fund and not out of other public money; for the making of payments towards the cost of the National Health Service and into the Redundancy and Maternity Pay Funds; and for paying benefit under the Industrial Injuries and Diseases (Old Cases) Act, 1975.

From April 6, 1987, the yearly Treasury supplement to the National Insurance Fund is equal to 7 per cent of all contributions (calculated so as to include those that would have been received if there had been no contracting out or statutory sick pay) after deducting the allocations to the National Health Service and the Redundancy and Maternity Pay Funds.

CONTRIBUTIONS

Contributions are of four classes:

Class 1 contributions are earnings-related, based on a percentage of the employee's earnings.

    (a) *primary Class 1* contributions are payable by employed earners and office-holders over age 16 with gross earnings at or above the lower earnings limit of £39·00 per week. For those with gross earnings at or above this level, contributions are payable on *all* earnings up to an upper limit of £295 per week. "Gross earnings" include overtime pay, commission, bonus, etc., without deduction of any superannuation contributions.

Women who marry for the first time no longer have a right to elect not to pay the full contribution rate. Married women and widows who before May 12, 1977, elected not to pay contributions at the full rate retain the right to pay a reduced rate over the same earnings range, which covers industrial injuries benefits and a contribution to the National Health Service. They lose this right if, after April 5, 1978, there are two consecutive tax years in which they have no earnings on which primary Class 1 contributions are payable and in which they have not been at any time self-employed earners. No primary contributions are due on earnings paid for a period on or after the employee's pension age, even when retirement is deferred.

    (b) *secondary Class 1* contributions are payable by employers of employed earners, and by the appropriate authorities in the case of office-holders. On Oct. 6, 1985, the upper earnings limit for employers' contributions was abolished and secondary contributions are payable on *all* the employee's earnings if they reach or exceed £39·00 per week.

Primary contributions are deducted from earnings by the employer, and are paid, together with the employer's contributions, to the Inland Revenue along with income tax collected under the PAYE system, so dispensing with contribution cards for employed earners. On Oct. 6, 1985 several lower percentage rates of contribution for lower paid employees and their employers were introduced.

Class 2 contributions are flat-rate, paid weekly by self-employed earners over age 16. Those with earnings below £2,125 a year for the tax year 1987–88 can apply for exception from liability to pay Class 2 contributions. People who while self-employed are excepted from liability to pay contributions on the grounds of small earnings may pay either Class 2 or Class 3 contributions voluntarily. Self-employed earners (whether or not they pay Class 2 contributions) may also be liable to pay Class 4 contributions based on profits or gains within certain limits. There are special rules for those who are concurrently employed and self-employed. Married women and widows can no longer choose not to pay Class 2 contributions. Those who elected not to pay Class 2 contributions before May 12, 1977, retain the right until there is a period of two consecutive tax years after April 5, 1978 in which they were not at any time either self-employed earners or had earnings on which primary Class 1 contributions were payable.

Class 2 contributions may be paid by direct debit through a bank or National Giro account or by stamping a contribution card.

Class 3 contributions are voluntary flat-rate contributions payable by persons over school-leaving age who would otherwise be unable to qualify for retirement pension and certain other benefits because they have an insufficient record of Class 1 or Class 2 contributions. Married women and widows who on or before May 11, 1977, elected not to pay Class 1 (full rate) or Class 2 contributions cannot pay Class 3 contributions while they retain this right.

Payment may be made by stamping a contribution card or by direct debit through a bank Giro account.

Class 4 contributions are payable by self-employed earners, whether or not they pay Class 2 contributions, on annual profits or gains from a trade, profession or vocation chargeable to income tax under Schedule D, where these fall between £4,590 and £15,340 a year. The maximum Class 4 contribution, payable on profits or gains of £15,340 or more, is £677·25.

Class 4 contributions are generally assessed and collected by the Inland Revenue along with Schedule D income tax. Self-employed persons under 16, or who at the beginning of a tax year are over pension age even where retirement is deferred, are not liable to pay Class 4 contributions. There are special rules for people who have more than one job, or who pay Class 1 contributions on earnings which are chargeable to income tax under Schedule D.

Regulations state the cases in which earners may be excepted from liability to pay contributions, and the conditions upon which contributions are credited to persons who are excepted. Leaflet NI 208 is obtainable from local Social Security offices.

The Secretary of State for Social Services is empowered by the Social Security Acts to alter certain rates of contributions by order approved by both Houses of Parliament, and is required by the same enactments to make annual reviews of the general level of earnings in order to determine whether such an order should be made.

For the period April 6, 1987 to April 5, 1988 the earnings brackets determining Class 1 contributions are:

Weekly earnings
£

a	0 — 39·00
b	39·00 — 64·99
c	65·00 — 99·99
d	100·00 — 149·99
e	150·00 — 295·00
f	over 295·00

Contribution rates for the period April 6, 1987 to April 5, 1988 are:

Class 1 contributions—not contracted out

Earnings bracket	Percentage of reckonable income		
	Employee's rate standard reduced		Employer's rate
a	0	0	0
b	5	3·85	5
c	7	3·85	7
d	9	3·85	9
e	9	3·85	10·45
f	9	3·85	10·45

Class 1 contributions—contracted out (*see* also p. 1211)

Employee's rates

Earnings bracket	On first £39·00		On earnings from £39·00–£295·00	
	standard	reduced	standard	reduced
a	0	0	0	0
b	5	3·85	2·85	3·85
c	7	3·85	4·85	3·85
d, e, f.	9	3·85	6·85	3·85

Employer's rates

Earnings bracket	On first £39·00	On earnings from £39·00–£295·00	On any earnings over £295·00
a	0	0	0
b	5	0·9	0
c	7	2·9	0
d	9	4·9	0
e	10·45	6·35	0
f	10·45	6·35	10·45

	Weekly flat rate
Class 2 contributions	£3·85
Class 3 contributions	£3·75
	Percentage of profits or gains
Class 4 contributions	6·3

THE STATE EARNINGS RELATED PENSION SCHEME

The Social Security Pensions Act, 1975, which came into force in April, 1978, aims to reduce reliance upon means-tested supplementary benefit in old age, in widowhood and in chronic ill-health by providing better pensions; to ensure that occupational pension schemes which are contracted out of part of the State scheme fulfil the conditions of a good scheme; that pensions are adequately protected against inflation; and that in both the State and occupational schemes men and women are treated equally. Retirement, widow's and invalidity pensions under the new scheme started in April 1979. Since April 6, 1979, flat-rate retirement and other State pensions have been augmented for employed earners by additional pensions related to earnings, but it will be twenty years before these additional pensions become payable at the full rate.

Under the scheme retirement, invalidity and widow's pensions for employees are related to the earnings on which national insurance contributions have been paid. For employees of either sex with a complete insurance record the scheme provides a category A retirement pension in two parts, a basic and an additional component. The basic pension corresponds to the old personal flat-rate national insurance pension. The additional component is 1¼ per cent of average earnings between the lower weekly earnings limit for Class 1 contribution liability and the upper earnings limit for each year of such earnings under the scheme, and will thus build up to 25 per cent in twenty years. When the number of years exceeds twenty, pensions will be based on contributors' twenty best years of earnings between age 16 and pension age (65 for men, 60 for women). Actual earnings are to be revalued in terms of the earnings level current in the last complete tax year before pension age (or death or incapacity). Both components of pensions in payment will be uprated annually in line with the movement of prices. Graduated retirement pensions in payment, and rights to such pensions earned by people who are still working, will be brought into the annual review of benefits.

Self-employed persons pay contributions towards the basic pension. The non-employed and employees with earnings below the lower limit may contribute voluntarily for basic pension. Although no primary Class 1 contributions or Class 2 or Class 4 contributions are payable by persons who work beyond pension age (65 for men, 60 for women), the employer's liability for secondary Class 1 contributions continues if earnings are at or above the lower earnings limit. Class 4 contributions are still payable up to the end of the tax year during which pension age is reached.

Widows will get the whole or part of additional pensions earned by their husbands with their widowed mother's allowances or widow's pensions; and can add to the retirement pensions earned by their own contributions any additional pensions earned by their husbands up to the maximum payable on one person's contributions. Men whose wives die when they are both over pension age can add together their own and their wives' pension rights in the same way as widows. Among the steps taken to give women equal treatment in benefit provision the State scheme permits years of home responsibilities to count towards satisfying the contribution conditions for retirement pension, widowed mother's allowance and widow's pension (and the "half-test" by which a married woman who married before age 55 could not qualify for a Category A retirement pension unless she had contributed on earnings at the basic level in at least half the years between marriage and pension age has been abolished with effect from Dec. 22, 1984). The range of short-term social security benefits and industrial injury benefits under the Social Security Act, 1975, continues with only minor changes.

Contracted Out and Personal Pension Schemes.— Members of occupational pension schemes which meet the standards laid down in the Social Security Pensions Act, 1975, can be contracted-out of the earnings related part of the state scheme relating to retirement and widows' benefits. Regulations made under the Act require employers to consult employees and their organisations and inform them of their intention to contract out. (Leaflets relating to pensions and guidance for employers about contracting-out are available from local Social Security offices.) The Act also contains provisions ensuring equal access to membership of schemes for men and women.

Until April 6, 1988, occupational pension schemes can only contract out if they promise a pension that is related to earnings. These are known as contracted-out salary related schemes. They must provide a pension that is not less than the guaranteed minimum pension (G.M.P.), which is broadly equivalent to the state earnings related pension. However, new options have been introduced by the Social Security Act, 1986. From April 6, 1988, occupational pension schemes which promise a minimum level of contributions will also be able to contract out. These are known as contracted-out money purchase schemes. They provide a pension based on the value of the fund built up in the scheme.

In addition, from July 1988 employees whose employers do not provide a pension scheme will be able to start their own personal pension instead of staying in the state earnings related pension scheme. From April 6, 1988, this choice will be open to all employees even if their employer does have a pension scheme. A personal pension, like a contracted-out money purchase scheme, provides a pension based on the value of the fund built up in the scheme.

The decision on whether or not an occupational pension scheme may become contracted-out lies with the Occupational Pension Board, an independent statutory body who have a general responsibility for supervising contracting-out. They also consider and approve personal pension schemes which can be used instead of state additional pension.

The State earnings related pension payable to a member of a contracted-out salary related scheme, or his widow, will be reduced by the amount of G.M.P. payable (which in the case of a widow must be at least half of the late husband's G.M.P. entitlement). Members of contracted-out money purchase schemes and personal pension schemes, or their widows, have no G.M.P. entitlement as such. But the state earnings related pension payable will be reduced by an amount equivalent to a G.M.P. (or widow's G.M.P.).

From April 6, 1988 contracted-out salary related schemes must also provide a widower's G.M.P. which must be at least half of the late wife's G.M.P. entitlement built up from April 6, 1988. Contracted-out money purchase schemes and personal pension schemes must provide half-rate widower's benefit.

In contracted-out schemes, both the employee and the employer pay the full ordinary rate of contribution on the first £39·00 (1987–88 figure) of earnings but earnings above that amount attract a lower rate of contribution from the employee, and from the employer where the employee's earnings are under £295·00 (1987–88 figure): where the employee's earnings exceed this amount, the full ordinary rate of contribution is payable only by the employer, the employee has no liability for contributions on these earnings (*see also* p. 1210).

An employee who chooses a personal pension in place of S.E.R.P.S. or their employer's pension scheme must pay National Insurance contributions at the full ordinary rate (the employers share must also be paid at the same rate). The D.H.S.S. pay the difference between the lower contracted-out rate and the full ordinary rate for the personal pension scheme.

BENEFITS

The benefits payable under the Social Security Acts are as follows:

(1) Contributory Benefits:
    Unemployment benefit.
    Sickness benefit.
    Invalidity pension and allowance.
    Maternity benefit.
    Widow's benefit, comprising widow's allowance, widowed mother's allowance and widow's pension.
    Retirement pensions, categories A and B.

(2) Non-contributory Benefits:
    Child benefit.
    One parent benefit.
    Guardian's allowance.
    Invalid care allowance.
    Attendance allowance.
    Severe disablement allowance.
    Mobility allowance.
    Retirement pensions, categories C and D.
    Supplementary benefits.
    Family income supplement.

(3) Benefits for Industrial Injuries and Diseases.

Leaflets relating to the various benefits are obtainable from local Social Security offices.

The Social Security Acts empower the Secretary of State to increase certain rates of benefit by order approved by both Houses of Parliament, and require him to increase certain rates by such an order if an annual review shows that they have not retained their value in relation to the general level of prices obtaining in Great Britain.

The latest order providing for increases in benefit rates took effect from the week commencing April 6, 1987.

CONTRIBUTORY BENEFITS

Entitlement to the contributory benefits (except invalidity benefit) depends on contribution conditions being satisfied either by the claimant or by some other person (depending on the kind of benefit). The class or classes of contribution which for this purpose are relevant to each benefit are as follows:

Short-term benefits
Unemployment benefit	Class 1
Sickness benefit	Class 1 or 2
Maternity benefit	Class 1 or 2
Widow's allowance*	Class 1, 2 or 3

*(to be replaced by Widow's payment from April 1988).

Other benefits
Widowed mother's allowance	
Widow's pension	Class 1, 2 or 3
Category A retirement pension	
Category B retirement pension	

The system of contribution conditions relates to yearly levels of earnings on which contributions have been paid. The contribution conditions for different benefits are set out in summary form in leaflets available at local Social Security offices.

Unemployment Benefit

Benefit is payable in a period of interruption of employment for up to 312 days (a year, excluding Sundays). Spells of unemployment and sickness not separated by more than 8 weeks count as one period of interruption of employment. A person who has exhausted benefit requalifies when he has again worked as an employed earner for at least 16 hours a week for 13 weeks. These weeks need not be consecutive nor fall within the same year.

Disqualifications.—There are disqualifications from receiving benefit, *e.g.* for a period not exceeding thirteen weeks if a person has lost his employment through his misconduct, or has voluntarily left his employment without just cause, or has, without good cause, refused an offer of suitable employment or training.

Sickness Benefit

Sickness benefit is payable for up to 28 weeks of sickness in a period of interruption of employment and is then replaced by invalidity benefit (*see* below).

Disqualifications.—There are disqualifications from receiving sickness or invalidity benefit for a period not exceeding six weeks if a person has become incapable of work through his own misconduct or if he fails without good cause to attend for or submit himself to prescribed medical or other examination or treatment, or observe prescribed rules of behaviour.

Since April 6, 1986, employers are responsible for paying Statutory Sick Pay (S.S.P.) to their employees for up to 28 weeks of sickness in any period of incapacity for work. S.S.P. replaces the employee's entitlement to State Sickness Benefit which is not payable as long as any S.S.P. liability remains. S.S.P. is subject to P.A.Y.E. and to N.I. deductions. Employers can recover the S.S.P. they have paid out and can also withhold an extra amount to compensate themselves for the N.I. contributions they have paid on S.S.P. from the payments of N.I. they make each month to the Collector of Taxes. Employees who cannot get S.S.P. can claim State Sickness Benefit instead.

Invalidity Benefit

Normally, after 28 weeks of sickness, sickness benefit is replaced by an invalidity pension. In addition an invalidity allowance is payable if incapacity for work begins more than five years before pension age. The allowance varies according to the age on falling sick, and if still in payment at pension age will continue as an addition to retirement pension. From Sept. 16, 1985 invalidity allowance is reduced or withdrawn completely if there is entitlement to an additional earnings-related pension and/or a guaranteed minimum pension.

Maternity Benefit

Statutory maternity pay (S.M.P.) is administered by employers but there is still a state maternity allowance scheme for women who are self-employed or otherwise do not qualify for S.M.P.

In general, employers pay S.M.P. to pregnant women who have been employed by them for at least six months and earned at least the lower earnings limit for the payment of N.I. contributions. For those who have been employed for at least two years, payment of S.M.P. for the first six weeks is related to earnings, followed by up to twelve weeks at a standard rate of £32·85. Those who have been employed for at least six months but less than two years receive payment at standard rate only for the 18 weeks. Part-time working women also qualify for the earnings-related element if employed for at least five years. Women have some choice in deciding when to begin maternity leave but S.M.P. is not payable for any week in which work is done.

A woman may qualify for maternity allowance (M.A.) if she has been working and paying contributions at the full rate for at least 26 weeks in the 52-week period which ends 15 weeks before the baby is due. She also has an element of choice in deciding when to stop work and receive M.A., which is not payable for any period whe works.

Widow's Benefits

Only the late husband's contributions of any class count for widow's benefit in any of its three forms.

Widow's Allowance.—A woman who at her husband's death is under 60 (or over 60, if he had not retired), receives a cash allowance during the first 26 weeks of widowhood, with increases for each child, in addition to child benefit. Widow's Allowance will be replaced by Widow's payment (a single payment) from April 1988.

Widowed Mother's Allowance.—When the 26 weeks of widow's allowance have elapsed, a widow who is left with one or more dependent children receives a weekly cash allowance with increases for each child, in addition to child benefit. A widowed mother's personal allowance is payable to widows who, when their widow's or widowed mother's allowance ends, have living with them a son or daughter under 19, who has left school.

Widow's Pension.—A widow receives this pension when widow's allowance ends, if she was over 50 at the time of her husband's death; or when her widowed mother's allowance or widowed mother's personal allowance ends, if she is then over 50 (40 if widowed before February 4, 1957).

Flat-rate widow's pensions on a graduated scale were introduced in April 1971 for women who are widowed between the ages of 40 and 50 (to be raised to 45 and 55 from April 1988), or who cease to be entitled to a widowed mother's allowance between those ages.

Widow's benefit of any form ceases upon remarriage.

Retirement Pension
Categories A and B

A *Category A pension* is payable for life to men or women on their own contributions if (a) they are over pension age (65 for a man and 60 for a woman), and (b) they have retired from regular employment. Men aged 70 or over and women aged 65 or over are not required to satisfy condition (b).

Where a person does not retire at 65 (60 for a woman) or later cancels retirement, and does not draw a Category A pension, the weekly rate of pension is increased, when he or she finally retires or reaches·the age of 70 (65 for a woman), in respect of weeks when pension is foregone during the five years after reaching minimum pension age. Details of the increase in the rate of pension due to deferred retirement are given in leaflet NP32, available at D.H.S.S. offices. A married man can also earn extra pension for his wife.

A *Category B pension* is normally payable for life to a woman on her husband's contributions when he has retired, or is over 70, and has qualified for his own Category A pension, and she has reached 60 and retired from regular work or has reached 65. It is also payable on widowhood after 60 whether or not the late husband had retired and qualified for his own pension. The weekly pension is payable at the rate of the increase for a wife while the husband is alive, and at the single person's rate on widowhood after 60. Where a woman is widowed before she reaches 60, a Category B pension is paid to her on reaching 60 at the same weekly rate as her widow's pension if she retires. If a woman qualifies for a pension of each category she receives whichever pension is the larger. Details of the increase in the rate of pension due to deferred retirement are given in leaflet NP32A, available at D.H.S.S. offices.

A man aged 65 to 70, or a woman aged 60 to 65, who has qualified for pension will have it reduced if he or she earns more than a certain amount. Where an adult dependant is living with the claimant, an Adult Dependents Allowance will only be payable if the dependent's earning do not exceed the standard rate of unemployment benefit for a single person under pensionable age (*see* below). For the purpose of the dependency rule only, earnings will include payments by way of occupational pension. The earnings of a separated spouse affect the increase of retirement pension if they exceed £23·75 a week.

Unemployment, sickness or invalidity benefit is payable to men between 65 and 70 and women between 60 and 65 who have not retired from regular work and who would have been entitled to a retirement pension if they had retired at pension age. This applies in the case of sickness and invalidity benefit if incapacity for work is the result of an industrial accident or prescribed disease. These rates of benefit for people over pension age are shown in leaflet N.I. 196. A retirement pension will be increased by the amount of any invalidity allowance the pensioner was getting within the period of 8 weeks and one day before reaching minimum pension age. An age addition of 25p per week is payable if a retirement pensioner is aged 80 or over. (For attendance allowance and invalidity care allowance, *see* Non-contributory Benefits).

Graduated Pension

The graduated pension scheme under which national insurance contributions and retirement pensions were graduated within specified limits, according to earnings, was discontinued in April, 1975, under the Social Security Act, 1975. Any graduated pension which an employed person over 18 and under 70 (65 for a woman) had earned by paying graduated contributions between April 6, 1961, when the scheme started and April 5, 1975, will be paid when the contributor retires, or at 70 (65 for a woman), in addition to any retirement pension for which he or she qualifies.

Graduated pension is at the rate of 5·17p a week for each "unit" of graduated contributions paid by the employee (half a unit or more counts as a whole unit). A unit of contributions is £7·50 for men, and £9·00 for women, of graduated contributions paid.

A wife can get a graduated pension in return for her own graduated contributions, but not for her husband's. A widow gets a graduated addition to her retirement pension equal to half of any graduated additions earned by her late husband, plus any additions earned by her own graduated contributions. If a person defers retirement beyond 65 (60 for a woman), half the graduated pension he or she has forgone by deferring retirement for any period before April 6, 1979, will be treated as extra graduated contributions paid, and will count towards further graduated pension on retirement or at 70 (65 for a woman). From April 6, 1979, graduated pension will normally be increased by one-seventh of one per cent for each week of deferred retirement.

Rates of Benefits
(from week commencing April 6, 1987)

Benefit	Weekly rate £
Unemployment Benefit—standard rate	
Person under pension age	31·45
Increase for wife/other adult dependent	19·40
Person over pension age*	39·50
Increase for wife/other adult dependent	23·75
Sickness Benefit—standard rate	
Person under pension age	30·05
Increase for wife/other adult dependent	18·60
Person over pension age*	37·85
Increase for wife/other adult dependent	22·70
Invalidity Pension	
Person (under or over pension age)	39·50
Increase for wife or adult dependent	23·75
Invalidity Allowance*	
(maximum amounts payable)	
higher rate	8·30
middle rate	5·30
lower rate	2·65
Maternity Allowance	30·05
Widow's Allowance*	55·35
Widowed Mother's Allowance* and Widow's Pension*	39·50
Retirement pension*—*categories A and B*	
Single person	39·50
Increase for wife or adult dependent	23·75
Earnings limit for retirement pensioners	75·00

* These benefits attract an increase for each dependent child (in addition to child benefit) of £8·05.

NON-CONTRIBUTORY BENEFITS
Child Benefit

Child benefit is payable for all children in a family within the age limits, including the first or only child. There is an additional payment for the first or only child in certain one-parent families.

Guardian's Allowance

Where the parents of a child are dead, the person who has the child in his family may claim a guardian's allowance in addition to child benefit. The allowance in exceptional circumstances, is payable on the death of only one parent.

Invalid Care Allowance

Invalid care allowance is payable to persons of working age, who are not gainfully employed because they are regularly and substantially engaged in caring for a severely disabled person who is receiving attendance allowance or constant attendance allowance with either a war or services pension, industrial disablement workman's compensation, or an allowance under the Pneumoconiosis, Byssinosis and Miscellaneous Diseases Benefit Scheme.

Mobility Allowance

The allowance is, subject to certain conditions, payable to persons who are suffering from such physical disablement that they are unable to walk or virtually unable to walk, and their handicap is likely to last for at least a year. It can be claimed by persons over the age of 5 and under 65 (for this purpose a claim may be made up to 12 months from that birthday) and may be retained to age 75.

Severe Disablement Allowance

Persons of working age who have been continuously incapable of work for a period of at least 28 weeks but who do not qualify for a contributory invalidity pension may be entitled to severe disablement allowance. People who first become incapable of work after their 20th birthday must be at least 80 per cent disabled.

Attendance Allowance

Attendance allowance is payable to the severely disabled, as determined by the Attendance Allowance Board. The full rate is paid to those in need of a great deal of attention or supervision both by day and by night. The allowance is paid at the lower rate to those whose need for attention or supervision arises either by day or by night. There is a six-month qualifying period.

Non-contributory Retirement Pension
Categories C and D

A *Category C pension* is provided, subject to a residence test, for persons who were over pensionable age on July 5, 1948, and for women whose husbands are so entitled if they are over pension age and have retired from regular work, with increases for adult and child dependents. A *Category D pension* is provided for others when they reach 80 if they are not already getting a retirement pension of any category or if they are getting that pension at less than these rates. An age addition of 25p per week is payable if persons entitled to retirement pension or their dependants are aged 80 or over.

Rates of Benefits
(from week commencing April 6, 1987)

Benefit	Weekly rate £
Child Benefit (per child).............	7·25
One Parent Benefit	
First or only child of certain lone parents........................	4·70
Guardian's Allowance	8·05
Severe Disablement Allowance*	23·75
Increase for wife/other adult dependent	14·20
Mobility Allowance	22·10
Invalid Care Allowance*	23·75
Increase for wife/other adult dependent	14·20
Attendance Allowance	
higher rate	31·60
lower rate	21·10
Retirement Pension—Categories C* and D.	
Single person	23·75
Increase for wife/other adult dependent	14·20
(not payable with Category D pension)	

*These benefits attract an increase for each dependent child (in addition to child benefit) of £8·50.

SUPPLEMENTARY BENEFITS

The Supplementary Benefits scheme is operated under the provisions of the Supplementary Benefits Act, 1976, as amended by the Social Security Acts, 1980 and 1986. Leaflets explaining in detail the calculation of income and capital resources and of each category of requirements (normal requirements, additional requirements and certain housing costs) are available from social security offices. The benefit payable is the amount, assessed under the provisions of the Act and regulations made thereunder, by which the claimant's resources fall short of his requirements. Claimants will be sent a written notice showing how their benefit has been worked out, as is done for family income supplement.

The supplementary pension may be claimed by persons of pension age (65 for men, 60 for women) and the supplementary allowance normally by persons aged 16 or over but under pension age, who are not in full-time work. Benefit can be paid on top of retirement pension or other benefits or of earnings from part-time work.

Supplementary allowance is paid at two rates: the ordinary and the long-term scale rates. The long-term rates apply to all beneficiaries who are aged over 60, and also younger beneficiaries who are not required to be available for work, after they have been in receipt of supplementary allowance or another qualifying benefit continuously for at least one year. Otherwise, supplementary benefit is paid at the ordinary rate.

There is an addition of £1·25 to the standard scale rates for blind people. Claimants and dependents aged 80 or over qualify for an addition of 25p to long-term rates. Additional payments are made for certain housing costs.

FAMILY INCOME SUPPLEMENT

The supplement is payable to families, including one parent families, with at least one dependent child under 16 (or over 16 if still at school), whose total family income is below the "prescribed amount" if the man or woman is employed or self-employed, and normally so engaged, in remunerative full-time work (*i.e.*, 30 or more hours per week, 24 in the case of single parents). "Total income" includes the gross earnings of the claimant and his wife, but excludes child benefit or children's income, except for children's maintenance. The supplement is one-half of the amount by which the family's total income falls below the "prescribed amount", subject to a maximum payment; odd amounts are rounded up to the next 10p above, and the minimum amount payable is 20p a week. Usually the supplement is awarded for 52 weeks and is not affected if the claimant's circumstances change during that time. Claim forms (FIS 1) can be obtained at a Social Security Office or a Post Office. (From April 1988 Family Income Supplement will be replaced by Family Credit, payable to low-income working families.)

Rates of Benefits
(from week commencing April 6, 1987)

	Weekly rate £
SUPPLEMENTARY ALLOWANCES/PENSION	
Ordinary scale rate	
Couple	49·35
Single householder	30·40
Non-householder aged 18 and over ..	24·35
aged 16–17........	18·75
Any other person aged 11–15	15·60
under 11	10·40
Long-term scale rate	
Couple	61·85
Single householder	38·65
Non-householder aged 18 and over ..	30·95
aged 16–17........	23·70
Any other person aged 11–15	15·60
under 11	10·40
Boarders' personal expenses	
Ordinary scale rates	
Couple	20·00
Single person	10·00
Dependent child 18–19	10·00
16–17	6·00
11–15	5·15
under 11	3·35

Long-term scale rates
Couple .... 22·30
Single person .... 11·15

Residents in private and voluntary
residential care and nursing homes. 9·25

Board and lodging limits (depending on
* area † type of home)
Ordinary board and lodging* ..... 45·00–70·00
Hostels .... 70·00
Residential care homes .... 130·00–190·00
Nursing homes† .... 175·00–230·00
(The limits for residential care and nursing homes in
London can be increased by up to £17·50)

Heating additions
Lower rate .... 2·20
Higher rate .... 5·55
Central heating additions
Lower rate .... 2·20
Higher rate .... 4·40
(claims or entitlement to central heating addition
must predate Aug. 5, 1985).
Estate rate heating additions
Lower rate .... 4·40
Higher rate .... 8·80

Housing Benefit Needs Allowances
Single person .... 48·90
Single handicapped person .... 54·50
Couple/single parent .... 72·15
Couple, one handicapped/single handi-
capped parent .... 77·75
Couple, both handicapped .... 80·45
Dependent child addition .... 14·75
Pensioner addition .... 0·85

FAMILY INCOME SUPPLEMENT
Prescribed amount of income
Family with one child—under 11 ..... 100·70
aged 11–15 .... 101·75
aged 16 and over .... 102·80
Family with more than one child
For each additional child—under 11. 11·90
aged 11–15 .... 12·95
aged 16 and over .... 14·00
Maximum amount payable
Family with one child—under 11 ..... 25·85
aged 11–16 .... 26·40
aged 16 and over .... 26·90
Family with more than one child
For each additional child—under 11. 2·60
aged 11–15 .... 3·15
aged 16 and over .... 3·65

DETERMINATION OF CLAIMS AND QUESTIONS

With a few exceptions, claims and questions
relating to Social Security benefits are decided by
statutory authorities who act independently of
D.H.S.S. and Department of Employment. The first
of the statutory authorities, the Adjudication Officer,
determines entitlement to benefit. A claimant who
is dissatisfied with that decision has the right of
appeal to a Social Security Appeal Tribunal. There is
a further right of appeal to a Social Security
Commissioner against the Tribunal's decision but
leave to appeal must first be obtained. Appeals to the
Commissioner must be on a point of law. Provision is
also made for the determination of certain questions
by the Secretary of State for Social Services.

Disablement questions are decided by adjudicating
medical authorities or Medical Appeal Tribunals.
Appeal to the Commissioner against a tribunal's
decision is with leave and on a point of law only.

Leaflet NI 246 which is available from D.H.S.S.
offices, explains how to appeal.

INDUSTRIAL INJURIES AND DISEASES BENEFITS

The Industrial Injuries scheme, administered under the Social Security Act 1975 and subsequent Acts
and Regulations, provides a range of benefits designed
to compensate for disablement resulting from an
industrial accident (i.e. an accident arising out of
and in the course of an employed earner's employment) or from a prescribed disease due to the nature
of a person's employment. Rates of benefit are
increased periodically.

Determination of Claims and Questions.—Provision is made for the determination of certain
questions by the Secretary of State for Social Services,
and of "disablement questions" by a medical board
(or a single doctor) or, on appeal, by a medical appeal
tribunal. An appeal on a point of law against a
medical appeal tribunal decision is determined by the
Social Security Commissioner. Claims for benefit and
certain questions arising in connection with a claim
for or award of benefit (*e.g.* whether the accident
arose out of and in the course of the employment) are
determined by an adjudication officer appointed by
the Secretary of State, or a Social Security Appeal
Tribunal, or in certain circumstances, on further
appeal, by the Commissioners.

Special schemes under the Industrial Injuries and
Diseases (Old Cases) Act 1975 provide supplementary
allowances to those entitled to receive weekly
payments of workmen's compensation for loss of
earnings due to injury at work, or disease contracted
during employment before July 5, 1948 when the
Industrial Injuries scheme was introduced. Other
schemes under the Act provide allowances to those
who contracted slowly developing diseases during
employment before July 1948 where neither workmen's compensation nor Industrial Injuries Benefits
are payable.

Benefits

Disablement Benefit is normally payable 15 weeks
(90 days) after the date of accident or onset of disease
if the employed earner suffers from loss of physical or
mental faculty such that the resulting disablement is
assessed at not less than 14 per cent. The amount of
disablement benefit payable varies according to the
degree of disablement (in the form of a percentage)
assessed by an adjudicating medical authority or
medical appeal tribunal.

Disablement assessed at less than 14 per cent. does
not normally attract basic benefit except for certain
progressive chest diseases. A weekly pension is
payable where the assessment of disablement is
between 14 and 100 per cent. (assessments of 14 to 19
per cent are payable at the 20 per cent rate). Payment
can be made for a limited period or for life.

The basic rates are applicable to adults and to
juveniles entitled to an increase for a child or adult
dependent; other juveniles receive lower rates.

Basic rates of pension are not related to the
pensioner's loss of earning power, and are payable
whether he is in work or not. If disablement is
assessed at one per cent. or more, loss of earnings may
be compensated by a reduced earnings allowance.
This may be paid even if basic disablement pension is
not paid because disablement is assessed at less than
14 per cent. There is provision also for increases of
pension if the pensioner requires constant attendance
or if his disablement is exceptionally severe. A
pensioner may draw S.S.P., sickness or invalidity
benefit as appropriate, in addition to disablement
pension, during spells of incapacity for work.

Death Benefit in the form of a pension, a gratuity
or a weekly allowance for a limited period, available
for widows and other dependents in fatal cases,
depends in amount upon their relationship to the

deceased and their circumstances at the time of death and not upon the deceased's earnings. A widow who was living with her husband at the time of his death receives a higher rate of pension for the first 26 weeks, and thereafter a lower rate of pension according to circumstances.

Regulations impose certain obligations on claimants and beneficiaries and on employers, including, in the case of claimants for disablement benefit, that of submitting to medical examination.

Rates of Benefits
(from April 6, 1987)

	Weekly rate £
Disablement Benefit/Pension	
Degree of disablement—100 per cent.	64·50
90	58·05
80	51·60
70	45·15
60	38·70
50	32·25
40	25·80
30	19·35
20	12·90
Unemployability supplement*	39·50
Addition for adult dependent (subject to earnings rule)	23·75
Special Hardship allowance (maximum)	25·80
Constant Attendance allowance (normal maximum rate)	25·80
Exceptionally severe disablement allowance	25·80
Industrial death benefit widow's pension*	
First 26 weeks	55·35
Higher permanent rate	40·05
Lower permanent rate	11·85

* These benefits attract an increase for each dependent child (in addition to child benefit) of £8·05.

FINANCE

The National Insurance Fund receives all social security contributions (less only the National Health Service and Redundancy Fund and Maternity Pay Fund allocations and the National Insurance Surcharge for taxation purposes) together with the Consolidated Fund supplement; and it bears the cost of all contributory benefits provided by the Social Security Acts and the cost of administration.

Approximate receipts and payments of the National Insurance Fund for the year ended March 31, 1986, were as follows:

Receipts	£'000
Balance, April 1, 1985	5,002,915
Contributions under the Social Security Acts (net of S.S.P.)	20,790,280
Consolidated Fund Supplement	2,163,000
Income from Investments	540,952
Other receipts	1,778
	28,498,853

Payments	£'000	£'000
Benefit:—		
Unemployment benefit.	1,588,688	
Sickness benefit	266,725	
Invalidity benefit	2,348,439	
Maternity allowance	164,430	
Widow's benefit	800,230	
Guardian's allowance and child's special allowance	1,442	
Retirement pension	16,582,660	
Death grant	18,282	
Industrial injuries benefits		
Disablement benefits	407,202	
Death benefit	58,499	
Other industrial injury benefits	4,516	
Pensioners lump sum payments	105,048	
Payments in lieu of benefit forgone	8,906	
		22,356,067
Transfers to Northern Ireland		60,000
Administration		809,890
Other payments		1,709
Write offs		
Balance, March 31, 1986		5,271,187
		28,498,853

WAR PENSIONS

War pensions are awarded under The Naval, Military and Air Forces, Etc. (Disablement and Death) Service Pensions Order 1983, which was a consolidation of the previous Royal Warrants, Orders in Council and Orders by Her Majesty.

The D.H.S.S. award war pensions in respect of the periods Aug. 4, 1914 to Sept. 30, 1921 and subsequent to Sept. 3, 1939 (including present members of the armed forces). The D.H.S.S. also have special schemes for the Merchant Navy, Naval Auxiliary personnel, civil defence, civilians, Home Guard, Polish armed forces under British command and Polish resettlement forces.

War pensions for the period Oct. 1, 1921 to Sept. 2, 1939 are dealt with by the Ministry of Defence who are also responsible for the Armed Forces Pension Scheme.

ELIGIBILITY

War disablement pension is awarded for the disabling effects of any injury, wound or disease which is attributable to, or aggravated by, conditions of service in the armed forces. It cannot be paid until the serviceman has left the armed forces.

War widows pension is awarded where death occurs as a result of service. Where a war disablement pensioner was receiving constant attendance allowance at the time of his death, or would have been receiving it if he were not in hospital, his widow has automatic entitlement to a war widow's pension, regardless of the cause of death.

Claims.—Where a claim is made no later than 7 years after the termination of service, the claimant does not have to prove that the disablement or death on which the claim is based is related to service and receives the benefit of any reasonable doubt. Where a claim is made more than 7 years after the termination of service the claimant has to show that disablement or death is related to service. However, the claim succeeds if reliable evidence is produced which raises a reasonable doubt whether disablement or death is related to service. There is no time limit for making a claim for war pension.

Payment.—Rank additions are normally paid with war pensions where the rank held was above that of private (or equivalent).

When a war disablement pensioner is sick, unemployed or retired, the appropriate social security benefits are paid in addition to the war pension. Any sickness, invalidity or unemployment benefit or retirement pension for which a war widow qualifies on her own contributions, and any graduated retirement benefit, can be paid in addition to her war pension or temporary allowance. A war pensioner or war widow who claims supplementary benefit has the first £4 of pension disregarded. A similar provision operates for housing benefit but the local authority may, at its discretion, disregard any or all of the balance. A special tax free Christmas bonus of £10.00 is payable to war disablement pensioners who are in receipt of unemployability supplement, constant attendance allowance, have retired, or are aged over 70 (65 for women); and to all war widows.

A reduced weekly rate is payable to war widows below the rank of Lieutenant-Colonel who are under the age of 40, without children and capable of maintaining themselves. This is increased to the standard rate at age 40.

D.H.S.S. is responsible for the payment of war pensions, and provision of necessary treatment for accepted disablement, to pensioners who reside overseas. They receive the same pension rates as war pensioners in this country and benefit from the same annual upratings.

BASIC DISABLEMENT PENSION

Disablement is assessed by comparison of the disabled person's condition with that of a normal, healthy person of the same age and sex, without taking into account the disabled person's earnings or occupation, and is expressed on a percentage scale up to 100 per cent. Disablement above 20 per cent is assessed in steps of 10 per cent. For assessment of less than 20 per cent a lump sum is payable. Maximum assessment does not necessarily imply total incapacity.

A 100 per cent disabled pensioner may receive an allowance of 60p a week for his dependent. Where disablement is less than 100 per cent the allowance is proportionate to the degree of disablement. The allowance is no longer paid under the social security scheme, but it still being paid to war pensioners.

SUPPLEMENTARY ALLOWANCES

A number of supplementary allowances may be awarded to a war pensioner which are intended to meet the various needs which may result from disablement or death and take account of its particular effect on the pensioner. Decisions on supplementary allowances are made on a discretionary basis on behalf of the Secretary of State and there is no provision for a statutory right of appeal against them. However, war pensioners may have any aspect of their pension position discussed by their local War Pensions Committees, which may be able to arrange help or make representations to the war pensions branch of the D.H.S.S.

Unemployability supplement, with additional allowances for dependants, may be paid to a war pensioner who is so seriously disabled as to be unemployable. In addition, an invalidity allowance may be payable if the incapacity for work began more than 5 years before normal retirement age.

Allowance for lowered standard of occupation may be awarded to a partially disabled pensioner whose pensioned disablement permanently prevents him from following his pre-service occupation and from doing another job of equivalent financial standard. The allowance, together with the basic war disablement pension, must not exceed pension at the 100 per cent rate.

Constant attendance allowance may be awarded to a war pensioner who is so severely handicapped by the nature of his pensioned disablement, assessed at not less than 80 per cent, that he must depend to a greater or lesser extent upon the attendance of some other person. There are four rates of the allowance and these vary according to the amount of time attendance is needed.

Exceptionally severe disablement allowance is paid to pensioners who are receiving constant attendance allowance on a permanent basis at either of the two highest rates.

Severe disablement occupational allowance is paid to those pensioners who qualify for constant attendance allowance at either of the two highest rates and who, despite their handicap, are normally in employment. This allowance is not payable if the pensioner is in receipt of unemployability supplement.

Comforts allowance is payable at one of two rates. The higher rate is paid to those pensioners who are receiving both constant attendance allowance and unemployability supplement. When only one of these allowances is in payment the lower rate can be paid under certain conditions where only constant attendance allowance is in payment.

Clothing allowance may be awarded where the pensioned disablement causes exceptional wear and tear of clothing. It is payable at two rates, depending on the degree of wear and tear caused.

Mobility supplement is intended to help those war pensioners who have problems in walking caused wholly or mainly by their pensioned disablement.

Treatment allowance may be paid to a pensioner receiving medical treatment in hospital or at home if the treatment is for the pensioned disablement, is necessary because of the continuing effects of service, and is of a kind which prevents the pensioner from working for more than seven days. The allowance replaces the disablement pension and is paid at the 100 per cent rate.

Age allowance may be awarded to those war pensioners aged 65 or over whose war disablement is assessed at 40 per cent or more. It is payable at four rates, depending on the degree of disablement.

Widows age allowance is paid at three different rates according to age (65-69, 70-79 and over 80).

Widows child's allowance may be paid in addition to child benefit.

Rent allowance may be paid to a widow who receives a war widows pension and maintains a home for a child eligible for an allowance.

Education allowance may be payable to a war disablement pensioner or war widow in respect of a dependent child if the D.H.S.S. is satisfied that the education is suitable for the child and that the family circumstances are such as to require an allowance.

Temporary allowance for widows may be payable in the form of a special allowance for the first 26 weeks of widowhood for widows of war pensioners receiving constant attendance allowance or unemployability supplement. After 26 weeks the widow will get any war widows pension or national insurance widows benefit to which she is entitled.

Funeral grant may be payable where the pensioner dies from his personal disablement. Claims should be made within three months of the funeral.

PENSION APPEALS TRIBUNALS

There are independent Pensions Appeal Tribunals which hear appeals against the decisions of the

D.H.S.S. on entitlement, and assessment of disablement, in respect of 1939 War and subsequent service cases. There are now no rights of appeal in the 1914 War disablement cases, the great majority of which were given final assessment in the 1920s with a 12 months right of appeal at the time. An appeal by a 1914 war widow must be made within twelve months of the date on which the rejection of the claim is notified.

WAR PENSIONERS WELFARE SERVICE

The D.H.S.S. operates a war pensioners welfare service to advise and assist war pensioners on any matters affecting their welfare. Welfare officers are attached to War Pensioners' Welfare Offices located in the major towns, and work closely with central and local Government agencies as well as the various ex-service organisations. The service is available on call to any war pensioner who needs it. In addition the service takes the initiative in arranging regular visits in certain cases.

Rates of Pensions and Allowances
(from week commencing April 6, 1987)

Disablement pension (for Private or equivalent rank)	Weekly rates £
Degree of disablement—	
100 per cent	64.50
90 per cent	58.05
80 per cent	51.60
70 per cent	45.15
60 per cent	38.70
50 per cent	32.25
40 per cent	25.80
30 per cent	19.35
20 per cent	12.90

Unemployability supplement	
Personal allowance	41.95
Increase for wife/other adult dependent	23.75
Increase for child	8.05
Allowance for lowered standard of occupation (maximum)	25.80
Constant attendance allowance	
Exceptional rate	51.60
Intermediate rate	38.70
Normal maximum	25.80
Half and quarter day	12.90
Exceptionally severe disablement allowance	25.80
Severe disablement occupational allowance	12.90
Comforts allowance	
Higher rate	11.10
Lower rate	5.55
Clothing allowance (**per annum**)	
Higher rate	88.00
Lower rate	56.00
Mobility supplement	24.05
Age allowance	
Disablement assessment—	
40–50 per cent	4.50
50–70 per cent	7.00
70–90 per cent	10.05
over 90 per cent	14.00
Widow's pension	
(widow of Private or equivalent rank)	
Standard rate	51.35
Childless widow under 40	11.85
Widow's age allowance	
Age—65–69	5.50
70–79	11.00
80 and over	13.85
Rent allowance (maximum)	19.55

PRINCIPAL NEWSPAPERS

DAILY NEWSPAPERS

National

Daily Express, 121–128 Fleet St., EC4P 4JT.

Daily Mail, Northcliffe House, EC4 0JA.

The Daily Mirror, Holborn Circus, EC1P 1DQ.

Daily Telegraph, 181 Marsh Wall, E14 9SR.

Financial Times, Bracken House, 10 Cannon St., EC4P 4BY.

The Guardian, 119 Farringdon Rd., EC1R 3ER.

The Independent, 40 City Rd., EC1Y 2DB.

Morning Star, 75 Farringdon Rd., EC1M 3JX.

Racing Post, 120 Combe Lane, Raynes Park, SW20 0BA.

Sporting Life, Alexander House, 81–89 Farringdon Road, EC1M 3LH.

The Star, Great Ancoats Street, Manchester M60 4HB.

The Sun, Virginia St., E1 9BD.

The Times, 1 Pennington St., E1 9XN.

Today, Allen House, 70 Vauxhall Bridge Road, SW1V 2RP.

ABERDEEN—Press and Journal and Evening Express, P.O. Box 43, Lang Stracht, Mastrick, AB9 8AF.

BARROW—North-Western Evening Mail, Abbey Road, LA14 5QS.

BATH—Bath and West Evening Chronicle, 33–34 Westgate Street, BA1 1EW.

BELFAST—Belfast Telegraph, 124–144 Royal Avenue, BT1 1EB; Irish News, and Belfast Morning News, 113–117 Donegall Street, BT1 2GE; News Letter, 51–59 Donegall St., BT1 2GB.

BIRMINGHAM—Birmingham Post, and Birmingham Evening Mail, P.O. Box 18, 28 Colmore Circus, B4 6AX.

BLACKBURN—Lancashire Evening Telegraph, New Telegraph House, High Street, BB1 1HT.

BLACKPOOL—W. Lancs. Ev. Gazette, Victoria Street, FY1 4RG.

BOLTON—Evening News, Mealhouse Lane, BL1 1DE.

BOURNEMOUTH—Evening Echo, Richmond Hill, BH2 6HH.

BRADFORD—Telegraph and Argus, P.O. Box 234, Hall Ings, BD1 1JR.

BRIGHTON—Evening Argus, 89 North Road, BN1 4AU.

BRISTOL—Evening Post and Western Daily Press, Temple Way, Old Market, BS99 7HD.

BURTON—Burton Mail, 65–68 High Street, DE14 1LE.

CAMBRIDGE—Cambridge Evening News, 51 Newmarket Road, CB5 8EJ.

CARDIFF—South Wales Echo, and Western Mail, Thomson House, Havelock St., CF1 1WR.

CARLISLE—Evening News and Star, Newspaper House, Dalston Road, CA2 5UA.

CHELTENHAM—Gloucestershire Echo, 1 Clarence Parade, GL50 3NZ.

COLCHESTER—Evening Gazette, Oriel House, 43–44 North Hill, CO1 1TZ.

COVENTRY—Coventry Evening Telegraph, Corporation Street, CV1 1FP.

DARLINGTON—Northern Echo, Priestgate, DL1 1NP.

DERBY—Derby Evening Telegraph, Northcliffe House, DE1 2DW.

DUNDEE—Courier and Advertiser, and Evening Telegraph and Post, 7 Bank Street, DD1 9HU.

EDINBURGH—The Scotsman, and Evening News, 20 North Bridge, EH1 1YT.

EXETER—Express and Echo, Sidwell House, Sidwell Street, EX4 6RS.

GLASGOW—Daily Record, 40 Anderston Quay, G3 8DA; Evening Times, and Glasgow Herald, 195 Albion Street, G1 1QP.

GLOUCESTER—Citizen, St. John's Lane, GL1 2AY.

GREENOCK—Greenock Telegraph, 2 Crawford Street, PA15 1LH.

GRIMSBY—Evening Telegraph, 80 Cleethorpe Road, DN31 3EF.

GUERNSEY—Guernsey Evening Press and Star, P.O. Box 57, Braye Road, Vale.

HALIFAX—Evening Courier, P.O. Box 19, Courier Buildings, HX1 2SF.

HARTLEPOOL—The Mail, Clarence Rd., TS24 8BU.

HUDDERSFIELD—Huddersfield Daily Examiner, Ramsden Street, HD1 2TD.

HULL—Hull Daily Mail, 84–86 Jameson Street, HU1 3LF.

IPSWICH—East Anglian Daily Times, and Evening Star, 30 Lower Brook St., IP4 1AN.

JERSEY—Evening Post, P.O. Box 582, Five Oaks, St. Saviour.

KETTERING—Northamptonshire Evening Telegraph, Northfield Avenue, NN16 9JN.

LEAMINGTON SPA—Leamington & District Morning News, P.O. Box 45, Tachbrook Road, CV31 3EP.

LEEDS—Yorkshire Evening Post, and Yorkshire Post, Wellington Street, LS1 1RF.

LEICESTER—Leicester Mercury, St. George Street, LE1 9FQ.

LINCOLN—Lincolnshire Echo, Brayford Wharf East, LN5 7AT.

LIVERPOOL—Liverpool Daily Post, and Liverpool Echo, P.O. Box 48, Old Hall Street, L69 3EB.

LONDON—The London Standard, and The Evening News, 118 Fleet Street, EC4P 4JT.

MAIDSTONE—Kent Evening Post, Messenger House, New Hythe Lane, Larkfield, ME20 6SG.

MANCHESTER—Manchester Evening News, 164 Deansgate, M60 2RD.

MIDDLESBROUGH—Evening Gazette, Borough Rd., TS1 3AZ.

NEWCASTLE—Evening Chronicle, and Journal, Thomson House, Groat Market, NE1 1ED.

NEWPORT—South Wales Argus, Cardiff Road, Maesglas, NP9 1QW.

NORTHAMPTON—Chronicle and Echo, Upper Mounts, NN1 3HR.

NORWICH—Eastern Daily Press, and Eastern Evening News, Prospect House, Rouen Road, NR1 1RE.

NOTTINGHAM—Evening Post, Forman St., NG1 4AB.

NUNEATON—Nuneaton Evening Tribune, Watling House, Whitacre Road, CV11 6BJ.

OLDHAM—Evening Chronicle, 172 Union Street, OL1 1EQ.

OXFORD—Oxford Mail, Newspaper House, Osney Mead, OX2 0EJ.

PAISLEY—Paisley Daily Express, Hellenic House, 87–97 Bath St., Glasgow, G2 2DZ.

PETERBOROUGH—Peterborough Evening Telegraph, Oundle Road, Woodston, PE2 9QR.

PLYMOUTH—Western Morning News, and Western Evening Herald, Leicester Harmsworth House, 65 New George Street, PL1 1RE.

PORTSMOUTH—The News, The News Centre, Hilsea, PO2 9SX.

PRESTON—Lancashire Evening Post, 127 Fishergate, PR1 2DN.

READING—Evening Post, 8 Tessa Road, RG1 8NS.

SCARBOROUGH—Scarborough Evening News, 17–23 Aberdeen Walk, YO11 1BB.

SCUNTHORPE—Scunthorpe Evening Telegraph, Telegraph House, Doncaster Road, DN15 7RE.

SHEFFIELD—Star, York Street, S1 1PU.

SOUTH SHIELDS—Shields Gazette, P.O. Box 4, Chapter Row, NE33 1BL.

SOUTHAMPTON—Southern Evening Echo, 45 Above Bar, SO9 7BA.

STOKE-ON-TRENT—Evening Sentinel, Sentinel House, Etruria, ST1 5SS.

SUNDERLAND—Echo, Pennywell Industrial Estate, SR4 9ER.

SWANSEA—South Wales Evening Post, Adelaide Street, SA1 1QT.

SWINDON—Evening Advertiser, Newspaper House, 100 Victoria Road, SN1 3BE.

TELFORD—Shropshire Star, Ketley, TF1 4HU.

TORQUAY—Herald Express, Harmsworth House, Barton Hill Road, TQ2 8JN.

WEYMOUTH—Dorset Evening Echo, 57 St. Thomas Street, DT4 8EU.

WOLVERHAMPTON—Express and Star, 50–53 Queen Street, WV1 3BU.

WORCESTER—Evening News, Berrow's House, WR2 5JX.

YORK—Yorkshire Evening Press, 15 Coney Street, YO1 1YN.

SUNDAY NEWSPAPERS

Mail on Sunday—Northcliffe House, EC4Y 0JA.

News of the World—1 Pennington Street, E1 9BH.

News on Sunday, Caxton House, 13–16 Borough Rd., SE1 0AL.

Observer—8 St. Andrew's Hill, EC4V 5JA.

Sunday Express—121–128 Fleet St., EC4P 4JT.

Sunday Independent—Burrington Way, Honicknowle, Plymouth, PL5 3LN.

Sunday Mail—40 Anderston Quay, Glasgow G3 8DA.

Sunday Mercury—P.O. Box 60, 28 Colmore Circus, Birmingham B4 6AZ.

Sunday Mirror—Holborn Circus, EC1P 1DQ.

Sunday News—51–59 Donegall St., Belfast BT1 2GB.

Sunday People—Holborn Circus, EC1P 1DQ.

Sunday Post—Courier Place, Dundee DD1 9QJ.

Sunday Sun—Thomson House, Groat Market, Newcastle on Tyne NE1 1ED.

Sunday Telegraph—181 Marsh Wall, E14 9SR.

Sunday Times—1 Pennington Street, E1 9XW.

RELIGIOUS PAPERS

[*W.*=Weekly; *M.*=Monthly; *Q.*=Quarterly]

Baptist Times—4 Southampton Row, WC1B 4AB. *W.*

British Weekly and Christian Record—11 Carteret St., SW1H 9DJ. *W.*

Catholic Herald—Herald House, Lambs Passage, Bunhill Row, EC1Y 8TQ. *W.*

Challenge, the Good News Paper—Revenue Buildings, Chapel Rd., Worthing, West Sussex BN11 1BQ. *M.*

Christian Herald—27 Chapel Road, Worthing, West Sussex BN11 1EG. *W.*

Church of England Newspaper—11 Carteret St., SW1H 9DJ. *W.*

Church of Ireland Gazette—48 Bachelor's Walk, Lisburn, Co. Antrim. *W.*

Church Times—7 Portugal St., WC2A 2HP. *W.*

English Churchman & St. James's Chronicle—P.O. Box 217, SE5 8NP. *Alt. W.*

Friend—Drayton House, 30 Gordon St., WC1H 0BQ. *W.*

Inquirer—1–6 Essex St., WC2R 3HY. *Alt. W.*

Jewish Chronicle—25 Furnival St., EC4A 1JT. *W.*

Jewish Gazette—18 Cheetham Parade, Manchester M8 6DJ. *W.*

Jewish Telegraph—Telegraph House, 11 Park Hill, Bury Old Road, Prestwich, Manchester M25 8HH. *W.*

Life and Work—Church of Scotland, 121 George St., Edinburgh EH2 4YN. *M.*

Methodist Recorder—122 Golden Lane, EC1Y 0TL. *W.*

Orthodox News—64 Prebend Gardens, W6 0XU. *M.*

Tablet—48 Great Peter St., SW1P 2HB. *W.*

Today—37 Elm Road, New Malden, Surrey KT3 3HB. *M.*

Universe, The—33–39 Bowling Green Lane, EC1R 0AB. *W.*

War Cry—101 Queen Victoria St., EC4P 4EP. *W.*

PERIODICALS, MAGAZINES AND REVIEWS

[*W.*=Weekly; *M.*=Monthly; *Q.*=Quarterly]

Amateur Gardening—Westover House, West Quay Road, Poole, Dorset BH15 1JG. *W.*

Amateur Photographer—Prospect House, 9–15 Ewell Road, Cheam, Surrey SM3 8BZ. *W.*

Angler's Mail—King's Reach Tower, Stamford St., SE1 9LS. *W.*

Antiquaries' Journal—Oxford U. Press, Walton Street, Oxford OX2 6DP. *Twice a year.*

Antique Collector—72 Broadwick St., W1V 2BP. *M.*

Apollo Magazine—22 Davies Street, W1Y 1LH. *M.*

Art and Artists—43B Gloucester Road, Croydon, Surrey CR0 2DH. *M.*

Autocar—38–42 Hampton Road, Teddington, Middlesex TW11 0JE. *W.*

Books and Bookmen—43 Museum Street, WC1A 1LY, *M.*

Boxing News—P.O. Box 94, W4 2ER *W.*

Brain—Oxford U. Press, Walton Street, Oxford OX2 6DP. *Alt. M.*

Brides & Setting-up Home—Vogue House, Hanover Square, W1R 0AD. *Alt. M.*

British Birds—Fountains, Park Lane, Blunham, Bedford MK44 3NJ. *M.*

British Book News—The British Council, 65 Davies Street, W1Y 2AA. *M.*

Bunty—2 Albert Square, Dundee, DD1 9QJ. *W.*

Burlington Magazine, The.—6 Bloomsbury Square, WC1A 2LP. *M.*

Buses—Coombelands House, Addlestone, Weybridge, Surrey KT15 1HY. *M.*

Cage and Aviary Birds—Prospect House, 9–15 Ewell Road, Cheam, Surrey SM3 8BZ. *W.*

Camper—38–42 Hampton Road, Teddington, Middlesex TW11 0JE. *M.*

Caravan Magazine—Link House, Dingwall Avenue, Croydon, Surrey CR9 2TA. *M.*

Classical Quarterly—Oxford U. Press, Walton Street, Oxford OX2 6DP. *Twice a Year.*

Classical Review—Oxford U. Press, Walton Street, Oxford OX2 6DP. *Twice a Year.*

Coal News—Hobart House, Grosvenor Place, SW1X 7AE. *M.*

Coin and Medal News—Crossways Rd., Grayshott, Hindhead, Surrey GU26 6HF. *M.*

Coin Monthly—Sovereign House, Brentwood, Essex CM14 4SE. *M.*

Company—72 Broadwick Street, W1V 2BP. *M.*

Contemporary Review— 61 Carey St., WC2A 2JG. *M.*

Cosmopolitan—72 Broadwick Street, W1V 2BP. *M.*

Country Homes and Interiors—25 Newman Street, W1P 3HA. *M.*

Country Life—King's Reach Tower, Stamford Street, SE1 9LS. *W.*

Countryman, The—Sheep Street, Burford, Oxford OX8 4LH. *Q.*

Cricketer International, The—Beech Hangar, Ashurst, Tunbridge Wells, Kent TN3 9ST. *M.*

Criminologist—P.O. Box 18, Bognor Regis, West Sussex. *Q.*

Cycling Weekly—Prospect House, 9–15 Ewell Road, Cheam, Surrey SM3 8BZ. *W.*

Daltons Weekly—Apex Tower, High Street, New Malden, Surrey KT3 4EE. *W.*

Dance and Dancers—436 Gloucester Road, Croydon, Surrey. *M.*

Dancing Times—Clerkenwell House, 45–47 Clerkenwell Green, EC1R 0BE. *M.*

Dog World—9 Tufton Street, Ashford, Kent TN23 1QN. *W.*

Do It Yourself—Link House, Dingwall Avenue, Croydon CR9 2TA. *M.*

Drama—9 Fitzroy Square, W1P 6AE. *Q.*

Drive & Trail—Automobile Association, Fanum House, Basingstoke, Hants RG21 2EA. *M.*

Economic Journal—Basil Blackwell Ltd., 108 Cowley Road, Oxford OX4 1JF. *Q.*

Economica—London School of Economics, Houghton St., WC2A 2AE. *Q.*

Economist, The—25 St. James's St., SW1A 1HG. *W.*

Edinburgh Gazette (*Official*)—Government Bookshop, 13A Castle Street, Edinburgh EH2 3AR. *Twice a week.*

Elle—4–12 Lower Regent Street, SW1Y 4PE. *M.*

Encounter—44 Great Windmill Street, W1V 7PA. *Ten times a year.*

English Historical Review, The—Westgate House, The High, Harlow, Essex CM20 1NE. *Q.*

Everywoman—34A Islington Green, N1 8DU.

Exchange and Mart—25 West Street, Poole, Dorset BH15 1LL. *W.*

Family Circle—38 Hans Crescent, SW1X 0LZ. *M.*

Field, The—Tallis House, Tallis Street, EC4. *W.*

Freethinker, The—702 Holloway Rd., N19 3NL. *M.*

Garden News—Bushfield House, Orton Centre, Peterborough PE2 0UW. *W.*

Geographical Magazine, 1 Kensington Gore, SW7 2AR. *M.*

Golf Illustrated—47 Dartford Road, Sevenoaks, Kent TN13 3TE. *Alt. W.*

Golf Monthly—1 Park Circus, Glasgow G3 6AS.

Good Housekeeping—72 Broadwick Street, W1V 2BP. *M.*

Good Housekeeping's Country Living—72 Broadwick Street, W1V 2BP. *M.*

Good Motoring—352 Lewisham High Street, SE13 6LE. *Alt. M.*

Gramophone—177–179 Kenton Road, Harrow, Mddx. HA3 0HA *M.*

Granta—44A Hobson Street, Cambridge, CB1 1NL. *Q.*

Greece and Rome—Oxford U. Press, Walton Street, Oxford OX2 6DP. *Twice a year.*

Guiding—17–19 Buckingham Palace Road, SW1W 0PT. *M.*

Harpers and Queen—72 Broadwick St., W1V 2BP. *M.*

History—59A Kennington Park Road, SE11 4JH. *Three times a year.*

History Today—83–84 Berwick St., W1V 3PJ. *M.*

Homes and Gardens—King's Reach Tower, Stamford Street, SE1 9LS. *M.*

Homoeopathy—27A Devonshire St., W1N 1RJ *Alt. M.*

Horse and Hound—King's Reach Tower, Stamford Street, SE1 9LS. *W.*

House and Garden—Vogue House, Hanover Square, W1R 0AD. *M.*

Ideal Home—King's Reach Tower, Stamford Street, SE1 9LS. *M.*

Illustrated London News—Sea Container House, 20 Upper Ground, SE1 9PF. *M.*

In Britain—B.T.A., Thames Tower, Black's Road, W6 9EL. *M.*

International Affairs—P.O. Box 63, Westbury House, Bury Street, Guildford GU2 5BH. *Q.*

Jazz Journal International—35 Great Russell Street, WC1B 3PP. *M.*

Kennel Gazette—1 Clarges St., W1Y 8AB. *M.*

Labour Research— 78 Blackfriars Rd., SE1 8HF. *M.*

Lady—39–40 Bedford St., Strand, WC2E 9ER. *W.*

Land and Liberty—177 Vauxhall Bridge Road, SW1V 1EU. *Alt. M.*

Liberal News—1 Whitehall Place, SW1A 2HE. *W.*

Light (*Psychic*)—16 Queensberry Place, SW7 2EB. *Q.*

Listener, The—35 Marylebone High Street, W1M 4AA *W.*

Living—38 Hans Crescent, SW1X 0LZ. *M.*

Local Government Chronicle—11–12 Bury St., EC3A 5AP. *W.*

London Gazette (*Official*)—H.M.S.O., P.O. Box 276, SW8 5DT. *Four times a week.*

London Magazine—30 Thurloe Place, S.W.7. *M.*

London Review of Books—Tavistock House, Tavistock Square, WC1H 9JZ. *Alt. W.*

London Weekly Diary of Social Events—10 College Approach, Greenwich, SE10 9HY. *W.*

Look Now—25 Newman Street, W1P 3PE. *M.*

Melody Maker (MM)—168–173 High Holborn, WC1V 7AU. *W.*

Meteorological Magazine—Met. Office, London Road, Bracknell, Berkshire, RG12 2SZ. *M.*

Mind—Oxford U. Press, Walton Street, Oxford OX2 6DP. *Q.*

Model Boats—P.O. Box 35, Wolsey House, Wolsey Road, Hemel Hempstead, Herts. HP2 4SS *M.*

Model Railway Constructor—Coombelands House, Addlestone, Weybridge, Surrey KT15 1HY. *M.*

Modern Languages—Regents College, Inner Circle, Regents Park, NW1 4NS. *Q.*

Month—114 Mount Street, W1Y 6AH. *M.*

Monthly Digest of Statistics (*Official*)—H.M.S.O., P.O. Box 276, SW8 5DT. *M.*

Mother—12–18 Paul Street, EC2A 4JS. *M.*

Motor Cycle News—P.O. Box 11, Huxloe Place, High Street, Kettering NN16 8SS. *W.*

Municipal Review and AMA News—35 Great Smith Street, SW1P 3BJ. *Ten times a year.*

Museums Bulletin—34 Bloomsbury Way, WC1A 2SF. *M.*

Music and Letters—Oxford U. Press, Walton Street, Oxford OX2 6DP. *Q.*

My Weekly—2 Albert Square, Dundee DD1 9QJ. *W.*

Nature—4 Little Essex Street, WC2R 3LF. *W.*

Nautical Magazine—4–10 Darnley Street, Glasgow G41 2SD. *M.*

Navy International—Hunters Moon, Hogspudding Lane, Newdigate, Dorking, Surrey. *M.*

New Homes News—10 East Road, N1 6AU. *M.*

N.M.E.—Commonwealth House, 1–19 New Oxford Street, WC1A 1NG. *W.*

New Scientist—Commonwealth House, 1–19 New Oxford Street, WC1A 1NG. *W.*

New Society—5 Sherwood Street, W1V 7RA. *W.*

New Statesman—14–16 Farringdon Lane, EC1R 3AU. *W.*

19—King's Reach Tower, Stamford Street, SE1 9LS. *M.*

Notes and Queries—Oxford U. Press, Walton Street, Oxford OX2 6DP. *Q.*

Nursery World—24–25 Cowcross Street, EC1M 6DQ. *Alt. W.*

Opera—6 Woodland Rise, N10 3UH. *M.*

Options—25 Newman Street, W1 3PE. *M.*

Our Dogs—5 Oxford Road, Station Approach, Manchester M60 1SX. *W.*

Over 21—Greater London House, Hampstead Road, NW1 7QZ. *M.*

Parents—116 Newgate Street, EC1A 7AE. *M.*

Parliamentary Debates (Lords) (Hansard)—H.M.S.O., P.O. Box 276, SW8 5DT. *Daily during Session.*

Parliamentary Debates (Commons) (Hansard)—H.M.S.O., P.O. Box 276, SW8 5DT. *Daily during Session.*

People's Friend—2 Albert Square, Dundee DD1 9QJ. *W.*

Philosophy—Cambridge U. Press, Shaftesbury Road, Cambridge CB2 2RU. *Q.*

Pins and Needles—66 Great Cumberland Place, W1H 7FD. *M.*

Playhour—King's Reach Tower, Stamford Street, SE1 9LS. *W.*

Plays and Players—30–32 Southampton Street, WC2E 7HR. *M.*

Poetry Review—21 Earl's Court Square, SW5 9DE. *Q.*

Political Quarterly—108 Cowley Road, Oxford OX4 1JF. *Q.*

Pony—104 Ash Road, Sutton, Surrey SM3 9LD. *M.*

Poultry World—Carew House, Wallington, Surrey SM6 0DX. *M.*

Practical Boat Owner—Westover House, West Quay Road, Poole, Dorset BH15 1JG. *M.*

Practical Caravan—38–42 Hampton Road, Teddington, Middx. TW11 0JE. *M.*

Practical Gardening—Bushfield House, Orton Centre, Peterborough PE2 0UW. *M.*

Practical Householder—Cambridge House, 373–375 Euston Road, NW1. *M.*

Progress (*Braille Type*)—338–346 Goswell Road, EC1V 7JE. *M.*

Punch—23–27 Tudor Street, EC4 0HR. *W.*

Racing Calendar—42 Portman Square, W1H 0EN. *W.*

Radio Control Models and Electronics—Wolsey House, Wolsey Road, Hemel Hempstead, Herts. HP2 4SS. *M.*

Radio Times—35 Marylebone High Street, W1M 4AA. *W.*

Railway Magazine—Prospect House, 9–15 Ewell Road, Cheam, Surrey SM3 8BZ. *M.*

Railway World—Coombelands House, Addlestone, Weybridge KT15 1HY. *M.*

Reader's Digest—25 Berkeley Square, W1X 6AB. *M.*

Riding—8 Stamford Hill, N16 6XZ. *M.*

Ritz Newspaper—35 Britannia Row, N1 8QH. *M.*

Scots Independent—51 Cowane St., Stirling. *M.*

Scottish Field—302 St. Vincent Street, Glasgow G2 5NL. *M.*

Scouting—Baden-Powell House, Queen's Gate, SW7 5JS. *M.*

Seafarer, The—202 Lambeth Road, SE1 7JW. *Q.*

She—72 Broadwick St., W1V 2BP. *M.*

Shoot!—King's Reach Tower, Stamford Street, SE1 9LS. *W.*

Shooting Times and Country Magazine—10 Sheet Street, Windsor SL4 1BG. *W.*

Sociological Review—11 New Fetter Lane, EC4P 4EE. *Q.*

Spare Rib—27 Clerkenwell Close, EC1R 0AT. *M.*

Spectator, The—56 Doughty Street, WC1N 2LL. *W.*

Strad, The—8 Lower James Street, W1R 4DN. *M.*

Studio International—Tower House, Southampton Street, WC2E 7LS. *Q.*

Tatler—Vogue House, Hanover Square, W1R 0AD. *M.*

Tennis World—184 High Street, Berkhamsted, Herts. HP4 3AP. *M.*

35 mm Photography—1 Golden Square, W1R 3AB. *M.*

This England—Alma House, Rodney Road, Cheltenham, Glos. GL50 1YQ. *Q.*

Time—Time and Life Building, New Bond Street, W1Y 0AA. *W.*

Times Educational Supplement, The—Priory House, St. John's Lane, EC1M 4BX. *W.*

Times Higher Education Supplement, The—Priory House, St. John's Lane, EC1M 4BX. *W.*

Times Literary Supplement, The—Priory House, St. John's Lane, EC1M 4BX. *W.*

Tribune—308 Gray's Inn Road, WC1X 8DY. *W.*

Trout & Salmon—Bretton Court, Bretton, Peterborough PE3 8DZ. *M.*

True Romances—12–18 Paul Street, EC2A 4JS. *M.*

True Story Magazine—12–18 Paul Street, EC2A 4JS. *M.*

TV Times—247 Tottenham Court Road, W1P 0AU. *W.*

Vacher's Parliamentary Companion—113 High Street, Berkhamsted, Herts. HP4 2DJ. *Q.*

Vogue—Vogue House, Hanover Square, W1R 0AD. *M.*

Weather—James Glaisher House, Grenville Place, Bracknell, Berks. RG12 1BX. *M.*

Weekend—Carmelite House, EC4Y 0JA. *W.*

Welsh Nation—51 Cathedral Road, Cardiff CF1 9HD. *M.*

West Africa—52–54 Gray's Inn Road, WC1X 8LT. *W.*

Woman—King's Reach Tower, Stamford Street, SE1 9LS. *W.*

Woman & Home—King's Reach Tower, Stamford Street, SE1 9LS. *M.*

Woman's Journal—King's Reach Tower, Stamford Street, SE1 9LS. *M.*

Woman's Own—King's Reach Tower, Stamford Street, SE1 9LS. *W.*

Woman's Realm—King's Reach Tower, Stamford Street, SE1 9LS. *W.*

Woman's Weekly—King's Reach Tower, Stamford Street, SE1 9LS. *W.*

Woman's World—25 Newman Street, W1P 3HA. *M.*

World Today, The—Chatham House, St. James's Square, SW1Y 4LE. *M.*

Yachting Monthly—King's Reach Tower, Stamford Street, SE1 9LS.

Yachting World—Prospect House, 9–15 Ewell Road, Cheam, Surrey SM3 8BZ. *M.*

Yachts and Yachting—196 Eastern Esplanade, Southend-on-Sea SS1 3AB. *Alt. W.*

Your Model Railway—P.O. Box 35, Wolsey House, Wolsey Road, Hemel Hempstead, Herts. HP2 4SS. *M.*

TRADE, PROFESSIONAL AND BUSINESS JOURNALS

[*W.* = Weekly; *M.* = Monthly; *Q.* = Quarterly]

Accountancy—40 Bernard Street, WC1N 1LD. *M.*

Accountant, The—17 Scarbrook Rd., Croydon CR0 1SQ. *W.*

Accountants' Magazine—27 Queen Street, Edinburgh EH2 1LA. *M.*

Administrator—16 Park Crescent, W1N 3PA. *M.*

Agricultural Machinery Journal—Carew House, Wallington, Surrey SM6 0DX. *M.*

Anti-Corrosion Methods and Materials—127 Stanstead Road, SE23 1JE. *M.*

Antique Dealer and Collectors Guide—King's Reach Tower, Stamford Street, SE1 9LS. *M.*

Architects' Journal—9 Queen Anne's Gate, SW1H 9BY. *W.*

Architectural Review—9 Queen Anne's Gate, SW1H 9BY. *M.*

Artist, The—102 High Street, Tenterden, Kent TN30 6HT. *M.*

Author, The—84 Drayton Gardens, SW10 9SD. *Q.*

Bakers' Review—Penn Place, Rickmansworth, Herts WD3 1SN. *M.*

Banker, The—102–108 Clerkenwell Road, EC1M 5SA. *M.*

Banking World—Orbit House, 9 New Fetter Lane, EC4A 1AR. *M.*

Bookseller, The—12 Dyott Street, WC1A 1DF. *W.*

Brewers' Guardian—209 Central Markets, Smithfield, EC1A 9LH. *M.*

British Baker—P.O. Box 109, Maclaren House, 19 Scarbrook Rd., Croydon CR9 1QH. *W.*

British Business—Dept. of Trade and Industry, Millbank Tower, SW1P 4QU. *W.*

British Clothing Manufacturer—100 Avenue Road, NW3 3TP. *Q.*

British Dental Journal—64 Wimpole Street, W1M 8AL. *Alt. W.*

British Food Journal—Peterson House, Northbank, Droitwich, Worcs. WR9 9BL. *Alt. M.*

British Jeweller—27 Frederick Street, Birmingham B1 3HJ. *M.*

British Journal for the Philosophy of Science—Farmers Hall, Aberdeen AB9 2XT. *Q.*

British Journal of Photography—28 Great James Street, WC1N 3HL. *W.*

British Medical Journal—B.M.A. House, Tavistock Square, WC1H 9JR. *W.*

British Printer—76 Oxford Street, W1N 9FD. *M.*

British Sugar Beet Review—P.O. Box 26, Oundle Road, Peterborough PE2 9QU. *Q.*

British Tax Review—11 New Fetter Lane, EC4P 4EE. *Alt. M.*

British Veterinary Journal—1 Vincent Square, SW1P 2PN. *Alt. M.*

Brushes and Brushmaking International—Penn House, Penn Place, Rickmansworth WD3 1SN. *Alt. M.*

Builders Merchants Journal—Sovereign Way, Tonbridge, Kent TN9 1RW. *Twenty times a year.*

Building—Builder House, 1 Pemberton Row, EC4P 4HL. *W.*

Cabinet Maker and Retail Furnisher—Sovereign Way, Tonbridge, Kent TN9 1RW. *W.*

Campaign—22 Lancaster Gate, W2 3LY. *W.*

Carpet and Floorcoverings Review—Sovereign Way, Tonbridge, Kent TN9 1RW. *Alt. W.*

Caterer and Hotelkeeper—Quadrant House, The Quadrant, Sutton, Surrey SM2 5AS. *W.*

Chemist and Druggist—Sovereign Way, Tonbridge, Kent TN9 1RW. *W.*

Chemistry and Industry—14 Belgrave Square, SW1X 8PS. *Twice a month.*

Chemistry in Britain—Burlington House, W1V 0BN. *M.*

Child Education—Marlborough House, Holly Walk, Leamington Spa, Warwickshire CV32 4LS. *M.*

Chiropodist, The—53 Welbeck Street, W1M 7HE. *M.*

Civil Engineering—30 Calderwood St., SE18 6QH. *M.*

Club Mirror—Maclaren House, Scarbrook Road, Croydon CR9 1QH. *M.*

Colliery Guardian—Queensway House, 2 Queensway, Redhill, Surrey RH1 1QS. *M.*

Commerce International—Queensway House, 2 Queensway, Redhill, Surrey RH1 1QS. *M.*

Commercial Motor—Quadrant House, The Quadrant, Sutton, Surrey SM2 5AS. *W.*

Computer Survey—33–35 Bowling Green Lane, EC1R 0DA. *Alt. M.*

Concrete—11 Grosvenor Crescent, SW1X 7EE. *M.*

Containerisation International—72 Broadwick Street, W1V 2BP. *M.*

Contract Journal—Carew House, Wallington, Surrey SM6 0DX. *W.*

Control and Instrumentation—30 Calderwood Street, SE18 6QH. *M.*

C.S.E. News (Camping and Sports Equipment)—4 Spring Street, W2 3RB. *M.*

Dairy Farmer—Wharfedale Road, Ipswich 1PI 4LG. *M.*

Dairy Industries International—33-35 Bowling Green Lane, EC1R 0DA. *M.*

Design—The Design Centre, 28 Haymarket, SW1Y 4SU. *M.*

Director, The—10 Belgrave Square, SW1X 8PH. *M.*

Dock and Harbour Authority—19 Harcourt Street, W1H 2AX. *M.*

Drapers Record—100 Avenue Road, NW3 3TP. *W.*

Education—21-27 Lamb's Conduit Street, WC1N 3NL. *W.*

Education Equipment—Sovereign Way, Tonbridge, Kent TN9 1RW. *M.*

Electrical & Electronic Trader—Quadrant House, Sutton, Surrey SM2 5AS. *W.*

Electrical and Radio Trading—Quadrant House, The Quadrant, Sutton, Surrey SM2 5AS. *W.*

Electrical Review—Quadrant House, The Quadrant, Sutton, Surrey SM2 5AS. *W.*

Electrical Times—Quadrant House, The Quadrant, Sutton, Surrey SM2 5AS. *M.*

Electronic Engineering—Morgan-Grampian House, 30 Calderwood Street, SE18 6QH. *16 times a year.*

Electronics Weekly—Quadrant House, The Quadrant, Sutton, Surrey SM2 5AS. *W.*

Embroidery—P.O. Box 42B, East Molesey, Surrey KT8 9BB. *Q.*

Engineer, The—Morgan-Grampian House, 30 Calderwood Street, SE18 6QH. *M.*

Engineering—28 Haymarket, SW1Y 4SU. *M.*

Engineer's Digest—33-35 Bowling Green Lane, EC1R 0DA. *Ten times a year.*

Estates Gazette—151 Wardour St., W1V 4BN. *W.*

Export News—The International Export Association, Bourne, Lincs. *Q.*

Fairplay International Shipping Weekly—52-54 Southwark Street, SE1 1UJ. *W.*

Farmers Weekly—Carew House, Wallington, Surrey SM6 0DX. *W.*

Fire—Queensway House, 2 Queensway, Redhill, Surrey RH1 1QS. *M.*

Fire and Security Protection—Stanley House, 9 West Street, Epsom, Surrey KT18 7RL. *M.*

Fish Friers Review—289 Dewsbury Road, Leeds LS11 5HW. *M.*

Fish Trader—Queensway House, 2 Queensway, Redhill, Surrey RH1 1QS. *W.*

Flight International—Quadrant House, The Quadrant, Sutton, Surrey SM2 5AS. *W.*

Food Trade Review—29 High Street, Green Street Green, Orpington, Kent BR6 6LS. *M.*

Forestry and British Timber—Sovereign Way, Tonbridge, Kent TN9 1RW. *M.*

Foundry Trade Journal—Queensway House, 2 Queensway, Redhill, Surrey RH1 1QS. *Alt. M.*

Frozen and Chilled Foods—Queensway House, 2 Queensway, Redhill, Surrey RH1 1QS. *M.*

Fuel—Westbury House, Bury Street, Guildford GU2 5BH. *M.*

Funeral Service Journal—Boundary House, Cricketfield Road, Uxbridge, Middx UB8 1TB. *M.*

Fur Weekly News—122 Lea Bridge Road, E5 9RB. *W.*

Gas Marketing—Sovereign Way, Tonbridge, Kent TN9 1RW. *M.*

Gas World—Sovereign Way, Tonbridge, Kent TN9 1RW. *M.*

Gifts International—Sovereign Way, Tonbridge, Kent TN9 1RW. *M.*

Glass—Queensway House, 2 Queensway, Redhill, Surrey RH1 1QS. *M.*

Grocer, The—5-7 Southwark Street, SE1 1RQ. *W.*

Grower, The—50 Doughty Street, WC1N 2LP. *W.*

Hair and Beauty—Quadrant House, The Quadrant, Sutton, Surrey SM2 5AS. *M.*

Hairdressers' Journal International—Quadrant House, The Quadrant, Sutton SM2 5AS. *W.*

Handy Shipping Guide—230-234 Long Lane, SE1 4QE. *W.*

Hardware Trade Journal—Sovereign Way, Tonbridge, Kent TN9 1RW. *W.*

Harpers Sports & Leisure—2 Silverdale Road, Bushey, Watford WD2 2LZ. *Every three weeks.*

Harpers Wine and Spirit Gazette—Harling House, 47-51 Great Suffolk Street, SE1 0BS. *W.*

Health Visitor—BMA House, Tavistock Square, WC1H 9JR. *M.*

Heating and Ventilating Engineer—Penn House, Penn Place, Rickmansworth, Herts. WD3 1SN. *Alt. M.*

Hospital & Health Services Review—Westgate House, The High, Harlow, Essex. *Alt. M.*

Ice Cream & Frozen Confectionery—90-94 Gray's Inn Road, WC1X 8AH. *M.*

Industrial Society—3 Carlton House Terrace, SW1Y 5DG. *Q.*

Insurance Mail—44 Fleet Street, EC4Y 1BS. *M.*

International Journal of Advertising—1 Vincent Square, SW1P 2PN. *Q.*

Investors Chronicle—Greystoke Place, Fetter Lane, EC4A 1ND. *W.*

Journal of The Chemical Society—Burlington House, W1V 0BN. *In six parts (each M).*

Journalist, The—314 Gray's Inn Rd., WC1X 8DP. *M.*

Justice of the Peace—East Row, Little London, Chichester, W. Sussex PO19 1PG. *W.*

Knitting and Haberdashery Review—80A South Street, Romford, Essex RM1 1RX. *Alt. M.*

Lancet—7 Adam Street, WC2N 6AD. *W.*

Law Quarterly Review—11 New Fetter Lane, EC4P 4EE. *Q.*

Law Reports, The—3 Stone Buildings, Lincoln's Inn, WC2A 3XN. *M.*

Law Society's Gazette—113 Chancery Lane, WC2A 1PL. *W.*

Leather—Sovereign Way, Tonbridge, Kent TN9 1RW. *M.*

Legal Executive, The—Kempston Manor, Kempston, Bedford MK42 7AB. *M.*

Library Review—302 St. Vincent Street, Glasgow G2 5NL. *Q.*

Litho Week—38-42 Hampton Road, Teddington, Middx. TW11 0JE. *W.*

Lloyd's Loading List—Sheepen Place, Colchester, Essex CO3 3LP. *W.*

Locomotive Journal—9 Arkwright Road, NW3 6AB. *M.*

London Corn Circular—54 Wentworth Crescent, Ash Vale, Aldershot, Hants. GU12 5LF. *W.*

Machinery and Production Engineering—Franks Hall, Horton, Kirby, Kent DA4 9LL. *Alt. W.*

Machinery Market—6 Blyth Road, Bromley, Kent BR1 3RX. *W.*

Management Accounting—63 Portland Place, W1N 4AB. *M.*

Management Decision—62 Toller Lane, Bradford BD8 9BY. *Alt. M.*

Management Today—30 Lancaster Gate, W2 3LP. *M.*

Manufacturing Chemist—Morgan-Grampian House, 30 Calderwood Street, SE18 6QH. *M.*

Marketing—22 Lancaster Gate, W2 3LY. *W.*

Materials Reclamation Weekly—Maclaren House, 19 Scarbrook Road, Croydon CR9 1QH. *W.*

Meat Trades' Journal—100 Avenue Road, NW3 3TP. *W.*

Medico-Legal Journal—5 New Square, Lincoln's Inn, WC2A 3RJ. *Q.*

Men's Wear—100 Avenue Road, NW3 3TP. *W.*

Metal Bulletin—Park House, Park Terrace, Worcester Park, Surrey KT4 7HY. *Twice a week.*

Metallurgia—Queensway House, 2 Queensway, Redhill, Surrey RH1 1QS. *M.*

Metals and Minerals International—5 Pond St., NW3 2PN. *Q.*

Milk Industry—19 Cornwall Terrace, NW1 4QP. *M.*

Mining Journal—60 Worship Street, EC2A 2HD. *W.*

Mining Magazine—60 Worship Street, EC2A 2HD. *M.*

Model Engineer—P.O. Box 35, Wolsey House, Hemel Hempstead, Herts. HP2 4SS. *Alt. W.*

Modern Law Review—11 New Fetter Lane, EC4P 4EE. *Alt. M.*

Modern Railways—Coombelands House, Addlestone, Weybridge, Surrey KT15 1HY. *M.*

Motor—Prospect House, 9–15 Ewell Road, Cheam, Surrey SM3 8BZ. *W.*

Motor Boat and Yachting—Prospect House, 9–15 Ewell Road, Cheam, Surrey SM3 8BZ. *M.*

Motorcycle Trader—Penn House, Penn Place, Rickmansworth, Herts. WD3 1SN. *M.*

Motor Trader—Quadrant House, The Quadrant, Sutton, Surrey SM2 5AS. *W.*

Motor Transport—Quadrant House, The Quadrant, Sutton, Surrey SM2 5AS. *W.*

Musical Times, The—8 Lower James Street, W1R 4DN. *M.*

National Builder—82 New Cavendish Street, W1M 8AD. *M.*

Natural Gas—Sovereign Way, Tonbridge, Kent TN9 1RW. *Alt. M.*

New Law Journal—9–12 Bell Yard, WC2A 2JR. *W.*

Nuclear Engineering International—Quadrant House, The Quadrant, Sutton, Surrey SM2 5AS. *M.*

Nurseryman & Garden Centre—Kenwood High Street, Cranbrook, Kent TN17 3DR. *Alt. W.*

Nursing Times & Nursing Mirror—4 Little Essex St., WC2R 3LF. *W.*

Off Licence News—5–7 Southwark St., SE1 1RQ. *W.*

Optician, The—Quadrant House, The Quadrant, Sutton, Surrey SM2 5AS. *W.*

Optometry Today—233–234 Blackfriars Road, SE1 8NW. *Alt. W.*

Packaging—Penn House, Penn Place, Rickmansworth, Herts. WD3 1SN. *M.*

Packaging Week—Sovereign Way, Tonbridge, Kent TN9 1RW. *W.*

Paint & Resin—Penn House, Penn Place, Rickmansworth, Herts. WD3 1SN. *M.*

Painting and Decorating—Penn Place, Rickmansworth, Herts. WD8 1SN. *Eight times a year.*

Paper—Sovereign Way, Tonbridge, Kent TN9 1RW. *Alt. W.*

Personnel Management—1 Hills Place, W1R 1AG. *M.*

Pharmaceutical Journal, The—1 Lambeth High Street, SE1 7JN. *W.*

Photographer, The—1 Gayford Road, W12 9BY. *M.*

Physics Bulletin—Techno House, Redcliffe Way, Bristol BS1 6NX. *M.*

Physics Education—Techno House, Redcliffe Way, Bristol BS1 6NX. *Seven times a year.*

Physics in Technology—Techno House, Redcliffe Way, Bristol BS1 6NX. *Alt. M.*

Plumbing and Heating Equipment News—Peterson House, Northbank, Droitwich, Worcs. WR9 9BL. *M.*

Police Review—14 St. Cross Street, EC1N 8FE. *W.*

Post Magazine and Insurance Monitor—58 Fleet Street, EC4Y 1JU. *W.*

Power Farming—Carew House, Wallington, Surrey SM6 0DX. *M.*

Practical Wireless—Enefco House, The Quay, Poole, Dorset B15 1PP. *M.*

Practical Woodworking—King's Reach Tower, Stamford Street, SE1 9LS. *M.*

Practitioner, The—30 Calderwood Street, SE18 6QH. *M.*

Precision Toolmaker—Queensway House, 2 Queensway, Redhill, Surrey RH1 1QS. *Q.*

Printing World—Sovereign Way, Tonbridge, Kent TN9 1RW. *W.*

Product Finishing—127 Stanstead Road, SE23 1JE. *M.*

Public Law—11 New Fetter Lane, EC4P 4EE. *Q.*

Public Ledger, The—12 Greycaine Road, Watford WD2 4JP *Daily and W.*

Public Service—1 Mabledon Place, WC1H 9AJ. *M.*

Quarry Management—7 Regent Street, Nottingham NG1 5BY. *M.*

Quarterly Journal of Experimental Psychology, The—319 City Road, EC1V 1LJ. *Q.*

Quarterly Journal of Medicine—Oxford U. Press, Walton Street, Oxford OX2 6DP. *M.*

Railway Gazette International—Quadrant House, The Quadrant, Sutton, Surrey SM2 5AS. *M.*

Rating and Valuation Reporter—2 Paper Buildings, Temple, EC4. *M.*

Resale Weekly—1–23 Queen's Road West, E13 0PE. *W.*

Retail Jeweller—100 Avenue Road, NW3 3TP. *Alt. W.*

Retail Newsagent Tobacconist Confectioner—60–66 Saffron Hill, EC1N 8QX. *W.*

Review, The: Worldwide Reinsurance—33–35 Bowling Green Lane, EC1R 0DA. *Alt. W.*

Review of English Studies—Oxford U. Press, Walton Street, Oxford OX2 6DP. *Q.*

Safety at Sea—Queensway House, 2 Queensway, Redhill, Surrey RH1 1QS. *M.*

Scottish Farmer, The—302–304 St. Vincent Street, Glasgow G2 5NL. *W.*

Scottish Grocer—36 North Frederick Street, Glasgow G1 2BT. *W.*

Service Station—1A Dunvegan Road, SE9 1RZ. *M.*

Sheet Metal Industries—Queensway House, 2 Queensway, Redhill, Surrey RH1 1QS. *M.*

Shipping World & Shipbuilder—42–43 Lower Marsh, SE1 7RQ. *M.*

Shoe & Leather News—84–88 Great Eastern Street, EC2A 3ED. *W.*

Soap, Perfumery and Cosmetics—33–35 Bowling Green Lane, EC1R 0DA. *M.*

Solicitors' Journal—21–27 Lamb's Conduit Street, WC1N 3NJ. *W.*

Sports Retailing—Sovereign Way, Tonbridge, Kent TN9 1RW.*Alt. W.*

Stage and Television Today—47 Bermondsey Street, SE1 3XT. *W.*

Stamp News—6 London Street, W2 1HR. *Alt. W.*

Structural Engineer, The—11 Upper Belgrave St., SW1X 8BH. *M. (Part A), Q. (Part B).*

Surveyor—Public Works Weekly—Carew House, Wallington, Surrey SM6 0DX. *W.*

Tableware International—Queensway House, 2 Queensway, Redhill, Surrey RH1 1QS. *M.*

Taxation—17 Scarbrook Rd., Croydon CR0 1SQ. *W.*

Teacher, The—Derbyshire House, Lower Street, Kettering, Northants. NN16 8BB. *W.*

Teaching History—59A Kennington Park Road, SE11 4JH. *Three times a year.*

Television—King's Reach Tower, Stamford Street, SE1 9LS. *M.*

Textile Horizons—10 Blackfriars Street, Manchester M3 5DR. *M.*

Textile Month—76 Kirkgate, Bradford BD1 1TB. *M.*

Timber Trades Journal & Wood Processing—Sovereign Way, Tonbridge, Kent TN9 1RW. *W.*

Tobacco—Queensway House, 2 Queensway, Redhill, Surrey RH1 1QS. *M.*

Town and Country Planning—17 Carlton House Terrace, SW1Y 5AH. *M.*

Town Planning Review—Dept. of Civic Design, Liverpool University, L69 3BX. *Q.*

Toy Trader—Penn House, Penn Place, Rickmansworth, Herts. WD3 1SN. *M.*

Trade Marks Journal—25 Southampton Buildings, WC2A 1AY. *W.*

Traffic Engineering and Control—29 Newman Street, W1P 3PE. *M.*

U.K. Press Gazette—244–249 Temple Chambers, Temple Avenue, EC4Y 0DT. *W.*

Ultrasonics—Westbury House, Bury Street, Guildford, Surrey GU2 5BH. *Alt. M.*

Weekly Law Reports—3 Stone Buildings, Lincoln's Inn, WC2A 3XN. *W.*

Welding and Metal Fabrication—Queensway House, 2 Queensway, Redhill, Surrey RH1 1QS. *Five times a year.*

Which?—14 Buckingham Street, WC2N 6DS. *M.*

Whitaker's Books of the Month and Books to Come—12 Dyott Street, WC1A 1DF. *M.*

Whitaker's Classified Monthly Book List—12 Dyott Street, WC1A 1DF. *M.*

Wire Industry—110–112 Station Road East, Oxted, Surrey RH8 0QA. *M.*

Woodworker—1 Golden Square, W1R 3AB. *M.*

Woodworking Crafts—170 High Street, Lewes, E. Sussex BN7 1YE. *Q.*

World Crops—Yew Tree House, Horne, Horley, Surrey RH6 9JP. *Alt. M.*

World's Fair—2 Daltry Street, Oldham OL1 4BB. *W.*

NORTHERN IRISH NEWSPAPERS

London Offices

Ballymena Guardian—30 Fleet Street, EC4Y 1AH.

Banbridge Chronicle—30–32 Fleet Street, EC4Y 1AH.

Belfast Telegraph—Pemberton House, East Harding Street, EC4A 3AS.

Coleraine Chronicle—30 Fleet Street, EC4Y 1AH.

Derry Journal—30 Fleet Street, EC4Y 1AH.

Down Recorder—30 Fleet Street, EC4Y 1AH.

Impartial Reporter & Farmers' Journal (Enniskillen)—30 Fleet Street, EC4Y 1AH.

Irish News—70 Hatton Garden, EC1N 8JT.

Irish Weekly—70 Hatton Garden, EC1N 8JT.

Mid Ulster Mail—30 Fleet Street, EC4Y 1AH.

Northern Constitution (Coleraine)—30 Fleet Street, EC4Y 1AH.

Strabane Weekly News—30 Fleet Street, EC4Y 1AH.

Tyrone Constitution—30 Fleet Street, EC4Y 1AH.

Ulster Gazette (Armagh)—30 Fleet Street, EC4Y 1AH.

Ulster Herald (Omagh)—147 Fleet Street, EC4A 2HN.

REPORTING AND NEWS AGENCIES IN LONDON

ASSOCIATED PRESS LTD.,
12 Norwich Street, EC4A 4BP. 01–353 1515.

BRENARD PRESS LTD.,
Building 221, Heathrow Airport, TW6 2BU. 01–759 1235.

CENTRAL PRESS FEATURES LTD.,
161 Fleet Street, EC4A 2AR. 01–353 7131.

EXCHANGE TELEGRAPH CO. LTD.,
East Harding Street, EC4P 4HB. 01–353 1080.

HAYTERS
4–5 Gough Square, EC4A 3DE. 01–353 0971.

NATIONAL PRESS AGENCY LTD.,
8–16 Great New Street, EC4P 4ER. 01–353 1030.

PARLIAMENTARY AND COMMON MARKET NEWS SERVICES,
19 Kingsdowne Road, Surbiton, KT6 6JZ. 01–399 2049.

PRESS ASSOCIATION LTD.,
85 Fleet Street, EC4P 4BE. 01–353 7440.

REUTERS LTD.,
85 Fleet Street, EC4P 4AJ. 01–250 1122.

UNITED PRESS INTERNATIONAL LTD.,
8 Bouverie Street, EC4Y 8BB. 01–353 2282.

UNIVERSAL NEWS SERVICES, LTD.,
Gough Square, Fleet St., EC4 4DP. 01–353 5200.

POSTAL AND TELECOMMUNICATIONS INFORMATION

GENERAL POSTAL REGULATIONS

Export Restrictions.—Under Department of Trade and Industry regulations the exportation of some goods by post is prohibited except under Department of Trade licence. Enquiries in the matter should be addressed to the Export Data Branch, Overseas Trade Divisions, Department of Trade and Industry, 1 Victoria Street, London, SW1H 0ET. Tel. 01–215 7877.

Prohibited Articles.—Among prohibitions are offensive or dangerous things, packets likely to impede the P.O. sorters, and certain kinds of advertisement.

Certificate of Posting.—Issued free on request at the time of posting.

Recorded Delivery (inland). Charge: 22p.—This service provides for a record of posting and delivery and is available for inland letters. Advice of delivery, a further 21p at time of posting. No compensation is payable in respect of money or jewellery sent by this service.

Unpaid Mail.—All unpaid or underpaid letters are treated as second class mail. The recipient will be charged the amount of underpayment plus 10p per item. The same rates apply to unpaid or underpaid parcels.

Undelivered Mail.—Undelivered mail is returned to the sender without charge provided the return address is indicated either on the outside of the envelope or inside. If the sender's address is not available, items not containing property are destroyed; however, if the packet contains something of intrinsic value, it is retained for up to three months pending reclaim before being disposed of. Perishable items within this category are dealt with as requisite. Exceptionally, items in the minimum weight step on which a rebate of postage has been allowed are destroyed unopened unless there is a return address shown on the outside of the cover. In addition, undeliverable second class mail in the minimum weight step, which, upon opening, is found to consist only of newspapers, magazines or commercial advertising material is also destroyed. *British packets undelivered abroad:* instructions for disposal are required if parcel is undeliverable and must be given at the time of posting. A parcel which cannot be delivered will be returned to sender at his expense.

International Reply Coupons, for the purpose of prepaying replies to letters, are exchangeable abroad for stamps representing the minimum surface mail letter rate from the country concerned to the U.K. Cost: 55p each.

Poste Restante (solely for the convenience of travellers, and for three months only in any one town).—A packet may be addressed as a rule to any post office except town sub-offices, and should have the words "Poste Restante" or "to be called for" in the address. If addressed to initials, fictitious names, or Christian name only, it is treated as undeliverable. Applicants must furnish sufficient particulars to ensure delivery to the proper person. Redirection from a Poste Restante is undertaken for up to three months. Letters at a seaport for an expected ship are kept 2 months; otherwise letters are kept for 2 weeks—or for 1 month if originating from abroad—at the end of which time they are treated as undeliverable, unless bearing a request for return at or before the end of the period.

Redirection.—(1) By agent of addressee: *Packets other than parcels, business reply and Freepost items* may be reposted free not later than the day after delivery (not counting Sundays and public holidays) if unopened and not tampered with, and if original addressee's name is unobscured. *Parcels* may be redirected free of charge within the same time limits, only if the original and the substituted address are both within the same local parcel delivery area (or within the London Postal Area). *Registered packets,* which must be taken to a post office, are *re-registered* free only up to day after delivery. (2) By the Post Office: Requests for redirection of *letters,* etc., should be on printed forms, obtainable from any post office, and must be signed by the person to whom the letters are to be addressed. The fees for redirection are as follows:—redirection for an initial period of up to one calendar month, £2·50; redirection for a period of up to three calendar months, commencing before the first anniversary of redirection, £5·75; redirection for a period of up to twelve calendar months, commencing before the first anniversary of redirection, £14·00; redirection for a period of up to 12 calendar months where redirection has already been in operation for 12 months or more, £47·00. A fee is payable for each different surname on the application form. Additional postage is generally due on redirected parcels (*see* above).

Registration, Inland (First Class letters only).—All packets intended for registration must be handed to an officer of the Post Office, and a certificate of posting obtained. The fees for registration (exclusive of first class postage) are: £1·20 covering compensation up to £650; £1·35, £1,350; £1·50, £1,850 (maximum). (No legal right to compensation exists in respect of registered letters sent to and from Irish Republic or the Channel Islands.) Compensation Fee (C.F.) parcels, fees: 30p up to £60 compensation; 40p up to £125; 60p up to £225; 75p up to £350. Advice of delivery, a further 20p at time of posting, 50p after time of posting.

Compensation in respect of money of any kind (coin, notes, orders, cheques, stamps, etc.) is only given if the money is sent by registered letter post in one of the special envelopes sold officially. Compensation cannot be paid for loss or damage in the case of any packet containing anything not legally transmissible by post; and for fragile articles only if they have been adequately packed. No compensation is paid for deterioration due to delay of perishable articles or for damage to exceptionally fragile articles, liquids or semi-liquids sent by letter or parcel post to or from Irish Republic, whether registered or not.

Compensation, Inland.—The ordinary mail services are not designed as compensation services. However, compensation up to a maximum limit of £20·00 may be paid where it can be shown that a letter or parcel was damaged or lost in the post. The onus of making up properly any packet sent by post and of packing adequately any article or articles enclosed therein lies on the sender, and the Post Office does not accept any responsibility for loss arising from faulty or inadequate packing. No compensation may be claimed for consequential injury or damage arising in respect of anything sent by post unless the item is registered and covered by Consequential Loss Insurance. This special insurance is arranged with certain Lloyds underwriters. Ask for details at the post office. The service is available only to U.K. addresses. *Recorded delivery packets:* maximum compensation £20 provided no contents inadmissible. Fee 22p.

Registration, Overseas (except for parcels and printed paper items posted in bulk), is in force to all countries with the exception of British Indian Ocean Territory or Republic of Maldives. No compensation is payable for the loss of or damage to valuable articles or other items sent in an unregistered letter. Fee £1·20. If claimed within a year compensation is paid to the sender for entire loss of registered packets while in the custody of a country in the Universal Postal Union, subject to certain conditions. Compensation is also payable for the partial or complete loss of or damage to the contents of registered items in the service with certain countries (*see* Post Office Guide for list).

Insurance, Overseas, may be effected on packets to many countries at the following rates:—£1·20 for up to £140 cover; 20p for each additional £100 up to £3·00 for £1,400. For H.M. Ships abroad and also members of H.M. Army and Air Force overseas using closed Forces addresses (e.g., British Forces Post Office followed by a number) only packets are insurable, up to £100. Fee £1·20. Packets containing valuable papers, (banknotes, etc.), documents (press, etc.) and, in some cases, valuable articles such as jewellery, can be insured as letters, or as parcels if the country of destination does not accept dutiable goods in the letter post.

The Post Office Guide should be consulted for details of the conditions of Insurance.

Compensation up to a maximum of £13·00 for parcels up to 5 kg. in weight, £20·00 for parcels up to 10 kg., £25·00 for parcels up to 15 kg. and £30·00 for parcels up to 20 kg may be given for loss or damage in the U.K. to uninsured parcels to or from most overseas countries, if certificate of posting is produced.

No compensation will be paid for any loss or damage due to the act of the Queen's Enemies.

Cash on Delivery Service, Inland (not to or from Irish Republic, nor to H.M. Ships).—A sum (Trade Charge) up to £350 can, under certain conditions, be collected from addresses and remitted to sender of a parcel containing an invoice. Invoice values over £50 are only collected at Post Office premises. Fee (extra to normal postage and registration charges): 75p for customers under contract; £1·00 for other customers. C.O.D. enquiry fee: 75p.

Cash on Delivery, Overseas.—Applicable to parcels only, but not all countries, nor to H.M. Naval and Military Forces and R.A.F. serving overseas. A fee, starting at £2.50 per parcel, must be prepaid in addition to the postage for outward parcels. For inward parcels the delivery fee is 70p. The Trade Charge (amount to be collected) may not exceed £1,500, but to most non-European countries the limit is lower. Addressee has also to pay on delivery, besides Customs, if any, a further fee (£1 in U.K.) not prepayable. If Trade Charge cannot be collected, special rules for undeliverable C.O.D. parcels apply.

Datapost.—A guaranteed service for the delivery of important documents and packages. Datapost Sameday provides same day collection and delivery in many areas. Datapost Overnight offers next day delivery nationwide. Items may be collected or handed in at post offices. Contractual arrangements may be made for regular consignments. There are also equally reliable and secure Datapost links with a number of overseas countries. Further details are available at local Head Post Offices or on Freephone Datapost.

Swiftair.—Express delivery of air mail letters and packets anywhere in the world. Items normally arrive at least one day in advance of normal air mail. Items should be handed in at a post office counter. Cost: normal postage plus £1·50.

Intelpost.—A public facsimile transmission service linking many towns and cities in the U.K. and also with international connections. Documents up to A4 size can be transmitted and received within minutes and the service can be used with hand delivery and collection services. Further details are available at local Head Post Offices or on Freephone Intelpost.

Royal Mail Special Delivery.—Offers special messenger treatment where necessary to ensure next day delivery of first class letters and packets. Special fee of £1·50 refunded if next working day delivery is not achieved provided items are posted before latest recommended posting times.

Express Delivery.—This service from the office of delivery by special messenger is available to or from certain countries. In some countries the service is restricted to certain towns. Fee payable in addition to postage, £1·50.

Business Reply and Freepost (Inland, excluding Irish Republic).—These services enable a person or firm to receive replies to advertisements, letters from clients, etc. without prepayment of postage, the addressee paying the postage together with a handling charge of 0·5p per item delivered. A licence costing £20 p.a. must be obtained to use either service and these are available from Head Postmasters who will also provide any further information required.

Postage Forward Parcel Service.—This service enables a person or firm to receive parcels from clients without prepayment of postage, the addressee pays a fee of 10p on each parcel in addition to postage. A special label is used for this service. A licence costing £25 p.a., to use the service must first be obtained from the local Head Postmaster.

Articles for the Blind (Inland, including Irish Republic).—Books, papers, literature and specified articles specially adapted for the use of the blind are admissible subject to certain conditions. A packet should bear on the outside the indication "Articles for the Blind" and the name and address of the sender. Packets must be capable of easy examination in the post. Postage free up to a maximum weight of 7 kg.

Blind Literature, Overseas (in other respects treated as Printed Papers).—Papers, periodicals and books, if printed in special type (also plates for embossing blind literature, and voice recordings and special paper intended solely for the use of the blind) subject to certain conditions of posting, marked outside "Literature for the Blind (Cécogrammes)", with name and address of sender. Packets must be capable of easy examination in the post. They may be sent post free up to 7 kg by surface route to all parts and free by air mail up to 1 kg to Europe; the air mail charge to other countries is 1p per 50 g up to 7 kg.

Small Packets Post, Overseas.—For the transmission of goods (including trade samples) in the same mails as Printed Papers up to 1 kg. Must be packed so that they can easily be opened for examination unless permission for sealing has been obtained from the Post Office. Registration is allowed; not insurance. Available to all countries, but to some countries there is a limit of 500 g. A customs declaration is required.

Newspaper Post, Inland.—For newspapers "registered at the P.O.".

Copies of registered newspapers may be posted by the publishers or their agents in wrappers open at both ends, in unsealed envelopes approved by the Post Office for the purpose or without covers and tied with string which can be removed without cutting. Wrappers and envelopes must be prominently marked NEWSPAPER POST in the top left-hand corner and be easily removable for the purpose of examination. No writing or additional printing is permitted, other than the words "with compliments", name and address of sender, request for return if undeliverable and a reference to a page. Items receive first class letter service.

Newspapers posted by the public or supplements to registered newspapers despatched apart from their ordinary publications are transmitted under the conditions governing the first or second class letter services.

STAMPS, ENVELOPES, POSTCARDS, &c.

POSTAGE STAMPS are sold in values of 1p, 2p, 3p, 4p, 5p, 10p, 13p, 18p, 20p, 22p, 24p, 26p, 28p, 31p, 34p, 50p, 75p, £1, £1·50, £2, and £5.

Books of stamps costing 50p and £1 are available from electronic vending machines at some main post offices. At all other vending machines, books to the value of 50p are available. At post office counters, books are sold containing 10 stamps at 18p (£1·80) and 10 at 13p (£1·30). Rolls of 13p and 18p stamps are sold: mixed value rolls are only available on special order from post offices.

REGISTERED LETTER ENVELOPES printed with a £1·38 stamp (£1·20 for registration and 18p for postage) are in three sizes: G, 156 mm × 95 mm, £1·35 each; H, 203 mm × 120 mm, £1·38 each; K, 292 mm × 152 mm, £1·46 each.

FORCES AEROGRAMMES, 13p.

ENVELOPES printed with 13p stamp: (220 mm × 110 mm) 17p each. With 18p stamp: (220 mm × 110 mm) 22p each.

Aerogrammes to all destinations, 26p.

Printed postage stamps cut out of envelopes, postcards, lettercards, air letter forms or newspaper-wrappers may be used as adhesive stamps in payment of postage or telegrams provided they are not imperfect, mutilated or defaced in any way.

POSTAL ORDERS

Postal Orders (British pattern) are issued and paid at nearly all post offices in the United Kingdom during the ordinary hours of business on weekdays. They are also issued and/or paid in many countries overseas. These countries are listed in the Post Office Guide which may be seen at any post office transacting postal order business. Transmission of postal orders to any other country is prohibited except to members of H.M. Forces. British postal orders are paid and issued in the Channel Islands and the Isle of Man and paid in the Irish Republic. They are printed, with a counterfoil, for denominations of 25p, 30p, 40p, 50p, 60p, 70p, 80p, 90p and £1, followed by £1 steps to £10 and £20. Adhesive unmarked British Postage Stamps not exceeding two in number, if affixed in the space provided, may increase the value of an order by not more than 9p. Fees: 22p on each order up to £1, 36p on each order £2–£10, and 55p on £20. The name of the payee must be inserted. If not presented within six months of the last day of the month of issue orders must be sent to the local Head Postmaster or, in London, to the District Postmaster, to ascertain whether the order may still be paid.

TELEMESSAGE

Telemessages can be sent by telephone or telex to anywhere in the UK for 'hard copy' delivery the next working day, including Saturdays. To achieve this, a Telemessage must be telephoned/telexed before 10 p.m. Monday to Saturday (7 p.m. Sundays and Bank Holidays). Dial 100 (190 in London) and ask for the Telemessage Service or see the telex directory for dialling codes.

A Telemessage costs £4·50 for the first 50 words and £2·50 for each subsequent group of 50 words—the name and address are free. A sender's copy costs 85p. A wide selection of colourful cards is available for special occasions at 80p per card. All prices are subject to VAT. Telemessage has a number of services for businesses. Details are available on 0800 282298 (free).

Telemessage is also available to the U.S.A. For next working day delivery in America a Telemessage must be filed by 10 p.m. U.K. time Monday to Saturday (7 p.m. Sundays and Bank Holidays). U.S. addresses must include the ZIP code. Charges are £7·25 for the first 50 words and £3·60 for each subsequent group of 50 words—the name and address are free. All charges are subject to VAT.

INTERNATIONAL TELEGRAMS

International Telegrams are available to most countries. Dial 0800 282298 (free) for full details and tariffs.

MARITIME COMMUNICATIONS

British Telecom International provides world-wide communication services for shipping, aircraft, oil and gas platforms and some remote land stations, HF, MF and VHF radio frequency bands are used as well as satellite. Services include telephone, telex, morse telegraphy and data transmission.

RADIOTELEGRAMS

To Ship.—Telegrams can be accepted by telex or telephone. *Telex.*—Calls use Telex 46441 (answer-back 46441 BTGKA G). Callers should provide the name of the radio station through which the message should be delivered. *Telephone.*—The number of the coastal station through which the call is to be made should be given where known. If unknown, callers should ask for Portishead Radio (0278-781111).

From Ship.—Long-wave communications are handled by Portishead Radio, medium-wave by coastal stations and on V.H.F. telegrams are dictated by Radiotelephone.

Charges.—(per word excl. VAT). To ship from the U.K.: 60p per word plus £2.00 per message. From ship to U.K.: 46p per word.

Further information is available from 0278-781111 (long-range services) or 01-583 9418 (medium range).

RADIOTELEPHONE SERVICE

To Ship.—Calls are normally made through the coast stations and callers should ask the local exchange telephone operator for Ships' Radio-Telephone Service adding, if known, the telephone number and name of the coast station through which the call should be made. If the name of the coast station is not known, the caller will be connected to Portishead Radio (0278-781111). When connected to the coast station operator, the caller should ask for SHIPS RADIO TELEPHONE DEPARTMENT, stating name and position of ship, and name or title of person being called.

From Ship.—Long range service is only available through Portishead Radio. Medium/short range services are available through all other coast stations.

Charges.—(per min. excluding VAT). To ship from U.K.: V.H.F. 72p; M.F. £1·26; H.F. £2·58.

From ship to U.K.: V.H.F. 72p; M.F. 84p; H.F. £1·72.

Further information and prices of calls from ship to other countries available from 0278-781111 (long range) or 01-583 9416 (short and medium range).

RADIOTELEX

To Ship.—Telexes must be sent to Portishead Radio Telex section (Telex 46116). For radio telex enquiries, use Telex 46506. Providing a ship has lodged its details with Portishead Radio, customers can dial direct to the vessel using telex 46300 (answer-back 46116 BTGKA G). When connected the caller must give the answer-back response and then follow the given prompts. For Phonetex messages dial the operator and ask for Portishead Radio.

From Ship.—The automatic system allows ships direct access to national and international telex routes.

Charges.—(per min. excluding VAT). To and from ship for the U.K.: M.F. £1·10; H.F. £1·70.

INMARSAT

The Inmarsat service provides for suitably equipped ships *via* its Coast Earth Station at Goonhilly which covers the Atlantic Ocean Region, while reciprocal arrangements with Norway and Singapore provide access to the Indian and Pacific Ocean Regions respectively.

Further information and details of charges are available from 01-936 4996.

AERONAUTICAL RADIO SERVICE

British Telecom International's Skyphone service provides a public air-to-ground telephone service through Portishead Radio. Further details are available from 01-936 4993.

INLAND TELEPHONES

The quarterly rental for an exclusive business exchange line is £25·55 and £13·95 for a residential exclusive exchange line. For shared service, in which two subscribers share one line but have practically the same facilities as those provided by individual lines, each customer pays £1·20 per quarter less than for exclusive line service. Full self-dialling (STD) facilities are provided on all exchanges. Local and dialled national calls from these exchanges are charged in 4·4p units when made from ordinary lines, in 10p units when made from payphones and 10p minimum charge from press-button payphones with 2p incremental units. All charges are subject to VAT. VAT on call charges from ordinary lines is charged as a percentage of the total on quarterly bills and VAT on calls from payphones is included in the unit fee. The length of time per unit depends on the distance of the call and time of day, from six minutes for a cheap rate local call to 18 seconds for distances over 56 kilometres at peak rate.

Operator-connected calls from ordinary lines have a three minute minimum charge (and thereafter by the minute) which varies with distance and time of day, but those from payphones are charged in 3 minute periods at the coinbox tariff. For calls that have to be passed through the operator because a dialled call had failed, the charge is equivalent to the dialled rate, subject normally to the three minute minimum. Generally higher charges apply to other operator connected calls including special services calls and those to mobile phones, the Irish Republic and the Channel Isles. All calls are cheaper if made before 8 a.m., after 6 p.m. or at weekends. Personal calls (to specified person) £1·75 extra from ordinary lines and £2·10 from payphones, if the person cannot be found nothing further is charged. For fuller information *see* Preface to Phone Book or Dialling Code Booklet.

INTERNATIONAL TELEPHONES

The charges are the same for calls originating in any part of Great Britain, Northern Ireland and the Isle of Man. All U.K. customers have had access to International Direct Dialling from this country since 1982 and can dial direct to numbers on most exchanges in over 170 countries worldwide. The number of places abroad to which calls may be dialled direct is still increasing. Callers should consult their dialling codes booklets or International Telephone Guide for information on how to make calls.

Directly dialled calls are charged in units of time costing 4·4p, plus VAT. Countries fall under one of eight charge bands. Cheaper rates are available at certain times for all calls except those in Charge Band G. Further details of international call charges and services may be found in the International Telephone Guide, available from British Telecom District Offices, or by dialling 100 and asking for Freefone BTI.

TELEX SERVICE

There are now 211 countries that can be reached by Telex from the UK; 197 of them by Direct Dial.

For most customers Direct Dialled calls to all international destinations are charged in six second units costing between 2·3p and 13·2p depending upon the country called. Calls via the operator are charged in one minute steps with a three minute minimum, plus a surcharge of £1·30 per call.

Calls made via British Telecom's Telex Plus store and forward facility attract normal Telex charges plus a surcharge of 10p for inland delivered messages and 20p for international delivered messages.

INTERNATIONAL DATA TRANSMISSION SERVICES

(i) Public Switched Telephone Network

BTI International Business Services offer data transmission over the public switched telephone network using International Direct Dialling (IDD). Calls are charged at the same rate as for telephone calls.

BTI has reached agreement with 70 countries for such use of the telephone network.

(ii) Analogue Private Circuits

International private circuits are available for data transmission and are provided in accordance with the recommendations of the International Telephone & Telegraph Consultative Committee (CCITT).

(iii) International Packet Switching Service (IPSS)

IPSS provides service with over 90 networks in 63 countries (June 1987) in Australasia, Europe, North and South America, the Caribbean and the Middle and Far East.

PRESTEL

Prestel, British Telecommunications' public videotex service, links adapted television screens to computers through ordinary telephone lines so information and two-way services can be delivered directly into offices and homes. Over 99 per cent of the U.K. telephone population can now use Prestel at local call rates, and over 74,000 terminals are attached to the network. Information on Prestel (from over 1,200 different sources) can be updated by the minute and is available 24 hours a day.

In addition, by using "Gateways", private computers can be linked to Prestel sets via Prestel computers. This facility makes possible services such as home banking, and for travel agents confirmed reservations of airline tickets.

Because the system is two-way, all customers can send messages, make bookings or request information at the touch of a button. There are well over 330,000 frames (or "pages") of information available.

BRITISH TELECOM

81 Newgate Street EC1A 7AJ
[01-356 5000]

British Telecom became a public limited company on August 6, 1984. It operates some 17·5 million residential and 4·5 million business telephone lines and 111,500 telex lines.
Chairman and Chief Executive, I. Vallance.

	1985–6	1986–7
	£m.	£m
Turnover	8,387	9,424
Main services income	7,657	8,387
Sales and other operating income	730	1,037
Total expenditure including interest	6,559	7,357
Profit on ordinary activities	1,810	2,067
Tax on profit	743	754
*Preference dividend	63	56
Profit attributable to shareholders	1,004	1,257
*Ordinary dividend	450	508
Retained profit	554	749
Capital expenditure	1,973	2,107
Fixed assets	10,714	11,500

* Result of privatisation.

POST OFFICE FINANCIAL RESULTS,
etc.

	1985–86 (£m.)	1986–87 (£m.)
POST OFFICE GROUP		
Turnover	3,247·5	3,473·3
Trading profit before tax	167·0	170·0
POSTS		
Turnover	3,159·0	3,367·4
Trading profit before tax	150·3	150·3
GIROBANK		
Turnover	292·2	328·0
Trading profit before tax	19·4	23·1

BASIC RATE OF INLAND LETTER POST

1840	1d	Sept. 1975	8½p
1918	1½d	June 1977	9p
1940	2½d	Aug. 1979	10p
1957	3d	Feb. 1980	12p
1965	4d	Jan. 1981	14p
1968*	5d	Feb. 1982	15½p
1971	3p	April 1983	16p
1973	3½p	Sept. 1984	17p
1974	4½p	Oct. 1986	18p
1975	7p		

(*Two-tier postal system introduced—subsequent figures are for 1st class letter post)

DUTY AND TAX-FREE ALLOWANCES

You are entitled to the allowances in either of the columns below (but not both) for any category of goods, as represented by the boxes (*see* Notes on Allowances). Passengers under 17 are not, however, entitled to tobacco and drinks allowances.

Column 1
Goods obtained duty and tax free in the E.C., or duty and tax free on a ship or aircraft, or goods obtained outside the E.C.

Column 2
Goods obtained duty and tax paid in the E.C.

Tobacco goods	
200 cigarettes	
or	
100 cigarillos	double if you live
or	outside Europe
50 cigars	
or	
250 grammes of tobacco	

Tobacco goods
300 cigarettes
or
150 cigarillos
or
75 cigars
or
400 grammes of tobacco

Alcoholic drinks
2 litres of still table wine

Alcoholic drinks
5 litres of still table wine

plus

1 litre over 22% vol. (e.g. spirits and strong liqueurs)
or
2 litres not over 22% vol. (e.g. low strength liqueurs, fortified wine or sparkling wine)
or
A further 2 litres of still table wine

plus

1½ litres over 22% vol. (e.g. spirits and strong liqueurs)
or
3 litres not over 22% vol. (e.g. low strength liqueurs, fortified wine, or sparkling wine)
or
A further 3 litres of still table wine

Perfume
50 grammes (60 cc or 2 fl oz)

Perfume
75 grammes (90 cc or 3 fl oz)

Toilet water
250 cc (9 fl oz)

Toilet water
375 cc (13 fl oz)

Other goods
£32 worth

Other goods
£250 worth

N.B. A maximum of 50 litres of beer and 25 lighters may be imported duty-free, subject to the limitations of the 'Other goods' monetary allowance.

If you are visiting the United Kingdom for less than six months, you are also entitled to bring in, free of duty and tax, all personal effects (except tobacco goods, alcoholic drinks and perfume) which you intend to take with you when you leave.

NOTES ON ALLOWANCES

(1) The countries of the European Community are Belgium, Denmark, France, West Germany, Greece, the Irish Republic, Italy, Luxembourg, the Netherlands, Portugal, Spain (but not the Canary Islands), and the United Kingdom (but not the Channel Islands).
(2) The allowances apply only to goods carried and cleared by you at the time of your arrival.
(3) The allowances do not apply to goods brought in for sale or for other commercial purposes.
(4) Reduced allowances apply to certain persons crossing the Irish land boundary and to seamen and aircrew members.
(5) Whisky, gin, rum, brandy, vodka and most liqueurs normally exceed 22% vol. (38.8° proof) but advocaat, cassis, fraise, suze and aperitifs may be less. Fortified wines include port, sherry, vermouth and madeira. Sparkling wines include champagne, perelada, spumante and semi-sparkling wines. Still table wines include claret, Sauterne, Graves and Chianti. Burgundy, Chablis, hock and Moselle may be either sparkling or still, depending on manufacture.
(6) You may not mix goods obtained duty and tax free or outside the E.C. with goods of the same category (as represented by the boxes) obtained duty and tax paid in the E.C. to obtain the higher allowance. E.g. you will not get the higher allowance for Tobacco goods if *any* of the items in that category were obtained duty and tax free or outside the E.C.
(7) Where there are alternative quantities within a category of goods they may be apportioned. For example, 150 cigarettes (half allowance) plus 75 cigarillos (half allowance).
(8) One litre is approximately 1¾ pints or 35 fl oz.
(9) A cigarillo is a cigar with a maximum weight of 3 grammes.

PROHIBITED AND RESTRICTED GOODS

The customs officer will be able to provide full information. This is a list of more frequently met items:
Controlled drugs, such as opium, heroin, morphine, cocaine, cannabis, amphetamines, lysergide (LSD) and barbiturates.
Firearms (including gas pistols, electric shock batons and similar weapons), ammunition and explosives (including fireworks).
Flick knives.
Counterfeit currency.
Horror comics. Indecent or obscene books, magazines, films and other articles.

Radio transmitters (walkie-talkies, Citizen's Band radios etc.) not approved for use in the U.K.

Meat and poultry, and most of their products (whether or not cooked), including ham, bacon, sausage, pâté, eggs and milk.

Plants, parts thereof and plant produce, including trees and shrubs, potatoes and certain other vegetables, fruit, bulbs and seeds.

Animals and birds, whether alive or dead (e.g. stuffed), certain fish and fish eggs, whether live or dead, or bees; certain articles derived from rare species including furskins, ivory, reptile leather and goods made from them.

N.B.: Cats, dogs and other mammals must not be landed unless a British import licence (rabies) has previously been issued.

EXPORT CONTROL

The following are some of the goods subject to export control and should be declared to the customs officer.

There are formalities to be completed in respect of these goods prior to your arrival at the port of exportation and further information is available through any local office of Customs and Excise (address in the telephone directory).

● Controlled drugs.
● Firearms and ammunition.
● Photographic material over 60 years old and valued at £400 or more.
● Portraits (including sculptures) of British historical personages which are over 50 years old and valued at £4,000 or more.
● Antiques, collectors' items, etc. (including paintings and other works of art) over 50 years old and valued at £16,000 or more.
● Certain archaeological material.
● Most live animals and birds, and items made from animals occurring wild in the U.K.

BRITISH PASSPORT REGULATIONS

Applications for United Kingdom Passports must be made on the forms obtainable at any of the Passport Offices (addresses given below) or at any main Post Office (except in Northern Ireland).

London.—Clive House, 70–78 Petty France, SW1H 9HD.

Liverpool.—India Buildings, Water Street, Liverpool L2 0QZ.

Newport, Gwent.—Olympia House, Upper Dock Street, Newport NPT 1XA.

Peterborough.—Passport Office, 55 Westfield Road, Peterborough PE3 6TG.

Glasgow.—3 Northgate, 96 Milton Street, Cowcaddens, Glasgow G4 0BT.

Belfast.—Passport Office, Hampton House, 47–53 High Street, Belfast BT1 2QS.

Hours. The above offices are open Mon.-Fri. 9 a.m. to 4.30 p.m. The Passport Office, London, is also open for cases of special emergency (*e.g.* death or serious illness) arising outside normal office hours between 4.30 p.m. and 6.00 p.m. and on Saturdays between 10 a.m. and noon.

Completed forms of application should be sent to one of the six Passport Offices, with photographs, supporting documents and the fee of £15 (£22·50 if particulars of spouse included), in the form of a cheque or postal order which should be crossed and made payable to the Passport Office.

A passport cannot be issued or extended on behalf of *a person already abroad*; such person should apply to the nearest British High Commission or Consulate.

United Kingdom Passports are granted to:—

(i) British Citizens.
(ii) British Dependent Territories Citizens.
(iii) British Nationals (overseas).
(iv) British Overseas Citizens.
(v) British Subjects.
(vi) British Protected Persons.

A passport granted to a child under 16 will normally be valid for an initial period of five years, after which it may be extended for a further five years with no extra charge. A passport granted to a person over 16 will normally be valid for 10 years and will not be renewable. Thereafter, or if at any time the Passport contains no further space for visas, a new Passport must be obtained.

A passport including particulars of the *holder's spouse* is not available for his/her use when he/she is travelling alone. A spouse's particulars may *only* be added at the time of issue of a passport.

Children who have reached the age of sixteen years require separate passports. Their applications must be signed by one of their parents.

Completed passport applications should be count-

ersigned by a Member of Parliament, Justice of the Peace, Minister of Religion, a professionally qualified person (*e.g.* Doctor, Engineer, Lawyer, Teacher), Bank Officer, established Civil Servant, Police Officer or a person of similar standing who has personally known the applicant for at least two years, and who is either a British citizen, a British Dependent Territories citizen, British overseas citizen, a British subject or a citizen of a Commonwealth country. A relative must not countersign the application. The applicant's birth certificate or previous British Passport, and other evidence in support of the statements made in the application must be produced.

In the case of children under the age of 16 requiring a separate passport, an application should be made by one of the parents on form (B).

If the applicant for a passport is a British national by naturalization or registration, the Certificate of Naturalization or registration must be produced with the application, unless the applicant holds a previous United Kingdom Passport issued after registration or naturalization.

United Kingdom Passports are generally available for travel to all countries. The possession of a passport does not, however, exempt the holder from compliance with any immigration regulations in force in British or foreign countries, or from the necessity of obtaining a visa where required.

Photographs

Duplicate unmounted photographs of applicant (and wife/husband, if to be included in the passport) must be sent. These photographs should be printed on normal thin photographic paper. They should measure 45 mm. by 35 mm. (1·77 in. by 1·38 in.) and should be taken full face without a hat. One photograph should be certified as a true likeness of the applicant by the person who countersigns the application form.

Extension of Passports

Applications for the extension of United Kingdom passports which have been valid for less than ten years must be made on Form D.

94-Page Passports

On May 1, 1973, a new type of passport became available. Intended to meet the needs of frequent travellers who fill standard passports well before the ten-year validity has expired, it contains 94 pages, is valid for ten years and costs £30 (£45 if particulars of spouse included).

British Visitors' Passports

A simplified form of travel document is available for British Citizens, British Dependent Territories Citizens or British Overseas Citizens wishing to pay short visits (not exceeding three months) to certain foreign countries, *viz.*

Andorra; Austria; Belgium; Bermuda; Denmark; Finland; France (incl. Corsica); Greece (& the Greek Islands); W. Germany (incl. West Berlin by air only); Gibraltar; Iceland; Italy; Liechtenstein; Luxembourg; Malta; Monaco; Netherlands; Norway; Portugal (incl. Madeira & Azores); San Marino; Spain (incl. Balearic & Canary Islands); Sweden; Switzerland; Tunisia; Turkey.

A fee of £7·50 (£11·25 if particulars of spouse included) is charged for the issue of a British Visitors' Passport, which is valid for 12 months, cannot be amended and is not renewable; on expiry application should be made for a new passport if required. Particulars of an applicant's spouse and/or children under 16 years can be included at the time of issue only at no extra cost. A child of 8 years of age and over is eligible to hold a British Visitors' Passport.

Applications for, or including, a person under 18 years of age (unless married or serving in H.M. Forces) must be countersigned by the legal guardian.

British Visitors' Passports are obtainable by application on Form VP (from any main Post Office except in Northern Ireland). Applicants in England, Scotland and Wales should take the completed form in person to any main Post Office which will normally issue the passport without further delay; applicants in Northern Ireland to the Passport Office, Belfast from whom application forms may be obtained. British Visitors' Passports are not obtainable from Passport Offices other than Belfast.

Two recent passport photographs will be required of the applicant and of his/her spouse, if to be included; photographs of children are not required. Size of photographs must be 50 mm. by 38 mm (2 in. × 1½ in.). They should be unmounted and must be printed on normal thin photographic paper. No visas are required on British Visitors' Passports. Applicants must also produce for the purpose of identification a N.H.S. Medical Card, birth certificate or retirement pension book.

VISAS

Visa regulations are liable to change and enquiries should be made at the Consulate or Embassy concerned (addresses and telephone numbers are given in the Commonwealth and Foreign Countries sections).

For entry into the following countries a visa or permit may be required: Afghanistan; Albania; Algeria; Angola; Antigua; Argentina; Austria; Bahrain; Benin; Bermuda; Bolivia; Brazil; Brunei; Bulgaria; Burkina; Burma; Burundi; Cameroon Republic; Cape Verde; Central African Republic; Chad; Chile; China; Colombia; Congo; Costa Rica; Côte d'Ivoire; Cuba; Czechoslovakia; Djibouti; Dominica; Dominican Republic; Ecuador; Egypt; El Salvador; Equatorial Guinea; Ethiopia; Finland; Gabon; German Democratic Republic; Federal Re-

public of Germany; Gibraltar; Grenada; Guatemala; Guinea; Guinea Bissau; Haiti; Honduras; Hong Kong; Hungary; Indonesia; Iran; Iraq; Israel; Japan; Jordan; Korea; Kuwait; Laos; Lebanon; Liberia; Libya; Madagascar; Mali; Mauritania; Mexico; Mongolia; Morocco; Mozambique; Nepal; Nicaragua; Niger; Oman; Pakistan; Panama; Paraguay; Peru; Philippines; Poland; Qatar; Romania; Rwanda; St. Lucia; St. Vincent and the Grenadines; Saudi Arabia; Senegal; Somali Democratic Republic; South Africa; Sudan; Sweden; Switzerland; Syria; Thailand; Togo; Tunisia; Turkey; United Arab Emirates; Uruguay; U.S.A.; U.S.S.R.; Venezuela; Vietnam; Yemen Arab Republic; People's Democratic Republic of Yemen; Yugoslavia; Zaire.

WORK AND BUSINESS OVERSEAS

A passport issued after December 31, 1982 showing the holder's national status as British citizen will secure for the holder the right to take employment or to establish himself in business or other self-employed activity in another member state of the European Community (except Spain and Portugal). A passport bearing the endorsement "holder has the right of abode in the United Kingdom" where the holder so qualifies will also secure the same right. Employment permits are required in most other countries, even for casual labour. The nearest representative of the country concerned should be consulted. Local Employment Offices have a booklet entitled "Working abroad".

Those planning to travel abroad on export business

are advised to contact the British Overseas Trade Board, 1 Victoria Street, London S.W.1 or its Regional Offices in London S.W.1, Birmingham, Bristol, Leeds, Manchester, Newcastle upon Tyne and Nottingham. *Wales*: Welsh Office Industry Department, New Crown Building, Cathays Park, Cardiff; *Scotland*: Scottish Export Office, Alhambra House, 45 Waterloo Street, Glasgow; *Northern Ireland*: Industrial Development Board for Northern Ireland, I.D.B. House, 64 Chichester Street, Belfast. These offices will send advance notification of the visit to the Commercial Section of the relevant Consulate or Embassy, and can offer advice and information about the markets to be visited.

VACCINATION

In very general terms vaccination for protection against cholera, typhoid and polio are recommended for all countries outside Europe, except North America, Australia and New Zealand. Protection, in the form of tablets, is advised for malaria similarly.

Vaccination against yellow fever is essential for entry into Angola, Benin, Burkina, Cameroon, Central African Republic, Chad, Congo, Côte d'Ivoire, French Guyana, Gambia, Ghana, Mali, Mauritania, Niger, Nigeria, Panama, Rwanda, São Tomé and Principé, Senegal, Sierra Leone, Togo and Uganda, and is recommended for most other African and South American countries. Fuller details are set out

in D.H.S.S. leaflet SA 35 "Protect your health abroad". For up-to-date information about vaccination requirements, contact one of the following health departments: *England*—International Relations Division, D.H.S.S., Alexander Fleming House, Elephant and Castle, London SE1 6BY (01-407 5522 ext. 6749), Communicable Disease Surveillance Centre, 61 Colindale Avenue, London NW9 5EQ (01-200 4400); *Wales*—Welsh Office, Cathays Park, Cardiff CF1 3NQ (0222-825111 ext. 3336); *Scotland*—Scottish Home and Health Department, St. Andrew's House, Edinburgh EH1 3DE (031-5568501 ext. 2438) Communicable Diseases (Scotland) Unit, Ruchill Hospital, Bilsland

Drive, Glasgow G20 9NB (041-946 7120); *Northern Ireland*—D.H.S.S., Dundonald House, Upper Newtownards Road, Belfast BT4 3SF (0232-63939 ext. 2593).

Your doctor should be consulted at least eight weeks before departure, and will advise you and arrange vaccinations. If children will be travelling outside Europe, North America, Australia and New Zealand the doctor should be informed, especially if they have not completed their full course of childhood immunization.

Details of free or reduced cost medical treatment when visiting other European countries, Hong Kong or New Zealand are set out in leaflet SA 30 "Medical costs abroad", available from some travel agents, local D.H.S.S. offices or the D.H.S.S. Leaflets Unit, P.O. Box 21, Stanmore, Middx. HA7 1AY.

VEHICLE LICENCES, ETC.

Since October 1, 1974, registration and first licensing of vehicles has been done through local offices (known as Vehicle Registration Offices) of the Department of Transport's Driver and Vehicle Licensing Centre in Swansea. The records of existing vehicles are held at Swansea. Local facilities for relicensing are available as follows:—

(i) with a licence reminder (form V11) in person at any Post Office which deals with vehicle licensing or post it to the Head Post Office, shown on the form.

(ii) with a vehicle licence application (form V10). You may normally apply either in person at any "licensing" Post Office if you have the Registration Document or post it to the Head Postmaster at one of the Head Post Offices listed on the back of the V10. If you do not have the Registration Document, you must complete form V62, application for a Registration Document. Please read the notes on the back of the form first.

Details of the present duties chargeable on motor vehicles are available at Post Offices and Vehicle Registration Offices. The Vehicles (Excise) Act, 1971 provides *inter alia* that any vehicle kept on a public road but not used on roads is chargeable to excise duty as if it were in use.

Rates of duty for motor car and motor cycle licences are shown below. For Hackney Carriages the rates of duty are: Hackney Carriage with seating capacity not exceeding 20 persons, £52·50; additional for each person above 20 (excluding the driver) for which the vehicle has seating capacity, £1·05.

Type of Vehicle	Exceeding	Not Exceeding	12 Months	6 Months
			£	£
MOTOR CARS				
Those first registered before January 1, 1947	—	—	60·00	33·00
Other than above	—	—	100·00	55·00
MOTOR CYCLES				
With or without sidecar	—	150 c.c.	10·00	—
With or without sidecar	150 c.c.	250 c.c.	20·00	—
With or without sidecar	250 c.c.	—	40·00	22·00
If first licensed before 1 Jan. 1933 and weighs not more than 101·6 kgs.	250 c.c.	—	20·00	—
THREE WHEELERS				
Other than pedestrian-controlled	—	150 c.c.	10·00	—
Other than pedestrian-controlled	150 c.c.	—	40·00	22·00
PEDESTRIAN-CONTROLLED VEHICLES (Other than mowing machines)				
Three wheeled	—	150 c.c.	10·00	—
Three wheeled	150 c.c.	—	20·00	—
More than three wheels			20·00	—

Driving Licences—Fees

On or after 1.9.86

FULL LICENCE

First full licence .... £15·00*

Renewal of full licence if last full licence was:

(i) Issued before 1.1.76 .... £15·00*

(ii) Issued after 1.1.76 (not being an exchange licence and no additional entitlement claimed) .... free

On or after 1.9.86

PROVISIONAL LICENCE

First provisional licence .... £15·00*

First renewal of provisional licence issued before 1.10.82 .... £15·00

DUPLICATE LICENCE................... £5·00

EXCHANGE LICENCE .... £5·00

* Once you have paid for *either* a provisional *or* a full licence all renewals are free except where additional entitlement is required.

Driving Test—Fees

For cars .... £15·00

For motor cycles, part I .... £17·94*

part II .... £15·00

*When conducted by the Department of Transport. Appointed motor cycle training organisations, who conduct the majority of part I tests within the framework of their own training courses, are free to set their own fee.

Driving tests for invalid carriages are free.

M.o.T. Testing

Cars, motor cycles, motor caravans, light goods and dual-purpose vehicles more than 3 years old must be covered by an effective vehicle test certificate (often called the M.o.T. certificate). Copies of the legislation governing M.o.T. testing can be obtained from any bookshop which stocks H.M.S.O. publications. The legislation comprises The Road Traffic Act 1972 (Sections 44 and 45), The Motor Vehicles (Test) Regulations 1981, The Motor Vehicles (Extension) Order 1981, and The Motor Vehicles (Production of Test Certificate) Regulations 1969.

DIARY OF EVENTS IN 1988

This diary is based on information (available at the time of going to press) supplied by the British Tourist Authority, *inter alia*. The horse-racing fixtures are the copyright of The Jockey Club.

SHOWS, PAGEANTS AND EXHIBITIONS

Jan. 6–17	London International Boat Show	Earls Court, London
Feb. 11–14	Cruft's Dog Show	Earls Court, London
March 8–April 3	*Daily Mail* Ideal Home Exhibition	Earls Court, London
March 28–31	The London International Book Fair	Olympia, London
May 12–15	Royal Windsor Horse Show	Home Park, Windsor
May 24–27	Chelsea Flower Show	Royal Hospital, Chelsea, London
June 10–July 10	York Mystery Plays	York
June 11	Trooping the Colour	Horse Guards Parade, London
July 4–7	Royal International Agricultural Show	Stoneleigh, Warwicks.
July 13–30	Royal Tournament	Earls Court, London
Aug. 11	Battle of Flowers	Jersey
Aug. 12–Sept. 3	Edinburgh Military Tattoo	Edinburgh Castle
Sept. 3	Braemar Royal Highland Gathering	Braemar, Grampian
Sept. 16–24	Southampton International Boat Show	Mayflower Park, Southampton
Oct. 22—30	Motor Show	National Exhibition Centre, Birmingham
Nov. 6	London to Brighton Veteran Car Run	Hyde Park to Brighton
Nov. 12	Lord Mayor's Procession and Show	City of London
Dec. 5–8	Royal Smithfield Show and Agricultural Machinery Exhibition	Earls Court, London

MUSIC AND DRAMA FESTIVALS

May 27–June 12	Bath Festival	Bath, Avon
May–Aug.	Glyndebourne Festival Opera Season	Glyndebourne, nr. Lewes
May–Sept.	Chichester Festival Theatre Season	Chichester, W. Sussex
June 10–26	Aldeburgh Festival	Aldeburgh, Suffolk
July 22–Sept. 17	Promenade Concerts Season	Royal Albert Hall
July 30–Aug. 8	Royal National Eisteddfod of Wales	Newport, Gwent
Aug. 14–Sept. 3	Edinburgh International Festival	Edinburgh
Aug. 21–26	Three Choirs Festival	Hereford

HORSE RACING

March 17	Cheltenham Gold Cup	Cheltenham
March 26	Lincoln Handicap	Doncaster
April 9	Grand National	Liverpool
April 28	One Thousand Guineas	Newmarket
April 30	Two Thousand Guineas	Newmarket
June 1	The Derby	Epsom
June 2	Coronation Cup	Epsom
June 4	The Oaks	Epsom
June 14–17	Royal Ascot	Ascot
July 23	King George VI and Queen Elizabeth Diamond Stakes	Ascot
Sept. 10	St. Leger	Doncaster
Oct. 1	Cambridgeshire	Newmarket
Oct. 15	Cesarewitch	Newmarket

OTHER SPORTS

Feb. 6	Rugby Union: England v. Wales	Twickenham, London
Feb. 13–28	Winter Olympics	Calgary, Canada
Feb. 20	Rugby Union: Wales v. Scotland	Cardiff Arms Park
March 5	Rugby Union: Scotland v. England	Murrayfield, Edinburgh
March 19	Rugby Union: England v. Ireland	Twickenham, London
April 14–17	Badminton Horse Trials	Badminton, Avon
April 17	London Marathon	London
May 14	Football: F.A. Cup Final	Wembley Stadium, London
May 30–June 4	Golf: British Amateur Championship	Porthcawl, Mid Glamorgan
June 4, 6, 8, 10	International TT Motorcycle Races	Isle of Man
June 20–July 3	Lawn Tennis Championships	Wimbledon, London
June 29–July 3	Henley Royal Regatta	Henley-on-Thames
July 14–17	Golf: Open Championship	Lytham St. Anne's, Lancs.
July 31–Aug. 7	Cowes Week	Cowes, Isle of Wight
Sept. 17–Oct. 2	Olympic Games	Seoul, S. Korea
Oct. 3–8	Horse of the Year Show	Wembley Arena, London